HARRAP'S
SPANISH
and ENGLISH
DICTIONARY

Paola Andrea Osorio H.
August 27/09

Mc
Graw
Hill

New York Chicago San Francisco Lisbon London Madrid Mexico City
Milan New Delhi San Juan Seoul Singapore Sydney Toronto

The **McGraw·Hill** Companies

Library of Congress Cataloging-in-Publication Data

Harrap's Spanish and English dictionary / [project manager and editor, Teresa Alvarez.]
     p.   cm.
    ISBN 0-07-144072-0 (pbk. : alk. paper)
     1. Spanish language—Dictionaries—English.   2. English language—
Dictionaries—Spanish.   I. Title: Spanish and English dictionary.   II. Alvarez
García, Teresa.   III. Harrap (Firm)

PC4640.H37   2005
463'.21—dc22   2005050526

1 2 3 4 5 6 7 8 9 10 11 12 13 14 15 16 17 18   DOC/DOC   0 9 8

ISBN 978-0-07-160879-4
MHID   0-07-160879-6

McGraw-Hill books are available at special quantity discounts to use as premiums
and sales promotions or for use in corporate training programs. To contact a
representative, please visit the Contact Us pages at www.mhprofessional.com.

The pages within this book were
printed on paper containing
100% Recycled Fiber,
40% Post-Consumer.

Contents

Contributors

Editors
Teresa Álvarez
Liam Rodger

with
Talia Bugel
José A. Gálvez
Orin Hargraves
Elena Ron

Proofreaders
Val McNulty
Alison Sadler

Publishing Manager
Patrick White

Prepress Manager
Sharon McTeir

Prepress
Clair Simpson

Preface

The Harrap's Spanish and English Dictionary aims to provide comprehensive coverage of the essential vocabulary of both languages, including a wide variety of idiomatic expressions, slang and colloquial language and literary terms. The result is an easy-to-use guide to current Spanish and English, with accurate, clearly-labeled translations.

The dictionary will find a place in school and workplace alike and therefore contains the broadest possible range of vocabulary, from fields as diverse as finance, education, medicine, the sciences and computing. Encyclopedic information is also covered, with a wide selection of geographical and other proper names featuring in the book.

Extra help is provided in the form of a useful supplement in the center of the book which contains an extensive Spanish grammar and detailed Spanish verb tables.

Abbreviations

abbr, abrev	abbreviation, abreviatura	*Ecuad*	Ecuador
adj	adjective, adjetivo	*Educ*	education, educación
adv	adverb, adverbio	*Elec*	electricity, electricidad
Agr	agriculture, agricultura	*Ent*	entomology, entomología
algn	alguien (somebody)	*Equit*	equitación, horse riding
Am	Latin America,	*esp*	especially, especialmente
	Hispanoamérica	*Esp*	Spain, España
Anat	anatomy, anatomía	*Espec*	termino especializado
Andes	Andean Spanish, español		(specialist term)
	andino (Bolivia, Chile,	*Euph, Euf*	euphemism, eufemismo
	Colombia, Ecuador, Peru)	*f*	feminine, femenino
Archit	architecture (arquitectura)	*Fam*	informal use, familiar uso
Arg	Argentina	*Farm*	farmacia (pharmacy)
Argot	muy informal (slang)	*Ferroc*	ferrocarril (rail)
Arquit	arquitectura (architecture)	*Fig*	figurative use, uso figurado
art	article, artículo	*Filos*	filosofía (philosophy)
Astrol	astrology, astrología	*Fin*	finance, finanzas
Astron	astronomy, astronomía	*Fís*	física (physics)
Astronaut,	space travel, astronáutica	*Fml*	formal use, uso formal
Astronáut		*Fot*	fotografía (photography)
Athlet, Atlet	athletics, atletismo	*fpl*	feminine plural, plural femenino
Austral	Australia	*Ftb*	soccer, fútbol
Aut	cars, automoción	*Furn*	furniture (muebles)
aux	auxiliary, auxiliar	*fut*	future, futuro
Av	aviation, aviación	*gen*	generally, generalmente
Bill	billiards, billar	*Geog*	geography, geografía
Biol	biology, biología	*Geol*	geology, geología
Bol	Bolivia	*Geom*	geometry, geometría
Bot	botany, botánica	*ger*	gerund, gerundio
Box	boxing, boxeo	*Guat*	Guatemala
Br	Britain, Gran Bretaña	*Hist*	history, historia
CAm	Central America, América	*Hond*	Honduras
	Central	*Hortic*	horticulture, horticultura
Can	Canada, Canadá	*Hum*	humorous, humorístico
Carib	Caribbean, Caribe	*imperat*	imperative, imperativo
Carp	carpentry, carpintería	*imperf*	imperfecto (imperfect)
Chem	chemistry (química)	*impers*	impersonal
Cin	cinema, cine	*Impr*	imprenta (printing)
Col	Colombia	*Ind*	industry, industria
Com	commerce, comercio	*indef*	indefinite, indefinido
Comptr	computing (informática)	*indic*	indicativo (indicative)
conj	conjunction, conjunción	*Inform*	informática (computing)
Constr	construction, construcción	*Ins*	insurance (seguros)
Cost	costura (sewing)	*interj*	interjection, interjección
CRica	Costa Rica	*interr*	interrogative, interrogativo
CSur	Cono Sur (Argentina, Uruguay,	*inv*	invariable
	Paraguay, Chile)	*Ir*	Ireland, Irlanda
Culin	cocina, cookery	*Iron, Irón*	ironic, irónico
def	definite, definido	*Jur*	law, derecho
dem	demonstrative, demostrativo	*Knit*	knitting (tricotar)
Dep	deporte (sport)	*Ling*	linguistics, lingüística
Econ	economics, economía	*Lit*	literature, literatura

loc	locución (phrase)
m	masculine, masculino
Math, Mat	mathematics, matemáticas
Med	medicine, medicina
Metal	metallurgy, metalurgia
Meteor	meteorology, meteorología
Méx	Mexico, México
m,f/mf	masculine or feminine, masculino o femenino
m,fpl/mfpl	masculine or feminine plural, masculino o femenino plural
Mil	military, militar
Min	mining, mineralogy, minas, mineralogía
Mit	mitología (mythology)
mpl	masculine plural, plural masculino
Mueb	muebles (furniture)
Mus, Mús	music, música
Myth	mythology (mitología)
n	noun, nombre
Naut, Náut	shipping, náutica
neut	neutro (neuter)
nf	feminine noun, nombre femenino
nfpl	plural feminine noun, nombre femenino plural
Nic	Nicaragua
nm	masculine noun, nombre masculino
nm,f/nmf	masculine or feminine noun, nombre masculino o femenino
nmpl	masculine plural noun, nombre masculino plural
npl	plural noun, nombre plural
Offens, Ofens	offensive, ofensivo
Opt, Ópt	optics, óptica
Orn	ornithology, ornitología
Pan	Panama, Panamá
Par	Paraguay
Parl	parliament, parlamento
Pej	pejorative (peyorativo)
pers	personal
Pey	peyorativo (pejorative)
Pharm	pharmacy (farmacia)
Philos	philosophy (filosofía)
Phot	photography (fotografía)
Phys	physics (física)
pl	plural
Pol	politics, política
poss, pos	possessive, posesivo
pp	past participle, participio pasado
pref	prefix, prefijo
prep	preposition, preposición
pres	present, presente
PRico	Puerto Rico
Print	printing (imprenta)
pron	pronoun (pronombre)
Prov	proverb, proverbio
Psych, Psic	psychology, psicología
pt	past tense, pretérito
Quím	química (chemistry)
Rad	radio
Rail	rail (ferrocarril)
RDom	Dominican Republic, República Dominicana
rel	relative, relativo
Rel	religion, religión
RP	Río de la Plata (Argentina, Uruguay, Paraguay)
Salv	El Salvador
SAm	América del Sur
sb	somebody (alguien)
Sch	school (escuela)
Scot	Scotland, Escocia
Seg	seguros (insurance)
Sew	sewing (costura)
sing	singular
Spec	specialist term (termino especializado)
sth	something (algo)
subj	subjunctive, subjuntivo
superl	superlative, superlativo
Taur	tauromaquia (bullfighting)
Teat	teatro (theatre)
Tech, Téc	technology, técnica
Tel	telecommunications, telecomunicaciones
Ten	tennis, tenis
Tex	textiles, textil
Theat	theatre (teatro)
Tip	tipografía (typography)
Tricot	tricotar (knitting)
TV	television, televisión
Typ	typography (tipografía)
Univ	university, universidad
Urug	Uruguay
US	United States, Estados Unidos
usu	usually, usualmente
v	verb, verbo
Ven	Venezuela
vi	intransitive verb, verbo intransitivo
vpr	verbo pronominal (reflexive verb)
vt	transitive verb, verbo transitivo
Vulg	vulgar
Zool	zoology, zoología

All other labels are written in full

Spanish Pronunciation Guide

The pronunciation of most Spanish words is predictable as there is a close match between spelling and pronunciation. The table below gives an explanation of that pronunciation. In the dictionary text therefore, pronunciation is only given when the word does not follow these rules, usually because it is a word of foreign origin. In these cases, the IPA (International Phonetic Alphabet) is used (see column 2 of the table below).

Letter in Spanish	IPA Symbol	Example in Spanish	Pronunciation (example in English)
Vowels			
Note that all vowel sounds in Spanish are shorter than in English			
a	a	**a**la	Similar to the sound in "f**a**ther" but more central
e	e	**e**có	Similar to the sound in "m**e**t"
i	i	**i**r**i**s	Like the vowel sound in "m**ea**t" but much shorter
o	o	**o**s**o**	Like the start of "**o**we" without the 'w' sound at the end
u	u	**u**va	Like the vowel sound in "s**oo**n" but much shorter
Semiconsonants			
"i" in the diphthongs: ia, ie, io, iu	j	h**i**ato, h**i**elo, av**i**ón, v**i**uda	**y**es
"u" in the diphthongs: ua, ue, ui, uo	w	s**u**ave, f**u**ego, h**u**ida	**w**in
Consonants			
b	b	**b**om**b**a (at beginning of word or after m)	**b**oom
	β	a**b**ajo (all other contexts)	A "**b**" pronounced without quite closing the lips completely
c	θ (in Spain)	**c**eña (before e) **c**inco (before i)	**th**anks (in Spain)
	s (in Latin America and southern Spain)		**s**un (in Latin America and southern Spain)
	k	**c**asa (all other contexts)	**c**at
ch	tʃ	cau**ch**o	ar**ch**

Letter in Spanish	IPA Symbol	Example in Spanish	Pronunciation (example in English)
d	d	**d**on**d**e (at beginning of word or after n) al**d**ea (after l)	**d**ay
	ð	a**d**orno (all other contexts)	Similar to the sound in "mo**th**er" but less strong
f	f	**f**uria	**f**ire
g	χ	**g**ema (before e) **g**irasol (before i)	Like an "**h**" but pronounced at the back of the throat (similar to Scottish "lo**ch**")
	g	**g**ato (at beginning of word) len**g**ua (after n)	**g**oose
	ɣ	a**g**ua (all other contexts)	Like a "**w**" pronounced while trying to say "**g**"
j	χ	**j**abalí	Like an "**h**" but pronounced at the back of the throat (similar to Scottish "lo**ch**")
l	l	**l**ado	**l**ake
ll	j	**ll**uvia	**y**es
	ʒ		In some regions (eg the Rio de la Plata area of South America) it is pronounced like the "**s**" in "plea**s**ure
m	m	**m**ano	**m**an
n	n	**n**ulo	**n**o
	ŋ	ma**n**co, fa**n**go (before c and g)	parki**ng**
ñ	ŋ	a**ñ**o	o**ni**on
p	p	**p**a**p**a	**p**ool
r	r	dora**d**o (in between vowels) habla**r** (at end of syllable or word)	A rolled "**r**" sound (similar to Scottish "**r**")
	rr	**r**osa (at beginning of word) al**r**ededor (after l) en**r**edo (after n)	A much longer rolled "**r**" sound (similar to Scottish "**r**")
rr	rr	a**rr**oyo	A much longer rolled "**r**" sound (similar to Scottish "**r**")
s	s	**s**aco	**s**ound
sh	ʃ	**sh**ow	**sh**ow
t	t	**t**ela	**t**ea

Letter in Spanish	IPA Symbol	Example in Spanish	Pronunciation (example in English)
v	b	in**v**ierno (after "n")	**b**oom
	β	a**v**e (all other contexts)	A "**b**" pronounced without quite closing the lips completely
x	ks	e**x**amen	e**x**tra
y	j	a**y**er	**y**es
	ʒ		In some regions (eg the Rio de la Plata area of South America) it is pronounced like the "**s**" in "plea**s**ure"
z	θ (in Spain)	**z**apato	**th**anks (in Spain)
	s (in Latin America and southern Spain)		**s**un (in Latin America and southern Spain)

Pronunciación del Inglés

Para ilustrar la pronunciación inglesa, en este diccionario utilizamos los símbolos del AFI (Alfabeto Fonético Internacional). En el siguiente cuadro, para cada sonido del inglés hay ejemplos de palabras en inglés y palabras en español donde aparece un sonido similar. En los casos en los que no hay sonido similar en español, ofrecemos una explicación de cómo pronunciar.

Carácter AFI	Ejemplo en inglés	Ejemplo en español
Consonantes		
[b]	**b**a**bb**le	**b**e**b**é
[d]	**d**ig	**d**e**d**o
[dʒ]	**g**iant, **j**ig	se pronuncia como "**ll**" en el Río de la Plata pero con una "**d**" adelante, o como "**gi**" en italiano - **Gi**ovanna
[f]	**f**it, **ph**ysics	**f**aro
[g]	**g**rey, bi**g**	**g**ris
[h]	**h**appy	"**h**" aspirada
[j]	**y**ellow	se pronuncia como "**y**" o "**ll**" en España - **y**o, **ll**uvia
[k]	**c**lay, **k**i**ck**	**c**a**s**a
[l]	**l**ip	**l**abio
	pi**ll**	pape**l**
[m]	**m**u**mm**y	**m**a**m**á
[n]	**n**ip, pi**n**	**n**ada
[ŋ]	si**ng**	se pronuncia como "**n**" antes de "**c**" - ba**n**co
[p]	**p**i**p**	**p**a**p**á
[r]	**r**ig, w**r**ite	sonido entre "**r**" y "**rr**"
[s]	**s**ick, **sc**ience	**s**apo
[ʃ]	**sh**ip, na**ti**on	**sh**ow
[t]	**t**ip, bu**tt**	**t**ela
[tʃ]	**ch**ip, ba**tch**	cau**ch**o
[θ]	**th**ick	**z**apato (como se pronuncia en España)
[ð]	**th**is	se pronuncia como la "**d**" de "ha**d**a" pero más fuerte
[v]	**v**ague, gi**v**e	se pronuncia como "**v**" de **v**ida, con los dientes apoyados sobre el labio inferior
[w]	**w**it, **w**hy	**wh**isky
[z]	**z**ip, phy**s**ics	"**s**" con sonido zumbante
[ʒ]	plea**s**ure	se pronuncia como "**y**" o "**ll**" en el Río de la Plata - **y**o, **ll**uvia
[χ]	lo**ch**	**j**ota

Carácter AFI	Ejemplo en inglés	Ejemplo en español
Vocales		
En inglés, las vocales marcadas con dos puntos son mucho más alargadas		
[æ]	ra**g**	se pronuncia "**e**" con posición bucal para "**a**"
[ɑ:]	la**rge**	"**a**" muy alargada
[ʌ]	c**u**p	"**a**" breve y cerrada
[e]	s**e**t	se pronuncia como "**e**" de **e**lef**a**nte pero más corta
[ɜ:]	c**ur**tain, w**e**re	se pronuncia como una "**e**" larga con posición bucal entre "**o**" y "**e**"
[ə]	utt**er**	se pronuncia como "**e**" con posición bucal para "**o**"
[ɪ]	b**i**g, w**o**men	"**i**" breve, a medio camino entre "**e**" e "**i**"
[i:]	l**ea**k, w**ee**	"**i**" muy alargada
[ɒ]	l**o**ck	"**o**" abierta
[ɔ:]	w**a**ll, c**o**rk	"**o**" cerrada y alargada
[ʊ]	p**u**t, l**oo**k	"**u**" breve
[u:]	m**oo**n	"**u**" muy alargada
Diptongos		
[aɪ]	wh**y**, h**igh**, l**ie**	**ai**re
[aʊ]	h**ow**	**au**ra
[eə]	b**ear**	"**ea**" pronunciado muy brevemente y con sonido de "**e**" más marcado que el de "**a**"
[eɪ]	d**ay**, m**a**ke, m**ai**n	r**ei**na
[əʊ]	sh**ow**, g**o**	"**ou**" como en COU
[ɪə]	h**ere**, g**ear**	h**ie**lo pronunciado con el sonido de "**i**" más marcado y alargado que el de "**e**"
[ɔɪ]	b**oy**, s**oi**l	v**oy**
[ʊə]	p**oor**	c**ue**rno pronunciado con el sonido de "**u**" más marcado y alargado que el de "**e**"

English-Spanish
Inglés-Español

A

A, a [eɪ] *n* (**a**) *(the letter)* A, a *f*; **a for ace** a de as; *Fig* **from A to Z** de principio a fin (**b**) *Mus* la *m*

A *(abbr* **ampère)** amperio *m*, A

a [eɪ, *unstressed* ə] *indef art (before vowel or silent h* **an**) (**a**) *(in general)* un, una; **a man/a woman** un hombre/una mujer; **an idea** una idea; **a woman has to be strong** las mujeres tienen que ser fuertes; **I didn't understand a word** no entendí ni jota; **he has a big nose** tiene la nariz grande (**b**) *(omitted in Spanish)* **half a litre/an hour** medio litro/media hora; **Bangor, a city in Wales** Bangor, ciudad de Gales; **let's have a drink/a snack** vamos a beber/comer algo; **he's a doctor** es médico; **many a time** muchas veces; **she got in without an invitation** entró sin invitación; **what a coincidence!** ¡qué casualidad!; **what a day!** ¡vaya día!; **what a pity** qué pena *or* lástima (**c**) *(each)* **60 pence a kilo** 60 peniques el kilo; **to eat grapes two at a time** comer las uvas de dos en dos; **three times a week** tres veces a la *or* por semana (**d**) *(a certain)* un/una tal; **a Mr Rees phoned** llamó un tal Sr. Rees; **in a sense** hasta cierto punto

AA [eɪˈeɪ] *n* (**a**) *(abbr* **Alcoholics Anonymous)** Alcohólicos *mpl* Anónimos, AA (**b**) *(abbr* **Automobile Association)** = asociación automovilística británica, *Esp* ≃ RACE *m*, *Arg* ≃ ACA *m*

AAA [eɪeɪˈeɪ] *n* (**a**) *Br (abbr* **Amateur Athletic Association)** Asociación *f* Atlética Amateur, AAA (**b**) *(abbr* **American Automobile Association)** = asociación automovilística estadounidense, *Esp* ≃ RACE *m*, *Arg* ≃ ACA *m*

aardvark [ˈɑːdvɑːk] *n* cerdo *m* hormiguero

AB [eɪˈbiː] *n* (**a**) *Br (abbr* **able-bodied (seaman))** marinero *m* de primera (**b**) *US (abbr* **artium baccalaureus)** Licenciado(a) *m,f* en Filosofía y Letras, Lic en Fil y Let

aback [əˈbæk] *adv* **to be taken a.** sorprenderse; *Fam* quedarse de una pieza (**by** por)

abacus [ˈæbəkəs] *n (pl* **abacuses** *or* **abaci** [ˈæbəsaɪ]) ábaco *m*

abandon [əˈbændən] **1** *n* desenfreno *m*; **with reckless a.** desenfrenadamente
2 *vt (child, family)* abandonar; *(job)* dejar; *(project)* renunciar a; **the match was abandoned because of rain** se suspendió el partido a causa de la lluvia; **to a. ship** abandonar el barco

abase [əˈbeɪs] *vt* humillar, degradar; **to a. oneself** humillarse, degradarse

abashed [əˈbæʃt] *adj* desconcertado(a), confuso(a)

abate [əˈbeɪt] *vi (anger)* apaciguarse; *(flood)* decrecer; *(storm, wind)* amainar

abatement [əˈbeɪtmənt] *n* reducción *f*, supresión *f*; **noise a. campaign** campaña *f* contra el ruido (en el medio ambiente)

abattoir [ˈæbətwɑːr] *n* matadero *m*

abbess [ˈæbɪs] *n* abadesa *f*

abbey [ˈæbɪ] *n* abadía *f*

abbot [ˈæbət] *n* abad *m*

abbreviate [əˈbriːvɪeɪt] *vt* abreviar

abbreviation [əbriːvɪˈeɪʃən] *n* abreviatura *f*

ABC¹ [eɪbiːˈsiː] *n* abecé *m*, abecedario *m*, alfabeto *m*; **an ABC of hotels** una guía completa de hoteles

ABC² [eɪbiːˈsiː] *n* (**a**) *(abbr* **American Broadcasting Company)** = compañía americana de radiodifusión, ABC (**b**) *(abbr* **Australian Broadcasting Commission)** = comisión australiana de radiofusión, ABC

abdicate [ˈæbdɪkeɪt] **1** *vt (throne)* abdicar; *(right, responsibility)* renunciar; **he abdicated in favour of his son** abdicó en su hijo
2 *vi (monarch)* abdicar

abdication [æbdɪˈkeɪʃən] *n (of throne by monarch)* abdicación *f*; *(of right, responsibility)* renunciación *f*

abdomen [ˈæbdəmən] *n* abdomen *m*, vientre *m*

abdominal [æbˈdɒmɪnəl] *adj* abdominal, de vientre, ventral

abduct [æbˈdʌkt] *vt* raptar, secuestrar

abduction [æbˈdʌkʃən] *n* rapto *m*, secuestro *m*

abductor [æbˈdʌktər] *n* secuestrador(a) *m,f*

aberrant [æˈberənt] *adj (behaviour)* anormal; *(example, specimen)* aberrante

aberration [æbəˈreɪʃən] *n* aberración *f*, defecto *m*; **mental a.** desvarío *m*

abet [əˈbet] *vt Jur* **to aid and a. sb** ser cómplice de algn

abeyance [əˈbeɪəns] *n* desuso *m*; **to be in/fall into a.** estar en/caer en desuso

abhor [əbˈhɔːr] *vt (pt & pp* **abhorred)** aborrecer, detestar

abhorrence [əbˈhɒrəns] *n* aborrecimiento *m*; **to have an a. of sth** aborrecer algo

abhorrent [əbˈhɒrənt] *adj* aborrecible, odioso(a); **it is a. to me** lo aborrezco

abide [əˈbaɪd] *vt (pt & pp* **abode** *or* **abided)** *(tolerate)* tolerar, aguantar; **I can't a. him** no le puedo ver, me cae muy mal; **I can't a. it** no lo aguanto

abide by *vt (promise)* cumplir con; *(rules)* atenerse a

abiding [əˈbaɪdɪŋ] *adj (interest, impression)* duradero(a); **my a. memory of Spain is ...** mi recuerdo más destacado de España es ...

ability [əˈbɪlɪtɪ] *n (capability)* capacidad *f*, aptitud *f*; *(talent)* talento *m*, dotes *fpl*; **a pupil of great a.** un alumno de grandes dotes; **she did it to the best of her a.** lo hizo lo mejor que pudo; **to have the a. to do sth** tener (la) capacidad para hacer algo

abject ['æbdʒekt] adj (state) miserable; (apology) rastrero(a); **a. poverty** miseria f

ablaze [ə'bleɪz] adj & adv en llamas, ardiendo; **to be a.** arder; Fig **a. with light** resplandeciente de luz

able ['eɪbəl] adj (person) (capable) capaz; (piece of work) (satisfactory) bien hecho(a); **is he a. to swim ten miles?** ¿es capaz de nadar diez millas?; **will you be a. to come on Tuesday?** ¿podrás venir el martes?

able-bodied [eɪbəl'bɒdɪd] adj sano(a), robusto(a) ❑ **a.-b. seaman** marinero m de primera

ablutions [ə'blu:ʃənz] npl Fml & Hum **to perform one's a.** lavarse

ABM [eɪbiː'em] n (abbr **anti-ballistic missile**) misil m antibalístico

abnormal [æb'nɔ:məl] adj anormal

abnormality [æbnɔ:'mælɪtɪ] n anormalidad f; Biol anomalía f; Med deformidad f

abnormally [æb'nɔ:məlɪ] adv anormalmente; **a. large/quiet** excepcionalmente grande/tranquilo

aboard [ə'bɔ:d] **1** adv a bordo; **to go a.** (ship) embarcarse, subir a bordo; (train) subir; **all aboard!** (ship) ¡pasajeros a bordo!; (train) ¡viajeros al tren!
2 prep a bordo de; **a. ship** a bordo del barco, en barco; **a. the train** en el tren

abode [ə'bəʊd] **1** pt & pp see **abide**
2 n **of no fixed a.** sin domicilio fijo

abolish [ə'bɒlɪʃ] vt (law, custom, distinction) abolir, suprimir; (slavery, death penalty) abolir

abolition [æbə'lɪʃən] n (of law, custom, distinction) abolición f, supresión f; (of slavery, death penalty) abolición f

abominable [ə'bɒmɪnəbəl] adj deplorable, abominable; **the A. Snowman** el abominable hombre de las nieves

abominably [ə'bɒmɪnəblɪ] adv abominablemente; **a. rude** terriblemente grosero(a) (**towards** hacia)

abomination [əbɒmɪ'neɪʃən] n abominación f; **it's an a.** es un escándalo

aboriginal [æbə'rɪdʒɪnəl] adj aborigen

aborigine [æbə'rɪdʒɪnɪ] n aborigen mf australiano(a)

abort [ə'bɔ:t] **1** vt Med (foetus) hacer abortar; Fig (plan etc) archivar, cancelar; Comptr cancelar
2 vi Med abortar

abortion [ə'bɔ:ʃən] n Med aborto m; **a. law** ley f del aborto; **to have an a.** abortar

abortionist [ə'bɔ:ʃənɪst] n abortista mf

abortive [ə'bɔ:tɪv] adj Fig (attempt, plan etc) fracasado(a)

abound [ə'baʊnd] vi **to a. in** or **with** abundar en

about [ə'baʊt] adv & prep **(a)** (concerning) acerca de, sobre; **a book a. Keats** un libro sobre Keats; **I've come a. the washing machine** vengo por lo de la lavadora; **to be worried a. sth** estar preocupado(a) por algo; **to enquire a. sth** preguntar por algo; **to speak a. sth** hablar de algo; **tell me all a. it** cuéntamelo todo; **what's it all a.?** (what's happening?) ¿qué pasa?; (what does it mean?) ¿qué quiere decir?; (story, play etc) ¿de qué (se) trata?; **what a. it?** (what do you think?) ¿qué te parece?; (so what?) ¿y qué?; **you know all a. it** ya estás muy enterado(a); Fam **how a. a game of tennis?** ¿qué te parece un partido de tenis?; Fam **how a. a cup of coffee?** ¿quieres un café?, ¿te Esp apetece or Carib Col Méx provoca un café? **(b)** (around) por todas partes, de un lado para otro; **don't leave things lying a.** no dejes las cosas por ahí; **he's somewhere a.** está aquí por algún lado; **there are a lot of crazy people a.** anda mucha gente loca suelta; **there's a lot of violence a.** hoy en día hay mucha violencia; **there's nobody a.** no hay nadie; **to be up and a.** estar levantado(a); (after illness) hacer vida normal; **to look a.** mirar a su alrededor; **to rush a.** correr de un lado para otro; **we went for a walk a. the town** dimos una vuelta por el pueblo; Fam **bring me a cup of tea while you're a. it** y traeme un té, de paso **(c)** (approximately) más o menos, casi, a eso de; **it's a. 3 o'clock** son más o menos las 3; **it's a. time you got up** ya es hora de que te levantes; **it's just a. finished** está casi terminado; **on or a. the 5th of May** hacia el día 5 de mayo; **she's a. 40** tendrá unos 40 años; Iron **a. time too!** ¡a buenas horas! **(d)** Mil **a turn!** ¡media vuelta! **(e)** (just ready) **I'm a. to do it now** lo voy a hacer ahora; **it's a. to start** está a punto de empezar; **they'll be just a. arriving** estarán al llegar **(f)** **to go a. (doing) sth** hacer algo; **how do you go a. opening a bank account?** ¿qué hay que hacer para abrir una cuenta bancaria?

about-face [əbaʊt'feɪs], Br **about-turn** [əbaʊt'tɜ:n] **1** n media vuelta f; **to do an a.-f.** hacer media vuelta; Fig cambiar de idea por completo
2 vi Mil dar media vuelta; Fig (change opinion) cambiar de idea por completo

above [ə'bʌv] adv & prep **(a)** (higher, higher than) encima de, sobre, arriba; **a voice from a.** una voz desde lo alto; **his voice was heard a. the noise** se oyó su voz por encima del ruido or a pesar de tanto ruido; **100 metres a. sea level** 100 metros sobre el nivel del mar; **it's a. the door** está encima de la puerta; **the flat a.** el piso de arriba; **the River Miño a. Orense** el río Miño antes de pasar por Orense; **the shelf a. the sink** el estante de encima del fregadero; **the town seen from a.** el pueblo visto desde arriba or a vista de pájaro **(b)** (greater, greater than) superior (a); **amounts a. $10** cantidades superiores a los 10 dólares; **tickets numbered 200 and a.** entradas a partir del número 200; **to be a. sb in rank/status** estar por encima de algn en rango/jerarquía; Fig **a policy imposed from a.** una política impuesta desde arriba **(c)** Fig (beyond) **a. all** sobre todo, encima de todo; **a. reproach** intachable; **he's not a. stealing** es capaz incluso de robar; **she's a. all that** está muy encima de todo esto; **it's a. me** está por encima de mis posibilidades, es demasiado difícil para mí **(d)** (in book etc) más arriba; **see paragraph 6 a.** véase el párrafo 6 más arriba

above-board [ə'bʌvbɔ:d] adj (scheme) legítimo(a); (person) honesto(a)

above-mentioned [ə'bʌvmenʃənd] adj arriba citado(a), susodicho(a)

Abp (abbr **Archbishop**) Arzobispo m

abrasion [ə'breɪʒən] n abrasión f

abrasive [ə'breɪsɪv] **1** adj (substance) abrasivo(a); Fig (voice, wit, etc) cáustico(a)
2 n abrasivo m

abreast [ə'brest] adv **to walk 3 abreast** ir de 3 en fondo; Fig **to keep a. of things** mantenerse al día, estar al tanto de las cosas

abridged [ə'brɪdʒd] adj (book) abreviado(a), resumido(a)

abroad [ə'brɔ:d] adv **(a)** (foreign places) en el or al extranjero; **to be a.** estar en el extranjero; **to go a.** irse al extranjero; **to live a.** vivir en el extranjero **(b)** (extensively) **the news spread a.** la noticia se divulgó rápidamente; **there's a rumour a. that ...** corre el rumor que ...

abrupt [ə'brʌpt] adj (manner) brusco(a); (tone, voice) áspero(a); (change, stop) repentino(a), súbito(a)

abruptly [ə'brʌptlɪ] adv (act) bruscamente; (speak) con aspereza; (change, stop) repentinamente

ABS [eɪbiː'es] n Aut (abbr **antilock braking system**) ABS m

abscess ['æbses] n (general) absceso m; (on gum) flemón m

abscond [əb'skɒnd] vi huir, fugarse; **he absconded with the money** se fugó con el dinero

abseil ['æbseɪl] *vi* hacer rappel; **to a. down sth** bajar algo haciendo rappel

abseiling ['æbseɪlɪŋ] *n* rappel *m*; **to go a.** ir a hacer rappel

absence ['æbsəns] *n (of person)* ausencia *f; (of thing)* falta *f; Jur* **she was sentenced in her a.** fue juzgada en rebeldía; **in the a. of any details …** a falta de datos …; *Fig* **a. of mind** distracción *f*

absent ['æbsənt] **1** *adj* ausente; *Mil* **a. without leave** ausente sin permiso; **to be a. from school** faltar a clase; *Fig* **an a. look** una mirada distraída
   2 [æb'sent] *vt* **to a. oneself** ausentarse

absentee [æbsən'tiː] *n* ausente *mf* □ **a. landlord** *Esp* absentista *m,f, Am* ausentista *m,f*

absenteeism [æbsən'tiːɪzəm] *n Esp* absentismo *m, Am* ausentismo *m*

absently ['æbsəntlɪ] *adv (distractedly)* distraídamente

absent-minded [æbsənt'maɪndɪd] *adj* distraído(a), despistado(a)

absent-mindedness [æbsənt'maɪndɪdnɪs] *n* distracción *f*, despiste *m*

absolute ['æbsəluːt] *adj (majority, power)* absoluto(a); *(certain)* completo(a); *(confidence, failure)* total; *(truth)* puro(a); *(proof)* incontrovertible; **it's an a. disgrace** es una auténtica vergüenza

absolutely [æbsə'luːtlɪ] **1** *adv (completely)* completamente, totalmente; **a. wrong** totalmente equivocado(a); **a. not** en absoluto; **you're a. right** tienes toda la razón
   2 *interj* **a.!** ¡desde luego!, ¡claro!, ¡por supuesto!

absolution [æbsə'luːʃən] *n Rel* absolución *f*

absolve [əb'zɒlv] *vt* absolver (**from** de)

absorb [əb'zɔːb] *vt (liquid, costs)* absorber; *(heat, sound, blow)* amortiguar; *(energy, time)* ocupar; *Fig* **to be absorbed in sth** estar absorto(a) en algo

absorbent [əb'zɔːbənt] *adj* absorbente; *US* **a. cotton** algodón *m* hidrófilo

absorbing [əb'zɔːbɪŋ] *adj (book, work)* absorbente; **it's an a. hobby** es un pasatiempo que distrae mucho

abstain [əb'steɪn] *vi* abstenerse (**from** de)

abstainer [əb'steɪnər] *n* abstemio(a) *m,f*

abstemious [əb'stiːmɪəs] *adj* abstemio(a), sobrio(a)

abstention [əb'stenʃən] *n* abstención *f*

abstinence ['æbstɪnəns] *n* abstinencia *f*

abstract ['æbstrækt] **1** *adj* abstracto(a); **an a. painting** una pintura de estilo abstracto
   2 *n (of thesis etc)* resumen *m; (painting)* abstracto *m;* **to talk in the a.** hablar en términos abstractos
   3 [æb'strækt] *vt (summarize)* abstraer; *Euph (steal)* sustraer

abstraction [æb'strækʃən] *n* abstracción *f*

abstruse [əb'struːs] *adj* abstruso(a), embrollado(a)

absurd [əb'sɜːd] *adj* absurdo(a); **it's a.!** ¡qué disparate!; **don't be a.!** ¡no seas ridículo(a)!

absurdity [əb'sɜːdɪtɪ] *n* disparate *m*, locura *f*

abundance [ə'bʌndəns] *n* abundancia *f;* **in a.** en abundancia, abundantemente

abundant [ə'bʌndənt] *adj* abundante, rico(a) (**in** en)

abundantly [ə'bʌndəntlɪ] *adv* abundantemente, en abundancia; **it's a. clear** está clarísimo, es evidente; **she made it a. clear to me that she was offended** me constató claramente que se sentía ofendida

abuse **1** [ə'bjuːs] *n* **(a)** *(ill-treatment)* malos tratos *mpl; (misuse) (of power, confidence)* abuso *m* **(b)** *(insults)* insultos *mpl*, improperios *mpl*, injurias *fpl;* **to shower a. on sb** colmar a algn de insultos *or* injurias
   2 [ə'bjuːz] *vt* **(a)** *(ill-treat)* maltratar; *(misuse)* abusar de **(b)** *(insult)* insultar, injuriar

abuser [ə'bjuːzər] *n* **(a)** *(misuser)* **alcohol a.** alcohólico(a) *m,f;* **drug a.** drogodependiente *mf* **(b)** *(of child)* pederasta *m*

abusive [əb'juːsɪv] *adj (insulting)* insultante, grosero(a), ofensivo(a); **to use a. language** decir groserías *or* injurias

abysmal [ə'bɪzməl] *adj (poverty, conditions)* extremo(a); *Fam (very bad) (weather, film, food etc)* fatal, pésimo(a)

abyss [ə'bɪs] *n* abismo *m; Fig* **to be on the edge of the a.** estar *or* encontrarse al borde del abismo

Abyssinia [æbɪ'sɪnɪə] *n Formerly* Abisinia

Abyssinian [æbɪ'sɪnɪən] *adj & n Formerly* abisinio(a) *(m,f)*

AC ['eɪsiː] *Elec (abbr* **alternating current)** corriente *f* alterna

a/c *Fin (abbr* **account)** cuenta *f*, cta.

acacia [ə'keɪʃə] *n Bot* acacia *f* □ **false a.** acacia *f* falsa, robinia *f*

academic [ækə'demɪk] **1** *adj Educ* académico(a), escolar; *(career)* universitario(a); *(question, discussion)* teórico(a); **a. year** año escolar
   2 *n* académico(a) *m,f*, profesor(a) *m,f* de universidad

academy [ə'kædəmɪ] *n (society)* academia *f; Scot Educ* instituto *m* de enseñanza media; **Royal A. (of Arts)** Real Academia (de Bellas Artes) □ **military a.** escuela *f* militar; **a. of music** conservatorio *m*

accede [æk'siːd] *vi (throne)* acceder (**to** a); *(petition, request)* consentir (**to** en), acceder (**to** a)

accelerate [æk'seləreɪt] **1** *vt (engine)* acelerar; *(step)* apretar, apresurar
   2 *vi (car, engine)* acelerar

acceleration [ækselə'reɪʃən] *n Aut* aceleración *f*

accelerator [æk'seləreɪtər] *n Aut* acelerador *m*

accent ['æksənt] *n* acento *m;* **he has a Scottish a.** tiene acento escocés; *Fig* **fashion with the a. on comfort** la moda con especial atención al confort

accentuate [æk'sentʃʊeɪt] *vt (word)* acentuar; *(difference etc)* subrayar

accept [ək'sept] **1** *vt (cheque, gift, invitation)* aceptar; *(theory)* admitir, aprobar; *(person)* aceptar, acoger; **do you a. that …?** ¿estás de acuerdo en que …?; **it's the accepted thing** es la norma, es lo normal; **to a. defeat** admitir la derrota
   2 *vi* aceptar

acceptable [ək'septəbəl] *adj (satisfactory)* aceptable; *(tolerable)* admisible; *(welcome)* grato(a); **that isn't (socially) a.** eso no se hace *or* no se admite (entre gente educada)

acceptance [ək'septəns] *n (act of accepting)* aceptación *f*, admisión *f; (good reception)* aprobación *f*, acogida *f;* **a. speech** discurso *m* de agradecimiento *(al recibir un premio)*

access ['ækses] *n* acceso *m;* **a. road** carretera *f or* camino *m* de acceso; **to have/gain a. to sth** tener/conseguir libre acceso a algo; *Comptr* **a. code** código *m* de acceso

accessibility [əksesə'bɪlɪtɪ] *n* accesibilidad *f*

accessible [ək'sesəbəl] *adj (place, position)* accesible; *(person)* asequible

accession [ək'seʃən] *n* **(a)** *(of monarch)* subida *f* (al trono) **(b)** *(acquisition) (in library etc)* adquisición *f*

accessorize [ək'sesəraɪz] *vt* complementar

accessory [ək'sesərɪ] *n* **(a)** *Jur* cómplice *mf;* **a. before/after the fact** cómplice instigador/encubridor **(b) accessories** accesorios *mpl; (for outfit)* complementos *mpl*

accident ['æksɪdənt] *n (misadventure)* accidente *m;* **to have an a.** tener *or* sufrir un accidente; **it was an a. on my part** lo hice sin querer □ **car a.** accidente *m* de carretera; **industrial a.** accidente laboral; **road a.** accidente *m* de carretera **(b)** *(coincidence)* casualidad *f;* **by a.** por casualidad; **it was quite by a.** fue una pura casualidad

accidental [æksɪ'dentəl] *adj (by chance)* fortuito(a); *(unexpected)* imprevisto(a)

accidentally [æksɪ'dentəlɪ] *adv (by chance)* por casualidad; **he did it a.** *(unintentionally)* lo hizo sin querer

accident-prone ['æksɪdəntprəʊn] *adj* propenso(a) a los accidentes

acclaim [ə'kleɪm] **1** *n* aclamación *f*
2 *vt* aclamar

acclamation [æklə'meɪʃən] *n* aclamación *f*, alabanza *f*

acclimate [ə'klaɪmət] *vt US see* **acclimatize**

acclimated ['æklɪmeɪtɪd] *adj US see* **acclimatized**

acclimation [æklɪ'meɪʃən] *n US see* **acclimatization**

acclimatization [əklaɪmətaɪ'zeɪʃən] *n* aclimatación *f*

acclimatize [ə'klaɪmətaɪz] *vt* aclimatar; **to a. oneself** aclimatarse

acclimatized [ə'klaɪmətaɪzd] *adj* aclimatado(a); **to become a.** aclimatarse

accolade ['ækəleɪd] *n* elogio *m*

accommodate [ə'kɒmədeɪt] *vt* **(a)** *(guests etc)* alojar, hospedar; **the hotel can a. 100 guests** el hotel tiene capacidad para cien huéspedes **(b)** *(satisfy, provide for)* **to a. sb's wishes** complacer a algn; **whatever you need, we try to a. you** procuramos facilitarle cualquier cosa que necesite **(c)** *(adapt)* **to a. oneself to a new situation** amoldarse *or* adaptarse a una nueva situación

accommodating [ə'kɒmədeɪtɪŋ] *adj (obliging)* complaciente; *(understanding)* comprensivo(a)

accommodation [əkɒmə'deɪʃən] *n* **(a)** *(lodgings)* alojamiento *m*; *(space)* sitio *m*; **do you have any a. for tonight?** ¿tiene *or* quedan habitaciones libres para esta noche?; **overnight a.** camas *fpl*; **we don't have the a. for so many people** no tenemos sitio para tanta gente **(b)** *(agreement)* acuerdo *m*; **to reach an a.** llegar a un acuerdo sobre algo **(c)** *US* **accommodations** *(lodgings)* alojamiento *m*

accompaniment [ə'kʌmpənɪmənt] *n* acompañamiento *m*

accompanist [ə'kʌmpənɪst] *n Mus* acompañante *mf*

accompany [ə'kʌmpənɪ] *vt* acompañar; **to be accompanied by sb** ir acompañado de algn; *Mus* **to a. sb on the piano** acompañar a algn al piano

accompanying [ə'kʌmpənɪŋ] *adj* **the a. documents** los documentos adjuntos

accomplice [ə'kʌmplɪs] *n* cómplice *mf*

accomplish [ə'kʌmplɪʃ] *vt (aim)* conseguir, lograr, realizar; *(task, mission)* llevar a cabo; **what have you accomplished?** ¿qué has conseguido?

accomplished [ə'kʌmplɪʃt] *adj (musician)* dotado(a), experto(a)

accomplishment [ə'kʌmplɪʃmənt] *n* **(a)** *(fulfilment) (of task)* realización *f*; *(of duty)* cumplimiento *m* **(b)** **accomplishments** *(talents)* talentos *mpl*, dotes *fpl*

accord [ə'kɔːd] **1** *n (agreement)* acuerdo *m*; **of her *or* his own a.** espontáneamente, voluntariamente; **with one a.** de común acuerdo, de una voz
2 *vt (honour, permission)* conceder
3 *vi (agree)* concordar (**with** con)

accordance [ə'kɔːdəns] *n* **in a. with** de acuerdo con, conforme a

according [ə'kɔːdɪŋ] *prep* **a. to** según; **a. to instructions** con arreglo a las instrucciones; **a. to them** según ellos; **everything went a. to plan** todo salió conforme a los planes; **lined up a. to age** alienados por edades

accordingly [ə'kɔːdɪŋlɪ] *adv* **(a)** *(appropriately)* en consecuencia; **to act a.** obrar según y conforme **(b)**

(therefore) así pues, por consiguiente; **a. I rang her** así pues, la llamé

accordion [ə'kɔːdɪən] *n Mus* acordeón *m*

accost [ə'kɒst] *vt (person)* abordar

account [ə'kaʊnt] *n* **(a)** *(report)* informe *m*; **by all accounts** al decir de todos; **to bring *or* call sb to a.** pedirle cuentas a algn; **to give sb an a. of sth** informar a algn de algo **(b)** *(importance)* importancia *f*; *(consideration)* consideración *f*; *(advantage)* provecho *m*; **I was fearful on her a.** sufría por ella; **it's of no a.** no tiene importancia; **on a. of** a causa de; **on no a.** bajo ningún concepto; **to take a. of sth, take sth into a.** tener algo en cuenta; **to turn sth to good a.** sacar provecho de *or* aprovechar algo **(c)** *Com* cuenta *f*; **to keep the accounts** llevar las cuentas *or* la contabilidad; **to open/close an a.** abrir/cancelar una cuenta; *Fig* **to settle accounts with sb** ajustar cuentas con algn ▫ **a. number** número *m* de cuenta; **bank a.** cuenta *f* bancaria; **charge a.** cuenta *f* abierta; **current/deposit a.** cuenta *f* corriente/de ahorros; **joint a.** cuenta *f* indistinta

account for *vt (explain)* explicar, dar cuentas de; **everyone has been accounted for** no falta nadie; **I can't a. for it** no me lo explico; **there's no accounting for tastes** sobre gustos no hay nada escrito

accountability [ə'kaʊntəbɪlɪtɪ] *n* responsabilidad *f*

accountable [ə'kaʊntəbəl] *adj* **to be a. to sb for sth** ser responsable ante algn de algo; **I'm not a. to them** no tengo por qué darles explicaciones a ellos

accountancy [ə'kaʊntənsɪ] *n* contabilidad *f*

accountant [ə'kaʊntənt] *n Esp* contable *mf*, *Am* contador(a) *m,f*; **chartered a.** *Esp* censor(a) *m,f* jurado(a) de cuentas, *Am* contador(a) *m,f* público(a)

accounting [ə'kaʊntɪŋ] *n* contabilidad *f*; **a. period** período *m* contable

accreditation [əkredɪ'teɪʃən] *n* **(a)** *(credentials) (for ambassador, envoy)* credencial *f*, acreditación *f* **(b)** *(recognition) (for school, course)* reconocimiento *m*, homologación *f*

accredited [ə'kredɪtɪd] *adj* acreditado(a), autorizado(a)

accrue [ə'kruː] *vi (interest)* acumularse; **interest will a. at a rate of 10 per cent** le corresponderá un interés del 10 por ciento

acct *Fin (abbr* **account)** cuenta *f*, cta.

accumulate [ə'kjuːmjʊleɪt] **1** *vt* acumular
2 *vi* acumularse

accumulation [əkjuːmjʊ'leɪʃən] *n* acumulación *f*, amontonamiento *m*; **an a. of things** un montón de cosas

accuracy ['ækjʊrəsɪ] *n (of figure, number, instrument)* exactitud *f*, precisión *f*; *(of shot, criticism)* certeza *f*; *(of translation)* fidelidad *f*

accurate ['ækjʊrɪt] *adj (figure, number)* exacto(a), preciso(a); *(shot, criticism)* certero(a); *(answer)* correcto(a); *(comment, observation)* acertado(a); *(instrument, watch)* de precisión; *(translation)* fiel

accurately ['ækjʊrətlɪ] *adv (calculate, measure, remember)* exactamente; *(translate)* fielmente

accusation [ækjʊ'zeɪʃən] *n* acusación *f*

accusative [ə'kjuːzətɪv] *adj & n* acusativo *(m)*

accuse [ə'kjuːz] *vt* acusar; **they accused Peter of stealing the money** acusaron a Peter de robar el dinero

accused [ə'kjuːzd] *n Jur* **the a.** *(man)* el acusado; *(woman)* la acusada

accuser [ə'kjuːzər] *n* acusador(a) *m,f*

accusing [ə'kjuːzɪŋ] *adj (look, tone)* acusador(a)

accusingly [ə'kjuːzɪŋlɪ] *adv* acusatoriamente, en un tono acusador

accustom [ə'kʌstəm] *vt* acostumbrar; **to a. sb to (doing) sth** acostumbrar a algn a (hacer) algo; **to be accustomed to doing sth** estar acostumbrado(a) a hacer algo; **to get accustomed to sth** acostumbrarse a algo

AC/DC ['eɪsi:'di:si:] *n* Elec (abbr **alternating current/ direct current**) corriente *f* alterna/continua

ace [eɪs] *n* (**a**) Cards 'as *m*; **a. of clubs/spades** as de tréboles/picas; **to play one's a.** jugar su mejor baza; Fig **to have an a. up one's sleeve** guardar un as en la manga (**b**) Fig as *m*; **he's an a. driver** es un as del volante (**c**) Ten (service) ace *m*

acerbic [ə'sɜːbɪk] *adj (wit)* acerbo(a), mordaz

acerbity [ə'sɜːbɪtɪ] *n (of wit)* acerbidad *f*

acetate ['æsɪteɪt] *n* acetato *m*

acetic acid [æ'si:tɪk'æsɪd] *n* ácido *m* acético

acetone ['æsɪtəʊn] *n* acetona *f*

ache [eɪk] **1** *n (pain)* dolor *m*; **aches and pains** achaques *mpl*
2 *vi (hurt)* doler; **it makes my head a.** me da dolor de cabeza; **my back aches** me duele la espalda; Fig **I was aching to tell them** ansiaba decírselo

achieve [ə'tʃiːv] *vt (attain)* conseguir, lograr, alcanzar; *(complete, accomplish)* llevar a cabo, realizar

achievement [ə'tʃiːvmənt] *n (attainment, success)* logro *m*; *(completion)* realización *f*; *(feat)* hazaña *f*, éxito *m*; **what an a.!** ¡vaya hazaña!

achiever [ə'tʃiːvər] *n* triunfador(a) *m,f*

aching ['eɪkɪŋ] *adj (head, limbs)* dolorido(a); **with an a. heart** con gran dolor

acid ['æsɪd] **1** *adj* Chem ácido(a), *(taste)* agrio(a); Fig (remark, wit) mordaz
2 *n* (**a**) Chem ácido *m* (**a**) **a. rain** lluvia *f* ácida; Fig **a. test** prueba *f* decisiva (**b**) *(drugs)* ácido *m*

acidic [ə'sɪdɪk] *adj* ácido(a)

acidity [ə'sɪdɪtɪ] *n (of chemical, taste)* acidez *f*; Fig (of tone, remark) sarcasmo *m*

acknowledge [ək'nɒlɪdʒ] *vt* (**a**) *(recognize) (person, truth)* reconocer; *(claim, defeat)* admitir; *(present)* agradecer, dar las gracias por; *(letter, invoice)* acusar recibo de (**b**) *(greet)* saludar

acknowledged [ək'nɒlɪdʒd] *adj (expert, authority)* de reconocido prestigio

acknowledgement [ək'nɒlɪdʒmənt] *n* (**a**) *(recognition)* reconocimiento *m*; *(admission)* admisión *f*; *(of letter, invoice)* & Comptr acuse *m* de recibo (**b**) **acknowledgements** *(in preface)* menciones *fpl*

ACLU ['eɪsi:elju:] *n* US (abbr **American Civil Liberties Union**) = organización americana para la defensa de las libertades civiles

acme ['ækmɪ] *n* colmo *m*, punto *m* culminante, apogeo *m*

acne ['æknɪ] *n* acné *m*

acolyte ['ækəlaɪt] *n* Rel acólito *m*; Fig seguidor(a) *m,f*

acorn ['eɪkɔːn] *n* bellota *f*

acoustic [ə'ku:stɪk] **1** *adj* acústico(a); **a. guitar** guitarra *f* acústica
2 acoustics *npl* acústica *f sing*

acquaint [ə'kweɪnt] *vt* (**a**) *(with facts)* **to a. sb with the facts** informar a algn de or sobre los detalles; **to a. oneself with sth** familiarizarse con algo; **to be acquainted with the procedure** estar al corriente de como se procede (**b**) *(person)* **to be acquainted with sb** conocer a algn; **they are acquainted** se conocen; **they're getting acquainted** se van conociendo

acquaintance [ə'kweɪntəns] *n* (**a**) *(familiarity) (with facts etc)* conocimiento *m*; *(with person)* conocimiento *m*,

relación *f*; **to make sb's a.** conocer a algn (**b**) *(person)* conocido(a) *m,f*; **he's an a. of ours** le conocemos

acquiesce [ækwɪ'es] *vi* consentir (**in** en), conformarse (**in** con)

acquiescence [ækwɪ'esəns] *n* consentimiento *m*, conformidad *f*

acquiescent [ækwɪ'esənt] *adj* conforme

acquire [ə'kwaɪər] *vt (get)* obtener, adquirir; *(possessions, property)* adquirir; *(territories)* tomar posesión de; *(habit, reputation)* adquirir, contraer; **to a. a taste for sth** tomarle gusto a algo

acquired [ə'kwaɪəd] *adj (characteristic, habit)* adquirido(a); **it's an a. taste** es un placer adquirido con el tiempo; **a. immune deficiency syndrome** síndrome *m* de inmunodeficiencia adquirida

acquisition [ækwɪ'zɪʃən] *n* adquisición *f*

acquisitive [ə'kwɪzɪtɪv] *adj* codicioso(a), acaparador(a)

acquit [ə'kwɪt] *vt (pt & pp* **acquitted**) (**a**) Jur **to a. sb of sth** absolver a algn de algo (**b**) **to a. oneself well** comportarse or defenderse bien

acquittal [ə'kwɪtəl] *n* Jur absolución *f*

acre ['eɪkər] *n* acre *m* (= 40,47 áreas)

acrid ['ækrɪd] *adj (smell, taste)* acre; Fig (remark, manner) cáustico(a), mordaz

acrimonious [ækrɪ'məʊnɪəs] *adj (remark, manner)* cáustico(a), mordaz; *(dispute)* enconado(a), amargo(a)

acrimony ['ækrɪmənɪ] *n* acritud *f*, aspereza *f*

acrobat ['ækrəbæt] *n* acróbata *mf*

acrobatic [ækrə'bætɪk] *adj* acrobático(a)

acrobatics [ækrə'bætɪks] *npl* acrobacia *f sing*

acronym ['ækrənɪm] *n* siglas *fpl*, acrónimo *m*

across [ə'krɒs] **1** *adv* (**a**) *(from one side to the other)* de un lado a otro; **the river is 30 metres a.** el río mide 30 metros de ancho; **to go** or **come a.** atravesar; **to lay sth a.** poner algo transversalmente or de través; **to run/jump a.** atravesar corriendo/de un salto; Fig **to put one's point of view a. to sb** exponer su punto de vista a algn; Fig **we couldn't get it a. to him** no logramos hacerle comprender (**b**) *(in crossword)* horizontalmente
2 *prep* (**a**) *(from one side to the other of)* a través de; **to go a. the bridge/the street** cruzar or atravesar el puente/la calle (**b**) *(on the other side of)* al otro lado de; **they live a. the road** viven enfrente; **our house is a. the park** nuestra casa se encuentra al otro lado del parque

across-the-board [əkrɒsðə'bɔːd] *adj* generalizado(a), indiscriminado(a)

acrylic [ə'krɪlɪk] *adj* acrílico(a)

act [ækt] **1** *n* (**a**) *(action)* acto *m*, acción *f*; **an a. of aggression/violence** una agresión/violencia; **an a. of folly** una tontería, una locura; **an a. of kindness** un gesto de amabilidad; **to catch sb in the a.** sorprender a algn en flagrante; Fam pillar a algn con las manos en la masa ▫ **a. of God** caso *m* de fuerza mayor (**b**) Jur **a. (of** Br **parliament** or US **Congress)** ley *f* (**c**) Theat *(part of play)* acto *m*; *(turn in circus, show)* número *m*; Fig **to put on an a.** fingir, disimular; Fig **to get in on the a.** *(get involved)* apuntarse, Am anotarse
2 *vt* Theat *(part)* hacer el papel de, interpretar; *(character)* representar; Fig **to a. the fool** hacer el tonto, hacer tonterías; Fig **to a. big** presumir
3 *vi* (**a**) Theat hacer teatro, ser actor/actriz; Cin hacer cine, ser estrella de cine; Fig *(pretend)* fingir, disimular; **to a. dumb** hacerse el sueco (**b**) *(behave)* comportarse; *(react)* reaccionar; **why did she a. like that?** ¿por qué se comportó así? (**c**) *(take action)* actuar, obrar, tomar medidas; **to a. for** or **on behalf of sb** representar a algn, obrar en

nombre de algn; **to a. on sb's advice** seguir el consejo de algn; **to a. with the best of intentions** obrar con las mejores intenciones (**d**) *(work)* funcionar; *(drug, medicine etc)* actuar; **to a. as a brake** servir de freno; **to a. as an incentive/a deterrent** servir de incentivo/disuasivo (**e**) **to a. as director/secretary** hacer de director/de secretaria

act out *vt (feelings)* exteriorizar

act up *vi Fam (machine)* funcionar mal; *(child)* dar guerra; *(injury, wound etc)* doler

acting ['æktɪŋ] **1** *adj* interino(a), en funciones **2** *n* (**a**) *(profession)* profesión *f* de actor, teatro *m*; **he's done some a.** ha hecho algo de teatro; **she wants to do a.** quiere hacer teatro *or* ser actriz (**b**) *(performance)* actuación *f*, interpretación *f*, representación *f*; *Fig* **it's only a.** es pura comedia

action ['ækʃən] *n* (**a**) *(functioning)* funcionamiento *m*, marcha *f*; *(deed)* acción *f*, hecho *m*; *Theat Cin* acción, historia *f*; *Mil* acción de combate; *Mil* **killed in a.** muerto en batalla; **the a. takes place in Africa** la acción transcurre en África; **to be out of a.** *(machine)* estar estropeado(a) *or* averiado(a); *(person)* estar fuera de servicio; **to put sth into a.** poner algo en marcha; **to take a.** tomar medidas; *Prov* **actions speak louder than words** hechos son amores y no buenas razones; *Com* **a. plan** plan *m* de acción; **a. stations** *(positions)* puestos *mpl* de combate (**b**) *Jur* demanda *f*, proceso *m*; **to bring an a. against sb** entablar una demanda contra algn (**c**) *Br TV* **a. replay** repetición *f* (de la jugada)

actionable ['ækʃənəbəl] *adj Jur* susceptible de procesamiento

action-packed ['ækʃənpækt] *adj (movie, novel)* lleno(a) de acción

activate ['æktɪveɪt] *vt* activar

active ['æktɪv] *adj (person, life, volcano)* activo(a); *(energetic)* vigoroso(a), enérgico(a); *(interest)* vivo(a); *(law)* vigente; *Mil* **on a. service** *or US* **duty** en servicio activo; **to take an a. part in sth** tomar parte activa en algo; *Ling* **a. voice** voz *f* activa; *Comptr* **a. window** ventana *f* activa

actively ['æktɪvlɪ] *adv* activamente; **to be a. involved in sth** estar metido(a) en algo

activist ['æktɪvɪst] *n* activista *mf*

activity [æk'tɪvɪtɪ] *n (movement) (of person)* actividad *f*; *(of street, office etc)* movimiento *m*, bullicio *m*; **outdoor activities** actividades al aire libre; **social activities** vida *f* social

actor ['æktər] *n* actor *m*

actress ['æktrɪs] *n* actriz *f*

actual ['æktʃʊəl] *adj* real, verdadero(a); **his a. address** su dirección verdadera; **in a. fact** en realidad; **let's look at an a. case** veamos un caso concreto

actually ['æktʃʊəlɪ] *adv (really)* en efecto, realmente; *(even)* incluso, hasta; *(well, in fact)* pues, de hecho; **he a. paid for our meal!** ¡y hasta nos pagó la comida!; **well a. I'm not hungry** pues no tengo hambre; **what a. happened?** ¿qué pasó realmente?

actuary ['æktʃʊərɪ] *n* actuario *m*

actuate ['æktʃʊeɪt] *vt* mover, motivar; **to be actuated by** ser movido(a) *or* motivado(a) por

acumen ['ækjʊmən] *n* perspicacia *f*

acupuncture ['ækjʊpʌŋktʃər] *n* acupuntura *f*

acute [ə'kju:t] *adj (illness)* agudo(a); *(pain)* intenso(a); *(hearing, smell)* muy fino(a); *(danger, situation, shortage)* grave, crítico(a); *(person, mind)* perspicaz, sagaz; *(angle)* agudo(a); *Ling* **a. accent** acento *m* agudo

acutely [ə'kju:tlɪ] *adv (suffer)* intensamente; **to be a. aware of sth** ser perfectamente consciente de algo

AD [eɪ'di:] *(abbr* **Anno Domini** in the year of our Lord) después de Cristo, d.de C.

ad [æd] *n Fam* anuncio *m*

Adam ['ædəm] *n* Adán *m*; *Anat* **A.'s apple** nuez *f* de la garganta; *Fam* **I don't know him from A.** no le conozco de nada

adamant ['ædəmənt] *adj* firme, inflexible; **to be a. about sth** mantenerse firme en algo

adamantly ['ædəməntlɪ] *adv* rotundamente, categóricamente

adapt [ə'dæpt] **1** *vt* adaptar, ajustar, acomodar (**to** a); **a play adapted from a novel** una obra adaptada de una novela; **to a. oneself to sth** adaptarse *or* amoldarse a algo **2** *vi* adaptarse, acomodarse, amoldarse; **to a. to a situation** adaptarse a una situación

adaptability [ədæptə'bɪlɪtɪ] *n* capacidad *f* de adaptación

adaptable [ə'dæptəbəl] *adj (instrument, tool)* ajustable; *(person)* adaptable; **he's very a.** se amolda fácilmente a las circunstancias

adaptation [ædəp'teɪʃən] *n (adjustment)* adaptación *f*; *(of play, text)* versión *f*

adapter *n*, **adaptor** [ə'dæptər] *n Elec* ladrón *m*

ADC [eɪdɪ'si:] *n Mil (abbr* **aide-de-camp**) edecán *m*

add [æd] **1** *vt (numbers)* sumar; *(one thing to another)* añadir, agregar **2** *vi (count)* sumar

add to *vt* ampliar, aumentar

add up 1 *vt (numbers)* sumar **2** *vi (numbers)* sumar; *Fig (make sense)* tener sentido; **it doesn't a. up** no tiene sentido, no lo entiendo; **it doesn't a. up to much** no es gran cosa

added ['ædɪd] *adj* adicional

adder ['ædər] *n* víbora *f*

addict ['ædɪkt] *n* adicto(a) *m,f*; **drug a.** drogadicto(a) *m,f*, toxicómano(a) *m,f*; **heroin a.** heroinómano(a) *m,f*; *Fam* **football a.** hincha *mf*; *Fam* **television a.** fanático(a) *m,f* de la televisión

addicted [ə'dɪktɪd] *adj* adicto(a); **to become a. to sth** enviciarse con algo

addiction [ə'dɪkʃən] *n (to gambling etc)* vicio *m*; *(to drugs)* adicción *f*

addictive [ə'dɪktɪv] *adj* que crea dependencia, que causa adición; **smoking is a.** el fumar crea hábito

Addis Ababa ['ædɪs'æbəbə] *n* Addis Abeba

addition [ə'dɪʃən] *n (adding)* el añadir; *Math* adición *f*, suma *f*; *(increase)* aumento *m*, adición *f*; **an a. to the family** un nuevo miembro de la familia; **additions to the staff** aumento *m* del personal; **in a. to** además de

additional [ə'dɪʃənəl] *adj* adicional, suplementario(a), supletorio(a); **that's an a. reason for going** eso es una razón de más para ir

additive ['ædɪtɪv] *n* aditivo *m*

add-on ['ædɒn] *n (pl* **add-ons**) *Comptr* extra *m*

address [ə'dres] **1** *n* (**a**) *(on letter)* dirección *f*, señas *fpl*; *Comptr* dirección *f*; **a. book** libreta *f* de direcciones (**b**) *(speech)* discurso *m*, conferencia *f*; **election a.** discurso electoral (**c**) **form of a.** tratamiento *m* **2** *vt* (**a**) *(send) (letter)* dirigir, poner la dirección en; **the letter was incorrectly addressed** la carta llevaba la dirección incorrecta (**b**) *(speak to)* dirigirse (**to** a); **to a. an assembly** pronunciar un discurso ante una asamblea; *Pol Parl* **to a. the floor** tomar la palabra (**c**) *(use form of address)* tratar de; **they addressed me as sister** me trataron de *or* me llamaron hermana

addressee [ædre'si:] *n* destinatario(a) *m,f*

Adelaide ['ædɪleɪd] n Adelaida

Aden ['eɪdən] n Adén

adenoidal [ædɪ'nɔɪdəl] adj gangoso(a)

adenoids ['ædɪnɔɪdz] npl Med vegetaciones fpl (adenoideas)

adept [ə'dept] **1** adj experto(a), ducho(a) (**at** en); **to be a. at doing sth** ser experto(a) en hacer algo
2 n experto(a); **to be an a. in sth** ser experto(a) en algo

adequate ['ædɪkwɪt] adj (enough) bastante, suficiente; (satisfactory) apropiado(a), adecuado(a), idóneo(a); **to feel/prove a.** to a task (person) sentirse/mostrarse competente para hacer una tarea

adequately ['ædɪkwətlɪ] adv (sufficiently) suficientemente; (satisfactorily) apropiadamente

adhere [əd'hɪər] vi (stick) pegarse (**to** a)

adhere to vt (cause, policy) adherirse a; (contract, promise) cumplir con; (regulations) observar; (belief) aferrarse a

adherence [əd'hɪərəns] n (to cause etc) adhesión f; (to beliefs) fidelidad f

adherent [əd'hɪərənt] n (supporter) partidario(a) m,f; (to religious beliefs) adepto(a) m,f

adhesion [əd'hi:ʒən] n (a) (stickiness) adherencia f (b) (to belief, plan) adhesión f (**to** a), apoyo m (**to** a)

adhesive [əd'hi:sɪv] **1** adj adhesivo(a), adherente; (sticky) pegajoso(a) ❑ **a. tape** cinta f adhesiva, celo m
2 n adhesivo m, pegamento m

ad hoc [æd'hɒk] adj a propósito; **an ad h. committee** un comité especial

ad infinitum [ædɪnfɪ'naɪtəm] adv a lo infinito, sin fin; **it goes on ad i.** no tiene fin

adjacent [ə'dʒeɪsənt] adj (building) contiguo(a), (land) colindante; (country) limítrofe; Geom **a. angle** ángulo m adyacente; **a. to** contiguo(a) a

adjective ['ædʒektɪv] n adjetivo m

adjoin [ə'dʒɔɪn] **1** vt (building) ser contiguo(a) a; (land) lindar con
2 vi (building) estar contiguo(a); (land) colindar

adjoining [ə'dʒɔɪnɪŋ] adj (buildings) contiguo(a); (land) colindante; **the a. room** la habitación de al lado

adjourn [ə'dʒɜ:n] **1** vt (postpone) aplazar, suspender; (court, session etc) levantar; **the meeting was adjourned** se levantó la sesión; **the trial is adjourned until after lunch** se aplaza el juicio hasta después de comer
2 vi (meeting etc) aplazarse (**until** hasta); suspenderse; (parliament) disolverse; Fam **let's a. to the sitting room** pasemos or vamos al salón

adjournment [ə'dʒɜ:nmənt] n (of trial, meeting etc) aplazamiento m, suspensión f

adjudge [ə'dʒʌdʒ] vt **to a. sb guilty** declarar a algn culpable; **to a. sb the winner** proclamar a algn ganador

adjudicate [ə'dʒu:dɪkeɪt] vt (contest etc) juzgar, actuar de juez or de árbitro

adjudication [ədʒu:dɪ'keɪʃən] n (of contest) fallo m

adjudicator [ə'dʒu:dɪkeɪtər] n juez mf, árbitro(a) m,f

adjunct ['ædʒʌŋkt] n adjunto m, accesorio m, añadidura f

adjust [ə'dʒʌst] **1** vt (machine, piece of furniture) ajustar; (engine) arreglar; Fig (methods) variar; **to a. oneself to sth** adaptarse a algo
2 vi (person) adaptarse (**to** a), amoldarse (**to** a)

adjustable [ə'dʒʌstəbəl] adj ajustable

adjusted [ə'dʒʌstɪd] adj equilibrado(a)

adjustment [ə'dʒʌstmənt] n (**a**) (act of adjusting) (machine etc) ajuste m; (person) adaptación f; **period of a.** período m de adaptación (**b**) (change) cambio m, modificación f

ad lib [æd'lɪb] **1** adv (speak) sin preparación; (continue) a voluntad
2 adj (speech, performance) improvisado(a)
3 ad-lib vt (pt & pp ad-libbed) improvisar
4 ad-lib vi improvisar; (actor) meter morcillas

Adm. (**a**) (abbr **Admiral**) Almirante m, Almte. (**b**) (abbr **Admiralty**) Almirantazgo m

adman ['ædmæn] n (pl admen ['ædmen]) agente m publicitario

admin ['ædmɪn] n Fam (work) papeleo m

administer [əd'mɪnɪstər] vt (country) gobernar; (goods, company) administrar; (justice, laws) aplicar; **to a. an oath to sb** tomar juramento a algn

administration [ədmɪnɪ'streɪʃən] n (**a**) (management, running) (of company, institution, funds) administración f (**b**) (giving) (of punishment, justice) administración f (**c**) (administrative department) gestión f, administración f (**d**) US (government) administración f, gobierno m

administrative [əd'mɪnɪstrətɪv] adj administrativo(a)

administrator [əd'mɪnɪstreɪtər] n administrador(a) m,f

admirable [æd'mərəbəl] adj admirable, digno(a) de admiración

admiral ['ædmərəl] n almirante m

admiration [ædmə'reɪʃən] n admiración f

admire [əd'maɪər] vt admirar; **to a. oneself** contemplarse con satisfacción

admirer [əd'maɪərər] n admirador(a) m,f; (wooer) pretendiente mf

admiring [əd'maɪərɪŋ] adj (look) lleno(a) de admiración

admiringly [əd'maɪərɪŋlɪ] adv (look) con admiración

admissible [əd'mɪsəbəl] adj admisible, aceptable

admission [əd'mɪʃən] n (**a**) (to school, hospital) ingreso m, CSur internación f; (price) entrada f; **'free a.'** 'entrada libre or gratis' (**b**) (acknowledgement) reconocimiento m; (confession) confesión f; **that's an a. of failure** eso es reconocer el fracaso

admit [əd'mɪt] vt (pt & pp admitted) (**a**) (allow to enter) (person) dejar entrar, admitir; (to hospital) admitir; **an invitation which admits two people** una entrada para dos personas; **'dogs are not admitted'** 'no se admiten perros'; **to be admitted to hospital** ser ingresado(a) en el hospital (**b**) (acknowledge) reconocer, admitir; (crime, guilt) confesar; **I must a. it's difficult** debo reconocer que es difícil

admittance [əd'mɪtəns] n (entry) entrada f; **'no admittance'** 'se prohíbe la entrada', 'prohibida la entrada'; **to gain a.** lograr entrar

admittedly [əd'mɪtɪdlɪ] adv la verdad es que, lo cierto es que; **a., it was dark when I saw him** reconozco que era de noche cuando le vi

admonish [əd'mɒnɪʃ] vt (scold) amonestar, reprender; **to a. sb for (doing) sth** amonestar or reprender a algn por (hacer) algo

ad nauseam [æd'nɔ:zɪæm] adv hasta la saciedad

ado [ə'du:] n **without further a.** sin más; Prov **much a. about nothing** mucho ruido y pocas nueces

adobe [ə'dəʊbɪ] n (clay) adobe m

adolescence [ædə'lesəns] n adolescencia f

adolescent [ædə'lesənt] n adolescente mf

adopt [ə'dɒpt] vt (child, method, tone of voice) adoptar; (suggestion) aceptar

adopted [ə'dɒptɪd] adj adoptado(a); **a. child** hijo(a) m,f adoptivo(a)

adoption [ə'dɒpʃən] n adopción f; **country of a.** país m adoptivo

adorable [ə'dɔːrəbəl] *adj* adorable; *Fam* encantador(a); **what an a. little dog!** ¡qué perrito más lindo!

adoration [ædə'reɪʃən] *n* adoración *f*

adore [ə'dɔːr] *vt (worship)* adorar; *Fam (love) (person)* querer muchísimo a; **I a. your new hairstyle** me encanta tu nuevo peinado; **we a. eating out** nos encanta comer fuera

adorn [ə'dɔːn] *vt* adornar, embellecer

adornment [ə'dɔːnmənt] *n* adorno *m*

ADP [eɪdiː'piː] *n Comptr (abbr* **automatic data processing**) proceso *m or* procesamiento *m* automático de datos

adrenalin(e) [ə'drenəlɪn] *n* adrenalina *f*

Adriatic [eɪdrɪ'ætɪk] *adj* adriático(a); **the A. (Sea)** el (mar) Adriático

adrift [ə'drɪft] *adv* **to come a.** *(boat)* irse a la deriva; *(rope)* soltarse, desatarse; *Fig (plans)* **to go a.** ir a la deriva

adroit [ə'drɔɪt] *adj* hábil, mañoso(a), diestro(a)

adroitly [ə'drɔɪtlɪ] *adv* hábilmente

adulation [ædjʊ'leɪʃən] *n* adulación *f*

adult ['ædʌlt] **1** *adj (person)* adulto(a), mayor; *(film, education)* para adultos
2 *n* adulto(a) *m,f*, persona *f* mayor

adulterate [ə'dʌltəreɪt] *vt* adulterar

adulteration [ə'dʌltə'reɪʃən] *n* adulteración *f*

adulterer [ə'dʌltərər] *n* adúltero *m*

adulteress [ə'dʌltrɪs] *n* adúltera *f*

adulterous [ə'dʌltərəs] *adj* adúltero(a)

adultery [ə'dʌltərɪ] *n* adulterio *m*

adulthood ['ædʌlthʊd] *n* edad *f* adulta

advance [əd'vɑːns] **1** *n* **(a)** *(movement)* avance *m*; *Fig (progress)* adelanto *m*, progreso *m*; **the latest advances in medicine** los últimos adelantos en medicina; **to arrive half an hour in a.** llegar media hora antes; **to book tickets in a.** reservar entradas con anticipación; **to have sth ready in a.** tener algo preparado de antemano; **to make advances** *(move forward)* avanzar; *Fig (to a person)* insinuarse **(to** a); **to pay in a.** pagar por adelantado **(b)** *(loan)* adelanto *m*, anticipo *m*
2 *adj (before time)* adelantado(a), anticipado(a); *Mil* **a. party** *or* **guard** avanzadilla *f*; *Cin Theat* **a. bookings** reservas *fpl* por adelantado; *Print* **a. copy** ejemplar *m* de anticipo; **a. notice** previo aviso *m*
3 *vt* **(a)** *(move forward) (troops)* avanzar; *(time, date)* adelantar; *Fig (promote) (arts, sciences)* fomentar, promover; *(interest)* promover; *(cause)* favorecer **(b)** *(propose) (idea)* proponer; *(suggestion)* hacer; *(opinion)* dar **(c)** *Fin (salary)* adelantar, anticipar; *(loan)* prestar
4 *vi (move forward)* avanzar, adelantarse; *(troops)* avanzar; *Fig (make progress) (person)* hacer progresos; *(technology etc)* progresar, adelantarse; *(gain promotion)* ascender

advanced [əd'vɑːnst] *adj (developed) (civilization)* avanzado(a); *(child, student)* adelantado(a); *(course)* superior; **to be a. in years** estar entrado(a) en años; *Educ* **A. level** = examen final o diploma en una asignatura de los estudios preuniversitarios

advancement [əd'vɑːnsmənt] *n (progress)* adelanto *m*, progreso *m*; *(promotion)* ascenso *m*

advantage [əd'vɑːntɪdʒ] *n* ventaja *f*; *Ten* **a. Velasco** ventaja para Velasco; **he has the a. of being tall** tiene la ventaja de ser alto; **it would be to your a. if you went** saldrías ganando si te fueras; **to show sth off to a.** hacer lucir algo; **to take a. of sb/sth** abusar de algn/aprovechar algo; **to turn sth to a.** sacar partido de algo

advantageous [ædvən'teɪdʒəs] *adj* ventajoso(a), conveniente **(to** para)

advent ['ædvent] *n (arrival)* llegada *f*; *(coming) (of Christ)* advenimiento *m*; **A.** Adviento □ **A. calendar** calendario *m* de Adviento

adventure [əd'ventʃər] *n* aventura *f*; **a. story** historia *f or* novela *f* de aventuras

adventurer [əd'ventʃərər] *n* **(a)** *(person fond of adventure)* aventurero(a) *m,f* **(b)** *(dishonest person)* sinvergüenza *mf*

adventurous [əd'ventʃərəs] *adj (person)* aventurero(a); *(plan, decision)* aventurado(a), arriesgado(a)

adverb ['ædvɜːb] *n* adverbio *m*

adversarial [ædvə'seərɪəl] *adj Jur* de adversarios, = basado en el enfrentamiento de dos partes

adversary ['ædvəsərɪ] *n* adversario(a) *m,f*, contrario(a) *m,f*

adverse ['ædvɜːs] *adj (effect)* desfavorable; *(conditions, decision)* adverso(a); *(winds)* contrario(a)

adversely ['ædvɜːslɪ] *adv* desfavorablemente

adversity [əd'vɜːsɪtɪ] *n* adversidad *f*

advert ['ædvɜːt] *n Br Fam* anuncio *m*

advertise ['ædvətaɪz] **1** *vt* anunciar; **to a. sth in the newspaper** anunciar algo en el periódico
2 *vi* hacer publicidad; *(in newspaper)* poner un anuncio; **to a. for sth/sb** buscar algo/a algn mediante un anuncio

advertisement [əd'vɜːtɪsmənt] *n (on television)* anuncio *m*, spot *m* publicitario; *(in newspaper)* anuncio *m*; **advertisements** publicidad *f* sing, anuncios *mpl*

advertiser ['ædvətaɪzər] *n* anunciante *mf*

advertising ['ædvətaɪzɪŋ] **1** *n* publicidad *f*, propaganda *f*; *(in newspaper)* anuncios *mpl*
2 *adj* publicitario(a); **a. agency** agencia *f* de publicidad; **a. campaign** campaña *f* publicitaria

advice [əd'vaɪs] *n* consejos *mpl*; **a piece of a.** un consejo; **to ask for sb's a.** pedir consejos a algn; **to take legal a. on a matter** consultar el caso con un abogado; **to take sb's a.** seguir los consejos de algn

advisable [əd'vaɪzəbəl] *adj* aconsejable, conveniente; **it's a. for us to start again** mejor si volvemos a empezar

advise [əd'vaɪz] *vt (give advice)* aconsejar, recomendar; *(on business, financial matters)* asesorar; **I a. you to do it** te aconsejo que lo hagas; **we don't a. it** no lo recomendamos *or* aconsejamos

adviser [əd'vaɪzər] *n* consejero(a) *m,f*; *(in business, financial matters)* asesor(a) *m,f*

advisory [əd'vaɪzərɪ] *adj (in business etc)* consultivo(a), asesor(a)

advocate 1 ['ædvəkɪt] *n Scot Jur* abogado(a) *m,f* defensor(a); *Fig (supporter)* defensor(a) *m,f*
2 ['ædvəkeɪt] *vt (reform)* abogar por; *(plan)* apoyar

AEC [eiː'siː] *n US (abbr* **Atomic Energy Commission**) = comisión americana para la energía nuclear

Aegean [ɪ'dʒiːən] *n* **the A. (Sea)** el (mar) Egeo

aegis ['iːdʒɪs] *n* **under the a. of** bajo el patrocinio de

aeon ['iːən] *n* eón *m*, eternidad *f*

aerate ['eəreɪt] *vt (liquid)* airear, gasificar; *(blood)* oxigenar

aerial ['eərɪəl] **1** *adj* aéreo(a); **a. photograph** aerofoto *f*
2 *n (for radio, television)* antena *f*

aerie ['eərɪ] *n US see* **eyrie**

aero- ['eərəʊ] *pref* aero-

aerobatics [eərəʊ'bætɪks] *n sing & pl* acrobacia *f* aérea

aerobic [eə'rəʊbɪk] **1** *adj (exercise)* aeróbico(a)
2 *n* **aerobics** aerobic *m*, aeróbic *m*

aerodrome ['eərədrəʊm] *n Br* aeródromo *m*

aerodynamics [eərəʊdar'næmɪks] *n* **(a)** *(science)* aerodinámica *f* **(b)** *pl (qualities)* aerodinámica *f* sing

aerogram(me) ['eərəʊgræm] *n* aerograma *m*

aeronautics [eərə'nɔːtɪks] *n* aeronáutica *f*

aeroplane ['eərəpleɪn] *n Br* avión *m*

aerosol ['eərəsɒl] *n* aerosol *m*, atomizador *m*

aerospace ['eərəuspeɪs] **1** *n* aire *m* y espacio *m* extraterrestre

2 *adj* **a. industry** industria *f* aeroespacial

aesthetic [iːs'θetɪk] *adj* estético(a)

aesthetics [iːs'θetɪks] *n* estética *f*

afar [ə'faːr] *adv* lejos; **from a.** desde lejos

affable ['æfəbəl] *adj* afable, amable

affair [ə'feər] *n (matter)* asunto *m*; *(event)* acontecimiento *m*; **to put one's affairs in order** arreglar sus asuntos personales; **the wedding was a big a.** la boda fue todo un acontecimiento; **that's my a.** eso es asunto mío ❑ **business affairs** negocios *mpl*; **foreign affairs** asuntos *mpl* exteriores; **love a.** aventura *f* amorosa

affect [ə'fekt] *vt* **(a)** *(influence) (person, health)* afectar; *(prices, decision, future etc)* influir en; *Med (attack) (organ, people)* afectar *or* atacar a; **countries affected by cholera** países afectados *or* atacados por el cólera; **it affects us all** nos afecta a todos; **will the delay a. the price?** ¿influirá el retraso en el precio? **(b)** *(touch emotionally)* afectar, conmover, emocionar; **to be affected by sth** conmoverse *or* emocionarse por algo; **we were greatly affected by her death** su muerte nos afectó mucho

affectation [æfek'teɪʃən] *n (false behaviour)* afectación *f*, amaneramiento *m*

affected [ə'fektɪd] *adj* **(a)** *(unnatural)* afectado(a), amanerado(a) **(b)** *(influenced)* afectado(a), influido(a); *Med* atacado(a) **(by** por) **(c)** *(touched emotionally)* afectado(a), conmovido(a), emocionado(a) **(by** por) **(d)** *(pretended)* fingido(a)

affection [ə'fekʃən] *n* afecto *m*, cariño *m*

affectionate [ə'fekʃənɪt] *adj* afectuoso(a), cariñoso(a)

affectionately [ə'fekʃənətlɪ] *adv* afectuosamente, cariñosamente, con cariño

affidavit [æfɪ'deɪvɪt] *n Jur* declaración *f* escrita y jurada

affiliate [ə'filɪət] **1** *n* filial *f*

2 [ə'filɪeɪt] *vt* afiliar **(to** *or* **with** a)

affiliated [ə'filɪeɪtɪd] *adj* afiliado(a), asociado(a); **to be** *or* **become a.** afiliarse **(to, with** a), asociarse **(to, with** a); **a. company** (empresa *f*) filial *f*

affiliation [əfilɪ'eɪʃən] *n* afiliación *f*

affinity [ə'fɪnɪtɪ] *n (connexion)* afinidad *f*, punto *m* de contacto; *(liking)* simpatía *f*; **there's a great a. between them** les une una gran simpatía

affirm [ə'fɜːm] *vt* afirmar, sostener

affirmation [æfə'meɪʃən] *n* afirmación *f*

affirmative [ə'fɜːmətɪv] **1** *adj* afirmativo(a); *US* **a. action** discriminación *f* positiva

2 *n* afirmativa *f*; **he answered in the a.** contestó que sí

affix [ə'fɪks] *vt (stamp)* poner, pegar

afflict [ə'flɪkt] *vt* afligir; **to be afflicted with** sufrir *or* padecer de

affliction [ə'flɪkʃən] *n (suffering)* aflicción *f*; *(grief)* pena *f*; *(illness)* mal *m*

affluence ['æfluəns] *n* opulencia *f*

affluent ['æfluənt] *adj* opulento(a), rico(a); **the a. society** la sociedad del consumo

afford [ə'fɔːd] *vt* **(a)** *(be able to buy)* darse *or* permitirse el lujo de; **I can't a. a new car** no puedo pagar un coche nuevo; **she can a. it** se lo puede permitir **(b)** *(be able to do)* permitirse; **I can a. to leave it for a few days** no pasa nada si lo dejo unos días; **you can't a. to miss the opportunity** no puedes perderte la ocasión

affordable [ə'fɔːdəbəl] *adj (price, purchase)* asequible

affray [ə'freɪ] *n* refriega *f*, reyerta *f*

affront [ə'frʌnt] **1** *n* afrenta *f*, ofensa *f*

2 *vt* afrentar, ofender; **to be affronted** ofenderse

Afghan ['æfgæn] **1** *n* **(a)** *(person)* afgano(a) *m,f* **(b)** *(dog)* (galgo *m*) afgano *m*

2 *adj* afgano(a); **A. hound** galgo *m* afgano

Afghanistan [æf'gænɪstɑːn] *n* Afganistán

aficionado [əfɪsɪə'nɑːdəu] *(pl* **aficionados**) *n* aficionado(a) *m,f*

afield [ə'fiːld] *adv* **far a.** muy lejos

AFL-CIO [eɪefelsiːaɪ'əu] *n US (abbr* **American Federation of Labor and Congress of Industrial Organizations)** = federación estadounidense de sindicatos

afloat [ə'fləut] *adv* a flote; **to keep a.** mantenerse a flote

afoot [ə'fut] *adv* **there's a plan a.** hay un proyecto en marcha; **there's something strange a.** se está tramando algo

aforementioned [ə'fɔːmenʃənd] *adj*, **aforesaid** [ə'fɔːsed] *adj* susodicho(a), arriba citado(a)

afraid [ə'freɪd] *adj* **(a)** *(frightened)* **to be a.** tener miedo **(of** sb a algn; **of** sth de algo); **I'm a. of it** me da miedo; **we were a. to go in** nos daba miedo entrar **(b)** *(sorry)* **I'm a. he's out** lo siento pero no está; **I'm a. not** me temo que no; **I'm a. so** me temo que sí, eso me temo; **I'm a. you're wrong** me temo que estás equivocado(a)

afresh [ə'freʃ] *adv* de nuevo, otra vez; **to start a.** volver a empezar

Africa ['æfrɪkə] *n* África ❑ **South A.** Sudáfrica

African ['æfrɪkən] *adj & n* africano(a) *(m,f)*; **A. American** afroamericano(a) *(m,f)*

Afrikaans [æfrɪ'kɑːnz] *n* afrikaans *m*

Afro ['æfrəu] *adj & n Fam (hairstyle)* afro *(m)*

Afro-American [æfrəuə'merɪkən] *adj & n* afroamericano(a) *(m,f)*

Afro-Caribbean ['æfrəukærɪ'bɪən] *adj & n* afrocaribeño(a) *(m,f)*

aft [ɑːft] *adv Naut* en popa; **to go a.** ir en popa

after ['ɑːftər] **1** *adv* después; **soon a.** poco después; **the day/week a.** el día/la semana siguiente; **to come a.** seguir; **to run a.** perseguir

2 *prep* **(a)** *(later)* después de, al cabo de; **a. a few weeks** al cabo de unas semanas; **come a. lunch** ven después de comer; *US* **it's twenty a. five** son las cinco y veinte; **soon a. arriving** al poco rato de llegar; **the day a. tomorrow** pasado mañana **(b)** *(behind)* detrás de, tras; **a. you!** ¡usted primero!, ¡pase usted!; **it comes a. 'M' in the alphabet** sigue a la 'M' en el alfabeto; **she came day a. day** vino día tras día; **they went in one a. the other** entraron uno tras otro; *Fam* **the police are a. them** la policía anda tras ellos **(c)** *(about, concerning)* por; **I see what you're a.** ya veo lo que buscas; **they asked a. you** preguntaron por ti; **what's he a.?** ¿qué pretende? **(d)** *(like)* **he takes a. his uncle** se parece a su tío; *Br* **she was named a. her grandmother** le llamaron como su abuela

3 *conj* después de, después que; **I came a. you left** vine después de que te marchases

afterbirth ['ɑːftəbɜːθ] *n* placenta *f*

aftercare ['ɑːftəkeər] *n (after hospital)* convalecencia *f*; *(after prison)* vigilancia *f*

after-dinner ['ɑːftədɪnər] *adj (speaker, speech)* de sobremesa

after-effect ['ɑːftərɪfekt] *n* efecto *m* secundario

afterglow ['ɑːftəgləu] *n (of sunset)* luz *f* del crepúsculo; *(of pleasant feeling)* regusto *m* placentero

after-hours [ˈæftərˈaʊəz] *adv (after closing time)* después de cerrar; *(after work)* después del trabajo

afterlife [ˈɑːftəlaɪf] *n* vida *f* después de la muerte

aftermath [ˈɑːftəmæθ] *n* secuelas *fpl*, consecuencias *fpl*, repercusiones *fpl*

afternoon [ɑːftəˈnuːn] *n* tarde *f*; **good a.!** ¡buenas tardes!; **in the a.** por la tarde

afters [ˈɑːftəz] *npl Fam (dessert)* postre *m*; **what's for a.?** ¿qué hay de postre?

after-sales service [ɑːftəseɪlzˈsɜːvɪs] *n* Com servicio *m* posventa

after-school [ˈɑːftəskuːl] *adj (activities)* extraescolar *(después de las clases)*

aftershave (lotion) [ˈɑːftəʃeɪv (ˈləʊʃən)] *n* loción *f* para después del afeitado *or Méx* rasurado

aftersun [ˈɑːftəsʌn] *adj* **a. cream/lotion** crema *f*/loción *f* para después del sol

aftertaste [ˈɑːftəteɪst] *n* regusto *m*

after-tax [ˈɑːftətæks] *adj (profits, salary)* después de impuestos

afterthought [ˈɑːftəθɔːt] *n* ocurrencia *f* tardía

afterwards [ˈɑːftəwədz] *adv* después, más tarde

again [əˈgen] *adv* **(a)** *(another time)* otra vez, de nuevo; **don't do it a.** no lo vuelvas a hacer; **I'm well a.** ya estoy bien; **I tried a. and a.** lo intenté repetidas veces; **to begin a.** volver a empezar; **to do sth a.** volver a hacer algo; **never a.!** ¡nunca más!; **now and a.** de vez en cuando; **once a.** otra vez; *Fam* **come a.?** ¿cómo? **(b)** *(besides)* además; **then a.** por otra parte

against [əˈgenst] *prep* **(a)** *(touching)* contra; **put the ladder a. the wall** coloca la escalera en la pared; **to lean a. sth** apoyarse contra algo **(b)** *(opposing)* contra, en contra (de); **a. the grain** a contrapelo; *Fig* **it goes a. the grain** esto va contra mis principios; **his height is a. him** su estatura no le ayuda nada; **it's a. the law** es ilegal, va en contra de la ley; **my father is a. it** mi padre se opone **(c)** **6 votes in favour, 4 a.** 6 votos a favor, 4 en contra; **to fight a. sth** luchar contra algo; **to work a. the clock** trabajar contra reloj **(d)** **as a.** en contraste con, comparado con; **she had two, as a. my one** ella tenía dos, y yo solamente uno

agape [əˈgeɪp] *adj (open-mouthed)* boquiabierto(a)

age [eɪdʒ] **1** *n* **(a)** *(of person)* edad *f*; **he doesn't look his a.** no representa la edad que tiene; **she's 18 years of a.** tiene 18 años; **the 20–30 a. group** las personas de edades comprendidas entre los 20 y 30 años; **to be under a.** ser menor de edad; **to come of a.** llegar a la mayoría de edad; **what a. are you?** ¿qué edad tienes? ▫ **a. limit** límite *m* de edad; **a. of consent** edad *f* núbil; **old a.** vejez *f* **(b)** *(period)* edad *f*, época *f*, era *f*; **the Middle Ages** la Edad Media; **the Golden A.** el Siglo de Oro; **the Iron A.** la Edad de Hierro **(c)** *Fam (very long time)* eternidad *f*; **it's ages since I last saw her** hace siglos que no la veo; **I've been waiting ages for you** hace una eternidad que te estoy esperando
2 *vt & vi* envejecer

aged¹ [eɪdʒd] *adj* de *or* a la edad de; **Anne, a. 26** Anne, de 26 años; **he died a. 80** murió a la edad de 80 años

aged² [ˈeɪdʒɪd] **1** *adj (very old)* anciano(a)
2 the a. *npl* los ancianos, la gente *sing* muy mayor

ageing [ˈeɪdʒɪŋ] **1** *adj (person)* envejecido(a), viejo(a); *(thing)* viejo(a)
2 *n (process)* envejecimiento *m*

ageism [ˈeɪdʒɪzəm] *n* discriminación *f* por motivos de edad

ageless [ˈeɪdʒlɪs] *adj (person)* siempre joven; *(beauty etc)* eterno(a)

agency [ˈeɪdʒənsɪ] *n* **(a)** *Com* agencia *f*; *US (delegation)*

representación *f*, delegación *f*; **advertising/employment/travel a.** agencia de publicidad/de trabajo/de viajes **(b)** **by the a. of** por medio de

agenda [əˈdʒendə] *n* programa *m*, orden *m* del día; **what's on the a. today?** ¿qué programa tenemos para hoy?

agent [ˈeɪdʒənt] *n* **(a)** *(person)* agente *mf*; *(representative)* representante *mf*, delegado(a) *m,f*; **estate/insurance a.** agente inmobiliario/de seguros; **to be a free a.** actuar *or* trabajar por cuenta propia *or* por libre **(b)** *(instrument)* agente *m*, causa *f*

age-old [ˈeɪdʒəʊld] *adj (custom etc)* viejo(a), antiquísimo(a), milenario(a)

agglomeration [əglɒməˈreɪʃən] *n* aglomeración *f*, concentración *f*

aggravate [ˈægrəveɪt] *vt (worsen)* agravar, empeorar; *Fam (annoy)* molestar

aggravating [ˈægrəveɪtɪŋ] *adj* **(a)** *(worsening)* agravador(a) **(b)** *Fam (annoying)* molesto(a)

aggravation [ægrəˈveɪʃən] *n* **(a)** *(worsening)* agravamiento *m*, empeoramiento *m* **(b)** *Fam (annoyance)* fastidio *m*, molestia *f*

aggregate [ˈægrɪgɪt] *n* **(a)** *(total)* conjunto *m*, total *m*; **on a.** en conjunto, en total **(b)** *(stones)* conglomerado *m*

aggression [əˈgreʃən] *n* agresión *f*

aggressive [əˈgresɪv] *adj (violent)* agresivo(a), violento(a); *(dynamic)* dinámico(a)

aggressively [əˈgresɪvlɪ] *adv (violently)* agresivamente; *(dynamically)* dinámicamente

aggressiveness [əˈgresɪvnɪs] *n (hostility)* agresividad *f*; *(vigour)* acometividad *f*, agresividad *f*

aggressor [əˈgresər] *n* agresor(a) *m,f*

aggrieved [əˈgriːvd] *adj* apenado(a); **to be a. about sth** estar herido(a) por algo

aggro [ˈægrəʊ] *n Fam see* **aggravation (b)**

aghast [əˈgɑːst] *adj (shocked)* espantado(a), horrorizado(a); **to be a. at the thought of sth** quedarse horrorizado(a) *or* pasmado(a) de pensar en algo

agile [*Br* ˈædʒaɪl, *US* ˈædʒəl] *adj* ágil

agility [əˈdʒɪlɪtɪ] *n* agilidad *f*

agitate [ˈædʒɪteɪt] **1** *vt (shake)* agitar; *Fig (disturb, worry)* inquietar, perturbar
2 *vi* **to a. about/against sth** hacer campaña a favor de/en contra de algo

agitated [ˈædʒɪteɪtɪd] *adj (person)* inquieto(a), perturbado(a), nervioso(a); **to be a. about sth** estar inquieto(a) *or* nervioso(a) por algo

agitation [ædʒɪˈteɪʃən] *n* **(a)** *(anxiety)* inquietud *f*, perturbación *f*, nerviosismo *m* **(b)** *Pol* agitación *f*

agitator [ˈædʒɪteɪtər] *n Pol* agitador(a) *m,f*, alborotador(a) *m,f*

aglow [əˈgləʊ] *adj (glowing)* resplandeciente, brillante; **to be a.** resplandecer, brillar

AGM [eɪdʒiːˈem] *n Br (abbr* **annual general meeting***)* junta *f* general anual

agnostic [ægˈnɒstɪk] *n* agnóstico(a) *m,f*

agnosticism [ægˈnɒstɪsɪzəm] *n* agnosticismo *m*

ago [əˈgəʊ] *adv* hace; **a long time a.** hace mucho tiempo; **a short while a.** hace un ratito; **as long a. as 1910** ya en 1910; **a week a.** hace una semana; **how long a. was it that you last saw him?** ¿cuánto tiempo hace que no le ves?

agog [əˈgɒg] *adj (expectant)* ansioso(a), curioso(a); **the whole town was a.** en todo el pueblo había una gran expectación

agonize [ˈægənaɪz] *vi* angustiarse, atormentarse (**over** por)

agonizing ['ægənaɪzɪŋ] *adj (pain)* atroz, horroroso(a); *(decision)* angustioso(a)

agony ['ægənɪ] *n (great pain)* dolor *m* muy fuerte; *(anguish)* angustia *f*; **he was in a. with his back** tenía un dolor insoportable de espalda; **it was a. having to wait** fue horroroso tener que esperar ❑ **a. column** consultorio *m* del corazón

agoraphobia [ægərə'fəʊbɪə] *n* agorafobia *f*

agoraphobic [ægərə'fəʊbɪk] *adj & n* agorafóbico(a) *(m,f)*

agrarian [ə'greərɪən] *adj* agrario(a)

agree [ə'griː] **1** *vi* (**a**) *(be in agreement)* estar de acuerdo; *(reach agreement)* ponerse *or* quedar de acuerdo; *(consent)* consentir; **don't you a.?** ¿no te parece?; **I agreed to see him on Monday** quedé en verle el lunes; **to a. about** *or* **on (doing) sth** ponerse de acuerdo en (hacer) algo; **to a. to do sth** consentir en hacer algo; **to a. with sb** estar de acuerdo con algn; **we agreed to differ** acordamos conservar cada uno sus propias opiniones (**b**) *(harmonize) (things, adjectives)* concordar; *(people)* congeniar

2 *vt* convenir, acordar; **I a. that she should come** estoy de acuerdo en que venga; **it was agreed that he would pay** se acordó que pagaría; **to a. a price/the terms of a contract** convenir un precio/los términos de un contrato

agree with *vt (of food)* sentar bien; *(of climate)* convenir; **raw onion doesn't a. with me** la cebolla cruda no me sienta bien

agreeable [ə'griːəbəl] *adj (pleasant)* agradable; *(person)* simpático(a); *(in agreement)* de acuerdo, conforme; **to be a. to (doing) sth** consentir en (hacer) algo

agreed [ə'griːd] *adj (price, time)* fijado(a)

agreement [ə'griːmənt] *n (arrangement)* acuerdo *m*, arreglo *m*; *Pol (treaty)* pacto *m*; *Com* contrato *m*, trato *m*; **by mutual a.** de común acuerdo; **to be in a. with sb** estar de acuerdo con algn; **to come to** *or* **reach an a. with sb** llegar a un acuerdo *or* ponerse de acuerdo con algn

agricultural [ægrɪ'kʌltʃərəl] *adj* agrícola(o); *(college)* de agricultura

agriculturalist [ægrɪ'kʌltʃərəlɪst] *n* ingeniero(a) *m,f* agrónomo(a)

agriculture ['ægrɪkʌltʃər] *n* agricultura *f*

agronomy [ə'grɒnəmɪ] *n* agronomía *f*

aground [ə'graʊnd] *adv Naut* encallado(a), varado(a); **to run a.** encallar, varar

ahead [ə'hed] *adv (in front)* adelante, delante; *(early)* antes, con antelación; *Naut* **full speed a.!** ¡avante toda!; **go a.!** ¡adelante!; **to go a. (of)** *(in race, opinion poll)* ir por delante (de); *(in match)* ir ganando (a); **to go a.** adelantar, ir adelante; *Fig* **to go a. with sth** llevar algo adelante; *Fig* **to get a.** triunfar, tener éxito; *Fig* **to look a.** pensar en el futuro; **to plan a.** planear el futuro; *(anticipate)* anticipar

ahem [ə'hem] *interj* ¡ejem!

ahoy [ə'hɔɪ] *interj Naut* **ship a.!** ¡barco a la vista!

AI [eɪ'aɪ] *n* (**a**) *(abbr* **artificial intelligence)** inteligencia *f* artificial (**b**) *(abbr* **artificial insemination)** inseminación *f* artificial

aid [eɪd] **1** *n (help)* ayuda *f*; *(rescue)* auxilio *m*, socorro *m*; **in a. of** a beneficio de, en pro de; **to come to the a. of sb** acudir en ayuda *or* en auxilio de algn; *Br Fam* **what's all this in a. of?** ¿a qué viene todo esto? ❑ **a. worker** cooperante *mf*; *Educ* **audiovisual a.** ayuda *f* audiovisual; **hearing a.** audífono *m*

2 *vt* ayudar; *Jur* **to a. and abet sb** ser cómplice de algn

aide [eɪd] *n Pol* ayudante *mf*, consejero(a) *m,f*

aide-de-camp [eɪddə'kɒŋ] *n (pl* **aides-de-camp)** *Mil* edecán *m*

AIDS [eɪdz] *n (abbr* **Acquired Immune Deficiency Syndrome)** SIDA *m*; **A. virus** virus *m* del SIDA; **A.-related complex** CAS *m*, complejo *m* asociado al sida

ailing ['eɪlɪŋ] *adj* enfermizo(a), achacoso(a)

ailment ['eɪlmənt] *n* enfermedad *f* (leve), achaque *m*

aim [eɪm] **1** *n (with weapon)* puntería *f*; *Fig (target)* propósito *m*, objetivo *m*; **he has no a. in life** no tiene objetivos en la vida; **to miss one's a.** errar el tiro; **to take a.** apuntar; **what's her a.?** ¿qué se propone?

2 *vt (gun)* apuntar (**at** a, hacia); *(stone)* lanzar (**at** a, hacia); *Fig (attack, action)* dirigir (**at** a, hacia)

aim at *vt (target)* tirar para; *Fig* **to a. at doing sth** querer *or* tener pensado hacer algo

aim to *vt* **to a. to do sth** tener la intención de *or* pensar *or* proponer hacer algo

aimless ['eɪmlɪs] *adj* sin objeto, sin propósito

aimlessly ['eɪmlɪslɪ] *adv (wander)* sin rumbo fijo

ain't [eɪnt] *Fam* (**a**) = **is not, am not, are not** (**b**) = **has not, have not**

air [eər] **1** *n* (**a**) *(mixture of gases, atmosphere)* aire *m*; **fresh a.** aire fresco; **in the open a.** al aire libre; **to go out for a breath of a.** salir a tomar el aire; **to send a letter by a.** mandar una carta por avión; **to travel by a.** viajar en avión; **to throw sth up in the a.** arrojar *or* lanzar algo al aire; *Fig* **it's still in the a. at the moment** todavía queda por resolver; *Fig* **there's something in the a.** se está tramando algo; *Fig* **to be walking on a.** estar en la gloria; *Fig* **to vanish into thin a.** esfumarse ❑ *Aut* **a. bag** airbag *m*; **a. base** base *f* aérea; **a. bed** colchón *m* hinchable *or* neumático; **a. brake** freno *m* neumático; **a. conditioner** acondicionador *m* de aire; **a. conditioning** aire *m* acondicionado; **a. fare** (precio *m* del) *Esp* billete *m* *or* *Am* boleto *m* *or* *Am* pasaje *m*; **a. filter** filtro *m* del aire; **A. Force** Fuerzas *fpl* Aéreas; **a. freight** transporte *m* aéreo; **a. freshener** ambientador *m*; **a. gun** pistola *f* de aire comprimido; **a. hostess** azafata *f* (de vuelo), *Am* aeromoza *f*; **a. lane** ruta *f* aérea; **a. letter** carta *f* aérea; **a. pocket** bache *m* aéreo; **a. pollution** contaminación *f* atmosférica, polución *f* ambiental; **a. pressure** presión *f* atmosférica; **a. raid** ataque *m* aéreo; **a. show** demostración *f* or exhibición *f* aérea; **a. shuttle** puente *m* aéreo; **a. steward** auxiliar *m* de vuelo; **a. stewardess** auxiliar *f* de vuelo, azafata *f* de vuelo, *Am* aeromoza *f*; **a. terminal** terminal *f* aérea; **a. traffic control** control *m* de tráfico aéreo; **a. traffic controller** controlador(a) *m,f* aéreo(a) (**b**) *Rad TV* **to be on the a.** *(programme)* estar emitiendo; *(person)* estar transmitiendo; **to go off the a.** *(programme)* cerrar la emisión; *(person)* dejar de transmitir (**c**) *Mus* aire *m*, tonada *f* (**d**) *(appearance, feeling)* aire *m*, aspecto *m*; **there was an a. of expectancy about the meeting** había cierta expectación entre los asistentes a la reunión; **to put on airs (and graces)** darse tono, presumir

2 *vt (bed, clothes)* airear; *(room, cupboard)* ventilar; *Fig (grievance)* airear; *(knowledge)* hacer alarde de

airborne ['eəbɔːn] *adj (aircraft)* en vuelo, en el aire; *Mil (troops)* aerotransportado(a); **soon we were a.** pronto estuvimos volando

airbrush ['eəbrʌʃ] **1** *n* aerógrafo *m*

2 *vt (photograph)* retocar *(con aerógrafo)*

air-conditioned ['eəkɒndɪʃənd] *adj* climatizado(a), con aire acondicionado

air-conditioning ['eəkən'dɪʃənɪŋ] *n* aire *m* acondicionado

aircraft ['eəkrɑːft] *n inv* avión *m* ❑ **a. carrier** portaviones *m inv*

aircrew ['eəkruː] *n* tripulación *f* del avión

airdrome ['eədrəʊm] *n US* aeródromo *m*

airfield ['eəfi:ld] n campo m de aviación
airhead ['eəhed] n Fam cabeza mf de chorlito, simple mf
airing ['eərɪŋ] n to give a room/clothes an a. ventilar un cuarto/airear la ropa; Fig the subject needs a good a. hace falta someter el tema a una buena discusión ❑ a. cupboard armario m caliente para secar la ropa
air-kiss ['eəkɪs] vi besar al aire
airless ['eəlɪs] adj (room) mal ventilado(a); (atmosphere) cargado(a)
airlift ['eəlɪft] **1** n puente m aéreo
  2 vt transportar por avión
airline ['eəlaɪn] n línea f aérea; **a. pilot** piloto mf comercial
airlock ['eəlɒk] n (in pipe) bolsa f de aire; (in spacecraft) esclusa f de aire
airmail ['eəmeɪl] n correo m aéreo; **by a.** por avión; **a. letter** carta f por vía aérea
airplane ['eəpleɪn] n US avión m
airport ['eəpɔ:t] n aeropuerto m
air-sea rescue ['eəsi:'reskju:] n rescate m marítimo desde el aire
airship ['eəʃɪp] n aeronave f
airsick ['eəsɪk] adj mareado(a); **to be a.** marearse en avión
airsickness ['eəsɪknɪs] n mareos mpl (en avión)
airspace ['eəspeɪs] n espacio m aéreo
airspeed ['eəspi:d] n velocidad f relativa or aerodinámica
airstrip ['eəstrɪp] n pista f de aterrizaje
airtight ['eətaɪt] adj hermético(a)
airtime ['eətaɪm] n Rad TV tiempo m de emisión
airwaves ['eəweɪvz] npl his voice came over the a. su voz llegó a través de las ondas
airworthy ['eəwɜ:ðɪ] adj (airworthier, airworthiest) en condiciones de vuelo
airy ['eərɪ] adj (airier, airiest) (well-ventilated) bien ventilado(a); (vague, carefree) ligero(a), despreocupado(a)
airy-fairy [eərɪ'feərɪ] adj (impractical) poco realista
aisle [aɪl] n (in church) nave f lateral; (in theatre, bus) pasillo m; Fam **they were rolling in the aisles** se troncharon de risa; **a. seat** (in plane) asiento m de pasillo
ajar [ə'dʒɑ:r] adj & adv entreabierto(a)
aka [eɪkeɪ'eɪ] adv (abbr also known as) alias
akimbo [ə'kɪmbəʊ] adj & adv en jarras; **with armas a.** con los brazos en jarras
akin [ə'kɪn] adj parecido(a) a, semejante a; **my lifestyle is a. to yours** mi forma de vivir se parece a la tuya
alabaster ['æləbɑ:stər] n alabastro m
alacrity [ə'lækrɪtɪ] n with a. con presteza
alarm [ə'lɑ:m] **1** n **(a)** (warning signal) alarma f, alerta m; **to give** or **raise the a.** dar la alarma ❑ **a. clock** despertador m; **burglar a.** alarma f antirrobo; **false a.** falsa alarma f **(b)** (fear) temor m, inquietud f, alarma f; **to cause a.** provocar temor
  2 vt alarmar, asustar; **to be alarmed at sth** asustarse por or de algo
alarming [ə'lɑ:mɪŋ] adj alarmante
alarmist [ə'lɑ:mɪst] n alarmista mf
alas [ə'læs] interj ¡ay!, ¡ay de mí!
Albania [æl'beɪnɪə] n Albania
Albanian [æl'beɪnɪən] **1** n **(a)** (person) albanés(esa) m,f **(b)** (language) albanés m
  2 adj albanés(esa)
albatross ['ælbətrɒs] n albatros m inv
albeit [ɔ:l'bi:ɪt] conj aunque, no obstante; **things are**

changing, a. slowly las cosas están cambiando, aunque lentamente
albino [æl'bi:nəʊ] adj & n albino(a) (m,f)
album ['ælbəm] n álbum m
albumen ['ælbjʊmɪn] n albúmina f
alchemy ['ælkəmɪ] n alquimia f
alcohol ['ælkəhɒl] n alcohol m, alcool m; **he doesn't drink a.** no bebe alcohol, es abstemio
alcoholic [ælkə'hɒlɪk] adj & n alcohólico(a) (m,f)
alcoholism ['ælkəhɒlɪzəm] n alcoholismo m
alcove ['ælkəʊv] n nicho m, hueco m
alder ['ɔ:ldər] n Bot aliso m
ale [eɪl] n cerveza f; **brown/pale a.** cerveza negra/rubia
alert [ə'lɜ:t] **1** adj (person) (quick to act) alerta, vigilante; (lively) despierto(a), despabilado(a); (mind) vivo(a)
  2 n alerta m; **to be on the a.** estar alerta
  3 vt **to a. sb to sth** alertar or avisar a algn de algo
alertness [ə'lɜ:tnɪs] n (watchfulness) actitud f vigilante; (liveliness) vivacidad f
Aleutian [ə'lu:ʃən] adj & n aleutiano(a) (m,f) ❑ **A. Islands** Islas fpl Aleutianas
A-level ['eɪlevəl] n Br Educ (abbr **Advanced level**) ≃ Curso m de Orientación Universitaria, COU m
Alexandria [ælɪg'zændrɪə] n Alejandría
alfalfa [æl'fælfə] n alfalfa f
alfresco [æl'freskəʊ] adj & adv al aire libre
algae ['ældʒi:] npl Bot algas fpl
algebra ['ældʒɪbrə] n álgebra f
Algeria [æl'dʒɪərɪə] n Argelia
Algerian [æl'dʒɪərɪən] adj & n argelino(a) (m,f)
Algiers [æl'dʒɪəz] n Argel
algorithm ['ælgərɪðəm] n Comptr algoritmo m
alias ['eɪlɪəs] **1** n alias m, apodo m
  2 adv alias, apodado(a)
alibi ['ælɪbaɪ] n (pl **alibis**) coartada f
Alice band ['ælɪsbænd] n cinta f para el cabello
alien ['eɪlɪən] **1** adj (foreign) extranjero(a); (from space) extraterrestre; (stranger) ajeno(a); **such behaviour is a. to him** semejante comportamiento es ajeno a él
  2 n (foreigner) extranjero(a) m,f; (from space) extraterrestre mf; (stranger) ajeno(a) m,f
alienate ['eɪlɪəneɪt] vt **(a) to a. sb** ofender a algn, ganarse la antipatía de algn; **to a. oneself from sb** alejarse de algn **(b)** Jur enajenar
alienated ['eɪlɪəneɪtɪd] adj **they feel a. from society** se sienten marginados de la sociedad
alienation [eɪlɪə'neɪʃən] n (feeling of not belonging) alienación f; (separation) alejamiento m
alight¹ [ə'laɪt] adj (on fire) ardiendo(a), encendido(a); **to be a.** (fire) estar ardiendo; (light) estar encendido(a); **to catch a.** incendiarse; **to set sth a.** prender fuego a algo
alight² [ə'laɪt] vi (get off) apearse, bajar (**from** de); (bird) posarse (**on** en)
align [ə'laɪn] vt alinear; **to a. oneself with sb** alinearse con algn
alignment [ə'laɪnmənt] n alineación f; **out of a. with** mal alineado(a) con
alike [ə'laɪk] **1** adj (similar) parecidos(as), semejantes; (the same) iguales; **they're all a.!** ¡son todos iguales!
  2 adv (in the same way) de la misma manera, igualmente; **dressed a.** vestidos(as) iguales; **summer and winter a.** tanto en verano como en invierno

alimentary [ælɪ'mentərɪ] *adj* alimenticio(a); *Anat* **a. canal** tubo *m* digestivo

alimony ['ælɪmənɪ] *n Jur* pensión *f* alimenticia, alimentos *mpl*

alive [ə'laɪv] *adj (living)* vivo(a), con vida; *(lively)* vivaz, vivaracho(a), activo(a); *Fig (teeming)* lleno(a) **(with** de); *(aware)* consciente **(to** de); **look a.!** ¡anímate!, ¡despabílate!; **to be a.** estar vivo(a) *or* con vida; *Fig* **to come a.** *(party etc)* animarse; *(person)* despabilarse; **she's a. to the risks** es consciente de los riesgos; **to keep the conversation a.** mantener (viva) la conversación

alkali ['ælkəlaɪ] *n (pl* **alkalis** *or* **alkalies)** álcali *m*

alkaline ['ælkəlaɪn] *adj* alcalino(a)

all [ɔːl] **1** *adj* todo(a), todos(as); **a. children** todos los niños; **a. the town** todo el pueblo, el pueblo entero; **a. year** (durante) todo el año; **a. kinds of things** todo tipo de cosas; **at a. hours** a todas horas; **at a. times** siempre; **by a. accounts** según se dice; **in a. honesty** con toda franqueza, francamente; **John of a. people** John entre todos; **of a. the cheek!** ¡qué carota!, ¡qué jeta!; **on a. fours** a gatas; **she works a. the time** siempre está trabajando; *Fam* **to be a. in** estar hecho(a) polvo, *Méx* estar camotes □ *Rel* **A. Saints' Day** Día *m* de Todos los Santos; **A. Souls' Day** Día *m* de los Santos Difuntos

2 *pron* todo(a), todos(as); **after a.** al fin y al cabo, después de todo; **a. but Paul are here** todos menos Paul están aquí; **a. of his work** toda su obra; **a. of us** todos(as) nosotros(as); **a. who saw it** todos los que lo vieron; **a. you can do is wait** lo único que puedes hacer es esperar; **it costs $50 in a.** cuesta 50 dólares en total; **I don't like it at a.** no me gusta en absoluto; **is that a.?** ¿eso es todo?; **it wasn't a. that good** no era nada del otro mundo; **most of** *or* **above a.** sobre todo; **not at a.** en absoluto; **once and for a.** de una vez para siempre; **thanks — not at a.** gracias — de nada; **that's a.** ya está; **that's a. there is** se acabó; **the score was one a.** empataron a uno; **they watched a. of it** lo miraron en su totalidad; **they will arrive late, if they come at a.** llegarán tarde, si es que vienen; **we ate a. of it** nos lo comimos todo

3 *adv* todo, completamente; **a. alone** completamente solo(a); **a. at once** *(suddenly)* de repente; *(altogether)* de una vez; **a. over the place** por todas partes; **a. along the valley** a lo largo del valle; **a. the better** tanto mejor; **a. the same** de todos modos; **he knew a. along** lo sabía desde el principio; **I'd like to go a. the same** a pesar de todo, me gustaría ir; **if it's a. the same to you** si no te importa; **I'm a. for it** me parece estupendo; **I'm not a.** that tired no estoy tan cansado(a) como eso; **it's a. but impossible** es casi imposible; **it's a. the same to me** me da igual; **I've a. but finished** me falta poco para terminar; **painted a. in red** pintado(a) todo(a) de rojo; **there were ten a. told** había diez en total; *Fam* **she's not a. there** es un poco tonta

4 *n* todo *m*; **to give one's a.** darse por completo

Allah ['ælə] *n* Alá *m*

all-American [ɔːlə'merɪkən] *adj* típico americano(a), típico(a) estadounidense

all-around ['ɔːlərəʊnd] *adj US (artist, athlete, picture etc)* completo(a), polifacético(a)

allay [ə'leɪ] *vt (fears, doubts)* clamar, apaciguar

all-clear ['ɔːl'klɪər] *n (after air-raid)* señal *f* de que pasó el peligro; *(for project)* luz *f* verde

all-day ['ɔːl'deɪ] *adj* de todo el día

allegation [ælɪ'geɪʃən] *n* alegato *m*

allege [ə'ledʒ] *vt* alegar, pretender **(that** que)

alleged [ə'ledʒd] *adj* presunto(a); **the a. criminal** el presunto criminal

allegedly [ə'ledʒɪdlɪ] *adv* supuestamente

allegiance [ə'liːdʒəns] *n* lealtad *f*; **to swear a. to the crown** rendir homenaje a la corona

allegorical [ælɪ'gɒrɪkəl] *adj* alegórico(a)

allegory ['ælɪgərɪ] *n* alegoría *f*

all-embracing [ɔːlɪm'breɪsɪŋ] *adj* general, global

allergen ['ælədʒən] *n* alergeno *m*

allergic [ə'lɜːdʒɪk] *adj* alérgico(a) **(to** a)

allergy ['ælədʒɪ] *n* alergia *f*

alleviate [ə'liːvɪeɪt] *vt (pain)* aliaviar, mitigar

alleviation [əliːvɪ'eɪʃən] *n* alivio *m*

alley ['ælɪ] *n* callejón *m*, callejuela *f*; **blind a.** callejón sin salida

alleyway ['ælɪweɪ] *n* callejón *m*, callejuela *f*

alliance [ə'laɪəns] *n* alianza *f*; **to enter into an a. with sb** aliarse con algn

allied ['ælaɪd] *adj Pol* aliado(a); *(connected)* relacionado(a), asociado(a) **(with, to** con)

alligator ['ælɪgeɪtər] *n* caimán *m*

all-important [ɔːlɪm'pɔːtənt] *adj* trascendental, de suma importancia

all-in ['ɔːlɪn] *adj (price)* todo incluido, global □ *Sport* **a.-in wrestling** lucha *f* libre

all-inclusive ['ɔːlɪn'kluːsɪv] *adj (price, holiday)* con todo incluido

all-in-one ['ɔːlɪn'wʌn] *adj (garment)* de una pieza

alliteration [əlɪtə'reɪʃən] *n* aliteración *f*

all-night ['ɔːlnaɪt] *adj (café, cinema etc)* abierto(a) toda la noche; *(vigil)* que dura toda la noche

allocate ['æləkeɪt] *vt (time, accommodation)* asignar; *(money)* destinar **(to** para)

allocation [ælə'keɪʃən] *n* **(a)** *(distribution)* (of time, accommodation) asignación *f*; *(of money)* distribución *f* **(b)** *(amount allocated)* cuota *f*

allot [ə'lɒt] *vt (pt & pp* **allotted)** *(time, money)* asignar

allotment [ə'lɒtmənt] *n* **(a)** *(of time, money)* asignación *f*. **(b)** *Br (plot of land)* parcela *f*, huerta *f* de ocio *(arrendada por el ayuntamiento para cultivo)*

all-out ['ɔːlaʊt] **1** *adj (effort)* supremo(a); *(attack)* concentrado(a); *(strike)* total

2 *adv* **to go a.-o. to do sth** emplearse a fondo para hacer algo

allow [ə'laʊ] *vt* **(a)** *(permit)* permitir, dejar; *(a request)* acceder a; **a. me!** ¡permítame!; **are we allowed to smoke here?** ¿se puede fumar aquí?; **to a. sb to do sth** permitir *or* dejar que algn haga algo; **you are not allowed to go in** está prohibido *or* se prohíbe entrar **(b)** *(allot) (time)* dejar, conceder; *(money)* destinar; **to a. a week to finish the job** dejar una semana para terminar el trabajo; **to a. sb time to pay** conceder a algn tiempo para pagar

allow for *vi* tener en cuenta, tomar en consideración; **allowing for delays** teniendo en cuenta los retrasos

allowable [ə'laʊəbəl] *adj (expense)* deducible

allowance [ə'laʊəns] *n (payment)* pensión *f*, subvención *f*; *(of food)* ración *f*; *(discount)* descuento *m*, rebaja *f*; *US (pocket money)* paga *f*; **to make allowances for sb/sth** disculpar a algn/tener algo en cuenta □ **family a.** subsidio *m* familiar; **tax a.** desgravación *f* fiscal; **travel a.** dietas *fpl* de viaje

alloy ['ælɔɪ] *n* aleación *f*

all-party ['ɔːl'pɑːtɪ] *adj (committee, initiative)* de todos los partidos

all-powerful ['ɔːl'paʊəfʊl] *adj* todopoderoso(a)

all-purpose ['ɔːlpɜːpəs] *adj* multiuso; **a. cleaner/adhesive** limpiador *m*/adhesivo *m* multiuso

all right [ɔːl'raɪt] **1** *adj (okay)* bien; **it's a. r., but it's nothing special** está bien, pero no es nada especial; **don't worry, you'll soon be a. r.** no te preocupes, pronto te encontrarás bien; **thank you very much — that's a. r.** muchas gracias — de nada; *Br Fam* **she's a bit of a. r.** está buenísima

2 *adv* **(a)** *(well)* bien; **is the car going a. r.?** ¿va bien el coche? **(b)** *(definitely)* ciertamente, sin duda; **he's dead a. r.** está muerto y bien muerto **(c)** *(agreement)* de acuerdo, *Esp* vale; **I'll give you a ring tomorrow — a. r.** te llamaré mañana — de acuerdo *or Esp* vale

all-round [ɔːl'raʊnd] *adj (artist, athlete, picture etc)* completo(a), polifacético(a)

all-rounder [ɔːl'raʊndər] *n Br* polifacético(a) *m,f*, persona *f* que hace de todo

all-singing all-dancing [ɔːl'sɪŋɪŋɔːl'dɑːnsɪŋ] *adj Hum* **(a)** *(versatile)* multiusos *inv*, todoterreno **(b)** *(extravagant)* **the conference was an a.-s. a.-d. affair** el congreso resultó una celebración por todo lo alto

allspice ['ɔːlspaɪs] *n* pimienta *f* inglesa

all-star [ɔːlstɑːr] *adj Theat Cin* **a.-s. cast** reparto *m* estelar

all-time ['ɔːltaɪm] *adj* **an a.-t. low** una baja sin antecedente; *Theat Cin* **the a.-t. greats** los grandes de siempre

allude [ə'luːd] *vi* aludir, hacer alusión *or* referencia **(to** a)

allure [ə'ljʊər] *n* atractivo *m*, encanto *m*

alluring [ə'ljʊərɪŋ] *adj (person)* atractivo(a); *(thing)* tentador(a)

allusion [ə'luːʒən] *n* alusión *f*, referencia *f*

allusive [ə'luːsɪv] *adj* alusivo(a)

alluvial [ə'luːvɪəl] *adj* aluvial

all-weather ['ɔːl'weðər] *adj* para cualquier tiempo

ally ['ælaɪ] **1** *n* aliado(a) *m,f*
2 *vt (pt & pp* **allied) to a. oneself to/with sb** aliarse a/con algn

almanac ['ɔːlmənæk] *n* almanaque *m*

almighty [ɔːl'maɪtɪ] *adj (all-powerful)* todopoderoso(a), omnipotente; *Fam (great, terrible)* **an a. din** un ruido de mil demonios
2 the A. *n* El Todopoderoso

Almohade ['ælməheɪd] *n Hist* almohade *m*

almond ['ɑːmənd] *n (nut)* almendra *f* □ **a. tree** almendro *m*

almost ['ɔːlməʊst] *adv* casi, por poco; **it's a. noon** es casi mediodía; **he a. cried** por poco llora

alms [ɑːmz] *npl* limosna *f sing*

aloft [ə'lɒft] *adv* arriba, en lo alto; *Naut* en la arboladura

alone [ə'ləʊn] **1** *adj* solo(a); **can I speak to you a.?** ¿puedo hablar contigo a solas?; **I can't afford a bicycle, let a. a car** no me puedo pagar una bicicleta, y muchos menos un coche; **I did it a.** lo hice yo solo; **leave it a.!** ¡no lo toques!; **leave me a.** déjame en paz, déjame tranquilo; **to be a.** estar solo(a); **you're not a. in thinking like that** no eres el único que piensa así
2 *adv* solamente, sólo; **they a. know** sólo ellos lo saben

along [ə'lɒŋ] **1** *adv (forward, on)* **come a.!** ¡anda, ven!; **he'll be a. in 10 minutes** llegará dentro de 10 minutos; **move a. please!** ¡circulen, por favor!; **she came a. with us** vino con nosotros, nos acompañó; **the whole family was there, a. with the dog** estaba allí toda la familia, junto con el perro; **to go** *or* **move a.** avanzar
2 *prep (the length of)* a lo largo de, por; **he walked a. the street** anduvo por la calle; **their house is a. here** su casa está por aquí; **there are trees a. the path** hay árboles a lo largo del camino

alongside [ə'lɒŋsaɪd] **1** *adv Naut* de costado; **to come a.** atracar

2 *prep* al lado de; *Naut* al costado de; **to come a. the quay** atracar en el muelle

aloof [ə'luːf] **1** *adj (person)* distante, reservado(a)
2 *adv* a distancia; **to keep oneself a.** mantenerse a distancia **(from** de)

aloofness [ə'luːfnɪs] *n* distanciamiento *m*, reserva *f*

aloud [ə'laʊd] *adv* en voz alta

alpha ['ælfə] *n* alfa *f*; *Phys* **a. rays** radiación *f or* rayos *mpl* alfa; *Comptr* **a. version** versión *f* alfa

alphabet ['ælfəbet] *n* alfabeto *m*

alphabetical [ælfə'betɪkəl] *adj* alfabético(a)

alphabetically [ælfə'betɪklɪ] *adv* por orden alfabético

alpine ['ælpaɪn] *adj (club, hotel)* alpino(a); *(scenery)* alpestre

Alps ['ælps] *npl* **the A.** los Alpes

al-Qaeda [æl'kaɪdə] *n* Al-Qaeda *n*

already [ɔːl'redɪ] *adv* ya; **I've a. seen it,** *US* **I a. saw it** ya lo he visto, *Am* ya lo vi

alright [ɔːl'raɪt] *adj & adv see* **all right**

Alsatian [æl'seɪʃən] *n (dog)* pastor *m* alemán

also ['ɔːlsəʊ] *adv* también, además; **not only milk but a. butter** no solamente leche sino también mantequilla

also-ran ['ɔːlsəʊræn] *n (horse)* caballo *m* no clasificado; *Fam (person)* nulidad *f*

alt **(a)** *(abbr* **altitude)** altitud *f*, alt. **(b)** *Comptr* **a. key** tecla *f* alt

altar ['ɔːltər] *n* altar *m*; **a. boy** monaguillo *m*

alter ['ɔːltər] **1** *vt (change) (plan)* cambiar, retocar; *(project)* modificar; *(opinion)* cambiar de; *(clothing)* arreglar, retocar; *(timetable)* revisar
2 *vi* cambiar, cambiarse; **we found it greatly altered** lo encontramos muy cambiado

alteration [ɔːltə'reɪʃən] *n (to plan)* cambio *m*; *(to project)* modificación *f*; *(to clothing)* arreglo *m*, retoque *m*; *(to timetable)* revisión *f*; *Archit* **alterations** reformas *fpl*, obras *fpl*

altercation [ɔːltə'keɪʃən] *n* altercado *m*, disputa *f*

alter ego ['æltə'riːgəʊ] *n (pl* **alter egos)** álter ego *m*

alternate [ɔːl'tɜːnɪt] **1** *adj* alterno(a); **on a. days** cada dos días, un día sí y otro no
2 ['ɔːltəneɪt] *vt* alternar
3 *vi* **to a. with sb/sth** alternar con algn/algo

alternately [ɔːl'tɜːnətlɪ] *adv* alternativamente; **a. hot and cold** ahora caliente, ahora frío

alternating ['ɔːltəneɪtɪŋ] *adj* alterno(a); *Elec* **a. current** corriente *f* alterna

alternative [ɔːl'tɜːnətɪv] **1** *adj* alternativo(a); **an a. proposal** una contrapropuesta; **a. energy** energía *f* alternativa; **a. medicine** medicina *f* alternativa
2 *n* alternativa *f*, opción *f*; **I have no a. but to accept** no tengo más remedio que aceptar; **let's look at the alternatives** miremos las alternativas

alternatively [ɔːl'tɜːnətɪvlɪ] *adv* por otra parte, o bien; **a. you could walk** o bien podrías ir andando

alternator ['ɔːltəneɪtər] *n Aut Elec* alternador *m*

although [ɔːl'ðəʊ] *conj* aunque; **a. it's late** aunque es tarde

altitude ['æltɪtjuːd] *n* altitud *f*; **a. sickness** mal *m* de altura, *Andes* soroche *m*

alto ['æltəʊ] *adj & n (pl* **altos)** *Mus (male singer, instrument)* alto *(m)*; *(female singer)* contralto *(f)*

altogether [ɔːltə'geðər] *adv (in total)* en conjunto, en total; *(completely)* enteramente, completamente, del todo; **we weren't a. happy with the result** no quedamos del todo satisfechos con el resultado; *Fam* **in the a.** *(naked)* en cueros

altruism ['æltru:ɪzəm] *n* altruismo *m*

altruist ['æltru:ɪst] *n* altruista *mf*

altruistic [æltrʊ'ɪstɪk] *adj* altruista

aluminium [æljʊ'mɪnɪəm] *n, US* **aluminum** [ə'lu:mɪnəm] *n* aluminio *m*

alumnus [ə'lʌmnəs] *n (pl* **alumni** [ə'lʌmnaɪ]) *US* antiguo alumno *m*

always ['ɔ:lweɪz] *adv* siempre; **he's a. working** siempre está trabajando; **I will a. love you** te quiero para siempre; **you can a. take the train** *(as a last resort)* como último recurso puedes ir en tren

AM [eɪ'em] *n* (**a**) *Rad (abbr* **amplitude modulation)** modulación *f* de amplitud, AM (**b**) *US see* **MA**

am [æm] *1st person sing pres see* **be**

a.m. [eɪ'em] *(abbr* **ante meridiem)** (before noon), de la mañana

amalgam [ə'mælgəm] *n* amalgama *f*

amalgamate [ə'mælgəmeɪt] **1** *vt (metals)* amalgamar; *(companies)* fusionar
2 *vi (metals)* amalgamarse; *(companies)* fusionarse

amalgamation [əmælgə'meɪʃən] *n* fusión *f*, unión *f*

amass [ə'mæs] *vt (fortune)* amasar; *(money)* amontonar; *(information)* acumular

amateur ['æmətər] **1** *n* amateur *mf*, aficionado(a) *m,f*; *Pej* chapucero(a) *m,f*
2 *adj (painter etc)* aficionado(a); *(work etc)* de aficionado(a); *Pej* chapucero(a), poco profesional

amateurish ['æmətərɪʃ] *adj* chapucero(a), inexperto(a)

amateurism ['æmətərɪzəm] *n* (**a**) *Sport* amateurismo *m* (**b**) *Pej (of work, performance)* chapucería *f*

amaze [ə'meɪz] *vt* asombrar, pasmar; **to be amazed at sth** quedarse pasmado(a) de algo

amazement [ə'meɪzmənt] *n* asombro *m*, sorpresa *f*; **they watched in a.** miraron asombrados; **to my a., they arrived** para gran sorpresa mía, llegaron

amazing [ə'meɪzɪŋ] *adj* asombroso(a), extraordinario(a), increíble

Amazon ['æməzən] *n* (**a**) **the A.** *(river)* el Amazonas; *(region)* la Amazonia (**b**) *(female warrior)* amazona *f*

ambassador [æm'bæsədər] *n* embajador(a) *m,f*

amber ['æmbər] **1** *n* ámbar *m*
2 *adj* ambarino(a); *(traffic light)* amarillo(a)

ambiance ['æmbɪəns] *n see* **ambience**

ambidextrous [æmbɪ'dekstrəs] *adj* ambidextro(a), ambidiestro(a)

ambience ['æmbɪəns] *n* ambiente *m*

ambient ['æmbɪənt] *adj (temperature)* ambiente, ambiental; *(noise, lighting)* ambiental

ambiguity [æmbɪ'gju:ɪtɪ] *n* ambigüidad *f*, doble sentido *m*

ambiguous [æm'bɪgjʊəs] *adj* ambiguo(a)

ambition [æm'bɪʃən] *n* ambición *f*; **her a. is to be famous** ambiciona ser famosa; **to have a.** tener ambición

ambitious [æm'bɪʃəs] *adj (person)* ambicioso(a); *(plan)* grandioso(a)

ambivalent [æm'bɪvələnt] *adj* ambivalente

amble ['æmbəl] *vi (horse)* amblar; *(person)* deambular, andar a paso lento

ambulance ['æmbjʊləns] *n* ambulancia *f* ❑ **a. man** ambulanciero *m*

ambush ['æmbʊʃ] **1** *n* emboscada *f*
2 *vt* tender una emboscada a; *Fig* atacar por sorpresa

ameba [ə'mi:bə] *n (pl* **amebas** *or* **amebi** [ə'mi:bi:]) *US* ameba *f*

amebic [ə'mi:bɪk] *US adj see* **amoebic**

amen [ɑ:'men] *interj* amén

amenable [ə'mi:nəbəl] *adj* susceptible, sumiso(a); **a. to reason** razonable; **he isn't a. to reason** no se deja convencer

amend [ə'mend] **1** *vt (text, law)* enmendar; *(error)* subsanar, corregir
2 *vi (text, law)* enmendarse; *(error)* subsanarse, corregirse

amendment [ə'mendmənt] *n* enmienda *f*

amends [ə'mendz] *npl* **to make a. to sb for sth** compensar a algn por algo

amenity [ə'mi:nɪtɪ] *n (facility, service)* servicio *m*; **amenities** comodidades *fpl*, servicios *mpl*

America [ə'merɪkə] *n (continent)* América; *(USA)* (los) Estados Unidos ❑ **Central A.** América Central, Centroamérica; **North A.** América del Norte, Norteamérica; **South A.** América del Sur, Sudamérica; **(the) United States of A.** (los) Estados Unidos

American [ə'merɪkən] **1** *n (gen)* americano(a) *m,f*; *(of USA)* norteamericano(a) *m,f*, estadounidense *mf*; **Central A.** centroamericano(a) *m,f*; **North A.** norteamericano(a) *m,f*; **South A.** sudamericano(a) *m,f*
2 *adj (gen)* americano(a); *(of USA)* norteamericano(a), estadounidense; **Central A.** centroamericano(a); **North A.** norteamericano(a); **South A.** sudamericano(a); **A. football** fútbol *m* americano; **A. Indian** amerindio(a) *m,f*

Americanism [ə'merɪkənɪzəm] *n* americanismo *m*

Americanization [əmerɪkənaɪ'zeɪʃen] *n* americanización *f*

amethyst ['æmɪθɪst] *n* amatista *f*

amiable ['eɪmɪəbəl] *adj* amable, afable, simpático(a) (**to, towards** con)

amicable ['æmɪkəbəl] *adj (relationship, agreement, etc)* amistoso(a), amigable

amid(st) ['æmɪd(st)] *prep* entre, en medio de

amino acid [ə'mi:nəʊ'æsɪd] *n* aminoácido *m*

amiss [ə'mɪs] *adj & adv* mal; **there's sth a.** algo anda mal; **to take sth a.** tomar algo a mal

ammonia [ə'məʊnɪə] *n* amoníaco *m*

ammunition [æmjʊ'nɪʃən] *n* municiones *fpl*; *Fig (in argument etc)* argumentos *mpl*

amnesia [æm'ni:ʒə] *n* amnesia *f*

amnesty ['æmnɪstɪ] *n* amnistía *f*

amniotic [æmnɪ'ɒtɪk] *adj* amniótico(a); **a. fluid** líquido *m* amniótico

amoeba [ə'mi:bə] *n (pl* **amoebas** *or* **amoebae** [ə'mi:bi:]) ameba *f*

amoebic [ə'mi:bɪk] *adj* amebiano(a); **a. dysentery** disentería *f* amebiana

amok [ə'mɒk] *adv* **to run a.** *(person)* volverse loco(a), destruirlo todo a su paso; *Fig (inflation etc)* desbocarse

among(st) [ə'mʌŋ(st)] *prep* entre; **he was a. those chosen** se encontraba entre los elegidos; **they quarrel a. themselves** se pelean entre ellos; **the money was divided a. them** se repartieron el dinero entre sí

amoral [eɪ'mɒrəl] *adj* amoral

amorous ['æmərəs] *adj* cariñoso(a), tierno(a)

amorphous [ə'mɔ:fəs] *adj* amorfo(a)

amount [ə'maʊnt] *n (quantity)* cantidad *f*; *(of money)* suma *f*; *(of bill)* importe *m*; **don't worry, you'll have any a. of time** no te preocupes, tendrás muchísimo tiempo; **the work requires a certain a. of patience** el trabajo exige mucha paciencia

amount to *vt* ascender *or* subir a; *Fig* equivaler a, significar; **her debts a. to $500** sus deudas ascienden a 500 dólares; *Fig* **it amounts to a go-ahead** equivale a una autorización; *Fig* **it amounts to the same thing** eso viene a ser lo mismo; *Fig* **it doesn't a. to much** no llega a ser gran cosa

amp ['æmp] *n Fam*, **ampere** ['æmpeər] *n Elec* amperio *m*; **13 a. plug** enchufe *m* de 13 amperios

ampersand ['æmpəsænd] *n Typ* = signo '&' que significa and

amphetamine [æm'fetəmi:n] *n* amfetamina *f*

amphibian [æm'fɪbɪən] *adj & n* anfibio(a) *(m)*

amphibious [æm'fɪbɪəs] *adj* anfibio(a)

amphitheatre, *US* **amphitheater** ['æmfɪθɪətər] *n* anfiteatro *m*

ample ['æmpəl] *adj (enough)* bastante; *(more than enough)* abundante; *(large)* amplio(a); **a. resources** grandes recursos; **a. time** mucho tiempo

amplification [æmplɪfɪ'keɪʃən] *n (of sound)* amplificación *f*; *(of remark)* ampliación *f*

amplifier ['æmplɪfaɪər] *n* amplificador *m*

amplify ['æmplɪfaɪ] *vt (pt & pp* **amplified)** *(sound)* amplificar; *(statement etc)* ampliar

amplitude ['æmplɪtju:d] *n Phys (of wave, signal)* amplitud *f* ◻ *Rad* **a. modulation** modulación *f* de la amplitud

amply ['æmplɪ] *adv (sufficiently)* bastante, suficientemente; *(abundantly)* abundantemente; *(greatly)* ampliamente; **we were a. rewarded** nos recompesaron plenamente

amputate ['æmpjuteɪt] *vt* amputar

amputation [æmpju'teɪʃən] *n* amputación *f*

amputee [æmpju'ti:] *n* amputado(a) *m,f*

Amsterdam ['æmstədæm] *n* Amsterdam

Amtrak ['æmtræk] *n* = compañía ferroviaria estado-unidense

amuck [ə'mʌk] *adv see* amok

amuse [ə'mju:z] *vt* divertir, entretener, distraer; **to a. oneself (by) doing sth** entretenerse haciendo algo; **to be amused by sth** encontrar algo divertido; **to keep sb amused** entretener a algn

amusement [ə'mju:zmənt] *n (enjoyment)* diversión *f*, distracción *f*; *(laughter)* risa *f*; *(pastime)* pasatiempo *m*; **much to our a.** para gran regocijo nuestro ◻ **a. arcade** salón *m* de juegos; **a. park** parque *m* de atracciones

amusing [ə'mju:zɪŋ] *adj (fun)* divertido(a), entretenido(a); *(funny)* gracioso(a); **I found it very a.** me reí mucho; **the a. thing is ...** lo gracioso del caso es ...

an [æn, *unstressed* ən] *indef art see* a

anabolic steroid [ænəbɒlɪk'stɪərɔɪd] *n* esteroide *m* anabolizante

anachronism [ə'nækrənɪzəm] *n* anacronismo *m*

anaconda [ænə'kɒndə] *n* anaconda *f*

anaemia [ə'ni:mɪə] *n* anemia *f*

anaemic [ə'ni:mɪk] *adj Med* anémico(a); *Fig (weak)* débil

anaesthesia [ænɪs'θi:zɪə] *n* anestesia *f*

anaesthetic [ænɪs'θetɪk] *n* anestesia *f*; **local/general a.** anestesia local/general *or* total

anaesthetist [ə'ni:sθətɪst] *n* anestesista *mf*

anaesthetize [ə'ni:sθətaɪz] *vt* anestesiar

anagram ['ænəgræm] *n* anagrama *m*

anal ['eɪnəl] *adj* anal

analgesic [ænəl'dʒi:sɪk] *adj & n* analgésico(a) *(m)*

analog ['ænəlɒg] *n US see* analogue

analogous [ə'næləgəs] *adj* **a. to** *or* **with** análogo(a) *or* semejante a

analogue ['ænəlɒg] *n* análogo *m* ◻ **a. computer** *Esp* ordenador *m or Am* computador *m* analógico; **a. watch** reloj *m* analógico

analogy [ə'nælədʒɪ] *n* analogía *f*, semejanza *f*; **to draw an a. with sth/between two things** señalar una semejanza con algo/entre dos cosas

analyse ['ænəlaɪz] *vt* analizar; *(psychoanalyse)* sicoanalizar

analysis [ə'nælɪsɪs] *n (pl* **analyses** [ə'nælɪsi:z]) análisis *m inv*; *(psychoanalysis)* sicoanálisis *m*; **in the final a.** a fin de cuentas

analyst ['ænəlɪst] *n* analista *mf*; *(psychoanalyst)* sicoanalista *mf*

analytic(al) [ænə'lɪtɪk(əl)] *adj* analítico(a)

analyze ['ænəlaɪz] *vt US see* analyse

anarchic [ə'nɑ:kɪk] *adj* anárquico(a)

anarchist ['ænəkɪst] *n* anarquista *mf*

anarchistic [ænə'kɪstɪk] *adj* anarquista

anarchy ['ænəkɪ] *n* anarquía *f*

anathema [ə'næθəmə] *n Rel* anatema *m*; *Fig (curse)* maldición *f*; **the very idea was a. to him** le repugnaba sólo de pensarlo

anatomical [ænə'tɒmɪkəl] *adj* anatómico(a)

anatomy [ə'nætəmɪ] *n* anatomía *f*

ANC [eɪen'si:] *n (abbr* **African National Congress)** ANC *m*, Congreso *m* Nacional Africano

ancestor ['ænsestər] *n* antepasado *m*

ancestral [æn'sestrəl] *adj* ancestral; **a. home** casa *f* solariega

ancestry ['ænsestrɪ] *n (ancestors)* ascendencia *f*; *(line)* solera *f*, abolengo *m*; **of noble a.** de rancio abolengo

anchor ['æŋkər] **1** *n Naut* ancla *f*; *Fig* ancora *f*, seguridad *f*; **to drop a.** echar el ancla; **to weigh a.** levar anclas, zarpar

2 *vt Naut* anclar; *Fig (fix securely)* sujetar

3 *vi Naut* anclar, echar el ancla

anchorman ['æŋkəmən] *n (pl* **anchormen)** *(in radio, TV programme)* presentador *m*, locutor *m*

anchorwoman ['æŋkəwʊmən] *n (pl* **anchorwomen)** *(in radio, TV programme)* presentadora *f*, locutora *f*

anchovy [*Br* 'æntʃəvɪ, *US* æn'tʃəʊvɪ] *n (pl* **anchovy** *or* **anchovies)** *(salted)* anchoa *f*; *(fresh)* boquerón *m*

ancient ['eɪnʃənt] *adj (custom, ruins, civilization)* antiguo(a); *(monument)* histórico(a); *Fam (very old)* viejísimo(a); **a. history** historia *f* antigua; **A. Rome** la antigua Roma; **the a. world** el mundo antiguo

ancillary [æn'sɪlərɪ] *adj & n* auxiliar *(mf)*; **a. staff** *(in hospital)* personal *m* auxiliar

and [ænd, *unstressed* ənd, ən] *conj* y; *(before* **i-**, **hi-)** e; **a hundred a. one** ciento uno; **a. so on** etcétera; **Bill a. Pat** Bill y Pat; **Chinese a. Indian** chino e indio; **come a. see us** ven a vernos; **four a. a half** cuatro y medio; **she cried a. cried** no paró de llorar; **try a. help me** trata de ayudarme; **wait a. see** espera a ver; **worse a. worse** cada vez peor

Andalusia [ændə'lu:zɪə] *n* Andalucía

Andalusian [ændə'lu:zɪən] *adj* andaluz(uza)

Andean [æn'di:ən, 'ændɪən] *adj* andino(a)

Andes ['ændi:z] *npl* **the A.** los Andes

Andorra [æn'dɔ:rə] *n* Andorra

Andorran [æn'dɔ:rən] *adj & n* andorrano(a) *(m,f)*

androgynous [æn'drɒdʒɪnəs] *adj* andrógino(a)

anecdotal [ænɪk'dəʊtəl] *adj* anecdótico(a)

anecdote ['ænɪkdəʊt] *n* anécdota *f*

anemia [ə'ni:mɪə] n US see **anaemia**

anemic [ə'ni:mɪk] adj US see **anaemic**

anemone [ə'nemənɪ] n Bot anémona f, □ **sea a.** anémona f de mar

aneroid ['ænərɔɪd] adj aneroide

anesthesia [ænɪs'θi:zɪə] n US see **anaesthesia**

anesthesiologist [ænɪsθiːzɪ'ɒlədʒɪst] n US see **anaesthetist**

anesthetic [ænɪs'θetɪk] n US see **anaesthetic**

anesthetize [ə'ni:sθətaɪz] vt US see **anaesthetize**

anew [ə'nju:] adv de nuevo

angel ['eɪndʒəl] n ángel m; Fam (nice person) encanto m, cielo m, sol m; **be an a.** sé amable; **you're an a.!** ¡eres un cielo! □ **guardian a.** ángel m custodio or de la guarda

Angeleno [ændʒə'li:nəʊ] n (pl **Angelenos**) = habitante o nativo de Los Angeles

angelfish ['eɪndʒəlfɪʃ] n (a) (saltwater fish) chiribico m (b) (freshwater fish) escalar m (c) (shark) angelote m

angelic [æn'dʒelɪk] adj (face) angelical; (smile, expression) angélico(a)

angelica [æn'dʒelɪkə] n Culin angélica f

anger ['æŋgər] 1 n cólera f, ira f; **fit of a.** ataque m de cólera; **to act/speak in a.** obrar llevado(a) por la cólera/ hablar con indignación
   2 vt encolerizar, enojar

angina (pectoris) [æn'dʒaɪnə ('pektərɪs)] n Med angina f (del pecho)

Angle ['æŋgəl] n Hist anglo(a) m,f

angle[1] ['æŋgəl] n Math ángulo m; Fig punto m de vista, perspectiva f; **a new a. to the story** una nueva perspectiva de la historia; **at an a. of 45** en ángulo de 45 grados □ **a. bracket** (for shelving) escuadra f (en ángulo); Typ paréntesis m angular; **right a.** ángulo m recto

angle[2] ['æŋgəl] vi (fish) pescar con caña; Fig **to a. for an invitation** intentar hacerse con una invitación

Anglepoise lamp® ['æŋgəlpɔɪz'læmp] n lámpara f de escritorio articulable, Esp flexo m

angler ['æŋglər] n pescador(a) m,f de caña □ **a. fish** rape m

Anglican ['æŋglɪkən] adj & n anglicano(a) (m,f)

Anglicism ['æŋglɪsɪzəm] n anglicismo m

anglicize ['æŋglɪsaɪz] vt anglicanizar

angling ['æŋglɪŋ] n pesca f con caña

Anglo-American ['æŋgləʊə'merɪkən] adj angloamericano(a)

Anglophile ['æŋgləʊfaɪl] n anglófilo(a) m,f

Anglo-Saxon [æŋgləʊ'sæksən] adj & n anglo-sajón(ona) (m,f)

Angola [æŋ'gəʊlə] n Angola

Angolan [æŋ'gəʊlən] adj & n angoleño(a) (m,f)

angora [æŋ'gɔːrə] n Tex angora f □ **a. goat/rabbit** cabra f/ conejo m de angora

angrily ['æŋgrɪlɪ] adv airadamente, con esp Esp enfado or esp Am enojo

angry ['æŋgrɪ] adj (**angrier, angriest**) (person) esp Esp enfadado(a), esp Am enojado(a); (voice, letter, look, words) airado(a); (wound) inflamado(a); (sky) tormentoso(a); (voice) airado(a); **to get a. with sb about sth** esp Esp enfadarse or esp Am enojarse con algn por algo

anguish ['æŋgwɪʃ] n angustia f

anguished ['æŋgwɪʃt] adj angustiado(a)

angular ['æŋgjʊlər] adj (shape) angular; (face, features) anguloso(a)

animal ['ænɪməl] 1 adj animal
   2 n animal m; Fig bestia f; **a. rights** derechos mpl de los animales

animate ['ænɪmɪt] 1 adj vivo(a), animado(a)
   2 ['ænɪmeɪt] vt animar; Fig estimular

animated ['ænɪmeɪtɪd] adj (lively) animado(a), vivo(a); **a. cartoons** dibujos mpl animados; **to become a.** animarse

animation [ænɪ'meɪʃən] n (liveliness) animación f, vivacidad f

animator ['ænɪmeɪtər] n animador(a) m,f

animosity [ænɪ'mɒsɪtɪ] n animosidad f

aniseed ['ænɪsiːd] n anís m

Ankara ['æŋkərə] n Ankara

ankle ['æŋkəl] n tobillo m □ **a. boots** botines mpl; **a. socks** calcetines mpl cortos

anklebone ['æŋkəlbəʊn] n hueso m del tobillo

ankle-deep ['æŋkəl'diːp] adj hasta los tobillos; **she was a. in mud** estaba metida en barro hasta los tobillos

ankle-length ['æŋkəlleŋθ] adj **a. sock** calcetines mpl cortos

anklet ['æŋklət] n (ankle bracelet) pulsera f para el tobillo

annals ['ænəlz] npl anales mpl

annex [æ'neks] 1 vt (territory) anexar
   2 ['æneks] n US see **annexe**

annexation [ænek'seɪʃən] n anexión f

annexe, US **annex** ['æneks] n (building) (edifico m) anexo m

annihilate [ə'naɪəleɪt] vt aniquilar

annihilation [ənaɪə'leɪʃən] n aniquilación f

anniversary [ænɪ'vɜːsərɪ] n aniversario m □ **wedding a.** aniversario m de bodas

anno Domini ['ænəʊ'dɒmɪnaɪ] adv después de Cristo

annotate ['ænəteɪt] vt (book etc) hacer anotaciones en, comentar; **an annotated edition** una edición crítica

annotation [ænə'teɪʃən] n anotación f; **annotations** notas fpl

announce [ə'naʊns] vt (arrival, wedding) anunciar; (news) comunicar, participar; (fact, statement) hacer saber, declarar; **she announced that she was going home** declaró que se iba a casa; **to a. the winner** (in competition etc) proclamar or anunciar al ganador

announcement [ə'naʊnsmənt] n (of arrival, wedding) anuncio m; (news) comunicación f, participación f; (statement) declaración f; **announcements** (in newspaper) anuncios mpl; **to make an a. about sth** anunciar or comunicar or participar algo

announcer [ə'naʊnsər] n TV Rad locutor(a) m,f

annoy [ə'nɔɪ] vt fastidiar, esp Esp enfadar, esp Am enojar; **he only does it to a.** lo hace sólo para fastidiar; **to be annoyed with sb about** or **because of sth** estar molesto(a) or esp Esp enfadado(a) or esp Am enojado(a) con algn por algo; **to get annoyed** molestarse, esp Esp enfadarse, esp Am enojarse

annoyance [ə'nɔɪəns] n (feeling) esp Esp enfado m, esp Am enojo m; (annoying thing) molestia f, fastidio m

annoying [ə'nɔɪɪŋ] adj molesto(a), irritante; **how a.!** ¡qué fastidio!

annual ['ænjʊəl] 1 adj anual; Com **a. turnover** volumen m de negocio anual
   2 n (book) anuario m; (plant) anual m, planta f anual

annually ['ænjʊəlɪ] adv anualmente, cada año

annuity [ə'njuːɪtɪ] n (pension) renta f vitalicia

annul [ə'nʌl] vt (pt & pp **annulled**) (contract, marriage) anular

annulment [ə'nʌlmənt] *n (of contract, marriage)* anulación *f*

anode ['ænəʊd] *n Elec* ánodo *m*

anodyne ['ænədaın] **1** *adj (bland)* anodino(a), neutro(a) **2** *n (comforter)* calmante *m*

anoint [ə'nɔint] *vt* ungir, untar (**with** con)

anomalous [ə'nɒmələs] *adj* anómalo(a)

anomaly [ə'nɒməlı] *n* anomalía *f*

anon¹ [ə'nɒn] *adv Literary & Hum (soon)* dentro de poco, ahora

anon² [ə'nɒn] *(abbr* **anonymous)** anónimo(a)

anonymity [ænə'nımıtı] *n* anonimato *m*

anonymous [ə'nɒnıməs] *adj* anónimo(a); **a. letter** anónimo *m*; **to remain a.** conservar el anonimato

anonymously [ə'nɒnıməslı] *adv* anónimamente

anorak ['ænəræk] *n* anorak *m*

anorexia [ænɒ'reksıə] *n Med* anorexia *f* ❑ **a. nervosa** anorexia *f* nerviosa

anorexic [ænə'reksık] *adj Med* anoréxico(a)

another [ə'nʌðər] **1** *adj (additional)* otro(a); *(different)* (otro(a)) distinto(a); **a. one** otro(a); **a. orange** otra naranja; **in a. few days** dentro de unos pocos días; **in a. 10 years** en otros 10 años; **one way or a.** de una forma o de otra; **that's a. matter** eso es harina de otro costal; **they say he's a. Picasso** según dicen, él es otro Picasso; **we'll do it a. time** lo haremos en otra ocasión; **without a. word** sin más

2 *pron* otro(a); **have a.** toma otro(a); **to love one a.** quererse el uno al otro *or* los unos a los otros; **we help one a.** nos ayudamos mutuamente

ANSI ['ænsı] *n (abbr* **American National Standards Institute)** ⇒ instituto estadounidense que crea estándares de calidad en el ámbito tecnológico

answer ['ɑːnsər] **1** *n (to letter, telephone call)* contestación *f*; *(to question)* respuesta *f*; *(to problem)* solución *f*, arreglo *m*; *(to criticism)* explicación *f*, justificación *f*; **in a. to your letter** contestando a su carta; **in a. to your question** en respuesta a su pregunta; **the only a. is to spend less** la única solución es gastar menos; **there's no a.** *(on telephone)* no contestan; *(at door)* no abren

2 *vt (letter)* contestar a; *(person, question)* contestar *or* responder a; *(criticism)* explicar, justificar; **to a. the door** abrir la puerta a algn; **to a. the telephone** contestar *or Esp* coger el teléfono

3 *vi* contestar, responder

answer back *vi* replicar; **don't a. back!** ¡no repliques!, ¡no seas respondón!

answer for *vt* responder de; **to a. to sb for sth** ser responsable ante algn de algo; **he's got a lot to a. for** es responsable de muchas cosas

answer to *vt (name)* responder a; *(description)* corresponder a; **it answers to the name of Shandy** atiende por Shandy

answerable ['ɑːnsərəbəl] *adj (responsible)* responsable; *(question)* que tiene solución; **he's a. to no one** no tiene que dar cuentas a nadie; **to be a. to sb for sth** ser responsable ante algn de algo

answering machine ['ɑːnsərıŋməʃiːn], *Br* **answerphone** ['ɑːnsəfəʊn] *n* contestador *m* (automático)

ant [ænt] *n* hormiga *f* ❑ **a. hill** hormiguero *m*

antacid [ænt'æsıd] *n* antiácido *m*

antagonism [æn'tægənızəm] *n* antagonismo *m*, rivalidad *f* (**between** entre), hostilidad *f* (**towards** hacia)

antagonist [æn'tægənıst] *n* antagonista *mf*, adversario(a) *m,f*

antagonistic [æntægə'nıstık] *adj* hostil, agresivo(a) (**to, towards** con)

antagonize [æn'tægənaız] *vt* enemistarse con, provocar la enemistad de

Antarctic [ænt'ɑːktık] **1** *adj* antártico(a) ❑ **A. Ocean** océano *m* Antártico **2 the A.** *n (polar region)* la zona antártica

Antarctica [ænt'ɑːktıkə] *n* Antártida

ante ['æntı] *n* **to up the a.** *Fam (in gambling, conflict)* elevar la apuesta

ante- ['æntı] *pref* ante-

anteater ['æntiːtər] *n* oso *m* hormiguero

antecedent [æntı'siːdənt] *n* antecedente *m*; **antecedents** *(past family)* antepasados *mpl*; *(past events)* antecedentes *mpl*

antedate [æntı'deıt] *vt (document, cheque)* antedatar, poner fecha anterior a; *(building, invention, etc)* anteceder, ser anterior a; **this building antedates that one by 50 years** este edificio es cincuenta años más antiguo o aquél

antelope ['æntıləʊp] *n (pl* **antelope** *or* **antelopes)** antílope *m*

antenatal [æntı'neıtəl] *adj* antenatal; *(clinic)* prenatal

antenna [æn'tenə] *n (a) (pl* **antennae** [æn'teniː]) *(of animal, insect)* antena *f* (b) *(pl* **antennas)** *TV Rad* antena *f*

anteroom ['æntıruːm] *n* antesala *f*; *(waiting room)* sala *f* de espera

anthem ['ænθəm] *n Mus Rel* motete *m* ❑ **national a.** himno *m* nacional

anthology [æn'θɒlədʒı] *n* antología *f*

anthracite ['ænθrəsaıt] *n* antracita *f*

anthrax ['ænθræks] *n Med* carbunco *m*, ántrax *m inv*

anthropological ['ænθrəpə'lɒdʒıkəl] *adj* antropológico(a)

anthropologist [ænθrə'pɒlədʒıst] *n* antropólogo(a) *m,f*

anthropology [ænθrə'pɒlədʒı] *n* antropología *f*

anti ['æntı] *adj Fam* en contra; **she's very a.** está muy en contra

anti- ['æntı] **1** *pref* anti-, contra- **2** *prep* en contra de

anti-abortion ['æntıə'bɔːʃən] *adj* antiabortista

anti-aircraft [æntı'eəkrɑːft] *adj* antiaéreo(a)

antibacterial [æntıbæk'tiːrıəl] *adj* antibacteriano(a)

antibiotic [æntıbaı'ɒtık] *n* antibiótico *m*

antibody ['æntıbɒdı] *n* anticuerpo *m*

Antichrist ['æntıkraıst] *n* Anticristo *m*

anticipate [æn'tısıpeıt] *vt (a) (expect)* esperar; **do you a. any problems?** ¿crees que surgirá algún problema?; **it was better than I anticipated** era mejor de lo que esperaba (b) *(predict)* prever; *(problems)* anticipar; *(get ahead of)* anticiparse a, adelantarse a

anticipation [æntısı'peıʃən] *n (expectation)* esperanza *f*; *(expectancy)* ilusión *f*; **in a. of good weather** esperando el buen tiempo; **we waited in eager a.** esperamos con gran ilusión

anticlimax [æntı'klaımæks] *n* anticlímax *m*; *(disappointment)* decepción *f*

anticlockwise [æntı'klɒkwaız] *adv* en sentido contrario a las agujas del reloj

antics ['æntıks] *npl (foolish behaviour)* payasadas *fpl*; *(naughtiness)* travesuras *fpl*

anticyclone [æntı'saıkləʊn] *n* anticiclón *m*

antidepressant [æntıdı'presənt] *adj & n* antidepresivo (*m*)

antidote ['æntɪdəʊt] *n Med* antídoto *m*; *Fig* remedio *m*, solución *f*

anti-dumping ['æntɪ'dʌmpɪŋ] *adj (laws, legislation)* antidumping

anti-establishment ['æntɪɪs'tæblɪʃmənt] *adj* en contra del orden establecido

antifreeze ['æntɪfriːz] *n* anticongelante *m*

antiglare ['æntɪ'gleər] *adj* (**a**) *US (mirror, finish)* antirreflector(a), antirreflejante (**b**) *Comptr* **a. filter** filtro *m* de pantalla

antiglobalization ['æntɪgləʊbəlaɪ'zeɪʃən] *n* antiglobalización *f*

Antigua [æn'tiːgə] *n* Antigua

Antigua and Barbuda [æn'tiːgɑnbɑ:'bjuːdə] *n* Antigua y Barbuda

antihistamine [æntɪ'hɪstəmɪn] *n* antihistamínico *m*

anti-inflammatory [æntɪɪn'flæmətərɪ] **1** *n* antiinflamatorio *m*
2 *adj* antiinflamatorio(a); **a. drug** antiinflamatorio *m*

Antilles [æn'tɪliːz] *npl* **the A.** las Antillas □ **Greater A.** Grandes Antillas; **Lesser A.** Pequeñas Antillas

antinuclear [æntɪ'njuːklɪər] *adj* antinuclear

antipathy [æn'tɪpəθɪ] *n* antipatía *f*, ojeriza *f* (**to, towards** a, hacia)

antiperspirant [æntɪ'pɜːspɪrənt] *n* antitranspirante *m*

antipodean [æntɪpə'diːən] **1** *n Hum (Australian)* australiano(a) *m,f*
2 *adj* (**a**) *Geog* antípoda, de las antípodas (**b**) *Hum* australiano(a)

antipodes [æn'tɪpədiːz] *npl (point)* antípoda *m sing*; *Br* **the A.** Australia y Nueva Zelanda

antiquarian [æntɪ'kweərɪən] **1** *adj* **a. bookseller** librero *m* de viejo
2 *n* anticuario(a) *m,f*

antiquated ['æntɪkweɪtɪd] *adj* anticuado(a)

antique [æn'tiːk] **1** *adj (furniture etc)* antiguo(a), de época
2 *n* antigüedad *f* □ **a. dealer** anticuario(a) *m,f*; **a. shop** tienda *f* de antigüedades

antiquity [æn'tɪkwɪtɪ] *n (ancient times)* antigüedad *f*; *(ancient monument)* monumento *m* antiguo or histórico; **of great a.** muy antiguo(a)

anti-Semitic [æntɪsɪ'mɪtɪk] *adj* antisemita, antisemítico(a)

anti-Semitism [æntɪ'semɪtɪzəm] *n* antisemitismo *m*

antiseptic [æntɪ'septɪk] *adj & n* antiséptico(a) *(m)*

antisocial [æntɪ'səʊʃəl] *adj (delinquent) (behaviour)* antisocial; *(unsociable) (person)* insociable

antiterrorist ['æntɪ'terərɪst] *adj* antiterrorista

antitheft ['æntɪ'θeft] *adj (device etc)* antirrobo *inv*

antithesis [æn'tɪθɪsɪs] *n (pl* **antitheses** [æn'tɪθɪsiːz]*)* antítesis *f*

antivirus ['æntɪ'vaɪrəs] *adj* antivirus; *Comptr* **a. program** programa *m* antivirus

antler ['æntlər] *n* cuerna *f*; **antlers** cornamenta *f*

antonym ['æntənɪm] *n* antónimo *m*

Antwerp ['æntwɜːp] *n* Amberes

anus ['eɪnəs] *n* ano *m*

anvil ['ænvɪl] *n* yunque *m*

anxiety [æŋ'zaɪɪtɪ] *n (concern)* inquietud *f*, desasosiego *m*; *(worry)* preocupación *f*; *(fear)* ansiedad *f*, angustia *f*; *(eagerness)* ansia *f*, ansias *fpl*; **it's a great a. to us** nos preocupa muchísimo

anxious ['æŋkʃəs] *adj (concerned)* inquieto(a); *(worried)* preocupado(a); *(fearful)* angustiado(a); *(eager)* ansioso(a),

deseoso(a); **an a. moment** un momento de angustia; **a. to please** deseoso(a) de complacer; **to be a. about sth** estar preocupado(a) por algo

anxiously ['æŋkʃəslɪ] *adv (worriedly)* con inquietud or preocupación; *(eagerly)* ansiosamente

any ['enɪ] **1** *adj (in questions)* algún(una); *(in negative clauses)* ningún(una); *(no matter which)* cualquier(a); *(every)* todo(a); **a. doctor will tell you the same thing** cualquier médico te dirá lo mismo; **are there a. seats left on the express?** ¿quedan plazas en el expreso?; **at a. moment** en cualquier momento; **have you a. apples?** ¿tienes manzanas?; **have you a. money?** ¿tienes (algo de) dinero?; **I don't have a. time** no tengo tiempo; **in a. case** en todo caso, de todas formas; **she did it without a. difficulty** lo hizo sin ninguna dificultad
2 *pron (in questions)* alguno(a); *(in negative clauses)* ninguno(a); *(no matter which)* cualquiera; **have they got a.?** ¿tienen alguno?; **I don't want a.** no quiero ninguno(a); **I need some paper, have you a.?** necesito papel, ¿tienes?; **you can use a. (one)** usa el/la que quieras
3 *adv* **we don't go a. longer** ya no vamos más; **is there a. more?** ¿hay más?; **I used to like it but not a. more** antes me gustaba pero ya no; **is it a. good?** ¿sirve para algo?

anybody ['enɪbɒdɪ] *pron (in questions)* alguien, alguno(a); *(in negative clauses)* nadie, ninguno(a); *(no matter who)* cualquiera, cualquier persona; **a. but me** cualquiera menos yo; **a. will tell you** so cualquiera te lo dirá; **a. would think he was poor** cualquiera diría que es pobre; **bring a. you like** trae a quien quieras; **do you see a. over there?** ¿ves a alguien allí?; **I can't find a.** no encuentro a nadie; **it's a.'s guess** quién sabrá; **we don't know a. else** no conocemos a nadie más

anyhow ['enɪhaʊ] *adv* (**a**) *(in spite of that)* en todo caso, de todas formas; *(changing the subject)* bueno, pues; **a., I said to him ...** bueno, pues le dije ...; **a., they arrived eventually** de todas formas al final llegaron (**b**) *(carelessly)* desordenadamente, de cualquier modo or forma; **don't just leave it a.** no lo dejes de cualquier forma

anyone ['enɪwʌn] *pron see* **anybody**

anyplace ['enɪpleɪs] *adv US Can see* **anywhere**

anything ['enɪθɪŋ] **1** *pron (in questions)* algo, alguna cosa; *(in negative clauses)* nada; *(no matter what)* cualquier cosa, **a. but that** cualquier cosa menos eso; **a. else?** ¿algo más?; **can I do a. for you?** ¿puedo ayudarte en algo?; **don't think a. of it** no tiene importancia; **hardly a.** casi nada; **he's a. but shy** tímido no es; **if a., I'd buy the big one** de comprar uno compraría el grande
2 *adv Fam* **as easy/hard as a.** de lo más fácil/difícil; **is this a. like what you wanted?** ¿viene a ser éste lo que tu querías?; **to run/work like a.** correr/trabajar a más no poder

anyway ['enɪweɪ] *adv see* **anyhow**

anywhere ['enɪweər] *adv* (**a**) *(in questions) (situation)* en algún sitio, en alguna parte; *(movement)* a algún sitio or alguna parte; **could it be a. else?** ¿podría estar en otro sitio?; **did you go a. yesterday?** ¿fuiste a alguna parte ayer? (**b**) *(in negative clauses) (situation)* en ningún sitio or ninguna parte; *(movement)* a ningún sitio or ninguna parte; *(no matter where)* dondequiera, donde sea, a or en cualquier parte; **go a. you like** ve a donde quieras; **she isn't a. near as clever as her sister** no es ni con mucho tan inteligente como su hermana; **she'll look for a job a. she can** buscará un trabajo donde sea; **we aren't a. near finished** no hemos terminado ni mucho menos; **we couldn't find a shop open a.** no encontramos una tienda abierta en ningún sitio

aorta [eɪ'ɔːtə] *n (pl* **aortas** or **aortae** [eɪ'ɔːtiː]*)* aorta *f*

apart [ə'pɑːt] *adv* (**a**) *(in pieces)* aparte; **to come** or **fall a.**

deshacerse; *(unstuck)* despegarse; **to take sth a.** desmontar algo (**b**) *(distant)* alejado(a); *(separate)* aparte, separado(a); **the chairs are too far a.** las sillas están demasiado separadas; **they live a.** viven separados; **to be poles a.** ser polos opuestos; **you can't tell the twins a.** no se puede distinguir los mellizos el uno del otro (**c**) *(except for)* aparte de; **joking a.** bromas aparte; **a. from a few scratches he was unhurt** aparte de algunos rasguños salió ileso; **a. from the fact that it was late** dejando aparte el hecho de que era tarde

apartheid [ə'pɑːtheɪt] *n* apartheid *m*

apartment [ə'pɑːtmənt] *n* (**a**) *US (dwelling)* apartamento *m, Esp* piso *m, Arg* departamento *m* ❏ **a. building** bloque *m* de apartamentos (**b**) *(room)* estancia *f,* habitación *f*

apathetic [æpə'θetɪk] *adj* apático(a)

apathy ['æpəθɪ] *n* apatía *f*

ape [eɪp] **1** *n (anthropoid)* antropomorfo *m,* antropoideo *m; (loosely)* mono *m,* simio *m*
2 *vt* imitar, copiar

Apennines ['æpənaɪnz] *npl* **the A.** los Apeninos

apéritif [ə'perɪtiːf] *n* aperitivo *m*

aperture ['æpətʃər] *n (hole, crack)* resquicio *m,* rendija *f; Phot* abertura *f*

APEX ['eɪpeks] *Av (abbr* **Advance Purchase Excursion)** APEX

apex ['eɪpeks] *n (pl* **apexes** *or* **apices** ['eɪpɪsiːz]) *(top)* ápice *m; (of triangle)* vértice *m; Fig* cumbre *f*

aphasia [ə'feɪzɪə] *n Med* afasia *f*

aphid ['eɪfɪd] *n* afidio *m*

aphorism ['æfərɪzəm] *n* aforismo *m*

aphrodisiac [æfrə'dɪzɪæk] **1** *adj* afrodisíaco(a)
2 *n* afrodisíaco *m*

apiece [ə'piːs] *adv* cada uno(a); **they cost 100 euros a.** cuestan 100 euros la unidad; **we were given two a.** nos dieron dos para cada uno

aplenty [ə'plentɪ] *adv* en abundancia; **there was wine a.** corría el vino a raudales

aplomb [ə'plɒm] *n* aplomo *m,* sangre *f* fría

apocalypse [ə'pɒkəlɪps] *n* apocalipsis *m inv*

apocalyptic [əpɒkə'lɪptɪk] *adj* apocalíptico(a)

Apocrypha [ə'pɒkrɪfə] *npl* libros *mpl* apócrifos de la Biblia

apocryphal [ə'pɒkrɪfəl] *adj* apócrifo(a)

apogee ['æpədʒiː] *n* apogeo *m*

apolitical [eɪpə'lɪtɪkəl] *adj* apolítico(a)

apologetic [əpɒlə'dʒetɪk] *adj (remorseful)* compungido(a); **he was very a.** pidió mil perdones; **to be a. towards sb about sth** pedirle a algn perdón por algo

apologetically [əpɒlə'dʒetɪklɪ] *adv* disculpándose, pidiendo perdón

apologist [ə'pɒlədʒɪst] *n Fml* apologista *mf,* defensor(a) *m,f* (**for** de)

apologize [ə'pɒlədʒaɪz] *vi (say sorry)* disculparse, pedir perdón; *(for absence)* presentar sus excusas; **they apologized to us for the delay** nos pidieron perdón por el retraso, se disculparon con nosotros por el retraso

apology [ə'pɒlədʒɪ] *n* disculpa *f,* excusa *f;* **I owe you an a.** tengo que pedirte perdón; **please accept our apologies** le rogamos nos disculpe; **to offer one's apologies** presentar sus excusas, disculparse; *Fam* **what an a. for a meal!** ¡vaya porquería *or Esp* birria de comida!

apoplectic [æpə'plektɪk] *adj Med* apopléctico(a); *Fam* **to be a. with rage** ponerse furioso(a)

apoplexy ['æpəpleksɪ] *n Med* apoplegía *f*

apostasy [ə'pɒstəsɪ] *n* apostasía *f*

apostle [ə'pɒsəl] *n* apóstol *m*

apostolic(al) [æpə'stɒlɪk(əl)] *adj* apostólico(a)

apostrophe [ə'pɒstrəfɪ] *n* apóstrofo *m*

apotheosis [əpɒθɪ'əʊsɪs] *n (pl* **apotheoses** [əpɒθɪ'əʊsiːz]) apoteosis *f inv*

appal, *US* **appall** [ə'pɔːl] *vt (pt & pp* **appalled)** horrorizar; **to be appalled by sth** quedar horrorizado(a) por algo

Appalachians [æpə'leɪtʃɪənz] *npl* los (montes) Appalaches

appalling [ə'pɔːlɪŋ] *adj (horrifying)* horroroso(a); *Fam (very bad)* pésimo(a), fatal

apparatus [æpə'reɪtəs] *n (pl* **apparatuses** *or* **apparatus)** *(instrument)* aparato *m; (equipment)* equipo *m; (in gymnasium)* aparatos de gimnasia; **a piece of a.** un aparato ❏ **breathing a.** aparato *m* respiratorio; **scientific a.** utensilios *mpl* de laboratorio

apparel [ə'pærəl] *n Literary (garb)* atuendo *m,* atavío *m*

apparent [ə'pærənt] *adj (obvious)* evidente, manifiesto(a); *(seeming)* aparente; **it's a. that he's wrong** está claro *or* es evidente que está equivocado; **her a. indifference** su aire de indiferencia; **to become a.** ponerse de manifiesto, quedar claro

apparently [ə'pærəntlɪ] *adv (obviously)* evidentemente; *(seemingly)* aparentemente, por lo visto; **a. not** parece que no

apparition [æpə'rɪʃən] *n (appearance)* aparición *f; (spirit)* aparición *f,* fantasma *m,* espectro *m*

appeal [ə'piːl] **1** *n* (**a**) *(request)* ruego *m,* solicitud *f; (plea)* súplica *f;* **an a. for help/money** una solicitud de ayuda/dinero; **to make an a. for sth** pedir *or* solicitar algo (**b**) *(attraction)* atractivo *m,* encanto *m; (interest)* interés *m;* **that type of music has lost its a.** esa clase de música ha perdido su encanto ❏ **sex a.** atractivo *m* sexual (**c**) *Jur* apelación *f,* recurso *m;* **to lodge an a.** presentar una apelación, interponer un recurso ❏ **right of a.** derecho *m* de apelación
2 *vt US Jur* **to a. a decision** entablar recurso de apelación contra una decisión
3 *vi* (**a**) *(plead)* rogar, suplicar (**to** a); **to a. for help** pedir *or* solicitar ayuda; **to a. to sb's better nature** apelar a los sentimientos humanitarios de algn (**b**) *(attract)* atraer; *(interest)* interesar; **it doesn't a. to me** no me atrae (**c**) *Jur* apelar, recurrir; **to a. against** *(decision, sentence)* interponer recurso de apelación contra, recurrir (**d**) *Sport* apelar; **to a. to the referee** apelar al árbitro

appealing [ə'piːlɪŋ] *adj (moving)* conmovedor(a); *(attractive)* atractivo(a), bonito(a); *(tempting)* atrayente, tentador(a)

appear [ə'pɪər] *vi* (**a**) *(become visible)* aparecer; *(publicly)* presentarse; *(on stage)* actuar; **she appeared round the corner** apareció por la esquina; **to a. before a court/a committee** comparecer ante un tribunal/un comité; **to a. in the shops** salir a la venta; **to a. on behalf of sb** aparecer en nombre de algn; **to a. on television** salir en la televisión (**b**) *(seem)* parecer; **he appears relaxed** parece relajado; **she appears to be right** parece que tiene razón; **so it appears** según parece; **there appears to have been a mistake** parece que ha habido un error

appearance [ə'pɪərəns] *n* (**a**) *(becoming visible)* aparición *f; (publicly)* presentación *f; (on stage)* actuación *f; (before court, committee)* comparecencia *f; (of book etc)* publicación *f; (in shops)* salida *f* a la venta; **to make one's first a.** debutar; **to put in an a.** hacer acto de presencia (**b**) *(look)* apariencia *f,* aspecto *m;* **by** *or* **to all appearances** al parecer, a todas luces; **don't judge by appearances** no juzgues según las apariencias; **smart in a.** de aspecto elegante; **to keep up appearances** guardar las apariencias

appease [əˈpiːz] *vt (anger)* apaciguar, aplacar; *(curiosity, hunger)* satisfacer

appeasement [əˈpiːzmənt] *n Pol* **policy of a.** política *f* de pacificación

append [əˈpend] *vt* añadir (**to** a)

appendage [əˈpendɪdʒ] *n* apéndice *m*, añadidura *f*

appendicitis [əpendɪˈsaɪtɪs] *n Med* apendicitis *f*

appendix [əˈpendɪks] *n (pl* **appendixes** *or* **appendices** [əˈpendɪsiːz]) apéndice *m*; **to have one's a.** taken out operarse de apendicitis

appetite [ˈæpɪtaɪt] *n* apetito *m* (**for** para); *Fig* deseo *m*, ganas *fpl* (**for** de); **it will spoil your a.** te quitará el apetito; **to have a good** *or* **healthy a.** tener buen apetito; **to whet one's a.** abrirse el apetito

appetizer [ˈæpɪtaɪzər] *n (drink)* aperitivo *m*; *(snack)* aperitivo *m*, tapa *f*, pincho *m*

appetizing [ˈæpɪtaɪzɪŋ] *adj* apetitoso(a)

applaud [əˈplɔːd] **1** *vt* aplaudir; *Fig (actions, decision)* aprobar
2 *vi* aplaudir, palmotear

applause [əˈplɔːz] *n* aplausos *mpl*

apple [ˈæpəl] *n (fruit)* manzana *f*; *Fig* **she's the a. of his eye** la cuida como si fuera la niña de los ojos ❑ **a. core** corazón *m* de la manzana; **a. pie** tarta *f* de manzana; **a. tree** manzano *m*; **cooking a.** manzana *f* para asar

applecart [ˈæplkɑːt] *n* **to upset the a.** *(spoil plan)* estropearlo todo

apple-pie [ˈæpəlpaɪ] *adj Fam* **in a.-p. order** arreglado(a), ordenadito(a)

appliance [əˈplaɪəns] *n* aparato *m*, dispositivo *m*; **electrical appliances** electrodomésticos *mpl*

applicable [əˈplɪkəbəl] *adj* aplicable; **it's a. only to students** se aplica *or* se refiere *or* se extiende sólo a estudiantes; **this rule is a. only after 6 o'clock** esta norma sólo es aplicable a partir de las 6

applicant [ˈæplɪkənt] *n (for post)* candidato(a) *m,f*; *(to court, for tickets)* solicitante *mf*

application [æplɪˈkeɪʃən] *n* (**a**) *(of cream, ointment)* aplicación *f*; **for external a. only** para uso externo (**b**) *(request) (for post, tickets, to court, etc)* solicitud *f*, petición *f*; *Com* **samples on a.** pídanos muestras ❑ **a. form** solicitud *f*; **job a.** solicitud *f* de empleo (**c**) *(effort)* aplicación *f*; **she lacks a.** no se aplica (**d**) *Comptr* aplicación *f*, programa *m*

applied [əˈplaɪd] *adj* aplicado(a); **a. mathematics** matemática *f* aplicada

appliqué [æˈpliːkeɪ] *n Sew* aplicación *f*

apply [əˈplaɪ] *(pt & pp* **applied**) **1** *vt (cream, ointment, paint)* aplicar; *(brake)* echar; *(rule)* aplicar; *(law)* recurrir a; *(force)* usar; *(discoveries, knowledge)* aplicar; **to a. oneself to a task** dedicarse a una tarea; **to a. one's mind to sth** concentrarse en algo
2 *vi* (**a**) *(refer)* aplicarse, referirse (**to** a); **does it a. in this case?** ¿se aplica en este caso?; **this rule does not a. to children** esta norma no se aplica a los niños (**b**) *(ask) (for job)* presentar una solicitud; *(for information, to court)* presentar una petición

apply for *vt (post)* solicitar; *(information, tickets)* pedir

appoint [əˈpɔɪnt] *vt* (**a**) *(choose) (person)* nombrar; *(committee)* elegir; **he was appointed Treasurer** le nombraron Tesorero (**b**) *(fix) (time, place, etc)* fijar, señalar

appointed [əˈpɔɪntɪd] *adj Fml (agreed) (place, hour)* fijado(a); **at the a. time** a la hora señalada

appointment [əˈpɔɪntmənt] *n* (**a**) *(to post)* nombra-

miento *m*; *(post)* cargo *m*, puesto *m*; **to make an a.** nombrar a algn (**b**) *(meeting)* cita *f*, compromiso *m*; **to have/make an a. with sb** tener una cita/citarse con algn; *(at doctor's)* tener/pedir hora con algn; **to keep an a.** acudir a una cita

apportion [əˈpɔːʃən] *vt (food, money)* distribuir, repartir; *Fig (blame)* repartir

appraisal [əˈpreɪzəl] *n* evaluación *f*, valoración *f*; **to make an a. of sth** evaluar algo

appraise [əˈpreɪz] *vt* evaluar, valorar

appreciable [əˈpriːʃəbəl] *adj (difference)* apreciable; *(loss)* sensible; *(sum)* importante

appreciably [əˈpriːʃəblɪ] *adv* sensiblemente

appreciate [əˈpriːʃeɪt] **1** *vt* (**a**) *(be thankful for) (help, advice etc)* apreciar, agradecer; **I would a. it if you didn't do that** te agradecería que no hicieras eso (**b**) *(understand) (difficulty, difference)* entender, reconocer; **I a. the problem** entiendo el problema; **do you a. the danger involved?** ¿te das cuenta del peligro que representa? (**c**) *(value)* apreciar, valorar; **to a. classical music/fine wine** saber apreciar la música clásica/el buen vino
2 *vi (increase in value)* cobrar valor, aumentarse en valor

appreciation [əpriːʃɪˈeɪʃən] *n* (**a**) *(of help, advice)* aprecio *m*, agradecimiento *m*, gratitud *f*; *(of difficulty, difference)* comprensión *f*; *(of music, wine etc)* aprecio *m*; *(appraisal) (of play)* evaluación *f*, comentario *m*; *(of situation)* evaluación *f*; **as a token of our a.** en señal de nuestra gratitud; **to show one's a.** mostrar su aprecio (**b**) *(increase in value)* aumento *m* en valor

appreciative [əˈpriːʃɪətɪv] *adj (thankful)* agradecido(a); *(responsive)* apreciativo(a), sensible; *(audience)* atento(a); **to be a. of sb's efforts** agradecerle los esfuerzos a algn

apprehend [æprɪˈhend] *vt* (**a**) *(arrest)* detener, apresar (**b**) *Fml (understand)* comprender

apprehension [æprɪˈhenʃən] *n* (**a**) *(arrest)* detención *f* (**b**) *(fear)* aprensión *f*, temor *m*, recelo *m*; **he did it with a certain amount of a.** lo hizo con cierto recelo

apprehensive [æprɪˈhensɪv] *adj (fearful)* aprensivo(a), receloso(a); **to be a. about sth** temer por algo

apprehensively [æprɪˈhensɪvlɪ] *adv* con aprensión, con recelo

apprentice [əˈprentɪs] **1** *n* aprendiz(iza) *m,f*
2 *vt* **to a. sb to a firm** colocar *or* poner a algn de aprendiz en una empresa; **to be apprenticed to a firm** estar de aprendiz en una empresa

apprenticeship [əˈprentɪsʃɪp] *n* aprendizaje *m*

appro [ˈæprəʊ] *n (abbr* **approval)** *Fam* **to get sth on a.** adquirir algo sin compromiso de compra

approach [əˈprəʊtʃ] **1** *n* (**a**) *(coming near)* acercamiento *m*; *(of season)* llegada *f*; *(to town etc)* acceso *m*, entrada *f*; **the approaches to the city** los alrededores de la ciudad; *Fig* **to make approaches to sb about sth** abordar *or* dirigirse a algn sobre algo ❑ **a. road** vía *f* de acceso (**b**) *(to problem etc)* enfoque *m*, planteamiento *m*; **his a. to the problem was different** su manera de enfocar el problema era distinta
2 *vt (come near to)* acercarse a; *(city)* entrar en; *(be similar to)* aproximarse a; *Fig (tackle) (problem etc)* abordar, enfocar; *(person)* abordar a, dirigirse a; **his ideas are approaching fanaticism** sus ideas se aproximan al fanatismo; **she's approaching forty** tiene casi cuarenta años; **temperatures approaching 40°C** temperaturas llegando a las 40 grados centígrados; **to a. sb about sth** dirigirse a algn sobre algo; **we approached the house** nos acercamos a la casa
3 *vi* acercarse

approachable [əˈprəʊtʃəbəl] *adj (person)* abordable, afable

approaching [ə'prəʊtʃɪŋ] *adj (event)* próximo(a); *(traffic)* en dirección opuesta; **the a. car** el coche que viene de frente

approbation [æprə'beɪʃən] *n* aprobación *f*; **a look of a.** una mirada aprobatoria

appropriate¹ [ə'prəʊprɪɪt] *adj (suitable) (clothing, style, etc)* apropiado(a), adecuado(a), apto(a); *(convenient) (moment, comment, etc)* oportuno(a); **you must contact the a. authority** tendrás que dirigirte a la autoridad competente

appropriate² [ə'prəʊprɪeɪt] *vt (allocate) (money etc)* asignar, destinar; *(steal)* apropiarse de

appropriately [ə'prəʊprɪətlɪ] *adv (suitably)* de una forma apropiada *or* adecuada; *(conveniently)* convenientemente

appropriation [əprəʊprɪ'eɪʃən] *n (allocation)* asignación *f*; *(seizure)* apropiación *f*

approval [ə'pruːvəl] *n (approbation)* aprobación *f*, visto *m* bueno; **to give one's a. to sth** dar el visto bueno a algo; *Com* **to get sth on a.** adquirir algo sin compromiso de compra; **a. rating** *(of product, politician)* índice *m* de aceptación *or* popularidad

approve [ə'pruːv] *vt (plans etc)* aprobar, sancionar, dar el visto bueno a; *Br Formerly* **approved school** reformatorio *m*

approve of *vt* aprobar, estar de acuerdo con, consentir en; **I don't a. of his friends** no me agradan sus amigos

approving [ə'pruːvɪŋ] *adj (look etc)* aprobatorio(a), de aprobación

approvingly [ə'pruːvɪŋlɪ] *adv* en aprobación; **she smiled a.** hizo una sonrisa de aprobación

approx. [ə'prɒks] **(a)** *(abbr* **approximate)** aproximado(a) **(b)** *(abbr* **approximately)** aproximadamente, aprox.

approximate [ə'prɒksɪmɪt] **1** *adj* aproximado(a) **2** [ə'prɒksɪmeɪt] *vt* aproximarse a, acercarse a

approximately [ə'prɒksɪmətlɪ] *adv* aproximadamente; **it's a. 10 miles away** está a 10 millas más o menos de distancia

approximation [əprɒksɪ'meɪʃən] *n* aproximación *f*; **a rough a. of the cost** una estimación aproximada del coste

APR [eɪpɪ'ɑː] *n Fin (abbr* **annual percentage rate)** TAE *m or f*

Apr *(abbr* **April)** abril *m*, abr.

apricot ['eɪprɪkɒt] *n (fruit) Esp* albaricoque *m*, *Andes RP* damasco *m*, *Méx* chabacano *m* ❏ **a. tree** *Esp* albaricoquero *m*, *Andes RP* damasco *m*, *Méx* chabacano *m*

April ['eɪprəl] *n* abril *m*; **to play an A. Fool on sb** hacerle una inocentada a algn; **A. Fool!** ¡inocente! ❏ **A. Fools' Day** día *m* uno de abril, ≃ día *m* de los Inocentes (28 de diciembre); *see also* **May**

apron ['eɪprən] *n (for cook, cleaner)* delantal *m*; *(for workman)* mandil *m*; *Av* pista *f* de servicio; *Fam* **he's tied to his wife's/mother's a. strings** está pegado a las faldas de su mujer/de su madre ❏ *Theat* **a. stage** proscenio *m*

apropos [æprə'pəʊ] **1** *adj (suitable)* oportuno(a), acertado(a)
2 *adv* **a. of her new job** y hablando de su nuevo trabajo

apse [æps] *n* ábside *m*

apt [æpt] *adj* **(a)** *(suitable)* apropiado(a), conveniente; *(remark, reply)* acertado(a), oportuno(a); *(word, name)* justo(a); *(description)* exacto(a); *(student)* dotado(a), inteligente **(b)** *(inclined)* **to be a. to do sth** ser propenso(a) *or* tender a hacer algo; **he's a. to forget** tiende a *or* suele olvidar

apt. *(abbr* **apartment)** apartamento *m*, piso *m*

aptitude ['æptɪtjuːd] *n (ability)* capacidad *f* ❏ **a. test** prueba *f* de aptitud

aptly ['æptlɪ] *adv* acertadamente

aptness ['æptnɪs] *n (of remark etc)* lo acertado, lo oportuno

aqualung ['ækwəlʌŋ] *n* botella *f* de oxígeno

aquamarine [ækwəmə'riːn] **1** *n Min* aguamarina *f*; *(colour)* color *m* de aguamarina
2 *adj* de color de aguamarina

aquaplane ['ækwəpleɪn] **1** *n* esquí *m* acuático
2 *vi Sport* hacer esquí acuático; *Aut* patinar

aquarium [ə'kweərɪəm] *n* acuario *m*

Aquarius [ə'kweərɪəs] *n Astrol Astron* Acuario *m*

aquatic [ə'kwætɪk] *adj* acuático(a)

aqueduct ['ækwɪdʌkt] *n* acueducto *m*

aquiline ['ækwɪlaɪn] *adj* aguileño(a)

Arab ['ærəb] *adj & n* árabe *(mf)*

arabesque [ærə'besk] *n* arabesco *m*

Arabia [ə'reɪbɪə] *n* Arabia

Arabian [ə'reɪbɪən] *adj* árabe, arábigo(a); **the A. Gulf** el golfo Arábigo

Arabic ['ærəbɪk] **1** *adj* árabe, arábigo(a); **A. literature/numerals** literatura *f*/numeración *f* arábiga
2 *n (language)* árabe *m*

arable ['ærəbəl] *adj (land)* cultivable, de cultivo

Aragon ['ærəgən] *n* Aragón

Aragonese [ærəgə'niːz] *adj & n* aragonés(esa) *(m,f)*

arbiter ['ɑːbɪtər] *n (referee)* árbitro *m*

arbitrary ['ɑːbɪtrərɪ] *adj (choice, decision)* arbitrario(a)

arbitrate ['ɑːbɪtreɪt] *vt & vi* arbitrar **(between** entre)

arbitration [ɑːbɪ'treɪʃən] *n* arbitraje *m*; **they agreed to submit the dispute to a.** acordaron someter la cuestión a arbitraje

arbitrator ['ɑːbɪtreɪtər] *n* árbitro *m*

arc [ɑːk] *n* arco *m* ❏ **a. lamp, a. light** arco *m* voltaico; **a. welding** soldadura *f* por arco

arcade [ɑː'keɪd] *n Archit (arches)* arcos *mpl*; *(passageway)* pasaje *m* ❏ **amusement a.** salón *m* de juegos; **shopping a.** galerías *fpl* (comerciales)

arch¹ [ɑːtʃ] **1** *n* **(a)** *Archit* arco *m*; *(vault)* bóveda *f* **(b)** *Anat* empeine *m*; **fallen arches** pies *mpl* planos
2 *vt (back)* arquear, doblar; **to a. one's back** arquear la espalda

arch² *adj* **a. enemy** mayor enemigo(a) *m,f*

arch- ['ɑːtʃ] *pref* archi-

archaeological [ɑːkɪə'lɒdʒɪkəl] *adj* arqueológico(a)

archaeologist [ɑːkɪ'ɒlədʒɪst] *n* arqueólogo(a) *m,f*

archaeology [ɑːkɪ'ɒlədʒɪ] *n* arqueología *f*

archaic [ɑː'keɪɪk] *adj* arcaico(a)

archaism ['ɑːkeɪɪzəm] *n* arcaísmo *m*

archangel ['ɑːkeɪndʒəl] *n* arcángel *m*

archbishop [ɑːtʃ'bɪʃəp] *n* arzobispo *m*; **the A. of York** el Arzobispo de York

arched [ɑːtʃt] *adj Archit* arqueado(a); *(vaulted)*, abovedado(a)

archeological [ɑːkɪə'lɒdʒɪkəl] *adj US see* **archaeological**

archeologist [ɑːkɪ'ɒlədʒɪst] *n US see* **archaeologist**

archeology [ɑːkɪ'ɒlədʒɪ] *n US see* **archaeology**

archer ['ɑːtʃər] *n* arquero(a) *m,f*

archery ['ɑːtʃərɪ] *n* tiro *m* al arco

archetypal ['ɑːkɪtaɪpəl] *adj* arquetípico(a)

archetype ['ɑːkɪtaɪp] *n (original)* arquetipo *m*; *(example)* modelo *m*

archipelago [ɑːkɪ'pelɪgəʊ] *n (pl* **archipelagos** *or* **archipelagoes)** archipiélago *m*

architect ['ɑːkɪtekt] *n* arquitecto(a) *m,f*

architectural [ɑːkɪ'tektʃərəl] *adj* arquitectónico(a)

architecture ['ɑːkɪtektʃər] *n* arquitectura *f*

archive ['ɑːkaɪv] *n also Comptr* archivo *m*

archway ['ɑːtʃweɪ] *n (arch)* arco *m; (vault)* bóveda *f; (in church)* atrio *m; (passage)* pasaje *m*

arctic ['ɑːktɪk] **1** *adj (conditions, weather)* ártico(a); *Fam (very cold)* glacial
2 the A. *n* el Ártico ❑ **A. Circle** círculo *m* polar Ártico; **A. Ocean** océano *m* Ártico

ardent ['ɑːdənt] *adj (admirer, supporter, lover)* apasionado(a); *(desire)* ardiente

ardour, *US* **ardor** ['ɑːdər] *n (passion)* pasión *f,* ardor *m; (zeal)* fervor *m*

arduous ['ɑːdjʊəs] *adj (climb, journey)* arduo(a), penoso(a); *(task, work)* difícil

are [ɑːr] *2nd person sing pres, 1st, 2nd, 3rd person pl pres see* **be**

area ['eərɪə] *n (surface)* area *f,* superficie *f; (space)* espacio *m,* extensión *f; (region)* región *f; (of town, city)* zona *f; Fig (field) of knowledge etc)* campo *m,* terreno *m;* **an a. of 10 square metres** una superficie de 10 metros cuadrados; **disaster a.** zona del desastre; *Fig* **his personal life is a disaster a.** tiene una vida personal desastrosa; **it's a grey a.** es un campo poco trabajado ❑ *US Tel* **a. code** prefijo *m* local; *Com* **a. sales manager** representante *mf* regional; *Sport* **penalty a.** área *f* de castigo; **postal a.** distrito *m* postal; *Educ* **subject a.** especialidad *f*

arena [ə'riːnə] *n (stadium)* estadio *m; (bullring)* plaza *f; (circus)* pista *f, Fig (stage)* palestra *f,* campo *m* de batalla

aren't [ɑːnt] **(a)** = **are not (b)** a. I? = am I not?

Argentina [ɑːdʒən'tiːnə] *n* Argentina

Argentine ['ɑːdʒəntaɪn] **1** *n (person)* argentino(a) *m,f; Old-fashioned* **the A.** *(country)* (la) Argentina
2 *adj* argentino(a)

Argentinian [ɑːdʒən'tɪnɪən] *adj & n* argentino(a) *(m,f)*

argon ['ɑːgɒn] *n Chem* argón *m*

arguable [ɑːgjʊəbəl] *adj* discutible **(that, whether** que)

arguably ['ɑːgjʊəblɪ] *adv* it's a. the best hay quienes dicen que es el mejor

argue ['ɑːgjuː] **1** *vt (reason) (case etc)* discutir, debatir; *(point of view, position)* mantener; **she argued that it wouldn't be practical** sostenía que no sería factible
2 *vi (quarrel)* discutir, reñir; *(reason)* argumentar, razonar; **don't a., just do it** hazlo y no discutas; **to a. for** abogar por; **to a. against sth** ponerse en contra de algo; **to a. about sth with sb** discutir algo con algn, reñir con algn por algo

argument ['ɑːgjʊmənt] *n (reason)* argumento *m,* razonamiento *m* **(for** en pro de, a favor de; **against** en contra de); *(quarrel)* discusión *f,* disputa *f,* riña *f;* **let's say $50 for the sake of a.** pongamos 50 dólares por decir algo; **to follow sb's (line of) a.** seguir el razonamiento de algn; **to have an a. with sb** discutir *or* reñir con algn

argumentative [ɑːgjʊ'mentətɪv] *adj* discutidor(a)

argy-bargy ['ɑːdʒɪ'bɑːdʒɪ] *n Fam* agarrada *f,* trifulca *f*

aria ['ɑːrɪə] *n Mus* aria *f*

arid ['ærɪd] *adj* árido(a)

aridity [ə'rɪdɪtɪ] *n* aridez *f*

Aries ['eəriːz] *n Astrol Astron* Aries *m*

arise [ə'raɪz] *vi (pt* **arose** [ə'rəʊz]; *pp* **arisen** [ə'rɪzən]) *Literary (get up)* levantarse; *(happen)* surgir, presentarse; **problems have arisen** han surgido problemas; **difficulties which a. from lack of time** dificultades que provienen de la falta de tiempo; **should the occasion/need a.** si se presenta la ocasión/si hace falta

aristocracy [ærɪ'stɒkrəsɪ] *n* aristocracia *f*

aristocrat [*Br* 'ærɪstəkræt, *US* ə'rɪstəkræt] *n* aristócrata *mf*

aristocratic [*Br* ærɪstə'krætɪk, *US* ərɪstə'krætɪk] *adj* aristocrático(a)

arithmetic [ə'rɪθmətɪk] *n* aritmética *f* ❑ **mental a.** cálculo *m* mental

arithmetical [ærɪθ'metɪkəl] *adj* aritmético(a)

ark [ɑːk] *n* arca *f;* **Noah's A.** el arca de Noé

arm [ɑːm] **1** *n* **(a)** *Anat* brazo *m; (of garment)* manga *f; (of chair)* brazo; **he took my a.** me agarró del brazo; **to walk a. in a.** ir cogidos(as) del brazo; *Fig* **to keep sb at a.'s length** mantener a algn a distancia; *Fig* **to welcome sb with open arms** recibir a algn con los brazos abiertos; **a. wrestling** los pulsos, *Am* la pulseada **(b)** *Mil* **arms** armas *fpl; Fig Fam* **to be up in a. about sth** estar furioso(a) por algo ❑ **a. race** carrera *f* armamentística; **coat of a.** *(in heraldry)* escudo *m,* blasón *m*
2 *vt (person, country)* armar; **to a. oneself against sth** armarse contra algo

armadillo [ɑːmə'dɪləʊ] *n (pl* **armadillos***)* armadillo *m*

Armageddon [ɑːmə'gedən] *n* apocalipsis *m inv*

armaments ['ɑːməmənts] *npl (weapons)* armamentos *mpl,* material *m sing* bélico

armband ['ɑːmbænd] *n Mil etc* brazalete *m; (for swimming)* flotador *m*

armchair ['ɑːmtʃeər] *n* sillón *m*

armed ['ɑːmd] *adj* armado(a) ❑ **a. forces** fuerzas *fpl* armadas; **a. robbery** robo *m* a mano armada

Armenia [ɑː'miːnɪə] *n* Armenia

Armenian [ɑː'miːnɪən] *adj & n* armenio(a) *(m,f)*

armful ['ɑːmfʊl] *n* brazada *f*

armhole ['ɑːmhəʊl] *n (of garment)* sisa *f*

armistice ['ɑːmɪstɪs] *n* armisticio *m;* **A. Day** = día en que se conmemora el final de la primera Guerra Mundial

armour, *US* **armor** ['ɑːmər] *n Mil (on vehicle)* blindaje *m;* **(suit of) a.** armadura *f*

armoured car, *US* **armored car** [ɑːməd'kɑːr] *n* carro *m* blindado

armour-plated, *US* **armor-plated** ['ɑːməpleɪtɪd] *adj* acorazado(a)

armoury, *US* **armory** ['ɑːmərɪ] *n* armería *f,* arsenal *m*

armpit ['ɑːmpɪt] *n* axila *f,* sobaco *m*

armrest ['ɑːmrest] *n* reposabrazos *m inv*

arm-twisting ['ɑːm'twɪstɪŋ] *n Fam* it took a bit of a.-t., but I got him to agree tuve que apretarle las clavijas un poco, pero logré que cediese

arm-wrestle ['ɑːm'resəl] *vi* to a.-w. with sb echar un pulso con algn

army ['ɑːmɪ] *n* ejército *m;* **to join the a.** alistarse, hacerse militar; **to be in the a.** ser militar; *Fig* **an a. of workers** un ejército de trabajadores

aroma [ə'rəʊmə] *n* aroma *m,* olor *m*

aromatic [ærə'mætɪk] *adj* aromático(a)

arose [ə'rəʊz] *pt see* **arise**

around [ə'raʊnd] **1** *adv (in the vicinity)* alrededor; **all a.** por todos los lados; **are the children a.?** ¿están los niños por aquí?; **computers have been a. for some time** hace bastante tiempo que la gente tiene ordenadores; **he looked a.** miró (a su) alrededor; **let me show you a.** ven que te enseñe (la casa *etc*); **to fool a.** hacer el tonto *or* el indio; **to rush a.** correr de un lado para otro; **to turn a.** *Esp* dar(se) la vuelta, *Am* darse vuelta; *Fam* **he's been a.** ha corrido mucho mundo

  2 *prep* (**a**) *(in the vicinity of)* alrededor de; **a. the corner** a la vuelta de la esquina; **a. the world** por todo el mundo; **is there a bank a. here?** ¿hay un banco por aquí? (**b**) *(approximately)* aproximadamente, a eso de; **it's a. 10 o'clock** son a eso de las 10

around-the-clock [ə'raʊndðə'klɒk] **1** *adj* continuo(a), 24 horas al día

  2 *adv* (durante) las 24 horas del día

arousal [ə'raʊzəl] *n* excitación *f*

arouse [ə'raʊz] *vt (wake up) (person)* despertar; *Fig (desire)* despertar; *(suspicion)* levantar; *(person) (incite)* estimular; *(sexually)* excitar

arr. *Rail (abbr* **arrival)** llegada *f*

arraign [ə'reɪn] *vt Jur* hacer comparecer, citar

arraignment [ə'reɪnmənt] *n Jur* acusación *f*

arrange [ə'reɪndʒ] **1** *vt* (**a**) *(put into order) (books, furniture)* ordenar, colocar; *(hair, flowers)* arreglar; *Mus* adaptar (**b**) *(plan) (visit, outing)* organizar, planear; *(agree on)* quedar en; **to a. a time** fijar una hora; **it was arranged that ...** se acordó que ...; **we arranged to meet in the hotel** quedamos en vernos en el hotel; **arranged marriage** boda *f* arreglada

  2 *vi (make plans)* hacer preparativos *or* planes, arreglarlo; **he's arranged for a taxi to come** ha avisado a un taxi para que venga; **I shall a. for him to be there** lo arreglaré para que pueda asistir; **we arranged for flowers to be bought** mandamos comprar flores

arrangement [ə'reɪndʒmənt] *n* (**a**) *(display)* colocación *f*; *Mus* adaptación *f* ❏ **flower a.** adorno *m* floral (**b**) *(agreement)* acuerdo *m*, arreglo *m*; **appointments by a.** visitas *fpl* a horas convenidas; **I'm pleased with the a.** me gusta el arreglo; **to come to an a. with sb about sth/to do sth** llegar a un acuerdo con algn sobre algo/para hacer algo (**c**) **arrangements** *(plans)* planes *mpl*; *(preparations)* preparativos *mpl*; *(projects)* proyectos *mpl*; **to make a. to do sth** hacer planes *or* preparativos *or* proyectos para hacer algo; **what are your holiday a.?** ¿qué proyectos de vacaciones tienes?

arrant ['ærənt] *adj* total, absoluto(a)

array [ə'reɪ] *n (collection)* colección *f*; **a great a. of goods** un gran surtido de productos

arrears [ə'rɪəz] *npl (money, work)* atrasos *mpl*; **to be in a. with the rent** estar atrasado(a) con el alquiler *or Méx* con la renta; **to be paid in a.** cobrar con retraso

arrest [ə'rest] **1** *n* (**a**) *(of criminal)* detención *f*; **to be under a.** quedar detenido(a) (**b**) *(of machine)* paro *m* ❏ *Med* **cardiac a.** paro *m* cardíaco

  2 *vt (criminal)* detener; *Fig (development, progress)* frenar, detener·

arresting [ə'restɪŋ] *adj* llamativo(a), que llama la atención

arrival [ə'raɪvəl] *n* llegada *f*; **a new a.** un(a) recién llegado(a); *(in class etc)* un nuevo miembro; *(in family)* un(a) recién nacido(a); **I'll phone on a.** llamaré al llegar

arrive [ə'raɪv] *vi* llegar (**at, in** a); *Fig (succeed)* triunfar; **to a. unexpectedly** llegar de improviso

arrive at *vt (reach) (decision, agreement)* llegar a; *(price)* fijar

arrogance ['ærəgəns] *n* arrogancia *f*

arrogant ['ærəgənt] *adj* arrogante, altanero(a)

arrogantly ['ærəgəntlɪ] *adv* eon arrogancia

arrow ['ærəʊ] *n* flecha *f* ❏ *Comptr* **a. key** tecla *f* de dirección *or* de movimiento del cursor

arrowhead ['ærəʊhed] *n* punta *f* de flecha

arse ['ɑːs] *n Br Vulg* (**a**) *(buttocks)* culo *m* (**b**) *(stupid person) Esp* gilipollas *mf inv, Am* pendejo(a) *m,f, RP* boludo(a) *m,f*

arsenal ['ɑːsənəl] *n* arsenal *m*

arsenic ['ɑːsənɪk] *n* arsénico *m*

arson ['ɑːsən] *n* incendio *m* provocado

arsonist ['ɑːsənɪst] *n* pirómano(a) *m,f*, incendiario(a) *m,f*

art [ɑːt] *n* (**a**) *(painting, drama etc)* arte *m*; *(drawing)* dibujo *m*; **the arts** las bellas artes; **arts and crafts** artes *fpl* y oficios *mpl*; **a. exhibition** exposición *f* de arte; **a. school** escuela *f* de bellas artes ❏ **a. gallery** galería *f* (de arte); **a. nouveau** art *m* nouveau; **fine a.** arte *f*; **work of a.** obra *f* de arte (**b**) *(skill)* habilidad *f*, arte *m*; **there's an a. to driving in thick snow** conducir en mucha nieve requiere su técnica; **the a. of conversation** saber conversar (**c**) **arts** *(branch of knowledge)* letras *fpl*; **a. and science** ciencias y letras ❏ *Univ* **Faculty of A.** Facultad *f* de Filosofía y Letras

artefact ['ɑːtɪfækt] *n* artefacto *m*

arterial [ɑː'tɪərɪəl] *adj Anat* arterial; *(road)* principal

arteriosclerosis [ɑːtɪərɪəʊsklɪ'rəʊsɪs] *n (pl* **arterioscleroroses** [ɑːtɪərɪəʊsklɪ'rəʊsiːz]) arteriosclerosis *f inv*

artery ['ɑːtərɪ] *n Anat* arteria *f*; *(road)* vía *f* principal; *(railway)* línea *f* principal

artesian well [ɑːtiːzɪən'wel] *n* pozo *m* artesiano

artful ['ɑːtfʊl] *adj (cunning)* mañoso(a), ladino(a), astuto(a)

arthritic [ɑː'θrɪtɪk] *adj* artrítico(a)

arthritis [ɑː'θraɪtɪs] *n* artritis *f*

artichoke ['ɑːtɪtʃəʊk] *n* (**globe**) **a.** alcachofa *f*, *RP* alcaucil *m*; **Jerusalem a.** aguaturma *f*, cotufa *f*

article ['ɑːtɪkəl] **1** *n* (**a**) *(thing)* artículo *m*, cosa *f*; *Press* artículo; *Jur* artículo, cláusula *f* ❏ **a. of clothing** prenda *f* de vestir; *Ling* **definite/indefinite a.** artículo *m* definido/ indefinido; *Press* **leading a.** editorial *m* (**b**) **articles** contrato *m sing* de aprendizaje

  2 *vt* **to be articled to** *or* **with a firm of solicitors** ser abogado(a) en aprendizaje con un gabinete de abogados

articled ['ɑːtɪkəld] *adj* **a. clerk** abogado(a) *m,f* en prácticas

articulate¹ [ɑː'tɪkjʊlɪt] *adj (speech)* claro(a); *(person)* que se expresa bien *or* con facilidad

articulate² [ɑː'tɪkjʊleɪt] *vt & vi* articular; *(words)* pronunciar ❏ **articulated lorry** camión *m* articulado

articulately [ɑː'tɪkjʊlətlɪ] *adv (speak, explain)* claramente

articulation [ɑːtɪkjʊ'leɪʃən] *n* articulación *f*

artifact ['ɑːtɪfækt] *n see* **artefact**

artifice ['ɑːtɪfɪs] *n (cunning)* astucia *f*, ingenio *m*; *(clever trick)* artificio *m*, estratagema *f*

artificial [ɑːtɪ'fɪʃəl] *adj (light, flowers, flavouring)* artificial; *(hair, limb)* postizo(a); *(smile)* falso(a) ❏ **a. insemination** inseminación *f* artificial, *Comptr* **a. intelligence** inteligencia *f* artificial; **a. respiration** respiración *f* artificial

artificially [ɑːtɪ'fɪʃəlɪ] *adv* de un modo artificial

artillery [ɑː'tɪlərɪ] *n Mil* artillería *f*

artisan ['ɑːtɪzæn] *n* artesano(a) *m,f*

artist ['ɑːtɪst] *n* artista *mf*; *(painter)* pintor(a) *m,f*

artistic [ɑː'tɪstɪk] *adj* artístico(a); **he's a.** tiene talento artístico

artistry ['ɑːtɪstrɪ] *n* arte *m*, talento *m* artístico

artless ['ɑːtlɪs] *adj (simple)* sencillo(a), simple

artwork ['ɑːtwɜːk] *n (in book, magazine)* ilustraciones *fpl*

arty ['ɑːtɪ], *US* **artsy** ['ɑːtsɪ] *adj* (**artier, artiest**, *US* **artsier, artsiest**) *Fam (person)* que se las da de artista

Aryan ['eərɪən] *adj & n* ario(a) *(m,f)*

as [æz, *unstressed* əz] **1** *adj & conj* **(a)** *(comparison)* **as ... as
... tan ... como ...**; *(distance)* **as far as** hasta; *Fig* **as far as I'm
concerned** por lo que a mi respecta; **as many as** tantos(as)
como; **as much as** tanto(a); **as tall as me** tan alto(a) como
yo; **as opposed to** a diferencia de; **at the same time as us**
a la (misma) vez que nosotros; **from as little as $18 a
week** desde tan sólo dieciocho dólares por semana; **I did
as much as I could** hice todo que pude; **I'll stay as long as I
can** me quedo tanto como puedo; **just as big** igual de
grande; **there were as many as 500** hubo hasta 500; **the
same as** igual que, el mismo que; **we now pay $100, as
against last year's $80** ahora nos cuesta 100 dólares,
comparado con los 80 del año pasado **(b)** *(manner)* como;
as a motorist, I can't agree como conductor, no estoy de
acuerdo; **as a rule** por regla general; **as you know, it isn't
true** como ya sabéis, no es verdad; **as you like** como
quieras; **do as I say, not as I do** haz lo que yo te digo, no lo
que yo hago; **he's working as a doctor** está trabajando de
médico; **I thought as much** ya me lo suponía; **it serves as
a table** sirve de mesa; **leave it as it is** déjalo tal como está;
she was dressed as a gypsy iba vestida de gitana; *Theat*
with Núria Espert as Phaedra con Núria Espert en el
papel de Fedra **(c)** *(while, when)* mientras (que); **as a child,
she was very bright** de niña era muy espabilada; **as I was
eating** mientras comía; **as we were leaving we saw Pat**
al salir vimos a Pat **(d)** *(though)* ya que, aunque; **be that as
it may** por mucho que así sea; **much as I like it I can't
afford to buy it** por mucho que me guste, no me lo puedo
comprar; **young as he is** aunque es joven **(e)** *(because)*
como, puesto que, ya que; **as he was out, we left a
message** como no estaba, dejamos un recado; **I'll come
early as I want to see your mother** vendré temprano
porque quiero ver a tu madre **(f)** *(and so)* como, igual que;
as well también; **I like fish, as does my wife** me gusta el
pescado y a mi mujer también **(g)** *(purpose)* para; **so as to
do sth** para hacer algo; **they left early so as to avoid the
traffic** salieron temprano para evitar el tráfico **(h)**
(concerning) en cuanto a; **as for my brother** en cuanto a
mi hermano, por lo que se refiere a mi hermano **(i)** **as from,
as of** a partir de; **as of tomorrow** a partir de mañana,
empezando mañana **(j)** **he did it as if his life depended
on it** lo hizo como si su vida dependiera de ello; **it looks as
if the concert is off** parece ser que no habrá concierto;
she spoke as though (she was) tired habló como si
estuviera atontada; *Fam* **as if I cared!** ¿y a mí qué? **(k)** **as
it is** *(in fact)* de por sí; **as it is we won't finish till
tomorrow** tal como van las cosas no terminaremos hasta
mañana; **it's late enough as it is, without stopping for a
meal** ya es muy tarde, no hay tiempo para parar a comer;
as it were por así decirlo, como si dijéramos **(l)** **as long as**
(only if) siempre que, con tal de que; **I'll come as long as it
isn't for long** vendré siempre que no sea por mucho rato;
I'll go as long as you come too yo iré con tal de que vayas
tú también **(m)** **as regards** en cuanto a, por lo que se refiere
a; **as usual** como siempre; **as yet** aún, todavía; **there's no
news as yet** no hay noticias todavía
2 *rel pron* **such as** como por ejemplo, tal como; **fruits
such as apples and pears** frutas tales como manzanas y
peras

ASA [eɪes'eɪ] *n Br* (*abbr* **Advertising Standards Authority**)
= organismo regulador de la publicidad

asap [eɪeseɪ'piː] *adv* (*abbr* **as soon as possible**) cuanto
antes, lo antes posible

asbestos [æz'bestəs] *n* amianto *m*, asbesto *m*

asbestosis [æzbes'təʊsɪs] *n Med* amiantosis *f*

ascend [ə'send] **1** *vt (mountain)* subir a, ascender; *(throne)*
subir *or* acceder a
2 *vi* subir, ascender

ascendancy [ə'sendənsɪ] *n* ascendiente *m*, dominio *m*

ascendant [ə'sendənt] *n* ascendiente *m*; **to be in the a.**
estar en auge, predominar

Ascension [ə'senʃən] *n Rel* Ascensión ❑ **A. Day** Día *m* de
la Ascensión; **A. Island** Ascensión

ascension [ə'senʃən] *n Rel* ascensión *f*

ascent [ə'sent] *n (slope)* subida *f*, cuesta *f*; *(act of going up)*
subida *f*, ascenso *m*

ascertain [æsə'teɪn] *vt* averiguar, enterarse de

ascetic [ə'setɪk] **1** *adj* ascético(a)
2 *n* asceta *mf*

asceticism [ə'setɪsɪzəm] *n* ascetismo *m*

ASCII ['æskɪ] *n Comptr* (*abbr* **American Standard Code
for Information Interchange**) ASCII *m*

ascribe [ə'skraɪb] *vt* **to a. sth to sb/sth** atribuir *or*
imputar algo a algn/algo

ASEAN ['æzɪæn] *n* (*abbr* **Association of South-East Asian
Nations**) ASEAN *f*

aseptic [ə'septɪk] *adj* aséptico(a)

asexual [eɪ'seksjʊəl] *adj* asexual

ash¹ [æʃ] *n Bot* fresno *m* ❑ **mountain a.** serbal *m* silvestre

ash² [æʃ] *n* ceniza *f* ❑ **a. bin**, *US* **a. can** cubo *m* de la
basura; *Rel* **A. Wednesday** miércoles *m* inv de ceniza

ashamed [ə'ʃeɪmd] *adj* avergonzado(a), *Am salvo RP*
apenado(a); **he was too a. to answer** le daba vergüenza
or Am salvo RP pena contestar; **I'm a. of you** ¡me
avergüenzas!, *Am salvo RP* ¡me das pena!; **it's nothing to
be a. of** no es motivo para avergonzarse *or Am salvo RP*
apenarse; **she was a. of her behaviour** estaba avergon-
zada *or Am salvo RP* apenada de su comportamiento; **you
ought to be a. of yourself!** ¡no te da vergüenza!, *Am salvo
RP* ¡debería darte pena!

ashen ['æʃən] *adj (face)* pálido(a), lívido(a)

ashore [ə'ʃɔːr] *adv Naut* en tierra; **to go a.** desembarcar

ashtray ['æʃtreɪ] *n* cenicero *m*

Asia ['eɪʒə] *n* Asia ❑ **A. Minor** Asia Menor

Asian ['eɪʒən] **1** *n* asiático(a) *m,f*; *Br (person from Indian
sub-continent)* = persona de la India, Paquistán o
Bangladesh
2 *adj* asiático(a); *Br (from Indian sub-continent)* = de la
India, Paquistán o Bangladesh; *US* **A. American** =
americano(a) de origen asiático

Asiatic [eɪsɪ'ætɪk] *adj & n* asiático(a) *(m,f)*

aside [ə'saɪd] **1** *adv* al lado, aparte; **to cast a.** echar a un
lado; **to put** *or* **set sth a.** apartar *or* reservar algo; **to stand
a.** hacerse a un lado, apartarse; **to take sb a.** llevarle a algn
a un lado
2 *prep US* **a. from** *(apart from)* aparte de; *(as well as)*
además de
3 *n Theat* aparte *m*; **to say in an a.** decir un aparte

asinine ['æsɪnaɪn] *adj* estúpido(a), imbécil

ask [ɑːsk] *vt* **1** *(a) (inquire)* preguntar; **to a. sb a question**
hacer una pregunta a algn; **to a. sb the time** preguntar la
hora a algn; **don't a. me!** ¡yo qué sé!, ¡ni idea!; **I only asked!**
¡sólo era por saber! **(b)** *(request)* pedir, solicitar; **I asked
them to go** les pedí que se fueran; **I asked permission to
leave** pedí permiso para marcharme; **she asked me to
post it** me pidió que lo echara al buzón; **she asked to see
the manager** dijo que quería hablar con el encargado;
that's asking a lot eso es mucho pedir **(c)** *(invite)* invitar;
we didn't go to the party because we weren't asked no
fuimos a la fiesta porque no nos invitaron
2 *vi (inquire)* preguntar; *(request)* pedir

ask after *vt* **to a. after sb** preguntar por algn

ask back *vt* **to a. sb back** devolver la invitación a algn

ask for *vt (help, advice)* pedir, solicitar; *(person)* preguntar por, buscar; *(price)* pedir por; **he asked for a grant** solicitó una beca; **how much are they asking for the car?** ¿cuánto piden por el coche?; **it's someone asking for Clare** preguntan por Clare; **that's asking for trouble** eso es buscarse problemas; **you asked for it** ¡te lo buscaste!

ask out *vt* **to a. sb out** invitar a algn a salir

ask round *vt* **to a. sb round (to one's home)** invitar a algn a casa

askance [ə'skæns] *adv* **to look a. at sth/sb** mirar algo/a algn con recelo

askew [ə'skjuː] **1** *adj* ladeado(a)
2 *adv* de lado, de través

asking ['ɑːskɪŋ] *n* **it's yours for the a.** si lo pides, es tuyo; **a. price** precio *m* de salida

ASL [eɪes'el] *n US (abbr* **American Sign Language)** = lenguaje de signos para sordos

asleep [ə'sliːp] *adj (person)* dormido(a); *(limb)* adormecido(a); **to be fast** *or* **sound a.** estar profundamente dormido(a); **to fall a.** quedarse dormido(a); **my foot is a.** se me ha dormido el pie

asocial [eɪ'səʊʃəl] *adj* asocial

asp [æsp] *n* áspid *m*

asparagus [ə'spærəgəs] *n inv (plant)* espárrago *m*; *(shoots)* espárragos *mpl*

aspect ['æspekt] *n* **(a)** *(of question, situation)* aspecto *m*; **to examine all the aspects of a problem** estudiar un problema bajo todos los aspectos **(b)** *(of building)* orientación *f*; **a house with a south-facing a.** una casa orientada al sur

aspen ['æspən] *n Bot* álamo *m* temblón

asperity [æ'sperɪtɪ] *n* aspereza *f*

aspersions [ə'spɜːʃənz] *npl* **to cast a. on sb** difamar a algn

asphalt ['æsfælt] *n* asfalto *m* ❏ **a. road** carretera *f* asfaltada

asphyxia [æs'fɪksɪə] *n* asfixia *f*

asphyxiate [æs'fɪksɪeɪt] **1** *vt* asfixiar; **to be asphyxiated** morir asfixiado(a)
2 *vi* asfixiarse, morir asfixiado(a)

asphyxiation [æsfɪksɪ'eɪʃən] *n* asfixia *f*

aspic ['æspɪk] *n Culin* gelatina *f*; **chicken in a.** pollo *m* en gelatina

aspidistra [æspɪ'dɪstrə] *n Bot* aspidistra *f*

aspirant [ə'spaɪərənt] *n* aspirante *mf*

aspirate¹ ['æspɪreɪt] *vt & vi Ling* aspirar

aspirate² ['æspɪrɪt] *n Ling* aspirado *m*

aspiration [æspə'reɪʃən] *n* **(a)** *(ambition)* aspiración *f*, ambición *f* **(b)** *Ling* aspiración *f*

aspire [ə'spaɪər] *vi* **to a. to do sth** aspirar a hacer algo

aspirin® ['æsprɪn] *n (pl* **aspirin** *or* **aspirins)** aspirina® *f*

aspiring [ə'spaɪərɪŋ] *adj* **to be an a. actor** aspirar a ser actor

ass¹ [æs] *n Zool* asno(a) *m,f*, burro(a) *m,f*; *Fam Fig (stupid person)* burro(a) *m,f*; **to make an a. of oneself** hacer el ridículo

ass² [æs] *n US Vulg* culo *m*

assail [ə'seɪl] *vt (attack)* atacar **(with** con); *Fig* asaltar; **assailed by doubts** asaltado(a) por las dudas

assailant [ə'seɪlənt] *n (attacker)* agresor(a) *m,f*, atacante *mf*

assassin [ə'sæsɪn] *n* asesino(a) *m,f*

assassinate [ə'sæsɪneɪt] *vt* asesinar

assassination [əsæsɪneɪ'ʃən] *n* asesinato *m*

assault [ə'sɔːlt] **1** *n Mil* ataque *m* **(on** a, contra), asalto *m* **(on** sobre); *Jur* agresión *f*, violencia *f* ❏ **a. and battery** lesiones *fpl*; *Mil* **a. course** pista *f* de entrenamiento; **indecent a.** ofensa *f* al pudor
2 *vt Mil* asaltar, atacar; *Jur* agredir; *(sexually)* violar; **to be assaulted** ser agredido(a)

assemble [ə'sembəl] **1** *vt (people)* reunir, juntar; *(furniture)* montar
2 *vi (people)* reunirse, juntarse

assembly [ə'semblɪ] *n (meeting)* reunión *f*, asamblea *f*; *Br Sch* = reunión de todos los profesores y los alumnos al principio de la jornada escolar; *(of machine, furniture)* montaje *m*, ensamblaje *m* ❏ *Comptr* **a. language** lenguaje *m* ensamblador; *Ind* **a. line** cadena *f* de montaje; **right of a.** derecho *m* de reunión

assent [ə'sent] **1** *n (agreement)* asentimiento *m*; *(consent)* consentimiento *m*; *(approval)* aprobación *f*
2 *vi (agree)* asentir **(to** a); *(consent)* consentir **(to** en)

assert [ə'sɜːt] *vt (declare)* afirmar, mantener; **he asserted that ...** mantuvo que ...; **to a. oneself** imponerse; **to a. one's rights** hacer valer sus derechos

assertion [ə'sɜːʃən] *n (declaration)* afirmación *f*, declaración *f*; *(of a right)* reivindicación *f*

assertive [ə'sɜːtɪv] *adj* enérgico(a), dinámico(a)

assertiveness [ə'sɜːtɪvnəs] *n* afirmación *f* personal, autoafirmación *f*; **a. training** cursos *mpl* de afirmación personal

assess [ə'ses] *vt (estimate value)* valorar, tasar; *(calculate) (damages, price)* calcular, fijar; *(tax)* gravar; *Fig (evaluate) (effect etc)* evaluar, juzgar

assessment [ə'sesmənt] *n (of value)* valoración *f*, tasación *f*; *(of damages, price)* cálculo *m*; *(of taxes)* gravamen *m*; *Fig (evaluation)* evaluación *f*, juicio *m*

assessor [ə'sesər] *n* asesor(a) *m,f* ❏ **tax a.** tasador(a) *m,f*

asset ['æset] *n* **(a)** *(valuable quality)* calidad *f* positiva, ventaja *f*; **her greatest a. is her sense of humour** lo mejor que tiene es su sentido del humor; **he's an a. to the firm** es una valiosa aportación a la empresa **(b)** *Fin* **assets** bienes *mpl* ❏ **current a.** activo *m* disponible; **fixed a.** bienes *mpl* raíces

asset-stripping ['æsetstrɪpɪŋ] *n Fin* = acaparamiento de activos de una empresa en crisis para su posterior reventa

asshole ['æshəʊl] *n US Vulg* **(a)** *(anus)* ojete *m* **(b)** *(unpleasant person)* hijo(a) *m,f* de puta, cabrón(ona) *m,f*

assiduous [ə'sɪdjʊəs] *adj* asiduo(a)

assiduously [ə'sɪdjʊəslɪ] *adv* asiduamente

assign [ə'saɪn] *vt (allot) (task, duty)* asignar, señalar; *(give) (property etc)* ceder; **to a. sb to a job** asignar *or* designar a algn para un trabajo

assignation [æsɪg'neɪʃən] *n (secret meeting)* cita *f* a escondidas

assignment [ə'saɪnmənt] *n (allocation)* asignación *f*; *(task)* tarea *f*; *(mission)* misión *f*; *(appointment)* cita *f*

assimilate [ə'sɪmɪleɪt] *vt (food, facts)* asimilar; **to be assimilated into** asimilarse *or* incorporarse a

assimilation [əsɪmɪ'leɪʃən] *n* asimilación *f*

assist [ə'sɪst] **1** *vt (help)* ayudar; **to a. sb in doing** *or* **to do sth** ayudar a algn a *or* en hacer algo; *Jur* **he's assisting the police with their inquiries** le está interrogando la policía
2 *vi* ayudar; **to a. in sth/in doing sth** ayudar en algo/en hacer algo

assistance [ə'sɪstəns] *n (help)* ayuda *f*, auxilio *m*; **can I be of any a.?** ¿puedo ayudarle?; *(in shop)* ¿qué quería?; **to come to sb's a.** acudir en ayuda *or* en auxilio de algn

assistant [ə'sɪstənt] *n* ayudante *mf* ❏ **a. manager** subdirector(a) *m,f*; **a. master/mistress** *(in school)* profesor(a) *m,f* (de instituto); **laboratory a.** ayudante *mf* de laboratorio; **shop a.** dependiente(a) *m,f*

assizes [ə'saɪzɪz] *npl Br Jur* sesión *f sing* de un tribunal

assoc. (**a**) (*abbr* **association**) asociación *f* (**b**) (*abbr* **associated**) asociado(a)

associate¹ [ə'səʊʃɪeɪt] **1** *vt (connect) (ideas)* relacionar, asociar; *(companies)* asociar; **to be associated with sth** estar relacionado(a) con algo, estar involucrado(a) en algo **2** *vi (person)* relacionarse, tratar (**with** con)

associate² [ə'səʊʃɪɪt] **1** *adj (company, etc)* associado(a); *(member)* correspondiente **2** *n (colleague)* colega *mf; (partner)* socio(a) *m,f; (accomplice)* cómplice *mf; (member)* socio(a) *m,f*

associated [ə'səʊʃɪeɪtɪd] *adj* asociado(a); **a. company** empresa *f* asociada

association [əsəʊsɪ'eɪʃən] *n (partnership)* asociación *f; (company, organization)* sociedad *f; (connection)* asociación *f,* conexión *f;* **to set up an a.** formar una sociedad; **in a. with** asociado(a) con; **a. of ideas** asociación de ideas; **it has pleasant associations for me** me trae buenos recuerdos ❑ **a. football** fútbol *m*

assonance ['æsənəns] *n* asonancia *f*

assorted [ə'sɔːtɪd] *adj* surtido(a), variado(a)

assortment [ə'sɔːtmənt] *n* surtido *m,* variedad *f*

asst. (*abbr* **assistant**) ayudante *mf,* ayte.

assuage [ə'sweɪdʒ] *vt (pain)* aliviar; *(thirst)* saciar, apagar

assume [ə'sjuːm] *vt* (**a**) *(power, authority)* asumir; *(attitude, name)* adoptar; **to a. power** tomar el poder; **an assumed name** un nombre falso (**b**) *(suppose)* suponer, dar por sentado(a); **we can a. that the story is true** es de suponer que la historia es de verdad, **assuming that they arrive on time** suponiendo que lleguen a la hora

assumption [ə'sʌmpʃən] *n* (**a**) *(of power, authority)* toma *f;* **a. of office** toma de posesión, entrada *f* en funciones (**b**) *(supposition)* suposición *f,* supuesto *m;* **on the a. that we succeed** suponiendo que tengamos éxito (**c**) *Rel* **the A.** la Asunción

assurance [ə'ʃʊərəns] *n* (**a**) *(guarantee)* garantía *f;* **to give one's a. that ...** asegurar *or* prometer que ... (**b**) *(confidence)* confianza *f,* aplomo *m* (**c**) *Br (insurance)* seguro *m* ❑ **life a.** seguro *m* de vida

assure [ə'ʃʊər] *vt* asegurar; **I can a. you of that** se lo puedo asegurar; **she will do it, I a. you** te aseguro que lo hará

assured [ə'ʃʊəd] *adj* seguro(a), asegurado(a); **you can rest a. that ...** puede estar totalmente seguro(a) de que ...

assuredly [ə'ʃʊərɪdlɪ] *adv (undoubtedly)* sin duda

Assyria [ə'sɪrɪə] *n Hist* Asiria

Assyrian [ə'sɪrɪən] *adj & n Hist* asirio(a) *(m,f)*

aster ['æstər] *n Bot* áster *f*

asterisk ['æstərɪsk] *n* asterisco *m*

astern [ə'stɜːn] *adv* a popa

asteroid ['æstərɔɪd] *n* asteroide *m*

asthma ['æsmə] *n* asma *f*

asthmatic [æs'mætɪk] *adj & n* asmático(a) *(m,f)*

astigmatism [ə'stɪɡmətɪzəm] *n* astigmatismo *m*

astonish [ə'stɒnɪʃ] *vt* asombrar, pasmar; **you a. me!** ¡no me digas!, ¡fíjate tú!

astonished [ə'stɒnɪʃt] *adj (look, reaction)* de asombro, asombrado(a); **he looked a.** pareció asombrado; **I was a.** me quedé pasmado(a)

astonishing [ə'stɒnɪʃɪŋ] *adj* asombroso(a), pasmoso(a); **I find it a. that ...** me asombra que ...

astonishingly [ə'stɒnɪʃɪŋlɪ] *adv* asombrosamente

astonishment [ə'stɒnɪʃmənt] *n* asombro *m;* **a look of a.** una expresión de desconcierto; **to my a.** para gran sorpresa mía

astound [ə'staʊnd] *vt* asombrar, pasmar; **you a. me** me dejas de piedra

astounded [ə'staʊndɪd] *adj* atónito(a), pasmado(a); **I was a.** me quedé atónito(a) *or* pasmado(a)

astounding [ə'staʊndɪŋ] *adj* asombroso(a), pasmoso(a)

astral ['æstrəl] *adj* estelar

astray [ə'streɪ] *adv* **to go a.** *(be lost)* extraviarse; *Fig (make a mistake)* equivocarse; *(decline morally)* ir por mal camino; **to lead sb a.** llevar a algn por mal camino

astride [ə'straɪd] *prep* a horcajadas sobre; **to sit a. a chair** sentarse a caballo *or* a horcajadas sobre una silla

astringent [ə'strɪndʒənt] *adj & n* astringente *(m)*

astrologer [ə'strɒlədʒər] *n* astrólogo(a) *m,f*

astrological [æstrə'lɒdʒɪkəl] *adj* astrológico(a); **a. chart** carta *f* astral

astrology [ə'strɒlədʒɪ] *n* astrología *f*

astronaut ['æstrənɔːt] *n* astronauta *mf*

astronomer [ə'strɒnəmər] *n* astrónomo(a) *m,f*

astronomical [æstrə'nɒmɪkəl] *adj* astronómico(a)

astronomically [æstrə'nɒmɪklɪ] *adv Fam (increase)* astronómicamente, desorbitadamente; **it's a. expensive** tiene un precio astronómico

astronomy [ə'strɒnəmɪ] *n* astronomía *f*

astrophysics [æstrəʊ'fɪzɪks] *n* astrofísica *f*

Astroturf® ['æstrəʊtɜːf] *n Sport* (césped *m* de) hierba *f* artificial

Asturian [æ'stʊərɪən] *n & adj* asturiano(a) *(m,f)*

Asturias [æ'stʊərɪəs] *n* Asturias

astute [ə'stjuːt] *adj* astuto(a)

astutely [ə'stjuːtlɪ] *adv* astutamente

astuteness [ə'stjuːtnɪs] *n (of person)* astucia *f,* sagacidad *f*

asunder [ə'sʌndər] *adv Literary* **to tear sth a.** hacer pedazos algo

asylum [ə'saɪləm] *n* (**a**) *(protection)* asilo *m;* **to seek political a.** pedir asilo político; **a. seeker** solicitante *mf* de asilo (**b**) *mental* **a.** manicomio *m*

asymmetrical [æsɪ'metrɪkəl] *adj* asimétrico(a)

at [æt] *prep* (**a**) *(position)* a, en; **at home** en casa; **at school** en el colegio *or* la escuela; **at the door/window** a la puerta/la ventana; **at the top** en lo alto; **at work** en el trabajo; **he's at work** está trabajando; **to knock at the door** llamar a la puerta (**b**) *(direction)* a; **to look at sth/sb** mirar algo/a algn; **to shoot at sb** disparar contra algn; **to shout at sb** gritarle a algn (**c**) *(time)* a; **at Christmas** por Navidades, en Navidad; **at Easter** en Semana Santa; **at 4 o'clock** a las 4; **at first** al principio; **at last** por fin; **at once** en seguida; **at that time** en aquel momento, entonces; **at the moment** ahora (**d**) *(manner)* a, en; **at all events** en cualquier caso; **at best/worst** en el mejor/peor de los casos; **at hand** a mano; **at least** por lo menos; **at peace** en paz; **not at all** *(absolutely not)* en absoluto; *(don't mention it)* de nada; **to be at a loss for words** no saber qué decir; **to be good at sth** ser fuerte en algo (**e**) *(cause)* **to be angry at sb** estar *esp Esp* enfadado(a) *or esp Am* enojado(a) con algn; **to be surprised at sth** sorprenderse de algo; **to laugh at sb** reírse de algn (**f**) *(rate)* a; **they retail at 100 euros each** se venden a 100 euros la unidad; **two at a time** de dos en dos; *Fam* **it isn't a very good one at that** ni siquiera es bueno (**g**) **while you're at it, could you make a cup of tea?** ¿y de paso, podrías hacer un té?; **she's at it again** *(doing the same thing)* ya está otra vez con lo mismo; **they've**

been hard at it all morning *(working hard)* han estado dando el callo toda la mañana

atavistic [ætə'vɪstɪk] *adj* atávico(a)

ate [et, eɪt] *pt see* eat

atheism ['eɪθɪɪzəm] *n* ateísmo *m*

atheist ['eɪθɪɪst] *n* ateo(a) *m,f*

Athenian [ə'θiːnɪən] *adj & n* ateniense *(mf)*

Athens ['æθɪnz] *n* Atenas

athlete ['æθliːt] *n* atleta *mf* ▫ *Med* **a.'s foot** pie *m* de atleta

athletic [æθ'letɪk] **1** *adj* atlético(a); *(sporty)* deportista
  2 athletics *npl Br (track and field)* atletismo *m*; *US* deportes *mpl*

atishoo [ə'tɪʃuː] *interj* ¡achís!

Atlantic [ət'læntɪk] *adj* **the A. (Ocean)** el (océano) Atlántico

atlas ['ætləs] *n* atlas *m*; **world a.** atlas del mundo

ATM [eɪtiː'em] *n (abbr* **automated telling machine***)* cajero *m* automático

atmosphere ['ætməsfɪər] *n (air)* atmósfera *f; Fig (ambience)* ambiente *m*; **a tense a.** un ambiente de tensión; **the earth's a.** la atmósfera terrestre

atmospheric [ætməs'ferɪk] **1** *adj (pressure etc)* atmosférico(a)
  2 atmospherics *npl Rad* perturbaciones *fpl* atmosféricas, parásitos *mpl*

atoll ['ætɒl] *n Geog* atolón *m*

atom ['ætəm] *n* átomo *m; Fig* pizca *f* ▫ **a. bomb** bomba *f* atómica

atomic [ə'tɒmɪk] *adj* atómico(a) ▫ **a. energy** energía *f* atómica; **a. warfare** guerra *f* atómica

atomizer ['ætəmaɪzər] *n* atomizador *m*

atone [ə'təʊn] *vt (crime, sin)* **to a. for** expiar; *(mistake)* reparar

atonement [ə'təʊnmənt] *n (for crime, sin)* expiación *f; (for mistake)* reparación *f*

atrocious [ə'trəʊʃəs] *adj (wicked, cruel)* atroz; *Fam (very bad)* fatal, malísimo(a)

atrociously [ə'trəʊʃəslɪ] *adv* **(a)** *(cruelly)* atrozmente, despiadadamente **(b)** *Fam (very badly)* de pena; **a. bad** malísimo, pésimo

atrocity [ə'trɒsɪtɪ] *n* atrocidad *f*

atrophy ['ætrəfɪ] **1** *n Med* atrofia *f*
  2 *vi* atrofiarse

attach [ə'tætʃ] *vt (tie)* atar; *(stick)* pegar; *(fasten)* sujetar; *(document) & Comptr* adjuntar; **she's attached to the embassy** está agregada a la embajada; **the attached letter** la carta adjunta; **to a. importance to sth** conceder *or* dar importancia a algo; **to a. oneself to a group** unirse *or* pegarse a un grupo; *Fig (be fond of)* **to be attached to sb/sth** encariñarse a algn/algo; *Fig* **Tom's very attached to that old pullover** Tom le tiene mucho cariño a ese viejo jersey

attaché [ə'tæʃeɪ] *n Pol* agregado(a) *m,f* ▫ **a. case** maletín *m*; **cultural a.** agregado(a) *m,f* cultural

attachment [ə'tætʃmənt] *n* **(a)** *Tech (piece)* accesorio *m*, dispositivo *m; (action)* acoplamiento *m* **(b)** *(fondness)* cariño *m*, apego *m* **(to** por**) (c)** *Comptr* archivo *m* adjunto, anexo *m*

attack [ə'tæk] **1** *n* **(a)** *(assault)* ataque *m*, asalto *m; Fig (criticism)* ataque *m*; **an a. on sb's life** un atentado contra la vida de algn; **to come under a.** ser agredido(a); **to launch an a. on sb** lanzar un ataque sobre algn **(b)** *Med* ataque *m; (of fever)* acceso *m; (of nerves)* crisis *f* ▫ **heart a.** infarto *m*
  2 *vt (assault)* atacar, asaltar; *Fig (problem)* abordar, enfrentar; *(job)* emprender; *Fig (criticize)* atacar, criticar; *Fig (theory)* impugnar

attacker [ə'tækər] *n* asaltante *mf*, agresor(a) *m,f*

attain [ə'teɪn] *vt (ambition, aim)* lograr; *(rank, age)* llegar a

attainable [ə'teɪnəbəl] *adj (goal, ambition)* alcanzable

attainment [ə'teɪnmənt] *n (achievement)* logro *m; (skill)* talento *m*; **the a. of his goals** la realización de sus metas

attempt [ə'tempt] **1** *n (try)* intento *m*, tentativa *f;* **at the second/third a.** a la segunda/tercera; **to make an a. to do sth** procurar *or* intentar hacer algo; **at least make an a. to smile** por lo menos procura sonreír; **an a. on sb's life** un atentado contra la vida de algn
  2 *vt (task, problem etc)* intentar; **to a. to do sth** tratar de *or* intentar hacer algo; *Jur* **attempted murder/rape** intento *m* de asesinato/violación

attend [ə'tend] **1** *vt (be present at) (meeting, school etc)* asistir a; *(care for) (patient)* atender, cuidar; *(wait on)* servir; *(bride)* acompañar
  2 *vi (be present)* asistir; *(pay attention)* atender, prestar atención; **he'll a. if he's free** irá si se encuentra libre

attend to *vt (business, job, etc)* atender a, ocuparse de; *(in shop)* **to a. to a customer** servir a un cliente

attendance [ə'tendəns] *n (being present)* asistencia *f; (those present)* asistentes *mpl*; **regular a.** asiduidad *f;* **there was a good a.** asistió mucha gente

attendant [ə'tendənt] *n (in cinema, theatre)* acomodador(a) *m,f; (in museum)* guía *mf; (in car park)* vigilante(a) *m,f, (at wedding)* acompañante *mf; (bridesmaid)* dama *f* de honor

attention [ə'tenʃən] *n* **(a)** *(in general)* atención *f;* **for the a. of Miss Jones** a la atención de la Srta. Jones; **pay a.!** ¡atiende!; **to attract sb's a.** llamar la atención de algn; **to pay a. to sb/sth** atender *or* prestar atención a algn/algo **(b)** *Mil* **a.!** ¡firmes!; **to stand to a.** estar firmes, cuadrarse

attentive [ə'tentɪv] *adj (listener, class)* atento(a); *(helpful)* solícito(a); **to be a. to** *or* **towards sb** ser solícito(a) con algn

attentively [ə'tentɪvlɪ] *adv* atentamente

attest [ə'test] **1** *vt (verify)* atestiguar; *Jur (document, signature)* legalizar
  2 *vt (bear witness to)* **to a. to** dar testimonio a

attic ['ætɪk] *n* desván *m*

attire [ə'taɪər] *n Fml* traje *m*; **formal a.** traje de ceremonia

attitude ['ætɪtjuːd] *n (opinion, way of behaving)* actitud *f; (position of body)* postura *f;* **an a. of mind** un estado de ánimo; **don't take that a.** no te pongas así; *Com* **a. survey** = estudio de la actitud del personal en materia laboral

attn *Com (abbr* **(for the) attention of** *)* a la atención de

attorney [ə'tɜːnɪ] *n* **(a)** *US (lawyer)* abogado(a) *m,f* ▫ **district a.** fiscal *mf* **(b) A. General** *(in England, Wales and Northern Ireland)* ≃ fiscal *mf* general del Estado; *(in United States)* ≃ Ministro(a) *m,f* de Justicia **(c)** *Jur* **power of a.** poderes *mpl*

attract [ə'trækt] *vt* atraer; **to a. attention** llamar la atención; **to a. a waiter's attention** llamar a un camarero; **to be attracted to sb/sth** sentirse atraído(a) por algn/algo

attraction [ə'trækʃən] *n* **(a)** *(power)* atracción *f;* **to feel a. towards sb** sentirse atraído(a) por algn; **what's the a.?** ¿porqué te atrae? **(b)** *(attractive thing)* atractivo *m; (charm)* encanto *m; (incentive)* aliciente *m*; **the job has many attractions** el trabajo tiene muchos alicientes; **the main a.** el número fuerte

attractive [ə'træktɪv] *adj (person)* atractivo(a), guapo(a); *(idea, proposition)* interesante, atrayente

attractively [ə'træktɪvlɪ] *adv* atractivamente, de modo atrayente

attributable [ə'trɪbjʊtəbəl] *adj* atribuible, imputable **(to** a**)**

attribute¹ ['ætrɪbjuːt] *n (quality)* atributo *m*

attribute² [ə'trɪbjuːt] *vt* atribuir; **the poem is attributed to Keats** el poema se atribuye a Keats

attributive [ə'trɪbjʊtɪv] *adj Ling* atributivo(a)

attrition [ə'trɪʃən] *n* **war of a.** guerra *f* de agotamiento *or* de desgaste

attuned [ə'tjuːnd] *adj* **to be a. to sb's way of thinking** entender la forma de pensar de algn

atypical [eɪ'tɪpɪkəl] *adj* atípico(a), anormal

AU [eɪ'juː] *n (abbr of* **African Union)** UA *f*

aubergine ['əʊbəʒiːn] *n Br* berenjena *f*

auburn ['ɔːbən] *adj (hair)* castaño rojizo *inv*

auction ['ɔːkʃən] **1** *n* subasta *f*; **to put sth up for a.** poner algo a subasta ❑ **a. room** sala *f* de subastas; **a. sale** subasta *f*

   2 *vt* subastar

auctioneer [ɔːkʃə'nɪər] *n* subastador(a) *m,f*

audacious [ɔː'deɪʃəs] *adj (daring)* audaz, intrépido(a); *(bold)* atrevido(a); *(impudent)* descarado(a)

audacity [ɔː'dæsɪtɪ] *n (daring)* audacia *f*, intrepidez *f*, *(boldness)* atrevimiento *m*; *(impudence)* descaro *m*

audible ['ɔːdɪbəl] *adj* audible, perceptible al oído; **it was barely** *or* **scarcely a.** apenas se le oía

audibly ['ɔːdɪblɪ] *adv* audiblemente; *(clearly)* claramente

audience ['ɔːdɪəns] *n* (**a**) *(spectators etc)* público *m*, espectadores *mpl*; *(at concert, conference)* auditorio *m*; *(television)* telespectadores *mpl* ❑ **a. participation** participación *f* del público (**b**) *(meeting)* audiencia *f*; **to be granted an a. with sb** ser recibido(a) en audiencia por algn

audio ['ɔːdɪəʊ] *adj* **a. book** audiolibro *m*; **a. cassette** cinta *f* de audio; **a. equipment** equipo *m* de sonido

audio-visual [ɔːdɪəʊ'vɪzjʊəl] *adj* audiovisual ❑ **a.-v. aids** ayudas *fpl or* medios *mpl* audiovisuales

audit ['ɔːdɪt] **1** *n Fin* revisión *f* de cuentas, intervención *f*

   2 *vt* (**a**) *Fin* revisar, intervenir (**b**) *US (class, lecture)* asistir de oyente a

audition [ɔː'dɪʃən] **1** *n Theat Cin* prueba *f*; **to hold auditions for a part** probar gente para un papel

   2 *vt* **to a. sb for a part** probar a algn para un papel

   3 *vi* **to a. for a part** presentarse a una prueba para un papel

auditor ['ɔːdɪtər] *n Com* revisor(a) *m,f* de cuentas, interventor(a) *m,f*

auditorium [ɔːdɪ'tɔːrɪəm] *n (pl* **auditoriums** *or* **auditoria** [ɔːdɪ'tɔːrɪə]) auditorio *m*, sala *f*

auditory ['ɔːdɪtrɪ] *adj* auditivo(a)

Aug *(abbr* **August)** agosto *m*, ago.

augment [ɔːg'ment] *vt* aumentar

augur ['ɔːgər] *vi* **to a. well/ill for sth** ser buen/mal agüero para algo

August ['ɔːgəst] *n* agosto *m*; *see also* **May**

august [ɔː'gʌst] *adj Literary (distinguished)* augusto(a)

aunt [ɑːnt] *n* tía *f*; **her a. and uncle** sus tíos ❑ **A. Sally** objeto *m* de burla

auntie, aunty ['ɑːntɪ] *n Fam* tita *f*

AUP [eɪjuː'piː] *n Comptr (abbr* **Acceptable Use Policy)** = código de conducta definido por un proveedor de acceso a Internet

au pair [əʊ'peər] *n* **au p. (girl)** (chica *f*) au pair *f*

aura ['ɔːrə] *n (pl* **auras** *or* **aurae** ['ɔːriː]) *(of person)* aura *f*; *Rel* aureola *f*; *(of place)* sensación *f*

aural ['ɔːrəl] *adj* auditivo(a), del oído

auricle ['ɔːrɪkəl] *n Anat* aurícula *f*

aurora [ə'rɔːrə] *(pl* **auroras** *or* **aurorae** [ə'rɔːriː]) *n Astron* aurora *f*; **a. australis** aurora *f* austral; **a. borealis** aurora *f* boreal

auspices ['ɔːspɪsɪz] *npl* **under the a. of** bajo los auspicios de, patrocinado(a) por

auspicious [ɔː'spɪʃəs] *adj* propicio(a), de buen augurio; **an a. start** un feliz comienzo

auspiciously [ɔː'spɪʃəslɪ] *adv* felizmente

Aussie ['ɒzɪ] *adj & n Fam* australiano(a) *(m,f)*

austere [ɒ'stɪər] *adj* austero(a), sobrio(a)

austerity [ɒ'sterɪtɪ] *n* austeridad *f*; *Pol* **economic a.** restricciones *fpl*

Australasia [ɒstrə'leɪʒə] *n* Australasia

Australasian [ɒstrə'leɪʒən] *adj* de Australasia

Australia [ɒ'streɪlɪə] *n* Australia

Australian [ɒ'streɪlɪən] *adj & n* australiano(a) *(m,f)*

Austria ['ɒstrɪə] *n* Austria

Austrian ['ɒstrɪən] *adj & n* austríaco(a) *(m,f)*

authentic [ɔː'θentɪk] *adj* auténtico(a)

authentically [ɔː'θentɪklɪ] *adv* auténticamente

authenticate [ɔː'θentɪkeɪt] *vt (document etc)* probar la autenticidad de

authenticity [ɔːθen'tɪsɪtɪ] *n* autenticidad *f*

author ['ɔːθər] *n* autor(a) *m,f*

authoritarian [ɔːθɒrɪ'teərɪən] *adj* autoritario(a)

authoritative [ɔː'θɒrɪtətɪv] *adj (reliable)* autorizado(a), digno(a) de crédito, fidedigno(a); *(authoritarian)* autoritario(a)

authority [ɔː'θɒrɪtɪ] *n (power, right)* autoridad *f*; *(governing body)* autoridad; *(expert)* autoridad, experto(a) *m,f*; **the authorities** las autoridades; **to be an a. on sth** ser experto(a) *or* una autoridad en algo; **to be in** *or* **have a. over sb** tener autoridad sobre algn; **I have it on good a. that ...** sé de buena fuente que ...; **who is in a. here?** ¿quién manda aquí? ❑ *Pol* **local a.** ayuntamiento *m*

authorization [ɔːθəraɪ'zeɪʃən] *n* autorización *f*

authorize ['ɔːθəraɪz] *vt (person)* autorizar; *(payment etc)* aprobar; **to a. sb to do sth** autorizar a algn a *or* para hacer algo

authorized ['ɔːθəraɪzd] *adj* **a. dealer** distribuidor *m* autorizado

autism ['ɔːtɪzəm] *n* autismo *m*

autistic [ɔː'tɪstɪk] *adj* autístico(a), autista

auto ['ɔːtəʊ] *n US Can* auto *m*, automóvil *m*

auto- ['ɔːtəʊ] *pref* auto-

autobiographical [ɔːtəbaɪə'græfɪkəl] *adj* autobiográfico(a)

autobiography [ɔːtəʊbaɪ'ɒgrəfɪ] *n* autobiografía *f*

autocracy [ɔː'tɒkrəsɪ] *n* autocracia *f*

autocrat ['ɔːtəkræt] *n* autócrata *mf*

autocratic [ɔːtə'krætɪk] *adj* autocrático(a)

Autocue® ['ɔːtəkjuː] *n Br TV* teleapuntador *m*

autodialler ['ɔːtəʊdaɪələr] *n* (dispositivo *m* de) marcación *f* automática

autofocus ['ɔːtəʊfəʊkəs] *n* autofocus *m*, autofoco *m*

autograph ['ɔːtəgrɑːf] **1** *n (signature)* autógrafo *m*

   2 *vt (sign)* firmar; *(book, photo)* dedicar

automat ['ɔːtəmæt] *n US* = restaurante en el que la comida se obtiene de máquinas expendedoras

automate ['ɔːtəmeɪt] *vt* automatizar

automated telling machine ['ɔːtəmeɪtɪd'telɪŋməʃiːn] *n*, **automatic telling machine** [ɔːtə'mætɪk-'telɪŋməʃiːn] *n* cajero *m* automático

automatic [ɔːtəˈmætɪk] **1** adj (washing machine, car, gun etc) automático(a) ⬜ **a. pilot** piloto m automático
2 n (car) coche m or Am carro m automático; (gun) pistola f automática

automatically [ɔːtəˈmætɪklɪ] adv automáticamente

automation [ɔːtəˈmeɪʃən] n automatización f

automaton [ɔːˈtɒmətɒn] n (pl **automatons** or **automata** [ɔːˈtɒmətə]) (robot) autómata m; Fig (person) autómata mf

automobile [ˈɔːtəməbiːl] n US automóvil m

autonomous [ɔːˈtɒnəməs] adj autónomo(a)

autonomy [ɔːˈtɒnəmɪ] n autonomía f

autopsy [ˈɔːtəpsɪ] n autopsia f

auto-save [ˈɔːtəʊseɪv] Comptr **1** n autoguardado m
2 vt guardar automáticamente

autumn [ˈɔːtəm] n otoño m

autumnal [ɔːˈtʌmnəl] adj otoñal, de otoño

auxiliary [ɔːgˈzɪljərɪ] **1** adj auxiliar
2 n (**a**) (helper) auxiliar mf, ayudante mf; Mil **auxiliaries** tropas fpl auxiliares (**b**) Ling (verb) auxiliar m

Av., av. (abbr **Avenue**) Avenida f, Av., Avda.

av. (abbr **average**) promedio

a-v, A-V, AV [eɪˈviː] (abbr **audio-visual**) audio-visual

avail [əˈveɪl] **1** n **to no a.** en vano
2 vt **to a. oneself of sth** aprovecharse de algo

availability [əveɪləˈbɪlɪtɪ] n disponibilidad f

available [əˈveɪləbəl] adj (thing) disponible; (person) libre; **is Mr Marshall a.?** ¿está libre el Sr. Marshall?; **it's a. in green and blue** lo hay en verde y en azul; **there are no tickets a.** están agotadas las localidades; **to make sth a. to sb** poner algo a la disposición de algn

avalanche [ˈævəlɑːnʃ] n avalancha f

avant-garde [ævɒnˈgɑːd] adj vanguardista

avarice [ˈævərɪs] n avaricia f

avaricious [ævəˈrɪʃəs] adj avaro(a)

Ave (abbr **Avenue**) Avenida f, Av., Avda.

avenge [əˈvendʒ] vt vengar; **to a. oneself on sb** vengarse en algn

avenue [ˈævɪnjuː] n (road) avenida f, paseo m; Fig vía f, posibilidad f

aver [əˈvɜːr] vt (pt & pp **averred**) Fml aseverar

average [ˈævərɪdʒ] **1** n promedio m, media f; **above/below a.** por encima de/debajo de la media; **on a.** por término medio
2 adj medio(a), mediano(a); (result, conditions) regular
3 vt sacar la media dè; **he averages 8 hours' work a day** hace un promedio de 8 horas de trabajo al día

average out at vt salir en un promedio de

averse [əˈvɜːs] adj opuesto(a), reacio(a); **to be a. to sth** ser reacio(a) a algo; **he's not a. to an occasional glass of wine** no rechaza una copa de vino de vez en cuando

aversion [əˈvɜːʃən] n (feeling) aversión f; (thing) bestia f negra; **it's my pet a.** es lo que más odio; **to have an a. to sth** odiar algo, sentir repugnancia hacia algo; **a. therapy** terapia f de aversión

avert [əˈvɜːt] vt (turn away) (eyes, thoughts) apartar (**from** de); (prevent) (accident) impedir; (danger) evitar

aviary [ˈeɪvjərɪ] n pajarera f

aviation [eɪvɪˈeɪʃən] n aviación f

avid [ˈævɪd] adj (reader) voraz; **to be a. for sth** ser ávido(a) por algo

avidly [ˈævɪdlɪ] adv vorazmente, con voracidad

avocado [ævəˈkɑːdəʊ] n (pl **avocados**) (also **avocado pear**) aguacate m, Andes RP palta f

avoid [əˈvɔɪd] vt (object) evitar; (person) esquivar; (question) eludir; (answer) evadir; (argument, danger) evitar; **to a. doing sth** evitar hacer algo, procurar no hacer algo

avoidable [əˈvɔɪdəbəl] adj evitable

avow [əˈvaʊ] vt reconocer, confesar, declarar

avowal [əˈvaʊəl] n confesión f, declaración f

avowed [əˈvaʊd] adj confesado(a), declarado(a)

await [əˈweɪt] vt esperar, Esp aguardar; **a warm welcome awaited her** le esperaba una calurosa acogida; **parcels awaiting delivery** paquetes mpl para repartir

awake [əˈweɪk] **1** adj despierto(a); **coffee keeps me a.** el café me desvela; **to be a.** estar despierto(a); **to lie a.** desvelar; **wide a.** totalmente despierto(a)
2 vt (pt **awoke, awaked**; pp **awoken, awaked**) despertar; Fig (memories etc) despertar, traer
3 vi Fig **to a. to the dangers/consequences of sth** darse cuenta del peligro/de las consecuencias de algo

awaken [əˈweɪkən] vt & vi (pt **awakened**; pp **awoken**) see awake **2** & **3**

awakening [əˈweɪkənɪŋ] n despertar m; Fig **a rude a.** un brusco despertar

award [əˈwɔːd] **1** n (prize) premio m; (medal) condecoración f; (trophy) trofeo m; Jur indemnización f; Educ (grant) beca f
2 vt (prize) conceder, otorgar; (medal) dar, conferir; Jur (damages) adjudicar

award-winner [əˈwɔːdwɪnər] n (person) galardonado(a) m,f; (film, book) obra f galardonada or premiada

award-winning [əˈwɔːdwɪnɪŋ] adj premiado(a)

aware [əˈweər] adj (knowledgeable) enterado(a), informado(a); **not that I'm a. of** que yo sepa no; **politically a.** políticamente consciente; **to be a. of sth** ser consciente de algo; **to become a. of sth** darse cuenta de algo

awareness [əˈweənɪs] n conciencia f (**of** de)

awash [əˈwɒʃ] adj inundado(a) (**with** de)

away [əˈweɪ] adv **a long way a.** lejos; **far a.** lejos; **go a.!** ¡fuera de aquí!; (familiar form) ¡vete!, ¡lárgate!; (polite form) ¡váyase!; **it's 3 miles a.** está a 3 millas de distancia; **keep a. from the fire!** ¡no te acerques al fuego!; **right a.** (at once) en seguida, ahora mismo; **to be a.** (absent) estar ausente; (out) estar fuera; (travelling) estar de viaje; **to die a.** (sound) desvanecerse; **to give sth a.** (thing) regalar algo; (secret) revelar algo; **to go a.** irse, largarse; Sport **to play a.** jugar fuera; **to put sth a.** guardar algo; **to sign one's rights a.** ceder sus derechos; **to stand a. from sth** mantenerse a distancia de algo; **to turn a.** volver la cara; **to work a.** (continue working) seguir trabajando

awe [ɔː] n (fear) temor m; (amazement) asombro m; **to be or stand in a. of sb** ser intimidado(a) por algn

awe-inspiring [ˈɔːɪnspaɪərɪŋ] adj impresionante, imponente; **an a.-i. sight** un espectáculo grandioso

awesome [ˈɔːsəm] adj (incredible) sobrecogedor(a); US Fam (wonderful) alucinante, Andes RP macanudo(a), Méx padrísimo(a)

awestruck [ˈɔːstrʌk] adj sobrecogido(a), impresionado(a)

awful [ˈɔːfʊl] adj Fam espantoso(a), horroroso(a); **an a. noise** un escándalo, un ruido de mil demonios; **an a. lot of work** muchísimo trabajo; **how a.!** ¡qué horror!; **what a. weather!** ¡qué tiempo tan horrible!

awfully [ˈɔːfəlɪ] adv Fam terriblemente; **I'm a. sorry** lo siento muchísimo; **it's a. funny** es graciosísimo, es de lo más divertido

awhile [əˈwaɪl] adv **wait a.** espera un poco

awkward [ˈɔːkwəd] adj (person) (clumsy) torpe; (difficult) difícil, pesado(a); (object) incómodo(a); (moment, time) inoportuno(a); (situation) embarazoso(a); (problem) difícil;

an **a. silence** un silencio embarazoso; **a. to handle** difícil de manejar; **he's being a.** está poniendo reparos

awl [ɔːl] *n* lezna *f*

awning ['ɔːnɪŋ] *n (on ship)* toldo *m*, toldilla *f; (on shop etc)* marquesina *f*

awoke [ə'wəʊk] *pt see* **awake**

awoken [ə'wəʊkən] *pp see* **awake**

AWOL ['eɪwɒl] *adj Mil (abbr* **absent without leave**) **to be A.** estar ausente sin permiso; *Fig* **to go A.** desaparecer así como así

awry [ə'raɪ] *adv* **to go a.** salir mal

axe, *US* **ax** [æks] **1** *n* hacha *f; Fig* **to have an a. to grind** tener un interés creado *or* personal

  2 *vt Fig (jobs, costs)* reducir; *(plan)* cancelar; *(person)* despedir

axiom ['æksɪəm] *n* axioma *m*

axiomatic [æksɪə'mætɪk] *adj* axiomático(a); **it's a.** está claro

axis ['æksɪs] *n (pl* **axes** ['æksiːz]) *Geom etc* eje *m*

axle ['æksəl] *n* eje *m*, árbol *m* ❑ *Aut* **rear a.** eje *m* trasero; **a. shaft** palier *m*

ayatollah [aɪə'tɒlə] *n Rel* ayatolá *m*

azalea [ə'zeɪljə] *n Bot* azalea *f* .

Azerbaijan [æzəbaɪ'dʒɑːn] *n* Azerbaiyán

Azerbaijani [æzəbaɪ'dʒɑːnɪ], **Azeri** [ə'zeərɪ] *adj & n* azerbaiyano(a) *(m,f)*

Azores [ə'zɔːz] *npl* **the A.** las Azores

Aztec ['æztɛk] *adj & n* azteca *(mf)*

azure ['eɪʒər] *adj & n* azul *(m)* celeste

B

B, b [biː] *n* **(a)** *(the letter)* B, b *f* ❑ **B movie** película *f* de serie B; *Br* **B road** carretera *f* secundaria **(b)** *Mus* si *m* ❑ **B flat** si *m* bemol

b *(abbr* **born)** nacido(a)

BA [biːˈeɪ] *n* *(abbr* **Bachelor of Arts)** Licenciado(a). *m,f* en Filosofía y Letras, Lic en Fil y Let

baa [baː] **1** *n* balido *m*
  2 *vi* balar

babble [ˈbæbəl] **1** *n* **(a)** *(of baby)* balbuceo *m*; *(of adult)* barboteo *m*, parloteo *m* **(b)** *(of brook)* murmullo *m*
  2 *vi* **(a)** *(baby)* balbucear; *(adult)* barbotear, farfullar, parlotear **(b)** *(brook)* murmurar

babbling [ˈbæblɪŋ] **1** *n see* **babble**
  2 *adj* **(a)** *(baby)* balbuceante; *(adult)* farfullador(a) **(b)** *(brook)* murmurador(a)

babe [beɪb] *n* **(a)** *(baby)* bebé *m*, *Andes RP* guagua *mf*; **b. in arms** niño *m* de pecho **(b)** *Fam (woman)* nena *f*, bombón *m* **(c)** *Fam (term of address)* cariño, cielo **(d)** *US Fam (attractive man)* guaperas *m inv*, *Chile* pepito *m*, *Col* bollo *m*

baboon [bəˈbuːn] *n Zool* zambo *m*, babuino *m*, papión *m*

baby [ˈbeɪbɪ] *n* **(a)** *(infant)* bebé *m*, *Andes RP* guagua *mf*; *(young child)* niño(a) *m,f*; **the b. of the family** el benjamín; **to have a b.** tener un niño; *Fam* **that's your b.** eso es cosa tuya; *Fam* **to be left holding the b.** cargar con el muerto, pagar el pato ❑ **b. boom** explosión *f* de la natalidad; **b. brother** hermanito *m*; **b. buggy,** *US* **b. carriage** cochecito *m* de niño; **b. doll** *(toy)* muñeca *f*; **b. face** cara *f* de niño; **b. sister** hermanita *f*; **b. sling** canguro *m*; **b. snatcher** *(woman)* ladrona *f* de bebés; **b. talk** habla *f* infantil; **b. tooth** diente *m* de leche **(b)** *(animal)* cría *f* **(c)** *Fam (darling)* querido(a) *m,f* **(d)** *Mus* **b. grand** piano *m* de media cola

baby-battering [ˈbeɪbɪbætərɪŋ] *n* malos tratos *mpl* a los niños

baby-face(d) [ˈbeɪbɪfeɪs(t)] *adj* con cara de niño

Babygro® [ˈbeɪbɪɡrəʊ] *(pl* **Babygros)** *n* pelele *m*

babyhood [ˈbeɪbɪhʊd] *n* infancia *f*

babyish [ˈbeɪbɪʃ] *adj* infantil

Babylon [ˈbæbɪlən] *n* Babilonia

Babylonian [bæbɪˈləʊnɪən] *adj & n* babilonio(a) *(m,f)*

baby-minder [ˈbeɪbɪmaɪndər] *n* niñera *f*

baby-scales [ˈbeɪbɪskeɪlz] *n* pesabebés *m inv*

baby-sit [ˈbeɪbɪsɪt] *vi* *(pt & pp* **baby-sat)** cuidar a niños, *Esp* hacer de canguro, *Am* hacer de babysitter

baby-sitter [ˈbeɪbɪsɪtər] *n Esp* canguro *mf*, *Am* babysitter *mf*

baby-sitting [ˈbeɪbɪsɪtɪŋ] *n* hacer *m* de canguro

baby-walker [ˈbeɪbɪwɔːkər] *n Br* tacataca *m*, tacatá *m*, andador *m*

baccalaureate [bækəˈlɔːrɪət] *n (at school)* bachillerato *m*

bachelor [ˈbætʃələr] *n* **(a)** *(single man)* soltero *m*; **old b.** solterón *m* ❑ **b. girl** soltera *f*; *Fam* **b. pad** picadero *m*, *RP* bulín *m*; *US* **b. party** despedida *f* de soltero **(b)** *Univ* licenciado(a) *m,f* ❑ **b. of Arts** licenciado(a) *m,f* en Filosofía y Letras; **B. of Science** licenciado(a) *m,f* en Ciencias

bacillus [bəˈsɪləs] *n (pl* **bacilli** [bəˈsɪlaɪ]) *Biol* bacilo *m*

back [bæk] **1** *n* **(a)** *(of person)* espalda *f*; *(of animal)* lomo *m*; **b. to b.** espalda con espalda; **b. to front** al revés; **to fall on one's b.** caer(se) de espaldas; *Fig* **to be glad to see the b. of sb** alegrarse de que algn se vaya; *Fig* **to break the b. of a job** hacer la parte más difícil de un trabajo; *Fig* **to do sth behind sb's b.** hacer algo a espaldas de algn; *Fig* **to get sb's b. up** fastidiar a algn, poner negro a algn; *Fig* **to have one's b. to the wall** estar en un aprieto; *Fig* **to put one's b. into sth** deslomarse en hacer algo; *Fam* **get off my b.!** ¡deja de fastidiarme!; **b. pain** dolor *m* de espalda **(b)** *(of book)* lomo *m*; *(of chair)* respaldo *m*; *(of cheque)* dorso *m*; *(of coin)* reverso *m*; *(of hand)* dorso *m*, revés *m*; *(of head)* parte *f* posterior; *(of house, car)* parte *f* de atrás; **at the b. (of),** *US* **in b. (of)** *(behind)* en la parte de atrás (de), detrás (de); *(to the rear of)* al fondo (de); **the dress fastens at the b.** el vestido se abrocha por detrás; *Fig* **he knows Leeds like the b. of his hand** conoce Leeds como la palma de la mano; *Fig* **who is at the b. of all this?** ¿quién está detrás de todo esto? **(c)** *(of garden, stage, cupboard)* fondo *m*; *Fam* **in the b. of beyond** en el quinto pino, *Chile* en la punta del cerro, *Col* en la Patagonia, *RP* donde el diablo perdió el poncho **(d)** *Ftb (position)* defensa *f*; *(player)* defensa *m*

  2 *adj* **(a)** *(in space)* trasero(a), de atrás ❑ *Aut* **b. axle** eje *m* trasero; **b. door** *(house)* puerta *f* de atrás; *(tradesman's entrance)* puerta *f* de servicio; *Fig* **to get in by the b. door** conseguir algo por enchufe; **b. garden** jardín *m (en la parte de atrás de una casa)*; **b. road** carretera *f* secundaria; **b. room** cuarto *m* trasero; **b. seat** asiento *m* de detrás; *Fig* **to take a b. seat** pasar al segundo plano; **the b. streets** pasar las callejuelas; *Aut* **b. wheel** rueda *f* trasera **(b)** *(in arrears)* atrasado(a) ❑ *Press* **b. number** número *m* atrasado; **b. pay** atrasos *mpl*; **b. rent** alquiler *m* atrasado, *Am* renta *f* atrasada

  3 *adv* **(a)** *(to the rear)* atrás, detrás; *(towards the rear)* hacia atrás; **b. and forth** de acá para allá; **stand b.!** ¡atrás! **(b)** *(in return)* **to hit b.** devolver el golpe; *Fig* contestar a una denuncia *or* acusación; **he hit b. at his critics** replicó a sus detractores **(c)** *(to starting point)* **as soon as you get b.** tan pronto como vuelvas; **to be b.** estar de vuelta; **to call sb b.** volver a llamar a algn; *Tel* volver a llamar a algn; **to come b.** volver, *Am salvo RP* regresar; **to put sth b.** *(replace)* devolver algo a su sitio; *(delay)* aplazar algo; **to put the**

clock b. retrasar el reloj (**d**) *(in time)* **as far b. as 1950** ya en 1950; **some years b.** hace unos años

4 *vt* (**a**) *(support)* apoyar, respaldar (**b**) *Fin* financiar (**c**) *(bet)* apostar por (**d**) *(car, bus, lorry)* dar marcha atrás a, hacer marcha atrás con; **he tried to b. the car into the garage** intentó meter el coche en el garaje marcha atrás

5 *vi* (**a**) *(move backwards)* retroceder (**b**) *Aut (car, bus)* ir marcha atrás, dar marcha atrás; **she backed into a tree** chocó por detrás con un árbol

back away *vi* retirarse

back down *vi* echarse atrás, claudicar

back off *vi* echarse atrás, desistir

back on to *vt* dar a

back out *vi* (**a**) *Aut* salir marcha atrás (**b**) *(withdraw)* retractarse, volverse atrás

back up 1 *vt* (**a**) *(support)* respaldar (**b**) *Comptr (file)* hacer una copia de seguridad de

2 *vi* (**a**) *(move backwards)* retroceder; *(in car)* ir marcha atrás (**b**) *Comptr* hacer copias de seguridad

backache ['bækeɪk] *n* dolor *m* de espalda, dolor *m* de riñones

backbencher ['bækbentʃər] *n* *Br Parl* diputado(a) *m,f* que no es ministro

backbite ['bækbaɪt] *vi* (*pt* **backbit** ['bækbɪt]; *pp* **backbitten** ['bækbɪtən]) chismorrear

backbiter ['bækbaɪtər] *n* murmurador(a) *m,f*

backbiting ['bækbaɪtɪŋ] *n* murmuración *f*, maledicencia *f*

backbone ['bækbəʊn] *n* *Anat* columna *f*; *Fig* **he's got no b.** le faltan agallas

backbreaking ['bækbreɪkɪŋ] *adj* agotador(a), matador(a)

backchat ['bæktʃæt] *n* *Br Fam* impertinencias *fpl*; **I don't want any more b. from you** ¡deja de contestarme!, ¡no seas respondón!

backcloth ['bækklɒθ] *n* *Theat* telón *m* de fondo

backcomb ['bækkəʊm] *vt* cardar

backdate [bæk'deɪt] *vt* antedatar

backdated [bæk'deɪtɪd] *adj* con efecto retroactivo; **b. pay rise** aumento *m* de sueldo con efecto retroactivo

backdrop ['bækdrɒp] *n* *Theat* telón *m* de fondo

backer ['bækər] *n* (**a**) *Fin* promotor(a) *m,f* (**b**) *Pol* partidario(a) *m,f* (**c**) *(person who bets)* apostante *mf*

backfire [bæk'faɪər] **1** *vi* (**a**) *Aut* petardear (**b**) *Fig* salir rana, fallar; **our plan backfired** nos salió el tiro por la culata

2 *n* *Aut* petardeo *m*

backgammon ['bækgæmən] *n* backgammon *m*

background ['bækgraʊnd] *n* (**a**) *(in scene, painting, view)* fondo *m*; **on a yellow b.** sobre un fondo amarillo; **to stay in the b.** quedarse en segundo plano ❑ **b. music** música *f* de fondo (**b**) *(origin)* origen *m*; *(past)* pasado *m*; *(education)* formación *f*; **from a working-class b.** de clase obrera (**c**) *(circumstances)* antecedentes *mpl* (**d**) *(atmosphere)* ambiente *m*; **against a b. of political unrest** en un ambiente de malestar político

backhand ['bækhænd] *n* (**a**) *Sport* revés *m* ❑ **b. volley** volea *f* de revés (**b**) *(handwriting)* letra *f* inclinada hacia la izquierda

backhanded ['bækhændɪd] *adj* equívoco(a), ambiguo(a); **a b. compliment** un cumplido ambiguo

backhander ['bækhændər] *n* (**a**) *(blow with hand)* revés *m* (**b**) *Br Fam (bribe)* soborno *m*, *Andes RP* coima *f*, *CAm Méx* mordida *f*

backing ['bækɪŋ] *n* (**a**) *(support)* apoyo *m*; *Com Fin*

respaldo *m* financiero (**b**) *(of picture)* soporte *m* (**c**) *Mus* acompañamiento *m*; **b. vocals** coros *mpl*

backlash ['bæklæʃ] *n* reacción *f* violenta y repentina

backlit ['bæklɪt] *adj Comptr* retroiluminado(a)

backlog ['bæklɒg] *n* acumulación *f* (de cosas); **to have a b. of work** tener un montón de trabajo atrasado

backpack ['bækpæk] *n* mochila *f*

backpacker ['bækpækər] *n* mochilero(a) *m,f*; *(hiker)* excursionista *mf*

backpacking ['bækpækɪŋ] *n* **to go b.** viajar con mochila; *(hiking)* ir de excursión

backpedal ['bækpedəl] *vi* (*pt & pp* **backpedalled**) *Fam* dar marcha atrás

backrest ['bækrest] *n* respaldo *m*

back-seat ['bæksiːt] *adj Aut* **b.-s. driver** =pasajero que da consejos innecesarios al conductor

backside [bæk'saɪd] *n* *Fam* trasero *m*, culo *m*

backslash ['bækslæʃ] *n* *Comptr* barra *f* invertida

backslide ['bækslaɪd] *vi* reincidir

backsliding ['bækslaɪdɪŋ] *n* reincidencia *f*

backspace ['bækspeɪs] *n* *Comptr* (tecla *f* de) retroceso *m*

backstage [bæk'steɪdʒ] *adv Theat* entre bastidores

backstairs ['bæksteəz] *n* escalera *f* de servicio ❑ **b. gossip** comadreo *m*; **b. influence** enchufe *m*

backstreet ['bækstriːt] *n* callejuela *f*; **the backstreets** *(of city)* las zonas deprimidas; **b. abortion** aborto *m* clandestino

backstroke ['bækstrəʊk] *n* *Swimming* espalda *f*

backtalk ['bæktɔːk] *n* *US Fam* impertinencias *fpl*; **I don't want any more b. from you** ¡deja de contestarme!, ¡no seas respondón!

back-to-back [bæktə'bæk] **1** *adj (in time)* **b.-to-b. meetings** reuniones *fpl* seguidas

2 *adv* (**a**) *(physically)* espalda con espalda (**b**) *(consecutively)* sucesivamente; **to watch two films b.-to-b.** ver dos películas seguidas

backtrack ['bæktræk] *vi* volver hacia atrás; *Fig* volverse or echarse atrás

backup ['bækʌp] *n* (**a**) *(support)* apoyo *m*, respaldo *m* (**b**) *Comptr* **b. copy/file** copia *f* de seguridad; **b. system** sistema *m* de apoyo (**c**) *US Aut* caravana *f*

backward ['bækwəd] **1** *adj* (**a**) *(movement)* hacia atrás (**b**) *(country)* subdesarrollado(a); *(child)* atrasado(a) (**c**) *Comptr* **b. compatible** compatible con versiones anteriores

2 *adv esp US* atrás, hacia atrás

backwardness ['bækwədnɪs] *n* *(of country)* subdesarrollo *m*; *(of child)* atraso *m*, retraso *m*

backwards ['bækwəds] *adv* hacia atrás, al revés; **to walk b.** andar de espaldas; **to walk b. and forwards** andar de acá para allá

backwash ['bækwɒʃ] *n* (**a**) *(of boat)* estela *f* (**b**) *Fig (of event, situation)* repercusiones *fpl*

backwater ['bækwɔːtər] *n* (**a**) *(of river)* remanso *m*, aguas *fpl* estancadas (**b**) *(isolated place)* zona *f* estancada, lugar *m* atrasado; **Jibrovia is a cultural b.** Jibrovia está muy atrasado culturalmente

backyard [bæk'jɑːd] *n* *Br (enclosed area)* patio *m* trasero; *US (garden)* jardín *m* trasero

bacon ['beɪkən] *n* tocino *m*, panceta *f*, *Esp* bacon *m*; **streaky b.** tocino entreverado; *Fam* **to bring home the b.** *(provide)* ganarse los garbanzos *or* el pan; *(be successful)* llevarse la palma; *Fam* **to save sb's b.** salvarle el pellejo a algn

bacteria [bæk'tɪərɪə] *npl* (*sing* **bacterium**) bacterias *fpl*

bacterial [bæk'tɪərɪəl] *adj* bacteriano(a)

bactericide [bæk'tɪərɪsaɪd] *n* bactericida *m*

bacteriological [bæktɪərɪə'lɒdʒɪkəl] *adj* bacteriológico(a)

bacteriologist [bæktɪərɪ'ɒlədʒɪst] *n* bacteriólogo(a) *m,f*

bacteriology [bæktɪərɪ'ɒlədʒɪ] *n* bacteriología *f*

bacterium [bæk'tɪərɪəm] *n (pl* **bacteria**) bacteria *f*

bad [bæd] **1** *adj* (**worse, worst**) (**a**) *(poor, inferior)* malo(a); **a b. translation** una mala traducción; **he's a b. driver** conduce muy mal; **she's b. at mathematics** se le dan mal las matemáticas; **to go from b. to worse** ir de mal en peor; **b. cheque** cheque *m* sin fondos; **b. feeling** animadversión *f*; **b. luck** mala suerte *f* (**b**) *(decayed)* podrido(a); **to go b.** echarse a perder, estropearse (**c**) *(unfortunate)* **he'll come to a b. end** acabará mal; **it's too b. that ...** qué lástima que ...; **that's too b.!** ¡qué pena!; **to be in a b. way** estar en un mal paso (**d**) *(wicked)* malo(a); *(naughty)* travieso(a); **a b. word** un taco; **to use b. language** ser mal hablado(a); *Fam* **she's a b. lot** es un elemento de mucho cuidado (**e**) *(unpleasant)* **b. blood** *(mutual resentment)* mala sangre *f*; **b. joke** broma de mal gusto; **b. manners** mala educación *f*, malos modales *mpl*; **b. news** malas noticias; **b. smell** mal olor; **they had a b. time** lo pasaron muy mal; **to be in a b. mood** estar de mal humor; **to be on b. terms with sb** estar a malas con algn (**f**) *(serious) (accident, mistake)* grave; *(headache)* fuerte; **to have a b. cold** estar muy acatarrado(a) (**g**) *(harmful)* nocivo(a); **to be b. for one's health** ser perjudicial para la salud (**h**) *(ill)* enfermo(a), malo(a); **she's very b. today** hoy está muy mal; **to have a b. leg** tener problemas con la pierna, dolerle la pierna a uno (**i**) **b. coin** moneda falsa; **b. debt** deuda incobrable

2 *n* lo malo; **to take the b. with the good** aceptar lo bueno y lo malo; **I'm a thousand dollars to the b.** he perdido mil dólares

baddie *n*, **baddy** ['bædɪ] *n Cin Fam* malo *m*

bade [beɪd] *pt see* **bid**

badge [bædʒ] *n* (**a**) *(emblem)* insignia *f*; *(metal disc)* chapa *f* (**b**) *Fig* símbolo *m*, señal *f*

badger ['bædʒər] **1** *n Zool* tejón *m*

2 *vt* acosar, importunar, fastidiar; **to b. sb with questions** acosar a algn con preguntas

bad-looking [bæd'lʊkɪŋ] *adj* **he's not b.-l.** no está nada mal

badly ['bædlɪ] *adv* (**a**) *(not well)* mal; **he did b. in the exam** le salió mal el examen; **to be b. off** andar mal de dinero; **b. dressed** mal vestido(a) (**b**) *(seriously)* gravemente; **b. injured** gravemente herido(a), herido(a) de gravedad; **b. damaged** gravemente dañado(a) (**c**) *(very much)* mucho; **to miss sb b.** echar mucho de menos a algn; **we need it b.** nos hace mucha falta

bad-mannered [bæd'mænəd] *adj* maleducado(a)

badminton ['bædmɪntən] *n Sport* bádminton *m*

badmouth ['bædmaʊθ] *vt US Fam* hablar mal de

badness ['bædnɪs] *n* (**a**) *(of person)* maldad *f* (**b**) *(of road)* mal estado *m*

bad-tempered [bæd'tempəd] *adj* gruñón(ona) ; **to be b.-t.** *(in temperament)* tener mal genio; *(temporarily)* estar de mal humor

baffle ['bæfəl] **1** *vt* desconcertar, confundir

2 *n* baffle *m*, pantalla *f* acústica

baffling ['bæflɪŋ] *adj* incomprensible, enigmático(a)

BAFTA ['bæftə] *n (abbr* **British Academy of Film and Television Arts**) = organización que anualmente concede premios a personalidades del cine y de la televisión británicos

bag [bæg] **1** *n* (**a**) *(large)* bolsa *f*; *(handbag)* bolso *m*, *Andes* *RP* cartera *f*, *Méx* bolsa *f*; **to pack one's bags and go** liar el petate; *Fig* **to be a b. of bones** estar esquelético(a) *or Esp* en los huesos; *Fam* **bags of** montones de; *Fam* **I've got bags of them** tengo la tira; *Fam* **they've got bags of time** tienen tiempo de sobra ❑ **b. snatcher** tironero(a) *m,f*; **diplomatic b.** valija *f* diplomática; **shopping b.** bolsa *f* de la compra; **sleeping b.** saco *m* de dormir; **travel b.** bolsa *f* de viaje (**b**) *(hunting)* caza *f*; *Fam* **it's in the b.** está en el bote, es cosa hecha (**c**) *Br Slang Pej (woman)* **old b.** bruja *f* (**d**) **bags** *(under eyes)* ojeras *fpl* (**e**) *Fam* **bags** pantalones *mpl*

2 *vt (pt & pp* **bagged**) (**a**) *(put in bag)* guardar en una bolsa, embolsar (**b**) *(in hunting)* cazar (**c**) *Br Fam (claim)* pedirse, *Esp* pillar; **he always bags the best seat** siempre consigue *or Esp* coge el mejor asiento

bagatelle [bægə'tel] *n* (**a**) *(trifle)* bagatela *f*, fruslería *f* (**b**) *(pinball)* millón *m*

bagel ['beɪgəl] *n* = tipo de rosca de pan compacto de origen judío

bagful ['bægfʊl] *n* bolsa *f*, saco *m*

baggage ['bægɪdʒ] *n* (**a**) *(luggage)* equipaje *m* ❑ **b. allowance** equipaje *m* permitido; *US Rail* **b. car** furgón *m* de equipajes; **b. reclaim** recogida *f* de equipajes; *US* **b. room** consigna *f* (**b**) *Mil* bagaje *m*

baggy ['bægɪ] *adj* (**baggier, baggiest**) holgado(a); **b. trousers** pantalones anchos; **my trousers have gone b. at the knees** mis pantalones han dado de sí por las rodillas

Baghdad [bæg'dæd] *n* Bagdad

bagpiper ['bægpaɪpər] *n* gaitero(a) *m,f*

bagpipes ['bægpaɪps] *npl* gaita *f* sing; **to play the b.** tocar la gaita

baguette [bæ'get] *n* barra *f* de pan

bah [bɑː] *interj* ¡bah!

Bahamas [bə'hɑːməz] *npl* **the B.** las Bahamas

Bahamian [bə'heɪmɪən] *adj & n* bahameño(a) *(m,f)*

Bahrain [bɑː'reɪn] *n* Bahrein

Bahraini [bɑː'reɪnɪ] *adj & n* bahreiní *(mf)*

bail¹ [beɪl] *n Jur* fianza *f*; **on b.** bajo fianza; **to jump b.** huir estando bajo fianza; **to release sb on b.** poner a algn en libertad bajo fianza; **to stand** *or US* **post b. for sb** salir fiador por algn

bail out *vt* (**a**) *Jur* conseguir la libertad de algn bajo fianza; *Fig (person)* sacar de un apuro; *Fam* echar un cable a (**b**) *Av* saltar en paracaídas de un avión

bail² [beɪl] *vi Naut* achicar (**out -**)

bail³ [beɪl] *n (in cricket)* travesaño *m*

bailiff ['beɪlɪf] *n* (**a**) *Jur* alguacil *m* (**b**) *(steward)* administrador *m*

bain-marie [bænmə'riː] *n Culin* baño *m* maría

bairn [beən] *n Scot* niño(a) *m,f*

bait [beɪt] **1** *n* (**a**) *Fishing* cebo *m*, carnada *f* (**b**) *Fig* cebo *m*, señuelo *m*; *Fishing & Fig* **to swallow the b., rise to the b.** tragar el anzuelo, picar

2 *vt* (**a**) *(hook)* cebar (**b**) *(torment)* hostigar

baize [beɪz] *n* bayeta *f*; **green b.** *(on games tables)* tapete *m* verde

bake [beɪk] **1** *vt* (**a**) *(cake etc)* cocer al horno (**b**) *(harden)* endurecer

2 *vi Fam* hacer mucho calor; **it's baking in here!** ¡hace un calor terrible aquí dentro!

baked ['beɪkt] *adj* al horno; **freshly b. bread** pan recién hecho ❑ **b. beans** alubias *fpl* con tomate *or Méx* jitomate; **b. potato** *Esp* patata *f* or *Am* papa *f* al horno *(con piel)*

baker ['beɪkər] *n* panadero(a) *m,f*; *(pastrycook)* pastelero(a) *m,f* ❑ **b.'s (shop)** panadería *f*; **b.'s dozen** docena *f* de fraile

bakery ['beɪkərɪ] *n* panadería *f*

baking ['beɪkɪŋ] *n* cocción *f* ❑ **b. dish** fuente *f* para horno; **b. powder** levadura *f* en polvo; **b. tin** molde *m*

balaclava [bælə'klɑːvə] *n* **b. (helmet)** pasamontañas *m inv*

balance ['bæləns] **1** *n* (a) *(scales)* balanza *f*; *Fig* **to hang in the b.** estar en juego, estar en la balanza (b) *(equilibrium)* equilibrio *m*; *Pol* **b. of power** equilibrio *m* de fuerzas; **to lose one's b.** perder el equilibrio; *Fig* trastornarse; **to throw sb off his b.** hacerle perder el equilibrio a algn; *Fig* desconcertar a algn (c) *Fin* saldo *m* de una cuenta ❑ **b. due** saldo *m* deudor; **b. in hand** saldo *m* disponible; **b. of payments** balanza *f* de pagos; **b. sheet** balance *m*; **credit b.** saldo *m* acreedor (d) *(remainder)* resto *m* (e) *(of clock)* volante *m*

2 *vt* (a) *(object)* poner en equilibrio (**on** en) (b) *Fin (budget)* equilibrar; *(account)* saldar; **to b. the books** hacer el balance (c) *(weigh up)* sopesar, comparar

3 *vi* (a) *(physically)* estar *or* mantenerse en equilibrio (b) *Fin (tally)* cuadrar

balance out *vi* compensarse

balanced ['bælənst] *adj* equilibrado(a); **a b. diet** una alimentación equilibrada

balancing act ['bælənsɪŋ'ækt] *n* **to do a political b. a.** hacer malabarismos en política

balcony ['bælkənɪ] *n* (a) *Archit* balcón *m* (b) *Theat* anfiteatro *m*

bald [bɔːld] *adj* (a) *(person)* calvo(a); **b. eagle** águila *f* calva; **b. patch** calva *f*; **to go b.** quedarse calvo; *Fam* **to be as b. as a coot** estar más calvo que una bola de billar (b) *(tyre)* desgastado(a) (c) *(style)* escueto(a), sencillo(a); **a b. statement of facts** una mera descripción de los hechos

balderdash ['bɔːldədæʃ] *n Fam* tonterías *fpl*, disparates *mpl*

bald-headed [bɔːld'hedɪd] *adj* calvo(a)

balding ['bɔːldɪŋ] *adj* medio calvo(a)

baldly ['bɔːldlɪ] *adv* francamente

baldness ['bɔːldnɪs] *n* (a) *(of person)* calvicie *f* (b) *(of tyre)* desgaste *m* (c) *(of style)* sencillez *f*

bale[1] [beɪl] **1** *n Com (of goods)* bala *f*, fardo *m*; *(of cotton)* bala *f*, paca *f*

2 *vt* embalar, empacar

bale[2] [beɪl] *vt see* **bail**[2]

bale out 1 *vi* (a) *Naut* achicar (b) *Av* saltar en paracaídas de un avión

2 *vt Fig (person)* sacar de apuro; *Fam* echar un cable a

Balearic [bælɪ'ærɪk] *adj* balear, baleárico(a); **the B. Islands** las Islas Baleares

baleful ['beɪlfʊl] *adj* funesto(a), siniestro(a)

Bali ['bɑːlɪ] *n* Bali

Balinese [bælɪ'niːz] *adj* balinés(esa)

balk [bɔːk] **1** *vt* poner obstáculos a; *(project, plan)* frustrar

2 *vi (horse)* plantarse (**at** en); *(person)* **to b. at doing sth** negarse *or* resistirse a hacer algo

Balkan ['bɔːlkən] *adj* balcánico(a); **the B. States, the Balkans** los Balcanes

ball[1] [bɔːl] **1** *n* (a) *(for tennis, golf, cricket)* pelota *f*; *(for basketball, soccer)* balón *m*; *Bill* bola *f*; **to play b.** jugar a la pelota; *Fig* **the b. is in your court** ahora te toca a ti; *Fig* **to keep the b. rolling** mantener; *Fig* **to play b. with sb** cooperar con algn; *Fig* **to start the b. rolling** poner las cosas en marcha; *Fam* **to be on the b.** ser un espabilado ❑ *Tech* **b. bearing** rodamiento *m* de bolas, cojinete *m* de bolas; *Ten* **b. boy, b. girl** recogepelotas *mf inv* (b) *(of paper)* bola *f*; *(of wool)* ovillo *m* (c) *Anat* **b. of the foot** metatarso *m* (d) *US* béisbol *m* ❑ **b. game** partido *m* de béisbol; *Fig* **it's a whole new b. game** es otra historia; **b. park** campo *m* de béisbol; *Fam* **a b. park figure** una cifra aproximativa (e) *Vulg Offens* **balls** huevos *mpl*, cojones *mpl*; **b.!** ¡y una mierda!; **he's got a lot of b.** tiene huevos, tiene cojones

2 *vt US Vulg Esp* follarse a, *Am* cogerse a, *Méx* chingarse a

ball up *vt US Vulg (task, activity)* cagar, pifiar, joder

ball[2] [bɔːl] *n* baile *m* de etiqueta; *Fam* **to have a b.** pasarlo en grande

ballad ['bæləd] *n* (a) *Lit* balada *f* (b) *Mus* balada *f*, copla *f*

ball-and-socket joint [bɔːlənd'sɒkɪtdʒɔɪnt] *n Tech* articulación *f* de rótula

ballast ['bæləst] *n* (a) *Naut* lastre *m* (b) *Rail* balasto *m*

ballcock ['bɔːlkɒk] *n Tech* llave *f* de bola, llave *f* de flotador

ballerina [bælə'riːnə] *n* bailarina *f*

ballet ['bæleɪ] *n* ballet *m*, baile *m* clásico ❑ **b. dancer** bailarín(ina) *m,f*; **b. shoe** zapatilla *f* de ballet

ballistic [bə'lɪstɪk] *adj* balístico(a); **b. missile** misil *m* balístico

ballistics [bə'lɪstɪks] *n* balística *f*

balloon [bə'luːn] **1** *n* (a) *(for party)* globo *m*; *Av* **hot-air b.** globo aerostático; **to go up in a b.** montar en un globo; *Fig* **to go down like a lead b.** ser un fracaso total (b) *(in cartoon)* bocadillo *m*

2 *vi* hincharse (**out, up** -); *Fig* aumentar rápidamente

ballooning [bə'luːnɪŋ] *n* aerostación *f*

balloonist [bə'luːnɪst] *n* aeróstata *mf*

ballot ['bælət] **1** *n* (a) *(vote)* votación *f*; **to take a b. on sth** someter algo a votación ❑ **b. box** urna *f*; **b. paper** papeleta *f* (de voto), *Chile Méx* voto *m*, *Col* tarjetón *m*, *RP* boleta *f*; **postal b.** votación *f* por correo; **secret b.** votación *f* secreta (b) *(paper)* papeleta *f*

2 *vi* votar (**for** por)

3 *vt* someter a votación, hacer votar; **the union has balloted its members on the issue** el sindicato ha sometido el asunto a la votación de sus miembros

ballpen ['bɔːlpen] *n Fam* boli *m*

ballpoint (pen) ['bɔːlpɔɪnt ('pen)] *n* bolígrafo *m*, *Carib Méx* pluma *f*, *Col Ecuad* estereográfico *m*, *CSur* lapicera *f*

ballroom ['bɔːlruːm] *n* salón *m* de baile; **b. dancing** baile *m* de salón

balls-up ['bɔːlzʌp], *US* **ball-up** ['bɔːlʌp] *n Vulg* cagada *f*; **he's made a real b.-up of the project!** en este proyecto, la ha cagado

ballyhoo [bælɪ'huː] *n Fam* (a) *(fuss)* jaleo *m*, alboroto *m* (b) *(noisy publicity)* propaganda *f* sensacionalista

balm [bɑːm] *n* bálsamo *m*

balmy ['bɑːmɪ] *adj* (**balmier, balmiest**) *(like balm)* balsámico(a); *(fragrant)* fragante; *(weather)* suave

baloney [bə'ləʊnɪ] *n Fam* tonterías *fpl*

balsa ['bɔːlsə] *n* balsa *f*

balsam ['bɔːlsəm] *n* bálsamo *m*

Baltic ['bɔːltɪk] *adj* báltico(a); **the B. (Sea)** el (mar) Báltico

balustrade ['bæləstreɪd] *n* balaustrada *f*, barandilla *f*

bamboo [bæm'buː] *n Bot* bambú *m*; **b. shoots** brotes *mpl* de bambú

bamboozle [bæm'buːzəl] *vt Fam* (a) *(puzzle)* dejar perplejo (b) *(trick)* burlar, embaucar

ban [bæn] **1** *n* prohibición *f*

2 *vt* (*pt & pp* **banned**) (a) *(prohibit)* prohibir (b) *(exclude)* excluir (c) *(from driving)* suspender; **he was banned from driving for six months** le retiraron el carnet durante seis meses

banal [bə'nɑːl] *adj* banal, trivial

banality [bə'nælɪtɪ] *n* banalidad *f*, trivialidad *f*

banally [bəˈnɑːlɪ] *adv* trivialmente

banana [bəˈnɑːnə] *n* (**a**) *(fruit)* plátano *m*, *RP* banana *f*; *Fam* **to be bananas** *(mad)* estar como una cabra *or Méx* destrompado *or RP* de la nuca; *Fam* **to go bananas** *(angry)* ponerse hecho(a) un basilisco, *Chile RP* rayarse ❑ *Pol* **b. republic** república *f* bananera; **b. skin** *(of fruit)* piel *f* de plátano *or CAm Col* banano *or RP* banana *or Ven* cambur; *Fig* trampa *f* potencial; *Culin* **b. split** postre *m* de plátano, helado y jarabe (**b**) *(tree)* plátano *m*, banano *m*

band [bænd] **1** *n* (**a**) *(strip of material)* tira *f*, faja *f*; *(ribbon)* cinta *f* ❑ **elastic b.** goma *f* elástica (**b**) *(stripe)* raya *f*, franja *f* (**c**) *Rad* banda *f* ❑ **frequency b.** banda *f* de frecuencia (**d**) *(group)* grupo *m*; *(of youths)* pandilla *f*; *(of thieves)* banda *f* (**e**) *Mus* banda *f* ❑ **jazz b.** orquesta *f* de jazz; **military b.** banda *f* militar; **pop b.** conjunto *m*

  2 *vi* **to b. together** unirse, juntarse

bandage [ˈbændɪdʒ] *Med* **1** *n* venda *f*

  2 *vt* vendar

Band-Aid® [ˈbændeɪd] *n US Esp* tirita® *f*, *Am* curita *f*

bandit [ˈbændɪt] *n* bandido *m* ❑ **one-armed b.** máquina *f* tragaperras

bandleader [ˈbændliːdər] *n* líder *mf* *(de un grupo musical)*

bandmaster [ˈbændmɑːstər] *n* director *m* de una banda

bandsman [ˈbændzmən] *n* (*pl* **bandsmen**) músico *m* de banda

bandstand [ˈbændstænd] *n* quiosco *m* de música

bandwagon [ˈbændwægən] *n Fig* **to jump on the b.** subirse al tren

bandwidth [ˈbændwɪdθ] *n Comptr* ancho *m* de banda

bandy [ˈbændɪ] **1** *vt* (*pt & pp* **bandied**) *(words, ideas)* intercambiar

  2 *adj* (**bandier, bandiest**) torcido(a) hacia fuera; **with b. legs** patizambo(a)

bandy about *vt* *(rumours, ideas)* propagar, difundir

bandy-legged [ˈbændɪleg(ɪ)d] *adj* patizambo(a)

bane [beɪn] *n* perdición *f*, ruina *f*; **it's the b. of my life** me está amargando la vida

bang [bæŋ] **1** *n* (**a**) *(blow)* golpe *m* (**b**) *(noise)* ruido *m*; *(explosion)* estallido *m*; *(of gun)* estampido *m*, detonación *f*; **supersonic b.** estampido supersónico; **to go off with a b.** estallar; *Fam Fig* ser un exitazo; **to shut the door with a b.** dar un portazo

  2 *vt* (**a**) *(hit)* golpear, dar golpes en; **to b. one's head** darse un golpe en la cabeza; **to b. sth shut** cerrar algo de golpe; *Fam* **to b. one's head against a brick wall** hacer esfuerzos en vano (**b**) *Vulg (have sex with)* follar

  3 *vi* golpear, dar golpes; **to b. at the door** dar golpes en la puerta; **to b. shut** cerrarse de golpe

  4 *interj (blow)* ¡zas!; *(crash)* ¡cataplum!; **b., b.!** *(of gun)* ¡pum, pum!

  5 *adv Fam* justo; **b. in the middle** justo en medio; **b. on time** justo a tiempo

bang about, bang around *vi Fam* hacer mucho ruido

banger [ˈbæŋər] *n* (**a**) *(firework)* petardo *m* (**b**) *Br Fam (sausage)* salchicha *f* (**c**) *Br Fam (car)* **old b.** cacharro *m* viejo

Bangkok [bæŋˈkɒk] *n* Bangkok

Bangladesh [bæŋgləˈdeʃ] *n* Bangladesh

Bangladeshi [bæŋgləˈdeʃɪ] **1** *adj* de Bangladesh

  2 *n* habitante *mf* de Bangladesh

bangle [ˈbæŋgəl] *n* ajorca *f*, brazalete *m*

bang-on [ˈbæŋˈɒn] *adj & adv* **to hit sth b.-on** dar en el clavo; **her answers were b.-on** sus respuestas dieron en el clavo

bangs [bæŋz] *npl US* flequillo *m*, *Am* cerquillo *m (corto)*

banish [ˈbænɪʃ] *vt* desterrar

banishment [ˈbænɪʃmənt] *n* destierro *m*

banister [ˈbænɪstər] *n* barandilla *f*, pasamanos *m inv*

banjo [ˈbændʒəʊ] *n* (*pl* **banjos** *or* **banjoes**) *Mus* banjo *m*

bank¹ [bæŋk] **1** *n* (**a**) *Com Fin* banco *m* ❑ **b. account** cuenta *f* bancaria; **b. balance** saldo *m* bancario, haberes *mpl* bancarios; **b. bill** letra *f* de cambio, *US* billete *m* de banco; **b. charges** comisión *f* bancaria, gastos *mpl* bancarios; **b. clerk** empleado(a) *m,f* de banca; **b. credit** crédito *m* bancario; **b. draft** letra *f* bancaria; *Br* **b. holiday** fiesta *f* nacional; **b. loan** préstamo *m or* crédito *m* bancario; **b. manager** director *m* de banco; **b. rate** tipo *m or Am* tasa *f* de interés bancario; **b. statement** extracto *m* de cuenta; **merchant b.** banco *m* mercantil; **savings b.** caja *f* de ahorros; **World B.** Banco *m* Mundial (**b**) *(in gambling)* banca *f*; **to break the b.** hacer saltar la banca (**c**) *(store)* banco *m* ❑ *Med* **blood b.** banco *m* de sangre; *Comptr* **data b.** banco *m* de datos

  2 *vt Com Fin* depositar, ingresar

  3 *vi Com Fin* **to b. with** tener una cuenta en

bank on *vt* contar con

bank² [bæŋk] **1** *n* (**a**) *(mound)* loma *f*; *(embankment)* terraplén *m*; *(slope)* pendiente *f*; **b. of snow** montón *m* de nieve (**b**) *(of river)* ribera *f*; *(edge)* orilla *f*; **on the banks of the Thames** a orillas del Támesis

  2 *vt (heap up)* amontonar; *Av* ladear

  3 *vi Av* ladearse

bank up *vt (fire)* avivar

bank³ [bæŋk] *n* hilera *f*, fila *f*; *Elec* **b. of lights** batería *f* de luces

bankable [ˈbæŋkəbəl] *adj (actor, actress)* taquillero(a), de éxito

bankbook [ˈbæŋkbʊk] *n* libreta *f or* cartilla *f* de ahorros

banker [ˈbæŋkər] *n* banquero(a) *m,f*

banking [ˈbæŋkɪŋ] *n* banca *f*; **to be in b.** ser banquero(a) ❑ **b. hours** horario *m* de los bancos; **b. house** banco *m*

banknote [ˈbæŋknəʊt] *n* billete *m* de banco

bankroll [ˈbæŋkrəʊl] *US* **1** *n* fondos *mpl*

  2 *vt Fam* financiar

bankrupt [ˈbæŋkrʌpt] **1** *adj* quebrado(a), en quiebra, insolvente; **to go b.** quebrar

  2 *n* quebrado *m*

  3 *vt* hacer quebrar, llevar a la bancarrota

bankruptcy [ˈbæŋkrʌptsɪ] *n Com* quiebra *f*, bancarrota *f*

banner [ˈbænər] *n* *(in demonstration, festival)* pancarta *f*; *(flag)* bandera *f*; *Fig* **under the b. of socialism** en nombre del socialismo ❑ *Press* **b. headlines** grandes titulares *mpl*

bannister [ˈbænɪstər] *n see* **banister**

banns [bænz] *npl* amonestaciones *fpl*; **to publish the b.** correr las amonestaciones

banquet [ˈbæŋkwɪt] **1** *n* banquete *m*

  2 *vi* banquetear

banshee [bænˈʃiː] *n Ir* hada *f* que anuncia la muerte

bantam [ˈbæntəm] *n (cock)* gallo *m*; *(hen)* gallina *f* de Bantam

bantamweight [ˈbæntəmweɪt] *n Box* peso *m* gallo

banter [ˈbæntər] **1** *n* bromas *fpl*, chanzas *fpl*

  2 *vi* bromear

bap [bæp] *n Br* = panecillo blando redondo

baptise [bæpˈtaɪz] *vt see* **baptize**

baptism [ˈbæptɪzəm] *n* (**a**) *(sacrament)* bautismo *m* (**b**) *(christening)* bautizo *m*

baptismal [bæpˈtɪzməl] *adj* **b. certificate** partida *f* de bautismo; **b. font** pila *f* bautismal

Baptist [ˈbæptɪst] *n* baptista *mf*, bautista *mf*

baptistry ['bæptɪstrɪ] *n* bautisterio *m*

baptize [bæp'taɪz, *US* 'bæptaɪz] *vt* bautizar

bar [bɑːr] **1** *n* (**a**) *(of iron, gold)* barra *f*; *(of chocolate)* tableta *f*; *(of soap)* pastilla *f*; **b. chart** gráfico *m* de barras; *Comptr* **b. code** código *m* de barras (**b**) *(of cage, prison)* barrote *m*; *Fam* **to be behind bars** estar a la sombra (**c**) *(in river, bay)* barra *f*, bajío *m*, medano *m* (**d**) *(obstacle)* obstáculo *m*; *(barrier)* barrera *f* ❏ **colour b.** segregación *f* racial (**e**) *Jur (dock)* banquillo *m*; *(court)* tribunal *m*; **the prisoner at the b.** el acusado, la acusada (**f**) *Jur* **the B.** *Br (barristers)* = conjunto de los abogados que ejercen en tribunales superiores; *US (lawyers in general)* la abogacía; *Br* **to be called to the B.** entrar en el colegio de abogados (**g**) *(room in pub etc)* bar *m*; *(counter)* barra *f*, mostrador *m* ❏ **singles b.** bar *m* de solteros (**h**) *(in gymnastics)* barra *f*; **horizontal b.** barra fija (**i**) *Mus* compás *m*

2 *vt (pt & pp barred)* (**a**) *(door)* atrancar; *Aut (road)* cortar; *(window)* poner barrotes a (**b**) *(exclude)* excluir (**from** de) (**c**) *(prohibit)* prohibir; **no holds barred** todo vale; **she was barred from the club** le prohibieron la entrada en el club

3 *prep* salvo, a excepción de; **b. none** sin excepción

barb [bɑːb] **1** *n* (**a**) *(point)* lengüeta *f* (**b**) *(gibe)* observación *f* mordaz

2 *vt* poner lengüetas en un dardo

Barbados [bɑː'beɪdɒs] *n* Barbados

barbarian [bɑː'beərɪən] *adj & n* bárbaro(a) *(m,f)*

barbaric [bɑː'bærɪk] *adj* bárbaro(a); **fox hunting is b.** la caza de zorros es una barbaridad

barbarism ['bɑːbərɪzəm] *n* barbarie *f*

barbarity [bɑː'bærɪtɪ] *n* barbaridad *f*

barbarous ['bɑːbərəs] *adj* bárbaro(a)

Barbary ['bɑːbərɪ] *n Hist* Berbería *f* ❏ *Zool* **B. ape** mona *f* de Berbería *or* de Gibraltar

barbecue ['bɑːbɪkjuː] **1** *n* barbacoa *f*, *Andes RP* asado *m*; **b. sauce** salsa *f* para barbacoa

2 *vt* asar a la parrilla

barbed [bɑːbd] *adj* (**a**) *(arrow)* con lengüeta; **b. wire** alambre *m* de púas (**b**) *Fig (remark)* mordaz

barbel ['bɑːbəl] *n (fish)* barbo *m*

barber ['bɑːbər] *n* barbero(a) *m,f*, peluquero(a) *m,f*; **b.'s (shop)** barbería *f*, peluquería *f*

barbershop ['bɑːbəʃɒp] *n US* barbería *f*; **b. quartet** cuarteto *m* de voces

barbiturate [bɑː'bɪtjʊrɪt] *n Med* barbitúrico *m*

Barcelona [bɑːsɪ'ləʊnə] *n* Barcelona

bard [bɑːd] *n Literary* bardo *m*

bare [beər] **1** *adj* (**a**) *(naked)* desnudo(a); *(head)* descubierto(a); *(foot)* descalzo(a); *(room)* sin muebles; *(landscape)* raso(a); *(style)* escueto(a); *Elec* **b. wire** cable descubierto; **to lay b.** poner al descubierto; **with his b. hands** sólo con las manos (**b**) *(basic)* mero(a); **the b. minimum** lo mínimo; **to earn a b. living** ganar lo justo para vivir

2 *vt (make naked)* desnudar; *(uncover)* descubrir; **to b. one's head** descubrirse; *Fig* **to b. one's soul** desnudar el alma

bareback(ed) ['beəbæk(t)] *adj & adv* **to ride b.** montar un caballo a pelo

barefaced ['beəfeɪst] *adj* desvergonzado(a); **b. lie** mentira descarada

barefoot ['beəfʊt] *adj & adv* descalzo(a); **to go b.** ir descalzo

bareheaded [beə'hedɪd] *adj* descubierto(a), sin sombrero

barely ['beəlɪ] *adv* apenas; **I b. know you** apenas te conozco

bareness ['beənɪs] *n* desnudez *f*; *(of style)* sencillez *f*, claridad *f*

bargain ['bɑːgɪn] **1** *n* (**a**) *(agreement)* trato *m*, pacto *m*; *(deal)* negocio *m*; **into the b.** por añadidura, además; **it's a b.!** ¡trato hecho!; **to drive a hard b.** imponer condiciones duras; **to make** *or* **strike a b.** cerrar un trato (**b**) *(cheap purchase)* ganga *f*, oportunidad *f*; **it's a real b.** es una verdadera ganga ❏ **b. basement** sección *f* de oportunidades; **b. offer** oferta *f*; **b. price** precio *m* de oferta

2 *vi* (**a**) *(negotiate)* negociar; **the union bargained with the management for more pay** el sindicato negoció el aumento de salario con la patronal (**b**) *(haggle)* regatear; **to b. over the price of sth** regatear el precio de algo

bargain for *vt* esperar, contar con; **I didn't b. for that** no contaba con eso

bargaining ['bɑːgɪnɪŋ] *n* (**a**) *(negotiation)* negociación *f* ❏ *Ind* **collective b.** negociación *f* sobre el convenio colectivo (**b**) *(about price)* regateo *m*

barge [bɑːdʒ] **1** *n* gabarra *f*

2 *vt Fam* **to b. into** *(room)* irrumpir en; *(person)* tropezar con

barge in *vi Fam* (**a**) *(go in)* entrar sin permiso (**b**) *(interfere)* entrometerse

bargee [bæ'dʒiː] *n* gabarrero *m*

bargepole ['bɑːdʒpəʊl] *n Br* pértiga *f*; *Fam* **I wouldn't touch it with a b.** no lo quiero ni regalado, no lo cogería ni con pinzas

barhop ['bɑːhɒp] *vi US* ir de copas *or* de bares

baritone ['bærɪtəʊn] *adj & n Mus* baritono *(m)*

barium ['beərɪəm] *n Chem* bario *m* ❏ *Med* **b. meal** sulfato *m* de bario

bark¹ [bɑːk] **1** *n* ladrido *m*; **his b. is worse than his bite** perro ladrador poco mordedor

2 *vi (dog)* ladrar; *Fam* **to b. up the wrong tree** ir descaminado(a)

3 *vt* gritar; **to b. (out) an order** gritar una orden

bark² [bɑːk] **1** *n Bot* corteza *f*

2 *vt* rasguñar; **she barked her shins on the desk** se hizo un rasguño en la espinilla con el borde de la mesa

bark³ [bɑːk] *n US Naut* barco *m* de vela; *Literary* barco *m*

barkeep(er) ['bɑːkiːp(ər)] *n US* camarero(a) *m,f*, *Am* mesero(a) *m,f*, *RP* mozo(a) *m,f*

barking ['bɑːkɪŋ] *n* ladridos *mpl*

barley ['bɑːlɪ] *n* cebada *f* ❏ **b. sugar** azúcar *m* cande; *Culin* **pearl b.** cebada *f* perlada

barmaid ['bɑːmeɪd] *n esp Br* camarera *f*, *Am* mesera *f*, *RP* moza *f*

barman ['bɑːmən] *n (pl barmen)* camarero *m*, *Am* mesero *m*, *RP* mozo *m*

barmy ['bɑːmɪ] *adj (barmier, barmiest)* *Br Fam* chalado(a), chiflado(a)

barn [bɑːn] *n* (**a**) *Agr* granero *m* ❏ **b. dance** baile *m* popular (**b**) *Pej (large house)* caserón *m*

barnacle ['bɑːnəkəl] *n Zool* percebe *m*

barnstorm ['bɑːnstɔːm] *vi US* hacer campaña electoral por los pueblos

barnstorming ['bɑːnstɔːmɪŋ] *adj (speech, performance)* apoteósico(a)

barnyard ['bɑːnjɑːd] *n* corral *m*

barometer [bə'rɒmɪtər] *n* barómetro *m*

barometric [bærə'metrɪk] *adj* barométrico(a)

baron ['bærən] *n* (**a**) *(nobleman)* barón *m* (**b**) *(powerful businessman)* barón *m*, magnate *m* ❏ **oil b.** magnate *m* del petróleo; **the press barons** los barones de la prensa

baroness ['bærənɪs] *n* baronesa *f*

baronet ['bærənɪt] *n* baronet *m*

baronial [bə'rəʊnɪəl] *adj* de barón

baroque [bə'rɒk] *adj* barroco(a)

barque [bɑːk] *n Naut* barco *m* de vela; *Literary* barco *m*

barrack¹ ['bærək] **1** *n (usu pl) Mil* cuartel *m sing*; **confined to barracks** bajo arresto en el cuartel
2 *vt Mil* acuartelar

barrack² ['bærək] *vt Br (heckle)* abuchear

barrack-room ['bærəkruːm] *n Mil* dormitorio *m* de cuartel ❑ **b.-r. language** lenguaje *m* de cuartel

barracuda [bærə'kjuːdə] *n* barracuda *f*

barrage ['bærɑːdʒ] *n* (a) *(dam)* presa *f* (b) *Mil* barrera *f* de fuego; (c) *Fig (of questions)* bombardeo *m*, lluvia *f*

barrel ['bærəl] *n* (a) *(of wine)* tonel *m*, cuba *f*, *(of beer, oil)* barril *m*; *Fig* **to scrape the bottom of the b.** tocar fondo, estar a las últimas; *Fam* **to have sb over a b.** tener contra las cuerdas a algn ❑ **biscuit b.** caja *f* de galletas (b) *(firearm)* cañón *m* (c) *Mus* **b. organ** organillo *m*

barren ['bærən] *adj* estéril

barrenness ['bærənes] *n* esterilidad *f*

barrette [bə'ret] *n US* pasador *m*

barricade [bærɪ'keɪd] **1** *n* barricada *f*
2 *vt* levantar *or* montar barricadas; **to b. oneself in** parapetarse

barrier ['bærɪər] *n* (a) *(fence, gate)* barrera *f* (b) *Fig (hindrance)* barrera *f*, obstáculo *m*; **a b. to progress** un obstáculo para el progreso ❑ **b. method** método *m* de barrera; **b. reef** banco *m* de coral, barrera *f* de coral; **sound b.** barrera *f* del sonido

barring ['bɑːrɪŋ] *prep* salvo, excepto; **b. accidents** salvo imprevistos

barrister ['bærɪstər] *n Br* abogado(a) *m,f (que ejerce en tribunales superiores)*

barrow ['bærəʊ] *n* (a) *(wheelbarrow)* carretilla *f* (b) *Br (handcart)* carretilla *f*, carrito *m* ❑ **b. boy** vendedor *m* ambulante de fruta (c) *(burial mound)* túmulo *m*

barstool ['bɑːstuːl] *n* taburete *m* de bar

Bart [bɑːt] *(abbr* **Baronet)** baronet *m*

bartender ['bɑːtendər] *n US* camarero(a) *m,f*, *Am* mesero(a) *m,f*, *RP* mozo(a) *m,f*

barter ['bɑːtər] **1** *n* trueque *m*, permuta *f*
2 *vt* trocar **(for** por)

basalt ['bæsɔːlt] *n* basalto *m*

base [beɪs] **1** *n (bottom)* base *f*; *(foot)* pie *m*; *Archit (of column)* basa *f* ❑ **air b.** base *f* aérea; **b. camp** campo *m* base, campamento *m* permanente; *US* **b. pay** salario *m or* sueldo *m* mínimo; **b. rate** *(interest rate)* tipo *m or Am* tasa *f* de interés básico; *US* **b. salary** salario *m or* sueldo *m* mínimo; **naval b.** base *f* naval; **submarine b.** base *f* submarina
2 *vt* (a) *(argument, system)* basar, fundar **(on** en) (b) *Mil (troops)* estacionar
3 *adj* (a) *(low, despicable)* bajo(a), vil, despreciable; **b. motives** móviles despreciables (b) *(metals)* común

baseball ['beɪsbɔːl] *n Sport* béisbol *m*; **b. cap** gorra *f* de visera

baseboard ['beɪsbɔːd] *n US Archit* zócalo *m*

Basel ['bɑːzəl] *n* Basilea

baseless ['beɪslɪs] *adj* infundado(a), que carece de fundamento

baseline ['beɪslaɪn] *n Ten* línea *f* de saque

basement ['beɪsmənt] *n* sótano *m*; **b. flat** (apartamento *m or Esp* piso *m or Am* departamento *m* del) sótano *m*

baseness ['beɪsnɪs] *n* bajeza *f*, vileza *f*

bases ['beɪsiːz] *npl see* **basis**

bash [bæʃ] **1** *n* (a) *(heavy blow)* golpetazo *m* (b) *(dent)* bollo *m*; **his car has had a b.** tiene el coche abollado (c) *Br Fam (attempt)* intento *m*; **to have a b. at sth** intentar hacer algo
2 *vt (hit)* golpear, aporrear; **she bashed her head against the wall** se dio con la cabeza contra la pared; *Fam* **to b. sb's head in** romperle la crisma a algn

bash up *vt Br Fam* dar una paliza a

bashful ['bæʃfʊl] *adj* tímido(a)

bashfulness ['bæʃfʊlnɪs] *n* timidez *f*

basic ['beɪsɪk] **1** *adj* básico(a), fundamental; **b. pay** sueldo *m* base; **b. vocabulary** vocabulario *m* elemental
2 basics *npl* lo fundamental, lo esencial, la base

basically ['beɪsɪklɪ] *adv* fundamentalmente, esencialmente

basil [*Br* 'bæzəl, *US* 'beɪzəl] *n Bot* albahaca *f*

basilica [bə'zɪlɪkə] *n* basílica *f*

basilisk ['bæzɪlɪsk] *n* basilisco *m*

basin ['beɪsən] *n* (a) *(washbowl)* palangana *f*, jofaina *f*; *(for washing up)* barreño *m*; *(in bathroom)* lavabo *m*, *Am* lavamanos *m inv*; *Culin (dish)* cuenco *m*, taza *f*, fuente *f* (b) *Geog (of river)* cuenca *f*

basis ['beɪsɪs] *n (pl* **bases** ['beɪsiːz]) base *f*; **on the b. of** en base a

bask [bɑːsk] *vi* tostarse; **to b. in the sun** tomar el sol, estar tumbado al sol; *Fig* **to b. in sb's favour** gozar del favor de algn

basket ['bɑːskɪt] *n* cesta *f*, cesto *m* ❑ **b. chair** sillón *m* de mimbre; **b. maker** cestero(a) *m,f*; **shopping b.** cesta *f* de la compra; **wastepaper b.** papelera *f*

basketball ['bɑːskɪtbɔːl] *n Sport* baloncesto *m* ❑ **b. player** baloncestista *mf*, *Am* basquetbolista *mf*

basketwork ['bɑːskɪtwɜːk] *n* cestería *f*

Basle [bɑːl] *n* Basilea

Basque [bæsk, bɑːsk] **1** *adj* vasco(a) ❑ **B. Country** País Vasco, Vascongadas, Euskadi
2 *n* (a) *(person)* vasco(a) *m,f* (b) *(language)* vasco *m*, vascuence *m*, euskera *m*

bas-relief ['bæsrɪliːf] *n* bajorrelieve *m*

bass¹ [bæs] *n inv (fish) (seawater)* lubina *f*, róbalo *m*; *(freshwater)* perca *f*

bass² [beɪs] **1** *n* (a) *(singer)* bajo *m* (b) *(notes)* graves *mpl*; **turn up the b. a little** sube los graves un poco ❑ **b. clef** clave *f* de fa; **b. drum** bombo *m*; **b. guitar** guitarra *f* baja; **b. player** bajista *m,f*; **double b.** violón *m*, contrabajo *m*
2 *adj* bajo(a)

basset ['bæsɪt] *n Zool* basset *m*; **b. (hound)** perro *m* basset

bassist ['beɪsɪst] *n Mus* bajista *mf*

bassoon [bə'suːn] *n Mus* fagot *m*

bassoonist [bə'suːnɪst] *n* fagotista *mf*

bastard ['bɑːstəd, 'bæstəd] **1** *n* (a) *(illegitimate child)* (hijo(a) *m,f)* bastardo(a) *m,f* (b) *Fam* **the poor b.'s broken his leg** el pobre desgraciado se ha roto la pierna; **this car's a b. to start** este coche es la hostia de difícil de arrancar; **you lucky b.!** ¡qué suerte tienes, cabrón! (c) *Offens* cabrón *m*, hijo *m* de puta; **he's a real b.!** ¡es un hijo de puta!
2 *adj* bastardo(a)

bastardize ['bɑːstədaɪz, 'bæstədaɪz] *vt* corromper

baste¹ [beɪst] *vt Culin* regar con grasa

baste² [beɪst] *vt (sew)* hilvanar

bastion ['bæstɪən] *n* baluarte *m*, bastión *m*

bat¹ [bæt] **1** *n (for cricket, baseball)* bate *m*; *(for table tennis)* pala *f*, paleta *f*; *Br Fam* **to do sth off one's own b.** hacer algo por cuenta propia
2 *vi (pt & pp* **batted)** *(in baseball, cricket)* batear

bat² [bæt] n *(animal)* murciélago m; *Fam* **to have bats in the belfry** estar mal de la azotea

bat³ [bæt] vt *(pt & pp* **batted**) *(blink)* pestañear; *Fam* **without batting an eyelid** sin inmutarse, sin pestañear

batch [bætʃ] n *(bread)* hornada f; *(goods)* lote m, serie f, remesa f; *Mil (recruits)* partida f, grupo m ❑ *Comptr* **b. processing** procesamiento m por lotes

bated ['beɪtɪd] adj **with b. breath** sin respirar

bath [bɑːθ] **1** n **(a)** *(action)* baño m; **to give sb a b.** bañar a algn; **to have** or **take a b.** bañarse; **to run a b.** llenar una bañera de agua ❑ **b. mat** alfombra f de baño; **b. salts** sales fpl de baño; **b. towel** toalla f de baño **(b)** *(tub)* bañera f, *Am* tina f **(c)** *Phot Ind* baño m **(d)** *Br* **(swimming) baths** piscina f, *Méx* alberca f, *RP* pileta f
2 vt *(baby)* bañar
3 vi bañarse

bathe [beɪð] **1** vi **(a)** *(swim)* bañarse **(b)** *US (wash)* bañarse, tomar un baño
2 vt **(a)** *Med (wound)* lavar **(b)** *(cover)* empapar; **he was bathed in sweat** estaba empapado de sudor; *Fig* **the room was bathed in sunlight** el sol bañaba la habitación
3 n *(in the sea, river)* baño m; **let's go for a b.** vamos a bañarnos

bather ['beɪðər] n bañista mf

bathing ['beɪðɪŋ] n baño m; **no b!** ¡prohibido bañarse! ❑ **b. cap** gorro m de baño; **b. costume** traje m de baño, bañador m, *RP* malla f; **b. trunks** bañador m (de hombre)

bathos ['beɪθɒs] n *Lit* = paso de lo sublime a lo común

bathrobe ['bɑːθrəʊb] n albornoz m

bathroom ['bɑːθruːm] n cuarto m de baño; **b. scales** báscula f de baño; **b. suite** = conjunto de bañera, lavabo e inodoro

bathtub ['bɑːθtʌb] n bañera f, *Am* tina f

batik [bə'tiːk] n batik m

batman ['bætmən] n *(pl* **batmen**) *Br Mil* ordenanza m

baton ['bætən, 'bætɒn] n **(a)** *Mus* batuta f **(b)** *Br (truncheon)* porra f ❑ **b. charge** carga f con la porra **(c)** *Athlet (in relay race)* testigo m

batsman ['bætsmən] n *(pl* **batsmen**) *(in cricket)* bateador m

batswoman ['bætswʊmən] n *(pl* **batswomen** ['bætswɪmɪn]) *(in cricket)* bateadora f

battalion [bə'tæljən] n *Mil* batallón m

batten¹ ['bætən] **1** n *Naut* listón m
2 vt listonar

batten down vt **to b. down the hatches** sujetar las escotillas con listones

batten² ['bætən] vi cebarse, enriquecerse (**on** de, a costa de)

batter¹ ['bætər] vt aporrear, apalear; **to b. down a door** derribar una puerta a golpes; **to b. sb to death** matar a algn a palos

batter² ['bætər] n *(in baseball, cricket)* bateador(a), m,f

batter³ ['bætər] *Culin* **1** n pasta f (para rebozar); **fish in b.** pescado rebozado
2 vt rebozar

battered ['bætəd] adj *(car)* abollado(a), desvencijado(a); *(hat)* estropeado(a); *(person)* maltratado(a); **b. baby** niño maltratado; **b. wives** mujeres maltratadas or apaleadas

battering ['bætərɪŋ] n paliza f; **to take a b.** recibir golpes or una paliza ❑ *Mil* **b. ram** ariete m

battery ['bætərɪ] n **(a)** *Elec (for torch, radio)* pila f; *Aut* batería f; **the b. has gone flat** se ha descargado la batería ❑ **storage b.** acumulador m; **b. charger** cargador m de pilas/baterías **(b)** *Mil* batería f **(c)** *Agr (for hens)* batería f ❑ **b.**

farming avicultura f intensiva; **b. hens** gallinas fpl de batería **(d)** *Jur* **assault and b.** lesiones fpl, agresión f

battle ['bætəl] **1** n batalla f, combate m; *Fig* lucha f (**for** por); **that's half the b.** ya llevamos medio camino andado; **the B. of Hastings** la batalla de Hastings; **to do b., fight a b.** librar batalla; **to fight a losing b.** luchar por una causa perdida ❑ **b. cry** *Mil* grito m de guerra; *Fig* lema m; **b. royal, pitched b.** batalla f campal
2 vi luchar (**for** por; **against** contra)

battle-axe, *US* **battle-ax** ['bætəlæks] n **(a)** *Mil* hacha f de guerra **(b)** *Fam (woman)* arpía f, bruja f

battledress ['bætəldres] n uniforme m *(de campaña)*

battlefield ['bætəlfiːld] n campo m de batalla

battle-hardened ['bætəlˈhɑːdənd] adj curtido(a)

battlements ['bætəlmənts] npl almenas fpl

battle-scarred ['bætəlˈskɑːd] adj *(place)* minado(a) por la guerra or la batalla

battleship ['bætəlʃɪp] n acorazado m

batty ['bætɪ] adj **(battier, battiest)** *Fam (crazy)* loco(a); *(eccentric)* excéntrico(a)

bauble ['bɔːbəl] n chuchería f

baulk [bɔːlk] vt & vi *see* **balk**

bauxite ['bɔːksaɪt] n bauxita f

Bavaria [bə'veərɪə] n Baviera

Bavarian [bə'verɪən] adj & n bávaro(a) *(m,f)*

bawdy ['bɔːdɪ] adj **(bawdier, bawdiest)** obsceno(a); **a b. joke** un chiste verde

bawl [bɔːl] vi gritar, chillar

bawl out vt gritar, vociferar; *US Fam* **to b. sb out** echar una bronca a algn

bay¹ [beɪ] n *Geog* bahía f; *(large)* golfo m; **B. of Biscay** golfo m de Vizcaya; **B. of Bengal** golfo m de Bengala

bay² [beɪ] n **(a)** *Archit (recess)* hueco m ❑ **b. window** ventana f saledizia **(b)** *(area) Naut* **cargo b.** bodega f de carga; *Com* **loading b.** cargadero m; *Aut* **parking b.** lugar m de aparcamiento **(c)** *Comptr* hueco m, bahía f

bay³ [beɪ] n *Bot* laurel m ❑ *Culin* **b. leaf** hoja f de laurel

bay⁴ [beɪ] n *Zool* caballo m bayo

bay⁵ [beɪ] **1** vi *(dog)* ladrar, aullar
2 n ladrido m; *Fig* **at b.** acorralado(a); *Fig* **to keep sb at b.** mantener a algn a raya

bayonet ['beɪənɪt] n *Mil* bayoneta f

bazaar [bə'zɑːr] n **(a)** *(market)* bazar m oriental **(b)** *(Church)* **b.** *(charity sale)* venta f benéfica, rastrillo m benéfico

bazooka [bə'zuːkə] n *Mil* bazuca f

B & B [biːənˈbiː] n *Br (abbr* **bed and breakfast**) cama f y desayuno m

BBC [biːbiːˈsiː] n *(abbr* **British Broadcasting Corporation**) = compañía británica de radiofusión, BBC f

BBQ ['bɑːbɪkjuː] n *Fam (abbr* **barbecue**) barbacoa f, *Andes RP* asado m; **B. sauce** salsa f (para) barbacoa

BC [biːˈsiː] **(a)** *(abbr* **before Christ**) antes de Cristo, a.de.C., antes de Jesucristo, a.de.J.C. **(b)** *(abbr* **British Council**) = consejo británico (para la promoción de la cultura británica en el extranjero)

be [biː, *unstressed* bɪ] **1** vi *(present 1st person sing* **am**; *3rd person sing* **is**; *2nd person sing & all persons pl* **are**; *pt 1st & 3rd persons sing* **was**; *2nd person sing & all persons pl* **were**; *pp* **been**) **(a)** *(permanent characteristic, essential quality)* ser; **he is very tall** es muy alto; **Madrid is the capital** Madrid es la capital; **sugar is sweet** el azúcar es dulce; **they are intelligent** son inteligentes; *Math* **three and two are five** tres y dos son cinco; **to be or not to be** ser o no ser **(b)** *(nationality,* *religion, occupation)* ser; **he's Italian** es italiano; **she's a Catholic** es católica; **they are both doctors** ambos son médicos **(c)** *(origin, ownership, authorship)* ser; *(price) (established)* costar, valer; *(variable)* estar a, valer; *(total)* ser; **a return ticket is £24** un billete de ida y vuelta cuesta £24; **how much is a kilo of cod?** ¿a cuánto está el kilo de bacalao?, ¿cuánto vale el kilo de bacalao?; **how much is a single room?** ¿cuánto cuesta una habitación individual?; **how much is it?** ¿cuánto es?; **it's £5 for adults and £2 for children, so that's £14** son £5 para (los) adultos y £2 para (los) niños, así que son £14; **peaches are 25 pence each** los melocotones están a *or* valen 25 peniques la unidad; **I am from Boston** soy de Boston; **the car is Domingo's** el coche es de Domingo; **this painting is by Goya** este cuadro es de Goya **(d)** *(temporary state)* estar; **how are you? — I'm very well, thank you** ¿cómo estás? — estoy muy bien, gracias; **she's tired** está cansada; **this soup is cold** esta sopa está fría; **to be cold/afraid/hungry** tener frío/miedo/hambre; **to be in danger** estar en peligro; **to be in a fix** estar en un apuro; **to be very lucky** tener mucha suerte **(e)** *(location)* estar; **Aberdeen is in Scotland** Aberdeen está en Escocia; **the ashtray is on the table** el cenicero está encima de la mesa **(f)** *(age)* tener; **how old are you?** ¿cuántos años tienes?; **she is thirty (years old)** tiene treinta años

2 *v aux* **(a)** *(with pres p)* estar; **he is writing a letter** está escribiendo una carta; **she was singing** cantaba; **they are always laughing at us** siempre se ríen de nosotros; **they are leaving tomorrow** se van mañana; **we have been waiting for a long time** hace mucho que esperamos **(b)** *(passive)* ser; **he was murdered** fue asesinado; **it was invented by an Australian** lo inventó un australiano; **she is allowed to smoke** se le permite fumar; **what's to be done?** ¿qué se puede hacer? **(c)** *(expectation, intention, obligation)* **I am to see him this afternoon** debo verle esta tarde; **you are not to smoke here** no se puede fumar aquí

3 *v impers* **(a)** *(with* there) haber; **there is, there are** hay; **there was, there were** había; **there will be** habrá; **there would be** habría; **there have been a lot of complaints** ha habido muchas quejas; **there is lots to see** hay mucho que ver; **there weren't any potatoes** no había patatas; **there were ten of us** éramos diez **(b)** *(with* it) **it is essential that we go** es imprescindible que vayamos; **it's late** es tarde, se hace tarde; **it is said/thought that** se dice/piensa que; **it was easy to learn** era fácil de aprender; **who is it? — it's me** ¿quién es? — soy yo; **what is it?** ¿qué hay?, ¿qué pasa? **(c)** *(weather)* **it's foggy/misty** hay niebla/neblina; **it's cold/cool/hot** hace frío/fresco/calor; **it's sunny/windy** hace sol/viento **(d)** *(time)* ser; **it's one o'clock/half past one** es la una/una y media; **it's four o'clock/twenty to four** son las cuatro/cuatro menos veinte **(e)** *(date)* **it's the 11th/Tuesday today** hoy es el día 11/martes, hoy estamos a día 11/a martes **(f)** *(in tag questions)* ¿verdad?, ¿no?; **it's lovely, isn't it?** ¿es mono, no?, ¿verdad que es mono?; **you're happy, aren't you?** ¿estás contento, verdad? **(g)** *(unreal conditions)* **if I was/were you ...** yo en tu lugar ...; **if you were a millionaire ...** si fueras millonario ... **(h)** *pres & past perfect (visit, go)* estar, ir; **I've been to Paris** he estado en París

beach [biːtʃ] **1** *n* playa *f*; **on the b.** en la playa; **b. ball** balón *m or* pelota *f* de playa; *US* **b. recliner** tumbona *f*
2 *vt* varar

beachcomber ['biːtʃkəʊmər] *n* **(a)** *(person)* raquero(a) *m,f* **(b)** *(wave)* ola *f*

beachhead ['biːtʃhed] *n Mil* cabeza *f* de playa

beachwear ['biːtʃweər] *n* ropa *f* de playa

beacon ['biːkən] *n* **(a)** *(fire)* almenara *f* **(b)** *Av Naut* baliza *f* **(c)** *(lighthouse)* faro *m*

bead [biːd] *n* **(a)** *(of rosary, necklace etc)* cuenta *f*; **glass b.**

abalorio *m*; **string of beads** collar *m* **(b)** *(drop of liquid)* gota *f*; **beads of sweat** gotas de sudor **(c)** **beads** *(rosary)* rosario *m sing*; **to say** *or* **tell one's b.** rezar el rosario

beading ['biːdɪŋ] *n Archit* astrágalo *m*

beady ['biːdɪ] *adj* (**beadier, beadiest**) *(eyes)* pequeños y brillantes

beady-eyed ['biːdɪaɪd] *adj (observant)* atento(a), vigilante

beagle ['biːgəl] *n Zool* beagle *m*

beak [biːk] *n* **(a)** *(of bird)* pico *m* **(b)** *Fam (nose)* nariz *f* ganchuda

beaker ['biːkər] *n* **(a)** *(cup, tumbler)* taza *f* alta, jarra *f* **(b)** *Chem* vaso *m* de precipitación

be-all ['biːɔːl] *n Fam* **the be-a. and end-all** lo único importante, la razón de existir

beam [biːm] **1** *n* **(a)** *Archit* viga *f* **(b)** *(of light)* rayo *m*; *Phys* haz *m*; *Rad (signal)* onda *f* dirigida; *Fam* **to be off b.** estar equivocado **(c)** *(in gymnastics)* barra *f* fija, barra *f* de equilibrio **(d)** *(smile)* sonrisa *f* radiante **(e)** *Naut (width of ship)* manga *f*; *Fam* **broad in the b.** ancho de caderas
2 *vi* **(a)** *(sun)* brillar **(b)** *(smile)* sonreír
3 *vt* **(a)** *(broadcast)* difundir, emitir **(b)** *(transmit)* transmitir

beaming ['biːmɪŋ] *adj (smiling)* radiante

bean [biːn] *n* **(a)** *Bot Esp* alubia *f*, *Esp* judía *f*, *Am* salvo *RP* frijol *m*, *Andes RP* poroto *m*; *Fam* **not to have a b.** no tener un centavo *or Esp* duro *or Méx RP* peso; *Fam* **to be full of beans** rebosar vitalidad; *Fam* **to spill the beans** descubrir el pastel ❑ *Culin* **baked beans** frijoles *mpl* cocidos en salsa de tomate; **b. curd** tofu *m*; **broad b.** haba *f*; **butter b.** = tipo de frijol blanco; **coffee b.** grano *m* de café; **French b.** *Esp* judía *f* verde, *Bol RP* chaucha *f*, *Chile* poroto *m* verde, *Carib Col* habichuela *f*, *Méx* ejote *m*; **kidney b.** *Esp* alubias *fpl*, *Esp* judías *fpl*, *Am* salvo *RP* frijoles *mpl*, *Andes RP* porotos *mpl* **(b)** *Br Fam (chap)* hombre *m*; **thank you, old b.!** ¡gracias, hombre!

beanbag ['biːnbæg] *n (for juggling)* bola *f* de malabares; *(for sitting on)* puf *m* relleno de bolitas

beanfeast ['biːnfiːst] *n Br Fam* francachela *f*

beanpole ['biːnpəʊl] *n* **(a)** *(stick)* palo *m*, estaca *f* **(b)** *Fam (person)* larguirucho(a) *m,f*

beansprout ['biːnspraʊt] *n* brote *m* de soja

beanstalk ['biːnstɔːk] *n* tallo *m* de *Esp* judía *or Am* salvo *RP* frijol *or Andes RP* poroto

bear¹ [beər] **1** *vt (pt* **bore**; *pp* **borne**) **(a)** *(carry) (inscription, signature)* llevar **(b)** *(support) (weight)* soportar, aguantar, sostener **(c)** *(endure)* soportar, aguantar; **I can't b. him** no lo soporto; **I couldn't b. it any longer** ya no aguantaba más **(d)** *(produce) (fruit)* dar; *Fin (interest)* devengar **(e)** *(show) (scar etc)* llevar; **to b. a resemblance to** parecerse a **(f)** *(hold)* **to b. a grudge against sb** guardar rencor a algn; **to b. in mind** tener presente, tener en cuenta **(g)** *(render, supply)* **to b. witness** atestiguar, dar testimonio **(h)** *(pp* **born**) *(passive only, not followed by* **by**) *(give birth to) (child)* dar a luz; **he was born in Wakefield** nació en Wakefield
2 *vi* **(a)** *(turn) (car, road)* girar, torcer; **to b. left** girar a la izquierda; *(ship)* **to b. north** dirigirse hacia el norte

bear down *vi (press)* apoyarse **(on** en); *Naut (approach)* correr **(on** sobre)

bear out *vt (confirm)* confirmar

bear up *vi (endure)* resistir; **b. up!** ¡ánimo!

bear with *vt* tener paciencia con; **b. with me** ten paciencia conmigo

bear² [beər] *n* **(a)** *Zool* oso *m* ❑ **b. cub** osezno *m*; *Astron* **Great B.** Osa *f* Mayor; **Little B.** Osa *f* Menor; **polar b.** oso *m* polar; **teddy b.** osito *m* de peluche **(b)** *Fin* bajista *mf*; *Fin* **b. market** mercado *m* a la baja

bearable ['beərəbəl] *adj* soportable

beard [bɪəd] *n* barba *f*; **to have a b.** llevar barba

bearded ['bɪədɪd] *adj* barbudo(a)

beardless ['bɪədlɪs] *adj (youth)* imberbe; *(man)* barbilampiño

bearer ['beərər] *n* **(a)** *(porter)* portador(a) *m,f*; **b. of sad news** portador(a) de malas noticias **(b)** *(of cheque)* portador(a) *m,f*; *(of passport)* titular *mf*; *(of office)* poseedor(a) *m,f*

bearing ['beərɪŋ] *n* **(a)** *(posture)* porte *m*; **of noble b.** de noble porte **(b)** *(relevance)* relación *f*, conexión *f*; **to have a b. on** estar relacionado(a) con **(c)** *Tech* cojinete *m*, soporte *m* **(d)** *Naut* **bearings** posición *f*, orientación *f*; **to get one's b.** orientarse; **to lose one's b.** desorientarse

bearish ['beərɪʃ] *adj Fin* de tendencia bajista

beast [biːst] *n* **(a)** *(animal)* bestia *f*; **wild b.** fiera *f* □ **b. of burden** bestia *f* de carga; **b. of prey** depredador *m* **(b)** *(unpleasant person)* bestia *f*, bruto *m* **(c)** **beasts** *(cattle)* reses *fpl*, ganado *m* sing

beastly ['biːstlɪ] *adj* (**beastlier, beastliest**) *Fam* asqueroso(a), abominable; **what b. weather!** ¡qué tiempo más feo!

beat [biːt] **1** *vt* (*pt* **beat**, *pp* **beaten**) **(a)** *(hit)* (*person*) pegar, azotar, golpear; *(clothes)* sacudir; *(metal)* martillear; **it's off the beaten track** está en un lugar muy apartado; **to b. a drum** tocar un tambor; *Fam* **to b. one's brains (out)** estrujarse el cerebro; *Fam* **b. it!** ¡lárgate!; *Fam* **to b. sb's brains out** matar a algn a palizas **(b)** *Culin* batir; **add the eggs and b. well** añada los huevos y bata bien **(c)** *(defeat)* batir, vencer; **we b. them 5–2** les ganamos 5 a 2; *Fig* **that beats everything!** ¡eso ya es el colmo!; *Fam* **to b. sb hollow, b. the pants off sb** aplastar a algn **(d)** *(hunting) (game)* batir **(e)** *Mil* **to b. a retreat** batirse en retirada **(f)** *Mus (indicate) (time)* marcar, llevar **(g)** *(anticipate)* llegar antes que; **he left early to b. the heavy traffic** se marchó temprano para evitar los atascos; *Fam* **I b. you to it** te gané **(h)** *Slang (puzzle)* extrañar; **it beats me how she stands him** es que no entiendo como lo aguanta; **it beats me that they refused to come** me extraña cantidad que se negaran a venir

2 *vi* **(a)** *(heart)* latir **(b)** *(strike, pound)* dar golpes; **someone's beating at the door** alguien da golpes en la puerta; *Fig* **to b. about the bush** andarse por las ramas

3 *n* **(a)** *(of heart)* latido *m* **(b)** *Mus* ritmo *m*, compás *m* **(c)** *Br (of policeman)* ronda *f*; **to walk one's b.** hacer la ronda

4 *adj Fam (exhausted)* agotado(a), rendido(a); **I'm dead b.** estoy rendido(a)

beat back *vt* rechazar; **to b. back the tears** reprimir las lágrimas

beat down 1 *vi (rain)* azotar; *(sun)* caer a plomo
2 *vt (price)* regatear

beat off *vt (attack)* rechazar

beat up *vt Fam* dar una paliza a

beaten ['biːtən] **1** *pp see* **beat**
2 *adj* **b. earth** tierra *f* batida; *Fig* **off the b. track** retirado(a)

beaten-up ['biːtənʌp] *adj Fam (vehicle)* desvencijado(a), destartalado(a)

beater ['biːtər] *n* **(a)** *Culin* batidora *f* **(b)** *Hunt* batidor *m*, ojeador *m*

beatification [bɪætɪfɪ'keɪʃən] *n Rel* beatificación *f*

beatify [bɪ'ætɪfaɪ] *vt* (*pt & pp* **beatified**) *Rel* beatificar

beating ['biːtɪŋ] *n* **(a)** *(thrashing)* paliza *f* **(b)** *(defeat)* derrota *f*; **to take a b.** sufrir una derrota; *Fam* **that idea**

takes some **b.** esa idea es inmejorable **(c)** *(of drum)* toque *m* **(d)** *(of heart)* latido *m* **(e)** *(of wings)* aleteo *m*

beatitude [bɪ'ætɪtjuːd] *n Rel* beatitud *f*; **the Beatitudes** las Bienaventuranzas

beatnik ['biːtnɪk] *n* hippy *mf*, pasota *mf*

beat-up ['biːtʌp] *adj Fam (vehicle)* desvencijado(a), destartalado(a)

beaut [bjuːt] *n Fam* **what a b.!** ¡qué preciosidad *or Am* preciosura!

beautician [bjuː'tɪʃən] *n* esteticista *mf*, esteticienne *f*

beautiful ['bjuːtɪfʊl] *adj (woman)* bonita, *esp Esp* guapa; *(child, animal)* bonito(a), precioso(a); *(music, dress, landscape)* hermoso(a), precioso(a); *(smell, taste)* delicioso(a) □ **b. people** gente *f* guapa

beautifully ['bjuːtɪfʊlɪ] *adv* de maravilla; **they behaved b.** se portaron de maravilla; **you put that b.!** ¡yo no lo habría dicho *or* expresado mejor!, ¡muy bien dicho!

beautify ['bjuːtɪfaɪ] *vt* (*pt & pp* **beautified**) embellecer, adornar

beauty ['bjuːtɪ] *n* belleza *f*, hermosura *f* □ **b. contest** concurso *m* de belleza; **b. parlour** salón *m* de belleza; **b. queen** miss *f*; **b. salon** salón *m* de belleza; **b. spot** *(on face)* lunar *m*; *(place)* lugar *m* pintoresco

beaver ['biːvər] **1** *n Zool* castor *m*; *Fig* **to work like a b.** trabajar como un negro □ *Fam* **eager b.** lanzado(a) *m,f*
2 *vi* **to b. away at sth** meterse de lleno en algo

became [bɪ'keɪm] *pt see* **become**

because [bɪ'kɒz] **1** *conj* porque; **I'm hot b. I've been playing tennis** tengo calor porque he estado jugando al tenis
2 *prep* **b. of** a causa de, debido a; **he lost his job b. of his wife** perdió el empleo por culpa de su mujer

beck [bek] *n* **to be at sb's b. and call** estar a (la entera) disposición de algn

beckon ['bekən] *vt & vi* llamar (con la mano); **to b. to sb** hacer señas a algn

become [bɪ'kʌm] **1** *vi* (*pt* **became**; *pp* **become**) **(a)** *(come to be)* (*doctor, priest etc*) hacerse; *(mayor, officer)* llegar a ser; *(angry, sad)* volverse, ponerse; **the palace became a hotel** el palacio se convirtió en hotel; **to b. accustomed to** acostumbrarse a **(b)** *(fall to)* acontecer; **what has b. of them?** ¿qué ha sido de ellos?
2 *vt (suit)* sentar bien a, favorecer; **that hat really becomes you** ese sombrero te sienta muy bien **(b)** *(be appropriate)* ser propio de; **it doesn't b. you to say that** no te conviene decir eso

becoming [bɪ'kʌmɪŋ] *adj* **(a)** *(dress)* favorecedor(a), que sienta bien **(b)** *(behaviour)* conveniente, apropiado(a)

BEd [biː'ed] *n Univ (abbr* **Bachelor of Education)** *(qualification)* licenciatura *f* en ciencias de la educación; *(person)* licenciado(a) *m,f* en ciencias de la educación

bed [bed] **1** *n* **(a)** *(for sleeping)* cama *f*; **double b.** cama de matrimonio; **single b.** cama individual; **to get into b.** meterse en la cama; **to get out of b.** levantarse de la cama; **to go to b.** acostarse; **to make the b.** hacer la cama; **to put to b.** acostar; *Press (magazine etc)* cerrar; **to take to one's b.** guardar cama; *Fam* **to get out of b. on the wrong side** levantarse con el pie izquierdo □ *Br* **b. and breakfast** *(service)* cama *f* y desayuno *m*; *(sign)* pensión; **b. linen** ropa *f* de cama; **bunk b.** litera *f*; **spare b.** cama *f* adicional *or* supletoria **(b)** *(of river)* lecho *m*, cauce *m*; *(of sea)* fondo *m* **(c)** *Geol* capa *f*, yacimiento *m* **(d)** *(flower)* **b.** macizo *m*, cuadro *m*, arriate *m*; *Fam* **a b. of roses** un lecho de rosas
2 *vt* (*pt & pp* **bedded**) *Slang* acostarse con

bed down *vi* acostarse

bedazzle [bɪ'dæzəl] *vt (impress)* deslumbrar, impresionar

bedbug ['bedbʌg] *n (insect)* chinche *mf*

bedclothes ['bedkləʊðz] *npl*, **bedding** ['bedɪŋ] *n* ropa *f* de cama

bedding ['bedɪŋ] *n (sheets, blankets)* ropa *f* de cama

bedevil [bɪ'devəl] *(pt & pp* **bedevilled***, US* **bedeviled)** *vt* to be bedevilled by problems tener muchos problemas; to be bedevilled by bad luck tener la negra, estar maldito(a)

bedfellow ['bedfeləʊ] *n* compañero(a) *m,f* de cama

bedlam ['bedləm] *n (uproar)* algarabía *f*, alboroto *m*, jaleo *m*

Bedouin ['beduɪn] *adj & n* beduino(a) *(m,f)*

bedpan ['bedpæn] *n* orinal *m* (de cama)

bedpost ['bedpəʊst] *n* pilar *f* de la cama

bedraggled [bɪ'drægəld] *adj (wet)* mojado(a); *(dirty)* ensuciado(a)

bedridden ['bedrɪdən] *adj* postrado(a) en cama

bedrock ['bedrɒk] *n* **(a)** *Geol* roca *f* de fondo **(b)** *Fig* fondo *m*; to get down to b. ir al grano

bedroll ['bedrəʊl] *n* petate *m*

bedroom ['bedru:m] *n* dormitorio *m*, habitación *f*, cuarto *m* , *CAm Col Méx* recámara *f*; **master b.** dormitorio *or* cuarto *or CAm Col Méx* recámara principal

bedside ['bedsaɪd] *n* cabecera *f*; **at sb's b.** al lado de *or* junto a la cama de alguien ◻ *Med* **b. manner** comportamiento *m* para con los enfermos; **b. table** mesilla *f* de noche, *Andes* velador *m*, *Méx* buró *m*, *RP* mesa *f* de luz

bedsit ['bedsɪt] *n Fam*, **bedsitter** [bed'sɪtər] *n Br* cuarto *m* de alquiler

bedsore ['bedsɔ:r] *n* úlcera *f* de decúbito

bedspread ['bedspred] *n* cubrecama *f*, colcha *f*

bedstead ['bedsted] *n* (armazón *m or f* de la) cama *f*

bedtime ['bedtaɪm] *n* hora *f* de acostarse; **b. story** cuento *m* (contado antes de acostarse)

bed-wetting ['bedwetɪŋ] *n Med* enuresis *f*

bee [bi:] *n* abeja *f*, *Br Fam* **the b.'s knees** lo ideal; *Fam* **to have a b. in one's bonnet** tener una idea fija *or* una obsesión ◻ **queen b.** abeja *f* reina *or* maestra; **worker b.** abeja *f* neutra *or* obrera

Beeb [bi:b] *n Fam* **the B.** la BBC

beech [bi:tʃ] *n Bot* haya *f* ◻ **copper b.** haya *f* cobriza

beechnut ['bi:tʃnʌt] *n* hayuco *m*

beef [bi:f] **1** *n Culin* carne *f* de vaca, *Am* carne *f* de res ◻ *Agr* **b. cattle** ganado *m* vacuno; **b. tea** caldo *m* de carne de vaca; **roast b.** rosbif *m*

2 *vi Fam* quejarse (**about** de)

beef up *vt Fam* reforzar

beefburger ['bi:fbɜ:gər] *n* hamburguesa *f*

beefeater ['bi:fi:tər] *n* alabardero *m* de la Torre de Londres

beefsteak ['bi:fsteɪk] *n Culin* filete *m*, bistec *m*, *RP* bife *m*

beefy ['bi:fɪ] *adj* (**beefier, beefiest**) *Fam (muscular)* fornido(a), *Esp* muy cachas

beehive ['bi:haɪv] *n* colmena *f*

beekeeper ['bi:ki:pər] *n* apicultor(a) *m,f*

beeline ['bi:laɪn] *n Fam* atajo *m*; **to make a b. for sth** ir directo hacia algo

been [bi:n, bɪn] *pp see* **be**

beep [bi:p] *n (noise) (of apparatus)* pitido *m*; *(of horn)* pito *m*

beeper [bi:pər] *n (pager)* buscapersonas *m inv*, *Esp* busca *m*, *Méx* localizador *m*, *RP* radiomensaje *m*

beer [bɪər] *n* cerveza *f*; **a glass of b.** una caña; **draught b.** cerveza de barril

beery ['bɪərɪ] *adj* (**beerier, beeriest**) que huele *or* sabe a cerveza

beeswax ['bi:zwæks] *n* cera *f* de abejas

beet [bi:t] *n* remolacha *f*, *US (beetroot)* remolacha *f*, *Méx* betabel *m*; **(sugar) b.** remolacha *f* azucarera

beetle ['bi:təl] *n Zool* escarabajo *m*

beetle off *vi Fam* escabullirse

beetroot ['bi:tru:t] *n Br* remolacha *f*, *Méx* betabel *m*

befall [bɪ'fɔ:l] **1** *vt (pt* **befell** [bɪ'fel]*; pp* **befallen** [bɪ'fɔ:lən]) acontecer a

2 *vi* acontecer, ocurrir

befit [bɪ'fɪt] *vt (pt & pp* **befitted**) convenir a, corresponder a

befitting [bɪ'fɪtɪŋ] *adj* conveniente, propio(a)

before [bɪ'fɔ:r] **1** *conj* **(a)** *(earlier than)* antes de que (+ *subj)*, antes de (+ *infin*); **b. leaving** antes de salir; **I'll see her b. she goes** la veré antes de que se vaya **(b)** *(rather than)* antes que (+ *infin*); **he'd die b. he asked for money** antes moriría que pedir dinero

2 *prep* **(a)** *(place)* delante de; *(in the presence of)* ante; **b. God** ante Dios; **to appear b. court** comparecer ante el juez **(b)** *(order, time)* antes de; **b. Christ** antes de Jesucristo; **b. long** dentro de poco; **b. 1950** antes de 1950; **b. tax** antes de deducir los impuestos; **I saw it b. you** lo vi antes que tú; **ladies b. gentlemen** las señoras primero; **that was b. my time** eso fue antes de que yo naciera **(c)** *(preference)* **death b. defeat** antes morir que entregarse

3 *adv* **(a)** *(time)* antes; **I have met him b.** ya lo conozco; **not long b.** poco antes; **the night b.** la noche anterior **(b)** *(place)* delante, por delante

beforehand [bɪ'fɔ:hænd] *adv* **(a)** *(earlier)* antes; **tell me b.** déjame saberlo antes; **they left 10 minutes b.** se fueron diez minutos antes **(b)** *(in advance)* de antemano, con anticipación; **to pay b.** pagar por adelantado

befriend [bɪ'frend] *vt* trabar amistad con; **he befriended her** le ofreció su amistad

befuddled [bɪ'fʌdəld] *adj* **(a)** *(confused)* perplejo(a) **(b)** *(by alcohol)* atontado(a)

beg [beg] **1** *vt (pt & pp* **begged**) **(a)** *(ask for) (money etc)* pedir **(b)** *(beseech)* rogar, suplicar; **he begged her to help him** le rogó que le ayudara; **I b. to differ** no estoy de acuerdo, no estoy conforme; **I b. to inform you that** tengo el honor de informarles que; **I b. you!** ¡se lo suplico!; **I b. your pardon!** ¡perdone usted!, ¡perdón!; **I b. your pardon?** ¿cómo ha dicho usted?; **to b. the question** hacer una petición de principio

2 *vi* **(a)** *(solicit)* mendigar; **to b. for money** pedir limosna; *(dog)* pedir; *Fam* **it's going begging** no lo quiere nadie **(b)** *(beseech)* **to b. for help/mercy** implorar ayuda/compasión

began [bɪ'gæn] *pt see* **begin**

beget [bɪ'get] *vt (pt* **begot***; pp* **begotten)** *(children)* engendrar

beggar ['begər] **1** *n* **(a)** *(mendicant)* mendigo(a) *m,f*, pordiosero(a) *m,f*; *Prov* **beggars can't be choosers** los pobres no escogen **(b)** *Br Fam Euph (chap)* tío *m*, tipo *m*; **he's a lucky b.!** ¡qué suerte tiene el tío!; **poor b.!** ¡pobre diablo!; **what a silly b.!** ¡qué tío más tonto!

2 *vt* **(a)** *(impoverish)* arruinar, empobrecer **(b)** *(defy)* sobrepasar; **it beggars description** es imposible describirlo

beggarly ['begəlɪ] *adj* miserable; mezquino(a); **a b. wage** un sueldo irrisorio

begin [bɪ'gɪn] **1** *vt (pt* **began***; pp* **begun)** empezar, comenzar; **he began a letter to his mother** empezó una carta a su madre; **I cannot b. to thank you** no encuentro palabras para agradecerle; **she can't b. to level up to the rest** no puede ni mucho menos compararse con los demás;

they began a campaign against him iniciaron una campaña en contra suya; **to b. a new life** comenzar una nueva vida; **to b. doing** or **to do sth** empezar a hacer algo

2 vi empezar, comenzar; **classes b. at nine** las clases empiezan a las nueve; **to b. again** volver a empezar; **to b. at the beginning** empezar por el principio; **to b. on sth** emprender algo; *(initially)* **to b. with ...** para empezar..., en primer lugar...; **to b. with sth** empezar con algo

beginner [bɪˈɡɪnər] n principiante mf; **English for beginners** inglés para principiantes

beginning [bɪˈɡɪnɪŋ] n **(a)** *(start)* principio m, comienzo m; **at the b. of May** a principios de mayo; **at the b. of the month** a principios de mes; **from b. to end** desde el principio hasta el final; **from the b.** desde el principio; **in the b.** al principio; **the b. of the civil war** el comienzo de la guerra civil; **the b. of the end** el principio del fin; **to make a b.** empezar **(b)** *(origin, cause)* origen m, causa f; **the b. of the incident** el origen del incidente; **the beginnings of the cold war** los orígenes de la guerra fría

begone [bɪˈɡɒn] interj Literary & Hum ¡fuera de aquí!, ¡vade retro!

begonia [bɪˈɡəʊnjə] n Bot begonia f

begot [bɪˈɡɒt] pt see **beget**

begotten [bɪˈɡɒtən] pp see **beget**

begrudge [bɪˈɡrʌdʒ] vt **(a)** *(resent)* **she begrudges spending money on clothes** le duele gastar dinero en ropa **(b)** *(envy)* envidiar; **to b. sb sth** envidiarle algo a algn

beguile [bɪˈɡaɪl] vt **(a)** *(deceive)* engañar; **he beguiled me out of my money** me timó **(b)** *(charm, seduce)* seducir

beguiling [bɪˈɡaɪlɪŋ] adj **(a)** *(deceiving)* engañoso(a), tramposo(a) **(b)** *(seducing)* seductor(a)

begun [bɪˈɡʌn] pp see **begin**

behalf [bɪˈhɑːf] n nombre m; **on** or US **in b. of** en nombre de; **a collection on b. of orphans** una colecta en favor de los huérfanos; **don't worry on my b.** no te preocupes por mí; **I thanked them on her b.** les di las gracias de su parte; **on b. of everyone** en nombre de todos; **to plead on sb's b.** abogar por algn

behave [bɪˈheɪv] vi **(a)** *(person)* portarse, comportarse; **b. yourself!** ¡pórtate bien!; **she behaved herself all afternoon** se portó bien toda la tarde; **to b. well/badly** portarse bien/mal **(b)** *(machine)* funcionar

behaviour, US **behavior** [bɪˈheɪvjər] n **(a)** *(of person)* comportamiento m, conducta f; **to be on one's best b.** portarse lo mejor posible **(b)** *(of machine)* funcionamiento m

behavioural, US **behavioral** [bɪˈheɪvjərəl] adj conductista, behaviorístico(a) □ **b. science** ciencia f de la conducta

behaviourism, US **behaviorism** [bɪˈheɪvjərɪzəm] n conductismo m, behaviorismo m

behaviourist, US **behaviorist** [bɪˈheɪvjərɪst] adj conductista, behaviorístico(a)

behead [bɪˈhed] vt decapitar, descabezar

beheld [bɪˈheld] pt & pp see **behold**

behest [bɪˈhest] n instancia f; **at the b. of** a petición de, a instancia de

behind [bɪˈhaɪnd] **1** prep **(a)** *(at the back of)* detrás de; **b. sb's back** a espaldas de algn; **b. the house** detrás de la casa; **b. the scenes** entre bastidores; **she left a bitter memory b. her** dejó tras ella un recuerdo amargo; **to be b. sb** apoyar a algn; **we're solidly b. you** te apoyamos de todo corazón; **what is b. all this?** ¿qué hay detrás de todo esto?; **what is there b. that smile?** ¿qué hay tras esa sonrisa?; **what motive was there b. the crime?** ¿qué

motivo había para el crimen?; *Fig* **to put sth b. one** olvidarse de algo, dejar algo atrás **(b)** *(less advanced than)* **b. the times** anticuado(a); **Paul is b. the rest of the class in maths** Paul está por debajo del resto de la clase en matemáticas; **that country is b. Japan in the data-processing field** ese país es inferior al Japón en el campo de la informática; **to be b. schedule** *(work)* ir atrasado(a); *(plane, train)* llevar retraso

2 adv **(a)** *(in the rear)* detrás, atrás; **I've left my umbrella b.** se me ha olvidado el paraguas; **to approach sb from b.** acercarse a algn por detrás; **to attack sb from b.** atacar a algn por la espalda; **to fall** or **lag b.** quedarse atrás; **to leave sb behind** dejar atrás a algn; **to stay b.** quedarse **(b)** *(late)* **to be b. with one's payments** estar atrasado(a) en los pagos; **to be b. with one's work** tener trabajo atrasado

3 n Fam trasero m, culo m

behindhand [bɪˈhaɪndhænd] **1** adj retrasado(a), atrasado(a)

2 adv en retraso

behind-the-scenes [bɪˈhaɪndðəsiːnz] adj de entre bastidores; **b.-t.-s. talks** negociaciones de entre bastidores

behold [bɪˈhəʊld] vt (pt & pp **beheld**) Literary *(see)* percibir; *(observe)* contemplar; **b.!** ¡mirad!, ¡he aquí!

beholden [bɪˈhəʊldən] adj agradecido(a) **(to** a); **he is b. to nobody for anything** no le debe nada a nadie

beholder [bɪˈhəʊldər] n Prov **beauty is in the eye of the b.** el amor depende del color del cristal con que se mire

beige [beɪʒ] adj & n beige (m inv), Esp beis (m inv)

Beijing [beɪˈʒɪŋ] n Pekín

being [ˈbiːɪŋ] n **(a)** *(living thing)* ser m □ **human b.** ser m humano **(b)** *(existence)* existencia f; **to come into b.** nacer

Beirut [beɪˈruːt] n Beirut

belabour, US **belabor** [bɪˈleɪbər] vt apalear; **to b. sb with insults** poner verde a algn

Belarus [belɑˈruːs] n Bielorrusia

belated [bɪˈleɪtɪd] adj tardío(a)

belay [bɪˈleɪ] vt **(a)** Naut *(line)* amarrar **(b)** *(mountaineering)* *(climber)* asegurar

belch [beltʃ] **1** vi *(person)* eructar

2 vt *(chimney etc)* *(smoke, flames)* vomitar, arrojar

3 n eructo m, regüeldo m

beleaguered [bɪˈliːɡəd] adj *(city)* sitiado(a), asediado(a); *(person)* acosado(a), asediado(a)

Belfast [belˈfɑːst] n Belfast

belfry [ˈbelfrɪ] n campanario m

Belgian [ˈbeldʒən] adj & n belga (mf)

Belgium [ˈbeldʒəm] n Bélgica

Belgrade [belˈɡreɪd] n Belgrado

belie [bɪˈlaɪ] vt **(a)** *(contradict)* desmentir, contradecir **(b)** *(disguise)* falsear **(c)** *(disappoint)* defraudar

belief [bɪˈliːf] n **(a)** *(conviction)* creencia f; **beyond b.** increíble; **religious/political beliefs** creencias religiosas/políticas **(b)** *(opinion)* opinión f; **it's my b. that ...** estoy convencido de que ...; **to the best of my b.** que yo sepa, a mi entender **(c)** Rel *(faith)* fe f **(d)** *(confidence)* confianza f **(in** en)

believable [bɪˈliːvəbəl] adj creíble, verosímil

believe [bɪˈliːv] **1** vi **(a)** *(have faith in)* creer; **I b. in God** creo en Dios **(b)** *(be in favour of)* ser partidario(a) de; **she believes in having a good breakfast** es de las que cree que un buen desayuno es importante **(c)** *(think, suppose)* creer; **I b. so** creo que sí

2 vt creer; **b. me!** ¡créeme!; **don't you b. it!** ¡no te lo creas!; **I can't b. it of her** me parece imposible que ella hiciera tal cosa; **she is believed to be in Brazil** se supone que está en Brasil

believer [bɪˈliːvər] n (a) Rel creyente mf; I'm no b. in miracles yo no creo en los milagros (b) (supporter) he's a great b. in telling the truth es partidario de decir la verdad

belittle [bɪˈlɪtəl] vt despreciar; to b. oneself rebajarse, quitarse importancia

Belize [beˈliːz] n Belice

Belizean [beˈliːzən] adj & n belicense (mf), beliceño(a) (m,f)

bell [bel] n (of church, school) campana f; (handbell) campanilla f; (decorative) cascabel m; (on animal) cencerro m; (on door, bicycle, device) timbre m; **to ring the b.** tocar el timbre; Fig **that rings a b.** eso me suena □ **b. jar** or **glass** campana f, fanal m; US **b. pepper** pimiento m (morrón); **b. tower** campanario m

belladonna [beləˈdɒnə] n Bot belladona f

bell-bottoms [ˈbelbɒtəmz] npl pantalones mpl acampanados

bellboy [ˈbelbɔɪ] n US botones m inv

belle [bel] n (beautiful woman) belleza f

belles-lettres [belˈletrə] npl bellas or buenas letras fpl

bellhop [ˈbelhɒp] n US botones m inv

bellicose [ˈbelɪkəʊs] adj belicoso(a), pendenciero(a)

belligerence [bɪˈlɪdʒərəns] n agresividad f

belligerent [bɪˈlɪdʒərənt] adj agresivo(a)

bellow [ˈbeləʊ] 1 vi (bull) bramar; (person) bramar, rugir 2 n (of bull) bramido m; (of person) bramido m, rugido m

bellows [ˈbeləʊz] npl (pair of) b. fuelle m sing

bell-ringer [ˈbelrɪŋər] n campanero(a) m,f

belly [ˈbelɪ] n (a) (of person) vientre m, barriga f, Chile guata f, Fam tripa f □ **b. dance** danza f del vientre; Swimming **b. flop** panzada f; Fam **b. laugh** carcajada f (b) (of animal, plane) panza f □ Av **b. landing** aterrizaje m sobre la panza

bellyache [ˈbelɪeɪk] 1 n Fam dolor m de barriga 2 vi (complain) rezongar, quejarse, Méx repelar (**about** de)

bellybutton [ˈbelɪbʌtən] n Fam ombligo m

bellyful [ˈbelɪfʊl] n panzada f, hartazgo m; Slang **to have had a b.** estar harto(a), estar hasta las narices (**of** de)

belong [bɪˈlɒŋ] vi (a) (be the property of) pertenecer (**to** a); **this book belongs to him** este libro le pertenece, este libro es suyo (b) (be a member) ser socio(a) (**to** de); **to b. to a club** ser socio de un club; Pol **to b. to a party** ser miembro de un partido (c) (have a proper place) corresponder; **put it back where it belongs** ponlo en su sitio; **she felt she didn't b.** no se sentía cómoda; **this chair belongs in the other room** esta silla va en la otra habitación; **this record doesn't b. in this cover** esta funda no corresponde a este disco

belonging [bɪˈlɒŋɪŋ] n **to have a sense of b.** sentirse (como) en casa

belongings [bɪˈlɒŋɪŋz] npl efectos mpl personales, pertenencias fpl

Belorussian [beləʊˈrʌʃən] adj & n bielorruso(a) (m,f)

beloved [bɪˈlʌvɪd, bɪˈlʌvd] 1 adj amado(a), querido(a); **b. by all** querido(a) de todos 2 n amado(a) m,f

below [bɪˈləʊ] 1 prep debajo de; **b. sea level** por debajo del nivel del mar; **b. (the) average** por debajo de la media; **b. the knee** (skirt) por debajo de la rodilla; **he lives b. us** vive debajo de nosotros; **temperatures b. normal** temperaturas inferiores a las normales; **ten degrees b. zero** diez grados bajo cero 2 adv abajo; **above and b.** arriba y abajo; **here b.** aquí abajo; **see b.** (on document etc) véase más abajo; **the shops b.** las tiendas de abajo

belt [belt] 1 n (a) (round waist) cinturón m; **blow below the b.** golpe m bajo; Fig **to tighten one's b.** apretarse el cinturón □ Sport **black b.** cinturón m negro; Aut Av **safety b., seat b.** cinturón m de seguridad; **please fasten your seat belts** abróchense los cinturones de seguridad, por favor (b) Tech **correa** f, cinta f □ **conveyor b.** cinta f transportadora; Aut **fan b.** correa f del ventilador (c) (area) zona f □ US **cotton b.** zona f algodonera; **green b.** franja f de protección, zona f rural no urbanizable 2 vt Slang pegar una paliza

belt along vi Fam ir a todo gas

belt out vt Fam (song) cantar a voz en grito

belt up vi Br Fam callarse; **b. up!** ¡cierra el pico!, ¡cállate la boca!

beltway [ˈbeltweɪ] n US carretera f de circunvalación, ronda f (de circunvalación)

bemoan [bɪˈməʊn] vt (loss, fate) lamentar, llorar

bemused [bɪˈmjuːzd] adj perplejo(a)

bench [bentʃ] n (a) (seat) banco m; **to sit on a b.** sentarse en un banco (b) (work table) banco m (c) Parl escaño m (d) Br Jur **the b.** (judges) la magistratura; **to be on the b.** ser juez or magistrado (e) Sport banquillo m (f) Geol banco m

benchmark [ˈbentʃmɑːk] n (for comparison) punto m de referencia □ Comptr **b. test** prueba f comparativa

bend [bend] 1 vt (pt & pp bent) (metal) curvar, doblar; (envelope) doblar; (back) encorvar; (head) inclinar; (knee, elbow) doblar; **do not b.** (on envelope) no doblar; **on bended knee** de rodillas; Fam **to b. the rules** hacer una excepción 2 vi (a) (metal) curvarse, doblarse; (road) torcerse, desviarse (b) **to b. (over)** (person) (stoop down) inclinarse, agacharse; Fam **he bends over backwards to please her** hace lo imposible por complacerla 3 n (a) (in river, road) curva f; (in pipe) recodo m, ángulo m; Br Slang **round the b.** loco(a) perdido(a); **hairpin b.** curva f cerrada (b) Med **the bends** aeroembolismo m sing, enfermedad f sing de los buzos

bend back vi inclinarse hacia atrás

bend down vi inclinarse

bend forward vi inclinarse hacia adelante

bender [ˈbendər] n Fam **to go on a b.** irse de juerga

beneath [bɪˈniːθ] 1 prep (below) bajo, debajo de; **b. the bushes** entre los arbustos; **to marry b. oneself** casarse con algn de clase inferior; Fig **it's b. him** es indigno de el; **b. contempt** (completamente) despreciable 2 adv debajo

Benedictine [benɪˈdɪktɪn] 1 n (a) Rel (monk) benedictino(a) m,f (b) [benɪˈdɪktiːn] (liqueur) benedictino m 2 adj Rel benedictino(a)

benediction [benɪˈdɪkʃən] n Rel bendición f

benefactor [ˈbenɪfæktər] n benefactor m, bienhechor m

benefactress [ˈbenɪfæktrɪs] n benefactora f, bienhechora f

benefice [ˈbenɪfɪs] n Rel beneficio m

beneficent [bɪˈnefɪsənt] adj (person) benefactor(a); (thing) benéfico(a)

beneficial [benɪˈfɪʃəl] adj (a) (doing good) benéfico(a); **b. climate** clima m benéfico (b) (advantageous) beneficioso(a), provechoso(a)

beneficiary [benɪˈfɪʃərɪ] n beneficiario(a) m,f

benefit [ˈbenɪfɪt] 1 vt (US pt & pp benefitted) beneficiar 2 vi beneficiarse, aprovecharse, sacar provecho (**from** or **by** de) 3 n (a) (advantage) beneficio m, ventaja f, provecho m; **for the b. of** en beneficio de (b) Com (gain) beneficio m, ganancia f (c) (good) bien m; **I did it for your b.** lo hice por tu bien (d) *(allowance)* subsidio *m*; **unemployment b.** subsidio *m* or seguro *m* de desempleo ❑ **fringe b.** extra *m* (e) *(event)* función *f* benéfica ❑ *Sport* **b. match** partido *m* benéfico

Benelux ['benɪlʌks] *n* (el) Benelux; **the B. countries** los países del Benelux

benevolence [bɪ'nevələns] *n (kindness)* benevolencia *f*, bondad *f*; *(generosity)* caridad *f*

benevolent [bɪ'nevələnt] *adj* (a) *(kindly)* benévolo(a) (b) *(charitable)* caritativo(a); **b. society** sociedad de beneficiencia

Bengal [beŋ'gɔ:l] *n* Bengala ❑ **B. light** bengala *f*, luz *f* de Bengala

Bengali [beŋ'gɔ:lɪ] *adj & n* bengalí *(mf)*

benign [bɪ'naɪn] *adj* benigno(a); *Med* **b. tumour** tumor benigno

Benin [be'ni:n] *n* Benín

Beninese [benɪ'ni:z] *adj & n* benimeño(a) *(m,f)*

bent [bent] **1** *pt & pp see* **bend**
2 *adj* (a) *(curved)* curvado(a), doblado(a), torcido(a) (b) *(determined)* empeñado(a); **to be b. on doing sth** estar empeñado(a) en hacer algo (c) *Br Fam (corrupt)* deshonesto(a) (d) *Br Slang (homosexual)* maricón(ona)
3 *n* (a) *(inclination)* inclinación *f* (**towards** hacia); **to follow one's b.** hacer lo que le apetezca (b) *(aptitude)* facilidad *f* (**for** para)

Benzedrine® ['benzədri:n] *n Med* Bencedrina® *f*

benzene ['benzi:n] *n Chem* benceno *m*

benzine ['benzi:n] *n Chem* bencina *f*

bequeath [bɪ'kwi:ð] *vt Jur* legar

bequest [bɪ'kwest] *n Jur* legado *m*

berate [bɪ'reɪt] *vt (scold)* reganar

Berber ['bɜ:bər] *adj & n* bereber *(mf)*, berebere *(mf)*

bereaved [bɪ'ri:vd] **1** *adj* desconsolado(a)
2 the b. *npl* los allegados del (de la) difunto(a)

bereavement [bɪ'ri:vmənt] *n* (a) *(loss)* pérdida *f* (b) *(mourning)* duelo *m*, luto *m*

bereft [bɪ'reft] *adj* **b. of** privado(a) de

beret ['bereɪ] *n* boina *f*

bergamot ['bɜ:gəmɒt] *n Bot* (a) *(fruit)* bergamota *f* (b) *(tree)* bergamoto *m*

beriberi [berɪ'berɪ] *n Med* beriberi *m*

Berlin [bɜ:'lɪn] *n* Berlín ❑ **East B.** Berlín Este; **West B.** Berlín Oeste

Berliner [bɜ:'lɪnər] *n* berlinés(esa) *m,f*

Bermuda [bə'mju:də] *n* las (Islas) Bermudas; **B. shorts** bermudas *mpl*

Bern(e) [bɜ:n] *n* Berna

berry ['berɪ] *n Bot* baya *f*

berserk [bə'sɜ:k, bə'zɜ:k] *adj* enloquecido(a); **he'll drive me b.** me volverá loco(a); **to go b.** volverse loco(a)

berth [bɜ:θ] *Naut* **1** *n* (a) *(mooring place)* atracadero *m*, amarradero *m*; *Fig* **to give sb a wide b.** evitar a algn (b) *(on train, ship) (bed)* litera *f*
2 *vt (dock) (ship)* poner en dique
3 *vi* atracar

beryl ['berɪl] *n Min* berilo *m*

beseech [bɪ'si:tʃ] *vt (pt & pp* **beseeched** *or* **besought**) suplicar, implorar; **to b. sb to do sth** suplicar a algn que haga algo

beset [bɪ'set] *vt (pt & pp* **beset**) acosar; **it is b. with dangers** está plagado de peligros; **to be b. by temptations** estar acosado por las tentaciones

beside [bɪ'saɪd] *prep* (a) *(next to)* al lado de, junto a; *(near)*

cerca de (b) *(compared with)* comparado con, al lado de (c) *(away from)* **he was b. himself with joy** estaba loco de alegría; **that's b. the point** eso no viene al caso; **to be b. oneself** estar fuera de sí

besides [bɪ'saɪdz] **1** *prep* (a) *(in addition to)* además de; **who is coming b. Alan?** ¿quién viene además de Alan? (b) *(except)* excepto, menos; **no one b. me** nadie más que yo
2 *adv* además; **it's late and b., I'm tired** es tarde, y además estoy cansado

besiege [bɪ'si:dʒ] *vt* (a) *Mil (city)* sitiar, asediar (b) *Fig (person)* asediar, acosar

besmirch [bɪ'smɜ:tʃ] *vt Literary (face)* manchar; *(reputation)* mancillar

besom ['bi:zəm] *n* escoba *f*

besotted [bɪ'sɒtɪd] *adj* (a) *(infatuated)* locamente enamorado(a) (**with** de) (b) *(intoxicated)* atontado(a); **b. with drink** aturdido(a) por la bebida

besought [bɪ'sɔ:t] *pt & pp see* **beseech**

bespatter [bɪ'spætər] *vt* salpicar (**with** de)

bespectacled [bɪ'spektəkəld] *adj* con gafas, que lleva gafas

bespoke [bɪ'spəʊk] *adj esp Br* (a) *(suit)* hecho(a) a la medida (b) *(tailor)* que confecciona ropa a la medida

best [best] **1** *adj (superl of* **good**) mejor; **b. man** ≃ padrino *m* de boda; **her b. friend** su mejor amiga; **it's the b. film of the year** es la mejor película del año; **he's the b. (pupil) in the class** es el mejor (alumno) de la clase; **the b. thing would be to phone them** lo mejor sería llamarles; **we had to wait the b. part of a year** tuvimos que esperar casi un año; **with b. wishes from Mary** *(in letter)* con mis mejores deseos, Mary
2 *adv (superl of* **well**) mejor; **as b. I can** lo mejor que pueda; **I like this one b.** éste es el que más me gusta; **I sleep b. in winter** en invierno duermo mejor; **the world's b. dressed man** el hombre mejor vestido del mundo; **to come off b.** salir ganando; **we had b. go** es mejor que nos vayamos
3 *n* lo mejor; **all the b.!** ¡que te vaya bien!; **at b.** a lo más; **it's all for the b.** más vale que sea así; **one has to make the b. of it** hay que conformarse; **she wants the b. of both worlds** quiere tenerlo todo; **the b. of it is that ...** lo mejor del caso es que ...; **to be at one's b.** estar en plena forma, estar como nunca; **to do one's b.** hacer todo lo posible; **to do sth to the b. of one's ability** hacer algo lo mejor posible; **to get the b. out of sth** aprovechar algo al máximo; **to look one's b.** tener muy buen aspecto; **to make the b. of a bad job** poner al mal tiempo buena cara; **to make the b. of sth** sacar el mejor partido de algo; **to the b. of my knowledge** que yo sepa; **with the b. of them** como el que más

bestial ['bestɪəl] *adj* bestial

bestiality [bestɪ'ælɪtɪ] *n* bestialidad *f*

bestow [bɪ'stəʊ] *vt (favour etc)* conceder; *(honours, power)* otorgar (**on** a); *(title etc)* conferir (**on** a)

best-seller [best'selər] *n* superventas *m inv*, best-seller *m*

best-selling ['bestselɪŋ] *adj* **a b.-s. author** un autor de superventas *or* éxito

bet [bet] **1** *n* apuesta *f*; **to make** *or* **place a b.** hacer una apuesta; **to make a b. on sth** apostar a algo
2 *vt (pt & pp* **bet** *or* **betted**) apostar; **I b. you five dollars that ...** te apuesto cinco dólares a que ...
3 *vi* apostar (**on** a); *Fam* **you b.!** ¡y tanto!

beta ['bi:tə] *n (Greek letter)* beta *f* ❑ *Phys* **b. particle** partícula *f* beta; **b. ray** rayo *m* beta; *Comptr* **b. testing/version** pruebas *fpl*/versión *f* beta

betel ['bi:təl] *n Bot* betel *m*

bête noire [bet'nwɑ:r] *n (pl* **bêtes noires**) bestia *f* negra

Bethlehem ['beθlɪhem] n Belén

betide [bɪ'taɪd] vt Literary **woe b. you if ...!** ¡ay de ti si ...!

betray [bɪ'treɪ] vt (**a**) (person, country) traicionar (**b**) (spouse) engañar (**c**) (secret, fact) revelar; **to b. one's ignorance** demostrar or dejar ver la ignorancia

betrayal [bɪ'treɪəl] n (**a**) (of person, country) traición f; **b. of trust** abuso m de confianza (**b**) (of spouse) engaño m

betrayer [bɪ'treɪər] n traidor(a) m,f

betrothal [bɪ'trəʊðəl] n Literary desposorios mpl, esponsales mpl

betrothed [bɪ'trəʊðd] **1** adj prometido(a)
2 the b. npl los prometidos

better[1] ['betər] **1** adj (**a**) (comp of **good**) mejor; **a b. class of hotel** un hotel de más categoría; **Suzanne's a b. athlete than me** Suzanne es mejor atleta que yo; **that's b.!** ¡eso es!, ¡eso está mejor!; **the weather is b. than last week** hace mejor tiempo que la semana pasada; **to be no b. than ...** no ser más que ...; **to get b.** mejorar; Br Fam Hum **b. half** (spouse) media naranja f, costilla f (**b**) (healthier) mejor (de salud); **are you b.?** ¿te encuentras mejor?, ¿estás mejor?; **she was ill, but she's b. now** estuvo enferma, pero ahora está mejor (**c**) **b. off** (better) mejor; (richer) mejor situado(a); **you'd be b. off going home** lo mejor es que te vayas a casa; **they are b. off than we are** tienen más dinero que nosotros (**d**) (larger) mayor; **the b. part of the day** la mayor parte del día
2 adv (comp of **well**) (**a**) (gen) mejor; **all the b., so much the b.** tanto mejor; **b. and b.** cada vez mejor; **he knows b. than to make such a silly mistake** un error así no es propio de él; **he swims b. than me** nada mejor que yo; **the sooner the b.** cuanto antes mejor; Prov **b. late than never** más vale tarde que nunca (**b**) **had b.** más vale que (+ subj); **we had b. leave** más vale que nos vayamos (**c**) **to think b. of** (plan, idea) cambiar de; (person) tener en más consideración
3 n **this one is the b. of the two** éste es el mejor de los dos; **a change for the b.** una mejora; **for b. (or) for worse** (marriage) en lo bueno y en lo malo; (come what may) pase lo que pase; **to get the b. of sb** vencer a algn; **to respect one's (elders and) betters** respetar a los mayores
4 vt (**a**) (improve) mejorar; **he must b. himself** debe mejorar su situación (**b**) Com (surpass) superar

better[2], US **bettor** ['betər] n apostante mf, (committed) apostador(a) m,f

betterment ['betəmənt] n mejoría f

betting ['betɪŋ] n apuestas fpl □ Br **b. shop** quiosco m de apuestas; **b. slip** resguardo m de una apuesta

between [bɪ'twi:n] **1** prep entre; **b. now and October** de ahora a octubre; **b. the door and the window** entre la puerta y la ventana; **b. you and me** entre nosotros; **the supermarket is closed b. 1 and 2** el supermercado está cerrado de 1 a 2
2 adv en or por medio; **in b.** (position) en medio; (time) entretanto, mientras (tanto)

betwixt [bɪ'twɪkst] adv Old-fashioned & Literary entre; **b. and between** entre las dos cosas, ni una cosa ni la otra

bevel ['bevəl] **1** n bisel m
2 vt (pt & pp **bevelled**, US **beveled**) biselar

beverage ['bevərɪdʒ] n bebida f; **non-alcoholic b.** bebida sin alcohol

bevvy ['bevɪ] n Br Fam **to go for** or **have a b.** (go for a drink) tomarse una copa

bevy ['bevɪ] n bandada f

bewail [bɪ'weɪl] vt lamentar

beware [bɪ'weər] vi tener cuidado (**of** con); **b.!** ¡cuidado!, ¡ojo!; Com **'b. of imitations'** 'desconfíe de las imitaciones'; **b. of the dog** (sign) cuidado con el perro

bewilder [bɪ'wɪldər] vt desconcertar, confundir

bewildered [bɪ'wɪldəd] adj desconcertado(a), perplejo(a)

bewildering [bɪ'wɪldərɪŋ] adj desconcertante

bewilderment [bɪ'wɪldərmənt] n desconcierto m

bewitch [bɪ'wɪtʃ] vt (**a**) (cast a spell over) hechizar (**b**) (enchant) fascinar, encantar

bewitching [bɪ'wɪtʃɪŋ] adj fascinante

beyond [bɪ'jɒnd] **1** prep (**a**) (on the other side of) más allá de; **b. the mountains** más allá de las montañas; **b. the seas** allende los mares, acullá de los mares (**b**) (outside the scope of) más allá de; **b. belief** increíble; **b. doubt** sin lugar a dudas, indudablemente; **b. my reach** fuera de mi alcance; **it is b. me why ...** no comprendo por qué ...; **it's b. a joke** ya no tiene gracia; **she is b. caring** ya no le importa; **this task is b. me** no puedo con esta tarea; **to live b. one's means** vivir por encima de las posibilidades de uno
2 adv más allá, más lejos; **he owns the palace and the gardens b.** es dueño del palacio y de los jardines de más allá
3 the b. n el más allá

Bhutan [bu:'tɑ:n] n Bhután

bias ['baɪəs] n (**a**) (tendency) tendencia f, inclinación f (**towards** hacia) (**b**) (prejudice) prejuicio m (**c**) Sew sesgo m; **cut on the b.** cortado al sesgo

bias(s)ed ['baɪəst] adj parcial; **to be b. against sth/sb** tener prejuicio en contra de algo/algn

bib [bɪb] n (**a**) (for baby) babero m (**b**) (of apron, dungarees) peto m (**c**) (fish) faneca f

Bible ['baɪbəl] n Biblia f; **the Holy B.** la Santa Biblia □ Br Fam Pej **B. basher** proselitista mf fanático(a); US **B. Belt** = zona habitada por los integristas protestantes; **B. paper** papel m biblia; Fam Pej **B. thumper** proselitista mf fanático(a)

biblical ['bɪblɪkəl] adj bíblico(a)

bibliographer [bɪblɪ'ɒɡrəfər] n bibliógrafo(a) m,f

bibliographic(al) [bɪblɪəʊ'ɡræfɪk(əl)] adj bibliográfico(a)

bibliography [bɪblɪ'ɒɡrəfɪ] n bibliografía f

bibliophile ['bɪblɪəʊfaɪl] n bibliófilo(a) m,f

bicameral [baɪ'kæmərəl] adj Parl bicameral

bicameralism [baɪ'kæmərəlɪzəm] n Parl bicameralismo m

bicarbonate [baɪ'kɑ:bənɪt] n Chem bicarbonato m □ **b. of soda** bicarbonato m sódico or de sosa

bicentenary [baɪsen'ti:nərɪ] n, US **bicentennial** [baɪsen'tenɪəl] **1** adj bicentenario(a)
2 n bicentenario m

biceps ['baɪseps] n Anat bíceps m

bicker ['bɪkər] vi discutir, reñir

bickering ['bɪkərɪŋ] n discusiones fpl, riñas fpl

bicultural [baɪ'kʌltʃərəl] adj con dos culturas

bicycle ['baɪsɪkəl] **1** n bicicleta f; **b. pump** bomba f de aire; **b. rack** (on pavement) soporte m para estacionar bicicletas; (on car) baca f para bicicletas; **to go by b.** ir en bicicleta; **to ride a b.** montar en bicicleta
2 vi ir en bicicleta

bid [bɪd] **1** vt (pt bid or bade; pp bid or bidden ['bɪdən]) (**a**) (say) decir; **to b. sb farewell** despedirse de algn; **to b. sb welcome** dar la bienvenida a algn (**b**) (command) mandar, ordenar; **she bade him be quiet** le mandó que se callase (**c**) (invite) invitar; **he bade me sit down** me invitó a sentarme (**d**) (seem) parecer; **to b. fair** parecer probable (**e**) (at auction) (pt & pp bid) pujar, ofrecer (**f**) Bridge (pt & pp bid) subastar, cantar

2 vi (**a**) *(at auction)* pujar, hacer una oferta (**for** por) (**b**) *Bridge* declarar

3 n (**a**) *(offer)* oferta f; **b. price** *(on stock exchange)* precio m comprador (**b**) *(at auction)* puja f, postura f (**c**) *Bridge* subasta f (**d**) *(attempt)* intento m, tentativa f; **a b. for power** un intento por conseguir el poder

bidder ['bɪdər] n *(at auction)* postor(a) m,f; **the highest b.** el mejor postor

bidding ['bɪdɪŋ] n (**a**) *(at auction)* puja f, licitación f (**b**) *Bridge* subasta f (**c**) *(order)* orden f; **to do sb's b.** cumplir la orden de algn

biddy ['bɪdɪ] n *Fam (gossip)* **old b.** vieja f chismosa

bide [baɪd] vt *(pt bided or bode; pp bided)* esperar; **to b. one's time** esperar el momento oportuno

bidet ['biːdeɪ] n bidé m

biennial [baɪ'enɪəl] **1** adj bienal

2 n (**a**) *(plant)* planta f bienal (**b**) *(event)* bienal f

bier [bɪər] n *(stand)* féretro m, andas fpl

biff [bɪf] *Fam* **1** n puñetazo m

2 vt dar un puñetazo a

bifocal [baɪ'fəʊkəl] **1** adj bifocal

2 bifocals npl gafas fpl or Am anteojos mpl bifocales

big [bɪg] **1** adj (**bigger, biggest**) grande; *(before singular nouns)* gran; **a b. clock** un reloj grande; **a b. surprise** una gran sorpresa; **he's too b. for his boots** or US **for his britches** es muy fanfarrón; **my b. brother** mi hermano mayor; **she's bigger than me** es más alta que yo; **to get b.** *(gen)* hacerse grande; *(child)* crecer, hacerse mayor; **to have b. ideas** ver las cosas en grande; *Fam* **what's the b. idea?** ¿qué pretendes?; *Fam Iron* **that's b. of you** ¡qué amable eres conmigo!; *Fam Iron* **b. deal!** ¿y qué? □ **B. Brother** el Gran Hermano; *US Fam* **b. bucks** muchas pelas fpl; **b. business** los grandes negocios; **b. dipper** *(at fairground)* montaña f rusa; *US Astron* **B. Dipper** Osa f Mayor; *Br Aut* **b. end** cabeza f de biela; *Pol* **the B. Five** las Cinco Potencias or Superpotencias; **b. game** caza f mayor; *Fam* **b. gun, b. noise, b. shot** pez m gordo; *Fam* **b. time** éxito m profesional; **to make the b. time** tener éxito; **b. toe** dedo m gordo del pie; *Fam* **b. top** tienda f mayor del circo

2 adv (**a**) *(on a grand scale)* a gran escala; **to think b.** planear a lo grande; *Fam* **to talk b.** fanfarronear (**b**) *(well)* de manera excepcional; **his plans went over b. with the committee** sus planes tuvieron mucho éxito entre los miembros del comité

bigamist ['bɪgəmɪst] n bígamo(a) m,f

bigamous ['bɪgəməs] adj bígamo(a)

bigamy ['bɪgəmɪ] n bigamia f

big-boned [bɪg'bəʊnd] adj corpulento(a)

big-eared [bɪg'ɪəd] adj orejudo(a)

bighead ['bɪghed] n *Fam* creído(a) m,f, engreído(a) m,f

bigheaded [bɪg'hedɪd] adj creído(a), engreído(a)

big-hearted [bɪg'hɑːtɪd] adj generoso(a)

bighorn ['bɪghɔːn] n *Zool* carnero m de cuernos grandes *(oriundo de las Montañas Rocosas)*

bight [baɪt] n bahía f □ **Great Australian B.** Gran Bahía f Australiana

bigmouth ['bɪgmaʊθ] n *Fam* bocazas mf inv, Am bocón(ona) m,f

bigot ['bɪgət] n fanático(a) m,f, intolerante mf

bigoted ['bɪgətɪd] adj fanático(a), intolerante

bigotry ['bɪgətrɪ] n fanatismo m, intolerancia f

big-sounding [bɪg'saʊndɪŋ] adj altisonante

bigwig ['bɪgwɪg] n *Fam* pez m gordo

bike [baɪk] *Fam (abbr* **bicycle** or **motorbike**) **1** n (**a**)

(bicycle) bici f; **b. lane** carril-bici m; *Br* **on your b.!** *(go away)* ¡largo!, ¡piérdete! (**b**) *(motorcycle)* moto f

2 vi (**a**) *(bicycle)* ir en bici (**b**) *(motorcycle)* ir en moto

biker ['baɪkər] n *Fam* motero(a) m,f

bikeway ['baɪkweɪ] n *US* carril-bici m

bikini [bɪ'kiːnɪ] n bikini m

bilabial [baɪ'leɪbɪəl] adj *Ling* bilabial

bilateral [baɪ'lætərəl] adj *(agreement etc)* bilateral

bilberry ['bɪlbərɪ] n *Bot* arándano m

bile [baɪl] n (**a**) *Med* bilis f, hiel f; **b. stone** cálculo m biliar (**b**) *Fig (irritability)* bilis f, hiel f, mal genio m

bilge [bɪldʒ] n (**a**) *Naut (bottom)* pantoque m □ **b. keel** quilla f (**b**) *Naut (also pl) (cavity)* sentina f □ **b. water** agua f de sentina (**c**) *Fam (rubbish)* tonterías fpl, idioteces fpl

bilingual [baɪ'lɪŋgwəl] adj bilingüe

bilingualism [baɪ'lɪŋgwəlɪzəm] n bilingüismo m

bilious ['bɪlɪəs] adj (**a**) *Med* bilioso(a); **b. attack** cólico bilioso (**b**) *Fam (colour etc)* asqueroso(a) (**c**) *Fig (irritable)* bilioso(a), colérico(a)

Bill [bɪl] n *Br Slang* **the Old B.** *(police)* la poli

bill¹ [bɪl] **1** n (**a**) *(for electricity, services etc)* factura f; **the gas b.** la factura del gas (**b**) *esp Br (in restaurant, hotel)* cuenta f; **the b., please** la cuenta, por favor; *Fam* **to foot the b.** pagar la cuenta (**c**) *Parl* proyecto m de ley; **to pass a b.** aprobar un proyecto de ley (**d**) *US (banknote)* billete m de banco; **a ten-dollar b.** un billete de diez dólares (**e**) *(poster)* cartel m; **on the b.** en cartel; **post no bills** *(sign)* prohibido fijar carteles; *Theat* **to top the b.** encabezar el reparto; *Fam* **to fit the b.** venir como anillo al dedo (**f**) *(document)* documento m □ **b. of exchange** letra f de cambio; **b. of fare** menú m; *Naut* **b. of health** patente f de sanidad; *Fam* **the doctor gave him a clean b. of health** el médico certificó su buen estado de salud; **b. of lading** conocimiento m de embarque; *Pol* **B. of Rights** declaración f de derechos; *Jur* **b. of sale** contrato m or escritura f de venta

2 vt (**a**) *(send bill to)* facturar, extender una factura a (**b**) *Theat (schedule)* programar; **she is billed to appear as Joan of Arc** figura en el cartel en el papel de Juana de Arco; **the play is billed for next Monday** la obra se representará el lunes que viene

bill² [bɪl] n *(of bird)* pico m

billabong ['bɪləbɒŋ] n *Austral* rebalsa f, embalse m

billboard ['bɪlbɔːd] n *US (hoarding)* cartelera f

billet ['bɪlɪt] *Mil* **1** n alojamiento m, acantonamiento m

2 vt *(troops)* alojar, acantonar

billet-doux [bɪlɪ'duː] n *(pl* **billets-doux**) *Hum & Literary* carta f de amor

billfold ['bɪlfəʊld] n *US* cartera f, billetero m, billetera f

billhook ['bɪlhʊk] n *Agr* podadera f

billiard ['bɪljəd] n **billiards** billar m □ **b. ball** bola f de billar; **b. cue** taco m de billar; **b. room** sala f de billar; **b. table** mesa f de billar

billing ['bɪlɪŋ] n *Theat* **to get top b.** estar a la cabeza del reparto

billion ['bɪljən] n *(pl* **billion** or **billions**) mil millones mpl; *Br Old-fashioned* billón m

billionaire [bɪljə'neər] n multimillonario(a) m,f

billow ['bɪləʊ] **1** n (**a**) *(of water)* ola f (**b**) *(of smoke)* nube f

2 vi (**a**) *(sea)* ondear (**b**) *(sail)* hincharse, inflarse; **clouds of black smoke billowed from the burning building** grandes nubes de humo negro surgían del edificio en llamas

billowy ['bɪləʊɪ] adj *(sea)* ondoso(a); *(sail)* hinchado(a)

billposter ['bɪlpəʊstər] n, **billsticker** ['bɪlstɪkər] n cartelero(a) m,f

billycan ['bɪlɪkæn] *n Br Austral* cazo *m*

billy goat ['bɪlɪgəʊt] *n* macho *m* cabrío

billy-(h)o ['bɪlɪəʊ] *adj Br Fam* **like b.-(h)o** a más no poder, a toda pastilla

bimbo ['bɪmbəʊ] *(pl* **bimbos)** *n Fam Pej* = mujer atractiva y de pocas luces

bin [bɪn] *n* **(a)** *(for storage)* cajón *m*, arca *f* □ **bread b.** caja *f* del pan; *Slang* **loony b.** manicomio *m*; *Br* **wine b.** botellero *m* **(b)** *Br (for rubbish)* **(rubbish) b.** balde *m*, *Esp* cubo *m* de la basura; **waste-paper b.** papelera *f*, *Arg Méx* cesto *m*, *Carib* zafacón *m*, *Chile* papelero *m*, *Col* caneca *f*, *Méx* bote *m*

binary ['baɪnərɪ] *adj Math & Comptr* binario(a); **b. number** número binario

bind [baɪnd] **1** *vt (pt & pp* **bound) (a)** *(tie up) (hands, package etc)* atar; *Agr (cereal)* agavillar **(b)** *Med (bandage)* vendar **(c)** *Print (book)* encuadernar **(d)** *(require)* obligar; **the contract binds him to pay interest** el contrato le obliga a pagar intereses **(e)** *(cause to stick)* unir
   2 *vi (agreement)* tener fuerza obligatoria
   3 *n Fam* aprieto *m*; **to be in a b.** estar en un aprieto

bind over *vt Jur* obligar legalmente

binder ['baɪndər] *n* **(a)** *Agr* agavilladora *f* **(b)** *Print (person)* encuadernador(a) *m,f* **(c)** *(file)* carpeta *f*

binding ['baɪndɪŋ] **1** *adj* **(a)** *(promise)* comprometedor(a); *(decision)* obligatorio(a) **(b)** *Med (constipating)* que estriñe, astringente
   2 *n* **(a)** *Print* encuadernación *f* **(b)** *Sew* ribete *m* **(c)** *(on skis)* fijación *f*

bindweed ['baɪndwiːd] *n Bot* enredadera *f*

binge [bɪndʒ] *n Fam* borrachera *f*; **to go on a b.** irse de juerga

bingo ['bɪŋgəʊ] *n* bingo *m*; **to play b.** jugar al bingo □ **b. hall** (sala *f* de) bingo *m*

binocular [bɪˈnɒkjʊlər] **1** *adj* binocular; **b. vision** visión *f* binocular
   2 binoculars *npl* prismáticos *mpl*, gemelos *mpl*

biochemical [baɪəʊˈkemɪkəl] *adj* bioquímico(a)

biochemist [baɪəʊˈkemɪst] *n* bioquímico(a) *m,f*

biochemistry [baɪəʊˈkemɪstrɪ] *n* bioquímica *f*

biodegradable [baɪəʊdɪˈɡreɪdəbəl] *adj* biodegradable

biodiversity [baɪəʊdaɪˈvɜːsɪtɪ] *n* biodiversidad *f*

biofeedback [baɪəʊˈfiːdbæk] *n* bioretracción *f*

biographer [baɪˈɒɡrəfər] *n* biógrafo(a) *m,f*

biographical [baɪəˈɡræfɪkəl] *adj* biográfico(a)

biography [baɪˈɒɡrəfɪ] *n* biografía *f*

biological [baɪəˈlɒdʒɪkəl] *adj* biológico(a); **b. warfare** guerra biológica

biologist [baɪˈɒlədʒɪst] *n* biólogo(a) *m,f*

biology [baɪˈɒlədʒɪ] *n* biología *f*

bionic [baɪˈɒnɪk] *adj* biónico(a)

bionics [baɪˈɒnɪks] *n* biónica *f*

biophysical [baɪəʊˈfɪzɪkəl] *adj* biofísico(a)

biophysicist [baɪəʊˈfɪzɪsɪst] *n* biofísico(a) *m,f*

biophysics [baɪəʊˈfɪzɪks] *n* biofísica *f*

biopsy ['baɪɒpsɪ] *n Med* biopsia *f*

biorhythm ['baɪəʊrɪðəm] *n* biorritmo *m*

biosphere ['baɪəsfɪər] *n* biosfera *f*

biotech ['baɪəʊtek] **1** *n* biotecnología *f*
   2 *adj (industry, company)* de biotecnología

biotechnology [baɪəʊtekˈnɒlədʒɪ] *n* biotecnología *f*

bipartisan [baɪˈpɑːtɪzæn] *adj* bipartito(a)

bipartite [baɪˈpɑːtaɪt] *adj* **(a)** *(with two parts)* bipartido(a),

bipartito(a) (b) *(shared by two parties)* bipartito(a), bilateral; **b. agreement** acuerdo *m* bipartito

biped ['baɪped] **1** *n Zool* bípedo *m*
   2 *adj* bípedo(a)

biplane ['baɪpleɪn] *n Av* biplano *m*

birch [bɜːtʃ] **1** *n* **(a)** *Bot* abedul *m* **(b)** *(rod)* vara *f* (de abedul)
   2 *vt* azotar

bird [bɜːd] *n* **(a)** *Orn (small)* pájaro *m*; *(large)* ave *f*; *Fig Theat* **to give sb the b.** abuchear a algn; *Fig* **to kill two birds with one stone** matar dos pájaros de un tiro; *Slang* **to do b.** estar en el talego; *Prov* **a b. in the hand is worth two in the bush** más vale pájaro en mano que ciento volando; *Prov* **birds of a feather flock together** Dios los cría y ellos se juntan; **they're birds of a feather** son tal para cual; *Prov* **the early b. catches the worm** a quien madruga Dios le ayuda □ **b. of paradise** ave *f* del Paraíso; **b. of passage** ave *f* de paso; **b. of prey** ave *f* de rapiña; **night b.** ave *f* nocturna **(b)** *Br Fam (girl)* nena *f*, *Arg* piba *f*

birdbath ['bɜːdbɑːθ] *n* pila *f* para pájaros

bird-brained ['bɜːdbreɪnd] *adj Fam* **to be b.** ser un majadero; **a b. idea** una majadería

birdcage ['bɜːdkeɪdʒ] *n* jaula *f*

birdie ['bɜːdɪ] *n* **(a)** *Fam (bird)* pajarito *m* **(b)** *Golf* uno *m* bajo par, birdie *m*

birdseed ['bɜːdsiːd] *n* alpiste *m*

bird's-eye view [bɜːdzaɪˈvjuː] *n* vista *f* panorámica *or* de pájaro

bird-watcher ['bɜːdwɒtʃər] *n* ornitólogo(a) *m,f*, observador(a) *m,f* de pájaros

bird-watching ['bɜːdwɒtʃɪŋ] *n* ornitología *f*, observación *f* de pájaros

biretta [bɪˈretə] *n Rel* birrete *m*, birreta *f*

Biro® ['baɪrəʊ] *n Br* bolígrafo *m*, *Carib* pluma *f*, *Col Ecuad* esferográfico *m*, *CSur* lapicera *f*, *Méx* pluma *f* (atómica)

birth [bɜːθ] *n* **(a)** *(of baby etc)* nacimiento *m*; *Med (childbirth)* parto *m*; **Spanish by b.** español de nacimiento; **to give b. to a child** dar a luz a un niño □ **b. certificate** partida *f* de nacimiento; **b. control** *(family planning)* control *m* de la natalidad; *(contraception)* métodos *mpl* anticonceptivos; **b. rate** índice *m* de natalidad **(b)** *(descent, parentage)* linaje *m*, origen *m*; **of noble b.** de noble linaje

birthday ['bɜːθdeɪ] *n* cumpleaños *m inv*; **happy b.!** ¡feliz cumpleaños!; *Fam* **to be in one's b. suit** estar como Dios le trajo al mundo, estar en cueros □ **b. party** fiesta *f* de cumpleaños

birthmark ['bɜːθmɑːk] *n* antojo *m*, marca *f* de nacimiento

birthplace ['bɜːθpleɪs] *n* lugar *m* de nacimiento

birthright ['bɜːθraɪt] *n (individual)* derechos *mpl* de nacimiento, derechos *mpl* de primogenitura; *(heritage)* patrimonio *m*

birthstone ['bɜːθstəʊn] *n* = piedra preciosa que corresponde al mes de nacimiento y que trae suerte al portador

Biscay ['bɪskeɪ] *n* Vizcaya; **the Bay of B.** el golfo de Vizcaya

biscuit ['bɪskɪt] *n* **(a)** *Br (sweet, salted)* galleta *f*; *Fam* **that really takes the b.!** ¡eso ya es el colmo!, ¡eso realmente se lleva la palma! **(b)** *US (muffin)* bollo *m*, bizcocho *m* **(c)** *(colour)* beige *m*, *Esp* beis *m inv*

bisect [baɪˈsekt] *vt* bisegmentar; *Geom* bisecar

bisexual [baɪˈseksjʊəl] *adj* bisexual

bishop ['bɪʃəp] *n* **(a)** *Rel* obispo *m* **(b)** *Chess* alfil *m*

bishopric ['bɪʃəprɪk] *n Rel* obispado *m*

bismuth ['bɪzməθ] *n Chem* bismuto *m*

bison ['baɪsən] *n inv Zool* bisonte *m*

bistro ['bi:strəʊ] *n* restaurante *m* pequeño

bit¹ [bɪt] *n* (**a**) *(small piece)* trozo *m*, pedazo *m*; **a b. of cake** un trozo de pastel; **the table has come to bits** la mesa se ha roto; **to smash sth to bits** hacer añicos algo; **to take sth to bits** desmontar algo; *Fig* **he went to bits** se puso histérico; *Fig* **I'm every b. as keen as you** estoy tan entusiasmado(a) como tú; *Fig* **thrilled to bits** muy emocionado(a), entusiasmado(a); *Fig* **to do one's b.** hacer or poner de su parte; *Fam* **b. of all right** *(woman)* tía *f* buena; *(man)* tío *m* bueno ❑ *Theat* **b. part** papel *m* secundario (**b**) *(small quantity)* poco *m*; **a b. of sugar** un poco de azúcar; **a b. of advice** un consejo; **a b. of news** una noticia; **bits and pieces** trastos *mpl*; **he's a b. of a philosopher** es un poco filósofo; **she's got a b. of money put aside** tiene algo de dinero ahorrado; *Fig* **b. by b.** poco a poco; *Fig* **not a b. of it!** ¡ni hablar!; **are you angry? — not a b.!** ¿estás enfadado? — ¡en absoluto! (**c**) *(slightly, quite)* **a b.** un poco; **a b. longer** un ratito más; **a b. worried** un poco preocupado; **a good b.** bastante (**d**) *(coin)* moneda *f* ❑ *Br Hist* **threepenny b.** moneda *f* de tres peniques; *US* **two bits** 25 centavos

bit² [bɪt] *n* (*of bridle*) bocado *m*; *Fig* **to have the b. between one's teeth** haber tomado or *Esp* cogido carrerilla

bit³ [bɪt] *n* (*of tool*) broca *f*, filo *m*; (*of drill*) broca *f*, taladro *m*, barrena *f*

bit⁴ [bɪt] *n Comptr* bit *m*

bit⁵ [bɪt] *pt see* **bite**

bitch [bɪtʃ] **1** *n* (**a**) *Zool (female)* hembra *f*; *(dog)* perra *f* (**b**) *Fam (spiteful woman)* bruja *f*, arpía *f*; *(prostitute)* zorra *f*; *Slang Offens* **son of a b.** hijo *m* de puta or perra
2 *vi Fam* **to b. (about)** *(complain)* quejarse (de); *(criticize)* criticar, despellejar; **he's always bitching about his workmates** *(criticizing)* siempre está poniendo a parir or *RP* ponéndole el cuero a sus compañeros de trabajo

bitchy ['bɪtʃɪ] *adj* (**bitchier, bitchiest**) *Fam* malicioso(a), *Esp* puñetero(a)

bite [baɪt] **1** *n* (**a**) *(act)* mordisco *m* (**b**) *(wound)* mordedura *f*; (*insect*) **b.** picadura *f* (de insecto) (**c**) *(mouthful)* bocado *m*; **a b. of chocolate** un bocado de chocolate (**d**) *Fam (snack)* bocado *m*, piscolabis *m*; **she hasn't had a b. to eat all day** no ha probado bocado en todo el día (**e**) *Fig* mordacidad *f*, garra *f*
2 *vt* (*pt* **bit**; *pp* **bitten**) morder; *(insect)* picar; **to b. one's nails** morderse las uñas; *Fig* **to b. the dust** *(scheme, plan)* irse a pique or al garete or *RP* al cuerno; *Fam* **don't b. off more than you can chew** quien mucho abarca, poco aprieta; *Fam* **to b. sb's head off** echarle una bronca a algn; *Fam* **what's biting you?** ¿qué mosca te ha picado?; *Prov* **once bitten twice shy** gato escaldado del agua fría huye
3 *vi* (**a**) *(person, dog)* morder; *(insect, snake)* picar (**b**) *Fig (take effect)* surtir efecto; **the economic measures are beginning to b.** las medidas económicas están empezando a tener efecto (**c**) *Fishing* picar, morder el anzuelo (**d**) *US Fam (be bad)* ser una mierda

bite-sized ['baɪtsaɪzd] *adj*, **bitesize** ['baɪtsaɪz] *adj* del tamaño de un bocado

biting ['baɪtɪŋ] *adj (wind)* cortante; *Fig (criticism)* mordaz, cáustico(a)

bitmap ['bɪtmæp] *Comptr* **1** *adj* en mapa de bits
2 *n* mapa *m* de bits

bit-mapped ['bɪtmæpt] *adj Comptr* en mapa de bits

bitten ['bɪtən] *pp see* **bite**

bitter ['bɪtər] **1** *adj* (**a**) *(taste)* amargo(a); **b. lemon** limonada *f* amarga (**b**) *(weather)* glacial; *(wind)* cortante (**c**) *(memory)* amargo(a); *(person)* amargado(a); **the experience has made him feel b.** la experiencia le ha amargado

(**d**) *(struggle)* enconado(a); *(hatred)* implacable; **to the b. end** hasta el final
2 *n* (**a**) *Br (beer)* cerveza *f* amarga (**b**) **bitters** bíter *m*

bitterly ['bɪtəlɪ] *adv (extremely)* enormemente, terriblemente; **she was b. disappointed** sufrió una terrible decepción; **it's b. cold** hace un frío glacial

bittern ['bɪtən] *n Orn* avetoro *m* común

bitterness ['bɪtənɪs] *n* (**a**) *(taste)* amargor *m* (**b**) *(weather)* crudeza *f*, severidad *f* (**c**) *(person)* amargura *f*, rencor *m* (**d**) *(of struggle)* encono *m*

bittersweet [bɪtə'swiːt] *adj* agridulce

bitty ['bɪtɪ] *adj* (**bittier, bittiest**) fragmentario(a), incoherente

bitumen ['bɪtjʊmɪn] *n* betún *m*

bituminous [bɪ'tjuːmɪnəs] *adj* bituminoso(a)

bivouac ['bɪvʊæk, 'bɪvwæk] *Mil* **1** *n* vivaque *m*, vivac *m*
2 *vi* (*pt & pp* **bivouacked**) vivaquear

biweekly [baɪ'wiːklɪ] **1** *adj* (**a**) *(every two weeks)* quincenal (**b**) *(twice a week)* bisemanal
2 *adv* (**a**) *(every two weeks)* quincenalmente, cada quincena (**b**) *(twice a week)* dos veces por semana
3 *n* publicación *f* quincenal or bisemanal

bizarre [bɪ'zɑːr] *adj* (**a**) *(odd)* extraño(a), raro(a) (**b**) *(eccentric)* estrafalario(a), extravagante

blab [blæb] *vi* (*pt & pp* **blabbed**) (**a**) *Fam* parlotear, *Esp* largar, *Méx* platicar, *RP* chusmear; *(chatter)* **he's always blabbing** nunca para de hablar (**b**) *(let out a secret)* descubrir el pastel, chivarse

blabber ['blæbər] *vi Fam* parlotear, *Esp* largar, *Méx* platicar, *RP* chusmear

blabbermouth ['blæbəmaʊθ] *n Fam* cotorra *f*, bocazas *mf inv*, *Am* bocón(ona) *m,f*

black [blæk] **1** *adj* (**a**) *(colour)* negro(a); **a b. and white television** un televisor en blanco y negro; **as b. as coal** negro como el carbón; *Fig* **b. and blue** amoratado(a), lleno(a) de cardenales; *Fig* **to be in sb's b. books** estar en la lista negra de algn; *Fam* **to put sth down in b. and white** poner algo por escrito ❑ *Av* **b. box** caja *f* negra; **b. coffee** café *n* solo; *Br* **the B. Country** la región de los Midlands; *Hist* **the B. Death** la peste negra; **the b. economy** la economía negra; **b. eye** ojo *n* morado or a la funeral; *Astron* **b. hole** agujero *n* negro; **b. humour** humor *n* negro; **b. magic** magia *f* negra; *Br* **B. Maria** coche *m* celular, furgón *m* policial; **b. mark** mala nota *f*; **b. market** mercado *m* negro; **b. marketeer** estraperlista *mf*; **b. market goods** artículos *mpl* de estraperlo; *US* **B. Power** = movimiento a favor de los derechos de los negros; *Br* **b. pudding** morcilla *f*; **B. Sea** mar *m* Negro; *Br* **b. sheep** oveja *f* negra; *Aut* **b. spot** punto *m* negro (**b**) *(gloomy)* negro(a); **it was a b. day for the army** fue un día aciago para el ejército; **the outlook is b.** la perspectiva es negra
2 *n* (**a**) *(colour)* negro *m* (**b**) *(person)* negro(a) *m,f* (**c**) *(mourning)* luto *m*; **he was in b.** iba de luto
3 *vt* (**a**) *(make black)* ennegrecer; *Fig* **to b. sb's eye** ponerle a algn un ojo a la funerala (**b**) *(polish)* limpiar, lustrar (**c**) *Br (boycott)* boicotear

black out 1 *vt* (**a**) *(extinguish lights)* apagar las luces de; **the city was blacked out during the air raids** durante los bombardeos se apagaron todas las luces de la ciudad (**b**) *Rad TV (censor)* censurar
2 *vi (faint)* perder el conocimiento, desmayarse

black-and-white [blækən'waɪt] *adj (film, TV, illustration)* en blanco y negro

blackball ['blækbɔːl] **1** *n (veto)* veto *m*; *(negative vote)* voto *m* negativo or en contra
2 *vt* votar en contra de algn

blackberry ['blækbərɪ] *n Bot* zarzamora *f*, mora *f*; **to go blackberrying** ir a recoger moras

blackbird ['blækbɜ:d] *n Orn* mirlo *m*

blackboard ['blækbɔːd] *n* pizarra *f,* encerado *m, Am* pizarrón *m*

blackcurrant [blæk'kʌrənt] *n Bot* grosella *f* negra

blacken ['blækən] *vt* **(a)** *(make black)* ennegrecer, tiznar **(b)** *Fig (defame)* manchar

blackguard -['blægɑːd] *n* sinvergüenza *mf*

blackhead ['blækhed] *n Med* espinilla *f*

blackish ['blækɪʃ] *adj* negruzco(a)

blackjack ['blækdʒæk] *n* **(a)** *US (truncheon)* porra *f,* cachiporra *f* **(b)** *Cards* veintiuna *f*

blackleg ['blækleg] *n* esquirol *m*

blacklist ['blæklɪst] **1** *n* lista *f* negra
2 *vt* poner en la lista negra

blackmail ['blækmeɪl] **1** *n* chantaje *m*
2 *vt* hacer chantaje, chantajear

blackmailer ['blækmeɪlər] *n* chantajista *mf*

blackness ['blæknɪs] *n (colouring)* negrura *f, (darkness)* oscuridad *f*

blackout ['blækaʊt] *n* **(a)** *(of lights)* apagón *m* **(b)** *Rad TV (censorship)* censura *f* **(c)** *(fainting)* pérdida *f* de conocimiento

Blackshirt ['blækʃɜːt] *n Hist* camisa negra *m,* fascista *mf*

blacksmith ['blæksmɪθ] *n* herrero *m*

blackthorn ['blækθɔːn] *n* **(a)** *Bot* endrino *m* **(b)** *(stick)* bastón *m*

black-tie ['blæktaɪ] *adj* de etiqueta ❑ **b.-t. dinner** cena *f* de etiqueta

bladder ['blædər] *n Anat* vejiga *f* ❑ **gall b.** vesícula *f* biliar

blade [bleɪd] *n* **(a)** *(of grass)* brizna *f* **(b)** *(of knife, sword, razor)* hoja *f, (of ice skate)* cuchilla *f* ❑ **razor b.** hoja *f* de afeitar **(c)** *(of propeller)* pala *f,* paleta *f; (of oar)* pala *f*

blag [blæg] *vt (pt & pp blagged) Br Fam (steal)* robar

blah [blɑː] *Fam n (meaningless remarks, nonsense)* sandeces *fpl, Esp* chorradas *fpl, Am* pendejadas *fpl, RP* pavadas *fpl;* **b., b., b.** *(to avoid repetition)* y tal y cual, patatín patatán

blame [bleɪm] **1** *n* culpa *f;* **to put the b. for sth on sb** echar la culpa de algo a algn; **to take the b. for sth** asumir la responsabilidad de algo
2 *vt* culpar, echar la culpa a; **he is to b.** él tiene la culpa; **I don't b. Tom** la culpa no es de Tom; **I've only myself to b.** la culpa es sólo mía; **to be to b.** ser el culpable *or* el responsable, tener la culpa

blameless ['bleɪmlɪs] *adj (person)* inocente; *(conduct)* intachable

blameworthy ['bleɪmwɜːðɪ] *adj* culpable, censurable

blanch [blɑːntʃ] **1** *vt Culin (boil)* escaldar
2 *vi (go pale)* palidecer

blancmange [bləˈmɒnʒ] *n Culin* = budín dulce de aspecto gelatinoso a base de leche y maicena

bland [blænd] *adj* **(a)** *(climate)* suave, templado(a) **(b)** *(person)* agradable, amable **(c)** *(food)* soso(a)

blandishments ['blændɪʃmənts] *npl* halagos *mpl,* lisonjas *fpl*

blank [blæŋk] **1** *adj* **(a)** *(without writing)* en blanco; **leave a b. space** deja un espacio en blanco **(b)** *(empty)* vacío(a); **a. look** una mirada vacía; **my mind went b.** me quedé en blanco ❑ *Mil* **b. cartridge** cartucho *m* de fogueo; *Fin* **b. cheque** cheque *m* en blanco; *Lit* **b. verse** verso *m* blanco *or* suelto **(c)** *(absolute)* tajante, categórico(a); a **b. refusal** una negativa rotunda
2 *n* **(a)** *(space)* espacio *m* en blanco, blanco *m,* hueco *m;* **fill in the blanks** rellene los espacios en blanco; **his mind was a b.** se quedó en blanco; **to draw a b.** no tener éxito **(b)** *Mil* cartucho *m* de fogueo **(c)** *US (form)* impreso *m,* formulario *m*

blanket ['blæŋkɪt] **1** *n* **(a)** *(for bed)* manta *f, Am* cobija *f, Am* frazada *f;* **electric b.** manta eléctrica ❑ *Fam* **wet b.** aguafiestas *mf inv* **(b)** *Fig* capa *f,* manto *m;* **a b. of snow** una capa de nieve
2 *adj* general, comprensivo(a); **a b. agreement** un acuerdo general

blankly ['blæŋklɪ] *adv* **(a)** *(expressionless)* con la mirada vacía **(b)** *(without understanding)* sin comprender

blare [bleər] **1** *n* **(a)** *(loud noise)* estruendo *m* **(b)** *(of trumpet)* trompetazo *m*
2 *vi (trumpet)* sonar, resonar

blare out *vt (announce)* pregonar

blarney ['blɑːnɪ] *n Fam* coba *f,* labia *f*

blasé [*Br* 'blɑːzeɪ, *US* blɑːˈzeɪ] *adj* hastiado(a), de vuelta de todo

blaspheme [blæsˈfiːm] *vt & vi* blasfemar **(against** contra)

blasphemer [blæsˈfiːmər] *n* blasfemador(a) *m,f,* blasfemo(a) *m,f*

blasphemous ['blæsfɪməs] *adj* blasfemo(a)

blasphemy ['blæsfɪmɪ] *n* blasfemia *f*

blast [blɑːst] **1** *n* **(a)** *(of wind)* ráfaga *f; (of sand, water, compressed air)* chorro *m* **(b)** *Mus (of horn etc)* toque *m;* **at full b.** a toda marcha; **the radio was on full b.** la radio sonaba a todo volumen; **trumpet b.** trompetazo *m* **(c)** *(explosion)* explosión *f* ❑ **b. furnace** alto horno *m* **(d)** *(shock wave)* onda *f* expansiva, onda *f* de choque **(e)** *US Fam (good time)* **it was b.** lo pasamos genial, *Esp* fue una pasada
2 *vt* **(a)** *(blow up)* volar, hacer volar; *Br Fam* **b. (it)!** ¡maldita sea! **(b)** *Fig (destroy)* acabar con, arruinar **(c)** *Fig (criticize)* criticar

blast off *vi Astronaut* despegar

blasted ['blɑːstɪd] *adj* maldito(a), condenado(a); *Slang* **to get b.** *(on drugs)* ponerse ciego(a)

blasting ['blɑːstɪŋ] *n Min* voladura *f* ❑ **b. charge** carga *f* explosiva

blast-off ['blɑːstɒf] *n Astronaut* despegue *m*

blatant ['bleɪtənt] *adj (very obvious)* evidente, patente; *(shameless)* descarado(a); **a b. lie** una mentira patente

blatantly ['bleɪtəntlɪ] *adv* descaradamente, ostensiblemente; **b. obvious** más que evidente

blather ['blæðər] *vi US Fam* desbarrar, decir *Esp* paridas *or Am* pendejadas *or RP* pavadas

blaze[1] [bleɪz] **1** *n* **(a)** *(burst of flame)* llamarada *f* **(b)** *(fierce fire)* incendio *m* **(c)** *(of sun, light)* resplandor *m* **(d)** *(outburst)* ataque *m,* arranque *m; Fig* **in a b. of anger** en un arranque de cólera **(e)** *Fam* **go to blazes!** ¡vete a la porra!; **to run like blazes** ir como una bala; **to work like blazes!** trabajar como un demonio; **what the blazes are you doing here?** ¿qué demonios haces tú aquí?
2 *vi* **(a)** *(fire)* arder; *Fig* **to b. with anger** echar chispas **(b)** *(sun, light, jewels)* resplandecer, brillar; **the sun was blazing down** el sol pegaba con fuerza

blaze[2] [bleɪz] **1** *n Zool* estrella *f,* mancha *f* blanca
2 *vt* **to b. a trail** abrir un camino

blazer ['bleɪzər] *n* chaqueta *f* sport, blazer *m*

blazing ['bleɪzɪŋ] *adj* **(a)** *(building)* en llamas **(b)** *(sun)* abrasador(a); *(light)* brillante **(c)** *(rowdy)* violento(a); **a b. row** una discusión muy violenta

blazon ['bleɪzən] *vt (decorate)* ornar; *(broadcast)* proclamar

bleach [bliːtʃ] **1** *n* lejía *f, Arg* lavandina *f, CAm Chile Méx Ven* cloro *m, Col* clorol *m, Urug* jane *f*
2 *vt* **(a)** *(whiten)* blanquear; *(fade)* descolorir; **the sun has bleached the dress** el sol ha descolorido el vestido **(b)** *(hair)* decolorar, aclarar con agua oxigenada

bleachers ['bliːtʃəz] *npl US Sport (seats)* gradas *fpl,* graderío *m*

bleak¹ [bliːk] *adj* (**a**) *(countryside)* desolado(a) (**b**) *(weather)* frío(a), desapacible (**c**) *(future)* poco prometedor(a)

bleak² [bliːk] *n (fish)* alburno *m*

bleary ['blɪərɪ] *adj* (**blearier, bleariest**) *(eyes) (due to tears)* nublado(a); *(due to tiredness)* legañoso(a)

bleary-eyed [blɪərɪ'aɪd] *adj* con los ojos nublados/legañosos

bleat [bliːt] **1** *n* balido *m*
2 *vi* (**a**) *(animal)* balar (**b**) *Fam (person)* quejarse

bled [bled] *pt & pp see* **bleed**

bleed [bliːd] **1** *vi* (*pt & pp* **bled**) *Med* sangrar; **his nose is bleeding** le sangra la nariz; **to b. to death** morir desangrado(a); *Iron* **my heart bleeds for you** ¡qué pena me das!
2 *vt Med* sangrar; *Fam* **to b. sb white** *or* **dry** sacarle a algn hasta el último céntimo

bleeder ['bliːdər] *n Br Fam* imbécil *mf*, soplagaitas *mf inv*; **you lucky b.!** ¡menuda suerte tienes, macho!

bleeding ['bliːdɪŋ] **1** *n Med (blood-letting)* sangría *f; (loss of blood)* pérdida *f* de sangre, hemorragia *f*
2 *adj* (**a**) *Med* sangrante, que sangra (**b**) *Br Fam (for emphasis)* **you b. liar!** ¡pedazo de *or* *Méx* pinche mentiroso!; **you b. idiot!** ¡maldito *or* *Méx* pinche imbécil!

bleed-valve ['bliːdvælv] *n Tech* válvula *f* de desahogo

bleep [bliːp] **1** *n* bip *m*, pitido *m*
2 *vi* hacer bip, pitar
3 *vt Fam* **to b. sb** llamar a algn al buscapersonas *or Esp* busca *or Méx* localizador *or RP* radiomensaje

bleeper ['bliːpər] *n Br Fam* buscapersonas *m inv*, *Esp* busca *m*, *Méx* localizador *m*, *RP* radiomensaje *m*

blemish ['blemɪʃ] *n* (**a**) *(defect, flaw)* defecto *m*, imperfección *f; (on fruit)* maca *f*, *Fig* mancha *f*, *Fig* **without b.** sin tacha (**b**) *(on skin)* mancha *f*

blench¹ [blentʃ] *vi (flinch)* echarse atrás; **without blenching** sin pestañear

blench² [blentʃ] *vi (turn pale)* palidecer

blend [blend] **1** *n (mixture)* mezcla *f*, combinación *f*
2 *vt (mix)* mezclar, combinar; *(match)* casar, armonizar
3 *vi (mix)* mezclarse, combinarse; *(colours)* casar, armonizar

blender ['blendər] *n Culin Esp* batidora *f*, *Am* licuadora *f*

bless [bles] *vt* (*pt & pp* **blessed** *or* **blest**) (**a**) *(say blessing for)* bendecir; *Fam* **b. my soul!** ¡caramba!; *Fam* **b. you!** *(after a sneeze)* ¡salud!, *Esp* ¡Jesús!; *Fam* **God b. you!** ¡Dios te bendiga! (**b**) *(with gift)* dotar; **blessed with good eyesight** dotado(a) de buena vista; **they were blessed with five children** Dios les bendijo con cinco hijos

blessed ['blesɪd] *adj* (**a**) *Rel* bendito(a); **b. be Thy Name** bendito sea Tu Nombre; **the B. Sacrament** el Santísimo Sacramento; **the B. Virgin** la Santa Virgen (**b**) *(happy)* bienaventurado(a), feliz (**c**) *Fam (damned)* maldito(a), dichoso(a); **I don't know a b. thing about it** no tengo ni la más remota idea; **the whole b. day** todo el santo día; **where's that b. book?** ¿dónde estará ese maldito libro?

blessing ['blesɪŋ] *n* (**a**) *Rel* bendición *f*; **to give the b.** dar la bendición; *Fig* **the government gave its b. to the project** el gobierno aprobó el proyecto (**b**) *(advantage)* ventaja *f*; **a mixed b.** una ventaja relativa; **it's a b. in disguise** no hay mal que por bien no venga; **one must count one's blessings** se debe apreciar lo que uno tiene; **the blessings of civilization** las ventajas de la civilización

blest [blest] *pt & pp see* **bless**

blew [bluː] *pt see* **blow**

blight [blaɪt] **1** *n Agr* añublo *m*; *Fig* plaga *f*
2 *vt* (**a**) *Agr* tener añublo, atizonar (**b**) *Fig (spoil)* arruinar, destrozar; *(frustrate)* frustrar

blighter ['blaɪtər] *n Br Fam Old-fashioned (fellow)* tío *m*, tipo *m*, *Esp* gachó *m*; **you lucky b.!** ¡qué suerte tienes, tío!

Blighty ['blaɪtɪ] *n Br Fam Old-fashioned* Inglaterra

blimey ['blaɪmɪ] *interj Br Fam* ¡caramba!, ¡caray!, *Méx* ¡ay güey!, *RP* ¡miércoles!

blimp [blɪmp] *n Av* dirigible *m*

blind [blaɪnd] **1** *adj* (**a**) *(medical condition)* ciego(a); **a b. man** un ciego; **a b. woman** una ciega; **b. in one eye** tuerto(a); **b. man's buff** *(game)* la gallinita ciega; **to go b.** quedarse ciego; *Fig* **b. faith** fe ciega; *Fig* **b. obedience** obediencia ciega; *Fig* **to be b. to sth** no ver algo; **he is b. to the consequences** no ve las consecuencias; *Fig* **to turn a b. eye** hacer la vista gorda; *Fam* **to be as b. as a bat** no ver tres en un burro (**b**) *(bad visibility)* ciego(a) □ **b. alley** callejón *m* sin salida; *Aut* **b. corner** curva *f* sin visibilidad; *Fam* **b. date** cita *f* a ciegas; *Sport* **b. side** lado *m* estrecho; **b. spot** ángulo *m* muerto
2 *adv* a ciegas; *Av* **to fly b.** volar sin visibilidad; *Fam* **to get b. drunk** agarrar una curda; *Cards* **to go b.** apostar a ciegas
3 *n* (**a**) *Br (on window)* persiana *f* (**b**) *pl* **the b.** los ciegos; *Fig* **it's the b. leading the b.** es como un ciego conduciendo a otro ciego
4 *vt* (**a**) *(deprive of sight)* cegar, dejar ciego; *Fig* **blinded by ambition** cegado por la ambición (**b**) *(dazzle)* deslumbrar

blinder ['blaɪndər] *n Br Fam (excellent example)* **a b. of a goal** un golazo; **a b. of a shot** un tiro increíble; **the keeper played a b.** el portero *or Am* arquero hizo un paradón

blinders ['blaɪndəz] *npl US* anteojeras *fpl*

blindfold ['blaɪndfəʊld] **1** *n* venda *f*
2 *vt* vendar los ojos a
3 *adv* con los ojos vendados

blindfolded ['blaɪndfəʊldɪd] *adj & adv* con los ojos vendados

blinding ['blaɪndɪŋ] *adj* cegador(a), deslumbrante

blindly ['blaɪndlɪ] *adv* a ciegas, ciegamente

blindness ['blaɪndnɪs] *n Med* ceguera *f*; *Fig* ceguera *f*, obcecación *f*

blink [blɪŋk] **1** *n (of eyes)* parpadeo *m*; *Fam* **to be on the b.** estar averiado(a)
2 *vi* (**a**) *(eyes)* pestañear, parpadear (**b**) *(lights)* parpadear

blinkered ['blɪŋkəd] *adj (horse)* con anteojeras; *Fig (attitude)* de miras estrechas

blinkers ['blɪŋkəz] *npl* (**a**) *(on horse)* anteojeras *fpl* (**b**) *Aut* intermitentes *mpl* (**c**) *Fam (eyes)* ojos *mpl*

blinking ['blɪŋkɪŋ] *adj Br Fam (for emphasis)* condenado(a), dichoso(a)

blip [blɪp] *n Rad* pip *m*

bliss [blɪs] *n* felicidad *f*, dicha *f*; **it was b.!** ¡fue maravilloso!, ¡fue estupendo!

blissful ['blɪsfʊl] *adj (happy)* feliz, dichoso(a); *(marvellous)* maravilloso(a)

blissfully ['blɪsfʊlɪ] *adv* **b. happy** verdaderamente feliz

blister ['blɪstər] **1** *n* (**a**) *Med (on skin)* ampolla *f* (**b**) *(on paint)* burbuja *f*
2 *vt Med* ampollar, provocar ampollas
3 *vi Med* ampollarse

blistering ['blɪstərɪŋ] *adj (sun, heat)* abrasador(a), achicharrante; *(criticism, attack)* feroz, despiadado(a)

blithe [blaɪð] *adj* alegre

blithely ['blaɪðlɪ] *adv* alegremente

blithering ['blɪðərɪŋ] *adj Fam* **he's a b. idiot** es tonto perdido

blitz [blɪts] **1** *n* bombardeo *m* aéreo; *Fig* **to have a b. on sth** atacar algo
2 *vt* bombardear

blitzkrieg ['blɪtskriːg] *n* guerra *f* relámpago

blizzard ['blɪzəd] *n* ventisca *f*

bloated ['bləʊtɪd] *adj* hinchado(a), inflado(a); *Fig* **b. with pride** henchido de orgullo

bloater ['bləʊtər] *n Culin* arenque *m* ahumado

blob [blɒb] *n (of liquid)* gota *f*; *(of colour)* mancha *f*

bloc [blɒk] *n Pol* bloque *m*; **the Eastern B. countries** los países del bloque del Este

block [blɒk] **1** *n* (**a**) *(of ice, wood, stone)* bloque *m*; *(butcher's, executioner's)* tajo *m*; **building b.** *(toy)* cubo *m* de madera; **in b. capitals** en mayúsculas ❏ **b. diagram** diagrama *m* de bloques (**b**) *(building)* edificio *m*, bloque *m*; *Br* **a b. of flats** un bloque de apartamentos *or Esp* pisos (**c**) *(group of buildings)* manzana *f*; **to run round the b.** dar la vuelta a la manzana (**d**) *(obstruction)* bloqueo *m*, obstrucción *f*; **mental b.** un bloqueo mental (**e**) *(group, series)* bloque *m*; *Theat* **a b. of seats** un grupo de asientos; *Fin* **a b. of shares** una serie de acciones ❏ **b. booking** reserva *f* de grupo; **b. vote** voto *m* por delegación (**f**) *Tech* **b. and tackle** aparejo *m* de poleas (**g**) *Fam (head)* coco *m*; **to knock sb's b. off** romperle la crisma a algn

2 *vt* (**a**) *(obstruct)* bloquear, obstruir; *Aut* **'road blocked'** 'carretera cortada'; **to b. the way** cerrar el paso; **to b. (up) a pipe** obstruir una tubería (**b**) *Sport (player)* obstaculizar; *(ball)* bloquear (**c**) *Fin Parl* bloquear (**d**) *Theat (moves, scene)* = establecer los movimientos y las posiciones de los actores en escena (**e**) *Comptr* **to b. and copy** seleccionar y copiar

block up *vt* bloquear, obstruir; *(pipe)* **to get blocked up** obstruirse

blockade [blɒˈkeɪd] *n* bloqueo *m*; **to run a b.** romper *or* burlar un bloqueo

blockage ['blɒkɪdʒ] *n* obstrucción *f*

blockbuster ['blɒkbʌstər] *n Fam* (**a**) *Mil* bomba *f* de gran potencia (**b**) *(success)* exitazo *m*; *Cin TV* gran éxito *m* de taquilla; *(book)* éxito *m* de ventas

blockhead ['blɒkhed] *n Fam* zoquete *m*, *Esp* tarugo *m*

blockhouse ['blɒkhaʊs] *n Mil* blocao *m*, fortín *m*

blocking ['blɒkɪŋ] *n Theat* puesta *f* en escena, dirección *f* escénica

blog [blɒg] *n Comptr (abbr* **weblog***)* blog *m*, bitácora *f*

blogger ['blɒgər] *n* blogger *mf*, bitacorero(a) *m,f*

bloke [bləʊk] *n Br Fam* tipo *m*, *Esp* tío *m*

blond [blɒnd] **1** *n* rubio *m*, *Méx* güero *m*, *CAm* chele *m*, *Carib* catire *m*, *Col* mono *m*

2 *adj* rubio(a), *Méx* güero(a), *CAm* chele(a), *Carib* catire(a), *Col* mono(a)

blonde [blɒnd] *adj & n* rubia *(f)*, *Méx* güera *(f)*, *CAm* chela *(f)*, *Carib* catira *(f)*, *Col* mona *(f)* ❏ *Cin* **dumb b.** rubia *f* tonta

blood [blʌd] *n* (**a**) *Biol* sangre *f*; *Fig* **in cold b.** a sangre fría; *Fig* **to make sb's b. run cold** helarle la sangre a algn; *Fig* **to sweat b.** sudar sangre; *Fam* **it makes my b. boil** me hierve la sangre; *Fam* **it's like trying to get b. from a stone** es como querer sacar agua del desierto ❏ **b. bank** banco *m* de sangre; **b. cell** glóbulo *m*; **b. clot** coágulo *m*; **b. count** recuento *m* de glóbulos sanguíneos; **b. donor** donante *mf* de sangre; **b. group** grupo *m* sanguíneo; **b. orange** naranja *f* sanguina; **b. poisoning** envenenamiento *m* de la sangre; **b. pressure** tensión *f* arterial; **high/low b. pressure** hipertensión *f*/hipotensión *f*; **to have high/low b. pressure** tener la tensión alta/baja; *US* **b. pudding** morcilla *f*; **b. sports** deportes *mpl* cruentos; **b. sugar** (nivel *m* de) azúcar *m or f* en la sangre; **b. test** análisis *m* de sangre; **b. transfusion** transfusión *f* de sangre; **b. vessel** vaso *m* sanguíneo (**b**) *(race)* sangre *f*, raza *f*; **of Scottish b.** de descendencia escocesa; *Fig* **new b.** sangre *f* nueva; *Fam* **b. is thicker than water** son muy fuertes los

lazos de parentesco ❏ **b. brother** hermano *m* carnal; **b. relation** pariente *m* consanguíneo, parienta *f* consanguínea

blood-and-thunder [blʌdənˈθʌndər] *adj Cin Theat* emocionante, melodramático(a)

bloodbath ['blʌdbɑːθ] *n Fig* baño *m* de sangre, carnicería *f*

bloodcurdling ['blʌdkɜːdlɪŋ] *adj* espeluznante, horripilante

bloodhound ['blʌdhaʊnd] *n Zool* sabueso *m*

bloodless ['blʌdlɪs] *adj* (**a**) *(anaemic)* anémico(a) (**b**) *(without bloodshed)* sin derramamiento de sangre, incruento(a)

bloodletting ['blʌdletɪŋ] *n Med* sangría *f*; *Fig* carnicería *f*

blood-red ['blʌdred] *adj* de color rojo sangre

bloodshed ['blʌdʃed] *n* derramamiento *m* de sangre

bloodshot ['blʌdʃɒt] *adj (eyes)* inyectado(a) de sangre

bloodstain ['blʌdsteɪn] *n* mancha *f* de sangre

bloodstained ['blʌdsteɪnd] *adj* manchado(a) de sangre

bloodstream ['blʌdstriːm] *n* corriente *f* sanguínea

bloodsucker ['blʌdsʌkər] *n Zool* sanguijuela *f*

bloodthirsty ['blʌdθɜːstɪ] *adj* sanguinario(a)

bloody ['blʌdɪ] **1** *adj* (**bloodier, bloodiest**) (**a**) *(battle)* sangriento(a) (**b**) *(bloodstained)* manchado(a) de sangre (**c**) *Br Austral Slang (for emphasis)* condenado(a), *Esp* puñetero(a), *Méx* pinche; **they took no b. notice of me** no me hicieron ni puñetero caso; **where's that b. book?** ¿dónde está ese condenado libro?

2 *adv Br Austral Slang* **it's b. difficult** ¡joder, qué difícil!; **not b. likely!** ¡ni de coña *or RP* en pedo!, *Méx* ¡no mames!; **not b. once** ni una puñetera vez

bloody-minded [blʌdɪˈmaɪndɪd] *adj Br Fam* terco(a), tozudo(a)

bloody-mindedness [blʌdɪˈmaɪndɪdnɪs] *n Br Fam* terquedad *f*

bloom [bluːm] **1** *n* (**a**) *(flower)* flor *f*; **in full b.** en flor, florecido(a); *Fig* **in the b. of youth** en la flor de la juventud (**b**) *(on fruit)* vello *m*, pelusa *f*

2 *vi* (**a**) *(blossom)* florecer; *Fig* prosperar, florecer (**b**) *(look radiant)* resplandecer; **blooming with health** rebosante de salud

bloomer¹ ['bluːmər] *n Br (bread)* pan *m* casero

bloomer² ['bluːmər] *n Fam* metedura *f* de pata, plancha *f*

bloomers ['bluːməz] *npl* pololos *mpl*, bombachos *mpl*

blooming ['bluːmɪŋ] *adj* (**a**) *(blossoming)* floreciente (**b**) *(glowing)* resplandeciente, radiante (**c**) *Br Fam (for emphasis)* maldito(a), condenado(a)

blooper ['bluːpər] *n US Fam* metedura *f* de pata, plancha *f*

blossom ['blɒsəm] **1** *n (flower)* flor *f*; **in b.** en flor ❏ **orange b.** flor *f* de azahar

2 *vi* florecer; *Fig* **to b. out** alcanzar la plenitud

blot [blɒt] **1** *n (of ink)* borrón *m*, mancha *f*; *Fig* mancha *f*; *Fig* **to be a b. on the landscape** afear el paisaje

2 *vt (pt & pp* **blotted***)* (**a**) *(with ink)* emborronar; *Fam* **to b. one's copybook** manchar su reputación (**b**) *(dry with blotting paper)* secar

3 *vi (ink)* correrse

blot out *vt (memories)* borrar; *(view)* ocultar

blotch [blɒtʃ] **1** *n (on skin)* mancha *f*, rojez *f*

2 *vi* enrojecer

blotchy ['blɒtʃɪ] *adj* (**blotchier, blotchiest**) *(skin, face etc)* enrojecido(a); *(paint etc)* cubierto(a) de manchas

blotter ['blɒtər] *n* (**a**) *(blotting paper)* papel *m* secante (**b**) *US (record book)* registro *m*

blotting-paper ['blɒtɪŋpeɪpər] *n* papel *m* secante

blotto ['blɒtəʊ] *adj Br Fam* **to be b.** estar *Esp RP* mamado(a) *or Col* caído(a) *or Méx* cuete

blouse [blaʊz] *n* blusa *f*

blow¹ [bləʊ] *n* **(a)** *(hit)* golpe *m*; **b. with a hammer** martillazo *m*; **b. with the fist** puñetazo *m*; **to exchange blows** pegarse; **to come to blows** llegar a las manos; *Fig* a **b. by b.** account un relato minucioso; *Fig* **to strike sb a b.** asestar un golpe a algn **(b)** *(shock)* golpe *m*; **it was a terrible b. for her** fue un golpe duro para ella

blow² [bləʊ] *(pt* **blew**; *pp* **blown)** **1** *vi* **(a)** *(wind)* soplar; **it blew out of the window** voló por la ventana; **it's blowing hard** hace mucho viento; **to b. on one's fingers** soplarse los dedos; **to b. open/shut** abrirse/cerrarse de golpe; *Fig* **to b. hot and cold** jugar con dos barajas **(b)** *(whistle)* sonar **(c)** *Elec (fuse)* fundirse **(d)** *Aut (tyre)* reventar

2 *vt* **(a)** *(kiss)* mandar, enviar **(b)** *Mus (trumpet etc)* tocar; *(horn)* tocar; *(whistle)* pitar; *Fig* **to b. one's own trumpet** echarse flores, *RP* batirse el parche; **(c)** *(glass)* soplar **(d)** *(one's nose)* sonarse **(e)** *Elec (fuse)* fundir **(f)** *Fam (waste)* despilfarrar; **to b. all one's savings on a new car** ventilarse *or RP* fumarse todos sus ahorros en un coche nuevo; *Fam* **b. the expense!** ¡no importa el gasto! **(g)** *Fam Euph (damn)* **b. you!** ¡vete a hacer puñetas!; **well, I'm blowed!** ¡caray! **(h)** *Fam (lose)* pifiar; **he blew his chances of getting the job** perdió cualquier posibilidad de conseguir el empleo **(i)** *(explode)* volar, hacer explotar; **it blew the bank sky-high** hizo volar el banco por los aires; *Fig* **to b. sb's cover** descubrir la tapadera de algn; *Fam* **to b. the gaff** descubrir el pastel; *Fam* **to b. one's top** salirse de sus casillas

blow away *vt (wind)* arrastrarse, llevarse

blow down *vt* derribar

blow in *vt* derribar

blow off 1 *vt (remove)* quitar; *Fam (in anger)* **to b. sb's head off** volarle la cabeza a algn
2 *vi (hat)* salir volando

blow out 1 *vt (extinguish)* apagar
2 *vi* **(a)** *(become extinguished)* apagarse **(b)** *Aut (tyre)* reventar

blow over 1 *vt* derribar
2 *vi* **(a)** *(storm)* calmarse **(b)** *Fig (scandal)* olvidarse

blow up 1 *vt* **(a)** *(building)* volar **(b)** *(inflate)* inflar **(c)** *Phot* ampliar
2 *vi* **(a)** *(explode)* explotar **(b)** *Fam (lose one's temper)* salirse de sus casillas

blow-by-blow [bləʊbaɪˈbləʊ] *adj (account)* detallado(a), con todo lujo de detalles

blow-dry ['bləʊdraɪ] **1** *n* secado *m*
2 *vt* secar con secador de mano

blower ['bləʊər] *n* **(a)** **glass b.** soplador(a) *m,f* de vidrio **(b)** *Br Fam (telephone)* teléfono *m*; **to get on the b. to sb** llamar a algn por teléfono

blowfly ['bləʊflaɪ] *n Ent* moscarda *f*, mosca *f* azul

blowhole ['bləʊhəʊl] *n* **(a)** *(in tunnel)* ventilador *m* **(b)** *(in ice)* respiradero *m* **(c)** *(of whale)* orificio *m* nasal

blowjob ['bləʊdʒɒb] *n Vulg* chupada *f*, *Esp* mamada *f*; **to give sb a b.** chupársela *or Esp* comérsela a algn

blowlamp ['bləʊlæmp] *n Br* soplete *m*

blown [bləʊn] *pp see* **blow**

blowout ['bləʊaʊt] *n* **(a)** *Aut* reventón *m*, *Am* ponchadura *f* **(b)** *Slang* comilona *f*, *Esp* cuchipanda *f*

blowpipe ['bləʊpaɪp] *n (weapon)* cerbatana *f*

blowsy ['bləʊzɪ] *adj* **(blowsier, blowsiest)** *Fam* deseada y gorda

blowtorch ['bləʊtɔːtʃ] *n US* soplete *m*

blow-up ['bləʊʌp] *n Phot* ampliación *f*

blowy ['bləʊɪ] *adj* **(blowier, blowiest)** ventoso(a)

blowzy ['blaʊzɪ] *adj* **(blowzier, blowziest)** *(woman)* desaseada y gorda

blub [blʌb] *vi Br Fam (pt & pp* **blubbed)** lloriquear

blubber ['blʌbər] **1** *n Zool* grasa *f* de ballena
2 *vi Fam* lloriquear, llorar a moco tendido

bludgeon ['blʌdʒən] **1** *n* maza *f*, cachiporra *f*
2 *vt* aporrear; *Fig* **to b. sb into doing sth** forzar a algn a hacer algo

blue [bluː] **1** *adj* **(a)** *(colour)* azul; **b. with cold** amoratado(a) de frío; *Fig* **once in a b. moon** de higos a brevas, *RP* cada muerte de obispo; *Fig* **you can complain till you're b. in the face** te puedes quejar hasta desgañitarte; *Fam* **to be in a b. funk** tener canguelo; *Fam* **to scream b. murder** gritar como un loco ❏ *Med* **b. baby** niño *m* azul; **b. blood** sangre *f* azul; **b. cheese** queso *m* azul; **b. jeans** vaqueros *mpl*, tejanos *mpl*; **b. whale** ballena *f* azul **(b)** *(sad)* triste, melancólico(a); *(depressed)* deprimido(a); **to feel b.** sentirse deprimido **(c)** *(obscene)* verde; **b. joke** chiste *m* verde; **b. film** película *f* pornográfica
2 *n* **(a)** *(colour)* azul *m*; *Fam* **the boys in b.** los maderos, la bofia, la policía ❏ **navy b.** azul *m* marino; **sky b.** azul *m* celeste **(b)** *(in laundering)* añil *m*, azulete *m* **(c)** *Pol* conservador(a) *m,f* **(d)** *Br Univ Sport* jugador(a) *m,f* que representa a la universidad **(e)** **the b.** *(sea)* el mar; *(sky)* el cielo; **out of the b.** *(suddenly)* de repente; *(unexpectedly)* como llovido del cielo

bluebell ['bluːbel] *n Bot* campanilla *f*

blueberry ['bluːbərɪ] *n Bot* arándano *f*

bluebird ['bluːbɜːd] *n Orn* azulejo *m*

bluebottle ['bluːbɒtəl] *n Ent* moscarda *f*, mosca *f* azul

blue-chip ['bluːtʃɪp] *adj Fin (shares, company)* de gran liquidez, puntero(a)

blue-collar ['bluːkɒlər] *adj* **b.-c. worker** obrero(a) *m,f*

blue-eyed ['bluːaɪd] *adj* de ojos azules; *Br Fam* **he's mummy's b.-e. boy** es el niño mimado de mamá

blueprint ['bluːprɪnt] *n Archit* cianotipo *m*; *Fig* anteproyecto *m*

blues [bluːz] *n* **(a)** *Mus* **the b.** el blues **(b)** *Fam (sadness)* tristeza *f*, melancolía *f*; **to have the b.** sentirse deprimido

blue-sky ['bluːskaɪ] *adj US* **(a)** *(research)* puramente teórico(a) *or* especulativo(a) **(b)** *(stocks, shares)* fraudulento(a)

bluestocking ['bluːstɒkɪŋ] *n* sabionda *f*, marisabidilla *f*

bluetit ['bluːtɪt] *n Orn* herrerillo *m* común

bluff [blʌf] **1** *n* **(a)** *(trick)* bluff *m*, farol *m*, fanfarronada *f*; **to call sb's b.** hacer que algn ponga sus cartas encima de la mesa **(b)** *Geog (cliff)* acantilado *m*
2 *adj* **(a)** *(down-to-earth)* campechano(a); *(abrupt)* brusco(a); *(forthright)* francote(a) **(b)** *Geog (cliff)* escarpado(a)
3 *vi* tirarse un farol, fanfarronear; **to b. one's way through sth** hacer colar algo

bluffer ['blʌfər] *n* farolero(a) *m,f*, fanfarrón(ona) *m,f*

bluish ['bluːɪʃ] *adj* azulado(a)

blunder ['blʌndər] **1** *n* metedura *f or Am* metida *f* de pata; *Fam* plancha *f*
2 *vi* meter la pata *or* una plancha, cometer un planchazo; **to b. into sth** tropezar con algo

blunderbuss ['blʌndəbʌs] *n* trabuco *m*

blunderer ['blʌndərər] *n* torpe *mf*, metepatas *mf inv*

blunt [blʌnt] **1** *adj* **(a)** *(knife)* embotado(a), desafilado(a); *(pencil)* despuntado(a), romo(a); **b. instrument** instrumento contundente **(b)** *(direct, frank)* directo(a),

francote(a); *(statement, answer)* tajante, terminante, categórico(a)
2 *vt* **(a)** *(blade, pencil, scissors)* desafilar **(b)** *Fig (emotions, feelings)* embotar

bluntly ['blʌntlɪ] *adv* francamente, sin rodeos

bluntness ['blʌntnɪs] *n Fig* franqueza *f*

blur [blɜːr] **1** *n* aspecto *m* borroso; **everything was just a b.** veía todo borroso
2 *vt (pt & pp* **blurred***)* (windows)* empañar; *(shape)* desdibujar; *(vision, memory)* enturbiar; **his memory was blurred** no se acordaba de nada

blurb [blɜːb] *n (bumph)* propaganda *f*; *(on book)* resumen *m*, reseña *f*

blurred [blɜːd] *adj Phot TV* borroso(a)

blurt [blɜːt] *vt* **to b. out** dejar escapar, soltar

blush [blʌʃ] **1** *n* rubor *m*, sonrojo *m*
2 *vi* ruborizarse, ponerse colorado(a)

blusher ['blʌʃər] *n* colorete *m*

blushing ['blʌʃɪŋ] *adj* ruborizado(a)

bluster ['blʌstər] **1** *n Fig* fanfarronadas *fpl*, bravatas *fpl*
2 *vi* **(a)** *(sea, wind)* bramar **(b)** *Fig (person)* fanfarronear, echar bravatas

blustery ['blʌstərɪ] *adj* borrascoso(a); **a b. day** un día ventoso

BO [biː'əʊ] *n Fam (abbr* **body odour)** sobaquina *f*, olor *m* a sudor

boa ['bəʊə] *n* **(a)** *Zool (snake)* boa *f* ❑ **b. constrictor** boa *f* constrictor **(b)** *(of fur, feathers)* boa *m*

boar [bɔːr] *n Zool* verraco *m* ❑ **wild b.** jabalí *m*

board [bɔːd] **1** *n* **(a)** *(plank)* tabla *f*; *Theat* **to tread the boards** pisar las tablas **(b)** *(work surface)* tabla *f*, mesa *f*; *(blackboard)* pizarra *f*, encerado *m*; *(for games)* tablero *m* ❑ **chess b.** tablero *m* de ajedrez; **drawing b.** tablero *m* de dibujo; **it's back to the drawing b.!** ¡volvamos a empezar!; **ironing b.** tabla *f* de planchar; **notice b.**, *US* **bulletin b.** tablón *m* de anuncios **(c)** *Print* **in boards** en cartoné **(d)** *(meals)* pensión *f*; **full b.** pensión completa; **b. and lodging** *or US* **room** alojamiento *m* y comida **(e)** *(committee, council)* junta *f*, consejo *m*; **b. of directors** junta directiva, consejo de administración; *Br* **B. of Trade** = departamento ministerial responsable de la supervisión del comercio y de la promoción de las exportaciones; *US* **b. of trade** cámara *f* de comercio ❑ **b. meeting** reunión *f* del consejo, junta *f*; **b. room** sala *f* del consejo **(f)** *Naut* **on b.** a bordo; **to go on b.** subir a bordo **(g)** *Comptr* placa *f* **(h)** *Fig* **above b.** en regla; **is it all above b.?** ¿es legal?; **across-the-b.** general; **an across-the-b. pay increase** un aumento lineal del sueldo; **to let sth go by the b.** abandonar algo
2 *vt* **(a)** *(lodge)* alojar **(b)** *(ship, plane etc)* embarcar, embarcarse en, subir
3 *vi* **(a)** *(lodge)* alojarse; **he boarded with my sister** se alojó en casa de mi hermana **(b)** *(at school)* estar interno(a)

board up *vt* tapar

boarder ['bɔːdər] *n* **(a)** *(in boarding house)* huésped *mf* **(b)** *(at school)* interno(a) *m,f*, pensionista *mf*

boardgame ['bɔːdgeɪm] *n* juego *m* de mesa

boarding ['bɔːdɪŋ] **(a)** *(floor)* entablado *m* **(b)** *(embarkation)* embarque *m* ❑ **b. card, b. pass** tarjeta *f* de embarque **(c)** *(lodging)* alojamiento *m*, pensión *f* ❑ **b. house** casa *f* de huéspedes, pensión *f*; **b. school** internado *m*

boardroom ['bɔːdruːm] *n* sala *f* de juntas

boardsailing ['bɔːdseɪlɪŋ] *n US* windsurf *m*, windsurfing *m*

boardwalk ['bɔːdwɔːk] *n US* paseo *m* marítimo entarimado

boast [bəʊst] **1** *n* jactancia *f*, alarde *m*

2 *vi* jactarse, alardear **(about** de)
3 *vt* presumir de, alardear de; **the town boasts an Olympic swimming pool** la ciudad disfruta de una piscina olímpica

boaster ['bəʊstər] *n* jactancioso(a) *m,f*

boastful ['bəʊstfʊl] *adj* jactancioso(a)

boasting ['bəʊstɪŋ] *n* jactancia *f*

boat [bəʊt] *n* **(a)** *Naut* barco *m*; *(small)* barca *f*, bote *m*; *(launch)* lancha *f*; *(large)* buque *m*; **to go by b.** ir en barco; *Fig* **to burn one's boats** quemar las naves; *Fig* **to miss the b.** perder el tren; *Fig* **we're all in the same b.** todos estamos en el mismo barco ❑ **fishing b.** barco *m* de pesca; **rowing b.** bote *m* de remos; **sailing b.** barco *m* de vela, velero *m* **(b)** *Culin* **gravy b.** salsera *f*

boatbuilder ['bəʊtbɪldər] *n* constructor(a) *m,f* de barcos

boater ['bəʊtər] *n* canotié *m*, canotier *m*

boathouse ['bəʊthaʊs] *n* cobertizo *m* (para barcas)

boating ['bəʊtɪŋ] *n* paseo *m* en barco; **to go boating** dar un paseo en barco ❑ **b. club** club *m* náutico

boatload ['bəʊtləʊd] *n* barcada *f*; *Fam* montón *m*

boatman ['bəʊtmən] *n (pl* **boatmen)** barquero *m*

boatswain ['bəʊsən] *n* contramaestre *m*

boatwoman ['bəʊtwʊmən] *n (pl* **boatwomen** ['bəʊtwɪmɪn]**)** barquera *f*

boatyard ['bəʊtjɑːd] *n* astillero *m*

Bob [bɒb] *n Br Fam* **you just add a little water, and B.'s your uncle!** ¡le añades un poco de agua y listo!

bob [bɒb] **1** *n* **(a)** *(haircut)* pelo *m* a lo chico **(b)** *Br Fam inv (shilling)* chelín *m*; **five b.** cinco chelines **(c)** *(curtsey)* reverencia *f* **(d)** *Sport* trineo *m*
2 *vi (pt & pp* **bobbed)** **to b. up and down** balancearse, subir y bajar
3 *vt (hair)* cortar; **she's had her hair bobbed** le han cortado el pelo a lo chico

bobbin ['bɒbɪn] *n (of spinning machine)* bobina *f*; *(of sewing machine)* canilla *f*; *(for lace-making)* bolillo *m*

bobble ['bɒbəl] *n (on hat)* borla *f*

bobby ['bɒbɪ] *n (Br Fam (policeman)* poli *m* **(b)** *US* **b. pin** pasador *m* **(c)** *US* **b. socks, b. sox** calcetines *mpl*

bobby-soxer ['bɒbɪsɒksər] *n US* adolescente *f*, quinceañera *f*

bobsled ['bɒbsled] *n*, **bobsleigh** ['bɒbsleɪ] *n Sport* bobsleigh *m*, trineo *m*

bobtail ['bɒbteɪl] *adj* **(a)** *(tail)* cortada **(b)** *(horse)* rabicorto(a)

bod [bɒd] *n Br Fam (person)* tipo *m,f*, *Esp* tío(a) *m,f*

bode¹ [bəʊd] *pt see* **bide**

bode² [bəʊd] **1** *vt* presagiar
2 *vi* **to b. well/ill** ser de buen/mal agüero

bodice ['bɒdɪs] *n* **(a)** *(sleeveless undergarment)* corpiño *m* **(b)** *(of dress)* cuerpo *m*

bodily ['bɒdɪlɪ] **1** *adj* **(a)** físico(a); **b. harm** daños *mpl* corporales; **b. needs** necesidades *fpl* físicas
2 *adv* **to carry sb b.** llevar a algn en brazos

body ['bɒdɪ] *n* **(a)** *Anat* cuerpo *m*; *Fig* **to earn enough to keep b. and soul together** ganar lo justo para vivir ❑ **b. clock** reloj *m* biológico; **b. fascism** dictadura *f* del cuerpo; **b. language** expresión *f* corporal; **b. odour** olor *m* corporal; **b. piercing** perforaciones *fpl* en el cuerpo, piercing *m* **(b)** *(corpse)* cadáver *m*; *Fam* **over my dead b.!** ¡tendrás *etc* que pasar por encima de mi cadáver! ❑ **b. bag** bolsa *f* para cadáveres; *Mil* **b. count** *(of casualties)* número *m* de bajas; **b. snatcher** ladrón *m* de cadáveres **(c)** *Chem Phys* cuerpo *m* ❑ *Astron* **heavenly b.** cuerpo *m* celeste **(d)** *(main part)* parte *f* principal, parte *f* central **(e)** *Aut* carrocería *f*; *Av* fuselaje *m*; *Naut* casco *m* (**f**) *(organization)* organismo *m*; *(profession)* cuerpo *m*; **legislative b.** cuerpo *m* or órgano *m* legislativo; **the b. politic** el estado (**g**) *(group of people)* conjunto *m*, grupo *m*; **a large b. of students** un gran número de estudiantes (**h**) *(of wine)* cuerpo *m*

body-blow ['bɒdıbləʊ] *n Fig* golpe *m* duro

body-builder ['bɒdıbıldər] *n* culturista *mf*

body-building ['bɒdıbıldıŋ] *n* culturismo *m*

bodyguard ['bɒdıgɑːd] *n* guardaespaldas *mf inv*

bodystocking ['bɒdıstɒkıŋ] *n* body *m*

bodywork ['bɒdıwɜːk] *n Aut* carrocería *f*

Boer ['bəʊər] *adj & n* bóer *(mf)*; **the B. War** la guerra del Transvaal

boffin ['bɒfın] *n Br Fam Hum* sabio *m*, lumbrera *f*

bog [bɒg] *n* (**a**) *(marsh)* ciénaga *f*, pantano *m*; (**peat**) **b.** turbera *f* (**b**) *Br Slang (lavatory)* baño *m*, *Esp* tigre *m*, meódromo *m*

bog down *vt Fig* atascar; **to get bogged down** atascarse

bogey ['bəʊgı] *n* (**a**) *(spectre)* espectro *m*, fantasma *m* (**b**) *(bugbear)* pesadilla *f* (**c**) *Golf* bogey *m* (**d**) *Br Slang (mucus)* moco *m*

bogeyman ['bəʊgımæn] *n (pl* **bogeymen)** *Fam* **the b.** el hombre del saco, el coco

boggle ['bɒgəl] *vi* sobresaltarse; *Fam* **the mind boggles** ¡es alucinante!

boggy ['bɒgı] *adj* (**boggier, boggiest**) pantanoso(a)

bogie ['bəʊgı] *n Rail* carretón *m*, bogie *m*

Bogota [bɒgə'tɑː] *n* Bogotá

bogus ['bəʊgəs] *adj* falso(a); **b. company** compañía *f* fantasma; **b. policemen** policía *f* ful

bogy ['bəʊgı] *n see* **bogey**

Bohemia [bəʊ'hiːmıə] *n* Bohemia

Bohemian [bəʊ'hiːmıən] *adj & n* bohemio(a) *(m,f)*, bohemio(a) *(m,f)*

boil¹ [bɔıl] **1** *n Culin* **to be on the b.** hervir, estar hirviendo; **to come to the b.** empezar a hervir
2 *vt Culin (water)* hervir; *(food)* hervir, cocer; *(egg)* cocer, pasar por agua
3 *vi Culin* hervir, cocer; *Fig* **to b. with rage** estar furioso(a)

boil down *vi* reducirse (**to** a); *Fig* **it boils down to money** en el fondo es una cuestión de dinero; *Fig* **it all boils down to this** todo se reduce a esto

boil over *vi (milk)* salirse

boil² [bɔıl] *n Med* furúnculo *m*

boiled [bɔıld] *adj* hervido(a); **b. egg** huevo *m* pasado por agua

boiler ['bɔılər] *n* caldera *f*; **b. room** sala *f* de calderas ❏ *Br* **b. suit** mono *m* (de trabajo), *Am* overol *m*, *CSur Cuba* mameluco *m*

boilermaker ['bɔıləmeıkər] *n* calderero(a) *m,f*

boiling ['bɔılıŋ] *adj (water)* hirviente; **it's b. hot** *(food)* quema, está quemando; *(weather)* hace un calor agobiante ❏ **b. point** punto *m* de ebullición

boisterous ['bɔıstərəs] *adj* (**a**) *(person, party)* alborotador(a), bullicioso(a) (**b**) *(weather)* borrascoso(a), tempestuoso(a)

bold [bəʊld] *adj* (**a**) *(brave)* valiente, intrépido(a) (**b**) *(daring)* audaz, atrevido(a) (**c**) *(marked)* marcado(a), pronunciado(a); **b. features** rasgos marcados ❏ *Typ* **b. type** negrita *f* (**d**) *(impudent)* descarado(a); **to be as b. as brass** ser un(a) caradura, *Esp* tener más cara que espalda

bold-faced [bəʊld'feıst] *adj* descarado(a)

boldly ['bəʊldlı] *adv (bravely)* audazmente, con audacia

boldness ['bəʊldnıs] *n* (**a**) *(courage)* valor *m* (**b**) *(daring)* audacia *f*, osadía *f* (**c**) *(impudence)* descaro *m*

bolero¹ [bə'leərəʊ] *n Mus* bolero *m*

bolero² ['bɒlərəʊ] *n (jacket)* chaleco *m*

Bolivia [bə'lıvıə] *n* Bolivia

Bolivian [bə'lıvıən] *adj & n* boliviano(a) *(m,f)*

bollard ['bɒlɑːd] *n* (**a**) *Naut* bolardo *m*, noray *m* (**b**) *Br (traffic barrier)* bolardo *m*

bollocking ['bɒləkıŋ] *n Br Vulg* bronca *f*

bollocks ['bɒləks] *npl Br Vulg* cojones *mpl*, huevos *mpl*; **b.!** *(anger)* ¡cojones!; *(disagreement)* ¡y un huevo!, ¡y una mierda!

boloney [bə'ləʊnı] *n Fam* disparates *mpl*, tonterías *fpl*

Bolshevik ['bɒlʃəvık] *adj & n* bolchevique *(mf)*

Bolshevism ['bɒlʃıvızəm] *n* bolchevismo *m*, bolchevinismo *m*

Bolshevist ['bɒlʃəvıst] *adj & n* bolchevique *(mf)*

bolshie ['bɒlʃı] *adj Br Fam* (**a**) *Pol* rojo(a) (**b**) *(rebellious)* rebelde

bolster ['bəʊlstər] **1** *n (pillow)* cabezal *m*, travesaño *m*
2 *vt (strengthen)* reforzar; *(support)* sostener, apoyar

bolt [bəʊlt] **1** *n* (**a**) *(on door, window) (large)* cerrojo *m*; *(small)* pestillo *m* (**b**) *Tech* perno *m*, tornillo *m* (**c**) *(of lightning)* rayo *m* (**d**) *(for crossbow)* flecha *f*; *Fig* **a b. from the blue** un acontecimiento inesperado (**e**) *(dash)* huida *f*, fuga *f*; **to make a b. for it** huir, escaparse
2 *vt* (**a**) *(lock)* cerrar con cerrojo or pestillo, echar el cerrojo (**b**) *Tech* sujetar con pernos or tornillos (**c**) *Fam (food)* engullir
3 *vi (person)* largarse, escaparse; *(horse)* desbocarse
4 *adv* **b. upright** derecho; **to sit b. upright in bed** sentarse muy derecho en la cama

bomb [bɒm] **1** *n* bomba *f*; **to burst like a b.** caer como una bomba; **to plant a b.** poner una bomba; *Br Fam* **to go like a b.** *(vehicle etc)* andar como un rayo; *(party etc)* ser todo un éxito; *Br Slang* **to cost a b.** costar un ojo de la cara ❏ **atomic b.** bomba *f* atómica; **b. disposal squad** brigada *f* de artificieros; **car b.** coche-bomba *m*; **hydrogen b.** bomba *f* de hidrógeno; **letter b.** carta-bomba *f*; **b. scare** amenaza *f* de bomba; **b. shelter** refugio *m* antiaéreo; **b. site** sitio *m* bombardeado; **smoke b.** bomba *f* de humo; **stink b.** bomba *f* fétida
2 *vt (city etc)* bombardear; *(terrorists)* volar, colocar una bomba en
3 *vi US Fam (fail)* fracasar (estrepitosamente)

bomb along *vi Br Fam (go quickly)* ir a toda máquina or *Esp* pastilla

bombard [bɒm'bɑːd] *vt* (**a**) *(bomb)* bombardear (**b**) *Fig (attack)* bombardear; **she was bombarded with questions** la bombardearon a preguntas

bombardment [bɒm'bɑːdmənt] *n* bombardeo *m*

bombast ['bɒmbæst] *n* rimbombancia *f*, ampulosidad *f*

bombastic [bɒm'bæstık] *adj (language)* rimbombante, altisonante, pomposo(a)

bomber ['bɒmər] *n* (**a**) *Av* bombardero *m* ❏ **b. jacket** cazadora *f* or *CSur* campera *f* or *Méx* chamarra *f* de aviador (**b**) *(person)* terrorista *mf (que coloca bombas)*

bombing ['bɒmıŋ] *n* bombardeo *m*

bomb-proof ['bɒmpruːf] *adj* a prueba de bombas

bombshell ['bɒmʃel] *n* (**a**) *Mil* obús *m* (**b**) *Fig (surprise)* bomba *f*; **to fall like a b.** caer como una bomba (**c**) *Fam (attractive woman)* mujer *f* explosiva; **a blonde b.** una rubia explosiva

bombsight ['bɒmsaıt] *n* visor *m* de bombardeo

bona fide [bəʊnə'faɪdɪ] *adj* (*a*) *(genuine)* auténtico(a); **a b. f. document** un documento auténtico (**b**) *(in good faith)* de buena fe; **a b. f. offer** una oferta seria

bonanza [bə'nænzə] *n* (*a*) *(luck)* bonanza *f* (**b**) *Fig* mina *f* de oro

bonbon ['bɒnbɒn] *n* *(sweet)* caramelo *m*

bonce [bɒns] *n* *Br Slang (head)* coco *m*, mollera *f*, *Esp* tarro *m*

bond [bɒnd] **1** *n* (*a*) *(link, tie)* lazo *m*, vínculo *m*; **the bonds of friendship** los lazos de la amistad (**b**) *Fin* bono *m*, obligación *f*; **Treasury bonds** bonos *mpl* del Tesoro; **b. issue** emisión *f* de bonos (**c**) *Jur (bail)* fianza *f* (**d**) *(binding agreement)* acuerdo *m*, contrato *m* (**e**) *Com (warehouse)* depósito *m*; **to be in b.** estar en depósito (**f**) *US (guarantee)* garantía *f* (**g**) *Constr (of bricks)* aparejo *m* (**h**) **bonds** *(shackles)* cadenas *fpl*; **to be in b.** estar en cautiverio **2** *vt* (*a*) *(join, unite)* ligar (**b**) *Com (merchandise)* poner en depósito (**c**) *(guarantee) (employee etc)* garantizar (**d**) *Constr (bricks)* aparejar

bondage ['bɒndɪdʒ] *n* *(slavery)* esclavitud *f*, *(servitude)* servilismo *m*

bonded ['bɒndɪd] *adj* (*a*) *Fin (debt)* garantizado(a) (**b**) *Com (goods)* depositado(a), en depósito ❑ **b. warehouse** almacén *m* de depósito

bondholder ['bɒndhəʊldər] *n* *Fin* obligacionista *mf*

bonding ['bɒndɪŋ] *n* (lazos *mpl* de) unión *f*; *Hum* **they're doing a bit of male b.** están haciendo cosas de hombres

bone [bəʊn] **1** *n* (*a*) *Anat (of person, animal)* hueso *m*; *(in corset)* ballena *f*, *(in fish)* espina *f*; *Fig* **b. of contention** manzana *f* de la discordia; *Fig* **to feel sth in one's bones** tener un presentimiento de algo; *Fig* **to have a b. to pick with sb** tener que ajustar cuentas a algn; *Fig* **to make no bones about sth** no andarse con rodeos en un asunto; *Fam* **funny b.** hueso de la alegría ❑ **b. china** porcelana *f* fina; **b. meal** harina *f* de huesos (**b**) **bones** *(remains)* huesos *mpl*, restos *mpl*; **the bare b.** *(essentials)* el meollo *sing*, lo esencial **2** *vt* *Culin (meat, chicken)* deshuesar; *(fish)* quitar las espinas a

bone up *vi* *Fam* empollar; **to b. up on a subject** empollar una asignatura

bone-dry [bəʊn'draɪ] *adj* completamente seco(a)

bonehead ['bəʊnhed] *n* *US Slang* majadero(a) *m,f*, imbécil *mf*, *Esp* berzotas *mf inv*

bone-idle [bəʊn'aɪdl] *adj* muy vago(a), gandul(ula)

boner ['bəʊnər] *n* *Slang* metedura *f* de pata, plancha *f*, planchazo *m*, patinazo *m*

bonesetter ['bəʊnsetər] *n* ensalmador(a) *m,f*, curandero(a) *m,f*

boneshaker ['bəʊnʃeɪkər] *n* *Slang (car)* cacharro *m*, cafetera *f*

bonfire ['bɒnfaɪər] *n* hoguera *f*, fogata *f*; *Br* **B. Night** = fiesta del 5 de noviembre en que de noche se hacen hogueras y hay fuegos artificiales

bongo ['bɒŋgəʊ] *n* (*pl* **bongos** *or* **bongoes**) *Mus* **b. (drum)** bongó *m*, bongo *m*

bonhomie ['bɒnɒmiː] *n* afabilidad *f*

bonk [bɒŋk] *vt* *Fam (hit)* pegar

bonkers ['bɒŋkəz] *adj* *Br Slang* chalado(a); **to drive sb b.** volver tarumba a algn

Bonn [bɒn] *n* Bonn

bonnet ['bɒnɪt] *n* (*a*) *(child's)* gorra *f*, gorro *m*; *Hist (woman's)* toca *f* (**b**) *Br Aut* capó *m*, *CAm Méx* cofre *m*

bonny ['bɒnɪ] *adj* (**bonnier, bonniest**) *Scot (gen)* precioso(a); *(person)* majo(a), mono(a)

bonsai ['bɒnsaɪ] *n* bonsai *m*

bonus ['bəʊnəs] *n* (*a*) *(on wages, salary)* prima *f*; **b. scheme** sistema *m* de primas; **Christmas b.** prima de Navidad; **cost-of-living b.** plus *m* de carestía de vida (**b**) *Fin (on shares)* dividendo *m* extraordinario (**c**) *Br Ins (on policy)* beneficio *m*

bony ['bəʊnɪ] *adj* (**bonier, boniest**) *(person)* huesudo(a); *(fish)* lleno(a) de espinas

boo [buː] **1** *interj* ¡bu!; **not to say b.** no decir ni pío; **she wouldn't say b. to a goose** es muy tímido, *Esp* es un cortado **2** *n* abucheo *m*, pateo *m* **3** *vt* abuchear, patear

boob [buːb] *Slang* **1** *n* (*a*) *Br (silly mistake)* plancha *f*, planchazo *m*, metedura *f or Am* metida *f* de pata (**b**) *Br* **boobs** *(breasts)* tetas *fpl* (**c**) *US (person)* lelo(a) *m,f*, bobalicón(ona) *m,f*; **b. tube** *(television)* caja *f* tonta **2** *vi* *Br* tirarse una plancha, meter la pata

booby ['buːbɪ] *n* *(fool)* bobo(a) *m,f*, *Esp* memo(a) *m,f* ❑ **b. prize** premio *m* de consolación; **b. trap** trampa *f*; *Mil* trampa *f* explosiva

booby-trap ['buːbɪtræp] *vt* (*pt & pp* **booby-trapped**) *Mil* poner una trampa explosiva en; **booby-trapped car** coche *m* cebo

boogie ['buːgɪ] *vi* *Fam* bailar

boogie-woogie [buːgɪ'wuːgɪ] *n* *Mus* bugui-bugui *m*

boohoo [buː'huː] **1** *vi* (*pt & pp* **boohooed**) berrear **2** *interj* ¡buaaah!

book [bʊk] **1** *n* (*a*) *(printed volume)* libro *m*; **a b. on do-it-yourself** un libro sobre bricolaje; **economics is a closed b. to me** no sé nada de economía; **in my b.** según mi punto de vista; *Fig* **by the b.** según las reglas; *Fig* **to be in sb's bad books** estar en la lista negra de algn, estar a malas con algn, *RP* estar en malos términos con algn; *Fig* **to be in sb's good books** estar a buenas con algn, *RP* estar en buenos términos con algn; *Fig* **to take a leaf out of sb's b.** tomar ejemplo de algn ❑ **address b.** agenda *f*, libro *m* de direcciones; **b. club** círculo *m* de lectores; **b. end** sujetalibros *m inv*; **b. review** reseña *f* de libros; *Br* **b. token** vale *m* para comprar libros; **b. trade** sector *m* editorial; **complaints b.** libro *m* de reclamaciones; **exercise b.** cuaderno *m*; **reference b.** libro *m* de consulta; **savings b.** libreta *f* de ahorros; **telephone b.** guía *f* telefónica, listín *m* (telefónico) (**b**) *(of stamps)* carpeta *f*; *(of tickets)* taco *m*; *(of matches)* cajetilla *f* (**c**) *Com* **books** libros *mpl*, cuentas *fpl*; **to keep the b.** llevar las cuentas **2** *vt* (*a*) *(reserve) (room, passage)* reservar; **the hotel is fully booked** el hotel está completo (**b**) *(engage) (performer etc)* contratar (**c**) *(police)* poner una multa a; **he was booked for speeding** lo multaron por exceso de velocidad (**d**) *Br (soccer player)* amonestar (**e**) *US* **to b. it** *(leave)* largarse, *Esp* darse el piro

book into *vt (hotel)* reservar una habitación en

book out *vi (from hotel)* marcharse

book up *vt* reservar; *Av* **the flight is booked up** el vuelo está completo

bookable ['bʊkəbəl] *adj* que se puede(n) reservar; *Theat* **'seats b. in advance'** 'las localidades se pueden reservar con antelación'

bookbinder ['bʊkbaɪndər] *n* encuadernador(a) *m,f*

bookbinding ['bʊkbaɪndɪŋ] *n* encuadernación *f*

bookcase ['bʊkkeɪs] *n* librería *f*, estantería *f*

bookie ['bʊkɪ] *n* *Fam see* **bookmaker**

booking ['bʊkɪŋ] *n* (*a*) *esp Br (reservation)* reserva *f* ❑ *Theat Rail* **b. office** taquilla *f*, *Am* boletería *f* (**b**) *Theat (hiring) (of performer etc)* contratación *f*

bookish ['bʊkɪʃ] *adj* (a) *(fond of reading)* aficionado(a) a la lectura (b) *(academic) (view etc)* académico(a) (c) *(style)* libresco(a)

bookkeeping ['bʊkki:pɪŋ] *n* Fin contabilidad *f*

booklet ['bʊklɪt] *n* folleto *m*

bookmaker ['bʊkmeɪkər] *n* corredor(a) *m,f* de apuestas

bookmark ['bʊkmɑːk] **1** *n* (a) *(for book)* marcapáginas *m* (b) *Comptr* marcador *m*
   2 *vt Comptr (Web page)* añadir a la lista de marcadores

bookmobile ['bʊkməbiːl] *n US* bibliobús *m*, biblioteca *f* ambulante

bookplate ['bʊkpleɪt] *n* ex libris *m inv*

bookrest ['bʊkrest] *n* atril *m*

bookseller ['bʊkselər] *n* librero(a) *m,f*

bookshelf ['bʊkʃelf] *n* (*pl* **bookshelves** ['bʊkʃelvz]) estante *m*; **bookshelves** estantería *f sing*

bookshop ['bʊkʃɒp] *n* librería *f*

bookstall ['bʊkstɔːl] *n* *n (in street)* puesto *m* de libros; *Br (in railway station)* quiosco *m* de prensa

bookstand ['bʊkstænd] *n (for supporting book)* atril *m* (de pie); *(in railway station)* quiosco *m* de prensa

bookstore ['bʊkstɔːr] *n US* librería *f*

bookworm ['bʊkwɜːm] *n Fam* ratón *m* de biblioteca

boom¹ [buːm] **1** *n* (a) *(noise)* estampido *m*, trueno *m* (b) *(sudden prosperity)* boom *m*, auge *m* ❑ **b. town** ciudad *f* en pleno desarrollo
   2 *vi* (a) *(thunder)* retumbar, tronar; *(cannon)* tronar (b) *(prosper)* estar en auge

boom² [buːm] *n* (a) *Naut (mast)* botalón *m* (b) *Cin Rad (of microphone)* jirafa *f* ❑ **b. operator** jirafista *mf* (c) *(barrier across harbour)* barrera *f*

boomerang ['buːməræŋ] *n* bumerán *m*

booming ['buːmɪŋ] *adj* (a) *(resonant) (cannon)* que truena; *(voice, thunder)* que retumba (b) *(prosperous) (industry etc)* en auge

boon [buːn] *n (blessing)* bendición *f*; **the new computer is a real b.** el nuevo ordenador es una verdadera bendición

boor [bʊər] *n* patán *m*, paleto(a) *m,f*, palurdo(a) *m,f*

boorish ['bʊərɪʃ] *adj* tosco(a), paleto(a)

boost [buːst] **1** *n* (a) *(push)* empujón *m* (b) *Fig (encouragement)* estímulo *m*, empujón *m*
   2 *vt* (a) *(increase) (sales)* aumentar, incrementar (b) *(improve) (morale)* levantar; **to b. sb's confidence** subirle la moral a algn (c) *(promote) (product)* promover; *(business)* fomentar (d) *Elec (voltage)* elevar (e) *US Fam (steal)* afanar, *Esp* sisar

booster ['buːstər] *n* (a) *Elec* elevador *m* de voltaje (b) *Astronaut* **b. rocket** cohete *m* acelerador (c) *Rad TV (amplifier)* amplificador *m* (d) *Med* **b. (shot)** revacunación *f*

boot¹ [buːt] **1** *n* (a) *(footwear)* bota *f*; *(short)* botín *m*; *Fig* **he's too big for his boots** es muy creído; *Fig* **the b. is on the other foot** se ha dado la vuelta a la tortilla; *Fig* **to die with one's boots on** morir con las botas puestas; *Fig* **to lick sb's boots** hacer la pelota a algn; *Br Fam* **to put the b. in** pisotear; *Fam* **she got the b.** la echaron (del trabajo) ❑ *US Mil* **b. camp** campamento *m* de reclutas; **b. polish** betún *m* (b) *Br Aut* maletero *m*, *CAm Méx* cajuela *f*, *RP* baúl *m*
   2 *vt Fam* (a) *Ftb (kick) (ball)* chutar (b) **to b. (out)** *(expel)* echar a patadas; *(dismiss from employment)* dar la patada a, echar, despedir (c) *Comptr* arrancar
   3 *vi Comptr* **to b. (up)** arrancar

boot² [buːt] *n* **to b.** además; **he's handsome, and rich to b.** es guapo, y además, rico

bootblack ['buːtblæk] *n esp US* limpiabotas *mf inv*, *Am* lustrabotas *mf inv*

bootee ['buːtiː, buː'tiː] *n* (a) *(baby's)* peúco *m*, botita *f* de lana (b) *(woman's)* botín *m*

booth [buːð, buːθ] *n* (a) *(in language lab etc)* cabina *f* ❑ **telephone b.** cabina *f* telefónica (b) *(in market, fair)* puesto *m*

bootlace ['buːtleɪs] *n* cordón *m*

bootleg ['buːtleg] *adj (liquor etc)* de contrabando

bootlegger ['buːtlegər] *n* contrabandista *m*

bootlicker ['buːtlɪkər] *n Fam* lameculos *mf inv*, *Esp* pelota *mf*, *Méx* arrastrado(a) *m,f*, *RP* chupamedias *mf inv*

bootstrap ['buːtstræp] *n* (a) trabilla *f*, tirante *m*; *Fig* **he pulled himself up by his bootstraps** logró salir adelante por su propio esfuerzo (b) *Comptr* arranque *m*; **b. routine** secuencia *f* de arranque

booty ['buːtɪ] *n* botín *m*

booze [buːz] *Fam* **1** *n* bebida *f*, *Esp* priva *f*, *RP* chupi *m*; **to go on the b.** irse de juerga *or* de borrachera
   2 *vi* empinar el codo, *RP* chupar

boozer ['buːzər] *n Fam* (a) *(person)* borracho(a) *m,f*, *Am* tomador(a) *m,f* (b) *Br (pub)* tasca *f*, *Esp* bareto *m*

booze-up ['buːzʌp] *n Br Fam* borrachera *f*

boozy ['buːzɪ] *adj Fam (voice, breath)* de borracho(a)

bop¹ [bɒp] **1** *n* (a) *Mus* be-bop *m* (b) *Br Fam (dance)* baile *m*
   2 *vi* (*pt & pp* **bopped**) *Br Fam (dance)* bailar, menear el esqueleto

bop² [bɒp] *vt* (*pt & pp* **bopped**) *Fam (hit)* golpear

boracic [bə'ræsɪk] *adj Chem* bórico(a)

borage ['bɒrɪdʒ] *n Bot* borraja *f*

borax ['bɔːræks] *n* (*pl* **boraxes** *or* **boraces** ['bɔːrəsiːz]) *Chem* bórax *m*

Bordeaux [bɔː'dəʊ] *n* (a) *(city)* Burdeos (b) *(wine)* burdeos *m*

border ['bɔːdər] **1** *n* (a) *(edge)* borde *m*, margen *m* (b) *Sew* ribete *m* (c) *(frontier)* frontera *f*; **to cross the b.** cruzar la frontera; **to escape over the b.** pasar la frontera ❑ **b. incident** incidente *m* fronterizo; **b. town** pueblo *m* fronterizo (d) *(flower bed)* arriate *m*
   2 *vt Sew (edge)* ribetear

border on *vi* (a) *Geog* lindar con (b) *Fig* rayar en, bordear; **this borders on the ridiculous** esto raya en lo ridículo

bordering ['bɔːdərɪŋ] *adj* limítrofe; **Spain and France are b. countries** España y Francia son países limítrofes

borderland ['bɔːdəlænd] *n* zona *f* fronteriza

borderline ['bɔːdəlaɪn] **1** *n* (a) *(border)* frontera *f* (b) *(dividing line)* línea *f* divisoria
   2 *adj* (a) *(on the border)* fronterizo(a) (b) *Fig (case etc)* dudoso(a)

bore¹ [bɔːr] **1** *vt Tech* taladrar, barrenar, perforar
   2 *n* (a) *Tech (hole)* taladro *m* (b) *Mil (inside of gun barrel)* ánima *f*, alma *f*; *(calibre)* calibre *m*; **a 12-b. shotgun** una escopeta de calibre 12

bore² [bɔːr] **1** *vt* aburrir; **the film bored me to tears** la película fue aburridísima
   2 *n (person)* pesado(a) *m,f*, pelma *mf*, pelmazo(a) *m,f*; *(thing)* lata *f*, rollo *m*; **what a b.!** ¡qué rollo!

bore³ [bɔːr] *pt see* **bear¹**

bored [bɔːd] *adj* aburrido(a); **to be b. stiff** *or* **to tears** aburrirse como una ostra; **to be b. with sth** estar harto(a) de algo

boredom ['bɔːdəm] *n* aburrimiento *m*

borer ['bɔːrər] *n Tech (machine)* taladradora *f*; *(hand tool)* taladro *m*

boric ['bɔːrɪk] *adj Chem* bórico(a)

boring ['bɔːrɪŋ] *adj (uninteresting)* aburrido(a); *(tedious)* pesado(a), latoso(a); **a b. film** una película aburrida

born [bɔːn] **1** *pp see* **bear¹**; **to be b.** nacer; **I wasn't b. yesterday** no nací ayer; **she was b.** in 1900 nació en 1900; **to be b. again** volver a nacer; *Fam* **in all my b. days** en toda mi vida

2 *adj (having natural ability)* nato(a); **b. poet** poeta nato; **she's a b. leader** nació para mandar; *Fig* **b. fool** tonto(a) de remate

born-again ['bɔːnəgen] *adj* converso(a), renacido(a)

borne [bɔːn] *pp see* **bear¹**

Borneo ['bɔːnɪəʊ] *n* Borneo

borough ['bʌrə] *n* **(a)** *(local district)* barrio *m*, distrito *m* **(b)** *US (municipality)* municipio *m* **(c)** *esp Br (constituency)* distrito *m* electoral

borrow ['bɒrəʊ] **1** *vt* **(a)** *(take on loan)* tomar prestado; **can I b. your pen?** ¿me prestas *or Esp* dejas tu bolígrafo?; **to be living on borrowed time** estar a dos pasos de la muerte **(b)** *(appropriate) (ideas etc)* apropiarse

2 *vi* pedir *or* tomar prestado

borrower ['bɒrəʊər] *n (of money)* prestatario(a) *m,f*

borstal ['bɔːstəl] *n Br Formerly* reformatorio *m*

bosh [bɒʃ] *n' Fam* tonterías *fpl*, *Am* pendejadas *fpl*, *RP* pavadas *fpl*; **that's a load of b.** no son más que tonterías *or Am* pendejadas *or RP* pavadas

Bosnia ['bɒznɪə] *n* Bosnia

Bosnian ['bɒznɪən] **1** *n* bosnio(a) *m,f*

2 *adj* bosnio(a); **B. Croat** croata *m,f* de Bosnia; **B. Muslim** musulmán(ana) *m,f* de Bosnia; **B. Serb** serbio(a) *m,f* de Bosnia

bosom ['bʊzəm] *n* **(a)** *(breast)* pecho *m*; *(breasts)* pechos *mpl* □ **b. friend** amigo(a) *m,f* íntimo(a), amigo(a) *m,f* del alma **(b)** *Fig (centre)* seno *m*; **the b. of the family** el seno de la familia

bosomy ['bʊzəmɪ] *adj Fam (woman)* pechugona

Bosphorus ['bɒsfərəs] *n (strait)* **the B.** el Bósforo

boss [bɒs] **1** *n* **(a)** *(head)* jefe(a) *m,f*; *(factory owner etc)* patrón(ona) *m,f*, amo *m* **(b)** *esp US Pol* jefe *m*; *Pej* cacique *m*

2 *vt* **to b. sb about** *or* **around** mangonear a algn

boss-eyed ['bɒsaɪd] *adj Br Slang* bizco(a)

bossy ['bɒsɪ] *adj* **(bossier, bossiest)** *Fam* mandón(ona) , mangoneador(a)

Bostonian [bɒ'stəʊnɪən] *adj & n* bostoniano(a) *(m,f)*

bosun ['bəʊsən] *n Naut* contramaestre *m*

botanic(al) [bə'tænɪk(əl)] *adj* botánico(a) □ **b. garden** jardín *m* botánico

botanist ['bɒtənɪst] *n* botánico(a) *m,f*, botanista *mf*

botany ['bɒtənɪ] *n* botánica *f*

botch [bɒtʃ] **1** *vt* chapucear

2 *n* chapucería *f*, chapuza *f*; **to make a b. of sth** chapucear algo

botched [bɒtʃt] *adj* chapucero(a); **a b. job** una chapuza

botcher ['bɒtʃər] *n (person)* chapucero(a) *m,f*

both [bəʊθ] **1** *adj* ambos(as), los/las dos; **b. men are teachers** ambos (hombres) son profesores; **hold it with b. hands** sujétala con las dos manos; **she wants to have it b. ways** quiere tenerlo todo; **there were mistakes on b. sides** hubo errores por ambas partes

2 *pron* **b. (of them)** ambos(as), los/las dos; **b. of us** nosotros dos

3 *conj* a la vez; **it is b. sad and depressing** es triste y deprimente a la vez; **b. England and Spain are in Europe** tanto Inglaterra como España están en Europa

bother ['bɒðər] **1** *vt* **(a)** *(disturb)* molestar; *(be a nuisance*

to) dar la lata a; **don't b. me!** ¡déjame en paz! **(b)** *(worry)* preocupar; **his behaviour bothered me** me extrañó su comportamiento; *Fam* **I can't be bothered** no tengo ganas

2 *vi* molestarse; **don't b. about me** no te preocupes por mí; **don't b. to write** no se moleste en escribir; **he didn't b. shaving** no se molestó en afeitarse

3 *n* **(a)** *(disturbance)* molestia *f*; *(nuisance)* lata *f*; **to give sb a lot of b.** dar la lata a algn **(b)** *(trouble)* problemas *mpl*; **I had a spot of b. with the police** tuve un pequeño roce con la policía

4 *interj Br* ¡maldito sea!

bothersome ['bɒðəsəm] *adj* molesto(a), fastidioso(a)

Botox ['bəʊtɒks] *n* Botox *m*

Botswana [bɒt'ʃwɑːnə] *n* Botsuana

Botswanan [bɒt'ʃwɑːnən] *adj & n* botsuano(a) *(m,f)*

bottle ['bɒtəl] **1** *n* **(a)** *(of drink)* botella *f*; *(of perfume, ink)* frasco *m*; *Fam* **to take to** *or* **hit the b.** darse a la bebida □ **baby's b.** biberón *m*; **b. opener** abrebotellas *m inv*; **b. party** = fiesta en la que cada invitado lleva una botella de vino o de licor; **b. rack** botellero *m*; **hot-water b.** bolsa *f* de agua caliente **(b)** *Br Slang (nerve)* agallas *fpl*; **to have a lot of b.** tener muchas agallas

2 *vt (wine)* embotellar; *(fruit etc)* enfrascar, envasar

bottle out *vi Br Fam (lose one's nerve)* rajarse

bottle up *vt (restrain) (emotion etc)* reprimir, sofocar

bottle-bank ['bɒtəlbæŋk] *n* contenedor *m* de vidrio (para reciclar)

bottlebrush ['bɒtəlbrʌʃ] *n* escobilla *f*

bottled ['bɒtəld] *adj (beer, wine)* en botella, embotella-do(a); *(fruit)* envasado(a)

bottle-feed ['bɒtəlfiːd] *vt (pt & pp* **bottle-fed** ['bɒtəlfed]) *(baby)* criar con biberón

bottle-green ['bɒtəlgriːn] *adj* verde botella; **a b.-g. car** un coche verde botella

bottleneck ['bɒtəlnek] *n Aut* embotellamiento *m*, atasco *m*

bottler ['bɒtələr] *n* embotellador(a) *m,f*

bottling ['bɒtəlɪŋ] *n (of wine etc)* embotellado *m*

bottom ['bɒtəm] **1** *adj* **(a)** *(lowest)* más bajo(a); **b. price** precio más bajo □ *Br* **b. drawer** ajuar *m*; **b. floor** planta *f* baja; *Aut* **b. gear** primera *f* **(b)** *(last)* último(a); **to bet one's b. dollar** jugarse hasta la camisa □ **b. line** *Fin* saldo *m* final; *Fig* resultado *m* final **(c)** *(at the end)* del fondo; **the b. room** la habitación del fondo

2 *n* **(a)** *(lowest part)* parte *f* inferior; *(of river, sea, garden, street, corridor, bag, box)* fondo *m*; *(of bottle)* culo *m*; *(of page, hill)* pie *m*; *(of dress)* bajo *m*; *(of trousers)* bajos *mpl*; **false b.** *(of suitcase)* doble fondo; *Fin* **the b. has fallen out of the market** los precios han caído en *Esp* picado *or Am* picada; *Educ* **to be (at) the b. of the class** ser el último/la última de la clase; **to sink to the b.** irse a pique; **to touch b.** tocar fondo; *Fig* **to scrape the b. of the barrel** estar en las últimas; *Fam* **bottoms up!** ¡salud! **(b)** *(cause)* origen *m*, causa *f*; **to get to the b. of a matter** llegar al meollo de una cuestión; **who is at the b. of all this?** ¿quién está detrás de todo esto? **(c)** *(buttocks)* trasero *m*

bottom out *vi Fin* tocar fondo; **the recession is bottoming out** la recesión se está estabilizando

bottomless ['bɒtəmlɪs] *adj* **(a)** *(pit)* sin fondo; *(mystery)* insondable **(b)** *(supply)* inagotable

bottommost ['bɒtəmməʊst] *adj (lowest)* del fondo; *(last)* último(a)

botulism ['bɒtjʊlɪʒəm] *n Med* botulismo *m*

boudoir ['buːdwɑːr] *n* boudoir *m*, tocador *m*

bouffant ['buːfɒn] *adj* ahuecado(a)

bougainvillea [buːgən'vɪlɪə] *n Bot* buganvilla *f*

bough [baʊ] *n Bot* rama *f*
bought [bɔːt] *pt & pp see* **buy**
bouillabaisse [ˈbuːjəbes] *n Culin* (sopa *f*) bullabesa *f*
bouillon [ˈbuːjɒn] *n Culin* caldo *m* ❑ *US* **b. cube** pastilla *f* de caldo
boulder [ˈbəʊldər] *n* canto *m* rodado
boulevard [ˈbuːlvɑːr] *n* bulevar *m*
bounce [baʊns] **1** *vi* (**a**) *(ball)* botar, rebotar (**b**) *(jump) (person)* saltar; **he bounced into the room** irrumpió en la habitación; **stop bouncing on the bed!** ¡para de saltar encima de la cama! (**c**) *Slang (cheque)* ser rechazado (por el banco); **she gave him a cheque which bounced** le dio un cheque sin fondos (**d**) *Comptr (message)* rebotar
  2 *vt (ball)* hacer botar
  3 *n* (**a**) *(of ball)* bote *m* (**b**) *(jump)* salto *m*, brinco *m* (**c**) *(life, energy) (of person, hair)* vitalidad *f*; **she's full of b.** es muy dinámica
bounce back *vi (recover health)* recuperarse, recobrarse
bouncer [ˈbaʊnsər] *n Slang* gorila *m*
bouncing [ˈbaʊnsɪŋ] *adj (baby)* robusto(a), con nervio
bouncy [ˈbaʊnsɪ] *adj* (**bouncier, bounciest**) (**a**) *(ball)* elástico(a) (**b**) *(person)* dinámico(a), vital
bound¹ [baʊnd] **1** *pt & pp see* **bind**
  2 *adj* (**a**) *(tied up)* atado(a); **b. hand and foot** atado de pies y manos (**b**) *Print (book)* encuadernado(a); **b. in leather** encuadernado en piel (**c**) *(obliged)* obligado(a); **you're b. by the contract** estás obligado por el contrato (**d**) **b. (up)** *(linked)* vinculado(a), ligado(a) (**with** a); **it is b. up with government policy** está estrechamente vinculado a la política del gobierno (**e**) **to be b. to** *(+ infin) (certain)* ser seguro que *(+ fut)*; **he is b. to arrive on time** seguro que llegará a tiempo; **it's b. to happen** sucederá con toda seguridad; **it was b. to fail** estaba destinado al fracaso
bound² [baʊnd] **1** *vi* (**a**) *(jump)* saltar, moverse dando saltos (**b**) *(bounce) (ball)* botar
  2 *n* (**a**) *(jump)* salto *m* (**b**) *(bounce) (of ball)* bote *m*, rebote *m*
bound³ [baʊnd] *adj (destined)* **b. for** con destino *or* rumbo a; **to be b. for** dirigirse a; **this train is b. for London** este tren se dirige a Londres
boundary [ˈbaʊndərɪ] *n (border)* límite *m*, frontera *f*
bounder [ˈbaʊndər] *n Br Slang* sinvergüenza *mf*
boundless [ˈbaʊndlɪs] *adj* ilimitado(a), sin límites; *(universe)* infinito(a)
bounds [baʊndz] *npl (limits)* límites *mpl*; **beyond the b. of reality** más allá de la realidad; **her ambition knows no b.** su ambición no conoce límites; **the river is out of b.** está prohibido bajar al río
bounteous [ˈbaʊntɪəs] *adj*, **bountiful** [ˈbaʊntɪfʊl] *adj* (**a**) *(generous)* generoso(a) (**b**) *(abundant)* abundante, copioso(a)
bounty [ˈbaʊntɪ] *n* (**a**) *(generosity)* generosidad *f* (**b**) *(gift)* regalo *m*, presente *m* (**c**) *(reward)* prima *f*, gratificación *f*
bouquet [buːˈkeɪ, bəʊˈkeɪ] *n* (**a**) *(of flowers)* ramo *m* de flores, ramillete *m* (**b**) [buːˈkeɪ] *(of wine)* aroma *m*, bouquet *m*, buqué *m*
Bourbon [ˈbʊəbən] **1** *n* Borbón *m*
  2 *adj* Borbón, borbónico(a)
bourbon [ˈbɜːbən] *n US* whisky *m* americano, bourbon *m*
bourgeois [ˈbʊəʒwɑː] *adj & n* burgués(esa) *(m,f)*
bourgeoisie [bʊəʒwɑːˈziː] *n* burguesía *f*
bout [baʊt] *n* (**a**) *(of time)* rato *m*; *(of work)* turno *m*, tanda *f*; *(of illness)* ataque *m*; **drinking b.** juerga *f*, borrachera *f* (**b**) *Box* encuentro *m*, combate *m*
boutique [buːˈtiːk] *n* boutique *f*, tienda *f*

bovine [ˈbəʊvaɪn] **1** *adj* bovino(a)
  2 *n* bovino *m*
bovver [ˈbɒvər] *n Br Slang (rowdiness)* camorra *f*, *Esp* follón *m*; **b. boys** camorristas *mpl*, delincuentes *mpl*, *RP* camorreros *mpl*
bow¹ [baʊ] **1** *vi* (**a**) *(as greeting, sign of respect)* hacer una reverencia, inclinarse; **to b. and scrape** hacer zalemas *or* zalamerías (**b**) *(give in)* ceder; **to b. to the inevitable** someterse a lo inevitable
  2 *n (with head, body)* reverencia *f*; *Theat* **to take a b.** salir a saludar
bow out *vi* retirarse (**of** de)
bow² [bəʊ] **1** *n* (**a**) *Sport* arco *m* (**b**) *Mus (of violin)* arco *m*; *Fig* **to have more than one string to one's b.** ser una persona de recursos (**c**) *(knot)* lazo *m* ❑ **b. tie** pajarita *f*, *Arg* moñito *m*, *CAm Carib Col* corbatín *m*, *Chile* humita *f*, *Méx* corbata *f* de moño, *Urug* moñita *f* (**d**) *Archit* bóveda *f* ❑ **b. window** mirador *m*
  2 *vi (wall)* arquearse, combarse
bow³ [baʊ] *n esp Naut* proa *f*
bowdlerize [ˈbaʊdləraɪz] *vt (book etc)* expurgar
bowed [baʊd] *adj* (**a**) *(head, body)* inclinado(a) (**b**) **b. down** cargado(a) (**by** *or* **with** de); **b. down by sorrow** apenado(a)
bowel [ˈbaʊəl] *n* (**a**) *(intestine)* intestino *m* ❑ **b. movement** evacuación *f* intestinal (**b**) **bowels** entrañas *fpl*; *Fig* **the b. of the earth** las entrañas de la tierra
bower [ˈbaʊər] *n (arbour)* emparrado *m*, enramada *f*
bowl¹ [bəʊl] *n* (**a**) *(dish)* cuenco *m*; *(for soup)* tazón *m*, plato *m* hondo; *(for washing hands)* jofaina *f*, palangana *f*; *(for washing clothes, dishes)* barreño *m*; *(of toilet)* taza *f*; *(of pipe)* cazoleta *f*; **sugar b.** azucarero *m* (**b**) *Geol* cuenca *f*
bowl² [bəʊl] *Sport* **1** *n (ball)* bola *f*
  2 *vt (in cricket) (ball)* lanzar, tirar
  3 *vi* (**a**) *(play bowls)* jugar a los bolos (**b**) *(in cricket)* lanzar la pelota
bowl along *vi Fam (car)* deslizarse rápidamente
bowl out *vt (in cricket)* eliminar, poner fuera de juego
bowl over *vt* (**a**) *(knock down)* derribar (**b**) *Fig (astonish)* desconcertar; **he was bowled over by the news** quedó pasmado ante la noticia
bowlegged [ˈbəʊlegɪd] *adj* con las piernas arqueadas, estevado(a)
bowler¹ [ˈbəʊlər] *n (in cricket)* lanzador(a) *m,f*
bowler² [ˈbəʊlər] *n (hat)* bombín *m*, sombrero *m* hongo
bowlful [ˈbəʊlfʊl] *n* cuenco *m*, bol *m*
bowling [ˈbəʊlɪŋ] *n* (**a**) *(game)* bolos *mpl* ❑ **b. alley** bolera *f*; **b. green** campo *m* de bolos (**b**) *(in cricket)* lanzamiento *m* de la pelota
bowls [bəʊlz] *npl Sport* bolos *mpl*, bochas *fpl*
bowser [ˈbaʊzər] *n Av Naut* camión *m* cisterna
bowsprit [ˈbəʊsprɪt] *n Naut* bauprés *m*
bow-wow [ˈbaʊwaʊ] *n (baby talk)* guau-guau *m*
box¹ [bɒks] **1** *n* (**a**) *(container)* caja *f*; *(large)* cajón *m*; *(of chocolates)* caja *f*; *(of matches)* cajetilla *f*; *Av* **black b.** caja *f* negra; **Christmas b.** aguinaldo *m*; **jewellery b.** joyero *m*; **letter b.** buzón *m*; **post-office b.** apartado *m* de correos ❑ *Phot* **b. camera** cámara *f* de cajón; *Theat* **b. office** taquilla *f*; **b. office success** éxito *m* taquillero *or* de taquilla; **b. spanner** llave *f* de tubo (**b**) *Press* recuadro *m* (**c**) *Jur* (**witness**) **b.** barra *f* de los testigos (**d**) *Theat* palco *m*; **b. seat** asiento *m* de palco (**e**) *Equit (in stable)* box *m*; *(vehicle)* furgón *m* para el transporte de caballos (**f**) *Br Fam (television)* caja *f* tonta
  2 *vt* (**a**) *(pack)* embalar (**b**) *Naut* **to b. the compass** cuartear la aguja

box 60 **brandish**

box² [bɒks] *Sport* **1** *vi* boxear
2 *vt* **(a)** *(fight)* boxear con **(b)** *Fam (hit)* pegar; **to b. sb's ears** dar un cachete a algn, abofetear a algn
3 *n (punch on the ears)* cachete *m*, bofetada *f*

box³ [bɒks] *n Bot* boj *m*

boxer [bɒksər] *n* **(a)** *Box* boxeador *m* **(b)** *Zool (dog)* bóxer *m*

boxing ['bɒksɪŋ] *n Sport* boxeo *m*, *CAm Méx* box *m* ❑ **b. glove** guante *m* de boxeo; **b. match** encuentro *m* de boxeo; **b. ring** cuadrilátero *m*

Boxing Day ['bɒksɪŋdeɪ] *n Br* = el día de San Esteban (26 de diciembre)

box-office ['bɒksɒfɪs] *n* taquilla *f*, *Am* boletería *f*; **a b.-o. success** un éxito de taquilla *or Am* boletería

boxroom ['bɒksru:m] *n Br* = en una vivienda, cuarto pequeño sin ventana que se suele usar como trastero

boy [bɔɪ] *n* **(a)** *(child)* niño *m*, chico *m*, muchacho *m*; *(youth)* joven *m*; **old b.** *(former pupil)* antiguo alumno *m*; *(old man)* viejo *m*; *(old friend)* amigo *m*; **listen, old b.** escúchame, amigo; *Fam* **the boys** los amigotes; *Fam* **oh b.!** ¡vaya!; *Prov* **boys will be boys** así son los chicos ❑ **b. band** = grupo de música formado por chicos jóvenes; **b. scout** explorador *m* **(b)** *(son)* hijo *m*

boycott ['bɔɪkɒt] **1** *n* boicot *m*, boicoteo *m*
2 *vt* boicotear

boyfriend ['bɔɪfrend] *n (gen)* novio *m*; *(live-in)* compañero *m*

boyhood ['bɔɪhʊd] *n* niñez *f*, juventud *f*

boyish ['bɔɪʃ] *adj* juvenil, de muchacho

bozo ['bəʊzəʊ] *n (pl* bozos*) US Fam* zoquete *m*, tarugo *m*

bps [bi:pi:'es] *n Comptr (abbr* bits per second*)* bps

bra [brɑ:] *n* sostén *m*, *Esp* sujetador *m*, *Carib Col Méx* brasier *m*, *RP* corpiño *m*

brace [breɪs] **1** *n* **(a)** *(clamp)* abrazadera *f*; *Tech (of drill)* berbiquí *m*; *(for straightening teeth)* aparato *m* ❑ **b. and bit** berbiquí y barrena *f* **(b)** *Constr (gen)* riostra *f*; *(of wood)* puntal *m* **(c)** *Naut (rope)* braza *f* **(d)** *Typ* llave *f*, corchete *m* **(e)** *Mus (accolade)* corchete *m* **(f)** *(pair)* par *m*; **a b. of pheasants** un par de faisanes **(g)** *Br* **braces** tirantes *mpl*
2 *vt* **(a)** *(prop) (wall)* apuntalar **(b)** *(strengthen) (building)* reforzar **(c)** *(steady)* **to b. oneself** prepararse *or Chile Méx Ven* alistarse **(for** para)

brace up *vi* cobrar ánimo, animarse

bracelet ['breɪslɪt] *n* pulsera *f*

bracing ['breɪsɪŋ] *adj (of wind, climate) (cool)* fresco(a); *(stimulating)* tonificante

bracken ['brækən] *n Bot* helecho *m*

bracket ['brækɪt] **1** *n* **(a)** *(support)* soporte *m*; *(for lamp)* brazo *m*; *(for balcony)* ménsula *f*; *(shelf)* repisa *f* **(b)** *Typ (round)* paréntesis *m*; *(square)* corchete *m*; *(brace)* llave *f*; **in brackets** entre paréntesis **(c)** *(group)* grupo *m*, sector *m*; **the middle-income b.** el sector de ingresos medios
2 *vt* **(a)** *Ling (phrase etc)* poner entre paréntesis **(b)** *(group together)* agrupar, juntar

brackish ['brækɪʃ] *adj (water)* salobre

bradawl ['brædɔ:l] *n* lezna *f*, punzón *m*

brag [bræg] **1** *vi (pt & pp* bragged*)* jactarse (**about** de); **stop bragging!** ¡deja de fanfarronear!
2 *n* **(a)** *(bragging)* jactancia *f*, fanfarronería *f* **(b)** *(braggart)* fanfarrón(ona) *m,f*

braggart ['brægət] *n* fanfarrón(ona) *m,f*

Brahman ['brɑ:mən] *n (pl* Brahmans*),* **Brahmin** ['brɑ:mɪn] *n (pl* Brahmin *or* Brahmins*)* brahmán *m*, brahmín *m*

braid [breɪd] **1** *vt (hair, thread)* trenzar

2 *n* **(a)** *Sew.* galón *m*; **gold b.** galón de oro **(b)** *esp US* trenza *f*

Braille [breɪl] *n* Braille *m*; **books in B.** libros en Braille

brain [breɪn] **1** *n* **(a)** *Anat* cerebro *m*; **he was the brains behind the job** fue el cerebro del trabajo; **she's got cars on the b.** está obsesionada por los coches; **to blow one's brains out** saltarse *or* volarse la tapa de los sesos; **to pick sb's brains** aprovechar los conocimientos de algn; **to rack one's brains** devanarse los sesos; *Fam* **use your b.!** ¡usa la cabeza! ❑ *Med* **b. death** muerte *f* cerebral; *Fig* **b. drain** fuga *f* de cerebros; *US* **b. trust** consejeros *mpl* del gobierno; **b. tumour** tumor *m* cerebral; **b. wave** idea *f* genial; **electronic b.** cerebro *m* electrónico **(b)** *Fam* **brains** inteligencia *f*; **to have b.** ser inteligente, tener mucho seso ❑ **b. trust** asociación *f* de expertos **(c)** *Culin* **brains** sesos *mpl*
2 *vt Fam* **to b. sb** romperle la crisma a algn

brainchild ['breɪntʃaɪld] *n* invento *m*, idea *f* genial, genialidad *f*

brain-dead ['breɪnded] *adj* **(a)** *Med* clínicamente muerto(a) **(b)** *Pej* subnormal

brainless ['breɪnlɪs] *adj* tonto(a), memo(a)

brainpower ['breɪnpaʊər] *n* capacidad *f* intelectual

brainstorm ['breɪnstɔ:m] *n* **(a)** *(mental confusion)* cruce *m* de cables **(b)** *US (brain wave)* idea *f* genial

brainstorming ['breɪnstɔ:mɪŋ] *n* brainstorming *m*

brainwash ['breɪnwɒʃ] *vt* lavar el cerebro a; **she's been brainwashed** le han lavado el cerebro

brainwashing ['breɪnwɒʃɪŋ] *n* lavado *m* de cerebro

brainy ['breɪnɪ] *adj* (**brainier, brainiest**) *Fam* listo(a), inteligente

braise [breɪz] *vt Culin (meat)* estofar, *Andes Méx* ahogar

brake¹ [breɪk] **1** *n Aut (also pl)* freno *m*; **to apply/release the brakes** frenar/soltar el freno ❑ **b. blocks** pastillas *fpl* del freno; **b. drum** tambor *m* del freno; **b. fluid** líquido *m* para frenos; **b. light** luz *f* de freno; **b. lining** guarnición *f* del freno; **b. pedal** (pedal *m* del) freno *m*; **b. shoe** zapata *f* del freno
2 *vi* frenar, echar el freno

brake² [breɪk] *n Bot (bracken)* helecho *m*; *(thicket)* matorral *m*

braking ['breɪkɪŋ] *n* frenado *m* ❑ *Aut* **b. distance** distancia *f* de seguridad

bramble ['bræmbəl] *n Bot* zarza *f*, zarzamora *f*

bran [bræn] *n* salvado *m*, afrecho *m*

branch [brɑ:ntʃ] **1** *n* **(a)** *(of tree, family)* rama *f*; *(of road, railway)* ramal *m*; *(of river)* brazo *m*; *(of science, industry, arts)* rama *f*, ramo *m* **(b)** *Com* **b. (office)** sucursal *f*
2 *vi (road)* bifurcarse

branch off *vi* desviarse; **the road branches off to the left** la carretera se desvía hacia la izquierda

branch out *vi* diversificarse; **they have branched out into insurance** han ampliado su campo de acción a los seguros

brand [brænd] **1** *n* **(a)** *Com* marca *f* ❑ **b. image** imagen *m* de marca; **b. leader** marca *f* líder (en el mercado); **b. loyalty** fidelidad *f* a la marca; **b. name** marca *f* de fábrica; **b. recognition** reconocimiento *m* de marca **(b)** *(type)* clase *f*; **he has his own b. of humour** tiene un sentido del humor muy particular **(c)** *(on cattle)* hierro *m*
2 *vt* **(a)** *(animal)* marcar con hierro candente; *Fig* **to b. sb for life** dejar marcado a algn para toda la vida **(b)** *(label)* tildar; **to b. sb a traitor** tildar a algn de traidor

branding-iron ['brændɪŋaɪən] *n* hierro *m* candente *or* de marcar

brandish ['brændɪʃ] *vt* **(a)** *(weapon)* blandir **(b)** *Fig (threat etc)* esgrimir

brand-new [brænd'nju:] *adj* flamante, completamente nuevo(a)

brandy ['brændɪ] *n* brandy *m*, coñac *m*, *RP* cognac *m*; **cherry b.** aguardiente *m* de cerezas

brash [bræʃ] *adj* (**a**) *(impudent)* descarado(a), insolente (**b**) *(reckless)* temerario(a) (**c**) *(loud, showy)* chillón(ona)

brass [brɑːs] *n* (**a**) *(metal)* latón *m*; *Fig* **to be as bold as b.** tener mucha cara; *Fig* **the top b.** los peces gordos; *Br Fam* **it's not worth a b. farthing** no vale un real; *Fam* **to get down to b. tacks** ir al grano ❑ **b. rubbing** calco *m* sacado de una placa de latón (**b**) *Br Slang (money)* *Esp* pasta *f*, *Esp RP* guita *f*, *Am* plata *f*, *Méx* lana *f* (**c**) *Mus* instrumentos *mpl* de metal, metal *m* ❑ **b. band** banda *f*, charanga *f*, fanfarria *f*

brassière ['bræzɪər] *n* sostén *m*, *Esp* sujetador *m*, *Carib Col Méx* brasier *m*, *RP* corpiño *m*

brassy ['brɑːsɪ] *adj* (**brassier, brassiest**) (**a**) *(of brass)* de latón (**b**) *(harsh)* estridente (**c**) *(brazen)* descarado(a)

brat [bræt] *n Fam* mocoso(a) *m,f*; *Fam* **b. pack** camada *f* or hornada *f* de jóvenes promesas

bravado [brə'vɑːdəʊ] *n* (*pl* **bravadoes** *or* **bravados**) bravata *f*, baladronada *f*, fanfarronada *f*

brave [breɪv] **1** *adj* valiente, valeroso(a); **a b. attempt** un intento valeroso
2 *n US* (**Indian**) **b.** guerrero *m* indio
3 *vt* (**a**) *(face) (danger)* hacer frente a (**b**) *(defy) (death)* desafiar

bravely ['breɪvlɪ] *adv* valientemente

bravery ['breɪvərɪ] *n* valentía *f*, valor *m*, arrojo *m*

bravo [brɑː'vəʊ] *interj* ¡bravo!

bravura [brə'vjʊərə] *n* (*spirit, zest*) brío *m*, entrega *f*; *Mus* virtuosismo *m*; **a b. performance** *Mus* una virtuosa interpretación; *Fig* una brillante actuación

brawl [brɔːl] **1** *n* pendencia *f*, reyerta *f*
2 *vi* pelearse

brawler ['brɔːlər] *n* pendenciero(a) *m,f*, alborotador(a) *m,f*

brawn [brɔːn] *n* (**a**) *(strength)* fuerza *f* física (**b**) *Br Culin* queso *m* de cerdo

brawny ['brɔːnɪ] *adj* (**brawnier, brawniest**) musculoso(a), fornido(a)

bray [breɪ] **1** *n (of donkey)* rebuzno *m*
2 *vi* rebuznar

brazen ['breɪzən] *adj* (**a**) *(metal)* de latón (**b**) *(shameless)* descarado(a)

brazier ['breɪzɪər] *n (brass-worker)* brasero *m*

Brazil [brə'zɪl] *n* (el) Brasil

brazil [brə'zɪl] *n* **b. nut** nuez *f* del Brasil

Brazilian [brə'zɪlɪən] *adj & n* brasileño(a) *(m,f)*, *Am* brasilero(a) *(m,f)*

breach [briːtʃ] **1** *n* (**a**) *(in wall)* brecha *f*; *Fig* **to step into the b.** echar una mano (en una situación difícil) (**b**) *(violation etc)* incumplimiento *m*; **b. of confidence** abuso *m* de confianza; **b. of contract** incumplimiento de contrato; **b. of faith** falta *f* de lealtad; **b. of promise** incumplimiento de una promesa; **b. of the law** violación *f* de la ley; **b. of the peace** alteración *f* del orden público (**c**) *(break in relations)* ruptura *f*
2 *vt (law, contract)* violar

bread [bred] *n* (**a**) *(food)* pan *m*; **a loaf of b.** un pan, una barra de pan; **b. and butter** pan con mantequilla; **piece of b.** pedazo *m* de pan; **sliced b.** pan de molde; **slice of b.** rebanada *f* de pan; **stale b.** pan duro; **unleavened b.** pan ácimo; **white b.** pan blanco *or* candeal; **wholemeal b.** pan integral; *Fig* **our daily b.** el pan nuestro de cada día; *Fig* **to earn one's daily b.** ganarse el pan de cada día; *Fig* **to know which side one's b. is buttered on** saber dónde

aprieta el zapato, saber qué terreno se pisa ❑ *Br* **b. bin,** *US* **b. box** panera *f*; **b. knife** cuchillo *m* del pan; *Culin* **b. sauce** salsa *f* bechamel con pan rallado (**b**) *Slang (money)* *Esp* pasta *f*, *Esp RP* guita *f*, *Am* plata *f*, *Méx* lana *f*

bread-and-butter [bredən'bʌtər] *adj Fam* **b. issues** asuntos *mpl* básicos

breadbasket ['bredbɑːskɪt] *n* cesta *f* del pan

breadboard ['bredbɔːd] *n* tabla *f* (para cortar el pan)

breadcrumb ['bredkrʌm] *n* miga *f* de pan; **breadcrumbs** *Culin* pan *m sing* rallado

breadfruit ['bredfruːt] *n* (*pl* **breadfruits** *or* **breadfruit**) *Bot (tree)* árbol *m* del pan; *(fruit)* fruto *m* del árbol del pan

breadline ['bredlaɪn] *n Fam* miseria *f*; **to be on the b.** vivir en la miseria

breadstick ['bredstɪk] *n* colín *m*

breadth [bredθ] *n* (**a**) *(width)* anchura *f*, ancho *m*; **it is two metres in b.** tiene dos metros de ancho (**b**) *(extent)* amplitud *f*

breadwinner ['bredwɪnər] *n* cabeza *mf* de familia, el *or* la que gana el pan

break [breɪk] **1** *vt (pt* **broke** *pp* **broken**) (**a**) *(gen)* romper; **he broke his glasses** se le rompieron las gafas; *Med* **to b. a leg** fracturarse la pierna; *Sport* **to b. a record** batir un récord; **to b. cover** salir al descubierto; **to b. even** no tener ni ganancias ni pérdidas; **to b. open a door** derribar una puerta; *Av* **to b. the sound barrier** cruzar la barrera del sonido; *Fig* **to b. one's back** matarse a trabajar; *Fig* **to b. sb's heart** partirle el corazón a algn; *Fig* **to b. the ice** romper el hielo (**b**) *(fail to keep)* faltar a; **to b. a contract** romper un contrato; **to b. a promise** faltar a una promesa; **to b. one's word** faltar a su palabra; **to b. the law** violar la ley (**c**) *(destroy)* destrozar; *Fin* arruinar; **to b. a rebellion** sofocar una rebelión; *Pol* **to b. a strike** romper una huelga; **to b. sb's health** quebrantar la salud de algn; **to b. the bank** hacer saltar la banca (**d**) *(interrupt)* interrumpir; **to b. (short) a journey/one's holidays** cortar *or* interrumpir un viaje/las vacaciones; **to b. silence** romper el silencio (**e**) *(decipher) (code)* descifrar (**f**) *(cushion, soften) (fall, blow)* amortiguar (**g**) *(disclose)* desvelar; **she broke the news to him** le comunicó la noticia
2 *vi* (**a**) *(gen)* romperse; *(clouds)* dispersarse; *(waves)* romper; **it fell and broke** se cayó y se rompió (**b**) *(storm)* estallar (**c**) *(voice)* cambiar (**d**) *(health)* resentirse, quebrantarse (**e**) *(day)* rayar, romper; **when day breaks** al rayar el alba (**f**) *(news, story)* propalarse, divulgarse, propagarse (**g**) *Box* separarse
3 *n* (**a**) *(split, fracture)* rotura *f*; *(crack)* grieta *f*; *(opening)* abertura *f*; *(in the clouds)* claro *m* ❑ **b. dance** (dance) *m*; **b. of day** amanecer *m*; *Elec* **b. switch** interruptor *m* (**b**) *(in relationship)* ruptura *f* (**c**) *(pause)* pausa *f*, descanso *m*; *(in a journey)* alto *m*; *(at school)* recreo *m*; **to take a b.** descansar un rato; *(holiday)* tomar unos días libres; **without a b.** sin parar (**d**) *Fam (chance)* oportunidad *f*, *Am* chance *f*; **a lucky b.** un golpe de suerte; **give me a b.!** ¡deja de fastidiarme, quieres! (**e**) *Elec* corte *m*, interrupción *f*

break away *vi* (**a**) *(become separate)* desprenderse, separarse (**from** de) (**b**) *(escape)* escaparse

break down 1 *vt* (**a**) *(knock down) (door etc)* derribar (**b**) *(weaken) (resistance)* minar, acabar con (**c**) *Fin (prices)* desglosar
2 *vi* (**a**) *Aut* tener una avería; **we broke down on the motorway** el coche se nos averió en la autopista (**b**) *(end) (resistance)* acabar con (**c**) *(health)* debilitarse (**d**) *(weep)* ponerse a llorar

break in 1 *vt* acostumbrar; **to b. in a horse** domar un caballo; **to b. in a new employee** iniciar en su trabajo a un empleado nuevo; **to b. in new shoes** acostumbrarse a unos zapatos nuevos

2 *vi (burglar)* entrar por la fuerza, allanar

break into *vt* (**a**) *(burgle) (house)* entrar por la fuerza en, forzar, allanar; *(safe)* forzar (**b**) *(begin)* irrumpir en; **to b. into song** ponerse a cantar

break off 1 *vt* (**a**) *(detach)* romper, cortar (**b**) *Fig* romper; **to b. off negotiations** romper las negociaciones; **to b. off an engagement** romper un compromiso
2 *vi* (**a**) *(become detached)* desprenderse (**b**) *(talks)* interrumpirse (**c**) *(stop)* pararse

break out *vi* (**a**) *(prisoners)* escaparse (**b**) *(war, epidemic, fire)* estallar; *Med* **to b. out in a rash** salirle a uno una erupción (en la piel)

break through 1 *vt* (**a**) *(make one's way through) (crowd)* abrirse camino *or* paso por; *(barricade)* atravesar; *(cordon)* romper (**b**) *(sun) (clouds, fog)* atravesar, filtrarse a través de
2 *vi* abrirse camino *or* paso

break up 1 *vt* (**a**) *(object)* romper; *(earth)* mullir; *(car)* desguazar (**b**) *(disperse) (crowd)* disolver
2 *vi* (**a**) *(disintegrate)* hacerse pedazos (**b**) *(crowd)* dispersarse; *(meeting)* levantarse (**c**) *(marriage, relationship)* fracasar; *(couple)* separarse (**d**) *Educ* terminar; **the schools b. up next week** las vacaciones empiezan la semana que viene

break with *vt* *(past, family)* romper con

breakable ['breɪkəbəl] **1** *adj* frágil, quebradizo(a)
2 breakables *npl* objetos *mpl* frágiles

breakage ['breɪkɪdʒ] *n* (**a**) *(breaking)* rotura *f* (**b**) **breakages** *(broken articles)* objetos *mpl* rotos

breakaway ['breɪkəweɪ] *adj* disidente; **b. group** grupo de escisión

break-dance ['breɪkdɑːns] *vi* bailar el break (dance)

breakdown ['breɪkdaʊn] *n* (**a**) *Aut* avería *f*; *Br* **b. truck** grúa *f*, camión *m* grúa (**b**) *(crisis)* crisis *f*; *Med* **(nervous) b.** crisis *f* nerviosa (**c**) *(in communications)* ruptura *f*; **there was a b. in talks** hubo una ruptura en las negociaciones (**d**) *(analysis)* análisis *m*; *Fin* desglose *m*; **price b.** desglose de precios

breaker ['breɪkər] *n* (**a**) *(large wave)* ola *f* grande (**b**) *Tech (crusher)* trituradora *f* (**c**) *Elec (switch)* interruptor *m* automático (**d**) *Rad Slang* radioaficionado(a) *m,f*

break-even point [breɪk'iːvənpɔɪnt] *n Fin* punto *m* de equilibrio, umbral *m* de rentabilidad

breakfast ['brekfəst] **1** *n* desayuno *m*; **he likes b. in bed** le gusta desayunar en la cama; **she only has a cup of tea for b.** sólo desayuna una taza de té; **to have b.** desayunar
2 *vi* desayunar

break-in ['breɪkɪn] *n (burglary)* robo *m* (con allanamiento de morada)

breaking ['breɪkɪŋ] *n* (**a**) **b. point** *(of person, patience)* límite *m*; **my patience was at b. point** no podía más (**b**) *Jur* **b. and entering** allanamiento *m* de morada

breakneck ['breɪknek] *adj (speed, pace)* de vértigo

break-out ['breɪkaʊt] *n (from prison)* fuga *f*

breakthrough ['breɪkθruː] *n (major achievement)* adelanto *m*, avance *m*; **it was an important b. in the treatment of burns** fue un avance importante en el tratamiento de las quemaduras

break-up ['breɪkʌp] *n (disintegration)* desintegración *f*; *(of empire)* desmembramiento *m*; *(of marriage, relationship)* fracaso *m*; *(of couple)* separación *f*; *(of talks)* ruptura *f*

breakwater ['breɪkwɔːtər] *n* rompeolas *m inv*

bream [briːm] *n inv Zool* brema *f* □ **sea b.** pargo *m*; **gilthead b.** dorada *f*; **Ray's b.** japuta *f*, palometa *f*; **red b.** besugo *m*

breast [brest] *n* (**a**) *(chest)* pecho *m*; *(of woman)* pecho *m*, seno *m*; *(of chicken etc)* pechuga *f*; **b. pocket** bolsillo *m* or

CAm Méx Perú bolsa *f* superior; *Fig* **to make a clean b. of it** dar la cara (**b**) *(of hill)* repecho *m*

breastbone ['brestbəʊn] *n Anat* esternón *m*

breast-fed ['brestfed] **1** *pt & pp see* **breast-feed**
2 *adj (baby)* criado(a) con el pecho

breast-feed ['brestfiːd] *vt (pt & pp* **breast-fed)** *(baby)* criar el pecho a, amamantar a

breast-feeding ['brestfiːdɪŋ] *n* amamantamiento *m*

breastplate ['brestpleɪt] *n (of armour)* peto *m (de armadura)*

breaststroke ['breststrəʊk] *n Swimming* braza *f*

breath [breθ] *n* (**a**) *(gen)* aliento *m*; *(breathing)* respiración *f*; **bad b.** mal aliento; **in the same b.** al mismo tiempo; **out of b.** sin aliento; **take a deep b.** respire hondo; **to catch one's b.** recobrar el aliento; **to draw b.** respirar; **to get one's b. back** recobrar el aliento *or* la respiración; **under one's b.** en voz baja; *Fig* **to take sb's b. away** dejar pasmado a algn; *Fig* **to waste one's b.** gastar saliva en balde □ *Aut* **b. test** prueba *f* del alcohol (**b**) *(gust)* soplo *m* (de aire); **to go out for a b. of air** salir a tomar el aire; *Fig* **her presence was like a b. of fresh air** su presencia fue como una bocanada de aire fresco

breathalyse, *US* **breathalyze** ['breθəlaɪz] *vt* hacer la prueba del alcohol a

Breathalyser®, *US* **Breathalyzer®** ['breθəlaɪzər] *n Br* alcohómetro *m*, alcoholímetro *m*

breathe [briːð] **1** *vt (air etc)* respirar; **to b. again, b. a sigh of relief** dar un suspiro de alivio; **to b. heavily** resoplar; **to b. one's last** exhalar el último suspiro; *Fig* **don't b. a word of it!** ¡no digas ni una palabra a nadie!, ¡no digas ni mu!
2 *vi* respirar; **he's still breathing** vive aún, aún respira; **to b. in** aspirar; **to b. out** espirar; *Fig* **now we can b. again** ya podemos estar tranquilos; *Fig* **to b. down sb's neck** atosigar a algn

breather ['briːðər] *n Fam (rest)* (momento *m* de) respiro *m*, descanso *m*; **give me a b.** déjame respirar un momento; **to take a b.** tomarse un descanso *or* un respiro

breathing ['briːðɪŋ] *n* respiración *f* □ **b. apparatus** equipo *m* respiratorio; **b. space** pausa *f*, respiro *m*

breathless ['breθlɪs] *adj* sin aliento, jadeante

breathtaking ['breθteɪkɪŋ] *adj (scenery etc)* impresionante, asombroso(a)

breathy ['breθɪ] *adj* **to have a b. voice** tener la voz jadeante

bred [bred] *pt & pp see* **breed**

breech [briːtʃ] *n* (**a**) *(of gun)* recámara *f* (**b**) *Med* **b. baby** niño *m* que nace de nalgas

breeches ['brɪtʃɪz, 'briːtʃɪz] *npl* bombachos *mpl* □ **knee b., riding b.** pantalones *mpl* de montar

breech-loading ['briːtʃləʊdɪŋ] *adj (gun)* de retrocarga

breed [briːd] **1** *n* (**a**) *(of animal)* raza *f* (**b**) *Fig (class)* clase *f*, género *m*; **a new b. of writers** una nueva generación de escritores
2 *vt (pt & pp* **bred)** (**a**) *(animals)* criar (**b**) *Fig (ideas)* engendrar
3 *vi (animals)* reproducirse

breeder ['briːdər] *n* (**a**) *(person)* criador(a) *m,f* (**b**) *(animal)* reproductor(a) *m,f* (**c**) *Tech* **(fast) b. reactor** reactor *m* generador

breeding ['briːdɪŋ] *n* (**a**) *(of animals)* cría *f* □ **b. ground** criadero *m*; *Fig (for activity, behaviour)* caldo *m* de cultivo (**b**) *(of person)* educación *f*; **(good) b.** buena crianza *f*; **to lack b.** carecer de educación

breeze [briːz] **1** *n* brisa *f*; **sea b.** brisa marina □ *Br Constr* **b. block** bloque *m* de cemento
2 *vi* **to b. in/out** entrar/salir despreocupadamente

breezy ['bri:zɪ] *adj* (**breezier, breeziest**) (**a**) *(weather)* ventoso(a) (**b**) *(person, attitude)* despreocupado(a)

Bren gun ['brengʌn] *n Mil* fusil *m* ametrallador

brethren ['breðrɪn] *npl Rel* hermanos *mpl*

Breton ['bretən] **1** *adj & n* bretón(ona) *(m,f)*
2 *n (language)* bretón *m*

breve [bri:v] *n Ling Mus* breve *f*

breviary ['brevjərɪ] *n Rel* breviario *m*

brevity ['brevɪtɪ] *n* brevedad *f*

brew [bru:] **1** *vt* (**a**) *(beer)* hacer, elaborar (**b**) *Culin (hot drink)* preparar (**c**) *Fig (crisis etc)* tramar
2 *vi* (**a**) *(tea)* reposar; **let the tea b.** deja reposar el té (**b**) *Fig* prepararse; **a storm is brewing** se prepara una tormenta; *Fam* **something's brewing** algo se está cociendo
3 *n* (**a**) *(of tea)* infusión *f*; *Br Fam (drink of beer)* birra *f*, *Méx* cheve *f* (**b**) *(magic potion)* brebaje *m*; *(strange mixture)* mezcolanza *f*

brewer ['bru:ər] *n* cervecero(a) *m,f* ❑ **b.'s yeast** levadura *f* de cerveza

brewery ['bruərɪ] *n* fábrica *f* de cerveza, cervecería *f*

brewing ['bru:ɪŋ] **1** *adj* cervecero(a); **the b. industry** la industria cervecera
2 *n (of beer)* elaboración *f* de la cerveza

briar ['braɪər] *n Bot* brezo *m* ❑ **b. pipe** pipa *f* de brezo

bribe [braɪb] **1** *vt* sobornar
2 *n* soborno *m*, *Andes RP* coima *f*, *CAm Méx* mordida *f* **to take a b. from sb** dejarse sobornar por algn

bribery ['braɪbərɪ] *n (process)* soborno *m*

bric-a-brac ['brɪkəbræk] *n* baratijas *fpl*, chucherías *fpl*

brick [brɪk] **1** *n* (**a**) *Constr* ladrillo *m*; **b. wall** muro *m* de ladrillo; **solid b.** ladrillo macizo; *Fam* **to come down on sb like a ton of bricks** echar una bronca de miedo a algn; *Br Fam* **to drop a b.** meter la pata (**b**) *Br (child's block)* cubo *m* (de madera) (**c**) *(of ice, ice cream)* bloque *m* (**d**) *Br Fam Old-fashioned* **he's a b.** es un gran tipo
2 *vt* **to b. (in/over/up)** tapiar con ladrillos

brickbat ['brɪkbæt] *n* (**a**) *(missile)* trozo *m* de ladrillo (**b**) *(criticism)* crítica *f*

bricklayer ['brɪkleɪər] *n* albañil *m*

brick-red ['brɪk'red] *adj* (de) color teja

brickwork ['brɪkwɜ:k] *n* ladrillos *mpl*, enladrillado *m*

bridal ['braɪdəl] *adj* nupcial ❑ **b. suite** suite *f* nupcial

bride [braɪd] *n (on wedding day)* novia *f*; *(newly-married woman)* recién casada *f*; **the b. and groom** los novios

bridegroom ['braɪdgru:m] *n (on wedding day)* novio *m*; *(newly-married man)* recién casado *m*

bridesmaid ['braɪdzmeɪd] *n* dama *f* de honor

bride-to-be ['braɪdtə'bi:] *n* futura esposa *f*

bridge¹ [brɪdʒ] **1** *n (over river, of violin, for teeth)* puente *m*; *(of nose)* caballete *m*; *(of ship)* puente *m* de mando; **suspension b.** puente colgante
2 *vt* (**a**) *(river)* tender un puente sobre (**b**) *(distances etc)* acortar; *(gap)* llenar; *Fin US* **b. or *Br* bridging loan** crédito *m* a corto plazo

bridge² [brɪdʒ] *n Cards* bridge *m*

bridgehead ['brɪdʒhed] *n Mil* cabeza *f* de puente

bridle ['braɪdəl] **1** *n* brida *f*; *(bit)* freno *m*; **b. path** camino *m* de herradura
2 *vt (horse)* embridar, poner la brida a

brief [bri:f] **1** *adj* (**a**) *(short)* breve; **a b. pause** una breve pausa; **a b. stay** una estancia corta (**b**) *(concise)* conciso(a)
2 *n* (**a**) *(report)* informe *m*; *(summary)* resumen *m*; **in b.** en resumen (**b**) *Jur* expediente *m* (**c**) *Mil* instrucciones *fpl* (**d**) *Rel (letter)* breve *m* (**e**) **briefs** *(for men)* calzoncillos *mpl*, slip

m sing, *Chile* fundillos *mpl*, *Col* pantaloncillos *mpl*, *Méx* calzones *mpl*; *(for women) Esp* bragas *fpl*, *Chile Col Méx* calzones *mpl*, *Ecuad* follones *mpl*, *RP* bombacha *f*
3 *vt* (**a**) *(inform)* informar (**b**) *(instruct)* dar instrucciones a

briefcase ['bri:fkeɪs] *n* cartera *f*, portafolios *mpl*

briefing ['bri:fɪŋ] *n* (**a**) *(instructions)* instrucciones *fpl* (**b**) *(meeting)* reunión *f* informativa

briefly ['bri:flɪ] *adv* brevemente; **as b. as possible** con la mayor brevedad (posible)

briefness ['bri:fnɪs] *n* brevedad *f*

brier ['braɪər] *n see* **briar**

Brig [brɪg] *Mil (abbr* **Brigadier**) General *m* de Brigada, Gral. Brig.

brig [brɪg] *n Naut* bergantín *m*

brigade [brɪ'geɪd] *n Mil* brigada *f*

brigadier [brɪgə'dɪər] *n Mil Br* general *m* de brigada; *US* **b. general** general *m* de brigada

brigand ['brɪgənd] *n* bandido *m*, bandolero *m*

bright [braɪt] *adj* (**a**) *(light, sun, eyes)* brillante; *(colour)* vivo(a); *(day)* claro(a), despejado(a) (**b**) *(cheerful)* alegre, muy animado(a); **b. and early** muy temprano; **to look on the b. side** mirar el lado bueno de las cosas (**c**) *(clever)* listo(a), despierto(a), espabilado(a); **a b. idea** una idea luminosa; *Fam* **a b. spark** un espabilado (**d**) *(promising)* prometedor(a); **a b. future** un futuro prometedor, un brillante porvenir

brighten ['braɪtən] *vi* (**a**) *(prospects)* mejorarse (**b**) *(face, eyes)* iluminarse

brighten up 1 *vt* (**a**) *(make more attractive)* hacer más alegre; **the new carpet brightens up the room** la alfombra nueva anima mucho la habitación (**b**) *(polish) (metal)* pulir
2 *vi* (**a**) *(weather)* aclararse, despejarse (**b**) *(person)* animarse

bright-eyed ['braɪtaɪd] *adj* con los ojos brillantes; *Fig (enthusiasm)* vivo(a); *Fam* **b. and bushy-tailed** alegre y contento(a)

brightly ['braɪtlɪ] *adv* brillantemente; *(cleverly)* inteligentemente

brightness ['braɪtnɪs] *n* (**a**) *(light)* luminosidad *f*, intensidad *f*; *(sun)* resplandor *m*; *(of day)* claridad *f*; *(colour)* viveza *f* (**b**) *(cleverness)* inteligencia *f*

brilliance ['brɪljəns] *n* (**a**) *(light)* brillo *m*; *(colour)* viveza *f* (**b**) *(of person)* brillantez *f*

brilliant ['brɪljənt] *adj* (**a**) *(light)* brillante, reluciente (**b**) *(person)* brillante, admirable; *(idea)* luminoso(a), genial; **a b. writer** un escritor brillante (**c**) *Br Fam (very good)* genial, *Andes CSur* macanudo(a), *Méx* padre, *RP* bárbaro(a)
2 *n (diamond)* brillante *m*

brilliantine ['brɪljənti:n] *n* brillantina *f*

brim [brɪm] **1** *n* (**a**) *(of cup etc)* borde *m*; **full to the b.** lleno hasta el borde (**b**) *(of hat)* ala *f*
2 *vi* rebosar (**with** de); **her eyes brimmed with tears** las lágrimas cegaban sus ojos; **to be brimming with happiness** estar rebosante de alegría

brim over rebosar

brimful ['brɪmfʊl] *adj* hasta el borde; *Fig* **b. of health/ideas** pletórico(a) de salud/ideas

brimstone ['brɪmstəʊn] *n Min* azufre *m*; *Literary* **fire and b.** el infierno

brine [braɪn] *n* salmuera *f*

bring [brɪŋ] *vt (pt & pp* **brought**) (**a**) *(carry sth to sb)* traer; **b. me a cup of coffee** tráigame un café; **to b. bad luck** traer mala suerte; **to b. news** traer noticias (**b**) *(take sth or sb with you)* traer; **could you b. that book tomorrow?** ¿podrías traerme el libro mañana?; **he brought his camera** se trajo la máquina de hacer fotos; **she brought her boyfriend to the party** trajo a su novio a la fiesta □ *Br* **b.-and-buy sale** = venta de artículos de segunda mano *o* de fabricación casera (**c**) *(take to a different position)* llevar; **Tina brought her hand to her head** Tina se llevó la mano a la cabeza (**d**) *(cause)* llevar, provocar; **he brought it upon himself** se lo buscó; **the experience brought her to suicide** aquella experiencia la llevó al suicidio; **the war brought hunger to many homes** la guerra llevó el hambre a muchos hogares; **what brings you here?** ¿qué te trae por aquí? (**e**) *(persuade)* persuadir, convencer; **how did they b. themselves to do it?** ¿cómo llegaron a hacerlo?; **I can't b. myself to do it** no puedo resignarme a hacerlo; **she can't b. herself to believe it** no le cabe en la cabeza (**f**) *(lead)* llevar, conducir; **the path brings you to a wood** el camino lleva a un bosque; **this now brings us to the question of inflation** esto nos conduce a hablar de la inflación (**g**) *Jur* **to b. an action against** acusar; **to b. a complaint** hacer una reclamación; **to b. evidence against** presentar pruebas contra (**h**) *(sell for)* vender; **this old car will b. about £50** este coche viejo se venderá por unas £50

bring about *vt* causar, provocar, ocasionar; **to b. about a change** efectuar un cambio

bring along *vt* traer

bring back *vt* (**a**) *(return)* devolver (**b**) *(reintroduce)* volver a introducir; **they are trying to b. back the mini-skirt** quieren poner de moda la minifalda otra vez (**c**) *(make one remember)* traerle a la memoria; **it brings back my school days** me recuerda los días del colegio

bring down *vt* (**a**) *(from upstairs)* bajar (algo); **b. down the trunk from the attic** baja el baúl del desván (**b**) *(destroy)* derribar; **to b. down a government/a dictator** derribar un gobierno/un dictador; *Theat* **to b. the house down** hacer que el teatro se te venga abajo con los aplausos (**c**) *(reduce)* rebajar; **to b. down prices** hacer bajar los precios

bring forward *vt* (**a**) *(arrange to happen earlier)* adelantar (**b**) *(present)* presentar; **she brought forward some good ideas** presentó algunas ideas buenas (**c**) *Fin (in accounts)* pasar a otra cuenta; **brought forward** suma y sigue

bring in *vt* (**a**) *(yield)* dar; **tourism brings in £7 million a year** el turismo proporciona £7 millones cada año (**b**) *(show in)* hacer entrar (**c**) *(introduce) (a law, custom etc)* introducir; *(a fashion)* lanzar (**d**) *Agr (collect)* recoger (**e**) *Jur (verdict)* pronunciar

bring off *vt* lograr, conseguir

bring on *vt (cause an illness)* causar, provocar

bring out *vt* (**a**) *(publish)* publicar, sacar un libro (**b**) *(reveal) (error, colour)* recalcar; **that woman brings out the worst in me** esa mujer despierta lo peor que hay en mí (**c**) *(draw out)* ayudar a algn a tener confianza en sí mismo

bring round *vt* (**a**) *(revive)* hacer volver en sí (**b**) *(persuade)* convencer, persuadir; **to b. sb round to your point of view** convencer a algn, poner a algn de tu lado

bring to *vt* reanimar, hacer volver en sí

bring up *vt* (**a**) *(care for, educate)* criar, educar; **he was brought up by his grandmother** lo crió su abuela (**b**) *(raise) (a subject)* plantear (**c**) *(vomit)* devolver

brink [brɪŋk] *n (edge)* borde *m*; *Fig* **on the b. of ruin** al borde de la ruina; **on the b. of tears** a punto de llorar

brinkmanship ['brɪŋkmənʃɪp] *n Pol* política *f* de cuerda floja

briny ['braɪnɪ] *adj* (**brinier, briniest**) salado(a)

briquette [brɪ'ket] *n (of coal, peat)* briqueta *f*

brisk [brɪsk] *adj* enérgico(a); *(pace)* rápido(a); *(trade)* activo(a); *(weather)* fresco(a)

briskly ['brɪsklɪ] *adv* (**a**) *(efficiently)* enérgicamente; *(dismissively)* bruscamente (**b**) *(rapidly)* rápidamente

briskness ['brɪsknɪs] *n* energía *f*; *(of pace)* ligereza *f*; *(of trade)* actividad *f*

bristle ['brɪsl] **1** *n (hair)* cerda *f*
2 *vi* (**a**) *(animal's fur)* erizarse (**b**) *(show anger)* enfurecer (**at** -); **she bristled at the suggestion** mostró su enfado ante tal sugerencia

bristle with *vt (be full of)* estar lleno(a) de, erizar; **bristling with difficulties** sembrado *or* lleno de dificultades; **the street was bristling with policemen** la calle estaba llena de policía

Brit [brɪt] *n Fam* británico(a) *m,f*

Britain ['brɪtən] *n* (**Great**) **B.** Gran Bretaña

British ['brɪtɪʃ] **1** *adj* británico(a); **the B. Isles** las Islas Británicas
2 the B. *npl* los británicos

Britisher ['brɪtɪʃər] *n US* británico(a) *m,f*

Briton ['brɪtən] *n* (**a**) *Hist* britano(a) *m,f* (**b**) *(British citizen)* británico(a) *m,f*

Brittany ['brɪtənɪ] *n* Bretaña

brittle ['brɪtəl] *adj* quebradizo(a), frágil

brittleness ['brɪtəlnɪs] *n* fragilidad *f*

broach [brəʊtʃ] *vt* (**a**) *(subject)* abordar, sacar a colación (**b**) *(barrel, bottle)* abrir

broad [brɔːd] **1** *adj* (**a**) *(wide)* ancho(a); *(large)* extenso(a); **a b. smile** una sonrisa abierta; *US Sport* **b. jump** salto *m* de longitud; **she has a b. range of interests** tiene intereses muy variados; *Fig* **it's as b. as it's long** da lo mismo (**b**) *(clear)* obvio(a); **a b. hint** una indirecta inconfundible (**c**) *(daylight)* pleno(a) (**d**) *(not detailed)* general, básico(a); **a b. outline** un esquema general; **in the b. sense** en sentido amplio (**e**) *(accent)* marcado(a), cerrado(a); **in a b. Italian accent** en un marcado acento italiano
2 *n US Slang (woman)* tipa *f*, *Esp* tía *f*

broadband ['brɔːdbænd] **1** *n Tel* banda *f* ancha
2 *adj Comptr* de banda ancha

broad-brush ['brɔːd'brʌʃ] *adj* a grandes rasgos

broadcast ['brɔːdkɑːst] *Rad TV* **1** *n* emisión *f*; **live b.** retransmisión *f* en directo; **repeat b.** reposición *f*
2 *vt (pt & pp* **broadcast** *or* **broadcasted**) (**a**) *Rad TV* emitir, transmitir (**b**) *(make widely known)* propagar, difundir

broadcaster ['brɔːdkɑːstər] *n* locutor(a) *m,f*

broadcasting ['brɔːdkɑːstɪŋ] *n Rad* radiodifusión *f*; *TV* transmisión *f* □ *Rad* **b. station** emisora *f*

broaden ['brɔːdən] *vt (road)* ensanchar; **to b. one's horizons** ampliar (uno) sus horizontes; **travel broadens the mind** viajar amplía los horizontes

broadly ['brɔːdlɪ] *adv* en general, en términos generales; **b. speaking** hablando en términos generales

broad-minded [brɔːd'maɪndɪd] *adj* liberal, tolerante, de miras amplias

broad-mindedness [brɔːd'maɪndɪdnɪs] *n* tolerancia *f*, amplitud *f* de miras

broadness ['brɔːdnɪs] *n* anchura *f*

broadsheet ['brɔːdʃiːt] *n* folleto *m*

broad-shouldered [brɔːd'ʃəʊldəd] *adj* ancho(a) de espaldas

broadside ['brɔːdsaɪd] *n* (**a**) *(side of ship)* costado *m* (**b**) *(volley of shots)* andanada *f*; **to fire a b.** soltar una andanada (**c**) *(insults)* andanada *f*, reprensión *f*

brocade [brəʊ'keɪd] *n Tex* brocado *m*

broccoli ['brɒkəlɪ] *n Bot* brécol *m*, brócili *m*

brochette [brɒ'ʃet] *n Culin (skewer)* brocheta *f*, broqueta *f*, pinchito *m*

brochure ['brəʊʃər, 'brəʊʃʊər] *n* folleto *m*

brogue¹ [brəʊg] *n* zapato *m* grueso

brogue² [brəʊg] *n* acento *m* (irlandés) muy marcado

broil [brɔɪl] *vt US Culin* asar a la parrilla

broiler ['brɔɪlər] *n Culin* pollo *m*

broke [brəʊk] **1** *pt see* **break**
2 *adj Fam* **to be (flat) b.** estar sin un centavo *or Méx* sin un peso *or Esp* sin blanca

broken ['brəʊkən] **1** *pp see* **break**
2 *adj* (**a**) *(stick, cup etc)* roto(a); *(tool, machinery)* estropeado(a); *(bone)* fracturado(a); *(promise)* roto(a); *(sleep)* interrumpido(a) (**b**) *(home)* deshecho(a); *(man, woman)* destrozado(a); *(ground)* accidentado(a), desnivelado(a); **to speak b. English** chapurrear el inglés

broken-down ['brəʊkəndaʊn] *adj (car, engine)* averiado(a); *(machine)* estropeado(a)

broken-hearted [brəʊkən'hɑːtɪd] *adj Fig* con el corazón destrozado

broker ['brəʊkər] *n Fin* corredor *m*, agente *mf* de Bolsa, comisionista *mf* ❑ **insurance b.** agente *mf* de seguros

brokerage ['brəʊkərɪdʒ] *n Fin* corretaje *m*

brolly ['brɒlɪ] *n Br Fam* paraguas *m inv*

bromide ['brəʊmaɪd] *n Chem* bromuro *m*; *Fig Fml* **please do not come out with those old bromides** no me vengan con las mismas historias de siempre

bromine ['brəʊmiːn] *n Chem* bromo *m*

bronchial ['brɒŋkɪəl] *adj Anat* bronquial; **b. tubes** bronquios *mpl*

bronchitic [brɒŋ'kɪtɪk] *adj Med* bronquítico(a)

bronchitis [brɒŋ'kaɪtɪs] *n Med* bronquitis *f*

bronze [brɒnz] **1** *n* bronce *m* ❑ **B. Age** Edad *f* de Bronce
2 *adj* (**a**) *(material)* de bronce (**b**) *(colour)* bronceado(a)

bronzed [brɒnzd] *adj (suntanned)* bronceado(a)

brooch [brəʊtʃ] *n* broche *m*, alfiler *m*

brood [bruːd] **1** *n (birds)* cría *f*, nidada *f*; *Hum (children)* prole *m*
2 *vi (hen)* empollar; *Fig (ponder)* rumiar; **dark clouds were brooding over the city** oscuras nubes se cernían sobre la ciudad; *Fig* **to b. over a problem** darle vueltas a un problema

broody ['bruːdɪ] *adj* (**broodier, broodiest**) (**a**) *(hen)* clueca; *Br Fam (women)* con ganas de tener hijos (**b**) *(pensive)* pensativo(a) (**c**) *(moody)* melancólico(a)

brook¹ [brʊk] *n* arroyo *m*

brook² [brʊk] *vt (usu in negative)* soportar, aguantar; **she will b. no interference** no tolerará ni la más mínima ingerencia

broom [bruːm] *n* (**a**) *(sweeping-brush)* escoba *f*; *Fig* **a new b.** una persona con nuevas ideas (**b**) *Bot* retama *f*, hiniesta *f*

broomstick ['bruːmstɪk] *n* palo *m* de escoba

Bros. *Com (abbr* **Brothers**) Hermanos *mpl*, Hnos.

broth [brɒθ] *n Culin* caldo *m*

brothel ['brɒθəl] *n* burdel *m*

brother ['brʌðər] *n* (**a**) *(family member)* hermano *m*; **brothers and sisters** hermanos; **older b.** hermano mayor; **younger b.** hermano menor (**b**) *(colleague)* colega *m*, compañero *m*; *(comrade)* camarada *f* (**c**) *Rel* hermano *m* (**d**) *US Fam (fellow black male)* hermano *m*

brotherhood ['brʌðəhʊd] *n* (**a**) *(condition of brother)* fraternidad *f*, hermandad *f* (**b**) *(association)* gremio *m*; *Rel* cofradía *f*, hermandad *f*

brother-in-law ['brʌðərɪnlɔː] *n (pl* **brothers-in-law**) cuñado *m*, hermano *m* político

brotherly ['brʌðəlɪ] *adj* fraternal, fraterno(a); **b. love** amor fraternal

brought [brɔːt] *pt & pp see* **bring**

brow [braʊ] *n* (**a**) *(forehead)* frente *f* (**b**) *(eyebrow)* ceja *f* (**c**) *(of hill)* cima *f*, cumbre *f*

browbeat ['braʊbiːt] *vt (pt* **browbeat**; *pp* **browbeaten**) intimidar; **to b. sb into doing sth** obligar a algn a hacer algo

brown [braʊn] **1** *adj* marrón, *Am* café; *(hair, eyes)* castaño(a); *(skin) (tanned)* bronceado(a); *(natural)* moreno(a); **as b. as a berry** muy moreno ❑ **b. bread** pan *m* integral; *Com* **b. goods** equipamiento *m* audiovisual; **b. paper** papel *m* de estraza; **b. sugar** azúcar *m & f* moreno(a)
2 *n* marrón *m*, *Am* color *m* café; *(hair, eyes)* castaño *m*
3 *vt* (**a**) *Culin* dorar (**b**) *(tan)* broncear, poner moreno

browned-off [braʊnd'ɒf] *adj Br Fam* estar hasta las narices *or* hasta la coronilla (**with** de)

Brownie ['braʊnɪ] *n (in Guide Movement)* niña *f* exploradora

brownie ['braʊnɪ] *n US Culin* bizcocho *m* de chocolate con nueces

brownish ['braʊnɪʃ] *adj* pardusco(a)

brown-nose ['braʊnnəʊz] *vt Vulg* lamer el culo a

brownout ['braʊnaʊt] *n US* apagón *m* parcial

browse [braʊz] **1** *vi* (**a**) *(animal) (grass)* pacer; *(leaves)* ramonear (**b**) *(person in shop)* mirar; *(through book, magazine)* hojear; **I spend hours browsing in bookshops** me paso horas en las librerías hojeando libros
2 *vt Comptr* **to b. the Web** navegar por la Web
3 *n* ojeada *f*; **to have a b.** dar un vistazo *or* una ojeada (**in** a)

browser ['braʊzər] *n Comptr* navegador *m*

bruise [bruːz] **1** *n* morado *m*, contusión *f*, magulladura *f*, cardenal *m*; **I've got a b.** me ha salido un morado
2 *vt (body)* contusionar, magullar; *(fruit)* estropear, machucar; *Fig (feelings)* herir; **I feel bruised and upset by his accusation** me siento herido y afectado por su acusación
3 *vi (body)* magullarse; *(fruit)* estropearse

bruiser ['bruːzər] *n Fam* matón *m*

bruising ['bruːzɪŋ] **1** *n (bruises)* moratones *mpl*, moraduras *fpl*
2 *adj (encounter, impact)* duro(a), violento(a)

brunch [brʌntʃ] *n* desayuno-comida *m*, *RP* brunch *m*

Brunei [bruːˈnaɪ] *n* Brunei

brunette [bruːˈnet] *adj & n (woman)* morena *(f)*

brunt [brʌnt] *n* lo peor; **to bear** *or* **take the b.** llevar el peso, aguantar: **we bore the b. of the expense** llevamos la mayor parte del gasto

brush¹ [brʌʃ] **1** *n* (**a**) *(for hair, teeth, clothes)* cepillo *m*; *Art* pincel *m*; *(for house-painting)* brocha *f* ❑ **scrubbing b.** cepillo *m* de fregar; **shaving b.** brocha *f* de afeitar (**b**) *(act of brushing)* cepillado *m* (**c**) *Fig* **to have a b. with the law** tener un roce con la policía
2 *vt* (**a**) *(clean)* cepillar; *(floor)* barrer; **to b. one's hair** peinarse; **to b. one's teeth** limpiarse los dientes (**b**) *(touch lightly)* rozar; **her hair brushed his cheek** su pelo rozó su mejilla
3 *vi* rozar al pasar (**against** -)

brush aside *vt* dejar de lado

brush off *vt* no hacer caso a, *Esp* pasar de

brush up *vt* mejorar, revisar; **to b. up one's French** volver a estudiar francés

brush² [brʌʃ] *n (undergrowth)* broza *f*, maleza *f*

brushed [brʌʃt] *adj (cotton, nylon)* afelpado(a)

brush-off ['brʌʃɒf] *n Fam* **to give sb the b.-o.** mandar a algn a paseo

brushwood ['brʌʃwʊd] *n* maleza *f*

brushwork ['brʌʃwɜːk] *n Art* pincelada *f*, técnica *f* del pincel

brusque [bruːsk, brʊsk] *adj (person)* brusco(a); *(words)* áspero(a)

brusquely ['bruːsklɪ] *adv* bruscamente

brusqueness ['bruːsknɪs, 'brʊsknɪs] *n* brusquedad *f*

Brussels ['brʌsəlz] *n* Bruselas; **B. sprouts** coles *fpl* de Bruselas

brutal ['bruːtəl] *adj* brutal, cruel; *Fig* **the b. truth** la cruel verdad

brutality [bruːˈtælɪtɪ] *n* brutalidad *f*; *(behaviour)* crueldad *f*

brutalize ['bruːtəlaɪz] *vt (make cruel or insensitive)* embrutecer; *(ill-treat)* tratar con brutalidad

brutally ['bruːtəlɪ] *adv* brutalmente

brute [bruːt] **1** *adj* bruto(a), brutal; **b. force** fuerza bruta
   2 *n (animal)* bruto *m*, bestia *mf*; *(person)* bestia *f*; *Fam* **a b. of a job** un trabajo de locos

brutish ['bruːtɪʃ] *adj* **(a)** *(savage)* bestial **(b)** *(rough)* brutal **(c)** *(stupid)* bruto(a)

BSc [biːesˈsiː], *US* **BS** [biːˈes] *n (abbr* **Bachelor of Science)** Licenciado(a) *m,f* en Ciencias

BSE [biːesˈiː] *n (abbr* **bovine spongiform encephalopathy)** encefalopatía *f* espongiforme bovina *(enfermedad de las vacas locas)*

BST [biːesˈtiː] *n Br (abbr* **British Summer Time)** hora *f* británica de verano

BT [biːˈtiː] *n (abbr* **British Telecom)** Telecomunicaciones *fpl* británicas

Bt *(abbr* **Baronet)** baronet *m*

BTU [biːtiːˈjuː] *n (abbr* **British Thermal Unit)** unidad *f* calorífica británica, BTU *f*

bubble ['bʌbəl] **1** *n* burbuja *f* ❑ **b. bath** espuma *f* de baño; **b. gum** chicle *m*; *Comptr* **b. jet (printer)** impresora *f* de inyección; *Com* **b. pack** blíster *m*; **soap b.** pompa *f* de jabón
   2 *vi* burbujear; *Culin* borbotear; *Fig* **to b. over with happiness** rebosar de alegría

bubble-and-squeak [bʌbələnˈskwiːk] *n Br Culin* = guiso de col, patatas y carne

bubbly ['bʌblɪ] **1** *adj* **(bubblier, bubbliest)** efervescente, con burbujas; **she has a b. personality** tiene una personalidad muy vivaz
   2 *n Fam* champán *m*, cava *m*

bubonic [bjuːˈbɒnɪk] *adj Med* bubónico(a) ❑ **b. plague** peste *f* bubónica

buccaneer [bʌkəˈnɪər] *n* bucanero *m*

Bucharest [buːkəˈrest] *n* Bucarest

buck[1] [bʌk] **1** *n* **(a)** *Zool (male of species)* macho *m*; *(male deer)* ciervo *m*; *(male goat)* macho *m* cabrío; *Fam* **to pass the b. to sb** echarle el muerto a algn **(b)** *(in gymnastics)* potro *m* **(c)** *(young man)* galán *m*
   2 *vi (horse)* corcovear
   3 *vt Fam (avoid)* esquivar

buck up 1 *vt Fam* **b. your ideas up, laddie!** ¡espabílate, chico!
   2 *vi (cheer up)* animarse

buck[2] [bʌk] *n US Austral Fam* dólar *m*; **to make a fast** *or* a **quick b.** hacer dinero rápido

bucket ['bʌkɪt] **1** *n* balde *m*, *Esp* cubo *m*; **a b. of water** un balde *or Esp* cubo de agua; *Fam* **to kick the b.** estirar la pata, guiñarla; *Br Fam* **it rained buckets** llovía a cántaros *or*, *RP* a baldes; *Fam* **she cried buckets** lloraba como una Magdalena ❑ *Aut* **b. seat** asiento *m* envolvente; *Br* **b. shop** *(for air tickets)* = agencia de viajes que vende billetes de avión a bajo precio
   2 *vi Fam (rain)* llover a cántaros **(down** -); **it's been bucketing down all day** ha llovido a cántaros *or RP* a baldes todo el día

bucketful ['bʌkɪtfʊl] *n* balde *m or Esp* cubo *m*; **a b. of water** un cubo lleno de agua

buckle ['bʌkəl] **1** *n (on belt, shoe)* hebilla *f*
   2 *vt* abrochar con hebilla
   3 *vi* **(a)** *(wall, metal)* combarse, torcerse **(b)** *(knees)* doblarse

buckle down *vi Fam* dedicarse **(to** a), concentrarse **(to** en); **to b. down to work** ponerse a trabajar en serio

buckshee [bʌkˈʃiː] *Br Fam* **1** *adj* gratuito(a)
   2 *adv* gratis

buckshot ['bʌkʃɒt] *n* perdigón *m*, posta *f*

buckskin ['bʌkskɪn] *n* ante *m*

bucktooth [bʌkˈtuːθ] *n (pl* **buckteeth** ['bʌktiːθ]) diente *m* de conejo

bucktoothed [bʌkˈtuːθt] *adj* con dientes de conejo

buckwheat ['bʌkwiːt] *n Bot* alforfón *m*

bucolic [bjuːˈkɒlɪk] *adj* bucólico(a)

bud [bʌd] **1** *n Bot (shoot)* brote *m*; *(flower)* capullo *m*
   2 *vi Bot* brotar; *Fig* florecer

Budapest [bjuːdəˈpest] *n* Budapest

Buddha ['bʊdə] *n Rel* Buda *m*

Buddhism ['bʊdɪzəm] *n Rel* budismo *m*

Buddhist ['bʊdɪst] *adj & n Rel* budista *(mf)*

budding ['bʌdɪŋ] *adj Fam* en ciernes; **a b. gymnast** una gymnasta que promete

buddy ['bʌdɪ] *n US Fam Esp* colega *mf*, *Am* compadre, *Am* hermano(a), *Méx* cuate

budge [bʌdʒ] *vi* **(a)** *(move)* moverse; **this screw won't b.** este tornillo no se mueve **(b)** *(yield)* ceder; **she won't b.** no cederá

budgerigar ['bʌdʒərɪgɑːr] *n Orn* periquito *m*

budget ['bʌdʒɪt] **1** *n* presupuesto *m*; *Pol* **the B.** el presupuesto estatal; **b. deficit/surplus** déficit *m*/superávit *m* presupuestario ❑ **b. account** cuenta *f* presupuestaria
   2 *vi* hacer un presupuesto **(for** para)

budgetary ['bʌdʒətərɪ] *adj* presupuestario(a); **b. control** control presupuestario

budgie ['bʌdʒɪ] *n Br Fam see* **budgerigar**

Buenos Aires ['bwenəˈsaɪrɪz] *n* Buenos Aires

buff[1] [bʌf] **1** *n* **(a)** *(leather)* piel *f* de búfalo *or* de ante; *Fam* **in the b.** en cueros **(b)** *(colour)* amarillo *m*, color *m* de ante
   2 *adj* amarillo(a), de color de ante
   3 *vt* dar brillo

buff[2] [bʌf] *n Fam (enthusiast)* aficionado(a) *m,f*, entusiasta *mf* ❑ **film b.** cinéfilo(a) *m,f*

buffalo ['bʌfələʊ] *n (pl* **buffaloes** *or* **buffalo)** *Zool* búfalo *m*

buffer[1] ['bʌfər] **1** *n* **(a)** *(device)* amortiguador *m*; *Rail* tope *m*; *US Aut* parachoques *m inv*, *Méx* defensas *fpl*, *RP* paragolpes *m inv* ❑ *Pol* **b. state** estado *m* tapón; **b. zone** zona *f* intermedia **(b)** *Comptr* memoria *f* intermedia **(c)** *Chem* regulador *m*
   2 *vt (insulate from shock)* amortiguar

buffer[2] ['bʌfər] *n Br Fam* **old b.** viejo *m* chocho

buffet[1] ['bʊfeɪ] *n* **(a)** *(snack bar)* bar *m*; *(at railway station)* cantina *f* ❑ *Rail* **b. car** coche *m* restaurante **(b)** *(meal)* bufé *m*; **b. lunch** (almuerzo *m* tipo) bufé *m* **(c)** *(sideboard)* aparador *m*, cristalera *f*

buffet² ['bʌfɪt] **1** vt (hit) golpear; **the ship was buffeted by the waves** las olas golpeaban el barco
2 n (with fist) golpe m; (with hand) puñetazo m

buffeting ['bʌfɪtɪŋ] n **to take a b.** (ship) ser zarandeado(a); Fig (person) recibir muchos golpes

buffoon [bə'fuːn] n bufón m, payaso m

buffoonery [bə'fuːnərɪ] n payasada f, payasadas fpl

bug [bʌg] **1** n (a) (biting insect) bicho m (que pica); US (any insect) bicho m, insecto m (b) Fam (microbe) microbio m □ **the flu b.** el virus de la gripe (c) (hidden microphone) micrófono m oculto (d) Fam (enthusiasm) afición f; **he's caught the photography b.** le ha dado por la fotografía (e) Comptr error m
2 vt (pt & pp **bugged**) Fam (a) (in spying) **to b. a room** ocultar micrófonos en una habitación; Tel **to b. a telephone** intervenir or pinchar un teléfono (b) (annoy) fastidiar, molestar; **what's bugging her?** ¿qué mosca la ha picado?, ¿qué le pasa?

bugbear ['bʌgbeər] n tormento m, pesadilla f

bug-eyed ['bʌgeɪd] adj con ojos saltones

bug-free [bʌg'friː] adj Comptr sin errores

bugger ['bʌgər] **1** n Slang (a) Offens (person) cabrón(ona) m,f; **to play silly buggers** Esp hacer el gilipollas, hacerse Méx el pendejo or RP el pavo; Hum **you lucky b.!** ¡menuda suerte tienes, macho! (b) Br (unpleasant thing) **a b. of a job** una putada de trabajo
2 interj Slang Offens ¡joder!; **b. it!** ¡joder!, ¡mierda!
3 vt sodomizar

bugger about Br Vulg **1** vi Esp hacer el gilipollas, Am pendejear
2 vt hacer la puñeta; **they really buggered him about** se las hicieron pasar canutas

bugger off vi Br Slang Offens abrirse, Esp RP pirarse; **b. off!** ¡vete a la mierda!

bugger up vt Br Slang joder, jorobar; **the strike really buggered up our holiday** la huelga nos jodió las vacaciones

buggery ['bʌgərɪ] n sodomía f

bugging device ['bʌgɪŋdɪ'vaɪs] n (in room) micrófono m oculto; (in telephone line) aparato m de escucha telefónica

buggy ['bʌgɪ] n (a) (carriage) calesa f (b) US (pram) cochecito m (de niño) (c) Br (pushchair) sillita f (de niño)

bugle ['bjuːgəl] n Mus bugle m

bugler ['bjuːglər] n corneta m, clarín m

bug-ridden ['bʌgrɪdən] adj lleno(a) de bichos

build [bɪld] **1** vt (pt & pp **built**) construir; (nest) hacer; **English-built** de fabricación inglesa; Fig **to b. a society** fundar una sociedad
2 n (physique) tipo m, constitución f, físico m

build on vt (a) (add) añadir (b) (use as foundation) **she built on their achievements** siguió avanzando a partir de sus logros

build up 1 vt (a) (cover with buildings) urbanizar (b) (accumulate) acumular; **to b. up a collection** hacer una colección; **to b. up a reputation** labrarse una buena reputación
2 vi (traffic) aumentar

builder ['bɪldər] n constructor(a) m,f; (contractor) contratista mf

building ['bɪldɪŋ] n edificio m, construcción f □ **b. site** solar m; (under construction) obra f, Br **b. society** sociedad f hipotecaria

build-up ['bɪldʌp] n (a) (accumulation) aumento m; (gas) acumulación f, Mil (troops) concentración f (b) (publicity) propaganda f

built [bɪlt] pt & pp see **build**

built-in [bɪlt'ɪn] adj (a) Carp empotrado(a); **b.-in cupboard** armario empotrado (b) (incorporated) incorporado(a); **this system has b. safeguards** este sistema lleva medidas de seguridad incorporadas

built-up [bɪlt'ʌp] adj urbanizado(a); **a b.-up area** una zona urbanizada

bulb [bʌlb] n (a) Bot bulbo m (b) Elec (lightbulb) Esp bombilla f, Andes Méx foco m, CAm Carib bombillo m, RP lamparita f

bulbous ['bʌlbəs] adj bulboso(a)

Bulgaria [bʌl'geərɪə] n Bulgaria

Bulgarian [bʌl'geərɪən] **1** adj búlgaro(a)
2 n (a) (person) búlgaro m,f (b) (language) búlgaro m

bulge [bʌldʒ] **1** n (a) (lump, swelling) bulto m, abultamiento m (b) (increase) aumento m repentino; **the population b.** el rápido aumento de población
2 vi (swell) hincharse; (be full) estar repleto(a); **his pockets were bulging with sweets** tenía los bolsillos llenos de caramelos

bulging ['bʌldʒɪŋ] adj abultado(a); **b. eyes** ojos saltones or desorbitados

bulimia [buː'lɪmɪə] n Med bulimia f

bulk [bʌlk] **1** n (a) (mass) masa f, volumen m; Com (goods) **in b.** a granel, suelto(a), al por mayor; **to buy in b.** comprar algo en grandes cantidades or al por mayor; **b. mail** envío m (postal) masivo; **b. purchase** compra f al por mayor (b) (greater part) mayor parte f, mayoría f; **the b. of the people stayed in their seats** la mayoría de la gente permaneció en sus asientos
2 vi **to b. large** parecer grande

bulk-buying [bʌlk'baɪɪŋ] n Com compra f en grandes cantidades or al por mayor

bulkhead ['bʌlkhed] n Naut mamparo m

bulkiness ['bʌlkɪnɪs] n volumen m, magnitud f

bulky ['bʌlkɪ] adj (bulkier, bulkiest) (a) (large) voluminoso(a), pesado(a) (b) (difficult to handle) de difícil manejo

bull¹ [bʊl] n (a) Zool toro m; Fig **to take the b. by the horns** agarrar or Esp coger el toro por los cuernos; **like a b. in a china shop** como una elefante en una cristalería □ **b. elephant** elefante m macho (b) (speculator) Fin alcista mf; Fin **b. market** mercado m al alza (c) esp US Slang (rubbish) tonterías fpl; **it's a load of b.** no son más que tonterías

bull² [bʊl] n Rel (papal announcement) bula f

bulldog ['bʊldɒg] n Zool buldog m □ Br Com **b. clip** pinza f sujetapapeles

bulldoze ['bʊldəʊz] vt (land) nivelar; (building) derribar; Fam **to b. sb into doing sth** forzar a algn a hacer algo; **to b. one's way through a crowd** abrirse paso a codazos entre una muchedumbre

bulldozer ['bʊldəʊzər] n bulldozer m

bullet ['bʊlɪt] n (a) (for gun) bala f; **plastic b.** bala de plástico □ **b. hole** agujero m de bala; **b. wound** balazo m (b) Comptr & Typ topo m

bulletin ['bʊlɪtɪn] n boletín m, comunicado m □ Rad TV **news b.** (on radio) boletín m de noticias; (on television) telediario m; US & Comptr **b. board** tablón m de anuncios

bullet-proof ['bʊlɪtpruːf] adj a prueba de balas; **b.-p. vest** chaleco m antibalas

bullfight ['bʊlfaɪt] n corrida f de toros

bullfighter ['bʊlfaɪtər] n torero(a) m,f

bullfighting ['bʊlfaɪtɪŋ] n los toros; (art) tauromaquia f; **he loves b.** le encantan los toros

bullfinch ['bʊlfɪntʃ] n Orn camachuelo m común

bullfrog ['bʊlfrɒg] n Zool rana f toro

bullion ['bʊljən] n (gold, silver) lingote m

bullish ['bʊlɪʃ] *adj Fin (market)* en alza
bullock ['bʊlək] *n Zool* buey *m*
bullring ['bʊlrɪŋ] *n* plaza *f* de toros
bullrush ['bʊlrʌʃ] *n US (soft rush)* junco *m*
bull's-eye ['bʊlzaɪ] *n (of target)* centro *m* del blanco; **to score a b.-e.** dar en el blanco
bullshit ['bʊlʃɪt] *Vulg* **1** *n Esp* gilipolleces *fpl, Am* pendejadas *fpl, RP* boludeces *fpl*
 2 *vi* decir *Esp* gilipolleces *or Am* pendejadas *or RP* boludeces
bully ['bʊlɪ] **1** *n* matón(ona) *m,f; (at school) Esp* abusón(ona) *m,f, Am* abusador(a) *m,f*
 2 *vt (pt & pp* **bullied)** *(terrorize)* intimidar; *(bulldoze)* tiranizar
 3 *interj Iron* **b. for you!** ¡bravo!, ¡a mí qué!
bully-boy ['bʊlɪbɔɪ] *n* matón *m*; **b.-b. tactics** tácticas *fpl* de intimidación
bullying ['bʊlɪɪŋ] *n* intimidación *f*
bully-off [bʊlɪ'ɒf] *n Sport (in hockey)* saque *m*
bulrush ['bʊlrʌʃ] *n Br (reed mace)* anea *f*, espadaña *f*
bulwark ['bʊlwək] *n also Fig* bastión *m*
bum[1] [bʌm] *n Br Fam (bottom)* trasero *m*, culo *m, Am* cola *f*
bum[2] [bʌm] **1** *n* **(a)** *US Fam (tramp)* vagabundo *m* **(b)** *Fam (idler, good-for-nothing)* holgazán(ana) *m,f*, vago(a) *m,f*
 2 *adj Fam (poor quality)* malo(a), *Esp* cutre, *RP* berreta; *(useless)* inútil; *(damaged)* dañado(a), estropeado(a)
 3 *vi (pt & pp* **bummed)** *Fam* gorrear; **he bummed a pencil off me** me gorreó un lápiz
bum around *vi Fam* vagabundear, vaguear
bumble ['bʌmbəl] *vi* **(a)** *(move)* andar a tropezones **(b)** *(speak)* murmurar, refunfuñar
bumblebee ['bʌmbəlbiː] *n Ent* abejorro *m*
bumbling ['bʌmblɪŋ] *adj* torpe
bumf [bʌmf] *n Br Fam see* **bumph**
bummer ['bʌmər] *n Fam (annoying thing)* lata *f*, *RP* emboie *m, Ven* lava *f*; **what a b.!** ¡qué lata!
bump [bʌmp] **1** *n* **(a)** *(swelling)* chichón *m*; *(lump)* abolladura *f*, bollo *m*; *(on road etc)* bache *m* **(b)** *(blow)* choque *m*, golpe *m* **(c)** *(jolt)* sacudida *f*
 2 *vt* golpear; **to b. one's head** darse un golpe en la cabeza; **to b. one's head against the door** dar con la cabeza contra la puerta
 3 *vi* chocar, darse un golpe **(into** contra)
bump into *vt (meet)* tropezar con, encontrarse a; **fancy bumping into you here!** ¡qué casualidad encontrarte aquí!
bump off *vt Slang* liquidar, matar; **she bumped off her husband and ran off with the money** mató a su marido y escapó con el dinero
bump up *vt Fam* aumentar
bumper ['bʌmpər] **1** *adj* abundante; **a b. crop** una cosecha abundante; *Br* **b. issue** número *m* especial
 2 *n Br Aut* parachoques *m inv, Méx* defensas *fpl, RP* paragolpes *m inv*; **b. car** *(at fairground)* auto *m or* coche *m* de choque, *Méx* carrito *m* chocón, *RP* autito *m* chocador; **b. sticker** adhesivo *m* para parachoques *or Méx* defensas *fpl or RP* paragolpes *m inv*
bumph [bʌmf] *n Br Fam* papelotes *m*
bumpkin ['bʌmpkɪn] *n* palurdo(a) *m,f, Esp* paleto(a) *m,f*
bump-start ['bʌmpstɑːt] *vt* **to b.-s. a car** arrancar un coche empujando
bumptious ['bʌmpʃəs] *adj* presuntuoso(a), engreído(a), creído(a)
bumpy ['bʌmpɪ] *adj* **(bumpier, bumpiest)** *(road)* lleno(a) de baches; *(journey, flight)* muy zarandeado(a) *or* sacudido(a)

bun [bʌn] *n* **(a)** *Culin (bread)* panecillo *m*; *(sweet)* bollo *m*; *(small cake)* magdalena *f, Fig Slang* **she's got a b. in the oven** esta preñada **(b)** *(hair)* moño *m*
bunch [bʌntʃ] **1** *n (of herbs, keys)* manojo *m*; *(of flowers)* ramo *m*, ramillete *m*; *(of grapes)* racimo *m*; *(of people)* grupo *m*; *(gang)* pandilla *f*; **the best of a bad b.** el único del grupo que se salva
 2 *vi* juntarse, agruparse **(together** -)
bundle ['bʌndəl] **1** *n* **(of clothes)** bulto *m*, fardo *m*; *(of papers)* fajo *m*; *(of wood)* haz *m*; *Fam* **to be a b. of nerves** ser un manojo de nervios
 2 *vt* **(a)** *(make a bundle)* liar, atar; **to b. up clothes** meter ropa en un hatillo **(b)** *(push)* empujar; **the police bundled the thief into the car** la policía obligó al ladrón a meterse en el coche **(c)** *Comptr* **it comes bundled with over $2,000 worth of software** viene acompañado de software por valor de mas de 2.000 dólares
bundle off *vi* despachar, mandar; **he was bundled off to stay with friends** se lo sacaron de encima mandándolo a casa de unos amigos
bung [bʌŋ] **1** *n* **(a)** *(of barrel)* tapón *m* **(b)** *Br Fam (bribe)* soborno *m, Andes RP* coima *f, CAm Méx* mordida *f*
 2 *vt* **(a)** *Fam (throw)* echar, *Am* botar; **b. it there** échalo *or Am* bótalo ahí **(b)** *Fam (put)* meter, poner; **b. it here** ponlo aquí
bung up *vt Fam* atascar
bungalow ['bʌŋɡələʊ] *n* chalet *m*, chalé *m*
bunged up ['bʌŋɡdʌp] *adj Fam (pipe)* atascado(a); *(nose)* tapado(a); *(person)* acatarrado(a)
bungee jumping ['bʌndʒiː'dʒʌmpɪŋ] *n* puenting *m*
bunghole ['bʌŋhəʊl] *n* agujero *m* de barril
bungle ['bʌŋɡəl] *vt* chapucear, chafallar
bungler ['bʌŋɡlər] *n* chapucero(a) *m,f*
bungling ['bʌŋɡlɪŋ] **1** *adj* chapucero(a); *(ineptitude)* torpe
 2 *n* torpeza *f*
bunion ['bʌnjən] *n* juanete *m*
bunk[1] [bʌŋk] *n (bed)* litera *f*
bunk[2] [bʌŋk] *n Slang (nonsense)* tonterías *fpl*
bunk[3] [bʌŋk] *n Br Fam* **to do a b.** *Esp* darse el piro, *Esp* pirarse, *Méx* rajarse, *RP* tomarse el buque
bunk off *vi Slang (run away)* largarse, abrirse, pirarse; *(play truant)* hacer las campañas
bunker ['bʌŋkər] *n* **(a)** *(coal)* carbonera **(b)** *Mil* búnker *m*, refugio *m* subterráneo **(c)** *Br Golf* bunker *m*, trampa *f* de arena
bunkum ['bʌŋkəm] *n (nonsense)* tonterías *fpl*
bunny ['bʌnɪ] *n Fam (baby talk)* **b. (rabbit)** conejito *m* ◻ **b. girl** camarera *f* vestida de conejito
Bunsen burner ['bʌnsən'bɜːnər] *n* mechero *m* Bunsen
bunting[1] ['bʌntɪŋ] *n (material)* lanilla *f*; *(flags)* banderas *fpl; Naut* empavesada *f*
bunting[2] ['bʌntɪŋ] *n Orn* escribano *m* ◻ **corn b.** escribano *m* triguero; **reed b.** escribano *m* palustre
buoy [bɔɪ] *n Naut* boya *f*
buoy up *vt* alentar, animar; **he did his best to b. her up** hizo todo lo posible para animarla
buoyancy ['bɔɪənsɪ] *n* **(a)** *(of object)* flotabilidad *f* **(b)** *Fin (of market, prices)* tendencia *f* alcista **(c)** *(optimism)* optimismo *m*
buoyant ['bɔɪənt] *adj* **(a)** *(object)* flotante, boyante **(b)** *Fin (economy)* con tendencia alcista **(c)** *(optimistic)* optimista
burble ['bɜːbəl] *vi* **(a)** *(stream)* murmurar; *(baby)* hacer gorgoritos, balbucear **(b)** *(talk quickly and unclearly)* farfullar, mascullar; **she burbled her thanks and left** farfulló su agradecimiento y se fue

burden ['bɜːdən] **1** n (**a**) *(load)* carga f; **beast of b.** bestia f de carga; *Jur* **b. of proof** carga de la prueba (**b**) *Fig* carga f, peso m; **to be a b. to sb** ser una carga para algn
2 vt cargar (**with** con)

burdensome ['bɜːdənsəm] adj Fml oneroso(a)

bureau ['bjʊərəʊ] n *(pl* **bureaus** *or* **bureaux**) (**a**) Br *(desk)* escritorio m, mesa f (**b**) *(office)* agencia f, oficina f (**c**) US *(chest of drawers)* cómoda f (**d**) US Pol departamento m del Estado, agencia f del gobierno

bureaucracy [bjʊə'rɒkrəsɪ] n burocracia f
bureaucrat ['bjʊərəkræt] n burócrata mf
bureaucratic [bjʊərə'krætɪk] adj burocrático(a)

burgeon ['bɜːdʒən] vi Bot brotar, retoñar; Fig *(trade, relationship)* crecer, florecer

burger ['bɜːgər] n Fam hamburguesa f

burglar ['bɜːglər] n *(of houses and shops)* ladrón(ona) m,f ▫ **b. alarm** alarma f antirrobo

burglarize ['bɜːgləraɪz] vt US robar *(una casa o edificio)*

burglar-proof ['bɜːgləpruːf] adj a prueba de robo

burglary ['bɜːglərɪ] n robo m con allanamiento de morada

burgle ['bɜːgəl] vt robar *(una casa o un edificio)*

burgundy ['bɜːgəndɪ] adj *(colour)* (color) burdeos

burial ['berɪəl] n entierro m ▫ **b. ground** cementerio m, camposanto m

Burkina-Faso [bɜːkiːnə'fæsəʊ] n Burkina Faso

burlap ['bɜːlæp] n US Tex arpillera f

burlesque [bɜː'lesk] **1** adj burlesco(a)
2 n Lit género m burlesco

burly ['bɜːlɪ] adj (**burlier, burliest**) fornido(a), fuerte

Burma ['bɜːmə] n Birmania

Burmese [bɜː'miːz] **1** adj birmano(a)
2 n *(pl* **Burmese**) (**a**) *(person)* birmano(a) m,f (**b**) *(language)* birmano m

burn [bɜːn] **1** n quemadura f
2 vt *(pt & pp* **burnt** *or* **burned**) (**a**) *(fuel, building)* quemar; **she burnt her hand** se quemó la mano; **to be burned to death** morir carbonizado(a); Fam **to b. the midnight oil** quedarse hasta muy tarde (estudiando *or* trabajando) (**b**) Comptr *(CD-ROM)* estampar
3 vi (**a**) *(fire)* arder; *(building)* arder, quemarse; Culin quemarse (**b**) *(lamp, light)* estar encendido(a) *or* Am prendido(a) (**c**) *(sore)* escocer

burn down 1 vt *(building)* incendiar
2 vi incendiarse

burn out 1 vi (**a**) *(fire)* extinguirse (**b**) *(machines)* desgastarse, dejar de funcionar (**c**) *(people)* quemarse
2 vt Fig **you'll b. yourself out if you carry on working so hard** si trabajas así acabarás quemado

burn up 1 vt quemar energía
2 vi *(rocket etc)* consumirse completamente

burner ['bɜːnər] n quemador m; Fam Fig **to put sth on the back b.** dejar algo a un lado, aparcar algo ▫ **Bunsen b.** quemador m Bunsen

burning ['bɜːnɪŋ] **1** adj (**a**) *(on fire)* incendiado(a); *(hot)* abrasador(a) (**b**) *(passionate)* apasionado(a), ardiente; **b. desire** deseo ardiente (**c**) *(crucial, intense)* vital; **a b. question** una cuestión candente
2 n *(combustion)* combustión f; **there's a smell of b.** huele a quemado

burnish ['bɜːnɪʃ] vt *(polish)* bruñir

burn-out ['bɜːnaʊt] n (**a**) **I had a b.-o.** *(engine)* se me quemó; **what caused the b.-o.?** *(in electrical system)* ¿por qué se fundió? (**b**) Fam *(exhaustion)* agotamiento m

burnt [bɜːnt] **1** pt & pp see **burn**

2 adj Culin quemado(a); **b. almonds** almendras fpl tostadas

burnt-out [bɜːnt'aʊt] adj (**a**) *(volcano, etc)* apagado(a) (**b**) Fig *(worn-out) (person)* quemado(a); *(passion)* consumido(a)

burp [bɜːp] **1** n eructo m
2 vi eructar, regoldar
3 vt **to b. a baby** hacer eructar a un bebé

burr¹ [bɜːr] n Bot erizo m

burr² [bɜːr] n (**a**) *(humming)* zumbido m (**b**) *(pronunciation)* pronunciación f fuerte de la r; **she speaks with a West-Country b.** tiene un marcado acento del West Country

burrow ['bʌrəʊ] **1** n madriguera f; *(for rabbits)* conejera f
2 vi (**a**) *(person, animal)* excavar; Fig **to b. into an affair** escudriñar un asunto (**b**) *(search)* hurgar; **she burrowed around in the drawer looking for the other glove** removió todo el cajón buscando el otro guante

bursar ['bɜːsər] n Univ tesorero(a) m,f

bursary ['bɜːsərɪ] n Br beca f

burst [bɜːst] **1** n (**a**) *(explosion)* estallido m, explosión f; *(of tyre)* reventón m (**b**) *(sudden outbreak) (of activity, speed)* arranque m; *(of rage)* arrebato m; *(of applause)* salva f; Mil **b. of gunfire** ráfaga f de tiros; **b. of laughter** carcajada f
2 vt *(pt & pp* **burst**) *(balloon)* reventar; Fig **the river b. its banks** el río se salió de madre
3 vi (**a**) *(balloon, tyre, boil, pipe)* reventarse; *(shell)* estallar (**b**) *(dam)* romperse (**c**) *(enter suddenly)* irrumpir (**into** en)

burst into vi empezar a; **to b. into tears** echarse a llorar, deshacerse en lágrimas; **to b. into laughter** echarse a reír

burst open vi abrirse violentamente

burst out vi **to b. out laughing** soltar una carcajada; **to b. out crying** echarse *or* romper a llorar

bursting ['bɜːstɪŋ] adj estar lleno(a) a revantar; **the bar was b. with people** había un montón de gente en el bar; Fam **to be b. to do sth** reventar por hacer algo, ansiar hacer algo; **I'm b. to tell you** reviento si no te lo digo

Burundi [bə'rʊndɪ] n Burundi

Burundian [bə'rʊndɪən] adj & n burundés(esa) *(m,f)*

bury ['berɪ] vt *(pt & pp* **buried**) (**a**) *(inter)* enterrar (**b**) *(hide)* esconder, ocultar; **to be buried in thought** estar absorto en pensamientos; **to b. oneself in the country** refugiarse en el campo

bus [bʌs] **1** n *(pl* **buses**, US **busses**) (**a**) *(vehicle)* autobús m, Andes buseta f, Bol RP colectivo m, CAm Méx camión m, CAm Carib guagua f, Urug ómnibus m, Ven microbusete m ▫ **b. conductor** cobrador m, revisor m; **b. driver** conductor(a) m,f; **b. route** línea f de autobús; **b. station** estación f de autobuses, CAm Méx central f camionera; **b. stop** parada f de autobús (**b**) Comptr bus m
2 vt *(pt & pp* **bused**, US **bussed**) llevar *or* trasladar en autobús

bush [bʊʃ] n (**a**) Bot *(shrub)* arbusto m, matorral m; Fig **to beat about the b.** andarse con rodeos, andarse por las ramas (**b**) Austral **the b.** el monte ▫ Fam **b. telegraph** Esp radio f macuto, Cuba CRica Pan radio f bemba

bushed [bʊʃt] adj Fam *(exhausted)* molido(a), reventado(a)

bushel ['bʊʃəl] n *(measure)* Br = 36,35 litros, US = 35,23 litros; Fig **to hide one's light under a b.** ser muy modesto

bushman ['bʊʃmən] n *(pl* **bushmen**) bosquimán m

bushy ['bʊʃɪ] adj (**bushier, bushiest**) espeso(a), tupido(a); **b. eyebrows** cejas tupidas

business ['bɪznɪs] n (**a**) *(commerce)* negocio m, negocios mpl; **big b.** los grandes negocios; **b. is good** los negocios andan bien; **how's b.?** ¿cómo andan los negocios?; **to be away on b.** estar en viaje de negocios; **to do b. with sb**

negociar con algn; **to go into b.** dedicarse a los negocios ❏ **b. card** tarjeta *f* de visita; **b. deal** negocio *m*; **b. hours** horas *fpl* de oficina, horas *fpl* hábiles *or* laborables; **b. incubator** vivero *m* (de empresas); **b. lunch** comida *f* de trabajo; **b. management** gestión *for* administración *f* de empresas; **b. park** parque *m* empresarial; **b. plan** plan *m* económico; **b. relations** relaciones *fpl* comerciales; **b. school** escuela *f* de negocios; **b. studies** empresariales *fpl*; **b. trip** viaje *m* de negocios **(b)** *(firm)* negocio *m*, empresa *f*; **family b.** empresa familiar **(c)** *(matter)* asunto *m*, cuestión *f*; **a dreadful b.** un asunto lamentable; **I mean b.** estoy hablando en serio; **it's no b. of mine** no es asunto mío; **the b. of the day** el orden del día; **to make it one's b. to ...** encargarse de ...; **to get down to b.** ir al grano; **to go about one's b.** ocuparse de sus asuntos; **what a b.!** qué lío!; *Fam* **like nobody's b.** muy bien; *Fam* **mind your own b.** no te metas donde no te llaman

businesslike ['bɪznɪslaɪk] *adj (practical)* práctico(a), eficiente; *(methodical)* metódico(a); *(serious)* serio(a)

businessman ['bɪznɪsmən] *n (pl* **businessmen**) hombre *m* de negocios, empresario *m*

businesswoman ['bɪznɪswʊmən] *n (pl* **businesswomen** ['bɪznɪswɪmɪn]) mujer *f* de negocios, empresaria *f*

busk [bʌsk] *vi Br* cantar *or* tocar música en la calle

busker ['bʌskər] *n Br* músico(a) *m,f*, callejero(a) *or* ambulante

busman ['bʌsmən] *n Fam* **b.'s holiday** = día de fiesta en el que uno tiene que hacer el mismo trabajo que de costumbre

bust¹ [bʌst] *n* **(a)** *(of woman)* pecho *m*, busto *m* **(b)** *Art (sculpture)* busto *m*

bust² [bʌst] **1** *vt* **(a)** *Fam (damage)* estropear, *Esp* escacharrar; *(break)* destrozar **(b)** *Slang (person)* trincar; *(place)* hacer una redada en; **to b. sb for possession of drugs** pescar a algn por posesión ilegal de drogas
2 *adj* **(a)** *Fam (burst)* reventado(a); *(damaged)* estropeado(a); *(broken)* destrozado(a) **(b)** *Fam (bankrupt)* **to go b.** quebrar

bustard ['bʌstəd] *n Orn* **great b.** avutarda *f*; **little b.** sisón *m*

buster ['bʌstər] *n US Fam (term of address) Esp* tío *m*, *Esp* tronco *m*, *Méx* cuate *m*, *RP* boludo *m*; **who are you looking at, b.?** ¿tú qué miras, *Esp* tronco *or Méx* cuate *or RP* boludo?

bustle¹ ['bʌsəl] **1** *n (activity, noise)* bullicio *m*, trajín *m*
2 *vi* ir y venir **(about** -)

bustle² ['bʌsəl] *n (under skirt)* polisón *m*

bustling ['bʌslɪŋ] *adj* bullicioso(a)

bust-up ['bʌstʌp] *n* **(a)** *Br Fam (quarrel)* bronca *f*; **to have a b.-up** tener una bronca **(b)** *(of relationship)* ruptura *f*

busty ['bʌstɪ] *adj Fam* pechugona, tetona

busy ['bɪzɪ] **1** *adj* **(a)** *(person)* ocupado(a), atareado(a); *(day)* lleno(a); *(life)* ajetreado(a); *(street)* concurrido(a), bullicioso(a); **to be as b. as a bee** estar ocupadísimo; **to keep oneself b.** mantenerse ocupado **(b)** *US Tel (line)* ocupado(a); **the line is b.** (el teléfono) da ocupado, *Esp* (el teléfono) está comunicando
2 *vt (pt & pp* **busied)** ocuparse, dedicarse; **to b. oneself doing sth** ocuparse en hacer algo

busybody ['bɪzɪbɒdɪ] *n* entrometido(a) *m,f*

but [bʌt] **1** *conj* **(a)** *(in general)* pero; **b. yet** pero, a pesar de todo; **poor b. honest** pobre pero honrado; **there's no doubt b. he's guilty** no hay duda de que es culpable **(b)** *(after negative)* sino; **not two b. three** no dos sino tres; **she's not Spanish b. Portuguese** no es española sino portuguesa
2 *adv Fml (only)* no más que, sólo, solamente; **had we b. known** si lo hubiéramos sabido, de haberlo sabido; **he is b.**

a child no es más que un niño; **we can b. try** al menos podemos intentarlo
3 *prep* salvo, excepto, menos; **everyone b. her** todos menos ella; **b. for her we would have drowned** si no hubiera sido por ella, nos habríamos hogado; **he's anything b. handsome** es todo menos guapo; **the last b. one** el penúltimo

4 buts *npl* peros *mpl*; **ifs and b.** pegas *fpl*; **stop all your ifs and b.!** ¡no pongas más pegas!; **no b.** no hay peros que valgan

butane ['bjuːteɪn] *n Chem* butano *m* ❏ **b. gas** gas *m* butano

butch [bʊtʃ] *adj* **(a)** *Fam Offens (woman)* hombruno(a) **(b)** *(man) Fam* macho

butcher ['bʊtʃər] **1** *n* **(a)** carnicero(a) *m,f*; *Fig* carnicero(a); **b.'s (shop)** carnicería *f* **(b)** *butcher's Slang* mirada; **let's have a b.'s** déjame ver
2 *vt (animals)* matar; *(people)* matar, asesinar

butchery ['bʊtʃərɪ] *n* **(a)** *(work)* carnicería *f* **(b)** *(killing)* matanza *f*, carnicería *f*

butler ['bʌtlər] *n* mayordomo *m*

butt¹ [bʌt] *n* **(a)** *(end)* extremo *m*; *(of rifle)* culata *f*; *(of cigarette)* colilla *f* **(b)** *(target)* blanco *m*; **he was the b. of all the jokes** era el blanco de todas las bromas **(c)** *US Fam (bottom)* trasero *m*

butt² [bʌt] **1** *n (blow with head)* cabezazo *m*
2 *vt* **(a)** *(strike with head or horns)* topetar **(b)** *(shove)* **to b. your way somewhere** abrirte paso
▸ **butt in** *vi* entrar en la conversación

butt³ [bʌt] *n (barrel)* tonel *m*

butter ['bʌtər] **1** *n* mantequilla *f*, *RP* manteca *f*; **she looks as if b. wouldn't melt in her mouth** parece incapaz de matar una mosca, *Esp* parece como si no hubiera roto un plato en su vida ❏ **b. dish** mantequera *f*
2 *vt (bread)* untar con mantequilla *or RP* manteca; *(vegetables)* aderezar con mantequilla *or RP* manteca
▸ **butter up** *vt* dar coba a algn

buttercup ['bʌtəkʌp] *n Bot* ranúnculo *m*, botón *m* de oro

butterfingered ['bʌtəfɪŋgəd] *adj Fam* torpe, patoso(a)

butterfingers ['bʌtəfɪŋgəz] *n Fam* manazas *mf inv*

butterfly ['bʌtəflaɪ] *n* **(a)** *Ent* mariposa *f*; *Fig* **to have butterflies** tener los nervios de punta, estar muy nervioso **(b)** *Swimming* mariposa *f*

buttermilk ['bʌtəmɪlk] *n (by-product from butter making)* suero *m* de la leche; *US (curdled milk)* leche *f* cuajada *or* batida *(para beber)*

butt-naked ['bʌtneɪkɪd] *adj US Fam* en pelotas, en cueros

buttock ['bʌtək] *n* nalga *f*; **buttocks** nalgas *fpl*, trasero *m*; *(of horse)* grupa *f*

button ['bʌtən] **1** *n* **(a)** *Sew* botón *m* **(b)** *(on machine etc)* botón *m*, pulsador *m*; *Comptr (on screen)* botón *m*; **press the b.** apriete el botón **(c)** *US (badge)* chapa *f*
2 *vt* **to b. (up)** abrocharse

buttonhole ['bʌtənhəʊl] **1** *n* **(a)** *Sew* ojal *m* **(b)** *(flower)* = flor que se lleva en el ojal
2 *vt Fig (detain)* enganchar a

buttress ['bʌtrɪs] **1** *n* **(a)** *Archit* contrafuerte *m* ❏ **flying b.** arbotante *m* **(b)** *(support)* apoyo *m*, sostén *m*
2 *vt Archit* apuntalar, reforzar; *Fig* reforzar, apoyar

butty ['bʌtɪ] *n Fam (sandwich)* bocata *f*

buxom ['bʌksəm] *adj (woman) (with big breasts)* pechugona; *(robust)* macizorra, rolliza

buy [baɪ] **1** *n (purchase)* compra *f*; **a good b.** una ganga
2 *vt (pt & pp* **bought) (a)** *(purchase)* comprar; **she bought that car from a neighbour** compró ese coche a un vecino

(**b**) *(bribe)* comprar, sobornar (**c**) *Slang (believe)* tragar, aceptar, creer; **he won't b. it** no colará

buy off *vt* sobornar, comprar

buy out *vt Com* comprar la parte de

buy into *vt (company, scheme)* adquirir una parte *or* acciones de

buy up *vt* acaparar, comprar la totalidad de

buyer ['baɪər] *n* comprador(a) *m,f; Com* **it's a b.'s market** es un mercado que favorece al comprador ❏ **chief b.** jefe *m* de compras

buy-out ['baɪaʊt] *n Com* adquisición *f* (de todas las acciones)

buzz [bʌz] **1** *n* (**a**) *(of bee)* zumbido *m*; *(of conversation)* rumor *m*, runruneo *m*; *Fam* **b. word** palabra *f* de moda (**b**) *Fam (telephone call)* telefonazo *m*; dar a algn un toque *or* un telefonazo, *Méx* echar un fonazo a algn (**c**) *Slang* **skating gives me a real b.** esto de patinar me pone a cien

2 *vt Fam (telephone)* dar un toque
3 *vi (bee, room, head)* zumbar; *Br Fam* **b. off!** ¡lárgate!

buzzard ['bʌzəd] *n (hawk)* ratonero *m* común; *US (vulture)* buitre *m*

buzzer ['bʌzər] *n* zumbador *m*

buzzing ['bʌzɪŋ] *n* zumbido *m*

Bvd *US (abbr* **Boulevard)** bulevar

b & w *Phot Cin (abbr* **black and white)** b/n, blanco y negro

by [baɪ] **1** *prep* (**a**) *(indicating agent)* por; **composed by Bach** compuesto(a) por Bach; **it was built b. her father** fue construido por su padre (**b**) *(via)* por; **he left by the back door** salió por la puerta trasera (**c**) *(manner)* por; **by car** en coche; **by chance** por casualidad; **by heart** de memoria; **by oneself** solo(a); **by rail** en tren; **made by hand** hecho a mano, **you can obtain a ticket by filling in the coupon** puede conseguir una entrada llenando el cupón (**d**) *(amount)* por; **little by little** poco a poco; **they are sold by the dozen** se venden por docenas; **to be paid by the hour** cobrar por horas (**e**) *(extent)* **by far** con mucho; **he won by a foot** ganó por un pie (**f**) *(beside)* al lado de, junto a; **side by side** juntos, uno al lado del otro; **sit by me** siéntate a mi lado (**g**) *(past)* **to walk by a building** pasar por delante de un edificio (**h**) *(not later than)* para; **by now** ya; **by then** para entonces; **we have to be there by nine** tenemos que estar allí para las nueve (**i**) *(during)* de; **by day** de día; **by night** de noche (**j**) *(in an oath)* por; **by God!** ¡por Dios!; **she swears by herbal remedies** tiene una fe ciega en las hierbas medicinales (**k**) *Math* por; **to multiply six by four** multiplicar seis por cuatro (**l**)

(according to) según; **to go by the rules** actuar según las reglas (**m**) *(origin)* **English by blood** de sangre inglesa; **he had two children by his first wife** tuvo dos hijos con su primera esposa (**n**) *(rate)* **bit by bit** poco a poco; **day by day** día a día, día tras día (**o**) *(quoting something)* con, por; **what do you mean by that?** ¿qué quieres decir con eso?; **by 'Lesley' I assumed she meant Lesley Dent** supuse que por 'Lesley' quería decir Lesley Dent (**p**) *(in measurements)* por; **the room is twenty metres by ten** la habitación hace veinte metros por diez

2 *adv* (**a**) *(past)* **to go by** pasar; **she just walked by** pasó de largo (**b**) **by and by** con el tiempo

bye [baɪ] *n* (**a**) *Fam* ¡adiós!, ¡hasta luego!, *Am* ¡bye!, *Am* ¡chau! (**b**) **by the b.** por cierto, a propósito

bye-bye ['baɪbaɪ] *n Fam* ¡adiós!, ¡hasta luego!, *Am* ¡bye!, *Am* ¡chau!

by-election ['baɪɪlekʃən] *n Br Pol* = elección parcial en una sola circunscripción para cubrir un escaño dejado vacante

bygone [:qxbaɪgɒn] **1** *adj* pasado(a)
2 bygones *npl* **let b. be b.** lo pasado, pasado está *Am* lo pasado, pisado

by-law ['baɪlɔ:] *n* ley *f* municipal

byline ['baɪlaɪn] *n Press* pie *m* de autor

BYOB *(abbr* **bring your own bottle)** = en invitaciones a una fiesta o en restaurantes, siglas que invitan a llevar bebidas

bypass ['baɪpɑːs] **1** *n* (**a**) *(road)* carretera *f* de circunvalación (**b**) *Med* **b. surgery** cirugía *f* de by-pass
2 *vt* evitar; **let's b. Bristol, as we are in a hurry** como tenemos prisa no entramos en Bristol; **she bypassed the normal procedures by writing directly to the director** escribió al director desestimando el sistema usual

by-product ['baɪprɒdʌkt] *n Chem Ind* derivado *m*, subproducto *m*; *Fig* consecuencia *f*

byre [baɪər] *n Br* establo *m* para vacas

by-road ['baɪrəʊd] *n* carretera *f* secundaria

bystander ['baɪstændər] *n* espectador(a) *m,f*, mirón(ona) *m,f*

byte [baɪt] *n Comptr* byte *m*, octeto *m*

by-way ['baɪweɪ] *n* carretera *f* secundaria

byword ['baɪwɜːd] *n* (**a**) *(perfect example)* sinónimo *m*; **the film became a b. for modernity** la película se convirtió en un sinónimo de modernidad (**b**) *(common saying)* decir *m*

C

C, c [siː] *n* (**a**) *(the letter)* C, c *f* (**b**) *Mus* do *m*

C *(abbr* **Celsius** *or* **centigrade)** C

c (**a**) *(abbr* **cent(s))** céntimo(s) *m(pl)* (**b**) *(abbr* **century)** siglo *m*, s (**c**) *(abbr* **circa)** (about, approximately), hacia, h (**d**) *(abbr* **copyright)** propiedad *f* literaria, copyright *m*, c

c/a *(abbr* **current account)** cuenta *f* corriente, c/c

cab [kæb] *n US* taxi *m*; **by c.** en taxi ❑ **c. driver** taxista *mf*

cabaret ['kæbəreɪ] *n* cabaret *m*; **is there a c.?** ¿hay espectáculo?

cabbage ['kæbɪdʒ] *n* col *f*, repollo *m*, berza *f*; **red c.** (col *f*) lombarda *f* ❑ *Ent* **c. white** mariposa *f* de la col

cabbie ['kæbɪ] *n US Fam* taxista *mf*, *RP* tachero(a) *mf*

cabin ['kæbɪn] *n* (**a**) *(hut)* choza *f*, cabaña *f* (**b**) *Naut* camarote *m* ❑ **c. cruiser** yate *m* de motor (**c**) *(of lorry, plane)* cabina *f*; **c. crew** *(on plane)* personal *m* de a bordo, auxiliares *mfpl* de vuelo

cabinet ['kæbɪnɪt] *n* (**a**) *(piece of furniture)* armario *m*; *(glassfronted)* vitrina *f*; **filing c.** archivador *m*; **kitchen c.** armario de cocina (**b**) *(in government)* gabinete *m* ministerial, consejo *m* de ministros; **c. meeting** consejo *m* de ministros; **shadow c.** portavoces *mpl* de la oposición

cabinet-maker ['kæbɪnɪtmeɪkər] *n* ebanista *mf*

cable ['keɪbəl] **1** *n* (**a**) *(electrical)* cable *m* ❑ **c. car** funicular *m*; **c. TV** televisión *f* por cable (**b**) *(message)* cable *m*, cablegrama *m*
2 *vt & vi* cablegrafiar, telegrafiar

cabling ['keɪbəlɪŋ] *n* cables *mpl*

caboodle [kə'buːdəl] *n Fam* **the whole (kit and) c.** todo, *Esp* toda la pesca

caboose [kə'buːs] *n US* furgón *m* de equipajes

cacao [kə'kɑːəʊ] *n Bot* cacao *m*

cache [kæʃ] *n* (**a**) *(of drugs)* alijo *m* (**b**) *Comptr* caché *f* ❑ **c. memory** memoria *f* caché

cack-handed [kæk'hændɪd] *adj Fam* torpe, *Esp* patoso(a)

cackle ['kækəl] **1** *vi (hen)* cacarear; *(person)* carcajearse
2 *n (of hen)* cacareo *m*; *(of person)* risa *f* tonta; *Fam* **cut the c.** corta el rollo

cacophonous [kə'kɒfənəs] *adj* cacofónico(a)

cactus ['kæktəs] *n* (*pl* **cactuses** *or* **cacti** ['kæktaɪ]) *Bot* cactus *m*

CAD [kæd] *n (abbr* **computer-aided** *or* **-assisted design)** CAD *m*, diseño *m* asistido por *Esp* ordenador *or Am* computadora

cad [kæd] *n Br Fam Old-fashioned* canalla *m*

cadaver [kə'dævər] *n* cadáver *m*

cadaverous [kə'dævərəs] *adj* cadavérico(a)

CAD/CAM ['kæd'kæm] *n Comptr (abbr* **cómputer-aided** *or* **-assisted design/computer-aided manufacture)** CAD/CAM *m*

caddie ['kædɪ] *n Golf* cadi *m* ❑ **c. car, c. cart** carrito *m* de golf

caddy ['kædɪ] *n Br* = cajita lata o donde se guarda el té

cadence ['keɪdəns] *n* cadencia *f*

cadenza [kə'denzə] *n* cadencia *f*

cadet [kə'det] *n Mil* cadete *m* ❑ **c. corps** = organismo que, en algunas escuelas, enseña disciplina militar; **c. school** escuela *f* militar

cadge [kædʒ] *Fam* **1** *vt (cigarettes etc)* gorrear, *Esp Méx* gorronear, *RP* garronear; **to c. a lift from sb** conseguir que algn te lleve en coche *or CAm Méx Perú* dé aventón; **to c. money from sb** darle un sablazo a algn
2 *vi (gen)* gorronear; *(involving money)* dar un sablazo, sablear

cadger ['kædʒər] *n Br* gorrón(ona) *m,f*

cadmium ['kædmɪəm] *n Chem* cadmio *m*

caecum ['siːkəm] *n (pl* **caeca** ['siːkə]) *(intestino m)* ciego *m*

Caesarean [siː'zeərɪən] *n Med* cesárea *f*; **she had a c.** le hicieron una cesárea ❑ **C. section** operación *f* cesárea

café ['kæfeɪ] *n* cafetería *f*

cafeteria [kæfɪ'tɪərɪə] *n* cafetería *f*, autoservicio *m*

caffeine ['kæfiːn] *n* cafeína *f*; **c.-free** descafeinado(a)

caffeine-free ['kæfiːn'friː] *adj* descafeinado(a)

caftan ['kæftæn] *n see* **kaftan**

cage [keɪdʒ] **1** *n* (**a**) *(for bird etc)* jaula *f* (**b**) *Min* ascensor *m*
2 *vt* enjaular; *Fig* **to feel caged in** sentirse enjaulado(a), tener claustrofobia

cagey ['keɪdʒɪ] *adj* (**cagier, cagiest**) *Fam* reservado(a), disimulado(a)

cagoule [kə'guːl] *n Br (garment)* canguro *m*

cahoots [kə'huːts] *npl US Fam* **to be in c. (with sb)** estar conchabado(a) (con algn), *RP* estar metido(a) (con algn)

CAI [siːeɪ'aɪ] *n Comptr (abbr* **computer-aided** *or* **-assisted instruction)** enseñanza *f* asistida por *Esp* ordenador *or Am* computadora

cairn [keən] *n* (**a**) *(monument)* monumento *m* formado de piedras apiladas (**b**) *(boundary marker)* hito *m* formado por piedras

Cairo ['kaɪrəʊ] *n* (el) Cairo

cajole [kə'dʒəʊl] *vt* engatusar; **he cajoled me into lending him money** me engatusó para que le prestara dinero

cajolery [kə'dʒəʊlərɪ] *n* engatusamiento *m*

cake [keɪk] **1** *n* (**a**) *Culin* pastel *m*, *Esp* tarta *f*, *Col CSur* torta *f, Col* ponqué *m*; *(small)* pastel *m*; *Fam Fig* **it's a piece of c.** es facilísimo, está tirado *or* chupado, *RP* es un boleto; *Fam Fig* **to sell like hot cakes** venderse como rosquillas; *Prov* **you can't have your c. and eat it** no se puede estar en misa y repicando, *RP* no se puede chiflar y comer gofio ◻ **birthday c.** pastel *m* de cumpleaños; **c. shop** pastelería *f*; **fish c.** medallón *m or* croqueta *f* de pescado; **fruit c.** plum cake *m*; **sponge c.** bizcocho *m* (**b**) *(of soap)* pastilla *f*

2 *vi (mud)* endurecerse; **caked with ... cubierto(a) de ...**

CAL [kæl] *n (abbr* **computer-aided** *or* **-assisted learning**) enseñanza *f* asistida por *Esp* ordenador *or Am* computadora

cal *(abbr* **calorie(s))** caloría(s) *f(pl),* cal

calamine ['kæləmaɪn] *n* calamina *f*

calamitous [kə'læmɪtəs] *adj* calamitoso(a)

calamity [kə'læmɪtɪ] *n* calamidad *f*

calcification [kælsɪfɪ'keɪʃən] *n* calcificación *f*

calcify ['kælsɪfaɪ] **1** *vt (pt & pp* **calcified)** calcificar
2 *vi* calcificarse

calcium ['kælsɪəm] *n Chem* calcio *m*

calculate ['kælkjʊleɪt] **1** *vt* calcular; **it was calculated to upset the plans** se planeó con la intención de estropear los planes
2 *vi* contar (**on** cón)

calculated ['kælkjʊleɪtɪd] *adj* deliberado(a), premeditado(a)

calculating ['kælkjʊleɪtɪŋ] *adj* (**a**) **c. machine** calculador *m*, calculadora *f* (**b**) *Pej (person)* interesado(a)

calculation [kælkjʊ'leɪʃən] *n* cálculo *m*

calculator ['kælkjʊleɪtər] *n* calculador *m*, calculadora *f* ◻ **pocket c.** calculadora *f* de bolsillo

calculus ['kælkjʊləs] *n (a)* (*pl* **calculuses**) *Math* cálculo *m* matemático (*pl* **calculi** ['kælkjʊlaɪ]) *Med* cálculo *m*

caldron ['kɔːldrən] *n see* **cauldron**

calendar ['kælɪndər] *n* calendario *m* ◻ **c. year** año *m* natural, *Am* año *m* calendario

calf¹ [kɑːf] *n (pl* **calves)** *Zool* (**a**) *(of cattle)* becerro(a) *m,f,* ternero(a) *m,f;* **a cow in c.** una vaca preñada (**b**) *(of other animals)* cría *f*

calf² [kɑːf] *n (pl* **calves)** *Anat* pantorilla *f*

calfskin ['kɑːfskɪn] *n* piel *f* de becerro

caliber ['kælɪbər] *n US see* **calibre**

calibrate ['kælɪbreɪt] *vt (gun)* calibrar; *(thermometer)* graduar

calibration [kælɪ'breɪʃən] *n (of instrument)* calibrado *m,* calibración *f*

calibre ['kælɪbər] *n* (**a**) *(of gun)* calibre *m* (**b**) *Fig (of person)* calibre *m*

calico ['kælɪkəʊ] *n (pl* **calicos** *or* **calicoes)** *Tex* calicó *m*

California [kælɪ'fɔːnɪə] *n* California

Californian [kælɪ'fɔːnɪən] *adj & n* californiano(a) *(m,f)*

calipers ['kælɪpəz] *npl US see* **callipers**

calisthenics [kælɪs'θenɪks] *n US see* **callisthenics**

call [kɔːl] **1** *vt* (**a**) *(gen)* llamar; **c. me at eight o'clock** llámame a las ocho; **to c. sb a liar** llamar a algn embustero; **to c. sb names** poner verde a algn; **what's he called?** ¿cómo se llama?; *Fam* **let's c. it a day** vamos a dar esto por terminado, vamos a dejarlo; *Fam* **let's c. it £1** dejémoslo en una libra (**b**) *(summon) (meeting etc)* convocar; **to c. sth to mind** traer algo a la memoria (**c**) *Tel* **to c. sb (up)** llamar a algn (por teléfono); **to c. 999 in an emergency** en caso de emergencia llamar al 999 (**d**) *(expose)* **to c. sb's bluff** devolver la pelota a algn
2 *vi* (**a**) *(gen)* llamar; **to c. out for help** gritar pidiendo socorro *or* ayuda (**b**) *Tel* llamar, telefonear; **who's calling?**

¿de parte de quién? (**c**) *(visit)* pasar; **to c. at sb's (house)** pasar por casa de algn; **to c. for sth/sb** pasar a recoger algo/a algn; **to c. (in) on sb** ir a ver a algn (**d**) *(trains)* parar, hacer parada; **this train calls at every station** este tren para en todas las estaciones (**e**) *(require)* **to c. for** *(food)* pedir; *(measures, courage)* exigir; **that wasn't called for** eso no estaba justificado

3 *n* (**a**) *(cry)* llamada *f,* grito *m*; **a c. for help** un grito de socorro; **give me a c. when dinner is ready** llámame cuando esté lista la comida ◻ *Rad* **c. sign** indicativo *m*; *Theat* **curtain c.** salida *f* (a escena para recibir aplausos) (**b**) *(of bird)* reclamo *m* (**c**) *(short visit)* visita *f*; **to pay** *or* **make a c. on sb** visitar a *or* ir a ver a algn; *(measures, courage)* **to c. box** *Br* cabina *f* telefónica; *US* teléfono *m* de emergencia; **c. centre** centro *m* de atención telefónica; **c. waiting** llamada *f or Am* llamado *m* en espera (**e**) *Fin (demand)* solicitud *f*; **money payable on c.** dinero *m* (pagadero) a la vista; *Fig* **I have too many calls on my time** tengo demasiadas obligaciones (**f**) *Med* **to be on c.** estar de guardia (**g**) *(need)* motivo *m*; **there's no c. for you to worry** no hay motivo para que te preocupes

call away *vt* **to be called away on business** tener que ausentarse por motivos de trabajo

call back 1 *vt* (**a**) *(phone in reply)* llamar; *(phone again)* llamar otra vez (**b**) *Pol* cesar
2 *vi (phone in reply)* llamar; *(phone again)* llamar otra vez; *(visit again)* volver

call in 1 *vt* (**a**) *(doctor, police)* llamar (**b**) *(coins etc)* retirar de circulación; **to c. in a loan** exigir el pago de un empréstito
2 *vi* (**a**) *(visit)* ir a ver, visitar (**b**) *Naut* hacer escala (**at** en)

call off *vt* (**a**) *(strike etc)* suspender (**b**) *(dog)* llamar

call on *vt* (**a**) *(visit)* visitar, ir a ver a (**b**) **to c. on sb for support** recurrir *or* acudir a algn en busca de apoyo

call out 1 *vt* (**a**) *(shout)* gritar (**b**) *(summon) (troops)* hacer intervenir, sacar a la calle; *(doctor)* hacer venir; *(workers)* llamar a la huelga
2 *vi* gritar; **to c. out for sth** pedir algo en voz alta

call up *vt* (**a**) *Tel* llamar, *Am* hablar (**b**) *Mil* llamar a filas, reclutar (**c**) *Comptr (data, information)* visualizar

call upon *vt see* **call on** (**b**)

caller ['kɔːlər] *n* (**a**) *(visitor)* visitante *mf,* visita *f* (**b**) *Tel* persona *f* que llama

calligrapher [kə'lɪgrəfər] *n* calígrafo(a) *m,f*

calligraphy [kə'lɪgrəfɪ] *n* caligrafía *f*

calling ['kɔːlɪŋ] *n* vocación *f,* llamada *f; US* **c. card** tarjeta *f* de visita

callipers ['kælɪpəz] *npl* (**a**) *Tech* calibrador *m sing* (**b**) *Med* aparato *m sing* ortopédico

callisthenics [kælɪs'θenɪks] *n* gimnasia *f* sueca

callous ['kæləs] *adj* insensible, duro(a)

callously ['kæləslɪ] *adv* con dureza

callousness ['kæləsnɪs] *n* insensibilidad *f,* dureza *f*

call-up ['kɔːlʌp] *n Mil* llamamiento *m* a filas, reclutamiento *m*

callus ['kæləs] *n (pl* **calluses)** *Med* callo *m*

calm [kɑːm] **1** *adj* (**a**) *(still) (weather)* en calma; *(sea)* en calma, sereno(a) (**b**) *(relaxed)* sosegado(a), tranquilo(a); **keep c.!** ¡tranquilo(a)!, ¡calma!
2 *n* (**a**) *(of weather, sea)* calma *f* (**b**) *(tranquility)* serenidad *f,* sosiego *m,* tranquilidad *f*
3 *vt* calmar, sosegar, tranquilizar
4 *vi* **to c. (down)** calmarse, sosegarse, tranquilizarse

calming ['kɑːmɪŋ] *adj (influence, effect)* tranquilizador(a), tranquilizante; **her words had a c. effect on him** sus palabras consiguieron tranquilizarlo

calmly ['kɑːmlɪ] *adv* con calma, tranquilamente

calmness ['kɑːmnɪs] *n* calma *f*, sosiego *m*, tranquilidad *f*

Calor Gas® ['kæləgæs] *n Br* (gas *m*) butano *m*

calorie *n*, **calory** ['kælərɪ] *n* caloría *f*

calorific [kælə'rɪfɪk] *adj* calorífico(a)

calumny ['kæləmnɪ] *n (gen)* calumnia *f*; *Jur* difamación *f*

calvary ['kælvərɪ] *n Rel* calvario *m*

calve [kɑːv] *vi* parir (un becerro)

calves [kɑːvz] *npl see* **calf**[1] & **calf**[2]

calypso [kə'lɪpsəʊ] *n (pl* **calypsos)** *Mus* calipso *m*

CAM [sɪeɪ'em] *n Comptr (abbr* **computer-aided manufacture)** CAM *f*, fabricación *f* asistida por *Esp* ordenador *or Am* computadora

cam [kæm] *n Tech* leva *f*

camaraderie [kæmə'rɑːdərɪ] *n* compañerismo *m*

camber ['kæmbər] *n* combadura *f*, convexidad *f*

Cambodia [kæm'bəʊdɪə] *n* Camboya

Cambodian [kæm'bəʊdɪən] *adj & n* camboyano(a) *(m,f)*

camcorder ['kæmkɔːdər] *n* videocámara *f* (portátil)

came [keɪm] *pt see* **come**

camel ['kæməl] **1** *n* (**a**) *Zool* camello *m*, *f* (**b**) *(colour)* color *m* leonado

2 *adj (colour)* leonado(a)

camelhair ['kæməlheər] *n* pelo *m* de camello

camellia [kə'miːlɪə] *n Bot* camelia *f*

cameo ['kæmɪəʊ] *n (pl* **cameos)** camafeo *m*

camera ['kæmərə] *n* (**a**) *Phot* cámara *f or* máquina *f* fotográfica; *Cin TV* cámara *f*; **on c.** en cámara (**b**) *Jur* **in c.** a puerta cerrada

cameraman ['kæmərəmən] *n (pl* **cameramen)** cámara *mf*

camera-shy ['kæmrəʃaɪ] *adj* **she's extremely c.** le da muchísima vergüenza *or Am* pena que le hagan fotos/que le filmen

camerawoman ['kæmərəwʊmən] *n (pl* **camerawomen)** cámara *f*, operadora *f*

camerawork ['kæmərəwɜːk] *n* fotografía *f*

Cameroon [kæmə'ruːn] *n* Camerún

Cameroonian [kæmə'ruːnɪən] *adj & n* camerunés(esa) *(m,f)*

camisole ['kæmɪsəʊl] *n* combinación *f*

camomile ['kæməmaɪl] *n Bot* camomila *f*, manzanilla *f*; **c. tea** (infusión *f* de) manzanilla *f*

camouflage ['kæməflɑːʒ] **1** *n* camuflaje *m*

2 *vt* camuflar

camp[1] [kæmp] **1** *n* campamento *m*; **to break** *or* **strike c.** levantar el campamento ❑ *Mil* **army c.** campamento militar; **c. bed** cama *f* plegable; **c. follower** vivandero(a) *m,f*; **c. site** camping *m*, campamento *m*; **holiday c.** colonia *f* de verano *or* de vacaciones

2 *vi* **to c. (out)** acampar; **to go camping** ir de camping

camp[2] [kæmp] *adj Fam* (**a**) *(effeminate)* afeminado(a); *(affected)* amanerado(a) (**b**) *(homosexual)* marica (**c**) *(style)* cursi

campaign [kæm'peɪn] **1** *n* campaña *f*; **election c.** campaña electoral; **publicity c.** campaña publicitaria

2 *vi* **to c. for sb/sth** hacer una campaña en pro de *or* en favor de algn/de algo

campaigner [kæm'peɪnər] *n (gen)* defensor(a) *m,f* (**for** de); *Pol* militante *mf*

camper ['kæmpər] *n* (**a**) *(person)* campista *mf* (**b**) *US (vehicle)* caravana *f*

campfire ['kæmpfaɪər] *n* fogata *f*

campground ['kæmpgraʊnd] *n US* camping *m*

camphor ['kæmfər] *n Chem* alcanfor *m*

camping ['kæmpɪŋ] *n* **c. ground, c. site** camping *m*, campamento *m*

campus ['kæmpəs] *n (pl* **campuses)** campus *m*, ciudad *f* universitaria

camshaft ['kæmʃɑːft] *n Tech* árbol *m* de levas

can[1] [kæn] *v aux (pt* **could)** (**a**) *(be able to)* poder; **he could have come** podría haber venido; **I'll phone you as soon as I c.** te llamaré en cuanto pueda; **she can't do it** no puede hacerlo (**b**) *(know how to)* saber; **I c. drive** sé conducir; **they couldn't speak French** no sabían francés (**c**) *(be permitted to)* poder; **he cannot** *or* **can't go out tonight** no le dejan salir esta noche (**d**) *(be possible or likely)* poder; **she could have forgotten** puede (ser) que lo haya olvidado; **they can't be very poor** no deben ser muy pobres; **what c. it be?** ¿qué será?, ¿qué podrá ser? (**e**) *(not translated)* **c. I have two coffees, please** dos cafés, por favor; **you can't be serious!** ¡no hablarás en serio!

can[2] [kæn] **1** *n* (**a**) *(container) (of oil etc)* bidón *m* ❑ *US* **trash c.** cubo *m* de la basura; **watering c.** regadera *f* (**b**) *(container) (for food, drink)* lata *f*; *(for hairspray)* bote *m*; **a c. of beer/beans** una lata de cerveza/judías; *Fam Fig* **to carry the c.** pagar el pato (**c**) *US Fam (toilet)* baño *m*, *Esp* tigre *m* (**d**) *US Fam (prison)* cárcel *f*, *Esp* chirona *f*, *Andes RP* cana *f*, *Méx* bote *m*

2 *vt (pt & pp* **canned)** (**a**) *(fish, fruit)* envasar, enlatar (**b**) *US Fam* desestimar, pasar de; **they canned the whole idea** decidieron olvidarlo todo

Canada ['kænədə] *n* Canadá

Canadian [kə'neɪdɪən] *adj & n* canadiense *(mf)*

canal [kə'næl] *n Anat Geog* canal *m*

canapé ['kænəpeɪ] *n* canapé *m*

canary [kə'neərɪ] **1** *n Orn* canario *m*

2 *adj (colour)* **c. yellow** amarillo vivo

Canary Islands [kə'neərɪaɪləndz] *npl* (Islas *fpl*) Canarias *fpl*

cancel ['kænsəl] **1** *vt (pt & pp* **cancelled,** *US* **canceled)** (**a**) *(train, contract)* & *Comptr* cancelar; *Com* anular (**b**) *(revoke) (permission)* retirar; *(decree)* revocar (**c**) *(stamp)* matasellar

2 *vi* **to c. out** anular, contrarrestar; **they c. each other out** se anulan mutuamente

cancellation [kænsɪ'leɪʃən] *n (gen)* cancelación *f*; *Com* anulación *f*

Cancer ['kænsər] *n Astrol Astron* Cáncer *m*; *Geog* **the Tropic of C.** el Trópico de Cáncer

cancer ['kænsər] *n Med* cáncer *m*; **breast c.** cáncer de mama; **c. research** cancerología *f*

cancerous ['kænsərəs] *adj* canceroso(a)

candelabra [kændɪ'lɑːbrə] *n* candelabro *m*

candid ['kændɪd] *adj* franco(a), sincero(a); **he's being less than c.** oculta algo ❑ **c. camera** cámara *f* indiscreta

candidacy ['kændɪdəsɪ] *n* candidatura *f*

candidate ['kændɪdeɪt, 'kændɪdɪt] *n* (**a**) *(in election, for job)* candidato(a) *m,f* (**b**) *(in examination)* opositor(a) *m,f*

candidature ['kændɪdətʃər] *n see* **candidacy**

candidly ['kændɪdlɪ] *adv* con franqueza

candied ['kændɪd] *adj Culin* escarchado(a), confitado(a), *Col Méx* cristalizado(a), *RP* abrillantado(a)

candle ['kændəl] *n (gen)* vela *f*; *(in church)* cirio *m*; **to light/blow out a c.** encender/apagar una vela; *Fig* **to burn the c. at both ends** trabajar a marchas forzadas; *Fam*

she can't hold a c. to him ella no tiene ni punto de comparación con él ❑ **c. grease** sebo *m*

candlelight ['kændəllaɪt] *n* luz *f* de vela; **by c.** a la luz de las velas

candlelit [kændəllɪt] *adj (room)* iluminado(a) con velas; **a c. dinner** una cena a la luz de las velas

Candlemas ['kændəlməs] *n Rel* candelaria *f*

candlestick ['kændəlstɪk] *n (gen)* candelero *m*, palmatoria *f*; *(in church)* cirial *m*

candlewick ['kændəlwɪk] *n* **(a)** *Tex* tela *f* afelpada **(b)** *(wick)* pábilo *m*, mecha *f*

candour, *US* **candor** ['kændər] *n* franqueza *f*, sinceridad *f*

candy ['kændɪ] *n US* caramelo *m* ❑ **c. store** confitería *f*

candyfloss ['kændɪflɒs] *n Br (sweet)* algodón *m*

candy-striped ['kændɪstraɪpt] *adj* de rayas multicolores

cane [keɪn] **1** *n* **(a)** *Bot* caña *f* ❑ **c. sugar** azúcar *m* de caña; **raspberry c.** frambueso *m* **(b)** *(for furniture)* mimbre *m*, junco *m* ❑ **c. chair** silla *f* de mimbre **(c)** *(walking stick)* bastón *m*; *(for punishment)* palmeta *f*
2 *vt* castigar con la palmeta

canine ['keɪnaɪn] *adj* **(a)** *Zool* canino(a) **(b)** *Anat* **c. tooth** colmillo *m*

caning ['keɪnɪŋ] *n* castigo *m* con la palmeta

canister ['kænɪstər] *n* bote *m*

canker ['kæŋkər] *n Med* chancro *m*; *Fig* cáncer *m*

cannabis ['kænəbɪs] *n* hachís *m*, cannabis *m*

canned [kænd] *adj* **(a)** *(food)* enlatado(a), envasado(a); **c. beer** cerveza enlatada; **c. foods** conservas *fpl* **(b)** *Fam Pej* **c. music** música *f* grabada **(c)** *Slang (drunk) Esp* ciego, *Méx* cuete, *RP* en pedo

cannery ['kænərɪ] *n* fábrica *f* de conservas

cannibal ['kænɪbəl] *adj & n* caníbal *(mf)*, antropófago(a) *(m,f)*

cannibalism ['kænɪbəlɪzəm] *n* canibalismo *m*

cannibalize ['kænɪbəlaɪz] *vt (machinery)* desmontar para utilizar de nuevo las piezas

canning ['kænɪŋ] *n* enlatado *m* ❑ *US* **c. factory** fábrica *f* de conservas; **c. industry** industria *f* conservera

cannon ['kænən] **1** *n (pl* **cannons** *or* **cannon)** **(a)** *(in aircraft)* cañón *m* antiaéreo **(b)** *Hist* cañón *m*; *Fig Iron* **c. fodder** carne *f* de cañón **(c)** *Bill* carambola *f*
2 *vi* chocar **(into** contra)

cannonball ['kænənbɔːl] *n* bala *f* de cañón

cannot ['kænɒt, kæ'nɒt] *v aux see* **can**[1]

canny ['kænɪ] *adj* astuto(a)

canoe [kə'nuː] *n (gen)* canoa *f*; *Sport* piragua *f*

canoeing [kə'nuːɪŋ] *n* piragüismo *m*; **to go c.** ir a hacer piragüismo

canon ['kænən] *n Rel (decree, rule)* canon *m*

canonize ['kænənaɪz] *vt Rel* canonizar

canopy ['kænəpɪ] *n* **(a)** *(over head)* dosel *m*; *(ceremonial)* palio *m* **(b)** *(awning)* toldo *m* **(c)** *Av* carlinga *f*

cant [kænt] *n* **(a)** *(platitudes)* hipocresías *fpl* **(b)** *(jargon)* jerga *f*

can't [kɑːnt] *v aux see* **can**[1]

Cantab [kæn'tæb] *(abbr* **Cantabrigiensis)** *(of Cambridge University)* de la Universidad de Cambridge

Cantabria [kæn'tæbrɪə] *n* Cantabria

Cantabrian [kæn'tæbrɪən] *n* **1** *(person)* cántabro(a) *m,f*
2 *adj* cántabro(a); **the C. Mountains** la Cordillera Cantábrica; **the C. Sea** el (Mar) Cantábrico

cantaloup(e) ['kæntəluːp] *n* **c. (melon)** melón *m* francés

cantankerous [kæn'tæŋkərəs] *adj* intratable, irascible

canteen [kæn'tiːn] *n* **(a)** *(restaurant)* cantina *f* **(b)** *Br (set of cutlery)* juego *m* de cubiertos **(c)** *(flask)* cantimplora *f*

canter ['kæntər] *Equit* **1** *n* medio galope *m*
2 *vi* ir a medio galope

cantilever ['kæntɪliːvər] *n Archit* voladizo *m* ❑ **c. bridge** puente *m* con voladizos

Cantonese [kæntə'niːz] **1** *n (language)* cantonés *m*
2 *adj* cantonés(esa)

canvas ['kænvəs] *n* **(a)** *Tex* lona *f* **(b)** *(painting)* lienzo *m* **(c)** **under c.** *(in tent)* bajo lona; *Naut* a vela

canvass ['kænvəs] *vi* **(a)** *Pol* hacer propaganda electoral **(b)** *Com* hacer promoción, buscar clientes

canvasser ['kænvəsər] *n* **(a)** *Pol* persona *f* que hace propaganda electoral **(b)** *Com* promotor(a) *m,f* de un producto

canyon ['kænjən] *n Geog* cañón *m*; **the Grand C.** el Gran Cañón

CAP [siːeɪ'piː] *n (abbr* **Common Agricultural Policy)** PAC *f*

cap [kæp] **1** *n* **(a)** *(man's)* gorro *m*; *Fig* **c. in hand** con el sombrero en la mano; *Prov* **if the c. fits, wear it** el que se pica ajos come, si te das por aludido(a) peor para ti **(b)** *(soldier's)* gorra *f*; *(academic)* birrete *m*; *(nurse's)* cofia *f*; *(cardinal's)* capelo *m* **(c)** *Br Sport* **to get** *or* **win a c. for England** ser seleccionado(a) para el equipo de Inglaterra **(d)** *(cover) (of pen)* capuchón *m*; *(of bottle)* chapa *f* **(e)** *Geog* casquete *m* **(f)** *(for toy pistol)* fulminante *m* **(g)** *Med* **(Dutch) c.** diafragma *m*
2 *vt (pt & pp* **capped) (a)** *(hills etc)* coronar; *(bottle)* poner la chapa a; *Fig* **to c. it all** para colmo; *Fam* **to c. sb's joke** contar un chiste todavía mejor **(b)** *Br Sport* seleccionar

capability [keɪpə'bɪlɪtɪ] *n* habilidad *f*; **it was beyond my capabilities** estaba fuera de mis posibilidades

capable ['keɪpəbəl] *adj* **(a)** *(skilful)* competente, hábil **(b)** *(able)* capaz **(of** de)

capacious [kə'peɪʃəs] *adj* espacioso(a)

capacitor [kə'pæsɪtər] *n Elec* condensador *m* gerente

capacity [kə'pæsɪtɪ] *n* **(a)** *(of container)* capacidad *f*, cabida *f*; *Aut* **engine c.** cilindrada *f* **(b)** *(of bus, theatre)* capacidad *f*; **a seating c. of 300** capacidad *or* cabida para 300 personas; **there was a c. crowd** estaba totalmente lleno de gente; **to be filled to c.** estar al completo **(c)** *(ability)* capacidad *f* **(for** de); **at full c.** a pleno rendimiento **(d)** *(position)* puesto *m*; **in her c. as manageress** en su calidad de gerente

cape[1] [keɪp] *n (garment)* capa *f*

cape[2] [keɪp] *n Geog* cabo *m*, promontorio *m* ❑ **C. Horn** Cabo *m* de Hornos; **C. Town** Ciudad del Cabo; **C. Verde** Cabo Verde; **C. Verdean** caboverdiano(a) *m,f*

caper[1] ['keɪpər] **1** *n* **(a)** *(jump)* brinco *m* **(b)** *(prank)* travesura *f*
2 *vi (jump about)* brincar

caper[2] ['keɪpər] *n* **(a)** *Culin* alcaparra *f* **(b)** *Bot* alcaparro *m*

capercaillie [kæpə'keɪljɪ] *n Orn* urogallo *m*

capillary [kə'pɪlərɪ] *adj & n* capilar *(m)*

capital[1] ['kæpɪtəl] **1** *n* **(a)** *(town)* capital *f* **(b)** *Fin* capital *m*; *Fig* **to make c. (out) of sth** sacar provecho de algo ❑ **c. assets** activo *m* fijo, bienes *mpl* de capital; **c. expenditure** inversión *f* de capital; *Br* **c. investment** inversión *f* (de capital); *US* **c. stock** capital *m* escriturado **(c)** *(letter)* mayúscula *f*
2 *adj* **(a)** *(city)* capital **(b)** *Jur (punishment)* capital **(c)** *(very serious)* grave **(d)** *(primary)* primordial, prioritario(a) **(e)** *(letter)* mayúscula, *f*. **c. C** C mayúscula

capital[2] ['kæpɪtəl] *n Archit* capitel *m*

capitalism ['kæpɪtəlɪzəm] *n* capitalismo *m*

capitalist [ˈkæpɪtəlɪst] *adj & n* capitalista *(mf)*

capitalization [kæpɪtəlaɪˈzeɪʃən] *n Fin* capitalización *f*

capitalize [ˈkæpɪtəlaɪz] **1** *vi Fin* capitalizar; *Fig* **to c. on** sth sacar provecho *or* beneficio de algo
2 *vt (letter)* escribir con mayúscula

Capitol [ˈkæpɪtəl] *n US Pol* **the C.** el Capitolio

capitulate [kəˈpɪtjʊleɪt] *vi* capitular

capo [ˈkeɪpəʊ] *n (pl* **capos***) Mus* traste *m*

capon [ˈkeɪpən] *n* capón *m*

caprice [kəˈpriːs] *n* capricho *m*

capricious [kəˈprɪʃəs] *adj* caprichoso(a)

Capricorn [ˈkæprɪkɔːn] *n Astrol Astron* Capricornio' *m*; *Geog* **tropic of C.** trópico *m* de Capricornio

capsicum [ˈkæpsɪkəm] *n Bot* pimiento *m*

capsize [kæpˈsaɪz] **1** *vt Naut* hacer zozobrar
2 *vi* zozobrar

capstan [ˈkæpstən] *n Naut* cabrestante *m*

capsule [ˈkæpsjuːl] *n* cápsula *f* □ **space c.** cápsula *f* espacial

Capt. *Mil Naut (abbr* **Captain***)* Capitán *m*, Cap

captain [ˈkæptɪn] **1** *n* **(a)** *Naut Av* capitán *m* **(b)** *US (in police)* comisario(a) *m,f* **(c)** *Sport* capitán(ana) *m,f*
2 *vt* capitanear

captaincy [ˈkæptɪnsɪ] *n* capitanía *f*

caption [ˈkæpʃən] *n* **(a)** *(under picture)* leyenda *f* **(b)** *Cin* subtítulo *m*

captivate [ˈkæptɪveɪt] *vt* cautivar

captivating [ˈkæptɪveɪtɪŋ] *adj* encantador(a), seductor(a)

captive [ˈkæptɪv] **1** *n* cautivo(a) *m,f*
2 *adj* cautivo(a); **to hold sb c.** poner *or* mantener a algn en cautiverio; **a c. audience** un auditorio que escucha sin querer; **c. market** mercado *m* cautivo

captivity [kæpˈtɪvɪtɪ] *n* cautiverio *m*

captor [ˈkæptər] *n* captor(a) *m,f*

capture [ˈkæptʃər] **1** *vt* **(a)** *(fugitive)* capturar, apresar; *Mil (town)* tomar **(b)** *Com (market)* acaparar **(c)** *Fig (mood etc)* captar
2 *n* **(a)** *(seizure) (of fugitive)* captura *f*, apresamiento *m*; *(of town)* toma *f* **(b)** *(person)* prisionero(a) *m,f*

CAR [siːeɪˈɑːr] *n (abbr* **Central African Republic***)* República *f* Centroafricana

car [kɑːr] *n* **(a)** *Aut* coche *m*, *Am* carro *m*, *CSur* auto *m*; **racing c.** coche de carreras □ **c. crash** accidente *m* de coche; **c. ferry** transbordador *m* para coches; *Br* **c. park** parking *m*, estacionamiento *m*, *Esp* aparcamiento *m*; **c. wash** túnel *m* de lavado **(b)** *US Rail* coche *m*, vagón *m* □ **dining c.** coche *m* restaurante; **sleeping c.** coche *m* cama

carafe [kəˈræf, kəˈrɑːf] *n* garrafa *f*

caramel [ˈkærəməl] *n Culin* **(a)** *(burnt sugar)* caramelo *m*; **c. custard** flan *m* **(b)** *(sweet)* caramelo *m*

carat, *US* **karat** [ˈkærət] *n* kilate *m*; **24-c. gold** oro de 24 kilates

caravan [ˈkærəvæn] *n* **(a)** *Br (pulled by car)* caravana *f*, rulot *f* **(b)** *(in the desert)* caravana *f*

caravel [ˈkærəvel] *n Naut* carabela *f* ·

caraway [ˈkærəweɪ] *n* **(a)** *Bot* alcaravea *f* **(b)** *Culin* **c. seed** carvi *m*

carbohydrate [kɑːbəʊˈhaɪdreɪt] *n* hidrato *m* de carbono, carbohidrato *m*

carbolic [kɑːˈbɒlɪk] *adj Chem* **c. acid** fenol *m*

carbon [ˈkɑːbən] *n Chem* carbono *m* □ **c. copy** copia *f* hecha con papel carbón; *Fig* copia *f* exacta; **c. dioxide** bióxido *or* dióxido *m* de carbono; **c. paper** papel *m* carbón

carbonated [ˈkɑːbəneɪtɪd] *adj (drink)* efervescente

carbonize [ˈkɑːbənaɪz] *vt* carbonizar

carbuncle [ˈkɑːbʌŋkəl] *n* **(a)** *(gem)* granate *m* **(b)** *Med* carbunco *m*

carburettor [kɑːbjʊˈretər] *n*, *US* **carburetor** [ˈkɑːbjʊreɪtər] *n Aut* carburador *m*

carcass [ˈkɑːkəs] *n (of animal)* animal *f* muerto; *(at butcher's)* res *f* muerta; **(chicken) c.** huesos *mpl or* restos *mpl* (de pollo)

carcinogen [kɑːˈsɪnədʒen] *n Med* agente *m* cancerígeno

carcinogenic [kɑːsɪnəˈdʒenɪk] *adj Med* cancerígeno(a), carcinógeno(a)

carcinoma [kɑːsɪˈnəʊmə] *n Med* carcinoma *m*

card¹ [kɑːd] *n* **(a)** *(gen)* tarjeta *f*; *(piece of cardboard)* cartulina *f* □ **birthday/visiting c.** tarjeta de cumpleaños/de visita **(b)** *(in file)* ficha *f*, *(identity, membership)* carné *m*, carnet *m*, *CSur Méx* credencial *m*; *Br Ind Fig* **to get one's cards** ser despedido(a) □ **c. index** fichero *m*; *Com* **credit c.** tarjeta *f* de crédito **(c)** *Comptr* tarjeta *f* **(d)** *Cards* **game of cards** partida *f* (de cartas); **pack of cards** baraja *f*, naipes *mpl*, cartas *fpl*; **(playing) c.** naipe *m*, carta *f*; *Fig* **it is Br** on *or US* **in the cards that …** es más que probable que…; *Fig* **to lay one's cards on the table** poner las cartas boca arriba; *Fig* **to play one's cards right** jugar bien sus cartas □ **c. table** mesa *f* de juego; **c. trick** truco *m* con las cartas **(e)** *Fam Fig* **he's a real c.** este tío es la monda

card² [kɑːd] *vt (wool)* cardar

cardamom [ˈkɑːdəməm] *n*, **cardamon** [ˈkɑːdəmən] *n Bot* cardamono *m*

cardboard [ˈkɑːdbɔːd] *n* cartón *m* □ **c. box** caja *f* de cartón; **c. cutout** recortable *m*

card-carrying [ˈkɑːdkærɪŋ] *adj* **c. member** miembro *m or* socio(a) *m,f* (de pleno derecho)

cardiac [ˈkɑːdɪæk] *adj* cardíaco(a); **c. arrest** paro *m* cardíaco

cardigan [ˈkɑːdɪgən] *n* rebeca *f*, chaqueta *f* de punto

cardinal [ˈkɑːdɪnəl] **1** *n Rel* cardenal *m*
2 *adj* cardinal; **c. numbers** números *mpl* cardinales

cardiologist [kɑːdɪˈɒlədʒɪst] *n Med* cardiólogo(a) *m,f*

cardiology [kɑːdɪˈɒlədʒɪ] *n Med* cardiología *f*

cardiovascular [kɑːdɪəʊˈvæskjʊlər] *adj* cardiovascular

cardsharp [ˈkɑːdʃɑːp] *n*, **cardsharper** [ˈkɑːdʃɑːpər] *n* fullero(a) *m,f*, tramposo(a) *m,f* (en el juego de cartas)

care [keər] **1** *vi* **(a)** *(be concerned)* preocuparse **(about** por), importar; **he cares very much about social issues** le preocupan mucho los asuntos sociales; **I don't c. (at all)** no me importa (en absoluto); **she only cares about money** sólo le interesa el dinero; *Fam* **for all I c.** me trae sin cuidado; *Fam* **he couldn't c. less** le importa un bledo **(b)** *(like, want)* gustar; **would you c. to go to the theatre tonight?** ¿te gustaría ir al teatro esta noche?
2 *n* **(a)** *(attention, protection)* cuidado *m*, atención *f*; *(on letter)* **'c. of …'** 'al cuidado de …'; **medical c.** asistencia *f* médica; *Br Jur* **to take (a child) into c.** poner (a un niño) bajo la custodia de una institución; **to take c. of** *(child etc)* cuidar; *(business, matters)* ocuparse de, hacerse cargo de; **under the doctor's c.** al cuidado del médico; *Slang* **I'll take c. of him** ya me encargaré de él **(b)** *(carefulness)* cuidado *m*; **handle with c.** *(on parcel)* frágil; **take c.** *(be careful)* ten cuidado; *(as farewell)* ¡cuidate!; **take c. not to spill your tea** ten cuidado de no derramar el té **(c)** *(worry)* preocupación *f*; **free of c.** sin preocupaciones; **he hasn't a c. in the world** no hay nada que le preocupe

care for *vt* **(a)** *(look after)* cuidar; **well cared for** bien cuidado(a) **(b)** *(like, want)* gustar, interesar; **I don't c. much for television** la televisión no me interesa mucho; **she**

really cares for him él le importa mucho; **would you c. for a coffee?** ¿quiere un café?, ¿le *Esp* apetece *or Carib Col Méx* provoca *or Méx* antoja un café?

career [kə'rɪər] **1** *n (profession)* carrera *f*; **a c. in medicine** una carrera en medicina
2 *vi* correr a toda velocidad

careerist [kə'rɪərɪst] *n Pej* arribista *mf*

carefree ['keəfriː] *adj* despreocupado(a)

careful ['keəful] *adj (painstaking)* cuidadoso(a); *(cautious)* prudente; **a c. examination of sth** un examen minucioso de algo; **be c.!** ¡ojo!, ¡cuidado!; **be c. not to drop it** procura no dejarlo caer; **c. with one's money** ahorrador(a); *Pej* tacaño(a); **to be c.** tener cuidado; **you can't be too c.** hay que andar con mucho cuidado

carefully ['keəfulɪ] *adv (painstakingly)* cuidadosamente; *(cautiously)* con cuidado, con precaución

careless ['keəlɪs] *adj* descuidado(a), despreocupado(a); *(about clothes, appearance)* desaliñado(a); *(driving etc)* negligente; **a c. mistake** un descuido

carelessly ['keəlɪslɪ] *adv* descuidadamente, a la ligera

carelessness ['keəlɪsnɪs] *n* descuido *m*, despreocupación *f*

carer ['keərər] *n* = persona que cuida de un familiar enfermo o anciano, sin que necesariamente reciba compensación económica por ello

caress [kə'res] **1** *n* caricia *f*
2 *vt* acariciar

caret ['kærət] *n Typ Comptr* signo *m* de intercalación

caretaker ['keəteɪkər] *n Br (of building)* conserje *m*, portero(a) *m,f*; *(of school)* conserje *m* □ **c. government** gobierno *m* provisional

careworn ['keəwɔːn] *adj* agobiado(a) (de preocupaciones)

cargo ['kɑːgəʊ] *n (pl* **cargoes** *or US* **cargos)** carga *f*, cargamento *m* □ *Naut* **c. boat** buque *m* de carga, carguero *m*

Caribbean [kærɪ'bɪən, *US* kə'rɪbɪən] *adj* caribe, caribeño(a); **the C. (Sea)** el mar de las Antillas

caribou ['kærɪbuː] *n Zool* caribú *m*

caricature ['kærɪkətjʊər] **1** *n* caricatura *f*
2 *vt* caricaturizar

caricaturist ['kærɪkətjʊərɪst] *n* caricaturista *mf*

caries ['keəriːz] *n inv (in teeth)* caries *f*

caring ['keərɪŋ] *adj* solícito(a), dedicado(a)

carjack ['kɑːdʒæk] *vt Fam* **they were carjacked** se los llevaron secuestrados en el coche *or Am* carro *or CSur* auto

carjacking ['kɑːdʒækɪŋ] *n Fam* secuestro *m* de un coche *or Am* carro *or CSur* auto

carload ['kɑːləʊd] *n* **(a)** *(in car)* **we got them home in three carloads** los llevamos a casa en tres viajes **(b)** *US (by rail)* vagón *m (lleno)*

carmine ['kɑːmaɪn] **1** *n* carmín *m*
2 *adj* carmín, carmíneo(a)

carnage ['kɑːnɪdʒ] *n Fig* carnicería *f*

carnal ['kɑːnəl] *adj* carnal

carnation [kɑː'neɪʃən] *n Bot* clavel *m*

carnival ['kɑːnɪvəl] *n* carnaval *m*

carnivore ['kɑːnɪvɔːr] *n Zool* carnívoro(a) *m,f*

carnivorous [kɑː'nɪvərəs] *adj Zool* carnívoro(a)

carob ['kærəb] *n (substance)* extracto *m* de algarroba *(sucedáneo de chocolate)*

carol ['kærəl] *n Mus* villancico *m*

carouse [kə'raʊz] *vi* ir de juerga

carousel [kærə'sel] *n* **(a)** *US (at fair)* tiovivo *m* **(b)** *(at airport)* cinta *f* transportadora de equipajes

carp¹ [kɑːp] *n (pl* **carp** *or* **carps)** *(fish)* carpa *f*

carp² [kɑːp] *vi* refunfuñar, criticar

Carpathians [kɑː'peɪθɪənz] *npl* (Montes *mpl*) Cárpatos *mpl*

carpenter ['kɑːpɪntər] *n* carpintero(a) *m,f*

carpentry ['kɑːpɪntrɪ] *n* carpintería *f*

carpet ['kɑːpɪt] **1** *n* alfombra *f*, *Am* tapete *m*; **fitted c.** *Esp* moqueta *f*, *Am* alfombra *f*; *Fig* **to roll out the red c. for sb** acoger a algn con la máxima ceremonia; *Br Fam* **to be on the c.** llevarse una buena regañina *or Esp* bronca □ *Mil* **c. bombing** bombardeo *m* de saturación; **c. slippers** zapatillas *fpl*
2 *vt Esp* enmoquetar, *Am* alfombrar; *Fig* **carpeted with flowers** cubierto(a) de flores; *Br Fam* **to c. sb** echar una regañina *or Esp* bronca a algn

carpetbagger ['kɑːpɪtbægər] *n US Pol* = candidato(a) electoral no oriundo(a) de la zona que pretende representar

carpeting ['kɑːpɪtɪŋ] *n* alfombrado *m*; **wall-to-wall c.** *Esp* moqueta *f*, *Am* alfombra *f*

carpet-sweeper ['kɑːpɪtswiːpər] *n* cepillo *m* mecánico *(para alfombras)*

carport ['kɑːpɔːt] *n* plaza *f* de estacionamiento *or Esp* aparcamiento techado *(al lado de una casa)*

carriage ['kærɪdʒ] *n* **(a)** *(horse-drawn)* carruaje *m*; *Br Rail* vagón *m*, coche *m*; *(of gun)* cureña *f*; *(of typewriter)* carro *m* **(b)** *(of goods)* porte *m*, transporte *m* □ **c. free** franco *m* de porte; **c. paid** porte *m* pagado **(c)** *(bearing)* porte *m*

carriageway ['kærɪdʒweɪ] *n Br* carril *m*, calzada *f*; **dual c.** carretera *f* de dos carriles en cada sentido

carrier ['kærɪər] *n* **(a)** *(company, person)* transportista *mf*; *(on bicycle)* portaequipajes *m inv* □ *Av* **aircraft c.** portaaviones *m inv*; *Br* **c. bag** bolsa *f* de plástico *or* de papel; **c. pigeon** paloma *f* mensajera **(b)** *Med* portador(a) *m,f* **(c)** *Comptr & Tel* portadora *f*

carrion ['kærɪən] *n* carroña *f*

carrot ['kærət] *n* zanahoria *f*

carroty ['kærətɪ] *adj Fam (hair)* rojizo(a)

carry ['kærɪ] *(pt & pp* **carried)** **1** *vt* **(a)** *(gen)* llevar; *(money, passport, gun)* llevar (encima), *Méx* cargar; *Com (goods, load)* transportar; *(electricity)* conducir; *Archit (load)* sostener; **she carries herself very nicely** tiene buen porte; *Fig* **to c. a joke too far** llevar una broma demasiado lejos **(b)** *(have, bear)* llevar; *(stock)* tener; *(responsibility, penalty)* conllevar, implicar; *Press* **the newspaper carried the story on the front page** el periódico publicó la noticia en primera página; *Fig* **that argument doesn't c. any weight** ese argumento se cae por sí solo **(c)** *Math (in multiplication etc)* llevar **(d)** *Jur Parl (vote etc)* ganar; **the motion was carried** se aprobó la moción **(e)** *Med (disease)* ser portador(a) de; *(in pregnancy)* **she's carrying twins** está embarazada de gemelos **(f)** *Fig (spread)* extender; **he carried his style of music to the West** extendió su estilo musical a Occidente
2 *vi (sound, voice)* oírse, tener alcance

carry away *vt* llevarse; **to get carried away** exaltarse; *Fam* desmadrarse

carry forward *vt Fin* pasar a nueva columna; **carried forward** suma y sigue

carry off *vt (prize)* llevarse; *Fam* **to c. it off (well)** salir airoso(a)

carry on 1 *vt* continuar; *(conversation)* mantener; *(business)* llevar, dirigir
2 *vi* **(a)** *(continue)* continuar, seguir; **c. on!** ¡continúa!, ¡adelante! **(b)** *Fam (make a fuss)* hacer una escena,

exaltarse; **don't c. on about it** ¡no te enrolles! (**c**) *Fam (have liaison)* **to c. on with sb** tener un lío con algn

carry out *vt (plan, work)* llevar a cabo, realizar; *(test)* verificar; *(threat)* cumplir; *(repair)* hacer

carry through *vt (complete)* completar, finalizar

carryall ['kærɪɔːl] *n US* bolsa *f* de viaje

carrycot ['kærɪkɒt] *n Br* cuna *f* portátil *or* plegable

carry-on [kærɪ'ɒn] *n Br Fam* jaleo *m*, lío *m*; **what a c.-on!** ¡menudo lío!

carry-out ['kærɪ'aʊt] *n US Scot (food)* = comida preparada para llevar; *(restaurant)* = restaurante donde se vende comida para llevar

carsick ['kɑːsɪk] *adj* mareado(a) (en el coche); **he always gets c.** siempre se marea en coche

carsickness ['kɑːsɪknɪs] *n* mareo *m (en el coche)*; **he suffers from c.** se marea en el coche *or Am* carro *or CSur* auto

cart [kɑːt] **1** *n (horse-drawn)* carro *m*; *(handcart)* carretilla *f*; *US (in supermarket)* carrito *m*; *Prov* **to put the c. before the horse** empezar la casa por el tejado
2 *vt Fam (carry)* cargar con; **she spends Saturdays carting the children about** se pasa los sábados llevando y trayendo a los niños

cart off *vt Fam* llevarse a la fuerza

carte blanche [kɑːt'blɑːntʃ] *n* carta *f* blanca

cartel [kɑː'tel] *n Ind Fin* cártel *m*

carthorse ['kɑːthɔːs] *n* caballo *m* de tiro

cartilage ['kɑːtɪlɪdʒ] *n Anat* cartílago *m*

cartload ['kɑːtləʊd] *n* carretada *f*

cartographer [kɑː'tɒgrəfər] *n* cartógrafo(a) *m,f*

cartography [kɑː'tɒgrəfɪ] *n* cartografía *f*

carton ['kɑːtən] *n (of cream, yoghurt)* bote *m*; **a c. of cigarettes** un cartón de tabaco

cartoon [kɑː'tuːn] *n* (**a**) *(in newspaper)* viñeta *f*; *(strip)* tira *f* cómica, historieta *f* (**b**) *Art* cartón *m* (**c**) *(animated)* dibujos *mpl* animados

cartoonist [kɑː'tuːnɪst] *n (for newspaper, comic strip)* humorista *mf* gráfico(a); *(for cartoon film)* animador(a) *m,f*

cartridge ['kɑːtrɪdʒ] *n* (**a**) *Mil* cartucho *m*; **blank c.** cartucho sin bala *or* de fogueo □ **c. belt** canana *f*, cartuchera *f* (**b**) *(for pen)* recambio *m* □ **c. paper** papel *m* guarro (**c**) *(for camera)* cartucho *m* (**d**) *Comptr (disk)* cartucho *m*; **ink/toner c.** cartucho de tinta/tóner

cartwheel ['kɑːtwiːl] *n* (**a**) *(wheel)* rueda *f* de carreta (**b**) *(in gymnastics)* voltereta *f*; **to turn cartwheels** hacer volteretas

carve [kɑːv] *vt* (**a**) *(wood)* tallar; *(stone, metal)* cincelar, esculpir (**b**) *(meat)* trinchar

carver ['kɑːvər] *n* (**a**) *Art (of wood)* tallista *mf*; *(of stone)* escultor(a) *m,f* (**b**) *(knife)* cuchillo *m* de trinchar

carving ['kɑːvɪŋ] *n* (**a**) *Art* talla *f* (**b**) **c. knife** *(for meat)* cuchillo *m* de trinchar

cascade [kæs'keɪd] **1** *n* cascada *f*
2 *vi* caer a torrentes

case¹ [keɪs] *n* (**a**) *(gen)* caso *m*; **a c. in point** un buen ejemplo; **in any c.** en todo *or* en cualquier caso, de todas formas; **in c. of doubt** en caso de duda; **just in c.** por si acaso; **to make out a c. for sth** exponer los argumentos en favor de algo; **c. study** estudio *m* de caso (real) (**b**) *Med* caso *m*; **a c. of whooping cough** un caso de tosferina □ **c. history** historial *m* clínico (**c**) *Jur* causa *f*, proceso *m*; **the c. for the defence/prosecution** la defensa/acusación □ **c. law** ley *f* de casos, jurisprudencia *f* (**d**) *Ling* caso *m*; **the genitive c.** el (caso) genitivo (**e**) *Fam (person)* caso *m*; **he's a c.** es (todo) un caso

case² [keɪs] **1** *n* (**a**) *(suitcase)* maleta *f*, *RP* valija *f*; *(small)* estuche *m*; *(soft)* funda *f* □ **cigarette c.** cigarrera *f*; **glass c.** vitrina *f*; **pillow c.** funda *f* (de almohada); **spectacle c.** funda *f* de gafas; **watch c.** estuche *m* de reloj (**b**) *(box)* caja *f*; **a c. of wine** una caja de botellas de vino (**c**) *Typ* caja *f*; **lower c.** caja baja, minúscula *f*; **upper c.** caja alta, mayúscula *f*; *Comptr* **the address is c. sensitive** hay que respetar las mayúsculas y las minúsculas en la dirección
2 *vt Slang* **to c. the joint** reconocer el terreno

casement ['keɪsmənt] *n* ventana *f* de bisagras

caseworker ['keɪswɜːkər] *n* asistente(a) *m,f* social

cash [kæʃ] **1** *n* dinero *m* efectivo, metálico *m*; **hard c.** metálico; **petty c.** dinero para gastos menores; **to be short of c.** tener poco dinero; **to pay c.** pagar al contado *or* en efectivo □ **c. box** caja *f* (para el dinero); **c. card** tarjeta *f* (del cajero automático); **c. crop** cultivo *m* comercial; *Br* **c. desk** caja *f*; **to pay at the c. desk** pagar en (la) caja; *Fin* **c. flow** movimiento *m or* flujo *m* de efectivo; **c. machine** cajero *m* automático; **c. on delivery** entrega *f* contra reembolso; **c. price** precio *m* al contado; **c. register** caja *f* registradora
2 *vt (cheque)* cobrar, hacer efectivo(a)

cash in *vt* hacer efectivo(a)

cash in on *vt Fam Fig* aprovechar, sacar provecho de

cash up *vi Br* rendir cuentas

cash-and-carry [kæʃən'kærɪ] *adj & adv* de renta al por mayor y pago al contado

cashback ['kæʃbæk] *n (in supermarket)* = servicio que ofrece la posibilidad de sacar dinero de una cuenta en el momento de pagar con tarjeta de débito una compra; **would you like any cashback?** ¿quiere sacar dinero de la cuenta?

cash-book ['kæʃbʊk] *n* libro *m* de caja

cashew ['kæʃuː] *n* **c. (nut)** anarcado *m*

cashier¹ [kæ'ʃɪər] *n* cajero(a) *m,f*

cashier² [kæ'ʃɪər] *vt Mil* dar de baja a

cashmere ['kæʃmɪər] **1** *n Tex* cachemira *f*
2 *adj* de cachemira

cashpoint ['kæʃpɔɪnt] *n* cajero *m* automático

casino [kə'siːnəʊ] *n (pl* **casinos)** casino *m*

cask [kɑːsk] *n* tonel *m*, barril *m*

casket ['kɑːskɪt] *n* (**a**) *(small box)* cofre *m* (**b**) *(coffin)* ataúd *m*

Caspian ['kæspɪən] *adj* **the C. (Sea)** el mar Caspio

cassava [kə'sɑːvə] *n Bot* mandioca *f*

casserole ['kæsərəʊl] *n* (**a**) *(dish)* cacerola *f* (**b**) *Culin* guisado *m*; **chicken c.** pollo *m* a la cazuela

cassette [kæ'set] *n* casete *f* □ **c. player** casete *m*, magnetófono *m*; **c. recorder** casete *m*

cassock ['kæsək] *n Rel* sotana *f*

cast [kɑːst] **1** *vt (pt & pp* **cast)** (**a**) *(throw) (net, fishing line)* echar, arrojar; *(shadow, light)* proyectar; *(dice)* tirar; **to c. a glance at sb/sth** volver la mirada hacia algn/algo; *Naut* **to c. anchor** echar el ancla; **to c. a spell on sb** hechizar a algn; *Fig* **to c. one's eye over sth** echar una ojeada a algo (**b**) *(vote)* emitir (**c**) *(of snake)* **to c. its skin** mudar la piel (**d**) *Fig (set, put)* poner; **to c. doubt on sth** poner algo en duda; **to c. suspicion on sb** levantar sospechas sobre algn; *Fig* **the die is c.** la suerte está echada (**e**) *Tech (of metal)* moldear, vaciar □ **c. iron** hierro *m* fundido *or* colado (**f**) *Theat (play)* hacer el reparto de; **to c. an actor in the part of ...** asignar a un actor el papel de ...
2 *n* (**a**) *(throw)* lanzamiento *m* (**b**) *Tech (mould)* molde *m*; *(product)* pieza *f* (**c**) *Med* **(plaster) c.** escayola *f*, *esp Am* yeso *m*; **to have a c. in one's eye** tener un defecto ocular (**d**) *Theat* reparto *m*; **c. list** reparto *m*, lista *f* de actores

cast about for, cast around for *vi* buscar, andar buscando

cast away *vt Naut* **to be c. away** naufragar

cast off 1 *vt (clothes)* desechar, deshacerse de
2 *vi* (**a**) *(in knitting)* cerrar los puntos (**b**) *Naut* soltar (las) amarras

cast on *vi (in knitting)* montar los puntos

castanets [kæstə'nets] *npl* castañuelas *fpl*

castaway ['kɑːstəweɪ] *n* náufrago(a) *m,f*

caste [kɑːst] *n* casta *f*

caster ['kɑːstər] *n* (**a**) *Br* **c. sugar** azúcar *m* molido muy fino (**b**) *(wheel)* ruedecilla *f*

castigate ['kæstɪgeɪt] *vt Fml* castigar

Castile [kæ'stiːl] *n* Castilla

Castilian [kæ'stɪljən] **1** *adj* castellano(a)
2 *n* (**a**) *(person)* castellano(a) *m,f* (**b**) *(language)* **C. (Spanish)** castellano *m*

casting ['kɑːstɪŋ] *n* (**a**) *Tech* vaciado *m* (**b**) *Theat* reparto *m* de papeles (**c**) **c. vote** voto *m* de calidad

cast-iron ['kɑːstaɪən] *adj* de hierro fundido *or* colado; *Fig* irrefutable

castle ['kɑːsəl] **1** *n* (**a**) *(building)* castillo *m*; *Fig* **castles in the air** castillos en el aire (**b**) *Chess* torre *f*
2 *vi Chess* enrocar

cast-off ['kɑːstɒf] *adj* desechado(a)

castoffs ['kɑːstɒfs] *npl* ropa *f* sing vieja

castor¹ ['kɑːstər] *n Zool* castor *m* ❑ **c. oil** aceite *m* de ricino

castor² ['kɑːstər] *n see* **caster**

castrate [kæ'streɪt] *vt* castrar

castration [kæ'streɪʃən] *n* castración *f*

casual ['kæʒjʊəl] *adj* (**a**) *(meeting etc)* casual, fortuito(a) (**b**) *(worker)* ocasional, temporero(a) (**c**) *(clothes, shoes)* (de) sport (**d**) *(unimportant)* casual, de paso; **a c. remark** un comentario sin importancia (**e**) *(not serious)* despreocupado(a), informal; **he has a c. attitude to life** se lo trae todo sin cuidado; **c. sex** relaciones *fpl* sexuales ocasionales

casually ['kæʒjʊəlɪ] *adv* de paso, sin darle importancia

casualty ['kæʒjʊəltɪ] *n* (**a**) *Mil* baja *f*; **casualties** pérdidas *fpl* (**b**) *(injured)* herido(a) *m,f*; *Br Med* **c. (department)** departamento *m* de traumatología

CAT [kæt] *Med n (abbr* **Computerized Axial Tomography)** TAC *f*; **C. scan** escáner *m* (TAC)

cat [kæt] *n Zool* gato(a) *m,f*; **the c. family** los felinos; *Fig* **to be like a c. on a hot tin roof** *or* **on hot bricks** estar sobre ascuas, estar como un flan; *Fig* **to let the c. out of the bag** revelar el secreto, *Esp* descubrir el pastel; *Fig* **to play c. and mouse with sb** jugar con algn al gato y ratón; *Fig* **to put the c. among the pigeons** meter los perros en danza; *Fam* **there isn't room to swing a c.** no cabe ni un alfiler; *Fam Fig* **it's raining cats and dogs** llueve a cántaros ❑ **c. burglar** ladrón *m* que escala edificios para robar; **c. litter** arena *f* para gatos

cataclysm ['kætəklɪzəm] *n* cataclismo *m*

catacombs ['kætəkuːmz] *npl* catacumbas *fpl*

Catalan ['kætəlæn] **1** *adj* catalán(ana)
2 *n* (**a**) *(person)* catalán(ana) *m,f* (**b**) *(language)* catalán *m*

catalogue, *US* **catalog** ['kætəlɒg] **1** *n* catálogo *m*
2 *vt* catalogar

Catalonia [kætə'ləʊnɪə] *n* Cataluña

Catalonian [kætə'ləʊnɪən] *adj* catalán(ana)

catalyst ['kætəlɪst] *n* catalizador *m*

catamaran [kætəmə'ræn] *n Naut* catamarán *m*

catapult ['kætəpʌlt] **1** *n* (**a**) *Br (toy)* tiragomas *m inv*, tirador *m* (**b**) *(for aircraft)* catapulta *f*
2 *vt (aircraft)* catapultar
3 *vi* salir disparado(a)

cataract ['kætərækt] *n Med* catarata *f*

catarrh [kə'tɑːr] *n Med* catarro *m*

catastrophe [kə'tæstrəfɪ] *n* catástrofe *f*

catastrophic [kætə'strɒfɪk] *adj* catastrófico(a)

catatonic [kætə'tɒnɪk] *adj Med* catatónico(a)

catcall ['kætkɔːl] *n (in theatre etc)* silbido *m*, silbo *m*

catch [kætʃ] **1** *vt (pt & pp* **caught)** (**a**) *(grasp, take, capture)* atrapar, *Esp* coger, *Am* agarrar; *(fish)* pescar; *(mouse etc)* coger, atrapar; *(thief)* coger; **the bullet c. her in the heart** la bala le alcanzó en el corazón; **to c. fire** prender fuego, incendiarse, encenderse; **to c. hold of** agarrar, echar mano a; **to c. one's finger in a door** *Esp* pillarse *or* agarrarse el dedo con una puerta; **to c. sb's eye** llamar la atención de algn; **to c. sight of** entrever; *Fam* **you'll c. it!** ¡te la vas a *Esp* cargar *or Esp* ganar *or Méx RP* ligar! (**b**) *(surprise) Esp* pillar, *Esp* coger, *Am* pescar; **to c. sb doing sth** *Esp* coger *or Am* pescar a algn haciendo algo; **to get caught in a storm/the traffic** pillarle a uno una tormenta/el tráfico (**c**) *(train, bus)* tomar, *Esp* coger; *(person)* pillar, dar con; **I caught him as he was leaving the office** lo pillé saliendo de la oficina (**d**) *(understand, hear)* entender, oír; **I didn't quite c. that** no lo he entendido bien (**e**) *Med* **to c. a cold** resfriarse, *Esp* coger *or Méx* pescar un resfriado, *Andes RP* agarrarse *or* pescarse un resfrío; **to c. one's breath** *(hold)* sostener la respiración; *(recover)* recuperar el aliento
2 *vi (sleeve etc)* engancharse (**on** en); *(fire)* encenderse
3 *n* (**a**) *(of ball)* parada *f*; *(of fish)* presa *f*, captura *f* (**b**) *(on door)* pestillo *m* (**c**) *(drawback)* pega *f*; **c. question** pega *f*; **c.-22** círculo *m* vicioso (**d**) *(slogan)* **c. phrase** slogan *m* (**e**) *(game)* juego *m* de pelota

catch at *vt* agarrarse de, asirse a

catch on *vi Fam* (**a**) *(become popular)* ganar popularidad (**b**) *(understand)* entender, caer en la cuenta

catch out *vt Fam* **to c. sb out** *Esp* pillar *or Am* agarrar a algn

catch up *vi* (**a**) *(reach)* **to c. up with sb, to c. sb up** alcanzar a algn (**b**) *(make up for lost ground) (with news)* ponerse al corriente (**on** de); **to c. up on sleep** recuperar el sueño perdido; **to c. up with work** ponerse al día de trabajo

catch-all ['kætʃɔːl] *adj Fam* **a c.-a. term** un término que vale para todo *or* muy general

catcher ['kætʃər] *n Sport* receptor(a) *m,f* (de pelota)

catching ['kætʃɪŋ] *adj* (**a**) *(disease)* contagioso(a) (**b**) *(attractive)* atractivo(a), llamativo(a)

catchment ['kætʃmənt] *n* captación *f*; **c. area of a hospital/school** zona *f* de captación de un hospital/una escuela

catchphrase ['kætʃfreɪz] *n* coletilla *f*, latiguillo *m*

catchword ['kætʃwɜːd] *n* slogan *m*, lema *m*, reclamo *m*

catchy ['kætʃɪ] *adj* (**catchier, catchiest**) *Fam (tune)* pegadizo(a)

catechism ['kætɪkɪzəm] *n Rel* catequismo *m*

categoric(al) [kætɪ'gɒrɪk(əl)] *adj* categórico(a)

categorize ['kætɪgəraɪz] *vt* categorizar, clasificar

category ['kætɪgərɪ] *n* categoría *f*

cater ['keɪtər] *vi* (**a**) *(at wedding etc)* proveer comida (**b**) **to c. for** *(taste, needs)* atender a; **a TV channel that caters for minority groups** un canal de televisión dirigido a los grupos minoritarios

caterer ['keɪtərər] *n* proveedor(a) *m,f*

catering ['keɪtərɪŋ] n (gen) abastecimiento m (de comidas por encargo); (on plane) catering m

caterpillar ['kætəpɪlər] n (a) Ent oruga f (b) c. (tractor) tractor m de oruga

caterwaul ['kætəwɔːl] vi maullar, berrear

catfish ['kætfɪʃ] n (fish) barbo m

catgut ['kætɡʌt] n (a) Mus cuerda f de tripa (b) Med catgut m

catharsis [kə'θɑːsɪs] n catarsis f

cathartic [kə'θɑːtɪk] adj catártico(a)

cathedral [kə'θiːdrəl] n catedral f; c. city ciudad f catedralicia

Catherine wheel ['kæθrɪnwiːl] n (firework) rueda f

catheter ['kæθɪtər] n Med catéter m

cathode ['kæθəʊd] n cátodo m ❑ c. ray rayo m catódico; c.-ray tube tubo m de rayos catódicos

Catholic ['kæθəlɪk] adj & n Rel católico(a) (m,f)

catholic ['kæθəlɪk] adj (universal) católico(a), liberal; we have c. tastes nos gusta todo

Catholicism [kə'θɒlɪsɪzəm] n Rel catolicismo m

catkin ['kætkɪn] n Bot candelilla f, amento m

catnap ['kætnæp] n siestecilla f, Am siestita f

Catseye® ['kætsaɪ] n Br catafaro m

catsuit ['kætsuːt] n Br (clothing) mono m

catsup ['kætsʌp] n US ketchup m, catchup m

cattle ['kætəl] npl ganado m vacuno; c. crossing (roadsign) paso de ganado ❑ c. breeding cría f de ganado vacuno; c. market mercado m de ganado; c. shed cobertizo m para ganado; c. show feria f de ganado

cattle-grid ['kætəlɡrɪd] n reja f, rejilla f

cattleman ['kætəlmən] n (pl cattlemen) ganadero m

catty ['kætɪ] adj (cattier, cattiest) Fam (remark) malintencionado(a); (person) malicioso(a), criticón(ona)

CATV [siːeɪtiː'viː] n US (abbr community antenna television) (cable TV) televisión f por cable; (via shared aerial) antena f (colectiva) comunitaria

catwalk ['kætwɔːk] n pasarela f

Caucasian [kɔː'keɪzɪən] adj & n (a) (from the Caucasus) caucasiano(a) (m,f) (b) (by race) caucásico(a) (m,f)

Caucasus ['kɔːkəsəs] n Cáucaso

caucus ['kɔːkəs] n (pl caucuses) Br Pol comité m; US = congreso de los dos principales partidos de Estados Unidos

caught [kɔːt] pt & pp see catch

cauldron ['kɔːldrən] n caldero m

cauliflower ['kɒlɪflaʊər] n (a) Bot coliflor f (b) Box c. ear oreja f deformada por los golpes

causality [kɔː'zælɪtɪ] n causalidad f

cause [kɔːz] 1 n (a) (origin) causa f; the causes of poverty las causas de la pobreza (b) (reason) motivo m, razón f; she has no c. for complaint or to complain no tiene motivos para quejarse; to have good c. for doing sth tener razón en hacer algo, tener motivo para hacer algo (c) (purpose) causa f; for a good c. por una buena causa (d) Jur pleito m, causa f

2 vt causar; to c. damage/anxiety causar daño/ansiedad; to c. sb to do sth hacer que algn haga algo; it caused him to miss the train le hizo perder el tren

causeway ['kɔːzweɪ] n carretera f elevada

caustic ['kɔːstɪk] adj cáustico(a); Fig a c. remark un comentario mordaz ❑ c. soda sosa f or soda f cáustica

cauterization [kɔːtəraɪ'zeɪʃən] n Med cauterización f

cauterize ['kɔːtəraɪz] vt Med cauterizar

caution ['kɔːʃən] 1 n (a) (care, wariness) precaución f, cautela f, prudencia f (b) (warning) aviso m, advertencia f (c) Br Jur reprensión f; to give sb a c. amonestar a algn

2 vt advertir, amonestar

cautionary ['kɔːʃənərɪ] adj admonitorio(a); c. tales cuentos mpl morales

cautious ['kɔːʃəs] adj cauteloso(a), cauto(a), prudente

cautiously ['kɔːʃəslɪ] adv cautelosamente, con precaución or prudencia

cautiousness ['kɔːʃəsnɪs] n precaución f, prudencia f, cautela f

cavalcade [kævəl'keɪd] n (gen) desfile m; (on horseback) cabalgata f

cavalier [kævə'lɪər] 1 adj (manner) arrogante

2 n caballero m

cavalry ['kævəlrɪ] n Mil caballería f

cavalryman ['kævəlrɪmən] n (pl cavalrymen) Mil soldado m de caballería

cave [keɪv] n cueva f ❑ c. dweller cavernícola mf, troglodita mf; c. paintings pinturas fpl rupestres or prehistóricas

cave in vi (roof etc) derrumbarse, hundirse

caveat ['kævɪæt] n (a) Jur = demanda de notificación previa ante un tribunal (b) Fml (warning) salvedad f, reserva f; with the c. that ... con la salvedad de que ...

caveman ['keɪvmæn] n (pl cavemen) hombre m de las cavernas

cavern ['kævən] n caverna f

cavernous ['kævənəs] adj cavernoso(a)

caviar(e) ['kævɪɑːr] n caviar m

cavil ['kævɪl] vi (pt & pp cavilled, US caviled) poner reparos or pegas (at, about) a

caving ['keɪvɪŋ] n espeleología f

cavity ['kævɪtɪ] n (a) (hole) cavidad f ❑ Constr c. wall pared f de tabique doble (b) (in tooth) caries f inv

cavort [kə'vɔːt] vi retozar, brincar

caw [kɔː] 1 n graznido m

2 vi graznar

cayenne [keɪ'en] n Culin c. (pepper) (pimienta f de) cayena f

cayman ['keɪmən] n (a) (pl caymans) Zool caimán m (b) C. Islands Islas fpl Cayman

CB [siː'biː] Rad n (abbr Citizens' Band) banda f ciudadana

cc [siː'siː] (a) Com (abbr carbon copy (to)) copia f a papel carbón (a) (b) (abbr cubic centimetre(s)) centímetro(s) m(pl) cúbico(s), cc

CCTV [siːsiːtiː'viː] n (abbr closed-circuit television) circuito m cerrado de televisión

CD [siː'diː] n (abbr compact disc) disco m compacto, compact disc m, CD m ❑ CD player (lector m or reproductor m de) CD m; C. writer grabadora f de CD

CDI [siːdiː'aɪ] n Comptr (abbr compact disc interactive) CDI m

CD-R [siːdiː'ɑr] n Comptr (abbr compact disc recordable) disco m compacto regrabable

Cdr Mil (abbr Commander) Comandante m, Cte

Cdre Mil (abbr Commodore) Comodoro m

CD-ROM [siːdiː'rɒm] n Comptr (abbr compact disc read-only memory) CD-ROM m; C. drive unidad f de CD-ROM

CD-RW n (abbr compact disc rewritable) CD-RW m

CE Rel (abbr Church of England) Iglesia f Anglicana

cease [siːs] 1 vt suspender, cesar; Mil c. fire cesar el fuego

2 vi cesar; to c. doing or to do sth dejar de hacer algo

cease-fire [siːsˈfaɪər] *n Mil* alto *m* el fuego

ceaseless [ˈsiːslɪs] *adj* incesante

ceaselessly [ˈsiːslɪslɪ] *adv* incesantemente, sin parar

cecum [ˈsiːkəm] *US (pl* **ceca** [ˈsiːkə]) *n see* **caecum**

cedar [ˈsiːdər] *n Bot* cedro *m* ❑ **Atlas c.** cedro *m* del atlas; **c. of Lebanon** cedro *m* del Líbano; **western red c.** tuya *f* gigante

cede [siːd] *vt Jur* ceder

cedilla [sɪˈdɪlə] *n Ling* cedilla *f*

ceiling [ˈsiːlɪŋ] *n* **(a)** *(of room)* techo *m; Fam Fig* **to hit the c.** ponerse negro(a) **(b)** *(limit)* tope *m*, límite *m* ❑ *Com* **c. price** precio *m* tope

celebrate [ˈselɪbreɪt] **1** *vt (occasion)* celebrar, conmemorar; *Rel* **to c. Mass** celebrar la misa
  2 *vi* divertirse; **let's c.** vamos a celebrarlo *or* festejarlo

celebrated [ˈselɪbreɪtɪd] *adj* famoso(a), célebre

celebration [selɪˈbreɪʃən] *n* celebración *f*; **celebrations** *(of anniversary, victory)* actos *mpl* conmemorativos; **in c.** para celebrar; **this calls for a c.** esto hay que celebrarlo *or* festejarlo

celebrity [sɪˈlebrɪtɪ] *n* celebridad *f*, personaje *m* famoso

celery [ˈselərɪ] *n* apio *m*

celestial [sɪˈlestɪəl] *adj* **(a)** *(heavenly)* celestial **(b)** *Astron* celeste; **c. navigation** navegación *f* astronómica

celibacy [ˈselɪbəsɪ] *n* celibato *m*

celibate [ˈselɪbɪt] *adj & n* célibe *(mf)*

cell [sel] *n* **(a)** *(in prison, monastery)* celda *f* **(b)** *(of honeycomb)* celdilla *f* **(c)** *Biol Pol* célula *f* **(d)** *Elec* pila *f* **(e)** *Comptr (in spreadsheet)* celda *f*

cellar [ˈselər] *n* **(a)** *(basement)* sótano *m* **(b)** *(for wine)* bodega *f*

cellist [ˈtʃelɪst] *n Mus* violoncelista *mf*

cello [ˈtʃeləʊ] *n (pl* **cellos)** *Mus* violoncelo *m*

Cellophane® [ˈseləfeɪn] *n Br* celofán *m*

cellphone [ˈselfəʊn] *n* teléfono *m* móvil *or Am* celular

cellular [ˈseljʊlər] *adj* celular; **c. phone** teléfono *m* móvil *or Am* celular

cellulite [ˈseljʊlaɪt] *n* celulitis *f inv*

celluloid [ˈseljʊlɔɪd] *n* celuloide *m*

cellulose [ˈseljʊləʊs] *n* celulosa *f*

Celsius [ˈselsɪəs] *adj* centígrado(a)

Celt [kelt, selt] *n* celta *mf*

Celtic [ˈkeltɪk, ˈseltɪk] **1** *n (language)* celta *m*
  2 *adj* celta

cement [sɪˈment] **1** *n* cemento *m*; **c. mixer** hormigonera *f*
  2 *vt Constr (bind)* unir con cemento; *(cover)* revestir de cemento; *Fig (friendship)* cimentar

cemetery [ˈsemɪtrɪ] *n* cementerio *m*

cenotaph [ˈsenətɑːf] *n* cenotafio *m*

censer [ˈsensər] *n Rel* incensario *m*

censor [ˈsensər] **1** *n* censor(a) *m,f*
  2 *vt* censurar

censorious [senˈsɔːrɪəs] *adj (person)* censurador(a); *(look)* reprobatorio(a); **to be c. of** censurar

censorship [ˈsensəʃɪp] *n* censura *f*

censure [ˈsenʃər] **1** *n* censura *f*; **vote of c.** voto de censura
  2 *vt* censurar

census [ˈsensəs] *n (pl* **censuses)** censo *m*, padrón *m*; **to take a c.** realizar un censo

cent [sent] *n* **(a)** *(coin)* centavo *m*, céntimo *m* **(b)** **per c.** por ciento

centaur [ˈsentɔːr] *n Myth* centauro *m*

centenarian [sentɪˈneərɪən] *n* centenario(a) *m,f*

centenary [senˈtiːnərɪ], *US* **centennial** [senˈtenɪəl] *adj & n* centenario(a) *(m)*

center [ˈsentər] *n & vt US see* **centre**

centerfold [ˈsentəfəʊld] *n US see* **centrefold**

centerline [ˈsentəlaɪn] *n US see* **centreline**

centerpiece [ˈsentəpiːs] *n US see* **centrepiece**

centigrade [ˈsentɪgreɪd] *adj* centígrado(a); **37°C.** 37 grados centígrados

centigramme, *US* **centigram** [ˈsentɪgræm] *n* centigramo *m*

centilitre, *US* **centiliter** [ˈsentɪliːtər] *n* centilitro *m*

centimetre, *US* **centimeter** [ˈsentɪmiːtər] *n* centimetro *m*

centipede [ˈsentɪpiːd] *n Ent* ciempiés *m inv*

central [ˈsentrəl] *adj* central; **c. bank** banco *m* central; **the c. character** el personaje principal; *Pol* **c. government** gobierno central; **c. heating** calefacción central; *Aut* **c. locking** cierre *m* centralizado ❑ **C. African Republic** República Centroafricana; **C. America** Centroamérica; **C. American** centroamericano(a) *m,f*

centralization [sentrəlaɪˈzeɪʃən] *n* centralización *f*

centralize [ˈsentrəlaɪz] *vt* centralizar

centrally [ˈsentrəlɪ] *adv* **c. heated** con calefacción central; **c. situated** céntrico(a)

centre [ˈsentər] **1** *n* **(a)** *(gen)* centro *m*; **town c.** centro de la ciudad ❑ *Ftb* **c. forward** delantero *m* centro; *Ftb* **c. half** medio *m* centro; *Pol* **c. party** partido *m* centrista *or* de centro **(b)** **shopping c.** centro *m* comercial; **sports c.** centro *m* deportivo; **arts c.** centro *m* cultural **(c)** *Fig* **c. of interest/attention** centro *m* de interés/de todas las miradas
  2 *vt (attention etc)* centrar, concentrar **(on, upon** en, sobre)

centrefold [ˈsentəfəʊld] *n (of magazine)* página *f* central

centreline [ˈsentəlaɪn] *n (of tennis court, road)* línea *f* central; *(of geometrical figure)* eje *m*

centrepiece [ˈsentəpiːs] *n (table decoration)* centro *m* de mesa; *Fig* atracción *f* principal

centrifugal [senˈtrɪfjʊgəl, ˈsentrɪfjuːgəl] *adj* centrífugo(a)

centripetal [senˈtrɪpɪtəl, ˈsentrɪpiːtəl] *adj* centrípeto(a)

centrist [ˈsentrɪst] *adj & n Pol* centrista *(mf)*

centurion [senˈtjʊərɪən] *n Hist* centurión *m*

century [ˈsentʃərɪ] *n* **(a)** *(a hundred years)* siglo *m*; **the nineteenth c.** el siglo diecinueve **(b)** *(cricket score)* centena *f*

CEO [siːiːˈəʊ] *n (pl* **CEOs)** *Com (abbr* **chief executive officer)** director(a) *m,f*, gerente, consejero(a) *m,f* delegado(a)

ceramic [sɪˈræmɪk] **1** *n* cerámica *f*
  2 *adj* de cerámica; **c. tile** azulejo *m*, teja *f*

ceramics [sɪˈræmɪks] *n sing Art* cerámica *f*

cereal [ˈsɪərɪəl] *n* cereal *m*; **breakfast c.** cereales *mpl* para el desayuno

cerebellum [serɪˈbeləm] *(pl* **cerebella** [serɪˈbelə]) *n Anat* cerebelo *m*

cerebral [ˈserɪbrəl, sɪˈriːbrəl] *adj* **(a)** *Med* cerebral; **c. palsy** parálisis *f* cerebral **(b)** *(person)* cerebral

cerebrum [ˈserɪbrəm] *(pl* **cerebrums** *or* **cerebra** [ˈserɪbrə]) *n Anat* cerebro *m*

ceremonial [serɪˈməʊnɪəl] **1** *adj* ceremonioso(a), formal
  2 *n* ceremonial *m*

ceremonious [serɪˈməʊnɪəs] *adj* ceremonioso(a)

ceremony [ˈserɪmənɪ] *n* ceremonia *f*; **the marriage c.** la ceremonia nupcial; **with/without c.** con/sin ceremonia; *Fig* **he was sacked without c.** lo despidieron sin ningún miramiento; **there's no need to stand on c.** no hace falta cumplir con formalidades

cert [sɜːt] *n Fam* **it's a dead c.** no puede fallar, no cabe duda

certain ['sɜːtən] **1** *adj* (**a**) *(sure)* seguro(a); **he's c. to win** no cabe duda que ganará; **I'm c. she didn't pay** estoy seguro(a) (de) que no ha pagado; **to make c. of sth** asegurarse de algo (**b**) *(moderate)* cierto(a); **to a c. extent** hasta cierto punto (**c**) *(not known)* cierto(a); **a c. Miss Ward** una tal señorita Ward; **for c. reasons** por razones desconocidas (**d**) *(true)* cierto(a), verdadero(a)
  2 *adv* **for c.** seguro; **I know for c.** sé a ciencia cierta, sé con toda seguridad

certainly ['sɜːtənlɪ] *adv* naturalmente, desde luego, por supuesto; **c. not** por supuesto que no, de ninguna manera, ni hablar

certainty ['sɜːtəntɪ] *n* (*gen*) certeza *f*; *(assurance)* seguridad *f*

certifiable ['sɜːtɪfaɪəbəl] *adj* (**a**) *(attested)* que se puede certificar (**b**) *(mad)* demente

certificate [sə'tɪfɪkɪt] *n* (**a**) (*gen*) certificado *m*; *Educ* diploma *m*; **birth c.** partida *f* de nacimiento; **death c.** certificado· *m* de defunción; **medical c.** certificado *m* médico (**b**) *Fin* **savings c.** bono *m* de ahorro

certified ['sɜːtɪfaɪd] *adj* (*gen*) certificado(a); *(copy)* legalizado(a) ❏ *US* **c. mail** correo *m* certificado; *US* **c. public accountant** *Esp* censor(a) *m,f* jurado(a) de cuentas, *Am* contador(a) *m,f* público(a)

certify ['sɜːtɪfaɪ] *vt (pt & pp* **certified**) certificar; **this is to c. that ...** certifico que ...; **to c. sb (as being) insane** declarar enfermo(a) mental a algn

certitude ['sɜːtɪtjuːd] *n* certeza *f*

cervical ['sɜːvɪkəl, sə'vaɪkəl] *adj* (**a**) *(neck)* cervical (**b**) *(uterus)* del útero; **c. cancer** cáncer *m* del útero; **c. smear** frotis *m* cervical

cervix ['sɜːvɪks] *n (pl* **cervixes** *or* **cervices** [sə'vaɪsiːz]) *Anat* cuello *m* del útero

Cesarian [sɪ'zeərɪən] *n US see* **Caesarean**

cessation [se'seɪʃən] *n (of hostilities etc)* cese *m*

cesspit ['sespɪt] *n,* **cesspool** ['sespuːl] *n* pozo *m* negro

CET [siːiː'tiː] *n (abbr* **Central European Time**) = hora de Europa central

Ceylon [sɪ'lɒn] *n Formerly* Ceilán

cf (*abbr* **confer**) (compare), compárese, cfr.

CFC [siːef'siː] *n (pl* **CFCs**) *Chem (abbr* **chlorofluorocarbon**) CFC *m*, clorofluorocarbono *m*

CGI [siːdʒiː'aɪ] *n (abbr* **computer-generated images**) imágenes *fpl* generadas por *Esp* ordenador *or Am* computadora

ch (*abbr* **chapter**) capítulo *m*, cap., c.

Chad [tʃæd] *n* Chad

Chadian ['tʃædɪən] *adj & n* chadiano(a) *(m,f)*

chafe [tʃeɪf] **1** *vt* (**a**) *(make sore)* rozar, excoriar (**b**) *(warm up)* calentar
  2 *vi* (**a**) *(skin)* irritarse (**b**) *(person)* irritarse (**at** a causa de)

chaff¹ [tʃɑːf] *n* barcia *f*, granzas *fpl*; *(fodder)* paja *f*; *Fig* **to separate the wheat from the c.** separar el grano de la paja

chaff² [tʃɑːf] *vt* burlarse de

chaffinch ['tʃæfɪntʃ] *n Orn* pinzón *m* vulgar

chagrin ['ʃægrɪn] *n* disgusto *m*, desilusión *f*

chain [tʃeɪn] **1** *n* (*gen*) cadena *f*; *Fig (of events)* serie *f*; **c. of**

mountains cordillera *f*; *Com* **supermarket c.** cadena de supermercados; **to make a c.** *(people)* formar una cadena humana; **to pull the c.** *(in WC)* tirar de la cadena ❏ *US* **c. gang** cadena *f* de presidiarios; **c. letter** cadena *f* de cartas; **c. mail** cota *f* de malla; **c. reaction** reacción *f* en cadena; **c. saw** sierra *f* mecánica; *Knit* **c. stitch** cadeneta *f*; **c. store** cadena *f* de tiendas
  2 *vt* **to c. (up)** encadenar

chain-smoke ['tʃeɪnsməʊk] *vi* fumar un pitillo tras otro

chain-smoker ['tʃeɪn'sməʊkər] *n* fumador(a) *m,f* empedernido(a)

chair [tʃeər] **1** *n* (**a**) *Furn* silla *f*; *(with arms)* sillón *m*, butaca *f*; **high c.** trono *m*; **please take a c.** siéntese por favor (**b**) *(position)* presidencia *f*; *Univ* cátedra *f*; **to address the c.** dirigirse al presidente; **to be in the c., to take the c. (at a meeting)** presidir (una reunión)
  2 *vt (meeting)* presidir

chairlift ['tʃeəlɪft] *n* telesilla *m*

chairman ['tʃeəmən] *n (pl* **chairmen**) presidente *m*

chairmanship ['tʃeəmənʃɪp] *n* presidencia *f*

chairperson ['tʃeəpɜːsən] *n* presidente(a) *m,f*

chairwoman ['tʃeəwʊmən] *n (pl* **chairwomen**) presidenta *f*

chalet ['ʃæleɪ] *n* chalet *m*, chalé *m*

chalice ['tʃælɪs] *n* cáliz *m*

chalk [tʃɔːk] **1** *n Min* creta *f*, roca *f* caliza; *(for writing)* tiza *f*, *Méx* gis *m*; *Br Fam* **not by a long c.** ni mucho menos, ni por mucho; *Br Fam* **they are as different as c. and cheese** se parecen como un huevo a una manzana
  2 *vt* **to c. (out)** *(area etc)* marcar con tiza; *(plan)* trazar

chalk up *vt Fam (victory)* apuntarse; **c. it up to me!** ¡ponlo en mi cuenta!

chalkboard ['tʃɔːkbɔːd] *n US* pizarra *f*, encerado *m*, *Am* pizarrón *m*

chalky ['tʃɔːkɪ] *adj* (**chalkier, chalkiest**) cretáceo(a), calcáreo(a)

challenge ['tʃælɪndʒ] **1** *vt* (**a**) *(to game of football etc)* retar, desafiar; **to c. sb to do sth** retar a algn a que haga algo (**b**) *(person, authority)* poner a prueba; *(statement)* poner en duda (**c**) *Mil* dar el alto *or* quién vive a (**d**) *Jur* recusar
  2 *n* (**a**) (*gen*) reto *m*, desafío *m*; *Sport* desafío; **the job will be a real c. to her** el trabajo pondrá a prueba sus cualidades; **to take up a c.** aceptar un reto (**b**) *Mil* quién vive *m* (**c**) *Jur* recusación *f*

challenger ['tʃælɪndʒər] *n* desafiador(a) *m,f*; *Sport* aspirante *mf* a un título

challenging ['tʃælɪndʒɪŋ] *adj* *(idea)* provocativo(a); *(task)* que presenta un reto *or* un desafío

chamber ['tʃeɪmbər] *n* (**a**) *(hall)* cámara *f*; *Parl* **Lower/Upper C.** cámara baja/alta; **C. of Commerce** Cámara de Comercio (**b**) *Mus* **c. music** música *f* de cámara (**c**) *(of gun)* recámara *f* (**d**) *Br Jur* **chambers** despacho *m sing*, gabinete *m sing*

chambermaid ['tʃeɪmbəmeɪd] *n* doncella *f*, camarera *f*

chamberpot ['tʃeɪmbəpɒt] *n* orinal *m*, *Am* bacinica *f*

chameleon [kə'miːlɪən] *n Zool* camaleón *m*

chamois ['ʃæmwɑː] *n inv* (**a**) *Zool* gamuza *f* (**b**) ['ʃæmɪ] **c.** **(leather)** gamuza *f*

champ¹ [tʃæmp] **1** *vt (fodder)* mascar
  2 *vi Fam* mordisquear; *Fig* **to c. at the bit** comerle a uno la impaciencia

champ² [tʃæmp] *n Fam* campeón(ona) *m,f*

champagne [ʃæm'peɪn] *n* champán *m*

champion ['tʃæmpɪən] **1** *n* campeón(ona) *m,f*; **a c. swimmer** un campeón de natación; **world c.** campeón mundial; *Fig* **c. of human rights** defensor(a) *m,f* de los derechos humanos

2 *vt Fig (cause)* defender

championship ['tʃæmpɪənʃɪp] *n Sport* campeonato *m*

chance [tʃɑːns] **1** *n* (**a**) *(fate, fortune)* casualidad *f,* azar *m*; **by c.** por casualidad; **games of c.** juegos de azar; **on the c.** por si acaso; **to take a c.** arriesgarse, correr un riesgo; **I'm not taking any chances** no quiero arriesgarme □ **c. discovery** descubrimiento *m* fortuito; **c. meeting** encuentro *m* casual (**b**) *(likelihood)* posibilidad *f;* **I don't stand a c., I've got no c.** no tengo ni la más remota posibilidad; **(the) chances are that ...** lo más posible es que ... (**c**) *(opportunity)* oportunidad *f, Am* chance *f;* **to have an eye for the main c.** cuidar de sus propios intereses; **to miss a c.** perder una oportunidad

2 *vi* **c. on** *or* **upon** encontrar por casualidad; **to c. to do sth** hacer algo por casualidad; **I chanced to look** miré por casualidad

3 *vt* arriesgar; *Fam* **let's c. it** vamos a arriesgarnos

chancel ['tʃɑːnsəl] *n Archit Rel* presbiterio *m*

chancellor ['tʃɑːnsələr] *n* (**a**) *Pol (head of state, in embassy)* canciller *m* (**b**) *Univ Br* rector(a) *m,f* honorario(a); *US* rector(a) *m,f* (**c**) *Br* **C. of the Exchequer** ministro(a) *m,f* de Hacienda

chancy ['tʃɑːnsɪ] *adj* (**chancier, chanciest**) *Fam* arriesgado(a)

chandelier [ʃændɪ'lɪər] *n* araña *f* (de luces)

change [tʃeɪndʒ] **1** *vt* cambiar (de); *Aut* **to c. gear** cambiar de marcha *or* de velocidad; **to c. one's mind/the subject** cambiar de opinión/de tema; **to c. euros into dollars** cambiar euros en dólares; **to c. places with sb** cambiarse de sitio con algn; *Mil* **to c. the guard** cambiar la guardia; **to c. trains** transbordar, cambiar de tren; **to get changed** mudarse, cambiarse de ropa; *Fig* **to c. hands** cambiar de dueño(a)

2 *vi* cambiar, cambiarse; *Rail* **all c.!** ¡cambio de tren!; **I think he's changed** le veo cambiado; **to c. for the better/worse** mejorar/empeorar; **to c. into** convertirse *or* transformarse en

3 *n* (**a**) *(alteration)* cambio *m*; **c. for the better/worse** cambio beneficioso/desventajoso; **c. of address/occupation** cambio de domicilio/trabajo; **c. of clothes** muda *f* de ropa; **for a c.** para variar; *Aut* **gear c.** cambio de velocidades; **to ring the changes** variar; *Fig* **c. of heart** cambio de parecer; *Fig* **c. of scene** cambio de aires; *Euph* **the c. of life** la menopausia (**b**) *(money)* cambio *m*, *Esp* vueltas *fpl*, *Andes CAm Méx* sencillo *m*, *Carib Col* devuelta *f*, *RP* vuelto *m*; **keep the c.** quédese con el cambio *or Am* vuelto; **small c.** cambio *m*, suelto *m*; **to give c. for a pound** cambiar una libra; *Fam* **you won't get much c. out of him** no esperes gran cosa de él

change down *vi Aut* reducir (marcha)

change over *vi* cambiarse; *Br Sport* cambiar de campo

change up *vi Aut* cambiar a una velocidad *or* marcha superior

changeable ['tʃeɪndʒəbəl] *adj (weather)* variable; *(person)* inconstante, voluble

changeless ['tʃeɪndʒlɪs] *adj* inmutable

changeover ['tʃeɪndʒəʊvər] *n* (**a**) *(gen)* conversión *f* (**b**) *Mil* cambio *m*, relevo *m* (de la guardia) (**c**) *Sport (of runner etc)* relevo *m*

changing ['tʃeɪndʒɪŋ] **1** *n* (**a**) *(gen)* cambio *m* □ *Sport* **c. room** vestuario *m* (**b**) *Mil* cambio *m*, relevo *m* (de la guardia)

2 *adj* cambiante

channel ['tʃænəl] **1** *n* (**a**) *Geog* canal *m*; *(bed of river)* cauce *m*, lecho *m* □ **the C. Islands** las Islas Anglonormandas; **the**

English C. el Canal de la Mancha (**b**) *(administrative)* vía *f*, conducto *m*; **c. of communication** vía de comunicación; **through the official channels** por los conductos oficiales (**c**) *TV Rad* canal *m*, cadena *f*

2 *vt* *(pt & pp* **channelled**, *US* **channeled**) *Fig (ideas etc)* canalizar, encauzar

channel-hop ['tʃænəlhɒp], *US* **channel-surf** ['tʃænəlsɜːf] *vi Fam* zapear, hacer zapping

chant [tʃɑːnt] **1** *n* (**a**) *Rel* canto *m* litúrgico, cántico *m* (**b**) *(of demonstrators)* slogan *m*

2 *vt & vi* (**a**) *Rel* cantar (cánticos) (**b**) *(demonstrators)* corear, repetir

chaos ['keɪɒs] *n* caos *m*; **c. theory** teoría *f* del caos

chaotic [keɪ'ɒtɪk] *adj* caótico(a)

chap[1] [tʃæp] *n Fam* chico *m*, *Esp* tío *m*; **a good c.** un tío fenomenal *or* fantástico

chap[2] *(abbr* **chapter**) capítulo *m*, cap., c.

chapel ['tʃæpəl] *n Rel* capilla *f*; **c. of rest** capilla ardiente

chaperone ['ʃæpərəʊn] **1** *n* señora *f* de compañía, *Esp* carabina *f*, *Am* chaperona *f*

2 *vt Fam Esp* acompañar como carabina, *Am* ir de chaperona de

chaplain ['tʃæplɪn] *n Rel* capellán *m*

chaplaincy ['tʃæplɪnsɪ] *n* capellanía *f*

chapped [tʃæpt] *adj (lips)* cortado(a); *(skin)* agrietado(a)

chapter ['tʃæptər] *n* (**a**) *(of book)* capítulo *m*; *Fig* serie *f;* **to quote c. and verse** citar palabra por palabra (**b**) *US Fin* **c. 11** *(part of bankruptcy laws)* = sección de la ley de quiebras estadounidense que regula el proceso de declaración oficial de bancarrota

chapterhouse ['tʃæptəhaʊs] *n Rel* sala *f* capitular

char[1] [tʃɑːr] **1** *vt (pt & pp* **charred**) chamuscar, carbonizar

2 *vi* chamuscarse, carbonizarse

char[2] [tʃɑːr] *Br Fam* **1** *n* señora *f* de la limpieza

2 *vi (pt & pp* **charred**) trabajar como señora de la limpieza

character ['kærɪktər] *n* (**a**) *(personality)* carácter *m*; **a person of good c.** una persona de buena reputación; **to have a lot of c.** tener mucho carácter *or* mucha personalidad; **to have a strong c.** tener un carácter fuerte; *Fig* **to be in/out of c.** conformar/no conformar al tipo; *Fam* **she's quite a c.** es todo un carácter (**b**) *Fam (person)* tipo *m*; **a suspicious c.** un tipo de mucho cuidado (**c**) *(in novel, play)* personaje *m*; **c. actor** = actor especializado en personajes poco convencionales (**d**) *(letter)* carácter *m*; *Comptr* **c. set** juego *m* de caracteres

characteristic [kærɪktə'rɪstɪk] **1** *n* característica *f*

2 *adj* característico(a)

characterization [kærɪktəraɪ'zeɪʃən] *n* caracterización *f*

characterize ['kærɪktəraɪz] *vt* caracterizar

characterless ['kærɪktəlɪs] *adj* de poco carácter

charade [ʃə'rɑːd] *n* (**a**) *Br* farsa *f* (**b**) **charades** *(game)* charadas *fpl*

charcoal ['tʃɑːkəʊl] *n Min* carbón *m* vegetal □ *Art* **c. drawing** carboncillo *m*, dibujo *m* al carboncillo; *(colour)* **c. grey** gris *m* marengo *or* oscuro

chard [tʃɑːd] *n Bot* acelga *f*

charge [tʃɑːdʒ] **1** *vt* (**a**) *(price)* cobrar; *Com* **c. it to my account** cárguelo en mi cuenta; **how much do you c.?** ¿cuánto cobra?; **they c. $30 an hour** cobran 30 dólares la hora (**b**) *Jur* acusar; **to c. sb with a crime** acusar a algn de un crimen (**c**) *Mil* atacar, cargar contra (**d**) *Elec (battery)* cargar

2 *vi* (**a**) *Elec (battery)* cargar (**b**) *Mil* atacar, cargar (**c**) **to c. about** atado a lo loco; **to c. in** entrar alocadamente

3 *n* (**a**) *(cost)* precio *m*; **bank charges** comisión *f* (por servicio bancario); **extra c.** suplemento *m*; **free of c.** gratis, sin gasto alguno; **service c.** servicio *m* ❑ **c. account** cuenta *f* corriente; **c. card** tarjeta *f* de compra **(b)** *(responsibility)* cargo *m*; **to be in c. of** estar a cargo de; **to take c. of** hacerse cargo de; **who is in c.?** ¿quién es el encargado?; *Fig* **a nanny and her c.** una niñera y el niño a su cargo **(c)** *Jur* cargo *m*, acusación *f*; **to bring a c. against sb** formular una acusación contra algn; **to face a c. of ...** responder a una acusación de ... **(d)** *Mil (explosive)* carga *f* explosiva; *(by cavalry)* carga *f* **(e)** *Elec* carga *f*

chargeable ['tʃɑːdʒəbəl] *adj (expenses, debts)* **c. to** a cargo de

charged [tʃɑːdʒd] *adj Elec* cargado(a); *Fig (issue)* emotivo(a); **emotionally c.** con una carga afectiva

chargé d'affaires [ʃɑːʒeɪdæˈfeər] *n (pl* **chargés d'affaires)** *Pol* encargado(a) *m,f* de negocios

charger ['tʃɑːdʒər] *n* **(a)** *Elec* cargador *m* **(b)** *(horse)* caballo *m* de guerra

chariot ['tʃærɪət] *n* carro *m* (de guerra)

charisma [kəˈrɪzmə] *n* carisma *m*

charismatic [kærɪzˈmætɪk] *adj* carismático(a)

charitable ['tʃærɪtəbəl] *adj* **(a)** *(person)* caritativo(a); *(attitude)* comprensivo(a) **(b)** *(work, organization)* benéfico(a)

charity ['tʃærɪtɪ] *n* **(a)** *(quality)* caridad *f*; **to do sth out of c.** hacer algo por caridad; *Prov* **c. begins at home** *Esp* la caridad bien entendida empieza por uno mismo, *Esp* la caridad empieza por casa **(b)** *(organization)* institución *f* benéfica

charlady ['tʃɑːleɪdɪ] *n Br* señora *f* de la limpieza

charlatan ['ʃɑːlətən] *n (doctor)* curandero(a) *m,f*

charm [tʃɑːm] **1** *n* **(a)** *(quality)* encanto *m* **(b)** *(spell)* hechizo *m*; **lucky c.** amuleto *m*; **to work like a c.** funcionar a las mil maravillas ❑ **c. bracelet** pulsera *f* de dijes

2 *vt* encantar; *Fig* **she can c. the birds off the trees** es muy coqueta

charmer ['tʃɑːmər] *n* **(a)** *Fam* atractivo(a) *m,f*, simpático(a) *m,f*, encantador(a) *m,f* **(b)** *(of snakes)* encantador(a) *m,f*

charming ['tʃɑːmɪŋ] *adj* encantador(a)

charred [tʃɑːd] *adj* carbonizado(a)

chart [tʃɑːt] **1** *n* **(a)** *(of institution)* estatutos *mpl*; *(of company)* carta *f* de privilegios; *(of rights)* carta *f* **(b)** *Av Naut* fletamento *m*; **c. flight** vuelo *m* chárter

chart [tʃɑːt] **1** *n* **(a)** *Naut* carta *f* de marear; *Av* carta *f* de navegación **(b)** *(giving information)* tabla *f*; *(graph)* gráfico *m* ❑ *Med* **temperature c.** gráfico *m* de temperaturas; **weather c.** mapa *m* meteorológico or del tiempo **(c)** *Mus* **the charts** la lista de éxitos, el hit parade

2 *vt* **(a)** *Av Naut (on map)* trazar **(b)** *(information)* poner en un gráfico *or* una tabla

charter ['tʃɑːtər] **1** *n* **(a)** *(of institution)* estatutos *mpl*; *(of company)* carta *f* de privilegios; *(of rights)* carta *f* **(b)** *Av Naut* fletamento *m*; **c. flight** vuelo *m* chárter

2 *vt (plane, boat)* fletar

chartered accountant [tʃɑːtədəˈkaʊntənt] *n Br* censor(a) *m,f* jurado(a) de cuentas, *Am* contador(a) *m,f* público(a)

charwoman ['tʃɑːwʊmən] *n (pl* **charwomen)** *Br see* charlady

chary ['tʃeərɪ] *adj* **(charier, chariest)** *Fam (wary)* cauteloso(a), cauto(a); **to be c. of doing sth** tener cuidado al hacer algo

chase [tʃeɪs] **1** *vt* perseguir; *(hunt)* cazar

2 *vi Fam* **to c. about** *or* **around** correr de un lado para otro

3 *n* persecución *f*; *(hunt)* caza *f*; **to give c. to sb** dar caza a algn; *Fig* **a wild goose c.** una empresa descabellada

chaser ['tʃeɪsər] *n* **(a)** *Fam Fig* = copita de licor que se toma después de cerveza **(b)** *(that chases)* perseguidor(a) *m,f*

chasm ['kæzəm] *n Geog* sima *f*; *Fig* abismo *m*

chassis ['ʃæsɪ] *n (pl* **chassis** ['ʃæsɪz]) *Aut* chasis *m inv*

chaste [tʃeɪst] *adj* casto(a); *(style)* sobrio(a)

chasten ['tʃeɪsən] *vt (punish)* castigar

chastise [tʃæsˈtaɪz] *vt* castigar

chastisement ['tʃæstɪzmənt, tʃæsˈtaɪzmənt] *n* castigo *m*

chastity ['tʃæstɪtɪ] *n* castidad *f*; **c. belt** cinturón *m* de castidad

chat [tʃæt] **1** *n* **(a)** *(informal conversation)* charla *f*, *CAm Méx* plática *f*; **I'll have a c. with him** hablaré con él un ratito; *Br Rad TV* **c. show** coloquio *m*, entrevista *f* **(b)** *Comptr* charla *f*, chat *m*; **c. room** sala *f* de conversación

2 *vi (pt & pp* **chatted)** charlar, *CAm Méx* platicar **chatting away** dando palique

chat up *vt Br Fam* **to c. sb up** intentar ligar con algn *or* ligarse a algn, *RP* intentar levantar a algn

chattels ['tʃætəlz] *npl Jur* bienes *mpl* muebles

chatter ['tʃætər] **1** *vi (person)* chacharear, parlotear; *(bird)* piar, gorjear; *(teeth)* castañetear; *(monkeys)* chillar

2 *n (of person)* cháchara *f*, parloteo *m*; *(of birds)* gorjeo *m*; *(of teeth)* castañeteo *m*; *(of monkeys)* chillidos *mpl*

chatterbox ['tʃætəbɒks] *n Fam* parlanchín(ina) *m,f*

chatty ['tʃætɪ] *adj* **(chattier, chattiest)** parlanchín(ina), hablador(a)

chauffeur ['ʃəʊfər, ʃəʊˈfɜːr] *n Esp* chófer *m*, *Am* chofer *m*

chauffeur-driven ['ʃəʊfəˈdrɪvən] *adj* con *Esp* chófer *or Am* chofer

chauvinism ['ʃəʊvɪnɪzəm] *n* chovinismo *m*, chauvinismo *m*; **male c.** machismo *m*

chauvinist ['ʃəʊvɪnɪst] *adj & n* chovinista *(mf)*, chauvinista *(mf)*; **male c.** machista *m*

cheap [tʃiːp] **1** *adj* barato(a); *(fare)* económico(a); *(joke)* fácil; *Fig Pej (contemptible)* vil, bajo(a); **to be c.** ser barato(a), estar a buen precio; *Fig* **to feel c.** avergonzarse, sentir vergüenza; *Fam* **c. and nasty** barato(a) (y malo(a)); **c. rate** tarifa *f* reducida; *Fam* **dirt c.** tirado(a), baratísimo(a)

2 *n Br Fam* **on the c.** en plan barato; **to get sth on the c.** conseguir algo muy barato

3 *adv* barato

cheapen ['tʃiːpən] *vt* abaratar, rebajar el precio de; *Fig* degradar, rebajar

cheaply ['tʃiːplɪ] *adv* barato, en plan económico *or* barato

cheapness ['tʃiːpnɪs] *n* baratura *f*, lo barato

cheapskate ['tʃiːpskeɪt] *n Fam* roñica *mf*

cheat [tʃiːt] **1** *vt* engañar; **to c. sb out of sth** estafar algo a algn

2 *vi* **(a)** *(at games)* hacer trampa **(b)** *Fam (husband, wife)* poner cuernos **(on** a)

3 *n (trickster)* tramposo(a) *m,f*, fullero(a) *m,f*; *(involving money)* estafador(a) *m,f*

cheating ['tʃiːtɪŋ] *n (trickery)* trampa *f*, fullería *f*; *(involving money)* estafa *f*, timo *m*

Chechen ['tʃetʃen] *adj & n* checheno(a) *(m,f)*

Chechnya ['tʃetʃnɪə] *n* Chechenia

check [tʃek] **1** *vt* **(a)** *visar*, repasar; *(facts, statement)* comprobar, *Guat Méx* checar; *(passports, tickets)* revisar, controlar; *(luggage at customs)* registrar; *Aut (tyres, oil)* revisar; **to c. sth against a list** cotejar *or* comparar algo con una lista **(b)** *(anger, impulse)* contener, refrenar; *(growth, progress)* retrasar, retardar **(c)** *(stop, control)* detener; **to keep in c.** *(disease, feelings)* contener, controlar; *(enemy)* mantener a raya; **to keep imports in c.** poner freno a las importaciones **(d)** *Chess* dar jaque a

2 *vi* mirar, comprobar, *Guat Méx* checar; **I have to c. to**

see if I locked the car tengo que comprobar si he cerrado el coche

3 *n* (**a**) *(of documents, goods, people)* revisión *f*; *(of results, facts)* comprobación *f*, verificación *f*; **a c. on all people leaving the country** una revisión de todas las personas que salgan del país ❑ **c. list** lista *f* de cotejo (**b**) *Chess* jaque *m* (**c**) *(pattern)* cuadro *m* (**d**) *US see* **cheque**

check in *vi (at airport)* facturar; *Am* despachar; *(at hotel)* registrarse (**at** en)

check off *vt* ir tachando (de una lista); **c. the names off as I read them out** tacha los nombres a medida que los vaya leyendo

check out 1 *vi (from hotel)* dejar el hotel, pagar la cuenta y marcharse
   2 *vt (facts)* verificar, *Am* chequear, *Méx* checar

check up *vi* **to c. up on sb** hacer averiguaciones sobre algn; **to c. up on sth** averiguar *or* comprobar algo

checkbook ['tʃekbʊk] *n US see* **chequebook**

checked [tʃekt] *adj* a cuadros; **c. material** tela *f* a cuadros

checker ['tʃekər] *n US (cashier)* cajero(a) *m,f*

checkerboard ['tʃekəbɔːd] *n US see* **chequerboard**

checkered ['tʃekəd] *adj US see* **chequered**

checkers ['tʃekəz] *n US (game)* damas *fpl*

check-in ['tʃekɪn] *n* registro *m*; **c.-in desk** recepción *f*; **c. time** = hora a la que hay que facturar

checking account ['tʃekɪŋə'kaʊnt] *n US* cuenta *f* corriente

checkmate ['tʃekmeɪt] **1** *n Chess* jaque mate *m*
   2 *vt Chess* dar mate a; *Fig* poner en un callejón sin salida

checkout ['tʃekaʊt] *n (counter)* caja *f*

checkpoint ['tʃekpɔɪnt] *n* control *m*; **she passed the c. with no difficulty** pasó el control sin problemas

checkroom ['tʃekruːm, 'tʃekrʊm] *n US (for luggage)* consigna *f*

checkup ['tʃekʌp] *n Med* chequeo *m*, examen *m* médico

cheek [tʃiːk] **1** *n* (**a**) *Anat* mejilla *f*; **c. by jowl** lado a lado; *Fig* **to say sth tongue in c.** decir algo para burlarse; *Fig* **to turn the other c.** dar la otra mejilla (**b**) *Fam (nerve)* jeta *f*, cara *f*; **to have the c. of the devil** ser un caradura, *Esp* tener jeta; **what (a) c.!** ¡vaya jeta!
   2 *vt Br Fam (be impudent to)* ser descarado(a) con

cheekbone ['tʃiːkbəʊn] *n* pómulo *m*

cheeky ['tʃiːkɪ] *adj* (**cheekier, cheekiest**) *Fam* fresco(a), insolente, descarado(a)

cheep [tʃiːp] **1** *n (of bird)* pío *m*, piada *f*, gorjeo *m*
   2 *vi* piar, gorjear

cheer [tʃɪər] **1** *vi* aplaudir, aclamar
   2 *vt* (**a**) *(applaud with shouts)* vitorear, aclamar, ovacionar (**b**) *(make hopeful)* animar
   3 *n* viva *m*, vítor *m*; **loud cheers** una ovación cerrada; **three cheers** tres hurras; **to the cheers of the crowd** a los aplausos del público; *Fam* **cheers!** *(before drinking)* ¡salud!; *Br (thank you)* gracias; *Br (goodbye)* adiós, *Am* ¡chau!

cheer on *vt (athlete)* alentar

cheer up 1 *vi* alegrarse, animarse; **c. up!** ¡ánimo!, ¡alegra esa cara!
   2 *vt* **to c. sb up** alegrar *or* animar a algn; **your letter cheered me up** tu carta me dio ánimos

cheerful ['tʃɪəfʊl] *adj* (**a**) *(person)* alegre, animado(a) (**b**) *(place, colour)* alegre; *(tune, conversation)* animado(a) (**c**) *(willing)* contento(a)

cheerfully ['tʃɪəfʊlɪ] *adv* alegremente, con buena disposición

cheerfulness ['tʃɪəfʊlnɪs] *n* alegría *f*

cheerily ['tʃɪərɪlɪ] *adv* de buen humor

cheering ['tʃɪərɪŋ] *n* ovaciones *fpl*, vítores *mpl*

cheerio [tʃɪərɪ'əʊ] *interj Br Fam* ¡adiós!, ¡hasta luego!, *Am* ¡chau!

cheerleader ['tʃɪəliːdər] *n* = persona que inicia los vítores (en un partido)

cheerless ['tʃɪəlɪs] *adj (place)* triste; *(day)* melancólico(a), triste

cheery ['tʃɪərɪ] *adj* (**cheerier, cheeriest**) alegre, optimista

cheese [tʃiːz] *n Culin* queso *m*; **a piece of c.** un trozo de queso; *Fam* **say c.!** *(for photograph)* ¡sonríe!, *Esp* ¡(di) patata!, *Méx* ¡(di) rojo!, *RP* ¡decí (whisky)! ❑ **cottage c.** requesón *m*

cheeseboard ['tʃiːzbɔːd] *n (selection)* tabla *f* de quesos

cheeseburger ['tʃiːzbɜːgər] *n* hamburguesa *f* de *or* con queso

cheesecake ['tʃiːzkeɪk] *n Culin* tarta *f* de queso

cheesecloth ['tʃiːzklɒθ] *n Tex* estopilla *f*

cheesed off [tʃiːzd'ɒf] *adj Br Fam* **to be c. o.** estar hasta las narices *or* la coronilla (de)

cheeseparing ['tʃiːzpeərɪŋ] **1** *adj* tacaño(a)
   2 *n* tacañería *f*

cheesy ['tʃiːzɪ] *n Fam Pej (inferior)* de tres al cuarto, *Esp* cutre

cheetah ['tʃiːtə] *n Zool* guepardo *m*

chef [ʃef] *n* chef *m*

chemical ['kemɪkəl] **1** *n* sustancia *f* química, producto *m* químico
   2 *adj* químico(a); **c. weapons** armas *fpl* químicas

chemist ['kemɪst] *n* (**a**) *Chem* químico(a) *m,f* (**b**) *Br* **c.'s (shop)** farmacia *f*; **dispensing c.** farmacéutico(a) *m,f*

chemistry ['kemɪstrɪ] *n* química *f*

chemotherapy ['kiːməʊ'θerəpɪ] *n Med* quimioterapia *f*

cheque [tʃek] *n Fin* cheque *m*, talón *m*; **a c. for £50** un cheque de cincuenta libras; **blank c.** cheque en blanco; **to pay by c.** pagar con (un) cheque ❑ *Br* **c. card** = tarjeta que avala los cheques; **traveller's c.** cheque *m* de viaje

chequebook ['tʃekbʊk] *n* talonario *m* (de cheques) ❑ **c. journalism** periodismo *m* de exclusivas (a golpe de talonario)

chequerboard ['tʃekəbɔːd] *n* tablero *m* de damas

chequered ['tʃekəd] *adj (cloth)* a cuadros; *Fig* **a c. career** una carrera con altibajos ❑ *Sport* **c. flag** bandera *f* a cuadros

cherish ['tʃerɪʃ] *vt* (**a**) *(person)* querer, tenerle mucho cariño a (**b**) *Fig (hopes etc)* abrigar

cherry ['tʃerɪ] *n Bot* cereza *f* ❑ **c. brandy** licor *m* de cerezas; **c. red** *(colour)* rojo *m* cereza; **c. tree** cerezo *m*

cherub ['tʃerəb] *n (pl* **cherubs** *or* **cherubim** ['tʃerəbɪm]) querubín *m*

cherubic [tʃə'ruːbɪk] *adj* de querubín, de ángel

chervil ['tʃɜːvɪl] *n Bot* cerafolio *m*

chess [tʃes] *n* ajedrez *m*; **game of c.** partida *f* de ajedrez; **to play c.** jugar al ajedrez

chessboard ['tʃesbɔːd] *n* tablero *m* de ajedrez

chessman ['tʃesmən] *n (pl* **chessmen**) pieza *f* de ajedrez

chesspiece ['tʃespiːs] *n* pieza *f* de ajedrez

chest [tʃest] *n* (**a**) *Anat* pecho *m*; *Fig* **to get sth off one's c.** desahogarse (**b**) *(for linen)* arca *f*; *(for valuables)* cofre *m*; *(for shipping)* baúl *m*, caja *f*; **tea c.** cajón *m* de té ❑ **c. of drawers** cómoda *f*

chestnut ['tʃesnʌt] *n* (**a**) *Bot (tree, wood, colour)* castaño *m*; *(nut)* castaña *f* ❑ **horse c.** castaño *m* de las Indias; **Spanish c., sweet c.** castaño *m* (**b**) *(horse)* alazán(ana) *m,f* (**c**) *Fam (joke)* **an old c.** un chiste gastado

chesty ['tʃestɪ] *adj* (**chestier, chestiest**) (**a**) *(cough)* de pecho (**b**) *Fam (woman)* pechugona, tetona, *Méx* chichona

chevron ['ʃevrən] *n Mil* galón *m*

chew [tʃuː] *vt* masticar, mascar; **to c. the cud** rumiar; *Fam Fig* **to c. sth over** darle vueltas a algo

chewing gum ['tʃuːɪŋɡʌm] *n* chicle *m*, goma *f* de mascar

chewy ['tʃuːɪ] *adj* (**chewier, chewiest**) enganchoso(a), difícil de masticar *or* mascar

chic [ʃiːk] **1** *adj* elegante
2 *n* elegancia *f*

Chicana [tʃɪ'kɑːnə] *n US* chicana *f*

Chicano [tʃɪ'kɑːnəʊ] *n US* chicano *m*

chick [tʃɪk] *n* pollito *m*

chicken ['tʃɪkɪn] **1** *n* (**a**) *(bird)* gallina *f*; *(meat)* pollo *m*; *Fam* **she's no c.** tiene sus años; *Prov* **don't count your chickens before they hatch** *or* **are hatched** no hagas como en el cuento de la lechera ▫ *Slang* **c. feed** una miseria; **c. farming** avicultura *f*; *Culin* **c. stock** caldo *m* de gallina (**b**) *Slang (coward)* gallina *mf*, *Esp* miedica *mf*
2 *adj Slang (cowardly)* gallina
3 *vi Fam* **to c. out** amilanarse, acoquinarse, *Méx* ciscarse, *RP* achicarse

chickenpox ['tʃɪkɪnpɒks] *n Med* varicela *f*

chickpea ['tʃɪkpiː] *n Culin* garbanzo *m*

chickweed ['tʃɪkwiːd] *n Bot* pamplina *f*

chicory ['tʃɪkərɪ] *n* achicoria *f*

chide [tʃaɪd] *vt* (*pt* **chided** *or* **chid** [tʃɪd]; *pp* **chided** *or* **chidden** ['tʃɪdən]) regañar, reprender

chief [tʃiːf] **1** *n* (*gen*) jefe *m*; *(of tribe)* cacique *m*; *Com* **c. executive**, *US* **c. executive officer** consejero(a) *m,f* delegado(a), director(a) *m,f* gerente; *Mil* **c. of staff** jefe *m* del estado mayor; **commander in c.** comandante *m* en jefe
2 *adj* principal; **the c. engineer** el ingeniero principal

chiefly ['tʃiːflɪ] *adv (above all)* sobre todo; *(mainly)* principalmente

chieftain ['tʃiːftən] *n* cacique *m*, jefe *m*

chiffon [ʃɪ'fɒn, 'ʃɪfɒn] *n Tex* gasa *f*

chihuahua [tʃɪ'wɑːwə] *n Zool* chihuahua *m*

chilblain ['tʃɪlbleɪn] *n Med* sabañón *m*

child [tʃaɪld] *n* (*pl* **children**) niño(a) *m,f*; *(son)* hijo *m*; *(daughter)* hija *f*; **children's books** libros *mpl* para niños; **children's stories** cuentos *mpl* infantiles; *Fam* **that's c.'s play** eso es un juego de niños ▫ **c. abuse** = malos tratos y/o agresión sexual a menores; **c. labour** trabajo *m* de menores; *Br* **c. minder** persona *f* que cuida niños en su propia casa

child-bearing ['tʃaɪldbeərɪŋ] *n* maternidad *f*; **of c.-b. age** en edad de tener hijos

childbirth ['tʃaɪldbɜːθ] *n* parto *m*, alumbramiento *m*; **in c.-f.** de parto

childcare ['tʃaɪldkeər] *n* cuidado *m* de menores *or* niños

child-friendly ['tʃaɪld'frendlɪ] *adj* **a c.-f. restaurant** un restaurante en el que están bienvenidos los niños

childhood ['tʃaɪldhʊd] *n* infancia *f*, niñez *f*; **in one's second c.** en la segunda infancia

childish ['tʃaɪldɪʃ] *adj* pueril; **don't be c.!** ¡no seas niño!

childless ['tʃaɪldlɪs] *adj* **to be c.** no tener hijos; **a c. couple** una pareja sin hijos

childlike ['tʃaɪldlaɪk] *adj* infantil, ingenuo(a)

childproof ['tʃaɪldpruːf] *adj* **c. bottle** = botella que los niños no pueden abrir; **c. lock** *(in car)* cierre *m* de seguridad a prueba de niños

children ['tʃɪldrən] *npl see* **child**

Chile ['tʃɪlɪ] *n* Chile *m*

Chilean ['tʃɪlɪən] *adj & n* chileno(a) *(m,f)*

chill [tʃɪl] **1** *n* (**a**) *Med* resfriado *m*; **to catch a c.** resfriarse, enfriarse, coger frío (**b**) *(coldness)* fresco *m*, frío *m*; **there's a c. in the air** hace fresquito; **to take the c. off sth** entibiar *or* templar algo; *Fig* **to cast a c. over sb** caer como un jarro de agua fría sobre algn
2 *adj (wind etc)* frío(a)
3 *vt (meat)* refrigerar; *(wine)* enfriar; *Fig* **to be chilled to the bone** estar helado(a) de frío

chil(l)i ['tʃɪlɪ] *n* (*pl* **chil(l)ies**) *Culin* chile *m*, *Esp* guindilla *f*, *Andes RP* ají *m*

chilling ['tʃɪlɪŋ] *adj* glacial; *Fig (story, crime)* espeluznante

chilly ['tʃɪlɪ] *adj* (**chillier, chilliest**) frío(a); **to feel c.** sentir *or* tener frío; *Fig* **a c. reception** una acogida fría

chime [tʃaɪm] **1** *n* carillón *m*; *(peal)* repique *m* de campanas
2 *vt (bells)* tocar; *(clock)* dar; **the bells chimed six** las campanas tocaron las seis
3 *vi (bell)* repicar, tañer; *(clock)* sonar

chime in *vi Fam* intervenir, entrometerse

chimney ['tʃɪmnɪ] *n* chimenea *f*; *Fam* **he smokes like a c.** fuma como un carretero *or* *Méx* un chacuaco *or* *RP* un escuerzo ▫ **c. stack** fuste *m*; **c. sweep** deshollinador *m*

chimneypot ['tʃɪmnɪpɒt] *n* cañón *m*

chimp [tʃɪmp] *n*, **chimpanzee** [tʃɪmpæn'ziː] *n Zool* chimpancé *m*

chin [tʃɪn] *n* barbilla *f*, mentón *m*; **double c.** papada *f*; *Fam* **keep your c. up** no te desanimes

China ['tʃaɪnə] *n* (**a**) **(People's Republic of) C.** (República *f* Popular de la) China (**b**) *Bot* **C. tree** jabonero *m* de la China

china ['tʃaɪnə] *n* loza *f*; **bone c.** porcelana *f*

Chinese [tʃaɪ'niːz] **1** *adj* chino(a); **C. lantern** farolillo *m* de papel
2 *n* (**a**) *(person)* chino(a) *m,f* (**b**) *(language)* chino *m*

Chink [tʃɪŋk] *n Slang Pej* chino(a) *m,f*

chink¹ [tʃɪŋk] *n (opening)* resquicio *m*; *(crack)* grieta *f*

chink² [tʃɪŋk] **1** *vt (glasses, coins)* hacer sonar *or* tintinear
2 *vi* sonar, tintinear
3 *n* tintineo *m*

chintz [tʃɪnts] *n Tex* chintz *m*

chinwag ['tʃɪnwæg] *n Br Fam* charla *f*

chip [tʃɪp] **1** *n* (**a**) *(of wood)* astilla *f*; *(of stone)* lasca *f*; *(of china)* pedacito *m*, trocito *m*; *(in cup, dish)* desportilladura *f*; *(in furniture)* astilladura *f*; *Fam Fig* **a c. off the old block** de tal palo tal astilla; *Fam* **to have a c. on one's shoulder** estar amargado(a) (**b**) *Culin Br* **chips** *Esp* patatas *fpl* *or Am* papas *fpl* fritas; *US* **(potato) chips** *(crisps) Esp* patatas *fpl* *or Am* papas *fpl* fritas *(de bolsa)* ▫ *Br Fam* **chip shop** = tienda que vende pescado y patatas *or Am* papas fritas para llevar (**c**) *Tech Comptr* **silicon c.** chip *m* (**d**) *(in gambling)* ficha *f*; *Fam Fig* **when the chips are down** a la hora de la verdad
2 *vt (pt & pp* **chipped**) *(wood)* astillar; *(stone)* resquebrajar; *(china, glass)* desportillar, resquebrajar; *(paint)* descascarillar, desconchar
3 *vi (wood)* astillarse; *(stones)* resquebrajarse; *(china, glass)* desportillarse; *(paint)* descascarillarse, desconcharse

chip in *vi Fam* (**a**) *(in discussion)* meter baza, *Méx RP* meter la cuchara (**b**) *(with money)* contribuir, poner algo

chipboard ['tʃɪpbɔːd] *n* aglomerado *m*, madera *f* aglomerada

chipmunk ['tʃɪpmʌŋk] *n Zool* ardilla *f* listada

chiropodist [kɪ'rɒpədɪst] *n* podólogo(a) *m,f*, pedicuro(a) *m,f*, callista *mf*, *Am* podiatra *mf*

chiropody [kɪ'rɒpədɪ] *n Med* pedicura *f*

chirp [tʃɜːp] **1** vi (birds) gorjear; (insects) chirriar, cantar
2 n (of birds) gorjeo m; (of insects) chirrido m

chirpy ['tʃɜːpɪ] adj alegre, jovial

chisel ['tʃɪzəl] **1** n cincel m
2 vt (pt & pp **chiselled**, US **chiseled**) (a) (in woodwork, sculpture) tallar (b) Slang timar, estafar

chit[1] [tʃɪt] n nota f; (small invoice) vale m

chit[2] [tʃɪt] n Pej mocoso(a) m,f

chitchat ['tʃɪttʃæt] n Fam palique m, habladurías fpl, CAm Méx plática f

chivalrous ['ʃɪvəlrəs] adj caballeroso(a)

chivalry ['ʃɪvəlrɪ] n (a) (bravery etc) caballerosidad f (b) Hist caballería f

chives [tʃaɪvz] npl Bot cebolleta f sing

chloride ['klɔːraɪd] n Chem cloruro m

chlorinate ['klɔːrɪmeɪt] vt tratar con cloro

chlorine ['klɔːriːn] n cloro m

chloroform ['klɒrəfɔːm] n Chem cloroformo m

chlorophyll, US **chlorophyl** ['klɒrəfɪl] n Biol clorofila f

choc-ice ['tʃɒkaɪs] n Br helado m cubierto de chocolate

chock [tʃɒk] n calzo m, cuña f

chock-a-block [tʃɒkə'blɒk] adj Fam, **chock-full** [tʃɒk'fʊl] adj Fam hasta los topes, de bote en bote

chocolate ['tʃɒkəlɪt] **1** n chocolate m; **chocolates** (candy) bombones mpl; **bar of c.** chocolatina f, tableta f de chocolate; **drinking c.** chocolate m (en taza)
2 adj (cake etc) de chocolate; (colour) de color chocolate

choice [tʃɔɪs] **1** n elección f, selección f; **a big** or **wide c.** un gran surtido; **by c.** por gusto; **she's my c. for the post** es la candidata que yo recomiendo para el puesto; **to make a c.** escoger, elegir
2 adj selecto(a), de primera calidad

choir ['kwaɪər] n Mus coro m, coral f

choirboy ['kwaɪəbɔɪ] n Mus niño m de coro

choirmaster ['kwaɪəmɑːstər] n (a) Mus director m de coro (b) (in church) maestro m de capilla

choke [tʃəʊk] **1** vt (a) (person) ahogar, asfixiar (b) (obstruct) obstruir, atascar
2 vi ahogarse, asfixiarse; **to c. on food** atragantarse con la comida
3 n Aut stárter m

choke back vt (anger, tears) contener, tragarse

choker ['tʃəʊkər] n gargantilla f

cholera ['kɒlərə] n Med cólera m

cholesterol [kə'lestərɒl] n colesterol m

chomp [tʃɒmp] vt & vi masticar, mascar

choose [tʃuːz] **1** vt (pt chose; pp chosen) (a) (select) escoger, elegir; **to c. sb to be** or **as a candidate** designar a algn como candidato(a); Fig **the chosen few** los elegidos (b) (decide) optar por, decidir; **he chose not to do anything** decidió no hacer nada
2 vi escoger, elegir; **do as you c.** haz lo que quieras; **there's little to c. between them** son muy parecidos, tanto monta monta tanto; **there's little** or **not much to c. from** no hay dónde escoger

choos(e)y ['tʃuːzɪ] adj (choosier, choosiest) Fam exigente, difícil de complacer

chop[1] [tʃɒp] **1** vt (pt & pp chopped) (a) (wood, branch) cortar; **to c. a branch off a tree** cortar una rama de un árbol; **to c. a tree down** talar or cortar un árbol; **to c. sth up** cortar algo en pedazos (b) Culin (meat, onions) cortar a pedacitos
2 n (a) (blow) tajo m, golpe m; (with axe) hachazo m; Br Fam

to get the c. ser despedido(a) (del trabajo) (b) Culin chuleta f; **pork c.** chuleta de cerdo

chop[2] [tʃɒp] vi (pt & pp chopped) cambiar bruscamente; Br **to c. and change** cambiar or estar cambiando como el viento

chopper ['tʃɒpər] n (a) (for meat) tajadera f; Br (axe) hacha f pequeña (b) Fam helicóptero m

chopping ['tʃɒpɪŋ] n c. **block** (butcher's) tajo m, tajadera f; **c. board** tabla f (para cortar)

choppy ['tʃɒpɪ] adj (choppier, choppiest) (sea) picado(a)

chopsticks ['tʃɒpstɪks] npl palillos mpl

choral ['kɔːrəl] adj Mus coral; **c. society** orfeón m

choral(e) [kɒ'rɑːl] n Mus coral m

chord[1] [kɔːd] n (a) Math cuerda f (b) Fig (response) **it strikes a c.** (me) suena; Fig **to touch the right c.** conmover (a algn) (c) Anat see **cord**

chord[2] [kɔːd] n Mus (group of sounds) acorde m

chore [tʃɔːr] n quehacer m, tarea f; **to do the chores** hacer la limpieza de la casa

choreograph ['kɒrɪəgræf] vt coreografiar

choreographer [kɒrɪ'ɒgrəfər] n coreógrafo(a) m,f

choreography [kɒrɪ'ɒgrəfɪ] n coreografía f

chorister ['kɒrɪstər] n corista mf

chortle ['tʃɔːtəl] **1** vi reírse, reír con ganas
2 n risa f alegre

chorus ['kɔːrəs] n (pl choruses) Mus Theat coro m; (in a song) estribillo m; **in c.** a coro; **there was a c. of protest** todos protestaron a la vez ❑ **c. girl** corista f

chose [tʃəʊz] pt see **choose**

chosen ['tʃəʊzən] pp see **choose**

chough [tʃʌf] n Orn chova f piquirroja

chowder ['tʃaʊdər] n US Culin crema f de almejas or de pescado

Christ [kraɪst] n Rel Cristo m, Jesucristo m

christen ['krɪsən] vt Rel bautizar

christening ['krɪsənɪŋ] n Rel (sacrament) bautismo m; (celebration) bautizo m

Christian ['krɪstʃən] Rel **1** adj cristiano(a); **c. name** nombre m de pila
2 n cristiano(a) m,f

Christianity [krɪstɪ'ænɪtɪ] n Rel cristianismo m

Christmas ['krɪsməs] n Navidad f; **at C.** por Navidades; **Father C.** Papá Noel m, Santa Claus m; **merry C.** feliz Navidad ❑ **C. card** tarjeta f de Navidad; **C. cake** = pastel de Navidad a base de frutas; **C. carol** villancico m; **C. Day** día m de Navidad; **C. dinner** comida f de Navidad; **C. Eve** Nochebuena f; **C. tree** árbol m de Navidad

chrome [krəʊm] n cromo m

chromium ['krəʊmɪəm] n Chem cromo m; Tech **c. plated** cromado(a) ❑ Tech **c. plating** cromado m

chromosome ['krəʊməsəʊm] n Biol cromosoma m

chronic ['krɒnɪk] adj (a) (invalid) crónico(a); **to suffer from c. ill health** tener mala salud; **c. unemployment** desempleo m crónico, Esp paro m estructural, Am desocupación f crónica (b) Br Fam (very bad) chungo(a), de pena, Méx mugrero(a), RP de última

chronicle ['krɒnɪkəl] **1** n crónica f
2 vt hacer la crónica de

chronicler ['krɒnɪklər] n cronista mf

chronological [krɒnə'lɒdʒɪkəl] adj cronológico(a)

chronology [krə'nɒlədʒɪ] n cronología f

chronometer [krə'nɒmɪtər] n cronómetro m

chrysalis ['krɪsəlɪs] n (pl chrysalises) Ent crisálida f

chrysanthemum [krɪ'sænθəməm] *n Bot* crisantemo *m*

chub [tʃʌb] *n (fish)* cacho *m*

chubby ['tʃʌbɪ] *adj* (**chubbier, chubbiest**) llenito(a), gordinflón(ona) ; **c. cheeked** mofletudo(a)

chuck [tʃʌk] *vt Fam* tirar, *Am* botar **c. it (in)!** ¡déjalo!, ¡deja eso!; **to c. one's job in** *or* **up** botar al trabajo; **to c. sb out** echar a algn; *(from work)* poner a algn de patitas en la calle; **to c. sth away** *or* **out** tirar *or Am* botar algo

chuckle ['tʃʌkəl] **1** *vi* reír en silencio
  2 *n* sonrisita *f*

chug [tʃʌɡ] *vi (pt & pp* **chugged**) *(engine)* resoplar; *(while moving)* traquetear

chum [tʃʌm] *n* compinche *mf*, compañero(a) *m,f*

chummy ['tʃʌmɪ] *adj* (**chummier, chummiest**) *Fam* simpático(a); **to be c. with sb** ser amigo(a) de algn; **they're very c.** son carne y uña

chump [tʃʌmp] *n* (**a**) *Fam (idiot)* imbécil *m* (**b**) *(of meat)* **c. chop** chuletón *m* (**c**) *Br Slang (head)* coco *m*; **to be off one's c.** faltarle un tornillo a algn, *Esp* estar mal de la chaveta *or* azotea, *RP* estar del tomate

chunk [tʃʌŋk] *n Fam* cacho *m*, pedazo *m*

chunky ['tʃʌŋkɪ] *adj* (**chunkier, chunkiest**) *(wood)* grueso(a); *(marmalade)* con pedazos de fruta

church [tʃɜːtʃ] *n* iglesia *f*; **to go to c.** ir al oficio *or* a misa; *Fig* **to enter the c.** hacerse cura/pastor/monja ❑ **c. hall** sala *f* parroquial; **C. of England** Iglesia *f* Anglicana

churchgoer ['tʃɜːtʃɡəʊər] *n Rel* practicante *mf*

churchwarden [tʃɜːtʃ'wɔːdən] *n (in Church of England)* capillero *m*

churchyard ['tʃɜːtʃjɑːd] *n* cementerio *m*, campo *m* santo

churlish ['tʃɜːlɪʃ] *adj* grosero(a), maleducado(a)

churlishness ['tʃɜːlɪʃnɪs] *n* grosería *f*, mala educación *f*

churn [tʃɜːn] **1** *n* (**a**) *(for butter)* mantequera *f* (**b**) *Br (for milk)* lechera *f*
  2 *vt (butter)* hacer; *(cream)* batir
  3 *vi* revolverse, agitarse

churn out *vt Fam* producir en serie

churn up *vt* revolver, agitar

chute [ʃuːt] *n* (**a**) *(channel)* conducto *m* (**b**) *(slide)* tobogán *m*

chutney ['tʃʌtnɪ] *n Culin* conserva *f* (de frutas) picante

chutzpah ['hʊtspə] *n US Fam* descaro *m*, frescura *f*

CIA [siːaɪ'eɪ] *n (abbr* **Central Intelligence Agency**) Agencia *f* Central de Información, CIA *f*

ciabatta [tʃə'bɑːtə] *n* ciabatta *f*

cicada [sɪ'kɑːdə] *n (pl* **cicadas** *or* **cicadae** [sɪ'kɑːdiː]) *Ent* cigarra *f*

CID [siːaɪ'diː] *n Br (abbr* **Criminal Investigation Department**) = policía judicial británica

cider ['saɪdər] *n (alcoholic)* sidra *f*; *US (non-alcoholic) Esp* zumo *m or Am* jugo *m* de manzana

cig [sɪɡ] *n (abbr* **cigarette**) *Fam* pitillo *m*

cigar [sɪ'ɡɑːr] *n* puro *m*, cigarro *m*; *US* **c. store** ≃ estanco *m*

cigarette [sɪɡə'ret] *n* cigarrillo *m*; **a packet/carton of cigarettes** un paquete/un cartón de tabaco ❑ **c. case** pitillera *f*; **c. end** colilla *f*, *Am* pucho *m*; **c. holder** boquilla *f*; **c. lighter** encendedor, *m Esp* mechero *m*

C-in-C [siːɪn'siː] *n Mil (abbr* **Commander-in-Chief**) Comandante *m* en jefe

cinch [sɪntʃ] *n Fam* **it's a c.** está chupado *or* tirado

cinder ['sɪndər] *n* ceniza *f*, pavesa *f*

Cinderella [sɪndə'relə] *n* Cenicienta *f*

cine camera ['sɪnɪkæmərə] *n Br* cámara *f* cinematográfica

cinema ['sɪnɪmə] *n* cine *m*

cinematography [sɪnəmə'tɒɡrəfɪ] *n* fotografía *f*

cinnamon ['sɪnəmən] *n* canela *f*

cipher ['saɪfər] *n* (**a**) *(numeral)* cifra *f*; *(code)* código *m*; **in c.** cifrado(a) (**b**) *Fig (nonentity)* cero *m* a la izquierda, don nadie *m*

circa ['sɜːkə] *prep* hacia, alrededor de

circle ['sɜːkəl] **1** *n* (**a**) *(shape)* círculo *m*; *Geom* circunferencia *f*; *(of people)* corro *m*; *Fig* **to go round in circles** dar muchas vueltas (**b**) *(cycle)* ciclo *m*; *Fig* **to come full c.** completar un ciclo; *Fig* **vicious c.** círculo *m* vicioso (**c**) *(group)* círculo *m*; **a c. of friends** un círculo de amigos; **in business circles** en el mundo de los negocios (**d**) *Theat* piso *m*; **upper c.** segundo piso (**e**) *US* **traffic c.** glorieta *f*
  2 *vt (form a circle round)* rodear; *(move round)* girar en torno de
  3 *vi* dar vueltas

circuit ['sɜːkɪt] *n* (**a**) *(journey round)* recorrido *m*; **to make a c. of** recorrer (**b**) *Elec* circuito *m*; **short c.** cortocircuito *m* ❑ **c. breaker** cortacircuitos *m inv* (**c**) *Sport (events)* liga *f*; *Br (racing track)* circuito *m* (**d**) *Cin Theat* cadena *f* (**e**) *Br Jur* distrito *m*; **c. judge** juez *mf* de distrito

circuitous [sə'kjuːɪtəs] *adj* indirecto(a), tortuoso(a)

circular ['sɜːkjʊlər] **1** *adj* circular; **c. saw** sierra circular; **c. tour** circuito *m*
  2 *n* circular *f*

circulate ['sɜːkjʊleɪt] **1** *vt (news)* hacer circular
  2 *vi* circular; **circulating library** biblioteca *f* ambulante

circulation [sɜːkjʊ'leɪʃən] *n* (**a**) *(of blood)* circulación *f* (**b**) *Press (of newspaper)* tirada *f*; *(of news)* difusión *f*

circumcise ['sɜːkəmsaɪz] *vt Med* circuncidar

circumcision [sɜːkəm'sɪʒən] *n Med* circuncisión *f*

circumference [sə'kʌmfərəns] *n* circunferencia *f*

circumflex ['sɜːkəmfleks] *n* circumflejo *m*

circumlocution [sɜːkəmlə'kjuːʃən] *n* circunloquio *m*

circumnavigate [sɜːkəm'nævɪɡeɪt] *vt* circunnavegar

circumscribe ['sɜːkəmskraɪb] *vt* (**a**) *(restrict)* restringir, limitar (**b**) *Geom* circunscribir

circumspect ['sɜːkəmspekt] *adj* circunspecto(a), prudente, cauteloso(a), *Esp* comedido(a)

circumstance ['sɜːkəmstəns] *n (gen pl)* circunstancia *f*; **in** *or* **under no circumstances** en ningún caso, bajo ningún concepto; **in the circumstances** dadas las circunstancias; **it depends on your circumstances** depende de tu situación económica

circumstantial [sɜːkəm'stænʃəl] *adj* **c. evidence** prueba *f* indiciaria

circumvent [sɜːkəm'vent] *vt Fig (law)* burlar; *(plans)* frustrar

circus ['sɜːkəs] *n (pl* **circuses**) circo *m*

cirrhosis [sɪ'rəʊsɪs] *n Med* cirrosis *f*

cistern ['sɪstən] *n* cisterna *f*

citadel ['sɪtədəl] *n* ciudadela *f*; *Fig* bastión *f*

citation [saɪ'teɪʃən] *n* (**a**) *(quotation)* cita *f* (**b**) *Mil (award)* mención *f* (**c**) *Jur (summons)* citación *f*

cite [saɪt] *vt* (**a**) *(quote)* citar (**b**) *Mil* mencionar

citizen ['sɪtɪzən] *n (native)* ciudadano(a) *m,f*, súbdito(a) *m,f*

citizenship ['sɪtɪzənʃɪp] *n* ciudadanía *f*

citric ['sɪtrɪk] *adj* cítrico(a); **c. acid** ácido cítrico

citrus ['sɪtrəs] *adj* cítrico(a); **c. fruit** agrios *mpl*, cítricos *mpl*

city ['sɪtɪ] *n* (**a**) *(town)* ciudad *f* ❑ **c. centre** centro *m* de la ciudad; *Br* **c. hall** ayuntamiento *m* (**b**) *Br Fin* **the C.** la City (de Londres), = el barrio financiero y bursátil de Londres

civic ['sɪvɪk] *adj* cívico(a); **c. authorities** autoridades *fpl* municipales; *Br* **c. centre** centro *m* cívico; **c. duties** obligaciones *fpl* cívicas

civics ['sɪvɪks] *npl* educación *f* cívica

civil ['sɪvəl] *adj* (**a**) *(non-military etc)* civil ❑ **c. defence** defensa *f* civil; **c. disobedience** resistencia *f* pasiva; **c. law** derecho *m* civil; **c. rights** derechos *mpl* civiles; *Pol* **c. servant** funcionario(a) *m,f*; *Pol* **c. service** administración *f* pública; **c. war** guerra *f* civil (**b**) *(polite)* cortés, educado(a)

civilian [sɪ'vɪljən] *adj & n* civil *(mf)*

civility [sɪ'vɪlɪtɪ] *n* cortesía *f*

civilization [sɪvɪlaɪ'zeɪʃən] *n* civilización *f*

civilize ['sɪvɪlaɪz] *vt* civilizar

civilized ['sɪvɪlaɪzd] *adj* civilizado(a)

cl *(abbr* **centilitre(s))** centilitro(s) *m(pl)*, cl

clad [klæd] *Literary* **1** *pt & pp see* **clothe**
2 *adj* vestido(a)

claim [kleɪm] **1** *vt* (**a**) *(property, benefits, rights)* reclamar; *Jur (compensation)* exigir (**b**) *(assert)* afirmar, alegar, sostener
2 *n* (**a**) *(demand)* reclamación *f*; *(on insurance)* demanda *f* de indemnización, reclamación; *Jur* demanda, reclamación judicial; *Jur* **to lay c. to sth** reclamar el derecho a algo; **to make a c. for** reclamar; **to put in a c.** reclamar una indemnización; **to put in a c. for damages** demandar por daños (**b**) *(right)* derecho *m*; **to have a c. on sth** tener derecho a algo; *Fig* **his only c. to fame is …** su único mérito es … (**c**) *(assertion)* pretensión *f*, afirmación *f*; **he made a c. to be a millionaire** alegó que era millonario (**d**) *Min* concesión *f*

claimant ['kleɪmənt] *n* (*gen*) reclamante *mf*, pretendiente *mf*; *Jur* demandante *mf*

clairvoyance [kleə'vɔɪəns] *n* clarividencia *f*

clairvoyant [kleə'vɔɪənt] *n* clarividente *mf*

clam [klæm] *n Zool* almeja *f*

clam up *vi (pt & pp* **clammed)** *Fam* callarse

clamber ['klæmbər] *vi* trepar (**over** por)

clammy ['klæmɪ] *adj* (**clammier, clammiest**) *(weather)* húmedo(a), bochornoso(a); *(hands)* pegajoso(a)

clamor ['klæmər] *n US see* **clamour**

clamorous ['klæmərəs] *adj (demand)* clamoroso(a); *(crowd)* vociferante

clamour ['klæmər] **1** *n* clamor *m*, griterío *m*
2 *vi* clamar, vociferar; **to c. for** *(things)* pedir a gritos; *(justice)* clamar por

clamp [klæmp] **1** *n* (*in carpentry*) tornillo *m* de banco; *Tech* abrazadera *f*; **wheel c.** cepo *m*
2 *vt* sujetar con abrazaderas

clamp down on *vt (restrict)* restringir; *(suppress)* suprimir

clampdown ['klæmpdaʊn] *n* restricción *f*

clan [klæn] *n* clan *m*

clandestine [klæn'destɪn] *adj* clandestino(a)

clang [klæŋ] **1** *vi* sonar
2 *vt* hacer sonar
3 *n* sonido *m* metálico

clanger ['klæŋər] *n Br Fam* metedura *f* or *Am* metida *f* de pata, patinazo *m*; **to drop a c.** meter la pata

clank [klæŋk] **1** *n* sonido *m* seco y metálico
2 *vt (chains)* hacer sonar
3 *vi* sonar

clannish ['klænɪʃ] *adj* exclusivista

clansman ['klænzmən] *n (pl* **clansmen)** miembro *m* de un clan

clap¹ [klæp] **1** *vt (pt & pp* **clapped)** (**a**) *(person, performance)* aplaudir; **to c. one's hands** aplaudir; **to c. sb on the back** dar a algn una palmada en la espalda (**b**) *Fam* **to c. eyes on** ver; **to c. sb in prison** meter a algn en chirona, meter *Méx* en el bote or *RP* en cana a algn
2 *vi* aplaudir; **to c. to the music** seguir la música con las palmas
3 *n* (**a**) *(with hands)* palmada *f*; **to give sb a c.** aplaudir a algn (**b**) *(light blow)* palmada *f*, golpecito *m* con la mano (**c**) *(noise)* ruido *m* seco; **a c. of thunder** un trueno

clap² [klæp] *n Slang* gonorrea *f*

clapped-out [klæpt'aʊt] *adj Br Austral Fam* rendido(a)

clapper ['klæpər] *n* badajo *m*

clapping ['klæpɪŋ] *n* aplausos *mpl*

claptrap ['klæptræp] *n Fam* majaderías *fpl*, *Am* huevadas *fpl*, *Am* pendejadas *fpl*

claret ['klærət] *n* (**a**) *Br (wine)* clarete *m* (**b**) *(colour)* burdeos *m*

clarification [klærɪfɪ'keɪʃən] *n* aclaración *f*, clarificación *f*

clarify ['klærɪfaɪ] *vt (pt & pp* **clarified)** aclarar, clarificar

clarinet [klærɪ'net] *n Mus* clarinete *m*

clarinettist [klærɪ'netɪst] *n Mus* clarinetista *mf*

clarity ['klærɪtɪ] *n* claridad *f*

clash [klæʃ] **1** *vi* (**a**) *(cymbals)* sonar; *(swords)* chocar; *Fig* **to c. with sb** estar en desacuerdo con algn (**b**) *(colours)* desentonar (**c**) *(dates)* coincidir
2 *n* (**a**) *(sound)* sonido *m*, ruido *m*; **the c. of cymbals** el sonido de los platillos; *Fig* **a border c.** un encuentro fronterizo (**b**) *(fight)* choque *m*, encuentro *m*; *Fig (conflict)* conflicto *m*, desacuerdo *m*; **a c. of interest** un conflicto de intereses

clasp [klɑːsp] **1** *n* (**a**) *(on belt)* cierre *m*, hebilla *f*; *(on necklace)* broche *m* (**b**) *(grasp)* apretón *m* ❑ **c. knife** navaja *f*
2 *vt (object)* agarrar, asir; **to c. hands** juntar las manos

class [klɑːs] **1** *n* (**a**) *(kind)* clase *f*, especie *f*, género *m*; *Biol* **a c. of mammal** una clase de mamífero; *Fig* **in a c. of its own** sin par or igual (**b**) *(in society)* clase *f*; **he's working c.** es de la clase obrera ❑ *Pol* **c. struggle** lucha *f* de clases; **middle c.** clase *f* media, burguesía *f*; **social c.** clase *f* social; **upper c.** aristocracia *f* (**c**) *Educ* clase *f*; *US Educ* **c. of '84** promoción *f* de 1984; **evening classes** clases nocturnas; *Br Educ* **first-c. honours degree** título *m* con sobresaliente; **she's in my c.** está en or es de mi clase (**d**) *(of travel)* clase *f*; *Rail* **first/second c. ticket** billete *m* de primera/segunda (clase); **tourist c.** clase *f* turista
2 *vt* clasificar

class-conscious [klɑːs'kɒnʃəs] *adj* clasista, con conciencia de clase

classic ['klæsɪk] **1** *adj* clásico(a)
2 *n* (**a**) *(author)* autor *m* clásico; *(work)* obra *f* clásica (**b**) **the classics** *(literature)* las obras clásicas, los clásicos; *(languages)* clásicas *fpl*

classical ['klæsɪkəl] *adj* clásico(a); **c. music** música *f* clásica

classification [klæsɪfɪ'keɪʃən] *n* clasificación *f*

classified ['klæsɪfaɪd] *adj (information)* secreto(a); *Press* **c. advertisements** anuncios *mpl* por palabras

classify ['klæsɪfaɪ] *vt (pt & pp* **classified)** clasificar

classless ['klɑːslɪs] *adj* sin clases

classmate ['klɑːsmeɪt] *n* compañero(a) *m,f* de clase

classroom ['klɑːsruːm] *n* aula *f*, clase *f*

classy ['klɑːsɪ] *adj* (**classier, classiest**) *Slang* con clase, elegante

clatter ['klætər] **1** *vi (pots etc)* hacer ruido; *(things falling)* hacer estrépito; *(machinery)* traquetear; *(hoofs)* chacolotear **2** *n (of pots etc)* ruido *m*; *(of things falling)* estrépito *m*; *(of machinery)* traqueteo *m*; *(of hoofs)* chacoloteo *m*

clause [klɔːz] *n Ling Jur* cláusula *f*

claustrophobia [klɔːstrə'fəʊbɪə] *n* claustrofobia *f*

claustrophobic [klɔːstrə'fəʊbɪk] *adj (person)* que padece claustrofobia; *(situation)* claustrofóbico(a), que produce claustrofobia

clavicle ['klævɪkəl] *n Anat* clavícula *f*

claw [klɔː] **1** *n* **(a)** *Zool (of bird, lion)* garra *f*; *(of cat)* uña *f*; *(of crab)* pinza *f* **(b)** **c. hammer** martillo *m* de orejas **2** *vt* agarrar, arañar; *(tear)* desgarrar

claw away *vt* agarrar, arañar

claw back *vt (money)* lograr recuperar

clay [kleɪ] *n* arcilla *f* ❑ **c. pigeon** plato *m*; **c. pigeon shooting** tiro *m* al plato

clean [kliːn] **1** *adj* **(a)** *(not dirty)* limpio(a) **(b)** *(unmarked, pure)* correcto(a), sin defecto; **a c. copy** una copia en limpio; **they gave him a c. bill of health** lo declararon en perfecto estado de salud; **to have a c. record** no tener antecedentes penales; **to have a c.** *Br* **(driving) licence** *or US* **(driver's) license** no tener puntos de penalización en *Esp* el carné de conducir *or Am* la licencia para conducir; **(c)** *(shape)* limpio(a); **a c. cut** un corte limpio; **the building has c. lines** el edificio tiene unas líneas bien definidas **(d)** *(not obscene)* decente; **keep it c.!** ¡nada de groserías! **(e)** *Fig* **to make a c. breast of it** contarlo todo; **to make a c. sweep of it** arrasar **2** *adv* **(a)** *(fairly)* limpiamente; *Sport* **to play c.** jugar limpio; *Fam* **to come c.** confesarlo todo **(b)** *Fam (completely)* por completo; **it went c. through the middle** pasó justo por el medio; **they got c. away** desaparecieron por completo **3** *vt (room)* limpiar; **to c. one's teeth** lavarse los dientes **4** *n* limpieza *f*; **to give sth a c.** limpiar algo

clean out *vt* **(a)** *(room)* limpiar a fondo **(b)** *Slang (leave broke)* dejar limpio(a) *or Esp* sin blanca *or Am* sin un centavo

clean up *vt & vi* limpiar

clean-cut ['kliːnkʌt] *adj* **(a)** *(person)* limpio(a), pulcro(a) **(b)** *(decision)* claro(a), bien definido(a)

cleaner ['kliːnər] *n (person)* encargado(a) *m,f* de la limpieza; *Fam Fig* **to take sb to the c.'s** dejar limpio(a) *or* sin blanca a algn ❑ **c.'s (shop)** tintorería *f*

cleaning ['kliːnɪŋ] *n* limpieza *f* ❑ **c. lady** asistenta *f*, mujer *f* de la limpieza

cleanliness ['klenlɪnɪs] *n* limpieza *f*

clean-living ['kliːn'lɪvɪŋ] *adj* sano(a), sin vicios

cleanly ['kliːnlɪ] *adv* limpiamente

cleanse [klenz] *vt* limpiar

cleanser ['klenzər] *n* loción *f* limpiadora

clean-shaven [kliːn'ʃeɪvən] *adj (man)* sin barba ni bigote

cleansing ['klenzɪŋ] *n* limpieza *f* ❑ **c. lotion** leche *f* limpiadora

clear [klɪər] **1** *adj* **(a)** *(image, handwriting, instruction)* claro(a); *(road, view, day)* despejado(a); **c. conscience** conciencia *f* limpia; *Culin* **c. soup** consomé *m* **(b)** *(obvious, certain)* claro(a); **have I made myself c.?** ¿me explico con claridad?; **it's c. to me that ...** me parece evidente que ...; **to make sth c.** aclarar algo; *Fam* **I'm not very c. about it** no me aclaro **(c)** *(complete, definite)* neto(a), absoluto(a); **c. majority** mayoría absoluta; **c. profit** beneficio *m* neto; **he earns a c. $350 a week** gana 350 dólares semanales limpios; **three c. days** tres días completos **(d)** *(free)* libre; **c. of** libre de; **when the coast is c.** cuando el campo esté libre

2 *adv* **stand c.!** ¡apártese!; **to keep** *or* **stay c. of** evitar, apartarse de

3 *n* **in the c.** *(from danger)* fuera de peligro; *(from suspicion)* fuera de toda sospecha

4 *vt* **(a)** *(snow)* limpiar; *(room)* vaciar; *(pipe)* desatascar, *Am* destapar; *Com (stock, debt)* liquidar; *Comptr (data)* borrar; **to c. one's throat** aclararse la garganta; **to c. the table** quitar la mesa; **to c. the way** abrir (el) camino; *Fig* **to c. the air** aclarar las cosas **(b)** *(authorize)* autorizar; **c. it with the boss** pregúntaselo al jefe **(c)** *(pass)* pasar por encima de; *Sport (hurdle)* salvar, saltar sin tocar; **to c. customs** pasar por la aduana **(d)** *Jur* descargar; **to c. sb of a charge** exculpar a algn de un delito

5 *vi (weather, sky)* despejarse

clear away *vt (dishes etc)* quitar

clear off 1 *vt (debts)* liquidar **2** *vi Br Fam* largarse; **c. off!** ¡largo!, ¡fuera de (aquí)!

clear out 1 *vt (room)* limpiar a fondo; *(cupboard)* vaciar; *(old clothes)* tirar **2** *vi Fam* largarse

clear up 1 *vt* **(a)** *(tidy)* recoger; *(arrange)* ordenar, poner en orden **(b)** *(mystery)* resolver; *(misunderstanding)* aclarar **2** *vi* **(a)** *(tidy up)* recoger **(b)** *(weather)* despejarse; *(illness, problem)* desaparecer

clearance ['klɪərəns] *n* **(a)** *(of area)* despeje *m* ❑ *Com* **c. sale** liquidación *f* (de existencias) **(b)** *(space)* espacio *m* libre **(c)** *(authorization)* autorización *f*

clear-cut [klɪə'kʌt] *adj* claro(a), bien definido(a)

clear-headed [klɪə'hedɪd] *adj* lúcido(a), perspicaz

clearing ['klɪərɪŋ] *n* **(a)** *(in wood)* claro *m* **(b)** *(of rubbish)* limpieza *f*; *(of pipe)* desatasco *m* **(c)** *Fin (of cheque)* compensación *f*

clearing house ['klɪərɪŋ'haʊs] *n Fin* cámara *f* de compensación

clearly ['klɪəlɪ] *adv* **(a)** *(explain, write)* claramente, con claridad; *Fig* **to see c.** entender bien **(b)** *(obviously)* claramente

clearness ['klɪənɪs] *n* claridad *f*

clearout ['klɪəraʊt] *n* **I need to give my desk a c.** tengo que limpiar *or* ordenar mi escritorio

clear-sighted [klɪə'saɪtɪd] *adj Fig* clarividente, perspicaz

clearway ['klɪəweɪ] *n Br Aut* carretera *f* donde está prohibido parar

cleavage ['kliːvɪdʒ] *n* **(a)** *Fam (in dress)* escote *m* **(b)** *(split)* división *f*

cleave¹ [kliːv] *vt (pt* **cleft, cleaved** *or* **clove;** *pp* **cleft, cleaved** *or* **cloven)** dividir, partir (por la mitad)

cleave² [kliːv] *vi (cling)* adherirse (**to** a)

cleaver ['kliːvər] *n* cuchillo *f* de carnicero

clef [klef] *n Mus* clave *f*; **bass/treble c.** clave de fa/de sol

cleft [kleft] **1** *pt & pp see* **cleave¹** **2** *n* hendidura *f*, grieta *f* ❑ *Med* **c. palate** fisura *f* del paladar

clematis ['klemətɪs] *n Bot* clemátide *f*

clemency ['klemənsɪ] *n* clemencia *f*; **to appeal for c.** pedir clemencia

clementine ['kleməntaɪn] *n Br* clementina *f*

clench [klentʃ] *vt (teeth, fist)* apretar; **with clenched fist** con el puño cerrado

clergy ['klɜːdʒɪ] *n Rel* clero *m*

clergyman ['klɜːdʒɪmən] *n (pl* **clergymen)** *Rel* clérigo *m*

clergywoman ['klɜːdʒɪwʊmən] *n (pl* **clergywomen)** mujer *f* sacerdote

cleric ['klerɪk] *n Rel* eclesiástico *m*

clerical ['klerɪkəl] *adj* **(a)** *Rel* clerical, eclesiástico(a) ❑ **c.**

collar alzacuello *m* **(b)** *(administrative)* de oficina ❏ **c. staff** oficinistas *mfpl*

clerk [klɑːk, *US* klɜːrk] *n* **(a)** *(office worker)* oficinista *mf* ❏ **bank c.** empleado(a) *m,f* de banco; *Jur* **c. of the court** secretario(a) *m,f* de juzgado; *Constr* **c. of works** maestro *m* de obras **(b)** *US Com* dependiente(a) *m,f*

clever ['klevər] *adj* **(a)** *(person)* inteligente, listo(a), espabilado(a); **c. at maths** fuerte en matemáticas; **she's c. with her hands** es muy habilidosa, *Esp* es una manitas; **that was/wasn't very c. of you** lo hiciste muy bien/mal; **to be c. at sth** tener habilidad *or* aptitud para algo; *Fam* **he's too c. by half** se pasa de listo ❏ *Br Fam* **c. Dick** sabiondo(a) *m,f*, sabelotodo *mf*, *Esp* listillo(a) *m,f* **(b)** *(argument)* ingenioso(a), astuto(a)

cleverly ['klevəlɪ] *adv* con inteligencia; *(skilfully)* hábilmente

cleverness ['klevənɪs] *n* **(a)** *(intelligence)* inteligencia *f*, *(skill)* habilidad *f* **(b)** *(of argument)* ingenio *m*

cliché ['kliːʃeɪ] *n* cliché *m*, lugar *m* común

clichéd ['kliːʃeɪd] *adj* tópico(a); **a c. comment** *or* **remark** un tópico, un lugar común

click [klɪk] **1** *n (sound)* clic *m*; *(with the tongue)* chasquido *m*; *Comptr* clic *m*
2 *vt (tongue)* chasquear; **to c. one's heels** taconear
3 *vi* **(a)** *(realize)* captar; **suddenly I clicked** de pronto caí en la cuenta **(b)** *Fam* congeniar; **they clicked at once** enseguida congeniaron **(c)** *Comptr* hacer clic

clickable image ['klɪkəbəl'ɪmɪdʒ] *n Comptr* imagen *f* interactiva

clicking ['klɪkɪŋ] *n* chasquido *m*

client ['klaɪənt] *n (customer)* & *Comptr* cliente *mf*

clientele [kliːɒn'tel] *n* clientela *f*

client-server database ['klaɪəntsɜːvə'deɪtəbeɪs] *n Comptr* base *f* de datos cliente/servidor

cliff [klɪf] *n* acantilado *m*, precipicio *m*

cliffhanger ['klɪfhæŋər] *n* momento *m* de suspense *or Am* suspenso

climactic [klaɪ'mæktɪk] *adj* culminante

climate ['klaɪmɪt] *n* clima *m*

climatic [klaɪ'mætɪk] *adj* climático(a)

climax ['klaɪmæks] *n* **(a)** *(peak)* clímax *m*, punto *m* culminante **(b)** *(sexual)* orgasmo *m*

climb [klaɪm] **1** *vt* trepar a, subir a; **to c. a ladder** subir una escalera; **to c. a mountain** subir a una montaña; *Sport* escalar una montaña; **to c. (up) a tree** trepar a un árbol
2 *vi* subir, trepar; *(plants)* trepar; *Av* subir; *(sun)* ascender; *Fig (socially)* ascender, subir
3 *n* subida *f*, ascensión *f*

climb down *vi* bajar; *Fig* volverse atrás

climber ['klaɪmər] *n* **(a)** *Sport* alpinista *mf*, *Am* andinista *mf*; **(b)** *Bot* enredadera *f* **(c)** *Fig* **social c.** arribista *mf*

climbing ['klaɪmɪŋ] *n Sport* montañismo *m*, *Am* alpinismo *m* ❏ **c. frame** barras *fpl*

clinch [klɪntʃ] **1** *vt* resolver; **to c. a deal** cerrar un trato; *Fam* **that clinches it!** ¡ni una palabra más!, ¡se acabó!
2 *n Slang* abrazo *m* apasionado

cling [klɪŋ] *vi (pt & pp* **clung)** *(hang on)* agarrarse; *(clothes)* ajustarse; *(smell)* pegarse; **to c. together** unirse; *Fig* **to c. to an opinion** seguir fiel a una opinión

clinging ['klɪŋɪŋ] *adj (child)* enmadrado(a); *(person)* pegajoso(a); *(clothing)* ceñido(a), ajustado(a)

clingy ['klɪŋɪ] *adj* **(clingier, clingiest)** *see* **clinging**

clinic ['klɪnɪk] *n Med* **(a)** *(in state hospital)* ambulatorio *m*, dispensario *m* **(b)** *(specialized)* clínica *f*; **dental c.** clínica dental

clinical ['klɪnɪkəl] *adj* **(a)** *Med* clínico(a); **c. thermometer** termómetro *m* clínico **(b)** *(detached)* imparcial, frío(a)

clink¹ [klɪŋk] **1** *vi* tintinear
2 *vt* **to c. glasses (with sb)** chocar copas *or* hacer chinchín (con algn)
3 *n (of keys, glasses)* tintineo *m*

clink² [klɪŋk] *n Slang Esp* trena *f*, *Esp* trullo *m*, *Andes RP* cana *f*, *Méx* bote *m*

clinker ['klɪŋkər] *n* escoria *f* de hulla

clip¹ [klɪp] **1** *vt (pt & pp* **clipped)** **(a)** *(cut)* cortar; *(sheep's wool)* esquilar; *(ticket)* picar; *Fig* **to c. sb's wings** cortar las alas a algn **(b)** *Fam* dar un cachete a
2 *n* **(a)** *Cin (of film)* extracto *m*, escenas *fpl* **(b)** *(with scissors)* tijeretada *f* **(c)** *Br Fam Esp* cachete *m*, *Am* cachetada *f Comptr* **c. art** clip art *m*, dibujos *mpl* artísticos

clip² [klɪp] **1** *n (for hair)* pasador *m*, clip *m*; *(for paper)* clip *m*, sujetapapeles *m inv*; *(brooch)* alfiler *m* de pecho, clip *m*
2 *vt (pt & pp* **clipped)** sujetar (con un clip)

clipboard ['klɪpbɔːd] *n* carpeta *f* con sujetapapeles

clip-on ['klɪpɒn] *adj (earrings etc)* de clip

clipped [klɪpt] *adj Fig (speech)* entrecortado(a)

clipper ['klɪpər] *n Naut* clíper *m*

clippers ['klɪpəz] *npl (for hair)* maquinilla *f* para cortar el pelo; *(for nails)* cortauñas *m inv*; *(for hedge)* tijeras *fpl* de podar

clipping ['klɪpɪŋ] *n esp US* recorte *m*

clique [kliːk, klɪk] *n Pej* camarilla *f*

cliqu(e)y ['kliːkɪ] *adj* **(cliquier, cliquiest)**, **cliquish** ['kliːkɪʃ] *adj Pej* exclusivista

clitoris ['klɪtərɪs] *n Anat* clítoris *m*

cloak [kləʊk] **1** *n (garment)* capa *f*; *Fig* pretexto *m*; **under the c. of** so capa de
2 *vt* encubrir; **to c. in secrecy** rodear de secreto

cloak-and-dagger [kləʊkən'dægər] *adj (gen)* clandestino(a); *(films, books)* de intriga

cloakroom ['kləʊkruːm] *n (for coats, bags)* guardarropa *m*; *Br Euph (toilets)* servicios *mpl*

clobber¹ ['klɒbər] *vt Fam* **to c. sb** dar una paliza a algn

clobber² ['klɒbər] *n Br Slang* trastos *mpl*, cachivaches *mpl*

clock [klɒk] **1** *n (gen)* & *Comptr* reloj *m*; **it's five o'c.** son las cinco; **to put the c. forward/back** adelantar/atrasar el reloj; *Fig* **to work round the c.** trabajar día y noche ❏ **alarm c.** despertador *m*; *Comptr* **c. speed** velocidad *f* de reloj; **grandfather c.** reloj *m* de pie
2 *vt (race)* cronometrar

clock in, clock on *vi (at work)* fichar (a la entrada), *Am* marcar tarjeta (a la entrada)

clock off, clock out *vi (at work)* fichar (a la salida), *Am* marcar tarjeta (a la salida)

clock up *vt (mileage)* hacer

clockmaker ['klɒkmeɪkər] *n* relojero(a) *m,f*

clock-watcher ['klɒkwɒtʃər] *n Fam* empleado(a) *m,f* que sólo piensa en salir del trabajo

clockwise ['klɒkwaɪz] *adj* & *adv* en el sentido de las agujas del reloj

clockwork ['klɒkwɜːk] *n* mecanismo *m*; *Fig* **to go like c.** ir sobre ruedas ❏ **c. toy** juguete *m* de cuerda

clod [klɒd] *n* terrón *m*

clodhoppers ['klɒdhɒpəz] *npl Fam* zapatones *mpl*

clog [klɒg] **1** *vt (pt & pp* **clogged)** obstruir; *(pipe)* atascar; **to get clogged up** atascarse
2 *vi* **to c. (up)** obstruirse, atascarse
3 *n (footwear)* zueco *m*

cloister [ˈklɔɪstər] n claustro m

clone [kləʊn] **1** n Biol clon m; Comptr clónico m
2 vt Biol clonar

cloning [ˈkləʊnɪŋ] n Biol clonación f

close[1] [kləʊs] **1** adj (a) (in space, time) cercano(a); (print, weave) compacto(a); (encounter) cara a cara; (contact) directo(a); **c. to** cerca de; **c. together** juntos; Fig **at c. quarters** de cerca; Fig **we had a c. shave** nos libramos por los pelos (b) (of relationships) cercano(a); **c. friends** amigos íntimos; **c. relative** pariente cercano; **they're very c.** están muy unidos or muy compenetrados (c) (careful) (inspection, examination) detallado(a); (watch) atento(a); (translation) fiel, exacto(a); **to pay c. attention** prestar mucha atención (d) (resemblance) muy parecido(a); (contest, match, finish) reñido(a) (e) (room, air) cargado(a); (weather) sofocante, bochornoso(a) (f) (secretive) reservado(a); **she's very c.** es muy reservada; **to be c. about sth** ser reacio a hablar de algo (g) (mean) tacaño(a), Esp rácano(a), Carib Col Méx amarrado(a) (h) (hunting) **c. season** veda f
2 adv cerca; **they live c. by** or **c. at hand** viven cerca; **to come closer together** acercarse; **to follow c. behind sb** seguir a algn de cerca; **to stand c. together** estar apretados(as); Fig **to be c. on forty** andar rondando los cuarenta

close[2] [kləʊz] **1** vt (a) (shut) cerrar; Com **closing time** hora f del cierre (del comercio); Aut **'road closed to traffic'** 'carretera cerrada al tráfico'; Mil **to c. ranks** cerrar filas; Fig **to c. one's eyes to sth** cerrar los ojos a algo (b) (end) concluir, terminar, cerrar; (meeting) levantar; **the closing lines of the play** el final de la obra (c) Fin Com cerrar; **to c. a deal** cerrar un trato; **to c. an account** cerrar or liquidar una cuenta
2 vi (a) (shut) cerrar, cerrarse (b) (end) concluirse, terminarse
3 n fin m, final m, conclusión f; **to bring to a c.** concluir, terminar; **to draw to a c.** tocar a su fin

close down 1 vt (business) cerrar
2 vi (business) cerrar; Br Rad TV (broadcast) cerrar

close in vi (a) (days) acortarse; (night) caer (b) **to c. in on sb** rodear a algn

close up 1 vt (business) cerrar del todo
2 vi cerrarse; (wound) cicatrizar; Mil (ranks) apretarse

closed [kləʊzd] adj cerrado(a); Fig **a c. book** un tema que se desconoce ❑ **c. circuit television** televisión f por circuito cerrado; Ind **c. shop** empresa f que emplea solamente a miembros de un sindicato

close-down [ˈkləʊzdaʊn] n cierre m

close-fitting [kləʊsˈfɪtɪŋ] adj (garment) ajustado(a), ceñido(a)

close-knit [kləʊsˈnɪt] adj Fig unido(a)

closely [ˈkləʊslɪ] adv (a) (tightly, extremely) estrechamente, muy; **c. connected** estrechamente relacionado(a); **c. contested** (election, match) muy reñido(a); **they are c. related** (people) son parientes próximos; **they c. resemble each other** se parecen muchísimo (b) (attentively) con atención; **to follow** (events) **c.** seguir or observar de cerca (los acontecimientos); **to watch/listen c.** observar/ escuchar atentamente

closeness [ˈkləʊsnɪs] n (a) (nearness) proximidad f; (of connection, relationship) intimidad f; (of translation) fidelidad f (b) (of weather) falta f de aire

close-run [ˈkləʊsrʌn] adj (election, race) reñido(a)

close-set [kləʊsˈset] adj **c.-s. eyes** ojos mpl muy juntos

closet [ˈklɒzɪt] **1** n US armario m
2 vt Fig **to be closeted with sb** estar encerrado(a) con algn; **to c. oneself** recluirse

close-up [ˈkləʊsʌp] n Phot primer plano m; Fig retrato m

closing [ˈkləʊzɪŋ] n cierre m; Com **early c. day** día m de cierre temprano ❑ Fin **c. price** precio m al cierre; **c. time** hora f de cerrar

closure [ˈkləʊʒər] n cierre m

clot [klɒt] **1** n (a) (of blood) coágulo m; Med **c. on the brain** embolia f cerebral (b) Br Fam tonto(a) m,f, bobo(a) m,f
2 vi (pt & pp **clotted**) coagularse, cuajar; Culin **clotted cream** nata f cuajada

cloth [klɒθ] n (pl **cloths** [klɒθs, klɒðz]) (gen) tela f, paño m; (rag) trapo m; (tablecloth) mantel m ❑ Print **c. binding** encuadernación f en tela

clothe [kləʊð] vt (pt & pp **clothed** or **clad**) vestir (**in, with** de); Fig revestir, cubrir (**in, with** de)

clothes [kləʊðz] npl ropa f sing, vestidos mpl; **in plain c.** de paisano; **to put on one's c.** ponerse la ropa; **to take off one's c.** quitarse or Am sacarse la ropa; **with one's c. on/ off** vestido(a)/desnudo(a) ❑ **c. brush** cepillo m de la ropa; **c. hanger** percha f, colgador m; **c. horse** tendedero m plegable; **c. line** tendedero m; **c.** Br **peg** or US **pin** pinza f

clothing [ˈkləʊðɪŋ] n ropa f; **article of c.** prenda f de vestir; **the c. industry** la industria de la confección

cloud [klaʊd] **1** n nube f; Fig **a c. of insects** una nube de insectos; Fig **to be under a c.** estar bajo sospecha; Fam **to be on c. nine** está más contenta que un chico con zapatos nuevos or Esp que unas castañuelas; Prov **every c. has a silver lining** no hay mal que por bien no venga
2 vt nublar, anublar; **eyes clouded with tears** ojos nublados or empañados de lágrimas; Fig **to c. the issue** complicar el asunto
3 vi (sky) **to c. over** nublarse

cloudburst [ˈklaʊdbɜːst] n Meteor chaparrón m

cloud-cuckoo-land [ˈklaʊdˈkʊkuːlænd] n Br Fam **to be (living) in c.-c.-l.** estar en Babia or la luna

cloudiness [ˈklaʊdɪnɪs] n nubosidad f

cloudless [ˈklaʊdlɪs] adj despejado(a)

cloudy [ˈklaʊdɪ] adj (**cloudier, cloudiest**) (a) (sky) nublado(a) (b) (liquid) turbio(a)

clout [klaʊt] Fam **1** n (a) (blow) tortazo m (b) (influence) influencia f, fuerza f
2 vt dar or arrear un tortazo a

clove[1] [kləʊv] n Bot Culin (spice) clavo m

clove[2] [kləʊv] n Culin (of garlic) diente f

clove[3] [kləʊv] pt see **cleave**[1]

cloven [ˈkləʊvən] **1** pp see **cleave**[1]
2 adj **c. hoof** pezuña f hendida

clover [ˈkləʊvər] n Bot trébol m; Fam **to be in c.** vivir como un rey

cloverleaf [ˈkləʊvəliːf] n (pl **cloverleaves**) Bot hoja f de trébol

clown [klaʊn] **1** n payaso m
2 vi **to c. (about** or **around)** hacer el payaso

clowning [ˈklaʊnɪŋ] n payasadas fpl

cloy [klɔɪ] vi empalagar

cloying [ˈklɔɪɪŋ] adj (taste, smell) empalagoso(a)

club [klʌb] **1** n (a) (society) club m, círculo m; **sports c.** club deportivo; **youth c.** club juvenil; Fam **join the c.!** ¡ya somos dos! (b) (heavy stick) garrote m, porra f; Golf palo m ❑ Med **c. foot** pie m zopo (c) Cards (English pack) trébol m; (Spanish pack) bastos mpl (d) Culin **c. sandwich** sandwich m doble
2 vt (pt & pp **clubbed**) aporrear, dar or pegar garrotazos a
3 vi **to c. together** pagar entre varios

clubhouse [ˈklʌbhaʊs] n Sport sede f de un club

cluck [klʌk] **1** n cloqueo m
2 vi cloquear

clue [kluː] n (sign) indicio m; (to mystery) pista f; (in *crossword)* clave *f*; *Fam* **I haven't a c.** no tengo (ni) idea, no tengo la menor idea; *Pej* **he hasn't a c.** es muy despistado, no se entera

clue up *vt Fam* poner al tanto; **to be clued up** estar al tanto

clueless ['klu:lɪs] *adj* despistado(a), que no se entera de nada

clump [klʌmp] **1** *n* **(a)** *(of trees)* grupo *m*; *(of plants)* mata *f*, macizo *m* **(b)** *(noise)* ruido *m* de pisadas
2 *vi* andar ruidosamente

clumsiness ['klʌmsɪnɪs] *n* desmaña *f*, torpeza *f*

clumsy ['klʌmsɪ] *adj* (**clumsier, clumsiest**) desmañado(a), torpe; *(awkward)* tosco(a), basto(a)

clung [klʌŋ] *pt & pp see* **cling**

cluster ['klʌstər] **1** *n* **(a)** *(of trees, stars)* grupo *m*; *(of grapes)* racimo *m*; *(of plants)* macizo *m*; *(of flowers)* ramillete *m* ❑ **c. bomb** bomba *f* de dispersión *or* fragmentación **(b)** *Comptr* cluster *m*, bloque *m*
2 *vi* agruparse (**round** en torno a)

clutch [klʌtʃ] **1** *vt (bag)* agarrar; *(child, doll)* estrechar; **to c. at** echar mano a, tratar de agarrar; *Fig* **to c. at straws** aferrarse a cualquier cosa
2 *n* **(a)** *Aut* embrague *m*; **to let in/out the c.** embragar/desembragar **(b)** *(hold)* agarrón *m*; *Fig* **to fall into sb's clutches** caer en las garras de algn

clutter ['klʌtər] **1** *vt* **to c. (up)** llenar, atestar; **cluttered up with books** atestado(a) de libros
2 *n* desorden *m*, revoltijo *m*; **in a c.** desordenado(a), revuelto(a)

cluttered ['klʌtəd] *adj* revuelto(a)

cm *(abbr* **centimetre(s)**) centímetro(s), cm

CO [si:'əʊ] *n Mil (abbr* **Commanding Officer**) Comandante *m*, Cte

Co **(a)** *Com (abbr* **Company**) Compañía *f*, C., Ca, Cía. **(b)** *(abbr* **County**) condado *m*

co- [kəʊ] *pref* co-; **co-driver** copiloto *mf*

c/o [si:'əʊ] *(abbr* **care of**) en casa de, c/d

coach [kəʊtʃ] **1** *n* **(a)** *esp Br Aut* autobús *m*; *(carriage)* carruaje *m* ❑ *US* **c. class** *(on plane)* clase *f* turista; **c. tour** excursión *f* en autocar **(b)** *Rail* coche *m*, vagón *m* **(c)** *Sport* entrenador(a) *m*,*f*; *Educ (tutor)* profesor(a) *m*,*f* particular
2 *vt Sport* entrenar; *Educ* dar clases particulares a, preparar

coach-builder ['kəʊtʃbɪldər] *n* carrocero(a) *m*,*f*

coachwork ['kəʊtʃwɜːk] *n* carrocería *f*

coagulant [kəʊ'ægjʊlənt] *n Med* coagulante *m*

coagulate [kəʊ'ægjʊleɪt] **1** *vt* coagular
2 *vi* coagularse

coagulation [kəʊægjʊ'leɪʃən] *n* coagulación *f*

coal [kəʊl] *n Min* carbón *m*, hulla *f*; *Fig* **to carry coals to Newcastle** llevar leña al monte; *Fig* **to haul sb over the coals** echar un rapapolvo a algn ❑ **c. bunker** carbonera *f*; **c. gas** gas *m* de hulla; **c. merchant** carbonero *m*; **c. mine** mina *f* de carbón; **c. miner** minero(a) *m*,*f* (del carbón); **c. mining** explotación *f* hullera; **c. scuttle** cubo *m* para el carbón; **c. tar** alquitrán *m* de hulla

coalesce [kəʊə'les] *vi* fundirse; *(unite)* unirse

coalfield ['kəʊlfiːld] *n Min* yacimiento *m* de carbón

coalition [kəʊə'lɪʃən] *n Pol* coalición *f*

coarse [kɔːs] *adj* **(a)** *(material)* basto(a), tosco(a); *(skin)* áspero(a); *(salt)* grueso(a) **(b)** *(language)* grosero(a), ordinario(a)

coarse-grained ['kɔːsgreɪnd] *adj* de grano grueso

coarseness ['kɔːsnɪs] *n (gen)* tosquedad *f*; *(of manner)* grosería *f*, ordinariez *f*

coast [kəʊst] **1** *n* costa *f*, litoral *m*; *Fam Fig* **the c. is clear** no hay moros en la costa
2 *vi Aut* ir en punto muerto; *(on bicycle)* deslizarse sin pedalear

coastal ['kəʊstəl] *adj* costero(a)

coaster ['kəʊstər] *n* **(a)** *Br Naut* barco *m* de cabotaje **(b)** *(mat)* salvamanteles *m inv*

coastguard ['kəʊstgɑːd] *n esp Br* guardacostas *m inv*

coastline ['kəʊstlaɪn] *n* litoral *m*, costa *f*

coast-to-coast ['kəʊstə'kəʊst] *adj* de costa a costa

coat [kəʊt] **1** *n* **(a)** *(overcoat)* abrigo *m*; *(short)* chaquetón *m*, *Méx* chamarra *f*, *RP* campera *f* ❑ **c. hanger** percha *f* **(b)** *(of animal)* pelo *m*, pelaje *m* **(c)** *(of paint)* mano *f*, capa *f* **(d)** *(in heraldry)* **c. of arms** escudo *m* de armas
2 *vt* cubrir (**with** de); *(with liquid)* bañar (**with** en); *Culin (with egg, flour)* rebozar (**with** con)

coating ['kəʊtɪŋ] *n* capa *f*, baño *m*

coat-tails ['kəʊtteɪlz] *npl* frac *m*; *Fig* **on sb's c.** a la sombra de algn

co-author [kəʊ'ɔːθər] **1** *n* coautor(a) *m*,*f*
2 *vt* **to co-a. a book with sb** escribir un libro conjuntamente con algn

coax [kəʊks] *vt* engatusar; **to c. sb into doing sth** engatusar a algn para que haga algo; **to c. sth out of sb** sonsacar algo a algn

coaxing ['kəʊksɪŋ] *n* zalamerías *fpl*, halagos *mpl*

cob [kɒb] *n* mazorca *f*

cobalt ['kəʊbɔːlt] *n Chem* cobalto *m* ❑ **c. blue** azul *m* cobalto

cobble ['kɒbəl] *n* adoquín *m*

cobbled ['kɒbəld] *adj* adoquinado(a)

cobbler ['kɒblər] *n* zapatero *m*

cobblers ['kɒbləz] *npl Br Slang Vulg (testicles)* huevos *mpl*; **a load of old c.** *(nonsense) Esp* chorradas *fpl*, gilipolleces *fpl*, *Am* pendejadas *fp*, *RP* pelotudeces *fpl*; *(film etc)* una birria, un asco

cobra ['kəʊbrə] *n Zool* cobra *f*

cobweb ['kɒbweb] *n* telaraña *f*

cocaine [kə'keɪn] *n* cocaína *f*

coccyx ['kɒksɪks] *n* coxis *m*

cock [kɒk] **1** *n* **(a)** *Orn* gallo *m*; *(male bird)* macho *m*; **c. sparrow** gorrión *m* macho; *Fig* **c. and bull story** cuento *m* chino **(b)** *(on gun)* percutor *m*, percusor *m* **(c)** *Slang Vulg (penis) Esp* polla *f*, *Am* verga *f*, *Chile* pico *m*, *Méx* pito *m*, *RP* pija *f*
2 *vt (gun)* amartillar; *(ears)* erguir; *Fam* **to c. a snook at sb** burlarse de algn

cock up *vt Br Slang* cagar, *Méx* madrear

cockade [kɒ'keɪd] *n Mil* escarapela *f*

cock-a-doodle-doo [kɒkədu:dəl'du:] *interj* quiquiriquí

cock-a-hoop [kɒkə'hu:p] *adj Fam* contento(a) como unas pascuas

cock-a-leekie [kɒkə'li:kɪ] *n Scot Culin* sopa *f* de pollo y puerros

cock-and-bull story ['kɒkən'bʊlstɔːrɪ] *n Fam* cuento *m* chino

cockatoo [kɒkə'tu:, 'kɒkətu:] *n Orn* cacatúa *f*

cockcrow ['kɒkkrəʊ] *n* canto *m* del gallo; **at c.** al amanecer

cocked [kɒkt] *adj (hat)* de tres picos; *Slang* **to knock sb into a c. hat** dar cien vueltas a algn

cocker ['kɒkər] *n Zool* **c. spaniel** cocker *m*

cockerel ['kɒkərəl] *n Orn* gallo *m* joven

cockeyed ['kɒkaɪd] *adj Fam (lopsided)* torcido(a); *(scheme)* disparatado(a)

cockfight ['kɒkfaɪt] *n* pelea *f* de gallos

cockiness ['kɒkɪnɪs] *n* descaro *m*, engreimiento *m*, *Esp* chulería *f*

cockle ['kɒkəl] *n* berberecho *m*; *Fig* **it warmed the cockles of my heart** me llenó de alegría

cockney ['kɒknɪ] **1** *adj* del East End londinense
  2 *n* persona *f* del East End londinense

cockpit ['kɒkpɪt] *n* cabina *f* del piloto, carlinga *f*

cockroach ['kɒkrəʊtʃ] *n Ent* cucaracha *f*

cockscomb ['kɒkskəʊm] *n* cresta *f* de gallo

cocksure [kɒk'ʃʊər] *adj* presumido(a), creído(a)

cocktail ['kɒkteɪl] *n* (a) *Culin* cóctel □ **c. lounge** bar *m*; **c. party** cóctel *m*, aperitivo *m*; **fruit c.** macedonia *f* de frutas; **prawn c.** cóctel *m* de gambas (b) **Molotov c.** cóctel *m* Molotov

cockup ['kɒkʌp] *n Br Slang* chapuza *f*, chapucería *f*

cocky ['kɒkɪ] *adj* (**cockier, cockiest**) *Fam* gallito(a), engreído(a), *Esp* chulo(a)

cocoa ['kəʊkəʊ] *n* cacao *m* □ **c. butter** manteca *f* de cacao

coconut ['kəʊkənʌt] *n* (a) *(fruit)* coco *m* □ *Bot* **c. palm** cocotero *m* (b) *(fibre)* fibra *f* de coco □ **c. matting** estera *f* de fibra de coco

cocoon [kə'kuːn] *n Ent* capullo *m*

COD [siːəʊ'diː] *n Br (abbr* **cash on delivery**) entrega *f* contra reembolso, cóbrese a la entrega, CAE

cod [kɒd] *n (pl* **cod** *or* **cods**) *(fish)* bacalao *m* □ **c. liver oil** aceite *m* de hígado de bacalao; **salt c.** bacalao *m* seco

coddle ['kɒdəl] *vt* (a) *(child)* mimar (b) *Culin (eggs)* escaldar

code [kəʊd] **1** *n* (a) *(gen)* & *Comptr* código *m*; **c. of conduct** ética *f* profesional; *Aut* **highway c.** código de la circulación (b) *(symbol)* clave *f*; **Morse c.** alfabeto *m* Morse; **secret c.** clave secreta; **to break a c.** descifrar una clave (c) *Tel* **c. (number)**, *US* **area c. (number)** prefijo *m*; **postal c.** código *m* postal
  2 *vt (message)* cifrar, poner en clave; *Comptr* codificar

codeine ['kəʊdiːn] *n* codeína *f*

codfish ['kɒdfɪʃ] *n (fish)* bacalao *m*

codify ['kəʊdɪfaɪ] *vt (pt & pp* **codified**) codificar

codswallop ['kɒdzwɒləp] *n Br Slang* majaderías *fpl*, sandeces *fpl*, *Am* pendejadas *fpl*

co-ed [kəʊ'ed] *Fam* **1** *adj* mixto(a)
  2 *n* colegio *m* mixto

coeducation [kəʊedjʊ'keɪʃən] *n* enseñanza *f* mixta

coeducational [kəʊedjʊ'keɪʃənəl] *adj* mixto(a)

coefficient [kəʊɪ'fɪʃənt] *n Math* coeficiente *m*

coerce [kəʊ'ɜːs] *vt* coaccionar; **to c. sb into doing sth** coaccionar a algn a que haga algo

coercion [kəʊ'ɜːʃən] *n* coacción *f*

coercive [kəʊ'ɜːsɪv] *adj* coercitivo(a)

coexist [kəʊɪg'zɪst] *vi* coexistir

coexistence [kəʊɪg'zɪstəns] *n* coexistencia *f*

C of E [siːəv'iː] *n Br Rel (abbr* **Church of England**) Iglesia *f* Anglicana

coffee ['kɒfɪ] *n* café *m* □ **black c.** café *m Esp* solo *or Am* negro; **c. bar** cafetería *f*, snack bar *m*; **c. break** descanso *m*; **c. cup** taza *f* para café; **c. grinder, c. mill** molinillo *m* de café; **c. shop** cafetería *f*, café *m*; **c. table** mesita *f* de café; **high roast c.** café *m* torrefacto; **instant c.** café *m* instantáneo; **white c.** café *m* con leche

coffeepot ['kɒfɪpɒt] *n* cafetera *f*

coffer ['kɒfər] *n* arca *f*, caja *f* de caudales

coffin ['kɒfɪn] *n* ataúd *m*

cog [kɒg] *n Tech* diente *m*; *Fig* **to be just a c. in the machine** no ser más que una pieza del mecanismo

cogent ['kəʊdʒənt] *adj* lógico(a), válido(a)

cognac ['kɒnjæk] *n* coñac *m*

cognition [kɒg'nɪʃən] *n* cognición *f*, conocimiento *m*

cogwheel ['kɒgwiːl] *n Tech* rueda *f* dentada

cohabit [kəʊ'hæbɪt] *vi* cohabitar

cohabitation [kəʊhæbɪ'teɪʃən] *n* cohabitación *f*

cohere [kəʊ'hɪər] *vi* adherirse; *Fig* ser coherente, concordar

coherence [kəʊ'hɪərəns] *n* coherencia *f*

coherent [kəʊ'hɪərənt] *adj* coherente, lógico(a)

cohesion [kəʊ'hiːʒən] *n* cohesión *f*

cohesive [kəʊ'hiːsɪv] *adj* adherente, cohesivo(a)

coiffure [kwɑː'fjʊər] *n* peinado *m*

coil [kɔɪl] **1** *vt* **to c. (up)** enrollar
  2 *vi (snake)* enroscarse; **to c. up** hacerse un ovillo
  3 *n* (a) *(loop)* vuelta *f*; *(of rope)* rollo *m*; *(of hair)* rizo *m*; *(of smoke)* espiral *f* □ **c. spring** muelle *m* en espiral (b) *Br Med (contraceptive)* espiral *f* (c) *Elec* carrete *m*, bobina *f*

coin [kɔɪn] **1** *n* moneda *f*; **to toss a c.** echar a cara o cruz
  2 *vt* (a) *(money)* acuñar (b) *(invent) (word)* crear; *Fig* **to c. a phrase** por así decirlo *or* como se suele decir

coinage ['kɔɪnɪdʒ] *n* moneda *f*, sistema *m* monetario

coincide [kəʊɪn'saɪd] *vi* coincidir (**with** con)

coincidence [kəʊ'ɪnsɪdəns] *n* coincidencia *f*

coincidental [kəʊɪnsɪ'dentəl] *adj* casual

coincidentally [kəʊɪnsɪ'dentəlɪ] *adv* por casualidad *or* coincidencia, casualmente

coin-op ['kɔɪnɒp] *n Fam* lavandería *f* automática

coin-operated ['kɔɪnɒpəreɪtɪd] *adj* **c. machine** máquina *f* de monedas

coitus ['kəʊɪtəs] *n* coito *m*

Coke® [kəʊk] *n (abbr* **Coca-Cola®**) *Fam* coca *f*

coke¹ [kəʊk] *n (coal)* coque *m*

coke² [kəʊk] *n (abbr* **cocaine**) *Fam* coca *f*

Col *Mil (abbr* **Colonel**) Coronel *m*, Cnel.

col. (a) *(abbr* **colour**) color *m* (b) *(abbr* **column**) columna *f*, col

colander ['kʌləndər] *n* colador *m*

cold [kəʊld] **1** *adj* (a) *(gen)* frío(a); **I'm c.** tengo frío; **it's c.** *(weather)* hace frío; *(thing)* está frío(a); **to get c.** enfriarse; *Fig* **as c. as ice** helado(a); *Fig* **to get** *or* **have c. feet (about doing sth)** entrarle miedo a algn (de hacer algo); *Fam Fig* **to put into c. storage** aplazar, dejar en suspenso □ **c. calling** *(in marketing)* contacto *m* en frío *or* sin previo aviso; **c. cream** crema *f* hidratante; *US* **c. cuts** fiambres *mpl* y embutidos; *Meteor* **c. front** frente *m* frío; **c. meats** fiambres *mpl*; **c. storage** conservación *f* en frío (b) *Fig (unenthusiastic)* indiferente; **it leaves me c.** ni me va ni me viene (c) *Fig (unemotional, unfriendly)* frío(a); **in c. blood** a sangre fría; **to give sb the c. shoulder** tratar a algn con frialdad □ *Fig* **c. comfort** poco consuelo *m*; *Pol* **c. war** guerra *f* fría (d) *(unconscious)* inconsciente; **to knock sb out c.** dejar a algn inconsciente (de un golpe)
  2 *n* (a) *(low temperature)* frío *m*; **to feel the c.** ser friolero(a); **to be left out in the c.** quedarse al margen (b) *Med* catarro *m*, *Esp Méx* resfriado *m*, *Andes RP* resfrío *m*; **to catch a c.** coger un resfriado, resfriarse; acatarrarse; **to have a c.** estar acatarrado(a), tener un *Esp Méx* resfriado *or Andes RP* resfrío, **to catch a c.** agarrar *or Esp* coger *or Méx* pescar un resfriado, *Andes RP* agarrarse *or*

pescarse un resfrío □ *Med* **c. sore** herpes *m inv* labial, *Esp* calentura *f*, *Méx* fuego *m*

cold-blooded [kəʊld'blʌdɪd] *adj* (**a**) *(animal)* de sangre fría (**b**) *Fig (person)* frío(a), insensible; *(crime)* a sangre fría, premeditado(a)

cold-hearted [kəʊld'hɑːtɪd] *adj* frío(a), insensible

coldly ['kəʊldlɪ] *adv* fríamente, con frialdad

coldness ['kəʊldnɪs] *n* frialdad *f*

cold-shoulder ['kəʊld'ʃəʊldər] *vt* dar de lado a, dar la espalda a

coleslaw ['kəʊlslɔː] *n Culin* ensalada *f* de col

colic ['kɒlɪc] *n Med* cólico *m*

colitis [kɒ'laɪtɪs] *n Med* colitis *f*

collaborate [kə'læbəreɪt] *vi* colaborar (**with** con)

collaboration [kəlæbə'reɪʃən] *n* colaboración *f*

collaborator [kə'læbəreɪtər] *n* colaborador(a) *m,f*; *Pol* colaboracionista *mf*

collage [kɒ'lɑːʒ] *n Art* collage *m*

collagen ['kɒlədʒən] *n* colágeno *m*

collapse [kə'læps] **1** *vi* (**a**) *(break down)* derrumbarse; *(cave in)* hundirse, venirse abajo (**b**) *Fig (currency, prices)* caer en picado (**c**) *Med* sufrir un colapso (**d**) *(table, tent)* plegarse
   2 *vt (table)* plegar
   3 *n* (**a**) *(breaking down)* derrumbamiento *m*; *(caving in)* hundimiento *m* (**b**) *Fig (of currency, prices)* caída *f* en picado (**c**) *Med* colapso *m*

collapsible [kə'læpsəbəl] *adj* plegable, desmontable

collar ['kɒlər] **1** *n (of garment)* cuello *m*; *(for dog)* collar *m*; **detachable c.** cuello falso; *Fig* **blue c. worker** obrero *m* industrial; *Fig* **hot under the c.** enfadado(a), indignado(a)
   2 *vt Fam* pescar, agarrar

collarbone ['kɒləbəʊn] *n Anat* clavícula *f*

collate [kɒ'leɪt] *vt* cotejar

collateral [kɒ'lætərəl] **1** *n Fin* garantía *f* subsidiaria
   2 *adj* colateral □ *Mil* **c. damage** bajas *fpl* civiles *(en un bombardeo)*

collation [kɒ'leɪʃən] *n* cotejo *m*

colleague ['kɒliːg] *n* colega *mf*

collect [kə'lekt] **1** *vt* (**a**) *(gather)* recoger; *Fig* **to c. one's thoughts** poner en orden sus ideas (**b**) *(stamps, records)* coleccionar (**c**) *Fin (taxes etc)* recaudar
   2 *vi* (**a**) *(people)* reunirse, congregarse (**b**) *(for charity)* hacer una colecta (**for** para)
   3 *adj US* **c. call** llamada *f or Am* llamado *m* a cobro revertido
   4 *adv US* **to call sb c.** llamar *or Am* hablar a algn a cobro revertido

collected [kə'lektɪd] *adj* (**a**) *(composed)* sosegado(a), tranquilo(a) (**b**) *Lit* **c. works** obras *fpl* completas

collection [kə'lekʃən] *n* (**a**) *(of mail)* recogida *f*; *(of money)* colecta *f*; **to take up** *or* **make a c.** hacer *or* efectuar una colecta (**b**) *(of stamps)* colección *f* (**c**) *(of taxes)* recaudación *f* (**d**) *(group) (of people)* grupo *m*; *(heap)* montón *m*

collective [kə'lektɪv] **1** *adj (ownership, efforts)* colectivo(a) □ *Ind* **c. bargaining** negociaciones *fpl* colectivas; **c. farm** (granja *f*) cooperativa *f*; *Ling* **c. noun** sustantivo *m* colectivo
   2 *n (group)* comunidad *f*; *(business)* cooperativa *f*

collectively [kə'lektɪvlɪ] *adv* colectivamente; **they are c. known as ...** se los/las conoce como ...

collectivize [kə'lektɪvaɪz] *vt* colectivizar

collector [kə'lektər] *n* (**a**) *(of stamps etc)* coleccionista *mf* □ **c.'s item, c.'s piece** pieza *f* de coleccionista (**b**) *Fin* **tax c.** recaudador(a) *m,f* (de impuestos) (**c**) *(on bus etc)* **ticket c.** cobrador(a) *m,f*

college ['kɒlɪdʒ] *n Educ (school)* colegio *m*, escuela *f*; *Br (of university)* colegio mayor; *US (university)* universidad *f*; *Br* **c. of further education** = centro de enseñanza donde se pueden cursar estudios de formación profesional y bachillerato; **military c.** escuela militar; **teachers' training c.** escuela normal; **technical c.** escuela de formación profesional

collide [kə'laɪd] *vi* chocar, colisionar; *Fig* estar en conflicto (**with** con)

collie ['kɒlɪ] *n Zool* perro *m* pastor escocés, collie *m*

collier ['kɒlɪər] *n Br Min* minero *m*

colliery ['kɒljərɪ] *n Br Min* mina *f* de carbón

collision [kə'lɪʒən] *n* choque *m*, colisión *f*

colloquial [kə'ləʊkwɪəl] *adj* coloquial, familiar

colloquialism [kə'ləʊkwɪəlɪzəm] *n* expresión *f* coloquial

collude [kə'luːd] *vi* conspirar, confabularse

collusion [kə'luːʒən] *n* colusión *f*, conspiración *f*; **to act in c. with sb** conspirar con algn

collywobbles ['kɒlɪwɒbəlz] *npl Slang (upset stomach)* retortijones *mpl*; *Fig* **I've got the c.** estoy muy nervioso(a)

Cologne [kə'ləʊn] *n* Colonia

cologne [kə'ləʊn] *n* (agua *f* de) colonia *f*

Colombia [kə'lɒmbɪə] *n* Colombia

Colombian [kə'lɒmbɪən] *adj & n* colombiano(a) *(m,f)*

colon¹ ['kəʊlən] *n Typ* dos puntos *mpl*

colon² ['kəʊlən] *n Anat* colon *m*

colonel ['kɜːnəl] *n Mil* coronel *m*

colonial [kə'ləʊnɪəl] **1** *adj* colonial; **c. rule** gobierno colonial
   2 *n (person)* colono(a) *m,f*

colonialism [kə'ləʊnɪəlɪzəm] *n* colonialismo *m*

colonialist [kə'ləʊnɪəlɪst] *adj & n* colonialista *(mf)*

colonist ['kɒlənɪst] *n* colonizador(a) *m,f*

colonization [kɒlənaɪ'zeɪʃən] *n* colonización *f*

colonize ['kɒlənaɪz] *vt* colonizar

colonnade [kɒlə'neɪd] *n Archit* columnata *f*

colony ['kɒlənɪ] *n* colonia *f*

color ['kʌlər] *n & vt & vi US see* **colour**

color-blind ['kʌləblaɪnd] *adj US see* **colour-blind**

color-blindness ['kʌləblaɪndnɪs] *n US see* **colour-blindness**

color-coded [kʌlə'kəʊdɪd] *adj US see* **colour-coded**

colored ['kʌləd] *adj US see* **coloured**

colorful ['kʌləfʊl] *adj US see* **colourful**

coloring ['kʌlərɪŋ] *n US see* **colouring**

colorless ['kʌləlɪs] *adj US see* **colourless**

colossal [kə'lɒsəl] *adj* colosal

colour ['kʌlər] **1** *n* (**a**) *(gen)* color *m*; **in full c.** a todo color; **to have no c.** estar pálido(a); **what c. is it?** ¿de qué color es?; *Fig* **to be/feel off c.** no encontrarse/sentirse bien; *Fig* **to lose c.** palidecer; *Fam* **let's see the c. of your money!** ¡a ver, saca el dinero! □ **c. blindness** daltonismo *m*; **c. film** película *f* en color; **c. printing** cromolitografía *f*; **c. scheme** combinación *f* de colores; **c. television** televisión *f* en color; *Art* **water c.** acuarela *f* (**b**) *(race)* color *m* □ **c. bar** discriminación *f* racial; **c. problem** problema *m* del racismo (**c**) **colours** *Br Sport* colores *mpl*; *Mil (flag)* bandera *f sing*, enseña *f sing*; *Mil* **to salute the c.** saludar la bandera; *Fig* **to pass (an examination) with flying c.** salir airoso(a) *or* victorioso(a) de un examen; *Fig* **to show oneself in one's true c.** mostrarse como uno es de verdad
   2 *vt* colorear; **to c. sth red** colorear algo en rojo
   3 *vi* **to c. (up)** ruborizarse

colour-blind ['kʌləblaɪnd] *adj* daltónico(a)

colour-blindness ['kʌləblaɪndnɪs] *n* daltonismo *m*

colour-coded [kʌlə'kəʊdɪd] *adj* **the wires are c.** los cables están coloreados de acuerdo con un código

Coloured ['kʌləd] **1** *n* persona *f* de color
2 *adj* de color

coloured ['kʌləd] *adj (photograph)* en color; **straw-c.** de color paja

colourful ['kʌləfʊl] *adj* **(a)** *(with colour)* lleno(a) de color, vistoso(a) **(b)** *Fig (vivid)* vivo(a), lleno(a) de colorido; *(person)* pintoresco(a)

colouring ['kʌlərɪŋ] *n (colour)* tinta *m*, colorido *m*; *(dye)* colorante *m*

colourless ['kʌləlɪs] *adj* incoloro(a), sin color; *Fig* soso(a); **a c. life** una vida gris

colt [kəʊlt] *n* potro *m*

column ['kɒləm] *n* columna *f* ❏ *Press* **gossip c.** ecos *mpl* mundanos; *Anat* **spinal c.** columna *f* vertebral

columnist ['kɒləmnɪst] *n Press* columnista *mf*

coma ['kəʊmə] *n Med* coma *m*; **to go into a c.** caer en coma

comatose ['kəʊmətəʊs] *adj* en estado comatoso

comb [kəʊm] **1** *n* **(a)** *(for hair)* peine *m* **(b)** *Orn* cresta *f* **(c)** *(honeycomb)* panal *m*
2 *vt* **(a)** *(hair)* peinar; **to c. one's hair** peinarse **(b)** *Fig (area etc)* peinar, registrar a fondo

combat ['kɒmbæt] **1** *n* combate *m* ❏ *Mil* **c. duty** servicio *m* de frente; **c. zone** área *f* de combate; **single c.** duelo *m*
2 *vt (enemy, disease)* combatir
3 *vi* combatir **(against** contra)

combatant ['kɒmbətənt] *n* combatiente *mf*

combination [kɒmbɪ'neɪʃən] *n (gen)* combinación *f*; *(of people)* asociación *f* ❏ **c. lock** cerradura *f* de combinación

combine [kəm'baɪn] **1** *vt* combinar; **to c. business with pleasure** combinar el trabajo con la diversión
2 *vi (gen)* combinarse; *(companies)* asociarse; *(people)* unirse; *(workers)* sindicarse
3 ['kɒmbaɪn] *n* **(a)** *Com* asociación *f* **(b)** *Agr* **c. harvester** cosechadora *f*

combined [kəm'baɪnd] *adj* combinado(a), conjunto(a); **c. efforts** esfuerzos *mpl* combinados; *Mil* **c. operations** operaciones *fpl* conjuntas

combustible [kəm'bʌstəbəl] *adj* combustible

combustion [kəm'bʌstʃən] *n* combustión *f* ❏ **c. chamber** cámara *f* de combustión; **c. engine** motor *m* de combustión

come [kʌm] *vi (pt* came; *pp* come) **(a)** *(gen)* venir; *(arrive)* llegar; **c. and see us soon** ven a vernos pronto; **c. here** ven aquí; **c. with me** ven conmigo; **coming!** ¡voy!; **he comes every day** viene cada día; **to c. and go** ir y venir; **who comes next?** ¿quién va ahora?; *Fig* **in years to c.** en el futuro; *Fig* **to take things as they c.** tomarse las cosas con calma; *Fig* **I could see it coming** lo veía venir; *Fam* **you had it coming to you** te lo merecías **(b)** *(travel)* venir; **she's c. a long way** viene desde lejos; *Fig* **ha progresado mucho **(c)** *(appear)* venir, aparecer; **it comes in three colours** viene en tres colores; **that comes on page ten** eso se encuentra en la página diez; *Fig* **that comes easy to me** eso lo encuentro fácil **(d)** *(become)* **to c. apart/undone** desatarse/soltarse **(e)** *(occur, happen)* suceder; **how does the door c. to be open?** ¿cómo es que la puerta está abierta?; **nothing good will c. of it** acabará *or* terminará mal; **nothing much came of it** resultó ser poca cosa; **that's what comes of being too impatient** eso te pasa por ser demasiado impaciente; *Fam* **how c.?** ¿cómo es eso? **(f)** *(become aware of)* llegar a pensar; **I came to believe**

that ... llegué a creer que ...; **now that I c. to think of it** ahora que lo pienso **(g)** *Fam* **c. again?** ¿cómo?; **c. now! don't exaggerate** ¡anda! no exageres **(h)** *(subjunctive use)* **c. spring** cuando venga la primavera; *Fig* **c. what may** pase lo que pase **(i)** *Slang (have orgasm) Esp* correrse, *Am* venirse, *RP* irse

come about *vi* ocurrir, suceder; **how did it c. about that ...?** ¿cómo ocurrió que ...?

come across 1 *vt (thing)* encontrar por casualidad; **to c. across sb** encontrarse con algn por casualidad, tropezar con algn
2 *vi (make an impression)* **to c. across well/badly** causar buena/mala impresión

come after *vt & vi* seguir

come along *vi* **(a)** *(arrive)* venir, llegar; **c. along!** ¡vamos!, ¡date prisa! **(b)** *(make progress)* ir bien, progresar

come at *vt (attack)* atacar

come away *vi (leave)* salir; *(part)* separarse, desprenderse **(from** de); **c. away from there!** ¡sal de allí!

come back *vi* **(a)** *(return)* volver, regresar, *Col Méx* regresarse; **to c. back to what I was saying** volviendo a lo que decía **(b)** *US (retort)* replicar **(at** a)

come before *vt* **(a)** *(be more important than)* anteponerse a **(b)** *Jur (court)* comparecer ante

come by *vt* adquirir, conseguir

come down 1 *vt* bajar
2 *vi (gen)* bajar; *Av* aterrizar; *(rain)* caer; *(prices)* bajar; *(building)* venirse abajo, ser derribado(a); **it comes down to the ground** llega hasta el suelo; **to c. down with the flu** coger la gripe; *Fig* **to c. down in the world** venir a menos; *Fig* **to c. down on sb's side** ponerse de parte de algn

come forward *vi (advance)* avanzar; *(volunteer)* ofrecerse, presentarse

come in *vi* **(a)** *(enter)* entrar; **c. in!** ¡pase!, ¡adelante! **(b)** *(arrive) (train) (tide)* crecer, subir; *Athlet* **to c. in first/ second** llegar el primero/segundo; *Fam Fig* **where do I c. in?** y yo ¿qué pinto? **(c)** *(prove to be)* resultar; **to c. in handy** *or* **useful** venir bien, ser útil **(d)** **to c. in for** ser objeto de; **to c. in for criticism** ser blanco de críticas

come into *vt* **(a)** *(enter)* entrar en; *Jur* **to c. into force** entrar en vigor; *Fig* **I said the first thing that came into my head** dije lo primero que me vino a la cabeza; *Fig* **to c. into the world** venir al mundo **(b)** *(inherit)* heredar

come off 1 *vt (fall from)* caerse de; **to c. off a horse** caerse de un caballo; *Fam* **c. off it!** ¡venga ya!, ¡no te pases!
2 *vi* **(a)** *(fall)* caerse; *(stain, lid)* despegarse **(button)* caerse, despegarse **(b)** *Fam (take place)* pasar, ocurrir; *(succeed)* salir bien, tener éxito; **to c. off badly** salir mal

come on *vi* **(a)** *(hurry)* darse prisa; **c. on!** ¡venga!, ¡date prisa! **(b)** *(make progress)* ir bien, progresar **(c)** *(actor)* entrar en escena **(d)** *(rain, illness)* comenzar; **I have a cold coming on** tengo síntomas de resfriado; **it came on to rain** se puso a llover

come out *vi* **(a)** *(gen)* salir **(of** de), mostrarse; *(sun, book)* salir, aparecer; *(product)* estrenarse; *(facts)* revelarse **(b)** *(appear) (on stage)* entrar en escena; *(in society)* presentarse en sociedad **(c)** *(be removed) (stain)* quitarse; *(colour)* desteñir **(d)** *(declare oneself)* declararse; **to c. out against/ in favour of sth** declararse en contra/a favor de algo; *Br Ind* **to c. out (on strike)** hacer huelga, declararse en huelga; **to c. out with a remark** soltar un comentario **(e)** *(turn out)* resultar, salir; **the photos didn't c. out very well** las fotos no han salido muy bien; *Educ* **to c. out on top** ser el primero (de la clase) **(f)** *(be covered with)* **to c. out in a rash** salirle a uno una erupción *or* un sarpullido

come over 1 *vi* venir, llegar **(from** de); *Fig* **I've c. over to your way of thinking** me has convencido; *Fig* **to c. over**

well/badly causar buena/mala impresión; *Fam* **to c. over faint** *or* **funny** marearse, sentirse indispuesto(a)
  2 *vt* **(a)** *(hill etc)* aparecer en lo alto de **(b)** *Fam (feeling)* pasar; **what's c. over you?** ¿qué te pasa?

come round 1 *vt (corner)* dar la vuelta a
  2 *vi* **(a)** *(visit etc)* venir; *(festival)* volver; **c. round on Monday** ven a verme el lunes **(b)** *(regain consciousness)* volver en sí **(c)** *(accept)* **to c. round to sb's way of thinking** dejarse convencer por algn

come through 1 *vt* **(a)** *(cross)* atravesar, cruzar **(b)** *Fig (illness)* recuperarse de; *(operation, accident)* sobrevivir, salir con vida de
  2 *vi* **(a)** *(message)* llegar **(b)** *Fig (from illness)* recuperarse; *(from operation, accident)* sobrevivir, salir con vida

come to 1 *vt* **(a)** **to c. to one's senses** volver en sí; *Fig* recobrar la razón **(b)** *(amount to)* costar; **how much does it c. to?** ¿cuánto es?; **the lunch came to $30** la comida costó 30 dólares en total **(c)** *(arrive at, reach)* llegar a; **it came to my notice that ...** me enteré de que ...; **it comes to the same thing** viene a ser lo mismo; **the idea came to me that ...** me vino a la mente que ...; **to c. to an end** terminar, acabar; **what are things coming to?** ¿a dónde irá a parar todo esto?; *Fig* **if it comes to that** si hace falta; *Fig* **when it comes to religion** en cuanto a la religión; *Fam* **c. to that** a propósito
  2 *vi (regain consciousness)* volver en sí

come under *vt* **(a)** *Jur (person)* estar bajo la jurisdicción de **(b)** *(be part of)* estar comprendido(a) en; *Fig* **to c. under fire from sb** ser criticado(a) por algn; *Fig* **to c. under sb's influence** caer bajo la influencia de algn

come up 1 *vt* subir
  2 *vi* **(a)** *(rise)* subir; *(approach)* acercarse **(to a)**; **the water came up to his knees** el agua le llegaba hasta las rodillas **(b)** *(arise) (difficulty, question)* presentarse, surgir; *(number)* salir; **something's c. up** ha surgido algo; **to c. up with a solution** encontrar una solución; **to c. up against problems** encontrarse con problemas **(c)** *(rise) (plants)* brotar; *(sun)* salir **(d)** **to c. up to** igualar; **to c. up to sb's expectations** satisfacer a algn **(e)** *Jur* **to c. up before the courts** *(person)* comparecer ante el tribunal; *(case)* llegar ante el tribunal **(f)** *Fam (food)* **three chips, coming up!** ¡van tres de patatas fritas!

come upon *vt see* **come across**

comeback ['kʌmbæk] *n Fam* **(a)** *(of person)* reaparición *f*; **to make a c.** reaparecer **(b)** *(answer)* réplica *f*, respuesta *f*

comedian [kə'miːdɪən] *n* cómico *m*

comedienne [kəmiːdɪ'en] *n* cómica *f*

comedown ['kʌmdaʊn] *n Fam* desilusión *f*, revés *m*

comedy ['kɒmɪdɪ] *n* comedia *f*

come-hither ['kʌm'hɪðər] *adj Fam* **c. look** mirada *f* seductora

come-on ['kʌmɒn] *n Fam* **to give sb the c.** *(sexually)* intentar seducir a algn, *Esp* tirar los tejos a algn, *Méx* echarle los perros a algn, *RP* cargar a algn

comer ['kʌmər] *n* asistente *mf*; **first c.** primero(a) *m,f* (en llegar); **open to all comers** abierto a todos los que quieran asistir

comet ['kɒmɪt] *n Astron* cometa *m*

comeuppance [kʌm'ʌpəns] *n Fam* merecido *m*; **to get one's c.** llevarse su merecido

comfort ['kʌmfət] **1** *n* **(a)** *(well-being)* comodidad *f*; **creature comforts** comodidades *fpl*; **to live in c.** vivir cómodamente ❑ *US* **c. station** servicios *mpl*, *Esp* aseos *mpl*, *Am* baños *mpl*, *Am* lavatorios *mpl* **(b)** *(consolation)* consuelo *m*; **to take c. in** *or* **from sth** consolarse con algo; *Fig* **cold c.** triste consuelo
  2 *vt* consolar

comfortable ['kʌmfətəbəl] *adj (chair, clothes etc)* cómodo(a); *(atmosphere, temperature)* agradable; *Med (patient)* tranquilo(a); **he doesn't feel c. with us** no se encuentra a gusto con nosotros; **it's so c. here** aquí se está de maravilla; **make yourself c.** ponte cómodo(a); *Fig* **to win by a c. majority** ganar por amplia mayoría; *Fam* **c. income** buenos ingresos *mpl*

comfortably ['kʌmfətəblɪ] *adv* cómodamente; *Fam* **to be c. off** vivir cómodamente

comforter ['kʌmfətər] *n* **(a)** *(person)* consolador(a) *m,f* **(b)** *Br (scarf)* bufanda *f* **(c)** *esp Br (dummy)* chupete *m* **(d)** *US* edredón *m*

comforting ['kʌmfətɪŋ] *adj (gen)* consolador(a); *(news)* alentador(a), reconfortante

comfortless ['kʌmfətlɪs] *adj* incómodo(a)

comfy ['kʌmfɪ] *adj* (**comfier, comfiest**) *Fam* cómodo(a)

comic ['kɒmɪk] **1** *adj* cómico(a) ❑ *Theat* **c. opera** ópera *f* bufa; **c. strip** tira *f* cómica, historieta *f*
  2 *n* **(a)** *(person)* cómico(a) *m,f* **(b)** *Press Esp* tebeo *m*, *Am* revista *f* de historietas; *(for adults)* cómic *m*

comical ['kɒmɪkəl] *adj* cómico(a)

coming ['kʌmɪŋ] **1** *adj (day, year)* próximo(a); *(generation)* venidero(a), futuro(a)
  2 *n* venida *f*, llegada *f*; **comings and goings** idas y venidas; *Fig* **c. and going** ajetreo *m*, vaivén *m*; **c. out is often traumatic** *(as gay or lesbian)* declararse homosexual públicamente es a menudo traumático

comma ['kɒmə] *n Ling* coma *f* ❑ **inverted c.** comilla *f*

command [kə'mɑːnd] **1** *vt* **(a)** *(order)* mandar, ordenar; *Mil* mandar; **to c. sb to do sth** ordenar a algn que haga algo **(b)** *(respect)* imponer, infundir; *(sympathy)* merecer; *(money, resources)* disponer de; **it commanded a high price** se vendió muy caro; **to c. a view** tener vista
  2 *vi* mandar
  3 *n* **(a)** *(order)* orden *f*; *(authority)* mando *m*; **to be at sb's c.** estar a las órdenes de algn; **to have/take c. of** tener/tomar el mando de; **under his c.** a su mando **(b)** *(of language)* dominio *m*; **she has many languages at her c.** domina muchos idiomas **(c)** *(disposal)* disposición *f*; **to have a lot of money at one's c.** disponer de mucho dinero **(d)** *Comptr* comando *m*, instrucción *f*

commandant ['kɒmədænt] *n Mil* comandante *m*

commandeer [kɒmən'dɪər] *vt* requisar

commander [kə'mɑːndər] *n Mil* comandante *m*; *Naut* capitán *m* de fragata ❑ *Mil* **c. in chief** comandante *m* en jefe

commanding [kə'mɑːndɪŋ] *adj* dominante ❑ *Mil* **c. officer** comandante *m*

commandment [kə'mɑːndmənt] *n* mandamiento *m*

commando [kə'mɑːndəʊ] *n* (*pl* **commandos**) *Mil* comando *m*

commemorate [kə'meməreɪt] *vt* conmemorar

commemoration [kəmemə'reɪʃən] *n* conmemoración *f*

commemorative [kə'memərətɪv] *adj* conmemorativo(a)

commence [kə'mens] *vt & vi Fml* comenzar

commencement [kə'mensmənt] *n* **(a)** *Fml* comienzo *m* **(b)** *US Univ* ceremonia *f* de graduación

commend [kə'mend] *vt* **(a)** *(praise)* alabar, elogiar **(b)** *(entrust)* encomendar **(c)** *(recommend)* recomendar; **it has little to c. it** poco se puede decir a su favor

commendable [kə'mendəbəl] *adj* encomiable, recomendable

commendation [kɒmen'deɪʃən] *n* **(a)** *(praise)* elogio *m*, encomio *m* **(b)** *US (award)* medalla *f*

commensurate [kə'menʃərɪt] *adj* proporcional, equiparable; **c. to** or **with** en proporción con; **salary c. with experience** salario según experiencia

comment ['kɒment] **1** n comentario m, observación f; **no c.** sin comentario; **to cause c.** dar lugar a comentarios; **to make a c.** hacer un comentario or una observación

2 vi hacer comentarios; **to c. on sth** comentar algo, hacer comentarios sobre algo

commentary ['kɒməntərɪ] n comentario m

commentate ['kɒmənteɪt] vi Rad TV comentar, retransmitir

commentator ['kɒmənteɪtər] n Rad TV comentarista mf

commerce ['kɒmɜ:s] n comercio m

commercial [kə'mɜ:ʃəl] **1** adj comercial, mercantil ❑ **c. art** arte m publicitario; **c. college** escuela f de estudios administrativos; **c. traveller** viajante mf de comercio

2 n TV spot m, anuncio m televisivo

commercialism [kə'mɜ:ʃəlɪzəm] n Pej comercialidad f

commercialize [kə'mɜ:ʃəlaɪz] vt comercializar

commercially [kə'mɜ:ʃəlɪ] adv comercialmente

commie ['kɒmɪ] adj & n Fam Pej rojo(a) (m,f)

commiserate [kə'mɪzəreɪt] vi compadecerse (**with** de)

commiseration [kəmɪzə'reɪʃən] n conmiseración f

commissar ['kɒmɪsɑ:r] n Pol comisario m

commissariat [kɒmɪ'seərɪət] n Mil intendencia f

commission [kə'mɪʃən] **1** n (**a**) Mil (officer's) despacho m (de oficial); **into/out of c.** en/fuera de servicio (**b**) (of enquiry) comisión f; (job) encargo m (**c**) (payment) comisión f; **to sell (goods) on c.** vender (productos) a comisión

2 vt (**a**) Mil nombrar (**b**) (order) encargar; **to c. sb to do sth** encargar a algn que haga algo (**c**) Naut poner en servicio

commissionaire [kəmɪʃə'neər] n Br portero m de librea

commissioner [kə'mɪʃənər] n (official) comisario m; Jur **C. for Oaths** ≈ notario(a) m,f, CRica Ecuad RP ≈ escribano(a) m,f; **c. of police** comisario m jefe de policía

commit [kə'mɪt] vt (pt & pp **committed**) (**a**) (crime) cometer; **to c. suicide** suicidarse (**b**) (dedicate, give) dedicar; **to c. oneself (to do sth)** comprometerse (a hacer algo) (**c**) (entrust) **to c. sth to memory** aprenderse algo de memoria; **to c. sth to sb's care** confiar algo a algn (**d**) Jur **to c. for trial** citar ante los tribunales; **to c. to prison** encarcelar

commitment [kə'mɪtmənt] n compromiso m, obligación f

committal [kə'mɪtəl] n (**a**) (burial) entierro m (**b**) Jur **c. to prison** encarcelamiento m

committed [kə'mɪtɪd] adj comprometido(a)

committee [kə'mɪtɪ] n comisión f, comité m; **parliamentary c.** comisión parlamentaria; **to sit on a c.** ser miembro de una comisión or de un comité

commode [kə'məʊd] n (chair) silla f con orinal; (chest of drawers) cómoda f

commodious [kə'məʊdɪəs] adj espacioso(a)

commodity [kə'mɒdɪtɪ] n Com artículo m, producto m; **a basic c.** un artículo de primera necesidad; **c. market** mercado m de productos básicos

commodore ['kɒmədɔ:r] n Naut comodoro m

common ['kɒmən] **1** adj (**a**) (shared) común; **to have sth in c. with sb** tener algo en común con algn; **c. belief** creencia general; **that's c. knowledge** eso lo sabe todo el mundo ❑ Math **c. denominator** denominador m común; **c. factor** factor m común; Fig **c. ground** puntos mpl en común; Jur **c. law** derecho m consuetudinario; Formerly **C. Market** Mercado m Común; Br Educ **c. room** sala f de profesores/de estudiantes (**b**) (ordinary) corriente, frecuente; **a c. event** un hecho corriente; **the c. people** la

gente corriente; Fam **c. or garden** normal y corriente ❑ Med **c. cold** resfriado m or Andes RP resfrío m común; Ling **c. noun** nombre m común; **c. sense** sentido m común; US Fin **c. stock** acciones fpl ordinarias (**c**) (vulgar) ordinario(a), maleducado(a)

2 n (land) campo m or terreno m comunal

commoner ['kɒmənər] n plebeyo(a) m,f

common-law ['kɒmənlɔ:] adj **c. marriage** matrimonio m or unión f de hecho; **c. husband/wife** esposo m/esposa f de hecho

commonly ['kɒmənlɪ] adv comúnmente

commonplace ['kɒmənpleɪs] **1** adj ordinario(a), corriente

2 n (remark) tópico m, lugar m común

Commons ['kɒmənz] npl Br **the (House of) C.** (la Cámara de) los Comunes

Commonwealth ['kɒmənwelθ] n **the (British) C.** la Commonwealth, la Comunidad Británica de Naciones

commotion [kə'məʊʃən] n conmoción f, alboroto m, confusión f; **to cause a c.** armar un escándalo

communal ['kɒmjʊnəl] adj comunal, comunitario(a)

communally ['kɒmjʊnəlɪ] adv en comunidad; **c. owned** de propiedad comunitaria

commune¹ [kə'mju:n] vi (converse) conversar; (with nature) estar en comunión (**with** con)

commune² ['kɒmju:n] n comuna f, comunidad f

communicable [kə'mju:nɪkəbəl] adj Med transmisible

communicant [kə'mju:nɪkənt] n Rel comulgante mf

communicate [kə'mju:nɪkeɪt] **1** vi (**a**) (people) comunicarse (**with** con) (**b**) (rooms) comunicarse; **communicating door** puerta f que comunica

2 vt comunicar

communication [kəmju:nɪ'keɪʃən] n (**a**) (gen) comunicación f; **radio c.** comunicación por radio (**b**) (message) comunicado m (**c**) Br Rail **c. cord** timbre m de alarma (**d**) Comptr **communications protocol/software** protocolo m/software m de comunicaciones

communicative [kə'mju:nɪkətɪv] adj comunicativo(a)

communion [kə'mju:nɪən] n comunión f; Rel **to take c.** comulgar

communiqué [kə'mju:nɪkeɪ] n comunicado m oficial

communism ['kɒmjʊnɪzəm] n Pol comunismo m

communist ['kɒmjʊnɪst] adj & n comunista (mf)

community [kə'mju:nɪtɪ] n (gen) comunidad f; (people) colectividad f; **the immigrant c.** la comunidad de inmigrantes; **the local c.** el vecindario ❑ **c. centre** centro m social; **c. singing** canto m colectivo; **c. spirit** espíritu m comunitario

commute [kə'mju:t] **1** vi viajar diariamente al lugar de trabajo

2 vt Jur conmutar

commuter [kə'mju:tər] n persona f que viaja diariamente al lugar de trabajo

Comoros ['kɒmərəʊz] n Comoras

compact¹ [kəm'pækt] **1** adj (gen) compacto(a); (style) conciso(a) ❑ **c. disc** disco m compacto

2 ['kɒmpækt] n (**a**) (for powder) polvera f (**b**) US (automobile) utilitario m

compact² ['kɒmpækt] n Pol pacto m, convenio m

companion [kəm'pænjən] n (**a**) (mate) compañero(a) m,f ❑ **lady's c.** señora f de compañía (**b**) (handbook) guía f

companionable [kəm'pænjənəbəl] adj sociable, agradable

companionship [kəm'pænjənʃɪp] n compañerismo m

company ['kʌmpənɪ] *n* (**a**) *(gen)* compañía *f*; **to keep sb c.** hacer compañía a algn; **she's good c. for me** me hace mucha compañía; **to part c. with sb** separarse de algn; **we're expecting c.** esperamos visita; *Fig* **to get into bad c.** andar con malas compañías (**b**) *Com* empresa *f*, compañía *f*; **Smith & C.** Smith y Compañía ❏ **c. car** coche *m or Am* carro *or RP* auto de la empresa (**c**) *Mil Theat* compañía *f*; *Naut* **ship's c.** tripulación *f*

comparable ['kɒmpərəbəl] *adj* comparable (**to, with** con)

comparative [kəm'pærətɪv] **1** *adj* (*gen*) comparativo(a); *(relative)* relativo(a); *(subject)* comparado(a); **a c. study** un estudio comparativo; **he's a c. stranger** es prácticamente un desconocido; *Ling* **the c. form** el comparativo
 2 *n Ling* comparativo *m*

comparatively [kəm'pærətɪvlɪ] *adv* relativamente

compare [kəm'peər] **1** *vt* comparar (**to, with** con); **(as) compared with** en comparación con; *Fig* **to c. notes** cambiar impresiones
 2 *vi* comparar, compararse; **to c. favourably with sth** no desmerecer de algo, no perder por comparación con algo
 3 *n* **beyond c.** sin comparación

comparison [kəm'pærɪsən] *n* comparación *f*; **by** *or* **in c.** en comparación; **there's no c.** no se puede comparar, no tiene ni punto de comparación

compartment [kəm'pɑːtmənt] *n* (**a**) *(section)* comparti-miento *m*; *Naut* **watertight c.** compartimiento estanco (**b**) *Rail* departamento *m*

compass ['kʌmpəs] *n* (**a**) *(for finding direction)* brújula *f* (**b**) *Geom* **(pair of) compasses** compás *m* (**c**) *Fig (range)* espectro *m*, límites *mpl*

compassion [kəm'pæʃən] *n* compasión *f*

compassionate [kəm'pæʃənət] *adj* compasivo(a) ❏ *Mil* **c. leave** permiso *m* por asuntos personales

compassionately [kəm'pæʃənətlɪ] *adv* con compasión

compatibility [kəmpætə'bɪlɪtɪ] *n* compatibilidad *f*

compatible [kəm'pætəbəl] *adj* compatible (**with** con)

compatriot [kəm'pætrɪət] *n* compatriota *mf*

compel [kəm'pel] *vt* (*pt & pp* **compelled**) (**a**) *(oblige)* obligar; **to c. sb to do sth** obligar a algn a hacer algo; **to be compelled to do sth** verse obligado(a) a hacer algo (**b**) *(demand) (respect)* imponer; *(admiration)* despertar

compelling [kəm'pelɪŋ] *adj* irresistible; **a c. reason** una razón apremiante

compendium [kəm'pendɪəm] *n* (*pl* **compendiums** *or* **compendia** [kəm'pendɪə]) *Br (book)* compendio *m*

compensate ['kɒmpenseɪt] **1** *vt* compensar; **to c. sb for sth** indemnizar a algn de algo
 2 *vi* compensar; **to c. for sth** compensar algo

compensation [kɒmpen'seɪʃən] *n (gen)* compensación *f*; *(for loss)* indemnización *f*

compensatory [kɒmpen'seɪtərɪ] *adj* compensatorio(a)

compere ['kɒmpeər] *Br* **1** *n* presentador(a) *m,f*, animador(a) *m,f*
 2 *vt* presentar

compete [kəm'piːt] *vi* competir; **to c. for a prize** competir por un premio; **to c. with sb** competir con algn

competence ['kɒmpɪtəns] *n* (**a**) *(ability)* competencia *f*, aptitud *f* (**b**) *Jur (of court etc)* competencia *f*

competent ['kɒmpɪtənt] *adj* (**a**) *(person)* competente, apto(a) (**b**) *Jur* competente

competition [kɒmpɪ'tɪʃən] *n* (**a**) *(contest)* concurso *m*, competición *f*, *Am* competencia *f* (**b**) *Com* competencia *f*; **fierce c.** competencia feroz; **in c. with** en competencia con

competitive [kəm'petɪtɪv] *adj* (**a**) *(person)* que tiene espíritu competitivo ❏ **c. examination** oposición *f* (**b**) *Com (price, goods)* competitivo(a) ❏ **c. tendering** adjudicación *f* por concurso público

competitor [kəm'petɪtər] *n* competidor(a) *m,f*

compilation [kɒmpɪ'leɪʃən] *n* compilación *f*, recopila-ción *f*

compile [kəm'paɪl] *vt* compilar, recopilar

compiler [kəm'paɪlər] *n* (**a**) *(of book, information)* recopilador(a) *m,f*, compilador(a) *m,f*; *(of dictionary)* redactor(a) *m,f* (**b**) *Comptr* compilador *m*

complacency [kəm'pleɪsənsɪ] *n* complacencia *f*

complacent [kəm'pleɪsənt] *adj* satisfecho(a) de sí mismo(a), suficiente; **a c. attitude** una actitud de complacencia

complacently [kəm'pleɪsəntlɪ] *adv* de modo satisfecho

complain [kəm'pleɪn] *vi* quejarse (**of, about** de); **I can't** *or* **mustn't c.** no me puedo quejar

complaint [kəm'pleɪnt] *n* (**a**) *(gen)* queja *f*; *Com* reclamación *f*; **reason for c.** motivo *m* de queja (**b**) *Jur* demanda *f*; **to lodge a c.** presentar *or* entablar una demanda (**c**) *Med* enfermedad *f*

complement ['kɒmplɪmənt] **1** *n* (**a**) *Ling Math* complemento *m* (**b**) *Mil* efectivos *mpl*; *Naut* dotación *f*; **a full c.** la totalidad
 2 *vt* complementar

complementary [kɒmplɪ'mentərɪ] *adj* complementa-rio(a) ❏ **c. medicine** medicina *f* alternativa

complete [kəm'pliːt] **1** *adj* (**a**) *(entire)* completo(a); **is the work c. now?** ¿está terminado ya el trabajo?; **the c. works of Shakespeare** las obras completas de Shakespeare (**b**) *(absolute)* total; **he's a c. idiot** es tonto de remate; **she's a c. stranger** es totalmente desconocida
 2 *vt* completar, rellenar; **to c. a form** rellenar un formulario

completely [kəm'pliːtlɪ] *adv* completamente, por completo

completeness [kəm'pliːtnɪs] *n* (**a**) *(wholeness)* **they added a final volume to the series for c.** añadieron un último volumen para redondear la colección (**b**) *(thorough-ness)* **the c. of their victory/defeat** lo categórico de su victoria/derrota

completion [kəm'pliːʃən] *n* finalización *f*, terminación *f*; **near c.** casi terminado(a); **on c.** en cuanto se termine; *Jur* **on c. of contract** cuando se haya firmado el contrato

complex ['kɒmpleks] **1** *adj* complejo(a)
 2 *n* (**a**) *(group)* complejo *m*; **industrial c.** complejo industrial (**b**) *Psych* complejo *m*; **inferiority c.** complejo de inferioridad

complexion [kəm'plekʃən] *n* tez *f*, cutis *m*; *Fig* **that puts a different c. on things** así la cosa cambia de aspecto

complexity [kəm'pleksɪtɪ] *n* complejidad *f*

compliance [kəm'plaɪəns] *n* conformidad *f*, acuerdo *m*; **in c. with a request** en *or* de conformidad con una solicitud; **in c. with the law** de acuerdo con la ley

compliant [kəm'plaɪənt] *adj* sumiso(a)

complicate ['kɒmplɪkeɪt] *vt* complicar

complicated ['kɒmplɪkeɪtɪd] *adj* complicado(a)

complication [kɒmplɪ'keɪʃən] *n* complicación *f*

complicity [kəm'plɪsɪtɪ] *n* complicidad *f*

compliment ['kɒmplɪmənt] **1** *n* (**a**) *(praise)* cumplido *m*; **to pay sb a c.** hacerle un cumplido a algn (**b**) **compliments** saludos *mpl*; **to send sb one's c.** dar sus recuerdos *or* saludos *or CAm Col Ecuad* saludes a algn; **with my c.** de mi parte

2 ['kɒmplɪment] vt felicitar; **to c. sb on sth** felicitar a algn por algo

complimentary [kɒmplɪ'mentərɪ] adj **(a)** (praising) elogioso(a) **(b)** (free) gratis; **c. copy (of a book)** ejemplar m gratis; **c. ticket** invitación f

comply [kəm'plaɪ] vi (pt & pp **complied**) obedecer; **to c. with** (order) cumplir con; (request) acceder a

component [kəm'pəʊnənt] **1** n componente m
2 adj componente; **c. part** parte f, componente m

compose [kəm'pəʊz] vt **(a)** Mus Print componer; **to be composed of** componerse de **(b)** (calm) **to c. oneself** calmarse, serenarse

composed [kəm'pəʊzd] adj (calm) sereno(a), tranquilo(a)

composer [kəm'pəʊzər] n Mus compositor(a) m,f

composite ['kɒmpəzɪt] adj compuesto(a)

composition [kɒmpə'zɪʃən] n (gen) composición f; Educ (essay) redacción f

compositor [kəm'pɒzɪtər] n Print cajista mf

compos mentis [kɒmpəs'mentɪs] adj **to be c. m.** estar en su sano juicio

compost ['kɒmpɒst] n Agr abono m

composure [kəm'pəʊʒər] n calma f, serenidad f

compound¹ ['kɒmpaʊnd] **1** n Chem Ling compuesto m
2 [kəm'paʊnd] vt (things) componer, combinar; (problem) agravar; **compounded of** compuesto(a) de
3 ['kɒmpaʊnd] adj compuesto(a); Med (fracture) complicado(a); (word) compuesto(a) ❏ Fin **c. interest** intereses mpl compuestos

compound² ['kɒmpaʊnd] n (enclosure) recinto m

comprehend [kɒmprɪ'hend] vt comprender

comprehensible [kɒmprɪ'hensəbəl] adj comprensible

comprehension [kɒmprɪ'henʃən] n comprensión f; **that's beyond my c.** no llego a entenderlo

comprehensive [kɒmprɪ'hensɪv] **1** adj **(a)** (broad) (view, knowledge) amplio(a); (study, description) detallado(a), global **(b)** (insurance) a todo riesgo **(c)** Br Educ **c. school** ≃ instituto m de segunda enseñanza
2 n Br Educ ≃ instituto m de segunda enseñanza

compress [kəm'pres] **1** vt (squeeze) comprimir; Fig (text) condensar; Comptr comprimir
2 ['kɒmpres] n Med compresa f

compression [kəm'preʃən] n compresión f

compressor [kəm'presər] n compresor m

comprise [kəm'praɪz] vt (include) comprender; (consist of) constar de

compromise ['kɒmprəmaɪz] **1** n acuerdo m, término m medio; **the art of c.** el arte de la negociación; **to reach a c.** llegar a un acuerdo
2 vi llegar a un acuerdo, transigir
3 vt (person) comprometer; **to c. oneself** comprometerse

compromising ['kɒmprəmaɪzɪŋ] adj comprometido(a)

compulsion [kəm'pʌlʃən] n obligación f, coacción f; **under c.** bajo coacción

compulsive [kəm'pʌlsɪv] adj compulsivo(a)

compulsory [kəm'pʌlsərɪ] adj obligatorio(a)

compunction [kəm'pʌŋkʃən] n remordimiento m; **without c.** sin escrúpulos

computation [kɒmpjʊ'teɪʃən] n cálculo m

computational [kɒmpjʊ'teɪʃənəl] adj computacional

compute [kəm'pjuːt] vt & vi calcular

computer [kəm'pjuːtər] n Esp ordenador m, Am computadora f, Am computador m ❏ **c. literacy** conocimientos mpl de informática; **c. literate** con conocimientos de

informática; **c. program** programa m informático; **c. programmer** programador(a) m,f; **c. programming** programación f (de Esp ordenadores or Am computadoras); **c. science** informática f; **c. simulation** simulación f por Esp ordenador or Am computadora; **personal c.** ordenador m or Am computadora f or Am computador m personal

computer-aided [kəm'pjuːtəreɪdɪd], **computer-assisted** [kəm'pjuːtərə'sɪstɪd] adj **c.-a. design** diseño m asistido por Esp ordenador or Am computadora; **c.-a. instruction** or **learning** enseñanza f asistida por Esp ordenador or Am computadora; **c.-a. manufacture** fabricación f asistida por Esp ordenador or Am computadora

computerization [kəmpjuːtəraɪ'zeɪʃən] n informatización f, Am computarización f, Am computadorización f

computerize [kəm'pjuːtəraɪz] vt informatizar, Am computarizar, Am computadorizar

computing [kəm'pjuːtɪŋ] n informática f, Am computación f

comrade ['kɒmreɪd] n **(a)** (companion) compañero(a) m,f **(b)** Pol camarada mf

comradeship ['kɒmreɪdʃɪp] n camaradería f

Con Br Pol (abbr **Conservative**) conservador(a) m,f

con¹ [kɒn] Slang **1** vt (pt & pp **conned**) timar, estafar, RP cagar; **I've been conned!** ¡me han timado!
2 n timo m, estafa f, Andes RP truchada f ❏ **c. man** estafador m; **c. trick** timo m, Andes RP truchada f

con² [kɒn] n Fam contra m; **the pros and cons** los pros y los contras

concave ['kɒnkeɪv] adj cóncavo(a)

conceal [kən'siːl] vt (gen) ocultar (**from** de); (facts) encubrir; Fig (emotions) disimular

concealed [kən'siːld] adj oculto(a); **c. lighting** luz indirecta

concealment [kən'siːlmənt] n ocultación f, encubrimiento m; **in c.** oculto(a)

concede [kən'siːd] vt conceder; **to c. defeat** admitir la derrota, rendirse; **to c. victory** conceder la victoria

conceit [kən'siːt] n presunción f, vanidad f

conceited [kən'siːtɪd] adj presuntuoso(a), engreído(a), vano(a)

conceivable [kən'siːvəbəl] adj concebible

conceivably [kən'siːvəblɪ] adv posiblemente; **she may c. have done it** es posible que lo haya hecho

conceive [kən'siːv] **1** vt **(a)** (child, idea) concebir **(b)** (understand) comprender
2 vi **to c. of** concebir, imaginarse

concentrate ['kɒnsəntreɪt] **1** vt concentrar
2 vi concentrarse; **to c. on sth** concentrarse en algo, aplicarse a algo
3 n concentrado m

concentrated ['kɒnsəntreɪtɪd] adj (gen) concentrado(a); (efforts) intenso(a)

concentration [kɒnsən'treɪʃən] n concentración f ❏ **c. camp** campo m de concentración; **c. span** capacidad f de concentración

concentric [kən'sentrɪk] adj concéntrico(a)

concept ['kɒnsept] n concepto m

conception [kən'sepʃən] n Med concepción f; Fig (understanding) concepto m, idea f

conceptual [kən'septjʊəl] adj conceptual

conceptualize [kən'septjʊəlaɪz] vt formarse un concepto de

concern [kən'sɜːn] **1** vt **(a)** (affect) concernir, involucrar, afectar; **as far as I'm concerned** por lo que a mí se refiere; **it doesn't c. me** no me afecta; **'to whom it may c.'** 'a quien corresponda'; **where your interests are concerned** en cuanto a tus intereses (**b**) *(worry)* preocupar; **to c. oneself about** *or* **with** preocuparse por, tomarse interés por

2 *n* (**a**) *(affair)* interés *m*; **it's no c. of mine** no es asunto mío; **what c. is it of yours?** ¿a ti qué te importa? (**b**) *(worry)* preocupación *f*, inquietud *f*; **there's no cause for c.** no hay motivo para preocuparse; **to show c.** mostrar preocupación (**c**) *Com (business)* negocio *m*; **a going c.** un negocio en marcha

concerned [kən'sɜːnd] *adj* (**a**) *(affected)* afectado(a), involucrado(a); **everybody c.** los interesados; **the person c.** la persona a la cual nos referimos (**b**) *(worried)* preocupado(a) (**about** por)

concerning [kən'sɜːnɪŋ] *prep* referente a, con respecto a, en cuanto a

concert ['kɒnsət, 'kɒnsɜːt] *n* (**a**) *Mus* concierto *m* □ **c. hall** sala *f* de conciertos (**b**) *Fig* acuerdo *m*; **in c. with** de acuerdo con

concerted [kən'sɜːtɪd] *adj* concertado(a)

concertgoer ['kɒnsətgəʊər] *n* **a crowd of concertgoers** una multitud de asistentes al concierto

concertina [kɒnsə'tiːnə] *n Mus* concertina *f*

concerto [kən'tʃeətəʊ] *n (pl* **concertos** *or* **concerti** [kən'tʃeəti]) *Mus* concierto *m*

concession [kən'seʃən] *n* (**a**) *(gen)* concesión *f*, privilegio *m*; **tax c.** privilegio fiscal (**b**) *Com* reducción *f*

concessionary [kən'seʃənərɪ] *adj* (**a**) *(gen)* concesionario(a) (**b**) *Br Com (price)* rebajado(a)

conciliate [kən'sɪlɪeɪt] *vt* conciliar

conciliation [kənsɪlɪ'eɪʃən] *n* conciliación *f*

conciliatory [kən'sɪljətərɪ] *adj (gen)* conciliador(a), *(procedure)* conciliatorio(a)

concise [kən'saɪs] *adj* conciso(a)

concisely [kən'saɪslɪ] *adv* con concisión

concision [kən'sɪʒən] *n* concisión *f*, brevedad *f*

conclave ['kɒnkleɪv] *n Rel* cónclave *m*

conclude [kən'kluːd] **1** *vt (finish)* concluir, terminar
2 *vi* (**a**) *(finish)* concluir (**b**) *(deduce)* concluir, llegar a una conclusión

concluding [kən'kluːdɪŋ] *adj* final, concluyente

conclusion [kən'kluːʒən] *n* (**a**) *(resolution)* conclusión *f*; **a foregone c.** un final *or* un desenlace anticipado; **to reach a c.** llegar a una conclusión (**b**) *(end)* conclusión *f*; **in c.** en conclusión

conclusive [kən'kluːsɪv] *adj* concluyente

conclusively [kən'kluːsɪvlɪ] *adv* de manera concluyente

concoct [kən'kɒkt] *vt (dish)* confeccionar; *Fig (lie, plan)* fraguar, urdir; *Fig (excuse)* inventar

concoction [kən'kɒkʃən] *n (mixture)* mezcolanza *f*; *Pej (brew)* brebaje *m*

concord ['kɒnkɔːd] *n* concordia *f*, armonía *f*

concordance [kən'kɔːdəns] *n* (**a**) *(harmony)* concordancia *f* (**b**) *(book)* concordancias *fpl*

concourse ['kɒnkɔːs] *n* (**a**) *(of people)* concurrencia *f*, concurso *m* (**b**) *Rail* explanada *f*

concrete ['kɒnkriːt] **1** *n* hormigón *m*, *Am* concreto *m* □ **c. mixer** hormigonera *f*; **reinforced c.** hormigón *m* or cemento *m* armado
2 *adj* (**a**) *(definite)* específico(a), concreto(a) □ *Ling* **c. noun** sustantivo *m* concreto (**b**) *(made of concrete)* de hormigón

concubine ['kɒŋkjʊbaɪn] *n* concubina *f*

concur [kən'kɜːr] *vi (pt & pp* **concurred**) (**a**) *(agree)* **to c.**

with estar de acuerdo con (**b**) *(coincide)* coincidir, concurrir

concurrence [kən'kʌrəns] *n* (**a**) *(agreement)* acuerdo *m*, conformidad *f* (**b**) *(of events etc)* concurrencia *f*, concurso *m*

concurrent [kən'kʌrənt] *adj* concurrente, simultáneo(a)

concurrently [kən'kʌrəntlɪ] *adv* simultáneamente

concussed [kən'kʌst] *adj* conmocionado(a)

concussion [kən'kʌʃən] *n Med* conmoción *f* cerebral

condemn [kən'dem] *vt (gen)* condenar; *(house)* declarar en ruina; **the condemned cell** la celda de los condenados a muerte; **to c. sb to death** condenar a muerte a algn

condemnation [kɒndem'neɪʃən] *n* condena *f*

condensation [kɒnden'seɪʃən] *n (gen)* condensación *f*; *(on glass)* vaho *m*

condense [kən'dens] **1** *vt* condensar
2 *vi* condensarse

condensed [kən'denst] *adj (gen)* condensado(a); *Fig (reduced)* resumido(a); **c. milk** leche *f* condensada

condenser *n*, **condensor** [kən'densər] *n Tech* condensador *m*

condescend [kɒndɪ'send] *vi* condescender, dignarse; **to c. to sb** tratar a algn con condescendencia

condescending [kɒndɪ'sendɪŋ] *adj* condescendiente; **he's very c.** se da aires de superioridad

condescension [kɒndɪ'senʃən] *n* altivez *f*

condiment ['kɒndɪmənt] *n* condimento *m*

condition [kən'dɪʃən] **1** *n* (**a**) *(state)* condición *f*, estado *m*; **to be in good/bad c.** estar en buen/mal estado; **to be in no c. to do sth** no estar en condiciones de hacer algo (**b**) *(requirement)* condición *f*; **on c. that ...** a condición de que ...; **on no c.** de ningún modo; **on one c.** con una condición; **to make a c.** poner una condición (**c**) *Med* **heart c.** enfermedad *f* cardíaca; **to be out of c.** no estar en forma (**d**) **conditions** *(circumstances)* circunstancias *fpl*; **under favourable c.** en condiciones ventajosas □ **weather c.** condiciones *fpl* atmosféricas; **working c.** condiciones *fpl* de trabajo
2 *vt* condicionar

conditional [kən'dɪʃənəl] *adj* condicional; *Ling* **c. clause** oración *f* condicional

conditionally [kən'dɪʃənəlɪ] *adv (accept, grant)* condicionalmente

conditioner [kən'dɪʃənər] *n* acondicionador *m*; **hair c.** (crema *f*) suavizante *m* (para el pelo)

conditioning [kən'dɪʃənɪŋ] *n (psychological)* condicionamiento *m*

condo ['kɒndəʊ] *(pl* **condos**) *n US (apartment)* apartamento *m*, *Esp* piso *m*, *Arg* departamento *m (en propiedad)*; *(building)* = bloque de pisos poseídos por diferentes propietarios

condolences [kən'dəʊlənsɪz] *npl* pésame *m sing*; **please accept my c.** le acompaño en el sentimiento; **to send one's c.** dar el pésame

condom ['kɒndəm] *n* preservativo *m*, condón *m*

condominium [kɒndə'mɪnɪəm] *n (pl* **condominiums**) *US (apartment)* apartamento *m*, *Esp* piso *m*, *Arg* departamento *m (en propiedad)*; *(building)* = bloque de pisos poseídos por diferentes propietarios

condone [kən'dəʊn] *vt* consentir, perdonar

condor ['kɒndɔːr] *n Zool* cóndor *m*

conducive [kən'djuːsɪv] *adj* conducente; **to be c. to sth** favorecer algo

conduct ['kɒndʌkt] **1** *n (behaviour)* conducta *f*, comportamiento *m*; *(management)* dirección *f*
2 [kən'dʌkt] *vt (lead)* guiar, conducir; *(business)* conducir,

dirigir; *(orchestra)* dirigir; **a conducted tour** una visita acompañada; **to c. oneself** comportarse, portarse
   3 *vi Mus* dirigir

conduction [kən'dʌkʃən] *n Phys* conducción *f*

conductor [kən'dʌktər] *n* (**a**) *Br (on bus)* cobrador(a) *m,f*, *RP* guarda *m* (**b**) *US Rail* revisor(a) *m,f* (**c**) *Mus* director(a) *m,f* (**d**) *Phys* conductor *m*

conductress [kən'dʌktrɪs] *n Br (on bus)* cobradora *f*, *RP* guarda *f*

conduit ['kɒndjʊɪt] *n* conducto *m*

cone [kəʊn] *n* (**a**) *Geom* cono *m*; **c.-shaped** en forma de cono ◻ **ice-cream c.** cucurucho *m* (**b**) *Bot* piña *f*

confab ['kɒnfæb] *n Fam* plática *f*, charla *f*

confectioner [kən'fekʃənər] *n* confitero(a) *m,f*; **c.'s (shop)** confitería *f*; *US* **confectioners' sugar** azúcar *m* glas

confectionery [kən'fekʃənərɪ] *n* dulces *mpl*

confederacy [kən'fedərəsɪ] *n* confederación *f*

confederate [kən'fedərɪt] **1** *adj* confederado(a)
   2 *n* confederado *m*; *Jur* cómplice *m*
   3 [kən'fedəreɪt] *vt* confederar
   4 *vi* confederarse

confederation [kənfedə'reɪʃən] *n* confederación *f*

confer [kən'fɜːr] **1** *vt* (*pt & pp* **conferred**) conferir; **to c. a title on sb** conferir *or* otorgar un título sobre algn
   2 *vi* consultar (**about** sobre)

conference ['kɒnfərəns] *n* conferencia *f* ◻ *Tel* **c. call** multiconferencia *f*

confess [kən'fes] **1** *vi* confesar; *Rel* **to c. (oneself)** confesarse
   2 *vt* confesar, admitir; **to c. to having done sth** confesar haber hecho algo

confession [kən'feʃən] *n* confesión *f*; **on his own c.** según su propia confesión; *Rel* **to go to c.** confesarse

confessional [kən'feʃənəl] *n Rel* confesionario *m*

confessor [kən'fesər] *n Rel* confesor *m*

confetti [kən'fetɪ] *n* confeti *m*

confidant [kɒnfɪ'dænt] *n* confidente *m*

confidante [kɒnfɪ'dænt] *n* confidenta *f*

confide [kən'faɪd] **1** *vt* confiar
   2 *vi* confiarse; **to c. in sb** confiar en *or* fiarse de algn

confidence ['kɒnfɪdəns] *n* (**a**) *(trust)* confianza *f*; **to have every c. in sb** tener absoluta confianza en algn; **to take sb into one's c.** depositar su confianza en algn; *Pol* **vote of c./ no c.** voto *m* de confianza/de censura ◻ *Fam* **c. trick** engaño *m*, camelo *m* (**b**) *(self-assurance)* confianza *f*; **self-c.** confianza *or* seguridad *f* en sí mismo(a) (**c**) *(secret)* confidencia *f*; **in c.** en confianza; **to exchange confidences** hacerse confidencias

confident ['kɒnfɪdənt] *adj* seguro(a); **a c. smile** una sonrisa confiada; **in a c. tone** en un tono seguro *or* de seguridad

confidential [kɒnfɪ'denʃəl] *adj (secret)* confidencial; *(entrusted)* de confianza

confidentiality [kɒnfɪdenʃɪ'ælɪtɪ] *n* confidencialidad *f*

confidentially [kɒnfɪ'denʃəlɪ] *adv* confidencialmente, en confianza

confidently ['kɒnfɪdəntlɪ] *adv* con seguridad

confine [kən'faɪn] *vt* encerrar; *Fig* limitar; **confined space** espacio *m* reducido; **he's confined to bed** tiene que guardar cama; *Fig* **to c. oneself to sth** limitarse a algo

confinement [kən'faɪnmənt] *n* (**a**) *(prison)* prisión *f*, reclusión *f*; **to be in solitary c.** estar incomunicado(a) (**b**) *Med* parto *m*

confines ['kɒnfaɪnz] *npl* límites *mpl*; **within the c. of the home** en el ámbito del hogar

confirm [kən'fɜːm] *vt (verify, assert)* confirmar; *(ratify)* ratificar

confirmation [kɒnfə'meɪʃən] *n* confirmación *f*

confirmed [kən'fɜːmd] *adj* empedernido(a), inveterado(a)

confiscate ['kɒnfɪskeɪt] *vt* confiscar

confiscation [kɒnfɪs'keɪʃən] *n (gen)* confiscación *f*; *Com* comiso *m*, decomiso *m*

conflagration [kɒnflə'greɪʃən] *n* conflagración *f*, incendio *m*

conflict ['kɒnflɪkt] **1** *n* conflicto *m*
   2 [kən'flɪkt] *vi* estar en desacuerdo *or* oposición (**with** con), chocar (**with** con)

conflicting [kən'flɪktɪŋ] *adj (reports, evidence)* contradictorio(a); *(views)* incompatible, contrario(a)

confluence ['kɒnfluəns] *n* confluencia *f*

conform [kən'fɔːm] *vi* conformarse; **to c. to** *or* **with** *(customs)* ajustarse a; *(rules)* someterse a

conformist [kən'fɔːmɪst] *adj & n* conformista *(mf)*

conformity [kən'fɔːmɪtɪ] *n* conformidad *f*; **in c. with** conforme a, en conformidad con

confound [kən'faʊnd] *vt* (**a**) *(bewilder)* confundir, desconcertar (**b**) [kɒn'faʊnd] *(damn)* **c. it!** ¡maldito sea!; **you confounded fool!** ¡imbécil!

confront [kən'frʌnt] *vt (enemy, problem)* confrontar, hacer frente a, plantar cara a

confrontation [kɒnfrʌn'teɪʃən] *n* confrontación *f*

confuse [kən'fjuːz] *vt (person)* despistar, hacer confuso(a); *(thing)* confundir (**with** con); **to get confused** confundirse, hacerse un lío

confused [kən'fjuːzd] *adj (person)* confundido(a), despistado(a); *(mind, ideas)* confuso(a)

confusing [kən'fjuːzɪŋ] *adj* confuso(a)

confusingly [kən'fjuːzɪŋlɪ] *adv* confusamente; **c., both twins do exactly the same course at university** para mayor confusión, ambos gemelos cursan la misma carrera universitaria

confusion [kən'fjuːʒən] *n (gen)* confusión *f*, desconcierto *m*; *(of person)* despiste *m*; **to throw into c.** confundir, desconcertar

congeal [kən'dʒiːl] **1** *vt* coagular
   2 *vi* coagularse

congenial [kən'dʒiːnjəl] *adj (atmosphere etc)* agradable; *(person)* simpático(a), amable

congenital [kən'dʒenɪtəl] *adj* congénito(a); *Fig* **c. liar** mentiroso(a) *m,f* patológico(a)

conger ['kɒŋgər] *n Zool* **c. eel** congrio *m*

congested [kən'dʒestɪd] *adj* (**a**) *(street)* repleto(a) *or* lleno(a) de gente; *(city)* superpoblado(a) (**b**) *Med* congestionado(a)

congestion [kən'dʒestʃən] *n* (**a**) *(traffic)* retención *f*, aglomeración *f* (**b**) *Med* congestión *f*

conglomerate [kən'glɒmərət] *n* (**a**) *Com* conglomerado *m* de empresas (**b**) *Geol* conglomerado *m*

conglomeration [kənglɒmə'reɪʃən] *n* conglomeración *f*

Congo ['kɒŋgəʊ] *n* Congo

Congolese [kɒŋgə'liːz] *adj & n* congoleño(a) *(m,f)*

congratulate [kən'grætjʊleɪt] *vt* felicitar, dar la enhorabuena a

congratulations [kəngrætjʊ'leɪʃənz] *npl* felicitaciones *fpl*, enhorabuena *f sing*; **c.!** ¡felicidades!; **to offer c.** dar la enhorabuena

congratulatory [kən'grætjʊlətərɪ] *adj* de felicitación
congregate ['kɒŋgrɪgeɪt] *vi* congregarse
congregation [kɒŋgrɪ'geɪʃən] *n (group)* congregación *f*; *Rel* fieles *mpl*, feligreses *mpl*
congress ['kɒŋgres] *n* congreso *m*; *US* **C.** el Congreso
congressional [kən'greʃənəl] *adj US Pol* del Congreso; **c. elections** ≃ elecciones *fpl* legislativas
Congressman ['kɒŋgresmən] *n (pl* **Congressmen)** *US Pol* miembro *m* del Congreso, congresista *m*, *Am* congresal *m*
Congresswoman ['kɒŋgreswʊmən] *n (pl* **Congresswomen)** *US Pol* miembro *f* del Congreso, congresista *f*, *Am* congresal *f*
conical ['kɒnɪkəl] *adj* cónico(a)
conifer ['kɒnɪfər] *n Bot* conífera *f*
coniferous [kɒ'nɪfərəs] *adj* conífero(a)
conjectural [kən'dʒektʃərəl] *adj* conjetural
conjecture [kən'dʒektʃər] **1** *n* conjetura *f*, suposición *f*
  2 *vt* conjeturar, suponer
  3 *vi* hacer conjeturas
conjugal ['kɒndʒʊgəl] *adj* conyugal
conjugate ['kɒndʒʊgeɪt] *vt* conjugar
conjugation [kɒndʒʊ'geɪʃən] *n* conjugación *f*
conjunction [kən'dʒʌŋkʃən] *n* conjunción *f*; *Fig* **in c. with** conjuntamente con
conjunctivitis [kəndʒʌŋktɪ'vaɪtɪs] *n Med* conjuntivitis *f*
conjure ['kʌndʒər] **1** *vt* **to c. (up)** *(magician)* hacer aparecer; *Fig (memories etc)* evocar
  2 *vi* hacer juegos de manos; *Br Fig* **a name to c. with** un nombre todopoderoso
conjurer ['kʌndʒərər] *n* prestidigitador(a) *m,f*
conjuring ['kʌndʒərɪŋ] *n* **c. (tricks)** juegos *mpl* de manos
conjuror ['kʌndʒərər] *n see* **conjurer**
conk [kɒŋk] *Slang* **1** *vt* pegarle una piña a
  2 *n Br (nose)* napia *fpl*, narices *fpl*, *Esp* napias *fpl*
conk out *vi Fam* averiarse, *Am* descomponerse, *Méx* desconchinflarse
conker ['kɒŋkər] *n Fam* castaña *f* (de las Indias)
connect [kə'nekt] **1** *vt* **(a)** *(join)* juntar, unir; *(wires, cables)* empalmar; *(two cities)* unir, conectar; *Fig* **to be connected by marriage** estar emparentado(a) por matrimonio **(b)** *Tech (instal)* instalar; *Elec (to power supply)* enchufar, conectar **(c)** *Tel (call)* conectar, *Tel (person)* poner (en comunicación) **(d)** *Fig (associate)* asociar; **are they connected?** ¿tienen alguna relación entre sí?
  2 *vi* unirse; *(rooms)* comunicarse; *(train, flight)* enlazar *or* empalmar **(with** con)
connect up *vt (pipes, wires)* conectar
connected [kə'nektɪd] *adj (gen)* unido(a), conectado(a); *(events)* relacionado(a); *Fig* **to be well c.** *(person)* tener muchos contactos; *Fam* tener enchufe
connection *n,* **connexion** [kə'nekʃən] *n* **(a)** *(joint)* juntura *f,* unión *f* **(b)** *Elec Tech* conexión *f,* empalme *m* **(c)** *Tel* instalación *f,* conexión *f* **(d)** *Comptr* **c. kit** kit *m* de conexión **(e)** *Rail* correspondencia *f* **(f)** *Fig (of ideas)* relación *f; (regarding)* **in c. with** con respecto a **(g)** *Fig (person)* contacto *m; Fam* **to have connections** tener enchufe
connivance [kə'naɪvəns] *n* connivencia *f,* complicidad *f*
connive [kə'naɪv] *vi* conspirar; **to c. at** hacer la vista gorda con
conniving [kə'naɪvɪŋ] *adj* confabulador(a)
connoisseur [kɒnɪ'sɜːr] *n* conocedor(a) *m,f*
connotation [kɒnə'teɪʃən] *n* connotación *f*

conquer ['kɒŋkər] *vt (enemy, bad habit)* vencer; *(country)* conquistar
conquering ['kɒŋkərɪŋ] *adj* victorioso(a), conquistador(a)
conqueror ['kɒŋkərər] *n* conquistador *m,* vencedor *m*
conquest ['kɒŋkwest] *n* conquista *f*
consanguinity [kɒnsæŋ'gwɪnɪtɪ] *n* consanguinidad *f*
conscience ['kɒnʃəns] *n* conciencia *f;* **to have a clear** *or* **easy c.** tener la conciencia limpia; **to have a guilty c.** sentirse culpable; *Fig* **to have sth on one's c.** llevar *or* tener un peso en la conciencia
conscience-stricken ['kɒnʃənsstrɪkən] *adj* lleno(a) de remordimientos
conscientious [kɒnʃɪ'enʃəs] *adj* concienzudo(a) □ *Mil* **c. objector** objetor(a) *m,f* de conciencia
conscientiously [kɒnʃɪ'enʃəslɪ] *adv* concienzudamente, a conciencia
conscientiousness [kɒnʃɪ'enʃəsnɪs] *n* escrupulosidad *f*
conscious ['kɒnʃəs] *adj* **(a)** *Med* consciente; **to become c.** volver en sí **(b)** *(aware)* consciente; *(choice etc)* deliberado(a), intencional
consciousness ['kɒnʃəsnɪs] *n* **(a)** *Med* conocimiento *m;* **to lose/regain c.** perder/recuperar el conocimiento **(b)** *(awareness)* conciencia *f;* **c. raising** concienciación *f*
conscript ['kɒnskrɪpt] *Mil* **1** *n* recluta *m*
  2 [kən'skrɪpt] *vt* reclutar
conscription [kən'skrɪpʃən] *n* servicio *m* militar obligatorio
consecrate ['kɒnsɪkreɪt] *vt Rel* consagrar
consecration [kɒnsɪ'kreɪʃən] *n Rel* consagración *f*
consecutive [kən'sekjʊtɪv] *adj* consecutivo; **on four c. days** cuatro días seguidos
consensual [kən'sensjʊəl] *adj* **(a)** *(approach, politics)* consensuado(a) **(b)** *(sexual activity)* consentido(a) **(c)** *Jur (contract)* consensual
consensus [kən'sensəs] *n* consenso *m;* **the c. of opinion** la opinión general
consent [kən'sent] **1** *n* consentimiento *m;* **age of c.** edad *f* núbil; **by common c.** de común acuerdo
  2 *vi* consentir **(to** en); **I c.** lo consiento
consequence ['kɒnsɪkwəns] *n* consecuencia *f;* **in c.** por consiguiente; **to take the consequences** aceptar las consecuencias; *Fig* **it's of no c.** no tiene importancia
consequent ['kɒnsɪkwənt] *adj* consiguiente; **c. on** *or* **upon** consecutivo(a)
consequential [kɒnsɪ'kwenʃəl] *adj* consecuente
consequently ['kɒnsɪkwəntlɪ] *adv* por consiguiente, en consecuencia
conservation [kɒnsə'veɪʃən] *n* conservación *f* □ **c. area** zona *f* protegida
conservationist [kɒnsə'veɪʃənɪst] *n* ecologista *mf*
conservatism [kən'sɜːvətɪzəm] *n Pol* conservadurismo *m*
Conservative [kən'sɜːvətɪv] *Br Pol* **1** *adj* conservador(a); **the C. Party** el Partido Conservador
  2 *n* conservador(a) *m,f;* **the Conservatives** los conservadores
conservative [kən'sɜːvətɪv] *adj (estimate etc)* moderado(a), cauteloso(a), prudente
conservatoire [kən'sɜːvətwɑːr] *n Mus* conservatorio *m*
conservatory [kən'sɜːvətrɪ] *n* **(a)** *(greenhouse)* invernadero *m* **(b)** *Mus* conservatorio *m*
conserve [kən'sɜːv] **1** *vt* **(a)** *(guard)* conservar; **to c. one's**

strength reservar las fuerzas, reservarse (**b**) *Culin* poner en conserva

  2 [ˈkɒnsɜːv] *n Culin* conserva *f*

consider [kənˈsɪdər] *vt* (**a**) *(ponder on)* considerar; **all things considered** pensándolo bien; **to c. doing sth** pensar hacer algo (**b**) *(keep in mind)* tener en cuenta (**c**) *(regard, judge)* considerar; **he's considered to be an expert** le tienen por experto; **I c. myself happy** me considero feliz; *Fam* **c. it done!** ¡dalo por hecho!

considerable [kənˈsɪdərəbəl] *adj* considerable

considerably [kənˈsɪdərəblɪ] *adv* bastante; **this car is c. cheaper** este coche es mucho más barato

considerate [kənˈsɪdərɪt] *adj* considerado(a), atento(a)

considerately [kənˈsɪdərətlɪ] *adv* con consideración

consideration [kənsɪdəˈreɪʃən] *n* consideración *f*; **out of c. for** en consideración a; **the matter is under c.** se está estudiando *or* examinando el asunto; **without due c.** sin reflexión

considered [kənˈsɪdəd] *adj* considerado(a); **my c. opinion** mi opinión después de pensarlo bien

considering [kənˈsɪdərɪŋ] **1** *prep* teniendo en cuenta

  2 *adv Fam* **it's not so bad, c.** no está tan mal, después de todo

consign [kənˈsaɪn] *vt Com (goods)* consignar; *Fig* entregar, enviar

consignment [kənˈsaɪnmənt] *n Com* envío *m*, remesa *f* □ **c. note** talón *m* de expedición

consist [kənˈsɪst] *vi* consistir; **to c. of** consistir en, constar de

consistency [kənˈsɪstənsɪ] *n* (**a**) *(of actions)* consecuencia *f*, lógica *f* (**b**) *(of mixture)* consistencia *f*

consistent [kənˈsɪstənt] *adj* consecuente, lógico(a); **c. with** consecuente *or* de acuerdo con

consistently [kənˈsɪstəntlɪ] *adv (play, perform)* con regularidad; *(fail, deny, oppose)* constantemente

consolation [kɒnsəˈleɪʃən] *n* consuelo *m*, consolación *f* □ **c. prize** premio *m* de consolación

console[1] [kənˈsəʊl] *vt* consolar

console[2] [ˈkɒnsəʊl] *n Mus Tech* consola *f*

consolidate [kənˈsɒlɪdeɪt] **1** *vt* consolidar

  2 *vi* consolidarse

consolidation [kənsɒlɪˈdeɪʃən] *n* consolidación *f*

consoling [kənˈsəʊlɪŋ] *adj* consolador(a), reconfortante

consommé [ˈkɒnsɒmeɪ, kənˈsɒmeɪ] *n Culin* consomé *m*, caldo *m*

consonant [ˈkɒnsənənt] *n Ling* consonante *f*

consort [kənˈsɔːt] **1** *vi* asociarse (**with** con)

  2 [ˈkɒnsɔːt] *n* consorte *mf* □ **prince c.** príncipe *m* consorte

consortium [kənˈsɔːtɪəm] *n* (*pl* **consortia** [kənˈsɔːtɪə]) consorcio *m*

conspicuous [kənˈspɪkjʊəs] *adj (striking)* llamativo(a); *(easily seen)* visible; *(colour)* chillón(ona); *(mistake, difference)* evidente; *(remarkable)* que destaca; **in a c. position** a la vista de todos; **to make oneself c.** llamar la atención; *Fig* **to be c. by one's absence** brillar por su ausencia

conspiracy [kənˈspɪrəsɪ] *n* conspiración *f*, conjura *f* □ **c. theory** = teoría que sostiene la existencia de una conspiración, generalmente imaginaria

conspirator [kənˈspɪrətər] *n* conspirador(a) *m,f*

conspiratorial [kənspɪrəˈtɔːrɪəl] *adj* conspirador(a)

conspire [kənˈspaɪər] *vi* conspirar (**against** contra); *Fig* **everything conspired against him** todo se volvió en contra suya

constable [ˈkʌnstəbəl] *n Br* policía *m*, guardia *m*; **chief c.** jefe *m* de policía

constabulary [kənˈstæbjʊlərɪ] *n Br* comisaría *f*, policía *f*

constancy [ˈkɒnstənsɪ] *n* constancia *f*

constant [ˈkɒnstənt] **1** *adj (fixed)* constante, estable (**b**) *(continuous)* incesante, continuo(a) (**c**) *(loyal)* fiel, leal

  2 *n Math Phys* constante *f*

Constantinople [kɒnstæntɪˈnəʊpəl] *n Hist* Constantinopla

constellation [kɒnstɪˈleɪʃən] *n Astron* constelación *f*

consternation [kɒnstəˈneɪʃən] *n* consternación *f*; **in c.** consternado(a)

constipate [ˈkɒnstɪpeɪt] *vt* estreñir; **to be constipated** sufrir estreñimiento

constipation [kɒnstɪˈpɔːʃən] *n* estreñimiento *m*

constituency [kənˈstɪtjʊənsɪ] *n Pol* circunscripción *f* electoral

constituent [kənˈstɪtjʊənt] **1** *adj (component)* constituyente, constitutivo(a)

  2 *n* (**a**) *(part)* componente *m* (**b**) *Pol* votante *mf*, elector(a) *m,f*

constitute [ˈkɒnstɪtjuːt] *vt* constituir

constitution [kɒnstɪˈtjuːʃən] *n* constitución *f*

constitutional [kɒnstɪˈtjuːʃənəl] **1** *adj* constitucional

  2 *n (walk)* paseo *m*

constitutionally [kɒnstɪˈtjuːʃənəlɪ] *adv* según la constitución

constrained [kənˈstreɪnd] *adj* (**a**) *(obliged)* obligado(a); **to feel c. to do sth** sentirse obligado(a) a hacer algo (**b**) *(unnatural)* forzado(a)

constraint [kənˈstreɪnt] *n* coacción *f*; **to feel** *or* **show c. in sb's presence** sentirse coartado(a) ante algn

constrict [kənˈstrɪkt] *vt* apretar, oprimir, restringir

constriction [kənˈstrɪkʃən] *n* constricción *f*

construct [kənˈstrʌkt] *vt* construir

construction [kənˈstrʌkʃən] *n* (**a**) *(act, building)* construcción *f*; **under c.** en construcción □ **c. site** obra *f* (**b**) *Fig (interpretation)* interpretación *f*; **to put a wrong c. on sth** interpretar mal algo

constructive [kənˈstrʌktɪv] *adj* constructivo(a)

constructor [kənˈstrʌktər] *n* constructor *m*

construe [kənˈstruː] *vt* interpretar

consul [ˈkɒnsəl] *n Pol* cónsul *mf*

consular [ˈkɒnsjʊlər] *adj Pol* consular

consulate [ˈkɒnsjʊlɪt] *n Pol* consulado *m*

consult [kənˈsʌlt] *vt & vi* consultar (**about** sobre); **to c. with sb** consultar con algn

consultancy [kənˈsʌltənsɪ] *n* (**a**) *(of medical specialist)* = plaza de especialista hospitalario(a) (**b**) *Com* asesoría *f*, consultoría *f*

consultant [kənˈsʌltənt] *n* (**a**) *Med* especialista *mf* (**b**) *Com Ind* consultor(a) *m,f*, asesor(a) *m,f*

consultation [kɒnsəlˈteɪʃən] *n* consulta *f*

consultative [kənˈsʌltətɪv] *adj* consultivo(a)

consulting [kənˈsʌltɪŋ] *adj* (**a**) *Med* **c. room** consulta *f* (**b**) *Com Ind* asesor(a); **c. engineer** ingeniero *m* asesor

consumables [kənˈsjuːməbəlz] *npl* bienes *mpl* consumibles; *Comptr* consumibles *mpl*

consume [kənˈsjuːm] *vt* consumir; **consumed by fire** consumido(a) *or* devorado(a) por las llamas; *Fig* **to be consumed with envy/jealousy** estar muerto(a) de envidia/de celos

consumer [kənˈsjuːmər] *n* consumidor(a) *m,f* □ **c. advice**

orientación *f* al consumidor; **c. goods** bienes *mpl* de consumo

consumerism [kən'sju:mərɪzəm] *n* consumismo *m*

consuming [kən'sju:mɪŋ] *adj Fig* arrollador(a), devorador(a)

consummate 1 ['kɒnsəmeɪt] **1** *vt* consumar
2 ['kɒnsəmɪt] *adj* consumado(a), completo(a)

consummation [kɒnsə'meɪʃən] *n* consumación *f*

consumption [kən'sʌmpʃən] *n* **(a)** *(of food, energy)* consumo *m*; **fit for c.** apto(a) para el consumo **(b)** *Med* tisis *f*

cont (a) *(abbr* **contents**) contenido *m* **(b)** *(abbr* **continued**) sigue

contact ['kɒntækt] **1** *n* **(a)** *(gen)* contacto *m*; **to be in c. with** estar en contacto con; **to make c. with** *(touch)* tocar; *Fig* establecer contacto con, entrar en contacto con ❑ **c. lenses** lentes *fpl* de contacto, *Esp* lentillas *fpl*, *Méx* pupilentes **(b)** *(person)* contacto *m*, relación *f*; **she has a lot of contacts** tiene muchos contactos
2 *vt* ponerse en contacto con, comunicar con

contactable [kən'tæktəbəl] *adj* localizable

contagion [kən'teɪdʒən] *n* contagio *m*

contagious [kən'teɪdʒəs] *adj* contagioso(a)

contain [kən'teɪn] *vt* **(a)** *(hold)* contener **(b)** *(restrain)* reprimir; **to c. oneself** contenerse

container [kən'teɪnər] *n* **(a)** *(box, package)* recipiente *m*, caja *f*; *(wrapping)* envase *m* **(b)** *Com* contenedor *m* ❑ **c. lorry** camión *m* de transporte de contenedores; **c. ship** buque *m* de transporte de contenedores

contaminate [kən'tæmɪneɪt] *vt* contaminar

contamination [kəntæmɪ'neɪʃən] *n* contaminación *f*

contd *(abbr* **continued**) sigue

contemplate ['kɒntempleɪt] *vt* **(a)** *(consider)* considerar, pensar en **(b)** *(look at)* contemplar

contemplation [kɒntem'pleɪʃən] *n* contemplación *f*; **deep in c.** absorto(a), ensimismado(a)

contemplative ['kɒntempleɪtɪv, kən'templətɪv] *adj* contemplativo(a)

contemporaneous [kəntempə'reɪnɪəs] *adj* contemporáneo(a)

contemporary [kən'temprərɪ] *adj & n* contemporáneo(a) *(m,f)*

contempt [kən'tempt] *n* desprecio *m*; **to hold in c.** despreciar ❑ *Jur* **c. of court** desacato *m* a los tribunales

contemptible [kən'temptəbəl] *adj* despreciable

contemptuous [kən'temptjʊəs] *adj* despectivo(a), despreciativo(a)

contend [kən'tend] **1** *vi* contender, competir; **to c. for a prize/a position** competir por un premio/una posición; *Fig* **there are many problems to c. with** se han planteado muchos problemas
2 *vt* sostener, afirmar

contender [kən'tendər] *n* contendiente *mf*

content¹ ['kɒntent] *n* *(of book, pocket)* contenido *m*; **alcohol c.** grado *m* de alcohol; **some cereals have a high fibre c.** algunos cereales contienen mucha fibra; **table of contents** índice *m* de materias

content² [kən'tent] **1** *adj* contento(a), satisfecho(a); **he's quite c. to stay in the background** se conforma con quedarse en segundo plano
2 *vt* contentar; **to c. oneself** contentarse **(with** con)
3 *n* contento *m*; **to one's heart's c.** hasta quedar satisfecho(a), todo lo que uno quiera

contented [kən'tentɪd] *adj* contento(a), satisfecho(a); **a c. smile** una sonrisa de contento *or* de satisfacción

contention [kən'tenʃən] *n* **(a)** *(dispute)* controversia *f*; *Fig* **bone of c.** manzana *f* de la discordia **(b)** *(point)* punto *m* de vista; **my c. is that ...** mi opinión es que ...

contentious [kən'tenʃəs] *adj* contencioso(a)

contentment [kən'tentmənt] *n* contento *m*

contest 1 ['kɒntest] **1** *n Sport* competición *f*, prueba *f*; *(of music)* concurso *m*; *Fig* **it was a c. of wills** fue una lucha de poderes
2 [kən'test] *vt* **(a)** *(question, matter)* rebatir, refutar; *(decision, verdict)* impugnar; *Fig (will)* disputar **(b)** *Pol (seat)* luchar por

contestant [kən'testənt] *n* concursante *mf*

context ['kɒntekst] *n* contexto *m*

contextualize [kɒn'tekstjʊəlaɪz] *vt* contextualizar

continent ['kɒntɪnənt] *n* continente *m*; *Br* **(on) the C.** (en) Europa

continental [kɒntɪ'nentəl] *adj* **(a)** *Geol* continental; **c. climate** clima *m* continental; **c. shelf** plataforma *f* continental **(b)** *Br* **C.** europeo(a) ❑ **c. breakfast** desayuno *m* continental; **c. quilt** edredón *m* de pluma

contingency [kən'tɪndʒənsɪ] *n* contingencia *f*, eventualidad *f*; *Jur* **c. fee** honorarios *mpl* condicionales; **c. plans** planes *mpl* para casos de emergencia

contingent [kən'tɪndʒənt] **1** *adj* contingente, fortuito(a); **c. on** *or* **upon** dependiente de
2 *n* **(a)** *Mil (of troops)* contingente *m* **(b)** *(group)* representación *f*

continual [kən'tɪnjʊəl] *adj* continuo(a), constante

continuance [kən'tɪnjʊəns] *n* *(gen)* continuación *f*; *(duration)* duración *f*

continuation [kəntɪnjʊ'eɪʃən] *n (sequel etc)* continuación *f*; *(extension)* prolongación *f*

continue [kən'tɪnju:] *vt & vi* continuar, seguir; **please c.** siga, por favor; **to c. to do sth** seguir *or* continuar haciendo algo; **'to be continued'** 'continuará'

continuity [kɒntɪ'nju:ɪtɪ] *n* continuidad *f* ❑ *Cin* **c. girl/ man** secretaria *f*/secretario *m* de rodaje

continuous [kən'tɪnjʊəs] *adj* continuo(a); *Sch Univ* **c. assessment** evaluación *f* continua

contort [kən'tɔ:t] *vt (body)* retorcer; *(face)* contraer

contorted [kən'tɔ:tɪd] *adj* contorsionado(a), retorcido(a)

contortion [kən'tɔ:ʃən] *n* contorsión *f*

contortionist [kən'tɔ:ʃənɪst] *n* contorsionista *mf*

contour ['kɒntʊər] *n* contorno *m* ❑ **c. line** línea *f* de nivel; **c. map** mapa *m* topográfico

contraband ['kɒntrəbænd] *n* contrabando *m*

contraception [kɒntrə'sepʃən] *n* anticoncepción *f*

contraceptive [kɒntrə'septɪv] **1** *adj* anticonceptivo(a) ❑ **c. pill** píldora *f* anticonceptiva
2 *n* anticonceptivo *m*

contract 1 [kən'trækt] **1** *vi* **(a)** *Phys* contraerse **(b)** *(make agreement)* hacer un contrato; **to c. to do sth** comprometerse por contrato a hacer algo
2 *vt (marriage, illness, debts)* contraer
3 ['kɒntrækt] *n* contrato *m*; **breach of c.** incumplimiento *m* de contrato; **to enter into a c.** hacer un contrato ❑ **c. bridge** *(card game)* contrato *m*; **c. killer** asesino(a) *m,f* a sueldo; **marriage c.** capitulaciones *fpl* matrimoniales

contract out *Com* **1** *vt* **the cleaning service was contracted out** el servicio de limpieza lo lleva una contrata
2 *vi Br* excluirse, optar por salirse **(of** de)

contraction [kən'trækʃən] *n Phys* contracción *f*

contractor [kən'træktər] *n Constr* contratista *mf*

contractual [kən'træktjʊəl] *adj* contractual

contractually [kən'træktjʊəlɪ] *adv* contractualmente

contradict [kɒntrə'dɪkt] *vt* contradecir; *(deny)* desmentir

contradiction [kɒntrə'dɪkʃən] *n* contradicción *f*; **it's a c. in terms** no tiene lógica

contradictory [kɒntrə'dɪktərɪ] *adj* contradictorio(a)

contralto [kən'træltəʊ] *n {pl* **contraltos** *or* **contralti** [kən'træltɪ])* *Mus (voice)* contralto *m*; *(singer)* contralto *f*

contraption [kən'træpʃən] *n Fam* invento *m*, cacharro *m*

contrariness [kən'treərɪnɪs] *n* terquedad *f*, obstinación *f*

contrary ['kɒntrərɪ] **1** *adj* **(a)** *(opposite)* contrario(a); **a c. wind** un viento contrario **(b)** [kən'treərɪ] *(awkward)* terco(a), obstinado(a), que siempre lleva la contraria

2 *n* contrario *m*; **on the c.** todo lo contrario, al contrario; **unless I tell you to the c.** a menos que te diga lo contrario

3 *adv* contrariamente, en contra de; **c. to common belief** en contra de lo que se suele creer

contrast [kən'trɑːst] **1** *vi* contrastar, distinguirse

2 ['kɒntrɑːst] *n* contraste *m*; **to be in c. to** *or* **with** contrastar con

contrasting [kən'trɑːstɪŋ] *adj* opuesto(a)

contravene [kɒntrə'viːn] *vt Jur* contravenir

contravention [kɒntrə'venʃən] *n Jur* contravención *f*

contribute [kən'trɪbjuːt] **1** *vt (money)* contribuir; *(one's share)* pagar; *(ideas, information)* aportar

2 *vi* **(a)** *(gen)* contribuir; *(in discussion)* participar **(b)** *Press* colaborar **(to** en)

contribution [kɒntrɪ'bjuːʃən] *n* **(a)** *(of money)* contribución *f*; *(of ideas etc)* aportación *f* **(b)** *Press* colaboración *f*

contributor [kən'trɪbjʊtər] *n* **(a)** *(to fund)* contribuyente *mf* **(b)** *(to newspaper)* colaborador(a) *m,f*

contributory [kən'trɪbjʊtərɪ] *adj* contribuyente; **to be a c. cause of sth** contribuir a algo □ *Jur* **c. negligence** responsabilidad *f* de la víctima; **c. pension scheme** plan *m* privado de jubilación para los trabajadores de una empresa

contrite [kən'traɪt, 'kɒntraɪt] *adj* contrito(a)

contrition [kən'trɪʃən] *n Rel* contrición *f*

contrivance [kən'traɪvəns] *n* **(a)** *(device)* artefacto *m*, invento *m* **(b)** *(plan)* estratagema *m*

contrive [kən'traɪv] **1** *vt* inventar, idear

2 *vi* **to c. to do sth** buscar la forma de hacer algo

contrived [kən'traɪvd] *adj* artificial, forzado(a)

control [kən'trəʊl] **1** *vt (pt & pp* **controlled)** **(a)** *(gen)* controlar; *(person)* dominar, ejercer control sobre; *(animal)* dominar; *(vehicle)* manejar **(b)** *(feelings)* gobernar; **to c. oneself** *or* **one's temper** controlarse

2 *n* **(a)** *(power)* control *m*, mando *m*, dominio *m*; *(authority)* autoridad *f*; *Sport* dominio *m*; **birth c.** control de natalidad; **circumstances beyond our c.** circunstancias fuera de nuestro control; **out of c.** fuera de control; **parental c.** autoridad de los padres; **the situation is under c.** la situación está bajo control; **to be in c.** estar al mando *or* a cargo; **to be under c.** *(situation)* estar bajo control; **to bring under c.** *(fire, disease etc)* conseguir controlar; **to go out of c.** descontrolarse; **to keep a dog under c.** controlar un perro; **to lose c.** perder el control, perder los estribos; **we brought the fire under c.** conseguimos controlar el fuego □ **c. group** grupo *m* de control **(b)** *Tech* control *m*, mando *m* □ **remote c.** control *m* or mando *m* a distancia **(c)** *Aut Av (device)* mando *m*; *Rad TV* botón *m* de control; **dual controls** doble mando *m sing*; **to take over the controls** *Aut* tomar el volante; *Av* tomar los mandos □ **c. panel** tablero *m* de instrumentos; *Comptr* panel *m* de control; **c. room** sala *f* de control; *Av* **c. tower** torre *f* de control; **volume c.** botón *m* del volumen

controllable [kən'trəʊləbəl] *adj* controlable; **it's no longer c.** está fuera de control

controller [kən'trəʊlər] *n* **(a)** *Fin* interventor(a) *m,f* **(b)** *Rad TV* director(a) *m,f* de programación; *Av* **air traffic c.** controlador(a) *m,f* del tráfico aéreo

controlling [kən'trəʊlɪŋ] *adj* controlador(a); *Com* **c. interest** participación *f* mayoritaria

controversial [kɒntrə'vɜːʃəl] *adj* controvertido(a), polémico(a)

controversy ['kɒntrəvɜːsɪ, kən'trɒvəsɪ] *n* controversia *f*, polémica *f*

contusion [kən'tjuːʒən] *n Med* contusión *f*

conundrum [kə'nʌndrəm] *n Fml* enigma *m*, problema *m*

conurbation [kɒnɜː'beɪʃən] *n* conurbación *f*

convalesce [kɒnvə'les] *vi* convalecer

convalescence [kɒnvə'lesəns] *n* convalecencia *f*

convalescent [kɒnvə'lesənt] *adj* convaleciente; **c. home** clínica *f* de reposo

convection [kən'vekʃən] *n Phys Meteor* convección *f*

convector [kən'vektər] *n* estufa *f* de convección

convene [kən'viːn] **1** *vt (meeting)* convocar

2 *vi* reunirse

convenience [kən'viːnɪəns] *n* *(suitability)* conveniencia *f*, comodidad *f*; **all modern conveniences** todas las comodidades; **at your c.** cuando le convenga; **at your earliest c.** tan pronto como le sea posible; *Fig* **to make a c. of sb** abusar (la amabilidad) de algn □ **c. food** comida *f* precocinada; *Br* **public conveniences** servicio *m* público, *Esp* aseos *mpl*, *Am* baños *mpl* públicos

convenient [kən'viːnɪənt] *adj* *(time, arrangement)* conveniente, oportuno(a); *(place)* bien situado(a); **if it is c. for you** si te conviene, si te viene bien

convent ['kɒnvənt] *n Rel* convento *m*

convention [kən'venʃən] *n* **(a)** *(conference)* convención *f*, congreso *m* **(b)** *(custom)* convención *f* **(c)** *(treaty)* convención *f*

conventional [kən'venʃənəl] *adj* convencional, clásico(a) □ **c. warfare** guerra *f* convencional

converge [kən'vɜːdʒ] *vi* convergir **(on** en)

convergent [kən'vɜːdʒənt] *adj* convergente

conversant [kən'vɜːsənt] *adj Fml* familiarizado(a); **to be c. with a subject** ser versado(a) en una materia; **to become c. with** familiarizarse con

conversation [kɒnvə'seɪʃən] *n* conversación *f*, *CAm Méx* plática *f*; **in c.** conversando

conversational [kɒnvə'seɪʃənəl] *adj* coloquial; **c. English** inglés *m* coloquial; **c. style** estilo *m* familiar

conversationalist [kɒnvə'seɪʃənəlɪst] *n* hablador(a) *m,f*; **to be a good c.** brillar en la conversación

conversationally [kɒnvə'seɪʃənəlɪ] *adv* **he mentioned, quite c., that he had got a new job** como quien no quiere la cosa, mencionó que tenía un empleo nuevo

converse¹ [kən'vɜːs] *vi* conversar, hablar

converse² ['kɒnvɜːs] **1** *adj* opuesto(a)

2 the c. *n* lo opuesto

conversely [kən'vɜːslɪ] *adv* a la inversa

conversion [kən'vɜːʃən] *n* **(a)** *Math Rel* conversión *f* **(to a** in); **into** en) □ *Math* **c. table** tabla *f* de conversión **(b)** *(of house etc)* reconstrucción *f* **(c)** *Rugby* transformación *f*

convert [kən'vɜːt] **1** *vt* **(a)** *(gen)* & *Comptr* convertir **(b)** *Rugby* transformar

2 *vi* convertirse; **a settee that converts into a bed** un sofá que se convierte en cama

3 ['kɒnvɜːt] *n Rel* converso(a) *m,f*

converter [kən'vɜːtər] *n Tech Elec* convertidor *m*, transformador *m*

convertible [kən'vɜːtəbəl] **1** *adj* **(a)** *(gen)* convertible **(b)** *Aut* descapotable, *Am* convertible

  2 *n Aut* descapotable *m*, *Am* convertible *m*

convex ['kɒnveks, kɒn'veks] *adj* convexo(a)

convey [kən'veɪ] *vt* **(a)** *(transport, carry)* transportar, llevar **(b)** *(communicate) (sound)* transmitir; *(idea)* comunicar, expresar **(c)** *Jur* preparar escrituras de traspaso

conveyance [kən'veɪəns] *n* **(a)** *(carrying)* transporte *m*, transmisión *f* **(b)** *(means)* transporte *m*, vehículo *m*

conveyancing [kən'veɪənsɪŋ] *n Jur* preparación *f* de escrituras de traspaso

conveyor [kən'veɪər] *n (person)* transportista *mf* ❑ *Tech* **c. belt** cinta *f* transportadora

convict [kən'vɪkt] **1** *vt* declarar culpable **(of** de), condenar

  2 ['kɒnvɪkt] *n* presidiario(a) *m,f*

conviction [kən'vɪkʃən] *n* **(a)** *(belief)* creencia *f*, convicción *f*; **to carry c.** convencer **(b)** *Jur* condena *f*; **he has no previous convictions** no tiene antecedentes penales

convince [kən'vɪns] *vt* convencer; **to c. sb to do sth** convencer a algn para que haga algo

convincing [kən'vɪnsɪŋ] *adj* convincente

convincingly [kən'vɪnsɪŋlɪ] *adv* con convicción

convivial [kən'vɪvɪəl] *adj (sociable)* sociable; *(festive)* jovial, festivo(a)

conviviality [kənvɪvɪ'ælɪtɪ] *n* alegría *f*, jovialidad *f*

convocation [kɒnvə'keɪʃən] *n* **(a)** *(gen)* convocatoria *f* **(b)** *Br Univ* asamblea *f*

convoke [kən'vəʊk] *vt* convocar

convoluted ['kɒnvəluːtɪd] *adj* **(a)** *(argument)* complejo(a) **(b)** *Bot (leaf)* enrollado(a)

convoy ['kɒnvɔɪ] **1** *n* convoy *m*; **in** or **under c.** bajo escolta

  2 *vt* escoltar

convulse [kən'vʌls] *vt* convulsionar; **her face was convulsed with pain** tenía la cara distorsionada por el dolor; *Fam* **to be convulsed with laughter** troncharse de risa

convulsion [kən'vʌlʃən] *n* convulsión *f*; *Fam* **convulsions of laughter** ataques *mpl* de risa

convulsive [kən'vʌlsɪv] *adj* convulsivo(a)

coo [kuː] *vi (baby)* gorjear; *(pigeon)* arrullar

cooing ['kuːɪŋ] *n (of baby)* gorjeos *mpl*; *(of pigeon)* arrullo *m*

cook [kʊk] **1** *vt (chicken, potatoes)* cocinar, guisar; *(food, dinner)* preparar, hacer; **how long do you c. the meat (for)?** ¿cuánto tiempo pones a cocer la carne?; *Fam* **to c. up an excuse** inventarse una excusa; *Slang* **to c. the books** falsificar las cuentas

  2 *vi (person)* cocinar, guisar, cocer; *(food)* cocerse; **c. slowly** cocer a fuego lento; **I can't c.** no sé guisar; *Fam* **what's cooking?** ¿qué se cuece por aquí?, *Am* ¿qué andan tramando por acá?

  3 *n Culin* cocinero(a) *m,f*; **he's a good c.** guisa bien

cookbook ['kʊkbʊk] *n US* libro *m* de cocina

cooker ['kʊkər] *n* **(a)** *(apparatus)* cocina *f*, *Col Méx Ven* estufa *f* ❑ **gas c.** cocina *f* de gas **(b)** *Br (apple)* manzana *f* ácida para cocinar

cookery ['kʊkərɪ] *n* cocina *f* ❑ **c. book** libro *m* de cocina

cookie ['kʊkɪ] *n* **(a)** *US* galleta *f* **(b)** *Comptr* cookie *m*

cooking ['kʊkɪŋ] **1** *n* cocina *f*; **home c.** comida *f* casera

  2 *adj* **c. apple** manzana *f* ácida para cocinar

cookout ['kʊkaʊt] *n US* barbacoa *f*

cool [kuːl] **1** *adj* **(a)** *(gen)* fresco(a); *(drink)* refrescante; *(weather)* **it's c.** hace fresquito; **it's getting cooler** está

refrescando, refresca **(b)** *Fig (calm)* tranquilo(a); *(reserved)* frío(a); **a c. reception** una acogida fría; **c. as a cucumber** fresco(a) como una lechuga; **keep c.!** ¡tranquilo(a)! **(c)** *Fam (cheeky)* fresco(a), descarado(a); **a c. $10,000** la friolera de 10.000 dólares; **he's a c. customer** es un fresco *or* un caradura **(d)** *Fam (excellent)* genial, *Esp* guay, *Andes RP* macanudo(a), *Méx* padre

  2 *n* **(a)** *(coolness)* fresco *m*; **the c. of the evening** el frescor de la tarde **(b)** *Slang* calma *f*; **to lose** or **blow one's c.** perder la calma

  3 *vt (room, air)* refrescar; *(drink)* enfriar; *Fam* **to c. one's heels** hacer antesala

  4 *vi* enfriarse; **to c. down** *(engine, feelings)* enfriarse; *(person)* calmarse

  5 *adv Fam* **to play it c.** hacer como si nada

cool off *vi Fig (person)* calmarse; *(feelings)* enfriarse

coolant ['kuːlənt] *n* líquido *m* refrigerante

cooler ['kuːlər] *n* **(a)** *(box)* nevera *f* or *CSur* heladera *f* or *Méx* refrigerador *m* portátil **(b)** *Slang Esp* chirona *f*, *Andes RP* cana *f*, *Méx* bote *m*

cool-headed ['kuːl'hedɪd] *adj* **to be c.** tener la cabeza fría, tener serenidad

cooling ['kuːlɪŋ] *n Tech* refrigeración *f*, enfriamiento *m* ❑ **c. system** sistema *m* de refrigeración; *Fig* **c.-off period** período *m* de reflexión

coolly ['kuːlɪ] *adv* **(a)** *(gen)* fríamente **(b)** *Fam (cheekily)* descaradamente

coolness ['kuːlnɪs] *n* **(a)** *(of air etc)* frescor *m* **(b)** *Fig (calmness)* calma *f*, frialdad *f*; *(composure)* sangre *f* fría **(c)** *Fam* frescura *f*

coop [kuːp] **1** *n* gallinero *m*

  2 *vt* **to c. (up)** encerrar

co-op ['kəʊɒp] *n (abbr* **co-operative**) cooperativa *f*

co-operate [kəʊ'ɒpəreɪt] *vi* cooperar, colaborar

co-operation [kəʊɒpə'reɪʃən] *n* cooperación *f*

co-operative [kəʊ'ɒpərətɪv] **1** *adj* **(a)** *(helpful)* cooperador(a) **(b)** *(society)* cooperativo(a) ❑ **co-o. farm** cooperativa *f* agrícola

  2 *n* cooperativa *f*

co-opt [kəʊ'ɒpt] *vt Fml* nombrar como nuevo miembro

co-ordinate [kəʊ'ɔːdɪneɪt] **1** *vt* coordinar

  2 [kəʊ'ɔːdɪnɪt] *n* **(a)** *Math* coordenada *f* **(b)** **co-ordinates** *(clothes)* conjunto *m* sing

co-ordination [kəʊɔːdɪ'neɪʃən] *n* coordinación *f*

co-ordinator [kəʊ'ɔːdɪneɪtər] *n* coordinador(a) *m,f*

coot [kuːt] *n Orn* focha *f* común

co-owner ['kəʊ'əʊnər] *n* copropietario(a) *m,f*

cop[1] [kɒp] *Slang* **1** *n (policeman)* poli *m*

  2 *vt (pt & pp* **copped)** *Br* pescar, *Esp* pillar, *Am* agarrar; **you'll c. it** te vas a ganar una buena

cop out *vi* zafarse, *Esp* escaquearse, *RP* zafar

cop[2] [kɒp] *n Br Slang (value)* **it's not much c.** no es nada del otro jueves

cope [kəʊp] *vi* adaptarse, arreglárselas; **she's coping well** se las arregla or apaña bien; **to c. with** *(person, work)* poder con; *(problem)* hacer frente a

Copenhagen [kəʊpən'heɪgən] *n* Copenhague

copier ['kɒpɪər] *n* copiadora *f*

copilot ['kəʊpaɪlət] *n Av* copiloto *m*

copious ['kəʊpɪəs] *adj* copioso(a), abundante

cop-out ['kɒpaʊt] *n Fam* **to be a c.-o.** ser una forma de zafarse or *Esp* escaquearse or *RP* zafar

copper[1] [kɒpər] **1** *n* **(a)** *Min* cobre *m* **(b)** *Fam (money)* calderilla *f*, *Méx* morralla *f*, *RP* chirolas *fpl* **it cost only a few coppers** me costó cuatro perras

2 *adj (colour)* cobrizo(a) ❑ *Bot* **c. beech** haya *f* de hoja oscura

copper² ['kɒpər] *n Slang* poli *m*; **the coppers** la pasma

copperplate ['kɒpəpleɪt] *n* (**a**) *(plate)* lámina *f* de cobre (**b**) *(print)* grabado *m* en cobre (**c**) **c. (writing)** letra *f* caligrafiada

coppice ['kɒpɪs] *n* arboleda *f*, soto *m*

coproduction [kəʊprə'dʌkʃən] *n Cin* coproducción *f*

copse [kɒps] *n* arboleda *f*, soto *m*

copulate ['kɒpjʊleɪt] *vi* copular

copulation [kɒpjʊ'leɪʃən] *n* copulación *f*

copy ['kɒpɪ] **1** *n* (**a**) *(reproduction)* copia *f* ❑ **rough c.** borrador *m* (**b**) *(of book, magazine)* ejemplar *m* (**c**) *Print* manuscrito *m* (**d**) *Typ Fam* tema *m*, asunto *m*; **it makes good c.** es un asunto de interés

2 *vt (pt & pp copied) (notes)* copiar; *(imitate)* copiar, imitar; **to c. out a letter** copiar una carta

3 *vi (gen) & Comptr* copiar; *(photocopy)* fotocopiar

copybook ['kɒpɪbʊk] *n* cuaderno *m* (de caligrafía); *Fam* **to blot one's c.** manchar su reputación

copycat ['kɒpɪkæt] *n Fam* copión(ona) *m,f* ❑ **c. crime** = delito inspirado en otro similar

copyreader ['kɒpɪriːdər] *n US* corrector(a) *m,f* de estilo

copyright ['kɒpɪraɪt] *n* derechos *mpl* de autor, propiedad *f* literaria *or* intelectual

copywriter ['kɒpɪraɪtər] *n* redactor(a) *m,f* de textos publicitarios

cor [kɔːr] *interj Br Slang* ¡caramba!, *Esp* ¡jolines!

coral ['kɒrəl] *n* coral *m* ❑ **c. island** isla *f* coralina; **c. reef** arrecife *m* de coral; **the C. Sea** el mar del Coral

cord [kɔːd] *n* (**a**) *(string, rope)* cuerda *f*; *Elec* cordón *m* ❑ *Anat* **spinal c.** médula *f* espinal; **umbilical c.** cordón *m* umbilical; **vocal cords** cuerdas *fpl* vocales (**b**) *Tex (corduroy)* pana *f*; **cords** *(garment)* pantalones *mpl* de pana

cordial ['kɔːdɪəl] **1** *adj* cordial, afectuoso(a)

2 *n (drink)* licor *m*

cordless ['kɔːdlɪs] *adj* **c. kettle** = hervidor eléctrico con soporte independiente enchufado a la red; **c. phone** teléfono *m* inalámbrico

cordon ['kɔːdən] **1** *n* cordón *m*

2 *vt* acordonar; **to c. off a street** acordonar *or* aislar una calle

corduroy ['kɔːdərɔɪ] *n Tex* pana *f*

core [kɔːr] **1** *n (of apple, pear)* corazón *m*; *Elec Tech* núcleo *m*; *Pol Fig* **hard c.** los incondicionales; *Fig* **to the c.** hasta la médula ❑ *Sch* **c. curriculum** asignaturas *fpl* troncales

2 *vt (apple)* quitarle el corazón a

corer ['kɔːrər] *n Culin* deshuesadora *f*

coriander [kɒrɪ'ændər] *n Bot* coriandro *m*, culantro *m*

cork [kɔːk] **1** *n* (**a**) *(material)* corcho *m* ❑ *Bot* **c. oak** alcornoque *m* (**b**) *(stopper)* corcho *m*, tapón *m*; **to pull the c. out of a bottle** descorchar una botella

2 *vt (bottle)* poner el corcho a, taponar

corked [kɔːkt] *adj* que sabe a corcho

corkscrew ['kɔːkskruː] *n* sacacorchos *m inv*

cormorant ['kɔːmərənt] *n Orn* cormorán *m* grande

corn¹ [kɔːn] *n* (**a**) *(wheat)* trigo *m* (**b**) *(maize)* maíz *m*, *Andes RP* choclo *m* ❑ **c. bread** pan *m* de maíz *or Andes RP* choclo; **c. oil** aceite *m* de maíz; **c. on the cob** mazorca *f* de maíz

corn² [kɔːn] *n Med* callo *m*; *Br Fam* **to tread on sb's corns** disgustar *or* ofender a algn

corncob ['kɔːnkɒb] *n* mazorca *f* de maíz

cornea ['kɔːnɪə] *n Anat* córnea *f*

corner ['kɔːnər] **1** *n* (**a**) *(of street)* esquina *f*; *(bend in road)* curva *f*, recodo *m*; *(of table)* esquina *f*, pico *m*; **(just) round**

the c. a la vuelta de la esquina; **out of the c. of one's eye** con el rabillo del ojo; *Fig* **from all corners of the world** de todos los rincones del mundo; *Fig* **to cut corners** tomar un atajo ❑ *Ftb* **c. kick** córner *m*; **c.** *Br* **shop** *or US* **store** tienda *f* pequeña de barrio (**b**) *(of room)* rincón *m*; *Fig* **to be in a tight c.** estar en un aprieto; *Fig* **to drive sb into a c.** arrinconar *or* acorralar a algn ❑ **c. table** mesa *f* rinconera (**c**) *Com* monopolio *m*

2 *vt* (**a**) *(enemy)* arrinconar, acorralar (**b**) *Com (market)* acaparar, monopolizar

3 *vi Aut* tomar una curva

cornerstone ['kɔːnəstəʊn] *n (of building)* piedra *f* angular; *Fig* base *f*

cornet [*Br* 'kɔːnɪt, *US* kɔː'net] *n* (**a**) *Mus* corneta *f* (**b**) *Br (for ice cream)* cucurucho *m*

cornfield ['kɔːnfiːld] *n* (**a**) *Br (of wheat)* trigal *m* (**b**) *(of maize)* campo *m* de maíz

cornflakes ['kɔːnfleɪks] *npl* copos *mpl* de maíz

cornflour ['kɔːnflaʊər] *n Br* harina *f* de maíz *or Andes RP* choclo, maicena® *f*

cornflower ['kɔːnflaʊər] *n Bot* aciano *m*, azulina *f*

cornice ['kɔːnɪs] *n Archit* cornisa *f*

Cornish ['kɔːnɪʃ] *adj* de Cornualles ❑ *Br Culin* **C. pasty** = empanadilla de carne picada y verduras

cornstarch ['kɔːnstɑːtʃ] *n US see* **cornflour**

Cornwall ['kɔːnwəl] *n* Cornualles

corny ['kɔːnɪ] *adj* (**cornier, corniest**) *Fam (joke)* gastado(a), rancio(a); *(film)* hortera

corolla [kə'rɒlə] *n Bot* corola *f*

corollary [kə'rɒlərɪ] *n* corolario *m*

coronary ['kɒrənərɪ] *Med* **1** *adj* coronario(a); **c. thrombosis** trombosis *f* coronaria

2 *n* trombosis *f* coronaria

coronation [kɒrə'neɪʃən] *n* coronación *f*

coroner ['kɒrənər] *n Jur* juez *mf* de instrucción

Corp (**a**) *Mil (abbr* **corporal**) cabo *m* (**b**) *US (abbr* **Corporation**) sociedad *f* anónima, S.A.

corporal¹ ['kɔːpərəl] *adj* corporal; **c. punishment** castigo *m* corporal

corporal² ['kɔːpərəl] *n Mil* cabo *m*

corporate ['kɔːpərɪt] *adj* corporativo(a); **c. body** corporación *f*; **c. culture** cultura *f* empresarial; **c. responsibility/action** responsabilidad/acción colectiva

corporation [kɔːpə'reɪʃən] *n* (**a**) *(business)* sociedad *f* anónima (**b**) *(of city)* **(municipal) c.** ayuntamiento *m*

corps [kɔːr] *n (pl* **corps** [kɔːz]) cuerpo *m*; *Mil* **the medical c.** el cuerpo médico

corpse [kɔːps] *n* cadáver *m*

corpulence ['kɔːpjʊləns] *n* corpulencia *f*

corpulent ['kɔːpjʊlənt] *adj* corpulento(a)

corpuscle ['kɔːpʌsəl] *n* corpúsculo *m*, glóbulo *m*

corral [kə'rɑːl] *n US* corral *m*

correct [kə'rekt] **1** *vt* (**a**) *(mistake)* corregir, rectificar (**b**) *(child etc)* reprender

2 *adj* (**a**) *(free from error)* correcto(a), exacto(a); **you're quite c.** tienes toda la razón (**b**) *(behaviour)* formal

correction [kə'rekʃən] *n* corrección *f* ❑ **c. fluid** líquido *m* corrector

corrective [kə'rektɪv] *adj* correctivo(a)

correctness [kə'rektnɪs] *n* (**a**) *(accuracy)* exactitud *f* (**b**) *(of behaviour)* formalidad *f*

correlate ['kɒrɪleɪt] **1** *vt* poner en correlación, correlacionar

2 *vi* tener *or* guardar correlación (**with** con)

correlation [kɒrə'leɪʃən] n correlación f

correspond [kɒrɪ'spɒnd] vi (**a**) (one thing with another) corresponder; **A corresponds with B** A y B se corresponden; **to c. to** equivaler a (**b**) (by letter) escribirse, mantener correspondencia; **they c.** se escriben; **to c. with sb** mantener correspondencia con algn

correspondence [kɒrɪ'spɒndəns] n (**a**) (between two things) correspondencia f (**b**) (letters) correo m ❏ **c. course** curso m por correspondencia

correspondent [kɒrɪ'spɒndənt] n Press corresponsal mf ❏ **special c.** enviado(a) m,f especial

corresponding [kɒrɪ'spɒndɪŋ] adj (gen) correspondiente; (in accordance with) conforme

correspondingly [kɒrɪ'spɒndɪŋlɪ] adv igualmente

corridor ['kɒrɪdɔ:r] n pasillo m, corredor m; Fig **the corridors of power** las altas esferas del poder

corroborate [kə'rɒbəreɪt] vt corroborar

corroboration [kərɒbə'reɪʃən] n corroboración f

corrode [kə'rəʊd] **1** vt corroer
   2 vi corroerse

corrosion [kə'rəʊʒən] n corrosión f

corrosive [kə'rəʊsɪv] **1** adj corrosivo(a)
   2 n sustancia f corrosiva

corrugate ['kɒrʊgeɪt] vt Tech ondular; **corrugated iron** hierro ondulado

corrupt [kə'rʌpt] **1** adj (person) corrompido(a), corrupto(a); (actions) deshonesto(a); Comptr corrompido(a); **c. practices** corrupción f sing
   2 vt corromper

corruption [kə'rʌpʃən] n, **corruptness** [kə'rʌptnɪs] n corrupción f

corset ['kɔ:sɪt] n (garment) faja f

Corsica ['kɔ:sɪkə] n Córcega

Corsican ['kɔ:sɪkən] adj & n corso(a) (m,f)

cortège [kɔ:'teɪʒ] n cortejo m, comitiva f

cortex ['kɔ:teks] (pl **cortices** ['kɔ:tɪsi:z]) n corteza f

cortisone ['kɔ:tɪzəʊn] n cortisona f

Corunna [kə'rʌnə] n La Coruña

cos¹ [kɒs] n **c. (lettuce)** lechuga f romana

cos² Math (abbr **cosine**) cos

cosh [kɒʃ] Br **1** n porra f
   2 vt dar un porrazo a, aporrear

cosmetic [kɒz'metɪk] **1** n producto m de belleza, cosmético m
   2 adj cosmético(a); **c. surgery** cirugía plástica

cosmic ['kɒzmɪk] adj cósmico(a); **c. rays** rayos cósmicos

cosmonaut ['kɒzmənɔ:t] n Astron cosmonauta mf

cosmopolitan [kɒzmə'pɒlɪtən] adj cosmopolita

cosmos ['kɒzmɒs] n cosmos m

cosset ['kɒsɪt] vt mimar

cost [kɒst] **1** n (price) precio m, costo m, Esp coste m; (expense) gasto m; **at c. price** a precio de costo or Esp coste; **c. of living** coste or Esp coste de vida; **the c. of running a car** los gastos de mantenimiento de un coche; Jur **to pay costs** pagar las costas; **whatever the c.** cueste lo que cueste; Fig **to count the c.** considerar las desventajas ❏ Fin **c. accounting** contabilidad f de costes
   2 vt (**a**) (pt & pp **cost**) costar, valer; **how much does it c.?** ¿cuánto cuesta?, ¿cuánto vale?; **it c. me $150 to have the car repaired** me costó 150 dólares arreglar el coche; **whatever it costs** cueste lo que cueste; Fig **it costs the earth** cuesta una fortuna or un riñón (**b**) (pt & pp **costed**) Com Ind calcular el coste de

co-star ['kəʊstɑ:r] Cin Theat **1** n coprotagonista mf

2 vi (pt & pp **co-starred**) **to co-s. with sb** coprotagonizar con algn

Costa Rica [kɒstə'ri:kə] n Costa Rica

Costa Rican [kɒstə'ri:kən] adj & n costarricense (mf)

cost-conscious ['kɒst'kɒnʃəs] adj **to be c.** ser consciente de los costos or Esp costes

cost-cutting ['kɒst'kʌtɪŋ] **1** n reducción f de costos or Esp costes
   2 adj (drive, campaign) de reducción de costos or Esp costes

cost-effective [kɒstɪ'fektɪv] adj rentable

costing ['kɒstɪŋ] n Com Ind cálculo m de costos or Esp costes

costliness ['kɒstlɪnɪs] n (in price) alto precio m; (in value) lujo m

costly ['kɒstlɪ] adj (**costlier, costliest**) (dear) costoso(a), caro(a); (valuable) costoso(a)

costume ['kɒstju:m] n traje m ❏ **bathing c.** traje m de baño, Esp bañador m, RP malla f; **c. ball** baile m de disfraces; **c. jewellery** bisutería f; **fancy dress c.** disfraz m; **national c.** traje m típico; **swimming c.** traje m de baño, Esp bañador m, RP malla f

cosy ['kəʊzɪ] **1** adj (**cosier, cosiest**) (room, atmosphere) acogedor(a), (bed) calentito(a); **it's c. in here** aquí se está bien
   2 n **tea/egg c.** cubierta f para tetera/huevo pasado por agua

cot [kɒt] n (**a**) US (folding bed) catre m, cama f plegable (**b**) Br (for child) cuna f ❏ Med **c. death (syndrome)** muerte f inexplicable de un bebé en la cuna

coterie ['kəʊtərɪ:] n camarilla f

cottage ['kɒtɪdʒ] n (gen) casa f de campo; US (for holiday) chalet m ❏ Culin **c. cheese** requesón m; Br **c. hospital** hospital m rural; **c. industry** industria f casera; Br Culin **c. pie** = pastel de carne picada con puré de patatas

cotton ['kɒtən] n (**a**) Bot algodonero m; Tex algodón m, Am cotón m; **the c. industry** la industria algodonera ❏ US **c. candy** algodón m dulce; **c. dress** vestido m de algodón; Br **c. wool** algodón m hidrófilo, guata f (**b**) (thread) hilo m

cotton on vi Fam **to c. on to sth** caer en la cuenta de algo

couch [kaʊtʃ] **1** n Furn canapé m, sofá m; (in surgery) camilla f ❏ Fam **c. potato** = persona que se pasa el día apoltronada viendo la tele
   2 vt expresar, formular

couchette [ku:'ʃet] n Rail litera f

cougar ['ku:gər] n puma m

cough [kɒf] **1** vi toser
   2 n tos f; **to have a (bad) c.** tener (mucha) tos ❏ **c. drop** pastilla f para la tos; **c. mixture** jarabe m para la tos

cough up 1 vt escupir; Fam **to c. up the money** soltar la pasta
   2 vi escupir; Fam **c. up!** ¡suéltalo!

could [kʊd] v aux see **can¹**

couldn't-care-less ['kʊdəntkeə'les] adj **c.-c.-l. attitude** actitud f pasota

council ['kaʊnsəl] n (**a**) (assembly, body) consejo m ❏ Br **c. house** vivienda f de protección oficial; **town** or **city c.** consejo m municipal, ayuntamiento m (**b**) Rel concilio m

councillor, US **councilor** ['kaʊnsələr] n concejal mf

counsel ['kaʊnsəl] **1** n (**a**) (advice) consejo m; **to take c. with sb** consultar con algn; Fig **to keep one's own c.** guardar silencio (**b**) Jur (barrister) abogado(a) m,f; **c. for the defence** abogado defensor; **c. for the prosecution** fiscal mf
   2 vt (pt & pp **counselled**, US **counseled**) aconsejar

counselling, US **counseling** [ˈkaʊnsəlɪŋ] n orientación f

counsellor, US **counselor** [ˈkaʊnsələr] n (**a**) (adviser) asesor(a) m,f (**b**) US Jur abogado(a) m,f

count[1] [kaʊnt] **1** vt (**a**) (gen) contar; **six not counting the dog** seis sin contar el perro (**b**) Fig (consider) considerar; **to c. one's blessings, to c. oneself lucky** considerarse afortunado(a)
2 vi contar; (be valid) valer; **counting from tomorrow** a partir de mañana; **he doesn't c.** él no cuenta or no tiene importancia; **that doesn't c.** eso no vale; **to c. to ten** contar hasta diez; Fig **to c. against sb** perjudicar a algn
3 n (**a**) (gen) cuenta f; (total) recuento m; **to keep/lose c. of sth** llevar/perder la cuenta de algo ❑ Med **blood c.** recuento m de hemoglobina (**b**) Box **to be out for the c.** estar fuera de combate (**c**) Jur cargo m, acusación f

count in vt Fam incluir, contar con; **c. me in!** ¡yo me apunto!

count on, count upon vt contar con

count out vt (**a**) (banknotes) contar uno por uno (**b**) Fam no contar con; **c. me out!** ¡no cuentes conmigo!

count[2] [kaʊnt] n (nobleman) conde m

countable [ˈkaʊntəbəl] adj contable

countdown [ˈkaʊntdaʊn] n cuenta f atrás

countenance [ˈkaʊntɪnəns] **1** n (**a**) (face) semblante m, rostro m (**b**) (composure) compostura f
2 vt aprobar, dar aprobación a

counter[1] [ˈkaʊntər] n (**a**) (in shop) mostrador m; (in bank) ventanilla f; **to buy a medicine over the c.** comprar un medicamento sin receta médica; Fig **under the c.** clandestinamente (**b**) (in board games) ficha f

counter[2] [ˈkaʊntər] n contador m

counter[3] [ˈkaʊntər] **1** adv en contra; **c. to** en contra de; **to run c. to** ir en contra de
2 vt (attack) contestar a; (blow) parar; (tendency) contrarrestar
3 vi contestar, replicar

counteract [kaʊntərˈækt] vt contrarrestar

counterattack [ˈkaʊntərətæk] **1** n contraataque m
2 vt & vi contraatacar

counterbalance [ˈkaʊntəbæləns] **1** n contrapeso m
2 [kaʊntəˈbæləns] vt contrapesar, equilibrar

counterbid [ˈkaʊntəbɪd] n Fin (during takeover) contraoferta f

counterblast [ˈkaʊntəblɑːst] n dura réplica f

counterclockwise [kaʊntəˈklɒkwaɪz] adj & adv US en sentido contrario a las agujas del reloj

counter-culture [ˈkaʊntəkʌltʃər] n contracultura f

counterespionage [kaʊntərˈespɪənɑːʒ] n contraespionaje m

counterfeit [ˈkaʊntəfɪt] **1** adj falsificado(a); **c. coin** moneda falsa
2 n falsificación f
3 vt falsificar

counterfoil [ˈkaʊntəfɔɪl] n Br (of cheque) matriz f

counterintelligence [kaʊntərɪnˈtelɪdʒəns] n contraespionaje m

countermand [kaʊntəˈmɑːnd] vt (command) revocar; Com (order) anular

countermeasure [ˈkaʊntəmeʒər] n contramedida f

counteroffensive [ˈkaʊntərəfensɪv] n Mil contraofensiva f

counteroffer [ˈkaʊntərˈɒfər] n contraoferta f

counterpane [ˈkaʊntəpeɪn] n cubrecama m, colcha f

counterpart [ˈkaʊntəpɑːt] n homólogo(a) m,f, colega mf

counterpoint [ˈkaʊntəpɔɪnt] n Mus contrapunto m

counterproductive [kaʊntəprəˈdʌktɪv] adj contraproducente

counterproposal [ˈkaʊntəprəˈpəʊzəl] n contrapropuesta f

counter-revolution [kaʊntərevəˈluːʃən] n Pol contrarrevolución f

counter-revolutionary [kaʊntərevəˈluːʃənərɪ] adj contrarrevolucionario(a)

countersign [ˈkaʊntəsaɪn] vt refrendar

counterterrorism [kaʊntəˈterərɪzəm] n contraterrorismo m

counterweight [ˈkaʊntəweɪt] n contrapeso m; **to act as a c. (to sth)** servir de contrapeso (a algo), contrarrestar (algo)

countess [ˈkaʊntɪs] n condesa f

countless [ˈkaʊntlɪs] adj innumerable, incontable

country [ˈkʌntrɪ] n (**a**) (state, nation) país m; **native c.** patria f; Br Pol **to go to the c.** convocar elecciones (**b**) (rural area) campo m ❑ **c. and western (music)** música f country; **c. dancing** baile m country; **c. seat** finca f, hacienda f

countryfolk [ˈkʌntrɪfəʊk] n gente f del campo

countryman [ˈkʌntrɪmən] n (pl **countrymen**) (**a**) (rural) hombre m del campo (**b**) (compatriot) compatriota m

countryside [ˈkʌntrɪsaɪd] n (area) campo m; (scenery) paisaje m

countrywoman [ˈkʌntrɪwʊmən] n (pl **countrywomen**) (**a**) (rural) mujer f del campo (**b**) (compatriot) compatriota f

county [ˈkaʊntɪ] n condado m ❑ Br **c. town**, US **c. seat** capital f de condado

coup [kuː] n golpe m ❑ Pol **c. d'état** golpe m de estado

coupé [ˈkuːpeɪ] n Aut cupé m

couple [ˈkʌpəl] **1** n (**a**) (people) pareja f; **a married c.** un matrimonio; **a young c.** una pareja joven (**b**) (things) par m; **a c. un par**; Fam **a c. of times** un par de veces; Fam **when he's had a c.** cuando ha bebido más de la cuenta
2 vt Tech (wagons) enganchar; Fig **coupled with** junto a
3 vi (mate) aparearse

couplet [ˈkʌplɪt] n Lit (verso m) pareado m

coupling [ˈkʌplɪŋ] n Rail enganche m

coupon [ˈkuːpɒn] n (**a**) (gen) cupón m (**b**) Br Ftb boleto m

courage [ˈkʌrɪdʒ] n coraje m, valor m, valentía f; **he has the c. of his convictions** tiene el valor de atenerse a sus principios

courageous [kəˈreɪdʒəs] adj valeroso(a), valiente

courageously [kəˈreɪdʒəslɪ] adv valientemente

courgette [kʊəˈʒet] n Br Culin calabacín m, CSur zapallito m, Méx calabacita f

courier [ˈkʊərɪər] n (**a**) (messenger) mensajero(a) m,f (**b**) (guide) guía mf turístico(a)

course [kɔːs] **1** n (**a**) (onward movement) curso m, marcha f; (direction) curso m, dirección f; Naut rumbo m; (of river) curso m; Av trayectoria f; **to be on/off c.** seguir/perder el rumbo; **to change c.** cambiar de rumbo or dirección; **to set c.** poner rumbo (**b**) Fig curso m, marcha f; (of illness) desarrollo m; **his c. of action was to ...** su opción fue ...; **in due c.** a su debido tiempo; **in the c. of construction** en vías de construcción; **in the c. of our conversation** mientras hablábamos; **in the c. of time** con el tiempo; **let things take their c.** deja que todo siga su curso; **that will happen as a matter of c.** eso ya vendrá por sí solo; **the c. of events** el curso de los acontecimientos (**c**) (set, series) ciclo m, serie f; (of lectures) ciclo m; **a c. of treatment** un tratamiento (**d**) Educ (year-long) curso m; (short) cursillo m;

Univ asignatura *f*; **refresher c.** cursillo de reciclaje; **to take a c.** seguir *or* hacer un curso (**e**) *Constr* hilada *f*, *RP* hilera *f* (**f**) *Sport (for golf)* campo *m*; *(for racing)* pista *f*; *(for horseracing)* hipódromo *m* (**g**) *Culin* plato *m*; **first c.** entrada *f*, primer plato *m* (**h**) **of c.** claro, naturalmente, por supuesto; **of c. not!** ¡claro que no!

2 *vi (liquid)* correr, fluir

court [kɔːt] **1** *n* (**a**) *Jur* tribunal *m*; **high c.** tribunal supremo; **to settle out of c.** llegar a un acuerdo sin ir a juicio; **to take sb to c.** llevar a algn a los tribunales ❑ *Mil* **c. martial** consejo *m* de guerra; *Br* **c. of inquiry** comisión *f* de investigación; **c. of justice** tribunal *m* de justicia; **c. order** orden *f* judicial (**b**) *(royal)* corte *f* ❑ *Br* **c. shoe** escarpín *m* (**c**) *Sport* pista *f*, cancha *f*

2 *vt (woman)* festejar a, hacer la corte a; *Fig* **to c. and spark** pelar la pava; *Fig* **to c. danger** buscar el peligro; *Fig* **to c. disaster** exponerse al desastre

3 *vi (couple)* llevar *or* tener relaciones

courteous [ˈkɜːtɪəs] *adj* cortés, fino(a), educado(a)

courteously [ˈkɜːtɪəslɪ] *adv* cortésmente, con cortesía

courtesy [ˈkɜːtɪsɪ] *n* (**a**) *(politeness)* cortesía *f*, educación *f*; **he didn't have the c. to visit her** no tuvo la atención de visitarla (**b**) *(favour)* permiso *m*; **by c. of** con permiso de (**c**) *Aut* **c. light** luz *f* interior

courthouse [ˈkɔːthaʊs] *n US Jur* palacio *m* de justicia

courtier [ˈkɔːtɪər] *n* cortesano *m*

court-martial [ˈkɔːtmɑːʃəl] *vt (pt & pp* **court-martialled,** *US* **court-martialed)** someter a consejo de guerra

courtroom [ˈkɔːtruːm] *n Jur* sala *f* de justicia

courtship [ˈkɔːtʃɪp] *n (of people)* noviazgo *m*; *(of animals)* cortejo *m*

courtyard [ˈkɔːtjɑːd] *n* patio *m*

cousin [ˈkʌzən] *n* · primo(a) *m,f*; **first c.** primo(a) hermano(a)

cove [kəʊv] *n Geog* cala *f*, ensenada *f*

covenant [ˈkʌvənənt] **1** *n Jur* convenio *m*, pacto *m*; *Br (to charity)* = acuerdo para realizar regularmente una donación a una entidad benéfica la cual, además, recibe los impuestos con que haya sido gravada la cantidad donada

2 *vi* convenir **(with sb** con algn), comprometerse **(to do sth** a hacer algo)

Coventry [ˈkʌvəntrɪ] *n Fam* **to send sb to C.** hacer el vacío a algn

cover [ˈkʌvər] **1** *vt* (**a**) *(person, object)* cubrir **(with** de); *(floor, furniture)* revestir **(with** de); *(with lid)* tapar; *(book)* forrar (**b**) *(hide)* cubrir, disimular; *Fig* **to c. one's tracks** no dejar rastro (**c**) *(protect)* abrigar, proteger; **to c. oneself** protegerse a sí mismo (**d**) *(financially)* cubrir; **$10 should c. it** con diez dólares habrá bastante; **to c. expenses** cubrir gastos (**e**) *(distance)* recorrer, cubrir; **to c. a great deal of ground** hacer mucho camino (**f**) *Ins* asegurar, cubrir (contra riesgos); **he's covered against fire** tiene un seguro antiincendios (**g**) *Press* investigar, hacer un reportaje sobre (**h**) *(deal with)* tratar, abarcar (**i**) *(include)* incluir, comprender; **to c. all eventualities** tener en cuenta todas las eventualidades (**j**) *(aim at)* apuntar a; **to c. sb with a revolver** apuntar a algn con una pistola (**k**) *Sport (player)* marcar

2 *vi* **to c. for sb** encubrir a algn

3 *n* (**a**) *(gen)* cubierta *f*; *(lid)* tapa *f*; *(on bed)* manta *f*, colcha *f*; *(of chair, typewriter)* funda *f* (**b**) *(of book)* tapa *f*, cubierta *f*; *(of magazine)* portada *f*; *Fig* **to read a book from c. to c.** leer un libro de cabo a rabo ❑ **c. girl** modelo *f* de revista (**c**) *(in restaurant)* cubierto *m* ❑ **c. charge** precio *m* del cubierto (**d**) *(envelope)* sobre *m*; **under separate c.** por separado (**e**) *Ins* **full c.** cobertura *f* completa ❑ *Br* **c. note** seguro *m*

provisional (**f**) *Fig (protection)* abrigo *m*, protección *f*; **to take c.** abrigarse, refugiarse; **under c.** al abrigo; *(indoors)* bajo techo

cover up 1 *vt* (**a**) *(person, object)* cubrir (**b**) *Fig (crime)* encubrir; *(truth)* disimular

2 *vi* (**a**) *(person)* abrigarse, taparse (**b**) *Fig* **to c. up for sb** encubrir a algn

coverage [ˈkʌvərɪdʒ] *n* (**a**) *Press* reportaje *m* (**of** sobre); **news c.** reportaje *m* (**b**) *Ins* cobertura *f*

coveralls [ˈkʌvərɔːlz] *npl US (garment)* mono *m sing*, *Am* overol *m*

covering [ˈkʌvərɪŋ] **1** *n* cubierta *f*, envoltura *f*

2 *adj (letter)* explicatorio(a)

coverlet [ˈkʌvəlɪt] *n* cubrecama *m*, colcha *f*

covert [ˈkʌvət] *adj* disimulado(a), secreto(a)

cover-up [ˈkʌvərʌp] *n* disimulo *m*, encubrimiento *m*

covet [ˈkʌvɪt] *vt* codiciar

covetous [ˈkʌvɪtəs] *adj* codicioso(a)

cow[1] [kaʊ] *n* (**a**) *Zool* vaca *f*; *(of elephant, seal)* hembra *f*; *Fam* **till the cows come home** hasta que las ranas echen pelo ❑ **c. shed** establo *m* (**b**) *Pej (woman)* arpía *f*, bruja *f*

cow[2] [kaʊ] *vt* intimidar, acobardar

coward [ˈkaʊəd] *n* cobarde *mf*

cowardice [ˈkaʊədɪs] *n* cobardía *f*

cowardly [ˈkaʊədlɪ] *adj* cobarde

cowboy [ˈkaʊbɔɪ] *n* vaquero *m*

cower [ˈkaʊər] *vi* agacharse; *(with fear)* encogerse

cowhide [ˈkaʊhaɪd] *n* piel *f* de vaca, cuero *m*

cowl [kaʊl] *n* (**a**) *(hood)* capucha *f* (**b**) *(of chimney)* sombrerete *m*

co-worker [kəʊˈwɜːkər] *n US* compañero(a) *m,f* de trabajo

cowslip [ˈkaʊslɪp] *n Bot* primavera *f*, prímula *f*

cox [kɒks] **1** *n* timonel *m*

2 *vt (boat)* gobernar

3 *vi* servir de timonel

coy [kɔɪ] *adj* (**coyer, coyest**) *(shy)* tímido(a); *(demure)* coquetón(ona)

coyly [ˈkɔɪlɪ] *adv* tímidamente

coyness [ˈkɔɪnɪs] *n (shyness)* timidez *f*; *(evasiveness)* evasión *f*

coyote [kɔɪˈjəʊtɪ] *n* coyote *m*

cozy [ˈkəʊzɪ] *adj* (**cozier, coziest**) *US see* **cosy**

CPI [siːpiːˈaɪ] *n US Econ (abbr* **consumer price index)** IPC *m*, Índice *m* de Precios al Consumo

Cpl *Mil (abbr* **Corporal)** cabo *m*

CPU [siːpiːˈjuː] *n Comptr (abbr* **central processing unit)** CPU *f*, unidad *f* central de proceso

crab [kræb] *n* (**a**) *Zool* cangrejo *m*, *Am* jaiba *f* ❑ **fiddler c.** nécora *f*; **spider c.** centolla *f* (**b**) *Bot* **c. apple** manzana *f* silvestre

crabbed [ˈkræbɪd] *adj* (**a**) *(irritable)* irritable, tosco(a) (**b**) *(handwriting)* apretado(a)

crabby [ˈkræbɪ] *adj* (**crabbier, crabbiest**) *Fam* **to be c.** tener mala leche

crack [kræk] **1** *vt* (**a**) *(break) (cup)* rajar; *Med (bone)* fracturar; *(nut)* cascar; *(safe)* forzar; *(head)* golpearse (**b**) *(whip)* hacer restallar (**c**) *Fig (problem)* dar con la solución de; *(clue)* descifrar; *(joke)* contar, soltar (**d**) *Comptr (program)* desproteger

2 *vi* (**a**) *(glass)* rajarse, resquebrajarse (**b**) *(whip)* restallar; *(voice)* cascarse (**c**) *Fam* **to get cracking on** *or* **with sth** ponerse a hacer algo; **get cracking!** ¡a trabajar!, ¡manos a la obra!

3 n (**a**) (in cup) raja f; (in ice, wall, ground) grieta f (**b**) (of whip) restallido m; (of gun) detonación f; Fam Fig **he had a fair c. of the whip** ha tenido su oportunidad (**c**) Fam (blow) golpetazo m; **a c. on the head** un tostón en la cabeza (**d**) Fam (attempt) intento m; **to have a c. at sth** intentar hacer algo (**e**) Slang (wisecrack) réplica f aguda (**f**) Slang (drug) crack m (**g**) **the c. of dawn** el amanecer
4 adj Slang bestial, de primera; **a c. shot** un tirador de primera

crack down on vt castigar

crack up 1 vi (pathway etc) agrietarse; Fam Fig (person) desquiciarse, venirse abajo
2 vt Fam poner por los cielos; **it's not all that it's cracked up to be** no es tan bueno(a) como se dice

crackbrained ['krækbreɪnd] adj Fam chalado(a), chiflado(a)

crackdown ['krækdaʊn] n medidas fpl severas; **a c. on drugs/tax evasion** medidas severas contra las drogas/la evasión fiscal

cracked [krækt] adj Fam see **crackbrained**

cracker ['krækər] n (**a**) (biscuit) galleta f seca (**b**) (firework) buscapiés m inv (**c**) Comptr cracker mf, intruso(a) m,f

crackers ['krækəz] adj Br Fam see **crackbrained**

crackle ['krækəl] **1** vi crujir, chasquear
2 n crujido m, chasquido m

crackling ['kræklɪŋ] n Culin cortezas fpl de cerdo, Am chicharrones mpl

crackpot ['krækpɒt] **1** n chiflado(a) m,f
2 adj (person) chiflado(a); (idea) excéntrico(a), desorbitado(a)

crack-up ['krækʌp] n Fam (of person) hundimiento m, derrumbe m

cradle ['kreɪdəl] **1** n (baby's) cuna f; Tel soporte m; Constr andamio m volante; Fig **the c. of civilization** la cuna de la civilización; Fig **from the c. to the grave** toda la vida
2 vt (baby) acunar (en los brazos)

craft ['krɑːft] n (**a**) (occupation) oficio m; (art) arte m; (skill) destreza f, habilidad f; **arts and crafts** artesanía f (**b**) (cunning) astucia f, maña f (**c**) Naut embarcación f

craftily ['krɑːftɪlɪ] adv astutamente, con astucia or maña

craftiness ['krɑːftɪnɪs] n astucia f, maña f

craftsman ['krɑːftsmən] n (pl **craftsmen**) artesano m

craftsmanship ['krɑːftsmənʃɪp] n arte m, artificio m

crafty ['krɑːftɪ] adj (**craftier, craftiest**) astuto(a), taimado(a)

crag [kræg] n peña f, peñasco m

craggy ['krægɪ] adj (**craggier, craggiest**) (**a**) (place) peñascoso(a), escarpado(a) (**b**) (face) de facciones marcadas

crake [kreɪk] n Orn polluela f

cram [kræm] **1** vt (pt & pp **crammed**) (**a**) (room etc) atestar, henchir, atiborrar; **crammed with people** llenísimo(a) de gente; **to c. oneself with food** atiborrarse de comida (**b**) Educ Fam (subject) empollar
2 vi Educ Fam matarse estudiando, Esp empollar, RP tragar

cram-full [kræm'fʊl] adj Fam atiborrado(a), atestado(a)

cramp[1] [kræmp] n Med calambre m; **cramps** (gen) retortijones mpl; (menstrual) molestias fpl menstruales

cramp[2] [kræmp] vt (restrict) limitar; (development) poner trabas a; **to be cramped for space** estar abarrotado(a); Fam Fig **to c. sb's style** cortar el vuelo a algn

cramped [kræmpt] adj (**a**) (place) atestado(a), abarrotado(a) (**b**) (writing) apretado(a)

cranberry ['krænbərɪ] n Bot arándano m

crane [kreɪn] **1** n (**a**) Zool grulla f común (**b**) (device) grúa f (**c**) Ent **c. fly** típula f
2 vt estirar; **to c. one's neck (to see sth)** estirar el cuello (para ver algo)

cranium ['kreɪnɪəm] n (pl **craniums** or **crania** ['kreɪnɪə]) Anat cráneo m

crank [kræŋk] **1** n (**a**) Tech cigüeñal m (**b**) Tech (starting handle) manivela f (**c**) Fam (eccentric) maniático(a) m,f, pájaro m raro
2 vt **to c. (up)** (engine) arrancar con la manivela

crankshaft ['kræŋkʃɑːft] n Tech árbol m del cigüeñal

cranky ['kræŋkɪ] adj (**crankier, crankiest**) Fam excéntrico(a), chiflado(a)

cranny ['krænɪ] n grieta f; Fig **in every nook and c.** en todos los rincones

crap [kræp] Fam **1** n mierda f
2 adj Br (of poor quality) **it's c.!** ¡es una mierda!

crash [kræʃ] **1** vt (**a**) **to c. one's car** tener un accidente con el coche or Am carro or CSur auto (**b**) Fam colarse; **she crashed the party** se coló en la fiesta
2 vi (**a**) (car, plane) estrellarse; (collide) chocar; **to c. into** estrellarse contra, chocar con or contra (**b**) Com quebrar, hundirse (**c**) Comptr bloquearse, colgarse (**d**) Slang **to c. (out)** quedarse roque or frito(a)
3 n (**a**) (noise) estrépito m; **c.!** ¡patapún! (**b**) (collision) choque m, colisión f; **car/plane c.** accidente m de coche or Am carro or CSur auto/avión ▫ **c. barrier** barrera f; Fig **c. course** curso m intensivo; Fig **c. diet** régimen m riguroso; **c. helmet** casco m protector (**c**) Com quiebra f

crashing ['kræʃɪŋ] adj Fam enorme; **c. bore** pelma mf, pelmazo mf

crash-land [kræʃ'lænd] vi Av hacer un aterrizaje forzoso

crass [kræs] adj (person) grosero(a); (ignorance) indisculpable, garrafal

crate [kreɪt] **1** n caja f, cajón m (para embalaje)
2 vt embalar

crater ['kreɪtər] n Geol cráter m

cravat [krə'væt] n pañuelo m (de hombre)

crave [kreɪv] vt & vi ansiar; **to c. (for) sth** ansiar algo; (in pregnancy) antojar algo

craving ['kreɪvɪŋ] n (gen) ansia f; (in pregnancy) antojo m

crawfish ['krɔːfɪʃ] n (fish) langosta f

crawl [krɔːl] **1** vi (baby) gatear; (insect) arrastrarse; (vehicle) avanzar lentamente; Fig **to be crawling with vermin** estar plagado(a) de bichos; Fig **to c. to sb** arrastrarse a los pies de algn, lamer a algn; Fam Fig **it makes my flesh c.** me pone los pelos de punta
2 n (**a**) Aut velocidad f lenta; **to go at a c.** ir or avanzar lentamente (**b**) Swimming crol m; **to do the c.** nadar crol

crawler ['krɔːlər] n Slang cobista mf, adulador(a) m,f, Méx lambiscón(ona) m,f, RP chupamedias mf inv

crayfish ['kreɪfɪʃ] n Zool cangrejo m de río

crayon ['kreɪɒn] **1** n pastel m, lápiz m pastel ▫ Art **c. drawing** dibujo m al pastel
2 vt dibujar al pastel

craze [kreɪz] n manía f, moda f; **it's the latest c.** es la última moda, es lo que se lleva

crazed [kreɪzd] adj loco(a) (**with** de); **half c.** medio loco(a)

crazily ['kreɪzɪlɪ] adv Fam locamente

craziness ['kreɪzɪnɪs] n Fam locura f

crazy ['kreɪzɪ] adj (**crazier, craziest**) Fam loco(a), chalado(a); **like c.** como un(a) loco(a); **to drive sb c.** volver loco a algn ▫ Br **c. paving** pavimento m en mosaico

creak [kriːk] **1** vi (floor, stairs) crujir, hacer un crujido; (hinge) chirriar

2 *n (of floorboards, new boots)* crujido *m*; *(of hinge)* chirrido *m*

creaky ['kri:kı] *adj* (**creaker, creakiest**) *(floor)* que cruje; *(hinge)* chirriante

cream [kri:m] **1** *n* (**a**) *(of milk) Esp* nata *f*, *Am* crema *f*(de leche); **c. coloured** color crema; **c. of chicken soup** crema *f* de pollo; **whipped c.** nata *f* montada; *Fig* **the c.** la flor y nata ❑ **c. cheese** queso *m* cremoso; **double c.** nata *f* para montar (**b**) *(cosmetic)* crema *f*; **face/hand c.** crema para el cutis/las manos

2 *vt* (**a**) *(milk)* desnatar (**b**) *Culin* batir; **c. the butter and sugar** batir la mantequilla con el azúcar ❑ **creamed potatoes** puré *m* de patatas

cream off *vt Fig* seleccionar

creamery ['kri:mərı] *n* lechería *f*, mantequería *f*

creamy ['kri:mı] *adj* (**creamier, creamiest**) cremoso(a)

crease [kri:s] **1** *n (wrinkle)* arruga *f*; *(fold)* pliegue *m*; *(on trousers)* raya *f*

2 *vt (clothes)* arrugar; *(with iron)* hacer la raya

3 *vi* arrugarse

create [kri:'eıt] **1** *vt* (**a**) *(gen)* crear; *(sensation)* producir; *(difficulties)* crear; **to c. a diversion** distraer la atención (**b**) *(appoint)* nombrar

2 *vi Br Slang* ponerse hecho(a) una furia

creation [kri:'eıʃən] *n* creación *f*

creative [kri:'eıtıv] *adj* creativo(a) ❑ *Fin* **c. accounting** maquillaje *m* de cuentas, artificios *mpl* contables; **c. writing** creación *f* literaria

creativity [kri:eı'tıvıtı] *n* creatividad *f*

creator [kri:'eıtər] *n* creador(a) *m,f*

creature ['kri:tʃər] *n* (**a**) *(animal)* criatura *f* (**b**) *(human being)* ser *m*; **c. of habit** esclavo(a) *m,f* de los hábitos ❑ **c. comforts** comodidades *fpl*

crèche [kreıʃ, kreʃ] *n Br* guardería *f*

credence ['kri:dəns] *n* crédito *m*; **to give c. to** dar crédito a

credentials [krı'denʃəlz] *npl* credenciales *fpl*

credibility [kredı'bılıtı] *n* credibilidad *f* ❑ **c. gap** falta *f* de credibilidad

credible ['kredıbəl] *adj* creíble

credit ['kredıt] **1** *n* (**a**) *Com* crédito *m*; *(in accountancy)* haber *m*; **c. and debit** debe y haber; **on c.** a crédito ❑ **c. card** tarjeta *f* de crédito; **c. rating** clasificación *f* or grado *m* de solvencia; **c. sales** ventas *fpl* a crédito; **c. squeeze** restricciones *fpl* al crédito (**b**) *(acknowledgement)* reconocimiento *m*; **to give c. to sb for sth** reconocer algo a algn; *Fig* **c. where c. is due** reconocimiento al mérito (**c**) *(benefit)* honor *m*; **it does you c.** puedes estar orgulloso(a); **to be a c. to** hacer honor a (**d**) *Cin TV* **credits** ficha *f* sing técnica (**e**) *US Univ* punto *m*, crédito *m*

2 *vt* (**a**) *Com (sum to sb's account)* abonar, acreditar (**b**) *(believe)* creer; **you wouldn't c. it!** ¡no te lo creerías! (**c**) *Fig* atribuir; **he was credited with the invention of the new machine** se le atribuyó el invento de la nueva máquina; **to c. sb with common sense** creer que algn tiene sentido común

creditable ['kredıtəbəl] *adj* loable, digno(a) de crédito

creditor ['kredıtər] *n Com* acreedor(a) *m,f*

creditworthy ['kredıtwɜ:ðı] *adj* solvente

credulity [krı'dju:lıtı] *n* credulidad *f*

credulous ['kredjʊləs] *adj* crédulo(a)

creed [kri:d] *n* credo *m*

creek [kri:k] *n* (**a**) *Br (small bay)* cala *f* (**b**) *US Austral (stream)* riachuelo *m*; *Slang* **to be up the c.** estar jodido(a)

creel [kri:l] *n* nasa *f*

creep [kri:p] **1** *vi (pt & pp* **crept**) *(insect)* arrastrarse, trepar; *(cat)* deslizarse (sigilosamente); *(plant)* trepar; *Med* **creeping paralysis** parálisis *f* progresiva; **to c. into/out of a house** entrar sigilosamente en/salir sigilosamente de una casa; **to c. up on sb** sorprender a algn; *Fig* **it made my flesh c.** me dio escalofríos; *Fig* **middle age is creeping up on me** me estoy haciendo mayor

2 *n Fam* (**a**) *(unpleasant person)* asqueroso(a) *m,f*; *Br (obsequious person)* pelotillero *mf*, pelota *mf*, arrastrado(a) *m,f*, *Méx* lambiscón(ona) *m,f*, *RP* chupamedias *mf inv* (**b**) **to give sb the creeps** hacerle poner la carne de gallina a algn, dar asco a algn

creeper ['kri:pər] *n Bot* trepadora *f*

creeping ['kri:pıŋ] *adj (gradual)* paulatino(a); **c. privatization** privatización *f* gradual subrepticia

creepy ['kri:pı] *adj* (**creepier, creepiest**) *Fam* horripilante, espeluznante

creepy-crawly ['kri:pı'krɔ:lı] *n Br Fam* bicho *m*

cremate [krı'meıt] *vt* incinerar

cremation [krı'meıʃən] *n* incineración *f*

crematorium [kremə'tɔ:rıəm] *n (pl* **crematoriums** *or* **crematoria** [kremə'tɔ:rıə]) *(horno m)* crematorio *m*

crème [krem] *n* **c. caramel** flan *m*; **the c. de la c.** *(the best)* la flor y nata; **c. fraîche** *Esp* nata *f* or *Am* crema *f* fresca fermentada

creole ['kri:əʊl] **1** *adj* criollo(a)

2 *n* (**a**) *(person)* criollo(a) *m,f* (**b**) *(language)* criollo *m*

creosote ['kri:əsəʊt] *n Chem* creosota *f*

crepe [kreıp] *n* (**a**) *Tex* crepé *m*, crespón *m* (**b**) **c. paper** papel *m* crespón

crept [krept] *pt & pp see* **creep**

crescendo [krı'ʃendəʊ] *n Mus* crescendo *m*

crescent ['kresənt] **1** *n (shape)* medialuna *f*; *Br (street)* calle *f* en medialuna

2 *adj* creciente; **c. moon** luna *f* creciente

cress [kres] *n Bot* berro *m*

crest [krest] *n* (**a**) *(of cock, wave)* cresta *f*; *(on helmet)* penacho *m*, cimera *f*; *(of hill)* cima *f* (**b**) *(in heraldry)* blasón *m*

crested ['krestıd] *adj* crestado(a)

crestfallen ['krestfɔ:lən] *adj* abatido(a), desanimado(a)

Cretan ['kri:tən] *adj* cretense

Crete [kri:t] *n* Creta

cretin ['kretın] *n* cretino(a) *m,f*

cretinous ['kretınəs] *adj* cretino(a)

Creutzfeldt-Jakob disease ['krɔıtsfelt'jɑ:kɒbdı'zi:z] *n* enfermedad *f* de Creutzfeld(t)-Jakob

crevasse [krı'væs] *n* grieta *f*, fisura *f*

crevice ['krevıs] *n* grieta *f*, raja *f*, hendedura *f*

crew¹ [kru:] **1** *n Av Naut* tripulación *f*; *(team)* equipo *m*; *Fam* banda *f*, *Méx* bola *f*, *RP* barra *f*; *Cin* **camera c.** equipo *m* de filmación; **c. cut** *(hairstyle)* corte *m* al rape; **c.-neck sweater** jersey *m* con cuello redondo; **ground c.** personal *m* de tierra

2 *vi* tripular

crew² [kru:] *pt see* **crow²**

crib [krıb] **1** *n* (**a**) *(manger)* pesebre *m*; *(for baby)* cuna *f* (**b**) *Fam (plagiarism)* hurto *m*, plagio *m*

2 *vt (pt & pp* **cribbed**) *Fam* (**a**) *(steal)* hurtar (**b**) *(copy)* copiar, plagiar

crick [krık] *n Fam (in the neck)* torticolis *f*

cricket¹ ['krıkıt] *n Ent* grillo *m*

cricket² ['krıkıt] *n Sport* cricket *m*; *Br Fam* **that's not c.** eso no se hace ❑ **c. ball** pelota *f* de cricket; **c. bat** paleta *f* de cricket

cricketer ['krɪkɪtər] *n Sport* jugador(a) *m,f* de cricket

crikey ['kraɪkɪ] *interj Slang* ¡mecachis!, ¡ostras!

crime [kraɪm] *n Jur* delito *m*; **to prevent c.** prevenir la criminalidad ▫ **c. fiction** novelas *fpl* policíacas; **c. wave** ola *f* de delincuencia

criminal ['krɪmɪnəl] *adj & n* criminal *(mf)*; **C. Investigation Department** ≃ Brigada *f* de Investigación Criminal; **c. law** derecho *m* penal; **c. lawyer** abogado(a) *m,f* criminalista, penalista *mf*; **c. offender** infractor(a) *m,f*; **c. record** antecedentes *mpl* penales

criminality [krɪmɪ'nælɪtɪ] *n (in general)* delincuencia *f*; *(serious)* criminalidad *f*

criminalize ['krɪmɪnəlaɪz] *vt* penalizar

criminally ['krɪmɪnəlɪ] *adv* **the c. insane** los (delincuentes) psicópatas; **he was c. negligent** cometió un delito de negligencia

criminology [krɪmɪ'nɒlədʒɪ] *n* criminología *f*

crimp [krɪmp] *vt (hair)* rizar (con tenacillas)

crimson ['krɪmzən] *adj & n* carmesí *(m)*

cringe [krɪndʒ] *vi* abatirse, encogerse; **to c. before sb** rebajarse ante algn

cringing ['krɪndʒɪŋ] *adj (behaviour)* servil; *(gesture)* de servilismo

crinkle ['krɪŋkəl] **1** *vt (gen)* fruncir, arrugar; *(paper)* hacer pliegues en
2 *vi* arrugarse, plegarse

crinkly ['krɪŋklɪ] *adj* (**crinklier, crinkliest**) fruncido(a), arrugado(a); *(paper)* con pliegues

cripple ['krɪpəl] **1** *n* lisiado(a) *m,f*, mutilado(a) *m,f*
2 *vt* mutilar, dejar cojo(a); *Fig* paralizar

crippled ['krɪpəld] *adj* tullido(a), lisiado(a)

crippling ['krɪplɪŋ] *adj* **(a)** *(illness)* incapacitante **(b)** *(taxes, strike)* pernicioso(a)

crisis ['kraɪsɪs] *n (pl* **crises** ['kraɪsi:z]*)* crisis *f inv* ▫ **c. management** gestión *f* de crisis

crisp [krɪsp] **1** *adj (toast, biscuit, snow)* crujiente; *(lettuce)* fresco(a), tierno(a); *(banknote)* nuevo(a); *(air, weather)* frío(a) y seco(a); *Fig (style)* directo(a), resuelto(a)
2 *n Br Culin* **(potato) c.** *Esp* patata *f or Am* papa *f* frita (de bolsa); **burnt to a c.** achicharrado(a)

crispbread ['krɪspbred] *n Culin* biscote® *m*

crisply ['krɪsplɪ] *adv* decididamente

crispy ['krɪspɪ] *adj* (**crispier, crispiest**) *(crisp)* crujiente

crisscross ['krɪskrɒs] **1** *vi* entrecruzarse
2 *vt* entrecruzar
3 *n* líneas *fpl* entrecruzadas

criterion [kraɪ'tɪərɪən] *n (pl* **criterions** *or* **criteria** [kraɪ'tɪərɪə]*)* criterio *m*

critic ['krɪtɪk] *n* **(a)** *Art Theat* crítico(a) *m,f* **(b)** *(of person)* criticón(ona) *m,f*

critical ['krɪtɪkəl] *adj* **(a)** *(judging, analytical)* crítico(a); **a c. remark** un comentario de crítica; **to be c. of sb** criticar a algn **(b)** *(crucial)* crítico(a), crucial, decisivo(a)

critically ['krɪtɪklɪ] *adv* críticamente; **c. ill** gravemente enfermo(a)

criticism ['krɪtɪsɪzəm] *n* crítica *f*; **he doesn't like c.** no le gusta que le critiquen; **literary c.** crítica literaria

criticize ['krɪtɪsaɪz] *vt* criticar

critique [krɪ'ti:k] *n Lit Philos* crítica *f*

croak [krəʊk] **1** *n* **(a)** *(of frog)* canto *m*; *(of raven)* graznido *m* **(b)** *(of person)* voz *f* ronca
2 *vi* **(a)** *(frog)* croar; *(raven)* graznar **(b)** *(person)* hablar con voz ronca **(c)** *Slang (die)* estirar la pata

Croat ['krəʊæt], **Croatian** [krəʊ'eɪʃən] **1** *n* **(a)** *(person)* croata *mf* **(b)** *(language)* croata *m*
2 *adj* croata

Croatia [krəʊ'eɪʃə] *n* Croacia *f*

crochet ['krəʊʃeɪ] *Knit* **1** *vt* hacer a ganchillo *or Col CSur* crochet *or Méx* gancho
2 *vi* hacer ganchillo *or Col CSur* crochet *or Méx* gancho *m*
3 *n* ganchillo *m*, *Col CSur* crochet *m*, *Méx* gancho *m* ▫ **c. hook** aguja *f* de ganchillo

crock¹ [krɒk] *n (pot)* cántaro *m*

crock² [krɒk] *n Br Slang (old person)* carca *mf*, carroza *mf*; *(car)* trasto *m*, cacharro *m*

crockery ['krɒkərɪ] *n* loza *f*

crocodile ['krɒkədaɪl] *n* **(a)** *Zool* cocodrilo *m*; *Fig* **c. tears** lágrimas *fpl* de cocodrilo **(b)** *Br Fam (line)* fila *f* (de niños) de dos en dos

crocus ['krəʊkəs] *n Bot* azafrán *m*

croissant ['krwæsɒŋ] *n* croissant *m*

crone [krəʊn] *n* vieja *f*, bruja *f*

crony ['krəʊnɪ] *n* amiguete *mf*, compinche *mf*

cronyism ['krəʊnɪɪzəm] *n Pej* amiguismo *m*, enchufismo *m*

crook [krʊk] **1** *n* **(a)** *(of shepherd)* cayado *m*; *(bishop's)* báculo *m* **(b)** *Fam* caco *m*, delincuente *mf*
2 *vt (arm)* doblar

crooked ['krʊkɪd] *adj* **(a)** *(stick, picture)* torcido(a); *(path)* tortuoso(a) **(b)** *Fam (dishonest)* deshonesto(a)

croon [kru:n] *vt & vi* canturrear

crooner ['kru:nər] *n* cantante *m* de música ligera

crop [krɒp] **1** *n* **(a)** *(variety)* cultivo *m*; *(harvest)* cosecha *f*; *(of hair)* mata *f* ▫ **c. circle** = franja aplastada y circular de terreno cultivado, que aparece por causas supuestamente paranormales **(b)** *(of bird)* buche *m* **(c)** *(whip)* fusta *f* **(d)** *(haircut)* corte *m* al rape
2 *vt (pt & pp* **cropped***) (hair)* rapar, cortar al rape; *(grass)* pacer

crop up *vi Fam* surgir, presentarse

cropper ['krɒpər] *n Fam* **to come a c.** *(fall)* darse un porrazo *or Esp* batacazo *or Méx* madrazo; *(fail)* pinchar

croquet ['krəʊkeɪ] *n Sport* croquet *n*

croquette [krɒ'ket] *n Culin* croqueta *f*

cross [krɒs] **1** *n* **(a)** *(sign, shape)* cruz *f* ▫ **Red C.** Cruz *f* Roja **(b)** *(of breeds, animals)* cruce *m*, *Am* cruza *f* **(c)** *Sew* sesgo *m*; **cut on the c.** cortado(a) al sesgo **(d)** *Math* **c. section** sección *f* transversal
2 *vt* **(a)** *(street)* cruzar, atravesar; *(legs)* cruzar; *Br (cheque)* cruzar; **it crossed my mind that ...** se me ocurrió que ...; *Fam* **to keep one's fingers crossed** tocar madera ▫ *Tel* **crossed line** mala comunicación *f* **(b)** *Rel* santiguar(se); **to c. oneself** hacer la señal de la cruz; *Fam* **c. my heart!** ¡te lo juro! **(c)** *(thwart)* contrariar
3 *vi (gen)* cruzar; *(roads)* cruzarse; **to c. from Dover to Calais** hacer la travesía de Dover a Calais; **to c. into another country** pasar la frontera a otro país; **to c. over** atravesar, cruzar
4 *adj (annoyed) esp Esp* enfadado(a), *esp Am* enojado(a); **to get c. with sb** *esp Esp* enfadarse *or esp Am* enojarse con algn

cross off, cross out *vt* tachar, rayar

crossbar ['krɒsbɑ:r] *n* travesaño *m*

crossbow ['krɒsbəʊ] *n* ballesta *f*

crossbred ['krɒsbred] **1** *pt & pp see* **crossbreed**
2 *adj* híbrido(a)

crossbreed ['krɒsbri:d] **1** *n* mestizo *m*
2 *vt (pt & pp* **crossbred***)* cruzar

crosscheck ['krɒstʃek] **1** vt comprobar por otro sistema **2** n comprobación f adicional

cross-country ['krɒskʌntrɪ] **1** adj **(a)** (vehicle) todo-terreno inv **(b)** Sport de cros **2** n Sport **c.-c. race** cros m **3** [krɒs'kʌntrɪ] adv campo través

cross-examination [krɒsɪgzæmɪ'neɪʃən] n Jur interrogatorio m

cross-examine [krɒsɪg'zæmɪn] vt Jur (witness) interrogar

cross-eyed ['krɒsaɪd] adj bizco(a)

cross-fertilization ['krɒsfɜːtɪlaɪ'zeɪʃən] n **(a)** (between plants) polinización f cruzada **(b)** (cultural) mestizaje m (cultural); (of ideas) intercambio m

cross-fertilize [krɒs'fɜːtɪlaɪz] n **(a)** (plants) polinizar con fecundación cruzada **(b)** Fig favorecer el mestizaje (cultural) entre

crossfire ['krɒsfaɪər] n Mil fuego m cruzado

crossing ['krɒsɪŋ] n cruce m ❑ **pedestrian c.** paso m de peatones; **sea c.** travesía f

cross-legged [krɒs'legɪd] adj con las piernas cruzadas

crossly ['krɒslɪ] adv de mal humor

cross-over ['krɒsəʊvər] **1** n (of career) salto m, cambio m **2** adj Mus (style) híbrido(a), de fusión

cross-party ['krɒs pɑːtɪ] adj interpartidista

cross-platform [krɒs'plætfɔːm] adj Comptr multiplataforma inv

cross-purposes ['krɒs'pɜːpəsɪz] npl **they were at c. with each other** sin darse cuenta, estaban hablando de cosas distintas

cross-reference [krɒs'refərəns] n remisión f

crossroads ['krɒsrəʊdz] n encrucijada f

cross-section ['krɒs'sekʃən] n sección f transversal; **a c. of the population** una muestra representativa de la población

crosswind ['krɒswɪnd] n viento m lateral

crosswise ['krɒswaɪz] adv transversal, de través

crossword ['krɒswɜːd] n **c. (puzzle)** crucigrama m

crotch [krɒtʃ] n (of body, garment) entrepierna f

crotchet ['krɒtʃɪt] n Br Mus negra f

crotchety ['krɒtʃɪtɪ] adj Fam cascarrabias inv, gruñón(ona)

crouch [kraʊtʃ] vi **to c. (down)** agacharse

croup [kruːp] n Med crup m

croupier ['kruːpɪər] n (in casino) crupié mf, crupier mf

crouton ['kruːtɒn] n picatoste m, = dado de pan frito

crow¹ [krəʊ] n Orn cuervo m; Fig **as the c. flies** en línea recta; US Fig **to eat c.** humillarse ❑ **carrion c.** corneja f negra; **c.'s-feet** patas fpl de gallo; Naut **c.'s-nest** vigía f

crow² [krəʊ] **1** vi (pt **crowed** or **crew**; pp **crowed**) **(a)** (cock) cantar; (person) **to c. over sth** jactarse de algo **(b)** (baby) balbucir **2** n (cry of bird) canto m

crowbar ['krəʊbɑːr] n palanca f

crowd [kraʊd] **1** n **(a)** (large number of people) muchedumbre f, multitud f; (at sports match) público m; **to push through the c.** abrirse paso por entre la muchedumbre; Fig **to follow the c.** seguir a la mayoría; Fam **he's a real c. puller** atrae a las masas ❑ Cin **c. scene** escena f de masas **(b)** Fam (gang) pandilla f, Méx bola f, RP barra f **2** vt (streets, area) llenar, atestar **3** vi apiñarse, aglomerarse; **to c. in/out** entrar/salir en tropel; **to c. round sb** apiñarse alrededor de algn

crowded ['kraʊdɪd] adj atestado(a), lleno(a); **the**

animals were c. together los animales estaban todos apiñados

crown [kraʊn] **1** n **(a)** (headdress) corona f; (garland) guirnalda f; **the c. jewels** las joyas de la corona ❑ Br Jur **c. court** tribunal m superior; **C. Prince** príncipe m heredero **(b)** (of head) coronilla f; (of hat, tree) copa f; (on tooth) corona f **2** vt **(a)** (king, queen) coronar; **crowned heads** testas coronadas **(b)** (tooth) poner una corona a **(c)** Fam **to c. sb** dar un golpe en la cabeza a algn; Fam Fig **to c. it all** y para colmo, y para más inri

crowning ['kraʊnɪŋ] **1** adj supremo(a) **2** n coronación f

cruces ['kruːsiːz] npl see **crux**

crucial ['kruːʃəl] adj crucial, decisivo(a), crítico(a)

crucible ['kruːsɪbəl] n crisol m

crucifix ['kruːsɪfɪks] n crucifijo m

crucifixion [kruːsɪ'fɪkʃən] n crucifixión f

crucify ['kruːsɪfaɪ] vt (pt & pp **crucified**) crucificar

crude [kruːd] adj **(a)** (manners, style) tosco(a), grosero(a) **(b)** (unrefined) (oil) crudo(a); (tool) primitivo(a)

crudely ['kruːdlɪ] adv con crudeza, con tosquedad

crudeness ['kruːdnɪs] n, **crudity** ['kruːdɪtɪ] n crudeza f, tosquedad f

cruel [kruːəl] adj cruel (**to** con)

cruelly ['kruːəlɪ] adv cruelmente, con crueldad

cruelty ['kruːəltɪ] n crueldad f (**to** hacia)

cruet ['kruːɪt] n Culin **c. set** vinagreras fpl

cruise [kruːz] **1** vi **(a)** Naut hacer un crucero **(b)** Aut viajar or circular a velocidad constante; Av Naut viajar a velocidad de crucero **(c)** Fam ir de ligue or RP levante por **2** n **(a)** Naut crucero m **(b)** Mil **c. missile** misil m teledirigido

cruiser ['kruːzər] n Naut (barco m) crucero m

cruising ['kruːzɪŋ] adj **c. speed** Aut velocidad f constante; Av velocidad de crucero

crumb [krʌm] n miga f, migaja f; Fig **a c. of comfort** una pizca de consuelo

crumble ['krʌmbəl] **1** vt (bread) desmigar, desmenuzar **2** vi (wall, building) desmoronarse; (empire) derrumbarse; Fig (hopes) desvanecerse

crumbly ['krʌmblɪ] adj (**crumblier, crumbliest**) (bread, cake) que se desmigaja

crummy ['krʌmɪ] adj (**crummier, crummiest**) Fam malo(a), Esp cutre, Col coroncho(a), RP groncho(a)

crumpet ['krʌmpɪt] n Culin = torta pequeña que se come con mantequilla

crumple ['krʌmpəl] **1** vt (paper) estrujar; (clothes) arrugar **2** vi (material) arrugarse, estrujarse

crunch [krʌntʃ] **1** vt (food) ronchar, mascar; (with feet, tyres) hacer crujir **2** vi ronchar, crujir **3** n (of snow, gravel) crujido m; Fam **when it comes to the c.** a la hora de la verdad

crunchy ['krʌntʃɪ] adj (**crunchier, crunchiest**) crujiente, que cruje

crusade [kruː'seɪd] **1** n cruzada f **2** vi **to c. for/against** hacer una cruzada or campaña a favor/en contra de

crusader [kruː'seɪdər] n Hist cruzado m; (champion) campeón(ona) m,f

crush [krʌʃ] **1** vt **(a)** (mash, squash) aplastar; (wrinkle) arrugar; (grind) moler; (squeeze) exprimir; Fig **to c. people into a train** apiñar gente en un tren **(b)** Fig (defeat utterly) aplastar

2 *vi (clothes)* arrugarse, ajarse; *Fig* **to c. into a car** apretujarse en un coche

3 *n* (**a**) *(of people)* gentío *m*, aglomeración *f* (**b**) *Culin* jugo *m*; **orange c.** naranjada *f* (**c**) *Fam* enamoramiento *m*; **to have a c. on sb** estar loco(a) perdido(a) por algn

crushing ['krʌʃɪŋ] *adj Fig (defeat, reply)* aplastante

crust [krʌst] *n* (**a**) *(of bread)* corteza *f*, cuscurro *m*; *(of pastry)* pasta *f* (**b**) *Geol (of earth)* corteza *f*

crustacean [krʌ'steɪʃən] *adj & n Zool* crustáceo(a) *(m)*

crusty ['krʌstɪ] *adj* (**crustier, crustiest**) (**a**) *(bread)* crujiente (**b**) *Br (person)* malhumorado(a), gruñón(ona)

crutch [krʌtʃ] *n* (**a**) *Med* muleta *f*; *Fig* apoyo *m* (**b**) *Br see* **crotch**

crux [krʌks] *n* (*pl* **cruxes** *or* **cruces**) quid *m*, meollo *m*; **the c. of the matter** el quid de la cuestión

cry [kraɪ] **1** *vi* (*pt & pp* **cried**) (**a**) *(shout, call)* gritar; **to c. for help** pedir socorro a voces (**b**) *(weep)* llorar; **to c. over sth** lamentarse por algo; **to c. with joy** llorar de alegría; *Fig* **to c. for the moon** pedir peras al olmo; *Prov* **don't c. over spilt milk** a lo hecho, pecho

2 *vt* (*exclaim*) gritar; **'it's true!' he cried** '¡es cierto!' gritó; *Fig* **to c. wolf** dar una falsa alarma (**b**) *(weep)* **to c. one's eyes out** llorar a lágrima viva

3 *n* (**a**) *(call)* grito *m*; **to give a c.** gritar; *Fig* **it's a far c. from ...** tiene poco que ver con ... (**b**) *(weeping)* llanto *m*; **to have a good c.** desahogarse llorando

cry down *vt* despreciar, desacreditar

cry off *vi Fam* volverse atrás, rajarse

cry out *vi* gritar; **to c. out against** clamar contra; **to c. out for sth** pedir algo a gritos

crybaby ['kraɪbeɪbɪ] *n* niño(a) *m,f* llorón(ona)

crying ['kraɪɪŋ] **1** *n* (**a**) *(shouts)* gritos *mpl* (**b**) *(weeping)* llanto *m*

2 *adj* (**a**) *(child)* que llora (**b**) *Fig (need)* urgente, apremiante; *(injustice)* que clama al cielo; **it's a c. shame** es una vergüenza

crypt [krɪpt] *n Rel* cripta *f*

cryptic ['krɪptɪk] *adj* enigmático(a)

crystal ['krɪstəl] *n* cristal *m*; **a c. vase** un florero de cristal ❏ **c. ball** bola *f* de vidrio *or Esp* cristal; **c. gazing** predicciones *fpl* que se hacen mirando una bola de cristal

crystal-clear [krɪstəl'klɪər] *adj* claro(a) como el agua

crystalline ['krɪstəlaɪn] *adj* cristalino(a)

crystallize ['krɪstəlaɪz] **1** *vt* cristalizar; **crystallized fruits** frutas *fpl* confitadas *or Col Méx* cristalizadas *or RP* abrillantadas

2 *vi* cristalizarse

CST [siːes'tiː] *n US (abbr* **Central Standard Time**) = hora oficial en el centro de los Estados Unidos

ct (**a**) *(abbr* **carat**) quilate *m*, quil (**b**) *(abbr* **cent**) céntimo *m*, centavo *m*

cu (*abbr* **cubic**) cúbico(a)

cub [kʌb] *n* (**a**) *(animal)* cachorro *m* (**b**) *(junior scout)* niño *m* explorador

Cuba ['kjuːbə] *n* Cuba

Cuban ['kjuːbən] *adj & n* cubano(a) *(m,f)*

cubbyhole ['kʌbɪhəʊl] *n* chiribitil *m*

cube [kjuːb] **1** *n* (**a**) *(shape)* cubo *m*; *(of sugar)* terrón *m*; *Culin* **stock c.** pastilla *f* de caldo (**b**) *Math* cubo *m* ❏ **c. root** raíz *f* cúbica

2 *vt* (**a**) *Math* elevar al cubo (**b**) *Culin* cortar en dados

cubic ['kjuːbɪk] *adj* cúbico(a); **c. centimetre** centímetro *m* cúbico

cubicle ['kjuːbɪkəl] *n (gen)* cubículo *m*; *(at swimming pool)* caseta *f*

cubism ['kjuːbɪzəm] *n Art* cubismo *m*

cuckold ['kʌkəld] **1** *n* cornudo *m*

2 *vt* poner los cuernos a

cuckoo ['kʊkuː] **1** *n Orn* cuco *m* común; *(call)* cucú *m* ❏ **c. clock** reloj *m* de cuco *or RP* cucú

2 *adj Fam* lelo(a), majareta, *Méx* zafado(a)

cucumber ['kjuːkʌmbər] *n Culin* pepino *m*

cud [kʌd] *n* **to chew the c.** rumiar

cuddle ['kʌdəl] **1** *vt* abrazar, acariciar; *(baby)* acunar (en los brazos)

2 *vi* abrazarse; **to c. up to sb** acurrucarse contra algn

3 *n* abrazo *m* afectuoso *or* amoroso

cuddly ['kʌdlɪ] *adj* (**cuddlier, cuddliest**) *(child)* mimoso(a); **c. toy** muñeco *m* de peluche

cudgel ['kʌdʒəl] *n* porra *f*; *Fig* **to take up the cudgels for sb** salir en defensa de algn, *Am* quebrar una lanza por algn

cue[1] [kjuː] *n Theat* pie *m*; *Fig* **to take one's c. from sb** seguirle la corriente a algn

cue in *vt* indicar a, hacer una señal a

cue[2] [kjuː] *n Bill* taco *m* ❏ **c. ball** bola *f* blanca *or* con que se juega

cuff[1] [kʌf] *n (of sleeve)* puño *m*; *US (of trousers)* dobladillo *m*; *Fig* **to do sth off the c.** improvisar

cuff[2] [kʌf] **1** *vt* abofetear

2 *n* bofetada *f*

cufflinks ['kʌflɪŋks] *npl (for shirt)* gemelos *mpl*

cuisine [kwɪ'ziːn] *n* cocina *f*

cul-de-sac ['kʌldəsæk] *n* (*pl* **cul-de-sacs**) calle *f* sin salida

culinary ['kʌlɪnərɪ] *adj* culinario(a)

cull [kʌl] **1** *vt* (**a**) *(choose)* escoger (**b**) *(take out) (animals)* eliminar

2 *n (of animals)* eliminación *f*

culminate ['kʌlmɪneɪt] *vi* culminar; **to c. in** terminar en

culmination [kʌlmɪ'neɪʃən] *n* culminación *f*, punto *m* culminante, apogeo *m*

culottes [kjuː'lɒts] *npl (garment)* falda-pantalón *f sing*, *Am* pollera *f sing* pantalón

culpability [kʌlpə'bɪlɪtɪ] *n* culpabilidad *f*

culpable ['kʌlpəbəl] *adj* culpable

culprit ['kʌlprɪt] *n Jur* culpable *mf*

cult [kʌlt] *n* culto *m* ❏ **c. figure** ídolo *m*; **c. film/novel** película *f*/novela *f* de culto

cultivate ['kʌltɪveɪt] *vt* cultivar

cultivated ['kʌltɪveɪtɪd] *adj* (**a**) *(person)* culto(a) (**b**) *(grown, tended)* cultivado(a)

cultivation [kʌltɪ'veɪʃən] *n* cultivo *m* (de la tierra)

cultivator ['kʌltɪveɪtər] *n* (**a**) *(person)* cultivador(a) *m,f* (**b**) *Tech* cultivador *m*

cultural ['kʌltʃərəl] *adj* cultural

culturally ['kʌltʃərəlɪ] *adv* culturalmente

culture ['kʌltʃər] *n* (**a**) *(artistic activity, refinement)* cultura *f*; **ancient c.** cultura de la antigüedad ❏ **c. shock** choque *m* cultural (**b**) *Biol* cultivo *m*

cultured ['kʌltʃəd] *adj see* **cultivated**

cumbersome ['kʌmbəsəm] *adj (awkward)* incómodo(a); *(bulky)* voluminoso(a)

cum(m)in ['kʌmɪn] *n* comino *m*

cumulative ['kjuːmjʊlətɪv] *adj* acumulativo(a)

cunning ['kʌnɪŋ] **1** *adj* astuto(a), mañoso(a)

2 *n* astucia *f*, maña *f*

cunningly ['kʌnɪŋlɪ] *adv* con astucia *or* maña

cunt [kʌnt] *n Offens* coño *m*, *Col* cuca *f*, *Méx* paloma *f*, *Andes RP* concha *f*

cup [kʌp] **1** *n* **(a)** *(for drinking)* taza *f*; **a c. of tea** un té; *Fam* **it's not everyone's c. of tea** no es lo que les gusta a todos **(b)** *Sport* copa *f* ❑ **C. Final** final *f* de copa; **c. tie** partido *m* de copa
2 *vt* (*pt & pp* **cupped**) *(hands)* ahuecar (**round** alrededor de)

cupboard [ˈkʌbəd] *n Furn (for clothes, books)* armario *m*; *(on wall)* alacena *f*; *(for crockery)* aparador *m*

cupcake [ˈkʌpkeɪk] *n* ≃ magdalena *f*

cupful [ˈkʌpfʊl] *n* taza *f* (llena)

Cupid [ˈkjuːpɪd] *n* Cupido *m*

cupidity [kjuːˈpɪdɪtɪ] *n* codicia *f*

cupola [ˈkjuːpələ] *n Archit* cúpula *f*

cuppa [ˈkʌpə] *n Br Fam* **a c.** un té

cur [kɜːr] *n* **(a)** *(dog)* perro *m* de mala raza **(b)** *(person)* canalla *m*

curable [ˈkjʊərəbəl] *adj* curable

curate [ˈkjʊərɪt] *n Rel* cura *m* coadjutor

curative [ˈkjʊərətɪv] *adj & n* curativo(a) *(m)*

curator [kjʊəˈreɪtər] *n (of museum)* conservador(a) *m,f*, director(a) *m,f*

curb [kɜːb] **1** *n* **(a)** *(for horse)* barbada *f*; *Fig* **to put a c. on** poner freno a **(b)** *US (kerb)* bordillo *m* (de la acera), *Chile* solera *f*, *Col Perú* sardinel *m*, *CSur* cordón *m* (de la vereda), *Méx* borde *m* (de la banqueta)
2 *vt (horse)* refrenar; *Fig (public spending)* contener; *Fig (emotions)* controlar

curbstone [ˈkɜːbstəʊn] *n US see* **kerbstone**

curd [kɜːd] *n Culin* cuajada *f*; **lemon c.** crema *f* de limón

curdle [ˈkɜːdəl] **1** *vt (milk)* cuajar
2 *vi (milk)* cuajarse; *(sauce)* cortarse; *Fig* **his blood curdled** se le heló la sangre en las venas

cure [kjʊər] **1** *vt* **(a)** *(illness)* curar; *(habit)* quitar **(b)** *(fish)* curar; *(hide)* curtir
2 *n (remedy)* cura *f*, remedio *m*; *(recovery)* curación *f*, cura *f*

cure-all [ˈkjʊərɔːl] *n* panacea *f*

curettage [kjʊərɪˈtɑːʒ] *n Med* raspado *m*

curfew [ˈkɜːfjuː] *n* toque *m* de queda

curio [ˈkjʊərɪəʊ] *(pl* **curios***)* *n* curiosidad *f*, rareza *f*

curiosity [kjʊərɪˈɒsɪtɪ] *n* curiosidad *f*

curious [ˈkjʊərɪəs] *adj* **(a)** *(inquisitive)* curioso(a) **(b)** *(odd)* extraño(a), singular; *(object)* curioso(a), interesante; **the c. thing is that ...** lo curioso es que ...

curiously [ˈkjʊərɪəslɪ] *adv* curiosamente; **c. enough** aunque parezca mentira

curl [kɜːl] **1** *vt (hair)* rizar; *(lip)* fruncir
2 *vi (hair)* rizarse; *(smoke)* formar una espiral; *(dry leaves)* enrollarse; *(wave)* encresparse
3 *n (of hair)* rizo *m*, *Andes RP* rulo *m*; *(of smoke)* espiral *f*, voluta *f*; **soft c.** bucle *m*; **with a c. of the lips** con una mueca

curl up *vi* enroscarse, acurrucarse; *Fam* **to c. up with a good book** echarse acurrucado(a) leyendo un libro interesante

curler [ˈkɜːlər] *n (for hair)* rulo *m*, *Chile* tubo *m*, *RP* rulero *m*, *Ven* rollo *m*

curlew [ˈkɜːljuː] *n Orn* zarapito *m* ❑ **stone c.** alcaraván *m*

curling [ˈkɜːlɪŋ] **1** *n Sport* curling *m*
2 *adj* **c. tongs** *(for hair)* tenacillas *fpl* de rizar el pelo

curly [ˈkɜːlɪ] *adj* (**curlier, curliest***)* *(hair)* rizado(a), *Chile Col* crespo(a), *Méx* quebrado(a), *RP* enrulado(a)

currant [ˈkʌrənt] *n* **(a)** *Culin (dried grape)* pasa *f* (de

Corinto); **c. bun** bollo *m* con pasas **(b)** *(fruit, on bush)* grosella *f*; **c. bush** grosellero *m*

currency [ˈkʌrənsɪ] *n* **(a)** *Fin* moneda *f*; **foreign c.** divisa *f*, moneda extranjera; **hard c.** divisa *f* fuerte **(b)** *(acceptance)* aceptación *f*; *(idea etc)* **to gain c.** ganar fuerza, irse extendiendo

current [ˈkʌrənt] **1** *adj* **(a)** *(opinions, beliefs, tendency)* general; *(word, phrase)* actual; *(year, month)* en curso ❑ **c. affairs** actualidad *f sing* (política); *Fin* **c. assets** activo *m sing* disponible **(b)** *Br Fin (bank account)* corriente **(c)** **the c. issue** *or* **number** *(latest edition)* el último número
2 *n* **(a)** *(of gas, air, water)* corriente *f*; *Elec* **alternating/direct c.** corriente alterna/continua **(b)** *(trend)* corriente *f*

currently [ˈkʌrəntlɪ] *adv* actualmente, en la actualidad

curriculum [kəˈrɪkjʊləm] *n (pl* **curriculums** *or* **curricula** [kəˈrɪkjʊlə]*)* *Educ* plan *m* de estudios ❑ *esp Br* **c. vitae** currículum *m* (vitae)

curry[1] [ˈkʌrɪ] *n Culin* curry *m*; **chicken c.** pollo *m* al curry
2 *vt (pt & pp* **curried***)* preparar *or* guisar al curry

curry[2] [ˈkʌrɪ] *vt (pt & pp* **curried***)* **to c. favour with sb** congraciarse *or* insinuarse con algn

currycomb [ˈkʌrɪkəʊm] *n* almohaza *f*

curse [kɜːs] **1** *n* maldición *f*; *(oath)* palabrota *f*, *Fig* azote *m*, plaga *f*; *Fam* **to have the c.** *(woman)* tener la regla
2 *vt* maldecir; *Fig* **to be cursed with** *(illness)* sufrir de
3 *vi* blasfemar, maldecir; **to c. at sb** maldecir a algn

cursed [kɜːst] *adj* maldito(a)

cursor [ˈkɜːsər] *n Comptr* cursor *m*; **c. keys** (teclas *fpl* de) flechas *fpl*, teclas *fpl* (de desplazamiento) del cursor

cursorily [ˈkɜːsərəlɪ] *adv* precipitadamente, superficialmente

cursory [ˈkɜːsərɪ] *adj (glance, reading)* rápido(a), superficial

curt [kɜːt] *adj* brusco(a), seco(a)

curtail [kɜːˈteɪl] *vt (expenses)* reducir; *(text)* acortar, abreviar

curtain [ˈkɜːtən] **1** *n* cortina *f*; *Theat* telón *m*; *Fig (of smoke, fog)* velo *m*; **to draw the curtains** correr las cortinas; **to drop/raise the c.** bajar/alzar el telón; *Pol Fig* **the Iron C.** el telón de acero; *Fig* **to draw a c. over sth** correr un tupido velo sobre algo; *Fam* **take care or it'll be curtains for us** ten cuidado o será nuestra perdición ❑ *Theat* **c. call** llamada *f* a escena; **c. ring** anillo *m* (de cortina); **c. rod** varilla *f* de la cortina
2 *vt* poner cortinas a; **to c. off (an area)** esconder *or* dividir (una zona) con una cortina

curts(e)y [ˈkɜːtsɪ] **1** *n* reverencia *f*
2 *vi (pt & pp* **curtseyed** *or* **curtsied***)* hacer una reverencia (**to** a)

curvaceous [kɜːˈveɪʃəs] *adj Fam (woman)* cachas *inv*

curvature [ˈkɜːvətʃər] *n* curvatura *f*; *Med (of the spine)* encorvamiento *m*

curve [kɜːv] **1** *n (in road etc)* curva *f*; *(of woman)* redondez *f*; *Aut* **to take a c.** doblar una curva ❑ *US* **c. ball** *(in baseball)* bola *f* con mucho efecto
2 *vt* encorvar
3 *vi (road, river)* torcer, describir una curva

curved [kɜːvd] *adj* curvo(a), encorvado(a)

cushion [ˈkʊʃən] **1** *n* cojín *m*; *(large)* almohadón *m*; *(of billiard table)* banda *f* ❑ *Tech* **air c.** colchón *m* de aire; **c. cover** funda *f* de almohadón *or* de cojín
2 *vt (blow, impact)* amortiguar; **to c. sb against sth** proteger a algn de algo

cushy [ˈkʊʃɪ] *adj* (**cushier, cushiest***)* *Fam (job, life)* fácil, cómodo(a); **a c. number** una ganga *Esp* un chollo, *Méx* pan *m* comido

cussedness [ˈkʌsɪdnɪs] n Fam terquedad f; **out of sheer c.** por narices

custard [ˈkʌstəd] n **(a)** Culin natillas fpl ❑ **c. powder** polvos mpl para natillas **(b)** (fruit) **c. apple** chirimoya f

custodial [kʌˈstəʊdɪəl] adj Jur **c. sentence** pena f de cárcel

custodian [kʌsˈtəʊdɪən] n (of public building) conserje mf, guarda mf

custody [ˈkʌstədɪ] n custodia f; Jur **in c.** bajo custodia; **to take into c.** detener

custom [ˈkʌstəm] n **(a)** (habit, tradition) costumbre f, hábito m **(b)** Com (patronage) clientela f; **to lose c.** perder clientes or clientela; **to withdraw one's c. from a shop** dejar de ser cliente de una tienda

customary [ˈkʌstəmərɪ] adj acostumbrado(a), habitual

custom-built [kʌstəmˈbɪlt] adj hecho(a) por encargo

customer [ˈkʌstəmər] n cliente mf; Fam **an odd c.** un tipo raro ❑ Com **c. base** clientela f fija, clientes mpl fijos; Com **c. care** atención f al cliente; Com **c. loyalty** fidelidad f del cliente; Com **c. services (department)** (departamento m de) atención f al cliente

customize [ˈkʌstəmaɪz] vt personalizar, hacer por encargo

custom-made [kʌstəmˈmeɪd] adj (suit etc) hecho(a) a la medida

customs [ˈkʌstəmz] npl aduana f; **to go through c.** pasar la aduana ❑ **c. declaration** declaración f en la aduana; **c. duty** derechos mpl de aduana; **c. officer** agente mf de aduana; **c. post** puesto m aduanero

cut [kʌt] **1** vt (pt & pp **cut**) **(a)** (in general) cortar; (stone) tallar; (film) hacer cortes en; (record) grabar; **he's cutting a tooth** le está saliendo un diente; Aut **to c. a corner** tomar una curva muy cerrada; **to c. one's finger** cortarse el dedo; **to c. one's hair** cortarse el pelo (uno mismo); **to c. one's way through the jungle** abrirse paso por la selva; **to c. short a visit** acortar una visita; **to have one's hair c.** hacerse cortar el pelo; Comptr **to c. and paste sth** cortar y pegar algo; Fig **that cuts no ice** no convence; Fig **to c. a long story short** en resumidas cuentas; Fig **to c. corners** recortar presupuestos; Fig **to c. it fine** llegar or contar con el tiempo justo; Fig **to c. sb to the quick** herir a algn en lo más vivo **(b)** (reduce) reducir, rebajar; **to c. one's losses** cortar por lo sano **(c)** (divide up) dividir, partir; **to c. a cake into four** dividir un pastel en cuatro (partes) **(d)** (cards) cortar **(e)** **to c. sb dead** negarse a saludar a algn

2 n **(a)** Elec Med corte m; (in skin) cortadura f, (wound) herida f; (with knife) cuchillada f; Fig **a short c.** un atajo; Fig **the c. and thrust of politics** la esgrima política **(b)** (part cut off) parte f; (of meat) clase f de carne; Fam **to get one's c.** recibir su parte; Fam **a c. of the profits** una parte de los beneficios **(c)** (reduction) reducción f; Press (deletion) corte m **(d)** (of clothes, hair) corte m **(e)** (insult) desaire m, corte m **(f)** Cin corte m **(g)** Fig **to be a c. above sb** estar por encima de algn

3 adj cortado(a); (price) reducido(a); **well c.** (clothes) de buen corte; Fig **c. and dried** convenido(a) de antemano ❑ **c. glass** vidrio m or Esp cristal m tallado

4 vi **(a)** (in general) cortar; **cloth that cuts easily** tela que se corta fácilmente; Fig **that cuts both ways** eso es un arma de dos filos; Fam Fig **to c. loose** romper con todo **(b)** Cin **c.!** ¡corten!; **to c. to the next scene** pasar a la siguiente escena **(c)** **to c. across the fields** coger un atajo campo través

cut back vt (tree) talar; (plant) podar; (expenses) reducir; (production) disminuir

cut down vt (tree) talar, cortar; **to c. down on** (spending) reducir; **to c. down on smoking** fumar menos

cut in vi (in conversation) interrumpir; (driver) adelantar bruscamente

cut off vt (water supply etc) cortar; (place) aislar; (leg) amputar; (heir) excluir; Tel **I've been c. off** me han cortado (la comunicación); Fig **to c. sb off without a penny** desheredar a algn; Fig **to feel c. off** sentirse aislado(a)

cut out 1 vt **(a)** (from newspaper) recortar; Sew (dress) cortar; (person) **to be c. out for sth** estar hecho(a) para algo; Fam **he's got his work c. out** lo tiene difícil **(b)** (exclude, delete) suprimir; **to c. out alcohol** dejar el alcohol; Fam **c. that out!** ¡basta ya!

2 vi (engine) calarse, pararse

cut up 1 vt cortar en pedazos, partir; Culin cortar a pedacitos; Fam **he's very c. up about it** está profundamente afectado por ello

2 vi Br Fam **to c. up rough** enfadarse, ponerse agresivo(a), hacerse el Méx pendejo or RP pavo

cutaneous [kjuːˈteɪnɪəs] adj cutáneo(a)

cutback [ˈkʌtbæk] n reducción f (in de)

cute [kjuːt] adj mono(a), lindo(a); US Fam listillo(a)

cuticle [ˈkjuːtɪkəl] n cutícula f ❑ **c. remover** crema f or líquido m para quitar la cutícula

cutlery [ˈkʌtlərɪ] n cubiertos mpl, cubertería f sing

cutlet [ˈkʌtlɪt] n Culin chuleta f

cutoff [ˈkʌtɒf] n **c. date** fecha f tope; **c. point** límite m, tope m

cutout [ˈkʌtaʊt] n **(a)** (shape) figura f recortada **(b)** Elec cortacircuitos m inv

cut-price [kʌtˈpraɪs] adj (article) a precio rebajado; (shop) de rebajas

cutter [ˈkʌtər] n **(a)** (person) cortador(a) m,f; (of gems) lapidario(a) m,f; (of stone) cantero m **(b)** Naut cúter m, patrullero m

cutthroat [ˈkʌtθrəʊt] **1** n asesino(a) m,f, matón m

2 adj (cruel) cruel; (fierce) feroz

cutting [ˈkʌtɪŋ] **1** n Br (from newspaper) recorte m; Bot esqueje m; Tex retal m; Rail tajo m ❑ Cin **c. room** sala f de montaje

2 adj (edge) cortante; Fig (wind) penetrante; Fig (remark) mordaz; Fig **to be at the c. edge of** estar a la vanguardia de

cuttlefish [ˈkʌtəlfɪʃ] n Zool jibia f, sepia f

CV, cv [siːˈviː] n (abbr **curriculum vitae**) currículum m (vitae)

cwt. (abbr **hundredweight**) **(a)** (metric) 50 kg **(b)** (imperial) Br (112 lb) = 50,8 kg; US (100 lb) = 45,36 kg

cyanide [ˈsaɪənaɪd] n Chem cianuro m

cybercafe [ˈsaɪbəkæfe] n Comptr cibercafé m

cyberculture [ˈsaɪbəkʌltʃər] n Comptr cibercultura f

cybernetics [saɪbəˈnetɪks] n Comptr cibernética f

cyberpunk [ˈsaɪbəpʌŋk] n Comptr (science fiction) ciberpunk m

cyberspace [ˈsaɪbəspeɪs] n Comptr ciberespacio m

cyborg [ˈsaɪbɔːg] n Comptr ciborg m

cyclamen [ˈsɪkləmən] n Bot ciclamen m

cycle [ˈsaɪkəl] **1** n **(a)** (of events) ciclo m **(b)** (bicycle) bicicleta f; (motorcycle) moto f ❑ **c. track** pista f para bicicletas; **c. racing track** velódromo m

2 vi ir en bicicleta

cyclic(al) [ˈsaɪklɪk(əl), ˈsɪklɪk(əl)] adj cíclico(a)

cycling [ˈsaɪklɪŋ] n ciclismo m

cyclist [ˈsaɪklɪst] n ciclista mf

cyclone [ˈsaɪkləʊn] n Meteor ciclón m

cygnet [ˈsɪgnɪt] n Orn pollo m de cisne

cylinder ['sɪlɪndər] *n* (**a**) *Geom Tech* cilindro *m* (**b**) *(for gas)* bombona *f*; **oxygen c.** balón *m* de oxígeno

cylindrical [sɪ'lɪmdrɪkəl] *adj* cilíndrico(a)

cymbal ['sɪmbəl] *n Mus* címbalo *m*, platillo *m*

cynic ['sɪnɪk] *n* cínico(a) *m,f*

cynical ['sɪnɪkəl] *adj* cínico(a)

cynicism ['sɪnɪsɪzəm] *n* cinismo *m*

cypress ['saɪprəs] *n Bot* ciprés *m* ❏ **Italian c.** ciprés *m*; **swamp c.** ciprés *m* de los pantanos

Cypriot ['sɪprɪət] *adj & n* chipriota *(mf)*

Cyprus ['saɪprəs] *n* Chipre

cyst [sɪst] *n Med* quiste *m*

cystitis [sɪ'staɪtɪs] *n Med* cistitis *f*

czar [zɑːr] *n* zar *m*

Czech [tʃek] **1** *adj* checo(a); **C. Republic** República Checa **2** *n* (**a**) *(person)* checo(a) *m,f* (**b**) *(language)* checo *m*

Czechoslovak [tʃekəʊ'sləʊvæk] *adj & n Formerly* checoslovaco(a) *(m,f)*

Czechoslovakia [tʃekəʊsləʊ'vækɪə] *n Formerly* Checoslovaquia

Czechoslovakian [tʃekəʊsləʊ'vækɪən] *adj & n Formerly see* **Czechoslovak**

D

D, d [di:] *n (the letter)* D, d *f*

D [di:] *n Mus* re *m*

'd = would; had; **he'd seen** había visto; **I'd have gone** habría ido

DA [di:'eɪ] *n US Jur (abbr* **District Attorney***)* fiscal *mf* (del distrito)

dab¹ [dæb] **1** *n* (**a**) *(small quantity)* toque *m* (**b**) *Br Fam* **dabs** *(fingerprints)* huellas *fpl* digitales
  2 *vt (pt & pp* **dabbed***)* (**a**) *(apply)* aplicar (**b**) *(touch lightly)* tocar ligeramente; *(spilt liquid)* frotar

dab² [dæb] *n (fish)* ≃ acedia *f*

dab³ [dæb] *n Br Fam* **to be a d. hand** ser un manitas

dabble ['dæbəl] **1** *vi* interesarse superficialmente, tener afición; **to d. in politics** meterse en política
  2 *vt (in water)* chapotear

dabbler ['dæblər] *n Pej* pseudoaficionado(a) *m,f*, amateur *mf*; *(in politics)* politiquero(a) *m,f*

dachshund ['dækshund] *n* perro *m* salchicha

dad [dæd] *n Fam*, **daddy** ['dædɪ] *n Fam* papá *m*, papi *m*

daddy-longlegs [dædɪ'lɒŋlegz] *n inv Fam* (**a**) *Br (insect)* típula *f* (**b**) *US (harvestman)* segador *m*

daffodil ['dæfədɪl] *n Bot* narciso *m*

daft [dɑːft] *adj Br Fam* tonto(a), *Am* sonso(a), *Am* zonzo(a); **to be d. about sb/sth** estar loco(a) por algn/algo

dagger ['dægər] *n* puñal *m*, daga *f*; *Fig* **to be at daggers drawn (with sb)** estar a matar (con algn); *Fig* **to look** or *US* **shoot daggers at sb** fulminar a algn con la mirada

dago ['deɪɡəʊ] *n (pl* **dagos** or **dagoes***) Slang Offens* persona *f* de raza latina

dahlia ['deɪljə] *n Bot* dalia *f*

daily ['deɪlɪ] **1** *adj* diario(a), cotidiano(a); **our d. bread** el pan nuestro de cada día
  2 *adv* diariamente, a diario; **three times d.** tres veces al día
  3 *n* (**a**) *(newspaper)* diario *m* (**b**) *Br Fam (cleaning lady)* asistenta *f*

dainty ['deɪntɪ] **1** *adj* (**daintier, daintiest**) (**a**) *(lace, china, flower)* delicado(a), fino(a) (**b**) *(child)* precioso(a); *(figure, manners)* exquisito(a)
  2 dainties *npl (sweets)* golosinas *fpl*

dairy ['deərɪ] *n (on farm)* vaquería *f*; *(shop)* lechería *f*; **d. farming** industria *f* lechera; **d. produce** productos *mpl* lácteos

dais ['deɪɪs] *n (in hall etc)* tarima *f*; *(in official ceremony)* estrado *m*

daisy ['deɪzɪ] *n Bot* margarita *f*; *Fam Hum* **to be pushing up the daisies** estar criando malvas ❑ **d. chain** collar *m* de margaritas

daisywheel ['deɪzɪwiːl] *n (typewriter, printer)* margarita *f*

dale [deɪl] *n Literary* valle *m*, hondonada *f*

dally ['dælɪ] *vi (pt & pp* **dallied***) (be slow)* tardar (**over** en); *(waste time)* perder el tiempo; **don't d. about** no te entretengas

dally with *vt (idea, thought)* acariciar; *Old-fashioned (person)* flirtear con, coquetear con

Dalmatian [dæl'meɪʃən] *n Zool* perro *m* dálmata, dálmata *m*

dam¹ [dæm] **1** *n (barrier)* dique *m*; *(lake)* embalse *m*, presa *f*
  2 *vt (pt & pp* **dammed***) (water)* embalsar, represar, estancar; **to d. (up) a river** construir una presa sobre un río

dam up *vt Fig (emotion)* contener, reprimir

dam² [dæm] *n Zool (of lamb etc)* madre *f*

damage ['dæmɪdʒ] **1** *n* (**a**) *(gen)* daño *m*; *(to health, reputation)* perjuicio *m*; *(to relationship)* deterioro *m*; *Br Fam* **what's the d.?** la dolorosa, por favor; **d. limitation** limitación *f* de daños (**b**) *Jur* **damages** daños *mpl* y perjuicios *mpl*
  2 *vt (harm)* dañar, hacer daño a; *(spoil)* estropear; *(undermine)* perjudicar, causar deterioro en

damaging ['dæmɪdʒɪŋ] *adj* perjudicial

damask ['dæməsk] *n Tex* damasco *m*

dame [deɪm] *n* (**a**) *US Fam* mujer *f*, tía *f*, *CSur* mina *f*, *Méx* vieja *f* (**b**) *Br (title)* dama *f* (**c**) *Br (in pantomime)* vieja *f*

damn [dæm] **1** *vt (gen)* condenar; *Fam* (**I'm**) **damned if I know** (no tengo) ni idea
  2 *interj Fam* **d. (it)!** ¡maldito(a) sea!; **well, I'm** or **I'll be damned!** ¡vaya por Dios!, ¡mecachis!
  3 *n Fam* **I don't give a d.** me importa un rábano or un bledo
  4 *adj Fam* maldito(a), condenado(a); **it's a d. nuisance!** ¡vaya lata!
  5 *adv Fam* muy, sumamente; **I was d. lucky** tuve muchísima suerte; **you know d. well what I mean** sabes de sobra lo que quiero decir

damnation [dæm'neɪʃən] **1** *n Rel* condenación *f*
  2 *interj* ¡maldito(a) sea!

damned [dæmd] **1** *adj & adv see* **damn** 4 & 5
  2 the d. *npl Rel* los condenados

damnedest ['dæmdɪst] *n Fam* **to do one's d. to ...** hacer todo lo posible para ...

damning ['dæmɪŋ] *adj* (**a**) *(proof, evidence)* indiscutible, irrefutable (**b**) *(remark, criticism)* mordaz

damp [dæmp] **1** *adj (gen)* húmedo(a); *(wet)* mojado(a)
  2 *n* humedad *f*
  3 *vt* (**a**) *(for ironing)* humedecer (**b**) **to d. (down)** *(fire)*

sofocar; *Fig (violence)* reducir, frenar; *(enthusiasm)* desalentar

dampcourse ['dæmpkɔːs] *n Constr* aislante *m* hidrófugo

dampen ['dæmpən] *vt* humedecer; *Fig* reducir, frenar

damper ['dæmpər] *n* (**a**) *(in chimney)* regulador *m* de tiro (**b**) *Mus* sordina *f* (**c**) *Fam Fig (restraint)* freno *m*; *Fig* **to put a d. on sth** poner freno a algo

damsel ['dæmzəl] *n Literary* doncella *f*; **d. in distress** chica *f* en apuros

damson ['dæmzən] *n Bot (fruit)* ciruela *f* damascena; *(tree)* ciruelo *m* damasceno

dance [dɑːns] **1** *n* (**a**) *(gen)* baile *m*; *(classical, tribal)* danza *f*; *(formal)* baile *m* de etiqueta; *Br Fam Fig* **to lead sb a (merry) d.** traer a algn al retortero □ **d. band** orquesta *f* de baile; **d. floor** pista *f* de baile; **d. hall** salón *m* de baile

2 *vi* (**a**) *(gen)* bailar; **to d. about** dar saltos, brincar (**b**) *(leaves, waves)* danzar, agitarse, moverse

3 *vt (gen)* bailar; *Br Fig* **to d. attendance on sb** desvivirse por complacer a algn

dancer ['dɑːnsər] *n (by profession)* bailarín(ina) *m,f*; *(of flamenco)* bailador(a) *m,f*; *(person dancing)* bailador(a) *m,f*

dancing ['dɑːnsɪŋ] *adj* de baile; *Fig (eyes)* que baila □ **d. girl** corista *f*

dandelion ['dændɪlaɪən] *n Bot* diente *m* de león

dandruff ['dændrəf] *n* caspa *f*

dandy ['dændɪ] **1** *n Pej* dandy *m*, petimetre *m*

2 *adj* (**dandier, dandiest**) *US Fam* estupendo(a); **fine and d.** perfecto, de perlas

Dane [deɪn] *n* danés(esa) *m,f*

danger ['deɪndʒər] *n* (**a**) *(risk)* riesgo *m*; **there was a** or **some d. of war** amenazaba la posibilidad de una guerra (**b**) *(peril)* peligro *m*; **'d.'** 'peligro'; **out of d.** fuera de peligro; *Med* **to be on the d. list** estar en estado crítico, estar grave □ **d. money** or *US* **pay** prima *f* de peligrosidad

dangerous ['deɪndʒərəs] *adj (gen)* peligroso(a); *(risky)* arriesgado(a); *(harmful)* nocivo(a); *(illness)* grave

dangerously ['deɪndʒərəslɪ] *adv (gen)* peligrosamente

dangle ['dæŋgəl] **1** *vi (hang)* colgar, pender; *(swing)* balancearse; *Fam* **to keep sb dangling** tener a algn pendiente

2 *vt (arms, legs)* colgar; *(bait)* dejar colgado(a); *(swing)* balancear en el aire; *Fig* **bonuses were dangled before the workers** se intentaba persuadir a los trabajadores ofreciéndoles primas

Danish ['deɪnɪʃ] **1** *adj* danés(esa) □ *Culin* **D. pastry** brioche *m* danés

2 *n* (**a**) *pl* **the D.** los daneses (**b**) *(language)* danés *m*

dank [dæŋk] *adj* húmedo(a) y malsano(a)

Danube ['dænjuːb] *n* **the D.** el Danubio

dapper ['dæpər] *adj* pulcro(a), aseado(a)

dappled ['dæpəld] *adj (shade)* moteado(a); *(horse)* rodado(a)

dapple-grey [dæpəl'greɪ] *adj & n (horse)* torildo(a) *(m,f)*

dare [deər] **1** *vi* atreverse, osar; **don't you d. (to) tell him!** ¡no se te ocurra decírselo!; **he d. not** or **he doesn't d. be late** no se atreve a llegar tarde; **how d. you!** ¿cómo te atreves?, ¡qué cara tienes!; *esp Br* **I d. say** quizás, posiblemente; *Iron* ya (lo creo)

2 *vt (challenge)* desafiar; **hit me — I d. you!** ¡pégame! — ¡a que no te atreves!

3 *n* desafío *m*, reto *m*; **I did it as a d.** me lo tomé como un desafío

daredevil ['deədevəl] *adj & n* atrevido(a) *(m,f)*, temerario(a) *(m,f)*

daring ['deərɪŋ] **1** *adj* (**a**) *(bold)* audaz, osado(a), atrevi-

do(a) (**b**) *(unconventional)* original; *(shocking)* atrevido(a)

2 *n* atrevimiento *m*, osadía *f*

dark [dɑːk] **1** *adj* (**a**) *(unlit)* oscuro(a); **it gets d. by five** a las cinco ya es de noche (**b**) *(colour)* oscuro(a); *(hair, complexion)* moreno(a); *(eyes)* negro(a); *(glasses)* oscuro(a) (**c**) *Fig (gloomy)* triste; *(future)* negro(a), tenebroso(a); *(forebodings)* sombrío(a) □ **the D. Ages** la Edad de las tinieblas (**d**) *Fig (secret)* secreto(a), misterioso(a), oscuro(a); *Fig* **to be a d. horse** ser una incógnita (**e**) *Fig (sinister)* siniestro(a), tenebroso(a)

2 *n* (**a**) *(darkness)* oscuridad *f*, tinieblas *fpl*; **before/after d.** antes/después del anochecer (**b**) *Fig* **to be in the d. (about sth)** estar a oscuras or estar en tinieblas (sobre algo), no saber nada (sobre algo); **to keep sb in the d. (about sth)** no dar a conocer (algo) a algn

darken ['dɑːkən] **1** *vt (sky)* oscurecer; *(room, colour)* hacer más oscuro(a); *Fig* **never d. my door again!** ¡no vuelvas nunca a pisar (el umbral) de mi casa!

2 *vi (sky)* oscurecerse, ponerse más oscuro(a); *(sky)* nublarse; *Fig (face, eyes)* ensombrecerse

darkish ['dɑːkɪʃ] *adj (colour)* tirando a or bastante oscuro(a); *(complexion, hair)* tirando a or bastante moreno(a)

darkly ['dɑːklɪ] *adv (say, hint)* con tono sombrío

darkness ['dɑːknɪs] *n* oscuridad *f*, tinieblas *fpl*; **in d.** a oscuras

darkroom ['dɑːkruːm] *n Phot* cuarto *m* oscuro, cámara *f* oscura

darky *n*, **darkie** ['dɑːkɪ] *n Offens* negrito(a) *m,f*

darling ['dɑːlɪŋ] **1** *n* querido(a) *m,f*, cariño *m*, amor *m*; *Fig* **she's the d. of the press** es la favorita de los periodistas; *Fam* **be a d. and get me a drink** sé bueno(a) y tráeme algo para beber

2 *adj* (**a**) *(loved)* querido(a) (**b**) *Fam (charming)* encantador(a), precioso(a); **what a d. little baby!** ¡qué monada de criatura!

darn¹ [dɑːn] **1** *vt (sock etc)* zurcir

2 *n (in sock etc)* zurcido *m*

darn² [dɑːn] **1** *vt Fam Euph see* **damn 1**

2 *adj Fam Euph see* **damn 4**

3 *interj Fam Euph see* **damn 2**

darning ['dɑːnɪŋ] *n* (**a**) *(act)* zurcidora *f* □ **d. needle** aguja *f* de zurcir (**b**) *(before)* cosas *fpl* por zurcir; *(after)* cosas *fpl* zurcidas

dart [dɑːt] **1** *n* (**a**) *(missile)* dardo *m*, rehilete *m* (**b**) *(sudden rush)* movimiento *m* rápido; **to make a d. for sth** lanzarse or precipitarse hacia algo (**c**) *Sew* pinza *f* (**d**) **darts** *sing (game)* dardos *mpl*

2 *vi (rush suddenly)* lanzarse, precipitarse; *(run about)* corretear; *(fly about)* revolotear; **to d. in/out** entrar/salir corriendo

3 *vt (look, glance)* echar un vistazo

dartboard ['dɑːtbɔːd] *n* blanco *m* de tiro

dash¹ [dæʃ] **1** *n* (**a**) *(rush)* carrera *f*; *Fam* **to make a d. for it** echarse a correr (**b**) *esp US (race)* sprint *m*, esprint *m* (**c**) *(small amount)* poco *m*, poquito *m*; *(of salt, spice)* pizca *f*; *(of liquid)* chorrillo *m*, chorrito *m*, gota *f*; *Fig* nota *f*, toque *m* (**d**) *Typ* raya *f*; *(hyphen)* guión *m*; *(in Morse)* raya *f* (**e**) *(vitality)* brío *m*, dinamismo *m*; *(style)* elegancia *f*; *Fig* **to cut a d.** causar sensación

2 *vt* (**a**) *(throw)* lanzar, arrojar; **to d. sth to the ground** tirar algo al suelo (**b**) *(smash)* estrellar, romper; **to d. sth to pieces** hacer algo añicos; *Fig* **to dash sb's hopes** desvanecer las esperanzas de algn

3 *vi* (**a**) *(rush)* correr; **to d. around** or **about** correr de un lado a otro; **to d. away** or **out** salir corriendo or disparado(a); *Fam* **I must d.!** ¡me voy pitando! (**b**) **to d. against/over** *(waves etc)* estrellarse or romper contra/ sobre

dash off 1 *vt (letter, note)* escribir a la carrera *orAm* a todo apuro

2 *vi* salir corriendo *or* disparado(a)

dash² [dæʃ] *interj Br Fam* ¡mecachis!

dashboard ['dæʃbɔːd] *n Aut* tablero *m* de mandos, *Esp* salpicadero *m*

dashing ['dæʃɪŋ] *adj (appearance)* garboso(a), gallardo(a); *(performance)* dinámico(a), lleno(a) de brío

DAT [diːeɪˈtiː] *n (abbr digital audio tape)* cinta *f* digital de audio, DAT

data ['deɪtə, 'dɑːtə] *n* datos *mpl*, información *f* ◻ *Comptr* **d. bank** *or* **base** banco *m* de datos; **d. capture** recolección *f* de datos; *Comptr* **d. processing** *(act)* proceso *m* de datos; *(science)* informática *f*; *Br* **D. Protection Act** = ley de protección de datos

database ['deɪtəbeɪs] *n Comptr* base *f* de datos

date¹ [deɪt] **1** *n* **(a)** *(day)* fecha *f*; **at a later d.** más tarde; **out of d.** *(ideas)* anticuado(a), pasado(a) de moda; *(expression)* desusado(a); *(invalid)* caducado(a), vencido(a); **to d.** hasta la fecha; **what's the d. today?** ¿a qué fecha estamos hoy?, *Am* ¿a cómo estamos? *Fig* **to be up to d. (on sth)** estar al tanto *or* estar al corriente (de algo) ◻ **closing d.** fecha *f* tope *or* límite; **d. of birth** fecha *f* de nacimiento; **sell-by d.** *(on foods)* fecha *f* de caducidad; **d. stamp** sello *m* de fecha **(b)** *(meeting)* cita *f* ◻ **blind d.** cita *f* a ciegas; **d. rape** = violación por una persona a la que se ha conocido de forma circunstancial o en una cita **(c)** *US Fam (person dated)* pareja *f*; **who's your d.?** ¿con quién sales?, ¿con quién tienes cita?

2 *vt* **(a)** *(ruins etc)* datar **(b)** *(person)* demostrar la edad de, hacer parecer mayor **(c)** *US Fam (go out with)* salir con

3 *vi (ideas)* quedar anticuado(a), pasar de moda; *(expression)* caer en desuso; **to d. (from** *or* **back to)** remontar a, datar de

date² [deɪt] *n (fruit)* dátil *m* ◻ **d. palm** datilera *f*, palmera *f* datilera

dated ['deɪtɪd] *adj (ideas)* anticuado(a); *(fashion)* pasado(a) de moda; *(expression)* desusado(a)

date-stamp ['deɪtstæmp] *vt (book, letter)* fechar, poner fecha a

dating agency ['deɪtɪŋ'eɪdʒənsɪ] *n* agencia *f* de contactos

dative ['deɪtɪv] *n Ling* dativo *m*; **d. case** caso *m* dativo

daub [dɔːb] **1** *vt (with mud, paint, ink)* embadurnar **(with** con, de); *(with oil, grease)* untar **(with** con**)**

2 *vi Fam (paint badly)* pintorrear, pintarrajear

daughter ['dɔːtər] *n* hija *f*; **baby d.** nena *f*, hijita *f*; **only d.** hija *f* única; *Fig* **she was a true d. of her times** era hija de su tiempo ◻ *Biol* **d. cell** célula *f* hija

daughter-in-law ['dɔːtərɪnlɔː] *n (pl* **daughters-in-law)** nuera *f*, hija *f* política

daunt [dɔːnt] *vt* intimidar, desanimar, desalentar

daunting ['dɔːntɪŋ] *adj* desalentador(a), que inspira miedo

dauntless ['dɔːntlɪs] *adj esp Literary* intrépido(a), impávido(a)

dawdle ['dɔːdəl] *vi Fam (in walking)* andar despacio; *(waste time)* perder el tiempo, entretenerse

dawn [dɔːn] **1** *n* **(a)** *(daybreak)* alba *f*, amanecer *m*; **at (the) break of d.** al rayar el alba; **to work from d. till dusk** trabajar de sol a sol ◻ **d. chorus** canto *m* de los pájaros al amanecer; **d. raid** *(by soldiers, police)* incursión *f* de madrugada; *(on stock exhange)* = compra masiva de acciones al comienzo de la sesión **(b)** *(of life, civilization)* albores *mpl*, despertar *m*

2 *vi* **(a)** *(day)* amanecer **(b)** *Fig (age, hope)* comenzar, nacer **(c)** *Fig (truth)* **to d. (on** *or* **upon)** comprender poco a poco;

suddenly it dawned on him that ... de repente se dio cuenta *or* cayó en la cuenta de que ...

day [deɪ] *n* **(a)** *(24 hours)* día *m*; **any d. now** cualquier día de éstos, de un día a otro; **d. after d., d. in, d. out** día tras día; **d. by d.** diariamente, día a día; **every d.** todos los días, a diario; **every other d.** cada dos días, un día sí y otro no; **from one d. to the next** de un día para otro; **from this d. onward(s)** de hoy en adelante; **good d.!** ¡buenos días!; **in a few days' time** dentro de unos días; **once a d.** una vez al día; **one (fine) d., some d., one of these days** un día de éstos; **(on) the next** *or* **following d.** el *or* al día siguiente; **the d. after tomorrow** pasado mañana; **the d. before yesterday** anteayer; **the d. that ...** el día en que ...; **the other d.** el otro día; **this very d.** hoy mismo; **two years ago to the d.** hoy hace dos años; *Fig* **to live from d. to d.** vivir al día; *Fig* **to win the d.** llevarse la palma; *Fam* **from d. one** desde el primer momento; *Fam* **he's forty if he's a d.** tendrá los cuarenta años cumplidos; *Fam* **that'll be the d.!** ¡cuándo las ranas críen pelos será!; *Fam* **to call it a d.** *(finish)* dar por acabado un trabajo; *(give up)* darse por vencido(a); *Fam* **today was one of those days** hoy todo ha salido mal; *Fam* **to make sb's d.** poner contento(a) a algn ◻ **Christmas D.** día *m* de Navidad; *Br* **d. return (ticket)** *(on train, bus, etc)* billete *m* *or Am* boleto *m* de ida y vuelta para el mismo día; **d. trip** excursión *f* de un día **(b)** *(period of daylight)* día *m*; **a winter's d.** un día de invierno; **by d.** de día; **d. and night** continuamente, de día y de noche; **we had a d. in the country** fuimos un día de campo; **what an awful d.!** ¡qué día más malo! ◻ *Br* **d. care** servicio *m* de guardería (infantil); **d. nursery** guardería *f* (infantil); *Ind* **d. shift** *(time, staff)* turno *m* de día **(c)** *(period of work)* jornada *f*; **an eight-hour d.** una jornada de ocho horas; **paid by the d.** pagado(a) a jornal; *esp US* **to work days** trabajar de día; *Fig* **it's all in a d.'s work** son gajes del oficio ◻ **d. off** día *m* de fiesta **(d)** *(era)* época *f*; **in (the) olden days** antaño; **in those days** en aquellos tiempos; **the best poet of his d.** el mejor poeta de su tiempo; **the good old days** los buenos tiempos de antaño; **these days, in this d. and age** hoy (en) día; *Fig* **he's had his d. as an athlete** ya no sirve para ser atleta; *Fig* **it's still early days** aún es temprano

dayboy ['deɪbɔɪ] *n esp Br Educ* externo *m*

daybreak ['deɪbreɪk] *n* amanecer *m*, alba *f*; **at d.** al amanecer, al alba

daydream ['deɪdriːm] **1** *n (reverie)* ensueño *m*; *(vain, hope)* fantasía *f*, ilusión *f*

2 *vi (have reverie)* soñar despierto(a); *(hope vainly)* hacerse ilusiones

daygirl ['deɪgɜːl] *n Br Educ* externa *f*

daylight ['deɪlaɪt] *n* **(a)** *(sunlight)* luz *f* del día; **in broad d.** en pleno día; **in** *or* **by d.** de día; **it's still d.** aún es de día; *Fig* **to (begin to) see d.** (empezar a) ver las cosas claras; *esp Br Fam Fig* **it's d. robbery!** ¡es un robo *or* una estafa! **(b)** *Fam* **to beat/knock the (living) daylights out of sb** darle/pegarle a algn una paliza tremenda; **to scare the (living) daylights out of sb** pegarle a algn un susto de muerte

daytime ['deɪtaɪm] *n* día *m*; **in the d.** de día; **d. TV** programación *f* diurna *or* de día

day-to-day ['deɪtədeɪ] *adj* cotidiano(a), diario(a)

daze [deɪz] **1** *n* aturdimiento *m*; **in a d.** aturdido(a), atontado(a)

2 *vt* aturdir, atontar

dazed [deɪzd] *adj* aturdido(a), atontado(a)

dazzle ['dæzəl] **1** *n (momentary blindness)* deslumbramiento *m*; *(brightness)* resplandor *m*

2 *vt* deslumbrar

dB *Tech (abbr* **decibel(s))** decibel(es), decibelio(s) *m(pl)*, dB

DC [diːˈsiː] *n* **(a)** *Elec (abbr* **direct current)** corriente *f* continua **(b)** *(abbr* **District of Columbia)** DC, Distrito de Columbia

D-day ['di:deɪ] *n* día *m* D

deacon ['di:kən] *n* diácono *m*

deaconess ['di:kənɪs] *n* diaconisa *f*

deactivate [di:'æktɪveɪt] *vt* desactivar

dead [ded] **1** *adj* **(a)** *(gen)* muerto(a); *(matter)* inerte; **d. woman** muerta *f*; **he was shot d.** le mataron de un tiro *or* a tiros; **to be d.** estar muerto(a); **to drop (down) d.** caer muerto(a); *Fig* **to be d. to the world** *(asleep)* estar dormido(a) como un tronco; *(unconscious)* estar sin sentido; *Fam* **drop d.!** ¡vete al cuerno!; *Fam* **I wouldn't be seen d. in that hat!** no me pondría ese sombrero por nada del mundo; *Fam* **to be d. and buried, to be d. as a doornail** estar muerto(a) y bien muerto(a); *Fam Fig* **I'm absolutely d!** ¡estoy muerto(a)!, ¡estoy agotado(a)!; *Fam Fig* **over my d. body!** ¡moriré antes!; *Fam Fig* **to be d. from the neck up** estar más torpe que un arado ❑ **d. body** cadáver *m*; *Fam Fig* **d. duck** fracaso *m* total; **d. man** muerto *m*; **d. march** marcha *f* fúnebre; **the D. Sea** el mar Muerto; **d. weight** peso *m* muerto **(b)** *(match)* calado(a); *(machine)* averiado(a); *(telephone)* cortado(a) **(c)** *(out of use)* *(language)* muerto(a); *(custom)* desusado(a); *(topic, issue)* agotado(a); **(d)** *(numb)* entumecido(a); *(limb, foot, etc)* adormecido(a); **my leg's gone d.** se me ha dormido la pierna **(e)** *(total)* *(silence, secrecy)* total, completo(a), absoluto(a); **to come to a d. stop** pararse en seco ❑ **d. end** callejón *m* sin salida; *Fig* **d.-end job** trabajo *m* sin porvenir; *Sport* **d. heat** empate *m*, final *m* reñido; *Fam* **d. loss** nulidad *f*, inútil *m*, birria *f*

2 *adv* **(a)** *(totally)* completamente, absolutamente, totalmente; *Fam* **d. drunk** borracho(a) perdido(a); *Fam* **d. easy** sumamente fácil; *Aut* **'d. slow'** 'al paso'; *Fam* **to be d. (set) against** sth oponerse totalmente a algo; *Fam* **to be d. set on** sth/on doing sth empeñarse en algo/en hacer algo; *Fam* **you're d. right** tienes toda la razón **(b)** *(exactly)* justo; **d. in the centre** justo *or* precisamente en medio; **d. on time** a la hora en punto **(c)** *(suddenly)* abruptamente; **to stop d.** pararse en seco **(d)** *(very)* muy; *Fam* **d. beat, d. tired** muerto(a), rendido(a); *Fam* **it's d. easy!** ¡está chupado(a)!

3 *n* **(a)** **the d.** *npl* los muertos **(b)** *(depths)* **at d. of night** a altas horas de la noche; **in the d. of winter** en pleno invierno

deadbeat ['dedbi:t] **1** *n US Fam (drop-out)* pasota *mf*
2 *adj Fam (tired)* reventado(a), hecho(a) polvo

deaden ['dedən] *vt (impact, noise)* amortiguar; *Fig (pain, feeling)* calmar, aliviar

deadline ['dedlaɪn] *n (date)* fecha *f* tope; *(time)* hora *f* tope; **to meet a d.** acabar *or* entregar un trabajo dentro del plazo; **to work to deadlines** respetar plazos

deadlock ['dedlɒk] *n* punto *m* muerto, callejón *m* sin salida; **the talks reached d.** las discusiones llegaron a un punto muerto

deadly ['dedli] **1** *adj* **(deadlier, deadliest) (a)** *(gen)* mortal; *(weapon, gas)* mortífero(a); *(aim)* certero(a); *Rel* **the seven d. sins** los siete pecados capitales **(b)** *(absolute)* completo(a), total; **d. silence** silencio de muerte **(c)** *Fam (very dull)* aburridísimo(a)
2 *adv (extremely)* terriblemente, sumamente; **d. boring** aburridísimo(a)

deadpan ['dedpæn] *Fam* **1** *adj* **(a)** *(face)* sin expresión, inexpresivo(a) **(b)** *(humour, grin)* socarrón(ona), guasón(ona)
2 *adv* **(a)** *(look)* sin expresión **(b)** *(act)* de una manera socarrona

deadwood ['dedwʊd] *n Fig* persona *f* or cosa *f* inútil; **to prune out the d.** *(in organization)* echar al personal que ya no sirve; *(in text)* quitar el material que sobra

deaf [def] **1** *adj* sordo(a); **to be d. in one ear** estar sordo(a) de un oído; **to go d.** quedarse sordo(a); *Fig* **to turn a d. ear** hacerse el sordo; *Fam* **to be stone d., be as d. as a (door)post** estar más sordo(a) que una tapia ❑ **d. mute** sordomudo(a) *m*,*f*
2 the d. *npl* los sordos; **the d. and dumb** los sordomudos

deaf-aid ['defeɪd] *n Br* audífono *m*

deaf-and-dumb [defən'dʌm] *adj* sordomudo(a)

deafen ['defən] *vt* ensordecer

deafening ['defənɪŋ] *adj* ensordecedor(a)

deafness ['defnɪs] *n* sordera *f*

deal[1] [di:l] *n* madera *f* de abeto *or* de pino

deal[2] [di:l] **1** *n* **(a)** *Com Pol* trato *m*, pacto *m*; **a new d. for nurses** un programa de reformas para enfermeras; **business d.** negocio *m*, transacción *f*; **fair** *or* **square d.** trato *m* justo; **the d.'s on/off** vale/no vale el trato; **to do** *or* **make a d. with sb** *(transaction)* hacer *or* cerrar un trato con algn; *(agreement)* pactar algo con algn, llegar a un acuerdo con algn; *Iron* **big d!** ¡vaya cosa!; *Fam* **it's a d.!** ¡trato hecho!, ¡de acuerdo!; *Fam Fig* **he got a rough** *or* **raw d. from life** la vida le trató mal **(b)** *(amount)* cantidad *f*; **a good** *or* **great d. (of sth)** una gran parte *or* cantidad (de algo); **a good d. slower** mucho más despacio; **it means a good d. to me** me importa mucho, significa mucho para mí; *Fig* **to make a great d. of sth** dar a algn con mucha atención **(c)** *Cards* reparto *m*; **it's your d.** te toca a ti repartir

2 *vt (pt & pp dealt)* **(a)** *Cards* repartir **(to a)**, dar **(to a) (b)** *(give)* dar; **to d. sb a blow** asestarle un golpe a algn; *Fig* **the article dealt a blow for freedom** el artículo ganó la batalla de la libertad

3 *vi Cards* repartir, dar

deal in *vt (goods)* comerciar en, tratar en; *(illegal drugs)* traficar en *or* con

deal out *vt Cards* repartir, dar; *Fig* repartir

deal with *vt* **(a)** *(firm, person)* tratar con **(b)** *(subject, problem)* abordar, ocuparse de, encargarse de; *Com (order)* despachar; **it's not to be dealt with lightly** no se debe tomar a la ligera **(c)** *(subject, theme)* tratar de

dealer ['di:lər] *n* **(a)** *Com (in goods)* comerciante *mf*, negociante *mf*; *(in illegal drugs)* traficante *mf* **(b)** *Cards* repartidor(a) *m*,*f*

dealings ['di:lɪŋz] *npl* **(a)** *(relations)* trato *m* sing, relaciones *fpl* personales; **to have d. with sb** tener trato con algn **(b)** *Com (transactions)* negocios *mpl*, transacciones *fpl*

dealt [delt] *pt & pp see* **deal**[2]

dean [di:n] *n* **(a)** *Rel* deán *m* **(b)** *Univ* decano *m*

dear [dɪər] **1** *adj* **(a)** *(loved)* querido(a); **a d. friend** un amigo *or* una amiga entrañable; **my dearest wife** mi queridísima mujer; **to hold sth/sb d.** apreciar mucho algo/a algn, tener cariño a algo/algn **(b)** *(in letter)* Querido(a); *Fam* **D. Andrew** Querido Andrew; *Fml* **D. Madam** Estimada señora; *Fml* **D. Sir(s)** Muy señor(es) mío(s) **(c)** *(precious)* **it is very d.** to me le tengo un gran cariño **(d)** *Br (expensive)* caro(a); *(price)* elevado(a)
2 *adv (buy, sell)* caro; *Fig* **it cost me d.** me costó caro
3 *n* querido(a) *m*,*f*, cariño *m*, cielo *m*, chato(a) *m*,*f*; *Br* **be a d. and hold this** sé bueno y aguántame esto; **my d.** mi vida, mi amor; **she's a d.** es un amor *or* un cielo *or* un encanto; **(you) poor d.!** ¡pobrecito! ❑ *Fam (woman)* **old d.** viejecita *f*
4 *interj* **oh d.!, d. me!** *(surprise)* ¡vaya por Dios!, ¡caramba!; *(disappointment)* ¡qué pena!, ¡qué lástima!

dearie *n*, **deary** ['dɪəri] *n Br Fam* querido(a) *m*,*f*, chato(a) *m*,*f*

dearly ['dɪəli] *adv* mucho, muchísimo; **he loved her d.** le tenía gran cariño; **I'd d. love to know** me encantaría saberlo; *Fig* **he paid d. for his mistake** su error le costó caro

dearth [dɜ:θ] n Fml escasez f, falta f, carencia f

death [deθ] n (a) (gen) muerte f; Fml fallecimiento m, defunción f; **to bleed to d.** morir desangrado(a); **to die a natural/violent d.** morir de muerte natural/violenta; **to fight to the d.** luchar hasta la muerte; **to put sb to death** matar or dar muerte a algn; **to sentence** or **condemn sb to death** condenar a algn a muerte; Fig **he works his employees to d.** hace trabajar muy duro a sus trabajadores; Fig **that subject's been done to d.** es un tema muy trillado; Fig **to be at d.'s door** estar a las puertas de la muerte; Fam **he drank himself to d., drink was the d. of him** le mató la bebida; Fam **to be bored to d.** aburrirse como una ostra; Fam **to catch one's d. (of cold)** agarrar un resfriado de muerte; Fam **to be scared** or **frightened to d.** estar muerto(a) de miedo; Fam **to worry oneself to d.** estar muy preocupado(a); Fam **to be sick to d. of sb/sth** estar hasta la coronilla de algn/algo; Fam **to look like d. warmed** Br **up** or US **over** parecer un muerto viviente or un cadaver; Fam Fig **you'll be the d. of me!** ¡me vas a matar! ❏ **d. cell** celda f de los condenados a muerte; Jur **d. certificate** certificado m de defunción; Fig **d. knell** golpe m de gracia; **d. mask** mascarilla f; Jur **d. penalty** pena f de muerte; **d. rate** índice m de mortalidad; **d. rattle** estertor m de la muerte; **d. sentence** pena f de muerte; **d. squad** brigada f de muerte; **d. throes** agonía f; Fig **the firm was in its d. throes** la empresa estaba a punto de irse a pique; **d. toll** mortandad f, número m de muertos or de víctimas; Psych **d. wish** ganas fpl de morir (b) Fig (end) fin m

deathbed ['deθbed] n lecho m de muerte; **to be on one's d.** estar en el lecho de muerte

deathblow ['deθbləʊ] n golpe m mortal

deathly ['deθlɪ] adj (**deathlier, deathliest**) (silence) sepulcral; (pallor) cadavérico(a), de muerte; **d. pale** pálido(a) como un muerto

deathtrap ['deθtræp] n Fam (place) lugar m peligroso

deathwatch ['deθwɒtʃ] n velatorio m ❏ Ent **d. beetle** escarabajo m del reloj de la muerte

deb [deb] n Fam debutante f

debacle [deɪ'bɑːkəl] n debacle f, desastre m, catástrofe f

debar [dɪ'bɑːər] vt (pt & pp **debarred**) Fml excluir, prohibir, privar

debase [dɪ'beɪs] vt (a) (coinage) alterar (b) Fig desvalorizar, envilecer, degradar; (meaning, word) quitar el sentido de; **to d. oneself** rebajarse or humillarse

debasement [dɪ'beɪsmənt] n desvalorización f

debate [dɪ'beɪt] **1** n (gen) debate m; **a heated d.** una discusión acalorada; **it's a matter for d., the matter is open to d.** se podría discutir la cuestión
2 vt (a) (discuss) debatir (b) (wonder about) considerar, dar vueltas a; **to d. (with oneself) whether ...** preguntarse si ...
3 vi discutir; **to d. on** or **about sth** discutir sobre algo

debat(e)able [dɪ'beɪtəbəl] adj discutible

debater [dɪ'beɪtər] n participante mf en un debate

debating [dɪ'beɪtɪŋ] n debate m, discusión f ❏ **d. society** grupo m de discusión, tertulia f

debating society [dɪ'beɪtɪŋsə'saɪətɪ] n = asociación que organiza debates en una universidad o instituto

debauch [dɪ'bɔːtʃ] vt Fml corromper, pervertir, seducir

debauched [dɪ'bɔːtʃt] adj (person) libertino(a), inmoral; (life, behaviour) vicioso(a), licencioso(a)

debauchery [dɪ'bɔːtʃərɪ] n libertinaje m, corrupción f

debilitate [dɪ'bɪlɪteɪt] vt (weaken) debilitar; (exhaust) agotar

debilitating [dɪ'bɪlɪteɪtɪŋ] adj (gen) debilitante; (heat, climate) agotador(a)

debility [dɪ'bɪlɪtɪ] n decaimiento m, abatimiento m

debit ['debɪt] **1** n Fin débito m ❏ **d. balance** saldo m negativo
2 vt (account, person) cargar en cuenta; **to d. $20 against Mr Jones, to d. Mr Jones with $20** cargar la suma de veinte dólares en la cuenta del Sr. Jones

debonair [debə'neər] adj (cheerful) alegre, despreocupado(a); (elegant) garboso(a), elegante; (polite) cortés; (pleasant) afable

debrief [diː'briːf] vt interrogar, pedir un informe de

debriefing [diː'briːfɪŋ] n informe m

debris ['debriː, US də'briː] n sing (of building) escombros mpl; (of vehicle) restos mpl

debt [det] n deuda f; **to be deeply in d.** estar cargado(a) de deudas; **to get into d., to run up debts** contraer deudas; **to pay (off) one's debts** saldar las deudas; Fig **to be in sb's d.** estar en deuda con algn ❏ **d. collector** cobrador(a) m,f de morosos; **national d.** deuda f pública

debtor ['detər] n deudor(a) m,f

debug [diː'bʌg] vt (pt & pp **debugged**) (a) Comptr (program) eliminar fallos de (b) (telephone, room) quitar micrófonos ocultos de

debunk [diː'bʌŋk] vt Fam (idea, belief) desacreditar, desprestigiar; (institution) desmitificar; (expose) desenmascarar

debut ['debjuː, 'deɪbjuː] n debut m; **to make one's d.** debutar, estrenarse

debutante ['debjʊtɑːnt] n debutante f

Dec (abbr **December**) diciembre m, dic.

decade [de'keɪd, 'dekeɪd] n decenio m, década f

decadence ['dekədəns] n decadencia f

decadent ['dekədənt] adj decadente

decaffeinated [dɪ'kæfɪneɪtɪd] adj descafeinado(a)

decal ['diːkæl] n US calcomanía f

decalitre, US **decaliter** ['dekəliːtər] n decalitro m

decametre, US **decameter** ['dekəmiːtər] n decámetro m

decamp [dɪ'kæmp] vi Fam (go away) largarse, pirárselas

decant [dɪ'kænt] vt decantar

decanter [dɪ'kæntər] n jarra f, jarro m

decapitate [dɪ'kæpɪteɪt] vt decapitar

decapitation [dɪkæpɪ'teɪʃən] n decapitación f

decathlon [dɪ'kæθlɒn] n Sport decatlón m

decay [dɪ'keɪ] **1** n (of food, body) descomposición f, putrefacción f; (of teeth) caries f inv; (of buildings) ruina f, deterioro m, desmoronamiento m; Fig decadencia f, corrupción f; Fig **to fall into d.** entrar en decadencia
2 vi (gen) descomponerse, pudrirse; (teeth) cariarse, picarse; (buildings) deteriorarse, desmoronarse; Fig corromperse, estar en decadencia
3 vt (teeth) cariar

decease [dɪ'siːs] n Fml fallecimiento m, defunción f

deceased [dɪ'siːst] Fml **1** adj difunto(a), fallecido(a)
2 n **the d.** sing el difunto/la difunta, el fallecido/la fallecida; pl los difuntos/las difuntas, los fallecidos/las fallecidas

deceit [dɪ'siːt] n (a) (dishonesty) falta f de honradez, falsedad f (b) (trick) engaño m, mentira f

deceitful [dɪ'siːtfʊl] adj (person) falso(a), embustero(a), mentiroso(a); (words) falso(a), mentiroso(a); (behaviour) falso(a), engañoso(a)

deceitfully [dɪ'siːtfʊlɪ] adv **to obtain sth d.** conseguir algo con engaños

deceitfulness [dɪ'siːtfʊlnɪs] n falsedad f

deceive [dɪ'siːv] vt *(mislead)* engañar; *(lie to)* mentir; **to d. oneself** engañarse; **to d. sb into doing sth** engañar a algn para que haga algo

decelerate [diː'seləreɪt] vi reducir la velocidad, desacelerar

deceleration [diːselə'reɪʃən] vi deceleración f, desaceleración f; **d. lane** carril m de deceleración or de salida

December [dɪ'sembər] n diciembre m; *see also* **May**

decency ['diːsənsɪ] n (**a**) *(seemliness)* decencia f, decoro m; *(modesty)* pudor m; *(morality)* moralidad f; **to have a** or **some sense of d.** tener sentido del decoro (**b**) *(politeness)* educación f, cortesía f; **he did have the d. to apologize** tuvo suficiente educación como para disculparse; **to do sth out of common d.** hacer algo por cumplir

decent ['diːsənt] adj (**a**) *(dress, behaviour)* decente; *(person)* honrado(a), bueno(a), decente; **to do the d. thing** hacer lo correcto; *Fam* **are you d. yet?** *(dressed)* ¿estás presentable ya? (**b**) *(meal, wage)* adecuado(a), decente; *(price)* razonable (**c**) *Fam (kind)* simpático(a), bueno(a); **it's very d. of you to help** es muy amable de tu parte ayudar

decently ['diːsəntlɪ] adv (**a**) *(honourably)* decentemente, honradamente (**b**) *(adequately)* adecuadamente (**c**) *Fam (kindly)* con amabilidad

decentralization [diːsentrəlaɪ'zeɪʃən] n descentralización f

decentralize [diː'sentrəlaɪz] **1** vt descentralizar; **to become decentralized** descentralizarse
2 vi descentralizarse

deception [dɪ'sepʃən] n *(act, trick)* engaño m; *(lie)* mentira f

deceptive [dɪ'septɪv] adj engañoso(a), falso(a)

deceptively [dɪ'septɪvlɪ] adv **it looks d. simple** parece engañosamente sencillo(a)

decibel ['desɪbel] n *Tech* decibel m, decibelio m

decide [dɪ'saɪd] **1** vt (**a**) *(gen)* decidir; **I can't d. which one to choose** no sé cuál escoger; **that was what decided me** *(determined)* fue eso lo que me hizo tomar la decisión; *(convinced)* fue eso lo que me convenció; **to d. to do sth** decidir or determinar hacer algo (**b**) *(matter, question)* resolver, determinar; **that move decided the outcome** esa jugada determinó el resultado
2 vi *(reach decision)* decidirse, tomar una decisión; **it's for you to d.** tú eres quien decide; **to d. against sth** decidirse en contra de algo; **to d. in favour of sth** optar por algo

decide on vt *(choose)* optar por

decided [dɪ'saɪdɪd] adj (**a**) *(noticeable)* marcado(a), claro(a) (**b**) *(resolute)* decidido(a), resuelto(a); *(views)* categórico(a)

decidedly [dɪ'saɪdɪdlɪ] adv *Fml* (**a**) *(clearly)* indudablemente, sin duda; **he's d. better** se encuentra francamente mejor (**b**) *(resolutely)* decididamente, con resolución

decider [dɪ'saɪdər] n **the d.** *(goal, match)* el gol/partido/etc decisivo

deciding [dɪ'saɪdɪŋ] adj decisivo(a)

deciduous [dɪ'sɪdjʊəs] adj *Bot* de hoja caduca

decilitre, *US* **deciliter** ['desɪliːtər] n decilitro m

decimal ['desɪməl] **1** adj decimal; **to six d. places** hasta la sexta cifra ❑ **d. point** coma f (de fracción decimal)
2 n decimal m

decimalization [desɪməlaɪ'zeɪʃən] n *Br* conversión f al sistema decimal

decimalize ['desɪməlaɪz] vt *Br* convertir al sistema decimal

decimate ['desɪmeɪt] vt diezmar

decimation [desɪ'meɪʃən] n reducción f catastrófica

decimetre, *US* **decimeter** ['desɪmiːtər] n decímetro m

decipher [dɪ'saɪfər] vt descifrar

decision [dɪ'sɪʒən] n (**a**) *(conclusion)* decisión f; *Jur* fallo m; **to come to** or **reach a d.** llegar a una decisión; **to take** or **make a d.** tomar una decisión (**b**) *(resolution)* resolución f, determinación f

decision-making [dɪ'sɪʒənmeɪkɪŋ] n toma f de decisiones

decisive [dɪ'saɪsɪv] adj (**a**) *(resolute)* decidido(a), resuelto(a), firme (**b**) *(conclusive)* decisivo(a)

decisiveness [dɪ'saɪsɪvnɪs] n resolución f, firmeza f, determinación f

deck [dek] **1** n (**a**) *(of ship)* cubierta f; **on/below d.** en/bajo cubierta ❑ **d. chair** tumbona f (**b**) *(of bus, coach)* piso m; **top d.** piso de arriba (**c**) *esp US (of cards)* baraja f (**d**) *(of record player)* plato m, platina f ❑ **cassette d.** platina f
2 vt **to d. out** adornar, decorar; **she decked herself (out) in all her finery** se puso de punta en blanco

declaim [dɪ'kleɪm] vt & vi *Fml* declamar

declamatory [dɪ'klæmətərɪ] adj *Fml* declamatorio(a)

declaration [deklə'reɪʃən] n declaración f

declare [dɪ'kleər] **1** vt *(gen)* declarar; *(winner, innocence)* proclamar; *(war)* declarar; *(decision)* manifestar; *(in customs)* **have you anything to d.?** ¿tiene Ud. algo que declarar?
2 vi **to d. against/for sth** pronunciarse en contra de/a favor de algo; *Old-fashioned* **I (do) d.!** ¡demontre!

declared [dɪ'kleəd] adj *(opponent, supporter)* declarado(a), reconocido(a); *(intention)* manifiesto(a)

declassify [diː'klæsɪfaɪ] vt *(pt & pp* **declassified)** *(information etc)* levantar el secreto oficial de

declension [dɪ'klenʃən] n *Ling* declinación f

decline [dɪ'klaɪn] **1** n (**a**) *(decrease)* disminución f; *(amount)* baja f; **to be on the d.** *(gen)* ir disminuyendo, ser menos frecuente; *(traditions etc)* ir perdiéndose; *(prestige etc)* ir a menos (**b**) *(deterioration)* deterioro m, decadencia f; *(of health)* empeoramiento m; *(empire etc)* ocaso m; **to go** or **fall into d.** empezar a decaer
2 vi (**a**) *(decrease)* disminuir; *(strength etc)* declinar; *(amount)* bajar; *(business)* ir de baja (**b**) *(deteriorate)* deteriorarse; *(health)* empeorarse (**c**) *(refuse)* negarse (**d**) *Ling* declinarse
3 vt (**a**) *(refuse)* rehusar, rechazar; *(offer, invitation)* declinar (**b**) *Ling* declinar

declining [dɪ'klaɪnɪŋ] adj *(decreasing)* disminuyendo; *(deteriorating)* deteriorando

declutch [dɪ'klʌtʃ] vi *Aut* desembragar

decode [diː'kəʊd] vt descifrar

decolonize [diː'kɒlənaɪz] vt descolonizar

decompose [diːkəm'pəʊz] **1** vt (**a**) *(rot)* descomponer, pudrir (**b**) *Chem (separate)* descomponer
2 vi (**a**) *(rot)* descomponerse, pudrirse (**b**) *Chem (separate)* descomponerse

decomposition [diːkɒmpə'zɪʃən] n descomposición f, putrefacción f

decompress [diːkəm'pres] vt *Comptr (file)* descomprimir

decompression [diːkəm'preʃən] n descompresión f ❑ **d. chamber** cámara f de descompresión; **d. sickness** aeroembolismo m

decongestant [diːkən'dʒestənt] adj & n descongestionante (m)

deconstruct [diːkən'strʌkt] vt *Lit* deconstruir

deconstruction [diːkən'strʌkʃən] n *Lit* teoría f desconstructiva, desconstruccionismo m

decontaminate [di:kən'tæmɪneɪt] *vt* descontaminar

decontamination [di:kəntæmɪ'neɪʃən] *n* descontaminación *f*

décor ['deɪkɔ:r] *n*, **decor** ['dekɔ:r] *n* decoración *f*; *Theat* decorado *m*

decorate ['dekəreɪt] **1** *vt* (**a**) *(adorn)* decorar, adornar (**with** con) (**b**) *(paint)* pintar; *(wallpaper)* empapelar (**c**) *(honour)* condecorar
2 *vi (paint)* pintar; *(wallpaper)* empapelar

decorating ['dekəreɪtɪŋ] *n* decoración *f*; *(painting)* pintura *f*; *(wallpapering)* empapelamiento *m*

decoration [dekə'reɪʃən] *n* (**a**) *(decor)* decoración *f* ❑ **Christmas decorations** adornos *mpl* navideños (**b**) *(medal)* condecoración *f*

decorative ['dekərətɪv] *adj* decorativo(a), ornamental

decorator ['dekəreɪtər] *n* **(painter and) d.** pintor(a) *m,f (que también empapela)*

decorous ['dekərəs] *adj Fml* decoroso(a), correcto(a)

decorum [dɪ'kɔ:rəm] *n* decoro *m*

decoy ['di:kɔɪ] **1** *n* (**a**) *(bird)* cimbel *m*; *(artificial bird)* señuelo *m* (**b**) *Fig* señuelo *m*
2 *vt (person, ship, etc)* atraer con señuelo (**into** a)

decrease ['di:kri:s] **1** *n (strength)* disminución *f*, decrecimiento *m*; *(price, temperature)* baja *f*; *Fin* merma *f*; *(in weight, speed, size)* reducción *f*; **to be on the d.** ir disminuyendo
2 [dɪ'kri:s] *vi (gen)* disminuir; *(strength, intensity)* menguar; *(price, temperature)* bajar; *Fin* mermar, perder valor; *(weight, speed, size)* reducir; *Knit* menguar
3 *vt (gen)* disminuir, reducir; *(price, temperatures)* bajar; *(in knitting)* menguar

decreasing [dɪ'kri:sɪŋ] *adj* decreciente

decree [dɪ'kri:] **1** *n* (**a**) *Pol Rel* decreto *m*; **to issue a d.** promulgar un decreto (**b**) *esp US Jur* sentencia *f* ❑ **d. absolute** sentencia *f* definitiva de divorcio; **d. nisi** sentencia *f* provisional de divorcio
2 *vt Pol Rel* decretar; pronunciar

decrepit [dɪ'krepɪt] *adj* decrépito(a)

decriminalize [di:'krɪmɪnəlaɪz] *vt* despenalizar

decry [dɪ'kraɪ] *vt Fml* censurar, criticar

dedicate ['dedɪkeɪt] *vt (gen)* consagrar, dedicar; **to d. oneself/one's life to science** dedicarse/dedicar su vida a la ciencia

dedicated ['dedɪkeɪtɪd] *adj* ardiente, convencido(a); **d. to** entregado(a) a ❑ *Comptr* **d. line** línea *f* dedicada

dedication [dedɪ'keɪʃən] *n* (**a**) *(act)* consagración *f*, dedicación *f* (**b**) *(commitment)* entrega *f*, compromiso *m* (**c**) *(in book, on music)* dedicatoria *f*

deduce [dɪ'dju:s] *vt Fml* deducir, inferir, concluir (**from** de)

deducible [dɪ'dju:sɪbəl] *adj* deducible (**from** de)

deduct [dɪ'dʌkt] *vt* restar, descontar, deducir (**from** de)

deductible [dɪ'dʌktəbəl] *adj* deducible (**from** de)

deduction [dɪ'dʌkʃən] *n* (**a**) *(conclusion)* conclusión *f*, deducción *f*; *(reasoning)* deducción *f* (**b**) *(subtraction)* deducción *f*, descuento *m*

deductive [dɪ'dʌktɪv] *adj* deductivo(a)

deed [di:d] *n* (**a**) *Literary (act)* acto *m*; *(feat)* hazaña *f*, proeza *f*; *Fam* **to do one's good d. for the day** hacer su buena obra diaria (**b**) *Jur* escritura *f*; *esp Br* **to do sth by d. poll** hacer algo por escritura legal ❑ **d. box** caja *f* de caudales, caja *f* fuerte; **title deeds** título *m sing* de propiedad

deejay ['di:dʒeɪ] *n Fam* pinchadiscos *mf inv*, discjockey *mf*

deem [di:m] *vt Fml* considerar, juzgar

de-emphasize [di:'emfəsaɪz] *vt (need, claim, feature)* quitar énfasis *or* importancia a

deep [di:p] **1** *adj* (**a**) *(well, river etc)* profundo(a), hondo(a); *(wrinkle, gash)* profundo(a); *(breath)* hondo(a); **it's ten metres d.** tiene diez metros de profundidad; *Fam Fig* **to be thrown in at the d. end** hacer algo por primera vez; *Fam Fig* **to go off the d. end** salirse de casillas, perder los estribos (**b**) *(shelf etc)* de fondo; *(hem, border)* ancho(a) (**c**) *(sound, voice)* grave, bajo(a); *(disgrace, shame)* grande; *(silence, mystery)* profundo(a), completo(a); *(interest)* vivo(a); *(mourning)* riguroso(a); *(sigh)* hondo(a) (**d**) *(colour)* oscuro(a) (**e**) *(serious)* grave, serio(a); *Fam* pseudofilosófico(a)
2 *adv* (**a**) *(down)* profundamente; **to dig d.** cavar hondo; **he thrust his hand d. into his pocket** metió la mano hasta el fondo del bolsillo; **to sleep d.** dormir profundamente; *Fig* **d. down (inside me), I knew he was right** en *or* para mis adentros, sabía que tenía razón; *Fig* **to be d. in thought** estar absorto(a), estar ensimismado(a) (**b**) *(back)* lejos; **d. in the woods** en lo más profundo del bosque; **to look d. into sb's eyes** penetrar a algn con la mirada; *Fig* **nine d.** de nueve en fondo
3 *n Literary* **the d.** el piélago

deepen ['di:pən] **1** *vt (well etc)* profundizar, ahondar; *Fig (knowledge etc)* aumentar; *(colour, emotion)* intensificar; *(sound, voice)* hacer más grave
2 *vi (river etc)* hacerse más hondo *or* profundo; *Fig (knowledge etc)* aumentarse; *(colour, emotion)* intensificarse; *(sound, voice)* hacerse más grave

deep-freeze [di:p'fri:z] **1** *n* congelador *m*
2 *vt (pt* **deep-froze**, *pp* **deep-frozen**) *(food)* congelar

deep-fry [di:p'fraɪ] *vt (pt & pp* **deep-fried**) freír en mucho aceite

deeply ['di:plɪ] *adv* (**a**) *(gen)* profundamente; *(breathe)* hondo; **to be d. in debt** estar cargado(a) de deudas (**b**) *(very)* muy, profundamente, sumamente; **I was d. hurt** me hirió *or* me tocó en lo vivo

deep-rooted [di:p'ru:tɪd] *adj Fig* profundo(a), arraigado(a)

deep-sea ['di:psi:] *adj (fishing)* de altura *f*; *(fish)* de aguas profundas, de alta mar

deep-seated [di:p'si:tid] *adj Fig* profundo(a), arraigado(a)

deep-set [di:p'set] *adj (eyes)* hundido(a)

deep-vein ['di:p'veɪn] *adj* **d. thrombosis** trombosis *f* venosa profunda

deer [dɪər] *n inv Zool* ciervo *m*, venado *m* ❑ **red d.** ciervo *m* común

deface [dɪ'feɪs] *vt (break)* mutilar; *(mark)* desfigurar con garabatos; *(tear)* desgarrar

de facto [deɪ'fæktəʊ] *adj & adv Fml* de hecho

defamation [defə'meɪʃən] *n Fml* difamación *f*

defamatory [dɪ'fæmətərɪ] *adj Fml* difamatorio(a)

defame [dɪ'feɪm] *vt Fml* difamar

default [dɪ'fɔ:lt] **1** *vi* (**a**) *(not act)* faltar a sus compromisos, incumplir un acuerdo *or* una promesa (**b**) *(not appear) Sport* perder por incomparecencia; *Jur* estar en rebeldía (**c**) *(not pay)* suspender pagos
2 *n* (**a**) *(failure to act)* omisión *f*, negligencia *f* (**b**) *(failure to pay)* incumplimiento *m* de pago (**c**) *(failure to appear) Jur* rebeldía *f*, *Fml* ausencia *f*; **in d. of** a falta de, en ausencia de; *Sport* **to win by d.** ganar por incomparecencia del adversario (**d**) *Comptr* **d. drive** unidad *f* (de disco) por defecto *or* omisión; **d. settings** valores *mpl or* configuración *f* por defecto *or* omisión

defaulter [dɪ'fɔ:ltər] *n (on loan, rent)* moroso(a) *m*

defeat [dɪ'fiːt] **1** *vt* **(a)** *(gen)* derrotar, vencer; *(motion, bill)* rechazar **(b)** *Fig* frustrar; **to d. an outrage** hacer fracasar un atentado
2 *n* **(a)** *(of army, team)* derrota *f*; *(of motion)* rechazo *m* **(b)** *Fig* fracaso *m*

defeatism [dɪ'fiːtɪzəm] *n* derrotismo *m*

defeatist [dɪ'fiːtɪst] *adj & n* derrotista *(mf)*

defecate ['defɪkeɪt] *vi Fml* defecar

defecation [defɪ'keɪʃən] *n Fml* defecación *f*

defect 1 ['diːfekt] *n* **(a)** *(gen)* defecto *m*; *(flaw)* desperfecto *m*
2 [dɪ'fekt] *vi* desertar **(from** de); *(from country)* huir

defection [dɪ'fekʃən] *n (from or to party)* deserción *f*, defección *f*; *(from or to country)* huida *f*, fuga *f*

defective [dɪ'fektɪv] *adj* **(a)** *(faulty)* defectuoso(a); *(flawed)* con desperfectos; *(lacking)* incompleto(a), deficiente **(b)** *Ling* defectivo(a)

defector [dɪ'fektər] *n Pol* tránsfuga *mf*, trásfuga *mf*

defence [dɪ'fens] *n* **(a)** *(gen)* defensa *f*; *(of rights, wildlife)* protección *f*; **d. against air attack** protección *f* antiaérea; **to act in self-d.** actuar en defensa propia; *Br* **the Ministry of D.**, *US* **the Department of Defense** el Ministerio de Defensa; **to come to sb's d.** salir en defensa de algn ❏ **d. mechanism** mecanismo *m* de defensa; **d. spending** gastos *mpl* militares **(b)** *Jur* defensa *f*; **counsel for the d.** abogado(a) *m,f* defensor(a) **(c)** *Sport* [*Br* dɪ'fens, *US* 'diːfens] **the d.** la defensa

defenceless [dɪ'fenslɪs] *adj* indefenso(a)

defend [dɪ'fend] *vt* **(a)** *(gen)* defender **(from** de; **against** contra); *(rights, wildlife)* proteger **(from** de; **against** contra); **to d. oneself** defenderse **(b)** *Jur (accused, case)* defender **(c)** *(claim, action, decision)* defender, vindicar, justificar

defendant [dɪ'fendənt] *n Jur* demandado(a) *m,f*, acusado(a) *m,f*

defender [dɪ'fendə] *n (gen)* defensor(a) *m,f*; *Sport* defensa *mf*

defending [dɪ'fendɪŋ] *adj* **(a)** *Sport* defensor(a); **d. champion** campeón(ona) *m,f* titular **(b)** *Jur* **d. counsel** abogado(a) *m,f* defensor(a)

defense [dɪ'fens, 'diːfens] *n US see* **defence**

defenseless [dɪ'fenslɪs] *adj US see* **defenceless**

defensible [dɪ'fensəbəl] *adj* defendible, justificable

defensive [dɪ'fensɪv] *adj* defensivo(a); **to be on the d.** estar a la defensiva

defensively [dɪ'fensɪvlɪ] *adv (gen) & Sport* a la defensiva; **she answered d.** respondió en actitud defensiva

defer[1] [dɪ'fɜː] *vt (pt & pp* **deferred)** aplazar, retrasar

defer[2] [dɪ'fɜː] *vi (pt & pp* **deferred) to d. to sth/sb** deferir a algo/a algn

deference ['defərəns] *n Fml* deferencia *f*, respeto *m*, consideración *f*; **out of** *or* **in d. to sth/sb** por respeto *or* por deferencia a algo/a algn

deferential [defə'renʃəl] *adj Fml* deferente, respetuoso(a)

deferment [dɪ'fɜːmənt] *n*, **deferral** [dɪ'fɜːrəl] *n Fml* aplazamiento *m*

defiance [dɪ'faɪəns] *n* **(a)** *(challenge)* desafío *m*; **in d. of** a despecho de **(b)** *(resistence)* resistencia *f*, oposición *f*

defiant [dɪ'faɪənt] *adj (challenging)* de desafío, provocador(a); *(bold)* insolente

deficiency [dɪ'fɪʃənsɪ] *n* **(a)** *(lack)* deficiencia *f*, falta *f*, carencia *f* **(b)** *(shortcoming)* defecto *m*

deficient [dɪ'fɪʃənt] *adj* deficiente; **to be d. in sth** carecer de algo, estar falto(a) de algo

deficit ['defɪsɪt] *n Com Fin* déficit *m*

defile[1] [dɪ'faɪl] *vt Fml* **(a)** *(mind)* corromper; *(honour)* manchar; *(memory)* profanar; *(woman)* deshonrar **(b)** *(desecrate)* profanar

defile[2] [dɪ'faɪl, 'diːfaɪl] *n* desfiladero *m*

definable [dɪ'faɪnəbəl] *adj* definible

define [dɪ'faɪn] *vt* **(a)** *(explain)* definir, explicar; *(functions, duties, powers)* delimitar **(b)** *(show clearly)* definir, perfilar

defining [dɪ'faɪnɪŋ] *adj* **(a)** *(decisive)* decisivo(a) **(b)** *(distinctive)* definidor(a), distintivo(a)

definite ['defɪnɪt] *adj* **(a)** *(clear)* claro(a), preciso(a), categórico(a); *(improvement, progress)* notable **(b)** *(date, place)* determinado(a), fijo(a); **is it d.?** ¿es seguro?; **it's quite d. that ...** no hay *or* no cabe ninguna duda que ... **(c)** *Ling* **d. article** artículo *m* determinado

definitely ['defɪnɪtlɪ] **1** *adv (without doubt)* sin duda, seguramente; **he was d. drunk** no cabe duda que estaba borracho; **I'm d. going** yo voy, seguro
2 *interj* ¡desde luego!, ¡claro que sí!, ¡por supuesto!

definition [defɪ'nɪʃən] *n* **(a)** *(explanation)* definición *f*; **by d.** por definición **(b)** *(clarity)* nitidez *f*

definitive [dɪ'fɪnɪtɪv] *adj* definitivo(a)

deflate [dɪ'fleɪt] **1** *vt* **(a)** *(tyre, balloon)* desinflar, deshinchar **(b)** *Fig* rebajar; *Fig* **to d. sb** hacer bajar los humos a algn; **to feel deflated** sentirse desilusionado(a) **(c)** *Econ* reducir la inflación
2 *vi* **(a)** *(tyre, balloon)* desinflarse, deshincharse **(b)** *Econ* sufrir la deflación

deflation [dɪ'fleɪʃən] *n* **(a)** *Econ* deflación *f* **(b)** *Fig (disappointment)* decepción *f*, desilusión *f*

deflationary [dɪ'fleɪʃənərɪ] *adj Econ* deflacionista, deflacionario(a)

deflect [dɪ'flekt] **1** *vt (gen)* desviar; *Fig (attention)* desviar, distraer
2 *vi (gen)* desviarse

deflection [dɪ'flekʃən] *n* desviación *f*

deflower [diː'flaʊər] *vt Literary (of virginity)* desflorar, desvirgar

defogger [diː'fɒgər] *n US Aut* luneta *f* térmica, dispositivo *m* antivaho

defoliant [diː'fəʊlɪənt] *n Tech* defoliante *m*

defoliate [diː'fəʊlɪeɪt] *vt* defoliar, deshojar

deforestation [diːfɒrɪs'teɪʃən] *n* deforestación *f*

deform [dɪ'fɔːm] *vt* deformar, desfigurar

deformation [diːfɔː'meɪʃən] *n* deformación *f*

deformed [dɪ'fɔːmd] *adj* deforme

deformity [dɪ'fɔːmɪtɪ] *n* deformidad *f*

DEFRA ['defrə] *n (abbr* **Department of the Environment, Food and Rural Affairs)** = departamento del gobierno británico de medio ambiente, alimentación y asuntos rurales

defraud [dɪ'frɔːd] *vt* estafar

defray [dɪ'freɪ] *vt Fml* sufragar

defrost [diː'frɒst] **1** *vt* **(a)** *(freezer, food)* descongelar **(b)** *US (windscreen)* desempañar
2 *vi* descongelarse

deft [deft] *adj (skilful)* hábil, diestro(a); *(adroit)* experto(a)

defunct [dɪ'fʌŋkt] *adj (person)* difunto(a); *(thing)* en desuso

defuse [diː'fjuːz] *vt (bomb)* desactivar; *Fig* **to d. a situation** reducir la tensión de una situación

defy [dɪ'faɪ] *vt (pt & pp* **defied) (a)** *(person)* desafiar; *(law, order)* desobedecer, contravenir **(b)** *(challenge)* retar, desafiar; *Fig* **it defies reason** se escapa a la razón

degeneracy [dɪ'dʒenərəsɪ] *n* degeneración *f*, decadencia *f*

degenerate [dɪ'dʒɛnəreɪt] **1** vi degenerar (**into** en)
2 [dɪ'dʒɛnərɪt] adj & n degenerado(a) (m,f)

degeneration [dɪdʒɛnə'reɪʃən] n degeneración f

degenerative [dɪ'dʒɛnərɒtɪv] adj degenerativo(a)

degrade [dɪ'greɪd] vt degradar, envilecer; **to d. oneself by doing sth** rebajarse a hacer algo

degrading [dɪ'greɪdɪŋ] adj degradante

degree [dɪ'griː] n (**a**) (unit of measurement) grado m (**b**) (amount, extent) grado m, cantidad f; **a certain d. of skill** una cierta habilidad; **it involves a high d. of risk** es sumamente arriesgado(a); **to some d.** hasta cierto punto (**c**) (stage) punto m, etapa m; **first-d. burns** quemaduras fpl de primer grado; **to do sth by degrees** hacer algo poco a poco or paso a paso (**d**) (qualification) título m; **first d.** licenciatura f; **higher d.** (of Master) licenciatura f superior; (of doctor) doctorado m; **honorary d.** doctorado m 'honoris causa'; **to have/take a d. in science** ser licenciado(a)/ licenciarse en ciencias

dehumanize [diː'hjuːmənaɪz] vt deshumanizar

dehumidifier [diːhjuː'mɪdɪfaɪər] n deshumidificador m

dehydrate [diːhaɪ'dreɪt] vt deshidratar

dehydrated [diːhaɪ'dreɪtɪd] adj (person) deshidratado(a); (milk) en polvo; (vegetables) seco(a)

dehydration [diːhaɪ'dreɪʃən] n deshidratación f

de-ice [diː'aɪs] vt quitar el hielo a, deshelar

de-icer [diː'aɪsər] n (device) dispositivo m anticongelante; (chemical) anticongelante m

deify ['deɪfaɪ] vt (pt & pp **deified**) deificar

deign [deɪn] vi dignarse

deindustrialization [diːɪndʌstrɪəlaɪ'zeɪʃən] n desindustrialización f

deity ['deɪtɪ] n deidad f

dejected [dɪ'dʒɛktɪd] adj desalentado(a), desanimado(a), abatido(a)

dejectedly [dɪ'dʒɛktɪdlɪ] adv con desánimo

dejection [dɪ'dʒɛkʃən] n desaliento m, desánimo m, abatimiento m

dekko ['dɛkəʊ] n Br Fam ojeada f; **let's have a d. at the menu** echemos un vistazo al menú

delay [dɪ'leɪ] **1** vt (**a**) (make late) (flight, train) retrasar; (person) entretener; **delayed action** (of fuse, bomb, camera shutter) acción f retardada (**b**) (defer) aplazar; (payment) demorar, aplazar, diferir
2 vi (be late) tardar; **don't d.!** ¡no te entretengas!; **to d. in doing sth** demorarse en hacer algo
3 n (gen) retraso m, demora f; (to traffic) atasco m, embotellamiento m; **trains are subject to d.** es posible que los trenes lleguen con retraso or Am demora

delaying [dɪ'leɪɪŋ] adj dilatorio(a), prorrogativo(a)

delectable [dɪ'lɛktəbəl] adj Literary delicioso(a)

delegate ['dɛlɪgɪt] **1** n delegado(a) m,f ❑ **conference d.** congresista mf
2 ['dɛlɪgeɪt] vt (**a**) (command, responsibility) delegar (**to** en) (**b**) (to representative) delegar; **to d. sb to do sth** encargar a algn que haga algo
3 vi delegar responsabilidad

delegation [dɛlɪ'geɪʃən] n delegación f

delete [dɪ'liːt] vt (cross out) tachar (**from** de); (remove) suprimir (**from** de)

deleterious [dɛlɪ'tɪərɪəs] adj Fml nocivo(a)

deletion [dɪ'liːʃən] n (crossing out) tachadura f; (removal) supresión f

deli ['dɛlɪ] n Fam (shop) = tienda de ultramarinos de calidad

deliberate [dɪ'lɪbərɪt] **1** adj (**a**) (intentional) deliberado(a), intencionado(a); (studied) premeditado(a); **was it d.?** ¿fue a propósito? (**b**) (careful) prudente; (unhurried) pausado(a), lento(a)
2 [dɪ'lɪbəreɪt] vt (consider) deliberar, considerar, examinar
3 vi (consider) deliberar, reflexionar (**on, about** sobre)

deliberately [dɪ'lɪbərətlɪ] adv (**a**) (intentionally) a propósito, adrede (**b**) (carefully) prudentemente; (unhurriedly) pausadamente; **to speak d.** ser pausado(a) en el hablar

deliberation [dɪlɪbə'reɪʃən] n (**a**) (consideration) deliberación f, consideración f; **our deliberations produced little result** nuestras discusiones tuvieron poco resultado (**b**) (care) (unhurriedness) pausa f, lentitud f

delicacy ['dɛlɪkəsɪ] n (**a**) (exquisiteness) delicadeza f (**b**) (fragility) (of glass etc) fragilidad f; Fig (of health) debilidad f (**c**) (sensitivity) lo delicado (**d**) (tact) delicadeza f, consideración f, atención f, gentileza f (**e**) (food) manjar m (exquisito or delicioso)

delicate ['dɛlɪkɪt] adj (**a**) (exquisite) (gen) delicado(a); (embroidery, handiwork) fino(a); (touch) ligero(a) (**b**) (fragile) (china etc) frágil; Fig (health) delicado(a) (**c**) (sensitive) (question, matter) delicado(a); (instrument) sensible; (sense of smell or taste) fino(a) (**d**) (subtle) (colour) suave; (flavour) delicado(a), fino(a); (perfume) delicado(a)

delicately ['dɛlɪkətlɪ] adv (**a**) (exquisitely) delicadamente, con finura (**b**) (tactfully) con delicadeza or consideración (**c**) (precisely) con sensibilidad

delicatessen [dɛlɪkə'tɛsən] n (shop) = tienda de ultramarinos de calidad

delicious [dɪ'lɪʃəs] adj (food) delicioso(a); (taste, smell) exquisito(a); Fig (feeling) agradable; **it's d.!** ¡está buenísimo(a) or riquísimo(a)!

deliciously [dɪ'lɪʃəslɪ] adv deliciosamente

delight [dɪ'laɪt] **1** n (**a**) (great pleasure) gusto m, placer m, alegría f; **to take a d. in sth** encantarle algo (**b**) (source of pleasure) encanto m, delicia f; **that player's a d. to watch** da gusto ver ese jugador
2 vt encantar, dar gusto, deleitar
3 vi **to d. in doing sth** encantar hacer algo, deleitarse en or con hacer algo

delighted [dɪ'laɪtɪd] adj (gen) encantado(a), contentísimo(a); (smile, shout) de alegría; **d. to meet you** encantado(a) (de conocerle), mucho gusto (de conocerle); **I am d. with** or **by the result** el resultado me pone muy contento(a); **I'm d. to see you** me alegro mucho de verte

delightful [dɪ'laɪtfʊl] adj (house, person, film) encantador(a); (view, person) muy agradable; (meal, weather, conversation) delicioso(a); **how d.!** ¡qué delicia!

delightfully [dɪ'laɪtfʊlɪ] adv de una manera encantadora, deliciosamente

delimit [diː'lɪmɪt] vt delimitar

delineate [dɪ'lɪnɪeɪt] vt Fml (outline) delinear, esbozar, perfilar; Fig (describe) (plan, argument) perfilar, describir or explicar con todo detalle

delinquency [dɪ'lɪŋkwənsɪ] n delincuencia f ❑ **juvenile d.** delincuencia f juvenil

delinquent [dɪ'lɪŋkwənt] adj & n delincuente (mf)

delirious [dɪ'lɪrɪəs] adj (**a**) Med delirante; **to be d.** delirar, tener delirios, desvariar (**b**) Fig (audience) muy entusiasmado(a) or emocionado(a); **to be d. with joy** estar loco(a) de alegría

deliriously [dɪ'lɪrɪəslɪ] adv **to be d. happy** estar loco(a) de alegría

delirium [dɪ'lɪrɪəm] n (pl **deliriums** or **deliria** [dɪ'lɪrɪə]) Med & Fig delirio m, desvarío m

deliver [dɪ'lɪvər] vt (**a**) (take, mail) (goods) repartir, entregar (**to** a); *(message)* dar (**to** a); *(order)* despachar (**to** a); *Fig* **to d. the goods** cumplir con la obligación (**b**) *(give) (kick, push, blow)* dar; *Sport (shot, fast ball)* lanzar; *(speech, sermon, verdict)* pronunciar; *(lecture)* dar (**c**) *Med (baby)* asistir al parto; *Fml* **she was delivered of a son** dio a luz un niño; **the baby was delivered safely** el niño nació sano (**d**) *Fml (rescue)* liberar, rescatar (**from** de) (**e**) *(fulfil)* cumplir

deliverance [dɪ'lɪvərəns] *n Fml* liberación *f*, rescate *m*

delivery [dɪ'lɪvərɪ] *n* (**a**) *(of goods)* reparto *m*, entrega *f*; *(of mail)* reparto *m*; **cash on d.** entrega *f* contra reembolso; **special d.** correo *m* urgente; **to take d. of an order** recibir un pedido ❏ **d. boy** recadero *m*, chico *m* de los recados; **d. date** fecha *f* de entrega; **d. man** repartidor *m*; **d. note** albarán *m* de entrega; **d. van** furgoneta *f* de reparto (**b**) *(of speech etc)* declamacion *f*, pronunciación *f*, modo *m* de hablar (**c**) *(of baby)* parto *m*, alumbramiento *m* ❏ **d. room** sala *f* de partos

dell [del] *n Literary* valle *m* pequeño

delphinium [del'fɪnɪəm] *n Bot* espuela *f* de caballero

delta ['deltə] *n* (**a**) *(Greek letter)* delta *f*; **d. wing** *(of plane)* ala *f* supercrítica (**b**) *Geog* delta *m*; **the Nile d.** el delta del Nilo

delude [dɪ'lu:d] *vt* engañar; **don't d. yourself** no te hagas ilusiones, no te dejes engañar; **to d. sb into doing sth** engañar a algn para que haga algo

deluded [dɪ'lu:dɪd] *adj (mistaken, foolish)* engañado(a)

deluge ['delju:dʒ] **1** *n (flood)* inundación *f*; *(rain)* diluvio *m*; *Fig (of questions, complaints)* avalancha *f*, alud *m*
2 *vt Fml (flood)* inundar; *Fig* inundar (**with** de), abrumar (**with** con); **I was deluged with enquiries** me llovieron las preguntas

delusion [dɪ'lu:ʒən] *n* (**a**) *(state, act)* engaño *m* (**b**) *(false belief)* ilusión *f* (falsa); **delusions of grandeur** delirios *mpl* de grandeza; **he was under the d. that ...** pensaba equivocadamente que ...; *Psych* **to suffer from delusions** tener alucinaciones

delusive [dɪ'lu:sɪv] *adj* (**a**) *(misleading)* engañoso(a) (**b**) *(illusory)* ilusorio(a)

de luxe [də'lʌks, də'lʊks] *adj* de lujo *inv*

delve [delv] *vi* (**a**) *(search) (bag, pocket)* hurgar (**into** en) (**b**) *(gen)* investigar; *(subject)* profundizar, ahondar (**into** en); *(past, private affairs)* escarbar (**into** en)

demagogue, *US* **demagog** ['deməgɒg] *n Pol Pej* demagogo(a) *m,f*

demand [dɪ'mɑ:nd] **1** *n* (**a**) *(request) (gen)* solicitud *f*; *(for pay rise, rights etc)* reclamación *f*; *(need)* necesidad *f*; **by popular d.** a petición del público; **final d.** ultimo aviso *m*; **on d.** a petición (**b**) *(claim)* exigencia *f*; **the work makes great demands on me** me absorbe totalmente el trabajo; **to be in d.** ser solicitado(a); **to make demands on sb** pedir mucho de algn (**c**) *Econ* demanda *f*; **there's a big d. for this product** este producto tiene mucha demanda
2 *vt* (**a**) *(request firmly) (gen)* exigir; *(pay rise, rights)* reclamar; **to d. that ...** insistir en que ... (**b**) *(need)* exigir, requerir

demanding [dɪ'mɑ:ndɪŋ] *adj* (**a**) *(hard to please)* exigente (**b**) *(wearing)* agotador(a)

demarcation [di:mɑ:'keɪʃən] *n* demarcación *f* ❏ *Ind* **d. dispute** conflicto *m* (laboral) de competencias; **d. line** línea *f* de demarcación

demean [dɪ'mi:n] *vt Fml* **to d. oneself** rebajarse; **I won't d. myself by accepting** no me voy a humillar por aceptar

demeaning [dɪ'mi:nɪŋ] *adj Fml* humillante, vergonzoso(a)

demeanour, *US* **demeanor** [dɪ'mi:nər] *n Fml* (**a**) *(behaviour)* comportamiento *m*, conducta *f* (**b**) *(bearing)* porte *m*

demented [dɪ'mentɪd] *adj Med* demente, trastornado(a); *Fam* loco(a)

dementia [dɪ'menʃɪə] *n Med* demencia *f* ❏ **senile d.** demencia *f* senil

demerara [demə'reərə] *n* **d. (sugar)** azúcar *m or f* moreno/a

demerit [di:'merɪt] *n* (**a**) *Fml (fault, flaw)* demérito *m*, defecto *m*; **the merits and demerits of the system** las ventajas y desventajas del sistema (**b**) *US Sch Mil* falta *f* (en el historial)

demi- ['demɪ] *pref* medio-, semi-; *Myth* **d.-god** semidiós *m*

demilitarize [di:'mɪlɪtəraɪz] *vt* desmilitarizar

demise [dɪ'maɪz] *n Fml (death)* fallecimiento *m*, defunción *f*; *(of institution)* desaparición *f*; *Fig (of ambition etc)* fracaso *m*

demist [di:'mɪst] *vt Br Aut* desempañar

demo ['deməʊ] *n (pl* **demos**) *Fam* (**a**) *(protest)* manifestación *f* (**b**) *Comptr* demo *f*; **d. version** versión *f* demo *or* de demostración

demob [di:'mɒb] *vt (pt & pp* **demobbed**) *Br Mil Fam (abbr* **demobilize**) desmovilizar

demobilize [di:'məʊbɪlaɪz] *vt* desmovilizar

democracy [dɪ'mɒkrəsɪ] *n* democracia *f*

Democrat ['deməkræt] *n US Pol (politician, voter)* demócrata *m,f*; **the Democrats** *(party)* los demócratas, el partido demócrata

democrat ['deməkræt] *n* demócrata *mf*; *Pol* **Christian D.** democratacristiano/a *m,f*; **Social D.** social-demócrata *mf*

democratic [demə'krætɪk] *adj* democrático(a); *US Pol* **D. party** partido *m* demócrata

democratically [demə'krætɪklɪ] *adv* democráticamente, con democracia

demographic [demə'græfɪk] *adj* demográfico(a)

demography [dɪ'mɒgrəfɪ] *n* demografía *f*

demolish [dɪ'mɒlɪʃ] *vt (building etc)* derribar, echar abajo, demoler; *Fig (theory, proposal)* echar por tierra, destruir

demolition [demə'lɪʃən] *n* demolición *f*, derribo *m* ❏ **d. squad** equipo *m* de demolición

demon ['di:mən] *n* (**a**) *(devil, bad child)* demonio *m*, diablo *m* (**b**) *Fam (energetic person)* fiera *f*; *(skilful person)* hacha *m*

demoniacal [di:mə'naɪəkəl] *adj (laughter, urge)* demoniaco(a), diabólico(a)

demonic [dɪ'mɒnɪk] *adj* demoníaco(a)

demonstrable [dɪ'mɒnstrəbəl] *adj* demostrable

demonstrably [dɪ'mɒnstrəblɪ] *adv* claramente

demonstrate ['demənstreɪt] **1** *vt* (**a**) *(gen)* demostrar, probar; **to d. one's affection** dar prueba de su cariño (**b**) *(explain) (procedure, system)* demostrar, explicar; **he demonstrates microwave ovens** enseña cómo funcionan los hornos microondas
2 *vi Pol* manifestarse, hacer una manifestación

demonstration [demən'streɪʃən] *n* (**a**) *(proof)* demostración *f*, prueba *f* (**b**) *(explanation)* demostración *f*, explicación *f* (**c**) *Pol (march)* manifestación *f*; **to hold** *or* **stage a d.** manifestarse, hacer una manifestación

demonstrative [dɪ'mɒnstrətɪv] **1** *adj* franco(a), expansivo(a), que muestra sus sentimientos
2 *n Ling* demostrativo *m* ❏ **d. pronoun** pronombre *m* demostrativo

demonstrator ['demənstreɪtər] *n* (**a**) *Pol* manifestante *mf* (**b**) *Com* persona *f* que hace demostraciones

demoralize [dɪ'mɒrəlaɪz] *vt* desmoralizar; **to be** *or* **become demoralized** desmoralizarse

demoralizing [dɪ'mɒrəlaɪzɪŋ] *adj* desmoralizador(a), desmoralizante

demote [dɪ'məʊt] *vt* rebajar de graduación *or* de categoría; *Mil* degradar

demotion [dɪ'məʊʃən] *n* reducción *f* de categoría; *Mil* degradación *f*

demur [dɪ'mɜ:r] *Fml* **1** *vi* (*pt & pp* **demurred**) *(object)* oponerse, objetar; *(be reluctant)* vacilar (**at** ante); **I demurred at paying the bill** puse reparos a pagar la cuenta

2 *n* **without d.** sin reparo(s) *m(pl)*

demure [dɪ'mjʊər] *adj (modest)* recatado(a)

demurely [dɪ'mjʊəlɪ] *adv* recatadamente, con recato

demystify [di:'mɪstɪfaɪ] *vt* (*pt & pp* **demystified**) desembrollar, aclarar

den [den] *n* (**a**) *(of lions, wolves, etc)* guarida *f*; *Fig* **d. of vice** *or* **iniquity** antro *m* de perdición (**b**) *Fam (study)* estudio *m*

denationalize [di:'næʃənəlaɪz] *vt* privatizar, desnacionalizar

deniable [dɪ'naɪəbəl] *adj* refutable, negable

denial [dɪ'naɪəl] *n* (**a**) *(repudiation) (of charge)* mentís *m inv*, desmentido *m*; **he issued a firm d. of the report** desmintió rotundamente el informe (**b**) *(refusal) (of rights)* denegación *f*; *(of request)* negativa *f*, rechazo *m* (**c**) *(rejection) (of doctrine, principles)* negación *f*

denier ['denɪər] *n Tex* denier *m*

denigrate ['denɪgreɪt] *vt Fml* denigrar

denim ['denɪm] *n Tex* tela *f* vaquera; **denims** vaqueros *mpl*, *Andes Ven* bluyíns *mpl*, *Méx* pantalones *mpl* de mezclilla; **a pair of blue d.** unos vaqueros azules; **d. skirt** falda *f* tejana

denizen ['denɪzən] *n Literary* habitante *mf*

Denmark ['denmɑ:k] *n* Dinamarca

denomination [dɪnɒmɪ'neɪʃən] *n* (**a**) *Rel* confesión *f*, secta *f* (**b**) *Fin (of coins)* valor *m*

denominational [dɪnɒmɪ'neɪʃənəl] *adj Rel* confesional

denominator [dɪ'nɒmɪneɪtər] *n Math* denominador *m* ❑ **common d.** común denominador *m*

denote [dɪ'nəʊt] *vt* (**a**) *(show) (illness, satisfaction)* indicar, denotar; *(position, exit, weight)* marcar (**b**) *(mean)* significar

denouement [deɪ'nu:mɒn] *n* desenlace *m*

denounce [dɪ'naʊns] *vt* censurar, denunciar; **she denounced him as a fraud** le acusó de ser un impostor

dense [dens] *adj* (**a**) *(jungle etc)* denso(a), cerrado(a); *(crowd)* numeroso(a) (**b**) *(thick) (fog etc)* espeso(a) (**c**) *Fam (stupid)* torpe, estúpido(a)

densely ['denslɪ] *adv* densamente

density ['densɪtɪ] *n* densidad *f*; **the d. of the fog** lo espeso de la niebla

dent [dent] **1** *n (in metal)* abolladura *f*; *(in cushion, pillow)* hueco *m*; *Fig* **the trip made a d. in her savings** el viaje mermó sus ahorros

2 *vt (car)* abollar; *(cushion)* hacer un hueco en; *Fig* **to d. sb's confidence** hacer que algn pierda la confianza

dental ['dentəl] *adj* dental; **d. floss** hilo *m* dental; **d. hygienist** ayudante *mf or* asistente *mf* de dentista ❑ **d. surgeon** odontólogo(a) *m,f*; **d. surgery** *(place)* consultorio *m* odontológico, clínica *f* dental; *(treatment)* cirugía *f* dental

dentist ['dentɪst] *n* dentista *mf*

dentistry ['dentɪstrɪ] *n* odontología *f*

denture ['dentʃər] *n usu pl* dentadura *f* postiza

denude [dɪ'nju:d] *vt* despojar (**of** de); **hillsides denuded of soil** laderas erosionadas

denunciation [dɪnʌnsɪ'eɪʃən] *n* denuncia *f*, condena *f*, censura *f*

deny [dɪ'naɪ] *vt* (*pt & pp* **denied**) (**a**) *(repudiate)* negar;

(rumour, report) desmentir; *(charge)* rechazar; **he denied knowing her** *or* **that he knew her** afirmó que no la conocía; **there's no denying that ...** no se puede negar que ... (**b**) *(refuse)* negar, privar; **he denies her nothing** le consiente todo; **I was denied access** no me permitieron entrar; **to d. sb his/her rights** privar a algn de sus derechos (**c**) *Literary (disown) (person)* desconocer, negar a; *(faith)* rechazar

deodorant [di:'əʊdərənt] *n* desodorante *m*

deodorize [di:'əʊdəraɪz] *vt* desodorizar

dep (*abbr* **departure, departs, departing, departed**) salida *f*, sale, saliendo, salió

depart [dɪ'pɑ:t] *vi (leave)* marcharse, irse (**from** de); *Fig (deviate) (from subject)* desviarse (**from** de); *(from routine)* salirse (**from** de)

departed [dɪ'pɑ:tɪd] *Euph* **1** *adj* difunto(a)

2 the d. *npl* el difunto/la difunta, los difuntos/las difuntas

department [dɪ'pɑ:tmənt] *n* (**a**) *(division) (in office, bank etc)* sección *f*, servicio *m*; *(in hospital)* departamento *m*; *(in shop)* sección *f*, departamento *m*; *(in university etc)* departamento *m*, facultad *f*; *(in government)* ministerio *m*, departamento *m* ❑ *Com* **accounts d.** (sección *f* de) contabilidad *f*; **d. store** grandes almacenes *mpl*; **sales d.** (sección *f* de) ventas *fpl* (**b**) *Fam (responsibility)* campo *m*, esfera *f*; **pets aren't my d.** no me toca a mí cuidar los animales domésticos

departmental [di:pɑ:t'mentəl] *adj* departamental

departure [dɪ'pɑ:tʃər] *n* (**a**) *(leaving)* marcha *f*, partida *f* ❑ *(at airport, station)* **d. board** tablón *m* de salidas; *Av* **d. lounge** sala *f* de embarque; **d. time** hora *f* de salida (**b**) *Fig (from routine)* salida *f* (**from** de); *(from previous policy)* reorientación *f*

depend [dɪ'pend] *vi* (**a**) *(rely)* fiarse (**on, upon** de); **a friend you can d. on** un amigo *or* una amiga de confianza; **he'll forget, (you can) d. on it!** ¡se olvidará, puedes estar seguro(a)! (**b**) *impers (be determined by)* depender (**on, upon** de); **it depends on the weather** según el tiempo que haga; **that** *or* **it all depends** según, eso depende

dependable [dɪ'pendəbəl] *adj (person)* responsable, fiable, digno(a) de confianza; *(income)* seguro(a); *(car, machine)* fiable, *Am* confiable

dependant, *US* **dependent** [dɪ'pendənt] *n* dependiente *mf*

dependence [dɪ'pendəns] *n* (**a**) *(need)* dependencia *f* (**b**) *(trust)* confianza *f*

dependency [dɪ'pendənsɪ] *n Pol* dependencia *f*

dependent [dɪ'pendənt] **1** *adj (reliant)* dependiente; *Pol* **d. territories** territorios *mpl* anexos; **to be d. on sth** depender de algo (**b**) *Ling* subordinado(a) ❑ **d. clause** oración *f* subordinada

2 *n US see* **dependant**

depending [dɪ'pendɪŋ] *adv* **d. on** dependiendo de

depict [dɪ'pɪkt] *vt Art* representar, pintar, retratar; *Fig* describir, retratar

depiction [dɪ'pɪkʃən] *n (picture)* representación *f*; *(description)* descripción *f*

depilatory [dɪ'pɪlətərɪ] *n* depilatorio *m* ❑ **d. cream** crema *f* depilatoria

deplete [dɪ'pli:t] *vt Fml* reducir

depletion [dɪ'pli:ʃən] *n Fml* reducción *f*

deplorable [dɪ'plɔ:rəbəl] *adj* lamentable, deplorable

deplore [dɪ'plɔ:r] *vt* lamentar, deplorar

deploy [dɪ'plɔɪ] *vt Mil (troops, ships etc)* desplegar; *Fig (staff, resources)* utilizar

deployment [dɪ'plɔɪmənt] n despliegue m

depoliticize [di:pə'lɪtɪsaɪz] vt despolitizar

depopulate [di:'pɒpjʊleɪt] vt despoblar

depopulation [di:pɒpjʊ'leɪʃən] n despoblación f

deport [dɪ'pɔːt] vt expulsar, deportar (**from** de; **to** a)

deportation [di:pɔː'teɪʃən] n expulsión f, deportación f □ **d. order** orden f de expulsión

deportee [di:pɔː'tiː] n deportado(a) m,f

deportment [dɪ'pɔːtmənt] n Fml porte m

depose [dɪ'pəʊz] **1** vt (leader, president) deponer, destituir; (king) destronar
2 vi Jur declarar, prestar declaración, deponer

deposit [dɪ'pɒzɪt] **1** n (**a**) (gen) sedimento m; Min yacimiento m; (in wine) poso m, heces mpl; Chem precipitado m (**b**) (in bank etc) depósito m □ Br **d. account** cuenta f de ahorros (**c**) Com (on purchase) señal f; (on rented car, property) depósito m; (on house purchase) entrada f; Com **to put a d. on sth** dejar una señal para algo
2 vt (**a**) (leave) depositar (**b**) (put down) depositar, poner, colocar; **the taxi deposited me at the door** el taxi me dejó en la puerta (**c**) (store) (valuables etc) depositar; (luggage) dejar en consigna (**d**) (pay) (into account) Esp ingresar, Am depositar; (towards sth) pagar un depósito de

deposition [depə'zɪʃən] n (**a**) (of leader, president) deposición f, destitución f; (of king) destronamiento m (**b**) Jur (of witness) declaración f

depositor [dɪ'pɒzɪtər] n depositante mf

depot [Br 'depəʊ, US 'di:pəʊ] n (**a**) (gen) almacén m; Mil depósito m; (bus garage) cochera f (de autobuses); (rail siding) depósito m de locomotoras (**b**) US (bus station) estación f de autobuses, CAm Méx central f camionera; (railway station) estación f de ferrocarriles

deprave [dɪ'preɪv] vt depravar

depraved [dɪ'preɪvd] adj (person) depravado(a)

depravity [dɪ'prævɪtɪ] n depravación f

deprecate ['deprɪkeɪt] vt Fml desaprobar, censurar

deprecatory ['deprɪkətərɪ] adj desaprobatorio(a)

depreciate [dɪ'priːʃɪeɪt] vi depreciarse

depreciation [dɪpriːʃɪ'eɪʃən] n depreciación f, desvalorización f

depress [dɪ'pres] vt (**a**) (discourage) deprimir, desanimar, desalentar (**b**) Econ (reduce) (profits) reducir; (trade) dificultar; (prices, wages) disminuir, hacer bajar (**c**) Fml (press down) (switch, lever etc) apretar; (clutch, piano pedal) pisar

depressed [dɪ'prest] adj (**a**) (person) deprimido(a), desanimado(a), desalentado(a); **to get d.** desanimarse (**b**) Econ (area) deprimido(a); (stock market) paralizado(a), en crisis (**c**) (surface) hundido(a), deprimido(a)

depressing [dɪ'presɪŋ] adj deprimente; **I find it d.** me deprime

depression [dɪ'preʃən] n (**a**) (low spirits) depresión f (**b**) Econ crisis f inv económica (**c**) (hollow) depresión f (**d**) Meteor depresión f

depressive [dɪ'presɪv] adj depresivo(a)

deprivation [deprɪ'veɪʃən] n (hardship) privación f; (loss) pérdida f

deprive [dɪ'praɪv] vt (gen) privar (**of** de); (of office) destituir (**of** de)

deprived [dɪ'praɪvd] adj pobre, necesitado(a)

Dept (abbr **Department**) departamento m, dpt., dpto.; (in store) sección f

depth [depθ] n (**a**) (of pond, hole) profundidad f; (of cupboard, shelf) fondo m; (of hem, border) ancho m; **to be or get out of one's d.** (in water) perder pie; Fig (in conversation

etc) meterse en camisa de once varas □ Mil **d. charge** carga f de profundidad (**b**) Fig (of emotion, colour, gaze) intensidad f; (of shame, anxiety, silence, mystery) profundidad f; (of thought) complejidad f; **in the depths of the forest** en el corazón del bosque; **in the depths of night** a altas horas de la noche; **in the depths of winter** en pleno invierno; **to be in the depths of despair** estar completamente desesperado(a); **to study sth in d.** estudiar algo a fondo

deputation [depjʊ'teɪʃən] n inv delegación f

depute [dɪ'pjuːt] vt Fml (responsibility, power) delegar (**to** en); (person) diputar

deputize ['depjʊtaɪz] vi **to d. for sb** suplir a algn

deputy ['depjʊtɪ] n (**a**) (substitute) suplente mf, sustituto(a) m,f □ **d. chairman** vicepresidente m; **d. director** director(a) m,f adjunto(a); Educ **d. head** subdirector(a) m,f (**b**) Pol (representative) diputado(a) m,f

derail [dɪ'reɪl] vt hacer descarrilar

derailment [dɪ'reɪlmənt] n descarrilamiento m

deranged [dɪ'reɪndʒd] adj trastornado(a), loco(a)

derby ['dɑːbɪ] n (**a**) Sport prueba f; **donkey d.** carrera f de burros; Br **the D.** carrera f (anual) clásica de caballos (**b**) ['dɜːrbɪ] US sombrero m hongo, bombín m

deregulate [di:'regjʊleɪt] vt Com Econ liberalizar

deregulation [di:regjʊ'leɪʃən] n Com Econ liberalización f

derelict ['derɪlɪkt] adj abandonado(a), en ruinas

dereliction [derɪ'lɪkʃən] n (ruin) abandono m; Fml **d. of duty** incumplimiento m del deber

deride [dɪ'raɪd] vt ridiculizar, burlarse, mofarse

derision [dɪ'rɪʒən] n mofa f, burla f; **his views met with d.** se mofaron de sus opiniones; **laugh of d.** risa f burlona

derisive [dɪ'raɪsɪv] adj burlón(ona), irónico(a)

derisory [dɪ'raɪsərɪ] adj irrisorio(a), ridículo(a)

derivation [derɪ'veɪʃən] n derivación f

derivative [de'rɪvətɪv] **1** adj (art, writing) sin originalidad, poco original
2 n (of word, substance) derivado m

derive [dɪ'raɪv] Fml **1** vt sacar; **I d. comfort from my family** la familia es un consuelo para mí
2 vi (word) derivarse (**from** de); (skill) provenir (**from** de)

dermatitis [dɜːmə'taɪtɪs] n Med dermatitis f

dermatology [dɜːmə'tɒlədʒɪ] n Med dermatología f

derogatory [dɪ'rɒgətərɪ] adj (remark, article) despectivo(a); (meaning) peyorativo(a)

derrick ['derɪk] n (**a**) (crane) grúa f (**b**) (over oil well) torre f de perforación

desalination [di:sælɪ'neɪʃən] n desalinización f, desalación f

descant ['deskænt] n Mus contrapunto m

descend [dɪ'send] **1** vi (**a**) (come or go down) (gen) bajar, descender; Fig **night descended** se hizo de noche (**b**) **to d. on** (invade) (enemy) caer sobre, atacar; (area) invadir; Fig **they descended on us at lunchtime** se dejaron caer por casa a la hora del almuerzo (**c**) (lower yourself) (to gossip, rudeness) rebajarse (**to** a); **to d. to telling lies** recurrir a mentiras (**d**) (be related to) descender
2 vt (stairs) bajar

descendant [dɪ'sendənt] n descendiente mf

descent [dɪ'sent] n (**a**) (way down) descenso m, bajada f (**b**) (degeneration) caída f; **d. into poverty** caída en la miseria (**c**) (slope) declive m, pendiente f (**d**) (ancestry) ascendencia f, familia f; **she is of Russian d.** es de ascendencia rusa (**e**) (attack) incursión f

describe [dɪ'skraɪb] vt (**a**) (depict verbally) describir; **d. him to me** cuéntame cómo es; **I wouldn't d. her as an**

expert no la calificaría de experta (**b**) *Tech (arc, circle)* trazar

description [dɪ'skrɪpʃən] *n* (**a**) *(portrayal, account)* descripción *f*; **it was painful beyond d.** el dolor era indescriptible; **to beggar** *or* **defy d.** superar la descripción (**b**) *(type)* clase *f*; **fish of all descriptions** peces de toda clase; **transport of some d.** algún medio de transporte

descriptive [dɪ'skrɪptɪv] *adj* descriptivo(a)

desecrate ['desɪkreɪt] *vt* profanar

desecration [desɪ'kreɪʃən] *n* profanación *f*

desegregate [di:'segrɪgeɪt] *vt* suprimir la segregación racial

desensitize [di:'sensɪtaɪz] *vt (emotionally)* insensibilizar

desert¹ ['dezət] *n* desierto *m*; **the Sahara D.** el desierto del Sáhara ❑ **d. island** isla *f* desierta

desert² [dɪ'zɜ:t] **1** *vt (place, family)* abandonar; *(political party, attributes)* desertar
2 *vi Mil* desertar (**from** de)

deserted [dɪ'zɜ:tɪd] *adj* desierto(a)

deserter [dɪ'zɜ:tər] *n Mil* desertor(a) *m,f*

desertification [dɪzɜ:tɪfɪ'keɪʃən] *n* desertización *f*

desertion [dɪ'zɜ:ʃən] *n (gen)* abandono *m*; *Pol* defección *f*; *Mil* deserción *f*; *Jur* **divorce on the grounds of d.** divorcio *m* por abandono del domicilio conyugal

deserts [dɪ'zɜ:ts] *npl* merecido *m*; **to get one's just d.** llevarse su merecido

deserve [dɪ'zɜ:v] *vt (rest, punishment)* merecer, *Am* ameritar; *(prize, praise)* ser digno(a) de; **she got what she deserved** se llevó su merecido

deservedly [dɪ'zɜ:vɪdlɪ] *adv* con (toda) razón

deserving [dɪ'zɜ:vɪŋ] *adj (person)* de valía, que vale; *(action, cause)* meritorio(a); *Fml* **to be d. of praise/blame** ser digno(a) de elogio/censura

desiccated ['desɪkeɪtɪd] *adj Fml (gen)* desecado(a); *(skin)* deshidratado(a) ❑ *Culin* **d. coconut** coco *m* rallado

design [dɪ'zaɪn] **1** *n (a)* *Art* diseño *m*, dibujo *m*; **fashion d.** creación *f* or diseño *m* de modas (**b**) *(preliminary plan) (of building, vehicle)* plano *m*; *(of dress etc)* patrón *m*; *(of painting, sculpture)* boceto *m*; *(of course, test, computer program)* modelo *m* (**c**) *(general arrangement, form)* diseño *m*; *(of room, city centre)* disposición *f*; **the d. of the car was wrong** el coche estaba mal concebido; **the overall d.** el concepto *or* la idea general (**d**) *(decoration, pattern)* dibujo *m*, diseño *m*, motivo *m* ornamental *or* decorativo (**e**) *Fig (scheme)* plan *m*, intención *f*, proyecto *m*; **was it by accident or by d.?** ¿ocurrió por casualidad o bien a propósito?; *Fam* **to have designs on sth/sb** tener puestas las miras en algo/en algn
2 *vt* (**a**) *(draw, create) (gen)* diseñar; *(fashions)* crear (**b**) *(intend, plan)* concebir; **the oven is designed to switch itself off** el horno está programado para autodesconectarse
3 *vi Art* diseñar

designate ['dezɪgneɪt] **1** *vt* (**a**) *(appoint)* designar, nombrar (**b**) *Fml (mark, show) (boundary)* señalar, indicar
2 ['dezɪgnɪt] *adj* designado(a), nombrado(a)

designation [dezɪg'neɪʃən] *n Fml* (**a**) *(appointment)* nombramiento *m*; **his d. as minister** su designación como ministro (**b**) *(title)* denominación *f*

designer [dɪ'zaɪnər] *n* diseñador(a) *m,f* ❑ **d. clothes/drugs** ropa *f*/drogas *fpl* de diseño; *Hum* **d. stubble** barba *f* de tres días; *Tex* **dress** *or* **fashion d.** diseñador(a) *m,f* de modas, modisto(a) *m,f*; *Cin Theat* **set d.** escenógrafo(a) *m,f*

designing [dɪ'zaɪnɪŋ] *adj Pej* intrigante

desirability [dɪzaɪərə'bɪlɪtɪ] *n (of outcome)* conveniencia *f*; *(of person)* atractivo *m*

desirable [dɪ'zaɪərəbəl] *adj* (**a**) *(attractive) (asset, position, offer)* atractivo(a); *(residence)* de alto standing; *(woman)* deseable, seductora (**b**) *(advisable)* conveniente, prudente; **it is d. that safety helmets should be worn** es aconsejable llevar casco de seguridad; **make what changes you think are d.** haga los cambios que le parezcan oportunos

desire [dɪ'zaɪər] **1** *n* (**a**) *(longing)* deseo *m*, anhelo *m*, ansia *f*; *(sexual longing)* deseo *m*, instinto *m* sexual (**b**) *(wish)* deseo·*m*; **I haven't the slightest d. to go** no me apetece *or Carib Col Méx* provoca nada ir, *CSur* no tengo nada de ganas de ir
2 *vt* (**a**) *(long for)* desear, anhelar, ansiar; *(person)* desear (**b**) *(wish for)* desear; *Iron* **it leaves much** *or* **a lot** *or* **a great deal to be desired** deja mucho que desear

desirous [dɪ'zaɪərəs] *adj Fml* deseoso(a)

desist [dɪ'zɪst] *vi Fml* desistir (**from** de); **to d. from smoking** abstenerse de fumar

desk [desk] *n (in school)* pupitre *m*; *(in office etc)* escritorio *m* ❑ **cash d.** caja *f*; *US* **d. clerk** *(in hotel)* recepcionista *mf*; **d. job, d. work** trabajo *m* de oficina; **information d.** (oficina *f* de) información *f*; **news d.** redacción *f*; **reception d.** recepción *f*

deskilling [di:'skɪlɪŋ] *n* = pérdida de la aportación humana en un trabajo como resultado de la introducción de una nueva tecnología

desktop ['desktɒp] *n Comptr* **d. computer** *Esp* ordenador *m* or *Am* computadora *f* de sobremesa; **d. publishing** autoedición *f*

desolate ['desəlɪt] **1** *adj* (**a**) *(uninhabited)* deshabitado(a), desierto(a); desocupado(a), despoblado(a), solitario(a); *(barren)* yermo(a), desolado(a) (**b**) *(person) (forlorn)* desconsolado(a), afligido(a); *(friendless)* solitario(a)
2 ['desəleɪt] *vt Literary* desolar

desolation [desə'leɪʃən] *n* (**a**) *(of place)* desolación *f*; *(by destruction)* asolamiento *m* (**b**) *(of person)* desconsuelo *m*, aflicción *f*; **to feel a sense of d.** sentirse abandonado(a)

despair [dɪ'speər] **1** *n* desesperación *f*; **to drive sb to d.** desesperar a algn; *Fig* **he's the d. of his parents** es una cruz para sus padres
2 *vi* desesperar(se), perder la esperanza (**of** de); **don't d.!** ¡no te desanimes!, ¡ánimo!

despairing [dɪ'speərɪŋ] *adj* de desesperación, desesperado(a)

despairingly [dɪ'speərɪŋlɪ] *adv* con desesperación

despatch [dɪ'spætʃ] *n & vt see* **dispatch**

desperate ['despərɪt] *adj* (**a**) *(reckless)* desesperado(a); *(sight, struggle)* encarnizado(a); **to do something d.** cometer un acto de desesperación; **to get d.** estar a punto de desesperarse (**b**) *(critical, extreme) (situation)* desesperado(a), grave; *(need)* urgente, apremiante; *(conditions)* malísimo(a); **to be d. for sth/to do sth** necesitar algo/hacer algo con gran urgencia

desperately ['despərətlɪ] *adv (recklessly)* desesperadamente; *(struggle)* encarnizadamente; *(ill)* gravemente, de gravedad; *(in love)* locamente; *(difficult, serious)* sumamente; **he was d. in need of sleep** le hacía muchísima falta dormir

desperation [despə'reɪʃən] *n* desesperación *f*; **in d.** a la desesperada; **the children drove her to d.** los niños la volvían loca

despicable [dɪ'spɪkəbəl] *adj (person, act)* despreciable, vil; *(behaviour)* indigno(a)

despicably [dɪ'spɪkəblɪ] *adv* de una manera despreciable *or* vil

despise [dɪ'spaɪz] *vt* despreciar, menospreciar

despite [dɪ'spaɪt] *prep Fml* a pesar de

despondency [dɪ'spɒndənsɪ] n desánimo m, abatimiento m

despondent [dɪ'spɒndənt] adj abatido(a), desanimado(a), desalentado(a)

despondently [dɪ'spɒndəntlɪ] adv con desánimo, sin entusiasmo

despot ['despɒt] n déspota mf

despotic [dɪs'pɒtɪk] adj despótico(a)

despotism ['despətɪzəm] n despotismo m

dessert [dɪ'zɜːt] n Culin postre m ❏ **d. wine** vino m dulce

dessertspoon [dɪ'zɜːtspuːn] n cuchara for Ven cucharilla f de postre; (as measurement) cucharada f de las de postre

destabilize [diː'steɪbəlaɪz] vt desestabilizar

destination [destɪ'neɪʃən] n destino m ❏ Comptr **d. drive** unidad f (de disco) de destino

destined ['destɪnd] adj (a) (meant, fated) destinado(a); **he was d. to be king** estaba llamado a ser rey; **she was d. to meet him** el destino quiso que le conociera; **the attempt was d. to fail** el atentado estaba condenado al fracaso (b) (bound) con destino (**for** a)

destiny ['destɪnɪ] n destino m, sino m

destitute ['destɪtjuːt] adj indigente; **to be d.** estar en la miseria

destitution [destɪ'tjuːʃən] n indigencia f; **in d.** en la miseria

destroy [dɪ'strɔɪ] vt (a) (building, letter, area) destruir; (vehicle, old furniture) destrozar; (plans, hopes, chances) destruir, destrozar; (health, career, reputation) destruir, arruinar (b) Euph (kill) (sick or unwanted animal) matar, abatir; (insects, pests, vermin) aniquilar

destroyer [dɪ'strɔɪə] n Naut destructor m

destruction [dɪ'strʌkʃən] n (gen) destrucción f, ruina f; **the d. caused by floods** los destrozos or daños causados por las inundaciones

destructive [dɪ'strʌktɪv] adj (gale, fire etc) destructor(a); (power, tendency) destructivo(a), (child) destrozón(ona); (criticism) destructivo(a), perjudicial

destructiveness [dɪ'strʌktɪvnɪs] n (of gale etc) poder m destructor, destructividad f; (of criticism) poder m destructivo

desultorily ['desəltərɪlɪ] adv (randomly) vagamente

desultory ['desəltərɪ] adj Fml (a) (fitful, unplanned) (attempts) irregular; **he worked in a d. way** trabajaba sin orden ni concierto (b) (random) (remark, conversation) inconexo(a), vago(a)

detach [dɪ'tætʃ] vt (remove) separar, quitar (**from** de); Mil destacar (**from** de); **she detached herself from the group** se apartó del grupo

detachable [dɪ'tætʃəbəl] adj (gen) separable (**from** de); (collar) postizo(a)

detached [dɪ'tætʃt] adj (a) (separated) separado(a), suelto(a) ❏ esp Br **d. house** casa f or chalé m individual; Med **d. retina** retina f desprendida (b) (impartial) objetivo(a), desinteresado(a), imparcial; (unemotional) indiferente

detachment [dɪ'tætʃmənt] n (a) (impartiality) objetividad f, imparcialidad f; (aloofness) desapego m; **an air of d.** un aire de indiferencia (b) Mil destacamento m

detail [Br 'diːteɪl, US dɪ'teɪl] **1** n (a) (item, particular) detalle m, pormenor m; **attention to d.** preocupación f por los detalles; **to have an eye for d.** fijarse en los detalles; **without going into detail(s), we won the match** sin entrar en detalles or pormenores, ganamos el partido (b) **details** (information) información f sing; **please send full d. of your activities** rogamos envíe información completa

sobre sus actividades (c) Mil destacamento m
2 vt (a) (list) detallar, enumerar (b) Mil (appoint) destacar; **to d. sb for sth/to do sth** destacar a algn para algo/para hacer algo

detailed ['diːteɪld] adj (description) detallado(a), minucioso(a), pormenorizado(a)

detain [dɪ'teɪn] vt (a) Jur (hold) detener (b) (delay) retener; **I won't d. you any longer** no le entretengo más

detainee [diːteɪ'niː] n Jur detenido(a) m,f; Pol preso(a) m,f

detect [dɪ'tekt] vt (a) (error, movement) advertir, detectar; (sarcasm, difference) notar; (smell, sound) percibir (b) (discover) (substance, fraud) descubrir; (enemy ship) detectar; (position) localizar

detectable [dɪ'tektəbəl] adj (difference, flaw) detectable; **a barely d. scent of roses** un perfume de rosas que apenas se percibía

detection [dɪ'tekʃən] n (a) (noticing) (of error, substance) descubrimiento m; (of smell, sound) percepción f; **to escape d.** pasar inadvertido(a) (b) (discovery) (of criminal) descubrimiento m; (of enemy ship) detección f

detective [dɪ'tektɪv] n detective mf ❏ **d. story** novela f policíaca; **d. work** investigaciones fpl

detector [dɪ'tektə] n aparato m detector ❏ **metal d.** detector m de metales

détente [deɪ'tɒnt] n distensión f (entre países)

detention [dɪ'tenʃən] n (of suspect etc) detención f, arresto m; Educ **to give/get d.** castigar/quedar castigado(a) ❏ Jur **d. centre** centro m de internamiento

deter [dɪ'tɜːr] vt (pt & pp **deterred**) (dissuade) disuadir (**from** de); (stop) impedir, hacer desistir (**from** de); **he was not deterred** no se desanimaba

detergent [dɪ'tɜːdʒənt] n detergente m

deteriorate [dɪ'tɪərɪəreɪt] vi (gen) deteriorar, empeorar; (substance, friendship) deteriorar

deterioration [dɪtɪərɪə'reɪʃən] n (gen) empeoramiento m; (of substance, friendship) deterioro m

determination [dɪtɜːmɪ'neɪʃən] n (a) (resolution) resolución f, decisión f, determinación f; **with an air of d.** con un aire decidido (b) (settling) determinación f

determine [dɪ'tɜːmɪn] vt (a) (find out) (cause, meaning) determinar, averiguar; (position, speed) determinar, calcular (b) (settle) (date, price) fijar, determinar; (limit, boundary) determinar, definir (c) (influence) (reaction, expenditure) determinar, condicionar (d) Fml (decide) determinar, decidir, resolver

determined [dɪ'tɜːmɪnd] adj (person) decidido(a), resuelto(a); (attempt, effort) enérgico(a), persistente

determining [dɪ'tɜːmɪnɪŋ] adj (factor, influence) determinante, decisivo(a)

deterrent [dɪ'terənt] **1** adj disuasivo(a), disuasorio(a)
2 n fuerza f de disuasión, fuerza f disuasoria or disuasiva; **to act as a d.** disuadir, servir como fuerza disuasoria ❏ Mil **nuclear d.** arma f nuclear disuasoria

detest [dɪ'test] vt detestar, odiar, aborrecer

detestable [dɪ'testəbəl] adj detestable, odioso(a)

detestation [diːtes'teɪʃən] n odio m, aborrecimiento m

dethrone [diː'θrəʊn] vt destronar

detonate ['detəneɪt] **1** vt hacer detonar, hacer estallar, hacer explotar
2 vi detonar, estallar, explotar

detonation [detə'neɪʃən] n detonación f, explosión f

detonator ['detəneɪtə] n detonador m

detour ['diːtʊər] n desvío m; US (diversion of traffic) desviación f; **to make a d.** dar un rodeo

detoxification [diːtɒksɪfɪ'keɪʃən] n, Fam **detox**

['di:tɒks] *n* desintoxicación *f*; **d. centre/programme** centro *m*/programa *m* de desintoxicación

detoxify [di:'tɒksɪfaɪ] *vt (person)* desintoxicar

detract [dɪ'trækt] *vi* quitar mérito (**from** a)

detractor [dɪ'træktər] *n* detractor(a) *m,f*

detriment ['detrɪmənt] *n Fml* detrimento *m* (**to** de), perjuicio *m* (**to** de)

detrimental [detrɪ'mentəl] *adj Fml (gen)* perjudicial (**to** para); *(noxious)* nocivo(a) (**to** para)

detritus [dɪ'traɪtəs] *n Geol & Fig* detrito *m*, detritus *m inv*

deuce [dju:s] *n (in tennis)* cuarenta iguales *mpl*

Deutschmark ['dɔɪtʃmɑːk] *n Formerly* marco *m* alemán

devaluation [di:væljuː'eɪʃən] *n* devaluación *f*, desvalorización *f*

devalue [di:'væljuː] *vt* devaluar, desvalorizar

devastate ['devəsteɪt] *vt* (**a**) *(city, area)* devastar, asolar, destruir (**b**) *Fig (person)* anonadar, apabullar; **he was devastated by the news** 'se quedó *or* se sintió anonado por la noticia

devastating ['devəsteɪtɪŋ] *adj* (**a**) *(storm, fire)* devastador(a), asolador(a); *(wind, flood)* arrollador(a) (**b**) *Fig (argument)* apabullante, abrumador(a); *(charm, beauty)* fatal; *Fam* **you look d.!** ¡estás guapísimo(a)!, ¡estás irresistible!

devastatingly ['devəsteɪtɪŋlɪ] *adv (witty, simple)* extraordinariamente

devastation [devə'steɪʃən] *n* devastación *f*, asolación *f*, asolamiento *m*

develop [dɪ'veləp] **1** *vt* (**a**) *(cultivate) (gen)* desarrollar; *(trade, arts)* fomentar; *(skill, system)* perfeccionar (**b**) *(start) (roots)* echar; *(plan, programme)* elaborar, formar; *(illness)* contraer, coger; **he soon developed spots** pronto le empezaron a salir granos (**c**) *Fml (acquire) (talent, interest)* mostrar; *(habit)* contraer, adquirir; *(tendency)* revelar, manifestar; *(accent)* contraer; **to d. a taste/hatred for sth** agarrarle *or Esp* cogerle gusto/odio a algo (**d**) *(exploit) (natural resources)* aprovechar, explotar; *(region)* desarrollar, explotar; *Constr (site, area)* urbanizar; **the area will be developed soon** próximamente se urbanizará esta zona (**e**) *Phot* revelar

2 *vi* (**a**) *(grow) (body, muscles, industry)* desarrollarse; *(system)* perfeccionarse; *(feeling, interest)* aumentar, crecer; *(plot, theme)* elaborarse; **it developed from friendship into love** se transformó de amistad en amor (**b**) *Fml (appear)* aparecer; *(situation)* producirse

developer [dɪ'veləpər] *n* (**a**) *Phot* revelador *m* (**b**) *Constr* (**property) d.** inmobiliaria *f*, empresa *f* constructora

development [dɪ'veləpmənt] *n* (**a**) *(growth)* desarrollo *m*; *(of trade, arts)* fomento *m*; *(of skill, system)* perfección *f*; *(of plot, theme, plan)* elaboración *f*; *(of character, writer)* formación *f*; **at the peak** *or* **height of d.** en pleno desarrollo ❑ **d. aid** ayuda *f* al desarrollo; *Econ* **d. potential** potencial *m* de explotación (**b**) *(advance)* avance *m*; **the latest developments in science** los últimos descubrimientos de la ciencia (**c**) *(change)* cambio *m*; *(in situation, policy, attitude)* dirección *f*, rumbo *m*; **let's await developments** esperemos a ver lo que pasa; **there are no new developments** no hay ninguna novedad (**d**) *(exploitation)* explotación *f*, aprovechamiento *m* (**e**) *Constr* urbanización *f* ❑ *Br* **d. area** = área deprimida en la que el gobierno fomenta la creación de nuevas industrias; **housing d.** conjunto *m* residencial

developmental [dɪveləp'mentəl] *adj* de desarrollo

deviance ['di:vɪəns] *n* desviación *f*

deviant ['di:vɪənt] **1** *adj (behaviour, action)* anormal, irregular; *(sexuality)* pervertido(a)

2 *n* pervertido(a) *m,f*

deviate ['di:vɪeɪt] *vi* desviarse (**from** de)

deviation [di:vɪ'eɪʃən] *n (from norm, route)* desviación *f* (**from** de); *(from truth)* alejamiento *m*; **sexual d.** perversión *f* sexual

device [dɪ'vaɪs] *n* (**a**) *(object) (gen)* aparato *m*; *(mechanism)* mecanismo *m* ❑ *Comptr* **d. driver** controlador *m* de dispositivos *or* periféricos; **electronic d.** dispositivo *m* electrónico; **explosive d.** artefacto *m* explosivo; **orthopaedic d.** aparato *m* ortopédico (**b**) *(trick, scheme)* ardid *m*, estratagema *f*, plan *m*; **to leave sb to his own devices** dejar que algn se las apañe solo

devil ['devəl] *n* (**a**) *(evil spirit)* diablo *m*, demonio *m*; **d.'s advocate** abogado(a) *m,f* del diablo; **the D.** el Diablo, el Demonio; *Fig* **between the d. and the deep blue sea** entre la espada y la pared; *Fam* **it's the (very) d. to fix** es dificilísimo de arreglar; *Fam* **talk** *or* **speak of the d.!** ¡hablando del rey de Roma!; *Fam* **to have the luck of the d.** desafiar a la suerte y tener éxito; *Fam* **to run/work like the d.** correr/trabajar como un loco(a); *Fam* **where the d. did you put it?** ¿dónde demonios lo pusiste?; *Prov* **better the d. you know** más vale malo conocido (**b**) *Fam* **go on, be a d.!** ¡anda!, ¡atrévete!; *(child)* **little d.** diablillo *m*; **poor d.** *(unlucky person)* pobre *mf*, pobre diablo *m*; *(wretched person)* desgraciado(a) *m,f*; **you lucky d.!** ¡vaya suerte que tienes! (**c**) *Fam* **he had a** *or* **the d. of a job selling his car** sudó tinta para vender su coche; **it's a d. of a problem** menudo problemón

devilish ['devəlɪʃ] *adj* (**a**) *(wicked)* malvado(a), diabólico(a) (**b**) *(difficult)* diabólico(a)

devilishly ['devəlɪʃlɪ] *adv Fam* muy, sumamente; **we were d. lucky** tuvimos una gran suerte

devil-may-care ['devəlmeɪ'keər] *adj* despreocupado(a)

devilry ['devəlrɪ] *n* diablura *f*; **to be full of d.** ser de la piel del diablo

devious ['di:vɪəs] *adj* (**a**) *(winding) (path etc)* tortuoso(a) (**b**) *esp Pej (not straightforward) (person)* tortuoso(a), taimado(a), falso(a); *(mind)* tortuoso(a); *(process, argument)* intrincado(a), enrevesado(a); **by d. means** *(complicated)* por medios complicados; *(underhand)* por medios poco limpios; **she's very d.** disimula *or* finge a la perfección

deviousness ['di:vɪəsnɪs] *n (of person)* tortuosidad *f*, falsedad *f*; *(of argument)* intrincamiento *m*

devise [dɪ'vaɪs] *vt* idear, concebir, inventar

devoid [dɪ'vɔɪd] *adj* desprovisto(a) (**of** de); **d. of interest** falto(a) de interés

devolution [di:və'lu:ʃən] *n Pol* transmisión *f* de poderes; **the nationalists want d.** los nacionalistas quieren la autonomía

devolve [dɪ'vɒlv] **1** *vt Pol* delegar; *(autonomy)* descentralizar; **to d. government on** *or* **to the regions** dar autonomía a las regiones

2 *vi (duty, task)* **to d. on sth/sb** recaer sobre algo/algn, corresponder a algo/algn

devote [dɪ'vəʊt] *vt* dedicar; **she devoted her life to helping the poor** consagró su vida a la ayuda de los pobres

devoted [dɪ'vəʊtɪd] *adj* fiel, leal (**to** a); **he's d. to sport** tiene gran afición al deporte; **to be d. to sb** tenerle mucho cariño a algn

devotee [devə'ti:] *n* (**a**) *(of religion)* devoto(a) *m,f* (**b**) *(of theatre, sport)* aficionado(a) *m,f*; *Pol* partidario(a) *m,f*

devotion [dɪ'vəʊʃən] *n* (**a**) *(to friend, master)* lealtad *f*, fidelidad *f*; *(to family, wife)* cariño *m*, afecto *m*, amor *m*; *(to research, cause)* dedicación *f*, entrega *f*; **d. to duty** cumplimiento *m* fiel de su deber (**b**) *Rel* devoción *f*, fervor *m*; **devotions** oraciones *fpl*; **he was at his devotions** rezaba

devour [dɪ'vaʊər] vt (meal) devorar, zampar; (prey, book) devorar; Fig **I was devoured by jealousy** me devoraban or me consumían los celos

devout [dɪ'vaʊt] adj Rel devoto(a); (prayer, hope) sincero(a)

devoutly [dɪ'vaʊtlɪ] adv con devoción

dew [djuː] n rocío m

dewy ['djuːɪ] adj (**dewier, dewiest**) rociado(a), cubierto(a) de rocío

dewy-eyed [djuːr'aɪd] adj Fig (innocent) inocente, ingenuo(a); (loving) romántico(a), sentimental

dexterity [dek'sterɪtɪ] n (of hands, fingers) destreza f, habilidad f; (of movement) agilidad f

dext(e)rous ['dekstrəs] adj (skilful) diestro(a), hábil; (agile) ágil

DfE [diːef'iː] Br (abbr **Department for Education**) = ministerio británico de educación

DG [diː'dʒiː] n (abbr **director-general**) director(a) m,f general

DHTML [diːemʃtiːem'el] n Comptr (abbr **Dynamic Hyper Text Transfer Protocol**) DHTML m

diabetes [daɪə'biːtiːz, daɪə'biːtɪs] n Med diabetes f

diabetic [daɪə'betɪk] Med **1** adj (person) diabético(a); (diet, treatment) para diabéticos
  2 n diabético(a) m,f

diabolic [daɪə'bɒlɪk] adj diabólico(a), demoníaco(a)

diabolical [daɪə'bɒlɪkəl] adj (**a**) (evil) diabólico(a) (**b**) Br Fam (difficult) diabólico(a); (unbearable) (noise, delay, weather) insoportable, espantoso(a)

diadem ['daɪədem] n diadema f

diagnose ['daɪəgnəʊz] vt Med (condition) diagnosticar; Fig (fault) descubrir; **his illness was diagnosed as hepatitis** le diagnosticaron una hepatitis

diagnosis [daɪəg'nəʊsɪs] n (pl **diagnoses** [daɪəg'nəʊsiːz]) Med diagnóstico m; **to make** or **give a d.** hacer un diagnóstico

diagnostic [daɪəg'nɒstɪk] adj Med diagnóstico(a)

diagonal [daɪ'ægənəl] adj & n diagonal (f)

diagonally [daɪ'ægənəlɪ] adv (cut) en diagonal; (go across) diagonalmente

diagram ['daɪəgræm] n (gen) diagrama m; (of process, system) esquema m; (of workings) gráfico m, plano m

dial ['daɪəl, daɪl] **1** n (of clock, barometer) esfera f; (of radio, time-switch) dial m, cuadrante m; (of telephone) disco m, dial m; (of machine) botón m selector
  2 (pt & pp **dialled**, US **dialed**) vi & vt Tel marcar, Andes RP discar; (operator) llamar; **to d. a wrong number** equivocarse de número ❏ Br **dialling code** prefijo m; Br **dialling** or US **d. tone** tono m de marcar

dialect ['daɪəlekt] n Ling dialecto m

dialectic(al) [daɪə'lektɪkəl] adj dialéctico(a)

dialectic(s) [daɪə'lektɪk(s)] n dialéctica f

dialogue, US **dialog** ['daɪəlɒg] n diálogo m ❏ Comptr **d. box** cuadro m de diálogo

dial-up ['daɪlʌp] n Comptr conexión f telefónica or Spec por línea conmutada

dialysis [daɪ'ælɪsɪs] n Med diálisis f

diameter [daɪ'æmɪtər] n diámetro m

diametrically [daɪə'metrɪkəlɪ] adv diametralmente

diamond ['daɪəmənd] n (**a**) (gem) diamante m; Fig **rough d.** diamante m (en) bruto ❏ **d. jubilee** sexagésimo aniversario m; **d. wedding** bodas fpl de diamante (**b**) (shape) rombo m (**c**) Cards diamante m

diaper ['daɪəpər] n US pañal m

diaphanous [daɪ'æfənəs] adj diáfano(a)

diaphragm ['daɪəfræm] n Med Anat diafragma m

diarist ['daɪərɪst] n escritor(a) m,f de diarios

diarrhoea, US **diarrhea** [daɪə'rɪə] n diarrea f

diary ['daɪərɪ] n (**a**) (of thoughts, events) diario m; **to keep a d.** llevar un diario (**b**) Br (for appointments) agenda f ❏ **desk d.** agenda f de sobremesa

diatribe ['daɪətraɪb] n diatriba f (**against** contra or en contra de)

dice [daɪs] **1** npl dados mpl; **to shoot** or Br **play d.** jugar a los dados
  2 vt Culin cortar en cuadritos
  3 vi Fig **to d. with death** jugar con la muerte

dicey ['daɪsɪ] adj (**dicier, diciest**) Fam (risky) arriesgado(a); (dangerous) peligroso(a); (uncertain) dudoso(a)

dichotomy [daɪ'kɒtəmɪ] n Fml dicotomía f

dick [dɪk] n (**a**) US Fam (detective) sabueso(a) m,f (**b**) Vulg (penis) Esp polla f, esp Am verga f, Méx pito m, RP pija f

dicta ['dɪktə] npl see dictum

dictate [dɪk'teɪt] **1** vt (**a**) (letter) dictar (**b**) (order) dar
  2 vi (order about) dar órdenes; **I won't be dictated to!** ¡a mí no me manda nadie!
  3 ['dɪkteɪt] n (order) mandato m, orden f; Fig **the dictates of conscience** los dictados de la conciencia

dictation [dɪk'teɪʃən] n (**a**) (of letter, passage) dictado m; **to take d.** escribir al dictado (**b**) (by authority) mandato m

dictator [dɪk'teɪtər] n dictador(a) m,f

dictatorial [dɪktə'tɔːrɪəl] adj dictatorial

dictatorship [dɪk'teɪtəʃɪp] n dictadura f

diction ['dɪkʃən] n dicción f

dictionary ['dɪkʃənərɪ] n diccionario m ❏ **French d.** diccionario m de francés

dictum ['dɪktəm] n (pl **dictums** or **dicta**) (**a**) (formal statement) afirmación f, declaración f; Jur dictamen m (**b**) (saying) dicho m

did [dɪd] pt see do

didactic [dɪ'dæktɪk] adj didáctico(a)

diddle ['dɪdəl] vt Fam estafar, timar; **to d. sb out of sth** sacar algo a algn con maña

die[1] [daɪ] vi (pt & pp **died**) (**a**) (person, animal, plant) morir, morirse; **to be dying** estar agonizando(a); Fam Fig **I nearly died!, I could have died!** (of laughter) ¡casi me muero (de risa)!; (of shame) ¡casi me muero (de vergüenza or CAm Carib Col Méx pena)!; Fam Fig **to be dying for sth/to do sth** morirse por algo/de ganas de hacer algo (**b**) Fig (light, flame) extinguirse, agonizar; (day, wave) morir; (feeling) morir, desaparecer; (smile) desaparecer; Fig (habit, custom) **to d. hard** tardar en desaparecer (**c**) (machine, engine) calarse, pararse; (battery) agotarse; Tel **the phone** or **the line died** la línea se cortó

die away vi (sound) desvanecerse

die back vi (plant) morir hasta las raíces

die down vi (fire) extinguirse, apagarse; (wind, storm) amainar; (noise, excitement) disminuir

die off vi (members of group, family relations) morir uno por uno

die out vi (tribe, species) extinguirse, perderse

die[2] [daɪ] n (**a**) (pl **dies**) (for coins) cuño m, troquel m; Fig **the d. is cast** la suerte está echada (**b**) (pl **dice**) dado m

die-hard ['daɪhɑːd] n reaccionario(a) m,f, intransigente mf

diesel ['diːzəl] n (**a**) (oil, fuel) gasoil m, gasóleo m ❏ **d. engine** motor m diesel (**b**) Fam (vehicle) vehículo m diesel

diet ['daɪət] **1** n (**a**) (normal food) alimentación f, dieta f (**b**)

(selected food) régimen *m*; *Med* dieta *f*; **to be** *or* **go on a d.** estar a régimen
2 *vi* estar a régimen *or* a dieta

dietary ['daɪətərɪ] *adj* alimenticio(a), dietético(a); *(products)* de régimen; *Med* de dieta ❑ **d. fibre** fibra *f* alimenticia

dietician [daɪɪ'tɪʃən] *n Med* especialista *mf* en dietética, *Am* dietista *mf*

differ ['dɪfər] *vi* **(a)** *(be unlike)* ser distinto(a), diferir **(b)** *(disagree)* discrepar; **to agree to d.** quedarse cada uno con la suya; *Fml* **I beg to d.** permítame decir que no estoy de acuerdo

difference ['dɪfərəns] *n* **(a)** *(dissimilarity)* diferencia *f*; **a job with a d.** un trabajo fuera de lo normal; **it makes no d. (to me)** (me) da lo mismo, (me) da igual; **what d. does it make?** ¿qué más da? **(b)** *(disagreement)* desacuerdo *m*; **to settle one's differences** llegar a un acuerdo

different ['dɪfərənt] *adj* **(a)** *(unlike)* diferente, distinto(a); **that's quite a d. matter** ésa es otra cuestión, eso es harina de otro costal; **you look d.** pareces otro(a) **(b)** *(several)* distinto(a); **I spoke to d. people** hablé con varias personas

differential [dɪfə'renʃəl] *n Econ Math* diferencial *f*; *Br* **pay differentials** diferencia *f sing* salarial ❑ *Aut* **d. (gear)** diferencial *f*

differentiate [dɪfə'renʃɪeɪt] **1** *vt* distinguir, diferenciar **(from** de)
2 *vi* distinguir **(between** entre)

differently ['dɪfərəntlɪ] *adv* de otra manera

difficult ['dɪfɪkəlt] *adj (gen)* difícil; **I find it d. to believe (that ...)** me cuesta creer (que ...); **to make life d. for sb** hacerle la vida imposible a algn

difficulty ['dɪfɪkəltɪ] *n (trouble)* dificultad *f*; *(problem)* problema *m*; **to be in difficulties** estar en un apuro *or* un aprieto; **to get into difficulties** meterse en un lío; **to make difficulties** crear problemas, poner pegas; **with d.** difícilmente, a duras penas; **without d.** fácilmente, sin problema *or* problemas

diffidence ['dɪfɪdəns] *n* timidez *f*, falta *f* de confianza en uno(a) mismo(a)

diffident ['dɪfɪdənt] *adj* tímido(a)

diffuse *adj* ['dɪfjuːs] **1** *adj* **(a)** *(light)* difuso(a); *Fig (feeling)* vago(a) **(b)** *Pej (style, writer)* prolijo(a)
2 [dɪ'fjuːz] *vt (light, perfume)* difundir; *(heat)* desprender; *Fig (knowledge)* difundir, extender
3 *vi* difundirse

diffusion [dɪ'fjuːʒən] *n* difusión *f*

dig [dɪg] **1** *n* **(a)** *(poke)* codazo *m* **(b)** *Fam (gibe)* pulla *f*; *(hint)* indirecta *f* **(c)** *(in archeology)* excavación *f* **(d)** **digs** *Br (lodgings)* alojamiento *m sing*; *(room)* habitación *f sing* alquilada
2 *vt (pt & pp* **dug)** **(a)** *(earth, well)* cavar; *(tunnel, trench)* excavar; *(hole)* hacer; *(potatoes etc)* sacar; *Fig* **to d. one's own grave** cavar la (propia) tumba **(b)** *(thrust)* clavar, hincar; **I dug my feet into the sand** hundí los pies en la arena; *Fig* **to d. sb in the ribs** darle un codazo a algn; *Fam Fig* **to d. one's heels in** mantenerse en sus trece **(c)** *Fam (enjoy)* molar, gustar; *(understand)* ligar, comprender
3 *vi (person)* cavar, excavar; *(animal)* escarbar; *(in archeology)* excavar

dig in 1 *vt (compost etc)* enterrar **(b)** *Mil* **to d. oneself in** atrincherarse; *Fam Fig* **we're well dug into our new home** estamos bien instalados en nuestra casa nueva
2 *vi* **(a)** *Mil* atrincherarse **(b)** *Br Fam (start eating)* empezar a comer; *(serve oneself)* servirse; **d. in!** ¡al ataque!, ¡a comer!

dig out *vt (trapped person)* sacar, desenterrar; *Fig (old suit etc)* sacar, desenterrar; *Fig (information)* encontrar, descubrir

dig up *vt (weeds)* arrancar; *(buried object)* desenterrar; *(lawn)* roturar; *(pavement, road)* levantar; *Fig (scandal, facts)* sacar a relucir

digest 1 *n* ['daɪdʒest] *(summary)* resumen *m*
2 [dɪ'dʒest] *vt (food)* digerir; *Fig (facts, novel)* digerir, asimilar

digestible [dɪ'dʒestəbəl] *adj* digerible, digestible

digestion [dɪ'dʒestʃən] *n* digestión *f*

digestive [dɪ'dʒestɪv] *adj* digestivo(a) ❑ *Br* **d. biscuit** galleta *f* integral; **d. system** aparato *m* digestivo

digger ['dɪgər] *n (machine)* excavadora *f*; *(person)* excavador(a) *m,f*

digicam ['dɪdʒɪkæm] *n* cámara *f* digital

digit ['dɪdʒɪt] *n* **(a)** *Math* dígito *m* **(b)** *Fml Anat (finger, toe)* dedo *m*; *(thumb)* pulgar *m*

digital ['dɪdʒɪtəl] *adj Math Anat* digital ❑ **d. camera** cámara *f* digital; **d. radio** radio *f* digital; **d. television** televisión *f* digital

digitization [dɪdʒɪtaɪ'zeɪʃən] *n Comptr* digitalización *f*

dignified ['dɪgnɪfaɪd] *adj (manner)* solemne, serio(a); *(appearance)* majestuoso(a), señorial

dignify ['dɪgnɪfaɪ] *vt (pt & pp* **dignified)** dignificar

dignitary ['dɪgnɪtərɪ] *n Fml* dignatario *m*

dignity ['dɪgnɪtɪ] *n* dignidad *f*; **to stand on one's d.** hacerse respetar

digress [daɪ'gres] *vi Fml* apartarse **(from** de), desviarse **(from** de)

digression [daɪ'greʃən] *n Fml* digresión *f*

dike [daɪk] *n US see* **dyke**

dilapidated [dɪ'læpɪdeɪtɪd] *adj (gen)* en mal estado, muy estropeado(a); *(ruined)* derruido(a); *(falling apart)* desvencijado(a)

dilapidation [dɪlæpɪ'deɪʃən] *n (gen)* mal estado *m*; *(ruin)* estado *m* ruinoso

dilate [daɪ'leɪt] **1** *vi* dilatarse
2 *vt* dilatar

dilatory ['dɪlətərɪ] *adj Fml* lento(a), tardo(a); **to be d. in** *or* **about doing sth** tardar en hacer algo

dilemma [dɪ'lemə, daɪ'lemə] *n* dilema *m*; *Fig* **to be on the horns of a d.** estar entre la espada y la pared

dilettante [dɪlɪ'tɑːntɪ] *n (pl* **dilettantes** *or* **dilettanti** [dɪlɪ'tɑːntiː]) diletante *mf*

diligence ['dɪlɪdʒəns] *n* diligencia *f*

diligent ['dɪlɪdʒənt] *adj (worker, student)* diligente, aplicado(a), concienzudo(a); *(inquiries, search)* minucioso(a), esmerado(a)

diligently ['dɪlɪdʒəntlɪ] *adv* con diligencia, diligentemente

dill [dɪl] *n Bot* eneldo *m*

dilly-dally ['dɪlɪdælɪ] *vi Fam (loiter)* entretenerse; *(hesitate)* titubear, vacilar

dilute [daɪ'luːt] **1** *vt* diluir; *(wine, milk)* aguar; *Fig (effect, influence)* atenuar, suavizar
2 *vi* diluirse
3 *adj (solution)* diluido(a)

dilution [daɪ'luːʃən] *n (of liquid)* dilución *f*; *Fig (of effect)* atenuación *f*

dim [dɪm] **1** *adj* **(dimmer, dimmest)** **(a)** *(light)* difuso(a), débil, tenue; *(room, street)* oscuro(a); *(outline)* borroso(a); *(eyesight)* defectuoso(a); *Fig (memory)* vago(a), lejano(a); *Fig (prospects, future)* sombrío(a); **his eyes are growing d.** le falla la vista; *Fam* **to take a d. view of sth** ver algo con malos ojos **(b)** *Fam (stupid)* tonto(a), corto(a) de alcances, *Am* sonso(a), *Am* zonzo(a)

2 vt (pt & pp **dimmed**) (light) bajar; (sight, eyes) nublar, empañar; Fig (memory) borrar, difuminar; Fig (joy, hope) apagar
3 vi (light) bajarse; (daylight) oscurecerse; (sight, eyes) nublarse, empañarse; Fig (memory) borrarse, difuminarse; Fig (joy) apagarse

dime [daɪm] n US moneda f de diez centavos; Fam Fig **they're a d. a dozen** los hay a porrillo ❑ **d. store** tienda f de baratijas

dimension [daɪˈmenʃən] n dimensión f

dimensional [daɪˈmenʃənəl] adj dimensional

diminish [dɪˈmɪnɪʃ] **1** vt (a) (size, number) disminuir, reducir ❑ Jur **diminished responsibility** responsabilidad f disminuida (b) (person, importance) rebajar, menospreciar
2 vi (size, number) disminuir, reducirse

diminishing [dɪˈmɪnɪʃɪŋ] adj decreciente; **law of 'd. returns** ley f de los rendimientos decrecientes

diminution [dɪmɪˈnjuːʃən] n Fml disminución f, reducción f

diminutive [dɪˈmɪnjʊtɪv] **1** adj Fml diminuto(a)
2 n Ling diminutivo m

dimly [ˈdɪmlɪ] adv vagamente, de una manera confusa

dimmer [ˈdɪmər] n Elec **d. (switch)** regulador m de voltaje

dimness [ˈdɪmnɪs] n (a) (of light) palidez f; (of room) oscuridad f; Fig (of memory) imprecisión f (b) (of shape) lo borroso; (of eyesight) debilidad f (c) Fam (of person) torpeza f

dimple [ˈdɪmpəl] n hoyuelo m

dimwit [ˈdɪmwɪt] n Fam tonto(a) m,f, mentecato(a) m,f, imbécil mf

din [dɪn] **1** n (of crowd) alboroto m; (of machinery) ruido m ensordecedor
2 vi (pt & pp **dinned**) Fam **to d. sth into sb** meterle algo en la cabeza a algn

dine [daɪn] vi Fml cenar; **to d. on** or **off caviar** cenar caviar; **to d. out** cenar fuera, salir a cenar; **to wine and d. sb** invitar a algn a comer or a cenar

diner [ˈdaɪnər] n (a) (person) comensal mf (b) US (restaurant) restaurante m barato

dingbat [ˈdɪŋbæt] n (a) US Fam chalado(a) m,f (b) Comptr Typ (carácter m) dingbat m

ding-dong [ˈdɪŋdɒŋ] **1** n (a) (sound) din dan m, din don m (b) Fam (quarrel) riña f, (fight) pelea f
2 adj Fam (argument, contest) reñido(a), disputado(a)

dinghy [ˈdɪŋɪ] n Naut bote m (a) (rubber) d. bote m neumático; (sailing) d. bote m con vela

dingo [ˈdɪŋgəʊ] (pl **dingoes**) n dingo m

dingy [ˈdɪndʒɪ] adj (**dingier, dingiest**) (a) (street, house) oscuro(a), sórdido(a) (b) (dirty) sucio(a) (c) (colour) desteñido(a), descolorido(a)

dining [ˈdaɪnɪŋ] n **d. car** (on train) vagón m restaurante; **d. hall** (in school) comedor m; **d. room** comedor m; **d. table** mesa f de comedor

dining car [ˈdaɪnɪŋkɑːr] n Rail vagón m restaurante

dining room [ˈdaɪnɪŋruːm] n comedor m

dinky, dinkie [ˈdɪŋkɪ] adj (a) Br Fam (small and charming) lindo(a), chiquitín(ina) (b) US Pej (insignificant) vulgar, del montón

dinner [ˈdɪnər] n (at midday) comida f; (in evening) cena f; Fml **to attend a d.** asistir a una cena ❑ **d. jacket** smoking m; **d. service** vajilla f; **d. table** mesa f de comedor

dinosaur [ˈdaɪnəsɔːr] n dinosaurio m

dint [dɪnt] n **by d. of** a fuerza de

diocese [ˈdaɪəsɪs] n Rel diócesis f inv

dioxide [daɪˈɒksaɪd] n Chem bióxido m, dióxido m

dip [dɪp] **1** n (a) Fam (quick bathe) chapuzón m (b) (drop) (of road, land) pendiente f, declive m; (in ground) depresión f; (of price, temperature) caída f (c) (for sheep) baño m desinfectante (d) Culin (sauce) salsa f
2 vt (pt & pp **dipped**) (a) (put into liquid) bañar; (pen) mojar; (spoon, hand) meter (b) (disinfect) (sheep) bañar en desinfectante (c) Br Aut **to d. one's lights** poner luces de cruce
3 vi (drop) (road, land) bajar; Av bajar en picado; (prices, temperature) bajar; **the sun dipped below the horizon** el sol desapareció bajo el horizonte

dip into vt (a) (savings, capital) echar mano de (b) (book, magazine) hojear

diphtheria [dɪpˈθɪərɪə] n Med difteria f

diphthong [ˈdɪfθɒŋ] n Ling diptongo m

diploma [dɪˈpləʊmə] n diploma m

diplomacy [dɪˈpləʊməsɪ] n Pol & Fig diplomacia f; (tact) tacto m, discreción f

diplomat [ˈdɪpləmæt] n Pol & Fig diplomático(a) m,f

diplomatic [dɪpləˈmætɪk] adj Pol & Fig diplomático(a) ❑ Br **d. bag** valija f diplomática; **d. corps** cuerpo m diplomático

dipper [ˈdɪpər] n (a) US (ladle) cucharón m, cazo m (b) Orn mirlo m acuático

dipsomania [dɪpsəʊˈmeɪnɪə] n Med dipsomanía f

dipsomaniac [dɪpsəʊˈmeɪnɪæk] n Med dipsómano(a) m,f, dipsomaníaco(a) m,f

dipstick [ˈdɪpstɪk] n Aut indicador m de nivel del aceite

Dir (abbr **Director**) Director(a) m,f, Dir.

dire [daɪər] adj (a) (urgent) extremo(a), urgente (b) (serious) fatal, grave; **to be in d. straits** estar en una situación desesperada (c) (terrible) espantoso(a), terrible

direct [dɪˈrekt, ˈdaɪrekt] **1** adj (a) (route, flight, link) directo(a) ❑ Elec **d. current** corriente f continua; Com **d. mail** propaganda f por correo, correo m directo; Com **d. selling** venta f directa; Ling **d. speech** estilo m directo (b) (result, action) directo(a), inmediato(a); **to be a d. descendent of sb** ser descendiente por línea directa de algn (c) (person, manner) franco(a), sincero(a) (d) (exact) exacto(a); **the d. opposite (of sth)** todo or exactamente lo contrario (de algo); Fig **to make** or **score a d. hit** dar en el blanco
2 adv (go, write) directamente; (broadcast) en directo
3 vt (a) (send) dirigir; **can you d. me to a bank?** ¿me puede indicar dónde hay un banco? (b) (control) dirigir (c) Fml (order) mandar, ordenar

direction [dɪˈrekʃən, daɪˈrekʃən] n (a) (way) dirección f; **in every d., in all directions** en todas direcciones; **sense of d.** sentido m de la orientación; Fig **a step in the right d.** un paso hacia adelante (b) (control) dirección f; **under the d. of** bajo la dirección de (c) **directions** (to place) señas fpl; **d. for use** instrucciones fpl de uso, modo m de empleo

directional [dɪˈrekʃənəl, daɪˈrekʃənəl] adj Tech direccional

directive [dɪˈrektɪv, daɪˈrektɪv] n Fml directiva f, directriz f

directly [dɪˈrektlɪ, daɪˈrektlɪ] **1** adv (a) (above, opposite etc) exactamente, justo (b) (speak) francamente, sinceramente (c) (descend) directamente (d) (come) en seguida, dentro de poco
2 conj Fam en cuanto, tan pronto como

directness [dɪˈrektnɪs, daɪˈrektnɪs] n franqueza f, sinceridad f

director [dɪˈrektər, daɪˈrektər] n (a) (of operation, company) director(a) m,f; **board of directors** consejo m de administración, (junta f) directiva f ❑ **managing d.** director(a) m,f, gerente mf (b) (of film, programme) director(a) *m,f* □ *Br Jur* **D. of Public Prosecutions** Fiscal *mf* General del Estado

directorate [dɪˈrektərɪt, daɪˈrektərɪt] *n* consejo *m* de administración, (junta *f*) directiva *f*

directorial [dɪrekˈtɔːrɪəl, daɪrekˈtɔːrɪəl] *adj Theat Cin (career, debut)* como director(a); *(work)* de director(a)

directorship [dɪˈrektəʃɪp, daɪˈrektəʃɪp] *n* cargo *m* de director

directory [dɪˈrektərɪ, daɪˈrektərɪ] *n Tel* guía *f* telefónica, listín *m* (de teléfonos), *Am* directorio *m* de teléfonos □ *Tel Br* **d. enquiries,** *US* **d. assistance** (servicio *m* de) información *f,* **(street) d.** callejero *m*

dirge [dɜːdʒ] *n* canto *m* fúnebre

dirt [dɜːt] *n* **(a)** *(dirtiness)* suciedad *f; (filth, grime)* mugre *f; (grease)* porquería *f; (mud)* barro *m; Fam Fig* **to treat sb like d.** tratar a algn como a una zapatilla **(b)** *(earth)* tierra *f* □ **d. road** pista *f* de tierra; *Sport* **d. track** pista *f* de ceniza **(c)** *Fam (obscenity)* porquerías *fpl; (scandal)* chisme *m*

dirt-cheap [dɜːtˈtʃiːp] *adv & adj Fam* tirado(a)

dirtiness [ˈdɜːtɪnɪs] *n* suciedad *f*

dirty [ˈdɜːtɪ] **1** *adj* **(dirtier, dirtiest)** **(a)** *(not clean)* sucio(a); *(muddy)* embarrado(a); **a d. mark** una mancha; **to get d.** ensuciarse **(b)** *(dishonest)* sucio(a), deshonesto(a); *(dealer)* sin escrúpulos; *(player, fighter)* sucio(a), tramposo(a); *Br Fam* **to do the d. on sb** hacer a algn una mala jugada **(c)** *Fam (night, weather)* borrascoso(a), de perros; *(thief)* vil, despreciable; **to give sb a d. look** fulminar a algn con la mirada **(d)** *(story, joke)* verde; *(mind, sense of humour)* pervertido(a) □ *(insult)* insulto *m;* **d. old man** viejo *m* verde; *Fam* **d. weekend** aventura *f* de fin de semana; **d. word** palabrota *f*

2 *vt (pt & pp* **dirtied)** ensuciar

3 *adv* **(a)** *(play, fight)* sucio **(b)** *Br Fam (intensifier)* muy; **a d. great hole** un pedazo de agujero

dis [dɪs] *vt US see* **diss**

dis- [dɪs] *pref* des-

disability [dɪsəˈbɪlɪtɪ] *n* **(a)** *(handicap)* desventaja *f,* hándicap *m* **(b)** *(state)* incapacidad *f* (física *or* mental), invalidez *f* □ **d. allowance, d. pension** pensión *f* por invalidez

disable [dɪsˈeɪbəl] *vt* **(a)** *(physically)* dejar imposibilitado(a); *(mentally)* dejar incapacitado(a) **(b)** *(ship, gun)* inutilizar

disabled [dɪˈseɪbəld] **1** *adj* minusválido(a)
2 the d. *npl* los minusválidos

disabuse [dɪsəˈbjuːz] *vt Fml* desengañar

disadvantage [dɪsədˈvɑːntɪdʒ] *n* desventaja *f; (obstacle)* inconveniente *m;* **to be at a d.** estar en inferioridad de condiciones

disadvantaged [dɪsədˈvɑːntɪdʒd] *adj* desheredado(a), discriminado(a)

disadvantageous [dɪsædvɑːnˈteɪdʒəs] *adj* desfavorable

disaffected [dɪsəˈfektɪd] *adj* descontento(a)

disaffection [dɪsəˈfekʃən] *n* desafección *f*

disagree [dɪsəˈɡriː] *vi* **(a)** *(differ)* no estar de acuerdo **(with** con); **to d. on** *or* **over** *or* **about sth** no estar de acuerdo por algo **(b)** *(not match)* discrepar **(with** de, con), no corresponder **(with** a) **(c)** *(upset) (climate)* no convenir **(with** a); *(food)* sentar mal **(with** -)

disagreeable [dɪsəˈɡriːəbəl] *adj* desagradable

disagreement [dɪsəˈɡriːmənt] *n* **(a)** *(difference)* desacuerdo *m; (argument)* riña *f,* altercado *m* **(b)** *(non-correspondence)* discrepancia *f,* disconformidad *f*

disallow [dɪsəˈlaʊ] *vt Fml (goal)* anular; *(objection)* rechazar

disappear [dɪsəˈpɪər] *vi* desaparecer; *Fam (person)* esfumarse; **to d. from view** perderse de vista

disappearance [dɪsəˈpɪərəns] *n* desaparición *f*

disappoint [dɪsəˈpɔɪnt] *vt (person)* decepcionar, defraudar, desilusionar; *(hope, ambition)* frustrar

disappointed [dɪsəˈpɔɪntɪd] *adj (person)* decepcionado(a), desilusionado(a); *(hope, ambition)* frustrado(a); **to be d. in sth** sufrir *or* llevarse un desengaño con algo

disappointing [dɪsəˈpɔɪntɪŋ] *adj* decepcionante

disappointment [dɪsəˈpɔɪntmənt] *n* decepción *f,* desilusión *f*

disapproval [dɪsəˈpruːvəl] *n* desaprobación *f*

disapprove [dɪsəˈpruːv] *vi* desaprobar

disapproving [dɪsəˈpruːvɪŋ] *adj* de desaprobación

disarm [dɪsˈɑːm] **1** *vt* desarmar
2 *vi (country)* desarmarse

disarmament [dɪsˈɑːməmənt] *n* desarme *m;* **d. talks** conversaciones *fpl* para el desarme

disarming [dɪsˈɑːmɪŋ] *adj Fig* que desarma

disarray [dɪsəˈreɪ] *n Fml* **in d.** *(room, papers)* en desorden; *(hair)* desarreglado(a), desaliñado(a); *(thoughts)* confuso(a)

disassemble [dɪsəˈsembəl] *vt* desmontar, desarmar

disaster [dɪˈzɑːstər] *n* desastre *f,* catástrofe *f*

disastrous [dɪˈzɑːstrəs] *adj* desastroso(a), catastrófico(a)

disavow [dɪsəˈvaʊ] *vt Fml* negar, rechazar

disavowal [dɪsəˈvaʊəl] *n Fml* desmentido *m,* mentís *m*

disband [dɪsˈbænd] **1** *vt (group)* disolver, deshacer; *(army)* licenciar
2 *vi (group)* disolverse, deshacerse; *(army)* licenciarse

disbar [dɪsˈbɑːr] *vt Jur* expulsar de la abogacía, inhabilitar como abogado(a)

disbelief [dɪsbɪˈliːf] *n* incredulidad *f*

disbelieve [dɪsbɪˈliːv] *vt Fml* no creer, dudar

disburse [dɪsˈbɜːs] *vt Fml* desembolsar

disbursement [dɪsˈbɜːsmənt] *n* desembolso *m*

disc [dɪsk] *n (gen)* disco *m; Comptr* disquete *m* □ *Mus* **d. jockey** disc-jockey *mf,* pinchadiscos *mf inv*

discard [dɪsˈkɑːd] *vt (old things)* desechar, deshacerse de; *(idea, plan)* descartar, desechar, rechazar; *(playing card)* descartarse de

discern [dɪˈsɜːn] *vt Fml (shape)* percibir, distinguir; *(merit, difference)* distinguir, discernir; *(truth)* darse cuenta de

discernible [dɪˈsɜːnəbəl] *adj (shape)* visible; *(merit)* perceptible

discerning [dɪˈsɜːnɪŋ] *adj (person)* perspicaz; *(taste)* refinado(a)

discernment [dɪˈsɜːnmənt] *n (perception)* discernimiento *m,* perspicacia *f; (judgement)* buen criterio *m*

discharge [dɪsˈtʃɑːdʒ] *Fml* **1** *vt* **(a)** *(release)* verter; *(electric current, cargo)* descargar; *(smoke, pus)* echar, emitir; **factories d. waste into the sea** las fábricas vierten los residuos en el mar **(b)** *(allow to go) (prisoner)* liberar, soltar; *(patient)* dar de alta; *(soldier etc)* licenciar; *(injured soldier etc)* dar de baja; *(dismiss)* despedir **(c)** *(pay)* saldar **(d)** *(fulfil)* cumplir
2 *vi (release) (sewer, pipe)* verter, desembocar; *(chimney)* emitir; *(wound)* supurar
3 [ˈdɪstʃɑːdʒ] *n* **(a)** *(of electric current, load)* descarga *f; (of smoke)* emisión *f; (of gases)* escape *m; (of waste)* vertido *m; (from wound)* supuración *f* **(b)** *(of prisoner)* liberación *f,* puesta *f* en libertad; *(of patient)* alta *f; (of soldier etc)* licencia *f* (absoluta); *(of worker)* despido *m* **(c)** *(of debt)* descargo *m,* pago *m* **(d)** *(of duty)* cumplimiento *m;* **in the d. of her duties** en el ejercicio de sus funciones

disciple [dɪˈsaɪpəl] n discípulo(a) m,f
disciplinary [ˈdɪsɪplɪnərɪ] adj disciplinario(a)
discipline [ˈdɪsɪplɪn] **1** n, **(a)** *(training, behaviour)* disciplina f; **self-d.** autodisciplina f **(b)** *(punishment)* castigo m **(c)** Fml *(subject)* disciplina f
2 vt **(a)** *(punish) (child)* castigar; *(worker)* sancionar; *(official)* expedientar **(b)** *(train)* disciplinar
disclaim [dɪsˈkleɪm] vt Fml *(knowledge, responsibility)* negar tener; *(credit)* renunciar a, rechazar
disclaimer [dɪsˈkleɪmər] n Fml *(in contract etc)* (nota f de) rectificación f; *(denial)* renuncia f
disclose [dɪsˈkləʊz] vt **(a)** *(reveal)* revelar, dar a conocer **(b)** *(show)* mostrar, dejar ver
disclosure [dɪsˈkləʊʒər] n *(revelation)* revelación f
disco [ˈdɪskəʊ] n *(pl* discos) *(abbr* **discotheque)** Fam disco f, discoteca f
discography [dɪsˈkɒɡrəfɪ] n discografía f
discoloration [dɪskʌləˈreɪʃən] n descoloramiento m
discolour, US **discolor** [dɪsˈkʌlər] **1** vt descolorar
2 vi descolorarse
discomfiture [dɪsˈkʌmfɪtʃər] n Fml desconcierto m
discomfort [dɪsˈkʌmfət] n **(a)** *(lack of comfort)* incomodidad f **(b)** *(pain)* malestar m, molestia f **(c)** *(unease)* inquietud f, preocupación f
disconcert [dɪskənˈsɜːt] vt desconcertar, perturbar
disconcerting [dɪskənˈsɜːtɪŋ] adj desconcertante
disconnect [dɪskəˈnekt] vt *(gen)* desconectar **(from** de), *(gas or electricity supply)* cortar
disconnected [dɪskəˈnektɪd] adj *(speech)* deshilvanado(a); *(thoughts)* inconexo(a)
disconsolate [dɪsˈkɒnsəlɪt] adj *(gen)* desconsolado(a); *(look)* abatido(a)
discontent [dɪskənˈtent] n descontento m, disgusto m
discontented [dɪskənˈtentɪd] adj descontento(a), disgustado(a)
discontentment [dɪskənˈtentmənt] n see **discontent**
discontinue [dɪskənˈtɪnjuː] vt Fml *(gen)* abandonar; *(work)* interrumpir, suspender; Com **discontinued line** restos mpl de serie
discontinuity [dɪskɒntɪˈnjuːɪtɪ] n discontinuidad f; Fml interrupción f
discontinuous [dɪskənˈtɪnjʊəs] adj discontinuo(a), interrumpido(a)
discord [ˈdɪskɔːd] n **(a)** Fml discordia f, disensión f **(b)** Mus disonancia f
discordant [dɪsˈkɔːdənt] adj **(a)** *(views)* discordante; *(personalities)* discorde **(b)** Mus discordante
discotheque [ˈdɪskətek] n discoteca f
discount [ˈdɪskaʊnt] **1** n descuento m; **a ten per cent d., a d. of ten per cent** un descuento de diez por ciento
2 [dɪsˈkaʊnt] vt **(a)** *(price)* hacer descuento de, rebajar **(b)** *(view, suggestion, possibility)* descartar
discourage [dɪsˈkʌrɪdʒ] vt **(a)** *(dishearten)* desanimar, desalentar **(b)** *(deter) (investment)* no fomentar; *(advances)* rechazar, resistirse a; *(bad habit)* hacer desistir de
discouragement [dɪsˈkʌrɪdʒmənt] n **(a)** *(depression)* desánimo m, desaliento m **(b)** *(dissuasion)* desaprobación f **(c)** *(obstacle)* obstáculo m
discouraging [dɪsˈkʌrɪdʒɪŋ] adj desalentador(a), desmoralizador(a)
discourse [ˈdɪskɔːs, dɪsˈkɔːs] Fml **1** n *(spoken)* discurso m, plática f; *(written)* discurso m, tratado m; **d. analysis** análisis m inv del discurso
2 [dɪsˈkɔːs] vi disertar **(on** sobre), conversar **(on** sobre)

discourteous [dɪsˈkɜːtɪəs] adj Fml maleducado(a), descortés(esa)
discourtesy [dɪsˈkɜːtɪsɪ] n Fml descortesía f, falta f de educación
discover [dɪsˈkʌvər] vt *(gen)* descubrir; *(missing person, object)* encontrar, hallar; *(mistake, loss)* darse cuenta de; *(secret, reason)* aprender, enterarse de
discovery [dɪsˈkʌvərɪ] n descubrimiento m
discredit [dɪsˈkredɪt] **1** n descrédito m
2 vt *(person, régime)* desacreditar, desprestigiar; *(idea, theory)* poner en duda
discreditable [dɪsˈkredɪtəbəl] adj indigno(a), vergonzoso(a)
discreet [dɪsˈkriːt] adj *(gen)* discreto(a); *(distance, silence)* prudente; *(hat, house)* modesto(a)
discrepancy [dɪsˈkrepənsɪ] n *(stories, facts)* discrepancia f **(between** entre); *(figures)* diferencia f **(between** entre)
discrete [dɪsˈkriːt] adj Fml discreto(a)
discretion [dɪsˈkreʃən] n *(gen)* discreción f; *(prudence)* prudencia f; **at the d. of ...** a juicio de ...; **use your own d.** haz lo que te parezca *(bien)*
discretionary [dɪsˈkreʃənərɪ] adj Fml discrecional
discriminate [dɪsˈkrɪmɪneɪt] **1** vt distinguir **(from** de)
2 vi discriminar **(between** entre); **to d. against sth/sb** discriminar algo/a algn; **to d. in favour of sth/sb** dar un trato preferencial a algo/a algn
discriminating [dɪsˈkrɪmɪneɪtɪŋ] adj *(person)* entendido(a), exigente; *(taste)* refinado(a), fino(a)
discrimination [dɪskrɪmɪˈneɪʃən] n **(a)** *(bias)* discriminación f **(b)** *(distinction)* diferenciación f, distinción f **(c)** *(taste)* juicio m, buen gusto m, discernimiento m
discriminatory [dɪsˈkrɪmɪnətərɪ] adj discriminatorio(a)
discursive [dɪsˈkɜːsɪv] adj divagador(a)
discus [ˈdɪskəs] n *(pl* **discuses** or **disci** [ˈdɪskaɪ]) Sport disco m
discuss [dɪsˈkʌs] vt **(a)** *(talk about)* discutir; *(in writing)* tratar de; **to d. sth in detail** examinar algo a fondo **(b)** *(debate)* discutir
discussion [dɪsˈkʌʃən] n discusión f
disdain [dɪsˈdeɪn] Fml **1** n desdén m, desprecio m
2 vt desdeñar, despreciar; **he disdained to notice me** no se dignó a hacerme caso
disdainful [dɪsˈdeɪnfʊl] adj Fml desdeñoso(a), despectivo(a)
disease [dɪˈziːz] n enfermedad f; Fig mal m, enfermedad f
diseased [dɪˈziːzd] adj enfermo(a)
disembark [dɪsɪmˈbɑːk] vt & vi desembarcar **(from** de)
disembarkation [dɪsɪmbɑːˈkeɪʃən] n *(of people)* desembarco m; *(of goods)* desembarque m
disembodied [dɪsɪmˈbɒdɪd] adj incorpóreo(a)
disembowel [dɪsɪmˈbaʊəl] vt *(pt & pp* **disembowelled,** US **disemboweled)** desentrañar, destripar
disenchanted [dɪsɪnˈtʃɑːntɪd] adj desencantado(a), desilusionado(a)
disenchantment [dɪsɪnˈtʃɑːntmənt] n desencanto m, desilusión f
disengage [dɪsɪnˈɡeɪdʒ] **1** vt **(a)** *(free)* desprender, soltar **(b)** *(clutch, gears)* desembragar
2 vi *(troops)* retirar **(from** de)
disentangle [dɪsɪnˈtæŋɡəl] vt desenmarañar, desenredar
disfavour, US **disfavor** [dɪsˈfeɪvər] n Fml desaprobación f; **to fall into d.** caer en desgracia
disfigure [dɪsˈfɪɡər] vt desfigurar
disfigurement [dɪsˈfɪɡəmənt] n desfiguración f

disgorge [dɪsˈɡɔːdʒ] *vt (liquid, waste)* verter; *(smoke, fumes)* emitir

disgrace [dɪsˈɡreɪs] **1** *n* **(a)** *(loss of favour)* desgracia *f*; **to be in d.** *(official etc)* estar desacreditado(a); *(child)* estar castigado(a); **to fall into d.** caer en desgracia **(b)** *(shame)* vergüenza *f*, escándalo *m*
   2 *vt (family, name)* deshonrar, desacreditar

disgraceful [dɪsˈɡreɪsfʊl] *adj* vergonzoso(a); **it's d!** ¡es una vergüenza!, ¡es un escándalo!

disgruntled [dɪsˈɡrʌntəld] *adj (person, expression) (sulky)* contrariado(a), disgustado(a); *(bad-tempered)* malhumorado(a)

disguise [dɪsˈɡaɪz] **1** *n* disfraz *m*; **in d.** disfrazado(a); *Fig* **it's a blessing in d.** no hay mal que por bien no venga
   2 *vt* **(a)** *(person)* disfrazar **(as** de); *(voice, handwriting)* cambiar **(b)** *(feelings, views)* disfrazar, disimular, esconder; **there's no disguising the fact that ...** no se puede ocultar que ...

disgust [dɪsˈɡʌst] **1** *n* **(a)** *(loathing)* repugnancia *f*, asco *m*; **to fill sb with d.** repugnar a *or* dar asco a algn **(b)** *(strong disapproval)* indignación *f*
   2 *vt* **(a)** *(revolt)* repugnar, dar asco a **(b)** *(disapprove)* indignar, disgustar; **I'm disgusted with** *or* **at your rudeness** tu falta de educación me indigna

disgusting [dɪsˈɡʌstɪŋ] *adj* **(a)** *(loathsome) (sight, habit)* asqueroso(a), repugnante; *(smell)* nauseabundo(a); *(behaviour, state of affairs)* desagradable, intolerable, reprobable **(b)** *Fam (weather)* asqueroso(a), horrible

dish [dɪʃ] *n* **(a)** *(for serving)* fuente *f*; *(course)* plato *m*; **to wash** *or* **do the dishes** fregar los platos **(b)** *Fam (attractive man or woman)* bombón *m*

dish out *vt Fam (food)* servir; *(books, passes, advice)* repartir; **to d. it out (to sb)** *(punish)* castigar (a algn); *(criticize)* criticar (a algn)

dish up *vt (meal)* servir

disharmony [dɪsˈhɑːmənɪ] *n* discordia *f*

dishcloth [ˈdɪʃklɒθ] *n* paño *m* (de cocina), *CAm* secador *m*, *Chile* paño *m* de loza, *Col* limpión *m*, *Méx* trapón *m*, *RP* repasador *m*

dishearten [dɪsˈhɑːtən] *vt* desanimar, descorazonar, desalentar

disheartening [dɪsˈhɑːtənɪŋ] *adj* desalentador(a)

dishevelled, *US* **disheveled** [dɪˈʃevəld] *adj (hair)* despeinado(a); *(appearance, clothes)* desaliñado(a), desarreglado(a)

dishonest [dɪsˈɒnɪst] *adj (person, behaviour)* poco honrado(a), deshonesto(a); *(means)* fraudulento(a)

dishonesty [dɪsˈɒnɪstɪ] *n (of person, behaviour)* falta *f* de honradez; *(of means)* fraude *m*

dishonour, *US* **dishonor** [dɪsˈɒnər] **1** *n Fml* deshonra *f*
   2 *vt* **(a)** *(family, name)* deshonrar **(b)** *(cheque)* rechazar, negarse a pagar

dishonourable, *US* **dishonorable** [dɪsˈɒnərəbəl] *adj* deshonroso(a)

dishpan [ˈdɪʃpæn] *n US* balde *m*, palangana *f (para fregar los platos)*

dishrag [ˈdɪʃræɡ] *n US* bayeta *f*

dishtowel [ˈdɪʃtaʊəl] *n US* paño *m* (de cocina), *CAm* secador *m*, *Chile* paño *m* de loza, *Col* limpión *m*, *Méx* trapón *m*, *RP* repasador *m*

dishwasher [ˈdɪʃwɒʃər] *n (machine)* lavaplatos *m inv*, lavavajillas *m inv*; *(person)* lavaplatos *mf inv*

dishwater [ˈdɪʃwɒtər] *n* agua *f* de fregar (los platos); *Fig* **this coffee is like d.!** ¡este café está aguado *or Esp* es puro aguachirle *or RP* parece caldo de medias!

dishy [ˈdɪʃɪ] *adj* **(dishier, dishiest)** *Br Fam* guapo(a); **he's really d.** está buenísimo, está como un tren

disillusion [dɪsɪˈluːʒən] **1** *n* desilusión *f*
   2 *vt* desilusionar

disillusioned [dɪsɪˈluːʒənd] *adj* desencantado(a), desilusionado(a); **to be d. (with sb/sth)** estar desencantado(a) (con algn/algo)

disillusionment [dɪsɪˈluːʒənmənt] *n* desilusión *f*

disincentive [dɪsɪnˈsentɪv] *n* freno *m*

disinclination [dɪsɪnklɪˈneɪʃən] *n* aversión *f*

disinclined [dɪsɪnˈklaɪnd] *adj* **to be d. to do sth** no tener ganas de *or* interés por hacer algo

disinfect [dɪsɪnˈfekt] *vt* desinfectar

disinfectant [dɪsɪnˈfektənt] *n* desinfectante *m*

disinformation [dɪsɪnfəˈmeɪʃən] *n* desinformación *f*

disingenuous [dɪsɪnˈdʒenjʊəs] *adj* falso(a), poco sincero(a)

disinherit [dɪsɪnˈherɪt] *vt* desheredar

disintegrate [dɪsˈɪntɪɡreɪt] *vi* desintegrarse

disintegration [dɪsɪntɪˈɡreɪʃən] *n* desintegración *f*

disinter [dɪsɪnˈtɜːr] *vt Fml* desenterrar

disinterested [dɪsˈɪntrɪstɪd] *adj* desinteresado(a), imparcial, objetivo(a)

disinvestment [dɪsɪnˈvestmənt] *n Fin* desinversión *f*

disjointed [dɪsˈdʒɔɪntɪd] *adj* inconexo(a), sin relación

disk [dɪsk] *n US (gen)* disco *m*; *Comptr* disquete *m* ❏ **d. drive** disquetera *f*

diskette [dɪsˈket] *n Comptr* disquete *m*

dislike [dɪsˈlaɪk] **1** *n* antipatía *f*, aversión *f* **(for, of** a, hacia)
   2 *vt* tener antipatía *or* aversión a *or* hacia; **I d. her intensely** me cae muy mal *or* gorda

dislocate [ˈdɪsləkeɪt] *vt* **(a)** *(joint)* dislocar; **he dislocated his hip** se dislocó *or* se desencajó la cadera **(b)** *Fig (routine, plan)* trastornar, desarreglar

dislocation [dɪsləˈkeɪʃən] *n* dislocación *f*

dislodge [dɪsˈlɒdʒ] *vt* desalojar, sacar

disloyal [dɪsˈlɔɪəl] *adj* desleal

disloyalty [dɪsˈlɔɪəltɪ] *n* deslealtad *f*

dismal [ˈdɪzməl] *adj* **(a)** *(gloomy) (prospect)* sombrío(a); *(place, weather)* deprimente; *(person)* triste **(b)** *(hopeless)* lamentable

dismantle [dɪsˈmæntəl] **1** *vt (tent, clock)* desarmar, desmontar; *Fig (company, system)* desmantelar
   2 *vi (tent, clock)* desarmarse, desmontarse

dismay [dɪsˈmeɪ] **1** *n* consternación *f*
   2 *vt (concern)* consternar; *(discourage)* desanimar, desalentar

dismayed [dɪsˈmeɪd] *adj* consternado(a)

dismember [dɪsˈmembər] *vt* desmembrar

dismiss [dɪsˈmɪs] *vt* **(a)** *(put aside) (idea etc)* descartar; *(thought)* alejar; *(subject)* despachar **(b)** *Fml (sack) (employee)* despedir; *(official)* destituir **(c)** *(send away) (gen)* dar permiso para retirarse; *(butler etc)* despedir; *(troops)* hacer romper filas; **the teacher dismissed the class** el profesor dio por terminada la clase **(d)** *(reject)* rechazar; *Jur (appeal)* desestimar; *Jur (case, charge)* sobreseer

dismissal [dɪsˈmɪsəl] *n* **(a)** *(of idea, suggestion)* descarte *m*, abandono *m* **(b)** *(of employee)* despido *m*; *(of official)* destitución *f* **(c)** *(of claim)* rechazo *m*; *Jur* desestimación *f*

dismissive [dɪsˈmɪsɪv] *adj* despectivo(a)

dismount [dɪsˈmaʊnt] *vi Fml* desmontarse, apearse **(from** de)

disobedience [dɪsəˈbiːdɪəns] *n* desobediencia *f*

disobedient [dɪsəˈbiːdɪənt] adj desobediente

disobey [dɪsəˈbeɪ] vt & vi (person) desobedecer; (law, rules) contravenir, violar

disobliging [dɪsəˈblaɪdʒɪŋ] adj Fml (unhelpful) poco complaciente; (unpleasant) desagradable

disorder [dɪsˈɔːdər] n (a) (untidiness) desorden m (b) (riot) disturbio m, desórdenes mpl (c) (ailment) (of stomach etc) indisposición f; (of mind) trastorno m (nervioso); (of speech) defecto m

disordered [dɪsˈɔːdəd] adj (a) (untidy) desordenado(a), desarreglado(a) (b) (malfunctioning) (stomach) indispuesto(a); (mind) enfermo(a), trastornado(a)

disorderly [dɪsˈɔːdəlɪ] adj (a) (untidy) desordenado(a), desarreglado(a) (b) (unruly) desordenado(a); (meeting) alborotado(a); (conduct) escandaloso(a) ❏ Jur d. house casa f de lenocinio

disorganization [dɪsɔːɡənaɪˈzeɪʃən] n desorganización f

disorganized [dɪsˈɔːɡənaɪzd] adj (person) desorganizado(a); (schedule, system) desorganizado(a), caótico(a)

disorient [dɪsˈɔːrɪənt] vt, **disorientate** [dɪsˈɔːrɪenteɪt] vt desorientar

disorientation [dɪsɔːrɪənˈteɪʃən] n desorientación f

disown [dɪsˈəʊn] vt desconocer

disparage [dɪˈspærɪdʒ] vt menospreciar, despreciar

disparaging [dɪˈspærɪdʒɪŋ] adj despectivo(a)

disparate [ˈdɪspərɪt] adj Fml dispar, diferente

disparity [dɪsˈpærɪtɪ] n Fml disparidad f

dispassionate [dɪsˈpæʃənɪt] adj desapasionado(a)

dispassionately [dɪsˈpæʃənətlɪ] adv desapasionadamente, sin apasionamiento

dispatch [dɪˈspætʃ] 1 n (a) (message) mensaje m; (official message) despacho m; (journalist's report) noticia m, reportaje m; (military message) parte m ❏ d. box (for papers) valija f oficial; d. case portafolios m inv; d. rider mensajero m (b) (sending) (of mail, parcel) envío m; (of goods) consignación f; (of courier, message) despacho m, envío m (c) Fml (speed) prontitud f; to act with d. obrar con diligencia
2 vt (a) (send) (mail, parcel) expedir, remitir, enviar; (goods) expedir, consignar; (courier, message) despachar, enviar (b) Fam (finish quickly) (food) zampar; (job, business) despachar (c) Euph (kill) despachar, matar

dispel [dɪˈspel] vt (pt & pp **dispelled**) disipar

dispensable [dɪˈspensəbəl] adj innecesario(a), superfluo(a)

dispensary [dɪˈspensərɪ] n dispensario m

dispensation [dɪspenˈseɪʃən] n (a) Fml (handing out) administración f (b) (exemption) exención f; Rel dispensa f

dispense [dɪˈspens] vt (a) (supplies, funds) repartir, distribuir; Fig (justice) administrar; Fig (favours) conceder (b) Pharm preparar y despachar

dispense with vi (a) (do without) prescindir de, pasar sin (b) (make unnecessary) eliminar la necesidad de

dispenser [dɪˈspensər] n máquina f expendedora ❏ cash d. cajero m automático; soap d. dosificador m de jabón

dispensing chemist [dɪspensɪŋˈkemɪst] n Br farmacéutico(a) m,f

dispersal [dɪˈspɜːsəl] n dispersión f

disperse [dɪˈspɜːs] 1 vt dispersar
2 vi dispersarse; (fog) disiparse

dispirited [dɪˈspɪrɪtɪd] adj abatido(a), desanimado(a), desalentado(a)

displace [dɪsˈpleɪs] vt (a) (gen) desplazar; (bone) dislocar ❏ displaced person refugiado(a) m,f (b) (supplant) sustituir, reemplazar; (official) destituir

displacement [dɪsˈpleɪsmənt] n (a) (removal) desplazamiento m (b) (supplanting) sustitución f, reemplazo m (c) Tech desplazamiento m

display [dɪˈspleɪ] 1 n (of paintings, goods) exposición f; Comptr visualización f; (of feelings, skills) demostración f; (of strength, force) despliegue m, exhibición f ❏ Comptr d. terminal terminal f de ordenador; d. window escaparate m, Am vidriera f, Chile Col Méx vitrina f; Mil military d. desfile m or despliegue m militar
2 vt (a) (gen) mostrar; (china, medals) exhibir; (goods) exponer; (advert) colocar; Comptr visualizar (b) Fig Fml (feelings) demostrar, manifestar; (skill, courage) mostrar

displease [dɪsˈpliːz] vt Fml disgustar, desagradar, contrariar; (offend) ofender

displeasure [dɪsˈpleʒər] n Fml disgusto m, desagrado m; to voice one's d. expresar la desaprobación

disport [dɪˈspɔːt] vt Fml to d. oneself entretenerse

disposable [dɪˈspəʊzəbəl] adj (a) (throwaway) desechable, de usar y tirar (b) (available) disponible ❏ d. income poder m adquisitivo

disposal [dɪˈspəʊzəl] n (a) (removal) eliminación f ❏ bomb d. desactivación f de artefactos explosivos; waste d. recogida f de basuras; waste d. unit trituradora f de basura (b) (availability) disponibilidad f; at my d. a mi disposición (c) Fml (arrangement) colocación f (d) (sale) venta f; (of property) traspaso m

dispose [dɪˈspəʊz] 1 vi to d. of (remove) eliminar; (rubbish) tirar; (unwanted object) deshacerse de, (argument) echar por tierra; (problem, matter) resolver; (sell) vender; (property) traspasar; (free time) emplear; Euph (kill) liquidar, despachar
2 vt Fml (arrange) disponer

disposed [dɪˈspəʊzd] adj (inclined) dispuesto(a)

disposition [dɪspəˈzɪʃən] n (a) (temperament) carácter m, genio m, naturaleza f (b) (readiness) predisposición f (c) Fml (arrangement) disposición f

dispossess [dɪspəˈzes] Fml vt desposeer (of de)

dispossessed [dɪspəˈzest] npl the d. los desposeídos

disproportion [dɪsprəˈpɔːʃən] n desproporción f

disproportionate [dɪsprəˈpɔːʃənɪt] adj desproporcionado(a) (to a)

disprove [dɪsˈpruːv] vt refutar

disputable [dɪˈspjuːtəbəl] adj discutible

dispute [ˈdɪspjuːt] 1 n (a) (disagreement) discusión f, controversia f; beyond or without d. indiscutiblemente (b) (quarrel) disputa f ❏ industrial d. conflicto m laboral
2 [dɪˈspjuːt] vt (a) (claim, right) refutar (b) (territory) disputar (c) (matter, question) discutir; a hotly disputed affair un asunto muy controvertido
3 vi discutir (about, over de, sobre)

disqualification [dɪskwɒlɪfɪˈkeɪʃən] n descalificación f

disqualify [dɪsˈkwɒlɪfaɪ] vt (pt & pp **disqualified**) (a) Sport descalificar (b) (make ineligible) incapacitar

disquiet [dɪsˈkwaɪət] n preocupación f, inquietud f

disquieting [dɪsˈkwaɪətɪŋ] adj preocupante, inquietante

disquisition [dɪskwɪˈzɪʃən] n Fml disquisición f, razonamiento m

disregard [dɪsrɪˈɡɑːd] 1 n (lack of concern) indiferencia f; (for risk, safety) despreocupación f
2 vt descuidar; (ignore) ignorar

disrepair [dɪsrɪˈpeər] n mal estado m; in (a state of) d. en mal estado; (building) que amenaza ruina; (road) muy bacheado(a); to fall into d. deteriorarse

disreputable [dɪsˈrepjʊtəbəl] adj (person, area) de mala fama; (behaviour) vergonzoso(a), lamentable; (clothes) asqueroso(a)

disrepute [dɪsrɪ'pjuːt] n mala fama f, oprobio m

disrespect [dɪsrɪ'spekt] n falta f de respeto

disrespectful [dɪsrɪ'spektfʊl] adj irrespetuoso(a)

disrobe [dɪs'rəʊb] vi Fml desvestirse, desnudarse

disrupt [dɪs'rʌpt] vt (meeting, traffic) interrumpir; (order) trastornar; (schedule etc) desbaratar

disruption [dɪs'rʌpʃən] n (of meeting, traffic) interrupción f, (of order) trastorno m; (of schedule etc) desbaratamiento m

disruptive [dɪs'rʌptɪv] adj (behaviour, influence) perjudicial, nocivo(a); (person) que trastorna or desorganiza todo

diss [dɪs] vt US Fam faltar (al respeto) a

dissatisfaction [dɪssætɪs'fækʃən] n descontento m, insatisfacción f

dissatisfied [dɪs'sætɪsfaɪd] adj descontento(a), insatisfecho(a)

dissect [dɪ'sekt, daɪ'sekt] vt disecar

dissemble [dɪ'sembəl] vi Fml disimular

disseminate [dɪ'semɪneɪt] vt Fml diseminar, difundir, propagar

dissemination [dɪsemɪ'neɪʃən] n Fml diseminación f, difusión f, propagación f

dissension [dɪ'senʃən] n disensión f, discordia f

dissent [dɪ'sent] 1 n disenso m, disentimiento m
2 vi disentir (from de)

dissenter [dɪ'sentər] n Rel disidente mf

dissenting [dɪ'sentɪŋ] adj discrepante

dissertation [dɪsə'teɪʃən] n (gen) disertación f; Br (for higher degree) tesina f; US (doctoral) tesis f

disservice [dɪs'sɜːvɪs] n perjuicio m; to do sth/sb a d. perjudicar algo/a algn

dissidence ['dɪsɪdəns] n Pol disidencia f

dissident ['dɪsɪdənt] adj & n Pol disidente (mf)

dissimilar [dɪ'sɪmɪlər] adj distinto(a), diferente

dissimilarity [dɪsɪmɪ'lærɪtɪ] n desemejanza f, diferencia f

dissimulate [dɪ'sɪmjʊleɪt] Fml 1 vt (feelings) disimular
2 vi disimular

dissimulation [dɪsɪmjʊ'leɪʃən] n Fml disimulo m, disimulación f

dissipate ['dɪsɪpeɪt] 1 vt (a) (clear) disipar; (crowd) dispersar; Fig (doubt, fear) disipar, desvanecer (b) (waste) derrochar
2 vi (fog, cloud) disiparse; (crowd) dispersarse; Fig (doubt, fear) disiparse, desvanecerse

dissipated ['dɪsɪpeɪtɪd] adj disoluto(a)

dissipation [dɪsɪ'peɪʃən] n (a) (clearing) disipación f (b) (waste) derroche m (c) (debauchery) disolución f, libertinaje m

dissociate [dɪ'səʊʃɪeɪt] vt separar

dissolute ['dɪsəluːt] adj disoluto(a)

dissolution [dɪsə'luːʃən] n disolución f; (of agreement) rescisión f

dissolve [dɪ'zɒlv] 1 vt disolver
2 vi (a) (disintegrate) disolverse; Fig to d. in or into tears/laughter deshacerse en lágrimas/en risa (b) (disappear) desvanecerse, esfumarse

dissonance ['dɪsənəns] n (a) Mus disonancia f (b) (disagreement) discordancia f

dissonant ['dɪsənənt] adj (a) Mus disonante (b) (opinions) discordante

dissuade [dɪ'sweɪd] vt disuadir (from de)

distance ['dɪstəns] 1 n (a) (gen) distancia f; at a (good) d. (bastante) lejos; in the d. a lo lejos, en la lejanía; Fam it's no d. to the beach la playa está a la vuelta de la esquina or está a dos pasos; Fam to go/stay the d. (in race, competition)

acabar/completar la prueba ❏ **d. learning** educación f a distancia (b) Fig (coldness) distancia f; to keep sb at a d. tratar a algn con frialdad
2 vt distanciarse, alejarse

distant ['dɪstənt] adj (a) (place) distante, lejano(a), remoto(a), apartado(a); (time) lejano(a); (look) distraído(a); (cousin etc) lejano(a) (b) Fig (aloof) distante, frío(a)

distantly ['dɪstəntlɪ] adv (see, hear) a lo lejos, de lejos; (smile) con frialdad; (absent-mindedly) distraídamente

distaste [dɪs'teɪst] n aversión f

distasteful [dɪs'teɪstfʊl] adj (joke) de mal gusto; (idea) desagradable

distemper¹ [dɪ'stempər] n (paint) temple m

distemper² [dɪ'stempər] n (disease) moquillo m

distend [dɪ'stend] Fml 1 vt dilatar
2 vi dilatarse

distil, US **distill** [dɪ'stɪl] vt (pt & pp distilled) destilar

distillation [dɪstɪ'leɪʃən] n destilación f

distiller [dɪ'stɪlər] n destilador(a) m,f

distillery [dɪ'stɪlərɪ] n destilería f

distinct [dɪ'stɪŋkt] adj (a) (different) diferente, distinto(a); as d. from a diferencia de (b) (smell, likeness, change) marcado(a); (idea, sign, intention) claro(a), evidente; (tendency) bien determinado(a)

distinction [dɪ'stɪŋkʃən] n (a) (difference) diferencia f (b) (excellence) distinción f; an expert of d. un(a) experto(a) notable or distinguido(a); Iron I had the d. of coming last tuvo el gran honor de llegar el último (c) Educ sobresaliente m; he got two distinctions sacó dos sobresalientes

distinctive [dɪ'stɪŋktɪv] adj distintivo(a)

distinctly [dɪs'tɪŋktlɪ] adv (a) (clearly) (speak, hear) claramente, con claridad; I d. remember telling you recuerdo con toda claridad habértelo dicho (b) (decidedly) (better, easier) claramente; (stupid, ill-mannered) verdaderamente

distinguish [dɪ'stɪŋgwɪʃ] 1 vt (a) (differentiate) distinguir (from de) (b) (see, hear, taste) notar, percibir (c) (bring honour to) distinguirse, descollar, destacar
2 vi (differentiate) distinguirse

distinguishable [dɪ'stɪŋgwɪʃəbəl] adj distinguible

distinguished [dɪ'stɪŋgwɪʃt] adj (appearance) distinguido(a); (career, position) distinguido(a), eminente

distinguishing [dɪ'stɪŋgwɪʃɪŋ] adj distintivo(a), característico(a)

distort [dɪ'stɔːt] vt (a) (misrepresent) deformar, desfigurar; (words) distorsionar (b) (contort) distorsionar; (shape, object) deformar

distorted [dɪ'stɔːtɪd] adj (shape) deformado(a); (sound, guitar) distorsionado(a); Fig (account) distorsionado(a), tergiversado(a)

distortion [dɪ'stɔːʃən] n (a) (of case, motive, truth) deformación f, distorsión f (b) (of sound, image) distorsión f; (of shape) deformación f; (of features) alteración f

distract [dɪ'strækt] vt (person) distraer; (attention) desviar, apartar

distracted [dɪ'stræktɪd] adj distraído(a)

distracting [dɪ'stræktɪŋ] adj (a) (amusing) que distrae, ameno(a) (b) (annoying) molesto(a)

distraction [dɪ'strækʃən] n (a) (interruption) interrupción f, distracción f (b) (amusement) distracción f, entretenimiento m, diversión f (c) (confusion) confusión f; to drive sb to d. sacar a algn de quicio; to love sb to d. estar loco(a) por algn

distraught [dɪ'strɔːt] adj (anguished) afligido(a); (upset) turbado(a); (crazed) trastornado(a), enloquecido(a)

distress [dɪ'stres] **1** *n* (**a**) *(mental)* aflicción *f*, angustia *f*; *(physical)* dolor *m*; *(exhaustion)* agotamiento *m* (**b**) *(poverty)* miseria *f*; **in economic d.** en un apuro económico (**c**) *(danger)* peligro *m* ▫ **d. call, d. signal** señal *f* de socorro **2** *vt (upset)* dar pena a

distressed [dɪs'trest] *adj* angustiado(a), afligido(a); **to be d.** estar angustiado(a) *or* afligido(a)

distressing [dɪ'stresɪŋ] *adj* penoso(a)

distribute [dɪ'strɪbjuːt] *vt* distribuir, repartir

distribution [dɪstrɪ'bjuːʃən] *n* distribución *f* ▫ *Com* **d. network** red *f* de distribución

distributor [dɪ'strɪbjʊtər] *n* (**a**) *Com* distribuidor(a) *m,f* (**b**) *Aut* distribuidor *m*, *Esp* delco® *m*

district ['dɪstrɪkt] *n* *(of country)* región *f*; *(of town, city)* barrio *m*, distrito *m* ▫ *US Jur* **d. attorney** fiscal *m* (de un distrito judicial); *Br Formerly* **d. council** municipio *m*; *Br* **d. nurse** = enfermera que visita a los pacientes en sus casas; **federal d.** distrito *m* federal; **postal d.** distrito *m* postal

distrust [dɪs'trʌst] **1** *n* desconfianza *f*, recelo *m* **2** *vt* desconfiar, recelar

distrustful [dɪs'trʌstfʊl] *adj* desconfiado(a), receloso(a)

disturb [dɪ'stɜːb] *vt* (**a**) *(inconvenience)* molestar, estorbar; **'do not d.'** 'se ruega no molestar' (**b**) *(silence)* romper; *(sleep)* interrumpir; *Jur* **to d. the peace** alterar el orden público (**c**) *(worry)* perturbar, inquietar, preocupar (**d**) *(disarrange)* *(papers)* desordenar; *(lake, grass)* agitar, mover

disturbance [dɪ'stɜːbəns] *n* (**a**) *(worry)* preocupación *f*, inquietud *f*; *(nuisance)* molestia *f* (**b**) *(of routine)* alteración *f*, *(of plans)* desarreglo *m* (**c**) *(commotion)* disturbio *m*, alboroto *m*

disturbed [dɪ'stɜːbd] *adj* desequilibrado(a), inestable

disturbing [dɪ'stɜːbɪŋ] *adj* inquietante

disunity [dɪs'juːnɪti] *n* desunión *f*

disuse [dɪs'juːs] *n* desuso *m*

disused [dɪs'juːzd] *adj* abandonado(a)

ditch [dɪtʃ] **1** *n* *(gen)* zanja *f*; *(at roadside)* cuneta *f*; *(for irrigation)* acequia *f*; *(round earthworks)* foso *m*; *Fig* **to make a last-d. attempt to do sth** hacer un último esfuerzo para conseguir algo **2** *vt Fam (plane)* hacer un amerizaje forzoso; *(plan, friend)* abandonar; *(relationship, lover)* deshacerse de

dither ['dɪðər] *Fam Br* **1** *n* confusión *f* **2** *vi* vacilar, titubear; **stop dithering about!** ¡decídete ya de una vez!

ditherer ['dɪðərər] *n Fam* **he's such a terrible d.** es superindeciso

ditsy ['dɪtsi] *adj* alocado(a)

ditto ['dɪtəʊ] **1** *n* *(pl* **dittos***) (in list)* idem *m* **2** *adv Fam* lo mismo, idem; **I love chocolate — d.** me encanta el chocolate — a mí también

ditty ['dɪti] *n* cantinela *f*

diuretic [daɪjʊ'retɪk] *adj & n* diurético(a) *(m)*

diurnal [daɪ'ɜːnəl] *adj* diurno(a)

divan [dɪ'væn] *n Furn* diván *m* ▫ **d. (bed)** cama *f* turca

dive [daɪv] **1** *n* (**a**) *(into water)* zambullida *f*; *(of diver)* buceo *m*; *(of submarine, whale)* inmersión *f*; *(of plane)* picado *m*; *(of bird)* descenso *m*; *Sport* salto *m* (**b**) *Fam (bar etc)* antro *m* **2** *vi* (*US pt also* **dove**) (**a**) *(to plunge)* zambullirse, tirarse; *(plane)* bajar en picado; *Sport* saltar; *Fig* **he dived into the discussion** se metió de lleno en la discusión (**b**) *(diver)* bucear; *(submarine, whale)* sumergirse (**c**) *(person, animal)* meterse rápidamente, precipitarse hacia; **he dived for the phone** se precipitó hacia el teléfono; *Fig* **she dived into her pocket** se metió la mano rápidamente en el bolsillo

dive in *vi Fam (eat)* **d. in!** ¡a comer!, ¡al ataque!

diver ['daɪvər] *n* (**a**) *(person)* buceador(a) *m,f*; *(professional)* buzo *m*; *Sport* saltador(a) *m,f* (**b**) *Orn* colimbo *m* ▫ **black-throated d.** colimbo *m* ártico; **great northern d.** colimbo *m* grande; **red-throated d.** colimbo *m* chico

diverge [daɪ'vɜːdʒ] *vi* divergir; *(roads etc)* bifurcarse

divergence [daɪ'vɜːdʒəns] *n* divergencia *f*

divergent [daɪ'vɜːdʒənt] *adj* divergente

diverse [daɪ'vɜːs] *adj* (**a**) *(varied)* diverso(a), variado(a) (**b**) *(different)* distinto(a), diferente

diversification [daɪvɜːsɪfɪ'keɪʃən] *n Com* diversificación *f*

diversify [daɪ'vɜːsɪfaɪ] **1** *vt* (*pt & pp* **diversified**) diversificar **2** *vi* diversificarse

diversion [daɪ'vɜːʃən] *n* (**a**) *(distraction)* distracción *f* (**b**) *Br (detour)* desvío *m*

diversity [daɪ'vɜːsɪti] *n* diversidad *f*, variedad *f*

divert [daɪ'vɜːt] *vt* desviar

divest [daɪ'vest] *vt* **to d. sb of sth** quitar algo a algn, desvestir a algn de algo; *Fig* despojar a algn de algo

divide [dɪ'vaɪd] **1** *vt* (**a**) *(separate)* dividir, separar; *(classify)* dividir, clasificar, agrupar; **to d. sth in two** *or* **in half** partir algo por la mitad (**b**) *(share)* dividir, repartir (**c**) *Math* dividir; **d. 40 by 8** cuarenta dividido entre *or* por ocho **2** *vi* (**a**) *(separate) (road, stream)* dividirse, bifurcarse (**b**) *Fig (disagree)* dividirse, enfrentarse; *Prov* **d. and rule** divide y vencerás (**c**) *Br Parl* votar **3** *n* (**a**) *Fml (split)* división *f*, diferencia *f* (**b**) *US Geog* línea *f* divisoria de las aguas

divided [dɪ'vaɪdɪd] *adj* dividido(a); **to be d.** estar dividido(a); **a family d. against itself** una familia dividida; *US* **d. highway** autovía *f*

dividend ['dɪvɪdend] *n Com* dividendo *m*; *Fig* beneficio *m*, provecho *m*

dividers [dɪ'vaɪdəz] *npl* compás *m sing* de puntas

dividing [dɪ'vaɪdɪŋ] *adj* **d. line** línea *f* divisoria; **d. wall** muro *m* divisorio

divination [dɪvɪ'neɪʃən] *n* adivinación *f*, futurología *f*

divine [dɪ'vaɪn] *adj (gen)* divino(a); *Fam Fig (dress, house)* divino(a), precioso(a)

diving ['daɪvɪŋ] *n (from poolside, diving board)* salto *m* (de cabeza); *(scuba diving)* submarinismo *m*, buceo *m*; *(deep sea diving)* buceo *m* en alta mar; **d. bell** campana *f* de buzo; **d. board** trampolín *m*; **d. suit** traje *m* de buceo *or* de hombre rana

divinity [dɪ'vɪnɪti] *n* (**a**) *(subject)* teología *f* (**b**) *(quality, personage)* divinidad *f*

divisible [dɪ'vɪzəbəl] *adj* divisible

division [dɪ'vɪʒən] *n* (**a**) *(separation)* división *f*, separación *f*; *(classification)* clasificación *f* (**b**) *(sharing)* división *f*, reparto *m* ▫ **d. of labour** división *f* *or* distribución *f* del trabajo (**c**) *(of organization)* sección *f*; *Mil* división *f* (**d**) *Math* división *f* (**e**) *Br Parl* votación *f* (secreta) (**f**) *(in football)* división *f*

divisional [dɪ'vɪʒənəl] *adj (gen)* divisional; *Mil* de división

divisive [dɪ'vaɪsɪv] *adj* divisivo(a)

divorce [dɪ'vɔːs] **1** *n* divorcio *m*; *Fig* divorcio *m*; **to get a d.** obtener el divorcio; **to start d. proceedings** iniciar los trámites de divorcio **2** *vt* divorciar; *Fig* divorciar, separar; **she divorced him** se divorció de él **3** *vi* divorciarse

divorcé [dɪ'vɔːseɪ] *n*, **divorcée** [dɪvɔː'siː] *n* divorciado(a) *m,f*

divulge [daɪ'vʌldʒ] *vt Fml* divulgar, revelar

DIY [di:aɪ'waɪ] *n Br* (*abbr* **do-it-yourself**) bricolaje *m*

dizziness ['dɪzɪnɪs] *n (sickness)* mareo *m*; *(giddiness)* vértigo *m*

dizzy ['dɪzɪ] *adj* (**dizzier, dizziest**) (**a**) *(person) (unwell, giddy)* mareado(a); **d. spell** mareo *m* (**b**) *(height, pace)* vertiginoso(a)

DJ ['di:dʒeɪ] *n Fam* (**a**) *Br* (*abbr* **dinner jacket**) smoking *m* (**b**) (*abbr* **disc jockey**) pinchadiscos *m inv*, disc-jockey *mf*

Djibouti [dʒɪ'bu:tɪ] *n* Djibouti, Yibuti

DLitt [di:'lɪt] *n* (*abbr* **Doctor of Letters**) Doctor(a) *m,f* en Letras

DNA [di:en'eɪ] *n Chem* (*abbr* **deoxyribonucleic acid**) ácido *m* desoxirribonucleico, ADN *m*

do [du:, *unstressed* dʊ, də] *v aux* (*3rd person sing pres* **does**; *pt* **did**; *pp* **done**) (**a**) *(in negatives and questions)* (*not translated in Spanish*) **do you drive?** ¿tienes carnet de conducir?; **don't you want to come?** ¿no quieres venir?; **he does not** *or* **doesn't smoke** no fuma (**b**) *(emphatic)* (*not translated in Spanish*) **do come with us!** ¡ánimo, vente con nosotros!; **I do like your bag** me encanta tu bolso (**c**) *(substituting main verb)* (*not translated in Spanish*) **I don't believe him** — **neither do I** no le creo — yo tampoco; **I'll go if you do** si vas tú, voy yo; **I think it's dear, but he doesn't** a mí me parece caro pero a él no; **who went?** — **I did** ¿quién asistió? — yo (**d**) *(in question tags)* **he refused, didn't he?** dijo que no, ¿verdad?; **I don't like it, do you?** a mí no me gusta, ¿y a ti?

2 *vt* (**a**) *(gen)* hacer; *(task)* realizar, llevar a cabo; *(puzzle)* solucionar; *(duty)* cumplir con; **are you doing anything?** ¿estás ocupado(a)?; **he did nothing but laugh** no hizo más que reír; **that dress doesn't do much for you** ese vestido no te favorece; **to do business with sb** hacer negocios con algn; **to do one's best** *or* **all one can** hacer todo lo posible; **to do sth again** volver a hacer algo; **to do sth for sb** hacer algo por algn; **to do the cooking/cleaning** cocinar/limpiar; **we must do something about it** tenemos que ocuparnos de ello; **what can I do about it?** ¿qué quieres que haga?; **what can I do for you?** ¿en qué puedo servirle?; **what do you do (for a living)?** ¿a qué te dedicas?, ¿en qué trabajas?; **what's to be done?** ¿qué se puede hacer?; *Fam* **he's done it!** ¡lo ha conseguido!; *Fam* **you've done it now!** ¡me han hecho!; ¡buena la has hecho!; *Fam* **well done!** ¡enhorabuena!, ¡muy bien!; *Prov* **what's done is done** a lo hecho, pecho (**b**) *(produce, make, offer) (film)* hacer; *(meat, food)* dar, producir; **do you do sportswear?** ¿aquí venden *or* tienen ropa de deporte? (**c**) *(study)* estudiar (**d**) *(suffice)* bastar; **ten will do us** con diez tenemos suficiente *or* bastante (**e**) *(tour, visit)* recorrer, visitar, ver (**f**) *Aut (speed)* ir a; *(distance)* recorrer; **we were doing eighty** íbamos a ochenta (**g**) *Br Fam (injure)* **I'll do you if you don't shut up!** ¡como no te calles te voy a dar! (**h**) *Br Fam (swindle)* **I've been done!** ¡me han timado!

3 *vi* (**a**) *(act, perform, function)* hacer, actuar; **do as I tell you** haz lo que te digo; **you did right** hiciste bien (**b**) *(proceed)* **he did badly in the exams** los exámenes le fueron mal; **how are you doing?** ¿qué tal?, ¿cómo te van las cosas?; **how do you do?** *(greeting)* ¿cómo está usted?; *(answer)* mucho gusto, encantado(a) (de conocerle); **to do well** *(person)* tener éxito, salir adelante; *(business)* ir bien (**c**) *(suffice)* bastar; **will five dollars do?** ¿tendrás suficiente *or* bastante con cinco dólares?; *Fam* **that will do!** ¡basta ya!, ¡ya está bien! (**d**) *(be suitable)* servir; **this cushion will do for** *or* **as a pillow** este cojín servirá de almohada; **this won't do** esto no puede ser

4 *n* (*pl* **dos** *or* **do's** [du:z]) *Fam* (**a**) *Br (party)* fiesta *f*, guateque *m*; *(gathering)* celebración *f*; *(event)* ceremonia *f* (**b**) **do's and don'ts** reglas *fpl* de conducta

do away with *vt* (**a**) *(abolish)* abolir, suprimir; *(discard)* deshacerse de (**b**) *(kill)* asesinar

do down *vt Br Fam* (**a**) *(humiliate)* hacer quedar mal, rebajar (**b**) *(cheat)* estafar, timar

do for *Fam* **1** *vi (destroy, ruin)* arruinar, destrozar; *Fig* **I'm done for if I don't finish this** estoy perdido(a) si no acabo esto
2 *vi* llevar la casa a; **Amanda has been doing for them since their mother died** Amanda lleva la casa desde que murió su madre

do in *vt Slang* (**a**) *(kill)* matar, cargarse (**b**) *Br (exhaust)* agotar; **I'm done in** estoy hecho(a) polvo

do out *vt Fam* (**a**) *Br (clean)* limpiar a fondo; *(decorate)* decorar (**b**) **to do sb out of sth** quitarle algo a algn por engaño

do over *vt Fam* (**a**) *US (repeat)* repetir, volver a hacer, hacer de nuevo (**b**) *(redecorate)* decorar (**c**) *Br (thrash)* dar una paliza a

do up *vt* (**a**) *(wrap)* envolver (**b**) *(fasten) (belt etc)* abrochar; *(laces)* atar (**c**) *(dress up)* arreglar; **she was all done up** iba toda arreglada (**d**) *Fam (redecorate)* renovar, decorar

do with *vt* (**a**) *(need)* **I could do with a rest** un descanso me vendría muy bien *or* no me vendría nada mal (**b**) *(concern)* **to have** *or* **be to do with** tener que ver con, tratarse de

do without *vt* pasar sin, prescindir de; **I can't do without your help** no puedo pasar sin tu ayuda

DOA [di:əʊ'eɪ] *adj Med* (*abbr* **dead on arrival**) **he was D.** cuando llegó al hospital ya había muerto, *Esp* ingresó cadáver

DOB (*abbr* **date of birth**) = fecha de nacimiento

doc [dɒk] *n* (*abbr* **doctor**) *Fam* doctor *m*

docile ['dəʊsaɪl] *adj (person)* dócil, sumiso(a); *(animal)* manso(a)

dock[1] [dɒk] **1** *n Naut (gen)* muelle *m*; *(for cargo)* dársena *f*; **to work on** *or* **at the docks** trabajar en el puerto ◻ **dry d.** dique *m* seco
2 *vt* (**a**) *(ship)* atracar (**at** en) (**b**) *(spacecraft)* acoplar
3 *vi* (**a**) *(ship)* atracar (**b**) *(spacecraft)* acoplarse

dock[2] [dɒk] **1** *n (tail)* cola *f*, rabo *m*
2 *vt* (**a**) *(tail)* descolar, cortar la cola a (**b**) *(reduce)* deducir, descontar

dock[3] [dɒk] *n Jur* **the d.** el banquillo (de los acusados)

docker ['dɒkər] *n* estibador *m*

docket ['dɒkɪt] *Br* **1** *n (label)* rótulo *m*, etiqueta *f* ◻ **customs d.** recibo *m* de aduanas
2 *vt* rotular

dockland ['dɒklænd] *n* zona *f* del puerto

dockyard ['dɒkjɑ:d] *n* astillero *m*

doctor ['dɒktər] **1** *n* (**a**) *Med* médico(a) *m,f*, doctor(a) *m,f*; **D. Jane Wells** la doctora Jane Wells ◻ **family d.** médico(a) *m,f* de cabecera (**b**) *Univ* doctor(a) *m,f*; **D. of Law** doctor en derecho
2 *vt* (**a**) *Pej (tamper with) (figures, bill)* falsificar; *(text)* arreglar, amañar; *(food, drink)* adulterar (**b**) *Br (cat)* castrar, capar

doctoral ['dɒktərəl] *adj* doctoral

doctorate ['dɒktərɪt] *n Educ* doctorado *m*

doctrinaire [dɒktrɪ'neər] *adj* doctrinario(a)

doctrinal [dɒk'traɪnəl] *adj* doctrinal

doctrine ['dɒktrɪn] *n* doctrina *f*

docudrama ['dɒkjʊdrɑːmə] *n* docudrama *m*

document 1 *n (gen)* documento *m* ◻ *Comptr* **d. reader** digitalizador *m*, lector *m* de documentos; **legal d.** escritura *f* (pública); **travel documents** documentación *f* para viajar
2 *vt* documentar

documentary [dɒkjʊˈmentərɪ] *adj & n* documental *(m)*

documentation [dɒkjʊmenˈteɪʃən] *n* documentación *f*

dodder [ˈdɒdər] *vi Fam (old person)* andar con paso inseguro

doddle [ˈdɒdəl] *n Br Fam* it's a d. es pan comido

dodge [dɒdʒ] **1** *vt* **(a)** *(avoid) (blow etc)* esquivar; *(pursuer)* despistar, dar esquinazo a; *(queue etc)* evitar; *Fig* evitar, esquivar, soslayar **(b)** *Fam (evade) (tax)* evadir; *(class, meeting)* fumarse; *(punishment, commitment)* librarse or zafarse de
2 *vi (move aside)* echarse a un lado
3 *n* **(a)** *(movement)* regate *m*, evasión *f* **(b)** *Fam (trick)* truco *m*, astucia *f*; **to be up to all the dodges** sabérselas todas ❑ **tax d.** elusión *f* fiscal or de impuestos

Dodgem® [ˈdɒdʒəm] *n Br* **D. (car)** auto *m* or coche *m* de choque, *Méx* carrito *m* chocón, *RP* autito *m* chocador

dodgy [ˈdɒdʒɪ] *adj* **(dodgier, dodgiest)** *Br Fam* **(a)** *(risky)* arriesgado(a); *(tricky)* difícil, problemático(a) **(b)** *(person)* poco honesto(a), que no es de fiar

dodo [ˈdəʊdəʊ] *n (pl* **dodos** *or* **dodoes)** *Orn* dodo *m*; *Fam Fig* **as dead as a d.** muerto y bien muerto

doe [dəʊ] *n inv (of deer)* gama *f*; *(of rabbit)* coneja *f*; *(of hare)* liebre *f*

doer [ˈduːər] *n Fam* persona *f* dinámica

does [dʌz] *3rd person sing pres see* **do**

doesn't [ˈdʌzənt] = does not

doff [dɒf] *vt* **to d. one's cap to sb** descubrirse ante algn

dog [dɒg] **1** *n* **(a)** *Zool* perro(a) *m,f*; **to d -paddle** nadar como los perros; *Fig* **d. eat d.** competencia *f* despiadada; *Fig* **not to have a d.'s chance** no tener ni la más remota posibilidad; *Br Fam* **to be dressed (up) like a d.'s dinner** estar hecho(a) un cromo; *US Fam* **to put on the d.** darse pisto; *Fam Fig* **a d.'s life** una vida de perros; *Prov* **every d. has his day** a cada cerdo le llega su San Martín; *Prov* **let sleeping dogs lie** no enturbiar las aguas; *Prov* **you can't teach an old d. new tricks** loro viejo no aprende a hablar ❑ **d. collar** *(of dog)* collar *m* de perro; *Rel Fam* alcacuello *m*; **d. show** exhibición *f* canina; **guard d.** perro *m* guardián; **pedigree d.** perro *m* de raza **(b)** *(male canine)* macho *m*; *(fox)* zorro *m*; *(wolf)* lobo *m* **(c)** *Br Sport Fam* **the dogs** carreras *fpl* de galgos; *Fig* **to go to the dogs** arruinarse **(d)** *Fam (fellow)* **dirty d.** canalla *m*, sinvergüenza *m*; **lucky d.** tío *m* con suerte **(e)** *US Fam (disappointment)* desastre *m*, fracaso *m*
2 *vt (pt & pp* **dogged)** *(pursue)* seguir de cerca, acosar; **to d. sb's footsteps** seguir los pasos de algn; *Fig* **dogged by bad luck** perseguido(a) por la mala suerte

dogcart [ˈdɒgkɑːt] *n* coche *m* de un solo caballo

dog-eared [ˈdɒgɪəd] *adj (newspaper, book)* con los bordes de las páginas doblados; *(shabby)* sobado(a)

dogfight [ˈdɒgfaɪt] *n* **(a)** *Av* combate *m* aéreo **(b)** *(between dogs)* pelea *f* entre perros; *Fig* altercado *m*

dogfish [ˈdɒgfɪʃ] *n inv* cazón *m*, perro *m* marino

dogged [ˈdɒgɪd] *adj (refusal)* obstinado(a); *(determination)* tenaz, persistente

doggedly [ˈdɒgɪdlɪ] *adv* tenazmente, con tenacidad

doggerel [ˈdɒgərəl] *n sing Lit* aleluyas *fpl*

doggie [ˈdɒgɪ] *n see* **doggy**

doggo [ˈdɒgəʊ] *adv Br Fam* **to lie d.** permanecer escondido(a)

doggone [ˈdɒgɒn] *adj US Fam Euph see* **damn 4**

doggy [ˈdɒgɪ] **1** *n (child's talk)* perrito(a) *m,f* ❑ **d. bag** bolsa *f* para el perro
2 *adj* **(doggier, doggiest)** *(fond of dogs)* aficionado(a) a los perros

doghouse [ˈdɒghaʊs] *n US Fam* perrera *f*; *Fig* **to be in the d.** tener la negra

dogma [ˈdɒgmə] *n (pl* **dogmas** *or* **dogmata** [ˈdɒgmətə]) *Rel Pol* dogma *m*

dogmatic [dɒgˈmætɪk] *adj* dogmático(a)

do-gooder [duːˈgʊdər] *n Fam* persona *f* bien intencionada

dogsbody [ˈdɒgzbɒdɪ] *n Br Fam (drudge)* burro *m* de carga

dog-tired [ˈdɒgtaɪəd] *adj Fam* rendido(a), hecho(a) polvo

doh [dəʊ] *n Mus* do *m*

doily [ˈdɔɪlɪ] *n (of paper)* tapete *m* decorativo (de papel)

doing [ˈduːɪŋ] *n* **(a)** *(action)* obra *f*; **it was none of my d.** yo no tuve nada que ver; *Fig* **it took some d.** costó trabajo hacerlo **(b) doings** *(activities)* actividades *fpl*

do-it-yourself [duːɪtjəˈself] *n* bricolaje *m* ❑ **do-it-y. shop** tienda *f* de bricolaje

doldrums [ˈdɒldrəmz] *npl Fam Fig* **to be in the d.** *(person)* estar deprimido(a) or abatido(a) or *Am* con el ánimo por el piso; *(business, trade)* estar estancado(a)

dole [dəʊl] **1** *n Br Fam* subsidio *m* de desempleo, *Esp* paro *m*; **to be** or **go on the d.** estar en el paro ❑ *Fig* **the d. queue** los parados
2 *vt* **to d. (out)** repartir

doleful [ˈdəʊlfʊl] *adj* triste, afligido(a)

doll [dɒl] **1** *n* **(a)** *(toy)* muñeca *f* ❑ *Br* **doll's house** casa *f* de muñecas **(b)** *US Slang (girl)* muñeca *f*
2 *vt Slang* **to d. oneself up** *(girl etc)* ponerse guapa, arreglarse

dollar [ˈdɒlər] *n* dólar *m* ❑ **d. bill** billete *m* de un dólar

dollhouse [ˈdɒlhaʊs] *n US* casa *f* de muñecas

dollop [ˈdɒləp] *n Fam* cucharada *f*; *(of ice cream)* porción *f*

dolly [ˈdɒlɪ] *n* **(a)** *(child's talk)* muñeca *f* **(b)** *Br Slang* **d. (bird)** muñeca *f*

Dolomites [ˈdɒləmaɪts] *npl* **the D.** las Dolomitas

dolphin [ˈdɒlfɪn] *n Zool* delfín *m*

dolt [dəʊlt] *n* idiota *m,f*, tonto(a) *m,f*, mentecato(a) *m,f*

domain [dəˈmeɪn] *n* **(a)** *(sphere)* campo *m*, esfera *f*; **that's not my d.** no es de mi competencia **(b)** *(territory)* dominio *m* **(c)** *Comptr* dominio *m*; **d. name** nombre *m* de dominio

dome [dəʊm] *n Archit (roof)* cúpula *f*; *(ceiling)* bóveda *f*; *Fam Fig (head)* coronilla *f*

domestic [dəˈmestɪk] **1** *adj* **(a)** *(appliance, pet)* doméstico(a); **d. bliss** felicidad conyugal; **d. violence** violencia *f* doméstica ❑ *Br Educ* **d. science** economía *f* doméstica **(b)** *(home-loving)* hogareño(a), casero(a) **(c)** *(national) (flight, news)* nacional; *(trade, policy)* interior
2 *n* **d. (help)** servicio *m* doméstico

domesticate [dəˈmestɪkeɪt] *vt* **(a)** *(animal)* domesticar; *(plant)* aclimatar **(b)** *(make home-loving)* volver hogareño(a) or casero(a)

domesticated [dəˈmestɪkeɪtɪd] *adj (animal)* domesticado(a); *Fig Hum* **to be d.** *(person)* estar muy bien enseñado(a)

domesticity [dəʊmesˈtɪsɪtɪ] *n* vida *f* casera

domicile [ˈdɒmɪsaɪl] *n Jur* domicilio *m*

dominance [ˈdɒmɪnəns] *n* dominio *m*, control *m*

dominant [ˈdɒmɪnənt] *adj* dominante

dominate [ˈdɒmɪneɪt] *vt & vi* dominar

domineering [dɒmɪˈnɪərɪŋ] *adj Pej* dominante, autoritario(a); *(woman)* marimandona

Dominica [dəˈmɪnɪkə] *n* Dominica

Dominican [dəˈmɪnɪkən] *adj & n* **(a)** *(of Dominica)*

dominicano(a) *(m,f)* ❏ **D. Republic** República *f* Dominicana (**b**) *Rel* dominicano(a) *(m,f)*

dominion [dəˈmɪnjən] *n* dominio *m*

domino [ˈdɒmɪnəʊ] *n (pl* **dominoes**) *(piece)* ficha *f* de dominó; *(game)* **dominoes** dominó *m sing; Pol* **d. effect** efecto *m* dominó

don¹ [dɒn] *vt (pt & pp* **donned**) *Fml* ponerse

don² [dɒn] *n Br Univ* catedrático(a) *m,f*

donate [dəʊˈneɪt] *vt (money)* hacer un donativo de; *(books, clothes)* donar; *(property)* hacer donación de

donation [dəʊˈneɪʃən] *n* (**a**) *(gift)* donativo *m* (**b**) *(act)* donación *f*

done [dʌn] **1** *pp see* **do**
2 *adj* (**a**) *(finished)* terminado(a), acabado(a), completado(a); **I'm** *or* **I've d. with the matter** no quiero tener más que ver con el asunto; **it's over and d. with** se acabó; *Fam* **d.!** ¡trato hecho! (**b**) *Fam (tired)* rendido(a), agotado(a) (**c**) *(cooked) (meat)* hecho(a); *(vegetables)* cocido(a); **d. to a turn** en su punto (**d**) *Br (acceptable)* **it's not d. to ...** es de mal gusto ...; **it's the d. thing** es de rigor, es lo que se hace

donkey [ˈdɒŋkɪ] *n (animal, person)* burro(a) *m,f; Fam* **I haven't seen you for d.'s years** hace siglos que no te veo ❏ *Br* **d. jacket** chaqueta *f or Méx* chamarra *f or RP* chamarra *f* gruesa de obrero

donor [ˈdəʊnər] *n* donante *m*

don't [dəʊnt] = **do not**

don't know [ˈdəʊntˈnəʊ] *n* (**a**) *(answer)* no sé *m* (**b**) *(person)* = persona que no sabe o no contesta en un cuestionario

donut [ˈdəʊnʌt] *n US see* **doughnut**

doodah [ˈduːdɑː], *US* **doodad** [duːˈdæd] *n Fam* chisme *m, CAm Carib Col* vaina *f, RP* coso *m*

doodle [ˈduːdəl] *Fam* **1** *vi (write)* garabatear *(distraídamente); (draw)* hacer dibujos
2 *n (writing)* garabato *m; (drawing)* dibujo *m*

doom [duːm] **1** *n (fate)* destino *m (funesto); (ruin)* perdición *f; (death)* muerte *f*
2 *vt (destine)* destinar; *(condemn)* condenar; **doomed to failure** condenado(a) al fracaso

doomsday [ˈduːmzdeɪ] *n Rel* día *m* del juicio final; *Fam Fig* **till D.** para siempre

door [dɔːr] *n* (**a**) *(entrance)* puerta *f;* **front/back d.** puerta principal/trasera; **to answer the d.** ir a abrir la puerta; **to be at the d.** estar en la puerta; **to be on the d.** hacer de portero; **to knock at the d.** llamar a la puerta; **to see sb to the d.** acompañar a algn hasta la puerta *or* la salida; **to slam the d.** dar un portazo; *Fig* **behind closed doors** a puerta cerrada; *Fig* **to get in by the back d.** colarse por la puerta falsa; *Fig* **to lay sth at sb's d.** echar la culpa de algo a algn; *Fig* **to show sb the d.** echar a algn (a la calle); *Fig* **to shut** *or* **slam the d. in sb's face** darle a algn con la puerta en las narices ❏ **d. handle** manilla *f* (de la puerta); **d. knocker** picaporte *m;* **revolving d.** puerta *f* giratoria; **sliding d.** puerta *f* corredera (**b**) *(house, building)* casa *f;* **next d. (to)** (en) la casa de al lado (de); **two doors up/down (the street)** en la segunda casa calle arriba/abajo

doorbell [ˈdɔːbel] *n* timbre *m* (de la puerta)

do-or-die [ˈduːɔːˈdaɪ] *adj* **he has a d. approach to any challenge** ante cualquier reto va a por todas

doorkeeper [ˈdɔːkiːpər] *n* portero(a) *m,f*

doorknob [ˈdɔːnɒb] *n* pomo *m* (de la puerta)

doorman [ˈdɔːmən] *n (pl* **doormen**) portero *m*

doormat [ˈdɔːmæt] *n* felpudo *m*, esterilla *f; Fam Fig (person)* trapo *m*

doornail [ˈdɔːneɪl] *n Fam* **as dead as a d.** muerto(a) y bien muerto(a)

doorstep [ˈdɔːstep] *n* peldaño *m; Fig* **on one's d.** al lado de casa

doorstop [ˈdɔːstɒp] *n (to prevent over-opening)* tope *m* (de puerta); *(to prop open)* cuña *f* (de puerta)

door-to-door [dɔːtəˈdɔːr] *adj* a domicilio

doorway [ˈdɔːweɪ] *n* portal *m*, entrada *f;* **he stood in the d.** se quedó en la puerta

dope [dəʊp] **1** *n* (**a**) *Slang (illegal drug)* chocolate *m;* **to take** *or* **be on d.** drogarse ❏ **d. addict** drogadicto(a) *m,f* (**b**) *Fam (person)* tonto(a) *m,f*, bobo(a) *m,f*, *Am* sonso(a), *Am* zonzo(a) *m,f* (**c**) *Fam (news)* información *f* confidencial, soplo *m*
2 *vt (food, drink)* adulterar con drogas; *Sport (athlete, horse)* drogar, dopar

dop(e)y [ˈdəʊpɪ] *adj* (**dopier, dopiest**) *Fam* (**a**) *(sleepy)* medio dormido(a); *(fuddled)* atontado(a) (**b**) *Slang (silly)* tonto(a), bobo(a), *Am* sonso(a), *Am* zonzo(a)

Dordogne [dɔːˈdɔɪn] *n* Dordoña

dork [dɔːk] *n US Fam* petardo(a) *m,f*

dorm [dɔːm] *n Fam* dormitorio *m (colectivo)*

dormant [ˈdɔːmənt] *adj (gen)* inactivo(a); *Fig (rivalry)* latente; *Fig* **the idea lay d. in her mind** le bullía la idea en la cabeza

dormer [ˈdɔːmər] *n* **d. (window)** buhardilla *f*

dormitory [ˈdɔːmɪtərɪ] *n* (**a**) *(in school, hostel)* dormitorio *m* ❏ *Br* **d. suburb** *or* **town** ciudad *f* dormitorio (**b**) *US (in university)* residencia *f*, colegio *m* mayor

dormouse [ˈdɔːmaʊs] *(pl* **dormice** [ˈdɔːmaɪs]) *n* lirón *m*

dorsal [ˈdɔːsəl] *adj Anat* dorsal

DOS [dɒs] *n Comptr (abbr* **disk operating system**) DOS *m*

dosage [ˈdəʊsɪdʒ] *n Fml (amount)* dosis *f inv; (on medicine bottle)* posología *f*

dose [dəʊs] **1** *n (of medicine)* dosis *f inv; Fig* **a nasty d. of flu** un ataque fuerte de gripe *or Col Méx* gripa
2 *vt (patient)* medicar; **he's always dosing himself (up) with pills** siempre se está automedicando con pastillas

doss [dɒs] *vi Br Slang* dormir, clapar; **I'll just d. (down) on the sofa** me echaré a dormir *or* me acostaré en el sofá

dosser [ˈdɒsər] *n Br Slang* vago(a) *m,f*, gandul(ula) *m,f*

dosshouse [ˈdɒshaʊs] *n Br Slang* pensión *f* barata *or* de mala muerte

dossier [ˈdɒsɪeɪ] *n* expediente *m*, dossier *m;* **to keep a d. on sth/sb** abrir un expediente sobre algo/a algn

dot [dɒt] **1** *n* punto *m;* **at two on the d., on the d. of two** a las dos en punto; *Fam* **the year d.** el año de la pera *or RP* de ñaupa *or Chile* de ñauca
2 *vt (pt & pp* **dotted**) (**a**) *(letter)* poner el punto a; *Fam* **to d. one's i's and cross one's t's** poner los puntos sobre las íes (**b**) *(scatter)* esparcir, desparramar; **fields dotted with daisies** campos salpicados de margaritas

dotage [ˈdəʊtɪdʒ] *n* chochez *f;* **to be in one's d.** estar chocho(a)

dote [dəʊt] *vi* **to d. on** mimar, adorar

dotty [ˈdɒtɪ] *adj Fam (person)* chalado(a); **a d. idea** una chaladura; **to be d.** estar chalado(a); **he's d. about her** se le cae la baba con ella

double [ˈdʌbəl] **1** *adj (gen)* doble; *Tel* **d. six five nine** sesenta y seis cincuenta y nueve; **he's d. my age** me dobla la edad; **it's d. the price** cuesta dos veces más; **to reach d. figures** ascender a una cantidad de dos cifras; **written with a d. 't'** escrito(a) con dos tes; *Br Fam* **it's d. Dutch to me** me suena a chino; *Fam* **to do a d. take** reaccionar tarde ❏ **d. agent** agente *mf* doble; *Mus* **d. bass** contrabajo *m*; **d. bed** cama *f* de matrimonio; *C in Theat* **d. bill** programa *m* doble; **d. check** segundo repaso *m*, segunda verificación *f or* revisión *f*; **d. chin** papada *f*; *Br* **d. cream** *Esp* nata *f* para montar, *Am* crema *f* líquida enriquecida, *RP* crema *f* doble; **d. date** cita *f* de dos parejas; **d. figures** números *mpl* de dos cifras; **d. glazing** ventana *f* doble; *US Fin* **d. indemnity** = seguro de vida en el que se paga el doble del capital cuando el asegurado muere por accidente; **d. standard** doble moral *m*; **d. talk** palabras *fpl* ambiguas; **d. time** *(pay)* paga *f* doble; *(time)* horas *fpl* extra

2 *adv* doble; **sheets folded d.** sábanas dobladas por la mitad; **to be bent d.** estar encorvado(a)

3 *n* (**a**) *(lookalike)* imagen *f* viva, vivo retrato *m*; *C in Theat (substitute)* doble *m* (**b**) *(amount)* doble *m*; **to earn d.** ganar el doble, ganar dos veces más; *Fam* **at** *or* **on the d.** enseguida, corriendo (**c**) *Ten* **doubles** partido *m sing* de dobles; **men's/ ladies' d.** partido de dobles masculino/femenino

4 *vt* (**a**) *(gen)* doblar, duplicar; *Fig (efforts)* redoblar (**b**) *(bend, fold)* doblar; **she doubled the sheet (back** *or* **over)** dobló la sábana para hacer reborde

5 *vi* (**a**) *(increase)* doblarse, duplicarse (**b**) *(serve)* **to d. as sth/sb** hacer las veces de algo/de algn (**c**) *(turn sharply)* girar bruscamente

double back *vi* **to d. back on one's tracks** volver sobre sus pasos

double up 1 *vt (bend)* doblar; **to be doubled up with** *or* **in pain** retorcerse de dolor

2 *vi* (**a**) *(bend)* doblarse; **to d. up with laughter** mondarse *or* partirse de risa (**b**) *(share room)* compartir la habitación (**with** con)

double-barrelled, *US* **double-barreled** ['dʌbəl-bærəld] *adj* (**a**) *(gun)* de dos cañones (**b**) *Br (surname)* compuesto(a)

double-breasted ['dʌbəlbrestɪd] *adj (garment)* cruzado(a)

double-check [dʌbəl'tʃek] *vt & vi* repasar *or* verificar *or* revisar dos veces

double-click ['dʌbəl'klɪk] *Comptr* **1** *n* doble click *m*

2 *vt* hacer doble click en

3 *vi* hacer doble click (**on** en)

double-cross [dʌbəl'krɒs] *Fam* **1** *vt* engañar, traicionar

2 *n* engaño *m*, traición *f*

double-dealing [dʌbəl'di:lɪŋ] *n Fig* duplicidad *f*, doblez *f*

double-decker [dʌbəl'dekər] *n* (**a**) *Br* **d.-d. (bus)** autobús *m* de dos pisos (**b**) *US Fam* **d.-d. (sandwich)** sandwich *m* doble

double-edged [dʌbəl'edʒd] *adj* de doble filo

double-jointed [dʌbəl'dʒɔɪntɪd] *adj* con articulaciones dobles

double-lock ['dʌbəl'lɒk] *vt* cerrar con dos vueltas (de llave)

double-park [dʌbəl'pɑːk] *vt & vi Aut* estacionar(se) *or Esp* aparcar en doble fila

double-quick ['dʌbəl'kwɪk] *adv* rapidísimamente

doublethink ['dʌbəlθɪŋk] *n* (asunción *f* de) ideas *fpl* contradictorias

doubly ['dʌblɪ] *adv* doblemente, por partida doble

doubt [daʊt] **1** *n (gen)* duda *f*; *(uncertainty)* incertidumbre *f*; **beyond (all reasonable) d.** sin duda alguna, fuera de (toda) duda; **if** *or* **when in d.** en caso de duda; **no d.** sin duda, seguramente; **there's no d. about it** no cabe la menor duda; **there's some d. whether he'll go** no se sabe si irá; **to be in d. about sth** dudar algo; **to be in d., be open to d.** *(fact, integrity)* ser dudoso(a); *(outcome)* ser incierto(a); **to cast d. on sth** poner algo en duda *or* en tela de juicio

2 *vt* (**a**) *(distrust)* dudar de, desconfiar de (**b**) *(not be sure of)* dudar; **I d. if** *or* **whether he'll come** dudo que *or* no creo que venga; **I very much d. it** lo dudo mucho

doubter ['daʊtər] *n Pol Rel* escéptico(a) *m,f*

doubtful ['daʊtfʊl] *adj* (**a**) *(uncertain) (future)* dudoso(a), incierto(a); *(look, feeling)* dubitativo(a), de duda; **I'm a bit d. about it** no me convence del todo; **it's d. whether ...** no se sabe seguro si ... (**b**) *(questionable)* dudoso(a), sospechoso(a)

doubting ['daʊtɪŋ] *adj* escéptico(a), incrédulo(a); **a d. Thomas** un(a) escéptico(a) *or* incrédulo(a)

doubtless ['daʊtlɪs] **1** *adv* sin duda, seguramente

2 *adj* indudable

douche [duːʃ] *n Med (process)* irrigación *f*; *(instrument)* irrigador *m*

dough [dəʊ] *n* (**a**) *Culin (for bread)* masa *f*; *(for pastries)* pasta *f* (**b**) *Slang (money) Esp* pasta *f*, *Esp RP* guita *f*, *Am* plata *f*, *Méx* lana *f*

doughnut ['dəʊnʌt] *n* rosquilla *f*, dónut® *m* ❑ **jam/ cream d.** rosquilla *f* rellena de mermelada/nata

dour [daʊər] *adj* hosco(a)

Douro ['dəʊrəʊ] *n* **the D.** el Duero

douse [daʊs] *vt* (**a**) *(soak)* mojar (**b**) *(extinguish)* apagar

dove[1] [dʌv] *n* paloma *f* ❑ **collared d.** tórtola *f* turca; **stock d.** paloma *f* zurita; **turtle d.** tórtola *f* común

dove[2] [dəʊv] *pt US see* **dive**

dovetail ['dʌvteɪl] **1** *n Tech* **d. (joint)** cola *f* de milano

2 *vt Fig (plans)* sincronizar

dowager ['daʊədʒər] *n* (**a**) *(widow)* viuda *f* (de un noble); **d. countess** condesa *f* viuda (**b**) *Fam* vieja dama *f*

dowdy ['daʊdɪ] *adj* (**dowdier, dowdiest**) sin gracia, poco elegante *or* atractivo(a)

dowel ['daʊəl] *n* clavija *f*

down[1] [daʊn] **1** *prep* (**a**) *(to or at a lower level)* (hacia) abajo; **d. the hill/river** cuesta/río abajo; **he ran a finger d. the list** recorrió la lista con el dedo; **to go d. the road** bajar la calle (**b**) *(along)* por; **cut it d. the middle** córtalo por la mitad

2 *adv* (**a**) *(to lower level)* (hacia) abajo; *(to floor)* al suelo; *(to ground)* a tierra; **to drink sth d.** beberse hasta la última gota de algo; **to fall d.** caerse; **to go d.** *(price, person)* bajar; *(sun)* ponerse; *Fig* **to come d. in the world** venir a menos (**b**) *(at lower level)* abajo; **d. here/there** aquí/allí abajo; **face d.** boca abajo; **he's just d. from Scotland** acaba de llegar de Escocia; *Fig* **he can't keep food d.** no retiene la comida; *Fig* **to be d. with a cold** estar resfriado(a); *Fam Fig* **to feel d.** estar deprimido(a) ❑ *Br Fam* **d. under** en/a Australia y Nueva Zelanda *f* (**c**) *(of smaller size, volume)* **sales are d. by five percent** las ventas han bajado un cinco por ciento; **the tyres are d.** los neumáticos están desinflados; **to put prices d.** reducir los precios; *Fig* **I'm one dollar d.** me falta una dólar; **I'm d. to my last stamp** no me queda más que un solo sello (**d**) *(in writing)* **I'm d. for the French course** me he matriculado para el cursillo de francés; **to take** *or* **write sth d.** apuntar algo; **to be d. in writing** estar puesto(a) por escrito (**e**) *(in succession)* **d. through the ages** a través de los siglos; **from 1800 d. to the present day** desde 1800 hasta el día de hoy (**f**) *(as payment)* **to pay ten dollars d.** pagar diez dólares al contado como paga y señal

3 *adj* (**a**) *(train)* que va hacia las afueras; *(escalator, draught)* de bajada (**b**) *(payment)* al contado; *(on property)* de entrada (**c**) *Comptr* **to be d.** no funcionar; **d. time** *(in industry)* paro *m* técnico

4 *vt* (**a**) *(knock over)* derribar; *(defeat)* derrotar (**b**) *Fam (drink)* tomarse de un trago; *(food)* zamparse

5 *n* (**a**) *(misfortune)* desgracia *f*; **ups and downs** altibajos

mpl, vicisitudes *fpl* (**b**) *Fam (dislike)* **to have a d. on sb** guardarle rencor a algn, tenerle manía a algn
6 *exclam* **d.!** *(to dog)* ¡quieto!; **d. with taxes!** ¡abajo los impuestos!

down² [daʊn] *n* (**a**) *(on bird)* plumón *m* (**b**) *(on cheek, peach)* pelusa *f*, pelusilla *f*; *(on body)* vello *m*

down-and-out ['daʊnənaʊt] **1** *adj* en las últimas
2 *n* (*pl* **down-and-outs**) vagabundo(a) *m,f*

downbeat ['daʊnbiːt] *adj Fam (gloomy)* triste, deprimido(a)

downcast ['daʊnkɑːst] *adj* abatido(a), desalentado(a); **with d. eyes** con los ojos bajos

downer ['daʊnər] *n Slang (drug)* calmante *m*, sedante *m*; *Fig* **to be on a d.** estar depre

downfall ['daʊnfɔːl] *n (of régime)* caída *f*; *(of person)* perdición *f*, ruina *f*

downgrade ['daʊngreɪd] *vt* degradar

downhearted [daʊn'hɑːtɪd] *adj* desalentado(a), descorazonado(a)

downhill [daʊn'hɪl] **1** *adj (road etc)* en pendiente; *(skiing)* de descenso; *Fam* **after his first exam, the rest were all d.** después del primer examen, los demás le fueron sobre ruedas
2 *adv (slide)* cuesta abajo; **to go d.** *(gen)* ir cuesta abajo; *Fig (person, health)* desmejorar; *Fig (standards)* perderse

Downing Street ['daʊnɪŋstriːt] *n* Downing Street

down-in-the-mouth ['daʊnɪnðə'maʊθ] *adj* **to be d.-in-t.-m.** estar deprimido(a) *or* tristón(ona)

download ['daʊn'ləʊd] *Comptr* **1** *n* descarga *f*
2 *vt* bajar, descargar

downloadable [daʊn'ləʊdəbəl] *adj Comptr* descargable; **d. font** fuente *f* cargable

downloading [daʊn'ləʊdɪŋ] *n Comptr* descarga *f*

down-market [daʊn'mɑːkɪt] *adj Com* barato(a), de baja calidad

downpour ['daʊnpɔːr] *n* chaparrón *m*, aguacero *m*

downright ['daʊnraɪt] *Fam* **1** *adj (blunt)* tajante; *(categorical)* categórico(a); **a d. fool** un tonto de remate; **it's a d. lie** es una mentira y gorda
2 *adv (totally)* completamente

downshift ['daʊnʃɪft] *vi* (**a**) *US (change gear)* reducir (**b**) *(change lifestyle)* relajar el ritmo de vida

downsize ['daʊnsaɪz] *vt Com* hacer reajuste de plantilla en, reducir plantilla en

downsizing ['daʊnsaɪzɪŋ] *n* reajuste *m* de plantillas

Down's Syndrome ['daʊn'sɪndrəʊm] *n* síndrome *m* de Down

downstairs [daʊn'steəz] **1** *adv* abajo; *(to ground floor)* a la planta baja; **to go d.** bajar la escalera
2 *adj (rooms) (on ground floor)* de la planta baja

downstream [daʊn'striːm] *adv* río abajo

downswing ['daʊnswɪŋ] *n Econ* (fase *f* de) contracción *f*, bajón *m*

down-to-earth [daʊntʊ'ɜːθ] *adj* práctico(a), realista

downtown [daʊn'taʊn] *US* **1** *adv* al *or* en el centro (de la ciudad)
2 *adj* céntrico(a); **d. New York** el centro de Nueva York

downtrodden ['daʊntrɒdən] *adj* oprimido(a), pisoteado(a)

downturn ['daʊntɜːn] *n* baja *f*, reducción *f*

downward ['daʊnwəd] *adj (slope)* descendente; *(look)* hacia abajo; *Fin (tendency)* a la baja

downward(s) ['daʊnwəd(z)] *adv (gen)* hacia abajo; **face d.** boca abajo

dowry ['daʊərɪ] *n* dote *f*

dowse [daʊs] *vt see* **douse**

doyl(e)y ['dɔɪlɪ] *n see* **doily**

doz *(abbr* **dozen**) docena *f*, doc.

doze [dəʊz] **1** *vi* dormitar, echar una cabezada
2 *n* cabezada *f*; **to have a d.** echar una cabezada

doze off *vi* quedarse dormido(a), dormirse

dozen ['dʌzən] *n* docena *f*; **half a d./a d. eggs** media docena/una docena de huevos; **twenty pence a d.** veinte peniques la docena; *Fam* **dozens of** *(times)* miles de, cantidad de; *(things, people)* un montón de

dozy ['dəʊzɪ] *adj Fam (sleepy)* amodorrado(a), *(stupid)* bobo(a), idiota

DPhil [diː'fɪl] *n (abbr* **Doctor of Philosophy**) Doctor(a) *m,f* en Filosofía

DPP [diːpiː'piː] *n Br Jur (abbr* **Director of Public Prosecutions**) Director(a) *m,f* del Ministerio Público *or* Fiscal

Dr *Med Univ (abbr* **Doctor**) Doctor(a) *m,f*, Dr., Dra.

drab [dræb] *adj* (**drabber, drabbest**) (**a**) *(ugly)* feo(a); *(dreary)* monótono(a), gris (**b**) *(colour)* pardo(a)

drachma ['drækmə] *n (pl* **drachmas** *or* **drachmae** ['drækmiː]) *(coin)* dracma *f*

Draconian [drə'kəʊnɪən] *adj Pej* draconiano(a)

draft [drɑːft] **1** *n* (**a**) *(of letter, speech)* borrador *m*; *(of plot)* esbozo *m*, bosquejo *m* ▫ *Comptr* **d. quality** calidad *f* borrador (**b**) *(bill of exchange)* letra *f* de cambio, giro *m* (**c**) *US (conscription)* llamada *f* or *Am* llamado *m* a filas, reclutamiento *m* ▫ **d. dodger** prófugo *m* (**d**) *US see* **draught**
2 *vt* (**a**) *(letter)* hacer un borrador de; *(novel)* esbozar, bosquejar (**b**) *US Mil* reclutar

draft-proof ['drɑːftpruːf] *vt & adj US see* **draught-proof**

draft-proofing ['drɑːft'pruːfɪŋ] *n US see* **draught-proofing**

draftsman ['drɑːftsmən] *n (pl* **draftsmen**) *US see* **draughtsman**

draftsmanship ['drɑːftsmənʃɪp] *n US see* **draughtsmanship**

drafty ['drɑːftɪ] *adj (draftier, draftiest) US see* **draughty**

drag [dræg] **1** *vt (pt & pp* **dragged**) (**a**) *(pull)* arrastrar; **to d. sb out of bed** sacar a algn de la cama; *Fig* **to d. one's feet** *or* **heels (over sth)** dar largas (a algo); *Fig* **we couldn't d. ourselves away from the scene** nos fue imposible marcharnos del lugar (**b**) *(trawl)* dragar, rastrear (**c**) *Comptr* arrastrar; **d. and drop** arrastrar y soltar
2 *vi* (**a**) *(trail, be pulled)* arrastrarse (**b**) *(go slowly) (person)* rezagarse, quedarse atrás; *(film, time)* hacerse largo(a)
3 *n* (**a**) *Tech (force)* resistencia *f* (aerodinámica); *Fig (hindrance)* estorbo *m*; **to be a d. on progress** poner trabas al progreso ▫ **d. racing** = carreras de aceleración en coches preparados (**b**) *Fam (nuisance)* lata *f*; **the party was a d.** la fiesta fue un rollo (**c**) *Fam (on cigarette etc)* chupada *f*, *Esp* calada *f*, *Am* pitada *f* (**d**) *Slang* **to be in d.** *(man)* ir vestido de mujer ▫ **d. artist** travestí *mf*, travestí *m,f* (**e**) *US Slang (street)* calle *f*

drag off, drag away *vt* llevar *or* llevarse arrastrando

drag down *vt (depress)* deprimir, hundir

drag in *vt (subject)* arrastrar por los cabellos; **don't d. me into it** a mí no me metas

drag on *vi (war, strike)* prolongarse, hacerse interminable

drag out *vt (speech, meeting)* alargar, prolongar

drag up *vt Fam* (**a**) *(revive)* sacar a relucir (**b**) *Br (child)* criar a la buena de Dios

dragnet ['drægnet] *n (in deep-sea fishing)* red *f* de arrastre *or* barredera; *Fig (to catch criminals)* emboscada *f*

dragon ['drægən] *n Myth* dragón *m*; *Fam Fig (woman)* bruja *f*

dragonfly ['drægənflaɪ] *n* libélula *f*

dragoon [drə'guːn] **1** *n Mil* dragón *m*
2 *vt* **to d. sb into doing sth** obligar a algn a hacer algo

drain [dreɪn] **1** *n* **(a)** *(pipe) (for water)* desague *m*, desaguadero *m*; *(for sewage)* alcantarilla *f*; **the drains** el alcantarillado **(b)** *(grating)* alcantarilla *f*, sumidero *m*; *Fam Fig* **to go down the d.** *(money)* esfumarse; *(work)* echarse a perder; *(business)* fracasar **(c)** *Fig (on energy)* pérdida *f*, disminución *f* **(on** de); **the boys are a d. on her strength** los niños le dejan agotada
2 *vt* **(a)** *(dry out) (marsh etc)* drenar; *(reservoir, region)* desecar, desaguar **(b) to d. (off)** *(glasses etc)* escurrir **(c)** *(empty) (radiator)* vaciar; *(glass)* apurar; *Med (wound)* drenar
3 *vi* **(a)** *(crockery etc)* escurrirse; **the colour drained from her cheeks** quedó pálida **(b) to d. (away)** *(liquid)* irse; *Fig (run out)* agotarse; *Fig (disappear)* desaparecer

drainage ['dreɪnɪdʒ] *n (of marsh etc)* avenamiento *m*; *(of reservoir, region)* desagüe *m*, desecación *f*; *(of town etc)* alcantarillado *m*; *(of building)* desagüe *m*

drainboard ['dreɪnbɔːd] *n US see* **draining board**

drained [dreɪnd] *adj Fig (person)* exhausto(a)

draining board ['dreɪnɪŋbɔːd] *n* escurridero *m*, escurreplatos *m inv*

drainpipe ['dreɪnpaɪp] *n* tubo *m* de desagüe

drake [dreɪk] *n Orn* pato *m* (macho)

dram [dræm] *n Fam* trago *m* (de whisky)

drama ['drɑːmə] *n* **(a)** *(play)* obra *f* de teatro, drama *m*; *Fig* drama, *Fig* **human d.** drama humano **(b)** *Lit (subject)* teatro *m*

dramatic [drə'mætɪk] *adj* **(a)** *(change, reduction)* impresionante, notable; *(moment)* emocionante; *(entrance)* teatral, afectado(a) **(b)** *Theat* dramático(a), teatral

dramatics [drə'mætɪks] *n (acting)* teatro *m*; *esp Pej* afectación *f*

dramatist ['dræm'ətɪst] *n* dramaturgo(a) *m,f*

dramatization [dræmətaɪ'zeɪʃən] *n* adaptación *f* teatral, dramatización *f*

dramatize ['dræmətaɪz] **1** *vt* **(a)** *(adapt)* hacer una adaptación teatral de **(b)** *Pej (exaggerate)* dramatizar
2 *vi Pej* dramatizar, exagerar

drank [dræŋk] *pt see* **drink**

drape [dreɪp] **1** *vt* **(a)** *(cloth)* drapear; **chairs draped with** *or* **in sheets** sillas cubiertas con sábanas **(b)** *(part of body)* dejar colgado(a)
2 *n* **(a)** *(of fabric)* caída *f* **(b)** *US* cortina *f*

draper ['dreɪpər] *n Br* pañero(a) *m,f*; **d.'s (shop)** pañería *f*

drapery ['dreɪpərɪ] *n* **(a)** *(fabric)* tela *f*; *(hanging)* colgadura *f* **(b)** *Br (goods)* pañería *f* **(c)** *esp pl US* cortina *f*

drastic ['dræstɪk] *adj* **(a)** *(severe)* drástico(a), severo(a) **(b)** *(important)* radical, importante

dratted ['drætɪd] *adj Fam* dichoso(a), condenado(a)

draught [drɑːft] **1** *n* **(a)** *(of cold air)* corriente *f* (de aire); **to cause a d.** hacer aire **(b)** *(of liquid)* trago *m* **(c) d. (beer)** cerveza *f* de barril; **on d.** a presión **(d)** *Br (in game)* dama *f*, pieza *f*; **draughts** *(game)* damas *fpl* **(e)** *Naut* calado *m*
2 *adj* **(a)** *(animal)* de tiro **(b)** *(beer)* de barril, a presión

draughtboard ['drɑːftbɔːd] *n Br* tablero *m* de damas, damero *m*

draught-proof ['drɑːftpruːf] **1** *vt* hacer hermético(a)
2 *adj* hermético(a)

draught-proofing ['drɑːft'pruːfɪŋ] *n* aislamiento *m* (contra corrientes)

draughtsman ['drɑːftsmən] *n* *(pl* **draughtsmen**) delineante *mf*

draughtsmanship ['drɑːftsmənʃɪp] *n (drawing)* dibujo *m* lineal; *(skill)* ejecución *f* gráfica

draughty ['drɑːftɪ] *adj* **(draughtier, draughtiest)** lleno(a) de corrientes (de aire)

draw [drɔː] **1** *vt (pt* **drew***; pp* **drawn)** **(a)** *(sketch) (picture)* dibujar; *(line, circle)* trazar; *(map)* hacer **(b)** *(pull) (cart)* tirar de; *(train, carriage)* arrastrar; *(curtains) (open)* descorrer, correr; *(close)* correr, *Esp* echar, *RP* cerrar; *(blinds)* bajar; **he drew his hand over his eyes** se pasó la mano por los ojos; *Fig* **I was drawn into the discussion** me envolvieron en la discusión **(c)** *(take out) (remove, withdraw)* sacar, extraer; *(salary, wage)* cobrar; *Fin (cheque)* librar, extender; **to d. blood** hacer sangrar **(d)** *(attract) (crowd)* atraer; *(response)* provocar; *(attention)* llamar **(e)** *(derive)* atraer; *Fig (strength)* sacar **(f)** *Sport (equalize)* empatar **(g)** *(take in) (breath)* aspirar, respirar; *Fig* **to have no time to d. breath** estar ocupadísimo(a) **(h)** *(choose)* escoger; **to d. lots** echar a suertes; *Fam Fig* **to d. a blank** seguir sin saber algo **(i)** *(formulate) (comparison)* hacer; *(conclusion)* sacar
2 *vi* **(a)** *(sketch)* dibujar **(b)** *(move)* moverse, desplazarse; **the train drew into/out of the station** el tren entró en *or Am* a/salió de la estación; **to d. apart (from)** separarse (de); *Fig* echarse atrás (de); **to d. to an end** acabarse; **to d. towards** *or* **near** acercarse (a) **(c)** *(equalize)* empatar; **they drew two all** empataron a dos **(d)** *(produce draught) (chimney)* tirar
3 *n* **(a)** *(raffle)* sorteo *m*; **the luck of the d.** toca a quien toca **(b)** *(score)* empate *m* **(c)** *Fig (attraction)* atracción *f*

draw in *vi (days)* acortarse, hacerse más corto(a)

draw on *vt* **(a)** *(exploit) (savings)* utilizar, recurrir a; *(experience)* aprovecharse de **(b)** *(suck)* chupar

draw out *vt* **(a)** *(make long)* alargar **(b)** *(encourage to speak)* hacer hablar, desatar la lengua **(c)** *(withdraw)* sacar

draw up *vt* **(a)** *(contract)* preparar, hacer; *(plan)* esbozar **(b)** *(straighten up)* enderezarse

drawback ['drɔːbæk] *n* desventaja *f*, inconveniente *m*

drawbridge ['drɔːbrɪdʒ] *n* puente *m* levadizo

drawer ['drɔːər] *n* cajón *m*; **chest of drawers** cómoda *f*

drawers [drɔːz] *npl Old-fashioned (for men)* calzoncillos *mpl*, *Chile* fundillos *mpl*, *Col* pantaloncillos *mpl*, *Méx* cãizones *mpl*; *(for women) Esp* bragas *fpl*, *Esp* braga *f*, *CAm Carib Méx* blúmer *m*, *CAm* calzón *m*, *Méx* pantaleta *f*, *RP* bombacha *f*

drawing ['drɔːɪŋ] *n (picture, skill)* dibujo *m*; **rough d.** esbozo *m* ❑ **charcoal d.** dibujo *m* al carbón; **d. board** tablero *m* de dibujo; *Fam Fig* **to go back to the d. board** volver a empezar, empezar de nuevo; *Br* **d. pin** chincheta *f*, *Am* chinche *f*; *Fml* **d. room** sala *f* de estar, salón *m*

drawl [drɔːl] **1** *vt & vi* hablar arrastrando las palabras
2 *n* voz *f* cansina; *US* **a Southern d.** un acento sureño

drawn [drɔːn] **1** *pp see* **draw**
2 *adj (tired)* cansado(a), ojeroso(a); *(worried)* preocupado(a)

drawstring ['drɔːstrɪŋ] *n* cordón *m* ❑ **d. waist** cintura *f* (de pantalón etc) que se cierra con cordón

dread [dred] **1** *vt* temer, tener pavor a
2 *n* temor *m*, pavor *m*

dreaded ['dredɪd] *adj* temido(a), temible

dreadful ['dredfʊl] *adj* **(a)** *(shocking)* espantoso(a), terrible, atroz **(b)** *Fam (awful)* fatal, malísimo(a); **how d.!** ¡qué horror!

dreadfully ['dredfʊlɪ] *adv Fam (horribly)* terriblemente; *(very)* muy, sumamente; **it was d. hot** hacía un calor espantoso

dreadlocks ['dredlɒks] *npl* trenzas *fpl* rastafari

dream [driːm] **1** *n* **(a)** *(while asleep)* sueño *m*; *Fig (hope)* sueño *m* (dorado), deseo *m*, ilusión *f*; **bad d.** pesadilla *f*; **to have a d. about sth/sb** soñar con algo/algn; *Fig* **a d. come true** un sueño hecho realidad; *Fig* **she was happy beyond her wildest dreams** era más feliz de lo que jamás había soñado (**b**) *(while awake)* ensueño *m*; **to go round in a d.** tener la cabeza en las nubes ❑ **d. world** mundo *m* de ensueño (**c**) *Fam (marvel)* encanto *m*, maravilla *f*; **things turned out like a d.** todo salió a las mil maravillas

2 *vt (pt & pp* **dreamed** *or* **dreamt)** soñar, imaginar

3 *vi* soñar (**of, about** con); *Fam* **I wouldn't d. of it!** ¡ni pensarlo!

dream up *vt Fam Pej (excuse)* inventarse; *(plan)* idear

dreamboat ['dri:mbəʊt] *n Fam* bombón *m*

dreamer ['dri:mər] *n* soñador(a) *m,f*, visionario(a) *m,f*

dreamlike ['dri:mlaɪk] *adj (state)* de ensueño

dreamt [dremt] *pt & pp see* **dream**

dreamy ['dri:mɪ] *adj* (**dreamier, dreamiest**) (**a**) *(absent-minded)* distraído(a) (**b**) *(dreamlike) (state)* de ensueño; *(vision)* nebuloso(a) (**c**) *Fam (wonderful)* maravilloso(a), encantador(a)

dreary ['drɪərɪ] *adj* (**drearier, dreariest**) (**a**) *(gloomy)* melancólico(a), triste, deprimente (**b**) *Fam (boring)* aburrido(a), pesado(a)

dredge [dredʒ] *vt & vi* dragar, rastrear

dredge up *vt* (**a**) *(body)* sacar del agua (**b**) *Fam Fig* sacar a relucir

dredger ['dredʒər] *n Naut* draga *f*

dregs [dregz] *npl (of tea etc)* heces *fpl*, sedimento *m sing*, poso *m sing*; *Fig* **the d. of society** la hez de la sociedad

drench [drentʃ] *vt (person, clothes)* empapar, mojar; **to be drenched to the skin** estar calado(a) hasta los huesos

Dresden ['drezdən] *n* Dresde

dress [dres] **1** *n* (**a**) *(frock)* vestido *m* ❑ **wedding d.** traje *m* de novia (**b**) *(clothing)* ropa *f*, vestimenta *f* ❑ *Theat* **d. circle** piso *m* principal; *Theat* **d. rehearsal** ensayo *m* general; **d. shirt** camisa *f* de etiqueta; **evening d.** *(for men)* traje *m* de etiqueta; *(for women)* traje *m* de noche; **fancy d.** disfraz *m*

2 *vt* (**a**) *(person)* vestir; **he was dressed in a grey suit** llevaba (puesto) un traje gris; **to be dressed in green/silk** ir (vestido(a)) de verde/seda (**b**) *Culin (salad)* aderezar, *Esp* aliñar; *(poultry, crab)* aderezar (**c**) *Med (wound)* vendar (**d**) *(shop window)* arreglar, decorar

3 *vi* vestirse

dress down 1 *vt (rebuke)* echar una bronca a; *(scold)* regañar

2 *vi Br* vestirse de una manera informal

dress up 1 *vi (child)* disfrazarse (**as** de); *(partygoer)* ponerse *or* ir de tiros largos, ponerse guapo(a); *Fam* **to be dressed up to the nines** ir de punta en blanco

2 *vt Fig (truth)* disfrazar, hacer más aceptable

dresser ['dresər] *n* (**a**) *(in kitchen)* aparador *m* (**b**) *US (in bedroom)* tocador *m* (**c**) *Theat* ayudante *mf* de camerino (**d**) *Fam* **a smart/shabby d.** uno/una que viste bien/mal

dressing ['dresɪŋ] *n* (**a**) *Med (bandage)* vendaje *m* (**b**) *Culin (salad)* aderezo *m*, *Esp* aliño *m* (**c**) **d. gown** *(clothing)* bata *f*; **d. room** *Theat* camarino *m*; *Sport* vestuario *m*; **d. table** tocador *m*

dressing-down [dresɪŋ'daʊn] *n* **to give sb. a d.-d.** echarle una bronca *or Esp* un rapapolvo a algn

dressmaker ['dresmeɪkər] *n* modista *mf*

dressmaking ['dresmeɪkɪŋ] *n* costura *f*

dressy ['dresɪ] *adj* (**dressier, dressiest**) (**a**) *(elegant)* elegante, vistoso(a) (**b**) *Pej (person)* emperifollado(a)

drew [dru:] *pt see* **draw**

dribble ['drɪbəl] **1** *vi* (**a**) *(baby)* babear (**b**) *(liquid)* gotear; *Fig* **the pupils dribbled into class** los alumnos fueron entrando en la clase en pequeños grupos

2 *vt* (**a**) *(saliva etc)* dejar caer; **the baby dribbled milk down its chin** al niño le caía la leche por la barbilla (**b**) *Sport (ball)* driblar

3 *n (saliva)* saliva *f*, baba *f*; *(of water, blood)* gotas *fpl*, hilo *m*

dribs and drabs [drɪbzn'dræbz] *npl Fam* **in d. a. d.** poquito a poco, en pequeñas cantidades

dried [draɪd] *adj (fruit)* seco(a); *(milk)* en polvo

drier ['draɪər] *n see* **dryer**

drift [drɪft] **1** *vi* (**a**) *(boat)* dejarse llevar por la corriente; **the yacht drifted out to sea** el yate iba a la deriva hacia alta mar (**b**) *Fig (government)* ir a la deriva; *(person)* ir *or* vivir sin rumbo, vagar; **the conversation began to d.** la conversación empezó a apartarse del tema; **the pupils drifted away** los alumnos se marcharon poco a poco (**c**) *(snow etc)* amontonarse

2 *vt* amontonar

3 *n* (**a**) *(flow)* flujo *m*, dirección *f*; *Fig (of people)* desplazamiento *m*; *(of events)* tendencia *f*, movimiento *m* (**b**) *(of snow)* ventisquero *m*; *(of sand, cloud)* montón *m* (**c**) *Fig (meaning)* significado *m*, idea *f*

drifter ['drɪftər] *n* (**a**) *Fam Fig* persona *f* sin ocupación fija (**b**) *Naut* trainera *f*

driftwood ['drɪftwʊd] *n* madera *f* flotante

drill[1] [drɪl] **1** *n* (**a**) *(hand tool)* taladro *m*; *Min (machine)* barreno *m*, barrena *f* ❑ **dentist's d.** fresa *f*; **pneumatic d.** taladradora *f* (**b**) *esp Mil* instrucción *f* ❑ **fire d.** procedimiento *m* en caso de incendio; **safety d.** instrucciones *fpl* de seguridad

2 *vt* (**a**) *(wood etc)* taladrar; *(hole)* agujerear (**b**) *(train) (soldier)* instruir; **to d. pupils in pronunciation** hacer ejercicios de pronunciación con los alumnos; *Fig* **to d. sth into sb** hacer que algn entienda algo a fuerza de repetición

3 *vi* (**a**) *(by hand)* taladrar; *(for oil, coal)* perforar, sondar (**b**) *Mil* entrenarse

drill[2] [drɪl] *n Tex* dril *m*

drily ['draɪlɪ] *adv see* **dryly**

drink [drɪŋk] **1** *vt (pt* **drank**; *pp* **drunk**) (**a**) *(gen)* beber, *Am* tomar; *Fig* **he drank himself into a stupor** bebió hasta perder el conocimiento; *Fam* **to d. sb under the table** aguantar más bebiendo *or Am* tomando que otro (**b**) *Fig* **to d. (in)** *(scene)* apreciar; *(success)* saborear

2 *vi* beber, *Am* tomar; **to have something to d.** tomarse algo; **to d. to sth/sb** brindar por algo/algn; *Fam Fig* **to d. like a fish** beber *or Am* tomar como un cosaco

3 *n* (**a**) *(gen)* bebida *f*; *(alcoholic)* copa *f*; **I gave the dog a d.** di de beber al perro; **let's have a d.!** ¡vamos a tomar una copita!; **to take to d.** darse a la bebida ❑ **soft d.** refresco *m* (**b**) *Fam* **the d.** el *or* la mar

drinkable ['drɪŋkəbəl] *adj (water)* potable; *(wine, beer)* agradable al paladar

drink-driving ['drɪŋk'draɪvɪŋ] *n Br* **he was arrested for d.-d.** lo detuvieron por conducir *or Am* manejar en estado de embriaguez

drinker [drɪŋkər] *n* bebedor(a) *m,f*; **hard** *or* **heavy d.** bebedor(a) empedernido(a)

drinking ['drɪŋkɪŋ] *n* (**a**) *(drunkenness)* bebida *f* (**b**) **d. water** agua *f* potable; **d. fountain** fuente *f* de agua potable

drip [drɪp] **1** *n* (**a**) *(gen)* goteo *m* (**b**) *Med* gota a gota *m inv* (**c**) *Fam (person)* necio(a) *m,f*

2 *vi (pt & pp* **dripped)** gotear; **he was dripping with sweat** el sudor le caía a gotas

3 *vt* dejar caer gota a gota

drip-dry ['drɪpdraɪ] *adj* que no necesita planchado

dripping ['drɪpɪŋ] **1** *n Culin* pringue *m or f*, grasa *f* de carne asada

2 *adj* **I'm d.!** ¡estoy calado(a) hasta los huesos!

3 *adv* **d. wet** chorreando(a)

drive [draɪv] **1** vt (pt **drove**; pp **driven**) (**a**) (operate) (vehicle) conducir, Am manejar; (person) llevar or traer (en coche); **I'll d. you home** te llevaré a casa; **to d. a bus** ser conductor de autobús (**b**) (power) hacer funcionar, poner en movimiento; **driven by nuclear power** impulsado(a) por energía nuclear (**c**) (propel) (cattle etc) arrear; (enemy) acosar; (ball) mandar; **inflation drives prices up** la inflación hace subir los precios; **rain drove us back** la lluvia nos hizo volver atrás (**d**) (strike in) (stake) hincar; (rail) clavar; Fig **the accident drove it home to me that** ... el accidente me hizo comprender que ... (**e**) (compel) forzar, obligar; **he drives himself too hard** trabaja demasiado; **to d. sb mad** volver loco(a) a algn; **to d. sb to crime/despair** llevar a algn al crimen/a la desesperación (**f**) **to d. (off)** repeler, rechazar

2 vi Aut conducir, Am manejar; **can you d.?** ¿sabes conducir or Am manejar?; **we drove home** fuimos a casa en coche or Am carro or CSur auto

3 n (a) (trip) viaje m (en coche or Am carro or CSur auto); **to go for a d.** dar una vuelta en Esp coche, dar un paseo en Am carro or CSur auto; **it's an hour's d. (away)** está a una hora en coche or Am carro or CSur auto (**b**) (private road) calle f; (to house) camino m de entrada (**c**) (transmission) transmisión f; Aut tracción f; Aut **left-hand d.** conducción f por la izquierda □ **d. shaft** eje m de transmisión (**d**) Comptr unidad f de disco (**e**) Golf golpe m inicial; Ten golpe m fuerte (**f**) (campaign) campaña f □ Com **sales d.** promoción f (**g**) (need) necesidad f; (energy) energía f, vigor m, fuerza f, dinamismo m □ **sex d.** instinto m sexual

drive at vt Fig insinuar; **what are you driving at?** ¿qué insinúas?, ¿qué quieres decir?

drive-in ['draɪvɪn] n US (a) (cinema) autocine m (b) **d.-in bank** autobanco m

drivel ['drɪvəl] n Fam Esp chorradas fpl, CAm Méx babosadas fpl, Chile leseras fpl, Andes CSur macanas fpl; **to talk d.** decir Esp chorradas fpl or CAm Méx babosadas fpl or Chile leseras fpl or Andes CSur macanas fpl

driven ['drɪvən] pp see **drive**

driver ['draɪvər] n (a) (of car, bus) conductor(a) m,f; (of taxi) taxista mf; (of train) maquinista mf; (of lorry) camionero(a) m,f; (of racing car) piloto mf, corredor(a) m,f; US **d.'s license** Esp carné m or carnet m or permiso m de conducir, Bol Ecuad Perú brevet m, Carib licencia f de conducir, RP permiso m de conductor, Urug libreta f de manejar, Méx licencia f de manejar or para conducir (**b**) (golf club) driver m (**c**) Comptr controlador m

drive-through ['draɪvθru:] n = establecimiento que atiende a sus clientes a través de una ventana sin que tengan que salir del automóvil

driveway ['draɪvweɪ] n (to house) camino m de entrada

driving ['draɪvɪŋ] adj (a) Aut **d. school** autoescuela f; **d. test** examen m de Esp conducir or Am manejar; Br **d. licence** Esp carné m or carnet m or permiso m de conducir, Bol Ecuad Perú brevet m, Carib licencia f de conducir, RP permiso m de conductor, Urug libreta f de manejar, Méx licencia f de manejar or para conducir (**b**) (rain, wind) que azota (**c**) Fig (force) motriz; (personality) dinámico(a)

drizzle ['drɪzəl] **1** n llovizna f, Andes RP garúa f

2 vi lloviznar, chispear, Andes RP garuar

droll [drəʊl] adj (a) (amusing) gracioso(a), cómico(a) (**b**) (odd) curioso(a), extraño(a)

dromedary ['drɒmədərɪ] n Zool dromedario m

drone¹ [drəʊn] n Ent zángano m

drone² [drəʊn] **1** vi (plane, bee) zumbar; Fig **to d. on** hablar monótonamente

2 n (noise) (of bee, engine) zumbido m; (of traffic) ruido m sordo, runruneo m

drool [dru:l] vi (dribble) babear; Fig **she was drooling at the idea** se le caía la baba con sólo pensarlo

droop [dru:p] vi (flower) marchitarse; (shoulders) encorvarse; (eyelids) caerse; (head) inclinarse; Fig **her spirits drooped** se desanimó

droopy ['dru:pɪ] adj (**droopier, droopiest**) caído(a)

drop [drɒp] **1** n (**a**) (liquid) gota f; Fig **a d. in the ocean** una gota de agua en el mar; Fam Fig **to have had a d. too much** haber bebido or Am tomado más de la cuenta □ **eye drops** colirio m sing (**b**) (sweet) pastilla f (**c**) (descent) desnivel m (**d**) (fall) caída f; (in price) bajada f; (in sales) disminución f; (in temperature) descenso m; Fig **at the d. of a hat** sin más ni más (**e**) US Fam lugar m de reparto or de recogida (**f**) (airdrop) lanzamiento m

2 vt (pt & pp **dropped**) (a) (let fall) dejar caer; (let go of) soltar; (lower) bajar; (launch) lanzar; (reduce) disminuir; **don't d. it!** ¡que no se te caiga!; **to d. a hint** soltar una indirecta; Br Fam Fig **to d. a brick** or **a clanger** hacer una plancha, meter la pata (**b**) Fam (leave) dejar; **I'll d. you (off) here** te dejo aquí (**c**) (abandon) (subject, charge) dejar, abandonar; (idea, plan) abandonar, renunciar a; Fam (boyfriend etc) plantar, dejar plantado(a); Fam (friend) dejar de ver; **let's d. the subject** cambiemos de tema; **the matter was dropped** ahí quedó el asunto; Fam **d. it!** ¡basta ya!, ¡ya está bien! (**d**) (omit) (spoken syllable, word) no pronunciar, comerse; (written syllable, word) omitir; Sport **he was dropped from the team** le echaron del equipo; Ling **the article is dropped** no se usa el artículo (**e**) Sport perder (**f**) Knit soltar

3 vi (**a**) (fall) (object) caerse; (person) dejarse caer; (voice, price, temperature) bajar; (wind) amainar; (speed) disminuir; **to d. dead** caerse muerto(a); **to d. to one's knees** arrodillarse; Fam **d. dead!** ¡muérete!, RP ¡morite!; Fam **I'm fit to d.!** ¡estoy hecho(a) polvo! (**b**) (descend) bajar, descender

drop away vi (interest) disminuir

drop by vi Fam see **drop in 1**

drop in Fam **1** vi (visit) dejarse caer, pasar (**at** por)

2 vt (deliver) dejar (en casa de algn)

drop off vi (**a**) Fam (fall asleep) quedarse dormido(a), echar una cabezada (**b**) see **drop away**

drop out vi (leave) (school, college) dejar los estudios; (society) marginarse; (match, competition) retirarse; **he dropped out of the class** dejó el curso sin acabar

drop round vi & vt Fam see **drop in**

drop-down menu ['drɒpdaʊn'menju:] n Comptr menú m desplegable

droplet ['drɒplɪt] n gotita f

drop-off ['drɒpɒf] n (**a**) (decrease) descenso m (**b**) US (descent) descenso m

dropout ['drɒpaʊt] n Fam Pej (from school) estudiante mf que no termina el curso; (from society) marginado(a) m,f; **d. rate** (from university) índice m de abandono de los estudios

dropper ['drɒpər] n Med cuentagotas m inv

droppings ['drɒpɪŋz] npl excrementos mpl, cagadas fpl

dropsy ['drɒpsɪ] n Med hidropesía f

dross [drɒs] n Fam (rubbish) porquería f, basura f

drought [draʊt] n sequía f

drove [drəʊv] **1** pt see **drive**

2 (of cattle) manada f; Fig (of people) multitud f; Fig **in droves** en manada

drown [draʊn] **1** vt (a) (gen) ahogar; **he was drowned** murió ahogado; Fig **to d. one's sorrows** ahogar las penas (**b**) (place) inundar, anegar (**c**) Pej (food) ahogar; **a salad drowned in or with oil** una ensalada que nadaba en aceite (**d**) (sound) ahogar; **we were drowned out by the music** no nos podíamos oír por culpa de la música

2 *vi (person, animal)* ahogarse; **he drowned** murió ahogado

drowse [drauz] *vi* **to d. off** adormitarse

drowsiness ['drauzınıs] *n* somnolencia *f*

drowsy ['drauzı] *adj* (**drowsier; drowsiest**) (**a**) *(person, yawn)* soñoliento(a); **to feel d.** tener ganas de dormir (**b**) *(murmur, scene)* soporífero(a)

drudge [drʌdʒ] *n Pej (housewife)* esclava *f* de la casa; *(employee)* esclavo(a) *m,f* del trabajo

drudgery ['drʌdʒərı] *n* trabajo *m* duro y pesado

drug [drʌg] **1** *n* (**a**) *(medicine)* medicamento *m*, medicina *f* (**b**) *(narcotic)* droga *f*, estupefaciente *m*, narcótico *m*; **to be on** *or* **take drugs** drogarse ❑ **d. addict** drogadicto(a) *m,f*; **d. addiction** drogadicción *f*; **d. dealer** *(large-scale)* narcotraficante *m,f*, traficante *mf* de drogas; *(small-scale)* camello *mf*; **d. squad** brigada *f* de estupefacientes
2 *vt (pt & pp drugged) (person, animal)* drogar; *(food, drink)* echar una droga en, adulterar con drogas

druggist ['drʌgıst] *n US* farmacéutico(a) *m,f*

drugstore ['drʌgstɔːr] *n US* establecimiento *m*, donde se compran medicamentos, periódicos, etc

druid ['druːɪd] *n* druida *m*

drum [drʌm] **1** *n* (**a**) *(instrument)* tambor *m*; **to play the drums** tocar la batería ❑ *Mil* **d. major** tambor *m* mayor; *US* **d. majorette** majorette *f* (**b**) *(container)* bidón *m* (**c**) *Tech* tambor *m*
2 *vi (pt & pp drummed) Fig (rain, fingers, hooves)* tabalear
3 *vt Fig* (**a**) *(tap)* tamborilear, tabalear (**b**) *Fig* **to d. sth into sb** meterle algo en la cabeza de algn a fuerza de repetirlo

drum up *vt Fam (votes)* solicitar; *(business)* fomentar, atraer; *(support)* buscar

drumbeat ['drʌmbiːt] *n Mus* toque *m* del tambor

drummer ['drʌmər] *n Mus (in band)* tambor *mf*; *(in pop group)* batería *mf*, *Am* baterista *mf*

drumstick ['drʌmstık] *n* (**a**) *Mus* baqueta *f*, palillo *m* (de tambor) (**b**) *Culin* muslo *m* (de ave)

drunk [drʌŋk] **1** *pp see* **drink**
2 *adj* borracho(a); *Fig* borracho(a), ebrio(a); *Jur* **to be d. and disorderly** comportarse escandalosamente estando borracho(a); **to get d.** emborracharse; *Fam* **to be dead** *or* **blind d.** estar como una cuba, estar trompa; *Fig* **d. with happiness** embriagado(a) de alegría
3 *n* borracho(a) *m,f*

drunkard ['drʌŋkəd] *n* borracho(a) *m,f*

drunk-driving ['drʌŋk'draıvıŋ] *n US* **he was arrested for d.-d.** lo detuvieron por conducir *or Am* manejar en estado de embriaguez

drunken ['drʌŋkən] *adj (person)* borracho(a); *(party, argument)* acalorado(a) por el alcohol; **d. stupor** aturdimiento *f* de borrachos; **in a d. stupor** aturdido(a) por el alcohol

drunkometer [drʌŋ'kɒmıtər] *n US Fam* alcoholímetro *m*

dry [draı] **1** *adj* (**drier, driest** *or* **dryer, dryest**) (**a**) *(gen)* seco(a); **it was a d. day** hacía un tiempo seco ❑ **d. ice** nieve *f* carbónica, hielo *m* seco; **d. land** tierra *f* firme; **d. rot** putrefacción *f* de la madera; **d. run** ensayo *m* (**b**) *(wine etc)* seco(a) (**c**) *(wry)* agudo(a) (**d**) *Fam (thirsty)* sediento(a)
2 *vt (pt & pp dried)* secar
3 *vi* **to d. (off)** secar, secarse

dry-clean [draı'kliːn] *vt* limpiar *or* lavar en seco

dry-cleaner's [draı'kliːnəz] *n* tintorería *f*

dry-cleaning [draı'kliːnıŋ] *n (process)* limpieza *f* en seco; *(clothes)* **to collect the d.** recoger la ropa de la tintorería

dryer ['draıər] *n* secadora *f*

dryly ['draılı] *adv (coldly)* secamente, *(humorously)* con humor, con guasa

DSc [diːes'siː] *n (abbr* **Doctor of Science***)* Doctor(a) *m,f* en Ciencias, Dr. en Cien.

DTs [diː'tiːz] *npl (abbr* **delirium tremens***)* delírium tremens *m inv*

DTI [diːtiː'aı] *n Br (abbr* **Department of Trade and Industry***)* = Ministerio de Industria

DTP [diːtiː'piː] *n Comptr (abbr* **desktop publishing***)* autoedición *f*

dual ['djuəl] *adj* doble; *Br* **d. carriageway** *(road)* (tramo *m* de) autovía *f*; **to have d. nationality** tener doble nacionalidad; **d. ownership** copropiedad *f*

dual-purpose ['djuəl'pɜːpəs] *adj* de doble uso

dub¹ [dʌb] *vt (pt & pp dubbed) (subtitle)* doblar (**into** a)

dub² [dʌb] *vt (pt & pp dubbed)* (**a**) *(give nickname)* apodar (**b**) *(knight)* armar

dubbing ['dʌbıŋ] *n Cin* doblaje *m*

dubious ['djuːbıəs] *adj* (**a**) *(doubtful) (morals, activities)* dudoso(a), sospechoso(a); *(compliment)* ambiguo(a), equívoco(a) (**b**) *(doubting)* dudoso(a), indeciso(a); **to be d. about sth** tener dudas sobre algo

Dublin ['dʌblın] *n* Dublín

Dubliner ['dʌblınər] *adj & n* dublinés(esa) *(m,f)*

ducal ['djuːkəl] *adj* ducal

duchess ['dʌtʃıs] *n* duquesa *f*

duchy ['dʌtʃı] *n* ducado *m*

duck¹ [dʌk] *n Orn* pato(a) *m,f*; *Culin* pato *m*; *Fig* **to play ducks and drakes** hacer saltar piedras planas sobre el agua; *Fam Fig* **criticism was like water off a d.'s back to him** las críticas le eran indiferentes; *Fam Fig* **like a d. to water** como el pez en el agua ❑ *Orn* **mandarin d.** pato *m* mandarín; *Fig* **sitting d.** víctima *f* propiciatoria

duck² [dʌk] **1** *vt* (**a**) *(bow down) (head)* agachar (**b**) *(submerge)* zambullir (**c**) *(evade)* esquivar; *Fig* eludir
2 *vi* (**a**) *(bow down)* agacharse; **he ducked behind the door** se escondió detrás de la puerta (**b**) *(go under water)* zambullirse (**c**) *(evade blow)* esquivar (**d**) *Fam* **to d. (out)** rajarse

duckling ['dʌklıŋ] *n Orn Culin* patito *m*

duct [dʌkt] *n (for fuel etc)* conducto *m*; *Anat* canal *m*, conducto *m*

dud [dʌd] *Fam* **1** *adj* (**a**) *(tool, machine) (useless)* inútil, que no sirve; *(defective)* defectuoso(a), estropeado(a) (**b**) *(banknote)* falso(a); *(cheque)* sin fondos
2 *n (useless thing)* trasto *m* inútil, engañifa *f*; *(person)* desastre *m*; **this tape's a d.** esta cinta no sirve

dude [djuːd] *n US Fam* (**a**) *(city-dweller)* ciudadano *m* ❑ **d. ranch** rancho *m or* hacienda *f* para turistas (**b**) *(type) Esp* colega *m*, *Esp* tío *m*, *Am* salvo *RP* mano *m*, *RP* flaco *m*

dudgeon ['dʌdʒən] *n Fml* **in high d.** muy enojado(a)

due [djuː] **1** *adj* (**a**) *(expected)* esperado(a); **I'm due for a rise** me toca una subida de sueldo; **the train is d. (to arrive) at ten** el tren debe llegar a las diez; **when's the baby d.?** ¿para cuándo esperas tener el niño? (**b**) *Fml (proper)* debido(a); **after d. consideration** con las debidas consideraciones; **in d. course** a su debido tiempo (**c**) *(owing)* pagadero(a); **how much are you d.** *or* **is d. to you?** ¿cuánto te deben?; **to become d.** *(payment)* vencer ❑ **d. date** vencimiento *m*, plazo *m* (**d**) **to be d. to** deberse a, ser causado(a) por
2 *adv (north etc)* derecho hacia .
3 *n* (**a**) **to give sb his/her d.** dar a algn su merecido, ser justo(a) con algn (**b**) **dues** *(fee)* cuota *f sing*

duel ['djuːəl] **1** *n* duelo *m*
2 *vi (pt & pp duelled, US dueled)* batirse en duelo (**with** con)

duet [djuː'et] *n Mus* dúo *m*, duelo *m*; **to play/sing a d.** tocar/cantar a dúo

duff [dʌf] *adj Br Slang (defective)* defectuoso(a), estropeado(a); *(useless)* inútil, que no sirve

duff up *vt Br Slang (beat up)* dar una paliza a

duffel ['dʌfəl] *n see* **duffle**

duffer ['dʌfər] *n Fam (hopeless person)* zoquete *m*; **he's a d. at Latin** es un desastre para el latín

duffle ['dʌfəl] *n* **d. bag** petate *m*; **d. coat** trenca *f*

dug [dʌg] *pt & pp see* **dig**

dugout ['dʌgaʊt] *n* **(a)** *(canoe)* piragua *f* **(b)** *Mil (shelter)* refugio *m* subterráneo

duke [djuːk] *n* duque *m*

dukedom ['djuːkdəm] *n* ducado *m*

dull [dʌl] **1** *adj* **(a)** *(uninteresting) (job)* monótono(a), pesado(a); *(person, life, film)* pesado(a), aburrido(a), soso(a); *(place)* aburrido(a), sin interés **(b)** *(not bright) (light, colour)* apagado(a); *(weather, day)* gris, triste; *(sky)* cubierto(a) **(c)** *(muffled)* sordo(a), amortiguado(a), *Fig (ache, pain)* sordo(a) **(d)** *Fig (slow-witted)* tonto(a), torpe, *Am* sonso(a), *Am* zonzo(a)
2 *vt* **(a)** *(deaden) (pain)* aliviar; *(sound)* amortiguar **(b)** *Fig (faculty)* embotar

dullness ['dʌlnɪs] *n* **(a)** *(tedium)* **the d. of the book/ speech** lo aburrido que era el libro/discurso **(b)** *(lack of intelligence)* necedad *f*, torpeza *f* **(c)** *(listlessness)* apatía *f* **(d)** *(of tool, blade)* embotamiento *m*; *(of sound, pain)* lo amortiguado **(e)** *(of colour, surface, eyes)* falta *f* de brillo

dully ['dʌlɪ] *adv* **(a)** *(boringly)* pesadamente **(b)** *(not brightly)* pálidamente, sin brillo

duly ['djuːlɪ] *adv Fml* **(a)** *(properly)* debidamente; **I d. paid my share** pagué mi parte como era debido **(b)** *(as expected)* como era de esperar; *(in due course)* a su debido tiempo

dumb [dʌm] **1** *adj* **(a)** *Med (unspeaking)* mudo(a); **deaf and d.** sordomudo(a); *Fig* **to be struck d. (with surprise)** quedarse de una pieza □ **d. waiter** *(lift)* montaplatos *m inv* **(b)** *Fam (stupid)* tonto(a), estúpido(a); **to act d.** hacerse el tonto □ *Pej* **d. blonde** rubia *f* or *Méx* güera *f* sin cerebro
2 the d. *npl* los mudos

dumbbell ['dʌmbel] *n* **(a)** *Sport* pesa *f* **(b)** *US Fam* tonto(a) *m,f*, imbécil *mf*

dumbfounded [dʌm'faʊndɪd] *adj* pasmado(a)

dumbing (down) ['dʌmɪŋ(daʊn)] *(of population, youth, electorate)* reducción *f* del nivel cultural; *(of newspaper, programme)* empobrecimiento *m* de contenidos

dumbly ['dʌmlɪ] *adv* sin decir nada

dummy ['dʌmɪ] *n* **(a)** *(sham)* substituto *m*, imitación *f* □ **d. run** ensayo *m*, prueba *f* **(b)** *(model) (in shop window)* maniquí *m*; *(of ventriloquist)* muñeco *m* **(c)** *Br (for baby)* chupete *m* **(d)** *Cards* **d. (hand)** mano *f* muerta **(e)** *Fam (fool)* tonto(a) *m,f*

dumbstruck ['dʌmstrʌk] *adj see* **dumbfounded**

dump [dʌmp] **1** *n* **(a)** *(tip) (for refuse)* vertedero *m*, basurero *m*; *(for old cars)* cementerio *m* (de coches) **(b)** *Fam Pej (place)* lugar *m* de mala muerte; *(town)* poblacho *m*; *(dwelling)* tugurio *m* **(c)** *Mil (store)* depósito *m*
2 *vt* **(a)** *(unload) (rubbish)* tirar, *Am* botar; *(truck contents)* descargar □ **d. truck** volquete *m* **(b)** *(leave)* dejar, abandonar, tirar; *Fam (boyfriend etc)* plantar; *Fam (passenger)* dejar; *Com (goods)* inundar el mercado con **(c)** *Comptr (transfer)* copiar de memoria interna, vaciar de memoria

dumper-truck ['dʌmpətrʌk] *n* volquete *m*

dumping ['dʌmpɪŋ] *n* vertido *m* □ *(tip)* **d. ground** vertedero *m*, basurero *m*

dumpling ['dʌmplɪŋ] *n Culin (in stew)* = bola de masa hervida; *(as dessert)* = tipo de budín relleno

dumps [dʌmps] *npl Fam* **to be (down) in the d.** estar con la moral por los suelos, *Am* estar con el ánimo por el piso

dumpy ['dʌmpɪ] *adj* **(dumpier, dumpiest)** *Fam* rechoncho(a), regordete

dunce [dʌns] *n Fam* tonto(a) *m,f*

dune [djuːn] *n* **(sand) d.** duna *f*

dung [dʌŋ] *n (of horse, cow)* excrementos *mpl*; *(as manure)* estiércol *m*

dungarees [dʌŋgə'riːz] *npl (overalls)* mono *m sing*; *(fashion garment, playsuit)* peto *m sing*

dungeon ['dʌndʒən] *n* calabozo *m*, mazmorra *f*

dunghill ['dʌŋhɪl] *n* estercolero *m*

dunk [dʌŋk] *vt Fam (bread, biscuit)* mojar

dunno [də'nəʊ] *Fam* = **don't know**

duo ['djuːəʊ] *n (pl* **duos)** *Mus* dúo *m*, duet *m*; *Fam* pareja *f*

duodenal [djuːə'diːnəl] *adj Anat* duodenal

duodenum [djuːə'diːnəm] *n* duodeno *m*

dupe [djuːp] **1** *vt* engañar, timar; **to d. sb into doing sth** embaucar a algn para que haga algo
2 *n* ingenuo(a) *m,f*, simple *mf*

duplex ['djuːpleks] *n US (house)* casa *f* adosada □ *US* **d. apartment** dúplex *m inv*

duplicate 1 ['djuːplɪkeɪt] *vt* **(a)** *(copy) (document, key)* sacar copia/s de, duplicar; *(film, tape)* reproducir **(b)** *(repeat) (work)* repetir; *(reproduce)* reproducir
2 ['djuːplɪkɪt] *n (copy)* copia *f*, duplicado *m*; **in d.** por duplicado

duplication [djuːplɪ'keɪʃən] *n* repetición *f*

duplicator ['djuːplɪkeɪtər] *n* multicopista *m*

duplicity [djuː'plɪsɪtɪ] *n Fml* doblez *f*, falsedad *f*, duplicidad *f*

durability [djʊərə'bɪlɪtɪ] *n* durabilidad *f*

durable ['djʊərəbəl] *adj* duradero(a)

duration [djʊ'reɪʃən] *n Fml* duración *f*

duress [djʊ'res] *n Fml* coacción *f*

during ['djʊərɪŋ] *prep* durante; **I work d. the day** trabajo de día

dusk [dʌsk] *n Fml* crepúsculo *m*; **at d.** al anochecer

dust [dʌst] **1** *n (gen)* polvo *m*; *Fig* **to allow the d. to settle** esperar que se calme la borrasca; *Fam* **to bite the d.** *(person)* morder el polvo; *(plan)* irse a pique □ **coal d.** polvo *m* de carbón; *Geog* **d. bowl** región *f* de sequía, zona *f* semi-árida; **d. cloud** polvareda *f*; *(of book)* **d. cover, d. jacket** sobrecubierta *f*
2 *vt* **(a)** *(room, furniture)* quitar el polvo a; **to d. oneself off** or **down** sacudirse el polvo **(b)** *(cake, plant)* espolvorear

dustbin ['dʌstbɪn] *n Br* cubo *m* or *Am* bote *m* de la basura

dustcart ['dʌstkɑːt] *n Br* camión *m* de la basura

duster ['dʌstər] *n Br (for housework)* trapo *m* or paño *m* (para quitar el polvo); *(for blackboard)* borrador *m* □ **feather d.** plumero *m*

dusting ['dʌstɪŋ] *n* **(a)** *(of room, furniture)* **to do the d.** limpiar or quitar el polvo **(b)** *(with sugar)* **give the cake a d. of cocoa** espolvorear el pastel con cacao

dustman ['dʌstmən] *n (pl* **dustmen)** *Br* basurero *m*

dustpan ['dʌstpæn] *n* recogedor *m*

dustsheet ['dʌstʃiːt] *n* guardapolvo *m (funda)*

dust-up ['dʌstʌp] *n Br Fam (fight)* pelea *f*, riña *f*; *(argument)* discusión *f*, altercado *m*

dusty ['dʌstɪ] *adj* **(dustier, dustiest)** **(a)** *(track)* polvoriento(a); *(room)* lleno(a) de polvo; *(clothes etc)* cubierto(a) de polvo; *Fig* **d. answer** evasiva *f* **(b)** *(colour)* ceniciento(a)

Dutch [dʌtʃ] **1** *adj* holandés(esa) □ *Fig* **D. cap** diafragma *m*; *Culin* **D. cheese** queso *m* de bola; *Fam* **D. courage** valor *m* que da la bebida
2 *n* **(a)** *pl* **the D.** los holandeses **(b)** *(language)* holandés *m*

3 *adv Fig* **to go D. (with sb)** pagar cada uno lo suyo, *Esp* pagar a escote

Dutchman ['dʌtʃmən] *n* (*pl* **Dutchmen**) holandés *m*; *Fam* **if that car starts, I'm a D.** que me maten si ese coche arranca

Dutchwoman ['dʌtʃwʊmən] *n* (*pl* **Dutchwomen**) holandesa *f*

dutiable ['djuːtɪəbəl] *adj (goods)* sujeto(a) a derechos de aduanas

dutiful ['djuːtɪfʊl] *adj (son, daughter)* obediente, bien mandado(a)

dutifully ['djuːtɪfʊlɪ] *adv* obedientemente, sin rechistar

duty ['djuːtɪ] *n* (**a**) *(obligation)* deber *m*, obligación *f*; **he went out of a sense of d.** asistió para cumplir *or* por cumplido; **to do one's d.** cumplir con su deber (**b**) *(task)* función *f*, cometido *m*; **to make it one's d. to ...** encargarse de ...; **to take up one's duties** entrar en funciones (**c**) *(availability)* **to be on d.** *(gen)* estar de servicio; *Med Mil* estar de guardia; **to do night d.** tener el turno de noche (**d**) *(tax)* impuesto *m* □ **customs d.** derechos *mpl* de aduana, aranceles *mpl*; **stamp d.** póliza *f*

duty-bound ['djuːtɪbaʊnd] *adj* moralmente obligado(a)

duty-free ['djuːtɪfriː] **1** *adj (shop, goods)* libre de impuestos
2 *adv* sin pagar impuestos
3 *n* duty-free *m*

duvet ['duːveɪ] *n Br* edredón *m* □ **d. cover** funda *f* (de edredón)

DVD [diːviːˈdiː] *n Comptr* (*abbr* **Digital Versatile Disk**, **Digital Video Disk**) DVD *m*; **D. player** reproductor *m* de DVD

DVT [diːviːˈtiː] *n* (*abbr* **deep-vein thrombosis**) TVP *f*

dwarf [dwɔːf] **1** *n* (*pl* **dwarfs** *or* **dwarves** [dwɔːvz]) (**a**) *(person)* enano(a) *m*,*f* (**b**) *Bot* **d. geranium** geranio *m* enano
2 *vt* achicar, hacer parecer pequeño(a)

dweeb [dwiːb] *n US Fam* petardo(a) *m*,*f*

dwell [dwel] *vi* (*pt & pp* **dwelled** *or* **dwelt**) *Fml* morar, vivir

dwell on, dwell upon *vt* hablar extensamente de; **let's not d. on it** olvidémoslo, cambiemos de tema

dweller ['dwelər] *n* habitante *mf* □ **cave d.** cavernícola *mf*

dwelling ['dwelɪŋ] *n Fml & Hum* morada *f*, vivienda *f*

dwelt [dwelt] *pt & pp see* **dwell**

dwindle ['dwɪndəl] *vi* menguar, disminuir; **to d. away to nothing** quedar reducido(a) a nada

dwindling ['dwɪndlɪŋ] *adj (interest, number)* cada vez más reducido(a); *(capital)* en disminución

DWP [diːdʌbəljuːˈpiː] *n* (*abbr* **Department for Work and Pensions**) = ministerio británico de seguridad social y empleo

dye [daɪ] **1** *n (substance)* tinte *m*, colorante *m*
2 *vt* (*pres p* **dyeing**; *pt & pp* **dyed**) *(gen)* teñir; **to d. one's hair black** teñirse el pelo de negro

dyed-in-the-wool [daɪdɪnðəˈwʊl] *adj Pej* acérrimo(a), inflexible, intransigente

dying ['daɪɪŋ] **1** *adj (person)* moribundo(a) *m*,*f*, agonizante *mf*; *Fig (custom)* en vías de desaparición; **to my d. day** hasta que me muera
2 the d. *npl* los moribundos, los agonizantes

dyke [daɪk] *n* (**a**) *(bank)* dique *m*, barrera *m*; *(causeway)* terraplén *m* (**b**) *Slang Offens (lesbian)* tortillera *f*

dynamic [daɪˈnæmɪk] **1** *adj Phys & Fig* dinámico(a); *(person)* dinámico(a), emprendedor(a)
2 *n Tech* dinámica *f*

dynamics [daɪˈnæmɪks] *n Phys* dinámica *f*

dynamism ['daɪnəmɪzəm] *n Fig* dinamismo *m*, energía *f*

dynamite ['daɪnəmaɪt] **1** *n* dinamita *f*; *Fam Fig (star, news)* sensación *f*; **his ideas are political d.** sus ideas son políticamente explosivas
2 *vt (building)* dinamitar, volar con dinamita

dynamo ['daɪnəməʊ] *n* (*pl* **dynamos**) *Elec & Fig* dínamo *m*, dinamo *m*

dynastic [dɪˈnæstɪk] *adj* dinástico(a)

dynasty ['dɪnəstɪ] *n* dinastía *f*

dysentery ['dɪsəntrɪ] *n Med* disentería *f*

dysfunctional [dɪsˈfʌŋkʃənəl] *adj (family, relationship)* disfuncional

dyslexia [dɪsˈleksɪə] *n Med* dislexia *f*

dyslexic [dɪsˈleksɪk] *adj* disléxico(a)

E (*abbr* East) Este, E

E, e [iː] *n* (**a**) *(the letter)* E, e *f* (**b**) *Mus* mi *m* ❑ **E flat** mi *m* bemol

each [iːtʃ] **1** *adj* cada; **e. and every one (of us)** todos y cada uno de nosotros; **e. day/month** todos los días/meses; **e. person** cada cual; **e. time I see him** cada vez que lo veo

 2 *pron* (**a**) *(both, all)* cada uno(a); **e. to his own** cada uno a lo suyo; **two dollars e.** dos dólares cada uno; **we bought one e.** nos compramos uno cada uno (**b**) *(reciprocal)* **e. other** a cada uno, el uno al otro; **they hate e. other** se odian; **we write to e. other** nos escribimos

eager [ˈiːgər] *adj* (**a**) *(anxious)* impaciente, ansioso(a); **e. to begin** impaciente por empezar (**b**) *(desirous)* deseoso(a); **e. to please** deseoso(a) de quedar bien; **to be e. for success** codiciar el éxito (**c**) *(keen)* apremiante; **he gave me an e. look** me dirigió una mirada apremiante ❑ *Fam* **e. beaver** trabajador(a) *m,f* incansable

eagerly [ˈiːgəlɪ] *adv* (**a**) *(anxiously)* con impaciencia (**b**) *(keenly)* con afán *or* ilusión

eagerness [ˈiːgənɪs] *n* (**a**) *(anxiety)* impaciencia *f* (**b**) *(enthusiasm)* afán *m*, ilusión *f*

eagle [ˈiːgəl] *n Zool* águila *f*

eagle-eyed [iːgəlˈaɪd] *adj* que tiene vista de lince

eaglet [ˈiːglɪt] *n Zool* aguilucho *m*

ear [ɪər] *n* (**a**) *Anat* oreja *f*; *(sense of hearing)* oído *m*; *Mus* **to have a good e.** tener buen oído; **to play sth by e.** tocar algo de oído; *Fig* **it goes in one e. and out the other** por un oído entra y por otro sale; *Fig* **to be all ears** ser todo oídos; *Fig* **to keep one's e. to the ground** estar al corriente; *Fam* **up to one's ears** hasta aquí; *Fam* **I'm up to my ears in work** estoy agobiado de trabajo ❑ *Med* **e., nose, and throat specialist** otorrinolaringólogo(a) *m,f* (**b**) *Bot (of corn)* espiga *f*; **e. of wheat/barley** espiga de trigo/cebada

earache [ˈɪəreɪk] *n* dolor *m* de oídos; *Fam* **to give sb a e.** dar dolor de cabeza a algn

eardrum [ˈɪədrʌm] *n Anat* tímpano *m*

earful [ˈɪəfʊl] *n Fam* **to give sb an e.** decirle a algn cuatro verdades

earl [ɜːl] *n* conde *m*

earldom [ˈɜːldəm] *n* condado *m*

earlobe [ˈɪələʊb] *n Anat* lóbulo *m*

early [ˈɜːlɪ] (**earlier, earliest**) **1** *adj* (**a**) *(before the usual time)* temprano(a), prematuro(a); **due to his e. arrival** debido a que llegó antes de lo previsto; **e. death** muerte prematura; **to book e.** reservar con tiempo; **to have an e. night** acostarse pronto; **you're e.!** ¡qué temprano has venido! ❑ **e. bird** madrugador(a) *m,f*; **e. retirement** jubilación *f* anticipada (**b**) *(at first stage, period)* **at an e. age** siendo joven; **e. Gothic** Gótico primitivo; **e. on** al principio; **e. strawberries** fresas tempranas; **e. train** tren que sale temprano; **e. work** obra de juventud; **in her e. forties** a los cuarenta y pocos; **it's still e. days** aún es pronto; *Prov* **the e. bird catches the worm** a quien madruga Dios le ayuda ❑ **e. man** el hombre primitivo; **e. warning system** sistema *m* de alerta roja (**c**) *(in the near future)* **an e. reply** una respuesta pronta; **at the earliest** cuanto antes; **at the earliest opportunity** lo antes posible; **could I have an earlier date?** ¿no podría ser antes?

 2 *adv* (**a**) *(before the expected time)* temprano, *Esp* pronto; **earlier on** antes; **five minutes e.** con cinco minutos de adelanto; **to leave e.** irse temprano *or Esp* pronto (**b**) *(near the beginning)* **as e. as 1914** ya en 1914; **as e. as possible** tan pronto como sea posible; **e. on in the book** al comienzo del libro; **in e. July** a principios de julio

earmark [ˈɪəmɑːk] *vt* destinar, reservar (**for** para, a)

earn [ɜːn] *vt* (**a**) *(money)* ganar; **money well earned** dinero bien merecido; **to e. one's living** ganarse la vida (**b**) *(obtain, get as deserved)* ganarse; **it earned him the respect of ...**, le valió el respeto de ...; **to e. a place at university** conseguir una plaza en la universidad (**c**) *Fin* **to e. interest** cobrar interés *or* intereses

earnest [ˈɜːnɪst] **1** *adj* serio(a), formal

 2 *n* **in e.** de veras, en serio; **he said it in e.** lo dijo en serio

earnestly [ˈɜːnɪstlɪ] *adv* (**a**) *(sincerely)* seriamente (**b**) *(zealously)* con gran interés

earnestness [ˈɜːnɪstnɪs] *n* seriedad *f*; **in all e.** muy seriamente

earning power [ˈɜːnɪŋˈpaʊər] *n* capacidad *f* de ingresos

earnings [ˈɜːnɪŋz] *npl* ingresos *mpl*; **e. related** *(pensions, benefits)* proporcional a los ingresos

earphones [ˈɪəfəʊnz] *npl* auriculares *mpl*

earpiece [ˈɪəpiːs] *n* auricular *m*

earplug [ˈɪəplʌg] *n* tapón *m* (para los oídos)

earring [ˈɪərɪŋ] *n Esp* pendiente *m*, *Am* arete *m*

earshot [ˈɪəʃɒt] *n* **out of e.** fuera del alcance del oído; **within e.** al alcance del oído

ear-splitting [ˈɪəsplɪtɪŋ] *adj* ensordecedor(a)

earth [ɜːθ] **1** *n* (**a**) *(gen)* tierra *f*; *Fig* **he promised the e.** prometió el oro y el moro; *Fig* **it costs the e.** cuesta un ojo de la cara; *Fig* **to be down to e.** tocar de pies en el suelo, tener los pies en el suelo; *Fig* **to be the salt of the e.** ser de fiar; *Fig* **to come down to e.** despertarse; *Fam* **where/why on e. ...?** ¿pero dónde/porqué demonios ...? ❑ **e. mother** *(in mythology)* madre tierra *f*, diosa *f* de la fecundidad; *Fig (woman)* madraza *f*; **e. sciences** ciencias

fpl de la Tierra (**b**) *(of fox, badger)* madriguera *f*; **to run to e.** acorralar (**c**) *Br Elec* toma *f* de tierra
2 *vt Br Elec* conectar a tierra

earthen ['ɜːðən] *adj* (**a**) *(gen)* de tierra (**b**) *(of clay)* de arcilla, de barro

earthenware ['ɜːðənweər] **1** *n* loza *f*
2 *adj* de barro

earthling ['ɜːθlɪŋ] *n* terrícola *mf*

earthly ['ɜːθlɪ] *adj* (**earthlier, earthliest**) *(worldly)* material, terrenal; *Fam* **it's no e. use** no sirve absolutamente para nada; *Fam* **we don't have an e. (chance)** no tenemos la más mínima posibilidad

earthquake ['ɜːθkweɪk] *n* terremoto *m*

earthshattering ['ɜːθʃætərɪŋ] *adj* trascendental; **e. news** noticia bomba

earthworks ['ɜːθwɜːks] *n* terraplén *m*

earthworm ['ɜːθwɜːm] *n Zool* lombriz *f*

earthy ['ɜːθɪ] *adj* (**earthier, earthiest**) (**a**) *(of colour, taste)* terroso(a) (**b**) *(bawdy)* tosco(a), grosero(a)

earwax ['ɪəwæks] *n* cera *f* de los oídos, cerumen *m*

earwig ['ɪəwɪg] *n Ent* tijereta *f*

ease [iːz] **1** *n* (**a**) *(freedom from discomfort)* calma *f*, tranquilidad *f*, *Mil* posición *f* de descanso; **at e.** relajado(a); **to set sb's mind at e.** tranquilizar a algn; **to take one's e.** ponerse cómodo (**b**) *(lack of difficulty)* facilidad *f*; **with e.** con facilidad (**c**) *(affluence)* comodidad *f*; **a life of e.** una vida cómoda *or* fácil (**d**) *(lack of restraint)* **e. of manner** naturalidad *f*, desenvoltura *f*, espontaneidad *f*
2 *vt* (**a**) *(pain)* aliviar (**b**) *(move gently)* deslizar, correr

ease off, ease up *vi* (**a**) *(decrease)* ceder, disminuir (**b**) *(slow down)* ir más despacio

easel ['iːzəl] *n* caballete *m*

easily ['iːzɪlɪ] *adv* (**a**) *(without difficulty)* fácilmente (**b**) *(beyond question)* **e. the best** con mucho el mejor

easiness ['iːzɪnɪs] *n* (**a**) *(simplicity)* facilidad *f* (**b**) *(of manner etc)* naturalidad *f*

east [iːst] **1** *n* este *m* □ **the Far E.** el Lejano Oriente; **the Middle E.** el Oriente Medio
2 *adj* este, del este, oriental; *Formerly* **E. Germany** Alemania Oriental
3 *adv* en dirección este, al *or* hacia el este; **heading e.** rumbo al este; **to face** *or* **look e.** estar orientado(a) al este

eastbound ['iːstbaʊnd] *adj* con rumbo al este, en dirección este

Easter ['iːstər] *n* Semana *f* Santa, Pascua *f* □ **E. egg** huevo *m* de Pascua; **E. Sunday** Domingo *m* de Pascua *or* de Resurrección

easterly ['iːstəlɪ] *adj* (**a**) *(from the east)* del este; **e. wind** viento del este (**b**) *(to the east)* hacia al este; **in an e. direction** en dirección este

eastern ['iːstən] *adj* oriental, del este □ **E. Europe** Europa *f* Oriental *or* del Este; *US* **E. Standard Time** hora *f* oficial en la costa este de los EE.UU.

eastward ['iːstwəd] *adj & adv* hacia el este

eastwards ['iːstwədz] *adv* hacia el este

easy ['iːzɪ] (**easier, easiest**) **1** *adj* (**a**) *(simple)* fácil, sencillo(a); **e. to please** poco exigente; *Fam* **it's as e. as pie** es pan comido, está chupado, *RP* es un boleto *or* una papa □ *Com* **e. payments, e. terms** facilidades *fpl* de pago (**b**) *(unworried, comfortable)* cómodo(a), tranquilo(a); **at an e. pace** con calma, tranquilamente; **a life of e.** la vida tranquila *or* cómoda; **in e. stages** poco a poco, de forma escalonada; **to have an e. mind** estar tranquilo(a); *Fig* **to be on e. street** no tener problemas económicos; *Fam* **I'm e.!** me da lo mismo □ **e. chair** butacón *m* (**c**) *(colour)* agradable; **e. on the eyes** agradable a la vista

2 *adv* **go e. on the cakes/wine** deja algún pastel/algo de vino; **go e. with that knife** ten cuidado con ese cuchillo; **it's easier said than done** es más fácil decirlo que hacerlo; *Fam* **to take things e.** tomarse la vida con calma; *Fam* **take it e.!** ¡tranquilo!

easy-going [iːzɪ'gəʊɪŋ] *adj* (**a**) *(calm)* tranquilo(a) (**b**) *(lax)* despreocupado(a); *(undemanding)* poco exigente

eat [iːt] (*pt* **ate** [et, eɪt]; *pp* **eaten**) **1** *vt* *(gen)* comer; **to e. one's breakfast** desayunar; *Fig* **to e. one's heart out** consumirse de pena; *Fig* **to e. one's words** tragarse lo dicho; *Fam* **what's eating you?** ¿qué te preocupa?, *RP* ¿qué te pica?
2 *vi* comer; *Fig* **he had them eating out of his hand** comían en la palma de su mano; *Fam* **to e. like a horse** comer como una vaca

eat away *vt* *(gen)* desgastar; *(metal)* corroer

eat into *vt* (**a**) *(wood)* roer (**b**) *Fig (savings)* consumir

eat out *vi* comer fuera

eat up *vt* (**a**) *(meal)* terminar (**b**) *Fig (petrol)* consumir; *(miles)* tragar; *(money)* llevarse, tragar

eatable ['iːtəbəl] *adj* comible, comestible

eaten ['iːtən] *pp see* **eat**

eater ['iːtər] *n Fam* **to be a big e.** ser de buen comer, ser comilón(ona); **to be a slow e.** ser lento(a) comiendo

eatery ['iːtərɪ] *n US* restaurante *m*

eau de Cologne [əʊdəkə'ləʊn] *n* colonia *f*, agua *f* de colonia

eaves [iːvz] *npl* alero *m sing*

eavesdrop ['iːvzdrɒp] *vi* (*pt & pp* **eavesdropped**) escuchar disimuladamente

eavesdropper ['iːvzdrɒpər] *n* curioso(a) *m,f*

ebb [eb] **1** *n* reflujo *m*; **e. and flow** flujo y reflujo; *Fig* **to be at a low e.** estar decaído(a)
2 *vi* (**a**) *(tide)* bajar; **to e. and flow** subir y bajar (**b**) *Fig* **e. away** decaer, disminuir

Ebola virus ['ebələ'vaɪrəs] *n* virus *m* del Ébola

ebony ['ebənɪ] **1** *n Bot* ébano *m*
2 *adj* de ébano

e-book ['iːbʊk] *n Comptr* libro *m* electrónico

ebullience [ɪ'bʌljəns] *n* exaltación *f*, entusiamo *m*

ebullient [ɪ'bʌljənt] *adj* exaltado(a), entusiasta

eccentric [ɪk'sentrɪk] **1** *adj* (**a**) *(person)* excéntrico(a), estrafalario(a), extravagante (**b**) *Math (circle)* excéntrico(a)
2 *n (person)* excéntrico(a) *m,f*, persona *f* extravagante

eccentricity [eksen'trɪsɪtɪ] *n* excentricidad *f*, extravagancia *f*

ecclesiastic [ɪkliːzɪ'æstɪk] **1** *adj* eclesiástico(a)
2 *n* eclesiástico *m*, clérigo *m*, sacerdote *m*

ecclesiastical [ɪkliːzɪ'æstɪkəl] *adj* eclesiástico(a)

echelon ['eʃəlɒn] *n (status)* nivel *m*, escalafón *m*; *Mil* **in e.** en escalafón

echo ['ekəʊ] **1** *n* (*pl* **echoes**) eco *m* □ **e. chamber** cámara *f* acústica; **e. sounder** sonda *f* acústica
2 *vt (repeat)* repetir; **to e. sb's words** repetir las palabras de algn; **to e. sb's opinions** hacerse eco de las opiniones de algn
3 *vi* resonar, hacer eco

éclair [eɪ'kleə, ɪ'kleə] *n Culin (cake)* palo *m* de nata, pastel *m* petisú; **chocolate e.** bombón *m* de chocolate y caramelo

eclectic [ɪ'klektɪk] *adj* ecléctico(a)

eclecticism [ɪ'klektɪsɪzəm] *n* eclecticismo *m*

eclipse [ɪ'klɪps] **1** *n* eclipse *m*
2 *vt* eclipsar

eco-friendly ['iːkəʊfrendlɪ] *adj* ecológico(a)

ecological [i:kə'lɒdʒɪkəl] adj ecológico(a)

ecologically [i:kə'lɒdʒɪklɪ] adv ecológicamente

ecologist [ɪ'kɒlədʒɪst] n ecólogo(a) m,f, ecologista mf

ecology [ɪ'kɒlədʒɪ] n ecología f

e-commerce ['i:kɒmɜːs] n comercio m electrónico

economic [i:kə'nɒmɪk] adj (gen) económico(a); (profitable) rentable; **e. migrant** emigrante mf(económico(a))

economical [i:kə'nɒmɪkəl] adj (gen) económico(a); (cheap) barato(a); **to be e. with sth** economizar en algo

economically [i:kə'nɒmɪklɪ] adv económicamente

economics [i:kə'nɒmɪks] n sing (a) (science) economía f; Educ (ciencias fpl) económicas fpl (b) (financial aspect) aspecto m económico

economist [ɪ'kɒnəmɪst] n economista mf

economize [ɪ'kɒnəmaɪz] vi economizar, ahorrar

economy [ɪ'kɒnəmɪ] n (a) (science) economía f; Pol **the e.** la economía, el sistema económico ◻ **black e.** economía f sumergida (b) (saving) economía f, ahorro m; Av **e. class** (clase f) turista f; **I always fly e. class** siempre viajo en clase turista; Com **e. sized** de tamaño familiar; **that's a false e.** esto no es un ahorro

ecosystem ['i:kɒsɪstəm] n ecosistema m

ecotax ['i:kəʊtæks] n ecotasa f, impuesto m ecológico

ecoterrorism ['i:kəʊterərɪzəm] n terrorismo m ecológico, ecoterrorismo m

ecotourism ['i:kəʊtɔːrɪzəm] n ecoturismo m, turismo m verde or ecológico

ecstasy ['ekstəsɪ] n éxtasis m; **to go into ecstasies over** extasiarse ante

ecstatic [ek'stætɪk] adj extático(a)

Ecuador ['ekwədɔːr] n Ecuador

Ecuadoran ['ekwədɔːrən], **Ecuadorian** [ekwə'dɔːrɪən] adj & n ecuatoriano(a) (m,f)

ecumenical [i:kjʊ'menɪkəl] adj ecuménico(a)

eczema ['eksɪmə] n Med eczema mf

ed. [ed] (a) (abbr **edition**) edición f, ed (b) (abbr **editor**) editor(a) m,f (c) (abbr **edited**) editado(a)

eddy ['edɪ] **1** n remolino m
2 vi (pt & pp eddied) formar remolinos, arremolinarse

Eden ['iːdən] n Edén m

edge [edʒ] **1** n borde m; (of knife) filo m; (of coin) canto m; (end) extremidad f; (of water) orilla f; **a knife with a blunt e.** un cuchillo con el canto desafilado; **he lives on the e. of town** vive en las afueras de la ciudad; **to have the e. on or over sb** llevar ventaja a algn; **to take the e. off one's appetite** quitar el hambre; Fig **to be on e.** tener los nervios de punta; Fig **to set sb's teeth on e.** crispar los nervios a algn; Fig **to live on the e.** vivir peligrosamente
2 vt Sew ribetear; **to e. sth with lace** poner un borde de encaje a algo
3 vi **to e. closer** acercarse lentamente; **to e. forward** avanzar poco a poco; Fig (prices) **to e. up** subir gradualmente

edge out vt (displace) eliminar, apartar; **to e. sb out** empujar a algn, poner la zancadilla a algn

edgeways ['edʒweɪz] adv de lado; Fig **I couldn't get a word in e.** no pude meter baza

edging ['edʒɪŋ] n borde m; Sew ribete m

edgy ['edʒɪ] adj (edgier, edgiest) nervioso(a)

edible ['edɪbəl] adj comestible

edict ['iːdɪkt] Hist n edicto m; Jur decreto m

edification [edɪfɪ'keɪʃən] n edificación f

edifice ['edɪfɪs] n gran edificio m; Fig **the whole e. of his argument fell down** su argumento se vino abajo

edify ['edɪfaɪ] vt (pt & pp **edified**) edificar

edifying ['edɪfaɪɪŋ] adj edificante

Edinburgh ['edɪnbrə] n Edimburgo

edit ['edɪt] **1** n Comptr (menu heading) edición f
2 vt (a) (prepare for printing) preparar para la imprenta (b) (rewrite) corregir; **to e. sth out** suprimir algo (c) Press dirigir la redacción de, ser redactor(a) de (d) Cin Rad TV montar; (cut) cortar, reducir (e) Comptr editar

editing ['edɪtɪŋ] n Cin montaje m

edition [ɪ'dɪʃən] n edición f; **first e.** primera edición

editor ['edɪtər] n (a) (of book) editor(a) m,f, autor(a) m,f de la edición (b) Press redactor(a) m,f; **e. in chief** redactor(a) jefe; (newspaper) director(a) m,f (c) Cin TV montador(a) m,f (d) Comptr (software) editor m

editorial [edɪ'tɔːrɪəl] **1** adj editorial; **e. staff** redacción f
2 n editorial m

educate ['edjʊkeɪt] vt educar; **he was educated in Italy** se formó en Italia; **she was educated at Oxford University** estudió en la universidad de Oxford

educated ['edjʊkeɪtɪd] adj culto(a), cultivado(a); **e. speech** lenguaje m culto

education [edjʊ'keɪʃən] n (a) (teaching, schooling) enseñanza f; **she received a good e.** recibió una buena preparación ◻ **adult e.** enseñanza f para adultos; **further e.** enseñanza f superior; **Ministry of E.** Ministerio m de Educación; **primary/secondary e.** enseñanza f primaria/secundaria (b) (training) formación f (c) (studies) estudios mpl (d) (culture) cultura f

educational [edjʊ'keɪʃənəl] adj educativo(a), educacional ◻ **e. film** película f educativa; **e. publisher** editor(a) m,f de libros de texto; **e. reform** reforma f educativa

education(al)ist [edjʊ'keɪʃən(əl)ɪst] n pedagogo(a) m,f, educador(a) m,f

educator ['edjʊkeɪtər] n educador(a) m,f, pedagogo(a) m,f

Edwardian [ed'wɔːdɪən] adj eduardiano(a)

eel [iːl] n Zool anguila f

eerie ['ɪərɪ] adj (eerier, eeriest) siniestro(a), escalofriante

eerily ['ɪərɪlɪ] adv de forma espeluznante; **it was e. silent** había un silencio sobrecogedor

efface [ɪ'feɪs] vt borrar

effect [ɪ'fekt] **1** n (a) (gen) efecto m; **in e.** efectivamente; **to come into e.** entrar en vigor; **to have an e. on** afectar a; **to have the desired e.** producir el efecto esperado; **to no e.** sin resultado alguno; **to take e.** (drug) surtir efecto; (law) entrar en vigor; **words to that e.** algo por el estilo (b) (impression) impresión f, efecto m; Fig **for e.** para impresionar (c) **effects** efectos mpl ◻ **personal e.** enseres mpl personales; **side e.** efectos mpl secundarios; **sound e.** efectos mpl sonoros; **special e.** efectos mpl especiales
2 vt (produce) efectuar; (cause) provocar

effective [ɪ'fektɪv] adj (a) (successful) eficaz; **to be e.** ser eficaz (b) (active, real) efectivo(a); **e. power** poder efectivo (c) (impressive) impresionante (d) (striking) llamativo(a)

effectively [ɪ'fektɪvlɪ] adv (a) (successfully) eficazmente (b) (in fact) en efecto, de hecho

effectiveness [ɪ'fektɪvnɪs] n eficacia f

effectuate [ɪ'fektjuːeɪt] vt efectuar, realizar, llevar a cabo

effeminacy [ɪ'femɪnəsɪ] n afeminación f, afeminamiento m

effeminate [ɪ'femɪnɪt] adj afeminado(a)

effervesce [efə'ves] vi (a) (liquid) burbujear, estar en efervescencia (b) (person) estar en plena efervescencia

effervescence [efə'vesəns] n efervescencia f

effervescent [efə'vesənt] *adj* efervescente

effete [ɪ'fi:t] *adj* débil, cansado(a), agotado(a)

efficacious [efɪ'keɪʃəs] *adj* eficaz

efficacy ['efɪkəsɪ] *n* eficacia *f*

efficiency [ɪ'fɪʃənsɪ] *n* (**a**) *(of person)* eficacia *f*, eficiencia *f*, competencia *f* (**b**) *(of machine)* rendimiento *m*

efficient [ɪ'fɪʃənt] *adj* (**a**) *(person)* eficaz, eficiente, competente (**b**) *(system, method)* eficaz, eficiente (**c**) *(machine)* de buen rendimiento

effigy ['efɪdʒɪ] *n* efigie *f*

effluent ['efluənt] *n* aguas *fpl* residuales, vertidos *mpl*, residuos *mpl*

effort ['efət] *n* (**a**) *(gen)* esfuerzo *m*; **to make an e.** hacer un esfuerzo, esforzarse (**b**) *(attempt)* tentativa *f*, intento *m*, conato *m*; **it was a good e.** fue un buen intento

effortless ['efətlɪs] *adj* fácil, sin esfuerzo

effortlessly ['efətlɪslɪ] *adv* fácilmente, sin esfuerzo

effrontery [ɪ'frʌntərɪ] *n* descaro *m*, desfachatez *f*, desvergüenza *f*

effusion [ɪ'fju:ʒən] *n* efusión *f*

effusive [ɪ'fju:sɪv] *adj* efusivo(a)

effusively [ɪ'fju:sɪvlɪ] *adv* efusivamente

EFL [i:ef'fel] *n* (*abbr* **English as a Foreign Language**) inglés *m* como lengua extranjera

EFT [i:ef'ti:] *n* Comptr (*abbr* **electronic funds transfer**) TEF *f*, transferencia *f* electrónica de fondos

EFTA ['eftə] *n* (*abbr* **European Free Trade Association**) EFTA *f*, AELC *f*, Asociación *f* Europea de Libre Comercio

EFTPOS ['eftpɒs] *n* Comptr (*abbr* **electronic funds transfer at point of sale**) transferencia *f* (electrónica de fondos) en el punto de venta

eg [i:'dʒi:] (*abbr* **exempli gratia**) (for example), por ejemplo, p. ej

egalitarian [ɪgælɪ'teərɪən] *adj* igualitario(a)

egalitarianism [ɪgælɪ'teərɪənɪzəm] *n* igualitarismo *m*

egg [eg] **1** *n* huevo *m*, CAm Méx blanquillo *m*; Fig **to be a bad e.** ser una mala persona; Fam **to have e. on one's face** quedar en ridículo; Fam Fig **to put all one's eggs in one basket** jugárselo todo a una carta, Am poner todos los huevos en la misma canasta ▫ Culin **boiled e.** huevo *m* pasado por agua; **e. cup** huevera *f*; **e. custard** natillas *fpl*; **e. timer** reloj *m* de arena; **e. white** clara *f* de huevo; **e. yolk** yema *f* de huevo; **fried e.** huevo *m* frito; Fig **nest e.** ahorrillos *mpl*; **poached e.** huevo *m* escalfado; **scrambled eggs** huevos *mpl* revueltos

2 *vt* **to e. sb on (to do sth)** empujar *or* animar a algn (a hacer algo)

egghead ['eghed] *n* Pej intelectual *mf*

eggnog [eg'nɒg] *n* Culin ponche *m* de huevo

eggplant ['egplɑ:nt] *n* US berenjena *f*

egg-shaped ['egʃeɪpt] *adj* ovoide

eggshell ['egʃel] *n* cáscara *f* de huevo; **e. finish** *(of paint)* acabado *m* mate

egg-whisk ['egwɪsk] *n* Br Culin batidor *m*

egis ['i:dʒɪs] *n* US **under the e. of** bajo el patrocinio de

ego ['i:gəʊ, 'egəʊ] *n* (**a**) Psych ego *m* ▫ **alter ego** *m*; Fam **e. trip** autobombo *m* (**b**) Fam amor *m* propio; **to boost sb's e.** levantar la moral a algn; **to deflate sb's e.** bajar los humos a algn; **to have a big e.** tener mucho ego

egocentric [i:gəʊ'sentrɪk] *adj* egocéntrico(a)

egoism ['i:gəʊɪzəm] *n* egoísmo *m*

egoist ['i:gəʊɪst] *n* egoísta *mf*

egotism ['i:gəʊtɪzəm] *n* egotismo *m*

egotist ['i:gəʊtɪst] *n* egotista *mf*

egotistic(al) [i:gəʊ'tɪstɪk(əl)] *adj* egotista

Egypt ['i:dʒɪpt] *n* Egipto

Egyptian [ɪ'dʒɪpʃən] *adj & n* egipcio(a) *(m,f)*

eiderdown ['aɪdədaʊn] *n* edredón *m*

eight [eɪt] **1** *adj* ocho *inv*

2 *n* ocho *m inv*; Fam **to have one over the e.** llevar una copa de más; *see also* **seven**

eighteen [eɪ'ti:n] **1** *adj* dieciocho *inv*

2 *n* dieciocho *m inv*; *see also* **seven**

eighteenth [eɪ'ti:nθ] **1** *adj* decimoctavo(a)

2 *n* (**a**) *(in series)* decimoctavo(a) *m,f* (**b**) *(fraction)* decimoctavo *m*, decimoctava parte *f*; *see also* **seventh**

eighth [eɪtθ] **1** *adj* octavo(a); US Mus **e. note** corchea *f*

2 *n* (**a**) *(in series)* octavo(a) *m,f* (**b**) *(fraction)* octavo *m*, octava parte *f*; *see also* **seventh**

eightieth ['eɪtɪɪθ] **1** *adj* octogésimo(a)

2 *n* (**a**) *(in series)* octogésimo(a) *m,f* (**b**) *(fraction)* octogavo *m*, octogésima parte *f*; *see also* **seventh**

eighty ['eɪtɪ] **1** *adj* ochenta *inv*

2 *n* ochenta *m inv*; *see also* **seven**

Eire ['eərə] *n* Formerly Eire *(hoy la República de Irlanda)*

either ['aɪðər, 'i:ðər] **1** *pron* (**a**) *(affirmative)* cualquiera; **e. of them will do** cualquiera de los dos sirve; **e. of us** cualquiera de nosotros dos (**b**) *(negative)* ninguno, ninguna, ni el uno ni el otro, ni la una ni la otra; **I don't want e. of them** no quiero ninguno de los dos

2 *adj (both)* cada, los dos, las dos; **on e. side** en ambos lados, a cada lado; **in e. case** en cualquier de los dos casos

3 *conj* o; **e. ... or ...** o ... o ...; **e. Friday or Saturday** o (bien) el viernes o el sábado; **you e. like it or you don't** o te gusta o no te gusta

4 *adv (after negative)* tampoco; **I don't want to do it e.** yo tampoco quiero hacerlo, yo no quiero hacerlo tampoco

either-or ['aɪðərɔ:r] *adj* **to be in an e. situation** tener que elegir (entre lo uno o lo otro)

ejaculate [ɪ'dʒækjʊleɪt] *vi* (**a**) *(emit semen)* eyacular (**b**) *(exclaim)* exclamar

ejaculation [ɪdʒækjʊ'leɪʃən] *n* (**a**) *(of semen)* eyaculación *f* (**b**) *(exclamation)* exclamación *f*

eject [ɪ'dʒekt] **1** *vt* expulsar, echar

2 *vi* Av eyectar, eyectarse

ejection [ɪ'dʒekʃən] *n* (**a**) *(of troublemaker, CD, video)* expulsión *f* (**b**) Av eyección *f*

ejector [ɪ'dʒektər] *n* Av **e. seat** asiento *m* eyectable

eke [i:k] *vt* **to e. out a living** ganarse la vida a duras penas

elaborate [ɪ'læbəreɪt] **1** *vt* (**a**) *(devise)* elaborar, desarrollar; **to e. a plan** elaborar un proyecto (**b**) *(explain)* explicar detalladamente

2 *vi* explicarse; **to e. on sth** explicar algo con más detalles; **he refused to e.** se negó a dar más detalles

3 [ɪ'læbərɪt] *adj* (**a**) *(complicated)* complicado(a) (**b**) *(detailed)* detallado(a); *(of style, work of art)* trabajado(a), esmerado(a)

elaborately [ɪ'læbərətlɪ] *adv* (**a**) *(in a complicated way)* de modo complicado (**b**) *(in detail)* detalladamente (**c**) *(carefully)* cuidadosamente

elaboration [ɪlæbə'reɪʃən] *n* elaboración *f*

élan [eɪ'lɑ:n, eɪ'læn] *n* brío *m*, vivacidad *f*, impetuosidad *f*

elapse [ɪ'læps] *vi* transcurrir, pasar

elastic [ɪ'læstɪk] **1** *adj* elástico(a); Fig flexible ▫ **e. band** goma *f* elástica

2 *n* elástico *m*

elasticated [ɪ'læstɪkeɪtɪd] *adj* con elástico, RP elastizado(a)

elasticity [ɪlæ'stɪsɪtɪ] *n* elasticidad *f*; *Fig* flexibilidad *f*

Elastoplast® [ɪ'lɑːstəplɑːst] *n Br* tirita® *f*, *Am* curita *f*

elated [ɪ'leɪtɪd] *adj* eufórico(a), satisfecho(a), muy contento(a)

elation [ɪ'leɪʃən] *n* júbilo *m*, regocijo *m*, euforia *f*

elbow ['elbəʊ] **1** *n* (**a**) *Anat* codo *m*; *Fig* **e. grease** sudor *m*; *Fig* **e. room** espacio *m*, sitio *m* (**b**) *(bend)* recodo *m*
  2 *vt* **to e. one's way through** abrirse paso a codazos; **to e. sb** dar un codazo a algn; *Fig* **to e. sb out** empujar *or* echar a algn

elder[1] ['eldər] **1** *adj* mayor; **e. statesman** viejo estadista; **my e. brother** mi hermano mayor
  2 *n (respected person)* mayor *m*; **the village elders** los ancianos del pueblo; **you must respect your elders** hay que respetar a tus mayores

elder[2] ['eldər] *n Bot* saúco *m*

elderberry ['eldəberɪ] *n Bot* baya *f* del saúco

elderflower ['eldəflaʊər] *n* flor *f* de saúco

elderly ['eldəlɪ] *adj* anciano(a); **the e.** los ancianos

eldest ['eldɪst] **1** *adj* mayor; **their e. sister** su hermana mayor
  2 *n* el/la mayor; **my e. has gone to work in London** mi hijo/hija mayor (se) ha ido a trabajar a Londres

elect [ɪ'lekt] **1** *vt* (**a**) *Pol* elegir (**b**) *(choose)* decidir; **he elected not to go on holiday** decidió no ir de vacaciones
  2 *adj* electo(a); **the president e.** el presidente electo
  3 the e. *npl* los elegidos

election [ɪ'lekʃən] **1** *n (action)* elección *f*; *(event)* elecciones *fpl*; **to hold an e.** convocar elecciones □ **general e.** elecciones *fpl* generales
  2 *adj* electoral □ **e. campaign** campaña *f* electoral

electioneering [ɪlekʃə'nɪərɪŋ] **1** *adj* electoralista
  2 *n* electoralismo *m*

elective [ɪ'lektɪv] *adj (assembly)* electivo(a); *Univ (course)* optativo(a), opcional

elector [ɪ'lektər] *n* elector(a) *m,f*

electoral [ɪ'lektərəl] *adj* electoral □ **e. roll, e. register** censo *m* electoral

electorate [ɪ'lektərɪt] *n* electorado *m*

Electra [ɪ'lektrə] *n* Electra *f*; *Psych* **E. complex** complejo *m* de Electra

electric [ɪ'lektrɪk] *adj* eléctrico(a); *Fig* **the atmosphere was e.** el ambiente estaba electrizado □ **e. blanket** manta *f* eléctrica; **e. chair** silla *f* eléctrica; **e. motor** electromotor *m*; **e. shock** electrochock *m*, electrochoque *m*; **to get an e. shock** recibir una descarga eléctrica; **e. storm** tormenta *f* eléctrica

electrical [ɪ'lektrɪkəl] *adj* eléctrico(a) □ **e. engineer** ingeniero(a) *m,f* electrotécnico(a); **e. engineering** ingeniería *f* eléctrica, electrotecnia *f*

electrically [ɪ'lektrɪklɪ] *adv* por electricidad; **e. operated** *or* **powered** electroaccionado(a)

electrician [ɪlek'trɪʃən] *n* electricista *mf*

electricity [ɪlek'trɪsɪtɪ] *n* electricidad *f* □ **e. supply** suministro *m* eléctrico

electrics [ɪ'lektrɪks] *npl (house)* instalación *f* sing eléctrica; *(equipment, apparatus)* sistema *m* sing eléctrico

electrification [ɪlektrɪfɪ'keɪʃən] *n* electrificación *f*

electrify [ɪ'lektrɪfaɪ] *vt (pt & pp* **electrified**) (**a**) *(provide supply)* electrificar; **they are going to e. the railway network** van a electrificar la red ferroviaria (**b**) *Fig (excite)* electrizar

electrifying [ɪ'lektrɪfaɪɪŋ] *adj Fig* electrizante

electrocardiogram [ɪlektrəʊ'kɑːdɪəʊgræm] *n Med* electrocardiograma *m*

electrocardiograph [ɪlektrəʊ'kɑːdɪəʊgrɑːf] *n* electrocardiógrafo *m*

electrocute [ɪ'lektrəkjuːt] *vt* electrocutar; **she was electrocuted** se electrocutó

electrocution [ɪlektrə'kjuːʃən] *n* electrocución *f*

electrode [ɪ'lektrəʊd] *n* electrodo *m*

electroencephalogram [ɪlektrəʊen'sefələgræm] *n Med* electroencefalograma *m*

electroencephalograph [ɪlektrəʊen'sefələgrɑːf] *n Med* electroencefalógrafo *m*

electrolysis [ɪlek'trɒlɪsɪs] *n* electrólisis *f*

electrolyte [ɪ'lektrəʊlaɪt] *n* electrólito *m*

electrolyze [ɪ'lektrəʊlaɪz] *vt* electrolizar

electromagnet [ɪlektrəʊ'mægnɪt] *n* electroimán *m*

electromagnetic [ɪlektrəʊmæg'netɪk] *adj* electromagnético(a) □ **e. field** campo *m* electromagnético

electron [ɪ'lektrɒn] *n* electrón *m* □ **e. microscope** microscopio *m* electrónico

electronic [ɪlek'trɒnɪk] *adj* electrónico(a) □ *Fin* **e. banking** banca *f* electrónica, (servicio *m* de) telebanco *m*; **e. funds transfer** transferencia *f* electrónica de fondos; *Comptr* **e. mail** correo *m* electrónico

electronically [ɪlek'trɒnɪklɪ] *adv* electrónicamente

electronics [ɪlek'trɒnɪks] *n* (**a**) *(science)* electrónica *f* (**b**) *(of machine)* componentes *mpl* electrónicos

electroshock [ɪlektrəʊ'ʃɒk] *n Med* **e. therapy** *or* **treatment** terapia *f* por tratamiento *m* de electrochoque

elegance ['elɪgəns] *n* elegancia *f*

elegant ['elɪgənt] *adj* elegante

elegantly ['elɪgəntlɪ] *adv* con elegancia

elegiac [elə'dʒaɪək] *adj* elegiaco(a), elegíaco(a)

elegy ['elɪdʒɪ] *n Lit* elegía *f*

element ['elɪmənt] *n* (**a**) *(gen)* elemento *m*; **an e. of surprise** un elemento de sorpresa; **the human e.** el factor humano (**b**) *(part of a whole)* parte *f*, componente *m*; **an e. of truth** una parte de verdad; **the reactionary elements of the party** la fracción reaccionaria del partido (**c**) *(electrical)* resistencia *f* (**d**) *Chem* elemento *m* (**e**) *Meteor* **the elements** los elementos, las fuerzas de la naturaleza; *Fig* **to brave the elements** hacer frente a los elementos (**f**) *(ideal environment)* *Fam Fig* **to be in one's element** estar en su elemento

elemental [elɪ'mentəl] *adj* elemental, básico(a)

elementary [elɪ'mentərɪ] *adj* (**a**) *(basic)* elemental, fundamental; **e. arithmetic** matemáticas elementales □ *Br Educ* **e. school** escuela *f* primaria (**b**) *(not developed)* rudimentario(a) (**c**) *(easy)* fácil

elephant ['elɪfənt] *n Zool* elefante *m*; **cow e.** elefanta *f*; *Fig* **white e.** cosa *f* inútil; *Fam* **to have a memory like an e.** tener una memoria de elefante

elephantiasis [elɪfən'taɪəsɪs] *n Med* elefantiasis *f*

elephantine [elɪ'fæntaɪn] *adj* (**a**) *(huge)* mastodóntico(a), descomunal (**b**) *(clumsy)* torpe, patoso(a)

elevate ['elɪveɪt] *vt* (**a**) *(mind, tone of conversation)* elevar (**b**) *(in rank)* ascender, promover

elevated ['elɪveɪtɪd] *adj* elevado(a) □ **e. railway** ferrocarril *m or* tren *m* elevado

elevation [elɪ'veɪʃən] *n* (**a**) *(height)* altitud *f* (**b**) *(in rank)* ascenso *m* (**c**) *Archit* alzado *m* (**d**) *Geog (hill)* elevación *f*; *(above sea level)* altitud *f*

elevator ['elɪveɪtər] *n* (**a**) *US* ascensor *m* □ **goods e.** montacargas *m inv* (**b**) *Av* timón *m* de profundidad

eleven [ɪ'levən] **1** *adj* once *inv*
  2 *n (number)* once *m inv*; *Sport* equipo *m*, once *m*; *see also* **seven**

eleven-plus [ɪˈlevənplʌs] *n Br Educ Formerly* = prueba selectiva que podían realizar los alumnos británicos a la edad de 11 años para acceder a una **grammar school** y así encaminar su educación secundaria con miras a la universidad

elevenses [ɪˈlevənzɪz] *npl Br Fam* bocadillo *m* de las once, *Am* onces *fpl*

eleventh [ɪˈlevənθ] **1** *adj* undécimo(a), onceavo(a); *Fig* **at the e. hour** *Esp* en el *or Am* a último momento, *Am* en el último minuto
  2 *n* (**a**) *(in series)* undécimo(a) *m,f* (**b**) *(fraction)* undécima parte *f; see also* **seventh**

elf [elf] *n* (*pl* **elves** [elvz]) elfo *m*

elfin [ˈelfɪn] *adj* delicado(a), angelical

elicit [ɪˈlɪsɪt] *vt* provocar, obtener

elide [ɪˈlaɪd] *vt Ling* elidir

eligibility [elɪdʒəˈbɪlɪtɪ] *n* elegibilidad *f,* idoneidad *f*

eligible [ˈelɪdʒəbəl] *adj (fulfilling requirements)* idóneo(a), apto(a); **an e. young man** un buen partido; **he isn't e. to vote** no tiene derecho al voto; **you are e. for a grant** tienes derecho a una beca, cumples los requisitos para obtener una beca

eliminate [ɪˈlɪmɪneɪt] *vt* eliminar

elimination [ɪlɪmɪˈneɪʃən] *n* eliminación *f*

eliminatory [ɪˈlɪmɪnətərɪ] *adj* eliminatorio(a); *Sport* **e. round** eliminatoria *f*

elision [ɪˈlɪʒən] *n Ling* elisión *f*

élite [ɪˈliːt] *n* elite *f*

élitism [ɪˈliːtɪzəm] *n* elitismo *m*

élitist [ɪˈliːtɪst] *adj* elitista

elixir [ɪˈlɪksər] *n* elixir *m*

Elizabethan [ɪlɪzəˈbiːθən] *adj & n* isabelino(a) *(m,f)*

elk [elk] *n Zool* alce *m*

ellipse [ɪˈlɪps] *n Math* elipse *f*

ellipsis [ɪˈlɪpsɪs] *n* (*pl* **ellipses** [ɪˈlɪpsiːz]) *Ling Lit* elipsis *f*

elm [elm] *n Bot* olmo *m* ❑ **Dutch e. disease** grafiosis *f,* enfermedad *f* holandesa del olmo

elocution [eləˈkjuːʃən] *n* elocución *f*

elongate [ˈiːlɒŋɡeɪt] *vt* alargar, extender

elope [ɪˈləʊp] *vi* fugarse para casarse

elopement [ɪˈləʊpmənt] *n* fuga *f* para casarse

eloquence [ˈeləkwəns] *n* elocuencia *f*

eloquent [ˈeləkwənt] *adj* elocuente

else [els] *adv* (**a**) *(other, different)* más, otro(a); **anyone e.** alguien más; **anything e.?** ¿algo más?; **everything e.** todo lo demás; **no-one e.** nadie más; **someone e.** otro(a); **something e.** otra cosa, algo más; **somewhere e.** en otra parte; **what e.?** ¿qué más?; **where e.?** ¿en qué otro sitio? (**b**) *Fam (otherwise)* **or e.** si no; **do as I tell you or e.** haz lo que te digo, si no (ya verás)

elsewhere [els'weər] *adv* en otro sitio, en otra parte

ELT [iːelˈtiː] *n* (*abbr* **English Language Teaching**) enseñanza *f* del inglés

elucidate [ɪˈluːsɪdeɪt] *vt* aclarar, dilucidar, poner en claro

elucidation [ɪluːsɪˈdeɪʃən] *n* aclaración *f,* dilucidación *f*

elude [ɪˈluːd] *vt* (**a**) *(escape)* eludir, escapar; **his name eludes me** no consigo acordarme de su nombre (**b**) *(avoid)* esquivar

elusive [ɪˈluːsɪv] *adj* (**a**) *(difficult to find)* esquivo(a), escurridizo(a) (**b**) *(evasive)* evasivo(a)

elver [ˈelvər] *n Zool* angula *f*

elves [ˈelvz] *pl see* **elf**

emaciated [ɪˈmeɪsɪeɪtɪd] *adj (body)* enflaquecido(a); *(of face)* demacrado(a); **to become e.** *(go thin)* enflaquecer; *(waste away)* demacrarse

emaciation [ɪmeɪsɪˈeɪʃən] *n (of body)* enflaquecimiento *m*; *(of face)* demacración *f*

e-mail [ˈiːmeɪl] *n* correo *m* electrónico ❑ **e. account** cuenta *f* de correo (electrónico); **e. address** dirección *f* de correo (electrónico)

emanate [ˈemaneɪt] *vi* emanar (**from** de), provenir (**from** de)

emancipate [ɪˈmænsɪpeɪt] *vt* emancipar

emancipation [ɪmænsɪˈpeɪʃən] *n* emancipación *f*

emasculate [ɪˈmæskjʊleɪt] *vt* (**a**) *(debilitate, weaken)* debilitar (**b**) *Med (castrate)* emacular, castrar

emasculation [ɪmæskjʊˈleɪʃən] *n* emasculación *f,* castración *f*

embalm [ɪmˈbɑːm] *vt* embalsamar

embalmer [ɪmˈbɑːmər] *n* embalsamador(a) *m,f*

embankment [ɪmˈbæŋkmənt] *n* (**a**) *(de tierra)* terraplén *m* (**b**) *(river)* dique *m*

embargo [emˈbɑːɡəʊ] **1** *n* (*pl* **embargoes**) prohibición *f,* embargo *m*; **to put an e. on sth** prohibir algo
  2 *vt* (*pt & pp* **embargoed**) (**a**) *(forbid)* prohibir (**b**) *(seize)* embargar

embark [emˈbɑːk] **1** *vt (merchandize)* embarcar
  2 *vi (boat, ship)* embarcar, embarcarse; *Fig* **to e. upon** emprender

embarkation [embɑːˈkeɪʃən] *n* embarque *m*

embarrass [ɪmˈbærəs] *vt* avergonzar, azorar, *Am salvo RP* apenar

embarrassed [ɪmˈbærəst] *adj* avergonzado(a), *Am salvo RP* apenado(a)

embarrassing [ɪmˈbærəsɪŋ] *adj* embarazoso(a), violento(a); **it's an e. situation** es una situación violenta

embarrassment [ɪmˈbærəsmənt] *n* vergüenza *f,* *Am salvo RP* pena *f;* **to be an e. to sb** ser motivo de vergüenza *or Am salvo RP* pena para algn

embassy [ˈembəsɪ] *n* embajada *f*

embattled [ɪmˈbætəld] *adj* acosado(a); **to be e.** estar acosado(a)

embed [ɪmˈbed] *vt* (*pt & pp* **embedded**) (**a**) *(jewels etc)* incrustar (**b**) *Fig* fijar, grabar; **it's embedded in my memory** lo tengo grabado en la memoria

embellish [ɪmˈbelɪʃ] *vt (decorate)* adornar, embellecer; *Fig (story, facts)* adornar

embellishment [ɪmˈbelɪʃmənt] *n* adorno *m*

ember [ˈembər] *n* brasa *f,* ascua *f,* rescoldo *m*

embezzle [ɪmˈbezəl] *vt* desfalcar, malversar

embezzlement [ɪmˈbezəlmənt] *n* desfalco *m,* malversación *f*

embezzler [ɪmˈbezələr] *n* desfalcador(a) *m,f,* malversador(a) *m,f*

embitter [ɪmˈbɪtər] *vt* amargar

embittered [ɪmˈbɪtəd] *adj* amargado(a), resentido(a)

emblem [ˈembləm] *n* emblema *m*

embodiment [ɪmˈbɒdɪmənt] *n* encarnación *f,* personificación *f*

embody [ɪmˈbɒdɪ] *vt* (*pt & pp* **embodied**) (**a**) *(include)* incorporar, abarcar (**b**) *(personify)* encarnar, personificar

embolden [ɪmˈbəʊldən] *vt* envalentonar

embolism [ˈembəlɪzəm] *n Med* embolia *f*

emboss [ɪmˈbɒs] *vt (gen)* grabar en relieve; *(leather, metal)* repujar

embossed [ɪmˈbɒst] *adj (gen)* en relieve; *(leather, metal)* repujado(a); **e. letterhead** membrete *m* en relieve

embrace [ɪmˈbreɪs] **1** *vt* (**a**) *(gen)* abrazar (**b**) *(occasion)* aprovechar (**c**) *(accept)* aceptar, adoptar (**d**) *(cover, include)* abarcar
2 *vi* abrazarse; **they embraced** se abrazaron
3 *n* abrazo *m*

embroider [ɪmˈbrɔɪdər] *vt* (**a**) *Sew* bordar (**b**) *Fig (story, truth)* adornar, embellecer

embroidery [ɪmˈbrɔɪdərɪ] *n* (**a**) *Sew* bordado *m* (**b**) *Fig* adorno *m*

embroil [ɪmˈbrɔɪl] *vt* enredar, liar; **to become embroiled in sth** enredarse en algo, liarse en algo

embryo [ˈembrɪəʊ] *n* embrión *m*

embryonic [embrɪˈɒnɪk] *adj Fig* embrionario(a)

emend [ɪˈmend] *vt* corregir, enmendar

emendation [iːmenˈdeɪʃən] *n* corrección *f*, enmienda *f*

emerald [ˈemərəld] **1** *n (stone)* esmeralda *f*; *(colour)* esmeralda *m*
2 *adj* (color) esmeralda; **the E. Isle** Irlanda

emerge [ɪˈmɜːdʒ] *vi (gen)* salir; *(problem)* surgir; **it emerged that ...** resultó que ...

emergence [ɪˈmɜːdʒəns] *n* aparición *f*, surgimiento *m*

emergency [ɪˈmɜːdʒənsɪ] *n* (**a**) *(gen)* emergencia *f*; **in an e.** en caso de emergencia □ *US* **e. brake** freno *m* de mano; **e. exit** salida *f* de emergencia; *Av* **e. landing** aterrizaje *m* forzoso; **e. measures** medidas *fpl* de urgencia; *Aut* **e. stop** frenazo *m* en seco *Pol* **state of e.** estado *m* de excepción (**b**) *Med* urgencia *f*, caso *m* de urgencia □ *US Med* **e. room** sala *f* de urgencias

emergent [ɪˈmɜːdʒənt] *adj* emergente □ **e. nation** país *m* en vías de desarrollo

emeritus [ɪˈmerɪtəs] *adj* emérito(a)

emery [ˈemərɪ] *n* esmeril *m* □ **e. board** lima *f* de uñas

emetic [ɪˈmetɪk] **1** *adj* emético(a), vomitivo(a)
2 *n* emético *m*, vomitivo *m*

emigrant [ˈemɪgrənt] *n* emigrante *mf*

emigrate [ˈemɪgreɪt] *vi* emigrar

emigration [emɪˈgreɪʃən] *n* emigración *f*

émigré [ˈemɪgreɪ] *n* emigrado(a) *m,f*

eminence [ˈemɪnəns] *n* eminencia *f*; *Rel* **Your/His E.** Su Eminencia; *Fig* **grey e.** eminencia gris

eminent [ˈemɪnənt] *adj (distinguished)* eminente; *(outstanding)* destacado(a)

emirate [ˈemɪrɪt] *n* emirato *m*

emissary [ˈemɪsərɪ] *n* emisario(a) *m,f*

emission [ɪˈmɪʃən] *n* emisión *f*

emit [ɪˈmɪt] *vt (pt & pp emitted) (signal)* emitir; *(smell)* despedir; *(sound)* producir

emolument [ɪˈmɒljʊmənt] *n (gen pl)* emolumentos *mpl*, honorarios *mpl*

emoticon [ɪˈmɒtɪkɒn] *n Comptr* emoticono *m*

emotion [ɪˈməʊʃən] *n* emoción *f*

emotional [ɪˈməʊʃənəl] *adj* (**a**) *(concerning the emotions)* emocional, sensible (**b**) *(moving)* emotivo(a), conmovedor(a)

emotionalism [ɪˈməʊʃənəlɪzəm] *n* emotividad *f*, sentimentalismo *m*, sensiblería *f*

emotionally [ɪˈməʊʃənəlɪ] *adv* emotivamente; **to be e. involved with sb** tener una relación sentimental con algn; **e. deprived** privado(a) de cariño

emotive [ɪˈməʊtɪv] *adj* emotivo(a)

empathize [ˈempəθaɪz] *vi* identificarse (**with** con)

empathy [ˈempəθɪ] *n* empatía *f*

emperor [ˈempərər] *n* emperador *m*

emphasis [ˈemfəsɪs] *n (pl* **emphases** [ˈemfəsiːz])* énfasis *m*; **in this school the e. is on languages** en este colegio ponemos especial énfasis en los idiomas; **to put** *or* **place e. on sth** hacer hincapié en algo, subrayar algo, poner algo de relieve

emphasize [ˈemfəsaɪz] *vt (give importance to)* subrayar, hacer hincapié en; *(specify)* poner de relieve; *(insist)* insistir; *(highlight)* hacer resaltar; **I must e. that ...** debo insistir que ...; **the dress emphasizes her figure** el vestido realza su figura

emphatic [emˈfætɪk] *adj (forceful)* enfático(a), enérgico(a); *(convinced)* categórico(a); **e. denial** negación rotunda; **he was most e.** fue muy categórico

emphatically [emˈfætɪklɪ] *adv* enfáticamente, enérgicamente, categóricamente

emphysema [emfɪˈsiːmə] *n* enfisema *m*

empire [ˈempaɪər] *n* imperio *m*; **the British/Roman E.** el Imperio Británico/Romano

empirical [emˈpɪrɪkəl] *adj* empírico(a)

empiricism [emˈpɪrɪsɪzəm] *n* empirismo *m*

emplacement [ɪmˈpleɪsmənt] *n* emplazamiento *m*

employ [ɪmˈplɔɪ] **1** *vt* (**a**) *(worker)* emplear, contratar (**b**) *(make use of)* emplear, usar (**c**) *(time)* ocupar
2 *n* empleo *m*; **to be in the e. of sb** ser empleado de algn

employed [ɪmˈplɔɪd] *adj* empleado(a), con empleo

employee [emˈplɔɪiː, emplɔɪˈiː] *n* empleado(a) *m,f*

employer [ɪmˈplɔɪər] *n* empresario(a) *m,f*, patrón(ona) *m,f*

employment [ɪmˈplɔɪmənt] *n* empleo *m*, trabajo *m* □ **e. agency** agencia *f* de colocaciones; *Formerly* **e. exchange** bolsa *f* de trabajo; **full e.** pleno empleo *m*

emporium [emˈpɔːrɪəm] *n (pl* **emporia** [emˈpɔːrɪə])* gran almacén *m*, *Am* emporio *m*

empower [ɪmˈpaʊər] *vt* autorizar, habilitar

empowering [ɪmˈpaʊərɪŋ] *adj* emancipador(a); **an e. experience** una experiencia que hace sentir fuerte

empress [ˈemprɪs] *n* emperatriz *f*

emptiness [ˈemptɪnɪs] *n* vacío *m*

empty [ˈemptɪ] **1** *adj* (**emptier, emptiest**) vacío(a); **an e. house** una casa deshabitada; **an e. look** una mirada vacía; **to do sth on an e. stomach** hacer algo en ayunas *or* con el estómago vacío □ **e. promises** promesas *fpl* vanas
2 *vt* vaciar
3 *vi* (**a**) *(gen)* vaciarse (**b**) *(river)* desembocar (**into** en)
4 **empties** *npl* envases *mpl*, cascos *mpl*

empty-handed [emptɪˈhændɪd] *adj* con las manos vacías

empty-headed [emptɪˈhedɪd] *adj* (**a**) *(dim-witted)* tonto(a), cabeza hueca *or* de chorlito (**b**) *(frivolous)* frívolo(a)

emu [ˈiːmjuː] *n Orn* emú *m*

emulate [ˈemjʊleɪt] *vt* emular

emulation [emjʊˈleɪʃən] *n* emulación *f*

emulsification [ɪmʌlsɪfɪˈkeɪʃən] *n* emulsificación *f*

emulsify [ɪˈmʌlsɪfaɪ] *vt (pt & pp* **emulsified**)* emulsionar

emulsion [ɪˈmʌlʃən] *n* emulsión *f* □ **e. paint** pintura *f* mate

enable [ɪˈneɪbəl] *vt* (**a**) *(allow)* permitir (**b**) *Comptr (function)* ejecutar; *(device)* activar, hacer operativo(a)

enact [ɪˈnækt] *vt (play)* representar; *(law, scene)* promulgar

enamel [ɪˈnæməl] **1** *n* esmalte *m*
2 *vt (pt & pp* **enamelled**, *US* **enameled**)* esmaltar

enamoured, *US* **enamored** [ɪˈnæməd] *adj* enamorado(a); **to be e. of** *or* **by sth** encantarle algo a algn

encamp [ɪn'kæmp] *vt* acampar

encampment [ɪn'kæmpmənt] *n Mil* campamento *m*

encapsulate [ɪn'kæpsjʊleɪt] *vt* encapsular, encerrar

encase [ɪn'keɪs] *vt* encajonar, encerrar; **to be encased in** estar revestido(a) de

encephalitis [ensefə'laɪtɪs] *n Med* encefalitis *f*

enchant [ɪn'tʃɑːnt] *vt (gen)* encantar, cautivar; *(cast spell on)* hechizar

enchanter [ɪn'tʃɑːntər] *n* hechicero *m*

enchanting [ɪn'tʃɑːntɪŋ] *adj* encantador(a)

enchantment [ɪn'tʃɑːntmənt] *n* encanto *m*, hechizo *m*

enchantress [ɪn'tʃɑːntrɪs] *n* hechicera *f*

enchilada [entʃɪ'lɑːdə] *n US Fam* **the whole e.** *(everything)* todo, toda la pesca *or RP* la bola

encircle [ɪn'sɜːkəl] *vt* rodear, cercar

encl (a) *(abbr* **enclosure)** material *m* adjunto **(b)** *(abbr* **enclosed)** adjunto(a)

enclave ['enkleɪv] *n* enclave *m*

enclose [ɪn'kləʊz] *vt* **(a)** *(surround)* rodear, cercar **(b)** *(fence in)* encerrar; *Rel* **an enclosed order** una orden de clausura **(c)** *(in an envelope)* adjuntar; **enclosed herewith** adjunto a la presente; **please find enclosed** le enviamos adjunto *or* anexo; **the enclosed document** el documento adjunto

enclosure [ɪn'kləʊʒər] *n* **(a)** *(act)* cercamiento *m*, encierro *m* **(b)** *(fenced area)* cercado *m* **(c)** *(in an envelope)* documento *m* adjunto, anexo *m* **(d)** *(racecourse)* recinto *m*

encode [en'kəʊd] *vt* cifrar, codificar; *Comptr* codificar

encompass [ɪn'kʌmpəs] *vt* abarcar

encore ['ɒŋkɔːr] **1** *interj* ¡otra!, ¡bis!
2 *n* repetición *f*, bis *m*; **to give an e.** repetir, bisar

encounter [ɪn'kaʊntər] **1** *n (fight, meeting)* encuentro *m*
2 *vt (meet)* encontrar, encontrarse con; *(problems)* tropezar con

encourage [ɪn'kʌrɪdʒ] *vt* **(a)** *(urge)* animar **(b)** *(help to develop)* fomentar, favorecer

encouragement [ɪn'kʌrɪdʒmənt] *n* estímulo *m*, aliento *m*

encouraging [ɪn'kʌrɪdʒɪŋ] *adj (smile)* alentador(a); *(news)* prometedor(a), halagüeño(a)

encroach [ɪn'krəʊtʃ] *vt* **to e. on** *(territory)* invadir; *(rights)* usurpar, abusar; *(time, freedom)* quitar

encroachment [ɪn'krəʊtʃmənt] *n* invasión *f*, usurpación *f*

encrusted [ɪn'krʌstɪd] *adj* incrustado(a) **(with** de)

encumber [ɪn'kʌmbər] *vt (impede)* estorbar; *(debts)* gravar

encumbrance [ɪn'kʌmbrəns] *n* estorbo *m*; *Fin Jur* gravamen *m*

encyclical [ɪn'sɪklɪkəl] *n Rel* encíclica *f*

encyclop(a)edia [ensaɪkləʊ'piːdɪə] *n* enciclopedia *f*

encyclop(a)edic [ensaɪkləʊ'piːdɪk] *adj* enciclopédico(a)

end [end] **1** *n* **(a)** *(of stick)* punta *f*; *(of street)* final *m*; *(of table)* extremo *m*; *Fig* **to jump in at the deep e.** meterse de cabeza; *Fig* **to make ends meet** llegar a final de mes; *Fig* **to make sb's hair stand on e.** ponerle a algn los pelos de punta; *Fam* **to get the wrong e. of the stick** tomar el rábano de las hojas, *RP* agarrar para el lado de los tomates **(b)** *(conclusion)* fin *m*, final *m*; **in the e.** al final; **for hours/weeks on e.** hora/semana tras hora/semana; **no e. of problems** un sinfín de problemas, cantidad de problemas; **there's no e. to it** esto no se acaba nunca; **that's the e.!** ¡es el colmo!; **to bring an e. to sth** poner fin a algo, acabar con

algo; **to draw to an e.** acabarse; **to put an e. to** acabar con; *Fig* **the e. of the line** *or* **road** el acabóse; *Fig* **to the bitter e.** hasta el último suspiro ❑ *Com Comptr* **e. user** usuario(a) *m,f* final **(c)** *(aim)* objetivo *m*, fin *m*; **to achieve one's e.** alcanzar su objetivo; **to no e.** en vano; **the e. justifies the means** el fin justifica los medios ❑ **e. product** producto *m* final; **loose ends** cabos *mpl* sueltos **(d)** *(remnants)* resto *m*, cabo *m*
2 *vt* acabar, terminar, concluir; *Fam* **to e. it all** suicidarse
3 *vi* acabarse, terminarse; **at what time does the film e.?** ¿a qué hora (se) termina la película?

▸ **end up** *vi* terminar, acabar; **he'll e. up with no money** acabará sin dinero; **it ended up in the dustbin** fue a parar en el cubo de la basura; **to e. up doing sth** terminar por hacer algo

endanger [ɪn'deɪndʒər] *vt* poner en peligro

endangered [ɪn'deɪndʒəd] *adj Zool* en peligro; **e. species** especie *f* en peligro (de extinción)

endear [ɪn'dɪər] *vt* **to e. oneself to sb** hacerse querer por algn; **her outspokenness did not e. her to her boss** su franqueza no le ganó el favor del jefe

endearing [ɪn'dɪərɪŋ] *adj* simpático(a), atractivo(a)

endearment [ɪn'dɪəmənt] *n* palabra *f* or frase *f* cariñosa

endeavour, *US* **endeavor** [ɪn'devər] **1** *n* esfuerzo *m*, empeño *m*
2 *vt* intentar, procurar; **to e. to do sth** procurar hacer algo

endemic [en'demɪk] *adj* endémico(a)

ending ['endɪŋ] *n* final *m*

endive ['endaɪv] *n Bot* **(a)** *esp US (chicory)* endibia *f* **(b)** *(like lettuce)* escarola *f*

endless ['endlɪs] *adj (wait etc)* interminable, eterno(a), sin fin; *(resources)* inagotable

endocrine ['endəʊkrɪn] *adj* endocrino(a) ❑ **e. gland** glándula *f* endocrina

endocrinologist [endəʊkrɪ'nɒlədʒɪst] *n* endocrinólogo(a) *m,f*

endocrinology [endəʊkrɪ'nɒlədʒɪ] *n* endocrinología *f*

endorphin [en'dɔːfɪn] *n* endorfina *f*

endorse [ɪn'dɔːs] *vt* **(a)** *Fin* endosar **(b)** *(approve)* aprobar; *(support)* apoyar

endorsement [ɪn'dɔːsmənt] *n* **(a)** *Fin* endoso *m* **(b)** *Br Aut* infracción *f* anotada **(c)** *(approval)* aprobación *f*; *(support)* respaldo *m*, apoyo *m*

endow [ɪn'daʊ] *vt* dotar; **to be endowed with** estar dotado(a) de

endowment [ɪn'daʊmənt] *n (donation)* donación *f* ❑ *Ins* **e. policy** póliza *f* diferida

endpaper ['endpeɪpər] *n Print* guarda *f*

endurable [ɪn'djuːərəbəl] *adj* soportable

endurance [ɪn'djuərəns] *n* resistencia *f* ❑ **e. test** prueba *f* de resistencia

endure [ɪn'djuər] **1** *vt (bear)* aguantar, soportar
2 *vi (last)* durar, perdurar

enduring [ɪn'djuərɪŋ] *adj* duradero(a)

enema ['enɪmə] *n Med* enema *m*

enemy ['enəmɪ] *adj & n* enemigo(a) *(m,f)*; **to make enemies** hacerse enemigos ❑ *Mil* **e. forces** fuerzas *fpl* enemigas

energetic [enə'dʒetɪk] *adj* enérgico(a)

energetically [enə'dʒetɪklɪ] *adv* enérgicamente

energize ['enədʒaɪz] *vt (invigorate)* dar energías a

energy ['enədʒɪ] *n* energía *f*; **to save e.** ahorrar energía ❑ **e. crisis** crisis *f* energética

energy-saving ['enədʒɪseɪvɪŋ] *adj* que ahorra energía

enervate ['enəveɪt] *vt* enervar, debilitar

enervating ['enəveɪtɪŋ] *adj* enervador(a), enervante

enfeeble [ɪn'fiːbəl] *vt* debilitar, enervar

enfold [ɪn'fəʊld] *vt* envolver

enforce [ɪn'fɔːs] *vt (law)* hacer cumplir; *(compel)* imponer; *(argument)* reforzar, enfatizar

enforcement [ɪn'fɔːsmənt] *n* aplicación *f*

enfranchise [ɪn'fræntʃaɪz] *vt* Pol conceder el derecho de votar a; *(slave)* liberar

engage [ɪn'geɪdʒ] *vt* (a) *(hire)* contratar (b) *(attention)* atraer, llamar; **to engage sb in conversation** entablar conversación con algn (c) *Tech* engranar; *Aut* **to e. the clutch** embragar

engaged [ɪn'geɪdʒd] *adj* (a) *(to be married)* prometido(a); **to get e.** prometerse (b) *Br (busy)* ocupado(a); *Tel* **it's e.** está ocupado *or Esp* comunicando

engagement [ɪn'geɪdʒmənt] *n* (a) *(to be married)* petición *f* de mano; *(period)* noviazgo *m* ❑ **e. ring** anillo *m* de compromiso (b) *(business appointment)* cita *f*; **prior e.** cita *f* previa (c) *Mil* combate *m*

engaging [ɪn'geɪdʒɪŋ] *adj* simpático(a), atractivo(a), agradable

engender [ɪn'dʒendər] *vt* engendrar

engine ['endʒɪn] *n* (a) *(combustion)* motor *m* ❑ **e. room** sala *f* de máquinas; **steam e.** máquina *f* de vapor (b) *Rail* locomotora *f* ❑ *Br* **e. driver** maquinista *mf*; **fire e.** coche *m* de bomberos

engineer [endʒɪ'nɪər] **1** *n* (a) *(in general)* ingeniero(a) *m,f* ❑ **civil e.** ingeniero(a) *m,f* de caminos; **chemical e.** ingeniero *m,f* químico(a) (b) *US Rail* maquinista *mf*
2 *vt* Fig *(contrive)* maquinar, tramar

engineering [endʒɪ'nɪərɪŋ] *n* ingeniería *f* ❑ **electrical e.** electrotecnia *f*; **civil e.** ingeniería *f* civil

England ['ɪŋglənd] *n* Inglaterra

English ['ɪŋglɪʃ] **1** *adj* inglés(esa)
2 *n* (a) *(language)* inglés *m* (b) *pl* **the E.** los ingleses

Englishman ['ɪŋglɪʃmən] *n (pl* **Englishmen)** inglés *m*

English-speaking ['ɪŋglɪʃspiːkɪŋ] *adj* de habla inglesa

Englishwoman ['ɪŋglɪʃwʊmən] *n (pl* **Englishwomen** ['ɪŋglɪʃwɪmɪn]) inglesa *f*

engorged [ɪn'gɔːdʒd] *adj* Med congestionado(a)

engrave [ɪn'greɪv] *vt* grabar

engraver [ɪn'greɪvər] *n* grabador(a) *m,f*

engraving [ɪn'greɪvɪŋ] *n* (a) *(art)* grabación *f* (b) *(picture, plate)* grabado *m*

engrossed [ɪn'grəʊst] *adj* absorto(a) **(in** en)

engrossing [ɪn'grəʊsɪŋ] *adj* fascinante, apasionante

engulf [ɪn'gʌlf] *vt* tragarse, sumergir, hundir

engulfed [ɪn'gʌlft] *adj* hundido(a) **(in** en)

enhance [ɪn'hɑːns] *vt (beauty)* realzar; *(power)* aumentar; *(chances)* mejorar

enigma [ɪ'nɪgmə] *n* enigma *m*

enigmatic [enɪg'mætɪk] *adj* enigmático(a)

enjoy [ɪn'dʒɔɪ] **1** *vt* (a) *(take pleasure in)* disfrutar de; **did you e. the film?** ¿te gustó la película?; **to e. oneself** pasarlo bien, divertirse (b) *(benefit from)* gozar de; **to e. good health** gozar de buena salud
2 *vi* US **e.!** ¡qué lo pases bien!

enjoyable [ɪn'dʒɔɪəbəl] *adj* agradable, divertido(a)

enjoyment [ɪn'dʒɔɪmənt] *n* placer *m*, gusto *m*; **to spoil sb's e.** quitarle el gusto a algn

enlarge [ɪn'lɑːdʒ] **1** *vt* extender, ampliar; *Phot* ampliar
2 *vi* ampliarse; **to e. upon a subject** extenderse sobre un tema

enlargement [ɪn'lɑːdʒmənt] *n* Phot ampliación *f*

enlarger [ɪn'lɑːdʒər] *n* Phot ampliadora *f*

enlighten [ɪn'laɪtən] *vt* iluminar; **to e. sb on sth** aclararle algo a algn

enlightened [ɪn'laɪtənd] *adj* (a) *(learned)* culto(a); *(informed)* bien informado(a) (b) Hist ilustrado(a); **e. despotism** despotismo ilustrado

enlightenment [ɪn'laɪtənmənt] *n* aclaración *f*; **the Age of E.** el Siglo de las Luces

enlist [ɪn'lɪst] **1** *vt* Mil reclutar; **to e. sb's help** conseguir ayuda de algn
2 *vi* Mil alistarse

enlisted [ɪn'lɪstɪd] *adj* alistado(a); US **e. man** soldado raso, soldado de tropa

enliven [ɪn'laɪvən] *vt* animar, avivar

en masse [ɒn'mæs] *adv* en masa

enmesh [ɪn'meʃ] *vt* enredar

enmity ['enmɪtɪ] *n* enemistad *f*, hostilidad *f*

enormity [ɪ'nɔːmɪtɪ] *n* (a) *(hugeness)* enormidad *f*, inmensidad *f* (b) *(atrocity)* atrocidad *f*, monstruosidad *f*

enormous [ɪ'nɔːməs] *adj* enorme, inmenso(a), descomunal

enormously [ɪ'nɔːməslɪ] *adv* enormemente; **I enjoyed myself e.** lo pasé genial

enough [ɪ'nʌf] **1** *adj* bastante, suficiente; **e. books** bastantes libros; **e. money** bastante dinero; **have we got e. gas?** ¿tenemos suficiente gasolina?
2 *adv* bastante; **fair e.** de acuerdo; **large e.** bastante grande; **oddly** *or* **curiously e. ...** lo curioso es que ...; **sure e.** en efecto, sin duda alguna
3 *n* lo bastante, lo suficiente; **e. to live on** lo suficiente para vivir; **it isn't e.** no basta; **more than e.** más que suficiente; *Fam* **e. is e.** ya está, ¡basta!; *Fam* **I've had e.!** estoy harto!

en passant [ɒnpæ'sɒn] *adv* de paso

enquire [ɪn'kwaɪər] *vi (information)* preguntar; *Jur* **to e. into a case** investigar un caso

enquiry [ɪn'kwaɪərɪ] *n* (a) *(question)* pregunta *f*; **enquiries** información *f*; **to make an e.** preguntar (b) *(investigation)* investigación *f*; **they conducted an e. into the affair** investigaron el asunto

enrage [ɪn'reɪdʒ] *vt* enfurecer

enraptured [ɪn'ræptʃəd] *adj* embelesado(a); **to be e.** estar embelesado(a)

enrich [ɪn'rɪtʃ] *vt* enriquecer; **enriched with vitamin C** enriquecido(a) con vitamina C

enriching [ɪn'rɪtʃɪŋ] *adj* enriquecedor(a)

enrol, *US* **enroll** [ɪn'rəʊl] *(pt & pp* **enrolled) 1** *vt* matricular
2 *vi* matricularse, inscribirse, apuntarse

enrolment, *US* **enrollment** [ɪn'rəʊlmənt] *n* matrícula *f*

en route [ɒn'ruːt] *adv* en *or* por el camino; **en r. to Soria** camino de Soria

ensconce [ɪn'skɒns] *vt* **to e. oneself** aposentarse

ensemble [ɒn'sɒmbəl] *n* Mus conjunto *m*

enshrine [ɪn'ʃraɪn] *vt* Fig conservar religiosamente

ensign ['ensaɪn] *n* (a) *(flag)* bandera *f*, pabellón *m* (b) *US (naval officer)* alférez *m* de fragata

enslave [ɪn'sleɪv] *vt* esclavizar

enslavement [ɪn'sleɪvmənt] *n* esclavitud *f*

ensnare [ɪn'sneər] *vt (animal, criminal)* capturar

ensue [ɪn'sjuː] *vi* (a) *(follow)* seguir (b) *(result)* resultar **(from** de)

ensuing [ɪnˈsjuːɪŋ] *adj* consiguiente, subsiguiente

en suite [ˈɒnˈswiːt] *n* **with an e. bathroom, with bathroom e.** con cuarto de baño privado

ensure [ɪnˈʃʊər] *vt* asegurar

entail [ɪnˈteɪl] *vt* (**a**) *(give rise to)* ocasionar, acarrear (**b**) *(involve)* suponer, implicar (**c**) *Jur* vincular

entangle [ɪnˈtæŋɡəl] *vt* *(general)* enredar; **he became entangled in the net** se enredó en la red; *Fig* **to get entangled in sth** enredarse en algo; *Fig* **they became entangled in political affairs** se vieron involucrados en asuntos políticos

entanglement [ɪnˈtæŋɡəlmənt] *n* enredo *m*; *Fig* complicación *f*

enter [ˈentər] **1** *vt* (**a**) *(go into)* entrar en; *Fig* *(join)* ingresar en, hacerse socio de (**b**) *(write down)* apuntar, anotar, dar entrada a (**c**) *(register)* inscribir; **to e. a car for a race** inscribir un coche en una carrera; **to e. one's name for a course** matricularse en un curso (**d**) *Comptr* dar entrada a
  2 *vi* entrar; **to e. for a race** tomar parte en *or* participar en una carrera

enter into *vt* (**a**) *(agreement)* concertar, firmar; *(negotiations)* iniciar (**with** con); *(bargain)* cerrar (**b**) *(relations)* establecer (**with** con); *(marriage)* contraer (**with** con) (**c**) *(conversation)* entablar (**with** con)

enterprise [ˈentəpraɪz] *n* empresa *f*; **a dangerous e.** una empresa peligrosa; **a man of e.** un hombre de empresa ❑ **free e.** libre empresa *f*; **private e.** la empresa *or* iniciativa privada; **public e.** el sector público

enterprising [ˈentəpraɪzɪŋ] *adj* emprendedor(a)

entertain [entəˈteɪn] **1** *vt* (**a**) *(amuse)* divertir (**b**) *(consider)* considerar; **to e. an idea** abrigar una idea; **to e. a proposal** estudiar una propuesta; **to e. the hope that ...** abrigar la esperanza que ...
  2 *vi* tener invitados; **they e. a lot** invitan con mucha frecuencia

entertainer [entəˈteɪnər] *n* (**a**) *(gen)* animador(a) *m,f* (**b**) *Theat* artista *mf*

entertaining [entəˈteɪnɪŋ] **1** *adj* divertido(a), entretenido(a)
  2 *n* **the secretary has to do a lot of e.** la secretaria tiene que hacer muchas relaciones publicas

entertainment [entəˈteɪnmənt] *n* (**a**) *(gen)* diversión *f*, entretenimiento *m* ❑ **e. allowance** gastos *mpl* de representación (**b**) *Theat* espectáculo *m*

enthral, *US* **enthrall** [ɪnˈθrɔːl] *vt* (*pt & pp* **enthralled**) cautivar

enthralling [ɪnˈθrɔːlɪŋ] *adj* cautivador(a), fascinante

enthrone [ɪnˈθrəʊn] *vt* entronizar

enthronement [ɪnˈθrəʊnmənt] *n* entronización *f*

enthuse [ɪnˈθjuːz] **1** *vi* entusiasmarse (**over** por)
  2 *vt* estimular, animar

enthusiasm [ɪnˈθjuːzɪæzəm] *n* entusiasmo *m*

enthusiast [ɪnˈθjuːzɪæst] *n* entusiasta *mf*, apasionado(a) *m,f*; **she's a real opera e.** es una entusiasta de la ópera

enthusiastic [ɪnθjuːzɪˈæstɪk] *adj* (**a**) *(person)* entusiasta; **to be e. about sth** entusiasmarse por algo (**b**) *(praise)* entusiástico(a), caluroso(a); **an e. welcome** un recibimiento caluroso

enthusiastically [ɪnθjuːzɪˈæstɪklɪ] *adv* con entusiasmo, entusiasmado(a)

entice [ɪnˈtaɪs] *vt* seducir, atraer

enticing [ɪnˈtaɪsɪŋ] *adj* atractivo(a), tentador(a)

entire [ɪnˈtaɪər] *adj* entero(a), todo(a); **it wasn't an e. success** no fue un éxito absoluto; **the e. community** la comunidad entera; **the e. population** toda la población

entirely [ɪnˈtaɪəlɪ] *adv* (**a**) *(completely)* enteramente, totalmente; **I e. agree** estoy totalmente de acuerdo (**b**) *(solely)* únicamente, exclusivamente; **the group was made up e. of Germans** el grupo estaba formado exclusivamente de alemanes

entirety [ɪnˈtaɪərɪtɪ] *n* totalidad *f*; **in its e.** en su totalidad

entitle [ɪnˈtaɪtəl] *vt* (**a**) *(allow)* dar derecho a; **it will e. you to travel free** le dará derecho a viajar gratis; **to be entitled to** tener derecho a (**b**) *(book etc)* titular; **the film was entitled ...** la película se titulaba ...

entitlement [ɪnˈtaɪtəlmənt] *n* derecho *m*

entity [ˈentɪtɪ] *n* entidad *f*

entomologist [entəˈmɒlədʒɪst] *n* entomólogo(a) *m,f*

entomology [entəˈmɒlədʒɪ] *n* entomología *f*

entourage [ɒntʊˈrɑːʒ] *n* séquito *m*

entrails [ˈentreɪlz] *npl Anat* tripas *fpl*; *Fig* entrañas *fpl*

entrance¹ [ˈentrəns] *n* (**a**) *(act of entering)* entrada *f*; *Theat* entrada *f* en escena, aparición *f*; **to make one's e.** entrar en escena ❑ **e. fee** *(museum etc)* entrada *f*; *(organization)* cuota *f*, inscripción *f* (**b**) *(door)* entrada *f*, puerta *f* ❑ **e. hall** vestíbulo *m*; **main e.** puerta *f* principal (**c**) *(admission)* admisión *f*, ingreso *m* ❑ **e. examination** examen *m* de ingreso

entrance² [ɪnˈtrɑːns] *vt* arrebatar, extasiar, encantar

entranced [ɪnˈtrɑːnst] *adj* *(delighted)* encantado(a); *(ecstatic)* extasiado(a)

entrancing [ɪnˈtrɑːnsɪŋ] *adj* fascinante, encantador(a)

entrant [ˈentrənt] *n* *(competition)* participante *mf*; *(applicant)* aspirante *mf*

entrapment [ɪnˈtræpmənt] *n Jur* incitación *f* al delito

entreat [ɪnˈtriːt] *vt Fml* suplicar, rogar; **I entreated them not to do it** les rogué que no lo hicieran

entreaty [ɪnˈtriːtɪ] *n* súplica *f*, ruego *m*

entrée [ˈɒntreɪ] *n Culin* (**a**) *Br (first course)* entrada *f* (**b**) *US (main course)* plato *m* principal

entrench [ɪnˈtrentʃ] *vt Fig* reafirmar, consolidar

entrenched [ɪnˈtrentʃt] *adj* firmemente enraizado(a)

entrepreneur [ɒntrəprəˈnɜːr] *n* (**a**) *(business person)* empresario(a) *m,f* (**b**) *(middle person)* intermediario(a) *m,f*

entrepreneurial [ɒntrəprəˈnɜːrɪəl] *adj* empresarial

entropy [ˈentrəpɪ] *n* entropía *f*

entrust [ɪnˈtrʌst] *vt* encargar (**with** de); **to e. sth to sb** dejar algo al cuidado de algn

entry [ˈentrɪ] *n* (**a**) *(entrance)* entrada *f* ❑ *Jur* **forcible e.** allanamiento *m* de morada; *Aut* **no e.** dirección *f* prohibida (**b**) *(in dictionary)* entrada *f*, artículo *m* (**c**) *(competition)* participante *mf* ❑ **e. fee** *(museum etc)* entrada *f*; *(organization)* cuota *f*, inscripción *f*

entwine [ɪnˈtwaɪn] **1** *vt* entrelazar; **to become entwined** entrelazarse, enredarse
  2 *vi* entrelazarse, enredarse

enumerate [ɪˈnjuːməreɪt] *vt* enumerar

enumeration [ɪnjuːməˈreɪʃən] *n* enumeración *f*

enunciate [ɪˈnʌnsɪeɪt] *vt Ling* pronunciar, articular

envelop [ɪnˈveləp] *vt* envolver

envelope [ˈenvələʊp] *n* (**a**) *(letters)* sobre *m*; *(cover)* funda *f*; **airmail e.** sobre de avión (**b**) *Av* envoltura *f*

enviable [ˈenvɪəbəl] *adj* envidiable

envious [ˈenvɪəs] *adj* envidioso(a); **to feel e.** tener envidia

enviously [ˈenvɪəslɪ] *adv* con envidia, envidiosamente

environment [ɪnˈvaɪərənmənt] *n* *(natural surroundings)* medio ambiente *m*; *(atmosphere)* ambiente *m*; **in a work e.** en un entorno laboral

environmental [ɪnvaɪərən'mentəl] *adj Ecol* del medio ambiente, ambiental; *Fig* contextual ❏ **e. disaster** catástrofe *f* ecológica; **e. pollution** contaminación *f* del medio ambiente

environmentalist [ɪnvaɪrən'mentəlɪst] *n* ecologista *mf*

environmentally [ɪnvaɪrən'mentəlɪ] *adv* ecológicamente, desde el punto de vista ecológico; **e. friendly** ecológico(a), que no daña el medio ambiente

environs [ɪn'vaɪrənz] *npl* alrededores *mpl*

envisage [ɪn'vɪzɪdʒ] *vt* **(a)** *(imagine)* imaginar **(b)** *(foresee)* prever; **I don't e. going before Christmas** no pienso ir antes de Navidad

envision [ɪn'vɪʒən] *vt* imaginar

envoy ['envɔɪ] *n* enviado(a) *m,f*; **special e.** enviado especial

envy ['envɪ] **1** *n* envidia *f*; **to be green with e.** estar corroido(a) por la envidia; **to be the envy of** ser la envidia de
2 *vt* envidiar, tener envidia de

enzyme ['enzaɪm] *n Biol* enzima *m*

eon ['iːən] *n US* eón *m*, eternidad *f*

EPA [iːpiː'eɪ] *n (abbr* **Environmental Protection Agency)** = agencia gubernamental estadounidense encargada de la protección medioambiental

epaulette, *US* **epaulet** ['epəlét] *n Mil* charretera *f*, hombrera *f*

ephemeral [ɪ'femərəl] *adj* efímero(a)

epic ['epɪk] **1** *n* epopeya *f*
2 *adj* épico(a); **it reached e. proportions** alcanzó dimensiones colosales

epicentre, *US* **epicenter** ['episentər] *n* epicentro *m*

epicure ['epɪkjʊər] *n Fml* gastrónomo(a) *m,f*

epicurean [epɪkjʊ'riːən] *adj & n Fml* epicúreo(a) *(m,f)*

epidemic [epɪ'demɪk] **1** *n Med* epidemia *f*; *Fig (wave)* ola *f*
2 *adj* epidémico(a)

epidermis [epɪ'dɜːmɪs] *n* epidermis *f*

epidural [epɪ'djuːrəl] *n Med* (anestesia *f*) epidural *f*

epiglottis [epɪ'glɒtɪs] *n Anat* epiglotis *f*

epigram ['epɪgræm] *n Lit* epigrama *m*

epigraph ['epɪgrɑːf] *n* epígrafe *m*

epilepsy ['epɪlepsɪ] *n Med* epilepsia *f*

epileptic [epɪ'leptɪk] *adj & n Med* epiléptico(a) *(m,f)*

epilogue, *US* **epilog** ['epɪlɒg] *n* epílogo *m*

Epiphany [ɪ'pɪfənɪ] *n Rel* Epifanía *f*, Día *m* de Reyes

episcopal [ɪ'pɪskəpəl] *adj* episcopal

episcopalian [ɪpɪskə'peɪliən] *adj & n* episcopaliano(a) *(m,f)*

episode ['epɪsəʊd] *n* episodio *m*; *TV* capítulo *m*

episodic [epɪ'sɒdɪk] *adj* episódico(a)

epistle [ɪ'pɪsəl] *n* epístola *f*; *Rel* **the E. to the Ephesians** la Epístola a los Efesios

epitaph ['epɪtɑːf] *n* epitafio *m*

epithet ['epɪθet] *n Ling* epíteto *m*

epitome [ɪ'pɪtəmɪ] *n Fml* personificación *f*; **she was the e. of generosity** era la personificación de la generosidad

epitomize [ɪ'pɪtəmaɪz] *vt Fml* personificar, ejemplificar

epoch ['iːpɒk] *n* época *f*

epoch-making ['iːpɒkmeɪkɪŋ] *adj* histórico(a)

equable ['ekwəbəl] *adj* **(a)** *(person)* ecuánime **(b)** *(climate)* uniforme, regular

equal ['iːkwəl] **1** *adj* igual; **of e. value** de igual valor; **other things being e.** si todo sigue igual; **she doesn't feel e. to going to the party** no se siente con fuerzas para ir a

la fiesta; **to be e. to the occasion** estar a la altura de las circunstancias; **with e. indifference** con la misma indiferencia ❏ **e. distance** equidistancia *f*; **e. opportunities employer** empresa *f* que contrata sin ningún tipo de discriminación; **e. pay** igualdad *f* de salarios; **e. rights** igualdad *f* de derechos
2 *n* igual *mf*; **to treat sb as an e.** tratar a algn de igual a igual
3 *vt (pt & pp* **equalled,** *US* **equaled) (a)** *Math* ser igual a, equivaler; **three and two equals five** tres más dos son cinco ❏ **equals sign** signo *m* igual **(b)** *(match)* igualar; **very few people can e. him at diplomacy** muy pocos le igualan en la diplomacia

equality [iː'kwɒlɪtɪ] *n* igualdad *f*

equalize ['iːkwəlaɪz] **1** *vi Ftb* igualar, empatar
2 *vt* igualar

equalizer ['iːkwəlaɪzər] *n Ftb* gol *m* del empate, igualada *f*

equally ['iːkwəlɪ] *adv* igualmente; **e. pretty** igual de bonito(a); **to share sth e.** dividir algo en partes iguales

equanimity [ekwə'nɪmɪtɪ] *n* ecuanimidad *f*

equate [ɪ'kweɪt] *vt* equiparar, comparar **(to** a, con)

equation [ɪ'kweɪʒən, ɪ'kweɪʃən] *n Math* ecuación *f*; **simple e.** ecuación de primer grado

equator [ɪ'kweɪtər] *n Geog* ecuador *m*

equatorial [ekwə'tɔːrɪəl] *adj* ecuatorial

equerry ['ekwərɪ] *n* caballerizo *m* de la casa real

equestrian [ɪ'kwestrɪən] **1** *adj* ecuestre
2 *n (man)* jinete *m*; *(woman)* amazona *f*

equidistant [iːkwɪ'dɪstənt] *adj* equidistante

equilateral [iːkwɪ'lætərəl] *adj* equilátero(a) ❏ **e. triangle** triángulo *m* equilátero

equilibrium [iːkwɪ'lɪbrɪəm] *n* equilibrio *m*

equine ['ekwaɪn] *adj* equino(a)

equinox ['iːkwɪnɒks] *n Astron* equinoccio *m* ❏ **autumnal e.** equinoccio *m* de otoño; **vernal e.** equinoccio *m* de primavera

equip [ɪ'kwɪp] *vt (pt & pp* **equipped)** *(supply)* equipar **(with** con); *(person)* proveer **(with** de)

equipment [ɪ'kwɪpmənt] *n (materials)* equipo *m*; *(act of equipping)* aprovisionamiento *m*, equipamiento *m* ❏ **e. allowance** gastos *mpl* de equipamiento; **office e.** material *m* de oficina

equipped [ɪ'kwɪpt] *adj* **to be e. with** *(machine)* estar dotado(a) de; *(person)* estar provisto(a) de; **he was ill e. to deal with them** no estaba preparado para enfrentarse con ellos

equitable ['ekwɪtəbəl] *adj* equitativo(a)

equities ['ekwɪtɪz] *npl Fin* acciones *fpl* ordinarias

equity ['ekwɪtɪ] *n* **(a)** *(general)* equidad *f* **(b)** *Br* **E.** = sindicato de actores

equivalence [ɪ'kwɪvələns] *n* equivalencia *f*

equivalent [ɪ'kwɪvələnt] **1** *adj* equivalente; **to be e. to** equivaler a, ser equivalente a
2 *n* equivalencia *f*

equivocal [ɪ'kwɪvəkəl] *adj* equívoco(a)

equivocation [ɪkwɪvə'keɪʃən] *n* evasivas *fpl*, ambigüedades *fpl*

ER [iː'ɑːr] *n* **(a)** *US Med (abbr* **Emergency Room)** (sala *f* de) urgencias *fpl* **(b)** *Br (abbr* **Elizabeth Regina)** = emblema de la reina Isabel

era ['ɪərə] *n* era *f*

eradicate [ɪ'rædɪkeɪt] *vt (eliminate)* erradicar; *(take out)* extirpar; *(uproot)* desarraigar

eradication [ɪrædɪ'kaɪʃən] n extirpación f, destrucción f, aniquilación f

erase [Br ɪ'reɪz, US ɪ'reɪs] vt borrar

eraser [Br ɪ'reɪzər, US ɪ'reɪsər] n goma f de borrar

erasure [ɪ'reɪʒə] n Fml borradura f

erect [ɪ'rekt] **1** adj (a) (upright) erguido(a), derecho(a); **to hold one's head e.** levantar la cabeza (b) (penis) erecto(a) **2** vt (monument) levantar, eregir

erection [ɪ'rekʃən] n (a) (building) construcción f (b) (penis) erección f

ergonomic [i:gə'nɒmɪk] adj ergonómico(a)

ergonomically [ɜːgə'nɒmɪklɪ] adv ergonómicamente; **e. designed** con diseño ergonómico

ergonomics [ɜːgəʊ'nɒmɪks] n ergonomía f

Eritrea [erɪ'treɪə] n Eritrea

Eritrean [erɪ'treɪən] adj & n eritreo(a) (m,f)

ermine ['ɜːmɪn] n armiño m

erode [ɪ'rəʊd] vt (a) Geol (rock, soil) erosionar (b) (metal) corroer, desgastar; Fig (power) desgastar; (confidence) minar

erogenous [ɪ'rɒdʒɪnəs] adj erógeno(a) □ **e. zones** zonas fpl erógenas

erosion [ɪ'rəʊʒən] n (a) Geol erosión f (b) (metal) corrosión f, desgaste m; Fig desgaste f

erotic [ɪ'rɒtɪk] adj erótico(a)

erotica [ɪ'rɒtɪkə] npl obras fpl eróticas

eroticism [ɪ'rɒtɪsɪzəm] n erotismo m

err [ɜːr] vi errar; **to e. on the side of caution** pecar de prudente

errand ['erənd] n recado m, Am mandado m; **to run an e.** hacer un recado □ **e. boy** recadero m

errata [ɪ'rɑːtə] npl Typ fe f sing de erratas; see **erratum**

erratic [ɪ'rætɪk] **1** adj (a) (performance, behaviour) irregular; (weather) muy variable (b) (person) caprichoso(a) **2** n Geol errático m

erratically [ɪ'rætɪklɪ] adv de manera irregular

erratum [ɪ'rɑːtəm] n (pl **errata**) Typ errata f

erroneous [ɪ'rəʊnɪəs] adj erróneo(a), equivocado(a)

error ['erər] n error m, equivocación f; **he saw the e. of his ways** reconoció sus errores; **in e.** por error; Comptr **e. message** mensaje m de error; **typing e.** falta de mecanografía

error-free ['erəfriː] adj sin error

ersatz ['ɜːzæts] adj sucedáneo(a)

Erse [ɜːs] n gaélico m irlandés

erstwhile ['ɜːstwaɪl] **1** adj antiguo(a) **2** adv Literary antiguamente

eruct [ɪ'rʌt] vi eructar

erudite ['erʊdaɪt] adj & n erudito(a) (m,f)

erudition [erʊ'dɪʃən] n erudición f

erupt [ɪ'rʌpt] vi (a) (volcano) entrar en erupción; (sudden movement) irrumpir; (violence) estallar; **to e. in anger** montar en cólera (b) Med (rash) brotar; (tooth) salir

eruption [ɪ'rʌpʃən] n (a) (volcano) erupción f; (violence) estallido m, explosión f (b) Med erupción f

escalate ['eskəleɪt] **1** vt (a) (war) agravar, intensificar (b) (prices) aumentar **2** vi (a) (war) agravarse, intensificarse (b) (prices) aumentarse (c) (change) convertirse (**into** en)

escalation [eskə'leɪʃən] n (a) (of war) agravación f, intensificación f, escalada f (b) (of prices) subida f, aumento m

escalator ['eskəleɪtər] n escalera f mecánica

escalope ['eskɒlɒp] n Culin escalopa f, escalope m

escapade ['eskəpeɪd] n aventura f

escape [ɪs'keɪp] **1** n (a) (of person) huida f, evasión f; (of prisoner) fuga f, evasión f; **to make one's e.** escapárse; Fam **to have a narrow e.** salvarse por los pelos □ Jur **e. clause** cláusula f de excepción; Av Naut **e. hatch** escotilla f de salvamento; Comptr **e. key** tecla f de escape; **e. route** vía f de escape; **fire e.** escalera f de incendios (b) (of gas, fluid) fuga f, escape m □ **e. valve** válvula f de escape **2** vi (person, gas, fluid) escaparse (**from** de) **3** vt (a) (avoid) evitar, huir de; **he narrowly escaped being hit** se libró del golpe por poco; **to e. punishment** librarse del castigo (b) Fig (elude) **her name escapes me** ahora mismo no recuerdo su nombre; **it escaped my notice** me pasó desapercibido; **nothing escapes him** no se le escapa una

escapee [ɪskeɪ'piː] n fugitivo(a) m,f

escapism [ɪ'skeɪpɪzəm] n evasión f; **this novel is pure e.** esta novela es pura evasión

escapist [ɪ'skeɪpɪst] **1** adj de evasión, evasionista **2** n soñador(a) m,f, escapista mf

escapologist [eskə'pɒlədʒɪst] n escapista mf

escarpment [ɪ'skɑːpmənt] n (fortress) escarpa f; (slope) escarpadura f, escarpa f

eschew [ɪs'tʃuː] vt evitar, abstenerse de

escort ['eskɔːt] **1** n (a) (companion) acompañante mf (b) (military, police) escolta f; **under police e.** escoltado(a) por la policía **2** [ɪs'kɔːt] vt (a) (accompany) acompañar; **to e. sb home** acompañar a algn a casa (b) (protect) escoltar

Eskimo ['eskɪməʊ] adj & n (pl **Eskimos** or **Eskimo**) esquimal (mf)

ESL [iːes'el] n (abbr **English as a Second Language**) = inglés como segunda lengua

esophagus [iː'sɒfəgəs] n (pl **esophagi** [iː'sɒfədʒaɪ] US Anat esófago m

esoteric [esəʊ'terɪk] adj esotérico(a)

ESP [iːes'piː] n (a) (abbr **extrasensory perception**) percepción f extrasensorial (b) (abbr **English for Specific Purposes**) (cursos mpl de) inglés m especializado

espadrille [espə'drɪl] n alpargata f

espagnolette [espænjə'let] n falleba f

especial [ɪ'speʃəl] adj especial, particular; **of e. importance** de especial importancia

especially [ɪs'peʃəlɪ] adv especialmente, sobre todo

esperantist [espə'ræntɪst] n esperantista mf

Esperanto [espə'ræntəʊ] n esperanto m

espionage ['espɪənɑːʒ] n espionaje m

esplanade [esplə'neɪd] n paseo m marítimo

espouse [ɪ'spaʊz] vt Fml (a) (cause) abrazar, adoptar (b) (marry) casarse con

espresso [e'spresəʊ] n café m □ **e. coffee** café m exprés or Esp solo or Am negro

esprit de corps [espriːdə'kɔːr] n espíritu m de camadería, fraternidad f

Esq (abbr **Esquire**) Derek Wilson, **E.** (Sr.) D. Derek Wilson

esquire [ɪ'skwaɪər] n Br señor m; **Timothy Whiteman E.** Sr. Don Timothy Whiteman

essay ['eseɪ] **1** n (a) Educ redacción f, composición f (b) Lit ensayo m (c) (attempt) intento m **2** [e'seɪ] vt (a) (test) probar (b) (attempt) intentar

essayist ['eseɪɪst] n Lit ensayista mf

essence ['esəns] n (a) (fundamental) esencia f; **in e.**

esencialmente; **speed is of the e.** la rapidez es esencial; **the e. of the matter** el quid de la cuestión (**b**) *(perfume)* esencia *f,* perfume *m*

essential [ɪˈsenʃəl] **1** *adj* esencial, fundamental, imprescindible ◻ **e. oil** aceite *m* esencial

2 *n* (**a**) *(fundamental)* elemento *m* esencial (**b**) *(vital)* necesidad *f* básica (**c**) **essentials** *(basic foodstuffs)* products primarios *or* de primera necesidad; *(basic issues)* cuestiones básicas

essentially [ɪˈsenʃəlɪ] *adv* esencialmente, fundamentalmente

EST [iːesˈtiː] *n US (abbr* **Eastern Standard Time)** hora *f* del meridiano 75 al oeste de Greenwich

establish [ɪˈstæblɪʃ] *vt (a) (found)* establecer, fundar, crear; *(business)* montar; *(habit)* consolidar; *(theory)* sentar; **to e. a precedent** sentar un precedente; **to e. oneself** establecerse; **to e. one's rights** hacer constar sus derechos (**b**) *Jur* **to e. a fact/sb's innocence** probar un hecho/la inocencia de algn; **to e. the truth** demostrar la verdad

established [ɪˈstæblɪʃt] *adj (person)* establecido(a); *(habit)* arraigado(a), consolidado(a); *(fact)* conocido(a) ◻ **e. church** iglesia *f* oficial del Estado

establishment [ɪˈstæblɪʃmənt] *n* (**a**) *(creation)* establecimiento *m* (**b**) *Com* negocio *m,* establecimiento *m* (**c**) *Pol* **the E.** el sistema

estate [ɪˈsteɪt] *n* (**a**) *(land)* finca *f* ◻ *Br* **e. agent** *(person)* agente *mf* inmobiliario(a); *(office)* agencia *f* inmobiliaria; *Br Aut* **e. car** ranchera *f, Esp* coche *m* familiar (**b**) *Br (development)* zona *f* urbanizada ◻ **council e.** viviendas *fpl* de protección oficial; **housing e.** urbanización *f;* **industrial e. polígono** *m* industrial, **trading e.** zona *f* comercial (**c**) *(property)* propiedad *f,* bienes *mpl* (**d**) *(inheritance)* herencia *f*

esteem [ɪˈstiːm] **1** *n* aprecio *m,* respeto *m;* **to hold sb in great e.** apreciar mucho a algn

2 *vt* (**a**) *(person)* apreciar a (**b**) *(regard)* considerar

esteemed [ɪˈstiːmd] *adj* apreciado(a), estimado(a)

esthetic [esˈθetɪk] *adj US* estético(a)

esthetics [esˈθetɪks] *n US* estética *f*

estimate [ˈestɪmɪt] **1** *n (calculation)* cálculo *m;* *(likely cost of work)* presupuesto *m;* **rough e.** cálculo aproximado

2 [ˈestɪmeɪt] *vt* calcular; *Fig* pensar, creer

estimation [estɪˈmeɪʃən] *n* (**a**) *(opinion)* juicio *m,* opinión *f;* **in my e.** a mi juicio (**b**) *(esteem)* estima *f*

Estonia [esˈtəʊnɪə] *n* Estonia

Estonian [esˈtəʊnɪən] **1** *n* (**a**) *(person)* estonio(a) *m,f* (**b**) *(language)* estonio *m*

2 *adj* estonio(a)

estrange [ɪˈstreɪndʒ] *vt* alejar; **to become estranged** alejarse (**from** de)

estranged [ɪsˈtreɪndʒd] *adj* separado(a); **to be e. (from)** estar separado(a) (de)

estrangement [ɪˈstreɪndʒmənt] *n Fml* alejamiento *m;* **the e. from his wife** el alejamiento de su mujer

estrogen [ˈiːstrədʒən] *n US Biol* estrógeno *m*

estuary [ˈestjʊərɪ] *n Geog* estuario *m*

ETA [iːtiːˈeɪ] *n (abbr* **estimated time of arrival)** hora *f* prevista de llegada

et al [etˈæl] *(abbr* **et alii)** et al.

etc [etˈsetrə] *adv (abbr* **et cetera)** etc., etcétera

etch [etʃ] *vt Art* grabar al agua fuerte

etching [ˈetʃɪŋ] *n Art* aguafuerte *f*

eternal [ɪˈtɜːnəl] *adj* eterno(a), incesante ◻ **e. triangle** triángulo *m* amoroso

eternally [ɪˈtɜːnəlɪ] *adv* eternamente, siempre

eternity [ɪˈtɜːnɪtɪ] *n* eternidad *f*

ethane [ˈiːθeɪn, ˈeθeɪn] *n Chem* etano *m*

ethanol [ˈethənɒl, ˈiːθənɒl] *n Chem* etanol *m*

ether [ˈiːθər] *n Chem* éter *m*

ethereal [ɪˈθɪərɪəl] *adj* etéreo(a)

ethic [ˈeθɪk] *n* ética *f*

ethical [ˈeθɪkəl] *adj* ético(a)

ethically [ˈeθɪklɪ] *adv* éticamente

ethics [ˈeθɪks] *n* ética *f,* moralidad *f;* **medical e.** ética profesional médica

Ethiopia [iːθɪˈəʊpɪə] *n* Etiopía

Ethiopian [iːθɪˈəʊpɪən] *adj & n* etíope (*mf*)

ethnic [ˈeθnɪk] *adj* étnico(a) ◻ **e. cleansing** limpieza *f* étnica; **e. minority** minoría *f* étnica

ethnicity [eθˈnɪsɪtɪ] *n* etnicidad *f*

ethnocentric [eθnəʊˈsentrɪk] *adj* etnocéntrico(a)

ethnographer [eθˈnɒɡəfər] *n* etnógrafo(a) *m,f*

ethnography [eθˈnɒɡrəfɪ] *n* etnografía *f*

ethnologist [eθˈnɒlədʒɪst] *n* etnólogo(a) *m,f*

ethnology [eθˈnɒlədʒɪ] *n* etnología *f*

ethos [ˈiːθɒs] *n* carácter *m* distintivo

ethyl [ˈiːθaɪl, ˈeθɪl] *n Chem* etilo *m* ◻ **e. alcohol** alcohol *m* etílico

ethylene [ˈeθɪliːn] *n Chem* etileno *m*

e-ticket [ˈiːˈtɪkɪt] *n Esp* billete *m or Am* boleto *m or Am* pasaje *m* electrónico

etiquette [ˈetɪket] *n* protocolo *m,* etiqueta *f,* buenos modales *mpl* ◻ **professional e.** ética *f* profesional

etymological [etɪməˈlɒdʒɪkəl] *adj* etimológico(a)

etymologist [etɪˈmɒlədʒɪst] *n* etimólogo(a) *m,f*

etymology [etɪˈmɒlədʒɪ] *n* etimología *f*

EU [iːˈjuː] *n (abbr* **European Union)** UE *f*

eucalyptus [juːkəˈlɪptəs] *n Bot* eucalipto *m*

Eucharist [ˈjuːkərɪst] *n Rel* Eucaristía *f*

eulogize [ˈjuːlədʒaɪz] *vt* elogiar

eulogy [ˈjuːlədʒɪ] *n* elogio *m*

eunuch [ˈjuːnək] *n* eunuco *m*

euphemism [ˈjuːfɪmɪzəm] *n* eufemismo *m*

euphemistic [juːfɪˈmɪstɪk] *adj* eufemístico(a)

euphonic [juːˈfɒnɪk] *adj* eufónico(a)

euphony [ˈjuːfənɪ] *n* eufonía *f*

euphoria [juːˈfɔːrɪə] *n* euforia *f*

euphoric [juːˈfɒrɪk] *adj* eufórico(a)

Eurasian [jʊəˈreɪʒən] *adj & n* euroasiático(a) (*m,f*)

eureka [jʊˈriːkə] *interj* ¡eureka!

eurhythmics [juːˈrɪðmɪks] *n US* gimnasia *f* rítmica

euro [ˈjʊərəʊ] (*pl* **euros**) *n Fin (European currency)* euro *m*

Eurocentric [jʊərəʊˈsentrɪk] *adj* eurocéntrico(a)

Eurocheque [ˈjʊərəʊtʃek] *n* eurocheque *m* ◻ **E. card** tarjeta *f* de eurocheque

eurocommunism [jʊərəʊˈkɒmjʊnɪzəm] *n* eurocomunismo *m*

Eurocrat [ˈjʊərəkræt] *n* eurócrata *mf*

Eurocurrency [ˈjʊərəʊkʌrənsɪ] *n Fin* eurodivisa *f*

eurodollar [ˈjʊərəʊdɒlər] *n Fin* eurodólar *m*

euro-MP [ˈjʊərəʊemˈpiː] *n* eurodiputado(a) *m,f*

Europe [ˈjʊərəp] *n* Europa

European [jʊərəˈpɪən] *adj & n* europeo(a) (*m,f*) ◻ **E. Commission** Comisión *f* Europea; *Formerly* **E. Economic Community** Comunidad *f* Económica Europea; **E.**

Parliament Parlamento *m* Europeo; **E. Union** Unión *f* Europea

Europhile ['jʊərəʊfaɪl] *adj & n* europeísta *(mf)*

Eurosceptic [jʊərəʊ'skeptɪk] *n Br* euroescéptico(a) *m,f*

Eustachian tube [ju:steɪʃən'tju:b] *n Anat* trompa *f* de Eustaquio

euthanasia [ju:θə'neɪzɪə] *n* eutanasia *f*

evacuate [ɪ'vækjʊeɪt] *vt* evacuar, desalojar

evacuation [ɪvækjʊ'eɪʃən] *n* evacuación *f*, desalojamiento *m*

evacuee [ɪvækjʊ'i:] *n* evacuado(a) *m,f*

evade [ɪ'veɪd] *vt* evadir, evitar; **to e. the issue** eludir la cuestión

evaluate [ɪ'væljʊeɪt] *vt* (**a**) *(calculate)* evaluar, calcular; **to e. damages** juzgar la cuantía de los daños (**b**) *Math* hallar el valor numérico de

evaluation [ɪvæljʊ'eɪʃən] *n* evaluación *f*

evanescent [evə'nesənt] *adj* evanescente

evangelical [i:væn'dʒelɪkəl] *adj* evangélico(a)

evangelism [ɪ'vændʒɪlɪzəm] *n* evangelismo *m*

evangelist [ɪ'vændʒɪlɪst] *n* evangelista *mf*; **Saint John the E.** San Juan Evangelista

evangelize [ɪ'vændʒɪlaɪz] *vt* evangelizar

evaporate [ɪ'væpəreɪt] **1** *vt* evaporar ❑ **evaporated milk** leche *f* evaporada
 2 *vi* evaporarse, *Fig* desvanecerse

evaporation [ɪvæpə'reɪʃən] *n* evaporación *f*

evasion [ɪ'veɪʒən] *n* (**a**) *(gen)* evasión *f* ❑ **e. of duty** incumplimiento *m* del deber; **tax e.** evasión *f* fiscal *or* capital (**b**) *(evasive answer)* evasiva *f*

evasive [ɪ'veɪsɪv] *adj* evasivo(a)

eve [i:v] *n* víspera *f*; **on the e. of** en vísperas de

even ['i:vən] **1** *adj* (**a**) *(smooth)* liso(a); *(level)* llano(a) (**b**) *(regular)* regular, uniforme; **e. temper** carácter *m* apacible; **to keep an e. pace** mantener un ritmo constante (**c**) *(equally balanced)* igual, igualado(a); *(Sport)* **to be e.** estar igualado(a) *or* empatado(a); *Fin* **to break e.** cubrir gastos; **to get e. with sb** desquitarse con algn; **to stand an e. chance** tener tantas posibilidades de éxito como de fracaso (**d**) *(number)* par; **odd or e.** par o impar (**e**) *(at the same level)* a nivel (**f**) *(quantity)* exacto(a), redondo(a)
 2 *adv* (**a**) *(for emphasis)* incluso, hasta, aun; **e. now** incluso ahora; **e. so** aun así; **e. the children knew** hasta los niños lo sabían; **e. when it rains** incluso cuando llueve (**b**) *(negative)* ni siquiera; **she can't e. write her name** ni siquiera sabe escribir su nombre; **without e. speaking** sin hablar siquiera (**c**) *(before comparative)* aun, todavía; **that would be e. worse** eso sería aun peor (**d**) **e. as** en el mismo momento en que, mientras; **e. as he wrote the letter** mientras escribía la carta; **e. if** incluso si; **e. though** aunque, aun cuando
 3 *vt* nivelar, igualar; *Fig* **to e. a score with sb** desquitarse con algn

even-handed [i:vən'hændɪd] *adj* imparcial

evening ['i:vnɪŋ] *n* (**a**) *(early)* tarde *f*; *(late)* noche *f*; **in the e.** por la tarde; **tomorrow e.** mañana por la tarde; **yesterday e.** ayer por la tarde ❑ *Educ* **e. class** clase *f* nocturna; **e. dress** *(man)* traje *m* de etiqueta; *(woman)* traje *m* de noche; **e. paper** periódico *m* de la tarde; *Cin Theat* **e. performance** función *f* de noche; *Rel* **e. service** misa *f* vespertina (**b**) *(greeting)* **good e.!** *(early)* ¡buenas tardes!; *(late)* ¡buenas noches!

evenly ['i:vənlɪ] *adv* (**a**) *(uniformly)* de modo uniforme (**b**) *(fairly)* equitativamente, igualmente (**c**) *(tone of voice)* en el mismo tono

evenness ['i:vənnɪs] *n* (**a**) *(equal)* uniformidad *f* (**b**) *(fairness)* ecuanimidad *f*

evensong ['i:vənsɒŋ] *n Rel* vísperas *fpl*

event [ɪ'vent] *n* (**a**) *(happening)* suceso *m*, acontecimiento *m*; **in the normal course of events** si todo sigue su curso normal; **it was quite an e.** fue todo un acontecimiento; **programme of events** programa *m* de actos (**b**) *(case)* caso *m*; **at all events** en todo caso; **in the e. of fire** en caso de incendio; **in the e. of his refusing** en (el) caso de que no acepte (**c**) *Sport* prueba *f* ❑ **track events** atletismo *m* en pista

eventful [ɪ'ventfʊl] *adj* lleno(a) de acontecimientos, agitado(a); **an e. day** *(busy)* un día agitado; *(memorable)* un día memorable

eventual [ɪ'ventʃʊəl] *adj* *(ultimate)* final; *(resulting)* consiguiente; *(possible)* posible

eventuality [ventʃʊ'ælɪtɪ] *n* eventualidad *f*; **to prepare for all eventualities** prepararse para cualquier eventualidad

eventually [ɪ'ventʃəlɪ] *adv* finalmente, con el tiempo; **we e. managed to find a telephone box** finalmente encontramos una cabina telefónica

ever ['evər] *adv* (**a**) *(never)* nunca, jamás; **nothing e. happens** nunca pasa nada; **stronger than e.** más fuerte que nunca (**b**) *(interrogative)* *(sometimes)* alguna vez; **have you e. been there?** ¿has estado allí alguna vez?; *Fam* **did you e.?** ¡habrase visto! (**c**) *(always)* siempre; **for e.** para siempre; **for e. and e.** para siempre jamás; **Scotland for e.!** ¡viva Escocia! (**d**) *(emphasis)* **how e. did you manage it?** ¿cómo diablos lo conseguiste?; **what e. shall we do now?** ¿qué demonios hacemos ahora?; **why e. not?** ¿por qué no?; *Fam* **e. so, e. such** muy; **e. so difficult** terriblemente difícil; **e. so little** muy poco; **thank you e. so much** muchísimas gracias

evergreen ['evəgri:n] *Bot* **1** *adj* de hoja perenne
 2 *n* árbol *m* or planta *f* de hoja perenne ❑ **e. oak** encina *f*

everlasting [evə'lɑːstɪŋ] *adj* eterno(a), perpetuo(a)

evermore [evə'mɔːr] *adv* eternamente; **for e.** para siempre

every ['evrɪ] *adj* (**a**) *(each)* cada; **e. now and then** de vez en cuando; **e. other day** cada dos días, *Am* día por medio (**b**) *(all)* todos(as); **e. citizen** todo ciudadano, todos los ciudadanos; **e. day** todos los días; **e. Saturday** todos los sábados (**c**) *(intensive)* **I have e. confidence in her** tengo plena confianza en ella; **you had e. right to be angry** tenías todo el derecho a estar *esp Esp* enfadado *or esp Am* enojado

everybody ['evrɪbɒdɪ] *pron* todo el mundo, todos(as)

everyday ['evrɪdeɪ] *adj* diario(a), de todos los días; corriente; **an e. occurrence** un suceso cotidiano; **it's an e. event** es un suceso ordinario ❑ **e. clothes** ropa *f* de todos los días

everyone ['evrɪwʌn] *pron* todo el mundo, todos(as)

everything ['evrɪθɪŋ] *pron* todo; **e. needs washing** hace falta lavarlo todo; **he eats e.** come de todo; **she means e. to me** ella lo es todo para mí

everywhere ['evrɪweər] *adv* en todas partes, por todas partes

evict [ɪ'vɪkt] *vt* desahuciar

eviction [ɪ'vɪkʃən] *n* desahucio *m*

evidence ['evɪdəns] **1** *n* (**a**) *(proof)* evidencia *f*; **there is no e. against her** no hay ninguna prueba en contra suya (**b**) *Jur* testimonio *m*, declaración *f*; **to call sb in e.** llamar a algn como testigo; **to give e.** prestar declaración, declarar como testigo; **to turn King's** *or* **Queen's** *or US* **State's e.** = inculpar a un cómplice ante un tribunal a cambio de recibir un trato indulgente (**c**) *(sign)* indicio *m*, señal *f*; **in e.** visible; **to be in e.** estar a la vista, hacerse notar

2 vt **(a)** (prove) demostrar, probar **(b)** Jur (witness) declarar; (give proof of) justificar

evident ['evɪdənt] adj evidente, patente, manifiesto(a)

evidently ['evɪdəntlɪ] adv evidentemente, al parecer

evil ['i:vəl] **1** adj **(a)** (wicked) malo(a), malvado(a) **(b)** (harmful) malo(a), nocivo(a) **(c)** (unfortunate) aciago(a), de mal agüero **(d)** (nasty) geniudo(a); **he's got an e. temper** tiene muy mal genio

2 n mal m; **to speak e. of sb** hablar mal de algn

evil-doer ['i:vəldʊər] n persona f malvada

evil-minded [i:vəl'maɪndɪd] adj malvado(a), malpensado(a)

evince [ɪ'vɪns] vt Fml evidenciar

evocation [evə'keɪʃən] n evocación f

evocative [ɪ'vɒkətɪv] adj evocador(a)

evoke [ɪ'vəʊk] vt evocar, provocar

evolution [i:və'lu:ʃən] n evolución f

evolutionary [i:və'lu:ʃənərɪ] adj evolutivo(a)

evolve [ɪ'vɒlv] **1** vi (species) evolucionar; (ideas) desarrollarse

2 vt **(a)** (gen) desarrollar **(b)** (gas, heat) desprender

evolvement [ɪ'vɒlvmənt] n (of ideas, plans) desarrollo m; (of gas, heat) desprendimiento m

ewe [ju:] n Zool oveja f

ex¹ [eks] prep **(a)** **e. dividend** sin dividendo, sin cupón **(b)** **e. factory** franco fábrica

ex² [eks] n **her e.** su ex marido; **his e.** su ex mujer

ex- [eks] pref ex, antiguo(a); **ex-minister** ex ministro m

exacerbate [ɪg'zæsəbeɪt] vt exacerbar, agravar

exact [ɪg'zækt] **1** adj (accurate, precise) exacto(a); (of description, definition) preciso(a); **an e. mind** una mente clara or precisa; **this e. spot** este mismo lugar

2 vt exigir

exacting [ɪg'zæktɪŋ] adj exigente

exactitude [ɪg'zæktɪtju:d] n exactitud f

exactly [ɪg'zæktlɪ] adv exactamente; **e.!** ¡exacto!

exactness [ɪg'zæktnəs] n exactitud f

exaggerate [ɪg'zædʒəreɪt] vi & vt exagerar

exaggerated [ɪg'zædʒəreɪtɪd] adj exagerado(a)

exaggeration [ɪgzædʒə'reɪʃən] n exageración f

exalt [ɪg'zɔ:lt] vt Fml exaltar

exaltation [egzɔ:l'teɪʃən] n Fml exaltación f

exalted [ɪg'zɔ:ltɪd] adj (high) elevado(a)

exam [ɪg'zæm] n Educ examen m

examination [ɪgzæmɪ'neɪʃən] n **(a)** Educ examen m; **to sit an e.** hacer un examen; **to take an e.** examinarse ❑ **entrance e.** examen m de ingreso **(b)** Med reconocimiento m **(c)** Jur interrogatorio m

examine [ɪg'zæmɪn] vt **(a)** (education) examinar; (at customs) registrar **(b)** Med reconocer, examinar **(c)** Jur (witness) interrogar

examinee [ɪgzæmɪ'ni:] n examinado(a) m,f

examiner [ɪg'zæmɪnər] n examinador(a) m,f

example [ɪg'zɑ:mpəl] n (gen) ejemplo m; (specimen) ejemplar m; **for e.** por ejemplo; **to make an e. of sb** dar un castigo ejemplar a algn; **to set an e.** dar ejemplo

exasperate [ɪg'zɑ:spəreɪt] vt exasperar

exasperated [ɪg'zɑ:spəreɪtɪd] adj exasperado(a)

exasperating [ɪg'zɑ:spəreɪtɪŋ] adj exasperante

exasperation [ɪgzɑ:spə'reɪʃən] n exasperación f

excavate ['ekskəveɪt] vt excavar

excavation [ekskə'veɪʃən] n excavación f

excavator ['ekskəveɪtər] n **(a)** (machine) excavadora f **(b)** (person) excavador(a) m,f

exceed [ek'si:d] vt exceder, sobrepasar; **to e. one's income** gastar más de lo que uno gana

exceedingly [ɪk'si:dɪŋlɪ] adv extremadamente, sumamente; **e. pleased** contentísimo(a)

excel [ɪk'sel] (pt & pp excelled) **1** vi sobresalir

2 vt superar; **to e. oneself** superarse

excellence ['eksələns] n excelencia f

excellency ['eksələnsɪ] n excelencia f; **His E.** Su Excelencia

excellent ['eksələnt] adj excelente, sobresaliente

excelsior [ɪk'selsɪɔ:r] n US virutas fpl

except [ɪk'sept] **1** prep excepto, salvo, con la excepción de; **e. for the little ones** excepto los pequeños; **e. that ...** sólo que ..., salvo que ...

2 vt excluir; **present company excepted** exceptuando a los aquí presentes

exception [ɪk'sepʃən] n **(a)** (gen) excepción f; **the e. proves the rule** la excepción confirma la regla; **to make an e. of** hacer una excepción de, exceptuar; **with the e. of** a excepción de; **without e.** sin excepción **(b)** (objection) objeción f; **to take e. to sth** ofenderse por algo

exceptionable [ɪk'sepʃənəbəl] adj censurable

exceptional [ɪk'sepʃənəl] adj excepcional, extraordinario(a)

exceptionally [ɪk'sepʃənəlɪ] adv extraordinariamente; **e., more time may be allowed** en casos excepcionales se dará más tiempo

excerpt [ek'sɜ:pt] n extracto m

excess [ɪk'ses] **1** n exceso m; **in e.** en exceso; **in e. of** superior a; **to eat to e.** comer con exceso

2 ['ekses] adj excedente ❑ Av **e. baggage** exceso m de equipaje; Econ **e. demand** exceso m de demanda; Rail **e. fare** suplemento m; **e. postage** franqueo m excesivo; **e. profits tax** impuestos mpl sobre beneficios excesivos; Econ **e. supply** exceso m de oferta

excessive [ɪk'sesɪv] adj excesivo(a)

excessively [ɪk'sesɪvlɪ] adv excesivamente, en exceso

exchange [ɪks'tʃeɪndʒ] **1** n **(a)** (gen) cambio m, intercambio m; **e. of ideas** intercambio de ideas; **in e. for** a cambio de **(b)** Fin cambio m ❑ **bill of e.** letra f de cambio; **e. control** control m de divisas; **foreign e.** divisas fpl; **rate of e., e. rate** tipo m or Am tasa de cambio **(c)** Hist lonja f ❑ **corn e.** lonja f de granos; Br Formerly **labour e.** oficina f de desempleo, bolsa f de trabajo; Fin **Stock E.** Bolsa f **(d)** Tel **(telephone) e.** central f telefónica

2 vt **(a)** (gen) cambiar; **to e. blows** golpearse; **to e. greetings** saludarse; **to e. words** cruzar unas palabras **(b)** (prisoners) canjear

exchangeable [ɪks'tʃeɪndʒəbəl] adj cambiable, canjeable

exchequer [ɪks'tʃekər] n Br **the E.** el Tesoro (público); ≃ Hacienda f ❑ **Chancellor of the E.** ≃ Ministro m de Hacienda

excise¹ ['eksaɪz] n impuesto m sobre el consumo ❑ **E. duty** derechos mpl de aduana; **E. officer** agente mf de aduana; Br **the Commissioners of Customs and E.** la Oficina de Control de Derechos de Aduana y de Importación

excise² [ɪk'saɪz] vt extirpar

excision [ɪk'sɪʒən] n Med extirpación f, excisión f

excitable [ɪk'saɪtəbəl] adj (temperamental) excitable; (nervous) nervioso(a)

excite [ɪk'saɪt] vt **(a)** (stimulate) excitar; **to get excited** ponerse nervioso(a) **(b)** (move) emocionar **(c)** (enthuse) entusiasmar; **don't get too excited about it** no te hagas demasiadas ilusiones; **to get excited** entusiasmarse **(d)** *(arouse)* provocar, levantar, despertar; **his speech excited suspicion** su discurso despertó sospechas

excitement [ɪkˈsaɪtmənt] *n* **(a)** *(stimulation)* excitación *f* **(b)** *(emotion)* emoción *f* **(c)** *(commotion)* agitación *f*, revuelo *m*; **to cause great e.** causar sensación; **what's all the e. about?** ¿a qué se debe tanto alboroto?

exciting [ɪkˈsaɪtɪŋ] *adj* apasionante, emocionante; **how e.!** ¡qué ilusión!

exclaim [ɪkˈskleɪm] **1** *vi* exclamar
2 *vt* gritar

exclamation [eksklə'meɪʃən] *n* exclamación *f* ❏ *Br* **e. mark**, *US* **e. point** signo *m* de admiración

exclamatory [ɪkˈsklæmətərɪ] *adj* exclamatorio(a)

exclude [ɪkˈskluːd] *vt* **(a)** *(leave out)* excluir **(b)** *(from club)* no admitir

excluding [ɪkˈskluːdɪŋ] *prep* excepto, con exclusión de

exclusion [ɪkˈskluːʒən] *n* exclusión *f*; **to the e. of** con exclusión de

exclusive [ɪkˈskluːsɪv] **1** *adj* **(a)** *(sole)* exclusivo(a) ❏ **e. interview** entrevista *f* en exclusiva; **e. rights** derechos *mpl* exclusivos **(b)** *(select)* selecto(a); *(club)* cerrado(a)
2 *n Press* exclusiva *f*
3 *adv* **e. of** excluyendo, sin tener en cuenta

exclusively [ɪksˈkluːsɪvlɪ] *adv* exclusivamente

excommunicate [ekskəˈmjuːnɪkeɪt] *vt* excomulgar

excommunication [ekskəmjuːnɪˈkeɪʃən] *n* excomunión *f*

excrement [ˈekskrɪmənt] *n* excremento *m*

excrescence [ɪkˈskresəns] *n* excrecencia *f*

excreta [ɪkˈskriːtə] *npl* excrementos *mpl*

excrete [ɪkˈskriːt] *vt* excretar

excretion [ɪkˈskriːʃən] *n* excreción *f*

excruciating [ɪkˈskruːʃɪeɪtɪŋ] *adj* insoportable

excruciatingly [ɪksˈkruːʃɪeɪtɪŋlɪ] *adv* atrozmente, horriblemente; **it's e. funny** es para morirse de risa

excursion [ɪkˈskɜːʃən] *n* excursión *f* ❏ **e. ticket** billete *m* or *Am* boleto *m* reducido

excursionist [ɪkˈskɜːʃənɪst] *n* excursionista *mf*

excusable [ɪkˈskjuːzəbəl] *adj* perdonable, disculpable

excuse [ɪkˈskjuːz] **1** *vt* **(a)** *(forgive)* perdonar, disculpar; **e. me!** ¡oiga, por favor!, con permiso; **e. my saying so** perdone mi atrevimiento; **may I be excused for a moment?** ¿puedo salir un momento? **(b)** *(exempt)* dispensar, eximir; *Mil* rebajar; **he was excused kitchen duty** lo rebajaron del servicio de cocina **(c)** *(justify)* justificar; **that does not e. your behaviour** eso no justifica tu comportamiento
2 [ɪkˈskjuːs] *n* excusa *f*; **to make an e.** dar excusas

ex-directory [eksdɪˈrektərɪ] *adj Br Tel* que no se encuentra en la guía telefónica; **the Minister's number is ex-d.** el número de teléfono del Ministro no figura en la guía *or Esp* en el listín *or Am* en el directorio

execrable [ˈeksɪkrəbəl] *adj Fml (abysmal)* execrable; *(awful)* abominable

execute [ˈeksɪkjuːt] *vt* **(a)** *(carry out)* ejecutar; *(order)* cumplir; *(task)* realizar, llevar a cabo **(b)** *Jur* cumplir; **to e. a will** cumplir un testamento **(c)** *(put to death)* ejecutar **(d)** *Mus* interpretar **(e)** *Comptr* ejecutar

execution [eksɪˈkjuːʃən] *n* **(a)** *(carrying out)* ejecución *f*; *(of order)* cumplimiento *m*; *(of task)* realización *f* **(b)** *Jur* cumplimiento *m* **(c)** *(putting to death)* ejecución *f* **(d)** *Mus* interpretación *f*

executioner [eksɪˈkjuːʃənər] *n* verdugo *m*

executive [ɪgˈzekjʊtɪv] **1** *adj* ejecutivo(a) ❏ **E. Board** consejo *m* de dirección; *US* **E. officer** segundo comandante *m*; **e. power** poder *m* ejecutivo; *US* **e. privilege** = exención de la obligación de revelar el contenido de documentos internos por parte del ejecutivo del gobierno
2 *n* ejecutivo(a) *m,f*

executor [ɪgˈzekjʊtər] *n Jur* albacea *m*

executrix [ɪgˈzekjʊtrɪks] *n Jur* albacea *f*

exemplary [ɪgˈzemplərɪ] *adj* ejemplar; **an e. pupil** un alumno ejemplar

exemplify [ɪgˈzemplɪfaɪ] *vt* (*pt & pp* **exemplified**) ejemplificar, servir de ejemplo para

exempt [ɪgˈzempt] **1** *vt* eximir, dispensar **(from** de); **he was exempted from national service** le eximieron del servicio militar
2 *adj* exento(a), libre; **e. from tax** libre de impuesto; **e. from taxation** exento(a) de impuestos

exemption [ɪgˈzempʃən] *n* exención *f* (**from** de)

exercise [ˈeksəsaɪz] **1** *n* ejercicio *m*; **to take e.** hacer ejercicio, hacer deporte ❏ **e. bike** bicicleta *f* estática; *Educ* **e. book** cuaderno *m*
2 *vt* **(a)** *(influence, rights, duties)* ejercer; **to e. care** tener cuidado, proceder con cuidado **(b)** *(dog)* sacar de paseo **(c)** *(mind)* inquietar; **this matter has much exercised the minds of scientists** este asunto ha inquietado mucho a los científicos
3 *vi* hacer ejercicio, entrenarse

exert [ɪgˈzɜːt] *vt (influence)* ejercer; **to e. oneself** esforzarse

exertion [ɪgˈzɜːʃən] *n* esfuerzo *m* (excesivo)

exfoliate [eksˈfəʊlɪeɪt] **1** *vt* exfoliar
2 *vi* exfoliarse

ex gratia [eksˈgreɪʃə] *adj Fml (payment)* discrecional

exhale [eksˈheɪl] *vt (air)* exhalar; *(smell)* despedir
2 *vi (breathe out)* exhalar

exhaust [ɪgˈzɔːst] **1** *vt* **(a)** *(tire)* agotar; **to e. oneself** agotarse **(b)** *(use up)* agotar; **we have exhausted all the possibilities** hemos agotado todas las posibilidades **(c)** *(empty)* vaciar
2 *n (gases)* gases *mpl* de combustión; *(pipe)* escape *m* ❏ *Aut* **e. pipe** tubo *m* or *RP* caño *m* de escape; **e. valve** válvula *f* de escape

exhausted [ɪgˈzɔːstɪd] *adj* agotado(a)

exhausting [ɪgˈzɔːstɪŋ] *adj* agotador(a)

exhaustion [ɪgˈzɔːstʃən] *n* agotamiento *m*

exhaustive [ɪgˈzɔːstɪv] *adj* exhaustivo(a), completo(a); **an e. inquiry** una investigación minuciosa

exhibit [ɪgˈzɪbɪt] **1** *n* **(a)** *Art* objeto *m* expuesto **(b)** *Jur* prueba *f* instrumental
2 *vt* **(a)** *Art* exponer **(b)** *(manifest)* mostrar, presentar

exhibition [eksɪˈbɪʃən] *n* **(a)** *(display)* muestra *f*, demostración *f*; **to make an e. of oneself** dar el espectáculo **(b)** *Art* exposición *f*; **to be on e.** estar actualmente expuesto(a) **(c)** *Com (trade fair)* feria *f*

exhibitionism [eksɪˈbɪʃənɪzəm] *n* exhibicionismo *m*

exhibitionist [eksɪˈbɪʃənɪst] *adj & n* exhibicionista *(mf)*

exhibitor [ɪgˈzɪbɪtər] *n* expositor(a) *m,f*

exhilarate [ɪgˈzɪləreɪt] *vt* alegrar, animar

exhilarated [ɪgˈzɪləreɪtɪd] *adj* muy animado(a)

exhilarating [ɪgˈzɪləreɪtɪŋ] *adj* estimulante

exhilaration [ɪgzɪləˈreɪʃən] *n* regocijo *m*, alegría *f*

exhort [ɪgˈzɔːt] *vt* exhortar

exhortation [ɪgzɔːˈteɪʃən] *n Fml* exhortación *f*

exhumation [ekshjʊˈmeɪʃən] *n* exhumación *f*

exhume [eks'hjʊm] *vt* exhumar, desenterrar

exigency ['eksɪdʒənsɪ, ɪg'zɪdʒənsɪ] *n (need)* exigencia *f;* *(emergency)* caso *m* de emergencia

exigent ['eksɪdʒənt] *adj (demanding)* exigente; *(urgent)* urgente

exiguous [ɪg'zɪgjʊəs] *adj* exiguo(a)

exile ['eksaɪl] **1** *n* (**a**) *(banishment)* exilio *m*, destierro *m* (**b**) *(person)* exiliado(a) *m,f* ❏ **tax e.** exiliado(a) *m,f* fiscal
2 *vt* exiliar, desterrar

exist [ɪg'zɪst] *vi* (**a**) *(gen)* existir (**b**) *(stay alive)* subsistir; **to e. on bread** subsistir a base de pan

existence [ɪg'zɪstəns] *n* existencia *f;* **to be in e.** existir; **to come into e.** nacer

existential [egzɪ'stenʃəl] *adj Philos* existencial

existentialism [egzɪ'stenʃəlɪzəm] *n Philos* existencialismo *m*

existentialist [egzɪ'stenʃəlɪst] *adj & n Philos* existencialista *(mf)*

existing [eg'zɪstɪŋ] *adj* existente, actual; **in the e. circumstances** en las circunstancias actuales

exit ['eksɪt] **1** *n* (**a**) *(gen)* salida *f* ❏ **emergency e.** salida *f* de emergencia; *Pol* **e. poll** sondeo *m* a la salida de los colegios electorales; **e. visa** visado *m* or *Am* visa *f* de salida; **fire e.** salida *f* de emergencia (**b**) *Theat* salida *f*, mutis *m*; **to make one's e.** salir
2 *vi Theat* salir (de escena), hacer mutis; **e. Macbeth** sale Macbeth

exodus ['eksədəs] *n* éxodo *m; Fam* **there was a general e.** se fueron todos

ex officio [eksə'fɪʃɪəʊ] *adj & adv* ex-oficio

exogamy [ek'sɒgəmɪ] *n* exogamia *f*

exonerate [ɪg'zɒnəreɪt] *vt Fml* exonerar, dispensar (**from** de)

exoneration [ɪgzɒnə'reɪʃən] *n Fml* exoneración *f*, dispensa *f*

exorbitant [ɪg'zɔːbɪtənt] *adj* exorbitante, desorbitado(a), excesivo(a)

exorcise ['eksɔːsaɪz] *vt (demon)* exorcizar; *Fig (memory)* borrar

exorcism ['eksɔːsɪzəm] *n* exorcismo *m*

exorcist ['eksɔːsɪst] *n* exorcista *mf*

exotic [ɪg'zɒtɪk] *adj* exótico(a)

expand [ɪk'spænd] **1** *vt* (**a**) *(enlarge)* ampliar; **he expanded his business** amplió su negocio (**b**) *(gas, metal)* dilatar
2 *vi* (**a**) *(grow)* ampliarse, crecer (**b**) *(metal)* dilatarse (**c**) *(become more friendly)* abrirse

expand on *vt* ampliar; **could you e. on your theory a little?** ¿podría ampliar un poco su teoría?

expandable [ɪks'pændəbəl] *adj Comptr* expandible; **4MB e. to 64MB** 4MB expandibles a 64MB

expanded [ɪks'pændɪd] *adj Comptr* ampliado(a); **e. polystyrene** poliestireno *m* expandido

expanding [ɪk'spændɪŋ] *adj* en expansión

expanse [ɪk'spæns] *n* extensión *f*

expansion [ɪk'spænʃən] *n* (**a**) *(size)* ampliación *f*, expansión *f* (**b**) *(gas, metal)* dilatación *f* (**c**) *(trade)* desarrollo *m* (**d**) *Comptr* **e. card** tarjeta *f* de ampliación (de memoria)

expansionism [ɪk'spænʃənɪzəm] *n* expansionismo *m*

expansive [ɪk'spænsɪv] *adj* expansivo(a), comunicativo(a)

expatriate [eks'pætrɪət] **1** *adj & n* expatriado(a) *(m,f)*
2 [eks'pætrɪeɪt] *vt* expatriar, desterrar

expatriation [ekspætrɪ'eɪʃən] *n* expatriación *f*

expect [ɪk'spekt] **1** *vt* (**a**) *(anticipate)* esperar; **I expected as much** ya me lo esperaba; **I fully expected to see them** estaba seguro de verlos; **I half-expected that to happen** suponía que iba a ocurrir; **I knew what to e.** sabía a qué atenerme (**b**) *(demand)* esperar, contar con; **I e. you to be punctual** cuento con que seas puntual; **I wouldn't have expected such behaviour from her** no esperaba tal comportamiento por su parte (**c**) *(suppose)* suponer, imaginar; **I e. she's in the office** me imagino que estará en la oficina; **I e. so** supongo que sí
2 *vi Fam* **to be expecting** estar embarazada

expectancy [ɪk'spektənsɪ] *n* expectación *f* ❏ **life e.** esperanza *f* de vida

expectant [ɪk'spektənt] *adj* ilusionado(a) ❏ **e. mother** mujer *f* embarazada

expectation [ekspek'teɪʃən] *n* esperanza *f;* **beyond e.** por encima de lo esperado; **contrary to e.**, **against e.** contrariamente a lo que se esperaba; **in e. of** con la esperanza de; **not to come up to sb's expectations, to fall short of sb's expectations** no alcanzar las expectativas de algn

expectorant [ɪk'spektərənt] *n* expectorante *m*

expectorate [ɪk'spektəreɪt] *vt & vi* expectorar, escupir

expediency [ɪk'spiːdɪənsɪ] *n* conveniencia *f*, oportunidad *f*

expedient [ɪk'spiːdɪənt] **1** *adj* conveniente, oportuno(a)
2 *n* expediente *m*, recurso *m*

expedite ['ekspɪdaɪt] *vt* (**a**) *(speed up)* acelerar (**b**) *(business)* despachar

expedition [ekspɪ'dɪʃən] *n* expedición *f* ❏ **rescue e.** expedición *f* de salvamento

expeditionary [ekspɪ'dɪʃənərɪ] *adj* expedicionario(a) ❏ **e. force** cuerpo *m* expedicionario

expeditious [ekspɪ'dɪʃəs] *adj* expeditivo(a)

expel [ɪk'spel] *vt (pt & pp expelled)* expulsar

expend [ɪk'spend] *vt* gastar, emplear

expendable [ɪk'spendəbəl] *adj* prescindible

expenditure [ɪk'spendɪtʃər] *n* gasto *m*, desembolso *m*

expense [ɪk'spens] *n* gasto *m*; **all expenses paid** con todos los gastos pagados; **at great e.** pagándolo caro; **he went on the trip at his own e.** pagó el viaje de su propio bolsillo; **to go to a lot of e.** gastar mucho dinero; **to spare no e.** no escatimar gastos; *Fig* **at my e.** a costa mía; *Fig* **at the e. of** a expensas de, a costa de ❏ *Com* **e. account** cuenta *f* de gastos de representación

expensive [ɪk'spensɪv] *adj* caro(a), costoso(a); *Fig* **it was an e. mistake** el error costó muy caro

experience [ɪk'spɪərɪəns] **1** *n* experiencia *f;* **an unforgettable e.** una experiencia inolvidable; **he has a lot of e. as a doctor** es un médico con mucha experiencia
2 *vt (sensation, situation)* experimentar; *(difficulty)* padecer, tener; *(loss)* sufrir

experienced [ɪk'spɪərɪənst] *adj* experimentado(a), con experiencia (**at, in** en); **you've got to be very e.** se necesita mucha experiencia

experiment [ɪk'sperɪmənt] **1** *n* experimento *m*; **as an e.** como experimento
2 *vi* experimentar, hacer experimentos (**on, with** con)

experimental [ɪksperɪ'mentəl] *adj* experimental

expert ['ekspɜːt] **1** *adj* experto(a); **e. opinion** opinión de un experto
2 *n* experto(a) *m,f*, especialista *mf*; **to be an e. on the subject** ser experto(a) en la materia ❏ *Comptr* **e. system** sistema *m* experto

expertise [ekspɜː'tiːz] *n* pericia *f*, habilidad *f*, competencia *f*

expertly [ˈekspɜːtlɪ] *adv* expertamente

expiate [ˈekspɪeɪt] *vt Fml* expiar

expiation [ekspɪˈeɪʃən] *n Fml* expiación *f*

expire [ɪkˈspaɪər] *vi* (**a**) *Euph (die)* expirar; *(come to an end)* terminar (**b**) *Com Ins* vencer; *(ticket)* caducar (**c**) *(breathe out)* espirar

expiry [ɪkˈspaɪərɪ] *n* expiración *f*, terminación *f*; *(bill of exchange)* vencimiento *m* ❑ **e. date** fecha *f* de caducidad

explain [ɪkˈspleɪn] **1** *vt* *(gen)* explicar; *(clarify)* aclarar; **that explains it** así se explica; **to e. oneself** explicarse, justificarse
  2 *vi* explicarse

explain away *vt* dar razones por, justificar; **he found it difficult to e. away the high number of accidents** le fue difícil justificar el gran número de accidentes

explanation [eksplə'neɪʃən] *n* *(gen)* explicación *f*; *(clarification)* aclaración *f*

explanatory [ɪkˈsplænətərɪ] *adj* explicativo(a), aclaratorio(a)

expletive [ɪkˈspliːtɪv] *n Fml* palabrota *f*, *Esp* taco *m*

explicable [ɪkˈsplɪkəbəl] *adj* explicable

explicit [ɪkˈsplɪsɪt] *adj* explícito(a)

explicitly [ɪksˈplɪsɪtlɪ] *adv* explícitamente

explode [ɪkˈspləʊd] **1** *vt* (**a**) *(bomb)* hacer explotar; *(mine)* hacer volar (**b**) *Fig (theory)* refutar; *(rumour)* desmentir
  2 *vi* *(bomb)* estallar, explotar; *Fig* **to e. with** *or* **in anger** montar en cólera; *Fig* **to e. with** *or* **into laughter** estallar de risa

exploit 1 [ˈeksplɔɪt] *n* proeza *f*, hazaña *f*
  2 [ek'splɔɪt] *vt* explotar, aprovecharse de

exploitation [eksplɔɪˈteɪʃən] *n* explotación *f*

exploitative [eks'plɔɪtətɪv] *adj* explotador(a)

exploration [eksplə'reɪʃən] *n* exploración *f*

exploratory [ek'splɒrətərɪ] *adj* exploratorio(a)

explore [ɪkˈsplɔːr] *vt & vi* explorar

explorer [ɪkˈsplɔːrər] *n* explorador(a) *m,f*

explosion [ɪkˈspləʊʒən] *n* explosión *f*; **e. of anger** ataque *m* de rabia *or* genio ❑ **population e.** explosión *f* demográfica

explosive [ɪkˈspləʊsɪv] **1** *adj* explosivo(a); *Fig* **he's got an e. temper** se enfurece por cualquier cosa ❑ **e. issue** asunto *m* delicado
  2 *n* explosivo *m*

exponent [ɪkˈspəʊnənt] *n* (**a**) *(gen)* exponente *m*; *(supporter)* defensor(a) *m,f*; *(expert)* experto(a) *m,f*; **he is the leading e. of the theory** es el principal defensor de la teoría (**b**) *(performer)* intérprete *mf* (**c**) *Math* exponente *m*

export 1 [ɪkˈspɔːt] *vt* exportar
  2 [ˈekspɔːt] *n* (**a**) *Com (trade)* exportación *f* ❑ **e. duty** aranceles *mpl* de exportación; **e. licence** licencia *f* de exportación; **e. subsidy** ayudas *fpl* a la exportación (**b**) *Com (commodity)* artículo *m* de exportación

exportation [ekspɔːˈteɪʃən] *n* exportación *f*

exporter [eks'pɔːtər] *n* exportador(a) *m,f*

exporting [eks'pɔːtɪŋ] *adj* exportador(a)

expose [ɪkˈspəʊz] *vt* (**a**) *(uncover)* exponer; *(secret)* revelar; *(plot)* descubrir; **to e. oneself** exhibirse desnudo(a); *(habitually)* practicar el exhibicionismo; **to e. oneself to danger** exponerse al peligro (**b**) *Phot* exponer

exposé [eks'pəʊzeɪ] *n* revelación *f*, desenmascaramiento *m*

exposed [ɪkˈspəʊzd] *adj* (**a**) *(shown)* expuesto(a) (**b**) *(house, place)* desabrigado(a), al descubierto

exposition [ekspə'zɪʃən] *n* (**a**) *(exhibition)* exposición *f* (**b**) *(account)* explicación *f*

expostulate [ɪk'spɒstjʊleɪt] *vi Fml* protestar, discutir, reconvenir

exposure [ɪkˈspəʊʒər] *n* (**a**) *(to light, cold, heat)* exposición *f*; **to die of e.** morir de frío (**b**) *Phot* fotografía *f* ❑ **e. meter** fotómetro *m*; **e. time** tiempo *m* de exposición (**c**) *(revealing)* revelación *f*; *(of criminal)* descubrimiento *m*; **fear of e.** temor *m* al escándalo ❑ **indecent e.** exhibicionismo *m* (**d**) *(of house)* situación *f*, orientación *f*

expound [ɪk'spaʊnd] *vt* exponer

express [ɪkˈspres] **1** *adj* (**a**) *(explicit)* expreso(a), claro(a); **for the e. purpose of ...** con el propósito expreso de ... (**b**) *Br (letter, parcel)* urgente; **send it by e. delivery** envíalo por correo urgente ❑ *Rail* **e. train** expreso *m*
  2 *n Rail* expreso *m*
  3 *vt* (**a**) *(opinion)* expresar; **to. e. oneself** *(speak, write thoughts)* expresarse (**b**) *(fruit juice)* exprimir
  4 *adv* urgente; **send it e.** mándalo urgente

expression [ɪkˈspreʃən] *n* expresión *f*; *Math* señal *f*

expressive [ɪkˈspresɪv] *adj* expresivo(a)

expressly [ɪksˈpreslɪ] *adv Fml* expresamente

expresso [e(k)s'presəʊ] *(pl* **expressos)** *n* café *m* solo

expropriate [eks'prəʊprɪeɪt] *vt* expropiar

expropriation [eksprəʊprɪˈeɪʃən] *n* expropiación *f*

expulsion [ɪkˈspʌlʃən] *n* expulsión *f*

expunge [ɪks'pʌndʒ] *vt* borrar, eliminar

expurgate [ˈekspəɡeɪt] *vt* expurgar

expurgation [ekspə'ɡeɪʃən] *n* expurgación *f*

exquisite [ɪk'skwɪzɪt] *adj* exquisito(a), perfecto(a)

exquisitely [eks'kwɪzɪtlɪ] *adv* exquisitamente

ex-serviceman [eks'sɜːvɪsmən] *n* *(pl* **ex-servicemen)** *Mil* ex combatiente *m*

extant [ek'stænt] *adj* existente

extempore [ɪk'stempərɪ] **1** *adj Fml* improvisado(a)
  2 *adv* de improviso, improvisadamente

extemporize [ɪk'stempəraɪz] *vt & vi Fml* improvisar

extend [ɪk'stend] **1** *vt* (**a**) *(space) (enlarge)* ampliar; *(lengthen)* alargar; *(increase)* aumentar; **she wants to e. her country house** quiere ampliar su casa de campo; *Fig* **the prohibition was extended to cover cigarettes** extendieron la prohibición a los cigarrillos (**b**) *(give, offer)* rendir, dar; **he extended the letter to the manager** hizo entrega de la carta al director; **to e. an invitation to sb** invitar a algn; **to e. a welcome to sb** recibir a algn (**c**) *(time) (prolong)* prolongar, alargar; **I asked them to e. my travel insurance** solicité que prorrogaran el seguro de viaje; **regular maintenance extends a car's life** el mantenimiento regular alarga la vida de un coche; **to e. a stay** prolongar una estancia
  2 *vi* (**a**) *(stretch)* extenderse; **his lands extended as far as the great desert** sus tierras se extendían hasta el gran desierto (**b**) *(last)* extenderse, prolongarse, durar, alargarse; **the winter extended well into March** el invierno se alargó hasta bien entrado marzo

extended family [ɪks'tendɪd'fæmɪlɪ] *n* clan *m* familiar

extension [ɪk'stenʃən] *n* (**a**) *(gen)* extensión *f*, prolongación *f*; *(of time)* prórroga *f* (**b**) *Tel* extensión *f*, *RP* interno *m* **e. 33 please** con la extensión *or RP* el interno 33 por favor (**c**) *Constr* anexo *m*

extensive [ɪk'stensɪv] *adj* *(length, quality)* extenso(a); *(space)* amplio(a)

extensively [ɪks'tensɪvlɪ] *adv* (**a**) *(widely)* extensamente (**b**) *(frequently)* frecuentemente, con frecuencia

extent [ɪk'stent] *n* (**a**) *(area)* extensión *f* (**b**) *(degree)* punto *m*; **to a certain e., to some e.** hasta cierto punto; **to a large e.** en gran parte; **to a lesser e.** en menor grado; **to**

such an e. hasta tal punto (**c**) *(limit)* límite *m*; **I've reached the e. of my patience** he llegado al límite de mi paciencia

extenuating [ɪk'stenjʊeɪtɪŋ] *adj Jur* atenuante ❑ **e. circumstances** circunstancias *fpl* atenuantes

exterior [ɪk'stɪərɪər] **1** *adj* exterior, externo(a)
2 *n* exterior *m*

exterminate [ɪk'stɜːmɪneɪt] *vt* exterminar

extermination [ɪkstɜːmɪ'neɪʃən] *n* exterminación *f*, exterminio *m*

exterminator [ɪk'stɜːmɪneɪtər] *n* exterminador(a) *m,f*

external [ek'stɜːnəl] *adj* (**a**) *(gen)* externo(a), exterior; *Med* **for e. use only** sólo para uso externo ❑ *Pol* **e. affairs** asuntos *mpl* exteriores (**b**) *Univ* por libre

externalize [ɪks'tɜːnəlaɪz] *vt (feelings, emotions)* exteriorizar

extinct [ɪk'stɪŋkt] *adj* (**a**) *(species)* extinguido(a); **to become e.** extinguirse (**b**) *(volcano)* extinguido(a), apagado(a)

extinction [ɪk'stɪŋkʃən] *n* extinción *f*

extinguish [ɪk'stɪŋgwɪʃ] *vt* extinguir, apagar

extinguisher [ɪk'stɪŋgwɪʃər] *n Esp* extintor *m*, *Am* extinguidor *m*

extirpate ['ekstəpeɪt] *vt* extirpar

extol, *US* **extoll** [ɪk'stəʊl] *vt (pt & pp* **extolled**) ensalzar, alabar

extort [ɪk'stɔːt] *vt (promise, confession)* arrancar; *(money)* sacar

extortion [ɪk'stɔːʃən] *n (of money)* extorsión *f*

extortionate [ɪk'stɔːʃənɪt] *adj* exorbitante, desorbitado(a)

extortionately [ɪks'tɔːʃənɪtlɪ] *adv* **to be e. expensive** tener un precio abusivo *or* exorbitante

extra ['ekstrə] **1** *adj* extra, más; *(spare)* de sobra; **e. charge** suplemento *m*; **I've got two e. tickets** me sobran dos entradas; **the wine is e.** el vino se cobra aparte, el vino no está incluido
2 *adv* extra; **e. fine** finísimo(a), extra fino; **e. strong** fortísimo(a), extra fuerte
3 *n* (**a**) *(additional charge)* suplemento *m* (**b**) *Cin* extra *mf* (**c**) *(newspaper)* edición *f* especial

extract ['ekstrækt] **1** *n* (**a**) *(concentrate)* extracto *m*; **meat e.** extracto de carne (**b**) *(from book)* fragmento *m*
2 [ɪk'strækt] *vt (tooth, information)* extraer, sacar; *(confession)* arrancar

extraction [ɪk'strækʃən] *n* (**a**) *(removal)* extracción *f* (**b**) *(descent)* origen *m*; **to be of Spanish e.** ser de origen español

extractor [ɪk'stræktər] *n* extractor *m* ❑ **e. fan** extractor *m* de humos

extracurricular [ekstrəkə'rɪkjʊlər] *adj Educ* extraescolar, fuera del programa de estudios

extradite ['ekstrədaɪt] *vt* extraditar, extradir

extradition [ekstrə'dɪʃən] *n* extradición *f*

extrajudicial ['ekstrədʒuː'dɪʃəl] *adj* extrajudicial

extramarital [ekstrə'mærɪtəl] *adj* fuera del matrimonio, extramatrimonial

extramural [ekstrə'mjʊərəl] *adj Br Univ* **e. course** curso *m* para estudiantes libres

extraneous [ɪk'streɪnɪəs] *adj Fml* ajeno(a), extraño(a)

extraordinarily [ɪks'trɔːdənərɪlɪ] *adv* extraordinariamente

extraordinary [ɪk'strɔːdənərɪ] *adj* (**a**) *(special, additional)* extraordinario(a), fuera de lo común (**b**) *(strange)* raro(a); **what an e. thing!** ¡qué cosa más rara!

extrapolate [ɪk'stræpəleɪt] *vt* (**a**) *Math* extrapolar (**b**) *(guess)* extrapolar

extrapolation [ɪkstræpə'leɪʃən] *n* extrapolación *f*

extrasensory perception ['ekstrə'sensərɪpə'sepʃən] *n* percepción *f* extrasensorial

extraterrestrial ['ekstrətɪ'restrɪəl] *adj & n* extraterrestre *(mf)*

extravagance [ɪk'strævɪgəns] *n (spending)* derroche *m*, despilfarro *m*; *(behaviour)* extravagancia *f*, exageración *f*

extravagant [ɪk'strævɪgənt] *adj (wasteful)* derrochador(a), despilfarrador(a); *(excessive)* exagerado(a); *(luxurious)* lujoso(a), suntuoso(a)

extravaganza [ɪkstrævə'gænzə] *n Theat* farsa *f*, fantasía *f*

Extremadura [ekstrəmə'djuːrə] *n* Extremadura

extreme [ɪk'striːm] **1** *adj* extremo(a); **an e. case** un caso excepcional; **to hold e. views** tener opiniones muy radicales ❑ **e. sports** deportes *mpl* extremos; *Rel* **E. Unction** Extremaunción *f*
2 *n* extremo *m*; **in the e.** en sumo grado, en extremo; **to go from one e. to the other** pasar de un extremo a otro; **to go to extremes** llegar a extremos

extremely [ɪks'triːmlɪ] *adv* extremadamente, sumamente; **e. annoyed/pleased** enfadadísimo(a)/contentísimo(a); **I'm e. sorry** lo siento de veras

extremism [ɪk'striːmɪzəm] *n* extremismo *m*

extremist [ɪk'striːmɪst] *n* extremista *mf*

extremity [ɪk'stremɪtɪ] *n* (**a**) *(extreme)* extremidad *f*, extremo *m* (**b**) **extremities** *(hands, feet)* extremidades *fpl*

extricate ['ekstrɪkeɪt] *vt* librar, sacar; **to e. oneself** lograr salir (**from** de)

extrovert ['ekstrəvɜːt] *adj & n* extrovertido(a) *(m,f)*

extrude [ɪk'struːd] *vt Tech* expulsar

exuberance [ɪg'zjuːbərəns] *n (effusiveness)* exuberancia *f*; *(vitality)* euforia *f*

exuberant [ɪg'zjuːbərənt] *adj (excessive)* exuberante; *(energetic)* eufórico(a)

exude [ɪg'zjuːd] *vt (sweat, sap)* exudar, rezumar; *Fig (health, confidence)* rebosar

exult [ɪg'zʌlt] *vi* regocijarse

exultant [ɪg'zʌltənt] *adj* jubiloso(a), regocijado(a), triunfante

exultation [ɪgzʌl'teɪʃən] *n* exultación *f*, júbilo *m*

eye [aɪ] **1** *n* (**a**) *Anat* ojo *m*; *Fig* **anyone with half an e. can see she's wrong** cualquiera con dos dedos de frente puede ver que está equivocada; *Fig* **as far as the e. can see** hasta donde alcanza la vista; *Fig* **before** *or* **under my very eyes** delante de mis propios ojos; *Fig* **I couldn't believe my eyes** no podía creerlo; *Fig* **in the eyes of** según; *Fig* **in the eyes of the law this is illegal** según la ley esto es ilegal; *Fig* **in the mind's e.** en la imaginación; *Fig* **in the twinkling of an e.** en un abrir y cerrar de ojos; *Fig* **my e. fell upon ...** me di cuenta de ...; *Fig* **not to take one's eyes off sth/sb** no quitar *or Andes RP* sacar la vista de encima a algo/algn; *Fig* **to be very much in the public -e.** aparecer mucho en público; *Fig* **to catch sb's e.** llamar la atención a algn; *Fig* **to do sth with one's eyes open** hacer algo sabiendo lo que le espera a uno; *Fig* **to have an e. for** tener buen ojo para; *Fig* **to have eyes in the back of one's head** saber *or* darse cuenta de todo, *RP* tener ojos en la nuca; *Fig* **to make eyes at sb** dirigir miraditas a algn; *Fig* **to my e.** en mi opinión; *Fig* **to only have eyes for ...** sólo tener ojos para ...; *Fig* **to open sb's eyes** abrirle los ojos a algn; *Fig* **to shut one's eyes to sth** hacer la vista gorda a algo; *Fig* **to see e. to e. with sb** estar de acuerdo con algn; *Fig* **to turn a blind e.** hacer la vista gorda (**to** a); *Fig.* **with an e. to** con el propósito de, con miras a; *Fig* **with the naked e.** a simple vista; *Fam* **to keep an e. on sth/sb** vigilar algo/a algn; *Fam* **to keep an e. out for sth/sb** tener un ojo pendiente de algo/algn; *Fam* **to keep one's eyes open** *or* **peeled** *or* **skinned** estar ojo alerta; *Fam Fig* **I'm up to my eyes in work** estoy hasta aquí de trabajo; *Prov* **an e. for an e. (a tooth for a tooth)** ojo por ojo (diente por diente) ❏ **black e.** ojo *m* a la funerala; **e. contact** contacto *m* visual; **glass e.** ojo *m* de cristal; **private e.** detective *mf* privado(a) **(b)** *(of needle, potato, hurricane)* ojo *m*

2 *vt* mirar, observar; **to e. sb up and down** mirar a algn de arriba abajo

eyeball ['aɪbɔːl] *n* globo *m* ocular

eyebrow ['aɪbraʊ] *n* ceja *f*

eyecatching ['aɪkætʃɪŋ] *adj* llamativo(a)

eyeful ['aɪfʊl] *n Fam* **to get an e.** echar un vistazo

eyeglass ['aɪglɑːs] *n* monóculo *m*; *US* **eyeglasses** *(spectacles)* gafas *fpl*

eyelash ['aɪlæʃ] *n* pestaña *f*

eyelet ['aɪlɪt] *n* ojete *m*

eyelid ['aɪlɪd] *n* párpado *m*

eyeliner ['aɪlaɪnə] *n* lápiz *m* de ojos

eye-opener ['aɪəʊpənər] *n* revelación *f*, gran sorpresa *f*

eyepatch ['aɪpætʃ] *n* parche *m*

eyepiece ['aɪpiːs] *n* ocular *m*

eyeshade ['aɪʃeɪd] *n* visera *f*

eyeshadow ['aɪʃædəʊ] *n* sombra *f* de ojos

eyesight ['aɪsaɪt] *n* vista *f*; **my e. is failing** me está fallando la vista

eyesore ['aɪsɔːr] *n* monstruosidad *f*; **to be an e.** ofender a la vista

eyestrain ['aɪstreɪn] *n* vista *f* cansada; **to suffer from e.** tener la vista cansada

eyetooth ['aɪtuːθ] *n* (*pl* **eyeteeth** ['aɪtiːθ]) *Anat* colmillo *m*; *Fam* **I would give my eyeteeth to ...** daría un ojo de la cara por ...

eyewash ['aɪwɒʃ] *n Med* colirio *m*; *Fam* **it's all e.** eso son disparates

eyewitness ['aɪwɪtnɪs] *n* testigo *mf* ocular

eyrie ['ɪərɪ] *n* aguilera *f*

F

F, f [ef] *n* (**a**) *(the letter)* F, f *f* (**b**) *Mus* fa *m*

F *(abbr* **Fahrenheit***)* Fahrenheit, F

f [ef] *Ling (abbr* **feminine***)* femenino, f

FA [efˈeɪ] *n* (**a**) *Br Sport (abbr* **Football Association**) Federación *f* de fútbol (**b**) *Vulg Offens (abbr* **fuck all**) *(virtually nothing)* una mierda; *(absolutely nothing)* ni una mierda

fab [fæb] *adj (abbr* **fabulous***) Br Fam* genial,*Esp* chachi

fable [ˈfeɪbəl] *n* fábula *f*; **Aesop's fables** las fábulas de Esopo

fabled [ˈfeɪbəld] *adj* (**a**) *(legendary)* fabulado(a); **ghosts are f. to appear at midnight** cuenta la leyenda que los fantasmas aparecen a media noche (**b**) *(fictitious)* ficticio(a)

fabric [ˈfæbrɪk] *n* (**a**) *Tex* tela *f*, tejido *m* (**b**) *Constr* fábrica *f*, estructura *f*; *Fig* **the f. of society** la estructura de la sociedad

fabricate [ˈfæbrɪkeɪt] *vt* (**a**) *(build, invent)* fabricar; *(story, lie)* inventar (**b**) *(forge)* falsificar

fabrication [fæbrɪˈkeɪʃən] *n Fig* invención *f*; **it is pure f.** es pura invención *or* ficción

fabulous [ˈfæbjʊləs] *adj* fabuloso(a)

façade, **facade** *n* [fəˈsɑːd] *Archit* fachada *f*; *Fig* **it's all a f.** es pura fachada

face [feɪs] **1** *n* (**a**) *Anat* cara *f*, rostro *m*; **a serious f.** una cara seria; **a smiling f.** un semblante risueño; **f. to f.** cara a cara; **he never forgets a f.** es muy buen fisonomista; **I told him to his f.** se lo dije en la cara; **she laughed in my f.** se me rió en la cara; **she slammed the door in my f.** me dió con la puerta en las narices; *Fam* **shut your f.!** ¡cierra el pico!; **to look sb in the f.** mirarle a algn a la cara; *Fig* **to fall flat on one's f.** caerse de bruces; *Fig* **to show one's f.** asomar la cara ❑ **f. cloth** paño *m*; **f. cream** crema *f* de belleza; **f. pack** mascarilla *f* facial (**b**) *(expression)* cara *f*, expresión *f*; **to pull a long f.** poner una cara larga; **to keep a straight f.** mantenerse serio(a); **to pull faces** hacer muecas (**c**) *(surface)* superficie *f*; *(card, coin)* cara *f*; *(dial)* cuadrante *m*; *(watch)* esfera *f*; *(cliff)* cara *f*; *(world)* faz *f*, superficie *f*; *(cards)* **f. down** boca abajo; **f. up** boca arriba; *(fig)* **in the f. of danger** ante el peligro ❑ **coal f.** frente *m* de carbón; **f. value** valor *m* nominal; **f. worker** minero *m* del frente (**d**) *(appearance)* aspecto *m*; **on the f. of it** a primera vista; **to lose f.** desprestigiarse; **to save f.** salvar las apariencias; **to take sth at f. value** entender algo sólo en su sentido literal

2 *vt* (**a**) *(building etc) (look onto)* dar a, mirar hacia; *(be opposite)* estar enfrente de (**b**) *(confront)* encontrarse delante de; **the country is facing a crisis** el país se halla frente a una crisis; **the problem facing us** el problema que se nos plantea; **we are faced with the prospect of ...** nos encontramos ante la perspectiva de ... (**c**) *(meet resolutely)* hacer frente a; **he won't f. the facts** no quiere enfrentarse con la realidad; **let's f. it** hay que reconocerlo; **to f. up to** hacer cara a, enfrentarse con, afrontar; **to f. the consequences** afrontar las consecuencias; *Fam* **to f. the music** dar la cara (**d**) *(tolerate)* soportar, aguantar; **I can't f. another meat pie** no puedo con otra empanada (**e**) *Constr (wall)* revestir (**with** de) (**f**) *Sew* forrar (**with** de)

3 *vi* **f. this way** vuélvase de este lado; **to f. on to** dar a; **to f. towards** mirar hacia

face-ache [ˈfeɪseɪk] (**a**) *n (pain)* neuralgia *f* (**b**) *Fam (ugly person)* feto *m*

faceless [ˈfeɪslɪs] *adj* sin cara, anónimo(a)

facelift [ˈfeɪslɪft] *n* (**a**) *Med* lifting *m* (**b**) *Fig (building)* renovación *f*, modernización *f*

face-off [ˈfeɪsɒf] *n (confrontation)* enfrentamiento *m* (a cara de perro)

face-saving [ˈfeɪsseɪvɪŋ] *adj* **f.-s. exercise** maniobra *f* para salvar las apariencias

facet [ˈfæsɪt] *n* faceta *f*, aspecto *m*

facetious [fəˈsiːʃəs] *adj* bromista, chistoso(a), gracioso(a)

face-to-face [feɪstəˈfeɪs] **1** *adj (meeting)* cara a cara

2 *adv* cara a cara, frente a frente; **to meet sb f.** encontrarse frente a frente con algn

facial [ˈfeɪʃəl] **1** *adj* facial

2 *n* tratamiento *m* facial

facile [ˈfæsaɪl] *adj (easy)* fácil; *(simplistic)* superficial

facilitate [fəˈsɪlɪteɪt] *vt* facilitar

facilitator [fəˈsɪlɪteɪtər] *n (person)* promotor(a) *m,f*

facility [fəˈsɪlɪti] *n* (**a**) *(ease)* facilidad *f* (**b**) **facilities** *(means)* facilidades *fpl* ❑ **credit f.** facilidades *fpl* de crédito (**c**) **facilities** *(rooms, equipment)* instalaciones *fpl* ❑ **cooking f.** derecho *m* a cocina; **sports f.** instalaciones *fpl* deportivas

facing [ˈfeɪsɪŋ] **1** *n* (**a**) *Constr* revestimiento *m* (**b**) *Sew* guarnición *f* (**c**) **facings** vueltas *fpl*

2 *adj* de enfrente; **f. page** página *f* opuesta

facsimile [fækˈsɪmɪli] **1** *n* (**a**) *(exact copy)* facsímil *m*, facsímile *m* (**b**) *(message)* facsímil *m*, telefax *m*, fax *m* (**c**) *(machine)* facsímil *m*, fax *m*

2 *vt* mandar *or* enviar por fax

fact [fækt] *n* (**a**) *(event, happening)* hecho *m*; **a story based on f.** una historia basada en un hecho real; **as a matter of f.** de hecho; **facts and figures** datos *mpl* y cifras *fpl*; **hard facts** hechos *mpl* innegables; **the f. that he confessed** el hecho de que confesara; **to stick to facts** atenerse a los hechos (**b**) *(reality)* realidad *f*; **f. and fiction** lo real y lo ficticio; **in f., in point of f.** en realidad; **it is a f. of life that ...** es un hecho ineludible que ...; **the f. is that ...** el hecho es que ...; **the f. remains that ...** sigue siendo un hecho que ...;

Euph **the facts of life** el misterio de la vida; **we know for a f. that ...** sabemos a ciencia cierta que ...

fact-finding ['fæktfaɪndɪŋ] *adj* investigador(a); **a f.-f. mission** una misión investigadora

faction¹ ['fækʃən] *n (group)* facción *f*

faction² ['fækʃən] *n Lit Fam* historia *f* novelada, reportaje *m* novelado

factitive ['fæktɪtɪv] *adj Ling* factitivo(a)

factor ['fæktər] *n* (a) *(element)* factor *m* (b) *Math* factor *m*; **highest common f.** máximo común divisor *m*

factorize ['fæktəraɪz] *vt Math* dividir en factores

factory ['fæktərɪ] *n* fábrica *f, Am* planta *f* ❑ **f. worker** obrero(a) *m,f,* operario(a) *m,f* de fábrica

factotum [fæk'təʊtəm] *n* factótum *m*

factual ['fæktʃʊəl] *adj* factual, objetivo(a); **a f. analysis** un análisis de los hechos; **a f. error** un error de hecho

faculty ['fækəltɪ] *n* (a) *(power)* facultad *f*; **he has all his faculties** tiene todas sus facultades (b) *Univ* facultad *f* (c) *US Univ* profesorado *m*, cuerpo *m* docente

fad [fæd] *n Fam* (a) *(fashion, craze)* moda *f* pasajera (b) *(whim)* capricho *m*; *(mania)* manía *f*

faddy ['fædɪ] *adj* (**faddier, faddiest**) *Fam* caprichoso(a)

fade [feɪd] **1** *vt (colour, material)* descolorar, desteñir
2 *vi* (a) *(colour, material)* descolorarse, desteñirse (b) *(flower)* marchitarse (c) *(light)* apagarse

fade away *vi* desvanecerse; **all hope has faded away** todas las esperanzas se desvanecieron

fade in *vt*, **fade out** *vt Cin TV* fundir

faded ['feɪdɪd] *adj* (a) *(colour, material)* descolorido(a), desteñido(a) (b) *(flower)* marchito(a)

fade-in ['feɪdɪn] *n*, **fade-out** ['feɪdaʊt] *n Cin TV* fundido *m*

faeces ['fiːsiːz] *npl* heces *fpl*

fag [fæg] *n* (a) *Br Fam (nuisance)* pesadez *f*, lata *f*; **what a f.!** ¡qué latazo! (b) *Br Fam (cigarette)* pitillo *m* (c) *US Slang (homosexual)* maricón *m, Méx* tortillón *m, RP* trolo *m* (d) *Br Sch Slang* fámulo *m*

fag-end ['fægend] *n Fam* colilla *f, Am* pucho *m*

fagged [fægd] *adj Fam* rendido(a), molido(a)

faggot ['fægət] *n* (a) *(wood)* haz *m* de leña (b) *Br Culin* albondiguilla *f* (c) *US Slang Offens* maricón *m, Méx* tortillón *m, RP* trolo *m*

faggy ['fægɪ] *adj US Slang Offens* maricón

Fahrenheit ['færənhaɪt] *n* Fahrenheit *m*; **ten degrees F.** diez grados Fahrenheit

fail [feɪl] **1** *n* (a) *Educ* suspenso *m, Am* reprobado *m* (b) **without f.** *(definitely)* sin falta
2 *vt* (a) *(let down)* fallar; **his memory failed him** le falló la memoria; **words f. me** no encuentro palabras (b) *Educ (exam) Esp* suspender, *Am* reprobar; **she failed biology** la suspendieron en biología
3 *vi* (a) *(show, film)* fracasar, fallar; *(brakes, lights)* fallar; *(crops)* perderse; **the attempt failed** el intento fracasó (b) *Com (business)* quebrar; **it can't f.** no puede fallar; **if all else fails** si te falla todo (c) *Educ Esp* suspender, *Am* reprobar; (d) *(be unable)* no lograr; **he failed to score** no logró marcar; **I f. to see why** no veo por qué (e) *(forget, neglect)* dejar de; **don't f. to come** no deje de venir; **she never fails to attend** nunca falta (f) *(health)* deteriorarse; **her sight is failing** le falla la vista; **his heart failed** le falló el corazón

failed [feɪld] *adj* fracasado(a); **a f. actress** una actriz fracasada

failing ['feɪlɪŋ] **1** *n* (a) *(shortcoming)* defecto *m, Esp* fallo *m, Am* falla *f* (b) *(weakness)* debilidad *f*, flaqueza *f*
2 *prep* a falta de

fail-safe ['feɪlseɪf] *adj* **f.-s. device** dispositivo *m* de seguridad

failure ['feɪljə] *n (lack of success)* fracaso *m*; **the meal was a complete f.** la comida fue un fracaso total (b) *Com* quiebra *f* (c) *Educ* suspenso *m* (d) *(person)* fracasado(a) *m,f*; **he was a f. as a writer** como escritor fue un fracaso (e) *Tech (breakdown)* fallo *m*, avería *f, Am* falla *f* ❑ **brake f.** fallo *m* de los frenos; *Med* **heart f.** paro *m* cardíaco; **power f.** apagón *m* (f) *(inability, neglect)* **her f. to answer the question** el hecho de que no contestara a la pregunta; **f. to attend will be punished** se castigará la falta de asistencia; **f. to observe the rules** incumplimiento *m* de las reglas

fain [feɪn] *adv Literary* de buena gana; **I would f. have stayed at home** me habría quedado en casa tranquilamente

faint [feɪnt] **1** *adj* (a) *(sound, voice)* débil, tenue; *(colour)* pálido(a); *(outline)* borroso(a); *(idea, recollection)* vago(a); **a f. resemblance** un ligero parecido; **f. hope** pocas esperanzas; **I haven't the faintest idea** no tengo la más mínima idea (b) *Med (giddy)* mareado(a); **to feel f.** sentirse mareado(a)
2 *n Med* desmayo *m*
3 *vi Med* desmayarse

faint-hearted [feɪnt'hɑːtɪd] *adj* pusilánime, temeroso(a)

faintly ['feɪntlɪ] *adv (with little strength)* débilmente; *(unclearly)* vagamente

faintness ['feɪntnɪs] *n* (a) *(of sound, light)* levedad *f* (b) *Med* mareos *mpl*, desfallecimientos *mpl*

fair¹ [feər] **1** *adj* (a) *(impartial)* imparcial; *(just)* justo(a), equitativo(a); **I have had my f. share of problems** yo ya he tenido bastantes problemas; **I paid my f. share** pagué mi parte; **it's not f.** no hay derecho; **to give sb a f. hearing** escuchar imparcialmente a algn; **to give sb f. warning** avisar debidamente a algn; *Fam* **f. do's** seamos justos; *Fam* **f. enough!** de acuerdo *or Esp* vale, está bien ❑ **f. play** juego *m* limpio (b) *(hair)* rubio(a), *Méx* güero(a), *Bol* choco(a), *Col* mono(a), *Ven* catire(a); *(skin)* claro(a); *(complexion)* blanco(a) (c) *Meteor* bueno(a), bonancible (d) *Literary (beautiful)* bello(a), hermoso(a); **the f. sex** el bello sexo (e) *(quite good)* **a f. number** un buen número; **he has a f. chance** tiene bastantes probabilidades; *Fam* **f. to middling** mediano, regular (f) **f. copy** copia *f* en limpio
2 *adv* **it hit me f. and square on the chin** me dio en pleno mentón; **they beat us f. and square** nos ganaron merecidamente; **to play f.** jugar limpio

fair² [feər] *n* (a) *Br (funfair)* feria *f* (b) **trade f.** feria *f* de muestras

fairground ['feəgraʊnd] *n* feria *f*

fair-haired [feə'heəd] *adj* rubio(a), *Méx* güero(a), *Bol* choco(a), *Col* mono(a), *Ven* catire(a)

fairly ['feəlɪ] *adv* (a) *(justly)* justamente, con equidad (b) *(moderately)* bastante; **f. rich** bastante rico(a) (c) *Fam (really, utterly)* **it's f. tipping it down** ciertamente llueve mucho

fair-minded [feə'maɪndɪd] *adj* imparcial, justo(a)

fairness ['feənɪs] *n* (a) *(justice)* justicia *f*, equidad *f*; **in all f.** para ser justos (b) *(hair)* color *m* rubio; *(complexion)* blancura *f*, palidez *f*

fair-sized [feə'saɪzd] *adj* bastante grande

fair-skinned [feə'skɪnd] *adj* de piel blanca *or* pálida

fairway ['feəweɪ] *n Golf* calle *f*

fair-weather friend ['feəweðə'frend] *n* amigo(a) *m,f* sólo para lo bueno

fairy ['feərɪ] *n* (a) *(in folklore)* hada *f* ❑ **f. godmother** hada *f* madrina; **f. tale** cuento *m* de hadas; **f. tale ending** desenlace *m* feliz (b) *Slang Offens* marica *m*

fairyland ['feərɪlænd] n Fig lugar m de ensueño

fairy-lights ['feərɪlaɪts] npl bombillas fpl de colorines

fait accompli [feɪtə'kɒmpliː] n (pl **faits accomplis** [feɪtsə'kɒmpliː]) Fml hecho m consumado

faith [feɪθ] n (a) Rel fe f; **the Catholic f.** la fe católica (b) (trust) fe f, confianza f; **in good/bad f.** de buena/mala fe; **to break f. with sb** ser desleal a algn; **to have f. in sb** tener fe or confiar en algn

faithful ['feɪθfʊl] **1** adj (a) (loyal) fiel, leal (**to** a, con) (b) (accurate) fiel, exacto(a)
2 the f. npl Rel los fieles

faithfully ['feɪθfʊlɪ] adv (a) (loyally) fielmente, lealmente (b) (accurately) fielmente (c) (in letter) **yours f.** le saluda atentamente

faithfulness ['feɪθfʊlnɪs] n (a) (loyalty) fidelidad f, lealtad f (**to** a) (b) (accuracy) fidelidad f, exactitud f

faith-healer ['feɪθhiːlər] n curandero(a) m,f por fe

faith-healing ['feɪθhiːlɪŋ] n curación f por fe

fake [feɪk] **1** adj falso(a), falsificado(a)
2 n (a) (object) falsificación f, copia f (b) (person) impostor(a) m,f, farsante mf, tramposo(a) m,f
3 vt (a) (forge) falsificar (b) (feign) fingir, simular
4 vi (pretend) fingir, simular

falcon ['fɔːlkən] n Orn halcón m

Falklands ['fɔːkləndz] npl **the F.** las (Islas) Malvinas

fall [fɔːl] **1** n (a) (of person, besieged city) caída f ⊃ US Fam **f. guy** cabeza f de turco (b) Pol (of government, politician, empire) caída f (c) (of rock) desprendimiento m; **f. of snow** nevada f (d) (decrease) baja f, disminución f; **an unexpected f. in prices** un inesperado descenso de los precios (e) US otoño m; **in the f.** en otoño (f) (usu pl) cascada f; **Niagara Falls** las cataratas del Niágara
2 vi (pt **fell**; pp **fallen**) (a) (trip, tumble) caerse; **she fell off her bicycle** se cayó de la bicicleta; **the stress falls on the first syllable** el acento cae en la primera sílaba; **they f. into two categories** se dividen en dos categorías; Fig **Christmas Day falls on a Sunday** el día de Navidad cae en domingo; Fig **night was falling** anochecía; Fig **to f. from grace** caer en desgracia; Fig **to f. into line** aceptar las reglas; Fig **to f. into sb's hands** caer en manos de algn; Fig **to f. prey to** ser víctima de; Fig **to f. short (of)** no alcanzar (b) (in battle) caer, morir (c) (temperature, prices) bajar (d) (become) **to f. asleep** dormirse, **to f. ill** caer enfermo(a), enfermar, RP Ven enfermarse; **to f. in love** enamorarse; **to f. to pieces** hacerse pedazos

fall about vi troncharse or mondarse or partirse de risa

fall away vi desaparecer

fall back vi Mil retirarse

fall back on vt (resort to) echar mano a, recurrir a

fall behind vi (in race) quedarse atrás; **to f. behind with one's work** retrasarse en el trabajo

fall down vi (a) (picture etc) caerse (b) (building) derrumbarse, hundirse (c) (argument) fallar

fall for vt (a) (fall in love with) enamorarse de, prendarse de (b) (be tricked by) dejarse engañar por; Fam **she fell for it** picó, se lo tragó

fall in vi (a) (roof) desplomarse, caerse (b) Mil formar filas, ponerse en fila

fall off vi (a) (drop off) caer; **her ring fell off** se le cayó el anillo (b) (come off) desprenderse (c) (diminish) bajar, disminuir, decaer; **sales have fallen off** las ventas han bajado

fall out vi (a) (hair) caerse (b) Mil romper filas (c) (quarrel) pelearse, reñirse (**with** con)

fall over vi caerse; Fig **to f. over oneself to do sth** volcarse en algo

fall through vi (plan) fracasar

fallacious [fə'leɪʃəs] adj Fml falso(a), erróneo(a)

fallacy ['fæləsɪ] n falacia f

fallen ['fɔːlən] **1** pp see **fall**
2 adj caído(a); Old-fashioned **a f. woman** una mujer perdida
3 the f. npl Mil los caídos

fallibility [fælɪ'bɪlɪtɪ] n falibilidad f

fallible ['fælɪbəl] adj falible

Fallopian [fə'ləʊpɪən] adj Anat **F. tube** trompa f de Falopio

fall-out ['fɔːlaʊt] n (radioactive) **f.-o.** lluvia f radioactiva ⊃ **f.-o. shelter** refugio m antiatómico

fallow ['fæləʊ] (a) adj Agr en barbecho; **to lie f.** estar en barbecho (b) Zool **f. deer** gamo m

false [fɔːls] adj falso(a); **under f. pretences** por fraude ⊃ **f. alarm** falsa alarma f; **f. bottom** doble fondo m; Mus **f. note** nota f falsa; Sport **f. start** salida f nula; **f. statement** declaración f falsa; **f. step** paso m en falso; **f. teeth** dentadura f postiza, Col RDom caja f de dientes

falsehood ['fɔːlshʊd] n (lie) falsedad f, mentira f

falsely ['fɔːlslɪ] adv falsamente

falseness ['fɔːlsnɪs] n (untruthfulness) falsedad f

falsetto [fɔːl'setəʊ] n (pl **falsettos**) Mus falsete m ⊃ **a f. voice** una voz de falsete

falsies ['fɔːlsɪz] npl Fam (breasts) postizos mpl, rellenos mpl

falsification [fɔːlsɪfɪ'keɪʃən] n falsificación f

falsify ['fɔːlsɪfaɪ] vt (pt & pp **falsified**) (records, accounts) falsificar; (misrepresent) (story, issue) falsear

falter ['fɔːltər] vi (hesitate) titubear, vacilar; (voice) fallar

faltering ['fɔːltərɪŋ] adj titubeante, vacilante; **with f. voice** con voz temblorosa

fame [feɪm] n fama f

famed [feɪmd] adj famoso(a), célebre (**for** por)

familiar [fə'mɪlɪər] adj (a) (common, usual) familiar, conocido(a); **his face is f.** su cara me suena; **it's the old f. story** es la misma historia de siempre (b) (aware, knowledgeable) al corriente; **to make oneself f. with sth** familiarizarse con algo; **I'm f. with the details** estoy al corriente de los detalles (c) (intimate) **to be on f. terms with sb** tener confianza con algn; **to get too f. with sb** tomarse demasiadas libertades con algn

familiarity [fəmɪlɪ'ærɪtɪ] n (a) (awareness, knowledge) familiaridad f (**with** con), conocimiento m (**with** de) (b) (intimacy) familiaridad f, confianza f; Prov **f. breeds contempt** el que no te conozca que te compre

familiarize [fə'mɪljəraɪz] vt (a) (acquaint) **to f. oneself with sth** familiarizarse con algo (b) (divulge) popularizar; **the press have familiarized the word 'yuppie'** la prensa ha popularizado la palabra 'yuppie'

family ['fæmɪlɪ] n familia f; **she is one of the f.** es como de la familia; Fam **it runs in the f.** viene de familia; Fam **to be in the f. way** estar en estado ⊃ Br Formerly **f. allowance** subsidio m familiar; **f. doctor** médico m de cabecera; **f. life** vida f familiar; **f. man** hombre m hogareño; US **f. name** apellido m; **f. planning** planificación f familiar; **f. ties** lazos mpl familiares; **f. tree** árbol m genealógico

famine ['fæmɪn] n hambre f, escasez f de alimentos; **f. relief** ayuda f humanitaria contra el hambre

famished ['fæmɪʃt] adj Fam muerto(a) de hambre

famous ['feɪməs] adj famoso(a), célebre (**for** por)

famously ['feɪməslɪ] adv Fam estupendamente; **they get on f.** se llevan estupendamente bien

fan [fæn] **1** n (a) (cooling device) (hand-held) abanico m; Elec ventilador *m* ❑ *Aut* **f. belt** correa *f* del ventilador; **f. heater** estufa *f* de aire (**b**) *(person)* aficionado(a) *m,f*; *(of pop star, entertainer, etc)* admirador(a) *m,f*; **a cinema f.** un aficionado al cine ❑ **f. club** club *m* de admiradores; **f. mail** cartas *fpl* de los admiradores; **football f.** hincha *mf*

2 *vt* (**a**) *(with fan)* abanicar; **to f. oneself** abanicarse (**b**) *(fire)* avivar (**c**) *Fig (passions)* atizar, avivar

fan out *vi (troops)* desplegarse en abanico

fanatic [fə'nætɪk] *adj* & *n* fanático(a) *(m,f)*

fanatical [fə'nætɪkəl] *adj* fanático(a)

fanaticism [fə'nætɪsɪzəm] *n* fanatismo *m*

fanciable ['fænsɪəbəl] *adj Fam* atractivo(a), *Esp* resultón(ona)

fancier ['fænsɪər] *n* aficionado(a) *m,f*; **pigeon f.** colombófilo(a) *m,f*

fanciful ['fænsɪfʊl] *adj* (**a**) *(person)* caprichoso(a), poco realista (**b**) *(idea)* fantástico(a)

fancy ['fænsɪ] **1** *adj* (**fancier, fanciest**) *(jewels, hat)* de fantasía; *(gadget)* sofisticado(a); *(party)* encopetado(a); *(hotel)* lujoso(a); *(food, decoration)* con muchas florituras; *Pej* **a f. car** *Esp* un coche muy pera ❑ **f. cakes** pastelitos *mpl* finos; **f. dress** disfraz *m*; **in f. dress** disfrazado(a); **f. dress ball** baile *m* de disfraces; **f. goods** artículos *mpl* de fantasía; **f. prices** precios *mpl* exorbitantes

2 *n* (**a**) *(imagination)* fantasía *f*, imaginación *f*; **flights of f.** ilusiones *fpl*; *Fam* **it tickled my f.** me cayó en gracia (**b**) *(whim)* capricho *m*, antojo *m*; **to take a f. to sb** cogerle cariño a algn; **to take a f. to sth** encapricharse con algo; **what takes your f.?** ¿qué se le antoja? ❑ **f. man** amigo *m*, amante *m*; **f. woman** amiga *f*, amante *f*

3 *vt (pt & pp fancied)* (**a**) *(imagine)* imaginarse, figurarse; *Fam* (**just**) **f. that!** ¡fíjate!; *Fam* **f. Liverpool losing!** parece mentira que haya perdido el Liverpool; *Fam* **f. seeing you here!** ¡qué casualidad verte por aquí! (**b**) *(like, want)* apetecer; **do you f. a drink?** *Esp* ¿te apetece algo de beber?, *Carib Col Méx* te provoca algo de beber?, *RP* ¿querés algo de tomar?; **take whatever you f.** coja lo que quiera; *Br Fam* **I f. her** esta chica me gusta (**c**) *(think highly of)* **I don't f. her chances** no creo que tenga muchas posibilidades; *Fam* **to f. oneself** ser creído(a) *or* presumido(a); **he fancies himself as a singer** se las da de cantante

fancy-free [fænsɪ'friː] *adj* sin compromiso; *Fam* **footloose and f.-f.** soltero(a) *m,f* y sin compromiso

fanfare ['fænfeər] *n Mus* fanfarria *f*, toque *m* de trompetas

fang [fæŋ] *n Zool* colmillo *m*

fanlight ['fænlaɪt] *n* montante *m* en abanico

fanny ['fænɪ] *n* (**a**) *(US Fam (buttocks)* pompis *m*, culo *m* ❑ **f. pack** riñonera *f* (**b**) *Br Vulg (vagina) Esp* coño *m*, *Andes RP* concha *f*, *Méx* paloma *f*

fantasize ['fæntəsaɪz] *vi* fantasear

fantastic [fæn'tæstɪk] *adj* fantástico(a), fabuloso(a)

fantasy ['fæntəsɪ] *n* fantasía *f*

FAO [efeɪ'əʊ] *n* (*abbr* **Food and Agriculture Organization**) FAO *f*, Organización *f* para la Agricultura y la Alimentación

far [fɑːr] (**farther** *or* **further, farthest** *or* **furthest**) **1** *adj* (**a**) *(distant)* lejano(a); *Fig* **it's a f. cry from student life** dista mucho de la vida estudiantil ❑ **the F. East** el Lejano Oriente (**b**) *(more remote)* **at the f. side** en el lado opuesto; **at the f. end** en el otro extremo (**c**) *Pol (extreme)* extremo(a); **the f. left** la extrema izquierda

2 *adv* (**a**) *(distant)* lejos; **as f. as the eye can see** hasta donde alcanza la vista; **f. and wide** por todas partes; **f. off** a lo lejos; **farther back/forward** más atrás/adelante; **farther north/south** más al norte/sur; **how f. is it?** ¿a qué distancia está?; **how f. is it to Cardiff?** ¿cuánto hay de

aquí a Cardiff?; **how much farther is it?** ¿cuánto camino nos queda?; **not f. from here** no muy lejos de aquí; **very f.** lejísimos; *Fig* **as f. as I can** en lo que puedo; **as f. as I'm concerned** por lo que a mí respecta *or* me toca; **as f. as I know** que yo sepa; **as f. as possible** en lo posible; *Fig* **f. from complaining, he seemed pleased** lejos de quejarse, parecía contento; *Fig* **he went so f. as to swear** llegó a jurar; *Fig* **how f. can we believe him?** ¿hasta qué punto podemos creerle?; *Fig* **I'm f. from satisfied** no estoy satisfecho ni mucho menos; *Fig* **in so f. as ...** en la medida en que ...; *Fig* **ten dollars won't go f.** diez dólares no alcanzarán para mucho; *Fam* **she will go f.** llegará lejos; *Fam* **to be f. away** estar en las nubes; *Fam* **to go too f.** pasarse de la raya, propasarse (**b**) *(in time)* **as f. back as I can remember** hasta donde alcanza mi memoria; **as f. back as the fifties** ya en los años cincuenta; **f. into the night** hasta muy entrada la noche; **so f.** hasta ahora, hasta aquí; **so f. so good** por ahora bien; **so f. this year** en lo que va de año (**c**) *(much)* mucho; **by f.** con mucho; **by f. the best** con mucho el mejor; **f. beyond** mucho más allá; **f. cleverer** mucho más listo(a); **f. too much** demasiado; **you're not f. wrong** casi aciertas; *Fam* **f. gone** borracho(a)

faraway ['fɑːrəweɪ] *adj* lejano(a), remoto(a); **a f. look** una mirada distraída

farce [fɑːs] *n Theat* farsa *f*; *Fig* farsa *f*; **what a f.!** ¡menudo cuento!

farcical ['fɑːsɪkəl] *adj* absurdo(a), ridículo(a)

fare [feər] **1** *n* (**a**) *(ticket price)* tarifa *f*, precio *m* del billete *or* del viaje; *(for boat)* pasaje *m*; **fares please!** ¡billetes por favor!; **half f.** medio billete (**b**) *(passenger)* viajero(a) *m,f*, pasajero(a) *m,f* (**c**) *(food)* comida *f* ❑ **bill of f.** lista *f* de platos, menú *m*

2 *(progress) vi* **how did you f.?** ¿qué tal te fue?

farewell [feə'wel] **1** *interj Literary* ¡adiós!

2 *n* despedida *f*; **to bid sb f.** despedirse de algn ❑ **f. dinner** cena *f* de despedida; **f. speech** discurso *m* de despedida

far-fetched ['fɑː'fetʃt] *adj* rebuscado(a), inverosímil

far-flung ['fɑː'flʌŋ] *adj* (**a**) *(distant)* lejano(a) (**b**) *(widespread)* vasto(a)

farm [fɑːm] **1** *n* granja *f*, *Am* hacienda *f*, explotación *f* agrícola, *RP* estancia *f* ❑ **f. labourer** peón *m*, labriego(a) *m,f*; **f. produce** productos *mpl* agrícolas; **fish f.** criadero *m*, piscifactoría *f*

2 *vt* cultivar, labrar

3 *vi* cultivar la tierra

farm out *vt* encargar fuera

farmer ['fɑːmər] *n* agricultor(a) *m,f*, granjero(a) *m,f*, *Am* hacendado(a) *m,f*

farmhand ['fɑːmhænd] *n* peón *m*, labriego(a) *m,f*

farmhouse ['fɑːmhaʊs] *n* granja *f*, casa *f* de labranza, *Am* hacienda *f*

farming ['fɑːmɪŋ] **1** *n* (**a**) *(agriculture)* agricultura *f* (**b**) *(the land)* cultivo *m*, labranza *f*

2 *adj* agrícola

farmland ['fɑːmlænd] *n* terreno *m* agrícola

farmyard ['fɑːmjɑːd] *n* corral *m*

Faroe ['feɪrəʊ] *n* **the F. Islands, the Faroes** las islas Feroe

far-off ['fɑːrɒf] *adj* lejano(a), remoto(a)

far-out ['fɑː'raʊt] *adj Fam (strange)* raro(a); **f.!** ¡súper!, *Esp* ¡chachi!

far-reaching [fɑː'riːtʃɪŋ] *adj* de gran alcance

farrier ['færɪər] *n* herrero *m*

Farsi ['fɑːsiː] *n (language)* persa *m* (moderno)

far-sighted [fɑː'saɪtɪd] *adj* (**a**) *(person, decision)* previsor(a), con visión de futuro (**b**) *US (long-sighted)* hipermétrope

far-sightedness [fɑːˈsaɪtɪdnɪs] *n* (**a**) *(of person, decision)* visión *f* de futuro (**b**) *US (long-sightedness)* hipermetropía *f*

fart [fɑːt] *Vulg* **1** *n* pedo *m*
  2 *vi* echarse *or* tirarse un pedo

farther [ˈfɑːðər] *adj & adv comp see* **far**

farthest [ˈfɑːðɪst] *adj & adv superl see* **far**

farthing [ˈfɑːðɪŋ] *n Br Formerly* cuarto *m* de penique; *Fam* **it isn't worth a brass f.** no vale un real

fascinate [ˈfæsɪneɪt] *vt* fascinar

fascinating [ˈfæsɪneɪtɪŋ] *adj* fascinador(a), fascinante

fascination [fæsɪˈneɪʃən] *n* fascinación *f*

fascism [ˈfæʃɪzəm] *n Pol* fascismo *m*

fascist [ˈfæʃɪst] *adj & n Pol* fascista *(mf)*

fashion [ˈfæʃən] **1** *n* (**a**) *(manner)* manera *f*, modo *m*; **in her own f.** a su manera; **after a f.** *(somehow)* más o menos; *(in the manner of)* **after the f. of Dickens** imitando a Dickens (**b**) *(latest style)* moda *f*; **it's all the f.** está muy de moda; **this year waistcoats are the f.** este año se llevan mucho los chalecos; **to be a slave to f.** ser un esclavo de la moda; **to be in f.** estar de moda; **to be out of f.** no estar de moda; **to come into f.** ponerse de moda; **to go out of f.** pasar de moda ❏ **f. designer** diseñador(a) *m,f* de modas; **f. magazine** revista *f* de modas; **f. parade** desfile *m* de modelos; **f. victim** adicto(a) *m,f* a la moda
  2 *vt (metal)* labrar; *(clay)* formar

fashionable [ˈfæʃənəbəl] *adj* de moda; **to be f.** estar de moda

fast¹ [fɑːst] **1** *adj* (**a**) *(quick)* rápido(a), veloz; **the f. train** el tren rápido; *Aut* **the f. lane** el carril de alta velocidad; *Fig* **to live in the f. lane** vivir deprisa; **at a f. and furious pace** a una velocidad vertiginosa; *Fam Fig* **to be a f. worker** ser un ligón; *Fam* **to pull a f. one on sb** jugarle una mala pasada a algn ❏ **f. food** comida *f* rápida; **f. woman** (mujer *f*) ligera *f* de cascos (**b**) *(tight, inflexible)* firme; seguro(a); **hard and f. rules** reglas estrictas (**c**) *(colour)* sólido(a) (**d**) *(clock)* adelantado(a)
  2 *adv* (**a**) *(rapidly)* rápido; **how f.?** ¿a qué velocidad?; **to drive f.** correr; *Fam* **not so f.!** ¡un momento! (**b**) *(securely)* firmemente; **f. asleep** profundamente dormido(a); **stuck f.** bien pegado(a); *Fig (with determination)* **to stand f.** mantenerse firme

fast² [fɑːst] **1** *n* ayuno *m*
  2 *vi* ayunar

fasten [ˈfɑːsən] **1** *vt* (**a**) *(attach)* sujetar; *(fix)* fijar; **to f. one's eyes on** fijar los ojos en (**b**) *(do up, secure) (belt)* abrochar; *(bag, suitcase)* asegurar; *(shoelaces)* atar; *(window)* echar el pestillo a; *(papers)* **to f. (together)** sujetar
  2 *vi (door)* cerrarse; *(dress)* abrocharse; *Fig* **to f. on to** apropiarse de

fastener [ˈfɑːsənər] *n* (**a**) *(window)* cierre *m* (**b**) *(necklace, dress)* cierre *m*, broche *m* ❏ **zip f.** cremallera *f*

fast-forward [ˈfɑːstˈfɔːwəd] **1** *n* avance *m* rápido
  2 *vt (cassette)* pasar hacia delante

fastidious [fæˈstɪdɪəs] *adj* quisquilloso(a), melindroso(a)

fastidiousness [fæsˈtɪdɪəsnɪs] *n* melindres *mpl*, remilgos *mpl*

fast-track [ˈfɑːsttræk] **1** *n* vía *f* rápida
  2 *vt* hacer por la vía rápida

fat [fæt] **1** *adj* (**fatter, fattest**) (**a**) *(obese)* gordo(a); **to get f.** engordar ❏ *US Fam* **F. cat** pez *m* gordo (**b**) *(thick)* grueso(a) (**c**) *(meat)* que tiene mucha grasa (**d**) *Fig (profit)* hermoso(a), jugoso(a); *Fam Iron* **that was a f. lot of good!** ¡pues sí que ha valido de mucho!; **that was a f. lot of help!** ¡valiente ayuda!
  2 *n* grasa *f*; *Fam* **the f.'s in the fire** se va a armar la de Dios; *Fig* **to live off the f. of the land** vivir a cuerpo de rey ❏ **f. content** materia *f* grasa; **cooking f.** manteca *f* de cerdo

fatal [ˈfeɪtəl] *adj* (**a**) *(accident, illness, blow)* mortal (**b**) *(ill-fated)* fatal, funesto(a) (**c**) *(fateful)* fatídico(a)

fatalist [ˈfeɪtəlɪst] *n* fatalista *mf*

fatalistic [feɪtəˈlɪstɪk] *adj* fatalista

fatality [fəˈtælɪtɪ] *n* víctima *f* mortal; **there were no fatalities** no hubo muertos

fatally [ˈfeɪtəlɪ] *adv* mortalmente; **f. wounded** mortalmente herido(a)

fate [feɪt] *n* (**a**) *(destiny)* destino *m*, suerte *f*; **his f. is decided** su suerte está decidida; **let us see what f. has in store** veamos lo que nos depara la suerte; **to meet one's f.** encontrarse uno con su destino; **to tempt f.** tentar a la suerte (**b**) *Myth* **the Fates** las Parcas

fated [ˈfeɪtɪd] *adj* (**a**) *(destined)* predestinado(a) (**b**) *(doomed)* condenado(a)

fateful [ˈfeɪtful] *adj* fatídico(a), aciago(a); **on this f. day in 1936** este día aciago en 1936

fat-free [ˈfætfriː] *adj* **a f.-f. diet** un régimen sin grasas

father [ˈfɑːðər] **1** *n* (**a**) *(parent)* padre *m*; **my f. and mother** mis padres; **to be a f. to sb** ser un padre para algn; *Prov* **like f. like son** de tal palo, tal astilla ❏ *Rel* **Christmas** Papa *m* Noel; **f. figure** figura *f* paterna (**b**) *Rel* padre *m*; **F. McSweeney** el padre McSweeney; **Our F.** Padre Nuestro; **the Holy F.** el Santo Padre
  2 *vt* engendrar

fatherhood [ˈfɑːðəhud] *n* paternidad *f*

father-in-law [ˈfɑːðərɪnlɔː] *n (pl* **fathers-in-law)** suegro *m*

fatherland [ˈfɑːðəlænd] *n* patria *f*

fatherly [ˈfɑːðəlɪ] *adj* paternal

father-to-be [ˈfɑːðətəˈbiː] *(pl* **fathers-to-be)** *n* futuro padre *m*

fathom [ˈfæðəm] **1** *n Naut (measure)* braza *f*
  2 *vt* comprender, penetrar en

fathom out *vt* averiguar, comprobar; **I can't f. it out** no me lo explico; **to f. out a mystery** desentrañar un misterio

fatigue [fəˈtiːg] **1** *n* (**a**) *(tiredness)* fatiga *f*, cansancio *m* ❏ *Tech* **metal f.** fatiga *f* del metal (**b**) *Mil* faena *f* ❏ **f. dress** traje *m* de faena
  2 *vt* fatigar, cansar

fatso [ˈfætsəʊ] *n (pl* **fatsos** *or* **fatsoes)** *Fam Offens* gordo(a) *m,f*

fatted [ˈfætɪd] *adj Fig* cebado(a); *Fig* **to kill the f. calf** echar la casa por la ventana

fatten [ˈfætən] *vt (animal)* cebar; *(person)* engordar

fattening [ˈfætənɪŋ] *adj* que hace engordar; **milk is f.** la leche engorda

fatty [ˈfætɪ] **1** *adj* (**fattier, fattiest**) (**a**) *(food)* graso(a) (**b**) *Anat (tissue)* adiposo(a)
  2 *n Fam (person)* gordinflón(ona) *m,f*

fatuous [ˈfætjʊəs] *adj* fatuo(a), necio(a)

faucet [ˈfɔːsɪt] *n US Esp* grifo *m*, *Chile Col Méx* llave *f*, *RP* canilla *f*

fault [fɔːlt] **1** *n* (**a**) *(defect)* defecto *m*; **generous to a f.** generoso(a) en exceso; **he has many faults** tiene muchos defectos (**b**) *(in merchandise)* defecto *m*, desperfecto *m*; **to find f. with** poner reparos a; **to find f. with sb** criticar a algn (**c**) *(culpability)* culpa *f*; **it's their f.** es culpa suya; **to be at f.** tener la culpa; **whose f. is it?** ¿quién tiene la culpa? (**d**) *(mistake)* error *m*, falta *f* (**e**) *Geol* falla *f* (**f**) *Ten* falta *f*

2 vt criticar; **her behaviour cannot be faulted** su conducta es intachable

fault-finding ['fɔːltfaɪndɪŋ] adj criticón(ona)

faultless ['fɔːltlɪs] adj intachable, impecable, perfecto(a)

faultlessly ['fɔːltlɪslɪ] adv perfectamente

faulty ['fɔːltɪ] adj (**faultier, faultiest**) defectuoso(a)

faun [fɔːn] n (mythological creature) fauno m

fauna ['fɔːnə] n (pl **faunas** or **faunae** ['fɔːniː]) Zool fauna f

faux pas [fəʊ'pɑː] n inv Fml (mistake) paso m en falso; (blunder) metedura f or Am metida f de pata

favour, US **favor** ['feɪvər] **1** n (**a**) (approval) favor m; **to be in f. of doing sth** estar a favor de hacer algo; **to be in f. with sb** gozar del favor de algn; **to fall out of f. with sb** perder el favor de algn; **to vote in f. of sth** votar a favor de algo (**b**) (service) favor m; **to ask sb a f.** pedirle un favor a algn; Fam **do me a f.!** ¡venga ya!; Br Fam **do me a f. and shut up** hazme el favor de callarte (**c**) (advantage) favor m; **an error in my f.** un error a mi favor; **1-0 in our f.** 1-0 a favor nuestro

2 vt (**a**) (bias) favorecer; Prov **fortune favours the brave** la fortuna sonríe a los audaces (**b**) (approve) estar a favor de

favourable, US **favorable** ['feɪvərəbəl] adj favorable, propicio(a)

favourably, US **favorably** ['feɪvərəblɪ] adv favorablemente; **f. disposed towards sb** bien dispuesto(a) hacia algn

favoured, US **favored** ['feɪvəd] adj favorecido(a); **the f. few** la minoría selecta

favourite, US **favorite** ['feɪvərɪt] **1** adj favorito(a), preferido(a), predilecto(a)

2 n Sport favorito(a) m,f

favouritism, US **favoritism** ['feɪvərɪtɪzəm] n favoritismo m

fawn[1] [fɔːn] **1** adj (de) color café claro

2 n (**a**) Zool cervato m (**b**) (colour) color m café claro

fawn[2] [fɔːn] vi (**a**) (dog) hacer fiestas (**on** a) (**b**) (person) adular (**on** a), lisonjear (**on** a)

fawning ['fɔːnɪŋ] adj adulador(a), lisonjero(a), servil

fax [fæks] **1** n (message) facsímil m, telefax m, fax m; (machine) facsímil m, fax m □ Comptr **f. modem** módem m fax; **f. number** número m de fax

2 vt mandar or enviar por fax

faze [feɪz] vt Fam desconcertar

FBI [efbiːˈaɪ] n US (abbr **Federal Bureau of Investigation**) FBI m

FC [efˈsiː] n Br Sport (abbr **Football Club**) Club m de Fútbol, CF

fealty ['fiːəltɪ] n fidelidad f; **to swear f.** jurar fidelidad

fear [fɪər] **1** n miedo m, temor m; **for f. of losing** por temor a perder; **have no f.!** ¡no temas!; **I ran for f. that it might rain** corrí por miedo de que lloviera; **there's no f. of that happening** no hay peligro de que ocurra eso; **to go in f. of one's life** temer por su vida; Fam **no f.!** ¡ni pensarlo!; Méx ¡ya mero!; Fam Fig **to put the f. of God into sb** darle un susto mortal a algn

2 vt temer, tener miedo a; **he's to be feared** es de temer; **I f. it's too late** me temo que ya es tarde; **to f. the worst** temer lo peor

3 vi temer (**for** por)

fearful ['fɪəfʊl] adj (**a**) (person) temeroso(a) (**b**) (frightening) horrible, espantoso(a)

fearless ['fɪəlɪs] adj intrépido(a), impávido(a)

fearlessly ['fɪəlɪslɪ] adv con intrepidez

fearlessness ['fɪəlɪsnɪs] n intrepidez f, impavidez f

fearsome ['fɪəsəm] adj terrible, espantoso(a)

feasibility [fiːzəˈbɪlɪtɪ] n viabilidad f □ **f. study** estudio m de viabilidad

feasible ['fiːzəbəl] adj (**a**) (practicable) factible; (possible) viable (**b**) (plausible) verosímil

feast [fiːst] **1** n (**a**) (large meal) banquete m, festín m; **it was a real f.** fue una verdadera comilona (**b**) Rel **f. day** día m de fiesta □ **movable f.** fiesta f movible

2 vt festejar; Fig **to f. one's eyes on sth** regalarse la vista con algo

3 vi banquetear; Fig **to f. on sth** regalarse con algo

feat [fiːt] n proeza f, hazaña f; **f. of endurance** prueba f de resistencia

feather ['feðər] **1** n pluma f; Fig **that's a f. in his cap** es un triunfo para él; Fig **they're birds of a f.** son de la misma calaña; Fam **you could have knocked me down with a f.** me quedé patidifuso; Prov **birds of a f. flock together** Dios los cría y ellos se juntan □ **f. bed** colchón m de plumas; **f. duster** plumero m

2 vt Fam **to f. one's nest** hacer su agosto

feather-brained ['feðəbreɪnd] adj despistado(a), insensato(a)

feathered ['feðəd] adj con plumas; Hum **f. friend** pájaro m

featherweight ['feðəweɪt] n Box peso m pluma

feature ['fiːtʃər] **1** n (**a**) (face) rasgo m, facción f; **he has typically Basque features** sus facciones son típicamente vascas (**b**) (characteristic) rasgo m, característica f (**c**) Cin **f. film** largometraje m (**d**) Press crónica f especial □ **f. writer** cronista mf

2 vt (**a**) (give prominence to) poner de relieve (**b**) Cin tener como protagonista; **the film features Cantinflas** es una película de Cantinflas

3 vi (**a**) (appear) constar, figurar; **his name features in the list** su nombre figura en la lista (**b**) (in film) figurar

featureless ['fiːtʃəlɪs] adj monótono(a)

Feb [feb] n (abbr **February**) febrero m, feb

February ['februərɪ] n febrero m; **in F.** en febrero; see also May

feckless ['feklɪs] adj débil, incapaz

Fed [fed] n US Slang agente mf de FBI

fed [fed] **1** pt & pp see **feed**

2 f. up adj Fam harto(a) (**with** de)

federal ['fedərəl] adj federal

federation [fedəˈreɪʃən] n federación f

fedora [fɪˈdɔːrə] n = sombrero flexible de fieltro

fee [fiː] n (lawyer, doctor) honorarios mpl; **what are your fees?** ¿cuánto cobra por visita? □ **entrance f.** entrada f; **membership f.** cuota f de socio; **retaining f.** anticipo m; Ftb **transfer f.** prima f de traslado; Univ **tuition fees** derechos mpl de matrícula

feeble ['fiːbəl] adj (person) débil; (excuse, argument) de poco peso; (voice, light) tenue, débil

feeble-minded [fiːbəlˈmaɪndɪd] adj imbécil, mentecato(a)

feebleness ['fiːbəlnɪs] n debilidad f

feed [fiːd] **1** vt (pt & pp **fed**) (**a**) (give food to) dar de comer a, alimentar; Fig (fire, passions) avivar; **to f. a baby** (breast-feed) amamantar a un bebé; (with bottle) dar el biberón a un bebé (**b**) Comptr Elec alimentar, suministrar (**c**) (insert) introducir; **to f. a parking meter** meter monedas en un parquímetro; **to f. data into a computer** introducir datos en un ordenador

2 vi comer, alimentarse (**on** de); (cows, sheep) pacer

3 n (**a**) (food, meal) comida f; Fam comilona f □ Agr **cattle f.** pienso m (**b**) Tech alimentación f □ **f. pipe** tubo m de alimentación

feed up *vt (animal)* cebar; *(make fat)* engordar

feedback ['fiːdbæk] *n* **(a)** *Elec* realimentación *f* **(b)** *Fig* reacción *f,* impresión *f*

feeder ['fiːdər] *n Tech* alimentador *m*

feeding ['fiːdɪŋ] *n* alimentación *f* ❑ **f. bottle** biberón *m*

feel [fiːl] **1** *vi (pt & pp* **felt)** **(a)** *(emotionally, physically)* sentirse, encontrarse; **f. free to return** vuelva cuando quiera; **how does it 'f. to be rich?** ¿qué se siente al ser rico?; **how do you f.?** ¿qué tal te encuentras?; **I f. bad about it** me da pena; **I f. like a new man** me siento como nuevo; **she felt a failure** se sentía hundida; **I f. sorry for him** le compadezco; **I'm not feeling myself** no me encuentro del todo bien; **to f. happy** sentirse feliz; **to f. cold/sleepy** tener frío/sueño; *Fam* **to f. up to sth** sentirse con ánimos *or* con fuerzas para hacer algo **(b)** *(seem)* parecer; **it felt good to do nothing** daba gusto no hacer nada; **your hand feels cold** tienes la mano fría; **it feels like leather** parece piel; **it feels like rain** parece que va a llover; **it feels like summer** parece verano **(c)** *(perceive, sense)* sentir; **he feels uncomfortable** se siente incómodo; **the atmosphere felt tense** el ambiente era tenso **(d)** *(opinion)* opinar, pensar; **how do you f. about this?** ¿qué opinas de esto?; **I f. sure that ...** estoy seguro de que ...; **they f. strongly about apartheid** tienen opiniones muy concretas sobre el apartheid **(e)** *(fancy)* apetecer; **I f. like an ice cream** *Esp* me apetece *or Carib Col Méx* me provoca *or Méx* se me antoja *or CSur* me tomaría un helado; **to f. like doing sth** tener ganas de hacer algo

2 *vt* **(a)** *(touch)* tocar, palpar; **f. my hand** toca mi mano; **to f. one's way** andar a tientas; *Fig* tantear el terreno **(b)** *(emotion, sensation)* sentir; **they felt the wind on their faces** sentían el viento en sus caras **(c)** *(believe)* creer; **we f. it is our duty** creemos que es nuestro deber **(d)** *(notice)* notar, apreciar; **we won't f. the effects of this until next year** no notaremos los efectos hasta el año que viene

3 *n* **(a)** *(touch, sensation)* tacto *m*; **I recognize it by the f.** lo reconozco al tacto; *Fig* **to get the f. for sth** acostumbrarse *or Esp* cogerle el truco *or Am* agarrarle la onda *or RP* encontrarle la vuelta a algo **(b)** *(atmosphere)* ambiente *m*; **this place has a certain f. about it** este lugar tiene un ambiente especial

feel for *vt* **(a)** *(search for)* buscar; **he felt around in the dark for the light switch** buscó el interruptor de la luz a tientas en la oscuridad; **she felt for her keys in her bag** buscó sus llaves en la bolsa **(b)** *(have sympathy for)* **f. for you** lo siento mucho por ti

feeler ['fiːlər] *n Ent* antena *f; Fig* **to put one's feelers out** tantear el terreno

feeling ['fiːlɪŋ] **1** *n* **(a)** *(emotion)* sentimiento *m*, emoción *f*; **a f. of guilt** un sentimiento de culpabilidad; **ill f.** resentimiento *m*, rencor *m* **(b)** *(concern, compassion)* compasión *f*, ternura *f*; **to have no f.** ser duro(a) *or* insensible **(c)** *(impression)* impresión *f*; **I had the f. that ...** tuve la impresión de que ... **(d)** *(consciousness, sensitivity)* sensibilidad *f*; **artistic f.** sensibilidad artística; **he has a f. for music** tiene sensibilidad para la música; **he has no f. in his fingers** no tiene sensibilidad en los dedos; **the pianist played with a lot of f.** el pianista tocó ·con mucho sentimiento **(e)** *(opinion)* sentir *m*, opinión *f*; **the general f. is that ...** la opinión general es que ...; **to express one's feelings** expresar sus opiniones **(f)** **feelings** sentimientos *mpl; Fig* **f. ran high** la gente estaba exaltada; *Fam* **no hard f.** no nos guardemos rencor **(g)** **feelings** *(thoughts)* sentimientos *mpl*, pensamientos *mpl*; **to have mixed f.** tener sentimientos enfrentados; **to hide one's f.** ocultar sus sentimientos

2 *adj* sensible, compasivo(a); **a f. person** una persona compasiva

fee-paying ['fiːpeɪɪŋ] *adj (school)* de pago

feet [fiːt] *npl see* **foot**

feign [feɪn] *vt* fingir, aparentar; **to f. illness** fingirse enfermo(a)

feint [feɪnt] *Sport* **1** *n* finta *f*
2 *vi* fintar

feline ['fiːlaɪn] *Zool adj & n* felino(a) *(m,f)*

fell¹ [fel] *pt see* **fall**

fell² [fel] *adj Pqet (fierce)* feroz; **at one f. swoop** de un solo golpe

fell³ [fel] *n Br Geog (hill)* monte *m*; *(moor)* páramo *m*

fell⁴ [fel] *vt (cut down) (trees)* talar; *Fig (enemy)* matar, derribar

fell⁵ [fel] *n (animal)* piel *f*

felling ['felɪŋ] *n* tala *f*

fellow ['feləʊ] *n* **(a)** *(companion)* compañero(a) *m,f,* camarada *mf*; **come in, my dear f.!** ¡adelante, hombre!; *Fig* **to be hail f. well met with sb** tratar a algn con falsa simpatía ❑ **f. citizen** conciudadano(a) *m,f*; **f. countryman, f. countrywoman** compatriota *mf*; **f. men** prójimos *mpl*; **f. passenger/student/worker** compañero(a) *m,f,* de viaje/estudios/trabajo **(b)** *Fam (chap, guy)* tipo *m*, *Esp* tío *m*, *RP* flaco *m* **a strange f.** un tío raro; **poor f.!** ¡pobrecito! **(c)** *(of society)* socio(a) *m,f* **(d)** *Univ* miembro *mf* del claustro de profesores

fellowship ['feləʊʃɪp] *n* **(a)** *(comradeship)* compañerismo *m*, camaradería *f* **(b)** *(organization)* asociación *f*, sociedad *f* **(c)** *Univ (scholarship)* beca *f*

felon ['felən] *n Jur* criminal *mf*

felony ['felənɪ] *n* crimen *m*, delito *m* mayor

felt¹ [felt] *pt & pp see* **feel**

felt² [felt] *n Tex* fieltro *m* ❑ **f. hat** sombrero *m* de fieltro

felt-tip(ped) ['felttɪp(t)] *adj* **f.-t. pen** rotulador *m*, *Méx* plumón *m*, *RP* marcador *m*

fem [fem] *Ling (abbr* **feminine)** femenino, f

female ['fiːmeɪl] **1** *adj* **(a)** *Zool* hembra; **a f. giraffe** una jirafa hembra; **a f. hedgehog** un erizo hembra **(b)** *(person)* femenino(a); **the f. sex** el sexo femenino; **a f. voice** una voz de mujer

2 *n* **(a)** *Zool* hembra *f* **(b)** *(woman)* mujer *f; (girl)* chica *f*

feminine ['femɪnɪn] **1** *adj* femenino(a)
2 *n Ling* femenino *m*

femininity [femɪ'nɪnɪtɪ] *n* feminidad *f*

feminism ['femɪnɪzəm] *n* feminismo *m*

feminist ['femɪnɪst] *adj & n* feminista *(mf)*

femur ['fiːmər] *n (pl* **femurs** *or* **femora** ['femərə]) *Anat* fémur *m*

fen [fen] *n Geog* pantano *m*

fence [fens] **1** *n* **(a)** *(barrier)* cerca *f*, valla *f; Equit* valla *f; Fig* **to sit on the f.** ver los toros desde la barrera **(b)** *Slang* perista *mf*
2 *vi Sport* practicar la esgrima

fence in *vt* meter en un cercado

fence off *vt* separar mediante cercas

fencer ['fensər] *n* jugador(a) *m,f* de esgrima

fencing ['fensɪŋ] *n* **(a)** *(surround)* cercado *m*, vallado *m* **(b)** *(material)* material *m* para cercas **(c)** *Sport* esgrima *f* ❑ **f. foil** florete *m*

fend [fend] *vi* **to f. for oneself** valerse por sí mismo(a)

fend off *vt (blow)* parar, desviar; *(question)* esquivar; *(attack)* rechazar

fender ['fendər] *n* **(a)** *(fireplace)* pantalla *f* **(b)** *US Aut Esp RP* guardabarros *m inv*, *Andes CAm Carib* guardafango *m*, *Méx* salpicadera *f* **(c)** *Naut* defensa *f*

feng shui ['fəŋʃɔi:] n feng shui m

fennel ['fenəl] n Bot hinojo m

ferment ['fɜ:ment] **1** n fermento m; Fig **in a state of f.** agitado(a)
 2 [fə'ment] vt & vi fermentar

fermentation [fɜ:men'teiʃən] n fermentación f

fern [fɜ:n] n Bot helecho m

ferocious [fə'rəuʃəs] adj feroz

ferocity [fə'rɒsiti] n ferocidad f

ferret ['ferit] **1** n Zool hurón m
 · **2** vi Fam huronear, husmear

ferret out vt Fam conseguir, descubrir

Ferris wheel ['feris'wi:l] n noria f

ferrous ['ferəs] adj de hierro, ferroso(a); **f. metals** metales ferrosos

ferry ['feri] **1** n **(a)** (small) barca f de pasaje **(b)** (large, for cars) transbordador m, ferry m
 2 vt transportar

ferryman ['ferimən] n (pl **ferrymen**) barquero m

fertile ['fɜ:tail] adj fértil, fecundo(a); Fig fértil, fecundo(a); **a f. imagination** una imaginación fecunda

fertility [fə'tiliti] n (of soil) fertilidad f, fecundidad f; (of living thing) fertilidad f □ Med **f. treatment** tratamiento m de fertilidad

fertilization [fɜ:tilai'zeiʃən] n **(a)** (soil) fertilización f **(b)** Biol fecundación f

fertilize ['fɜ:tilaiz] vt **(a)** (soil) fertilizar, abonar **(b)** (egg) fecundar

fertilizer ['fɜ:tilaizər] n Agr abono m, fertilizante m

fervent ['fɜ:vənt] adj ferviente, fervoroso(a)

fervid ['fɜ:vid] adj exaltado(a), apasionado(a)

fervour, US **fervor** ['fɜ:vər] n fervor m

fester ['festər] vi Med supurar, enconarse

festival ['festivəl] n (event) festival m; (celebration) fiesta f □ **film f.** festival m de cine; Rel **harvest f.** fiesta f (de acción de gracias) de la cosecha

festive ['festiv] adj festivo(a); **the f. season** las fiestas de Navidad

festivity [fes'tiviti] n regocijo m; **the festivities** las fiestas, los festejos

festoon [fe'stu:n] **1** n guirnalda f, festón m
 2 vt adornar

feta ['fetə] n **f. (cheese)** queso m feta

fetal ['fi:təl] adj US see **foetal**

fetch [fetʃ] vt **(a)** (go and get) buscar, ir a buscar, ir por **(b)** (bring) traer; **why did you f. me?** ¿para qué me has hecho venir?; (to dog) **f.!** ¡busca!; **to f. and carry for sb** ser el machaca de algn **(c)** (sell for) alcanzar; **how much did it f.?** ¿por cuánto se vendió?

fetching ['fetʃiŋ] adj atractivo(a)

fete [feit] **1** n fiesta f
 2 vt festejar

fetid ['fetid] adj fétido(a), hediondo(a)

fetish ['fetiʃ] n fetiche m; Fig veneración f, culto m

fetishism ['fetiʃizəm] n fetichismo m

fetishist ['fetiʃist] n fetichista mf

fetlock ['fetlɒk] n Zool espolón m

fetter ['fetər] **1** npl **fetters** grillos mpl, cadenas fpl; **to be in fetters** estar encadenado(a)
 2 vt encadenar

fettle ['fetəl] n Fam condición f, forma f; **in fine f.** (health) en plena forma; (spirit) de buen humor

fetus ['fi:təs] n US see **foetus**

feud [fju:d] **1** n enemistad f duradera; **family f.** disensión f familiar
 2 vi disentir, pelear

feudal ['fju:dəl] adj feudal

feudalism ['fju:dəlizəm] n feudalismo m

fever ['fi:vər] n Med fiebre f; Fig fiebre f; **to have a f.** tener fiebre; **gambling f.** la fiebre del juego

feverish ['fi:vəriʃ] adj Med febril, calenturiento(a); Fig febril; **to be f.** tener fiebre; **f. excitement** emoción febril

feverishness ['fi:vəriʃnis] n estado m febril

few [fju:] **1** adj **(a)** (small number) **for the past f. years** durante estos últimos años; **in the next f. days** dentro de unos días **(b)** (not many) pocos(as); **he has f. friends** tiene pocos amigos; **he is one of the f. people who know** es uno de los pocos que saben **(c)** (some) algunos(as), unos(as) cuantos(as); **a f. books** unos or algunos libros; **she has fewer books than I thought** tiene menos libros de lo que pensaba **(d)** (rare) muy pocos(as); **f. and far between** escaso(a), raro(a) **(e)** **as f. as** solamente
 2 pron **(a)** (not many) pocos(as); **few of them** pocos de entre ellos; **there are too f.** no hay suficientes; **there are precious f. of them left** quedan muy pocos; **the fewer the better** cuantos menos mejor **(b)** (some) **a f.** algunos(as), unos(as) cuantos(as); **a f. of them** algunos de ellos; **quite a f.** un buen número; **I've only a f. left** sólo me quedan unos cuantos; **the chosen f.** los seleccionados, la crema; **there were no fewer than ten** había no menos de diez; **who has the fewest?** ¿quién tiene menos?; Fam **to have had a f. too many** haber bebido unas copas de más

fez [fez] n (pl **fezzes**) n fez m

fiancé [fi'ænsei] n novio m, prometido m

fiancée [fi'ænsei] n novia f, prometida f

fiasco [fi'æskəʊ] n (pl Br **fiascos**, US **fiascoes**) fiasco m, fracaso m

fib [fib] Fam **1** n bola f, Esp trola f
 2 vi (pt & pp **fibbed**) contar bolas, Esp decir trolas

fibber ['fibər] n Fam mentiroso(a) m,f, Am cuentero(a) m,f

fibre, US **fiber** ['faibər] n fibra f □ **f. optics** transmisión f por fibra óptica; **man-made f.** fibra f artificial; Fig **moral f.** nervio m, carácter m

fibreglass, US **fiberglass** ['faibəgla:s] n fibra f de vidrio

fibre-optic, US **fiber-optic** [faibə'rɒptik] adj de fibra óptica

fibrositis [faibrə'saitis] n Med fibromatosis f

fibrous ['faibrəs] adj fibroso(a)

fickle ['fikəl] adj inconstante, voluble

fickleness ['fikəlnis] n inconstancia f, volubilidad f

fiction ['fikʃən] n **(a)** Lit novela f, narrativa f; **works of f.** novelas fpl **(b)** (invention) ficción f

fictional ['fikʃənəl] adj **(a)** Lit novelesco(a) **(b)** (imaginative) ficticio(a)

fictitious [fik'tiʃəs] adj ficticio(a), fingido(a)

fiddle ['fidəl] Fam **1** n **(a)** (violin) violín m (en música folk); Fig **to play** or **be second f.** ser de segunda categoría; Fig **as fit as a f.** más sano(a) que una manzana, fuerte como un roble **(b)** esp Br (shady deal) estafa f, trampa f; **he's on the f.** está haciendo trampas □ **tax f.** evasión f fiscal
 2 vt Br **(a)** (cheat) estafar **(b)** (accounts) falsificar
 3 vi tocar el violín

fiddle about, fiddle around vi **(a)** (delay) perder tiempo **(b)** (fidget) juguetear (**with** con)

fiddler ['fidlər] n Fam **(a)** (musician) violinista mf (en música folk) **(b)** (swindler) tramposo(a) m,f

fiddlesticks ['fɪdəlstɪks] *interj Old-fashioned* ¡paparruchas!

fiddly ['fɪdlɪ] *adj* (**fiddlier, fiddliest**) *Br Fam* delicado(a), poco manejable

fidelity [fɪ'delətɪ] *n* fidelidad *f* ❑ **high f.** alta fidelidad *f*

fidget ['fɪdʒɪt] **1** *vi* moverse, no poder estarse quieto(a); **stop fidgeting!** ¡estáte quieto!
  2 *vt* jugar (**with** con)
  3 *n* argadillo(a) *m,f*

fidgety ['fɪdʒɪtɪ] *adj* inquieto(a)

field [fiːld] **1** *n* (**a**) *(meadow)* campo *m*, prado *m* (**b**) *Mil* campo *m*; **in the f.** en campaña; *Fig* **to have a f. day** disfrutar de lo lindo ❑ **f. day** día *m* de maniobras; **f. glasses** gemelos *mpl* (de campaña); **f. marshal** mariscal *m* de campo; **f. of battle** campo *m* de batalla (**c**) *Sport* campo *m*, *Am* cancha *f*; **to take the f.** salir al campo ❑ *US* **f. hockey** hockey *m* sobre hierba *or Am* césped; **playing f.** campo *m* de deportes (**d**) *Geol Min* yacimiento *m*, yacimientos *mpl* ❑ **oil f.** yacimiento *m* petrolífero (**e**) *Elec Phys* campo *m* ❑ *Opt* **f. of vision** campo *m* visual (**f**) *(subject, area)* campo *m*, terreno *m*; **it's outside my f.** no es de mi competencia; **the f. of medicine** el campo de la medicina; **what's your f.?** ¿cuál es su especialidad? ❑ **f. study** *(scientific)* estudio *m* de campo; **f. trip** viaje *m* de estudios; **f. work** trabajo *m* de campo (**g**) *Comptr* campo *m*
  2 *vt Sport* (**a**) *(ball)* parar y devolver (**b**) *(present)* presentar; **to f. a strong team** presentar un equipo fuerte
  3 *vi Sport (in baseball, cricket)* parar y devolver la pelota, *Am* fildear

fielder ['fiːldər] *n Sport* jugador(a) *m,f*, que no batea, *Am* fildeador(a) *m,f*

fieldmouse ['fiːldmaʊs] *n* (*pl* **fieldmice** ['fiːldmaɪs]) *Zool* ratón *m* del campo

fiend [fiːnd] *n* (**a**) *(devil)* demonio *m*, diablo *m* (**b**) *Fam (fanatic)* fanático(a) *m,f*; **she's a fresh air f.** es una fanática del aire fresco

fiendish ['fiːndɪʃ] *adj Fam (cruel)* diabólico(a), malvado(a); *Fig (difficult)* enrevesado(a)

fiendishly ['fiːndɪʃlɪ] *adv (difficult, clever)* endiabladamente, endemoniadamente

fierce [fɪəs] *adj* (**a**) *(animal, look)* feroz (**b**) *(argument)* acalorado(a) (**c**) *(heat, competition)* intenso(a), fuerte (**d**) *(wind)* fuerte, violento(a)

fiercely ['fɪəslɪ] *adv (glare)* fieramente; *(fight)* ferozmente; *(condemn, defend)* vehementemente, apasionadamente; *(resist)* con furia

fierceness ['fɪəsnɪs] *n* (**a**) *(of animal, look)* ferocidad *f* (**b**) *(of heat, competition)* intensidad *f* (**c**) *(of wind)* fuerza *f*

fiery ['faɪərɪ] *adj* (**fierier, fieriest**) *(temper)* fogoso(a); *(speech)* acalorado(a); *(colour)* encendido(a)

fiesta [fɪ'estə] *n* fiesta *f*

FIFA ['fiːfə] *n (abbr* **Fédération Internationale de Football Association)** FIFA *f*

fife [faɪf] *n Mus* pífano *m*

fifteen [fɪf'tiːn] **1** *adj* quince *inv*; **f. books** quince libros; **she is f.** tiene quince años
  2 *n* (**a**) *(number)* quince *m inv* (**b**) *Rugby* equipo *m*; *see also* **seven**

fifteenth [fɪf'tiːnθ] **1** *adj* decimoquinto(a); **the f. of August** el quince de agosto
  2 *n* (**a**) *(in series)* decimoquinto(a) *m,f* (**b**) *(fraction)* quinzavo *m*; *see also* **seventh**

fifth [fɪfθ] **1** *adj* quinto(a); *Pol* **f. column** quinta columna; **the f. of May** el cinco de mayo
  2 *n* (**a**) *(in series)* quinto(a) *m,f* (**b**) *(fraction)* quinto *m*; *see also* **seventh**

fifth-former ['fɪfθfɔːmər] *n Br Sch Formerly* alumno(a) *m,f* del quinto curso

fiftieth ['fɪftɪɪθ] **1** *adj* quincuagésimo(a) *m,f*
  2 *n* (**a**) *(in series)* quincuagésimo(a) *m,f* (**b**) *(fraction)* cincuentavo *m*; *see also* **seventh**

fifty ['fɪftɪ] **1** *adj* cincuenta *inv*; **the Fifties** los años cincuenta; **she's in her fifties** tiene unos cincuenta años
  2 *n* cincuenta *m inv*; *see also* **seventy** *and* **seven**

fifty-fifty ['fɪftɪ'fɪftɪ] **1** *adj* **a f.-f. chance** una probabilidad del cincuenta por ciento
  2 *adv* **to go f.-f.** ir a medias

fig[1] [fɪg] *n Bot* (**a**) *(fruit)* higo *m*; *Fam* **I don't give** *or* **care a f.** me importa un pimiento *or* comino (**b**) *(tree)* higuera *f*

fig[2] [fɪg] *(abbr* **figure)** figura *f*, fig

fight [faɪt] **1** *vt* (*pt & pp* **fought**) (**a**) *(physical violence)* pelear(se) contra, luchar contra; *Box* pelear contra; *Fig (corruption, decision)* combatir, luchar contra; **to f. one's way through (the crowds)** luchar por abrirse camino (entre la multitud); *Fig* **to f. a losing battle** luchar por una causa perdida (**b**) *Mil (battle)* librar; *(war)* hacer (**c**) *(contest)* recurrir contra, presentar un recurso contra; **to f. a case** defenderse contra un cargo *or* un pleito
  2 *vi* (**a**) *(physically)* pelear(se), luchar; *Box* pelear, combatir (**b**) *(quarrel)* pelearse, reñir; **to f. over sth** disputarse la posesión de algo (**c**) *Fig (struggle)* luchar (**for/against** por/contra); **to f. on** seguir luchando; **to f. for one's life** luchar por la vida; **to f. shy of** evitar
  3 *n* (**a**) *(physical violence)* pelea *f*, lucha *f*; *Box* combate *m*; **a f. to the death** una lucha a muerte; **to pick a f. with sb** meterse con algn; **to start a f.** armar una pelea (**b**) *(quarrel)* pelea *f*, riña *f* (**c**) *Fig (struggle)* lucha *f*; **the f. against poverty** la lucha contra la pobreza (**d**) *(spirit)* combatividad *f*; **there's no f. left in him** no le queda ánimo para luchar

fight back 1 *vt (tears)* contener
  2 *vi* (**a**) *(recover a position)* resistir (**b**) *(in argument)* defenderse

fight off *vt* (**a**) *(attack)* rechazar (**b**) *Fig (illness)* cortar

fight out *vt* discutir; **a meeting with management to f. out the overtime issue** una reunión con la dirección para llegar a una decisión sobre las horas extras

fighter ['faɪtər] *n* (**a**) *(person)* combatiente *mf*; *Box* púgil *m* (**b**) *Fig* luchador(a) *m,f* ❑ *Av* **f. (plane)** (avión *m* de) caza *m*; **f. bomber** cazabombardero *m*; **f. pilot** piloto *m* de caza

fighting ['faɪtɪŋ] **1** *adj* **he's got a f. chance** tiene verdaderas posibilidades; **to be f. fit** estar en plena forma
  2 *n* (**a**) *(brawling)* peleas *fpl* (**b**) *Mil* combates *mpl*, enfrentamientos *mpl*

fig-leaf ['fɪgliːf] *n* (*pl* **fig-leaves** ['fɪgliːvz]) hoja *f* de parra

figment ['fɪgmənt] *n* **it's a f. of your imagination** es un producto de tu imaginación

figurative ['fɪgərətɪv] *adj* figurado(a)

figuratively ['fɪgərətɪvlɪ] *adv* **f. speaking** en sentido figurado

figure ['fɪgər, *US* 'fɪgjər] **1** *n* (**a**) *(form, outline)* forma *f*, silueta *f*; **a human f.** una figura humana ❑ **f. skating** patinaje *m* artístico (**b**) *(body shape)* figura *f*; **a fine f. of a man** un hombre bien plantado; **she has a good f.** tiene buen tipo; **to keep a good f.** guardar la línea (**c**) *(bearing)* **to cut a fine f.** tener buena presencia (**d**) *(character)* figura *f*, personaje *m*; **she was a key f. in the negotiations** fue una figura clave en las negociaciones (**e**) *(statue)* figura *f* (**f**) *(in book)* grabado *m*, dibujo *m* (**g**) *Ling* **f. of speech** figura *f* retórica (**h**) *Geom* figura *f* (**i**) *Math* cifra *f*, guarismo *m*; **in round figures** en números redondos; **he's good at figures** se le dan bien los números; *Fam* **to put a f. to sth** ponerle precio a algo ❑ *TV* **viewing figures** cifras *fpl* de los telespectadores

2 *vt US Fam* imaginarse, suponer; **I f. it's time to go** me imagino que ya es hora de marchar

3 *vi* **(a)** *(appear)* figurar, constar; **his name figures on the list** su nombre figura en la lista **(b)** *US Fam (make sense)* **that figures** eso tiene sentido

figure on *vt US* esperar, contar con

figure out *vt Fam (person)* comprender; *(problem)* resolver; **I can't f. it out** no me lo explico

figurehead ['fɪgəhed] *n Naut* mascarón *m* de proa; *Fig* figura *f* decorativa

figure-hugging ['fɪgəhʌgɪŋ] *adj* muy ceñido(a)

Fiji ['fiːdʒiː] *n* Fiji

Fijian [fiːˈdʒiːən] *n* fijiano(a) *m,f*

filament ['fɪləmənt] *n Elec* filamento *m*

filch [fɪltʃ] *vt Fam* afanar, *Esp* mangar

file [faɪl] **1** *n* **(a)** *(tool)* lima *f* **(b)** *(folder)* carpeta *f* **(c)** *(archive)* archivo *m*, expediente *m*; **to be on f.** estar archivado(a) ❏ **card-index f.** fichero *m*; **police f.** archivos *mpl* policiales **(d)** *Comptr* archivo *m* ❏ **f. management** gestión *f* de archivos *or* ficheros; **f. manager** administrador *m* de archivos; **f. server** servidor *m* de ficheros *or* archivos **(e)** *(line)* fila *m*; **in single f.** en fila india

2 *vt* **(a)** *(smooth)* limar; **to f. one's nails** limarse las uñas **(b)** *(put away)* archivar; *(in card-index)* fichar **(c)** *Jur* presentar; **to f. a petition for divorce** entablar demanda de divorcio

3 *vi Mil* **to f. past** desfilar

filet ['fɪlɪt] *n US see* fillet

filial ['fɪlɪəl] *adj* filial

filibuster ['fɪlɪbʌstər] **1** *n US Pol* filibustero(a) *m,f*, obstruccionista *mf*

2 *vi* practicar el filibusterismo

3 *vt (law, project)* obstruir

filibustering ['fɪlɪbʌstərɪŋ] *n US Pol* filibusterismo *m*, obstruccionismo *m*

filigree ['fɪlɪgriː] *n* filigrana *f*

filing ['faɪlɪŋ] *n* (a) *(of records)* clasificación *f* ❏ **f. cabinet** archivador *m*, clasificador *m*; *(for cards)* fichero *m*; **f. clerk** archivero(a) *m,f* **(b)** *(of metal)* **filings** limaduras *fpl*

Filipino [fɪlɪˈpiːnəʊ] *n* filipino(a) *m,f*

fill [fɪl] **1** *vt* **(a)** *(space)* llenar **(with** de); **to f. a glass** llenar un vaso; **to f. a gap** llenar un vacío **(b)** *(time)* llenar, ocupar **(c)** *(post, requirements)* cubrir **(d)** *(load)* cargar **(e)** *Culin* rellenar **(f)** *(tooth)* empastar, *RP* emplomar

2 *vi* llenarse **(with** de); **his eyes filled with tears** sus ojos se llenaron de lágrimas

3 *n Literary* saciedad *f*; **to eat one's f.** comer hasta hartarse; *Fam* **I've had my f. of him** estoy harto de él

fill in 1 *vt* **(a)** *(space, hole)* rellenar; **to f. in a form** rellenar un formulario **(b)** *(inform) Fam* poner al corriente **(on** de); **could you f. me in on the affair?** ¿me podrías poner al corriente del asunto? **(c)** *(time)* pasar; **how shall we f. in the afternoon?** ¿cómo vamos a pasar la tarde?

2 *vi* sustituir; **to f. in for sb** sustituir a algn

fill out 1 *vt US (form)* rellenar

2 *vi Fam* engordar

fill up 1 *vt (glass)* llenar (hasta el borde); *Aut Fam* **f. her up!** ¡llénelo!

2 *vi* llenarse; **the room filled up quickly** la sala se llenó rápidamente; *Aut* **to f. up with** *Br* **petrol** *or US* **gas** llenar el depósito de gasolina

filler ['fɪlər] *n (for cracks)* masilla *f*; *(to increase size)* relleno *m*

fillet ['fɪlɪt] **1** *n Culin* filete *m*; **f. of sole** filete de lenguado; **f. steak** filete *m*

2 *vt* cortar en filetes

filling ['fɪlɪŋ] **1** *adj* que llena mucho; **rice is very f.** el arroz llena mucho

2 *n* **(a)** *(stuffing)* relleno *m*; *Culin* **cake with lemon f.** pastel *m* relleno de limón ❏ *Br Aut* **f. station** gasolinera *f* **(b)** *(in tooth)* empaste *m*

fillip ['fɪlɪp] *n Fam* estímulo *m*

filly ['fɪlɪ] *n Zool* potra *f*

film [fɪlm] **1** *n* **(a)** *esp Br Cin* película *f*, film(e) *m*; **on f.** filmado(a), en película ❏ **f. industry** industria *f* cinematográfica; **f. star** estrella *f* de cine; **f. studio** estudio *m* de cine; **silent f.** película *f* muda **(b)** *(of dust, oil)* capa *f* **(c)** *Phot* película *f* ❏ **colour f.** película *f* en color

2 *vt Cin* filmar

3 *vi Cin* rodar

film over *vi* nublarse

filmgoer ['fɪlmgəʊər] *n* aficionado(a) *m,f* al cine, espectador(a) *m,f* de cine

film-strip ['fɪlmstrɪp] *n* cortometraje *m*

filo pastry ['fiːləʊˈpeɪstrɪ] *n* hojaldre *m* griego

filter ['fɪltər] **1** *n (for liquids, on cigarette)* & *Comptr* filtro *m* ❏ *Phot* **colour f.** filtro *m* de color; **f. coffee** café *m* de filtro; **f. paper** papel *m* de filtro; *Aut* **oil f.** filtro *m* de aceite

2 *vt* filtrar

3 *vi* filtrarse; **the sun filtered through the curtains** el sol se filtraba entre las cortinas; *Fig* **the news filtered through** se filtraron las noticias

filter-tip ['fɪltətɪp] *n* **(a)** *(of cigarette)* boquilla *f*, filtro *m* **(b)** *(cigarette)* cigarrillo *m* con filtro

filth [fɪlθ] *n* **(a)** *(dirt)* porquería *f*, suciedad *f* **(b)** *Fig (language, thoughts)* porquerías *fpl*, marranadas *fpl* **(c)** *Slang* bofia *f*, pasma *f*, maderos *mpl*

filthy ['fɪlθɪ] *adj (filthier, filthiest)* **(a)** *(dirty)* puerco(a), asqueroso(a), sucio(a) **(b)** *(obscene)* obsceno(a), grosero(a); **a f. mind** una mente sucia

fin [fɪn] *n Zool Av* aleta *f*

final ['faɪnəl] **1** *adj* **(a)** *(last)* último(a), final; **f. call** último aviso; *Sport* **the f. score** el resultado final; *(payment)* **f. demand** último aviso *m* de pago **(b)** *(definitive)* definitivo(a); **and that's f.** y no hay más que hablar

2 *n* **(a)** *Sport* final *f* ❏ **cup f.** final *f* de la copa **(b)** *Univ* **finals** *Br* exámenes *mpl* de fin de carrera; *US* exámenes *mpl* finales

finale [fɪˈnɑːlɪ] *n Mus* final *m*; *Fig* **grand f.** apoteosis *f*

finalist ['faɪnəlɪst] *n* finalista *mf*

finality [faɪˈnælɪtɪ] *n (of words, statement)* rotundidad *f*, irrevocabilidad *f*; *(of death)* carácter *m* irreversible

finalize ['faɪnəlaɪz] *vt (plans, arrangements)* ultimar; *(date)* fijar

finally ['faɪnəlɪ] *adv* **(a)** *(lastly)* por último, finalmente **(b)** *(at last)* por fin **(c)** *(definitively)* definitivamente

finance ['faɪnæns, fɪˈnæns] **1** *n* **(a)** *(subject)* finanzas *fpl* ❏ **f. company** sociedad *f* financiera; **high f.** altas finanzas *fpl*; **Minister of F.** ministro(a) *m,f* de Economía; **public f.** hacienda *f* pública **(b)** **finances** *(funds)* fondos *mpl*

2 *vt* financiar

financial [faɪˈnænʃəl, fɪˈnænʃəl] *adj* financiero(a) ❏ **f. affairs** asuntos *mpl* financieros; **f. crisis** crisis *f* económica; **f. planning** planificación *f* financiera; **f. reform** reforma *f* fiscal; **f. statement** balance *m* (general); **f. success** éxito *m* financiero; *Br* **f. year** *(for budget)* ejercicio *m* (económico); *(for tax)* año *m* fiscal

financially [faɪˈnænʃəlɪ, fɪˈnænʃəlɪ] *adv* económicamente

financier [faɪˈnænsɪər, fɪˈnænsɪər] *n* financiero(a) *m,f*

financing ['faɪnænsɪŋ, fɪˈnænsɪŋ] *n* financiación *f*

finch [fɪntʃ] *n Orn* pinzón *m*

find [faɪnd] **1** vt (pt & pp **found**) **(a)** (locate, come across) encontrar; **I couldn't f. him** no pude localizarlo; **they were nowhere to be found** no los encontramos en ningún sitio; **we found ourselves without a car** nos encontramos sin coche **(b)** (think) encontrar; **I f. her very nice** la encuentro muy simpática; **we f. the car a bit small** el coche nos resulta un poco pequeño **(c)** (discover) descubrir; **it has been found that ...** se ha comprobado que ...; **you'll f. that I'm right** ya verás or RP vas a ver cómo llevo razón **(d)** Jur declarar; **to f. sb guilty/not guilty** declarar culpable/inocente a algn **(e)** (obtain, manage) encontrar, conseguir; **he found his way in** logró introducirse; **he's been working there for one week and hasn't found his feet yet** lleva una semana trabajando allí y todavía no se ha situado; **I can't f. the courage to tell him** no tengo valor para decírselo; **I found him a job** le encontré un trabajo; **I found it impossible to get away** me resultó imposible irme; **to f. one's tongue** soltarse a hablar; **to f. one's way** encontrar el camino; **this found its way into my bag** esto vino a parar a mi bolso **(f)** Br Old-fashioned **thirty pounds, all found** treinta libras, todo incluido

2 n hallazgo m

find out 1 vt **(a)** (enquire) averiguar; **f. out his address** averigüe or entérese de su dirección; **I phoned to f. out the dates** llamé para preguntar las fechas **(b)** (discover) descubrir; **I found out that he had lied** descubrí que había mentido; **to f. sb out** descubrirle el juego a algn

2 vi **(a)** (enquire) averiguar; **to f. out about sth** informarse sobre algo **(b)** (discover) enterarse de; **when I found out ...** cuando lo supe ...

finder ['faɪndər] n **the f. of the money should contact the police** quien encuentre el dinero ha de llamar a la policía; Fam **finders keepers** = si yo lo encontré, es para mí

findings ['faɪndɪŋz] npl conclusiones fpl, resultados mpl

fine [faɪn] **1** n multa f

2 vt multar; **he was fined fifty dollars** le pusieron una multa de cincuenta dólares

3 adj **(a)** (delicate etc) fino(a) **(b)** (subtle) sutil; **a f. distinction** una diferencia sutil; **he's got it down to a f. art** lo hace a la perfección; **not to put too f. a point on it** hablando sin rodeos **(c)** (excellent) excelente; **a f. effort** un gran esfuerzo; **a f. pianist** un excelente pianista; **a f. piece of work** un trabajo excelente; **f. clothes** ropa elegante **(d)** (weather) bueno(a); **it was f.** hacia buen tiempo **(e)** **the f. arts** las bellas artes **(f)** (all right) bien; **I'm f.** estoy bien; **that's f. by me** ¡me parece bien!, ¡por mí, Esp vale or Arg dale or Méx órale!; **(g)** Iron **a f. mess** menudo lío; **you're a f. friend** ¡vaya amigo estás hecho!; **you're a f. one!** ¡estás tú bueno!; **you're a f. one to talk!** ¡mira quién habla!

4 adv Fam muy bien; **it suits me f.** me viene muy bien; **the patient's doing f.** el enfermo va muy bien; Fig **to cut it f.** ser muy justo de tiempo, llegar con el tiempo justo

5 interj muy bien, Esp vale, Arg dale, Méx órale

finely ['faɪnli] adv **(a)** (small pieces) finamente; **f. chopped** picado(a) fino **(b)** Tech Aut (delicately) **f. tuned** a punto **(c)** (elegantly) **f. dressed** vestido(a) con elegancia

finery ['faɪnəri] n galas fpl; **in all her f.** vestida con sus mejores galas

finesse [fɪ'nes] n **(a)** (delicacy) finura f, delicadeza f **(b)** (cunning) astucia f; (tact) sutileza f

fine-tuning ['faɪn'tjuːnɪŋ] n ajuste m

finger ['fɪŋgər] **1** n Anat dedo m (de la mano); Fam **he didn't lift a f. to help** no movió ni un dedo para ayudar; Fam **I didn't lay a f. on her** no la toqué en absoluto; Br Fam **pull your f. out!** ¡muévete!, RP ¡mueve las bolas!; Fam **to have a f. in every pie** estar metido(a) en todo; Fam **to keep one's fingers crossed** esperar que todo salga bien; Fam **to put two fingers up** hacer un corte de mangas; Fam

you've put your f. on it has dado en el clavo □ **f. bowl** lavadedos m inv; **index f.** dedo m índice; **little f.** dedo m meñique; **middle f.** dedo m corazón

2 vt tocar; Pej manosear

fingering ['fɪŋgərɪŋ] n Mus digitación f

fingernail ['fɪŋgəneɪl] n uña f

fingerprint ['fɪŋgəprɪnt] **1** n huella f digital or dactilar

2 vt tomar las huellas digitales a

fingertip ['fɪŋgətɪp] n punta f or yema f del dedo; Fig **to have sth at one's fingertips** saberse algo al dedillo

finicky ['fɪnɪki] adj **(a)** (person) quisquilloso(a), melindroso(a) **(b)** (job) delicado(a)

finish ['fɪnɪʃ] **1** n **(a)** (end) fin m, conclusión f; (of race) llegada f; **a close f.** un final muy reñido; **a fight to the f.** una lucha hasta el final; **to be in at the f.** estar presente en el final **(b)** (surface) acabado m □ **matt/glossy f.** acabado m mate/brillo

2 vt **(a)** (complete) acabar, terminar; **to f. doing sth** terminar de hacer algo **(b)** (use up, eat up) acabar, agotar; **f. (up) your potatoes** cómete las patatas **(c)** Fam (exhaust) agotar

3 vi acabar, terminar; **she finished by saying ...** terminó diciendo ...; **she has finished with her boyfriend** ha roto con el novio; Sport **to f. second** llegar el segundo

finish off 1 vt **(a)** (complete) terminar completamente **(b)** (use up) acabar, terminar; **let's f. off the wine** acabémonos el vino **(c)** (kill) Fam rematar, despachar

2 vi acabar

finish up 1 vt acabar, agotar

2 vi ir a parar; **she finished up in jail** fue a parar a la cárcel

finished ['fɪnɪʃt] adj **(a)** (product) acabado(a); **hand f.** acabado(a) a mano **(b)** Fam (exhausted) agotado(a), rendido(a) **(c)** Fam (burnt-out) quemado(a); **he's f. as a footballer** como futbolista está acabado

finishing ['fɪnɪʃɪŋ] adj **to put the f. touch(es) to sth** darle los últimos toques a algo □ Sport **f. line** or **post** (línea f de) meta f; **f. school** escuela f privada de modales para señoritas

finite ['faɪnaɪt] adj finito(a) □ Ling **f. verb** verbo m conjugable

Finland ['fɪnlənd] n Finlandia

Finn [fɪn] n finlandés(esa) m,f

Finnish ['fɪnɪʃ] **1** adj finlandés(esa)

2 n (language) finlandés m

fiord [fjɔːd, 'fiːɔːd] n Geog fiordo m

fir [fɜː] n Bot abeto m □ **Douglas f.** abeto m de Douglas; **silver f.** abeto m (blanco)

fire ['faɪər] **1** n **(a)** (element, in hearth) fuego m; **to light a f.** encender un fuego; **to sit by the f.** sentarse al calor de la lumbre **(b)** (accident etc) incendio m, fuego m; **f.!** ¡fuego!; **to be on f.** estar ardiendo or en llamas; **to catch f.** incendiarse; **to set f. to sth** prenderle fuego a algo, incendiar algo; Fig **to get on like a house on f.** llevarse de maravilla; Fig **to play with f.** jugar con fuego □ **f. alarm** alarma f de incendios; esp Br **f. brigade**, US **f. department** (cuerpo m de) bomberos mpl; **f. door** puerta f cortafuegos; **f. drill** simulacro m de incendio; Br **f. engine** coche m de bomberos; **f. escape** escalera f de incendios; **f. exit** salida f de emergencia; **f. extinguisher** Esp extintor m, Am extinguidor m; **f. fighting** extinción f de incendios; **f. fighting equipment** equipo m contra incendios; **f. insurance** seguro m contra incendios; **f. raiser** incendiario(a) m,f; **f. station** parque m de bomberos; US **f. truck** coche m de bomberos; US **f. warden** = responsable en caso de incendios forestales **(c)** Br (heater) estufa f □ **electric/gas f.** estufa f eléctrica/de gas **(d)** Mil fuego m;

heavy f. fuego nutrido; *Mil* **to come under f.** estar bajo el fuego; *Fig* ser el blanco de las críticas; **to open f.** abrir fuego ❑ **f. power** capacidad *f* ofensiva

2 *vt* **(a)** *(discharge) (arm)* disparar **(at a);** *(rocket)* lanzar; *Fig* **to f. questions at sb** bombardear a algn a preguntas **(b)** *Fam (dismiss)* despedir; **she was fired after they caught her stealing** le despidieron despúes de encontrarla robando **(c)** *(pottery)* cocer

3 *vi* **(a)** *(shoot)* disparar, hacer fuego **(at** sobre); **f.!** ¡fuego! **(b)** *Aut* encenderse, *Am* prenderse **(c)** *Fig* **f. away!** ¡adelante!

firearm ['faɪərɑ:m] *n* arma *f* de fuego

firebrand ['faɪəbrænd] *n* **(a)** *(torch)* tea *f* **(b)** *(person)* revoltoso(a) *m,f*

firebreak ['faɪəbreɪk] *n* cortafuego *m*

firecracker ['faɪəkrækər] *n* petardo *m*

firefighter ['faɪəfaɪtər] *n* bombero(a) *m,f*

firefly ['faɪəflaɪ] *n* luciérnaga *f*

fireguard ['faɪəgɑ:d] *n* pantalla *f* (de chimenea)

firelight ['faɪəlaɪt] *n* luz *f* del fuego

firelighter ['faɪəlaɪtər] *n* *(to start a fire)* astilla *f* para encender *or Am* prender el fuego; *(firebrand)* tea *f*

fireman ['faɪəmən] *n* *(pl* **firemen)** bombero *m*

fireplace ['faɪəpleɪs] *n* *(whole structure)* chimenea *f*; *(hearth)* hogar *m*

fireproof ['faɪəpru:f] *adj* incombustible

fireside ['faɪəsaɪd] *n* hogar *m*; **by the f.** al calor de la lumbre ❑ **f. chair** sillón *m*; **f. chat** tertulia *f*

firewall ['faɪəwɔ:l] *n Comptr* cortafuegos *m inv*

firewood ['faɪəwʊd] *n* leña *f*

fireworks ['faɪəwɜ:ks] *npl* fuegos *mpl* artificiales; *Fig* **there will be f.** se va a armar la gorda

firing ['faɪərɪŋ] *n Mil* tiroteo *m* ❑ **f. line** línea *f* de fuego; **f. squad** pelotón *m* de fusilamiento

firm [fɜ:m] **1** *adj* **(a)** *(steady, definite)* firme; **f. decision** firme decisión *f*; **f. foundation** base *f* sólida; **f. offer** oferta *f* en firme; **to stand f.** mantenerse firme **(b)** *(strict)* **to be f. with sb** tratar a algn con firmeza; **to rule with a f. hand** gobernar con mano dura

2 *n Com* empresa *f*, firma *f*

firmly ['fɜ:mlɪ] *adv* firmemente

firmness ['fɜ:mnɪs] *n* firmeza *f*

first [fɜ:st] **1** *adj* primero(a); *(before masculine singular noun)* primer; **at f. sight** a primera vista; **Charles the F.** Carlos Primero; **for the f. time** por primera vez; **f. thing in the morning** a primera hora de la mañana; **in the f. place** en primer lugar ❑ *Med* **f. aid** primeros auxilios *mpl*; **f. aid box** botiquín *m*; *Univ* **f. degree** licenciatura *f*; **f. edition** primera edición *f*; **f. floor** *Br* primer piso *m*, *US* planta *f* baja; *Aut* **f. gear** primera *f* (marcha); **f. name** nombre *m* de pila; *Theat* **f. night** noche *f* de estreno; *Jur* **f. offender** delincuente *m,f* sin antecedentes penales

2 *adv (before anything else)* primero; **finish your work f.** primero acaba el trabajo; **f. and foremost** ante todo; **f. of all** en primer lugar; **f. things f.** primero es lo primero; **her career comes f.** para ella su carrera es lo primero; **I'd die f.!** ¡antes morir!; *Sport* **to come f.** llegar el primero *or* la primera; *(in exam)* sacar la mejor nota; **when I f. saw her** cuando la vi por primera vez; *Fam* **f. come, f. served** los primeros primero

3 *n* **(a) the f.** el primero, la primera; **to be the f. to do sth** ser el primero *or* la primera en hacer algo; **the f. of April** el *Esp* uno *or* el primero de abril **(b)** *(at the beginning)* **at f.** al principio; **from the (very) f.** desde el principio **(c)** *Aut* primera *f* (marcha); **in f.** en primera **(d)** *Br Univ* **to get a f.** sacar una matrícula de honor

first-born ['fɜ:stbɔ:n] *n & adj* primogénito(a) *(m,f)*

first class [fɜ:st'klɑ:s] *adv Rail* en primera; **to travel f. c.** viajar en primera

first-class [fɜ:stklɑ:s] *adj* de primera clase; **f.-c. hotel** hotel de primera categoría; **f.-c. sportsman** deportista fuera de serie; **f.-c. ticket** billete de primera clase

first-degree ['fɜ:stdɪ'gri:] *adj* **(a)** *Med (burns)* de primer grado **(b)** *US Jur (murder)* en primer grado

first-former ['fɜ:stfɔ:mər] *n Br Sch Formerly* alumno(a) del primer curso

first-generation ['fɜ:stdʒenə'reɪʃən] *adj* de primera generación

first-hand ['fɜ:sthænd] *adv & adj* de primera mano; **f.-h. information** información *f* de primera mano

firstly ['fɜ:stlɪ] *adv* primero, en primer lugar

first-rate ['fɜ:streɪt] *adj* excelente, de primera

fiscal ['fɪskəl] *adj* fiscal

fish [fɪʃ] **1** *n* *(pl* **fish** *or* **fishes) (a)** *Zool* pez *m*; *Fig* **he's a queer f.** es un tipo raro; *Fig* **like a f. out of water** como pez fuera del agua, *RP* como sapo de otro pozo; *Fam* **to drink like a f.** beber como una esponja, *Am* tomar como un barril sin fondo ❑ **f. farm** piscifactoría *f*; **f. farming** piscicultura *f*; *Br* **f. finger** palito *m* de pescado; **f. hook** anzuelo *m*; **f. shop** pescadería *f*; *US Can* **f. stick** palito *m* de pescado; **f. tank** pecera *f* **(b)** *Br Culin* pescado *m*; **f. and chips** pescado frito con *Esp* patatas *or Am* papas fritas

2 *vi* pescar; **to f. for trout** pescar truchas; *Fig* **to f. in one's pocket for sth** buscar algo en el bolsillo *or CAm Perú Méx* la bolsa; *Fig* **to f. for compliments** buscar los elogios

3 *vt (river)* pescar en; *Fig* **to f. a sock out of the drawer** sacar un calcetín del cajón

fishbone ['fɪʃbəʊn] *n* espina *f*, raspa *f*

fishcake ['fɪʃkeɪk] *n Culin* medallón *m* de pescado y patata

fisherman ['fɪʃəmən] *n* *(pl* **fishermen)** pescador *m*

fishery ['fɪʃərɪ] *n* pesquería *f*, pesquera *f*

fishing ['fɪʃɪŋ] *n* pesca *f*; **to go f.** ir de pesca ❑ **deep-sea f.** pesca *f* de altura; **f. net** red *f* de pesca; **f. rod** caña *f* de pescar; **f. tackle** aparejo *m* de pescar

fish-knife ['fɪʃnaɪf] *n* *(pl* **fish-knives** ['fɪʃnaɪvz]) cuchillo *m* de pescado

fishmonger ['fɪʃmʌŋgər] *n Br* pescadero(a) *m,f*; **fishmonger's (shop)** pescadería *f*

fishnet ['fɪʃnet] *n* malla *f* ❑ **f. tights** leotardo *m* de malla gruesa

fishwife ['fɪʃwaɪf] *n* *(pl* **fishwives** ['fɪʃwaɪvz]) *Fig Pej* verdulera *f*

fishy ['fɪʃɪ] *adj* (**fishier, fishiest**) de pescado; **f. smell** olor a pescado; *Fam Fig* **there's something f. going on** aquí hay gato encerrado

fission ['fɪʃən] *n Phys* fisión *f*

fissure ['fɪʃər] *n* **(a)** *(in mountain, rock)* grieta *f* **(b)** *Anat* fisura *f*

fist [fɪst] *n* puño *m*; **to shake one's f. at sb** amenazar a algn con el puño

fistful ['fɪstfʊl] *n* puñado *m*

fisticuffs ['fɪstɪkʌfs] *npl* pelea *f* a puñetazos

fit¹ [fɪt] **1** *vt (pt & pp* **fitted) (a)** *(correct size)* quedar bien a; **that suit doesn't f. you** ese traje no te queda bien **(b)** *Sew* probar; **he is being fitted for a jacket** le están probando una chaqueta **(c)** *(slot)* encajar, poner; **this key doesn't f. the lock** esta llave no es de esta cerradura **(d)** *(put, install)* poner, colocar; **a car fitted with a radio** un coche provisto de radio; **to have a shelf fitted** hacer colocar un estante **(e)** *Fig (correspond)* encajar con, estar de acuerdo con; **she**

doesn't f. the description no responde a la descripción (**f**) *(make suitable)* *Fml* **to f. sb for sth** capacitar a algn para algo

2 *vi* (**a**) *(be right size)* caber; **all my belongings f. into the room** todas mis pertenencias caben en la habitación; **the door doesn't f. properly** la puerta no ajusta bien; **these trousers f. well** estos pantalones se ponen muy bien; **to f. like a glove** *(clothes)* quedar como un guante; *(others)* ir muy bien (**b**) *(correspond)* cuadrar; **the facts don't f.** los hechos no cuadran; *Fig* **his face didn't f.** no encajó

3 *adj* (**a**) *(suitable)* apto(a), adecuado(a) (**for** para); **a feast f. for a king** un banquete digno de un rey; **are you f. to drive?** ¿estás en condiciones de conducir?; **is he a f. person for the job?** ¿es la persona adecuada para el puesto?; **she's not f. to teach** no vale para la enseñanza; **that's all he's f. for** no sirve para nada más; **to see** *or* **think f. to do sth** juzgar oportuno hacer algo (**b**) *(healthy)* en forma, en plena forma; **to get/keep fit** ponerse/ mantenerse en forma; *Prov* **f. as a fiddle** en plena forma (**c**) *Fam (ready)* **he was f. to burst with excitement** desbordaba de entusiasmo

4 *n* ajuste *m*; *Sew* corte *m*; **to be a good f.** encajar bien; **the jacket is a good f.** la americana te viene bien

fit in 1 *vi* (**a**) *(match)* adaptarse; **he didn't f. in with his colleagues** no encajó con sus compañeros de trabajo (**b**) *(tally)* cuadrar (**with** con); **her story didn't f. in with the rest** su historia no cuadraba con las otras; **it's all fitting into place** ahora empiezo a entenderlo

2 *vt (find time for)* encontrar un hueco para; **the director tried to f. me in on Monday** el director intentó encontrar un hueco para verme el lunes; **we couldn't f. it all in** no tuvimos tiempo para todo

~~**fit out** *vt* equipar; **they fitted him out for the expedition** le equiparon para la expedición; **they fitted out the office** amueblaron el despacho~~

fit² [fɪt] *n* (**a**) *Med* ataque *m*, acceso *m*; **a f. of coughing** un acceso de tos; **epileptic f.** ataque epiléptico; *Fam* **he'll have a f.** le va a dar un ataque (**b**) *Fig* ataque *m*, arrebato *m*; **f. of anger** arranque *m* de cólera; **f. of enthusiasm** arrebato *m* de entusiasmo; **f. of jealously** ataque *or* arrebato *m* de celos; *Fig* **by fits and starts** a trompicones; *Br* **to go into fits of laughter** troncharse de risa

fitful ['fɪtfʊl] *adj* irregular, discontinuo(a)

fitfully ['fɪtfʊlɪ] *adv* a rachas

fitness ['fɪtnɪs] *n* (**a**) *(aptitude)* aptitud *f*, capacidad *f* (**b**) *(health)* (buen) estado *m* físico ❑ *Sport* **f. test** examen *m* de forma física

fitted ['fɪtɪd] *adj* empotrado(a) ❑ *Br* **f. carpet** moqueta *f*, *Am* alfombra *f*; *Br* **f. cupboard** armario *m* empotrado

fitter ['fɪtər] *n* ajustador(a) *m,f*

fitting ['fɪtɪŋ] **1** *adj* (*appropriate*) apropiado(a), oportuno(a); **it was f. that he won** era justo que ganara

2 *n* (**a**) *(dress)* prueba *f* ❑ **f. room** probador *m* (**b**) *(usu pl)* accesorio *m*; **light fittings** apliques *mpl* eléctricos; **bathroom fittings** sanitarios *mpl*

five [faɪv] **1** *adj* cinco *inv*; **f. cups** cinco tazas; **f. hundred** quinientos(as); **f. thousand men** cinco mil hombres; **f.-day week** semana *f* laboral de cinco días

2 *n* cinco *m inv*; *see also* **seven**

fiver ['faɪvər] *n Fam* billete *m* de cinco libras *or* dólares

five-star ['faɪvstɑː] *adj* de cinco estrellas; **f.-s. hotel** hotel *m* de cinco estrellas

five-year ['faɪvjɪər] *adj* que dura cinco años; **f.-y. plan** plan *m* quinquenal

fix [fɪks] **1** *n* (**a**) *Fam (difficulty)* aprieto *m*, apuro *m*; **to be in a f.** estar en un apuro (**b**) *(drugs) Slang* dosis *f*, pico *m*

2 *vt* (**a**) *(fasten)* fijar, asegurar; *Fig* fijar (**on** en); **she fixed her eyes on me** clavó sus ojos en mí; *Fig* **they fixed the**

blame on me me echaron la culpa (**b**) *(establish) (date, price)* fijar; *(limit)* señalar; **let's f. a price** fijemos un precio (**c**) *(arrange)* arreglar; **he'll f. it with the boss** se las arreglará con el jefe; *Fam* **how are you fixed for money?** qué tal andas de dinero?; **there's nothing fixed yet** no hay nada decidido todavía (**d**) *Sport (dishonestly)* amañar, *Am* arreglar; **the game was fixed for them to win** les arreglaron el partido para que ganasen (**e**) *(repair)* arreglar, componer (**f**) *US (food, drink)* preparar (**g**) *Phot* fijar (**h**) *(tidy)* arreglar; **she fixed her hair** se arregló el pelo

fix up *vt (arrange)* arreglar; **it's all fixed up** ya está todo arreglado; **to f. sb up with sth** proveer a algn de algo

fixated [fɪk'seɪtɪd] *adj* obsesionado(a) (**on** con)

fixation [fɪk'seɪʃən] *n* idea *f* fija, obsesión *f*; **to have a f. about sth.** estar obsesionado(a) por algo

fixed [fɪkst] *adj* (**a**) *(unchanging)* fijo(a); **of no f. abode** sin domicilio fijo **f. assets** activo *m* fijo *or* inmovilizado; **f. income** renta *f* fija (**b**) *Fam (election, contest) Esp* amañado(a), *Am* arreglado(a) **a f. match** un partido arreglado

fixedly ['fɪksɪdlɪ] *adv* fijamente

fixer ['fɪksər] *n Phot* fijador *m*

fixture ['fɪkstʃər] *n* (**a**) *Br Sport* encuentro *m* (**b**) **fixtures** *(in building)* accesorios *mpl*

fizz [fɪz] **1** *n* burbujeo *m*

2 *vi* burbujear

fizziness ['fɪzɪnɪs] *n* efervescencia *f*

fizzle ['fɪzəl] *vi (hiss)* chisporrotear

fizzle out *vi* quedar en nada; **their interest in the matter fizzled out within a week** su interés en el tema ~~se desvaneció en una semana~~

fizzy ['fɪzɪ] *adj (fizzier, fizziest) (water)* gaseoso(a), con gas; *(wine)* espumoso(a)

fjord [fjɔːd, 'fiːɔːd] *n Geog* fiordo *m*

flab [flæb] *n Fam* michelines *mpl*

flabbergasted ['flæbəgɑːstɪd] *adj* pasmado(a); **I was f.** quedé pasmado

flabby ['flæbɪ] *adj (flabbier, flabbiest)* fofo(a)

flaccid ['flæsɪd] *adj* fláccido(a)

flag [flæg] **1** *n* (**a**) *(of country)* bandera *f*, *Naut* pabellón *m*; *Fig* **to show the f.** hacer acto de presencia; **to keep the f. flying** ser patriótico(a), representar uno a su propio país ❑ **F. Day** *(in United States)* = día de la bandera, 14 de junio (**b**) *(for charity)* banderita *f* ❑ *Br* **f. day** día *m* de la banderita

2 *vt (pt & pp flagged) (mark)* señalar; *Fig* **to f. down a car** hacer señales a un coche para que pare

3 *vi (interest)* decaer; *(conversation)* languidecer; **after working on the same material his attention began to f.** después de trabajar el mismo material su atención empezó a decaer

flagellate ['flædʒəleɪt] *vt Fml* flagelar

flagged [flægd] *adj (floor)* enlosado(a)

flagging ['flægɪŋ] **1** *n (on floor)* enlosado *m*

2 *adj (strength, enthusiasm)* debilitado(a); *(conversation, interest)* decreciente

flagon ['flægən] *n (jug)* jarro *m*; *(bottle)* botella *f* grande

flagpole ['flægpəʊl] *n* asta *f* de bandera

flagrant ['fleɪgrənt] *adj* flagrante

flagship ['flægʃɪp] *n Naut* buque insignia *m*

flagstone ['flægstəʊn] *n* losa *f*

flail [fleɪl] **1** *n (agricultural implement)* mayal *m*

2 *vt* agitar; **she flailed her fists at him** trató inútilmente de golpearle

3 *vi* agitarse; **I managed to avoid his flailing fists** conseguí evitar sus puñetazos

flair [fleər] *n* instinto *m*, facilidad *f*, talento *m*, don *m*; **he has a f. for languages** tiene un don especial para los idiomas

flak [flæk] *n* (**a**) *Mil* fuego *m* antiaéreo (**b**) *Fam* críticas *fpl* negativas; **the decision came in for a lot of f.** la decisión fue duramente criticada

flake [fleɪk] **1** *n* (*of snow*) copo *m*; (*of skin, soap*) escama *f*; (*of paint*) desconchón *m*
2 *vi* (*skin*) descamarse; (*paint*) desconcharse

flake out *vi Fam* caer rendido(a); **I ran five miles and then flaked out** corrí cinco millas y después no me tenía en pie

flaky [ˈfleɪkɪ] *adj* (**flakier, flakiest**) (**a**) (*surface*) que se desconcha ▫ *Culin* **f. pastry** hojaldre *m* (**b**) *US Fam* (*eccentric*) raro(a)

flamboyant [flæmˈbɔɪənt] *adj* llamativo(a), extravagante

flame [fleɪm] *n* (**a**) (*of fire*) llama *f*; **to go up in flames** incendiarse; **to burst into flames** estallar en llamas; *Fam* **an old f.** un antiguo amor (**b**) *Comptr* llamarada *f*

flameproof [ˈfleɪmpruːf] *adj* ininflamable, ignífugo(a)

flamethrower [ˈfleɪmθrəʊər] *n* lanzallamas *m inv*

flaming [ˈfleɪmɪŋ] *adj* (**a**) (*burning*) en llamas (**b**) *Br Fam* maldito(a), *Méx* pinche, *RP* bendito(a); **where's the f. key?** ¿dónde está la maldita llave?

flamingo [fləˈmɪŋɡəʊ] *n* (*pl* **flamingos** *or* **flamingoes**) *Orn* flamenco *m*

flammable [ˈflæməbəl] *adj* inflamable

flan [flæn] *n Culin* tarta *f* rellena; **fruit f.** tarta de fruta

Flanders [ˈflɑːndəz] *n* Flandes

flange [flændʒ] *n* pestaña *f*, reborde *m*

flank [flæŋk] **1** *n* (**a**) (*of animal*) ijada *f*, ijar *m* (**b**) *Mil* flanco *m*
2 *vt* flanquear, bordear; **the road was flanked with** *or* **by trees** la carretera estaba bordeada de árboles

flannel [ˈflænəl] *n* (**a**) *Tex* franela *f* ▫ **f. trousers** pantalón *m* de franela (**b**) *Br* (*face cloth*) toallita *f*

flap [flæp] **1** *vt* (*pt & pp* **flapped**) (*wings, arms*) batir
2 *vi* (*wings*) aletear; (*flag*) ondear (**b**) *Fam* inquietarse
3 *n* (**a**) (*of envelope, book, pocket*) solapa *f*; (*of tent*) faldón *m* ▫ **cat f.** gatera *f* (**b**) (*of wing*) aletazo *m* (**c**) *Fam* pánico *m*; **to get into a f.** ponerse nervioso(a)

flapjack [ˈflæpdʒæk] *n Culin* (**a**) *Br* (*biscuit*) galleta *f* (**b**) *US* (*pancake*) hojuela *f*, tortita *f*

flare [fleər] **1** *n* (**a**) (*flame*) llamarada *f* (**b**) *Mil Naut* bengala *f*, cohete *m* de señales
2 *vi* (**a**) (*fire*) llamear (**b**) *Fig* (*person*) encolerizarse (**c**) (*trouble*) estallar

flared [fleəd] *adj* acampanado(a); **f. trousers** pantalones *mpl* acampanados

flares [fleəz] *npl* (*trousers*) pantalones *mpl* de campana; **a pair of f.** unos pantalones de campana

flash [flæʃ] **1** *n* (**a**) (*of light*) destello *m*; **f. of lightning** relámpago *m*; *Fig* **quick as a f.** como un relámpago; *Fig* **in a f.** en un decir Jesús ▫ **f. flood** inundación *f* repentina; **f. point** (*of situation*) momento *m* de máxima tensión; (*region*) zona *f* conflictiva (**b**) (*burst*) ráfaga *f*, *Fig* **a f. in the pan** un triunfo *or* éxito fugaz; *Fig* **f. of inspiration** momento *m* de inspiración (**c**) *Rad TV* (**news**) **f.** flash *m*, noticia *f* de última hora (**d**) *Phot* flash *m*
2 *adj Br Fam* llamativo(a), ostentoso(a)
3 *vt* (**a**) (*shine*) (*torch, light*) dirigir; *Fig* **to f. a smile at sb** lanzarle una sonrisa a algn (**b**) *Rad TV* transmitir (**c**) (*show quickly*) **he flashed his card** enseñó rápidamente su carnet
4 *vi* (**a**) (*sudden light*) destellar; (*shine*) brillar (**b**) (*move quickly*) mover muy rapidamente; **a car flashed past un**

coche pasó como un rayo; *Fig* **it flashed across** *or* **through** *or* **into my mind that ...** se me ocurrió de repente que ...

flashback [ˈflæʃbæk] *n Cin Lit* escena *f* retrospectiva

flashcube [ˈflæʃkjuːb] *n Phot* cubo *m* flash

flasher [ˈflæʃər] *n Br Slang* exhibicionista *m*

flashing [ˈflæʃɪŋ] *adj* (*light*) intermitente

flashlight [ˈflæʃlaɪt] *n* (**a**) *US* (*torch*) linterna *f* (**b**) *Br Phot* flash *m*

flashy [ˈflæʃɪ] *adj* (**flashier, flashiest**) *Fam* chillón(ona), ostentoso(a)

flask [flɑːsk, flæsk] *n Chem* matraz *m*; (**hip**) **f.** petaca *f*; (**thermos**) **f.** termo *m*

flat [flæt] **1** *adj* (**flatter, flattest**) (**a**) (*surface*) llano(a), plano(a); **to lay sth f.** tender algo; **to lie f.** tenderse ▫ **f. feet** pies *mpl* planos (**b**) (*beer*) sin gas (**c**) *Aut* (*battery*) descargado(a); (*tyre*) desinflado(a) (**d**) (*rate*) fijo(a) ▫ **f. rate** precio *m* fijo (**e**) (*categorical*) rotundo(a); **a f. refusal** una negativa rotunda (**f**) (*dull*) monótono(a), soso(a); **a f. party** una fiesta sosa (**g**) *Mus* bemol; **B. f.** si *m* bemol
2 *adv* (**a**) **to fall f. on one's face** caerse de bruces (**b**) (*exactly*) **in ten seconds f.** en diez segundos justos (**c**) *Fam* **to be f. broke** estar sin un *Esp* duro *or* *Méx* quinto, *RP* estar en lampa y la vía; *Fam* **to go f. out** ir a todo gas
3 *n* (**a**) (*surface*) superficie *f* plana (**b**) *Br* (*apartment*) apartamento *m*, *Esp* piso *m*, *Arg* departamento *m* (**c**) *US Aut Fam* rueda *f* desinflada (**d**) *Geog* **mud flats** marismas *fpl*

flat-chested [flætˈtʃestɪd] *adj* de poco pecho, liso(a)

flatfish [ˈflætfɪʃ] *n* pez *m* (de cuerpo) plano

flat-footed [flætˈfʊtɪd] *adj* **to be f.-f.** tener los pies planos

flatlet [ˈflætlɪt] *n Br* piso *m* pequeño, apartamento *m*

flatly [ˈflætlɪ] *adv* categóricamente, rotundamente

flatmate [ˈflætmeɪt] *n Br* compañero(a) *m,f* de apartamento *or* *Esp* piso *or* *Arg* departamento

flatness [ˈflætnəs] *n* (**a**) (*of surface*) lo llano (**b**) (*dullness*) monotonía *f*, sosería *f*

flat-screen [ˈflætskriːn] *adj* de pantalla plana

flatten [ˈflætən] *vt* (**a**) (*make level*) allanar, aplanar (**b**) (*crush*) aplastar

flatter [ˈflætər] *vt* (**a**) (*person*) adular, halagar; **I am flattered to be invited** me siento halagado por su invitación (**b**) (*clothes, portrait*) favorecer; **that hairstyle flatters her** ese peinado le favorece mucho (**c**) **to f. oneself** hacerse ilusiones; **don't f. yourself** no te hagas ilusiones

flatterer [ˈflætərər] *n* adulador(a) *m,f*

flattering [ˈflætərɪŋ] *adj* (**a**) (*words*) halagüeño(a), lisonjero(a) (**b**) (*dress, portrait*) favorecedor(a), que favorece

flattery [ˈflætərɪ] *n* adulación *f*, halagos *mpl*

flatulence [ˈflætjʊləns] *n* flatulencia *f*

flatulent [ˈflætjʊlənt] *adj Med* flatulento(a); *Fig* (*speech, style*) rimbombante, campanudo(a)

flaunt [flɔːnt] *vt* ostentar, hacer alarde de; **to f. oneself** pavonearse

flautist [ˈflɔːtɪst] *n* flautista *mf*

flavour, *US* **flavor** [ˈfleɪvər] **1** *n* (*of food*) & *Fig* sabor *m*; **her stories have a Mediterranean f.** sus relatos tienen un sabor mediterráneo
2 *vt Culin* sazonar (**with** con), condimentar (**with** con)

flavoured, *US* **flavored** [ˈfleɪvəd] *adj* con sabor a; **strawberry f. ice cream** helado *m* con sabor a fresa

flavouring, *US* **flavoring** [ˈfleɪvərɪŋ] *n* condimento *m*, aderezo *m*; **artificial f.** aroma *m* artificial

flavourless, *US* **flavorless** [ˈfleɪvəlɪs] *adj* insípido(a)

flaw [flɔː] *n (failing)* defecto *m, Esp* fallo *m, Am* falla *f;* *(fault)* desperfecto *m*

flawed [flɔːd] *adj* defectuoso(a)

flawless ['flɔːlɪs] *adj (immaculate)* sin defecto, sin tacha, perfecto(a)

flax [flæks] *n Bot* lino *m*

flaxen ['flæksən] *adj* **f. hair** pelo muy rubio

flay [fleɪ] *vt* **(a)** *(flog)* desollar; *(animal)* despellejar **(b)** *Fig (argument)* criticar; **to f. sb alive** desollar a algn vivo(a)

flea [fliː] *n* pulga *f* □ **f. market** rastro *m*, mercado *m* de trastos viejos; *Br Fam Pej* **f. pit** cine *m or* teatro *m* de mala muerte

fleabag ['fliːbæg] *n* **(a)** *Br Fam Pej* cochino(a) *m,f* **(b)** *US* hotelucho *m*

fleabite ['fliːbaɪt] *n* picadura *f* de pulga

flea-bitten ['fliːbɪtən] *adj Fam* sucio(a), desharrapado(a)

fleck [flek] *n (speck)* mota *f*, punto *m*

flecked [flekt] *adj (speckled)* moteado(a); *(spattered)* salpicado(a) **(with** de)

fled [fled] *pt & pp see* **flee**

fledg(e)ling ['fledʒlɪŋ] **1** *n Orn* volantón *m*, volandero *m*
2 *adj Fig* novato(a)

flee [fliː] **1** *vt (pt & pp fled)* huir de; **to f. the country** huir del país
2 *vi* huir **(from** de); **city dwellers f. to the coast in the summer** los habitantes de la ciudad huyen hacia la costa en verano

fleece [fliːs] **1** *n* **(a)** *(sheep's coat)* lana *f* **(b)** *(sheared)* vellón *m; Myth* **the Golden F.** el Vellocino de Oro
2 *vt Fam (cheat)* desollar, desplumar

fleecy ['fliːsɪ] *adj* **(fleecier, fleeciest) (a)** *(woollen)* lanoso(a) **(b)** *(soft, fluffy)* suave; **f. clouds** nubes *fpl* aborregadas

fleet¹ [fliːt] *n Naut* flota *f* □ **fishing f.** flota *f* pesquera; *(of cars)* escuadra *f; Br* **F. Air Arm** Armada *f* Aérea de la Flota

fleet² [fliːt] *adj Literary* rápido(a), veloz; **f. of foot** de pies ligeros

fleeting ['fliːtɪŋ] *adj (brief, passing)* fugaz, efímero(a)

fleetingly ['fliːtɪŋlɪ] *adv* fugazmente

Flemish ['flemɪʃ] **1** *adj* flamenco(a)
2 *n (language)* flamenco *m*

flesh [fleʃ] *n* **(a)** *(of person)* carne *f; Fig* **I saw David Bowie in the f.** vi a David Bowie en persona; *Fig (kin)* **she's your own f. and blood** es de tu propia sangre; *Fig* **the pleasures of the f.** los placeres de la carne; *Fig* **to be of f. and blood** ser de carne y hueso; *Fig* **to put f. on sth** *(fill out)* dar forma a algo □ **f. wound** herida *f* superficial **(b)** *(of fruit)* carne *f*, pulpa *f*

flesh-coloured, *US* **flesh-colored** ['fleʃkʌləd] *adj* de color carne

fleshy ['fleʃɪ] *adj* **(fleshier, fleshiest)** carnoso(a)

flew [fluː] *pt see* **fly**

flex [fleks] **1** *n Br Elec* cable *m*
2 *vt (body, knees)* doblar; *(muscles)* flexionar

flexibility [fleksɪ'bɪlɪtɪ] *n* flexibilidad *f*

flexible ['fleksɪbəl] *adj* flexible

flexitime ['fleksɪtaɪm] *n* horario *m* flexible

flick [flɪk] **1** *n* **(a)** *(jerk)* movimiento *m* rápido *or* brusco; *(with finger)* capirotazo *m;* **with the flick of a wrist** con un movimiento rápido de la muñeca; **with a f. of the tail** de un coletazo; **at the f. of a switch** solo con apretar un botón **(b)** *Br Fam Old-fashioned* **the flicks** *(cinema)* el cine
2 *vt* **(a)** *(button, switch)* darle a **(b)** *(whip)* chasquear **(c)** *(with finger)* dar un capirotazo a; **to f. sth at sb** tirarle algo a algn con un capirotazo

flick off *vt (brush)* sacudirse de encima; *(ash)* tirar; *(light)* apagar

flick on *vt (light)* encender, *Am* prender

flick through *vt (book etc)* hojear

flicker ['flɪkər] **1** *n* **(a)** *(gen)* parpadeo *m; (light)* titileo *m* **(b)** *Fig (trace)* indicio *m*, rastro *m;* **a f. of hope** una pizca de esperanza; **not a f. of interest** ni un ápice de interés
2 *vi (eyes)* parpadear; *(flame)* vacilar, titilar

flick-knife ['flɪknaɪf] *n (pl* **flick-knives** ['flɪknaɪvz]**)** navaja *f* automática

flier ['flaɪər] *n Av* aviador(a) *m,f* □ *Fig* **high f.** ambicioso(a) *m,f*

flight [flaɪt] *n* **(a)** *(act of flying)* vuelo *m;* **how long is the f.?** ¿cuánto dura el vuelo?; **is there a f. to Malaga?** ¿hay algún vuelo a Málaga?; *Fig* **f. of fancy** vuelo *m* de la imaginación □ **charter f.** vuelo *m* chárter; **f. attendant** auxiliar *mf* de vuelo; **f. deck** *(of plane)* cabina *f* del piloto; *(of aircraft carrier)* cubierta *f* de vuelo; **f. path** trayectoria *f* de vuelo; **f. recorder** registrador *m* de vuelo **(b)** *(of ball)* trayectoria *f* **(c)** *(flock of birds)* bandada *f* **(d)** *(running away)* huida *f*, fuga *f;* **to take f.** darse a la fuga **(e)** *(of stairs)* tramo *m;* **the office is three flights up** el despacho está tres pisos más arriba

flightiness ['flaɪtɪnɪs] *n* ligereza *f*

flightless ['flaɪtlɪs] *adj Zool* **f. bird** ave *f* no voladora

flighty ['flaɪtɪ] *adj* **(flightier, flightiest)** casquivano(a)

flimsiness ['flɪmzɪnɪs] *n* **(a)** *(thinness)* ligereza *f*, finura *f* **(b)** *(brittleness)* fragilidad *f*

flimsy ['flɪmzɪ] **1** *adj* **(flimsier, flimsiest) (a)** *(cloth)* ligero(a); *(paper)* fino(a) **(b)** *(structure)* poco sólido(a) **(c)** *(excuse)* flojo(a), malo(a)
2 *n* papel *m* cebolla

flinch [flɪntʃ] *vi* **(a)** *(wince)* estremecerse; **without flinching** sin pestañear **(b)** *(shy away)* **to f. from sth** retroceder ante algo

fling [flɪŋ] **1** *vt (pt & pp flung)* *(hurl, toss)* arrojar, tirar; **he flung his hat onto the table** lanzó su sombrero sobre la mesa; **she flung herself into his arms** se dejó caer en sus brazos; **to f. a door open** abrir una puerta de golpe; **to f. oneself at sb** arrojarse sobre algn; **to f. sb out** echar a algn a patadas; *Fig* **she flung insults at him** le lanzó una sarta de insultos; *Fig* **to f. oneself into sth** entregarse a algo
2 *n* **(a)** *(throw)* lanzamiento *m* **(b)** *Fam (good time)* juerga *f;* **to have one last f.** correrse la última juerga **(c)** *Fam (affair)* lío *m;* **to have a f.** echar una cana al aire

fling off *vt (clothes)* quitarse rápidamente

fling on *vt (clothes)* ponerse rápidamente

fling out *vt* tirar, *Am* botar; **we flung out all the old furniture** tiramos todos los muebles viejos

flint [flɪnt] *n* **(a)** *(stone)* pedernal *m*, sílex *m* **(b)** *(in cigarette lighter)* piedra *f*

flintlock ['flɪntlɒk] *n (gun)* escopeta *f or* fusil *m* de chispa

flip [flɪp] **1** *n (flick)* capirotazo *m*, capirote *m*, papirotazo *m* □ **f. chart** flip chart *m*, pizarra *f* de conferencia *(con bloc)*; **f. side** *(of record)* cara *f* B
3 *vt (pt & pp flipped)* **(a)** *(toss)* tirar *or* echar (al aire); *US* **to f. a coin** echar a cara o cruz **(b)** *(flick) (button, switch)* darle a
4 *vi Fam (freak)* perder los estribos

flip-flop ['flɪpflɒp] *n Br (footwear)* chancleta *f*

flippancy ['flɪpənsɪ] *n (frivolity)* liviandad *f*, ligereza *f*, falta *f* de seriedad

flippant ['flɪpənt] *adj (frivolous)* liviano(a), ligero(a), poco serio(a)

flipper ['flɪpər] *n* aleta *f*

flirt [flɜːt] **1** n coqueto(a) m,f; ligón(ona) m,f

  2 vi flirtear, coquetear; Fig **to f. with an idea** acariciar una idea; **to f. with death** jugar con la muerte

flirtation [flɜː'teɪʃən] n flirteo m, coqueteo m, ligue m

flirtatious [flɜː'teɪʃəs] adj coqueto(a)

flit [flɪt] **1** n Br Fam **to do a moonlight f.** irse a la chita callando

  2 vi (pt & pp **flitted**) (buzz, whizz) revolotear; **to f. in and out** ir y venir sin hacer ruido

float [fləʊt] **1** n **(a)** Fishing corcho m, flotador m **(b)** (Swimming) flotador m **(c)** (money) cambio m **(d)** (in procession) carroza f ▫ Br **milk f.** furgoneta f de repartir la leche

  2 vt **(a)** (ship) flotar **(b)** Fin (shares) emitir; (currency, business) hacer flotar

  3 vi (gen) flotar; **to f. to the surface** salir a la superficie; (glide) **she floated into the room** entró en la habitación elegantemente

float around vi (rumour) circular

floating ['fləʊtɪŋ] adj flotante; (population) flotante; Pol (voter) indeciso(a) ▫ Tech **f. axle** eje m flotante; Fin **f. currency** moneda f flotante

flock [flɒk] **1** n **(a)** Zool rebaño m; Orn bandada f **(b)** Rel (congregation) grey f **(c)** (crowd) multitud f, tropel m **(d)** Tex borra f

  2 vi acudir en masa; **to f. together** congregarse, reunirse; Fig **they flocked to the exhibition** acudieron en masa or tropel a la exposición

floe [fləʊ] n témpano m (de hielo)

flog [flɒg] vt (pt & pp **flogged**) **(a)** (beat) azotar; Fam Fig (idea) **flogged to death** pasado(a) de moda, demasiado usado(a); Fam Fig **to f. a dead horse** querer hacer lo imposible; Fam Fig **to f. oneself to death** matarse trabajando **(b)** Br Slang (sell) vender

flogging ['flɒgɪŋ] n azotaina f, paliza f

flood [flʌd] **1** n inundación f; (of river) riada f; Fig (of people) torrente m, riada f, tropel m; (of light) torrente m, chorro m

  2 vt inundar; **to be flooded** inundarse; Com **to f. the market with products** inundar el mercado de productos

  3 vi (river) desbordarse; Fig **to f. in** entrar a raudales; **letters came flooding in** hubo una avalancha de cartas

floodgate ['flʌdgeɪt] n compuerta f

flooding ['flʌdɪŋ] n inundaciones fpl

floodlight ['flʌdlaɪt] n Elec foco m

floodlit ['flʌdlɪt] adj iluminado(a) con focos

floor [flɔːr] **1** n **(a)** (of room) suelo m, piso m; **to take the f.** salir a bailar ▫ **dance f.** pista f de baile; **f. polish** cera f (de suelos) **(b)** Geog (of ocean, forest, etc) fondo m **(c)** (storey) piso m ▫ **first f.** Br primer piso m, US planta f baja; **f. show** espectáculo m de cabaret; **ground f.** planta f baja **(d)** Parl hemiciclo m

  2 vt (knock down) derribar; Fig dejar perplejo(a)

floorboard ['flɔːbɔːd] n tabla f (del suelo)

floorcloth ['flɔːklɒθ] n bayeta f

floozie, floozy ['fluːzɪ] n Fam pelandusca f

flop [flɒp] **1** n Fam fracaso m

  2 vi (pt & pp **flopped**) **(a)** (fall) dejarse caer; **to f. down on the bed** tumbarse en la cama **(b)** Fam fracasar

floppy ['flɒpɪ] adj (**floppier, floppiest**) blando(a); flojo(a) ▫ Comptr **f. disc** disco m flexible, disquete m

flora ['flɔːrə] n Bot flora f

floral ['flɔːrəl] adj floral

Florence ['flɒrəns] n Florencia

florentine ['flɒrentaɪn] adj & n florentino(a) (m,f)

florid ['flɒrɪd] adj Fml **(a)** (style etc) florido(a), recargado(a) **(b)** (complexion) rojizo(a)

florist ['flɒrɪst] n florista mf; **f.'s** floristería f

floss [flɒs] **1** n (dental) **f.** hilo m dental

  2 vt **to f. one's teeth** limpiarse los dientes con hilo dental

flotation [fləʊ'teɪʃən] n (buoyancy) flotabilidad f

flotilla [flə'tɪlə] n Naut flotilla f

flotsam ['flɒtsəm] n Naut **f. and jetsam** desechos mpl arrojados al mar; Fig gente f sin oficio ni beneficio

flounce¹ [flaʊns] **1** n gesto m exagerado or de enfado

  2 vi moverse desahogadamente; **to f. in/out** entrar/salir airadamente

flounce² [flaʊns] n Sew volante m, Chile vuelo m, RP Ven volado m

flounder¹ ['flaʊndər] n (fish) platija f

flounder² ['flaʊndər] vi **(a)** (struggle) forcejear; Fig enredarse **(b)** (dither) no saber que decir or hacer; Fig vacilar

flour ['flaʊər] n harina f ▫ **f. mill** molino m de harina

flourish ['flʌrɪʃ] **1** n **(a)** (gesture) ademán m, gesto m; **he entered the room with a f.** entró en la habitación haciendo un gesto teatral **(b)** (of sword) floreo m; (under signature) rúbrica f; (in writing) plumada f **(c)** Mus (on guitar) floreo m; (fanfare) toque m de trompeta **(d)** (speech, singing) floritura f

  2 vt **(a)** (brandish, wave) agitar, ondear **(b)** Mus florear

  3 vi **(a)** (thrive, bloom) prosperar, florecer **(b)** (plant) crecer, medrar

flourishing ['flʌrɪʃɪŋ] adj floreciente, próspero(a)

flout [flaʊt] vt Jur desacatar

flow [fləʊ] **1** n **(a)** (of liquid, electricity) flujo m; (of river) corriente f; **he interrupted me when I was in full f.** me interrumpió en pleno discurso **(b)** (of traffic) circulación f **(c)** Fin (of capital) movimiento m **(d)** (of people, goods) afluencia f; **to go along with the f.** seguir la corriente

  2 vi **(a)** (blood, water, etc) fluir, manar; **the Douro flows into the Atlantic** el Duero desemboca en el Atlántico **(b)** (sea) subir **(c)** (traffic) circular **(d)** Fig (ideas, information, people) correr ▫ **f. chart** diagrama m de flujo; Comptr organigrama m

flower ['flaʊər] **1** n **(a)** Bot flor f; **in f.** en flor; **bunch of flowers** ramo m de flores ▫ **f. arranging** arte m or decoración f floral; **f. bed** arriate m, parterre m; **f. show** exposición f de flores **(b)** Fig flor f; **in the f. of youth** en la flor de la juventud

  2 vi (blossom, bloom) florecer

flowered ['flaʊəd] adj (patterned) floreado(a)

flowering ['flaʊərɪŋ] **1** adj **f. plant** planta f florida

  2 n Fig (blossoming) floración f, florecimiento m

flowerpot ['flaʊəpɒt] n maceta f, tiesto m

flowery ['flaʊrɪ] adj (pattern) de flores; Fig (style) florido(a); **a f. apron** un delantal de flores

flowing ['fləʊɪŋ] adj (water) que fluye; (hair) suelto(a); (dress) de mucho vuelo; (style) fluido(a), suelto(a); (shape, movement) natural

flown [fləʊn] pp see **fly**

flu [fluː] n (abbr **influenza**) gripe f, Am gripa f

fluctuate ['flʌktjʊeɪt] vi fluctuar

fluctuating ['flʌktjʊeɪtɪŋ] adj fluctuante

fluctuation [flʌktjʊ'eɪʃən] n fluctuación f, variación f

flue [fluː] n Archit conducto m de humos; (chimney) cañón m; (stove) orificios mpl de ventilación

fluency ['fluːənsɪ] n fluidez f; **f. in Russian** dominio m del ruso

fluent ['fluːənt] adj **(a)** (articulate, eloquent) fluido(a), elocuente (**b**) *(languages)* **he speaks f. German** habla el alemán con soltura

fluently ['fluːəntlɪ] *adv* con soltura

fluff [flʌf] **1** *n (down, material)* pelusa *f*
2 *vt Fam* hacer mal *or* a destiempo; *Theat (bungle)* equivocar; **to f. one's lines** equivocarse en su papel

fluff up, fluff out *vt (cushion)* sacudir; *(hair, feathers)* encrespar, erizar, ensortijar; **the cock fluffed up his feathers** el gallo se encrespó

fluffy ['flʌfɪ] *adj* (**fluffier, fluffiest**) *(pillow)* mullido(a); *(toy)* de peluche; *(cake)* esponjoso(a)

fluid ['fluːɪd] **1** *adj* (**a**) *(movement, shape)* natural, con soltura (**b**) *(flexible, variable)* flexible; *(politics etc)* incierto(a)
2 *n* fluido *m*, líquido *m* ◻ **f. mechanics** mecánica *f* de fluidos; **f. ounce** onza *f* líquida

fluidity [fluː'ɪdɪtɪ] *n* fluidez *f*; *(movement, shape)* soltura *f*

fluke [fluːk] *n Fam* chiripa *f*, churra *f*; **by a f.** por *or* de chiripa

fluk(e)y ['fluːkɪ] *adj* (**flukier, flukiest**) *Fam (lucky)* **a f. goal** un gol de churro *or* por churra

flume [fluːm] *n* tobogán *m*

flummox ['flʌməks] *vt Fam* desconcertar, despistar; **his question left me flummoxed** su pregunta me dejó parado

flung [flʌŋ] *pt & pp see* **fling**

flunk [flʌŋk] *vt & vi US Fam Esp* catear, *Am* reprobar, *Méx* tronar, *RP* desaprobar; **I've flunked history** me han suspendido en historia

flunk out *vi US Fam Esp* suspender, *Am* reprobar

flunk(e)y ['flʌŋkɪ] *n* (**a**) *Fam* mayordomo *m*, lacayo *m* (**b**) *Pej (sycophant)* lameculos *mf inv*, pelota *mf*

fluorescence [fluə'resəns] *n* fluorescencia *f*

fluorescent [fluə'resənt] *adj (glowing)* fluorescente ◻ **f. lighting** alumbrado *m* fluorescente

fluoride ['fluəraɪd] *n Chem* fluoruro *m*

flurry ['flʌrɪ] *n* (**a**) *(wind)* ráfaga *f*; *(whirl)* **f. of snow** nevato *m* (**b**) *Fig (bustle, excitement)* agitación *f*; **a f. of terrorism** una oleada de terrorismo

flush [flʌʃ] **1** *adj* (**a**) *(level)* nivelado(a); **f. with** a ras de (**b**) *Fam (replete)* desahogado(a); **to be f.** andar bien de dinero
2 *n* (**a**) *(blush)* rubor *m*; *Med* **hot flushes** sofocos *mpl*; **f. of anger** acceso *m* de cólera; **in the first f. of victory** en la euforia inicial de la victoria (**b**) *Cards (poker)* color *m* ◻ **Royal f.** escalera *f* real
3 *vt* (**a**) *(clean)* limpiar con agua; **to f. the lavatory** tirar la cadena (del wáter); **to f. sth down the lavatory** tirar algo al wáter (**b**) **to f. out** *(enemy, prey)* hacer salir; **the police flushed out the kidnappers** la policía hizo salir a los secuestradores
4 *vi* (**a**) **the loo won't f.** la cisterna del wáter no funciona (**b**) *(blush)* ruborizarse; **to f. with anger** ponerse rojo(a) de ira

flushed [flʌʃt] *adj (cheeks)* rojo(a), encendido(a); *Fig* **f. with success** emocionado(a) ante el éxito

fluster ['flʌstər] *vt (bother)* molestar, marear; **to get flustered** ponerse nervioso(a)

flute [fluːt] *n* flauta *f*

fluted ['fluːtɪd] *adj Archit* acanalado(a)

flutist ['fluːtɪst] *n US* flautista *mf*

flutter ['flʌtər] **1** *vi* (**a**) *(leaves, birds)* revolotear; *Fig (flit)* **she fluttered about the room** revoloteaba por la habitación (**b**) *(flag)* ondear
2 *vt* **to f. one's eyelashes** parpadear
3 *n (flap)* agitación *f*; **to be in a f.** estar nervioso(a) (**b**) *Br Fam (gambling)* apuesta *f* pequeña

fluvial ['fluːvɪəl] *adj* fluvial

flux [flʌks] *n (flow)* flujo *m*; *(instability)* inestabilidad *f*; *Fig* **to be in a state of f.** estar cambiando constantemente

fly¹ [flaɪ] **1** *vt (pt* **flew;** *pp* **flown)** (**a**) *Av* pilotar (**b**) *(merchandise, troops)* transportar (**c**) *(travel)* sobrevolar; **to f. the Atlantic** sobrevolar el Atlántico (**d**) *(hoist)* izar (**e**) *(kite)* hacer volar
2 *vi* (**a**) *(bird, plane)* volar; *Fig* **the bird has flown** el pájaro voló (**b**) *(go by plane)* ir en avión (**c**) *(flag)* estar izado(a) (**d**) *(sparks)* saltar; **the door flew open** la puerta se abrió de golpe (**e**) *(rush)* irse volando, irse a toda prisa; **I must f.** me voy volando; **the train flew past** el tren pasó volando; **to f. into a rage** montar en cólera; *Fam Fig* **to f. off the handle** salirse de sus casillas (**f**) **to f. at sb** *(attack)* lanzarse sobre algn; **to let f. at sb** asestarle un golpe a algn, empezar a insultar a algn; (**g**) *(fall)* caerse; *Fam* **to go flying** caerse; **he slipped and went flying** resbaló y se cayó; *Fam* **to send sb flying** mandar a algn por los aires
3 *n* (**a**) *(also* **f. sheet**) *(paper)* hoja *f* suelta; *(of tent)* doble techo *m* (**b**) *(flies)* bragueta *f* sing

fly² [flaɪ] *n* (**a**) *Ent* mosca *f*; *Fig* **she wouldn't hurt a f.** es incapaz de matar una mosca; *Fam Fig* **there are no flies on him** no se chupa el dedo; *Fam Fig* **they're dropping like flies** caen como moscas ◻ **f. spray** spray *m* matamoscas, matamoscas *m inv* (**b**) *Fishing (bait)* mosca *f*

fly³ [flaɪ] *adj* (**flier, fliest**) *Br Fam* avispado(a), astuto(a)

flyby ['flaɪbaɪ] *n (pl* **flybys**) *US Av* desfile *m* aéreo

fly-by-night ['flaɪbaɪnaɪt] *adj Fam* de poca confianza

flycatcher ['flaɪkætʃər] *n Orn* papamoscas *m inv* ◻ **pied f.** papamoscas *m inv* cerrojillo; **spotted f.** papamoscas *m inv* gris

flyer ['flaɪər] *n see* **flier**

fly-fishing ['flaɪfɪʃɪŋ] *n* pesca *f* con moscas *or* al lanzado

flying ['flaɪɪŋ] **1** *adj (soaring)* volante; *(rapid)* rápido(a); *Sport* **a f. start** una salida lanzada; **a f. visit** una visita relámpago; *Fig* **to come out of an affair with f. colours** salir airoso(a) de un asunto; *Fig* **to get off to a f. start** empezar con buen pie ◻ *Archit* **f. buttress** arbotante *m*; *Austral* **f. doctor** médico *mf* que viaja en avión para visitar a sus pacientes; **f. fish** pez *m* volador; **f. picket** piquete *m* (informativo); **f. saucer** platillo *m* volante; **f. squad** patrulla *f* volante
2 *n* (**a**) *(action)* vuelo *m* (**b**) *(aviation)* aviación *f*; **fear of f.** miedo *m* a volar ◻ **f. school** escuela *f* de aviación; **f. hours** horas *fpl* de vuelo

flyleaf ['flaɪliːf] *n (pl* **flyleaves** ['flaɪliːvz]) *(of book)* guarda *f*

fly-on-the-wall ['flaɪɒnðə'wɔːl] *adj* **a f. documentary** = un documental en el que la cámara actúa con la mayor discreción posible para mostrar un retrato realista

flyover ['flaɪəʊvər] *n Br* paso *m* elevado

flypaper ['flaɪpeɪpər] *n* tira *f* de papel matamoscas, matamoscas *m inv*

flypast ['flaɪpɑːst] *n Br Av* desfile *m* aéreo

flyweight ['flaɪweɪt] *n Box* peso *m* mosca

FM [e'fem] *n Rad (abbr* **frequency modulation**) FM *f*, frecuencia *f* modulada

foal [fəʊl] *Zool* **1** *n* potro(a) *m,f*; **in f.** *(mare)* preñada
2 *vi (mare)* parir

foam [fəʊm] **1** *n (froth)* espuma *f* ◻ **f. bath** espuma *f* de baño; **f. rubber** (goma *f*) espuma *f*; **shaving f.** espuma *f* de afeitar
2 *vi (bubble)* hacer espuma; *(froth)* **to f. at the mouth** echar espumarajos; *Fig* echar espumarajos de cólera

foamy ['fəʊmɪ] *adj* (**foamier, foamiest**) espumoso(a)

fob [fɒb] *n (chain)* cadenilla *f* de reloj

fob off *vt Fam* colocar (**on** a); *(unload on)* **he fobbed off his old radio on a stranger** le colocó su radio vieja a un desconocido; **to f. sb off with excuses** darle largas a algn

focaccia [fə'kætʃə] *n* focaccia *f*

focal ['fəʊkəl] *adj* focal ❑ *Opt* **f. point** foco *m*; *Fig* punto *m* de referencia

focus ['fəʊkəs] **1** *vt (pt & pp* **focused** *or* **focussed)** *Phot Phys* enfocar; **all eyes were focused on him** todas las miradas recayeron sobre él
2 *vi Phot* enfocar; *Fig* centrarse; **to f. on sth** *Phot* enfocar algo; *Fig* centrarse en algo
3 *n* (**a**) *(pl* **focuses** *or* **focusses** *or* **foci** ['fəʊsaɪ]) *Phys Opt* foco *m*; **to be in f./out of f.** estar enfocado(a)/ desenfocado(a) (**b**) *Fig* foco *m*, centro *m*; **to be the f. of attention** ser el centro de la atención ❑ *Com Pol* **f. group** grupo *m* de discusión

focus(s)ing ['fəʊkəsɪŋ] *n* enfoque *m*

fodder ['fɒdər] *n* forraje *m*, pienso *m* ❑ *Fig Iron* **cannon f.** carne *f* de cañón

foe [fəʊ] *n Fml* enemigo(a) *m,f*

foetal ['fiːtəl] *adj* fetal; **f. position** posición *f* fetal

foetus ['fiːtəs] *n Biol* feto *m*

fog [fɒg] **1** *n* niebla *f*, bruma *f*, neblina *f*
2 *vt (pt & pp* **fogged)** *(glass)* empañar; *Fig* **to f. the issue** complicar el asunto

fog up *vi* empañarse

fogbound ['fɒgbaʊnd] *adj* inmovilizado(a) *or* paralizado(a) por la niebla

fogey ['fəʊgɪ] *n (pl* **fogeys)** *Fam* carca *mf*, persona *f* chapada a la antigua, *Am* carcamán *mf*; **old f.** cascarrabias *mf inv*

foggy ['fɒgɪ] *adj* (**foggier, foggiest**) nubloso(a), brumoso(a); **a f. day** un día de niebla; **it is f.** hay niebla; *Fam* **I haven't the foggiest (idea)** no tengo la más mínima idea

foghorn ['fɒghɔːn] *n* sirena *f* (de niebla)

foglamp ['fɒglæmp] *n*, *US* **foglight** ['fɒglaɪt] *n Aut* faro *m* antiniebla

foible ['fɔɪbəl] *n (peculiarity)* extravagancia *f*; *(fad)* manía *f*; *(weakness)* punto *m* flaco, debilidad *f*

foil [fɔɪl] **1** *n* (**a**) *Metal* hoja *f* de metal ❑ **aluminium f.** papel *m* de aluminio; *Fam* papel *m* de plata (**b**) *(sword)* florete *m* (**c**) *(counterweight, contrast)* contraste *m*; **to act as a f.** to hacer resaltar, realzar
2 *vt (plot)* frustrar

foist [fɔɪst] *vt Fam* **to f. sth on sb** colocarle algo a algn; **to f. oneself on sb** pegarse a algn

fold [fəʊld] **1** *n* (**a**) *(for sheep)* redil *m*, aprisco *m* (**b**) *(crease)* pliegue *m*
2 *vt* plegar, doblar; **to f. up a chair** plegar una silla; **to f. one's arms** cruzar los brazos
3 *vi* **to f. (up)** *(chair etc)* plegarse, doblarse; *Com* quebrar

folder ['fəʊldər] *n* (**a**) *(file, document wallet)* carpeta *f*; *(ring binder)* carpeta *f* de anillas (**b**) *Comptr* carpeta *f*

folding ['fəʊldɪŋ] *adj* plegable ❑ **f. ladder** escalera *f* de tijera; **f. table** mesa *f* plegable

foldout ['fəʊldaʊt] *n (in a book)* (página *f*) desplegable *m*

foliage ['fəʊlɪdʒ] *n* follaje *m*

folic acid ['fɒlɪk'æsɪd] *n* ácido *m* fólico

folio ['fəʊlɪəʊ] *n* (**a**) *(sheet)* folio *m* (**b**) *(volume)* libro *m* en folio

folk [fəʊk] **1** *npl* (**a**) *(people)* gente *f*; **old f.** la gente mayor (**b**) *Fam* **folks** *(friends)* amigos *mpl*; **hello f.!** ¿qué tal chicos? (**c**) *Fam* **folks** *(family)* padres *mpl*; **one's f.** la familia
2 *adj* popular ❑ **f. customs** costumbres *fpl* populares; **f.**

music música *f* folk; **f. singer** cantante *mf* de música folk; **f. song** canción *f* tradicional, canción *f* folk

folklore ['fəʊklɔːr] *n* folklore *m*

follicle ['fɒlɪkəl] *n* folículo *m*

follow ['fɒləʊ] **1** *vt (gen)* seguir; *(pursue)* perseguir; *(film, events)* seguir; *(advice, example, orders, etc)* seguir; *(understand)* comprender; *(way of life)* llevar; *(hobby, faith)* seguir; *(profession)* ejercer; **do you f. the rock scene?** ¿te interesa el rock?; *Ftb* **he follows Hull City** es un seguidor del Hull City; **I don't f. you** no te entiendo; **she is being followed** la están siguiendo; **they f. a life of total abstinence** llevan una vida de abstinencia total; *Fam* **f. your nose** sigue todo recto
2 *vi* (**a**) *(come after, ensue)* seguir; **as follows** a saber; **to f. close behind** seguir muy cerca; **and to f., a delicious paella** y a continuación, una deliciosa paella (**b**) *(result)* resultar; **it follows that ...** resulta que ..., se sigue que ...; **that doesn't f.** eso no es lógico (**c**) *(understand)* entender, comprender, seguir; **do you f.?** ¿entiendes?, ¿me sigues?

follow about, follow around *vt* seguir por todas partes

follow on *vi* (**a**) *(continue)* venir detrás (**b**) *(result)* ser la consecuencia lógica (**from** de)

follow out *vt (plan)* ejecutar

follow through, follow up *vt (idea)* llevar a cabo; *(clue)* investigar

follower ['fɒləʊər] *n* seguidor(a) *m,f*, partidario(a) *m,f*

following ['fɒləʊɪŋ] **1** *adj* siguiente; **the f. day** al día siguiente
2 *n* seguidores *mpl*, partidarios *mpl*, admiradores *mpl*; **he has a large f.** tiene muchos admiradores
3 *pron* **listen to the f.** escuche lo siguiente

follow-my-leader [fɒləʊmaɪ'liːdər], *US* **follow-the-leader** ['fɒləʊðə'liːdə(r)] *n* juego *m* de seguir al rey

follow-up ['fɒləʊʌp] *n* continuación *f*

folly ['fɒlɪ] *n* locura *f*, desatino *m*

foment [fə'ment] *vt* instigar

fond [fɒnd] *adj* (**a**) *(loving)* cariñoso(a), tierno(a) (**b**) *(partial to)* aficionado(a); **to be f. of sth** tenerle mucho cariño a algn; **she is f. of music** tiene afición a la música; **to be f. of doing sth** ser aficionado(a) a hacer algo (**c**) *(hope)* fervoroso(a)

fondle ['fɒndəl] *vt* acariciar

fondly ['fɒndlɪ] *adv (naïvely)* ingenuamente; **I f. believed that we could win** creí ingenuamente que podíamos ganar

fondness ['fɒndnɪs] *n* (**a**) *(love)* cariño *m* (**for** a) (**b**) *(liking)* afición *f* (**for** a)

fondue ['fɒndjuː] *n Culin* fondue *f*

font [fɒnt] *n* (**a**) *Rel* pila *f* (**b**) *Comptr Typ* fuente *f*

food [fuːd] *n* comida *f*, alimento *m*; **f. and drink** comida y bebida *f*; **I like Greek f.** me gusta la comida griega; **I'm off my f.** he perdido el apetito; *Fig* **to give sb f. for thought** darle a algn en qué pensar ❑ *Biol* **f. chain** cadena *f* trófica *or* alimentaria; **f. court** = plaza o zona de un centro comercial dedicada al consumo de comida rápida; **f. department** sección *f* de alimentación; **f. poisoning** intoxicación *f* alimenticia; **f. processor** robot *m* de cocina; **f. supplies** víveres *mpl*

foodie ['fuːdɪ] *n Fam* sibarita *mf* de la cocina

foodstuffs ['fuːdstʌfs] *npl* alimentos *mpl*, productos *mpl* alimenticios

fool [fuːl] **1** *n* (**a**) *(stupid person)* idiota *mf*; **don't be a f.** no seas tonto; **to feel a f.** sentirse ridículo(a); **to make a f. of sb** poner a algn en ridículo; **to play the f.** hacer el tonto ❑ **f.'s errand** trabajo *m* inútil; **f.'s paradise** mundo *m* irreal *or* de ensueño (**b**) *Culin* ≃ mousse *f* de fruta (**c**) *(jester)* bufón(ona) *m,f*

2 *US adj* tonto(a); **what a f. thing to say** ¡vaya estupidez decir aquello!

3 *vt (deceive)* engañar

4 *vi* (**a**) *(joke)* bromear (**b**) *(mess around)* **to f. about** or **around** hacer el tonto

foolhardy ['fu:lhɑ:dɪ] *adj* (**foolhardier, foolhardiest**) temerario(a); *(person)* intrépido(a)

foolish ['fu:lɪʃ] *adj (silly)* tonto(a); *(unwise)* estúpido(a); **that would be f.** eso sería imprudente; **to do sth f.** hacer una tontería; **to look f.** parecer ridículo(a)

foolishness ['fu:lɪʃnɪs] *n* estupidez *f*

foolproof ['fu:lpru:f] *adj (plan, method, device)* infalible; **a f. machine** una máquina fácil de usar y segura

foolscap ['fu:lskæp] *n Print* pliego *m*, folio *m*

foosball ['fu:zbɔ:l] *n US* fútbol *m* de mesa, *Esp* futbolín *m*, *Arg* metegol *m*, *Chile* taca-taca *m*, *Méx Urug* futbolito *m*

foot [fʊt] **1** *n* (*pl* **feet** [fi:t]) (**a**) *Anat* pie *m*; *Zool* pata *f*; **to be on one's feet** estar de pie or *Am* parado(a); *(after illness)* haberse levantado; **to go on f.** ir a pie or caminando or *Esp* andando; **to leap to one's feet** levantarse de un salto; **to set f. in** entrar en; **wipe your feet** límpiate los pies; *Fig* **he didn't put a f. wrong** no se equivocó; *Fig* **to drag one's feet** hacerse el remolón or el roncero; *Fig* **to fall on one's feet** tener buena suerte; *Fig* **to find one's feet** acostumbrarse, situarse; *Fig* **to have one's feet on the ground** ser realista; *Fig* **to put one's best f. forward** esmerarse; *Fig* **to stand on one's own two feet** valerse por sí mismo(a), ser independiente; *Fam Fig* **to get off on the wrong f.** empezar con mal pie; *Fam Fig* **to have** or **get cold feet** tener miedo; *Fam Fig* **to put one's f. down** *(be firm) Esp* ponerse serio(a), *Am* no ceder; *(refuse)* negarse *Esp* en redondo or *Am* rotundamente, *(drive faster)* apretar el acelerador, pisar fuerte; *Fig* **to put one's f. in it** meter la pata; *Fam Fig* **to put one's feet up** descansar □ **f. soldier** soldado *m* de infantería (**b**) *(of stairs, hill)* pie *m*; **at the f. of the page** a pie de página; **at the f. of the bed** a los pies de la cama (**c**) *(of shoe, stocking)* pie *m* (**d**) *Mus* pie *m* (**e**) *(in poetry)* pie *m*

2 *vt* (**a**) **to f. it** ir a pie (**b**) *(pay)* pagar; **to f. the bill** pagar la cuenta

footage ['fʊtɪdʒ] *n Cin* metraje *m*

foot-and-mouth disease [fʊtən'maʊθdɪzi:z] *n* fiebre *f* aftosa

football ['fʊtbɔ:l] *n* (**a**) *Br (soccer)* fútbol *m* □ **bar f.** futbolín *m*; **f. ground** estadio *m* de fútbol; **f. match** partido *m* de fútbol; **f. pools** quinielas *fpl* (**b**) *US (American football)* fútbol *m* americano □ **f. game** partido *m* de fútbol americano; **f. stadium** estadio *m* de fútbol americano (**c**) *(ball)* balón *m*

footballer ['fʊtbɔ:lər] *n* futbolista *mf*

footbridge ['fʊtbrɪdʒ] *n* puente *m* para peatones

footer ['fʊtər] *n Comptr Typ* pie *m* de página

foothills ['fʊthɪlz] *npl Geog* estribaciones *fpl*

foothold ['fʊthəʊld] *n* hueco *m* para apoyar el pie; *Fig* **to gain a f.** afianzarse en una posición

footing ['fʊtɪŋ] *n* (**a**) *(balance)* equilibrio *m*; **to lose one's f.** perder el equilibrio (**b**) *Fig* base *f*, nivel *m*; **on a friendly f.** en plan amistoso; **on an equal f.** en igualdad

footlights ['fʊtlaɪts] *npl Theat* candilejas *fpl*

footling ['fʊtlɪŋ] *adj Fam* fútil, trivial

footloose ['fʊtlu:s] *adj* libre de ataduras; **to be f. and fancy-free** ser libre como el viento

footman ['fʊtmən] *n (pl* **footmen**) lacayo *m*

footnote ['fʊtnəʊt] *n* nota *f* a pie de página

footpath ['fʊtpɑ:θ] *n (track)* sendero *m*, camino *m*

footprint ['fʊtprɪnt] *n* huella *f*, pisada *f*

footrest ['fʊtrest] *n (on motorbike)* reposapiés *m inv*

footsie ['fʊtsɪ] *n Fam* **to play f. with sb** = acariciar a algn con el pie por debajo de la mesa

footsore ['fʊtsɔ:r] *adj* con los pies doloridos

footstep ['fʊtstep] *n* paso *m*, pisada *f*; *Fig* **to follow in sb's footsteps** seguir los pasos de algn, imitar a algn

footstool ['fʊtstu:l] *n* escabel *m*, reposapiés *m inv*

footwear ['fʊtweər] *n* calzado *m*

footwork ['fʊtwɜ:k] *n Sport* juego *m* de pies

fop [fɒp] *n Pej* lechuguino *m*

foppish ['fɒpɪʃ] *adj* afeminado(a)

for [fɔ:r] **1** *prep* (**a**) *(intended)* para; **curtains f. the bedroom** cortinas para el dormitorio; **f. sale** en venta; **it's not f. eating** no es para comer; **it's time f. bed** es hora de acostarse (**b**) *(representing)* por; **a cheque f. twenty dollars** un cheque (por valor) de veinte dólares; **'fag' is slang f. homosexual** en argot homosexual es maricón; **J f. John** J de Juan; **the MP f. Oxford** el diputado por Oxford; **what's the Spanish f. 'rivet'?** ¿cómo se dice 'rivet' en español? (**c**) *(purpose)* para; **it's good f. the digestion** es bueno para la digestión; **this knob is f. the volume** este botón es el del volumen; **to study f. an exam** estudiar para un examen; **what's this f.?** ¿para qué sirve esto? (**d**) *(because of)* por; **but f. that** a no ser por eso; **famous f. its cuisine** famoso(a) por su cocina; **I couldn't hear f. the noise** no pude oír nada por el ruido; **if it weren't f. him** si no fuera por él; **to jump f. joy** saltar de alegría (**e**) *(on behalf of)* por; **I can do it f. myself** puedo hacerlo yo solo; **I speak f. everybody** hablo por todos; **open the door f. me** ábreme la puerta; **the campaign f. peace** la campaña por la paz; **to die f. one's country** morir por la patria; **will you do it f. me?** ¿lo harás por mí? (**f**) *(during)* por, durante; **I hadn't seen him f. two years** hacía dos años que no le veía; **I lent it to her f. a year** se lo presté por un año; **I shall stay f. two weeks** me quedaré dos semanas; **I was ill f. a month** estuve enfermo durante un mes; **I've been here f. a month** llevo or *Am* tengo un mes aquí (**g**) *(distance)* por; **I walked f. ten kilometres** caminé diez kilómetros (**h**) *(at a point in time)* para; **can you do it f. tomorrow?** puedes hacerlo para mañana?; **f. my birthday** para mi cumpleaños; **f. the first/last time** por primera/última vez; **we have a meeting arranged f. next Thursday** hemos convenido un mitin para el jueves que viene (**i**) *(destination)* para; **he left f. France** partió para Francia; **the train f. London** el tren para or de Londres (**j**) *(amount of money)* por; **I got the car f. five hundred dollars** conseguí el coche por quinientos dólares; **the painting went f. six million** la pintura se vendió por seis millones (**k**) *(in favour of)* en favor de; **are you f. or against?** ¿estás a favor o en contra?; **I'm all f. telling the truth** soy partidario de decir la verdad; **to vote f. sth/sb** votar por algo/algn; **we argued f. a stop to the violence** insistimos en la necesidad de acabar con la violencia; **who's f. a drink?** ¿quién quiere una copa? (**l**) *(to obtain)* para; **f. further details apply to ...** para mayor información diríjanse a ...; **to run f. the bus** correr para coger el autobús; **to send sb f. water** mandar a algn a por agua (**m**) *(with respect to, concerning)* en cuanto a; **are you all right f. money?** ¿qué tal andas de dinero?; **as f. him** en cuanto a él; **f. all I care** por mí; **f. all I know** que yo sepa; **f. all the good it has done us** teniendo en cuenta lo poco que nos ha servido; **f. one thing** para empezar (**n**) *(despite)* a pesar de; **f. all his faults** con or a pesar de todos sus defectos; **f. all that** aún así, con todo y eso; **he's tall f. his age** está muy alto para su edad (**o**) *(instead of)* por; **can you go f. me?** puede ir por mí? (**p**) *(towards)* hacia, por; **affection f. sb** cariño hacia

algn; **his love f. you** su amor por ti; **respect f. sb** respeto para con algn **(q)** *(as)* por; **to leave sb f. dead** dar a algn por muerto(a); **what do you use f. fuel?** ¿qué utilizan como combustible? **(r)** *(in exchange)* por; **f. every success there are two failures** por cada éxito hay dos fracasos; **to exchange one thing f. another** cambiar una cosa por otra; **to buy/sell sth f. five dollars** comprar/vender algo por cinco dólares **(s)** *(+ object + infin)* **there's no reason f. us to quarrel** no hay motivo para que riñamos; **he signalled f. the car to stop** hizo señas al coche para que parara; **it's time f. you to go** es hora de que te marches; **it's best f. you to leave** más vale que te vayas; **it would be a pity f. you to resign** sería una lástima que dimitieras; **it's easy f. him to say that** le es fácil decir eso **(t)** *(exclamation)* **oh f. a drink!** ¡ojalá tuviera una copa!; **that's politicians f. you!** ¡mira cómo son los políticos!; *Fam* **he's f. it!** ¡se la va a cargar!, *RP* ¡se va a ligar una!
  2 *conj (since, as)* ya que, puesto que

forage ['fɒrɪdʒ] **1** *n Agr* forraje *m*
  2 *vi* hurgar, fisgar; **to f. about in a drawer** hurgar en un cajón

foray ['fɒreɪ] *n* **(a)** *(raid)* correría *f*, incursión *f*; *(plundering)* saqueo *m* **(b)** *(excursion)* excursión *f*

forbade [fɔːbæd, fɔːˈbeɪd] *pt see* **forbid**

forbear [fɔːˈbeər] *vt (pt* **forbore**; *pp* **forborne)** abstenerse **(from** de)

forbearance [fɔːˈbeərəns] *n* paciencia *f*, comprensión *f*

forbid [fəˈbɪd] *vt (pt* **forbade;** *pp* **forbidden** [fəˈbɪdən]) prohibir; *Rel* **forbidden fruit** fruta *f* prohibida; **smoking is forbidden** está prohibido fumar; **to f. sb to do sth** prohibirle a algn hacer algo

forbidding [fəˈbɪdɪŋ] *adj* **(a)** *(stern)* severo(a); *(bleak)* inhóspito(a) **(b)** *(task)* difícil, peligroso(a)

forbore [fɔːˈbɔːr] *pt,* **forborne** [fɔːˈbɔːn] *pp see* **forbear**

force [fɔːs] **1** *n* **(a)** *(power, influence)* fuerza *f*; **by f. of habit** por la fuerza de la costumbre; **the forces of nature** las fuerzas de la naturaleza **(b)** *(strength, violence)* fuerza *f*; **brute f.** fuerza bruta; **the f. of the earthquake** la fuerza del terremoto; **by f. a** or por la fuerza; **by sheer f.** a viva fuerza **(c)** *Mil* cuerpo *m* ❑ **the (armed) forces** las fuerzas armadas; **the police f.** la policía; *Fig* **to join forces** unirse; *Ind* **labour f.** mano *f* de obra; **to turn up in f.** llegar en gran número **(d)** *(law etc)* **to come into f.** entrar en vigor
  2 *vt* **(a)** *(oblige, coerce)* forzar, obligar; **I was forced to do it** me obligaron a hacerlo; **to f. sb to do sth** forzar a algn a hacer algo; **to f. sth on sb** obligar a algn a aceptar algo **(b)** *(break open, prise)* forzar

force back *vt* **(a)** *(enemy)* hacer retroceder **(b)** *(tears, emotions)* contener

force down *vt* **(a)** *(plane)* obligar a aterrizar **(b)** *(food)* tragar a duras penas

forced [fɔːst] *adj* **(a)** *(labour, march)* forzado(a) ❑ *Av* **f. landing** aterrizaje *m* forzoso **(b)** *(smile, laugh)* forzado(a)

force-feed ['fɔːsfiːd] *vt (pt & pp* **force-fed** ['fɔːsfed]) alimentar a la fuerza

forceful ['fɔːsful] *adj* **(a)** *(person, manner)* enérgico(a), contundente **(b)** *(argument)* convincente

forceps ['fɔːseps] *npl Med* fórceps *m sing*

forcible ['fɔːsəbəl] *adj Jur* **f. entry** *Esp* allanamiento *m* de morada, *Am* invasión *m* de domicilio

forcibly ['fɔːsɪblɪ] *adv* a or por la fuerza

ford [fɔːd] *Geog* **1** *n* vado *m*
  2 *vt* vadear

fore¹ [fɔːr] **1** *adj Naut* delantero(a); **f. and aft** de popa a proa
  2 *n* parte *f* delantera; *Fig* **to come to the f.** empezar a destacar

fore² [fɔːr] *interj Golf* ¡atención!

forearm ['fɔːrɑːm] *n* antebrazo *m*

forebear ['fɔːbeər] *n (usu pl)* antepasado *m*

foreboding [fɔːˈbəʊdɪŋ] *n* presentimiento *m*

forecast ['fɔːkɑːst] **1** *n* previsión *f*; pronóstico *m* ❑ **weather f.** parte *m* meteorológico
  2 *vt (pt & pp* **forecast** *or* **forecasted)** pronosticar

foreclose [fɔːˈkləʊz] *vt Fin* **to f. a mortgage** ejecutar una hipoteca

forecourt ['fɔːkɔːt] *n (of garage)* área *f* de servicio

forefathers ['fɔːfɑːðəz] *npl* antepasados *mpl*

forefinger ['fɔːfɪŋgər] *n* (dedo *m*) índice *m*

forefront ['fɔːfrʌnt] *n* vanguardia *f*; **to be in the f.** estar a la vanguardia

forego [fɔːˈgəʊ] *vt Fml (pt* **forewent**; *pp* **foregone)** sacrificar; **she forewent her holiday to be with her family** no se marchó de vacaciones para estar con su familia

foregoing [fɔːˈgəʊɪŋ] *adj* precedente; *(aforementioned)* susodicho(a)

foregone ['fɔːgɒn] **1** *pp see* **forego**
  2 *adj* **a f. conclusion** un resultado inevitable

foreground ['fɔːgraʊnd] *n* primer plano *m*

forehand ['fɔːhænd] *n (tennis stroke)* derecha *f*

forehead ['fɒrɪd, 'fɔːhed] *n* frente *f*

foreign ['fɒrɪn] *adj* **(a)** *(from abroad)* extranjero(a); **f. language** lengua extranjera; **f. travel** viajes al or en el extranjero ❑ **f. aid** *(to another country)* ayuda *f* al exterior; *(from another country)* ayuda *f* extranjera *or* del exterior; *Journ* **f. correspondent** corresponsal *mf* (en el extranjero); **the F. Legion** la Legión Extranjera **(b)** *(trade, policy)* exterior; *Pol* **f. affairs** política *f* exterior, asuntos *mpl* exteriores; *Econ* **f. debt** deuda *f* exterior *or* externa; *Fin* **f. exchange** divisas *fpl*; *Br* **the F. Office** el Ministerio de Asuntos *or Am* Relaciones Exteriores **(c)** *(strange, extraneous)* ajeno(a); *Med* **f. body** cuerpo extraño

foreigner ['fɒrɪnər] *n* extranjero(a) *m,f*

foreleg ['fɔːleg] *n* pata *f* delantera

foreman ['fɔːmən] *n (pl* **foremen) (a)** *Ind* capataz *m* **(b)** *Jur* presidente *m* del jurado

foremost ['fɔːməʊst] *adj* primero(a), principal; **first and f.** ante todo

forename ['fɔːneɪm] *n* nombre *m* de pila

forensic [fəˈrensɪk] *adj* forense ❑ **f. evidence** pruebas *fpl* forenses; **f. medicine** medicina *f* forense

foreplay ['fɔːpleɪ] *n* juego *m* amoroso *(antes del coito)*

forerunner ['fɔːrʌnər] *n* precursor(a) *m,f*

foresaw [fɔːrˈsɔː] *pt see* **foresee**

foresee [fɔːˈsiː] *vt (pt* **foresaw**; *pp* **foreseen)** prever

foreseeable [fɔːˈsiːəbəl] *adj* previsible; **in the f. future** en un futuro próximo; **for the f. future** por mucho tiempo

foreseen [fɔːˈsiːn] *pp see* **foresee**

foreshadow [fɔːˈʃædəʊ] *vt* presagiar, anunciar

foresight ['fɔːsaɪt] *n* previsión *f*; **lack of f.** imprevisión *f*; **to have f.** ser previsor(a)

foreskin ['fɔːskɪn] *n Anat* prepucio *m*

forest ['fɒrɪst] *n (large)* selva *f*; *(small)* bosque *m* ❑ **f. fire** incendio *m* forestal

forestall [fɔːˈstɔːl] *vt (plan)* anticiparse a; *(danger)* prevenir

forester ['fɒrɪstər] *n* guardabosques *m inv*

forestry ['fɒrɪstrɪ] *n* silvicultura *f*, selvicultura *f*

foretaste ['fɔːteɪst] *n* anticipo *m*, anticipación *f* **(of** de)

foretell [fɔː'tel] *vt* (*pt* & *pp* **foretold**) presagiar, pronosticar

forethought ['fɔːθɔːt] *n* previsión *f*; *Jur* premeditación *f*

foretold [fɔː'təʊld] *pt* & *pp see* **foretell**

forever [fə'revər] *adv* (**a**) *(eternally)* siempre (**b**) *(for good)* para siempre (**c**) *Fam (ages)* siglos *mpl*, mucho tiempo; **I've been reading this book f.** llevo siglos leyendo este libro (**d**) *(constantly)* siempre; **they're f. digging up the roads** no paran de hacer obras (**e**) *(long live)* ¡viva!; **Liverpool f.!** ¡viva el Liverpool!

forewarn [fɔː'wɔːn] *vt* prevenir; *Prov* **forewarned is forearmed** hombre prevenido vale por dos

forewent [fɔː'went] *pt see* **forego**

forewoman ['fɔːwʊmən] *n* (*pl* **forewomen** ['fɔːwɪmɪn]) (**a**) *Ind* encargada *f* (**b**) *Jur* presidenta *f* del jurado

foreword ['fɔːwɜːd] *n Lit* prefacio *m*, prólogo *m*

forfeit ['fɔːfɪt] **1** *adj* perdido(a)
2 *n (penalty)* pena *f*, multa *f*; *(in games)* prenda *f*; **to pay a f.** pagar prenda
3 *vt* perder; *(declare)* comisar; **he was forced to f. all his property** tuvo que renunciar a todas sus propiedades

forfeiture ['fɔːfɪtʃər] *n* pérdida *f*

forgave [fɔː'geɪv] *pt see* **forgive**

forge [fɔːdʒ] **1** *n* (**a**) *(fire)* fragua *f* (**b**) *(blacksmith's)* herrería *f*
2 *vt* (**a**) *(counterfeit)* falsificar (**b**) *(metal)* forjar; *Fig* **to f. a friendship/an alliance** forjar una amistad/una alianza
3 *vi* **to f. ahead** hacer grandes progresos

forged [fɔːdʒd] *adj (banknote, letter)* falso(a), falsificado(a)

forger ['fɔːdʒər] *n* falsificador(a) *m,f*

forgery ['fɔːdʒərɪ] *n* falsificación *f*

forget [fə'get] **1** *vt* (*pt* **forgot**, *pp* **forgotten**) olvidar, olvidarse de; **and don't you f. it!** ¡no lo olvides!; **f. it!** ¡déjalo!; **I forgot that ...** olvidé que ..., se me olvidó que ...; **I forgot to close the window** se me olvidó cerrar la ventana; **I shall never f. you** nunca me olvidaré de ti; **I've forgotten my key** he olvidado la llave; **never to be forgotten** inolvidable; **not forgetting ...** sin olvidar ...; **to f. how to do sth** olvidar cómo se hace algo; **to f. oneself** perder los estribos, no poderse contener
2 *vi* olvidar; **I f.** no me acuerdo; **it's is hard to f.** es difícil olvidarlo

forgetful [fə'getfʊl] *adj* olvidadizo(a), despistado(a)

forgetfulness [fə'getfʊlnɪs] *n* falta *f* de memoria; *(overlooking)* despiste *m*

forget-me-not [fə'getmɪnɒt] *n Bot* nomeolvides *f inv*

forgivable [fə'gɪvəbəl] *adj* perdonable

forgive [fə'gɪv] *vt* (*pt* **forgave**; *pp* **forgiven** [fə'gɪvən]) *(pardon)* perdonar, excusar; **f. my brother's impoliteness** disculpe la mala educación de mi hermano; **to f. sb sth** perdonarle algo a algn

forgiveness [fə'gɪvnɪs] *n* (**a**) *(pardon)* perdón *m* (**b**) *(mercy)* clemencia *f*

forgiving [fə'gɪvɪŋ] *adj* (**a**) *(easy-going)* dispuesto(a) a perdonar (**b**) *(merciful)* clemente

forgo [fɔː'gəʊ] *vt* (*pt* **forwent**; *pp* **forgone** [fɔː'gɒn]) *see* **forego**

forgot [fə'gɒt] *pt*, **forgotten** [fə'gɒtən] *pp see* **forget**

fork [fɔːk] **1** *n* (**a**) *Agr* horca *f*, horquilla *f* (**b**) *(cutlery)* tenedor *m*, *Am* trinche *m* (**c**) *(of bicycle, motorbike)* horquilla *f* (**d**) *(in road)* bifurcación *f* (**e**) *Mus* **tuning f.** diapasón *m*
2 *vi (roads)* bifurcarse

fork out *vt Fam (money)* aflojar, *Esp* apoquinar, *RP* garpar

forked [fɔːkt] *adj* bifurcado(a) □ *Meteor* **f. lightning** relámpago *m* en zigzag

fork-lift truck [fɔːklɪf'trʌk] *n* carretilla *f* elevadora de horquilla

forlorn [fə'lɔːn] *adj* (**a**) *(forsaken)* abandonado(a) (**b**) *(desolate, wretched)* triste, melancólico(a) (**c**) *(without hope)* desesperado(a)

form [fɔːm] **1** *n* (**a**) *(type)* clase *f*, tipo *m* (**b**) *(shape)* forma *f*; **in book f.** en forma de libro; **in the f. of a cross** en forma de cruz; **what f. does the disease take?** ¿cómo se manifiesta la enfermedad? (**c**) *(formality)* formas *fpl*; **for f.'s sake** para guardar las formas; **it's bad f.** es de mala educación (**d**) *(document)* impreso *m*, formulario *m*, *Méx* forma *f*; **application f.** formulario *m* or *Méx* forma *f* de solicitud (**e**) *(condition)* forma *f*; **to be on f./on top f./off f.** estar en forma/en plena forma/en baja forma; *(mood)* **to be in good f.** estar de buen humor; **true to f.** como es de esperar (**f**) *Br Educ (class)* clase *f*; *(year)* curso *f*; *Formerly* **the first/second f.** el primer/segundo grado (**g**) *(bench)* banco *m* (**h**) *(style)* forma *f*; **sculpture is an ancient art f.** la escultura es una forma de arte muy antigua (**i**) *Ling* forma *f*
2 *vt* formar; **to f. a ring** formar un corro; **to f. a government** formar un gobierno; **to f. an impression** formarse una impresión; **to f. part of sth** formar parte de algo
3 *vi* formarse; **a crowd formed outside the town hall** se juntó una multitud frente al ayuntamiento

formal ['fɔːmal] *adj* (**a**) *(public, official)* formal, oficial; **a f. application** una solicitud en forma; **f. education** educación convencional (**b**) *(conventional) (party, dress)* de etiqueta; *(visit)* de cumplido (**c**) *(ordered)* formal, ordenado(a) (**d**) *(person, language)* formalista, ceremonioso(a)

formality [fɔː'mælɪtɪ] *n* formalidad *f*; **it's just a f.** son sólo formalidades

formalize ['fɔːməlaɪz] *vt* formalizar

formally ['fɔːməlɪ] *adv* formalmente, oficialmente; **f. dressed** vestido(a) de etiqueta

format ['fɔːmæt] **1** *n* formato *m*
2 *vt* (*pt* & *pp* **formatted**) *Comptr* formatear

formation [fɔː'meɪʃən] *n* *(arrangement)* formación *f*; *(development)* formación *f*; *(establishment)* creación *f* □ *Av* **f. flying** vuelo *m* en formación; *Mil* **in battle f.** en formación de combate

formative ['fɔːmətɪv] *adj* formativo(a), **f. years** años *mpl* de formación

formatting ['fɔːmætɪŋ] *n* *Comptr (of text)* formato *m*

former ['fɔːmər] *adj* (**a**) *(time)* anterior; **f. glories** glorias pasadas (**b**) *(one-time)* antiguo(a); *(person)* ex; **the f. champion** el excampeón; **the hotel was a f. convent** el hotel era un antiguo convento (**c**) *(first)* aquél, aquélla, primero(a); **Peter and Lisa came, the f. wearing a hat** vinieron Peter y Lisa, aquél llevaba sombrero

formerly ['fɔːməlɪ] *adv* antiguamente

Formica® [fɔː'maɪkə] *n* formica® *f*

formidable ['fɔːmɪdəbəl] *adj (prodigious)* formidable; *(daunting, intimidating)* terrible

formula ['fɔːmjʊlə] *n* (*pl* **formulae** ['fɔːmjʊliː] *or* **formulas**) (**a**) *(in general)* fórmula *f* (**b**) *US (baby milk)* leche *f* maternizada

formulate ['fɔːmjʊleɪt] *vt* formular

fornicate ['fɔːnɪkeɪt] *vt Fml* fornicar

forsake [fə'seɪk] *vt* (*pt* **forsook** [fə'sʊk]; *pp* **forsaken** [fɔː'seɪkən]) *Literary* (**a**) *(abandon, desert)* abandonar (**b**) *(give up)* renunciar a

fort [fɔːt] *n Mil* fortaleza *f*, fuerte *m*; *Fam Fig* **to hold the f.** quedarse vigilando

forte ['fɔːteɪ] **1** n *(strong point)* fuerte m; **music is not my f.** la música no es mi fuerte
2 adv Mus forte

forth [fɔːθ] adv **and so f.** y así sucesivamente; **to go back and f.** ir de acá para allá; Fml *(onwards)* **from that day f.** desde aquel día en adelante; Fml **to set f.** ponerse en camino

forthcoming [fɔːθ'kʌmɪŋ] adj **(a)** *(event)* próximo(a), de próxima aparición **(b)** *(available)* **no money was f.** no hubo oferta de dinero **(c)** *(communicative)* comunicativo(a); **he wasn't very f.** estaba poco dispuesto a hablar

forthright ['fɔːθraɪt] adj *(blunt, frank)* franco(a); *(direct)* directo(a)

forthwith [fɔːθ'wɪθ] adv Fml en el acto

fortieth ['fɔːtɪəθ] **1** adj cuadragésimo(a)
2 n **(a)** *(in series)* cuadragésimo(a) m,f **(b)** *(fraction)* cuarentavo m; see also **seventh**

fortification [fɔːtɪfɪ'keɪʃən] n Mil fortificación f

fortify ['fɔːtɪfaɪ] vt *(pt & pp* **fortified)** Mil fortificar; Fig fortalecer; **fortified wine** vino m licoroso

fortitude ['fɔːtɪtjuːd] n fortaleza f, fuerza f

fortnight ['fɔːtnaɪt] n Br quincena f; **a f.'s holiday** dos semanas de vacaciones

fortnightly ['fɔːtnaɪtlɪ] Br **1** adj quincenal
2 adv cada quince días

fortress ['fɔːtrɪs] n fortaleza f, fuerte m; *(city)* plaza f fuerte

fortuitous [fɔː'tjuːɪtəs] adj Fml *(accidental)* accidental, casual; *(lucky)* fortuito(a)

fortunate ['fɔːtʃənɪt] adj afortunado(a); **she was f.** tuvo suerte; **it was f. that he came** fue una suerte que viniera; **how f.!** ¡qué suerte!

fortunately ['fɔːtʃənətlɪ] adv afortunadamente, por suerte or fortuna

fortune ['fɔːtʃən] n **(a)** *(luck)* suerte f; **he had the good f. to escape** tuvo la suerte de escapar **(b)** *(fate)* fortuna f; **the wheel of f.** la rueda de la fortuna; **to tell sb's f.** decir or echar la buenaventura a algn; Fml **f. smiled on them** la suerte les sonrió □ US **f. cookie** galleta f de la buenaventura **(c)** *(money)* fortuna f; **to make one's f.** hacer (una) fortuna; Fam **it cost a f.** costó un dineral; Fam **to be worth a f.** valer una fortuna

fortune-teller ['fɔːtʃəntelər] n echador(a) m,f de la buenaventura, adivino(a) m,f

forty ['fɔːtɪ] **1** adj cuarenta inv; Fam **to have f. winks** echar una siestecita
2 n cuarenta m inv; see also **seventy** and **seven**

forum ['fɔːrəm] n *(pl* **forums** or **fora** ['fɔːrə]) *(place)* foro m; Comptr fórum m

forward ['fɔːwəd] **1** adv **(a)** *(also* **forwards)** *(direction and movement)* hacia delante; **leaning f.** inclinado(a) hacia delante; **to go f.** ir hacia adelante; **to step f.** dar un paso adelante **(b)** Fig **carried f.** suma y sigue; **to come f. (with help)** ofrecerse (para ayudar) **(c)** *(time)* **from this day f.** de ahora or de aquí en adelante; **to bring sth f.** adelantar algo; **to look f. to sth** esperar algo con ilusión; **to put the clock f.** adelantar el reloj **(d)** Naut hacia la proa
2 adj **(a)** *(movement)* hacia adelante; **a f. movement** un movimiento hacia adelante; *(position)* delantero(a), frontal; **the f. section** la sección delantera □ **f. planning** planificación f a largo plazo **(b)** *(person)* fresco(a), descarado(a)
3 n Sport delantero(a) m,f
4 vt **(a)** *(send on)* remitir; **please f.** remítase al destinatario **(b)** Fml *(send goods)* expedir, enviar; **the goods will be forwarded on receipt of payment** se enviarán las mercancías contra recibo del pago **(c)** Fml *(further)*

adelantar, fomentar; **he tried to f. his career by ...** intentó promocionarse haciendo ...

forward-looking ['fɔːwədlʊkɪŋ] adj previsor(a)

forwent [fɔː'went] pt see **forego**

fossil ['fɒsəl] n fósil m □ **f. fuel** combustible m fósil

fossilized ['fɒsɪlaɪzd] adj fosilizado(a)

foster ['fɒstər] **1** vt **(a)** *(child)* criar **(b)** Fml *(cherish)* *(hopes, ideas)* abrigar; *(promote)* *(relations, business)* fomentar
2 adj adoptivo(a) □ **f. child** hijo(a) m,f adoptivo(a); **f. father** padre m adoptivo; **f. mother** madre f adoptiva; **f. parents** padres mpl adoptivos

fostering ['fɒstərɪŋ] n acogida f familiar *(de un niño)*

fought [fɔːt] pt & pp see **fight**

foul [faʊl] **1** adj **(a)** *(smell)* fétido(a); *(taste)* asqueroso(a) **(b)** Literary *(deed)* vil, atroz; **f. temper/weather** humor m/ tiempo m de perros **(c)** *(language)* grosero(a), obsceno(a) **(d)** *(illegal)* **by fair means or f.** por las buenas o por las malas, por fas o por nefas; **to fall f. of the law** tener líos con la policía □ Sport **f. play** juego m sucio; Jur **f. play is suspected** se sospecha que se haya cometido un acto criminal
2 n Sport falta f
3 vt **(a)** *(dirty)* ensuciar; *(air)* contaminar **(b)** *(block a device)* atascar; *(get entangled with)* enredarse en **(c)** Sport cometer una falta contra

foul up vt Fam estropear, fastidiar; **he fouled up the whole plan** echó por tierra todo el plan

foul-mouthed [faʊl'maʊðd] adj malhablado(a)

foul-smelling [faʊl'smelɪŋ] adj hediondo(a)

foul-up ['faʊlʌp] n Fam metedura f or Am metida f de pata

found¹ [faʊnd] pt & pp see **find**

found² [faʊnd] vt **(a)** *(establish)* fundar **(b)** *(base)* fundar, fundamentar **(on** en); **founded on fact** basado(a) en hechos

found³ [faʊnd] vt Tech fundir

foundation [faʊn'deɪʃən] n **(a)** *(establishment)* fundación f □ **f. stone** primera piedra f; **(b)** *(basis)* fundamento m, base f, without f. sin fundamento □ **f. course** curso m común **(c)** *(cosmetic)* **f. (cream)** maquillaje m de fondo **(d)** Constr **foundations** cimientos mpl; **to lay the foundations** poner los cimientos

founder¹ ['faʊndər] n fundador(a) m,f

founder² ['faʊndər] vi **(a)** Fml *(sink)* hundirse, irse a pique **(b)** Fig *(plan, hopes)* fracasar, malograrse; **the project foundered because of a lack of finance** el proyecto se malogró por falta de financiación

founding father ['faʊndɪŋ'fɑːðər] n padre m fundador

foundling ['faʊndlɪŋ] n Literary expósito(a) m,f

foundry ['faʊndrɪ] n Ind fundición f

fount¹ [faʊnt] n Print fuente f

fount² [faʊnt] n Literary Fig fuente f; **it was the f. of all knowledge** era la fuente de todos los conocimientos

fountain ['faʊntɪn] n *(structure)* fuente f; *(jet)* surtidor m; **drinking f.** fuente de agua potable □ **f. pen** pluma f *(estilográfica)*, CSur lapicera f fuente

four [fɔːr] **1** adj cuatro inv; **to the f. corners of the earth** de una punta a otra del mundo
2 n cuatro m inv; **on all fours** a gatas; see also **seven**

four-by-four ['fɔːbaɪ'fɔːr] n *(vehicle)* todoterreno m

four-door ['fɔːdɔːr] adj Aut de cuatro puertas

foureyes ['fɔːraɪz] n Slang Pej cuatro ojos mf inv, Esp gafotas mf inv, Méx cuatro lámparas mf inv, RP anteojudo(a) m,f

fourfold ['fɔːfəʊld] **1** adj **a f. increase (in)** cuatro veces más (de)
2 adv cuatro veces

four-legged ['fɔː'legɪd] *adj* cuadrúpedo(a); *Hum* **f. friend** amigo *m* cuadrúpedo

four-letter ['fɔːletər] *adj* **f.-l. word** palabrota *f*, *Esp* taco *m*

four-poster [fɔː'pəʊstər] *n* **f.-p. (bed)** cama *f* con colgadura

foursome ['fɔːsəm] *n* grupo *m* de cuatro personas

fourteen [fɔː'tiːn] **1** *adj* catorce *inv*
2 *n* catorce *m inv*; *see also* **seven**

fourteenth [fɔː'tiːnθ] **1** *adj* decimocuarto(a); **the f. century** el siglo catorce
2 *n* **(a)** *(in series)* decimocuarto(a) *m,f* **(b)** *(fraction)* catorceavo *m*; *see also* **seventh**

fourth [fɔːθ] **1** *adj* cuarto(a); **the f. of June** el cuatro de junio
2 *n* **(a)** *(in series)* cuarto(a) *m,f* **(b)** *(fraction)* cuarto *m* **(c)** *Aut* cuarta velocidad; *see also* **seventh**

fourth-former ['fɔːθfɔːmər] *n Br Sch Formerly* alumno(a) *m,f* del cuarto curso

fourthly ['fɔːθlɪ] *adv* en cuarto lugar

four-wheel drive ['fɔːwiːl'draɪv] *n* tracción *f* a las cuatro ruedas

fowl [faʊl] *n* aves *fpl* de corral

fox [fɒks] **1** *n* **(a)** *Zool* zorro(a) *m,f*; **f. hunt** caza *f* de zorros **(b)** *Fig Pej* zorro *m*
2 *vt* **(a)** *(perplex)* dejar perplejo(a), desorientar **(b)** *(deceive)* engañar

foxglove ['fɒksglʌv] *n* digital *f*, dedalera *f*

foxhound ['fɒkshaʊnd] *n* perro *m* raposero

fox-hunting ['fɒkshʌntɪŋ] *n* caza *f* del zorro

foxtrot ['fɒkstrɒt] *n Mus* fox-trot *m*

foxy ['fɒksɪ] *adj* **(foxier, foxiest)** *Fam* **(a)** *(wily)* astuto(a), zorro(a) **(b)** *US (sexy)* sexy

foyer ['fɔɪeɪ, 'fɔɪə] *n Cin Theat* vestíbulo *m*; *US (house)* vestíbulo *m*

Fr (a) *Rel (abbr* **Father)** Padre *m*, P., Pe **(b)** *(abbr* **French)** francés(esa), fr

fracas ['frækɑː] *n* gresca *f*, reyerta *f*

fractal ['fræktəl] *n* fractal *m*

fraction ['frækʃən] *n Math* fracción *f*, quebrado *m*; **a f. of a second** una fracción de segundo; **a f. smaller** un poquitín más pequeño

fractional ['frækʃənəl] *adj* fraccional; *Fig* ínfimo(a)

fractionally ['frækʃənəlɪ] *adv* ligeramente

fractious ['frækʃəs] *adj* irritable

fracture ['fræktʃər] *Med Tech* **1** *n* fractura *f*
2 *vt* fracturar; **to f. a leg** fracturarse una pierna
3 *vi* fracturarse

fragile ['frædʒaɪl] *adj* **(a)** *(object, alliance)* frágil; **this glass is f.** esta copa es frágil **(b)** *Fig (health)* frágil, delicado(a); **the morning after the party he felt f.** al día siguiente de la fiesta se encontraba mal

fragility ['frædʒɪlɪtɪ] *n* fragilidad *f*

fragment ['frægmənt] **1** *n* fragmento *m*
2 [fræg'ment] *vi* fragmentarse

fragmentary ['frægməntərɪ] *adj* fragmentario(a)

fragrance ['freɪgrəns] *n* fragancia *f*, aroma *m*, perfume *m*

fragrant ['freɪgrənt] *adj* fragante, aromático(a)

frail [freɪl] *adj* frágil, delicado(a)

frailty ['freɪltɪ] *n* fragilidad *f*, delicadeza *f*; **human frailties** las flaquezas humanas

frame [freɪm] **1** *n* **(a)** *(window, door, picture)* marco *m*; *(building, machine)* armazón *f*; *(bed)* armadura *f*; *(bicycle)* cuadro *m*; *(spectacles)* montura *f*; *Fig* **f. of mind** estado *m* de ánimo **(b)** *(human, animal)* cuerpo *m* **(c)** *Cin TV* fotograma *m* **(d)** *(snooker)* jugada *f*, set *m*
2 *vt* **(a)** *(picture)* enmarcar; *Fig* **a doorway framed by roses** una puerta encuadrada por rosas **(b)** *(formulate a question)* formular; *(a plan)* elaborar **(c)** *Fam (innocent person)* incriminar

framework ['freɪmwɜːk] *n (structure)* armazón *f*; *Fig* estructura *f*; **within the f. of ...** dentro del marco de ...

franc [fræŋk] *n Fin* franco *m*

France [frɑːns] *n* Francia

franchise ['fræntʃaɪz] *n* **(a)** *Pol* derecho *m* al voto **(b)** *Com* concesión *f*, licencia *f*

Franciscan [fræn'sɪskən] *adj & n* franciscano(a) *(m,f)*

francophile ['fræŋkəfaɪl] *adj & n* francófilo(a) *(m,f)*

Frank [fræŋk] *n Hist* franco(a) *m,f*

frank [fræŋk] **1** *adj* franco(a), sincero(a)
2 *vt Br (mail)* franquear

Frankfurt ['fræŋkfɜːrt] *n* Francfort

frankfurter ['fræŋkfɜːtər] *n (sausage)* salchicha *f* de Francfort

franking ['fræŋkɪŋ] *n* franqueo *m* ▫ **f. machine** máquina *f* franqueadora

frankly ['fræŋklɪ] *adv* francamente

frankness ['fræŋknɪs] *n* franqueza *f*

frantic ['fræntɪk] *adj (anxious)* desesperado(a); *(hectic)* frenético(a); **to be f. with worry** estar preocupadísimo(a)

frantically ['fræntɪklɪ] *adv* desesperadamente; **shouting f.** gritando como un loco *or* un poseso

fraternal [frə'tɜːnəl] *adj* fraterno(a), fraternal

fraternity [frə'tɜːnɪtɪ] *n* **(a)** *(brotherliness)* fraternidad *f* **(b)** *(society)* asociación *f*; *the legal/medical f.* cofradía *f* **(c)** *US Univ* = asociación de estudiantes que suele funcionar como club social; **f. house** = residencia perteneciente a dicha asociación

fraternize ['frætənaɪz] *vi* fraternizar **(with** con)

fratricide ['frætrɪsaɪd] *n Fml Jur (action)* fratricidio *m*; *(person)* fratricida *mf*

fraud [frɔːd] *n* **(a)** *(act)* fraude *m*, engaño *m* **(b)** *Jur* fraude *m* **(c)** *(person)* impostor(a) *m,f*

fraudulent ['frɔːdjʊlənt] *adj* fraudulento(a)

fraught [frɔːt] *adj* **(a)** *(full)* lleno(a) **(with** de), cargado(a) **(with** de); **f. with difficulties** cargado(a) de dificultades **(b)** *(tense)* nervioso(a), tenso(a)

fray¹ [freɪ] *vi* **(a)** *(cloth)* deshilacharse **(b)** *(temper)* crisparse; **his temper frequently frayed** se irritaba a menudo

fray² [freɪ] *n* combate *m*; *Fig* **to enter the f.** salir a la palestra

frayed [freɪd] *adj (cloth)* deshilachado(a); *(temper)* crispado(a); **to have f. nerves** tener los nervios crispados

frazzle ['fræzəl] *n Fam* **to be worn to a f.** estar hecho(a) polvo; **burnt to a f.** carbonizado(a), quemado(a); **she was burnt to a f. in the midday sun** se achicharró bajo el sol del mediodía

freak [friːk] **1** *n* **(a)** *(monster)* monstruo *m*; **a f. of nature** un accidente de la naturaleza **(b)** *Slang (eccentric)* estrafalario(a) *m,f* **(c)** *Slang (fan)* fanático(a) *m,f*; **she's a jazz f.** es una fanática del jazz
2 *adj* **(a)** *(unexpected)* inesperado(a), imprevisto(a); **f. result** resultado inesperado **(b)** *(unusual)* insólito(a), extraño(a); **f. storm** tormenta insólita

freak out *vi Slang* fliparse, alucinarse

freakish ['friːkɪʃ] *adj* **(a)** *(unexpected)* inesperado(a), imprevisto(a) **(b)** *(unusual)* insólito(a), extraño(a) **(c)** *(abnormal)* anormal, monstruoso(a) **(d)** *(eccentric)* estrafalario(a), excéntrico(a)

freaky ['fri:kɪ] *adj Fam* muy raro(a)

freckle ['frekəl] *n* peca *f*

freckled ['frekəld] *adj* pecoso(a), lleno(a) de pecas

freckly ['freklɪ] *adj* (**frecklier, freckliest**) pecoso(a), lleno(a) de pecas

free [fri:] **1** *adj* (**a**) *(at liberty)* libre; **as f. as a bird** libre como un pájaro; **feel f.!** ¡con toda confianza!; **of his own f. will** por voluntad propia; **to be f. to do sth** ser libre de hacer algo; **to give sb a f. hand** darle carta blanca a algn; **to set sb f.** poner en libertad a algn, liberar a algn; **to work f.** soltarse □ **f. access** entrada *f* libre; **f. fall** caída *f* libre; *Ftb* **f. kick** golpe *m* franco, saque *m* de falta; **f. love** amor *m* libre; *Econ* **f. market** libre mercado *m*; **f. speech** libertad *f* de expresión; **f. will** libre albedrío *m*; **f. translation** traducción *f* libre; **the f. world** el mundo libre (**b**) *Com* **f. port** puerto *m* franco; **f. trade** libre cambio *m*, (**c**) *(not occupied)* libre; **when will you be f.?** ¿cuándo estará libre?; **is that seat f.?** ¿está libre ese asiento? □ **f. time** tiempo *m* libre (**d**) *(gratis)* **f. (of charge)** gratuito(a), gratis; **admission f.** entrada *f* gratuita *or* libre □ **f. gift** obsequio *m*; **f. pass** pase *m*; **f. sample** muestra *f* gratuita (**e**) *(exempt)* libre. (**from** de); **trouble f.** sin problemas (**f**) *(generous)* generoso(a); **she's too f. with her money** es una manirrota (**g**) *(relaxed)* desenvuelto(a); **f. and easy** despreocupado(a)

2 *adv* (**a**) *(gratis)* gratis, gratuitamente; **to travel f.** viajar gratis *or* de balde; *Fam* **for f.** gratis (**b**) *(loose)* suelto(a); **the dogs run f. in the garden** los perros andan sueltos *or* libres en el jardín

3 *vt* (**a**) *(liberate)* poner en libertad; *(release)* liberar (**b**) *(let loose, work loose)* soltar (**c**) *(untie)* soltar, desatar (**d**) *(exempt)* eximir (**from** de)

freedom ['fri:dəm] *n* (**a**) *(liberty)* libertad *f*; **f. of choice** libertad de elección; **f. of the press** libertad de prensa; **to have complete f. to do sth** tener plena libertad para hacer algo; **f. of the city** ciudadanía *f* de honor □ **f. fighter** luchador(a) *m,f* por la libertad (**b**) *(exemption)* exención *f*

free-for-all ['fri:fərɔ:l] *n* bronca *f*, gresca *f*, *Méx* agarrón *m*

freehand ['fri:hænd] *adv* a mano alzada; **to draw f.** dibujar a mano alzada

freehold ['fri:həʊld] *Jur* **1** *n* derecho *m* de dominio absoluto
2 *adj* en propiedad absoluta

freelance ['fri:lɑ:ns] **1** *adj* independiente
2 *n* colaborador(a) *m, f* externo(a), free-lance *mf*
3 *vi* trabajar por su cuenta

freelancer ['fri:lɑ:nsər] *n* colaborador(a) *m,f* externo(a), free-lance *mf*

freeloader ['fri:ləʊdər] *n Fam* gorrero(a) *m,f*, *Esp Méx* gorrón(ona) *m,f*, *RP* garronero(a) *m,f*

freely ['fri:lɪ] *adv* (**a**) *(without limitation)* libremente; **to come and go f.** ir y venir con toda libertad (**b**) *(openly)* abiertamente, francamente

freemason ['fri:meɪsən] *n* francmasón(ona) *m,f*, masón(ona) *m,f*

freemasonry ['fri:meɪsənrɪ] *n* francmasonería *f*, masonería *f*

free-range ['fri:reɪndʒ] *adj Br* de granja; **f.-r. eggs** huevos *mpl* de granja

freestanding [fri:'stændɪŋ] *adj* independiente

freestyle ['fri:staɪl] *n Swimming* estilo *m* libre; **the hundred metres f.** los cien metros libres

freethinker [fri:'θɪŋkər] *n* librepensador(a) *m,f*

freeware ['fri:weər] *n Comptr* freeware *m*, programa *m* de dominio público *(y gratuito)*

freeway ['fri:weɪ] *n US* autopista *f*

freewheel [fri:'wi:l] *vi* (**a**) *(on bicycle)* andar a rueda libre (**b**) *Aut* ir en punto muerto

freeze [fri:z] **1** *vt* *(pt* **froze**; *pp* **frozen**) (**a**) *(liquid, food)* congelar (**b**) *Econ (money)* congelar (**c**) *Cin TV (image)* congelar
2 *n Meteor* helada *f* □ *Econ* **price f.** congelación *f* de precios
3 *vi* (**a**) *(liquid)* helarse; *(food)* congelarse; **I'm freezing** estoy helado; **to f. to death** morirse de frío (**b**) *Fig (stand still)* quedarse inmóvil; *(from shock)* quedarse paralizado(a) (**c**) *Comptr* bloquearse

freeze over, freeze up *vi* helarse

freeze-dried ['fri:zdraɪd] *adj* liofilizado(a); **f.-d. coffee** café liofilizado

freeze-dry ['fri:zdraɪ] *vt* (*pt & pp* **freeze-dried**) liofilizar

freeze-frame ['fri:z'freɪm] *n Cin* imagen *f* congelada

freezer ['fri:zər] *n* congelador *m*

freezing ['fri:zɪŋ] **1** *adj* (**a**) *Meteor* glacial; **f. fog** niebla *f* glacial; *Fam* **it's f. cold** hace un frío que pela (**b**) *Phys* **f. point** punto *m* de congelación; **above/below f. point** sobre/bajo cero
2 *n (of food, prices)* congelación *f*

freight [freɪt] *n* (**a**) *(transport)* transporte *m* □ **air/sea f.** transporte *m* aéreo/marítimo de mercancías (**b**) *(goods)* flete *m*, carga *f* □ *US* **f. car** wagon *m* de mercancías; *US* **f. elevator** montacargas *m inv*; **f. train** tren *m* de mercancías; **f. plane** avión *m* de carga (**c**) *(price)* flete *m*

freighter ['freɪtər] *n Av Naut* buque *m* *or* avión *m* de carga, carguero *m*

French [frentʃ] **1** *adj* francés(esa); **to take F. leave** despedirse a la francesa □ **F. bean** *Esp* judía *f* verde, *Bol RP* chaucha *f*, *Chile* poroto *m* verde, *Carib Col* habichuela *f*, *Méx* ejote *m*; **F. dressing** vinagreta *f*; *US* **F. fries** *Esp* patatas *fpl* *or Am* papas *fpl* fritas; **F. Horn** trompa *f* de pistones; **F. kiss** beso *m* con lengua; *Br Old-fashioned* **F. letter** condón *m*; **F. window** puerta *f* vidriera
2 *n* (**a**) *(language)* francés *m*; **F. teacher** profesor(a) *m,f* de francés (**b**) *pl* **the F.** los franceses

French-Canadian [frentʃkə'neɪdɪən] **1** *adj* franco-canadiense
2 *n* francocanadiense *mf*

Frenchman ['frentʃmən] *n (pl* **Frenchmen**) francés *m*

French-speaking ['frentʃspi:kɪŋ] *adj* de habla francesa, francófono(a)

Frenchwoman ['frentʃwʊmən] *n (pl* **Frenchwomen** ['frentʃwɪmɪn]) francesa *f*

frenetic [frɪ'netɪk] *adj* frenético(a)

frenzied ['frenzɪd] *adj* (**a**) *(wild)* frenético(a) (**b**) *(mad)* enloquecido(a)

frenzy ['frenzɪ] *n* frenesí *m*; **to be in a f.** estar frenético(a)

frequency ['fri:kwənsɪ] *n* (**a**) *(rate)* frecuencia *f* (**b**) *Rad* frecuencia *f*; **high/low f.** alta/baja frecuencia

frequent ['fri:kwənt] **1** *adj* frecuente, habitual
2 [frɪ'kwent] *vt (visit)* frecuentar

frequently ['fri:kwəntlɪ] *adv* frecuentemente, con frecuencia, a menudo

fresco ['freskəʊ] *n (pl* **frescoes**) *Art* fresco *m*

fresh [freʃ] **1** *adj* (**a**) *(new)* nuevo(a); **f. clues** nuevos indicios; **open a f. packet** abre otro paquete; **to make a f. start** volver a empezar (**b**) *(recent)* fresco(a); **have you got any f. news?** ¿traes noticias frescas? (**c**) *(air)* puro(a); **in the f. air** al aire libre (**d**) *(not salt)* dulce; **f. water** agua *f* dulce (**e**) *(not tired)* fresco(a); **as f. as a daisy** tan fresco(a) como una rosa (**f**) *(not frozen, untreated)* natural, fresco(a); **f. eggs** huevos frescos; **f. bread** pan del día (**g**) *(complexion)* sano(a) (**h**) *US Fam (cheeky)* fresco(a); **don't get f. with me!** ¡basta de familiaridades!

2 *adv* recién; **f. from university** recién salido(a) de la universidad

freshen ['freʃən] *vi (wind)* refrescar

freshen up *vi* lavarse y arreglarse, asearse

fresher ['freʃər] *n Br Univ* estudiante *mf* de primer año, novato(a) *m,f*

freshly ['freʃlɪ] *adv* recién, recientemente; **f. made sandwiches** bocadillos recién preparados

freshman ['freʃmən] *n Univ* estudiante *mf* de primer año, novato(a) *m,f*

freshness ['freʃnɪs] *n* **(a)** *(brightness)* frescura *f* **(b)** *(newness)* novedad *f*

freshwater ['freʃwɔːtər] *adj* de agua dulce

fret¹ [fret] *vi (pt & pp* **fretted)** *(worry)* preocuparse **(about** por)

fret² [fret] *n Mus (guitar)* traste *m*

fretful ['fretfʊl] *adj* **(a)** *(worried)* preocupado(a) **(b)** *(complaining)* quejumbroso(a) **(c)** *(tearful)* lloroso(a)

fretsaw ['fretsɔː] *n* segueta *f*, sierra *f* de calar

fretwork ['fretwɜːk] *n* calado *m*

Freudian ['frɔɪdɪən] *adj* freudiano(a); **F. slip** lapsus *m* freudiano

FRG [efɑːˈdʒiː] *n (abbr* **Federal Republic of Germany)** República *f* Federal de Alemania, RFA *f*

Fri *(abbr* **Friday)** viernes *m*, viern

friar ['fraɪər] *n Rel* fraile *m*

fricative ['frɪkətɪv] *Ling* **1** *adj* fricativo(a) **2** *n* fricativa *f*

friction ['frɪkʃən] *n (resistance, conflict)* fricción *f*; *(chafing)* roce *m*

Friday ['fraɪdɪ] *n* viernes *m*; **on F.** el viernes; **on Fridays** los viernes; **Good F.** Viernes Santo; *see also* **Saturday**

fridge [frɪdʒ] *n (abbr* **refrigerator)** *esp Br Fam* nevera *f*, *Esp* frigorífico *m*, *Méx* refrigerador *m*, *RP* heladera *f*

fridge-freezer ['frɪdʒ'friːzər] *n* combi *m*, *Esp* frigorífico-congelador *m*

fried [fraɪd] *adj* frito(a); **f. egg** huevo frito

friend [frend] *n* amigo(a) *m,f*, compañero(a) *m,f*, amistad *f*; **a family f.** un amigo de la familia; *Prov* **a f. in need is a f. indeed** en la necesidad se conoce a los amigos; **a f. of mine** un(a) amigo(a) mío(a); **a school f.** un(a) compañero(a) de clase; **he has lots of friends** tiene muchos amigos *or* muchas amistades; **she's friends with John** es amiga de John; **to have friends in high places** tener enchufes; **to make friends with sb** trabar amistad con algn; **to make friends again** *(after a quarrel)* hacer las paces; **we're just good friends** sólo somos amigos

friendliness ['frendlɪnɪs] *n* amabilidad *f*, simpatía *f*

friendly ['frendlɪ] *adj* **(friendlier, friendliest) (a)** *(person)* simpático(a), amable; **she's very f.** es muy simpática; **they became f.** se hicieron amigos; **to be on f. terms with sb** estar en buenos términos con algn □ **f. advice** consejo *m* de amigo; *Mil* **f. fire** fuego *m* del propio bando; **f. nation** nación *f* amiga **(b)** *(atmosphere)* acogedor(a)

friendship ['frendʃɪp] *n* amistad *f*, relación *f*

fries [fraɪz] *npl US* **(French) f.** *Esp* patatas *fpl* *or Am* papas *fpl* fritas

Friesian ['friːʒən] *adj & n* frisón(ona) *(m,f)*

frieze [friːz] *n Art* friso *m*

frigate ['frɪgɪt] *n Naut* fragata *f*

frigging ['frɪgɪn] *adj Vulg Esp* puñetero(a), *Méx* pinche, *RP* reverendo(a)

fright [fraɪt] *n* **(a)** *(fear)* miedo *m*; **to take f.** asustarse **(b)** *(shock)* susto *m*; **to get a f.** pegarse un susto; **to give sb a f.** darle un susto a algn; **the f. of one's life** un susto de muerte **(c)** *Fam (person)* adefesio *m*; **she looks a f.** está hecha un adefesio

frighten ['fraɪtən] *vt* asustar, espantar; **to f. the life/wits out of sb** dar a algn un susto *Esp* de muerte *or Méx* de la madre *or RP* de miércoles

frighten away, frighten off *vt* espantar, ahuyentar

frightened ['fraɪtənd] *adj* asustado(a); **easily f.** asustadizo(a); **f. to death** muerto(a) de miedo; **to be f. of sb** tenerle miedo a algn; **to be f. to do sth** tener miedo de hacer algo

frightening ['fraɪtənɪn] *adj* espantoso(a)

frightful ['fraɪtfʊl] *adj* espantoso(a), horroroso(a); **I'm in a f. hurry** tengo una prisa tremenda

frightfully ['fraɪtfʊlɪ] *adv* tremendamente, terriblemente; **I'm f. sorry** lo siento muchísimo

frigid ['frɪdʒɪd] *adj* **(a)** *Med* frígido(a) **(b)** *(climate)* glacial, muy frío(a); *Fig (manner, atmosphere)* glacial

frigidity ['frɪdʒɪdɪtɪ] *n Med* frigidez *f*

frill [frɪl] *n* **(a)** *(dress)* volante *m* **(b)** *Fig* **frills** *(decorations)* adornos *mpl*; *(extras)* pretensiones *fpl*; **with no f.** sencillo(a), sin adornos; **with all the f.** con toda la pompa

frilly ['frɪlɪ] *adj* **(frillier, frilliest)** *(dress etc)* con volantes

fringe [frɪndʒ] **1** *n* **(a)** *Br (of hair)* flequillo *m* **(b)** *Tex* fleco *m* **(c)** *(edge)* borde *m*; *(of city)* periferia *f*; *Fig* **on the f. of society** al margen de la sociedad; **the lunatic f.** los elementos fanáticos □ **f. benefits** extras *mpl*; **f. group** grupo *m* marginal; **f. theatre** teatro *m* experimental **2** *vt* **(a)** *Sew* poner un fleco a **(b)** *Fig (border)* bordear; **a lake fringed by trees** un lago rodeado de árboles

Frisbee® ['frɪzbɪ] *n* frisbee® *m*

Frisian ['frɪʒən] *adj & n* frisón(ona) *(m,f)*

frisk [frɪsk] **1** *vt (search)* registrar, cachear **2** *vi (frolic)* retozar, juguetear, corretear

frisky ['frɪskɪ] *adj* **(friskier, friskiest) (a)** *(children, animals)* retozón(ona), juguetón(ona) **(b)** *(adult)* vivo(a), vital

fritter ['frɪtər] *n Culin* buñuelo *m*; **apple f.** buñuelo *m* de manzana

fritter away *vt* malgastar

frivolity [frɪˈvɒlɪtɪ] *n* frivolidad *f*

frivolous ['frɪvələs] *adj (flippant)* frívolo(a); *(useless)* sin importancia

frizz [frɪz] **1** *n* pelo *m* crespo *or* rizado **2** *vt* rizar **3** *vi* rizarse

frizzy ['frɪzɪ] *adj* **(frizzier, frizziest)** crespo(a), muy rizado(a)

fro [frəʊ] *adv* **to go to and f.** ir y venir (de un lado para otro)

frock [frɒk] *n* vestido *m* □ **f. coat** levita *f*

Frog [frɒg] *n Br Slang Pej* franchute(a) *m,f*, *Esp* gabacho(a) *m,f*

frog [frɒg] *n* rana *f*; **frogs' legs** ancas *fpl* de rana; *Fig* **to have a f. in one's throat** tener carraspera

frogman ['frɒgmən] *n (pl* **frogmen)** hombre *m* rana

frogmarch ['frɒgmɑːtʃ] *vt* llevar a la fuerza sujetándole los brazos; llevar en volandas

frogspawn ['frɒgspɔːn] *n Br* huevos *mpl* de rana

frolic ['frɒlɪk] *vi* retozar, juguetear

from [frɒm, *unstressed* frəm] *prep* **(a)** *(time)* desde, a partir de; **f. her childhood onwards** desde la infancia; **f. now on** a partir de ahora; **f. one o'clock to two o'clock** desde la una hasta las dos; **f. that time onwards** desde entonces, desde aquel momento; **f. time to time** de vez en cuando (**b**) *(price, number)* desde, de; **dresses f. thirty dollars** vestidos desde treinta dólares; **choose a number f. one to ten** elige un número del uno a diez (**c**) *(source, origin)* de; **a letter f. her father** una carta de su padre; **f. a woman's point of view** desde el punto de vista de una mujer; **f. English into Spanish** del inglés al español; **f. far and wide** desde los lugares más remotos; **f. head to foot** de los pies a la cabeza; **he's f. Malaga** es de Málaga; **I heard it f. Daniel** me lo dijo Daniel; **she jumped (down) f. the wall** saltó del muro; **the train f. Bilbao** el tren procedente de Bilbao; **things went f. bad to worse** las cosas fueron de mal en peor; **tell her f. me that ...** dile de mi parte que ...; **to go f. door to door** ir de puerta en puerta (**d**) *(distance)* de; **the town is four miles f. the coast** el pueblo está a cuatro millas de la costa (**e**) *(out of)* de; **bread is made f. flour** el pan se hace con harina; **he recited the poem f. memory** recitó el poema de memoria (**f**) *(remove, subtract)* a; **he took the book f. the child** le quitó *or Andes RP* sacó el libro al niño; *Math* **take three f. five** restar tres a cinco (**g**) *(according to)* según, por; **f. what the author said** según lo que dijo el autor; **speaking f. my own experience** hablando por experiencia propia (**h**) *(position)* desde, de; **f. here** desde aquí; **f. the top of the mountain** desde la cima de la montaña (**i**) *(distinguish)* entre; **can you tell margarine f. butter?** ¿puedes distinguir entre la margarina y la mantequilla?

frond [frɒnd] *n* fronda *f*

front [frʌnt] **1** *n* (**a**) *(general)* parte *f* delantera; **from the f.** por delante, de frente; **in f. of** delante de, *Am* adelante de; **in f.** delante; *Fam* **up f.** con antelación; *Fam* **we want the money up f.** primero, queremos ver el dinero (**b**) *(of building)* fachada *f* (**c**) *Mil Pol* frente *m*; **he was sent to the f.** le mandaron al frente; **popular f.** frente *m* popular (**d**) *Meteor* frente *m*; **cold f.** frente *m* frío (**e**) *Br (seaside)* paseo *m* marítimo, *Arg* costanera *f*, *Cuba* malecón *m*, *Urug* rambla *f* (**f**) *(activity)* asunto *m*; **has she made any progress on the work f.?** ¿ha progresado en el trabajo? (**g**) *Fig (cover)* **she put on a brave f.** hizo de tripas corazón; **they used him as a f. for smuggling heroin** lo utilizaban como una tapadera para pasar heroína

2 *adj* delantero(a), de delante ❏ *Br Parl* **f. bench** = cada una de las dos primeras filas de escaños ocupados por los ministros y sus homólogos en la oposición; *Br Parl* **f. bencher** = diputado con cargo ministerial en el gobierno u homólogo en la oposición; **f. door** puerta *f* principal *or* de entrada; **f. page** *(of newspaper)* portada *f*, primera plana *f*; **f. room** salón *m*; *Aut* **f. seat** asiento *m* de delante *or* delantero

3 *vi* **to f. on(to)** dar a; **the house fronts onto the river** la casa da al río

frontage [ˈfrʌntɪdʒ] *n* fachada *f*

frontal [ˈfrʌntəl] *adj* frontal; **f. attack** ataque *m* frontal

frontier [ˈfrʌntɪər] **1** *n* frontera *f*; *Fig* **the frontiers of scientific knowledge** las fronteras de la ciencia

2 *adj* fronterizo(a); **f. post** puesto *m* fronterizo

frontispiece [ˈfrʌntɪspiːs] *n* frontispicio *m*

front-page [ˈfrʌntpeɪdʒ] *adj* de primera página; **f.-p. news** noticias *fpl* de primera plana

frontrunner [ˈfrʌntrʌnər] *n* favorito(a) *m,f*

frost [frɒst] **1** *n* (**a**) *(frozen dew)* escarcha *f* (**b**) *(freezing weather)* helada *f*

2 *vt* (**a**) *(freeze)* helar (**b**) *US Culin* glasear

frost over *vi* cubrirse de escarcha

frostbite [ˈfrɒstbaɪt] *n Med* congelación *f*

frostbitten [ˈfrɒstbɪtən] *adj Med* congelado(a); **her fingers were f.** tenía los dedos congelados

frosted [ˈfrɒstɪd] *adj* (**a**) *(glass)* esmerilado(a) (**b**) *US Culin* recubierto(a) de azúcar glas

frostiness [ˈfrɒstɪnɪs] *n Fig* frialdad *f*

frosting [ˈfrɒstɪŋ] *n US (on cake)* glaseado *m*

frosty [ˈfrɒstɪ] *adj* (**frostier, frostiest**) (**a**) *(weather)* de helada; **a f. night** una noche de helada (**b**) *Fig* glacial; **a f. reception** una acogida glacial

froth [frɒθ] **1** *n* (**a**) *(gen)* espuma *f* (**b**) *(from mouth)* espumarajos *mpl*

2 *vi* espumar; **to f. at the mouth** echar espumarajos por la boca

frothy [ˈfrɒθɪ] *adj* (**frothier, frothiest**) espumoso(a), con mucha espuma

frown [fraʊn] **1** *vi* fruncir el ceño; **he frowned as he read the latest news** frunció el ceño al leer las últimas noticias

2 *n* ceño *m*

frown upon *vt* desaprobar; **his behaviour was frowned upon** desaprobaron su comportamiento

froze [frəʊz] *pt see* **freeze**

frozen [ˈfrəʊzən] **1** *pp see* **freeze**

2 *adj* (**a**) *(liquid, lake)* helado(a); *Fam* **I'm f. stiff** estoy helado; *Fam* **my feet are f.** tengo los pies helados (**b**) *(food)* congelado(a); **f. peas** guisantes *mpl or Méx* chícharos *mpl* congelados, *Am* arvejas *fpl* congeladas

frugal [ˈfruːgəl] *adj* frugal; **she lived a f. life** llevaba una vida austera; **we sat down to a f. supper** tuvimos una cena frugal

frugality [fruːˈgælɪtɪ] *n* frugalidad *f*

fruit [fruːt] **1** *n* (**a**) *Bot* fruto *m*; **to bear f.** dar fruto; **f. tree** árbol *m* frutal (**b**) *(for eating)* fruta *f*; **there's f. for dessert** de postre tenemos fruta ❏ **f. bowl** frutero *m*; **f. cake** pastel *m* con fruto seco; **f. dish** frutero *m*; *Br* **f. machine** máquina *f* tragaperras; **f. salad** macedonia *f* de frutas (**c**) **fruits** *(rewards)* frutos *mpl*; **to reap the f. of such hard work** cosechar los frutos de tan duro trabajo

2 *vi* dar fruto

fruitful [ˈfruːtfʊl] *adj* fructífero(a); *Fig* provechoso(a)

fruition [fruːˈɪʃən] *n Fml* fruición *f*; **to come to f.** realizarse

fruitless [ˈfruːtlɪs] *adj* infructuoso(a), inútil, vano(a); **a f. task** un trabajo infructuoso

fruitlessly [ˈfruːtlɪslɪ] *adv* infructuosamente

fruity [ˈfruːtɪ] *adj* (**fruitier, fruitiest**) (**a**) *(taste)* con sabor a fruta (**b**) *Fam (voice)* pastoso(a) (**c**) *Fam (joke)* picante, verde

frump [frʌmp] *n Fam (woman)* adefesio *m*

frumpish [ˈfrʌmpɪʃ] *adj* (**a**) *(old-fashioned)* anticuado(a), pasado(a) de moda (**b**) *(ideas)* chapado(a) a la antigua

frustrate [frʌˈstreɪt] *vt* frustrar; **the bad weather frustrated our plans** el mal tiempo frustró nuestros planes

frustrated [frʌˈstreɪtɪd] *adj* frustrado(a); **he felt f.** se sentía frustrado

frustrating [frʌsˈtreɪtɪŋ] *adj* frustrante

frustration [frʌˈstreɪʃən] *n* frustración *f*

fry[1] [fraɪ] **1** *vt (pt & pp* **fried**) freír

2 *vi* freírse; *Fig* asarse; *Fig* **you'll f. in this sun without suncream** te achicharrarás bajo este sol sin crema bronceadora

fry[2] [fraɪ] *npl (fish)* alevines *mpl*; *(children)* gente *f* menuda; **small f.** gente *f* de poca monta

fryer [ˈfraɪər] *n* **(deep fat) f.** freidora *f*

frying pan [ˈfraɪɪŋpæn] *n, US* **fry-pan** [ˈfraɪpæn] *n* sartén *f*; *Fig* **to jump out of the frying p. into the fire** salir de Guatemala y entrar en Guatepeor

fry-up [ˈfraɪʌp] *n Br Fam* fritura *f*

ft (**a**) *(abbr* **foot**) pie *m* (**b**) *(abbr* **feet**) pies *mpl*

FTP [eftiːˈpiː] *n Comptr (abbr* **File Transfer Protocol**) FTP *m*, protocolo *m* de transferencia de ficheros

fuchsia ['fju:ʃə] *n Bot* fucsia *f*

fuck [fʌk] *Vulg* **1** *vt & vi* joder, *Am* coger, *Méx* chingar; **f. (it)!** ¡carajo!, *Esp* ¡joder!; **f. you!** ¡que te den por culo!, *Méx* ¡chinga tu madre!, *RP* ¡andate a la puta que te parió!
 2 *n* **I don't give a f.** me importa un carajo *or* una mierda; **shut the f. up!** ¡cállate de una puta vez!

fuck off *vi* largarse, pirarse, abrirse, *RP* tomarse el raje; **f. off!** *Esp* ¡vete a tomar por (el) culo!, *Méx* ¡vete a la chingada!, *RP* ¡andate a la puta que te parió!

fuck up *vt* joder; **the poor bloke's really fucked up** está muy jodido el pobre

fucker ['fʌkər] *n Vulg* cabrón(ona) *m,f*, hijo(a) *m,f* de puta *or Méx* de la chingada

fucking ['fʌkɪŋ] *Vulg* **1** *adj* **f. idiot!** ¡gilipollas!, *Am* ¡pendejo!, *RP* ¡boludo!; **where are my f. keys?** ¿dónde coño están las llaves?
 2 *adv (intensifier)* **a f. good film** una película de puta madre

fuddy-duddy ['fʌdɪdʌdɪ] *n* persona *f* chapada a la antigua

fudge [fʌdʒ] **1** *n Culin* = dulce hecho con azúcar, leche y mantequilla
 2 *vt* **(a)** *(fiddle)* amañar **(b)** *(dodge)* eludir; **to f. the issue** eludir el problema

fuel ['fjʊəl] **1** *n* combustible *m*; *(for engines)* carburante *m*; *Fig* **to add f. to the fire** echar leña al fuego ❑ *Aut* **f. gauge** indicador *m* del nivel de gasolina *or RP* nafta; **f. tank** depósito *m* de combustible
 2 *vt (pt & pp* **fuelled**, *US* **fueled)** *(plane)* abastecer de combustible; *(car)* echar gasolina a; *Fig (ambition)* estimular; *Fig (difficult situation)* empeorar
 3 *vi* repostar

fuel-efficient ['fjʊəlɪˈfɪʃənt] *adj* de poco consumo

fug [fʌg] *n Br Fam* aire *m* viciado

fugitive ['fju:dʒɪtɪv] **1** *n Fml* fugitivo(a) *m,f*, prófugo(a) *m,f*
 2 *adj (fleeing)* fugitivo(a); *Fig (transient)* fugaz, efímero(a), pasajero(a)

fugue [fju:g] *n Mus* fuga *f*

fulcrum ['fʊlkrəm] *n (pl* **fulcrums** *or* **fulcra** ['fʊlkrə]*) Tech* fulcro *m*, punto *m* de apoyo

fulfil, *US* **fulfill** [fʊlˈfɪl] *vt (pt & pp* **fulfilled)** **(a)** *(carry out) (task, ambition)* realizar; *(promise)* cumplir; *(role, function)* desempeñar **(b)** *(satisfy) (requirements, wishes)* satisfacer

fulfilment, *US* **fulfillment** [fʊlˈfɪlmənt] *n* **(a)** *(of ambition)* realización *f*; **a sense of f.** un sentimiento de realización **(b)** *(of duty, promise)* cumplimiento *m*

full [fʊl] **1** *adj* **(a)** *(filled)* lleno(a); **don't talk with your mouth f.** no hables con la boca llena; **f. of** lleno(a) de; **f. of beans** rebosante de salud *or* de alegría; **f. of gratitude** muy agradecido(a); **f. to the brim** lleno(a) hasta los topes; **I'm f. (up)** no puedo más; **the bottle is f.** la botella está llena; **to be f. of oneself** ser un(a) engreído(a); **to lead a very f. life** llevar una vida muy ajetreada **(b)** *(complete, entire)* completo(a); **at f. speed** a toda velocidad; **f. particulars** todos los detalles; **f. report** informe completo; **f. text** texto íntegro; **in f. uniform** en uniforme completo; **the hotel is f.** el hotel está completo; **to come f. circle** volver al punto de partida; *Fam* **f. blast** a todo gas, *RP* a todo vapor; *Fam* **in f. swing** en pleno auge ❑ **f. board** pensión *f* completa; **f. employment** pleno empleo *m*; *Theat* **f. house** agotadas las localidades; **f. moon** luna *f* llena; **f. stop** punto *m*, punto *m* y seguido *or* aparte **(c)** *(parts of body) (face)* lleno(a); *(figure)* relleno(a) **(d)** *(clothes) (loose-fitting)* ancho(a); *(too big)* flojo(a); **f. skirt** falda *f* con vuelo; **f. sleeve** manga *f* ancha
 2 *n* **in f.** en su totalidad; **name in f.** nombre y apellidos completos; **the bill must be paid in f.** hay que pagar la factura en su totalidad; **to enjoy life to the f.** disfrutar al máximo de la vida
 3 *adv* **f. well** perfectamente, muy bien

fullback ['fʊlbæk] *n Sport* defensa *m* central; *(rugby)* zaguero *m*

full-blown ['fʊlˈbləʊn] *adj* autentico(a)

full-bodied ['fʊlˈbɒdɪd] *adj (wine)* con cuerpo

full-cream ['fʊlˈkri:m] *adj* **f. milk** leche *f* entera

full-fledged ['fʊlˈfledʒd] *adj US* hecho(a) y derecho(a)

full-grown ['fʊlˈgrəʊn] *adj* **(a)** *(tree)* crecido(a) **(b)** *(person, animal)* adulto(a)

full-length ['fʊlˈleŋθ] *adj* **(a)** *(film)* de largo metraje ❑ **f.-l. feature film** largometraje *m* **(b)** *(mirror, portrait)* de cuerpo entero; *(skirt)* largo(a)

fullness ['fʊlnɪs] *n* **(a)** *(abundance)* plenitud *f*, abundancia *f*; **in the f. of time** en su momento **(b)** *(of skirt)* amplitud *f*

full-on ['fʊlˈɒn] *adj Fam (argument)* en serio; **to have f. sex** llegar hasta el final

full-page ['fʊlˈpeɪdʒ] *adj* de una página; **f.-p. advertisement** anuncio a toda página

full-scale ['fʊlˈskeɪl] *adj* **(a)** *(model etc)* de tamaño natural **(b)** *(thorough)* completo(a), total; **f.-s. search** registro *m* a fondo, búsqueda *f* minuciosa; **f.-s. war** guerra *f* generalizada *or* total

full-time ['fʊlˈtaɪm] **1** *adj* de jornada completa; **looking after two children is a f.-t. job** cuidar a dos niños requiere una dedicación total
 2 **f. t.** *adv* **to work f. t.** hacer una jornada completa

fully ['fʊlɪ] *adv* completamente, enteramente; **I f. agree with you** estoy completamente de acuerdo contigo

fully-fledged ['fʊlˈfledʒd] *adj Br* hecho(a) y derecho(a)

fully-grown ['fʊlˈgrəʊn] *adj see* **full-grown**

fulmar ['fʊlmər] *n Orn* fulmar *m*

fulminate ['fʌlmɪneɪt] *vi* tronar, arremeter (**against** contra)

fulsome ['fʊlsəm] *adj Fml* excesivo(a), exagerado(a)

fumble ['fʌmbəl] *vi* hurgar; **to f. for sth** buscar algo a tientas; **to f. with sth** manejar algo con torpeza

fume [fju:m] **1** *n (usu pl)* humo *m*, vapores *mpl*
 2 *vi* echar humo; *Fig* **she was fuming (with rage)** estaba que se subía por las paredes

fumigate ['fju:mɪgeɪt] *vt* fumigar

fumigation [fju:mɪˈgeɪʃən] *n* fumigación *f*

fun [fʌn] **1** *n* **(a)** *(amusement)* diversión *f*; **figure of f.** hazmerreír *m*; **have f.!** ¡que lo pases muy bien!; **in** *or* **for f.** en broma; **to have f.** divertirse, pasarlo bien; **to make f. of** *or* **to poke f. at sb** reírse de algn; *Fam* **to have f. and games** pasárselo en grande **(b)** *(humour)* gracia *f*; **I can't see the f. in it** no le veo la gracia
 2 *adj* divertido(a); **he's great f.** es muy divertido; *US Fam* **f. clothes** ropa graciosa; *US Fam* **to have a f. time** pasarlo bomba

function ['fʌŋkʃən] **1** *n* **(a)** *(purpose)* función *f*; **to fulfil a f.** desempeñar una función; **in my f. as treasurer** en mi calidad de tesorero **(b)** *(working)* funcionamiento *m* **(c)** *(ceremony)* acto *m*, ceremonia *f*; *(party)* recepción *f* **(d)** *Comptr Math* función *f*; **f. key** tecla *f* de función
 2 *vi* funcionar

functional ['fʌŋkʃənəl] *adj* funcional, práctico(a); **f. clothes** ropa práctica

functionality [fʌŋkʃəˈnælɪtɪ] *n* funcionalidad *f*

functionary ['fʌŋkʃənərɪ] *n* funcionario(a) *m,f*

fund [fʌnd] **1** *n* **(a)** *Com* fondo *m*; **school building f.** fondo para la construcción del colegio ❑ **International Monetary F.** Fondo *m* Monetario Internacional **(b)** *Fig*

(source) fuente *f*; **f. of wisdom** fuente *f* de sabiduría **(c) funds** fondos *mpl*; *(securities)* fondos *mpl* públicos
2 *vt (finance)* financiar

fundamental [fʌndə'mentəl] **1** *adj (central, basic)* fundamental, básico(a); *(elementary)* elemental
2 fundamentals *npl* **the f.** los fundamentos; **they need to know the f. before setting sail** es necesario conocer las cuatro reglas básicas antes de lanzarse al mar

fundamentalism [fʌndə'mentəlɪzəm] *n Rel* fundamentalismo *m*

fundamentally [fʌndə'mentəlɪ] *adv* básicamente, fundamentalmente

funding ['fʌndɪŋ] *n* fondos *mpl*, financiación *f*; *Am* financiamiento *m*

fund-raiser ['fʌndreɪzər] *n (person)* recaudador(a) *m,f* de fondos; *(event)* acto *m* para recaudar fondos

funeral ['fjuːnərəl] *n* entierro *m*, funerales *mpl*; **to attend sb's f.** asistir a los funerales de algn; *Fam Fig* **that's her f.** allá ella *or* con su pan se lo coma ❑ **f. director** encargado(a) *m,f* de la funeraria; *US* **f. home** funeraria *f*; **f. march** marcha *f* fúnebre; **f. parlour** funeraria *f*; **f. procession** cortejo *m* fúnebre; **f. service** misa *f* de cuerpo presente; **state f.** exequias *fpl* nacionales

funereal [fjuː'nɪərɪəl] *adj* fúnebre

funfair ['fʌnfeər] *n Br* feria *f*, parque *m* de atracciones

fungal ['fʌŋgəl] *adj* fúngico(a), de los hongos

fungi ['fʌŋgaɪ] *pl see* **fungus**

fungicide ['fʌŋgɪsaɪd] *n* fungicida *m*

fungus ['fʌŋgəs] *n (pl* **funguses** *or* **fungus** *or* **fungi** ['fʌŋgiː] *or* ['fʌŋgaɪ]) **(a)** *Bot* hongo *m* **(b)** *Med* fungo *m*

funicular [fjuː'nɪkjʊlər] *adj & n* funicular *(m)*

funky ['fʌŋkɪ] *adj* **(funkier, funkiest)** *Mus* vibrante

fun-loving ['fʌnlʌvɪŋ] *adj* amante de las diversiones

funnel ['fʌnəl] **1** *n* **(a)** *(for liquids)* embudo *m* **(b)** *Naut* chimenea *f*
2 *vt (pt & pp* **funnelled,** *US* **funneled)** *(liquid)* verter por un embudo; *Fig (funds, energy)* encauzar

funnily ['fʌnɪlɪ] *adv Fam* de forma extraña; **f. enough** aunque parezca extraño

funny ['fʌnɪ] *adj* **(funnier, funniest) (a)** *(peculiar, strange)* raro(a), extraño(a); **he's a f. character** es un tipo raro; **that's f., I can't remember** ¡qué raro! no lo recuerdo; **the f. thing about it is that …** lo curioso del caso es que ❑ *Fam* **f. farm** manicomio *m, Esp* frenopático *m* **(b)** *(amusing)* divertido(a), gracioso(a); **I found it very f.** me hizo mucha gracia; **are you trying to be f.?** ¿me estás tomando el pelo?; **don't get f. with me!** ¡no te hagas el gracioso conmigo! ❑ **f. bone** hueso *m* de la alegría **(c)** *(malfunctioning) Fam* estropeado(a); **the radio's gone f.** la radio se ha estropeado **(d)** *Fam (ill)* enfermo(a), mal; **I feel a bit f.** me encuentro un poco mal **(e)** *Fam (dishonest)* dudoso(a); **f. business** negocios *mpl* sucios; **I don't want any f. business!** ¡nada de trucos!

fur [fɜːr] **1** *n* **(a)** *(of living animal)* pelo *m*, pelaje *m* **(b)** *(of dead animal)* piel *f* **(c)** *(on tongue)* sarro *m*, saburra *f* **(d)** *Br (in kettle)* sarro *m*
2 *adj* de piel, de pieles; **f. coat** abrigo *m* de pieles
3 *vi (pt & pp* **furred)** calcificarse; **an iron furs (up) if you don't clean it regularly** una plancha se calcifica si no la limpias a menudo

furious ['fjʊərɪəs] *adj* **(a)** *(angry)* furioso(a); **to be f. with sb** estar muy enfadado(a) con algn **(b)** *(vigorous)* violento(a), furioso(a); **she was in a f. mood** estaba de un humor de perros

furlong ['fɜːlɒŋ] *n (measurement)* = 201 metros

furnace ['fɜːnɪs] *n* horno *m*; **blast f.** alto horno

furnish ['fɜːnɪʃ] *vt* **(a)** *(house)* amueblar **(with** con); **furnished bedsitter** estudio amueblado **(b)** *Fml (supply) (food)* suministrar, proveer; *(details)* facilitar, proporcionar

furnishings ['fɜːnɪʃɪŋz] *npl (furniture, fittings)* muebles *mpl*, mobiliario *m*

furniture ['fɜːnɪtʃər] *n* muebles *mpl*, mobiliario *m*; **a piece of f.** un mueble ❑ **f. polish** cera *f* or abrillantador *m* para muebles, *CSur* lustramuebles *m inv*; *Br* **f. remover** empleado(a) *m,f* de una empresa de mudanzas; **f. shop** tienda *f* de muebles; **f. van** camión *m* de mudanzas

furore [fjʊ'rɔːrɪ] *n, US* **furor** ['fjʊərɔːr] *n* ola *f* de protestas *or* de entusiasmo

furrier ['fʌrɪər] *n* peletero(a) *m,f*

furrow ['fʌrəʊ] **1** *n* **(a)** *Agr* surco *m* **(b)** *(on forehead)* arruga *f*
2 *vt* **(a)** *Agr* surcar **(b)** *(forehead)* arrugar

furry ['fɜːrɪ] *adj* **(furrier, furriest) (a)** *(hairy)* peludo(a) **(b)** *(tongue, kettle)* sarroso(a)

further ['fɜːðər] **1** *adj see also* **far (a)** *(new)* nuevo(a); **until f. notice** hasta nuevo aviso; **until f. orders** hasta nueva orden **(b)** *(additional)* otro(a), adicional; **f. detail** más detalles; **we have no f. use for it** ya no nos sirve **(c)** *(later)* posterior, ulterior ❑ *Br* **f. education** estudios *mpl* superiores
2 *adv* **(a)** *(more)* más; **f. back** más allá; **f. along** más adelante; **she heard nothing f.** no volvió a saber nada más; **to go f. into sth** estudiar algo más a fondo; **nothing was f. from my thoughts** nada estaba más lejos de mi pensamiento **(b)** *Fml Com* con referencia, referente; **f. to your letter of the 9th** con referencia a su carta del 9 del corriente **(c)** *Fml (besides)* además; **I disagree with the new company policy, and f., it does not cover any of the points discussed initially** no estoy de acuerdo con la nueva política de la empresa y además no incluye ninguno de los puntos acordados inicialmente
3 *vt (peace, development)* fomentar, promover

furthermore ['fɜːðə'mɔːr] *adv Fml* además

furthermost ['fɜːðəməʊst] *adj Literary* más lejano(a)

furthest ['fɜːðɪst] *adj see also* **far**; más, más lejano(a)

furtive ['fɜːtɪv] *adj* furtivo(a)

fury ['fjʊərɪ] *n* **(a)** *(rage)* furia *f*, furor *m* **(b)** *(energy)* furor *m*; **to work like f.** trabajar como un loco **(c)** *Myth* **the Furies** las Furias

furze [fɜːz] *n Bot* aulaga *f*

fuse [fjuːz] **1** *n* **(a)** *Elec* fusible *m*, plomo *m*; **f. box** caja *f* de fusibles **(b)** *(of bomb) (lead)* mecha *f*; *(detonator)* espoleta *f*; **to light the f.** encender la mecha
2 *vi* **(a)** *Br Elec* fundirse; **the lights fused** se fundieron los plomos **(b)** *Fig (merge)* fusionarse; **the two organizations fused after the talks** las dos organizaciones se fusionaron después de las negociaciones **(c)** *(melt)* fundirse
3 *vt* **(a)** *Br Elec* **if you're not careful you'll f. the lights** si no vas con cuidado fundirás los plomos **(b)** *Fig (merge)* fundir **(c)** *(melt)* fundir

fuselage ['fjuːzɪlɑːʒ] *n Av* fuselaje *m*

fusilier [fjuːzɪ'lɪər] *n Mil* fusilero *m*

fusillade [fjuːzɪ'leɪd] *n* tiroteo *m*; *Fig (questions, criticisms)* lluvia *f*

fusion ['fjuːʒən] *n* fusión *f*

fuss [fʌs] **1** *n* **(a)** *(commotion)* jaleo *m*, alboroto *m*; **what's all the f. about?** ¿por qué tanto jaleo?; **to kick up a f.** armar un escándalo; *Fig* **a lot of f. about nothing** mucho ruido y pocas nueces **(b)** *(complaints)* quejas *fpl*; **stop making a f.** deja ya de quejarte; **there's no need to make such a f.** no es para tanto **(c)** *(attention)* atenciones *fpl*; **to make a f. of sb** mimar a algn; **he always makes a real f. of Maggie** se deshace por Maggie
2 *vi* preocuparse **(about** por)

fuss over *vt* mimar excesivamente, preocuparse excesivamente por

fusspot ['fʌspɒt] *n Fam* quisquilloso(a) *m,f,* tiquismiquis *mf*

fussy ['fʌsɪ] *adj* (**fussier, fussiest**) *(nitpicking)* quisquilloso(a); *(thorough)* exigente

fusty ['fʌstɪ] *adj* (**fustier, fustiest**) (**a**) *(old-fashioned)* chapado(a) a la antigua (**b**) *(musty)* mohoso(a)

futile ['fjuːtaɪl] *adj* inútil, vano(a)

futility [fjuː'tɪlɪtɪ] *n* inutilidad *f*

futon ['fuːtɒn] *n* futón *m*

future ['fjuːtʃər] **1** *n* (**a**) *(time)* futuro *m*; **in the f.** en el futuro, en lo sucesivo; **in the near f.** en un futuro próximo; **in the not too distant f.** en un futuro no muy lejano; **we'll be more careful in f.** de aquí en adelante tendremos más

cuidado (**b**) *(prospects)* futuro *m*, porvenir *m*; **that job has no f.** ese trabajo no tiene porvenir (**c**) *Ling* futuro *m* (**d**) *Fin* **futures** futuros *mpl*

2 *adj* futuro(a); **her f. husband** su futuro marido

futuristic [fjuːtʃə'rɪstɪk] *adj* futurista

fuzz¹ [fʌz] **1** *n (hair)* vello *m*

2 *vt* rizar

fuzz² [fʌz] *n Slang (police)* **the f** la poli, *Esp* la pasma, *Méx* los pitufos, *RP* la cana

fuzzy ['fʌzɪ] *adj* (**fuzzier, fuzziest**) (**a**) *Fam (hair)* muy rizado(a) (**b**) *(blurred)* borroso(a); **the photo was f.** la foto era borrosa

fwd *(abbr* **forward(s)**) adelante

FYI *(abbr* **for your information**) para tu información

G

G, g [dʒi:] *n* (**a**) *(the letter)* G, g *f* (**b**) G *Mus* sol *m*; **G major** sol *m* mayor

g [dʒi:] *(abbr* **gramme**) g

gab [gæb] *Fam* **1** *n* palique *m*; **to have the gift of the g.** tener un pico de oro
2 *vi* (*pt & pp* **gabbed**) charlar

gabardine ['gæbədi:n] *n* gabardina *f*, impermeable *m*

gabble ['gæbəl] **1** *n* chapurreo *m*, farfulla *f*
2 *vi* chapurrear, hablar atropelladamente, farfullar

gaberdine ['gæbədi:n] *n see* **gabardine**

gable ['geɪbəl] *n Archit* aguilón *m*, gablete *m*; **g. end** hastial *m*

Gabon [gə'bɒn] *n* Gabón

Gabonese [gæbə'ni:z] *adj & n* gabonés(esa) *(m,f)*

gad [gæd] *vi* (*pt & pp* **gadded**) **to g. about** callejear

gadabout ['gædəbaʊt] *n Fam* callejero(a) *m,f,* azotacalles *mf inv,* juerguista *mf*

gadfly ['gædflaɪ] *n Ent* tábano *m*

gadget ['gædʒɪt] *n* artilugio *m*, aparato *m*, dispositivo *m*; *Fam* chisme *m*

gadgetry ['gædʒɪtrɪ] *n* artilugios *mpl*; *Fam* chismes *mpl*

Gael [geɪl] *n* = persona de origen celta oriunda de Irlanda o el Noroeste de Escocia

Gaelic ['geɪlɪk] **1** *adj* gaélico(a)
2 *n (language)* gaélico *m*

gaff¹ [gæf] *n Fishing* garfio *m*

gaff² [gæf] *n Fam* disparate *m*; **to blow the g.** descubrir el pastel

gaffe [gæf] *n* metedura *f or Am* metida *f* de pata, plancha *f*, planchazo *m*, patinazo *m*; **to make a g.** meter la pata, patinar

gaffer ['gæfər] *n Br Fam* (**a**) *(boss)* jefe *m* (**b**) *(man)* tío *m*

gag [gæg] **1** *n* (**a**) *(for the mouth)* mordaza *f* (**b**) *Fam Theat* morcilla *f, (joke)* gag *m*, chiste *m*
2 *vt* (*pt & pp* **gagged**) amordazar; **they tied him up and gagged him** le ataron y le amordazaron
3 *vi* tener náuseas

gaga ['gɑːgɑː] *adj Br Fam* chocho(a)

gage [geɪdʒ] *n & vt US see* **gauge**

gaggle ['gægəl] *n* manada *f*; **g. of geese** manada de ocas; *Fig* **a g. of journalists** una horda de periodistas

gaiety ['geɪətɪ] *n* alegría *f*, regocijo *m*, animación *f*

gaily ['geɪlɪ] *adv* alegremente; **g. coloured** de colores vivos *or* alegres

gain [geɪn] **1** *n* (**a**) *(profit)* ganancia *f*, beneficio *m*; **they hoped to make a financial g. from the company** esperaban obtener beneficios de la compañía (**b**) *(increase)* aumento *m*; **weight g.** aumento de peso
2 *vt* (**a**) *(obtain)* ganar; **what did he g. from such hard work?** ¿qué consiguió con tanto esfuerzo?; *Fig* **to g. ground** ganar terreno (**b**) *(increase)* incrementar, aumentar; **to g. speed** ganar velocidad, acelerar; **to g. weight** aumentar de peso
3 *vi (clock)* adelantar

gainful ['geɪnfʊl] *adj Fam* beneficioso(a), lucrativo(a)

gainfully ['geɪnfʊlɪ] *adv* **to be g. employed** tener un trabajo remunerado

gainsay [geɪn'seɪ] *vt* (*pt & pp* **gainsaid**) *Fml (gen negative)* negar; **there's no gainsaying they were right** no se puede negar que tenían razón *or* estaban en lo cierto

gait [geɪt] *n* porte *m*, manera *f* de caminar *or Esp* andar, andares *mpl*

gaiter ['geɪtər] *n (gen pl)* polaina *f*

gal¹ [gæl] *n Fam* chavala *f*, chica *f*, muchacha *f*, tía *f*

gal² [gæl] *(pl* **gal** *or* **gals**) *abbr* **gallon** galón *m*

gala ['gɑːlə, 'geɪlə] *n* gala *f*, fiesta *f*; *Br Sport* **swimming g.** festival *m* de natación

galactic [gə'læktɪk] *adj* galáctico(a)

Galapagos [gə'læpəgəs] *n* **the G. Islands** las Islas Galápagos

galaxy ['gæləksɪ] *n Astron* galaxia *f*

gale [geɪl] *n* vendaval *m*, viento *m* fuerte; *Fig* **gales of laughter** carcajadas *fpl*

Galicia [gə'lɪsɪə] *n (in Spain)* Galicia

Galician [gə'lɪʃɪən, gə'lɪʃən] **1** *adj* gallego(a)
2 *n* (**a**) *(person)* gallego(a) *m,f* (**b**) *(language)* gallego *m*

gall [gɔːl] **1** *n Fam* descaro *m*, caradura *f*
2 *vt* molestar, irritar

gallant ['gælənt] *adj* (**a**) *(brave)* valiente (**b**) *(also* [gə'lænt]) *(chivalrous)* galante

gallantry ['gæləntrɪ] *n* (**a**) *(bravery)* valentía *f*, gallardía *f*, valor *m* (**b**) *(politeness)* galantería *f*

galleon ['gælɪən] *n Naut* galeón *m*

gallery ['gælərɪ] *n* (**a**) *(gen)* galería *f*; **art g.** galería de arte (**b**) *Theat* gallinero *m*; **to play to the g.** actuar para la galería (**c**) *Parl (court)* tribuna *f* (**d**) *(mine)* galería *f*

galley ['gælɪ] *n* (**a**) *(ship)* galera *f*; **g. slave** galeote *m* (**b**) *Naut (kitchen)* cocina *f* (**c**) *Print* **g. (proof)** galerada *f*

Gallic ['gælɪk] *adj Fml (French)* francés(esa), *(of Gaul)* gálico(a)

Gallicism ['gælɪsɪzəm] *n Ling* galicismo *m*

galling ['gɔːlɪŋ] *adj* irritante

gallivant ['gælɪvænt] *vi Fam* callejear

gallon ['gælən] *n* galón *m* (≃ 4,55 litros; *US* 3,79 litros)

gallop ['gæləp] **1** n galope m; **at a g.** al galope; **at full g.** a galope tendido

2 vi galopar, ir al galope; **to g. away** alejarse al galope

galloping ['gæləpɪŋ] adj galopante □ Med **g. consumption** tisis f galopante

gallows ['gæləʊz] npl horca f sing, patíbulo m sing, cadalso m sing

gallstone ['gɔ:lstəʊn] n Med cálculo m biliar

Gallup poll ['gæləppəʊl] n encuesta f, sondeo m

galore [gə'lɔ:r] adv Fam en cantidad, en abundancia; **money g.** dinero en abundancia; **whisky g.** whisky a granel

galosh [gə'lɒʃ] n chanclo m

galumph [gə'lʌmf] vi Fam corretear; **to g. about** dar saltos de alegría

galvanization [gælvənaɪ'zeɪʃən] n galvanización f

galvanize ['gælvənaɪz] vt (metal) galvanizar; Fig **to g. sb into action** galvanizar a algn

galvanized ['gælvənaɪzd] adj galvanizado(a)

Gambia ['gæmbɪə] n Gambia

Gambian ['gæmbɪən] adj & n gambiano(a) (m,f)

gambit ['gæmbɪt] n (a) Chess gambito m (b) Fig (move) táctica f, maniobra f, estratagema f

gamble ['gæmbəl] **1** n (a) (risk) riesgo m; (risky undertaking) empresa f arriesgada; **they took a real g. when they decided to employ him** arriesgaron mucho cuando decidieron contratarlo (b) (bet, wager) jugada f, apuesta f

2 vi (a) (bet) jugar; **to g. away a fortune** perder una fortuna en el juego (b) (take a risk) arriesgarse; **they gambled on the assumption that nobody would come** tomaron el riesgo de pensar que nadie vendría

gambler ['gæmblər] n jugador(a) m,f

gambling ['gæmblɪŋ] n juego m □ **g. house** casa f de juego

gambol ['gæmbəl] vi (pt & pp **gambolled**, US **gamboled**) saltar, brincar

game [geɪm] **1** n (a) (gen) juego m; **g. of chance** juego de azar; Fig **the g. is up** se acabó; Fig **to give the g. away** enseñar las cartas; Fig **to play the g.** jugar limpio; Fig **two can play at that g.** donde las dan las toman; Fig **what's his g.?** ¿qué pretende?; Fig **to play silly games** hacer el tonto □ **g. show** concurso m televisivo (b) (match etc) partido m; (bridge) partida f; **to be off one's g.** no estar en forma (c) **games** Sport juegos mpl, Br Sch deportes mpl; **Olympic G.** Juegos Olímpicos, Olimpiadas fpl (d) (hunting) caza f; Fig presa f; **big g.** caza mayor; **g. bag** morral m; **g. reserve** coto m de caza; Fig **he was easy g.** fue una presa fácil

2 adj (ready) listo(a); **g. for** listo(a) para, preparado(a) para; **g. for anything** listo(a) para todo

gamekeeper ['geɪmki:pər] n guardabosque mf

gamely ['geɪmlɪ] adv resueltamente

gamey ['geɪmɪ] adj see **gamy**

gamma ['gæmə] n gamma f □ Biol **g. globulin** gammaglobulina f; Phys **g. rays** rayos mpl gamma

gammon ['gæmən] n Br jamón m ahumado or curado

gammy ['gæmɪ] adj (**gammier, gammiest**) Br Fam lisiado(a), tullido(a); **g. leg** pata f coja or Andes RP renga or Esp chula

gamut ['gæmət] n gama f, serie f; **to run the g. of ...** experimentar todas las posibilidades de ...

gamy ['geɪmɪ] adj (of flavour) de or a caza

gander ['gændər] n Orn ganso m

gang [gæŋ] n (of criminals) banda f; (of youths) pandilla f; (of workers) cuadrilla f, brigada f, equipo m; Fam (of friends) grupo m, pandilla f, cuadrilla f

gang up vi Fam unirse (**on** contra), confabularse (**on** contra)

ganger ['gæŋər] n Br Fam capataz m

Ganges ['gændʒi:z] n **the G.** el Ganges

gangland ['gæŋlænd] n Fam hampa f, submundo m, bajos fondos mpl

gangling ['gæŋglɪŋ] adj Fam larguirucho(a)

ganglion ['gæŋglɪən] n Med ganglio m

gangplank ['gæŋplæŋk] n Naut plancha f

gangrene ['gæŋgri:n] n Med gangrena f

gangrenous ['gæŋgrɪnəs] adj gangrenoso(a); **to go g.** gangrenarse

gangsta ['gæŋstə] n (a) (music) **g. (rap)** gangsta m (b) (rapper) gangsta mf

gangster ['gæŋstər] n gángster m

gangway ['gæŋweɪ] n Naut Theat pasarela f, pasillo m; **g.!** ¡abran paso!

gannet ['gænɪt] n Orn alcatraz m; Fig comilón m

gantry ['gæntrɪ] n (a) Tech puente m transversal □ **g. crane** grúa f de pórtico (b) Astronaut torre f de lanzamiento (c) (for barrel) caballete m

gaol [dʒeɪl] n & vt Br see **jail**

gap [gæp] n (a) (hole) abertura f, hueco m; (crack) brecha f; (space) espacio m; (blank space) blanco m; (in traffic) claro m; **to bridge** or **fill a g.** rellenar un hueco (b) Geol desfiladero m (c) (in time) intervalo m; (emptiness) vacío m □ **g. year** = año que muchos jóvenes utilizan, una vez concluida la educación secundaria y antes de ingresar a la universidad, para viajar por el mundo o trabajar (d) (gulf) diferencia f; **age g.** diferencia de edades; Econ **trade g.** déficit m comercial (e) (deficiency) laguna f; **there were gaps in his knowledge of English** su inglés presentaba ciertas lagunas

gape [geɪp] vi (person) quedarse boquiabierto(a), mirar boquiabierto(a); (thing) abrir, quedar abierto(a)

gaping ['geɪpɪŋ] adj Fig profundo(a); **a g. wound** una herida tremenda or profunda

garage ['gærɑ:ʒ, 'gærɪdʒ, US gə'rɑ:ʒ] n (a) (for storing cars) garaje m, Am cochera f □ US **g. sale** = mercadillo en casa de un particular (b) (for repairs) taller m mecánico (c) (filling station) gasolinera f, estación f de servicio

garb [gɑ:b] n Fml atuendo m, atavío m

garbage ['gɑ:bɪdʒ] n (a) US (household waste) basura f □ **g. can** cubo m or Am bote m de la basura; **g. collector** basurero(a) m,f; **g. truck** camión m de la basura (b) Fig (nonsense) Esp chorradas fpl, Am pendejadas

garbled ['gɑ:bəld] adj embrollado(a); **g. account** relato confuso; **she left a g. message** dejó un recado incomprensible

garden ['gɑ:dən] **1** n jardín m □ **g. centre** centro m de jardinería, vivero m, plantel m; **G. of Eden** Edén m; **g. party** recepción f al aire libre; **vegetable g.** huerto m

2 vi (usually continuous) cuidar el jardín; **John's gardening** John está trabajando en el jardín

gardener ['gɑ:dənər] n jardinero(a) m,f

gardenia [gɑ:'di:nɪə] n Bot gardenia f

gardening ['gɑ:dənɪŋ] n jardinería f; **his mother does the g.** su madre es la que cuida el jardín

garfish ['gɑ:fɪʃ] n (fish) aguja f

gargle ['gɑ:gəl] **1** n (a) (act) gárgaras fpl (b) (liquid) gargarismo m

2 vi hacer gárgaras, gargarizar

gargoyle ['gɑ:gɔɪl] n Archit gárgola f

garish ['geərɪʃ] adj (colour) chillón(ona), llamativo(a); (light) cegador(a), deslumbrante

garland ['gɑːlənd] **1** *n* guirnalda *f*
2 *vt* adornar con guirnaldas

garlic ['gɑːlɪk] *n Culin Hortic* ajo *m*; **a clove of g.** un diente de ajo; **prawns in g.** gambas *fpl* al ajillo ❑ **g. bread** pan *m* de ajo

garment ['gɑːmənt] *n* prenda *f*

garnet ['gɑːnɪt] *n Min* granate *m*

garnish ['gɑːnɪʃ] *Culin* **1** *n* guarnición *f*
2 *vt* guarnecer

Garonne [gæ'rɒn] *n* Garona

garret ['gærɪt] *n* buhardilla *f*, ático *m*

garrison ['gærɪsən] *Mil* **1** *n* guarnición *f*; **g. town** ciudad *f* de guarnición
2 *vt* guarnecer; **to g. a town** guarnecer una ciudad; **to g. troops in a town** acuartelar tropas en una ciudad

garrotte [gə'rɒt] **1** *n* garrote *m*
2 *vt* dar garrote a, ejecutar con garrote

garrulous ['gærʊləs] *adj* gárrulo(a), locuaz, parlanchín(ina)

garter ['gɑːtər] *n* (**a**) *(for stockings)* liga *f* ❑ *US* **g. belt** liguero *m* (**b**) *Br* **the Order of the G.** la Orden de la Jarretera

gas [gæs] **1** *n* (*pl* **gases** *or* **gasses**) (**a**) *(substance)* gas *m* ❑ **Calor g.** gas *m* butano; **g. chamber** cámara *f* de gas; **g. cooker** cocina *f or Col Méx Ven* estufa *f* de gas; **g. fire** estufa *f* de gas; **g. mask** careta *f* antigás; **g. meter** contador *m* del gas; **g. ring** hornillo *m* de gas; **natural g.** gas *m* natural; **tear g.** gas *m* lacrimógeno (**b**) *Med* anestesia *f*; **I had g.** me anestesiaron ❑ **laughing g.** gas *m* hilarante (**c**) *US (gasoline)* gasolina *f*, *RP* nafta *f*; **g. station** gasolinera *f*; *Fam* **step on the g.!** ¡pisa a fondo!; *Slang* **g. guzzler** coche *m* que chupa mucha gasolina (**d**) *Fam* **it was a real g.** lo pasamos bomba
2 *vt* (*pt & pp* **gassed**) *(asphyxiate)* asfixiar con gas
3 *vi Fam (talk)* charlotear, darle a la sinhueso

gasbag ['gæsbæg] *n Fam Offens* cotorra *f*

gaseous ['gæsɪəs, 'gæʃɪəs] *adj* gaseoso(a)

gash [gæʃ] **1** *n* herida *f* profunda
2 *vt* hacer un corte en; **he gashed his forehead** se hizo una herida en la frente

gasket ['gæskɪt] *n Tech* junta *f*; *Fam* **to blow a g.** salirse de sus casillas

gasoline ['gæsəliːn] *n US* gasolina *f*

gasometer [gæ'sɒmɪtər] *n* gasómetro *m*

gasp [gɑːsp] **1** *n* (**a**) *(cry)* grito *m* (**b**) *(breath)* boqueada *f*; *Fig* **to be at one's last g.** estar en las últimas
2 *vi* (**a**) *(in surprise)* quedar boquiabierto(a) (**b**) *(breathe)* jadear; **to g. for air** hacer esfuerzos para respirar

gassy ['gæsɪ] *adj* (**gassier, gassiest**) gaseoso(a)

gastric ['gæstrɪk] *adj* gástrico(a); *Med* **g. flu** fiebre *f* gástrica; **g. juice** jugo *m* gástrico; **g. ulcer** úlcera *f* gástrica

gastritis [gæs'traɪtɪs] *n Med* gastritis *f*

gastro-enteritis [gæstrəʊentə'raɪtɪs] *n Med* gastroenteritis *f*

gastronome ['gæstrənəʊm] *n* gastrónomo(a) *m,f*

gastronomic [gæstrə'nɒmɪk] *adj* gastronómico(a)

gastronomy [gæs'trɒnəmɪ] *n* gastronomía *f*

gasworks ['gæswɜːks] *n* fábrica *f or Am* planta *f* de gas

gate [geɪt] *n* (**a**) *(door)* puerta *f*, verja *f*; **garden g.** puerta de jardín (**b**) *(at airport)* puerta *f* (**c**) *Sport (attendance)* entrada *f*; **g. (money)** taquilla *f*, recaudación *f*

gâteau ['gætəʊ] *n* (*pl* **gâteaux** ['gætəʊz]) *Culin* pastel *m*, *Esp* tarta *f*, *Col CSur* torta *f*

gatecrash ['geɪtkræʃ] *Fam* **1** *vi* colarse, entrar de gorra
2 *vt* colarse en, entrar de gorra en

gatecrasher ['geɪtkræʃər] *n Fam* persona *f* que se cuela

gatekeeper ['geɪtkiːpər] *n* (*of park, castle*) guarda *mf*; *(of house, estate)* portero(a) *m,f*

gatepost ['geɪtpəʊst] *n* poste *m*; *Fam Fig* **between you, me and the g.** entre nosotros

gateway ['geɪtweɪ] *n* (**a**) *(entrance)* entrada *f*, puerta *f*; *Fig* camino *m*, pasaporte *m*; *Fig* **the g. to success** el camino *or* pasaporte hacia el éxito (**b**) *Comptr* pasarela *f*

gather ['gæðə] **1** *vt* (**a**) *(collect)* juntar; *(pick)* coger; *(pick up)* recoger (**b**) *(bring together)* reunir, juntar (**c**) *(harvest)* cosechar (**d**) *(gain)* ganar, cobrar; **to g. speed** ir ganando velocidad; **to g. strength** cobrar fuerzas (**e**) *(understand)* suponer, deducir; **I g. that ...** tengo entendido que ... (**f**) *Sew* fruncir
2 *vi* (**a**) *(come together)* reunirse, juntarse (**b**) *(form)* formarse; **a crowd gathered** se formó una muchedumbre; **a storm is gathering** amenaza tormenta

gather round *vi* acercarse, agruparse

gather up *vt* recoger

gathering ['gæðərɪŋ] **1** *adj* creciente; **g. darkness** oscuridad *f* creciente; **g. gloom** tristeza *f* creciente
2 *n* reunión *f*; **a family g.** una reunión familiar

GATT [gæt] *n* (*abbr* **General Agreement on Tariffs and Trade**) GATT *m*

gauche [gəʊʃ] *adj* (**a**) *(clumsy)* torpe, desmañado(a) (**b**) *(tactless)* sin tacto, torpe

gaucheness ['gəʊʃnɪs] *n* (**a**) *(clumsiness)* torpeza *f* (**b**) *(tactlessness)* falta *f* de tacto, falta *f* de delicadeza

gaudily ['gɔːdɪlɪ] *adv* llamativamente; **g. dressed** vestido(a) de forma llamativa

gaudy ['gɔːdɪ] *adj* (**gaudier, gaudiest**) chillón(ona), llamativo(a)

gauge [geɪdʒ] **1** *n* (**a**) *(measure)* medida *f* estándar; *(of gun, wire)* calibre *m* (**b**) *Rail* ancho *m* de vía; **narrow g.** de vía estrecha (**c**) *(calibrator)* indicador *m*, calibre *m*, calibrador *m*; **oil g.** indicador *m* del nivel de aceite; **tyre g.** manómetro *m* para neumáticos (**d**) *Fig (indication)* indicación *f*, muestra *f*
2 *vt* (**a**) *(measure)* medir, calibrar (**b**) *Fig (judge)* calcular, determinar, juzgar

Gaul [gɔːl] *n Hist* (**a**) *(country)* Galia *f* (**b**) *(inhabitant)* galo(a) *m,f*

gaunt [gɔːnt] *adj* (**a**) *(lean)* demacrado(a) (**b**) *(desolate)* lúgubre

gauntlet ['gɔːntlɪt] *n Hist* guantelete *m*; *(glove)* guante *m*; *Fig* **to run the g. of ...** estar sometido(a) a ...; *Fig* **to take up the g.** recoger el guante; *Fig* **to throw down the g.** arrojar el guante, *Am* desafiar a algn

gauze [gɔːz] *n* gasa *f*

gave [geɪv] *pt see* **give**

gavel ['gævəl] *n* martillo *m*

gawk [gɔːk] *vi Fam* papar moscas, mirar a las musarañas; **to g. at sth/sb** mirar con cara de tonto(a) algo/a algn

gawky ['gɔːkɪ] *adj* (**gawkier, gawkiest**) desgarbado(a)

gawp [gɔːp] *vi Fam* quedarse papando moscas; **to g. at sth/sb** mirar boquiabierto(a) algo/a algn

gay [geɪ] **1** *adj* (**gayer, gayest**) (**a**) *(homosexual)* gay, homosexual; *(woman)* lesbiana (**b**) **g. rights** derechos *mpl* de los homosexuales (**b**) *esp Old-fashioned (happy)* alegre; **g. bachelor** soltero *m* libre y sin compromiso
2 *n (man)* gay *m*, homosexual *m*; *(woman)* lesbiana *f*

gaze [geɪz] **1** *n* mirada *f* fija
2 *vi* mirar fijamente

gazebo [gə'ziːbəʊ] *n* (*pl* **gazebos** *or* **gazeboes**) belvedere *m*

gazelle [gæˈzel] n (pl **gazelles** or **gazelle**) Zool gacela f

gazette [gəˈzet] n gaceta f; US periódico m

GB [dʒiːˈbiː] (**a**) (abbr **Great Britain**) Gran Bretaña (**b**) Comptr (abbr **gigabyte**) GB m

GCSE [dʒiːsiːesˈiː] n Br (abbr **General Certificate of Secondary Education**) = certificado de enseñanza secundaria

Gdns (abbr **Gardens**) ≃ calle f sing, c/

GDP [dʒiːdiːˈpiː] n Econ (abbr **gross domestic product**) producto m interior bruto, PIB m

GDR [dʒiːdiːˈɑː(r)] n Formerly (abbr **German Democratic Republic**) RDA

gear [ɡɪər] **1** n (**a**) (equipment) equipo m ❏ **camping g.** equipo m de acampada; **fishing g.** aparejo m de pesca; Av **landing g.** tren m de aterrizaje (**b**) Fam (belongings) cosas fpl (**c**) Fam (clothing) ropa f; **punk g.** ropa punk (**d**) Tech engranaje m (**e**) Aut velocidad f, marcha f; **out of g.** en punto muerto; **to change g.** cambiar de velocidad ❏ **first g.** primera f (velocidad f); **g.** Br **lever** or US **shift** palanca f de cambios
2 vt ajustar, adaptar; **a policy geared to the needs of the people** una política adaptada a las necesidades del pueblo

gearbox [ˈɡɪəbɒks] n Aut caja f de cambios

gearstick [ˈɡɪəstɪk] n, US **gearshift** [ˈɡɪəʃɪft] n Aut palanca f de cambios

gee [dʒiː] interj (**a**) US Fam ¡caramba!, ¡ostras! (**b**) (to horse) **g. up!** ¡arre!

gee-gee [ˈdʒiːdʒiː] n Fam caballito m

geese [ɡiːs] npl see **goose**

geezer [ˈɡiːzər] n Br Fam tipo m, Esp tío m; **an old g.** un vejestorio

Geiger counter [ˈɡaɪɡər] n contador m Geiger

gel [dʒel] **1** n (**a**) Chem gel m (**b**) (for hair) gel m moldeador, gomina f
2 vi (pt & pp **gelled**) (**a**) Chem gelificarse (**b**) Fig (ideas etc) cuajar
3 vt (hair) engominar; **to g. one's hair** engominarse el pelo

gelatin n, **gelatine** [ˈdʒelətiːn] n gelatina f

gelatinous [dʒɪˈlætɪnəs] adj gelatinoso(a)

geld [ɡeld] vt capar, castrar

gelding [ˈɡeldɪŋ] n caballo m castrado

gelignite [ˈdʒelɪɡnaɪt] n gelignita f, gelinita f

gem [dʒem] n (**a**) (jewel) piedra f preciosa, gema f (**b**) Fig (person) joya f, alhaja f

Gemini [ˈdʒemɪnaɪ] n Astrol Astron Géminis m sing

gemstone [ˈdʒemstəʊn] n piedra f preciosa, gema f

Gen Mil (abbr **General**) General m, Gral., Genl

gen [dʒen] n Br Fam información f, datos mpl; **to get the g. on sth** informarse sobre algo

gender [ˈdʒendə] n Ling género m

gene [dʒiːn] n Biol gene m, gen m

genealogical [dʒiːnɪəˈlɒdʒɪkəl] adj genealógico(a)

genealogist [dʒiːnɪˈælədʒɪst] n genealogista mf

genealogy [dʒiːnɪˈælədʒɪ] n genealogía f

general [ˈdʒenərəl] **1** adj general; **a g. idea** una idea general; **as a g. rule** por regla general; **a word in g. use** una palabra de uso corriente; **in g.** en general, generalmente; **in the g. interest** en beneficio de todos, para el bien de todos; **the g. public** el público ❏ **g. anaesthetic** anestesia f general; Pol **G. Assembly** Asamblea f General; US **g. delivery** lista f de correos; **g. knowledge** conocimientos mpl generales; Br Med **g.**

practice medicina f general; Br Med **g. practitioner (GP)** médico m de cabecera; US **g. store** tienda f (que vende de todo); **g. strike** huelga f general
2 n Mil general m

generality [dʒenəˈrælɪtɪ] n generalidad f

generalization [dʒenərəlaɪˈzeɪʃən] n generalización f

generalize [ˈdʒenərəlaɪz] vt & vi generalizar

generally [ˈdʒenrəlɪ] adv generalmente, por lo general, en general; **g. speaking** hablando en términos generales

general-purpose [ˈdʒenərəlˈpɜːpəs] adj de uso general

generate [ˈdʒenəreɪt] vt (**a**) Elec generar (**b**) Fig (produce) generar, engendrar, producir

generating [ˈdʒenəreɪtɪŋ] adj generador(a); **g. station** central generadora

generation [dʒenəˈreɪʃən] n generación f; **from g. to g.** de generación en generación; **the younger g.** los jóvenes, la juventud, la nueva generación ❏ **g. gap** abismo m or conflicto m or diferencia f generacional

generator [ˈdʒenəreɪtər] n Elec generador m

generic [dʒɪˈnerɪk] adj genérico(a)

generosity [dʒenəˈrɒsɪtɪ] n generosidad f

generous [ˈdʒenərəs] adj (lavish) generoso(a); (plentiful) copioso(a); **a g. helping** una buena ración

generously [ˈdʒenərəslɪ] adv generosamente

Genesis [ˈdʒenɪsɪs] n Rel Génesis m

genesis [ˈdʒenɪsɪs] n (pl **geneses** [ˈdʒenɪsiːz]) génesis f, origen m

genetic [dʒɪˈnetɪk] adj genético(a) ❏ **g. engineering** ingeniería f genética; **g. fingerprinting** identificación f genética

genetically [dʒɪˈnetɪklɪ] adv genéticamente; **g. modified** transgénico(a), modificado(a) genéticamente

geneticist [dʒɪˈnetɪsɪst] n genetista mf

genetics [dʒɪˈnetɪks] n genética f

Geneva [dʒɪˈniːvə] n Ginebra

Genevan [dʒɪˈniːvən] adj & n ginebrino(a) (m,f)

genial [ˈdʒiːnɪəl, ˈdʒiːnjəl] adj cordial, amable, simpático(a)

geniality [dʒiːnɪˈælɪtɪ] n cordialidad f, amabilidad f, simpatía f

genie [ˈdʒiːnɪ] n duende m, genio m

genital [ˈdʒenɪtəl] adj genital

genitalia [dʒenɪˈteɪlɪə] npl Fml (órganos mpl) genitales mpl

genitals [ˈdʒenɪtəlz] npl órganos mpl genitales

genitive [ˈdʒenɪtɪv] adj & n Ling genitivo (m)

genius [ˈdʒiːnjəs, ˈdʒiːnɪəs] n (pl **geniuses**) (**a**) (person) genio m; **a work of g.** una obra genial; **to be a g.** ser un genio (**b**) (gift) don m; **to have a g. for business** tener un don especial para los negocios

Genoa [ˈdʒenəʊə] n Génova

genocide [ˈdʒenəʊsaɪd] n genocidio m

Genoese [dʒenəʊˈiːz] adj & n, **Genovese** [dʒenəˈviːz] adj & n genovés(esa) (m,f)

genre [ˈʒɑːnrə] n Art Lit género m; **dramatic g.** género dramático

gent [dʒent] n (abbr **gentleman**) Br Fam señor m, caballero m; Com **gents' footwear** calzado m para caballero; **the gents** el baño or Esp el servicio or CSur la toilette de caballeros; **where's the gents?** ¿dónde están los servicios (de caballeros)?

genteel [dʒenˈtiːl] adj (refined) fino(a), distinguido(a); Pej afectado(a), cursi

Gentile ['dʒentaɪl] *adj & n (not Jewish)* no judío(a) *(m,f)*; *(Christian)* cristiano(a) *(m,f)*; *(pagan)* pagano(a) *(m,f)*, gentil *(mf)*

gentle ['dʒentəl] *adj* **(a)** *(person)* dulce, tierno(a); *(breeze)* suave; *(movement)* suave, palisado(a) **(b)** *(noble)* noble; **of g. birth** de buena cuna

gentleman ['dʒentəlmən] *n (pl* **gentlemen)** caballero *m*; **g.'s agreement** acuerdo *m* entre caballeros; **he's a real g.** es todo un caballero; **ladies and gentlemen!** ¡señoras y señores!

gentleness ['dʒentəlnɪs] *n (mildness)* ternura *f*; *(kindness)* amabilidad *f*

gentlewoman ['dʒentəlwomən] *n Hist* dama *f*, señora *f*

gently ['dʒentlɪ] *adv (movement)* con cuidado

gentry ['dʒentrɪ] *n* pequeña nobleza *f*, alta burguesía *f*

genuflect ['dʒenju:flekt] *vi Rel* hacer una genuflexión

genuflection *n*, **genuflexion** [dʒenju:'flekʃən] *n* genuflexión *f*

genuine ['dʒenjʊɪn] *adj* **(a)** *(authentic, true)* auténtico(a), genuino(a), verdadero(a); **the painting was discovered to be g.** el cuadro resultó ser un original **(b)** *(sincere)* sincero(a); **his feelings for her were g.** sus sentimientos hacía ella eran sinceros; **they were g. people** era buena gente

genuinely ['dʒenjʊɪnlɪ] *adv* auténticamente, realmente, sinceramente; **they were g. surprised** estaban realmente sorprendidos

genus ['dʒiːnəs] *n (pl* **genuses** *or* **genera** ['dʒenərə]) *Biol* género *m*

geocentric [dʒiːəʊ'sentrɪk] *adj* geocéntrico(a)

geodesic [dʒiːəʊ'diːzɪk] *adj Geom* geodésico(a)

geographer [dʒɪ'ɒɡrəfər] *n* geógrafo(a) *m,f*

geographic(al) [dʒɪə'ɡræfɪk(əl)] *adj* geográfico(a)

geography [dʒɪ'ɒɡrɑfɪ, 'dʒɒɡrəfɪ] *n* geografía *f*

geologic(al) [dʒɪə'lɒdʒɪk(əl)] *adj* geológico(a)

geologist [dʒɪ'ɒlədʒɪst] *n* geólogo(a) *m,f*

geology [dʒɪ'ɒlədʒɪ] *n* geología *f*

geomagnetic [dʒiːəʊmæɡ'netɪk] *adj* geomagnético(a)

geomagnetism *n*

geometric(al) [dʒɪə'metrɪk(əl)] *adj* geométrico(a)

geometrician [dʒɪɒmɪ'trɪʃən] *n* geómetra *mf*

geometry [dʒɪ'ɒmɪtrɪ] *n* geometría *f*

geomorphic [dʒiːəʊ'mɔːfɪk] *adj Geol* geomórfico(a)

geophysical [dʒiːəʊ'fɪzɪkəl] *adj* geofísico(a)

geophysics [dʒiːəʊ'fɪzɪks] *n* geofísica *f*

geopolitical [dʒiːəʊpə'lɪtɪkəl] *adj* geopolítico(a)

geopolitics [dʒiːəʊ'pɒlɪtɪks] *n* geopolítica *f*

Georgia ['dʒɔːdʒə] *n* Georgia

Georgian ['dʒɔːdʒən] *adj & n* georgiano(a) *(m,f)*

georgic ['dʒɔːdʒɪk] *n Lit* geórgica *f*

geothermal [dʒiːəʊ'θɜːməl] *adj* geotérmico(a)

geranium [dʒɪ'reɪnɪəm] *n Bot* geranio *m*

gerbil ['dʒɜːbɪl] *n Zool* gerbo *m*, jerbo *m*

geriatric [dʒerɪ'ætrɪk] *adj Med* geriátrico(a)

geriatrician [dʒerɪə'trɪʃən] *n Med* geriatra *mf*

geriatrics [dʒerɪ'ætrɪks] *n Med* geriatría *f*

germ [dʒɜːm] *n* **(a)** *Biol* germen *m*; *Fig* germen *m*, principio *m*; **wheat g.** germen del trigo **(b)** *Med* microbio *m* ❑ **g. warfare** guerra *f* bacteriológica

German ['dʒɜːmən] **1** *adj* **(a)** *(from Germany)* alemán(ana), germano(a); *Formerly* **G. Democratic Republic** República *f* Democrática Alemana **(b)** *Med* **G. measles** rubeola *f*

2 *n* **(a)** *(from Germany)* alemán(ana) *m,f*, germano(a) *m,f*;

(East) germanooriental *mf*; *(West)* germanooccidental *mf* **(b)** *(language)* alemán *m*

Germanic [dʒɜː'mænɪk] *adj* germánico(a), germano(a)

Germany ['dʒɜːmənɪ] *n* Alemania; **East G.** Alemania Oriental, Alemania del Este; **West G.** Alemania Occidental

germ-free ['dʒɜːmfriː] *adj* esterilizado(a)

germicidal [dʒɜːmɪ'saɪdəl] *adj* germicida

germicide ['dʒɜːmɪsaɪd] *n* germicida *m*

germinate ['dʒɜːmɪneɪt] *vi* germinar

germination [dʒɜːmɪ'neɪʃən] *n* germinación *f*

gerontocracy [dʒerɒn'tɒkrəsɪ] *n Pol* gerontocracia *f*

gerontologist [dʒerɒn'tɒlədʒɪst] *n Med* gerontólogo(a) *m,f*

gerontology [dʒerɒn'tɒlədʒɪ] *n Med* gerontología *f*

gerrymander ['dʒerɪmændər] *vt Pol* = alterar los límites de un distrito electoral para que un partido obtenga mejores resultados

gerund ['dʒerənd] *n Ling* gerundio *m*

gestate ['dʒesteɪt] *vi* gestar

gestation [dʒe'steɪʃən] *n* gestación *f*

gestatorial [dʒestə'tɔːrɪəl] *adj* **g. chair** silla *f* gestatoria

gesticulate [dʒe'stɪkjʊleɪt] *vi* gesticular

gesticulation [dʒestɪkjʊ'leɪʃən] *n* gesticulación *f*

gesture ['dʒestʃər] **1** *n* gesto *m*, ademán *m*; *Fig* gesto *m*, detalle *m*; **as a g. of friendship** en señal de amistad; **it's an empty g.** es pura formalidad

2 *vi* gesticular, hacer gestos

get [get] **1** *vt (pt & pp* **got**; *US pp* **gotten)** **(a)** *(obtain, acquire)* obtener, conseguir; **he got the best marks in the class** obtuvo las mejores notas de la clase; **I got it for nothing** me lo dieron gratis; **she got a first in her degree** sacó matrícula en la carrera; **she got a job at the school** obtuvo un trabajo en el colegio; **to g. a bank loan** obtener un crédito; **to g. a divorce** obtener el divorcio; **to g. one's own way** salirse con la suya **(b)** *(earn)* ganar; **he gets paid on Fridays** cobra los viernes **(c)** *(fetch)* traer; **g. my coat** tráigame el abrigo; **g. the police!** ¡llama a la policía! **(d)** *(receive)* recibir; **he got a prize for the best picture** recibió un premio por el mejor cuadro; **she got chocolates for Christmas** le regalaron bombones por Navidad; *Fam* **he got the sack** le despidieron; *Fam* **she got five years for armed robbery** le echaron cinco años por robo a mano armada **(e)** *(catch)* tomar, *Esp* coger, *Am* agarrar; **(f)** *Tel* **can you g. me New York?** ¿me puede comunicar *o Esp* poner con NuevaYork?; **g. me Mr Brown** póngame con el Sr. Brown **(g)** *(prepare)* preparar; **can I g. you a drink?** ¿quiere beber algo?, ¿le pongo algo para beber?; **to g. lunch** preparar la comida **(h)** *(ask)* pedir; **g. him to call me** dile que me llame **(i)** *(make do sth)* conseguir; **I can't g. the radio to work** no consigo arreglar la radio; **they got him to return the money** le convencieron para que devolviese el dinero; **to g. sb to agree to sth** conseguir que algn acepte algo **(j)** *(have sth done)* **he must g. his hair cut** tiene que cortarse el pelo; **they got the house painted** hicieron pintar la casa **(k)** *(wound)* dar, alcanzar; **they got him in the chest** le dieron en el pecho **(l)** *(understand)* entender, ligar; **I don't g. it** no lo entiendo; **do you g. the joke?** ¿entiendes *or Am* cachas la broma? **(n)** *Fam (record)* **did you g. that?** ¿lo ha apuntado?

2 *vi* **(a)** *(become)* ponerse; **to g. angry** *esp Esp* enfadarse, *esp Am* enojarse; **to g. dark** anochecer; **to g. dressed** vestirse; **to g. drunk** emborracharse; **to g. late** hacerse tarde; **to g. married** casarse; **to g. used to doing sth** acostumbrarse a hacer algo; **to g. wet** mojarse **(b)** *(go)* ir; **can you g. there by train?** ¿se puede ir en tren?; *Fig* **we are not getting anywhere** así no vamos a ninguna parte;

Fam **where has he got to?** ¿dónde se ha metido? **(c)** *(arrive)* llegar; **she'll g. here at three** llegará a las tres **(d) to g. to** *(come to)* llegar a; **to g. to know sb** llegar a conocer a algn; **we got to like him in the end** llegamos a quererle al final; **when I got to know ...** al enterarme ...

get about *vi* **(a)** *(person)* desplazarse **(b)** *(news etc)* difundirse

get across *vt* **(a)** *(cross) (street)* cruzar; *(bridge)* atravesar **(b)** *(idea etc)* hacer comprender

get ahead *vi* adelantar, progresar

get along *vi* **(a)** *(leave)* marcharse; **I'll have to be getting along** tengo que marcharme **(b)** *(manage)* arreglárselas; **to g. along without sth** pasarse sin algo; *Fam* **g. along with you!** ¡déjate de memeces!

get around 1 *vi* **(a)** *(person)* desplazarse **(b)** *(travel)* viajar **(b)** *(news)* difundirse

2 *vt (problem)* evitar

get around to *vt* tener tiempo para; **I never got around to doing it** al final no lo hice

get at *vt* **(a)** *(reach)* alcanzar; **I can't g. at it** no lo alcanzo, no llego a cogerlo **(b)** *(ascertain)* descubrir; **they want to g. at the truth** quieren descubrir la verdad **(c)** *(insinuate)* insinuar; **what are you getting at?** ¿qué estás insinuando?, ¿a dónde quieres llegar? **(d)** *(criticize)* criticar; *(tease)* meterse con; **she's always getting at me** siempre me está pinchando

get away *vi* escaparse; *Fam* **to g. away from it all** alejarse del mundanal ruido

get away with *vt* salir impune de; **she got away with stealing the money** salió impune del robo

get back 1 *vi* **(a)** *(return)* regresar, volver; **they got b. at nine** regresaron a las nueve **(b)** *(move backwards)* **g. back!** ¡atrás!

2 *vt (recover) (money, strength, etc)* recuperar; *Fam* **to g. one's own back on sb** vengarse de algn

get behind *vi* atrasarse

get by *vi* **(a)** *(manage)* arreglárselas; **she can g. by in French** sabe defenderse en francés **(b)** *(pass)* pasar; **let me g. by** déjame pasar

get down 1 *vt (depress)* deprimir; **don't let it g. you down** no te desanimes

2 *vi (descend)* bajar; **g. down off the table!** ¡bájate de la mesa!; **to g. down on one's knees** arrodillarse

get down to *vt* ponerse a; **to g. down to work** ponerse a trabajar; **to g. down to the facts** ir al grano

get in 1 *vi* **(a)** *(arrive)* llegar; **when the train gets in** cuando llegue el tren **(b)** *Pol* ser elegido(a); **the labour party got in at the last elections** el partido laborista ganó las últimas elecciones

2 *vt* **(a)** *(buy)* comprar; **to g. in a supply of sth** hacer provisión de algo **(b)** *(collect)* recoger, recolectar; **they wanted to g. the harvest in** querían recoger la cosecha; *Fam* **he couldn't g. a word in edgeways** no pudo meter baza

get into *vt* **(a)** *Pol* **to g. into parliament** ser elegido(a) diputado(a) **(b)** *Fig* **to g. into bad habits** adquirir malas costumbres; **to g. into trouble** meterse en un lío; *Fam* **what's got into him?** ¿qué mosca le ha picado?

get off 1 *vt* **(a)** *(bus, train, etc)* bajarse de **(b)** *(remove)* quitar(se), *Andes RP* sacar; **he couldn't g. the paint off his trousers** no podía quitar *or Andes RP* sacar la pintura de los pantalones; *Fig* **to g. sth off one's hands** quitarse algo de encima

2 *vi* **(a)** *(descend from vehicle)* bajarse; **he got off the table** se bajó de la mesa; *Fam* **to tell sb where to g. off** mandar a algn a hacer puñetas; *Fam* **g. off!** ¡fuera! **(b)** *(depart)* salir; **I must be getting off now** tengo que irme **(c)** *(begin)*

empezar; **to g. off to a good start** empezar bien *or* con buen pie; *Fig* **I couldn't g. off to sleep** no pude conciliar el sueño **(d)** *(escape)* escaparse; **to g. off lightly** salir bien librado(a)

get off with *vt Br* ligar con; **Richard got off with Anne on Saturday night** Richard ligó con Anne el sábado por la noche

get on 1 *vt (board)* subir a, subirse a

2 *vi* **(a)** *(board)* subirse **(b)** *(make progress)* hacer progresos; *(succeed)* tener éxito; **how are you getting on?** ¿qué tal estás?, ¿cómo te van las cosas? **(c)** *(have good relationship)* llevarse bien; **to g. on well with sb** llevarse bien con algn; **we g. on well together** nos entendemos muy bien **(d)** *(continue)* seguir; **to g. on with one's work** seguir trabajando **(e)** *(time)* **it's getting on for eleven** son casi las once; **she's getting on in years** está envejeciendo; **time's getting on** se está haciendo tarde

get on to *vt* **(a)** *(find a person)* localizar; **you should g. on to her straight away** deberías localizarla enseguida, deberías ponerte en contacto con ella enseguida **(b)** *(continue)* pasar a; **let's now g. on to the question of pay** ahora tratemos la cuestión de dinero

get out 1 *vt (object)* sacar; *(nail)* arrancar; *(stain)* quitar, *Andes RP* sacar

2 *vi* **(a)** *(room, building, etc)* salir **(of** de); *(train)* bajar, bajarse **(of** de) **(b)** *(escape)* escaparse **(of** de); **to g. out of an obligation** librarse de un compromiso **(c)** *(stop)* **to g. out of the habit of doing sth** perder la costumbre de hacer algo **(d)** *(news etc)* difundirse; *(secret)* hacerse público

get over *vt* **(a)** *(recover from) (illness)* recuperarse de; *(loss)* sobreponerse a; **I can't g. over him** no le puedo olvidar; **you'll g. over it** con el tiempo se te pasará **(b)** *(overcome) (obstacle)* salvar; *(difficulty)* vencer **(c)** *(convey)* hacer comprender, comunicar

get over with *vt* acabar; **to g. sth over with** acabar con algo

get round 1 *vt* **(a)** *(problem)* salvar; *(difficulty)* vencer **(b)** *(rule, law)* soslayar, evitar **(c)** *(win over)* persuadir, convencer; **she knows how to g. round him** sabe cómo llevarlo

2 *vi (news)* difundirse; **if news gets round about this, we'll suffer** si se difunden noticias sobre esto, tendremos problemas

get round to *vi* **to. g. round to doing sth** llegar a hacer algo; **if I g. round to it** si tengo tiempo

get through 1 *vi* **(a)** *(message, news)* llegar **(b)** *Educ* aprobar; *Sport* **to g. through to the final** llegar a la final **(c)** *Tel* **to g. through to sb** conseguir comunicar con algn **(d)** *(law)* aprobar; **if this law gets through ...** si aprueban esta ley ...

2 *vt* **(a)** *(finish)* acabar, terminar; **to g. through a lot of work** trabajar mucho **(b)** *(consume)* consumir; **he got through fifty dollars in two days** se gastó cincuenta dólares en dos días; **we got through a bottle of milk** nos bebimos una botella entera de leche **(c)** *Educ (pass)* aprobar; **to g. through an exam** aprobar un examen **(d)** *(make understand)* hacer entender or comprender; **I can't g. it through to her that ...** no consigo hacerle comprender que ...

get together 1 *vi (people)* juntarse, reunirse

2 *vt* **(a)** *(people)* juntar, reunir; **he got them all together before making the announcement** reunió a todos antes de anunciarlo **(b)** *(assemble)* montar; **they got the machine together** consiguieron montar la máquina **(c)** *(money)* reunir; **they managed to g. enough money together to go on holiday** reunieron suficiente dinero para irse de vacaciones

get up 1 *vi (rise)* levantarse; **to g. up out of bed** levantarse de la cama

2 vt **(a)** *(wake up)* despertar; **get me up at six** despiértame a las seis **(b)** *(disguise)* **to g. oneself up as ...** disfrazarse de ..., vestirse de ...; **he was got up as a clown** iba disfrazado de payaso **(c)** *(organize)* montar, organizar

get up to vt hacer; **to g. up to mischief** hacer de las suyas; **what are they getting up to?** ¿qué estarán haciendo?

get-at-able [get'ætəbəl] adj Fam accesible

getaway ['getəwei] n fuga f; **to make one's g.** fugarse □ **g. car** coche m utilizado en una fuga

get-rich-quick ['get'rɪtʃ'kwɪk] adj Fam **a g. scheme** un proyecto para enriquecerse rápidamente

get-together ['getəgeðər] n *(meeting)* reunión f; *(party)* fiesta f

get-up ['getʌp] n Fam atuendo m, atavío m; *(disguise)* disfraz m

get-up-and-go [getʌpənd'gəʊ] n Fam *(energy)* dinamismo m, iniciativa f

get-well card [get'welkɑːd] n tarjeta f con la inscripción 'que te mejores'

geyser ['giːzə, US 'gaɪzər] n **(a)** Geog géiser m **(b)** *(water heater)* calentador m de agua

Ghana ['gɑːnə] n Ghana

Ghanian ['gɑːnɪən] adj & n, **Ghanaian** [gɑː'neɪən] adj & n ghanés(esa) (m,f)

ghastly ['gɑːstlɪ] adj **(ghastlier, ghastliest)** horrible, horroroso(a), espantoso(a), atroz

Ghent [gent] n Gante

gherkin ['gɜːkɪn] n pepinillo m

ghetto ['getəʊ] n *(pl* **ghettos** *or* **ghettoes)** ghetto m, gueto m □ **g. blaster** *(cassette player)* radiocasete m portátil *(de gran tamaño)*

ghost [gəʊst] **1** n **(a)** *(spirit)* fantasma m; Fig **not the g. of a chance** ni la más remota posibilidad; Fam **to give up the g.** entregar el alma □ **g. story** cuento m de fantasmas; **g. town** pueblo m abandonado or fantasma **(b)** Rel **the Holy G.** el Espíritu Santo

2 vt **to g. a book for sb** escribir un libro para algn

ghostly ['gəʊstlɪ] adj **(ghostlier, ghostliest)** fantasmal, espectral

ghost-write ['gəʊstraɪt] vt Lit escribir para otro, hacer de negro

ghost-writer ['gəʊstraɪtər] n Lit negro(a) m,f

ghoul [guːl] n **(a)** *(evil spirit)* espíritu m maligno **(b)** *(person)* persona f de gustos macabros

ghoulish ['guːlɪʃ] adj macabro(a)

GHQ [dʒiːeɪtʃ'kjuː] n *(abbr* **General Headquarters)** Cuartel m General

GHz Elec *(abbr* **gigahertz)** GHz

GI [dʒiː'aɪ] n US Fam soldado m raso

giant ['dʒaɪənt] **1** n gigante m

2 adj gigante, gigantesco(a) □ **g. panda** (oso m) panda m, panda m gigante

Gib [dʒɪb] n Fam *(abbr* **Gibraltar)** Gibraltar

gibbering ['dʒɪbərɪŋ] adj incoherente, desvariado(a); Fam **a g. idiot** un perfecto idiota

gibberish ['dʒɪbərɪʃ] n galimatías m inv

gibbet ['dʒɪbɪt] n horca f

gibbon ['gɪbən] n Zool gibón m

gibe [dʒaɪb] **1** n mofa f, comentario m sarcástico, sarcasmo m

2 vi mofarse **(at** de), burlarse **(at** de)

giblets ['dʒɪblɪts] npl menudillos mpl

Gibraltar [dʒɪ'brɔːltər] n Gibraltar; **the Rock of G.** el Peñón de Gibraltar; **the Straits of G.** el Estrecho de Gibraltar

Gibraltarian [dʒɪbrɔːl'teərɪən] adj & n gibraltareño(a) (m,f)

giddiness ['gɪdɪnɪs] n mareo m, vértigo m

giddy ['gɪdɪ] adj **(giddier, giddiest)** mareado(a); **it makes me g.** me da vértigo; **to feel g.** sentirse mareado(a)

GIF [dʒɪf] n Comptr *(abbr* **Graphics Interchange Format)** GIF m, formato m de intercambio de gráficos

gift [gɪft] n **(a)** *(present)* regalo m; Com obsequio m **(b)** *(give-away)* ganga f; **g. shop** tienda f de artículos de regalo; Br **g. token** vale m; **that car was a g. at that price** ese coche te ha salido que ni regalado; Fam Fig **he thinks he's God's g.** se cree el Rey del Mambo; Prov **never look a g. horse in the mouth** a caballo regalado no le mires el diente **(c)** *(talent)* don m; **to have a g. for music** estar muy dotado(a) para la música; Fam **to have the g. of the gab** tener un pico de oro

gifted ['gɪftɪd] adj dotado(a)

gift-wrapped ['gɪftræpt] adj envuelto(a) para regalo

gig [gɪg] n Slang Mus actuación f

gigabyte ['dʒɪgəbaɪt, gigəbait] n Comptr gigabyte m

gigahertz ['dʒɪgəhɜːts, 'gɪgəhɜːts] n Elec gigahercio m

gigantic [dʒaɪ'gæntɪk] adj gigantesco(a), descomunal

giggle ['gɪgəl] **1** n **(a)** *(chuckle)* risita f, risa f tonta; **I got the giggles** me dio la risa **(b)** esp Br *(lark)* broma f, diversión f; **the film's a right g.** la película es divertida; **we all dressed up like clowns for a g.** nos disfrazamos de payaso para reír un rato

2 vi reírse tontamente

giggly ['gɪglɪ] adj **two g. girls at the back of the class** dos niñas soltando risitas al fondo de la clase

gigolo ['dʒɪgələʊ] n *(pl* **gigolos)** gigolo m

gild [gɪld] vt *(pt & pp* **gilded** or **gilt)** dorar; Fig **to g. the lily** *(gen)* sobrecargar; *(decoration)* poner demasiadas florituras a

gill¹ [dʒɪl] n *(measurement)* cuarto m de pinta *(≃ 0,142 litros)*

gill² [gɪl] n *(of fish)* branquia f, agalla f; Fam **to look pale** or **green about the gills** tener mala cara

gilt [gɪlt] **1** pt & pp see **gild**

2 adj dorado(a)

3 n *(colour)* dorado m

gilt-edged ['gɪltedʒd] adj Fin **g.-e. securities** or **stock** Br títulos mpl de deuda pública, valores mpl del Estado; US valores mpl de máxima garantía

gimlet ['gɪmlɪt] n Tech barrena f de cola, broca f

gimmick ['gɪmɪk] n *(action)* truco m; *(device)* reclamo m; **advertising g.** reclamo m publicitario

gimmicky ['gɪmɪkɪ] adj con truco, superficial

gin [dʒɪn] n ginebra f; **g. and tonic** gin tonic m

ginger ['dʒɪndʒər] **1** n **(a)** Bot jengibre m; **g. ale** ginger ale m **(b)** Pol **g. group** grupo m de presión

2 adj **(a)** *(flavour)* de jengibre **(b)** *(hair)* pelirrojo(a)

gingerbread ['dʒɪndʒəbred] n pan m o galleta f de jengibre

gingerly ['dʒɪndʒəlɪ] adv cautelosamente

gingernut ['dʒɪndʒənʌt] n galleta f de jengibre

gingersnap ['dʒɪndʒəsnæp] n US galleta f de jengibre

gingham ['gɪŋəm] n Tex guinga f, guingán m

gingivitis [dʒɪndʒɪ'vaɪtɪs] n Med gingivitis f

gipsy ['dʒɪpsɪ] adj & n gitano(a) (m,f)

giraffe [dʒɪ'rɑːf] n Zool jirafa f

gird [gɜːd] vt *(pt & pp* **girded** or **girt)** **(a)** *(fasten)* ceñir **(b)**

to g. oneself (up) *(for fight etc)* prepararse; *Fig* **to g. up one's loins** prepararse para la lucha **(c)** *(encircle)* rodear

girder ['gɜːdər] *n Constr* viga *f*

girdle ['gɜːdəl] **1** *n* **(a)** *(clothes)* faja *f* **(b)** *Anat* pelvic g. pelvis *f*
2 *vt Literary* rodear

girl [gɜːl] *n* **(a)** *(gen)* chica *f*, muchacha *f*, joven *f*; *(child)* niña *f*; **g. Friday** chica *f* para todo; *Br* **g. guide** *US* **g. scout** exploradora *f* **(b)** *(daughter)* hija *f* **(c)** *(pupil)* alumna *f*; **old girls' reunion** reunión *f* de las antiguas alumnas **(d)** *(sweetheart)* novia *f*

girlfriend ['gɜːlfrend] *n* **(a)** *(fiancée)* novia *f* **(b)** *(companion)* amiga *f*, compañera *f*

girlhood ['gɜːlhʊd] *n (childhood)* niñez *f*; *(youth)* juventud *f*

girlie ['gɜːlɪ] *adj Fam* **g. magazines** revistas *fpl* de destape

girlish ['gɜːlɪʃ] *adj* **(a)** *(of girl)* de niña **(b)** *(effeminate)* afeminado(a)

giro ['dʒaɪrəʊ] *n Br* giro *m* (postal) ❏ **g. account** cuenta *f* de giros postales; **g. (cheque)** cheque *m* de giros postales

girt [gɜːt] *pt & pp see* **gird**

girth [gɜːθ] *n (of tree)* contorno *m*; *(of person)* barriga *f*

gist [dʒɪst] *n* esencia *f*; **the g.** lo esencial; **did you get the g. of what he was saying?** ¿cogiste la idea de lo que decía?; **the g. of the matter** el quid de la cuestión

give [gɪv] **1** *n (elasticity)* elasticidad *f*
2 *vt (pt* **gave**; *pp* **given) (a)** *(gen)* dar; **to g. a cry** lanzar un grito; **to g. a sigh** dar un suspiro; **to g. a start** asustarse, pegar un salto; **to g. sth a shake** sacudir algo **(b)** *(deliver, pass on)* entregar; *Tel* **could you please g. me** Anne Smith póngame con Anne Smith, por favor; **g. him our love** dale un abrazo de nuestra parte; **to g. sb a message** dar un recado a algn; **to g. sb a present** regalar algo a algn; **to g. sth to sb** dar algo a algn **(c)** *(provide)* dar, suministrar; **to g. sb sth to eat** dar de comer a algn; **to g. sb one's support** apoyar a algn; *(pay)* pagar, dar; **how much did he g. for it?** ¿cuánto pagó por ello?; *Fig* **I'd g. anything to go** daría cualquier cosa por poder ir **(e)** *(perform etc) (concert)* dar; *(speech)* pronunciar; **g. us a song!** ¡cántanos algo! **(f)** *(dedicate)* dedicar, consagrar; **to g. some thought to a matter** reflexionar sobre un asunto **(g)** *(grant)* otorgar; **to g. sb one's attention** prestar atención a algn **(h)** *(cause)* ocasionar, causar; **to g. sb to understand that ...** dar a entender a algn que ... **(i)** *(yield)* ceder; *Fam* **I'll g. you that** te doy la razón **(j)** **to g. way** *Aut* ceder el paso; *Fig* ceder, concedcr; *(ground)* hundirse; *(ladder)* romperse; *(legs)* doblarse; **'g. way'** ceda el paso' **(k)** *(expressions) Fam* **don't g. me that!** ¡no me vengas con esas!; *Fam* **g. me English cooking every time** para mí no hay nada como la cocina inglesa; *Fam* **I'll g. you (what for)!** ¡te vas a enterar!
3 *vi* **(a)** *(concede)* **to g. and take** hacer concesiones mutuas; **to g. as good as one gets** devolver golpe por golpe **(b)** *(yield)* ceder; *(cloth, elastic)* dar de sí

give away *vt* **(a)** *(gen)* distribuir, repartir; *(present)* regalar; *(prize)* entregar; *Fam Fig* **to g. the bride away** llevar a la novia al altar **(b)** *(disclose, divulge)* revelar, descubrir; **to g. the game away** descubrir el pastel **(c)** *(betray)* traicionar, denunciar; **his smile gave him away** su sonsrisa le traicionó

give back *vt (return)* devolver

give in 1 *vi* **(a)** *(admit defeat)* darse por vencido(a); *(surrender)* rendirse; **I g. in!** ¡me rindo! **(b)** *(yield)* ceder; **to g. in to** ceder ante
2 *vt (hand in)* entregar

give off *vt (smell, heat, etc)* despedir, emitir

give onto *vt* dar a; **her apartment gives onto a rubbish tip** su piso da a un vertedero de basuras

give out 1 *vt* **(a)** *(distribute)* distribuir, repartir **(b)** *(announce)* anunciar
2 *vi (supplies)* agotarse; *(break down)* sufrir una avería; *Fam Fig* **my patience is giving out** se me está acabando la paciencia

give over 1 *vt (hand over)* entregar; *(devote)* dedicar; **land given over to agriculture** terreno dedicado a la agricultura
2 *vi Br Fam* **g. over!** ¡basta ya!

give up 1 *vt* **(a)** *(renounce)* dejar; *(idea)* abandonar, renunciar a; **to g. up smoking** dejar de fumar **(b)** *(betray)* traicionar; **my friends would never g. me up** mis amigos nunca me traicionarían **(c)** *(one's life)* dar; **many young men gave up their lives for their country** muchos jovenes dieron su vida por el país **(d)** *(abandon)* **the victims were given up for dead** se dieron las víctimas por muertas
2 *vi* **(a)** *(admit defeat)* darse por vencido(a), rendirse; **don't g. up** no te desanimes; **I g. up!** ¡me rindo! **(b)** *(hand over)* entregar; **to g. oneself up to the police** entregarse a la policía

give up on *vt* **he gave up on the idea of becoming a successful writer** abandonó la idea de ser un escritor famoso

give up to *vt* **to g. oneself up to** dedicarse enteramente a; **she gave her whole life up to helping the needy** entregó su vida a ayudar a los necesitados

give-and-take ['gɪvən'teɪk] *n* toma y daca *m*

giveaway ['gɪvəweɪ] *n* **(a)** *(disclosure)* revelación *f* involuntaria; *Fam* **it's a dead g.** salta a la vista **(b)** *(gift)* regalo *m*; **g. price** precio *m* de saldo; **when I bought that I got a chocolate as a g.** cuando compré esto me dieron una chocolatina de regalo

given ['gɪvən] **1** *pp see* **give**
2 *adj* **(a)** *(particular, fixed)* dado(a); **at a g. time** en un momento determinado; *US* **g. name** nombre *m* de pila **(b)** *(inclined, prone)* **g. to** dado(a) a, propenso(a) a
3 *conj* **(a)** *(considering)* dado(a); **g. his resources, he's done pretty well** teniendo en cuenta sus medios lo ha hecho bastante bien **(b)** *(if)* si; **g. the chance, he could do just as well as the others** si tuviera la oportunidad, lo podría hacer tan bien como los otros

gizmo ['gɪzməʊ] *n Br Fam* chisme *m*

gizzard ['gɪzəd] *n (of bird)* molleja *f*

Gk *(abbr* **Greek)** griego(a) *m,f*

glacé ['glæseɪ] *adj Culin* confitado(a), escarchado(a), *Col Méx* cristalizado(a), *RP* abrillantado(a) **g. cherry** cereza *f* confitada

glacial ['gleɪsɪəl] *adj* **(a)** *Geol* glaciar; **g. deposits** depósitos *mpl* glaciares **(b)** *(icy)* glacial; *Fig (cold)* glacial; **g. wind** viento *m* glacial; *Fig* **g. look** mirada *f* glacial

glacier ['glæsɪər] *n Geol* glaciar *m*

glad [glæd] *adj* **(gladder, gladdest)** *(delighted)* contento(a); *(happy)* alegre; **he'll be only too g. to help you** tendrá mucho gusto en ayudarle; **I'm g. you came** me alegro de que hayas venido; **to be g.** alegrarse ❏ **g. rags** ropa *f* sing de fiesta

gladden ['glædən] *vt* alegrar

glade [gleɪd] *n (clearing)* claro *m*; **a g. in the forest** un claro en el bosque

gladiator ['glædɪeɪtər] *n Hist* gladiador *m*

gladiolus [glædɪ'əʊləs] *n (pl* **gladioli** [glædɪ'əʊlaɪ]) *Bot* gladiolo *m*

gladly ['glædlɪ] *adv* con mucho gusto

gladness ['glædnɪs] *(delight)* satisfacción *f*; *(happiness)* alegría *f*

glamor ['glæmər] *n US see* **glamour**

glamorize ['glæmərɑɪz] *vt* embellecer, hacer más atractivo(a); **films can sometimes g. war** en algunas ocasiones, el cine puede hacer que la guerra resulte atractiva

glamorous ['glæmərəs] *adj* **(a)** *(attractive, stunning)* atractivo(a), encantador(a); **his wife looked very g. in her silk dress** su esposa estaba muy llamativa con el vestido de seda **(b)** *(fashionable)* prestigioso(a); **the group played many g. venues** el grupo actuó en muchos locales prestigiosos

glamour ['glæmər] *n* **(a)** *(attraction)* atractivo *m*; *(charm)* encanto *m*; **a g. girl** una belleza, un bombón, *Am* una muñequita **(b)** *(beauty)* belleza *f* sofisticada

glance [glɑːns] **1** *n* mirada *f*, vistazo *m*, ojeada *f*; **at a g.** de un vistazo; **at first g.** a primera vista

2 *vi* **(a)** *(look)* echar una mirada *or* un vistazo *or* una ojeada **(at** a); **to g. sideways** mirar de reojo **(b)** *(newspaper etc)* **to g. through** ojear

glance off *vt (ball etc)* rebotar de

glancing ['glɑːnsɪŋ] *adj (blow)* oblicuo(a)

gland [glænd] *n Anat* glándula *f*

glandular ['glændjʊlər] *adj* glandular □ *Med* **g. fever** mononucleosis *f* infecciosa

glare [gleər] **1** *n* **(a)** *(light)* luz *f* deslumbrante; *Aut (dazzle)* deslumbramiento *m* **(b)** *(look)* mirada *f* feroz

2 *vi* **(a)** *(dazzle)* deslumbrar **(b)** *(look)* lanzar una mirada furiosa, mirar airadamente **(at** a)

glaring ['gleərɪŋ] *adj* **(a)** *(light)* deslumbrante; *(colour)* chillón(ona) **(b)** *(obvious)* evidente; **a g. mistake** un error que salta a la vista

glass [glɑːs] *n (pl* **glasses) (a)** *(material)* vidrio *m*, *Esp* cristal *m*; **pane of g.** cristal *m*; *Prov* **people who live in g. houses shouldn't throw stones** el que esté libre de pecado que tire la pimera piedra □ **cut g.** cristal *m* tallado; **g. bead** abalorio *m*; **g. case** campana *f* de cristal; *Fig* **g. ceiling** *(in career)* barreras *fpl* laborales *or* profesionales; **g. door** puerta *f* de cristal; **g. eye** ojo *m* de vidrio *or Esp* cristal; **g. fibre** fibra *f* de vidrio; **g. industry** industria *f* del vidrio; **stained g.** vidrio *m* de color **(b)** *(drinking vessel)* vaso *m*; **a g. of water** un vaso de agua; **wine g.** copa *f* (para vino) **(c)** *Old-fashioned* **looking g.** espejo *m* **(d)** *(barometer)* barómetro *m* **(e)** **glasses** gafas *fpl*, *Am* anteojos *mpl*, *Am* lentes *mpl*; **to wear g.** llevar gafas □ **field g.** gemelos *mpl*

glass-blower ['glɑːsbləʊər] *n* soplador(a) *m,f* de vidrio

glass-blowing ['glɑːsbləʊɪŋ] *n* soplado *m* de vidrio

glasshouse ['glɑːshaʊs] *n Br* **(a)** *Hortic* invernadero *m* **(b)** *Slang Mil* prisión *f* militar

glassware ['glɑːsweər] *n* cristalería *f*

glassworks ['glɑːswɜːks] *n* fábrica *f* de vidrio

glassy ['glɑːsɪ] *adj* **(glassier, glassiest) (a)** *(like glass)* vítreo(a); *(water)* cristalino(a) **(b)** *Fig (eyes)* vidrioso(a)

glaucoma [glɔːˈkəʊmə] *n Med* glaucoma *m*

glaze [gleɪz] **1** *(varnish)* barniz *m*; *(for pottery)* vidriado *m*

2 *vt* **(a)** *(windows)* poner cristales a **(b)** *(varnish)* barnizar; *(ceramics)* vidriar **(c)** *Culin* glasear

glazed [gleɪzd] *adj (eyes)* de mirada ausente

glazier ['gleɪzɪər] *n* vidriero(a) *m,f*

glazing ['gleɪzɪŋ] *n* cristales *mpl*; **double g.** doble cristal *m*

gleam [gliːm] **1** *n (of light)* destello *m*; *Fig* **a g. of hope** un rayo de esperanza

2 *vi* brillar, relucir

gleaming ['gliːmɪŋ] *adj* brillante, reluciente

glean [gliːn] *vt* **(a)** *Agr* espigar **(b)** *Fig (cull)* recoger, cosechar; **we gleaned very little information from the lecture** pudimos extraer muy poca información de la conferencia

glee [gliː] *n* **(a)** *(delight)* alegría *f*, júbilo *m*, regocijo *m* **(b)** *Mus* **g. club** coral *f*

gleeful ['gliːfʊl] *adj* alegre, jubiloso(a)

gleefully ['gliːfʊlɪ] *adv* con alegría, con júbilo

glen [glen] *n Scot Ir Geog* cañada *f*

glib [glɪb] *adj* **(glibber, glibbest)** *Pej (person)* con mucha labia, *CAm Ecuad Méx* labioso(a)

glibly ['glɪblɪ] *adv* con labia

glide [glaɪd] *vi* **(a)** *(slip, slide)* deslizarse **(b)** *Av* planear

glider ['glaɪdər] *n Av* planeador *m*

gliding ['glaɪdɪŋ] *n Av* planeo *m*; *Sport* vuelo *m* sin motor

glimmer ['glɪmər] **1** *n* **(a)** *(light)* luz *f* tenue **(b)** *(reflection)* reflejo *m* **(c)** *Fig (trace)* resquicio *m*, indicio *m*; **g. of hope** resquicio de esperanza

2 *vi* **(a)** *(shine)* brillar tenuemente **(b)** *(water)* espejear, relucir

glimpse [glɪmps] **1** *n* vislumbre *f*, visión *f* momentánea; **to catch a g. of** vislumbrar

2 *vt (catch sight of)* vislumbrar, entrever; *(perceive)* darse cuenta de, comprender; **he glimpsed a difficult week ahead** vio que le esperaba una semana muy difícil

glint [glɪnt] **1** *n (twinkle)* destello *m*, centelleo *m*; **he had a g. in his eye** le brillaban los ojos

2 *vi (glisten)* destellar, centellear

glisten ['glɪsən] *vi* relucir, brillar

glitter ['glɪtər] **1** *n* brillo *m*

2 *vi* relucir, brillar; *Prov* **all that glitters is not gold** no es oro todo lo que reluce

glitterati [glɪtəˈrɑːtɪ] *npl Fam* famosos *mpl*, *Esp* gente *f* guapa, *Méx* popis *mpl*, *RP* crema *f*

glittering ['glɪtərɪŋ] *adj* reluciente, brillante, resplandeciente

glitz [glɪts] *n* boato *m*, pompa *f*

gloat [gləʊt] *vi* jactarse; **to g. over** *(news)* saborear; **to g. over another's misfortune** recrearse con la desgracia de otro

global ['gləʊbəl] *adj* **(a)** *(of the world)* mundial □ **g. economy** economía *f* global; **g. warming** cambio *m* climático, calentamiento *m* global **(b)** *(overall)* global; **g. view** vista *f* global, vista *f* de conjunto

globalization [gləʊbəlɑɪˈzeɪʃən] *n* mundialización *f*, globalización *f*

globe [gləʊb] *n* **(a)** *(sphere)* esfera *f*, bola *f* **(b)** *(earth)* globo *m* terrestre; *(model)* globo *m* (terráqueo)

globe-trotter ['gləʊbtrɒtər] *n* trotamundos *mf inv*

globular ['glɒbjʊlər] *adj* globular

globule ['glɒbjuːl] *n (droplet)* glóbulo *m*

gloom [gluːm] *n* **(a)** *(obscurity)* penumbra *f* **(b)** *(melancholy)* melancolía *f*, tristeza *f* **(c)** *(pessimism)* desolación *f*, pesimismo *m*

gloomy ['gluːmɪ] *adj* **(gloomier, gloomiest) (a)** *(dark)* oscuro(a), tenebroso(a); *(weather)* gris **(b)** *(dismal)* deprimente **(c)** *(despondent)* pesimista, desalentador(a); *(sad)* melancólico(a), triste; **the future looks g.** el futuro pinta negro; **to feel g.** verlo todo negro

glorified ['glɔːrɪfaɪd] *adj Pej* pretencioso(a); **the castle was just a g. old house** resultó ser una casa con pretensiones de castillo

glorify ['glɔːrɪfaɪ] *vt (pt & pp* **glorified)** *(God)* glorificar; *(extol)* alabar

glorious ['glɔːrɪəs] *adj (momentous)* glorioso(a); *(splendid)* magnífico(a), espléndido(a); **the weather is g. at the moment** hace un tiempo espléndido

glory ['glɔːrɪ] **1** *n (gen)* gloria *f*; *Fig (splendour)* esplendor *m*; *Fig (triumph)* triunfo *m*; **to be in one's g.** estar en la gloria; **to live on past glories** vivir de glorias pasadas
2 *vi (pt & pp gloried)* **to g. in sth** jactarse de algo

gloss [glɒs] **1** *n* (**a**) *(explanation)* glosa *f* (**b**) *(sheen)* brillo *m*; *Fig (polish)* lustre *m* ❑ **g. (paint)** pintura *f* brillante *or* esmalte
2 *vi* glosar

gloss over *vt Fig* encubrir

glossary ['glɒsərɪ] *n* glosario *m*

glossy ['glɒsɪ] *adj* (**glossier, glossiest**) lustroso(a), brillante ❑ *Press* **g. magazine** revista *f* de lujo

glottal stop ['glɒtəl'stɒp] *n* oclusión *f* glotal

glottis ['glɒtɪs] *n Anat* glotis *f*

glove [glʌv] *n* guante *m*; *Fig* **to fit like a g.** sentar como un guante ❑ *Aut* **g. compartment** guantera *f*; *Br* **g. puppet** polichinela *f*, pulchinela *f*

glow [gləʊ] **1** *n* (**a**) *(of jewel)* brillo *m*; *(of fire, metal)* incandescencia *f*; *(of sun)* arrebol *m*; *(heat)* calor *m*; *(light)* luz *f* (**b**) *(in cheeks)* rubor *m* (**c**) *Fig (thrill)* bienestar *m*, satisfacción *f*
2 *vi* (**a**) *(jewel, sun)* brillar; *(fire)* arder; *(metal)* estar al rojo vivo (**b**) *Fig* **to. g. with** rebosar de; **to g. with health** rebosar de salud

glower ['glaʊər] *vi* poner cara de enfadado(a), fruncir el ceño

glowing ['gləʊɪŋ] *adj* (**a**) *(fire, metal)* incandescente; *(metal)* al rojo vivo; *(fire, colour)* vivo(a); *(light)* brillante (**b**) *(cheeks)* encendido(a) (**c**) *(report)* entusiasta; *(style)* cálido(a)

glowworm ['gləʊwɜːm] *n Zool* luciérnaga *f*, gusano *m* de luz

glucose ['gluːkəʊz] *n Chem* glucosa *f*

glue [gluː] **1** *n* pegamento *m*, cola *f*; *(drug)* **to sniff g.** inhalar cola
2 *vt* pegar (**to** a); **to g. sth together** pegar algo; *Fam Fig* **his eyes were glued to the screen** tenía los ojos pegados a la pantalla

glue-sniffing ['gluːsnɪfɪŋ] *n* inhalación *f* de cola

glum [glʌm] *adj* (**glummer, glummest**) triste, abatido(a), desanimado(a); **don't look so g.** no estés tan serio

glumly ['glʌmlɪ] *adv* con desánimo

glut [glʌt] **1** *n* superabundancia *f*, exceso *m*
2 *vt* (*pt & pp* **glutted**) (**a**) *(swamp)* saturar; **the market is glutted with hifi equipment** el mercado está invadido de equipos de alta fidelidad (**b**) **to g. oneself with** *or* **on** *(overeat)* hartarse or saciarse de

gluten ['gluːtən] *n* gluten *m*

gluten-free ['gluːtən'friː] *adj* sin gluten

glutinous ['gluːtɪnəs] *adj* pegajoso(a), glutinoso(a)

glutton ['glʌtən] *n* glotón(ona) *m,f*; *Fam Fig* **he's a g. for punishment, he studies ten hours a day** es un masoquista, estudia diez horas cada día; *Fam Fig* **to be a g. for work** ser un trabajador incansable

gluttonous ['glʌtənəs] *adj* glotón(ona), goloso(a)

gluttony ['glʌtənɪ] *n* glotonería *f*, gula *f*

glycerine, *US* **glycerin** ['glɪsərɪn] *n* glicerina *f*

GM [dʒiː'em] *adj* (*abbr* **genetically modified**) transgénico(a), modificado(a) genéticamente; **GM food** (alimentos *mpl*) transgénicos *mpl*

gm (*abbr* **gram**) gramo *m*, gr

GMT [dʒiːem'tiː] *n* (*abbr* **Greenwich Mean Time**) Hora *f* media de Greenwich, GMT

gnarled [nɑːld] *adj* nudoso(a)

gnash [næʃ] *vt* **to g. one's teeth** hacer rechinar los dientes

gnat [næt] *n* mosquito *m*

gnaw [nɔː] *vt & vi (chew)* roer; *Fig (nag)* corroer; **he had a great sense of sadness gnawing away inside** una terrible sensación de tristeza le corroía por dentro

gnawing ['nɔːɪŋ] *adj (hunger, anxiety)* constante; *(pain)* insistente

gnome [nəʊm] *n* gnomo *m*

GNP [dʒiːen'piː] *n Econ* (*abbr* **gross national product**) producto *m* nacional bruto, PNB *m*

go [gəʊ] **1** *vi* (*3rd person sing pres* **goes**; *pt* **went**; *pp* **gone**) (**a**) *(gen)* ir; **to come and go** ir y venir; **to go by car/by train/on foot** ir en coche/en tren/a pie; **to go for a walk** (ir a) dar un paseo; **to g. on a journey** ir de viaje; **to go shopping** ir de compras; **to go to Scotland** ir a Escocia; **to go to the cinema** ir al cine; **you go first** vete tú primero; *Fig* **to go too far** ir demasiado lejos, pasarse (de la raya); *Fig* **I wouldn't go so far as to say that** yo no diría tanto (**b**) *(depart)* irse, marcharse; *(train, bus)* salir; **let's go!** ¡vámonos!; **we must be going** tenemos que irnos; *Sport* **ready, steady, go!** ¡preparados, listos, ya! (**c**) *(disappear)* desaparecer; **her voice has gone** se ha quedado afónica; **my umbrella has gone** ha desaparecido mi paraguas; **these flowers will have to go** habrá que tirar estas flores (**d**) *(function)* funcionar, marchar; *(car)* **it goes at fifty miles an hour** alcanza las cincuenta millas por hora; **to make an engine go** hacer funcionar un motor; *Fig* **to get things going** poner las cosas en marcha; *Fig* **to keep going** mantenerse a flote (**e**) *(sell)* venderse; **going, going, gone!** ¡a la una, a las dos, a las tres!; **it went for $250** se vendió por 250 dólares; **shoes going cheap** zapatos a precios de rebaja (**f**) *(become)* quedarse, volverse; **to go blind** quedarse ciego(a); **to go mad** volverse loco(a); **to go red** ruborizarse (**g**) *(progress)* ir, marchar, andar; **everything went well** todo salió bien; **how did the meeting go?** ¿qué tal la reunión?; **how's it going?** ¿cómo va todo?, qué tal te van las cosas?; **I hope it goes well for you** que te vaya bien; **the way things are going** tal como van las cosas (**h**) *(future)* **to be going to** *(in the future)* ir a; *(be on the point of)* estar a punto de; **she's just going to leave** va a salir; **we were just going to do it now** estábamos a punto de hacerlo (**i**) *(fit)* caber; **it won't go into the box** no cabe en la caja; **three into two won't go** dos dividido entre tres no cabe (**j**) *(be kept)* guardarse; **where do the cups go?** ¿dónde se guardan las tazas? (**k**) *(be available)* quedar; **I'll take whatever's going** me conformo con lo que hay; **is there any tea going?** ¿queda algo de té?; **there are few jobs going** hay poco trabajo (**l**) *(be acceptable)* valer; **anything goes** todo vale, todo está permitido; **that goes without saying** eso es evidente (**m**) *(break)* romperse; *(yield)* ceder; *(blow)* fundirse; **the fuses went** se fundieron los plomos; **to go at the seams** descoserse (**n**) *(make) (noise, gesture)* hacer; **go like this with your hands** haz así con las manos; **how does that song go?** ¿cómo hace aquella canción?; **it went bang** hizo pum (**o**) *(time)* pasar; **it's just gone seven** acaban de dar las siete; **there are only two weeks to go** sólo (nos) quedan dos semanas; **time goes (by) so quickly** el tiempo pasa volando; *Fam* **she's six months gone** está embarazada de seis meses (**p**) *(be won)* **the prize went to Paul** el premio fue a parar a Paul (**q**) *(be inherited)* pasar (**to** a); **the house went to her daughter** la casa pasó a su hija (**r**) *(say)* decir; **and I went ...** y yo dije ...; **as the saying goes** según el dicho; **there he goes again** otra vez con la misma canción (**s**) *(release)* **to let sth go** soltar algo; *Fam Fig* **to let oneself go** *(lose inhibitions)* dejarse llevar; *(neglect appearance)* descuidarse (**t**) *(have a turn)* **it's my turn to go** ahora me toca a mí (**u**) *US* **to go** *(to take away)* para llevar

2 vt (**a**) (travel, cover) hacer, recorrer; **they went six miles** hicieron seis millas (**b**) **to go it alone** apañárselas solo; **to go one better than sb** superar a algn

3 n (**a**) (energy) energía f, dinamismo m; **he's always on the go** no para nunca; **it's all go!** ¡no hay quien pare!; **she's got lots of go** tiene mucha marcha (**b**) (try) intento m; **to have a go at sth** probar suerte con algo (**c**) (turn) turno m; **it's your go** te toca a ti (**d**) (success) **to make a go of sth** tener éxito en algo; **no go** nada que hacer (**e**) (fashion) moda f; **it's all the go** está muy de moda (**f**) (start) **I knew from the word go** lo sabía desde el principio (**g**) (criticism) **to have a go at sb** criticar a algn

go about 1 vt (**a**) (task) emprender; **how do you go about it?** ¿cómo hay que hacerlo? (**b**) (regular activity) continuar; **to go about one's business** ocuparse de sus asuntos

2 vi (**a**) (circulate) circular; (rumour) correr; (illness) haber, correr (**b**) Naut virar

go after vt (pursue) perseguir, andar tras

go against vt (oppose) ir en contra de; (verdict) ser desfavorable a

go ahead vi (**a**) (proceed) proceder; **go ahead!** ¡adelante!; **to go ahead with a scheme** llevar un proyecto adelante (**b**) (preceed) preceder; **we'll go on ahead** iremos delante

go along 1 vt (street etc) pasar por

2 vi (progress) progresar; **things are going along fine** las cosas van muy bien; Fam **I made it up as I went along** lo iba pensando a medida que lo hacía

go along with vt (**a**) (agree) estar de acuerdo con (**b**) (accompany) acompañar

go around vi (**a**) (rumour) correr; (illness) haber, correr (**b**) (suffice) llegar, haber; **there's enough to go around** hay para todos (**c**) (associate oneself) salir; **I don't like the people they go around with** no me gusta la gente con la que salen (**d**) (habit) estar continuamente; **she was always going around talking about people behind their backs** siempre estaba criticando a la gente a sus espaldas

go at vt Fig (attack) atacar; **he went at the wine** se abalanzó sobre el vino

go away vi marcharse

go back vi (**a**) (return) volver, regresar (**b**) Fig (date from) datar; **the church goes back to the Middle Ages** la iglesia data de la Edad Medieval

go back on vt (break) no cumplir; **to go back on one's word** faltar a su palabra

go back to vt (resume) volver a

go before vi (**a**) (precede) preceder (**b**) (in court) (person, matter) comparecer ante

go by vi (elapse) pasar; **as time goes by** con el tiempo; **in days gone by** en otros tiempos

go down vi (**a**) (gen) ir; (descend) bajar; (sun) ponerse; (ship) hundirse; **to go down on all fours** gatear (**b**) (tyre) desinflarse (**c**) (diminish) disminuir; (temperature) bajar; **to go down in value** perder su valor (**d**) (be received) ser acogido(a); **to go down well** ser bien acogido(a) (**e**) Br Univ dejar la universidad

go down as vi (be recorded, remembered) **this must go down as one of the worst days of my life** este día pasará a la historia como uno de los peores de mi vida

go down with vt (contract) agarrar, Esp coger; **to go down with flu** agarrar or Esp coger una gripe

go for vt (**a**) (attack) lanzarse sobre, atacar; Fam Fig **go for it!** ¡a por ello! (**b**) (fetch) intentar conseguir, Esp ir a por; (**c**) Fam (favour, like) **I don't go much for that** eso no me dice gran cosa (**d**) Fam valer para; **that goes for me too** esto también va por mí

go in vi (enter) entrar; (sun) esconderse

go in for vt (exam) presentarse a; (pastime, hobby) dedicarse a; Fam **we don't go in for that sort of thing** esas cosas no nos van

go into vt (**a**) (enter) entrar en; **to go into fits of laughter** troncharse de risa; **to go into journalism** dedicarse al periodismo (**b**) (study) examinar; (matter) investigar (**c**) (energy, money) invertirse en; **a lot of money went into the project** se invirtió mucho dinero en el proyecto (**d**) (crash) chocar; **my car went into yours** choqué contra tu coche or Am carro or CSur auto

go off 1 vi (**a**) (leave) irse, marcharse; Theat hacer mutis; **she went off to post a letter** salió a echar una carta (**b**) (bomb) explotar; (gun) dispararse; (alarm) sonar (**c**) (food) estropearse, pasarse; (milk) cortarse (**d**) (event) salir; **it went off very well** salió muy bien; **it went off without a hitch** transcurrió sin problemas (**e**) Fam (go to sleep) dormirse

2 vt Fam **to go off sth** perder el gusto or el interés por algo; **I've gone off him** ya no me gusta

go off with vt Fam (elope) escaparse con (un(a) amante)

go on vi (**a**) (continue) seguir, continuar; **after University she went on to work in the media** después de la universidad pasó a trabajar en los medios de comunicación; **this is enough to be going on with** de momento esto va bien así; Fam **to go on talking** seguir hablando; Fam **to go on and on about sth** machacar un tema; (complain) quejarse constantemente de algo; Fam **don't go on!** ¡no insistas!; Fam **she's always going on about it** siempre está con la misma canción; Fam **to go on at sb** dar el tostón a algn (**b**) (happen, take place) pasar, ocurrir; **what's going on?** ¿qué pasa? (**c**) (time) transcurrir, pasar; **as time goes on I get more impatient** a medida que pasa el tiempo me voy impacientando más (**d**) (light etc) encenderse; **the heating goes on automatically at eight o'clock** la calefacción se enciende automáticamente a las ocho (**e**) (age) estar a punto de cumplir; **he's sixteen going on seventeen** está a punto de cumplir los diecisiete (**f**) Fam **go on!** (incredulity) ¡no me digas!, ¡vaya!; (persuasion) ¡vamos!, Esp ¡venga!, Méx ¡ándale!, RP ¡dale!

go out vi (**a**) (leave) salir; **she doesn't go out much** apenas sale; **to go out for a meal** comer or cenar fuera; **to go out on strike** declararse en huelga (**b**) (boy and girl) salir juntos (**c**) (fire, light) apagarse (**d**) (tide) bajar (**e**) (información) propagarse; TV Rad transmitirse, retransmitirse; **the film goes out on Friday on BBC 1** la película se emite el viernes por el canal 1 de la BBC (**f**) **to go (all) out** (set out) ir a por todas; **they went all out to win** hicieron todo lo posible para ganar (**g**) Sport (cup-tie) perder la eliminatoria

go over 1 vt (revise) repasar; (examine) estudiar, examinar

2 vi (**a**) (approach) **to go over** to acercarse a; **they went over to help them** se acercaron para ayudarles **to go over to the enemy** pasarse al enemigo (**b**) (switch to) cambiar a, pasar a; **in the seventies we went over to the decimal system** en los años setenta pasamos a usar el sistema decimal

go round vi (**a**) (revolve) girar, dar vueltas (**b**) **to go round to sb's house** pasar por casa de algn

go through 1 vi (**a**) (bill, law) ser aprobado(a), (deal) ser concluido(a), ser llevado(a) a cabo (**b**) Sport (cup-tie) pasar la eliminatoria

2 vt (**a**) (examine) examinar; (search) registrar; **to go through sb's pockets** registrar los bolsillos a algn (**b**) (rehearse) ensayar (**c**) (spend) gastar; **he went through five hundred dollars on his holidays** se gastó quinientos dólares en sus vacaciones (**d**) (list, plan, story, etc) explicar (**e**) (endure) resistir, sufrir; **after their divorce they went**

through a lot lo pasaron muy mal después del divorcio

go through with vt llevar a cabo; **I don't think I can go through with this marriage** no creo que pueda llevar bien esto de la boda

go towards vi contribuir a; **this money will go towards the down payment for the house** este dinero se reserva para el pago de la casa

go under vi (a) (ship) hundirse (b) (business) fracasar

go up vi (a) (price, temperature, stairs) subir (b) Univ ingresar en la universidad (c) (approach) acercarse; **to go up to sb** acercarse a algn (d) (go) ir; **they always go up the pub before Sunday lunch** siempre van al pub los domingos a mediodía (e) (in a lift etc) subir (f) (explode) explotar; **the oil refinery could go up any minute** la refinería puede explotar en cualquier momento; **to go up in flames** ser pasto de las llamas (g) Theat (curtain) levantarse; **the curtain goes up at seven thirty** se levanta el telón a las siete y media (h) Sport (be promoted) subir, promocionarse; **United went up with City** el United se promocionó junto al City

go with vi (a) (accompany) ir con; **the car goes with the job** el coche va con el puesto (b) (colours) hacer juego con, armonizar con (c) Fam (sexually) ir con, dormir con

go without 1 vt (not have) prescindir de, quedarse sin
2 vi **if there's no bread we'll have to go without** tendremos que prescindir del pan si no lo hay

goad [gəʊd] vt aguijonear; **to g. sb into doing sth** acosar a algn para que haga algo

goad on vt (spur on) incitar

go-ahead [ˈgəʊəhed] Fam **1** n luz f verde; **to give sth/sb the go-a.** dar luz verde a algo/algn
2 adj (enterprising) dinámico(a), emprendedor(a)

goal [gəʊl] n (a) Sport gol m; **to score a g.** marcar un gol ❏ Ftb **g. area** área f (de meta); **g. kick** saque m de puerta; **g. line** línea f meta; **(g.) post** poste m; **g. posts** portería f, meta f, Am arco m; **g. scorer** goleador(a) m,f, **leading g. scorer** pichichi m (b) (aim, objective) meta f, objetivo m, fin m

goalie [ˈgəʊlɪ] n Sport Fam portero(a) m,f, guardameta mf, Am arquero(a) m,f, Am guardavallas mf inv, RP golero(a) m,f

goalkeeper [ˈgəʊlkiːpər] n Sport portero(a) m,f, guardameta mf, Am arquero(a) m,f, Am guardavallas mf inv, RP golero(a) m,f

goat [gəʊt] n Zool (female) cabra f; **he-g.** macho m cabrío; **old g.** viejo(a) m,f pesado(a); Fam **it gets my g.** me pone negro, or RP de la nuca, me saca de quicio; Br Fam **to act or play the g.** hacer el indio, hacer el ganso

goatee [gəʊˈtiː] n perilla f

goatherd [ˈgəʊthɜːd] n cabrero(a) m,f

goatskin [ˈgəʊtskɪn] n piel f de cabra

gob¹ [gɒb] n Br Slang boca f; **shut your g.!** ¡cierra el pico!, ¡cállate la boca!

gob² [gɒb] Br Slang **1** n lapo m, sipiajo m
2 vi escupir

gobble¹ [ˈgɒbəl] vt (food) engullir

gobble² [ˈgɒbəl] vi (turkey) gluglutear

gobbledegook n, **gobbledygook** [ˈgɒbəldɪguːk] n Fam parrafada f; **the minister just gave us a mouthful of g.** el ministro sólo soltó una parrafada incomprensible

go-between [ˈgəʊbɪtwiːn] n (a) (mediator) intermediario(a) m,f, mediador(a) m,f (b) (between lovers) alcahueta f

goblet [ˈgɒblɪt] n copa f

goblin [ˈgɒblɪn] n duende m

gobstopper [ˈgɒbstɒpər] n Br = caramelo grande y redondo

goby [ˈgəʊbɪ] n (fish) chanquete m

go-cart [ˈgəʊkɑːt] n (a) (toy) coche m de juguete (b) (handcart) carretilla f de mano

god [gɒd] n (a) (divine being) dios m; **for G.'s sake!** ¡por Dios!; **G. Dios;** **(my) G.!** ¡Dios mío!; **G. forbid** ¡no lo permita Dios!; **G. only knows** sabe Dios; **G. willing** si Dios quiere (b) Theat Fam **the gods** el gallinero

godchild [ˈgɒdtʃaɪld] n (pl **godchildren** [ˈgɒdtʃɪldrən]) ahijado(a) m,f

goddam(n) [ˈgɒdæm], **goddamned** [ˈgɒdæmd] Fam **1** adj maldito(a), Esp dichoso(a), Méx pinche; **he's a g. fool!** ¡es un maldito imbécil!
2 adv **that was g. stupid!** ¡eso fue una auténtica estupidez!
3 interj **g. (it)!** ¡maldita sea!, Méx ¡híjole!, RP ¡miércoles!

goddaughter [ˈgɒdɔːtər] n ahijada f

goddess [ˈgɒdɪs] n diosa f

godfather [ˈgɒdfɑːðər] n padrino m

God-fearing [ˈgɒdfɪərɪŋ] adj timorato(a), que teme a Dios

godforsaken [ˈgɒdfəseɪkən] adj (person) dejado(a) de la mano de Dios; (place) poco interesante, remoto(a)

godless [ˈgɒdlɪs] adj (a) (wicked) descreído(a) (b) (atheist) ateo(a)

godmother [ˈgɒdmʌðər] n madrina f

godparents [ˈgɒdpeərənts] npl padrinos mpl

godsend [ˈgɒdsend] n regalo m inesperado; **those fifty dollars were a g.** los cincuenta dólares me vinieron como llovidos del cielo

godson [ˈgɒdsʌn] n ahijado m

go-getter [ˈgəʊgetər] n Fam ambicioso(a) m,f

goggle [ˈgɒgəl] vi mirar con ojos desorbitados; **to g. at sth** mirar algo con los ojos como platos; TV Fam **the g. box** la caja tonta

goggles [ˈgɒgəlz] npl gafas fpl or CSur antiparras fpl protectoras, **don't forget your g. if you go swimming** si vas a la piscina, no te olvides las gafas

going [ˈgəʊɪŋ] **1** adj (a) (price) actual, corriente; **the g. rate** el precio medio (b) (business) **a g. concern** un negocio que marcha bien (c) **to get** or **be g.** marcharse; **we must be g.** tenemos que irnos (d) **to keep g.** resistir, aguantar
2 n (a) (departure) ida f, salida f (b) (pace) paso m, ritmo m; **that was good g.!** ¡qué rápido!; Fam **when the g. gets tough the tough get g.** cuando las cosas se ponen difíciles la reacción del valiente es hacerles frente (c) (condition of terrain) estado m del camino; Fig **the g. was rough** encontraron muchos obstáculos; Fig **to get out while the g. is good** dejar de hacer algo antes que sea demasiado tarde

going-over [gəʊɪŋˈəʊvər] n Fam (a) (check) inspección f (b) (beating) paliza f, **to give sb a g.-o.** darle una paliza a algn

goings-on [gəʊɪŋzˈɒn] npl Fam actividades fpl, tejemanejes mpl

goitre, US **goiter** [ˈgɔɪtər] n Med bocio m

go-kart [ˈgəʊkɑːt] n Sport kart m

gold [gəʊld] **1** n (metal) oro m; (colour) dorado m; **the g. rush** la fiebre del oro; Fig **to have a heart of g.** tener un corazón de oro ❏ **g. bullion** lingotes mpl de oro; **g. digger** buscador(a) m,f de oro; **g. dust** oro m en polvo; **g. leaf** pan m de oro; **g. medal** medalla f de oro; **g. mine** mina f de oro; **g. plate** vajilla f de oro; **g. reserves** reservas fpl de oro
2 adj (made of gold) de oro; (colour) oro, dorado(a)

goldcrest [ˈgəʊldkrest] n Orn reyezuelo m sencillo

golden [ˈgəʊldən] adj (made of gold) de oro; (colour)

dorado(a); *Fig* **a g. opportunity** una excelente oportunidad ❏ *Myth* **G. Age** Edad *f* de Oro; *Esp Lit* Siglo *m* de Oro; *Orn* **g. eagle** águila *f* real; *Com* **g. handcuffs** contrato *m* blindado; *Fig* **g. handshake** indemnización *f* de despido; **g. hello** = cuantiosa gratificación ofrecida como incentivo para ingresar en una empresa; **g. wedding** bodas *fpl* de oro; *Myth* **the G. Fleece** el Vellocino de oro

goldfinch [ˈɡəʊldfɪntʃ] *n Orn* jilguero *m*

goldfish [ˈɡəʊldfɪʃ] *n* (*pl* **goldfish** *or* **goldfishes**) pez *m* de colores ❏ **g. bowl** pecera *f*

gold-plated [ɡəʊldˈpleɪtɪd] *adj* dorado(a), chapado(a) en oro

goldsmith [ˈɡəʊldsmɪθ] *n* orfebre *m*

golf [ɡɒlf] *n Sport* golf *m*; **to play g.** jugar al golf ❏ **g. ball** pelota *f* de golf; **g. club** (*stick*) palo *m* de golf; (*place*) club *m* de golf; **g. course** campo *m* de golf

golfer [ˈɡɒlfər] *n Sport* golfista *mf*, jugador(a) *m,f* de golf

golfing [ˈɡɒlfɪŋ] **1** *adj* de golf; **g. holiday** vacaciones para jugar al golf
2 *n* jugar al golf; **their husbands go g. every weekend** sus maridos van a jugar al golf cada fin de semana

golly [ˈɡɒlɪ] *interj* ¡vaya!; *Fam* **by g.** sea como sea; **by g. I'm going to have a good time** sea como sea me lo voy a pasar bien

gondola [ˈɡɒndələ] *n* góndola *f*

gondolier [ɡɒndɒˈlɪər] *n* gondolero *m*

gone [ɡɒn] **1** *pp see* go
2 *adj* desaparecido(a); **g. are the days when you can walk the streets at night safely** quedan lejos los tiempos en los que se podía caminar por las calles de noche con seguridad
3 *prep* **it'll be g. six by the time he gets here** serán las seis pasadas cuando llegue

goner [ˈɡɒnər] *n Fam* enfermo *m* terminal

gong [ɡɒŋ] *n* gong *m*, batintín *m*

gonorrhoea, *US* **gonorrhea** [ɡɒnəˈrɪə] *n Med* gonorrea *f*

goo [ɡuː] *n Fam* (**a**) (*gunge*) sustancia *f* pegajosa (**b**) *Fig* (*sentimentality*) cursilería *f*, *Esp* cursiladas *fpl*

good [ɡʊd] **1** *adj* (**better, best**) (**a**) (*of positive or pleasing qualities*) (*before noun*) buen(a); (*after noun*) bueno(a); (*land*) bueno(a), rico(a), fértil; **a g. book** un buen libro; **g. afternoon**, **g. evening** buenas tardes; **g. morning** buenos días; **g. night** buenas noches; **it looks g.** tiene buen aspecto *or* buena pinta; **it's too g. to be true** es demasiado bueno para ser cierto; **it was g. to get your letter** me hizo mucha ilusión recibir tu carta; **that's a g. one!** ¡no me digas!, *Esp* ¡venga ya!; **this cake is very g.** este pastel está riquísimo; **to be as g. as new** estar como nuevo(a); **to feel g.** sentirse bien; **to have a g. time** pasarlo bien; **to smell g.** oler bien; **with all g. wishes** con mis *or* nuestros mejores deseos ❏ *Rel* **G. Friday** Viernes *m* Santo (**b**) (*person*) (*kind*) amable; (*generous*) generoso(a); **it's very g. of you** es muy amable de tu parte; **to be g. to sb** ser amable con algn; **would you be g. enough to open the window?** ¿sería tan amable de abrir la ventana? (**c**) (*beneficial*) bueno(a); (*healthy*) sano(a); **to drink more than is g. for one** beber más de la cuenta; **yoghurt is g. for you** el yogur es muy sano (**d**) (*well-behaved*) bueno(a); (*morally correct*) correcto(a), responsable; **be g.!** ¡pórtate bien!; **you can trust her, she's a g. woman** puedes confiar en ella, es una buena mujer; *Fam Fig* **her son was as g. as gold** su hijo se portó como un ángel (**e**) (*skilled*) bueno(a), hábil; **he's g. at languages** tiene facilidad para los idiomas; **she's g. with her hands** es muy hábil con las manos, *Esp* es muy manitas; **they're g. with children** tienen don para los niños; (**f**) (*attractive*) bueno(a), bonito(a); **g. handwriting**

buena letra; **he's earning g. money** gana un buen sueldo; **red looks g. on you** el rojo te favorece mucho; **she has a very g. figure** tiene un tipo estupendo ❏ **g. looks** atractivo *m sing*, belleza *f sing* (**g**) (*valid*) válido(a); **it's as g. as an offer** equivale a una oferta; **it's as g. a way as any** es una manera como otra cualquiera; **she's as g. as you** ella vale tanto como tú (**h**) (*at least*) **a g.** como mínimo, por lo menos; **a g. fifty kilometres** unos cincuenta kilómetros por lo menos (**i**) (*considerable*) bueno(a); (*sufficient*) bastante; **a g. amount of food** bastante comida; **a g. many people** bastante gente; **to give sb a g. telling off** echar una buena bronca a algn; **to give sth a g. clean** limpiar algo a fondo; **we waited a g. while** esperamos un buen rato (**j**) (*just, fair*) **to give as g. as one gets** devolver golpe por golpe; **to make g.** (*injustice*) reparar; (*loss*) compensar; (*one's word*) cumplir; (*succeed in life*) triunfar (**k**) (*reliable*) de confianza, bueno(a); **a g. butcher's** una carnicería de confianza (**l**) (*satisfying*) bueno(a); **a g. rest** un buen descanso (**m**) (*propitious*) bueno(a), propicio(a); **a g. time to go on holiday** un buen momento para ir de vacaciones (**n**) (*honourable*) bueno(a); **she comes from a g. family** es de buena familia (**o**) (*suitable*) bueno(a); **a g. pair of gloves and a g. coat** unos buenos guantes y un buen abrigo (**p**) (*character*) bueno(a), agradable; **he's in a g. mood** está de buen humor (**q**) (*profitable*) *Fam* **to be on to a g. thing** tenerlo bien montado
2 *n* (**a**) (*gen*) bien *m*; **g. and evil** el bien y el mal; **he's up to no g.** está tramando algo malo; **to come to no g.** acabar *or* *RP* terminar mal; **to do g.** hacer el bien (**b**) (*people*) **the g.** los buenos, la buena gente; **he's no g. as a doctor** no es buen médico (**c**) (*advantage*) bien *m*, provecho *m*; **for the common g.** en bien de todos; **for your own g.** para tu propio bien; **if it's any g.** si te sirve de algo; **it's no g. waiting** no sirve de nada esperar; **it will do you g.** te hará bien; **what's the g. of that?** ¿de qué sirve eso? (**d**) *Jur* **goods** (*possessions*) bienes *mpl* ❏ **consumer g.** bienes *mpl* de consumo; **g. and chattels** muebles y enseres *mpl*, efectos *mpl* personales (**e**) *Com* **goods** artículos *mpl*, géneros *mpl*, mercancías *fpl*; **knitted g.** género *m* de punto; *Fam* **to deliver the g.** cumplir su palabra ❏ *Br* **g. train** tren *m* de mercancías
3 *adv* (*forever*) **she's gone for g.** se ha ido para siempre
4 *interj* **g.!** ¡bravo!, ¡muy bien!

goodbye [ɡʊdˈbaɪ] **1** *interj* ¡adiós!
2 *n* adiós *m*, despedida *f*; **to say g. to sb** despedirse de algn

good-for-nothing [ˈɡʊdfənʌθɪŋ] *adj & n* inútil (*mf*)

good-hearted [ɡʊdˈhɑːtɪd] *adj* de buen corazón, bueno(a)

good-humoured, *US* **good-humored** [ɡʊdˈhjuːməd] *adj* (*discussion*) afable; (*joke, remark*) sin mala intención

good-looking [ɡʊdˈlʊkɪŋ] *adj Esp* guapo(a), *Am* lindo(a) **he's very g.-l.** es muy guapo

good-natured [ɡʊdˈneɪtʃəd] *adj* amable, bondadoso(a)

goodness [ˈɡʊdnɪs] *n* (**a**) (*of heart*) bondad *f*; **my g.!** ¡Dios mío!, ¡madre mía!; **thank g.!** ¡gracias a Dios!; **for g. sake!** ¡por Dios!; **I wish to g. you'd shut up!** ¡ojalá te callaras! (**b**) (*quality*) calidad *f*

good-tempered [ɡʊdˈtempəd] *adj* de buen carácter; (*pleasant*) apacible

goodwill [ɡʊdˈwɪl] *n* (**a**) (*benevolence, willingness*) buena voluntad *f* (**b**) *Com* (*reputation*) buen nombre *m*

goody [ˈɡʊdɪ] **1** *n Fam* (**a**) *Cin* bueno(a) *m,f*; **the goodies and the baddies** los buenos y los malos (**b**) *Culin* dulce *m*, golosina *f*
2 *interj* (*baby-talk*) **g.!** ¡qué bien!

goody-goody [ˈɡʊdɪɡʊdɪ] *adj & n Fam* (*pl* **goody-goodies**) santurrón(ona) (*m,f*)

gooey ['guːɪ] adj (**gooier, gooiest**) Fam (**a**) (sticky) pegajoso(a) (**b**) Fig (slushy) sentimental, sentimentaloide

goof [guːf] US Fam **1** n (person) bobo(a) m,f; (thing) metedura f or Am metida f de pata
2 vi (blunder) meter la pata

goof off vi US Fam (skive) perder el tiempo

goofy ['guːfɪ] adj (**goofier, goofiest**) Fam (**a**) (of teeth) Br dentudo(a); **to have g. teeth** tener dientes de conejo (**b**) US (crazy) alocado(a), estúpido(a)

goon [guːn] n Fam (**a**) Br (stupid person) bobo(a) m,f, lerdo(a) m,f (**b**) US (thug) matón m

goose [guːs] n (pl **geese** [giːs]) (**a**) Orn ganso m, oca f; Fig **the golden g.** la gallina de los huevos de oro; Fam Fig **to cook sb's g.** hacerle la pascua a algn ❑ Br **g. pimples**, US **g. bumps** carne f de gallina; **barnacle g.** barnacla f cariblanca; **Canada g.** barnacla f canadiense; **greylag g.** ánsar m común (**b**) Fam (silly person) tonto(a) m,f, bobo(a) m,f

gooseberry ['guzbərɪ] n Bot uva f espina, grosella f espinosa; Br Fam **to play g.** hacer de carabina or de sujetavelas, Méx hacer mal tercio, RP estar de paleta ❑ **g. bush** grosellero m espinoso

gooseflesh ['guːsfleʃ] n carne f de gallina; **the cold air raised g. on her arms** con el aire frío se le puso la carne de gallina

goose-step ['guːsstep] Mil **1** n paso m de la oca
2 vi ir a paso de la oca

gopher ['gəʊfər] n (ground squirrel) ardilla f de tierra

Gordian ['gɔːdɪən] adj Fml **G. knot** nudo m gordiano, problema m grave

gore[1] [gɔːr] n sangre f derramada

gore[2] [gɔːr] vt (bull) cornear, dar cornadas a

gorge [gɔːdʒ] **1** n Geog desfiladero m, garganta f
2 vt & vi (food) **to g. (oneself)** atiborrarse (**on** de), hartarse (**on** de)

gorgeous ['gɔːdʒəs] adj (fantastic) magnífico(a), estupendo(a); (marvellous) espléndido(a); (person) atractivo(a), guapísimo(a)

gorilla [gə'rɪlə] n Zool gorila m

gormless ['gɔːmlɪs] adj Br Fam idiota, Esp memo(a)

gorse [gɔːs] n Bot tojo m, aulaga f

gory ['gɔːrɪ] adj (**gorier, goriest**) sangriento(a); **a g. horror film** una película sangrienta or de vísceras; **I'd rather you spared me the g. details** puedes ahorrarte los detalles escabrosos

gosh [gɒʃ] interj Fam ¡vaya!, Esp ¡jolines!, Méx ¡híjole!

goshawk ['gɒshɔːk] n Orn azor m

gosling ['gɒzlɪŋ] n ansarón m

go-slow ['gəʊ'sləʊ] n Br huelga f de celo

gospel ['gɒspəl] n Rel **the G.** el Evangelio; **the G. according to Saint Mark** el Evangelio según San Marcos; Fam **it's the g. truth** es la pura verdad ❑ **g. singer** cantante m,f (de) gospel

gossamer ['gɒsəmər] n (**a**) (cobweb) telaraña f (**b**) Tex gasa f

gossip ['gɒsɪp] **1** n (**a**) (rumour) chismorreo m, Esp cotilleo m, comadreo m ❑ Press **g. column** ecos mpl de sociedad (**b**) (person) chismoso(a) m,f, Esp cotilla m,f
2 vi (natter) chismorrear, contar chismes, Esp cotillear

gossipy ['gɒsɪpɪ] adj Fam (style) familiar; (person) chismoso(a)

got [gɒt] pt & pp see **get**

Goth [gɒθ] n Hist godo(a) m,f

Gothic ['gɒθɪk] adj (**a**) (race) godo(a) (**b**) Art gótico(a)

gotta ['gɒtə] Fam = **got to**

gotten ['gɒtən] US pp see **get**

gouache [gʊ'ɑːʃ] n Art aguada f, pintura f a la aguada

gouge [gaʊdʒ] **1** n Carp gubia f
2 vi Carp **to g. out** escoplear con gubia; Fig **to g. out sb's eyes** arrancarle los ojos a algn

goulash ['guːlæʃ] n gulach m

gourd [gʊəd] n calabaza f, Bol CSur zapallo m, Col Ven ahuyama f

gourmand ['gʊəmənd] n goloso(a) m,f, glotón(ona) m,f

gourmet ['gʊəmeɪ] n gourmet mf, gastrónomo(a) m,f

gout [gaʊt] n Med gota f

Gov (**a**) (abbr **Governor**) Gobernador(a) m,f, Gobr (**b**) (abbr **Government**) Gobierno m, Gob, Gobno

govern ['gʌvən] vt (**a**) (gen) gobernar (**b**) (determine) dictar, guiar

governess ['gʌvənɪs] n institutriz f

governing ['gʌvənɪŋ] adj gobernante, gobernador(a); **g. body** consejo m de administración

government ['gʌvənmənt] **1** n gobierno m; **local g.** gobierno municipal
2 adj del gobierno, del Estado, gubernamental

governmental [gʌvən'mentəl] adj gubernamental

governor ['gʌvənər] n (**a**) (ruler, of US state) gobernador(a) m,f (**b**) (of prison) director(a) m,f (**c**) (of school) administrador(a) m,f (**d**) Fam jefe m

governorship ['gʌvənəʃɪp] n gobernación f

Govt (abbr **Government**) Gobierno m, Gob, Gobno

gown [gaʊn] n (**a**) (dress) vestido m largo; **dressing g.** bata f (**b**) Jur Univ (robe) toga f

GP [dʒiː'piː] n Br Med (abbr **general practioner**) médico(a) m,f de cabecera

GPO [dʒiːpiː'əʊ] n Br Formerly (abbr **General Post Office**) Oficina f Central de Correos

gr (abbr **gramme(s)**) g

grab [græb] **1** n agarrón m; **to make a g. for sth** intentar agarrar algo; Fam **to be up for grabs** estar libre, estar disponible
2 vt (pt & pp **grabbed**) (**a**) (gen) agarrar, coger; **to g. hold of sb** agarrarse a algn; Fam **the police grabbed him** le pilló la policía (**b**) Fig pillar; **I think I'll g. a few hours sleep before I go out** creo que antes de salir me echaré una siesta (**c**) Fig (interest) hacer ilusión a; **how does that g. you?** ¿qué te parece?; **the idea of going to Egypt really grabbed him** la idea de ir a Egipto le estusiasmaba

grace [greɪs] **1** n (**a**) (favour) gracia f; **by the g. of God** por la gracia de Dios; **in a state of g.** en estado de gracia; Fig **to fall from g.** caer en desgracia (**b**) (prayer) bendición f de la mesa; **to say g.** bendecir la mesa (**c**) (courtesy) cortesía f, delicadeza f; **he had the g. to apologize** tuvo la cortesía de pedir perdón; **it's her saving g.** es lo que la salva; **to do sth with good g.** hacer algo de buena gana (**d**) (delay, reprieve) plazo m, demora f; **five days' g.** un plazo de cinco días (**e**) (refinement, elegance) gracia f, elegancia f; (tact) tacto m (**f**) (in title) **Your G.** (gen) (Su) Excelencia; (bishop) (Su) Ilustrísima (**g**) **graces** (manners) buenos modales mpl
2 vt (**a**) (adorn) adornar (**b**) (honour) honrar

graceful ['greɪsfʊl] adj (beautiful) lleno(a) de gracia, elegante; (movement) garboso(a)

gracefully ['greɪsfʊlɪ] adv (**a**) (beautifully) con gracia, con elegancia (**b**) (accept, decline) con cortesía

gracefulness ['greɪsfʊlnɪs] n gracia f

gracious ['greɪʃəs] adj (**a**) (elegant) elegante; **g. living** vida f elegante or de lujo (**b**) (courteous) cortés, educado(a) (**c**) (kind) amable
2 interj **good g. (me)!, goodness g.!** ¡santo cielo!

graciously ['greɪʃəslɪ] *adv* (a) *(elegantly)* elegantemente (b) *(kindly)* amablemente

graciousness ['greɪʃəsnɪs] *n* (a) *(elegance)* elegancia *f* (b) *(affability)* amabilidad *f*

gradation [grə'deɪʃən] *n* gradación *f*

grade [greɪd] **1** *n* (a) *(degree, quality)* grado *m*; *(rank)* categoría *f*; *Mil* rango *m* (b) *US Educ (mark)* nota *f*; **to get good grades** sacar buenas notas (c) *US Educ (class, form)* clase *f*; **g. school** escuela primaria (d) *(level)* nivel *m*; **to make the g.** llegar al nivel deseado, tener éxito, triunfar (e) *US (slope)* pendiente *f* (f) *US Rail* **g. crossing** paso *m* a nivel
2 *vt (classify)* clasificar; *US* **to g. essays** calificar los trabajos

gradient ['greɪdɪənt] *n (graph)* declive *m*; *(hill)* cuesta *f*, pendiente *f*; **a g. of one in five** una pendiente de veinte por ciento

gradual ['grædjʊəl] *adj* gradual, progresivo(a)

gradualism ['grædjʊəlɪzəm] *n* transformación *f* gradual

gradually ['grædjʊəlɪ] *adv* poco a poco, progresivamente

graduate ['grædjʊɪt] **1** *n Univ* licenciado(a) *m,f*; *US (from high school)* bachiller *mf* ❑ *US* **g. school** escuela *f* para graduados
2 ['grædjʊeɪt] *vi* (a) *Br Univ* licenciarse, graduarse; *(from high school)* sacar el bachillerato (**in** en) (b) *(progress)* pasar; **start with a small one and then g. to a bigger one** empezar con uno pequeño y después pasar a uno mayor

graduated ['grædʊeɪtɪd] *adj (thermometer)* graduado(a); **g. income tax** impuesto *m* sobre la renta progresivo

graduation [grædjʊ'eɪʃən] *n (gen)* graduación *f*; *Univ* **g. ceremony** ceremonia *f* de entrega de los títulos

graffiti [græ'fiːtiː] *npl* grafiti *mpl*

graft [grɑːft] **1** *n* (a) *Agr Med* injerto *m* ❑ **skin g.** injerto *m* de piel (b) *Br Fam (work)* trabajo *m*; **the job involves a lot of hard g.** en ese trabajo hay que trabajar mucho *or Esp* currar a tope *or Méx* chambear duro *or RP* laburar como loco (c) *US (bribery)* soborno *m*
2 *vt Agr Med* injertar (**on to** en)
3 *vi Br Fam* trabajar mucho, *Esp* currar a tope, *Méx* chambear duro, *RP* laburar como loco

Grail [greɪl] *n Lit* grial *m*; **the Holy G.** el Santo Grial

grain [greɪn] *n* (a) *(cereals)* cereales *mpl* (b) *(seed, particle)* grano *m*; *Fig* **there's not a g. of truth in it** no tiene ni pizca de verdad (c) *(in wood)* fibra *f*; *(in stone)* veta *f*; *(in leather)* flor *f*; *Fig* **it goes against the g. for me to do** *(gen) Fig* me cuesta mucho hacer eso

grainy ['greɪnɪ] *adj* (**grainier, grainiest**) *Phot* granuloso(a), con mucho grano

gram [græm] *n* gramo *m*

grammar ['græmər] *n* gramática *f*; **English g.** la gramática inglesa ❑ **g. (book)** libro *m* de gramática; *Br* **g. school** instituto *m* de segunda enseñanza *(al que sólo se accede después de superar un examen de ingreso)*

grammarian [grə'meərɪən] *n* gramático(a) *m,f*

grammatical [grə'mætɪkəl] *adj* gramatical, gramático(a)

grammatically [grə'mætɪklɪ] *adv* gramaticalmente

gramme [græm] *n Br* gramo *m*

gramophone ['græməfəʊn] *n* gramófono *m*, gramola *f*

granary ['grænərɪ] *n Agr* granero *m*

grand [grænd] **1** *adj* (a) *(gen)* grande; *(before sing noun)* gran; **g. ideas** grandes ideas ❑ **G. Canary** Gran Canaria *f*; *Br Jur* **g. jury** gran jurado *m*; **g. piano** piano *m* de cola; *Aut* **G. Prix** Gran Premio *m* (b) *(splendid)* grandioso(a), magnífico(a); *(impressive)* impresionante (c) *(complete)* global ❑ **g. total** total *m* (d) *Fam (wonderful)* genial, *Méx*

padre, *RP* bárbaro; **that would be g.!** ¡eso sería estupendo!; **to have a g. time** pasarlo en grande
2 *n* (a) *(piano)* piano *m* de cola (b) *Slang* mil libras *fpl*, *US* mil dólares *mpl*

grandad ['grændæd] *n Fam* abuelito *m*, *Esp* yayo *m*

grandchild ['græntʃaɪld] *n* (*pl* **grandchildren** ['græntʃɪldrən]) nieto(a) *m,f*

granddaughter ['grændɔːtər] *n* nieta *f*

grandeur ['grændʒər] *n* grandeza *f*, grandiosidad *f*

grandfather ['grænfɑːðər] *n* abuelo *m* ❑ **g. clock** reloj *m* de caja

grandiloquent [græn'dɪləkwənt] *adj Fml* grandilocuente

grandiose ['grændɪəʊs] *adj* grandioso(a), imponente

grandma ['grænmɑː] *n Fam* abuelita *f*, *Esp* yaya *f*

grandmaster ['grændmɑːstər] *n Chess* gran maestro *m*

grandmother ['grænmʌðər] *n* abuela *f*

grandpa ['grænpɑː] *n Fam* abuelito *m*, *Esp* yayo *m*

grandparents ['grænpeərənts] *npl* abuelos *mpl*

grandson ['grænsʌn] *n* nieto *m*

grandstand ['grænstænd] *n Sport* tribuna *f*

grange [greɪndʒ] *n* finca *f*, cortijo *m*

granite ['grænɪt] *n Min* granito *m*

granite-like ['grænɪtlaɪk] *adj Min* granítico(a)

granny, grannie ['grænɪ] *n Fam* abuelita *f*, *Esp* yaya *f*

grant [grɑːnt] **1** *vt* (a) *(allow) (interview etc)* conceder (b) *(concede, bestow)* conceder, otorgar (c) *(admit)* admitir, reconocer; **I g. that you were right** reconozco que tenías razón; **to take sb for granted** no apreciar a algn en lo que vale; **to take sth for granted** dar algo por sentado
2 *n Educ* beca *f*; *(subsidy)* subvención *f*

granular ['grænjʊlər] *adj* granular

granulate ['grænjʊleɪt] **1** *vt Chem* granular
2 *vi* granularse

granulated ['grænjʊleɪtɪd] *adj* granulado(a) ❑ **g. sugar** azúcar *m* granulado

granulation [grænjʊ'leɪʃən] *n* granulación *f*

granule ['grænjuːl] *n* gránulo *m*

grape [greɪp] *n Bot* uva *f*; **a bunch of grapes** un racimo de uvas; *Fam* **sour grapes!** ¡te aguantas! ❑ **g. harvest** vendimia *f*; **g. juice** zumo *m* *or Am* jugo *m* de uva, mosto *m*

grapefruit ['greɪpfruːt] *n* (*pl* **grapefruit** *or* **grapefruits**) pomelo *m*, *Am* toronja *f*

grapevine ['greɪpvaɪn] *n Bot* vid *f*; *(against wall)* parra *f*; *Fam* **I heard it on** *or* **through the g.** me enteré por ahí

graph [grɑːf, græf] *n* gráfica *f* ❑ **g. paper** papel *m* cuadriculado

graphic ['græfɪk] *adj* gráfico(a) ❑ **g. arts** artes *fpl* gráficas; **g. designer** grafista *mf*; *Elec* **g. equalizer** ecualizador *m* gráfico; **g. novel** novela *f* ilustrada

graphically ['græfɪklɪ] *adv (describe, portray)* gráficamente

graphics ['græfɪks] *n* (a) *(study)* grafismo *m* (b) *pl Comptr* gráficas *fpl*

graphite ['græfaɪt] *n Min* grafito *m*

graphologist [græ'fɒlədʒɪst] *n* grafólogo(a) *m,f*

graphology [græ'fɒlədʒɪ] *n* grafología *f*

grapple ['græpəl] **1** *vi (struggle)* luchar cuerpo a cuerpo (**with** con); *Fig* **to g. with a problem** intentar resolver un problema
2 *n (hook)* garfio *m*

grappling hook ['græplɪŋ'hʊk], **grappling iron** ['græplɪŋ 'aɪən] *n Naut* rezón *m*

grasp [grɑːsp] **1** vt (**a**) (seize) agarrar, asir (**b**) (understand) comprender, captar

2 n (**a**) (grip) asimiento m; (clasp) apretón; **to have a strong g.** agarrar muy fuerte; **to lose one's g.** soltarse (**b**) (understanding) comprensión f, alcance m; **it's beyond my g.** está fuera de mi alcance; **to have a good g. of sth** comprender algo bien, dominar algo; **within sb's g.** al alcance de algn

grasping ['grɑːspɪŋ] adj ávaro(a), codicioso(a)

grass [grɑːs] **1** n (**a**) (plant) hierba f, yerba f; (lawn) césped m; (pasture) pasto m; **'keep off the g.'** 'prohibido pisar el césped'; Fig **he doesn't let the g. grow under his feet** no pierde el tiempo ❑ Ten **g. court** pista f de hierba; Sport **g. hockey** hockey m sobre hierba; Pol **g. roots** base f (popular); Zool **g. snake** culebra f; **g. widow** mujer f cuyo marido está ausente; **g. widower** hombre m cuya mujer está ausente; (for the summer) Rodríguez m (**b**) Slang (drug) hierba f, maría f

2 vi Br Slang (inform) soplar, Esp chivarse (**on** a)

grass over vi cubrirse de hierba or yerba

grasshopper ['grɑːshɒpər] n saltamontes m inv

grassland ['grɑːslænd] n prado m, pasto m

grass-roots ['grɑːsruːts] adj Pol de base; **at g.-r. level** a nivel popular; **g.-r. militant** militante mf de base

grassy ['grɑːsɪ] adj (**grassier, grassiest**) cubierto(a) de hierba

grate[1] [greɪt] **1** vt (**a**) Culin rallar (**b**) (teeth etc) hacer rechinar

2 vi chirriar; (teeth) rechinar; Fig **to g. on one's nerves** crisparle a uno los nervios

grate[2] [greɪt] n (**a**) (in fireplace etc) rejilla f (**b**) (fireplace) chimenea f (**c**) Constr rejilla f, reja f

grateful ['greɪtfʊl] adj (person) agradecido(a), (letter etc) de agradecimiento; **I am very g. to you** te lo agradezco mucho, te estoy muy agradecido; **to be g. for** agradecer; **with g. thanks** con agradecimiento

gratefully ['greɪtfʊlɪ] adv con agradecimiento

grater ['greɪtər] n Culin rallador m

gratification [grætɪfɪ'keɪʃən] n (**a**) (pleasure) placer m, satisfacción f (**b**) Fig (reward) recompensa f, gratificación f

gratify ['grætɪfaɪ] vt (pt & pp **gratified**) (**a**) (please) complacer, gratificar (**b**) (yield to) sucumbir a

gratifying ['grætɪfaɪɪŋ] adj grato(a), gratificante

gratin ['grætɪŋ] n Culin gratén m; **au g.** al gratén

grating[1] ['greɪtɪŋ] n rejilla f, reja f

grating[2] ['greɪtɪŋ] adj (noise) chirriante, rechinante; (voice) chillón(ona); (tone) áspero(a)

gratis ['grætɪs] adv gratis

gratitude ['grætɪtjuːd] n agradecimiento m, gratitud f

gratuitous [grə'tjuːɪtəs] adj gratuito(a)

gratuitously [grə'tjuːɪtəslɪ] adv gratuitamente

gratuitousness [grə'tjuːɪtəsnɪs] n gratuidad f

gratuity [grə'tjuːɪtɪ] n (reward) gratificación f, (tip) propina f

grave[1] [greɪv] n (tomb) sepultura f, sepulcro m, tumba f; Fig **to make sb turn in his/her grave** hacer que algn se retuerza en su tumba; Fam **to have one foot in the g.** tener un pie en la tumba, estar en las últimas

grave[2] [greɪv] adj (**a**) (serious) (look etc) serio(a); (situation) grave (**b**) [grɑːv] Ling grave; **g. accent** acento grave

gravedigger ['greɪvdɪgər] n sepulturero m, enterrador m

gravel ['grævəl] n grava f, gravilla f, guijo m; **g. path** camino m de grava

gravely ['greɪvlɪ] adv gravemente

graven ['greɪvən] adj (in the Bible) **g. image** ídolo m

gravestone ['greɪvstəʊn] n lápida f sepulcral or mortuoria

graveyard ['greɪvjɑːd] n cementerio m

gravitate ['grævɪteɪt] vi (**a**) Phys gravitar (**b**) Fig (be drawn) sentirse atraído(a) (**towards** por)

gravitation [grævɪ'teɪʃən] n Phys gravitación f

gravitational [grævɪ'teɪʃənəl] adj (force, field) gravitatorio(a); **g. pull** atracción f gravitatoria

gravity ['grævɪtɪ] n (**a**) Phys gravedad f; **the law of g.** la ley de la gravedad ❑ **centre of g.** centro m de gravedad; **specific g.** peso m específico (**b**) (of situation) gravedad f

gravy ['greɪvɪ] n Culin salsa f, jugo m (de la carne) ❑ **g. boat** salsera f; Slang **g. train** Esp chollo m, Am chance m

gray [greɪ] adj & n (**grayer, grayest**) US see **grey**

grayling ['greɪlɪŋ] n Orn tímalo m

graze[1] [greɪz] vi pacer, pastar

graze[2] [greɪz] **1** vt rasguñar, rozar, arañar

2 n rasguño m, roce m, arañazo m

grazing ['greɪzɪŋ] n (tierra f de) pasto m

grease [griːs] **1** n grasa f ❑ **g. gun** pistola f engrasadora, engrasador m

2 vt Tech engrasar, untar; Slang **to g. sb's palm** untar a algn, Andes RP coimear a algn, CAm Méx dar una mordida a algn

greasepaint ['griːspeɪnt] n Theat maquillaje m

greaseproof paper ['griːspruːf'peɪpə(r)] n Br papel m graso

greasy ['griːsɪ] adj (**greasier, greasiest**) (**a**) (oily) grasiento(a); (hair, food) graso(a) ❑ Br Slang **g. spoon** restaurante m de mala muerte (**b**) (slippery) resbaladizo(a) (**c**) Fam (ingratiating) cobista, pelota

great [greɪt] **1** adj (**a**) (big, large) grande; (before sing noun) gran; (pain, heat) fuerte, intenso(a); (determination) fuerte; **a g. many** muchos(as); **a g. number of** un gran número de ❑ **G. Britain** Gran Bretaña; Zool **G. Dane** gran danés m (**b**) (important) grande, importante; **a g. writer** un gran escritor; **the G. War** la Gran Guerra, la Primera Guerra Mundial (**c**) Fam (excellent) genial, Méx padre, RP bárbaro(a); **g.!** ¡estupendo!; **he's g. at tennis** juega al tenis de maravilla; **she's g. one for museums** le encantan los museos; **there was a g. big crash** se oyó un ruido de narices; **to have a g. time** pasarlo en grande

2 n (person) grande m

3 adv Fam muy bien, estupendamente; **she's doing just g.** le va todo muy bien

great-aunt [greɪt'ɑːnt] n tía f abuela

greatcoat ['greɪtkəʊt] n abrigo m, gabán m

great-grandchild [greɪt'grænt∫aɪld] n (pl **great-grandchildren** [greɪt'grænt∫ɪldrən]) bisnieto(a) m,f, biznieto(a) m,f

great-granddaughter [greɪt'grændɔːtər] n bisnieta f, biznieta f

great-grandfather [greɪt'grænfɑːðər] n bisabuelo m

great-grandmother [greɪt'grænmʌðər] n bisabuela f

great-grandparents ['greɪt'grænpeərənts] npl bisabuelos mpl

great-grandson [greɪt'grænsʌn] n bisnieto m, biznieto m

great-great-grandfather [greɪtgreɪt'grænfɑːðər] n tatarabuelo m

great-great-grandmother [greɪtgreɪt'grænmʌðər] n tatarabuela f

greatly ['greɪtlɪ] adv muy, mucho; **it is g. improved** ha mejorado mucho; **you are g. mistaken** estás muy equivocado

greatness ['greɪtnɪs] *n (importance)* grandeza *f; (size)* magnitud *f*

great-uncle [greɪt'ʌŋkəl] *n* tío *m* abuelo

grebe [gri:b] *n Orn* somormujo *m* ❑ **great crested g.** somormujo *m* lavanco

Grecian ['gri:ʃən] *adj* helénico(a), griego(a)

Greece [gri:s] *n* Grecia

greed [gri:d] *n,* **greediness** ['gri:dɪnɪs] *n* (**a**) *(for food)* gula *f,* glotonería *f* (**b**) *(for money)* codicia *f,* avaricia *f*

greedy ['gri:dɪ] *adj* (**greedier, greediest**) (**a**) *(for food)* glotón(ona), goloso(a) (**b**) *(for money)* codicioso(a), ávido(a) (**for** de)

Greek [gri:k] **1** *adj* griego(a)
  2 *n* (**a**) *(person)* griego(a) *m,f;* **the G.** los griegos (**b**) *(language)* griego *m;* **ancient/modern G.** griego clásico/ moderno; *Fam* **it's (all) G. to me** me suena a chino

green [gri:n] **1** *n* (**a**) *(colour)* verde *m* (**b**) *(stretch of grass)* césped *m; Golf* campo *m,* green ❑ **village g.** terreno *m* comunal, plaza *f* (del pueblo) (**c**) **greens** *(vegetables)* verdura *f* sing, verduras *fpl*
  2 *adj* (**a**) *(colour)* verde; *Fig* **to give a project the g. light** dar luz verde a un proyecto; **to have** *Br* **g. fingers** *or US* **a g. thumb** tener buena mano para *or Esp* con las plantas ❑ **g. bean** judía *f* verde, *Bol RP* chaucha *f, Carib Col* habichuela *f, Chile* poroto *m* verde, *Méx* ejote *m;* **g. belt** zona *f* verde; *Ins* **g. card** carta *f* verde; **g. pepper** pimiento *m* verde; **g. salad** ensalada *f* verde (**b**) *(unripe)* verde; *(uncured)* sin curar (**c**) *(pale)* pálido(a), lívido(a); **to go** *or* **turn g.** ponerse pálido(a) (**d**) *(jealous)* envidioso(a); **she was g. with envy** se la comía la envidia (**e**) *(inexperienced)* verde, novato(a); *(gullible)* crédulo(a), ingenuo(a) (**f**) *Pol (ecologist)* verde; **G. Party** Partido *m* Verde, Partido *m* Ecologista

greenback ['gri:nbæk] *n US Slang* billete *m,* verde *m*

greenery ['gri:nərɪ] *n* verde *m,* follaje *m*

green-eyed ['gri:naɪd] *adj Fig* envidioso(a), celoso(a)

greenfly ['gri:nflaɪ] *n* pulgón *m*

greengage ['gri:ngeɪdʒ] *n Bot* ciruela *f* claudia

greengrocer ['gri:ngrəʊsər] *n Br* verdulero(a) *m,f,* frutero(a) *m,f;* **g.'s (shop)** verdulería *f,* frutería *f*

greenhorn ['gri:nhɔ:n] *n* novato(a) *m,f*

greenhouse ['gri:nhaʊs] *n* invernadero *m* ❑ *Meteor* **g. effect** efecto *m* invernadero

greenish ['gri:nɪʃ] *adj* verdoso(a)

Greenland ['gri:nlənd] *n* Groenlandia ❑ **G. Sea** mar *m* de Groenlandia

Greenlander ['gri:nləndər] *n* groenlandés(esa) *m,f*

Greenlandic [gri:n'lændɪk] *adj* groenlandés(esa)

greenness ['gri:nnɪs] *n* verdor *m*

greenroom ['gri:nru:m] *n Theat* camerino *m*

green-thumbed ['gri:n'θʌmd] *adj US* con buena mano para *or Esp* con las plantas

Greenwich ['grɪnɪdʒ, 'grenɪtʃ] *n* **G. Mean Time** la hora media de Greenwich

greet [gri:t] *vt* (**a**) *(wave at)* saludar (**b**) *(receive)* recibir; *(welcome)* dar la bienvenida a

greeting ['gri:tɪŋ] *n* (**a**) *(gen)* saludo *m;* **greetings on your birthday!** ¡felicidades en el día de tu cumpleaños!; **greetings to all!** ¡saludos a todos!, ¡recuerdos a todos! ❑ *US* **g.** *or Br* **greetings card** tarjeta *f* de felicitación (**b**) *(reception)* recibimiento *m; (welcome)* bienvenida *f*

gregarious [grɪ'geərɪəs] *adj* gregario(a), sociable

Gregorian [grɪ'gɔ:rɪən] *adj* gregoriano(a) ❑ *Mus* **G. chant** canto *m* gregoriano

gremlin ['gremlɪn] *n* duende *m*

Grenada [gre'neɪdə] *n* Granada

grenade [grɪ'neɪd] *n Mil* granada *f* ❑ **hand g.** granada *f* de mano

Grenadian [gre'neɪdɪən] *adj & n* granadino(a) *(m,f)*

grenadier [grenə'dɪər] *n Mil* granadero *m*

grenadine[1] [grenə'di:n] *n Tex* granadina *f*

grenadine[2] ['grenədi:n] *n (syrup)* granadina *f*

grew [gru:] *pt see* **grow**

grey [greɪ] *Br* **1** *adj* (**greyer, greyest**) (**a**) *(colour)* gris; *(hair)* cano(a); *(sky)* nublado(a); **to go g.** *(sky)* nublarse; *(hair)* encanecer, volverse cano ❑ **g. matter** materia *f* gris (**b**) *(gloomy)* gris, triste
  2 *n* (**a**) *(colour)* gris *m* (**b**) *(horse)* caballo *m* tordo

grey-haired ['greɪheəd] *adj Br* de pelo cano, canoso(a)

Greyhound® [{'greɪhaʊnd] *n US* **G. (bus)** = autobús de largo recorrido

greyhound ['greɪhaʊnd] *n Zool* galgo *m*

greyish ['greɪɪʃ] *adj Br (gen)* grisáceo(a); *(hair)* entrecano(a)

grid [grɪd] *n* (**a**) *(on map etc)* cuadrícula *f* (**b**) *Tech (of electricity, water, etc)* red *f* nacional de suministro (**c**) *see* **gridiron**

griddle ['grɪdəl] *n Culin* plancha *f*

gridiron ['grɪdaɪən] *n* (**a**) *Culin* parrilla *f* (**b**) *US Ftb* campo *m* de fútbol

gridlock ['grɪdlɒk] *n US (traffic jam)* atasco *m,* embotellamiento *m*

grief [gri:f] *n* dolor *m,* pena *f; Fam* **to come to g.** *(car, driver)* sufrir un accidente; *(plans)* irse al traste; *Fam* **good g.!** ¡Dios mío!

grief-stricken ['gri:fstrɪkən] *adj* desconsolado(a)

grievance ['gri:vəns] *n* (**a**) *(wrong)* motivo *m* de queja, agravio *m* ❑ *Ind* **g. procedure** juicio *m* de faltas (**b**) *(resentment)* queja *f;* **to air one's grievances** desahogarse

grieve [gri:v] **1** *vt* apenar, dar pena a; **it grieves me to hear it** me da pena saberlo
  2 *vi* apenarse, afligirse; **to g. for sb** llorar la muerte de algn; **to g. over sth** lamentar algo

grievous ['gri:vəs] *adj (loss)* cruel, penoso(a); *(injury etc)* fuerte, doloroso(a); *(offence)* grave ❑ *Br Jur* **g. bodily harm** lesiones *fpl* corporales graves (de pronóstico reservado)

griffin ['grɪfɪn] *n Myth* grifo *m*

grill [grɪl] **1** *vt* (**a**) *Culin* asar a la parrilla; **grilled steak** bistec *m* a la parrilla (**b**) *Fam (interrogate)* interrogar duramente
  2 *n* (**a**) *(gridiron)* parrilla *f; Br (over cooker)* parrilla *f,* grill *m* (**b**) *Culin (dish)* parrillada *f,* asado *m* a la parrilla; **mixed g.** parrillada *f* de carne

grill(e) [grɪl] *n (grating)* reja *f,* verja *f,* enrejado *m; (latticework)* rejilla *f* ❑ *Aut* **radiator g.** calandra *f*

grilling ['grɪlɪŋ] *n Fam (interrogation)* **to give sb a g.** acribillar a algn a preguntas

grillroom ['grɪlru:m] *n (restaurant)* asador *m*

grim [grɪm] *adj* (**grimmer, grimmest**) (**a**) *(sinister)* macabro(a); *(landscape)* lúgubre; *(smile, laughter)* sardónico(a) (**b**) *(manner)* severo(a); *(expression)* ceñudo(a) (**c**) *(resolute)* inflexible, inexorable; **he held on like g. death** se agarró como si su vida dependiera de ello; **with g. determination** con una voluntad de hierro (**d**) *Fam (unpleasant)* desagradable; **g. reality** la dura realidad; **to feel g.** encontrarse *Esp* fatal *or Am* pésimo

grimace [grɪ'meɪs, 'grɪməs] **1** *n* mueca *f*
  2 *vi* hacer una mueca

grime [graɪm] *n* mugre *f,* suciedad *f*

grimly ['grɪmlɪ] *adv* (**a**) *(derisively)* sardónicamente (**b**) *(resolutely)* inexorablemente

grimy ['graɪmɪ] *adj* (**grimier, grimiest**) mugriento(a), sucio(a)

grin [grɪn] **1** *vi* (*pt & pp* **grinned**) sonreír abiertamente; *Fam* **to g. and bear it** poner al mal tiempo buena cara
   2 *n* sonrisa *f* abierta; *(ironic)* sonrisa *f* burlona

grind [graɪnd] **1** *vt* (*pt & pp* **ground**) *(mill)* moler; *(crush)* triturar; *(sharpen)* afilar; **to g. one's teeth** hacer rechinar los dientes; *Fig* **to have an axe to g.** tener intereses personales
   2 *vi* (**a**) *(wheels, gears)* chirriar; *Fig* **to g. to a halt** *(vehicle)* pararse ruidosamente; *(production etc)* pararse poco a poco (**b**) *Fam (swot)* empollar, machacar
   3 *n* (**a**) *Fam (routine)* trabajo *m* pesado; **the daily g.** la rutina cotidiana; **what a g.!** ¡qué rollo!, ¡qué lata! (**b**) *US Slang (student)* empollón(ona) *m,f*

grind down *vt sep Fig (oppress)* oprimir; **to g. down the opposition** acabar con la oposición

grind out *vt* (**a**) *(words)* decir gruñendo (**b**) *(tune)* machacar

grinder ['graɪndər] *n (for coffee, pepper)* molinillo *m*; *(crusher)* trituradora *f*

grinding ['graɪndɪŋ] *n* rechinamiento *m*

grindstone ['graɪndstəʊn] *n* muela *f*; *Fig* **to keep one's nose to the g.** trabajar sin levantar cabeza

gringo ['grɪŋgəʊ] *n* (*pl* **gringos**) *US Pej* gringo(a) *m,f*

grip [grɪp] **1** *n* (**a**) *(hold)* asimiento *m*; *(handshake)* apretón *m*; *(of tyre)* adherencia *f*; **to have a firm g. on sth** agarrar bien algo (**b**) *Fig (control)* dominio *m*, control *m*; **get a g. on yourself!** ¡tranquilízate!; **to come** *or* **get to grips with a problem** superar un problema; **to lose one's g.** perder el control (**c**) *(handle)* asidero *m*; *(of weapon)* empuñadura *f* (**d**) *US (bag)* bolsa *f* de viaje (**e**) *(hairgrip)* pasador *m*, horquilla *f*
   2 *vt* (*pt & pp* **gripped**) (**a**) *(gen)* agarrar, asir; *(weapon)* empuñar; *(hand)* apretar (**b**) *Fig (film, story)* captar la atención de; **to be gripped by fear** ser presa del miedo
   3 *vi (tyres)* adherirse a la carretera

gripe [graɪp] **1** *vi Fam (complain)* quejarse, refunfuñar
   2 *n* (**a**) *Med (pain)* retortijón *m*, cólico *m* ❑ *Br* **g. water** calmante *m* para el cólico infantil (**b**) *Fam (complaint)* queja *f*

gripping ['grɪpɪŋ] *adj (film, story)* apasionante

grisly ['grɪzlɪ] *adj* (**grislier, grisliest**) espeluznante, horripilante

grist [grɪst] *n* grano *m*; *Fam* **it's all g. to the mill** todo ayuda

gristle ['grɪsəl] *n* cartílago *m*, ternilla *f*

gristly ['grɪslɪ] *adj* (**gristlier, gristliest**) cartilaginoso(a), ternilloso(a)

grit [grɪt] **1** *n* (**a**) *(sand)* arena *f*; *(gravel)* grava *f* (**b**) *(sandstone)* arenisca *f*, asperón *m* (**c**) *Fam (courage)* valor *m*; **she's got g.** tiene agallas
   2 *vt* (*pt & pp* **gritted**) (**a**) *Br (cover with grit)* cubrir de arena *or* grava (**b**) *Fig* hacer rechinar; **to g. one's teeth** apretar los dientes

grits [grɪts] *npl US Culin* (**hominy**) **g.** maíz *m sing* molido

gritty ['grɪtɪ] *adj* (**grittier, grittiest**) (**a**) *(courageous)* valiente, duro(a) (**b**) *(sandy)* arenoso(a); *(gravelly)* cubierto(a) de grava

grizzle ['grɪzəl] *vi Br Fam* (**a**) *(whine)* lloriquear (**b**) *(complain)* refunfuñar

grizzled ['grɪzəld] *adj* gris, entrecano(a), canoso(a)

grizzly ['grɪzlɪ] *adj* (**grizzlier, grizzliest**) gris, pardo(a) ❑ *Zool* **g. bear** oso *m* pardo

groan [grəʊn] **1** *n* (**a**) *(of pain)* gemido *m*; *(tree etc)* crujido *m* (**b**) *Fam (of disapproval)* gruñido *m*
   2 *vi* (**a**) *(in pain)* gemir; *(plank, table)* crujir (**b**) *Fam (complain)* quejarse (**about** de), gruñir

grocer ['grəʊsər] *n* tendero(a) *m,f*; *Br* **g.'s (shop)** *Esp* tienda *f* de comestibles, *CSur* almacén *m*, *Col Méx* tienda *f* de abarrotes

groceries ['grəʊsərɪz] *npl* comestibles *mpl*

grocery ['grəʊsərɪ] *n (shop) Esp* tienda *f* de comestibles, *CSur* almacén *m*, *Col Méx* tienda *f* de abarrotes ❑ *esp US* **g. store** supermercado *m*

grog [grɒg] *n* grog *m*, ponche *m*

groggy ['grɒgɪ] *adj* (**groggier, groggiest**) *Fam* (**a**) *Box* grogui; *Fig (unsteady)* grogui, atontado(a); *(reeling)* tambaleante (**b**) *(weak)* débil

groin [grɔɪn] *n Anat* ingle *f*

groom [gru:m] **1** *n* (**a**) *(for horses)* mozo *m* de cuadra (**b**) *(bridegroom)* novio *m*
   2 *vt (horse)* almohazar; *(clothes, appearance)* cuidar; **well groomed** bien arreglado(a); *Fig* **to g. sb for a post** preparar a algn para un puesto

grooming ['gru:mɪŋ] *n (smart, neat appearance)* buena presencia *f*

groove [gru:v] *n (furrow etc)* ranura *f*; *(of record)* surco *m*

groovy ['gru:vɪ] *adj* (**groovier, grooviest**) *Fam Esp* chachi, *Méx* padre, *RP* bárbaro(a)

grope [grəʊp] *vi* (**a**) *(search about)* andar a tientas; **to g. for sth** buscar algo a tientas (**b**) *Slang (fondle)* meter mano a, sobar

gross [grəʊs] **1** *adj* (**a**) *(coarse)* basto(a), grosero(a); *(joke)* verde (**b**) *(fat)* muy gordo(a), obeso(a) (**c**) *(flagrant) (injustice)* flagrante; *(ignorance)* craso(a) (**d**) *Com Econ (profit, weight, income)* bruto(a) ❑ **g. domestic product** producto *m Esp* interior *or Am* interno bruto; **g. margin** beneficio *m or* margen *m* bruto; **g. national product** producto *m* nacional bruto
   2 *n* (**a**) *(pl* **gross**) *(unit)* gruesa *f*, doce docenas *fpl*; *Com* **by the g.** (a) por mayor, en grueso (**b**) *(pl* **grosses**) totalidad *f*
   3 *vt (gain)* recaudar (en bruto); **he grosses $60,000 a year** tiene unos ingresos brutos de 60 mil dólares al año

gross out *vt US Slang* revolver el estómago a

grossly ['grəʊslɪ] *adv* enormemente; **g. exaggerated** muy exagerado(a); **g. unfair** totalmente injusto(a)

grotesque [grəʊ'tesk] *adj* grotesco(a)

grotto ['grɒtəʊ] *n* (*pl* **grottos** *or* **grottoes**) gruta *f*

grotty ['grɒtɪ] *adj* (**grottier, grottiest**) *Br Slang* malo(a), *Esp* cutre, *Méx* gacho(a), *RP* roñoso(a); **to feel g.** sentirse *Esp* fatal *or Am* pésimo

grouch [graʊtʃ] **1** *vi Fam* refunfuñar, quejarse
   2 *n (person)* gruñón(ona) *m,f*, cascarrabias *mf*

grouchy ['graʊtʃɪ] *adj* (**grouchier, grouchiest**) refunfuñón(ona), quejica

ground¹ [graʊnd] **1** *n* (**a**) *(surface)* suelo *m*, tierra *f*; **at g. level** al nivel del suelo; **stony g.** suelo pedregoso; **to fall to the g.** caer al suelo; **to get off the g.** *(plane)* despegar; *Fig (scheme)* realizarse; **to sit on the g.** sentarse en el suelo; **to touch g.** tocar fondo; *Fig* **above g.** vivo(a); *Fig* **to go to g.** esconderse; *Br Fam* **it suits me down to the g.** me viene de perlas ❑ *Av* **g. control** control *m* de tierra; *Br* **g. floor** planta *f* baja; *Mil* **g. forces** ejército *m* de tierra; *Av* **g. staff** personal *m* de tierra; **g. swell** mar *m* de fondo; *Fig* marejada *f* (**b**) *(terrain)* terreno *m*; **to gain/lose g.** ganar/ perder terreno; *Fig* **to break new** *or* **fresh g.** abrir nuevos horizontes; *Fig* **to hold** *or* **stand one's g.** mantenerse firme ❑ **breeding g.** semillero *m*; **football g.** campo *m* de fútbol, estadio *m* (**c**) *US Elec* toma *f* de tierra (**d**) **grounds** *(gardens)* jardines *mpl*, parque *m sing* (**e**) **grounds** *(reason)* motivo *m sing*, razón *f sing*; **g. for divorce** motivo de divorcio; **on health g.** por motivos de salud (**f**) **grounds** *(sediment)* poso *m sing*, sedimento *m sing*
   2 *vt* (**a**) *Av* obligar a quedarse en tierra; *Naut* varar (**b**) *US*

Elec conectar con tierra (**c**) *(teach)* enseñar los conocimientos básicos a; **to be well grounded in** ser muy entendido(a) en

ground² [graʊnd] **1** *pt & pp see* **grind**
 2 *adj (coffee)* molido(a); *US (meat)* picado(a)

groundbreaking ['graʊndbreɪkɪŋ] *adj* innovador(a)

groundcloth ['graʊndklɒθ] *n US (of tent)* suelo *f*

groundhog ['graʊndhɒg] *n Zool* marmota *f* ❑ *US* **G. Day** día *m* dos de febrero

grounding ['graʊndɪŋ] *n* base *f*, conocimientos *mpl*; **to have a good g. in** tener buenos conocimientos de

groundless ['graʊndlɪs] *adj* sin fundamento, infundado(a)

groundnut ['graʊndnʌt] *n Br Esp* cacahuete *m*, *Am* maní *m*, *CAm Méx* cacahuate *m*

groundsheet ['graʊndʃiːt] *n Br (of tent)* suelo *f*

groundsman ['graʊndzmən] *n (pl* **groundsmen**) *Sport* encargado *m* de campo

groundswell ['graʊndswel] *n* oleada *f*

groundwork ['graʊndwɜːk] *n* trabajo *m* preparatorio *or* preliminar

group [gruːp] **1** *n (gen)* grupo *m*, conjunto *m* ❑ *Med* **blood g.** grupo *m* sanguíneo; **g. dynamics** dinámica *f* de grupo; *Med* **g. practice** gabinete *m* médico; *Psych* **g. therapy** psicoterapia *f* de grupo; *Pol* **pressure g.** grupo *m* de presión
 2 *vt* agrupar, juntar (**into** en)
 3 *vi* **to g. (together)** agruparse, juntarse

grouper ['gruːpər] *n (fish)* mero *m*

groupie ['gruːpɪ] *n Slang* = fan que intenta ligar con los miembros de un grupo de rock

grouse¹ [graʊs] *n (pl* **grouse** *or* **grouses**) *Orn* urogallo *m* ❑ **red g.** lagópodo *m* escocés

grouse² [graʊs] *Fam* **1** *vi* quejarse (**about** de)
 2 *n* queja *f*, motivo *m* de queja

grout [graʊt] *n Constr* lechada *f*

grove [grəʊv] *n* arboleda *f*, bosquecillo *m*; **orange g.** naranjal *m*

grovel ['grɒvəl] *vi (pt & pp* **grovelled**, *US* **groveled**) *(humble)* humillarse, rebajarse (**to** ante); *(crawl)* arrastrarse (**to** ante)

grovelling, *US* **groveling** ['grɒvəlɪŋ] *adj* servil, rastrero(a)

grow [grəʊ] **1** *vt (pt* **grew**; *pp* **grown**) *(cultivate)* cultivar; **to g. a beard** dejarse (crecer) la barba
 2 *vi* (**a**) *(gen)* crecer; *(increase)* aumentar (**b**) *(become)* hacerse, volverse; **to g. accustomed to** acostumbrarse a; **to g. dark** oscurecer; **to g. into a woman** hacerse mujer; **to g. old** envejecer

grow on *vt* llegar a gustar

grow out of *vt* (**a**) *(become too big for)* **he's grown out of his shirt** se le ha quedado pequeña la camisa (**b**) *Fig (phase etc)* superar

grow up *vi (become adult)* crecer, hacerse mayor; **they grew up together** se criaron juntos; *Fam* **g. up!** ¡no seas niño *or Esp* crío!

grower ['grəʊər] *n* cultivador(a) *m,f*

growing ['grəʊɪŋ] *adj (child)* que crece; *(problem etc)* creciente; **he's a g. boy** el niño crece cada día más ❑ **g. pains** *Med* dolores *mpl* producidos por el crecimiento; *Fig* problemas *mpl* iniciales

growl [graʊl] **1** *vi* (**a**) *(dog)* gruñir (**b**) *(person)* refunfuñar
 2 *vt* decir refunfuñando
 3 *n* gruñido *m*

growling ['graʊlɪŋ] *n* gruñidos *mpl*

grown [grəʊn] **1** *pp see* **grow**
 2 *adj* crecido(a), adulto(a)

grown-up ['grəʊnʌp] *adj & n* adulto(a) *(m,f)*; **the grown-ups** los mayores

growth [grəʊθ] *n* (**a**) *(gen)* crecimiento *m*; *(increase)* aumento *m*; *(development)* desarrollo *m*; **economic g.** desarrollo económico; **three days' g. of beard** barba *f* de tres días; **g. industry** industria *f* en expansión (**b**) *Med* bulto *m*, tumor *m*

grub [grʌb] **1** *vi (pt & pp* **grubbed**) **to g. about** *or* **around** hurgar, rebuscar (**in** entre)
 2 *n* (**a**) *(larva)* larva *f*, gusano *m* (**b**) *Slang (food)* comida *f*, *Esp* manduca *f*, *RP* morfi *m*; **g.'s up!** ¡a comer! (**c**) *Fam (drudge)* chupatintas *mf inv*

grubbiness ['grʌbɪnɪs] *n* suciedad *f*

grubby ['grʌbɪ] *adj* (**grubbier**, **grubbiest**) sucio(a), mugriento(a)

grudge [grʌdʒ] **1** *n* rencor *m*, resentimiento *m*; **to bear sb a g.** guardar rencor a algn
 2 *vt* (**a**) *(give unwillingly)* dar a regañadientes (**b**) *(envy)* envidiar; **he grudges me my success** me envidia el éxito

grudging ['grʌdʒɪŋ] *adj* **he felt g. respect for her** sentía respeto por ella a pesar de sí mismo; **to be g. in one's praise** ser reacio(a) a alabar

grudgingly ['grʌdʒɪŋlɪ] *adv* a regañadientes, de mala gana

gruel ['gruːəl] *n Culin* gachas *fpl*

gruelling, *US* **grueling** ['gruːəlɪŋ] *adj* agotador(a), duro(a), penoso(a)

gruesome ['gruːsəm] *adj* espantoso(a), horrible, horripilante

gruff [grʌf] *adj (manner)* brusco(a); *(voice)* áspero(a)

gruffly ['grʌflɪ] *adv* en un tono brusco

gruffness ['grʌfnɪs] *n* brusquedad *f*, aspereza *f*

grumble ['grʌmbəl] **1** *vi* quejarse (**about** de), refunfuñar
 2 *n* queja *f*; **to have a g. about sth** quejarse de algo

grumbler ['grʌmblər] *n* refunfuñón(ona) *m,f*, quejica *mf*, gruñón(ona) *m,f*

grumbling ['grʌmblɪŋ] **1** *adj* gruñón(ona), refunfuñón(ona); *Fam* **g. appendix** apendicitis *f* crónica
 2 *n* quejas *fpl*

grump [grʌmp] *n Fam (person)* gruñón(ona) *m,f*

grumpily ['grʌmpɪlɪ] *adv* con mal humor, de mala gana

grumpy ['grʌmpɪ] *adj* (**grumpier**, **grumpiest**) gruñón(ona), malhumorado(a)

grunge [grʌndʒ] *n (music)* (música *f*) grunge *m*

grungy ['grʌndʒɪ] *adj* (**grungier**, **grungiest**) *US Fam* asqueroso(a), *Esp* cutre, *Méx* gacho(a), *RP* roñoso(a)

grunt [grʌnt] **1** *vi* gruñir
 2 *vt* decir gruñendo
 3 *n* (**a**) *(of pig, person)* gruñido *m* (**b**) *US Fam (foot soldier)* soldado *mf* de infantería

gryphon ['grɪfn] *n see* **griffin**

Guadaloupe [gwɑːdəˈluːp] *n* Guadalupe

Guam [gwɑːm] *n* Guam

guarantee [gærənˈtiː] **1** *n (gen)* garantía *f*; *(certificate)* certificado *m* de garantía; *Com* **a six-month g.** una garantía de seis meses; **there's no g. that they will come** no hay ninguna garantía de que vengan; **under g.** bajo garantía
 2 *vt (gen)* garantizar; *(assure)* asegurar; *(take responsibility for)* responder de; **I can't g. it** no te lo puedo asegurar; **it is guaranteed for five years** está garantizado por cinco años

guarantor [gærənˈtɔːr] *n* garante *mf*

guard [gɑːd] **1** *vt* (**a**) *(protect)* defender, proteger; *(keep watch over)* vigilar; **a closely guarded secret** un secreto bien guardado (**b**) *(control)* guardar

2 *vi* protegerse (**against** de, contra); **g. against doing that** guárdate de hacer eso

3 *n* (**a**) *(act)* guardia *f*; **to be on g.** estar de guardia; **to be on one's g.** estar en guardia; **to catch sb off his g.** agarrar *or Esp* coger a algn desprevenido; **to put sb on his g.** poner en guardia a algn (**b**) *Mil (sentry)* guardia *mf*; *(body of sentries)* guardia *f*; **g. of honour** guardia de honor; **the changing of the g.** el relevo de la guardia; **the Guards** la guardia; **to mount** *or* **stand g.** montar la guardia ◻ **g. dog** perro *m* guardián (**c**) *US (in prison)* funcionario(a) *m,f* de prisiones, guardián(ana) *m,f* (**d**) *Br Rail* jefe *m* de tren ◻ **g.'s van** furgón *m* de cola (**e**) *(on machine)* seguro *m*, dispositivo *m* de seguridad ◻ **fire g.** pantalla *f*

guarded [ˈɡɑːdɪd] *adj* cauteloso(a), precavido(a)

guardedly [ˈɡɑːdɪdlɪ] *adv* cautelosamente, con cautela

guardhouse [ˈɡɑːdhaʊs] *n* (**a**) *(headquarters)* cuerpo *m* de guardia (**b**) *(prison)* prisión *f* militar

guardian [ˈɡɑːdɪən] *n* (**a**) *(defender)* guardián(ana) *m,f* ◻ **g. angel** ángel *m* de la guarda (**b**) *Jur (of minor)* tutor(a) *m,f*

guardrail [ˈɡɑːdreɪl] *n* pasamanos *m inv*, *Esp* barandilla *f*

guardsman [ˈɡɑːdzmən] *n* *(pl* **guardsmen**) *Br Mil* guardia *m*

Guatemala [ɡwɑːtəˈmɑːlə] *n* Guatemala

Guatemalan [ɡwɑːtəˈmɑːlən] *adj & n* guatemalteco(a) *(m,f)*

guava [ˈɡwɑːvə] *n* *Bot* guayaba *f* ◻ **g. tree** guayabo *m*

gubernatorial [ɡuːbənəˈtɔːrɪəl] *adj* *Fml* del/de la gobernador(a); **a g. candidate/election** un candidato/ unas elecciones a gobernador

gudgeon¹ [ˈɡʌdʒən] *n* *(fish)* gobio *m*

gudgeon² [ˈɡʌdʒən] *n* *Tech (of axle)* gorrón *m*

Guernsey [ˈɡɜːnzɪ] *n* Guernesey

guer(r)illa [ɡəˈrɪlə] *n* guerrillero(a) *m,f* ◻ **g. warfare** guerra *f* de guerrillas

guess [ɡes] **1** *vt & vi* (**a**) *(gen)* adivinar; **g. what happened today!** ¡adivina lo que ha pasado hoy!; **I guessed as much** me lo imaginaba; **to g. right/wrong** acertar/no acertar; **to keep sb guessing** mantener a algn en la incertidumbre (**b**) *US Fam* creer, pensar, suponer; **I g. so** supongo que sí

2 *n* *(gen)* conjetura *f*, suposición *f*; *(estimate)* cálculo *m*, suposición *f*; **at a rough g.** a ojo de buen cubero; **have a g.!** ¡a ver si aciertas!; **it's anyone's g.** no se sabe; **to have** *or* **make a g.** intentar adivinar

guessing game [ˈɡesɪŋɡeɪm] *n* (juego *m* de las) adivinanzas *fpl*

gues(s)timate [ˈɡestɪmɪt] *n* *Fam* cálculo *m* aproximado

guesswork [ˈɡeswɜːk] *n* conjetura *f*; **it's all g.** es pura conjetura

guest [ɡest] *n* *(at home)* invitado(a) *m,f*; *(in hotel)* cliente(a) *m,f*, huésped(eda) *m,f*; **g. of honour** invitado(a) de honor; *Fam* **be my g.!** ¡estás en tu casa! ◻ **g. artist** artista *mf* invitado(a); **g. room** cuarto *m* de los invitados; **g. worker** = extranjero con permiso de trabajo

guesthouse [ˈɡesthaʊs] *n* *Br* casa *f* de huéspedes

guffaw [ɡʌˈfɔː] **1** *n* carcajada *f*

2 *vi* reírse a carcajadas

GUI [ˈɡuːɪ] *n* *Comptr (abbr* **Graphical User Interface**) interfaz *f* gráfica

Guiana [ɡaɪˈænə] *n* Guayana ◻ **French G.** Guayana Francesa

Guianan [ɡaɪˈænən] *adj & n*, **Guianese** [ɡaɪəˈniːz] *adj & n* guayanés(esa) *(m,f)*

guidance [ˈɡaɪdəns] *n* orientación *f*, consejos *mpl*; **for your g.** a título de información; *Educ* **vocational g.** orientación profesional

guide [ɡaɪd] **1** *vt* guiar, orientar, dirigir; **to be guided by** dejarse guiar por

2 *n* (**a**) *(person)* guía *mf* ◻ *Br* (**girl**) **g.** exploradora *f*; **g. dog** perro *m* lazarillo (**b**) *(guidebook)* guía *f* (**c**) *(example)* ejemplo *m*; **it's a rough g.** es una aproximación; **reason is my g.** me dejo guiar por la razón

guidebook [ˈɡaɪdbʊk] *n* guía *f*

guided [ˈɡaɪdɪd] *adj* dirigido(a) ◻ *Mil* **g. missile** misil *m* teledirigido; **g. tour** visita *f* con guía

guideline [ˈɡaɪdlaɪn] *n* directiva *f*, directriz *f*, pauta *f*; **to serve as a g.** servir de gobierno *or* de directriz

guiding [ˈɡaɪdɪŋ] *adj* que sirve de guía; *(principle)* directivo(a); *Fig* **g. light, g. star** lumbrera *f*

guild [ɡɪld] *n* gremio *m*

guile [ɡaɪl] *n* *(cleverness)* sagacidad *f*; *(cunning)* astucia *f*

guileless [ˈɡaɪlɪs] *adj* inocente, ingenuo(a)

guillemot [ˈɡɪlɪmɒt] *n* *Orn* arao *m* común

guillotine [ˈɡɪlətiːn] **1** *n* guillotina *f*

2 *vt* guillotinar

guilt [ɡɪlt] *n* (**a**) *(gen)* culpa *f*; **g. feelings** sentimiento de culpabilidad (**b**) *Jur* culpabilidad *f*

guilty [ˈɡɪltɪ] *adj* (**guiltier, guiltiest**) culpable (**of** de); **to feel g.** sentirse culpable; **to have a g. conscience** remorderle a uno la conciencia; *Jur* **to plead g./not g.** declararse culpable/inocente

Guinea [ˈɡɪnɪ] *n* Guinea ◻ **Equatorial G.** Guinea Ecuatorial; **g. fowl** gallina *f* de Guinea; *Zool* **g. pig** conejillo *m* de Indias, cobaya *m*, cobayo *m*; *Fig* **to act as a g. pig** servir de conejillo de Indias

guinea [ˈɡɪnɪ] *n* *Br (coin)* guinea *f* (= 21 chelines)

Guinea-Bissau [ɡɪnɪbɪˈsaʊ] *n* Guinea Bissau

Guinean [ˈɡɪnɪən] *adj & n* guineano(a) *(m,f)*

guipure [ɡɪˈpjʊər] *n* *Tex* guipur *m*

guise [ɡaɪz] *n* apariencia *f*; **under the g. of** so pretexto de

guitar [ɡɪˈtɑːr] *n* guitarra *f*

guitarist [ɡɪˈtɑːrɪst] *n* guitarrista *mf*, guitarra *mf*

gulch [ɡʌltʃ] *n* *US (valley)* garganta *f*, hoz *f*

gulf [ɡʌlf] *n* (**a**) *Geog* golfo *m* ◻ **G. of Bothnia** Golfo *m* de Botnia; **G. of Guinea** Golfo *m* de Guinea; **G. of Lions** Golfo *m* de León; **G. of Mexico** Golfo *m* de Méjico; **G. Stream** corriente *f* del Golfo de Méjico; **Persian G.** golfo *m* Pérsico (**b**) *Fig* abismo *m*

gull [ɡʌl] *n* *Orn* gaviota *f* ◻ **black-headed g.** gaviota *f* reidora; **common g.** gaviota *f* cana; **herring g.** gaviota *f* argéntea; **little g.** gaviota *f* enana

gullet [ˈɡʌlɪt] *n* esófago *m*

gull(e)y [ˈɡʌlɪ] *n* *(pl* **gulleys** *or* **gullies**) barranco *m*, hondonada *f*

gullibility [ɡʌləˈbɪlɪtɪ] *n* credulidad *f*, tragaderas *fpl*

gullible [ˈɡʌləbəl] *adj* crédulo(a)

gulp [ɡʌlp] **1** *n* trago *m*; **in one g.** de un trago

2 *vt* tragar; **to g. back tears** tragarse las lágrimas; **to g. sth down** *(drink)* tomarse algo de un trago; *(food)* engullir algo

3 *vi* (**a**) *(swallow air)* tragar aire (**b**) *Fig (with fear)* tragar saliva

gum¹ [ɡʌm] **1** *n* (**a**) *(natural substance)* goma *f*, chicle *m* ◻ **chewing g.** chicle *m*, goma *f* de mascar; **g. arabic** goma *f* arábiga (**b**) *(glue)* goma *f*, pegamento *m* (**c**) *Bot (gumtree)* gomero *m* ◻ **sweet g.** ocozol *m*, liquidámbar *m* americano

2 *vt* *(pt & pp* **gummed**) pegar con goma

gum up *vt* *Fam* estropear

gum² [ɡʌm] *n* *Anat* encía *f* ◻ **g. disease** gingivitis *f inv*

gumboil [ˈɡʌmbɔɪl] *n* *Med* flemón *m*

gumboots ['gʌmbuːts] *npl* botas *fpl* de agua *or* goma *or* *Méx Ven* caucho

gummed [gʌmd] *adj* engomado(a), gomoso(a)

gummy ['gʌmɪ] *adj* (**gummier, gummiest**) (**a**) *(sticky)* pegajoso(a) (**b**) *(gummed)* engomado(a), gomoso(a)

gumption ['gʌmpʃən] *n* *Br Fam* caletre *m*, mollera *f*, cacumen *m*

gumtree ['gʌmtriː] *n* *Bot* gomero *m*; *Fam* **to be up a g.** estar en un aprieto

gun [gʌn] **1** *n* *(gen)* arma *f* de fuego; *(handgun)* pistola *f*, revólver *m*; *(rifle)* fusil *m*, rifle *m*, escopeta *f*; *(cannon)* cañón *m*; **he was carrying a g.** iba armado; *Fam* **the big guns** los peces gordos; *Fam* **to jump the g.** adelantarse; *Fam* **to stick to one's guns** mantenerse en sus trece; *Slang* **to go great guns** ir a toda pastilla ❑ **g. carriage** cureña *f*; **g. dog** perro *m* de caza; **g. laws** legislación *f* sobre armas de fuego; **g. licence** licencia *f* de armas; **machine g.** ametralladora *f*; **spray g.** pistola *f*, pulverizador *m*; **sub-machine-g.** metralleta *f*

   2 *vt* *(pt & pp* **gunned**) *Aut (engine)* hacer zumbar

gun down *vt* matar a tiros

gun for *vt (hunt down)* andar a la caza de

gunboat ['gʌnbəʊt] *n* *Naut* cañonero *m*, (lancha *f)* cañonera *f* ❑ *Fig* **g. diplomacy** diplomacia *f* de cañón

gunfight ['gʌnfaɪt] *n* tiroteo *m*

gunfire ['gʌnfaɪər] *n* *(gen)* fuego *m*, tiros *mpl*; *(shellfire)* cañoneo *m*; *(shooting)* tiroteo *m*

gung-ho ['gʌŋ'həʊ] *adj (enthusiastic)* exaltado(a); *(eager for war)* belicoso(a); **to be g. about sth** lanzar las campanas al vuelo con relación a algo

gunk [gʌŋk] *n* *Fam* porquería *f*, *Esp* pringue *f*

gunman ['gʌnmən] *n (pl* **gunmen**) pistolero *m*, gángster *m*

gunner ['gʌnər] *n* *Mil* artillero *m*

gunnery ['gʌnərɪ] *n* *Mil* artillería *f*

gunpoint ['gʌnpɔɪnt] *n* **at g.** a punta de pistola

gunpowder ['gʌnpaʊdər] *n* pólvora *f*

gunrunner ['gʌnrʌnər] *n* traficante *mf* de armas

gunrunning ['gʌnrʌnɪŋ] *n* tráfico *m* de armas

gunshot ['gʌnʃɒt] *n* disparo *m*, tiro *m* ❑ **g. wounds** heridas *fpl* de bala

gunsmith ['gʌnsmɪθ] *n* armero *m*

gunwale ['gʌnəl] *n* *Naut* regala *f*, borda *f*

gurgle ['gɜːgəl] **1** *vi (baby)* gorjear; *(liquid, gas)* gorgotear; *(stream)* murmurar

   2 *n (of baby)* gorjeo *m*; *(of liquid, gas)* gorgoteo *m*, gluglú *m*; *(of stream)* murmullo *m*

gurnard ['gɜːnəd] *n (pl* **gurnard** *or* **gurnards**) *(fish)* red **g.** arete *m*, cuco *m*, rubio *m*

guru ['gʊruː, 'guːruː] *n* gurú *m*

gush [gʌʃ] **1** *vi* (**a**) *(spurt, pour)* manar, correr (**b**) *Fig* **to g. over sb** enjabonar a algn

   2 *n* (**a**) *(of water etc)* chorro *m*; *(of words)* torrente *m* (**b**) *Fig* efusión *f*, sentimentalismo *m*

gushing ['gʌʃɪŋ] *adj* (**a**) *(liquid, gas)* que brota, que sale a chorros (**b**) *Fig (person)* efusivo(a)

gusset ['gʌsɪt] *n* *Sew* escudete *m*

gust [gʌst] *n (of wind)* ráfaga *f*, racha *f*; *(of rain)* chaparrón *m*

gusto ['gʌstəʊ] *n* entusiasmo *m*, placer *m*; **to eat with g.** comer con ganas

gusty ['gʌstɪ] *adj* (**gustier, gustiest**) *(wind)* racheado(a)

gut [gʌt] **1** *n* (**a**) *Anat (intestine)* intestino *m*, tripa *f* (**b**) *(catgut)* cuerda *f* de tripa (**c**) **guts** *(entrails)* entrañas *fpl*, tripas *fpl* (**d**) *Slang* **guts** agallas *fpl*; **to have g.** tener agallas; *Fam* **she hates his g.** no lo puede ni ver; *Fam* **to sweat** *or* **work one's g. out** dejarse la piel en algo, trabajar como un negro

   2 *vt* *(pt & pp* **gutted**) (**a**) *(fish etc)* destripar, limpiar (**b**) *(destroy)* destruir por dentro; **fire gutted the building** el fuego destruyó el interior del edificio

   3 *adj* *Fam* visceral; **g. reaction** reacción visceral

gutsy ['gʌtsɪ] *adj* (**gutsier, gutsiest**) *Slang (courageous)* con agallas; *(determined)* lanzado(a)

gutta-percha [gʌtə'pɜːtʃə] *n* gutapercha *f*

gutter ['gʌtər] **1** *n (in street)* arroyo *m*, cuneta *f*; *(on roof)* canal *m*, canalón *m*; *Fig* **the g.** los barrios bajos; *Fig* **to rise from the g.** salir del arroyo *or* de la nada ❑ *Fig* **g. press** prensa *f* amarilla

   2 *vi (candle)* derretirse

guttural ['gʌtərəl] *adj* gutural

guy¹ [gaɪ] *n* *Fam* tipo *m*, *Esp* tío *m*; **he's a great g.** es un chico estupendo ❑ **tough g.** tío *m* duro, matón *m*; **wise g.** sabihondo *m*, sabelotodo *m* inv

guy² [gaɪ] *n (rope)* viento *m*, cuerda *f*

Guyana [gaɪ'ænə] *n* Guyana

Guyanan [gaɪ'ænən] *adj & n*, **Guyanese** [gaɪə'niːz] *adj & n* guyanés(esa) *(m,f)* guayanés(esa) *(m,f)*

guzzle ['gʌzəl] *vt & vi Fam (food etc)* engullirse, zamparse, tragarse; *(car)* tragar mucho

guzzler ['gʌzlər] *n* *Fam (person)* tragón(ona) *m,f*, comilón(ona) *m,f*, glotón(ona) *m,f*

gym [dʒɪm] *Fam* (**a**) *(gymnasium)* gimnasio *m* (**b**) *(gymnastics)* gimnasia *f* ❑ **g. shoes** zapatillas *fpl* de deporte

gymkhana [dʒɪm'kɑːnə] *n* *Equit* gymkhana *f*

gymnasium [dʒɪm'neɪzɪəm] *n* *(pl* **gymnasiums** *or* **gymnasia** [dʒɪm'neɪzɪə]*)* gimnasio *m*

gymnast ['dʒɪmnæst] *n* gimnasta *mf*

gymnastic [dʒɪm'næstɪk] *adj* gimnástico(a)

gymnastics [dʒɪm'næstɪks] *n* gimnasia *f*

gynaecological, *US* **gynecological** [gaɪnɪkə'lɒdʒɪkəl] *adj Med* ginecológico(a)

gynaecologist, *US* **gynecologist** [gaɪnɪ'kɒlədʒɪst] *n* *Med* ginecólogo(a) *m,f*

gynaecology, *US* **gynecology** [gaɪnɪ'kɒlədʒɪ] *n* *Med* ginecología *f*

gyp [dʒɪp] *n* *Br Fam* **my tooth/leg is giving me g.** la muela/pierna me está matando

gypsum ['dʒɪpsəm] *n* yeso *m*

gypsy ['dʒɪpsɪ] *adj & n* gitano(a) *(m,f)*

gyrate [dʒaɪ'reɪt] *vi* girar, dar vueltas

gyration [dʒaɪ'reɪʃən] *n* giro *m*, vuelta *f*

gyratory ['dʒaɪrətərɪ] *adj* giratorio(a)

gyrocompass ['dʒaɪrəʊkʌmpəs] *n* girocompás *m*

gyroscope ['dʒaɪrəskəʊp] *n* giroscopio *m*, giróscopo *m*

gyroscopic [dʒaɪrə'skɒpɪk] *adj* giroscópico(a)

H

H, h [eɪtʃ] *n (the letter)* H, h *f*

H *(abbr* **hydrogen)** hidrógeno *m*, H

ha *(abbr* **hectare)** hectárea *f*, ha

habeas corpus [ˈheɪbɪəsˈkɔːpəs] *n Jur* habeas corpus

haberdasher [ˈhæbədæʃər] *n* (**a**) *Br (draper)* mercero(a) *m,f; (shop)* **h.'s** mercería *f* (**b**) *US (men's outfitter)* propietario(a) *m,f* de una tienda *f* de ropa para caballeros

haberdashery [hæbəˈdæʃərɪ] *n* (**a**) *Br (sewing items, shop)* mercería *f* (**b**) *US (men's clothes)* ropa *f* de caballero; *(shop)* tienda *f* de confección de caballero

habit [ˈhæbɪt] *n* (**a**) *(custom)* hábito *m*, costumbre *f*; **bad h.** vicio *m*; **out of h.** por costumbre; **to be in the h. of** tener la costumbre de; **to get into the h. of** coger la costumbre de, acostumbrarse a; **to get out of the h. of** perder la costumbre de; **to kick the h.** dejar el vicio; **to make a h. of sth** hacer de algo una costumbre (**b**) *(garment) Rel* hábito *m*

habitable [ˈhæbɪtəbəl] *adj* habitable

habitat [ˈhæbɪtæt] *n* hábitat *m*

habitation [hæbɪˈteɪʃən] *n Fml* habitación *f*; **unfit for human h.** inhabitable

habit-forming [ˈhæbɪtfɔːmɪŋ] *adj* que crea hábito *or* dependencia

habitual [həˈbɪtjuəl] *adj (customary)* habitual, acostumbrado(a); *(of drinker, smoker, liar)* inveterado(a), empedernido(a)

habitually [həˈbɪtjuəlɪ] *adv* por costumbre, habitualmente

habituate [həˈbɪtjʊeɪt] *vt Fml* habituar (**a** to), acostumbrar (**a** to); **to become habituated to sth** habituarse a algo

habitué [həˈbɪtjʊeɪ] *n Fml* parroquiano(a) *m,f* habitual

hack¹ [hæk] **1** *n (cut)* corte *m*, tajo *m; (with an axe)* hachazo *m; (notch)* mella *f, (kick)* patada *f*, puntapié *m*
   2 *vt (with knife, axe)* cortar, rajar; *(notch)* mellar; *(kick)* dar un puntapié a; *Comptr* **to h. into a computer system** introducirse ilegalmente en un sistema informático

hack about *vt (text, article)* cortar, mutilar

hack² [hæk] **1** *n* (**a**) *(hired horse)* caballo *m* de alquiler; *(worn-out horse)* rocín *m*, jamelgo *m* (**b**) *Fam (writer)* escritorzuelo(a) *m,f; (journalist)* gacetillero(a) *m,f*, periodista *mf* de poca categoría
   2 *adj Fam (work)* mecánico(a), rutinario(a)
   3 *vi Fam* montar a caballo

hacker [ˈhækər] *n Comptr* pirata *mf* informático(a), hacker *mf*

hacking¹ [ˈhækɪŋ] **1** *n Comptr* piratería informática
   2 *adj (cough)* seco(a), áspero(a)

hacking² *adj* de montar ❑ **h. jacket** chaqueta *f* de montar

hackles [ˈhæklz] *npl Zool (of bird)* collar *m*, plumas *fpl* del cuello; *(of mammal)* pelo *m* del cuello; *Fig* **to put sb's h. up** poner negro(a) a algn

hackneyed [ˈhæknɪd] *adj* gastado(a), trillado(a)

hacksaw [ˈhæksɔː] *n* sierra *f* para metales

had [hæd] *pt & pp see* **have**

haddock [ˈhædək] *n (pl* **haddocks** *or* **haddock)** *(fish)* abadejo *m*

haemoglobin [hiːməʊˈɡləʊbɪn] *n Med* hemoglobina *f*

haemophilia [hiːməʊˈfɪlɪə] *n Med* hemofilia *f*

haemophiliac [hiːməʊˈfɪlɪæk] *adj & n Med* hemofílico(a) *(m,f)*

haemorrhage [ˈhemərɪdʒ] *n Med* hemorragia *f*

haemorrhoids [ˈhemərɔɪdz] *npl Med* hemorroides *fpl*

haft [hɑːft] *n (of knife)* mango *m; (of sword)* puño *m*, empuñadura *f*

hag [hæɡ] *n Pej* bruja *f*, arpía *f*

haggard [ˈhæɡəd] *adj* ojeroso(a)

haggis [ˈhæɡɪs] *n Scot Culin* = guiso hecho con las asaduras del cordero

haggish [ˈhæɡɪʃ] *adj* de bruja

haggle [ˈhæɡəl] *vi* regatear; **to h. over** *or* **about the price of sth** regatear el precio de algo

haggling [ˈhæɡəlɪŋ] *n* regateo *m*

hagiography [hæɡɪˈɒɡrəfɪ] *n* hagiografía *f*

Hague [heɪɡ] *n* **The H.** La Haya

hah [hɑː] *interj*, **ha ha** [hɑːˈhɑː] *interj* ¡ja ja!

hail¹ [heɪl] **1** *n Meteor (ice)* granizo *m; (storm)* granizada *f; Fig* **a h. of bullets/insults** una lluvia de balas/insultos
   2 *vi* granizar

hail² [heɪl] **1** *n (greeting)* saludo *m* ❑ *Rel* **H. Mary** avemaría *f*
   2 *vt* (**a**) *(call)* llamar (**b**) *(taxi)* llamar (**c**) *(acclaim)* aclamar, proclamar
   3 *vi* (**a**) *Meteor* granizar (**b**) *(originate)* ser nativo(a) (**from** de), ser (**from** de)

hailstone [ˈheɪlstəʊn] *n* granizo *m*

hailstorm [ˈheɪlstɔːm] *n* granizada *f*

hair [heər] *n (strand)* pelo *m*, cabello *m; (mass)* pelo *m*, cabellos *npl*, cabellera *f; (on arm, leg)* vello *m*; **to have long h.** tener melena, tener el pelo largo; **to have one's h. cut** cortarse el pelo; *Fig* **to let one's h. down** desmadrarse; *Fig* **to make sb's h. stand on end** poner los pelos de punta a algn; *Fig* **to split hairs** hilar muy delgado; *Fig* **to tear one's h. out** estar desesperado(a); *Fam* **keep your h. on!** ¡tranquilo!, ¡no es para tanto!; *Fam Fig* **it gets in my h.** lo odio ❑ **h's breadth** anchura *f* de un pelo; **h. gel** gel *m* moldeador, *Esp* gomina *f*; *Br* **h. slide** pasador *m*

hairband ['heəbænd] *n* cinta *f* (para el pelo)

hairbrush ['heəbrʌʃ] *n* cepillo *m* (para el pelo)

haircut ['heəkʌt] *n* corte *m* de pelo; **to have a h.** cortarse el pelo

hairdo ['heədu:] *n Fam* peinado *m*

hairdresser ['heədresər] *n* peluquero(a) *m,f*; **h.'s (shop)** peluquería *f*

hairdressing ['heədresɪŋ] *n (profession)* peluquería *f*

hairdryer *n*, **hairdrier** ['heədraɪər] *n* secador *m* (de pelo)

hairgrip ['heəgrɪp] *n Br* horquilla *f*, *Andes CAm Méx* gancho *m*

hairless ['heəlɪs] *adj* sin pelo, calvo(a)

hairline ['heəlaɪn] **1** *adj* muy fino(a); **a h. crack** una raja pequeña
2 *n* nacimiento *m* del pelo; **receding h.** entradas *fpl*

hairnet ['heənet] *n* redecilla *f*

hairpiece ['heəpi:s] *n* postizo *m*, peluquín *m*

hairpin ['heəpɪn] *n* horquilla *f*, *Andes CAm Méx* gancho *m* ❑ *Aut* **h. bend** curva *f* muy cerrada

hair-raising ['heəreɪzɪŋ] *adj* espeluznante, que pone los pelos de punta

hair-remover ['heərɪmu:vər] *n* depilatorio *m*

hair-splitting ['heəsplɪtɪŋ] *Pej* **1** *adj* sutil
2 *n* sutilezas *fpl*

hairspray ['heəspreɪ] *n* laca *f* (para el pelo)

hairstyle ['heəstaɪl] *n* peinado *m*, corte *m* de pelo

hairy ['heərɪ] *adj* (**hairier, hairiest**) (**a**) *(with hair)* peludo(a) (**b**) *Fig (frightening)* enervante, espantoso(a)

Haiti ['heɪtɪ, hɑ:'i:tɪ] *n* Haití

Haitian ['heɪʃən, hɑ:'i:ʃən] **1** *adj* haitiano(a)
2 *n* (**a**) *(person)* haitiano(a) *m,f* (**b**) *(language)* haitiano *m*

hake [heɪk] *n* (*pl* **hakes** *or* **hake**) *(fish)* merluza *f*; *(young)* pescadilla *f*

halcyon ['hælsɪən] *adj Fml* **h. days** los brillantes y tranquilos días de la juventud

hale [heɪl] *adj* sano(a); **h. and hearty** fuerte y sano

half [hɑ:f] **1** *n* (*pl* **halves**) *(section)* media parte *f*, mitad *f*; *Sport (period)* parte *f*, mitad *f*, tiempo *m*; *(position)* medio *m*; *Br (ticket) (for child) Esp* billete *m or Am* boleto *m* infantil; **he's four and a h.** tiene cuatro años y medio; **to cut/rip/ break in h.** cortar/rasgar/romper por la mitad; *Fig* **my better** *or* **other h.** mi media naranja; *Hum* **to go halves with sb** ir a medias con algn; *Fam* **I've a problem and a h.** ¡vaya problema que tengo! ❑ *Sport* **first/second h.** primer/ segundo tiempo *m*, primera/segunda parte *for* mitad *f*; *Ftb* **centre h.** (defensa *m*) central *m*

2 *adj* medio(a); **h. a dozen/an hour** media docena/hora; **he is h. German** es medio alemán ❑ **h. board** media pensión *f*; **h. fare** media tarifa *f*, medio billete *m*; **h. measures** medias tintas *fpl*; *US Mus* **h. note** blanca *f*; *Br* **h. term** medio trimestre *m*; **h. year** semestre *m*, medio año *m*

3 *adv* medio, a medias; **h. asleep** medio dormido(a); **h. and h.** mitad y mitad; *Fam* **I was h. expecting you not to come** casi creía que no ibas a venir; *Br Fam* **would you like a beer? — not h.!** ¿quieres una cerveza? — ¡hombre, claro!; *Fam Iron* **he's too clever by h.** es un poco desmasiado listillo, ¿sabes?

half-baked [hɑ:f'beɪkt] *adj* (**a**) *Culin* medio cocido(a) (**b**) *Fig (of idea, plan)* mal concebido(a), poco serio(a)

half-breed ['hɑ:fbri:d] *adj & n* mestizo(a) *(m,f)*

half-brother ['hɑ:fbrʌðər] *n* hermanastro *m*

half-caste ['hɑ:fkɑ:st] *adj & n* mestizo(a) *(m,f)*

half-closed [hɑ:f'kləʊzd] *adj* entreabierto(a)

half-cock [hɑ:f'kɒk] *n (of gun)* **at h.-c.** con el seguro echado

half-day [hɑ:f'deɪ] *n* media jornada *f*

half-empty [hɑ:f'emptɪ] *adj* medio vacío(a)

half-full ['hɑ:f'fʊl] *adj* medio lleno(a)

half-hearted [hɑ:f'hɑ:tɪd] *adj* poco entusiasta

half-heartedly ['hɑ:f'hɑ:tɪdlɪ] *adv* sin entusiasmo, sin ganas

half-hour [hɑ:f'aʊər] *n* media hora *f*

half-hourly [hɑ:f'aʊəlɪ] *adv* cada media hora

half-life ['hɑ:flaɪf] *n Chem* media vida *f*

half-mast [hɑ:f'mɑ:st] *n* **at h.-m.** *(flag)* a media asta

half-open [hɑ:f'əʊpən] *adj (eyes, window)* entreabierto(a), entornado(a)

halfpenny ['heɪpnɪ] *n Formerly* (*pl* **halfpennies** *or* **halfpence** ['heɪpens]) medio penique *m*

half-price [hɑ:f'praɪs] *adv* a mitad de precio

half-sister ['hɑ:fsɪstər] *n* hermanastra *f*

half-time [hɑ:f'taɪm] *n Sport* descanso *m*

half-tone ['hɑ:ftəʊn] *n* (**a**) *Print* medio tono *m*, media tinta *f* (**b**) *Mus* semitono *m*

half-truth ['hɑ:f'tru:θ] *n* verdad *f* a medias

halfway [hɑ:f'weɪ] *adv* a medio camino, a mitad de camino; *Fig* **to meet sb h.** llegar a un arreglo con algn

half-way ['hɑ:fweɪ] *adj* medio(a), intermedio(a); **the h.- w. point** el punto intermedio; **h.-w. house** *(for former prisoners, addicts)* centro *m* de reinserción; *Fig (compromise)* término *m* medio

half-wit ['hɑ:fwɪt] *n* tonto(a) *m,f*, imbécil *mf*

halfwitted [hɑ:f'wɪtɪd] *adj (person)* idiota, *Esp* memo(a); **a h. idea** una bobada, *Esp* una memez

half-yearly ['hɑ:fjɪəlɪ] *adj* semestral

halibut ['hælɪbət] *n* (*pl* **halibuts** *or* **halibut**) *(fish)* mero *m*

hall [hɔ:l] *n* (**a**) *(lobby)* entrada *f*, vestíbulo *m* ❑ **h. stand**, *US* **h. tree** percha *f* (**b**) *(building)* sala *f* ❑ *Br Univ* **h. of residence** residencia *f* universitaria, *Esp* colegio *m* mayor; **town** *or* **city h.** ayuntamiento *m* (**c**) *(estate)* mansión *f*, casa *f* de campo señorial

hallmark ['hɔ:lmɑ:k] *n* (**a**) *(on gold, silver)* contraste *m* (**b**) *Fig* sello *m*

hallo [hə'ləʊ] *interj* ¡hola!

hallowed ['hæləʊd] *adj (holy)* santo(a), santificado(a), bendito(a); *Fig* reverenciado(a); **h. be Thy name** santificado sea Tu nombre

Hallowe('en [hæləʊ'i:n] *n* víspera *f* de Todos los Santos

hallucinate [hə'lu:sɪneɪt] *vi* alucinar

hallucination [həlu:sɪ'neɪʃən] *n* alucinación *f*

hallucinatory [hə'lu:sɪnətrɪ] *adj* alucinante

hallucinogenic [həlu:sɪnəʊ'dʒenɪk] *adj* alucinógeno(a)

hallway ['hɔ:lweɪ] *n* vestíbulo *m*

halo ['heɪləʊ] *n* (*pl* **haloes** *or* **halos**) (**a**) *Astron* halo *m* (**b**) *Rel* aureola *f*

halogen ['hælədʒən] *n* halógeno(a); **h. lamp** lámpara *f* halógena

halt [hɔ:lt] **1** *n (stop)* alto *m*, parada *f*; **to call a h. to sth** atajar algo, acabar con algo; **to come to a h.** *(stop)* pararse; *(interrupt)* interrumpirse
2 *vt* parar, detener
3 *vi* pararse, detenerse
4 *interj* ¡alto!

halter ['hɔ:ltər] *n Equit* ronzal *m*, cabestro *m*

halterneck ['hɔ:ltənek] *adj* vestido *m* escotado por detrás

halting ['hɔːltɪŋ] *adj (speech)* vacilante; *(steps)* titubeante

halve [hɑːv] *vt (a) (cut in half)* partir por la mitad; *(reduce by half)* reducir a la mitad **(b)** *(share)* compartir **(c)** *Golf* empatar

halves [hɑːvʒ] *pl see* **half**

ham¹ [hæm] *n Culin* jamón *m* ❑ **boiled h.** jamón *m* cocido *or* en dulce *or Esp* de York; **Parma** *or* **cured h.** jamón *m* serrano

ham² [hæm] **1** *n* **(a)** *Rad* radioaficionado(a) *m,f* **(b)** *Theat (actor)* comicastro(a) *m,f*, histrión *m; (acting)* histrionismo *m*
  2 *vt (pt & pp* **hammed)** *Theat* **to h. it up** sobreactuar
  3 *vi* sobreactuar

Hamburg ['hæmbɜːg] *n* Hamburgo

hamburger ['hæmbɜːgər] *n Culin* hamburguesa *f*

ham-fisted [hæm'fɪstɪd] *adj* torpe, *Esp* manazas; **he's very h.-f.** es muy manazas

hamlet ['hæmlɪt] *n* aldea *f*, pueblecito *m*

hammer ['hæmər] **1** *n* **(a)** *(tool)* martillo *m; Pol* **the h. and sickle** la hoz y el martillo; *Fig* **to come under the h.** salir a subasta; *Fig* **to fight h. and tongs** luchar a brazo partido **(b)** *Mus (of piano)* macillo *m* **(c)** *(of gun)* percursor *m* **(d)** *Sport* lanzamiento *m* de martillo
  2 *vt* **(a)** *(gen)* martillar, martillear; *(nail)* clavar; *Fig* **to h. home** insistir sobre *or* en; *Fig* **to h. sth into sb** meterle algo en la cabeza a algn **(b)** *Fam (defeat)* dar una paliza a, *Esp* machacar **(c)** *(slate)* machacar; *(criticize)* criticar
  3 *vi (gen)* martillar, martillear, dar golpes; **to h. at the door** golpear la puerta; *Fig* **it's been hammering down** no ha parado de llover

hammer away *vi* trabajar constantemente

hammer out *vt (agreement)* lograr, alcanzar; **to h. it out** llegar a un acuerdo

hammerhead ['hæməhed] *n (fish)* pez *m* martillo

hammering ['hæmərɪŋ] *n* **(a)** *(knocking)* martilleo *m* **(b)** *Fam* paliza *f*; **to give sb a h.** darle una paliza a algn; **to take a h.** recibir una paliza

hammock ['hæmək] *n* hamaca *f; Naut* coy *m*

hamper¹ ['hæmpər] *n* cesta *f* ❑ **Christmas h.** cesta *f* de Navidad

hamper² ['hæmpər] *vt* estorbar, obstaculizar, impedir, dificultar

hamster ['hæmstər] *n Zool* hámster *m*

hamstring ['hæmstrɪŋ] **1** *n Anat* tendón *m* de la corva
  2 *vt (pt & pp* **hamstrung** ['hæmstrʌŋ]) limitar, perjudicar

hand [hænd] **1** *n* **(a)** *(part of body)* mano *f*; **by h.** a mano; **(close) at h.** a mano, muy cerca; **hands off!** ¡manos fuera!; **hands up!** ¡manos arriba!; **on the one/other h.** por una/ otra parte; **to walk h. in h.** andar cogidos *or* ir de la mano; *Fig* **a free h.** carta *f* blanca; *Fig* **to get out of h.** descontrolarse; *Fig* **the job in h.** lo que nos ocupa; *Fig* **to ask for sb's h.** pedir la mano de algn; *Fig* **to be on h.** estar a mano; *Fig* **to bite the h. that feeds you** morder la mano que nos da de comer; *Fig* **to change hands** cambiar de manos; *Fig* **to do sth out of h.** hacer algo sin pensarlo; *Fig* **to have the upper h.** llevar ventaja; *Fig* **to have a h. in** intervenir en; *Fig* **to have sth to h.** tener algo a la mano; *Fig* **to have time in h.** sobrarle a uno tiempo; *Fig* **to keep one's h. in** no perder la práctica; *Fig* **to know sth like the back of one's h.** conocer algo como la palma de la mano; *Fig* **to live from h. to mouth** vivir al día; *Fig* **to play (right) into sb's hands** ponerse a merced de algn; *Fig* **to take sb in h.** ocuparse de algn; *Fig* **to turn one's h. to** meterse en, dedicarse a; *Fig* **to wash one's hands** lavarse las manos; *Fig* **to wait h. and foot on sb** ser el esclavo de algn; *Fig* **to work h. in glove** colaborar; *Fam Fig* **to have one's hands full** tener mucho que hacer; *Fam Fig* **to give** *or* **lend sb a h.** echarle una mano a algn ❑ **h. grenade** granada *f* de mano

(b) *(worker)* trabajador(a) *m,f; Naut* tripulante *m;* **all hands on deck!** ¡toda la tripulación a cubierta! ❑ *Agr* **farm h.** peón *m* **(c)** *(of clock etc)* manecilla *f*, aguja *f* **(d)** *(applause)* aplauso *m;* **to give sb a big h.** dedicar a algn una gran ovación **(e)** *Cards* mano *f*, partida *f; Fig* **to show one's h.** poner las cartas sobre la mesa **(f)** *(handwriting)* letra *f;* **to write by h.** escribir a mano
  2 *vt (give)* dar, entregar; *Fam Fig* **I have to h. it to you** tengo que reconocerlo

hand around *vt* repartir, ofrecer, pasar

hand back *vt* devolver

hand down *vt* dejar en herencia

hand in *vt (homework, document)* entregar; *(resignation, notice)* presentar, notificar

hand on *vt (give)* pasar

hand out *vt* repartir, distribuir

hand over *vt* entregar

hand round *vt* repartir

handbag ['hændbæg] *n Br Esp* bolso *m*, *Col CSur* cartera *f*, *Méx* bolsa *f*

handball ['hændbɔːl] *n Sport* balonmano *m*

handbook ['hændbʊk] *n* manual *m*, guía *f*

handbrake ['hændbreɪk] *n Br Aut* freno *m* de mano

handclap ['hændklæp] *n* aplauso *m*

handcuff ['hændkʌf] **1** *vt* esposar
  2 handcuffs *npl* esposas *fpl*

hand-drier ['hænd'draɪər] *n* secador *m* de manos, secamanos *m inv*

handful ['hændfʊl] *n* puñado *m*

handgun ['hændgʌn] *n* pistola *f*

hand-held ['hænd'held] *adj (camera)* de mano, portátil ❑ **h.-h. computer** *Esp* ordenador *m or Am* computadora *f* de bolsillo

handicap ['hændɪkæp] **1** *n* **(a)** *(physical, mental)* minusvalía *f*, disminución *f*, deficiencia *f* **(b)** *(Sport)* hándicap *m*, desventaja *f*
  2 *vt (pt & pp* **handicapped)** impedir, obstaculizar, handicapar

handicapped ['hændɪkæpt] **1** *adj* **(a)** *Med (physically)* minusválido(a); *(mentally)* retrasado(a) **(b)** *Sport* en desventaja **(c)** *Fig* desfavorecido(a)
  2 the h. *npl* los minusválidos

handicraft ['hændɪkræft] *n (art)* artesanía *f; (articles)* (objetos *mpl* de) artesanía, artesanado *m*

handiwork ['hændɪwɜːk] *n (work)* trabajo *m*, obra *f; (craft)* artesanía *f*

handkerchief ['hæŋkətʃiːf] *n* pañuelo *m*

handle ['hændəl] **1** *n (of knife)* mango *m; (of cup, bag)* asa *f; (of door, stick)* pomo *m; (of lever)* palanca *f; (of drawer)* tirador *m; Fam Fig* **to fly off the h.** salirse de sus casillas
  2 *vt* **(a)** *(gen)* manejar, manipular; *(on parcel)* **'h. with care'** 'frágil' **(b)** *(situation, subject)* manejar; *(problem, responsibility)* encargarse de; *(people)* tratar; *Fam (put up with)* soportar, aguantar
  3 *vi* manejarse; *(car)* comportarse

handlebars ['hændəlbɑːz] *npl (of bicycle, motorbike)* manillar *m sing*, *Am* manubrio *m sing*

handler ['hændlər] *n* cuidador(a) *m,f* ❑ **baggage h.** mozo *m* de equipajes; **dog h.** cuidador(a) *m,f* de perros

handmade [hænd'meɪd] *adj* hecho(a) a mano

handmaiden ['hændmeɪdən] *n* **(a)** *Old-fashioned* doncella *f* **(b)** *Fig* algo *m* de segunda

hand-me-down ['hændmɪdaʊn] *n Fam* prenda *f* de segunda mano *or* usada

hand-out ['hændaʊt] *n* **(a)** *(leaflet)* folleto *m*; *Pol* octavilla *f*; *Press* nota *f or* comunicado *m* de prensa **(b)** *(charity)* limosna *f*, caridad *f*

handover ['hændəʊvər] *n* entrega *f*

hand-picked [hænd'pɪkt] *adj* cuidadosamente escogido(a)

handrail ['hændreɪl] *n* pasamanos *m inv*, baranda *f*, *Esp* barandilla *f*

handset ['hændset] *n (of telephone)* auricular *m*

hands-free ['hænz'fri:] *adj (phone, dialling)* de manos libres

handshake ['hændʃeɪk] *n* apretón *m* de manos

hands-off ['hæn'zɒf] *adj (approach, style)* no intervencionista

handsome ['hænsəm] *adj* **(a)** *(of person) Esp* guapo(a), *Am* lindo(a); *(beautiful)* bonito(a), bello(a); *(elegant)* elegante **(b)** *(substantial)* considerable

handsomely ['hænsəmlɪ] *adv* **(a)** *(elegantly)* elegantemente, con elegancia **(b)** *(substantially)* substancialmente

hands-on ['hæn'zɒn] *adj* **he has a h.-on management style** le gusta implicarse en todos los aspectos del negocio; **h.-on training** formación *f* práctica

handspring ['hændsprɪŋ] *n* voltereta *f*

handstand ['hændstænd] *n* **to do a h.** hacer el pino

hand-to-hand ['hændtəhænd] *adj* **h.-to-h. combat** combate cuerpo a cuerpo

hand-to-mouth ['hæntə'maʊθ] **1** *adj* **a h.-to-m. existence** una existencia precaria
     2 *adv* **to live h.-to-m.** vivir de forma precaria

handwash ['hændwɒʃ] **1** *vt* lavar a mano
     2 *n* **I'm doing a h.** voy a lavar unas cosas a mano

handwriting ['hændraɪtɪŋ] *n* letra *f*

handwritten ['hændrɪtən] *adj* escrito(a) a mano

handy ['hændɪ] *adj* **(handier, handiest)** **(a)** *(useful)* útil, práctico(a); *(nearby)* a mano, cercano(a); *Fam* **to come in h.** ser útil, venir bien; **to keep h.** tener a mano **(b)** *(dextrous)* hábil, habilidoso(a)

hang [hæŋ] **1** *vt (pt & pp* **hung) (a)** *(gen)* colgar **(b)** *(wallpaper)* pegar; *(room)* empapelar, decorar **(c)** *(head)* bajar, inclinar **(d)** *(pt & pp* **hanged)** ahorcar
     2 *vi* **(a)** *(be suspended)* colgar **(from** de), pender **(from** de); *(in air)* flotar; *(material, clothing)* caer, colgar; *Fig* **to h. in the air** flotar en el aire; **the problem was left hanging in the air** el problema quedó sin solución; *US Fam* **h. loose!** ¡tranqui, tranqui!; *Fam Fig* **we've got this exam hanging over us** tenemos pendiente este examen **(b)** *(criminal)* ser ahorcado(a); **to h. oneself** ahorcarse
     3 *n* **(a)** *(of material, clothing)* caída *f* **(b)** *Fam (trick)* truquillo *m*; **to get the h. of sth** pillar el truco *or Esp* el tranquillo a algo, *Méx* pescar algo, *RP* agarrar la mano a algo

hang about, hang around *Fam* **1** *vt (frequent)* frecuentar, andar por
     2 *vi* **(a)** *(be slow)* perder el tiempo; *Fig* **he doesn't h. around** es muy rápido **(b)** *(wait)* esperar; **h. about!** ¡espera!

hang back *vi* **(a)** *(place, race, etc)* quedarse atrás **(b)** *Fig* vacilar

hang down *vi (hair)* caer, colgar

hang on *vi* **(a)** *(hold)* agarrarse; *Fig* **we hung on his every word** estábamos pendientes de cada una de sus palabras **(b)** *(wait)* esperar; **h. on!** ¡espérate!; *US Fam* **h. on in there!** ¡aguanta tío!

hang onto *vt* agarrarse a; *Fig* **h. onto it** guárdalo

hang out 1 *vt (washing etc)* colgar, tender

2 *vi Slang (frequent)*; **where do they h. out?** ¿qué lugares frecuentan?; *US Fam* **to let it all h. out** desmadrarse

hang together *vi* **(a)** *(friends)* mantenerse unidos **(b)** *(ideas, argument)* ser coherente

hang up 1 *vt (coat, picture, telephone)* colgar; *Fig* **to h. up one's boots** colgar las botas
     2 *vi (on telephone)* colgar

hangar ['hæŋər] *n Av* hangar *m*

hanger ['hæŋər] *n* percha *f*

hanger-on [hæŋər'ɒn]. *n (pl* **hangers-on)** *Fam* lapa *f*, parásito(a) *m,f*

hang-glider ['hæŋglaɪdər] *n* ala *f* delta

hang-gliding ['hæŋglaɪdɪŋ] *n* vuelo *m* libre

hanging ['hæŋɪŋ] **1** *adj* colgante ◻ **h. bridge** puente *m* colgante
     2 *n* **(a)** *(execution)* ejecución *f* en la horca **(b) (wall) h.** colgadura *f*

hangman ['hæŋmən] *n (pl* **hangmen)** verdugo *m*

hangnail ['hæŋneɪl] *n* padrastro *m*, pellejo *m*

hang-out ['hæŋaʊt] *n Slang (bar etc)* local *m*; *(pad)* guarida *f*

hangover ['hæŋəʊvər] *n* **(a)** *(remnant)* resto *m*, vestigio *m* **(b)** *(after drinking)* resaca *f*

hang-up ['hæŋʌp] *n (pl* **hang-ups)** *Fam (worries)* preocupación *f*, inhibición *f*; *(complex)* complejo *m*

hanker ['hæŋkər] *vi* desear; **to h. after** *or* **for sth** anhelar *or* ansiar algo

hankering ['hæŋkərɪŋ] *n* deseo *m*, anhelo *m*, ansia *f*

hankie *n*, **hanky** ['hæŋkɪ] *n Fam* pañuelo *m*

hanky-panky [hæŋkɪ'pæŋkɪ] *n Fam* (mal) rollo *m*

haphazard [hæp'hæzəd] *adj* caótico(a), desordenado(a)

haphazardly [hæp'hæzədlɪ] *adv* sin orden ni concierto

hapless ['hæplɪs] *adj Fml* desdichado(a), infortunado(a)

happen ['hæpən] *vi (occur)* suceder, ocurrir, pasar, producirse; **as it happens** lo que pasa es que; **if you h. to see my friend** si por casualidad ves a mi amigo; **I h. to know that it is true** me consta que es verdad

happening ['hæpənɪŋ] *n* acontecimiento *m*

happily ['hæpɪlɪ] *adv (with pleasure)* felizmente, con alegría; *(fortunately)* afortunadamente

happiness ['hæpɪnɪs] *n* felicidad *f*

happy ['hæpɪ] *adj* **(happier, happiest)** *(cheerful)* feliz, contento(a), alegre; *(fortunate)* afortunado(a); **h. birthday!** ¡feliz cumpleaños!; **we're not h. with the decision** no nos convence la decisión ◻ **h. ending** desenlace *m* feliz; **h. medium** término *m* medio

happy-go-lucky [hæpɪgəʊ'lʌkɪ] *adj* despreocupado(a); **a h.-go-l. fellow** un viva la virgen

hara-kiri [hærə'kɪrɪ] *n* harakiri *m*

harangue [hə'ræŋ] **1** *vt* arengar
     2 *n* arenga *f*

harass ['hærəs] *vt* acosar, atormentar

harassed ['hærəst, hə'ræst] *adj* agobiado(a)

harassment ['hærəsmənt, hə'ræsmənt] *n* hostigamiento *m*, acoso *m*

harbinger ['hɑ:bɪndʒər] **1** *n (person)* precursor(a) *m,f*; *(thing)* presagio *m*
     2 *vt* anunciar, presagiar

harbour, *US* **harbor** ['hɑ:bər] **1** *n* puerto *m*
     2 *vt* **(a)** *(criminal)* encubrir **(b)** *(doubts, suspicions)* abrigar; **to h. a grudge** guardar rencor

hard [hɑ:d] **1** *adj* **(a)** *(not soft)* duro(a), firme; *(solid)* sólido(a); *Fam Fig* **as h. as nails** más duro(a) que una piedra; *Fam Fig* **he's a h. nut** es un hueso duro de roer ◻

Ten **h. court** pista *f* (de tenis) dura; *Comptr* **h. disk** disco *m* duro; *Comptr* **h. return** retorno *m* manual; *Br* **h. shoulder** arcén *m*, *Méx* acotamiento *m*, *RP* banquina *f* **(b)** *(difficult)* difícil, duro(a); **h. of hearing** duro(a) de oído; *Fig* **we'll be h. pushed** *or* **pressed** *or* **put to finish today** difícilmente acabaremos hoy; *Fam Fig* **to have a h. time** pasarlo mal **(c)** *(harsh, severe)* duro(a), severo(a); *(strict)* estricto(a), rígido(a); **a h. winter** un invierno riguroso; *Pol* **to take a h. line** tomar medidas severas; *Fig* **h. and fast** *(information)* fidedigno(a); *(rule)* fijo(a); *Fig* **to be h. hit** resultar gravemente afectado(a); *Fig* **to be h. on sb** ser severo(a) con algn; *Fam Fig* **to drive a h. bargain** ser muy duro(a) negociando ▫ **h. drugs** droga *f* dura; **h. labour** trabajos *mpl* forzados; *Pol* **h. left** extrema izquierda *f*; **h. porn** pornografía *f* dura; *Pol* **h. right** extrema derecha *f*; *Com* **h. sell** promoción *f* de venta agresiva **(d)** *(inveterate, incorrigible)* incorregible; **a h. drinker** un bebedor inveterado; **a h. worker** un trabajador concienzudo **(e)** *(unfortunate)* malo(a); **h. luck!** ¡mala suerte! **(f)** *(real)* real; **h. evidence** pruebas *fpl* definitivas ▫ *Com* **h. cash** dinero *m* en metálico; *Comptr* **h. copy** copia *f* impresa, listado *m*; *Pol* **h. core** núcleo *m*; *Com* **h. currency** divisa *f* fuerte **(g)** *US* **h. cider** sidra *f*

2 *adv* **(a)** *(forcibly)* fuerte **(b)** *(with application)* mucho, fijamente, concienzudamente; *Fig* **to be h. on sb's heels** pisar los talones a algn **(c)** *(with pain)* con dolor, duramente; **he took it very h.** fue un golpe muy duro para él; **to be h. done by** ser tratado(a) injustamente **(d)** *Fam Fig* **to be h. up** estar en apuros *or Am* problemas; *Fam* **I'm a bit h. up for cash** ando mal de dinero

hard-and-fast ['hɑːdən'fɑːst] *adj* **there are no h.-a.-f. rules** no hay reglas fijas

hardback ['hɑːdbæk] *n Print* edición *f* en tela *or* de tapas duras

hard-bitten ['hɑːdbɪtən] *adj* tenaz, duro(a)

hardboard ['hɑːdbɔːd] *n* chapa *f* de madera, contrachapado *m*

hard-boiled ['hɑːdbɔɪld] *adj* **(a)** *(of egg)* duro(a) **(b)** *Fig (of person)* duro(a), insensible

hard-core ['hɑːdkɔːr] *adj* irreductible, incondicional; **h.-c. supporter** partidario(a) *m,f* acérrimo(a)

hard-earned [hɑːd'ɜːnd] *adj* ganado(a) con mucho esfuerzo

harden ['hɑːdən] **1** *vt* endurecer; *Fig* **to h. sb's heart** insensibilizar el corazón de algn
2 *vi* endurecerse

hardened ['hɑːdənd] *adj* endurecido(a); *(criminal)* habitual

hard-headed [hɑːd'hedɪd] *adj* realista, poco sentimental

hard-hearted [hɑːd'hɑːtɪd] *adj* cruel, insensible

hard-hitting [hɑːd'hɪtɪŋ] *adj (criticism, report)* contundente

hardliner [hɑːd'laɪnər] *n Pol* duro(a) *m,f*, partidario(a) *m,f* de la línea dura

hardly ['hɑːdlɪ] *adv* apenas, casi; **h. anyone/ever** casi nadie/nunca; **h.!** ¡qué va!; **he had h. begun when ...** apenas había comenzado cuando ...; **I can h. believe it** apenas lo puedo creer

hardness ['hɑːdnɪs] *n* **(a)** *(gen)* dureza *f* **(b)** *(difficulty)* dificultad *f* **(c)** *(insensitivity)* insensibilidad *f*

hard-nosed [hɑːd'nəʊʃd] *adj Fam* realista, poco sentimental

hard-pressed [hɑːd'prest] *adj* en aprietos

hardship ['hɑːdʃɪp] *n* privación *f*, apuro *m*

hardware ['hɑːdweər] *n* **(a)** *(goods)* ferretería ▫ **h.** *Br* **shop** *or US* **store** ferretería *f* **(b)** *Mil* armamento *m* **(c)** *Comptr* hardware *m*

hardwearing [hɑːd'weərɪŋ] *adj* duradero(a), resistente

hard-won [hɑːd'wʌn] *adj* ganado(a) a pulso

hardworking ['hɑːd'wɜːkɪŋ] *adj* trabajador(a)

hardy ['hɑːdɪ] *adj* **(hardier, hardiest)** *(of person)* robusto(a), fuerte; *(of plant)* resistente

hare [heər] **1** *n (pl* **hares** *or* **hare)** *Zool* liebre *f*; *Fam* **mad as a March h.** loco(a) como una cabra
2 *vi Br* **to h. off** *or* **away** salir disparado(a)

harebrained ['heəbreɪnd] *adj* estúpido(a), absurdo(a)

harelip ['heəlɪp] *n Med* labio *m* leporino

harem [hɑː'riːm] *n* harén *m*

haricot ['hærɪkəʊ] *n Culin* **h. (bean)** alubia *f* blanca, *Esp* judía *f* blanca, *Am* salvo *RP* frijol *m* blanco, *Andes RP* poroto *m* blanco

hark [hɑːk] *vi Literary* escuchar

hark back *vi* recordar

harlequin ['hɑːlɪkwɪn] *n* arlequín *m*

harlot ['hɑːlət] *n Literary* ramera *f*

harm [hɑːm] **1** *n* daño *m*, perjuicio *m*; **there's no h. in it** no hay de malo en ello; **to be out of h.'s way** estar a salvo; **you will come to no h.** no te pasará nada; *Fam* **no h. done** tranquilo, no pasa nada
2 *vt* dañar, hacer daño a, perjudicar

harmful ['hɑːmfʌl] *adj* nocivo(a) **(to** para), perjudicial **(to** para)

harmless ['hɑːmlɪs] *adj* inocuo(a), inofensivo(a)

harmonic [hɑː'mɒnɪk] **1** *adj* armónico(a)
2 *n* armónico *m*

harmonica [hɑː'mɒnɪkæ] *n* armónica *f*

harmonious [hɑː'məʊnɪəs] *adj* armonioso(a)

harmonize ['hɑːmənaɪz] *vt & vi* armonizar

harmony ['hɑːmənɪ] *n* armonía *f*

harness ['hɑːnɪs] **1** *n (for horse)* guarniciones *fpl*, arreos *mpl*; *Fig* **to die in h.** morir con las botas puestas; *Fig* **to work in h.** colaborar
2 *vt* **(a)** *(horse)* enjaezar, poner los arreos a **(b)** *Fig (resources, energy, etc)* aprovechar

harp [hɑːp] *n Mus* arpa *f*

harp on *vi Fam* hablar sin parar

harpist ['hɑːpɪst] *n Mus* arpista *mf*

harpoon [hɑː'puːn] **1** *n* arpón *m*
2 *vt* arponear

harpsichord ['hɑːpsɪkɔːd] *n Mus* clavicordio *m*

harpy ['hɑːpɪ] *n Literary* arpía *f*

harrier¹ ['hærɪər] *n* **(a)** *(hound)* perro *m* de caza **(b)** *Sport* corredor(a) *m,f* de cros

harrier² ['hærɪər] *n Orn* aguilucho *m*

harrow ['hærəʊ] *n Agr* grada *f*

harrowing ['hærəʊɪŋ] *adj* angustioso(a); *(experience)* terrible

harry ['hærɪ] *vt (pt & pp* **harried)** acosar

harsh [hɑːʃ] *adj (gen)* severo(a), duro(a); *(voice)* áspero(a); *(sound)* discordante

harshly ['hɑːʃlɪ] *adv (gen)* severamente, duramente; *(sound)* con discordancia

harshness ['hɑːʃnɪs] *n (gen)* severidad *f*, dureza *f*; *(hardness, roughness)* aspereza *f*; *(discordancy)* discordancia *f*

hart [hɑːt] *n Zool* ciervo *m*

harvest ['hɑːvɪst] **1** *n (gen)* cosecha *f*, siega *f*; *(of grapes)* vendimia *f*; *Fig* cosecha *f*
2 *vt* cosechar, recoger

harvester ['hɑːvɪstər] *n* **(a)** *(person)* segador(a) *m,f* **(b)** *(machine)* segadora *f*, cosechadora *f*

has [hæs] *3rd person sing pres see* **have**

has-been ['hæzbiːn] *n Fam* vieja gloria *f*

hash¹ [hæʃ] *n* **(a)** *Culin* guiso *m* de carne con *Esp* patatas *or Am* papas; *Andes Méx* ahogado *m* de carne con papas; *Fam Fig* **to make a h. of sth** estropear algo ❑ *US* **h. browns** = fritura de *Esp* patata *or Am* papa y cebolla **(b)** *(symbol)* **h. mark** *Comptr Typ* = el símbolo '#'; *(on telephone)* almohadilla *f*, numeral *m*; *(in music)* sostenido *m*

hash² [hæʃ] *n Slang* hachís *m*

hashish ['hæʃiːʃ] *n* hachís *m*

hasp [hɑːsp] *n (of lock)* cierre *m*; *(of door)* pestillo *m*; *(of window)* falleba *f*

hassle ['hæsəl] *Fam* **1** *n* **(a)** *(nuisance)* rollo *m*, molestia *f* **(b)** *(problem)* problema *m*, lío *m* **(c)** *(wrangle)* bronca *f*, discusión *f*
2 *vt* molestar, fastidiar; **don't h. me** déjame en paz

hassock ['hæsək] *n Rel* cojín *m*

haste [heɪst] *n Fml* prisa *f*, *Am* apuro *m*; **to make h.** apresurarse, *Am* apurarse; *Prov* **more h. less speed** vísteme despacio que tengo prisa

hasten ['heɪsən] **1** *vt Fml* apresurar, acelerar el paso de
2 *vi* apresurarse, *Am* apurarse

hastily ['heɪstɪlɪ] *adv* **(a)** *(quickly)* de prisa **(b)** *(rashly)* sin reflexionar, a la ligera, precipitadamente

hastiness ['heɪstɪnɪs] *n* prisa *f*, precipitación *f*

hasty ['heɪstɪ] *adj* (**hastier, hastiest**) **(a)** *(hurried)* apresurado(a), rápido(a) **(b)** *(rash)* precipitado(a), ligero(a)

hat [hæt] *n* sombrero *m*; *Fig* **I'll eat my h. if ...** que me ahorquen si ...; *Fig* **I take my h. off to him** lo admiro; *Fig* **to keep sth under one's h.** guardar un secreto; *Fam Fig* **that story is old h.** esa historia es muy vieja; *Fam Fig* **to talk through one's h.** decir tonterías

hatband ['hætbænd] *n* cinta *f* de sombrero

hatbox ['hætbɒks] *n* sombrerera *f*

hatch¹ [hætʃ] *n* escotilla *f*; *Fam* **down the h.!** ¡salud! ❑ **serving h.** ventanilla *f*

hatch² [hætʃ] **1** *vt* **(a)** *(eggs, chicks)* empollar, incubar **(b)** *Fig (scheme, plan)* tramar, idear
2 *vi* **to h.(out)** salirse del huevo, romper el cascarón

hatchback ['hætʃbæk] *n Aut* coche *m* con portón trasero

hatchery ['hætʃərɪ] *n* criadero *m*

hatchet ['hætʃɪt] *n* hacha *f*; *Fig* **to bury the h.** enterrar el hache de guerra, hacer las paces ❑ **h. man** matón *m*

hate [heɪt] **1** *n* odio *m*; *Fig* **pet h.** bestia *f* negra ❑ **h. mail** = cartas que contienen amenazas o fuertes críticas; *US Fam* **h. sheet** = publicación de carácter xenófobo, racista, antihomosexual, etc.
2 *vt* **(a)** *(detest)* odiar, aborrecer, no soportar **(b)** *(regret)* lamentar; **I h. to say this but ...** lamento decirte esto pero ...

hateful ['heɪtfʌl] *adj* odioso(a)

hatpin ['hætpɪn] *n* alfiler *m* de sombrero

hatred ['heɪtrɪd] *n* odio *m*

hatstand ['hætstænd] *n* percha *f* (para sombreros)

haughtiness ['hɔːtɪnɪs] *n* altanería *f*, arrogancia *f*, altivez *f*

haughty ['hɔːtɪ] *adj* (**haughtier, haughtiest**) altanero(a), arrogante, engreído(a)

haul [hɔːl] **1** *n* **(a)** *(pull)* tirón *m*, estirón *m* **(b)** *(journey)* trayecto *m* **(c)** *Fishing* redada *f* **(d)** *(loot)* botín *m*
2 *vt* **(a)** *(gen)* tirar; *(drag)* arrastrar; *Naut* halar; *(car)* remolcar **(b)** *(transport)* acarrear

haul up *vt Fam (to court)* llevar

haulage ['hɔːlɪdʒ] *n* transporte *m*, acarreo *m*

haulier ['hɔːljər], *US* **hauler** ['hɔːlər] *n* transportista *mf*

haunch [hɔːntʃ] *n* **(a)** *Anat* cadera *f*; **to sit on one's haunches** ponerse en cuclillas **(b)** *Culin* pernil *m*

haunt [hɔːnt] **1** *n* lugar *m* predilecto; *(of criminals, animals)* guarida *f*
2 *vt* **(a)** *(of ghost)* aparecer en **(b)** *Fig* perseguir, atormentar **(c)** *(frequent)* frecuentar

haunted ['hɔːntɪd] *adj* encantado(a), embrujado(a)

haunting ['hɔːntɪŋ] *adj* obsesionante

Havana [hə'vænə] *n* La Habana ❑ **H. cigar** habano *m*

have [hæv] **1** *vt* (*3rd person sing pres* **has**) (*pt & pp* **had**) **(a)** *(possess)* tener; **you got a car?** *US* **do you h. a car?** ¿tienes coche?; **if you like it h. it** si te gusta, quédate con él; **we h. jobs at the same school** trabajamos a la misma escuela; **you h. a way with children** tienes una buena mano con los niños; *Fig* **to put** *or* **give all one has into sth** hacer todo lo que uno pueda **(b)** *(get, experience, suffer)* pasar, tener; **to h. a fright** *or* **a shock** asustarse; **to h. a holiday** tomarse unas vacaciones; *Fam Fig* **I've had it** *(will be in trouble)* me la voy a cargar; *(tired etc)* estoy hecho polvo; *Fam Fig* **I've had it with smoking** voy a dejar de fumar porque ya estoy harto; *Fam Fig* **the radio's had it** la radio ya no va **(c)** *(partake of drink)* tomar; **to h. a cigarette** fumarse un cigarrillo; **to h. breakfast/lunch/tea/dinner** desayunar/comer/merendar/cenar **(d)** *(engage in)* **to h. a bath/shower/shave** bañarse/ducharse/afeitarse; **to h. a game of football** jugar un partido de fútbol; **to h. a nap** echar una siesta; *Br Vulg* **to h. it off** *or* **away (with sb)** echar un polvo (con algn) **(e)** *(obligation)* **to h.** tener que, deber; **we h. to speak in French** debemos hablar francés **(f)** *(make happen)* hacer que; **I'll h. someone come round** haré que venga alguien; **they had me washing up** tuve que lavar los platos **(g)** *(receive)* (people, mail) tener, recibir; **to h. people round** invitar a gente; **you h. my permission** tienes mi permiso **(h)** *(borrow)* pedir prestado; *(use)* utilzar, emplear; **can I h. your pen a moment?** ¿me dejas tu bolígrafo un momento? **(i)** *(party, meeting)* hacer, celebrar; **they had an exhibition last year** montaron una exposición el año pasado **(j)** *(give birth to)* dar a luz a; **to h. a baby** tener un niño **(k)** *(allow, tolerate)* permitir; **we won't h. it** no lo consentiremos **(l)** *(hold)* tener; **he had his head in his hands** tenía la cabeza entre las manos; *Fig* **to h. sth against sb** tener algo en contra de algn **(m)** *(according to)* según; **legend has it that ... según la leyenda ... (n)** *Fam (cheat, deceive)* engañar; **I've been had!** ¡me han timado! **(o)** *(preference)* **you'd better stay** más vale que te quedes; *Fig* **to h. done with sth** acabar con algo

2 *v aux* **(a)** *(compound)* haber; **he hasn't eaten yet** no ha comido aún; **she had broken the window** había roto el cristal; **we h. lived here for ten years** hace diez años que vivimos aquí; **I had been waiting for half an hour** hacía media hora que esperaba, llevaba media hora esperando; *(emphatic)* **you h. forgotten your gloves —so I h.!** te has olvidado los guantes —¡ay, sí!, es verdad; **you haven't swept the floor —I h.!** no has barrido el suelo —¡sí que lo he barrido! **(b)** *(have + just)* acabar de; **she's just arrived** acaba de llegar; **we'd just gone out** acabábamos de salir

have in *vt* **(a)** *(invite)* invitar, recibir; *(call)* llamar **(b)** *Fam (hold against)* **to h. it in for sb** tenerla tomada con algn

have on *vt* **(a)** *(wear)* llevar puesto(a), vestir; **to h. nothing on** estar desnudo(a) **(b)** *(plan to do)* tener planeado(a), tener que hacer; **I h. nothing on** estoy libre **(c)** *Fam (fool)* engañar; **to h. sb on** tomarle el pelo *or Esp Carib Méx* vacilar a algn

have out *vt* **(a)** *(extract)* sacar; **to h. one's appendix out** operarse de apendicitis **(b)** *Fam (clear up)* **to h. it out with sb** ajustar cuentas con algn

have over *vt (invite)* recibir, invitar

have up *vt Br Fam Jur* **to be had up (for sth)** tener que ir a juicio (por algo)

haven ['heɪvən] *n* (**a**) *Naut* puerto *m* (**b**) *Fig* refugio *m*, asilo *m*; **a h. of peace** un remanso de paz

have-nots ['hævnɒts] *npl* desposeídos *mpl*, pobres *mpl*

haversack ['hævəsæk] *n* mochila *f*

havoc ['hævək] *n* estragos *mpl*; **to play h. with** hacer estragos en

haw [hɔ:] *n Bot* baya *f* del espino

Hawaii [hə'waɪɪ] *n* Hawai

Hawaiian [hə'waɪən] *adj & n* hawaiano(a) *(m,f)*

hawk¹ [hɔ:k] *n Orn Pol* halcón *m*; *Fig* **to have eyes like a h.** tener ojos de lince

hawk² [hɔ:k] *vt* (**a**) *(in the street)* vender en la calle; *(door-to-door)* vender de puerta en puerta (**b**) *(gossip, news)* divulagar, pregonar

hawk-eyed ['hɔ:kaɪd] *adj* con ojos de lince

hawkish ['hɔ:kɪʃ] *adj Pol* partidario(a) de la línea dura *(en política exterior)*

hawser ['hɔ:zər] *n Naut* guindaleza *f*

hawthorn ['hɔ:θɔ:n] *n Bot* majuelo *m*, espino *m* albar

hay [heɪ] *n Bot* heno *m*; **to make h.** secar la paja; *Fam* **to hit the h.** irse al catre; *Prov* **make h. while the sun shines** la ocasión la pintan calva ❏ *Med* **h. fever** fiebre *f* del heno

hayfork ['heɪfɔ:k] *n Agr* bieldo *m*

haymaker ['heɪmeɪkər] *n* segador(a) *m,f*

haymaking ['heɪmeɪkɪŋ] *n Agr* siega *f* del heno

haystack ['heɪstæk] *n* almiar *m*; *Fig* **to look for a needle in a h.** buscar una aguja en un pajar

haywire ['heɪwaɪər] *adj Fam* en desorden, confuso(a); **to go h.** *(machine etc)* estropearse; *(person)* volverse loco(a)

hazard ['hæzəd] **1** *n* (**a**) *(risk)* peligro *m*, riesgo *m* (**b**) *Golf* obstáculo *m*
2 *vt Fml* arriesgar, poner en peligro; **to h. a guess** intentar adivinar

hazardous ['hæzədəs] *adj* arriesgado(a), peligroso(a)

haze [heɪz] *n* (**a**) *(mist)* neblina *f* (**b**) *Fig (blur)* confusión *f*

hazel ['heɪzəl] **1** *n Bot (tree)* avellano *m*
2 *adj (de color)* avellana

hazelnut ['heɪzəlnʌt] *n Bot* avellana *f*

hazily ['heɪzɪlɪ] *adv* vagamente, con poca claridad

hazy ['heɪzɪ] *adj* (**hazier, haziest**) nebuloso(a); *Fig* vago(a)

H-bomb ['eɪtʃbɒm] *n* bomba *f* H

HE *(abbr* **His/Her Excellency**) Su Excelencia *mf*, S.E.

he [hi:] **1** *pers pron* él; **he did it** ha sido él; **he who** el que
2 *adj* macho; **he-goat** macho cabrío

head [hed] **1** *n* (**a**) *Anat* cabeza *f*; *(mind)* mente *f*; **from h. to toe** de pies a cabeza; **she got** *or* **took it into her h. to ...** se le ocurrió la idea de ...; *Fig* **off the top of one's h.** así de entrada; *Fig* **on your own h. be it** allá se las compongas; *Fig* **ten dollars a** *or* **per h.** diez dólares por cabeza; *Fig* **to be h. over heels in love** estar locamente enamorado(a); *Fig* **to do sth standing on one's h.** hacer algo con los ojos cerrados; *Fig* **to go over sb's h.** pasar por encima de algn; *Fig* **to keep one's h.** mantener la calma; *Fig* **to keep one's h. above water** mantenerse a flote; *Fig* **to lose one's h.** perder la cabeza; *Fam* **champagne goes to my h.** el champán se me sube a la cabeza; *Fam* **he couldn't get it into his thick h.** no le entraba en la cabezota; *Fam* **success went to his h.** se le subió el éxito a cabeza; *Fam* **to be off one's h.** estar chiflado(a); *Fam Fig* **this philosophy stuff is over my h.** de todo este rollo de la filosofía no entiendo nada; *Fam Fig* **to bite sb's h. off** echar una bronca a algn; *Fam Fig* **to cry one's h. off** llorar a moco tendido; *Fam Fig*

to get one's h. around sth alcanzar a comprender algo; **to laugh one's h. off** reírse a mandíbula batiente; *Prov* **two heads are better than one** cuatro ojos ven más que dos ❏ **crowned h.** testa *f* coronada; **h. start** ventaja *f* (**b**) *(end, top, etc) (of table)* cabecera *f*; *(of nail, pin, etc)* cabeza *f*; *(of beer)* espuma *f*; *(of arrow)* punta *f*; *(of cabbage)* cogollo *m*; *(of page)* principio *m*; *(of tape recorder)* cabezal *m*; *(of spot, boil)* punta *f*; *(of water, steam)* presión *f*; *Fig* **to come to a h.** llegar a un momento decisivo (**c**) *(chief, boss)* cabeza *m*; *(of company)* director(a) *m,f*; *(of family)* cabeza *f* ❏ *Br Sch* **h. (teacher)** director(a) *m,f* (**d**) *(cattle)* res *f* (**e**) *(of coin)* cara *f*; **heads or tails?** ¿cara o cruz?, *Chile Col* ¿cara o sello?, *Méx* ¿águila o sol?, *RP* ¿cara o ceca?; *Fam Fig* **I can't make h. or tail of it** no entiendo ni jota (**f**) *Geog (headland)* cabo *m*, punta *f* (**g**) *Press* título *m*, titular *m*
2 *adj* principal ❏ **h. office** oficina *f* central
3 *vt* (**a**) *(list, company, procession, etc)* encabezar (**b**) *Ftb* rematar de cabeza (**c**) *(title)* titular
4 *vi* dirigirse, ir

head for *vt* dirigirse hacia; *Fig* **they're heading for big trouble** van a tener muchos problemas

head off 1 *vi* marcharse, irse
2 *vt (divert)* desviar, interceptar; *(avert)* evitar

headache ['hedeɪk] *n* dolor *m* de cabeza; *Fig* quebradero *m* de cabeza

headband ['hedbænd] *n* cinta *f* (para la cabeza)

headboard ['hedbɔ:d] *n* cabecera *f*

headdress ['heddres] *n* tocado *m*

header ['hedər] *n Ftb* cabezazo *m*

head-first ['hed'fɜ:st] *adv* de cabeza

headgear ['hedgɪər] *n* tocado *m*

head-hunt ['hed'hʌnt] *vt Com* captar, cazar *(altos ejecutivos)*

head-hunter ['hedhʌntər] *n* cazador(a) *m,f* de cabezas; *Fam Fig* cazatalentos *mf inv*

heading ['hedɪŋ] *n* *(of chapter)* título *m*; *(of letter)* membrete *m*

headlamp ['hedlæmp] *n Aut* faro *m*

headland ['hedlənd] *n Geog* punta *f*, cabo *m*

headlight ['hedlaɪt] *n Aut* faro *m*

headline ['hedlaɪn] **1** *n* titular *m*, *Méx RP* encabezado *m*; **to hit the headlines** ser noticia de primera plana
2 *vt* poner en los titulares

headlong ['hedlɒŋ] *adj & adv* de cabeza; **to rush h. into sth** lanzarse a hacer algo sin pensar

headmaster ['hed'mɑ:stər] *n Sch* director *m*

headmistress [hed'mɪstrɪs] *n Sch* directora *f*

head-on ['hedɒn] **1** *adj* frontal; **a h.-on collision** un choque frontal
2 [hed'ɒn] *adv* de frente

headphones ['hedfəʊns] *npl* auriculares *mpl*, cascos *mpl*

headquarters ['hedkwɔ:təz] *npl* (**a**) *(of organization)* oficina *f* central, sede *f* (**b**) *Mil* cuartel *m* general

headrest ['hedrest] *n* cabecero *m*, cabezal *m*

headroom ['hedru:m] *n* altura *f* libre

headscarf ['hedsɑ:f] *n* (*pl* **headscarves** ['hedskɑ:vz]) pañuelo *m*

headset ['hedset] *n* auriculares *mpl*

headship ['hedʃɪp] *n Educ* dirección *f*

headstand ['hedstænd] *n* posición *f* de la cabeza

headstone ['hedstəʊn] *n* (**a**) *(gravestone)* lápida *f* mortuoria (**b**) *Archit (keystone)* piedra *f* angular

headstrong ['hedstrɒŋ] *adj* testarudo(a), cabezota

head-up display ['hedʌpdɪs'pleɪ] n *(in aircraft, car)* pantalla f virtual a la altura de la vista

headway ['hedweɪ]'n progreso m; **to make h.** avanzar, progresar

headwind ['hedwɪnd] n viento m de proa

headword ['hedwɜːd] n entrada f, lema m

heady ['hedɪ] adj **(headier, headiest)** embriagador(a); **a h. drink** una bebida fuerte

heal [hiːl] vi *(wound)* cicatrizar; **to h. up** curarse
2 vt *(illness)* curar

healer ['hiːlər] n curador(a) m,f

health [helθ] n salud f; Fig prosperidad f; **to drink (to) sb's h.** beber a la salud de algn; **to be in good/bad h.** estar bien/mal de salud; **your good h.!** ¡salud! □ Br **h. centre** centro m médico; **h. farm** centro m para curas de adelgazamiento; **h. foods** alimentos mpl naturales; **h. food shop** tienda f de alimentos naturales; Fin **h. insurance** seguro m de enfermedad; **h. officer** inspector(a) m,f de Sanidad; **h. visitor** enfermero(a) m,f visitante; Br **the H. Service** = el sistema de sanidad pública británico

healthful ['helθfʊl] adj esp US saludable, sano(a)

healthy ['helθɪ] adj **(healthier, healthiest)** *(in good health)* sano(a); *(good for health)* saludable; *(thriving)* próspero(a); *(attitude etc)* sensato(a); Fig **to have a h. outlook on sth** tener ideas sanas sobre algo

heap [hiːp] **1** n montón m; Fig **to be at the bottom of the h.** ser el último mono; Fam **heaps of** montones de, cantidad de; Fam **I've got heaps to do** tengo un montón de cosas que hacer
2 vt amontonar; Fig *(presents, praises)* colmar; Culin **a heaped** or US **heaping spoonful** una cucharada colmada

hear [hɪər] vt *(pt & pp* **heard** [hɜːrd]*)* **(a)** *(perceive)* oír; **do you h. (me)?** ¿me oyes?; **h. h.!** ¡muy bien!; **to have heard of sb** haber oído hablar de algn; Fig **I can't h. myself think** me van a estallar los oídos; Hum **have you heard the one about the Englishman who ...?** ¿conoces el chiste del inglés que ...? **(b)** *(listen to)* escuchar; **did you h. the ten o'clock news?** ¿escuchaste las noticias de las diez?; **I won't h. of it!** ¡ni hablar! **(c)** *(find out)* enterarse; **I've heard he's ill** me han dicho que está enfermo; **to h. from sb** tener noticias de algn **(d)** Jur *(case)* ver; *(evidence)* oír

hear out vt escuchar hasta el final

hearer ['hɪərər] n oyente mf

hearing ['hɪərɪŋ] n **(a)** *(sense)* oído m; **hard of h.** duro(a) de oído, sordo(a); **within h. (distance)** al alcance del oído □ **h. aid** audífono m **(b)** Jur audiencia f; Fig **to give sb a fair h.** escuchar a algn, dejar hablar a algn

hearsay ['hɪəseɪ] n rumores mpl □ Jur **h. evidence** pruebas fpl basadas en rumores

hearse [hɜːs] n coche m or carroza f fúnebre

heart [hɑːt] n **(a)** Anat corazón m; **to have h. trouble** padecer del corazón □ **h. attack** infarto m de miocardio or de corazón; Med **h. transplant** trasplante m de corazón **(b)** *(centre of feelings)* corazón m; **a broken h.** un corazón destrozado or roto; **a change of h.** un cambio de opinión; **at h.** en el fondo; **have a h.!** ¡ten piedad!; **to pour out your h.** abrir el corazón; **to take sth to h.** tomarse algo a pecho; **to wear your h. on your sleeve** llevar el corazón en la mano **(c)** *(courage and determination)* valor m, corazón m; **he had his h. in his mouth** tenía el corazón en un puño or Am en la boca; **her h. sank** se le cayó el alma a los pies; **his h. wasn't in it** no ponía interés en ello; **to lose h.** desanimarse **(d)** *(character and attitudes)* corazón m; **he's a man after my own h.** es un hombre de los que me gustan; **she's got her h. in the right place** es buena persona; **to have a good** or **kind h.** tener buen corazón **(e)** *(core, centre)*

meollo m; *(of lettuce)* cogollo m; **in the h. of winter** en pleno invierno; **to get to the h.** profundizar **(of** en) **(f)** Cards corazón m; **the ace of hearts** el as de corazones

heartache ['hɑːteɪk] n dolor m, tristeza f

heartbeat ['hɑːtbiːt] n latido m del corazón

heart-breaking ['hɑːtbreɪkɪŋ] adj que parte el corazón, desgarrador(a)

heart-broken ['hɑːtbrəʊkən] adj hundido(a); **he's h.-b.** tiene el corazón destrozado

heartburn ['hɑːtbɜːn] n ardor m de estómago, acedía f

hearten ['hɑːtən] vt animar

heartening ['hɑːtənɪŋ] adj alentador(a)

heartfelt ['hɑːtfelt] adj sincero(a); **my h. thanks** mi sincero agradecimiento

hearth [hɑːθ] n **(a)** *(of fireplace)* chimenea f, hogar m **(b)** Fml *(home)* hogar m □ **h.-rug** alfombrilla f de chimenea

heartily ['hɑːtɪlɪ] adv **(a)** *(enthusiastically)* **to welcome h.** recibir cordialmente; **to laugh h.** reírse de buena gana **(b)** *(thoroughly)* completamente; **we h. agree** estamos totalmente de acuerdo; Fam **I'm h. sick of it** estoy hasta la coronilla de ello

heartland ['hɑːtlænd] npl núcleo m; **Britain's industrial h. was devastated by the depression** la recesión asoló el núcleo or el corazón industrial de Gran Bretaña

heartless ['hɑːtlɪs] adj cruel, insensible

heartlessly ['hɑːtlɪslɪ] adv sin corazón, cruelmente

heart-rending ['hɑːtrendɪŋ] adj conmovedor(a), desgarrador(a)

heart-searching ['hɑːtsɜːtʃɪŋ] n **after much h.-s.** tras un profundo examen de conciencia

heartstrings ['hɑːtstrɪŋz] npl corazón m sing; **it tugs at your h.** llega hasta lo más hondo, toca la fibra sensible

heartthrob ['hɑːtθrɒb] n ídolo m

heart-to-heart [hɑːttə'hɑːt] n conversación f íntima y franca

heart-warming ['hɑːtwɔːmɪŋ] adj conmovedor(a)

hearty ['hɑːtɪ] adj **(heartier, heartiest)** *(person)* francote; *(meal)* abundante; *(welcome)* cordial; **to have a h. appetite** ser de buen comer

heat [hiːt] n **(a)** *(warmth)* calor m; *(heating)* calefacción f □ Med **h. rash** sarpullido m **(b)** Sport eliminatoria f, serie f; **dead h.** empate m **(c)** Zool celo m; **in** or Br **on h.** en celo
2 vt calentar
3 vi calentarse

heat up vi **(a)** *(warm up)* calentarse **(b)** *(increase action and excitement)* acalorarse; **the atmosphere in the square started to h. up as the demonstrators came closer** el ambiente de la plaza comenzó a hacerse más tenso a medida que se acercaban los manifestantes

heated ['hiːtɪd] adj **(a)** *(of room)* con calefacción **(b)** Fig *(of argument)* acalorado(a); **to become** or **get h. about sth** acalorarse por algo

heater ['hiːtər] n calentador m; **gas/water h.** calentador de gas/agua

heath [hiːθ] n Bot **(a)** *(land)* brezal m **(b)** *(plant)* brezo m

heathen ['hiːðən] adj & n pagano(a) *(m,f)*

heather ['heðər] n Bot brezo m

heating ['hiːtɪŋ] n calefacción f □ **central h.** calefacción f central

heatstroke ['hiːtstrəʊk] n Med insolación f

heatwave ['hiːtweɪv] n ola f de calor

heave [hiːv] **1** n *(pull)* tirón m; *(push)* empujón m
2 vt **(a)** *(lift)* levantar; *(haul)* tirar, Am salvo RP jalar; *(push)*

empujar (**b**) *(throw)* lanzar, arrojar; *Fig* **to h. a sigh of relief** dar un suspiro de alivio

3 *vi* (**a**) *(rise and fall) (gen)* subir y bajar; *(chest)* jadear; **her shoulders heaved with emotion** sus hombros se movían por la emoción (**b**) *(retch)* tener náuseas (**c**) *Naut* (*pt & pp* **hove**) cabecear

heave to *vi* (*pt & pp* **hove to**) *Naut* ponerse al pairo

heaven ['hevən] *n* (**a**) *(place)* cielo *m*; *(state)* gloria *f*, paraíso *m*; **to be in seventh h.** estar en el séptimo cielo; *Fam* **that hotel is h. on earth** ese hotel es el paraíso en la tierra; *Fam* **to stink to high h.** heder *or* oler a perro muerto (**b**) *(in exclamations)* **heavens!** ¡cielos!; **good heavens!** ¡por Dios!; **thank h.!** ¡gracias a Dios!; *Fam* **h. knows!** ¡no tengo ni idea!; *Fam* **h. knows I've worked hard enough!** ¡hambre, he trabajado bastante! (**c**) **heavens** *(sky)* cielo *m sing*; **the h. opened** empezó a llover a cántaros

heavenly ['hevənlı] *adj* celestial; *Fig* divino(a) □ *Astron* **h. body** cuerpo *m* celeste

heaven-sent [hevən'sent] *adj* de lo más oportuno(a), llovido(a) del cielo; **the opportunity is h.-s.** es la ocasión perfecta

heavenward(s) ['hevənwəd(z)] *adv* hacia el cielo

heavily ['hevılı] *adv* pesadamente; **he was fined h.** le pusieron una multa muy fuerte; **it rained/snowed h.** llovió/nevó mucho; **the country relied h. on its tourist trade** el país dependía principalmente de la industria turística; **to sleep h.** dormir profundamente

heaviness ['hevınıs] *n (quality)* pesadez *f*; *(weight)* peso *m*

heavy ['hevı] **1** *adj* (**heavier, heaviest**) *(weight)* pesado(a); *(rain, meal)* fuerte, pesado(a); *(traffic)* denso(a); *(atmosphere)* cargado(a); *(loss, expense)* grande; **a h. fine** una multa grande; **h. going** duro(a); **is it h.?** ¿pesa mucho?; **she is a h. sleeper** tiene el sueño muy profundo; **to be a h. drinker/smoker** beber/fumar mucho; **to have a h. heart** tener el corazón oprimido □ **h. industry** industria *f* pesada; *Mus* **h. metal** rock *m* duro *or* heavy

2 *n Slang* gorila *m*

heavy-duty ['hevıdju:tı] *adj (clothes, footwear)* de faena, resistente; *(machinery)* sólido(a), para grandes cargas

heavy-handed ['hevıhændıd] *adj (clumsy)* torpe; *(severe)* autoritario(a)

heavyweight ['hevıweıt] *n Box* peso *m* pesado

Hebrew ['hi:bru:] **1** *adj* hebreo(a)

2 *n* (**a**) *(person)* hebreo(a) *m,f* (**b**) *(language)* hebreo *m*

Hebrides ['hebrıdi:z] *npl* **the H.** las (Islas) Hébridas

heck [hek] *interj Fam* ¡jolín!; *Fam* **a h. of a noise** un ruido de mil demonios; *Fam* **what the h.!** ¿qué diablos importa?

heckle ['hekəl] *vt Pol Theat* interrumpir, provocar

heckler ['heklər] *n Pol Theat* altercador(a) *m,f*, follonero(a) *m,f*

heckling ['heklıŋ] *n Pol Theat* altercado *m*, gresca *f*

hectare ['hekta:r] *n* hectárea *f*

hectic ['hektık] *adj* agitado(a); **a h. day** un día ajetreado

hectogram ['hektəʊgræm] *n* hectogramo *m*

hector ['hektər] *vt* intimidar, tiranizar

hectoring ['hektərıŋ] *adj* tiránico(a)

hedge [hedʒ] **1** *n* seto *m* vivo; *Fig* barrera *f*; *Fig* **a h. against inflation** una barrera contra la inflación

2 *vt* cercar o separar con un seto; **to be hedged in by** *or* **around with** *(be surrounded)* estar rodeado(a) de; *Fig* **to h. one's bets** cubrirse

3 *vi (in discussion)* contestar con evasivas

hedgehog ['hedʒhɒg] *n* erizo *m*

hedgerow ['hedʒrəʊ] *n* seto *m* vivo

hedonism ['hedənızəm] *n* hedonismo *m*

heebie-jeebies [hi:bı'dʒi:bız] *npl Fam* **it gives me the h.-j.** me da canguelo *or Méx* mello *or RP* cuiqui

heed [hi:d] *Fml* **1** *vt* prestar atención a, hacer caso de

2 *n* atención *m*; **to pay h. to, take h. of** hacer caso de

heedless ['hi:dlıs] *adj* desatento(a), despreocupado(a)

heedlessly ['hi:dlıslı] *adv* despreocupadamente, a la ligera

hee-haw ['hi:hɔ:] *n* rebuzno *m*

heel¹ [hi:l] **1** *n* (**a**) *Anat* talón *m*; *(of sock, stocking)* talón *m*; *(of shoe)* tacón *m*, *Am* taco *m*; *(of palm of hand)* pulpejo *m*; *Fig* **to bring sb to h.** meter a algn en cintura; *Fig* **to dig one's heels in** negarse a cambiar; *Fig* **down at h.** desharrapado(a); *Fig* **head over heels in love** locamente enamorado(a); *Fig* **to take to one's heels** darse a la fuga; *Fig* **to be on sb's heels** pisarle los talones a algn; *Fam* **to cool** *or* **kick one's heels** esperar impacientemente □ **high heels** zapatos *mpl* de tacón *or Am* taco alto (**b**) *Slang* sinvergüenza *mf*

2 *vt* poner tacón *or Am* taco a

heel² [hi:l] *vi Naut* escorar

heel over *vi* ladearse

heeled [hi:ld] *adj* de tacón; *Fam Fig* **well-h.** adinerado(a)

hefty ['heftı] *adj* (**heftier, heftiest**) (**a**) *(big and powerful) (of person)* robusto(a), fornido(a); *(of package)* pesado(a); **a h. punch** un puñetazo fuerte (**b**) *(large amount)* grande; **a h. sum of money** una fuerte suma

heifer ['hefər] *n* novilla *f*, vaquilla *f*

height [haıt] *n* (**a**) *(gen)* altura *f*; **to be afraid of heights** tener vértigo; **to gain/lose h.** subir/bajar (**b**) *(of person)* estatura *f*; **what h. are you?** ¿cuánto mides? (**c**) *Fig (most intense or successful part)* **it's the h. of fashion** es la última moda; **the h. of ignorance** el colmo de la ignorancia (**d**) *Geog* cumbre *f*

heighten ['haıtən] *vt (intensify)* realzar; *(increase)* aumentar

heinous ['heınəs] *adj Fml* atroz

heir [eər] *n* heredero *m*; **to be h. to** ser heredero de □ *Jur* **h. apparent** heredero *m* forzoso; **h. presumptive** presunto heredero *m*

heiress ['eərıs] *n* heredera *f*

heirloom ['eəlu:m] *n* reliquia *f* or joya *f* de familia

heist [haıst] *n US Fam* golpe *m*, robo *m*

held [held] *pt & pp see* **hold**

helicopter ['helıkɒptər] *n* helicóptero *m*

helipad ['helıpæd] *n* helipuerto *m*

heliport ['helıpɔ:t] *n* helipuerto *m*

helium ['hi:lıəm] *n Chem* helio *m*

hell [hel] *n* (**a**) *(gen)* infierno *m*; **come h. or high water** pase lo que pase; *Fig* **to go h. for leather** ir como si se le llevara el diablo; *Fam* **like h.!** *Esp* ¡ni de coña!, *Méx* ¡ya mero!, *RP* ¡ni en joda!; *Fam* **she gave him h.** se las hizo pasar negras *or Esp* canutas; *Fam* **there'll be h. to pay** habrá problemas; *Fam* **to play h. with** estropear; *Fam* **what the h. are you doing?** ¿qué diablos *or Esp* leches estás haciendo?; *Offens* **go** *or* **get to h.!** ¡vete a la mierda! (**b**) *Fam* **a h. of a** mucho(a); **a h. of a noise** un ruido excesivo; **a h. of a party** una fiesta estupenda; **one h. of a guy** un tío genial; **she's had a h. of a day** ha tenido un día horrible; **they paid a h. of a lot** pagaron *Esp* una porrada de *or Méx* un chorro de *or RP* un toco de dinero; **to have a h. of a time** *(good)* pasárselo como Dios *or RP* como los dioses; *(bad)* pasarlas negras *or Esp* moradas

hell-bent [hel'bent] *adj* empeñado(a); **he's h.-b. on destruction** está empeñado en destruirse *or* destruirlo

hellhole ['helhəʊl] *n Fam (place)* infierno *m*, agujero *m* infecto

hellish ['helɪʃ] *adj Fam* infernal

hellishly ['helɪʃlɪ] *adv Fam* muy; **a h. difficult job** una faena muy difícil

hello [hə'ləʊ, 'heləʊ] *interj* (**a**) *(as greeting)* ¡hola! (**b**) *Tel (answering)* ¿sí?, *Esp* ¿diga?, *Esp* ¿dígame?, *Am* ¿aló?, *Carib RP* ¿oigo?, *Méx* ¿bueno?, *RP* ¿hola?; *(calling)* ¡oiga! (**c**) *(showing surprise)* ¡vaya!; **hello!, what's this?** ¡vaya!, ¿qué pasa?

hell-raiser ['helreɪzər] *n Fam* camorrista *mf*

helm [helm] *n Naut* timón *m*; **to be at the h.** llevar el timón

helmet ['helmɪt] *n* casco *m* ❑ **crash h.** casco *m* protector

helmsman ['helmzmən] *n (pl* **helmsmen**) timonel *m*

help [help] **1** *n* (**a**) *(gen)* ayuda *f*; **h!** ¡socorro!; *Br* **there's no h. for it** no tenemos más remedio; **to ask for h.** pedir socorro *or* ayuda ❑ *Comptr* **h. menu** menú *m* de ayuda (**b**) **(daily) h.** asistenta *f*
2 *vt* (**a**) *(gen)* ayudar; **can you h. me?** ¿me quieres ayudar?; *(in shop etc)* **may I h. you?** ¿qué desea?; **your advice didn't h. at all** tus consejos no sirvieron de nada (**b**) *(alleviate)* aliviar; **this new medicine will h. your cold** este nuevo medicamento te aliviará el resfriado (**c**) *(serve)* **h. yourself!** ¡sírvete!; **to h. oneself to more food** servirse más comida; *Fam* **he helped himself to my purse** me birló el monedero (**d**) *(assist)* **can I h. you up with that case?** ¿puedo echar una mano para subir esa maleta?; **he helped her into her coat** la ayudó a ponerse el abrigo (**e**) *(avoid)* evitar; **I can't h. it** no lo puedo remediar; **I couldn't h. laughing** no pude por menos que reír; **it can't be helped** no lo podemos evitar

help out *vt* ayudar; **to h. sb out** echarle una mano a algn

helper ['helpər] *n* ayudante(a) *m,f*, auxiliar *mf*

helpful ['helpfʊl] *adj (of person)* amable; *(of thing)* útil, práctico(a)

helpfully ['helpfʊlɪ] *adv* amablemente

helping ['helpɪŋ] **1** *n* porción *f*, ración *f*; **who wants a second h.?** ¿quién quiere repetir?
2 *adj* **to give sb a h. hand** echarle una mano a algn

helpless ['helplɪs] *adj (defenceless)* desamparado(a); *(powerless)* incapaz, impotente; **a h. child** un niño indefenso

helplessly ['helplɪslɪ] *adv* inútilmente, en vano

helplessness ['helplɪsnɪs] *n (defencelessness)* desamparo *m*; *(powerlessness)* impotencia *f*

helpline ['helplaɪn] *n* teléfono *m* de asistencia *or* ayuda

Helsinki [hel'sɪŋkɪ] *n* Helsinki

helter-skelter [heltə'skeltər] **1** *n Br (at fairground)* tobogán *m*
2 *adj* atropellado(a)
3 *adv* atropelladamente, deprisa y corriendo

hem [hem] **1** *n Sew* dobladillo *m*
2 *vt (pt & pp* **hemmed)** *Sew* hacer un dobladillo a

hem in *vt* cercar *or* rodear

he-man ['hi:mæn] *n (pl* **he-men** ['hi:men]) machote *m*, *Esp* hombretón *m*

hemisphere ['hemɪsfɪər] *n* hemisferio *m*; **northern/ southern h.** hemisferio norte/sur

hemispherical [hemɪs'ferɪkəl] *adj* hemisférico(a)

hemline ['hemlaɪn] *n* bajo *m*; **hemlines are lower this year** los vestidos se llevan más largos este año

hemlock ['hemlɒk] *n Bot* (**a**) *(plant)* cicuta *f* (**b**) *(tree)* tsuga *f* ❑ **eastern h.** tsuga *f* del Canadá; **western h.** tsuga *f* heterófila

hemoglobin [hi:məʊ'gləʊbɪn] *n US Med see* **haemoglobin**

hemophilia [hi:məʊ'fɪlɪə] *n US Med see* **haemophilia**

hemophiliac [hi:məʊ'fɪlɪæk] *adj & n US Med see* **haemophiliac**

hemorrhage ['hemərɪdʒ] *n US Med see* **haemorrhage**

hemorrhoids ['hemərɔɪdz] *npl US Med see* **haemorrhoids**

hemp [hemp] *n* (**a**) *Bot* cáñamo *m* (**b**) *(drug)* hachís *m*, marihuana *f*

hemstitch ['hemstɪtʃ] **1** *n Sew* vainica *f*
2 *vt Sew* hacer una vainica a

hen [hen] *n* gallina *f* ❑ *Fam* **h. party** *or Br* **night** *(before wedding)* despedida *f* de soltera

hence [hens] *adv Fml* (**a**) *(from now)* de aquí a; **six months h.** de aquí a seis meses (**b**) *(consequently)* por lo tanto, de ahí *or* aquí que; **he is upset, h. his long face** está disgustado, de ahí que tenga cara larga

henceforth [hens'fɔ:θ] *adv Fml* de ahora en adelante

henchman ['hentʃmən] *n (pl* **henchmen**) *Pej* secuaz *m*

henhouse ['henhaʊs] *n* gallinero *m*

henna ['henə] *n Bot* alheña *f*

henpecked ['henpekt] *adj Fam* **a h. husband** un calzonazos

hepatic [hɪ'pætɪk] *adj Med* hepático(a)

hepatitis [hepə'taɪtɪs] *n Med* hepatitis *f*

heptagon ['heptəgən] *n* heptágono *m*

heptagonal [hep'tægənəl] *adj* heptagonal

her [hɜ:r, *unstressed* hə] **1** *poss adj (one thing)* su; *(more than one)* sus; *(to distinguish)* de ella; **are they h. books or his?** ¿los libros son de ella o de él?; **h. car** su coche; **h. children** sus hijos; **she has cut h. finger** se ha cortado el dedo
2 *pers pron* (**a**) *(direct object)* la; **I saw h. recently** la vi hace poco; **they can't help h.** no la pueden ayudar (**b**) *(indirect object)* le; *(with other third person pronouns)* se; **he gave h. money** le dio dinero; **they handed it to h.** se lo entregaron (**c**) *(after prep)* ella; **for h.** para ella; **with h.** con ella (**d**) *(as subject) Fam* ella; **look, it's h.!** ¡mira, es ella!

herald ['herəld] **1** *n* heraldo *m*; *Fig* precursor *m*
2 *vt* anunciar

heraldic [he'rældɪk] *adj* heráldico(a)

heraldry ['herəldrɪ] *n* heráldica *f*

herb [hɜːb, *US* ɜːrb] *n Bot Culin* hierba *f* ❑ **h. tea** infusión *f* de hierbas

herbaceous [hɜː'beɪʃəs, *US* ɜːr'beɪʃəs] *adj* herbáceo(a); **h. border** arriate *m* de plantas

herbal ['hɜːbəl, *US* 'ɜːrbəl] *adj* herbario(a); **h. remedies** curas *fpl* de hierbas

herbalist ['hɜːbəlɪst, *US* 'ɜːrbəlɪst] *n* herbolario(a) *m,f*

herbicide ['hɜːbɪsaɪd, *US* 'ɜːrbɪsaɪd] *n* herbicida *m*

herbivore ['hɜːbɪvɔːr, *US* 'ɜːrbɪvɔːr] *n Zool* herbívoro(a) *m,f*

herbivorous [hɜː'bɪvərəs, *US* ɜːr'bɪvərəs] *adj Zool* herbívoro(a)

herd [hɜːd] **1** *n (of cattle)* manada *f*; *(of goats)* rebaño *m*; *(of pigs)* piara *f*; *Fig (large group)* manada *f*, multitud *f*; *Fig* **to go with the h.** ir con las masas ❑ **h. instinct** instinto *m* gregario
2 *vt (collect)* juntar en manada; *(drive forward)* guiar *or* conducir en manada; **the tourists were herded into the coach** los turistas se apiñaron en el autobús
3 *vi (animals)* reunirse rebaño *or* manada; *(people)* apiñarse

herdsman ['hɜːdzmən] *n (pl* **herdsmen**) *(of cattle)* vaquero *m*; *(of sheep)* pastor *m*

here [hɪər] **1** adv aquí; **come h.** ven aquí; **h.!** ¡presente!; **h. and there** aquí y allá; **h. goes!** ¡vamos a ver!; **h. he comes** ya viene; **here's to success!** ¡brindemos por el éxito!; **h. you are!** ¡toma!, ¡ten!; **that's neither h. nor there** eso no tiene nada que ver
2 interj ¡oye!, ¡oiga!; **look h., you can't do that!** ¡oiga, que no se permite hacer eso!
3 n **the h. and now** el presente, el aquí y ahora
hereafter [hɪər'ɑːftər] Fml **1** adv de ahora en adelante
2 the h. n la otra vida, el más allá
hereby [hɪə'baɪ] adv Fml por la presente; **I h. declare that ...** afirmo por la presente que ...
hereditary [hɪ'redɪtərɪ] adj hereditario(a)
heredity [hɪ'redɪtɪ] n herencia f
herein [hɪər'ɪn] adv Fml (inside) aquí dentro; (in document) aquí mencionado(a)
heresy ['herəsɪ] n herejía f
heretic ['herətɪk] n hereje mf
heretical [hɪ'retɪkəl] adj herético(a)
herewith [hɪə'wɪð] adv Fml adjunto(a); **the letter enclosed h.** la carta adjunta
heritage ['herɪtɪdʒ] n patrimonio m; Jur herencia f
hermaphrodite [hɜː'mæfrədaɪt] adj & n hermafrodita (mf)
hermetic [hɜː'metɪk] adj hermético(a)
hermetically [hɜː'metɪklɪ] adv herméticamente; **h. sealed** con cierre hermético
hermit ['hɜːmɪt] n ermitaño(a) m,f, eremita m ◻ **hermit crab** ermitaño m, paguro m
hermitage ['hɜːmɪtɪdʒ] n ermita f
hernia ['hɜːnɪə] n Med hernia f
hero ['hɪərəʊ] n (pl heroes) héroe m; (in novel) personaje m principal, protagonista m ◻ **h. worship** idolatría f
heroic [hɪ'rəʊɪk] **1** adj heroico(a)
2 heroics npl grandilocuencia f
heroically [hɪ'rəʊɪklɪ] adv heroicamente
heroin ['herəʊɪn] n heroína f ◻ **h. addict** heroinómano(a) m,f
heroine ['herəʊɪn] n heroína f; (in novel) personaje m principal, protagonista f
heroism ['herəʊɪzəm] n heroísmo m
heron ['herən] n Orn garza f, garza f real
herpes ['hɜːpiːz] n Med herpes m
herring ['herɪŋ] n (pl herring or herrings) arenque m; Fig **a red h.** una divagación, una pista falsa
herringbone ['herɪŋbəʊn] n espiga f ◻ **h. tweed** cheviot m de espiga
hers [hɜːz] poss pron (a) (attribute) (one thing) suyo(a); (more than one) suyos(as); (to distinguish) de ella; **a friend of h.** un amigo suyo; **the book is h.** el libro es suyo or de ella; **they are h. not his** son de ella, no de él (b) (noun reference) (one thing) el suyo, la suya; (more than one) los suyos, las suyas; **of all the houses h. is the nicest** de todas las casas la suya es la más bonita
herself [hɜː'self] pers pron (a) (reflexive) se; **she dressed h.** se vistió; **she wasn't h.** no se encontraba bien (b) (alone) ella misma; **she did it (by) h.** lo hizo ella misma or por sí sola; **she was by h.** estaba sola (c) (emphatic) ella misma; **she told me so h.** eso dijo ella
hertz [hɜːts] n Phys hertz m, hercio m
hesitant ['hezɪtənt] adj vacilante, indeciso(a); **h. steps** pasos mpl titubeantes
hesitantly ['hezɪtəntlɪ] adv indecisamente
hesitate ['hezɪteɪt] vi vacilar; **don't h. to call/ask**

llámame/pídemelo con toda confianza; **without hesitating** sin vacilar
hesitation [hezɪ'teɪʃən] n vacilación f, indecisión f; **without h.** sin vacilar
hessian ['hesɪən] n arpillera f
heterogeneous [hetərəʊ'dʒiːnɪəs] adj heterogéneo(a)
heterosexual [hetərəʊ'seksjʊəl] adj & n heterosexual (mf)
het up [het'ʌp] adj Br Fam nervioso(a); **to get h. up about sth** ponerse nervioso(a) por algo
heuristic [hjʊə'rɪstɪk] adj heurístico(a)
hew [hjuː] vt (pt hewed; pp hewed or hewn [hjuːn]) tallar
hexagon ['heksəgən] n hexágono m
hexagonal [hek'sægənəl] adj hexagonal
hey [heɪ] interj ¡oye!, ¡oiga!
heyday ['heɪdeɪ] n auge m, apogeo m; **in his h.** en sus mejores años
HF Rad (abbr high frequency) alta frecuencia f, AF f
HGV [eɪtʃdʒiː'viː] n Br Aut (abbr heavy goods vehicle) vehículo m de carga pesada
hi [haɪ] interj Fam ¡hola!
hiatus [haɪ'eɪtəs] n (pl hiatuses or hiatus) (a) Ling hiato m (b) Fml laguna f, pausa f
hibernate ['haɪbəneɪt] vi hibernar
hibernation [haɪbə'neɪʃən] n hibernación f
hibiscus [haɪ'bɪskəs] n Bot hibisco m
hiccough ['hɪkʌp] n & vi see hiccup
hiccup ['hɪkʌp] **1** n (a) (sound) hipo m; **to have hiccups** tener hipo (b) Fam (minor problem) pega f, fallo m
2 vi (pt & pp hiccuped, hiccupped) (repeatedly) tener hipo, (once) hipar
hick [hɪk] adj & n US Fam pueblerino(a) (m,f), Esp paleto(a) (m,f), Méx paisa (mf), RP pajuerano(a) (m,f)
hickey ['hɪkɪ] n US Fam (lovebite) marca f (de un beso), Esp chupetón m, Am chupón m
hickory ['hɪkərɪ] n (tree, wood) nogal m americano
hid [hɪd] pt see hide
hidden ['hɪdən] **1** adj oculto(a); **to be h.** estar oculto(a); **h. agenda** objetivo m secreto; **h. economy** economía f sumergida
2 pp see hide
hide[1] [haɪd] **1** vt (pt hid; pp hidden) (conceal) esconder; (obscure) ocultar; **she hid her feelings** ocultó sus sentimientos; **to h. the truth from sb** ocultar la verdad a algn
2 vi esconderse, ocultarse
3 n Br (for birdwatching) puesto m de observación
hide[2] [haɪd] n (animal skin) piel f; Fam (of person) pellejo m; Fig **I haven't seen h. nor hair of him** no le he visto el pelo últimamente; Fig **to have a h. like an elephant** ser totalmente insensible
hide-and-seek [haɪdən'siːk] n escondite m, Am escondidas fpl; **to play h.-a.-s.** jugar al escondite
hidebound ['haɪdbaʊnd] adj chapado(a) a la antigua
hideous ['hɪdɪəs] adj (a) (horrific) horroroso(a); **a h. crime** un crimen atroz (b) (extremely ugly) espantoso(a), repelente
hideously ['hɪdɪəslɪ] adv horrorosamente
hide-out ['haɪdaʊt] n escondrijo m, escondite m
hiding[1] ['haɪdɪŋ] n huida f; **to go into h.** esconderse
hiding[2] ['haɪdɪŋ] n Fam paliza f; **to give sb a good h.** darle una buena paliza a algn
hierarchic(al) [haɪə'rɑːkɪk(əl)] adj jerárquico(a)

hierarchy ['haɪərɑːkɪ] *n* jerarquía *f*

hieroglyphics [haɪərə'glɪfɪks] *npl* jeroglíficos *mpl*

hi-fi ['haɪfaɪ] *n* hifi *m* ❑ **hi-fi equipment** equipo *m* de alta fidelidad

higgledy-piggledy [hɪgəldɪ'pɪgəldɪ] **1** *adj* desordenado(a), hecho(a) un lío
2 *adv* a la buena de Dios

high [haɪ] **1** *adj* (**a**) *(tall)* alto(a); **h. building** edificio alto; **h. ceiling** techo alto; **how h. is that wall?** ¿qué altura tiene esa pared?; **it's three feet h.** tiene tres pies de alto; *Fig* **to leave sb h. and dry** dejar plantado(a) a algn; *Fig* **to search h. and low for sth** buscar algo por todas partes ❑ **h. chair** silla *f* alta para niños; *Swimming* **h. diving** salto *m* de palanca; *Athlet* **h. jump** salto *m* de altura *or Am* alto; *Br Fam Fig* **she's for the h. jump** se la va a cargar (**b**) *(elevated, intense)* alto(a), elevado(a); *Med* **h. blood pressure** presión *or* tensión alta; **h. prices** precios elevados; *Fam* **to be in h. spirits** estar alegre *or* de buen humor (**c**) *(great, important)* alto(a), importante; **a h. position in life** un alto standing; **h. wind** viento *m* fuerte; **to have a h. opinion of sb** hablar muy bien de algn; **to have friends in h. places** estar bien relacionado(a) ❑ **H. Commissioner** Alto Comisario *m*; **H. Court** Tribunal *m* Supremo; **h. fidelity** alta fidelidad *f*; **h. priest** sumo sacerdote *m*; **h. road** carretera *f* principal; *Educ* **h. school** instituto *m* de enseñanza media; *Br* **h. tea** merienda-cena *f*; *Br* **the H. Street** la Calle Mayor (**d**) *Mus (of note)* alto(a) (**e**) *(excellent)* bueno(a); **a h. standard** un nivel alto; **h. principles** buenos principios; *Fam* **the h. life** la buena vida; *Fam* **to have a h. old time of it** pasarlo en grande (**f**) *(of food)* pasado(a); *(of game)* manido(a) (**g**) *Slang (drugged)* colocado(a), flipado(a), *RP* entregado(a)
2 *adv* alto; **feelings ran h.** los ánimos estaban exaltados; **to bet** *or* **stake h.** apostar fuerte; **to fly h.** volar a gran altura
3 *n* (**a**) *(high point)* récord *m*, punto *m* máximo; **to reach an all-time h.** batir el récord; *Fam* **to be on a h.** estar a las mil maravillas (**b**) *US Meteor* temperatura *f* alta

highball ['haɪbɔːl] *n US (drink)* highball

highbrow ['haɪbraʊ] *adj & n* intelectual *(mf)*

high-class ['haɪklɑːs] *adj* de alta categoría

higher ['haɪər] *adj* superior ❑ **h. education** enseñanza *f* superior

highfalutin(g) [haɪfə'luːtɪŋ] *adj Fam* pomposo(a), presumido(a), presuntuoso(a)

high-flier *n*, **high-flyer** [haɪ'flaɪər] *n Fig* persona *f* ambiciosa

high-flying ['haɪflaɪɪŋ] *adj Fig* ambicioso(a)

high-frequency [haɪ'friːkwənsɪ] *adj Rad* de alta frecuencia

high-handed [haɪ'hændɪd] *adj* autoritario(a), despótico(a)

high-heeled ['haɪhiːld] *adj* de tacón alto *or Am* taco alto

highland ['haɪlənd] **1** *adj* montañoso(a) ❑ **h. cattle** ganado *m* vacuno de las montañas
2 highlands *npl Geog* tierras *npl* altas

highlander ['haɪləndər] *n* montañés(esa) *m,f*

high-level ['haɪlevəl] *adj (talks, delegation)* de alto nivel

highlight ['haɪlaɪt] **1** *n* (**a**) *Art* toque *m* de luz (**b**) *(in hair)* reflejo *m* (**c**) *(the most interesting)* atracción *f* principal
2 *vt* (**a**) *(problem, difference)* poner de relieve, destacar; **the talk highlighted the problem** el discurso puso de relieve el problema (**b**) *(a text)* marcar con un rotulador fosforescente

highlighter ['haɪlaɪtər] *n (pen)* rotulador *m* fluorescente, *Col RP* resaltador *m*, *Méx* marcador *m*

highly ['haɪlɪ] *adv* (**a**) *(very)* muy, sumamente; **h. pleased**

muy contento(a); *Culin* **h. seasoned** muy picante (**b**) *(favourably)* muy bien; **to speak h. of sb** hablar muy bien de algn

highly-strung [haɪlɪ'strʌŋ] *adj* muy nervioso(a)

high-minded [haɪ'maɪndɪd] *adj* noble, magnánimo(a); *Pej* altivo(a)

Highness ['haɪnɪs] *n* alteza *mf*; **Your H.** Su Alteza

high-performance ['haɪpə'fɔːməns] *adj* de alto rendimiento

high-pitched ['haɪpɪtʃt] *adj* estridente, agudo(a)

high-powered ['haɪpaʊəd] *adj (of engine)* de gran potencia; *(of person)* dinámico(a)

high-pressure ['haɪ'preʃər] *adj (substance, container)* gran presión

high-profile ['haɪ'prəʊfaɪl] *adj (person)* prominente, destacado(a); *(campaign)* de gran alcance

high-ranking ['haɪræŋkɪŋ] *adj* superior, de alta categoría; **h.-r. official** alto funcionario

high-resolution ['haɪrezə'luːʃən] *adj (screen, graphics)* de alta resolución

high-rise ['haɪraɪz] *adj* **h.-r. building** rascacielos *m inv*

highroad ['haɪrəʊd] *n Old-fashioned* carretera *f* principal; *Fig* **the h. to success** la vía directa hacia el éxito

high-speed ['haɪspiːd] *adj* rápido(a), de gran velocidad; *Phot* **h.-s. lens** objetivo ultrarrápido; *Rail* **h.-s. train** supertrén *m*

high-spirited [haɪ'spɪrɪtɪd] *adj (of person)* muy animado(a); *(of horse)* fogoso(a)

high-strung [haɪ'strʌŋ] *adj US* muy nervioso(a)

hightail ['haɪteɪl] *vt US Fam* **to h. it** largarse corriendo, *Esp RP* pirarse, pirárselas

high-tech ['haɪtek] *adj* de alta tecnología

highway ['haɪweɪ] *n US (main road)* carretera *f*; *(freeway)* autopista *f* ❑ *Br* **H. Code** código *m* de la circulación

highwayman ['haɪweɪmən] *n (pl* **highwaymen**) salteador *m* de caminos, bandido *m*

hijack ['haɪdʒæk] **1** *vt* secuestrar
2 *n* secuestro *m*

hijacker ['haɪdʒækər] *n* secuestrador(a) *m,f*; *(of planes)* pirata *mf* del aire

hijacking ['haɪdʒækɪŋ] *n* secuestro *m*

hike [haɪk] **1** *n* (**a**) *(walk)* excursión *f*; **to go for** *or* **on a h.** hacer una excursión a pie (**b**) *(increase)* subida *f*
2 *vi* ir de excursión, hacer una excursión

hiker ['haɪkər] *n* excursionista *mf*

hiking ['haɪkɪŋ] *n* **to go h.** ir de excursión, hacer una excursión

hilarious [hɪ'leərɪəs] *adj* graciosísimo(a), hilarante, para morirse de risa

hilariously [hɪ'leərɪəslɪ] *adv* hilarantemente; **h. funny** graciosísimo(a)

hilarity [hɪ'lærɪtɪ] *n* hilaridad *f*

hill [hɪl] *n* (**a**) *(small mountain)* colina *f*, cerro *m*; *Fam* **as old as the hills** más viejo que Matusalén (**b**) *(slope)* cuesta *f*

hillbilly ['hɪlbɪlɪ] *n US Pej* paleto(a) *m,f*

hillock ['hɪlək] *n (small hill)* collado *m*, colina *f* pequeña; *(mound)* montículo *m*

hillside ['hɪlsaɪd] *n* ladera *f*

hilltop ['hɪltɒp] *n* cima *f*

hilly ['hɪlɪ] *adj* (**hillier, hilliest**) accidentado(a)

hilt [hɪlt] *n* puño *m*, empuñadura *f*; *Fam* **I'll support him up to the h.** le daré mi apoyo total; *Fam* **mortgaged up to the h.** hipotecado(a) al máximo

him [hɪm] *pers pron* **(a)** *(direct object)* lo, le; **hit h.!** ¡pégale!; **she loves h.** lo quiere **(b)** *(indirect object)* le; *(with other third person pronouns)* se; **give h. the money** dale el dinero; **give it to h.** dáselo; **I gave h. my book** le di mi libro **(c)** *(after prep)* él; **he had no money on h.** no llevaba dinero encima; **he took his luggage with h.** se llevó el equipaje; **it's not like h. to say that** no es muy propio de él decir eso **(d)** *(as subject) Fam* él; **it's h.** es él

Himalayan [hɪmə'leɪən] *adj* himalayo(a)

Himalayas [hɪmə'leɪəz] *npl* **the H.** el Himalaya *sing*

himself [hɪm'self] *pers pron* **(a)** *(reflexive)* se; **he hurt h.** se hizo daño; **he's not h. today** hoy no se encuentra bien **(b)** *(unaided, alone)* solo, por sí mismo; **he lives by h.** vive solo **(c)** *(emphatic)* él mismo; **he said so h.** eso dijo él

hind[1] [haɪnd] *adj* trasero(a); **h. legs** patas traseras; *Fam* **to talk the h. legs off a donkey** hablar por los codos

hind[2] [haɪnd] *n Zool* cierva *f*

hinder ['hɪndər] *vt* dificultar, entorpecer, estorbar; **to h. sb from doing sth.** impedir a algn hacer algo; **noise hinders my concentration** el ruido me impide concentrarme; **the rain hindered our journey** la lluvia dificultó nuestro viaje

Hindi ['hɪndɪ] *n (language)* hindi *m*

hindquarters ['haɪndkwɔːtəz] *npl* cuartos *mpl* traseros

hindrance ['hɪndrəns] *n* obstáculo *m*, estorbo *m*

hindsight ['haɪndsaɪt] *n* retrospectiva *f*

Hindu [hɪn'duː, 'hɪnduː] *adj & n* hindú *(mf)*

Hinduism ['hɪnduɪzəm] *n* hinduismo *m*

hinge [hɪndʒ] **1** *n* **(a)** *(of door, lid, box)* bisagra *f*, gozne *m*; *Fig* eje *m* **(b)** *(for stamp collecting)* fijasellos *m inv* **2** *vt* engoznar

hinge on *vt* depender de; **everything hinged on his reaction** todo dependía de su reacción

hinged ['hɪndʒd] *adj* de bisagra

hint [hɪnt] **1** *n* **(a)** *(indirect suggestion)* indirecta *f*; **to drop a h.** lanzar *or* tirar una indirecta; **to take the h.** darse por aludido(a) **(b)** *(clue)* pista *f*; **give us a h.** danos una pista **(c)** *(sign, trace)* pizca *f*; *Culin* **a h. of garlic** una pizca de ajo; **there wasn't the slightest h. of cold** no hacía ni pizca de frío **(d)** *(advice)* sugerencia *f*, consejo *m*; **hints for travellers** consejos para el viajero **2** *vi* **(a)** *(suggest indirectly)* lanzar *or* soltar indirectas **(b)** *(imply)* **to h. at** insinuar; **he hinted at a possible change in policy** aludió a un posible cambio de política; **what was she hinting at?** ¿qué estaba insinuando?

hinterland ['hɪntəlænd] *n Geog* interior *m*

hip[1] [hɪp] *n Anat* cadera *f* **h. flask** petaca *f*; **h. joint** articulación *f* de la cadera

hip[2] [hɪp] *n Bot* escaramujo *m*

hip[3] [hɪp] *adj Slang* moderno(a), a la última, *Am* de onda

hip[4] [hɪp] *interj* **h., h., hooray!** ¡hurra!, ¡viva!

hipbone ['hɪpbəʊn] *n Anat* hueso *m* de la cadera

hippie ['hɪpɪ] *adj & n Fam* hippy *(mf)*

hippo ['hɪpəʊ] *n Fam* hipopótamo *m*

hippopotamus [hɪpə'pɒtəməs] *n (pl* **hippopotamus** *or* **hippopotami** [hɪpə'pɒtəmaɪ]) hipopótamo *m*

hippy ['hɪpɪ] *adj & n Fam see* **hippie**

hipsters ['hɪpstəz] *npl* pantalones *mpl* de cintura baja, pantalones *mpl* por la cadera

hire ['haɪər] **1** *n Br (of car, room, suit)* alquiler *m*, *Méx* renta *f*; *(cost) (of car, boat)* alquiler *m*; **bicycles for h.** se alquilan *or Méx* rentan bicicletas; **taxi for h.** taxi *m* libre **car h.** alquiler *m* de coches *or Méx* carros *or CSur* autos; *Br* **h. purchase** compra *f* a plazos; **we bought it on h. purchase** lo compramos a plazos

2 *vt* **(a)** *Br (car, room, suit)* alquilar, *Méx* rentar; **we hired skates** alquilamos patines **(b)** *(lawyer, worker)* contratar; **they hired her for the job** la contrataron para el puesto

hire out *vt Br (boat, bicycle)* alquilar, *Méx* rentar; *(one's services)* ofrecer

hired ['haɪəd] *adj* alquilado(a), de alquiler, *Méx* rentado(a) **Jur h. assassin** asesino(a) *m,f* a sueldo; **h. hand** *(on farm)* jornalero(a) *m,f*

hireling ['haɪəlɪŋ] *n Pej* mercenario(a) *m,f*

hirsute ['hɜːsjuːt] *adj Fml* hirsuto(a)

his [hɪz] **1** *poss adj (one thing)* su; *(more than one)* sus; *(to distinguish)* de él; **h. book** su libro; **h. house** su casa; **h. friends** sus amigos; **he washed h. face** se lavó la cara; **he broke h. leg** se rompió la pierna; **is it h. dog or hers?** ¿el perro es de él o de ella?

2 *poss pron* **(a)** *(attribute) (one thing)* suyo(a); *(more than one)* suyos(as); *(to distinguish)* de él; **is the umbrella h. or hers?** ¿el paraguas es de él o de ella?; **the cigarettes are h.** el tabaco es suyo **(b)** *(noun reference) (one thing)* el suyo, la suya; *(more than one)* los suyos, las suyas; **my car is blue and h. is red** mi coche es azul y el suyo es rojo

Hispanic [hɪ'spænɪk] **1** *adj* hispánico(a) **2** *n US* hispano(a) *m,f*, latino(a) *m,f*

Hispanicist [hɪs'pænɪsɪst] *n see* **Hispanist**

Hispaniola [hɪspən'jəʊlə] *n* la Española

Hispanist ['hɪspənɪst] *n* hispanista *mf*

Hispanophile [hɪs'pænəfaɪl] *n* hispanófilo(a) *m,f*

hiss [hɪs] **1** *n (gen)* siseo *m*; *(of steam)* silbido *m*; *Theat* silbido *m* **2** *vt* sisear, silbar; *Theat* **the actors were booed and hissed** silbaron y abuchearon a los actores

hissing ['hɪsɪŋ] *n (gen)* siseo *m*; *(of steam)* silbido *m*; **a h. noise** un pitido

histamine ['hɪstəmiːn] *n Biol* histamina *f*

histology [hɪ'stɒlədʒɪ] *n Med* histología *f*

historian [hɪ'stɔːrɪən] *n* historiador(a) *m,f*

historic [hɪ'stɒrɪk] *adj* histórico(a); **a(n) h. day** un día memorable

historical [hɪ'stɒrɪkəl] *adj* histórico(a) **h. novel** novela *f* histórica

historically [hɪs'tɒrɪklɪ] *adv* históricamente

history ['hɪstərɪ] *n* historia *f*; **to go down in h.** pasar a la historia; *Med* **to have a h. of ...** haber tenido *or* sufrido ... **H. of Art** Historia *f* del Arte

hit [hɪt] **1** *n* **(a)** *(blow)* golpe *m* **(b)** *(shot)* tiro *m*; *Mil* impacto *m*; **direct h.** impacto directo **h. list** lista *f* negra; *Fam* **h. man** asesino(a) *m,f* a sueldo; **h. squad** banda *f* de asesinos **(c)** *(success)* éxito *m*, acierto *m*; **he made a h. with them** les cayó muy simpático; **smash h.** exitazo *m*, éxito rotundo **h. musical** comedia *f* musical con éxito; **h. parade** hitparade *m*, lista *f* de éxitos; **h. record** disco *m* con éxito **(d)** *Fig (damaging remark)* pulla *f* **(e)** *Comptr* acceso *m*, visita *f*

2 *vt (pt & pp* **hit)** **(a)** *(strike)* golpear, pegar; **he h. me** me pegó; **he was h. in the leg** le dieron en la pierna; **she h. the dog with the stick** le pegó un bastonazo al perro; **the car h. the kerb** el coche chocó contra el bordillo; **to h. sth back** devolver algo; *Fig* **it suddenly h. me** de repente me di cuenta; *Fig* **to h. the nail on the head** dar en el clavo; *Fam Fig* **it hits you in the eye** salta a la vista; *Fam Fig* **to h. below the belt** dar un golpe bajo; *Fam Fig* **to h. it off with sb** caer bien a algn; *Fam Fig* **to h. the bottle** darse a la bebida; *Fam Fig* **to h. the roof** poner el grito en el cielo; *Fam* **to h. the hay** irse al catre **(b)** *(affect badly)* afectar; **the company was h. by high inflation** la empresa sufrió a causa de la alta inflación **(c)** *(reach)* alcanzar; **to h. the headlines** ser noticia; *Fam* **to h. the road** irse, ponerse en camino; *Fam* **we h. bad weather** nos tocó mal tiempo

hit back *vi* (a) *(strike in return)* devolver los golpes (b) *(reply to criticism)* vengarse

hit on, hit upon *vt* dar con; **they h. on an interesting solution** dieron con una solución interesante; **we h. on the idea of ...** se nos ocurrió la idea de ...

hit out *vi* (a) *(try to hit)* atacar; **to h. out at sb** atacar a algn (b) *(attack verbally)* atacar

hit-and-miss [hɪtən'mɪs] *adj* al azar, casual

hit-and-run [hɪtən'rʌn] *adj Aut* que se da a la fuga; **h.-a.-r. driver** = conductor que huye tras atropellar a alguien

hitch [hɪtʃ] **1** *n* obstáculo *m*, dificultad *f*; **a technical h.** un incidente técnico; **without a h.** sin problema alguno

2 *vt* (a) *(fasten)* atar; **they hitched on another wagon** añadieron otro vagón (b) *Fam (hitch-hike)* **they hitched a lift into town** llegaron a dedo *or CAm Méx Perú* se fueron de aventón a la ciudad

3 *vi Fam* hacer autostop *or* dedo; *CAm Méx Perú* ir de *or* pedir aventón

hitch up *vt* remangarse; **to h. up one's trousers** arremangarse los pantalones

hitched ['hɪtʃt] *adj Fam* **to get h.** casarse

hitch-hike ['hɪtʃhaɪk] *vi* hacer autoestop *or* dedo, *CAm Méx Perú* ir de *or* pedir aventón

hitch-hiker ['hɪtʃhaɪkər] *n* autostopista *mf*

hi-tech ['haɪtek] *adj* de alta tecnología

hither ['hɪðər] *adv Literary* acá; **h. and thither** acá y acullá

hitherto [hɪðə'tuː] *adv Fml* hasta ahora, hasta la fecha

hit-or-miss [hɪtɔː'mɪs] *adj* al azar, casual

HIV [eɪtʃaɪ'viː] *n Med (abbr* **human immunodeficiency virus)** virus *m* de inmunodeficiencia humana; **to be diagnosed H. positive/negative** dar seropositivo(a) seronegativo(a) en la prueba del SIDA

hive [haɪv] *n* colmena *f*; *Fig* lugar *m* muy activo

hive off *vt (sell)* desprenderse de

hives [haɪvz] *npl Med* urticaria *f sing*

hiya [haɪjə] *interj Fam* **h.!** ¡hola!, ¿qué hay?

HM [eɪtʃ'em] *n (abbr* **His/Her Majesty)** Su Majestad *mf*, S.M.

HMS [eɪtʃem'es] *n Br Naut (abbr* **His/Her Majesty's Ship)** = título que precede a los nombres de buques de la marina británica

hoard [hɔːd] **1** *n (provisions)* reservas *fpl*; *(money, jewels etc)* tesoro *m*; *Fam* **a h. of things** un montón de cosas

2 *vt (objects)* acumular, amontonar; *(money)* atesorar

hoarder ['hɔːdər] *n* acumulador(a) *m,f*

hoarding ['hɔːdɪŋ] *n* (a) *Br (display board)* valla *f* publicitaria (b) *Constr (temporary fence)* valla *f*

hoarfrost ['hɔːfrɒst] *n* escarcha *f*

hoarse [hɔːs] *adj* ronco(a); **to be h.** tener la voz ronca

hoarsely ['hɔːslɪ] *adv* roncamente

hoarseness ['hɔːsnɪs] *n* ronquera *f*

hoary ['hɔːrɪ] *adj* (**hoarier, hoariest**) (a) *(white)* canoso(a) (b) *(very old)* viejo(a); **a h. old joke** un chiste muy pasado

hoax [həʊks] **1** *n (joke)* broma *f* pesada; *(trick)* engaño *m*; **to play a h. on sb** gastarle una broma a algn

2 *vt* gastar una broma a, engañar

hob [hɒb] *n* (a) *(of cooker)* fuego *m*, *Esp Andes Méx* hornilla *f*, *RP* hornalla *f*; (b) *(by fireplace)* repisa *f*

hobble ['hɒbəl] **1** *vi (walk with difficulty)* andar con dificultad, cojear, *Andes RP* renguear

2 *vt (fetter) (animal)* manear

hobby ['hɒbɪ] *n* hobby *m*, pasatiempo *m* favorito; **his h. is carpentry** dedica su tiempo libre a la carpintería

hobbyhorse ['hɒbɪhɔːs] *n* (a) *(toy)* caballito *m* de juguete (b) *Fig (fixed idea)* caballo *m* de batalla, tema *m* preferido; **he's on his h. again** ya sacó el tema de siempre

hobgoblin [hɒb'gɒblɪn] *n* duende *m*

hobnail(ed) boot ['hɒbneɪl(d)'buːt] *n* bota *f* de suela claveteada

hobnob ['hɒbnɒb] *vi Fam* codearse; **to h. with the rich** codearse con los ricos

hobo ['həʊbəʊ] *n US (pl* **hobos** *or* **hoboes)** vagabundo(a) *m,f*

hock¹ [hɒk] *n Anat Zool* jarrete *m*

hock² [hɒk] *n* vino *m* del Rin

hock³ [hɒk] *US Fam* **1** *vt* empeñar

2 *n* **in h.** empeñado(a)

hockey ['hɒkɪ] *n Br (on grass)* hockey *m* (sobre hierba *or Am* césped); *US (on ice)* hockey (sobre hielo) ❑ *US* **field h.** hockey *m* sobre hierba *or Am* césped

hocus-pocus [həʊkəs'pəʊkəs] *n* trampa *f*

hod [hɒd] *n* capacho *m* de albañil ❑ **h. carrier** peón *m* de albañil

hodge-podge ['hɒdʒpɒdʒ] *n US see* **hotch-potch**

hoe [həʊ] **1** *n* azada *f*, azadón *m*

2 *vt* azadonar

hog [hɒg] *n* (a) *Br (castrated pig)* cerdo *m* castrado; *US (pig)* cerdo *m*, puerco *m*, marrano *m*, *Am* chancho *m*; *Fam* **to go the whole h.** tirar *or Am* salvo *RP* botar la casa por la ventana ❑ *US* **h. cholera** peste *f* porcina (b) *Fam Pej (undesireable person)* indeseable *mf*

2 *vt (pt & pp* **hogged)** *Fam* acaparar; **to h. the limelight** monopolizar la atención

Hogmanay [hɒgməˈneɪ] *n Scot* Nochevieja *f*

hogwash ['hɒgwɒʃ] *n inv Fam* tonterías *fpl*, disparates *mpl*

hoi polloi [hɔɪpə'lɔɪ] *n inv Pej* **the h. p.** la gentuza, el populacho

hoist [hɔɪst] **1** *n* (a) *(crane)* grúa *f* (b) *(lift)* montacargas *m inv*

2 *vt* levantar, subir; **to h. the flag** izar la bandera

hoity-hoity [hɔɪtɪˈtɔɪtɪ] *adj Fam Pej* presumido(a)

hold [həʊld] **1** *vt (pt & pp* **held)** (a) *(keep in hand)* aguantar, tener (en la mano), asir, sostener; *(grip)* coger, sujetar, *Am* agarrar; *(support) (weight etc)* soportar, aguantar; *(opinion)* sostener; **h. my books** aguántame los libros; **to h. sb** abrazar a algn; **to h. sb's hand** cogerle la mano a algn; *Aut* **to h. the road** agarrarse a la carretera; *Fig* **she can h. her own in French** se defiende en francés; *Fig* **to h. one's head high** mantener la cabeza alta (b) *(contain)* dar cabida a; **the chapel holds a hundred people** caben cien personas en la capilla; **the jug holds a litre** la jarra tiene capacidad para un litro; *Fig* **to h. water** resultar cierto *or* válido; *Fig* **who knows what the future holds** quién sabe lo que nos espera en el futuro (c) *(have) (meeting etc)* celebrar; *(conversation)* mantener; **the concert was held in the school** el concierto se celebró en el colegio (d) *(reserve)* guardar, reservar; **they will h. our tickets until this afternoon** nos guardarán las entradas hasta esta tarde (e) *(occupy)* ocupar; **to h. office** ocupar un puesto *or* un cargo (f) *(consider)* considerar; **I h. you responsible** te considero responsable (g) *(restrain)* retener; **he was held for two hours at the police station** estuvo detenido durante dos horas en la comisaría; **to h. one's breath** contener la respiración; **to h. one's tongue** callarse; **to h. sb hostage** retener a algn como rehén; *Fig* **there was no holding her** no había manera de disuadirle; *Fam* **h. it!** ¡espera! (h) *Tel* **to h. the line** mantenerse al habla, no colgar

2 *vi* (a) *(rope etc)* aguantar, resistir (b) *Fig (offer, promise)* ser válido(a), valer; **the rules h. (good) for everyone** las reglas valen para todos

3 *n* (**a**) *(grip)* asimiento *m*; **to catch** *or* **get h. of** coger, agarrar; *Fig* **to get h. of** encontrar, localizar; **can you get h. of a newspaper?** ¿puedes conseguir un periódico?; **where can I get h. of you?** ¿dónde te puedo localizar? (**b**) *(control)* control *m*; **to have a firm h. on spending** controlar rigurosamente los gastos; **to have a h. over sb** influir mucho en algn, tener control sobre algn (**c**) *(in wrestling)* llave *f* (**d**) *Naut* bodega *f*

hold back *vt* (**a**) *(restrain) (crowd)* contener; *(feelings)* reprimir; *(truth)* ocultar; *(suspect)* retener (**b**) *(store)* guardar

2 *vi* (**a**) *(hesitate)* vacilar, no atreverse (**b**) *(abstain)* abstenerse

hold down *vt* (**a**) *(control)* dominar (**b**) *Fam (job)* desempeñar; **she couldn't h. down a job** perdía todos los empleos

hold forth *vi* hablar detenidamente (**on** sobre)

hold off 1 *vt (keep apart)* mantener a distancia

2 *vi (refrain)* refrenarse, retenerse; **he held off from buying new shares** aplazó *or* postergó la compra de nuevas acciones; **I hope the rain holds off** espero que no llueva

hold on *vi* (**a**) *(keep a firm grasp)* agarrarse bien; **h. on tight!** ¡agárrate fuerte! (**b**) *(wait)* esperar; *Tel* **h. on!** ¡no cuelgue!

hold out 1 *vt (hand etc)* ofrecer, tender

2 *vi* (**a**) *(last) (things)* durar; *(person)* resistir; **will supplies h. out?** ¿nos llegarán *or* alcanzarán las provisiones? (**b**) **to h. out for** insistir en; **they held out for more pay** persistieron en su demanda de aumento de sueldo

hold over *vt (meeting etc)* aplazar

hold up *vt* (**a**) *(attack and rob) (train)* asaltar; *(bank etc)* atracar (**b**) *(delay)* retrasar; **we were held up for half an hour** sufrimos media hora de retraso (**c**) *(raise)* levantar; **h. your hand up** levanta la mano (**d**) *(support) (weight)* sostener, sujetar

hold with *vt* estar de acuerdo con; **I don't h. with such ideas** no comulgo con esas ideas

holdall ['həʊldɔːl] *n esp Br* bolsa *f (de viaje o de deporte)*

holdback ['həʊldbæk] *n Fig* inconveniente *m*

holder ['həʊldər] *n* (**a**) *(handle)* asidero *m* (**b**) *(receptacle)* receptáculo *m*, recipiente *m* ❑ **cigarette h.** boquilla *f* (**c**) *(owner)* poseedor(ora) *m,f*; *(bearer)* portador(ora) *m,f*; *(of passport)* titular *mf* ❑ *Sport* **record h.** plusmarquista *mf*, recordman *mf*

holding ['həʊldɪŋ] **1** *n* (**a**) *(property)* propiedad *f*; *(land)* terreno *m*, propiedad *f* (**b**) *Fin* valor *m* en cartera ❑ **h. company** holding *m*

2 *adj* de control

hold-up ['həʊldʌp] *n* (**a**) *(robbery)* atraco *m* (**b**) *(delay)* retraso *m*, *Am* demora *f*; *(in traffic)* atasco *m*

hole [həʊl] **1** *n* (**a**) *(small)* agujero *m*; *(large)* hoyo *m*; *(in the road)* bache *m*; *Slang* **to be in a h.** estar en un apuro (**b**) *Golf* hoyo *m* ❑ **h. in one** hoyo *m* en uno (**c**) *Slang (of place)* antro *m*

2 *vi Golf* meter la pelota en el hoyo

hole up *vi (animal)* hibernar; *Fig* esconderse

holiday ['hɒlɪdeɪ] **1** *n* (**a**) *(one day) Esp* (día *m* de) fiesta *f*, *Am* feriado *m*; **Monday is a h.** el lunes es fiesta ❑ **h. atmosphere** ambiente *m* festivo (**b**) *esp Br (vacation)* vacaciones *fpl*; **paid holidays** vacaciones pagadas; **to be/go on h.** estar/ir de vacaciones; **to take a h.** coger unas vacaciones; **we usually spend our summer holidays in France** solemos veranear en Francia ❑ **h. pay** paga *f* extra *(de vacaciones)*; **h. resort** lugar *m* turístico

2 *vi Br (gen)* pasar las vacaciones; *(in summer)* veranear

holiday-maker ['hɒlɪdeɪmeɪkər] *n esp Br (gen)* turista *mf*; *(in summer)* veraneante *mf*

holier-than-thou ['həʊlɪəðən'ðaʊ] *adj* gazmoño(a)

holiness ['həʊlɪnɪs] *n* santidad *f*; **His H. Pope John Paul II** Su Santidad el Papa Juan Pablo II

holistic [həʊ'lɪstɪk] *adj* holístico(a); **h. medicine** medicina holística

Holland ['hɒlənd] *n* Holanda

hollandaise [hɒlən'deɪz] *adj Culin* **h. sauce** salsa *f* holandesa

holler ['hɒlər] *vi Fam* gritar, dar voces

hollow ['hɒləʊ] **1** *adj* (**a**) *(sound, object)* hueco(a) (**b**) *(cheeks, eyes)* hundido(a) (**c**) *Fig (insincere)* falso(a); *(empty)* vacío(a); **a h. laugh** una risa falsa; **h. promises** promesas vacías

2 *n (gen)* hueco *m*; *Geog* hondonada *f*

3 *vt* **to h. (out)** vaciar, hacer un hueco en

holly ['hɒlɪ] *n Bot* acebo *m*

hollyhock ['hɒlɪhɒk] *n Bot* malvarrosa *f*

holocaust ['hɒləkɔːst] *n* holocausto *m*; **nuclear h.** holocausto nuclear

hologram ['hɒləɡræm] *n* holograma *m*

holster ['həʊlstər] *n* pistolera *f*

holy ['həʊlɪ] *adj* (**holier, holiest**) (**a**) *(sacred)* sagrado(a), santo(a) ❑ **H. Communion** Sagrada Comunión *f*; **H. Ghost** Espíritu *m* Santo; *Fam Pej* **H. Joe** meapilas *mf inv*; **H. Land** Tierra *f* Santa; **h. orders** órdenes *fpl* sagradas; **H. See** Santa Sede *f*; **h. war** guerra *f* santa; **H. Week** Semana *f* Santa (**b**) *(blessed) (of bread, water)* bendito(a)

homage ['hɒmɪdʒ] *n* homenaje *m*; **to pay** *or* **do h. to sb** rendir homenaje a algn

home [həʊm] **1** *n* (**a**) *(house)* casa *f*, hogar *m*; *Fml* domicilio *m*; **at h.** en casa; *Fig* a gusto; **h. sweet h.** hogar dulce hogar; *Br* **a h. from h.,** *US* **a h. away from h.** un segundo hogar; *Fig* **make yourself at h.!** ¡estás en tu casa!; *Fig* **to feel at h.** estar a gusto ❑ **h. address** domicilio *m*; **h. banking** telebanco *m*; *Comptr* **h. page** *(initial page)* portada *f* de página Web, página *f* inicial *or* de inicio; *(personal page)* página *f* personal; *US Sch* **h. room** = aula donde cada alumno debe presentarse todas las mañanas; **h. shopping** telecompra *f*; **h. shopping channel** teletienda *f* (**b**) *(institution)* asilo *m* ❑ **h. nursing h.** clínica *f*; **old people's h.** asilo *m or* residencia *f* de ancianos (**c**) *(country etc)* tierra *f*, patria *f*; **he is far from h.** está lejos de su tierra (**d**) *Zool* hábitat *m* (**e**) *Sport* casa *f*; **to play at h.** jugar en casa ❑ *US (in baseball)* **h. base, h. plate** base *f* del bateador; **h. run** carrera *f* completa

2 *adj* (**a**) *(domestic)* casero(a), del hogar; **h. cooking** cocina casera; **h. comforts** comodidades del hogar ❑ *Br* **h. help** asistenta *f*; *US* **h. improvements** reformas *fpl* del hogar; **h. life** vida *f* de familia (**b**) *Pol* interior, del interior; **h. affairs** asuntos interiores ❑ *Br* **H. Office** Ministerio *m* del Interior; **h. rule** autonomía *f*; *Br* **H. Secretary** Ministro(a) *m,f* del Interior (**c**) *(native)* natal; **h. town** pueblo natal, patria chica (**d**) *Sport* de *or* en casa; **h. game** partido en casa; **h. team** equipo de casa

3 *adv* en casa, a casa, de casa; **to be (at) h.** estar en casa; **to go h.** irse *or* volver a casa; **to leave h.** irse de casa; *Fig* **to bring sth h. to sb** hacer comprender algo a algn; *Fam* **it's nothing to write h. about** no es nada del otro jueves

homeboy ['həʊmbɔɪ] *n US Fam* (**a**) *(man from one's home town, district)* paisano *m* (**b**) *(friend)* amiguete *m*, *Esp* colega *m*, *Méx* cuate *m* (**c**) *(fellow gang member)* compinche *m*, *Méx* CAm cuate *m*

homecoming ['həʊmkʌmɪŋ] *n* regreso *m* a casa

home-grown ['həʊmɡrəʊn] *adj (produced in the region)* del país; *(in one's garden)* de cosecha propia, casero(a)

homeland ['həʊmlænd] *n (gen)* patria *f*; *(birthplace)* tierra *f* natal

homeless ['həʊmlɪs] **1** *adj* sin techo
2 the h. *npl* los sin techo

home-loving ['həʊmlʌvɪŋ] *adj* casero(a), hogareño(a)

homely ['həʊmlɪ] *adj* (**homelier, homeliest**) (**a**) *Br (warm, domesticated) (of person)* casero(a); *(of atmosphere)* familiar (**b**) *US (ugly)* feúcho(a)

home-made ['həʊmmeɪd] *adj* hecho(a) en casa, de fabricación casera

homemaker ['həʊmmeɪkər] *n* ama *f* de casa

homeopath ['həʊmɪəpæθ] *n US Med see* **homoeopath**

homeopathic [həʊmɪəʊ'pæθɪk] *adj* homeopático(a)

homeopathy [həʊmɪ'ɒpəθɪ] *n US Med see* **homoeopathy**

homesick ['həʊmsɪk] *adj* nostálgico(a); **to be h.** tener nostalgia *or Esp* morriña; **to be h. for one's family** echar en falta la familia

homesickness ['həʊmsɪknɪs] *n* nostalgia *f*, *Esp* morriña *f*

homestead ['həʊmsted] *n* granja *f*, *Am* estancia *f*, *Am* hacienda *f*

homeward(s) ['həʊmwəd(z)] *adv* hacia casa

homework ['həʊmwɜːk] *n* deberes *mpl*; **to do one's h.** hacer los deberes; **what do we have for h.?** ¿qué tenemos de deberes?

homeworker ['həʊmwɜːkər] *n* teletrabajador(a) *m,f*, persona *f* que trabaja desde su propio domicilio

homicidal [hɒmɪ'saɪdəl] *adj* homicida

homicide ['hɒmɪsaɪd] *n* (**a**) *(crime)* homicidio *m* (**b**) *(criminal)* homicida *mf*

homily ['hɒmɪlɪ] *n* homilía *f*

homing ['həʊmɪŋ] *adj* (**a**) *Mil* buscador(a); **h. device** cabeza *f* buscadora (**b**) *Zool* **h. pigeon** paloma *f* mensajera

homo ['həʊməʊ] *n Fam (homosexual)* marica *m*

homoeopath ['həʊmɪəpæθ] *n Med* homeópata *mf*

homoeopathy [həʊmɪ'ɒpəθɪ] *n Med* homeopatía *f*

homogeneous [hɒmə'dʒiːnɪəs] *adj* homogéneo(a)

homogenization [hɒmɒdʒɪnaɪ'zeɪʃən] *n* homogeneización *f*

homogenize [hɒ'mɒdʒɪnaɪz] *vt* homogeneizar; **homogenized milk** leche homogeneizada

homogenous [hə'mɒdʒɪnəs] *adj see* **homogeneous**

homologate [hɒ'mɒləgeɪt] *vt* homologar

homological [həʊmə'lɒdʒɪkəl] *adj*, **homologous** [həʊ'mɒləgəs] *adj* homólogo(a)

homology [həʊ'mɒlədʒɪ] *n* homología *f*

homonym ['hɒmənɪm] *n* homónimo *m*

homophobia [hɒmə'fəʊbɪə] *n* homofobia *f*

homophobic [hɒmə'fəʊbɪk] *adj* homófobo(a)

homophone ['hɒməfəʊn] *n* homófono *m*

homosexual [həʊməʊ'seksjʊəl] *adj & n* homosexual *(mf)*

homosexuality [həʊməʊseksjʊ'ælɪtɪ] *n* homosexualidad *f*

Hon (**a**) *(abbr* **Honorary)** *(member)* honorario(a), *(Secretary, Treasurer)* no remunerado(a) (**b**) *(abbr* **Honourable)** ilustre señor(a)

honcho ['hɒntʃəʊ] *n esp US Fam* **the head h.** el/la mandamás

Honduran [hɒn'djʊərən] *adj & n* hondureño(a) *(m,f)*

Honduras [hɒn'djʊərəs] *n* Honduras

hone [həʊn] **1** *n* piedra *n* de afilar
2 *vt* afilar

honest ['ɒnɪst] **1** *adj* (**a**) *(trustworthy)* honrado(a), recto(a); **an h. face** una cara abierta; *Fam* **to do an h. day's work**

hacer una buena jornada (**b**) *(sincere)* sincero(a), franco(a); **give me your h. opinion** dime sinceramente lo que opinas; **the h. truth** la pura verdad; **to be h., I don't know what to say** sinceramente, no sé qué decir (**c**) *(fair)* justo(a), decente
2 *adv Fam* **h. (to God)!** ¡te lo prometo!

honestly ['ɒnɪstlɪ] *adv (fairly etc)* honradamente; *(question)* ¿de verdad?; *(exclamation)* ¡hay que ver!; *Fig* de verdad, a decir verdad; **h., it doesn't matter** de verdad or créeme, no tiene importancia; **h., it's the truth** es la verdad, te lo juro

honesty ['ɒnɪstɪ] *n* honradez *f*, rectitud *f*

honey ['hʌnɪ] *n* (**a**) *(substance)* miel *f* (**b**) *US Fam (endearment)* cariño *m*

honeycomb ['hʌnɪkəʊm] *n* panal *m*

honeyed ['hʌnɪd] *adj* meloso(a), dulzón(ona); **h. words** palabras melosas or dulces

honeymoon ['hʌnɪmuːn] **1** *n* luna *f* de miel, viaje *m* de novios
2 *vi* pasar la luna de miel, hacer el viaje de novios

honeymooner ['hʌnɪmuːnər] *n* recién casado(a) *m,f*

honeysuckle ['hʌnɪsʌkəl] *n Bot* madreselva *f*

honied ['hʌnɪd] *adj see* **honeyed**

honk [hɒŋk] **1** *n* (**a**) *(of goose)* graznido *m* (**b**) *(of car horn)* bocinazo *m*
2 *vi* (**a**) *(goose)* graznar (**b**) *Aut* tocar la bocina
3 *vt (car horn)* tocar

honky ['hɒŋkɪ] *n US Slang Pej* = término ofensivo para referirse a un blanco

honor ['ɒnər] *n & vt US see* **honour**

honorable ['ɒnərəbəl] *adj US see* **honourable**

honorarium [ɒnə'reərɪəm] *n (pl* **honorariums** or **honoraria** [ɒnə'reərɪə]) honorarios *mpl*

honorary ['ɒnərərɪ] *adj (of member)* honorario(a); *(of duties)* honorífico(a); *Univ* **to receive an h. degree** ser nombrado(a) doctor(a) honoris causa

honour ['ɒnər] **1** *n* (**a**) *(virtue)* honor *m*, honra *f*; **in h. of** en honor de; **to defend one's h.** defender su honra; **to do h. to** *(pay homage to)* rendir honores a; *(be a credit to)* honrar; **to do the honours** hacer los honores; **to have the h. of doing sth** tener el honor de hacer algo (**b**) *(title)* **Her H., His H., Your H.** Su Señoría *f* (**c**) *Mil* **honours** honores *mpl* (**d**) **Honours degree** licenciatura *f* superior
2 *vt* (**a**) *(respect)* honrar (**b**) *(fulfil) (obligation)* cumplir; *Fin* **to h. a cheque** aceptar y pagar un talón bancario; **to h. one's word** cumplir con su palabra

honourable ['ɒnərəbəl] *adj* (**a**) *(of person)* honrado(a); *Parl* **the h. gentleman** el señor diputado (**b**) *(of actions)* honorífico(a), honroso(a); **h. mention** mención honorífica

Hons [ɒnz] *Br Educ (abbr* **Honours)** Licenciado *m* Superior

hooch [huːtʃ] *n US Slang* alcohol *m (destilado clandestinamente)*

hood¹ [hʊd] *n* (**a**) *(of garment)* capucha *f*; **Little Red Riding H.** Caperucita *f* Roja (**b**) *Br (of car, pram)* capota *f* (**c**) *US (car bonnet)* capó *m*, *CAm Méx* cofre *m*

hood² [hʊd] *n US Slang (gangster)* matón(ona) *m,f*

hooded ['hʊdɪd] *adj* (**a**) *(of person, garment)* con capucha; **a h. bank robber** un atracador encapuchado (**b**) *(of falcon)* encapirotado(a)

hoodlum ['huːdləm] *n US* matón(ona) *m,f*

hoodwink ['hʊdwɪŋk] *vt* engañar, *Esp* timar; **I've been hoodwinked** me han engañado

hoof [huːf] **1** *n (pl* **hoofs** or **hooves** [huːvz]) *(of horse)* casco *m*; *(of cow, sheep)* pezuña *f*
2 *vt Slang* **to h. it** ir a pata, ir con el coche de San Fernando

hoofed [huːft] *adj* ungulado(a)

hoofer [ˈhuːfər] *n US Slang* bailarín(ina) *m,f* de claqué

hoo-ha [ˈhuːhɑː] *n Fam* alboroto *m*; **there was a great h.-ha** se armó un follón enorme

hook [hʊk] **1** *n* **(a)** *(gen)* gancho *m*; *Knit* **crochet h.** ganchillo *m*; *Sew* **hooks and eyes** corchetes *mpl*; *Tel* **to take the phone off the h.** descolgar el teléfono; *Fig* **by h. or (by) crook** por las buenas o por las malas; *Slang* **off the h.** limpio(a); *Slang* **on the h.** *(waiting)* a la espera; *(in trouble)* en la mierda **(b)** *Fishing* anzuelo *m* **(c)** *Box* gancho *m* **2** *vt* **(a)** *(fasten)* enganchar; **her skirt got hooked on a nail** se le enganchó la falda en un clavo **(b)** *(of bull etc)* clavar **(c)** *Fishing* pescar, coger **(d)** *Box* pegar haciendo un gancho **(e)** *Slang (steal)* birlar, mangar

hook up *vt & vi Rad TV Comptr* conectar (**with** con)

hooka(h) [ˈhʊkə] *n* narguile *m*

hooked [hʊkt] *adj* **(a)** *(hook-shaped)* ganchudo(a); *(nose)* aquilino(a) **(b)** *Slang (attracted)* prendado(a), enca-riñado(a); *(addicted)* enganchado(a) (**on** a); **to get h.** engancharse; **he's h. on heroin** está enganchado al caballo

hooker [ˈhʊkər] *n* **(a)** *Br Rugby* talonador(a) *m,f* **(b)** *US Slang (prostitute)* puta *f*

hook(e)y [ˈhʊki] *n US Can Fam* **to play h.** faltar a clase, *Esp* hacer novillos, *Col* capar clase, *Méx* irse de pinta, *RP* hacerse la rabona

hook-up [ˈhʊkʌp] *n* **(a)** *Comptr* conexión *f* **(b)** *Rad TV* = emisión transmitida a varios lugares

hooligan [ˈhuːlɪgən] *n Slang* vándalo(a) *m,f*, *Esp* gamberro(a) *m,f*

hooliganism [ˈhuːlɪgənɪzəm] *n Slang* vandalismo *m*, *Esp* gamberrismo *m*

hoop [huːp] *n (gen)* aro *m*; *(of barrel)* fleje *m*; *(of wheel)* llanta *f*; *Fig* **to put sb through the hoops** hacérselo pasar mal a algn

hoopoe [ˈhuːpuː] *n Orn* abubilla *f*

hoorah [huːˈrɑː] *interj*, **hooray** [huːˈreɪ] *interj* ¡hurra!

hoot [huːt] **1** *n* **(a)** *(of owl, train, wind)* ululato *m*; *Fam* **hoots of laughter** carcajadas *fpl*, risotadas *fpl*; *Fam* **I don't care a h.** me importa un pepino **(b)** *(of car horn)* bocinazo *m* **(c)** *Fam* = cosa *or* persona *f* divertida; *Fam* **it was a h.** fue divertidísimo **2** *vi* **(a)** *(owl)* ulular **(b)** *(car)* dar un bocinazo, tocar la bocina; *(train)* silbar; *(siren)* pitar

hootch [huːtʃ] *n US Slang see* hooch

hooter [ˈhuːtər] *n* **(a)** *(of car)* bocina *f*; *(siren)* sirena *f* **(b)** *Slang (nose)* narizota *f*

Hoover® [ˈhuːvər] *Br* **1** *n* aspiradora *f* **2** *vt* **to h.** pasar la aspiradora a

hooves [huːvz] *pl see* hoof

hop¹ [hɒp] **1** *vi (pt & pp* **hopped)** saltar, dar saltitos; **to h. on one leg** andar a la pata coja; *Fam* **h. in!** *(into car)* ¡sube!; *Fam* **to h. on the bus/train** subirse al autobús/tren **2** *vt* **(a)** *US Fam (train etc)* coger **(b)** *Br Slang* **h. it!** ¡lárgate!, ¡esfúmate! **(c)** *Av* cruzar **3** *n* **(a)** *(small jump)* brinco *m*, saltito *m*; **in one h.** de un salto; *Fam* **to be on the h.** estar muy atareado(a); *Br Fam* **to catch sb on the h.** agarrar *or Esp* coger desprevenido(a) a algn **(b)** *Fam (dance)* baile *m*, bailongo *m* **(c)** *Av Fam* vuelo *m* corto

hop² [hɒp] *n Bot* lúpulo *m*

hope [həʊp] **1** *n (gen)* esperanza *f*; *(false)* ilusión *f*; **don't build up your hopes** no te hagas ilusiones; **to have high hopes** tener grandes esperanzas; **to have little h. of doing sth** tener pocas posibilidades de hacer algo; *Fam* **not a h.!, some h.!** ¡ni hablar!, ¡qué va! ❑ *US* **h. chest** ajuar *m*

2 *vt & vi* esperar; **I h. not** espero que no; **I h. so** espero que sí; **I h. to have an answer tomorrow** espero tener una respuesta para mañana; **I'm hoping for a letter** espero carta; **we h. you're well** esperamos que estés bien

hopeful [ˈhəʊpfʊl] **1** *adj (confident)* optimista; *(promising)* esperanzador(a), prometedor(a); **she's h. that ...** tiene esperanzas de que ...

2 *n* persona *f* que promete; **young h.** joven *mf* promesa

hopefully [ˈhəʊpfʊli] *adv* **(a)** *(confidently)* con esperanza, con optimismo **(b)** *Fam (it is hoped)* esperamos, se espera; **h., the weather will be fine** se espera que haga buen tiempo

hopeless [ˈhəʊplɪs] *adj* desesperado(a); **a h. case** un caso perdido; **it's h.** es imposible; *Fam* **to be h. at sports** ser nulo(a) *or Esp* un(a) negado(a) para los deportes

hopelessly [ˈhəʊplɪsli] *adv* sin esperanza, deses-peradamente; **h. in love** locamente enamorado(a); **h. lost** completamente perdido(a)

hopper [ˈhɒpər] *n (funnel)* tolva *f*

hop-picker [ˈhɒpɪkər] *n* recogedor(a) *m,f* de lúpulo

hop-picking [ˈhɒpɪkɪŋ] *n* cosecha *f* del lúpulo

hopping [ˈhɒpɪŋ] **1** *n* saltos *mpl*, brincos *mpl*

2 *adj Fam* **h. mad** rabioso(a); **she's h. mad** está que trina, está que bota, *Méx* está como agua para chocolate

hopscotch [ˈhɒpskɒtʃ] *n* infernáculo *m*

horde [hɔːd] *n* **(a)** *(crowd)* multitud *f*, *Am* horda *f* **(b)** *(nomadic group)* horda *f*

horizon [həˈraɪzən] *n* horizonte *m*

horizontal [hɒrɪˈzɒntəl] *adj* horizontal

horizontally [hɒrɪˈzɒntəli] *adv* horizontalmente

hormonal [hɔːˈməʊnəl] *adj* hormonal

hormone [ˈhɔːməʊn] *n Biol* hormona *f*, hormón *m*

horn [hɔːn] *n* **(a)** *Zool* cuerno *m*, asta *f*; *(of snail)* tentáculo *m*; *Fig* **to take the bull by the horns** agarrar *or* coger al toro por los cuernos **(b)** *Mus (gen)* instrumento *m* de viento; *(primitive)* cuerno *m*; *Fam* trompeta *f*; *Fig* **on the horns of a dilemma** entre la espada y la pared; *US Fig* **to blow one's own h.** vanagloriarse ❑ **French h.** trompa *f*; **hunting h.** cuerno *m* de caza **(c)** *(of gramophone)* pabellón *m*, bocina *f* **(d)** *Aut* bocina *f*; **to honk** *or* **sound the h.** dar un bocinazo **(e)** *Br Slang Vulg* erección *f*

horned [hɔːnd] *adj (of cattle etc)* con cuernos

hornet [ˈhɔːnɪt] *n Ent* avispón *m*; *Fig* **to stir up a h.'s nest** meterse en un avispero

hornpipe [ˈhɔːnpaɪp] *n* **(a)** *Mus (instrument)* chirimía *f* **(b)** *Br (dance)* = baile folklórico marinero

horn-rimmed [ˈhɔːnrɪmd] *adj (spectacles)* con montura de concha

horny [ˈhɔːni] *adj* (**hornier, horniest**) **(a)** *(of hands)* calloso(a) **(b)** *Slang (sexually aroused)* *Esp Méx* cachondo(a), *Esp* calentorro(a), *CAm Col Méx Ven* arrecho(a), *RP* caliente

horology [hɒˈrɒlədʒi] *n* relojería *f*

horoscope [ˈhɒrəskəʊp] *n* horóscopo *m*

horrendous [hɒˈrendəs] *adj* horrendo(a), horroroso(a)

horrible [ˈhɒrəbəl] *adj* horrible, horroroso(a); **the weather was h.** hizo un tiempo horroroso; *Fam* **what a h. man!** ¡qué hombre más antipático!

horribly [ˈhɒrɪbli] *adv* horriblemente; **it was h. hot** hacía un calor insoportable

horrid [ˈhɒrɪd] *adj (horrible)* horrible, horroroso(a); *(unkind)* antipático(a)

horrific [həˈrɪfɪk] *adj* horrendo(a)

horrify [ˈhɒrɪfaɪ] *vt (pt & pp* **horrified)** espantar, horrorizar; **she was horrified at the thought** se horrorizaba sólo de pensarlo

horror ['hɒrər] *n* horror *m*, terror *m*; **it fills me with h.** me llena de terror; **to have a h. of sth** tener horror a algo; *Fam* **a little h.** un diablillo □ **h. film** película *f* de miedo *or* de terror

horrors ['hɒrəz] *interj* ¡qué horror!

horror-stricken ['hɒrəstrɪkən] *adj*, **horror-struck** ['hɒrəstrʌk] *adj* horrorizado(a)

hors d'oeuvre [ɔː'dɜːvr] *n* (*pl* **hors d'oeuvre** *or* **hors d'oeuvres**) *Culin* entremés *m*

horse [hɔːs] **1** *n* (**a**) *Zool* caballo *m*; *Fig* **hold your horses!** ¡echa el freno!, ¡alto ahí!; *Fig* **to beat** *or* **flog a dead h.** machacar en hierro frío; *Fig* **to get sth straight from the h.'s mouth** saber algo de buena tinta; *Fam Fig* **to get on one's high h.** darse ínfulas □ **h. doctor** veterinario *m*; *Zool Fam* **h. family** grupo *m or* familia *f* de los ecuestres; **h. race** carrera *f* de caballos; *Fig* **h. sense** sentido *m* común (**b**) *(gym apparatus)* potro *m* (**c**) *Tech* caballete *m* (**d**) *Bot* **h. chestnut** *(tree)* castaño *m* de Indias; *(fruit)* castaña *f* de Indias (**e**) *Slang (heroin)* caballo *m*

  2 *vi Fam* **to h. around** *or* **about** hacer el indio

horseback ['hɔːsbæk] *n* **on h.** a caballo □ *US Can* **h. riding** equitación *f*

horsebox ['hɔːsbɒks] *n Br* furgón *m* para caballos

horse-drawn ['hɔːsdrɔːn] *adj* de tiro, de caballos

horseflesh ['hɔːsfleʃ] *n* carne *f* de caballo

horsefly ['hɔːsflaɪ] *n Ent* tábano *m*

horsehair ['hɔːsheər] *n* crin *m* (de caballo) □ **h. mattress** colchón *m* de crin (de caballo)

horseman ['hɔːsmən] *n* (*pl* **horsemen**) jinete *m*, caballista *m*; *(professional)* yoquey *m*

horsemanship ['hɔːsmənʃɪp] *n* equitación *f*

horseplay ['hɔːspleɪ] *n* payasadas *fpl*; **to indulge in h.** hacer el payaso

horsepower ['hɔːspaʊər] *n Aut* caballo *m* (de vapor)

horseradish ['hɔːsrædɪʃ] *n Bot* rábano *m* rusticano

horseshoe ['hɔːsʃuː] *n* herradura *f*

horsewoman ['hɔːswʊmən] *n* (*pl* **horsewomen** ['hɔːswɪmɪn]) amazona *f*, caballista *f*

hors(e)y ['hɔːsɪ] *adj* (**horsier, horsiest**) (**a**) *(horse-like)* caballuno(a); **h. features** rasgos caballunos (**b**) *(interested in horses)* aficionado(a) a los caballos

horticultural [hɔːtɪ'kʌltʃərəl] *adj* hortícola, hortelano(a)

horticulture ['hɔːtɪkʌltʃər] *n* horticultura *f*

hose[1] [həʊz] **1** *n (pipe)* manguera *f*

  2 *vt* **to h. (down)** *(with water)* regar con una manguera; *(wash)* lavar con una manguera

hose[2] [həʊz] *n* (*pl* **hose** *or* **hosen** ['həʊzən]) *(socks)* calcetines *mpl*; *(stockings)* medias *fpl*

hosepipe ['həʊzpaɪp] *n* manguera *f*

hosiery ['həʊzɪərɪ] *n Com* medias *fpl* y calcetines *mpl*

hospice ['hɒspɪs] *n* residencia *f* geriátrica *or* de ancianos

hospitable ['hɒspɪtəbəl, hɒs'pɪtəbəl] *adj* hospitalario(a); **h. atmosphere** ambiente acogedor

hospitably [hɒs'pɪtəblɪ] *adv* con hospitalidad

hospital ['hɒspɪtəl] *n* hospital *m*

hospitality [hɒspɪ'tælɪtɪ] *n* hospitalidad *f*

hospitalize ['hɒspɪtəlaɪz] *vt* hospitalizar

Host [həʊst] *n Rel* hostia *f*

host[1] [həʊst] **1** *n* (**a**) *(at home)* anfitrión *m* (**b**) *Theat TV* presentador *m* (**c**) *Biol Zool* huésped *m* (**d**) *Comptr* **h. (computer)** host *m*, sistema *m* central

  2 *vt Theat TV (show)* presentar

host[2] [həʊst] *n (large number)* montón *m*; **a h. of things** la tira de cosas

hostage ['hɒstɪdʒ] *n* rehén *m*; **to hold sb h.** tener a algn como rehén

hostel ['hɒstəl] *n* (**a**) **(youth) h.** albergue *m* juvenil (**b**) *esp Br (for students, nurses)* residencia *f*; *(for the homeless)* albergue *m*, hogar *m*

hostess ['həʊstɪs] *n* (**a**) *(at home etc)* anfitriona *f* (**b**) *(in club)* camarera *f* (**c**) *Theat TV* presentadora *f* (**d**) *Av* **(air) h.** azafata *f*

hostile ['hɒstaɪl, *US* 'hɒstəl] *adj* hostil, enemigo(a); **to be h. to change** ser hostil a los cambios

hostility [hɒ'stɪlɪtɪ] *n* hostilidad *f*; *Mil* **hostilities have now ceased** han cesado las hostilidades

hosting ['həʊstɪŋ] *n Comptr* hospedaje *m*

hot [hɒt] *adj* (**hotter, hottest**) (**a**) *(gen)* caliente; **h. water** agua caliente; *Fig* **to blow h. and cold** cambiar continuamente de actitud □ *Tel Fig* **h. line** teléfono *m* rojo; *US Aut Slang* **h. rod** coche *m or Am* carro *m or Chile RP* auto *m* trucado; **h. spot** *(nightclub)* club *m* nocturno; *US* **h. tub** jacuzzi® *m* (**b**) *Meteor* caluroso(a); **it's very h.** hace mucho calor; **to feel h.** tener calor □ *Fig* **h. air** palabrería *f* (**c**) *Culin (not cold)* caliente; **h. meals** comidas calientes □ **h. dog** perrito *m* caliente (**d**) *Culin (spicy)* picante; **h. sauce** salsa picante; **not a very h. chicken curry** un pollo al curry no muy picante (**e**) *(temper)* fuerte; *Fam* **to get h. under the collar** ponerse nervioso(a) (**f**) *Fam (fresh)* de última hora; **h. news** noticia *f* de última hora (**g**) *Fam (good)* bueno(a), enterado(a); **ask Frank, he's h. on that subject** pregúntaselo a Frank, sabe bastante de eso; **it's not so h.** no mata; **she's h. stuff** está buena, está como un tren (**h**) *(popular)* popular; **a very h. play** una obra muy taquillera (**i**) *(dangerous)* peligroso(a); *Fig* **to get oneself into h. water** meterse en un lío; *Fig* **to make things h. for sb** hacerle la vida difícil a algn □ *Fam* **h. potato** asunto *m* delicado; *Fam* **h. seat** primera fila *f*; *Fam* **h. spot** punto *m* caliente

hot up *vi Fam Esp* calentarse, *Am* ponerse bravo(a); **things are hotting up** la cosa se está poniendo al rojo vivo

hot-air balloon ['hɒteəbə'luːn] *n* globo *m* de aire caliente, aerostato *m*

hotbed ['hɒtbed] *n Fig* hervidero *m*

hot-blooded ['hɒtblʌdɪd] *adj* de sangre caliente; *Fig* **to be h.-b.** tener la sangre caliente

hotch-potch ['hɒtʃpɒtʃ] *n Br Fam* revoltijo *m*, *Esp* batiburrillo *m*

hotel [həʊ'tel] *n* hotel *m*

hotelier [həʊ'teljeɪ] *n*, **hotel-keeper** [həʊ'telkiːpər] *n* hotelero(a) *m,f*

hotfoot ['hɒtfʊt] *adv* a toda prisa

hothead ['hɒthed] *n Fam* cabeza *mf* loca

hot-headed [hɒt'hedɪd] *adj* impetuoso(a), impulsivo(a)

hothouse ['hɒthaʊs] *n Hortic* invernadero *m*

hotly ['hɒtlɪ] *adv (to reply, protest)* acaloradamente; **h. contested** reñidamente disputado(a)

hotplate ['hɒtpleɪt] *n (cooker)* placa *f* de cocina; *(to keep food warm)* calientaplatos *m inv*

hotpot ['hɒtpɒt] *n Br Culin* estofado *m*, *Am* ahogado *m*

hots [hɒts] *npl Slang* **she had the h. for Fred** Fred la ponía a cien *or* muy caliente, *RP* estaba recaliente con Fred

hotshot ['hɒtʃɒt] *n US Slang* as *m*, *Esp* hacha *m*

hot-tempered [hɒt'tempəd] *adj* de genio vivo

hot-water ['hɒtwɔːtər] *adj* de agua caliente □ **h.-w. bottle** bolsa *f* de agua caliente

houmous ['huːməs] *n see* **hummus**

hound [haʊnd] **1** *n Zool* perro *m* de caza

  2 *vt* acosar, perseguir; **he was hounded by the press** fue acosado por la prensa

hour ['aʊər] n hora f; **a quarter of an h.** un cuarto de hora; **every h.** cada hora; **half an h.** media hora; **on the h.** a la hora en punto; **sixty miles an h.** sesenta millas por hora; **the clock struck the h.** el reloj dio la hora; **to be paid by the h.** cobrar por horas; **what are the visiting hours?** ¿cuáles son las horas de visita?; *Fig* **his h. had come** había llegado su hora; *Fig* **the small hours** la madrugada; *Fig* **to take hours to do sth** tardar *or Am* demorar horas en hacer algo; *Fig* **until all hours (of the night)** hasta la madrugada ❑ **h. hand** manecilla f; **lunch h.** hora f de comer; **rush h.** hora f punta

hourly ['aʊəlɪ] **1** adj cada hora; **an h. train service** un tren cada hora
   2 adv por horas; **to be paid h.** cobrar por horas

house [haʊs] **1** (a) (gen) casa f; *Fml* domicilio m; **at my h.** en mi casa; **doll's h.** casa de muñecas; **to move h.** mudarse de casa, trasladarse; *Fig* **on the h.** cortesía de la casa; *Fig* **to keep open h.** ser muy hospitalario(a); *Fam* **to get on with sb like a h. on fire** llevarse de maravilla con algn ❑ *Br* **h. agent** agente m inmobiliario; *Jur* **h. arrest** arresto m domiciliario; **h. guest** invitado(a) m,f de la casa; *Med* **h. physician** interno(a) m,f; **h. plant** planta f de interior; *Med* **h. surgeon** cirujano m interno (b) *Pol* cámara f ❑ **H. of Commons** Cámara f de los Comunes; **H. of Lords** Cámara f de los Lores; *US* **H. of Representatives** Cámara f de Representantes; **Houses of Parliament** Parlamento m (c) (company) empresa f ❑ **publishing h.** editorial f (d) *Theat* sala f; *Fig* **to bring the h. down** ser un exitazo ❑ **first h.** primera sesión f; **full h.** lleno m; **'h. full'** 'agotadas las localidades' (e) *Br Sch* = división que se hace de los alumnos de cada curso para la realización de actividades no académicas
   2 [haʊz] vt (gen) alojar; (give housing to) proveer de vivienda, (store) guardar; (fit) dar cabida a

houseboat ['haʊsbəʊt] n casa f flotante

housebound ['haʊsbaʊnd] adj **to be h.** estar confinado(a) en casa

housebreaker ['haʊsbreɪkər] n ladrón(ona) m,f

housebreaking ['haʊsbreɪkɪŋ] n *Jur* robos mpl de casas

housebroken ['haʊsbrəʊkən] adj *US (dog)* = que ya ha aprendido a no hacer sus necesidades en casa; *Hum (husband)* bien enseñado

housecoat ['haʊskəʊt] n bata f

housefly ['haʊsflaɪ] n mosca f (doméstica)

houseful ['haʊsfʊl] n **we have a h. of guests** tenemos la casa llena de invitados

household ['haʊshəʊld] n casa f, hogar m; *Fig* **to become a h. name** ser archiconocido(a) or popular ❑ **h. expenses** gastos mpl de la casa; **h. products** productos mpl domésticos

householder ['haʊshəʊldər] n dueño(a) m,f de la casa

house-hunting ['haʊshʌntɪŋ] n búsqueda f de vivienda

househusband ['haʊshʌzbənd] n *Fam* amo m de casa

housekeeper ['haʊskiːpər] n ama f de llaves

housekeeping ['haʊskiːpɪŋ] n administración f de la casa ❑ **h. money** dinero m para los gastos de casa

housemaid ['haʊsmeɪd] n criada f ❑ *Med* **h.'s knee** hidrartrosis f

houseman ['haʊsmən] n (pl **housemen**) *Br Med* interno m

housemaster ['haʊsmɑːstər] n *Br Educ* = profesor a cargo de una **house** (división para actividades no académicas)

housemistress ['haʊsmɪstrɪs] n *Br Educ* = profesora a cargo de una **house** (división para actividades no académicas)

house-proud ['haʊspraʊd] adj **she's very h.** es una mujer muy de su casa

houseroom ['haʊsruːm] n sitio m en casa; **I wouldn't give it h.** no lo tendría ni en casa

house-sit ['haʊssɪt] vi quedarse cuidando la casa (**for** de)

house-to-house ['haʊstə'haʊs] adj de casa en casa; **h.-to-h. salesman** vendedor a domicilio

house-trained ['haʊstreɪnd] adj esp *Br (dog)* = que ya ha aprendido a no hacer sus necesidades en casa; *Hum (husband)* bien enseñado

house-warming ['haʊswɔːmɪŋ] n **h.-w. (party)** = fiesta que se da al estrenar casa

housewife ['haʊswaɪf] n (pl **housewives** ['haʊswaɪvz]) ama f de casa

housework ['haʊswɜːk] n trabajo m doméstico, quehaceres mpl domésticos

housing ['haʊzɪŋ] n vivienda f ❑ *Br* **h. estate** (public housing) = urbanización con viviendas de protección oficial; (private housing) urbanización f; *US* **h. project** = urbanización con viviendas de protección oficial; *Pol* **Ministry of H.** Ministerio m de la Vivienda

hove [həʊv] pt & pp see **heave**

hovel ['hɒvəl] n *Esp* chabola f, *Méx* jacal m, *CSur Ven* rancho m

hover ['hɒvər] vi (a) (bird) cernerse; (aircraft) permanecer inmóvil (en el aire); **the eagle hovered over its prey** el águila se cernía sobre su presa (b) (person) cernerse; **to h. between one thing and another** vacilar entre una cosa y otra

hovercraft ['hɒvəkrɑːft] n *Naut* hovercraft m

how [haʊ] adv (a) (direct question) ¿cómo?; **h. are you?** ¿cómo estás?; **h. did it happen?** ¿cómo ocurrió?; **h. do you do** mucho gusto; *Fam* **and h.!** ¡y tanto!; *Fam* **h. come?** ¿por qué?; *Fam* **h.'s that for an answer?** ¿qué te parece? (b) (indirect question) cómo; **I don't know h. to tell you** no sé cómo decírtelo (c) (very) qué; **h. funny!** ¡qué divertido!; **h. long the film was!** ¡qué larga que fue la película! (d) (suggestion) **h. about ...?** ¿y si ...?; **h. about a stroll?** ¿qué te parece un paseo?; **h. about going out for a meal?** ¿quieres salir a comer?, ¿te *Esp* apetece or *Carib Col Méx* provoca salir a comer? (e) (quantity) cuánto; **h. old is she?** ¿cuántos años tiene?, ¿qué edad tiene?; **h. tall are you?** ¿cuánto mides de altura? (f) (quantity) **h. many?** ¿cuántos(as)?; **h. much?** ¿cuánto(a)?; **I don't know h. many people there were** no sé cuánta gente había

howdy ['haʊdɪ] interj *US Fam* ¡hola!, ¿qué hay?, *CAm Col Méx* ¡quihubo!

however [haʊ'evər] adv (a) (nevertheless) no obstante, sin embargo; **h., he was right** sin embargo, tenía razón (b) (with adjective) por; **h. difficult it may be** por difícil que sea; **h. much** por más que, por mucho que (+ subj); **h. much you insist ...** por más que insistas ... (c) (how) ¿cómo?; **h. did you manage to do it?** ¿cómo diablos conseguiste hacerlo?

howl [haʊl] **1** n (a) (cry) aullido m (b) *Slang* (funny thing, person) **to be a h.** ser la monda
   2 vi aullar; *Fam* **to h. with laughter** reír a carcajadas

howl down vt abuchear

howler ['haʊlər] n *Fam* error m grave; **to make a h.** cometer una falta garrafal

howling ['haʊlɪŋ] n (of dogs, wolves) aullido m; (of wind) rumor m

HP, hp [eɪtʃ'piː] n (a) *Br* (abbr **hire purchase**) compra f a plazos (b) (abbr **horsepower**) caballos mpl de vapor, cv mpl

HQ [eɪtʃ'kjuː] n *Mil* (abbr **headquarters**) cuartel m general; *Fig* centro m de operaciones

hr (*pl* **hrs**) *abbr* **hour** hora *f*, h

HRH [eɪtʃɑːrˈeɪtʃ] *n Br* (*abbr* **His/Her Royal Highness**) Su Alteza *mf*Real, S.A.R.

HRT [eɪtʃɑːˈtiː] *n Med* (*abbr* **hormone replacement therapy**) terapia *f* hormonal sustitutiva

HTML [eɪtʃtiːemˈel] *n Comptr* (*abbr* **Hyper Text Markup Language**) HTML *m*

HTTP [eɪtʃtiːtiːˈpiː] *n Comptr* (*abbr* **Hyper Text Transfer Protocol**) HTTP *m*

hub [hʌb] *n* (**a**) *Aut* cubo *m* (**b**) *Fig* eje *m*, centro *m*

hubbub [ˈhʌbʌb] *n* alboroto *m*, jaleo *m*

hubby [ˈhʌbɪ] *n Fam* marido *m*

hubcap [ˈhʌbkæp] *n Aut* tapacubos *m inv*

huckleberry [ˈhʌkəlberɪ] *n Bot* arándano *m*

huddle [ˈhʌdəl] **1** *n* grupo *m*; **a h. of people** un grupo cerrado de gente; *Fam* **to go into a h. about sth** conferenciar en secreto sobre algo
    2 *vi* **to h. (up** *or* **together)** acurrucarse

Hudson Bay [hʌdsənˈbeɪ] *n* Bahía *f* de Hudson

hue[1] [hjuː] *n* (*colour*) tinte *m*; (*shade*) matiz *m*; *Fig* color *m*

hue[2] [hjuː] *n* **h. and cry** fuerte protesta *f*

huff [hʌf] **1** *n Fam* **to be in a h.** estar mosqueado(a)
    2 *vi* **to h. (and puff)** resoplar

huffy [ˈhʌfɪ] *adj* (**huffier, huffiest**) *Fam* **to be h.** (*in bad mood*) estar mosqueado(a); (*by nature*) ser un(a) refunfuñón(ona), ser muy picajoso(a)

hug [hʌg] **1** *vt* (*pt & pp* **hugged**) (**a**) (*embrace*) abrazar, dar un abrazo a; *Fig* **to h. oneself** sentirse satisfecho(a) de sí mismo(a) (**b**) *Fig* (*coast, kerb*) pegarse a
    2 *n* abrazo *m*

huge [hjuːdʒ] *adj* enorme; **a h. building** un edificio inmenso; **a h. success** un exitazo

hugely [ˈhjuːdʒlɪ] *adv* enormemente

huh [hʌ] *interj* (*showing surprise*) ¡vaya!, ¡caramba!; (*inquiry*) ¿eh?, ¿qué?

hulk [hʌlk] *n* (**a**) *Naut* casco *m* (**b**) (*thing, person*) armatoste *m*

hulking [ˈhʌlkɪŋ] *adj* grueso(a), pesado(a)

hull [hʌl] **1** *n* (**a**) *Naut* casco *m* (**b**) *Bot* (*shell*) cáscara *f*; (*pod*) vaina *f*
    2 *vt* (*fruit, peas*) desvainar

hullabal(l)oo [hʌləbəˈluː] *n Fam* follón *m*, escándalo *m*, jaleo *m*

hullo [hʌˈləʊ] *interj Br see* **hello**

hum [hʌm] **1** *vt* (*pt & pp* **hummed**) (*tune*) tararear
    2 *vi* (**a**) (*bees, engine*) zumbar; (*sing*) tararear; *Fig* **to h. and haw** vacilar al hablar (**b**) *Br Slang* (*smell*) apestar
    3 *n* (*of bees, engine*) zumbido *m*

human [ˈhjuːmən] **1** *adj* humano(a) ◻ **h. being** ser *m* humano; **h. error** error *m* humano; **h. race** raza *f* humana; **h. resources** recursos *mpl* humanos; **h. rights** derechos *mpl* humanos; **h. shield** escudo *m* humano
    2 *n* ser *m* humano

humane [hjuːˈmeɪn] *adj* humano(a); **toward a more h. society** hacia una sociedad más humana ◻ *Univ* **h. studies** humanidades *fpl*

humanely [hjuːˈmeɪnlɪ] *adv* con humanidad, de una forma humana

humanism [ˈhjuːmənɪzəm] *n* humanismo *m*

humanist [ˈhjuːmənɪst] *adj & n* humanista (*mf*)

humanitarian [hjuːmænɪˈteərɪən] **1** *adj* humanitario(a), filantrópico(a)
    2 *n* filántropo(a) *m,f*

humanity [hjuːˈmænɪtɪ] *n* (**a**) (*mankind*) género *m*

humano, raza *f* humana (**b**) (*virtue*) humanidad *f* (**c**) *Univ* **the humanities** las humanidades

humankind [hjʊmənˈkaɪnd] *n* humanidad *f*, raza *f* humana

humanly [ˈhjuːmənlɪ] *adv* humanamente; **to do everything h. possible** hacer todo lo posible

humanoid [ˈhjuːmənɔɪd] *n* humanoide *mf*

humble [ˈhʌmbəl] **1** *adj* humilde; **in my h. opinion** en mi modesta opinión; *Fig* **to eat h. pie** reconocer su error
    2 *vt* humillar

humbleness [ˈhʌmbəlnɪs] *n* humildad *f*

humbly [ˈhʌmblɪ] *adv* humildemente

humbug [ˈhʌmbʌg] *n* (**a**) *Fam* (*trick*) burla *f*, camelo *m*; **it's all h.** son tonterías (**b**) (*trickster*) embaucador(a) *m,f*, camelista *mf*, farsante *mf* (**c**) *Br* (*mint*) **h.** caramelo *m* de menta

humdinger [ˈhʌmdɪŋər] *n Fam* **a h. of a movie** una película bestial *or* genial *or* *Méx* padrísima

humdrum [ˈhʌmdrʌm] *adj* monótono(a), aburrido(a)

humerus [ˈhjuːmərəs] *n* (*pl* **humeri** [ˈhjuːməraɪ]) *Anat* húmero *m*

humid [ˈhjuːmɪd] *adj* húmedo(a)

humidifier [hjuːˈmɪdɪfaɪər] *n* humidificador *m*

humidity [hjuːˈmɪdɪtɪ] *n* humedad *f*

humiliate [hjuːˈmɪlɪeɪt] *vt* humillar

humiliation [hjuːmɪlɪˈeɪʃən] *n* humillación *f*

humility [hjuːˈmɪlɪtɪ] *n see* **humbleness**

hummingbird [ˈhʌmɪŋbɜːd] *n Orn* colibrí *m*

hummus [ˈhʊməs] *n* hum(m)us *m inv*, puré *m* de garbanzos

humongous, humungous [hjuːˈmʌŋgəs] *adj Fam* grandísimo(a), *Esp* gansísimo(a)

humor [ˈhjuːmər] *n US see* **humour**

humorist [ˈhjuːmərɪst] *n* humorista *mf*

humorless [ˈhjuːmələs] *US adj see* **humourless**

humorous [ˈhjuːmərəs] *adj* (*of writer*) humorístico(a); (*of person, story*) gracioso(a), divertido(a)

humour [ˈhjuːmər] **1** *n* (**a**) (*comedy*) humor *m*; **to see the h. in sth** verle la gracia a algo ◻ **sense of h.** sentido *m* del humor (**b**) (*mood*) humor *m*; **ill/good h.** mal/buen humor; **out of h.** de mal humor; **to be in good/bad h.** estar de buen/mal humor
    2 *vt* seguir el humor a

humourless [ˈhjuːmələs] *adj* serio(a), con poco sentido del humor

hump [hʌmp] **1** *n* (**a**) (*on back*) joroba *f*; *Br Fam* **to have the h.** estar deprimido(a) *or* chafado(a) (**b**) (*small hill*) montículo *m*
    2 *vt esp Br Slang* acarrear

humpback [ˈhʌmpbæk] *n* jorobado(a) *m,f* ◻ *Br Constr* **h. bridge** puente *m* peraltado

humungous [hjuːˈmʌŋgəs] *adj see* **humongous**

humus [ˈhjuːməs] *n Agr* mantillo *m*, humus *m*

Hun [hʌn] *n Hist* huno(a) *m,f*

hunch [hʌntʃ] **1** *n Fam* presentimiento *m*; **to act on one's hunches** actuar por intuición; **to have a h.** tener una corazonada
    2 *vt* **to h. one's back** encorvarse

hunchback [ˈhʌntʃbæk] *n* (*person*) jorobado(a) *m,f*

hundred [ˈhʌndrəd] **1** *n* (*pl* **hundred** *or* **hundreds**) cien *m*, ciento *m*; (*rough number*) centenar *m*; **by the hundred** a centenares; **five h.** quinientos; **hundreds of soldiers** centenares de soldados; **hundreds of trees** cientos de árboles; **she lived in the sixteen hundreds** vivió en el siglo diecisiete; **to live to be a h.** llegar a los cien años

2 *adj* cien; **a h. people** cien personas; **a h. per cent** cien por cien, ciento por ciento, *Am* cien por ciento; **a h. and twenty-five books** ciento veinticinco libros; **two h. chairs** doscientas sillas; *Fig* **to agree one h. per cent with sb** estar totalmente de acuerdo con algn

hundredth ['hʌndrədθ] **1** *adj* centésimo(a); **for the h. time** por centésima vez

2 *n* centésimo *m*, centésima parte *f*

hundredweight ['hʌndrədweɪt] *n* (*pl* **hundredweight** *or* **hundredweights**) (*metric*) 50kg; (*imperial*) *Br* = 50,8 kg; *US* = 45,36 kg

hung [hʌŋ] **1** *pt & pp see* **hang**

2 *adj* (**a**) **h. jury** = jurado cuyos miembros no se ponen de acuerdo (**b**) *Fam* **h. over** con resaca; **he's still h. over from yesterday** aún tiene resaca de lo de ayer (**c**) *Fam* **h. up** acomplejado(a); *Slang* **h. up on sth/sb** obsesionado(a) con algo/algn (**d**) *Slang (man)* **well h.** bien dotado *or Méx* dado *or RP* armado

Hungarian [hʌŋ'geərɪən] *adj & n* húngaro(a) *(m,f)*

Hungary ['hʌŋgərɪ] *n* Hungría

hunger ['hʌŋgər] **1** *n* hambre *f* ❏ **h. strike** huelga *f* de hambre

2 *vi Fig* tener hambre, estar hambriento(a) (**for** de); ansiar (**for** *or* **after** -)

hungry ['hʌŋgrɪ] *adj* (**hungrier**, **hungriest**) hambriento(a); **to be h.** tener hambre; **to go h.** pasar hambre; **to make h.** dar hambre a, abrir el apetito a

hunk [hʌŋk] *n* (**a**) (*large piece*) trozo *m* grueso, buen pedazo *m*; **a h. of bread** un buen pedazo de pan (**b**) *Slang* **a h. (of a man)** un machote

hunt [hʌnt] **1** *n* (**a**) (*gen*) caza *f*; (*expedition*) partida *f* de caza (**b**) (*search*) búsqueda *f*; **they're on the h. for the killer** van en busca del asesino

2 *vi* (**a**) (*for game*) cazar (**b**) (*search*) buscar; **to h. for sth/ sb** buscar algo/a algn; *Fam* **we hunted high and low for it** lo buscamos por todas partes

3 *vt* cazar

hunt down *vt* perseguir, ir a la caza de

hunt out, hunt up *vt* (*look for*) buscar; (*find*) encontrar

hunter ['hʌntər] *n* (**a**) (*person*) cazador(a) *m,f*; *Fig* **bargain h.** persona *f* que busca gangas en las rebajas; *Fig* **fortune h.** (*gen*) aventurero *m*; (*through marriage*) cazadotes *m inv* (**b**) *Zool* (*horse*) caballo *m* de caza

hunting ['hʌntɪŋ] *n* (*gen*) caza *f*; (*expedition*) cacería *f*; *Fig* **a happy h. ground for stamp collectors** un buen mercado para los coleccionistas de sellos ❏ **fox h.** caza *f* del zorro; **h. ground** terreno *m or* coto *m* de caza; **h. knife** navaja *f* de monte

huntsman ['hʌntsmən] *n* (*pl* **huntsmen**) cazador *m*

hurdle ['hɜːdəl] **1** *n* (**a**) *Athlet* valla *f*, *Am* obstáculo *m*; **the 100 metres hurdles** los 100 metros valla (**b**) *Fig* obstáculo *m*

2 *vt Athlet* (*barrier etc*) saltar

hurdler ['hɜːdlər] *n Athlet* corredor(a) *m,f* de vallas *or Am* obstáculos

hurdling ['hɜːdlɪŋ] *n Athlet* carrera *f* de vallas *or Am* obstáculos

hurdy-gurdy ['hɜːdɪgɜːdɪ] *n Mus* organillo *m*

hurl [hɜːl] *vt* (*object*) arrojar, lanzar; **to h. oneself (from** de); *Fig* **to h. abuse at sb** soltar una retahíla de insultos a algn, decir de todo a algn

hurling ['hɜːlɪŋ] *n Sport* = juego irlandés parecido al hockey y al lacrosse

hurly-burly ['hɜːlɪbɜːlɪ] *n Fam* alboroto *m*

hurrah [hʊ'rɑː] *interj*, **hurray** [hʊ'reɪ] *interj* ¡hurra!, ¡olé!; **h. for John!** ¡viva John!

hurricane ['hʌrɪkən, *US* 'hʌrɪkeɪn] *n* huracán *m* ❏ **h. lamp** farol *m*

hurried ['hʌrɪd] *adj* apresurado(a), hecho(a) de prisa; **a h. letter** una carta escrita deprisa; **a h. visit** una visita apresurada

hurriedly ['hʌrɪdlɪ] *adv* deprisa, apresuradamente

hurry ['hʌrɪ] **1** *vi* (*pt & pp* **hurried**) darse prisa, apresurarse, *Am* apurarse; **he hurried through his work** trabajó a toda prisa a; **h. (up)!** ¡date prisa!, *Am* ¡apúrate!

2 *vt* meter prisa a, *Am* apurar; **don't h. us** no nos metas prisa; **he was hurried (off) to hospital** le llevaron urgentemente al hospital; **to h. a meal** comer deprisa

3 *n* prisa *f*, *Am* apuro *m*; **are you in a h. for it?** ¿le corre prisa?; **there's no h. for it** no corre prisa; **to be in a h.** tener prisa *or Am* apuro ; **to do sth in a h.** hacer algo deprisa *or* rápido; **to leave in a h.** salir corriendo; **what's your h.?** ¿tanta prisa *or Am* tanto apuro tienes?; *Fig* **I won't do it again in a h.** la próxima vez me lo pensaré dos veces

hurt [hɜːt] **1** *vt* (*pt & pp* **hurt**) (**a**) (*physically*) hacer daño a; (*wound*) herir; **she has h. her foot** se ha hecho daño en el pie; **to h. oneself** hacerse daño, lastimarse (**b**) (*mentally*) herir, ofender; **her words h. me** sus palabras me hirieron; **to h. sb's feelings** ofender a algn

2 *vi* (**a**) (*physically*) doler; **my arm hurts** me duele el brazo; **where does it h. most?** ¿dónde le duele más? (**b**) (*mentally*) escocer, doler; **the truth always hurts** la verdad siempre duele (**c**) *Fam* venir or ir mal; **it doesn't h. to go out once in a while** no viene mal salir de vez en cuando; **it wouldn't h. for you to help** no iría mal que echaras una mano

3 *n* (**a**) (*physical*) herida *f* (**b**) (*mental*) daño *m*, mal *m*

4 *adj* (**a**) (*physically*) herido(a) (**b**) (*mentally*) dolido(a); **a h. look** una mirada dolida

hurtful ['hɜːtfʊl] *adj* doloroso(a), hiriente; **a h. remark** una observación hiriente

hurtle ['hɜːtəl] *vi* lanzarse, precipitarse; **to h. down** precipitarse *or* caer violentamente

husband ['hʌzbənd] *n* marido *m*, esposo *m*

husbandry ['hʌzbəndrɪ] *n* agricultura *f*

hush [hʌʃ] **1** *vt* callar, silenciar; **to h. a matter up** echar tierra a un asunto

2 *n* silencio *m* ❏ *Slang* **h. money** soborno *m*, cohecho *m*, *RP* coima *f*

3 *interj* ¡silencio!, ¡chito!

hush-hush [hʌʃ'hʌʃ] *adj Fam* confidencial, secreto(a)

husk [hʌsk] **1** *n* (*of nuts, cereals*) cáscara *f*; (*of peas, beans*) vaina *f*

2 *vt* pelar

huskiness ['hʌskɪnɪs] *n* ronquera *f*

husky¹ ['hʌskɪ] *adj* (**huskier**, **huskiest**) ronco(a); **a h. voice** una voz profunda

husky² ['hʌskɪ] *n Zool* perro *m* esquimal

hussar [hʊ'zɑːr] *n Mil* húsar *m*

hussy ['hʌsɪ] *n Fam* (*woman*) fresca *f*

hustings ['hʌstɪŋz] *npl Pol* (**a**) (*platform*) tribuna *f sing* electoral (**b**) (*election*) elecciones *fpl*; **at the h.** durante la campaña electoral

hustle ['hʌsəl] **1** *vt* (**a**) (*jostle*) empujar, dar empujones a (**b**) *Fam* apurar, apremiar (**c**) *Slang* apañarse, hacerse con

2 *n* apaño *m*, bullicio *m*; **h. and bustle** ajetreo *m*

hustler ['hʌslər] *n* (**a**) (*swindler*) estafador(a) *m,f*, *Esp* timador(a) *m,f* (**b**) *US Slang* (*prostitute*) puto(a) *m,f*

hut [hʌt] *n* (*gen*) cabaña *f*; (*garden shed*) cobertizo *m*; *Mil* barraca *f*

hutch [hʌtʃ] *n* (**a**) (*cage*) jaula *f* ❏ **rabbit h.** conejera *f* (**b**) *Fam Pej* ratonera *f*

hyacinth ['haɪəsɪnθ] n Bot jacinto m
hybrid ['haɪbrɪd] adj & n híbrido(a) (m,f)
hydrangea [haɪ'dreɪndʒə] n Bot hortensia f
hydrant ['haɪdrənt] n boca f de riego ❑ **fire h.** boca f de incendio
hydraulic [haɪ'drɒlɪk] adj hidráulico(a); **h. power** fuerza hidráulica ❑ **h. brake** freno m hidráulico; **h. suspension** suspensión f hidráulica
hydraulics [haɪ'drɒlɪks] n hidráulica f
hydric ['haɪdrɪk] adj hídrico(a)
hydro[1] ['haɪdrəʊ] n (pl **hydros**) Br (spa) balneario m, estación f termal
hydro[2] ['haɪdrəʊ] adj (abbr **hydroelectric**) hidroeléctrico(a)
hydrocarbon [haɪdrəʊ'kɑːbən] n Chem hidrocarburo m
hydrochloric [haɪdrəʊ'klɒrɪk] adj Chem clorhídrico(a) ❑ **h. acid** ácido m clorhídrico
hydroelectric [haɪdrəʊɪ'lektrɪk] adj hidroeléctrico(a) ❑ **h. power station** central f hidroeléctrica
hydroelectricity [haɪdrəʊɪlek'trɪsɪti] n hidroelectricidad f
hydrofoil ['haɪdrəfɔɪl] n hidroala f, RP alíscafo m
hydrogen ['haɪdrɪdʒən] n Chem hidrógeno m ❑ **h. bomb** bomba f de hidrógeno; **h. chloride** ácido m clorhídrico; **h. peroxide** agua f oxigenada
hydrographer [haɪ'drɒgrəfər] n hidrógrafo(a) m,f
hydrography [haɪ'drɒgrəfi] n hidrografía f
hydrolysis [haɪ'drɒlɪsɪs] n Chem hidrólisis f
hydrophobia [haɪdrə'fəʊbɪə] n Med hidrofobia f
hydroplane ['haɪdrəʊpleɪn] n Av hidroavión m, hidroplano m
hydroponics [haɪdrəʊ'pɒnɪks] n hidroponía f
hydrotherapy [haɪdrəʊ'θerəpɪ] n Med hidroterapia f
hyena [haɪ'iːnə] n Zool hiena f ❑ **laughing h.** hiena f manchada
hygiene ['haɪdʒiːn] n higiene f
hygienic [haɪ'dʒiːnɪk] adj higiénico(a)
hygienically [haɪ'dʒiːnɪklɪ] adv con higiene, de un modo higiénico
hygrometer [haɪ'grɒmɪtər] n higrómetro m
hymen ['haɪmen] n Anat himen m
hymn [hɪm] n himno m ❑ **h. book** cantoral m
hymnal ['hɪmnəl] n cantoral m
hype[1] [haɪp] Slang **1** vi **to h. (up)** (shoot up) chutarse; (get high) colocarse
   2 vt estimular, excitar; Fig **hyped up** excitado(a)
hype[2] [haɪp] n Slang campaña f publicitaria, movida f
hyper ['haɪpər] adj Fam (overexcited) acelerado(a)
hyper- ['haɪpər] pref hiper-; **hyperactive** hiperactivo(a)

hyperactive [haɪpə'ræktɪv] adj hiperactivo(a)
hyperbola [haɪ'pɜːbələ] n (pl **hyperbolas** or **hyperbole** [haɪ'pɜːbəliː]) hipérbola f
hyperbole [haɪ'pɜːbəlɪ] n hipérbole f
hypercritical [haɪpə'krɪtɪkəl] adj hipercrítico(a)
hypermarket ['haɪpəmɑːkɪt] n Br hipermercado m
hypersensitive [haɪpə'sensɪtɪv] adj hipersensible
hypertension [haɪpə'tenʃən] n Med hipertensión f
hypertext ['haɪpətekst] n Comptr hipertexto m
hyphen ['haɪfən] n guión m
hyphenate ['haɪfəneɪt] vt (gen) escribir con guión; (write together) unir con guión; (separate) separar con guión
hypnosis [hɪp'nəʊsɪs] n (pl **hypnoses** [hɪp'nəʊsiːz]) Med hipnosis f
hypnotic [hɪp'nɒtɪk] adj hipnótico(a)
hypnotism ['hɪpnətɪzəm] n hipnotismo m
hypnotist ['hɪpnətɪst] n hipnotizador(a) m,f
hypnotize ['hɪpnətaɪz] vt hipnotizar
hypo ['haɪpəʊ] n Phot fijador m
hypo- ['haɪpəʊ] pref hipo-
hypoallergenic [haɪpəæləː'dʒenɪk] adj (cosmetics etc) hipoalérgico(a)
hypochondria [haɪpə'kɒndrɪə] n hipocondría f
hypochondriac [haɪpə'kɒndrɪæk] adj & n hipocondríaco(a) (m,f)
hypocrisy [hɪ'pɒkrəsɪ] n hipocresía f
hypocrite ['hɪpəkrɪt] n hipócrita mf
hypocritical [hɪpə'krɪtɪkəl] adj hipócrita
hypodermic [haɪpə'dɜːmɪk] adj Med hipodérmico(a); **h. needle/syringe** aguja/jeringa hipodérmica
hypotension [haɪpəʊ'tenʃən] n Med hipotensión f
hypotenuse [haɪ'pɒtɪnjuːz] n Geom hipotenusa f
hypothermia [haɪpəʊ'θɜːmɪə] n Med hipotermia f
hypothesis [haɪ'pɒθɪsɪs] n (pl **hypotheses** [haɪ'pɒθɪsiːz]) hipótesis f
hypothesize [haɪ'pɒθəsaɪz] **1** vt plantear como hipótesis, conjeturar
   2 vi plantear hipótesis, conjeturar
hypothetic(al) [haɪpə'θetɪk(əl)] adj hipotético(a)
hysterectomy [hɪstə'rektəmɪ] n Med histerectomía f
hysteria [hɪ'stɪərɪə] n Psych histeria f
hysterical [hɪ'sterɪkəl] adj histérico(a); **h. laughter** risa convulsiva
hysterically [hɪs'terɪklɪ] adv histéricamente
hysterics [hɪ'sterɪks] npl (**a**) (attack) ataque m de histeria (**b**) Fam (of laughter) ataque m de risa; **to have h.** mondarse de risa
Hz (abbr **hertz**) hercio(s) m(pl), Hz

I

I [aɪ] *pers pron* yo; **I know her** la conozco; **I know him but you don't** yo lo conozco pero tú no

I, i [aɪ] *n (the letter)* I, i *f*

IAEA [aɪeɪiː'eɪ] *n (abbr* **International Atomic Energy Agency)** AIEA *f*

IATA [aɪ'ɑːtə] *n (abbr* **International Air Transport Association)** Asociación *f* del Transporte Aéreo Internacional, IATA *f*

Iberia [aɪ'bɪərɪə] *n* Iberia

Iberian [aɪ'bɪərɪən] **1** *adj* ibérico(a)
2 *n Hist (person)* ibero(a) *m,f*

ibex ['aɪbeks] *n* íbice *m*, cabra *f* montés

ICBM [aɪsiːbiː'em] *n Mil (abbr* **intercontinental ballistic missile)** proyectil *m* balístico intercontinental, PBI *m*

ice [aɪs] **1** *n (frozen water)* hielo *m*; *(ice cream)* helado *m*; **a lemon ice** un helado de limón; *Fig* **my feet are like i.** tengo los pies helados; *Fig* **to break the i.** romper el hielo; *Fig* **to cut little** *or* **no i. with sb** dejar frío(a) a algn; *Fig* **to put** *or* **keep sth on i.** *(project)* postergar algo; *(suggestion, idea)* tener algo de reserva; *Fig* **to skate on thin i.** pisar un terreno resbaladizo ❑ **black i.** hielo *m* invisible; **i. age** glaciación *f*; **i. axe** pico *m or* piqueta *f* (de alpinista); **i. cream** helado *m*; **i.-cream parlour** heladería *f*; **i. cube** cubito *m* de hielo; **i. floe** témpano *m*; **i. hockey** hockey *m* sobre hielo; *Br* **i. lolly** polo *m*, *Am* paleta *f* (helada), *RP* palito *m* (de agua) ; **i. pack** bolsa *f* de hielo; **i. rink** pista *f* de patinaje; **i. show** espectáculo *m* sobre hielo; **i. skate** patín *m* de cuchilla
2 *vt* **(a)** *(drink)* poner hielo en **(b)** *(cake etc)* alcorzar, glasear

ice over, ice up *vi (pond etc)* helarse; *(windscreen, plane wings)* cubrirse de hielo

iceberg ['aɪsbɜːg] *n* iceberg *m*, témpano *m*

icebound ['aɪsbaʊnd] *adj (harbour, road)* obstruido(a) *or* bloqueado(a) por el hielo; *(ship)* atrapado(a) por el hielo

icebox ['aɪsbɒks] *n* **(a)** *Br (compartment of fridge)* congelador *m* **(b)** *US (fridge)* nevera *f*, *RP* heladera *f*, *Méx* refrigerador *m*

icebreaker ['aɪsbreɪkər] *n Naut* rompehielos *m inv*

icecap ['aɪskæp] *n* casquete *m* glaciar

ice-cold ['aɪskəʊld] *adj* helado(a)

iced [aɪst] *adj* **(a)** *(drink)* con hielo **(b)** *(cake etc)* glaseado(a)

Iceland ['aɪslənd] *n* Islandia

Icelander ['aɪsləndər] *n* islandés(esa) *m,f*

Icelandic [aɪs'lændɪk] **1** *adj* islandés(esa)
2 *n (language)* islandés *m*

ice-skate ['aɪsskeɪt] *vi* patinar sobre hielo

ice-skater ['aɪsskeɪtər] *n* patinador(a) *m,f* sobre hielo

ice-skating ['aɪsskeɪtɪŋ] *n* patinaje *m* sobre hielo

icicle ['aɪsɪkəl] *n* carámbano *m*

icing ['aɪsɪŋ] *n Culin* alcorza *f*, glaseado *m*; *Fig* **the i. on the cake** remate *m*, guinda *f* ❑ *Br* **i. sugar** azúcar *m Esp Méx* glas *or Esp* de lustre *or Chile* flor *or Col* pulverizado *or RP* impalpable

icon ['aɪkɒn] *n* icono *m*

iconoclast [aɪ'kɒnəklæst] *n* iconoclasta *mf*

iconoclastic [aɪkɒnə'klæstɪk] *adj* iconoclasta

ICRC [aɪsiːɑː'siː] *n (abbr* **International Committee of the Red Cross)** CICR *m*

icy ['aɪsɪ] *adj* **(icier, iciest) (a)** *(road etc)* helado(a), cubierto(a) de hielo **(b)** *Fig (hands, feet)* helado(a); *(wind, smile)* glacial

ID [aɪ'diː] *n (abbr* **identification, identity)** identificación *f*, identidad *f*; **ID card** documento *m* nacional de identidad, *Esp* DNI *m*

I'd [aɪd] = **I would; I had**

idea [aɪ'dɪə] *n* **(a)** *(thought)* idea *f*; *(opinion)* idea *f*, opinión *f*; *(concept)* concepto *m*; **I haven't the faintest** *or* **foggiest i.** no tengo ni la menor *or* la más mínima idea; **I've got an i.** tengo una idea, se me ocurre una idea; **the (very) i. of it!** ¡vaya *or* qué ocurrencia!; **to put ideas into sb's head** meter ideas en la cabeza a algn; **vague i.** ligera idea; **what gave you that i.?** ¿cómo se te ocurrió pensar eso? **(b)** *(aim)* idea *f*, intención *f*; **the i. is to save money** la idea es ahorrar dinero; *Fam* **that's the i.!** ¡eso es!, ¡así se hace!; *Fam* **what's the big i.?** ¿a qué viene eso? **(c)** *(impression)* impresión *f*, idea *f*; **some i. (of) what it's about** una idea aproximada de lo que se trata; **to have an i. that ...** tener la impresión (de) que ...

ideal [aɪ'dɪəl] **1** *adj* ideal
2 *n* **(a)** *(example)* ideal *m* **(of** de) **(b)** *(principle)* ideal *m*, principio *m*

idealism [aɪ'dɪəlɪzəm] *n* idealismo *m*

idealist [aɪ'dɪəlɪst] *n* idealista *mf*

idealistic [aɪdɪə'lɪstɪk] *adj* idealista

idealize [aɪ'dɪəlaɪz] *vt* idealizar

ideally [aɪ'dɪəlɪ] *adv* **(a)** *(perfectly)* idealmente, perfectamente; **they're i. suited (to each other)** forman una pareja perfecta, están hechos el uno para el otro **(b)** *(in the best conditions)* en el mejor de los casos, de ser posible, si es posible; **i., we should start now** lo ideal sería que empezáramos ahora

identical [aɪ'dentɪkəl] *adj* idéntico(a); **i. twins** gemelos(as) *mfpl* idénticos(as) *or* monocigóticos(as)

identification [aɪdentɪfɪ'keɪʃən] *n* **(a)** *(gen)* identificación *f* ❑ *Br* **i. parade** rueda *f* de identificación *or* reconocimiento **(b)** *(papers etc)* documentación *f*

identify [aɪ'dentɪfaɪ] **1** vt (pt & pp **identified**) (**a**) (suspect, body) identificar (**b**) (cause, source) descubrir, averiguar (**c**) (associate) he was identified with the Labour Party se le relacionaba con el partido laborista **2** vi (hero, cause) identificarse (**with** con)

identifying mark [aɪ'dentɪfaɪŋ'mɑːk] n seña f de identidad

Identikit® [aɪ'dentɪkɪt] n **I. picture** retrato m robot

identity [aɪ'dentɪtɪ] n identidad f ▫ **i. card** carné m de identidad, Esp DNI m; **i. crisis** crisis f inv de identidad; **proof of i.** prueba f de identidad

ideological [aɪdɪə'lɒdʒɪkəl] adj ideológico(a)

ideology [aɪdɪ'ɒlədʒɪ] n ideología f

idiocy ['ɪdɪəsɪ] n idiotez f

idiom ['ɪdɪəm] n (**a**) (expression) modismo m, locución f, frase f hecha (**b**) Fig (style) lenguaje m, estilo m

idiomatic [ɪdɪə'mætɪk] adj idiomático(a); **i. expression** modismo m, locución f, frase f hecha

idiosyncrasy [ɪdɪəʊ'sɪŋkrəsɪ] n idiosincrasia f

idiosyncratic [ɪdɪəʊsɪŋ'krætɪk] adj idiosincrásico(a)

idiot ['ɪdɪət] n (**a**) (stupid person) idiota mf, tonto(a) m,f, imbécil mf (**b**) Med Pej (imbecile) idiota mf, subnormal mf

idiotic [ɪdɪ'ɒtɪk] adj (person, behaviour) idiota, imbécil, tonto(a); (joke, plan) estúpido(a)

idle ['aɪdəl] **1** adj (**a**) (lazy) perezoso(a), holgazán(ana), vago(a); Fam **he's bone i.** no da golpe (**b**) (at leisure) ocioso(a); **i. moment** momento m libre; **I went out of i. curiosity** fui por pura curiosidad (**c**) (not working) (person) desempleado(a), sin trabajo; (machinery) parado(a); (capital) improductivo(a) (**d**) (gossip, talk) frívolo(a); (threat, hope) vano(a); (fear, suspicion) infundado(a) **2** vi (engine) funcionar en vacío

idle away vt (time) desperdiciar

idleness ['aɪdəlnɪs] n (**a**) (laziness) pereza f, holgazanería f, vagancia f (**b**) (leisure) ociosidad f (**c**) (unemployment) desempleo m, paro m; (stoppage) paro m (**d**) (groundlessness) falta f de base; (of gossip etc) frivolidad f, (of threat etc) futilidad f

idly ['aɪdlɪ] adv (**a**) (inactively) ociosamente; **to stand i. by** estar sin hacer nada (**b**) (casually) despreocupadamente

idol ['aɪdəl] n ídolo m

idolatry [aɪ'dɒlətrɪ] n idolatría f

idolize ['aɪdəlaɪz] vt idolatrar

idyll ['ɪdɪl] n idilio m

idyllic [ɪ'dɪlɪk] adj idílico(a)

ie ['aɪ'iː] (abbr **id est**) (that is to say), esto es, a saber, i.e

if [ɪf] **1** conj (**a**) (supposing) si; **as if** como si; **as if by magic** como por ensalmo; **it's not as if I'm rich** no soy rico, ni mucho menos; **if at all** si acaso; **if ever** raras veces, por no decir nunca; **if I were rich** si fuera rico(a); **if necessary** (en) caso de que sea necesario; **if not** sino; **if so** si es así, de ser así; **if I were you** yo en tu lugar, yo que tú; **I would appreciate it if you could come** te agradecería que vinieras; **she's tall if anything** es más bien alta (**b**) (whenever) si, cuandoquiera que; **if you need help, ask** siempre que necesites ayuda, pídela (**c**) (although) aunque, si bien; **the film's good, if a bit long** la película es buena aunque un poco larga (**d**) (whether) si; **I don't know if I can go** no sé si puedo ir (**e**) (in exclamations) **if only I'd known!** ¡si lo hubiera sabido!, ¡de haberlo sabido!; **if only she were here!** ¡ojalá estuviera aquí!; **well, if it isn't David!** ¡pero si es David! **2** n **ifs and buts** Esp pegas fpl, Am peros mpl; **it's a big if** es muy dudoso

iffy ['ɪfɪ] adj (**iffier, iffiest**) Fam dudoso(a)

igloo ['ɪgluː] n (pl **igloos**) iglú m

ignite [ɪg'naɪt] **1** vt encender, prender fuego a **2** vi encenderse, prender

ignition [ɪg'nɪʃən] n ignición f; Aut encendido m, arranque m ▫ **i. key** llave f de contacto

ignoble [ɪg'nəʊbəl] adj innoble, vil, infame

ignominious [ɪgnə'mɪnɪəs] adj ignominioso(a), vergonzoso(a)

ignominy ['ɪgnəmɪnɪ] n Fml ignominia f, oprobio m

ignoramus [ɪgnə'reɪməs] n ignorante mf

ignorance ['ɪgnərəns] n ignorancia f; **to be in i. of sth** ignorar or desconocer or no saber algo; **to keep sb in i. of sth** ocultarle algo a algn, tener a algn en la ignorancia (de algo)

ignorant ['ɪgnərənt] adj ignorante (**of** de); **to be i. of the facts** ignorar or desconocer los hechos

ignore [ɪg'nɔːr] vt (warning, remark) no hacer caso de, hacer caso omiso de; (behaviour, fact) pasar por alto; (letter, message) dejar sin contestar; **whenever we met, he ignored me** siempre que nos encontrábamos, solía hacer como si no me viera

iguana [ɪ'gwɑːnə] n Zool iguana f

ilk [ɪlk] n **of that i.** de esa clase or índole

I'll [aɪl] = **I shall**; **I will**

ill [ɪl] **1** adj (**a**) (sick) enfermo(a); **to fall** or **be taken i.** caer or ponerse enfermo(a); **to feel i.** encontrarse or sentirse mal; **to look i.** hacer mala cara, tener mal aspecto (**b**) (bad) malo(a); **i. feeling** resentimiento; **i. will** mala voluntad; **I bear you no i. will** no le guardo ningún rencor; **to suffer from i. health** estar mal de salud, ser enfermizo(a); Prov **it's an i. wind (that blows nobody any good)** no hay mal que por bien no venga **2** n (evil) mal m; (misfortune) desgracia f **3** adv difícilmente; **I can i. afford it** a duras penas puedo permitírmelo; **to be i. received** ser mal recibido(a)

ill-advised [ɪləd'vaɪzd] adj (person) mal aconsejado(a), imprudente; (act, remark) desatinado(a), poco acertado(a); **you'd be i.-a. to go** harías mal en ir

ill-bred [ɪl'bred] adj maleducado(a), malcriado(a)

ill-considered [ɪlkən'sɪdəd] adj poco pensado(a), imprudente

ill-disposed [ɪldɪ'spəʊzd] adj mal or poco dispuesto(a); **to be i.-d. towards sb** tenerla tomada con algn

illegal [ɪ'liːgəl] adj ilegal

illegality [ɪlɪ'gælɪtɪ] n ilegalidad f

illegible [ɪ'ledʒɪbəl] adj ilegible

illegitimacy [ɪlɪ'dʒɪtɪməsɪ] n ilegitimidad f

illegitimate [ɪlɪ'dʒɪtɪmɪt] adj ilegítimo(a)

ill-equipped [ɪlɪ'kwɪpt] adj mal equipado(a); Fig mal preparado(a)

ill-fated [ɪl'feɪtɪd] adj fatal, desdichado(a), desafortunado(a)

ill-founded [ɪl'faʊndɪd] adj (fear, suspicion) infundado(a); (hope, ambition) vano(a)

ill-gotten ['ɪlgɒtən] adj Fml **i.-g. gains** bienes mpl mal adquiridos

illiberal [ɪ'lɪbərəl] adj (narrow-minded) intolerante

illicit [ɪ'lɪsɪt] adj ilícito(a)

ill-informed [ɪlɪn'fɔːmd] adj mal informado(a)

illiteracy [ɪ'lɪtərəsɪ] n analfabetismo m

illiterate [ɪ'lɪtərɪt] **1** adj (**a**) (person) (unlettered) analfabeto(a); Fam (uneducated) ignorante, inculto(a) (**b**) (style) (poor) inculto(a), pobre **2** n (unlettered person) analfabeto(a) m,f

ill-mannered [ˌɪlˈmænəd] *adj* maleducado(a)

illness [ˈɪlnɪs] *n* enfermedad *f*

illogical [ɪˈlɒdʒɪkəl] *adj* ilógico(a)

ill-suited [ɪlˈsuːtɪd] *adj* que no congenian

ill-timed [ɪlˈtaɪmd] *adj* inoportuno(a)

ill-treat [ɪlˈtriːt] *vt* maltratar

ill-treatment [ɪlˈtriːtmənt] *n* malos tratos *mpl*, maltrato *m*

illuminate [ɪˈluːmɪneɪt] *vt* **(a)** *(light up)* iluminar, alumbrar **(b)** *Fig (clarify)* aclarar **(c)** *(manuscript)* iluminar

illuminating [ɪˈluːmɪneɪtɪŋ] *adj (experience, book)* instructivo(a); *(remark)* revelador(a)

illumination [ɪluːmɪˈneɪʃən] *n* **(a)** *(lighting up)* iluminación *f*, alumbrado *m* **(b)** *Fig (clarification)* aclaración *f* **(c)** *Br* **illuminations** *(coloured lights)* iluminación *f* sing **(d)** *(of manuscript)* iluminación *f*

illusion [ɪˈluːʒən] *n* ilusión *f*; **to be under the i. that ...** estar equivocado(a) *or* engañarse pensando que ...

illusive [ɪˈluːsɪv] *adj*, **illusory** [ɪˈluːsərɪ] *adj* ilusorio(a)

illustrate [ˈɪləstreɪt] *vt (gen)* ilustrar; *Fig (point, theory)* aclarar

illustration [ɪləˈstreɪʃən] *(gen)* ilustración *f*; *Fig (clarification)* aclaración *f*; *(example)* ejemplo *m*

illustrative [ˈɪləstrətɪv] *adj (gen)* ilustrativo(a), ilustrador(a); *Fig (example)* aclaratorio(a)

illustrator [ˈɪləstreɪtər] *n* ilustrador(a) *m,f*

illustrious [ɪˈlʌstrɪəs] *adj* ilustre

ILO [aɪelˈəʊ] *n (abbr* **International Labour Organization)** Organización *f* Internacional del Trabajo, OIT *f*

I'm [aɪm] = **I am**

image [ˈɪmɪdʒ] *n* **(a)** *(gen)* imagen *f*; *Fam* **he's the living** *or* **spitting i. of his father** es el vivo retrato de su padre **(b)** *(reputation)* imagen *f*, fama *f*, reputación *f*

image-conscious [ˈɪmɪdʒˈkɒnʃəs] *adj* preocupado(a) por la propia imagen

imagery [ˈɪmɪdʒərɪ] *n Lit* imágenes *fpl*

imaginable [ɪˈmædʒɪnəbəl] *adj* imaginable, concebible

imaginary [ɪˈmædʒɪnərɪ] *adj* imaginario(a)

imagination [ɪmædʒɪˈneɪʃən] *n (gen)* imaginación *f*; *(inventiveness)* inventiva *f*; **don't let your i. run away with you** no te dejes llevar por la imaginación; **it's a figment of your i.** son imaginaciones *or Am* fantasías tuyas

imaginative [ɪˈmædʒɪnətɪv] *adj (person)* imaginativo(a), de gran inventiva; *(writing, decor)* lleno(a) de imaginación *or* fantasía

imagine [ɪˈmædʒɪn] **1** *vt* **(a)** *(visualize)* imaginar; **I can't i. what it is** no tengo ni idea de lo que es **(b)** *(think)* suponer, figurarse, imaginarse
2 *vi* **just i.!** ¡imagínate!, ¡fíjate!

imbalance [ɪmˈbæləns] *n* falta *f* de equilibrio, desequilibrio *m*

imbecile [ˈɪmbɪsiːl] *n* imbécil *mf*

imbibe [ɪmˈbaɪb] *vt* **(a)** *Fml (alcohol etc)* beber **(b)** *Fig (ideas, knowledge)* asimilar, empaparse de, absorber

imbue [ɪmˈbjuː] *vt Fml* **to i. sb with sth** imbuir a algn de algo; **imbued with hope** lleno(a) de esperanza

IMF [aɪemˈef] *n Econ (abbr* **International Monetary Fund)** Fondo *m* Monetario Internacional, FMI *m*

imitate [ˈɪmɪteɪt] *vt (gen)* imitar, copiar; *Pej* parodiar, remedar

imitation [ɪmɪˈteɪʃən] **1** *n (gen)* imitación *f*, copia *f*; *Pej* parodia *f*, remedo *m*; *Com* **'beware of imitations'** 'desconfíe de las imitaciones'
2 *adj* de imitación

imitative [ˈɪmɪtətɪv] *adj* imitativo(a)

imitator [ˈɪmɪteɪtər] *n* imitador(a) *m,f*

immaculate [ɪˈmækjʊlɪt] *adj* *(clean)* inmaculado(a); *(tidy)* perfectamente ordenado(a); *(clothes, appearance)* impecable; *(work)* perfecto(a); *Rel* **the I. Conception** la Inmaculada Concepción, la Purísima

immaterial [ɪməˈtɪərɪəl] *adj* irrelevante; **it's i. to me whether ...** me trae sin cuidado *or* me es indiferente si ...; **my views are i.** lo que opino yo no tiene nada que ver *or* no viene al caso

immature [ɪməˈtjʊər] *adj* inmaduro(a)

immaturity [ɪməˈtjʊərɪtɪ] *n* inmadurez *f*, falta *f* de madurez

immeasurable [ɪˈmeʒərəbəl] *adj* inconmensurable, incalculable

immeasurably [ɪˈmeʒərəblɪ] *adv (long, high)* inmensamente, infinitamente; *(better, improved)* infinitamente, sumamente

immediacy [ɪˈmiːdɪəsɪ] *n* **(a)** *(urgency)* urgencia *f*, carácter *m* urgente **(b)** *(closeness)* inmediación *f*, proximidad *f*

immediate [ɪˈmiːdɪət] *adj* **(a)** *(instant)* inmediato(a); *(urgent)* urgente; **i. need** primera necesidad; **to have i. rapport (with sb)** simpatizar en seguida (con algn); **to take i. action** actuar inmediatamente **(b)** *(close) (area, family)* cercano(a), próximo(a); *(danger)* inminente; **the i. vicinity** las inmediaciones **(c)** *(direct) (cause)* primero(a), principal; *(heir)* en línea directa

immediately [ɪˈmiːdɪətlɪ] **1** *adv* **(a)** *(at once)* inmediatamente, de inmediato, en seguida, en el acto; **i. after arriving** inmediatamente después de llegar; **I i. left** acto seguido, me marché **(b)** *(directly)* directamente; **i. in front of/behind** directamente delante/detrás
2 *conj* en cuanto, tan pronto como; **i. I sat down, the waiter came** en cuanto me senté vino el camarero

immemorial [ɪmɪˈmɔːrɪəl] *adj* inmemorial

immense [ɪˈmens] *adj* inmenso(a), enorme

immensely [ɪˈmenslɪ] *adv (rich, gifted)* enormemente; *(interesting, difficult)* sumamente; **to enjoy oneself i.** disfrutar muchísimo, pasarlo en grande

immensity [ɪˈmensɪtɪ] *n* inmensidad *f*

immerse [ɪˈmɜːs] *vt* sumergir, hundir (**in** en); *Fig* **to be immersed in one's work** estar absorto(a) en el trabajo

immersion [ɪˈmɜːʃən] *n (in water etc)* inmersión *f*, sumersión *f*; *Fig (in work etc)* absorción *f*, enfrascamiento *m* ❑ **i. course** cursillo *m* intensivo; *Br* **i. heater** calentador *m* de inmersión

immigrant [ˈɪmɪgrənt] *adj & n* inmigrante *(mf)*

immigrate [ˈɪmɪgreɪt] *vi* inmigrar

immigration [ɪmɪˈgreɪʃən] *n* inmigración *f*; **to go through i.** pasar por el control de pasaportes ❑ **i. control** control *m* de pasaportes

imminence [ˈɪmɪnəns] *n Fml* inminencia *f*

imminent [ˈɪmɪnənt] *adj* inminente

immobile [ɪˈməʊbaɪl] *adj* inmóvil, sin movimiento

immobility [ɪməʊˈbɪlɪtɪ] *n* inmovilidad *f*

immobilize [ɪˈməʊbɪlaɪz] *vt* inmovilizar; *Fig* **he was immobilized by lack of funds** su proyecto estaba paralizado por falta de fondos

immoderate [ɪˈmɒdərɪt] *adj Fml (views, conduct)* desmedido(a); *(desire, appetite)* descomunal, desaforado(a); *(demands)* excesivo(a)

immodest [ɪˈmɒdɪst] *adj* **(a)** *(indecent)* indecente; *(act)* desvergonzado(a), descarado(a), impúdico(a) **(b)** *(presumptuous)* presumido(a), creído(a), engreído(a)

immodesty [ɪˈmɒdɪstɪ] n (a) *(indecency)* indecencia f, falta f de pudor; *(of act)* descaro m (b) *(presumption)* presunción f, engreimiento m

immoral [ɪˈmɒrəl] adj inmoral; **i. earnings** ganancias fpl ilícitas

immorality [ɪməˈrælɪtɪ] n inmoralidad f

immortal [ɪˈmɔːtəl] adj *(soul, god)* inmortal; *(fame, memory)* imperecedero(a), perdurable

immortality [ɪmɔːˈtælɪtɪ] n inmortalidad f

immortalize [ɪˈmɔːtəlaɪz] vt inmortalizar

immovable [ɪˈmuːvəbəl] adj (a) *(fixed)* inamovible; *(feast)* fijo(a) (b) *Fig (person)* inconmovible, inflexible; *(impassive)* impasible, inmutable

immune [ɪˈmjuːn] adj *(gen)* inmune; *(exempt)* exento(a); **to be i. from attack** no correr riesgo de ser atacado(a) □ *Med* **i. system** sistema m inmunológico

immunity [ɪˈmjuːnɪtɪ] n *(gen)* inmunidad f; *(exemption)* exención f □ **diplomatic i.** inmunidad f diplomática

immunization [ɪmjʊnaɪˈzeɪʃən] n *Med* inmunización f

immunize [ˈɪmjʊnaɪz] vt *Med* inmunizar **(against** contra)

immunodeficiency [ɪmjʊnəʊdəˈfɪʃənsɪ] n inmunodeficiencia f

immunology [ɪmjʊˈnɒlədʒɪ] n inmunología f

immutable [ɪˈmjuːtəbəl] adj *Fml* inmutable, inalterable

imp [ɪmp] n *(small devil)* diablillo m, duendecillo m; *Fig (mischievous child)* diablillo m, pillo(a) m,f

impact [ˈɪmpækt] n *(gen)* impacto m; *(crash)* choque m; *(influence)* efecto m; **on i.** al chocar; *Fig* **the poem had** or **made a great i. on me** el poema me produjo un gran impacto, el poema me impresionó mucho

impacted [ɪmˈpæktɪd] adj *(tooth)* impactado(a)

impair [ɪmˈpeər] vt *(health, efforts)* perjudicar, debilitar; *(sight etc)* dañar; *(quality)* alterar; *(efficiency)* disminuir

impale [ɪmˈpeɪl] vt *(with sword etc)* atravesar

impart [ɪmˈpɑːt] vt *Fml (news, information)* comunicar, hacer saber; *(skill, knowledge)* impartir, transmitir; *(flavour)* desprender

impartial [ɪmˈpɑːʃəl] adj imparcial

impartiality [ɪmpɑːʃɪˈælɪtɪ] n imparcialidad f

impassable [ɪmˈpɑːsəbəl] adj *(road, ground)* intransitable, impracticable; *(barrier)* infranqueable

impasse [æmˈpɑːs] n impasse m, punto m muerto

impassioned [ɪmˈpæʃənd] adj *(gen)* apasionado(a), exaltado(a); *(debate)* acalorado(a)

impassive [ɪmˈpæsɪv] adj *(expressionless)* impasible, impávido(a), imperturbable; *(indifferent)* indiferente

impatience [ɪmˈpeɪʃəns] n impaciencia f

impatient [ɪmˈpeɪʃənt] adj *(intolerant)* impaciente; *(fretful)* irritable, nervioso(a); *(eager)* impaciente, ansioso(a); **to get i. with sb** perder la paciencia con algn

impeach [ɪmˈpiːtʃ] vt *US Jur* iniciar un proceso de destitución or un impeachment contra

impeachment [ɪmˈpiːtʃmənt] n *Jur* denuncia f, acusación f; *(trial)* proceso m

impeccable [ɪmˈpekəbəl] adj impecable

impecunious [ɪmpɪˈkjuːnɪəs] adj falto(a) de dinero, necesitado(a)

impede [ɪmˈpiːd] vt *(prevent)* impedir; *(hinder)* estorbar, dificultar; *(obstruct)* poner obstáculos or trabas a

impediment [ɪmˈpedɪmənt] n *(gen)* impedimento m; *(obstacle)* estorbo m, obstáculo m; **speech i.** defecto m del habla

impel [ɪmˈpel] vt *(pt & pp* **impelled)** *(compel)* obligar **(to** a); *(urge)* incitar **(to** a)

impending [ɪmˈpendɪŋ] adj *Fml* inminente

impenetrable [ɪmˈpenɪtrəbəl] adj *(gen)* impenetrable; *Fig (mystery, thoughts)* insondable; *(character, smile)* inescrutable

imperative [ɪmˈperətɪv] **1** adj (a) *Fml (gen)* imperativo(a); *(tone, voice)* imperioso(a) (b) *(urgent)* urgente, apremiante (c) *(authoritative)* perentorio(a), autoritario(a) (d) *Ling* imperativo(a)
2 n *Ling* imperativo m

imperceptible [ɪmpəˈseptəbəl] adj *(gen)* imperceptible; *(difference, change)* insensible

imperfect [ɪmˈpɜːfɪkt] **1** adj (a) *(gen)* imperfecto(a); *(goods, sight)* defectuoso(a) (b) *Ling* imperfecto(a)
2 n *Ling* imperfecto m

imperfection [ɪmpəˈfekʃən] n imperfección f, defecto m

imperial [ɪmˈpɪərɪəl] adj (a) *(power etc)* imperial (b) *(weight, measure)* **i. gallon** galón m británico or inglés (= 4,543 litres)

imperialism [ɪmˈpɪərɪəlɪzəm] n imperialismo m

imperialist [ɪmˈpɪərɪəlɪst] adj & n imperialista *(mf)*

imperil [ɪmˈperɪl] vt *(pt & pp* **imperilled,** *US* **imperiled)** *Fml* poner en peligro, arriesgar

imperious [ɪmˈpɪərɪəs] adj imperioso(a), autoritario(a)

imperishable [ɪmˈperɪʃəbəl] adj imperecedero(a)

impermeable [ɪmˈpɜːmɪəbəl] adj impermeable

impersonal [ɪmˈpɜːsənəl] adj impersonal

impersonate [ɪmˈpɜːsəneɪt] vt *(gen)* hacerse pasar por; *(famous people)* imitar

impersonation [ɪmpɜːsəˈneɪʃən] n imitación f

impersonator [ɪmˈpɜːsəneɪtər] n imitador(a) m,f

impertinence [ɪmˈpɜːtɪnəns] n impertinencia f, descaro m

impertinent [ɪmˈpɜːtɪnənt] adj impertinente, descarado(a)

imperturbable [ɪmpəˈtɜːbəbəl] adj imperturbable

impervious [ɪmˈpɜːvɪəs] adj (a) *(rock etc)* impermeable (b) *Fig (person)* insensible **(to** a); **to be i. to reason** no atender a razones

impetuosity [ɪmpetjʊˈɒsɪtɪ] n impetuosidad f

impetuous [ɪmˈpetjʊəs] adj impetuoso(a), impulsivo(a), irreflexivo(a)

impetus [ˈɪmpɪtəs] n ímpetu m; *Fig* impulso m

impinge [ɪmˈpɪndʒ] vi *Fml* afectar **(on** a), repercutir **(on** en), hacerse sentir **(on** en)

impish [ˈɪmpɪʃ] adj travieso(a), pícaro(a)

implacable [ɪmˈplækəbəl] adj implacable

implant [ɪmˈplɑːnt] **1** vt (a) *Med (tissue, hormone)* implantar, injertar (b) *Fig (principles, ideas)* inculcar
2 [ˈɪmplɑːnt] n *Med* implantación f, injerto m

implausible [ɪmˈplɔːzəbəl] adj inverosímil, poco probable

implement [ˈɪmplɪmənt] **1** n *(tool)* herramienta f; *(instrument)* instrumento m □ **farm implements** aperos mpl de labranza
2 [ˈɪmplɪment] vt *(decision, plan)* llevar a cabo, realizar, poner en práctica; *(promise)* cumplir; *(law, policy)* aplicar

implementation [ɪmplɪmenˈteɪʃən] n *(of plan, agreement, proposal)* puesta f en práctica

implicate [ˈɪmplɪkeɪt] vt implicar **(in** en), comprometer **(in** en)

implication [ɪmplɪˈkeɪʃən] n *(gen) Esp* implicación f, *Am* implicancia f; *(consequence)* consecuencia f

implicit [ɪmˈplɪsɪt] adj (a) *(implied)* implícito(a), tácito(a)

(b) *(belief, trust)* absoluto(a); *(faith, obedience)* incondicional, ciego(a)

implied [ɪmˈplaɪd] *adj* implícito(a), tácito(a)

implore [ɪmˈplɔːr] *vt* implorar, suplicar

imploring [ɪmˈplɔːrɪŋ] *adj* suplicante, de súplica

imploringly [ɪmˈplɔːrɪŋlɪ] *adv (look)* de modo suplicante; *(beg)* en tono suplicante

imply [ɪmˈplaɪ] *vt (pt & pp* **implied)** **(a)** *(involve)* implicar, presuponer, suponer **(b)** *(hint)* insinuar, dar a entender; *(mean)* significar, querer decir

impolite [ɪmpəˈlaɪt] *adj* maleducado(a), descortés

impoliteness [ɪmpəˈlaɪtnɪs] *n* mala educación *f*, falta *f* de educación, descortesía *f*

imponderable [ɪmˈpɒndərəbəl] **1** *adj* imponderable **2 imponderables** *npl* imponderables *mpl*

import [ˈɪmpɔːt] **1** *n* **(a)** Com *(gen pl)* *(commodity)* artículo *m* importado, importación *f*; *(act)* importación *f* ❏ **i. duty** derechos *mpl* de importación **(b)** *Fml (meaning)* sentido *m*, significado *m* **(c)** *Fml (importance)* importancia *f* **2** [ɪmˈpɔːt] *vt* Com importar

importance [ɪmˈpɔːtəns] *n (gen)* importancia *f*; *(standing)* envergadura *f*; **a matter of the utmost i.** un asunto de suma importancia; **he's full of his own i.** se cree muy importante, es muy engreído; **of little i.** de poca monta *or* importancia; **to attach great i. to sth** dar *or* otorgar mucha importancia a algo

important [ɪmˈpɔːtənt] *adj (gen)* importante; *(influential)* de envergadura; **it's not i.** no importa, no tiene importancia

importantly [ɪmˈpɔːtəntlɪ] *adv* **(a)** *(speak, say)* dándose aires **(b) it's hard work and more i., badly-paid** el trabajo es difícil y, lo que es más, está mal pagado

importer [ɪmˈpɔːtər] *n* Com importador(a) *m,f*

import-export [ˈɪmpɔːtˈekspɔːt] *n* **i.-e. (trade)** importación *f* y exportación, comercio *m* exterior

importunate [ɪmˈpɔːtjʊnɪt] *adj* Fml importuno(a), molesto(a)

importune [ɪmˈpɔːtjuːn] *vt* importunar, molestar

impose [ɪmˈpəʊz] **1** *vt (force)* imponer **(on, upon** a) **2** *vi (take advantage)* **to i. on** *or* **upon** abusar de, aprovecharse de

imposing [ɪmˈpəʊzɪŋ] *adj* imponente, impresionante

imposition [ɪmpəˈzɪʃən] *n* **(a)** *(of tax, fine, beliefs)* imposición *f* **(b)** *(unfair demand)* imposición *f*, abuso *m*; **it's rather an i.** es pedir demasiado; **would it be an i. if ...?** ¿le molestaría si ...?

impossibility [ɪmpɒsəˈbɪlɪtɪ] *n* imposibilidad *f*

impossible [ɪmˈpɒsəbəl] **1** *adj (gen)* imposible; *(person)* insoportable, inaguantable; **it's not i. that ...** existe la posibilidad de que ...; **to make life i. for sb** hacerle la vida imposible a algn **2 the i.** *n* lo imposible; **to ask/do the i.** pedir/hacer lo imposible

impossibly [ɪmˈpɒsɪblɪ] *adv (gen)* de manera insoportable; **i. difficult** de una dificultad insuperable; **the train was i. late** el tren llevaba un retraso increíble; **to behave i.** comportarse de una manera insoportable

impostor, *US* **imposter** [ɪmˈpɒstər] *n* impostor(a) *m,f*

impotence [ˈɪmpətəns] *n* impotencia *f*

impotent [ˈɪmpətənt] *adj* impotente

impound [ɪmˈpaʊnd] *vt* Jur confiscar, incautarse, embargar

impoverished [ɪmˈpɒvərɪʃt] *adj (person, country)* empobrecido(a), necesitado(a); *(soil, resources)* agotado(a)

impracticable [ɪmˈpræktɪkəbəl] *adj* no factible, irrealizable, impracticable

impractical [ɪmˈpræktɪkəl] *adj (person)* poco *or* nada práctico(a); *(project, solution, etc)* poco viable *or* factible

imprecise [ɪmprɪˈsaɪs] *adj* impreciso(a)

imprecision [ɪmprɪˈsɪʒən] *n* imprecisión *f*, falta *f* de precisión

impregnable [ɪmˈpregnəbəl] *adj (fortress)* inexpugnable; *Fig (position)* inexpugnable, invulnerable

impregnate [ˈɪmpregneɪt] *vt* **(a)** *(soak)* impregnar **(with** de), empapar **(with** de) **(b)** *Fml (fertilize)* fecundar

impresario [ɪmprəˈsɑːrɪəʊ] *n (pl* **impresarios)** empresario(a) *m,f*

impress· [ɪmˈpres] *vt* **(a)** *(make an impression on)* impresionar; **I was not impressed with the film** la película me dejó frío; **to i. sb favourably/unfavourably** hacerle *or* causarle a algn buena/mala impresión **(b)** *(mark)* imprimir, marcar **(into, on** en); *(pattern)* estampar **(into, on** en); *Fig* **her advice is impressed on my memory** sus consejos están grabados en mi memoria; *Fig* **to i. sth on sb** convencer a algn de la importancia de algo

impression [ɪmˈpreʃən] *n* **(a)** *(gen)* impresión *f*; **good/bad i.** buena/mala impresión; **to be under** *or* **have the i. that ...** tener la impresión de que ...; **what's your i. of her?** ¿qué te parece ella?; **to give the i. of ...** dar la impresión de ... **(b)** *(imprint)* impresión *f*, marca *f*, señal *f*; *(in snow etc)* huella *f*; *(in wax, plaster)* hueco *m* **(c)** *(imitation)* imitación *f*; **to do impressions** hacer imitaciones **(d)** *Print (printing)* impresión *f*; *(number of copies)* edición *f*, tirada *f*

impressionable [ɪmˈpreʃənəbəl] *adj* impresionable

Impressionism [ɪmˈpreʃənɪzəm] *n* Art impresionismo *m*

impressionist [ɪmˈpreʃənɪst] *adj & n* Art impresionista *(mf)*

impressionistic [ɪmpreʃənˈɪstɪk] *adj* Art impresionista

impressive [ɪmˈpresɪv] *adj* impresionante

imprint 1 [ɪmˈprɪnt] *vt (mark)* dejar huella, marcar **(on, in** en); *(stamp)* imprimir, estampar **(on, in** en); *Fig* **his words were imprinted on my mind** sus palabras quedaron grabadas en mi memoria **2** [ˈɪmprɪnt] *n* **(a)** *(mark)* marca *f*; *(left by foot etc)* huella *f*; *(stamp)* marca *f*, sello *m* **(b)** *(publisher's name)* pie *m* de imprenta

imprison [ɪmˈprɪzən] *vt* encarcelar, meter en la cárcel

imprisonment [ɪmˈprɪzənmənt] *n* encarcelamiento *m* ❏ **life i.** cadena *f* perpetua

improbability [ɪmprɒbəˈbɪlɪtɪ] *n (of event)* improbabilidad *f*; *(of story, explanation)* inverosimilitud *f*

improbable [ɪmˈprɒbəbəl] *adj (event)* improbable; *(story, explanation)* inverosímil

impromptu [ɪmˈprɒmptjuː] **1** *adj (speech, party)* improvisado(a); *(visit, trip)* imprevisto(a) **2** *adv (spontaneously)* improvisamente, sin preparación; *(unexpectedly)* de improviso, de repente

improper [ɪmˈprɒpər] *adj* **(a)** *(gen)* impropio(a); *(conditions, method)* inadecuado(a) **(b)** *(indecent)* indecente, indecoroso(a); *(behaviour, suggestion)* deshonesto(a) **(c)** *(wrong) (use, diagnosis)* incorrecto(a)

improperly [ɪmˈprɒpəlɪ] *adv* **(a)** *(dress, behave)* impropiamente **(b)** *(speak)* mal; *(behave)* con indecencia, deshonestamente **(c)** *(use, diagnose)* incorrectamente

impropriety [ɪmprəˈpraɪtɪ] *n* Fml impropiedad *f*, falta *f* de decoro

improve [ɪmˈpruːv] *vt* **(a)** *(make better)* mejorar; *(looks, appearance)* favorecer a, caer bien a; *(beauty)* realzar; *(skill, knowledge)* perfeccionar; *(property)* hacer mejoras en; *(mind)* cultivar **(b)** *(increase)* aumentar; **to i. one's chances** ampliar (uno) sus probabilidades *or* posibilidades **2** *vi* **(a)** *(become better)* mejorar, mejorarse; *(skill,* *knowledge)* perfeccionarse; **to i. with keeping** mejorar con el tiempo (**b**) *(increase)* aumentar, subir

improve on *vt (gen)* superar, sobrepasar; *(offer, bid)* sobrepujar; **can you i. on my suggestion?** ¿se le ocurre algo mejor?

improved [ɪmˈpruːvd] *adj (system, design)* mejorado(a); **he is much i.** ha mejorado mucho

improvement [ɪmˈpruːvmənt] *n* (**a**) *(making better)* mejora *f*, mejoramiento *m; (in aim, skill)* perfeccionamiento *m;* **home improvements** reformas *fpl* domésticas; **my new car is an i. on my old one** mi coche nuevo es mejor que el que tenía antes; **there's room for i.** deja algo que desear; **to show (signs of) i.** hacer progresos, ir mejorando (**b**) *(increase)* aumento *m*

improvident [ɪmˈprɒvɪdənt] *adj Fml* (**a**) *(wasteful)* derrochador(a), despilfarrador(a), pródigo(a) (**b**) *(lacking foresight)* imprevisor(a)

improvisation [ɪmprəvaɪˈzeɪʃən] *n* improvisación *f*

improvise [ˈɪmprəvaɪz] *vt & vi* improvisar

imprudent [ɪmˈpruːdənt] *adj* imprudente

impudence [ˈɪmpjʊdəns] *n* insolencia *f*, frescura *f*, descaro *m*

impudent [ˈɪmpjʊdənt] *adj* insolente, fresco(a), descarado(a)

impugn [ɪmˈpjuːn] *vt Fml* impugnar

impulse [ˈɪmpʌls] *n (gen)* impulso *m; Fig* impulso *m*, estímulo *m;* **to act on (an) i.** dejarse llevar por un impulso; **to give in** *or* **to yield to an i.** obedecer *or* ceder a un impulso ◻ *Com* **i. buy** compra *f* por impulso

impulsive [ɪmˈpʌlsɪv] *adj* impulsivo(a), irreflexivo(a)

impunity [ɪmˈpjuːnɪtɪ] *n* impunidad *f;* **to break the law with i.** romper *or* quebrantar la ley impunemente *or* con impunidad

impure [ɪmˈpjʊər] *adj* (**a**) *(acts)* impuro(a); *(thoughts, motives)* impúdico(a), deshonesto(a) (**b**) *(air, water, etc)* contaminado(a); *(milk, oil, etc)* adulterado(a)

impurity [ɪmˈpjʊərɪtɪ] *n* (**a**) *(of act)* deshonestidad *f*, falta *f* de pudor (**b**) *(gen pl) (in air, substance)* impureza *f*

impute [ɪmˈpjuːt] *vt Fml* **to i. sth to sth/sb** *(crime, blame)* imputar *or* achacar algo a algo/algn; *(false motives)* atribuir algo a algo/algn

in¹ *(pl* **in** *or* **ins)** *abbr* **inch(es)** pulgada(s) *f(pl)*

in² [ɪn] **1** *prep* (**a**) *(place)* en; *(within)* dentro de; **a pain in one's back** un dolor de espalda; **in bed** en la cama; **in England** en Inglaterra; **in prison** en la cárcel; **in the distance** a lo lejos; **in the wardrobe** en el armario; **the light in the kitchen** la luz de la cocina (**b**) *(motion)* en; **I threw it in the fire** lo eché al fuego; **put it in your bag** métalo en tu bolso; **she arrived in Paris** llegó a París; **he fell in the river** se cayó al río (**c**) *(time) (during)* en, durante; **I haven't seen her in years** hace años que no la veo; **in May** en mayo; **in my youth** en mi juventud; **in 1945 en 1945**; **in spring** en primavera; **in the daytime** durante el día; **in the morning** por la mañana; **at ten in the morning** a las diez de la mañana; **in the sixties** en los sesenta (**d**) *(time) (within)* en; **I arrived in time** llegué a tiempo; **phone me in ten minutes** llámame dentro de diez minutos (**e**) *(time) (after)* al cabo de; **in a while he returned** volvió al cabo de un rato; **you'll learn in time** con el tiempo aprenderás (**f**) *(manner)* en; **in all honesty** con toda franqueza; **in alphabetical order** en orden alfabético; **in a loud voice** en voz alta; **in cash** en efectivo, en metálico; **in fashion** de moda; **in French** en francés; **in an odd way** de una manera rara; **in this way** de este modo; **in rows** en filas; **in writing** por escrito; **packed in sixes** envasado en cajas de seis; **they arrived in (their) thousands** llegaron a millares; **write in pencil** escribe con

lápiz (**g**) *(wearing)* en; **dressed in blue** vestido(a) de azul; **in jeans** en tejanos *or* vaqueros; **in uniform** de uniforme; **the man in a tie** el señor de la corbata; **you look good in black** el negro te sienta bien (**h**) *(weather)* a, en; **in darkness** en la oscuridad; **in daylight** a la luz del día; **in the rain** bajo la lluvia; **in the shade** a la sombra; **in the sun** al sol; **in this heat** con este calor (**i**) *(state, condition)* en; **blind in the right eye** ciego(a) del ojo derecho; **carved in wood** tallado(a) en madera; **he's in his sixties** anda por los sesenta; **in a good/bad mood** de buen/mal humor; **in bloom** *or* **flower** en flor; **in danger** en peligro; **in love** enamorado(a); **in good/bad condition** en buenas/malas condiciones; **in public/private** en público/privado; **in silence** en silencio; **to live in poverty** vivir en la miseria (**j**) *(ratio, measurement, numbers)* de; **cut in half** cortado(a) por la mitad; **in threes** de tres en tres; **one in six** uno de cada seis; **ten pence in the pound** diez peniques por libra; **two metres in length/width/depth/height** dos metros de largo/ancho/profundo/alto; **we were ten in number** éramos diez (**k**) *(profession)* en; **to be in insurance** trabajar en seguros; **to be in medicine** dedicarse a la medicina; **to be in the army** ser militar (**l**) *(person)* en; **he has it in him to win** es capaz de ganar; **you have a good friend in me** en mí tienes un buen amigo (**m**) *(after superlative)* de; **the smallest car in the world** el coche más pequeño del mundo (**n**) *(before present participle)* al; **in so doing** con ello, gracias a ello; **in spending so much** al gastar tanto (**o**) *(phrases)* **in all** en total; **in itself/himself/herself** en sí; **in that ...** dado que ..., ya que ...

2 *adv* **all in** *(price etc)* todo incluido; **in here/there** aquí/allí dentro; **let's go in** vamos adentro; **on the way in** al entrar; **to be in** *(at home)* estar (en casa); *(at work)* estar; *(train, plane, etc)* haber llegado; *(tide)* estar alta; *Sport (ball)* estar en juego; *(harvest)* estar recogido(a); *Pol (in power)* estar en el poder; *Fam (in fashion)* estar de moda; **applications must be in by the 3rd** el plazo para presentar las solicitudes finaliza el día 3; **my luck is in** estoy de suerte; **to go in and out** entrar y salir; **to invite sb in** invitar a algn a entrar; *Fam* **to be all in** estar agotado(a) *or* rendido(a); *Fam* **to be** *or* **get in on sth** estar al tanto de *or* enterado(a) de algo; *Fam* **to be** *or* **keep (well) in with sb** tener (mucha) confianza con algn; *Fam* **to have it in for sb** *Esp* tenerla tomada *or* *Méx* traerla *or* *RP* agarrársela con algn; *Fam* **we're in for a storm** vamos a tener tormenta; *Fam* **you're in for a surprise** te espera una sorpresa; *Fam* **you're in for it!** ¡la que te espera!

3 *adj Fam* (**a**) *(fashionable) (place)* de moda; *(clothes, jewellery)* del último grito; **the in crowd to be with** la gente in *or* de moda con la que hay que codearse (**b**) *(private)* particular; **an in joke** una broma privada

4 *n Fam* **ins and outs** detalles *mpl*, complicaciones *fpl*; **without going into all the ins and outs of the matter ...** sin entrar en los pormenores del caso ...

inability [ɪnəˈbɪlɪtɪ] *n* incapacidad *f*

inaccessibility [ɪnæksesəˈbɪlɪtɪ] *n* inaccesibilidad *f*

inaccessible [ɪnækˈsesəbəl] *adj* inaccesible

inaccuracy [ɪnˈækjʊrəsɪ] *n (gen)* inexactitud *f; (gen pl)* error *m*, incorrección *f*

inaccurate [ɪnˈækjʊrɪt] *adj (gen)* inexacto(a); *(statement)* erróneo(a); *(figures, total)* incorrecto(a)

inaction [ɪnˈækʃən] *n* inacción *f*

inactive [ɪnˈæktɪv] *adj* inactivo(a)

inactivity [ɪnækˈtɪvɪtɪ] *n* inactividad *f*

inadequacy [ɪnˈædɪkwəsɪ] *n* (**a**) *(lack)* insuficiencia *f* (**b**) *(inability)* incompetencia *f*, incapacidad *f* (**c**) *(defect)* defecto *m*, imperfección *f*

inadequate [ɪnˈædɪkwɪt] *adj* (**a**) *(lacking)* insuficiente (**b**) *(not capable)* incapaz, incompetente; *(unsuitable)* inade-

cuado(a); **socially i.** inadaptado(a) (**c**) *(defective)* defec-
tuoso(a), imperfecto(a)

inadmissible [ɪnəd'mɪsəbəl] *adj* inadmisible, intolerable; *Jur (evidence etc)* improcedente

inadvertent [ɪnəd'vɜːtənt] *adj* involuntario(a)

inadvertently [ɪnəd'vɜːtəntlɪ] *adv* involuntariamente,
sin querer

inadvisable [ɪnəd'vaɪzəbəl] *adj* imprudente, inconveniente, poco aconsejable

inalienable [ɪn'eɪljənəbəl] *adj Fml (right)* inalienable

inane [ɪ'neɪn] *adj (comment etc)* necio(a), fatuo(a);
(question, conversation) tonto(a), estúpido(a)

inanimate [ɪn'ænɪmɪt] *adj* inanimado(a)

inanity [ɪ'nænɪtɪ] *n (of comment etc)* necedad *f*, fatuidad *f*;
(of question, conversation) tontería, *f*, estupidez *f*

inapplicable [ɪnə'plɪkəbəl] *adj* inaplicable (**to** a); **delete
where i.** táchese lo que no proceda

inappropriate [ɪnə'prəʊprɪət] *adj (time, remark)*
inoportuno(a), inconveniente; *(clothes, behaviour)* no or
poco apropiado(a), impropio(a); **it would be i. for you to
attend** no estaría bien que Ud. asistiera

inapt [ɪn'æpt] *adj Fml* inadecuado(a), impropio(a)

inarticulate [ɪnɑː'tɪkjʊlɪt] *adj (cry, sound)* inar-
ticulado(a); *(words)* mal pronunciado(a); **she was i. with
rage** estaba tan *esp Esp* enfadada *or esp Am* enojada que no
podía ni hablar

inasmuch as [ɪnəz'mʌtʃəz] *conj Fml* (**a**) *(since, because)*
puesto que, visto que, ya que (**b**) *(in so far as)* en la medida
en que, en tanto que

inattention [ɪnə'tenʃən] *n* inatención *f*, desatención *f*,
falta *f* de atención

inattentive [ɪnə'tentɪv] *adj* desatento(a), poco atento(a),
distraído(a)

inaudible [ɪn'ɔːdəbəl] *adj* inaudible, imperceptible

inaugural [ɪn'ɔːgjʊrəl] *adj* inaugural, de apertura, de
inauguración

inaugurate [ɪn'ɔːgjʊreɪt] *vt* (**a**) *(event, scheme)* inaugurar
(**b**) *(president etc)* investir; **he was inaugurated president**
fue investido como presidente

inauguration [ɪnɔːgjʊ'reɪʃən] *n* (**a**) *(of event, scheme)*
inauguración *f* (**b**) *(of president etc)* toma *f* de posesión,
investidura *f*

inauspicious [ɪnɔː'spɪʃəs] *adj Fml (start, moment)* poco
propicio(a); *(circumstances)* desfavorable, adverso(a)

inauthentic [ɪnɔː'θentɪk] *adj* no auténtico(a), falso(a)

inborn [ɪn'bɔːn] *adj* innato(a)

inbred [ɪn'bred] *adj* (**a**) *(quality)* innato(a) (**b**) *(family)*
endogámico(a), nacido(a) de padres consanguíneos

in-built [ɪn'bɪlt] *adj (tendency, weakness)* inherente;
(feature) incorporado(a); **his height gives him an i.
advantage** su altura le proporciona una ventaja de entrada

Inc, inc [ɪŋk] *US Com (abbr* **Incorporated**) ≃ sociedad *f*
anónima, S.A.

Inca ['ɪŋkə] **1** *adj* inca, incaico(a), incásico(a)
    2 *n* inca *mf*

incalculable [ɪn'kælkjʊləbəl] *adj (loss, assets)* incalculable; *(mood)* imprevisible

incandescent [ɪnkæn'desənt] *adj* incandescente

incantation [ɪnkæn'teɪʃən] *n* conjuro *m*

incapable [ɪn'keɪpəbəl] *adj* (**a**) *(unable)* incapaz (**of** de)
(**b**) *(incompetent)* incompetente

incapacitate [ɪnkə'pæsɪteɪt] *vt Fml* incapacitar (**for**
para)

incapacity [ɪnkə'pæsɪtɪ] *n* incapacidad *f*

in-car ['ɪnkɑːr] *adj* de automóvil; **an i. stereo** un
autorradio

incarcerate [ɪn'kɑːsəreɪt] *vt Fml* encarcelar

incarceration [ɪnkɑːsə'reɪʃən] *n Fml* encarcelamiento *m*,
encarcelación *f*

incarnate [ɪn'kɑːneɪt] *adj* encarnado(a); **beauty i.** la
belleza personificada; **the devil i.** el mismísimo diablo

incarnation [ɪnkɑː'neɪʃən] *n* encarnación *f*

incautious [ɪn'kɔːʃəs] *adj* incauto(a)

incendiary [ɪn'sendɪərɪ] **1** *adj* incendiario(a)
    2 *n* (**a**) *(bomb)* bomba *f* incendiaria (**b**) *(person)*
incendiario(a) *m,f*, pirómano(a) *m,f*

incense¹ ['ɪnsens] *n* incienso *m*

incense² [ɪn'sens] *vt* enfurecer, poner furioso(a), sacar de
quicio

incensed [ɪn'senst] *adj* enfurecido(a); **to get** *or* **become
i.** enfurecerse

incentive [ɪn'sentɪv] *n* (**a**) *(stimulus)* incentivo *m*, estímulo
m, aliciente *m*; **to give sb an i.** incentivar a algn (**b**)
(payment) incentivo *m*, plus *m* or prima *f* de rendimiento

inception [ɪn'sepʃən] *n Fml* comienzo *m*, principio *m*

incessant [ɪn'sesənt] *adj (rain, noise)* incesante, inin-
terrumpido(a); *(complaints, demands)* constante, con-
tinuo(a)

incessantly [ɪn'sesəntlɪ] *adv* sin cesar *or* parar

incest ['ɪnsest] *n* incesto *m*

incestuous [ɪn'sestjʊəs] *adj* incestuoso(a); *Fig (profession, group)* endogámico(a), cerrado(a)

inch [ɪntʃ] *n* pulgada *f* (= 2,54 cm); *Fig* **he's every i. a hero**
es todo un héroe; *Fig* **I know every i. of the city** conozco
todos los rincones de la ciudad; *Fig* **i. by i.** poco a poco; *Fig*
she wouldn't budge *or* **give an i.** no quería ceder ni un
ápice; *Fig* **the car missed me by inches** por poco me
atropelló el coche; *Prov* **give him an i. and he'll take a
mile** *or* **a yard** le das la mano y te coge *or* se toma el pie

inch along, inch forward *vi* avanzar poco a poco

inch through *vt & vi* pasar poco a poco

incidence ['ɪnsɪdəns] *n* frecuencia *f*, extensión *f*

incident ['ɪnsɪdənt] *n* incidente *m*, incidencia *f*; **the visit
passed (off) without i.** la visita se desarrolló sin
incidentes

incidental [ɪnsɪ'dentəl] **1** *adj (accessory)* incidental,
accesorio(a), secundario(a); *(risk, danger)* inherente (**to** a),
propio(a) (**to** de); **i. music** música *f* de fondo
    2 incidentals *npl (gastos mpl)* imprevistos *mpl*

incidentally [ɪnsɪ'dentəlɪ] *adv* a propósito, dicho sea de
paso, por cierto

incinerate [ɪn'sɪnəreɪt] *vt* incinerar, quemar

incineration [ɪnsɪnə'reɪʃən] *n* incineración *f*, quema *f*

incinerator [ɪn'sɪnəreɪtər] *n* incinerador *m*

incipient [ɪn'sɪpɪənt] *adj Fml* incipiente

incision [ɪn'sɪʒən] *n Med* incisión *f*

incisive [ɪn'saɪsɪv] *adj (comment)* incisivo(a), mordaz,
agudo(a); *(reply)* tajante; *(mind)* penetrante

incisor [ɪn'saɪzər] *n* diente *m* incisivo, incisivo *m*

incite [ɪn'saɪt] *vt (violence)* incitar, provocar, instigar;
(crowd) incitar, provocar (**to** a); **to i. sb to do sth** incitar a
algn a hacer algo

incitement [ɪn'saɪtmənt] *n* incitación *f*, provocación *f*,
instigación *f*

incivility [ɪnsɪ'vɪlɪtɪ] *n Fml* descortesía *f*, falta *f* de cortesía

incl (**a**) *(abbr* **including**) incl. (**b**) *(abbr* **inclusive**) incl.

inclement [ɪn'klemənt] *adj Fml (weather)* inclemente

inclination [ɪnklɪ'neɪʃən] *n* **(a)** *(tendency)* inclinación *f*, tendencia *f* **(to** a); **he shows no i. to leave** no da señales de querer marcharse; **my i. is to stay** yo prefiero quedarme **(b)** *(slope)* inclinación *f*, pendiente *f* **(c)** *(bow)* inclinación *f*

incline [ɪn'klaɪn] **1** *vt* **(a)** *(tend)* **to be inclined to** tender a, tener tendencia a, inclinarse por; **if you feel so inclined** si quieres; **it is romantic but I'm that way inclined** es romántico pero es que yo soy así; **she's inclined to be mean** tiene tendencia a la tacañería **(b)** *(head)* inclinar, bajar; *(body)* inclinar
2 *vi* *(slope)* inclinarse, estar inclinado(a)
3 ['ɪnklaɪn] *n* *(slope)* pendiente *f*, inclinación *f*; **steep i.** cuesta *f* empinada

include [ɪn'klu:d] *vt* *(gen)* incluir **(in** en); *(in range, series, price)* comprender **(in** en); **the team includes two women** el equipo incluye dos mujeres; **he lost everything, his wallet included** perdió todo incluso su cartera

including [ɪn'klu:dɪŋ] *prep* incluso, inclusive; **I stayed up to and i. Friday** me quedé hasta el viernes inclusive; **there are five desserts, i. ice cream** hay cinco postres, incluido helado; **we have six children i. the baby** tenemos seis hijos contando el bebé

inclusion [ɪn'klu:ʒən] *n* inclusión *f*

inclusive [ɪn'klu:sɪv] *adj* inclusivo(a); **all-i. price** precio *m* (con) todo incluido; **pages six to ten i.** de la página seis a la diez, ambas inclusive; **the rent is i. of bills** el alquiler incluye el importe de las facturas

incognito [ɪnkɒg'ni:təʊ] **1** *n* incógnito(a) *m,f*
2 *adv* *(travel etc)* de incógnito

incoherence [ɪnkəʊ'hɪərəns] *n* incoherencia *f*; *(of speech)* ininteligibilidad *f*

incoherent [ɪnkəʊ'hɪərənt] *adj* **(a)** *(unconnected)* incoherente, inconexo(a), deshilvanado(a) **(b)** *(unintelligible)* incoherente, ininteligible

income ['ɪnkʌm] *n* *(gen)* ingresos *mpl*; *(from investment)* réditos *mpl*; **earned i.** ingresos profesionales *or* salariales; **I live on a monthly i. of $800** vivo de un sueldo de 800 dólares mensuales; **to live within one's i.** vivir de acuerdo con lo que se gana; **unearned** *or* **private i.** rentas *fpl* particulares ❑ **i. tax** impuesto *m* sobre la renta; **i. tax return** declaración *f* de impuestos

incoming ['ɪnkʌmɪŋ] *adj* *(flight, train)* de llegada; *(passenger)* que llega; *(president, government)* nuevo(a), recién elegido(a); *(tide)* ascendente; *(mail, message, call)* recibido(a)

incommunicado [ɪnkəmju:nɪ'kɑ:dəʊ] *adj* incomunicado(a)

in-company ['ɪnkʌmpəni] *adj esp Br* **i. training** formación *f* en el lugar de trabajo

incomparable [ɪn'kɒmpərəbəl] *adj* incomparable, inigualable, sin par

incomparably [ɪn'kɒmpərəblɪ] *adv* sin comparación; **i. better than ...** muchísimo mejor que ...

incompatibility [ɪnkəmpætə'bɪlɪtɪ] *n* incompatibilidad *f*; **divorce on grounds of i.** divorcio *m* por incompatibilidad de caracteres

incompatible [ɪnkəm'pætəbəl] *adj* incompatible **(with** con)

incompetence [ɪn'kɒmpɪtəns] *n* incompetencia *f*, incapacidad *f*, ineptitud *f*

incompetent [ɪn'kɒmpɪtənt] *adj* incompetente, incapaz, inepto(a)

incomplete [ɪnkəm'pli:t] *adj* *(series, account)* incompleto(a); *(task)* inacabado(a), sin terminar

incomprehensible [ɪnkɒmprɪ'hensəbəl] *adj* incomprensible

incomprehension [ɪnkɒmprɪ'henʃən] *n* incomprensión *f*

inconceivable [ɪnkən'si:vəbəl] *adj* inconcebible

inconclusive [ɪnkən'klu:sɪv] *adj* *(debate, vote, meeting)* no decisivo(a); *(reasoning)* poco convincente; *(proof)* no concluyente

incongruity [ɪnkɒŋ'gru:ɪtɪ] *n* incongruencia *f*

incongruous [ɪn'kɒŋgrʊəs] *adj* incongruente, incongruo(a), fuera de lugar

inconsequential [ɪnkɒnsɪ'kwenʃəl] *adj* de poca importancia, sin trascendencia

inconsiderable [ɪnkən'sɪdərəbəl] *adj* insignificante

inconsiderate [ɪnkən'sɪdərɪt] *adj* desconsiderado(a), inconsiderado(a), desatento(a); **how i. of you!** ¡qué falta de consideración por tu parte!

inconsistency [ɪnkən'sɪstənsɪ] *n* *(gen)* inconsecuencia *f*, inconsistencia *f*, falta *f* de lógica; *(contradiction)* contradicción *f*

inconsistent [ɪnkən'sɪstənt] *adj* *(gen)* inconsecuente, inconsistente; *(contradictory)* contradictorio(a), ilógico(a); **your evidence is i. with the facts** su testimonio no concuerda con los hechos

inconsolable [ɪnkən'səʊləbəl] *adj* inconsolable, desconsolado(a)

inconspicuous [ɪnkən'spɪkʊəs] *adj* *(not noticeable)* que pasa desapercibido(a) *or* inadvertido(a); *(discrete)* discreto(a); **to make oneself i.** pasar desapercibido(a), no llamar la atención

incontestable [ɪnkən'testəbəl] *adj* incontestable, indiscutible

incontinence [ɪn'kɒntɪnəns] *n Med* incontinencia *f*

incontinent [ɪn'kɒntɪnənt] *adj Med* incontinente

incontrovertible [ɪnkɒntrə'vɜ:təbəl] *adj Fml* incontrovertible

inconvenience [ɪnkən'vi:nɪəns] **1** *n* *(gen)* inconveniente *f*, *(annoyance)* molestia *f*, incomodidad *f*; *(difficulty)* dificultad *f*; **to put sb to i.** molestar *or* incomodar a algn; **to go to great i.** sufrir muchos inconvenientes
2 *vt* *(annoy)* molestar, causar molestia a; *(cause difficulty)* incomodar

inconvenient [ɪnkən'vi:nɪənt] *adj* *(gen)* molesto(a); *(place)* mal situado(a); *(time)* inoportuno(a), mal escogido(a); *(arrangement, design)* poco práctico(a)

incorporate [ɪn'kɔ:pəreɪt] *vt* *(integrate)* incorporar **(in, into** a); *(include)* incluir **(in, into** en); *(contain)* contener; **a lawyer was incorporated into the team** se incorporó un abogado al equipo

incorporated [ɪn'kɔ:pəreɪtɪd] *adj US Com (company)* legalmente constituido(a) en sociedad anónima

incorrect [ɪnkə'rekt] *adj* **(a)** *(answer)* incorrecto(a), equivocado(a); *(view)* erróneo(a); **you're i. in thinking that ...** te equivocas al pensar que ...; **(b)** *(behaviour)* incorrecto(a); *(dress)* impropio(a), inadecuado(a)

incorrigible [ɪn'kɒrɪdʒəbəl] *adj* incorregible

increase ['ɪnkri:s] **1** *n* *(gen)* aumento *m*; *(in number, birthrate)* incremento *m*; *(in price, temperature)* subida *f*, alza *f*; **to be on the i.** estar en aumento *or* en alza
2 [ɪn'kri:s] *vt* *(gen)* aumentar; *(price, temperature)* subir; **to i. one's efforts** redoblar sus esfuerzos; **to i. one's speed** acelerar el paso
3 *vi* *(gen)* aumentar; *(temperature)* subir; **to i. in price** subir *or* aumentar de precio; **to i. in weight/size** aumentar de peso/tamaño

increasing [ɪn'kri:sɪŋ] *adj* creciente

increasingly [ɪn'kri:sɪŋlɪ] *adv* cada vez más

incredible [ɪnˈkredəbəl] *adj* increíble; **it's i. that ...** parece mentira que ...

incredulity [ɪnkrɪˈdjuːlɪtɪ] *n* incredulidad *f*

incredulous [ɪnˈkredjʊləs] *adj* incrédulo(a); **i. smile** sonrisa *f* de incredulidad

increment [ˈɪnkrɪmənt] *n* aumento *m*, incremento *m* □ **unearned i.** plusvalía *f*

incriminate [ɪnˈkrɪmɪneɪt] *vt* incriminar, inculpar

incriminating [ɪnˈkrɪmɪneɪtɪŋ] *adj* incriminatorio(a), incriminador(a)

incubate [ˈɪnkjʊbeɪt] **1** *vt (egg)* incubar, empollar; *(virus)* incubar
 2 *vi (egg, virus)* incubarse

incubation [ɪnkjʊˈbeɪʃən] *n* incubación *f*

incubator [ˈɪnkjʊbeɪtər] *n* incubadora *f*

inculcate [ˈɪnkʌlkeɪt] *vt Fml* inculcar (**in** en)

incumbent [ɪnˈkʌmbənt] **1** *n (gen)* titular *mf*
 2 *adj Fml* **to be i. on sb to do sth** incumbir *or* corresponder a algn hacer algo

incur [ɪnˈkɜːr] *vt (pt & pp* **incurred**) *(blame, displeasure)* incurrir en; *(risk)* correr; *(debt, expenses)* contraer; *(loss)* sufrir

incurable [ɪnˈkjʊərəbəl] *adj (disease)* incurable; *Fig (loss)* irremediable; *(optimist)* incorregible

incursion [ɪnˈkɜːʃən] *n* incursión *f*

Ind *Br Pol (abbr* **Independent)** independiente *(mf)*

indebted [ɪnˈdetɪd] *adj (gen)* endeudado(a); *Fig (grateful)* agradecido(a); *Fig* **I am i. to you for your help** le agradezco su ayuda; *Fig* **to be i. to sb** estar en deuda con algn

indebtedness [ɪnˈdetɪdnɪs] *n (gen)* deuda *f*; *Fig* agradecimiento *m*

indecency [ɪnˈdiːsənsɪ] *n* indecencia *f*, obscenidad *f*

indecent [ɪnˈdiːsənt] *adj* indecente, indecoroso(a) □ *Jur* **i. assault** atentado *m* contra el pudor; *Jur* **i. exposure** exhibicionismo *m*

indecipherable [ɪndɪˈsaɪfərəbəl] *adj Fml* indescifrable

indecision [ɪndɪˈsɪʒən] *n* indecisión *f*, irresolución *f*

indecisive [ɪndɪˈsaɪsɪv] *adj* (**a**) *(person, manner)* indeciso(a), irresoluto(a) (**b**) *(evidence, victory)* poco concluyente, no decisivo(a)

indeed [ɪnˈdiːd] *adv* (**a**) *Fml (in fact)* efectivamente, en efecto, realmente, en realidad; **I was i. late but ...** de acuerdo que llegué tarde pero ... (**b**) *(intensifying use)* realmente; **I'm very sorry i.** lo siento de veras *or* de verdad; **it's very hard i.** es sumamente *or* verdaderamente difícil; **look at my new car! —car i.!, it's a banger!** mira mi coche nuevo —¿coche dices?, ¡pero si es una cafetera!; **thank you very much i.** muchísimas gracias; **that is i. a problem** eso sí (que) es un problema; **you'll come then? —i. I won't!** ¿entonces, vendrás? —¡ni hablar!, ¡claro que no!

indefatigable [ɪndɪˈfætɪgəbəl] *adj Fml* incansable, infatigable

indefensible [ɪndɪˈfensəbəl] *adj* (**a**) *(place)* indefenso(a), indefendible, indefensible, indefensable (**b**) *Fig (view)* insostenible; *(behaviour)* injustificable, inexcusable

indefinable [ɪndɪˈfaɪnəbəl] *adj* indefinible

indefinite [ɪnˈdefɪnɪt] *adj* (**a**) *(vague)* indefinido(a), vago(a), impreciso(a) (**b**) *(indeterminate)* indefinido(a), indeterminado(a); **i. strike** huelga indefinida (**c**) *Ling* indefinido(a), indeterminado(a); **i. article** artículo *m* indeterminado *or* indefinido

indefinitely [ɪnˈdefɪnɪtlɪ] *adv* indefinidamente

indelible [ɪnˈdeləbəl] *adj* indeleble, imborrable

indelicate [ɪnˈdelɪkɪt] *adj* (**a**) *(indecent)* indelicado(a), poco delicado(a) (**b**) *(tactless)* indiscreto(a)

indemnify [ɪnˈdemnɪfaɪ] *vt (pt & pp* **indemnified)** indemnizar (**for** de, por)

indemnity [ɪnˈdemnɪtɪ] *n* (**a**) *(insurance)* indemnidad *f* (**b**) *(compensation)* indemnización *f*, reparación *f*, compensación *f*

indent [ɪnˈdent] **1** *vt Typ* sangrar
 2 *vi Br Com* **to i. for sth** hacer un pedido de algo

indentation [ɪndenˈteɪʃən] *n* (**a**) *Typ* sangría *f* (**b**) *(of edge)* muesca *f*; *(of coastline)* quebradura *f*, *(of surface)* depresión *f*, hundimiento *m*, abolladura *f*

indented [ɪnˈdentɪd] *adj* (**a**) *Typ* sangrado(a) (**b**) *(coastline)* quebrado(a); *(surface)* abollado(a)

independence [ɪndɪˈpendəns] *n* independencia *f* □ *US* **I. Day** día *m* de la Independencia *(4 July)*

independent [ɪndɪˈpendənt] *adj* independiente; *Br* **i. school** colegio *m* no subvencionado por el estado; **to become i.** independizarse; **to have i. means** vivir de renta

independently [ɪndɪˈpendəntlɪ] *adv* independientemente (**of** de)

in-depth [ˈɪndepθ] *adj* minucioso(a), exhaustivo(a)

indescribable [ɪndɪˈskraɪbəbəl] *adj (gen)* indescriptible; *(spectacle, grandeur)* inenarrable; *(emotion)* indecible

indestructible [ɪndɪˈstrʌktəbəl] *adj* indestructible

indeterminable [ɪndɪˈtɜːmɪnəbəl] *adj* indeterminable

indeterminate [ɪndɪˈtɜːmɪnɪt] *adj* indeterminado(a)

index [ˈɪndeks] **1** *n (pl* **indexes** *or* **indices)** (**a**) *(in book etc)* índice *m*; *(in library)* índice *m*, catálogo *m* □ **card i.** fichero *m*; **i. card** ficha *f* (**b**) *Math* índice *m*, exponente *m*; *Econ* índice *m*; **cost-of-living i.** índice del coste de la vida (**c**) *(forefinger)* **i. finger** dedo *m* índice
 2 *vt (book etc)* poner un índice a; *(collection)* catalogar, clasificar

index-linked [ˈɪndekslɪŋkt] *adj* sujeto(a) al aumento del coste de la vida

India [ˈɪndɪə] *n* (la) India

Indian [ˈɪndɪən] **1** *adj (of America)* indio(a), amerindio(a), *Am* indígena; *(of India)* indio(a), hindú □ **I. elephant** elefante *m* asiático; **I. ink** tinta *f* china; **I. Ocean** Océano *m* Índico; **I. Summer** veranillo *m* de San Martín
 2 *n (person) (of America)* indio(a) *m,f*, amerindio(a) *m,f*, *Am* indígena *mf*; *(of India)* indio(a) *m,f*, hindú *mf* □ **Red I.** piel roja *mf*; **West I.** antillano(a) *m,f*

indicate [ˈɪndɪkeɪt] **1** *vt* indicar
 2 *vi Br Aut* poner el intermitente; **to i. left/right** indicar a la izquierda/derecha

indication [ɪndɪˈkeɪʃən] *n* indicio *m*, señal *f*; **there's every i. that** *or* **all the indications are that he'll win** todo hace suponer que ganará; **this gives some i. of his strength** esto da una idea de su fuerza

indicative [ɪnˈdɪkətɪv] **1** *adj* indicativo(a)
 2 *n Ling* indicativo *m*

indicator [ˈɪndɪkeɪtər] *n .(gen)* indicador *m*; *Br Aut* intermitente *m* □ **i. board** *(at station, in airport)* panel *m* de información

indices [ˈɪndɪsiːz] *npl see* **index**

indict [ɪnˈdaɪt] *vt Jur* acusar (**for** de), procesar (**for** por)

indictable [ɪnˈdaɪtəbəl] *adj Jur* encausable, procesable

indictment [ɪnˈdaɪtmənt] *n Jur* acusación *f*, procesamiento *m*; **to bring an i. against sb** procesar a algn; *Fig* **a damning i. of his books** una crítica feroz de sus libros

indie [ˈɪndɪ] *adj Fam (music, band)* independiente, indie

indifference [ɪnˈdɪfərəns] *n* indiferencia *f*

indifferent [ɪnˈdɪfərənt] *adj* **(a)** *(uninterested)* indiferente; it's quite i. **to me** me trae sin cuidado **(b)** *(mediocre)* pobre, regular ·

indigenous [ɪnˈdɪdʒɪnəs] *adj Fml* indígena, nativo(a)

indigestible [ɪndɪˈdʒestəbəl] *adj* indigesto(a); *Fig* **this book is very i.** este libro es muy indigesto

indigestion [ɪndɪˈdʒestʃən] *n* indigestión *f*, empacho *m*; **milk gives me i.** la leche se me indigesta, la leche me sienta mal; **to suffer from i.** tener una indigestión *or* un empacho; **you'll get i.!** ¡te vas a indigestar!

indignant [ɪnˈdɪɡnənt] *adj (person)* indignado(a); *(look, tone)* de indignación; **to get i. about sth** indignarse por algo

indignation [ɪndɪɡˈneɪʃən] *n* indignación *f*

indignity [ɪnˈdɪɡnɪtɪ] *n* indignidad *f*

indigo [ˈɪndɪɡəʊ] **1** *n (pl* **indigos** *or* **indigoes)** añil *m* **2** *adj* (de color) añil

indirect [ɪndɪˈrekt] *adj* indirecto(a) □ *Ling* **i. object** complemento *m or* objeto *m* indirecto; *Ling* **i. speech** estilo *m* indirecto; **i. taxation** impuestos *mpl* indirectos

indirectly [ɪndɪˈrektlɪ] *adv* indirectamente

indiscipline [ɪnˈdɪsɪplɪn] *n* indisciplina *f*

indiscreet [ɪndɪˈskriːt] *adj* indiscreto(a), poco discreto(a), imprudente

indiscretion [ɪndɪˈskreʃən] *n* indiscreción *f*, imprudencia *f*

indiscriminate [ɪndɪˈskrɪmɪnɪt] *adj (punishment, shooting)* indiscriminado(a); *(praise, reading)* sin criterio, sin discernimiento

indispensable [ɪndɪˈspensəbəl] *adj* indispensable, imprescindible

indisposed [ɪndɪˈspəʊzd] *adj Fml* **(a)** *(ill)* indispuesto(a) **(b)** *(disinclined)* poco dispuesto(a); **i. to help** con pocas ganas de ayudar

indisposition [ɪndɪspəˈzɪʃən] *n Fml* indisposición *f*

indisputable [ɪndɪˈspjuːtəbəl] *adj* indiscutible, incontestable, irrefutable

indissoluble [ɪndɪˈsɒljʊbəl] *adj Fml* indisoluble

indistinct [ɪndɪˈstɪŋkt] *adj (gen)* indistinto(a); *(memory)* confuso(a), vago(a); *(shape etc)* borroso(a)

indistinguishable [ɪndɪˈstɪŋɡwɪʃəbəl] *adj* indistinguible

individual [ɪndɪˈvɪdjʊəl] **1** *adj* **(a)** *(separate)* individual; *(for one)* particular, propio(a); *(personal)* personal; **each i. note** cada una de las notas, cada nota por separado **(b)** *(characteristic)* personal, particular; *(original)* original; **she has a highly i. style of dressing** es muy original en el vestir **2** *n Fam (person)* individuo *m*, tipo *m*, tío(a) *m,f*; **private i.** particular *m*

individualist [ɪndɪˈvɪdjʊəlɪst] *n* individualista *mf*

individuality [ɪndɪvɪdjʊˈælɪtɪ] *n* individualidad *f*

individually [ɪndɪˈvɪdjʊəlɪ] *adv* individualmente; **he spoke to us all i.** nos habló a todos uno por uno

indivisible [ɪndɪˈvɪzəbəl] *adj Math* indivisible

Indo- [ˈɪndəʊ] *pref* indo-

indoctrinate [ɪnˈdɒktrɪneɪt] *vt* adoctrinar

indoctrination [ɪndɒktrɪˈneɪʃən] *n* adoctrinamiento *m*

indolence [ˈɪndələns] *n Fml* indolencia *f*

indolent [ˈɪndələnt] *adj Fml* indolente, perezoso(a)

indomitable [ɪnˈdɒmɪtəbəl] *adj Fml* indomable, indómito(a)

Indonesia [ɪndəʊˈniːzɪə] *n* Indonesia

Indonesian [ɪndəʊˈniːzɪən] **1** *adj* indonesio(a)

2 *n* **(a)** *(person)* indonesio(a) *m,f* **(b)** *(language)* indonesio *m*

indoor [ˈɪndɔːr] *adj (aerial, plant)* interior; *(clothes, shoes)* de andar por casa, casero(a); *(hobby)* casero(a) □ **i. football** fútbol *m* sala; **i. games** juegos *mpl* de salón; **i. pool** piscina *f or Méx* alberca *f or RP* pileta *f* cubierta

indoors [ɪnˈdɔːz] *adv (inside)* dentro (de casa); *(at home)* en casa; **i. the house had been painted** el interior de la casa había sido pintado; **let's go i.** vamos adentro; **to stay i.** quedarse en casa

induce [ɪnˈdjuːs] *vt* **(a)** *(persuade)* inducir, persuadir **(b)** *(cause)* producir, causar; *Med (labour)* provocar

inducement [ɪnˈdjuːsmənt] *n* incentivo *m*, estímulo *m*, aliciente *m*; **as an added i.** para mayor estímulo; **material inducements** incentivo *m sing* económico

induction [ɪnˈdʌkʃən] *n* **(a)** *Med (of labour)* inducción *f* **(b)** *Elec* inducción *f* **(c)** *(reasoning)* inducción *f* **(d)** *(into new job, group)* iniciación *f*

inductive [ɪnˈdʌktɪv] *adj* inductivo(a)

indulge [ɪnˈdʌldʒ] **1** *vt* **(a)** *(child etc)* mimar, consentir; *(person)* complacer; **to i. oneself** darse gusto **(b)** *(whim)* ceder a, consentir, satisfacer; *(passion)* dar rienda suelta a **2** *vi* **(a)** *Fam (drink)* beber (demasiado) **(b)** *(luxuries)* darse el gusto (**in** de), complacerse (**in** en); *(vices)* entregarse (**in** a), abandonarse a (**in** a); **to i. in a nap** permitirse el lujo de una siesta

indulgence [ɪnˈdʌldʒəns] *n* **(a)** *(of child etc)* mimo *m*, consentimiento *m*; *(of attitude)* indulgencia *f*, tolerancia *f* **(b)** *(of whim)* satisfacción *f*, gratificación *f*; **to allow** *or* **permit oneself small indulgences** permitirse pequeños lujos; *Fam* **it's sheer self-i.!** ¡es puro vicio!

indulgent [ɪnˈdʌldʒənt] *adj* indulgente

industrial [ɪnˈdʌstrɪəl] *adj (gen)* industrial; *(accident)* de trabajo, laboral; *(disease)* profesional; *Br* **to take i. action** declararse en huelga □ **i. disease** enfermedad *f* laboral; *Br* **i. dispute** conflicto *m* laboral; **i.** *Br* **estate** *or US* **park** polígono *m* industrial; **i. relations** relaciones *fpl* laborales; **i. unrest** conflictividad *f* laboral; **i. waste** residuos *mpl* industriales

industrialist [ɪnˈdʌstrɪəlɪst] *n* industrial *mf*, empresario(a) *m,f*

industrialization [ɪndʌstrɪəlaɪˈzeɪʃən] *n* industrialización *f*

industrialize [ɪnˈdʌstrɪəlaɪz] **1** *vt (country, area)* industrializar; **to become industrialized** industrializarse **2** *vi* industrializarse

industrious [ɪnˈdʌstrɪəs] *adj* trabajador(a)

industry [ˈɪndəstrɪ] *n* **(a)** *(business)* industria *f* □ **heavy i.** industria *f* pesada; **light i.** industria *f* ligera; **steel i.** industria *f* siderúrgica **(b)** *(diligence)* diligencia *f*, aplicación *f*

inebriated [ɪnˈiːbrɪeɪtɪd] *adj* ebrio(a), embriagado(a)

inedible [ɪnˈedəbəl] *adj* incomible, incomestible

ineffable [ɪnˈefəbəl] *adj Fml* inefable

ineffective [ɪnɪˈfektɪv] *adj (cure, method)* ineficaz, inútil; *(person)* incapaz, incompetente; **the strike was i.** la huelga no surtió efecto

ineffectiveness [ɪnɪˈfektɪvnɪs] *n (of cure, method)* ineficacia *f*; *(of person)* incapacidad *f*, incompetencia *f*

ineffectual [ɪnɪˈfektʃʊəl] *adj (aim, protest)* ineficaz, inútil; *(person)* incapaz, incompetente

inefficiency [ɪnɪˈfɪʃənsɪ] *n (gen)* ineficacia *f*; *(of person)* ineptitud *f*, incompetencia *f*

inefficient [ɪnɪˈfɪʃənt] *adj (gen)* ineficaz, ineficiente; *(person)* inepto(a), poco eficiente

inelastic [ɪnɪˈlæstɪk] *adj (material, principles)* rígido(a)

inelegant [ɪnˈelɪgənt] *adj* poco elegante

ineligible [ɪnˈelɪdʒəbəl] *adj* inelegible (**for** para); **to be i. to vote** no tener derecho al voto

inept [ɪnˈept] *adj* (**a**) *(person)* inepto(a); *(treatment, attempt)* inepto(a), inapropiado(a) (**b**) *(absurd) (remark, behaviour)* estúpido(a)

ineptitude [ɪnˈeptɪtjuːd] *n* ineptitud *f*, incapacidad *f*

inequality [ɪnɪˈkwɒlɪtɪ] *n* desigualdad *f*

inequitable [ɪnˈekwɪtəbəl] *adj Fml* injusto(a)

inert [ɪnˈɜːt] *adj* (**a**) *Chem (gas etc)* inerte (**b**) *(position)* inerte, inmóvil

inertia [ɪnˈɜːʃə] *n* inercia *f*

inescapable [ɪnɪˈskeɪpəbəl] *adj* ineludible, inevitable

inessential [ɪnɪˈsenʃəl] **1** *adj* no esencial, innecesario(a)
  2 inessentials *npl* detalles *mpl or* cosas *fpl* sin importancia

inestimable [ɪnˈestɪməbəl] *adj (gen)* inestimable; *(value, cost)* incalculable

inevitability [ɪnevɪtəˈbɪlɪtɪ] *n* inevitabilidad *f*

inevitable [ɪnˈevɪtəbəl] *adj* inevitable; *Fam* **his i. jokes** sus chistes de siempre

inevitably [ɪnˈevɪtəblɪ] *adv* inevitablemente

inexact [ɪnɪgˈzækt] *adj* inexacto(a)

inexcusable [ɪnɪkˈskjuːzəbəl] *adj* inexcusable, imperdonable, injustificable

inexhaustible [ɪnɪgˈzɔːstəbəl] *adj* inagotable

inexorable [ɪnˈeksərəbəl] *adj Fml* inexorable

inexpensive [ɪnɪkˈspensɪv] *adj* económico(a), barato(a)

inexperience [ɪnɪkˈspɪərɪəns] *n* inexperiencia *f*, falta *f* de experiencia

inexperienced [ɪnɪkˈspɪərɪənst] *adj* inexperto(a)

inexpert [ɪnˈekspɜːt] *adj* inexperto(a), inhábil, torpe

inexplicable [ɪnɪkˈsplɪkəbəl] *adj* inexplicable

inexpressible [ɪnɪkˈspresəbəl] *adj Fml* inexpresable, indecible, inefable

inexpressive [ɪnɪkˈspresɪv] *adj* inexpresivo(a)

inextricably [ɪneksˈtrɪkəblɪ] *adv* inseparablemente

infallibility [ɪnfæləˈbɪlɪtɪ] *n* infalibilidad *f*

infallible [ɪnˈfæləbəl] *adj* infalible

infamous [ˈɪnfəməs] *adj* infame, ruin

infamy [ˈɪnfəmɪ] *n* infamia *f*

infancy [ˈɪnfənsɪ] *n (childhood)* infancia *f*, niñez *f*; *Fig (first stage)* infancia *f*; **a nation in its i.** una nación joven

infant [ˈɪnfənt] *n (baby)* bebé *m*; *(small child)* niño(a) *m,f* pequeño(a) □ *Br* **i. school** colegio *m* de párvulos, escuela *f* infantil

infanticide [ɪnˈfæntɪsaɪd] *n (murder)* infanticidio *m*; *(murderer)* infanticida *mf*

infantile [ˈɪnfəntaɪl] *adj* infantil

infantry [ˈɪnfəntrɪ] *n Mil* infantería *f*

infantryman [ˈɪnfəntrɪmən] *n (pl* infantrymen) *Mil* soldado *m* de infantería

infatuated [ɪnˈfætjʊeɪtɪd] *adj* encaprichado(a)

infatuation [ɪnfætjʊˈeɪʃən] *n* encaprichamiento *m*

infect [ɪnˈfekt] *vt (cut, spot)* infectar; *(food, water)* contaminar; *(person)* contagiar; *Fig* **she infected us with her optimism** nos contagió su optimismo

infection [ɪnˈfekʃən] *n (of cut etc)* infección *f*; *(of air, food)* contaminación *f*; *(with illness)* infección *f*, contagio *m*; **source of i.** foco *m* infeccioso *or* de infección

infectious [ɪnˈfekʃəs] *adj (disease)* infeccioso(a), contagioso(a); *Fig* contagioso(a)

infer [ɪnˈfɜːr] *vt (pt & pp* inferred) inferir (**from** de), deducir (**from** de)

inference [ˈɪnfərəns] *n* inferencia *f*; **to draw inferences from sth** sacar conclusiones de algo

inferior [ɪnˈfɪərɪər] **1** *adj* inferior (**to** a)
  2 *n Pej* inferior *mf*

inferiority [ɪnfɪərɪˈɒrɪtɪ] *n* inferioridad *f*

infernal [ɪnˈfɜːnəl] *adj* infernal

inferno [ɪnˈfɜːnəʊ] *n (pl* infernos) *Literary* infierno *m*; *Fig* **the house was a raging i.** la casa ardía en llamas

infertile [ɪnˈfɜːtaɪl] *adj* estéril

infertility [ɪnfəˈtɪlɪtɪ] *n* esterilidad *f*

infest [ɪnˈfest] *vt* infestar, plagar (**with** de); **shark-infested seas** mares *mpl* infestados de tiburones

infestation [ɪnfesˈteɪʃən] *n* infestación *f*, plaga *f*

infidelity [ɪnfɪˈdelɪtɪ] *n* infidelidad *f*

infield [ˈɪnfiːld] *n Sport (in baseball)* diamante *m* (interior)

infielder [ˈɪnfiːldər] *n Sport (in baseball)* jugador *m* (del diamante) interior

infighting [ˈɪnfaɪtɪŋ] *n Fig* luchas *fpl* internas

infiltrate [ˈɪnfɪltreɪt] *vt* infiltrarse en

infiltration [ɪnfɪlˈtreɪʃən] *n* infiltración *f*

infiltrator [ˈɪnfɪltreɪtər] *n* infiltrado(a) *m,f*, espía *mf*

infinite [ˈɪnfɪnɪt] *adj (gen)* infinito(a); *(love, patience, etc)* sin límites; **an i. variety of jobs** un sinfín de empleos

infinitely [ˈɪnfɪnɪtlɪ] *adv* infinitamente; **i. better** muchísimo mejor; **i. tiny** pequeñísimo(a)

infinitesimal [ɪnfɪnɪˈtesɪməl] *adj* infinitesimal, infinitésimo(a)

infinitive [ɪnˈfɪnɪtɪv] *n Ling* infinitivo *m*

infinity [ɪnˈfɪnɪtɪ] *n (gen)* infinidad *f*; *Math* infinito *m*

infirm [ɪnˈfɜːm] **1** *adj (ailing)* enfermizo(a); *(weak)* débil, endeble
  2 the i. *npl* los inválidos

infirmary [ɪnˈfɜːmərɪ] *n (hospital)* hospital *m*, clínica *f*; *(in monastery etc)* enfermería *f*

infirmity [ɪnˈfɜːmɪtɪ] *n Fml (ailment)* enfermedad *f*; *(weakness)* debilidad *f*; **the infirmities of old age** los achaques de la vejez

inflame [ɪnˈfleɪm] *vt (anger, passion)* encender, inflamar; *(curiosity)* excitar, avivar; *(crowd)* excitar; **to be inflamed with rage** rabiar

inflamed [ɪnˈfleɪmd] *adj Med* inflamado(a); **to become i.** inflamarse

inflammable [ɪnˈflæməbəl] *adj (material, fuel)* inflamable; *Fig (situation)* explosivo(a)

inflammation [ɪnfləˈmeɪʃən] *n Med* inflamación *f*

inflammatory [ɪnˈflæmətərɪ] *adj* incendiario(a)

inflatable [ɪnˈfleɪtəbəl] *adj* inflable

inflate [ɪnˈfleɪt] **1** *vt (tyre etc)* hinchar, inflar; *Fig (prices)* inflar
  2 *vi* hincharse, inflarse

inflated [ɪnˈfleɪtɪd] *adj* (**a**) *(tyre etc)* hinchado(a), inflado(a); *Fig (prices)* inflacionista, inflacionario(a) (**b**) *Pej (view, idea)* exagerado(a); **to have an i. opinion of oneself** ser muy engreído(a)

inflation [ɪnˈfleɪʃən] *n Econ* inflación *f*

inflationary [ɪnˈfleɪʃənərɪ] *adj Econ* inflacionista, inflacionario(a)

inflect [ɪnˈflekt] **1** *vt* (**a**) *(voice)* modular (**b**) *Ling (noun)* declinar; *(verb)* conjugar
  2 *vi* (**a**) *(voice)* modularse (**b**) *Ling (noun)* declinarse; *(verb)* conjugarse

inflected [ɪnˈflektɪd] *adj Ling* flexional

inflection [ɪnˈflekʃən] *n Ling* inflexión *f,* flexión *f*

inflexibility [ɪnfleksəˈbɪlɪtɪ] *n* inflexibilidad *f*

inflexible [ɪnˈfleksəbəl] *adj* inflexible

inflexion [ɪnˈflekʃən] *n see* **inflection**

inflict [ɪnˈflɪkt] *vt (blow)* dar, asestar (**on** a); *(damage, wound, suffering)* causar (**on** a); *(punishment, defeat)* infligir, imponer (**on** a); *(view, opinion)* imponer (**on** a); **to i. oneself** *or* **one's company on sb** imponer su presencia a algn

in-flight [ˈɪnflaɪt] *adj Av (meal, entertainment)* durante el vuelo

influence [ˈɪnfluəns] **1** *n* influencia *f;* **to have** *or* **be a strong i. on sb** tener mucha influencia sobre algn; **under the i. of drink/drugs** bajo la influencia del alcohol/de las drogas; *Fam* **to be under the i.** llevar una copa de más
   2 *vt* influir en *or* con; **to be easily influenced** ser influenciable

influential [ɪnfluˈenʃəl] *adj* influyente, acreditado(a)

influenza [ɪnfluˈenzə] *n Med* gripe *f,* *Col Méx* gripa *f*

influx [ˈɪnflʌks] *n* afluencia *f,* oleada *f*

info [ˈɪnfəʊ] *n (abbr* **information)** *Fam* información *f*

infomercial [ˈɪnfəʊmɜːʃəl] *n TV* publirreportaje *m*

inform [ɪnˈfɔːm] **1** *vt (gen)* informar, notificar, *CAm Méx* reportar (**of, about** de, sobre); *(police)* avisar (**of, about** de); **keep me informed** téngame al corriente
   2 *vi* **to i. against** *or* **on** denunciar, delatar

informal [ɪnˈfɔːməl] *adj* (**a**) *(occasion, behaviour)* sin ceremonia, sin etiqueta, informal; *(discussion)* entre amigos, de confianza; *(language, treatment)* familiar (**b**) *(unofficial)* extraoficial, no oficial

informality [ɪnfɔːˈmælɪtɪ] *n* (**a**) *(of occasion, behaviour)* sencillez *f;* *(of treatment)* familiaridad *f* (**b**) *(of announcement)* carácter *m* no oficial

informally [ɪnˈfɔːməlɪ] *adv (hold talks, inform)* extraoficialmente; *(dress, behave)* informalmente, de manera informal

informant [ɪnˈfɔːmənt] *n Fml* informante *mf*

information [ɪnfəˈmeɪʃən] *n* (**a**) *(news, facts)* información *f;* **a piece of i.** una información, un dato ▫ **classified i.** información *f* secreta *or* reservada; **i. bureau** centro *m* de información; **i. desk** información *f* (**b**) *Comptr* datos *mpl* ▫ **i. processing** proceso *m* de datos; **i. retrieval** recuperación *f* de la información; **i. science** informática *f;* **i. superhighway** autopista *f* de la información; **i. technology** informática *f* (**c**) *US Tel* información *f,* *Am* informaciones *fpl*

informative [ɪnˈfɔːmətɪv] *adj* informativo(a)

informed [ɪnˈfɔːmd] *adj (gen)* informado(a), enterado(a); *(up-to-date)* al corriente, al tanto; **i. guess** suposición *f* bien fundada

informer [ɪnˈfɔːmər] *n (gen)* delator(a) *m,f;* *(to the police)* informador(a) *m,f,* soplón(ona) *m,f,* chivato(a) *m,f*

infotainment [ɪnfəʊˈteɪnmənt] *n TV* programas *mpl* informativos de entretenimiento

infra dig [ɪnfrəˈdɪg] *adj Fam (behaviour, situation)* indigno(a); *(clothes)* impropio(a)

infrared [ɪnfrəˈred] *adj* infrarrojo(a)

infrastructure [ˈɪnfrəstrʌktʃər] *n* infraestructura *f*

infrequent [ɪnˈfriːkwənt] *adj Fml* poco frecuente, raro(a)

infringe [ɪnˈfrɪndʒ] **1** *vt Fml (law, rule)* infringir, transgredir, violar; *(copyright)* no respetar
   2 *vi* **to i. on** *or* **upon** *(rights)* violar, usurpar; *(privacy)* invadir, estorbar

infringement [ɪnˈfrɪndʒmənt] *n Fml (of law, rule)*

infracción *f,* transgresión *f,* violación *f;* *(of rights)* violación *f,* usurpación *f*

infuriate [ɪnˈfjʊərɪeɪt] *vt* poner furioso(a), enfurecer; **you i. me!** ¡me pones negro!, ¡me sacas de quicio!

infuriating [ɪnˈfjʊərɪeɪtɪŋ] *adj* exasperante

infuse [ɪnˈfjuːz] *vt* (**a**) *(herbs, tea)* hacer una infusión de (**b**) *Fig (courage etc)* infundir

infusion [ɪnˈfjuːʒən] *n (drink)* infusión *f,* tisana *f*

ingenious [ɪnˈdʒiːnɪəs] *adj (skilful)* ingenioso(a); *(inspired)* genial

ingenuity [ɪndʒɪˈnjuːɪtɪ] *n* ingenio *m,* ingeniosidad *f,* inventiva *f;* **to test one's i.** aguzar el ingenio

ingenuous [ɪnˈdʒenjʊəs] *adj* ingenuo(a)

inglorious [ɪnˈglɔːrɪəs] *adj* vergonzoso(a)

ingot [ˈɪŋgət] *n* lingote *m*

ingrained [ɪnˈgreɪnd] *adj (dirt)* incrustado(a); *Fig (habit, belief)* arraigado(a)

ingratiate [ɪnˈgreɪʃɪeɪt] *vt Pej* **to i. oneself with sb** darle coba a algn

ingratiating [ɪnˈgreɪʃɪeɪtɪŋ] *adj* zalamero(a), obsequioso(a)

ingratitude [ɪnˈgrætɪtjuːd] *n* ingratitud *f*

ingredient [ɪnˈgriːdɪənt] *n Culin* ingrediente *m;* *Fig* componente *m,* elemento *m*

ingrowing [ˈɪngrəʊɪŋ] *adj* **i. nail** uñero *m,* uña *f* encarnada

inhabit [ɪnˈhæbɪt] *vt Fml* vivir en, habitar, ocupar, poblar

inhabitable [ɪnˈhæbɪtəbəl] *adj* habitable

inhabitant [ɪnˈhæbɪtənt] *n* habitante *mf*

inhabited [ɪnˈhæbɪtɪd] *adj* habitado(a)

inhalant [ɪnˈheɪlənt] *n* inhalación *f,* medicamento *m* para inhalar

inhale [ɪnˈheɪl] **1** *vt (gas, vapour)* inhalar; *(air)* aspirar, respirar; *(cigarette smoke)* tragar
   2 *vi (smoker)* tragar el humo; *(patient)* aspirar, respirar

inhaler [ɪnˈheɪlər] *n* inhalador *m*

inherent [ɪnˈhɪərənt] *adj* inherente, intrínseco(a); **the risks i. in climbing** los riesgos propios del montañismo

inherit [ɪnˈherɪt] *vt* heredar (**from** de)

inheritance [ɪnˈherɪtəns] *n (wealth, title)* herencia *f;* *(act)* sucesión *f;* **to come into an i.** heredar ▫ **i. tax** impuesto *m* sobre sucesiones

inhibit [ɪnˈhɪbɪt] *vt (freedom, activity)* limitar, restringir; *(feeling, reaction)* reprimir, inhibir; *(person)* cohibir; *(sales, growth)* limitar; **to i. sb from doing sth** impedir a algn de hacer algo

inhibited [ɪnˈhɪbɪtɪd] *adj* cohibido(a)

inhibition [ɪnhɪˈbɪʃən] *n* cohibición *f,* inhibición *f*

inhospitable [ɪnhɒˈspɪtəbəl] *adj (gen)* inhospitalario(a); *(climate, place)* inhóspito(a)

in-house [ˈɪnhaʊs] **1** *adj* **in-h. staff** personal *m* en plantilla; **in-h. training** formación *f* en el lugar de trabajo
   2 *adv* **the work was done in-h.** el trabajo se hizo en la misma empresa

inhuman [ɪnˈhjuːmən] *adj* inhumano(a)

inhumane [ɪnhjuːˈmeɪn] *adj* inhumano(a)

inhumanity [ɪnhjuːˈmænɪtɪ] *n* falta *f* de humanidad, inhumanidad *f*

inimical [ɪˈnɪmɪkəl] *adj Fml (person)* hostil; *(conditions, methods)* desfavorable; *(interest)* perjudicial

inimitable [ɪˈnɪmɪtəbəl] *adj* inimitable

iniquitous [ɪˈnɪkwɪtəs] *adj Fml* inicuo(a), injusto(a)

iniquity [ɪˈnɪkwɪtɪ] *n Fml* iniquidad *f,* injusticia *f*

initial [ɪˈnɪʃəl] **1** adj inicial, primero(a); **in the i. stages** al principio

2 n inicial f, letra f inicial; **initials** (of name) iniciales fpl; (of abbreviation etc) siglas fpl

3 vt (pt & pp **initialled**, US **initialed**) firmar con las iniciales

initially [ɪˈnɪʃəlɪ] adv al principio, en primer lugar

initiate [ɪˈnɪʃɪeɪt] vt (**a**) (gen) iniciar; (struggle, talks) iniciar, entablar; (plan, reform) promover; (lawsuit) entablar (**b**) (admit) (into society) admitir (**into** en); (into knowledge) iniciar (**into** en)

initiation [ɪnɪʃɪˈeɪʃən] n (**a**) (start) iniciación f, principio m (**b**) (admission) admisión f, iniciación f

initiative [ɪˈnɪʃətɪv] n iniciativa f; **on one's own i.** por iniciativa propia

inject [ɪnˈdʒekt] vt (**a**) (drug etc) inyectar; (person) poner una inyección a; **to i. sb with a vaccine** vacunar a algn (**b**) Fig (capital) invertir; (life, hope) infundir

injection [ɪnˈdʒekʃən] n (**a**) Med inyección f; **to give sb an i.** poner una inyección a algn (**b**) Fig (of capital) inversión f; (of life, hope) inyección f

injudicious [ɪndʒʊˈdɪʃəs] adj Fml poco discreto(a), imprudente

injunction [ɪnˈdʒʌŋkʃən] n Jur interdicto m, entredicho m; **to issue/take out an i.** dar/obtener una orden or un mandato

injure [ˈɪndʒər] vt (**a**) (gen) herir, lesionar, lastimar; **to i. oneself** hacerse daño (**b**) Fig (feelings) herir; (health, economy, reputation) perjudicar

injured [ˈɪndʒəd] **1** adj (**a**) (gen) lesionado(a), lastimado(a), herido(a) (**b**) Fig (feelings) herido(a); (look, tone) ofendido(a)

2 the i. npl los heridos

injurious [ɪnˈdʒʊərɪəs] adj Fml perjudicial

injury [ˈɪndʒərɪ] n (**a**) (hurt) herida f, lesión f; **to do oneself an i.** esp Esp hacerse daño, esp Am lastimarse ◻ Br Sport **i. time** (tiempo m de) descuento m (**b**) Fig (harm) daño m, perjuicio m

injustice [ɪnˈdʒʌstɪs] n injusticia f; **to do sb an i.** ser injusto(a) con algn

ink [ɪŋk] n tinta f ◻ **invisible i.** tinta f simpática

ink in vt repasar con tinta

inkling [ˈɪŋklɪŋ] n (idea) idea f, noción f, impresión f; (suspicion) sospecha f; (sign) señal m, indicio m; **I hadn't an i. that he was married** no tenía la menor idea de que estaba casado

inkpad [ˈɪŋkpæd] n almohadilla f

inkwell [ˈɪŋkwel] n tintero m

inky [ˈɪŋkɪ] adj (**inkier, inkiest**) (**a**) (fingers etc) manchado(a) de tinta (**b**) Fig (night etc) negro(a)

inlaid [ɪnˈleɪd] **1** pt & pp see **inlay**

2 adj (wood) taraceado(a); (iron, gold) damasquinado(a); (marquetry) adornado(a) con marquetería; (ivory, gems) incrustado(a)

inland [ˈɪnlənd] **1** adj (del) interior ◻ Br **the I. Revenue** ≃ Hacienda f, Esp ≃ la Agencia Tributaria, Méx ≃ el Servicio de Administración Tributaria

2 [ɪnˈlænd] adv (**a**) (live) en el interior (**b**) (travel) tierra adentro, hacia el interior

in-laws [ˈɪnlɔːz] npl Fam familia f sing política

inlay [ˈɪnleɪ] **1** n (**a**) (in wood) taracea f; (in metal) damasquinado m; (of marquetry) marquetería f (**b**) (in tooth) empaste m, Am emplomadura f, Chile tapadura f, Col calza f

2 [ɪnˈleɪ] vt (pt & pp **inlaid**) (wood) taracear; (iron, gold) damasquinar; (ivory, gem) incrustar

inlet [ˈɪnlet] n (**a**) (in coastline) ensenada f, cala f; (between

islands) brazo m de mar (**b**) (in pipe, machine) entrada f, admisión f

inmate [ˈɪnmeɪt] n (gen) residente mf, habitante mf; (of prison) preso(a) m,f, interno(a) m,f; (of hospital) enfermo(a) m,f, hospitalizado(a) m,f; (of asylum, camp) internado(a) m,f

inmost [ˈɪnməʊst] adj see **innermost**

inn [ɪn] n (with lodging) posada f, mesón m, fonda f; (in country) venta f; (pub) taberna f

innards [ˈɪnədz] npl entrañas fpl, tripas fpl

innate [ɪˈneɪt] adj innato(a)

inner [ˈɪnər] adj (**a**) (room, region) interior; (structure, organization) interno(a) ◻ **i. city** = área céntrica y degradada de una ciudad; **i. ear** oído m interno; **i. tube** cámara f de aire (**b**) Fig (thoughts, feelings) interior, íntimo(a); (peace etc) profundo(a)

innermost [ˈɪnəməʊst] adj (**a**) (room, recess) más interior (**b**) Fig (thoughts, feelings) más íntimo(a), más secreto(a)

innings [ˈɪnɪŋz] n (in cricket) turno m para batear, Am inning m; Br Fam Fig **to have had a good i.** haber disfrutado de una vida larga y feliz

innkeeper [ˈɪnkiːpər] n (of lodging house) posadero(a) m,f, mesonero(a) m,f; (of pub) tabernero(a) m,f

innocence [ˈɪnəsəns] n inocencia f

innocent [ˈɪnəsənt] adj & n inocente (mf)

innocuous [ɪˈnɒkjʊəs] adj inocuo(a), inofensivo(a)

innovate [ˈɪnəveɪt] vi innovar

innovation [ɪnəˈveɪʃən] n innovación f, novedad f

innovative [ˈɪnəvətɪv] adj, **innovatory** [ɪnəˈveɪtərɪ] adj innovador(a)

innovator [ˈɪnəveɪtər] n innovador(a) m,f

innuendo [ɪnjʊˈendəʊ] n (pl **innuendoes** or **innuendos**) indirecta f, insinuación f

innumerable [ɪˈnjuːmərəbəl] adj innumerable

innumerate [ɪˈnjuːmərət] adj falto(a) de conocimientos de aritmética

inoculate [ɪˈnɒkjʊleɪt] vt inocular, vacunar

inoculation [ɪnɒkjʊˈleɪʃən] n inoculación f, vacuna f

inoffensive [ɪnəˈfensɪv] adj inofensivo(a)

inoperable [ɪnˈɒpərəbəl] adj Med inoperable

inoperative [ɪnˈɒpərətɪv] adj inoperante

inopportune [ɪnˈɒpətjuːn] adj inoportuno(a)

inordinate [ɪˈnɔːdɪnɪt] adj Fml (**a**) (uncontrolled) desmesurado(a), desmedido(a) (**b**) (excessive) excesivo(a)

inorganic [ɪnɔːˈgænɪk] adj inorgánico(a)

inpatient [ˈɪnpeɪʃənt] n interno(a) m,f, internado(a) m,f

input [ˈɪnpʊt] **1** n (of capital, resources) inversión f; (of power) entrada f; Comptr (of data) input m

2 (pt & pp **input**) vt Comptr entrar, introducir

inquest [ˈɪnkwest] n encuesta f judicial; Fam Fig investigación f

inquire [ɪnˈkwaɪər] **1** vt (ask) preguntar; (find out) averiguar; Fml **to i. sth of sb** preguntar algo a algn

2 vi (ask) preguntar (**about** por); (find out) informarse (**about** de), pedir informes (**about** sobre); **'i. within'** 'razón aquí'

inquire after vt (person, person's health) preguntar por

inquire into vt (case, matter) investigar, indagar

inquiring [ɪnˈkwaɪərɪŋ] adj (look etc) de interrogación; (mind) curioso(a), inquisidor(a)

inquiry [ɪnˈkwaɪərɪ] n (**a**) (question) pregunta f; **'all inquiries to ...'** 'dirigirse a ...'; **'inquiries'** 'información'; **to make inquiries (about sth)** pedir informes (sobre algo) ◻ **i. desk** información f (**b**) (investigation) investigación f, encuesta *f*; **to set up** *or* **open an i.** abrir una investigación; **we are making inquiries** estamos investigando

inquisition [ɪnkwɪˈzɪʃən] *n* investigación *f*, inquisición *f*; *Hist* **the (Spanish) I.** la Inquisición

inquisitive [ɪnˈkwɪzɪtɪv] *adj (curious)* curioso(a), inquisidor(a); *(questioning)* preguntón(ona)

inquisitively [ɪnˈkwɪzɪtɪvlɪ] *adv* con curiosidad

inroads [ˈɪnrəʊdz] *npl* **the firm is making i. into the market** la empresa está ganando terreno *or* se está abriendo camino en el mercado; **to make i. on one's free time** quitarle a uno sus horas libres; **to make i. into one's capital** reducir *or* mermar su capital

insane [ɪnˈseɪn] **1** *adj (person)* loco(a), demente; *(act)* insensato(a); **to go i.** enloquecer, volverse loco(a); *Fig* **to drive sb i.** volver loco(a) a algn; *Fam* **what an i. idea!** ¡vaya locura! □ *US* **i. asylum** manicomio *m*
2 *npl* **the i.** los enfermos mentales

insanely [ɪnˈseɪnlɪ] *adv Fig* **i. jealous** loco(a) de celos

insanitary [ɪnˈsænɪtərɪ] *adj* insalubre, antihigiénico(a)

insanity [ɪnˈsænɪtɪ] *n* **(a)** *Med (madness)* demencia *f*, locura *f* **(b)** *Fig (stupidity)* locura *f*, insensatez *f*

insatiable [ɪnˈseɪʃəbəl] *adj* insaciable

inscribe [ɪnˈskraɪb] *vt (name, tombstone)* inscribir, grabar; *(book, photo)* dedicar; *(name, initials)* inscribir

inscription [ɪnˈskrɪpʃən] *n (on stone, coin)* inscripción *f*; *(in book, on photo)* dedicatoria *f*

inscrutable [ɪnˈskruːtəbəl] *adj* inescrutable, insondable, impenetrable

insect [ˈɪnsekt] *n* insecto *m* □ **i. bite** picadura *f*

insecticide [ɪnˈsektɪsaɪd] *n* insecticida *m*

insecure [ɪnsɪˈkjʊər] *adj* inseguro(a)

insecurity [ɪnsɪˈkjʊərɪtɪ] *n* inseguridad *f*

inseminate [ɪnˈsemɪneɪt] *vt* inseminar

insensible [ɪnˈsensəbəl] *adj Fml* **(a)** *(unconscious)* inconsciente, sin conocimiento **(b)** *(unaware)* inconsciente **(c)** *(unfeeling)* insensible

insensitive [ɪnˈsensɪtɪv] *adj* insensible

insensitivity [ɪnsensɪˈtɪvɪtɪ] *n* insensibilidad *f*

inseparable [ɪnˈsepərəbəl] *adj* inseparable

insert [ˈɪnsɜːt] **1** *n (in journal etc)* encarte *m*
2 [ɪnˈsɜːt] *vt (gen)* introducir, meter (**in, into** en); *(clause, text)* incluir, insertar (**in, into** en); *(advertisement)* poner (**in, into** en)

insertion [ɪnˈsɜːʃən] *n (gen)* introducción *f*; *(of clause, text)* inclusión *f*, inserción *f*; *(in newspaper)* anuncio *m*

inset [ˈɪnset] *n (in map, picture)* recuadro *m*

inshore [ˈɪnʃɔːr] **1** *adj (fishing, navigation)* costero(a); *(wind)* de mar
2 [ɪnˈʃɔːr] *adv (fish, sail)* cerca de la costa; *(blow)* hacia la costa

inside [ɪnˈsaɪd] **1** *n* **(a)** *(interior)* interior *m*, parte *f* interior; **gloves with fur on the i.** guantes *mpl* forrados de piel; **on/ from the i.** por/de dentro; **to know sb i. out** conocer muy bien a algn; **to know sth i. out** conocer algo al dedillo; *Aut* **to overtake on the i.** *(in Britain)* adelantar por la izquierda; *(in the US, Europe, etc)* adelantar por la derecha; **to turn sth i. out** volver algo al revés; *Fam* **someone on the i. told me** me lo dijo alguien de dentro **(b)** *Fam* **insides** tripas *fpl*
2 [ˈɪnsaɪd] *adj* interior; *Sport* **i. forward** interior *mf*; *Aut* **i. lane** carril *m* interior; *Sport* **i. left/right** interior *mf* izquierda/derecha; *Fam* **i. information** información *f* confidencial *or* privilegiada; *Fam* **i. story** *(of scandal)* revelaciones *fpl* íntimas; *(of event)* relato *m* de uno de los protagonistas; *Fam* **the robbery was an i. job** el robo fue organizado por alguien de dentro

3 [ɪnˈsaɪd] *adv (be, stay)* dentro, *Am* adentro; *(run etc)* hacia *or* para adentro; **please come** *or* **step i.** pase, por favor; **to come** *or* **go i.** entrar; **we looked i. and outside** miramos por dentro y por fuera; *Fig* **to feel funny i.** tener una sensación rara en el estómago; *Br Fam* **he spent a year i.** pasó un año en *Esp* chirona *or* Andes Cuba RP cana *or* Méx Ven bote
4 *prep* **(a)** *(place)* dentro de; *Aut* **to be travelling i. the speed limit** circular dentro del límite de velocidad **(b)** *Fam* **i. (of)** *(time)* en menos de, dentro de

insider [ɪnˈsaɪdər] *n* persona *f* enterada □ *Jur Fin* **i. dealing** *or* **trading** uso *m* indebido de información privilegiada y confidencial para operaciones comerciales

insidious [ɪnˈsɪdɪəs] *adj* insidioso(a)

insight [ˈɪnsaɪt] *n* **(a)** *(perception)* penetración *f*, perspicacia *f* **(b)** *(understanding)* idea *f*; **to get an i. into sth** hacerse una idea de algo

insignia [ɪnˈsɪgnɪə] *n inv* insignia *f*

insignificance [ɪnsɪgˈnɪfɪkəns] *n* insignificancia *f*

insignificant [ɪnsɪgˈnɪfɪkənt] *adj* insignificante

insincere [ɪnsɪnˈsɪər] *adj* poco sincero(a), insincero(a), falso(a)

insincerity [ɪnsɪnˈserɪtɪ] *n* falta *f* de sinceridad, insinceridad *f*, falsedad *f*

insinuate [ɪnˈsɪnjʊeɪt] *vt* **(a)** *(hint)* insinuar, dar a entender **(b)** *Fml (introduce)* **to i. oneself into sb's favour** ganarse arteramente el favor de algn

insinuation [ɪnsɪnjʊˈeɪʃən] *n* insinuación *f*, indirecta *f*

insipid [ɪnˈsɪpɪd] *adj* insípido(a), soso(a), insulso(a)

insist [ɪnˈsɪst] **1** *vi (gen)* insistir (**on, upon** en); *(argue)* obstinarse (**on, upon** en); **I i. on coming** insisto en ir
2 *vt* **to i. that …** insistir en que …

insistence [ɪnˈsɪstəns] *n* insistencia *f*, empeño *m*; **at my i.** ante mi insistencia

insistent [ɪnˈsɪstənt] *adj* **(a)** *(person)* insistente, obstinado(a); **I was most i. about it** insistí mucho en ello **(b)** *(demand, noise)* persistente

in so far as [ɪnsəʊˈfɑːrəz] *adv* en la medida en que, en tanto que

insole [ˈɪnsəʊl] *n (of shoe)* plantilla *f*

insolence [ˈɪnsələns] *n* insolencia *f*, descaro *m*, frescura *f*

insolent [ˈɪnsələnt] *adj* insolente, descarado(a), fresco(a)

insoluble [ɪnˈsɒljʊbəl] *adj* insoluble, indisoluble

insolvency [ɪnˈsɒlvənsɪ] *n* insolvencia *f*

insolvent [ɪnˈsɒlvənt] *adj* insolvente

insomnia [ɪnˈsɒmnɪə] *n* insomnio *m*

insomniac [ɪnˈsɒmnɪæk] *n* insomne *mf*

insomuch as [ɪnsəʊˈmʌtʃəz] *conj* **(a)** *(inasmuch as)* puesto que, visto que, ya que **(b)** *(to such an extent that)* hasta tal punto que

insouciance [ɪnˈsuːsɪəns] *n Fml* despreocupación *f*, indiferencia *f*

Insp *(abbr* **Inspector)** Inspector(a) *m*,*f*, Inspec

inspect [ɪnˈspekt] *vt* **(a)** *(gen)* inspeccionar, examinar, revisar; *(luggage etc)* registrar **(b)** *(troops)* pasar revista a; *(school)* inspeccionar

inspection [ɪnˈspekʃən] *n* **(a)** *(gen)* inspección *f*, examen *m*, revisión *f*; *(of luggage etc)* registro *m*; **to make a detailed i. of sth** examinar algo minuciosamente **(b)** *(of troops)* revista *f*; *(of school)* (visita *f* de) inspección *f*

inspector [ɪnˈspektər] *n (of schools, factories)* inspector(a) *m*,*f*; *Br (on bus, train)* revisor(a) *m*,*f* □ *Br* **(police) i.** inspector(a) *m*,*f* de policía; *Br* **tax i.** inspector(a) *m*,*f* de hacienda

inspectorate [ɪnˈspektərɪt] n cuerpo m de inspectores
inspiration [ɪnspɪˈreɪʃən] n inspiración f; **to get** or **draw i. from sth/sb** inspirarse en algo/algn
inspirational [ɪnspɪˈreɪʃənəl] adj inspirador(a)
inspire [ɪnˈspaɪər] vt (**a**) (feeling, novel) inspirar; **to i. respect in sb, to i. sb with respect** infundir respeto a algn (**b**) (effort) estimular, animar; **it inspired me to try harder** me animó a esforzarme más
inspired [ɪnˈspaɪəd] adj inspirado(a)
inspiring [ɪnˈspaɪərɪŋ] adj inspirador(a)
Inst (abbr **Institute**) Instituto m, Inst
instability [ɪnstəˈbɪlɪtɪ] n inestabilidad f
install, US **instal** [ɪnˈstɔːl] vt (pp & pp **installed**) (**a**) (fit) instalar; Fml **to i. oneself in an armchair** instalarse en un sillón (**b**) (appoint) nombrar
installation [ɪnstəˈleɪʃən] n (**a**) (of equipment) instalación f (**b**) (appointment) nombramiento m
instalment, US **installment** [ɪnˈstɔːlmənt] n (**a**) (of payment) plazo m; **to pay by** or **in instalments** pagar a plazos ▫ **annual i.** anualidad f; US **i. plan** venta f or compra f a plazos or Am en cuotas; **monthly i.** mensualidad f (**b**) (of novel, programme) entrega f; (of journal) fascículo m
instance [ˈɪnstəns] n ejemplo m, caso m; **for i.** por ejemplo; **in the first i.** en primer lugar; **in this i.** en este caso
instant [ˈɪnstənt] **1** n (moment) instante m, momento m; **do it this i.!** ¡hazlo ahora mismo!; **in an i.** (soon) de un momento a otro; (quickly) en un instante; **not an i. too soon** justo a tiempo; **the i. I saw you** en cuanto te vi
2 adj (gen) inmediato(a); (coffee, meal) instantáneo(a); **I took an i. liking to him** me cayó bien enseguida; US TV **i. replay** repetición f (a cámara lenta)
instantaneous [ɪnstənˈteɪnɪəs] adj instantáneo(a)
instantly [ˈɪnstəntlɪ] adv inmediatamente, al instante; **he died i.** su muerte fue instantánea
instead [ɪnˈsted] **1** adv en lugar de eso, en cambio
2 prep **i. of** en vez de, en lugar de; **I went i. of her** fui yo en su lugar
instep [ˈɪnstep] n empeine m
instigate [ˈɪnstɪgeɪt] vt instigar
instigation [ɪnstɪˈgeɪʃən] n instigación f
instigator [ˈɪnstɪgeɪtər] n instigador(a) m,f
instil, US **instill** [ɪnˈstɪl] vt (pt & pp **instilled**) (idea, habit) inculcar (**in** a, en); (courage, respect) infundir (**in** a)
instinct [ˈɪnstɪŋkt] n instinto m; **to have an i. for sth/for doing sth** tener un don para algo/para hacer algo
instinctive [ɪnˈstɪŋktɪv] adj instintivo(a), intuitivo(a)
institute [ˈɪnstɪtjuːt] **1** n (gen) instituto m; (centre) centro m; (professional body) asociación f, colegio m
2 vt Fml (**a**) (system, rules) establecer; (society) fundar, empezar (**b**) (start) iniciar, empezar; (proceedings) entablar
institution [ɪnstɪˈtjuːʃən] n (**a**) (act) institución f, creación f (**b**) (organization) institución f, organismo m (**c**) (home) asilo m; (asylum) manicomio m (**d**) (habit, custom) institución f, tradición f
institutional [ɪnstɪˈtjuːʃənəl] adj institucional
institutionalize [ɪnstɪˈtjuːʃənəlaɪz] vt (**a**) (practice) institucionalizar (**b**) (person) meter en un asilo or manicomio
in-store [ˈɪnstɔːr] adj Com **i. advertising** publicidad f en el punto de venta; **i. promotion** promoción f en el punto de venta
instruct [ɪnˈstrʌkt] vt (**a**) (teach) instruir, enseñar (**b**) (order) mandar; **I am instructed to say that ...** me han encargado decir que ...

instruction [ɪnˈstrʌkʃən] n (**a**) (teaching) instrucción f, enseñanza f; **driving i.** clases fpl de conducir (**b**) **instructions** instrucciones fpl; **'instructions for use'** 'modo de empleo'; **on the instructions of the boss** por orden del jefe; **i. manual** manual m de instrucciones
instructive [ɪnˈstrʌktɪv] adj instructivo(a), formativo(a)
instructor [ɪnˈstrʌktər] n (gen) instructor(a) m,f; (of driving) profesor(a) m,f; (of sport) monitor(a) m,f; US (university lecturer) profesor(a) m,f de universidad
instructress [ɪnˈstrʌktrɪs] n (gen) instructora f; (of driving) profesora f; (of sport) monitora f
instrument [ˈɪnstrəmənt] n instrumento m ▫ Aut Av Naut **i. panel** tablero m de mandos
instrumental [ɪnstrəˈmentəl] adj (**a**) Mus instrumental (**b**) Fml **to be i. in sth/in doing sth** contribuir decisivamente a algo/a hacer algo
instrumentalist [ɪnstrəˈmentəlɪst] n Mus instrumentista mf
instrumentation [ɪnstrəmenˈteɪʃən] n (**a**) Aut Av Naut instrumentos mpl (**b**) Mus instrumentación f
insubordinate [ɪnsəˈbɔːdɪnɪt] adj insubordinado(a), indisciplinado(a)
insubordination [ɪnsəbɔːdɪˈneɪʃən] n insubordinación f, indisciplina f
insubstantial [ɪnsəbˈstænʃəl] adj (gen) insubstancial; (meal) poco nutritivo(a); (structure) poco sólido(a), poco seguro(a); (evidence) flojo(a)
insufferable [ɪnˈsʌfərəbəl] adj insoportable, inaguantable, insufrible
insufferably [ɪnˈsʌfrəblɪ] adv **i. rude** extremadamente grosero(a)
insufficient [ɪnsəˈfɪʃənt] adj insuficiente
insular [ˈɪnsjʊlər] adj (**a**) Geog insular (**b**) Fig Pej estrecho(a) de miras
insularity [ɪnsjʊˈlærɪtɪ] n (**a**) Geog insularidad f (**b**) Fig Pej estrechez f de miras
insulate [ˈɪnsjʊleɪt] vt aislar (**against, from** de)
insulating tape [ˈɪnsjʊleɪtɪŋteɪp] n Br Elec cinta f aislante
insulation [ɪnsjʊˈleɪʃən] n aislamiento m
insulin [ˈɪnsjʊlɪn] n insulina f
insult **1** n (words) insulto m; (action) afrenta f, ofensa f, ultraje m; Fig **to add i. to injury** para colmo
2 [ɪnˈsʌlt] vt insultar, ofender
insulting [ɪnˈsʌltɪŋ] adj insultante, ofensivo(a)
insuperable [ɪnˈsuːpərəbəl] adj insuperable
insurance [ɪnˈʃʊərəns] n seguro m; **to take out i.** hacerse or contratar un seguro ▫ **fire i.** seguro m contra incendios; **fully comprehensive i.** seguro m a todo riesgo; **i. broker** agente mf or Am corredor(a) m,f de seguros; **i. claim** reclamación f or Col CSur reclamo m al seguro; **i. company** compañía f de seguros; **i. cover** cobertura f del seguro; **i. policy** póliza f (de seguro); **i. premium** prima f (de seguro); **i. value** valor m asegurado; **life i.** seguro m de vida; **private health i.** seguro m médico privado; **third party i.** seguro m a terceros
insure [ɪnˈʃʊər] vt asegurar (**against** contra); **to i. oneself** or **one's life** hacerse un seguro de vida
insured [ɪnˈʃʊəd] adj & n asegurado(a) (m,f)
insurer [ɪnˈʃʊərər] n asegurador(a) m,f
insurgent [ɪnˈsɜːdʒənt] adj & n insurgente (mf), insurrecto(a), (m,f)
insurmountable [ɪnsəˈmaʊntəbəl] adj (problem etc) insuperable; (barrier) infranqueable
insurrection [ɪnsəˈrekʃən] n insurreción f

intact [ɪn'tækt] *adj* intacto(a)

intake ['ɪnteɪk] *n* (**a**) *Tech (of air, water)* entrada *f*; *(of electricity, water, gas)* toma *f* (**b**) *(of food, calories)* consumo *m* (**c**) *(of students, recruits)* número *m* de admitidos *or* inscritos

intangible [ɪn'tændʒɪbəl] *adj* intangible

integer ['ɪntɪdʒər] *n Math* (número *m*) entero *m*

integral ['ɪntɪɡrəl] **1** *adj* (**a**) *(intrinsic)* integrante (**b**) *(whole)* íntegro(a) (**c**) *Math* integral
  2 *n Math* integral *f*

integrate ['ɪntɪɡreɪt] **1** *vt* integrar (**into, with** en), incorporar (**into, with** a)
  2 *vi* integrarse (**into, with** en), incorporarse (**into, with** a)

integrated ['ɪntɪɡreɪtɪd] *adj* integrado(a)

integration [ɪntɪ'ɡreɪʃən] *n* integración *f*

integrity [ɪn'teɡrɪtɪ] *n* integridad *f*, honradez *f*

intellect ['ɪntɪlekt] *n* inteligencia *f*, intelecto *m*

intellectual [ɪntɪ'lektʃʊəl] *adj & n* intelectual *(mf)*

intelligence [ɪn'telɪdʒəns] *n* (**a**) *(gen)* inteligencia *f* ❑ *Comptr* **artificial i.** inteligencia *f* artificial; **i. quotient** cociente *m* intelectual (**b**) *(information)* espionaje *m*, información *f* ❑ **i. officer** oficial *m* del servicio de información

intelligent [ɪn'telɪdʒənt] *adj* inteligente

intelligentsia [ɪntelɪ'dʒentsɪə] *n* intelectualidad *f*

intelligible [ɪn'telɪdʒəbəl] *adj* inteligible, comprensible

intemperate [ɪn'tempərɪt] *adj Fml (behaviour, habits)* inmoderado(a); *(drunkard)* dado(a) a la bebida; *(climate)* riguroso(a)

intend [ɪn'tend] *vt* (**a**) *(mean)* tener la intención de, proponerse, querer; **I i. you to be happy** quiero que seas feliz; **I intended no harm** no lo hice con mala intención; **it was intended as a joke** era sólo una broma; **to i. to do sth, i. doing sth** tener el propósito de hacer algo; **was that intended?** ¿fue intencionado? (**b**) *(destine)* **to i. sth for sb** destinar algo a algn; **that place was intended for me** ese sitio estaba reservado para mí; **the film is intended for children** la película es para niños

intended [ɪn'tendɪd] **1** *adj* (**a**) *(deliberate)* intencionado(a), deliberado(a) (**b**) *(planned)* previsto(a), proyectado(a); **it had the i. effect** consiguió el efecto deseado
  2 *n Old-fashioned or Hum* prometido(a) *m,f*

intense [ɪn'tens] *adj (gen)* intenso(a), fuerte; *(look)* penetrante; *(person)* muy serio(a); *(difficulty)* enorme, sumo(a)

intensely [ɪn'tenslɪ] *adv (extremely)* enormemente, sumamente; **to dislike sb i.** tener una fuerte aversión a algn

intensifier [ɪn'tensɪfaɪər] *n Ling* intensivo *m*, intensificador *m*

intensify [ɪn'tensɪfaɪ] **1** *vt (pt & pp* **intensified)** *(search)* intensificar; *(effort)* redoblar; *(production, pollution)* aumentar
  2 *vi* intensificarse, aumentar

intensity [ɪn'tensɪtɪ] *n* intensidad *f*

intensive [ɪn'tensɪv] *adj (course, farming)* intensivo(a); *(activity, study)* profundo(a) ❑ *Med* **i. care unit** unidad *f* de cuidados intensivos, unidad *f* de vigilancia *or Méx RP* terapia *f* intensiva

intent [ɪn'tent] **1** *adj* (**a**) *(absorbed)* absorto(a); *(gaze etc)* atento(a) (**b**) *(resolved)* decidido(a); **to be i. on doing sth** estar resuelto(a) *or* decidido(a) a hacer algo
  2 *n Fml* intención *f*, propósito *m*; **to all intents and purposes** a todos los efectos

intention [ɪn'tenʃən] *n* intención *f*, propósito *m*

intentional [ɪn'tenʃənəl] *adj* deliberado(a), intencional; **it wasn't i.** fue sin querer

intentionally [ɪn'tenʃənəlɪ] *adv* a propósito, adrede

inter [ɪn'tɜːr] *vt (pt & pp* **interred)** *Fml* enterrar

inter- ['ɪntər] *pref* inter-, entre-

interact [ɪntər'ækt] *vi* actuar recíprocamente, interactuar

interaction [ɪntər'ækʃən] *n* interacción *f*

interactive [ɪntər'æktɪv] *adj* interactivo(a) ❑ **i. television** televisión *f* interactiva

intercede [ɪntə'siːd] *vi* interceder (**with** con)

intercept [ɪntə'sept] *vt* interceptar

interception [ɪntə'sepʃən] *n* interceptación *f*

interceptor [ɪntə'septər] *n Av* avión *m* interceptor

intercession [ɪntə'seʃən] *n* intercesión *f*, mediación *f*

interchange ['ɪntətʃeɪndʒ] **1** *n* (**a**) *(exchange)* intercambio *m* (**b**) *(on motorway)* cruce *m*
  2 [ɪntə'tʃeɪndʒ] *vt* intercambiar (**with** con)

interchangeable [ɪntə'tʃeɪndʒəbəl] *adj* intercambiable

intercity [ɪntə'sɪtɪ] *adj Rail* interurbano(a), de largo recorrido

intercom ['ɪntəkɒm] *n* interfono *m*

intercommunicate [ɪntəkə'mjuːnɪkeɪt] *vi* comunicarse

interconnect [ɪntəkə'nekt] *vt* interconectar

intercontinental [ɪntəkɒntɪ'nentəl] *adj* interconti-nental ❑ **i. ballistic missile** misil *m* balístico interconti-nental

intercourse ['ɪntəkɔːs] *n* (**a**) *(dealings)* trato *m* (**b**) *(sexual)* relaciones *fpl* sexuales, coito *m*

interdependent [ɪntədɪ'pendənt] *adj* interdependiente

interest ['ɪntrɪst] **1** *n* (**a**) *(curiosity)* interés *m*; **is this of i. to you?** ¿te interesa esto?; **my main i. is travel** viajar es lo que más me interesa; **to have** *or* **take an i. in sth/sb** interesarse por algo/algn; **to lose i. in sth/in doing sth** perder el interés por algo/en hacer algo (**b**) *(advantage)* provecho *m*, beneficio *m*; **in the i. of peace** en pro de la paz; **it's not in my (best) i.** yo no salgo ganando; **to act in one's own i.** obrar en beneficio propio; **to have a vested i. in sth** tener interés personal en algo (**c**) *Com (share)* participación *f*, interés *m*; **he has a controlling i. in the firm** tiene la mayor parte de las acciones de la empresa (**d**) *Fin* interés *m*, rédito *m*; **a loan at six per cent i.** un préstamo a un interés del seis por ciento; **i.-free loan** préstamo sin intereses ❑ **i. rate** tipo *m or Am* tasa *f* de interés; **simple/compound i.** interés *m* simple/compuesto
  2 *vt* interesar; **to be interested in sth/sb** interesarse en *or* por algo/algn; *Fml* **can I i. you in a drink?** ¿le gustaría tomar algo?

interested ['ɪntrɪstɪd] *adj* interesado(a)

interest-free ['ɪntrɪst'friː] *adj (loan, credit)* sin intereses

interesting ['ɪntrɪstɪŋ] *adj* interesante

interestingly ['ɪntrɪstɪŋlɪ] *adv* **i. enough ...** lo curioso (del caso) es que ...

interface ['ɪntəfeɪs] *n Comptr* interface *f*, interfaz *f*; *Fig* terreno *m* común

interfere [ɪntə'fɪər] *vi* (**a**) *(meddle)* entrometerse, meterse (**in** en; **between** entre); **to i. with** *(hinder)* dificultar; *(spoil)* estropear; *(prevent)* impedir; **don't i. with my papers** no toques mis papeles (**b**) *Rad TV* interferir (**with** con) (**c**) *Euph (person)* abusar (**with** de)

interference [ɪntə'fɪərəns] *n* (**a**) *(meddling)* intromisión *f*, entrometimiento *m*, injerencia *f* (**b**) *(hindrance)* dificultad *f*, estorbo *m* (**c**) *Rad TV* interferencia *f*

interfering [ɪntə'fɪərɪŋ] *adj* entrometido(a)

interim ['ɪntərɪm] **1** *n Fml* **in the i.** en el ínterin, mientras tanto
  2 *adj* interino(a), provisional, *Am* provisorio(a)
interior [ɪn'tɪərɪər] **1** *adj (gen)* interior
  2 *n* interior *m*, parte *f* interior ❑ **i. design** interiorismo *m*; **i. designer** interiorista *mf*
interject [ɪntə'dʒekt] *vt* interponer
interjection [ɪntə'dʒekʃən] *n* (**a**) *(act, remark)* interposición *f* (**b**) *Ling* interjección *f*
interlink [ɪntə'lɪŋk] *vt* entrelazar
interlock [ɪntə'lɒk] **1** *vt (fingers)* entrelazar; *(cogs)* engranar; *(units, parts)* enganchar
  2 *vi (fingers)* entrelazarse; *(cogs)* engranarse; *(units)* engancharse
interlocutor [ɪntə'lɒkjʊtər] *n Fml* interlocutor(a) *m,f*
interloper ['ɪntələʊpər] *n* intruso(a) *m,f*
interlude ['ɪntəluːd] *n* (**a**) *(break)* intervalo *m*, pausa *f* (**b**) *Cin Theat* descanso *m*, intermedio *m* (**c**) *Mus* interludio *m*
intermarriage [ɪntə'mærɪdʒ] *n (within family)* matrimonio *m* entre parientes; *(between races, tribes, etc)* matrimonio *m* mixto
intermediary [ɪntə'miːdɪərɪ] *n* intermediario(a) *m,f*
intermediate [ɪntə'miːdɪɪt] *adj* intermedio(a)
interment [ɪn'tɜːmənt] *n Fml* entierro *m*
interminable [ɪn'tɜːmɪnəbəl] *adj* inacabable, interminable, sin fin
intermingle [ɪntə'mɪŋgəl] *vi* entremezclarse
intermission [ɪntə'mɪʃən] *n US Cin Mus Theat* descanso *m*, intermedio *m*
intermittent [ɪntə'mɪtənt] *adj* intermitente
intern [ɪn'tɜːn] **1** *vt* internar, recluir
  2 ['ɪntɜːn] *n US Med* médico(a) *m,f* interno(a) residente
internal [ɪn'tɜːnəl] *adj* (**a**) *(gen)* interior; *(dispute, injury)* interno(a) ❑ *Fin* **i. audit** auditoría *f* interna; *US* **i. medicine** medicina *f* interna (**b**) *Pol (domestic)* interior ❑ *US* **the I. Revenue Service** ≃ Hacienda *f*, *Esp* ≃ la Agencia Tributaria, *Méx* ≃ el Servicio de Administración Tributaria
internalize [ɪn'tɜːnəlaɪz] *vt* interiorizar, *Am* internalizar
internally [ɪn'tɜːnəlɪ] *adv* interiormente; *Med* **'not to be taken i.'** 'uso externo'
international [ɪntə'næʃənəl] **1** *adj* internacional; **the i. date line** la línea de cambio de fecha
  2 *n Sport (player)* internacional *mf*; *(match)* partido *m* internacional
internationalize [ɪntə'næʃənəlaɪz] *vt* internacionalizar; **to become internationalized** internacionalizarse
internee [ɪntɜː'niː] *n* preso(a), *m,f*, interno(a) *m,f*
Internet ['ɪntənet] *n Comptr* **the I.** Internet ❑ **I. address** dirección *f* de Internet; **I. banking** banca *f* por Internet; **I. connection** conexión *f* a Internet
internment [ɪn'tɜːnmənt] *n* internamiento *m*
internship ['ɪntɜːnʃɪp] *n US Med Esp* ≃ MIR *m*, *Am* internado *m*
interpersonal [ɪntə'pɜːsənəl] *adj* interpersonal
interplay ['ɪntəpleɪ] *n* interacción *f*
Interpol ['ɪntəpɒl] *n* Interpol *f*
interpolate [ɪn'tɜːpəleɪt] *vt Fml* interpolar, intercalar
interpose [ɪntə'pəʊz] *vt Fml* interponer
interpret [ɪn'tɜːprɪt] **1** *vt (gen)* interpretar; *(understand)* interpretar, entender
  2 *vi* actuar *or* hacer de intérprete
interpretation [ɪntɜːprɪ'teɪʃən] *n* interpretación *f*
interpretative [ɪn'tɜːprɪtətɪv], **interpretive** [ɪn'tɜː-

pritɪv] *adj* interpretativo(a) ❑ **i. centre** centro *m* de interpretación
interpreter [ɪn'tɜːprɪtər] *n* intérprete *mf*
interracial [ɪntə'reɪʃəl] *adj* interracial
interrelated [ɪntərɪ'leɪtɪd] *adj* estrechamente relacionado(a)
interrogate [ɪn'terəgeɪt] *vt* interrogar
interrogation [ɪnterə'geɪʃən] *n* interrogatorio *m*
interrogative [ɪntə'rɒgətɪv] *Ling* **1** *adj* interrogativo(a)
  2 *n (word)* palabra *f* interrogativa; *(phrase)* oración *f* interrogativa
interrogator [ɪn'terəgeɪtər] *n* interrogador(a) *m,f*
interrogatory [ɪntə'rɒgətərɪ] *adj* interrogativo(a)
interrupt [ɪntə'rʌpt] *vt & vi* interrumpir
interruption [ɪntə'rʌpʃən] *n* interrupción *f*
intersect [ɪntə'sekt] **1** *vt* (**a**) *(road etc)* cortar, cruzar (**b**) *Geom* intersecar
  2 *vi* (**a**) *(road etc)* cruzarse (**b**) *Geom* intersecarse
intersection [ɪntə'sekʃən] *n* (**a**) *(crossroads)* cruce *m*; *(junction)* bocacalle *f* (**b**) *(act)* intersección *f*
intersperse [ɪntə'spɜːs] *vt* esparcir, entremezclar; **sunny intervals interspersed with showers** claros con intervalos de lluvia
interstate ['ɪntəsteɪt] **1** *n US* autopista *f (que une un estado con otro)*
  2 *adj* entre estados
intertwine [ɪntə'twaɪn] **1** *vt* entrelazar (**with** con)
  2 *vi* entrelazarse (**with** con)
interval ['ɪntəvəl] *n* (**a**) *(of time, space)* intervalo *m* (**between** entre); **at intervals** *(time, space)* a intervalos; *(time)* de vez en cuando (**b**) *Br Cin* intermedio *m*, descanso *m*; *Theat* entreacto *m*, intermedio *m* (**c**) *Mus* intervalo *m*
intervene [ɪntə'viːn] *vi* (**a**) *(person)* intervenir (**in** en) (**b**) *(event)* sobrevenir, ocurrir (**c**) *(time)* transcurrir, mediar
intervening [ɪntə'viːnɪŋ] *adj (years, months)* mediante, transcurrido(a); *(miles)* intermedio(a); **in the i. period** en el ínterin
intervention [ɪntə'venʃən] *n* intervención *f*
interview ['ɪntəvjuː] **1** *n (gen)* entrevista *f*; *(by media)* interviú *f*; **to give an i.** conceder una entrevista
  2 *vt* entrevistar
interviewee [ɪntəvjuː'iː] *n* entrevistado(a) *m,f*
interviewer ['ɪntəvjuːər] *n* entrevistador(a) *m,f*
interweave [ɪntə'wiːv] *vt (pt* **interwove** [ɪntə'wəʊv]; *pp* **interwoven** [ɪntə'wəʊvən]) entretejer
intestate [ɪn'testeɪt] *adj* intestado(a)
intestinal [ɪn'testɪnəl] *adj* intestinal
intestine [ɪn'testɪn] *n (gen pl)* intestino *m* ❑ **large/small i.** intestino *m* grueso/delgado
intimacy ['ɪntɪməsɪ] *n (closeness)* intimidad *f*, familiaridad *f*; *Euph (sex)* relaciones *fpl* íntimas; *(act, remark)* **intimacies** intimidades *fpl*
intimate¹ ['ɪntɪmɪt] **1** *adj (gen)* íntimo(a); *(knowledge)* profundo(a); **to be i. with sb** *(friendly)* intimar con algn; *Euph (having sex)* tener relaciones (íntimas) con algn
  2 *n (person)* amigo(a) *m,f* íntimo(a)
intimate² ['ɪntɪmeɪt] *vt Fml* insinuar, dar a entender
intimately ['ɪntɪmɪtlɪ] *adv* íntimamente
intimation [ɪntɪ'meɪʃən] *n Fml (sign)* indicio *m*; *(hint)* sugerencia *f*, indirecta *f*; **to have an i. of sth** presentir algo
intimidate [ɪn'tɪmɪdeɪt] *vt* intimidar; **to i. sb into doing sth** convencer a algn con amenazas de que haga algo
intimidating [ɪn'tɪmɪdeɪtɪŋ] *adj* atemorizante, amenazador(a)

intimidation [ɪntɪmɪˈdeɪʃən] *n* intimidación *f*

into [ˈɪntuː, *unstressed* ˈɪntə] *prep* (**a**) *(motion)* en, dentro de, a, contra, con; **he fell i. the water** se cayó al agua; *(met by chance)* **I bumped i. a friend** me topé con un amigo; **it crashed i. a tree** chocó contra un árbol; **to get i. a car/train** subir a un coche/tren; **to go i. a house** entrar en *or Am* a una casa; **to go i. town** ir al centro (**b**) *(state, condition)* en, a; **buds develop i. flowers** los capullos se convierten en flores; **he grew i. a man** se hizo un hombre; **to burst i. tears** deshacerse en lágrimas; **to change pounds i. euros** cambiar libras en *or* por euros; **to translate sth i.** French traducir algo al francés (**c**) *(time, age)* **she's well i. her fifties** tiene los cincuenta bien cumplidos; **to work i. the night** trabajar hasta muy avanzada la noche (**d**) *Math* **to divide sth i. three** dividir algo en *or* entre tres; **two i. ten goes five** diez entre dos caben a *or* son cinco (**e**) *Fam* **to be i. sth** ser aficionado(a) de algo; **I'm really i. cycling** me chifla *or* me encanta el ciclismo

intolerable [ɪnˈtɒlərəbəl] *adj* intolerable, inaceptable, inadmisible, inaguantable

intolerance [ɪnˈtɒlərəns] *n* intolerancia *f*, intransigencia *f*

intolerant [ɪnˈtɒlərənt] *adj* intolerante, intransigente

intonation [ɪntəʊˈneɪʃən] *n* entonación *f*

intone [ɪnˈtəʊn] *vt* decir solemnemente

intoxicated [ɪnˈtɒksɪkeɪtɪd] *adj (drunk)* borracho(a), ebrio(a)

intoxicating [ɪnˈtɒksɪkeɪtɪŋ] *adj (inebriating)* embriagador(a) □ **i. liquor** bebida *f* alcohólica

intoxication [ɪntɒksɪˈkeɪʃən] *n (drunkenness)* embriaguez *f*, borrachera *f*

intractable [ɪnˈtræktəbəl] *adj Fml (person)* intratable; *(problem)* insoluble

intranet [ˈɪntrənet] *n Comptr* intranet *f*

intransigence [ɪnˈtrænsɪdʒəns] *n Fml* intransigencia *f*, intolerancia *f*

intransigent [ɪnˈtrænsɪdʒənt] *adj Fml* intransigente, intolerante

intransitive [ɪnˈtrænsɪtɪv] *adj Ling* intransitivo(a)

intrastate [ˈɪntrəˈsteɪt] *adj US* intraestatal

intrauterine [ɪntrəˈjuːtəraɪn] *adj Med* intrauterino(a) □ **i. device** dispositivo *m* intrauterino

intravenous [ɪntrəˈviːnəs] *adj Med* intravenoso(a)

in-tray [ˈɪntreɪ] *n* bandeja *f* de asuntos pendientes

intrepid [ɪnˈtrepɪd] *adj* intrépido(a), audaz

intricacy [ˈɪntrɪkəsɪ] *n (gen pl)* complejidad *f*

intricate [ˈɪntrɪkɪt] *adj* intrincado(a), complejo(a), complicado(a)

intrigue [ɪnˈtriːg, ˈɪntriːg] **1** *n* intriga *f*; *Hum* **amorous intrigues** amoríos *mpl*, aventuras *fpl*

2 [ɪnˈtriːg] *vt* intrigar, fascinar

3 *vi* intrigar, conspirar (**against** contra)

intriguing [ɪnˈtriːgɪŋ] *adj* intrigante, fascinante, curioso(a)

intrinsic [ɪnˈtrɪnsɪk] *adj Fml* intrínseco(a)

intrinsically [ɪnˈtrɪnsɪklɪ] *adv* intrínsecamente

intro [ˈɪntrəʊ] *n (abbr* **introduction)** *Fam* presentación *f*

introduce [ɪntrəˈdjuːs] *vt* (**a**) *(person, programme)* presentar (**to** a); **let me i. my son** permítame presentar a mi hijo, le presento a mi hijo (**b**) *(bring in)* introducir (**into, to** en); *Com (range, product)* lanzar (**into, to** a); *Pol (act, law)* presentar; *(topic, question)* proponer, sugerir, plantear

introduction [ɪntrəˈdʌkʃən] *n* (**a**) *(of person, programme)* presentación *f*; *(in book, speech)* introducción *f*; **letter of i.** carta *f* de recomendación; **my i. to art** mi iniciación *f* en el

arte; *Fam* **to make** *or* **do the introductions** hacer las presentaciones (**b**) *(bringing in)* introducción *f*; *Com (of product)* lanzamiento *m*; *Pol (of act)* presentación *f*; *(of topic)* planteamiento *m*

introductory [ɪntrəˈdʌktərɪ] *adj (gen)* introductorio(a); *(remarks)* preliminar; *Com (price, offer)* de lanzamiento

introspection [ɪntrəˈspekʃən] *n* introspección *f*

introspective [ɪntrəˈspektɪv] *adj* introspectivo(a)

introvert [ˈɪntrəvɜːt] *n* introvertido(a) *m,f*

introverted [ˈɪntrəvɜːtɪd] *adj* introvertido(a)

intrude [ɪnˈtruːd] *vi (interfere)* entrometerse, inmiscuirse (**into, on** en); *(disturb)* estorbar; **I don't wish to i. (on you)** no quiero molestar(te)

intruder [ɪnˈtruːdər] *n* intruso(a) *m,f*

intrusion [ɪnˈtruːʒən] *n (into place)* intrusión *f*; *(on privacy, mood)* invasión *f*

intrusive [ɪnˈtruːsɪv] *adj (neighbour etc)* entrometido(a); *(presence, noise)* que molesta *or* estorba

intuition [ɪntjuˈɪʃən] *n* intuición *f*

intuitive [ɪnˈtjuːɪtɪv] *adj* intuitivo(a)

inundate [ˈɪnʌndeɪt] *vt* inundar (**with** de); *Fig* **we were inundated with complaints** recibimos un montón de quejas

inure [ɪˈnjʊər] *vt Fml* acostumbrar (**to** a), habituar (**to** a)

invade [ɪnˈveɪd] *vt* invadir

invader [ɪnˈveɪdər] *n* invasor(a) *m,f*

invalid¹ [ˈɪnvəlɪd] *n (disabled person)* inválido(a) *m,f*, minusválido(a) *m,f*; *(sick person)* enfermo(a) *m,f* □ **i. chair** silla *f* de ruedas

invalid² [ɪnˈvælɪd] *adj* inválido(a), no válido(a), nulo(a)

invalidate [ɪnˈvælɪdeɪt] *vt (result, agreement)* invalidar, anular; *(argument)* refutar, demostrar el error de

invaluable [ɪnˈvæljʊəbəl] *adj* inestimable, inapreciable

invariable [ɪnˈveərɪəbəl] *adj* invariable, constante

invariably [ɪnˈveərɪəblɪ] *adv* invariablemente

invasion [ɪnˈveɪʒən] *n* invasión *f*

invasive [ɪnˈveɪsɪv] *adj Med* invasivo(a)

invective [ɪnˈvektɪv] *n Fml* invectivas *fpl*, improperios *mpl*

inveigh [ɪnˈveɪ] *vi Fml* **to i. against sth/sb** censurar *or* condenar algo/a algn

inveigle [ɪnˈviːgəl, ɪnˈveɪgəl] *vt Fml* **to i. sb into sth/into doing sth** embaucar *or* persuadir a algn para que haga algo

invent [ɪnˈvent] *vt* inventar

invention [ɪnˈvenʃən] *n* (**a**) *(machine etc)* invento *m*, invención *f* (**b**) *(creativity)* invención *f*, fantasía *f*; *(lie)* mentira *f*

inventive [ɪnˈventɪv] *adj* inventivo(a)

inventiveness [ɪnˈventɪvnɪs] *n* inventiva *f*

inventor [ɪnˈventər] *n* inventor(a) *m,f*

inventory [ˈɪnvəntərɪ] *n* inventario *m*; **to draw up an i. of sth** inventariar algo

inverse [ɪnˈvɜːs] *Fml* **1** *adj* inverso(a)

2 the i. *n* lo inverso, lo contrario

inversion [ɪnˈvɜːʃən] *n* inversión *f*

invert [ɪnˈvɜːt] *vt* invertir, volver del revés

invertebrate [ɪnˈvɜːtɪbrɪt] *Zool* **1** *adj* invertebrado(a)

2 *n* invertebrado *m*

inverted [ɪnˈvɜːtɪd] *adj* **i. commas** comillas *fpl*; **in i. commas** entre comillas

invest [ɪnˈvest] **1** *vt* (**a**) *(money)* invertir (**in** en); *Fig (time, energy)* emplear, invertir (**in** en) (**b**) *Fml (right, power, etc)*

investir; **to i. sb with sth** conferir algo a algn
2 *vi* hacer una inversión, invertir dinero (**in** en); *Fam* **I must i. in a new watch** me tengo que comprar un reloj nuevo

investigate [ɪnˈvestɪɡeɪt] *vt (crime, subject)* investigar; *(cause, possibility)* examinar, estudiar

investigation [ɪnvestɪˈɡeɪʃən] *n (of crime, subject)* investigación *f; (of cause, possibility)* examen *m*, estudio *m*

investigative [ɪnˈvestɪɡətɪv] *adj* investigador(a) ❏ **i. journalism** periodismo *m* de investigación

investigator [ɪnˈvestɪɡeɪtər] *n* investigador(a) *m,f* ❏ **private i.** detective *m* privado

investigatory [ɪnˈvestɪɡeɪtərɪ] *adj* de investigación

investiture [ɪnˈvestɪtʃər] *n* investidura *f*

investment [ɪnˈvestmənt] *n* inversión *f* ❏ **i. bank** banco *m* de inversiones; **i. trust** sociedad *f* or fondo *m* de inversión

investor [ɪnˈvestər] *n* inversor(a), *m,f*, inversionista *mf*

inveterate [ɪnˈvetərɪt] *adj* empedernido(a)

invidious [ɪnˈvɪdɪəs] *adj (gen)* odioso(a); *(task, role)* ingrato(a), desagradable; *(comparison, choice)* injusto(a)

invigilate [ɪnˈvɪdʒɪleɪt] *vt & vi Br (exam)* vigilar

invigilator [ɪnˈvɪdʒɪleɪtər] *n Br (in exam)* vigilante *mf*

invigorated [ɪnˈvɪɡəreɪtɪd] *adj* tonificado(a), vigorizado(a)

invigorating [ɪnˈvɪɡəreɪtɪŋ] *adj* tónico(a), vigorizante, estimulante

invincibility [ɪnvɪnsɪˈbɪlɪtɪ] *n* invencibilidad *f*

invincible [ɪnˈvɪnsəbəl] *adj* invencible

inviolable [ɪnˈvaɪələbəl] *adj Fml* inviolable

inviolate [ɪnˈvaɪəlɪt] *adj Fml* inviolado(a); **to remain i.** permanecer intacto(a)

invisibility [ɪnvɪzɪˈbɪlɪtɪ] *n* invisibilidad *f*

invisible [ɪnˈvɪzəbəl] *adj* invisible ❏ *Fin* **i. assets** activos *mpl* invisibles or intangibles; *Fin* **i. earnings** (ganancias *fpl*) invisibles *mpl*

invitation [ɪnvɪˈteɪʃən] *n* invitación *f*

invite [ɪnˈvaɪt] **1** *vt* (**a**) *(guest)* invitar, convidar (**to** a); *(candidate, participant)* pedir, invitar; **to i. sb over** or **round for supper** invitar a algn a casa a cenar; **I was invited for interview** me pidieron que fuera a entrevistarme con ellos (**b**) *(comments, questions, offers)* solicitar; *(criticism, disaster)* provocar; **to i. trouble** buscarse problemas
2 [ˈɪnvaɪt] *n Fam* invitación *f*

inviting [ɪnˈvaɪtɪŋ] *adj (attractive)* atractivo(a), tentador(a), atrayente; *(food)* apetitoso(a)

invoice [ˈɪnvɔɪs] *Com* **1** *n* factura *f*; **to draw up** or **make out an i.** extender una factura
2 *vt* facturar

invoke [ɪnˈvəʊk] *vt Fml* invocar

involuntarily [ɪnˈvɒləntərəlɪ, ˌɪnvɒlənˈteərəlɪ] *adv* involuntariamente; **she smiled i.** sonrió sin querer

involuntary [ɪnˈvɒləntərɪ] *adj* involuntario(a)

involve [ɪnˈvɒlv] *vt* (**a**) *(concern)* implicar, comprometer, involucrar (**in** en); **I don't want to get involved in your problems** no quiero mezclarme en tus líos; **is there money involved?** ¿hay dinero de por medio?; **the changes don't i. me** los cambios no me afectan; **the issues involved** las cuestiones en juego; **the people involved** los interesados; **to be involved in an accident** sufrir un accidente; **to be deeply involved in sth** estar muy metido(a) en algo (**b**) *(entail)* suponer, implicar; *(trouble, risk)* acarrear; **the post involves travel** el puesto exige viajar; **what's involved?** ¿de qué se trata?

involved [ɪnˈvɒlvd] *adj* (**a**) *(complicated)* complicado(a),

complejo(a), enrevesado(a) (**b**) *Fam (romantically attached)* enredado(a)

involvement [ɪnˈvɒlvmənt] *n* (**a**) *(participation)* participación *f; (in crime)* implicación *f*, complicidad *f; (in scandal)* compromiso *m*; **American i. in the Middle East** intervención *f* americana en el Oriente Medio (**b**) *Fam (romance)* enredo *m*

invulnerable [ɪnˈvʌlnərəbəl] *adj* invulnerable

inward [ˈɪnwəd] **1** *adj* interior ❏ *Econ* **i. investment** inversión *f* del exterior
2 *adv see* **inwards**

inward-looking [ˈɪnwədˈlʊkɪŋ] *adj (person)* introvertido(a); *(community)* cerrado(a)

inwardly [ˈɪnwədlɪ] *adv* interiormente, por dentro; **to laugh i.** reír para sus adentros

inwards [ˈɪnwədz] *adv* hacia dentro

in-your-face [ˈɪnjɔːˈfeɪs] *adj Fam (style)* descarado(a); *(movie, advert)* impactante, fuerte

iodine [ˈaɪədiːn] *n* yodo *m*

ion [ˈaɪən] *n* ion *m*

Ionian [aɪˈəʊnɪən] *adj* **I. Sea** mar Jónico

ionize [ˈaɪənaɪz] *vt* ionizar

iota [aɪˈəʊtə] *n* pizca *f*, ápice *m*

IOU [aɪəʊˈjuː] *n (abbr* **I owe you**) pagaré *m*

IP [aɪˈpiː] *n Comptr (abbr* **Internet Protocol**) IP **address** dirección *f* IP

IPA [aɪpiːˈeɪ] *n (abbr* **International Phonetic Alphabet**) Alfabeto *m* Fonético Internacional, AFI *m*

IQ [aɪˈkjuː] *n (abbr* **intelligence quotient**) coeficiente *m* de inteligencia, CI *m*

IRA [aɪɑːrˈeɪ] *n* (**a**) *(abbr* **Irish Republican Army**) Ejército *m* Republicano irlandés, IRA *m* (**b**) *US (abbr* **individual retirement account**) cuenta *f* de retiro or jubilación

Iran [ɪˈrɑːn] *n* Irán

Iranian [ɪˈreɪnɪən] **1** *adj* iraní *mf*
2 *n* (**a**) *(person)* iraní *mf* (**b**) *(language)* iraní *m*

Iraq [ɪˈrɑːk] *n* Irak

Iraqi [ɪˈrɑːkɪ] *adj & n* iraquí *(mf)*

irascible [ɪˈræsɪbəl] *adj Fml*, irascible, colérico(a)

irate [aɪˈreɪt] *adj* airado(a), furioso(a)

IRBM [aɪeɪbiːˈem] *n Mil (abbr* **intermediate-range ballistic missile**) proyectil *m* balístico de alcance intermedio, PBAI *m*

ire [ˈaɪər] *n Literary* ira *f*, cólera *f*

Ireland [ˈaɪələnd] *n* Irlanda ❏ **Northern I** Irlanda del Norte; **Republic of I.** República de Irlanda

iridescent [ɪrɪˈdesənt] *adj Fml* iridiscente, irisado(a)

iris [ˈaɪərɪs] *n* (**a**) *Anat* iris *m inv* (**b**) *Bot* lirio *m*

Irish [ˈaɪrɪʃ] **1** *adj* irlandés(esa) ❏ **I. coffee** café *m* irlandés; **I. Sea** mar *m* de Irlanda; **I. setter** setter *m* irlandés
2 *n* (**a**) *(language)* irlandés *m* (**b**) *pl* **the I.** los irlandeses

Irishman [ˈaɪrɪʃmən] *n (pl* **Irishmen**) irlandés *m*

Irishwoman [ˈaɪrɪʃwʊmən] *n (pl* **Irishwomen** [ˈaɪrɪʃwɪmɪn]) irlandesa *f*

irk [ɜːk] *vt* fastidiar, molestar

irksome [ˈɜːksəm] *adj* fastidioso(a), molesto(a); **how i.!** ¡qué lata!

iron [ˈaɪən] **1** *n* (**a**) *Min* hierro *m*; **the i. and steel industry** la industria siderúrgica; *Fig* **a will of i., an i. will** una voluntad de hierro; *Fig* **to have an i. constitution** ser de hierro; *Fig* **to have several/too many irons in the fire** traer varias/demasiadas cosas entre manos; *Prov* **strike while the i. is hot** a hierro candente batir de repente ❏ **cast i.** hierro or colado; *Pol* **I. Curtain** telón *m* de acero, *Am*

cortina f de hierro; **i. foundry** fundición f (de hierro); *Med* **i. lung** pulmón *m* de acero; **i. ore** mineral *m* de hierro; **scrap i.** chatarra f; **wrought i.** hierro *m* forjado (**b**) *(for clothes)* plancha f ❏ **steam i.** plancha f de vapor (**c**) *(for golf)* hierro *m* (**d**) **irons** *(fetters)* grillos *mpl*, grilletes *mpl*; **to clap sb in i.** encadenar a algn
  2 *vt (clothes)* planchar

iron out *vt* (**a**) *(crease)* planchar (**b**) *Fam Fig (problem)* resolver; *(objection)* quitar

ironic(al) [aɪˈrɒnɪk(əl)] *adj* irónico(a)

ironing [ˈaɪənɪŋ] *n* (**a**) *(act)* **to do the i.** planchar ❏ **i. board** tabla f de planchar (**b**) *(clothes to be ironed)* ropa f por planchar; *(clothes ironed)* ropa f planchada

ironmonger [ˈaɪənmʌŋgər] *n Br* ferretero(a) *m,f* ❏ **i.'s (shop)** ferretería f

irony [ˈaɪrənɪ] *n* ironía f; **the i. (of it) is that ...** lo más curioso *or* gracioso es que ...

irradiate [ɪˈreɪdɪeɪt] *vt Med* irradiar

irrational [ɪˈræʃənəl] *adj* irracional

irreconcilable [ɪrekənˈsaɪləbəl] irreconciliable, inconciliable

irredeemable [ɪrɪˈdiːməbəl] *adj Fml (gen)* irredimible, irremediable; *(fault)* irreparable, incorregible

irrefutable [ɪrɪˈfjuːtəbəl] *adj Fml* irrefutable

irregular [ɪˈregjʊlər] *adj* (**a**) *(gen)* irregular; *(abnormal)* anormal (**b**) *(uneven)* desigual

irregularity [ɪregjʊˈlærɪtɪ] *n* (**a**) *(abnormality)* irregularidad f (**b**) *(unevenness)* desigualdad f

irrelevance [ɪˈreləvəns] *n*, **irrelevancy** [ɪˈreləvənsɪ] *n* (**a**) *(state)* falta f de pertinencia (**b**) *(remark)* observación f fuera de lugar *or* que no viene al caso

irrelevant [ɪˈreləvənt] *adj* no pertinente, ajeno(a); **i. remark** comentario *m* fuera de lugar; **that's i.** eso no viene al caso *or* no tiene nada que ver

irreligious [ɪrɪˈlɪdʒəs] *adj Fml* irreligioso(a)

irremediable [ɪrɪˈmiːdɪəbəl] *adj Fml* irreparable, irremediable

irreparable [ɪˈrepərəbəl] *adj* irreparable

irreplaceable [ɪrɪˈpleɪsəbəl] *adj* irremplazable, insustituible

irrepressible [ɪrɪˈpresəbəl] *adj* incontenible, incontrolable

irreproachable [ɪrɪˈprəʊtʃəbəl] *adj Fml* irreprochable, intachable

irresistible [ɪrɪˈzɪstəbəl] *adj* irresistible

irresolute [ɪˈrezəluːt] *adj Fml* indeciso(a), vacilante, irresoluto(a)

irrespective [ɪrɪˈspektɪv] *adj* **i. of** sin tomar en consideración, sin tener en cuenta

irresponsible [ɪrɪˈspɒnsəbəl] *adj* irresponsable

irretrievable [ɪrɪˈtriːvəbəl] *adj (object)* irrecuperable; *(mistake, harm)* irreparable; *(loss, situation)* irremediable

irreverence [ɪˈrevərəns] *n* irreverencia f, falta f de respeto

irreverent [ɪˈrevərənt] *adj* irreverente, irrespetuoso(a)

irreversible [ɪrɪˈvɜːsəbəl] *adj (process)* irreversible; *(judgement, decision)* irrevocable

irrevocable [ɪˈrevəkəbəl] *adj* irrevocable, inalterable

irrigate [ˈɪrɪgeɪt] *vt Agr* regar, irrigar

irrigation [ɪrɪˈgeɪʃən] *n Agr* riego *m*, irrigación f ❏ **i. channel** acequia f, canal *m* de riego; **i. system** sistema *m* de regadío

irritable [ˈɪrɪtəbəl] *adj* irritable, de mal humor

irritant [ˈɪrɪtənt] *n* (**a**) *Med* agente *m* irritante (**b**) *Fig Fml* motivo *m* de irritación, molestia f

irritate [ˈɪrɪteɪt] *vt* (**a**) *(annoy)* irritar, fastidiar, molestar (**b**) *Med* irritar, inflamar

irritated [ˈɪrɪteɪtɪd] *adj also Med* irritado(a); **don't get i.!** *Esp* ¡no te enfades!, *Am* ¡no te enojes!

irritating [ˈɪrɪteɪtɪŋ] *adj* (**a**) *(habit, delay)* irritante, fastidioso(a), molesto(a) (**b**) *Med* irritante

irritation [ɪrɪˈteɪʃən] *n* (**a**) *(annoyance)* fastidio *m*, molestia f; *(ill humour)* mal humor *m* (**b**) *Med* irritación f

IRS [aɪɑːˈres] *n US (abbr* **Internal Revenue Service**) **the I.** Hacienda, *Esp* ≃ la Agencia Tributaria, *Méx* ≃ el Servicio de Administración Tributaria

is [ɪz] *3rd person sing pres see* **be**

ISBN [aɪesbiːˈen] *n (abbr* **International Standard Book Number**) ISBN *m*

ISDN [aɪesdiːˈen] *n Comptr (abbr* **integrated services digital network**) RDSI f; **ISDN modem** módem *m* RDSI

Islam [ˈɪzlɑːm] *n* Islam *m*

Islamic [ɪzˈlæmɪk] *adj* islámico(a)

island [ˈaɪlənd] *n* isla f; *Aut* **(traffic)** i. isla f, refugio *m*

islander [ˈaɪləndər] *n* isleño(a) *m,f*

isle [aɪl] *n Literary* isla f; **the British Isles** las Islas Británicas

isn't [ˈɪzənt] = **is not**

ISO [aɪesˈəʊ] *n (abbr* **International Standards Organization**) ISO f, Organización f Internacional de Normalización

isobar [ˈaɪsəʊbɑːr] *n* isobara f

isolate [ˈaɪsəleɪt] *vt* aislar (**from** de)

isolated [ˈaɪsəleɪtɪd] *adj* aislado(a)

isolation [aɪsəˈleɪʃən] *n* aislamiento *m*; **to deal with sth in i.** tratar algo por separado; **to live in i.** vivir aislado(a) ❏ *Med* **i. ward** pabellón *m or* sala f de aislamiento *or* de enfermedades contagiosas

isolationism [aɪsəˈleɪʃənɪzəm] *n Pol* aislacionismo *m*

isosceles [aɪˈsɒsɪliːz] *adj* isósceles; **i. triangle** triángulo *m* isósceles

isotope [ˈaɪsətəʊp] *n* isótopo *m*

Israel [ˈɪzreɪəl] *n* Israel

Israeli [ɪzˈreɪlɪ] **1** *adj* israelí
  2 *n (pl* **Israelis**) israelí *mf*

Israelite [ˈɪzrɪəlaɪt] *adj & n Hist* israelita *(mf)*

issue [ˈɪʃuː] **1** *n* (**a**) *(matter)* cuestión f, asunto *m*, tema *m*; **let's not make an i. of it** no riñamos por esto; **side i.** cuestión secundaria; **the point at i.** el tema en discusión; **to avoid** *or* **evade the i.** andar con rodeos; **to cloud** *or* **confuse the i.** complicar la cosa; **to face the i.** hacer frente al problema; **to force the i.** forzar una decisión; **to raise an i.** plantear un tema; **to take i. with sb (over sth)** manifestar su desacuerdo con algn (en algo) (**b**) *(of book)* tirada f; *(of banknotes, stamps)* emisión f; *(of passport)* expedición f (**c**) *(copy) (of journal etc)* ejemplar *m*; **back i.** número *m* atrasado (**d**) *(of equipment, supplies)* distribución f, reparto *m* (**e**) *Fml (outcome)* resultado *m*, consecuencia f (**f**) *(offspring)* prole f, descendencia f; **to die without i.** morir sin descendencia
  2 *vt* (**a**) *(book)* publicar; *(banknotes, stamps)* emitir; *(passport)* expedir (**b**) *(equipment, supplies)* distribuir, repartir; **to i. sb with sth** *or* **sth to sb** suministrar algo a algn (**c**) *(order, instructions)* dar; *Jur (warrant)* dictar
  3 *vi Fml (blood)* brotar (**from** de); *(smoke)* salir (**from** de)

Istanbul [ɪstænˈbuːl] *n* Estambul

isthmus [ˈɪsməs] *n* istmo *m*

IT [aɪˈtiː] *n Comptr (abbr* **information technology**) informática f

it [ɪt] *pers pron* (**a**) *(subject)* él, ella, ello *(often omitted)*; **it's here** está aquí (**b**) *(direct object)* lo, la; **I don't believe it** no me lo creo; **I liked the house and bought it** me gustó la casa y la compré (**c**) *(indirect object)* le; **give it a kick** dale una patada (**d**) *(after prep)* él, ella, ello; **are you afraid of it?** ¿te da miedo?; **I saw the beach and ran towards it** vi la playa y fui corriendo hacia ella; **we'll talk about it later** ya hablaremos de ello (**e**) *(abstract)* ello; **let's get down to it!** ¡vamos a ello! (**f**) *(impersonal)* **he had a bad time of it** lo pasó mal; **it's late** es tarde; **it's me** soy yo; **it's raining** llueve, está lloviendo; **it's said that ...** se dice que ...; **it's two miles to town** son dos millas de aquí al pueblo; **how's it going?** ¿qué tal?; **that's it!** *(agreeing)* ¡eso mismo!, ¡precisamente!; *(finishing)* ¡se acabó!; *(disapproving)* ¡basta ya!; **the worst of it is that ...** lo peor del caso es que ...; **this is it!** ¡ha llegado la hora *or* el momento!; **who is it?** ¿quién es?; *Fam* **she thinks she's it** se da mucho tono

Italian [ɪˈtæljən] **1** *adj* italiano(a)
   2 *n* (**a**) *(person)* italiano(a) *m,f* (**b**) *(language)* italiano *m*

italic [ɪˈtælɪk] *n Typ* cursiva *f*; **i. script** letra *f* cursiva

italicize [ɪˈtælɪsaɪz] *vt* poner en cursiva

Italy [ˈɪtəlɪ] *n* Italia

itch [ɪtʃ] **1** *n* picor *m*, picazón *f*; *Fig* **an i. to travel** unas ganas locas de viajar
   2 *vi* (**a**) *(skin)* picar; **my hand itches** me pica la mano (**b**) *Fig* **to be itching for sth/to do sth** tener muchas ganas de algo/de hacer algo, estar impaciente por algo/por hacer algo

itchy [ˈɪtʃɪ] *adj* (**itchier, itchiest**) *(scalp, material)* que pica; **I've got an i. nose** me pica la nariz; *Fam Fig* **to have i. feet** *(travel)* tener muchas ganas de viajar; *(move off or away)* tener muchas ganas de largarse

item [ˈaɪtəm] *n* (**a**) *(object)* *(in list)* artículo *m*; *(in collection)* pieza *f*; **i. of clothing** prenda *f* de vestir (**b**) *(subject)* *(on agenda)* punto *m*, asunto *m*; *(on bill)* partida *f*, asiento *m*; *(in show)* número *m*; **news i.** noticia *f*

itemize [ˈaɪtəmaɪz] *vt (contents)* hacer una lista de; *(bill)* detallar

itinerant [ɪˈtɪnərənt] *adj Fml* itinerante, ambulante

itinerary [aɪˈtɪnərərɪ] *n* itinerario *m*, ruta *f*

it'll [ˈɪtəl] = **it will**

its [ɪts] *poss adj (one thing)* su; *(more than one)* sus; **the bear hurt i. paw** el oso se lastimó la pata; **the club and i. members** el club y sus socios

itself [ɪtˈself] *pers pron* (**a**) *(reflexive)* se; **the cat scratched i.** el gato se arañó (**b**) *(emphatic)* él *or* ella *or* ello mismo(a); *(after prep)* sí (mismo(a)); **in i.** en sí, de por sí; **it works by i.** funciona solo; **she's kindness i.** es la bondad misma

IUD [aɪjuːˈdiː] *Med n* (*abbrs of* **intrauterine device**) dispositivo *m* intrauterino, DIU *m*

IVF [aɪviːˈef] *n Med* (*abbr* **in vitro fertilization**) fertilización *f* in vitro

ivory [ˈaɪvərɪ] *n (substance)* marfil *m*; *(colour)* color *m* marfil ❑ **I. Coast** Costa *f* de Marfil

ivy [ˈaɪvɪ] *n* (**a**) *Bot* hiedra *f*, yedra *f* (**b**) *US* **I. League** = grupo de ocho universidades privadas y de categoría del nordeste de Estados Unidos

J

J, j [dʒeɪ] *n (the letter)* J, j *f*

jab [dʒæb] **1** *n* (**a**) *(stab)* pinchazo *m*; *(poke)* golpe *m* seco; *(with elbow)* codazo *m* (**b**) *Br Fam (injection)* pinchazo *m*
2 *vt (pt & pp* **jabbed)** *(with sharp object)* pinchar; *(with fist)* dar un puñetazo a; *(with elbow)* dar un codazo a

jabber ['dʒæbər] *Fam* **1** *vt* decir atropelladamente, farfullar
2 *vi (chatter)* charlotear, charlar; *(speak quickly)* farfullar, chapurrear, hablar atropelladamente

jacaranda [dʒækə'rændə] *n Bot* jacarandá *m*

Jack [dʒæk] *n* **every man J.** todo quisque; *Br Fam* **I'm all right, J.** ande yo caliente y ríase la gente

jack [dʒæk] *n* (**a**) *Aut* gato *m*; *Tech* cric *m* (**b**) *Cards* jota *f*; *(Spanish pack)* sota *f* (**c**) *(bowls)* boliche *m* (**d**) *Elec (plug)* clavija *f*; *(socket)* clavijero *m* (**e**) **j. rabbit** *(North American hare)* liebre *f* americana

jack in *vt Br Fam* dejar

jack up *vt Aut* levantar (con el gato); *Fig (prices)* aumentar

jackal ['dʒækɔːl] *n Zool* chacal *m*

jackass ['dʒækæs] *n Fam* burro(a) *m,f*, imbécil *mf*

jackboot ['dʒækbuːt] *n* (**a**) *Mil* bota *f* militar (**b**) *Fam Fig* represión *f*, tiranía *f*

jackdaw ['dʒækdɔː] *n Orn* grajilla *f*

jacket ['dʒækɪt] *n* (**a**) *(clothing)* chaqueta *f*; *(of suit)* americana *f*, *Am* saco *m*; *(bomber jacket)* cazadora *f*, *CSur* campera *f*, *Méx* chamarra *f*; **bed j.** mañanita *f*; **dinner j** esmoquin *m*, smoking *m* (**b**) *(of book)* sobrecubierta *f* (**c**) *US (record)* funda *f* (**d**) *Culin* **j. potatoes** patatas *fpl* or *Am* papas *fpl* al horno

jackhammer ['dʒækhæmər] *n* martillo *m* perforador

jack-in-the-box ['dʒækɪnðəbɒks] *n (pl* **jack-in-the-boxes)** caja *f* sorpresa

jack-knife ['dʒæknaɪf] **1** *n (pl* **jack-knives** ['dʒæknaɪvz]) navaja *f*
2 *vi (lorry)* colear

jack-of-all-trades [dʒækəv'ɔːltreɪdz] *n (pl* **jacks-of-all-trades)** persona *f* mañosa or de muchos oficios; **j.-of-a.-t., master of none** hombre de muchos oficios, maestro de ninguno

jack-o'-lantern ['dʒækə'læntən] *n US (Halloween lantern)* = farolillo hecho con una calabaza hueca y una vela dentro

jackpot ['dʒækpɒt] *n* (premio *m*) gordo *m*; *Fam* **I hit the j.** me tocó el premio gordo

Jacobean [dʒækə'bɪən] *adj* jacobita

Jacobin ['dʒækəbɪn] *adj & n* jacobino(a) *(m,f)*

Jacuzzi® [dʒə'kuːzɪ] *n (pl* **Jacuzzis)** jacuzzi® *m*, baño *m* de burbujas

jade [dʒeɪd] *n Min* jade *m*

jaded ['dʒeɪdɪd] *adj* (**a**) *(tired)* agotado(a), molido(a) (**b**) *(of palate)* hastiado(a), saciado(a), harto(a)

jagged ['dʒægɪd] *adj* dentado(a), mellado(a)

jaguar [*Br* 'dʒægjʊər, *US* 'dʒægwɑːr] *n Zool* jaguar *m*

jail [dʒeɪl] **1** *n* cárcel *f*, prisión *f*; **to be in j.** estar en la cárcel, estar encarcelado(a); **to go to j.** ir a la cárcel
2 *vt* encarcelar, meter en la cárcel

jailbird ['dʒeɪlbɜːd] *n Fam* (preso(a) *m,f*) reincidente *mf*

jailbreak ['dʒeɪlbreɪk] *n* fuga *f*, evasión *f*

jailer ['dʒeɪlər] *n* carcelero(a) *m,f*

jailhouse ['dʒeɪlhaʊs] *n US* cárcel *f*

jailor ['dʒeɪlər] *n see* **jailer**

Jakarta [dʒə'kɑːtə] *n* Yakarta

jalop(p)y [dʒə'lɒpɪ] *n Fam Aut* cacharro *m*

jam¹ [dʒæm] *n Culin* mermelada *f*; *Fam* **that's money for j.** ¡qué chollo! ❑ **j. roll** rollo *m* de bizcocho con mermelada

jam² [dʒæm] **1** *n* (**a**) *(blockage)* atasco *m*; **traffic j.** embotellamiento *m*, atasco *m* (**b**) *Fam (fix)* apuro *m*; **in a j.** en un apuro (**c**) *Mus* **j. session** sesión *f* de jazz improvisada
2 *vt (pt & pp* **jammed)** (**a**) *(cram)* meter a la fuerza, embutir; **jammed with people** atestado(a) de gente; **jammed with things** atiborrado(a) de cosas (**b**) *(block)* atascar, obstruir; *Rad (transmission)* interferir
3 *vi* (**a**) *(door)* atascarse, *Am* trancarse; *(brakes)* agarrotarse (**b**) *Mus* = tocar en una sesión de jazz improvisada

jam on *vt Aut* **to j. on the brakes** frenar en seco

Jamaica [dʒə'meɪkə] *n* Jamaica

Jamaican [dʒə'meɪkən] *adj & n* jamaicano(a) *(m,f)*, jamaiquino(a) *(m,f)*

jamb [dʒæm] *n* jamba *f*

jamboree [dʒæmbə'riː] *n* (**a**) *(scout meeting)* congreso *m* internacional de exploradores (**b**) *Fam (party)* juerga *f*

jammed [dʒæmd] *adj* atestado(a), relleno(a)

jamming ['dʒæmɪŋ] *n Rad* interferencia *f*

jammy ['dʒæmɪ] *adj* (**jammier, jammiest**) (**a**) *Br Fam (lucky)* **what a j. shot!** ¡vaya potra or *Méx* chance or *RP* tarro tienes!; **you j. bugger!** ¡qué suerte tienes tío! (**b**) *Fam* pegajoso(a), pringoso(a)

jam-packed [dʒæm'pækt] *adj Fam (people)* atestado(a); *(things)* atiborrado(a)

Jan [dʒæn] *(abbr* **January)** enero *m*, ene, eno

jangle ['dʒæŋgəl] **1** *vt (keys etc)* hacer sonar
2 *vi* tintinear

janitor ['dʒænɪtər] *n US Scot* portero *m*, conserje *m*

January ['dʒænjʊərɪ] *n* enero *m*; *see also* **May**

Jap [dʒæp] n Fam = término ofensivo para referirse a los japoneses, RP ponja mf

Japan [dʒə'pæn] n (el) Japón; **the Sea of J.** el mar del Japón

Japanese [dʒæpə'niːz] **1** adj japonés(esa), nipón(ona); **the J.** los japoneses
   2 n (person) japonés(esa) m,f, nipón(ona) m,f; (language) japonés m

jape [dʒeɪp] **1** n broma f
   2 vi bromear

jar¹ [dʒɑːr] n (a) (glass) tarro m, pote m; (earthenware) tinaja f; (jug) jarra f (b) Br Fam **to have a j.** tomar una caña or copa

jar² [dʒɑːr] vi (pt & pp **jarred**) (a) (sounds) chirriar; Fig **to j. on one's nerves** ponerle a uno los nervios de punta, crispar los nervios a uno (b) (colours, appearance) chocar, desentonar

jargon ['dʒɑːgən] n jerga f, argot m, jerigonza f; **political j.** jerga política

jarring ['dʒɑːrɪŋ] adj (a) (of sounds) discordante, disonante (b) (of colours) que chocan or desentonan (c) (of opinion) discorde, discordante

jasmin(e) ['dʒæzmɪn] n Bot jazmín m

jasper ['dʒæspər] n Min jaspe m

jaundice ['dʒɔːndɪs] n Med ictericia f

jaundiced ['dʒɔːndɪst] adj (a) Med ictérico(a) (b) Fig (bitter) amargado(a), resentido(a); **to take a j. view of things** ver las cosas por el lado malo

jaunt [dʒɔːnt] **1** n (a) (walk) paseo m (b) (trip) excursión f, viaje m corto
   2 vi (walk) pasear; (go on a trip) viajar

jauntiness ['dʒɔːntɪnɪs] n (a) (sprightliness) garbo m (b) (liveliness) viveza f (c) (ease) desenvoltura f

jaunty ['dʒɔːntɪ] adj (jauntier, jauntiest) (a) (sprightly) garboso(a); **j. gait** paso airoso (b) (lively) vivaz (c) (easy-going) desenvuelto(a); **a j. manner** un aire desenvuelto

Java ['dʒɑːvə] n Java

Javanese [dʒɑːvə'niːz] adj & n javanés(esa) (m,f); **the J.** los javaneses

javelin ['dʒævəlɪn] n Sport jabalina f; **j. throwing** lanzamiento m de jabalina

jaw [dʒɔː] **1** n (a) Anat mandíbula f; Zool mandíbula f, quijada f; Fig **the jaws of death** las garras de la muerte (b) Tech **jaws** mordaza f sing
   2 vi Fam charlar, estar de palique, darle a la sinhueso, CAm Méx platicar

jawbone ['dʒɔːbəʊn] n Anat maxilar m, mandíbula f

jay [dʒeɪ] n Orn arrendajo m (común)

jaywalker ['dʒeɪwɔːkər] n peatón m imprudente

jazz [dʒæz] **1** n Mus jazz m; **modern j.** jazz moderno; Fam **and all that j.** y otras cosas por el estilo ❑ **j. band** conjunto m de jazz
   2 adj de jazz, jazzístico(a)

jazz up vt alegrar; (premises) arreglar, modernizar; **she turned up all jazzed up** se presentó vestida de forma muy llamativa

jazzman ['dʒæzmæn] n (pl jazzmen) músico m de jazz

jazzy ['dʒæzɪ] adj (jazzier, jazziest) Fam (a) (showy) llamativo(a) (b) (brightly coloured) de colores chillones (c) Mus del estilo de jazz, jazzístico(a)

jealous ['dʒeləs] adj (a) (gen) celoso(a); **to be j. of ...** tener celos de ... (b) (envious) envidioso(a)

jealously ['dʒeləslɪ] adv (a) (gen) celosamente (b) (enviously) con envidia

jealousy ['dʒeləsɪ] n (a) (resentment) celos mpl (b) (envy) envidia f, celos mpl

jeans [dʒiːnz] npl (pantalones mpl) vaqueros mpl, Andes Ven bluyín m, Col bluejeans mpl, Méx pantalones mpl de mezclilla

jeep [dʒiːp] n Aut jeep m, todo terreno m inv

jeer [dʒɪər] **1** n (a) (boo) abucheo m; (mocking) mofa f, burla f (b) **jeers** (insults) insultos mpl
   2 vi (boo) abuchear; (mock) burlarse

jeering ['dʒɪərɪŋ] **1** adj burlón(ona), sarcástico(a)
   2 n (booing) abucheo m; (mocking) mofa f, burla f

jeez [dʒiːz] interj US Slang ¡jolín!, ¡caray!

Jehovah [dʒɪ'həʊvə] n Rel Jehová m ❑ **J.'s Witness** testigo mf de Jehová

jejunum [dʒɪ'dʒuːnəm] n Anat yeyuno m

jell [dʒel] n see gel

jellied ['dʒelɪd] adj Culin en gelatina

Jell-O® ['dʒeləʊ] n US jalea f

jelly ['dʒelɪ] n (a) Br (dessert) gelatina f, jalea f (b) US (jam) mermelada f, confitura f ❑ **j. bean** US pastilla f de goma; US **j. roll** brazo m de gitano (c) (of meat) gelatina f de carne; (d) Fig **when he saw her, his legs turned to j.** cuando la vió, las piernas empezaron a temblarle

jellyfish ['dʒelɪfɪʃ] n (pl jellyfish or jellyfishes) Zool medusa f

jemmy ['dʒemɪ] n Br palanqueta f

jeopardize ['dʒepədaɪz] vt poner en peligro, arriesgar; (agreement etc) comprometer

jeopardy ['dʒepədɪ] n riesgo m, peligro m

Jericho ['dʒerɪkəʊ] n Jericó

jerk¹ [dʒɜːk] **1** n (a) (jolt) sacudida f (b) (pull) tirón m (c) Pej (idiot) majadero(a) m,f, imbécil mf; (nuisance) pelmazo(a) m,f
   2 vt (a) (shake) sacudir (b) (pull) tirar; **to j. oneself free** soltarse de un tirón
   3 vi (move suddenly) dar una sacudida; **the car jerked forward** el coche avanzaba a tirones

jerk off vi Vulg hacerse una paja

jerk² [dʒɜːk] n Culin cecina f

jerkin ['dʒɜːkɪn] n (a) Hist jubón m (b) (sleeveless) chaleco m

jerky¹ ['dʒɜːkɪ] adj (jerkier, jerkiest) (movement) espasmódico(a), nervioso(a)

jerky² ['dʒɜːkɪ] n Culin see jerk²

jerrican ['dʒerɪkæn] n bidón m

Jerry ['dʒerɪ] n Fam alemán m; (soldier) soldado m alemán

jerry-builder ['dʒerɪbɪldər] n Constr chapucero(a) m,f

jerry-built ['dʒerɪbɪlt] adj chapucero(a), construido(a) de cualquier manera

Jersey ['dʒɜːzɪ] n (a) (island) Jersey (b) Zool vaca f

jersey ['dʒɜːzɪ] n (a) (sweater) suéter m, Esp jersey m, Col saco m, RP pulóver m (b) Tex tejido m de punto, Am jersey m

Jerusalem [dʒə'ruːsələm] n (a) (city) Jerusalén (b) (vegetable) **J. artichoke** aguaturma f, pataca f

jest [dʒest] **1** n (a) (fun, joking) burla f, broma f; **spoken in j.** dicho(a) en broma (b) (joke) chiste m
   2 vi bromear

jester ['dʒestər] n bromista mf; Hist bufón m

Jesuit ['dʒezjʊɪt] adj & n Rel jesuita (m); **J. school** colegio m de jesuitas

Jesus ['dʒiːzəs] n Jesús m; **J. Christ** Jesucristo m; Offens **J. Christ!** ¡joder!

jet¹ [dʒet] **1** n (a) (stream of water) chorro m (b) (water spout) surtidor m; **gas j.** mechero m de gas ❑ Meteor **j. stream** corriente f a chorro (c) Av reactor m; **j. propelled**

de propulsión a reacción *or* chorro ❑ **j. engine** reactor *m*; **j. lag** desfase *m* horario, jet lag *m*
  2 *vi* (*pt & pp* **jetted**) *Fam* viajar, volar

jet² [dʒet] *n Min* azabache *m*; **j. black** negro(a) como el azabache

jet-lagged ['dʒetlægd] *adj* afectado(a) por el desfase horario, con jet lag

jetsam ['dʒetsəm] *n Naut* echazón *m*, carga *f* arrojada al mar; *Fig* desechos *mpl*

jet-set ['dʒetset] *n* **the j.-s.** la alta sociedad, la jet-set, *Am* el jet-set

jetski ['dʒetskiː] *n* moto *f* náutica *or* acuática

jetsom ['dʒetsəm] *n see* jetsam

jettison ['dʒetɪsən] *vt Naut* tirar *or* echar *or Am* salvo *RP* botar por la borda; *Fig* deshacerse de, tirar; *(project etc)* abandonar

jetty ['dʒetɪ] *n Naut* muelle *m*, malecón *m*

Jew [dʒuː] *n* judío(a) *m,f*

jewel ['dʒuːəl] *n* (**a**) *(ornament)* joya *f*, alhaja *f*; *(stone)* piedra *f* preciosa; *(in watch)* rubí *m* (**b**) *Fig (person)* joya *f*, perla *f*

jeweller, *US* **jeweler** ['dʒuːələr] *n* joyero(a) *m,f*; **j.'s (shop)** joyería *f*

jewellery, *US* **jewelry** ['dʒuːəlrɪ] *n* joyas *fpl*, alhajas *fpl*; **costume j.** bisutería *f*

Jewess ['dʒuːɪs] *n* judía *f*

Jewish ['dʒuːɪʃ] *adj* judío(a)

Jewry ['dʒʊərɪ] *n Fml (people)* los Judíos, el Pueblo Judío; *(religion)* judaísmo *m*

jib¹ [dʒɪb] *vi* (*pt & pp* **jibbed**) (**a**) *(horse)* plantarse (**b**) *Br (person)* oponerse, oponerse

jib² [dʒɪb] *n* (**a**) *Tech (of crane)* aguillón *m* (**b**) *Naut* foque *m* ❑ **j. boom** botalón *m*

jibe [dʒaɪb] *n & vi see* gibe

jiffy ['dʒɪfɪ] *n Fam* momento *m*, instante *m*; **in a j.** en un santiamén; **just a j.!** ¡un momento! ❑ **j. bag**® sobre *m* acolchado

jig [dʒɪg] **1** *n* (**a**) *Mus* giga *f* (**b**) *Tech* calibre *m*, gálibo *m*
  2 *vi* (*pt & pp* **jigged**) bailar

jiggery-pokery [dʒɪgərɪ'pəʊkərɪ] *n Br Fam* tejemaneje *m*, trampas *fpl*

jiggle ['dʒɪgəl] **1** *vt* sacudir, dar meneos a, menear
  2 *vi* **to j. about** menearse

jigsaw ['dʒɪgsɔː] *n* (**a**) *(puzzle)* rompecabezas *m inv* (**b**) *Tech* sierra *f* de vaivén

jihad [dʒɪ'hæd] *n* guerra *f* santa', yihad *f* (islámica)

jilt [dʒɪlt] *vt Fam* dejar plantado(a), dar calabazas a

jimjams ['dʒɪmdʒæmz] *npl Fam* nervios *mpl*, mieditis *f sing*

jimmy ['dʒɪmɪ] *n US see* jemmy

jingle ['dʒɪŋgəl] **1** *n* (**a**) *(sound)* tintineo *m* (**b**) *Rad TV* = canción que acompaña un anuncio
  2 *vt* hacer sonar
  3 *vi* tintinear

jingling ['dʒɪŋglɪŋ] *n* tintineo *m*

jingo ['dʒɪŋgəʊ] *n* patriotero(a) *m,f*, jingoísta *mf*; **by j.!** ¡pardiez!, ¡caray!

jingoism ['dʒɪŋgəʊɪzəm] *n* patriotería *f*, jingoísmo *m*

jingoistic [dʒɪŋgəʊ'ɪstɪk] *adj* patriotero(a), jingoísta

jink [dʒɪŋk] *vi Fam* zigzaguear

jinks [dʒɪŋks] *npl* juerga *f sing*; **high j.** jolgorio *m sing*; **to get up to high j.** ponerse en plan de juerga

jinx [dʒɪŋks] **1** *n Fam (person)* gafe *mf*, cenizo *m*; **to be a j.** *(person)* ser un gafe; *(bad luck)* ser mala suerte; **to put a j. on sb** embrujar a algn, *Esp* gafar a algn, *Méx* echarle la sal a algn, *RP* enyetar a algn
  2 *vt* gafar

jinxed [dʒɪŋkst] *adj Fam Esp* gafado(a), *Méx* salado(a)

JIT [dʒɪt] *adj Ind (abbr* **just in time)** **J. production** producción *f* 'justo a tiempo' *(con minimización de stocks)*

jitters ['dʒɪtəz] *npl* **the j.** canguelo *m*, *Méx* mello *m*, *RP* cuiqui *m*; **to get/have the j.** entrar el canguelo *or Méx* mello *or RP* cuiqui a uno

jittery ['dʒɪtərɪ] *adj* nervioso(a); **to be j.** tener miedo *or* canguelo

jiu-jitsu [dʒuː'dʒɪtsuː] *n see* ju-jitsu

jive [dʒaɪv] *Mus* **1** *n* swing *m*
  2 *vi* bailar el swing

Jnr *US (abbr* **Junior)** hijo, el más joven

job [dʒɒb] *n* (**a**) *(piece of work)* trabajo *m*; *(task)* & *Comptr* tarea *f*; **to do a j.** hacer un trabajo; **to do a good j.** hacer un buen trabajo; **to do odd jobs** hacer trabajillos; **to give sth/sb up as a bad j.** darse por vencido(a); **to make a good/bad j. of sth** hacer algo bien/mal; **to make the best of a bad j.** poner a mal tiempo buena cara; **you should be on the j.** deberías estar trabajando en este momento; *Br Fam* **just the j.!** ¡perfecto! ¡justo lo que nos hacía falta! ❑ **odd j. man** hombre *m* que hace de todo (**b**) *(occupation, post)* (puesto *m* de) trabajo *m*, empleo *m*; *(trade)* oficio *m*; **he's got a j. as a waiter** trabaja de camarero; **to have a good j.** tener un buen puesto; **to have j. satisfaction** sentirse realizado(a) en su trabajo; **to look for a j.** buscar empleo; **to lose one's j.** perder el empleo; **she knows her j.** conoce (bien) su oficio; *Br Fam* **jobs for the boys** enchufismo *m* ❑ *US* **j. action** huelga *f* de celo; *US* **J. Center** oficina *f* de empleo; **j. hunting** búsqueda *f* de empleo; **j. sharing** trabajo *m* compartido a tiempo partido (**c**) *Fam (difficult task)* esfuerzo *m*, trabajo *m*; **we had a j. to ...** nos costó (trabajo) ... (**d**) *Fam (robbery)* golpe *m*, robo *m* (**e**) *(duty)* deber *m*; **it's his j. to ...** él está encargado de ... (**f**) *Br Fam (state of affairs)* **it's a good j.!** ¡menos mal!; **it's a good j. that ...** menos mal que ... (**g**) *Fam (specimen)* modelo *m*; **that motorbike's a lovely j.** esa moto es una máquina finísima (**h**) *Fam (finished piece of work)* trabajo *m*, obra *f*; **he did a good paint j. on the house** hizo un buen trabajo pintando la casa

jobber ['dʒɒbər] *n* (**a**) *(middleman)* intermediario *m,f* (**b**) *(Stock Exchange)* corredor(a) *m,f* de Bolsa

jobbing ['dʒɒbɪŋ] *adj Br (carpenter, electrician)* a destajo ❑ **j. printer** impresor *m* que se dedica al mundo comercial

Jobcentre ['dʒɒbsentə(r)] *n Br* oficina *f* de empleo

jobless ['dʒɒblɪs] *adj* sin trabajo, *Am* desocupado(a), *Esp* parado(a)

job lot [dʒɒb'lɒt] *n* lote *m* mixto vendido a bajo precio

job-share ['dʒɒbʃeər] **1** *n* empleo *m* compartido
  2 *vi* compartir un empleo

jock [dʒɒk] *n US Fam (athlete)* deportista *m*

jockey ['dʒɒkɪ] **1** *n* jinete *m*, jockey *m*
  2 *vi* luchar para conseguir una posición aventajada; *(in hierarchy)* ascender, escalar; **to j. for position** escalar puestos

Jockey® shorts ['dʒɒkɪʃɔːts] *npl US* calzoncillos *mpl*, *Chile* fundillos *mpl*, *Col* pantaloncillos *mpl*, *Méx* calzones *mpl*, *Méx* chones *mpl*

jockstrap ['dʒɒkstræp] *n* suspensorio *m*

jocose [dʒə'kəʊs] *adj* jocoso(a), gracioso(a), divertido(a)

jocular ['dʒɒkjʊlər] *adj* jocoso(a), gracioso(a)

jodhpurs ['dʒɒdpəz] *npl Equit* pantalón *m sing* de montar

Joe [dʒəʊ] *n US Fam* **he's an ordinary J.** es un tipo del montón; *Br* **J. Bloggs** *or* **Public,** *US* **J. Blow** *or* **Schmo** el ciudadano de a pie *or RP* común y silvestre

jog [dʒɒg] **1** *n* trote *m;* **slow j.** trote corto; *Sport* **to go for a j.** hacer footing
2 *vt (pt & pp* **jogged)** empujar; *Fig (memory)* refrescar; **to j. sb's elbow** dar un golpe en el codo a algn
3 *vi Sport* hacer footing; **to j. along** *or* **on** andar a trote corto; *Fig (progress slowly)* avanzar poco a poco; *Fig (manage)* ir tirando

jogger ['dʒɒgər] *n Sport* = persona que practica el footing

jogging ['dʒɒgɪŋ] *n Sport* footing *m;* **to go j.** hacer footing □ *Br* **j. bottoms,** *US* **j. pants** pantalones *mpl* de *Esp* chándal *or RP* jogging *or Ven* mono, *Méx* pants *mpl*

Johannesburg [dʒəʊˈhænɪsbɜːg] *n* Johannesburgo

John [dʒɒn] *n* Juan *m;* **J. Bull** = personificación de Inglaterra; **J. the Baptist** San Juan Bautista

john [dʒɒn] *n US Fam* wáter *m,* retrete *m,* servicio *m*

John Dory [dʒɒnˈdɔːrɪ] *n (fish)* pez *m* de San Pedro

join [dʒɔɪn] **1** *vt* (**a**) *(gen)* juntar; **they joined the tables** juntaron las mesas; **to j. forces with sb** unir fuerzas con algn (**b**) *(of road)* empalmar con; *(of river)* desembocar en; **the road joins the motorway here** la carretera empalma con la autopista aquí (**c**) *(meet, accompany)* reunirse con; **will you j. us for a drink?** ¿quiere tomar una copa con nosotros? (**d**) *(take one's place in) (team, group)* unirse a; *(institution)* entrar en; *(army)* alistarse en; **Mr Serrano joined the company last month** el Sr. Serrano se incorporó a la compañía el mes pasado (**e**) *(become a member of) (party)* afiliarse a; *(club)* hacerse socio(a) de
2 *vi* (**a**) *(gen)* unirse (**b**) *(roads)* empalmar; *(rivers)* confluir; **the Wharfe and the Ouse j. near Cawood** el Wharfe y el Ouse confluyen cerca de Cawood (**c**) *(become a member) (party)* afiliarse; *(club)* hacerse socio(a)
3 *n* (**a**) *(gen)* juntura *f* (**b**) *Sew* costura *f*

join in 1 *vi (game etc)* participar, tomar parte; *(debate, discussion)* intervenir
2 *vt (game etc)* participar en, tomar parte en; *(debate)* intervenir en; **they all joined in the singing** todos se pusieron a cantar

join up 1 *vt (of two things)* juntar
2 *vi* (**a**) *(roads)* unirse (**b**) *Mil* alistarse

joiner ['dʒɔɪnər] *n Br* carpintero(a) *m,f*

joinery ['dʒɔɪnərɪ] *n* carpintería *f*

joint [dʒɔɪnt] **1** *n* (**a**) *(gen)* juntura *f,* unión *f; Tech* articulación *f,* *(woodwork, pipes)* ensambladura *f; Anat* articulación *f;* **out of j.** dislocado(a); *Br* **to put sb's nose out of j.** *(upset)* desairar a algn (**b**) *Culin (piece of meat)* corte *m* de carne para asar; *(once roasted)* asado *m* (**c**) *Slang (nightclub etc)* garito *m,* antro *m* (**d**) *Slang (drug)* porro *m* (**e**) *US Slang (prison) Esp* chirona *f, Andes RP* cana *f, Méx* bote *m*
2 *vt Culin (chicken etc)* descuartizar
3 *adj* colectivo(a) □ **j. (bank) account** cuenta *f* (bancaria) conjunta; **j. agreement** acuerdo *m* mutuo; **j. author** coautor(a) *m,f;* **j. effort** esfuerzo *m* colectivo; **j. ownership** copropiedad *f;* **j. statement** declaración *f* conjunta; **j. venture** empresa *f* común

jointed ['dʒɔɪntɪd] *adj* articulado(a)

jointly ['dʒɔɪntlɪ] *adv* conjuntamente, en común

joist [dʒɔɪst] *n Archit* vigueta *f*

joke [dʒəʊk] **1** *n* (**a**) *(funny story)* chiste *m; (prank)* broma *f;* **he can't take a j.** no sabe aguantar una broma; **it's getting beyond a j.** está pasando de castaño a oscuro, ya no tiene gracia; **she did it for a j.** lo hizo en broma; **to make a j. of everything** reírse de todo; **to play a practical j. on sb** gastarle una broma pesada a algn; **to tell a j.** contar un chiste; *Fam* **it's no j.** no tiene gracia (**b**) *Fam (person, thing)*

hazmerreír *m,* payaso(a) *m,f; Fam* **the j. is on you** tú pagarás el pato
2 *vi* estar de broma; **I'm not joking** lo digo en serio; **joking apart** bromas aparte; **to j. about sth** reírse de algo; **you must be joking!** ¡no hablarás en serio!

joker ['dʒəʊkər] *n* (**a**) *(clown)* bromista *mf,* guasón(ona) *m,f* (**b**) *Cards* comodín *m*

jokey ['dʒəʊkɪ] *adj* jocoso(a)

jokily ['dʒəʊkɪlɪ] *adv* en tono de broma

jokingly ['dʒəʊkɪŋlɪ] *adv* en broma

jolly ['dʒɒlɪ] **1** *adj* (**jollier, jolliest**) (**a**) *(happy)* jovial, alegre (**b**) *(tipsy)* piripi, achispado(a)
2 *adv Fam Br* (**a**) *(very)* **it was j. cold** hacía mucho frío; **j. good!** *Méx* ¡padre!, *RP* ¡bárbaro!; **j. useful** de lo más práctico; **she played j. well** jugó muy bien (**b**) **j. well** *(really)* decididamente; **I'm j. well not going** desde luego, yo no voy
3 *vt* animar; **to j. sb along** animar a algn

jolt [dʒəʊlt] **1** *n* (**a**) *(jerk)* sacudida *f; (pull)* tirón *m; Fig (fright)* susto *m;* **it gave me a j.** me dio un susto
2 *vi* moverse a sacudidas; **the car jolted along** el coche iba dando botes
3 *vt (usually passive)* sacudir; **she was jolted out of her daydreaming by a sudden scream** un grito repentino la hizo volver a la realidad

Jordan ['dʒɔːdən] *n* (**a**) *(river)* Jordán *m* (**b**) *(country)* Jordania

Jordanian [dʒɔːˈdeɪnɪən] *adj & n* jordano(a) *(m,f)*

josh [dʒɒʃ] *vt Fam (tease)* tomar el pelo a

joss-stick ['dʒɒstɪk] *n* varita *f* de incienso, pebete *m*

jostle ['dʒɒsəl] **1** *vt (bump)* empujar; **he jostled his way through the crowd** se abrió paso a empujones entre la multitud
2 *vi* (**a**) *(bump)* dar empujones (**b**) *(compete)* competir; **they jostled for the prize** compitieron por el premio

jot [dʒɒt] **1** *n* jota *f,* pizca *f;* **I don't care a j.** me importa un bledo; **not a j.** ni jota
2 *vt (pt & pp* **jotted)** apuntar, anotar

jot down *vt* apuntar, anotar

jotter ['dʒɒtər] *n Br* bloc *m*

jottings ['dʒɒtɪŋz] *npl* notas *fpl,* apuntes *mpl*

joule [dʒuːl] *n Elec Phys* julio *m*

journal ['dʒɜːnəl] *n* (**a**) *(periodical)* boletín *m,* revista *f* (**b**) *(diary)* diario *m* (**c**) *(newspaper)* periódico *m*

journalese [dʒɜːnəˈliːz] *n* jerga *f* periodística, lenguaje *m* periodístico

journalism ['dʒɜːnəlɪzəm] *n* periodismo *m*

journalist ['dʒɜːnəlɪst] *n* periodista *mf*

journalistic [dʒɜːnəˈlɪstɪk] *adj* periodístico(a)

journey ['dʒɜːnɪ] **1** *n* (**a**) *(trip)* viaje *m;* **to go on a j.** salir de viaje (**b**) *(distance)* trayecto *m;* **a twenty-mile j.** un trayecto de veinte millas; **it's a two-day j. from here** son dos días de viaje desde aquí
2 *vi Fml* viajar

joust [dʒaʊst] *vi Hist* justar, justear

jovial ['dʒəʊvɪəl] *adj* jovial

jowl [dʒaʊl] *n (of animal)* quijada *f; Fig* **cheek by j.** muy unidos(as)

joy [dʒɔɪ] *n* (**a**) *(happiness)* alegría *f* (**b**) *(pleasure)* placer *m;* **it's a j. to see him** da gusto verle (**c**) *Br Fam (luck, use)* suerte *f;* **you won't get any j. out of it, it doesn't work** no conseguirás nada, no funciona

joyful ['dʒɔɪfʊl] *adj* alegre, contento(a)

joyless ['dʒɔɪlɪs] *adj* triste

joyous ['dʒɔɪəs] *adj Literary* alegre, jubiloso(a)

joyride ['dʒɔɪraɪd] *n Fam* paseo *m* en un coche *or Am* carro *or esp CSur* auto robado

joystick ['dʒɔɪstɪk] *n* (**a**) *Av* palanca *f* de mando (**b**) *(of video game)* joystick *m*

JP [dʒeɪ'piː] *n Br Jur* (*abbr* **Justice of the Peace**) juez *m* de paz

Jr *abbr see* **Jnr**

jubilant ['dʒuːbɪlənt] *adj* jubiloso(a), alborozado(a)

jubilation [dʒuːbɪ'leɪʃən] *n* júbilo *m*, regocijo *m*, alborozo *m*

jubilee ['dʒuːbɪliː] *n* festejos *mpl*; **golden j.** *(general sense)* quincuagésimo aniversario *m*; *(wedding anniversary)* bodas *fpl* de oro

Judaic(al) [dʒuː'deɪk(əl)] *adj* judaico(a)

Judaism ['dʒuːdeɪɪzəm] *n* judaísmo *m*

Judas ['dʒuːdəs] *n* **J. tree** árbol *m* del amor *or* de Judas, ciclamor *m*

judder ['dʒʌdər] *vi Br* dar sacudidas, dar botes, vibrar

judge [dʒʌdʒ] **1** *n Jur* juez *mf*, jueza *f*; *(competition)* jurado *m*; **to be a good j.** saber juzgar; **to be a good j. of character** saber juzgar a las personas

2 *vt* (**a**) *Jur (case)* juzgar; *(accused)* declarar (**b**) *(estimate, consider)* calcular, considerar; **he judged the distance badly** calculó mal la distancia; **I j. him the best** le considero el mejor; **I j. him to be about 45** le calculo unos 45 años (**c**) *(competition)* adjudicar, decidir; **she judged the poetry competition** fue miembro del jurado en el concurso de poesía (**d**) *(assess)* juzgar; **never j. a person just by their appearance** no juzgues nunca a una persona sólo por su aspecto

3 *vi* juzgar, formarse una opinión; **judging from what you say** a juzgar por lo que dices

judg(e)ment ['dʒʌdʒmənt] *n* (**a**) *Jur (sentence)* sentencia *f*, fallo *m*; **to pass j.** pronunciar sentencia; **to sit in j. on a case** deliberar en un juicio (**b**) *(opinion)* juicio *m*, opinión *f*; **to do sth against one's better j.** hacer algo sin estar completamente convencido(a); **to pass j.** comentar, opinar (**on** sobre); **to reserve j.** no opinar (**on** sobre), reservarse la opinión; **to the best of my j.** por lo que puedo juzgar, a mi entender (**c**) *(ability)* discernimiento *m*, buen juicio *m*; **a person of sound j.** una persona con capacidad de juicio (**d**) *Jur (trial)* juicio *m*; **the Last J.** el Juicio Final

judg(e)mental [dʒʌdʒ'mentəl] *adj* **to be j.** hacer juicios a la ligera

judicial [dʒuː'dɪʃəl] *adj* judicial; **j. inquiry** investigación *f* judicial

judiciary [dʒuː'dɪʃɪərɪ] *n* magistratura *f*, judicatura *f*

judicious [dʒuː'dɪʃəs] *adj Fml* juicioso(a), sensato(a)

judiciousness [dʒuː'dɪʃəsnɪs] *n Fml* juicio *m*, sensatez *f*, sentido *m* común

judo ['dʒuːdəʊ] *n* judo *m*

judoka [dʒuː'dəʊkæ] *n* judoka *mf*

jug [dʒʌg] *n* (**a**) *Br (container)* jarra *f*; **milk j.** jarra de leche (**b**) *Slang (prison) Esp* chirona *f*, *Andes RP* cana *f*, *Méx* bote *m*; **in j.** en la cárcel *or Esp* chirona *or Andes RP* la cana *or Méx* el bote

2 *vt Culin* estofar; **jugged hare** estofado *m* de liebre

juggernaut ['dʒʌgənɔːt] *n Br Aut* camión *m* pesado

juggle ['dʒʌgəl] *vi* (**a**) *(perform)* hacer juegos malabares (**with** con) (**b**) *Fig (organize)* reorganizar; **to j. with figures** jugar con las cifras

juggler ['dʒʌglər] *n* malabarista *mf*

jugular ['dʒʌgjʊlər] *adj Anat* yugular *f*

juice [dʒuːs] *n* (**a**) *(gen) Esp* zumo *m*, *Am* jugo *m*; *(of citrus fruits)* zumo *m*; **tomato j.** jugo de tomate; **gastric j.** jugo gástrico (**b**) *US Fam (gasoline)* gasolina *f*, *Esp* gasofa *f*, *RP* nafta *f* (**c**) *Anat* **juices** jugos *mpl*; **digestive j.** jugos digestivos

juicer ['dʒuːsər] *n* exprimidor *m*

juiciness ['dʒuːsɪnɪs] *n* jugosidad *f*

juicy ['dʒuːsɪ] *adj* (**juicier, juiciest**) (**a**) *(succulent)* jugoso(a); **j. orange** naranja jugosa (**b**) *Fam Fig* verde, picante; **a j. story** una historia picante

ju-jitsu [dʒuː'dʒɪtsuː] *n* jiu-jitsu *m*

jukebox ['dʒuːkbɒks] *n* máquina *f* de discos

Jul *(abbr* **July**) julio *m*, jul

July [dʒuː'laɪ] *n* julio *m*; **in J.** en julio; *see also* **May**

jumble ['dʒʌmbəl] **1** *n* revoltijo *m*, revoltillo *m*, mezcolanza *f* □ *Br* **j. sale** bazar *m* *or* mercadillo *m* de caridad

2 *vt* mezclar, revolver

jumbo ['dʒʌmbəʊ] **1** *adj* enorme, gigante

2 *n* (**a**) *Av* **j. (jet)** jumbo *m* (**b**) *Zool Fam* elefante *m*

jump [dʒʌmp] **1** *n* (**a**) *(leap)* salto *m*; *Sport* **the horse cleared the third j.** el caballo pasó el tercer obstáculo □ *Br Aut* **j. leads** pinzas *fpl* *or* cables *mpl* (de arranque) de batería; *US* **j. rope** *Esp* comba *f*, *Am* cuerda *f* de saltar; **j. suit** mono *m*; **high j.** salto *m* de altura; **long j.** salto *m* de longitud (**b**) *(sudden increase)* salto *m*, subida *f* repentina; **there was a sudden j. in prices in December** hubo una subida repentina de los precios en diciembre (**c**) *(step)* paso *m*; **they made a huge j. forward in the plans for the pedestrian precinct** dieron un paso gigante para adelantar el proyecto de la zona peatonal

2 *vi* (**a**) *(leap)* saltar, dar un salto; *Aut* **j. in!** ¡sube!; **he jumped into the taxi** subió de un salto al taxi; **Ingrid jumped off the wall** Ingrid saltó del muro; **to j. down from a wall** bajarse de un muro; **to j. into the water** tirarse al agua; **to j. out of the window** tirarse por la ventana; **to j. up and down** dar brincos; *Fig* **to j. for joy** saltar de alegría; *Fig* **to j. from one subject to another** saltar de un tema a otro; *Fig* **to j. to conclusions** sacar conclusiones precipitadas; *Fam* **j. to it!** ¡hazlo ya!; *Fam Fig* **to j. down sb's throat** echarle una bronca *or* un rapapolvo a algn (**b**) *Fig (start)* sobresaltarse; **he jumped out of his skin when he heard the noise** se pegó un susto de muerte cuando oyó el ruido; **her heart jumped when she saw the telegram** el corazón le dio un vuelco cuando vio el telegrama; **to make sb j.** darle un susto a algn, asustar a algn (**c**) *(increase)* dar un salto, aumentar de golpe; **the price of gasoline jumped sharply last month** el precio de la gasolina aumentó bruscamente el mes pasado

3 *vt* (**a**) *(leap)* saltar; **the horse jumped the fence** el caballo saltó la valla; **to j. the gun** *Sport* tomar la salida en falso; *Fam Fig* precipitarse; **to j.** *Br* **the queue** *or US* **the line** colarse (**b**) *Equit* hacer saltar; **to j. a horse over a fence** hacer saltar una valla a un caballo (**c**) *(miss out)* saltarse; **he jumped the question** se saltó la pregunta (**d**) *(of train) Fam* **to j. a train** coger un tren sin pagar (**e**) *Aut Fam* saltarse; **to j. the lights** saltarse el semáforo, *RP* comerse la luz roja

jump at *vt* aceptar sin pensarlo; **she jumped at the offer** aceptó la oferta sin pensarlo

jump on *vt* criticar, reñir; **she jumped on me for telling Sylvia** me riñó por habérselo contado a Sylvia

jumped-up ['dʒʌmptʌp] *adj Br* arribista, advenedizo(a)

jumper ['dʒʌmpər] *n* (**a**) *Br (sweater)* suéter *m*, *Esp* jersey *m*, *Col* saco *m*, *RP* pulóver *m* (**b**) *US (dress) Esp* pichi *m*, *CSur Méx* jumper *m*

jumpiness ['dʒʌmpɪnɪs] *n Fam* nerviosismo *m*

jumping-off place ['dʒʌmpɪŋ'ɒf'pleɪs] *n*, **jumping-off point** ['dʒʌmpɪŋ'ɒf'pɔɪnt] *n* punto *m* de partida

jump-jet ['dʒʌmpdʒet] *n Av* avión *m or* reactor *m* de despegue vertical

jump-start ['dʒʌmpstɑːt] *vt (car)* arrancar utilizando pinzas de batería

jumpy ['dʒʌmpɪ] *adj* (**jumpier, jumpiest**) *Fam* nervioso(a)

Jun (a) *(abbr* **June**) junio *m*, jun (b) *abbr see* **Jnr**

junction ['dʒʌŋkʃən] *n* (a) *(of roads)* cruce *m* (b) *Rail Elec* empalme *m*; **j. box** caja *f* de empalme

juncture ['dʒʌŋktʃər] *n Fml* coyuntura *f*; **at this j.** en esta coyuntura

June [dʒuːn] *n* junio *m*; **(on) 5th J.** el cinco de junio; *see also* **May**

jungle ['dʒʌŋgəl] *n* jungla *f*, selva *f*; *Fig* laberinto *m*; **the concrete j.** la jungla de asfalto

junior ['dʒuːnjər] **1** *adj* (a) *(son of)* hijo; **David Hughes j.** David Hughes hijo (b) *(young) US* **j. high (school)** *(between 11 and 15)* escuela *f* secundaria; *Br* **j. school** *(between 7 and 11)* escuela *f* primaria; *Sport* **j. team** equipo *m* juvenil (c) *(lower in rank)* subalterno(a) ❑ **j. members** miembros *mpl* de menor antigüedad *or* más recientes; **j. officer** oficial subalterno

2 *n* (a) *(person of lower rank)* subalterno(a) *m,f* (b) *(younger person)* menor *mf*; **she's my j. by five years** tiene cinco años menos que yo, le llevo cinco años (c) *Br Educ* alumno(a) *m,f* de EGB; *US* estudiante *mf* de penúltimo año

juniper ['dʒuːnɪpər] *n Bot* enebro *m*, junípero *m*

junk [dʒʌŋk] *n* (a) *Fam (old furniture etc)* trastos *mpl* ❑ *Fin* **j. bond** bono *m* basura; *Fam* **j. food** comida *f* de plástico; **j. heap** vertedero *m*; *Fam* **j. mail** propaganda *f* (por correo); **j. shop** baratillo *m*, tienda *f* de artículos usados (b) *(boat)* junco *m* (c) *(drug) Slang* heroína *f*

junket ['dʒʌŋkɪt] *n* (a) *Culin* requesón *m*, cuajada *f* (b) *US Can (visit)* visita *f* oficial

junketing ['dʒʌŋkɪtɪŋ] *n Fam* fiesta *f*; **to go j.** irse de fiesta

junkie ['dʒʌŋkɪ] *n Slang* yonqui *mf*

junky ['dʒʌŋkɪ] *n see* **junkie**

junkyard ['dʒʌŋkjɑːd] *n (for metal)* chatarrería *f*, depósito *m* de chatarra

junta ['dʒʌntə, *US* 'hʊntə] *n Mil Pol* junta *f*, junta *f* militar

Jupiter ['dʒuːpɪtər] *n Astron Myth* Júpiter *m*

jurisdiction [dʒʊərɪs'dɪkʃən] *n Fml* jurisdicción *f*; **it doesn't come within our j.** no es de nuestra competencia

jurisprudence [dʒʊərɪs'pruːdəns] *n Fml* jurisprudencia *f*

jurist ['dʒʊərɪst] *n Fml* jurista *mf*

juror ['dʒʊərər] *n* jurado(a) *m,f*, miembro *m* de un jurado

jury ['dʒʊərɪ] *n* jurado *m*, tribunal *m*; **to serve on a j.** ser miembro de un jurado ❑ **j. box** tribuna *f* del jurado, banco *m* del jurado

just [dʒʌst] **1** *adj (fair)* justo(a); *(deserved)* merecido(a); *Fml (well-founded)* justificado(a); **a j. sentence** una sentencia justa; **a j. war** una guerra justificada; **it is only j. that ...** es justo que ...; **it was a j. reward for all his hard work** fue un justo premio a todos sus esfuerzos

2 *adv* (a) *(recently)* **to have j.** acabar de; **he had j. arrived** acababa de llegar; **the film has j. started** la película acaba de empezar (b) *(at this very moment)* ahora mismo, en este momento; **a plane is j. taking off** un avión está despegando en este mismo momento; **he was j. leaving when Rosa arrived** estaba a punto de salir cuando llegó Rosa; **I'm j. coming!** ¡ya voy!; **I'm j. leaving** me marcho ahora mismo; **j. as ...** cuando ..., justo al ...; **j. as I shut the door I realized I had left my keys inside** justo al cerrar la puerta me di cuenta de que había dejado las llaves en el interior; **j. as I was leaving** en el momento en que me marchaba (c) *(only)* solamente, nada más, sólo; **he is j. a boy** no es más que un niño; **j. in case** por si acaso; **j. those with tickets** únicamente los que llevan billetes; **these are j. a few examples of his work** estas son sólo algunas muestras de su trabajo; **they are j. good friends** sólo son buenos amigos; *Fam* **j. a minute** *or* **a moment** *or* **a second!** ¡un momento! (d) *(barely, very nearly)* por poco; **I j. managed it** por poco no lo consigo; **I only j. caught the bus** *Am* tomé *or Esp* cogí el autobús por los pelos; **j. about** casi; **j. enough** justo lo suficiente; **we'll j. make it** llegaremos justo a tiempo (e) *(emphatic)* **he's so good-looking —isn't he j.!** ¡es tan guapo! —¡ya lo creo!; **it's j. fantastic!** ¡es sencillamente fantástico!; **she's j. marvellous** es un encanto de mujer; **you'll j. have to wait** tendrás que esperar (f) *(exactly)* exactamente, justamente, justo; **it's j. what I wanted** es exactamente lo que quería; **j. as I thought** me lo figuraba; **she likes everything j. so** le gusta tenerlo todo perfecto; **that's j. it!** ¡precisamente!; *Fam* **it's j. my luck** vaya mala suerte tengo (g) *(equally)* tan, igual de; **my car's j. as fast as yours** mi coche es tan rápido como el tuyo

3 the j. *npl* los justos

justice ['dʒʌstɪs] *n* (a) *(fairness)* justicia *f*; **he was brought to j.** lo llevaron ante los tribunales; **let j. be done** que se haga justicia; **the portrait doesn't do her j.** el retrato no le hace justicia; **we did j. to the fantastic lunch** correspondimos lo mejor que pudimos a tan fantástica comida; **you didn't do yourself j. in the interview** no diste lo mejor de ti en la entrevista (b) *Jur (judge, magistrate)* juez *mf*; **J. of the Peace** juez de paz; *Br* **Mr J. Burke** el juez Burke

justifiable ['dʒʌstɪfaɪəbəl] *adj* justificable ❑ *Jur* **j. homicide** homicidio *m* justificado

justification [dʒʌstɪfɪ'keɪʃən] *n* (a) *(defence)* justificación *f*, razón *f*; **in j. of** en defensa de (b) *(of text)* justificación *f*

justified ['dʒʌstɪfaɪd] *adj* (a) *(right)* justificado(a); **to be j. in doing sth** tener razón en hacer algo (b) *(text)* justificado(a)

justify ['dʒʌstɪfaɪ] *vt* (*pt & pp* **justified**) (a) *(explain)* justificar; **he justified what he had done** justificó lo que había hecho (b) *(text)* justificar

justly ['dʒʌstlɪ] *adv* justamente, con justicia; **she was j. famous** alcanzó merecida fama

justness ['dʒʌstnɪs] *n (fairness)* justicia *f*

jut [dʒʌt] *vi* (*pt & pp* **jutted**) sobresalir; **to j. out from** sobresalir de; **to j. out over** proyectarse sobre

Jute [dʒuːt] *n Hist* yuto(a) *m,f*

jute [dʒuːt] *n Bot* yute *m*

juvenile ['dʒuːvənaɪl] **1** *adj* (a) *(young)* juvenil; *Jur* **j. court** tribunal de menores; **j. delinquent** delincuente juvenil (b) *(immature)* infantil; **don't be so j.!** ¡no seas tan infantil!

2 *n* menor *mf*, joven *mf*, adolescente *mf*

juxtapose [dʒʌkstə'pəʊz] *vt* yuxtaponer

juxtaposition [dʒʌkstəpə'zɪʃən] *n* yuxtaposición *f*

K

K, k [keɪ] *n (the letter)* K, k *f*

k [keɪ] (**a**) *(abbr* **kilo***)* kilo *m*, kilogramo *m*, kg (**b**) *Comptr (abbr* **kilobyte***)* K

Kabul [kəˈbʊl, ˈkɑːbəl] *n* Kabul

kaftan [ˈkæftæn] *n* caftán *m*

Kaiser [ˈkaɪzər] *n* káiser *m*

kale [keɪl] *n* col *f* rizada; *CSur* repollo *m* rizado

kaleidoscope [kəˈlaɪdəskəʊp] *n* caleidoscopio *m*

kamikaze [kæmɪˈkɑːzɪ] *adj & n* kamikaze *(mf)*

Kampuchea [kæmpʊˈtʃɪə] *n Formerly* Kampuchea

kangaroo [ˈkæŋgəˈruː] *n* canguro *m* ❑ **k. court** tribunal *m* desautorizado

kaolin [ˈkeɪəlɪn] *n Min* caolín *m*

kapok [ˈkeɪpɒk] *n* kapok *m*

kaput [kæˈpʊt] *adj Fam* estropeado(a); *(plan)* fastidiado(a); **my car's k.** tengo el coche estropeado

karaoke [kærɪˈəʊkɪ] *n* karaoke *m*

karat [ˈkærət] *n US* quilate *m*

karate [kəˈrɑːtɪ] *n Sport* kárate *m*

karma [ˈkɑːmə] *n Rel* karma *m*; *Fam Fig* **good/bad k.** buenas/malas vibraciones *or Am* ondas, *Esp* buen/mal rollo

Kashmir [kæʃˈmɪər] *n* Cachemira

Kat(h)mandu [kætmænˈduː] *n* Katmandú

kayak [ˈkaɪæk] *n* kayac *m*

Kázak(h)stan [kæzækˈstɑːn] *n* Kazajistán

kebab [kəˈbæb] *n Culin* pincho *m* moruno, brocheta *f*

keel [kiːl] *n Naut* quilla *f*; *Fig* **to be on an even k.** estar en equilibrio

keel over *vi (boat)* zozobrar; *Fam (person)* desmayarse

keen¹ [kiːn] *adj* (**a**) *(eager)* entusiasta; **he's a k.** golfer, **he's k. on golf** es muy aficionado al golf; *Fam* **he's k. on your sister** le gusta tu hermana (**b**) *(intense)* profundo(a); **she took a k. interest in international affairs** tomó un gran interés por los asuntos internacionales (**c**) *(sharp, acute) (mind, senses)* agudo(a); *(look)* penetrante; *(wind)* cortante; *(blade)* afilado(a); *(competition)* fuerte (**d**) *Br (price)* competitivo(a)

keen² [kiːn] *vi* lamentar

keenly [ˈkiːnlɪ] *adv (intensely)* profundamente; *(eagerly)* con entusiasmo

keenness [ˈkiːnɪs] *n* (**a**) *(enthusiasm)* entusiasmo *m*, afición *f* (**b**) *(intensity)* intensidad *f*, fuerza *f* (**c**) *(sharpness)* agudeza *f*, penetración *f*

keep [kiːp] *n* (**a**) *(maintenance)* manutención *f*; **to earn one's k.** ganarse el cocido *or* el pan (**b**) *(tower)* torreón *m* (**c**) *Fam* **for keeps** para siempre

2 *vt (pt & pp* **kept***)* (**a**) *(cause to remain)* tener, mantener; *(letters, memories, silence)* guardar; **to k. one's looks** conservarse bien; **to k. sb awake** mantener despierto(a) a algn; **to k. sb informed** tener a algn al corriente; **to k. sb in the dark about sth** ocultarle algo a algn; **to k. sth in mind** tener a algo en cuenta *or* en mente (**b**) *(retain possession of)* quedarse con; **he can't k. a job for more than six months** es incapaz de conservar un trabajo más de seis meses; **k. it, it's for you** quédatelo, es tuyo; **k. the change** quédese con el cambio (**c**) *(detain)* detener, retener; **the rain kept them at home** la lluvia les retuvo en casa; **to k. sb waiting** hacer esperar a algn (**d**) *(maintain, support)* mantener; *(animals)* criar; **badly kept road** carretera en mal estado (**e**) *(observe, fulfil) (the law)* observar; *(a promise)* cumplir; *(holidays)* guardar (**f**) *(conceal, reserve) (secret, place)* guardar; **k. this to yourself** no se lo digas a nadie (**g**) *(write) (diary, accounts)* llevar; *Educ* **to k. the register** pasar lista (**h**) *(prevent, delay)* **to k. sb from doing sth** impedir a algn hacer algo; **I don't know what kept me from slapping him** no sé qué me impidió darle una bofetada; **the noise keeps me from sleeping** el ruido me impide dormir (**i**) *(own, manage)* tener; *(shop, hotel)* llevar; **to k. house** llevar la casa (**j**) *(stock)* tener, vender; **we don't k. cigars** no vendemos puros

3 *vi* (**a**) *(remain)* mantenerse; **k. calm!** ¡tranquilo!; **k. quiet!** ¡cállate!; **k. still!** ¡estate quieto!; **to k. fit** mantenerse en forma; **to k. going** seguir adelante; *Fig* ir tirando; **to k. in touch** no perder el contacto; **to k. smiling** seguir sonriendo (**b**) *(do frequently)* **he keeps phoning me** no deja de llamarme; **she keeps forgetting her keys** siempre se olvida las llaves (**c**) *(food)* conservarse

keep at *vt (persevere)* **k. at it!** ¡no te desanimes!; **the boss kept us at it all day** el jefe nos hizo trabajar en ello todo el día

keep away 1 *vt* mantener a distancia

2 *vi* mantenerse a distancia; **to k. away from drink** abstenerse de beber

keep back *vt* (**a**) *(hold back) (enemy)* contener; **his ill-health kept him back at school** su mala salud le impidió progresar en el colegio (**b**) *(withhold) (truth, information)* ocultar, callar; *(money, food, etc)* retener

keep down *vt* (**a**) *(limit)* limitar; **to k. expenses down** limitar los gastos; **to k. prices down** mantener los precios bajos (**b**) *(oppress)* contener (**c**) *(prevent vomiting)* **I can't even k. water down** vomito hasta el agua que bebo

keep in *vt (detain)* no dejar salir, impedir salir; **he was kept in after school** le dejaron castigado

keep in with *vi* cultivar la amistad de

keep off 1 *vt (bar from)* prohibir; *(prevent from touch or reference)* no tocar; *(avoid consuming)* no comer, no beber; **k. off the grass** prohibido pisar la hierba; **please k. off that**

subject le ruego que no toque ese tema
 2 *vi* the rain kept off no llegó a llover
keep on 1 *vt* (**a**) *(clothes etc)* no quitarse; **to k. an eye on sth/sb** vigilar algo/a algn; *Fam* **k. your shirt on!** ¡no pierdas la calma! (**b**) *(continue to employ)* no despedir
 2 *vi (continue to do)* seguir; **she kept on walking** siguió andando
keep on about *vt Fam Pej* no parar de hablar de; **he keeps on about money** no para de hablar del dinero
keep on at *vt Fam* no dejar tranquilo(a)
keep out 1 *vt* no dejar pasar
 2 *vi* no entrar; **k. out!** ¡prohibida la entrada!
keep out of *vt* evitar; **I kept out of trouble** evité líos; **k. out of this!** ¡no te metas en esto!
keep to *vt* (**a**) *(observe) (law, promise)* cumplir; **to k. sb to his promise** obligar a algn a cumplir lo prometido; **to k. to a resolution** mantenerse firme en un propósito (**b**) *(restrict)* limitarse a; **k. to the point!** ¡ciñete a la cuestión! (**c**) *(remain, stay)* quedarse en; **he kept to his room all day** se quedó en su cuarto todo el día; **to k. oneself to oneself** no relacionarse con la gente; **to k. to the left** circular por la izquierda
keep up *vt* (**a**) *(maintain)* mantener; **to k. up appearances** guardar las apariencias; **to k. up the pace** mantener el ritmo (**b**) *(continue)* seguir; *Fam* **k. it up!** ¡sigue así! (**c**) *(prevent from sleeping)* mantener despierto(a); **I mustn't k. you up** ya debe ser tarde para ti
keep up with *vt* **to k. up with the times** estar al día; *Fig* **to k. up with the Joneses** no ser menos que el vecino
keeper ['ki:pər] *n* guarda *mf*, vigilante *m*; *(in library, record office)* archivero(a) *m,f*; *(in museum)* conservador(a) *m,f*
keeping ['ki:pɪŋ] *n* (**a**) *(care)* cargo *m*, cuidado *m*; **in sb's k.** al cuidado de algn; **to be in safe k.** estar en buenas manos (**b**) *(appropriate)* **in k. with** en armonía con; **out of k. with** en desacuerdo con
keepsake ['ki:pseɪk] *n* recuerdo *m*
keg [keg] *n* barril *m*
ken [ken] *n* **to be beyond sb's k.** estar fuera del alcance de algn
kennel ['kenəl] *n* (**a**) *(hut)* caseta *f* para perros (**b**) **kennels** *(for breeding)* granja *f sing* de perros; *(for boarding)* hotel *m sing* de perros
Kenya ['kenjə, 'ki:njə] *n* Kenia
Kenyan ['kenjən, 'ki:njən] *adj & n* keniata *(mf)*, keniano(a) *(m,f)*
kept [kept] *pt & pp see* **keep**
kerb [kɜ:b] *n Br* bordillo *m* (de la acera), *Chile* solera *f*, *Col Perú* sardinel *m*, *CSur* cordón *m* (de la vereda), *Méx* borde *m* (de la banqueta)
kerbstone ['kɜ:bstəʊn] *n Br* adoquín *m* (del bordillo)
kerchief ['kɜ:tʃɪf] *n Old-fashioned* pañuelo *m*
kerfuffle [kə'fʌfəl] *n Br Fam* lío *m*, *Esp* jaleo *m*
kernel ['kɜ:nəl] *n (of fruit, nut)* pepita *f*; *(of wheat)* grano *m*; *Fig* **the k. of the matter** el meollo de la cuestión
kerosene *n,* **kerosine** ['kerəsi:n] *n US* queroseno *m*, *Am* querosén *m* ❑ **k. lamp** lámpara *f* de petróleo
kestrel ['kestrəl] *n Orn* cernícalo *m* vulgar
ketch [ketʃ] *n Naut* queche *m*
ketchup ['ketʃəp] *n* ketchup *m*, salsa *f* de tomate
kettle ['ketəl] *n* tetera *f*, *Fig* **a fine k. of fish!** ¡menudo lío!; *Fam* **that's a different k. of fish** eso es harina de otro costal ❑ **electric k.** tetera *f* eléctrico
kettle-drum ['ketəldrʌm] *n Mus* timbal *m*
key [ki:] **1** *n* (**a**) *(for lock)* llave *f* ❑ **k. money** depósito *m*; **k. ring** llavero *m* (**b**) *(to code, mystery)* clave *f* (**c**) *(of piano,*

typewriter, computer) tecla *f* (**d**) *Mus* tono *m*; **minor k.** tono *m* menor; **to play off k.** desafinar (**e**) *Geog* cayo *m*
 2 *adj* clave; **k. industry** industria clave
key in *vt Comptr* teclear, *Am* tipear
keyboard ['ki:bɔ:d] *n* teclado *m* ❑ **k. player** teclista *mf*
keycard ['ki:kɑ:d] *n (for door)* tarjeta *f* de acceso
keyed up [ki:d'ʌp] *adj* nervioso(a), excitado(a)
keyhole ['ki:həʊl] *n* ojo *m* de la cerradura ❑ **k. surgery** cirugía *f* endoscópica
keynote ['ki:nəʊt] *n Mus* tónica *f*; *Fig* nota *f* dominante
keypad ['ki:pæd] *n Comptr* teclado *m* numérico
keystone ['ki:stəʊn] *n Archit* piedra *f* clave; *Fig* piedra *f* angular
keystroke ['ki:strəʊk] *n Comptr* pulsación *f*
kg *(abbr* **kilogram(s))** kilogramo(s) *m(pl)*, kg
khaki ['kæ:kɪ] *adj & n* caqui *(m)*
Khart(o)um [kɑ:'tu:m] *n* Jartum
kHz *Rad (abbr* **kilohertz)** kilohercio(s) *m(pl)*, kHz
kibbutz [kɪ'bʊts] *n (pl* **kibbutzim** [kɪbʊ'tsi:m]) kibutz *m*
kick [kɪk] **1** *n* (**a**) *(a blow) (from animal)* coz *f*; *(from person)* patada *f*, puntapié *m*; *(from gun)* culatazo *m*; *Fig* **to get a k. in the teeth** darse un canto en las narices; *Fam* **a drink with a k. in it** una bebida explosiva ❑ *Aut* **k. starter** arranque *m*, pedal *m* de arranque (**b**) *Fam (pleasure, thrill)* **I get a k. out of it** disfruto con ello; **to do sth for kicks** hacer algo por el simple placer de hacerlo
 2 *vi (animal)* cocear; *(person)* dar patadas; *(gun)* dar un culatazo; *Fam* **alive and kicking** vivito y coleando
 3 *vt* dar un puntapié a; **to k. the ball** chutar (el balón); *Fig* **to k. sb when they are down** dar la puntilla o rematar a algn; *Fig* **to k. up a fuss** *or* **a row** armar un escándalo; *Fam* **I could k. myself** ¡qué imbécil soy!; *Fam* **to k. a habit** dejar un vicio; *Fam* **to k. the bucket** estirar la pata, *CAm Méx* doblar *or* liar el petate
kick about *vi Fam (lie unnoticed, unused)* andar por ahí
kick around *Fam* **1** *vi (lie unnoticed, unused)* andar por ahí
 2 *vt (consider) (ideas, suggestions)* dar vueltas a
kick off *vi Fam* empezar; *Ftb* sacar
kick out *vt* echar a patadas, expulsar
kick up *vt Fam (fuss, row)* armar
kickback ['kɪkbæk] *n* (**a**) *(of gun)* culatazo *m* (**b**) *Fam* soborno *m*
kick-off ['kɪkɒf] *n Ftb* saque *m* inicial
kick-start ['kɪkstɑ:t] *vt (motorbike, engine)* arrancar a patada *(con el pedal)*; *Fig (economy)* reactivar
kid[1] [kɪd] *n* (**a**) *Zool* cabrito *m*; **k. gloves** guantes de cabritilla; *Fig* **to handle sb with k. gloves** tratar a algn con guante blanco (**b**) *Fam Esp* crío(a) *m,f*, *Arg* pibe(a) *m,f*, *CAm* chavalo(a) *m,f*, *Chile* cabro(a) *m,f*, *Col* chino(a) *m,f*, *Méx* chavo(a) *m,f*, *Urug* botija *mf*; **my k. brother** mi hermano pequeño; **that's k.'s stuff** eso está chupado, es cosa de niños (**c**) *Fam* **the kids** los críos, los chiquillos
kid[2] [kɪd] *Fam* **1** *vt (pt & pp* **kidded)** *(fool)* **to k. oneself** hacerse ilusiones
 2 *vi (joke)* estar de broma, tomar el pelo, *Esp Carib Méx* vacilar; **no kidding!** va en serio, no es broma; **you're kidding!** ¡no me digas!
kidnap ['kɪdnæp] *vt (pt & pp* **kidnapped)** secuestrar, raptar
kidnapper ['kɪdnæpər] *n* secuestrador(a) *m,f*, raptor(a) *m,f*
kidnapping ['kɪdnæpɪŋ] *n* secuestro *m*, rapto *m*
kidney ['kɪdnɪ] *n Anat Culin* riñón *m* ❑ *Med* **k. machine** riñón *m* artificial; *Med* **k. stone** cálculo *m* renal

kill [kɪl] **1** n *(act)* matanza f; *(animal)* pieza f; *Fig* **to be in at the k.** ser testigo

2 vt **(a)** *(gen)* matar; **to k. oneself** suicidarse, matarse; *Fig* **to k. time** pasar el rato, matar el tiempo; *Fig* **to k. two birds with one stone** matar dos pájaros de un tiro; *Fig* **to k. sb with kindness** proteger excesivamente a algn; *Fam* **to k. oneself laughing** morirse de risa **(b)** *Fam (hurt)* doler mucho a; **my feet are killing me** ¡ay, cómo me duelen los pies! **(c)** *Fam (stop)* acabar; **that mistake has killed his chances** ese error ha acabado con sus posibilidades

kill off vt exterminar, liquidar

killer ['kɪlər] n asesino(a) m,f □ **k. whale** orca f

killing ['kɪlɪŋ] **1** n matanza f, asesinato m; *Fig* **to make a k.** forrarse de dinero

2 adj Fam **(a)** *(tiring)* agotador(a) **(b)** *(funny)* para morirse, divertidísimo(a)

killjoy ['kɪldʒɔɪ] n aguafiestas mf inv

kiln [kɪln] n horno m

kilo ['kiːləʊ] n kilo m

kilobyte ['kɪləbaɪt] n Comptr kilobyte m

kilogram(me) ['kɪləʊgræm] n kilogramo m

kilohertz ['kɪləʊhɜːts] n kilohercio m

kilometre, US **kilometer** [kɪ'lɒmɪtər] n kilómetro m

kilowatt ['kɪləʊwɒt] n kilovatio m

kilt [kɪlt] n falda f or RP pollera f escocesa, kilt m

kilter ['kɪltər] n Fam **out of k.** *(machine part)* descuajeringado(a), Esp escacharrado(a), Méx madreado(a); *(schedule)* manga por hombro

kimono [kɪ'məʊnəʊ] n quimono m, kimono m

kin [kɪn] n familiares mpl, parientes mpl; **next of k.** pariente(s) m(pl) más cercano(a)

kind¹ [kaɪnd] **1** n **(a)** *(gen)* tipo m, clase f; **all kinds of** toda clase de; **chicha is a k. of beer** la chicha es una especie de cerveza; **nothing of the k.** nada por el estilo; **they are the k. you can eat** son de los que se puede comer; **they are two of a k.** son tal para cual; **what k. of car?** ¿qué tipo de coche? **(b) in k.** *(payment)* en especie; *(similar treatment)* con la misma moneda

2 adv Fam **k. of** en cierta manera; **I feel k. of sorry for him** en cierta manera le compadezco; **I k. of expected it** me lo temía; **she's k. of tired** está algo cansada

kind² ['kaɪnd] adj amable, simpático(a); **it's very k. of you** es usted muy amable; *Fml* **would you be so k. as to …?** ¿me haría usted el favor de …?

kinda ['kaɪndə] Fam = **kind of**

kindergarten ['kɪndəgɑːtən] n parvulario m, jardín m de infancia

kind-hearted [kaɪnd'hɑːtɪd] adj bondadoso(a), de buen corazón

kindle ['kɪndəl] vt *(fire)* encender; *Fig (emotion, interest, etc)* encender, despertar

kindliness ['kaɪndlɪnɪs] n bondad f, amabilidad f

kindling ['kɪndlɪŋ] n leña f

kindly ['kaɪndlɪ] **1** adj **(kindlier, kindliest)** amable, bondadoso(a)

2 adv **(a)** *(in a kind way)* Fml amablemente **(b)** *(in polite requests)* **k. remit a cheque** sírvase enviar cheque; **to look k. on** aprobar

kindness ['kaɪndnɪs] n bondad f, amabilidad f; **to do sb a k.** hacerle un favor a algn

kindred ['kɪndrɪd] **1** adj **(a)** *(related)* emparentado(a); **k. languages** idiomas emparentados **(b)** *(similar)* semejante, afín; **k. spirits** almas f pl gemelas

2 n Old-fashioned or Literary familiares mpl

kinetic [kɪ'netɪk] adj cinético(a)

king [kɪŋ] n *(gen)* rey m; *(draughts)* dama f; **K. John** el rey Juan; **the three kings** los Reyes Magos

kingdom ['kɪŋdəm] n reino m; **the animal k.** el reino animal

kingfisher ['kɪŋfɪʃər] n Orn martín m pescador

kingpin ['kɪŋpɪn] n Tech clavija f maestra; *Fig* persona f clave

king-size(d) ['kɪŋsaɪz(d)] adj extralargo(a)

kink [kɪŋk] n *(in rope, thread)* coca f, retorcimiento m; *(in hair)* rizo m; *(peculiarity)* manía f

kinky ['kɪŋkɪ] adj **(kinkier, kinkiest)** Fam *(strange)* raro(a); *(sexually)* pervertido(a)

kinship ['kɪnʃɪp] n parentesco m

kiosk ['kiːɒsk] n quiosco m

kip [kɪp] Br Fam **1** n **to have a k.** echar una cabezada
2 vi **to k. (down)** dormir

Kirg(h)izia [kɜː'giːzɪə] n, **Kirg(h)izstan** [kɜːgɪz'stæn] n Kirguizistán

kiss [kɪs] **1** n beso m; **the k. of life** el boca a boca

2 vt besar; **he kissed the child good night** besó al niño al darle las buenas noches; *Fam* **to k. sth goodbye** dar un beso de despedida a algo

3 vi besarse

kisser ['kɪsər] n Fam *(mouth)* morros mpl, boca f

kit [kɪt] n **(a)** *(equipment, gear)* equipo m; Mil avíos mpl, pertrechos mpl □ **first-aid k.** botiquín m; **tool k.** caja f de herramientas **(b)** *(clothing)* ropa f □ **riding k.** traje m de montar **(c)** *(toy model)* maqueta f, kit m

kit out vt equipar

kitbag ['kɪtbæg] n Mil Naut mochila f

kitchen ['kɪtʃɪn] n cocina f □ **k. sink** fregadero m, Chile Col Méx lavaplatos m inv, RP pileta f; *Fig* **they took everything but the k. sink** sólo les faltó llevarse las paredes; **k. unit** módulo m de cocina

kitchenette [kɪtʃɪ'net] n pequeña cocina f

kitchenware ['kɪtʃɪnweər] n batería f de cocina

kite [kaɪt] n **(a)** Orn milano m □ **red k.** milano m real **(b)** *(toy)* cometa f; CAm Méx papalote m, Chile volantín m, Par pandorga f, RP barrilete m; *Fig* **to fly a k.** sondear la opinión

kith [kɪθ] n **k. and kin** Literary parientes mpl y amigos mpl

kitsch [kɪtʃ] n kitsch m

kitten ['kɪtən] n gatito(a) m,f; *Fam* **I nearly had kittens** casi me muero del susto

kittiwake ['kɪtɪweɪk] n Orn gaviota f tridáctila

kitty¹ ['kɪtɪ] n Fam minino(a) m,f

kitty² ['kɪtɪ] n *(moneybox)* hucha f; Cards bote m

kiwi ['kiːwiː] **1** n **(a)** Orn kiwi m **(b)** *(fruit)* **k. (fruit)** kiwi m **(c)** *(person)* Fam neozelandés(esa) m,f

2 adj Fam neozelandés(esa)

kleptomania [kleptəʊ'meɪnɪə] n cleptomanía f

kleptomaniac [kleptəʊ'meɪnɪæk] n cleptómano(a) m,f

klutz [klʌts] n US Fam *(clumsy person)* torpe mf, Esp patoso(a) m,f

km *(pl* **km** *or* **kms)** abbr **kilometre(s)** kilómetro(s) m(pl), km

knack [næk] n maña f, truco m; **to get the k. of doing sth** pillarle or Esp cogerle or Am agarrarle el truco or el tranquillo a algo

knacker ['nækər] n Br matarife m

knackered ['nækəd] adj Br Fam **to be k.** estar reventado(a)

knapsack ['næpsæk] n mochila f

knave [neɪv] n Cards *(English pack)* jota f; *(Spanish pack)* sota f

knead [niːd] *vt (muscles)* masajear, dar un masaje a; *(bread etc)* amasar

knee [niː] **1** *n* (a) *Anat* rodilla *f*; **on one's knees** de rodillas; *Fig* **to bring sb to their knees** humillar a algn (b) *(of trousers)* rodillera *f*
2 *vt* dar un rodillazo a

kneecap ['niːkæp] *n Anat* rótula *f*

knee-deep ['niːdiːp] *adj* que llega hasta las rodillas; **he was k.-d. in water** estaba metido en el agua hasta las rodillas

knee-high ['niːhaɪ] *adj* hasta (la altura de) la rodilla; *Fam* **when I was k. to a grasshopper** cuando era pequeño *or* canijo *or Am* chiquito

kneejerk ['niːdʒɜːk] *adj (reaction, response)* reflejo(a)

kneel [niːl] *vi (pt & pp knelt)* **to k. (down)** arrodillarse

knee-length ['niːleŋθ] *adj* largo(a) hasta la rodilla; **a k.-l. skirt** una falda hasta la rodilla

kneepad ['niːpæd] *n* rodillera *f*

knees-up ['niːsʌp] *n inv Br Fam* fiesta *f*, juerga *f*

knell [nel] *n Literary* toque *m* de difuntos

knelt [nelt] *pt & pp see* **kneel**

knew [njuː] *pt see* **know**

knickerbockers ['nɪkəbɒkəz] *npl* bombachos *mpl*

knickers ['nɪkəz] *npl* (a) *(for women)* bragas *fpl, Chile Col Méx* calzones *mpl, Col* blúmers *mpl, Ecuad* follones *mpl, RP* bombacha *f; Fam* **to get one's k. in a twist** ponerse negro(a) (b) *US* bombachos *mpl*

knick-knack ['nɪknæk] *n* chuchería *f*

knife [naɪf] **1** *n (pl knives* [naɪvz]) cuchillo *m; Fig* **on a k. edge** pendiendo de un hilo; *Fam* **to get one's k. into sb** tenérsela jurada a algn
2 *vt* apuñalar, dar una puñalada a

knight [naɪt] **1** *n Hist* caballero *m; Chess* caballo *m*
2 *vt* armar caballero

knighthood ['naɪthʊd] *n* (a) *(rank)* título *m* de caballero (b) *(body of knights)* caballería *f*

knit [nɪt] **1** *vt (pt & pp knitted or knit)* (a) *(with wool etc)* tejer (b) *(join)* juntar (**together** -); *Fig* **to k. one's brow** fruncir el entrecejo *or* el ceño
2 *vi* (a) *(with wool)* hacer punto (b) *Med (bone)* soldarse

knitted ['nɪtəd] *adj* de punto

knitting ['nɪtɪŋ] *n (labor f de) punto m, Am* tejido *m* ❑ **k. machine** *Am* máquina *f* de tejer, *Esp* tricotosa *f*; **k. needle** aguja *f* de punto *or Am* tejer

knit-wear ['nɪtweə] *n* prendas *fpl* de punto *or Am* tejidas

knob [nɒb] *n* (a) *(of stick)* puño *m*, pomo *m; (of drawer)* tirador *m; (control button)* botón *m* (b) *(small portion)* trozo *m*, porción *f*

knobbly ['nɒblɪ] *adj (knobblier, knobbliest)* nudoso(a); **k. knees** rodillas huesudas

knock [nɒk] **1** *n* (a) *(sound, blow)* golpe *m*; **k., k., k.!** ¡toc, toc, toc!; **there was a k. at the door** llamaron a la puerta; **to get a nasty k.** darse un buen golpe (b) *Fig* revés *m*
2 *vt* (a) *(strike)* golpear; **to k. a hole in sth** abrir un agujero en algo; *Fig* **to k. one's head against a brick wall** darse de cabeza contra la pared; *Fig* **to k. sb for six** dejar pasmado(a) a algn (b) *Fam (criticize)* criticar
3 *vi* (a) *(hit)* dar golpes, golpear (**against, into** contra); *(at door)* llamar (**at** a); *Fam* **she's knocking on 70** tiene casi 70 años (b) *Aut (make a noise)* golpetear

knock about, knock around 1 *vt* (a) *(beat up)* pegar, maltratar (b) *(discuss) (ideas etc)* discutir
2 *vi Fam (to be present)* andar por ahí; **she has knocked about a bit** ha vivido mucho

knock back *vt Fam* (a) *(drink)* beber de un trago (b) *(cost)* costar

knock down *vt* (a) *(demolish)* derribar (b) *Aut (hit)* atropellar; **he was knocked down by a car** le atropelló un coche (c) *(reduce) (price)* rebajar

knock off 1 *vt* (a) *(cause to fall off)* tirar; **she knocked the vase off the table** tiró el florero de la mesa (b) *(reduce)* hacer una rebaja de, rebajar; **he knocked five dollars off it** lo rebajó en cinco dólares (c) *Fam (steal) Esp* mangar, *Am* volar (d) *Slang (kill)* **to k. sb off** liquidar a algn (e) *Fam* **k. it off!** *(stop it)* ¡basta ya!
2 *vi Fam* largarse; **they k. off at five** se piran a las cinco

knock out *vt* (a) *(make unconscious)* dejar sin conocimiento; *Box* poner fuera de combate, derrotar por K.O., noquear (b) *(surprise)* dejar pasmado(a); **she was knocked out by the news** se quedó de una pieza al oírlo

knock over *vt* volcar; *Aut* atropellar

knock up 1 *vt* (a) *Fam (wake)* despertar (b) *(make)* hacer deprisa (c) *US Fam Offens (make pregnant)* dejar preñada
2 *vi Ten* pelotear

knockabout ['nɒkəbaʊt] **1** *n* astracanada *f*
2 *adj (comedy, comedian)* bullanguero(a)

knockdown ['nɒkdaʊn] *n Fam* **at a k. price** a un precio de risa

knocker ['nɒkə] *n* aldaba *f*

knock-kneed [nɒk'niːd] *adj* patizambo(a), *Am* chueco(a)

knock-on effect ['nɒkɒn'fekt] *n* efecto *m* dominó

knockout ['nɒkaʊt] **1** *n* (a) *Box* K.O. *m*, fuera de combate *m*, knock-out *m* (b) *Fam* maravilla *f*; **she's a k.** es guapísima
2 *adj* (a) *Box* **k. blow** golpe *m* que pone fuera de combate (b) *Sport* **k. competition** competición *f or Am* competencia *f* de pruebas eliminatorias

knoll [nəʊl] *n Literary* loma *f*, montículo *m*

knot [nɒt] **1** *n* (a) *(gen)* nudo *m; (in ribbon)* lazo *m; (group)* grupo *m; Fig* **to tie oneself up in knots** hacerse un lío (b) *Naut (sea mile)* nudo *m*
2 *vt* anudar; **the rope must be knotted** hay que anudar la cuerda, hay que hacer un nudo a la cuerda

knotty ['nɒtɪ] *adj (knottier, knottiest)* nudoso(a); *Fig* **a k. problem** un problema espinoso

know [nəʊ] **1** *vt (pt knew; pp known)* (a) *(have knowledge or information of)* saber; **not to k. the first thing about sth** no saber ni jota de algo; **she knows how to ski** sabe esquiar; **to get to k. sth** enterarse de algo; **to k. one's own mind** saber lo que se quiere; **to k. sth by heart** saber algo de memoria; **to k. too much** saber más de la cuenta (b) *(be acquainted with)* conocer; **he has known better days** ha conocido tiempos mejores; **to k. sb by sight** conocer a algn de vista; *Fam* **I don't k. him from Adam** no tengo ni idea de quién es; **we got to k. each other at the party** nos conocimos en la fiesta (c) *(understand)* entender; **I don't k. a thing about cars** no entiendo nada de coches; **she was a very clever person, you k.** era muy inteligente, ¿entiendes?
2 *vi* saber; **as far as I k.** que yo sepa; **how should I k.!** ¡yo qué sé!; **I don't k. about that** eso no te lo puedo decir; **if only I'd known** de haberlo sabido antes; **not that I k. of** que yo sepa no; **something worth knowing** algo que merece la pena saber; **to k. better than to do sth** guardarse bien de hacer algo; **to let sb k.** avisar a algn; *Fam* **Heaven knows!** ¡sabe Dios!
3 *n Fam* **to be in the k.** estar en el ajo

knowable ['nəʊəbəl] *adj* conocible

know-all ['nəʊɔːl] *n Fam* sabelotodo *mf*, sabihondo(a) *m,f*

know-how ['nəʊhaʊ] *n Fam* conocimiento *m* práctico

knowing ['nəʊɪŋ] *adj (shrewd)* astuto(a); *(deliberate)* deliberado(a); **a k. smile** una sonrisa de complicidad

knowingly ['nəʊɪŋlɪ] *adv (shrewd)* a sabiendas; *(deliberately)* deliberadamente

know-it-all ['nəʊɪtɔːl] *n US Fam* sabelotodo *mf*, sabihondo(a) *m,f*

knowledge ['nɒlɪdʒ] *n* (a) *(understanding)* conocimiento *m*; **he has no k. of good and evil** no tiene conocimiento del bien o del mal; **it's a matter of common k.** es de sobra sabido; **lack of k.** falta *f* de conocimiento; **not to my k.** que yo sepa no; **without my k.** sin saberlo yo (b) *(learning)* conocimientos *mpl*; **my k. of German is poor** mis conocimientos del alemán son escasos; **scientific k.** conocimientos científicos; **to have a thorough k. of a subject** conocer un tema a fondo; **to improve one's k.** aumentar los conocimientos

knowledgeable ['nɒlɪdʒəbəl] *adj* erudito(a); **to be k. about a subject** ser muy entendido(a) en un tema

knowledgeably ['nɒlɪdʒəblɪ] *adv* eruditamente

known [nəʊn] **1** *pp see* **know**
  2 *adj* conocido(a)

knuckle ['nʌkəl] *n Anat* nudillo *m*; *Culin* hueso *m*; *Fam* **near the k.** rayando la indecencia

knuckle down *vi Fam* ponerse a trabajar *or* estudiar en serio

knuckle under *vi Fam* pasar por el aro

knuckleduster ['nʌkəldʌstər] *n* puño *m* americano

KO [keɪ'əʊ] *n (abbr* **knockout** *)* **Box** *Fam* fuera de combate *m*, K.O. *m*

koala [kəʊ'ɑːlə] *n Zool* koala *m*

kookie *adj,* **kooky** ['kʊkɪ] *adj* (**kookier, kookiest**) *US Fam* chalado(a), chiflado(a)

Koran [kɔː'rɑːn] *n Rel* Corán *m*

Korea [kə'riːə] *n* Corea

Korean [kə'riːən] *adj & n* coreano(a) *(m,f)*

kosher ['kəʊʃər] *adj* conforme a la ley judaica; *Fam* correcto(a)

kowtow ['kaʊ'taʊ] *vi also Fig* **to k. to sb** inclinarse ante algn

kph [keɪpiː'eɪtʃ] *(abbr* **kilometres per hour**) kilómetros *mpl* por hora, Km/h, km/h

Kraut [kraʊt] *n Slang Offens Esp* cabeza cuadrada *mf*, = término generalmente ofensivo para referirse a los alemanes

krypton ['krɪptɒn] *n Chem* kriptón *m*

kudos ['kjuːdɒs] *n* prestigio *m*

Kurd [kɜːd] *n* curdo(a) *m,f*

Kurdish ['kɜːdɪʃ] **1** *adj* curdo(a)
  2 *n (language)* curdo *m*

Kurdistan [kɜːdɪ'stɑːn] *n* Kurdistán

Kuwait [kʊ'weɪt] *n* Kuwait

Kuwaiti [kʊ'weɪtɪ] *adj & n* kuwaití *(mf)*

kW *(abbr* **kilowatt(s)**) kilovatio(s) *m(pl)*, Kw, kw

kWh *(abbr* **kilowatt-hours**) kilovatios-hora *m (pl)*, Kw/h, kw/h

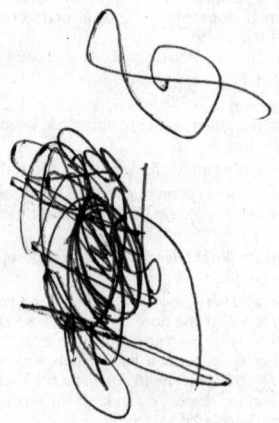

L, l [el] *n (the letter)* L, l *f*

L *Br Aut (abbr* **Learner driver)** ≃ conductor *m* en prácticas

Lab *Br (abbr* **Labour)** laborista

lab [læb] *n Fam (abbr* **laboratory)** laboratorio *m*

label ['leɪbəl] **1** *n* **(a)** *(tag)* etiqueta *f* ▫ *Mus* **record l.** ≃ casa *f* discográfica **(b)** *Fig* etiqueta *f,* calificación *f,* clasificación *f*
2 *vt (pt & pp* **labelled,** *US* **labeled) (a)** *(parcel)* poner etiqueta a, etiquetar **(b)** *Fig* calificar, clasificar

labial ['leɪbɪəl] *adj Ling* labial

labor ['leɪbər] *n & vi US Austral see* **labour**

laboratory [ləˈbɒrətərɪ, *US* ˈlæbrətɔːrɪ] *n* laboratorio *m* ▫ **l. assistant** ayudante *m,f* de laboratorio

labored ['leɪbəd] *adj US Austral see* **laboured**

laborer ['leɪbərər] *n US Austral see* **labourer**

laboring ['leɪbərɪŋ] *adj US Austral see* **labouring**

labor-intensive [leɪbərɪnˈtensɪv] *adj US Austral see* **labour-intensive**

laborious [ləˈbɔːrɪəs] *adj* laborioso(a), penoso(a), difícil

labor-saving ['leɪbərseɪvɪŋ] *adj US Austral see* **labour-saving**

labour ['leɪbər] **1** *n* **(a)** *(work)* trabajo *m; (task, job)* labor *f,* tarea *f,* faena *f.* **l. of love** trabajo *m* placentero *or* agradable ▫ *Jur* **hard l.** trabajos *mpl* forzados *or* forzosos; **l. camp** campo *m* de trabajos forzados *or* forzosos **(b)** *Ind (workforce)* mano *f* de obra ▫ **l. costs** costos *mpl or Esp* coste *m* de la mano de obra; **skilled l.** mano *f* de obra especializada **(c) labours** *(efforts)* esfuerzos *mpl* **(d)** *Br Pol* **the L. Party** el Partido Laborista; **to vote L.** votar a los laboristas **(e)** *Med (childbirth)* parto *m;* **to be in l.** estar de parto ▫ **l. pains** dolores *mpl or* contracciones *fpl* del parto
2 *adj Ind* laboral; **l. relations/disputes** relaciones/ conflictos laborales ▫ *US* **L. Day** Día *m* del Trabajador; *Br Formerly* **l. exchange** Bolsa *f* de Trabajo; **l. force** mano *f* de obra; *US* **l. laws** legislación *f* laboral; **l. market** mercado *m* laboral; *US* **l. union** sindicato *m*
3 *vi* **(a)** *(work)* trabajar (duro); *Fig* **to l. under a delusion** hacerse ilusiones, estar equivocado(a) **(b)** *(move etc) (person)* avanzar penosamente; *(engine)* funcionar con dificultad
4 *vt (stress, linger on)* machacar; *(a point)* insistir en

laboured ['leɪbəd] *adj* **(a)** *(breathing)* fatigoso(a) **(b)** *(style)* trabajoso(a), forzado(a)

labourer ['leɪbərər] *n (on roads etc)* peón *m* ▫ **farm l.** peón *m* agrícola, jornalero(a) *m,f,* bracero(a) *m,f*

labouring ['leɪbərɪŋ] *adj* **he did a number of l. jobs** trabajó de obrero en varias ocasiones

labour-intensive [leɪbərɪnˈtensɪv] *adj* que requiere mucha mano de obra

labour-saving ['leɪbəseɪvɪŋ] *adj* que ahorra trabajo; *(in kitchen)* **l.-s. devices** electrodomésticos *mpl*

labrador ['læbrədɔːr] *n (dog)* terranova *m,* labrador *m*

laburnum [ləˈbɜːnəm] *n Bot* laburno *m,* codeso *m*

labyrinth ['læbərɪnθ] *n* laberinto *m*

labyrinthine [læbeˈrɪnθaɪn] *adj* laberíntico(a)

lace [leɪs] **1** *n* **(a)** *(fabric)* encaje *m* **(b) laces** cordones *mpl*
2 *vt* **(a)** *(shoes)* atar (los cordones de) **(b)** *(add spirits to)* echar licor **(with** a)

lace up *vt* atar con cordones

lacerate ['læsəreɪt] *vt Med* lacerar

laceration [læsəˈreɪʃən] *n* laceración *f*

lace-up ['leɪsʌp] **1** *adj (shoes etc)* de cordones
2 *lace-ups npl* zapatos *mpl* de cordones

lachrymose ['lækrɪməʊs] *adj Literary* lacrimoso(a)

lack [læk] **1** *n* falta *f,* carencia *f,* escasez *f; for* **l. of** por falta de, a falta de; **there is no l. of enthusiasm** entusiasmo no falta
2 *vt* faltarle a uno, carecer de, no tener
3 *vi* **she lacked for nothing** no le faltaba nada

lackadaisical [lækəˈdeɪzɪkəl] *adj (lazy)* perezoso(a), vago(a); *(distracted)* distraído(a), despistado(a); *(indifferent)* indiferente, apático(a)

lackey ['lækɪ] *n Pej* lacayo *n*

lacklustre, *US* **lackluster** ['læklʌstər] *adj (eyes)* apagado(a), sin brillo; *(performance)* inexpresivo(a), sin brillo

laconic [ləˈkɒnɪk] *adj* lacónico(a)

lacquer ['lækər] **1** *n Constr* laca *f; (hair)* laca *f* para el pelo
2 *vt (furniture)* pintar con laca; *(hair)* poner laca a

lacrosse [ləˈkrɒs] *n Sport* lacrosse *f*

lactation [lækˈteɪʃən] *n* lactancia *f*

lactic ['læktɪk] *adj* láctico(a) ▫ **l. acid** ácido *m* láctico

lactose ['læktəʊs] *n Chem* lactosa *f*

lacuna [ləˈkjuːnə] *n (pl* **lacunae** [ləˈkjuːniː] *or* **lacunas)** laguna *f*

lacy ['leɪsɪ] *adj* **(lacier, laciest)** *(real)* de encaje; *(artificial)* parecido(a) al encaje

lad [læd] *n* **(a)** *(boy)* muchacho *m,* chaval *m, Arg* pibe *m, CAm Méx* chavo *m, Chile* cabro *m* ▫ **(stable) l.** mozo *m* de cuadra **(b)** *Br Fam (young man)* tipo *m, Esp* tío *m;* **come on, lads!** ¡vamos, muchachos!; *Fam* **the lads** los amigotes, la pandilla, *Méx* los cuates

ladder ['lædər] **1** *n* **(a)** *(for climbing)* escalera *f* (de mano); *Fig* escala *f,* jerarquía *f; Fig* **the evolutionary/social l.** la escala evolutiva/social ▫ **rope l.** escalera *f* de cuerda **(b)** *Br (in stocking)* carrera *f*

2 *vt Br (stocking)* hacer una carrera en
3 *vi Br (stocking)* hacerse una carrera

laddie ['lædɪ] *n esp Scot Fam* chaval *m*, muchacho *m*, chico *m*, joven *m*, *CAm Méx* chavalo *m*

laden ['leɪdən] *adj* cargado(a) (**with** de)

la-di-da [lɑːdɪ'dɑː] *adj Fam (accent, manner) Esp* pijo(a), *Méx* fresa, *RP* fifí

lading ['leɪdɪŋ] *n Com* flete *m*, mercancías *fpl*; **bill of l.** conocimiento *m* de embarque

ladle ['leɪdəl] **1** *n Culin* cucharón *n*
2 *vt Culin* servir con cucharón

ladle out *vt* repartir

lady ['leɪdɪ] *n* señora *f*, dama *f*; *Pol* **First L.** primera dama; **'Ladies'** *(WC)* 'Señoras', 'Damas'; **ladies and gentlemen!** ¡señoras y señores!; *(title)* **L. Brown** Lady Brown; **l. doctor** médica, doctora; *Theat* **leading l.** primera actriz; *Rel* **Our L.** Nuestra Señora; *Fam* **l. friend** amiguita; *Fam* **ladies' man** hombre mujeriego; *Br Fam Pej* **who does she think she is, L. Muck?** no sé quién se cree que es

ladybird ['leɪdɪbɜːd] *n*, *US Can* **ladybug** ['leɪdɪbʌg] *n* mariquita *f*, vaca *f* de San Antón

lady-in-waiting [leɪdɪn'weɪtɪŋ] *n (pl* **ladies-in-waiting)** dama *f* de honor

lady-killer ['leɪdɪkɪlər] *n* ladrón *n* de corazones, tenorio *m*, donjuán *m*

ladylike ['leɪdɪlaɪk] *adj* elegante, fino(a), distinguido(a)

ladyship ['leɪdɪʃɪp] *n* señoría *f*; **Her L., Your L.** su señoría

lag [læg] **1** *n* **(a)** *(delay)* retraso *m*; **time l.** retraso *m*, demora *f* **(b)** *Br Slang (convict)* presidiario *m*; **old l.** reincidente *m*
2 *vi (pt & pp* **lagged)** rezagarse; **to l. (behind)** quedarse atrás, retrasarse, rezagarse
3 *vt Tech* revestir

lager ['lɑːgər] *n* cerveza *f* rubia

lagging ['lægɪŋ] *n Tech* revestimiento *m* (calorífugo)

lagoon [lə'guːn] *n* laguna *f*

lah-di-dah [lɑːdɪ'dɑː] *adj see* **la-di-da**

laid [leɪd] *pt & pp* **lay**

laid-back [leɪd'bæk] *adj Fam* tranquilo(a), suave, *Esp* cachazudo(a)

lain [leɪn] *pp see* **lie**

lair [leər] *n* guarida *f*

laird [leəd] *n Scot (landowner)* terrateniente *m*

laissez-faire [leɪseɪ'feər] *n Pol* política *f* de no injerencia *or* no intervención

laity ['leɪtɪ] *n Rel* **the l.** los seglares, los laicos, los legos

lake [leɪk] *n* lago *m*

lama ['lɑːmə] *n Rel* lama *m*

lamb [læm] **1** *n (animal)* cordero *m*; *(meat)* carne *f* de cordero; *Fam* **poor l.!** ¡pobrecito! ❑ **l. chop** chuleta *f* de cordero; **l.'s wool** lana *f* de cordero
2 *vi (sheep)* parir

lambast [læm'bæst] *vt* vapulear

lambing ['læmɪŋ] *n* (tiempo *m* del) nacimiento *m* de los corderos

lambskin ['læmskɪn] *n* piel *f* de cordero

lamb's-wool ['læmswʊl] *adj* de lana de cordero, de lambswool

lame [leɪm] *adj* **(a)** *(person, animal)* cojo(a); **to be l.** *(temporarily)* estar cojo(a); *(permanently)* ser cojo(a); **l. in one leg** cojo(a) de una pierna ❑ *(person)* **l. duck** incapaz *mf* **(b)** *Fig (excuse)* poco convincente, débil; *(argument)* flojo(a); *(business)* fallido(a)

lamely ['leɪmlɪ] *adv Fig* sin convicción

lameness ['leɪmnɪs] *n* cojera *f*; *Fig* falta *f* de convicción, debilidad *f*

lament [lə'ment] **1** *n (grief)* lamento *n*; *Mus* endecha *f*.
2 *vt (death)* llorar, lamentar
3 *vi* llorar **(for** a), lamentarse **(over** de)

lamentable ['læməntəbəl] *adj* lamentable, deplorable

lamentation [læmən'teɪʃən] *n* lamentación *f*, lamento *m*

lamented [lə'mentɪd] *adj* llorado(a)

laminate ['læmɪneɪt] **1** *vt* laminar
2 ['læmɪnət] *n* laminado *m*

laminated ['læmɪneɪtɪd] *adj (metal)* laminado(a); *(glass)* inastillable; *(paper)* plastificado(a)

lamp [læmp] *n (gen)* lámpara *f*; *Aut Rail* faro *m* ❑ **street l.** farol *m*, farola *f*; **sun l.** lámpara *f* UVA *or* de rayos ultravioletas; **table l.** lámpara *f* de mesa

lamplight ['læmplaɪt] *n* luz *f* de lámpara

lamplit ['læmplɪt] *n* illuminado(a) con luz de lámpara

lampoon [læm'puːn] **1** *n* pasquín *m*, sátira *f*
2 *vt* satirizar

lamp-post ['læmppəʊst] *n* (poste *m* de) farol *m*, farola *f*

lamprey ['læmprɪ] *n (fish)* lamprea *f*

lampshade ['læmpʃeɪd] *n* pantalla *f*

lampstand ['læmpstænd] *n* pie *m* de lámpara

LAN [læn] *n Comptr (abbr* **local area network)** red *f* de área local

lance [lɑːns] **1** *n* **(a)** *(weapon)* lanza *f* ❑ *Br Mil* **l. corporal** cabo *m* interino **(b)** *Med* lanceta *f*
2 *vt Med* abrir con lanceta

lancet ['lɑːnsɪt] *n Med* lanceta *f*

land [lænd] **1** *n* **(a)** *(gen)* tierra *f*; *(soil)* suelo *m*, tierra *f*; **by l.** por tierra; *Naut* **l. ahoy!** ¡tierra a la vista!; **on dry l.** en tierra firme; *Fig* **to see how the l. lies** tantear el terreno ❑ **farm l.** tierras *fpl* de cultivo; *Mil* **l. forces** ejército *m* de tierra; **mass** gran extensión *f* de tierra; **l. reform** reforma *f* agraria; **waste l.** tierra *f* baldía **(b)** *(country)* país *m*, tierra *f*; *Esp (world)* mundo *m*; **foreign lands** tierras extranjeras; *Fig* **the l. of milk and honey** (la tierra de) Jauja; *Fam Fig* **to be in the l. of the living** seguir entre los vivos ❑ **native l.** tierra *f* natal, patria *f* **(c)** *(property)* tierras *fpl*; *(estate)* finca *f*, estancia *f*, hacienda *f* ❑ **l. register** registro *m* de la propiedad; **piece of l.** terreno *m*; **plot of l.** parcela *f*
2 *vt* **(a)** *(touch down)* hacer aterrizar **(b)** *(disembark)* desembarcar; *(unload)* descargar **(c)** *Fishing (catch)* sacar peces del agua, pescar **(d)** *Fam (succeed in obtaining)* conseguir; *(prize, contract, etc)* ganar, conseguir, obtener **(e)** *Fam (in jail)* llevar; **she got landed with the job** tuvo que cargar con el paquete; **to l. sb in trouble** causarle problemas a algn **(f)** *Fam (hit)* arrear; *(blow)* asestar
3 *vi* **(a)** *(plane)* aterrizar; *(bird)* posarse; *Av* **to l. on the moon** alunizar **(b)** *(disembark)* desembarcar **(c)** *(after jumping, falling)* caer **(in** sobre); *Fig* salir adelante; *Fig* **to l. on one's feet** caer de pies

land up *vi Fam* ir a parar

landed ['lændɪd] *adj* hacendado(a) ❑ **l. gentry** terratenientes *mpl*; **l. property** bienes *mpl* raíces

landfill site ['lændfɪl'saɪt] *n* = vertedero donde se entierran basuras

landing ['lændɪŋ] *n* **(a)** *(of staircase)* descansillo *m*, rellano *m* **(b)** *(of plane)* aterrizaje *m* ❑ **crash l.** aterrizaje *m* de emergencia; **forced l.** aterrizaje *m* forzoso; **l. gear** tren *m* de aterrizaje; **l. strip** pista *f* de aterrizaje **(c)** *(of passengers, troops)* desembarco *m* ❑ **l. card** tarjeta *f* de inmigración; *Mil* **l. craft** lancha *f* or barcaza *f* de desembarco; **l. net** salabre *m*; **l. stage** desembarcadero *m* **(d)** *Naut* embarcadero *m*

landlady ['lændleɪdɪ] *n (of flat, land)* dueña *f*, propietaria *f*; *(of boarding house)* patrona *f*; *(of pub)* dueña *f*

landlocked ['lændlɒkt] *adj (country)* sin salida al mar, interior

landlord ['lændlɔ:d] *n (of flat, land)* dueño *m*, propietario *m*; *(of pub)* patrón *m*, dueño *m*

landmark ['lændmɑ:k] *n* (**a**) *Geog Naut* señal *f*, marca *f*; *(well-known place)* lugar *m* muy conocido *or* famoso (**b**) *Fig* hito *m*

landmine ['lændmaɪn] *n Mil* mina *f* (de tierra)

landowner ['lændəʊnər] *n* terrateniente *mf*, propietario(a) *m,f*, hacendado(a) *m,f*

landscape ['lændskeɪp] **1** *n* (**a**) *(land, painting)* paisaje *m* ❏ **l. gardener** jardinero(a) *m,f* paisajista; **l. gardening** jardinería *f* paisajista; *Art* **l. painter** paisajista *mf*; **l. painting** paisaje *m* (**b**) *Comptr* **l. (orientation)** formato *m* apaisado
  2 *vt* ajardinar

landslide ['lændslaɪd] *n Geol* desprendimiento *m or* corrimiento *m* de tierras ❏ *Pol* **l. victory** triunfo *m* arrollador, victoria *f* arrolladora

landward ['lændwəd] *adj* hacia la tierra

lane [leɪn] *n* (**a**) *(in country)* camino *m*, sendero *m*, vereda *f*; *(in town)* callejuela *f*, callejón *m* (**b**) *(of motorway)* carril *m*, vía *f* ❏ **bus l.** carril-bus *m* (**c**) *Sport* calle *f* (**d**) *Naut* ruta *f* ❏ **shipping l.** ruta *f* marítima

language ['læŋgwɪdʒ] *n* (**a**) *(faculty, style, terminology)* lenguaje *m*; **bad l.** palabrotas *fpl*; **scientific l.** lenguaje científico; **to use bad l.** ser mal hablado(a); **watch your l.!** ¡cuida tu lenguaje!; *Fig* **we speak the same l.** hablamos el mismo idioma (**b**) *(of a country)* idioma *m*, lengua *f*; **dead l.** lengua muerta; **the English l.** el (idioma) inglés; **we study l. and literature** estudiamos lengua y literatura ❏ **l. laboratory** laboratorio *m* de idiomas; **l. school** escuela *f* or academia *f* de idiomas (**c**) *Comptr* lenguaje *m*

languid ['læŋgwɪd] *adj* lánguido(a)

languish ['læŋgwɪʃ] *vi (for love)* languidecer; *(project, plan, etc)* quedar abandonado(a), consumirse; *(in prison)* pudrirse

languishing ['læŋgwɪʃɪŋ] *adj* lánguido(a); *(attitude)* relajado(a)

languor ['læŋgər] *n* languidez *f*

languorous ['læŋgərəs] *adj* lánguido(a)

lank [læŋk] *adj (hair)* lacio(a)

lanky ['læŋkɪ] *adj* (**lankier, lankiest**) larguirucho(a)

lanolin(e) ['lænəlɪn] *n* lanolina *f*

lantern ['læntən] *n* farol *m*, linterna *f*

lantern-jawed ['læntəndʒɔːd] *adj Fam* chupado(a) de cara

Laos [laʊs] *n* Laos

Laotian ['laʊʃɪən] **1** *adj* laosiano(a)
  2 *n (person)* laosiano(a) *m,f*; *(language)* laosiano *m*

lap¹ [læp] *n Anat* regazo *m*; *(knees)* rodillas *fpl*; *(skirt)* falda *f*; *Fig* **it's in the l. of the gods** está en manos de los dioses; *Fig* **to live in the l. of luxury** vivir a cuerpo de rey ❏ **l. dancing** striptease *m (para un único cliente)*

lap² [læp] **1** *n Sport (circuit)* vuelta *f*; *(of journey)* etapa *f*, escala *f*; *Fig* trecho *m*, etapa ❏ **l. of honour** vuelta *f* de honor
  2 *vt (pt & pp* **lapped***) Sport (overtake)* doblar
  3 *vi (go round)* girar, dar la vuelta

lap³ [læp] **1** *vt (pt & pp* **lapped***) (cat)* beber a lengüetadas; *(waves)* lamer, besar
  2 *vi (waves)* **to l. against** lamer, besar

lap up *vt* (**a**) *(cat)* beber a lengüetadas (**b**) *Fig (wallow in)* disfrutar con; *(flattery)* recibir con estusiasmo (**c**) *Fig (believe)* tragar

lapdog ['læpdɒg] *n* perrito *m* faldero

lapel [lə'pel] *n (of jacket, coat)* solapa *f*

Lapland ['læplænd] *n* Laponia

Laplander ['læplændər] *n* lapón(ona) *m,f*

Lapp [læp] **1** *adj* lapón(ona)
  2 *n (language)* lapón *m*

lapping ['læpɪŋ] *n (of cat)* lamedura *f*, lametón *m*, lametazo *m*; *(of waves)* chapoteo *m*

lapse [læps] **1** *n* (**a**) *(of time)* lapso *m*, intervalo *m* (**b**) *(error)* error *m*, desliz *m*; *(when speaking)* lapso *m*, lapsus *m*; *(of memory)* fallo *m*
  2 *vi* (**a**) *(time) (pass)* pasar, transcurrir (**b**) *(contract, subscription) (expire)* caducar (**c**) *(person) (err)* cometer un error, equivocarse; *(fall back)* caer (**into** en); **to l. into silence** quedarse callado(a) (**d**) *Rel* perder la fe

lapsed [læpst] *adj* (**a**) *(contract etc)* caducado(a) (**b**) *(Catholic)* no practicante

laptop ['læptɒp] *n Comptr* **l. (computer)** *Esp* ordenador *m or Am* computadora *f* portátil

lapwing ['læpwɪŋ] *n Orn* avefría *f*

larceny ['lɑ:sənɪ] *n Br Jur* latrocinio *m*; *US* robo *m*, hurto *m*; **grand l.** robo importante; **petty l.** robo de menor cuantía

larch [lɑ:tʃ] *n Bot* alerce *m*

lard [lɑ:d] **1** *n Culin* manteca *f or RP* grasa *f* de cerdo
  2 *vt* (**a**) *Culin* poner manteca a (**b**) *Fig Pej (speech, style)* cargar, recargar

larder ['lɑ:dər] *n* despensa *f*; *Fam* **to raid the l.** saquear la dispensa

large [lɑ:dʒ] **1** *adj* (**a**) *(gen)* grande; *(amount, sum)* importante, considerable; *(meal, harvest)* abundante; *(family)* numeroso(a); *Com* **the l. size** la talla grande; *Fig* **as l. as life** en persona; *Fig* **to be larger than life** ser exagerado(a) (**b**) *(extensive)* amplio(a), extenso(a); **by and l.** por lo general
  2 *n (prisoner etc)* **to be at l.** estar libre *or* en libertad, andar suelto(a); **the public at l.** el público en general

largely ['lɑ:dʒlɪ] *adv (mainly)* en gran parte; *(chiefly)* principalmente

largeness ['lɑ:dʒnɪs] *n* (**a**) *(size)* gran tamaño *m*, magnitud *f*, amplitud *f* (**b**) *(importance)* importancia *f*

large-scale ['lɑ:dʒskeɪl] *adj (project, problem, etc)* de gran escala; *(map)* a gran escala

largesse [lɑ:'dʒes] *n Fml (generosity)* generosidad *f*

lark¹ [lɑ:k] *n Orn* alondra *f*; *Fig* **to rise** *or* **be up with the l.** madrugar ❏ **calandra l.** calandria *f* (común); **sky l.** alondra *f* común; **wood l.** totovía *f*

lark² [lɑ:k] *n Br Fam* (**a**) *(joke)* broma *f*; **what a l.!** ¡qué divertido!, ¡qué risa! (**b**) *(stupid thing)* tontería *f*

lark about, lark around *vi Fam* hacer el tonto

larkspur ['lɑ:kspɜ:r] *n Bot* espuela *f* de caballero

larva ['lɑ:və] *n (pl* **larvae** ['lɑ:vi:]) larva *f*

laryngitis [lærɪn'dʒaɪtɪs] *n Med* laringitis *f*

larynx ['lærɪŋks] *n Anat* laringe *f*

lasagne [lə'sænjə] *n* lasaña *f*

lascivious [lə'sɪvɪəs] *adj* lascivo(a), lujurioso(a)

lasciviousness [lə'sɪvɪəsnɪs] *n* lascivia *f*, lujuria *f*

laser ['leɪzər] *n* láser *m* ❏ **l. disc** láser disc *m*; *Comptr* **l. printer** impresora *f* láser; *Med* **l. surgery** cirugía *f* con láser

lash [læʃ] **1** *n* (**a**) *(eyelash)* pestaña *f* (**b**) *(whip)* látigo *m*; *(thong)* tralla *f* (**c**) *(blow with whip)* latigazo *m*, azote *m* (**d**) *(tail)* coletazo *m*
  2 *vt* (**a**) *(beat)* azotar (**b**) *(of sea)* azotar (**c**) *(lay into)* criticar (**d**) *(tail)* dar coletazos (**e**) *(tie, bind)* atar

lash down vt (fasten) atar, sujetar; Naut amarrar

lash out vi (a) (with fists) repartir golpes a diestro y siniestro; (verbally) criticar (**at** a) (**b**) Fam (spending spree) tirar or Am salvo RP botar la casa por la ventana; **to l. out on sth** permitirse el lujo de comprar algo

lashing ['læʃɪŋ] n (**a**) (beating) azotes mpl; (whipping) flagelación f (**b**) (rope) cuerda f, maroma f (**c**) Br Fam **lashings of** montones de, la tira de

lass [læs] n Fam chavala f, muchacha f, chica f, joven f

lassitude ['læsɪtjuːd] n lasitud f

lasso [læ'suː] **1** n (pl lassos or lassoes) lazo m
  2 vt capturar con lazo, CSur lacear

last¹ [lɑːst] **1** adj (**a**) (final) último(a), final; **she would be the l. person to do sth like that** eso me lo esperaría de cualquiera menos a ella; Rel **the L. Judgement** el Juicio Final; Rel **the l. rites** extremaunción f; Fam **if it's the l. thing I do** aunque sea lo último que haga; Fam **the l. straw** el colmo (**b**) (most recent) último(a); **the l. time** la última vez (**c**) (past) pasado(a); (previous) anterior; **l. but one** penúltimo(a); **l. month/Sunday** el mes/domingo pasado; **l. night** anoche, ayer por la noche; **l. week** la semana pasada; **the night before l.** anteanoche; **the year before l.** hace dos años
  2 adv (**a**) (last occasion) por última vez; **the last I heard …** lo último que sé …; **when I l. saw her** la última vez que la vi (**b**) (at the end) en último lugar; (in race etc) último; **at (long) l.** por fin, finalmente; **l. but not least** el último en orden pero no en importancia; **to come l.** llegar el último (**c**) (until the end) **to the last** hasta el final
  3 n (in queue) el último, la última; **the l. of the wine/cheese** (todo) lo que queda del vino/queso; **to have seen the l. of sb** haber visto a algn por última vez; **we'll never hear the l. of it** esto no nos lo dejarán olvidar nunca; Fig **to breathe one's l.** dar el último suspiro
  4 vi (**a**) (time) durar; (suffer, hold out) aguantar, resistir (**b**) (money, food) (be enough for) llegar, alcanzar
  5 vt (time) durar

last out vi (**a**) (continue) durar; (hold out) aguantar, resistir (**b**) (be enough for) llegar, alcanzar

last² [lɑːst] n (shoemaker's) horma f

last-ditch ['lɑːstdɪtʃ] adj (effort, attempt) último(a); (desperate) desesperado(a)

lasting ['lɑːstɪŋ] adj duradero(a), perdurable

lastly ['lɑːstlɪ] adv por último, finalmente

last-minute ['lɑːstmɪnɪt] adj de última hora

latch [lætʃ] n picaporte m, pestillo m

latch onto vt (cling) pegarse a; **to l. onto sb** pegarse a algn; **to l. onto an idea** agarrarse or aferrarse a una idea

latchkey ['lætʃkiː] n Fam llavín m □ **l. child** niño m cuyos padres trabajan

late [leɪt] **1** adj (**a**) (not on time) tardío(a); (hour) avanzado(a); (arrival) tardío(a); **to be five minutes l.** llegar con cinco minutos de retraso or Am demora; **to be l.** (not arrive on time) llegar tarde; (be detained) retrasarse; **to be l. in doing sth** tardar en hacer algo (**b**) (far on in time) tarde; **in l. autumn** a finales del otoño; **in the l. afternoon** a última hora de la tarde; **in the l. nineteenth century** a finales del siglo diecinueve; **it's getting l.** se hace tarde; **she's in her l. twenties** tiene casi treinta años, ronda los treinta; **to keep l. hours** acostarse tarde (**c**) (dead) difunto(a), fallecido(a), finado(a)
  2 adv (**a**) (not on time) tarde; **to arrive l.** llegar tarde; Prov **better l. than never** más vale tarde que nunca (**b**) (far on in time) tarde; **l. at night** a altas horas de la noche; **l. into the night** hasta muy entrada la noche; **l. in life** a una edad avanzada; **to stay up l.** acostarse muy tarde; Fam Fig **it's a bit l. in the day** ya es tarde (**c**) (recently) recién; **as l. as 1950**

todavía en 1950; **as l. as yesterday** ayer mismo; **of l.** últimamente, recientemente

latecomer ['leɪtkʌmər] n tardón(ona) m,f

lately ['leɪtlɪ] adv últimamente, recientemente; **until l.** hasta hace poco

lateness ['leɪtnɪs] n (**a**) (of person, train) retraso m; (of delivery) atraso m (**b**) (of hour) lo avanzado

late-night ['leɪtnaɪt] adj de noche, de madrugada; **the l.-n. film** la película de media noche or de madrugada, la sesión golfa

latent ['leɪtənt] adj (**a**) (heat, infection) latente (**b**) (desire etc) oculto(a)

later ['leɪtər] **1** adj (comp of late) (**a**) (subsequent) más tarde; **at a l. stage** más adelante; **in her l. novels** en sus novelas posteriores (**b**) (more recent) más reciente
  2 adv (comp of late) más tarde, después; **five years l.** cinco años después; **I'll do it l.** lo haré luego; **l. on** más adelante, más tarde, después; **no l. than Monday** el lunes a más tardar; **see you l.!** ¡hasta luego!; **sooner or l.** tarde o temprano

lateral ['lætərəl] adj lateral □ **l. thinking** pensamiento m lateral, = capacidad para darse cuenta de aspectos no inmediatamente evidentes de los problemas

latest ['leɪtɪst] **1** adj (superl of late) (most recent) último(a), más reciente
  2 n **the l.** (**a**) (most recent news, style) lo último; **have you heard the l.?** ¿te enteraste de lo último?; **it's the l. in kitchen furniture** es el último grito en muebles de cocina (**b**) (final date) **Friday at the l.** el viernes a más tardar

latex ['leɪteks] n (pl latexes or latices ['lætɪsiːz]) Bot látex m

lath [lɑːθ] n listón m

lathe [leɪð] n Tech torno m □ **l. operator** tornero m, m,f

lather ['lɑːðər] **1** n (**a**) (of soap) espuma f (**b**) (horse's sweat) sudor m; Fam **to work oneself into a l.** ponerse histérico(a)
  2 vt (with soap) enjabonar
  3 vi enjabonarse, sacar espuma

Latin ['lætɪn] **1** adj & n latino(a) (m,f); **the L. Quarter** el barrio latino; **L. America** América f Latina, Latinoamérica f; **L. American** latinoamericano(a) (m,f)
  2 n (language) latín m

latitude ['lætɪtjuːd] n latitud f

latrine [lə'triːn] n letrina f, retrete n

latter ['lætər] **1** adj (**a**) (last) último(a) (**b**) (second of two) segundo(a); **the l. half of the week** la segunda mitad de la semana
  2 pron éste(a); **the former … the l. …** aquél or aquélla … éste or ésta …

latter-day ['lætədeɪ] adj moderno(a), actual, de hoy

latterly ['lætəlɪ] adv recientemente, últimamente

lattice ['lætɪs] n enrejado m, rejilla f, celosía f □ **l. window** ventana f de celosía

latticework ['lætɪswɜːk] n enrejado m

Latvia ['lætvɪə] n Letonia

Latvian ['lætvɪən] **1** n (**a**) (person) letón(ona) m,f (**b**) (language) letón m
  2 adj letón(ona)

laud [lɔːd] vt Fml or Literary loar, elogiar

laudable ['lɔːdəbəl] adj loable

laudanum ['lɔːdənəm] n láudano m

laugh [lɑːf] **1** n (gen) risa f; (guffaw) carcajada f; **to do sth for a l.** or **for laughs** hacer algo en broma or para divertirse; **to have a good l.** reírse mucho; Fig **to have the last l.** ser el último en reír; Fam **what a l.!** ¡qué risa!; Fam Fig **he's a good l.** es muy divertido

2 *vi* reír, reírse; **it makes me l.** me da risa; **to burst out laughing** echarse a reír; *Fam* **to l. all the way to the bank** regocijarse de un éxito económico; *Fam* **you've got to l., haven't you?** es mejor tomárselo a risa; *Fam Fig* **to l. on the other side of one's face** arrepentirse; *Fam Fig* **to l. one's head off** partirse de risa; *Prov* **he who laughs last laughs** *Br* **longest** or *US* **best** quien ríe el último ríe mejor

laugh at *vt* **to l. at sth/sb** reírse de algo/algn

laugh about *vi* **to l. about sth/sb** reírse de algo/algn

laugh off *vt* tomar a risa

laughable ['lɑːfəbəl] *adj (situation, suggestion)* ridículo(a), absurdo(a); *(amount, offer)* irrisorio(a)

laughing ['lɑːfɪŋ] **1** *adj* risueño(a); **it's no l. matter** no es para tomárselo a risa □ **l. gas** gas *m* hilarante
2 *n (gen)* risas *fpl*; *(loud)* carjadas *fpl*

laughingly ['lɑːfɪŋlɪ] *adv* **(a)** *(cheerfully)* con risas **(b)** *(absurdly)* absurdamente, risiblemente

laughing-stock ['lɑːfɪŋstɒk] *n* hazmerreír *m inv*

laughter ['lɑːftər] *n* risa *f*

launch [lɔːntʃ] **1** *n* **(a)** *(vessel)* lancha *f* **(b)** *see* **launching**
2 *vt* **(a)** *(rocket, new product)* lanzar **(b)** *(ship, boat)* botar; *(lifeboat)* echar al mar **(c)** *(film, play)* estrenar **(d)** *(company)* crear, fundar **(e)** *Mil* desatar, iniciar; *Fig (scheme)* iniciar; *(attack)* iniciar **(against** contra) **(f)** *Comptr* lanzar

launch into *vt (speech etc)* lanzarse a, enfrascarse en

launch out into *or* **on** *vt* emprender, lanzarse a

launcher ['lɔːntʃər] *n Mil* lanzador *m* □ **grenade l.** lanzagranadas *m inv*; **rocket l.** lanzacohetes *m inv*

launching ['lɔːntʃɪŋ] *n* **(a)** *(of rocket, new product)* lanzamiento *m*; *Fig (trigger, catalyst)* trampolín *m* □ **l. pad** plataforma *f* de lanzamiento **(b)** *(of ship)* botadura *f* □ **l. ramp** rampa *f* de lanzamiento **(c)** *(of film, play)* estreno *m* **(d)** *(of new company)* creación *f*, fundación *f*

launchpad ['lɔːntʃpæd] *n* plataforma *f* de lanzamiento

launder ['lɔːndər] *vt* **(a)** *(wash and iron)* lavar y planchar **(b)** *Fig (money)* blanquear

Laund(e)rette, [lɔːn'dret] *n, US* **Laundromat**® ['lɔːndrəmæt] *n* lavandería *f* automática

laundry ['lɔːndrɪ] *n* **(a)** *(place)* lavandería *f* **(b)** *(dirty clothes or linen)* ropa *f* sucia, colada *f*; *(clean clothes)* ropa *f* lavada; **to do the l.** lavar la ropa, *Esp* hacer la colada □ **l. basket** cesto *m* de la ropa sucia

laurel ['lɒrəl] *n Bot* laurel *m* □ **l. wreath** corona *f* de laureles; *Fam Fig* **to rest on one's laurels** dormirse en los laureles

lava ['lɑːvə] *n* lava *f*

lavatory ['lævətərɪ] *n* **(a)** *(toilet)* excusado *m*, wáter *m* □ **l. paper** papel *m* higiénico, *Chile* confort *m* **(b)** *(room)* cuarto *m* de baño, servicio *m*, *Am* baño *m*; **public l.** servicios *mpl*, aseos *mpl*

lavender ['lævəndər] **1** *n Bot* espliego *m*, lavanda *f* □ **l. water** agua *f* de lavanda
2 *adj (colour)* de color lavanda

lavish ['lævɪʃ] **1** *adj* **(a)** *(generous)* pródigo(a), generoso(a) **(b)** *(abundant)* abundante **(c)** *(luxurious, extravagant)* lujoso(a), espléndido(a)
2 *vt (praise)* colmar (**on** de); *(care, attention)* prodigar (**on** a)

law [lɔː] *n* **(a)** *(governing customs, actions)* ley *f*; **by** or **in l.** según la ley; **l. and order** el orden público; **to be above the l.** estar por encima de la ley; **to go to l.** recurrir a la justicia; **to keep within the l.** obrar según la ley; **to lay down the l.** dictar la ley; *Fig* **to be a l. unto oneself** dictar sus propias leyes; *Fig* **to take the l. into one's own hands** tomarse la justicia por su mano **(b)** *(as subject)* derecho *m*; **civil/criminal l.** derecho civil/penal □ **l. court** tribunal *m* de

justicia; *US* **l. school** facultad *f* de derecho **(c)** *Philos Phys* ley *f* **(d)** *Fam* **the l.** la poli, la bofia, la pasma

law-abiding ['lɔːæbaɪdɪŋ] *adj* observante *or* respetuoso(a) de la ley

law-breaker ['lɔːbreɪkər] *n* infractor(a) *m,f* or violador(a) *m,f* de la ley

law-breaking ['lɔːbreɪkɪŋ] *n* infracción *f* or violación *f* de la ley

lawful ['lɔːfʊl] *adj (gen)* legal; *(permitted by law)* lícito(a); *(legitimate)* legítimo(a)

lawless ['lɔːlɪs] *adj (without law)* ilegal; *(law-breaking)* anárquico(a); *(ungovernable)* ingobernable

lawlessness ['lɔːlɪsnɪs] *n* anarquía *f*, desorden *m*

lawmaker ['lɔːmeɪkər] *n* legislador(a) *m,f*

lawn [lɔːn] *n* **(a)** *(grass)* césped *m* □ *Sport* **l. tennis** tenis *m* sobre hierba **(b)** *Tex* linón *m*

lawnmower ['lɔːnməʊər] *n* cortacéspedes *m inv*

lawsuit ['lɔːsjuːt] *n* pleito *m*, juicio *m*, proceso *m*

lawyer ['lɔːjər] *n* abogado(a) *m,f*; *Ind* **labour l.** abogado(a) *m,f* laboralista; **l.'s office** bufete *m* de abogados; **l.'s fees** honorarios *mpl* de abogado(a)

lax [læks] *adj* **(a)** *(not strict)* laxo(a), relajado(a); *(not demanding)* poco exigente **(b)** *(careless)* descuidado(a); *(negligent)* negligente **(c)** *(loose, not taut)* suelto(a), flojo(a)

laxative ['læksətɪv] *adj & n* laxante *(m)*

laxity ['læksɪtɪ] *n* **(a)** *(lacking stricture)* laxitud *f*, relajación *f*, relajamiento *m*; *(undemanding)* falta *f* de exigencia **(b)** *(carelessness)* descuido *m*; *(negligence)* negligencia *f*

lay¹ [leɪ] *adj* **(a)** *Rel* seglar, laico(a) □ **l. preacher** predicador(a) *m,f* seglar **(b)** *(non-specialist)* lego(a), profano(a)

lay² [leɪ] **1** *vt (pt & pp* **laid)** **(a)** *(place, put)* poner, colocar; *(bricks, carpet)* poner; *(cable, trap)* tender; *(basis, foundations)* echar; *(bomb)* colocar; **she laid the baby in its cot** acostó al bebé en la cuna; *Fam Fig* **don't l. a finger on it!** ¡no lo toques!; *Fam Fig* **I've never laid eyes on him before** es la primera vez que lo veo; *Fam Fig* **just wait until I lay my hands on him!** espera a que lo pille or atrape **(b)** *(prepare)* preparar; *(fire)* hacer; *(table)* poner; *(curse)* lanzar **(c)** *(leave) (trail)* dejar; **to l. oneself open to criticism** exponerse a las críticas **(d)** *(eggs)* poner **(e)** *Vulg Esp* echar un polvo con, *Am* cogerse a, *Méx* chingarse a **(f)** *(set down)* asentar; *(bet)* hacer; *(charge)* presentar; *(blame)* echar; *(emphasis)* hacer; **to l. claim to sth** hacer valer su derecho a algo
2 *vi (hen)* poner huevos
3 *n Vulg* = la persona con la cual uno se acuesta

lay aside *vt (gen)* dejar a un lado; *(principles)* dejar de lado; *Fig (emotions, feelings)* olvidar

lay before *vt (plan, accusation, etc)* presentar a

lay by *vt (save)* guardar; *(money)* ahorrar

lay down *vt* **(a)** *(put down)* posar, dejar a un lado; *(let go)* dejar, soltar **(b)** *(title etc)* renunciar **(c)** *(surrender)* deponer; **to l. down one's arms** rendir *or* deponer las armas; *Literary* **to l. down one's life for sb** dar la vida por algn **(d)** *(plan)* formular **(e)** *(establish, dictate)* fijar, imponer; *(principles, guidelines)* sentar

lay in *vt (store up)* proveerse de, abastecerse de

lay into *vt Fam (attack) (physically)* dar una paliza a; *(verbally)* arremeter contra

lay off **1** *vt* **(a)** *(dismiss, make redundant)* despedir **(b)** *Fam (cease)* dejar de
2 *vt Fam* dejar en paz
3 *vi Fam* **l. off!** ¡deja de fastidiarme!, ¡ya está bien!, ya vale, ¿no?

lay on *vt* **(a)** *(provide) (transport)* organizar; *(food)* preparar (**b**) *(spread)* aplicar; *Fam (exaggerate)* **to l. it on (thick)** cargar las tintas, exagerar (**c**) *Fam* **to l. one on sb** *(hit)* pegar a algn (**c**) *Fam Br (trick)* engañar, timar; **to l. one on sb** hacer una jugarreta a algn

lay out *vt* (**a**) *(open out)* extender, tender, desplegar (**b**) *(arrange)* disponer, distribuir, colocar; *(body)* amortajar (**c**) *(ideas, information)* presentar, exponer (**d**) *(plan) (road)* trazar; *(garden)* diseñar (**e**) *Fam (money)* gastar, desembolsar (**f**) *Fam (knock out)* derribar, turbar

lay over *vi US* hacer noche

lay up *vt* (**a**) *(store)* guardar, almacenar (**b**) *(accumulate)* acumular, amasar; **to l. up trouble for oneself** crearse problemas (**c**) *Fam* **to be laid up** tener que guardar cama, estar enfermo(a)

lay³ [leɪ] *pt of* **lie²**

lay⁴ [leɪ] *n Lit Old-fashioned (ballad)* romance *m*

layabout ['leɪəbaʊt] *n Br Fam* holgazán(ana) *m,f*, gandul(ula) *m,f*, *Méx* flojo(a), *RP* fiaca *mf*

lay-by ['leɪbaɪ] *n Br Aut* área *f* de descanso

layer ['leɪər] **1** *n* (**a**) *(of paint etc)* capa *f*; *(of rock)* estrato *m* (**b**) *(hen)* gallina *f* ponedora

  2 *vt* **to have one's hair layered** cortarse el pelo a capas

layman ['leɪmən] *n* (*pl* **laymen**) (**a**) *Rel* seglar *m*, laico *m* (**b**) *(non-specialist)* lego *m*, profano *m*

lay-off ['leɪɒf] *n* despido *m*

layout ['leɪaʊt] *n* (**a**) *(arrangement)* disposición *f*, distribución *f*; *(presentation)* presentación *f*; *Typ* composición *f*, formato *m* (**b**) *(plan)* diseño *m*, trazado *m*

laywoman ['leɪwʊmən] *n* (*pl* **laywomen** ['leɪwɪmɪn]) (**a**) *Rel* seglar *f*, laica *f* (**b**) *(non-specialist)* lega *f*, profana *f*

laze [leɪz] *vi* holgazanear, gandulear

laze about, laze around *vi* no hacer nada

laziness ['leɪzɪnɪs] *n* pereza *f*, holgazanería *f*, gandulería *f*

lazy ['leɪzɪ] *adj* (**lazier, laziest**) perezoso(a), holgazán(ana), vago(a); **at a l. pace** a paso lento

lazybones ['leɪzɪbəʊnz] *n inv Fam* perezoso(a) *m,f*, gandul(ula) *m,f*, vago(a) *m,f*

lb *(abbr* **pound***)* libra *f*

LCD [elsiː'diː] *n Elec Comptr (abbr* **liquid crystal display***)* LCD, pantalla *f* de cristal líquido

lead¹ [led] *n* (**a**) *(metal)* plomo *m*; *Fam* **to swing the l.** gandulear ◻ *Med* **l. poisoning** saturnismo *m*; **white l.** albayalde *m*, plomo *m* blanco (**b**) *Slang (bullets)* plomo *m* (**c**) *(in pencil)* mina *f*

lead² [liːd] **1** *n* (**a**) *(front position)* delantera *f*; *(advantage)* ventaja *f*; **to be in the l.** ir en cabeza; **to take the l.** *(race)* ponerse a la cabeza, tomar la delantera; *(score)* adelantarse (**b**) *(clue)* pista *f* (**c**) *Theat (principal role)* primer papel *m* ◻ **l. singer** cantante *mf* principal (**d**) *Cards* mano *f*; **it's your l.** tú llevas la mano; *Fig* **to follow sb's l.** seguirle el ejemplo de algn (**e**) *(leash)* correa *f* (**f**) *Elec* cable *m*

  2 *vt* (*pt & pp* **led**) (**a**) *(conduct)* llevar, conducir, dirigir; **to l. the way** enseñar el camino (**b**) *(be the leader of)* dirigir, encabezar, liderar; *Br Mus (orchestra)* ser el primer violín de; *US* dirigir; *Fig* **to l. the field** ir en cabeza (**c**) *(influence)* **she is easily led** se deja llevar fácilmente; **this leads me to believe that** esto me lleva a creer que (**d**) *(life)* llevar; **to l. a dog's life** llevar una vida de perros (**e**) *Cards* salir con

  3 *vi* (**a**) *(road)* llevar, conducir, ir (**to** a); *(door)* dar (**to** a) (**b**) *(go first)* ir delante; *(in procession)* ir a la cabeza; *(in race)* llevar la delantera (**c**) *Cards* salir (**d**) *(result)* **to l. to** resultar en, llevar a; **it led to nothing** no llevó a nada

lead away *vt* llevar

lead off *vi* (**a**) *(road, corridor, etc)* salir, bifurcarse; *(room, door)* dar a (**from** de) (**b**) *(conversation, performance, etc)* empezar

lead on 1 *vi (go ahead)* ir adelante; **l. on!** ¡adelante!

  2 *vt (deceive)* engañar, timar

lead up to *vt* llevar a, conducir a

leaded ['ledɪd] *adj (window)* emplomado(a) *(gasoline)* con plomo

leaden ['ledən] *adj Literary (of lead)* de plomo; *(sky)* plomizo(a); *(food)* pesado(a)

leader ['liːdər] *n* (**a**) *(of party etc)* jefe(a) *m,f*, líder *mf*, dirigente *mf*; *(of race)* líder *mf*; **she was a born l.** nació para mandar (**b**) *Mus (of orchestra) Br* primer violín *m*; *US* director(a) *m,f* (**c**) *Br Press* editorial *m*, artículo *m* de fondo

leadership ['liːdəʃɪp] *n* (**a**) *(command)* dirección *f*, mando *m*; *Pol* liderato *m*, liderazgo *m*; *Fig* dotes *mpl* de mando (**b**) *(leaders)* dirigentes *mpl*, dirección *f*

lead-free ['ledfriː] *adj (petrol, paint)* sin plomo

lead-in ['liːdɪn] *n TV Rad* introducción *f*, presentación *f*

leading ['liːdɪŋ] *adj* (**a**) *(most important)* principal, primero(a) ◻ *Press* **l. article** *Br (editorial)* editorial *m*; *US (main story)* artículo *m* principal (**b**) *(outstanding)* destacado(a), notable; *Fam* **the l. light** el cerebro gris (**c**) **l. question** pregunta *f* tendenciosa

leaf [liːf] *n* (*pl* **leaves** [liːvz]) (**a**) *(of plant)* hoja *f*; **gold l.** pan *m* de oro; **to be in/come into l.** tener/echar hojas (**b**) *(of book)* hoja *f*, página *f*; *Fig* **to take a l. out of sb's book** tomar el ejemplo de algn; **to turn over a new l.** hacer borrón y cuenta nueva, volver la página (**c**) *(of table)* hoja *f* abatible

leaf through *vt* hojear

leaflet ['liːflɪt] **1** *n (single sheet)* octavilla *f*, panfleto *m*; *(brochure)* folleto *m*

  2 *vt* distribuir octavillas *or* folletos en

leafy ['liːfɪ] *adj* (**leafier, leafiest**) frondoso(a)

league [liːg] *n* (**a**) *(alliance)* liga *f*, alianza *f*; *(association)* sociedad *f*; **L. of Nations** Sociedad de las Naciones; *Fam* **to be in l. with sb** estar conchabado(a) con algn (**b**) *Sport* liga *f*; *Fam* **they are in a completely different l.** no hay comparación entre los dos ◻ **l. championship** campeonato *m* de liga (**c**) *(measure)* legua *f*

leak [liːk] **1** *n* (**a**) *(hole)* agujero *m*; *(in roof)* gotera *f*; *(in boat)* vía *f* de agua (**b**) *(escape) (of gas, liquid)* fuga *f*, escape *m*; *(of information)* filtración *f* (**c**) *Fam* **to take** *or Br* **have a l.** echar una meadita

  2 *vi* (**a**) *(container)* tener un agujero; *(pipe)* tener un escape; *(roof)* gotear; *(boat)* hacer agua; *(shoes)* dejar entrar el agua (**b**) *(gas, liquid)* salirse, fugarse, escaparse; *(information)* filtrarse; *(news)* trascender

  3 *vt (pipe etc)* dejar salir, dejar escapar (**b**) *(information, secret, etc)* filtrar, pasar (**to** a)

leakage ['liːkɪdʒ] *n (loss)* pérdida *f*

leaky ['liːkɪ] *adj* (**leakier, leakiest**) *(container)* agujereado(a); *(roof)* que tiene goteras; *(ship)* que hace agua; *(shoes)* que dejan entrar el agua

lean¹ [liːn] *adj (meat)* magro(a), sin grasa; *(person)* flaco(a), delgado(a); *(harvest)* malo(a), escaso(a); *Fig* **the l. years** los años de escasez, las vacas flacas

lean² [liːn] **1** *vi* (*pt & pp* **leaned** *or Br* **leant**) (**a**) *(building, tree)* inclinarse, ladearse (**b**) *(for support)* apoyarse; **to l. on/ against** apoyarse en/contra; *Fig* **to l. on** *or* **upon sb** *(pressurize)* presionar a algn; *(depend)* depender de algn

  2 *vt (ladder, bicycle, etc)* apoyar, recostar (**on** en)

lean back *vi* reclinarse, recostarse

lean forward *vi* inclinarse hacia delante

lean out *vi* asomarse

lean over *vi* inclinarse

leaning ['liːnɪŋ] **1** *adj* inclinado(a)

  2 *n Fig (tendency)* inclinación *f*, tendencia *f*, propensión *f*

leant [lent] *Br pt & pp see* **lean**

lean-to ['li:ntu:] *n (hut)* cobertizo *m*

leap [li:p] **1** *n (jump)* salto *m*, brinco *m*; *Fig* salto *m*, paso *m*; **a l. forward** *or* **ahead** un paso hacia adelante, un avance; *Fig* **a l. in the dark** un salto en el vacío ❏ **l. year** año *m* bisiesto

2 *vi (pt & pp* **leaped** *or* **leapt)** *(jump)* saltar, brincar; **to l. for joy** dar saltos de alegría; **to l. over a fence** saltarse una valla; **to l. to one's feet** levantarse de un salto; *Fig* **her heart leapt** su corazón dio un vuelco; *Fig* **Jones leapt from tenth to fourth** Jones dio un salto de la décima a la cuarta posición; *Fig* **the words leapt off the page at me** las palabras saltaba a la vista

leap at *vt Fig (gen)* aprovechar; *(chance)* no dejar escapar

leap up *vi* **(a)** *(person) (off ground)* saltar; *(to one's feet)* levantarse de un salto **(b)** *(flame)* brotar, saltar

leapfrog ['li:pfrɒg] **1** *n* pídola *f*

2 *vi (pt & pp* **leapfrogged)** jugar a la pídola

leapt [lept] *pt & pp see* **leap**

learn [lɜ:n] **1** *vt (pt & pp* **learned** *or Br* **learnt)** **(a)** *(in school etc)* aprender; **to l. (how) to ski** aprender a esquiar; **to l. sth by heart** aprenderse algo de memoria **(b)** *(find out about)* enterarse de, saber

2 *vi* **(a)** *(in school etc)* estudiar, aprender; **to l. from experience** aprender por experiencia; **to l. by** *or* **from one's mistakes, to l. the hard way** aprender de sus errores **(b)** *(find out)* enterarse; **to l. about** *or* **of** enterarse de, saber

learned ['lɜ:nɪd] *adj (person)* culto(a), erudito(a), leído(a); *(journal etc)* erudito(a)

learner ['lɜ:nər] *n (beginner)* principiante *mf; (student)* estudiante *mf; Aut* **l. driver** aprendiz(iza) *m,f* de conductor; **to be a slow l.** tener dificultades para aprender

learning ['lɜ:nɪŋ] *n (knowledge)* conocimientos *mpl; (erudition)* saber *m* ❏ **l. curve** curva *f* de aprendizaje

learnt [lɜ:nt] *Br pt & pp see* **learn**

lease [li:s] **1** *n* contrato *m* de arrendamiento; *Fig* **to give sb a new l. on** *or Br* **of life** dar nueva vida a algn

2 *vt* arrendar; *(rent)* alquilar

leasehold ['li:shəʊld] **1** *n* derechos *mpl* de arrendamiento

2 *adj (property)* arrendado(a)

leash [li:ʃ] *n* correa *f*

leasing ['li:sɪŋ] *n* **(a)** *(gen)* arrendamiento *m*, arriendo *m*; *(renting)* alquiler *m* **(b)** *Fin* leasing *m*

least [li:st] *(superl of* **little)** **1** *adj* menor, mínimo(a); **he has the l. time** él es quien menos tiempo tiene

2 *adv* menos; **it's the l. known of his novels** es su novela menos conocida; **l. of all him** él menos que nadie; **they are the ones who go l.** son ellos quienes van menos

3 *n* lo menos; **at l.** por lo menos; *(in number)* al menos; **it's the l. we can do** es lo menos que podemos hacer; **not in the l.!** ¡en absoluto!, ¡no faltaba más!, ¡cómo no!; **not in the l.** en lo más mínimo; **that's the l. of my worries** eso es lo de menos; **to say the l.** no decir más

leather ['leðər] **1** *n* cuero *m*, *Esp Méx* piel *f* ❏ **patent l.** charol *m*

2 *adj* de cuero *or Esp Méx* piel

leather-bound ['leðəbaʊnd] *adj (book)* encuadernado(a) en cuero *or Esp Méx* piel

leathery ['leðərɪ] *adj (skin)* curtido(a); *(meat)* correoso(a)

leave¹ [li:v] **1** *vt (pt & pp* **left)** **(a)** *(go away from)* dejar, abandonar; *(go out of)* salir de; **he left his wife to live with his mistress** abandonó a su mujer para ir a vivir con su amante; **he left school at 16** dejó de estudiar a los 16 años; **I usually l. home at eight** normalmente salgo de casa a las

ocho; **she left home after a family row** se marchó de casa después de una discusión familiar; **the car left the road** el coche se salió de la carretera; **they left him to his fate** lo abandonaron a su suerte; **to l. the table** levantarse de la mesa **(b)** *(allow to remain)* dejar; **it leaves much to be desired** deja mucho que desear; **l. her to herself** déjala que lo haga a su manera; **l. him alone!** *Fam* **l. him be!** ¡déjale en paz!; **she leaves the cleaning to me** a mí me deja encargarme de la limpieza; **to l. a tip/a message** dejar una propina/un recado; **to l. the door open** dejar la puerta abierta; *Fam* **l. it to me** yo me encargo; *Fam* **let's l. it at that!** ¡dejémoslo así! **(c)** *(bequeath)* dejar, legar **(d)** *(be survived by)* dejar; **he leaves a wife and three children** deja una viuda y tres hijos **(e)** *(forget)* dejarse, olvidarse; **he left his umbrella on the bus** se dejó el paraguas en el autobús **(f)** *Math* dar; **3 from 9 leaves 6** 9 menos 3 son 6, de 3 a 9 van 6 **(g)** *to be left* quedar; **I have two biscuits left** me quedan dos galletas; **it's all the money we have left** es todo el dinero que nos queda; **there's nobody/nothing left** no queda nadie/nada **(h)** *to be left over* sobrar; **there are three serviettes left over** sobran tres servilletas

2 *vi (go away)* irse, marcharse; *(go out)* salir; **he left without saying goodbye** se fue sin despedirse; **the train is leaving in five minutes** el tren sale dentro de cinco minutos

leave about *vt* dejar tirado(a); **he always leaves his clothes about** siempre deja la ropa tirada por ahí

leave behind *vt* **(a)** *(gen)* dejar atrás **(b)** *(forget)* dejarse, olvidarse

leave off 1 *vt* **(a)** *(stop)* dejar de; **to l. off smoking** dejar de fumar **(b)** *(clothes)* dejar de llevar

2 *vi (finish)* acabar; **where did we l. off?** ¿dónde acabamos?

leave on *vt* **(a)** *(clothes)* dejar puesto(a) **(b)** *(lights, radio)* dejar encendido(a)

leave out *vt* **(a)** *(keep in the open)* dejar fuera; *(put out)* *(books, clothes, etc)* dejar a mano; *(food, meal, etc)* dejar preparado(a); **you shouldn't l. the car out in the rain** no deberías dejar el coche a la intemperie cuando llueve **(b)** *(omit)* omitir, saltarse; *Fig* **to feel left out** sentirse excluido(a)

leave² [li:v] *n* **(a)** *(permission)* permiso *m*; **by** *or* **with your l.** con su permiso; **without so much as a by your l.** sin pedir permiso a nadie **(b)** *(time off)* vacaciones *fpl; Mil* permiso *m*; **annual l.** vacaciones anuales; *Mil* **to be on l.** estar de permiso; **to go on sick l.** darse de baja por enfermedad ❏ **l. of absence** excedencia *f*; **maternity l.** baja *f* por maternidad; **sick l.** baja *f* por enfermedad **(c)** *(farewell)* despedida *f*; **to take one's l. of sb** despedirse de algn; *Fig* **to take French l.** despedirse a la francesa; *Fig* **to take l. of one's senses** perder la razón *or* la cabeza

leaven ['levən] *n*, **leavening** ['levənɪŋ] *n* levadura *f*

leaves [li:vz] *npl see* **leaf**

leave-taking ['li:vteɪkɪŋ] *n* despedida *f*

leaving ['li:vɪŋ] *n* **(a)** *(departure)* salida *f* **(b)** **leavings** *(remains)* restos *mpl*; *(of food)* sobras *fpl*

Lebanese [lebə'ni:z] *adj & n* libanés(esa) *(m,f)*

Lebanon ['lebənən] *n* **(the) L.** (el) Líbano

lecher ['letʃər] *n* sátiro *m*, obseso *m*

lecherous ['letʃərəs] *adj* lascivo(a), lujurioso(a)

lechery ['letʃərɪ] *n* lascivia *f*, lujuria *f*

lectern ['lektən] *n (gen)* atril *m*; *(in church)* facistol *m*

lecture ['lektʃər] **1** *n* **(a)** *(by visiting speaker)* conferencia *f*, charla *f; Univ* clase *f*; **to give a l.** dar una conferencia (**on** sobre) ❏ **l. hall, l. room, l. theatre** *(gen)* sala *f* de conferencias; *Univ* aula *f*; **l. notes** apuntes *mpl* **(b)** *(reproof)* sermón *m*, reprimenda *f*

2 *vi (visiting speaker)* dar una conferencia *or* conferencias; *Univ* dar *or Am* dictar clases; **he lectured on animal life** dio conferencias sobre la vida animal; **she lectures to advanced students** da clases a los alumnos más avanzados
3 *vt (reproach)* sermonear, echar una reprimenda a; **they were lectured for being late** les echaron una reprimenda por haber llegado tarde

lecturer ['lektʃərər] *n (visiting speaker)* conferenciante *mf, Am* conferencista *mf; Br Univ* profesor(a) *m,f*

lectureship ['lektʃəʃɪp] *n Br Univ* cargo *m* de profesor

LED [eliː'diː] *n Elec (abbr* **light-emitting diode)** LED *m,* diodo *m* emisor de luz

led [led] *pt & pp see* **lead²**

ledge [ledʒ] *n* **(a)** *(shelf)* repisa *f; (of window)* antepecho *m,* alféizar *m* **(b)** *(on mountain)* saliente *m*

ledger ['ledʒər] *n Com* libro *m* mayor

lee [liː] **1** *n* **(a)** *Naut* sotavento *m,* socaire *m* **(b)** *Fig* abrigo *m;* **in the l. of** al abrigo de
2 *adj Naut* de sotavento

leech [liːtʃ] *n* **(a)** *Zool* sanguijuela *f* **(b)** *Fig (person)* sanguijuela *f,* parásito(a) *m,f;* **to cling like a l.** pegarse como una lapa

leek [liːk] *n Bot* puerro *m*

leer [lɪər] **1** *vi* mirar con lascivia, echar una mirada lasciva
2 *n* mirada *f* lasciva

leery ['lɪərɪ] *adj* **(leerier, leeriest)** *Slang* **(a)** *(suspicious)* receloso(a) **(b)** *(wary)* cauteloso(a); **to be l. of** tener cuidado con

lees [liːz] *npl* heces *fpl,* poso *m*

leeward ['liːwəd] *Naut* **1** *adj* de sotavento; **L. Islands** Islas de Sotavento
2 *n* sotavento *m*
3 *adv* a sotavento

leeway ['liːweɪ] *n* **(a)** *(freedom)* libertad *f;* **this gives me a certain amount of l.** esto me da cierto margen de libertad **(b)** *Naut Av* deriva *f* **(c)** *Fig (backlog)* tiempo *m* perdido, atraso *m;* **to make up l.** recuperar el tiempo perdido

left¹ [left] **1** *adj* **(a)** *(gen)* izquierdo(a) **(b)** *Pol* de izquierdas □ **l. wing** izquierda *f*
2 *adv* a la izquierda, hacia la izquierda; **turn l. at the lights** gira a la izquierda después del semáforo
3 *n* **(a)** *(gen)* izquierda *f;* **on the l.** a mano izquierda **(b)** *Pol* izquierda *f;* **the far l.** la extrema izquierda; **to be on the l.** ser de izquierdas

left² [left] *pt & pp see* **leave¹**

left-click ['leftklɪk] **1** *vt* hacer click con el botón izquierdo en
2 *vi* hacer click con el botón izquierdo **(on** en)

left-field ['left'fiːld] *adj US Fam (bizarre)* raro(a), extravagante

left-hand ['lefthænd] *adj* izquierdo(a); *Aut* **l.-h. drive** con el volante a la izquierda; **on the l.-h. side** a mano izquierda

left-handed [left'hændɪd] *adj* **(a)** *(person)* zurdo(a); *(object)* para zurdos; **l.-h. scissors** tijeras para zurdos **(b)** *(ambiguous)* de doble filo, ambiguo(a)

left-hander [left'hændər] *n* **(a)** *(blow)* golpe *m* con la izquierda **(b)** *(person)* zurdo(a) *m,f*

leftist ['leftɪst] *adj & n* izquierdista *(mf)*

left-luggage [left'lʌgɪdʒ] *n Br* **l.-l. office** consigna *f*

leftover ['leftəʊvər] **1** *adj* sobrante, restante, de sobras
2 leftovers *npl* sobras *fpl,* restos *mpl*

left-wing ['leftwɪŋ] *adj* de izquierdas, izquierdista

left-winger ['left'wɪŋər] *n Pol* izquierdista *mf*

lefty ['leftɪ] *n Fam Pol* izquierdoso(a) *m,f,* izquierdista *mf, RP* zurdo(a) *m,f*

leg [leg] **1** *n* **(a)** *(of person)* pierna *f; (of animal)* pata *f; Culin (of lamb)* pierna *f; (of chicken)* muslo *m; (of table, chair)* pata *f,* pie *m; (of trousers)* pernera *f;* **to give sb a l. up** ayudar a algn a subir; **to stretch one's legs** estirar las piernas; *Fig* **he hasn't got a l. to stand on** no tiene en qué basarse; *Fig* **to be on one's last legs** estar en las últimas; *Fam* **to shake a l.** *(hurry)* espabilarse; *(dance)* bailotear; *Fam* **to show a l.** levantarse por la mañana; *Fam Fig* **to pull sb's l.** tomar el pelo a algn **(b)** *(stage)* etapa *f*
2 *vt (pt & pp* **legged)** *Fam* **to l. it** *(walk)* ir a pata; *(rush)* ir volando

legacy ['legəsɪ] *n* herencia *f,* legado *m; Fig* herencia *f,* patrimonio *m*

legal ['liːgəl] *adj* **(a)** *(gen)* legal; *(legitimate)* legítimo(a); *(permitted by law)* lícito(a) □ **l. tender** moneda *f* de curso legal **(b)** *(relating to the law)* jurídico(a), legal; **the l. profession** la abogacía; **to take l. action against sb** entablar un pleito contra algn □ **l. adviser** asesor *m* jurídico, asesoría *f* jurídica; **l. aid** asesoramiento *m* jurídico para los pobres; **l. costs** costas *fpl;* **l. eagle** *(successful lawyer)* = abogado de éxito, especialmente joven, brillante y dinámico; *US* **l. holiday** fiesta *f* nacional

legalistic [liːgə'lɪstɪk] *adj* legalista

legality [lɪ'gælɪtɪ] *n* legalidad *f*

legalize ['liːgəlaɪz] *vt* legalizar

legally ['liːgəlɪ] *adv* legalmente; **l. responsible** responsable ante la ley

legate ['legɪt] *n Rel* legado *m*

legation [lɪ'geɪʃən] *n (diplomatic mission)* legación *f*

legend ['ledʒənd] *n* leyenda *f; Fig* **to become a l. in one's own time** ser una leyenda viva

legendary ['ledʒəndərɪ] *adj* legendario(a)

leggings ['legɪŋz] *npl* polainas *fpl*

leggy ['legɪ] *adj* **(leggier, leggiest)** **(a)** *(long-legged)* zanquilargo(a), patilargo(a); *(with shapely legs)* con bonitas piernas **(b)** *(plant)* muy crecido(a)

legibility [ledʒə'bɪlɪtɪ] *n* legibilidad *f*

legible ['ledʒəbəl] *adj* legible

legion ['liːdʒən] *n* legión *f;* **the Foreign L.** la Legión Extranjera

legionnaire [liːdʒə'neər] *n* legionario *m* □ *Med* **l.'s disease** enfermedad *f* del legionario

legislate ['ledʒɪsleɪt] *vi* legislar

legislation [ledʒɪs'leɪʃən] *n* legislación *f*

legislative ['ledʒɪslətɪv] *adj* legislativo(a)

legislator ['ledʒɪsleɪtər] *n* legislador(a) *m,f*

legislature ['ledʒɪsleɪtʃər] *n* asamblea *f* legislativa, legislatura *f*

legitimacy [lɪ'dʒɪtɪməsɪ] *n* legitimidad *f*

legitimate [lɪ'dʒɪtɪmɪt] *adj* legítimo(a); *(valid)* válido(a)

legitimize [lɪ'dʒɪtɪmaɪz] *vt* legitimar

legless ['leglɪs] *adj Br Fam (drunk) Esp Méx* pedo, *Col* caído(a), *Méx* cuete, *RP* en pedo

leg-pull ['legpʌl] *n Br Fam* broma *f,* tomadura *f* de pelo

legroom ['legruːm] *n* espacio *m* para las piernas

legume ['legjuːm] *n Bot* legumbre *f*

leg-warmers ['legwɔːməz] *npl* calientapiernas *fpl*

leisure ['leʒər, *US* 'liːʒər] *n* ocio *m,* tiempo *m* libre; **at l.** *(with free time)* con tiempo libre; *(calmly)* con calma; **do it at your l.** hazlo cuando tengas tiempo; **to live a life of l.** vivir como un rey □ **l. activities** pasatiempos *mpl;* **l. centre** polideportivo *m;* **l. wear** ropa *f* de sport

leisurely ['leʒəlɪ, *US* 'liːʒəlɪ] *adj (unhurried)* con calma, sin prisa; *(slow)* lento(a)

leitmotif *n*, **leitmotiv** ['laɪtməʊtiːf] *n* leitmotiv *m*, tema *m* central

lemming ['lemɪŋ] *n Zool* lemming *m*

lemon ['lemən] **1** *n* **(a)** *(fruit)* limón *m* ▫ **l. cheese**, *Br* **l. curd** crema *f* de limón; **l. ice** granizado *m* de limón; **l. juice** zumo *m* de limón; *Br* **l. squash** limonada *f*; **l. squeezer** exprimidor *m*, exprimelimones *m inv*; **l. tea** té *m* con limón; **l. tree** limonero *m* **(b)** *Br Slang (halfwit)* primo(a) *m,f* **(c)** *Slang (old car)* cacharro *m*
2 *adj (colour)* de color limón

lemonade [lemə'neɪd] *n* **(a)** *(still)* limonada *f* **(b)** *Br (fizzy) Esp Arg* gaseosa *f*, *Am* gaseosa *f* de lima *or* limón

lemur ['liːmər] *n* lémur *m*

lend [lend] *vt (pt & pp* lent*) (money etc)* prestar, dejar; *Fig (impart, contribute)* dar, prestar, dotar de; **can you l. me your pen?** ¿me dejas tu bolígrafo?; **her ideas lent intelligence to the meeting** sus ideas dotaron de inteligencia a la reunión; **to l. oneself** *or* **itself to sth** prestarse a *or* para algo; *Fam* **can you l. me a hand?** ¿me echas una mano?; *Fam Fig* **to l. an ear to sb** escuchar a algn

lender ['lendər] *n Fin* prestamista *mf*

lending ['lendɪŋ] *n* **l. library** biblioteca *f* pública

length [leŋθ] *n* **(a)** *(dimension)* longitud *f*, largo *m*; **it is five metres in l.** tiene *or* mide cinco metros de largo; **what l. is it?** ¿cuánto tiene *or* mide de largo?; *Fig* **throughout the l. and breadth of the country** a lo largo y ancho del país **(b)** *(duration)* duración *f*; **for what l. of time?** ¿por cuánto tiempo?; **the l. of a visit** la duración de una visita **(c)** *(piece) (of string, tubing)* trozo *m*; *(of cloth)* largo *m* **(d)** *(distance)* largo *m*, distancia *f*; *(of swimming pool)* largo *m*; *(stretch of road)* tramo *m*; **she walked the l. of the river** anduvo a lo largo del río; *Sport* **to win by a l.** ganar por un largo; *Fig* **to go to any lengths to achieve sth** hacer lo que sea para conseguir algo; *Fig* **to go to great lengths** tomarse mucha molestia; *Fig* **to keep sb at arm's l.** mantener las distancias con algn **(e)** **at l.** *(finally)* finalmente, a la larga; *(in depth)* a fondo, con detalle; **to explain sth at l.** explicar algo con todo detalle; **to talk at l.** hablar largo y tendido

lengthen ['leŋθən] **1** *vt* **(a)** *(skirt etc)* alargar **(b)** *(lifetime)* prolongar, extender
2 *vi (days)* crecer

lengthways ['leŋθweɪz] *adv*, **lengthwise** ['leŋθwaɪz] *adv* a lo largo, longitudinalmente

lengthy ['leŋθɪ] *adj* **(lengthier, lengthiest)** *(gen)* largo(a); *(film, illness)* de larga duración; *(meeting, discussion)* prolongado(a)

lenience ['liːnɪəns] *n*, **leniency** ['liːnɪənsɪ] *n* lenidad *f*, clemencia *f*, indulgencia *f*

lenient ['liːnɪənt] *adj* indulgente

leniently ['liːnɪəntlɪ] *adv* con indulgencia, benevolamente

Leningrad ['lenɪŋgræd] *n Formerly* Leningrado

lens [lenz] *n* **(a)** *(of eye)* cristalino *m* **(b)** *(of spectacles)* lente *m or f* ▫ **contact lenses** *Am* lentes *mpl* de contacto, *Esp* lentillas *fpl*, *Méx* pupilentes *fpl* **(c)** *Phot* objetivo *m*

Lent [lent] *n Rel* Cuaresma *f*

lent [lent] *pt & pp see* **lend**

lentil ['lentɪl] *n* lenteja *f*; **l. soup** sopa de lentejas

Leo ['liːəʊ] *n Astrol Astron* Leo *m*, León *m*

leopard ['lepəd] *n* leopardo *m*

leopard-skin ['lepədskɪn] *adj* de piel de leopardo

leotard ['liːətɑːd] *n (for dance, gym)* leotardo *m*, malla *f*, maillot *m*; *(as underwear)* leotardo *m*

leper ['lepər] *n Med* leproso(a) *m,f*

leprechaun ['leprəkɔːn] *n Ir* duende *m*

leprosy ['leprəsɪ] *n Med* lepra *f*

leprous ['leprəs] *adj Med* leproso(a)

lesbian ['lezbɪən] *adj & n* lesbiana (*f*)

lesion ['liːʒən] *n Med* lesión *f*

Lesotho [lɪ'suːtʊ] *n* Lesotho

less [les] **1** *adj (comp of* little*)* menos; **he is earning l. money than last year** gana menos dinero que el año pasado
2 *pron* menos; **at a price of l. than ten pence** a un precio inferior a diez peniques; **in l. than an hour** en menos de una hora; **nothing l. than** nada menos que; **the l. said about it, the better** cuanto menos se diga mejor; **they see l. of each other these days** se ven menos estos días; *Fam* **it was signed by the President, no l.** lo firmó el mismísimo presidente
3 *adv* menos; **l. and l.** cada vez menos; **she's l. intelligent than her brother** es menos inteligente que su hermano; **still l.** menos aún; *Fig* **to think l. of** tener en menos consideración
4 *prep* menos; **a year l. two days** un año menos dos días; **she earns a thousand dollars, l. tax** gana mil dólares, sin descontar los impuestos

lessee [le'siː] *n* arrendatario(a) *m,f*

lessen ['lesən] **1** *vt* disminuir, reducir
2 *vi* disminuir, reducirse

lessening ['lesənɪŋ] *n* disminución *f*, reducción *f*

lesser ['lesər] *adj* menor; **to a l. extent** en menor grado; **to choose the l. of two evils** escoger el mal menor

lesser-known ['lesə'nəʊn] *adj* menos conocido(a)

lesson ['lesən] *n* **(a)** *(session)* clase *f*; *(in book)* lección *f*; **Spanish lessons** clases de español; *Fig* **let that be a l. to you** que eso te sirva de lección **(b)** *Rel* lectura *f*

lessor ['lesɔːr, le'sɔːr] *n* arrendador(a) *m,f*

lest [lest] *conj Fml* **(a)** *(in order not to)* para (que) no; **l. we forget** para que no lo olvidemos **(b)** *(for fear that)* por miedo a que; **he kept quiet l. he should be discovered** no hizo ruido por miedo a que le descubrieran

let¹ [let] **1** *vt (pt & pp* let*)* **(a)** *(allow)* dejar, permitir; **he l. me borrow his car** me dejó el coche; **l. me know if you want one** avísame si quieres uno; **to l. go of sth** soltar algo; **to l. loose** soltar, dejar suelto(a); **to l. sb by** dejar pasar a algn; **to l. sb know** avisar a algn; *Fig* **to l. oneself go** dcjarse ir **(b)** *Br (rent out)* alquilar, *Méx* rentar; **'to l.'** 'se alquila', *Méx* 'se renta' **(c)** *Med (blood)* sangrar **(d)** **l. alone** ni mucho menos; **he can't walk, l. alone run** no puede andar, ni mucho menos correr
2 *v aux* **l. him wait** que espere; **l. me alone!, l. me be!** ¡déjame en paz!; **l. me go!** ¡suéltame!; **l. me tell you sth** déjame decirte una cosa; **l. us pray** oremos; **l.'s go!** ¡vamos!, ¡vámonos!; **l.'s see** a ver; **l. X equal Y** pongamos que X es igual a Y
3 *n Br (renting of house etc)* alquiler *m*; **short l.** alquiler *m or Méx* renta *f* por un periodo corto

let down *vt* **(a)** *(lower)* bajar; *(lengthen)* alargar; *Fam Fig* **to l. one's hair down** desmelenarse, echar una cana al aire **(b)** *(deflate)* desinflar, deshinchar **(c)** *(fail)* fallar, defraudar, decepcionar; **the car l. us down** nos falló el coche; **to be l. down** llevarse un chasco *or* un disgusto; **to feel l. down** sentirse defraudado(a)

let in *vt* **(a)** *(admit)* dejar entrar, hacer pasar; **her mother l. me in** me abrió su madre; **these shoes l. the water in** estos zapatos dejan entrar el agua; **to l. oneself in** abrir la puerta uno(a) mismo(a) **(b)** **to l. oneself in for** meterse en; **to l. oneself in for trouble** meterse en un lío **(c)** **to l. in on**; **to l. sb in on a secret** revelar un secreto a algn

let off *vt* **(a)** *(leave off)* dejar; **could you l. me off at the**

station? ¿puedes dejarme en la estación? **(b)** *(bomb)* hacer explotar; *(fireworks)* hacer estallar **(c)** *(liquid, air)* soltar, emitir; *Fam Fig* **to l. off steam** desfogarse, desahogarse **(d)** *Fam* **to l. sb off** *(pardon)* perdonar a algn; *(free)* dejar a algn en libertad; **he was l. off with a warning** le dejaron marcharse tras una amonestación

let on *vi Fam (pretend)* hacer ver; *(reveal)* contar, revelar; **don't l. on, will you?** no digas nada, por favor; **he l. on that he knew nothing** hizo ver que no sabía nada

let out *vt* **(a)** *(release) (prisoner)* soltar, poner en libertad; *(news)* divulgar; *(secret)* revelar; *Fam* **that lets me out** eso me deja limpio **(b)** *(air, water)* dejar salir; **to l. air out of a tyre** desinflar un neumático **(c)** *(sound, cry)* soltar **(d)** *Sew (widen)* ensanchar **(e)** *(rent out)* alquilar

let through *vt* dejar pasar

let up *vi* cesar, parar; **when will this rain l. up?** ¿cuándo dejará de llover?; *Fam* **l. up on me, will you?** déjame en paz, ¿quieres?

let² [let] *n Ten* let *m*

letdown ['letdaʊn] *n* decepción *f*, chasco *m*; **what a l.!** ¡qué desilusión!

lethal ['liːθəl] *adj* mortal, letal ▫ **l. weapon** arma *f* mortífera

lethargic [lɪ'θɑːdʒɪk] *adj* letárgico(a), aletargado(a)

lethargy ['leθədʒɪ] *n* letargo *m*

letter ['letər] *n* **(a)** *(of alphabet)* letra *f*; **the l. 'S'** la letra 'S'; *Fig* **to the l.** al pie de la letra ▫ **capital l.** mayúscula *f*; **small l.** minúscula *f* **(b)** *(written message)* carta *f*; **covering l.** carta adjunta; **registered l.** carta certificada ▫ **l. bomb** carta bomba; *Br* **l. box** buzón *m*; *Br* **l. card** carta-tarjeta *f*; **l. of attorney** poderes *mpl*; *Com* **l. of credit** carta *f* de crédito; **l. of introduction** carta *f* de presentación *or* de recomendación **(c)** **letters** *(learning)* letras *fpl*; **man of l.** hombre *m* de letras

letter-carrier ['letəkærɪər] *n US* cartero(a) *m,f*

letterhead ['letəhed] *n* membrete *m*

lettering ['letərɪŋ] *n* inscripción *f*, rótulo *m*

letter-opener ['letərəʊpenər] *n* abrecartas *m inv*

letterpress ['letəpres] *n* **(a)** *(method)* impresión *f* tipográfica **(b)** *(text)* texto *m* impreso

letter-writer ['letəraɪtər] *n* escritor(a) *m,f* de cartas; **he isn't much of a l.-w.** no es muy amigo de escribir cartas

lettuce ['letɪs] *n* lechuga *f*

let-up ['letʌp] *n Fam* descanso *m*, tregua *f*, respiro *m*

leukaemia, *US* **leukemia** [luː'kiːmɪə] *n Med* leucemia *f*

levee ['levɪ] *n US* dique *m*

level ['levəl] **1** *adj* **(a)** *(flat) (surface, ground)* llano(a), plano(a); *(even)* a nivel, nivelado(a); *(equal)* igual, parejo(a), igualado(a); *Culin* **a l. spoonful of** una cucharada rasa de; **to be l. with** estar a nivel de; **to draw l.** igualar **(with** a); *Fig* **to do one's l. best** hacer todo lo posible ▫ *Br Rail* **l. crossing** paso *m* a nivel **(b)** *(steady) (temperature)* estable; *(tone)* uniforme; *Fig* **to keep a l. head** no perder la cabeza **2** *vt (pt & pp* **levelled,** *US* **leveled) (a)** *(make level)* nivelar, allanar **(b)** *(raze)* rasar, igualar, arrasar **(c)** *(aim)* dirigir; **to l. a blow at sb** asestar un golpe a algn; **to l. a weapon at sb** apuntar un arma a algn; *Fig* **to l. an accusation against sb** dirigir una acusación a algn **(d)** *(survey)* nivelar **3** *n* **(a)** *(horizontal plane)* nivel *m*; **at sea l.** a nivel del mar; **to be on a l. with** estar al mismo nivel que; *Fig* **to find one's (own) l.** estar con los suyos; *Fam* **to be on the l.** *(be honest)* ser de fiar; *(be truthful)* decir la verdad, hablar en serio **(b)** *(instrument)* nivel *m* ▫ *Constr* **spirit l.** nivel *m* (de burbuja de aire)

level off, level out *vi* **(a)** *(ground)* nivelarse **(b)** *(prices)* estabilizarse **(c)** *(aircraft)* enderezarse, recuperar la estabilidad

level with *vt Fam* ser franco(a) con

level-headed [levəl'hedɪd] *adj* sensato(a), equilibrado(a)

lever ['liːvər, *US* 'levər] **1** *n* palanca *f* **2** *vt* apalancar; **to l. sth out** alzar algo con palanca

leverage ['liːvərɪdʒ] *n* apalancamiento *m*; *Fig (influence)* influencia *f*

leveret ['levərɪt] *n Zool* lebrato *m*

levitate ['levɪteɪt] **1** *vt* hacer levitar **2** *vi* levitar

levitation [levɪ'teɪʃən] *n* levitación *f*

levity ['levɪtɪ] *n* ligereza *f*, frivolidad *f*

levy ['levɪ] **1** *vt (pt & pp* **levied)** *(impose, collect) (tax)* recaudar; *(fine)* imponer **2** *n (of tax)* recaudación *f*; *(of fine)* imposición *f*

lewd [luːd] *adj (person)* lascivo(a), lujurioso(a); *(story, song)* obsceno(a); *(joke)* verde

lewdness ['luːdnɪʃ] *n (of person)* lascivia *f*; *(of song etc)* obscenidad *f*

lexical ['leksɪkəl] *adj* léxico(a)

lexicographer [leksɪ'kɒgrəfər] *n* lexicógrafo(a) *m,f*

lexicography [leksɪ'kɒgrəfɪ] *n* lexicografía *f*

lexicology [leksɪ'kɒlədʒɪ] *n* lexicología *f*

lh *(abbr* **left hand)** *(mano f)* izquierda *f*

liability [laɪə'bɪlɪtɪ] *n* **(a)** *Jur (responsibility)* responsabilidad *f* **(b)** *(handicap)* estorbo *m*, carga *f*; *Fam* **he's a real l.** es un cero a la izquierda **(c)** **liabilities** *Fin (debts)* deudas *fpl*, pasivo *m sing*; **assets and l.** activo *m sing* y pasivo *m sing*

liable ['laɪəbəl] *adj* **(a)** *Jur (responsible)* responsable; *(susceptible)* sujeto(a), obligado(a); **he is l. for military service** está obligado a hacer el servicio militar; **l. to a fine** expuesto(a) a una multa; **l. to duties** sujeto(a) a impuestos; **to be l. for** ser responsable de, responder de **(b)** *(likely)* propenso(a); **to be l. to do sth** tener tendencia a hacer algo, ser propenso(a) a hacer algo; **he's l. to change his mind** puede que cambie de idea; **it's l. to happen** es muy probable que así suceda

liaise [lɪ'eɪz] *vi* comunicarse **(with** con), establecer contacto **(with** con)

liaison [lɪ'eɪzɒn] *n* **(a)** *(coordination)* enlace *m*, coordinación *f* ▫ **l. committee** comité *m* de enlace; **l. officer** oficial *mf* de enlace **(b)** *(love affair)* aventura *f*, amorío *m*

liar ['laɪər] *n* mentiroso(a) *m,f*, embustero(a) *m,f*

lib [lɪb] *n Fam (abbr* **liberation)** liberación *f*

libel ['laɪbəl] *Jur* **1** *n (defamation)* difamación *f*, calumnia *f*; *(written)* libelo *m* ▫ **l. suit** pleito *m* por difamación **2** *vt (pt & pp* **libelled,** *US* **libeled)** difamar, calumniar

libellous, *US* **libelous** ['laɪbələs] *adj* difamatorio(a), calumnioso(a)

liberal ['lɪbərəl] **1** *adj* **(a)** *(gen)* liberal ▫ *Br* **l. arts** letras *fpl*; **l. education** educación *f* liberal; *Pol* **L. Party** Partido *m* Liberal **(b)** *(abundant)* abundante **2** *n Pol* **L.** liberal *mf*

liberalism ['lɪbərəlɪzəm] *n* liberalismo *m*

liberalize ['lɪbərəlaɪz] *vt* liberalizar

liberally ['lɪbərəlɪ] *adv* generosamente

liberal-minded ['lɪbərəlmaɪndɪd] *adj* liberal, tolerante, de amplias miras

liberate ['lɪbəreɪt] *vt (gen)* liberar; *(prisoner etc)* poner en libertad, libertar; **liberated woman** mujer liberada

liberation [lɪbə'reɪʃən] *n* liberación *f* ▫ **l. movement** movimiento *m* de liberación; *Rel* **l. theology** teología *f* de la liberación; **women's l.** liberación f de la mujer

liberator ['lɪbəreɪtər] n liberador(a) m,f, libertador(a) m,f

Liberia [laɪˈbɪərɪə] n Liberia

Liberian [laɪˈbɪərɪən] adj & n liberiano(a) (m,f)

libertarian [lɪbəˈteərɪən] adj & n libertario(a) (m,f)

liberty ['lɪbətɪ] n libertad f; **at l.** libre, en libertad; **to be at l. to say sth** ser libre de decir algo, tener derecho a decir algo; **to take liberties with sb** tomarse libertades con algn; **to take the l. of doing sth** tomarse la libertad de hacer algo; Fam **what a l.!** ¡qué cara!

libido [lɪˈbiːdəʊ] n (pl **libidos**) libido f

Libra ['liːbrə] n Astrol Astron Libra f

librarian [laɪˈbreərɪən] n bibliotecario(a) m,f

library ['laɪbrərɪ] n biblioteca f □ **l. book** libro m de biblioteca; **l. ticket** carnet m de biblioteca; **mobile l.** biblioteca f móvil, bibliobús m; **newspaper l.** hemeroteca f; **public l.** biblioteca f pública; **reference l.** biblioteca f de consulta

libretto [lɪˈbretəʊ] n (pl **librettos** or **libretti** [lɪˈbretiː]) Mus libreto m

Libya ['lɪbɪə] n Libia

Libyan ['lɪbɪən] adj & n libio(a) (m,f)

lice [laɪs] npl see **louse**

licence ['laɪsəns] n (a) (permit) licencia f, permiso m; Br (driving) l., US (driver's) license carné m or permiso m de Esp conducir or RP conductor, licencia f Carib de conducir or Méx para conducir; **gun l.** licencia f de armas □ Aut **l. number** matrícula f; US Aut **license plate** (placa f de) matrícula f (b) (freedom) libertad f, (excessive freedom) licencia f □ **poetic l.** licencia f poética

license ['laɪsəns] **1** vt autorizar
2 n US see **licence**

licensed ['laɪsənst] adj autorizado(a); Br **l. premises** local m autorizado para la venta de bebidas alcohólicas

licensee [laɪsənˈsiː] n (gen) concesionario(a) m,f; (of pub) dueño(a) m,f

licentious [laɪˈsenʃəs] adj licencioso(à), disoluto(a)

lichen ['laɪkən] n Bot liquen m

lick [lɪk] **1** vt (a) (with tongue) lamer; **to l. one's lips** lamerse; Fig (in anticipation) relamerse; Fam **to l. sth into shape** poner algo a punto; Fam Fig **to l. sb's boots** hacer la pelota a algn (b) Fam (beat) dar una paliza a
2 n lamedura f, lengüetada f, lengüetazo m; Fam **a l. of paint** una mano de pintura; Fam **at full l.** a todo gas; Fam **to give oneself a l. and a promise** lavarse rápidamente

licking ['lɪkɪŋ] n Fam paliza f

licorice ['lɪkərɪs, 'lɪkərɪʃ] n US see **liquorice**

lid [lɪd] n (a) (cover) tapa f, tapadera f; Br Fam **that puts the (tin) l. on it!** ¡eso ya es el colmo!; Fam Fig **to take the l. off a scandal** destapar un escándalo; Slang **to flip one's l.** ponerse hecho(a) una furia (b) (of eye) párpado m

lie¹ [laɪ] **1** vi (pt & pp **lied**) mentir; Fam **to l. one's head off** mentir como un bellaco
2 n mentira f; **it's a pack of lies** es pura mentira; **to give the l. to** desmentir; **to tell lies** mentir □ **l. detector** detector m de mentiras; Fig **white l.** mentira f piadosa

lie² [laɪ] **1** vi (pt **lay**, pp **lain**) (a) (act) echarse, acostarse, tumbarse, tenderse; (state) estar echado(a), estar acostado(a), estar tumbado(a), estar tendido(a); (be buried) yacer (b) (be situated) estar, encontrarse, hallarse, situarse; **the city lies to the north** la ciudad está al norte; **the fault lies with him** la culpa es suya; **the problem lies in her intransigence** el problema está en or radica en su intransigencia; **the valley lay before us** el valle se extendía ante nosotros (c) (remain) quedarse; **to l. still**

quedarse inmóvil; Fig **to l. low** permanecer escondido(a)
2 n (position) posición f, situación f; (direction) dirección f, orientación f; **the l. of the land** la topografía del terreno; Fig **el estado de las cosas**

lie about, lie around vi (person) estar tumbado(a); (things) estar tirado(a)

lie back vi (in an armchair) recostarse

lie down vi acostarse, echarse, tumbarse, tenderse; Fig **to take sth lying down** aceptar algo sin chistar

lie in vi Fam (stay in bed) levantarse tarde

Liechtenstein ['lɪktənstaɪn] n Liechtenstein

lie-down ['laɪdaʊn] n Br Fam **to have a l.** echarse un rato

lie-in ['laɪɪn] n Br Fam **to have a l.-in** levantarse tarde

lieu [ljuː, luː] n lugar m; **in l. of** en lugar de

Lieut Mil (abbr **Lieutenant**) Teniente m, Tente., Tte.

lieutenant [Br lefˈtenənt, US luːˈtenənt] n (a) Mil teniente m □ **l. colonel** teniente m coronel; **l. general** teniente m general (b) (non-military) lugarteniente m

life [laɪf] n (pl **lives** [laɪvz]) (a) (gen) vida f; **human l.** la vida humana; **it's a matter of l. and death** es cuestión de vida o muerte; **to bring sb back to l.** resucitar a algn; **to come to l.** cobrar vida; Fig **for dear l.** con toda la fuerza, a más no poder; Fam **as large as l.** de carne y hueso □ **l. belt** cinturón m salvavidas; **l. cycle** ciclo m vital; **l. force** fuerza f vital; **l. imprisonment** cadena f perpetua; **l. insurance** seguro m de vida; **l. jacket** chaleco m salvavidas; **l. sciences** ciencias fpl naturales or biológicas; **l. style** estilo m de vida (b) (individual) vida f; **at my time of l.** a mi edad; **his early l.** su juventud; **run for your l.!** ¡sálvese quien pueda!; **to take one's own l.** suicidarse; **to take sb's l.** matar a algn; Fig **he had the time of his l.** se lo pasó como nunca; Fam **he can't play the piano to save his l.** es un negado para el piano; Fam **never in my l. have I seen such a thing** en mi vida he visto tal cosa; Fam **not on your l.!** ¡ni hablar! □ **l. story** biografía f (c) (way of life) vida f; **urban l.** la vida urbana; Fig **to see l.** ver mundo; Fam **how's l.?** ¿qué tal (la vida)?; Fam **this is the l.!** ¡esto sí que es vivir!; Fam **to lead the l. of Riley** pegarse la gran vida (d) (of machine, battery) vida f, duración f (e) (liveliness) vida f, vitalidad f, vivacidad f; Fam Fig **to be the l. (and soul) of the party** ser el alma de la fiesta (f) Art **still l.** bodegón m, naturaleza f muerta

life-and-death ['laɪfəndeθ] adj a vida o muerte; **l.-and-d. struggle** lucha a vida o muerte

lifeblood ['laɪfblʌd] n sangre f vital, Fig alma f, nervio m

lifeboat ['laɪfbəʊt] n (on ship) bote m salvavidas; (on shore) lancha f de socorro

lifeguard ['laɪfgɑːd] n socorrista mf

lifeless ['laɪflɪs] adj sin vida, exánime, inánime

lifelike ['laɪflaɪk] adj (gen) natural; (portrait) fiel

lifeline ['laɪflaɪn] n (rope) cuerda f de salvamento; Fig cordón m umbilical

lifelong ['laɪflɒŋ] adj de toda la vida, de siempre □ Educ **l. learning** aprendizaje m a continuo

life-or-death ['laɪfɔːˈdeθ] adj (choice, decision) de vida o muerte; (struggle) a vida o muerte

lifer ['laɪfər] n Fam (prisoner) condenado(a) m,f a cadena perpetua

life-saver ['laɪfseɪvər] n Fam **it was a l.** (provided relief) me salvó la vida

life-saving ['laɪfseɪvɪŋ] **1** n socorrismo m, salvamento m
2 adj de salvamento

life-size(d) ['laɪfsaɪz(d)] adj (de) tamaño natural

life-support ['laɪfsəpɔːt] n Med **l. machine** or **system** equipo m de ventilación or respiración asistida

life-threatening ['laɪfθretnɪŋ] adj Med **l. condition** or

disease enfermedad *f* mortífera *or* que puede ocasionar la muerte; **l. situation** situación *f* de peligro mortal

lifetime ['laɪftaɪm] *n* vida *f*; **in his l.** durante su vida; **it's the chance of a l.** es una ocasión única; *Fam* **never in a l.!** ¡nunca en la vida!; *Fam* **we had to wait a l.** tuvimos que esperar una eternidad

lift [lɪft] **1** *vt* **(a)** *(raise) (weight)* levantar; *(head etc)* levantar, alzar; *(baby)* levantar en brazos; *(take up)* subir; *(pick up)* coger; *Fam* **he never lifts a finger in the house** no mueve ni un dedo para ayudar en casa **(b)** *Av Mil (troops)* transportar **(c)** *(ban, restriction)* levantar **(d)** *Fam (steal)* afanar, *Esp* birlar, *Méx* volar; *(plagiarize)* copiar, plagiar
  2 *vi (disappear)* disiparse
  3 *n* **(a)** *(act)* levantamiento *m* **(b)** *Br (elevator)* ascensor *m* ❑ **goods l.** montacargas *m inv*; **l. attendant** ascensorista *mf*; **l. shaft** hueco *m* del ascensor; **ski l.** telesquí *m* **(c)** *Br (free ride)* **to give sb a l.** llevar a algn (en el coche), *CAm Méx Perú* dar aventón a algn; **to hitch a l.** hacer autostop **(d)** *Fig (boost)* estímulo *m*; **the news gave her a l.** la noticia le subió la moral

lift down *vt* bajar

lift off 1 *vt* levantar, quitar
  2 *vi Astronaut* despegar

lift out *vt* sacar

lift up *vt* levantar, alzar; *Fig (spirits)* exaltar, elevar

lift-off ['lɪftɒf] *n Astronaut* despegue *m*

ligament ['lɪgəmənt] *n Anat* ligamento *m*

light¹ [laɪt] **1** *n* **(a)** *(gen)* luz *f*; **against the l.** a trasluz; **by the l. of the moon** a la luz de la luna; **electric l.** luz eléctrica; **to stand in sb's l.** quitarle la luz a algn; *Fig* **in the l. of** en vista de; *Fig* **to bring sth to l.** sacar algo a luz; *Fig* **to come to l.** salir a luz; *Fig* **to see things in a new l.** ver las cosas bajo otro aspecto ❑ **l. bulb** bombilla *f*, *CAm Méx RP* foco *m*, *RP* lamparita *f*, *Andes CAm* bombillo *m*; *Phot* **l. meter** fotómetro *m*; *Comptr* **l. pen** lápiz *m* óptico; **l. year** año *m* luz **(b)** *(lamp)* luz *f*, lámpara *f*; *(traffic light)* semáforo *m*; *Aut (headlight)* faro *m*; **the lights were (at) green** el semáforo estaba en verde; **to turn on the l.** encender *or Am* prender la luz; *Fam Fig* **to go out like a l.** quedarse planchado(a) *or Esp* traspuesto(a) ❑ *Aut* **parking lights** luces *fpl* de estacionamiento; *Aut* **tail lights** pilotos *mpl*; **traffic lights** semáforo *m sing* **(c)** *(flame)* fuego *m*, lumbre *f*; **to set l. to sth** prender fuego a algo; **to strike a l.** encender una cerilla; *Fam* **have you got a l.?** ¿tiene fuego?
  2 *vt* *(pt & pp* **lighted** *or* **lit)** **(a)** *(illuminate)* iluminar, alumbrar **(b)** *(ignite)* encender, *Am* prender
  3 *vi (fire)* encenderse, prenderse
  4 *adj* **(a)** *(bright)* claro(a); **it's growing l.** se hace de día **(b)** *(not dark) (colour, eyes)* claro(a), pálido(a); *(hair)* rubio(a); *(complexion)* blanco(a); **l. green** verde claro

light up 1 *vt* iluminar, alumbrar
  2 *vi* **(a)** *(sky, display)* iluminarse **(b)** *Fam* encender un cigarrillo

light² [laɪt] **1** *adj (not heavy)* ligero(a); *(rain)* fino(a); *(breeze)* suave; *Fig (wound, sentence, etc)* leve; **l. ale** cerveza clara; *Fig* **to be a l. sleeper** tener el sueño ligero; *Fig* **to be l. on one's feet** ser ligero(a) de pies; *Fig* **to make l. of sth** dar poca importancia a algo; *Fig* **with a l. heart** con el corazón alegre; *Fam* **to be l. on sth** andar mal de algo ❑ *Fig* **l. fingers** uñas *fpl* largas; *Mil* **l. horse** caballería *f* ligera; **l. opera** opereta *f*; **l. reading** lectura *f* fácil
  2 *adv* **to travel l.** ir ligero(a) de equipaje, viajar con poco equipaje

lighten¹ ['laɪtən] **1** *vt* **(a)** *(colour)* aclarar **(b)** *(illuminate)* iluminar
  2 *vi (colour)* aclararse

lighten² ['laɪtən] *vt* **(a)** *(weight)* aligerar **(b)** *Fig (mitigate)* aliviar, mitigar; *(heart)* alegrar

lighter¹ ['laɪtər] *n* **(cigarette) l.** encendedor *m*, *Esp* mechero *m*

lighter² ['laɪtər] *n Naut (barge)* barcaza *f*, gabarra *f*

light-fingered ['laɪtfɪŋgəd] *adj* de uñas largas

light-footed ['laɪtfʊtɪd] *adj* ligero(a) de pies

light-haired ['laɪtheəd] *adj* rubio(a), de pelo claro

light-headed [laɪt'hedɪd] *adj* **(a)** *(dizzy)* mareado(a) **(b)** *(frivolous)* frívolo(a)

light-hearted ['laɪthɑːtɪd] *adj* alegre, despreocupado(a)

lighthouse ['laɪthaʊs] *n* faro *m* ❑ **l. keeper** farero(a) *m,f*

lighting ['laɪtɪŋ] *n* **(a)** *(act)* iluminación *f* **(b)** *(system)* alumbrado *m*

lightly ['laɪtlɪ] *adv* **(a)** *(not heavily)* ligeramente; **l. clad** ligero(a) de ropa **(b)** *(not seriously)* a la ligera; **to get off l.** salir casi indemne; **to take sth l.** tomar algo a la ligera

lightness¹ ['laɪtnɪs] *n (brightness) (of room)* luminosidad *f*, claridad *f*; *(of colour)* claridad *f*

lightness² ['laɪtnɪs] *n (of weight)* ligereza *f*

lightning ['laɪtnɪŋ] *n (flash)* relámpago *m*; *(stroke)* rayo *m*; *Fig* **as quick as l., like l.** como un rayo ❑ **l. conductor, l. rod** pararrayos *m inv*; **l. strike** huelga *f* relámpago; **l. visit** visita *f* relámpago

lightweight ['laɪtweɪt] **1** *adj* **(a)** *(suit etc)* ligero(a) **(b)** *Box* de peso ligero
  2 *n Box* peso *m* ligero

Ligurian [lɪ'gjʊərɪən] *adj* **the L. Sea** el mar Ligur

like¹ [laɪk] **1** *adj* **(a)** *(similar)* parecido(a), semejante, similar; **umbrellas, walking-sticks and l. objects** paraguas, bastones y otros objetos parecidos; *Fig* **they are as l. as two peas (in a pod)** son como dos gotas de agua **(b)** *(equal)* igual, equivalente; *Elec* **l. poles** polos iguales
  2 *adv* **(a)** *(likely)* probable; **(as) l. as not** a lo mejor, probablemente **(b)** *Fam (as it were)* como; **because he's an orphan l.** porque es huérfano, ¿sabes?; **he looked scared, l.** parecía como asustado
  3 *prep* **(a)** *(similar to)* como, parecido(a) a; *(the same as)* igual que; **he thinks l. us** piensa como nosotros; **it costs something l. $50** cuesta alrededor de los 50 dólares; **it looks l. a bullet wound** parece un balazo; **it looks l. rain** parece que va a llover; **it's not l. her to do that** no es propio de ella hacer eso; **it's nothing l. Rioja wine** no se parece en nada al vino de Rioja; **I've never seen anything l. it** nunca he visto cosa igual; **l. that** así; **people l. that** ese tipo de gente; **she's l. her mother** se parece a su madre; **something l. that** algo por el estilo; **that's just l. a man!** ¡eso es muy típico de los hombres!; **the actual profit is more l. forty per cent** el beneficio real es más bien del cuarenta por ciento; **what's he l.?** ¿cómo es?, ¿qué tal es?; **what's the weather l.?** ¿qué tiempo hace?; *Fam* **that's more l. it!** ¡así es!, ¡así se hace!; *Prov* **l. father l. son** de tal palo tal astilla **(b)** *(want, wish)* querer, gustar; *(prefer)* preferir; **how do you l. your coffee?** ¿cómo quiere el café?; **I didn't l. to disturb them** no quería molestarles; **I should l. a chat with your father** me gustaría hablar con
  4 *n* cosa *f* parecida; **brushes, combs and the l.** cepillos, peines y cosas por el estilo; **it's too good for the likes of him** es demasiado bueno para personas como él; **I've never seen the l. of it** nunca he visto cosa igual

like² [laɪk] **1** *vt* **(a)** *(take pleasure in)* **do you l. chocolate?** ¿te gusta el chocolate?; **he likes dancing** le gusta bailar; **how do you l. London?** ¿qué (tal) te parece Londres?; **I don't l. him at all** ése no me gusta nada, ése me cae muy mal; **she likes children** le gustan los niños; **they l. each other** se caen bien; **to l. sth better** preferir algo; *Fam Iron* **well, I l. that!** ¡qué cara! **(b)** *(want, wish)* querer, gustar;

tu padre; **whether you l. it or not** quieras o no (quieras), te guste o no te guste; **would you l. a drink?** ¿quieres tomar algo?, ¿te apetece tomar algo?; **would you l. him to wait?** ¿quiere que espere?

2 *vi* querer; **as you l.** como quieras; **if you l.** si quieres; **whenever you l.** cuando quieras

3 *n* gusto *m*; **likes and dislikes** gustos, preferencias

likeable ['laɪkəbəl] *adj* simpático(a), agradable

likelihood ['laɪklɪhʊd] *n*, **likeliness** ['laɪklɪnɪs] *n* probabilidad *f*; **in all l.** con toda probabilidad; **there's little l. of finding it** es poco probable que lo encontremos

likely ['laɪklɪ] **1** *adj* (**likelier, likeliest**) probable; **a l. outcome** un resultado probable; **he's l. to cause trouble** es probable que cause problemas; **he's the man most l. to succeed in the job** es el hombre más indicado para el trabajo; *Fam Iron* **that's a l. story!** ¡esto es puro cuento!; **where are you l. to be this afternoon?** ¿dónde piensas estar esta tarde?

2 *adv* probablemente; **as l. as not** a lo mejor; **not l.!** ¡ni hablar!

like-minded [laɪk'maɪndɪd] *adj* de la misma opinión

liken ['laɪkən] *vt* comparar (**to** con)

likeness ['laɪknɪs] *n* (**a**) *(similarity)* semejanza *f*, parecido *m*; **in his l.** a su semejanza □ **family l.** aire *m* de familia (**b**) *(portrait)* retrato *m*

likewise ['laɪkwaɪz] *adv* (**a**) *(also)* también, asimismo (**b**) *(the same)* lo mismo, igualmente; **to do l.** hacer lo mismo

liking ['laɪkɪŋ] *n (for thing)* gusto *m*, afición *f*; *(for person)* simpatía *f*; *(for friend)* cariño *m*; **is it to your l.?** ¿te gusta?; **to take a l. to sth** tomar *or Esp* coger gusto a algo, aficionarse a algo; **to take a l. to sb** tomar *or Esp* coger simpatía a algn; **to have a l. for sth** ser aficionado(a) a algo

lilac ['laɪlək] **1** *n* (**a**) *Bot* lila *f* (**b**) *(colour)* lila *m*

2 *adj* lila, de color lila

Lilo® ['laɪləʊ] *n (pl* **Lilos**) *Br* colchón *m* inflable *or* de aire

lilt [lɪlt] *n (in voice)* melodía *f*; *(in song)* ritmo *m* alegre

lilting ['lɪltɪŋ] *adj (voice)* melodioso(a), cantarín(ina); *(song)* rítmico(a)

lily ['lɪlɪ] *n Bot* lirio *m*, azucena *f* □ **l. of the valley** lirio *m* de los valles, muguete *m*; **water l.** nenúfar *m*

lily-livered ['lɪlɪlɪvəd] *adj* cobarde, miedoso(a)

lima bean ['liːmə'biːn] *n Esp* judía *f* blanca (limeña), *Am salvo RP* frijol *m* blanco, *Andes RP* poroto *m* blanco

limb [lɪm] *n* (**a**) *Anat* miembro *m* (**b**) *(of tree)* rama *f*; *Fig* **to be out on a l.** *(in danger)* estar en peligro; *Br (isolated)* estar aislado(a)

limber ['lɪmbər] *adj (person)* ágil; *(thing)* flexible

limber up 1 *vi* (**a**) *Sport* entrar en calor (**b**) *Fig* prepararse, entrenarse (**for** para)

2 *vt* calentar

limbo ['lɪmbəʊ] *n (pl* **limbos**) (**a**) *Rel* limbo *m* (**b**) *Fig* olvido *m*; **to be** *or* **remain in l.** caer en el olvido

lime¹ [laɪm] *n Chem* cal *f*

lime² [laɪm] *n Bot (citrus fruit)* lima *f*, *Méx* limón *m*; *(citrus tree)* limero *m*, *Méx* limonero *m* □ **l. juice** *Esp* zumo *m Am* jugo *m* de lima

lime³ [laɪm] *n Bot (linden)* tilo *m* □ **broad-leaved l.** tilo *m* de hoja grande; **European l.** tilo *m* común; **silver l.** tilo *m* plateado; **weeping silver l.** tilo *m* péndulo

lime-green [laɪm'griːn] *adj* de color verde lima

limekiln ['laɪmkɪln] *n* calera *f*, horno *m* de cal

limelight ['laɪmlaɪt] *n* luz *f* de calcio; *Fig* **to be in the l.** estar en el candelero, ser el centro de la atención pública

limerick ['lɪmərɪk] *n* quintilla *f* humorística

limestone ['laɪmstəʊn] *n* piedra *f* caliza

limey ['laɪmɪ] *n US Can Fam* inglés(esa) *m,f*

limit ['lɪmɪt] **1** *n* (**a**) *(boundary)* límite *m*, frontera *f*; **to be off limits** estar en zona prohibida (**b**) *(restriction)* límite *m*; *(maximum)* máximo *m*; *(minimum)* mínimo *m*; *Aut* **speed l.** límite *m* de velocidad; *Aut* **'speed limit 40'** 'velocidad máxima 40'; **within limits** dentro de ciertos límites; *Fam* **that's the l.!** ¡eso es el colmo!; *Fam* **you really are the l.!** ¡eres imposible!

2 *vt (restrict)* limitar, restringir; **she has limited herself to two slices of bread a day** ya no se permite más de dos rebanadas de pan al día

limitation [lɪmɪ'teɪʃən] *n* limitación *f*, restricción *f*

limited ['lɪmɪtɪd] *adj* limitado(a), restringido(a) □ **l. edition** edición *f* limitada; *Com* **l. (liability) company** sociedad *f* limitada, sociedad *f* anónima

limiting ['lɪmɪtɪŋ] *adj* restrictivo(a)

limitless ['lɪmɪtlɪs] *adj* ilimitado(a), sin límites

limo ['lɪməʊ] *(pl* **limos**) *n Fam* limusina *f*

limousine ['lɪməziːn, lɪmə'ziːn] *n Aut* limousine *f*, limusina *f*

limp¹ [lɪmp] **1** *vi* cojear

2 *n* cojera *f*; **to walk with a l.** cojear

limp² [lɪmp] *adj* (**a**) *(floppy)* flojo(a), fláccido(a), fofo(a); *(relaxed)* relajado(a); **let your body go l.** relaja el cuerpo (**b**) *(weak)* débil

limpet ['lɪmpɪt] *n* (**a**) *Zool* lapa *f* (**b**) *Mil* **l. mine** mina *f* magnética

limpid ['lɪmpɪd] *adj* límpido(a), claro(a)

limply ['lɪmplɪ] *adv (weakly)* lánguidamente

limp-wristed [lɪmp'rɪstɪd] *adj Pej* amariposado(a), afeminado(a)

linchpin ['lɪntʃpɪn] *n* (**a**) *Tech* pezonera *f* (**b**) *Fig* eje *m*, pieza *f* clave

linctus ['lɪŋktəs] *n (pl* **linctuses**) jarabe *m* para la tos

linden ['lɪndən] *n Bot* tilo *m*

line¹ [laɪn] *n* (**a**) *(gen)* línea *f*; *(made with pen etc)* raya *f*; **to draw a l. under sth** subrayar algo; *Fig* **to draw the l. at sth** decir basta a algo; *Fig* **to know where to draw the l.** saber cuándo hay que parar □ **l. drawing** dibujo *m* lineal (**b**) *(of writing)* línea *f*, renglón *m*; *(of poetry)* verso *m*; **new l.** punto y aparte; *Theat* **to learn one's lines** aprenderse el papel; *Fig* **to read between the lines** leer entre líneas; *Fam* **drop me a l.** mándame cuatro líneas □ *Typ* **l. spacer** interlineador *m* (**c**) *(of descent)* línea *f*, linaje *m* (**d**) *(row)* fila *f*, línea *f*; *(of trees)* hilera *f*; *US (queue)* cola *f*; *US* **to stand in l.** hacer cola; *Fig* **he's in l. for presidency** está bien situado en la carrera por la presidencia; *Fig* **to be in l.** corresponder, coincidir (**with** con); *Fig* **to be out of l.** no corresponder, no coincidir (**with** con); *Fam* **to bring sb into l.** pararle los pies a algn; *Fam* **to step out of l.** salirse de las reglas □ *Ind* **assembly l.** línea *f* de montaje; **l. dancing** baile *m* en línea, = baile al ritmo de música country en el que los participantes se colocan en hileras y dan los mismos pasos; *Com Ind* **l. manager** gerente *mf or* jefe(a) *m,f* de línea (**e**) *(rope)* cuerda *f*; *(wire)* cable *m* □ **fishing l.** sedal *m*, hilo *m*; **washing l.** cuerda *f* para tender la ropa (**f**) *Tel* línea *f*; **hold the l.!** ¡no cuelgue!, ¡no se retire! □ *Fig* **hot l.** teléfono *m* rojo (**g**) *Comptr* **to be off/on l.** estar desconectado(a)/conectado(a) (**h**) *(route)* vía *f*; *Br Rail (track)* vía *f*, línea *f*; **lines of communication** vías de comunicación; *Fig* **to reach** *or* **come to the end of the l.** llegar al final □ *Br Rail* **branch l.** ramal *m* (**i**) *(boundary)* límite *m*; *Sport (on court, field)* línea *f* □ *US* **State l.** límite *m* del Estado (**j**) *Mil* línea *f*; **l. of fire** línea de fuego; **to be in the front l.** estar en primera línea (**k**) *(company)* empresa *f*, compañía *f*; **bus l.** línea *f* de autobuses; **shipping l.** compañía naviera (**l**) *Fig (course,* direction) línea f; **l. of argument** argumento m; **l. of vision** campo m visual; **something along those lines** algo por el estilo; **to be in l. with** ser conforme a; **to be on the right lines** ir por buen camino; **to take a strong l. on sth** tener una actitud firme sobre algo; **to toe the (party) l.** seguir la línea (del partldo), Fig **all along the l.** (at every stage) desde el principio; (in detail) con todo detalle (**m**) Fam (speciality) especialidad f, rama f; **it's not my l.** no es lo mío; **what's his l.?** ¿qué hace? (**n**) (range of goods) surtido m; Com **it's a new l.** es una línea nueva (**o**) Fam (story) rollo m, cuento m; **don't give me that l.** no me vengas otra vez con ese rollo (**p**) Slang (of cocaine etc) línea f

line² [laɪn] vt (**a**) Tech (pipe etc) revestir; Sew forrar; (walls) llenar; Fam **to l. one's pockets** forrarse (**b**) (border) bordear (**with** con)

line up 1 vt (**a**) (arrange in rows) poner en fila (**b**) (organize) organizar; **he has something lined up for this evening** tiene algo organizado para esta noche

2 vi (people) ponerse en fila; (troops) formar; (in queue) hacer cola

lineage ['lɪnɪɪdʒ] n linaje m

linear ['lɪnɪər] adj (gen) lineal; (of length) de longitud ❑ **l. perspective** perspectiva lineal; Comptr **l. programming** programación f lineal

lined [laɪnd] **1** pt & pp see **line²**

2 adj (**a**) (paper) rayado(a); (face) arrugado(a) (**b**) (garment) forrado(a), con forro

linen ['lɪnɪn] n (**a**) (fabric) hilo m, lino m (**b**) (clothes) ropa f; (sheets, tablecloths, etc) ropa f blanca, lencería f; Fig **don't wash your dirty l. in public** los trapos sucios se lavan en casa ❑ **bed l.** ropa f de cama; **dirty l.** ropa f sucia; **l. basket** cesto m de la ropa sucia; **l. room** lencería f; **table l.** mantelería f

liner¹ ['laɪnər] n Naut transatlántico m

liner² ['laɪnər] n (lining) forro m, revestimiento m ❑ **dustbin l.** bolsa f de la basura; **nappy l.** metedor m

linesman ['laɪnzmən] n (pl linesmen) Sport juez m de línea

line-up ['laɪnʌp] n Sport formación f, alineación f ❑ Theat **star l.-up** reparto m estelar

linger ['lɪŋɡər] vi (gen) tardar; (dawdle) rezagarse; (smell, doubt) persistir, tardar en desaparecer; Fig (memory) perdurar; **to l. over doing sth** tardar en hacer algo

lingerie ['lænʒəriː] n Fml ropa f íntima, ropa f interior (de mujer)

lingering ['lɪŋɡərɪŋ] adj (death) lento(a); (doubt) persistente; (look) fijo(a)

lingo ['lɪŋɡəʊ] n (pl lingoes) Fam (**a**) (language) lengua f, idioma m (**b**) (jargon) jerga f

lingua ['lɪŋɡwə] n (pl linguas or linguae ['lɪŋɡwiː]) Ling **l. franca** lingua f franca

linguist ['lɪŋɡwɪst] n (**a**) (specialist in linguistics) lingüista mf (**b**) Fam (speaker of various languages) políglota mf

linguistic [lɪŋ'ɡwɪstɪk] adj lingüístico(a)

linguistics [lɪŋ'ɡwɪstɪks] n lingüística f

liniment ['lɪnɪmənt] n linimento m

lining ['laɪnɪŋ] n Tech (of pipes etc) revestimiento m interior; (of garment) forro m

link [lɪŋk] **1** n (**a**) (of chain) eslabón m; Fig **missing l.** eslabón perdido; Fig **weak l.** punto m débil (**b**) (connection) conexión f, enlace m; Fig (tie) lazo m, vínculo m; **air/rail l.** enlace aéreo/ferroviario; **cultural/economic links** lazos culturales/económicos (**c**) Comptr enlace m, vínculo m (**d**) **links** campo m sing de golf

2 vt (join) unir, enlazar, conectar; Fig unir, vincular, relacionar; **to l. arms** tomarse del brazo

link up 1 vt Comptr conectar

2 vi (roads, travellers) encontrarse (**with** con)

linkage ['lɪŋkɪdʒ] n (act) conexión f, concatenación f

linkman ['lɪŋkmən] n (pl linkmen) TV Rad presentador m

link-up ['lɪŋkʌp] n Tel TV enlace m, conexión f; (meeting) encuentro m, reunión f; (of spaceships) acoplamiento m

linnet ['lɪnɪt] n Orn pardillo m

lino ['laɪnəʊ] n Fam linóleo m, linóleum m

linoleum [lɪ'nəʊlɪəm] n linóleo m, linóleum m

linseed ['lɪnsiːd] n linaza f

lint [lɪnt] n Med hilas fpl

lintel ['lɪntəl] n Archit dintel m

lion ['laɪən] n león m; Fig **the l.'s share** la parte del león

lioness ['laɪənɪs] n leona f

lion-hearted [laɪən'hɑːtɪd] adj valiente

lip [lɪp] n (**a**) Anat labio m; Fig **his name is on everybody's lips** todos hablan de él; Fig **my lips are sealed** soy una tumba; Fig **to bite one's l.** disimular, morderse la lengua; Fig **to keep a stiff upper l.** no inmutarse, poner al mal tiempo buen cara ❑ **l. gloss** brillo m de labios (**b**) Fam (cheek) impertinencia f; **less of your l.!** ¡basta de impertinencias! (**c**) (of jug) pico m

liposuction ['lɪpəʊsʌkʃən] n liposucción f

lip-read ['lɪpriːd] vt & vi (pt & pp lip-read ['lɪpred]) leer en los labios

lip-reading ['lɪpriːdɪŋ] n lectura f en los labios

lip-service ['lɪpsɜːvɪs] n jarabe m de pico, palabrería f

lipstick ['lɪpstɪk] n (substance) carmín m, pintalabios m inv; (stick) lápiz m or Esp barra f de labios, CSur lápiz m rouge, Méx bilet m

liquefy ['lɪkwɪfaɪ] **1** vt (pt & pp liquefied) licuar

2 vi licuarse

liqueur [lɪ'kjʊər] n licor m

liquid ['lɪkwɪd] **1** adj líquido(a); Fig (eyes) claro(a) ❑ Fin **l. assets** activo m líquido

2 n líquido m

liquidate ['lɪkwɪdeɪt] vt Fin liquidar; Euph (murder) liquidar

liquidation [lɪkwɪ'deɪʃən] n Fin liquidación f; **to go into l.** entrar en liquidación

liquidator ['lɪkwɪdeɪtər] n Fin liquidador(a) m,f

liquidity [lɪ'kwɪdɪtɪ] n Fin liquidez f

liquidize ['lɪkwɪdaɪz] vt Culin licuar

liquidizer ['lɪkwɪdaɪzər] n Br Culin Esp batidora f, Am licuadora f

liquor ['lɪkər] n US alcohol m, bebidas fpl, alcohólicas; **hard l.** bebidas fpl de alta graduación alcohólica ❑ **l. store** bodega f, tienda f de bebidas alcohólicas

liquorice ['lɪkərɪs, 'lɪkərɪʃ] n regaliz m

Lisbon ['lɪzbən] n Lisboa f

lisp [lɪsp] **1** n ceceo m

2 vi cecear

lissom(e) ['lɪsəm] adj Literary esbelto(a), elegante

list¹ [lɪst] **1** n (gen) lista f; (catalogue) catálogo m; Med **to be on the danger l.** estar grave; Fig **to enter the lists** entrar en acción ❑ Com **l. price** precio m de catálogo; **price/waiting l.** lista f de precios/espera; **wine l.** carta f de vinos

2 vt (make a list of) hacer una lista de; (put on a list) poner en una lista; **it is not listed** no figura en la lista or Am en el directorio; Br Archit **listed building** edificio de interés histórico

list² [lɪst] Naut **1** n escora f

2 vi escorar

listen ['lɪsən] vi (gen) escuchar, oír; (pay attention) prestar atención, hacer caso; **l.!** ¡escucha!, ¡oye!; **to l. to reason** atender a razones.

listen in vi (telephone etc) escuchar, espiar

listen out vi estar atento(a) a (**for** a)

listener ['lɪsənər] n oyente mf; (to the radio) radioyente mf, radioescucha mf

listeria [lɪ'stɪərɪə] n Med (illness) listeriosis f inv; (bacteria) listeria f

listing ['lɪstɪŋ] n listado m

listless ['lɪstlɪs] adj decaído(a), apático(a)

listlessness ['lɪstlɪsnɪs] n apatía f, desgana f

Lit. [lɪt] Fam (abbr **Literature**) literatura f

lit [lɪt] pt & pp see **light**[1]

litany ['lɪtənɪ] n letanía f

liter ['liːtər] n US see **litre**

literacy ['lɪtərəsɪ] n alfabetización f

literal ['lɪtərəl] adj literal

literally ['lɪtərəlɪ] adv literalmente; (really) verdaderamente, auténticamente

literary ['lɪtərərɪ] adj literario(a)

literate ['lɪtərɪt] adj alfabetizado(a).

literature ['lɪtərɪtʃər] n (a) (writings) literatura f (b) (secondary) bibliografía f (c) Fam (bumph etc) folletos mpl informativos

lithe [laɪð] adj Fml ágil

lithium ['lɪθɪəm] n Chem litio m

lithograph ['lɪθəgrɑːf] n litografía f

lithography [lɪ'θɒgrəfɪ] n litografía f

Lithuania [lɪθjʊ'eɪnɪə] n Lituania

Lithuanian [lɪθjʊ'eɪnɪən] **1** adj lituano(a)
  2 n (person) lituano(a) m,f; (language) lituano m

litigant ['lɪtɪgənt] n litigante mf

litigate ['lɪtɪgeɪt] **1** vi Jur litigar
  2 vt Jur pleitear

litigation [lɪtɪ'geɪʃən] n Jur litigio m, pleito m

litigious [lɪ'tɪdʒəs] adj Fml litigante, litigioso(a)

litmus ['lɪtməs] n Chem **l. paper** papel m de tornasol; Fig **l. test** prueba f contundente

litre ['liːtər] n litro m

litter ['lɪtər] **1** n (a) (rubbish) basura f; (papers) papeles mpl □ Br **l. bin** papelera f; **l. lout** = persona que tira papeles en la vía pública (b) Zool (off-spring) camada f (c) (stretcher) camilla f (d) (for animals) (to sleep) cesto m (para dormir); (to defecate) pajaza f
  2 vt ensuciar; **books and magazines littered the floor** el suelo estaba lleno de libros y revistas

litterbug ['lɪtəbʌg] n US Can = persona que tira papeles en la vía pública

littered ['lɪtəd] adj cubierto(a) (**with** de), lleno(a) (**with** de)

little ['lɪtəl] **1** adj (a) (small) pequeño(a); **a l. dog** un perrito; **a l. house** una casita; **do you fancy a l. drink?** ¿quieres un trago de algo?; Fam **poor l. thing!** ¡pobrecillo! □ **l. finger** dedo m meñique (b) (not much) poco(a); **he has l. money** tiene poco dinero (c) (young) pequeño(a); **I have three l. girls** tengo tres niñas pequeñas
  2 pron poco m; **l. by l.** poco a poco; **l. or nothing** casi nada; **save me a l.** guárdame un poco; **a l. cheese** un poco de queso; **stay a l. (bit) longer** quédate un ratito más
  3 adv poco; **as l. as possible** lo menos posible; **I see her very l.** la veo muy poco; **I did she know that ...** no tenía la menor idea de que ...; **they were a l. surprised** se quedaron algo sorprendidos

littoral ['lɪtərəl] n & adj Geog litoral (m)

liturgical [lɪ'tɜːdʒɪkəl] adj litúrgico(a)

liturgy ['lɪtədʒɪ] n liturgia f

livable ['lɪvəbəl] adj (house) habitante; (life) llevadero(a)

live[1] [lɪv] **1** vi vivir; **as long as I l.** mientras yo viva; **long l. the King!** ¡viva el Rey!; **to l. and learn** vivir para ver; **to l. and let l.** vivir y dejar vivir
  2 vt vivir; **to l. an interesting life** llevar or tener una vida interesante; **to l. a lie** vivir en la mentira; **to l. a part** identificarse con un personaje

live by vt adherirse a, seguir los dictados de

live down vt conseguir que se olvide

live for vt vivir para

live in vi (student) ser interno(a); (maid) vivir con la familia

live off vt vivir de, alimentarse de; **to l. off the land** vivir de la tierra; **to l. off the state** vivir del cuento

live on 1 vt (food, money, etc) vivir de
  2 vi (a) (memory) persistir (b) (survive) sobrevivir

live out 1 vt (finish) acabar; **to l. out one's days** acabársele a uno sus días
  2 vi (a) (student) ser externo(a); (maid) no vivir con la familia (b) Fam **to l. out of a suitcase** ir de hotel en hotel; Fam **to l. out of cans** vivir (a base) de latas

live through vt vivir (durante)

live together vi Fam vivir juntos

live up vt Fam **to l. it up** pasarlo bien

live up to vt (promises) cumplir con; (principles) vivir de acuerdo con; (expectations) **not to l. up to one's expectations** no ser lo que se esperaba

live with vt (a) (cohabit with) vivir con (b) Fig (accept) aceptar

live[2] [laɪv] **1** adj (a) (living) vivo(a); **a real l. prince** un príncipe de verdad; Fig **a l. issue** un tema de actualidad or candente (b) TV Rad en directo, en vivo (c) Mil (ammunition) real; (bomb) sin explotar; Elec (wire) con corriente; Fam **he's a real l. wire!** ¡éste no para nunca!
  2 adv (broadcast, perform) en directo, en vivo

lived-in ['lɪvdɪn] adj (home, room) acogedor(a), con un toque humano; **a l. face** un rostro curtido

live-in ['lɪvɪn] adj (chauffeur, nanny) interno(a); **she has a l. lover** su amante vive con ella

livelihood ['laɪvlɪhʊd] n sustento m; **to earn one's l.** ganarse la vida

liveliness ['laɪvlɪnɪs] n (of person) viveza f, vivacidad f; (of event) animación f

lively ['laɪvlɪ] adj (**livelier, liveliest**) (person) vivo(a), enérgico(a); (place) animado(a); Fig (interest) estusiasmado(a); Fam **look l.!** ¡date prisa!; Fam **things are getting l.** las cosas se están poniendo interesantes

liven ['laɪvən] **1** vt **to l. up** animar
  2 vi **to l. up** animarse

liver ['lɪvər] n Anat Culin hígado m

liverish ['lɪvərɪʃ] adj Fam empachado(a), RP descompuesto(a)

livery ['lɪvərɪ] n librea f

lives [laɪvz] npl see **life**

livestock ['laɪvstɒk] n (cattle) ganado m; **l. farming** ganadería f

livid ['lɪvɪd] adj (a) (pallid) lívido(a); (lead-coloured) plomizo(a) (b) Fam (angry) furioso(a)

living ['lɪvɪŋ] **1** adj vivo(a); Literary **a l. death** una muerte en vida; **not a l. soul** ni un alma; **the greatest l. poet** el mejor poeta contemporáneo
  2 n (a) (way of life) vida f; **clean l.** vida respetable; **to earn**

or **make one's l.** ganarse la vida; **what does she do for a l.?** ¿cómo se gana la vida? ❏ **l. conditions** condiciones de vida; **l. expenses** dietas; **l. room** sala *f* de estar, living *m*; **l. space** espacio vital; **l. standards** nivel *m* de vida; **l. wage** sueldo *m* mínimo **(b)** *(alive)* vivo *m*; **the l.** los vivos; *Fam Fig* **she's still in the land of the l.** sigue viva ❏ **l. will** testamento *m* en vida **(c)** *Rel* beneficio *m*

lizard ['lɪzəd] *n Zool (large)* lagarto *m*; *(small)* lagartija *f*

llama ['lɑːmə] *n Zool* llama *f*

lo [ləʊ] *interj* **lo and behold…** hete aquí que…

load [ləʊd] **1** *n (cargo etc)* carga *f*; *(weight)* peso *m*; *Elec Tech* carga *f*; **to lighten the l.** aligerar la carga; *Fig* **you have taken a l. off my mind** me has quitado *or* Am sacado un peso de encima; *Fam* **get a l. of this!** ¡no te lo pierdas!, *Esp* ¡al loro con esto!; *Fam* **loads of** montones de, un montón de; **I've got loads to tell you** tengo un montón de cosas que contarte; *Fam* **that's a l. of rubbish!** ¡no son más que tonterías!

2 *vt (vehicle, gun)* & *Comptr* cargar

3 *vi* cargar

load down *vt* cargar; **we were loaded down with presents** íbamos cargados de regalos; *Fig* **to be loaded down with** *(work, worries)* estar agobiado(a) de

load up *vi* & *vt* cargar

loaded ['ləʊdɪd] *adj* **(a)** *(vehicle, gun)* cargado(a) **(with** de); *Fig* **a l. question** una pregunta tendenciosa **(b)** *Fam* rico(a); **to be l.** estar forrado(a) **(c)** *(dice)* trucado(a); *Fig* **the dice are l. against me** tengo pocas posibilidades **(d)** *US Fam (drunk) Esp RP* mamado(a), *Méx* hasta atrás

loading ['ləʊdɪŋ] *n (gen)* carga *f*; **l. bay** cargadero *m*

loaf¹ [ləʊf] *n (pl* **loaves** [ləʊvz]*)* pan *m*; **a l. of bread** *(unsliced)* un pan de molde, *Col* un pan tajado, *RP* un pan lactal; *(sliced)* un pan de molde

loaf² [ləʊf] *vi* **to l. (about** *or* **around)** holgazanear, gandulear

loafer ['ləʊfər] *n Fam* **(a)** *(person)* holgazán(ana) *m,f*, gandul(ula) *m,f*, vago(a) *m,f* **(b)** *US* **loafers** *(shoes)* mocasines *mpl*

loam [ləʊm] *n (soil)* marga *f*

loan [ləʊn] **1** *n (gen)* préstamo *m*; *Fin* empréstito *m*; **on l.** prestado(a); *(footballer)* cedido(a); *Fin* **to raise a l.** hacer un empréstito ❏ **l. shark** prestamista *mf*; **l. word** préstamo *m* (lingüístico)

2 *vt* prestar

loath [ləʊθ] *adj* reacio(a); **to be l. to do sth** estar poco dispuesto(a) a hacer algo

loathe [ləʊð] *vt* aborrecer, odiar

loathing ['ləʊðɪŋ] *n* aborrecimiento *m*, odio *m*

loathsome ['ləʊðsəm] *adj* odioso(a), repugnante, asqueroso(a)

loaves [ləʊvz] *npl see* **loaf**

lob [lɒb] **1** *n Ten* lob *m*

2 *vt* **(a)** *(pt & pp* **lobbed***)* *Ten* hacer un lob a **(b)** *Fam (throw)* lanzar, tirar

lobby ['lɒbɪ] **1** *n* **(a)** *(entrance hall)* vestíbulo *m* **(b)** *(pressure group)* grupo *m* de presión, lobby *m*; *(campaign)* campaña *f*; **the anti-nuclear l.** el grupo en contra de las armas nucleares

2 *vt (pt & pp* **lobbied***)* presionar; **to l. an MP** ejercer presiones sobre un diputado

3 *vi* ejercer presiones, cabildear

lobbying ['lɒbɪɪŋ] *n Pol* presiones *fpl* políticas

lobbyist ['lɒbɪɪst] *n Pol* activista *mf* de un grupo de presión

lobe [ləʊb] *n Anat* lóbulo *m*

lobotomy [ləʊ'bɒtəmɪ] *n Med* lobotomía *f*

lobster ['lɒbstər] *n (pl* **lobster** *or* **lobsters***)* *Zool* bogavante *m* ❏ *Norway* **l.** cigala *f*; **l. pot** nasa *f*, langostera *f*; **spiny l.** langosta *f*

local ['ləʊkəl] **1** *adj (gen)* local; *(person)* del pueblo, del barrio; *(wine)* de la región, del país ❏ *Med* **l. anaesthetic** anestésico *m* local; *Tel* **l. call** llamada *f* urbana, *Am* llamado *m* urbano; **l. colour** ambientación *f*; **l. government** gobierno *m* municipal; **l. time** hora *f* local

2 *n Fam* **(a)** *(person)* vecino(a) *m,f*; **the locals** los vecinos, la gente del barrio **(b)** *Br (pub)* bar *m* del barrio

locale [ləʊ'kɑːl] *n Fml (place)* lugar *m*; *(scene)* escenario *m*

locality [ləʊ'kælɪtɪ] *n* localidad *f*

localize ['ləʊkəlaɪz] *vt Fml* localizar

locally ['ləʊkəlɪ] *adv* en *or* de la localidad, en el *or* del lugar

locate [ləʊ'keɪt] *vt Fml* **(a)** *(situate)* situar, ubicar **(b)** *(find)* localizar, encontrar

location [ləʊ'keɪʃən] *n* **(a)** *(place)* lugar *m*, situación *f* **(b)** *(placing)* ubicación *f* **(c)** *Cin* **l. shots** exteriores *mpl*; **they're on l. in Australia** están rodando en Australia

loc. cit. [lɒk'sɪt] *(abbr* **loco citato***)* (in the place cited), en el lugar citado, loc. cit., l. c.

loch [lɒx, lɒk] *n Scot Geog* lago *m*

loci ['ləʊsaɪ] *npl see* **locus**

lock¹ [lɒk] **1** *n* **(a)** *(on door, drawer, etc)* cerradura *f*; *(bolt)* cerrojo *m*; *(padlock)* candado *m*; *Aut (on steering wheel)* retén *m*; **to force the l.** forzar la cerradura; **under l. and key** bajo llave, bajo siete llaves; *Fam Fig* **l., stock and barrel** completamente **(b)** *(on canal)* esclusa *f* **(c)** *(in wrestling)* llave *f* **(d)** *Aut (steering)* ángulo *m* de giro

2 *vt* **(a)** *(door, padlock)* cerrar; *Fig* **they were locked in each other's arms** quedaron fuertemente abrazados **(b)** *Comptr* bloquear

3 *vi (door etc)* cerrarse; *(wheels)* trabarse

lock away *vt* guardar bajo llave

lock in *vt (prisoners etc)* encerrar

lock out *vt* **(a)** *(gen)* cerrar la puerta a, dejar fuera a; **I've locked myself out** he olvidado la llave dentro **(b)** *Ind* **the workers were locked out** hubo un cierre patronal

lock up *vt (house)* cerrar; *(valuables)* dejar bajo llave; *(jail)* meter en la cárcel

lock² [lɒk] *n Literary (of hair)* mecha *f*, mechón *m*

locker ['lɒkər] *n* **(a)** *(cupboard)* armario *m* ropero *m*, taquilla *f* ❏ *US* **l. room** vestuarios *mpl* **(b)** *(chest)* cajón *m*

locket ['lɒkɪt] *n (with picture)* medallón *m*; *(with hair)* guardapelo *m*

lockjaw ['lɒkdʒɔː] *n Old-fashioned* tétanos *m*

lockout ['lɒkaʊt] *n Ind* cierre *m* patronal, lockout *m*

locksmith ['lɒksmɪθ] *n* cerrajero *m*

lockup ['lɒkʌp] *n (police cells)* cárcel *f*; *Br (garage)* garaje *m*, *Am* cochera *f*; *Br (shop)* tienda *f* pequeña

locomotion [ləʊkə'məʊʃən] *n* locomoción *f*

locomotive [ləʊkə'məʊtɪv] *n Rail* locomotora *f*

locum ['ləʊkəm] *n Br* suplente *mf*

locus ['ləʊkəs] *n (pl* **loci***)* lugar *m*

locust ['ləʊkəst] *n Ent* langosta *f*

locution [ləʊ'kjuːʃən] *n Ling* locución *f*

lodge [lɒdʒ] **1** *n* **(a)** *(gamekeeper's)* casa *f* del guarda; *(porter's)* portería *f*; *(hunter's)* refugio *m* **(b)** *(masonic)* logia *f* **(c)** *(beaver's den)* madriguera *f*

2 *vt* **(a)** *(accommodate)* alojar, hospedar **(b)** *(complaint)* presentar

3 *vi* **(a)** *(live)* alojarse, hospedarse **(b)** *(jam, become fixed)* posarse, meterse **(in** en); *Fig* **he had strange thoughts lodged in his mind** tenía algunas extrañas ideas metidas en la cabeza

lodger ['lɒdʒər] *n* huésped(eda) *m,f*

lodging ['lɒdʒɪŋ] *n* alojamiento *m*, hospedaje *m* ❏ **l. house** casa *f* de huéspedes

loft [lɒft] **1** *n (attic)* desván *m*, buhardilla *f* ❏ *Agr* **hay l.** pajar *m*
2 *vt Sport (ball)* lanzar al aire

lofty ['lɒftɪ] *adj* (**loftier, loftiest**) *Literary* (**a**) *(high)* alto(a); *Fig (sentiments etc)* altivo(a) (**b**) *Pej (haughty)* arrogante, altivo(a)

log [lɒg] **1** *n* (**a**) *(tree-trunk)* tronco *m*; *(for fuel)* leño *m*; *Fig* **to sleep like a l.** dormir como un tronco ❏ **l. cabin** cabaña *f* de troncos (**b**) *(record)* registro *m*; *Naut* diario *m* de a bordo (**c**) *Math Fam* logaritmo *m* (**d**) *Comptr* **l. file** registro *m* de actividad
2 *vt (pt & pp* **logged***) (record)* registrar, apuntar

log in, log on *vi Comptr* entrar (en sistema)

log out, log off *vi Comptr* salir (del sistema), abandonar el sistema

loganberry ['ləʊgənbərɪ] *n Bot (fruit)* zarza *f* frambuesa *or* de Logan

logarithm ['lɒgərɪðəm] *n Math* logaritmo *m*

log-book ['lɒgbʊk] *n Naut* diario *m* de a bordo; *Av* diario *m* de vuelo; *Aut* documentación *f* (del coche)

loggerheads ['lɒgəhedz] *npl* **to be at l. with sb** estar peleado(a) con algn

logic ['lɒdʒɪk] *n* lógica *f*

logical ['lɒdʒɪkəl] *adj* lógico(a)

logically ['lɒdʒɪklɪ] *adv* lógicamente

logician [lɒ'dʒɪʃən] *n* lógico(a) *m,f*

login ['lɒgɪn] *n Comptr* conexión *f*; **l. name** nombre *m* del usuario

logistic(al) [lə'dʒɪstɪk(əl)] *adj* logístico(a)

logistics [lə'dʒɪstɪks] *npl* logística *f*

logo ['ləʊgəʊ] *n*, **logotype** ['ləʊgəʊtaɪp] *n* logotipo *m*

loin [lɔɪn] *n* (**a**) *(of animal)* ijada *f*, ijar *m*; *Fig* **to gird up one's loins** prepararse para la lucha (**b**) *Culin (of pork)* lomo *m*; *(of beef)* solomillo *m*

loincloth ['lɔɪnklɒθ] *n* taparrabos *m inv*

Loire [lwɑːr] *n* Loira

loiter ['lɔɪtər] *vi (hang about)* holgazanear; *(lag behind)* rezagarse, retrasarse; *(prowl)* merodear

loiterer ['lɔɪtərər] *n* gandúl(ula) *m,f*, holgazán(ana) *m,f*; *(suspicious person)* merodeador(a) *m,f*

loll [lɒl] *vi (tongue, head)* colgar

loll about, loll around *vi (sit lazily)* repantigarse; *(laze about)* holgazanear, hacer el vago, no dar golpe

lollipop ['lɒlɪpɒp] *n (disc)* piruleta *f*; *(ball) Esp* chupachups® *m inv*; *(disc, ball) Chile* chupete *m, Col* colombina *f, Méx* paleta *f, RP* chupetín *m, Ven* chupeta *f* **ice(d) l.** polo *m* ❏ *Br Fam* **l. lady/man** guardia *mf* (que para el tráfico para que puedan cruzar los colegiales)

lollop ['lɒləp] *vi Fam* moverse torpe y lentamente

lolly ['lɒlɪ] *n Br Fam* (**a**) *(sweet) (disc)* piruleta *f*; *(ball) Esp* chupachups® *m inv*; *(disc, ball) Chile* chupete *m, Col* colombina *f, Méx* paleta *f, RP* chupetín *m, Ven* chupeta *f* **ice(d) l.** polo *m* (**b**) *Fam (money) Esp* pasta *f, Am* plata *f, Méx* lana *f*

London ['lʌndən] **1** *n* Londres
2 *adj* londinense, de Londres

Londoner ['lʌndənər] *n* londinense *mf*

lone [ləʊn] *adj (solitary)* solitario(a); *(single)* solo(a), único(a)

loneliness ['ləʊnlɪnɪs] *n* soledad *f*

lonely ['ləʊnlɪ] *adj* (**lonelier, loneliest**) (**a**) *(person)* solo(a), solitario(a) ❏ **l. hearts club** agencia *f* matrimonial (**b**) *(place)* solitario(a), aislado(a)

loner ['ləʊnər] *n* solitario(a) *m,f*

lonesome ['ləʊnsəm] *adj US see* **lonely**

long¹ [lɒŋ] **1** *adj* (**a**) *(size, distance)* largo(a); **how l. is the table?** ¿cuánto tiene de largo la mesa?; **it's three metres l.** tiene tres metros de largo; *Sport* **l. jump** salto *m* de longitud *or Chile Col* largo *or RP* en largo; **the l. way round** el camino más largo; *Fig* **to pull a l. face** poner cara larga (**b**) *(time)* mucho(a); **a l. time** mucho tiempo, mucho; **at l. last** por fin; **how l. is the film?** ¿cuánto tiempo dura la película?; **we were a l. time in getting here** tardamos *or Am* demoramos mucho en llegar ❏ **l. life milk** leche *f* de larga conservación
2 *adv* mucho, mucho tiempo; **all day l.** todo el día; **as l. as the exhibition lasts** mientras dure la exposición; **as l. as or so l. as you don't mind** con tal que no te importe; **before l.** dentro de poco; **(for) how much longer is he going to stay?** ¿cuánto tiempo más va a quedarse?; **how l. have you been here?** ¿cuánto tiempo llevas *or Méx Ven* tienes aquí?; **how l. did you live in Spain?** ¿durante cuánto tiempo viviste en España?; **I can't wait any longer** no puedo esperar más; **keep it as l. as you like** quédatelo el tiempo que quieras; *Fam* **so l.!** ¡hasta luego!
3 *n* **the l. and the short of the matter is ...** el caso es que ...

long² [lɒŋ] *vi* añorar; **to l. for** *(yearn)* desear con ansia, anhelar; *(nostalgically)* añorar con ansia; **to l. to do sth** tener muchas ganas de hacer algo

long³ [lɒŋ] *Geog (abbr* **longitude***)* longitud *f*, long

longboat ['lɒŋbəʊt] *n Naut* chalupa *f*, lancha *f*

longbow ['lɒŋbəʊ] *n Mil* arco *m*

long-distance ['lɒŋdɪstəns] *adj* de larga distancia ❏ *Tel* **l.-d. call** conferencia *f* interurbana; *Sport* **l.-d. runner** corredor(a) *m,f* de fondo

long-drawn-out [lɒŋdrɔːn'aʊt] *adj* interminable

longevity [lɒn'dʒevɪtɪ] *n* longevidad *f*

longhand ['lɒŋhænd] *n* escritura *f* a mano

longing ['lɒŋɪŋ] *n (desire)* deseo *m*, ansia *f*, anhelo *m*; *(nostalgia)* nostalgia *f*, añoranza *f*

longingly ['lɒŋɪŋlɪ] *adv (with desire)* ansiosamente; *(nostalgically)* con nostalgia

longish ['lɒŋɪʃ] *adj Fam* bastante largo(a), más bien largo(a)

longitude ['lɒndʒɪtjuːd] *n* longitud *f*

longitudinal [lɒndʒɪ'tjuːdɪnəl] *adj* longitudinal

long johns ['lɒŋdʒɒnz] *npl* calzones *mpl* largos

long-lost ['lɒŋlɒst] *adj* perdido(a) tiempo atrás; **his l.-l. brother returned** regresó su hermano al que no veía desde hacía mucho tiempo

long-playing ['lɒŋpleɪɪŋ] *adj* de larga duración; **l.-p. record** elepé *m*

long-range ['lɒŋreɪndʒ] *adj* (**a**) *(missile etc)* de largo alcance (**b**) *(weather forecast)* de largo plazo; *Fam (plans etc)* para las próximas semanas, para los meses que vienen

longshoreman ['lɒŋʃɔːmən] *n US (pl* **longshoremen***)* estibador *m*, descargador *m* de muelle

long-sighted [lɒŋ'saɪtɪd] *adj* (**a**) *Med* présbita (**b**) *Fig* previsor(a), perspicaz

long-standing ['lɒŋstændɪŋ] *adj* viejo(a), antiguo(a), de hace mucho tiempo

long-suffering ['lɒŋsʌfrɪŋ] *adj* sufrido(a)

long-term ['lɒŋtɜːm] *adj* a largo plazo

longtime ['lɒŋtaɪm] *adj* viejo(a), antiguo(a), de hace mucho tiempo

long-winded [lɒŋ'wɪndɪd] *adj (person)* prolijo(a), pedante; *(story)* interminable

loo [lu:] *n Br Fam* excusado *m*, wáter *m*, baño *m*, servicios *mpl*

loofah ['lu:fə] *n* esponja *f* de lufa

look [lʊk] **1** *n* (a) *(glance)* mirada *f*; **have** *or* **take a l. in the cupboard** mira en el armario; **he had a strange l. in his eye** tenía una mirada extraña; **let me have** *or* **take a l.** déjeme ver; **to have a l. around a place** visitar un lugar; **to have a l. for sth** buscar algo; **to have** *or* **take a l. at** *(peep)* echar una mirada *or* vistazo a; *(examine)* examinar (b) *(appearance)* aspecto *m*, apariencia *f*; **by the l. of him** a juzgar por su aspecto; **by the l. of things** según parece; **I don't like the l. of it** me da mala espina (c) *(fashion)* moda *f*, estilo *m* (d) **(good) looks** belleza *f*; **he had it all: looks, money, and prospects** lo tenía todo; era guapo, tenía dinero y buen futuro; **she has her mother's looks** es tan guapa como su madre

  2 *vi* (a) *(glance etc)* mirar, *Am* ver; *Fam* **l. here!** ¡oye!; *Prov* **l. before you leap** antes de que te cases mira lo que haces (b) *(seem)* parecer; **he looks well** tiene buena cara; **it looks delicious** tiene un aspecto buenísimo; **how does the hat l.?** ¿qué te parece el sombrero?; **it looks good on you** te va muy bien; **she looks tired** parece cansada; *Fam* **l. lively!** ¡espabílate! (c) *(be similar)* **to l. like** parecer; **it looks like rain** parece que va a llover; **she looks like her father** se parece a su padre

  3 *vt* (a) *(gen)* mirar; **to l. sb in the face** mirar a algn a la cara; **to l. sb up and down** mirar a algn de arriba abajo (b) *(seem)* parecer; **she doesn't l. herself today** tiene mala cara hoy

look after *vt (pay attention to)* cuidar a, cuidar de, ocuparse de; *(supervise)* vigilar; **l. after yourself!** ¡cuídate!, *Am* ¡que estés bien!; *Fam Iron* **he can l. after himself** sabe arreglárselas

look ahead *vi* mirar hacia adelante; *Fig* mirar al futuro

look at *vt* mirar; *Fig* **it depends an how you l. at it** depende de como se enfoca la cuestión; *Fig* **to l. at him, you wouldn't think he was rich** no tiene aspecto de persona rica; *Fig* **whichever way you l. at it** desde cualquier punto de vista

look away *vi* apartar la mirada

look back *vi* (a) *(in space)* mirar hacia atrás; *Fig* **since then he has never looked back** desde entonces ha ido prosperando (b) *(remember)* recordar

look down *vi* bajar la mirada; *Fig* **to l. down on sth/sb** despreciar algo/a algn

look for *vt* (a) *(search)* buscar (b) *(expect)* esperar; **we're looking for two points** esperamos ganar dos puntos

look forward to *vt* esperar con ansia; *(in letter)* **I l. forward to hearing from you** espero noticias suyas

look in *vi (visit)* hacer una visita rápida; **to l. in on sb** pasar por casa de algn

look into *vt* examinar, estudiar, investigar

look on *vt (consider)* considerar

  2 *vi (not participate etc)* mirar, hacer de espectador(a)

look onto *vt* dar a

look out *vi* (a) *(window etc)* **to l. out of** mirar por; **the bedroom looks out onto the garden** el dormitorio da al jardín (b) *(take care)* **l. out!** ¡cuidado!, ¡ojo!

look out for *vt* (a) *(await)* esperar, estar alerta; **l. out for that film** estate al tanto de esta película (b) *Fam* **to l. out for oneself** velar por los intereses propios

look over *vt (examine)* revisar, examinar; *(place)* inspeccionar, registrar

look round 1 *vi (gen)* mirar alrededor; *(turn head)* volver

la cabeza; **don't l. round!** ¡no mires atrás!; **to l. round for sb** buscar a algn

  2 *vt (visit) (city etc)* visitar, recorrer

look through *vt* (a) *(window etc)* mirar por; *Fam Fig* **he just looked through me** me pasó de largo (b) *(leaf through)* hojear; *(examine)* examinar, revisar; *(check)* registrar

look to *vt* (a) *(take care of)* cuidar de, velar por, ocuparse de (b) *(turn to)* recurrir a, contar con; **they always looked to their father for advice** siempre buscaban los consejos de su padre (c) *(make sure)* asegurar; **l. to it that you get here on time** asegúrate de que llegues a tiempo (d) *(foresee)* contemplar; **certain ecologists l. to the future with great pessimism** ciertos ecologistas tienen una visión muy pesimista del futuro

look up 1 *vi* (a) *(glance upwards)* alzar la vista (b) *(improve)* mejorar; **things are looking up** se nota una mejora en las cosas

  2 *vt* (a) *(look for)* buscar; **he looked the word up (in a dictionary)** buscó la palabra (en un diccionario) (b) *(visit)* ver, ir a visitar; **when I go to Madrid I'll l. him up** cuando vaya a Madrid iré a verle

look upon *vt (consider)* considerar

look up to *vt (person)* respetar

lookalike ['lʊkəlaɪk] *n* sosia *m*

looker ['lʊkər] *n* (a) **l. (on)** espectador(a) *m,f* (b) *Fam (woman)* belleza *f*

look-in ['lʊkɪn] *n Fam* ocasión *f*, oportunidad *f*; **he won't get a l.-in** no le harán ni caso

lookout ['lʊkaʊt] *n* (a) *(person)* centinela *mf*, guardia *mf* (b) *(place)* mirador *m*, atalaya *f* (c) *(watch)* **to be on the l. for** estar al acecho de; **to keep a l.** estar ojo avizor (d) *Br Fam* **that's his l.!** ¡eso es asunto suyo!, ¡allá él!

loom¹ [lu:m] *n* telar *m*

loom² [lu:m] *vi (stand tall)* surgir, aparecer; *Fig (threaten)* amenazar; **to l. large** cobrar mucha importancia

loom up *vi (problems, buildings, etc)* surgir

loony ['lu:nɪ] *adj* **(loonier, looniest)** *Fam* loco(a), chiflado(a) ❑ **l. bin** manicomio *m*

loop [lu:p] **1** *n* (a) *(in rope)* lazo *m*, lazada *f* (b) *(contraceptive)* esterilete *m* (c) *Comptr* bucle *m*

  2 *vt* (a) *(string)* enrollar; **to l. a rope around sth** pasar una cuerda alrededor de algo (b) *Av* **to l. the l.** rizar el rizo

  3 *vi (road etc)* serpentear

loophole ['lu:phəʊl] *n* (a) *(in wall)* aspillera *f* (b) *Fig (in law etc)* escapatoria *f*; **tax l.** laguna *f* impositiva

loopy ['lu:pɪ] *adj* **(loopier, loopiest)** *Fam* loco(a), chiflado(a), *Méx* zafado(a)

loose [lu:s] **1** *adj* (a) *(not secure) (knot, rope, screw)* flojo(a), holgado(a); *(tooth)* que se mueve; *(bowels)* suelto(a); *(papers, hair)* suelto(a); *(tongue)* suelto(a), desatado(a); *(clothes)* suelto(a); *(baggy)* holgado(a); **l. skin** carnes *fpl* fofas; **to break l.** escaparse; **to come l.** *(shoelace etc)* desatarse; *(part)* desprenderse; **to cut** *or* **let l.** soltar, dejar; **to set sb l.** soltar a algn, poner en libertad a algn; *US Fam* **to stay** *or* **hang l.** relajarse; *Fig* **to tie up l. ends** dejar cabo suelto; *Fam* **to be at a l. end** no saber qué hacer para distraerse ❑ *Br* **l. cover** funda *f*; **l. end** cabo *m* suelto (b) *(not packaged) (goods)* suelto(a), a granel; **l. tobacco** tabaco *m* en hebras; **l. change** suelto *m*, dinero *m* suelto (c) *(not connected)* *Elec* desconectado(a); *Fig (ideas)* inconexo(a) (d) *(not exact)* inexacto(a), vago,a; *(translation)* libre (e) *(lax)* relajado(a); **a l. woman** una mujer fácil; **l. living** vida *f* alegre

  2 *n Fam (prisoner etc)* **to be on the l.** andar suelto(a)

  3 *vt Literary* (a) *(animal, person)* dejar en libertad, soltar (b) *(bring about)* provocar

loose-fitting [luːsˈfɪtɪŋ] *adj (gen)* suelto(a); *(clothes)* holgado(a), amplio(a)

loose-leaf [luːsˈliːf] *adj (album, folder)* de hojas sueltas

loosely [ˈluːslɪ] *adv* (a) *(approximately)* aproximadamente (b) *(vaguely)* vagamente

loosen [ˈluːsən] 1 *vt (slacken)* aflojar, soltar; *(belt)* desabrochar; *Fig (restrictions)* flexibilizar (b) *(untie)* desatar; *Fig* the wine loosened his tongue el vino le hizo hablar más de la cuenta
2 *vi* (a) *(slacken)* aflojarse, soltarse (b) *(become untied)* desatarse

loosen up *vi* (a) *Sport* desentumecerse (b) *Fam (relax)* relajarse

looseness [ˈluːsnɪs] *n* (a) *(of knot, rope)* aflojamiento *m*, soltura *f* (b) *(of clothes)* holgura *f* (c) *(of morals, discipline)* disipación *f*, *Esp* relajo *m* (d) *(vagueness)* vaguedad *f*, falta *f* de precisión

loot [luːt] 1 *n* (a) *(booty)* botín *m* (b) *Fam (money) Esp* pasta *f*, *Am* plata *f*, *Méx* lana *f*
2 *vt* saquear

looter [ˈluːtər] *n* saqueador(a) *m,f*

looting [ˈluːtɪŋ] *n* saqueo *m*

lop [lɒp] *vt (pt & pp lopped)* podar; to l. branches off a tree podar un árbol

lop off *vt* cortar

lope [ləʊp] 1 *vi* andar a zancador *or* con paso largo
2 *n* zancada *f*, paso *m* largo

lop-eared [ˈlɒpɪəd] *adj* de orejas gachas

lopsided [lɒpˈsaɪdɪd] *adj (gen)* ladeado(a), torcido(a); *(table)* cojo(a); *(view)* descentrado(a)

loquacious [lɒˈkweɪʃəs] *adj Fml* locuaz

loquacity [lɒˈkwæsɪtɪ] *n Fml* locuacidad *f*

lord [lɔːd] 1 *n* (a) *(ruler)* señor *m*; *(British peer)* lord *m*; *Br Parl* the House of Lords la Cámara de los Lores; the L. Mayor el señor alcalde; *Fig* to live like a l. vivir a cuerpo de rey *or* como un pachá (b) *Rel* the L. El Señor; good L.! ¡Dios mío!; the L.'s Prayer el Padrenuestro (c) *Jur (judge)* señoría *mf*; yes, my l. sí, señoría
2 *vt* to l. it over sb tratar despóticamente a algn

lordship [ˈlɔːdʃɪp] *n Br* señoría *f*, señorío *m*; His L., Your L. su señoría

lore [lɔːr] *n* saber *m* popular, tradición *f*

lorry [ˈlɒrɪ] *n Br* camión *m*; *Fam Fig* to fall off the back of a l. ser de trapicheo, *Méx* ser chueco(a), *RP* ser trucho(a) □ l. driver camionero(a) *m,f*; l. load carga *f*

lose [luːz] 1 *vt (pt & pp lost)* (a) *(gen)* perder; to l. one's way perderse; *Fig* to l. face perder prestigio *or* carisma; *Fig* to l. one's voice quedarse afónico; *Fam Fig* we're losing sight of the problem nos estamos desviando del problema; *Fam Fig* you've got nothing to l. no tienes nada que perder (b) *(wipe out)* destrozar; to be lost at sea perecer en el mar (c) *(shed)* perder; she's lost six kilos ha adelgazado seis kilos; to l. weight perder peso, adelgazar; the patient has lost a lot of blood el paciente ha perdido mucha sangre (d) *(be dismissed)* costar, hacer perder; his attitude lost him the job su actitud le costó el puesto de trabajo (e) *(make a loss)* perder (f) *(through death)* perder; to l. a child perder a un hijo; to l. one's life perder la vida, perecer (g) *(time)* perder; *(clock, watch)* atrasar; his alarm clock loses three minutes a day su despertador se atrasa tres minutos por día
2 *vi* (a) *(gen)* perder; to l. to sb perder contra algn; to l. out salir perdiendo; United lost 6-0 el United perdió 6-0 (b) *(clock, watch)* atrasarse

lose out *vi* sufrir (to a costa de)

loser [ˈluːzər] *n* perdedor(a) *m,f*; to be a good/bad l.

saber/no saber perder; *Fam* she's a born l. tiene mala suerte; *Fam* to be on a l. tener todas las de perder

losing [ˈluːzɪŋ] *adj (team etc)* vencido(a), derrotado(a); to be on the l. side ser entre los perdedores; *Fig* to fight a l. battle luchar por una causa perdida

loss [lɒs] *n (gen)* pérdida *f*; heat/weight l. pérdida de calor/peso; l. of memory/vision pérdida de memoria/ vista; there was a great l. of life hubo muchas víctimas; *Com* to make a l. perder; *Com* to sell sth at a l. vender algo con pérdida; *Fig* to be at a l. estar perdido(a) *or* desorientado(a); *Fig* to be at a l. for words quedarse de una pieza; to be at a l. what to do no saber qué hacer; *Fig* to cut one's losses reducir pérdidas; *Fam* it's your l. sales perdiendo tú; *Fam* she's a dead l. es un desastre *or* una calamidad □ *Com* l. leader reclamo *m* de ventas

lost [lɒst] 1 *pt & pp see* lose
2 *adj* (a) *(gen)* perdido(a); to get l. perderse; to make up for l. time recuperar el tiempo perdido; *Fam* get l.! ¡vete a la porra! □ l. cause causa *f* perdida; l. property objetos *mpl* perdidos; l. property office *US* l. and found department oficina *f* de objetos perdidos (b) *(disoriented)* desorientado(a); *(distracted)* distraído(a), despistado(a); to be l. for words quedarse de una pieza; to be l. in thought estar ensimismado(a) (c) *(wasted)* inútil

lot [lɒt] *n* (a) *(fortune, fate)* suerte *f*, destino *m*; *Fig* the common l. la suerte común; *Fig* to throw in one's l. with sb unirse a la suerte de algn (b) *(for choosing)* sorteo *m*; to draw *or* cast lots for sth sortear algo, echar algo a suertes (c) *US (plot of land)* parcela *f*, terreno *m* □ *US* parking l. estacionamiento *m*, *Esp* aparcamiento *m* (d) *(in an auction)* lote *m* (e) *Fam (group of people)* grupo *m* de gente; are your l. coming too? ¿los tuyos también vienen?; they never speak to us l. nunca hablan con nosotros; they're a nice l. es gente maja (f) *(everything)* todo *m*; he ate the l. se lo comió todo; that's the l. eso es todo (g) *(large amount, number)* a l. of *(much)* mucho(a); *(many)* muchos(as); a l. of people mucha gente, muchas personas; he feels a l. better se encuentra mucho mejor; she reads a l. lee mucho; such a l. of tanto(a), tantos(as); thanks a l.! ¡muchísimas gracias!; *Iron* ¡y gracias!; what a l. of children! ¡cuántos niños! (h) *Fam* lots of un montón de, montones de, cantidad de, la mar de; lots of concentration mucha concentración

loth [ləʊθ] *adj see* loath

lotion [ˈləʊʃən] *n* loción *f*

lottery [ˈlɒtərɪ] *n* lotería *f* □ l. ticket billete *m or Am* boleto *m* de lotería

lotto [ˈlɒtəʊ] *n (boardgame)* lotería *f*

lotus [ˈləʊtəs] *n Bot* loto *m* □ l. position postura *f* del loto

lotus-eater [ˈləʊtəsiːtər] *n* vividor(a) *m,f*

loud [laʊd] 1 *adj* (a) *(voice)* alto(a), fuerte; *(noise)* fuerte; *(laugh)* estrepitoso(a); *(applause)* clamoroso(a); *(protests, party)* ruidoso(a); *Fig* I can hear you l. and clear te oigo perfectamente (b) *(flashy) (colour)* chillón(ona), llamativo(a) (c) *(vulgar) (behaviour etc)* de mal gusto, cursi, hortera
2 *adv* alto, fuerte; to say/read/think out l. decir/leer/ pensar en voz alta

loud-hailer [laʊdˈheɪlər] *n Br* megáfono *m*

loudly [ˈlaʊdlɪ] *adv* alto

loudmouth [ˈlaʊdmaʊθ] *n Pej* chismoso(a) *m,f*, *(mujer)* verdulera *f*

loud-mouthed [ˈlaʊdmaʊθt] *adj* gritón(ona)

loudness [ˈlaʊdnɪs] *n (of noise)* fuerza *f*, intensidad *f*

loudspeaker [laʊdˈspiːkər] *n* altavoz *m*, *Am* altoparlante *m*, *Méx* bocina *f*

lounge [laʊndʒ] 1 *n Br (sitting-room)* salón *m*, sala *f* de estar; *(in pub)* salón *m* ❏ **departure l.** sala *f* de espera

2 *vi* holgazanear, gandulear; **to l. on the sofa** repantigarse en el sofá

lounge about *vi* holgazanear, gandulear

lounger ['laʊndʒər] *n* tumbona *f*

louse [laʊs] *n* (**a**) *(pl* **lice** [laɪs]*) (insect)* piojo *m* (**b**) *(pl* **louses**) *Fam (person)* canalla *mf*, sinvergüenza *mf*

louse up *vt Fam (spoil)* echar a perder, estropear

Lousiana [luːzɪˈænə] *n* Luisiana

lousy ['laʊzɪ] *adj* (**lousier, lousiest**) *Fam (dreadful)* pésimo(a), horroroso(a); **a l. day** un día de perros; **a l. trick** una cochinada; **I feel l.** me encuentro *Esp* fatal *or Am* pésimo

lout [laʊt] *n* salvaje *m*, *Esp* gamberro *m*

loutish ['laʊtɪʃ] *adj* grosero(a), *Esp* gamberro(a)

louvre, *US* **louver** ['luːvər] *adj* persiana *f*

lovable ['lʌvəbəl] *adj* adorable, encantador(a)

love [lʌv] **1** *n* (**a**) *(between lovers or members of a family)* amor *m* (**for** por); *(affection)* cariño *m* (**for** por); *(passion)* pasión *f* (**for** por), afición *f* (**for** a); **for the l. of it** por amor al arte; **give my l. to David** dale un abrazo de mi parte a David; **it was l. at first sight** fue un flechazo; **not for l. or money** por nada del mundo; **to be in l. with sb** estar enamorado(a) de algn; **to fall in l.** enamorarse; **to make l.** hacer el amor; *Old-fashioned* **to make l. to sb** *(court)* hacer la corte a algn; *(in letter)* **(with) l. (from)** Mary un abrazo afectuoso, Mary; *Fig* **there's no l. lost between them** no se pueden ver ❏ **l. affair** amorío *m*; *Euph* **l. child** hijo(a) *m,f* natural; **l. letter** carta *f* de amor; **l. life** vida *f* sentimental; *(sexual)* vida *f* sexual; **l. story** historia *f* de amor (**b**) *(person)* amor *m* cariño *m*; *Fam* chato(a) *m,f*; *Br* **my l.** mi amor, amor mío; *Fam* **thanks, l.** gracias, guapa *or Am* mamita (**c**) *Ten (nil)* **forty l.** cuarenta a cero ❏ **l. game** juego *m* a cero

2 *vt* querer, amar; *(sport etc)* ser muy aficionado(a) a; **he loves cooking** le encanta cocinar; **we'd l. to go with you** nos gustaría mucho acompañaros

lovebirds ['lʌvbɜːdz] *npl Iron* enamorados *mpl*, tortolitos *mpl*

love-hate [lʌvˈheɪt] *adj* **a l. relationship** una relación de amor y odio

loveless ['lʌvlɪs] *adj* sin amor

loveliness ['lʌvlɪnɪs] *n* encanto *m*, belleza *f*

lovelorn ['lʌvlɔːn] *adj Literary or Hum* apesadumbrado(a) *(por amor)*

lovely ['lʌvlɪ] *adj* (**lovelier, loveliest**) *(pleasing, charming)* encantador(a); *(beautiful)* precioso(a), *Am* lindo(a); *(person)* bello(a), *Esp* guapo(a), *Am* lindo(a); *(delicious)* delicioso(a), riquísimo(a); **we had a l. time** lo pasamos en grande

love-making ['lʌvmeɪkɪŋ] *n* (**a**) *(courtship)* galanteo *m* (**b**) *(sexual intercourse)* relaciones *fpl* sexuales

lover ['lʌvər] *n* (**a**) *(sexual partner)* amante *mf* (**b**) *(enthusiast)* amante *mf*, aficionado(a) *m,f*, amigo(a) *m,f*; **he's a l. of fine food** es un amante de la buena comida

lovesick ['lʌvsɪk] *adj* enfermo(a) de amor

lovey-dovey [lʌvɪˈdʌvɪ] *adj Iron* zalamero(a), empalagoso(a)

loving ['lʌvɪŋ] *adj (affectionate)* cariñoso(a), afectuoso(a); *(in letter)* **your l. daughter, Emma** un abrazo afectuoso de tu hija Emma

low¹ [ləʊ] **1** *adj* (**a**) *(not high)* bajo(a); *(bridge, voice, sun)* bajo(a); *(neckline)* escotado(a); *(tide, level)* bajo(a); *Culin* **cook on a l. light** *or* **gas** cocinar a fuego lento; *Fig* **to keep a l. profile** ser discreto(a) ❏ *Geog* **the L. Countries** los Países Bajos (**b**) *(in number or quantity)* bajo(a), poco(a); **l. prices** precios bajos; **l. tar cigarettes** cigarrillos bajos en nicotina; **l. temperatures** temperaturas bajas; **we're l. on**

supplies no tenemos muchas provisiones (**c**) *(poor)* pobre, bajo(a); **a l. standard of living** un bajo nivel de vida (**d**) *(battery)* gastado(a) ❏ **l. frequency** baja frecuencia *f* (**e**) *(depressed)* deprimido(a); **morale among the soldiers was l.** había muy poco entusiasmo entre los soldados; **to feel l.** sentirse deprimido(a) (**f**) *(reprehensible)* malo(a); **a l. trick** una mala jugada

2 *adv* bajo; **our supplies are running l.** se nos están acabando las provisiones; **to aim l.** apuntar bajo; **to fly l.** volar bajo; *Fig* **to be laid l. with flu** tener que guardar cama a causa de la gripe; *Fig* **to lie l.** permanecer escondido(a)

3 *n* (**a**) *Meteor* depresión *f*, área *f* de baja presión (**b**) *(low point)* punto *m* más bajo; **to reach an all-time l.** tocar fondo

low² [ləʊ] *vi (cow)* mugir

lowbrow ['ləʊbraʊ] **1** *adj* poco culto(a)

2 *n* persona *f* de poca cultura

low-budget [ləʊˈbʌdʒɪt] *adj (film, holiday)* de bajo presupuesto

low-calorie [ləʊˈkælərɪ] *adj* bajo(a) en calorías

low-cost [ləʊˈkɒst] *adj (mortgage)* de bajo costo *or Esp* coste; *(flight)* económico(a)

low-cut [ləʊˈkʌt] *adj (dress)* escotado(a)

lowdown ['ləʊdaʊn] *n Fam* pormenores *mpl*; **to give sb the l. on sth** dar informes confidenciales a algn sobre algo

low-down ['ləʊdaʊn] *adj* bajo(a), vil

lower ['ləʊər] **1** *adj (comp of* **low**) inferior; **the l. jaw** la mandíbula inferior ❏ *Typ* **l. case** caja *f* baja, minúscula *f*; **l. class** clase *f* baja

2 *adv comp see* **low**

3 *vt* (**a**) *(voice, radio)* bajar; *(lifeboat)* lanzar; *(flag)* arriar (**b**) *(reduce)* reducir, bajar, disminuir; *(price)* rebajar, bajar; *Fig* **to l. oneself** rebajarse (**c**) *(weaken)* debilitar

lower-case ['ləʊəˈkeɪs] *Typ* **1** *n* minúsculas *fpl*, *Spec* caja *f*

2 *adj* en minúsculas, *Spec* en caja baja

lower-class ['ləʊəklɑːs] *adj* de clase baja

lowest ['ləʊɪst] **1** *adj (superl of* **low**) más bajo(a); *(price, speed)* mínimo(a) ❏ *Math* **l. common denominator** mínimo común denominador *m*

2 *n* mínimo *m*; **at the l.** como mínimo; *Fig* **the l. of the low** lo peor que hay

low-key [ləʊˈkiː] *adj (calm)* de baja intensidad; *(informal)* sin ceremonia

lowland ['ləʊlənd] *adj* de las tierras bajas

lowlands ['ləʊləndz] *npl* tierras *fpl* bajas; *Geog* **the L.** las Tierras Bajas de Escocia

low-level ['ləʊlevəl] *adj* de bajo nivel

lowly ['ləʊlɪ] *adj* (**lowlier, lowliest**) humilde, modesto(a)

low-necked ['ləʊnekt] *adj (dress)* escotado(a), con escote

low-pitched ['ləʊpɪtʃt] *adj* grave

low-profile [ləʊˈprəʊfaɪl] *adj (talks, visit)* discreto(a); **the police maintained a l. presence throughout** la presencia de la policía fue discreta todo el tiempo

low-spirited [ləʊˈspɪrɪtɪd] *adj* desanimado(a)

loyal ['lɔɪəl] *adj* leal, fiel

loyalist ['lɔɪəlɪst] *n* leal *mf*; *Hist* legitimista *mf*

loyally ['lɔɪəlɪ] *adv* lealmente, fielmente

loyalty ['lɔɪəltɪ] *n* lealtad *f*, fidelidad *f* ❏ **l. card** tarjeta *f or* carné *m* de fidelización

lozenge ['lɒzɪndʒ] *n* (**a**) *Med* pastilla *f* (**b**) *Geom* rombo *m*

LP [elˈpiː] *n (abbr* **long-playing record**) disco *m* de larga duración, LP *m*

L-plate ['elpleɪt] n Br Aut (placa f de) la ele

LSD [eles'di:] n (abbr **lysergic acid diethylamide**) dietilamida f del ácido lisérgico, LSD m

Lt abbr see **Lieut**

lt (abbr **litres**) l.

Ltd Br Com (abbr **Limited (Liability)**) (responsabilidad f) Limitada, Ltda

lubricant ['lu:brɪkənt] n lubricante m, lubrificante m

lubricate ['lu:brɪkeɪt] vt (gen) lubricar; (engine) engrasar

lubrication [lu:brɪ'keɪʃən] n engrase m

lubricious [lu:'brɪʃəs] adj Literary lascivo(a), lujurioso(a)

lucerne [lu:'sɜ:n] n Bot alfalfa f brasileña

lucid ['lu:sɪd] adj lúcido(a), claro(a)

lucidity [lu:'sɪdɪtɪ] n lucidez f, claridad f

luck [lʌk] n suerte f; **bad** or **hard** or **tough l.!** mala suerte; **good l.!**, **best of l.!** ¡(buena) suerte!; **no such l.!** ¡ojalá!; **this pen brings me good l.** este bolígrafo me da buena suerte; **to be in l.** estar de suerte, estar con suerte; **to be down on one's l.** tener muy mala suerte; **to be out of l.** estar de malas; Fig **as l. would have it ...** la suerte quiso que ...; Fig **to have l. on one's side** tener la suerte de su parte; Fig **to push one's l.** tentar la suerte; Fig **to try one's l.** probar fortuna; Fam **any l.?** ¿qué?, ¿cómo te ha ido?; Fam **I've got to do the dishes, worse l.** ¡vaya suerte que tengo! me toca lavar los platos; Fam **with any** or **a bit of l.**, **he'll phone this evening** con un poco de suerte llamará esta tarde

luckily ['lʌkɪlɪ] adv por suerte, afortunadamente

luckless ['lʌklɪs] adj Fml infortunado(a), desgraciado(a), desafortunado(a)

lucky ['lʌkɪ] adj (luckier, luckiest) (person) afortunado(a), que tiene suerte; (day) favorable, de buen agüero; (move) oportuno(a); (charm) que trae suerte; **a l. break** una oportunidad; **how l.!** ¡qué suerte!; **I'm wearing my l. shirt** visto mi camisa de la suerte; **it's your l. day!** hoy estás de suerte; **to be born l.** haber nacido con buena estrella; **to have a l. escape** escaparse por los pelos; **you'll be l. to get the job** no veo muy claro que consigas el trabajo; Fig **third time l.** a la tercera va la vencida; Fam **l. you!**, **l. devil!** ¡que suerte tienes!; Fam **l. you phoned when you did** menos mal que llamaste; Fam Fig **to thank one's l. stars** dar gracias a Dios; Fam Iron **you'll be l.!**, **you should be so l.!** ¡ya veremos! □ Br **l. dip** caja f de las sorpresas

lucrative ['lu:krətɪv] adj lucrativo(a)

ludicrous ['lu:dɪkrəs] adj absurdo(a), ridículo(a)

ludo ['lu:dəʊ] n (game) parchís m

lug [lʌg] vt (pt & pp **lugged**) Fam (heave) arrastrar, transportar con dificultad

luggage ['lʌgɪdʒ] n equipaje m □ **l. rack** Aut baca f, portaequipajes m inv; Rail red f, redecilla f; Br Rail **l. van** furgón m de equipaje

lughole ['lʌghəʊl] n Br Fam oreja f, Esp soplillo m

lugubrious [lʊ'gu:brɪəs] adj Literary lúgubre

lukewarm ['lu:kwɔ:m] adj (water etc) tibio(a); Fig (reception etc) poco entusiasta

lull [lʌl] **1** n (in storm, wind) calma f, recalmón m; (in activity, fighting) respiro m, tregua f; Fig **the l. before the storm** una tensa calma que anuncia la tempestad
2 vt (cause to sleep, relax, etc) adormecer; (deceive) **to l. sb into a false sense of security** infundir una falsa seguridad a algn

lullaby ['lʌləbaɪ] n canción f de cuna, nana f, arrullo m

lumbago [lʌm'beɪgəʊ] n Med lumbago m

lumbar ['lʌmbər] adj Anat lumbar

lumber ['lʌmbər] **1** n (a) Br (junk) trastos mpl viejos □ **l. room** trastero m (b) US (timber) maderos mpl, madera f
2 vt (a) (encumber) abarrotar, atestar (**with** de) (b) Fam cargar (**with** de); **he lumbered me with his little brother** tuve que cargar con el hermano pequeño (c) US (fell) (trees) talar
3 vi **to l. (about** or **along)** (move clumsily) moverse pesadamente

lumberjack ['lʌmbədʒæk] n leñador m

lumberyard ['lʌmbəjɑ:d] n almacén m de madera

luminary ['lu:mɪnərɪ] n Literary luminario(a) m,f

luminosity [lu:mɪ'nɒsɪtɪ] n Literary luminosidad f

luminous ['lu:mɪnəs] adj luminoso(a)

lump [lʌmp] **1** n (a) (of coal etc) trozo m, pedazo m; (of sugar, earth) terrón m; (in sauce) grumo m; Med (swelling) bulto m, protuberancia f; Fam Fig (in throat) nudo m □ **l. sum** cantidad f global, suma f global (b) Fam (person) bobo(a) m,f
2 vt Fam (endure) aguantar; **he'll just have to l. it** que se aguante

lump together vt juntar, agrupar, amontonar

lumpy ['lʌmpɪ] adj (lumpier, lumpiest) (bed) lleno(a) de bultos; (sauce) grumoso(a), lleno(a) de grumos; Culin **to go l.** hacerse grumos

lunacy ['lu:nəsɪ] n locura f; Fam **it's sheer l.!** ¡es una locura!

lunar ['lu:nər] adj lunar □ **l. eclipse** eclipse m lunar; Astronaut **l. landing** alunizaje m; **l. month** mes m lunar

lunatic ['lu:nətɪk] adj & n loco(a) (m,f) □ **l. asylum** manicomio m; Pej **the l. fringe** el sector más radical y fanático

lunch [lʌntʃ] **1** n comida f, almuerzo m; **to have l.** comer, almorzar □ **l. hour** hora f de comer; US **l. pail** tartera f, fiambrera f, Méx RP vianda f; Br **pub l.** comida f servida en pub
2 vi comer, almorzar

lunchbox ['lʌntʃbɒks] n (container) tartera f, fiambrera f, Méx RP vianda f

luncheon ['lʌntʃən] n Fml comida f, almuerzo m □ Br **l. voucher** vale m de comida; (pork) **l. meat** carne f de cerdo troceada, chopped m

lunchtime ['lʌntʃtaɪm] n hora f de comer or del almuerzo

lung [lʌŋ] n pulmón m □ Med iron **l.** pulmón m de acero; **l. cancer** cáncer m del pulmón

lunge [lʌndʒ] **1** n arremetida f, embestida f
2 vi (also **l. forward**) arremeter, lanzarse; **to l. (out) at sb** arremeter contra algn, abalanzarse sobre algn

lupin, US **lupine** ['lu:pɪn] n Bot altramuz m, lupino m

lurch [lɜ:tʃ] **1** n (a) (of vehicle) sacudida f, bandazo m; (person) tambaleo m (b) Fam **to leave sb in the l.** dejar plantado(a) a algn
2 vi (vehicle) dar sacudidas, dar bandazos; (person) tambalearse; **to l. along** (vehicle) ir dando sacudidas or bandazos; (person) ir tambaleándose

lure [lʊər] **1** n (a) (decoy) señuelo m; (bait) cebo m (b) Fig (charm) aliciente m, atractivo m
2 vt atraer or convencer con engaños; **nothing could l. him away from the game** era imposible distraerlo del partido

lurid ['lʊərɪd] adj (a) (gruesome) espeluznante, horripilante (b) (sensational) sensacionalista (c) (gaudy) chillón(ona)

lurk [lɜ:k] vi (a) (lie in wait) estar al acecho (b) (hidden) esconderse, estar escondido(a); Fig **a doubt still lurked in his mind** aún le atormentaba una duda

luscious ['lʌʃəs] *adj (food)* delicioso(a), exquisito(a); *(person)* encantador(a)

lush [lʌʃ] *adj (vegetation)* exuberante; *(place, life, etc)* lujoso(a)

lust [lʌst] **1** *n* **(a)** *(sexual desire)* lujuria *f* **(b)** *(craving)* ansia *f*; *(greed)* codicia *f*
  2 *vi* **to l. after sth/sb** codiciar algo/desear a algn

luster ['lʌstər] *n US see* **lustre**

lustful ['lʌstfʊl] *adj* lujurioso(a), lascivo(a); *(look)* lleno(a) de deseo

lustre ['lʌstər] *n* lustre *m*, brillo *m*

lustrous ['lʌstrəs] *adj* lustroso(a), brillante

lusty ['lʌstɪ] *adj* (**lustier, lustiest**) *(person)* fuerte, robusto(a); *(cry)* fuerte

lute [luːt] *n Mus* laúd *m*

Lutheranism ['luːθərənɪzəm] *n Hist* luteranismo *m*

lutist ['luːtɪst] *n* tañedor(a) *m,f* de laúd

Luxembourg ['lʌksəmbɜːg] *n* Luxemburgo

Luxembourger ['lʌksəmbɜːgər] *n* luxemburgués(esa) *m,f*

luxuriance [lʌgˈzjʊərɪəns] *n (of plants)* exuberancia *f*; *(of hair etc)* abundancia *f*

luxuriant [lʌgˈzjʊərɪənt] *adj (plants)* exuberante; *(hair, etc)* abundante

luxuriate [lʌgˈzjʊərɪeɪt] *vi* disfrutar; **to l. in** deleitarse con

luxurious [lʌgˈzjʊərɪəs] *adj* lujoso(a), de lujo

luxury ['lʌkʃərɪ] *n* **(a)** *(gen)* lujo *m*; **l. flat** piso *m* de lujo ❑ **l. goods** artículos *mpl* de lujo **(b)** *(article)* artículo *m* de lujo

LW *Rad (abbr* **long wave)** onda *f* larga, OL *f*

lychee ['laɪtʃiː] *n* lichi *m*

lying ['laɪɪŋ] **1** *adj* mentiroso(a), falso(a)
  2 *n* mentira *f*, mentiras *fpl*

lymph [lɪmf] *n Anat* linfa *f* ❑ **l. gland** glándula *f* linfática

lymphatic [lɪmˈfætɪk] *adj* linfático(a)

lynch [lɪntʃ] *vt* linchar

lynching ['lɪntʃɪŋ] *n* linchamiento *m*

lynx [lɪŋks] *n Zool* lince *m*

lynx-eyed ['lɪŋksaɪd] *adj* con ojos de lince

lyre [laɪər] *n Mus* lira *f*

lyric ['lɪrɪk] **1** *adj* lírico(a)
  2 *n* **(a)** *(poem)* poema *m* lírico **(b)** **lyrics** *(words of song)* letra *f* sing

lyrical ['lɪrɪkəl] *adj* lírico(a); *Fam* **to wax l. about sth** entusiasmarse por algo

lyricism ['lɪrɪsɪzəm] *n* lirismo *m*

M

M, m [em] *n (the letter)* M, m *f*

M (**a**) *(on clothes etc)* (*abbr* **medium (size)**) (talla *f*) mediana (**b**) *Br* (*abbr* **motorway**) autopista *f*, A *f*

m (**a**) (*abbr* **male**) *(on forms etc)* varón *m*, v (**b**) *(on forms etc)* (*abbr* **married**) casado(a), c (**c**) *Ling* (*abbr* **masculine**) masculino *m*, m (**d**) (*abbr* **metre(s)**) *(distance, radio)* metro(s) *m(pl)*, m (**e**) (*abbr* **million(s)**) millón *m*, millones *mpl*, m

MA [em'eɪ] *n* (*abbr* **Master of Arts**) máster *m* or *Am* maestría *f* (en Humanidades)

ma [mɑː] *n Fam (mother)* mamá *f*

ma'am [mæm, mɑːm] *n Fml* señora *f*

macabre [mə'kɑːbrə] *adj* macabro(a)

macaroni [mækə'rəʊnɪ] *n Culin* macarrones *mpl* ❑ **m. cheese** macarrones *mpl* al gratén

macaroon [mækə'ruːn] *n Culin* mostachón *m*

macaw [mə'kɔː] *n Orn* guacamayo *m*, ara *m*

Mace® [meɪs] *n (spray)* aerosol *m* antivioladores

mace¹ [meɪs] *n (club, ceremonial staff)* maza *f* ❑ **m. bearer** macero *m*

mace² [meɪs] *n (spice)* macis *f inv*

Macedonia [mæsə'dəʊnɪə] *n* Macedonia

Macedonian [mæsə'dəʊnɪən] **1** *n* (**a**) *(person)* macedonio(a) *m,f* (**b**) *(language)* macedonio *m*
2 *adj* macedonio(a)

Mach [mæk, mɑːk] *n Av* **M. (number)** (número *m* de) Mach *m*

machete [mə'tʃeɪtɪ] *n* machete *m*

Machiavellian [mækɪə'velɪən] *adj* maquiavélico(a)

machinations [mækɪ'neɪʃənz] *npl* intrigas *fpl*, maquinaciones *fpl*

machine [mə'ʃiːn] **1** *n (gen)* máquina *f*, aparato *m*; *(machinery)* maquinaria *f*; *Fig* **they treat you like machines** te tratan como si fueras una máquina ❑ **drinks m.** distribuidor *m* automático de bebidas; **fruit m.** máquina *f* tragaperras; **m. gun** ametralladora *f*; *Comptr* **m. language** lenguaje *m* máquina; **m. shop** taller *m* de máquinas; **m. tool** máquina *f* herramienta; *Comptr* **m. translation** traducción *f* automática; **sewing m.** máquina *f* de coser; **washing m.** lavadora *f*
2 *vt Tech* trabajar a máquina; *Sew* coser a máquina

machine-gun [mə'ʃiːngʌn] *vt* (*pt & pp* **machine-gunned**) ametrallar

machine-readable [mə'ʃiːn'riːdəbəl] *adj Comptr (text, data)* legible para *Esp* el ordenador or *Am* la computadora

machinery [mə'ʃiːnərɪ] *n (machines)* maquinaria *f*; *(workings of machine)* mecanismo *m*; *Fig* **the bureaucratic m.** la maquinaria burocrática

machine-washable [mə'ʃiːn'wɒʃəbəl] *adj* lavable a máquina

machinist [mə'ʃiːnɪst] *n Tech* operario(a) *m,f*, mecánico(a) *m,f*

machismo [mæ'tʃɪzməʊ] *n* machismo *m*

macho ['mætʃəʊ] *Fam* **1** *adj (virile etc)* viril, macho; *(male chauvinist)* machista
2 *n (pl* **machos**) macho *m*; *Pej* machista *m*

mac [mæk] *n Br Fam (raincoat)* impermeable *m*, gabardina *f*

mackerel ['mækrəl] *n (pl* **mackerel** *or* **mackerels**) *(fish)* caballa *f*

mac(k)intosh ['mækɪntɒʃ] *n* impermeable *m*

macramé [mə'krɑːmɪ] *n* macramé *m*

macro ['mækrəʊ] *n (pl* **macros**) *Comptr* macro *m or f*; **m. virus** virus *m* de macro

macrobiotic [mækrəʊbaɪ'ɒtɪk] *adj* macrobiótico(a)

macrocosm ['mækrəkɒzəm] *n* macrocosmo *m*

macroeconomics [mækrəʊiːkə'nɒmɪks] *n* macroeconomía *f*

mad [mæd] *adj* (**madder, maddest**) (**a**) *(insane)* loco(a), demente; *Fig* loco(a); *(animal)* furioso(a); *(dog)* rabioso(a); **to be m.** estar loco(a); **to drive sb m.** volver loco(a) a algn; **to go m.** volverse loco(a), enloquecer; **you must be m.!** ¿estás loco?; **as m. as a hatter** *or* **as a March hare** más loco que una cabra (**b**) *(foolish)* loco(a); *(idea, plan)* disparatado(a), insensato(a) (**c**) *Fam (enthusiastic)* chiflado(a), loco(a); **to be m. about** *or* **on sth/sb** estar loco(a) por algo/algn, chiflarse por algo/algn (**d**) *esp US Fam (angry)* esp *Esp* enfadado(a), *esp Am* enojado(a); **to be m. with** *or* **at sb** estar muy *esp Esp* enfadado(a) *or esp Am* enojado(a) con algn (**e**) *(wild, uncontrolled) (gallop, race etc)* desenfrenado(a), frenético(a); **to be in a m. rush** ir como un loco, ir a toda prisa

madam ['mædəm] *n* (**a**) *(as form of address)* señora *f*; **Dear M.** *(in letter)* Muy señora mía, Estimada señora (**b**) *(brothel-keeper)* patrona *f*, ama *f* (**c**) *Fam (girl)* **a little m.** una niña precoz; *Pej* una niña sabihonda

madcap ['mædkæp] *adj (idea, plan etc)* disparatado(a), descabellado(a)

madden ['mædən] *vt (infuriate)* volver loco(a), enfurecer

maddening ['mædənɪŋ] *adj (infuriating)* exasperante, enloquecedor; **it's m.** es para volverse loco(a)

made [meɪd] *pt & pp see* **make**

Madeira [mə'dɪərə] *n* (**a**) *(island)* Madeira (**b**) *(wine)* madeira *m*, madera *m* ❑ *Culin* **M. cake** bizcocho *m*

made-to-measure [meɪdtə'meʒər] *adj (suit, curtains etc)* hecho(a) a (la) medida

made-up ['meɪdʌp] *adj* (**a**) *(face, person)* maquillado(a); *(eyes, lips)* pintado(a) (**b**) *(story, excuse)* inventado(a)

madhouse ['mædhaʊs] *n Fam (mental hospital)* manicomio *m*; *Fig* casa *f* de locos

madly ['mædlɪ] *adv* (**a**) *(gen)* como un loco, locamente (**b**) *(hurriedly)* apresuradamente, precipitadamente; *(frantically)* desesperadamente (**c**) *Fam (intensely, extremely)* terriblemente; **it's m. expensive** es carísimo; **to be m. in love with sb** estar locamente *or* perdidamente enamorado(a) de algn

madman ['mædmən] *n (pl* **madmen**) loco *m*

madness ['mædnɪs] *n (insanity)* locura *f*, demencia *f*; *Fig* locura *f*; **it's sheer m.** es una locura *or* un desvarío

Madonna [mə'dɒnə] *n* Virgen *f*

madrigal ['mædrɪgəl] *n Mus* madrigal *m*

madwoman ['mædwʊmən] *n (pl* **madwomen** ['mædwɪmɪn]) loca *f*

maelstrom ['meɪlstrəʊm] *n* remolino *m*, torbellino *m*

maestro ['maɪstrəʊ] *n (pl* **maestros**) maestro *m*

Mafia ['mæfɪə] *n* mafia *f*

mag [mæg] *n (abbr* **magazine**) *Fam* revista *f*

magazine [mægə'ziːn] *n* (**a**) *(periodical)* revista *f* (**b**) *(in rifle)* recámara *f* (**c**) *Mil (storehouse)* almacén *m*; *(for explosives)* polvorín *m*; *Naut* santabárbara *f*, pañol *m* de municiones

magenta [mə'dʒentə] **1** *n* magenta *f*
 2 *adj* (de color) magenta *inv*

maggot ['mægət] *n Zool* larva *f*, cresa *f*, gusano *m*

maggoty ['mægətɪ] *adj* agusanado(a), gusaniento(a)

Magi ['meɪdʒaɪ] *npl Rel* **the M.** los Reyes Magos

magic ['mædʒɪk] **1** *n* magia *f*; **as if by m.** como por arte de magia ❑ **black m.** magia *f* negra
 2 *adj* (**a**) *(spell, trick)* mágico(a); **m. spell** hechizo *m*, encanto *or* ❑ **m. wand** varita *f* mágica (**b**) *Fam (wonderful)* genial, *Esp* guay, *Méx* padrísimo(a), *RP* bárbaro(a)*

magical ['mædʒɪkəl] *adj* mágico(a)

magician [mə'dʒɪʃən] *n* (**a**) *(wizard)* mago(a) *m,f* (**b**) *(conjuror)* prestigiditador(a) *m,f*, ilusionista *mf*

magisterial [mædʒɪ'stɪərɪəl] *adj* magistral

magistrate ['mædʒɪstreɪt] *n Br Jur* juez *mf* de primera instancia ❑ **magistrates' court** juzgado *m* de primera instancia

magna cum laude ['mægnəkʊm'laʊdeɪ] *adv US Univ* **to graduate m.** = licenciarse con matrícula de honor

magnanimity [mægnə'nɪmɪtɪ] *n* magnanimidad *f*

magnanimous [mæg'nænɪməs] *adj* magnánimo(a)

magnate ['mægneɪt] *n* magnate *m*

magnesia [mæg'niːʃə] *n Chem* magnesia *f*

magnesium [mæg'niːzɪəm] *n Chem* magnesio *m*

magnet ['mægnɪt] *n* imán *m*

magnetic [mæg'netɪk] *adj (force, field, etc)* magnético(a); *Fig (personality)* carismático(a), magnético(a) ❑ **m. compass** brújula *f*; **m. field** campo *m* magnético; **m. north** norte *m* magnético; **m. tape** cinta *f* magnetofónica

magnetism ['mægnɪtɪzəm] *n (force)* magnetismo *m*; *Fig (of personality)* magnetismo *m*, carisma *m*

magnetize ['mægnɪtaɪz] *vt (object)* magnetizar, imanar, imantar; *Fig (person)* magnetizar

magnification [mægnɪfɪ'keɪʃən] *n* aumento *m*, ampliación *f*

magnificence [mæg'nɪfɪsəns] *n* magnificencia *f*, esplendor *m*

magnificent [mæg'nɪfɪsənt] *adj (outstanding)* magnífico(a), espléndido(a); *(sumptuous)* suntuoso(a)

magnify ['mægnɪfaɪ] *vt (pt & pp* **magnified**) (**a**) *(enlarge)* aumentar, ampliar (**b**) *Fig (exaggerate)* exagerar

magnifying glass ['mægnɪfaɪɪŋɡlɑːs] *n* lupa *f*

magnitude ['mægnɪtjuːd] *n (gen)* magnitud *f*; *Fig (importance)* magnitud *f*, envergadura *f*; **a problem of the first m.** un problema de mucha envergadura

magnolia [mæg'nəʊlɪə] *n Bot* (**a**) *(tree)* magnolio *m* (**b**) *(flower)* magnolia *f*

magnum ['mægnəm] *n* = botella de vino o champán de 1,5 litros

magpie ['mægpaɪ] *n Orn* urraca *f*

mahogany [mə'hɒɡənɪ] **1** *n* caoba *f*
 2 *adj* de caoba

maid [meɪd] *n* (**a**) *(servant)* criada *f*, sirvienta *f*, *Am* mucama *f*; *(in hotel)* camarera *f* ❑ **m. of honour** dama *f* de honor (**b**) *Literary (young girl)* doncella *f*; *Pej* **old m.** solterona *f*

maiden ['meɪdən] **1** *n Literary (young girl)* doncella *f*
 2 *adj* (**a**) *(unmarried)* soltera; **m. aunt** tía soltera ❑ **m. name** apellido de soltera (**b**) *(voyage, flight)* inaugural ❑ *Parl* **m. speech** primer discurso *m (de un parlamentario en el Parlamento)*

mail[1] [meɪl] **1** *n* correo *m*; **by m.** por correo ❑ **air m.** correo *m* aéreo; *Comptr* **m. merge** fusión *f* de correo; *Com* **m. order** venta *f* por correo; **m. train** tren *m* correo
 2 *vt esp US* enviar *or* mandar (por correo)

mail[2] [meɪl] *n* malla *f* ❑ **coat of m.** cota *f* de malla

mailbag ['meɪlbæɡ] *n* valija *f*, saca *f* de correo

mailbox ['meɪlbɒks] *n US* buzón *m* (de correos); *Comptr* buzón *m*

mailing ['meɪlɪŋ] *n (mailshot)* mailing *m*; **m. list** lista *f* de direcciones *(para envío de publicidad)*

mailing list ['meɪlɪŋlɪst] *n Com* lista *f* de direcciones

mailman ['meɪlmæn] *n (pl* **mailmen**) *US* cartero *m*

mailshot ['meɪlʃɒt] *n Br (leaflet)* carta *f* publicitaria; *(campaign)* mailing *m*

maim [meɪm] *vt* mutilar, lisiar

main [meɪn] **1** *adj (problem, idea, floor, door etc)* principal; *(square, mast, sail)* mayor; *(office)* central; **the m. body of the army** el grueso del ejército; **the m. thing is to keep calm** lo esencial *or* lo más importante es mantener la calma ❑ *Archit* **m. beam** viga *f* maestra; *Culin* **m. course** plato *m* principal; *Aut* **m. road** carretera *f* principal; **m. street** calle *f* mayor
 2 *n* (**a**) *(pipe, wire)* conducto *m* principal; *(sewer)* colector *m*; **the mains** *(water or gas system)* la cañería principal *or* maestra; *Elec* la red eléctrica; **a radio that works on battery or mains** una radio que funciona con pilas o con corriente; **to turn off the water at the mains** cerrar la llave principal del agua (**b**) **in the m.** *(on the whole)* en general, por regla general; *(for the most part)* en su mayoría

mainframe ['meɪnfreɪm] *n Comptr* **m. computer** *Esp* ordenador *m or* computadora *f* central

mainland ['meɪnlənd] *n* continente *m*; **m. Europe** Europa continental; **to reach the m.** llegar a tierra firme

main-line ['meɪnlaɪn] *adj Rail (train, station)* interurbano(a)

mainly ['meɪnlɪ] *adv (chiefly)* principalmente, sobre todo; *(for the most part)* en su mayoría

mainsail ['meɪnseɪl] *n Naut* vela *f* mayor

mainspring ['meɪnsprɪŋ] *n (of clock)* muelle *m* real; *Fig* motivo *m or* razón *f* principal

mainstay ['meɪnsteɪ] *n Naut* estay *m* mayor; *Fig* sustento *m*, sostén *m*

mainstream ['meɪnstriːm] *n* corriente *f* principal; **m.**

ideology la manera de pensar convencional, la ideología dominante

maintain [meɪnˈteɪn] *vt* (**a**) *(preserve) (order, balance)* mantener; *(living standard, conversation)* sostener; *(silence, appearances)* guardar; *(custom)* conservar; *(road, building, car, machine)* conservar en buen estado (**b**) *(support one's family etc)* mantener, sustentar (**c**) *(claim, assert)* mantener, sostener; **she maintains that it is untrue** sostiene que no es verdad

maintenance [ˈmeɪntənəns] *n* (**a**) *(gen)* mantenimiento *m* ▫ **m. costs** costos *mpl or Esp* costes *mpl* de mantenimiento; **m. man** encargado *m* de mantenimiento (**b**) *Jur (divorce allowance)* pensión *f*

maisonette [meɪzəˈnet] *n* dúplex *m*

maître d' [ˈmeɪtrəˈdiː] *n US* maître *mf* (d'hôtel)

maize [meɪz] *n* maíz *m, Andes RP* choclo *m*

Maj (**a**) *Mil (abbr* **Major**) comandante *m* (**b**) *Mus (abbr* **major**) mayor

majestic [məˈdʒestɪk] *adj* majestuoso(a)

majesty [ˈmædʒɪstɪ] *n* majestad *f*; **Her M. the Queen** Su Graciosa Majestad

major [ˈmeɪdʒər] **1** *adj* (**a**) *(gen)* principal, mayor; *(contribution, operation)* importante, considerable; *(issue)* de mucha envergadura; *(illness)* grave ▫ **m. league** *(in baseball)* = liga profesional de béisbol estadounidense; *Fig* **a m. league company** una de las grandes empresas del sector (**b**) *Mus (scale etc)* mayor; **in C m.** en do mayor

2 *n* (**a**) *Mil* comandante *m* ▫ **m. general** general *m* de división (**b**) *US Univ* especialidad *f*

3 *vi US Univ* **to m. in** especializarse en

Majorca [məˈjɔːkə] *n* Mallorca

Majorcan [məˈjɔːkən] *adj & n* mallorquín(ina) *(m,f)*

majority [məˈdʒɒrɪtɪ] *n* (**a**) *(of a group)* mayoría *f*; **he won by a m. vote** ganó por mayoría; **in the m. of cases** en la mayoría de los casos ▫ *US Pol* **m. leader** = líder de la formación mayoritaria en el senado o el congreso estadounidense; *Pol* **m. rule** gobierno *m* mayoritario; *Jur* **m. verdict** veredicto *m* mayoritario; (**b**) *Jur* **age of m.** mayoría *f* de edad

make [meɪk] **1** *vt (pt & pp* **made**) (**a**) *(gen)* hacer; *(build)* construir; *(manufacture)* fabricar, elaborar; *(create)* crear; *(clothes, curtains)* confeccionar; *(meal)* preparar; *(plans, journey, statement)* hacer; *(payment)* efectuar; *(speech)* pronunciar; *(decision)* tomar; *(mistake)* cometer; **'made in Ireland'** 'fabricado en Irlanda'; **made of gold** de oro; **to be made of** estar hecho(a) or compuesto(a) de, ser de; **to m. a noise** hacer ruido; **to m. love** hacer el amor (**to** con); *Fig* **to m. a clean breast of sth** confesar algo (**b**) *(render)* hacer, poner, volver; *(convert)* convertir, transformar (**into** en); *(appoint)* hacer, nombrar; **he made it clear that ...** dejó claro que ...; **it makes me sad** me pone triste; **it makes you look taller** te hace (parecer) más alto; **m. yourself at home** estás en tu casa; **to m. a fool of sb** dejar or poner en ridículo a algn; **to m. sb happy** hacer feliz a algn (**c**) *(force, compel)* hacer, obligar; *(cause)* hacer, causar; **to m. do with sth** arreglárselas con algo; **to m. sb do sth** obligar a algn a hacer algo; **what makes you say that?** ¿por qué dices eso? (**d**) *(earn)* ganar; *(profits)* sacar; **he makes $400 a week** gana 400 dólares a la semana; **to m. a living** ganarse la vida; **to m. a name for oneself** hacerse famoso(a); *Fig* **to m. the best of sth** sacar partido de algo (**e**) *(have qualities of)* ser, servir de; **it makes interesting reading** es interesante de leer; **she'll m. a good teacher** será una buena profesora (**f**) *(amount to)* ser, hacer, equivaler a; **5 and 5 m. 10** 5 y 5 son 10 (**g**) *(calculate, reckon)* calcular; **I m. it $20 in all** calculo que son 20 dólares en total; **what time do you m. it?** ¿qué hora tienes? (**h**) *(think)* pensar, opinar; **what do you m. of his behaviour?** ¿qué te parece su

conducta?; **I don't know what to m. of it** no lo acabo de entender; **it doesn't m. sense** no tiene sentido (**i**) *(reach)* alcanzar, llegar a; *(achieve)* alcanzar, conseguir; **she's made it!** ¡lo ha conseguido!; **we just made it to the airport** llegamos al aeropuerto con el tiempo justo; *Slang* **to m. it with sb** conseguir acostarse con algn (**j**) *(assure future or success of)* **it will m. or break her** será su consagración o su ruina; **that novel made him** esa novela le consagró; **you've got it made!** ¡tienes el éxito asegurado! (**k**) **to m. an early start** empezar temprano; **to m. a fresh start** volver a empezar

2 *vi* (**a**) *(gen)* hacer; **to m. certain** *or* **sure of sth** asegurarse de algo; **to m. good** triunfar; **to m. merry** divertirse (**b**) *(move)* dirigirse; **to m. after sb** perseguir a algn; **to m. at sb** abalanzarse sobre algn; **to m. towards a place** dirigirse hacia un lugar (**c**) *(appear to)* hacer como, simular; **she made as if to leave** hizo como si quisiera marcharse

3 *n* (**a**) *(brand)* marca *f*; **of German m.** de fabricación alemana (**b**) *Fam* **to be on the m.** *(seeking profit)* andar tras el dinero; *(seeking success)* ir a por todas; *(full of self-interest)* barrer para adentro; *(in search of sex)* ir a ligar *or RP* de levante

make for *vt* (**a**) *(move towards)* dirigirse hacia; *(attack)* atacar a, abalanzarse sobre (**b**) *(result in)* crear; *(contribute to)* contribuir a; **this makes for less work** esto genera menos trabajo

make out 1 *vt* (**a**) *(write out) (list, receipt)* hacer; *(report)* redactar; *(cheque)* extender (**b**) *(see, perceive)* distinguir, divisar; *(writing)* descifrar (**c**) *(understand)* comprender, entender (**d**) *(claim)* pretender; **she made out that she was a nurse** se hizo pasar por enfermera (**e**) *(present)* presentar; **to m. out a case for doing sth** presentar sus argumentos para hacer algo

2 *vi* (**a**) *(manage)* arreglárselas, apañárselas; **how did you m. out?** *(get on)* ¿qué tal te fue? (**b**) *US Fam (sexually)* meterse mano, *Esp* darse el lote

make up 1 *vt* (**a**) *(put together) (parcel, list)* hacer; *(prescription, bed)* preparar; *(dress, curtains)* confeccionar, hacer; *Typ (page)* componer; *(assemble)* montar; **to m. sth up into a parcel** empaquetar algo (**b**) *(invent)* inventar; **the whole thing is made up!** ¡es puro cuento! (**c**) *(apply cosmetics to)* maquillar; *(one's face)* maquillarse, pintarse; **to m. oneself up** maquillarse, pintarse (**d**) *(complete quantity, sum)* completar (**e**) *(compensate for) (loss)* compensar; *(deficit)* cubrir; *(lack)* suplir; *(lost time, ground)* recuperar (**f**) *(constitute)* componer, integrar, formar; *(represent)* representar; **the committee is made up of six teachers** el comité está compuesto de seis profesores; **they m. up 10 per cent of the population** representan un 10 por ciento de la población (**g**) **to m. up a quarrel** *or* **m. it up (with sb)** hacer las paces (con algn), reconciliarse (con algn) (**h**) **to m. up one's mind** decidirse

2 *vi* (**a**) *(friends)* hacer las paces, reconciliarse (**b**) *(apply cosmetics)* maquillarse, pintarse

make up for *vt (loss, damage)* compensar; *(lost time)* recuperar; *(lack)* suplir

make up to *vt* (**a**) **to m. up to sb** *(try to gain favour with)* congraciarse con algn; *(flatter)* halagar a algn (**b**) **to m. it up to sb for sth** compensar *or* indemnizar a algn por algo

make-believe [ˈmeɪkbɪliːv] **1** *n (fantasy)* fantasía *f*, invención *f*; *(pretence)* simulación *f*, fingimiento *m*; **that story is just m.-b.** esa historia es pura fantasía; **to live in a world of m.-b.** vivir en un mundo de ensueño

2 *adj (world)* imaginario(a), falso(a); *(game, toy)* de mentirijillas

makeover [ˈmeɪkəʊvər] *n* renovación *f or* cambio *m* de imagen

maker [ˈmeɪkər] *n* (**a**) *(manufacturer)* fabricante *mf*;

(builder) constructor(a) *m,f*; **the makers** los fabricantes, la fábrica (**b**) **the M.** el Creador; *Euph* **to meet one's M.** morirse

makeshift ['meɪkʃɪft] *adj (improvised)* improvisado(a); *(temporary)* provisional, temporal

make-up ['meɪkʌp] *n* (**a**) *(cosmetics)* maquillaje *m* ❑ **m.-up bag** neceser *m*; **m.-up remover** desmaquillador *m* (**b**) *(composition) (of team etc)* composición *f*; *(structure)* estructura *f*; *(character)* carácter *m*, temperamento *m* (**c**) *Typ (of page, book)* compaginación *f* (**d**) *Sew* confección *f*

making ['meɪkɪŋ] *n* (**a**) *(manufacture)* fabricación *f*; *(of clothes)* confección *f*; *(of bridge, machinery etc)* construcción *f*; *(of post)* creación *f*; *(preparation)* preparación *f*, elaboración *f*; **it is history in the m.** eso pasará a la historia; **the film was three years in the m.** se tardó tres años en hacer la película; **the novel was the m. of her** la novela marcó el inicio de su éxito (**b**) **to have the makings of ...** tener las características para llegar a ser ...; **he has the makings of a politician** tiene madera de político

malachite ['mæləkaɪt] *n Min* malaquita *f*

maladjusted [mælə'dʒʌstɪd] *adj Psych* inadaptado(a)

maladjustment [mælə'dʒʌstmənt] *n Psych* inadaptación *f*

malady ['mælədɪ] *n* mal *m*, enfermedad *f*

malaise [mæ'leɪz] *n Med & Fig* malestar *m*

malapropism ['mæləprɒpɪzəm] *n* gazapo *m*

malaria [mə'leərɪə] *n Med* paludismo *m*, malaria *f*

malark(e)y [mə'lɑːkɪ] *n Fam (ridiculous behaviour)* payasadas *fpl*, majaderías *fpl*; *(ridiculous explanation)* sandeces *fpl*, majaderías *fpl*

Malay [mə'leɪ] **1** *adj* malayo(a)
2 *n* (**a**) *(person)* malayo(a) *m,f* (**b**) *(language)* malayo *m*

Malaysia [mə'leɪzɪə] *n* Malasia *f*

Malaysian [mə'leɪzɪən] *adj & n* malasio(a) *(m,f)*

Maldives ['mɔːldiːvz] *npl* **the M.** las Maldivas

male [meɪl] **1** *adj (animal, plant)* macho; *(person, child)* varón; *(sex)* masculino; *Tech (screw, plug)* macho; *(ward, attire)* de hombres; *(manly)* varonil, viril ❑ *Pej* **m. chauvinism** machismo *m*; **m. nurse** enfermero *m*
2 *n (person)* varón *m*; *(animal, plant)* macho *m*

malevolence [mə'levələns] *n* malevolencia *f*

malevolent [mə'levələnt] *adj* malévolo(a)

malformation [mælfɔː'meɪʃən] *n* malformación *f*, deformidad *f*

malformed [mæl'fɔːmd] *adj* malformado(a), deforme

malfunction [mæl'fʌŋkʃən] **1** *n Esp* fallo *m*, *Am* falla *f*
2 *vi* funcionar mal *or* defectuosamente

malice ['mælɪs] *n (wickedness)* malicia *f*; *(evil intent)* maldad *f*; *(bitterness)* rencor *m*; **to bear sb m.** guardar rencor a algn; *Jur* **with m. aforethought** con premeditación

malicious [mə'lɪʃəs] *adj (wicked)* malévolo(a); *(bitter)* rencoroso(a)

malign [mə'laɪn] **1** *adj* perjudicial, pernicioso(a)
2 *vt (slander)* calumniar, difamar, hablar mal de

malignant [mə'lɪgnənt] *adj* (**a**) *(person)* malvado(a), malo(a); *(influence)* maligno(a); *(action)* perjudicial (**b**) *Med (tumour, disease)* maligno(a)

malinger [mə'lɪŋgər] *vi* fingirse enfermo(a)

malingerer [mə'lɪŋgərər] *n* enfermo(a) *m,f* fingido(a), calandria *mf*

mall [mɔːl, mæl] *n esp US* centro *m* comercial

mallard ['mælɑːd] *n (pl* mallard *or* mallards) *Orn* ánade *m* real

malleable ['mælɪəbəl] *adj (metal)* maleable; *Fig (person)* dócil

mallet ['mælɪt] *n* mazo *m*

mallow ['mæləʊ] *n Bot* malva *f*

malnourished [mæl'nʌrɪʃt] *adj* desnutrido(a)

malnutrition [mælnjuː'trɪʃən] *n* desnutrición *f*

malpractice [mæl'præktɪs] *n Jur* procedimiento *m* ilegal; *Med* negligencia *f* ❑ *esp US Jur* **m. suit** demanda *f* por negligencia (profesional)

malt [mɔːlt] **1** *n (grain)* malta *f* ❑ **m. whisky** whisky *m* de malta
2 *vt (grain)* hacer germinar

Malta ['mɔːltə] *n* Malta

malted ['mɔːltɪd] *adj* malteado(a)

Maltese [mɔːl'tiːz] *adj & n* maltés(esa) *(m,f)*

maltreatment [mæl'triːtmənt] *n* maltrato *m*, malos tratos *mpl*

mammal ['mæməl] *n Zool* mamífero *m*

mammary ['mæmərɪ] *adj Anat* mamario(a) ❑ **m. gland** mama *f*

mammography [mæ'mɒgrəfɪ] *n* mamografía *f*

mammoth ['mæməθ] **1** *n Zool* mamut *m*
2 *adj (huge)* descomunal, gigantesco(a); *Com* **'m. reductions'** 'super rebajas'

mammy ['mæmɪ] *n esp Ir US Fam* mamá *f*

Man [mæn] *n* the Isle of M. la Isla de Man

man [mæn] **1** *n (pl* men) (**a**) *(adult male person)* hombre *m*; **old m.** viejo *m*; *US* **the men's room** el servicio *or Am* los baños de caballeros; **the navy will make a m. of him** la marina le hará un hombre; **young m.** joven *m*; *Fig* **a m. about town** un gran vividor; *Fig* **a m. of the world** un hombre de mundo; *Fig* **the m. in the street** el hombre de la calle; *Fig* **to be a family m.** *(with children etc)* ser padre de familia; *(home-loving)* ser muy casero; *Fig* **to be m. enough for ...** ser lo suficientemente hombre como para ... ❑ **best m.** padrino *m* de boda; *Fam* **dirty old m.** viejo *m* verde; **m. Friday** factótum *m* (**b**) *(humanity)* **M.** el Hombre; *(person)* hombre *m*; *(human being)* ser *m* humano; **all men are equal** todos los hombres son iguales ❑ **Stone Age m.** el hombre de la Edad de Piedra (**c**) *(person, type)* hombre *m*, persona *f*; **he's a Bristol m.** es de Bristol; **he's the best m. for the job** es el hombre más indicado para el puesto; *Fig* **as one m.** todos a la vez; *Fig* **he's a m. of his word** es hombre de palabra; *Fig* **they are patriots to a m.** todos sin excepción son patriotas; *Fig* **to be one's own m.** ser dueño de sí mismo (**d**) *(husband)* hombre *m*, marido *m*; *(boyfriend)* compañero *m*; *(partner)* pareja *f*; **to live together as m. and wife** vivir como marido y mujer (**e**) *(male worker)* hombre *m*, empleado *m*; *(in factory)* obrero *m*; *(servant)* criado *m*; *(butler)* mayordomo *m*; *(soldier)* soldado *m*; **our m. in Madrid** nuestro representante en Madrid; *Fig* **right-hand m.** brazo *m* derecho (**f**) *(in chess)* pieza *f*; *(in draughts)* ficha *f*
2 *vt (pt & pp* manned) *(boat, plane)* tripular; *(post)* servir; *(gun)* manejar; **m. the lifeboats!** ¡todos a los botes!; **manned flight** vuelo *m* tripulado; **the telephone is manned 24 hours a day** el teléfono está en servicio las 24 horas del día
3 *interj Fam Esp* ¡tío!, *Am* ¡compadre!, *Am salvo RP* ¡mano!

manacles ['mænəkəlz] *npl* esposas *fpl*, grillos *mpl*

manage ['mænɪdʒ] **1** *vt* (**a**) *(company)* dirigir, llevar, administrar; *(property)* administrar; *(household)* llevar; *(money, affairs)* manejar; *(child, person)* llevar, manejar; *(animal)* domar (**b**) *(succeed)* conseguir; **to m. to do sth** lograr hacer algo; **to m. to get sth** conseguir algo; **can you m. to do it?** ¿lo puedes hacer?
2 *vi* (**a**) *(cope physically)* poder; **can you m.?** ¿puedes con

eso?; **could you m. another piece of cake?** ¿te apetece otro trozo de pastel?; **I can m., thanks** ya puedo, gracias **(b)** *(cope esp financially)* arreglárselas, apañarse; **to m. on very little money** arreglárselas *or* apañarse con muy poco dinero; **to m. without sth** prescindir de algo; **we're managing** vamos tirando

manageable ['mænɪdʒəbəl] *adj* manejable

management ['mænɪdʒmənt] *n* **(a)** *(of company, project etc)* dirección *f*, gestión *f* ❑ **m. consultant** consultor(a) *m,f* en administración de empresas; **m. studies** administración *f* de empresas **(b)** *(people in charge)* dirección *f*, gerencia *f*; *(board of directors)* junta *f* directiva, consejo *m* de administración; **the M. and the workers** la patronal y los trabajadores; **under new m.** bajo nueva dirección ❑ **m. buyout** = adquisición de una empresa por sus directivos

manager ['mænɪdʒər] *n* **(a)** *(of company, bank)* director(a) *m,f*, gerente *mf*; *(of estate)* administrador(a) *m,f*; *(head of department)* jefe(a) *m,f* **(b)** *(of actor, pop group etc)* manager *mf* **(c)** *Sport (of soccer team)* director(a) *m,f* técnico(a), manager *mf*; *(trainer)* entrenador(a) *m,f*

manageress [mænɪdʒə'res] *n* *(of shop, restaurant)* encargada *f*, jefa *f*; *(of company)* directora *f*, gerente *f*

managerial [mænɪ'dʒɪərɪəl] *adj* directivo(a), administrador(a); **m. staff** personal *m* directivo *or* gerente

managing ['mænɪdʒɪŋ] *adj* directivo(a) ❑ *esp Br* **m. director** director(a) *m,f* gerente; **m. editor** jefe(a) *m,f* de redacción, redactor(a) *m,f* jefe

Mancunian [mæŋ'kju:nɪən] **1** *adj* de Manchester
2 *n* habitante *mf* de Manchester

Mandarin ['mændərɪn] *n (language)* mandarín *m*

mandarin ['mændərɪn] *n* **(a)** *Bot* **m. (orange)** mandarina *f* **(b)** *Pej (official)* mandarín *m*

mandate ['mændeɪt] *n* mandato *m*

mandatory ['mændətərɪ] *adj Fml (compulsory)* obligatorio(a)

mandible ['mændɪbəl] *n Anat* mandíbula *f*

mandolin(e) ['mændəlɪn] *n Mus* mandolina *f*

mandrake ['mændreɪk] *n Bot* mandrágora *f*

mane [meɪn] *n (of horse)* crin *f*; *(of lion)* melena *f*

man-eater ['mæni:tər] *n* **(a)** *(animal)* devorador(a) *m,f* de hombres **(b)** *Fam (woman)* devoradora *f* de hombres

maneuver [mə'nu:vər] *n & vt US see* **manoeuvre**

maneuverable [mə'nu:vərəbəl] *adj US see* **manoeuvrable**

manfully ['mænfʊlɪ] *adv* valientemente

manganese [mæŋgə'ni:z] *n Chem* manganeso *m*

mange [meɪndʒ] *n Med* sarna *f*

manger ['meɪndʒər] *n (trough)* pesebre *m*; *Fig* **to be a dog in the m.** ser el perro del hortelano

mangetout [mɒnʒ'tu:] *n Bot* **m. (pea)** guisante *m* mollar

mangle¹ ['mæŋgəl] *n (for wringing)* escurridor *m*, rodillo *m*

mangle² ['mæŋgəl] *vt (crush)* aplastar; *(destroy by cutting)* destrozar, despedazar; *Fig* **a mangled version of events** una versión mutilada de los hechos

mango ['mæŋgəʊ] *n (pl* **mangoes** *or* **mangos)** *(tree, fruit)* mango *m*

mangy ['meɪndʒɪ] *adj* **(mangier, mangiest)** *(animal)* sarnoso(a); *Fam (carpet)* raído(a)

manhandle ['mænhændəl] *vt* **(a)** *(person)* maltratar **(b)** *(large object)* manipular

manhole ['mænhəʊl] *n* boca *f* de acceso ❑ **m. cover** *(in roof, boiler room)* tapa *f* de registro; *(in street)* recubrimiento *m*; *(of sewer)* tapa *f* de alcantarilla

manhood ['mænhʊd] *n* **(a)** *(state)* madurez *f*; *(age of majority)* mayoría *f* de edad; **to reach m.** llegar a la edad viril **(b)** *(manly qualities)* virilidad *f*, hombría *f* **(c)** *(men collectively)* hombres *mpl*

man-hour ['mænaʊər] *n Econ* hora-hombre *f*

manhunt ['mænhʌnt] *n* persecución *f*

mania ['meɪnɪə] *n Psych & Fig* manía *f*

maniac ['meɪnɪæk] *n* **(a)** *Psych* maníaco(a) *m,f*; *Fam* loco(a) *m,f* ❑ **sex m.** obseso *m* sexual **(b)** *Fam (enthusiast, fan)* fanático(a) *m,f*

maniacal [mə'naɪəkəl] *adj Psych* maníaco(a); *Fig* loco(a)

manic ['mænɪk] *adj* maníaco(a); **m. depression** depresión maníaca

manic-depressive [mænɪkdɪ'presɪv] *n Psych* **1** *adj (illness)* maníaco(a) depresivo(a)
2 *n* maníaco(a) *m,f* depresivo(a)

manicure ['mænɪkjʊər] **1** *n* manicura *f*; **to give sb a m.** hacer la manicura a algn
2 *vt* **to m. one's nails** arreglarse las uñas

manicurist ['mænɪkjʊərɪst] *n* manicuro(a) *m,f*

manifest ['mænɪfest] *Fml* **1** *adj (obvious)* manifiesto(a), evidente
2 *vt (show)* manifestar

manifestation [mænɪfe'steɪʃən] *n Fml* manifestación *f*

manifesto [mænɪ'festəʊ] *n (pl* **manifestos** *or* **manifestoes)** *Pol* manifiesto *m*

manifold ['mænɪfəʊld] **1** *adj Fml (many)* múltiples; *(varied)* diversos(as), variados(as)
2 *n Aut* colector *m* de escape

mani(l)la envelope [mə'nɪlə'envələʊp] *n* sobre *m* marrón de papel manila

manipulate [mə'nɪpjʊleɪt] *vt* **(a)** *(machine, vehicle etc)* manipular, manejar; *(knob, lever)* accionar; *Med (bones)* dar masajes a **(b)** *Fig* manipular; *(accounts etc)* falsificar

manipulation [mənɪpjʊ'leɪʃən] *n* **(a)** *(of machine, vehicle etc)* manipulación *f*, manejo *m*; *(of knob, lever)* accionamiento *m*; *Med (of bones)* masaje *m* **(b)** *Fig* manipulación *f*; *(of accounts etc)* manipulación *f*, falseamiento *m*

manipulative [mə'nɪpjʊlətɪv] *adj Pej* manipulador(a)

mankind [mæn'kaɪnd] *n* la humanidad

manliness ['mænlɪnɪs] *n* virilidad *f*, hombría *f*

manly ['mænlɪ] *adj* **(manlier, manliest)** varonil, viril, macho

man-made ['mænmeɪd] *adj (disaster)* provocado(a) por el hombre; *(lake)* artificial; *(fibres, fabric)* sintético(a)

manned [mænd] *adj (ship, aircraft etc)* tripulado(a)

mannequin ['mænɪkɪn] *n* **(a)** *(dummy)* maniquí *m* **(b)** *(fashion model)* modelo *f*

manner ['mænər] *n* **(a)** *(way, method)* manera *f*, modo *m*; **in this m.** de esta manera, así; **in a m. of speaking** por así decirlo, hasta cierto punto **(b)** *(way of behaving)* forma *f* de ser, comportamiento *m*; **to have an easy m.** tener un aire desenvuelto; **bedside m.** *(of doctor)* trato *m* **(c)** *Fml (type, class)* clase *f*, suerte *f*, índole *f*; **all m. of gifts** toda clase de regalos **(d)** **manners** *(social behaviour)* modales *mpl*, educación *f* sing; **(good) m.** buenos modales *mpl*; **bad m.** falta *f* sing de educación **(e)** **manners** *(of society)* costumbres *fpl*

mannered ['mænəd] *adj Fml (affected)* amanerado(a), afectado-a

mannerism ['mænərɪzəm] *n (gesture)* gesto *m*; *(affectation)* amaneramiento *m*

mannerly ['mænəlɪ] *adj* cortés, (bien) educado(a), formal

mannish ['mænɪʃ] *adj (appearance, behaviour etc)* hombruno(a)

manoeuvrable [mə'nu:vərəbəl] *adj* manejable

manoeuvre [mə'nu:vər] **1** *n* **(a)** *(gen)* maniobra *f* **(b)** *Fig (scheme)* maniobra *f*, estratagema *f*

  2 *vt (gen)* maniobrar; *(person)* manejar, manipular; **to m. sth into position** poner algo en posición

  3 *vi* maniobrar; *Fig* **we need room to m.** necesitamos un amplio margen de actuación

manometer [mə'nɒmɪtər] *n* manómetro *m*

manor ['mænər] *n (estate)* señorío *m* □ **m. house** casa *f* solariega

manpower ['mænpaʊər] *n Ind* mano *f* de obra; *Mil* soldados *mpl*

manservant ['mænsɜ:vənt] *n (pl* **menservants** *)* criado *m*, sirviente *m*

mansion ['mænʃən] *n* mansión *f*

manslaughter ['mænslɔ:tər] *n Jur* homicidio *m* involuntario

mantelpiece ['mæntəlpi:s] *n (shelf)* repisa *f* de chimenea; *(fireplace)* chimenea *f*

mantle ['mæntəl] *n* **(a)** *(cloak)* capa *f* **(b)** *Fig* manto *m*; *(layer)* capa *f*; **beneath a m. of snow** bajo una capa de nieve

man-to-man [mæntə'mæn] *adj* de hombre a hombre

mantra ['mæntrə] *n* mantra *m*; *Fig* estribillo *m*

manual ['mænjʊəl] **1** *adj (work etc)* manual

  2 *n (handbook)* manual *m*

manually ['mænjʊəlɪ] *adv* a mano, manualmente

manufacture [mænjʊ'fæktʃər] **1** *vt (gen)* fabricar; *(clothing)* confeccionar; *(foodstuffs)* elaborar; *Fig (excuse)* inventar

  2 *n (gen)* fabricación *f*; *(of clothing)* confección *f*; *(of foodstuffs)* elaboración *f*

manufacturer [mænjʊ'fæktʃərər] *n (maker)* fabricante *mf*

manufacturing [mænjʊ'fæktʃərɪŋ] *n Ind* fabricación *f*; **m. capacity** capacidad *f* de fabricación; **m. industries** industrias *fpl* manufactureras *or* de transformación

manure [mə'njʊər] **1** *n* abono *m*, estiércol *m*; **m. heap** estercolero *m*

  2 *vt* abonar, estercolar

manuscript ['mænjʊskrɪpt] *n* manuscrito *m*

many ['menɪ] **1** *adj (more, most)* mucho(a), muchos(as); **a good** *or* **great m. citizens** muchísimos(as) ciudadanos, un gran número de ciudadanos; **as m. ... as ...** tantos(as) ... como...; **as m. books as records** tantos libros como discos; **how m. days?** ¿cuántos días?; **m. people** muchas personas, mucha gente, muchos; **m. things** muchas cosas; **m. times, m. a time** muchas veces; **not m. books** pocos *or* no muchos libros; **one too m.** uno de más, uno de sobra; **so m. flowers!** ¡cuántas flores!; **too m.** demasiados(as); *Fam* **he has had one too m.** ha bebido *or* *Am* tomado una copa de más

  2 *pron* muchos(as); **m. came** vinieron muchos

  3 *n* muchos(as) *m,fpl*; **the m.** la mayoría

many-sided ['menɪsaɪdɪd] *adj* **(a)** *(figure)* multilateral, de muchos lados **(b)** *Fig (personality, talent)* polifacético(a); *(question)* complejo(a)

Maori ['maʊrɪ] *adj & n* maorí *(mf)*

map [mæp] **1** *n (of country, region)* mapa *m*; *(of town, bus, tube)* plano *m*; **m. of the world** mapamundi *m*; *Fig* **this will put our village on the m.** esto dará a conocer nuestro pueblo; *Fam* **his house is right off the m.** su casa está en el quinto pino □ **m. reference** coordenadas *fpl*; **weather m.** carta *f* meteorológica

  2 *vt (pt & pp* **mapped***) (area)* trazar un mapa de

map out *vt (route)* trazar en un mapa; *Fig (future etc)* proyectar, planear, organizar

maple ['meɪpəl] *n (tree, wood)* arce *m* □ **m. leaf** hoja *f* de arce; **m. syrup** jarabe *m* de arce

mapmaker ['mæpmeɪkər] *n* cartógrafo(a) *m,f*

mapmaking ['mæpmeɪkɪŋ] *n* cartografía *f*

Mar *(abbr* **March***)* marzo *m*

mar [mɑ:r] *vt (pt & pp* **marred***) (spoil)* estropear, echar a perder; **to m. sb's enjoyment** aguarle la fiesta a algn

maracas [mə'rækəz] *npl Mus* maracas *fpl*

marathon ['mærəθən] **1** *n* maratón *m*

  2 *adj Fig (speech etc)* maratoniano(a), larguísimo(a)

marauder [mə'rɔ:dər] *n* merodeador(a) *m,f*

marauding [mə'rɔ:dɪŋ] *adj* merodeador(a)

marble ['mɑ:bəl] **1** *n* **(a)** *(stone, statue)* mármol *m* **(b)** *(glass ball)* canica *f*; **to play marbles** jugar a canicas; *Fig Fam* **to have lost one's marbles** estar chiflado(a)

  2 *adj (floor, statue etc)* de mármol; *(industry)* del mármol □ **m. cutter** marmolista *mf*; **m. quarry** cantera *f* de mármol

marbled ['mɑ:bəld] *adj (paper)* jaspeado(a)

March [mɑ:tʃ] *n* marzo *m*; *see also* **May**

march [mɑ:tʃ] **1** *n* **(a)** *Mil* marcha *f*; *(walk)* caminata *f*; **it's three days' m. from here** está a tres días de marcha; **to be on the m.** estar en marcha; *Fig* **to steal a m. on sb** tomar la delantera a algn **(b)** *(demonstration)* manifestación *f*; **a peace m.** una manifestación a favor de la paz **(c)** *(of time, events)* marcha *f*, paso *m* **(d)** *Mus* marcha *f* □ **wedding m.** marcha *f* nupcial

  2 *vi* **(a)** *Mil* marchar, hacer una marcha; *(walk)* marchar, caminar; **forward** *or* **quick m.!** ¡frente!, ¡jar!; **to m. in** entrar decidido(a); **to m. out** salir enfadado(a); **to m. straight up to sb** abordar a algn; *Mil* **to m. past** desfilar **(b)** *(demonstrate)* manifestarse, hacer una manifestación

  3 *vt Mil* hacer marchar; **they marched him off to prison** se lo llevaron a la cárcel; **to m. sb off** llevarse a algn

marcher ['mɑ:tʃər] *n (in demonstration)* manifestante *mf*

marching orders ['mɑ:tʃɪŋɔ:dəz] *npl Fam* **to give sb his/her m. o.** mandar a paseo a algn, *Andes RP* mandar a algn a bañarse

marchioness ['mɑ:ʃənɪs] *n* marquesa *f*

march past ['mɑ:tʃpɑ:st] *n Mil* desfile *m*

mare [meər] *n Zool* yegua *f*

margarine [mɑ:dʒə'ri:n] *n*, *Br Fam* **marge** [mɑ:dʒ] *n* margarina *f*

margin ['mɑ:dʒɪn] *n* **(a)** *(on page)* margen *m*; **in the m.** al margen **(b)** *Fig* margen *m*, límite *m*; **to win by a narrow m.** ganar por poco □ **m. of error** margen *m* de error; *Com* **profit m.** margen *m* de beneficio

marginal ['mɑ:dʒɪnəl] *adj (gen)* marginal; *(improvement)* escaso(a), pequeño(a); **m. note** nota *f* al margen □ *Br Pol* **m. seat** = escaño que varios partidos pueden ganar en unas elecciones

marginalize ['mɑ:dʒɪnəlaɪz] *vt* marginar

marginally ['mɑ:dʒɪnəlɪ] *adv* ligeramente

marigold ['mærɪgəʊld] *n Bot* maravilla *f*, caléndula *f*

marijuana, **marihuana** [mærɪ'hwɑ:nə] *n* marihuana *f*, marijuana *f*

marina [mə'ri:nə] *n* puerto *m* deportivo

marinade [mærɪ'neɪd] *n Culin* **1** *n* adobo *m*

  2 ['mærmeɪd] *vt see* **marinate**

marinate ['mærɪneɪt] *vt Culin* adobar

marine [mə'ri:n] **1** *adj (life, flora etc)* marino(a), marítimo(a) □ **m. engineer** ingeniero(a) *m,f* naval; **m. insurance** seguro *m* marítimo

  2 *n (person)* marine *mf*, infante *mf* de marina, *Am* fusilero *m* naval; *Br* **the Marines,** *US* **the M. Corps** la infantería de marina

mariner ['mærɪnər] *n* marinero *m*

marionette [mærɪə'net] *n* marioneta *f*, títere *m*

marital ['mærɪtəl] *adj (relations, problems)* matrimonial, marital; *(bliss)* conyugal ❑ **m. status** estado *m* civil

maritime ['mærɪtaɪm] *adj* marítimo(a)

marjoram ['mɑːdʒərəm] *n Bot* mejorana *f*

mark¹ [mɑːk] **1** *n* **(a)** *(trace)* huella *f*; *(left by blow etc)* señal *f*; *(stain)* mancha *f*; **distinguishing marks** señas *fpl* de identidad; *Fig* **to leave one's m.** dejar su impronta; *Fig* **to make one's m.** distinguirse **(b)** *(symbol)* signo *m*, señal *f*; *(instead of signature)* cruz *f* ❑ **punctuation m.** signo *m* de puntuación **(c)** *(sign, token)* señal *f*, marca *f*; *(indication)* indicio *m*; *(proof)* prueba *f*; **as a m. of respect** en señal de respeto **(d)** *Sch (in exam etc)* nota *f*, calificación *f*; *Sport (of score)* tanto *m*; **to get high marks in English** sacar una buena nota en inglés **(e)** *(target)* blanco *m*; *(aim)* objetivo *m*; **to hit the m.** dar en el blanco; *Fig* dar en el clavo, acertar; *Fig* **to be up to the m.** estar a la altura (de las circunstancias); *Fig* **to be wide of the m.** estar lejos de la verdad **(f)** *Sport* línea *f* de salida; **on your marks!, get set!, go!** ¡preparados!, ¡listos!, ¡ya! **(g)** *Com (brand, trade name)* marca *f*; *(label)* etiqueta *f* **(h)** *Tech (model)* serie *f*; **a M. 3 engine** un motor de tercera serie

2 *vt* **(a)** *(make mark on)* marcar; *(stain)* manchar **(b)** *(indicate)* señalar, indicar; *(show)* mostrar, revelar; **it marks a change of direction** indica un cambio de dirección **(c)** *(exam, exercise) (correct)* corregir; *(give mark to)* puntuar, calificar; *(student)* dar notas a **(d)** *Com (add price)* indicar el precio de, poner precio a; *(label)* poner etiqueta a; **'10% off marked price'** 'descuento del 10% sobre el precio indicado' **(e)** *(pay attention to)* fijarse en, prestar atención a; **m. my words** fíjate en lo que te digo **(f)** *Br Sport (opponent)* marcar **(g)** *Mil* **to m. time** marcar el paso; *Fig (kill time)* hacer tiempo; *(await one's chance)* esperar el momento oportuno

mark down *vt* **(a)** *(note down)* apuntar **(b)** *Com (price)* rebajar; *(goods)* rebajar el precio de

mark off *vt* **(a)** *(separate)* separar, dividir, distinguir; *(area)* delimitar **(b)** *(tick off)* poner una señal a; *(cross out)* tachar

mark out *vt* **(a)** *(area)* delimitar; *(boundary)* trazar; *(field)* jalonar **(b)** *(single out)* distinguir; **to m. sb out for** destinar a algn a

mark up *vt (price)* aumentar

mark² [mɑːk] *n (unit of currency)* marco *m*

markdown ['mɑːkdaʊn] *n (of price)* rebaja *f*

marked [mɑːkt] *adj* **(a)** *(noticeable)* marcado(a), acusado(a); *(improvement, increase)* sensible, apreciable **(b)** **he is a m. man** lo tienen fichado

markedly ['mɑːkɪdlɪ] *adv (different)* marcadamente, acusadamente; *(better)* sensiblemente

marker ['mɑːkər] *n* **(a)** *(stake, pole)* jalón *m* **(b)** *(bookmark)* registro *m* **(c)** *Sport (person)* marcador(a) *m,f* **(d)** *Educ (person)* examinador(a) *m,f* **(e)** *(pen)* rotulador *m*, *Col* marcador *m*, *Méx* plumón *m*

market ['mɑːkɪt] **1** *n* **(a)** *(place)* mercado *m*, *RP* feria *f*, *CAm Méx* tianguis *m*; **Monday is m. day** el lunes hay mercado; **to go to m.** ir al mercado *or Fam* a la plaza ❑ **flea m.** rastrillo *m*, mercadillo *m*; **m. day** día *m* de mercado; *Br* **m. garden** *(small)* huerto *m*; *(large)* huerta *f*; **m. town** población *f* con mercado **(b)** *(trade)* mercado *m*; *(demand)* salida *f*, mercado *m*, demanda *f*; **to be on the m.** estar a la *or* en venta; **to come on to the m.** *(product)* salir al mercado, ponerse en venta ❑ **black m.** mercado *m* negro; *Formerly* **the Common M.** el Mercado Común; **domestic m., home m.** mercado *m* interior *or* nacional; **m. analyst**

analista *mf* de mercados; **m. forces** tendencias *fpl* del mercado; *Com* **m. leader** líder *mf* del mercado; **m. price** precio *m* de mercado; **m. research** estudio *m* de mercado; *Com* **m. share** cuota *f* de mercado; **open m.** mercado *m* libre; **overseas m.** mercado *m* exterior **(c)** *Fin* **stock m.** bolsa *f* or mercado *m* (de valores); **to play the stock m.** jugar a la bolsa

2 *vt (sell)* poner en venta, vender; *(launch)* lanzar al mercado; *(find outlet for)* dar salida a; *(promote)* promocionar

marketable ['mɑːkɪtəbəl] *adj* vendible, comerciable

marketing ['mɑːkɪtɪŋ] *n* marketing *m*, mercadotecnia *f* ❑ **m. campaign** campaña *f* de marketing *or* de publicidad; **m. department** departamento *m* de marketing; **m. director** director(a) *m,f* de marketing; **m. strategy** estrategia *f* comercial

marketplace ['mɑːkɪtpleɪs] *n (gen)* mercado *m*; *(square)* plaza *f*

marking ['mɑːkɪŋ] *n* **(a)** **markings** *(on animal)* marcas *fpl*, manchas *fpl*; *(on plane)* distintivo *m*; **m. ink** tinta *f* indeleble **(b)** *(of essay, exam)* corrección *f*; **I've got a lot of m. to do** tengo que corregir muchos exámenes

marksman ['mɑːksmən] *n (pl* **marksmen**) tirador *m*

marksmanship ['mɑːksmənʃɪp] *n* puntería *f*

mark-up ['mɑːkʌp] *n Com (increase)* subida *f*, aumento *m*; *(profit margin)* margen *m* comercial *or* de beneficio

marmalade ['mɑːməleɪd] *n* mermelada *f* (de cítricos)

maroon [mə'ruːn] **1** *n (color)* granate *m*

2 *adj* (de color) granate

marooned [mə'ruːnd] *adj* abandonado(a), bloqueado(a); **m. by the snow** bloqueado(a) por la nieve

marquee [mɑː'kiː] *n Br (tent)* carpa *f*, *US (of building)* marquesina *f*

marquess ['mɑːkwɪs] *n n* marqués *m*

marquetry ['mɑːkɪtrɪ] *n* marquetería *f*, taracea *f*

marquis ['mɑːkwɪs] *n* marqués *m*

marriage ['mærɪdʒ] *n (state, institution)* matrimonio *m*; *(wedding)* boda *f*, *RP* casamiento *m*, enlace *m* matrimonial, *Andes* matrimonio *m*; **an uncle by m.** un tío político ❑ **m. bureau** agencia *f* matrimonial; **m. certificate** certificado *m* de matrimonio; **m. of convenience** matrimonio *m* de conveniencia

marriageable ['mærɪdʒəbəl] *adj* casadero(a), en edad de casarse

married ['mærɪd] *adj (person, status)* casado(a); **to be m.** estar *or Am* ser casado(a) **(to con)**; **to get m.** casarse **(to con)** ❑ **m. life** vida *f* matrimonial *or* conyugal; **m. name** *(of woman)* apellido *m* de casada

marrow ['mærəʊ] *n* **(a)** *Anat (bone)* **m.** médula *f*, tuétano *m*; *Fig* meollo *m*; *Fig* **to be frozen to the m.** estar helado(a) hasta los tuétanos **(b)** *Br (vegetable)* = especie de calabacín de gran tamaño

marrowbone ['mærəʊbəʊn] *n Culin* caña *f* de vaca

marrowfat pea ['mærəʊfæt'piː] *n* = tipo de *Esp* guisante *or Am* arveja grande

marry ['mærɪ] *vt (pt & pp* **married**) *(take in marriage)* casarse con; *(give in marriage)* casar **(to con)**; *(unite in marriage)* casar; *Fig* **to m. (up)** unir

marry into *vi* emparentar vía matrimonio; **to m. into a wealthy family** emparentarse con una familia adinerada

marry off *vt* casar a; **to m. off one's daughters** casar a sus hijas

Mars [mɑːz] *n Astrol Astron Myth* Marte *m*

Marseilles [mɑː'seɪ] *n* Marsella *f*

marsh [mɑːʃ] *n (bog)* pantano *m* ❏ **salt m.** marisma *f*

marshal ['mɑːʃəl] **1** *n* **(a)** *Mil* mariscal *m* **(b)** *Br (at sports event, demonstration)* oficial *mf* **(c)** *US (sheriff)* sherif *m*, alguacil *m* **(d)** *US (of police department)* jefe *m* de policía; *(of fire department)* jefe *m* de bomberos

2 *vt (pt & pp* **marshalled,** *US* **marshaled) (a)** *Mil* formar **(b)** *(facts, arguments etc)* ordenar, poner en orden

marshland ['mɑːʃlənd] *n* tierra *f* pantanosa, pantanal *m*

marshmallow [mɑːʃ'mæləʊ] *n* **(a)** *Bot* malvavisco *m* **(b)** *(sweet)* esponja *f*, bombón *m* de merengue blando

marshy ['mɑːʃɪ] *adj* **(marshier, marshiest)** pantanoso(a)

marsupial [mɑː'suːpɪəl] *adj & n Zool* marsupial *(m)*

martial ['mɑːʃəl] *adj* marcial ❏ **m. arts** artes *fpl* marciales; **m. law** ley *f* marcial

Martian ['mɑːʃən] *adj & n* marciano(a) *(m,f)*

martin ['mɑːtɪn] *n Orn* avión *m*

Martini® [mɑː'tiːnɪ] *n* vermut *m*, Martini® *m*

Martinique [mɑːtɪ'niːk] *n* La Martinica

martyr ['mɑːtər] **1** *n* mártir *mf*; *Fig* **to make a m. of oneself** dárselas de mártir
2 *vt* martirizar

martyrdom ['mɑːtədəm] *n* martirio *m*

marvel ['mɑːvəl] **1** *n* maravilla *f*; *Fig* **it's a m. he survived** es un milagro que sobreviviera
2 *vi* **to m. at** maravillarse, asombrarse
3 *vt (pt & pp* **marvelled,** *US* **marveled) to m. that ...** maravillarse que ... + *subj*; **I m. at the fact that he can work so much** me sorprende *or* maravilla que pueda trabajar tanto

marvellous, *US* **marvelous** ['mɑːvələs] *adj* maravilloso(a), estupendo(a); **how m.!** ¡qué bien!, ¡fantástico!

Marxism ['mɑːksɪzəm] *n Pol* marxismo *m*

Marxist ['mɑːksɪst] *adj & n Pol* marxista *(mf)*

marzipan ['mɑːzɪpæn] *n Culin* mazapán *m*, pasta *f* de almendras

mascara [mæ'skɑːrə] *n* rímel *m*

mascot ['mæskət] *n* mascota *f*

masculine ['mæskjʊlɪn] **1** *adj (man)* masculino(a); *(woman)* hombruna
2 *n Ling* (género *m*) masculino *m*

masculinity [mæskjʊ'lɪnɪtɪ] *n* masculinidad *f*

mash [mæʃ] **1** *n* **(a)** *Fam Culin* puré *m* de *Esp* patatas *or Am* papas **(b)** *(for poultry, cattle etc)* afrecho *m*
2 *vt* **to m. (up)** *(crush)* triturar, machacar; *Culin* hacer un puré de; **mashed potatoes** puré *m* de *Esp* patatas *or Am* papas

mask [mɑːsk] **1** *n (gen)* máscara *f*; *(disguise)* máscara *f*, careta *f*; *(face pack)* mascarilla *f*
2 *vt (face)* enmascarar; *Fig (conceal)* encubrir, ocultar **(from** de)

masked [mɑːskt] *adj* enmascarado(a) ❏ **m. ball** baile *m* de máscaras

masking tape ['mɑːskɪŋteɪp] *n* cinta *f* adhesiva

masochism ['mæsəkɪzəm] *n* masoquismo *m*

masochist ['mæsəkɪst] *adj & n* masoquista *(mf)*

masochistic [mæsə'kɪstɪk] *adj* masoquista

mason ['meɪsən] *n* **(a)** *(builder)* albañil *m* **(b)** *(freemason)* masón *m*, francmasón *m*

masonic [mə'sɒnɪk] *adj* masónico(a)

masonry ['meɪsənrɪ] *n (stonework)* albañilería *f*, construcción *f*

masquerade [mæskə'reɪd] **1** *n (pretence)* farsa *f*, mascarada *f*, falacia *f*

2 *vi* disfrazarse; **to m. as a policeman** disfrazarse de *or* hacerse pasar por policía

mass¹ [mæs] *n Rel* misa *f*; **to hear m.** oír misa; **to say m.** decir misa ❏ **Low M.** misa *f* rezada; **Midnight M.** misa *f* del gallo; **Requiem M.** misa *f* de réquiem *or* difuntos

mass² [mæs] **1** *n* **(a)** *(gen)* masa *f*; **atomic m.** masa atómica **(b)** *(large quantity)* montón *m*; *(of people)* multitud *f*; **masses of clothes** montones de ropa; **the m. of people** la mayoría de gente ❏ *US* **m. transit** transporte *m* colectivo *or* público **(c) the masses** la masa, la gente en general
2 *adj* masivo(a), multitudinario(a); **a m. protest** una protesta multitudinaria ❏ **m. grave** fosa *f* común; **m. hysteria** histeria *f* colectiva; **m. media** medios *mpl* de comunicación (de masas); **m. production** fabricación *f* en serie
3 *vi (crowd)* congregarse, reunirse en gran número; *Mil (troops)* concentrarse; *(clouds)* amontonarse

massacre ['mæsəkər] **1** *n* masacre *f*, matanza *f*, carnicería *f*
2 *vt* asesinar en masa, masacrar

massage ['mæsɑːʒ, mæ'sɑːdʒ] **1** *n* masaje *m*
2 *vt* **(a)** *(body, scalp)* dar un masaje a **(b)** *Fig (figures, facts)* maquillar

masseur [mæ'sɜːr] *n* masajista *m*

masseuse [mæ'sɜːz] *n* masajista *f*

massive ['mæsɪv] *adj* **(a)** *(solid, weighty)* macizo(a), sólido(a) **(b)** *(huge)* enorme, descomunal; **a m. majority** una mayoría aplastante **(c)** *(imposing)* imponente

mass-produce [mæsprə'djuːs] *vt* fabricar en serie

mast [mɑːst] *n* **(a)** *Naut* mástil *m*, palo *m* **(b)** *Rad TV* torre *f*, poste *m*

mastectomy [mæ'stektəmɪ] *n Med* mastectomía *f*

master ['mɑːstər] **1** *n* **(a)** *(of dog, servant)* amo *m*; *(of household)* señor *m*; *(owner)* dueño *m*; **the m. of the house** el señor de la casa; *Fig* **to be m. of the situation** dominar la situación; *Fig* **to be one's own m.** ser dueño de sí mismo ❏ *Comptr* **m. file** archivo *m* maestro; **m. of ceremonies** maestro *m* de ceremonias **(b)** *Naut (of ship)* capitán *m*; *(of fishing boat)* patrón *m* **(c)** *Br (teacher)* maestro *m*, profesor *m*; **music m.** profesor de música **(d)** *Univ* **m.'s degree** licenciatura *f* con tesina **(e)** *(expert)* maestro *m* ❏ *Mus* **m. class** clase *f* magistral **(f)** *Old-fashioned* **the young m.** *(boy)* el señorito; **M. James Brown** *(as title)* el señor James Brown
2 *adj* **(a)** *(original)* original ❏ **m. copy** original *m*; **m. key** llave *f* maestra; **m. switch** interruptor *m* central **(b)** *(expert)* experto(a), maestro(a) ❏ **m. baker** maestro *m* panadero; **m. builder** maestro de obras
3 *vt* **(a)** *(control) (person, situation etc)* dominar; *(overcome)* superar, vencer **(b)** *(learn) (subject, skill)* llegar a dominar; *(craft)* llegar a ser experto en; **she will never m. the cello** no llegará nunca a dominar el violoncelo

masterful ['mɑːstəfʊl] *adj* **(a)** *(personality)* dominante; **he was so m.** tenía tal poderío **(b)** *(showing great skill)* magistral

masterly ['mɑːstəlɪ] *adj* magistral, genial; **in a m. way** con gran maestría, magistralmente

mastermind ['mɑːstəmaɪnd] **1** *n (person)* cerebro *m*, genio *m*
2 *vt (crime, operation)* dirigir, ser el cerebro de

masterpiece ['mɑːstəpiːs] *n* obra *f* maestra

masterstroke ['mɑːstəstrəʊk] *n* golpe *m* maestro

mastery ['mɑːstərɪ] *n* **(a)** *(control)* dominio *m* **(of** de); *(supremacy)* supremacía *f*, superioridad *f*; **to gain m. over** llegar a dominar **(b)** *(skill, expertise)* maestría *f*

masticate ['mæstɪkeɪt] *vt & vi* masticar

mastiff ['mæstɪf] *n (dog)* mastín *m*

mastitis [mæ'staɪtɪs] n Med mastitis f inv
masturbate ['mæstəbeɪt] **1** vt masturbar
  2 vi masturbarse
masturbation [mæstə'beɪʃən] n masturbación f
mat¹ [mæt] n **(a)** (rug) alfombrilla f; (doormat) felpudo m; (rush mat) estera f; (table mat) salvamanteles m inv; (drink mat) posavasos m inv; (under vase etc) tapete m; Sport colchoneta f **(b) a m. of hair** una mata de pelos
mat² [mæt] adj mate
match¹ [mætʃ] n fósforo m, Esp cerilla f, Am cerillo m; **box of matches** caja f de cerillas; **to strike a m.** encender una cerilla
match² [mætʃ] **1** n **(a)** Sport partido m, encuentro m; Box combate m; Ten match m ❏ **m. point** (in tennis) punto m de partido **(b)** (equal) igual mf; **he's no m. for his brother** no puede competir con su hermano; **she's more than a m. for you** te da cien vueltas; Fig **to meet one's m.** encontrar uno la horma de su zapato **(c)** (colours, clothes etc) **to be a good m.** hacer juego, armonizar; **the gloves are a good m. for the hat** los guantes hacen juego con el sombrero **(d)** (marriage) matrimonio m, casamiento m; **they are a good m.** hacen buena pareja
  2 vt **(a)** (equal, be the equal of) igualar; **there is nobody to m. him** no tiene par **(b)** (be in harmony with) (gen) armonizar; **they are well matched** (teams) van iguales or igualados; (couple) hacen buena pareja **(c)** (colours, clothes etc) hacer juego con, combinar con, casar con; (pair of socks, gloves) emparejar con, casar con; **the blouse does not m. the skirt** la blusa y la falda no hacen juego **(d)** (compare) equiparar; **to m. X with Y** equiparar X con Y **(e)** (confront) enfrentar; **to m. one team against another** enfrentar un equipo contra otro
  3 vi **(a)** (harmonize) hacer juego, estar a tono; **with handbag to m.** con (un) bolso a juego **(b) to m. up to** (equal) corresponder a; (live up to) estar a la altura de
matchbox ['mætʃbɒks] n caja f de Esp cerillas or Am cerillos
matching ['mætʃɪŋ] adj (jacket etc) que hace juego
matchless ['mætʃlɪs] adj sin par, sin igual
matchmaker ['mætʃmeɪkər] n casamentero(a) m,f
matchstick ['mætʃstɪk] n Esp cerilla f, Am cerillo m; **m. man** or **figure** monigote m (dibujo hecho con palotes)
mate¹ [meɪt] **1** n **(a)** (school companion, fellow worker) compañero(a) m,f, camarada mf, colega mf; Br Austral Fam (friend) amigo(a) m,f, Esp colega mf Mér cuate mf; Fam **many thanks, m.!** ¡muchas gracias, macho! **(b)** Zool (male) macho m; (female) hembra f **(c)** (assistant) ayudante mf; aprendiz(iza) m,f; **plumber's m.** ayudante ór aprendiz de fontanero **(d)** Naut piloto m; **first/second m.** primer/segundo oficial m
  2 vt Zool acoplar, aparear
  3 vi Zool acoplarse, aparearse
mate² [meɪt] Chess **1** n mate m
  2 vt dar jaque mate a
material [mə'tɪəriəl] **1** n **(a)** (substance) materia f; Fig **he's artist m.** tiene madera de artista **(b)** (cloth) tejido m, tela f **(c)** (ideas, information) material m, datos mpl, documentación f; **teaching m.** material (para usar en clase) **(d) materials** (ingredients, equipment) material msing, materiales mpl; **building m.** materiales para la construcción
  2 adj **(a)** (important, significant) importante, substancial; Jur **m. evidence** prueba f substancial or pertinente **(b)** (physical) material; **m. world** mundo m material
materialism [mə'tɪəriəlɪzəm] n materialismo m
materialist [mə'tɪəriəlɪst] adj & n materialista (mf)
materialistic [mətɪəriə'lɪstɪk] adj materialista
materialize [mə'tɪəriəlaɪz] vi **(a)** (hopes) realizarse,

hacerse realidad; (plan, idea) concretarse, tomar forma **(b)** (appear, show up) aparecer, presentarse
materially [mə'tɪəriəli] adv **(a)** (physically) materialmente **(b)** (essentially) esencialmente, en esencia **(c)** (noticeably) sensiblemente; (significantly) considerablemente
maternal [mə'tɜːnəl] adj (motherly) maternal; (uncle etc) materno(a)
maternity [mə'tɜːnɪti] n maternidad f ❏ **m. benefit** subsidio m por maternidad; **m. dress** vestido m premamá; **m. hospital** maternidad f; **m. leave** baja f por maternidad; **m. ward** pabellón m de maternidad
matey ['meɪti] adj (matier, matiest) Br Fam (person) simpático(a), bonachón(ona)
math [mæθ] n US matemáticas fpl
mathematical [mæθə'mætɪkəl] adj matemático(a); **to have a m. brain** estar dotado(a) para las matemáticas
mathematician [mæθəmə'tɪʃən] n matemático(a) m,f
mathematics [mæθə'mætɪks] n matemáticas fpl
maths [mæθs] n Br Fam mates fpl, matemáticas fpl
matinée ['mætɪneɪ] n Cin sesión f de tarde; Theat función f de tarde
mating ['meɪtɪŋ] n Zool acoplamiento m, apareamiento m ❏ **m. call** reclamo m; **m. season** época f de celo
matins ['mætɪnz] npl Rel maitines mpl
matriarch ['meɪtrɪɑːk] n matriarca f
matriarchal [meɪtrɪ'ɑːkəl] adj matriarcal
matriarchy ['meɪtrɪɑːki] n matriarcado m
matrices ['meɪtrɪsiːz] npl see matrix
matricide ['mætrɪsaɪd] n (act) matricidio m
matriculate [mə'trɪkjʊleɪt] Univ **1** vt matricular
  2 vi matricularse
matriculation [mətrɪkjʊ'leɪʃən] n Univ matrícula f, matriculación f; (entrance exam) examen m de selectividad
matrimonial [mætrɪ'məʊnɪəl] adj matrimonial
matrimony ['mætrɪməni] n (ceremony, sacrament) matrimonio m; (married life) vida f conyugal
matrix ['meɪtrɪks] n (pl matrixes or matrices) matriz f
matron ['meɪtrən] n **(a)** (in hospital) enfermera f jefe or jefa **(b)** (in school) ama f de llaves **(c)** (older married woman) matrona f
matronly ['meɪtrənli] adj matronil
matt [mæt] adj (colour, surface) mate
matted ['mætɪd] adj enmarañado(a)
matter ['mætər] **1** n **(a)** (substance) materia f, sustancia f ❏ **grey m.** materia f gris; **printed m.** impresos mpl; **reading m.** lecturas fpl, material m de lectura **(b)** Med (pus) pus m **(c)** (content) contenido m; **subject m.** tema m **(d)** (affair, question) asunto m, cuestión f; **as a m. of course** por rutina; **as a m. of fact** en realidad; **as matters stand** tal y como están las cosas; **business matters** negocios mpl; **it's a m. of five minutes** es cuestión or cosa de cinco minutos; **it's no laughing m.** no es cosa de risa; **that's another m.** eso es otra cosa; **to make matters worse** para colmo de desgracias **(e)** (problem, difficulty) problema m; **there's something the m.** pasa algo; **there's something the m. with my foot** me pasa algo en el pie; **there's nothing the m. with him** no le pasa nada; **what's the m.?** ¿qué pasa?, ¿qué ocurre?; **what's the m. with her?** ¿qué le pasa? **(f)** (importance) **no m.!** ¡no importa!; **no m. what he does** haga lo que haga; **no m. when** no importa cuando; **no m. where you go** dondequiera que vayas; **no m. how clever he is** por muy inteligente que sea; **no m. how much you work** por mucho que trabajes; **no m. how** como sea
  2 vi (be important) importar; **it doesn't m.** no importa, da igual; **what does it m.?** ¿y qué?

matter-of-fact ['mætərəvfækt] adj (person) práctico(a), realista; (account) realista; (style) prosaico(a); (voice) impersonal

matting ['mætɪŋ] n estera f

mattress ['mætrɪs] n colchón f

mature [mə'tʃʊər] **1** adj maduro(a); Fin vencido(a)
  2 vi madurar; Fin vencer
  3 vt madurar

maturity [mə'tʃʊərɪtɪ] n madurez f

maudlin ['mɔːdlɪn] adj (sentimental) sensiblero(a); (tearful) llorón(ona)

maul [mɔːl] vt (a) (wound) herir, agredir; **he was mauled by a lion** fue agredido por un león (b) (handle roughly) maltratar (c) Fig (criticize) vapulear

maundy ['mɔːndɪ] n Rel **M. Thursday** Jueves m Santo

Mauritius [mə'rɪʃəs] n Mauricio

mausoleum [mɔːsə'lɪəm] n mausoleo m

mauve [məʊv] adj & n (colour) malva (m)

maverick ['mævərɪk] adj & n (person) inconformista (mf); Pol disidente (mf)

mawkish ['mɔːkɪʃ] adj sensiblero(a), empalagoso(a)

max [mæks] (abbr **maximum**) máximo m, max.

maxim ['mæksɪm] n máxima f

maximize ['mæksɪmaɪz] vt llevar al máximo, maximizar

maximum ['mæksɪməm] **1** n (pl **maximums** or **maxima** ['mæksɪmə]) máximo m, máximum m; **as a m.** como máximo; **to the m.** al máximo
  2 adj máximo(a); **m. speed** velocidad f máxima

May [meɪ] n mayo m; **at the beginning/end of M.** a principios/finales de mayo; **during M.** durante el mes de mayo; **each** or **every M.** todos los años en mayo; **in M.** en mayo; **in the middle of M.** a mediados de mayo; **last/next M.** en mayo del año pasado/del año que viene; **(on) the first/sixteenth of M.** el primero/dieciséis de mayo; **she was born on 16th M. 1964** nació el 16 de mayo de 1964 ❑ **M. Day** el Primero or el Uno de Mayo

may¹ [meɪ] v aux (pt **might**) (a) (possibility, probability) poder, ser posible; **be that as it m.** sea como sea; **come what m.** pase lo que pase; **he m.** or **might come** puede que venga, es posible que venga, a lo mejor viene; **he m.** or **might have forgotten** puede que se haya olvidado; **I m.** or **might be wrong** quizás esté equivocado(a); **I'm afraid you m.** or **might be late** me temo que llegarás tarde; **you m.** or **might as well stay** más vale que te quedes; **you might have said something (to me)!** ¡habérmelo dicho!; **work as she might** por mucho que trabajara (b) (permission) poder; **if I m.** si me lo permite; **m. I?** ¿me permite?; **m. I come in?** ¿se puede (entrar or pasar)?; **m. we go now?** ¿podemos irnos ya?; **you m. smoke** pueden fumar (c) (wish) ojalá (+ subj); **m. you always be happy!** ¡ojalá seas siempre feliz!, ¡que siempre seas feliz!; **we hoped it might last** esperábamos que durase

may² [meɪ] n Bot (a) (blossom) flor f de espino (b) (tree) espino m

Maya ['maɪə], **Mayan** ['maɪən] adj & n maya (mf)

maybe ['meɪbiː] adv quizá, quizás, tal vez; **m. she'll phone today** quizá or quizás or tal vez llame hoy, a lo mejor llama hoy

Mayday ['meɪdeɪ] n Av Naut señal f de socorro, SOS m

mayfly ['meɪflaɪ] n Ent cachipolla f, efímera f

mayhem ['meɪhem] n (disturbance) alboroto m, bullicio m; (havoc) estragos mpl

mayonnaise [meɪə'neɪz] n Culin mayonesa f, mahonesa f

mayor [meər] n (man) alcalde m; (woman) alcaldesa f

mayoress ['meərɪs] n alcaldesa f

maypole ['meɪpəʊl] n mayo m

maze [meɪz] n laberinto m

MB [em'biː] n (abbr **Bachelor of Medicine**) licenciado(a) m,f en Medicina, Lic. en Med.

MBA [embiː'eɪ] n Univ (abbr **Master of Business Administration**) máster m en administración de empresas

MBO [embiː'əʊ] n Com (pl **MBOs**) (abbr **management buyout**) = adquisición de una empresa por sus directivos

MC [em'siː] n (abbr **Master of Ceremonies**) maestro m de ceremonias

MD [em'diː] n (a) (abbr **Doctor of Medicine**) doctor(a) m,f en Medicina, Dr. en Medicina (b) Fam (abbr **Managing Director**) director(a) m,f gerente

ME [em'iː] n Med (abbr **myalgic encephalomyelitis**) encefalomielitis f inv miálgica

me¹ [miː] pron (a) (as object) me; **he gave it to me, he gave me it** me lo dio; **listen to me** escúchame; **she knows me** me conoce (b) (after prep) mí; **it's for me** es para mí; **with me** conmigo (c) (emphatic) yo; **it's me** soy yo; **it's me, Alyson** soy Alyson; **what about me?** ¿y yo, qué?

me² [miː] n Mus mi m

meadow ['medəʊ] n prado m, pradera f

meagre, US **meager** ['miːgər] adj escaso(a), exiguo(a)

meal¹ [miːl] n (flour) harina f

meal² [miːl] n (food) comida f; **to have a m.** comer; Fam Fig **to make a m. of sth** recrearse en algo ❑ US **m. ticket** vale m de comida

mealtime ['miːltaɪm] n hora f de comer

mealy ['miːlɪ] adj (**mealier, mealiest**) (floury) harinoso(a)

mealy-mouthed [miːlɪ'maʊðd] adj Pej evasivo(a), embustero(a); **stop being m.-m. about it!** ¡déjate ya de rodeos!

mean¹ [miːn] vt (pt & pp **meant**) (a) (signify) significar, querer decir; **'casa' means 'house'** 'casa' significa 'house'; **that name means nothing to me** ese nombre no me suena; **this clock means a lot to me** este reloj significa mucho para mí; **what does 'gullible' m.?** ¿qué quiere decir 'gullible'?; **what do you m. by that?** ¿qué quieres decir con eso? (b) (intend) pensar, tener la intención de; (wish) querer; **he meant to do it tomorrow** tenía pensado hacerlo mañana; **I m. it** (te) lo digo en serio; **she didn't m. to do it** lo hizo sin querer; **she was meant to arrive on the 7th** tenía que or debía llegar el día 7; **they m. well** tienen buenas intenciones; **to m. business** hablar or actuar en serio (c) (involve, entail) suponer, implicar; **it means an outlay of $500** supone una inversión de 500 dólares (d) (refer to) referirse a; **do you m. me?** ¿te refieres a mí? (e) (destine) destinar (**for** a, para); **his remarks were meant for your mother** sus observaciones iban dirigidas a tu madre; **they are meant for each other** están hechos el uno para el otro

mean² [miːn] adj (**meaner, meanest**) (a) (miserly) tacaño(a), agarrado(a); **to be m. with one's money** mirar mucho por su dinero (b) (unkind) malo(a); (petty) mezquino(a); US (bad-tempered) malhumorado(a); **a m. trick** una mala pasada or jugada; **don't be so m.!** ¡no seas tan malo!; **to be m. to sb** tratar mal a algn (c) (inferior) pobre, mediocre; (origins) humilde, pobre (d) **no m.** (difficult) (achievement) difícil, hazañoso(a); (excellent) de primera; **it was no m. feat** fue toda una hazaña; **she's no m. photographer** es una excelente fotógrafa, es una fotógrafa de primera (e) US Fam (good) genial, Esp guay, Am salvo RP chévere, Méx padre, RP macanudo(a); **he plays a m. game of pool** juega al billar de vicio

mean³ [miːn] **1** adj (average) medio(a); **m. temperature** temperatura f media
  2 n (a) (average) promedio m; Math media f (b) (middle term) término m medio

meander [mɪ'ændər] **1** *vi (river)* serpentear; *(person)* vagar, andar sin rumbo fijo; *Fig (digress)* divagar
2 meandro *m*

meanderings [mɪ'ændərɪŋz] *npl Fig (digressions)* divagaciones *fpl*

meaning [ˈmiːnɪŋ] *n* **(a)** *(sense of word etc)* sentido *m*, significado *m*; *(in dictionary)* acepción *f*; **double m.** doble sentido; **what is the m. of 'gazump'?** ¿qué significa 'gazump'?, ¿qué quiere decir 'gazump'?; **what's the m. of this?** y esto, ¿qué quiere decir?; *Fam* **do you get my m.?** ¿entiendes lo que te quiero decir? **(b)** *Fig* sentido *m*; **a world without m.** un mundo sin sentido

meaningful [ˈmiːnɪŋfʊl] *adj* significativo(a)

meaningless [ˈmiːnɪŋlɪs] *adj (devoid of sense)* sin sentido, que carece de sentido; *(absurd)* absurdo(a)

meanness [ˈmiːnnɪs] *n* **(a)** *(miserliness)* tacañería *f*, mezquindad *f* **(b)** *(nastiness)* mezquindad *f*, maldad *f*

means [miːnz] *n* **(a)** *sing or pl (method)* medio *m*, manera *f*; **a m. of transport** un medio de transporte; **by fair m. or foul** por las buenas o por las malas; **by m. of** por medio de, mediante; **the end does not justify the m.** el fin no justifica los medios **(b)** *pl (resources, wealth)* medios *mpl* (de vida), recursos *mpl* (económicos); **a woman of m.** una mujer acaudalada; **to live beyond one's m.** vivir por encima de sus posibilidades ❑ **m. test** comprobación *f* de medios de vida **(c)** **by all m.!** ¡por supuesto!, ¡naturalmente!; **by all m. telephone him** no dejes de llamarle; **by no m.** de ningún modo, de ninguna manera; **by any m.** de cualquier modo

mean-spirited [ˈmiːnˈspɪrɪtɪd] *adj* malintencionado(a)

meant [ment] *pt & pp see* **mean**[1]

meantime [ˈmiːntaɪm] **1** *adv* mientras tanto, entretanto
2 *n* **in the m.** mientras tanto

meanwhile [ˈmiːnwaɪl] *adv* mientras tanto, entretanto

measles [ˈmiːzəlz] *n Med* sarampión *m* ❑ **German m.** rubeola *f*

measly [ˈmiːzlɪ] *adj* **(measlier, measliest)** *Fam* miserable, mezquino(a)

measurable [ˈmeʒərəbəl] *adj* mensurable, medible

measure [ˈmeʒər] **1** *n* **(a)** *(system)* medida *f*; **liquid m.** medida para líquidos; **square/cubic m.** medida de superficie/de volumen **(b)** *(ruler)* regla *f*; metro *m* ❑ **tape m.** cinta *f* métrica, metro *m* **(c)** *(measured amount)* medida *f*; **to give full m.** dar la medida exacta; *Fig* **for good m.** para estar seguro(a) **(d)** *(degree, extent)* **in some m.** hasta cierto punto; **she had a m. of success** tuvo cierto éxito **(e)** *Mus* compás *m*, ritmo *m* **(f)** *(step, remedy)* medida *f*; **safety measures** medidas de seguridad
2 *vt (object, area)* medir; *(person)* tomar las medidas de

measure off *vt (area)* medir

measure up *vi* **to m. (up) (to sth)** estar a la altura (de algo); **he didn't m. up** no estuvo a la altura de las circunstancias

measured [ˈmeʒəd] *adj (step)* estudiado(a); *(tone)* mesurado(a); *(statement)* prudente, circunspecto(a); *(language)* moderado(a), comedido(a)

measurement [ˈmeʒəmənt] *n* **(a)** *(act of measuring)* medición *f* **(b)** *(length etc)* medida *f*; **to take sb's measurements** tomarle las medidas a algn

measuring [ˈmeʒərɪŋ] *n* medición *f* ❑ **m. tape** cinta *f* métrica, metro *m*

meat [miːt] *n* **(a)** *(food)* carne *f*; **cold m.** fiambre *m*; *Fig* **it is m. and drink to them** es lo que más les gusta ❑ **m. loaf** = pastel de carne picada horneado en un molde; *Culin* **m. pie** empanada *f* de carne **(b)** *Fig* esencia *f*, jugo *m*

meatball [ˈmiːtbɔːl] *n Culin* albóndiga *f*

meaty [ˈmiːtɪ] *adj* **(meatier, meatiest)** **(a)** *(fleshy)* carnoso(a); **m. smell** olor *m* a carne **(b)** *Fig (story)* jugoso(a), sustancioso(a)

Mecca [ˈmekə] *n* la Meca

mechanic [mɪˈkænɪk] *n (person)* mecánico(a) *m,f*

mechanical [mɪˈkænɪkəl] *adj (device, process, failure)* mecánico(a); *Fig (behaviour)* mecánico(a), maquinal ❑ **m. engineer** ingeniero(a) *m,f* mecánico(a) *or* industrial; **m. engineering** ingeniería *f* industrial

mechanics [mɪˈkænɪks] *n* **(a)** *sing (science)* mecánica *f* **(b)** *pl (technical aspects)* mecanismo *m sing*; *Fig* **the m. of politics** los mecanismos de la política

mechanism [ˈmekənɪzəm] *n* mecanismo *m*

mechanization [mekənaɪˈzeɪʃən] *n* mecanización *f*

mechanize [ˈmekənaɪz] *vt* mecanizar

MEd [emˈed] *n (abbr* **Master of Education)** *(title)* máster *m* en Pedagogía

medal [ˈmedəl] *n* medalla *f*; **gold/silver/bronze m.** medalla de oro/plata/bronce

medallion [mɪˈdæljən] *n* medallón *m*

medallist, *US* **medalist** [ˈmedəlɪst] *n Sport* medalla *f*, campeón *m*; **he was the 1988 Olympic gold m.** fue medalla de oro en los juegos olímpicos de 1988

meddle [ˈmedəl] *vi* entrometerse **(in** en); **to m. with sth** manosear algo

meddler [ˈmedlər] *n* entrometido(a) *m,f*

meddlesome [ˈmedəlsəm] *adj*, **meddling** [ˈmedəlɪŋ] *adj* entrometido(a)

media [ˈmiːdɪə] *npl* medios *mpl* de comunicación ❑ **m. coverage** cobertura *f* periodística; **m. man** periodista *m*; *Univ* **m. studies** ciencias *fpl* de la información, periodismo *m*

median [ˈmiːdɪən] **1** *adj* mediano(a)
2 *n Geom (line)* mediana *f*; *(quantity)* valor *m* mediano

mediate [ˈmiːdɪeɪt] *vi* mediar **(between** entre; **in** en)

mediation [miːdɪˈeɪʃən] *n* mediación *f*

mediator [ˈmiːdɪeɪtər] *n* mediador(a) *m,f*

medic [ˈmedɪk] *n Fam (doctor)* médico(a) *m,f*; *Univ* estudiante *mf* de medicina

Medicaid [ˈmedɪkeɪd] *n (in US)* = seguro médico estatal para personas con renta baja

medical [ˈmedɪkəl] **1** *adj (treatment, profession)* médico(a); *(book, student)* de medicina ❑ **m. advice** consejo *m* médico; **m. examination** reconocimiento *m* médico; *US* **m. examiner** médico(a) *m,f* forense; **m. insurance** seguro *m* médico *or* de enfermedad; **m. practitioner** médico(a) *m,f*; *Univ* **m. school** Facultad *f* de Medicina
2 *n* reconocimiento *m* médico

Medicare [ˈmedɪkeər] *n (in US)* = seguro médico para ancianos y algunos discapacitados

medicated [ˈmedɪkeɪtɪd] *adj (shampoo etc)* medicinal

medication [medɪˈkeɪʃən] *n* medicación *f*

medicinal [meˈdɪsɪnəl] *adj* medicinal

medicine [ˈmedsɪn, ˈmedɪsɪn] *n* **(a)** *(science)* medicina *f* **(b)** *(drugs etc)* medicina *f*, medicamento *m*; *Fig* **to give sb a taste of his own m.** pagar a algn con la misma moneda ❑ **m. chest** botiquín *m*

medieval [medɪˈiːvəl] *adj* medieval

mediocre [miːdɪˈəʊkər] *adj* mediocre

mediocrity [miːdɪˈɒkrɪtɪ] *n* mediocridad *f*

meditate [ˈmedɪteɪt] **1** *vi* meditar, reflexionar **(on** sobre)
2 *vt* meditar

meditation [medɪˈteɪʃən] *n* meditación *f*

meditative [ˈmedɪtətɪv] *adj* meditabundo(a), meditativo(a)

Mediterranean [medɪtə'reɪnɪən] **1** *adj* mediterráneo(a)
2 *n* **the M.** el Mediterráneo

medium ['miːdɪəm] **1** *adj (average)* mediano(a), regular;
of m. height de estatura mediana ❑ *Br Rad* **m. wave** onda
f media
2 *n (pl* **media**) **(a)** *(means)* medio *m; (to express ideas etc)*
medio de expresión; **the media** los medios de
comunicación; **through the m. of** por medio de **(b)**
(environment) medio *m* ambiente **(c) to strike a happy m.**
hallar el punto justo **(d)** *(pl* **mediums**) *(spiritualist)* médium
mf

medium-dry [miːdɪəm'draɪ] *adj (wines)* semiseco(a)

medium-range ['miːdɪəm'reɪndʃ] *adj (missile)* de
medio alcance; *(forecast)* a medio plazo

medium-sized [miːdɪəm'saɪzd] *adj* de tamaño mediano

medium-term ['miːdɪəm'tɜːm] *adj* a medio plazo

medlar ['medlər] *n Bot* níspero *m*

medley ['medlɪ] *n* **(a)** *(miscellany)* miscelánea *f; (mixture)*
mezcla *f; (of articles)* surtido *m* **(b)** *Mus* popurrí *m*

meek [miːk] *adj (quiet, gentle)* manso(a), sumiso(a), dócil;
(humble) humilde; **to be m. and mild** ser un corderito

meekness ['miːknɪs] *n (quietness, gentleness)* mansedumbre *f*, docilidad *f; (humility)* humildad *f*

meet [miːt] **1** *vt (pt & pp* met) **(a)** *(person) (by chance)*
encontrar, encontrarse con; *(by arrangement)* reunirse con,
citarse; *(in formal meeting)* entrevistarse con; *(see)* ver; *(pass
in street etc)* cruzar *or* topar con; *Fig* **to m. sb halfway** llegar
a un acuerdo con algn **(b)** *(get to know)* conocer; **I'd like you
to m. my mother** quiero presentarle a mi madre; **pleased
to m. you!** ¡encantado(a) de conocerle!, ¡mucho gusto! **(c)**
(await arrival of) esperar; *(collect)* ir *or* venir a buscar;
(receive) recibir, ir a recibir; **she'll m. us at the airport** irá
a buscarnos al aeropuerto **(d)** *(bus, train etc)* tener conexión
con, empalmar **(e)** *(danger, difficulty)* encontrar; *(opponent)*
enfrentarse con; **to m. one's death** encontrar la muerte,
morir **(f)** *(satisfy)* satisfacer; *(obligations)* cumplir con;
(expenses) costear, hacer frente a, correr con; *(bill, debt)*
pagar; *(deficit)* cubrir **(g) to m. sb's eye** cruzarse las
miradas; *Fig* **there's more to this than meets the eye** es
más complicado de lo que parece
2 *vi* **(a)** *(people) (by chance)* encontrarse; *(by arrangement)*
verse, reunirse; *(formal meeting)* entrevistarse; **we've
arranged to m. tomorrow** hemos quedado en vernos
mañana; **until we m. again!** ¡hasta la vista!, ¡hasta luego!
(b) *(get to know each other)* conocerse; **they met at school**
se conocieron en la escuela **(c)** *Sport* enfrentarse **(d)** *(join)*
unirse; *(rivers)* confluir; *(roads, railway lines)* empalmar;
our eyes met nuestras miradas se cruzaron; *Fam* **to make
ends m.** llegar a fin de mes
3 *n* **(a)** *Sport* reunión *f* **(b)** *(hunting)* partida *f* de caza

meet up *vi Fam (by chance)* encontrar, encontrarse **(with**
con); *(by arrangement)* reunirse **(with** con)

meet with *vt* **(a)** *(difficulty, problem)* encontrar, tropezar
con; *(loss, accident)* sufrir; *(success)* tener; **she met with a
warm welcome** fue acogida calurosamente **(b)** *esp US
(person)* reunirse con

meeting ['miːtɪŋ] *n* **(a)** *(chance encounter)* encuentro *m;
(prearranged)* cita *f; (formal)* entrevista *f* **(b)** *(of club,
committee etc)* reunión *f; (of assembly)* sesión *f; (of
shareholders, creditors)* junta *f; Pol (rally)* mitin *m;* **to hold a
m.** celebrar una reunión *or* una sesión; **to open/close a m.**
abrir/levantar la sesión ❑ **annual general m.** junta *f*
general anual; **business m.** reunión *f* de negocios; *Educ*
staff m. claustro *m* **(c)** *Sport* encuentro *m* **(d)** *(of two rivers)*
confluencia *f*

meeting place ['miːtɪŋpleɪs] *n* lugar *m* de encuentro *or*
de reunión

megabucks ['megəbʌks] *npl Fam* una millonada, *Esp* un
pastón, *Méx* un chingo de dinero, *RP* una ponchada de
pesos

megabyte ['megəbaɪt] *n Comptr* megabyte *m*, mega-
octeto *m*

megahertz ['megəhɜːts] *n* megahercio *m*

megalith ['megəlɪθ] *n* megalito *m*

megalomania [megələʊ'meɪnɪə] *n* megolomanía *f*

megalomaniac [megələʊ'meɪnɪæk] *adj & n* megaló-
mano(a) *(m,f)*

megaphone ['megəfəʊn] *n* megáfono *m*, altavoz *m*

megastar ['megəstɑːr] *n Fam* superestrella *f*

megastore ['megəstɔːr] *n* macrotienda *f*

megaton ['megətʌn] *n* megatón *m*

megawatt ['megəwɒt] *n* megavatio *m*

megrim ['miːgrɪm] *n (fish)* gallo *m*

melamine ['meləmiːn] *n* melamina *f*

melancholic [melən'kɒlɪk] *adj* melancólico(a)

melancholy ['melənkəlɪ] **1** *n* melancolía *f*
2 *adj* melancólico(a)

melanin ['melənɪn] *n* melanina *f*

melanoma [melə'nəʊmə] *n Med* melanoma *m*

mêlée ['meleɪ] *n (of people)* tumulto *m*, gentío *m; (fight)*
pelea *f* confusa

mellifluous [me'lɪflʊəs] *adj* melifluo(a)

mellow ['meləʊ] **1** *adj (flavour)* delicado(a); *(wine)*
añejo(a); *(colour, voice)* suave; *(person)* apacible, tierno(a)
2 *vi (fruit)* madurar; *(colour, voice)* suavizarse; *(person)*
enternecerse, ablandarse; **he has mellowed with age** ha
madurado con los años

melodic [mɪ'lɒdɪk] *adj* melódico(a)

melodious [mɪ'ləʊdɪəs] *adj* melodioso(a)

melodrama ['melədrɑːmə] *n* melodrama *m*

melodramatic [melədrə'mætɪk] *adj* melodramático(a)

melody ['melədɪ] *n* melodía *f*

melon ['melən] *n (honeydew etc)* melón *m; (watermelon)*
sandía *f*

melt [melt] **1** *vt (snow)* derretir; *(metal)* fundir; *Fig (sb's
heart)* ablandar
2 *vi (snow)* derretirse; *(metal)* fundirse; *Fig* ablandarse; **it
melts in one's mouth** se derrite en la boca; **to m. into
tears** deshacerse en lágrimas

melt away *vi (snow)* derretirse; *Fig (money)* desaparecer;
Fig (confidence) desvanecerse, esfumarse

melt down *vt (metal)* fundir

meltdown ['meltdaʊn] *n Phys (process)* = fusión
accidental del núcleo de un reactor; *(leak)* fuga *f* radiactiva

melting ['meltɪŋ] *n* **(a)** *(of snow)* derretimiento *m; (of
metal)* fundición *f;* **m. point** punto *m* de fusión **(b) m. pot**
crisol *m; Fig* **it's in the m. pot** está por decidir

member ['membər] *n* **(a)** *(person)* miembro *mf, (of society)*
miembro *mf*, socio(a) *m,f; (of party, union)* miembro *mf*,
afiliado(a) *m,f;* **'members only'** 'sólo para socios' ❑ *Br* **M.
of Parliament** diputado(a) *m,f;* **m. of staff** empleado(a)
m,f; (teacher) profesor(a) *m,f* **(b)** *Anat* miembro *m* ❑ **male m.**
miembro *m* viril

membership ['membəʃɪp] *n* **(a)** *(state)* calidad *f* de socio
or miembro; *(entry)* ingreso *m; Pol* afiliación *f* ❑ **m. card**
carnet *m* de socio; **m. (fee)** cuota *f* de socio **(b)** *(members)*
socios *mpl*, miembros *mpl; (number of members)* número *m*
de socios *or* miembros; *Pol* **the active m.** la militancia;
what is the m.? ¿cuántos socios hay?

membrane ['membreɪn] *n* membrana *f;* **mucus m.**
membrana mucosa

memento [mə'mentəʊ] *n* (*pl* **mementos** *or* **mementoes**) recuerdo *m*, recordatorio *m*

memo ['meməʊ] *n* (*pl* **memos**) (**a**) *(official note)* memorándum *m* (**b**) *(personal note)* nota *f*, apunte *m* ❑ **m. pad** bloc *m* de notas

memoir ['memwɑːr] *n* *(essay)* memoria *f*; **memoirs** *(biography)* memorias *fpl*, autobiografía *f*

memorabilia [meməra'bɪlɪə] *npl (things)* recuerdos *mpl*

memorable ['memərəbəl] *adj* memorable

memorably ['memərəblɪ] *adv* **as Dante so m.** said como dicen las memorables palabras de Dante

memorandum [memə'rændəm] *n* (*pl* **memorandums** *or* **memoranda**) (**a**) *Pol Com* memorándum *m* (**b**) *(personal note)* nota *f*, apunte *m*

memorial [mɪ'mɔːrɪəl] **1** *adj (plaque etc)* conmemorativo(a)
2 *n* monumento *m* conmemorativo; **war m.** monumento a los Caídos ❑ *US* **M. Day** Día *m* de Conmemoración a los Caídos

memorize ['meməraɪz] *vt* memorizar, aprender de memoria

memory ['memərɪ] *n* (**a**) *(faculty, of computer)* memoria *f*; *Med* **loss of m.** amnesia *f*; **to have a good/bad m.** tener buena/mala memoria; **to play sth from m.** tocar algo de memoria (**b**) *(recollection)* recuerdo *m*; **childhood memories** recuerdos de la infancia; **in m. of** en memoria de

men [men] *npl see* **man**

menace ['menɪs] **1** *n* (**a**) *(threat)* amenaza *f*; *(danger)* peligro *m* (**b**) *Fam (nuisance) (thing)* lata *f*; *(person)* pesado(a) *m,f*
2 *vt* amenazar

menacing ['menɪsɪŋ] *adj* amenazador(a)

menagerie [mɪ'nædʒərɪ] *n* colección *f* de animales *(privada)*

mend [mend] **1** *vt* (**a**) *(repair)* reparar, arreglar; *(clothes)* remendar; *(socks etc)* zurcir (**b**) **to m. one's ways** *(reform)* enmendarse, reformarse
2 *vi (recover)* mejorarse, reponerse
3 *n (patch)* remiendo *m*; *(darn)* zurcido *m*; *Fig* **to be on the m.** estar *or* ir mejorando

mendacious [men'deɪʃəs] *adj Fml* mendaz, mentiroso(a)

mending ['mendɪŋ] *n* (**a**) *(repair)* reparación *f*, arreglo *m*; *(darning)* zurcido *m* (**b**) *(clothes for mending)* ropa *f* por remendar *or* zurcir

menfolk ['menfəʊk] *npl Fam* **the m.** los hombres

menial ['miːnɪəl] **1** *adj (task)* servil, bajo(a)
2 *n (servant)* criado(a) *m,f*

meningitis [menɪn'dʒaɪtɪs] *n Med* meningitis *f*

menopausal [menə'pɔːzəl] *adj* menopáusico(a)

menopause ['menəpɔːz] *n* menopausia *f*

menservants ['mensɜːvənts] *npl see* **manservant**

menstrual ['menstruəl] *adj* menstrual ❑ **m. cycle** ciclo *m* menstrual

menstruate ['menstrueɪt] *vi* menstruar

menstruation [menstru'eɪʃən] *n* menstruación *f*, regla *f*

menswear ['menzweər] *n Com* ropa *f* de caballero

mental ['mentəl] *adj* (**a**) *(of the mind)* mental ❑ **m. age** edad *f* mental; **m. arithmetic** cálculo *m* mental; **m. home, m. hospital** hospital *m* psiquiátrico; **m. illness** enfermedad *f* mental; **m. patient** enfermo(a) *m,f* mental; **m. strain** tensión *f* nerviosa (**b**) *Br Fam (mad)* pirado(a), *CSur* rayado(a)

mentality [men'tælɪtɪ] *n* mentalidad *f*

mentally ['mentəlɪ] *adv* mentalmente; **to be m.**

handicapped ser un(a) disminuido(a) psíquico(a); **to be m. ill** padecer una enfermedad mental

menthol ['menθɒl] **1** *n* mentol *m*
2 *adj (sweet)* de menta; *(cigarette)* mentolado(a)

mention ['menʃən] **1** *n* mención *f*
2 *vt* mencionar, hacer mención de, aludir a; *Jur (in will)* mencionar; **don't m. it!** ¡de nada!, ¡no hay de qué!, ¡no faltaba más!; **I need hardly m. that ...** huelga decir que ...

mentor ['mentɔːr] *n* mentor *m*

menu ['menjuː] *n* (**a**) *(card)* carta *f*; *(fixed meal)* menú *m*; **today's m.** menú del día (**b**) *Comptr* menú *m*

meow [mɪ'aʊ] **1** *n* maullido *m*, miau *m*
2 *vi* maullar

MEP [emiː'piː] *n Br (abbr* **Member of the European Parliament)** miembro *mf* del Parlamento Europeo

mercantile ['mɜːkəntaɪl] *adj* mercantil, comercial

mercenary ['mɜːsɪnərɪ] *adj & n* mercenario(a) *(m,f)*

merchandise ['mɜːtʃəndaɪz] *n* mercancías *fpl*, géneros *mpl*

merchandising ['mɜːtʃəndaɪzɪŋ] *n Com* artículos *mpl* de promoción *or* promocionales

merchant ['mɜːtʃənt] *n Com Fin (trader)* comerciante *mf*, negociante *mf*; *(retailer)* detallista *mf*, minorista *mf* ❑ **m. bank** banco *m* comercial; **m. insurance** seguro *m* médico *or* de enfermedad; *Br* **m. navy** marina *f* mercante

merciful ['mɜːsɪfʊl] *adj* misericordioso(a), clemente, compasivo(a) **(towards** con)

mercifully ['mɜːsɪfʊlɪ] *adv (showing mercy)* con compasión; *(fortunately)* afortunadamente

merciless ['mɜːsɪlɪs] *adj* despiadado(a), sin piedad

mercurial [mɜː'kjʊərɪəl] *adj (person, temperament)* voluble, volátil

Mercury ['mɜːkjʊrɪ] *n Myth Astron* Mercurio *m*

mercury ['mɜːkjʊrɪ] *n* mercurio *m*, azogue *m*

mercy ['mɜːsɪ] *n* (**a**) *(compassion)* misericordia *f*, clemencia *f*, compasión *f*; **to be at the m. of sth/sb** estar a la merced de algo/algn; **to beg for m.** pedir clemencia; **to have m. on sb** tener compasión de algn (**b**) *Fam (good fortune)* suerte *f*; **it's a m. that more people weren't injured** es una suerte que no hubiera más heridos ❑ **m. killing** eutanasia *f*

mere [mɪər] *adj* mero(a), simple, puro(a)

merely ['mɪəlɪ] *adv* simplemente, solamente

meretricious [merɪ'trɪʃəs] *adj Fml (flashy)* de oropel, de relumbrón; *(deceptive)* engañoso(a)

merge [mɜːdʒ] **1** *vt (blend)* unir, combinar **(with** con); *Com (firms)* fusionar; *Comptr (files)* fusionar, unir
2 *vi* unirse, combinarse; *Com (firms)* fusionarse; **to m. into the background** perderse de vista

merger ['mɜːdʒər] *n Com* fusión *f*

meridian [mə'rɪdɪən] *n Astron Geog* meridiano *m*

meringue [mə'ræŋ] *n Culin* merengue *m*

merit ['merɪt] **1** *n* (**a**) *(worth)* mérito *m* (**b**) *(advantage)* ventaja *f*, mérito *m*; **to look into the merits of sth** examinar los pros y los contras de algo
2 *vt (deserve)* merecer, *Am* ameritar; **the plan merits consideration** el plan es digno de consideración

meritocracy [merɪ'tɒkrəsɪ] *n* meritocracia *f*

meritorious [merɪ'tɔːrɪəs] *adj Fml* meritorio(a)

merlin ['mɜːlɪn] *n Orn* esmerejón *m*

mermaid ['mɜːmeɪd] *n* sirena *f*

merman ['mɜːmæn] *n (pl* **mermen** ['mɜːmen]) tritón *m*

merrily ['merɪlɪ] *adv* alegremente

merriment ['merɪmənt] *n* alegría *f*, regocijo *m*

merry ['merɪ] *adj* (**merrier, merriest**) *(happy)* alegre; *(amusing)* divertido(a), gracioso(a); *Fam (tipsy)* alegre, achispado(a); **m. Christmas!** ¡felices Navidades!; **the more the merrier** cuantos(as) más mejor

merry-go-round ['merɪgəʊraʊnd] *n* tiovivo *m*, *Esp* caballitos *mpl*, *RP* calesita *f*

merry-making ['merɪmeɪkɪŋ] *n (fun)* juerga *f*; *(party)* fiesta *f*

mesh [meʃ] **1** *n* (**a**) *Tex* malla *f*; *Fig* red *f* ❏ **wire m.** tela *f* metálica (**b**) *Tech* engranaje *m*
2 *vt Tech* engranar; *(fit)* encajar

mesmerize ['mezməraɪz] *vt* hipnotizar

mess [mes] **1** *n* (**a**) *(confusion)* confusión *f*; *(disorder)* desorden *m*; **the house is a m.** la casa está patas arriba; *Fig* **he's a complete m.** es un desastre (**b**) *(difficult situation, mix-up)* lío *m*, follón *m*; **to get into a m.** meterse en un lío *or* un aprieto; **to make a m. of one's life** fracasar en la vida; **what a m.!** ¡vaya lío!, ¡vaya follón! (**c**) *(dirt)* suciedad *f*; *Euph (faeces)* porquería *f*; **to make a m. of one's clothes** ensuciarse la ropa (**d**) *Mil (food)* rancho *m*, comida *f* (**e**) *Mil (room)* comedor *m*
2 *vt* **to m. one's pants** cagarse encima

mess about, mess around *Fam* **1** *vi* fastidiar
2 *vi* (**a**) *(act the fool)* hacer el primo (**b**) *(idle)* gandulear; *(kill time)* matar el rato; *(potter about)* entretenerse

mess about with *vt (fiddle with)* tocar, manosear; **to m. about with sb** *(have affair with)* tener un lío *or* estar liado(a) con algn

mess up *vt Fam (untidy)* desordenar, dejar en desorden; *(dirty)* ensuciar; *Fam (spoil)* estropear, echar a perder

message ['mesɪdʒ] *n* (**a**) *(communication)* recado *m*; **to leave a m.** dejar un recado *or Am* mensaje (**b**) *(of story, film, etc)* mensaje *m*; *Fam* **to get the m.** comprender

messaging ['mesədʒɪŋ] *n (by mobile phone)* mensajería *f*

messenger ['mesɪndʒər] *n* mensajero(a) *m,f* ❏ **m. boy** chico *m* de los recados

Messiah [mɪ'saɪə] *n* Mesías *m*

messianic [mesɪ'ænɪk] *adj* mesiánico(a)

Messrs ['mesəz] *npl Com (abbr* **Messieurs**) Señores *mpl*, Sres.

mess-up ['mesʌp] *n Fam* lío *m*, follón *m*

messy ['mesɪ] *adj* (**messier, messiest**) (**a**) *(untidy)* desordenado(a), en desorden (**b**) *(confused)* confuso(a); *(involved)* lioso(a), enredado(a) (**c**) *(dirty)* sucio(a)

met [met] *pt & pp see* **meet**

metabolic [metə'bɒlɪk] *adj* metabólico(a)

metabolism [me'tæbəlɪzəm] *n* metabolismo *m*

metabolize [me'tæbəlaɪz] *vt* metabolizar

metal ['metəl] **1** *n* (**a**) metal *m*; **sheet m.** lámina *f* de metal ❏ **m. detector** detector *m* de metales; **m. polish** limpiametales *m inv* (**b**) *(on road)* grava *f*
2 *adj* metálico(a), de metal

metallic [mɪ'tælɪk] *adj* metálico(a) ❏ **m. blue** *(colour)* azul *m* metalizado

metallurgist [me'tælədʒɪst] *n* metalúrgico(a) *m,f*

metallurgy [me'tælədʒɪ] *n* metalurgia *f*

metalwork ['metəlwɜːk] *n* (**a**) *(craft)* metalistería *f* (**b**) *(objects)* objetos *mpl* de metal

metamorphosis [metə'mɔːfəsɪs] *n (pl* **metamorphoses** [metə'mɔːfəsiːz]) metamorfosis *f*

metaphor ['metəfər, 'metəfɔːr] *n* metáfora *f*

metaphoric(al) [metə'fɒrɪk(əl)] *adj* metafórico(a)

metaphysical [metə'fɪzɪkəl] *adj* metafísico(a)

metaphysics [metə'fɪzɪks] *n* metafísica *f*

mete [miːt] *vt* **to m. out** *(justice, rewards)* repartir; *(punishment)* imponer

meteor ['miːtɪər] *n* bólido *m*

meteoric [miːtɪ'ɒrɪk] *adj* meteórico(a); *Fig* **his m. rise to fame** su meteórico ascenso a la fama

meteorite ['miːtɪəraɪt] *n* meteorito *m*, aerolito *m*

meteorological [miːtɪərə'lɒdʒɪkəl] *adj* meteorológico(a)

meteorologist [miːtɪə'rɒlədʒɪst] *n* meteorólogo(a) *m,f*

meteorology [miːtɪə'rɒlədʒɪ] *n* meteorología *f*

meter¹ ['miːtər] *n* contador *m* ❏ **gas/electricity m.** contador *m* de gas/electricidad; **parking m.** parquímetro *m*

meter² ['miːtər] *n US see* **metre**

methadone ['meθədəʊn] *n* metadona *f*

methane ['miːθeɪn] *n Chem* metano *m*

methinks [mi'θɪŋks] *adv Archaic & Hum* me parece a mí

method ['meθəd] *n (manner, way)* método *m*; *(technique)* técnica *f*; *Fam* **there's m. in her madness** es menos loca de lo que parece ❏ *Theat Cin* **m. acting** interpretación *f* según el método de Stanislavski

methodical [mɪ'θɒdɪkəl] *adj* metódico(a), ordenado(a)

Methodism ['meθədɪzəm] *n Rel* metodismo *m*

Methodist ['meθədɪst] *adj & n Rel* metodista *(mf)*

methodology [meθə'dɒlədʒɪ] *n* metodología *f*

meths [meθs] *n Br Fam* alcohol *m* de quemar

Methuselah [mə'θjuːzələ] *n* Matusalén *m*; *Hum* **as old as M.** más viejo(a) que Matusalén

methylated spirits [meθɪleɪtɪd'spɪrɪts] *n Br* alcohol *m* desnaturalizado *(con metanol)*, alcohol *m* de quemar

meticulous [mə'tɪkjʊləs] *adj* meticuloso(a), minucioso(a)

metre ['miːtər] *n* metro *m*; **cubic/square m.** metro cúbico/cuadrado

metric ['metrɪk] *adj* métrico(a) ❏ **m. ton** tonelada *f* métrica

metrication [metrɪ'keɪʃən] *n* adopción *f* del sistema métrico

metronome ['metrənəʊm] *n* metrónomo *m*

metropolis [mɪ'trɒpəlɪs] *n* metrópoli *f*

metropolitan [metrə'pɒlɪtən] *adj* metropolitano(a)

mettle ['metəl] *n* ánimo *m*, valor *m*

mew [mjuː] *vi (cat)* maullar, miar

mewing ['mjuːɪŋ] *n* maullido *m*

mews [mjuːz] *n Br (backstreet)* = plazoleta o callejuela formada por antiguos establos convertidos en viviendas o garajes ❏ **m. flat/house** apartamento *m*/casa *f* de lujo en unas caballerizas reconvertidas

Mexican ['meksɪkən] *adj & n* mejicano(a) *(m,f)*, mexicano(a) *(m,f)*

Mexico ['meksɪkəʊ] *n* Méjico, México; **M. City** Ciudad de Méjico *or* México

mezzanine ['mezəniːn] *n* **m. (floor)** entresuelo *m*

MF *(abbr* **medium frequency**) frecuencia *f* modulada, FM *f*

mg *(abbr* **milligram(s), milligramme(s)**) miligramo(s) *m(pl)*, mg

Mgr *Rel (abbr* **Monsignor**) Monseñor *m*, Mons.

MHz *(abbr* **megahertz**) megahercio(s) *m(pl)*, MHz

mi [miː] *n Mus* mi *m*

MI5 [emaɪ'faɪv] *n Br (abbr* **Military Intelligence Section 5**) = servicio británico de espionaje interior

MI6 [emaɪˈsɪks] n Br (abbr **Military Intelligence Section 6**) = servicio británico de espionaje exterior

miaow [miːˈaʊ] **1** vi (cat) maullar, miar
2 interj ¡miau!
3 n maullido m, miau m

mica [ˈmaɪkə] npl mica f

mice [maɪs] npl see **mouse**

mickey [ˈmɪkɪ] n Br Fam **to take the m. (out of sb)** tomar el pelo (a algn)

micro [ˈmaɪkrəʊ] n (pl **micros**) Comptr Esp microordenador m, Am microcomputadora f

microbe [ˈmaɪkrəʊb] n microbio m

microbiologist [maɪkrəʊbaɪˈɒlədʒɪst] n microbiólogo(a) m,f

microbiology [maɪkrəʊbaɪˈɒlədʒɪ] n microbiología f

microchip [ˈmaɪkrəʊtʃɪp] n Comptr microchip m, microplaqueta f

microcomputer [maɪkrəʊkəmˈpjuːtər] n Esp microordenador m, Am microcomputador m

microcosm [ˈmaɪkrəʊkɒzəm] n microcosmo m

microdot [ˈmaɪkrəʊdɒt] n micropunto m

microelectronics [maɪkrəʊɪlekˈtrɒnɪks] n microelectrónica f

microfiche [ˈmaɪkrəʊfiːʃ] n microficha f

microfilm [ˈmaɪkrəʊfɪlm] n microfilm m ❑ **m. reader** lector m óptico

microorganism [ˈmaɪkrəʊˈɔːɡənɪzəm] n microorganismo m

microphone [ˈmaɪkrəfəʊn] n micrófono m

microprocessor [maɪkrəʊˈprəʊsesər] n microprocesador m

microscope [ˈmaɪkrəskəʊp] n microscopio m

microscopic [maɪkrəˈskɒpɪk] adj microscópico(a)

microsurgery [maɪkrəʊˈsɜːdʒərɪ] n microcirugía f

microwave [ˈmaɪkrəʊweɪv] n microonda f ❑ **m. oven** (horno m de) microondas m inv

microwaveable [ˈmaɪkrəʊˈweɪvəbəl] adj it's m. se puede cocinar en el microondas

mid [mɪd] adj medio(a); **(in) m. afternoon** a media tarde; **(in) m. April** a mediados de abril; **in the m. nineteen-sixties** a mediados de los sesenta; **to be in one's m. thirties** tener unos treinta y cinco años

midair [mɪdˈeər] adj (collision, explosion) en el aire; Fig **to leave sth in m.** dejar algo sin resolver

mid-Atlantic [ˈmɪdətˈlæntɪk] adj (accent) = a medio camino entre el inglés británico y el americano

midday [mɪdˈdeɪ] **1** n mediodía m; **at m.** a mediodía
2 adj de mediodía

middle [ˈmɪdəl] **1** adj (central) de en medio; (medium) mediano(a); **m. age** mediana edad f ❑ **the M. Ages** la Edad Media; **M. America** los estadounidenses tradicionalistas y conservadores; **the m. class** la clase media; **m. management** mandos mpl intermedios
2 n (a) (centre) centro m, medio m; (half-way point) mitad f; **in the m. of** en medio de, en el centro de; **in the m. of August** a mediados de agosto; **in the m. of winter** en pleno invierno; **to be in the m. of doing sth** estar metido en faena; Fam **in the m. of nowhere** en el quinto pino (b) Fam (waist) cintura f

middle-aged [mɪdəlˈeɪdʒd] adj de mediana edad

middlebrow [ˈmɪdəlbraʊ] adj (tastes, interests) del público medio; **a m. novelist** un/una novelista para el público medio

middle-class [mɪdəlˈklɑːs] adj de clase media; (bourgeois) burgués(esa)

middleman [ˈmɪdəlmæn] n (pl **middlemen** [ˈmɪdəlmen]) Com intermediario m

middle-of-the-road [mɪdələvðəˈrəʊd] adj (politics, views) moderado(a)

middle-size(d) [ˈmɪdəlsaɪz(d)] adj de tamaño mediano

middleweight [ˈmɪdəlweɪt] n Box peso m medio

middling [ˈmɪdlɪŋ] adj mediano(a), regular

midfield [mɪdˈfiːld] n Sport centrocampo m ❑ **m. player** centrocampista mf

midfielder [mɪdˈfiːldər] n Sport centrocampista mf

midge [mɪdʒ] n mosca f enana

midget [ˈmɪdʒɪt] **1** n enano(a) m,f
2 adj (very small) diminuto(a), pequeñísimo(a); (miniature) en miniatura

midi system [ˈmɪdɪˈsɪstəm] n (stereo) minicadena f

Midlands [ˈmɪdləndz] npl **the M.** la región central de Inglaterra

midlife crisis [ˈmɪdlaɪfˈkraɪsɪs] n crisis f inv de los cuarenta

midnight [ˈmɪdnaɪt] n medianoche f; Fam Fig **to burn the m. oil** quemarse las pestañas

midpoint [ˈmɪdpɔɪnt] n ecuador m

midriff [ˈmɪdrɪf] n Anat diafragma m

midshipman [ˈmɪdʃɪpmən] n. (pl **midshipmen**) Naut guardia m marina

midst [mɪdst] prep en medio de; **in our/their m.** entre nosotros/ellos; **in the m. of** en medio de

midstream [mɪdˈstriːm] n **in m.** (river) en medio de la corriente; (way) a mitad de camino

midsummer [mɪdˈsʌmər] n pleno verano m ❑ **M.'s Day** Día m de San Juan (24 de junio)

midterm [ˈmɪdˈtɜːm] n (a) Pol US **m. elections** = elecciones a mitad del mandato presidencial (b) Sch Univ de mitad de trimestre; **m. break** = vacaciones de mitad de trimestre

midway [ˈmɪdweɪ] **1** adv a medio camino, a mitad del camino
2 adj (point etc) intermedio(a)

midweek [ˈmɪdwiːk] **1** adv entre semana
2 adj (match, flight etc) de entre semana

Mid-West [ˈmɪdˈwest] n Medio Oeste m (de Estados Unidos)

Mid-Western [mɪdˈwestən] adj del Medio Oeste (de Estados Unidos)

midwife [ˈmɪdwaɪf] n (pl **midwives** [ˈmɪdwaɪvz]) comadrona f, partera f

midwifery [ˈmɪdwɪfərɪ] n Med obstetricia f

midwinter [mɪdˈwɪntər] **1** n pleno invierno m
2 adj de pleno invierno

miff [mɪf] vt Fam ofender, disgustar; **she was quite miffed about it** le sentó bastante mal

might¹ [maɪt] v aux see **may**

might² [maɪt] n Fml fuerza f, poder m; **with m. and main** a más no poder

mightily [ˈmaɪtɪlɪ] adv (a) (powerfully) con fuerza (b) Fam cantidad de, muy; **to be m. relieved** quedarse aliviadísimo(a)

mighty [ˈmaɪtɪ] **1** adj (**mightier, mightiest**) (a) (strong) fuerte; (powerful) poderoso(a) (b) (great) enorme
2 adv US Fam (very) un montón, Esp cantidad; **a m. long journey** un viaje muy largo or larguísimo

migraine [ˈmiːgreɪn, ˈmaɪgreɪn] n jaqueca f

migrant [ˈmaɪgrənt] **1** adj migratorio(a); **m. worker** trabajador(a) m,f inmigrante

2 *n* (**a**) *n (person)* emigrante *mf*, migrante *mf*; *(bird)* ave *f* migratoria (**b**) *Austral* inmigrante *mf*

migrate [maɪˈɡreɪt] *vi* emigrar

migration [maɪˈɡreɪʃən] *n* migración *f*

migratory [ˈmaɪɡrətərɪ] *adj* migratorio(a)

mike [maɪk] *n Fam (abbr* **microphone**) micro *m*

mil [mɪl] *n (millilitre)* mililitro *m*

Milan [mɪˈlæn] *n* Milán

mild [maɪld] **1** *adj (person, character)* apacible, dulce; *(climate, weather)* templado(a), suave; *(punishment)* leve; *(beer)* ligero(a); *(tobacco, taste)* suave
2 *n Br (beer)* cerveza *f* tostada *(suave)*

mildew [ˈmɪldjuː] *n (on paper, leather, food)* moho *m*; *(on plants)* mildiu *m*

mildly [ˈmaɪldlɪ] *adv (softly, gently)* suavemente; *(slightly)* ligeramente; **and that's putting it m.** y esto es decir poco

mildness [ˈmaɪldnɪs] *n (of person, character)* apacibilidad *f*, suavidad *f*, dulzura *f*; *(of climate, weather, taste)* suavidad *f*; *(of punishment)* levedad *f*

mile [maɪl] *n* milla *f (= 1609,34m)*; *Aut* **miles to the gallon** millas por galón; *Fig* **it stands out a m.** se ve a la legua; *Fam* **it's miles away** está lejísimos; *Fam* **this is miles better** este es muchísimo mejor ◻ **nautical m.** milla *f* marina

mileage [ˈmaɪlɪdʒ] *n (distance travelled)* distancia *f* en millas; *Aut* kilometraje *m*; **a car with a low m.** un coche con pocos kilómetros; *Fig* **to get a lot of m. out of sth** sacarle mucho partido a algo

mil(e)ometer [maɪˈlɒmɪtər] *n (in car)* cuentakilómetros *m inv*

milepost [ˈmaɪlpəʊst] *n* mojón *m*

milestone [ˈmaɪlstəʊn] *n (on road)* mojón *m*; *Fig* hito *m*

milieu [ˈmiːljɜː] *n (pl* **milieux** *or* **milieus**) medio *m* ambiente *m*, entorno *m*

militancy [ˈmɪlɪtənsɪ] *n* militancia *f*

militant [ˈmɪlɪtənt] *adj & n Pol* militante *(mf)*

militarism [ˈmɪlɪtərɪzəm] *n* militarismo *m*

militarist [ˈmɪlɪtərɪst] *n* militarista *mf*

militaristic [mɪlɪtəˈrɪstɪk] *adj* militarista

military [ˈmɪlɪtərɪ] **1** *adj* militar; **to do one's m. service** hacer el servicio militar ◻ **m. police** policía *f* militar
2 the m. *npl* los militares, las fuerzas armadas

militate [ˈmɪlɪteɪt] *vi Fig* **to m. against/in favour of** militar en contra/a favor de

militia [mɪˈlɪʃə] *n* milicia *f*

militiaman [mɪˈlɪʃəmən] *n (pl* **militiamen**) miliciano *m*

milk [mɪlk] **1** *n* leche *f*; *Fig* **it's no use crying over spilt m.** a lo hecho, pecho ◻ **condensed m.** leche *f* condensada; **m. chocolate** chocolate *m* con leche; **m. churn** lechera *f*; **m. products** productos *mpl* lácteos; **m. shake** batido *m* (de leche), *RP* licuado *m*; **m. tooth** diente *m* de leche; **powdered m.** leche *f* en polvo; **skimmed m.** leche *f* descremada *or* desnatada
2 *vt* (**a**) *(cow, goat)* ordeñar (**b**) *Fam* chupar; **they milked him of all his money** le chuparon hasta el último céntimo

milking [ˈmɪlkɪŋ] *n* ordeño *m* ◻ **m. machine** ordeñadora *f* mecánica

milkman [ˈmɪlkmən] *n (pl* **milkmen**) lechero *m*, repartidor *m* de la leche

milky [ˈmɪlkɪ] *adj* (**milkier, milkiest**) *(colour)* lechoso(a); **a m. coffee** un café con mucha leche ◻ *Astron* **M. Way** Vía *f* Láctea

mill [mɪl] **1** *n* (**a**) *(grinder)* molino *m*; *(for coffee, pepper)* molinillo *m*; *Tech (for metals)* fresadora *f*; *Fig* **they put me**

through the m. me hicieron pasarlas negras *or Esp* moradas (**b**) *(factory)* fábrica *f*; **cotton m.** hilandería *f*; **paper/steel m.** fábrica de papel/acero
2 *vt (grind)* moler; *Tech (metals)* fresar

mill about, mill around *vi (crowd)* arremolinarse, apiñarse

millennium [mɪˈleniəm] *n (pl* **millenniums** *or* **millennia** [mɪˈleniə]) milenio *m*, milenario *m*

miller [ˈmɪlər] *n* molinero(a) *m,f*; **m.'s thumb** *(fish)* cabezudo *m*

millet [ˈmɪlɪt] *n Bot* mijo *m*

millibar [ˈmɪlɪbɑːr] *n* milibar *m*

milligram(me) [ˈmɪlɪɡræm] *n* miligramo *m*

millilitre, *US* **milliliter** [ˈmɪliːliːtər] *n* mililitro *m*

millimetre, *US* **millimeter** [ˈmɪliːmiːtər] *n* milímetro *m*

milliner [ˈmɪlɪnər] *n* sombrerero(a) *m,f*; **m.'s (shop)** sombrerería *f*, tienda *f* de sombreros

millinery [ˈmɪlɪnərɪ] *n (hats)* sombreros *mpl* de señora

million [ˈmɪljən] *n* millón *m*; **one m. dollars** un millón de dólares; **two m. women** dos millones de mujeres; *Fam* **millions of** millones de

millionaire [mɪljəˈneər] *n* millonario(a) *m,f*

millionth [ˈmɪljənθ] *adj & n* millonésimo(a) *(m,f)*; *Fam* **for the m. time** por enésima vez

millipede [ˈmɪlɪpiːd] *n Ent* milpiés *m inv*

millstone [ˈmɪlstəʊn] *n* muela *f*, rueda *f* de molino; *Fig* **it's a m. round his neck** es su cruz

milometer [maɪˈlɒmɪtər] *n (in car)* cuentakilómetros *m inv*

mime [maɪm] **1** *n (art)* mímica *f*; *(play, performance)* pantomima *f*
2 *vt* imitar, remedar

mimic [ˈmɪmɪk] **1** *n (imitator)* mímico(a) *m,f*, remedador(a) *m,f*
2 *adj* mímico(a); **m. art** mímica *f*
3 *vt (pt & pp* **mimicked**) imitar, remedar

mimicry [ˈmɪmɪkrɪ] *n (art)* mímica *f*; *(imitation)* imitación *f*, remedo *m*

mimosa [mɪˈməʊzə] *n Bot* mimosa *f*

min (**a**) *(abbr* **minute(s)**) min., minuto *m* (**b**) *(abbr* **minimum**) mín., mínimo *m*

minaret [ˈmɪnəret] *n* alminar *m*, minarete *m*

mince [mɪns] **1** *n Br (meat)* carne *f Esp RP* picada *or Am* molida ◻ *Culin* **m. pie** pastel *m or Esp RP* torta *f* de picadillo de fruta
2 *vt (meat etc)* picar; *Fig* **he doesn't m. his words** no tiene pelos en la lengua
3 *vi (walk)* **to m. (along)** andar con pasos menuditos

mincemeat [ˈmɪnsmiːt] *n (dried fruit)* conserva *f* de picadillo de fruta; *US (meat)* carne *f Esp RP* picada *or Am* molida

mincer [ˈmɪnsər] *n (machine)* máquina *f* de picar carne, picadora *f* de carne

mincing [ˈmɪnsɪŋ] *adj (step)* menudito(a)

mind [maɪnd] **1** *n* (**a**) *(intellect)* mente *f*, *(intelligence)* inteligencia *f*; **peace of m.** tranquilidad *f* de espíritu; **state of m.** estado *m* de ánimo (**b**) *(mentality)* mentalidad *f*; **open m.** mentalidad abierta (**c**) *(brain)* cabeza *f*, cerebro *m*; **I can't get it out of my m.** no me lo puedo quitar *or Am* sacar de la cabeza; **to speak one's m.** hablar sin rodeos; **what kind of car do you have in m.?** ¿en qué clase de coche estás pensando? (**d**) *(sanity)* juicio *m*; **to lose one's m.** perder el juicio (**e**) *(opinion)* opinión *f*, parecer *m*; **to be in two minds (about sth)** estar indeciso(a) (acerca de algo); **to change one's m.** cambiar de opinión *or* parecer;

to make up one's m. decidirse; **to my m.** a mi parecer (**f**) *(intention)* intención *f*, propósito *m*; **to have a m. to do sth** tener intención de hacer algo (**g**) *(memory)* recuerdo *m*, memoria *f*; **it slipped my m.** lo olvidé por completo; **to bear sth in m.** tener algo en cuenta; **to bring/call sth to m.** recordar algo, traer algo a la memoria

2 *vt* (**a**) *(look after) (child)* cuidar; *(house)* vigilar (**b**) *(heed)* hacer caso de; *(be careful of)* tener cuidado con; **m. the step!** ¡ojo con el peldaño!; **m. your own business!** ¡no te metas donde no te llaman! (**c**) *(object to)* tener inconveniente en; **I don't m. going** no tengo inconveniente en ir; **I wouldn't m. a cup of coffee** me vendría bien un café; **never m.** no importa

3 *vi* (**a**) *(be careful)* tener cuidado; **m. (out)!** ¡cuidado!, ¡ojo!; **m. you ...** la verdad es que ...; **m. you, he is fifty** ten en cuenta que tiene cincuenta años; *Fam* **never you m.!** ¿a ti qué te importa? (**b**) *(object, express reluctance)* importar; **do you m. if I open the window?** ¿le molesta or importa que abre la ventana?; **never m.** *(don't worry)* no te preocupes; *(it doesn't matter)* no importa

mind out *vi Br* **m. out!** ¡cuidado!

mind-boggling ['maɪndbɒgəlɪŋ] *adj Fam* alucinante, acojonante

minded ['maɪndɪd] *adj* **if you were so m.** si te pusieras (a hacerlo); **he is commercially/mechanically m.** se le da muy bien el comercio/la mecánica

minder ['maɪndər] *n* (**a**) *Br Fam (bodyguard)* gorila *m*, *Méx* guarura *m* (**b**) *(for child)* niñera *f*; *(baby-sitter)* *Esp* canguro *mf*, *Méx* nana *f*, *Am* baby-sitter *f*

mindful ['maɪndfʊl] *adj* consciente

mindless ['maɪndlɪs] *adj* estúpido(a), absurdo(a); **to be m. of danger** ser inconsciente del peligro

mind-reader ['maɪndriːdər] *n* adivinador(a) *m,f* de pensamientos

mind-reading ['maɪndriːdɪŋ] *n* adivinación *f* de pensamientos

mine[1] [maɪn] *poss pron* (el) mío, (la) mía, (los) míos, (las) mías, lo mío; **a friend of m.** un amigo mío; **these gloves are m.** estos guantes son míos; **which is m.?** ¿cuál es el mío?

mine[2] [maɪn] **1** *n* (**a**) *(for coal, tin, diamonds)* mina *f* □ **coal/gold m.** mina *f* de carbón/de oro; **m. shaft** pozo *m* de extracción (**b**) *Mil Naut* mina *f*; *Fig* **he's a m. of information** es un pozo *or* una mina de información

2 *vt* (**a**) *(coal etc)* extraer (**b**) *Mil Naut (road, waterway)* sembrar minas en; *(ship) (blow up)* volar con minas

minefield ['maɪnfiːld] *n* campo *m* de minas

minelayer ['maɪnleɪər] *n Naut (ship)* minador *m*

miner ['maɪnər] *n* minero(a) *m,f*

mineral ['mɪnərəl] **1** *adj* mineral □ **m. water** agua *f* mineral

2 *n* mineral *m*

mineralogist [mɪnə'rælədʒɪst] *n* mineralogista *mf*

mineralogy [mɪnə'rælədʒɪ] *n* mineralogía *f*

minesweeper ['maɪnswiːpər] *n Naut* dragaminas *m inv*

mineworker ['maɪnwɜːkər] *n* minero(a) *m,f*

mingle ['mɪŋgəl] **1** *vt* mezclar

2 *vi* mezclarse; **to m. with the crowd** mezclarse con la multitud

mini ['mɪnɪ] *n (skirt)* minifalda *f*

miniature ['mɪnɪtʃər] **1** *n* miniatura *f*; **in m.** en miniatura

2 *adj* (en) miniatura □ **m. golf** minigolf *m*, golf *m* miniatura

miniaturize ['mɪnɪtʃəraɪz] *vt* miniaturizar

minibus ['mɪnɪbʌs] *n* microbús *m*

minicab ['mɪnɪkæb] *n Br* taxi *m (que sólo se puede pedir por teléfono)*

MiniDisc® ['mɪnɪdɪsk] *n Comptr* MiniDisc® *m*

minim ['mɪnɪm] *n Br Mus* blanca *f*

minima ['mɪnɪmə] *npl see* **minimum**

minimal ['mɪnɪməl] *adj* mínimo(a)

minimalism ['mɪnɪməlɪzəm] *n (in art, music, design)* minimalismo *m*

minimize ['mɪnɪmaɪz] *vt (problems, dangers)* minimizar, reducir al mínimo

minimum ['mɪnɪməm] **1** *adj* mínimo(a); *Econ* **m. wage** salario *m* mínimo

2 *n (pl* **minimums** *or* **minima)** mínimo *m*, mínimum *m*; **with a m. of effort** con el mínimo esfuerzo

mining ['maɪnɪŋ] **1** *n* (**a**) *(for coal, minerals)* minería *f*, explotación *f* de minas (**b**) *Mil Naut* minado *m*

2 *adj (industry, town)* minero(a) □ **m. engineer** ingeniero(a) *m,f* de minas

minion ['mɪnjən] *n Pej* lacayo *m*, subordinado(a) *m,f*

minipill ['mɪnɪpɪl] *n* = píldora anticonceptiva sin estrógenos

miniskirt ['mɪnɪskɜːt] *n* minifalda *f*

minister ['mɪnɪstər] **1** *n* (**a**) *Pol* ministro(a) *m,f*; *Br* **M. of Defence/Health** ministro de Defensa/Sanidad □ **Prime M.** primer(era) ministro(a) *m,f* (**b**) *Rel* pastor(a) *m,f*

2 *vi* **to m. to sb** atender *or* cuidar a algn

ministerial [mɪnɪ'stɪərɪəl] *adj Pol* ministerial; **m. office** cargo *m* de ministro

ministry ['mɪnɪstrɪ] *n* (**a**) *Pol* ministerio *m*; *Br* **M. of Transport** Ministerio de Transportes (Públicos) (**b**) *Rel* sacerdocio *m*; **to enter the m.** *(Catholics)* hacerse sacerdote; *(Protestants)* hacerse pastor

mink [mɪŋk] *n (animal, fur)* visón *m* □ **m. coat** abrigo *m* de visón

minnow ['mɪnəʊ] *n (fish)* piscardo *m*

minor ['maɪnər] **1** *adj* (**a**) *(smaller, lesser)* menor, más pequeño(a) (**b**) *(unimportant)* sin importancia, insignificante; *(defect)* pequeño(a); *(role, interest)* secundario(a); *(party)* minoritario(a); **m. expenses** gastos *mpl* menudos; *Sport* **m. league** = liga profesional estadounidense de béisbol de menor importancia que la liga nacional; *Fig* **a m. league company** una empresa de segunda (**c**) *Mus* menor; **G m.** Sol *m* menor; **m. key** tono *m* menor

2 *n* (**a**) *Jur* menor *mf* de edad (**b**) *Mus* tono *m* menor (**c**) *US Univ* asignatura *f* secundaria

Minorca [mɪ'nɔːkə] *n* Menorca

Minorcan [mɪ'nɔːkən] *adj & n* menorquín(ina) *(m,f)*

minority [maɪ'nɒrɪtɪ] **1** *n (smaller part, small group)* minoría *f* □ *Fin* **m. interest** participación *f* minoritaria; **m. opinion** opinión *f* de la minoría (**b**) *Jur* minoría *f* de edad

2 *adj (government, interest etc)* minoritario(a)

minstrel ['mɪnstrəl] *n* juglar *m*, trovador *m*

mint[1] [mɪnt] *n Fin* **the M.** la Casa de la Moneda; **in m. condition** en perfecto estado; *Fam* **to be worth a m.** valer un dineral

2 *vt (coin, words)* acuñar

mint[2] [mɪnt] *n* (**a**) *Bot* menta *f* (**b**) *(sweet)* pastilla *f* de menta

minuet [mɪnjʊ'et] *n Mus* minué *m*

minus ['maɪnəs] **1** *prep* (**a**) *Math* menor; **5m. 3** 5 menos 3; **m. 10 degrees** 10 grados bajo cero (**b**) *Fam (without)* sin; **he came back m. his wife** volvió sin su mujer

2 *adj (quantity, number)* negativo(a)

3 *n (quantity)* cantidad *f* negativa; **m. (sign)** signo *m* de menos

minuscule ['mɪnəskjuːl] *adj* minúsculo(a)

minute[1] ['mɪnɪt] *n* (**a**) *(of time)* minuto *m*; **at the last m.** a última hora; **10 (minutes) past 3** las 3 y 10 (minutos); **just a m.** (espera) un momento; **she could arrive any m. now** llegará de un momento a otro; **this very m.** ahora mismo ❑ **m. hand** *(on clock)* minutero *m* **(b)** *(note)* nota *f*, minuta *f*; **the minutes of the meeting** el acta de la reunión

minute² [maɪˈnjuːt] *adj (tiny)* diminuto(a), minúsculo(a); *(careful, exact)* minucioso(a), detallado(a)

minutely [maɪˈnjuːtlɪ] *adv (examine)* minuciosamente

minutiae [mɪˈnjuːʃɪiː] *npl* pequeños detalles *mpl*

mips [mɪps] *Comptr (abbr* **million instructions per second)** millón *m* de instrucciones por segundo

miracle [ˈmɪrəkəl] *n* milagro *m*; **by a m.** de *or* por milagro; **it's a m. that she survived** es un milagro que haya sobrevivido; **to work miracles** hacer milagros

miraculous [mɪˈrækjʊləs] *adj* milagroso(a); **to have a m. escape** salvarse de milagro

miraculously [mɪˈrækjʊləslɪ] *adv* milagrosamente, por milagro

mirage [mɪˈrɑːʒ] *n* espejismo *m*

mire [maɪər] *n (mud)* fango *m*, lodo *m*; *(muddy place)* lodazal *m*

mirror [ˈmɪrər] **1** *n* espejo *m*; *Fig* espejo *m*, reflejo *m*; **to look at oneself in the m.** mirarse en el espejo ❑ **driving m., rear-view m.** retrovisor *m*; **m. image** réplica *f*
2 *vt* reflejar

mirth [mɜːθ] *n (jollity)* alegría *f*; *(laughter)* risas *fpl*

misadventure [mɪsədˈventʃər] *n (misfortune)* desventura *f*; *Jur* **death by m.** muerte *f* accidental

misanthrope [ˈmɪzənθrəʊp] *n* misántropo(a) *m,f*

misanthropic [mɪzənˈθrɒpɪk] *adj* misantrópico(a)

misanthropist [mɪˈzænθrəpɪst] *n* misántropo(a) *m,f*

misanthropy [mɪˈzænθrəpɪ] *n* misantropía *f*

misapprehend [ˈmɪsæprɪˈhend] *vt* comprender *or* entender mal

misapprehension [mɪsæprɪˈhenʃən] *n* malentendido *m*, equivocación *f*

misappropriate [mɪsəˈprəʊprɪeɪt] *vt (funds)* malversar

misappropriation [ˈmɪsəprəʊprɪˈeɪʃən] *n (of funds)* malversación *f*

misbehave [mɪsbɪˈheɪv] *vi* portarse *or* comportarse mal

misbehaviour, *US* **misbehavior** [mɪsbɪˈheɪvjər] *n* mala conducta *f*, mal comportamiento *m*

misc *(abbr* **miscellaneous)** varios

miscalculate [mɪsˈkælkjʊleɪt] *vt & vi* calcular mal

miscalculation [mɪskælkjʊˈleɪʃən] *n* error *m* de cálculo

miscarriage [mɪsˈkærɪdʒ] *n* **(a)** *Med* aborto *m* (espontáneo) **(b) m. of justice** error *m* judicial

miscarry [mɪsˈkærɪ] *vi (pt & pp* **miscarried)** **(a)** *Med* abortar (espontáneamente) **(b)** *Fig (plan)* fracasar

miscast [mɪsˈkɑːst] *vt (pt & pp* **miscast)** *(actor)* dar un papel poco apropiado a

miscellaneous [mɪsɪˈleɪnɪəs] *adj* misceláneo(a), variado(a); **m. expenses** gastos *mpl* diversos

miscellany [mɪˈselənɪ] *n (mixture, assortment)* miscelánea *f*, *(of poems etc)* antología *f*

mischance [mɪsˈtʃɑːns] *n* mala suerte *f*, desgracia *f*

mischief [ˈmɪstʃɪf] *n* **(a)** *(naughtiness)* travesura *f*, diablura *f*; **she's full of m.** es muy traviesa; **to get into** *or* **up to m.** hacer diabluras *or* travesuras **(b)** *(evil)* malicia *f*, maldad *f* **(c)** *Br Fam Hum (injury)* **to do oneself a m.** hacerse daño

mischievous [ˈmɪstʃɪvəs] *adj* **(a)** *(naughty)* travieso(a); *(playful)* juguetón(ona) **(b)** *(wicked)* malicioso(a)

misconception [mɪskənˈsepʃən] *n* concepto *m* erróneo *or* falso

misconduct [mɪsˈkɒndʌkt] *n (misbehaviour)* mala conducta *f*; *Com* mala administración *f*; *(adultery)* adulterio *m*; **professional m.** error *m* profesional

misconstruction [mɪskənˈstrʌkʃən] *n* mala interpretación *f*

misconstrue [mɪskənˈstruː] *vt* interpretar mal

miscount [mɪsˈkaʊnt] *vt (votes etc)* contar mal

misdeed [mɪsˈdiːd] *n* delito *m*, fechoría *f*

misdemeanour, *US* **misdemeanor** [mɪsdɪˈmiːnər] *n (misdeed)* fechoría *f*; *Jur* delito *m* menor

misdiagnose [mɪsdaɪəgˈnəʊz] *vt Med* diagnosticar erróneamente

misdirect [mɪsdɪˈrekt] *vt (letter)* poner mal las señas en; *(operation)* dirigir mal; *(person)* orientar *or* informar mal; *(energies, efforts)* encaminar *or* encauzar mal

miser [ˈmaɪzər] *n* avaro(a) *m,f*

miserable [ˈmɪzərəbəl] *adj* **(a)** *(sad)* triste, deprimido(a); *(unfortunate)* desgraciado(a); **it makes me m.** me deprime muchísimo **(b)** *(unpleasant)* desagradable; *(weather)* malo(a); *(wretched, pathetic)* miserable, lamentable **(c)** *(paltry)* despreciable, miserable

miserably [ˈmɪzərəblɪ] *adv* **(a)** *(sadly)* tristemente; *(unfortunately)* desgraciadamente **(b)** *(pathetically)* miserablemente, lamentablemente

miserly [ˈmaɪzəlɪ] *adj* avaro(a), tacaño(a)

misery [ˈmɪzərɪ] *n* **(a)** *(sadness)* tristeza *f*; *(wretchedness)* desgracia *f*, desdicha *f*; **to make sb's life a m.** amargarle la vida a algn **(b)** *(suffering)* sufrimiento *m*, dolor *m*; **to put an animal out of its m.** acortarle la agonía a un animal; *Fig Hum* **go on, tell me, put me out of my m.** anda, dímelo, no me hagas esperar más **(c)** *(poverty)* pobreza *f*, miseria *f* **(d)** *Br Fam (person)* amargado(a) *m,f*

misfire [mɪsˈfaɪər] *vi (gun, car, plan)* fallar

misfit [ˈmɪsfɪt] *n (person)* inadaptado(a) *m,f*; *(outcast)* marginado(a) *m,f*

misfortune [mɪsˈfɔːtʃən] *n (unfortunate event)* desgracia *f*, infortunio *m*; *(bad luck)* desgracia *f*

misgiving [mɪsˈgɪvɪŋ] *n (doubt)* duda *f*, recelo *m*; *(fear)* temor *m*

misguided [mɪsˈgaɪdɪd] *adj* equivocado(a), desacertado(a)

mishandle [mɪsˈhændəl] *vt* llevar *or* manejar mal

mishap [ˈmɪshæp] *n* desgracia *f*, contratiempo *m*, accidente *m*; **without m.** sin novedad

mishear [mɪsˈhɪər] *vt & vi (pt & pp* **misheard** [mɪsˈhɜːd]) oír mal

mishmash [ˈmɪʃmæʃ] *n Fam* batiburrillo *m*, mezcolanza *f*, *Am* mejunje *m*

misinform [mɪsɪnˈfɔːm] *vt* informar mal

misinformation [mɪsɪnfəˈmeɪʃən] *n* falsa información *f*

misinterpret [mɪsɪnˈtɜːprɪt] *vt* interpretar mal

misinterpretation [mɪsɪntɜːprɪˈteɪʃən] *n* mala interpretación *f*

misjudge [mɪsˈdʒʌdʒ] *vt (person, situation)* juzgar mal; *(distance etc)* calcular mal

misjudg(e)ment [mɪsˈdʒʌdʒmənt] *n* error *m* de apreciación

mislay [mɪsˈleɪ] *vt (pt & pp* **mislaid** [mɪsˈleɪd]) extraviar, perder

mislead [mɪsˈliːd] *vt (pt & pp* **misled)** despistar, desorientar

misleading [mɪsˈliːdɪŋ] *adj (erroneous)* erróneo(a); *(deliberately)* engañoso(a)

misled [mɪsˈled] *pt & pp see* **mislead**

mismanage [mɪsˈmænɪdʒ] *vt* manejar mal, administrar mal

mismanagement [mɪsˈmænɪdʒmənt] *n* mal manejo *m*, mala administración *f*

misnomer [mɪsˈnəʊmər] *n* nombre *m* equivocado *or* inapropiado

misogynist [mɪˈsɒdʒɪnɪst] *n* misógino(a) *m,f*

misogyny [mɪˈsɒdʒɪnɪ] *n* misoginia *f*

misplace [mɪsˈpleɪs] *vt* (**a**) *(trust, affection)* encauzar mal (**b**) *(lose)* extraviar, perder

misplaced [mɪsˈpleɪst] *adj* (**a**) *(trust, affection)* inapropiado(a), equivocado(a); *(remark)* fuera de lugar (**b**) *(lost)* extraviado(a), perdido(a)

misprint [ˈmɪsprɪnt] *n* errata *f*, error *m* de imprenta

mispronounce [mɪsprəˈnaʊns] *vt* pronunciar mal

mispronunciation [mɪsprənʌnsɪˈeɪʃən] *n* mala pronunciación *f*

misquotation [mɪskwəʊˈteɪʃən] *n* cita *f* incorrecta *or* equivocada

misquote [mɪsˈkwəʊt] *vt* (**a**) *(accidentally)* citar equivocadamente (**b**) *(deliberately) (person)* tergiversar las palabras de; *(words)* tergiversar

misread [mɪsˈriːd] *vt* (*pt & pp* **misread** [mɪsˈred]) *(notice, timetable)* leer mal; *(misinterpret)* interpretar mal

misrepresent [mɪsreprɪˈzent] *vt* *(facts)* falsificar, desvirtuar; *(words)* tergiversar, desvirtuar

misrepresentation [mɪsreprɪzenˈteɪʃən] *n* falsificación *f*, tergiversación *f*

miss¹ [mɪs] *n* señorita *f*; **M. Fitzpatrick** la señorita Fitzpatrick; **M. World** Miss *f* Mundo; **thank you, m.** gracias, señorita

miss² [mɪs] **1** *n* (**a**) *(throw etc) Esp* fallo *m*, *Am* falla *f*; *(shot)* tiro *m* errado; *(failure)* fracaso *m*; *Fig* desacierto *m* (**b**) *Fam* **to give sth a m.** no asistir; **I'll give the party a m.** paso de ir a la fiesta ·

   2 *vt* (**a**) *(target)* no acertar en; *(shot, penalty) Esp* fallar, *Am* errar (**b**) *(fail to catch) (train etc)* perder; *(fail to see, hear, understand) (joke)* no entender, *Esp* no coger; *(fail to take) (opportunity)* perder, dejar pasar; **I missed what you said** no oí lo que dijiste; **you didn't m. much!** ¡no te perdiste gran cosa!; **you have missed the point** no has captado la idea; *Fig* **to m. the boat** perder el tren *or* la ocasión (**c**) *(avoid)* evitar; **that car just missed me** por poco me atropella ese coche *or Am* carro *or CSur* auto (**d**) *(not attend)* no asistir a; **to m. class** faltar a clase (**e**) *(omit, skip)* saltarse; *(disregard)*.pasar por alto; **you missed a page** te saltaste una página (**f**) *(sth just lost)* echar en falta; *(person)* echar de menos, *Am* extrañar; *(homeland)* añorar

   3 *vi* (**a**) *(throw etc)* fallar; *(shot)* errar (**b**) *(fail to attend)* faltar (**c**) *Aut (engine)* fallar (**d**) *(be lacking)* faltar; **is anything missing?** ¿falta algo?

miss out 1 *vt (omit)* saltarse; *(disregard)* pasar por alto

   2 *vi* **to m. out on** *(opportunity etc)* perderse, dejar pasar

missal [ˈmɪsəl] *n Rel* misal *m*

misshapen [mɪsˈʃeɪpən] *adj (badly formed)* deforme; *(out of shape)* deformado(a)

missile [ˈmɪsaɪl, *US* ˈmɪsəl] *n Mil* misil *m*; *(object thrown)* proyectil *m* ❑ **m. launcher** lanzamisiles *m inv*

missing [ˈmɪsɪŋ] *adj (lost)* perdido(a), extraviado(a); *(disappeared)* desaparecido(a); *(absent)* ausente; **m. link** eslabón *m* perdido; **m. person** desaparecido(a) *m,f*; **three cups are m.** faltan tres tazas

mission [ˈmɪʃən] *n* misión *f*; *Astronaut* **m. control** centro *m* de control; *Com* **m. statement** declaración *f* de (la) misión, misión *f*

missionary [ˈmɪʃənərɪ] **1** *adj* misional

   2 *n Rel* misionero(a) *m,f*

missis [ˈmɪsɪs] *n Fam* **the m.** *(wife)* la parienta, *Méx* la vieja, *RP* la doña

missive [ˈmɪsɪv] *n* misiva *f*

misspell [mɪsˈspel] *vt* (*pt & pp* **misspelled** *or* **misspelt** [mɪsˈspelt]) *(write)* escribir mal; *(say)* deletrear mal

misspent [ˈmɪsspent] *adj (youth)* malgastado(a)

mist [mɪst] **1** *n (fog)* niebla *f*; *(thin)* neblina *f*, calina *f*; *(at sea)* bruma *f*; *(on window etc)* vaho *m*; *Fig (of tears etc)* velo *m*

   2 *vi* **to m. over** *or* **up** *(countryside)* cubrirse de neblina; *(window etc)* empañarse; *Fig (eyes)* llenarse de lágrimas

mistake [mɪsˈteɪk] **1** *n (error)* equivocación *f*, error *m*; *(oversight)* descuido *m*; *(in test etc)* falta *f*; **by m.** por equivocación *or* descuido; *(unintentionally)* sin querer; **make no m. about it!** ¡que quede bien claro!; **to make a m.** equivocarse, cometer un error ❑ **spelling m.** falta *f* de ortografía

   2 *vt* (*pt* **mistook**; *pp* **mistaken**) (**a**) *(meaning, intention)* entender *or* interpretar mal (**b**) *(confuse)* confundir; **to m. Jack for Bill** confundir a Jack con Bill

mistaken [mɪsˈteɪkən] **1** *pp see* **mistake**

   2 *adj* equivocado(a), erróneo(a); **you are m.** estás equivocado(a)

mister [ˈmɪstər] *n* señor *m*; *Fam* **hey M.!** ¡oiga, señor!

mistime [mɪsˈtaɪm] *vt* **to m. sth** hacer algo a deshora *or* a destiempo

mistletoe [ˈmɪsəltəʊ] *n Bot* muérdago *m*

mistook [mɪsˈtʊk] *pt see* **mistake**

mistranslate [mɪstrænsˈleɪt] *vt* traducir erróneamente

mistranslation [mɪstrænsˈleɪʃən] *n* error *m* de traducción, mala traducción *f*

mistreat [mɪsˈtriːt] *vt* maltratar, tratar mal

mistress [ˈmɪstrɪs] *n* (**a**) *(of house, servant)* señora *f*, ama *f*; *(of dog)* dueña *f* (**b**) *(lover)* amante *f*, querida *f* (**c**) *(teacher) (in primary school)* maestra *f*; *(in secondary school)* profesora *f*

mistrial [mɪsˈtraɪəl] *n Jur* juicio *m* nulo

mistrust [mɪsˈtrʌst] **1** *n* desconfianza *f*, recelo *m*

   2 *vt* desconfiar de, dudar de

mistrustful [mɪsˈtrʌstfʊl] *adj* desconfiado(a), receloso(a); **to be m. of sth/sb** desconfiar de algo/algn

misty [ˈmɪstɪ] *adj* (**mistier, mistiest**) *(weather)* nublado(a), de niebla; *(window etc)* empañado(a)

misunderstand [mɪsʌndəˈstænd] *vt & vi* (*pt & pp* **misunderstood**) entender *or* comprender mal

misunderstanding [mɪsʌndəˈstændɪŋ] *n (misconception)* malentendido *m*, confusión *f*; *(disagreement)* desacuerdo *m*, diferencias *fpl*

misunderstood [mɪsʌndəˈstʊd] **1** *pt & pp see* **misunderstand**

   2 *adj (thing)* mal entendido(a); *(person)* incomprendido(a)

misuse [mɪsˈjuːs] **1** *n (of tool, resources, word)* mal uso *m*, mal empleo *m*; *(of funds)* malversación *f*; *(of authority, power)* abuso *m*

   2 [mɪsˈjuːz] *vt (tool, resources, word)* utilizar *or* emplear mal; *(funds)* malversar; *(authority, power)* abusar de

mite [maɪt] *n* (**a**) *(insect)* ácaro *m*, acárido *m* (**b**) *(small child)* chiquillo(a) *m,f*, criatura *f*; (**c**) *(small amount)* pizca *f*; *Fam* **he's a m. tired** está cansadito

miter [ˈmaɪtər] *n US see* **mitre**

mitigate [ˈmɪtɪgeɪt] *vt* mitigar, aliviar; *Jur* **mitigating circumstances** circunstancias *fpl* atenuantes

mitigation [mɪtɪˈgeɪʃən] *n (of effect, suffering)* atenuación *f*; *(of pain, anger, grief)* alivio *m*; *Jur* **to plead sth in m.** alegar algo como atenuante

mitre ['maɪtər] n (a) Rel mitra f (b) m. (joint) inglete m

mitt [mɪt] n manopla f; US **baseball m.** guante m de béisbol; **oven m.** manopla de cocina

mitten ['mɪtən] n (glove) manopla f; (fingerless glove) mitón m

mix [mɪks] **1** n (combination, blend) mezcla f; Culin **cake m.** preparado m para hacer un pastel

2 vt (blend) mezclar, combinar; (paste, concrete) amasar, mezclar; Culin (ingredients) mezclar; (eggs) batir; (cocktail) preparar; **to m. business with pleasure** compaginar los negocios con la diversión

3 vi (blend) mezclarse (**with** con); (go well together) ir bien juntos; (socially) (people) entenderse bien; Fig **oil and water don't m.** el queso y el chocolate no se comen juntos

mix in vt incorporar, añadir

mix up vt (**a**) (mix well) (ingredients) mezclar bien (**b**) (confuse, muddle up) (person) confundir (**with** con); (papers) revolver; **to get all mixed up** hacerse un lío (**c**) (involve) implicar; **to be mixed up in sth** estar metido(a) or enredado(a) en algo; **to get mixed up with sb** liarse con algn

mix-and-match ['mɪksən'mætʃ] adj **m.-a.-m. clothes** coordinados mpl

mixed [mɪkst] adj (assorted) surtido(a); (varied) variado(a); (feelings) contradictorio(a); (salad) mixto(a); (weather) variable; Sport **m. doubles** dobles mpl mixtos; Culin **m. grill** parrillada f; Br **m. school** (coeducational) colegio m mixto

mixed-media ['mɪkst'miːdɪə] adj Art multimedia inv

mixed-up [mɪkst'ʌp] adj (objects, papers etc) revuelto(a); (person) confuso(a), desorientado(a)

mixer ['mɪksər] n (**a**) Culin mezcladora f, batidora f (**b**) Constr **concrete m.** hormigonera f (**c**) Cin TV mezclador(a) m,f (**d**) (person) **to be a good m.** tener don de gentes

mixing ['mɪksɪŋ] n **m. bowl** cuenco m, bol m; Cin Mus **m. desk** mesa f de mezclas

mixture ['mɪkstʃər] n mezcla f ◻ Med **cough m.** jarabe m para la tos

mix-up ['mɪksʌp] n Fam (confusion) confusión f, lío m, enredo m

ml (abbr **millilitre(s)**) mililitro(s) m(pl), ml

MLitt [em'lɪt] n (abbr **Master of Letters**) Máster m en Letras

MLR [emel'ɑːr] n Fin (abbr **minimum lending rate**) tipo m activo mínimo de interés, Am tasa f activa mínima de interés

mm (abbr **millimetre(s)**) milímetro(s), m(pl), mm

mnemonic [nɪ'mɒnɪk] **1** adj mnemotécnico(a), nemo-técnico(a)

2 n mnemotécnica f, nemotécnica f

MO [em'əʊ] n (abbr **Medical Officer**) médico(a) m,f militar

moan [məʊn] **1** n (**a**) (groan) gemido m, quejido m (**b**) (complaint) queja f

2 vi (**a**) (groan) gemir (**b**) (complain) quejarse (**about** de)

moaner ['məʊnər] n quejica mf, Am quejoso(a) m,f

moaning ['məʊnɪŋ] n (**a**) (groaning) gemidos mpl; (of wind in trees) quejido m (**b**) (complaining) quejas fpl

moat [məʊt] n foso m

mob [mɒb] **1** n (crowds) multitud f, muchedumbre f, gentío m; (gang) pandilla f; (riff-raff) gentuza f, chusma f; US Slang **the M.** (Mafia) la mafia; **m. rule** ley f de la calle; **the m.** el populacho

2 vt (pt & pp **mobbed**) (crowd around) acosar, rodear; (attack) asaltar, atropellar

mobile ['məʊbaɪl, US 'məʊbəl] **1** adj móvil, movible; **are you m.?** ¿tienes coche or Am carro or CSur auto?; **m. home** caravana f, remolque m, RP casa f rodante; **m. phone** teléfono m móvil or Am celular

2 n (**a**) (hanging ornament) móvil m (**b**) Fam (mobile phone) móvil m, Am celular m

mobility [məʊ'bɪlɪtɪ] n movilidad f

mobilization [məʊbɪlaɪ'zeɪʃən] n movilización f

mobilize ['məʊbɪlaɪz] vt (troops, support) movilizar

mobster ['mɒbstər] n US Fam gángster m

moccasin ['mɒkəsɪn] n (shoe) mocasín m

mocha ['mɒkə] n moca m

mock [mɒk] **1** adj (**a**) (feelings) fingido(a), simulado(a); (modesty) falso(a) (**b**) (objects) de imitación (**c**) (events) de prueba; **m. battle** simulacro m de batalla

2 vi (make fun of) burlarse or mofarse de; (mimic) imitar

3 vi burlarse, mofarse (**at** de)

mockery ['mɒkərɪ] n (**a**) (ridicule, derision) burla f, mofa f (**b**) (travesty) parodia f; (farce) farsa f; **it makes a m. of the whole system** esto pone el sistema en ridículo

mocking ['mɒkɪŋ] adj burlón(ona)

mockingbird ['mɒkɪŋbɜːd] n Orn sinsonte m

mock-up ['mɒkʌp] n (model) maqueta f, modelo m a escala

MOD [eməʊ'diː] n Br (abbr **Ministry of Defence**) Ministerio m de Defensa

modal ['məʊdəl] **1** n verbo m modal

2 adj **m. verb** verbo m modal

mode [məʊd] n (**a**) (manner, way) modo m, estilo m (**b**) (fashion) moda f

model ['mɒdəl] **1** n (**a**) (solid representation) modelo m; (scale) **m.** maqueta f (**b**) (design) figurín m; (pattern) patrón m, modelo m (**c**) (fashion model) modelo mf, maniquí mf (**d**) (of car, machine etc) modelo m (**e**) Fig (perfect example) modelo m; **to act as a m. for** servir de pauta a

2 adj (**a**) (railway, car) en miniatura, de juguete; **m. aeroplane** aeromodelo m (**b**) (teacher, friend) ejemplar (**c**) (factory, school) modelo; **m. home** casa f piloto

3 vt (pt & pp **modelled**, US **modeled**) (**a**) (clay etc) modelar (**b**) (clothes) presentar (**c**) Fig imitar, copiar; **A is modelled on B** A se ha inspirado en B; **to m. oneself on sb** seguir el ejemplo de algn (**d**) Comptr simular por Esp ordenador or Am computadora

4 vi (**a**) (make clay models etc) modelar (**b**) (work as fashion model) trabajar de modelo; (pose for artist) posar

modelling, US **modeling** ['mɒdəlɪŋ] n (**a**) (of clay etc) modelado m (**b**) (profession) profesión f de modelo (**c**) Comptr modelado m

modem ['məʊdem] n Comptr modem m

moderate[1] ['mɒdərɪt] **1** adj (gen) moderado(a); (reasonable) razonable; (price) módico(a); (average) regular, mediano(a); (talent, ability) mediocre; (climate) templado(a); **to be a m. drinker** beber con moderación

2 n Pol moderado(a) m,f, centrista mf

moderate[2] ['mɒdəreɪt] **1** vt (demands, speed etc) moderar

2 vi (**a**) (diminish) moderarse; (wind, storm) calmarse, amainar (**b**) (act as moderator) arbitrar, servir de moderador

moderately ['mɒdərɪtlɪ] adv (expensive, good) media-namente; (eat, drink) con moderación

moderation [mɒdə'reɪʃən] n moderación f; **in m.** con moderación

moderator ['mɒdəreɪtər] n (mediator) moderador(a) m,f, árbitro m

modern ['mɒdən] adj moderno(a); **m. history/litera-ture** historia f/literatura f contemporánea; **m. languages** lenguas fpl modernas

modernism ['mɒdənɪzəm] n modernismo m

modernist ['mɒdənɪst] adj & n modernista (mf)

modernity [mɒ'dɜːnɪtɪ] n modernidad f

modernization [mɒdənaɪ'zeɪʃən] n modernización f

modernize ['mɒdənaɪz] **1** vt modernizar **2** vi modernizarse

modest ['mɒdɪst] adj (**a**) (not boastful) modesto(a) (**b**) (chaste) recatado(a) (**c**) (small) (sum of money, house etc) modesto(a), pequeño(a); (price) módico(a); (success) discreto(a)

modestly ['mɒdɪstlɪ] adv (**a**) (not boastfully) modestamente (**b**) (moderately) moderadamente (**c**) (chastely) recatadamente

modesty ['mɒdɪstɪ] n (**a**) (humility) modestia f (**b**) (chastity) recato m, pudor m

modicum ['mɒdɪkəm] n **a m. of** una pizca de, un mínimo de; **it requires a m. of know-how** requiere un mínimo de conocimientos

modification [mɒdɪfɪ'keɪʃən] n modificación f

modify ['mɒdɪfaɪ] vt (pt & pp modified) modificar

modular ['mɒdjʊlər] adj por módulos

modulate ['mɒdjʊleɪt] vt modular

modulation [mɒdjʊ'leɪʃən] n modulación f ❑ Rad frequency m. frecuencia f modulada

module ['mɒdjuːl] n módulo m

modus operandi ['məʊdəsɒpə'rændaɪ] n Fml modus m operandi

mogul ['məʊgʌl] n magnate m

mohair ['məʊheər] n mohair m

Mohammed [məʊ'hæmɪd] n Mahoma

Mohammedan [məʊ'hæmɪdən] adj & n musulmán(ana) (m,f)

moist [mɔɪst] adj (soil, skin, climate) húmedo(a); (cake) esponjoso(a)

moisten ['mɔɪsən] vt humedecer; **she moistened her lips** se humedeció los labios

moisture ['mɔɪstʃər] n (dampness) humedad f; (on glass) vaho m

moisturize ['mɔɪstʃəraɪz] vt (air) humedecer; (skin) hidratar; **moisturizing cream** crema f hidratante

moisturizer ['mɔɪstʃəraɪzər] n crema f or leche f hidratante

molar ['məʊlər] n muela f

molasses [mə'læsɪz] n melaza f

mold [məʊld] n US see **mould**

Moldavia [mɒl'deɪvɪə] n Moldavia

Moldavian [mɒl'deɪvɪən] adj & n moldavo(a) (m,f)

molder ['məʊldər] vi US see **moulder**

molding ['məʊldɪŋ] n US see **moulding**

Moldova [mɒl'dəʊvə] n see **Moldavia**

Moldovan [mɒl'dəʊvən] adj & n see **Moldavian**

moldy ['məʊldɪ] adj (moldier, moldiest) US see **mouldy**

mole¹ [məʊl] n (beauty spot) lunar m

mole² [məʊl] n (**a**) (animal) topo m (**b**) (spy) agente mf clandestino(a), infiltrado(a) m,f

molecular [məʊ'lekjʊlər] adj molecular

molecule ['mɒlɪkjuːl] n molécula f

molehill ['məʊlhɪl] n topera f; Fig **to make a mountain out of a m.** hacer una montaña de un grano de arena

molest [mə'lest] vt (annoy) importunar, acosar, vejar; Jur (sexually assault) acosar (sexualmente)

molestation [mɒle'steɪʃən] n (**a**) (sexual) abuso m sexual

(**b**) (pestering) hostigamiento m; (more violently) agresión f

mollify ['mɒlɪfaɪ] vt (pt & pp mollified) aplacar, calmar, apaciguar

mollusc, US **mollusk** ['mɒləsk] n Zool molusco m

mollycoddle ['mɒlɪkɒdəl] vt Fam mimar, consentir

Molotov cocktail [mɒlətɒf'kɒkteɪl] n cóctel m Molotov

molt [məʊlt] vi US see **moult**

molten ['məʊltən] adj fundido(a), derretido(a); **m. lava** lava líquida

mom [mɒm] n US Fam mamá f

moment ['məʊmənt] n (**a**) (instant) momento m, instante m; **a m. ago** hace un momento; **at the m.** en este momento; **at the last m.** a última hora; **for the m.** de momento; **I've just this m. seen them** acabo de verles ahora mismo; **in a m.** dentro de un momento; **to expect sb at any m.** esperar a algn de un momento a otro (**b**) (significance) importancia f, trascendencia f; **of great m.** de gran importancia

momenta [məʊ'mentə] npl see **momentum**

momentarily [məʊmən'terɪlɪ] adv (**a**) (for a short time) momentáneamente (**b**) (soon) de un momento a otro (**c**) US (very soon) dentro de poco

momentary ['məʊməntərɪ] adj momentáneo(a)

momentous [məʊ'mentəs] adj trascendental

momentum [məʊ'mentəm] n (pl **momentums** or **momenta**) Phys momento m; (speed) ímpetu m, velocidad f; Fig ímpetu m, impulso m; **to gather m.** cobrar velocidad

mommy ['mɒmɪ] n US Fam mamá f

Mon (abbr **Monday**) lunes m, lun.

Monaco ['mɒnəkəʊ] n Mónaco

monarch ['mɒnək] n monarca mf

monarchical [mə'nɑːkɪkəl] adj monárquico(a)

monarchist ['mɒnəkɪst] adj & n monárquico(a) (m,f)

monarchy ['mɒnəkɪ] n monarquía f

monastery ['mɒnəstərɪ] n monasterio m

monastic [mə'næstɪk] adj monástico(a)

Monday ['mʌndɪ] n lunes m; see also **Saturday**

Monegasque [mɒnə'gæsk] adj & n monegasco(a) (m,f)

monetarism ['mʌnɪtərɪzəm] n monetarismo m

monetarist ['mʌnɪtərɪst] adj & n monetarista (mf)

monetary ['mʌnɪtərɪ] adj monetario(a), **m. policy** política f monetaria

money ['mʌnɪ] n (cash) dinero m; (coin, currency) moneda f; **to be worth a lot of m.** (person) ser rico(a), tener mucho dinero; (thing) valer mucho dinero; **to get one's m.'s worth** sacar partido del dinero; **to make m.** (person) ganar or hacer dinero; (business etc) rendir bien; **to put m. on** apostar por; Fig **I'd put my m. on her** yo apostaría por ella; Br Fam **it's m. for old rope** es dinero regalado; Fam **to be in the m.** haber ganado mucha plata, Esp haberse hecho con un montón de pasta, Méx haber hecho un chorro de lana, RP haber juntado un toco de guita; Fam **to be made of m., to be rolling in m.** estar forrado(a) (de dinero) ❑ **m. market** mercado m de valores; **m. order** giro m postal; Econ **m. supply** oferta f or masa f monetaria; **paper m.** papel m moneda; **ready m.** dinero m contante; **spending m.** dinero m para gastos personales

money-back ['mʌnɪbæk] n **m.-b. guarantee** garantía f de devolución del dinero si el producto no es satisfactorio

moneybags ['mʌnɪbægz] n Fam ricachón(ona) m,f

moneybox ['mʌnɪbɒks] n Esp hucha f, esp Am alcancía f

moneyed ['mʌnɪd] adj adinerado(a), rico(a)

money-grubbing ['mʌnɪgrʌbɪŋ] adj Fam tacaño(a), rata

moneylender ['mʌnɪlendər] *n* prestamista *mf*

moneylending ['mʌnɪlendɪŋ] *n* préstamo *m*

moneymaker ['mʌnɪmeɪkər] *n* (**a**) *(product, business)* negocio *m* rentable (**b**) *Fam Pej (person)* pesetero(a) *m,f*

moneymaking ['mʌnɪmeɪkɪŋ] **1** *adj (business)* rentable, lucrativo(a)
  2 *n* ganancia *f*

money-spinner ['mʌnɪspɪnər] *n Fam see* **moneymaker (a)**

Mongol ['mɒŋgɒl] **1** *adj* mongol(ola), mogol(ola)
  2 *n* (**a**) *(person)* mongol(ola) *m,f*, mogol(ola) *m,f* (**b**) *(language)* mongol *m*, mogol *m*

Mongolia [mɒŋ'gəʊlɪə] *n* Mongolia

Mongolian [mɒŋ'gəʊlɪən] *adj & n* mongol(ola) *(m,f)*, mogol(ola) *(m,f)*

mongolism ['mɒŋgəlɪzəm] *n* mongolismo *m*

mongoose ['mɒŋguːs] *n (pl* **mongooses)** *Zool* mangosta *f*

mongrel ['mʌŋgrəl] *n (dog)* perro *m* mestizo; *Pej* perro *m* callejero

monied ['mʌnɪd] *adj see* **moneyed**

monies ['mʌnɪz] *npl Com Jur* fondos *mpl*

monitor ['mɒnɪtər] **1** *n* (**a**) *Rad (person)* escucha *mf* (**b**) *TV Comptr Med (screen)* monitor *m* (**c**) *Sch (prefect)* delegado(a) *m,f*, responsable *mf*
  2 *vt* (**a**) *(radio broadcast)* escuchar (**b**) *(check)* controlar; *(progress, events)* seguir de cerca

monitoring ['mɒnɪtərɪŋ] *n* (**a**) *(of radio broadcast)* escucha *f*; **m. station** estación *f* de escucha (**b**) *(checking)* control *m*, *Am* monitoreo *m*

monk [mʌŋk] *n* monje *m*

monkey ['mʌŋkɪ] *n* mono *m*, mico *m*; **female m.** mona *f*, mica *f*; *Fam* **little m.** *(child)* diablillo *m* ❑ *Fam* **m. business** *(mischief)* travesuras *fpl*; *(swindle)* trampas *fpl*; *Br* **m. nut** *Esp* cacahuete *m*, *Am* maní *m*, *CAm Méx* cacahuate *m*; *Fam (mischief)* **m. tricks** diabluras *fpl*, travesuras *fpl*; *US* **m. wrench** llave *f* inglesa

monkey about, monkey around *vi Fam* hacer tonterías, hacer el tonto; **to m. about** *or* **around with sth** juguetear con algo

monkfish ['mʌŋkfɪʃ] *n* rape *m*

mono ['mɒnəʊ] *n* **in m.** *(sound recording)* en mono(aural)

monochrome ['mɒnəkrəʊm] **1** *adj Art Comptr* monocromo(a); *(television, photo)* en blanco y negro
  2 *n* monocromía *f*

monocle ['mɒnəkəl] *n* monóculo *m*

monogamous [mɒ'nɒgəməs] *adj* monógamo(a)

monogamy [mɒ'nɒgəmɪ] *n* monogamia *f*

monogram ['mɒnəgræm] *n* monograma *m*

monolingual [mɒnəʊ'lɪŋgwəl] *adj* monolingüe

monolith ['mɒnəlɪθ] *n* monolito *m*

monolithic [mɒnə'lɪθɪk] *adj* monolítico(a)

monologue, *US* **monolog** ['mɒnəlɒg] *n* monólogo *m*

monoplane ['mɒnəʊpleɪn] *n* monoplano *m*

monopolize [mə'nɒpəlaɪz] *vt* (**a**) *Fin* monopolizar (**b**) *(attention etc)* acaparar

monopoly [mə'nɒpəlɪ] *n* monopolio *m*

monorail ['mɒnəʊreɪl] *n (train, system)* monorriel *m*, monocarril *m*

monosyllabic [mɒnəsɪ'læbɪk] *adj (word)* monosílabo(a); *(language, remark)* monosilábico(a)

monosyllable [mɒnə'sɪləbəl] *n* monosílabo *m*

monotheism ['mɒnəθɪɪzəm] *n* monoteísmo *m*

monotone ['mɒnətəʊn] *n* **in a m.** con una voz monótona

monotonous [mə'nɒtənəs] *adj* monótono(a)

monotony [mə'nɒtənɪ] *n* monotonía *f*

monoxide [mɒ'nɒksaɪd] *n Chem* monóxido *m* ❑ **carbon m.** monóxido *m* de carbono

monsoon [mɒn'suːn] *n Meteor* monzón *m*; **m. rains** lluvias *fpl* monzónicas

monster ['mɒnstər] **1** *n* monstruo *m*
  2 *adj Fam (huge)* enorme, gigantesco(a)

monstrosity [mɒn'strɒsɪtɪ] *n* monstruosidad *f*

monstrous ['mɒnstrəs] *adj* (**a**) *(huge)* enorme, gigantesco(a); *(hideous)* monstruoso(a) (**b**) *(outrageous)* escandaloso(a), monstruoso(a); *(unfair)* injusto(a); **it's m. that ...** es una vergüenza que ...

montage ['mɒntɑːʒ] *n Cin Phot* montaje *m*

Monte Carlo [mɒntɪ'kɑːləʊ] *n* Montecarlo

month [mʌnθ] *n* mes *m*; **a m. today** de aquí a un mes; **calendar m.** mes civil; **every m.** cada mes, todos los meses; **in the m. of June** en el mes de junio; **last/next m.** el mes pasado/que viene; **m.'s pay** sueldo *m* mensual, mensualidad *f*; **once a m.** una vez al mes; **the 10th of this m.** el 10 del corriente; *Fam* **never in a m. of Sundays** nunca jamás

monthly ['mʌnθlɪ] **1** *adj* mensual; **m. instalment** *or* **payment** mensualidad *f*; *Rail etc* **m. ticket** abono *m* mensual
  2 *n (periodical)* revista *f* mensual
  3 *adv (every month)* mensualmente, cada mes; *(pay)* al mes

monument ['mɒnjʊmənt] *n* monumento *m*

monumental [mɒnjʊ'mentəl] *adj* (**a**) *(large, impressive)* monumental; **m. mason** marmolista *mf* (**b**) *Fam (huge)* enorme, monumental; **a m. blunder** una metedura de pata garrafal

moo [muː] **1** *n (pl* **moos)** mugido *m*
  2 *vi* mugir

mooch [muːt] **1** *vi Fam* **to m. about** *or* **around** vagar, divagar
  2 *vt US Slang* **to m. sth off sb** *(cadge)* gorrear *or Esp Méx* gorronear *or RP* garronear algo a algn; *(steal)* birlar algo a algn

mood[1] [muːd] *n Ling* modo *m*

mood[2] [muːd] *n* humor *m*; **he's in one of his moods** está de malas; **to be in a good/bad m.** estar de buen/mal humor; **to be in the m. for (doing) sth** tener ganas de *or* estar de humor para (hacer) algo; **I'm not in the m. for jokes** no estoy para bromas ❑ **m. swing** cambio *m* repentino de humor

moodiness ['muːdɪnɪs] *n (changeable moods)* cambios *mpl* de humor; *(bad mood)* mal humor *m*; *(sadness)* melancolía *f*

moody ['muːdɪ] *adj* (**moodier, moodiest**) *(changeable)* de humor cambiadizo, lunático(a); *(bad-tempered)* malhumorado(a); *(sad)* melancólico(a); **she's very m.** siempre está con caras largas

moon [muːn] **1** *n* luna *f*; *Fig* **once in a blue m.** de higos a brevas; *Fam* **to be over the m.** estar en el séptimo cielo ❑ **full/new m.** luna *f* llena/nueva
  2 *adj* lunar ❑ **m. buggy** vehículo *m* lunar; **m. landing** alunizaje *m*
  3 *vi* **to m. about** *or* **around** perder el tiempo, mirar a las musarañas

moonbeam ['muːnbiːm] *n* rayo *m* de luna

moonlight ['muːnlaɪt] **1** *n* claro *m* de luna, luz *f* de la luna; **by m., in the m.** a la luz de la luna; **it was m.** había luna; *Br Fam* **to do a m. flit** largarse a la chita callando
  2 *vi Fam* estar pluriempleado(a)

moonlighter ['muːnlaɪtər] *n Fam* pluriempleado(a) *m,f*

moonlighting ['muːnlaɪtɪŋ] *n Fam* pluriempleo *m*

moonlit ['muːlɪt] *adj (landscape etc)* iluminado(a) por la luna; *(night)* de luna

moonshine ['muːnʃaɪn] *n* **(a)** *(nonsense)* bobadas *fpl*, pamplinas *fpl* **(b)** *US (alcohol)* = alcohol destilado ilegalmente

moonstone ['muːnstəʊn] *n Min* piedra *f* de la luna, adularia *f*

moonstruck ['muːnstrʌk] *adj Fam (crazy)* chiflado(a), tocado(a)

Moor [mɔːr] *n* moro(a) *m,f*

moor¹ [mʊər] *n (heath)* brezal *m*, páramo *m*

moor² *vt Naut (with ropes)* amarrar; *(with anchor)* anclar

moorhen ['mʊəhen] *n Orn* polla *f* de agua

mooring ['mʊərɪŋ] *n* **(a)** *(place)* amarradero *m* **(b) moorings** *(ropes etc)* amarras *fpl*

Moorish ['mʊərɪʃ] *adj* moro(a)

moorland ['mʊələnd] *n* brezal *m*, páramo *m*

moose ['muːs] *n inv Zool* alce *m*

moot [muːt] **1** *adj* **it's a m. point** es discutible **(whether** si)
  2 *vt (suggest)* plantear, proponer, sugerir; **it has been mooted that ...** se ha sugerido que ...

mop [mɒp] **1** *n (for floor)* fregona *f*, fregasuelos *m inv; Fam* **m. of hair** melena *f*, mata *f* de pelo
  2 *vt (pt & pp* **mopped)** *(floor)* fregar, limpiar; **to m. one's brow** enjugarse la frente

mop up *vt* **(a)** *(spilt liquids)* limpiar, enjugar; *(dry up)* secar; *Fig (profits, funds)* llevarse **(b)** *Mil (enemy forces)* acabar con, rematar

mope [məʊp] *vi* estar deprimido(a) *or* abatido(a)

mope about, mope around *vi* andar abatido(a)

moped ['məʊped] *n* ciclomotor *m*, vespa *f*

mopping-up [mɒpɪŋ'ʌp] *n Mil* **m.-up operation** operación *f* de limpieza

moral ['mɒrəl] **1** *adj* moral; **m. victory** victoria moral
  2 *n* **(a)** *(of story)* moraleja *f* **(b)** **morals** *(standards)* moral *f sing*, moralidad *f sing*

morale [mə'rɑːl] *n* moral *f*, estado *m* de ánimo; **her m. was very low** estaba muy baja de moral; **to raise sb's m.** subirle la moral a algn

moralist ['mɒrəlɪst] *n* moralista *mf*

moralistic [mɒrə'lɪstɪk] *adj* moralizador(a)

morality [mə'rælɪtɪ] *n* moralidad *f*

moralize ['mɒrəlaɪz] *vi* moralizar

morally ['mɒrəlɪ] *adv* moralmente; **m. right/wrong** moral/inmoral

morass [mə'ræs] *n (marsh)* cenagal *m*, pantano *m; Fig (mess)* lío *m*, embrollo *m*; **a m. of details** un laberinto *or* un mar de detalles

moratorium [mɒrə'tɔːrɪəm] *n (pl* **moratoriums** *or* **moratoria** [mɒrə'tɔːrɪə]) moratoria *f*

morbid ['mɔːbɪd] *adj Med* mórbido(a); *(mind)* morboso(a), enfermizo(a); *(curiosity)* malsano(a); *(depressed)* pesimista

morbidness ['mɔːbɪdnɪs] *n (medical, of mind)* morbosidad *f; (depression)* pesimismo *m*

mordant ['mɔːdənt] *adj (criticism etc)* mordaz

more [mɔːr] **1** *adj* más; **and what is m.** y además, y lo que es más; **is there any m. tea?** ¿queda más té?; **I've no m. money** no me queda más dinero; **m. people** más gente; **no m. crying!** ¡deja ya de llorar!
  2 *pron* más; **how many m.?** ¿cuántos más?; **I need some m.** necesito más; **it's m. than enough** basta y sobra;

many/much m. muchos(as)/mucho más; **m. than a hundred** más de cien; **the m. he has, the m. he wants** cuanto más tiene más quiere; **to see m. of sb** ver a algn más a menudo
  3 *adv* más; **I won't do it any m.** no lo volveré a hacer; **it's m. than a little surprising** es bastante sorprendente; **m. and m. difficult** cada vez más difícil; **m. or less the same** más o menos igual; **once m.** una vez más; **she doesn't live here any m.** ya no vive aquí; **still m.** todavía más

morello [mə'reləʊ] *n (pl* **morellos) m. (cherry)** guinda *f*

moreover [mɔː'rəʊvər] *adv* además, por otra parte

mores ['mɔːreɪz] *npl Fml* costumbres *fpl*, tradiciones *fpl*

morgue [mɔːg] *n* depósito *m* de cadáveres

moribund ['mɒrɪbʌnd] *adj* moribundo(a)

Mormon ['mɔːmən] *n Rel* mormón(ona) *m,f*

morning ['mɔːnɪŋ] **1** *n (of day)* mañana *f; (before dawn)* madrugada *f*; **early in the m.** muy de mañana; **in the m.** por la mañana; **in the early hours of the m.** de madrugada; **on Monday mornings** los lunes por la mañana; **tomorrow m.** mañana por la mañana; **good m.!** *(greeting)* ¡buenos días!; *Fam* **to have the m. after** feeling tener resaca
  2 *adj (walk, breeze)* matutino(a), de la mañana ❑ **m. dress** chaqué *m*; **m. paper** diario *m* de la mañana; **m. sickness** náuseas *fpl* del embarazo; **m. star** lucero *m* del alba, estrella *f* matutina

morning-after pill ['mɔːnɪŋ'ɑːftəpɪl] *n* píldora *f* del día después

mornings ['mɔːnɪŋs] *adv* por la mañana

Moroccan [mə'rɒkən] *adj & n* marroquí *(mf)*

Morocco [mə'rɒkəʊ] *n* Marruecos

moron ['mɔːrɒn] *n* **(a)** *Med* retrasado(a) *m,f* mental **(b)** *Fam* subnormal *mf*, *Am* zonzo(a) *m,f*

moronic [mə'rɒnɪk] *adj Fam (person)* subnormal, *Am* zonzo(a); *(expression, behaviour)* de subnormal, *Am* zonzo(a); **a m. comment** una memez

morose [mə'rəʊs] *adj* malhumorado(a), hosco(a)

morpheme ['mɔːfiːm] *n Ling* morfema *m*

morphia ['mɔːfiə] *n*, **morphine** ['mɔːfiːn] *n* morfina *f*

morphology [mɔː'fɒlədʒɪ] *n Biol Ling* morfología *f*

Morse [mɔːs] *n* **M. (code)** (alfabeto *m*) Morse *m*

morsel ['mɔːsəl] *n (of food)* bocado *m; Fig* trozo *m*, fragmento *m*

mortal ['mɔːtəl] **1** *adj (not immortal)* mortal; *(injury, fall)* fatal; **m. remains** restos *mpl* mortales; *Rel* **m. sin** pecado *m* mortal
  2 *n* mortal *mf*

mortality [mɔː'tælɪtɪ] *n* **(a)** *(condition)* mortalidad *f* **(b)** *(number of deaths)* mortalidad *f*; **infant m.** la mortalidad infantil; **m. (rate)** índice *m* or tasa *f* de mortalidad **(c)** *(number of victims)* mortandad *f*

mortally ['mɔːtəlɪ] *adv (offended etc)* mortalmente; **m. wounded** herido(a) de muerte

mortar ['mɔːtər] **1** *n* **(a)** *Constr (cement)* mortero *m*, argamasa *f; Fig* **to put one's money in bricks and m.** invertir dinero en asuntos inmobiliarios **(b)** *Mil (gun)* mortero *m* **(c)** *(bowl)* mortero *m*, almirez *m*; **pestle and m.** maja *f* y mortero
  2 *vt Mil* bombardear con morteros

mortarboard ['mɔːtəbɔːd] *n Univ (cap)* birrete *m*

mortgage ['mɔːgɪdʒ] **1** *n* hipoteca *f*; **m. repayment** pago *m* hipotecario; **to pay off a m.** levantar *or* redimir una hipoteca
  2 *vt (property, one's future)* hipotecar

mortice ['mɔːtɪs] *n see* **mortise**

mortician [mɔːˈtɪʃən] n US encargado(a) m,f de funeraria

mortification [mɔːtɪfɪˈkeɪʃən] n mortificación f

mortify [ˈmɔːtɪfaɪ] vt (pt & pp **mortified**) Rel mortificar; Fam **I was mortified** me sentí avergonzado(a)

mortise [ˈmɔːtɪs] n Carp muesca f, mortaja f; **m. lock** cerradura f embutida

mortuary [ˈmɔːtʃʊərɪ] n depósito m de cadáveres

mosaic [məˈzeɪɪk] n mosaico m; **m. floor** suelo m de mosaico

Moscow [ˈmɒskəʊ, US ˈmɒskaʊ] n Moscú

Moses [ˈməʊzɪz] n Moisés m ▫ **M. basket** moisés m

Moslem [ˈmɒzləm] adj & n musulmán(ana) (m,f)

mosque [mɒsk] n mezquita f

mosquito [mɒsˈkiːtəʊ] n (pl **mosquitoes** or **mosquitos**) Ent mosquito m, Am zancudo m; **m. bite** picadura f de mosquito ▫ **m. net** mosquitero m, mosquitera f

moss [mɒs] n Bot musgo m

mossy [ˈmɒsɪ] adj (**mossier, mossiest**) musgoso(a), cubierto(a) de musgo

most [məʊst] **1** adj (superl of **much, many**) (a) (greatest in quantity etc) más; **this house suffered (the) m. damage** esta casa fue la más afectada; **who made (the) m. mistakes?** ¿quién cometió más errores? (b) (the majority of) la mayoría de, la mayor parte de; **for the m. part** por lo general; **m. of the time** la mayor parte del tiempo; **m. people** la mayoría de la gente

2 pron (a) (greatest part) la mayor parte; **m. of it is finished** la mayor parte está terminada (b) (greatest number or amount) lo máximo, lo más; **there were 50 at the (very) m.** había 50 como máximo; **to make the m. of sth** aprovechar algo al máximo (c) (the majority of people) la mayoría; **m. voted in favour** la mayoría votó a favor

3 adv (superl of **much**) (a) (to form superl) más; **the m. intelligent student in the class** el estudiante más inteligente de la clase (b) (to the greatest degree) más; **what I like m.** lo que más me gusta (c) (very) muy, de lo más; **a m. amusing speech** un discurso de lo más divertido; **m. likely** muy probablemente; **she'll m. likely come** es muy probable que venga; **m. of all** (especially) sobre todo; **you have been m. kind** usted ha sido muy amable (d) US Fam casi; **m. everyone** casi todos

most-favoured nation, US most-favored nation [ˈməʊstfeɪvədˈneɪʃən] n Econ nación f más favorecida; **m.-f. n. status** estatus m inv de nación más favorecida

mostly [ˈməʊstlɪ] adv (a) (chiefly) principalmente, en su mayor parte (b) (generally) generalmente; (usually) normalmente

MOT [eməʊˈtiː] n Br (abbr **Ministry of Transport**) Ministerio m de Trasporte; **MOT test** inspección f técnica de vehículos, Esp ITV f, RP VTV f

motel [məʊˈtel] n motel m

moth [mɒθ] n mariposa f nocturna ▫ **clothes m.** polilla f

mothball [ˈmɒθbɔːl] n bola f de naftalina

motheaten [ˈmɒθiːtən] adj apolillado(a)

mother [ˈmʌðər] **1** n (a) (parent) madre f; **m. love** amor m materno or maternal; **unmarried m.** madre soltera ▫ **m. country** patria f, madre patria f; **M. Nature** Madre f Naturaleza; **M.'s Day** Día m de la Madre; **m.'s help** niñera f; **m. tongue** lengua f materna (b) Rel madre f; **M. Superior** madre superiora; **M. Teresa** la Madre Teresa

2 vt (care for) cuidar como una madre; Pej (spoil) mimar

motherboard [ˈmʌðəbɔːd] n Comptr placa f madre

motherfucker [ˈmʌðəfʌkər] n Vulg (person) hijo(a) m,f de puta, Méx hijo(a) m,f de la chingada

motherhood [ˈmʌðəhʊd] n maternidad f

mothering [ˈmʌðərɪŋ] n cuidados mpl maternales ▫ **M. Sunday** Día m de la Madre

mother-in-law [ˈmʌðərɪnlɔː] n (pl **mothers-in-law**) suegra f

motherland [ˈmʌðəlænd] n patria f, madre patria f

motherless [ˈmʌðəlɪs] adj huérfano(a) de madre

motherly [ˈmʌðəlɪ] adj maternal

mother-of-pearl [mʌðərəvˈpɜːl] n madreperla f, nácar m

mothers-in-law [ˈmʌðəzɪnlɔː] npl see **mother-in-law**

mother-to-be [mʌðətəˈbiː] n (pl **mothers-to-be**) futura madre f

mothproof [ˈmɒθpruːf] adj a prueba de polillas

motif [məʊˈtiːf] n Art Mus motivo m; (embroidered etc) adorno m; Fig (main subject) tema m

motion [ˈməʊʃən] **1** n (a) (movement) movimiento m; Cin **in slow m.** a cámara lenta; **to be in m.** estar en marcha; Fig **to go through the motions** hacer algo como es debido pero sin convicción ▫ US **m. picture** película f; **m. sickness** mareo m (b) (gesture) además m, señal f (c) Pol etc (proposal) moción f; **to carry a m.** aprobar una moción; **to second a m.** apoyar una moción (d) Br Fml (of bowel) deposición f, evacuación f

2 vt & vi hacer señas; **to m. (to) sb to do sth** hacer señas a algn para que haga algo

motionless [ˈməʊʃənlɪs] adj inmóvil

motivate [ˈməʊtɪveɪt] vt motivar

motivation [məʊtɪˈveɪʃən] n motivación f

motivational [məʊtɪˈveɪʃənəl] adj Psych **m. research** estudio m de la psicología del consumidor

motive [ˈməʊtɪv] **1** adj motor, motora or motriz ▫ **m. power** fuerza f motriz

2 n (reason) motivo m; Jur móvil m; **with the best of motives** con la mejor intención

motiveless [ˈməʊtɪvlɪs] adj sin motivo

motley [ˈmɒtlɪ] adj (**motlier, motliest**) (a) (multi-coloured) abigarrado(a), variopinto(a) (b) (varied) diverso(a), variado(a), heterogéneo(a)

motocross [ˈməʊtəkrɒs] n Sport motocross m, motocrós m

motor [ˈməʊtər] n (engine) motor m; Br Fam (car) coche m, automóvil m, Am carro m, CSur auto m; **the m. trade** la industria del automóvil ▫ **m. home** (caravan) auto-caravana f, rulot f, RP casa f rodante; **m. oil** aceite m para motores; **m. racing** carreras fpl de coches or Am carros or CSur autos; **m. show** salón m del automóvil

motorbike [ˈməʊtəbaɪk] n Fam motocicleta f, moto f

motorboat [ˈməʊtəbəʊt] n (lancha) motora f

motorcade [ˈməʊtəkeɪd] n desfile m de coches or Am carros or CSur autos

motorcar [ˈməʊtəkɑːr] n Br coche m, automóvil m

motorcoach [ˈməʊtəkəʊtʃ] n autocar m

motorcycle [ˈməʊtəsaɪkəl] n motocicleta f

motorcyclist [ˈməʊtəsaɪklɪst] n motociclista mf

motoring [ˈməʊtərɪŋ] **1** adj automovilístico(a), del automóvil; **m. accident** accidente m automovilístico; **m. holiday** vacaciones fpl en coche

2 n automovilismo m

motorist [ˈməʊtərɪst] n automovilista mf, conductor(a) m,f (de coche)

motorize [ˈməʊtəraɪz] vt motorizar

motorized [ˈməʊtəraɪzd] adj motorizado(a)

motorman [ˈməʊtəmən] n (pl **motormen**) (train driver) maquinista m, conductor m

motorway ['məʊtəweɪ] n Br autopista f

mottled ['mɒtəld] adj (skin, animal) con manchas; (surface) moteado(a), jaspeado(a)

motto ['mɒtəʊ] n (pl **mottoes** or **mottos**) lema m

mould¹ [məʊld] n (fungus) moho m

mould² [məʊld] **1** n Art Culin Tech molde m; Fig carácter m, temple m; **cast in the same m.** cortado(a) con el mismo patrón

   2 vt (figure) moldear; (clay) modelar; Fig **to m. oneself on sb** tomar a algn como modelo

moulder ['məʊldər] vi **to m. (away)** desmoronarse

moulding ['məʊldɪŋ] n Archit moldura f

mouldy ['məʊldɪ] adj (**mouldier, mouldiest**) (a) (food) mohoso(a); (clothes) lleno(a) de moho, apulgarado(a); **to go m.** enmohecerse; **to smell m.** oler a moho or humedad (b) Br Slang cochino(a), miserable

moult [məʊlt] vi (feathers, skin) mudar

mound [maʊnd] n (a) (of earth) montón m; (small hill) montículo m (b) Fig (pile) montón m

mount¹ [maʊnt] n (mountain) monte m; **M. Everest** (Monte) Everest m

mount² [maʊnt] **1** n (a) (horse) montura f (b) (base, support) soporte m, base f; (for photograph) marco m; (for jewel) engaste m, montura f

   2 vt (a) (horse) subirse or montar a; (bicycle) subir a, montar en; **the car mounted the pavement** el coche se subió a la acera (b) (exhibition) montar; (campaign) organizar, lanzar (c) (photograph) enmarcar; (jewel) engastar, montar (d) Mil **to m. guard** montar la guardia

   3 vi (a) (go up) subir; (get on horse, bike) montar (b) (increase) subir, aumentar

mount up vi (increase) subir, aumentar; (accumulate) amontonarse, acumularse

mountain ['maʊntɪn] **1** n montaña f; Fig (pile) montaña f, montón m

   2 adj Bot **m. ash** serbal m; **m. bike** bicicleta f de montaña; Zool **m. lion** puma m; **m. range** sierra f, cordillera f; **m. sickness** mal m de montaña

mountaineer [maʊntɪ'nɪər] n montañero(a) m,f, alpinista mf, Am andinista mf

mountaineering [maʊntɪ'nɪərɪŋ] n montañismo m, alpinismo m, Am andinismo m

mountainous ['maʊntɪnəs] adj (region) montañoso(a); Fig enorme

mountainside ['maʊntɪnsaɪd] n ladera f

mounted ['maʊntɪd] adj montado(a); **the m. police** la policía montada

mounting ['maʊntɪŋ] **1** n (for engine, gun) soporte m

   2 adj (cost, opposition) creciente

mourn [mɔːn] vt & vi **to m. (for) sb** llorar la muerte de algn

mourner ['mɔːnər] n doliente mf

mournful ['mɔːnfʊl] adj (person) triste, afligido(a); (voice, tone) triste, lúgubre

mourning ['mɔːnɪŋ] n luto m, duelo m; **to be dressed in m.** ir vestido(a) de luto; **to be in m. for sb** estar de luto por algn; **to go into m.** ponerse de luto

mouse [maʊs] n (pl **mice**) (a) Zool ratón m (b) Comptr Esp ratón m, Am mouse m ▫ **m. mat** alfombrilla f

mousetrap ['maʊstræp] n ratonera f

mousse [muːs] n (a) Culin mousse f (b) (for hair) (styling) **m.** espuma f (moldeadora)

moustache [mə'stɑːʃ] n bigote(s) m(pl)

mousy ['maʊsɪ] adj (**mousier, mousiest**) (a) (colour) pardusco(a); (hair) castaño claro (b) (shy) tímido(a)

mouth 1 n (pl **mouths** [maʊðz]) (a) Anat boca f; Fig **I got it straight from the horse's m.** lo sé de buena tinta; Fig **it made my m. water** se me hizo la boca agua; Fig **she has five mouths to feed** tiene cinco bocas que alimentar; Fig **to keep one's m. shut** no decir ni mu or Esp ni pío; Fam **shut your m.!** ¡cállate la boca!, ¡cierra el pico!; Fam **to be down in the m.** estar deprimido(a); Fam **to have a big m.** ser un(a) bocazas or Am chusmo(a); Fam **to shoot one's m. off** hablar más de la cuenta, ser un(a) bocazas or Am chusmo(a) (b) (of bottle) boca f; (of tube) abertura f; (of cave, tunnel etc) boca f, entrada f; (of river) desembocadura f

   2 [maʊð] vt (words) pronunciar, articular; (in affected manner) pronunciar con afectación; (insults) proferir

   3 vi mover los labios

mouth off vi Fam **to m. off about sth** echar un discurso sobre algo, hacerse el enterado en algo

mouthful ['maʊθfʊl] n (of food) bocado m; (of drink) sorbo m; (of air) bocanada f; **to be a bit of a m.** (name etc) ser largo or difícil de pronunciar; Br Fam **to give sb a m.** poner verde a algn

mouth organ ['maʊθɔːgən] n Mus armónica f

mouthpiece ['maʊθpiːs] n (a) Mus boquilla f (b) (of telephone) micrófono m (c) Fig (spokesman) portavoz m

mouth-to-mouth [maʊθtə'maʊθ] adj **m.-to-m. resuscitation** boca a boca m

mouthwash ['maʊθwɒʃ] n enjuage m bucal

mouthwatering ['maʊθwɔːtərɪŋ] adj muy apetitoso(a), que se le hace a uno la boca agua

movable ['muːvəbəl] adj movible, móvil

move [muːv] **1** n (a) (movement) movimiento m; **to be on the m.** (travel) viajar, desplazarse; Fig (army, country) estar en marcha; Fig (be busy) estar muy ocupado(a), no parar; **we must make a m.** debemos irnos ya; Fam **get a m. on!** ¡date prisa!, Am ¡apúrate! (b) (games) jugada f; (turn) turno m; **whose m. is it?** ¿a quién le toca jugar? (c) (step) paso m; (course of action) medida f; **to make the first m.** dar el primer paso; **what is the next m.?** ¿qué hay que hacer ahora? (d) (transfer) (to new home) mudanza f, traslado m; (to new job) traslado m

   2 vt (a) (gen) mover; (furniture etc) cambiar de sitio, trasladar; (steering wheel) girar; (transfer) trasladar; **m. that motorbike off the lawn!** ¡quita or Am saca esa moto del césped!; **to m. house** mudarse (de casa), trasladarse; **to m. job** cambiar de trabajo; **to m. sth closer** acercar algo (b) (in games) mover, jugar (c) (incite, motivate) inducir, mover; (persuade) persuadir; **I won't be moved** no me harán cambiar de parecer; **to m. sb to tears** hacer llorar a algn (d) (affect emotionally) conmover; **she is easily moved** es muy sensible (e) (resolution etc) proponer, Am mocionar; **I m. that the meeting be closed** propongo or Am mociono que se cierre la reunión

   3 vi (a) (change position) moverse, trasladarse, desplazarse; (change house) mudarse (de casa); (change post, department etc) trasladarse; **to start moving** ponerse en marcha; **don't m.!** ¡no te muevas!; **m. out of the way!** ¡quítate de en medio!, Am ¡sal del medio!; **to m. to another seat/job** cambiarse de asiento/trabajo; **keep moving!** ¡circulen! (b) (travel, go) ir; **it moves at high speed** va a gran velocidad (c) (leave) irse, marcharse; **it's time we were moving** es hora de irnos (d) (games) jugar, hacer una jugada; (game piece) moverse (e) (take action) tomar medidas (f) (progress) hacer progresos, adelantar

move about, move around 1 vt (object) cambiar de sitio or lugar; (employee) trasladar

   2 vi (be restless) moverse mucho; (walk to and fro etc) ir y venir, ir de acá para allá; (travel) viajar de un lugar a otro; **to m. about freely** circular libremente

move along 1 *vt (move forward)* hacer avanzar, adelantar; *(keep moving)* hacer circular
2 *vi (move forward)* avanzar, adelantarse; *(keep moving)* circular; **m. along!** *(to crowd)* ¡circulen!; *(to person on bench)* ¡córrete!, ¡haz sitio!

move away 1 *vt (object, person)* alejar, apartar (**from** de)
2 *vi* (**a**) *(move aside etc)* alejarse, apartarse (**b**) *(leave)* irse, marcharse (**c**) *(change house)* mudarse (de casa)

move back 1 *vt* (**a**) *(object)* mover hacia atrás; *(crowd etc)* hacer retroceder (**b**) *(to original place)* volver
2 *vi* (**a**) *(withdraw, retreat)* retroceder, retirarse (**b**) *(to original place)* volver

move down 1 *vt (person, object)* bajar
2 *vi* bajar

move forward 1 *vt* (**a**) *(person, vehicle etc)* avanzar, adelantar (**b**) *(clock)* adelantar
2 *vi* avanzar, adelantarse

move in 1 *vt (object)* llevar hacia dentro; *(furniture into new home etc)* instalar
2 *vi* (**a**) *(into new home)* instalarse (**b**) *(police etc) (approach)* acercarse; **to m. in on** acercarse a, avanzar hacia

move off 1 *vt (remove from)* sacar *or* quitar de
2 *vi* (**a**) *(go away)* irse, marcharse; *(train)* salir (**b**) *(set off)* ponerse en camino; *(car, train)* arrancar

move on 1 *vt* (**a**) *(keep moving) (people, cars etc)* circular (**b**) *(hands of clock)* adelantar
2 *vi* (**a**) *(keep moving) (people, cars etc)* circular; **m. on, please!** ¡circulen! (**b**) *(go forward)* avanzar; *(time)* pasar, transcurrir

move out 1 *vt (object)* sacar; *(troops)* retirar
2 *vi* (**a**) *(leave)* irse, marcharse; *(troops)* retirarse (**b**) *(leave house)* mudarse (**c**) *Aut* **to m. out in order to overtake** salirse para adelantar

move over 1 *vt* correr
2 *vi* correrse; **m. over!** ¡córrete!

move up 1 *vt* (**a**) *(object, person)* subir; *(bring closer)* acercar (**b**) *Fig (promote)* ascender; **to be moved up** *(pupil)* pasar a la clase superior
2 *vi* (**a**) *(go up)* subir (**b**) *Fig (be promoted)* ser ascendido(a), ascender (**c**) *(move along)* correrse

moveable ['muːvəbəl] *adj see* **movable**

movement ['muːvmənt] *n* (**a**) *(act, motion)* movimiento *m*; *(gesture with hand etc)* gesto *m*, ademán *m*; **back and forth m.** vaivén *m*; **to watch sb's movements** vigilar los movimientos *or* las actividades de algn (**b**) *(transport)* transporte *m*; *(of goods, employees)* traslado *m*; *(of troops)* desplazamiento *m* (**c**) *Pol Lit* movimiento *m*; *(trend)* tendencia *f*, corriente *f*; **the feminist m.** el movimiento feminista (**d**) *Com (of stock market)* actividad *f*; *(of prices)* variación *f* (**e**) *Tech (workings) (of clock, machine)* mecanismo *m* (**f**) *Mus (of symphony etc)* movimiento *m*, tempo *m*, tiempo *m* (**g**) *Med (of bowels)* evacuación *f*

mover ['muːvər] *n* (**a**) *Fam* **she's a lovely m.** tiene mucho garbo (**b**) *(in meeting etc)* proponedor(a) *m,f* (**c**) *US* mozo *m* de mudanzas

movie ['muːvɪ] *n* película *f*; **to go to the movies** ir al cine ❑ **m. camera** cámara *f* cinematográfica *or* de cine; **m. industry** industria *f* cinematográfica *or* del cine; **m. star** estrella *f* de cine; *US* **m. theater** cine *m*

moviegoer ['muːvɪɡəʊər] *n US* aficionado(a) *m,f* al cine

moving ['muːvɪŋ] *adj* (**a**) *(that moves)* móvil; *(in motion)* en movimiento; *(car etc)* en marcha ❑ **m. staircase** escalera *f* mecánica (**b**) *(causing motion)* motor(a), motriz; *Fig (motivating)* instigador(a), promotor (**c**) *Fig (touching)* conmovedor(a)

mow [məʊ] *vt (pt* **mowed**; *pp* **mown** *or* **mowed)** *(lawn)*

cortar, segar; *(corn, wheat)* segar; *Fig* **to m. down** *(kill etc)* matar, segar

mower ['məʊər] *n (for lawn)* segadora *f*, cortacésped *m or f*; *Agr* segadora *f*

mown [məʊn] *pp see* **mow**

Mozambican [məʊzæm'biːkən] *adj & n* mozambique-ño(a) *(m,f)*

Mozambique [məʊzəm'biːk] *n* Mozambique

Mozarab [məʊ'zærəb] *n* mozárabe *mf*

MP [em'piː] *n* (**a**) *Br (abbr* **Member of Parliament)** diputado(a) *m,f* (**b**) *Fam (abbr* **Military Police)** P.M., policía *f* militar

MP3 [empiː'θriː] *n (abbr* **MPEG-1 Audio Layer-3)** MP3 *m*; **M. player** reproductor *m* de MP3

MPEG ['empeɡ] *n Comptr (abbr* **Moving Pictures Expert Group)** MPEG *m*

mpg [empiː'dʒiː] *(abbr* **miles per gallon)** = litros de gasolina a los cien kilómetros

mph [empiː'eɪtʃ] *(abbr* **miles per hour)** millas *fpl* por hora

Mr ['mɪstər] *(abbr* **mister)** señor *m*, Sr.

MRBM [emɑːbiː'em] *n Mil (abbr* **medium-range ballistic missile)** proyectil *m* balístico de alcance intermedio, PBAI *m*

Mrs ['mɪsɪz] *abbr* señora *f*, Sra.

MS [em'es] *(abbr* **manuscript)** manuscrito *m*, ms.

Ms [məz] *(abbr* señora *f*, Sra., señorita *f*, Srta.

ms (**a**) *(abbr* **milliseconds)** ms, milisegundos *mpl* (**b**) *(abbr* **manuscript)** manuscrito *m*, ms.

MSc [emes'siː] *n (abbr* **Master of Science)** máster *m or Am* maestría *f* en Ciencias

MSG [emes'dʒiː] *n (abbr* **monosodium glutamate)** glutamato *m* monosódico

MST [emes'tiː] *n US (abbr* **Mountain Standard Time)** = hora oficial en la zona de las Montañas Rocosas en los Estados Unidos

Mt *(abbr* **Mount, Mountain)** monte *m*, montaña *f*

mth *(abbr* **month)** mes *m*, m/

much [mʌtʃ] (**more, most**) **1** *adj* mucho(a); **add twice as m. flour** añade el doble de harina; **as m. ... as** tanto(a) ... como; **as m. wine as you like** tanto vino como quieras; **how m. chocolate?** ¿cuánto chocolate?; **m. admiration** mucha admiración; **so m.** tanto(a); **so m. suffering** tanto sufrimiento; **too m.** demasiado(a); **m. love** *(at end of letter)* un fuerte abrazo
2 *adv* mucho; **as m. as** tanto como; **as m. as you like** todo lo que quieras; **as m. as possible** todo lo posible; **how m.?** ¿cuánto?; **how m. is it?** ¿cuánto es?, ¿cuánto vale?; **m. better/worse** mucho mejor/peor; **m. as I hate him** por mucho que le odie; **m. more** mucho más; **m. to my surprise** para gran sorpresa mía; **so m. the better** ¡tanto mejor!; **thank you very m.** muchísimas gracias; **they are m. the same** son más o menos iguales; **too m.** demasiado; **10 kilos too m.** 10 kilos de más; **very m.** muchísimo; **without so m. as** sin siquiera; *Fam* **that's a bit m.!** ¡eso ya es el colmo!
3 *pron* mucho; **I'll say this m. for her** tiene eso en su favor; **I thought as m.** lo suponía; **it's not up to m.** no vale gran cosa; **m. of the town was destroyed** gran parte de la ciudad quedó destrozada; **m. remains to be done** queda mucho por hacer; **they don't see m. of each other** se ven muy poco; **there isn't that m. of it** no hay tanto; **to be not m. of sth** *(no good at)* no ser muy bueno(a) en algo; *(not keen on)* no ser muy aficionado(a) a algo; **to make m. of sth** dar mucha importancia a algo

muchness ['mʌtʃnɪs] *n Fam* **it's much of a m.** viene a ser lo mismo

muck [mʌk] n (**a**) *(dirt)* suciedad *f; (mud)* lodo *m; (manure)* estiércol *m; Fam* caca *f* (**b**) *Fig* porquería *f;* **to make a m. of sth** meter la pata con algo, *Esp* hacer algo fatal *or* de pena

muck about, muck around *Br Fam* **1** *vi (idle)* gandulear, perder el tiempo; *(play the fool)* hacer el tonto; **to m. about with sth** *(fiddle with)* enredar *or Am* dar vueltas con algo
   2 *vt* **to m. sb about** fastidiar a algn ·

muck in *vi Br Fam (help)* arrimar el hombro, *Méx RP* dar una mano

muck out *vt (stable)* limpiar

muck up *vt* (**a**) *(dirty)* ensuciar (**b**) *Fig (spoil)* echar a perder; *(fail to achieve)* no conseguir, fracasar

muckraking [ˈmʌkreɪkɪŋ] n *Fam* cotilleo *m*

muck-up [ˈmʌkʌp] n *Fam (bungle)* chapuza; *(mess)* follón *m*, lío *m*

mucky [ˈmʌkɪ] *adj* (**muckier, muckiest**) *(dirty)* sucio(a); *(muddy)* lodoso(a)

mucous [ˈmjuːkəs] *adj* mucoso(a) □ **m. membrane** membrana *f* mucosa

mucus [ˈmjuːkəs] n moco *m*, mocosidad *f*

mud [mʌd] n lodo *m*, barro *m; (thick)* fango *m; Fig Hum* **it's as clear as m.** no queda nada claro; *Fam* **her name is m.** tiene muy mala fama; **to throw** *or* **sling m. at sb** poner a algn por los suelos □ **m. bath** baño *m* de lodo; **m. flat** marisma *f*

mudbank [ˈmʌdbæŋk] n banco *m* de arena

muddle [ˈmʌdəl] **1** n *(mess)* desorden *m; Fig (mix-up)* confusión *f,* embrollo *m*, lío *m;* **to be in a m.** *(things)* estar en desorden; *(person)* estar hecho un lío; **to get into a m.** *(things)* quedar en desorden; *(person)* hacerse un lío; **there was a m. over the dates** hubo un lío con las fechas
   2 *vt* **to m. (up)** *(person, facts)* confundir; **to get muddled up** liarse, hacerse un lío

muddle along *vi* actuar a la buena de Dios *or* al tuntún

muddle through *vi* arreglárselas, ingeniárselas

muddle-headed [ˈmʌdəlhedɪd] *adj (person)* despistado(a); *(plan, ideas)* confuso(a)

muddy [ˈmʌdɪ] *adj* (**muddier, muddiest**) *(path etc)* lodoso(a), fangoso(a); *(hands, shoes etc)* lleno(a) *or* cubierto(a) de barro *or* de lodo; *(river)* cenagoso(a); *(liquid)* turbio(a); *(complexion, colour)* terroso(a)

mudguard [ˈmʌdgɑːd] n *Br Esp RP* guardabarros *m inv, Andes CAm Carib* guardafango *m, Méx* salpicadera *f*

mudslinging [ˈmʌdslɪŋɪŋ] n *Fam* **the debate degenerated into m.** el debate degeneró en meras descalificaciones

muesli [ˈmjuːzlɪ] n muesli *m*

muezzin [muˈezɪn] n *Rel* almuecín *m*

muff¹ [mʌf] n *(for hands)* manguito *m;* **ear muffs** orejeras *fpl*

muff² [mʌf] *vt Fam* pifiar; **to m. it (up)** estropearlo, echarlo a perder

muffin [ˈmʌfɪn] n *Br (teacake)* tortita *f, ·US (cake)* magdalena *f*

muffle [ˈmʌfəl] *vt* (**a**) *(sound)* amortiguar, ensordecer (**b**) *(person)* **to m. (up)** abrigar; *(with scarf, hat)* embozar

muffled [ˈmʌfəld] *adj (sound)* sordo(a)

muffler [ˈmʌflər] n (**a**) *(scarf)* bufanda *f* (**b**) *US Aut* silenciador *m*

mufti [ˈmʌftɪ] n *Mil etc* **in m.** vestido(a) de paisano

mug¹ [mʌg] n *(large cup)* taza *f* alta, tazón *m; (beer tankard)* jarra *f*

mug² [mʌg] **1** n *Fam* (**a**) *Br Fam (gullible person)* bobo(a)

m,f; primo(a) *m,f, Am* zonzo(a) *m,f;* **it's a m.'s game** es cosa de tontos (**b**) *(face)* jeta *f,* hocico *m*
   2 *vt (pt & pp* **mugged**) *(attack)* atracar, asaltar

mug up *vi Br Fam (study)* **to m. up on sth** matarse estudiando algo, *Esp* empollar *or RP* tragar algo

mugger [ˈmʌgər] n *(attacker)* asaltante *mf*

mugging [ˈmʌgɪŋ] n *(attack)* asalto *m*

muggy [ˈmʌgɪ] *adj* (**muggier, muggiest**) *(weather)* bochornoso(a)

mugshot [ˈmʌgʃɒt] n *Fam (esp taken by police)* foto *f* de la cara

mulatto [mjuːˈlætəʊ] n *(pl* **mulattos** *or* **mulattoes**) mulato(a) *m,f*

mulberry [ˈmʌlbərɪ] n (**a**) *(fruit)* mora *f* (**b**) *(tree)* morera *f,* moral *m* (**c**) *(colour)* morado *m*

mulch [mʌltʃ] n *Agr* abono *m*, pajote *m*

mule¹ [mjuːl] n *(animal)* mulo(a) *m,f; Fig* **as stubborn as a m.** *(person)* más terco(a) que una mula

mule² [mjuːl] n *(slipper)* chinela *f*

mulish [ˈmjuːlɪʃ] *adj* terco(a), testarudo(a)

mull [mʌl] *vt (wine)* calentar con especias; **mulled wine** vino *m* caliente con especias

mull over *vi* **to m. over a matter** reflexionar sobre *or* reconsiderar un asunto

mullet [ˈmʌlɪt] n *(pl* **mullet** *or* **mullets**) *(fish)* **grey m.** mújol *m;* **red m.** salmonete *m*

multiaccess [mʌltɪˈækses] n *Comptr* acceso *m* múltiple; **m. system** sistema *m* multiacceso *or* de acceso múltiple

multichannel [mʌltɪˈtʃænəl] *adj (TV)* multicanal

multicoloured, *US* **multicolored** [ˈmʌltɪkʌləd] *adj* multicolor

multicultural [mʌltɪˈkʌltʃərəl] *adj* multicultural

multidisciplinary [ˈmʌltɪdɪsɪˈplɪnərɪ] *adj Educ* multidisciplinar

multiethnic [ˈmʌltɪˈeθnɪk] *adj* multiétnico(a)

multifaceted [ˈmʌltɪˈfæsɪtɪd] *adj* múltiple, con múltiples facetas

multifarious [mʌltɪˈfeərɪəs] *adj* múltiple, vario(a), diverso(a)

multi-functional [mʌltɪˈfʌŋkʃənəl] *adj* multifuncional

multilateral [mʌltɪˈlætərəl] *adj* multilateral

multilingual [mʌltɪˈlɪŋwəl] *adj* plurilingüe

multimedia [mʌltɪˈmiːdɪə] **1** n multimedia *f*
   2 *adj* multimedia *inv*

multimillion [mʌltɪˈmɪljən] *adj* **a m. pound/dollar project** un proyecto multimillonario

multimillionaire [mʌltɪmɪljəˈneər] n multimillonario(a) *m,f*

multinational [mʌltɪˈnæʃənəl] **1** *adj* multinacional
   2 n multinacional *f*

multiparty [mʌltɪˈpɑːtɪ] *adj* **m. democracy/system** democracia *f*/sistema *m* pluripartidista

multiple [ˈmʌltɪpəl] **1** *adj* múltiple; *Aut* **m. pile-up** colisión *f* múltiple □ *Med* **m. sclerosis** esclerosis *f* en placas *or* múltiple
   2 n *Math* múltiplo *m*

multiple-choice [ˈmʌltɪplˈtʃɔɪs] *adj* **m.-c. exam/ question** examen *m*/pregunta *f* (de) tipo test

multiplex [ˈmʌltɪpleks] n multicine *m*

multiplication [mʌltɪplɪˈkeɪʃən] n multiplicación *f* □ **m. sign** signo *m* de multiplicar; **m. table** tabla *f* de multiplicar

multiplicity [mʌltɪˈplɪsɪtɪ] n multiplicidad *f*

multiply ['mʌltɪplaɪ] **1** vt (pt & pp **multiplied**) Math multiplicar (**by** por)
 2 vi (reproduce) multiplicarse
multiprocessor [mʌltɪ'prəʊsesər] n Comptr multiprocesador m
multipurpose [mʌltɪ'pɜːpəs] adj multiuso inv
multiracial [mʌltɪ'reɪʃəl] adj multirracial
multistorey, US **multistory** [mʌltɪ'stɔːrɪ] adj (building) de varios pisos; **m. car park** parking m or Esp aparcamiento m or Col parqueadero m de varias plantas
multitasking ['mʌltɪtɑːskɪŋ] n (**a**) Comptr multitarea f (**b**) Ind movilidad f funcional
multitude ['mʌltɪtjuːd] n (crowd) multitud f, muchedumbre f
multi-user ['mʌltɪ'juːsər] adj Comptr multiusuario inv; **m. system** sistema m multiusuario
mum¹ [mʌm] n Br Fam mamá f
mum² [mʌm] adj **to keep m.** no decir ni pío, guardar silencio
mumble ['mʌmbəl] vt & vi musitar, hablar entre dientes
mumbo jumbo [mʌmbəʊ'dʒʌmbəʊ] n (pl **mumbo jumbos**) (gibberish) galimatías f inv
mummify ['mʌmɪfaɪ] vt (pt & pp **mummified**) momificar
mummy¹ ['mʌmɪ] n (body) momia f
mummy² ['mʌmɪ] n Br Fam (mother) mamá f
mumps [mʌmps] n Med paperas fpl
munch [mʌntʃ] vt & vi mascar, masticar
mundane [mʌn'deɪn] adj (**a**) (worldly) mundano(a) (**b**) Pej (ordinary) vulgar, banal; (job, life) rutinario(a)
municipal [mjuː'nɪsɪpəl] adj municipal
municipality [mjuːnɪsɪ'pælɪtɪ] n municipio m
munitions [mjuː'nɪʃənz] npl municiones fpl
mural ['mjʊərəl] **1** adj mural
 2 n pintura f mural, mural m
murder ['mɜːdər] **1** n (**a**) (killing) asesinato m, homicidio m; **m. case** caso m de homicidio; **the m. weapon** el arma homicida (**b**) Fam **it was m.!** ¡vaya pesadilla!; **she cried blue m.** gritó como si la estuvieran matando; **they get away with m.** hacen lo que les da la gana
 2 vt (**a**) (kill) asesinar, matar (**b**) Fam Fig (song etc) destrozar, estropear
murderer ['mɜːdərər] n asesino m, homicida m
murderess ['mɜːdərɪs] n asesina f, homicida f
murderous ['mɜːdərəs] adj (look, thoughts) asesino(a), homicida
murky ['mɜːkɪ] adj (**murkier, murkiest**) (**a**) (gen) oscuro(a), tenebroso(a); (water) turbio(a); (weather) nublado(a); (night) de niebla (**b**) Fig (business) turbio(a); (past) tenebroso(a)
murmur ['mɜːmər] **1** n (**a**) (of voice, stream) murmullo m, susurro m; (of traffic) rumor m ❑ Med **heart m.** soplo m cardiaco (**b**) (complaint) queja f; **he did it without a m.** lo hizo sin rechistar
 2 vt & vi murmurar
muscle ['mʌsəl] **1** n músculo m; **m. power** fuerza f; **he didn't move a m.** ni se inmutó
 2 vi Fam **to m. in on sth** entrometerse en asuntos ajenos
Muscovite ['mʌskəvaɪt] adj & n moscovita (mf)
muscular ['mʌskjʊlər] adj (pain, tissue) muscular; (person) musculoso(a)
Muse [mjuːz] n Myth musa f
muse [mjuːz] vi **to m. on** or **about sth** meditar algo, reflexionar sobre algo
museum [mjuː'zɪəm] n museo m

mush [mʌʃ] n (soft) papilla f; (porridge) gachas fpl; Fam (food overcooked) mazacote m
mushroom ['mʌʃruːm] **1** n Bot hongo m, Esp seta f; Culin champiñón m ❑ **m. cloud** hongo m atómico
 2 vi Fig (grow quickly) crecer de la noche a la mañana; (spread) multiplicarse
mushy ['mʌʃɪ] adj (**mushier, mushiest**) (**a**) (food) blando(a), en papilla; **m. peas** puré m de guisantes (**b**) Fam (sentimental) sentimentaloide
music ['mjuːzɪk] n música f; **to set a work to m.** poner música a una obra; Fig **to face the m.** dar la cara ❑ **chamber m.** música de cámara; **m. box** caja f de música; **m. hall** teatro m de variedades; **m. lover** melómano(a) m,f; **m. piracy** piratería f musical; **m. score** partitura f; **m. stand** atril m; **m. video** vídeo m or Am video m musical; **piped m.** música f ambiental
musical ['mjuːzɪkəl] **1** adj musical, de música; **to be m.** (gifted) estar dotado(a) para la música; (fond of music) ser aficionado(a) a la música; **to have a m. ear** tener buen oído para la música ❑ **m. instrument** instrumento m musical
 2 n comedia f musical
musician [mjuː'zɪʃən] n músico(a) m,f
musicologist [mjuːzɪ'kɒlədʒɪst] n musicólogo(a) m,f, musicógrafo(a) m,f
musings ['mjuːzɪŋz] npl meditaciones fpl, reflexiones fpl
musk [mʌsk] n (substance) almizcle m
musket ['mʌskɪt] n mosquete m
musketeer [mʌskɪ'tɪər] n mosquetero m
Muslim ['mʊzlɪm] adj & n musulmán(ana) (m,f)
muslin ['mʌzlɪn] n muselina f
musquash ['mʌskwɒʃ] n Zool ratón m amizclero, desmán m
mussel ['mʌsəl] n Zool mejillón m ❑ **m. bed** criadero m de mejillones
must¹ [mʌst] n (of grapes) mosto m
must² [mʌst] n (mould) moho m; (smell) olor m a humedad
must³ [mʌst] **1** v aux (**a**) (necessity, obligation) deber, tener que; **if I m.** si no hay más remedio; **one m. eat to live** hay que comer para vivir; **you m. arrive on time** tienes que or debes llegar a la hora; **you m. not do that again** no lo vuelvas a hacer (**b**) (probability) deber de; **he m. be ill** debe de estar enfermo; **it m. be four o'clock** serán las cuatro
 2 n Fam necesidad f; **this gadget is an absolute m. for do-it-yourself fanatics** es un aparato imprescindible para los aficionados al bricolage
mustache ['mʌstæʃ] n US see **moustache**
mustachioed [mə'stɑːʃɪəʊd] adj con bigotes, bigotudo(a)
mustard ['mʌstəd] n Bot Culin mostaza f ❑ **m. gas** gas m mostaza; **m. pot** mostacera f
muster ['mʌstər] **1** n Mil etc (gathering) asamblea f; (inspection) revista f; Fig **to pass m.** ser aceptable
 2 vt (supporters) reunir; (troops) formar; Fig **to m. (up) courage** or **strength** cobrar fuerzas
 3 vi (supporters) reunirse, juntarse; (troops) formar
mustiness ['mʌstɪnɪs] n olor m a humedad
mustn't ['mʌsənt] = must not
musty ['mʌstɪ] adj (**mustier, mustiest**) que huele a cerrado or a humedad
mutant ['mjuːtənt] adj & n mutante (mf)
mutate [mjuː'teɪt] **1** vt mudar, transformar
 2 vi sufrir mutación, transformarse
mutation [mjuː'teɪʃən] n mutación f
mute ['mjuːt] **1** adj (person, letter etc) mudo(a)

2 _n_ (**a**) _(person)_ mudo(a) _m,f_ ❑ **deaf m.** sordomudo(a) _m,f_ (**b**) _Mus_ sordina _f_

muted ['mju:tɪd] _adj (sound)_ sordo(a), apagado(a); _(colour)_ suave, apagado(a)

mutilate ['mju:tɪleɪt] _vt_ mutilar

mutilation [mju:tɪ'leɪʃən] _n_ mutilación _f_

mutineer [mju:tɪ'nɪər] _n_ amotinado(a) _m,f_

mutinous ['mju:tɪnəs] _adj (taking part in mutiny)_ amotinado(a); _Fig_ rebelde

mutiny ['mju:tɪnɪ] **1** _n_ motín _m_, rebelión _f_
   2 _vi_ amotinarse, rebelarse

mutt [mʌt] _n Fam_ (**a**) _(dog)_ perro _m_ callejero, chucho _m_, _RP_ pichicho _m_ (**b**) _(person)_ estúpido(a) _m,f_

mutter ['mʌtər] **1** _n (mumble)_ murmullo _m_
   2 _vt_ murmurar, decir entre dientes
   3 _vi (angrily)_ refunfuñar

muttering ['mʌtərɪŋ] _n_ rezongo _m_, refunfuño _m_

mutton ['mʌtən] _n Culin_ (carne _f_ de) cordero _m_; **shoulder of m.** paletilla _f_ de cordero

mutual ['mju:tʃʊəl] _adj (help, love etc)_ mutuo(a), recíproco(a); _(common, shared)_ común; **by m. consent** de común acuerdo; **our m. friend George** nuestro (común) amigo George; **the feeling is m.** lo mismo digo yo ❑ _US Fin_ **m. benefit society** mutualidad _f_, mutua _f_; _US Fin_ **m. fund** fondo _m_ común de inversión; **m. insurance** seguro _m_ mutuo

mutually ['mju:tʃʊəlɪ] _adv_ mutuamente; **at a m. agreed time** a una hora convenida entre los dos

Muzak® ['mju:zæk] _n_ música _f_ de fondo, _Esp_ hilo _m_ musical, _RP_ música _f_ funcional

muzzle ['mʌzəl] **1** _n_ (**a**) _(snout)_ hocico _m_ (**b**) _(device)_ bozal _m_; _(of gun)_ boca _f_
   2 _vt (dog)_ abozalar, poner un bozal a; _Fig (person, press etc)_ amordazar

muzzy ['mʌzɪ] _adj_ (**muzzier, muzziest**) (**a**) _(dizzy)_ mareado(a); _(groggy)_ atontado(a); _(tipsy)_ achispado(a) (**b**) _(blurred)_ borroso(a)

MW _(abbr_ **medium wave**_)_ onda _f_ media, OM _f_

my [maɪ] **1** _poss adj_ mi; **I washed my hair** me lavé el pelo; **my cousins** mis primos; **my father** mi padre; **my own car**

mi propio coche; **one of my friends** un amigo mío; **she twisted my arm** me torció el brazo
   2 _interj_ ¡caramba!, ¡caray!

Myanmar [maɪæn'mɑːr] _n (official name of Burma)_ Myanmar

myopia [maɪ'əʊpɪə] _n_ miopía _f_

myopic [maɪ'ɒpɪk] _adj_ miope

myriad ['mɪrɪəd] _n Literary_ miríada _f_

myrrh [mɜːr] _n_ mirra _f_

myrtle ['mɜːtəl] _n Bot_ arrayán _m_, mirto _m_

myself [maɪ'self] _pers pron_ (**a**) _(emphatic)_ yo mismo(a); **I did it all by m.** lo hice yo solo; **I saw it (for) m.** yo mismo lo vi; **my husband and m.** mi marido y yo (**b**) _(reflexive)_ me; **I hurt m.** me hice daño (**c**) _(after prep)_ mí (mismo(a)); **I kept it for m.** lo guardé para mí; **I said to m.** me dije para mí

mysterious [mɪ'stɪərɪəs] _adj_ misterioso(a)

mysteriously [mɪs'tɪərɪəslɪ] _adv_ misteriosamente

mystery ['mɪstərɪ] _n_ misterio _m_; **it's a m. to me how he managed to do it** no entiendo cómo consiguió hacerlo ❑ _Rel_ **m. play** auto _m_ sacramental, misterio _m_

mystic ['mɪstɪk] _adj & n_ místico(a) _(m,f)_

mystical ['mɪstɪkəl] _adj_ místico(a)

mysticism ['mɪstɪsɪzəm] _n_ misticismo _m_; _Lit_ mística _f_

mystification [mɪstɪfɪ'keɪʃən] _n (bewilderment)_ estupefacción _f_, desconcierto _m_; _(deliberate confusion)_ artimaña _f_, ardid _m_

mystify ['mɪstɪfaɪ] _vt (pt & pp_ **mystified**_)_ dejar perplejo(a), desconcertar; **I was completely mystified** me quedé pasmado(a)

mystique [mɪ'sti:k] _n_ mística _f_; **there's no m. about it** no tiene secretos

myth [mɪθ] _n (traditional story)_ mito _m_; **it's a complete m.** _(illusion)_ es pura fantasía

mythical ['mɪθɪkəl] _adj (legendary)_ mítico(a); _(imagined)_ imaginario(a), fantástico(a)

mythological [mɪθə'lɒdʒɪkəl] _adj_ mitológico(a)

mythology [mɪ'θɒlədʒɪ] _n_ mitología _f_

myxomatosis [mɪksəmə'təʊsɪs] _n_ mixomatosis _f_

N, n [en] *n (the letter)* N, n *f*

N *(abbr* **North)** Norte, N

NAACP [eneɪeɪsiːˈpiː] *n US (abbr* **National Association for the Advancement of Colored People)** = asociación americana para la defensa de los derechos de la gente de color

NAAFI [ˈnæfɪ] *n Br Mil (abbr* **Navy, Army and Air Force Institutes)** = servicio de tiendas y cantinas para las fuerzas armadas

nab [næb] *vt (pt & pp* **nabbed)** *Fam* pescar, pillar

nacre [ˈneɪkər] *n* nácar *m*, madreperla *f*

nadir [ˈnædɪər] *n* **(a)** *Astron* nadir *m* **(b)** *Fig* punto *m* más bajo

naff [næf] *adj Br Fam (tasteless)* ordinario(a), *Esp* hortera, *Esp* cutre, *Chile* cuico(a), *RP* terraja; *(of poor quality)* pobre, *Esp* cutre, *RP* terraja; *(comment, behaviour)* de mal gusto

NAFTA [ˈnæftə] *n (abbr* **North American Free Trade Agreement)** NAFTA *m*, TLC *m*

nag¹ [næg] *n (horse)* rocín *m*

nag² [næg] **1** *n (person)* gruñón(ona) *m,f*, regañón(ona) *m,f*
 2 *vt (pt & pp* **nagged)** *(annoy)* fastidiar, *Esp* dar la lata a; *(constantly complain)* dar la tabarra
 3 *vi* quejarse

nagger [ˈnægər] *n* regañón(ona) *m,f*

nagging [ˈnægɪŋ] **1** *adj* **(a)** *(complaining)* gruñón(ona), regañón(ona) **(b)** *(persistent)* continuo(a); **a n. pain** un dolor continuo
 2 *n* quejas *fpl*

nail [neɪl] **1** *n* **(a)** *(of finger, toe)* uña *f*; **to bite/clip/trim one's nails** comerse/cortarse/arreglarse las uñas; *Fig* **to be as hard as nails** *(tough)* ser muy fuerte *or* resistente; *(unsympathetic)* tener el corazón de piedra □ **n. clippers** cortaúñas *m inv*; **n. polish, n. varnish,** *US* **n. enamel** esmalte *m or* laca *f* de uñas **(b)** *(metal)* clavo *m*; *Fig* **to hit the n. on the head** dar en el clavo
 2 *vt* **(a)** *(in carpentry)* clavar, sujetar con clavos; **they nailed the picture to the wall** clavaron el cuadro en la pared **(b)** *Fam (catch, trap)* pillar, coger

nail-biting [ˈneɪlbaɪtɪŋ] *adj Fam (contest, finish)* de infarto, emocionantísimo(a); **after a n.-b. few hours, the hostages were released** después de varias horas de tensa espera liberaron a los rehenes

nailbrush [ˈneɪlbrʌʃ] *n* cepillo *m* de uñas

nailfile [ˈneɪlfaɪl] *n* lima *f* de uñas

nail-scissors [ˈneɪlsɪzəz] *npl* tijeras *fpl* de uñas

naïve [naɪˈiːv] *adj* ingenuo(a)

naively [naɪˈiːvlɪ] *adv* ingenuamente

naivety [naɪˈiːvtɪ] *n* ingenuidad *f*

naked [ˈneɪkɪd] *adj (body)* desnudo(a); *(light)* sin pantalla; *(flame)* sin protección; **n. from the waist up/down** desnudo de cintura para arriba/abajo; **barely visible to the n. eye** apenas visible a simple vista; *Fig* **the n. truth** la pura verdad

nakedness [ˈneɪkɪdnɪs] *n* desnudez *f*

namby-pamby [næmbɪˈpæmbɪ] *adj & n* ñoño(a) *(m,f)*

name [neɪm] **1** *n* **(a)** *(of person, thing)* nombre *m*; *(surname)* apellido *m*; **what's your n.?** ¿cómo te llamas?; **the house is in my father's n.** la casa está a nombre de mi padre; **this is a democracy in n. only** esto de democracia tiene solamente el nombre; **to call sb names** poner verde a algn; **to put one's n. down** apuntarse □ **n. day** santo *m*; **proper n.** nombre *m* propio; **stage n.** nombre *m* artístico **(b)** *(reputation)* fama *f*, reputación *f*; **she's a big n. in the fashion world** es una de las grandes figuras de la moda; **to have a bad/good n.** tener mala/buena reputación; **to make a n. for oneself** hacerse famoso(a)
 2 *vt* **(a)** *(give name to)* llamar, bautizar; **they named the ship 'Coronia'** bautizaron el buque con el nombre de 'Coronia' **(b)** *(appoint)* nombrar; **he was named Chief of Police** lo nombraron Jefe de Policía **(c)** *(mention)* mencionar; **to be named in a list** figurar en una lista

name-calling [ˈneɪmkɔːlɪŋ] *n* improperios *mpl*, insultos *mpl*

name-dropping [ˈneɪmdrɒpɪŋ] *n Fam* **to go in for n.-d.** dárselas de conocer a gente importante

nameless [ˈneɪmlɪs] *adj* anónimo(a); **to remain n.** permanecer en el anonimato

namely [ˈneɪmlɪ] *adv* a saber

nameplate [ˈneɪmpleɪt] *n* placa *f* con el nombre

namesake [ˈneɪmseɪk] *n* tocayo(a) *m,f*

Namibia [nəˈmɪbɪə] *n* Namibia

Namibian [nəˈmɪbɪən] *adj & n* namibio(a) *(m,f)*

naming [ˈneɪmɪŋ] *n* **(a)** *(choice of name)* elección *f* de un nombre **(b)** *(appointment)* nombramiento *m*

nan [næn] *n Br (baby talk)* abuelita *f*, *Esp* yaya *f*

nancy [ˈnænsɪ] *n Fam* afeminado *m* □ **n. boy** mariquita *m*

nanna [ˈnænə] *n see* **nan**

nanny [ˈnænɪ] *n* niñera *f*

nanny goat [ˈnænɪgəʊt] *n* cabra *f*

nanotechnology [ˈnænəʊtekˈnɒlədʒɪ] *n* nanotecnología *f*

nap¹ [næp] **1** *n (sleep)* siesta *f*; **to take** *or* **have a n.** echar la *or* una siesta
 2 *vi (pt & pp* **napped)** dormir la siesta; *Fig* **to catch sb napping** *Esp* coger *or Am* agarrar a algn desprevenido

nap² [næp] *n Tex* lanilla *f*, pelusa *f*

napalm ['neɪpɑːm] *n* napalm *m*

nape [neɪp] *n Anat* nuca *f*, cogote *m*

naphtha ['næfθə] *n Chem* nafta *f*

naphthalene ['næfθəliːn] *n Chem* naftalina *f*

napkin ['næpkɪn] *n* **(a) (table) n.** servilleta *f* ❏ **n. ring** servilletero *m* **(b)** *US (sanitary towel)* compresa *f*, *Am* toalla *f* higiénica

Naples ['neɪpəlz] *n* Nápoles

Napoleonic [nəpəʊlɪ'ɒnɪk] *adj* napoleónico(a)

nappy ['næpɪ] *n Br* pañal *m*

narc [nɑːk] *n US Fam* estupa *mf (agente de la brigada de estupefacientes)*

narcissi [nɑː'sɪsaɪ] *npl see* narcissus

narcissism [nɑː'sɪsɪzəm] *n* narcisismo *m*

narcissist ['nɑːsɪsɪst] *n* narcisista *mf*

narcissistic [nɑːsɪ'sɪstɪk] *adj* narcisista

narcissus [nɑː'sɪsəs] *n (pl* **narcissi** *or* **narcissuses)** *Bot* narciso *m*

narcotic [nɑː'kɒtɪk] **1** *adj* narcótico(a)
2 *n (drug)* narcótico *m*; *US (illegal drug)* narcótico *m*, estupefaciente *m*

nark [nɑːk] *Br Fam* **1** *n* soplón(ona) *m,f*, chivato(a) *m,f*
2 *vt (annoy)* fastidiar
3 *vi (inform the police)* dar el chivatazo

narrate [nə'reɪt] *vt* narrar, relatar

narration [nə'reɪʃən] *n* narración *f*, relato *m*

narrative ['nærətɪv] **1** *n Lit* narrativa *f*; *(story)* narración *f*
2 *adj* narrativo(a)

narrator [nə'reɪtər] *n* narrador(a) *m,f*

narrow ['nærəʊ] **1** *adj* **(a)** *(passage, road etc)* estrecho(a), angosto(a) **(b)** *(restricted)* reducido(a), restringido(a), limitado(a); **a n. circle of friends** un círculo reducido de amigos; **in the narrowest sense of the word** en el sentido más estricto de la palabra; **a n. majority** una mayoría escasa; **to have a n. escape** escaparse *or* librarse por los pelos **(c)** *(person)* de miras estrechas, cerrado(a)
2 narrows *npl (in river)* estrecho *m sing*
3 *vi* **(a)** *(become narrow)* estrecharse, hacerse más estrecho(a) **(b) to n. down** to reducirse a
4 *vt* estrechar, hacer más estrecho

narrow down *vt* reducir, limitar; **our choice was narrowed down to four applicants** tuvimos que escoger entre los cuatro candidatos que quedaban

narrow-gauge ['nærəʊɡeɪdʒ] *adj (railway)* de vía estrecha

narrowly ['nærəʊlɪ] *adv* **(a)** *(closely)* de cerca, minuciosamente **(b)** *(by a small margin)* por poco; **he n. avoided hitting the tree** faltó muy poco para que chocase contra el árbol

narrow-minded [nærəʊ'maɪndɪd] *adj* de miras estrechas

narrow-mindedness [nærəʊ'maɪndɪdnɪs] *n* estrechez *f* de miras

narrowness ['nærəʊnɪs] *n* estrechez *f*

narwhal ['nɑːwəl] *n Zool* narval *m*

NASA ['næsə] *n US (abbr* **National Aeronautics and Space Administration)** Administración *f* Nacional de Aeronáutica y del Espacio, NASA *f*

nasal ['neɪzəl] *adj* nasal; **a n. voice** una voz gangosa

nastiness ['nɑːstɪnɪs] *n* **(a)** *(unpleasantness)* carácter *m* desagradable **(b)** *(maliciousness)* mala intención *f*

nasturtium [nə'stɜːʃəm] *n Bot* capuchina *f*

nasty ['nɑːstɪ] *adj* **(nastier, nastiest) (a)** *(unpleasant)* desagradable; **a n. business** un asunto feo; **a n. habit** una

mala costumbre; **a n. remark** una observación desagradable; **a n. smell** un olor desagradable; **a n. trick** una mala jugada *or* pasada; **cheap and n.** hortera; **to smell n.** oler mal; **to taste n.** tener mal sabor; **to turn n.** *(weather, situation)* ponerse feo; **to have a n. mind** ser un mal pensado/una mal pensada **(b)** *(dirty)* sucio(a), asqueroso(a) **(c)** *(indecent)* obsceno(a) **(d)** *(unfriendly)* antipático(a); *(malicious)* mal intencionado(a), malévolo(a); *Br Fam* **he's a n. piece of work** es un asco de tío **(e)** *(dangerous)* peligroso(a); *(illness, accident)* grave; **a n. bend** una curva peligrosa; **a n. wound** una herida fea

nation ['neɪʃən] *n* nación *f*; **n. state** estado-nación *m*

national ['næʃnəl] **1** *adj* nacional ❏ **n. anthem** himno *m* nacional; **n. debt** deuda *f* pública; **n. grid** red *f* nacional de electricidad; **N. Insurance** seguridad *f* social; **n. park** parque *m* nacional; *Br Mil* **n. service** servicio *m* militar
2 *n* súbdito(a) *m,f*

nationalism ['næʃnəlɪzəm] *n* nacionalismo *m*

nationalist ['næʃnəlɪst] *adj & n* nacionalista *(mf)*

nationalistic [næʃənə'lɪstɪk] *adj* nacionalista

nationality [næʃə'nælɪtɪ] *n* nacionalidad *f*

nationalization [næʃnəlaɪ'zeɪʃən] *n* nacionalización *f*

nationalize ['næʃnəlaɪz] *vt* nacionalizar

nationally ['næʃnəlɪ] *adv* en el ámbito nacional; **to be n. renowned** ser conocido(a) en todo el país

nationwide ['neɪʃənwaɪd] *adj* de ámbito nacional; **n. appeal** llamamiento *m* a toda la nación; **n. tour** viaje *m* por todo el país; **n. scandal** escándalo *m* nacional

native ['neɪtɪv] **1** *adj* **(a)** *(place)* natal; **N. American** indio(a) *m,f* americano(a); **n. city** ciudad *f* natal; **n. land** patria *f*; **n. language** lengua *f* materna; **n. speaker** hablante *mf* nativo(a) **(b)** *(innate)* innato(a) **(c)** *(plant, animal)* originario(a) **(to** de)
2 *n* nativo(a) *m,f*, natural *mf*; *(original inhabitant)* indígena *mf*; **she's a n. of Edinburgh** es natural de Edimburgo

Nativity [nə'tɪvɪtɪ] *n Rel* Natividad *f*; *(Christmas)* Navidad *f*

NATO, Nato ['neɪtəʊ] *n (abbr* **North Atlantic Treaty Organization)** Organización *f* del Tratado del Atlántico Norte, OTAN *f*

natter ['nætər] *esp Br Fam* **1** *vi* charlar, *CAm Méx* platicar
2 *n* charla *f*, *CAm Méx* plática *f*; **to have a n.** charlar, *CAm Méx* platicar

nattily ['nætɪlɪ] *adv (smartly)* elegantemente; **n. dressed** bien vestido

natty ['nætɪ] *adj* **(nattier, nattiest)** *Fam* **(a)** *(clothes)* elegante; **to be a n. dresser** vestir bien **(b)** *(gadget etc)* ingenioso(a)

natural ['nætʃərəl] **1** *adj* **(a)** *(created by nature, not artificial)* natural ❏ **n. disaster** catástrofe *f* natural; **n. gas** gas *m* natural; **n. language** lenguaje *m* natural; **n. resources** recursos *mpl* naturales; **n. sciences** ciencias *fpl* naturales **(b)** *(normal)* normal; **it's only n. that ...** es lógico que ... ❏ **n. childbirth** parto *m* natural; **n. death** muerte *f* natural **(c)** *(born)* nato(a); **a n. actor** un actor nato **(d)** *(unaffected)* sencillo(a), natural
2 *n* **(a)** *(person)* **she's a n. for the job** es la persona ideal para el trabajo **(b)** *Mus* becuadro *m*

naturalism ['nætʃərəlɪzəm] *n* naturalismo *m*

naturalist ['nætʃərəlɪst] *adj & n* naturalista *(mf)*

naturalistic ['nætʃərəlɪstɪk] *adj* naturalista

naturalization [nætʃərəlaɪ'zeɪʃən] *n (of person)* naturalización *f* ❏ **n. papers** carta *f* sing de ciudadanía

naturally ['nætʃərəlɪ] *adv* **(a)** *(of course)* naturalmente, por supuesto, desde luego **(b)** *(by nature)* por naturaleza **(c)** *(in a relaxed manner)* con naturalidad

nature ['neɪtʃər] *n* **(a)** *(the natural world)* la naturaleza ❏

Mother N. la Madre Naturaleza; **n. lover** amante *mf* de la naturaleza; **n. reserve** reserva *f* natural; **n. study** historia *f* natural (**b**) *(character)* naturaleza *f*, carácter *m*; **by n.** por naturaleza; **it is in his n.** to be kind es bondadoso por naturaleza ❑ **human n.** la naturaleza humana (**c**) *(sort, kind)* índole *f*, género *m*, clase *f*; **things of this n.** cosas de esta índole

naturism ['neɪtʃərɪzəm] *n* naturismo *m*

naturist ['neɪtʃərɪst] *n* naturista *mf*

naught [nɔːt] *n* (**a**) *Literary (nothing)* nada *f*; **to bring to n.** frustrar; **to come to n.** fracasar (**b**) *US see* **nought**

naughtily ['nɔːtɪlɪ] *adv* **to behave n.** portarse mal

naughtiness ['nɔːtɪnɪs] *n* (**a**) *(behaviour)* mala conducta *f*, desobediencia *f* (**b**) *(of story)* picardía *f*

naughty ['nɔːtɪ] *adj* (**naughtier, naughtiest**) (**a**) *(child)* travieso(a) (**b**) *(risqué)* atrevido(a), picante

Nauru [nɑːˈuːruː] *n* Nauru

Nauruan [nɑːˈuːruːən] *adj & n* nauruano(a) *(m,f)*

nausea ['nɔːzɪə] *n* (**a**) *Med (sickness)* náusea *f* (**b**) *Fig (disgust)* asco *m*

nauseate ['nɔːzɪeɪt] *vt* (**a**) *Med (sickness)* dar náuseas a (**b**) *(disgust)* dar asco a

nauseating ['nɔːzɪeɪtɪŋ] *adj* nauseabundo(a), repugnante

nauseous ['nɔːzɪəs] *adj* nauseabundo(a); **to feel n.** sentir *or* tener náuseas

nautical ['nɔːtɪkəl] *adj* náutico(a); **n. mile** milla marítima

naval ['neɪvəl] *adj* naval ❑ **n. attaché** agregado *m* naval; **n. base** base *f* naval; **n. officer** oficial *mf* de marina; **n. power** potencia *f* marítima *or* naval

Navarre [nəˈvɑːr] *n* Navarra

Navarrese [nævəˈriːz] *adj & n* navarro(a) *(m,f)*

nave [neɪv] *n Archit* nave *f*

navel ['neɪvəl] *n Anat* ombligo *m* ❑ **n. orange** naranja *f* navel

navigable ['nævɪgəbəl] *adj (river)* navegable

navigate ['nævɪgeɪt] **1** *vt* (**a**) *Naut (river)* navegar por (**b**) *Naut (ship)* gobernar; *Av (aircraft)* pilotar
2 *vi* (**a**) *Naut* navegar (**b**) *Aut (in rally)* hacer de copiloto

navigation [nævɪˈgeɪʃən] *n Naut* navegación *f* ❑ **n. laws** código *m* marítimo

navigational [nævɪˈgeɪʃənəl] *adj* **n. equipment** equipo *m* de navegación

navigator ['nævɪgeɪtər] *n* (**a**) *Naut* navegante *mf*, oficial *mf* de derrota (**b**) *Aut Av* copiloto *mf*

navvy ['nævɪ] *Br n* peón *m* caminero

navy ['neɪvɪ] *n* (**a**) *(service)* armada *f*, marina *f* (de guerra) ❑ **merchant n.** marina *f* mercante; **n. blue** azul *m* marino; **a n. blue skirt** una falda azul marino; **N. Department** Ministerio *m* de la Marina (**b**) *(fleet)* flota *f*, armada *f*

Nazi ['nɑːtsɪ] *adj & n* nazi *(mf)*

Nazism ['nɑːtsɪzəm] *n* nazismo *m*

NB, nb [en'biː] *(abbr* **nota bene)** (note well), observa bien, N.B.

NBA [enbiːˈeɪ] *n US (abbr* **National Basketball Association)** NBA *f*

NBC [enbiːˈsiː] *n US (abbr* **National Broadcasting Company)** sociedad *f* nacional de radiodifusión, NBC *f*

NCO [ensiːˈəʊ] *n Br Mil (abbr* **non-commissioned officer)** suboficial *mf*

NE *(abbr* **North-East)** nordeste, NE

neap [niːp] *n* **n. (tide)** marea *f* muerta

Neapolitan [nɪəˈpɒlɪtən] *adj & n* napolitano(a) *(m,f)*

near [nɪər] **1** *adj* (**a**) *(space)* cercano(a); **the nearest stop** la parada más cercana; **the nearest way** el camino más corto ❑ *Aut* **the n. side** el lado del pasajero (**b**) *(time)* próximo(a); **in the n. future** en un futuro próximo (**c**) *Fig* cercano(a); **a n. relation** un pariente cercano; **it was a n. thing** poco faltó; **one's nearest and dearest** los más íntimos
2 *adv (space)* cerca; **do you live n.?** ¿vives cerca?; **far and n.** por todas partes; **n. at hand** a un paso, a mano; **the hotel is nowhere n. as good as it appears in the brochure** *(degree)* el hotel está muy lejos de ser tan bueno como parece en el folleto; **that's n. enough** *(close)* (ya) vale, está bien
3 *prep* cerca de; **n. death** cerca de la muerte; **n. here** cerca de aquí, aquí cerca; **n. the end of the film** hacia el final de la película
4 *vt* acercarse a; **she's nearing retirement** está a punto de jubilarse; **the ship is nearing port** el barco se está acercando al puerto

near- [nɪər] *pref* **n.-complete** casi completo(a); **n.-perfect** casi perfecto(a)

nearby [nɪəˈbaɪ] **1** *adj* cercano(a)
2 *adv* cerca

nearly ['nɪəlɪ] *adv* casi; **I n. died** por poco me muero; **it's n. seven** son casi las siete; **very n.** casi, casi; **we haven't n. enough to buy her a present** no alcanza ni con mucho para comprarle un regalo

nearly-new ['nɪəlɪ'njuː] *adj* casi como nuevo(a)

nearness ['nɪənɪs] *n* proximidad *f*

near-sighted [nɪəˈsaɪtɪd] *adj* miope, corto(a) de vista

near-sightedness [nɪəˈsaɪtɪdnɪs] *n* miopía *f*

neat [niːt] *adj* (**a**) *(room etc)* ordenado(a), limpio(a); *(handwriting)* claro(a); *(person) (appearance)* pulcro(a); *(habits)* ordenado(a); **n. and tidy** bienordenado(a) (**b**) *(clever)* hábil, ingenioso(a); **a n. trick** un truco ingenioso (**c**) *(whisky etc)* solo(a) (**d**) *US Fam (good)* genial, fenomenal

neatly ['niːtlɪ] *adv* (**a**) *(carefully)* cuidadosamente, con esmero (**b**) *(cleverly)* hábilmente

neatness ['niːtnɪs] *n* esmero *m*, pulcritud *f*

nebula ['nebjʊlə] *n (pl* **nebulae** ['nebjʊliː]) *Astron* nebulosa *f*

nebulous ['nebjʊləs] *adj Astron* nebuloso(a), *Fig* vago(a), impreciso(a)

necessarily [nesɪˈserɪlɪ] *adv* necesariamente, por fuerza

necessary ['nesɪsərɪ] **1** *adj* (**a**) *(essential)* necesario(a), esencial; **absolutely n.** imprescindible; **is it n. that we all go?, is it n. for all of us to go?** ¿es necesario que vayamos todos?; **to do what is n.** hacer todo lo necesario *or* lo que haga falta; **to do no more than is n.** no hacer más que lo (mínimo) indispensable; **if n.** si es preciso (**b**) *(unavoidable)* inevitable; **the n. consequence** la consecuencia inevitable
2 *n* lo necesario, lo esencial; **to do the n.** hacer lo necesario

necessitate [nɪˈsesɪteɪt] *vt* necesitar, exigir, requerir

necessitous [nɪˈsesɪtəs] *adj* necesitado(a), indigente

necessity [nɪˈsesɪtɪ] *n* (**a**) *(need)* necesidad *f*; **in case of n.** en caso de necesidad *or* urgencia; **out of n.** por necesidad; **to make a virtue of n.** hacer de la necesidad una virtud; *Prov* **n. is the mother of invention** la necesidad aviva el ingenio (**b**) *(article)* requisito *m* indispensable; **a phone is a n. these days** hoy en día el teléfono es indispensable (**c**) **necessities** artículos *mpl* de primera necesidad

neck [nek] **1** *n* (**a**) *Anat* cuello *m*; *(of animal)* pescuezo *m*; **to be n. and n.** ir parejos; **to be up to one's n. in debt** estar hasta el cuello de deudas; **to break one's n. working** matarse trabajando; **to crane one's n.** estirar el cuello; **to risk one's n.** jugarse el tipo *or* el cuello; **to stick one's n. out**

arriesgarse; **to win/lose by a n.** *(in horse racing)* ganar/ perder por una cabeza; **to wring sb's n.** retorcerle el pescuezo a algn ❏ **stiff n.** tortícolis *f* **(b)** *(of garment)* cuello *m* ❏ **low n.** escote *m*; **roll n.** cuello *m* vuelto *or* de cisne; **V n.** cuello *m* de pico **(c)** *(of bottle)* cuello *m* **(d)** *(of guitar)* mástil *m* **(e)** *Geog* istmo *m*
   2 *vi Fam (kiss)* besuquearse, *Esp* morrearse,' *(caress, hug)* manosearse, *Esp* magrearse

necking ['nekɪŋ] *n Fam (kissing)* besuqueo *m*, *Esp* morreo *m*; *(caressing, hugging)* manoseo *m*, *Esp* magreo *m*

necklace ['neklɪs] *n* collar *m*

neckline ['neklaɪn] *n (of dress)* escote *m*

necktie ['nektaɪ] *n US* corbata *f*

nectar ['nektər] *n* néctar *m*

nectarine ['nektəri:n] *n* nectarina *f*

née [neɪ] *adj* de soltera; **Mrs Williams, n. Brown** Sra. Williams, de soltera Brown

need [ni:d] **1** *n* **(a)** *(necessity)* necesidad *f*; **basic needs** necesidades elementales; **if n. be** si fuera necesario; **there's no n. for you to do that** no hace falta que hagas eso; **the urgent n. for ...** la acuciante necesidad de ...; **to be in n. of** necesitar **(b)** *(poverty)* indigencia *f*, necesidad *f*; **to be in n.** estar necesitado; **to help a friend in n.** sacar a un amigo de un apuro
   2 *vt* **(a)** *(have need of)* necesitar; **I n. a break** necesito un descanso; **they n. to be told everything** hay que decirles *or* explicárselo todo; *Fam* **that's all I n.** sólo me faltaba eso; *Fam* **what she needs is a good ticking off** lo que le hace falta es una buena bronca **(b)** *(expressing obligation)* **I didn't n. to pay, it was free** no tuve que pagar, era gratis; **I n. to see him** tengo que verle **(c)** *(require)* requerir, exigir; **it's a job that needs patience** es un trabajo que requiere paciencia
   3 *v aux* tener que, deber; **n. he go?** ¿tiene que ir?; **n. you shout so much?** ¿tienes que gritar tanto?; **you needn't have bothered to come, you could have phoned** no tenías que haberte molestado en venir, podrías haber llamado; **you needn't wait** no hace falta que esperes

needful ['ni:dfʊl] *adj* necesario(a); **to do what is n.** hacer lo necesario

needle ['ni:dəl] **1** *n* **(a)** *(gen)* aguja *f*; **to look for a n. in a haystack** buscar una aguja en un pajar; **to thread a n.** enhebrar una aguja **(b)** *Bot* hoja *f*; **the ground was covered with pine needles** la tierra estaba cubierta de pinaza **(c)** *Fam (friction)* pique *m*; **to get the n.** pincharse, *Esp* picarse
   2 *vt Fam* pinchar; **he's always needling me** nunca me deja en paz

needless ['ni:dlɪs] *adj* innecesario(a), inútil; **n. violence** violencia *f* gratuita; **n. to say** ni que decir tiene que, huelga decir

needlessly ['ni:dlɪslɪ] *adv* innecesariamente, inútilmente

needlework ['ni:dəlwɜ:k] *n (sewing)* costura *f*; *(embroidery)* bordado *m*

needs [ni:dz] *adv* necesariamente, forzosamente; **if n. must** si hace falta

need-to-know [ni:dtə'nəʊ] *adj* **information is given on a n.-t.-k. basis** se proporciona la información sólo a las personas que se considere que la necesitan

needy ['ni:dɪ] **1** *adj* **(needier, neediest)** necesitado(a)
   2 the n. *npl* los necesitados

ne'er-do-well ['neədu:wel] *n* vago(a) *m,f*

nefarious [nɪ'feərɪəs] *adj* infame

neg *(abbr* **negative)** negativo(a), negat

negate [nɪ'geɪt] *vt* **(a)** *(deny)* negar **(b)** *(nullify)* anular, invalidar

negation [nɪ'geɪʃən] *n* negación *f*

negative ['negətɪv] **1** *adj* negativo(a) ❏ **n. criticism** crítica *f* negativa; **n. result** resultado *m* negativo; **n. sign** *(minus)* signo *m* negativo
   2 *n* **(a)** *Ling* negación *f*; **to reply in the n.** contestar con una negativa **(b)** *Phot* negativo *m* **(c)** *Math* término *m* negativo

negatively ['negətɪvlɪ] *adv* negativamente

neglect [nɪ'glekt] **1** *vt* **(a)** *(not look after)* descuidar, desatender; **to n. one's health/house** descuidar la salud/ la casa; **to n. one's appearance** no arreglarse, dejarse ir; **to n. one's friends** olvidarse de los amigos **(b)** *(omit to do)* no cumplir con, faltar a; **to n. one's duty/obligations** no cumplir con su deber/sus obligaciones
   2 *n* negligencia *f*, descuido *m*, dejadez *f*; **in a state of n.** abandonado(a), descuidado(a); **n. of duty** incumplimiento de su deber; **through n.** por negligencia

neglectful [nɪ'glektfʊl] *adj* descuidado(a), negligente

negligée ['neglɪʒeɪ] *n* salto *m* de cama, negligé *m*

negligence ['neglɪdʒəns] *n* negligencia *f*, descuido *m*

negligent ['neglɪdʒənt] *adj* descuidado(a), negligente

negligible ['neglɪdʒɪbəl] *adj* insignificante

negotiable [nɪ'gəʊʃəbəl] *adj* **(a)** *(demand, salary)* negociable **(b)** *Fin (obstacle)* superable

negotiate [nɪ'gəʊʃɪeɪt] **1** *vt* **(a)** *(treaty, contract)* negociar **(b)** *Fin (sale, loan)* gestionar; *(bill of exchange)* negociar **(c)** *Fig (obstacle)* salvar, franquear; **to n. a bend** tomar una curva
   2 *vi* negociar; **he refused to n. with the terrorists** se negó a negociar con los terroristas

negotiating [nɪ'gəʊʃɪeɪtɪŋ] *adj* negociador(a); **the n. table** la mesa de negociaciones

negotiation [nɪgəʊʃɪ'eɪʃən] *n* negociación *f*; **to open negotiations** entablar negociaciones; **under n.** en negociación

negotiator [nɪ'gəʊʃɪeɪtər] *n* negociador(a) *m,f*

Negress ['ni:grɪs] *n Old-fashioned* negra *f*

Negro ['ni:grəʊ] *Old-fashioned* **1** *n (pl* **Negroes)** negro(a) *m,f*
   2 *adj* negro(a); **N. spiritual** *(song)* espiritual *m* negro

negroid ['ni:grɔɪd] *adj* negroide

neigh [neɪ] **1** *n* relincho *m*
   2 *vi* relinchar

neighbour, *US* **neighbor** ['neɪbər] *n (person)* vecino(a) *m,f*; *(country)* (país *m)* vecino *m*; *(fellow man)* prójimo *m*

neighbourhood, *US* **neighborhood** ['neɪbəhʊd] *n* **(a)** *(district)* vecindad *f*, barrio *m*; *(people)* vecindario *m* **(b)** *(of amount)* **in the n. of** alrededor de, aproximadamente

neighbouring, *US* **neighboring** ['neɪbərɪŋ] *adj* vecino(a); **n. country** país *m* vecino

neighbourly, *US* **neighborly** ['neɪbəlɪ] *adj* amable, de buen vecino

neither ['naɪðər, 'ni:ðər] **1** *adj & pron* ninguno de los dos, ninguna de las dos; **n. candidate is good enough** ninguno de los candidatos es suficientemente bueno; **n. (of them) has come** ninguno de los dos ha venido
   2 *adv & conj* **n. ... nor** ni ... ni; **n. young nor old** ni joven ni viejo; **n. you nor I** ni tú ni yo; *Fig* **it's n. here nor there** no viene al caso; **she was not there and n. was her sister** ella no estaba, ni su hermana tampoco

nemesis ['neməsɪs] *n Literary* verdugo *m*

neoclassical [ni:əʊ'klæsɪkəl] *adj* neoclásico(a)

neoclassicism [ni:əʊ'klæsɪsɪzəm] *n* neoclasicismo *m*

neofascism [ni:əʊ'fæʃɪzəm] *n* neofascismo *m*

neofascist [ni:əʊ'fæʃɪst] *adj & n* neofascista *mf*

neolithic [niːəʊ'lɪθɪk] *adj* neolítico(a)

neologism [niː'ɒlədʒɪzəm] *n* neologismo *m*

neon ['niːɒn] *n* neón *m* ◻ **n. light** luz *f* de neón; **n. sign** letrero *m* de neón

neo-Nazi [niːəʊ'nɑːtsɪ] *adj & n* neonazi *(mf)*

Nepal [nɪ'pɔːl] *n* Nepal

Nepalese [nepə'liːz] *adj & n* nepalés(esa) *(m,f)*; **the N.** los nepaleses

nephew ['nevjuː, 'nefjuː] *n* sobrino *m*

nephritis [nɪ'fraɪtɪs] *n* nefritis *f*

nepotism ['nepətɪzəm] *n* nepotismo *m*

Neptune ['neptjuːn] *n (planet, god)* Neptuno *m*

nerd [nɜːd] *n Fam* (**a**) *(boring person)* petardo(a) *m,f, RP* nerd *mf*; **a computer n.** un tipo raro obsesionado con los ordenadores (**b**) *(as insult)* bobo(a) *m,f,* gil *mf*

nerdy [nɜːdɪ] *adj Fam* de petardo(a) *or RP* nerd

nerve [nɜːv] *n* (**a**) *Anat* nervio *m*; **to be a bundle of nerves** estar hecho un manojo de nervios; **to get on sb's nerves** poner los nervios de punta a algn, poner nervioso a algn; **to have nerves of steel** tener nervios de acero ◻ **n. cell** neurona *f*; **n. centre** centro *m* nervioso; *Fig* punto *m* neurálgico; **n. gas** gas *m* nervioso (**b**) *(courage)* valor *m*; **to lose one's n.** rajarse (**c**) *Fam (cheek)* cara *f,* descaro *m,* caradura *f*; **he had the n. to phone me** tuvo el descaro de llamarme por teléfono; **what a n.!** ¡qué cara!

nerve-(w)racking ['nɜːvrækɪŋ] *adj* crispante, exasperante

nervous ['nɜːvəs] *adj* (**a**) *Anat* nervioso(a) ◻ **n. breakdown** depresión *f* nerviosa; **n. system** sistema *m* nervioso (**b**) *(on edge)* nervioso(a) (**c**) *(afraid)* miedoso(a); **to be n.** tener miedo (**d**) *(timid)* tímido(a)

nervously ['nɜːvəslɪ] *adv* nerviosamente, con miedo

nervousness ['nɜːvəsnɪs] *n (edginess)* nerviosismo *m,* nerviosidad *f; (fear)* miedo *m*

nervy ['nɜːvɪ] *adj* (**nervier, nerviest**) *Fam (tense)* nervioso(a)

nest [nest] *n* (**a**) *(of bird)* nido *m; (of hen)* nidal *m; (of wasp)* avispero *m; (of animal)* madriguera *f; Fig* **to feather one's n.** hacer su agosto ◻ **n. egg** ahorros *mpl,* ahorrillos *mpl* (**b**) *Fig (shelter)* nido *m,* refugio *m* ◻ **machine-gun n.** nido *m* de ametralladoras (**c**) *(set)* **n. of tables** mesas *fpl* de nido
  2 *vi* (**a**) *(birds)* anidar (**b**) *(egg collector)* ir a buscar nidos

nestle ['nesəl] **1** *vt* recostar; **to n. one's head against sb's shoulder** recostar la cabeza contra el hombro de algn
  2 *vi* (**a**) *(settle comfortably)* acomodarse, arrellanarse; **to n. up to sb** apretarse contra algn (**b**) *(lie sheltered)* esconderse, ocultarse

Net [net] *n Fam Comptr* **the N.** *(Internet)* la Red

net¹ [net] *n* (**a**) *(material, for fishing)* red *f; Sport* red, malla *f* ◻ **fishing n.** red *f* de pescar; **hair n.** redecilla *f;* **landing n.** manga *m;* **mosquito n.** mosquitero *m;* **n. curtains** visillos *mpl* (**b**) *(trap)* red *f,* trampa *f*
  2 *vt (pt & pp netted)* coger con red; *Fishing* pescar con red

net² [net] **1** *adj* neto(a); **n. price/profit/weight** precio *m*/ beneficio *m*/peso *m* neto
  2 *vt (pt & pp netted) (earn)* ganar neto; **he netted 100,000 dollars** ganó cien mil dólares netos

netball ['netbɔːl] *n Sport* baloncesto *m* femenino

Netherlands ['neðələndz] *npl* **the N.** Holanda, los Países Bajos

nethermost ['neðəməʊst] *adj Literary* inferior

netiquette ['netɪket] *n Comptr* netiqueta *f*

netting ['netɪŋ] *n* redes *fpl,* malla *f* ◻ **wire n.** alambrera *f*

nettle ['netəl] **1** *n Bot* ortiga *f* ◻ **n. rash** urticaria *f*
  2 *vt Fam* irritar, fastidiar, molestar

network ['netwɜːk] *n also Comptr* red *f; TV* cadena *f;* **road/rail n.** red de carreteras/ferrocarriles; **n. computer** *Esp* ordenador *m or Am* computadora *f* de red

networking ['netwɜːkɪŋ] *n Com* establecimiento *m* de contactos profesionales

neural ['njʊərəl] *adj Anat* neural

neuralgia [njʊə'rældʒə] *n Med* neuralgia *f*

neuritis [njʊə'raɪtɪs] *n Med* neuritis *f*

neurological [njʊərə'lɒdʒɪkəl] *adj Med* neurológico(a)

neurologist [njʊə'rɒlədʒɪst] *n Med* neurólogo(a) *m,f*

neurology [njʊ'rɒlədʒɪ] *n Med* neurología *f*

neuron ['njʊərɒn] *n Anat* neurona *f*

neurosis [njʊ'rəʊsɪs] *n (pl* **neuroses** [njʊə'rəʊsiːz]*) Med* neurosis *f*

neurosurgeon ['njʊərəʊ'sɜːdʒən] *n* neurocirujano(a) *m,f*

neurosurgery ['njʊərəʊ'sɜːdʒərɪ] *n Med* neurocirugía *f*

neurotic [njʊ'rɒtɪk] *adj & n Med* neurótico(a) *(m,f)*

neuter ['njuːtər] **1** *adj* neutro(a)
  2 *n Ling* neutro *m*
  3 *vt (geld)* castrar

neutral ['njuːtrəl] **1** *adj* neutro(a); *Pol* **to remain n.** permanecer neutral
  2 *n Aut* punto *m* muerto

neutrality [njuː'trælətɪ] *n* neutralidad *f*

neutralize ['njuːtrəlaɪz] *vt* neutralizar

neutron ['njuːtrɒn] *n Phys* neutrón *m* ◻ **n. bomb** bomba *f* de neutrones

never ['nevər] *adv* nunca, jamás; **he n. complains** nunca se queja; **n. again** nunca más, nunca jamás; **n. in all my life have I seen anything like it** jamás en la vida he visto nada parecido; *Fam* **n. mind** da igual, no importa; *Fam* **that will n. do!** ¡eso es inaceptable!; *Fam* **you n. forgot your keys!** ¡no me digas que te olvidaste las llaves!; *Fam* **well, I n. (did)!** ¡no me digas!

never-ending [nevər'endɪŋ] *adj* sin fin, interminable

nevermore [nevə'mɔːr] *adj* nunca más

never-never [nevə'nevər] *n* (**a**) *Br Fam* **to buy sth on the n.-n.** comprar algo a plazos (**b**) **N.-N. land** tierra *f* de Jauja

nevertheless [nevəðə'les] *adv* sin embargo, no obstante

new [njuː] *adj* nuevo(a); **a n. car/dress/suit** un coche/ vestido/traje nuevo; **as good as n.** como nuevo; **I'm n. to this job** soy nuevo en este trabajo ◻ **N. Age** = movimiento que gira en torno a las ciencias ocultas, medicinas alternativas, religiones orientales, etc.; **n. baby** recién nacido *m;* **N. Delhi** Nueva Delhi; **N. England** Nueva Inglaterra; **N. Englander** persona *f* de Nueva Inglaterra; **N. Guinea** Nueva Guinea; **N. Hampshire** Nueva Hampshire; **N. Jersey** Nueva Jersey; **n. man** hombre *m* moderno *(que ayuda en casa, etc);* **n. moon** luna *f* nueva; **N. Orleans** Nueva Orleáns; **ñ. potatoes** *Esp* patatas *fpl or Am* papas *fpl* nuevas, *Andes* chauchas *fpl;* **N. South Wales** Nueva Gales del Sur; **N. Year** año *m* nuevo; **N. Year's Day** día *m* del año nuevo; **N. Year's Eve** Noche *f* vieja, Nochevieja *f;* **N. York** Nueva York; **N. Yorker** neoyorquino(a) *m,f;* **N. Zealand** Nueva Zelanda; **N. Zealander** neocelandés(esa) *m,f*

newbie ['njuːbɪ] *n Comptr Fam* novato(a) *m,f*

newborn ['njuːbɔːn] *adj* recién nacido(a)

newcomer ['njuːkʌmər] *n* recién llegado(a) *m,f*

newfangled ['njuːfæŋɡəld] *adj* novedoso(a); **n.-f. ideas** ideas *fpl* novedosas

Newfoundland ['njuːfəndlənd] *n* Terranova

newish ['nju:ɪʃ] *adj Fam* casi nuevo(a)

newly ['nju:lɪ] *adv* recién, recientemente; **a n. painted house** una casa recién pintada

newlywed ['nju:lɪwed] *n* recién casado(a) *m,f*

news [nju:z] *n* noticias *fpl*; **a piece of n.** una noticia; **it's in the n.** es noticia; **the n.** *TV* el telediario, *Am* el noticiero, *Andes RP* el noticioso; *Rad* las noticias; **to break the n. to sb** dar una (mala) noticia a algn; *Fam* **it's n. to me** ahora me entero; *Prov* **no n. is good n.** sin noticias, buenas noticias ❑ **n. agency** agencia *f* de prensa *or* de información; **n. bulletin** noticiario *m*, boletín *m* informativo; **n. conference** rueda *f* de prensa; **n. correspondent** corresponsal *mf* de prensa; **n. clipping** recorte *m* de periódico; **n. item** noticia *f*

newsagent ['nju:zeɪdʒənt] *n Br* vendedor(a) *m,f* de periódicos

newscaster ['nju:zkɑːstər] *n US TV* locutor(a) *m,f* del telediario; *Rad* locutor(a) *m,f* del diario hablado

newsflash ['nju:zflæʃ] *n* noticia *f* de última hora

newsgroup ['nju:zgru:p] *n Comptr* grupo *m* de noticias

newsletter ['nju:zletər] *n* boletín *m* informativo

newspaper ['nju:zpeɪpər] *n* periódico *m*, diario *m*

newspaperman ['nju:zpeɪpəmæn] *n* (*pl* **newspapermen**) *(reporter)* periodista *m*, hombre *m* de prensa; *(proprietor)* propietario *m* de un periódico, hombre *m* de prensa

newsprint ['nju:zprɪnt] *n* papel *m* de periódico

newsreader ['nju:zri:dər] *TV Rad* presentador(a) *m,f* de los informativos

newsreel ['nju:zri:l] *n* noticiario *m*

newsroom ['nju:zrʊm] *n* sala *f* de redacción

news-stand ['nju:zstænd] *n* quiosco *m*, puesto *m* de periódicos

newsworthy ['nju:zwɜ:ðɪ] *adj* de interés periodístico

newsy ['nju:zɪ] *adj* (**newsier, newsiest**) *Fam* **a n. letter** una carta llena de noticias

newt [nju:t] *n Zool* tritón *m*

next [nekst] **1** *adj* (**a**) *(place)* vecino(a), de al lado; **the n. room** la habitación de al lado (**b**) *(time)* próximo(a); **the n. time** la próxima vez; **the n. day** el día siguiente; **n. day** al día siguiente; **n. Friday** el viernes que viene; **n. week** la semana que viene; **the week after n.** dentro de dos semanas (**c**) *(order)* siguiente, próximo(a); **the n. page** la página siguiente; **the n. stop** la próxima parada; **n. of kin** pariente *m* más cercano; **who's n.?** ¿quién es el siguiente?

2 *adv* (**a**) *(in time, order)* después, luego; **what did you do n.?** ¿que hiciste luego?; **what shall we do n.?** ¿qué hacemos ahora? (**b**) *(next time)* la próxima vez; **when n. we meet** la próxima vez que nos veamos

3 *prep* **n. to** al lado de, junto a; **n. to nothing** casi nada

next door [neks'dɔːr] *adj & adv* de al lado; **our n.-d. neighbour** el vecino/la vecina de al lado; **the house n. d.** la casa de al lado; **they live n. d.** viven en la casa de al lado

NFL [enef'el] *n US* (*abbr* **National Football League**) = una de las dos ligas nacionales de fútbol americano

NGO [endʒi:'əʊ] *n* (*pl* **NGOs**) (*abbr* **non-governmental organization**) ONG *f*, organización *f* no gubernamental

NHS [eneɪtʃ'es] *n Br* (*abbr* **National Health Service**) = la sanidad pública británica, *Esp* Insalud *m*

NI [en'aɪ] *n Br* (*abbr* **National Insurance**) SS *f*

niacin ['naɪəsɪn] *n* niacina *f*

nib [nɪb] *n* plumilla *f*

nibble ['nɪbəl] **1** *vt & vi* mordisquear; *(of fish)* picar; **to n. at sth** mordisquear algo

2 *n* (**a**) *(small bite)* **to have a n. at sth** dar un mordisquito a

or mordisquear algo (**b**) *Fam* **nibbles** *(snacks)* algo *m* de picar, *Méx* antojitos *mpl*

nibs [nɪbz] *n Fam Iron* **his n.** su señoría

Nicaragua [nɪkə'rægjʊə, nɪkə'rɑːgwə] *n* Nicaragua

Nicaraguan [nɪkə'rægjʊən, nɪkə'rɑːgwən] *adj & n* nicaragüense *(mf)*

Nice [niːs] *n* Niza

nice [naɪs] *adj* (**a**) *(pleasant) (person)* simpático(a), amable, *Esp* majo(a), *RP* dulce; *(thing)* agradable, bueno(a); **a n. meal** una buena comida; **a n. day** un día agradable; **how n. of you!** ¡qué amable eres!; **n. weather** buen tiempo; **n. and cool/warm** fresquito(a)/calentito(a); **to smell/taste n.** oler/saber bien (**b**) *(pretty) Esp* bonito(a), *Am* lindo(a); **a n. house** una casa *Esp* bonita *or Am* linda (**c**) *Iron* menudo(a); **a n. mess you've made!** ¡menudo lío has hecho!, ¡buena la has hecho! (**d**) *(subtle)* sutil; **a n. distinction** una distinción sutil (**e**) *(exact)* **these shoes are a n. fit** estos zapatos me sientan muy bien

nice-looking [naɪs'lʊkɪŋ] *adj Esp* guapo(a), *Am* lindo(a)

nicely ['naɪslɪ] *adv* muy bien; **that will do n.** así está muy bien; **she's doing n.** va bien

nicety ['naɪsɪtɪ] *n* (**a**) *(subtlety)* sutileza *f*, detalle *m* (**b**) **niceties** *(refinements)* lujos *mpl*, detalles *mpl*

niche [niːʃ] *n* (**a**) *Archit* hornacina *f*, nicho *m* (**b**) *Fig* hueco *m*; **to carve out a n. for oneself** hacerse un hueco ❑ *Com* **n. market** nicho *m* de mercado

nick[1] [nɪk] **1** *n* (**a**) *(notch)* muesca *f*, corte *m*; *(cut)* corte *m*, rasguño *m*; *Fam* **in the n. of time** en el momento preciso (**b**) *Br Fam (prison)* cárcel *f*, *Esp* chirona *f*, *Andes RP* cana *f*, *Méx* bote *m*

2 *vt Br Fam* (**a**) *(steal)* birlar, afanar, *Esp* mangar (**b**) *(arrest)* pillar, pescar

nick[2] [nɪk] *n Br Fam* **in good/poor n.** en buenas/malas condiciones

nickel ['nɪkəl] *n* (**a**) *(metal)* níquel *m* ❑ **n. silver** metal *m* blanco (**b**) *US* moneda *f* de cinco centavos

nicker ['nɪkər] *n inv Br Fam* libra *f* esterlina

nickname ['nɪkneɪm] **1** *n* *(derisory)* apodo *m*, mote *m*; *(affectionate)* diminutivo *m*

2 *vt* apodar, poner de apodo; **he was nicknamed 'Fatty'** le apodaron 'el Gordo'

nicotine ['nɪkəti:n] *n* nicotina *f* ❑ **n. patch** parche *m* de nicotina

nIece [ni:s] *n* sobrina *f*

niff [nɪf] *Br Fam* **1** *n* tufo *m*

2 *vt* apestar, *Esp* atufar

niffy ['nɪfɪ] *adj* (**niffier, niffiest**) *Br Fam* maloliente

nifty ['nɪftɪ] *adj* (**niftier, niftiest**) (**a**) *(smart)* elegante, chulo(a) (**b**) *(quick)* rápido(a); *(agile)* ágil (**c**) *(ingenious)* ingenioso(a)

Niger ['naɪdʒər] *n* Níger

Nigeria [naɪ'dʒɪərɪə] *n* Nigeria

Nigerian [naɪ'dʒɪərɪən] *adj & n* nigeriano(a) *(m,f)*

Nigerien [niː'ʒeərɪən] *adj & n* nigerino(a) *(m,f)*

niggardly ['nɪgədlɪ] *adj* *(miserly)* tacaño(a), avaro(a); *(meagre)* exiguo(a)

nigger ['nɪgər] *n Offens* = término generalmente ofensivo para referirse a un negro, *RP* grone *m*

niggle ['nɪgəl] *vi* reparar en nimiedades *or* pequeñeces

niggling ['nɪgəlɪŋ] *adj* *(trifling)* insignificante, de poca monta; *(irritating)* molesto(a)

nigh [naɪ] *adv* (**a**) *Literary* cerca; **the end is n.!** ¡el fin está cerca! (**b**) **well n. impossible** *(almost)* casi *or* prácticamente imposible

night [naɪt] *n* noche *f*; **all n.** toda la noche; **at n.** de noche;

last n. anoche; **late at n.** avanzada *or* bien entrada la noche; **the n. before last** anteanoche, antes de anoche; **tomorrow n.** mañana por la noche; **to have a n. out** salir por la noche ❑ **first n.** estreno *m*; **n. court** juzgado *m* de guardia; **n. flight** vuelo *m* nocturno; **n. life** vida *f* nocturna; **n. owl** trasnochador(a) *m,f*; **n. school** escuela *f* nocturna; **n. shift** turno *m* de noche

nightcap ['naɪtkæp] *n* bebida *f* antes de acostarse

nightclub ['naɪtklʌb] *n* club *m* nocturno, sala *f* de fiestas

nightdress ['naɪtdres] *n* camisón *m*

nightfall ['naɪtfɔːl] *n* anochecer *m*; **at n.** al anochecer, al caer la noche

nightgown ['naɪtgaʊn] *n*, **nightie** ['naɪtɪ] *n Fam* camisón *m*

nightingale ['naɪtɪŋgeɪl] *n Orn* ruiseñor *m*

nightlife ['naɪtlaɪf] *n* ambiente *m* nocturno; **there's not much n. here** no hay mucha marcha (nocturna) aquí

nightlight ['naɪtlaɪt] *n* lamparilla *f*

nightly ['naɪtlɪ] **1** *adj* **(a)** *(at night)* nocturno(a), de noche **(b)** *(every night)* de cada noche
  2 *adv* cada noche, todas las noches

nightmare ['naɪtmeər] *n* pesadilla *f*

nightmarish ['naɪtmeərɪʃ] *adj* de pesadilla

nights [naɪts] *adv Fam* de noche, por la noche; **to work n.** trabajar de noche

nightshade ['naɪtʃeɪd] *n Bot* hierba *f* mora ❑ **deadly n.** belladona *f*

nightshirt ['naɪtʃɜːt] *n* camisa *f* de dormir

nightspot ['naɪtspɒt] *n* club *m* nocturno, sala *f* de fiestas

nightstick ['naɪtstɪk] *n US* porra *f*

night-time ['naɪttaɪm] *n* noche *f*; **at n.-t.** por la noche

nihilism ['naɪɪlɪzəm] *n* nihilismo *m*

nihilistic [naɪɪ'lɪstɪk] *adj* nihilista

nil [nɪl] *n* cero *m*; *Br* **we won two n.** ganamos dos a cero

Nile [naɪl] *n* **the N.** el Nilo

nimble ['nɪmbəl] *adj* ágil, rápido(a); **n. feet** pies *mpl* ágiles

nincompoop ['nɪŋkəmpuːp] *n Fam* memo(a) *m,f*, tonto(a) *m,f*

nine [naɪn] **1** *adj* nueve *inv*; **n. hundred** novecientos(as); **n. thousand dollars** nueve mil dólares; **n. times** nueve veces; **n. times out of ten** en el noventa por ciento de los casos
  2 *n* nueve *m inv*; *Fam* **dressed up to the nines** de punta en blanco; *see also* **seven**

ninepins ['naɪnpɪnz] *npl* bolos *mpl*, juego *m* de bolos; **they went down like n.** cayeron como moscas

nineteen [naɪn'tiːn] *adj & n* diecinueve *(m) inv*; **to talk n. to the dozen** hablar por los codos; *see also* **seven**

nineteenth [naɪn'tiːnθ] *adj* decimonoveno(a) ❑ *Golf Slang* **the n. hole** el bar; *see also* **seventh**

ninetieth ['naɪntɪɪθ] *adj & n* nonagésimo(a) *(m,f)*

nine-to-five ['naɪntə'faɪv] **1** *adj* **a n.-to-f. job** un trabajo de oficina *(de nueve a cinco)*
  2 *adv* **to work n.-to-f.** trabajar de nueve a cinco, tener horario de oficina

ninety ['naɪntɪ] *adj & n* noventa *(m) inv*; **n.-nine times out of a hundred** casi siempre; **the nineties** los (años) noventa; *see also* **seventy**

ninth [naɪnθ] **1** *adj* noveno(a)
  2 *n* **(a)** *(in series)* noveno(a) *m,f* **(b)** *(fraction)* noveno *m*; *see also* **seventh**

Nip [nɪp] *n Slang Offens* = término ofensivo para referirse a los japoneses, *RP* ponja *mf*

nip¹ [nɪp] **1** *vt (pt & pp* **nipped)** **(a)** *(pinch)* pellizcar **(b)** *(bite)* morder; **to n. sth in the bud** cortar algo de raíz

  2 *vi Br Fam* **to n. in/out/up** entrar/salir/subir un momento; **n. across to the shop** ve un momento a la tienda
  3 *n* **(a)** *(pinch)* pellizco *m* **(b)** *(bite)* mordisco *m*, mordedura *f*; *Fig* **there's a n. in the air** hace fresquito

nip² [nɪp] *n (of drink)* copita *f*, *Esp* chupito *m*

nipper ['nɪpər] *n Br Fam* chavalín(ina) *m,f*, *CAm Méx* chavalo(a) *m,f*, *RP* pibito(a) *m,f*

nipple ['nɪpəl] *n* **(a)** *Anat (female)* pezón *m*; *(male)* tetilla *f* **(b)** *US (on baby's bottle)* tetilla *f*, tetina *f* **(c)** *Tech* **(greasing) n.** pezón *m* de engrase

nippy ['nɪpɪ] *adj* **(nippier, nippiest)** *Fam* **(a)** *(quick)* rápido(a); **look n.!** ¡date prisa! **(b)** *(cold)* fresquito(a); **it's a bit n. today** hoy hace fresquito

nirvana [nɪə'vɑːnə] *n Rel* nirvana *f*

nit¹ [nɪt] *n Zool* liendre *f*

nit² [nɪt] *n Br Fam* imbécil *mf*

nit-pick ['nɪtpɪk] *vi Fam* poner peros *or Esp* pegas, ser un(a) quisquilloso(a)

nit-picking ['nɪtpɪkɪŋ] *adj Fam* quisquilloso(a); **n.-p. details** nimiedades *fpl*

nitrate ['naɪtreɪt] *n Chem* nitrato *m*

nitric ['naɪtrɪk] *adj Chem* nítrico(a) ❑ **n. acid** ácido *m* nítrico

nitride ['naɪtraɪd] *n Chem* nitruro *m*

nitrite ['naɪtraɪt] *n Chem* nitrito *m*

nitrogen ['naɪtrədʒən] *n Chem* nitrógeno *m*

nitroglycerin(e) [naɪtrəʊ'glɪsəriːn] *n Chem* nitroglicerina *f*

nitrous ['naɪtrəs] *adj* nitroso(a)

nitty-gritty [nɪtɪ'grɪtɪ] *n Fam* **to get down to the n.-g.** ir al grano

nitwit ['nɪtwɪt] *n Fam* imbécil *mf*

no [nəʊ] **1** *adj* ninguno(a); **I have no idea** no tengo (ni) idea; **it's no good** *or* **use** no vale la pena; **make no mistake about it** no lo dudes; *Aut* **'no parking'** 'prohibido aparcar'; **no sensible person** ninguna persona razonable; **no two are the same** no hay dos (que sean) iguales; **she has no children** no tiene hijos; **she's no genius** no es ningún genio; **there is no such thing as ...** no existe ...; **there's no changing your mind now** ya no puedes cambiar de idea; *Fam* **n. end of ...** un mogollón *or* montón de ...; *Fam* **no way!** ¡ni hablar!, *Esp* ¡de eso nada!, *Am* ¡para nada!
  2 *n (pl* **noes)** no *m*; **ayes and noes** votos a favor y votos en contra; **she won't take no for an answer** no se dará por vencida, no aceptará un no por respuesta
  3 *adv* no; **come here! — no!** ¡ven aquí! — ¡no!; **it's no better than before** no está mejor que antes; **no longer** ya no; **no less than** no menos de; **to say no** decir que no

no. *(pl* **nos.)** *(abbr* **number)** número *m*, n., núm

Noah ['nəʊə] *n Rel* Noé *m* ❑ **N.'s ark** el arca *f* de Noé

nob [nɒb] *n Br Fam* pez *m* gordo

nobble ['nɒbəl] *vt Br Fam* **(a)** *(drug)* drogar **(b)** *(bribe)* comprar, untar, *Andes RP* coimear, *CAm Méx* dar la mordida

Nobel Prize ['nəʊbel'praɪz] *n* Premio *m* Nobel

nobility [nəʊ'bɪlɪtɪ] *n* nobleza *f*

noble ['nəʊbəl] **1** *adj* **(a)** *(aristocratic)* noble; **of n. birth** de noble cuna; **of n. descent** de noble alcurnia **(b)** *(sentiment)* noble; *(gesture)* magnánimo(a) **(c)** *(impressive)* magnífico(a), grandioso(a)
  2 *n (in feudal system)* noble *m*

nobleman ['nəʊbəlmən] *n (pl* **noblemen)** noble *m*

noblewoman ['nəʊbəlwʊmən] *n (pl* **noblewomen** ['nəʊbəlwɪmɪn]) noble *f*

nobody ['nəʊbədɪ] **1** *pron* nadie; **I told n.** no se lo dije a nadie; **n. came** no vino nadie; **n. else** nadie más; **n. knows the answer** no conoce la respuesta nadie
2 *n* nadie *m*; **he's a n.** es un don nadie

no-brainer ['nəʊ'breɪnər] *n US Fam* **it's a n.** está tirado

no-claims ['nəʊkleɪmz] *adj* **no-c. bonus** prima *f* de no siniestrabilidad

nocturnal [nɒk'tɜːnəl] *adj* nocturno(a)

nod [nɒd] **1** *n* (**a**) *(in greeting)* saludo *m* con la cabeza (**b**) *(in agreement)* señal *f* de asentimiento; *Br Fam* **as good as a wink** a buen entendedor pocas palabras bastan (**c**) **the land of N.** el mundo de los sueños
2 *vi (pt & pp nodded)* (**a**) *(in greeting)* saludar con la cabeza (**b**) *(in agreement)* asentir con la cabeza
3 *vt* **to n. one's head** inclinar la cabeza; *(in agreement)* asentir con la cabeza

nod off *vi* quedarse dormido-(a), dormirse

nodding ['nɒdɪŋ] *adj* **to have a n. acquaintance with sb** conocer a algn de vista

node [nəʊd] *n* (**a**) *Bot* nudo *m* (**b**) *Anat Med* nodo *m*

nodule ['nɒdjuːl] *n* nódulo *m*

no-fly zone [nəʊ'flaɪzəʊn] *n* zona *f* de exclusión aérea

no-frills [nəʊ'frɪlz] *adj* sin florituras

no-go [nəʊ'gəʊ] *adj* **no-go area** zona *f* prohibida

no-good ['nəʊgʊd] *Fam adj* inútil

no-holds-barred ['nəʊhəʊldz'bɑːd] *adj (report, documentary)* a fondo, sin restricciones

no-hoper [nəʊ'həʊpər] *n Br Fam* inútil *mf*

nohow ['nəʊhaʊ] *adv US Fam* ¡ni hablar!

noise [nɔɪz] *n* (**a**) *(sound, din)* ruido *m*; **to make a n.** hacer ruido □ **background n.** ruido *m* de fondo (**b**) *Fam* **a big n.** un pez gordo

noiseless ['nɔɪzlɪs] *adj* silencioso(a), sin ruido

noiselessly ['nɔɪzlɪslɪ] *adv* silenciosamente

noiseproof ['nɔɪzpruːf] *adj* insonorizado(a)

noisy ['nɔɪzɪ] *adj* **(noisier, noisiest)** ruidoso(a); **a n. machine/street** una máquina/calle ruidosa; **a n. crowd** una muchedumbre bulliciosa

nomad ['nəʊmæd] *n* nómada *mf*

nomadic [nəʊ'mædɪk] *adj* nómada

no-man's-land ['nəʊmænzlænd] *n* tierra *f* de nadie

nomenclature [nəʊ'menklətʃər, *US* 'nəʊmənkleɪtʃər] *n* nomenclatura *f*

nominal ['nɒmɪnəl] *adj* (**a**) *(in name only)* nominal (**b**) *(payment, rent)* simbólico(a)

nominally ['nɒmɪnəlɪ] *adv* nominalmente, de nombre solamente

nominate ['nɒmɪneɪt] *vt* (**a**) *(propose)* designar, proponer (**b**) *(appoint)* nombrar

nomination [nɒmɪ'neɪʃən] *n* (**a**) *(proposal)* propuesta *f*; **to accept/support a n.** aceptar/apoyar una candidatura (**b**) *(appointment)* nombramiento *m*

nominative ['nɒmɪnətɪv] *n Ling* nominativo *m*

nominee [nɒmɪ'niː] *n* nominado(a), *m,f,* persona *f* propuesta

non- [nɒn] *pref* no; **n.-Catholic** no católico(a)

non-aggression [nɒnə'greʃən] *n Pol* no agresión *f* □ **n.-a. pact** pacto *m* de no agresión

non-alcoholic [nɒnælkə'hɒlɪk] *adj* no alcohólico(a), sin alcohol

non-aligned [nɒnə'laɪnd] *adj Pol* no alineado(a) □ **n.-a. countries** países *mpl* no alineados

nonattendance [nɒnə'tendəns] *n* ausencia *f*

nonbinding [nɒn'baɪndɪŋ] *adj* no vinculante

nonchalance ['nɒnʃələns, *US* nɒnʃə'lɑːns] *n (indifference)* indiferencia *f*; *(calmness)* imperturbabilidad *f*

nonchalant ['nɒnʃələnt, *US* nɒnʃə'lɑːnt] *adj (indifferent)* indiferente; *(calm)* imperturbable, impasible

noncombatant [nɒn'kɒmbətənt] *adj & n* no combatiente *(mf)*

noncommissioned ['nɒnkəmɪʃənd] *adj Mil* **n. officer** suboficial *m*

noncommittal ['nɒnkəmɪtəl] *adj* evasivo(a), que no compromete a nada; **a n. reply** una respuesta poco comprometedora

non-compliance ['nɒnkəm'plaɪəns] *n Fml* incumplimiento *m* (**with de**)

nonconductor [nɒnkən'dʌktər] *n Elec Phys* aislante *m*

nonconformist [nɒnkən'fɔːmɪst] *n* inconformista *mf*

noncontributory [nɒnkən'trɪbjʊtərɪ] *adj* **a n. pension scheme** un plan de jubilación pagado por la empresa

non-dairy ['nɒndeərɪ] *adj* no lácteo(a)

nondescript [*Br* 'nɒndɪskrɪpt, *US* nɒndɪ'skrɪpt] *adj (person, place, building)* anodino(a); *(taste)* indefinido(a); **n. music** una música cualquiera

none [nʌn] **1** *pron* ninguno(a); **I know n. of them** no conozco a ninguno de ellos; **it is n. of her business** no tiene nada que ver con ella, no es asunto suyo; **n. at all** nada en absoluto; **n. of that in here!** ¡nada de esto aquí dentro!; **n. of the records is his** ninguno de los discos es suyo; **n. other than …** nada menos que …
2 *adv* de ningún modo, de ninguna manera; **she's n. the worse for it** no se ha visto afectada *or* perjudicada por ello; **n. too soon** a buena hora

nonentity [nɒ'nentɪtɪ] *n (person)* nulidad *f*, cero *m* a la izquierda

nonessential [nɒnɪ'senʃəl] **1** *n* **nonessentials** lo accesorio
2 *adj* accesorio(a), prescindible

nonetheless [nʌnðə'les] *adv* no obstante, sin embargo

nonevent [nɒnɪ'vent] *n* fracaso *m*; **the concert turned out to be a n.** aquello ni fue concierto ni fue nada

nonexecutive director [nɒnɪg'zekjʊtɪvdaɪ'rektər] *n* director(a) *m,f* no ejecutivo(a)

nonexistent [nɒnɪg'zɪstənt] *adj* inexistente

non-fat ['nɒnfæt] *adj (food)* sin grasa

nonfattening [nɒn'fætənɪŋ] *adj* que no engorda

nonfiction [nɒn'fɪkʃən] *n* literatura *f* no novelesca

nonflammable [nɒn'flæməbəl] *adj* incombustible, ininflamable

non-intervention ['nɒnɪntə'venʃən] *n* no intervención *f*

nonmember [nɒn'membər] *n* no socio(a) *m,f*

non-native ['nɒn'neɪtɪv] *adj* no nativo(a); **n.-n. speaker** hablante no nativo

non-negotiable [nɒnnɪ'gəʊʃɪəbəl] *adj* no negociable

no-no ['nəʊnəʊ] *n Fam* **that's a no-n.** eso ni se te ocurra

no-nonsense [nəʊ'nɒnsens] *adj (person)* recto(a), serio(a)

non-partisan [nɒn'pɑːtɪzæn] *adj* imparcial

nonpayment [nɒn'peɪmənt] *n* falta *f* de pago

non-person ['nɒn'pɜːsən] *n (pl non-persons)* politically, **she became a n.** políticamente hablando, dejó de existir

nonplussed [nɒn'plʌst] *adj* perplejo(a), anonadado(a)

non-profit-making [nɒn'prɒfɪtmeɪkɪŋ] *adj (organization)* sin fin lucrativo

non-racist [nɒnˈreɪsɪst] *adj* no racista

non-refundable [ˈnɒnrɪˈfʌndəbəl] *adj (deposit)* a fondo perdido, sin posibilidad de reembolso

nonresident [nɒnˈrezɪdənt] *n* no residente *mf*

nonreturnable [nɒnrɪˈtɜːnəbəl] *adj* no retornable

non-sectarian [ˈnɒnsekˈteərɪən] *adj* no sectario(a)

nonsense [ˈnɒnsəns] *n* tonterías *fpl*, disparates *mpl*; **to talk n.** decir tonterías; **that's n.** eso es absurdo

nonsensical [nɒnˈsensɪkəl] *adj* absurdo(a)

non sequitur [nɒnˈsekwɪtər] *n* incongruencia *f*

non-sexist [nɒnˈseksɪst] *adj* no sexista

nonsmoker [nɒnˈsməʊkər] *n* no fumador(a) *m,f*, persona *f* que no fuma

non-smoking [ˈnɒnsməʊkɪŋ] *adj (area, carriage)* de no fumadores; **this is a n. flight** no está permitido fumar en este vuelo

non-specialist [nɒnˈspeʃəlɪst] **1** *n* profano(a) *m,f*
2 *adj* no especializado(a)

non-standard [ˈnɒnˈstændəd] *adj* **(a)** *Ling* no normativo(a) **(b)** *(product, size)* fuera de lo común

nonstarter [nɒnˈstɑːtər] *n* **to be a n.** *Sport (competitor)* quedar descalificado(a); *Fig (person)* ser imposible

nonstick [nɒnˈstɪk] *adj (pan etc)* antiadherente

nonstop [nɒnˈstɒp] **1** *adj (train)* directo(a); *(flight)* sin escalas
2 *adv* sin parar; **to talk n.** hablar sin parar, no parar de hablar; **to fly n.** volar sin hacer escalas

nontaxable [nɒnˈtæksəbəl] *adj* exento(a) de impuestos, no imponible

nontoxic [nɒnˈtɒksɪk] *adj* no tóxico(a)

nontransferable [ˈnɒntrænsˈfɜːrəbəl] *adj* intransferible

nonverbal [nɒnˈvɜːbəl] *adj* no verbal; **n. communication** comunicación *f* no verbal

nonviolent [nɒnˈvaɪələnt] *adj* no violento(a)

noodle [ˈnuːdəl] *n* **(a)** *(pasta)* **noodles** tallarines *mpl (chinos)* **(b)** *US Fam (head)* coco *m*, mollera *f*

nook [nʊk] *n* rincón *m*, recoveco *m*

noon [nuːn] *n* mediodía *m*; **at n.** a mediodía

noonday [ˈnuːndeɪ] *n* **the n. sun** el sol de mediodía

no one [ˈnəʊwʌn] *pron* nadie; **no o. came** no vino nadie

noose [nuːs] *n (loop)* nudo *m* corredizo; *(hangman's)* soga *f*; *Fig* **to have one's head in the n.** estar con la soga al cuello

nope [nəʊp] *adv Fam* no

nor [nɔːr] *conj* ni, ni tampoco; **neither ... n.** ni ... ni; **neither you n.** I ni tú ni yo; **he neither drinks n. smokes** ni fuma ni bebe *or Am* toma; **n. do I** (ni) yo tampoco

Nordic [ˈnɔːdɪk] *adj* nórdico(a)

norm [nɔːm] *n* norma *f*; **to deviate from the n.** salirse de lo normal *or* de la norma

normal [ˈnɔːməl] **1** *adj* normal; **a n. person** una persona normal
2 *n* lo normal; **below n.** por debajo de lo normal

normality [nɔːˈmælɪtɪ] *n*, *US* **normalcy** [ˈnɔːməlsɪ] *n* normalidad *f*

normalization [nɔːməlaɪˈzeɪʃən] *n* normalización *f*

normalize [ˈnɔːməlaɪz] **1** *vt* normalizar
2 *vi* normalizarse

normally [ˈnɔːməlɪ] *adv* normalmente

Norman [ˈnɔːmən] *adj & n* normando(a) *(m,f)*

Normandy [ˈnɔːməndɪ] *n* Normandía

Norse [nɔːs] *Hist* **1** *adj* nórdico(a)
2 *n (language)* nórdico *m*

Norseman [ˈnɔːsmən] *n (pl* **Norsemen)** *Hist* vikingo *m*

north [nɔːθ] **1** *n* norte *m*; **the N.** el norte □ **N. Africa** África del Norte; **N. African** norteafricano(a) *(m,f)*; **N. America** América del Norte, Norteamérica; **N. American** norteamericano(a) *(m,f)*; **N. Carolina** Carolina del Norte; **N. Dakota** Dakota del Norte; **N. Pole** Polo *m* Norte; **the N. Sea** el Mar del Norte
2 *adv* hacia el norte, al norte; **to face n.** dar al norte
3 *adj* del norte; **the n. coast** la costa del norte; **n. wind** viento del norte

northbound [ˈnɔːθbaʊnd] *adj* con dirección norte; **a n. train** un tren que viaja hacia el norte

northeast [nɔːθˈiːst] *n* nordeste *m*, noreste *m*

northeasterly [nɔːθˈiːstəlɪ] *adj,* **northeastern** [nɔːθˈiːstən] *adj* del nordeste

northerly [ˈnɔːðəlɪ] *adj* norte, del norte; **n. wind** viento *m* del norte; **in a n. direction** en dirección norte; **the most n. point** el punto más septentrional

northern [ˈnɔːðən] *adj* del norte, septentrional □ **n. hemisphere** hemisferio *m* norte; **N. Ireland** Irlanda del Norte; **N. Irishman** norirlandés *m*; **N. Irishwoman** norirlandesa *f*; **n. lights** aurora *f* sing boreal

northerner [ˈnɔːðənər] *n* norteño(a), *mf*

North Korea [ˈnɔːθkəˈriːə] *n* Corea del Norte

North Korean [ˈnɔːθkəˈriːən] *adj & n* norcoreano(a) *(m,f)*

northward [ˈnɔːθwəd] *adj & adv* hacia el norte

northwards [ˈnɔːθwədz] *adv* hacia el norte

northwest [nɔːθˈwest] *n* noroeste *m*

northwesterly [nɔːθˈwestəlɪ] *adj,* **northwestern** [nɔːθˈwestən] *adj* del noroeste

Norway [ˈnɔːweɪ] *n* Noruega

Norwegian [nɔːˈwiːdʒən] **1** *adj* noruego(a)
2 *n* **(a)** *(person)* noruego(a) *m,f* **(b)** *(language)* noruego *m*

nose [nəʊz] **1** *n* **(a)** *Anat* nariz *f*; **my n. is bleeding** me sangra la nariz; **to blow one's n.** sonarse; *Fig (right)* **under sb's n.** delante de las propias narices de algn; *Fig* **to be as plain as the n. on one's face** estar tan claro como el agua; *Fig* **to lead sb by the n.** manejar a algn a su antojo; *Br Fam* **to get up sb's n.** fastidiar *or* jorobar a algn; *Fam* **to keep one's n. clean** no meterse en líos; *Fam* **to pay through the n.** pagar un dineral; *Fam* **to poke** *or* **stick one's n. into sth** meter la nariz *or* las narices en algo; *Fam* **to turn one's n. up at sth** despreciar algo **(b)** *(sense of smell)* olfato *m* **(c)** *(of car, plane)* morro *m*; **the cars stood n. to tail** los coches estaban parados en una caravana
2 *vi* avanzar poco a poco; **the car nosed (out) into the street** el coche asomó el morro para salir a la calle

nose about, nose around *vi* curiosear

nose out *vt (animal)* olfatear; *Fig (secret)* averiguar

nosebag [ˈnəʊzbæg] *n* morral *m*

nosebleed [ˈnəʊzbliːd] *n* hemorragia *f* nasal

nosedive [ˈnəʊzdaɪv] *Av* **1** *n Esp* picado *m*, *Am* picada *f*
2 *vi* caer en *Esp* picado *or Am* picada

nosegay [ˈnəʊzgeɪ] *n* ramillete *m* de flores

nosey [ˈnəʊzɪ] *adj see* **nosy**

nosh [nɒʃ] *n Br Fam Esp* manduca *f*, *Méx RP* papa *f*, *RP* morfi *m*

no-show [nəʊˈʃəʊ] *n (for flight)* pasajero *m* (con reserva) no presentado; *(at theatre)* reserva *f* no cubierta

no-smoking [nəʊˈsməʊkɪŋ] *adj (carriage, area)* de *or* para no fumadores

nostalgia [nɒˈstældʒə] *n* nostalgia *f*

nostalgic [nɒˈstældʒɪk] *adj* nostálgico(a)

nostril [ˈnɒstrɪl] *n Anat* orificio *m* nasal

nosy [ˈnəʊzɪ] *adj (***nosier, nosiest)** *Fam* entrometido(a); **n. parker** metomentodo *mf*

not [nɒt] *adv* no; **certainly n.** de ninguna manera; **he's n. in today** hoy no está; **I'm n. sorry to leave** no siento nada irme; **n. at all** en absoluto; **thank you — n. at all** gracias — no hay de qué, de nada; **n. one, but many** no uno sino muchos; **n. one (of them) said thank you** nadie me dio las gracias; **n. that I don't want to come** no es que no quiera ir; **n. too well** bastante mal; **n. without reason** no sin razón; *Fam* **n. likely!** ¡ni hablar!

notable ['nəʊtəbəl] *adj* notable; **a n. success** un éxito notable

notably ['nəʊtəblɪ] *adv* notablemente; **n. well done** admirablemente bien hecho; **she was n. absent** brilló por su ausencia

notary ['nəʊtərɪ] *n* notario(a) *m,f*, *Am* escribano(a) *m,f*

notation [nəʊ'teɪʃən] *n Mus* notación *f*

notch [nɒtʃ] **1** *n* muesca *f*, corte *m*
2 *vt* hacer una muesca, marcar con muescas

notch up *vt Fig* **to n. up a victory** apuntarse una victoria *or* un tanto

note [nəʊt] **1** *n* **(a)** *Mus* nota *f*; *(hint)* tono *m*, nota *f*; **a n. of bitterness** un tono de amargura **(b)** *Mus (key)* tecla *f*; **the black/white notes** las teclas negras/blancas; *Fig* **to strike the right n.** acertar, hacer *or* decir lo apropiado **(c)** *(on paper)* nota *f*; **I sent her a n.** le envié una nota; **there's a n. in the margin** hay una nota en el margen **(d)** *(notice)* **to take n. of** prestar atención a; **worthy of n.** digno de mención **(e)** *esp Br (banknote)* billete *m* de banco; **a ten pound n.** un billete de diez libras **(f)** **notes** apuntes *mpl*; **I'll have to look it up in my n.** tendré que mirarlo en mis apuntes; **to take n.** tomar apuntes
2 *vt* **(a)** *(write down)* apuntar, anotar; **she noted the details in her diary** apuntó los detalles en su agenda **(b)** *(see, notice)* notar, advertir, fijarse; **his reaction was noted by everyone** todos advirtieron su reacción

notebook ['nəʊtbʊk] *n* **(a)** *(small)* libreta *f*, *(bigger)* cuaderno *m* **(b)** *Comptr* **n. (computer)** *Esp* ordenador *m or Am* computadora *f* portátil

noted ['nəʊtɪd] *adj* notable, célebre; **she was n. for her strength** era famosa por su fuerza

notepad ['nəʊtpæd] *n* bloc *m* de notas

notepaper ['nəʊtpeɪpər] *n* papel *m* de cartas *or* de escribir

noteworthy ['nəʊtwɜːðɪ] *adj* digno(a) de mención

not-for-profit ['nɒtfər'prɒfɪt] *adj US* sin ánimo de lucro

nothing ['nʌθɪŋ] **1** *n* nada, no ... nada; **for n.** gratis; **it's n.** no es nada; **it's n. to be proud of** no es como para estar orgulloso; **it's n. to do with you** no tiene nada que ver contigo; **n. else** nada más; **n. happened today** hoy no pasó nada; **n. more** nada más; **sweet nothings** ternezas *fpl*; **there's n. in it** no es cierto; *Fam* **n. much** poca cosa; *Fam* **there's n. to it** es facilísimo; *Slang* **n. doing** ni hablar; *Esp* de eso nada, *Méx* ni un quinto
2 *adv* de ninguna manera, de ningún modo; **it's n. like as good as ...** no tiene ni *(punto de)* comparación con ...; **she looks n. like her sister** no se parece en nada a su hermana

nothingness ['nʌθɪŋnɪs] *n* nada *f*

notice ['nəʊtɪs] **1** *n* **(a)** *(warning)* aviso *m*; **a month's n.** un mes de plazo; **he gave a month's n.** presentó la dimisión con un mes de antelación; **at a moment's n.** sin antelación; **at short n.** con poca antelación; **until further n.** hasta nuevo aviso; **without n.** sin previo aviso ❑ **n. to quit** notificación *f* para desocupar una vivienda *or* un local **(b)** *(attention)* atención *f*; **it escaped my n.** se me escapó; **to come to sb's n.** llegar al conocimiento de uno; **to take no n. of sth** no hacer caso de algo; **to take n. of sth** prestar atención a algo **(c)** *(announcement)* anuncio *m*; **she put a n. in the shop window** puso un anuncio en el escaparate de

la tienda **(d)** *(sign)* letrero *m*, aviso *m*; **the n. says 'keep off the grass'** el letrero dice 'prohibido pisar el césped' **(e)** *(review)* reseña *f*
2 *vt* darse cuenta de, fijarse en, notar; **he didn't n.** no se dio cuenta; **I didn't n. the new curtains** no me fijé en las cortinas nuevas; **she noticed nothing strange** no notó nada extraño

noticeable ['nəʊtɪsəbəl] *adj* que se nota, evidente; **the stain isn't very n.** la mancha no se nota mucho; **it's hardly n.** casi no se nota; **a n. change** un cambio evidente

noticeably ['nəʊtɪsəblɪ] *adv* claramente, notablemente

noticeboard ['nəʊtɪsbɔːd] *n Br* tablón *m* de anuncios

notifiable [nəʊtɪ'faɪəbəl] *adj Med (disease)* de declaración médica obligatoria

notification [nəʊtɪfɪ'keɪʃən] *n* aviso *m*, notificación *f*

notify ['nəʊtɪfaɪ] *vt (pt & pp notified)* avisar, notificar; **she was notified that her car had been found** le notificaron que el coche había aparecido; **to n. the police of a burglary** denunciar un robo a la policía

notion ['nəʊʃən] *n* **(a)** *(idea, concept)* idea *f*, noción *f*; **he had little n. of what was being said** tenía muy poca idea de lo que se estaba diciendo; **her n. of friendship is different from mine** su concepto de la amistad es diferente del mío **(b)** *(whim)* capricho *m* **(c)** *US* **notions** *(sewing materials)* cosas *fpl* de costura

notional ['nəʊʃənəl] *adj* **(a)** *(vague)* teórico(a) **(b)** *(imaginary)* imaginario(a)

notoriety [nəʊtə'raɪətɪ] *n* mala fama *f*, mala reputación *f*

notorious [nəʊ'tɔːrɪəs] *adj* célebre, muy conocido(a); **a n. criminal** un criminal célebre

notoriously [nəʊ'tɔːrɪəslɪ] *adv* notoriamente; **they were n. ill-equipped** era de todos sabido que iban mal equipados

notwithstanding [nɒtwɪθ'stændɪŋ] **1** *prep* a pesar de
2 *adv* sin embargo, no obstante

nougat ['nuːgɑː] *n* turrón *m* blando

nought [nɔːt] *n* cero *m*; **n. point five** cero coma cinco ❑ **noughts and crosses** tres en raya *m*

noun [naʊn] *n Ling* nombre *m*, sustantivo *m* ❑ **proper n.** nombre *m* propio

nourish ['nʌrɪʃ] *vt* **(a)** *(person, animal)* alimentar, nutrir **(b)** *Fig (hopes)* abrigar

nourishing ['nʌrɪʃɪŋ] *adj* nutritivo(a), alimenticio(a)

nourishment ['nʌrɪʃmənt] *n* alimentación *f*, nutrición *f*

nous [naʊs] *n Br Fam* cacumen *m*

Nov *(abbr* **November)** noviembre *m*, nov., novbre

Nova Scotia [nəʊvə'skəʊʃə] *n* Nueva Escocia

novel¹ ['nɒvəl] *n* novela *f*

novel² ['nɒvəl] *adj* original, novedoso(a)

novelist ['nɒvəlɪst] *n* novelista *mf*

novelty ['nɒvəltɪ] *n* **(a)** *(thing, idea)* novedad *f*; **the n. of the situation** la novedad de la situación; **the n. will soon wear off** pronto dejará de ser una novedad **(b)** *(trinket)* novedad *f*, fantasía *f*

November [nəʊ'vembər] *n* noviembre *m*; **(on) the fifth of N.** el cinco de noviembre; *see also* **May**

novice ['nɒvɪs] *n* **(a)** *(beginner)* novato(a) *m,f*, principiante *mf* **(b)** *Rel* novicio(a) *m,f*

now [naʊ] **1** *adv* **(a)** *(at this moment)* ahora; **from n. on** de ahora en adelante; **it's my turn n.** ahora me toca a mí; **just n., right n.** ahora mismo; **n. and then, n. and again** de vez en cuando **(b)** *(for events in past)* ya, entonces; **everything was n. ready** ya estaba todo a punto **(c)** *(at present, these days)* actualmente, hoy (en) día **(d)** *(not related to time)* **n. (then)** ahora bien; **n. then, what's the problem?**

¿veamos, cuál es el problema?; **n., n.!** ¡vamos!, ¡ya está bien!

2 *conj* **n. (that)** ahora que, ya que; **n. that she is going to school** ahora que va al colegio; **n. that you mention it** ya que lo mencionas

3 *n* **until n.** hasta ahora; **he'll be home by n.** ya habrá llegado a casa; **goodbye for n.!** ¡hasta pronto!; **four days from n.** dentro de cuatro días

nowadays ['nauǝdeɪz] *adv* hoy, hoy (en) día, actualmente

nowhere ['nǝʊweǝr] *adv* en ningún lugar, en ningún sitio, en ninguna parte; **it's n. to be seen** no está en ninguna parte; **he's n. near the end** le falta mucho para terminar; **that will get you n.** eso no te servirá de nada; *Fam* **she lives in the middle of n.** vive en el quinto pino; **n. else** en ninguna otra parte; **to come out of n.** salir de la nada

noxious ['nɒkʃǝs] *adj* nocivo(a), perjudicial

nozzle ['nɒzǝl] *n* boca *f*, boquilla *f*

nr (*abbr* **near**) cerca de

NRA [enɑː'reɪ] *n US* (*abbr* **National Rifle Association**) = asociación estadounidense que se opone a cualquier restricción en el uso de armas de fuego

NSPCC [enespiːsiː'siː] *n Br* (*abbr* **National Society for the Prevention of Cruelty to Children**) = sociedad nacional para la protección de los niños

NT [en'tiː] *n Br* (*abbr* **National Trust**) = organización que vela por el patrimonio nacional

Nth (*abbr* **North**) norte, N

nth [enθ] *adj* **for the n. time** por enésima vez

nuance [nju:'ɑːns] *n* matiz *m*

nub [nʌb] *n* nudo *m*, meollo *m*; **the n. of the matter** el quid de la cuestión

nubile [nju:baɪl] *adj* núbil, casadero(a)

nuclear ['nju:klɪǝr] *adj* nuclear ❑ **n. arms** armas *fpl* nucleares; **n. disarmament** desarme *m* nuclear; **n. energy** energía *f* nuclear; **n. family** familia *f* nuclear; **n. fission** fisión *f* nuclear; **n. power** energía *f* nuclear; **n. power station** central *f* nuclear; **n. war(fare)** guerra *f* nuclear *or* atómica; **n. weapon** arma *f* nuclear *or* atómica; **n. winter** invierno *m* nuclear

nuclear-powered ['nju:klɪǝ'paʊǝd] *adj* nuclear; **n.-p. submarine** submarino *m* nuclear

nucleic [nju:'kliːɪk] *adj Biol Chem* nucleico(a); **n. acid** ácido *m* nucleico

nucleus ['nju:klɪǝs] *n* (*pl* **nuclei** ['nju:klɪaɪ]) núcleo *m*

nude [nju:d] **1** *adj* desnudo(a)
2 *n Art Phot* desnudo *m*; **in the n.** desnudo(a)

nudge [nʌdʒ] **1** *vt* dar un codazo a
2 *n* codazo *m*

nudism ['nju:dɪzǝm] *n* nudismo *m*

nudist ['nju:dɪst] *adj & n* nudista *(mf)* ❑ **n. colony** colonia *f* nudista

nudity ['nju:dɪtɪ] *n* desnudez *f*

nugget ['nʌgɪt] *n Min* pepita *f*; **gold n.** pepita de oro

nuisance ['nju:sǝns] *n* (**a**) (*annoying thing*) molestia *f*, pesadez *f*; **this weather is a n.** este tiempo es una pesadez; **what a n.!** ¡qué lata! (**b**) (*annoying person*) pesado(a) *m,f*; **to make a n. of oneself** dar la lata, ponerse pesado

nuke [nju:k] *Slang* **1** *n* (**a**) (*bomb*) bomba *f* nuclear *or* atómica (**b**) *US* (*power plant*) central *f* nuclear
2 *vt* atacar con armas nucleares

null [nʌl] *adj* nulo(a); **n. and void** nulo y sin valor

nullify ['nʌlɪfaɪ] *vt* (*pt & pp* **nullified**) anular

numb [nʌm] **1** *adj* (**a**) (*without feeling*) entumecido(a); **my**

leg has gone n. se me ha dormido la pierna; **n. with cold** entumecido de frío (**b**) *Fig* (*unable to move*) paralizado(a), petrificado(a); **n. with fear** paralizado de miedo
2 *vt* (**a**) (*with cold*) entumecer (de frío); (*with anaesthetic*) adormecer (**b**) *Fig (paralyse)* paralizar, dejar helado

number ['nʌmbǝr] **1** *n* (**a**) *Math* número *m*; **odd/even n.** número impar/par; **in round numbers** en números redondos ❑ *Comptr* **n. crunching** cálculos *mpl* (**b**) (*quantity*) **a n. of people** varias personas; **a large n. of** un gran número de (**c**) (*of page, house, etc*) número *m*; **she lives at n. four** vive en el (número) cuatro; *Tel* **have you got my n.?** ¿tienes mi (número de) teléfono?; *Tel* **you've got the wrong n.** se ha equivocado de número (**d**) **to be n. one** ser el primero *or* el mejor *or* el número uno; **to look after n. one** barrer para adentro (**e**) *Br (of magazine)* número *m*; **the June n.** el número de junio; **back n.** número atrasado (**f**) *Fam (clothing)* modelo *m*; **Kathy was wearing a black lace n.** Kathy llevaba un modelo de encaje negro (**g**) *Fam (job etc)* **a cushy n.** un chollo (**h**) *Mus Theat* número *m*
2 *vt* (**a**) (*put a number on*) numerar, poner número a; **the seats are numbered** los asientos llevan número (**b**) (*count*) contar; **his days are numbered** tiene los días contados; **I n. you among my friends** te cuento entre mis amigos

numbering ['nʌmbǝrɪŋ] *n* numeración *f*

numberplate ['nʌmbǝpleɪt] *n Br Aut* placa *f* de la matrícula

numbness ['nʌmnɪs] *n* (**a**) (*loss of feeling*) entumecimiento *m* (**b**) *Fig* parálisis *f*

numbskull ['nʌmskʌl] *n* idiota *mf*, *Esp* majadero(a) *m,f*

numeracy ['nju:mǝrǝsɪ] *n* conocimiento *m* básico de las matemáticas

numeral ['nju:mǝrǝl] *n* número *m*, cifra *f*; **Roman numerals** números romanos

numerate ['nju:mǝrǝt] *adj* **to be n.** tener un conocimiento básico de matemáticas

numerator ['nju:mǝreɪtǝr] *n Math* numerador *m*

numeric(al) [nju:'merɪk(ǝl)] *adj* numérico(a); **in n. order** por orden numérico ❑ *Comptr* **n. keypad** teclado *m* numérico

numerically [nju:'merɪklɪ] *adv* numéricamente; **the enemy was n. superior** el enemigo era numéricamente superior

numerous ['nju:mǝrǝs] *adj* numeroso(a); **n. friends** numerosos *or* muchos amigos; **on n. occasions** en innumerables ocasiones

numismatic [nju:mɪz'mætɪk] *adj* numismático(a)

numismatics [nju:mɪz'mætɪks] *n* numismática *f*

numismatist [nju:'mɪzmǝtɪst] *n* numismático(a) *m,f*

nun [nʌn] *n* monja *f*

nuncio ['nʌnsɪǝʊ] *n* (*pl* **nuncios**) *Rel* nuncio *m*

nunlike ['nʌnlaɪk] *adj* monjil

nunnery ['nʌnǝrɪ] *n* convento *m*

nuptial ['nʌpʃǝl] **1** *adj* nupcial; **n. mass** misa *f* nupcial
2 nuptials *npl Hum* casamiento *m*, boda *f*

nurse [nɜːs] **1** *n* enfermera *f*; **children's n.** niñera *f*; **male n.** enfermero *m*
2 *vt* (**a**) (*look after*) cuidar, atender; **to n. sb back to health** cuidar a algn durante una enfermedad; **to n. a cold** curarse un resfriado (**b**) (*baby*) acunar, mecer en los brazos; **he nursed his swollen ankle** cuidó de su tobillo hinchado (**c**) (*suckle*) amamantar, criar (**d**) *Fig (harbour)* guardar; **to n. a grievance** guardar rencor

nursemaid ['nɜːsmeɪd] *n* niñera *f*

nursery ['nɜːsǝrɪ] *n* (**a**) (*in house*) cuarto *m* de los niños ❑ **n. rhyme** poema *m* infantil (**b**) (*institution*) guardería *f* ❑ **day n.** guardería *f*; **n. school** parvulario *m*, jardín *m* de infancia (**c**) *Fig* semillero *m*, vivero *m* (**d**) *Sport* **n. slopes** pistas *fpl* para principiantes (**e**) *Hortic* vivero *m*

nurseryman ['nɜːsərɪmən] *n* (*pl* **nurserymen**) encargado *m* de un vivero, arbolista *m*

nursing ['nɜːsɪŋ] **1** *adj* (**a**) *(mother)* que amamanta (**b**) *Med* **n. home** *Br (where children are born)* maternidad *f*; *(for old people, war veterans)* residencia *f*; **n. staff** enfermeros *mpl* y enfermeras *fpl*, personal *m* sanitario
     2 *n* profesión *f* de enfermero(a)

nurture ['nɜːtʃər] *vt* nutrir, alimentar

nut [nʌt] *n* (**a**) *(fruit)* fruto *m* seco; *(walnut)* nuez *f*; *(peanut)* *Esp* cacahuete *m*, *Andes Carib RP* maní *m*, *CAm Méx* cacahuate *m*; *(hazelnut)* avellana *f*; *(almond)* almendra *f*; *Fig* **a tough n. to crack** un hueso duro de roer (**b**) *Slang (head)* coco *m*, chola *f*, melón *m*; **he's off his n.** está chalado (**c**) *Slang (mad person)* chiflado(a) *m,f*, *Esp* chalado(a) *m,f* (**d**) *Tech* tuerca *f*; **nuts and bolts** tuercas y pernios

nut-brown ['nʌtbraʊn] *adj* castaño(a), (de) color avellana

nutcase ['nʌtkeɪs] *n Slang* loco(a) *m,f*, chalado(a) *m,f*

nutcracker ['nʌtkrækər] *n* cascanueces *m inv*

nuthatch ['nʌthætʃ] *n Orn* trepador *m* azul

nuthouse ['nʌthaʊs] *n Fam* manicomio *m*, loquero *m*

nutmeg ['nʌtmeg] *n* nuez *f* moscada

nutrient ['njuːtrɪənt] **1** *adj* nutritivo(a)
     2 *n* alimento *m* nutritivo, sustancia *f* nutritiva

nutrition [njuːˈtrɪʃən] *n* nutrición *f*, alimentación *f*

nutritional [njuːˈtrɪʃənəl] *adj* nutritivo(a)

nutritious [njuːˈtrɪʃəs] *adj* nutritivo(a), alimenticio(a)

nuts [nʌts] *adj* chiflado(a), *Esp* majara; **to go n.** volverse loco; **he's n. about motorbikes** las motos le chiflan

nutshell ['nʌtʃel] *n* cáscara *f* (de fruto seco); *Fig* **in a n.** en pocas palabras

nutter ['nʌtər] *n Br Fam* loco(a) *m,f*, chalado(a) *m,f*

nutty ['nʌtɪ] *adj* (**nuttier, nuttiest**) (**a**) *Culin* que sabe a nuez (**b**) *Slang (crazy)* loco(a), chalado(a)

nuzzle ['nʌzəl] *vi* **to n. up to** arrimarse a

NW (*abbr* **North-West**) noroeste, NO

NY (*abbr* **New York**) Nueva York

nylon ['naɪlɒn] **1** *n* (**a**) *(material)* nilón *m*, nailon *m* (**b**) **nylons** medias *fpl* de nilón
     2 *adj* de nilón

nymph [nɪmf] *n Myth* ninfa *f*

nymphomania [nɪmfəˈmeɪnɪə] *n* ninfomanía *f*

nymphomaniac [nɪmfəˈmeɪnɪæk] *n* ninfómana *f*

NZ (*abbr* **New Zealand**) Nueva Zelanda

O

O, o [əʊ] *n* (**a**) *(the letter)* O, o *f* (**b**) *Math Tel* cero *m*

oaf [əʊf] *n* patán *m*, palurdo(a) *m,f*, zoquete *m,f*

oak [əʊk] *n Bot* roble *m* ❑ **common o.** carballo *m*, carvallo *m*; **cork o.** alcornoque *m*; **evergreen** *or* **holm o.** encina *f*; **o. apple** agalla *f*; **red o.** roble *m* americano; **sessile o.** roble *m* albar

oaken [ˈəʊkən] *adj* de roble

OAP [əʊeɪˈpiː] *n Br Fam* (*abbr* **old-age pensioner**) pensionista *mf*

oar [ɔːr] *n* (**a**) *(pole)* remo *m*; *Fig* **to put** *or* **stick one's o. in** entrometerse; *Fig* **to rest on one's oars** dormirse en los laureles (**b**) *(person)* remero(a) *m,f*

oarsman [ˈɔːzmən] *n* (*pl* **oarsmen**) remero *m*

OAS [əʊeɪˈes] *n* (*abbr* **Organization of American States**) OEA *f*, Organización *f* de Estados Americanos

oasis [əʊˈeɪsɪs] *n* (*pl* **oases** [əʊˈeɪsiːz]) oasis *m inv*

oat [əʊt] *n Bot* (**a**) *(plant)* avena *f* (**b**) **oats** avena *f sing*; *Fig* **to sow one's wild o.** correrla; *US Fam* **to feel one's o.** *(feel exuberant)* sentirse en la gloria ❑ **rolled o.** copos *mpl* de avena

oatcake [ˈəʊtkeɪk] *n* torta *f* de avena

oath [əʊθ] *n* (*pl* **oaths** [əʊðz]) (**a**) *Jur* juramento *m*; **o. of allegiance** juramento de fidelidad; **to swear** *or* **take an o.** prestar juramento; *Fam* **on my o.** palabra de honor (**b**) *(blasphemy)* blasfemia *f*, *(swearword)* palabrota *f*

oatmeal [ˈəʊtmiːl] *n* (**a**) *(meal)* harina *f* de avena (**b**) *US (porridge)* copos *mpl* de avena

obdurate [ˈɒbdjʊrɪt] *adj (obstinate)* obstinado(a), terco(a); *(unyielding)* inflexible, duro(a)

obedience [əˈbiːdɪəns] *n* obediencia *f*

obedient [əˈbiːdɪənt] *adj* obediente

obelisk [ˈɒbɪlɪsk] *n* obelisco *m*

obese [əʊˈbiːs] *adj* obeso(a)

obesity [əʊˈbiːsɪtɪ] *n* obesidad *f*

obey [əˈbeɪ] *vt (gen)* obedecer; *(law)* cumplir; *(need)* responder a

obfuscate [ˈɒbfʌskeɪt] *vt* ofuscar, oscurecer

obituary [əˈbɪtjʊərɪ] *n* necrología *f*, nota *f* necrológica ❑ **o. column** sección *f* necrológica

object¹ [ˈɒbdʒɪkt] *n* (**a**) *(thing)* objeto *m*, cosa *f* ❑ **o. glass** objetivo *m* (**b**) *(aim, purpose)* fin *m*, objeto *m*, objetivo *m*; **with this o.** con este fin ❑ **o. lesson** ejemplo *m* práctico (**c**) *Fam (focus of feelings etc)* ejemplo *m*; **he's an o. of pity** da lástima, es un triste espectáculo; **she's an o. of affection** inspira afecto (**d**) *(obstacle)* inconveniente *m*; **money is no o.** el dinero no es inconveniente (**e**) *Ling* complemento *m*, objeto *m*; **direct o.** complemento directo

object² [əbˈdʒekt] **1** *vt* objetar

2 *vi* oponerse, poner reparos (**to** a); **everyone objected to the decision** todos se opusieron a la decisión; *Fig* **do you o. to my smoking?** ¿le molesta que fume?

objection [əbˈdʒekʃən] *n* (**a**) *(argument against)* objeción *f*, reparo *m*; **she raised no objections** no puso reparo alguno; **to take o.** molestarse (**to** por) (**b**) *(drawback)* inconveniente *m*, obstáculo *m*; **provided there's no o.** si no hay inconveniente

objectionable [əbˈdʒekʃənəbəl] *adj (unacceptable)* inaceptable; *(unpleasant)* ofensivo(a), desagradable; **o. remarks** observaciones *fpl* inadmisibles

objective [əbˈdʒektɪv] **1** *adj* objetivo(a)

2 *n* (**a**) *(aim)* fin *m*, objetivo *m* (**b**) *Opt Phot* objetivo *m*

objectively [əbˈdʒektɪvlɪ] *adv* objetivamente

objectivity [ɒbdʒekˈtɪvɪtɪ] *n* objetividad *f*

objector [əbˈdʒektər] *n* objetante *mf*, objetor(a) *m,f* ❑ **conscientious o.** objetor(a) *m,f* de conciencia

obligation [ɒblɪˈgeɪʃən] *n* obligación *f*; **to be under an o. to sb** estarle muy agradecido(a) a algn; **to meet one's obligations** cumplir las obligaciones ❑ *Rel* **day of o.** fiesta *f* de guardar

obligatory [ɒˈblɪgətərɪ] *adj* obligatorio(a)

oblige [əˈblaɪdʒ] *vt* (**a**) *(compel)* obligar; **I'm obliged to do it** me veo obligado(a) a hacerlo (**b**) *(do a favour for)* ayudar a, hacer un favor a; **can you o. me with a pound?** ¿podrías prestarme una libra? (**c**) *(be grateful)* **to be obliged** estar agradecido(a); **I'm much obliged to you** le estoy muy agradecido

obliging [əˈblaɪdʒɪŋ] *adj* complaciente, amable

oblique [əˈbliːk] *adj* oblicuo(a), inclinado(a); *Fig* **an o. reference** una alusión indirecta

obliterate [əˈblɪtəreɪt] *vt* (**a**) *(efface)* borrar, obliterar (**b**) *(eliminate)* eliminar; *(destroy)* destruir, arrasar

obliteration [əblɪtəˈreɪʃən] *n* (**a**) *(effacing)* borradura *f* (**b**) *(elimination)* eliminación *f*, *(destruction)* destrucción *f*

oblivion [əˈblɪvɪən] *n* (**a**) *(being forgotten)* olvido *m*; **to sink into o.** caer en el olvido (**b**) *Jur* amnistía *f*

oblivious [əˈblɪvɪəs] *adj* inconsciente

oblong [ˈɒblɒŋ] **1** *adj* oblongo(a), rectangular

2 *n* rectángulo *m*

obnoxious [əbˈnɒkʃəs] *adj (of person)* repugnante, odioso(a); *(of smell)* nocivo(a), repugnante

oboe [ˈəʊbəʊ] *n Mus* oboe *m*

oboist [ˈəʊbəʊɪst] *n* oboe *m*, oboísta *mf*

obscene [əbˈsiːn] *adj* obsceno(a), indecente, escabroso(a)

obscenity [əbˈsenɪtɪ] *n* obscenidad *f*, indecencia *f*

obscure [əb'skjʊər] **1** adj **(a)** (unclear) oscuro(a), obscuro(a); (vague) confuso(a), vago(a); (hidden) recóndito(a) **(b)** (unimportant) (writer etc) desconocido(a) **(c)** (dark) oscuro(a), obscuro(a)
2 vt **(a)** (make unclear) ofuscar, obscurecer **(b)** (cover) oscurecer, obscurecer

obscurity [əb'skjʊərɪtɪ] n oscuridad f, obscuridad f

obsequious [əb'si:kwɪəs] adj servil

observable [əb'zɜ:vəbəl] adj visible, observable, apreciable

observance [əb'zɜ:vəns] n **(a)** (recognition) (of law, custom) observancia f **(b)** Rel **observances** prácticas fpl religiosas

observant [əb'zɜ:vənt] adj observador(a), atento(a)

observation [ɒbzə'veɪʃən] n **(a)** (watching) observación f; (surveillance) vigilancia f; **to escape o.** pasar inadvertido(a) ❑ Mil **o. post** puesto m de observación **(b)** (remark) observación f, comentario m; **to make an o.** hacer un comentario

observational [ɒbzə'veɪʃənəl] adj (study, techniques) de observación

observatory [əb'zɜ:vətərɪ] n **(a)** Astron observatorio m **(b)** (lookout) mirador m

observe [əb'zɜ:v] vt **(a)** (watch) observar; (in surveillance) vigilar; **she observes things keenly** se fija mucho en las cosas **(b)** (remark) advertir, señalar; **as Mr Brown has observed** como ha señalado el Sr. Brown **(c)** (notice) notar, observar **(d)** (keep) guardar, respetar

observer [əb'zɜ:vər] n observador(a) m,f

obsess [əb'ses] vt obsesionar; **to be obsessed** estar obsesionado(a), obsesionarse **(with, by** con)

obsession [əb'seʃən] n obsesión f, idea f fija

obsessive [əb'sesɪv] adj obsesivo(a)

obsolescence [ɒbsə'lesəns] n obsolescencia f

obsolescent [ɒbsə'lesənt] adj obsolescente

obsolete ['ɒbsəli:t, ɒbsə'li:t] adj obsoleto(a), caído(a) en desuso

obstacle ['ɒbstəkəl] n obstáculo m; Fig obstáculo m, impedimento m, inconveniente m ❑ Sport **o. race** carrera f de obstáculos

obstetric(al) [ɒb'stetrɪk(əl)] adj obstétrico(a)

obstetrician [ɒbstə'trɪʃən] n tocólogo(a) m,f, obstetra mf

obstetrics [ɒb'stetrɪks] n Med obstetricia f, tocología f

obstinacy ['ɒbstɪnəsɪ] n obstinación f, terquedad f, tenacidad f

obstinate ['ɒbstɪnɪt] adj **(a)** (of person) obstinado(a), tenaz, terco(a) **(b)** Med (pain) persistente; (illness) rebelde

obstreperous [əb'strepərəs] adj alborotado(a); **to get o. (about sth)** alborotarse (por algo)

obstruct [əb'strʌkt] vt **(a)** (block) (passage) obstruir, estorbar; (pipe etc) atascar, obstruir; (view) tapar; Med obstruir **(b)** (hinder) estorbar; (progress) dificultar; Parl **to o. a bill** obstaculizar la aprobación de un proyecto de ley; Sport **to o. a player** bloquear a un jugador

obstruction [əb'strʌkʃən] n **(a)** (gen) obstrucción f **(b)** (hindrance) estorbo m, obstáculo m

obstructive [əb'strʌktɪv] adj obstructor(a); **o. tactics** tácticas fpl de obstrucción

obtain [əb'teɪn] **1** vt (acquire) obtener, conseguir
2 vi (be valid) prevalecer, regir

obtainable [əb'teɪnəbəl] adj obtenible; **only o. at chemists** de venta exclusiva en farmacias

obtrude [əb'tru:d] **1** vi (interfere) entrometerse, imponerse
2 vt **(a)** (impose) imponer **(b)** (push out) extender

obtrusive [əb'tru:sɪv] adj **(a)** (interfering) entrometido(a) **(b)** (noticeable) llamativo(a); (smell) penetrante

obtuse [əb'tju:s] adj **(a)** (slow) obtuso(a), lento(a), torpe **(b)** Geom obtuso(a); **o. triangle** triángulo m obtusángulo

obverse ['ɒbvɜ:s] **1** adj del anverso
2 n anverso m

obviate ['ɒbvɪeɪt] vt (counter) (difficulty etc) obviar; (danger) evitar

obvious ['ɒbvɪəs] adj obvio(a), evidente, manifiesto(a); **an o. fact** un hecho patente; **it's the o. thing to do** es lo más indicado

obviously ['ɒbvɪəslɪ] adv evidentemente, claramente; **o.!** ¡claro!, ¡por supuesto!; **she is o. not telling the truth** es evidente que no está diciendo la verdad

occasion [ə'keɪʒən] **1** n **(a)** (gen) ocasión f; **on o.** en ocasiones, de vez en cuando; **on the o. of** con motivo de; **to rise to the o.** ponerse a la altura de las circunstancias **(b)** (opportunity) ocasión f, oportunidad f; **to take o. to do sth** aprovechar la oportunidad para hacer algo **(c)** (event) acontecimiento m; **let's make it an o.!** ¡vamos a celebrarlo! **(d)** (cause) motivo m; **I have no o. for complaint** no tengo motivo de queja
2 vt ocasionar, causar

occasional [ə'keɪʒənəl] adj **(a)** (not frequent) esporádico(a), eventual; Meteor **o. showers in Galicia** chubascos aislados en Galicia **(b)** (on special occasions) en o para ocasiones especiales

occasionally [ə'keɪʒənəlɪ] adv de vez en cuando, en ocasiones

occidental [ɒksɪ'dentəl] adj occidental

occluded front [ə'klu:dɪd'frʌnt] n Meteor frente m ocluido

occult [ɒ'kʌlt, 'ɒkʌlt] **1** adj oculto(a)
2 the o. n las ciencias ocultas, lo oculto

occupant ['ɒkjʊpənt] n (of house, flat, car) ocupante mf; (of job) titular mf

occupation [ɒkjʊ'peɪʃən] n **(a)** (job, profession) profesión f, ocupación f **(b)** (task) trabajo m **(c)** (of building, house, country) ocupación f; **army of o.** ejército m de ocupación

occupational [ɒkjʊ'peɪʃənəl] adj profesional, laboral, de oficio; **o. hazards** gajes mpl del oficio

occupied ['ɒkjʊpaɪd] adj ocupado(a); **to keep one's mind o. doing sth** distraerse haciendo algo

occupier ['ɒkjʊpaɪər] n Br ocupante mf; (tenant) inquilino(a) m,f

occupy ['ɒkjʊpaɪ] vt (pt & pp occupied) **(a)** (live in) ocupar, habitar, vivir en **(b)** (fill) emplear, ocupar; **to o. one's time in doing sth** dedicar su tiempo a hacer algo **(c)** (take possession of) ocupar, tomar posesión de

occur [ə'kɜ:r] vi (pt & pp occurred) **(a)** (happen) (event) ocurrir, suceder, acaecer; (change) producirse; **if another opportunity occurs** si se presenta otra ocasión **(b)** (be found) encontrarse, existir **(c)** (come to mind) ocurrir, ocurrirse, ofrecerse; **it occurred to me that ...** se me ocurrió que ...

occurrence [ə'kʌrəns] n **(a)** (event) acontecimiento m, suceso m; **an everyday o.** un hecho cotidiano; **it's a common o.** ocurre con frecuencia **(b)** (occurring) reincidencia f; **that's a habit of frequent o.** es un hábito que se muestra con frecuencia

ocean ['əʊʃən] n **(a)** Geog océano m; US (sea) mar m ❑ **o. currents** corrientes fpl oceánicas **(b)** Fam **oceans of** la mar de, montones de

ocean-going ['əʊʃəngəʊɪŋ] adj de alta mar

Oceania [əʊʃɪ'ɑ:nɪə] n Oceanía

Oceanian [əʊʃɪ'ɑ:nɪən] **1** adj de Oceanía
2 n persona f de Oceanía

oceanic [əʊʃɪˈænɪk] *adj* oceánico(a); **o. ridge** cresta *f* oceánica

oceanography [əʊʃəˈnɒɡrəfɪ] *n* oceanografía *f*

ocelot [ˈɒsɪlɒt, ˈəʊsɪlɒt] *n Zool* ocelote *m*

ochre, *US* **ocher** [ˈəʊkər] **1** *n* ocre *m*, sil *m* ❑ **red o.** almagre *m*; **yellow o.** ocre *m* amarillo
2 *adj* (de color) ocre

o'clock [əˈklɒk] *adv* **(it's) one o'c.** (es) la una; **(it's) two o'c.** (son) las dos; **the train leaves at six o'c.** el tren sale a las seis

OCR [əʊsiːˈɑːr] *n Comptr* **(a)** *(abbr* **optical character reader)** lector *m* óptico de caracteres **(b)** *(abbr* **optical character recognition)** reconocimiento *m* óptico de caracteres

Oct *(abbr* **October)** octubre *m*, oct.

octagon [ˈɒktəɡən] *n Geom* octágono *m*, octógono *m*

octagonal [ɒkˈtæɡənəl] *adj* octagonal, octogonal

octane [ˈɒkteɪn] *n* octano *m* ❑ **high-o. gasoline** supercarburante *m*; **o. number** octanaje *m*

octave [ˈɒktɪv] *n* octava *f*

octet [ɒkˈtet] *n Mus* octeto *m*

October [ɒkˈtəʊbər] *n* octubre *m*; **in O.** en octubre; **(on) the sixth of O.** el seis de octubre; *see also* **May**

octogenarian [ɒktəʊdʒɪˈneərɪən] *adj & n* octogenario(a) *(m,f)*, ochentón(ona) *(m,f)*

octopus [ˈɒktəpəs] *n Zool* pulpo *m*

octosyllable [ˈɒktəˈsɪləbəl] *n* octosílabo *m*

oculist [ˈɒkjʊlɪst] *n* oculista *mf*

OD [əʊˈdiː] *vi (pt & pp* **OD'd**, **OD'ed)** *Fam* meterse una sobredosis; *Fig* **I think I've rather OD'd on pizza** creo que me he pasado con la pizza

odd [ɒd] **1** *adj* **(a)** *(strange)* raro(a), extraño(a); **the o. thing is that ...** lo raro es que ... **(b)** *(occasional)* esporádico(a), eventual; **at o. times** de vez en cuando; **he writes the o. letter to me** me escribe de vez en cuando; **the o. customer** algún que otro cliente; **o. job** trabajillo *m* **(c)** *(extra)* adicional, de más; **a few o. coins** algunas monedas sueltas; *Fig* **to be the o. man out** estar de más **(d)** *Math (not even)* impar; **1 and 3 are o. numbers** el 1 y el 3 son números impares **(e)** *(unpaired)* desparejado(a), suelto(a); **an o. sock** un calcetín suelto
2 *adv* y pico; **there were twenty o. students there** había unos veinte y tantos alumnos
3 *n (number)* non *m*, impar *m*; **odds and evens** pares y nones

oddball [ˈɒdbɔːl] *Fam* **1** *n* pájaro *m* raro, estrafalario(a) *m,f*
2 *adj* estrafalario(a)

oddity [ˈɒdɪtɪ] *n* **(a)** *(thing)* cosa *f* rara, curiosidad *f*; *(person)* estrafalario(a) *m,f* **(b)** *(quality)* rareza *f*, peculiaridad *f*

odd-job man [ˈɒdʒɒbmən] *n (pl* **odd-job men)** = hombre que hace arreglos o apaños ocasionales

oddly [ˈɒdlɪ] *adv* de manera extraña, extrañamente; **o. enough** por extraño que parezca

oddness [ˈɒdnɪs] *n (strangeness)* rareza *f*, peculiaridad *f*; *(eccentricity)* extravagancia *f*

odds [ɒdz] *npl* **(a)** *(chances)* probabilidades *fpl*, posibilidades *fpl*; **he's fighting against the o.** lleva las de perder, está luchando contra fuerzas mayores; **the o. are in her favour** ella lleva ventaja; **the o. are that ...** lo más probable es que *(+ subj)* **(b)** *(in betting)* puntos *mpl* de ventaja; **the o. are five to one** las apuestas están cinco a uno; **to give** *or* **lay o.** ofrecer puntos de ventaja; *Br Fam* **it makes no o.** da lo mismo; *Fam* **what's the o.?** ¿qué más da? **(c)** **to be at o. with sb** *(disagree)* estar peleado(a) *or* reñido(a) con algn **(d)** **o. and ends** *(small things)* cositas *fpl*,

cosillas *fpl*; *(trinkets)* cachivaches *mpl*, chucherías *fpl*

odds-on [ˈɒdzɒn] *adj* seguro(a); **o.-on favourite** *(horse)* caballo *m* favorito; *(person)* favorito(a) *m,f*; **o.-on victory** victoria *f* segura

ode [əʊd] *n* oda *f*

odious [ˈəʊdɪəs] *adj* odioso(a), repugnante

odium [ˈəʊdɪəm] *n* **(a)** *(dislike, disapproval)* reprobación *f*, rechazo *m* **(b)** *(hatred)* odio *m*

odometer [ɒˈdɒmɪtər, əʊˈdɒmɪtər] *n US Aut* cuenta-kilómetros *m inv*

odontologist [ɒdɒnˈtɒlədʒɪst] *n* odontólogo(a) *m,f*

odontology [ɒdɒnˈtɒlədʒɪ] *n* odontología *f*

odour, *US* **odor** [ˈəʊdər] *n* **(a)** *(smell)* olor *m*; *(fragrance)* perfume *m*, fragancia *f* **(b)** *Fig* consideración *f*; **to be in good/bad o. with sb** estar bien/mal visto(a) por algn

odourless, *US* **odorless** [ˈəʊdəlɪs] *adj* inodoro(a)

odyssey [ˈɒdɪsɪ] *n* odisea *f*

OECD [əʊiːsiːˈdiː] *n (abbr* **Organization for Economic Co-operation and Development)** Organización *f* para la Cooperación y el Desarrollo Económico, OCDE *f*

Oedipus [ˈiːdɪpəs] *n* Edipo *m* ❑ **O. complex** complejo *m* de Edipo

oenology [iːˈnɒlədʒɪ] *n* enología *f*

oesophagus [iːˈsɒfəɡəs] *n (pl* **oesophagi** [iːˈsɒfəɡaɪ]) *Anat* esófago *m*

oestrogen [ˈiːstrədʒen] *n Biol* estrógeno *m*

of [ɒv, *unstressed* əv] *prep* **(a)** *(belonging to, part of)* de; **a friend of mine** un amigo mío; **a friend of my mother's** un amigo de mi madre; **it's no business of yours** no es asunto tuyo; **the end of the novel** el final de la novela; **the Queen of England** la reina de Inglaterra **(b)** *(containing)* de; **a bottle of wine** una botella de vino **(c)** *(origin)* de; **of good family** de buena familia **(d)** *(by)* de, por; **beloved of all** amado(a) por todos; **the works of Shakespeare** las obras de Shakespeare **(e)** *(quantity)* de; **there are four of us** somos cuatro; **there were twenty of them** fueron veinte; **two of them** dos de ellos **(f)** *(from)* de; *US* **a quarter of seven** las siete menos cuarto; **free of** libre de; **south of** al sur de; **within a year of his death** al año de su muerte **(g)** *(material)* de; **a dress (made) of silk** un vestido de seda **(h)** *(apposition)* de; **the city of Lisbon** la ciudad de Lisboa; **the topic of pollution** el asunto de la contaminación **(i)** *(characteristic)* de; **a man of no importance** un hombre de poca monta; **it's wrong of him not to come** hace mal en no venir; **that fool of a sergeant** el imbécil del sargento; **that's typical of her** muy propio de ella; **that's very cruel of him** es muy cruel por su parte; **that's very kind of you** es usted muy amable **(j)** *(with adj)* de; **hard of hearing** duro(a) de oído; **tired/guilty of sth** cansado(a)/culpable de algo **(k)** *(after superlative)* de; **king of kings** rey de reyes; **the bravest of them** el más valiente (de todos ellos); **the thing she wanted most of all** lo que más quería; **you, of all people** precisamente tú **(l)** *(cause)* por, de; **because of** a causa de; **of necessity** por necesidad; **to die of hunger** morir de hambre **(m)** *(concerning, about)* de, sobre; **to dream of sth/sb** soñar con algo/algn; **to think of sb** pensar en algn; **what do you think of her?** ¿qué opinas de ella?; **what of it?** ¿y qué? **(n)** *(with dates)* de; **the seventh of July** el siete de julio

off [ɒf] **1** *prep* **(a)** *(movement)* de; **she fell o. her horse** se cayó del caballo; **take it o. the table** quítalo de la mesa; **there's a button o. my jacket** le falta un botón a mi chaqueta **(b)** *(removal)* de; **I'll take something o. the price for you** se lo rebajaré un poco **(c)** *(distance, situation)* de; **a few kilometres o. the coast** a unos kilómetros de la costa; **a house o. the road** una casa apartada de la carretera; *Naut* **o. Calais** a la altura de Calais **(d)** *(away from)* fuera de; **the ship went o. course** el barco se desvió; *Sport* **to be o. form** no estar en forma **(e)** *(not inclined towards)* **I'm o. wine** he perdido el gusto al vino **(f)** *(free from)* libre de; **he took two days o. work** se tomó dos días libres; **I'm o. duty today** libro hoy; *Fig* **o. the record** extraoficialmente

2 *adv* **(a)** *(disengaged)* **he turned o. the radio** apagó la radio **(b)** *(absent)* fuera; **I can't take time o.** no puedo faltar al trabajo; **I have a day o.** tengo un día libre; **she's o. on Mondays** los lunes no viene *or* no trabaja; **to be o. sick** estar de baja por enfermedad **(c)** *(completely)* del todo, completamente; **this will kill o. any extra germs** esto rematará cualquier germen restante **(d)** *(away) (distance)* **his arrival is three days o.** faltan tres días para su llegada; **six miles o.** a seis millas; *Theat* **voice o.** voz en off **(e)** *(departure)* **I'm o. to London** me voy a Londres; **o. we go** vámonos; **she ran o.** se fue corriendo; *Sport* **they're o.!** ¡ya han salido! **(f)** *(removal)* **ten per cent o.** un descuento del diez por ciento; **to take one's shoes o.** quitarse *or Am* sacarse los zapatos **(g)** **o. and on, on and o.** de vez en cuando, a ratos **(h)** **hands o.!** ¡fuera las manos! **(i)** **right o.** acto seguido

3 *adj* **(a)** *(disconnected) (gas etc)* apagado(a); *(water)* cortado(a) **(b)** *(cancelled)* cancelado(a), suspendido(a); **their engagement is o.** han roto el compromiso **(c)** *(low)* bajo(a); *(unsatisfactory)* malo(a); **the o. season** la temporada baja □ **o. chance** posibilidad *f* **(d)** *(equipped, situated)* parado(a), situado(a); **how are you o. for money?** ¿cómo andas de dinero?; **to be badly o.** andar mal de dinero; **you're better/worse o.** así estás mejor/ peor **(e)** *(gone bad) (meat, fish)* malo(a), pasado(a), *RP* estropeado(a); *(milk)* agrio(a), cortado(a)

offal ['ɒfəl] *n (of chicken etc)* menudillos *mpl*; *(of cattle, pigs)* asaduras *fpl*, menudos *mpl*

offbeat ['ɒfbi:t] *adj* excéntrico(a), poco convencional

off-centre, *US* **off-center** ['ɒfsentər] *adj* descentrado(a)

off-chance ['ɒftʃɑ:ns] *n* **on the o.** por si acaso

off-colour, *US* **off-color** ['ɒfkʌlər] *adj* **(a)** *Br (ill)* indispuesto(a), malo(a) **(b)** *(risqué)* indecente, verde

offcut ['ɒfkʌt] *n (of wood)* recorte *m*; *(of cloth)* retal *m*; *(of carpet)* retazo *m*

off-duty ['ɒf'dju:tɪ] *adj (soldier)* de permiso; *(policeman)* fuera de servicio

offence [ə'fens] *n* **(a)** *Jur* delito *m* □ **minor o.** infracción *f*; **second o.** reincidencia *f* **(b)** *(insult)* ofensa *f*; **no o. meant** sin intención de ofenderle; **to give o.** ofender; **to take o. at sth** sentirse ofendido(a) por algo, ofenderse por algo **(c)** *Mil (attack)* ofensiva *f*, ataque *m*

offend [ə'fend] *vt* **(a)** *(hurt)* ofender; **to be easily offended** ser muy susceptible **(b)** *(disgust)* disgustar, repeler

offended [ə'fendɪd] *adj (insulted)* ofendido(a)

offender [ə'fendər] *n* **(a)** *Jur (criminal)* delincuente *mf*, infractor(a) *m,f* **(b)** *(insulter)* ofensor(a) *m,f*

offense [ə'fens] *n US see* **offence**

offensive [ə'fensɪv] **1** *adj* **(a)** *(insulting)* ofensivo(a), insultante **(b)** *(repulsive)* repugnante **(c)** *Mil* ofensivo(a)
2 *n Mil* ofensiva *f*

offer ['ɒfər] **1** *vt* **(a)** *(gen)* ofrecer; **to o. to do a job** ofrecerse para hacer un trabajo **(b)** *(propose)* proponer **(c)** *(provide)* proporcionar **(d)** *(bid)* ofrecer **(e)** *Rel* ofrecer, ofrendar
2 *vi* **(a)** *(arise)* presentarse **(b)** *(propose marriage)* proponer el matrimonio
3 *n* **(a)** *(gen)* oferta *f*, ofrecimiento *m*; *(proposal)* propuesta *f*; **o. of marriage** proposición *f* de matrimonio **(b)** *(bid)*

oferta *f*; **any offers?** ¿hay alguna oferta?, ¿le(s) interesa?; *Com* **on o.** de oferta

offering ['ɒfərɪŋ] *n* **(a)** *(gen)* ofrecimiento *m*; *(gift)* regalo *m*; **a peace o.** una prenda de paz **(b)** *Rel* ofrenda *f*; **burnt o.** holocausto *m*

offertory ['ɒfətərɪ] *n Rel* **(a)** *(hymn)* ofertorio *m* **(b)** *(collection)* colecta *f*

offhand [ɒf'hænd] **1** *adj* **(a)** *(abrupt)* brusco(a); *(inconsiderate)* descortés, desatento(a), desconsiderado(a); **in an o. way** sin ceremonias **(b)** *(impromptu)* improvisado(a)
2 *adv* de improviso; **I don't know o.** así sin pensarlo, no lo sé

office ['ɒfɪs] *n* **(a)** *(room)* despacho *m*, oficina *f*; *US (of doctor, dentist)* consulta *f*; *(building)* oficina *f* □ **box o.** taquilla *f*; **head o.** sede *f* central; **lawyer's o.** bufete *m*; **o. boy** recadero *m*; **o. hours** horas *fpl* de oficina; **o. work** trabajo *m* de oficina; **o. worker** oficinista *mf* **(b)** *Br Pol* ministerio *m* □ **Foreign O.** Ministerio *m* de Asuntos Exteriores **(c)** *US (federal agency)* agencia *f* gubernamental **(d)** *(position)* cargo *m*; **to hold o.** ocupar un cargo; **to leave o.** dimitir; **to seek o.** pretender *òr* aspirar a un cargo **(e)** *Pol (portfolio)* cartera *f* de ministro; **to be in o.** estar en el poder

officeholder ['ɒfɪshəoldər] *n* alto cargo *m*

officer ['ɒfɪsər] *n* **(a)** *Mil* oficial *mf* □ **customs o.** aduanero(a) *m,f* **(b)** **(police) o.** policía *mf*, agente *mf* de policía **(c)** *(in public administration)* oficial *mf*, funcionario(a) *m,f*; **Medical O. of Health** jefe(a) *m,f* de Sanidad **(d)** *(of company, society)* director(a) *m,f*

official [ə'fɪʃəl] **1** *adj* oficial
2 *n* oficial *mf*, funcionario(a) *m,f*

officialdom [ə'fɪʃəldəm] *n Pej (bureaucracy)* los funcionarios, la administración

officialese [əfɪʃə'li:z] *n* jerga *f* burocrática

officially [ə'fɪʃəlɪ] *adv* oficialmente

officiate [ə'fɪʃɪeɪt] *vi* **(a)** *(gen)* ejercer; **to o. as** ejercer de **(b)** *Rel* oficiar

officious [ə'fɪʃəs] *adj (ready)* oficioso(a); *(obtrusive)* entrometido(a)

offing ['ɒfɪŋ] *n* **(to be) in the o.** (ser) inminente

offish ['ɒfɪʃ] *adj Fam* altivo(a), distante

off-key ['ɒfki:] *adj* **(a)** *Mus (out of tune)* desafinado(a) **(b)** *Fig (discordant)* desentonado(a), discordante

off-licence ['ɒflaɪsəns] *n Br* = establecimiento de venta de bebidas alcohólicas

off-line ['ɒflaɪn] *adj Comptr (processing)* fuera de línea; *(printer)* desconectado(a)

off-load [ɒf'ləʊd] *vt (surplus goods)* colocar; **to o.-l. sth onto sb** colocarle algo a algn; **to o.-l. blame onto sb** descargar la culpa en algn

off-peak ['ɒfpi:k] *adj Elec Tel* reducido(a); **o.-p. charge** tarifa *f* reducida; **the o.-p. hours** *(on transport)* las horas de menos tránsito

offprint ['ɒfprɪnt] *n (article)* separata *f*

off-putting ['ɒfpʊtɪŋ] *adj Br Fam* desconcertante, chocante

off-screen ['ɒf'skri:n] *adj Cin TV* **their o.-s. relationship mirrored their love affair in the film** su relación detrás de la cámara era un reflejo de su aventura amorosa en la película

offset ['ɒfset] **1** *n* **(a)** *(counterbalance)* compensación *f* **(b)** *Typ* offset *m*
2 [ɒf'set] *vt (pt & pp* **offset)** **(a)** *(balance out)* compensar **(b)** *Typ* imprimir en offset

offshoot ['ɒfʃu:t] *n* **(a)** *Bot* renuevo *m*, vástago *m* **(b)** *Fig* *(of organization)* ramificación *f; (of discussion)* consecuencia *f,* resultado *m*

offshore [ɒf'ʃɔːr] **1** *adj* (**a**) *(from the coast) (breeze etc)* terral, que sopla de tierra (**b**) *(off the coast)* offshore, costa afuera ❏ **o. drilling** *(for oil)* perforación *f* costa afuera (**c**) *(overseas)* en el extranjero; **o. fund** fondo *m* colocado en paraíso fiscal; **o. investment** inversión *f* en un paraíso fiscal
2 *adv* mar adentro

offside [ɒf'saɪd] **1** *adj & adv* Ftb fuera de juego, offside, orsay
2 *n* Aut *(with left-hand drive)* lado *m* derecho; *(with right-hand drive)* lado *m* izquierdo

offspring ['ɒfsprɪŋ] *n inv* (**a**) *(child)* vástago *m,* descendiente *mf; (children)* progenitura *f,* descendencia *f* (**b**) *Fig* consecuencia *f,* resultado *m*

offstage [ɒf'steɪdʒ] *adj & adv* entre bastidores

off-the-cuff [ɒfðə'kʌf] *adj (remark)* espontáneo(a), improvisado(a)

off-the-peg [ɒfðə'peg] *adj esp Br* de confección; **an o.-t.-p. suit** un traje de confección

off-the-record [ɒfðə'rekəd] *adj* extraoficial, oficioso(a)

off-the-wall [ɒfðə'wɔːl] *adj Fam* estrafalario(a)

off-white ['ɒfwaɪt] *adj* blancuzco(a), blanquecino(a)

oft [ɒft] *adv Literary* a menudo

oft- [ɒft] *pref* **o.-repeated** muy repetido(a); **o.-quoted** muy citado(a)

often ['ɒfən, 'ɒftən] *adv* a menudo, con frecuencia; **as o. as not** con bastante regularidad; **every so o.** de vez en cuando, regularmente; **more o. than not** la mayoría de las veces

ogle ['əʊgəl] *vt & vi* **to o. (at) sb** comerse a algn con los ojos

ogre ['əʊgər] *n* ogro *m*

ogress ['əʊgrɪs] *n (frightening woman)* ogro *m*

oh [əʊ] *interj* ¡oh!, ¡ay!; **oh, my God!** ¡Dios mío!; **oh, really?** ¿de veras?

ohm [əʊm] *n Elec* ohmio *m*

OHMS [əʊeɪtʃem'es] *Br (abbr* **On His/Her Majesty's Service)** en el servicio de su majestad

oho [əʊ'həʊ] *interj (expressing triumph, surprise)* ¡ajajá!

oil [ɔɪl] **1** *n* (**a**) *(gen)* aceite *m; Fig* **to pour o. on troubled waters** templar los ánimos ❏ **cooking o.** aceite *m* comestible *or* para cocinar; **lubricating o.** aceite *m* lubricante; **o. drum** bidón *m; Aut* **o. gauge** indicador *m* (del nivel) del aceite; *Aut* **o. gun** bomba *f* de engrase; **o. lamp** lámpara *f* de aceite, quinqué *m;* **o. slick** mancha *f* de aceite, marea *f* negra; **olive o.** aceite *m* de oliva (**b**) *(petroleum)* petróleo *m;* **crude o.** crudo *m;* **the o. industry** la industria petrolera; **to strike o.** encontrar petróleo ❏ **o. company** compañía *f* petrolera; **o. refinery** refinería *f* de petróleo; **o. rig** plataforma *f* petrolera; **o. tanker** petrolero *m* (**c**) *Art (painting)* óleo *m,* pintura *f* al óleo ❏ **o. colour, o. paint** óleo *m;* **o. painting** *(picture)* cuadro *m* al óleo, óleo *m; Fam Fig* **she's no o. painting** no es exactamente una belleza
2 *vt* engrasar, lubricar, lubrificar; *Fig* **to o. the wheels** preparar el terreno; *Fam* **to o. sb's palm** untar la mano a algn

oil-bearing ['ɔɪlbeərɪŋ] *adj* petrolífero(a)

oilcan ['ɔɪlkæn] *n Aut* aceitera *f*

oilcloth ['ɔɪlklɒθ] *n* hule *m*

oilfield ['ɔɪlfiːld] *n* yacimiento *m* petrolífero

oilfired ['ɔɪlfaɪəd] *adj* de fuel-oil

oilskin ['ɔɪlskɪn] *n* (**a**) *(fabric)* hule *m* (**b**) **oilskins** chubasquero *m sing,* traje *m sing* de hule

oily ['ɔɪlɪ] *adj* (**oilier, oiliest**) *(gen)* aceitoso(a), grasiento(a); *(hair, skin)* graso(a)

oink [ɔɪŋk] *vi (pig)* gruñir

ointment ['ɔɪntmənt] *n* ungüento *m,* pomada *f*

O.K., okay [əʊ'keɪ] *Fam* **1** *interj* de acuerdo, *Esp* vale *or Am* ok *or Méx* ándale;
2 *adj* correcto(a), bien; **is it O.K. if ...?** ¿está bien si ...?
3 *n* visto *m* bueno, aprobación *f;* **to give the O.K.** dar el visto bueno
4 *vt (pt & pp* **O.K.ed** *or* **okayed)** dar el visto bueno a

okra ['ɒkrə] *n* quingombó *m,* okra *f*

old [əʊld] **1** *adj* (**a**) *(gen)* viejo(a); *(worn)* viejo(a), usado(a); *(wine)* añejo(a); *(stale) (bread)* duro(a), rancio(a), *RP* amenecido(a); *(food)* pasado(a), malo(a); **an o. man** un hombre mayor, un anciano; **to grow o.** envejecer; *Fam* **my o. man** *(husband)* mi *or* el pariente, *Méx* mi *or* el viejo, *RP* el don, el viejo; *(father)* mi *or* el viejo, *Méx* mi *or* el jefe ❏ **o. age** vejez *f; Br* **o.-age pensioner** pensionista *mf;* **O. Glory** *(US flag)* = la bandera estadounidense; **o. maid** soltera *f; Fam Pej* solterona *f;* **o. wives' tale** cuento *m* de viejas (**b**) *(age)* **how o. are you?** ¿cuántos años tienes?, ¿qué edad tienes?; **she's five years o.** tiene cinco años; **she's o. enough to do it** ya tiene edad para hacerlo (**c**) *Br (former)* **o. boy** antiguo alumno, ex-alumno (**d**) *(earlier)* antiguo(a) ❏ **o. country** madre patria *f; Rel* **O. Testament** Antiguo Testamento *m* (**e**) *(long-established, experienced)* viejo(a); **an o. dodge** un viejo truco; **an o. friend** un viejo amigo ❏ **o. hand, o. stager** veterano(a) *m,f* (**f**) *(cherished)* **good o. John!** ¡el bueno de John! (**g**) *Fam (intensifying)* **any o. how** de cualquier manera; **any o. thing** cualquier cosa
2 *n* (**a**) *(past) m;* **of o.** de antaño (**b**) **the o.** los viejos, los ancianos

olden ['əʊldən] *adj Literary* antiguo(a); **in o. times** en tiempos antiguos, antaño

old-established [əʊldɪ'stæblɪʃt] *adj* antiguo(a)

old-fashioned [əʊld'fæʃənd] *(outdated)* chapado(a) a la antigua, anticuado(a); *(unfashionable)* anticuado(a), pasado(a) de moda

old-time ['əʊldtaɪm] *adj* antiguo(a)

old-timer [əʊld'taɪmər] *n Fam* (**a**) *(experienced person)* veterano(a) *m,f* (**b**) *US (form of address)* abuelo *m*

old-world ['əʊldwɜːld] *adj* tradicional, de los tiempos antiguos

oleander [əʊlɪ'ændər] *n Bot* adelfa *f*

olfactory [ɒl'fæktərɪ, ɒl'fæktrɪ] **1** *adj* olfativo(a), olfatorio(a)
2 *n (nerve)* nervio *m* olfativo

oligarchy ['ɒlɪgɑːkɪ] *n* oligarquía *f*

olive ['ɒlɪv] **1** *n* (**a**) *(tree)* olivo *m; Fig* **to hold out the o. branch** proponer una reconciliación ❏ **o. grove** olivar *m* (**b**) *(fruit)* aceituna *f,* oliva *f;* **stuffed olives** aceitunas rellenas (**c**) *(wood)* olivo *m* (**d**) *(colour)* **o. (green)** verde *m* oliva
2 *adj (olive-growing)* olivarero(a)

olive-growing ['ɒlɪvgrəʊɪŋ] *adj* olivarero(a)

Olympiad [ə'lɪmpiæd] *n* Olimpíada *f,* Olimpiada *f*

Olympic [ə'lɪmpɪk] **1** *adj* olímpico(a) ❏ **O. Games** Juegos *mpl* Olímpicos
2 **the Olympics** *npl* los Juegos Olímpicos, la Olimpíada

Oman [əʊ'mɑːn] *n* Omán

Omani [əʊ'mɑːnɪ] *adj & n* omaní *(mf)*

ombudsman ['ɒmbʊdzmən] *n* defensor(a) *m,f* del pueblo

omelette, *US* **omelet** ['ɒmlɪt] *n Culin* tortilla *f, Am* tortilla *f* francesa; **Spanish o.** tortilla española *or* de patatas

omen ['əʊmen] *n* presagio *m,* agüero *m,* augurio *m;* **it's a**

good o. es un buen presagio; *Fig* **bird of ill o.** pájaro agorero *or* de mal agüero

ominous [ˈɒmɪnəs] *adj (foreboding evil)* de mal agüero, siniestro(a); *(prophetic)* agorero(a), inquietante

ominously [ˈɒmɪnəslɪ] *adv* de modo amenazante

omission [əʊˈmɪʃən] *n* omisión *f*; **sins of o.** faltas *fpl or* pecados *mpl* de omisión

omit [əʊˈmɪt] *vt (pt & pp **omitted**) (gen)* omitir; *(overlook)* pasar por alto, dejarse; *(forget)* olvidarse

omnibus [ˈɒmnɪbʌs, ˈɒmnɪbəs] *n (vehicle)* ómnibus *m*, autobús *m* ❑ **o. volume** *(book)* antología *f*

omnipotence [ɒmˈnɪpətəns] *n* omnipotencia *f*

omnipotent [ɒmˈnɪpətənt] **1** *adj* omnipotente
2 the O. *n* el Todopoderoso

omniscient [ɒmˈnɪsɪənt] *adj* omnisciente

omnivorous [ɒmˈnɪvərəs] *adj* omnívoro(a)

on [ɒn] **1** *prep* **(a)** *(position) (on top of)* sobre, encima de, en; **I hit him on the head** le di un golpe en la cabeza; **it's on the table** está encima de *or* sobre *or* en la mesa; **on page four** en la página cuatro; *Fig* **to swear on the Bible** jurar por la Biblia; *Fam* **have you got any money on you?** ¿llevas dinero *or Am* plata? **(b)** *(alongside)* en; **a town on the coast** un pueblo en la costa; **on shore** en tierra **(c)** *(attached to)* **a puppet on a string** un títere colgado de un hilo; **hanging on a nail/the wall** colgado de un clavo/la pared **(d)** *(direction)* en, a; **on the right** a la derecha; **on the way** en el camino; **on this side of the road** de este lado de la carretera **(e)** *(time)* **on April 3rd, on the 3rd of April** el tres de abril; **on a sunny day** un día de sol; **on Monday** el lunes; **on that occasion** en aquella ocasión; **on the following day** al día siguiente; **on the morning of the crime** la mañana del crimen; **on time** a tiempo **(f)** *(relayed through)* en; **I heard it on the radio** lo oí en la radio; **to play sth on the piano** tocar algo en el *or Esp* al piano; **what's on TV?** ¿qué ponen en la tele?; *Fam* **she's on the phone** está al teléfono **(g)** *(at the time of)* a; **on his arrival** al llegar él; **on leaving the office** al salir de la oficina; **on second thoughts** pensándolo bien **(h)** *(support, subsistence)* **she lives on bread** vive de pan; **to be on a diet** estar a régimen; **to be on drugs** drogarse; **to be on the pill** tomar la píldora; **to depend on** depender de **(i)** *(transport)* en, a; **on foot** a pie; **on horseback** a caballo; **on the train/plane** en el tren/avión; **on wheels** sobre ruedas **(j)** *(state, process)* en, de; **on holiday** de vacaciones; **on purpose** adrede, a propósito; **on sale** en venta; **on strike** en huelga; **she is here on business** está aquí por negocios; **to be on duty** estar de guardia; **to be on fire** arder, estar en llamas; **to go out on an errand** salir a hacer un recado **(k)** *(regarding)* sobre; **a lecture on numismatics** una conferencia sobre la numismática; **the new tax on tobacco** el nuevo impuesto sobre el *or Am* al tabaco; **they congratulated him on his success** le felicitaron por su éxito **(l)** *(under)* bajo; **on condition that ...** a condición de que ... *(+ subj)*; *Jur* **on a charge of** acusado(a) de; **on no account** bajo ningún concepto, de ninguna manera; **on pain of death** so pena de muerte **(m)** *(against)* contra; **an attack on the government** un ataque contra el Gobierno; **they marched on Washington** hicieron una marcha sobre Washington; *Fam* **the police have nothing on him** la policía no tiene ningún cargo contra él **(n)** *Fam (manner)* **on the cheap** en plan barato; **on the sly** a escondidas, a hurtadillas **(o)** *Fam (in detriment to)* **he told me on me** se chivó; **the car conked out on him** el coche se le escoñó **(p)** *(working for)* **he's on the Daily Telegraph** trabaja para el Daily Telegraph; **to be on the staff** estar en plantilla

2 *adv* **(a)** *(functioning)* **to be on** *(TV, radio, light)* estar encendido(a) *or Am* prendido(a); *(engine)* estar en marcha; **to put the brake on** echar el freno **(b)** *(covering)* encima,

puesto; **she had a coat on** llevaba un abrigo puesto; **on with your boots!** ¡ponte las botas!; **to have nothing on** estar *or* ir desnudo(a) **(c)** *Cin TV Theat* en cartelera; **that film was on last week** pusieron esa película la semana pasada; **what's on at the theatre?** ¿qué dan en el teatro?; *Fam* **have you anything on tonight?** ¿tienes algún plan para esta noche? **(d)** *(continued activity)* **and so on** y así sucesivamente; **go on!** ¡sigue!; **he talks on and on** habla sin parar; **she's always going on about her boss** se pasa el día hablando de su jefe; **to work on** seguir trabajando **(e)** *(time)* **from that day on** a partir de aquel día; **later on** más tarde; **he's getting on** se está haciendo viejo; **it's getting on for ten** son casi las diez; **well in April** muy entrado el mes de abril; **well on in years** entrado en años **(f)** *Fig* **to get on to sb** ponerse en contacto con algn; **to have sb on** tomarle el pelo a algn

3 *adj Fam* **(a)** *(of actor)* **to be on** salir a escena **(b)** *(definitely planned)* previsto(a); **the party's on for Friday** la fiesta se hará el viernes; **you're on!** ¡trato hecho! **(c)** *(charged to)* **the drinks are on me** invito yo; **the drinks are on the house** invita la casa **(d)** *Br Fam (acceptable)* **that attitude isn't on** esa actitud no vale **(e)** *Fam* **to be on** dar la lata a; **she's always on at me** no para de pincharme, me tiene manía **(f)** **on to** *(aware of)* enterado(a) de; **the police are on to him** la policía le tiene fichado

onboard [ˈɒnbɔːd] *adj* de a bordo ❑ **o. computer** *Esp* ordenador *m or Am* computadora *f* de a bordo

once [wʌns] **1** *adv* **(a)** *(one time)* una vez; **not o.** ni una sola vez; **o. a week** una vez por semana; **o. in a while** de vez en cuando; **o. more** una vez más; **o. or twice** un par de veces, una o dos veces; *Fig* **o. and for all** de una vez por todas; *Fig* **o. in a blue moon** de Pascuas a Ramos; *Prov* **o. a ... always a ...** genio y figura hasta la sepultura **(b)** *(formerly)* antes, en otro tiempo; **o. (upon a time) there was** érase una vez; **the o. famous actress** la antes famosa actriz **(c)** **at o.** en seguida, inmediatamente; **all at o.** de repente; **don't all speak at o.** no habléis todos a la vez

2 *conj* una vez que, en cuanto; **o. you've seen it** una vez que lo hayas visto

once-over [ˈwʌnsəʊvər] *n Fam* vistazo *m*

oncologist [ɒŋˈkɒlədʒɪst] *n* oncólogo(a) *m,f*

oncology [ɒŋˈkɒlədʒɪ] *n Med* oncología *f*

oncoming [ˈɒnkʌmɪŋ] *adj (event)* venidero(a), futuro(a); *(car, traffic)* que viene en dirección contraria

one [wʌn] **1** *adj* **(a)** *(a single)* un, una; **for o. thing** primero; **o. book** un libro **(b)** *(only)* único(a); **the o. and only** el único/la única; **the o. way of doing it** la única manera de hacerlo; *Fig* **neither o. thing nor the other** ni una cosa ni otra **(c)** *(same)* mismo(a); **all in o.** en una (sola) pieza; **it's all o.** es lo mismo; **o. and the same** el mismo/la misma; *Fig* **it's all o. to me** me da igual; *Fig* **to be made o.** unirse en matrimonio **(d)** *(indefinite)* un, una; **he'll come back o. day** un día volverá, volverá algún día; **o. stormy night** una noche de tormenta

2 *dem pron* **any o.** cualquiera; **that o.** ése/ésa; *(distant)* aquél/aquélla; **the blue ones** los azules/las azules; **the little ones** los pequeños/las pequeñas; **the o. on the table** el *or* la que está encima de la mesa; **the ones that, the ones who** los que; **the ones you want** los/las que quieras; **the red o.** el rojo/la roja; **this o.** éste/ésta; **which o.?** ¿cuál?; **which ones?** ¿cuáles?; *Fam* **he's a sharp o.** no se le escapa ni una; *Fam* **that's a good o.!** ¡ésa sí que es buena!; *Fam* **you're a o.!** ¡eres un caso!

3 *indef pron* **(a)** *(individual person, thing)* uno(a) *m,f*; **he's o. of the family** es de la familia; **I, for o., am against it** yo, por lo menos, estoy en contra; **I'm not o. to complain** no soy de los que se quejan; **o. at a time** de uno en uno, *Am* uno por uno; **o. by o.** uno por uno, uno tras otro; *Fig* **many a o.** mucha gente; *Fig* **o. and all** todo el mundo; *Fam* **I**

landed him o. le pegué un tortazo *or* una; *Fam* **to have o. for the road** tomar la última *or Esp* la espuela **(b)** *(indefinite person)* uno(a) *m,f;* **o. has to fight** uno tiene que luchar, hay que luchar; **o. never knows** nunca se sabe; **to cut o.'s finger** cortarse el dedo; **to give o.'s opinion** dar su opinión; *Fig* **it's enough to kill o.** es como para morirse **(c) o. another** el uno al otro; **they help o. another** se ayudan mutuamente; **they love o. another** se quieren

4 *n (digit)* uno *m;* **a hundred and o.** ciento uno; **at o. o'clock** a la una; **there's only o. left** sólo queda uno; **o. of two things** una de dos

one-act ['wʌnækt] *adj (of play)* de un (solo) acto

one-armed ['wʌnɑːmd] *adj* manco(a); *Br Fam Fig* **o.-a. bandit** (máquina *f*) tragaperras *f inv,* *RP* tragamonedas *f inv*

one-dimensional ['wʌndaɪ'menʃənəl] *adj Geom* unidimensional; *(character)* superficial

one-eyed ['wʌnaɪd] *adj* tuerto(a)

one-handed ['wʌnhændɪd] **1** *adj (one-armed)* manco(a) **2** *adv* con una mano

one-horse ['wʌnhɔːs] *adj Pej* de poca monta; **o.-h. town** pueblucho *m*

one-legged ['wʌnlegɪd] *adj* cojo(a), con una sola pierna

one-liner [wʌn'laɪnər] *n Fam (joke)* golpe *m*

one-man ['wʌnmæn] *adj* individual, de un solo hombre; **a o.-m. show** un espectáculo con un solo artista; *Fig* **to be a o.-m. show** llevarse la palma

oneness ['wʌnnɪs] *n* unidad *f*

one-night ['wʌnnaɪt] *adj* **o.-n. stand** *Theat* representación *f* única; *(encounter)* ligue *m or RP* levante *m* de una sola noche

one-off ['wʌnɒf] *adj Br Fam* único(a), fuera de serie, irrepetible

one-parent ['wʌnpeərənt] *adj* **o.-p. family** = familia en que sólo hay padre o madre

one-party ['wʌn'pɑːtɪ] *adj* unipartidista

one-piece ['wʌnpiːs] *adj* de una sola pieza

onerous ['ɒnərəs, 'əʊnərəs] *adj* oneroso(a); **an o. duty** una carga pesada

oneself [wʌn'self] *pron (pl* **oneselves** [wʌn'selvz]) **(a)** *(reflexive)* uno(a) mismo(a) *m,f,* sí mismo(a) *m,f;* **to speak of o.** hablar de sí mismo(a); **to talk to o.** hablar para sí, hablar a solas; **to wash o.** lavarse **(b)** *(alone)* uno(a) mismo(a) *m,f;* **by o.** solo(a); **one must do it o.** hay que hacérselo uno mismo **(c)** *(one's usual self)* el *or* la de siempre; **one isn't o. after such a shock** un golpe así trastorna a uno

one-sided ['wʌnsaɪdɪd] *adj (bargain)* desigual; *(judgement)* parcial; *(decision)* unilateral

one-storey(ed) ['wʌnstɔːrɪ(d)] *adj* de una planta; **o.-s. house** casa de planta baja

one-time ['wʌntaɪm] *adj* antiguo(a), ex-; **o.-t. mayor** exalcalde de

one-to-one ['wʌntəwʌn] *adj* de uno a uno; **on a o.-to-o. basis** con una correspondencia mutua

one-track ['wʌntræk] *adj Fam* **to have a o.-t. mind** ser monomaníaco(a), no pensar más que en una cosa

one-upmanship [wʌn'ʌpmənʃɪp] *n Fam* **it was pure o.-u.** todo era por quedar por encima de los demás

one-way ['wʌnweɪ] *adj* **(a)** *(ticket)* de ida **(b)** *(street)* de dirección única; *(agreement etc)* sin compromiso

ongoing ['ɒngəʊɪŋ] *adj* **(a)** *(in progress)* en curso, actual **(b)** *(developing)* en desarrollo

onion ['ʌnjən] *n* cebolla *f; Br Fam* **to know one's onions** saber lo que se trae entre manos ❑ **o. soup** sopa *f* de cebolla; **spring o.** cebollino *m,* cebolleta *f*

onionskin ['ʌnjənskɪn] *n* papel *m* cebolla

on-line ['ɒn'laɪn] *adj Comptr* en línea, on line; **to be on-l.** *(person)* estar conectado(a) (a Internet); **o. banking** banca *f* electrónica; **o. retailer** minorista *mf* online *or* en línea, tienda *f* virtual; **o. store** tienda *f* virtual

onlooker ['ɒnlʊkər] *n* espectador(a) *m,f,* mirón(ona) *m,f;* **there was a group of onlookers** hubo un grupo de gente que miraba

only ['əʊnlɪ] **1** *adj* único(a); **his one o. hope** su única esperanza; **I'm the o. one to receive a prize** soy el único que recibo un premio; **o. son** hijo único

2 *adv* **(a)** *(just, merely)* solamente, sólo; **I o. touched it** no hice más que tocarlo; **I've o. got three** sólo tengo tres; **'staff o.'** 'reservado al personal'; **you've o. to ask for it** no tienes más que pedirlo **(b)** *(not earlier than)* apenas; **he has o. just left** acaba de marcharse hace un momento; **o. yesterday** ayer mismo **(c)** **if o.** ojalá; **if o. I knew!** ¡ojalá lo supiera! **(d)** *(as intensifier)* **o. too glad!** ¡con mucho gusto!; **o. too pleased to** encantado(a) de

3 *conj* pero; **I would do it, o. I can't** lo haría, pero no puedo

ono ['əʊen'əʊ] *Br (abbr* **or nearest offer)** u oferta aproximada

on-off switch ['ɒn'ɒfswɪtʃ] *n* interruptor *m*

onomatopoeia [ɒnəmætə'piːə] *n* onomatopeya *f*

onrush ['ɒnrʌʃ] *n (of people)* riada *f,* oleada *f; (of water)* riada *f*

onset ['ɒnset] *n* **(a)** *(attack)* asalto *m,* arremetida *f* **(b)** *(start)* comienzo *m,* principio *m*

on-site ['ɒn'saɪt] *adj & adv* in situ

onslaught ['ɒnslɔːt] *n* ataque *m* violento, embestida *f*

on-stage 1 *adj* ['ɒnsteɪdʒ] de escena
2 *adv* [ɒn'steɪdʒ] en escena

onto ['ɒntʊ, *unstressed* 'ɒntə] *prep see* **on 2(f), 3(f)**

onus ['əʊnəs] *n (pl* **onuses)** responsabilidad *f;* **the o. is upon you to find a solution** a ti te incumbe encontrar una solución

onward ['ɒnwəd] **1** *adj* progresivo(a), hacia adelante
2 *adv* a partir de, en adelante; **from this time o.** de ahora en adelante

onwards ['ɒnwədz] *adv see* **onward 2**

onyx ['ɒnɪks] *n Min* ónice *m*

oodles ['uːdəlz] *npl Fam* montones *mpl;* **o. of money** un montón *or Col* un jurgo *or RP* un toco de dinero

oomph [ʊmf] *n Fam (enthusiasm)* nervio *m,* vigor *m; (sex appeal)* atractivo *m* sexual, sex-appeal *m*

oops [uːps] *interj (to child)* ¡arriba!, *Esp* ¡aúpa!; *(after mistake)* ¡uy!, ¡oh!

ooze[1] [uːz] **1** *vi* rezumar; **blood was oozing from the wound** brotaba sangre de la herida
2 *vt* rebosar; **she oozes confidence** rebosa confianza

ooze[2] [uːz] *n (mud)* cieno *m*

op [ɒp] *n* **(a)** *Fam (abbr* **operation)** operación *f* **(b)** *Mil (abbr* **operation) ops** maniobras *fpl*

opal ['əʊpəl] *n Min* ópalo *m*

opalescent [əʊpə'lesənt] *adj* opalescente

opaque [əʊ'peɪk] *adj* opaco(a)

op cit [ɒp'sɪt] *(abbr* **opere citato)** en la obra citada, ob. cit., op. cit.

OPEC ['əʊpek] *n (abbr* **Organization of Petroleum Exporting Countries)** Organización *f* de los Países Exportadores de Petróleo, OPEP *f*

open ['əʊpən] **1** *adj* **(a)** *(not closed) (gen)* abierto(a); *(wound)* abierto(a), sin cicatrizar; **half o.** entreabierto; **wide o.** abierto de par en par **(b)** *(not enclosed)* abierto(a);

in the o. air al aire libre, al descubierto; **o. field** descampado *m*; **o. view** vista despejada ❑ **o. prison** prisión *f* de régimen abierto (**c**) *(extended)* abierto(a), extendido(a); *Fig* **with o. arms** con los brazos abiertos (**d**) *(not covered) (car etc)* descubierto(a); *(pan)* destapado(a) (**e**) *(admitting customers, visitors)* abierto(a); **o. to the public** abierto al público; *Fig* **to keep o. house** tener las puertas abiertas a todo el mundo ❑ *Jur* **o. court** juicio *m* a puerta abierta; *Br* **o. day,** *US* **o. house** jornada *f* de puertas abiertas (**f**) *(not restricted)* abierto(a), libre; **o. competition** concurso libre; **o. letter** carta abierta ❑ *(hunting)* **o. season** temporada *f* de caza; **o. shop** empresa *f* de sindicación libre; *Br* **O. University** = universidad a distancia británica, *Esp* UNED *f* (**g**) *(unengaged)* libre (**h**) *(not hidden)* abierto(a), franco(a); **o. admiration** franca admiración; **o. secret** secreto a voces; **to be o. with sb** ser sincero(a) con algn (**i**) *(available) (post, job)* vacante (**j**) *(undecided)* sin decidir; **an o. question** una cuestión sin resolver; **let's leave it o.** dejémoslo sin concretar; *Av Rail* **o. ticket** billete *m* abierto ❑ *Jur* **o. verdict** veredicto *m* inconcluso (**k**) *(blatant)* manifiesto(a), patente (**l**) *(not biased)* sin prejuicios; **to keep an o. mind** no tener prejuicios (**m**) *(liable, susceptible)* abierto(a); **I am o. to suggestions** acepto cualquier sugerencia; *Sport* **o. goal** gol *m* cantado; **o. to attack** expuesto(a) a los ataques; **o. to criticism** que da lugar a críticas (**n**) *Fin (cheque, account)* abierto(a)

2 *vt* (**a**) *(gen)* abrir; *(unfold)* desplegar; *Mil* **to o. fire** abrir fuego; *Mil* **to o. ranks** romper filas; *Fig* **to o. one's heart to sb** sincerarse con algn (**b**) *(inaugurate, initiate) (shop)* abrir; *(exhibition etc)* inaugurar; *(negotiations)* iniciar; *(conversation)* entablar; *Fin (account)* abrir

3 *vi* (**a**) *(gen)* abrir, abrirse; **the bank opens at ten** el banco abre a las diez (**b**) *(render accessible)* dar a; **is there an exit opening on the street?** ¿hay una salida a la calle? (**c**) *(appear in view)* abrirse (**d**) *(start)* empezar, comenzar; *Theat Cin* estrenarse; **the story opens with a murder** la historia comienza con un asesinato (**e**) *Cards* abrir (**with** de)

4 *n* (**a**) *(open air)* campo *m*, aire *m* libre; **in the o.** al aire libre, al raso; *Fig* **to bring into the o.** hacer público; *Fig* **to come into the o.** declarar abiertamente (**b**) *Sport* open *m*

open out 1 *vt* abrir, desplegar, desdoblar

2 *vi (flowers)* abrirse; *(view)* extenderse

open up 1 *vt* (**a**) *(market etc)* abrir; *(possibilities)* crear (**b**) *Aut Fam* dar gas, acelerar

2 *vi (gen)* abrirse; *Fam* **o. up!** ¡ábreme!, ¡abre la puerta! (**b**) *(start)* empezar, comenzar, iniciarse (**c**) *(talk freely)* hablar con franqueza (**d**) *(become more lively)* animarse

open-air ['əʊpneər] *adj* al aire libre

open-and-shut [əʊpənən'ʃʌt] *adj* claro(a), evidente; **an o.-a.-s. case** un caso evidente

opencast ['əʊpnkɑːst] *adj Br Min* a cielo abierto

open-door ['əʊpəndɔːr] *adj Ind* no proteccionista

open-ended [əʊpən'endɪd] *adj (gen)* sin límites; *(contract)* ilimitado(a)

opener ['əʊpənər] *n* abridor *m*; **bottle o.** abrebotellas *m inv*; **tin o.,** *US* **can o.** abrelatas *m inv*

open-heart ['əʊpnhɑːt] *adj Med* de corazón abierto

open-hearted [əʊpən'hɑːtɪd] *adj* abierto(a), sincero(a)

opening ['əʊpnɪŋ] *n* (**a**) *(act)* apertura *f*; *Cin Theat* estreno *m*; **formal o.** inauguración *f* ❑ *Theat* **o. night** noche *f* de estreno; *Fin* **o. price** cotización *f* inicial; **o. speech** discurso *m* inaugural; *Br* **o. time** *(in pub)* hora *f* en que abren los bares (**b**) *(beginning)* comienzo *m* (**c**) *(aperture)* abertura *f*; *(gap)* brecha *f*; *US (in forest)* claro *m* (**d**) *Com (chance)* salida *f*, oportunidad *f* (**e**) *(vacancy)* puesto *m* vacante, vacante *f*

openly ['əʊpənlɪ] *adv (gen)* abiertamente; *(publicly)* públicamente, en público

open-minded [əʊpən'maɪndɪd] *adj* de mente abierta, sin prejuicios

open-mindedness [əʊpən'maɪndɪdnɪs] *n* falta *f* de prejuicios

open-mouthed [əʊpən'maʊθt] *adj* boquiabierto(a)

openness ['əʊpənnɪs] *n* franqueza *f*

open-plan ['əʊpənplæn] *adj Archit (office etc)* abierto(a)

opera¹ ['ɒprə] *n Mus* ópera *f* ❑ **o. glasses** prismáticos *mpl*, gemelos *mpl*; **o. house** ópera *f*, teatro *m* de la ópera; **o. singer** cantante *mf* de ópera

opera² ['ɒprə] *npl see* **opus**

operable ['ɒprəbəl] *adj Med* operable

operagoer ['ɒprəgəʊər] *n* **as regular operagoers will know. ...** como los asiduos *or* aficionados a la ópera ya sabrán ...

operand ['ɒpərænd] *n Math* operando *m*

operate ['ɒpəreɪt] **1** *vi* (**a**) *(function)* funcionar (**b**) *(act)* obrar, actuar (**c**) *Med* operar, hacer una intervención quirúrgica, intervenir; **to o. on sb for appendicitis** operar a algn de apendicitis

2 *vt* (**a**) *(switch on)* accionar; *(control)* hacer funcionar, manejar (**b**) *(manage) (business)* dirigir; *(mine)* explotar

operatic [ɒpə'rætɪk] *adj* de ópera, operístico(a)

operating ['ɒpəreɪtɪŋ] *n* (**a**) *Com Ind* operación *f*, funcionamiento *m* ❑ **o. costs** costos *mpl or Esp* costes *mpl* de explotación (**b**) *Med* operación *f* ❑ *US* **o. room** quirófano *m*; **o. table** mesa *f* de operaciones; *Br* **o. theatre** quirófano *m* (**c**) *Comptr* **o. system** sistema *m* operativo

operation [ɒpə'reɪʃən] *n* (**a**) *(of machine)* funcionamiento *m*; *(by person)* manejo *m*; **to be in o.** *(machine)* estar funcionando *or* en funcionamiento; *(law)* estar vigente *or* en vigor (**b**) *Math* operación *f* (**c**) *Mil* operación *f*, maniobra *f* (**d**) *Med* operación *f*, intervención *f* quirúrgica; **to undergo an o. for** ser operado(a) de

operational [ɒpə'reɪʃənəl] *adj* (**a**) *(of operations)* de operaciones (**b**) *(ready for use)* operativo(a), listo(a) para usar; *(in use)* en funcionamiento; **to be o.** estar en funcionamiento (**c**) *Mil* operacional, de servicio

operative ['ɒpərətɪv] **1** *adj* (**a**) *Jur (in force)* vigente; **to become o.** entrar en vigor (**b**) *(significant)* clave, significativo(a); **the o. word** la palabra clave (**c**) *Med* operatorio(a)

2 *n* operario(a) *m,f*

operator ['ɒpəreɪtər] *n* (**a**) *Ind* operario(a) *m,f* (**b**) *Tel* operador(a) *m,f*, telefonista *mf*; *Av Mil* **radio o.** radiotelegrafista *mf* (**c**) *(dealer)* negociante *mf*, agente *m*; **tour o.** agente de viajes; *Fam* **a slick o.** un tipo aprovechado (**d**) *Math* operador *m*

operetta [ɒpə'retə] *n Mus* opereta *f*

ophthalmic [ɒf'θælmɪk] *adj Br* **o. optician** óptico(a) *m,f*

ophthalmology [ɒfθæl'mɒlədʒɪ] *n Med* oftalmología *f*

opinion [ə'pɪnjən] *n* (**a**) *(belief)* opinión *f*; **in my o.** a mi parecer, en mi opinión, a mi juicio; **it's a matter of o.** es cuestión de opiniones; **to be of the o. that ...** opinar que ...; **to give one's o.** dar su opinión (**b**) *(evaluation, estimation)* opinión *f*, concepto *m*; **to have a high/low o. of sb** tener buen/mal concepto de algn; **public o.** la opinión pública; **what's your o. of him?** ¿qué piensas de él? ❑ **o. poll** encuesta *f*, sondeo *m*

opinionated [ə'pɪnjəneɪtɪd] *adj (obstinate)* terco(a), testarudo(a); *(dogmatic)* dogmático(a)

opium ['əʊpɪəm] *n* opio *m* ❑ **o. addict** opiómano(a) *m,f*, adicto(a) *m,f* al opio; **o. den** fumadero *m* de opio

opossum [ə'pɒsəm] *n Zool* zarigüeya *f*

opp (*abbr* **opposite**) enfrente

opponent [ə'pəʊnənt] *n* adversario(a) *m,f*, contrincante *mf*

opportune ['ɒpətjuːn] *adj* oportuno(a), propício(a); **an o. moment** un momento oportuno

opportunist [ɒpə'tjuːnɪst] *adj & n* oportunista *(mf)*

opportunistic [ɒpətjʊ'nɪstɪk] *n* oportunista; *Med* **o. infection** infección *f* oportunista

opportunity [ɒpə'tjuːnɪtɪ] *n* **(a)** *(gen)* oportunidad *f*, ocasión *f*; **if I get an o.** si se me presenta la ocasión; **to miss an o.** perder una oportunidad ❑ **equal o.** igualdad *f* de oportunidades **(b)** *(prospect)* perspectiva *f*; '**excellent opportunities for promotion'** *(advert)* 'excelentes perspectivas de promoción'

oppose [ə'pəʊz] *vt* oponerse a, ser contrario(a) a; *Pol* **to o. the motion** oponerse a la moción

opposed [ə'pəʊzd] **1** *adj* opuesto(a), contrario(a); **to be o. to sth** estar en contra de algo, oponerse a algo
2 as opposed to *prep* comparado(a) con, en comparación con

opposing [ə'pəʊzɪŋ] *adj* contrario(a), adversario(a); *Mil* **the o. forces** las fuerzas enemigas; *Sport* **the o. team** el equipo adversario

opposite ['ɒpəzɪt, 'ɒpəsɪt] **1** *adj* **(a)** *(facing)* de enfrente; *(page)* contiguo(a); **the house o.** la casa de enfrente **(b)** *(contrary)* opuesto(a), contrario(a), contrapuesto(a); **at the o. end** en el extremo opuesto; **in the o. direction** en dirección contraria; **o. poles** polos *mpl* opuestos; **to take the o. view** tomar la actitud contraria ❑ **o. number** colega *mf*, homólogo(a) *m,f*; **o. sex** sexo *m* opuesto
2 *n* antítesis *f*, contraposición *f*; **quite the o.!** ¡al contrario!; **she's the o. of her brother** es la antítesis de su hermano
3 *prep* enfrente de, frente a; **o. (to) the butcher's** frente a la carnicería
4 *adv* enfrente; **the church is o.** la iglesia está enfrente

opposition [ɒpə'zɪʃən] *n* **(a)** *(resistance)* oposición *f*, resistencia *f*; **they met with no o.** no encontraron resistencia **(b)** *(contrast)* contradicción *f*, contraposición *f*; **in o. to** en contra de, contrario a **(c)** *Br Pol* **the O.** la oposición; **the o. party** el partido de la oposición; **to be in o.** ser de la oposición

oppress [ə'pres] *vt* **(a)** *(treat cruelly)* oprimir **(b)** *(of anxiety, atmosphere)* agobiar, oprimir

oppressed [ə'prest] **1 the o.** *npl* los oprimidos
2 *adj* *(people, nation)* oprimido(a)

oppression [ə'preʃən] *n* **(a)** *(of a people)* opresión *f* **(b)** *(of the mind)* agobio *m*

oppressive [ə'presɪv] *adj* **(a)** *(gen)* opresivo(a) **(b)** *(atmosphere)* agobiante; *(heat)* sofocante

opt [ɒpt] *vi* optar; **to o. for** optar por; **we opted to decline the invitation** optamos por no ir

opt out *vi* desentenderse **(of** de**)**

optative ['ɒptətɪv] **1** *adj* optativo(a)
2 *n Ling* modo *m* optativo

optic ['ɒptɪk] *adj* óptico(a); *Anat* **o. nerve** nervio óptico

optical ['ɒptɪkəl] *adj* óptico(a); **o. fibre** fibra *f* óptica; **o. illusion** ilusión *f* óptica

optician [ɒp'tɪʃən] *n* óptico(a), *m,f*

optics ['ɒptɪks] *n* óptica *f*

optimal ['ɒptɪməl] *adj* óptimo(a)

optimism ['ɒptɪmɪzəm] *n* optimismo *m*

optimist ['ɒptɪmɪst] *n* optimista *mf*

optimistic(al) [ɒptɪ'mɪstɪk(əl)] *adj* optimista

optimistically [ɒptɪ'mɪstɪklɪ] *adv* con optimismo

optimize ['ɒptɪmaɪz] *vt* aprovechar al máximo, optimizar

optimum ['ɒptɪməm] **1** *n* grado *m* óptimo
2 *adj* óptimo(a); **o. conditions** condiciones *fpl* óptimas

option ['ɒpʃən] *n* opción *f*; **I have no o.** no tengo más remedio; **to keep** *or* **leave one's options open** no comprometerse; **with the o. on** con opción a

optional [ɒpʃənəl] *adj* optativo(a), facultativo(a) ❑ *Com* **o. extras** extras *mpl* opcionales; *Educ* **o. subject** (asignatura *f*) optativa *f*

opt-out ['ɒptaʊt] **1** *n* autoexclusión *f*
2 *adj* **o-o. clause** cláusula *f* de exclusión *or* de no participación

opulence ['ɒpjʊləns] *n* opulencia *f*

opulent ['ɒpjʊlənt] *adj* opulento(a)

opus ['əʊpəs] *(pl* **opuses** *or* **opera)** *n* opus *m*

OR *n* [əʊ'ɑːr] *US (abbr* **operating room)** quirófano *m*, sala *f* de operaciones; *US* **OR nurse** instrumentista *mf*

or [ɔːr, *unstressed* ər] *conj* **(a)** *(in general)* o; *(before a word beginning* **o** *or* **ho)** u; **keep still or I'll shoot** no se mueva o disparo; **or else** si no, o bien; **tell me whether you like it or not** dime si te gusta o no; **ten kilometres or so** unos diez kilómetros; **you may have either a bun or a piece of cake** puedes tomarte (o) una madalena o un trozo de pastel **(b)** *(with negative)* ni; **he can't read or write** no sabe leer ni escribir; **without money or luggage** sin dinero ni equipaje; *see also* **nor**

oracle ['ɒrəkəl] *n* oráculo *m*

oral ['ɔːrəl, 'ɒrəl] **1** *adj* oral; **o. contraceptive** anticonceptivo *m* oral; **o. hygiene** higiene *f* bucal; *Med* **o. vaccine** vacuna *f* por vía oral
2 *n* examen *m* oral

orally ['ɔːrəlɪ] *adv* oralmente; *Pharm* **to be taken o.** por vía oral

orange ['ɒrɪndʒ] **1** *n* **(a)** *(fruit)* naranja *f* ❑ *Bot* **o. blossom** azahar *m*; *Bot* **o. grove** naranjal *m*; **o. juice** *Esp* zumo *m* *or* *Am* jugo *m* de naranja; **o. tree** naranjo *m* **(b)** *(colour)* naranja *m*
2 *adj* naranja *inv*, de color naranja

orangeade [ɒrɪndʒ'eɪd] *n* naranjada *f*

orang-outang [ɔːræŋuː'tæŋ] *n Zool* orangután *m*

oration [ɔː'reɪʃən] *n* oración *f*, discurso *m*

orator ['ɒrətər] *n* orador(a) *m,f*

oratorical [ɒrə'tɒrɪkəl] *adj* oratorio(a)

oratory[1] ['ɒrətərɪ] *n (art of speaking)* oratoria *f*

oratory[2] ['ɒrətərɪ] *n Rel (chapel)* oratorio *m*, capilla *f*

orbit ['ɔːbɪt] **1** *n* **(a)** *Astron* órbita *f*; **to go into o.** entrar en órbita; **to put a satellite into o.** poner un satélite en órbita **(b)** *Fig* ámbito *m*, esfera *f*, órbita *f*; **the Russian o.** la esfera de influencia soviética
2 *vt* girar alrededor de
3 *vi* orbitar, girar

orbital ['ɔːbɪtəl] *adj* orbital, orbitario(a)

orchard ['ɔːtʃəd] *n* huerto *m* ❑ **apple o.** manzanal *m*

orchestra ['ɔːkɪstrə] *n* **(a)** *(musicians)* orquesta *f* ❑ **chamber o.** orquesta *f* de cámara; **o. pit** orquesta *f*, foso *m* **(b)** *US (in theatre)* platea *f*, patio *m* de butacas

orchestral [ɔː'kestrəl] *adj* orquestal

orchestration [ɔːkɪ'streɪʃən] *n* orquestación *f*

orchid ['ɔːkɪd] *n Bot* orquídea *f*

ordain [ɔː'deɪn] *vt* **(a)** *Rel* ordenar; **to be ordained** ordenarse **(b)** *(decree)* decretar, ordenar; **it was ordained by fate** el destino quiso que fuera así

ordeal [ɔː'diːl] *n* mala experiencia *f*, sufrimiento *m*

order ['ɔːdər] **1** *n* (**a**) *(sequence)* orden *m*, serie *f*; **in alphabetical o.** por orden alfabético; **in o. of importance** por orden de importancia; **in the wrong o., out of o.** sin orden; **to put in** *or* **into o.** poner en orden, ordenar (**b**) *(condition)* estado *m*, condiciones *fpl*; **in good o.** en buen estado, en condiciones; **is your passport in o.?** ¿tienes el pasaporte en regla?; **'out of o.'** 'no funciona' (**c**) *(peace)* orden *m*; **law and o.** orden público; **to call to o.** llamar al orden (**d**) *(class etc)* clase *f*; **the lower orders** las clases bajas, el proletariado (**e**) *Biol* orden *m* (**f**) *(command)* orden *f*; **to give orders** dar órdenes; **until further orders** hasta nueva orden; **we received an o. to withdraw** recibimos órdenes de retirarnos; *Fig* **to be the o. of the day** estar a la orden del día □ *Jur* **court o.** orden *f* judicial; **extradition o.** orden *f* de extradición (**g**) *(commission, instruction)* pedido *m*, encargo *m*; **to be on o.** estar pedido *or* encargado; **to place an o. with sb** hacer un pedido a algn; **to o.** a (la) medida; *Fam* **that's a tall o.** eso es mucho pedir □ **o. form** hoja *f* de pedido; **postal o.** giro *m* postal (**h**) *Rel* orden *f*; **to take (holy) orders** ordenarse (sacerdote) (**i**) *Hist (medal)* condecoración *f*; *(title)* orden *f* (**j**) *Archit* orden *m* (**k**) *(quality)* calidad *f*, categoría *f*; **of the highest o.** de primer orden, de primera calidad (**l**) *(kind)* índole *f*, tipo *m* (**m**) **in the o. of** del orden de, alrededor de, aproximadamente (**n**) **in o. that** para que, a fin de que; **in o. that she should arrive on time** para que llegara a tiempo; **in o. to** *(+ infin)* para, a fin de *(+ infin)*

2 *vt* (**a**) *(command)* ordenar, mandar; **she ordered me into the car** me ordenó que entrara en el coche; *Sport* **to o. a player off** expulsar a un jugador; **to o. sb about** *or* **around** mangonear a algn, gobernar a algn; **to o. sb to do sth** mandar *or* ordenar a algn hacer algo (**b**) *(request)* pedir; *Com* pedir, encargar; **to o. a dish** pedir un plato (**c**) *(organize)* ordenar, poner en orden

3 *interj* ¡orden!; **o. in the court!** ¡orden en la sala!

ordered ['ɔːdəd] *adj (organized)* ordenado(a)

orderliness ['ɔːdəlɪnɪs] *n* orden *m*, disciplina *f*

orderly ['ɔːdəlɪ] **1** *adj* (**a**) *(tidy etc)* ordenado(a); **he's very o.** es muy metódico (**b**) *(obeying)* disciplinado(a)
2 *n* (**a**) *Med* enfermero *m* (**b**) *Mil* ordenanza *m* □ **o. room** oficina *f*

ordinal ['ɔːdɪnəl] *adj & n* ordinal *(m)*

ordinance ['ɔːdɪnəns] *n Fml* ordenanza *f*, decreto *m*

ordinarily [ɔːdɪnərɪlɪ] *adv* normalmente

ordinary ['ɔːdənrɪ] **1** *adj (usual, normal)* usual, normal; *(average)* corriente, común; **an o. guy** un tipo corriente; **in the o. way** en la forma habitual, de la manera usual; **the o. citizen** el ciudadano de a pie, el hombre de la calle; **the o. Spaniard** el español medio □ *Br Naut* **o. seaman** marinero *m*; *Br* **o. shares** acciones *fpl* ordinarias
2 the o. *n* lo corriente, lo normal; **above the o.** sobresaliente; **out of the o.** fuera de lo común, excepcional, extraordinario(a)

ordinate ['ɔːdɪnɪt] *n Math* ordenada *f*

ordination [ɔːdɪ'neɪʃən] *n* ordenación *f*

ordnance ['ɔːdnəns] *n Br* **O. Survey** = servicio oficial de topografía y cartografía

ore [ɔːr] *n Min* mineral *m*, mena *f* □ **iron o.** mineral *m* de hierro

oregano [ɒrɪ'gɑːnəʊ] *n Bot* orégano *m*

organ ['ɔːgən] *n* (**a**) *Mus* órgano *m* □ **barrel o.** organillo *m* (**b**) *Anat* órgano *m* □ **o. donor** donante *mf* de órganos; **o. transplant** transplante *m* de órganos (**c**) *(agency)* órgano *m*; *(periodical)* órgano *m*, boletín *m*; **the party o.** el órgano del partido

organ-grinder ['ɔːgəngraɪndər] *n* organillero(a) *m,f*

organic [ɔː'gænɪk] *adj* orgánico(a); **o. chemistry** química *f* orgánica

organism ['ɔːgənɪzəm] *n* organismo *m*

organist ['ɔːgənɪst] *n Mus* organista *mf*

organization [ɔːgənaɪ'zeɪʃən] *n* organización *f*

organize ['ɔːgənaɪz] *vt* organizar; **to get organized** organizarse

organizer ['ɔːgənaɪzər] *n* organizador(a) *m,f*

orgasm ['ɔːgæzəm] *n* orgasmo *m*

orgy ['ɔːdʒɪ] *n* orgía *f*; *Fig* **an o. of colour** una explosión de colores

orient ['ɔːrɪənt] *n* **the O.** el Oriente

Oriental [ɔːrɪ'entəl] *adj & n* oriental *(mf)*

orientate ['ɔːrɪenteɪt] *vt* orientar

orientation [ɔːrɪen'teɪʃən] *n* orientación *f* □ **o. course** curso *m* orientativo

orienteering [ɒrɪən'tɪərɪŋ] *n* orientación *f (deporte de aventura)*

orifice ['ɒrɪfɪs] *n* orificio *m*

origin ['ɒrɪdʒɪn] *n* origen *m*; **country of o.** país natal *or* de origen

original [ə'rɪdʒɪnəl] **1** *adj* (**a**) *(first)* primero(a), original; **the o. inhabitants** los primeros habitantes □ *Rel* **o. sin** pecado *m* original (**b**) *(novel)* original, genuino(a)
2 *n* original *m*; **the o. is in the Prado** el original está en el Prado; **to read Cervantes in the o.** leer a Cervantes en versión original

originality [ərɪdʒɪ'nælɪtɪ] *n* originalidad *f*

originally [ə'rɪdʒɪnəlɪ] *adv* (**a**) *(at first)* en un principio, originariamente (**b**) *(with originality)* con originalidad

originate [ə'rɪdʒɪneɪt] **1** *vt* originar, crear, dar lugar a
2 *vi* **to o. from** *or* **in** tener su origen en, provenir de

Orkneys ['ɔːknɪz] *npl* (Islas) Órcadas

ornament ['ɔːnəmənt] **1** *n* ornamento *m*, adorno *m*
2 *vt* adornar, engalanar

ornamental [ɔːnə'mentəl] *adj* ornamental, decorativo(a)

ornate [ɔː'neɪt] *adj (gen)* vistoso(a); *(style)* sobrecargado(a)

ornithology [ɔːnɪ'θɒlədʒɪ] *n* ornitología *f*

orphan ['ɔːfən] **1** *n* huérfano(a) *m,f*
2 *vt* dejar huérfano(a); **she was orphaned** quedó huérfana

orphanage ['ɔːfənɪdʒ] *n* orfanato *m*

orthodontics [ɔːθə'dɒntɪks] *n* ortodoncia *f*

orthodontist [ɔːθə'dɒntɪst] *n* ortodontista *mf*

orthodox ['ɔːθədɒks] *adj* ortodoxo(a)

orthodoxy ['ɔːθədɒksɪ] *n* ortodoxia *f*

orthography [ɔː'θɒgrəfɪ] *n* ortografía *f*

orthopaedic, *US* **orthopedic** [ɔːθə'piːdɪk] *adj* ortopédico(a)

orthopaedics, *US* **orthopedics** [ɔːθəʊ'piːdɪks] *n* ortopedia *f*

orthopaedist, *US* **orthopedist** [ɔːθəʊ'piːdɪst] *n* ortopedista *mf*

OS [əʊ'es] (**a**) *Naut (abbr* **ordinary seaman)** marinero *m* (**b**) *Br Geol (abbr* **Ordnance Survey)** = servicio oficial de topografía y cartografía (**c**) *Comptr (abbr* **Operating System)** sistema *m* operativo

oscillate ['ɒsɪleɪt] *vi Elec Phys* oscilar; *Fig* oscilar, variar

osier ['əʊʒɪər] *n* mimbre *m* □ **o. bed** mimbrera *f*

Oslo ['ɒzləʊ] *n* Oslo

osmosis [ɒz'məʊsɪs] *n* ósmosis *f*, osmosis *f*

osprey ['ɒsprɪ, 'ɒspreɪ] *n Orn* águila *f* pescadora

ossification [ɒsɪfɪ'keɪʃən] *n* osificación *f*

ossify ['ɒsɪfaɪ] *vi* (*pt & pp* **ossified**) osificarse

ostensible [ɒ'stensɪbəl] *adj* (**a**) *(apparent)* ostensible (**b**) *(pretended)* aparentado(a), fingido(a)

ostensibly [ɒ'stensɪblɪ] *adv* aparentemente

ostentation [ɒsten'teɪʃən] *n* ostentación *f*

ostentatious [ɒsten'teɪʃəs] *adj* ostentoso(a)

osteoarthritis [ɒstɪəʊɑː'θraɪtɪs] *n Med* osteoartritis *f inv*, artritis *f inv* ósea

osteopath ['ɒstɪəpæθ] *n Med* osteópata *mf*

ostracism ['ɒstrəsɪzəm] *n* ostracismo *m*

ostracize ['ɒstrəsaɪz] *vt (from society)* condenar al ostracismo; *(from group)* aislar, excluir

ostrich ['ɒstrɪtʃ] *n Orn* avestruz *m*

other ['ʌðər] **1** *adj* (**a**) *(gen)* otro(a); **any o. member** cualquier otro miembro; **every o. day** cada dos días; **on the o. hand** por otra parte, por otro lado; **o. people have seen it** otros lo han visto; **o. people's property** los bienes ajenos; **the o. four** los otros cuatro; **the o. one** el otro/la otra; **the o. thing** lo otro (**b**) **or o.** u otro(a); **he must be somewhere or o.** debe de estar en alguna parte; **one or o. of us** alguno de nosotros

2 *pron* otro(a) *m,f*; **many others** otros muchos; **one after the o.** uno tras otro; **the others** los otros, los demás; **we see each o. quite often** nos vemos con bastante frecuencia

3 *adv* **she can't be o. than what she is** ella no puede ser de otra manera

otherwise ['ʌðəwaɪz] **1** *adv* (**a**) *(if not)* si no, de no ser así; **o. you'll have to do it on your own** si no, tendrás que hacerlo solo (**b**) *(differently)* de otra manera; **except where o. stated** excepto cuando se indique lo contrario; **he couldn't do o.** no podía obrar de otra manera; **if she's not o. engaged** si no tiene otro compromiso (**c**) *(in other respects)* por lo demás; **he's o. quite sane** aparte de eso está en su sano juicio

2 *adj* distinto(a); **the truth is o.** la verdad es bastante distinta

otherworldly [ʌðə'wɜːldlɪ] *adj* alejado(a) de este mundo, espiritual

otter ['ɒtər] *n (pl* **otters** *or* **otter)** *Zool* nutria *f*

Ottoman ['ɒtəmən] *adj & n* otomán(ana) *(m,f)*, otomano(a) *(m,f)*

ottoman ['ɒtəmən] *n (seat)* otomana *f*

OU [əʊ'juː] *n Br (abbr* **Open University)** = universidad a distancia británica, *Esp* UNED *f*

ouch [aʊtʃ] *interj* ¡ay!

ought [ɔːt] *v aux* (**a**) *(obligation)* deber; **I thought I o. to tell you** creí que debía decírtelo; **she o. to do it** debería hacerlo; **to behave as one o.** comportarse como es debido; **you oughtn't to eat so many cakes** no deberías comer tantos pasteles (**b**) *(vague desirability)* tener que, deber; **you o. to see the exhibition** deberías ver la exposición; **you o. to have seen it!** ¡si lo hubieras visto! (**c**) *(expectation)* **he o. to pass the exam** seguramente aprobará el examen; **that o. to do** con eso bastará

ounce [aʊns] *n (unit of weight)* onza *f (= 28,4 g)*; *US (fluid ounce)* onza *f* líquida *(= 29,6ml)*; *Fig* **he hasn't an o. of courage** no tiene ni pizca de valentía

our [aʊər] *poss adj* nuestro(a); **o. daughter** nuestra hija; **o. friends** nuestros amigos; **it's one of o. books** es un libro nuestro ❑ *Rel* **O. Father** Padrenuestro *m*; *Rel* **O. Lady** Nuestra Señora *f*

ours [aʊəz] *poss pron* (el) nuestro/(la) nuestra; **have you seen o.?** ¿has visto el nuestro?; **this table is o.** esta mesa

es nuestra; **of o.** nuestro(a); **a friend of o.** un amigo nuestro

ourselves [aʊə'selvz] *pers pron pl* (**a**) *(reflexive)* nos; **we can serve o.** nos podemos servir (**b**) *(emphatic)* nosotros mismos/nosotras mismas; **we did it o.** lo hicimos nosotros mismos; **we o. are to blame** la culpa es nuestra (**c**) **by o.** a solas; **all by o.** completamente solos

oust [aʊst] *vt* (**a**) *(from a post)* desbancar (**b**) *(from property etc)* expulsar, desalojar

out [aʊt] **1** *adv* (**a**) *(outside, away)* fuera; **o. you go!** ¡vete!, *RP* ¡andate!; **he's o. and about again** ya está bien otra vez; **a long way o. (of town)** muy lejos (de la ciudad); **o. at sea** en alta mar; **o. there** ahí fuera; *Naut* **the voyage o.** la ida; **to go o.** salir; **to throw sth o.** tirar *or Am salvo RP* botar algo (a la basura); **'way o.'** 'salida' (**b**) *(clearly)* claramente; **I told him straight o.** se lo dije muy claramente; **o. loud** en voz alta (**c**) *(to the end)* hasta el final; **hear me o.** escúchame hasta el final (**d**) **o. of** *(place)* fuera de; **get o. of here!** ¡sal de aquí!; **move o. of the way!** ¡quítate de en medio!; **o. of danger** fuera de peligro; **she's o. of town** está fuera de la ciudad; **to get money o. of sb** sacarle dinero a algn; **to go o. of the room** salir de la habitación; *Fig* **to feel o. of it** sentirse aislado; *Fam* **you must be o. of your mind** estás mal de la cabeza, estás loco; *Slang* **to be o. of it** no estar al tanto, no enterarse; *Prov* **o. of sight, o. of mind** ojos que no ven, corazón que no siente (**e**) **o. of** *Fig* fuera de; **o. of control** fuera de control, descontrolado(a); **o. of date** *(expired)* caducado(a); *(old-fashioned)* pasado(a) de moda; **o. of focus** desenfocado(a); *Pol* **o. of office** fuera del poder; **'o. of order'** 'no funciona'; **o. of print** agotado(a) (**f**) **o. of** *(cause, motive)* por; **he did it o. of spite** lo hizo por despecho; **o. of respect** por respeto (**g**) **o. of** *(made from)* de; **made o. of wood** hecho(a) de madera (**h**) **o. of** *(short of, without)* sin; **I'm o. of money** se me ha acabado el dinero, estoy sin dinero; **o. of breath** sin aliento; **to be o. of practice** faltarle práctica a algn; **to be o. of. work** estar parado(a) *or* sin trabajo; **we're o. of milk** nos hemos quedado sin leche, se nos ha acabado la leche (**i**) **o. of** *(among)* entre; **forty o. of fifty** cuarenta de cada cincuenta; **one o. of many** uno entre otros muchos

2 *adj* (**a**) **the sun is o.** *(in view)* ha salido el sol (**b**) *(unfashionable)* pasado(a) de moda; **hats are o. this year** los sombreros no se llevan *or Am* usan este año (**c**) *(not lit)* apagado(a); **the fire is o.** se ha apagado el fuego (**d**) *(not working)* estropeado(a); **the TV's o.** la tele no va (**e**) *(unconscious)* inconsciente; **to be o. cold** haber perdido completamente el conocimiento (**f**) **she's o.** *(not in)* ha salido, no está (**g**) *(intent)* **to be o. for** *or* **to** buscar; **he's o. for your blood** va a por ti; **I'm not o. to do that** no es ése mi propósito (**h**) *(on strike)* en huelga (**i**) *(published)* publicado(a); *(made public)* público(a); **the book is just o.** el libro acaba de salir; **the secret is o.** el secreto ha salido a luz (**j**) *Sport (ball)* fuera de juego; *(player)* eliminado(a); *(boxer)* fuera de combate (**k**) *(used up)* agotado(a), terminado(a); **the paper is o.** se ha terminado el papel (**l**) *(inaccurate)* equivocado(a); **I wasn't far o.** no andaba muy equivocado; **to be o. in one's calculations** equivocarse en los cálculos (**m**) *(not in office)* fuera del poder (**n**) *(completed)* acabado(a), terminado(a); **before the week is o.** antes de acabar la semana (**o**) *(in flower)* en flor

3 *prep* *(out of)* por; **he jumped o. the window** saltó por la ventana; **she ran o. the door** salió corriendo por la puerta

4 *n Fig* **the ins and outs of the matter** los pormenores del asunto

5 *interj (leave)* ¡fuera!; *Fam* **o. with it!** ¡suéltalo ya!

outage ['aʊtɪdʒ] *n Elec* **power o.** corte *m or* interrupción *f* del servicio eléctrico

out-and-out ['aʊtənaʊt] *adj* empedernido(a),

redomado(a); **he's an o.-a.-o. liar** es un mentiroso empedernido

outback ['aʊtbæk] n **the o.** el interior despoblado de Australia

outbid [aʊt'bɪd] vt (pt **outbid;** pp **outbid** or **outbidden** [aʊt'bɪdən]) (at auction) pujar más alto que, ofrecer más que

outboard ['aʊtbɔːd] adj Naut **o. motor** motor m fueraborda, fuera borda m

outbreak ['aʊtbreɪk] n (of war) comienzo m; (of spots) erupción f; (of disease) brote m, epidemia f; (of violence) ola f; (of anger) arrebato m; **at the o. of war** cuando estalló la guerra

outbuilding ['aʊtbɪldɪŋ] n (gen) dependencia f; (shed) cobertizo m

outburst ['aʊtbɜːst] n (of anger) explosión f, arrebato m; (of generosity) arranque m; **there was an o. of applause** irrumpieron en aplausos

outcast ['aʊtkɑːst] n marginado(a) m,f, proscrito(a) m,f

outclass [aʊt'klɑːs] vt superar (ampliamente)

outcome ['aʊtkʌm] n resultado m

outcrop ['aʊtkrɒp] n Geol afloramiento m

outcry ['aʊtkraɪ] n protesta f; **there was an o.** hubo fuertes protestas

outdated [aʊt'deɪtɪd] adj anticuado(a), obsoleto(a)

outdid [aʊt'dɪd] pt see **outdo**

outdistance [aʊt'dɪstəns] vt dejar atrás

outdo [aʊt'duː] vt (pt **outdid;** pp **outdone** [aʊt'dʌn]) (person) superar, sobrepasar; **not to be outdone** para no ser menos; **to o. sb** poderle a algn

outdoor ['aʊtdɔːr] adj (a) (gen) exterior, al aire libre; **o. swimming pool** piscina f or Méx alberca f or RP pileta f descubierta; **the o. life** la vida al aire libre ❏ Phot **o. shot** exterior m (b) (clothes) de calle

outdoors [aʊt'dɔːz] **1** adv fuera; **to eat o.** comer al aire libre
  2 n **the (great) o.** el aire libre, la naturaleza

outer ['aʊtər] adj exterior, externo(a); **o. garments** ropa exterior; **the o. suburbs** las afueras ❏ **o. space** espacio m sideral

outermost ['aʊtəməʊst] adj (layer) exterior

outfit ['aʊtfɪt] n (a) (kit, equipment) equipo m (b) (set of clothes) conjunto m; (uniform) uniforme m (c) Fam (group) grupo m, equipo m

outflank [aʊt'flæŋk] vt Mil sorprender por la espalda; Fig (outmanoeuvre) superar

outfox [aʊt'fɒks] vt ser más listo(a) que

outgoing ['aʊtgəʊɪŋ] **1** adj (a) (departing) saliente (b) (sociable) sociable, extrovertido(a)
  2 outgoings npl Br gastos mpl

outgrow [aʊt'grəʊ] vt (pt **outgrew** [aʊt'gruː]; pp **outgrown** [aʊt'grəʊn]) (game, toys) hacerse demasiado mayor para; **he has outgrown his protest phase** ya ha dejado atrás la fase de protestar; **he's outgrowing all his clothes** toda la ropa se le está quedando pequeña; **she'll o. it** se le pasará con la edad

outhouse ['aʊthaʊs] n see **outbuilding**

outing ['aʊtɪŋ] n excursión f

outlandish [aʊt'lændɪʃ] adj extravagante, estrafalario(a)

outlast [aʊt'lɑːst] vt (gen) durar más que; (outlive) sobrevivir a

outlaw ['aʊtlɔː] **1** n proscrito(a) m,f
  2 vt (ban) prohibir

outlay ['aʊtleɪ] n (pl **outlays**) n (expense) desembolso m

outlet ['aʊtlet, 'aʊtlɪt] n (a) (opening) salida f (b) (for

emotions) válvula f de escape (c) Com mercado m, salida f (d) (for water) desagüe m

outline ['aʊtlaɪn] **1** n (a) (draft) bosquejo m (b) (résumé) resumen m (c) (outer line) contorno m; (silhouette) perfil m (d) Art (sketch) boceto m, esbozo m; (of map) trazado m
  2 vt (a) (draw lines of) perfilar; **to be outlined against the sky** perfilarse en el cielo (b) (summarize) hacer un resumen de, resumir (c) (describe roughly) trazar las líneas generales de

outlive [aʊt'lɪv] vt (person, experience) sobrevivir a

outlook ['aʊtlʊk] n (a) (point of view) punto m de vista; (attitude) enfoque m (b) (prospect) perspectiva f, panorama m; Meteor previsión f; **the o. is not very promising** no es un panorama muy esperanzador

outlying ['aʊtlaɪɪŋ] adj (remote) alejado(a), aislado(a); (suburban) periférico(a); **o. districts** barrios mpl periféricos

outmanoeuvre, US **outmaneuver** [aʊtmə'nuːvər] vt superar estratégicamente

outmoded [aʊt'məʊdɪd] adj anticuado(a), pasado(a) de moda

outnumber [aʊt'nʌmbər] vt exceder en número; **we were outnumbered by them** eran más que nosotros

out-of-court ['aʊtəv'kɔːt] adj **an o.-of-c. settlement** un acuerdo sin acudir a los tribunales

out-of-doors [aʊtəv'dɔːz] adv see **outdoors I**

out-of-the-way [aʊtəvðə'weɪ] adj (a) (distant) apartado(a), aislado(a) (b) (uncommon) poco corriente, insólito(a)

out-of-work ['aʊtəv'wɜːk] adj sin trabajo, desempleado(a)

outpatient ['aʊtpeɪʃənt] n Med paciente mf externo(a); **outpatients' department** departamento de consulta externa

outperform [aʊtpə'fɔːm] vt rendir más que, ofrecer un mejor rendimiento que

outplacement ['aʊtpleɪsmənt] n recolocación f, = asesoramiento dirigido a facilitar la recolocación de empleados, generalmente subvencionado por la empresa que los despide

outpost ['aʊtpəʊst] n Mil avanzada f; (at frontier) puesto m fronterizo

output ['aʊtpʊt] n (a) (gen) producción f; (of machine) rendimiento m (b) Elec potencia f (c) Comptr salida f

outrage ['aʊtreɪdʒ] **1** n ultraje m, agravio m; **an o. against humanity** un atentado contra la humanidad; **it's an o.!** ¡es un escándalo!
  2 vt ultrajar, agraviar; **to be outraged by sth** indignarse por algo

outrageous [aʊt'reɪdʒəs] adj (gen) indignante; (crime) atroz; (behaviour) escandaloso(a); (clothes) extravagante; (price) exorbitante

outrageously [aʊt'reɪdʒəslɪ] adv de manera indignante; **o. expensive** terriblemente caro(a)

outreach 1 vt [aʊt'riːtʃ] (exceed) exceder, superar
  2 ['aʊtriːtʃ] n **o. worker** = trabajador social que presta asistencia a personas que pudiendo necesitarla no la solicitan

outright ['aʊtraɪt] **1** adj (a) (absolute) absoluto(a), total; **the o. winner** el ganador indiscutible (b) (straightforward) directo(a)
  2 [aʊt'raɪt] adv (a) (completely) por completo; **to buy sth o.** comprar algo en su totalidad (b) (directly) directamente, sin reserva (c) (immediately) en el acto

outset ['aʊtset] n comienzo m, principio m; **from the o.** de entrada, desde el principio

outside [aʊt'saɪd] **1** prep (a) (gen) fuera de; **o. the house**

fuera de la casa (**b**) *(beyond)* más allá de, fuera de; **o. office hours** fuera de las horas de trabajo (**c**) *(other than)* aparte de

2 ['aʊtsaɪd] *adj* (**a**) *(exterior)* exterior, externo(a); **the o. world** el mundo exterior; *Fig* **an o. opinion** una opinión ajena ▫ *Rad TV* **o. broadcast** emisión *f* desde fuera de los estudios (**b**) *(remote)* remoto(a)

3 [aʊt'saɪd] *adv* fuera, *Am* afuera; **she's o.** está fuera

4 *n* exterior *m*, parte *f* exterior; **from the o.** desde fuera *or Am* afuera; **on the o.** por fuera *or Am* afuera; *Fam* **at the o.** como mucho, como máximo

outsider [aʊt'saɪdə(r)] *n* (**a**) *(stranger)* extraño(a) *m,f*, forastero(a) *m,f*; *(intruder)* intruso(a) *m,f* (**b**) *(unlikely winner) (horse)* caballo *m* que no es el favorito; *Pol (person)* candidato(a) *m,f* con pocas posibilidades de ganar

outsize(d) ['aʊtsaɪz(d)] *adj (vegetables etc)* de gran tamaño; *(clothes)* de talla muy grande

outskirts ['aʊtskɜːts] *npl (of town)* afueras *fpl*

outsmart [aʊt'smɑːt] *vt Fam* burlar, engañar

outsourcing ['aʊtsɔːsɪŋ] *n Com* externalización *f*, subcontratación *f*, *Am* tercerización *f*, *Am* terciarización *f*

outspoken [aʊt'spəʊkən] *adj* directo(a), abierto(a); **to be very o.** no tener pelos en la lengua

outstanding [aʊt'stændɪŋ] *adj* (**a**) *(exceptional)* destacado(a), notable, sobresaliente; **an o. success** un éxito rotundo (**b**) *Com (unpaid)* sin pagar, pendiente; *(unresolved)* pendiente, por hacer

outstay [aʊt'steɪ] *vt* **to o. one's welcome** abusar de la hospitalidad, quedarse más tiempo del apropiado

outstretched [aʊt'stretʃt] *adj* extendido(a)

outstrip [aʊt'strɪp] *(pt & pp* **outstripped)** *vt* superar, aventajar

out-tray ['aʊttreɪ] *(pl* **out-trays)** *n* bandeja *f* de trabajos terminados

outvote [aʊt'vəʊt] *vt (person)* derrotar; *(proposal etc)* vencer; **to be outvoted** perder la votación

outward ['aʊtwəd] **1** *adj* (**a**) *(external)* exterior, externo(a) (**b**) *(of ship, voyage)* de ida; **the o. journey** el viaje de ida

2 *adv* hacia fuera, hacia afuera

outwardly ['aʊtwədlɪ] *adv* (**a**) *(apparently)* aparentemente; **o. calm** tranquilo en apariencia (**b**) *(externally)* por fuera

outwards ['aʊtwədz] *adv see* **outward 2**

outweigh [aʊt'weɪ] *vt* (**a**) *(prevail over)* prevalecer sobre, ser de más peso que (**b**) *(weigh more than)* pesar más que

outwit [aʊt'wɪt] *vt (pt & pp* **outwitted)** ser más astuto(a) que, burlar

ova ['əʊvə] *npl see* **ovum**

oval ['əʊvəl] **1** *adj* oval, ovalado(a)

2 *n* óvalo *m*

ovarian [əʊ'veərɪən] *adj Anat* ovárico(a); **o. cancer** cáncer *m* de ovario

ovary ['əʊvərɪ] *n Anat* ovario *m*

ovation [əʊ'veɪʃən] *n* ovación *f*; **to give sb a standing o.** tributar una ovación a algn, ovacionar a algn (puestos de pie)

oven ['ʌvən] *n* horno *m*; *Culin* **bake in a slow o.** cocer a baja temperatura

ovenproof ['ʌvənpruːf] *adj (dish etc)* refractario(a)

oven-ready ['ʌvənredɪ] *adj (chicken)* listo(a) para hornear

ovenware ['ʌvənweə(r)] *n* accesorios *mpl* para el horno

over ['əʊvə(r)] **1** *prep* (**a**) *(above)* encima de, *Am* arriba de; **her name is o. the door** su nombre está escrito encima de la puerta; **the plane flew o. the afflicted area** el avión

voló por encima de la zona afectada; *Fig* **what came o. you?** ¿qué te pasó?, ¿por qué reaccionaste así? (**b**) *(on top of)* sobre, encima de; **he put on a sweater o. his shirt** se puso un jersey encima de la camisa (**c**) *(across)* al *or Am* del otro lado de; **o. the border** al *or Am* del otro lado de la frontera; **the bridge o. the river** el puente que cruza el río; **the house o. the road** la casa de enfrente (**d**) *(during)* durante; **o. the last fifty years** en los últimos cincuenta años; **o. the weekend** durante el fin de semana; **she told me o. dinner** me lo dijo durante la cena (**e**) *(throughout)* por; **to travel o. France** viajar por Francia (**f**) **all o.** por todo(a); **all o. the house** por toda la casa; **famous all o. the world** famoso en el mundo entero; *Fig* **to be all o. sb** deshacerse en atenciones con algn (**g**) *(by the agency of)* por; **o. the phone** por teléfono; **o. the radio** por la radio (**h**) *(more than)* más de; **men o. twenty-five** hombres mayores de veinticinco años; **o. a century ago** hace más de un siglo; **o. and above** además de; **o. sixty dollars** más de sesenta dólares (**i**) *(about)* por; **to fight o. sth** pelearse por algo (**j**) *(recovered from)* recuperado(a) de; **he isn't o. the flu yet** aún no se ha repuesto de la gripe *or Am* gripa

2 *adv* (**a**) *(above, across)* **to flow o.** rebosar; **to cross o.** cruzar (la calle) (**b**) *(downwards)* **to fall o.** caerse; **to lean o.** inclinarse (**c**) *(somewhere else)* **o. there** allí *Am* allá; *Rad* **o. to you** corto; **why don't you come o. tomorrow?** ¿por qué no vienes a casa mañana? (**d**) *(throughout)* por; **all o.** en *or* por todas partes; **all the world o.** en el mundo entero; **I ache all o.** me duele todo (**e**) *(more)* más; **children of ten and o.** niños mayores de diez años; **there are about two hundred people or o.** hay unas doscientas personas o más (**f**) *(again)* otra vez; **o. and o. (again)** repetidas veces, una y otra vez; **to do sth o. (again)** volver a hacer algo; **to start all o. again** volver a empezar; **twice o.** dos veces seguidas (**g**) *(in excess)* de más; **it's two ounces o.** pesa dos onzas de más, sobran dos onzas

3 *adj* (**a**) *(finished)* acabado(a), terminado(a); **it's (all) o.** se acabó; **the danger is o.** ha pasado el peligro; **the performance is o.** la función ha terminado; **to get sth o. with** acabar con algo de una vez (**b**) *(remaining)* sobrante; **keep what is left o.** quédate con lo que sobra

4 *n (in cricket)* serie *f* de seis saques

over- ['əʊvə(r)] *pref* sobre-, super-

overact [əʊvər'ækt] *vt & vi Theat* exagerar

overall ['əʊvərɔːl] **1** *adj* total, global; **the o. price** el precio global

2 [əʊvər'ɔːl] *adv (on the whole)* por lo general, en conjunto

overalls ['əʊvərɔːlz] *npl Br (boiler suit)* mono *m* (de trabajo), *Am* overol *m*; *US (dungarees)* peto *m*, *CSur* mameluco *m*

overambitious [əʊvəræm'bɪʃəs] *adj* demasiado ambicioso(a)

overanxious [əʊvər'æŋkʃəs] *adj (too eager)* demasiado *or* excesivamente ansioso(a); **don't get o. about buying the house** no le des tantas vueltas a eso de comprar la casa

overate [əʊvər'eɪt] *pt see* **overeat**

overawe [əʊvər'ɔː] *vt* intimidar; **to be overawed** sobrecogerse

overbalance [əʊvə'bæləns] *vi* perder el equilibrio

overbearing [əʊvə'beərɪŋ] *adj (domineering)* dominante, autoritario(a); *(important)* significativo(a)

overblown [əʊvə'bləʊn] *adj* pomposo(a), exagerado(a)

overboard ['əʊvəbɔːd] *adv* por la borda; **man o.!** ¡hombre al agua!; **to fall o.** caer al agua; *Fam* **to go o.** pasarse; *Fam* **to go o. for sth** chiflarse por algo

overbooking [əʊvə'bʊkɪŋ] *n* overbooking *m*, = venta de más plazas de las disponibles

overburden [əʊvə'bɜːdən] *vt* sobrecargar, agobiar (**with** de)

overcame [əʊvə'keɪm] *pt see* **overcome**

overcast ['əʊvəkɑːst] *adj Meteor* nuboso(a), nublado(a), cubierto(a)

overcharge [əʊvə'tʃɑːdʒ] *vt* (**a**) *(charge too much)* cobrar demasiado (**b**) *(overload)* sobrecargar

overcoat ['əʊvəkəʊt] *n* abrigo *m*

overcome [əʊvə'kʌm] *vt* (*pt* **overcame**; *pp* **overcome**) (**a**) *(conquer)* vencer; **we shall o.** venceremos (**b**) *(overwhelm)* agobiar, abrumar; **he was o. by grief** estaba deshecho por el dolor (**c**) *(surmount)* salvar, superar

overcompensate [əʊvə'kɒmpenseɪt] *vi* **to o. for sth** compensar algo en exceso

overcomplicate [əʊvə'kɒmplɪkeɪt] *vt* complicar en exceso

overconfident [əʊvə'kɒnfɪdənt] *adj* presumido(a), creído(a)

overcook [əʊvə'kʊk] *vt* cocinar demasiado, pasar mucho

overcrowded [əʊvə'kraʊdɪd] *adj (room)* abarrotado(a), atestado(a) (de gente); *(country)* superpoblado(a)

overcrowding [əʊvə'kraʊdɪŋ] *n (of prisons etc)* hacinamiento *m*; *(of country)* superpoblación *f*

overdeveloped [əʊvədɪ'veləpt] *adj* (**a**) *(physique)* hiperdesarrollado(a) (**b**) *Phot* sobrerrevelado(a)

overdevelopment [əʊvədɪ'veləpmənt] *n* desarrollo *m* excesivo

overdo [əʊvə'duː] *vt (pt* **overdid** [əʊvə'dɪd]; *pp* **overdone**) (**a**) *(carry too far)* exagerar; *Fam* **don't o. it** no te pases (**b**) *Culin* cocer *or* asar demasiado

overdone [əʊvə'dʌn] **1** *pp see* **overdo**
2 *adj (meat)* muy hecho(a)

overdose ['əʊvədəʊs] *n* sobredosis *f*

overdraft ['əʊvədrɑːft] *n Fin (draft)* giro *m* en descubierto, sobregiro *m*; *(amount)* saldo *m* deudor

overdraw [əʊvə'drɔː] *vt (pt* **overdrew**; *pp* **overdrawn**) *Fin* girar en descubierto

overdrawn [əʊvə'drɔːn] *adj Fin (account)* en descubierto; **to be overdrawn** *(person)* tener la cuenta en descubierto; **to be $100 o.** tener un descubierto de 100 dólares

overdressed ['əʊvədrest] *adj* demasiado trajeado(a)

overdrew [əʊvə'druː] *pp see* **overdraw**

overdrive ['əʊvədraɪv] *n (in car)* superdirecta *f; Fig* **to go into o.** entregarse a una actividad frenética

overdue [əʊvə'djuː] *adj (rent, train etc)* atrasado(a); *(reform)* largamente esperado(a); *Com* vencido y sin pagar

overeat [əʊvər'iːt] *vi (pt* **overate**; *pp* **overeaten** [əʊər'iːtən]) comer en exceso

overemphasize [əʊvər'emfəsaɪz] *vt* hacer excesivo hincapié en, recalcar en exceso

overenthusiastic [əʊvərɪnθjuːzɪ'æstɪk] *adj* excesivamente entusiasta

overestimate [əʊvər'estɪmeɪt] **1** *vt* sobreestimar
2 [əʊvər'estɪmɪt] *n* sobreestimación *f*

overexcited [əʊvərɪk'saɪtɪd] *adj* demasiado emocionado(a) *or* entusiasmado(a)

overexertion [əʊvərɪg'zɜːʃən] *n* esfuerzo *m* excesivo

overexposure [əʊvərɪks'pəʊʒər] *n Phot* sobreexposición *f*

overextended [əʊvərɪk'stendɪd] *adj Fin* insolvente, con alto grado de pasivo

overfamiliar [əʊvəfə'mɪlɪər] *adj* (**a**) *(too intimate, disrespectful)* confianzudo(a); **to be o. with sb** ser demasiado confianzudo(a) con algn, tomarse demasiadas libertades con algn (**b**) *(conversant)* **I'm not o. with the system** no estoy muy familiarizado con el sistema

overfeed [əʊvə'fiːd] *vt (pt & pp* **overfed** [əʊvə'fed]) sobrealimentar

overflew [əʊvə'fluː] *pt see* **overfly**

overflow 1 [əʊvə'fləʊ] **1** *vi (river)* desbordarse; *(cup etc)* derramarse; *Fig* **to o. with joy** rebosar de alegría
2 ['əʊvəfləʊ] *n* (**a**) *(of river etc)* desbordamiento *m*; *(smaller)* derrame *m* ❑ **o. pipe** cañería *f* de desagüe (**b**) *Fig* exceso *m* ❑ **o. meeting** reunión *f* suplementaria; **population o.** exceso *m* de población (**c**) *Comptr* desbordamiento *m*

overfly [əʊvə'flaɪ] *vt (pt* **overflew**; *pp* **overflown** [əʊvə'fləʊn]) sobrevolar

overgrown ['əʊvəgrəʊn] *adj* (**a**) *(with grass etc)* cubierto(a) (de hierba) (**b**) *(in size)* demasiado grande

overhang [əʊvə'hæŋ] **1** *vt (pt & pp* **overhung**) *(project over)* sobresalir por encima de; *(hang over)* colgar por encima de
2 *n* ['əʊvəhæŋ] proyección *f*

overhanging ['əʊvəhæŋɪŋ] *adj (ledge, balcony)* sobresaliente; **we walked under the o. branches** caminamos bajo las crecidas ramas de los árboles

overhaul 1 [əʊvə'hɔːl] **1** *vt (machine, policy)* revisar
2 ['əʊvəhɔːl] *n (of machine, policy)* revisión *f*

overhead 1 [əʊvə'hed] **1** *adj* (por) encima de la cabeza; **o. cable** cable *m* aéreo
2 [əʊvə'hed] *adv* arriba, por encima de la cabeza
3 *n, US Com see* **overheads**

overheads ['əʊvəhedz] *npl Br Com* gastos *mpl* generales *or* indirectos

overhear [əʊvə'hɪər] *vt (pt & pp* **overheard** [əʊvə'hɜːd]) oír por casualidad *or* sin querer

overheat [əʊvə'hiːt] *vi* recalentarse, calentarse demasiado

overheated [əʊvə'hiːtɪd] *adj (engine, economy)* recalentado(a); *Fig (argument, person)* acalorado(a), agitado(a)

overhung [əʊvə'hʌŋ] *pt & pp see* **overhang**

overindulge [əʊvərɪn'dʌldʒ] **1** *vt (child)* consentir; **to o. oneself** *(drink, eat to excess)* atiborrarse, empacharse
2 *vi* atiborrarse, empacharse

overindulgent [əʊvərɪn'dʌldʒənt] *adj* (**a**) *(towards person)* demasiado indulgente (**b**) *(in food and drink)* **an o. weekend** un fin de semana de excesos

overjoyed [əʊvə'dʒɔɪd] *adj* rebosante de alegría; **he was o.** no cabía en sí de contento

overkill ['əʊvəkɪl] *n* **there's a danger of o.** se corre el peligro de caer en el exceso; **media o.** *(on TV, in newspapers)* cobertura *f* informativa exagerada

overland ['əʊvəlænd] *adj & adv* por tierra

overlap [əʊvə'læp] **1** *vi (pt & pp* **overlapped**) superponerse; *Fig* **our plans o.** nuestros planes coinciden parcialmente
2 *n (of planks, tiles)* superposición *f; Fig* coincidencia *f*

overleaf [əʊvə'liːf] *adv* al dorso; **see o.** véase al dorso

overload 1 [əʊvə'ləʊd] **1** *vt* sobrecargar
2 *n* sobrecarga *f*

overlong [əʊvə'lɒŋ] *adj* demasiado largo(a)

overlook [əʊvə'lʊk] *vt* (**a**) *(fail to notice)* pasar por alto, dejar pasar; **to o. an error** dejar pasar un error (**b**) *(ignore)* no hacer caso de; **we'll o. it this time** esta vez haremos la vista gorda (**c**) *(have a view of)* dar a, tener vista a; **the house overlooks the park** la casa da al parque (**d**) *(supervise) (job)* supervisar; *(person)* vigilar

overly ['əʊvəlɪ] *adv* demasiado; **I'm not o. impressed** no estoy del todo convencido

overmanning [əʊvə'mænɪŋ] *n Ind* exceso *m* de empleados

overmuch [əʊvə'mʌtʃ] *adv* en exceso

overnight [əʊvə'naɪt] **1** *adv* (**a**) *(during the night)* por la noche; **we stayed there o.** pasamos la noche allí; **will this meat keep o.?** ¿se conservará esta carne hasta mañana? (**b**) *(suddenly)* de la noche a la mañana
2 ['əʊvənaɪt] *adj* (**a**) *(of one night)* de (una) noche; **o. bag** bolsa de viaje; **o. journey** viaje de noche; **o. stay** *Esp Méx* estancia *or Am* estadía *f* de una (sola) noche (**b**) *(sudden)* repentino(a); **to be an o. success** saltar a la fama de la noche a la mañana

overpaid [əʊvə'peɪd] *pt & pp see* **overpay**

overpass ['əʊvəpæs] *n US Aut* paso *m* elevado

overpay [əʊvə'peɪ] *vt* (*pt & pp* **overpaid**) pagar demasiado

overpopulation [əʊvəpɒpjʊ'leɪʃən] *n* superpoblación *f*

overpower [əʊvə'paʊər] *vt* (**a**) *(subdue)* vencer, dominar (**b**) *(affect strongly)* sofocar, abrumar, agobiar

overpowering [əʊvə'paʊərɪŋ] *adj* *(emotion, heat)* tremendo(a), desmesurado(a); *(smell, taste)* fortísimo(a), intensísimo(a); *(desire)* irrefrenable, irreprimible

overpriced [əʊvə'praɪst] *adj* excesivamente caro(a)

overproduce [əʊvəprə'djuːs] *vt* producir en exceso

overproduction [əʊvəprə'dʌkʃən] *n* superproducción *f*

overqualified [əʊvə'kwɒlɪfaɪd] *adj* **to be o. (for a job)** tener más títulos de los necesarios (para un trabajo)

overran [əʊvə'ræn] *pt see* **overrun**

overrate [əʊvə'reɪt] *vt* sobreestimar, supervalorar; **an overrated restaurant** un restaurante que no merece la buena fama que tiene

overrated [əʊvə'reɪtɪd] *adj* sobrevalorado(a)

overreach [əʊvə'riːtʃ] *vt* **to o. oneself** extralimitarse

overreact [əʊvərɪ'ækt] *vi* reaccionar exageradamente

override [əʊvə'raɪd] *vt* (*pt* **overrode**; *pp* **overridden** [əʊvə'rɪdən]) (**a**) *(disregard)* hacer caso omiso de, no tener en cuenta (**b**) *(annul)* invalidar, anular (**c**) *(be more important than)* contar más que

overriding [əʊvə'raɪdɪŋ] *adj* *(importance)* primordial; *(belief, consideration, factor)* preponderante

overrode [əʊvə'rəʊd] *pt see* **override**

overrule [əʊvə'ruːl] *vt* invalidar, descalificar; *Jur* denegar

overrun [əʊvə'rʌn] **1** *vt* (*pt* **overran**; *pp* **overrun**) (**a**) *(invade)* invadir; **a garden o. with weeds** un jardín invadido por la mala hierba (**b**) *(extend beyond)* exceder, rebasar
2 *vi* rebasar el tiempo previsto

oversaw [əʊvə'sɔː] *pt see* **oversee**

overseas [əʊvə'siːz] **1** *adv* fuera del país; **to go o.** ir al extranjero; **to live o.** vivir en el extranjero
2 ['əʊvəsiːz] *adj* *(visitor)* extranjero(a); *(trade, debt)* exterior; *(travel)* al extranjero; **our o. office** nuestra sucursal en el extranjero

oversee [əʊvə'siː] *vt* (*pt* **oversaw**; *pp* **overseen** [əʊvə-'siːn]) supervisar

overseer ['əʊvəsiːər] *n* *(gen)* supervisor(a) *m,f*; *(foreman)* capataz *m*

overshadow [əʊvə'ʃædəʊ] *vt* *Fig* hacer sombra a, eclipsar

overshoot [əʊvə'ʃuːt] *vt* (*pt & pp* **overshot** [əʊvə'ʃɒt]) *Aut* **to o. a turning** pasarse un cruce; *Av* **to o. the runway** *(in the air)* aterrizar más allá de la pista; *(on land)* quedarse demasiado tiempo en la pista; *Fig* **to o. the mark** pasarse de la raya

oversight ['əʊvəsaɪt] *n* descuido *m*; **through o.** por descuido

oversimplify [əʊvə'sɪmplɪfaɪ] *vt* (*pt & pp* **oversimplified**) simplificar demasiado

oversize(d) [əʊvə'saɪz(d)] *adj* demasiado grande

oversleep [əʊvə'sliːp] *vi* (*pt & pp* **overslept** [əʊvə'slept]) dormirse, no despertar a tiempo

overspend [əʊvə'spend] *vi* (*pt & pp* **overspent** [əʊvə'spent]) gastar demasiado *or* más de la cuenta

overspill ['əʊvəspɪl] *n Br (population)* exceso *m* de población

overstaffing [əʊvə'stɑːfɪŋ] *n* exceso *m* de personal

overstate [əʊvə'steɪt] *vt* exagerar

overstatement [əʊvə'steɪtmənt] *n* exageración *f*

overstay [əʊvə'steɪ] *vt* **to o. one's welcome** abusar de la hospitalidad, quedarse más tiempo del apropiado

overstep [əʊvə'step] *vt* (*pt & pp* **overstepped**) pasar de; *Fig* **to o. the mark** pasarse de la raya

oversubscribed [əʊvəsəb'skraɪbd] *adj Fin* **the share offer was (five times) o.** la demanda superó (en cinco veces) la oferta de venta de acciones

overt ['əʊvɜːt, əʊ'vɜːt] *adj* (**a**) *(observable)* manifiesto(a), patente (**b**) *Jur (deliberate)* abierto(a)

overtake [əʊvə'teɪk] *vt* (*pt* **overtook**; *pp* **overtaken** [əʊvə'teɪkən]) (**a**) *Br Aut* adelantar, *SAm* rebasar (**b**) *(pass)* adelantarse a; *(surpass)* superar a (**c**) *(catch unawares)* sorprender (**d**) *(catch up with)* alcanzar

overtax [əʊvə'tæks] *vt* (**a**) *Fin* gravar en exceso (**b**) *Fig* exigir demasiado a

over-the-counter [əʊvəðə'kaʊntər] *adj Pharm* **o.-t.-c. drugs** = medicamentos que se pueden adquirir sin receta médica

overthrow [əʊvə'θrəʊ] *vt* (*pt* **overthrew** [əʊvə'θruː]; *pp* **overthrown** [əʊvə'θrəʊn]) *(government etc)* derribar, derrocar; *(project)* enervar, destruir

overtime [əʊvə'taɪm] **1** *n* (**a**) *(work)* horas *fpl* extras (**b**) *US Sport* prórroga *f*
2 *adv* **to work o.** hacer horas extras

overtly [əʊ'vɜːtlɪ] *adv* abiertamente

overtone ['əʊvətəʊn] *n* insinuación *f*, alusión *f*

overtook [əʊvə'tʊk] *pt see* **overtake**

overture ['əʊvətjʊər] *n* (**a**) *Mus* obertura *f* (**b**) *(proposal)* propuesta *f*; **peace overtures** propuestas de paz (**c**) *(introduction)* introducción *f*

overturn [əʊvə'tɜːn] **1** *vt* *(car etc)* volcar; *(boat)* hacer zozobrar
2 *vi* *(car etc)* volcar; *(boat)* zozobrar

overview ['əʊvəvjuː] *n* visión *f* general

overweight [əʊvə'weɪt] *adj* demasiado pesado(a); **to be o.** *(gen)* pesar demasiado; *(person)* estar gordo(a); **he's five pounds o.** pesa cinco libras de más

overwhelm [əʊvə'welm] *vt* (**a**) *(overcome)* aplastar, arrollar; *(overpower)* abrumar; **to be overwhelmed with joy** rebosar de alegría; **we were overwhelmed by the news** nos quedamos de piedra al saber la noticia (**b**) *(cover over)* inundar, sumergir

overwhelming [əʊvə'welmɪŋ] *adj (defeat)* aplastante, arrollador(a); *(desire etc)* irresistible; **o. majority** mayoría *f* aplastante

overwork [əʊvə'wɜːk] **1** *vi* trabajar demasiado
2 *vt* *(person)* forzar, hacer trabajar demasiado; *(excuse etc)* abusar de

overworked [əʊvə'wɜːkt] *adj* forzado(a); **an o. expression** una expresión muy gastada

overwrite ['əʊvəraɪt] *Comptr* **1** *n* **o. mode** función *f* de 'sobreescribir'
2 [əʊvə'raɪt] *vt* (*pt* **overwrote** [əʊvə'rəʊt]; *pp* **overwritten** [əʊvə'rɪtən]) sobreescribir

overwrought [əʊvə'rɔːt] *adj* (**a**) *(tense)* muy nervioso(a), con los nervios crispados (**b**) *(too elaborate)* forzado(a)

overzealous [əʊvə'zeləs] *adj* demasiado celoso(a)

ovulate ['ɒvjʊleɪt] *vi* ovular

ovulation [ɒvjʊ'leɪʃən] *n* ovulación *f*

ovum ['əʊvəm] *n (pl* **ova**) *Biol* óvulo *m*

ow [aʊ] *interj* ¡ay!

owe [əʊ] *vt* deber; **I o. my life to you** te debo la vida; **I still o. you for the gasoline** aún te debo lo de la gasolina; **she owes her fortune to hard work** se ha hecho rica a base de trabajar duro

owing ['əʊɪŋ] *adj* (**a**) *(due)* **the money o. to me** el dinero que se me debe (**b**) **o. to** debido a, a causa de; **o. to the rain** a causa de la lluvia

owl [aʊl] *n* (**a**) *Orn* lechuza *f*, búho *m* ❑ **barn o.** lechuza *f* común; **eagle o.** búho *m* real; **little o.** mochuelo *m* común (**b**) *Fig* **night o.** ave *f* nocturna

owlet ['aʊlɪt] *n Orn* mochuelo *m*

own [əʊn] **1** *adj* propio(a); **his o. money** su propio dinero; **in my o. time** en mi tiempo libre; **it's his o. fault** es culpa suya; **she makes all her o. clothes** se hace toda la ropa ella misma

2 *pron* (**a**) **my/your/his/***etc* **o.** lo mío/tuyo/suyo/*etc*; **for reasons of her o.** por razones personales; **he has a copy of his o.** tiene su propio ejemplar; **the house is my o.** la casa es mía; **this fruit has a flavour all its o.** esta fruta tiene un sabor inconfundible; *Fig* **he can hold his o.** se defiende, sabe defenderse; *Fig* **to come into one's o.** *(fulfil oneself)* realizarse; *(receive recognition)* ser reconocido(a); *Fam* **to get one's o. back** vengarse, tomarse la revancha (**b**) **on one's o.** *(without help)* uno(a) mismo(a); *(alone)* solo(a); **he did it on his o.** lo hizo él mismo; **I was left on my o.** me dejaron solo

3 *vt* poseer, ser dueño(a) de; **he owns three newspapers** es propietario de tres periódicos; **who owns this plot of land?** ¿a quién pertenece esta parcela?

own up *vt* **to o. up (to)** confesar, admitir; **to o. up to a mistake** reconocer un error

own-brand ['əʊn'brænd] *adj Br Com* = de la marca del supermercado que vende el producto

owner ['əʊnər] *n* propietario(a) *m,f*, dueño(a) *m,f*, poseedor(a) *m,f*; **'cars parked here at owners' risk'** 'estacionamiento *or Esp* aparcamiento permitido bajo responsabilidad del propietario' ❑ **joint o.** copropietario(a) *m,f*

owner-occupier ['əʊnər'ɒkjʊpaɪər] *n Br* propietario(a) *m,f* de la vivienda que habita

ownership ['əʊnəʃɪp] *n* propiedad *f*, posesión *f*; **under new o.** bajo nueva dirección

own-label ['əʊn'leɪbəl] *adj Com* del establecimiento; **o. product** producto *m* de marca blanca

ox [ɒks] *n (pl* **oxen**) buey *m*

oxcart ['ɒkskɑːt] *n* carro *m* de bueyes

oxen ['ɒksən] *npl see* **ox**

Oxfam ['ɒksfæm] *n (abbr* **Oxford Committee for Famine Relief**) OXFAM, = organización caritativa benéfica de ayuda al desarrollo

oxide ['ɒksaɪd] *n Chem* óxido *m*

oxidize ['ɒksɪdaɪz] **1** *vt* oxidar

2 *vi* oxidarse

Oxon ['ɒksən] *(abbr* **Oxoniensis**) (of Oxford University), de (la Universidad de) Oxford

oxtail ['ɒksteɪl] *n* rabo *m* de buey

oxyacetylene [ɒksɪə'setɪliːn] *n Chem* oxiacetileno *m* ❑ **o. torch** soplete *m* oxiacetilénico; **o. welding** soldadura *f* oxiacetilénica

oxygen ['ɒksɪdʒən] *n Chem* oxígeno *m* ❑ **o. mask** máscara *f* de oxígeno

oxymoron [ɒksɪ'mɔːrɒn] *n* oxímoron *m*, = figura del lenguaje consistente en yuxtaponer dos palabras aparentemente contradictorias

oyster ['ɔɪstər] *n (fish)* ostra *f*; **the o. industry** la industria ostrícola ❑ **o. bed, o. farm** criadero *m* de ostras; **o. pink** *(colour)* rosa *m* salmón

oystercatcher ['ɔɪstəkætʃər] *n Orn* ostrero *m*

oz *(pl* **oz** *or* **ozs**) *(abbr* **ounce(s)**) onza(s) *f(pl)*, oz *f*

ozone-friendly ['əʊzəʊn'frendlɪ] *adj* no perjudicial para la capa de ozono

P

P, p [piː] *n (the letter)* P, p *f*; *Fam* **to mind one's p's and q's** andar con cuidado

P *Aut (abbr* **Parking)** aparcamiento *m*, P

p (**a**) *(abbr* **page)** *(pl* **pp)** página *f*, pág., p. (**b**) [piː] *Br Fam (abbr* **penny, pence)** penique(s) *m(pl)*

PA [piːˈeɪ] *n* (**a**) *Fam (abbr* **personal assistant)** ayudante *mf* personal (**b**) *(abbr* **Press Association)** = asociación nacional de prensa (**c**) *(abbr* **public-address (system))** megafonía *f*, sistema *m* de altavoces

p.a. *(abbr* **per annum)** al año

PAC [piːˈeɪˈsiː] *n US Pol (abbr* **Political Action Committee)** = grupo de presión estadounidense para el apoyo de causas políticas

pace [peɪs] **1** *n* (**a**) *(step)* paso *m*; *(speed)* marcha *f*, velocidad *f*, ritmo *m*; **at a brisk p.** a buen paso; **20 paces away** a 20 pasos; **to keep p. with** seguir a; *Fig* avanzar al mismo ritmo que; **to quicken one's p.** acelerar el paso; **to set the p.** marcar el paso a; *Fig* marcar la pauta

2 *vt* (**a**) *(room, floor)* ir de un lado a otro de (**b**) *(runner)* marcar el paso a

3 *vi* **to p. up and down** ir de un lado a otro

pacemaker [ˈpeɪsmeɪkər] *n* (**a**) *Sport* liebre *f* (**b**) *Med* marcapasos *m inv*

Pacific [pəˈsɪfɪk] *adj* **the P. (Ocean)** el (océano) Pacífico

pacifier [ˈpæsɪfaɪər] *n US* chupete *m*

pacifism [ˈpæsɪfɪzəm] *n* pacifismo *m*

pacifist [ˈpæsɪfɪst] *adj & n* pacifista *(mf)*

pacify [ˈpæsɪfaɪ] *vt (pt & pp* **pacified)** *(person)* calmar, tranquilizar; *(country)* pacificar

pack¹ [pæk] **1** *n* (**a**) *(parcel)* paquete *m*; *(bundle)* bulto *m*; *(rucksack)* mochila *f*; *(on animal)* albarda *f*; *Fam* **to tell a p. of lies** contar una sarta de mentiras ◻ **p. ice** banco *m* de hielo (**b**) *US (of cigarettes)* paquete *m*, cajetilla *f* (**c**) *Br (of cards)* baraja *f* (**d**) *(of thieves)* banda *f*; *(of wolves, dogs)* manada *f*; *(of hounds)* jauría *f* (**e**) *Med* emplasto *m*, compresa *f*; **face** *or* **mud p.** mascarilla *f* (de lodo)

2 *vt* (**a**) *(goods)* embalar, envasar, empaquetar; **packed lunch** comida *f* fría para llevar (**b**) *(things in suitcase)* poner; **to p. one's bags** hacer las maletas; *Fig* marcharse (**c**) *(fill)* atestar, llenar; *(people)* meter; **the room was packed** la sala estaba abarrotada; *Fig* **to be packed in like sardines** estar apretados como sardinas (**d**) *(press down)* *(snow, soil)* apretar (**e**) *Fam Box* **to p. a hard punch** pegar duro; *Fig* jugar fuerte

3 *vi* (**a**) *(prepare baggage)* hacer las maletas or el equipaje; *Fam* **to send sb packing** mandar a paseo a algn (**b**) *(people)* apiñarse, apretarse (**into** en)

pack in *vt Fam* (**a**) *(give up)* dejar; **p. it in!** ¡déjalo ya! (**b**) *(pull in)* atraer; **the show is really packing them in** este espectáculo atrae a muchísimas personas

pack off *vt Fam* enviar, mandar; **to p. a child off to bed** mandar a un niño a la cama

pack up 1 *vt* (**a**) *(belongings)* meter en la maleta (**b**) *(give up)* dejar; **she's packed up smoking** ha dejado de fumar, ya no fuma

2 *vi Fam* (**a**) *(stop working)* terminar (**b**) *(machine etc)* estropearse, *Esp* escacharrarse, *Méx* desconchinflarse, *RP* hacerse bolsa

pack² [pæk] *vt (meeting, jury)* amañar, llenar de partidarios

package [ˈpækɪdʒ] **1** *n* (**a**) *(parcel)* paquete *m*; *(bundle)* bulto *m* ◻ *Fig* **p. holiday, p. tour** viaje *m* organizado todo incluido (**b**) *(of proposals etc)* paquete *m*; *(agreement)* acuerdo *m*, convenio *m* ◻ **p. deal** convenio *m* general

2 *vt (goods)* envasar, embalar

packaging [ˈpækɪdʒɪŋ] *n* envase *m*, embalaje *m*

packed [pækt] *adj* (**a**) *(crowded)* abarrotado(a) (**b**) **p. lunch** comida *f* preparada de casa *(para excursión, trabajo, colegio)*

packer [ˈpækər] *n* empaquetador(a) *m,f*, embalador(a) *m,f*

packet [ˈpækɪt] *n* (**a**) *(box)* cajita *f*, paquete *m*; *(of cigarettes)* cajetilla *f*; *(bag)* bolsa *f*; *(envelope)* sobre *m* (**b**) *Fam (fortune)* dineral *m*; **to cost a p.** costar un riñón *or* un ojo de la cara; **to make a p.** ganar una millonada *or Méx* un chorro de lana *or RP* una ponchada de guita

packhorse [ˈpækhɔːs] *n* caballo *m* de carga

packing [ˈpækɪŋ] *n* envase *m*, embalaje *m*; **p. case** caja *f* de embalar; **to do one's p.** hacer las maletas

pact [pækt] *n* pacto *m*; **to make a p. with sb** pactar con algn

pad¹ [pæd] **1** *n* (**a**) *(gen)* almohadilla *f*, cojinete *m*; *(of brake)* zapata *f*; *(filling)* relleno *m* ◻ **knee p.** rodillera *f*; **sanitary p.** compresa *f*; **shin p.** espinillera *f*; **shoulder p.** hombrera *f* (**b**) *(of paper)* bloc *m*, taco *m* ◻ **blotting p.** papel *m* secante; **writing p.** bloc *m* de cartas (**c**) *(platform)* plataforma *f* ◻ **launch p.** plataforma *f* de lanzamiento (**d**) *Zool Anat* almohadilla *f* (**e**) *Bot (large leaf)* hoja *f* grande (**f**) *Fam* casa *f*, piso *m*; **bachelor p.** piso de soltero

2 *vt (pt & pp* **padded)** *(chair, wall)* rellenar, acolchar; *(shoulders of garment)* poner hombreras a

pad out *vt Fig (speech etc)* meter paja en

pad² [pæd] *vi (pt & pp* **padded)** **to p. about** *or* **around** andar sin hacer ruido

padded [ˈpædɪd] *adj (shoulders of garment)* con hombreras; *(cell)* acolchado(a)

padding [ˈpædɪŋ] *n* (**a**) *(material)* relleno *m*, acolchado *m* (**b**) *Fig (in speech etc)* paja *f*

paddle¹ [ˈpædəl] **1** *n (oar)* pala *f*, remo *m*, canalete *m*; *Tech (blade on wheel)* alabe *m*, paleta *f*; *US (for table tennis)* pala *f* ◻ **p. boat** *or* **steamer** vapor *m* de ruedas

2 *vt (boat, canoe)* remar con pala *or* canalete en; *Fig* **to p. one's own canoe** arreglárselas solo(a)
3 *vi (in boat)* remar con pala *or* canalete
paddle² ['pædəl] **1** *vi* chapotear, mojarse los pies
2 *n* chapoteo *m*; **to go for** *or* **have a p.** chapotear, mojarse los pies
paddling pool ['pædəlɪŋpu:l] *n* piscina *for Méx* alberca *f or RP* pileta *f* para niños
paddock ['pædək] *n (field)* potrero *m*; *(in race course)* paddock *m*
Paddy ['pædɪ] *n Fam* irlandés *m*
paddy ['pædɪ] *n* arrozal *m*
padlock ['pædlɒk] **1** *n* candado *m*
2 *vt* cerrar con candado
padre ['pɑːdrɪ] *n Mil Fam* capellán *m*
paediatric [piːdɪ'ætrɪk] *adj* pediátrico(a)
paediatrician [piːdɪə'trɪʃən] *n* pediatra *mf*
paediatrics [piːdɪ'ætrɪks] *n* pediatría *f*
paedophile ['piːdəʊfaɪl] *n* pedófilo(a) *m,f*
paedophilia [piːdə'fɪlɪə] *n* pederastia *f*
pagan ['peɪgən] *adj & n* pagano(a) *(m,f)*
page¹ [peɪdʒ] **1** *n* **(a)** *(servant, at wedding)* paje *m*; *(of knight)* escudero *m* **(b)** *(at club)* botones *m inv*
2 *vt (call)* llamar por altavoz
page² [peɪdʒ] *n (of book)* página *f*; *(of newspaper)* plana *f*; **front p. news** noticias *fpl* de primera plana; **on p. six** en la página seis
pageant ['pædʒənt] *n (show)* espectáculo *m*; *(procession)* desfile *m*; *(on horses)* cabalgata *f*
pageantry ['pædʒəntrɪ] *n* pompa *f*, boato *m*
pageboy ['peɪdʒbɔɪ] *n* **(a)** *(servant, at wedding)* paje *m*; *(hairstyle)* **p. (haircut)** peinado *m* estilo paje **(b)** *(in hotel)* botones *m inv*
pager ['peɪdʒər] *n* buscapersonas *m inv, Esp* busca *m, Méx* localizador *m, RP* radiomensaje *m*
pagoda [pə'gəʊdə] *n* pagoda *f*
paid [peɪd] **1** *pt & pp see* **pay**
2 *adj* pagado(a); *Fig* **to put p. to sth** acabar con algo
paid-up [peɪd'ʌp] *adj, US* **paid-in** [peɪd'ɪn] *adj (member)* que ha pagado las cuotas
pail [peɪl] *n (gen)* cubo *m*; *(child's)* cubito *m*
pain [peɪn] **1** *n* **(a)** *(gen)* dolor *m*; *(grief)* sufrimiento *m*; **a severe p.** un dolor agudo; **aches and pains** achaques *mpl*; **I have a p. in my chest** me duele el pecho; **to be in great p.** sufrir mucho; **where is the p.?** ¿dónde te duele?; *Fam* **he's a p. (in the neck)** es un plomazo *or* pelmazo *or Méx* sangrón **(b)** *(punishment)* pena *f*; **on p. of death** so pena de muerte **(c)** **pains** esfuerzos *mpl*, esmero *m sing*; **to take p. over sth** esforzarse *or* esmerarse en algo
2 *vt (gen)* doler; *(grieve)* dar pena a, apenar; **it pains me to see her like this** me da pena verla así
pained [peɪnd] *adj* afligido(a), disgustado(a), ofendido(a)
painful ['peɪnfʊl] *adj* **(a)** *(physically)* doloroso(a), dolorido(a); *(mentally)* angustioso(a), que da pena; **it's my p. duty to tell you** es mi doloroso deber decírselo; **it's p. to watch them** da pena verles **(b)** *Fam (very bad)* malísimo(a), pésimo(a)
painfully ['peɪnfʊlɪ] *adv* **(a)** *(with pain)* dolorosamente, con dolor; **p. shy** lastimosamente tímido(a) **(b)** *Fam* lamentablemente, terriblemente
painkiller ['peɪnkɪlər] *n* analgésico *m*, calmante *m*
painless ['peɪnlɪs] *adj (childbirth)* indoloro(a), sin dolor; *Fig* sin esfuerzos or dificultades
painlessly ['peɪnlɪslɪ] *adv* sin causar dolor; *Fig* sin hacer esfuerzos

painstaking ['peɪnzteɪkɪŋ] *adj (person)* cuidadoso(a), concienzudo(a); *(care, research)* esmerado(a)
paint [peɪnt] **1** *n* pintura *f*; **coat of p.** capa *f* de pintura; **'wet paint'** 'recién pintado' ❑ **p. remover** quitapinturas *m inv*; **p. spray** pistola *f* (de pintar)
2 *vt* pintar; **to p. one's face** pintarse la cara; **to p. sth white** pintar algo de blanco; *Fig* **he isn't as black as he is painted** no es tan fiero el león como lo pintan; *Fig* **to p. the town red** irse de juerga
3 *vi* pintar, ser pintor(a)
paintball ['peɪntbɔːl] *n* paintball *m*, juegos *mpl* de guerra con pintura
paintbox ['peɪntbɒks] *n* caja *f* de pinturas
paintbrush ['peɪntbrʌʃ] *n Art* pincel *m*; *(for walls)* brocha *f*
painter¹ ['peɪntər] *n Art* pintor(a) *m,f*; *(decorator)* pintor(a) *m,f* (de brocha gorda)
painter² ['peɪntər] *n Naut* amarra *f*
painting ['peɪntɪŋ] *n Art (picture)* pintura *f*, cuadro *m*; *(activity)* pintura *f*; **oil p.** pintura al óleo; **p. and decorating** (pintura y) decoración *f* del hogar; **she likes p.** le gusta pintar
paint-stripper ['peɪntstrɪpər] *n* quitapinturas *f inv*
paintwork ['peɪntwɜːk] *n* pintura *f*
pair [peər] **1** *n (of gloves, socks, shoes)* par *m*; *(of people, cards)* pareja *f*; **a p. of scissors** unas tijeras; **a p. of pyjamas** un pijama; **a p. of trousers** un pantalón, unos pantalones; **to make a p.** hacer juego *or* pareja
2 *vt (animals)* aparear; *(people)* emparejar
3 *vi (animals)* aparearse; *(people)* emparejarse, formar pareja
pair off 1 *vt* emparejar
2 *vi* emparejarse, formar pareja (**with** con)
pajamas [pə'dʒæməz] *npl US see* **pyjamas**
Pakistan [pɑːkɪ'stɑːn] *n* Paquistán, Pakistán
Pakistani [pɑːkɪ'stɑːnɪ] *adj & n* paquistaní *(mf)*, pakistaní *(mf)*
PAL [pæl] *n TV (abbr* **phase alternation line)** (sistema *m)* PAL *m*
pal [pæl] *n Fam* amiguete(a) *m,f, Esp* colega *mf*
palace ['pælɪs] *n* palacio *m*
palatable ['pælətəbəl] *adj (tasty)* sabroso(a); *Fig (acceptable)* aceptable
palatal ['pælətəl] *adj & n* palatal *(f)*
palate ['pælɪt] *n* paladar *m*
palatial [pə'leɪʃəl] *adj* magnífico(a), suntuoso(a)
palaver [pə'lɑːvər] *n Br Fam* lío *m, Esp* follón *m*; **what a p.!** ¡qué lío *or Esp* follón!
pale¹ [peɪl] **1** *adj (complexion, skin)* pálido(a); *(colour)* claro(a); *(light)* débil, tenue; **to go** *or* **turn p.** ponerse pálido(a), palidecer ❑ *Br* **p. ale** cerveza *f* rubia
2 *vi* palidecer
pale² [peɪl] *n* estaca *f*; *Fig* **to be beyond the p.** ser inaceptable
paleness ['peɪlnɪs] *n* palidez *f*
Palestine ['pælɪstaɪn] *n* Palestina
Palestinian [pælɪ'stɪnɪən] *adj & n* palestino(a) *(m,f)*
palette ['pælɪt] *n* paleta *f* ❑ **p. knife** espátula *f*
paling ['peɪlɪŋ] *n* estacada *f*, valla *f*
palisade [pælɪ'seɪd] *n* **(a)** *(fence)* palizada *f*, estacada *f* **(b)** *US* **palisades** *(cliffs)* acantilado *m sing*
pall¹ [pɔːl] *n (on coffin)* paño *m* mortuorio; *Fig (covering)* manto *m*; *(of smoke)* cortina *f*
pall² [pɔːl] *vi* dejar de gustar, cansar, aburrir; **it never palls** nunca cansa

pallbearer ['pɔːlbeərər] *n* portador(a) *m,f* del féretro

pallet ['pælɪt] *n* (**a**) *Tech* plataforma *f* de carga (**b**) *(bed)* jergón *m*

palliative ['pælɪətɪv] *n* paliativo *m*

pallid ['pælɪd] *adj* pálido(a)

pallor ['pælər] *n* palidez *f*

pally ['pælɪ] *adj* (**pallier, palliest**) amigo(a); **to be p. with sb** ser amigo(a) de algn; **we're very p.** somos muy amigos

palm¹ [pɑːm] *n Bot (tree)* palmera *f*; *(leaf, branch)* palma *f* ❑ **coconut p.** cocotero *m*; **date p.** palma *f* datilera; **P. Sunday** domingo *m* de Ramos

palm² [pɑːm] *n Anat* palma *f*; **to read sb's p.** leer la mano a algn; *Fig* **to have sb in the p. of one's hand** tener a algn en la palma de la mano; *Fam* **to grease sb's p.** untar la mano a algn

palm off *vt* **to p. sth off onto sb** colocar *or* endosar algo a algn

palmist ['pɑːmɪst] *n* quiromántico(a) *m,f*

palmistry ['pɑːmɪstrɪ] *n* quiromancia *f*

palmtop ['pɑːmtɒp] *n Comptr* palmtop *m*, asistente *m* personal

palpable ['pælpəbəl] *adj* palpable

palpate ['pælpeɪt] *vt Med* palpar

palpitate ['pælpɪteɪt] *vi* palpitar

palpitation [pælpɪ'teɪʃən] *n* palpitación *f*

paltry ['pɔːltrɪ] *adj* (**paltrier, paltriest**) insignificante

pampas ['pæmpəz] *npl Geog* pampa *f sing*

pamper ['pæmpər] *vt* mimar, consentir

pamphlet ['pæmflɪt] *n* folleto *m*

pan¹ [pæn] **1** *n* (**a**) *(saucepan)* cazuela *f*, cacerola *f*; *Fam* **pots and pans** batería *f sing* (de cocina) ❑ **frying p.** sartén *f* (**b**) *(of scales)* platillo *m* (**c**) *Br (of lavatory)* taza *f*
2 *vt (pt & pp* **panned**) (**a**) *(gold)* lavar con batea (**b**) *Fam (criticize)* vapulear, *Esp* poner por los suelos
3 *vt* extraer oro

pan out *vi (turn out)* salir; *(be successful)* salir bien

pan² [pæn] *vt & vi (pt & pp* **panned**) *Cin* tomar vistas panorámicas

pan- [pæn] *pref* pan; **pan-American** panamericano(a)

panacea [pænə'sɪə] *n* panacea *f*

panache [pə'næʃ] *n* garbo *m*, salero *m*

Panama ['pænəmɑː] *n* Panamá; **P. Canal** Canal *m* de Panamá

panama ['pænəmɑː] *n* **p. (hat)** panamá *m*

Panamanian [pænə'meɪnɪən] *adj & n* panameño(a) *(m,f)*

pancake ['pænkeɪk] *n Culin* crepe *f* ❑ **P. Day** martes *m* de carnaval; *Av* **p. landing** aterrizaje *m* de emergencia

panchromatic [pænkrəʊ'mætɪk] *adj* pancromático(a)

pancreas ['pæŋkrɪəs] *n Anat* páncreas *m*

panda ['pændə] *n Zool* panda *m* ❑ *Br* **p. car** coche *m* or *Am* carro *m* or *CSur* auto *m* patrulla

pandemic [pæn'demɪk] *n Med* pandemia *f*

pandemonium [pændɪ'məʊnɪəm] *n* jaleo *m*, desmadre *m*; **there was p.** había mucho jaleo

pander ['pændər] *vi (to person)* consentir (**to** a), complacer (**to** a); *(to wishes)* acceder (**to** a)

pandora [pæn'dɔːrə] *n (fish)* pagel *m*

p & p [piːən'piː] *Br Com (abbr* **(cost of) postage and packing)** gastos *mpl* de embalaje y envío

pane [peɪn] *n* vidrio *m*, *Esp* cristal *m*

panel ['pænəl] *n* (**a**) *(of wall, door)* panel *m*; *(flat surface)* tablero *m*, tabla *f*; *(of instruments)* tablero *m*; *(of ceiling)* artesón *m* ❑ *Aut* **p. beater** planchista *mf*; **p. pin** clavo *m* or

alfiler *m* de espiga (**b**) *(team)* equipo *m*; *(jury)* jurado *m*; *Rad TV (contestants)* concursantes *mpl*; **p. game** concurso *m* por equipos

panelled, *US* **paneled** ['pænəld] *adj (door, wall)* con paneles; *(ceiling)* artesonado(a)

panelling, *US* **paneling** ['pænəlɪŋ] *n (of door, wall)* paneles *mpl*; *(of ceiling)* artesonado *m*

panellist, *US* **panelist** ['pænəlɪst] *n (judge)* miembro *mf* del jurado; *Rad TV (contestant)* concursante *mf*

pan-fry ['pænfraɪ] *vt (pt & pp* **pan-fried**) freír a la sartén

pang [pæŋ] *n (of pain, hunger)* punzada *f*; *(of childbirth)* dolores *mpl*; *Fig (of conscience)* remordimiento *m*

panic ['pænɪk] **1** *n* pánico *m*, miedo *m*; **the crowd was thrown into a p.** el pánico cundió entre la gente; **to get into a p.** dejarse llevar por el pánico *or* el miedo; *Fig* **to push the p. button** dejarse llevar por el pánico; *Fam* **it was p. stations** cundió el pánico
2 *vi (pt & pp* **panicked**) aterrarse, entrar el pánico; **I panicked** me entró el pánico
3 *vt* aterrar, infundir pánico a

panicky ['pænɪkɪ] *adj* asustadizo(a); **to get p.** dejarse llevar por el pánico *or* el miedo

panic-stricken ['pænɪkstrɪkən] *adj* preso(a) de pánico, aterrado(a)

pannier ['pænɪər] *n (for animal)* alforja *f*; *(for bicycle)* bolsa *f*

panorama [pænə'rɑːmə] *n (view)* panorama *m*; *Cin Phot* panorámica *f*

panoramic [pænə'ræmɪk] *adj* panorámico(a)

panpipes ['pænpaɪps] *npl Mus* siringa *f sing*

pansy ['pænzɪ] *n* (**a**) *Bot* pensamiento *m* (**b**) *Fam (effeminate man)* mariquita *m*

pant [pænt] **1** *n* jadeo *m*, resoplido *m*
2 *vi* jadear, resoplar; **to p. for breath** intentar recobrar el aliento

pantechnicon [pæn'teknɪkən] *n Br Old-fashioned* camión *m* de mudanzas

pantheon ['pænθɪən] *n Archit* panteón *m*

panther ['pænθər] *n Zool* pantera *f*

panties ['pæntɪz] *npl Esp* bragas *fpl*, *Chile Col Méx* calzones *mpl*, *Ecuad* follones *mpl*, *RP* bombacha *f*

pantomime ['pæntəmaɪm] *n Theat (play)* función *f* musical navideña; *(mime)* pantomima *f*

pantry ['pæntrɪ] *n* despensa *f*

pants [pænts] *npl* (**a**) *(underpants) (women's) Esp* bragas *fpl*, *Chile Col Méx* calzones *mpl*, *Ecuad* follones *mpl*, *RP* bombacha *f*; *(men's)* calzoncillos *mpl*, *Chile* fundillos *mpl*, *Col* pantaloncillos *mpl*, *Méx* calzones *mpl*, *Méx* chones *mpl* (**b**) *US (trousers)* pantalones *mpl*

panty ['pæntɪ] *n* **p. liner** protege-slips *m inv*, *RP Ven* protector *m* diario

pantyhose ['pæntɪhəʊz] *npl US (tights)* medias *fpl* panties; *(woollen)* leotardos *mpl*

pap [pæp] *n Fam Pej (nonsense)* bobadas *fpl*

papa *n* (**a**) [pə'pɑː] *Br Old-fashioned* papá (**b**) ['pɑːpə] *US* papá *m*, papi *m*

papacy ['peɪpəsɪ] *n* papado *m*, pontificado *m*

papal ['peɪpəl] *adj* papal, pontificio(a)

papaya [pə'paɪə] *n (tree)* papayo *m*; *(fruit)* papaya *f*

paper ['peɪpər] **1** *n* (**a**) *(material)* papel *m*; **a piece/sheet of p.** un trozo/una hoja de papel; **to put sth down on p.** poner algo por escrito; *Fig* **it isn't worth the p. it's written on** es papel mojado; *Fig* **on p.** en teoría, sobre el papel ❑ **brown p.** papel *m* de estraza; **cigarette p.** papel *m* de fumar; *Comptr* **p. feed** sistema *m* de alimentación de papel;

p. mill fábrica *for Am* planta *f* de papel; **p. money** papel *m* moneda; *Comptr* **p. tray** bandeja *f* del papel; **toilet p.** papel *m* higiénico; **wrapping p.** papel *m* de envolver; **writing p.** papel *m* de escribir **(b)** *Educ Univ (examination)* examen *m*; *(test)* prueba *f*; *(essay)* trabajo *m* (escrito); **to write a p. on a subject** hacer un trabajo sobre un tema ❑ **question p.** cuestionario *m*; **written p.** examen *m* escrito **(c)** *Pol* libro *m*; **white p.** libro blanco **(d)** *(newspaper)* periódico *m*, diario *m*; **to write for a p.** hacer de *or* ser periodista; **the papers** los periódicos, la prensa ❑ **p. round** reparto *m* de periódicos; *Br* **p. shop** tienda *f* de periódicos; **weekly p.** semanario *m* **(e)** **papers** *(documents)* papeles *mpl*, documentos *mpl* ❑ *Mil* **call-up p.** llamamiento *m* *sing* a filas; **identity p.** documentación *f sing*
  2 *vt (wall, room)* empapelar

paperback ['peɪpəbæk] *n* libro *m* en rústica

paperboy ['peɪbabɔɪ] *n* repartidor *m* de periódicos

paperclip ['peɪpəklɪp] *n* clip *m*, sujetapapeles *m inv*

papergirl ['peɪpəgɜːl] *n* repartidora *f* de periódicos

paperknife ['peɪpənaɪf] *n* cortapapeles *m inv*

paperless ['peɪpəlɪs] *adj* **the p. office** la oficina completamente informatizada

paper-thin ['peɪpəˈθɪn] *adj* muy fino(a)

paperweight ['peɪpəweɪt] *n* pisapapeles *m inv*

paperwork ['peɪpəwɜːk] *n* papeleo *m*

papery ['peɪpərɪ] *adj* parecido(a) al papel

papier-mâché [pæpjeɪˈmæʃeɪ] *n* cartón *m* piedra

papist ['peɪpɪst] *adj & n Pej* papista *(mf)*

paprika ['pæprɪkə] *n* pimentón *m* molido, paprika *f*

Papua ['pæpjʊə] *n* Papúa ❑ **P. New Guinea** Papúa Nueva Guinea

Papuan ['pæpjʊən] *adj & n* papú *(mf)*, papúa *(mf)*

par [pɑːr] *n (parity)* igualdad *f*; *Fin* par *f*; *Golf* par *m*; *Golf* **three under p.** tres bajo par; *Fig* **it's p. for the course** es lo normal en estos casos; *Fig* **to be on a p. with sb** estar en igualdad de condiciones con algn; *Fig* **to feel under** *or* **below p.** sentirse mal, estar en baja forma

para ['pærə] *(abbr* **paragraph***)* párrafo *m*, párr.

parable ['pærəbəl] *n* parábola *f*

parabola [pəˈræbələ] *n* parábola *f*

parabolic [pærəˈbɒlɪk] *adj* parabólico(a)

paracetamol [pærəˈsiːtəmɒl] *n* paracetamol *m*

parachute ['pærəʃuːt] **1** *n* paracaídas *m inv* ❑ **p. jump** salto *m* en paracaídas
  2 *vt (person, provisions etc)* lanzar en paracaídas
  3 *vi* **to p. (down)** saltar *or* lanzarse en paracaídas

parachutist ['pærəʃuːtɪst] *n* paracaidista *mf*

parade [pəˈreɪd] **1** *n* **(a)** *(procession)* desfile *m*; **carnival/ fashion p.** desfile de carrozas/de modelos; *Mil* **to be on p.** pasar revista ❑ **shopping p.** área *f* comercial; **p. ground** plaza *f* de armas **(b)** *Fig (display)* alarde *m*; **to make a p. of sth** hacer alarde de algo
  2 *vt* **(a)** *Mil* hacer desfilar **(b)** *Fig (flaunt) (knowledge, wealth)* alardear de, hacer alarde de
  3 *vi (troops)* pasar revista; *(demonstrators, procession)* desfilar

parade about, parade around *vi (show off)* pavonearse

paradigm ['pærədaɪm] *n* paradigma *m*

paradigmatic [pærədɪgˈmætɪk] *adj* paradigmático(a)

paradise ['pærədaɪs] *n* paraíso *m*; *Fig* **it's sheer p.** es un paraíso terrenal

paradox ['pærədɒks] *n* paradoja *f*

paradoxical [pærəˈdɒksɪkəl] *adj* paradójico(a)

paraffin ['pærəfɪn] *n* parafina *f* ❑ **liquid p.** aceite *m* de parafina; **p. heater** estufa *f* de parafina; **p. lamp** lámpara *f* de petróleo, quinqué *m*; **p. wax** parafina *f*

paragon ['pærəgən] *n* modelo *m*, dechado *m*

paragraph ['pærəgrɑːf] *n* párrafo *m*; **new p.** punto y aparte

Paraguay ['pærəgwaɪ] *n* Paraguay

Paraguayan [pærəˈgwaɪən] *adj & n* paraguayo(a) *(m,f)*

parakeet ['pærəkiːt] *n Orn* periquito *m*, perico *m*

paralegal [pærəˈliːgəl] *n US* ayudante *mf* de un abogado, *RP* procurador(a) *m,f*

parallel ['pærəlel] **1** *adj* paralelo(a) (**to, with** con); *Fig* comparable, análogo(a) (**to, with** a); **to be/run p. with sth** ser/correr paralelo(a) a algo ❑ *Sport* **p. bars** (barras *fpl*) paralelas *fpl*; *Comptr* **p. port** puerto *m* paralelo; *Comptr* **p. processing** procesado *m* en paralelo
  2 *n Geog* paralelo *m*; *Geom* paralela *f*; *Fig* paralelo *m*; *Fig* **to draw a p. between two things** establecer un paralelo entre dos cosas; **without p.** sin comparación
  3 *vt Fig* ser paralelo(a) *or* análogo(a) a, correr parejas con

parallelogram [pærəˈleləgræm] *n Geom* paralelogramo *m*

paralyse ['pærəlaɪz] *vt* paralizar; **the strike paralysed the railway system** la huelga paralizó la red ferroviaria; **to be paralysed in both legs** estar paralizado(a) de ambas piernas; *Fig* **to be paralysed with fear** quedarse paralizado(a) de miedo

paralysis [pəˈrælɪsɪs] *n (pl* **paralyses** [pəˈrælɪsiːz]) *Med* parálisis *f*; *Fig* paralización *f*

paralytic [pærəˈlɪtɪk] **1** *adj Med* paralítico(a); *Fam* **to be p.** estar como una cuba *or Méx* hasta atrás
  2 *n* paralítico(a) *m,f*

paralyze ['pærəlaɪz] *vt US see* **paralyse**

paramedic [pærəˈmedɪk] *n* auxiliar *mf* sanitario(a)

parameter [pəˈræmɪtər] *n* parámetro *m*

paramilitary [pærəˈmɪlɪtərɪ] *adj* paramilitar

paramount ['pærəmaʊnt] *adj* supremo(a); **of p. importance** de suma importancia

paranoia [pærəˈnɔɪə] *n Med* paranoia *f*

paranoiac [pærəˈnɔɪk] *adj & n*, **paranoid** ['pærənɔɪd] *adj & n* paranoico(a) *(m,f)*

paranormal [pærəˈnɔːməl] *adj* paranormal

parapet ['pærəpɪt] *n* parapeto *m*

paraphernalia [pærəfəˈneɪlɪə] *n* parafernalia *f*

paraphrase ['pærəfreɪz] **1** *n* paráfrasis *f inv*
  2 *vt* parafrasear

paraplegia [pærəˈpliːdʒə] *n Med* paraplejía *f*

paraplegic [pærəˈpliːdʒɪk] *adj & n Med* parapléjico(a) *(m,f)*

parasite ['pærəsaɪt] *n* parásito(a) *m,f*

parasitic(al) [pærəˈsɪtɪk(əl)] *adj* parásito(a), parasítario(a)

parasol ['pærəsɒl] *n* sombrilla *f*

paratrooper ['pærətruːpər] *n Mil* paracaidista *mf*

paratroops ['pærətruːps] *npl Mil* paracaidistas *mpl*

parboil ['pɑːbɔɪl] *vt* cocer a medias, sancochar

parcel ['pɑːsəl] **1** *n* **(a)** *(package)* paquete *m* ❑ **p. bomb** paquete *m* bomba; **p. post** servicio *m* de paquetes postales, *Andes RP* encomienda *f* **(b)** *(piece of land)* parcela *f*; *Fig* **to be part and p. of sth** formar parte esencial de algo
  2 *vt (pt & pp* **parcelled**, *US* **parceled***)* **to p. up** envolver, empaquetar, embalar

parcel out *vt* repartir, distribuir

parched [pɑːtʃt] *adj (land)* abrasado(a), reseco(a); *(lips,* *mouth)* seco(a); *Fig* **to be p.** estar muerto(a) de sed

Parcheesi® [pɑ:ˈtʃiːzɪ] *n US* parchís *m*

parchment [ˈpɑːtʃmənt] *n* pergamino *m* ❑ **p. paper** papel *m* pergamino

pardon [ˈpɑːdən] **1** *n (forgiveness)* perdón *m; Jur* indulto *m;* **I beg your p.!** *(in apology)* ¡discúlpeme!; **(I beg your) p.?** ¿cómo (dice)?; **to ask for p.** pedir perdón
 2 *vt (forgive)* perdonar, disculpar; *Jur* indultar; **p. me!** *(in apology)* ¡discúlpeme!; **p. me interrupting but ...** perdone que le interrumpa pero ...; **to p. sb sth** perdonar algo a algn

pardonable [ˈpɑːdənəbəl] *adj* perdonable, disculpable

pare [peər] *vt (fruit)* pelar, mondar; *(nails)* cortar

pare down *vt (reduce)* reducir

parent [ˈpeərənt] *n (father)* padre *m; (mother)* madre *f;* **parents** padres *mpl;* **p. company** empresa *f* matriz

parentage [ˈpeərəntɪdʒ] *n* familia *f,* origen *m;* **of humble p.** de padres humildes

parental [pəˈrentəl] *adj (paternal)* paterno(a); *(maternal)* materno(a); **p. guidance** consejos *mpl* paternales

parenthesis [pəˈrenθɪsɪs] *n (pl* **parentheses** [pəˈrenθɪsiːz]) paréntesis *m inv;* **in p.** entre paréntesis

parenthetical [pærənˈθetɪkəl] *adj* entre paréntesis

parenthood [ˈpeərənthʊd] *n* paternidad *f,* maternidad *f;* **planned p.** planificación *f* familiar; **the joys of p.** la alegría de tener hijos

parenting [ˈpeərəntɪŋ] *n* **p. skills** capacidad *f* para cuidar de los hijos

par excellence [pɑːrˈeksələns] *adv* por excelencia

pariah [pəˈraɪə] *n* paria *m*

parings [ˈpeərɪŋz] *npl* mondaduras *fpl*

Paris [ˈpærɪs] *n* París

parish [ˈpærɪʃ] *n Rel* parroquia *f; (civil)* municipio *m* ❑ **p. council** consejo *m* parroquial *or* municipal; **p. priest** párroco *m*

parishioner [pəˈrɪʃənər] *n* feligrés(esa) *m,f*

Parisian [pəˈrɪzɪən, *US* pəˈriːʒən] *adj & n* parisino(a) *(m,f),* parisiense *(mf)*

parity [ˈpærɪtɪ] *n (equality)* igualdad *f; Fin (of shares)* paridad *f*

park [pɑːk] **1** *n* parque *m,* jardín *m* (público) ❑ **amusement p.** parque *m* de atracciones; **car p.** aparcamiento *m,* parking *m; Col* parqueadero *m;* **national p.** parque *m* nacional; **p. bench** banco *m* del parque
 2 *vt (car)* estacionar, *Esp* aparcar; *Fam* **p. yourself down here** siéntate aquí

parka [ˈpɑːkə] *n* anorak *m*

park-and-ride [ˈpɑːkənˈraɪd] *n* = sistema de estacionamientos en la periferia de una ciudad conectados con el centro por transporte público

parking [ˈpɑːkɪŋ] *n* estacionamiento *m, Esp* aparcamiento *m, Col* parqueadero *m;* **'no p.'** 'prohibido estacionar *or Esp* aparcar', 'estacionamiento prohibido' ❑ **p. attendant** vigilante *mf* de estacionamiento *or Esp* aparcamiento; **p. lights** luces *fpl* de estacionamiento; *US* **p. lot** *Esp* aparcamiento *m,* parking *m, RP* playa *f* de estacionamiento, *Col* parqueadero *m;* **p. meter** parquímetro *m;* **p. offence** multa *f* por estacionamiento incorrecto; **p. space** *Esp* aparcamiento *m,* sitio *m or* hueco *m* para estacionar

Parkinson's disease [ˈpɑːkɪnsənzdɪˈziːz] *n* (síndrome *m* de) Parkinson *m*

parkland [ˈpɑːklænd] *n* prado *m*

parkway [ˈpɑːkweɪ] *n US* = carretera o avenida con árboles a los lados y en el medio

parky [ˈpɑːkɪ] *adj* **(parkier, parkiest)** *Br Fam* fresco(a); **it's a bit p.** hace fresquito

parlance [ˈpɑːləns] *n* lenguaje *m*

parley [ˈpɑːlɪ] **1** *n* parlamento *m*
 2 *vi* parlamentar

parliament [ˈpɑːləmənt] *n* parlamento *m;* **to get into p.** ser elegido(a) diputado(a) ❑ **Houses of P.** parlamento *m;* **Member of P.** diputado(a) *m,f*

parliamentarian [pɑːləmənˈteərɪən] *n* parlamentario(a) *m,f*

parliamentary [pɑːləˈmentərɪ] *adj* parlamentario(a)

parlour, *US* **parlor** [ˈpɑːlər] *n (in house)* salón *m,* salita *f; (shop)* salón, tienda *f* ❑ **funeral p.** funeraria *f*

Parmesan [pɑːmɪˈzæn] *n* **P. (cheese)** queso *m* parmesano

parochial [pəˈrəʊkɪəl] *adj* **(a)** *(of parish)* parroquial **(b)** *Pej (narrow-minded)* de miras estrechas, pueblerino(a)

parochialism [pəˈrəʊkɪəlɪzəm] *n Pej (of mentality)* provincialismo *m,* estrechez *f* de miras

parody [ˈpærədɪ] **1** *n* parodia *f*
 2 *vt (pt & pp* **parodied)** parodiar

parole [pəˈrəʊl] **1** *n Jur* libertad *f* condicional *or* bajo palabra; **to be on p.** estar libre bajo palabra ❑ **p. board** junta *f* de libertad condicional; **p. officer** = asistente social que supervisa a un preso en libertad bajo palabra y ante quien se presenta periódicamente
 2 *vt (prisoner)* poner en libertad condicional *or* bajo palabra

paroxysm [ˈpærəksɪzəm] *n* paroxismo *m*

parquet [ˈpɑːkeɪ] *n* parqué *m* ❑ **p. floor** suelo *m* de parqué

parrot [ˈpærət] *n* loro *m,* papagayo *m; Fig* **to repeat sth p. fashion** repetir algo como un loro

parry [ˈpærɪ] *vt (pt & pp* **parried)** *(blow)* parar, desviar; *Fig (question etc)* esquivar, eludir

parse [pɑːz] *vt Comptr Ling (sentence)* analizar gramaticalmente

parsimonious [pɑːsɪˈməʊnɪəs] *adj* tacaño(a), parco(a)

parsley [ˈpɑːslɪ] *n Bot* perejil *m*

parsnip [ˈpɑːsnɪp] *n Bot* chirivía *f*

parson [ˈpɑːsən] *n (vicar)* cura *m,* párroco *m* ❑ *Culin* **p.'s nose** rabadilla *f* (de pollo)

parsonage [ˈpɑːsənɪdʒ] *n* casa *f* parroquial, parroquia *f*

part [pɑːt] **1** *n* **(a)** *(portion, proportion, section)* parte *f; (piece)* parte, trozo *m; Rad TV (episode)* capítulo *m; Tech* pieza *f;* **a tenth p.** una décima parte; **for the most p.** en la mayor parte; *Cin Lit* **in p. two** en la segunda parte; *Ling* **parts of speech** partes de la oración; *Anat Euph* **private parts** partes pudendas; **she was away for the best p. of a week** estaba fuera durante la mayor parte de la semana; **spare parts** recambios *mpl,* piezas *fpl* de recambio, *Col Cuba RP* repuestos *mpl, Am* refacciones *fpl;* **the funniest/ saddest p. of it is that ...** lo más gracioso/triste del caso es que ...; *Culin* **two parts water to one p. wine** dos partes de agua y una de vino ❑ **p. owner** copropietario(a) *m,f* **(b)** *(rôle, participation)* papel *m,* parte *f; Cin Theat* papel; **bit p.** papel secundario; **to look the p.** encajar bien en el papel; **to play a p. in a film/play** hacer un papel en una película/ una obra de teatro; **to play a p. in sth** tener algo que ver con algo; **to take p. in sth** participar en algo; *Fig* **a man of many parts** un hombre de mucho talento; *Fig* **I want no p. in it** no quiero saber nada de ello **(c)** *(area, place)* parte *f,* lugar *m;* **in foreign parts** en el extranjero; **in these parts** por estos lugares **(d)** *(side)* parte *f;* **for my p** en cuanto a mí, por mi parte; **it was an oversight on the p. of my wife** fue un descuido por parte de mi mujer; **to take sb's p.**

tomar partido por algn, apoyar a algn; **to take sth in good p.** tomarse bien algo **(e)** *US (in hair)* raya *f, Col Méx Ven* carrera *m*

2 *adj (partial)* parcial; **the pullover is p. wool** el jersey tiene una parte de lana; **to take sth in p. exchange** aceptar algo como parte de un pago

3 *adv (partly)* en parte; **he's p. Scottish, p. Spanish** es mitad escocés, mitad español

4 *vt (separate)* separar; **they were parted during the war** la guerra los separó; **to p. company with sb** *(leave)* despedirse de algn; *(quarrel)* reñir con algn; **to p. one's hair** hacerse la raya *or Col Méx Ven* carrera (en el pelo)

5 *vi (separate)* separarse; *(say goodbye)* despedirse; **to p. (as) friends** se separaron amistosamente

part with *vi* separarse de; **I'm sorry to have to p. with it** siento perderlo *or* perderla

partake [pɑːˈteɪk] *vi (pt* **partook;** *pp* **partaken** [pɑːˈteɪkən]) *Fml* **to p. of** *(food)* comer; *(drink)* beber

parterre [pɑːˈteər] *adj US Theat* platea *f*

partial [ˈpɑːʃəl] *adj* parcial; **to be p. to sth** ser aficionado(a) a algo

partiality [pɑːʃɪˈælɪtɪ] *n (bias)* parcialidad *f; (liking)* afición *f,* gusto *m*

partially [ˈpɑːʃəlɪ] *adv* **(a)** *(partly)* parcialmente; **p. sighted** con visión parcial **(b)** *(with bias)* con parcialidad

participant [pɑːˈtɪsɪpənt] *n (gen)* participante *mf; (in competition)* concursante *mf*

participate [pɑːˈtɪsɪpeɪt] *vi* participar **(in** en)

participation [pɑːtɪsɪˈpeɪʃən] *n* participación *f*

participatory [pɑːtɪsɪˈpeɪtərɪ] *adj* participativo(a)

participle [ˈpɑːtɪsɪpəl] *n* participio *m* ◻ **past p.** participio *m* pasado; **present p.** participio *m* presente

particle [ˈpɑːtɪkəl] *n* partícula *f*

particular [pəˈtɪkjʊlər] **1** *adj* **(a)** *(special)* particular, especial; **for no p. reason** sin ninguna razón especial; **in this p. case** en este caso concreto; **it's of p. interest** es de especial interés; **nothing in p.** nada de especial; **that p. person** esa persona en particular **(b)** *(fussy)* exigente; **I'm not p.** me da igual; **she's very p. about her food** es muy especial para la comida

2 particulars *npl (details)* detalles *mpl,* pormenores *mpl;* **to receive full p. about sth** recibir información detallada sobre algo; **to take down sb's p.** tomar nota de los datos personales de algn

particularize [pəˈtɪkjʊləraɪz] **1** *vt* particularizar, especificar

2 *vi* entrar en detalles

particularly [pəˈtɪkjʊləlɪ] *adv (especially)* particularmente, especialmente; **I'm p. fond of peaches** me encantan los melocotones

parting [ˈpɑːtɪŋ] **1** *n* **(a)** *(separation)* separación *f,* despedida *f; Fig* **the p. of the ways** el momento de la separación *or* la despedida **(b)** *Br (in hair)* raya *f, Col Méx Ven* carrera *f*

2 *adj* de despedida; **a p. kiss** un beso de despedida; **his p. words were ...** sus palabras al despedirse fueron ...; *Fig* **p. shot** último comentario *m,* golpe *m* de gracia

partisan [pɑːtɪˈzæn, ˈpɑːtɪzæn] **1** *n* **(a)** *Mil* guerrillero(a) *m,f; (supporter)* partidario(a) *m,f*

2 *adj Mil* guerrillero(a); *(supporter)* partidario(a); *(of party)* partidista

partition [pɑːˈtɪʃən] **1** *n* **(a)** *(wall)* tabique *m;* **glass p.** tabique de cristal **(b)** *(of country)* partición *f,* división *f*

2 *vt (country)* partir, dividir

partition off *vt (room)* dividir *or* separar con tabiques

partly [ˈpɑːtlɪ] *adv (in part)* en parte, parcialmente; *(in a*

sense) en cierto sentido; **p. cooked** cocido(a) a medias; **we are p. to blame** somos culpables en parte

partner [ˈpɑːtnər] **1** *n* **(a)** *(gen)* compañero(a) *m,f; (dancing, in tennis)* pareja *f; (husband)* marido *m; (wife)* mujer *f* **(b)** *Com* socio(a) *m,f,* asociado(a) *m,f*

2 *vt* acompañar, ir de pareja de

partnership [ˈpɑːtnəʃɪp] *n* **(a)** *(marriage, relationship)* vida *f* en común **(b)** *Com* sociedad *f,* asociación *f; Com* **to go into p. with sb** asociarse con algn

partook [pɑːˈtʊk] *pt see* **partake**

partridge [ˈpɑːtrɪdʒ] *n Orn* perdiz *f* pardilla ◻ **rough-legged p.** perdiz *f* común

part-time [pɑːtˈtaɪm] **1** *adj (work etc)* de media jornada

2 *adv* media jornada, a tiempo parcial

part-timer [pɑːtˈtaɪmər] *n* trabajador(a) *m,f* a tiempo parcial

partway [ˈpɑːtweɪ] *adv* **I'm p. through it** *(book, task)* voy por la mitad; **this will go p. towards covering the costs** esto sufragará parte de los gastos

party [ˈpɑːtɪ] **1** *n* **(a)** *(celebration)* fiesta *f;* **to give** *or* **have** *or* **throw a p.** organizar una fiesta; **to give a dinner p.** invitar a gente a cenar ◻ **birthday p.** fiesta *f* de cumpleaños; *Fam* **p. pooper** aguafiestas *mf inv;* **tea p.** merienda *f;* **(b)** *(group)* grupo *m* ◻ **rescue p.** equipo *m* de rescate **(c)** *Pol* partido *m* ◻ **Conservative/Labour P.** partido *m* Conservador/Socialista; **p. leader** secretario(a) *m,f* general del partido; *Br* **p. political broadcast** emisión *f* de propaganda política **(d)** *Jur* parte *f,* interesado(a) *m,f;* **guilty/innocent p.** el *or* la culpable/inocente; **to be a p. to a crime** ser cómplice *mf* en un delito

2 *adj (clothes, atmosphere)* de fiesta, de gala; *Tel* **p. line** línea *f* compartida; **p. wall** pared *f* medianera

partygoer [ˈpɑːtɪɡəʊər] *n* **the streets were full of partygoers** las calles estaban llenas de gente que acudía a fiestas

pass [pɑːs] **1** *n* **(a)** *Geog (in mountains)* puerto *m,* desfiladero *m* **(b)** *(official permit)* permiso *m,* pase *m;* **rail/bus p.** abono *m or* pase *m* de tren/autobús **(c)** *(in exam)* aprobado *m;* **to get a p. in French** sacar un aprobado en francés **(d)** *Sport* pase *m; Ftb* **to make a p. with the ball** hacer un pase con *or* pasar la pelota **(e)** *Fam* **to make a p. at sb** intentar seducir *or Esp* tirar los tejos a algn, *RP* tirarse un lance con algn

2 *vt* **(a)** *(go past)* pasar; *(border)* cruzar, atravesar; *Aut (overtake)* adelantar; **to p. the police station** pasar por delante de la comisaría; **we passed him in the street** nos cruzamos con él por la calle **(b)** *(go, move)* pasar; *Sport (ball)* pasar; **to p. sb a chair, p. a chair to sb** pasar una silla a algn; **p. the salt, please** ¿me puedes pasar la sal, por favor? **(c)** *(exam)* aprobar; *(motion, plan, law)* aprobar; **to p. sb as fit for work** dar a algn de alta; *Jur* **to p. sentence** fallar, dictar sentencia; **to p. the censors** pasar la censura **(d)** *(time)* pasar; **it helps to p. the time** ayuda a pasar el rato; **to p. the time of day with sb** charlar *or CAm Méx* platicar un rato con algn **(e)** *(express)* expresar; **to p. an opinion** dar una opinión; **to p. a remark** hacer una observación *or* un comentario **(f)** *(expel)* **to p. water** orinar; **to p. wind** tener gases

3 *vi* **(a)** *(move past)* pasar; *(procession)* desfilar; *Aut (car)* adelantar; *(people)* cruzarse; *Sport* hacer un pase; **we passed on the stairs** nos cruzamos en la escalera **(b)** *(go, move)* pasar; *(pain)* remitir; *(anger, storm)* pasar, desaparecer; *(opportunity)* perderse; *(memory)* olvidarse; *(time)* pasar; **time passes quickly** el tiempo pasa rápido; **to p. into oblivion** pasar al olvido; **to p. out of sight** perderse a la vista **(c)** *(happen)* pasar, ocurrir; **all that has passed** todo lo que ha pasado *or* ocurrido; **it came to p. that ...** resultó que ...; **(d)** *(be accepted)* pasar por; **let it p.**

déjalo pasar; **what passes for good manners** lo que se considera buena educación (**e**) *(in exam)* aprobar, ser aprobado(a)

pass away *vi Euph* pasar a mejor vida

pass by 1 *vt* pasar de largo; **life has passed him by** ha disfrutado poco de la vida

   2 *vi* pasar cerca (de)

pass down *vt (hand down)* pasar, transmitir

pass for *vt* she could p. for our sister podría pasar por nuestra hermana

pass off 1 *vt* hacer pasar; **to p. oneself off as sth** hacerse pasar por algo; **to p. sth/sb off as sth** hacer pasar a algn/algo por algo

   2 *vi (happen)* pasar, transcurrir

pass on 1 *vt (hand on)* pasar, transmitir

   2 *vi* (**a**) *Euph (die)* pasar a mejor vida (**b**) *(proceed)* pasar a

pass out *vi* (**a**) *(faint)* desmayarse, perder el conocimiento (**b**) *Mil* graduarse

pass over *vt* (**a**) *(bridge, land etc)* atravesar, cruzar; *(aircraft)* volar por (**b**) *(disregard)* pasar por alto, hacer caso omiso de; **she was passed over in favour of her sister** eligieron a su hermana en vez de a ella

pass through 1 *vt (place)* pasar por, atravesar; *(barrier, border)* cruzar

   2 *vi* estar de paso; **I'm just passing through** sólo estoy de paso

pass up *vt (opportunity)* renunciar; *(offer)* rechazar

passable ['pɑːsəbəl] *adj* (**a**) *(road, bridge)* transitable (**b**) *(acceptable)* pasable, aceptable

passably ['pɑːsəblɪ] *adv* aceptablemente; **p. good** bastante bueno(a)

passage ['pæsɪdʒ] *n* (**a**) *(in street)* pasaje *m*; *(alleyway)* callejón *m*; *(hallway)* pasillo *m* (**b**) *(travelling)* paso *m*, tránsito *m*; *Naut* travesía *f*; **to grant sb a safe p.** darle a algn un salvoconducto; *Fig* **the p. of time** el paso del tiempo (**c**) *Mus Lit (piece)* pasaje *m*, trozo *m*

passageway ['pæsɪdʒweɪ] *n (interior)* pasillo *m*; *(exterior)* pasaje *m*

passbook ['pɑːsbʊk] *n* libreta *f* de banco

passé ['pɑːseɪ] *adj* pasado(a) de moda

passenger ['pæsɪndʒər] *n* pasajero(a) *m,f*, viajero(a) *m,f*

passer-by [pɑːsə'baɪ] *n (pl* **passers-by**) transeúnte *mf*

passing ['pɑːsɪŋ] **1** *n* (**a**) *(of car, train)* paso *m*; *(of time)* transcurso *m*; paso *m*; *Aut (overtaking)* adelantamiento *m*; **to mention sth in p.** mencionar algo de pasada (**b**) *(of law)* aprobación *f*

   2 *adj (car etc)* que pasa; *(glance)* rápido(a); *(thought)* pasajero(a); **a p. remark** una observación hecha de pasada

passion ['pæʃən] *n (gen)* pasión *f*; *(vehemence)* ardor *m*, vehemencia *f*; **crime of p.** crimen *m* pasional; **he has a p. for opera** le apasiona la ópera; *Rel* **the P.** la Pasión ❑ **p. fruit** granadilla *f*

passionate ['pæʃənɪt] *adj (gen)* apasionado(a); *(vehement)* ardiente, vehemente

passionflower ['pæʃənflaʊər] *n Bot* pasionaria *f*

passive ['pæsɪv] **1** *adj* pasivo(a); **p. resistance** resistencia *f* pasiva; **p. smoking** tabaquismo *m* pasivo

   2 *n Ling (voz f)* pasiva *f*

passively ['pæsɪvlɪ] *adv (gen)* pasivamente; *Ling* en voz pasiva

passkey ['pɑːskiː] *n* llave *f* maestra

Passover ['pɑːsəʊvər] *n Rel* Pascua *f* de los judíos

passport ['pɑːspɔːt] *n* pasaporte *m*

password ['pɑːswɜːd] *n Mil Comptr* contraseña *f*

past [pɑːst] **1** *n* pasado *m*; **in the p.** en el pasado, antes; **it's a thing of the p.** pertenece al pasado; **the p.** *(time)* el pasado; *(events)* lo pasado; *(tense)* el pretérito, el pasado; **to have a p.** tener antecedentes

   2 *adj (gen)* pasado(a); *(former)* anterior; **in p. years** en años anteriores; **in the p. weeks** en las últimas semanas; **to be a p. master at sth** ser experto(a) en algo ❑ *Ling* **p. participle** participio *m* pasado; **p. tense** pretérito *m*, pasado *m*

   3 *adv* por delante; **to drive p.** pasar en coche; **to run/walk p.** pasar corriendo/andando

   4 *prep (beyond)* más allá de; *(more than)* más de; **he's p. forty** pasa de los cuarenta (años); **it's five p. ten** son las diez y cinco; **it's just p. the postbox** está un poco más allá del buzón; **quarter/half p. two** las dos y cuarto/media; *Fam* **I'm p. caring** me trae sin cuidado; *Fam* **I wouldn't put it p. him** es capaz de cualquier cosa, no me extraña viniendo de él; *Fam* **she's p. going to discotheques** ya no tiene edad para ir de discotecas; *Fam* **to be p. it** estar muy carroza

pasta ['pæstə] *n* pasta *f*, pastas *fpl*

paste [peɪst] **1** *n* (**a**) *(gen)* pasta *f*; *(glue)* engrudo *m*; *Culin* pasta *f*; **anchovy p.** pasta de anchoas; **tomato p.** tomate *m* concentrado (**b**) *(jewellery)* bisutería *f*

   2 *vt (stick)* pegar; *(put paste on)* engomar, encolar; **to p. sth onto a wall** pegar algo a una pared

pasteboard ['peɪstbɔːd] *n* cartón *m*

pastel ['pæstəl] **1** *n (chalk)* pastel *m*; *(drawing)* pintura *f* al pastel; *(colour)* color *m* pastel

   2 *adj (drawing)* al pastel; *(colour)* pastel

pasteurization [pæstʃəraɪˈzeɪʃən] *n* pasteurización *f*

pasteurized ['pæstʃəraɪzd] *adj* pasteurizado(a)

pastiche [pæˈstiːʃ] *n* pastiche *m*

pastille ['pæstɪl] *n* pastilla *f*

pastime ['pɑːstaɪm] *n* pasatiempo *m*

pasting ['peɪstɪŋ] *n Fam* paliza *f*; **to give sb a p.** dar una paliza a algn

pastor ['pɑːstər] *n Rel* pastor *m*

pastoral ['pɑːstərəl] *adj* pastoril, pastoral; **p. care** tutoría *f* y orientación *f* individual

pastry ['peɪstrɪ] *n (dough)* pasta *f*; *(cake)* pastel *m*, *Col CSur* torta *f*; **pastries** pasteles, pastas

pasture ['pɑːstʃər] **1** *n* pasto *m*; **to put cattle out to p.** pastorear *or* apacentar el ganado; *Fig* **to put sth out to p.** tirar algo, deshacerse de algo; *Fig* **to move on to pastures new** buscar nuevos terrenos ❑ **p. land** pradera *f*

   2 *vt* apacentar

   3 *vi* pacer

pasty¹ ['pæstɪ] *n Culin* empanada *f*, pastel *m* de carne

pasty² ['peɪstɪ] *adj* (**pastier, pastiest**) pálido(a), blancuzco(a)

pat¹ [pæt] **1** *n* (**a**) *(touch)* toque *m*; *(caress)* caricia *f*; *(tap)* golpecito *m*, palmadita *f*; **to give a dog a p.** acariciar a un perro; **to give sb a p. on the back** dar a algn una palmadita en la espalda; *Fig (congratulate)* felicitar a algn (**b**) *(of butter)* porción *f*

   2 *vt (pt & pp* **patted**) *(touch)* tocar; *(caress)* acariciar; *(tap)* dar una palmadita en; **to p. sb on the back** dar a algn palmaditas en la espalda; *Fig* felicitar a algn

pat² [pæt] **1** *adv* de memoria; **to learn sth off p.** aprender algo de memoria; **to know sth off p.** saber algo al dedillo

   2 *adj (answer)* (glib) fácil; *(appropriate)* apropiado(a); **to give a p. answer** dar una respuesta fácil

patch [pætʃ] *n* (**a**) *(piece of material)* parche *m*; *(of land)* terreno *m*; *(of colour)* mancha *f*; *(of sky)* trozo *m*; *(of road)* trecho *m*; *Fig* **to go through/to hit a bad p.** pasar por/tener una mala racha; *Fam* **the film isn't a p. on the book**

no se puede comparar la película con· el libro (**b**) *(hole, garment)* poner un parche en

patch up *vt* (**a**) *(garment)* poner un parche en; *Fig* **a patched-up job** una chapuza (**b**) *(marriage, quarrel)* reconciliarse

patchwork ['pætʃwɜːk] **1** *n* labor *f* de retales; **p. quilt** edredón *m* de retazos *or* de patchwork
　2 *adj (quilt etc)* hecho(a) con retales distintos

patchy ['pætʃɪ] *adj* (**patchier, patchiest**) (**a**) *(colour, performance)* desigual (**b**) *(knowledge)* incompleto(a), parcial

pâté ['pæteɪ] *n* paté *m*, foie gras *m*

patent¹ ['peɪtənt] **1** *n Com* patente *f*; **to take out a p. on sth** sacar una patente de algo
　2 *adj* (**a**) *(obvious)* patente, evidente (**b**) *Com (patented)* patentado(a) ❑ **p. medicine** específico *m*
　3 *vt Com* patentar

patent² ['peɪtənt] *n* charol *m* ❑ **p. leather** charol *m*; **p. leather shoes** zapatos de charol

patently ['peɪtəntlɪ] *adv (obviously)* evidentemente; **it is p. obvious** está clarísimo

paternal [pə'tɜːnəl] *adj (fatherly)* paternal; *(through father's line)* paterno(a); **p. grandmother** abuela *f* paterna

paternalism [pə'tɜːnəlɪzəm] *adj* paternalista

paternalistic [pətɜːnə'lɪstɪk] *adj* paternalista

paternity [pə'tɜːnɪtɪ] *n* paternidad *f* ❑ *Jur* **p. suit** demanda *f* de paternidad; **p. test** prueba *f* de (la) paternidad

path [pɑːθ] *n (pl* **paths** [pɑːðz]*)* camino *m*, sendero *m*; *(route)* rumbo *m*, ruta *f*; *(of bullet, missile)* trayectoria *f*; **to clear a p. through the forest** abrir camino por el bosque; *Fig* **to be on the right p.** ir bien encaminado(a); *Fig* **to lead sb up the garden p.** llevar a algn al huerto

pathetic [pə'θetɪk] *adj (rousing pity)* patético(a); *Fam (hopeless)* malísimo(a), pésimo(a); **she was a p. sight** daba lástima *or* pena verla así; **the music was p.** la música era malísima

pathetically [pə'θetɪklɪ] *adv* patéticamente; *Fam* que da lástima *or* pena; **p. thin** tan flaco(a) que da lástima

pathological [pæθə'lɒdʒɪkəl] *adj* patológico(a)

pathologist [pə'θɒlədʒɪst] *n* patólogo(a) *m,f*

pathology [pə'θɒlədʒɪ] *n* patología *f*

pathos ['peɪθɒs] *n* patetismo *m*

pathway ['pɑːθweɪ] *n* camino *m*, sendero *m*

patience ['peɪʃəns] *n* (**a**) *(quality)* paciencia *f*; **to lose one's p. with sb** perder la paciencia con algn; **to try sb's p.** poner a la prueba la paciencia a algn; **you need p. for that** para eso hace falta tener paciencia (**b**) *Br Cards* solitario *m*; **to play p.** hacer solitarios

patient ['peɪʃənt] **1** *adj* paciente, sufrido(a); **to be p. with sb** tener paciencia con algn
　2 *n* paciente *mf*, enfermo(a) *m,f*

patiently ['peɪʃəntlɪ] *adv* pacientemente, con paciencia

patina ['pætɪnə] *n* pátina *f*

patio ['pætɪəʊ] *n (pl* **patios**) patio *m*

patriarch ['peɪtrɪɑːk] *n* patriarca *m*

patriarchal [peɪtrɪ'ɑːkəl] *adj* patriarcal

patrician [pə'trɪʃən] **1** *n* patricio *m*
　2 *adj* (**a**) *(upper-class)* patricio(a) (**b**) *(haughty)* altanero(a)

patrimony ['pætrɪmənɪ] *n* patrimonio *m*

patriot ['peɪtrɪət] *n* patriota *mf*

patriotic [pætrɪ'ɒtɪk] *adj (person)* patriota; *(speech, act)* patriótico(a)

patriotism ['pætrɪətɪzəm] *n* patriotismo *m*

patrol [pə'trəʊl] **1** *n* patrulla *f*; **to be on p.** estar de patrulla ❑ **p. car** coche *m or Am* carro *m or CSur* auto *m* patrulla; **p. leader** jefe(a) *m,f* de patrulla
　2 *vt (pt & pp* **patrolled**) *(area)* estar de patrulla en, patrullar por
　3 *vi* patrullar; *Fig* **to p. up and down** pasearse de un lado a otro

patrolman [pə'trəʊlmən] *n (pl* **patrolmen**) *US (policeman)* patrullero *m*, policía *m*

patron ['peɪtrən] *n* (**a**) *(benefactor)* patrón(ona) *m,f*; *(of charity, cause)* patrocinador(a) *m,f*; *(of arts)* mecenas *m inv* ❑ **p. saint** (santo/a *m,f*) patrón(ona) *m,f* (**b**) *Com (customer)* cliente(a) *m,f* habitual

patronage ['pætrənɪdʒ] *n* (**a**) *(of charity, cause)* patrocinio *m*; *(of arts etc)* mecenazgo *m*; *Pej (in politics, business)* enchufe *m*; **under the p. of** patrocinado(a) por (**b**) *Com (customers)* clientela *f* habitual

patronize ['pætrənaɪz] *vt* (**a**) *(arts etc)* fomentar, proteger (**b**) *Com (shop)* ser cliente(a) *m,f* habitual de; *(club etc)* frecuentar (**c**) *Pej (treat condescendingly)* tratar con condescendencia

patronizing ['pætrənaɪzɪŋ] *adj Pej* condescendiente

patter¹ ['pætər] **1** *n (noise) (of rain)* repiqueteo *m*, tamborileo *m*; *(of feet)* pasito *m*
　2 *vi (rain)* repiquetear, tamborilear; *(feet, person)* trotar, corretear

patter² ['pætər] *n Fam* parloteo *m*, labia *f*

pattern ['pætən] *n· (model)* modelo *m*, patrón *m*; *Sew* patrón; *(design)* diseño *m*, dibujo *m*; *(on material)* estampado *m*; *(sample)* muestra *f*; *Fig (of behaviour)* modelo *m*; *Fig* **the p. of events** el curso de los acontecimientos ❑ **p. book** libro *m* de muestras, muestrario· *m*; *Sew* catálogo *m* de modas

patterned ['pætənd] *adj (gen)* decorado(a) con dibujos; *(material)* estampado(a)

paunch [pɔːntʃ] *n* barriga *f*, panza *f*, *Chile* guata *f*; **to have a p.** tener barriga *or* panza

pauper ['pɔːpər] *n* pobre *mf* ❑ **p.'s grave** fosa *f* común

pause [pɔːz] **1** *n (gen)* pausa *f*; *(silence)* silencio *m*; *(rest)* descanso *m*; **there was a p. in the conversation** la conversación se interrumpió por un instante
　2 *vi (gen)* hacer una pausa; *(be silent)* callarse; *(rest)* descansar; **she paused for breath** se paró para recobrar el aliento

pave [peɪv] *vt (road)* pavimentar; *(courtyard, floor)* embaldosar, enlosar; *(with stones)* empedrar, adoquinar; *Fig* **to p. the way for sb/sth** preparar el terreno para algn/ algo

pavement ['peɪvmənt] *n Br (along street)* acera *f*, *CSur* vereda *f*, *CAm Méx* banqueta *f*; *US (road surface)* calzada *f*, pavimento *m*

pavilion [pə'vɪljən] *n* (**a**) *(at exhibition)* pabellón *m* (**b**) *Br Sport (changing rooms)* vestuarios *mpl*

paving ['peɪvɪŋ] *n (on road)* pavimento *m*; *(on courtyard, floor)* embaldosado *m*, enlosado *m*; *(with stones)* empedrado *m*, adoquinado *m* ❑ **p. stone** baldosa *f*, losa *f*

paw [pɔː] **1** *n Zool (foot)* pata *f*; *(claw) (of cat)* garra *f*; *(of lion)* zarpa *f*, *Fam (hand)* manaza *f*
　2 *vt* (**a**) *(animal)* tocar con la pata; *(lion)* dar zarpazos; **to p. the ground** *(horse)* piafar (**b**) *Pej (person)* manosear, sobar

pawn¹ [pɔːn] *n Chess* peón *m*; *Fig* **to be sb's p.** ser el juguete de algn

pawn² [pɔːn] **1** *n* prenda *f*; **to put sth in p.** dejar *or* entregar algo en prenda, empeñar algo
　2 *vt* empeñar

pawnbroker ['pɔːnbrəukər] *n* prestamista *mf*; **p.'s (shop)** monte *m* de piedad, casa *f* de empeños

pawnshop ['pɔːnʃɒp] *n* monte de piedad, casa *f* de empeños

pay [peɪ] **1** *n (wages)* paga *f*, sueldo *m*, salario *m*; **equal p.** igualdad *f* de salarios; **holidays with p.** vacaciones *fpl* pagadas; **to be in sb's p.** ser empleado(a) de algn ▫ **overtime p.** paga *f* extraordinaria; *Br* **p. packet,** *US* **p. envelope** sobre *m* de la paga; **p. rise** aumento *m* del sueldo; **p. slip** hoja *f* de salario

2 *vt (pt & pp* **paid)** **(a)** *(gen)* pagar; **how much did you p. for this?** ¿cuánto pagaste por esto?; **to be** *or* **get paid** cobrar; **to be well/badly paid** estar bien/mal pagado(a); **to p. interest/dividends** dar interés/beneficios; **to p. money into an account** *Esp* ingresar *or Am* depositar dinero en una cuenta; **to p. one's way** pagar su parte; **to p. sb money** pagar dinero a algn; **to p. sb to do sth** pagar a algn para que haga algo; **when will you be paid?** ¿cuándo cobrarás *or* te pagarán? **(b)** *(give, make) (attention)* prestar; *(homage)* rendir; *(visit)* hacer; **to p. one's respects to sb** saludar a algn; **to p. sb a compliment** halagar a algn **(c)** *(be profitable)* compensar; **it paid him to do it** le compensó hacerlo; *Fig* **it pays you to be honest** te compensa *or* vale la pena ser honrado(a)

3 *vi* **(a)** *(gen)* pagar; **to p. by cash/cheque** pagar al contado *or* en efectivo/con talón; **to p. for sth** pagar (por) algo; **to p. for sb to do sth** *or* **for sth to be done by sb** pagar para que algn haga algo; **they paid for us to attend** nos pagaron para que asistiéramos; **to p. in advance/in instalments** pagar por adelantado/a plazos; *Fam* **to p. through the nose for sth** pagar un ojo de la cara *or Esp* un riñón por algo **(b)** *Fig (suffer)* pagar; **you'll p. for this!** ¡me las pagarás! **(c)** *(be profitable)* ser factible *or* rentable; **the business doesn't p.** el negocio no es rentable; *Fig* **crime doesn't p.** el crimen no compensa

pay back *vt (money)* devolver, reembolsar; *Fig* **to p. sb back** vengarse de algn, pagar a algn con la misma moneda

pay in *vt (money, cheque) Esp* ingresar, *Am* depositar

pay off **1** *vt (debt)* liquidar, saldar; *(loan)* pagar; *(mortgage)* cancelar; **to p. sth off in instalments** pagar algo a plazos; *Ind* **to p. off an employee** despedir a un empleado con una indemnización

2 *vi (be successful)* dar resultado; **the plan paid off** el proyecto dio buen resultado

pay out *vt* **(a)** *(spend) (money)* desembolsar, gastar (**on** en); **to p. out money to sb** pagar dinero a algn **(b)** *Naut (rope)* soltar

pay up 1 *vt (bill, debt)* liquidar, saldar
2 *vi* pagar

payable ['peɪəbəl] *adj* pagadero(a); **to make a cheque p. to sb** extender un talón a favor de algn

pay-as-you-earn [peɪæzjuːˈɜːn] *n* retención *f* del impuesto sobre la renta

pay-as-you-go ['peɪəzjuˈɡəʊ] *n (with mobile phone)* prepago *m*

payback ['peɪbæk] *n* **(a)** *Fin* recuperación *f*, reembolso *m* **p. period** periodo *m* de amortización *or* reembolso **(b)** *US Fam (revenge)* venganza *f*, revancha *f*

paybed ['peɪbed] *n (in hospital)* cama *f* de pago

paycheque ['peɪtʃek] *n* sueldo *m*

payday ['peɪdeɪ] *n* día *m* de paga

PAYE [piːeɪwaɪˈiː] *n Br (abbr* **pay as you earn)** retención *f*. fiscal sobre el sueldo

payee [peɪˈiː] *n* portador(a) *m,f*, beneficiario(a) *m,f*

paying ['peɪɪŋ] *adj* de pago; **p. guest** huésped(eda) *m,f* de pago

paymaster ['peɪmɑːstər] *n* oficial *m* pagador

payment ['peɪmənt] *n (paying)* pago *m*; *(amount paid)* pago *m*, remuneración *f*; *(expense)* desembolso *m*; *(of cheque)* cobro *m*; **on p. of $10** mediante pago de *or* pagando 10 dólares; **to do sth without p.** hacer algo gratis *or* sin cobrar ▫ **advance p.** anticipo *m*; **cash p.** pago *m* al contado *or* en efectivo; **deferred p.** pago *m* a plazos; **down p.** entrada *f*; **monthly p.** mensualidad *f*, pago *m* mensual; **p. by instalments** pago *m* a plazos; **yearly p.** anualidad *f*, pago *m* anual

payoff ['peɪɒf] *n* **(a)** *(of debt)* liquidación *f*; *(reward)* recompensa *f* **(b)** *Fam (bribe)* soborno *m*, *Méx* mordida *f*, *RP* coima *f* **(c)** *Fam (outcome)* desenlace *m*

pay-per-view ['peɪpəˈvjuː] **1** *n* pago *m* por visión

2 *adj* **p.-p.-v. channel** canal *m* de pago por visión; **p. television** televisión *f* a la carta

payroll ['peɪrəʊl] *n* nómina *f*; **to be on a firm's p.** estar en la nómina de una empresa

PC [piːˈsiː] **1** *n (pl* **PCs) (a)** *Br (abbr* **Police Constable)** (agente *mf* de) policía *mf* **(b)** *(abbr* **personal computer)** PC *m*

2 *adj (abbr* **politically correct)** políticamente correcto(a)

pc **(a)** *(abbr* **per cent)** por ciento, p.c. **(b)** [piːˈsiː] *Fam (abbr* **postcard)** (tarjeta *f*) postal *f*

pd *(abbr* **paid)** pagado(a)

PDQ [piːdiːˈkjuː] *adv Fam (abbr* **Pretty Damn Quick)** por la vía rápida, rapidito

PE [piːˈiː] *n (abbr* **physical education)** educación *f* física

pea [piː] *n Bot Esp* guisante *m*, *Am* arveja *f*, *Carib Méx* chícharo *m*; *Fig* **to be as like as two peas in a pod** ser *or* parecerse como dos gotas de agua ▫ **sweet p.** guisante *m* de olor

peace [piːs] *n (gen)* paz *f*; *(calm)* tranquilidad *f*; **at** *or* **in p.** en paz; **leave us in p.** déjanos en paz; **p. of mind** tranquilidad de espíritu; **p. and quiet** tranquilidad, sosiego *m*; **to keep the p.** mantener la paz; *Jur* mantener el orden; **to make p.** *(people)* hacer las paces; *(countries)* firmar la paz ▫ **p. conference** conferencia *f* de paz; **P. Corps** = organización gubernamental estadounidense de ayuda al desarrollo con cooperantes sobre el terreno; **p. march** marcha *f* por la paz *or* pacifista; **p. movement** pacifismo *m*, movimiento *m* pacifista; *Fig* **p. offering** prenda *f* de paz; **p. talks** conversaciones *fpl* por la paz; **p. treaty** tratado *m* de paz

peaceable ['piːsəbəl] *adj* pacífico(a)

peaceful ['piːsfʊl] *adj (non-violent)* pacífico(a); *(calm)* tranquilo(a), sosegado(a)

peace-keeping ['piːskiːpɪŋ] *adj* pacificador(a) ▫ **p.-k. forces** fuerzas *fpl* de pacificación

peace-loving ['piːslʌvɪŋ] *adj* amante de la paz, pacífico(a)

peacemaker ['piːsmeɪkər] *n* pacificador(a) *m,f*

peacetime ['piːstaɪm] *n* tiempos *mpl* de paz

peach [piːtʃ] **1** *n* **(a)** *Bot (fruit)* melocotón *m*, *Am* durazno *m*; *Fam* **she's a p.** es una monada ▫ **p. tree** melocotonero *m* **(b)** *(colour)* melocotón *m*, *Am* durazno *m*

2 *adj* de color melocotón

peacock ['piːkɒk] *n* pavo *m* real

peahen ['piːhen] *n* pava *f* real

peak [piːk] *n* **(a)** *(of cap)* visera *f* **(b)** *(of mountain)* pico *m*; *(summit)* cima *f*, cumbre *f* **(c)** *Fig (highest point)* cumbre *f*, cúspide *f*; *(climax)* apogeo *m*; **she was at the p. of her career** estaba en pleno apogeo de su carrera ▫ **p. hours** horas *fpl* punta; *Ind* **p. output** máxima producción *f*, máximo rendimiento *m*; *Elec* **p. period** horas *fpl* de mayor consumo; **p. season** temporada *f* alta

peaked [piːkt] *adj (cap)* con visera

peaky ['pi:kɪ] *adj* (**peakier, peakiest**) *Br Fam* pachucho(a), *Am* flojo(a); **to look p.** estar paliducho(a), tener la cara pálida

peal [pi:l] **1** *n (of bells)* repique *m*; **p. of thunder** trueno *m*; **peals of laughter** carcajadas *fpl*
2 *vt (also* **p. out***) (bells)* repicar, tocar a vuelo
3 *vi (bells)* repicar, tocar a vuelo; *(thunder)* retumbar; *(organ)* sonar

peanut ['pi:nʌt] *n* cacahuete *m*, *Andes Carib RP* maní *m*, *CAm Méx* cacahuate *m*; *Fam* **it's peanuts** son migajas ❑ **p. butter** mantequilla *f or* manteca *f* de cacahuete *or Andes Carib RP* maní *or CAm Méx* cacahuate; **p. oil** aceite *m* de cacahuete *or Andes Carib RP* maní *or CAm Méx* cacahuate

pear [peər] *n (tree)* peral *m*; *(fruit)* pera *f*

pearl [pɜ:l] **1** *n* perla *f*; **real/cultured pearls** perlas finas/cultivadas; **mother of p.** nácar *m*, madreperla *f*; **string of pearls, p. necklace** collar *m* de perlas; *Fig* **pearls of wisdom** joyas *fpl* de sabiduría; **to cast pearls before swine** echar margaritas a los cerdos
2 *adj (necklace etc)* de perlas; *(button)* de nácar *or* madreperla; **p. barley** cebada *f* perlada; **p. diver** pescador(a) *m,f* de perlas; **p. oyster** ostra *f* perlífera

pearly ['pɜ:lɪ] *adj* (**pearlier, pearliest**) *(colour)* nacarado(a); *Hum* **the P. Gates** las puertas del paraíso

pear-shaped ['peəʃeɪpt] *adj* en forma de pera

peasant ['pezənt] *adj & n* campesino(a) *(m,f)*

peashooter ['pi:ʃu:tər] *n* cerbatana *f*

peat [pi:t] *n* turba *f* ❑ **p. bog** turbera *f*

peaty ['pi:tɪ] *adj* (**peatier, peatiest**) turboso(a)

pebble ['pebəl] *n* guijarro *m*, china *f*; *Fam* **you're not the only p. on the beach** no eres el único que cuenta

pebbledash ['pebəldæʃ] *n Br* enguijarrado *m (mampostería)*

pebbly ['peblɪ] *adj* (**pebblier, pebbliest**) *(stony)* pedregoso(a); *(beach)* guijarroso(a)

pecan [*Br* 'pi:kən, *US* pɪ'kæn] *n (tree)* pacanero *m*; *(nut)* pacana *f*

peccadillo [pekə'dɪləʊ] *n (pl* **peccadilloes** *or* **peccadillos**) pecadillo *m*, vicio *m* pequeño

peccary ['pekərɪ] *n Zool* pecarí *m*

peck [pet] **1** *n (of bird)* picotazo *m*; *Fam (little kiss)* besito *m*
2 *vt (bird)* picotear; *Fam (kiss)* dar un besito a
3 *vi (bird)* picotear; **to p. at sth** picotear algo; **to p. at one's food** picar la comida

pecker ['pekər] *n Slang* **(a)** *US (penis)* pito *m*, cola *f* **(b)** *Br (spirits)* **keep your p. up!** ¡ánimo!, ¡no te desanimes!

pecking order ['pekɪŋɔ:dər] *n Fig* jerarquía *f*

peckish ['pekɪʃ] *adj Fam* algo hambriento(a); **to feel p.** empezar a tener hambre

pecs [peks] *npl Fam (pectoral muscles)* pectorales *mpl*

pectin ['pektɪn] *n* pectina *f*

pectoral ['pektərəl] *Anat* **1 pectorals** *npl* pectorales *mpl*
2 *adj* pectoral

peculiar [pɪ'kju:lɪər] *adj* **(a)** *(strange)* extraño(a), raro(a); *(unwell)* indispuesto(a); **to feel p.** sentirse mal; **what a p. taste!** ¡qué sabor más raro! **(b)** *(particular)* característico(a), peculiar, propio(a); **customs p. to this region** costumbres propias de esta región

peculiarity [pɪkjʊlɪ'ærɪtɪ] *n* **(a)** *(oddity)* rareza *f*, cosa *f* extraña **(b)** *(characteristic)* característica *f*, peculiaridad *f*, particularidad *f*

peculiarly [pɪ'kju:lɪəlɪ] *adv (strangely)* de una forma extraña *or* rara; *(especially)* particularmente

pecuniary [pɪ'kju:nɪərɪ] *adj* pecuniario(a); **p. problems** problemas de dinero

pedagogical [pedə'gɒdʒɪkəl] *adj* pedagógico(a)

pedagogy ['pedəgɒdʒɪ] *n* pedagogía *f*

pedal ['pedəl] **1** *n* pedal *m* ❑ *Aut* **clutch p.** pedal *m* del embrague; *Mus* **loud p.** pedal *m* fuerte; **p. bin** cubo *m or* bote *m* de la basura con pedal; **p. boat** hidropedal *m*; **p. car** cochecito *m* con pedales; *Mus* **soft p.** sordina *f*
2 *vt (pt & pp* **pedalled**, *US* **pedaled**) *(bicycle, boat etc)* impulsar pedaleando
3 *vi* pedalear

pedalo ['pedələʊ] *(pl* **pedalos**) *n* patín *m*, hidropatín *m*

pedant ['pedənt] *n* pedante *mf*

pedantic [pɪ'dæntɪk] *adj* pedante

pedantry ['pedəntrɪ] *n* pedantería *f*

peddle ['pedəl] *vt Com* vender de puerta en puerta; **to p. drugs** traficar con drogas

peddler ['pedlər] *n* **(a)** *(pusher)* traficante *mf* de drogas **(b)** *US see* **pedlar**

pederast ['pedəræst] *n* pederasta *m*

pedestal ['pedɪstəl] *n* pedestal *m*, basa *f*; *Fig* **to put sb on a p.** poner a algn sobre un pedestal ❑ **p. lamp** lámpara *f* de pie

pedestrian [pɪ'destrɪən] **1** *n* peatón(ona) *m,f* ❑ **p. crossing** paso *m* de peatones; **p. precinct** zona *f* peatonal
2 *adj (dull)* pedestre, prosaico(a)

pedestrianize [pɪ'destrɪənaɪz] *vt* **to p. a road** hacer peatonal una calle

pediatric [pi:dɪ'ætrɪk] *adj US see* **paediatric**

pediatrician [pi:dɪə'trɪʃən] *n US see* **paediatrician**

pediatrics [pi:dɪ'ætrɪks] *n US see* **paediatrics**

pedicure ['pedɪkjʊər] *n* pedicura *f*, quiropedia *f*

pedigree ['pedɪgri:] **1** *n (ancestry)* linaje *m*; *(family tree)* árbol *m* genealógico; *(of animal)* pedigrí *m*
2 *adj (animal)* de raza, de casta

pedlar ['pedlər] *n Br Com* vendedor(a) *m,f* ambulante

pedophile ['pi:dəʊfaɪl] *US see* **paedophile**

pedophilia [pi:də'fɪlɪə] *US see* **paedophilia**

pee [pi:] *Fam* **1** *n* pis *m*; **to have a p.** hacer pis
2 *vi* hacer pis

peek [pi:k] **1** *n* mirada *f* rápida, ojeada *f*; **to have** *or* **take a p. at sth** echar una ojeada a algo, mirar algo a hurtadillas
2 *vi* **to p. at sth** echar una ojeada a algo, mirar algo a hurtadillas

peel [pi:l] **1** *n (skin)* piel *f*, mondadura *f*; *(of orange, lemon)* corteza *f*; **candied p.** piel confitada
2 *vt (fruit etc)* pelar, quitar la piel *or* la corteza de; *Fam* **to keep one's eyes peeled** estar ojo avizor
3 *vi (paint)* desconcharse; *(wallpaper)* despegarse; *(skin, person)* pelarse; **her back was peeling** se le pelaba la espalda

peel back *vt (layers etc)* quitar, despegar

peel off 1 *vt (skin of fruit)* pelar, quitar la piel *or* corteza de; *Fam (clothes)* quitarse, *Am* sacarse
2 *vi (paint)* desconcharse; *(wallpaper)* despegarse; *(clothes)* desnudarse

peeler ['pi:lər] *n Esp* pelapatatas *m inv*, *Am* pelapapas *m inv*

peelings ['pi:lɪŋz] *npl* peladuras *fpl*, mondaduras *fpl*

peep¹ [pi:p] *n (sound)* pío *m*; *Fig* **there hasn't been a p. out of them all day** no han dicho ni pío en todo el día

peep² [pi:p] **1** *n (glance)* ojeada *f*, vistazo *m*; *(furtive look)* mirada *f* furtiva; **to have** *or* **take a p. at sth** echar una ojeada *or* un vistazo a algo
2 *vi* **to p. at sth** echar una ojeada *or* un vistazo a algo; **to p. through the keyhole** mirar *or* espiar por el ojo de la cerradura; **to p. out from behind sth** dejarse ver detrás de algo

peephole ['pi:phəʊl] n mirilla f

Peeping Tom [pi:pɪŋ'tɒm] n Pej mirón m

peepshow ['pi:pʃəʊ] n mundonuevo m

peer[1] [pɪər] n (a) (contemporary, equal) par mf, igual mf ❏ **p. group** grupo m parejo (b) (noble) par m; **to be made a p.** adquirir un título de nobleza

peer[2] [pɪər] vi (look closely) mirar detenidamente; (shortsightedly) mirar con ojos de miope; **to p. over a wall** echar un vistazo por un muro

peerage ['pɪərɪdʒ] n título m de nobleza; **to give sb a p.** otorgar a algn un título de nobleza

peeress ['pɪərɪs] n paresa f

peerless ['pɪəlɪs] adj sin par, sin igual, incomparable

peeved [pi:vd] adj Fam fastidiado(a), de mal humor; **to be p. about sth** estar fastidiado(a) or de malhumor por algo

peevish ['pi:vɪʃ] adj malhumorado(a)

peevishly ['pi:vɪʃlɪ] adv con mal humor, malhumoradamente

peewit ['pi:wɪt] n Orn avefría f

peg [peg] **1** n Tech clavija f; (for coat, hat) percha f, gancho m, colgador m; **to buy clothes off the p.** comprar la ropa hecha; Fam Fig **to take sb down a p. or two** bajar los humos a algn ❏ **clothes p.** pinza f; **tent p.** estaca f; Mus **tuning p.** clavija f
2 vt (pt & pp **pegged**) (clothes) tender; (tent) fijar con estacas; Fin (prices) fijar, estabilizar

peg away at vt Fam Esp currar, Méx Perú Ven chambear, RP laburar

peg down vt (tent) sujetar con estacas

peg out 1 vt (clothes) tender; (boundary) marcar con estacas
2 vi Fam (die) estirar la pata, Méx petatearse

pegging ['pegɪŋ] n Sport **to be level p.** estar igualados(as)

pejorative [pɪ'dʒɒrətɪv] adj peyorativo(a), despectivo(a)

Pekinese [pi:kə'ni:z] adj & n pequinés(esa) (m,f)

Peking [pi:'kɪŋ] n Pekín

pelican ['pelɪkən] n Orn pelícano m ❏ Br **p. crossing** paso m de peatones

pellet ['pelɪt] n (small ball) bolita f; (for gun) perdigón m; Med píldora f

pell-mell [pel'mel] adv en confusión, en tropel

pelmet ['pelmɪt] n galería f de cortina

pelt[1] [pelt] n (skin) piel f, pellejo m

pelt[2] [pelt] **1** vt arrojar, tirar; **to p. sb with sth** tirar algo a algn; **he was pelted with stones** lo apedrearon; **he was pelted with abuse** le cubrieron de insultos
2 vi Fam (a) (rain) **it's pelting (down)** llueve a cántaros (b) (rush) correr a toda prisa or a toda velocidad; **to p. along** ir disparado(a) or como una flecha

pelvic ['pelvɪk] adj pélvico(a)

pelvis ['pelvɪs] n pelvis f

pen[1] [pen] **1** n (gen) pluma f; (ballpoint pen) bolígrafo m, Chile lápiz m (de pasta), Col Ecuad Ven esferográfica f, Méx pluma f, RP birome m; **to put p. to paper** tomar la pluma, escribir ❏ **felt-tip p.** rotulador m; **fountain p.** estilográfica f; **p. name** seudónimo m
2 vt (pt & pp **penned**) (letter) escribir; (article) redactar

pen[2] [pen] **1** n (for animals) corral m; (for sheep) aprisco m, redil m; (for bulls) toril m; (for children) parque m de niños
2 vt **to p. in** encerrar, acorralar

pen[3] [pen] n (abbr **penitentiary**) US Fam (prison) Esp trullo m, Andes Col RP cana f, Méx bote m

penal ['pi:nəl] adj penal ❏ **p. code** código m penal; **p.**

offence infracción f penal; **p. servitude** trabajos mpl forzados

penalize ['pi:nəlaɪz] vt (punish) castigar; Sport penalizar; (handicap) perjudicar; **the policy penalizes the poor** la política perjudica a los pobres

penalty ['penltɪ] n (punishment) pena f, castigo m; Sport penalización f; Ftb penalti m, penalty m, Am penal m; Fig (handicap) desventaja f; **on p. of death** so pena de muerte; **to pay the p. for sth** cargar con or pagar las consecuencias de algo ❏ **death p.** pena f de muerte; Ftb **p. area** área f de castigo; Jur **p. clause** cláusula f de penalización; Ftb **p. goal** gol m de penalti; Ftb **p. kick** (lanzamiento m de) penalti m or Am penal m

penance ['penəns] n penitencia f; **to do p. for sth** hacer penitencia por algo

pence [pens] npl see **penny**

penchant ['pɒnʃɒn] n inclinación f, predilección f; **to have a p. for sth** tener una predilección por algo

pencil ['pensəl] **1** n lápiz m; **to write in p.** escribir a lápiz ❏ **p. case** estuche m de lápices, plumero m; **p. drawing** dibujo m a lápiz; **p. sharpener** sacapuntas m inv
2 vt (pt & pp **pencilled**, US **penciled**) **to p. in** (write) escribir con lápiz; (draw) dibujar (con lápiz)

pendant ['pendənt] n colgante m, medallón m

pending ['pendɪŋ] **1** adj pendiente; **to be p.** estar pendiente, estar en trámites
2 prep (while) mientras; (until) hasta; **p. a decision** hasta que se tome una decisión; **p. their arrival** hasta que lleguen

pendulum ['pendjʊləm] n péndulo m

penetrate ['penɪtreɪt] **1** vt (go through) penetrar por; (infiltrate) infiltrar; Fig (reach) llegar hasta
2 vi (go through) atravesar; (get inside) penetrar; (permeate) trascender; Fig (be understood) entrar, penetrar

penetrating ['penɪtreɪtɪŋ] adj (look, thought) penetrante; (small) trascendente; (mind) perspicaz; (sound) agudo(a)

penetration [penɪ'treɪʃən] n (gen) penetración f; (permeation) trascendencia f; Fig (entry) entrada f

penfriend ['penfrend] n amigo(a) m,f por carta

penguin ['peŋgwɪn] n Orn pingüino m

penicillin [penɪ'sɪlɪn] n Med penicilina f

peninsula [pɪ'nɪnsjʊlə] n península f; **the Iberian P.** la Península Ibérica

peninsular [pɪ'nɪnsjʊlər] adj peninsular; Hist **the P. War** la guerra de la Independencia de España

penis ['pi:nɪs] n Anat pene m

penitence ['penɪtəns] n Rel penitencia f; (repentance) arrepentimiento m

penitent ['penɪtənt] **1** adj Rel penitente; (repentant) arrepentido(a)
2 n Rel penitente mf

penitentiary [penɪ'tenʃərɪ] n US penitenciaria f, cárcel f, penal m

penknife ['pennaɪf] n (pl **penknives** ['pennaɪvz]) navaja f, cortaplumas m inv

pennant ['penənt] n banderín m

penniless ['penɪlɪs] adj sin dinero, arruinado(a); **to be p.** estar sin un centavo or Esp duro

Pennines ['penaɪnz] n **the P.** los (montes) Peninos

penny ['penɪ] n (pl **pennies, pence**) (a) Br penique m; **a ten/twenty pence piece** una moneda de diez/veinte peniques; **he dropped three pennies** dejó caer tres peniques; **in for a p., in for a pound** preso por mil, preso por mil quinientos; **they haven't got a p. to their name** no tienen ni una perra gorda or Esp ni un duro; **to cost a**

pretty p. costar un dineral; *Fig* **the p. dropped** cayó en la cuenta; *Fig* **he turns up like a bad p.** mala hierba nunca muere; *Euph* **to spend a p.** ir a los servicios; *Fam* **they are two a p.** están muy vistos(as) **(b)** *US* centavo *m*

penny-pinching ['penɪpɪntʃɪŋ] *adj* tacaño(a)

penpal ['penpæl] *n US see* **penfriend**

pension ['penʃən] *n* pensión *f*; **to draw one's p.** cobrar la pénsión ❑ **old age p.** pensión *f* de vejez; **p. fund** caja *f* de pensiones; **retirement p.** jubilación *f*, pensión *f*; **p. scheme** plan *m* de jubilación

pension off *vt* jubilar

pensionable ['penʃənəbəl] *adj* **of p. age** en edad de jubilación

pensioner ['penʃənər] *n* pensionista *mf*, jubilado(a) *m,f*

pensive ['pensɪv] *adj (deep in thought)* pensativo(a); *(melancholy)* melancólico(a)

pensively ['pensɪvlɪ] *adv* con aire pensativo *or* melancólico

pentagon ['pentəgɒn] *n* pentágono *m*; *US Pol* **the P.** el Pentágono

pentathlon [pen'tæθlən] *n* pentatlón *m*

Pentecost ['pentɪkɒst] *n Rel* Pentecostés *m*

penthouse ['penthaʊs] *n* ático *m*, sobreático *m*

pent-up ['pentʌp] *adj (confined)* encerrado(a); *(repressed)* reprimido(a)

penultimate [pɪ'nʌltɪmɪt] *adj & n* penúltimo(a) *(m,f)*

penury ['penjʊrɪ] *n* miseria *f*, pobreza *f*; **to live in p.** vivir en la miseria

peony ['piːənɪ] *n Bot* peonía *f*

people ['piːpəl] **1** *npl* **(a)** *(gen)* gente *f sing*; *(individuals)* personas *fpl*; **many p.** mucha gente, muchas personas; **Mary of all p.!** María, ¿quién lo diría?; **old p.** las personas de la tercera edad, *Esp* las personas mayores; **old p.'s home** asilo *m* de ancianos; **other p.** los demás, otras personas; **p. say that ...** se dice que ...; **some p.** algunas personas; **some p. have all the luck!** ¡algunos nacen de pie!; **there were 500 p.** había 500 personas; **what a lot of p.!** ¡cuánta gente!; **young p.** los jóvenes, la juventud, la gente joven ❑ **p. carrier** monovolumen *m* **(b)** *(citizens)* ciudadanos *mpl*; *(inhabitants)* habitantes *mpl*; **city/country p.** la gente de la ciudad/del campo; **government by the p.** el gobierno del pueblo; **the p.** el pueblo; **the p. of Scotland** los habitantes de Escocia, los escoceses ❑ **p.'s tribunal** tribunal *m* popular *or* del pueblo **(c)** *(family)* familia *f*, gente *f*; **his p.** los suyos **(d)** *(nation)* pueblo *m*, nación *f*; **the Mexican p.** el pueblo mejicano

2 *vt* poblar

pep [pep] *n Fam* ánimo *m*, energía *f* ❑ **p. pill** estimulante *m*; **p. talk** discurso *m* enardecedor

pep up *vt Fam (pt & pp* **pepped)** *(gen)* animar; *(person)* dar ánimos a

pepper ['pepər] **1** *n (spice)* pimienta *f*; *(fruit)* pimiento *m*, *Méx* chile *m*, *RP* ají *m*, *Col Ven* pimentón *m* ❑ **black p.** pimienta *f* negra; **green p.** pimiento *m* verde; **p. mill** molinillo *m* de pimienta; **p. pot** pimentero *m*; **red p.** pimiento *m* rojo; **sweet p.** pimiento *m* morrón; **white p.** pimiento *f* blanca

2 *vt Culin* echar pimienta a; *Fig* **peppered with** salpicado(a) de; **peppered with bullets** acribillado(a) a balazos

pepperbox ['pepəbɒks] *n US* pimentero *m*

peppercorn ['pepəkɔːn] *n* grano *m* de pimienta

peppermint ['pepəmɪnt] *n Bot* hierbabuena *f*, menta *f*; *(sweet)* caramelo *m or* pastilla *f* de menta ❑ **p. tea** infusión *f* de menta

peppery ['pepərɪ] *adj (food)* con mucha pimienta; *(spicy)* picante; *Fig (person)* colérico(a), enojadizo(a)

peptic ['peptɪk] *n Med* péptico(a) ❑ **p. ulcer** úlcera *f* estomacal

per [pɜːr] *prep* por; **as p. usual** como de costumbre; **as p. your advice** según tus consejos; **5 times p. week** 5 veces a la semana; **p. cent** por ciento; **100 p. cent** cien por cien; **p. day/annum** al *or* por día/año; **p. head** *or* **capita** *or* **person** por cabeza, cada uno

perceive [pə'siːv] *vt (see)* percibir, ver; *(realize)* darse cuenta de; *(notice)* notar

percentage [pə'sentɪdʒ] *n* porcentaje *m*; **to get a p. on the sales** recibir un tanto por ciento de las ventas

perceptible [pə'septəbəl] *adj (visible)* perceptible, visible; *(audible)* audible; *(noticeable)* sensible

perceptibly [pə'septɪblɪ] *adv (visibly)* visiblemente; *(audibly)* audiblemente; *(noticeably)* sensiblemente

perception [pə'sepʃən] *n* percepción *f*

perceptive [pə'septɪv] *adj* perspicaz

perch¹ [pɜːtʃ] *n (fish)* perca *f*

perch² [pɜːtʃ] **1** *n (for bird)* percha *f*; *Fig (pedestal)* posición *f* elevada, pedestal *m*

2 *vt* poner *or* colocar arriba; **perched on a rock** encaramado(a) en una roca

3 *vi (bird)* posarse **(on** en); *(person)* colocarse en una posición elevada

percolate ['pɜːkəleɪt] **1** *vt* filtrar ❑ **percolated coffee** café *m* filtro

2 *vi (gen)* filtrarse

percolator ['pɜːkəleɪtər] *n* cafetera *f* de filtro

percussion [pə'kʌʃən] *n* percusión *f*; **p. instrument** instrumento *m* de percusión

percussionist [pə'kʌʃənɪst] *n* percusionista *mf*

peregrine falcon ['perɪgrɪn'fɔːlkən] *n Orn* halcón *m* peregrino

peremptory [pə'remptərɪ] *adj* perentorio(a)

perennial [pə'renɪəl] **1** *n Bot* planta *f* perenne

2 *adj (plant)* perenne; *(youthfulness)* eterno(a)

perfect ['pɜːfɪkt] **1** *adj* **(a)** *(gen)* perfecto(a); *(behaviour, reputation)* intachable ❑ *Mus* **p. pitch** tono *m* perfecto **(b)** *(ideal)* idóneo(a) **(c)** *(absolute, utter) (fool)* perdido(a); *(gentleman)* consumado(a); *(waste of time)* auténtico(a); **he's a p. stranger to us** nos es totalmente desconocido **(d)** *Ling* **p. tense** tiempo *m* perfecto

2 *n Ling* perfecto *m*

3 [pə'fekt] *vt* perfeccionar

perfection [pə'fekʃən] *n* perfección *f*; **done to p.** hecho(a) a la perfección

perfectionist [pə'fekʃənɪst] *n* perfeccionista *mf*

perfectly ['pɜːfɪktlɪ] *adv (faultlessly)* perfectamente; *(absolutely)* completamente; **p. obvious** clarísimo; **you're p. right** tienes toda la razón

perfidious [pə'fɪdɪəs] *adj* pérfido(a)

perforate ['pɜːfəreɪt] *vt* perforar ❑ **perforated line** línea *f* perforada; *Med* **perforated ulcer** úlcera *f* perforada

perforation [pɜːfə'reɪʃən] *n Med* perforación *f*; *(on stamps etc)* perforado *m*

perform [pə'fɔːm] **1** *vt* **(a)** *(task, work)* ejecutar, cumplir, realizar **(b)** *Mus (piece of music)* tocar, interpretar; *(song)* cantar; *Theat (play)* representar, dar

2 *vi* **(a)** *(machine)* funcionar, marchar; *(car etc)* andar, ir; *(person)* trabajar **(b)** *Mus* tocar, interpretar; *Theat (actor)* actuar; *(company)* dar una representación; *(in circus, show)* hacer un número

performance [pə'fɔːməns] *n* **(a)** *(of task etc)* ejecución *f*, cumplimiento *m*, realización *f* ❑ **p. appraisal** evaluación *f* del rendimiento **(b)** *Mus* interpretación *f*; *Theat* representación f; (in circus, show) número m; Sport (of team etc) actuación f; **a great p. by Arsenal** una magnífica actuación del Arsenal; Fam **what a p.!** ¡vaya lío! **(c)** (of machine etc) funcionamiento m, rendimiento m

performance-enhancing [pə'fɔːmənsen'hɑːnsɪŋ] adj que mejora el rendimiento

performance-related [pə'fɔːmənsrɪ'leɪtɪd] adj según el rendimiento

performer [pə'fɔːmər] n Mus intérprete mf; Theat artista mf, actor m, actriz f

performing [pə'fɔːmɪŋ] adj (dog, seal) amaestrado(a); **p. arts** artes fpl interpretativas

perfume ['pɜːfjuːm] **1** n perfume m
2 [pə'fjuːm] vt perfumar, echar perfume a

perfumery [pə'fjuːmərɪ] n perfumería f

perfunctory [pə'fʌŋktərɪ] adj (action) superficial; (person) negligente

perhaps [pə'hæps, præps] adv quizá, quizás, tal vez, Am talvez; **p./p. not** puede que sí/no; **p. she'll come** quizás vendrá, puede que venga

peril ['perɪl] n (risk) riesgo m; (danger) peligro m; **at your own p.** por su cuenta y riesgo

perilous ['perɪləs] adj (risky) arriesgado(a); (dangerous) peligroso(a)

perilously ['perɪləslɪ] adv peligrosamente; **we came p. close to falling** por poco nos caemos

perimeter [pə'rɪmɪtər] n perímetro m

period ['pɪərɪəd] **1** n (**a**) (length of time) período m, época f; (stage) etapa f; **for a p. of three years** durante (un período de) tres años; Meteor **sunny periods** claros mpl; **the holiday p.** el período or la temporada de vacaciones; **the post-war p.** la posguerra; **the Romantic p.** la época romántica (**b**) Educ (class) clase f; **free p.** hora f libre (**c**) US (full stop) punto m (**d**) (menstruation) **(menstrual) p.** regla f, período m; **to have one's p.** tener el período ❑ **p. pains** dismenorrea f sing
2 adj (dress) de época; (furniture) de época, clásico(a)

periodic [pɪərɪ'ɒdɪk] adj periódico(a) ❑ Chem **p. table** cuadro m de elementos

periodical [pɪərɪ'ɒdɪkəl] **1** adj periódico(a)
2 n revista f

periodically [pɪərɪ'ɒdɪklɪ] adv de vez en cuando

peripatetic [perɪpə'tetɪk] adj peripatético(a)

peripheral [pə'rɪfərəl] **1** adj periférico(a)
2 Comptr **peripherals** npl periféricos mpl

periphery [pə'rɪfərɪ] n periferia f

periscope ['perɪskəʊp] n periscopio m

perish ['perɪʃ] vi (**a**) (person) fallecer, perecer (**b**) (material) echarse a perder, estropearse

perishable ['perɪʃəbəl] **1** adj perecedero(a)
2 perishables npl productos mpl perecederos

perishing ['perɪʃɪŋ] adj Fam **it's p.** hace un frío que pela

peritonitis [perɪtə'naɪtɪs] n Med peritonitis f inv

periwinkle ['perɪwɪŋkəl] n Bot vincapervinca f; Zool caracol m de mar, bígaro m

perjure ['pɜːdʒər] vt **to p. oneself** jurar en falso, perjurar

perjury ['pɜːdʒərɪ] n perjurio m; **to commit p.** cometer perjurio

perk [pɜːk] n Br Fam beneficio m, gaje m

perk up 1 vt (liven up) animar, levantar el ánimo; **to p. oneself up** animarse
2 vi (person) animarse; (after illness) reponerse

perky ['pɜːkɪ] adj (**perkier, perkiest**) animado(a), alegre

perm [pɜːm] **1** n (abbr **permanent wave**) permanente f; **to have a p.** hacerse la permanente
2 vt **to p. sb's hair** hacer la permanente a algn; **to have one's hair permed** hacerse la permanente

permanence ['pɜːmənəns] n, **permanency** ['pɜːmənənsɪ] n permanencia f

permanent ['pɜːmənənt] adj (lasting) permanente, duradero(a); (address, job) fijo(a) ❑ **p. wave** permanente f

permanently ['pɜːmənəntlɪ] adv (forever) permanentemente; (always) siempre

permanganate [pə'mæŋɡənɪt] n permanganato m

permeate ['pɜːmɪeɪt] vt & vi penetrar, trascender (**through** por); Fig extenderse por

permissible [pə'mɪsəbəl] adj admisible, lícito(a); **it's not p.** no se permite

permission [pə'mɪʃən] n (gen) permiso m; (authorization) autorización f; **to ask for p. to do sth** pedir permiso para hacer algo; **to give sb p. to do sth** autorizar a algn para que haga algo; **with your p.** con su permiso

permissive [pə'mɪsɪv] adj permisivo(a)

permit ['pɜːmɪt] **1** n (gen) permiso m; Com permiso, licencia f; (pass) pase m ❑ **import/export p.** licencia f de importación/exportación; **residence p.** permiso m de residencia
2 [pə'mɪt] vt (pt & pp **permitted**) (gen) permitir; (authorize) autorizar; **to p. sb to do sth** permitir or autorizar a algn hacer algo
3 [pə'mɪt] vi permitir; **weather permitting** si el tiempo lo permite

permutation [pɜːmjʊ'teɪʃən] n permutación f

pernicious [pə'nɪʃəs] adj nocivo(a), perjudicial; Med pernicioso(a)

pernickety [pə'nɪkətɪ] adj Fam (person) quisquilloso(a); (job) delicado(a)

peroxide [pə'rɒksaɪd] n peróxido m ❑ **hydrogen p.** agua f oxigenada

perpendicular [pɜːpən'dɪkjʊlər] **1** adj (gen) perpendicular; (cliff) vertical
2 n perpendicular f

perpetrate ['pɜːpɪtreɪt] vt (crime) perpetrar, cometer

perpetrator ['pɜːpɪtreɪtər] n (of crime) autor(a) m,f

perpetual [pə'petʃʊəl] adj (constant) continuo(a); (endless) interminable; (eternal) perpetuo(a), eterno(a)

perpetually [pə'petʃʊəlɪ] adv (constantly) continuamente; (eternally) perpetuamente, eternamente

perpetuate [pə'petʃʊeɪt] vt perpetuar

perpetuity [pɜːpɪ'tjuːɪtɪ] n perpetuidad f; **in p.** a perpetuidad

perplex [pə'pleks] vt dejar perplejo(a) or confuso(a)

perplexed [pə'plekst] adj perplejo(a), confuso(a); **we were p. by her refusal** su negativa nos dejó perplejos

perplexing [pə'pleksɪŋ] adj que deja perplejo(a) or confuso(a)

perplexity [pə'pleksɪtɪ] n perplejidad f, confusión f

persecute ['pɜːsɪkjuːt] vt (for political or religious reasons) perseguir; (harass) atormentar, acosar

persecution [pɜːsɪ'kjuːʃən] n persecución f ❑ Psych **p. complex** complejo m persecutorio

persecutor ['pɜːsɪkjuːtər] n perseguidor(a) m,f

perseverance [pɜːsɪ'vɪərəns] n perseverancia f, persistencia f

persevere [pɜːsɪ'vɪər] vi perseverar, persistir; **to p. with sth/at doing sth** perseverar en algo/en hacer algo

persevering [pɜːsɪ'vɪərɪŋ] adj perseverante

Persia ['pɜːʒə] *n Formerly* Persia

Persian ['pɜːʃən] *adj* persa ❑ **P. Gulf** golfo *m* Pérsico

persist [pə'sɪst] *vi (insist)* empeñarse (**in** en); *(endure)* persistir; *(rain)* continuar; **to p. in doing sth** empeñarse en hacer algo

persistence [pə'sɪstəns] *n (insistence)* empeño *m*; *(durability)* persistencia *f*

persistent [pə'sɪstənt] *adj (person)* perseverante; *(cough, smell etc)* persistente; *(attempts, warnings etc) (continuous)* continuo(a); *(continual)* constante ❑ **p. offender** reincidente *mf*

persistently [pə'sɪstəntlɪ] *adv (determinedly)* con empeño; *(continually)* continuamente, constantemente

person ['pɜːsən] *n (pl* **people**) persona *f*; *(individual)* individuo *m*, tipo *m*; *Tel* **a p.** una llamada persona a persona; *Ling* **first p. singular/plural** primera persona del singular/plural; **in p.** en persona

personable ['pɜːsənəbəl] *adj (handsome)* bien parecido(a); *(pleasant)* amable

personage ['pɜːsənɪdʒ] *n* personaje *m*

personal ['pɜːsənəl] *adj* **(a)** *(private)* personal, particular; *(friend, life, hygiene)* íntimo(a) ❑ **p. assistant** secretario(a) *m,f* personal; **p. best** *(in sport)* plusmarca *f* (personal), récord *m* personal; **p. call** llamada *f* particular; **p. column** anuncios *mpl* personales; **p. effects** efectos *mpl* personales; **p. growth** desarrollo *m* personal; **p. organizer** agenda *f*; *Ling* **p. pronoun** pronombre *m* personal; **p. stereo** walkman® *m*; **p. trainer** preparador(a) *m,f* físico(a) personal **(b)** *(in person)* en persona; **to give sth one's p. attention** encargarse personalmente de algo, atender algo personalmente; **to make a p. appearance** hacer acto de presencia **(c)** *Pej (indiscreet)* indiscreto(a); **to get p. about sth** hacer alusiones personales acerca de algo; **to make p. remarks** ser indiscreto(a)

personality [pɜːsə'nælɪtɪ] *n* **(a)** *(nature)* personalidad *f* ❑ *Psych* **p. disorder** trastorno *m* de la personalidad **(b)** *(famous person)* personaje *m*

personally ['pɜːsənəlɪ] *adv (for my part)* personalmente; *(in person)* en persona; **don't take it p.** no lo tomes como algo personal; **p., I think ...** en cuanto a mí, pienso que ...

personification [pɜːsɒnɪfɪ'keɪʃən] *n* personificación *f*; **she's the p. of patience** es la paciencia personificada

personify [pɜː'sɒnɪfaɪ] *vt* personificar, encarnar

personnel [pɜːsə'nel] *n* personal *m* ❑ **p. department** departamento *m* de personal; **p. manager, p. officer** jefe(a) *m,f* de personal

perspective [pə'spektɪv] *n* perspectiva *f*; **to get** *or* **keep sth in p.** ver algo en perspectiva *or* objetivamente

Perspex® ['pɜːspeks] *n* plexiglás® *m*

perspicacious [pɜːspɪ'keɪʃəs] *adj* perspicaz

perspicacity [pɜːspɪ'kæsɪtɪ] *n* perspicacia *f*

perspiration [pɜːspə'reɪʃən] *n* transpiración *f*, sudor *m*; **to be bathed in p.** estar bañado(a) en sudor

perspire [pə'spaɪər] *vi* transpirar, sudar

persuade [pə'sweɪd] *vt* persuadir, convencer; **he isn't easily persuaded** no se deja convencer fácilmente; **to p. sb not to do sth** disuadir a algn de hacer algo; **to p. sb to do sth** persuadir *or* convencer a algn para que haga algo

persuasion [pə'sweɪʒən] *n* **(a)** *(act)* persuasión *f* **(b)** *(persuasiveness)* persuasiva *f*; **to use p. on sb** persuadir a algn ❑ **powers of p.** poder *m sing* de persuasión **(c)** *Pol Rel (opinion, belief)* credo *m*; *Art (movement)* tendencia *f*

persuasive [pə'sweɪsɪv] *adj* persuasivo(a), convincente

persuasively [pə'sweɪsɪvlɪ] *adv* de modo persuasivo *or* convincente

pert [pɜːt] *adj (cheeky)* pizpireta; *(stylishly neat)* coqueto(a)

pertain [pə'teɪn] *vi* estar relacionado(a) (**to** con)

pertinence ['pɜːtɪnəns] *n* pertinencia *f*

pertinent ['pɜːtɪnənt] *adj (relevant)* pertinente; **p. to** relacionado(a) con, a propósito de

perturb [pə'tɜːb] *vt* inquietar, perturbar

perturbing [pə'tɜːbɪŋ] *adj* inquietante, perturbador(a)

Peru [pə'ruː] *n* Perú

perusal [pə'ruːzəl] *n (reading with care)* lectura *f* detenida; *(browsing leisurely)* lectura *f* rápida *or* por encima

peruse [pə'ruːz] *vt (read with care)* leer detenidamente; *(browse through)* leer rápidamente *or* por encima

Peruvian [pə'ruːvɪən] *adj & n* peruano(a) *(m,f)*

pervade [pɜː'veɪd] *vt (smell)* penetrar, extenderse por; *(light)* difundirse por; *Fig (influence)* extenderse por

pervasive [pɜː'veɪsɪv] *adj (smell)* penetrante; *(influence)* extendido(a)

perverse [pə'vɜːs] *adj (wicked)* perverso(a); *(stubborn)* terco(a); *(contrary)* puñetero(a)

perversely [pə'vɜːslɪ] *adv (wickedly)* por perversidad; *(stubbornly)* tercamente; *(contrarily)* por llevar la contraria

perversion [pə'vɜːʃən] *n Med Psych* perversión *f*; *(of justice, truth)* tergiversación *f*

perversity [pə'vɜːsɪtɪ] *n (wickedness)* perversidad *f*; *(stubbornness)* terquedad *f*

pervert 1 *n* ['pɜːvɜːt] *Med Psych* pervertido(a) *m,f* (sexual) **2** [pə'vɜːt] *vt (gen)* pervertir; *(justice, truth)* tergiversar, desvirtuar

peseta [pə'seɪtə] *n Formerly* peseta *f*

pesky ['peskɪ] *adj US Fam* plomo(a), latoso(a), *Méx* sangrón(ona), *RP* hinchón(ona)

peso ['peɪsəʊ] *(pl* **pesos**) *n (Argentinian or Mexican currency)* peso *m*

pessary ['pesərɪ] *n* pesario *m*

pessimism ['pesɪmɪzəm] *n* pesimismo *m*

pessimist ['pesɪmɪst] *n* pesimista *mf*

pessimistic [pesɪ'mɪstɪk] *adj* pesimista; **to be p. about sth** ser pesimista en cuanto a algo

pessimistically [pesɪ'mɪstɪklɪ] *adv* con pesimismo

pest [pest] *n* **(a)** *Zool* insecto *m or* animal *m* nocivo, bicho *m*; *Bot* planta *f* nociva ❑ **p. control** control *m* de plagas **(b)** *Fam (person) (nuisance)* plomazo *m*, *Esp* latazo *m*

pester ['pestər] *vt* molestar, fastidiar

pesticide ['pestɪsaɪd] *n* pesticida *f*

pestilence ['pestɪləns] *n* pestilencia *f*, plaga *f*

pestilent ['pestɪlənt] *adj* latoso(a)

pestle ['pesəl] *n* maja *f*, mano *f* (de mortero *or* almirez)

pet [pet] **1** *n* **(a)** *(animal)* animal *m or* pájaro *m* doméstico ❑ **p. shop** tienda *f* de animales **(b)** *(favourite)* preferido(a) *m,f* ❑ **teacher's p.** alumno(a) *m,f* preferido(a) *or* enchufado(a) del maestro *or* de la maestra **(c)** *Fam (dear)* cariño *m*, chato(a) *m,f*; **he's a p.** es un cielo

2 *adj* **(a)** *(tame)* domesticado(a) **(b)** *(favourite)* preferido(a), favorito(a) ❑ **p. hate** bestia *f* negra; **p. name** nombre *m* cariñoso; **p. subject** tema *m* preferido, manía *f*

3 *vt (spoil) (child)* mimar, consentir; *(caress)* acariciar

4 *vi (sexually)* besuquearse, *Esp* darse *or* pegarse al lote, *Am* manosearse

petal ['petəl] *n* pétalo *m*

peter ['piːtər] *vi* **to p. out** *(gen)* acabarse, agotarse; *(supplies)* irse agotando; *(plans)* quedar en agua de borrajas; *(engine)* pararse

petite [pə'tiːt] *adj (woman)* menuda, chiquita

petition [pɪˈtɪʃən] **1** n petición f, solicitud f, demanda f, Am pedido m ❏ **divorce p.** demanda f de divorcio
 2 vt presentar una petición or Am un pedido a
 3 vi **to p. for sth** solicitar algo; **to p. for divorce** pedir el divorcio

petrel [ˈpetrəl] n Orn paíño m

petrify [ˈpetrɪfaɪ] vt (pt & pp **petrified**) Literary petrificar; Fig horrorizar, paralizar; Fig **they were petrified** se quedaron de piedra

petrochemical [petrəʊˈkemɪkəl] **1** adj petroquímico(a)
 2 n producto m petroquímico

petrodollar [ˈpetrəʊdɒlər] n petrodólar m

petrol [ˈpetrəl] n Br gasolina f, RP nafta f; Aut **to be heavy on p.** gastar mucha gasolina; Aut **to run out of p.** quedarse sin gasolina ❏ **high-octane p.** supercarburante m, gasolina f súper; **p. bomb** bomba f de petróleo; **p. can** bidón m de gasolina or RP nafta; **p. pump** surtidor m de gasolina; **p. station** gasolinera f, estación f de servicio, Andes grifo m; **p. tank** depósito m de la gasolina or RP de la nafta or del combustible

petroleum [pəˈtrəʊlɪəm] n petróleo m ❏ **p. jelly** vaselina f; **p. products** productos mpl petrolíferos

petticoat [ˈpetɪkəʊt] n (waist slip) enaguas fpl; (full length slip) combinación f

pettiness [ˈpetɪnɪs] n mezquindad f

petty [ˈpetɪ] adj (**pettier, pettiest**) (trivial) insignificante, sin importancia; (small-minded) mezquino(a) ❏ **p. cash** dinero m para gastos pequeños; **p. officer** sargento m de marina

petulance [ˈpetjʊləns] n mal humor m

petulant [ˈpetjʊlənt] adj malhumorado(a)

petulantly [ˈpetjʊləntlɪ] adv de mal humor

petunia [pɪˈtjuːnɪə] n Bot petunia f

pew [pjuː] n banco m de iglesia; Fam **take a p.!** ¡siéntate!

pewter [ˈpjuːtər] n peltre m

pH [piːˈeɪtʃ] n Chem pH m

phalanx [ˈfælæŋks] n Mil Hist falange f; Fig (of officials, journalists) pelotón m

phallic [ˈfælɪk] adj fálico(a)

phallus [ˈfæləs] n falo m

phantom [ˈfæntəm] adj & n fantasma (m)

Pharaoh [ˈfeərəʊ] n faraón m

pharmaceutical [fɑːməˈsjuːtɪkəl] adj farmacéutico(a)

pharmacist [ˈfɑːməsɪst] n farmacéutico(a) m,f

pharmacologist [fɑːməˈkɒlədʒɪst] n farmacólogo(a) m,f

pharmacology [fɑːməˈkɒlədʒɪ] n farmacología f

pharmacy [ˈfɑːməsɪ] n farmacia f

pharyngitis [færɪnˈdʒaɪtɪs] n faringitis f

pharynx [ˈfærɪŋks] n faringe f

phase [feɪz] **1** n (gen) fase f; Fig (stage) etapa f; **to be out of p.** estar fuera de fase, estar desfasado(a)
 2 vt **to p. sth in/out** introducir/retirar algo progresivamente

phased [feɪzd] adj (gradual) gradual; (in stages) escalonado(a)

PhD [piːeɪtʃˈdiː] n (abbr **Doctor of Philosophy**) Doctor(a) m,f en Filosofía

pheasant [ˈfezənt] n Orn faisán m (vulgar)

phenobarbitone [fiːnəʊˈbɑːbɪtəʊn] n fenobarbitona f

phenomena [fɪˈnɒmɪnə] npl see **phenomenon**

phenomenal [fɪˈnɒmɪnəl] adj fenomenal

phenomenally [fɪˈnɒmɪnəlɪ] adv fenomenalmente, extraordinariamente

phenomenon [fɪˈnɒmɪnən] n (pl **phenomenons** or **phenomena**) fenómeno m

pheromone [ˈferəməʊn] n feromona f

phew [fjuː] interj ¡uf!

phial [faɪəl] n frasco m

philanderer [fɪˈlændərər] n Fml tenorio m

philandering [fɪˈlændərɪŋ] Pej **1** n líos mpl amorosos
 2 adj mujeriego(a)

philanthropic [fɪlənˈθrɒpɪk] adj filantrópico(a)

philanthropist [fɪˈlænθrəpɪst] n filántropo(a) m,f

philanthropy [fɪˈlænθrəpɪ] n filantropía f

philately [fɪˈlætəlɪ] n filatelia f

philharmonic [fɪlhɑːˈmɒnɪk] adj filarmónico(a)

Philippine [ˈfɪlɪpiːn] adj & n filipino(a) (m,f)

Philippines [ˈfɪlɪpiːnz] npl **the P.** las (Islas) Filipinas

Philistine [ˈfɪlɪstaɪn] n filisteo(a) m,f

philologist [fɪˈlɒlədʒɪst] n filólogo(a) m,f

philology [fɪˈlɒlədʒɪ] n filología f

philosopher [fɪˈlɒsəfər] n filósofo(a) m,f

philosophical [fɪləˈsɒfɪkəl] adj (argument) filosófico(a); (person) filósofo(a); **to have a p. attitude towards sth** tener una actitud resignada frente a algo

philosophize [fɪˈlɒsəfaɪz] vi filosofar

philosophy [fɪˈlɒsəfɪ] n filosofía f

phlegm [flem] n flema f

phlegmatic [flegˈmætɪk] adj flemático(a)

phlegmatically [flegˈmætɪklɪ] adv con mucha flema, tranquilamente

phobia [ˈfəʊbɪə] n fobia f

phobic [ˈfəʊbɪk] adj **she's a bit p. about spiders** le tiene fobia a las arañas

Phoenicia [fəˈniːʃɪə] n Fenicia

Phoenician [fəˈniːʃən] adj & n fenicio(a) (m,f)

phoenix [ˈfiːnɪks] n Myth fénix m

phone [fəʊn] n see **telephone**

phonecard [ˈfəʊnkɑːd] n tarjeta f telefónica

phone-in [ˈfəʊnɪn] n Fam = programa de radio o televisión con línea telefónica abierta

phoneme [ˈfəʊniːm] n fonema m

phonetic [fəˈnetɪk] **1** adj fonético(a)
 2 phonetics n fonética f sing

phoney [ˈfəʊnɪ] **1** adj (**phonier, phoniest**) (thing) falso(a); (person) farsante
 2 n (thing) camelo m; (person) farsante mf

phonograph [ˈfəʊnəɡrɑːf] n US Old-fashioned gramófono m

phonology [fəˈnɒlədʒɪ] n fonología f

phony [ˈfəʊnɪ] n US see **phoney**

phosphate [ˈfɒsfeɪt] n fosfato m

phosphorescent [fɒsfəˈresənt] adj fosforescente

phosphorus [ˈfɒsfərəs] n fósforo m

photo [ˈfəʊtəʊ] n (abbr **photograph**) foto f ❏ **p. opportunity** = ocasión de aparecer fotografiado dando una buena imagen

photocopier [ˈfəʊtəʊkɒpɪər] n fotocopiadora f

photocopy [ˈfəʊtəʊkɒpɪ] **1** n fotocopia f
 2 vt (pt & pp **photocopied**) fotocopiar

photocopying [ˈfəʊtəʊkɒpɪŋ] n fotocopiado m; **there's some p. to do** hay que hacer algunas fotocopias

photoelectric [fəʊtəʊɪˈlektrɪk] adj fotoeléctrico(a) ❏ **p. cell** célula f fotoeléctrica, fotocélula f

photogenic [fəʊtəʊ'dʒenɪk] *adj* fotogénico(a)
photograph ['fəʊtəgræf, 'fəʊtəgrɑːf] **1** *n* fotografía *f*,
foto *f*; **black and white/colour p.** fotografía en blanco y
negro/en color; **to take a p.** *of sb/sth* hacer *or* sacar una
fotografía de algn/algo; **to have one's p. taken** sacarse
una fotografía ❑ **p. album** álbum *m* de fotos
 2 *vt* fotografiar, hacer *or* sacar fotografías *or* fotos de
photographer [fə'tɒgrəfər] *n* fotógrafo(a) *m,f*
photographic [fəʊtə'græfɪk] *adj* fotográfico(a)
photography [fə'tɒgrəfɪ] *n* fotografía *f*
photosensitive [fəʊtəʊ'sensɪtɪv] *adj* fotosensible
photostat ['fəʊtəʊstæt] *n* fotostato *m*
photosynthesis [fəʊtəʊ'sɪnθɪsɪs] *n* fotosíntesis *f inv*
phrasal verb [freɪzəl'vɜːb] *n* verbo *m* preposicional *or*
adverbial
phrase [freɪz] **1** *n (expression)* frase *f*, locución *f*; *Mus* frase
❑ **p. book** libro *m* de frases *or* expresiones; **stock p.** frase *f*
hecha
 2 *vt (express)* expresar; *Mus* frasear
phraseology [freɪzɪ'ɒlədʒɪ] *n* fraseología *f*
phrasing ['freɪzɪŋ] *n Mus* fraseo *m*
phrenology [frɪ'nɒlədʒɪ] *n* frenología *f*
Phrygian ['frɪdʒɪən] *adj & n* frigio(a) *(m,f)*
physical ['fɪzɪkəl] **1** *adj (of the body)* físico(a); *(of the world)*
material; *(of physics)* físico(a) ❑ **p. education** educación *f*
física; **p. examination** reconocimiento *m* físico; **p.**
exercises *or Br Fam* **jerks** ejercicios *mpl* físicos
 2 *n Fam* reconocimiento *m* físico
physically ['fɪzɪklɪ] *adv* físicamente; **it's p. impossible**
es materialmente imposible; **p. handicapped** minus-
válido(a); **the p. handicapped** los minusválidos; **to be p.**
fit estar en forma
physician [fɪ'zɪʃən] *n* médico(a) *m,f*
physicist ['fɪzɪsɪst] *n* físico(a) *m,f*
physics ['fɪzɪks] *n* física *f*
physiognomy [fɪzɪ'ɒnəmɪ] *n Fml* fis(i)onomía *f*
physiological [fɪzɪə'lɒdʒɪkəl] *adj* fisiológico(a)
physiology [fɪzɪ'ɒlədʒɪ] *n* fisiología *f*
physiotherapist [fɪzɪəʊ'θerəpɪst] *n* fisioterapeuta *mf*
physiotherapy [fɪzɪəʊ'θerəpɪ] *n* fisioterapia *f*
physique [fɪ'ziːk] *n* físico *m*
pianist ['pɪənɪst] *n* pianista *mf*
piano [pɪ'ænəʊ] *n (pl* **pianos)** piano *m*; **to play the p.** tocar
al piano ❑ **baby grand p.** piano *m* de media cola; **grand p.**
piano *m* de cola; **p. accordion** acordeónpiano *m*; **p. stool**
taburete *m* de piano; **p. tuner** afinador(a) *m,f* de pianos;
upright p. piano *m* vertical
pic [pɪk] *n Fam* foto *f*
piccolo ['pɪkələʊ] *n (pl* **piccolos)** *Mus* flautín *m*
pick [pɪk] **1** *n (a) (tool)* pico *m*, piqueta *f* **(b)** *(choice)* elección
f; **the p. of the bunch** la flor y nata; **take your p.** elige *or*
escoge el que quieras
 2 *vt* **(a)** *(choose)* elegir, escoger; *(team)* seleccionar; *Fig* **to**
p. a winner elegir *or* escoger bien **(b)** *(flowers, fruit)*
recoger, *Esp* coger **(c)** *(scratch)* escarbar, hurgar; *(pimple*
etc) rasgarse; **to p. one's nose** hurgarse la nariz; **to p. one's**
teeth mondarse *or* escarbarse los dientes (con un palillo);
to p. the bones of a chicken chupar los huesos de un
pollo; *Fig* **to p. holes in sth** encontrar defectos en algo; *Fig*
to p. sb's brains explotar los conocimientos de algn; **to p.**
sb's pocket robar algo del bolsillo de algn **(d)** *(lock)* forzar
(e) *US (pluck)* desplumar **(f)** *Mus (guitar, violin)* puntear **(g)**
to p. a fight *or* **quarrel with sb** buscar camorra con algn
 3 *vi* **to p. at one's food** comer sin ganas, picar la comida;
to p. and choose ser muy exigente

pick off *vt* **(a)** *(remove)* quitar *or Am* sacar **(b)** *(shoot)*
matar uno a uno
pick on *vt (persecute)* meterse con; **they always p. on her**
siempre se meten con ella
pick out *vt (a) (choose)* elegir, escoger **(b)** *(distinguish, see)*
distinguir; *(identify)* identificar; *(recognize)* reconocer **(c)**
Mus (tune) buscar, tocar de oído
pick up 1 *vt* **(a)** *(object on floor etc)* recoger, levantar; *(child)*
coger; *(telephone)* descolgar; *(stitches)* coger; **this tonic will**
p. you up este tónico te fortalecerá; **to p. oneself up**
levantarse, ponerse de pie; *Fig* reponerse; *Fig* **to p. up the**
bill quedarse con *or* pagar la cuenta; *Fig* **to p. up the**
pieces volver a empezar después de un fracaso **(b)** *(collect)*
(apples, toys, etc) recoger; *(shopping, person)* buscar, recoger;
to p. up a hitchhiker coger un autostopista; *Fam* **to p. up a**
boy on the beach ligar con un chico en la playa **(c)**
(increase) aumentar; *(points)* ganar; **to p. up speed**
acelerar la marcha **(d)** *(acquire)* conseguir, encontrar;
(learn) aprender **(e)** *Rad TV (station)* captar
 2 *vi* **(a)** *(improve) (health, situation)* mejorarse, ir
mejorando; *(prices)* subir **(b)** *(continue)* seguir; **we picked**
up where he had left off seguimos donde él se había
dejado
pickaxe, *US* **pickax** ['pɪkæks] *n* piqueta *f*, piocha *f*,
zapapico *m*
picket ['pɪkɪt] **1** *n* **(a)** *(stick)* estaca *f* **(b)** *Ind (strikers)*
piquete *m*; *Mil (sentry)* piquete; **to be on p. duty** estar de
guardia ❑ **p. fence** vallado *m*; **p. line** piquete *m*
 2 *vt* piquetear
 3 *vi* hacer piquete
pickings ['pɪkɪŋz] *npl (leftovers)* restos *mpl*, sobras *fpl*;
(profits) ganancias *fpl*
pickle ['pɪkəl] **1** *n* **(a)** *Culin* adobo *m*, escabeche *m*; **pickles**
(vegetables in vinegar) variantes *mpl*, encurtidos *mpl* **(b)** *Fam*
(mess) lío *m*, apuro *m*; **to be in a p.** estar en un apuro
 2 *vt Culin* conservar en adobo *or* escabeche ❑ **pickled**
onions cebollas *fpl* en vinagre
picklock ['pɪklɒk] *n* ganzúa *f*
pick-me-up ['pɪkmiːʌp] *n Med* tónico *m*, reconstituyente
m
pickpocket ['pɪkpɒkɪt] *n* carterista *mf*, ratero(a) *m,f*
pick-up ['pɪkʌp] *n* **(a)** *Br (on record player)* **p.-up (arm)**
brazo *m* (del tocadiscos) **(b)** **p.-up (truck)** furgoneta *f* **(c)** *US*
(acceleration) aceleración *f* **(d)** *Fam* ligue *m*, *RP Ven* levante
m
picky ['pɪkɪ] *adj Fam* exigente, escrupuloso(a)
picnic ['pɪknɪk] **1** *n* comida *f* campestre *or* de campo,
picnic *m*; **to go on a p.** hacer comida de campo, ir a comer
al campo; *Fam Fig* **it was no p.** no fue nada fácil ❑ **p.**
basket cesta *f* para picnic
 2 *vi (pt & pp* **picnicked)** hacer una comida campestre *or* de
campo
picnicker ['pɪknɪkər] *n* excursionista *mf*
Pict [pɪkt] *n Hist* picto(a) *m,f*
pictorial [pɪk'tɔːrɪəl] *adj (magazine)* ilustrado(a)
picture ['pɪktʃər] **1** *n* **(a)** *(painting)* cuadro *m*; *(drawing)*
dibujo *m*; *(portrait)* retrato *m*; *(photo)* foto *f*, *(illustration)*
ilustración *f*, lámina *f*; **to draw a p.** hacer un dibujo; **to**
paint a p. pintar un cuadro; **to take a p. of sb** sacar una
foto a algn; *Fig* **pretty as a p.** monísimo(a); *Fig* **she's the p.**
of health rebosa de salud ❑ **p. book** libro *m* ilustrado; **p.**
frame marco *m*; **p. gallery** galería *f* de arte; **p. messaging**
mensajería *f* de imágenes; **p. postcard** tarjeta *f* postal; **p.**
window ventanal *m* **(b)** *TV* imagen *m*; *Cin* película *f*; *Br* **to**
go to the pictures ir al cine **(c)** *(mental image)* imagen *f*; *Fig*
the other side of the p. la otra cara de la moneda; *Fig* **to**
paint a black p. of sth pintar algo muy negro; *Fig* **to put**

sb in the p. poner a algn al corriente; *Fam Fig* **do you get the p.?** ¿entiendes?

  2 *vt (imagine)* imaginarse, figurarse; **I can p. it as if it were yesterday** lo recuerdo como si fuera ayer

picturesque [pɪktʃə'resk] *adj* pintoresco(a)

pidgin ['pɪdʒɪn] *adj* macarrónico(a) ❑ **p. English** inglés *m* macarrónico

pie [paɪ] *n (of fruit)* tarta *f,* pastel *m; (of meat etc)* empanada *f,* pastel *m, Col CSur* torta *f; (pasty)* empanadilla *f; Fig* **it's p. in the sky** es pura fantasía

piece [piːs] *n* **(a)** *(of food) (large)* pedazo *m,* trozo *m'; (small)* cacho *m; (of paper, wood)* trozo *m; (of grass)* fragmento *m; (of one's work)* muestra *f; (part)* pieza *f;* **a 56 p. dinner service** una vajilla de 56 piezas; **a 500 p. jigsaw** un rompecabezas de 500 piezas; **a p. of advice** un consejo; **a p. of carelessness** un descuido; **a p. of furniture** un mueble; **a p. of land** *(for building)* una parcela; *(for farming)* un terreno; **a p. of luck** un golpe de suerte; **a p. of luggage** un bulto; **a p. of news** una noticia; **a p. of work** un trabajo; **in one p.** en un solo trozo; *Fig* sano(a) y salvo(a); **she arrived in one p.** llegó sana y salva; **to be in pieces** *(broken)* estar hecho(a) pedazos; *(dismantled)* estar desmontado(a); **to break sth into pieces** hacer algo pedazos; **to pull** *or* **tear sth to pieces** hacer algo trizas; **to take sth to pieces** desmontar algo; *Fig (criticize)* dejar algo por los suelos; *Fig* **to give sb a p. of one's mind** decir cuatro verdades a algn; *Fig* **to go to pieces** *(business etc)* venirse abajo; *(person)* perder el control (de sí mismo); *Fig* **to say one's p.** decir su parte; *Fam* **it's a p. of cake** es pan comido **(b)** *Lit Mus* obra *f,* pieza *f;* **a p. of music/poetry** una obra musical/un poema; **a 20 p. orchestra** una orquesta de 20 músicos **(c)** *(coin)* moneda *f;* **a 10 pence p.** una moneda de 10 peniques **(d)** *(in chess)* pieza *f; (in draughts)* ficha *f*

piece together *vt (facts)* reconstruir; *(evidence)* atar cabos; *(jigsaw)* hacer

piecemeal ['piːsmiːl] *adv (by degrees)* poco a poco, a etapas; *(unsystematically)* desordenadamente

piecework ['piːswɜːk] *n* trabajo *m* a destajo; **to be on p.** trabajar a destajo

pieceworker ['piːswɜːkər] *n* trabajador(a) *m,f* a destajo

pied [paɪd] *adj* de varios colores

pier [pɪər] *n* **(a)** *(jetty)* embarcadero *m,* muelle *m; (promenade)* paseo *m,* rompeolas *m inv* **(b)** *Archit (of bridge)* pila *f,* estribo *m*

pierce [pɪəs] *vt (with sharp instrument)* perforar, agujerear; *(with drill)* taladrar; *(penetrate)* penetrar en; *Fig* trascender; **to have one's ears pierced** hacerse los agujeros en las orejas

piercing ['pɪəsɪŋ] *adj (sound etc)* penetrante, agudo(a)

piety ['paɪtɪ] *n* piedad *f*

pig [pɪg] *n* **(a)** *Zool* cerdo *m,* puerco *m, Am* chancho *m; Fam (person)* cerdo(a) *m,f,* asqueroso(a) *m,f, Am* chancho(a) *m,f; (glutton)* comilón(ona) *m,f,* glotón(ona) *m,f, Am* chancho(a) *m,f; Fig* **he bought a p. in a poke** le dieron gato por liebre; *Fam* **to make a p. of oneself** ponerse las botas ❑ **p. farm** granja *f* porcina; **sucking p.** lechón *m,* cochinillo *m* **(b)** *(ingot)* lingote *m* ❑ **p. iron** hierro *m* en lingotes **(c)** *Slang Offens (policeman) Esp* madero *m, Andes* paco *m, Col* tombo *m, Méx* tamarindo *m, RP* cana *m;* **the pigs** la bofia, la pasma

pig out *vi US Fam* ponerse las botas

pigeon ['pɪdʒɪn] *n (gen)* paloma *f; Culin Sport* pichón *m; Fam* **that's your p.** eso es asunto tuyo ❑ **clay p. shooting** tiro *m* al pichón; **homing p.** paloma *f* mensajera; **p. breeding** paloma *f* colombofilia *f;* **p. fancier** colombófilo(a) *m,f*

pigeonhole ['pɪdʒɪnhəʊl] **1** *n* casilla *f*

  2 *vt* encasillar, clasificar

pigeon-toed [pɪdʒɪn'təʊd] *adj* patituerto(a)

piggery ['pɪgərɪ] *n (farm)* granja *f* porcina; *(sty)* pocilga *f*

piggy ['pɪgɪ] *n* cerdito(a) *m,f, Am* chanchito(a) *m,f* ❑ **p. bank** hucha *f, Am* alcancía *f* (en forma de cerdito), *CSur* chanchita *f*

piggyback ['pɪgɪbæk] *n & adv* **to give sb a p., carry sb p.** llevar a algn a cuestas

pigheaded [pɪg'hedɪd] *adj* terco(a), cabezota

piglet ['pɪglɪt] *n* cerdito *m,* lechón *m,* cochinillo *m*

pigment ['pɪgmənt] *n* pigmento *m*

pigmentation [pɪgmən'teɪʃən] *n* pigmentación *f*

pigmy ['pɪgmɪ] *n see* **pygmy**

pigskin ['pɪgskɪn] *n* piel *m* de cerdo *or* puerco *or Am* chancho

pigsty ['pɪgstaɪ] *n* pocilga *f*

pigtail ['pɪgteɪl] *n* trenza *f; (Chinese, bullfighter's)* coleta *f*

pike [paɪk] *n (fish)* lucio *m*

pilchard ['pɪltʃəd] *n* sardina *f*

pile¹ [paɪl] **1** *n* **(a)** *(of books, things)* montón *m;* **to put things into a p.** amontonar cosas; *Fig* **to make one's p.** hacer fortuna, forrarse; *Fam* **piles of work** montones de trabajo **(b)** *Fam (building)* caserón *m*

  2 *vt* amontonar; **a plate piled with food** un plato colmado de comida

  3 *vi* **to p. into** amontonarse *or* meterse en; **to p. on/off a bus** subir a/bajar de un autobús en tropel

pile on *vt Fam* **to p. it on** *(exaggerate)* exagerar, recargar las tintas

pile up 1 *vt (books, clothes)* amontonar; *(riches, debts)* acumular

  2 *vi* amontonarse, acumularse

pile² [paɪl] *n (on carpet)* pelo *m;* **thick p.** pelo largo

pile³ [paɪl] *n Archit* pilar *m,* pilote *m*

pile-driver ['paɪldraɪvər] *n* martinete *m*

piles [paɪlz] *npl Med* almorranas *fpl,* hemorroides *fpl*

pile-up ['paɪlʌp] *n Aut* choque *m* en cadena

pilfer ['pɪlfər] *vt & vi* hurtar

pilgrim ['pɪlgrɪm] *n* peregrino(a) *m,f*

pilgrimage ['pɪlgrɪmɪdʒ] *n* peregrinación *f,* romería *f;* **to go on** *or* **make a p.** ir en peregrinación *or* en romería

pill [pɪl] *n* píldora *f,* pastilla *f;* **to be on** *or* **take the p.** tomar la píldora (anticonceptiva)

pillage ['pɪlɪdʒ] **1** *n* pillaje *m,* saqueo *m*

  2 *vt & vi* pillar, saquear

pillar ['pɪlər] *n Archit* pilar *m,* columna *f; (of smoke etc)* columna; **to go from p. to post** ir de Herodes a Pilatos ❑ *Br* **p. box** buzón *m*

pillion ['pɪljən] *n* asiento *m* trasero (de una moto); **to ride p.** ir sentado(a) detrás

pillory ['pɪlərɪ] **1** *n* picota *f*

  2 *vt (pt & pp* **pilloried)** poner en la picota; *Fig* dejar en ridículo

pillow ['pɪləʊ] *n* almohada *f*

pillowcase ['pɪləʊkeɪs] *n,* **pillowslip** ['pɪləʊslɪp] *n* funda *f* de almohada

pilot ['paɪlət] **1** *n* piloto *m*

  2 *adj (trial)* piloto *inv,* experimental ❑ **p. light** piloto *m;* **p. scheme** proyecto *m* piloto

  3 *vt (aircraft, boat)* pilotar; *Fig* **to p. sth through** llevar algo a buen término

pimento [pɪ'mentəʊ] *n (pl* **pimentos)** *Culin* pimiento *m* morrón, *Méx* chile *m, RP* ají *m, Col Ven* pimentón *m*

pimp [pɪmp] *n* proxeneta *m, Esp* chulo *m, RP* cafiolo *m*

pimple ['pɪmpəl] *n (gen)* grano *m; (blackhead)* espinilla *f*

pimply ['pɪmplɪ] *adj* (**pimplier, pimpliest**) cubierto(a) de granos

PIN [pɪn] *n Fin (abbr* **personal identification number**) P. **(number)** PIN *m*

pin [pɪn] **1** *n (gen)* alfiler *m; Med* clavo *m; Tech* clavija *f; (in grenade)* seguro *m; (in bowling)* bolo *m; US (brooch)* broche *m; Fig* **as neat as a new p.** limpio(a) como un espejo; *Fig* **you could have heard a p. drop** se podía oír el vuelo de una mosca; *Fam* **for two pins I'd have walked out!** ¡por poco me marcho! ❏ **drawing p.** chincheta *f;* **hair p.** horquilla *f;* **p. money** alfileres *mpl;* **pins and needles** hormigueo *m;* **rolling p.** rodillo *m;* **safety p.** imperdible *m, Am* alfiler *m* de gancho, *CAm Méx* seguro *m; Elec* **three p. plug** clavija *f* de tres patillas

2 *vt (pt & pp* **pinned**) *(notice on board etc)* clavar con chinchetas; *(garment etc)* sujetar con alfileres; **to p. a hem** prender un dobladillo con alfileres; **to p. sb against a wall** tener a algn contra una pared; *Fig* **to p. one's hopes on sth** poner sus esperanzas en algo; *Fam* **to p. a crime on sb** endosar un delito a algn

pin down *vt* sujetar; *Fig* **to p. sb down** hacer que algn se comprometa

pin up *vt (notice etc)* clavar con chinchetas; *(hem etc)* prender con alfileres; *(hair)* recoger

pinafore ['pɪnəfɔːr] *n (apron)* delantal *m* ❏ **p. dress** pichi *m, CSur Méx* jumper *m*

pinball ['pɪnbɔːl] *n* flíper *m*, millón *m*

pincers ['pɪnsəz] *npl (on crab, lobster etc)* pinzas *fpl; (tool)* tenazas *fpl*

pinch [pɪntʃ] **1** *n* (a) *(nip)* pellizco *m;* **to give sb a p.** pellizcar a algn (b) *Fig (hardship)* apuro *m;* **at a p.** en caso de apuro; **to feel the p.** pasar apuros *or* estrecheces (c) *(small amount)* pizca *f;* **p. of salt** pizca de sal; *Fig* **to take sth with a p. of salt** admitir algo con reservas

2 *vt* (a) *(nip)* pellizcar; **these shoes p. my feet** estos zapatos me aprietan (los pies) (b) *Fam (steal)* afanar, *Esp* levantar (c) *Fam (arrest)* pescar

3 *vi (shoes)* apretar; **to p. and scrape** escatimar gastos

pinched [pɪntʃt] *adj* (a) *(face)* cansado(a); **p. with cold** muerto(a) de frio; **to look p.** tener mala cara (b) *(short)* **p. for time/money** escaso(a) de tiempo/dinero

pinch-hit ['pɪntʃ'hɪt] *vi US* (a) *(in baseball)* = sustituir a un bateador en un momento decisivo del partido (b) *Fig (substitute)* **to p. for sb** sustituir a algn *(en una emergencia)*

pincushion ['pɪnkʊʃən] *n* acerico *m*

pine[1] [paɪn] *n* pino *m* ❏ **p. cone** piña *f;* **p. forest** pinar *m;* **p. needle** aguja *f* de pino; **p. tree** pino *m;* **Scots p.** pino *m* albar; **stone p.** pino *m* manso *or* piñonero

pine[2] [paɪn] *vi* **to p. (away)** consumirse, morirse de pena; **to p. for sth/sb** echar de menos *or* añorar algo/a algn, *Am* extrañar algo/a algn

pineapple ['paɪnæpəl] *n* piña *f, RP* ananá *m*

ping [pɪŋ] **1** *n (sound)* sonido *m* metálico; *(of bullet)* silbido *m*
2 *vi (gen)* hacer un sonido metálico; *(bullet)* silbar

ping-pong ['pɪŋpɒŋ] *n* ping-pong *m,* tenis *m* de mesa

pinhead ['pɪnhed] *n Fam (stupid person)* majadero(a) *m,f*

pinion ['pɪnjən] *n Tech* piñón *m*

pink[1] [pɪŋk] **1** *n* (a) *(colour)* rosa *m;* **to be in the p. (of health)** rebosar de salud (b) *Bot* clavel *m*
2 *adj (colour)* rosa *inv; Pol Fam* rojillo(a); **to go** *or* **turn p.** ponerse colorado(a)

pink[2] [pɪŋk] **1** *vt Sew* cortar con tijeras dentadas
2 *vi Aut* picar

pinkie ['pɪŋkɪ] *n Scot US Fam* dedo *m* meñique

pinking shears ['pɪŋkɪŋʃiːəz] *npl* tijeras *fpl* dentadas

pinkish ['pɪŋkɪʃ] *adj* rosáceo(a)

pinnacle ['pɪnəkəl] *n (of building)* pináculo *m; (of mountain)* cima *f,* pico *m; Fig (of success)* cumbre *f*

pinny ['pɪnɪ] *n Br Fam* delantal *m*

pinpoint ['pɪnpɔɪnt] *vt* señalar

pinprick ['pɪnprɪk] *n* pinchazo *m*

pinstripe ['pɪnstraɪp] *adj* a rayas

pint [paɪnt] *n (measure)* pinta *f; Br Fam* **a p. (of beer)** una cerveza; **to go for a p.** salir a tomar una copa

pinta ['paɪntə] *n Br Fam* pinta *f* de leche

pint-sized ['paɪntsaɪzd] *adj* muy pequeño(a), minúsculo(a)

pin-up ['pɪnʌp] *n Fam* (a) *(poster)* = póster de actriz, actor, cantante o modelo atractivo(a) (b) *(person)* = actriz, actor, cantante o modelo considerado(a) atractivo(a)

pioneer [paɪə'nɪər] **1** *n (settler)* pionero(a) *m,f; (forerunner)* precursor(a) *m,f*
2 *vt* promover, iniciar

pioneering [paɪə'nɪərɪŋ] *adj* pionero(a)

pious ['paɪəs] *adj* piadoso(a), devoto(a); *Pej* beato(a); **a p. hope** un deseo bienintencionado

piously ['paɪəslɪ] *adv* piadosamente, con piedad

pip[1] [pɪp] *n (seed)* pepita *f, (of sunflower)* pipa *f*

pip[2] [pɪp] (a) *Br (sound)* señal *f* (corta) (b) *Fam (on dice, dominoes)* punto *m; Br (on uniform)* estrella *f* (c) *Br Fam* **to give sb the p.** sacar a algn de quicio

pip[3] [pɪp] *vt (pt & pp* **pipped**) *Br* **to p. sb at the post** ganar a algn en el último momento; **to be pipped at the post** perder por un pelo

pipe [paɪp] **1** *n* (a) *(for water, gas etc)* conducto *m,* tubería *f* (b) *Mus (flute)* flauta *f; (of organ)* caramillo *m; Scot Fam* **the pipes** la gaita (c) *(for smoking)* pipa *f;* **to smoke a p.** fumar en pipa; *Fam* **put that in your p. and smoke it!** *Esp* ¡toma del frasco, Carrasco!, *Am* ¡tómate esa! ❏ **p. cleaner** limpiapipas *m inv; Fig* **p. dream** sueño *m* imposible
2 *vt* (a) *(water)* llevar *or* transportar por tubería; *(oil)* transportar por oleoducto; *Culin (cream etc)* poner con manga; **piped music** hilo *m* musical
3 *vi Mus (on simple pipes)* tocar la flauta; *(on bagpipes)* tocar la gaita

pipe down *vi Fam* callarse

pipe up *vi Fam* hacerse oír

pipeline ['paɪplaɪn] *n (for water)* tubería *f,* cañería *f. (for gas)* gasoducto *m; (for oil)* oleoducto *m; Fig* **it's in the p.** está en trámites

piper ['paɪpər] *n* gaitero(a) *m,f*

piping ['paɪpɪŋ] **1** *n* (a) *(for water, gas etc)* tubería *f,* cañería *f* (b) *Sew* ribete *m* (c) *Culin (on cake)* adorno *m* (d) *Mus* música *f* de gaita
2 *adj* **p. hot** bien caliente

pipit ['pɪpɪt] *n Orn* bisbita *m* ❏ **meadow/tawny/tree p.** bisbita *m* común/campestre/arbóreo

piquancy ['piːkənsɪ] *n* gusto *m* picante

piquant ['piːkənt] *adj (taste)* picante; *(fig)* intrigante, estimulante

pique [piːk] *n* resentimiento *m,* despecho *m;* **to do sth in a fit of p.** hacer algo por resentimiento
2 *vt* picar, herir

piracy ['paɪərəsɪ] *n* piratería *f*

piranha [pɪ'rɑːnjə] *n (fish)* piraña *f*

pirate ['paɪrɪt] *n* pirata *m* ❏ **p. edition** edici[...] **radio** emisora *f* pirata; **p. ship** barco *m* pirata

pirouette [pɪrʊ'et] **1** *n* pirueta *f*
2 *vi* piruetear, hacer piruetas

Pisces ['paisi:z] n Astrol Astron Piscis m

piss [pɪs] Slang **1** vi mear; **it's pissing with rain** está lloviendo Esp que te cagas or Méx duro, RP caen soretes de punta

2 n meada f; **to have a p.** mear, echar una meada; Br Fig **to take the p. out of sb** burlarse or Esp cachondearse de algn

pissed [pɪst] adj Slang **(a)** Br (drunk) Esp Méx pedo inv, Col caído(a), RP en pedo; **p. off** cabreado(a), Méx enchilado(a) **(with** con) **(b)** US (angry) cabreado(a)

pistachio [pɪs'tɑ:ʃɪəʊ] n (pl **pistachios**) (nut) pistacho m ❑ **p. tree** pistachero m

pistol ['pɪstəl] n pistola f; **at p. point** a punta de pistola ❑ **p. shot** tiro m de pistola, pistoletazo m; Sport **starting p.** pistola f (para dar la señal de salida)

piston ['pɪstən] n pistón m, émbolo m ❑ **p. ring** aro m de pistón; **p. rod** biela f

pit¹ [pɪt] **1** n **(a)** (hole) hoyo m, foso m; (large) hoya f; (of stomach) boca f ❑ **orchestra p.** foso m de la orquesta **(b)** (coal mine) mina f de carbón; **to work down the p.** trabajar en las minas **(c)** Theat patio m de butacas, platea f **(d)** (mark on surface) hoyo m, picadura f **(e)** Aut (in garage) foso m de inspección; (in motor racing) foso m, box m **(f)** **the p.** (hell) el infierno **(g)** US (in stock exchange) corro m

2 vt (pt & pp **pitted**) **(a)** (mark) llenar de hoyos, picar; **pitted with** picado(a) de **(b)** (oppose, challenge) **to p. one's strength** or **wits against sb** medirse con algn

pit² [pɪt] **1** n (of cherry) hueso m, pipo m, RP carozo m; US (of peach, plum) hueso m, RP carozo m

2 vt (pt & pp **pitted**) (cherry, olive) deshuesar

pitapat [pɪtə'pæt] adv **to go p.** (rain) repiquetear; (feet, heart) golpetear

pitch¹ [pɪtʃ] **1** vt **(a)** Mus (sound) entonar; (instrument) afinar; Fig **the speech was pitched at a simple level** el discurso tuvo un tono asequible **(b)** (throw) lanzar, arrojar **(c)** (tent) armar

2 vi **(a)** **to p. and toss** (aircraft, ship) cabecear **(b)** **to p. forward** (fall) caerse hacia adelante

3 n **(a)** Mus (of sound) tono m; (of instrument) diapasón m; **to have perfect p.** tener el oído perfecto **(b)** (degree) grado m; (level) nivel m; **it reached such a p. that ...** llegó a tal punto or tal extremo que ... **(c)** (of aircraft, ship) cabeceo m **(d)** Sport (field) campo m, terreno m **(e)** Br (for market stall) puesto m; Fig (reserved place) terreno m; **to queer sb's p.** estropear los planes a algn **(f)** (slope of roof) pendiente f **(g)** (throw) lanzamiento m

pitch in vi Fam echar una mano

pitch into vt (attack) (physically) atacar; (verbally) criticar

pitch² [pɪtʃ] n (tar) brea f, pez f

pitch-black [pɪtʃ'blæk] adj, **pitch-dark** [pɪtʃ'dɑ:k] adj negro(a) como la boca de lobo

pitched [pɪtʃt] adj **(a)** (roof) pendiente **(b)** **p. battle** batalla f

pitcher¹ ['pɪtʃər] n (container) cántaro m, jarro m

pitcher² ['pɪtʃər] n US (in baseball) pitcher m

pitchfork ['pɪtʃfɔ:k] **1** n horca f

2 vt Fig **to p. sb into doing sth** forzar a algn a hacer algo sin ser preparado

piteous ['pɪtɪəs] adj lastimoso(a)

pitfall ['pɪtfɔ:l] n (difficulty) dificultad f; (obstacle) obstáculo m; (danger) peligro m

pith [pɪθ] n (of bone, plant) médula f; (of orange) piel f blanca; Fig (essence) meollo m ❑ **p. helmet** salacot m

pithead ['pɪthed] n Min bocamina f

:thy ['pɪθɪ] adj (**pithier, pithiest**) (bone, plant) ⁻uloso(a); Fig (advice, argument) contundente

pitiable ['pɪtɪəbəl] adj lamentable

pitiful ['pɪtɪfʊl] adj (producing pity) lastimoso(a), que da lástima; (terrible) lamentable, pésimo(a)

pitifully ['pɪtɪfʊlɪ] adv que da pena; **she's p. thin** está tan delgada que da pena verla

pitiless ['pɪtɪlɪs] adj despiadado(a), implacable

pitilessly ['pɪtɪlɪslɪ] adv despiadadamente

pittance ['pɪtəns] n miseria f

pitter-patter [pɪtə'pætər] n repiqueteo m; **to go p.-p.** repiquetear

pituitary [pɪ'tju:ɪtərɪ] adj **p. gland** glándula f pituitaria

pity ['pɪtɪ] **1** n **(a)** (compassion, sorrow) compasión f, piedad f; **for p.'s sake!** ¡por amor de Dios!; **to have** or **take p. on sb** compadecerse de algn **(b)** (regret) lástima f, pena f; **it's a p. he didn't pass** es una pena que no aprobó; **more's the p.** tanto peor; **what a p.!** ¡qué pena!, ¡qué lástima!

2 vt (pt & pp **pitied**) compadecerse de, sentir pena por; **I p. them** me dan pena

pitying ['pɪtɪɪŋ] adj compasivo(a)

pivot ['pɪvət] **1** n pivote m

2 vi girar sobre su eje; Fig **to p. on sth** depender de algo, girar sobre algo

pivotal ['pɪvətəl] adj crucial

pixel ['pɪksəl] n Comptr píxel m, elemento m de imagen

pixie ['pɪksɪ] n duendecillo m

pizza ['pi:tsə] n pizza f ❑ **p. parlour** pizzería f

Pk (abbr **Park**) parque m

pkt (abbr **packet**) paquete m

Pl (abbr **Place**) C/, calle f

placard ['plækɑ:d] n pancarta f

placate [plə'keɪt] vt aplacar, apaciguar, calmar

place [pleɪs] **1** n **(a)** (position) sitio m, lugar m; (area) área f; (in book) página f; (in queue) turno m; **in p. of Mary, in Mary's p.** en el lugar de María; **in your p. I'd have gone** yo en tu lugar habría ido; **there's no p. for that here** eso está de más aquí; **there's no p. like home** como tu casa no hay dos; **to be in/out of p.** estar en/fuera de su sitio; **to go from p. to p.** ir or andar de un lugar a otro; **to hold sth in p.** sujetar algo; **to put sth back in its p.** devolver algo a su sitio; **to take p.** tener lugar; Fig **to put sb in his p.** poner a algn en su lugar; Fig **you'll go places** irás lejos; Fam **all over the p.** por todas partes; Fam **here's the p.** aquí estamos ❑ **p. name** topónimo m **(b)** (seat) sitio m, plaza f; (space) espacio m; Theat localidad f; (on bus) asiento m; (at university, on course) plaza; (at table) plaza f; (place setting) cubierto m; **to change places with sb** intercambiar sitios con algn; **to feel out of p.** encontrarse fuera de lugar; **to lay a p. at table for sb** poner un cubierto para algn; **to get a p. at university** ser aceptado(a) para ingresar en la universidad; **to take sb's p.** sustituir a algn ❑ **p. mat** individual m **(c)** Fig (suitable occasion) sitio m, lugar m; **this isn't the p. to discuss religion** este no es el lugar más indicado para hablar de religión **(d)** (position on scale) posición f, lugar m; (social position) lugar, rango m; (in argument) lugar; **in the first/second p.** en el primer/ segundo lugar; **people in high places** gente f influyente; **to finish in last p.** llegar el último; **to take first/second p.** ganar el primer/segundo lugar; Fig **it isn't your p. to give advice** no te incumbe a ti dar consejos; Fig **to have friends in high places** tener enchufes; Fig **to know one's p.** conocer su lugar ❑ Math **decimal p.** punto m decimal **(e)** (house) casa f; (building) lugar m, sitio m; **come round to our p. for coffee** pasa por casa a tomar café; **we're going to his p.** vamos a su casa ❑ **p. of residence** domicilio m; **p. of work** lugar m de trabajo; **p. of worship** (church) iglesia f; (temple) templo m **(f)** (square, street) plaza f

2 *vt* **(a)** *(put)* poner, colocar; **p. the books on the shelves** coloca los libros en la estantería; **she placed a vase on the table** puso un florero en la mesa; **to be well/better placed to do sth** estar en buena/mejor situación para hacer algo; **to p. in order of preference** poner en orden de preferencia; *Fig* **it places me in an awkward position** me pone en una situación difícil *or* delicada **(b)** *Com* **to p. a bet** hacer una apuesta, apostar; **to p. an order with sb** hacer un pedido a algn **(c)** *(face, person)* recordar; **I know the face but I can't p. him** reconozco la cara pero no sé de qué **(d)** *(in job)* colocar en un empleo

placebo [pləˈsiːbəʊ] *n* (*pl* **placebos** *or* **placeboes**) *Med* placebo *m*

placement [ˈpleɪsmənt] *n* colocación *f*

placenta [pləˈsentə] *n* (*pl* **placentas** *or* **placentae** [pləˈsentiː]) placenta *f*

placid [ˈplæsɪd] *adj* apacible, tranquilo(a)

plagiarism [ˈpleɪdʒərɪzəm] *n* plagio *m*

plagiarize [ˈpleɪdʒəraɪz] *vt* plagiar

plague [pleɪg] **1** *n* *(of insects etc)* plaga *f*; *Med* peste *f*; *Fig* **to avoid sth like the p.** evitar algo por todos los medios
2 *vt* **to p. sb with requests** acosar a algn a peticiones

plaice [pleɪs] *n inv* *(fish)* platija *f*

plaid [plæd, pleɪd] **1** *n* *(cloth)* tejido *m* escocés
2 *adj* *(shawl)* de cuadros ❑ **p. skirt** falda *f* escocesa

plain [pleɪn] **1** *adj* **(a)** *(clear)* claro(a), evidente, obvio(a); **her attitude made it p. that she wasn't interested** su actitud puso de manifiesto que no estaba interesada; **it was p. that he was mistaken** quedó claro que estaba equivocado; *Fig* **he likes p. speaking** le gusta hablar con franqueza; *Fam* **as p. as the nose on your face** más claro no puede ser ❑ **p. language** palabras *fpl* claras **(b)** *(simple)* sencillo(a); *(chocolate)* amargo(a); *(flour)* sin levadura; *(material)* de un solo color; *(paper)* liso(a); *(person)* llano(a), *(stitch)* a la derecha; **in p. clothes** vestido(a) de paisano; **the p. truth** la verdad lisa y llana **(c)** *(unattractive)* sin atractivo *or* encanto **(d)** *(complete)* total; **it's p. foolishness** es una auténtica locura
2 *n* **(a)** *(in knitting)* punto *m* a la derecha **(b)** *Geog* llanura *f*, llano *m*

plainly [ˈpleɪnlɪ] *adv* *(clearly)* claramente; *(simply)* sencillamente; **to speak p.** hablar con franqueza

plainness [ˈpleɪnnɪs] *n* *(clearness)* claridad *f*, *(simplicity)* sencillez *f*; *(unattractiveness)* falta *f* de atractivo *or* encanto

plain-spoken [pleɪnˈspəʊkən] *adj* franco(a)

plaintiff [ˈpleɪntɪf] *n* demandante *mf*, querellante *mf*

plaintive [ˈpleɪntɪv] *adj* lastimero(a), triste

plait [plæt] **1** *n* trenza *f*
2 *vt* trenzar

plan [plæn] **1** *n* **(a)** *(scheme)* plan *m*, proyecto *m*; **everything went according to p.** todo salió como estaba previsto; **to draw up a p.** elaborar *or* hacer un proyecto; **to have a change of p.** cambiar de planes; **to make plans** hacer proyectos; *Fam* **the best p. would be to attend** lo mejor sería asistir ❑ **development p.** plan *m* de desarrollo; **five-year p.** plan *m* quinquenal **(b)** *(drawing, diagram)* plano *m*
2 *vt* *(pt & pp* **planned***)* *(make plans for)* *(future etc)* planear, proyectar; *(design, draw up plans for)* *(economy)* planificar; *(house etc)* hacer los planos de; *(intend)* pensar, tener la intención de; **it wasn't planned** no estaba previsto; **to p. one's family** planificarse la familia; **we p. to go out** pensamos salir
3 *vi* hacer planes; **she hadn't planned for so many guests** no había previsto tantos invitados; **to p. for the future** hacer planes *or* proyectos para el futuro; **to p. on doing sth** contar con hacer algo

plane¹ [pleɪn] **1** *n* **(a)** *Art Math* plano *m*; *Fig* nivel *m* **(b)** *Fam* avión *m*
2 *adj Geom.*plano(a)
3 *vi* *(glide)* planear

plane² [pleɪn] **1** *n* *(tool)* cepillo *m*
2 *vt* cepillar

plane³ [pleɪn] *n Bot* **p. (tree)** plátano *m* ❑ **London p.** plátano *m* común; **Oriental p.** plátano *m* oriental

planet [ˈplænɪt] *n* planeta *m*

planetarium [plænɪˈteərɪəm] *n* (*pl* **planetariums** *or* **planetaria** [plænɪˈteərɪə]) planetario *m*

planetary [ˈplænɪtərɪ] *adj* planetario(a)

plank [plæŋk] *n* *(piece of wood)* tabla *f*, tablón *m*; *Fig* *(principle)* punto *m*

plankton [ˈplæŋktən] *n* plankton *m*

planner [ˈplænər] *n* planificador(a) *m,f* ❑ **town p.** urbanista *mf*

planning [ˈplænɪŋ] *n* planificación *f* ❑ **family p.** planificación *f* familiar; **p. committee** servicio *m* de planning; *Br* **p. permission** permiso *m* de construcción *or* de obras; **town p.** urbanismo *m*

plant¹ [plɑːnt] **1** *n Bot* planta *f* ❑ **p. life** flora *f*; **p. pot** maceta *f*, tiesto *m*
2 *vt* *(flowers etc)* plantar; *(seeds, vegetables)* sembrar; *(bomb)* poner, colocar; *Fig* **to p. an idea in sb's mind** introducir una idea en la mente de algn; **to p. sth on sb** endosarle algo a algn

plant² [plɑːnt] *n Ind* *(factory)* planta *f*, fábrica *f*; *(machinery)* equipo *m*, maquinaria *f*

plantain [ˈplæntɪn] *n Bot* llantén *m*

plantation [plænˈteɪʃən] *n* plantación *f*

planter [ˈplɑːntər] *n* *(person)* plantador(a) *m,f*; *(machine)* plantadora *f*

plaque [plæk] *n* placa *f*

plasma [ˈplæzmə] *n* plasma *m*; *Comptr* **p. screen** pantalla *f* de plasma

plaster [ˈplɑːstər] **1** *n Constr* yeso *m*, argamasa *f*; *Med* escayola *f*; *Br* **sticking p.** esparadrapo *m*, tirita *f*, *Am* curita *f*; **to have one's leg in p.** tener la pierna escayolada ❑ **p. cast** *Art* vaciado *m* de yeso; *Med* enyesado *m*; **p. of Paris** yeso *m* mate
2 *vt* **(a)** *Constr* enyesar, enlucir **(b)** *Fig* *(cover)* cubrir; **the wall was plastered with slogans** la pared estaba cubierta de pintadas

plasterboard [ˈplɑːstəbɔːd] *n* cartón *m* yeso

plastered [ˈplɑːstəd] *adj Slang* borracho(a), trompa

plasterer [ˈplɑːstərər] *n* yesero(a) *m,f*

plastic [ˈplæstɪk, ˈplɑːstɪk] **1** *n* plástico *m*, materia *f* plástica; **plastics** materiales *mpl* plásticos; **the plastics industry** la industria del plástico
2 *(cup, bag etc)* de plástico; **it's p.** es de plástico; **the p. arts** las artes plásticas ❑ **p. bomb, p. explosive** plástico *m*; **p. surgeon** especialista *mf* en cirugía plástica; **p. surgery** cirugía *f* plástica

Plasticine® [ˈplæstɪsiːn] *n* arcilla *f* de moldear, plastilina *f*

plate [pleɪt] **1** *n* **(a)** *(dish)* plato *m*; *(plateful)* plato lleno **(of** de**)**; *(for church offering)* platillo *m*, bandeja *f*; *Fam Fig* **it was handed to him on a p.** se lo dieron en bandeja de plata; *Fig* **to have a lot on one's p.** tener mucha faena ❑ **p. rack** escurreplatos *m inv* **(b)** *(sheet)* placa *f* ❑ *Elec* **hot p.** placa *f* eléctrica; **gold p.** chapa *f* de oro; *(tableware)* vajilla *f* de oro; *Aut* **number p.** matrícula *f*, placa *f*; **p. glass** vidrio *m or* cristal *m* cilindrado; **silver p.** chapa *f* de plata; *(tableware)* vajilla *f* de plata **(c)** *Typ* *(illustration)* grabado *m*, lámina *f* **(d)** **dental p.** dentadura *f* postiza
2 *vt* chapar; *(with gold)* dorar; *(with silver)* platear; **gold/**

silver/chromium plated chapado(a) en oro/en plata/de cromo

plateau ['plætəʊ] n (pl **plateaus** or **plateaux** ['plætəʊz]) meseta f

platform ['plætfɔːm] n (**a**) (gen) plataforma f; (stage) estrado m; (at meeting) tribuna f; Rail andén m, vía f □ **p. ticket** billete m de andén (**b**) Pol (programme) programa m

platinum ['plætɪnəm] n platino m □ **p.-blond hair** pelo m rubio platino

platitude ['plætɪtjuːd] n lugar m común, tópico m

Platonic [plə'tɒnɪk] adj platónico(a)

platoon [plə'tuːn] n Mil pelotón m

platter ['plætər] n (dish) fuente f

plausibility [plɔːzɪ'bɪlɪtɪ] n plausibilidad f

plausible ['plɔːzəbəl] adj (excuse, argument) admisible, plausible

play [pleɪ] **1** vt (**a**) (game, sport) jugar a; **to p. a game of cards** echar una partida de cartas; **to p. ball** jugar a la pelota; Fig cooperar; **to p. cards** jugar a las cartas or a los naipes; **to p. hide-and-seek/chess/football** jugar al escondite/al ajedrez/al fútbol; **to p. games** jugar; Fin **to p. the Stock Exchange** jugar a la Bolsa; Fig **stop playing games!** ¡basta de tomar el pelo!; Fig **if you p. your cards right** si te espabilas; Fam **to p. a trick on sb** gastar una broma a algn; Fam **to p. a dirty trick on sb** jugar una mala pasada a algn; Fam **to p. it cool** tomárselo con calma (**b**) Sport (position) jugar de; (team) jugar contra; **Spain played Scotland** España jugó contra Escocia; **they played her in the team** la seleccionaron para el equipo; **to p. a shot** (in soccer) tirar; (in golf, tennis) golpear (**c**) Mus (instrument, tune) tocar; **to p. a record/tape** poner un disco/cassette; **to p. the piano/guitar** tocar el piano/la guitarra; **to p. sth by ear** tocar algo de oído; Fig **you'll have to p. it by ear** tendrás que improvisar (**d**) Theat (part) hacer (el papel) de; **to p. Ophelia** hacer de Ofelia; Fig **to p. a part in sth** intervenir or participar en algo; Fig **to p. the fool** hacer el indio or el tonto (**e**) (aim) dirigir.

2 vi (**a**) (children) jugar (**with** con); (animals) juguetear; **to go out to p.** salir a jugar; **to p. at doctors and nurses** jugar a médicos y enfermeras; Fig **to p. with an idea** dar vueltas a una idea; Fig **to p. with fire** jugar con fuego; Fam **what is she playing at?** ¿qué pretende? (**b**) Sport (at game, gamble) jugar; **he plays centre-forward** juega de centro delantero; **to p. against sb** jugar contra algn; **to p. at cards** jugar a las cartas or a los naipes; **to p. fair** jugar limpio; **to p. for money** jugar por dinero; Fig **to p. for time** tratar de ganar tiempo; Fig **to p. into sb's hands** hacerle el juego a algn; (joke) bromear; **he's just playing** lo hace en broma (**d**) Mus (person) tocar; (instrument) sonar (**e**) Theat (act) actuar; **to p. in a film** trabajar en una película; Fig **to p. to the gallery** actuar para la galería

3 n (**a**) (game, activity) juego m; **a p. on words** un juego de palabras; **to be at p.** estar jugando; Fig **it's child's p.** es coser y cantar (**b**) Sport juego m; (match) partido m; **fair/foul p.** juego limpio/sucio; **p. begins at 3 o'clock** el partido empieza a las 3; **to be in/out of p.** (ball) estar dentro/fuera de juego (**c**) Theat obra f de teatro; **films and plays** cine m sing y teatro m sing □ **radio/television p.** obra f para radio/televisión (**d**) Tech & Fig (movement) juego m; **there's a lot of p. in the steering wheel** el volante tiene mucho juego; Fig **to bring sth into p.** poner algo en juego; Fig **to give full p. to one's emotions** dar rienda suelta a las emociones; Fig **to make a p. for sth/sb** intentar conseguir algo/conquistar a algn

play about vi juguetear; **to p. about with sth** juguetear con algo

play along vi **to p. along with sb** seguirle la corriente or la pista a algn

play around vi (waste time) gandulear; (be unfaithful) tener líos

play back vt (volver a) poner

play down vt minimizar, quitar importancia a

play off 1 vt oponer; **to p. off one thing against another** oponer una cosa a otra
2 vi Sport jugar un partido de desempate

play on vt (**a**) (take advantage of) aprovecharse de; (exploit) explotar (**b**) (irritate) (nerves etc) atacar, exacerbar

play out vt (game etc) llevar a su fin; Fam **to be played out** estar agotado(a) or rendido(a)

play up 1 vt (exaggerate) exagerar
2 vi Br Fam (child etc) dar guerra; (machine) no funcionar bien

play-acting ['pleɪæktɪŋ] n teatro m, cuento m

playbill ['pleɪbɪl] n cartel m or Am afiche m anunciador

playboy ['pleɪbɔɪ] n playboy m

player ['pleɪər] n Sport jugador(a) m,f; Mus músico(a) m,f; Theat (man) actor m; (woman) actriz f □ **football p.** futbolista mf; **guitar p.** guitarrista mf; **tennis p.** tenista mf

playful ['pleɪfʊl] adj (person, animal) juguetón(ona), travieso(a); (mood) juguetón(ona)

playground ['pleɪɡraʊnd] n patio m de recreo

playgroup ['pleɪɡruːp] n jardín m de niños or de infancia, guardería f

playhouse ['pleɪhaʊs] n (**a**) (theatre) teatro m (**b**) (for children) casita f

playing ['pleɪɪŋ] n juego m, el jugar □ **p. card** carta f, naipe m; **p. field** campo m de deportes

playmate ['pleɪmeɪt] n compañero(a) m,f de juego

play-off ['pleɪɒf] n Sport partido m de desempate

playpen ['pleɪpen] n corral m or parque m (de niños)

playroom ['pleɪruːm] n cuarto m de juego

playschool ['pleɪskuːl] n jardín m de infancia, guardería f

plaything ['pleɪθɪŋ] n juguete m

playtime ['pleɪtaɪm] n recreo m

playwright ['pleɪraɪt] n dramaturgo(a) m,f

plaza ['plɑːzə] n US (shopping centre) centro m comercial

PLC, plc [piːel'siː] Br Com (abbr **Public Limited Company**) Sociedad f Anónima, S.A.

plea [pliː] n (request) petición f, súplica f; Am pedido m; (excuse) pretexto m, disculpa f; Jur alegato m; **to enter a p. of not guilty** declararse inocente □ US **p. bargaining** = negociación extrajudicial entre el abogado y el fiscal por la que el acusado acepta su culpabilidad en cierto grado a cambio de no ser juzgado por un delito más grave

plead [pliːd] **1** vt (US Scot pt & pp **pled** [pled]) (**a**) Jur defender; Fig abogar por; **to p. sb's case** defender en juicio a algn; Fig **to p. sb's cause** defender la causa de algn, hablar por algn (**b**) (give excuse) pretender; **to p. ignorance/poverty** alegar ignorancia/pobreza
2 vi (**a**) (beg) rogar, implorar, suplicar; **to p. for mercy** pedir clemencia (**b**) Jur declararse; **to p. for sb** intervenir a favor de algn; **to p. guilty/not guilty** declararse culpable/inocente; **to p. with sb for sth** rogar a algn que conceda algo; **to p. with sb to do sth** suplicar a algn que haga algo

pleading ['pliːdɪŋ] **1** n súplicas fpl (**for** a favor de); Jur defensa f, alegato m
2 adj (voice, look) suplicante

pleasant ['plezənt] adj (gen) agradable; (person) simpático(a), amable; (surprise) grato(a); **it's very p. here** aquí se está muy bien; **to have a p. time** pasar un buen rato

pleasantly ['plezəntlɪ] adv (smile, behave) con simpatía;

to be p. surprised estar gratamente sorprendido(a)

pleasantry ['plezəntrɪ] *n* cumplido *m*; **to exchange pleasantries** intercambiar cumplidos

please [pliːz] **1** *vt (give pleasure to)* gustar, agradar, complacer; *(satisfy)* satisfacer; **he did it to p. us** lo hizo para complacernos; **there's no pleasing her** no hay forma de contentarla; **this will p. you** esto te gustará; **to p. oneself** hacer lo que le da la gana; *Fml* **p. God he will come** si Dios quiere vendrá; *Fam* **p. yourself** como quieras
2 *vi (give pleasure)* complacer; *(give satisfaction)* satisfacer; **easy/hard to p.** poco/muy exigente; **to be eager to p.** estar deseoso(a) de complacer
3 *adv* por favor; **come in, p.** pase, por favor; **may I? — do** ¿me permite? — desde luego; **'p. do not smoke'** 'se ruega no fumar'; **p. don't go** no te vayas, te lo ruego; **yes, p.** sí, por favor

pleased [pliːzd] *adj (happy)* contento(a); *(satisfied)* satisfecho(a); **I'm p. for you** me alegro por ti; **I'm p. to see it** me alegra verlo; **p. to meet you!** ¡encantado(a)!, ¡mucho gusto!; **to be p. about sth** alegrarse de algo; **to be p. with oneself** estar satisfecho(a) de sí mismo(a); **to be p. with sb/sth** estar contento(a) con algn/algo; **we are p. to inform you that ...** tenemos el gusto de comunicarle que ...

pleasing ['pliːzɪŋ] *adj (pleasant)* agradable, grato(a); *(satisfactory)* satisfactorio(a)

pleasurable ['pleʒərəbəl] *adj* agradable, divertido(a)

pleasure ['pleʒər] *n* (a) *(feeling of enjoyment)* gusto *m*, placer *m*; *(source of enjoyment)* placer; **it gives me great p. to welcome you** me complace mucho darle la bienvenida; **it's a p. to talk to him** da gusto hablar con él; **'Mr and Mrs Smith request the p. of your company'** 'los Sres. Smith tienen el gusto de solicitar la compañía de usted'; **the pleasures of the flesh** los placeres de la carne; **to take great p. in doing sth** disfrutar mucho haciendo algo; **with p.** con mucho gusto ❑ **p. boat** barco *m* de recreo; **p. cruise** crucero *m*; **p. ground** parque *m* de atracciones; **p. trip** excursión *f* (b) *(will)* voluntad *f*; **at sb's p.** según la voluntad de algn; *Br* **to be detained at** *or* **during her Majesty's p.** quedar detenido(a) a disposición del Estado

pleasure-loving ['pleʒəlʌvɪŋ] *adj*, **pleasure-seeking** ['pleʒəsiːkɪŋ] *adj* hedonista

pleat [pliːt] **1** *n* pliegue *m*
2 *vt* plisar, hacer pliegues en

plebeian [plɪ'biːən] *adj* plebeyo(a); *Fig* ordinario(a)

plebiscite ['plebɪsɪt] *n* plebiscito *m*

plectrum ['plektrəm] *n* *(pl* **plectrums** *or* **plectra** ['plektrə]) púa *f*, plectro *m*

pledge [pledʒ] **1** *n (promise)* promesa *f*; *(token of love etc)* señal *f*; *(security, guarantee)* garantía *f*, prenda *f*; **as a p. of our friendship** en señal de nuestra amistad; *Fig* **to take the p.** hacer la promesa de no beber alcohol
2 *vt* (a) *(promise)* prometer; **he pledged his support** prometió su apoyo; **she pledged never to return** juró no regresar nunca; **to p. sb to secrecy** hacer jurar a algn guardar el secreto (b) *(pawn)* empeñar, dar en prenda

plenary ['pliːnərɪ, 'plenərɪ] *adj* plenario(a); **p. power** poder absoluto; **p. session** sesión plenaria

plenipotentiary [plenɪpə'tenʃərɪ] *adj & n* plenipoten-ciario(a) *(m,f)*

plentiful ['plentɪfʊl] *adj* abundante

plenty ['plentɪ] **1** *n* abundancia *f*; **p. of potatoes** patatas *fpl* en abundancia, muchas patatas; **p. of time/money** tiempo *m*/dinero *m* de sobra; **that's p.** es más que suficiente; **we've got p.** tenemos de sobra; **years of p.** años *mpl* de abundancia
2 *adv* *US Fam* **it's p. big enough** es bastante grande

plethora ['pleθərə] *n* plétora *f*

pleurisy ['plʊərɪsɪ] *n Med* pleuresía *f*

Plexiglas® ['pleksɪɡlɑːs] *n US* plexiglás® *m*

pliable ['plaɪəbəl] *adj* flexible

pliant ['plaɪənt] *adj* dócil

pliers ['plaɪəz] *npl* **(pair of) p.** alicates *mpl*, tenazas *fpl*

plight [plaɪt] *n* situación *f* grave

plimsolls ['plɪmsɒlz] *npl Br* playeras *fpl*, zapatos *mpl* de lona *or* de tenis

plinth [plɪnθ] *n* plinto *m*

PLO [piːe'ləʊ] *n (abbr* **Palestine Liberation Organization)** OLP *f*

plod [plɒd] *vi (pt & pp* **plodded)** andar con paso lento *or* pesado; **to p. along** ir andando con paso lento; *Fig* **to p. on** perseverar; *Fig* **to p. through a report** estudiar laboriosamente un informe

plodder ['plɒdər] *n* trabajador(a) *m,f or* estudiante *mf* tenaz

plodding ['plɒdɪŋ] *adj* tenaz, laborioso(a)

plonk¹ [plɒŋk] **1** *vt Fam* dejar caer; **p. yourself down** siéntate; **to p. books down on the table** dejar caer los libros sobre la mesa
2 *n (sound)* golpe *m* seco, ruido *m* sordo

plonk² [plɒŋk] *n Br Fam (cheap wine)* vinazo *m*, vinaza *f*

plop [plɒp] **1** *n* plaf *m*; **to go p.** hacer plaf
2 *vi (pt & pp* **plopped)** hacer plaf

plot¹ [plɒt] **1** *n (conspiracy)* complot *m*; *Theat Lit (story)* argumento *m*, trama *f*; *Fig* **the p. thickens** se complica la trama
2 *vt (course, position)* trazar; *(scheme)* fraguar
3 *vi* conspirar, maquinar, tramar; **to p. to kill sb** conspirar para matar a algn

plot² [plɒt] *n Agr* parcela *f*, terreno *m*; **a p. of land** un terreno, una parcela; *(for building)* un solar ❑ **vegetable p.** campo *m* de hortalizas

plotter ['plɒtər] *n (conspirator)* conspirador(a) *m,f*

plough [plaʊ] **1** *n Agr* arado *m*; *Astron* **the P.** el Carro, la Osa Mayor
2 *vt Agr* arar, labrar
3 *vi* (a) *Agr (till)* arar, labrar (b) *Fig (run)* **the car ploughed through the fence** el coche atravesó la valla; **to p. into sth** chocar *or* dar fuerte contra algo; *Fig* **to p. through a book** leer un libro con dificultad

plough back *vt (money, profits)* reinvertir

plough up *vt (field)* arar, surcar

ploughman ['plaʊmən] *n (pl* **ploughmen)** arador *m*, labrador *m* ❑ *Culin* **p.'s lunch** pan *m* y ensalada *f* con queso

plover ['plʌvər] *n Orn* **golden p.** chorlito *m* dorado común; **ringed p.** chorlitejo *m* grande

plow [plaʊ] *n US see* **plough**

plowman ['plaʊmən] *n (pl* **plowmen)** *US see* **plough-man**

ploy [plɔɪ] *n* truco *m*, estratagema *f*

pluck [plʌk] **1** *vt (gen)* arrancar **(out of, from** de); *(flowers)* coger; *(chicken etc)* desplumar; *Mus (guitar etc)* puntear; **to p. one's eyebrows** depilarse las cejas
2 *n (courage)* valor *m*, ánimo *m*, arrojo *m*

pluck up *vt* **to p. up courage** armarse de valor, cobrar ánimos

plucky ['plʌkɪ] *adj* **(pluckier, pluckiest)** valiente

plug [plʌɡ] **1** *n* (a) *(bath, sink etc)* tapón *m*; *(of cotton wool)* tampón *m* (b) *Elec* enchufe *m*, clavija *f*; *(socket)* toma *f* de corriente ❑ *Aut* **spark p.** bujía *f*. **2/3 pin p.** clavija *f* de dos/tres patillas, clavija *f* bipolar/tripolar (c) *Fam (publicity)* publicidad *f*; **to give sth a p.** promocionar algo
2 *vt (pt & pp* **plugged)** (a) *(hole etc)* tapar; *(tooth)* empastar;

Fig cerrar (**b**) *(insert)* introducir; *(plug)* enchufar (**c**) *Fam (publicize)* dar publicidad a, promocionar; *(push) (idea etc)* hacer hincapié en

plug away *vi* **to p. away at sth** perseverar en algo

plug in *vt & vi Elec* enchufar

plug up *vt (hole etc)* tapar

plug-and-play ['plʌgən'pleɪ] *adj Comptr* para enchufar y usar

plughole ['plʌghəʊl] *n* desagüe *m*, desaguadero *m*

plug-in ['plʌgɪn] *n Comptr* dispositivo *m* opcional

plum [plʌm] *n (fruit)* ciruela *f; (colour)* color *m* ciruela; *Fig* **a p. job** un *Esp* chollo *or Méx* churro *(de trabajo), RP* un laburazo □ *Culin* **p. pudding** budín *m* de pasas; **p. tree** ciruelo *m*

plumage ['pluːmɪdʒ] *n Orn* plumaje *m*

plumb [plʌm] **1** *n* plomo *m*, plomada *f* □ **p. line** *(in building)* plomada *f; (in sea)* sonda *f*
  2 *adj* a plomo, vertical; **out of p.** torcido(a), desnivelado(a)
  3 *adv US Fam* **it's p. crazy** es una locura; **p. in the middle** justo en medio *or* en el centro
  4 *vt (depths) (of sea)* sondar; *Fig (of mind, soul etc)* sondear, penetrar; *Fig* **to p. the depths of despair** estar completamente desesperado(a)

plumber ['plʌmər] *n* fontanero(a) *m,f, Méx RP Ven* plomero(a)

plumbing ['plʌmɪŋ] *n (occupation)* fontanería *f, Méx RP Ven* plomería *f; (system)* tubería *f*, cañería *f*

plume [pluːm] *n* penacho *m*

plummet ['plʌmɪt] *vi (bird, plane)* caer en picado *or Am* picada; *Fig (prices)* bajar vertiginosamente; *(morale)* caer a plomo

plummy ['plʌmɪ] *adj Fam (voice, accent)* engolado(a) *(propio de la clase alta británica)*

plump¹ [plʌmp] *adj (person)* relleno(a); *(baby)* rechoncho(a); *(animal)* gordo(a)

plump² [plʌmp] *vi* **to p. for sth** optar *or* decidirse por algo

plump down 1 *vt* dejar caer
  2 *vi* desplomarse

plump up *vt (cushions)* ahuecar, agitar

plunder ['plʌndər] **1** *vt* saquear, pillar
  2 *n (action)* saqueo *m*, pillaje *m; (loot)* botín *m*

plunge [plʌndʒ] **1** *vt (immerse)* sumergir; *(thrust)* arrojar; **to p. a knife into sth** clavar *or* hundir un cuchillo en algo; *Fig* **to be plunged into despair** estar hundido(a) en la desesperación
  2 *vi* (**a**) *(dive) (into water)* lanzarse, tirarse de cabeza, zambullirse; *(ship)* cabecear; *Fig (fall)* caer, hundirse; **to p. to one's death** tener una caída mortal (**b**) *Fin (shares, prices)* desplomarse
  3 *n (dive)* chapuzón *m*, zambullida *f; Fig (fall)* caída *f*, desplome *m*; **to take the p.** dar el paso decisivo

plunge into *vt* sumirse en, lanzarse a

plunger ['plʌndʒər] *n Tech* émbolo *m; (for blocked pipes)* desatascador *m*

plunging ['plʌndʒɪŋ] *adj (neckline)* escotado(a)

pluperfect [pluː'pɜːfɪkt] *n Ling* pluscuamperfecto *m*

plural ['plʊərəl] **1** *adj* plural
  2 *n* plural *m*; **in the p.** en el plural

pluralism ['plʊərəlɪzəm] *n* pluralismo *m*

plurality [plʊə'rælɪtɪ] *n* pluralidad *f; US* **a p. of** la mayoría de

plus [plʌs] **1** *prep* más; **there are four of them, p. the children** son cuatro, más los niños; **three p. four makes seven** tres más cuatro hacen siete
  2 *adj Math Elec* positivo(a); **a p. factor** un factor positivo, *Fam* **she's forty p.** ha pasado de las cuarenta □ **p. sign** signo *m* más
  3 *n Math* signo *m* más; *Fig (advantage)* ventaja *f*, factor *m* positivo; *Fam* plus *m*

plush [plʌʃ] **1** *n* felpa *f*, peluche *m*
  2 *adj Fam (luxurious)* lujoso(a)

Pluto ['pluːtəʊ] *n Astron Myth* Plutón *m*

plutonium [pluː'təʊnɪəm] *n* plutonio *m*

ply¹ [plaɪ] **1** *vt (pt & pp* **plied**) (**a**) *(use) (tool)* manejar, utilizar; *(sea route)* navegar por; **to p. one's trade** ejercer su oficio *or* profesión (**b**) *(overwhelm)* abrumar, acosar; **to p. sb with drinks** no parar de ofrecer copas a algn; **to p. sb with questions** acosar a algn con preguntas
  2 *vi (ship)* navegar; **to p. between Majorca and Barcelona** cubrir la línea *or* ir y venir de Mallorca a Barcelona; **to p. for hire** ir en busca de clientes

ply² [plaɪ] *n (of wood)* capa *f; (of wool)* cabo *m* □ **three-p. wool** lana *f* de tres cabos

plywood ['plaɪwʊd] *n* madera *f* contrachapada, contrachapado *m*

PM [piː'em] *n Br Fam (abbr* **Prime Minister**) Primer(a) Ministro(a) *m,f*

p.m. [piː'em] *(abbr* **post meridiem**) *(after noon),* después del mediodía; **at 2 p.m.** a las dos de la tarde

PMT [piːem'tiː] *n Med Fam (abbr* **premenstrual tension**) tensión *f* premenstrual

pneumatic [njʊ'mætɪk] *adj* neumático(a)

pneumonia [njuː'məʊnɪə] *n Med* pulmonía *f*

PO [piː'əʊ] *n* (**a**) *Naut (abbr* **Petty Officer**) contramaestre *m* (**b**) *Br (abbr* **postal order**) giro *m* postal, g.p. (**c**) *(abbr* **Post Office**) correos *mpl*

poach¹ [pəʊtʃ] **1** *vt* (**a**) **to p. fish/game** pescar/cazar en vedado (**b**) *Fig Fam (steal)* birlar, quitar
  2 *vi (for fish)* pescar en vedado; *(for game)* cazar en vedado; *Fig* **to p. on sb's territory** pisar los papeles a algn

poach² [pəʊtʃ] *vt Culin (egg)* escalfar; *(fish)* hervir; **poached egg** huevo *m* escalfado

poacher¹ ['pəʊtʃər] *n (of fish)* pescador *m* furtivo; *(of game)* cazador *m* furtivo

poacher² ['pəʊtʃər] *n (for eggs)* escalfador *m*

pocket ['pɒkɪt] **1** *n* (**a**) *(gen)* bolsillo *m*, *CAm Méx Perú* bolsa *f;* **he came in with his hands in his pockets** entró con las manos metidas en los bolsillos; **to dip into one's p.,** **put one's hand in one's p.** poner las manos en el bolsillo; **to go through sb's pockets** vaciar los bolsillos a algn; **to pay for sth out of one's own p.** pagar algo con su propio dinero; **to turn out one's pockets** vaciar los bolsillos; *Fig* **to be \$10 in/out of p.** salir ganando/perdiendo 10 dólares; *Fig* **to have sth/sb in one's p.** tener algo/a algn en el bolsillo; *Fig* **to line one's pockets** forrarse □ **p. dictionary** diccionario *m* de bolsillo; **p. handkerchief** pañuelo *m;* **p. money** dinero *m* de bolsillo (**b**) *(area) (of air)* bolsa *f; (of resistence)* foco *m*, rincón *m*
  2 *vt (money)* embolsar, meter en el bolsillo; **to p. the change** quedarse con el cambio; *Fig* **to p. one's pride** tragarse el orgullo

pocketbook ['pɒkɪtbʊk] *n US Esp* bolso *m, Col CSur* cartera *f, Méx* bolsa *f*

pocketknife ['pɒkɪtnaɪf] *n (pl* **pocketknives** ['pɒkɪtnaɪvz]) navaja *f*

pocket-sized ['pɒkɪtsaɪzd] *adj (tamaño m)* de bolsillo

pockmarked ['pɒkmɑːkt] *adj (face)* picado(a) de viruelas; *(surface)* acribillado(a) de agujeros

pod [pɒd] *n Bot* vaina *f*

podgy ['pɒdʒɪ] *adj Br* (**podgier, podgiest**) gordin-flón(ona), regordete

podia ['pəʊdɪə] *npl see* **podium**

podiatrist [pə'daɪətrɪst] *n US* podólogo(a) *m,f*

podiatry [pə'daɪətrɪ] *n US* podología *f*

podium ['pəʊdɪəm] *n* (*pl* **podiums** *or* **podia**) podio *m*

poem ['pəʊɪm] *n* poema *m*, poesía *f*

poet ['pəʊɪt] *n* poeta *mf*

poetic [pəʊ'etɪk] *adj* poético(a) ❏ **p. justice** justicia *f* divina; **p. licence** licencia *f* poética

poetical [pəʊ'etɪkəl] *adj* poético(a)

poetry ['pəʊɪtrɪ] *n* poesía *f* ❏ **p. reading** lectura *f or* recital *m* de poesías

pogrom ['pɒgrəm] *n* pogrom *m*

poignancy ['pɔɪnjənsɪ] *n* patetismo *m*

poignant ['pɔɪnjənt] *adj* patético(a), conmovedor(a)

point [pɔɪnt] **1** *n* (**a**) *(sharp end)* punta *f*; **at the p. of a gun** a mano armada; **to dance on points** *(in ballet)* bailar de puntas; **with a sharp p.** puntiagudo(a); *Fig* **not to put too fine a p. on it** hablando sin rodeos *or* con franqueza (**b**) *(place)* punto *m*, lugar *m*; **he's outspoken to the p. of being rude** es franco para no decir grosero; **p. of arrival/departure** punto de llegada/salida *or* partida; *Fig* **p. of contact** punto de contacto; *Fig* **p. of no return** punto de no volver atrás (**c**) *(quality)* cualidad *f*, punto *m*; **good/bad p.** cualidad buena/mala; **weak/strong p.** punto débil/fuerte (**d**) *(moment)* punto *m*; **at that p.** entonces, en aquel momento; **at the p. of death** al borde de la muerte; **from that p. onwards** desde entonces; **to be on the p. of doing sth** estar a punto de hacer algo ❏ **boiling/freezing/melting p.** punto *m* de ebullición/congelación/fusión (**e**) *(score) (in test, sport)* punto *m*, tanto *m*; **to score points** ganar *or* marcar puntos; *Box* **to win on points** ganar por puntos ❏ *Ten* **match p.** pelota *f* de match; **penalty p.** punto *m* de penalti; *Ten* **set p.** pelota *f* de partido (**f**) *(in argument)* punto *m*; **the main p.** lo esencial, el meollo; **to make one's p.** insistir en el argumento; **I see** *or* **take your p.** entiendo lo que quieres decir; **p. taken!** ¡ya, ya!; **it's a case in p.** es un ejemplo de esto; **in p. of fact** de hecho, en realidad; **to stretch a p.** hacer una excepción (**g**) *(purpose)* fin *m*, propósito *m*; **I don't see the p.** no veo el sentido; **it's to the p.** viene al caso; **that isn't the p., it's beside the p.** eso no viene al caso; **there's no p. in going** no merece la pena ir; **to come** *or* **get to the p.** llegar al meollo de la cuestión; **to make a p. of doing sth** poner empeño en hacer algo; **to miss the p. of sth** no seguir la corriente de algo; **what's the p.?** ¿para qué?; **what's the p. of it?** ¿qué sentido tiene? ❏ *Ten* **moot p.** punto *m* discutible (**h**) *(on scale)* punto *m*; *(on compass)* grado *m*, cuarta *f*; *(on thermometer)* punto *m*; *Fin (of shares etc)* entero *m*; *Math* **decimal p.** punto decimal; **six p. three** seis coma tres; *Fin* **the index is up 3 points** el índice ha subido de 3 puntos; *Fig* **up to a p.** hasta cierto punto (**i**) *(full stop)* punto *m* (**j**) *Geog* punta *f*, cabo *m* (**k**) *Elec* **power p.** toma *f* de corriente (**l**) *(police)* **to be on p. duty** dirigir la circulación (**m**) **points** *Aut* platinos *mpl*; *Rail* agujas *fpl*

2 *vt* (**a**) *(aim) (gun etc)* apuntar; *(indicate) (way etc)* señalar, indicar; **to p. a gun at sb** apuntar a algn con una pistola; **to p. one's finger** señalar con el dedo; **to p. one's toes** hacer puntas; *Fig* **to p. the finger at sb** acusar a algn; *Fig* **to p. the way** señalar el camino (**b**) *Constr (wall, house)* rejuntar

3 *vi* señalar, indicar; **the hands of the clock p. to ten o'clock** las manecillas del reloj marcan las diez; **to p. at sth/sb** señalar algo/a algn con el dedo; **to p. to** *or* **towards somewhere** indicar el camino hacia un lugar; *Fig* **everything points to her guilt** todo indica que ella es la culpable

point out *vt (show)* indicar, señalar; *(mistake)* señalar,

hacer notar; *(mention)* hacer notar; *(warn)* advertir; **they pointed out that it could be difficult** advirtieron que podría ser difícil

point up *vt* destacar, subrayar

point-blank [pɔɪnt'blæŋk] **1** *adj (shot)* a boca de jarro, a quemarropa; *(question)* hecho(a) de golpe y porrazo; *(refusal)* categórico(a), rotundo(a); **to shoot at p.-b. range** tirar a boca de jarro *or* a quemarropa

2 *adv (shoot)* a boca de jarro, a quemarropa; *(fire question)* de golpe y porrazo; *(refuse)* categóricamente, rotundamente

pointed ['pɔɪntɪd] *adj (sharp)* puntiagudo(a); *Fig (comment)* intencionado(a), significativo(a); *(cutting)* mordaz

pointedly ['pɔɪntɪdlɪ] *adv Fig (significantly)* con intención, de un modo significativo; *(cuttingly)* con mordacidad

pointer ['pɔɪntər] *n* (**a**) *(indicator)* indicador *m*, aguja *f*; *(for blackboard, map)* puntero *m* (**b**) *Zool (dog)* perro *m* de muestra (**c**) *(clue)* indicación *f*; *(piece of advice)* consejo *m*

pointless ['pɔɪntlɪs] *adj* sin sentido; **it's p.** carece de sentido; **it would be p. to accept** no serviría de nada aceptar

point-to-point [pɔɪnttə'pɔɪnt] *n Br Sport* **p.-to-p. race** carrera *f*

poise [pɔɪz] **1** *n (balance)* equilibrio *m*; *(bearing)* porte *m*; *(self-assured)* aplomo *m*

2 *vt (hold in balance)* equilibrar, balancear; **to be poised** estar equilibrado(a), cernerse; *Fig* **to be poised for action** estar listo(a) para la acción

poised [pɔɪzd] *adj* sereno(a)

poison ['pɔɪzən] **1** *n* veneno *m*; **to take p.** envenenarse; *Fam* **what's your p.?** ¿qué quieres tomar? ❏ **p. gas** gas *m* tóxico; *Bot* **p. ivy** hiedra *f* venenosa; **p. pen letter** anónimo *m* amenazador *or* insultante

2 *vt* envenenar, intoxicar; **to p. oneself** envenenarse; **to p. one's system** intoxicarse; *Fig* **to p. sb's mind** envenenar la mente de algn

poisoning ['pɔɪzənɪŋ] *n* envenenamiento *m*, intoxicación *f*; **to die of p.** morir envenenado(a) *or* intoxicado(a) ❏ **blood p.** envenenamiento *m* de la sangre; **food p.** intoxicación *f* por alimentos

poisonous ['pɔɪzənəs] *adj (plant, snake)* venenoso(a); *(drugs, gas)* tóxico(a); *Fig (rumour)* pernicioso(a)

poke [pəʊk] **1** *vt (with finger or stick)* dar con la punta del dedo *or* del bastón a; **to p. one's head out of the window** asomar la cabeza por la ventana; **to p. sb in the eye with one's finger** poner el dedo en el ojo de algn; **to p. sb with one's elbow** dar un codazo a algn; **to p. the fire** atizar el fuego; *Fig* **to p. fun at sb** burlarse de algn; *Fig* **to p. one's nose into sb else's business** meterse en asuntos ajenos

2 *n (jab) (with finger)* empujón *m*, golpe *m*; *(nudge)* codazo *m*; **to give sb a p. in the ribs** dar a algn un codazo en las costillas; **to give the fire a p.** atizar el fuego

poke about, poke around *vi* **to p. about** *or* **around in sb's handbag** fisgonear *or* hurgar en el bolso de algn

poke out *vt (eye)* sacar; **you nearly poked my eye out!** ¡casi me sacaste el ojo!

poker¹ ['pəʊkər] *n (for fire)* atizador *m*; *Fig* **as stiff as a p.** más tieso(a) que un palo

poker² ['pəʊkər] *n Cards* póquer *m*

poker-faced ['pəʊkəfeɪst] *adj Fam* de rostro impasible

poky ['pəʊkɪ] *adj* (**pokier, pokiest**) *Fam Pej* minúsculo(a); **a p. little house/room** una casucha/un cuartucho

Poland ['pəʊlənd] *n* Polonia

polar ['pəʊlər] *adj* polar ❏ **p. bear** oso *m* polar

polarity [pəʊ'lærɪtɪ] *n* polaridad *f*

polarization [pəʊləraɪ'zeɪʃən] *n* polarización *f*

polarize ['pəʊləraɪz] **1** *vt* polarizar
 2 *vi* polarizarse

Polaroid® ['pəʊlərɔɪd] *adj* polaroid

Pole [pəʊl] *n* polaco(a) *m,f*

pole¹ [pəʊl] *n* palo *m*, estaca *f*; *(for curtain)* bara *f* ❑ *Athlet* **p. vault** salto *m* de pértiga; **telegraph p.** poste *m* telegráfico; **tent p.** palo *m* de tienda; *Athlet* **vaulting p.** pértiga *f*

pole² [pəʊl] *n Elec Geog* polo *m*; *Fig* **to be poles apart** ser polos opuestos ❑ **North/South P.** Polo *m* Norte/Sur; **P. Star** estrella *f* polar

poleaxe, *US* **poleax** ['pəʊlæks] *vt* apalear

polecat ['pəʊlkæt] *n inv Zool (like weasel)* turón *m*; *US (skunk)* mofeta *f*

polemic [pə'lemɪk] *n* **(a)** *(controversy)* polémica *f* **(b)** *(speech, article)* diatriba *f*

polemical [pə'lemɪkəl] *adj* polémico(a)

police [pə'liːs] **1** *npl* policía *f sing*; **to call the p.** llamar a la policía; **to join the p.** meterse de policía ❑ *US* **p. academy** academia *f* de policía; **p. car** coche *m or Am* carro *m or CSur* auto *m*, de policía; *US* **p. commissioner** = ciudadano que preside un consejo civil encargado de supervisar la actuación de la policía; *Br* **p. constable** guardia *m*, policía *m*; *US* **p. department** jefatura *f* de policía; **p. escort** escolta *f* de policía; **p. force** cuerpo *m* de policía; **p. headquarters** jefatura *f* de policía; **p. officer** guardia *mf*, policía *mf*; **p. record** antecedentes *mpl* penales; **p. state** estado *m* policíaco; **p. station** comisaría *f*
 2 *vt* vigilar, mantener el orden en

policeman [pə'liːsmən] *n* (*pl* **policemen**) guardia *m*, policía *m*

policewoman [pə'liːswʊmən] *n* (*pl* **policewomen** [pə'liːswɪmɪn]) (mujer *f*) policía *f*

policy ['pɒlɪsɪ] *n* **(a)** *(course of action)* norma *f*, táctica *f*; *Pol* política *f*; **foreign p.** política exterior; **it's a good/bad p.** es buena/mala táctica; **it's a matter of p.** es cuestión de política; **our p. is to do this** tenemos por norma hacer esto **(b)** *Ins* **(insurance) p.** póliza *f* (de seguros); **to take out an insurance p.** hacerse un seguro, sacar una póliza ❑ **p. holder** asegurado(a) *m,f*

polio ['pəʊlɪəʊ] *n (abbr* **poliomyelitis)** *Med* poliomielitis *f*, polio *f*

Polish ['pəʊlɪʃ] **1** *adj* polaco(a)
 2 *n* **(a)** *pl* **the P.** los polacos **(b)** *(language)* polaco *m*

polish ['pɒlɪʃ] **1** *vt (metal, stone)* pulir; *(furniture, floors)* encerar; *(nails)* pintar con esmalte; *(shoes)* limpiar; *(silver)* sacar brillo a
 2 *n* **(a)** *(cream etc) (for furniture, floors)* cera *f*; *(for shoes)* betún *m*; *(for nails)* esmalte *m* **(b)** *(action)* pulimento *m*; **to give one's shoes a p.** limpiar los zapatos; **to give sth a p.** dar brillo a algo **(c)** *(shine)* brillo *m*, lustre *m*; *Fig (refinement)* refinamiento *m*, brillo *m*

polish off *vt Fam (work)* despachar, terminar con; *(food)* tragarse, zamparse

polish up *vt Fig* perfeccionar

polished ['pɒlɪʃt] *adj (metal, stone, silver)* pulido(a), lustroso(a); *(furniture, floors)* encerado(a); *(nails)* pintado(a); *(shoes)* limpio(a); *Fig (manners)* refinado(a); *(style)* pulido(a); *(performance)* impecable

polite [pə'laɪt] *adj* cortés, educado(a); **in p. society** entre gente educada; **to be p. to sb** tratar a algn con cortesía *or* educación

politely [pə'laɪtlɪ] *adv* cortésmente, educadamente, con cortesía *or* educación

politeness [pə'laɪtnɪs] *n* cortesía *f*, educación *f*

politic ['pɒlɪtɪk] *adj* prudente

political [pə'lɪtɪkəl] *adj* político(a) ❑ **p. asylum** asilo *m* político; **p. correctness** lo políticamente correcto; **p. science** ciencias *fpl* políticas

politically [pə'lɪtɪklɪ] *adv* políticamente; **p. correct** políticamente correcto(a)

politician [pɒlɪ'tɪʃən] *n* político(a) *m,f*

politicization [pəlɪtɪsaɪ'zeɪʃən] *n* politización *f*

politicize [pə'lɪtɪsaɪz] *vt* politizar

politics ['pɒlɪtɪks] **1** *n sing (subject)* política *f*; **to go into p.** dedicarse a la política; **to talk p.** hablar de política
 2 *npl (views)* posición *f sing or* postura *f sing* política; **what are his p.?** ¿cuál es su postura política?

polka ['pɒlkə] *n (pl* **polkas**) **(a)** *(dance)* polca *f* **(b)** **p. dot** dibujo *m* de puntos

poll [pəʊl] **1** *n* **(a)** *(voting)* votación *f*; **a heavy p.** una votación masiva; **to take a p. on sth** someter algo a votación; **the polls** las elecciones; **a defeat at the polls** una derrota electoral; **to go to the polls** acudir a las urnas **(b)** *(survey)* encuesta *f*; *(register)* registro *m* ❑ **opinion p.** sondeo *m* de opinión; **p. tax** = impuesto directo, individual y de tarifa única
 2 *vt (votes)* obtener; *(opinion)* sondear

pollen ['pɒlən] *n* polen *m* ❑ **p. count** índice *m* de polen en el aire

pollinate ['pɒlɪneɪt] *vt* polinizar

polling ['pəʊlɪŋ] *n* votación *f* ❑ **p. booth** cabina *f* electoral; **p. station** centro *m* electoral

pollster ['pəʊlstər] *n* encuestador(a) *m,f*

pollutant [pə'luːtənt] *n* (sustancia *f*) contaminante *m*

pollute [pə'luːt] *vt* contaminar, polucionar

polluter [pə'luːtər] *n (company)* empresa *f* contaminante; *(industry)* industria *f* contaminante

pollution [pə'luːʃən] *n* contaminación *f*, polución *f*; **environmental p.** contaminación del medio ambiente

polo ['pəʊləʊ] *n* **(a)** *Sport* polo *m* ❑ **water p.** waterpolo *m*, polo *m* acuático **(b)** *Br* **p. neck sweater** suéter *m or Esp* jersey *m or Col* saco *m or RP* pulóver *m* con cuello vuelto *or* cuello cisne

poltergeist ['pɒltəgaɪst] *n* duende *m*

poly ['pɒlɪ] *n Br Fam Formerly (abbr* **polytechnic)** (escuela *f*) politécnica *f*

poly- ['pɒlɪ] *pref* poli-, multi-

polyester [pɒlɪ'estər] *n* poliéster *m*

polyethylene [pɒlɪ'eθəliːn] *n US* polietileno *m*

polygamous [pə'lɪgəməs] *adj* polígamo(a)

polygamy [pə'lɪgəmɪ] *n* poligamia *f*

polyglot ['pɒlɪglɒt] *adj & n* polígloto(a) *(m,f)*

polygon ['pɒlɪgɒn] *n Geom* polígono *m*

polymer ['pɒlɪmər] *n Chem* polímero *m*

Polynesia [pɒlɪ'niːzɪə] *n* Polinesia

Polynesian [pɒlɪ'niːzɪən] *adj & n* polinesio(a) *(m,f)*

polyp ['pɒlɪp] *n Med* pólipo *m*

polyphonic [pɒlɪ'fɒnɪk] *adj Mus* polifónico(a)

polystyrene [pɒlɪ'staɪriːn] *n* poliestireno *m*

polytechnic [pɒlɪ'teknɪk] *n Br Formerly* escuela *f* politécnica, politécnico *m*

polythene ['pɒlɪθiːn] *n Br* polietileno *m* ❑ **p. bag** bolsa *f* de plástico

polyunsaturated [pɒlɪʌn'sætjʊreɪtɪd] *adj* poliinsaturado(a)

polyurethane [pɒlɪ'jʊərəθeɪn] *n* poliuretano *m*

pomegranate ['pɒmɪgrænɪt] *n Bot (fruit)* granada *f* ❑ **p. tree** granado *m*

pommy ['pɒmɪ] *n Austral Slang Pej* inglés(esa) *m,f*

pomp [pɒmp] *n* pompa *f*

pompom ['pɒmpɒm] *n*, **pompon** ['pɒmpɒn] *n* borla *f*, pompón *m*

pomposity [pɒm'pɒsɪtɪ] *n* pomposidad *f*

pompous ['pɒmpəs] *adj (person)* presumido(a); *(speech)* rimbombante; *(occasion)* pomposo(a)

ponce [pɒns] *n Br Slang Pej* proxeneta *m*, *Esp* chulo *m*, *RP* cafiolo *m*

poncho ['pɒntʃəʊ] *n (pl* **ponchos***)* poncho *m*

pond [pɒnd] *n* estanque *m*

ponder ['pɒndər] **1** *vt* considerar, sopesar
2 *vi* **to p. over sth** meditar *or* reflexionar sobre algo

ponderous ['pɒndərəs] *adj* pesado(a)

pong [pɒŋ] *Br Fam* **1** *n* hedor *m*, olor *m* a peste
2 *vi* heder, oler a peste, apestar

pontiff ['pɒntɪf] *n* pontífice *m*

pontificate [pɒn'tɪfɪkeɪt] *vi* pontificar

pontoon¹ [pɒn'tu:n] *n Constr* pontón *m* ❑ **p. bridge** puente *m* de pontones

pontoon² [pɒn'tu:n] *n Br Cards* veintiuna *f*, siete y medio *m*

pony ['pəʊnɪ] *n* poney *m* ❑ **p. trekking** excursión *f* en poney

ponytail ['pəʊnɪteɪl] *n* cola *f* de caballo

pooch [pu:tʃ] *n Fam* chucho *m*

poodle ['pu:dəl] *n Zool* caniche *m*

poof [pʊf] *n Br Slang Offens* marica *m*

pooh [pu:] *interj* ¡bah!

pooh-pooh [pu:'pu:] *vt* despreciar, descartar

pool¹ [pu:l] *n (of water, oil etc)* charco *m*; *(pond)* estanque *m*; *(in river)* pozo *m* ❑ **swimming p.** piscina *f*, *Méx* alberca *f*, *RP* pileta *f*

pool² [pu:l] **1** *n* **(a)** *Com (common fund)* fondo *m* común; *(services)* servicios *mpl* comunes ❑ **car p.** reserva *f* de coches; **typing p.** servicio *m* de mecanografía **(b)** *US (snooker)* billar *m* americano **(c)** *Br* **football pools** quinielas *fpl*, *Arg* Prode *m*, *Col CRica* totogol *m*; **to do the football p.** jugar a las quinielas *or Arg* al Prode *or Col CRica* al totogol
2 *vt (funds)* reunir, juntar; *(ideas, resources)* poner en común

poop [pu:p] *n US Fam* **1** *n (faeces)* cacas *fpl*; **to take a p.** hacer caca
2 *vi* hacer(se) caca

pooped [pu:pt] *adj Fam* hecho(a) migas *or* polvo

poor [pʊər, pɔ:r] **1** *adj (person)* pobre; *(quality)* malo(a), inferior; *(attempt)* poco satisfactorio(a); **he was knocked down by a car, the p. thing** le atropelló un coche, el pobre; **p. people** gente *f* pobre; **to be a p. traveller** soportar mal los viajes; **to be p. at French** estar flojo(a) en francés; **to be in p. health** estar mal de salud; **to have a p. memory** tener poca memoria; **to have a p. opinion of sth** tener una opinión poco favorable de algo; *Fam* **you p. thing!** ¡pobrecito!
2 the poor *npl* los pobres

poorly ['pʊəlɪ, 'pɔ:lɪ] **1** *adv (gen)* pobremente; *(badly)* mal; **p. dressed/attended** mal vestido(a)/asistido(a)
2 *adj (poorlier, poorliest) (ill)* mal, malo(a); **to be p.** estar *or* sentirse mal *or* malo(a)

pop¹ [pɒp] **1** *vt (pt & pp* **popped***)* **(a)** *(burst)* hacer reventar; *(cork)* hacer saltar **(b)** *Fam* **p. your coat on** ponte el abrigo; **she popped a chocolate into her mouth** se metió un bombón en la boca; **to p. one's head out of the window** asomar la cabeza por la ventana; *Fam* **to p. the question** declararse

2 *vi* **(a)** *(burst)* reventar; *(cork)* saltar; **her eyes nearly popped out of her head** le saltaron los ojos de sorpresa **(b)** *Fam (go quickly)* **I'm just popping over to Ian's** voy un momento a casa de Ian
3 *n* **(a)** *(noise)* pequeña explosión *f*; **to go p.** *(burst)* reventar; *(bang)* hacer pum **(b)** *Fam (drink)* gaseosa *f* **(c)** *Mus Fam* música *f* pop ❑ **p. festival** festival *m* de música pop; **p. singer** cantante *mf* pop

pop in *vi Fam* ir un momento a, pasar por; **p. in and see us** pásate a hacernos una visita

pop off *vi Fam* **(a)** *(leave)* irse, marcharse **(b)** *(die)* estirar la pata, *Esp* irse al otro barrio, *Méx* patatearse

pop² *US (father)* papá *m*

pop³ *(abbr* **population***)* población *f*

popcorn ['pɒpkɔ:n] *n* palomitas *fpl* de maíz, *RP* pochoclo *m*

pope [pəʊp] *n* papa *m*

popeyed ['pɒpaɪd] *adj* de ojos saltones

popgun ['pɒpɡʌn] *n* pistola *f* de juguete (de aire comprimido)

poplar ['pɒplər] *n Bot* álamo *m* ❑ **black p.** chopo *m* negro; **grey p.** álamo *m* cano; **Italian black p.** chopo *m* negro italiano; **Lombardy p.** chopo *m* lombardo, álamo *m* de Italia

poplin ['pɒplɪn] *n Tex* popelina *f*

popper ['pɒpər] *n Br Sew Fam* corchete *m*

poppet ['pɒpɪt] *n Br Fam* cielo *m*, encanto *m*; **she's a p.** es un cielo; **yes, my p.** sí, mi vida

poppy ['pɒpɪ] *n Bot* amapola *f* ❑ **p. seed** semilla *f* de amapola

poppycock ['pɒpɪkɒk] *n Fam Esp* majaderías *fpl*, *Am* zonceras *fpl*; **don't talk p.!** ¡no digas tonterías!

Popsicle® ['pɒpsɪkəl] *n US* polo *m*, *Am* paleta *f* helada, *Arg* palito *m* de agua

populace ['pɒpjʊləs] *n (people)* pueblo *m*; *(masses)* populacho *m*

popular ['pɒpjʊlər] *adj* **(a)** *(well-liked)* popular; *(person)* estimado(a); *(fashionable)* de moda; *(common)* corriente, común; **a p. colour** un color muy visto; **he's p. with his colleagues** sus colegas le estiman mucho; **you won't be p. with the neighbours if you do it** no ganarás la simpatía de los vecinos si lo haces **(b)** *(of or for the people)* popular; **by p. request** a petición *or Am* pedido popular *or* del público ❑ **p. opinion** opinión *f* general; **p. prices** precios *mpl* populares

popularity [pɒpjʊ'lærɪtɪ] *n* popularidad *f*; **p. rating** índice *m* de popularidad

popularize ['pɒpjʊləraɪz] *vt (music, fashion etc)* popularizar; *(idea etc) (make understandable)* vulgarizar

popularly ['pɒpjʊləlɪ] *adv* popularmente, generalmente; **it's p. believed that ...** la mayoría de la gente cree que ...

populate ['pɒpjʊleɪt] *vt* poblar; **thinly populated** muy poco poblado(a)

population [pɒpjʊ'leɪʃən] *n* población *f*; **the p. explosion** la explosión demográfica

populist ['pɒpjʊlɪst] *adj & n* populista *(mf)*

populous ['pɒpjʊləs] *adj* populoso(a), poblado(a)

pop-up menu ['pɒpʌp'menjuː] *n Comptr* menú *m* desplegable

porcelain ['pɔːslɪn] *n* porcelana *f*; **made of p.** de porcelana ❑ **p. cup** taza *f* de porcelana

porch [pɔːtʃ] *n (of church)* pórtico *m*; *(of house) US (veranda)* porche *m*; *Br (doorway)* zaguán *m*

porcupine ['pɔːkjʊpaɪn] *n Zool* puerco *m* espín

pore¹ [pɔːr] *vi* **to p. over sth** engolfarse en algo

pore² [pɔ:r] *n Anat* poro *m*

pork [pɔ:k] *n* (carne *f* de) cerdo *m* or puerco *m* or *Am* chancho *m* ❏ **p. butcher** charcutero(a) *m,f;* **p. chop** chuleta *f* de cerdo; **p. pie** empanada *f* de carne de cerdo; **p. sausage** salchicha *f*

porn [pɔ:n] *n Fam* (*abbr* **pornography**) porno *m*; **hard/ soft p.** pornografía *f* dura/blanda

porno [ˈpɔ:nəʊ] *adj Fam* porno

pornographic [pɔ:nəˈgræfɪk] *adj* pornográfico(a)

pornography [pɔ:ˈnɒgrəfɪ] *n* pornografía *f*

porous [ˈpɔ:rəs] *adj* poroso(a)

porpoise [ˈpɔ:pəs] *n Zool* marsopa *f*

porridge [ˈpɒrɪdʒ] *n Culin* gachas *fpl* de avena ❏ **p. oats** copos *mpl* de avena (para hacer gachas)

port¹ [pɔ:t] *n* (*town, harbour*) puerto *m*; **to come** or **put into p.** tomar puerto; *Fig* **any p. in a storm** la necesidad carece de ley ❏ **fishing/sea p.** puerto *m* pesquero/ marítimo; **free p.** puerto *m* franco; **home p.** puerto *m* de matrícula; **p. of call** puerto *m* de escala; **P. of Spain** Puerto España

port² [pɔ:t] *n Naut Av* (*larboard*) babor *m*

port³ [pɔ:t] *n* (*wine*) vino *m* de Oporto, oporto *m*

portable [ˈpɔ:təbəl] *adj* portátil

portal [ˈpɔ:təl] *n* (**a**) *Fml* (*entrance*) pórtico *m* (**b**) *Comptr* (*Web page*) portal *m*

Port-au-Prince [pɔ:təʊˈprɪns] *n* Puerto Príncipe

portend [pɔ:ˈtend] *vt Fml* augurar, presagiar

portent [ˈpɔ:tent] *n Fml* augurio *m*, presagio *m*

portentous [pɔ:ˈtentəs] *adj Fml* (*significant*) decisivo(a), relevante; (*threatening*) de mal agüero

porter [ˈpɔ:tər] *n* (**a**) (*in hotel, building, market*) portero(a) *m,f;* *Rail* mozo *m* de estación (**b**) *US Rail* mozo *m* de los coches-cama

portfolio [pɔ:tˈfəʊlɪəʊ] *n* (*pl* **portfolios**) (*file*) carpeta *f;* (*of artist, politician*) cartera *f;* **minister without p.** ministro(a) *m,f* sin cartera

porthole [ˈpɔ:thəʊl] *n Naut* portilla *f*

portion [ˈpɔ:ʃən] *n* (*part, piece*) parte *f*, porción *f;* (*of food*) ración *f*

portion out *vt* repartir, distribuir

portly [ˈpɔ:tlɪ] *adj* (**portlier, portliest**) corpulento(a), gordo(a)

portrait [ˈpɔ:trɪt, ˈpɔ:treɪt] *n* retrato *m*; **to have one's p. painted** hacerse (hacer) un retrato; **to paint sb's p.** retratar a algn ❏ **p. painter** retratista *mf*

portray [pɔ:ˈtreɪ] *vt* (*paint portrait of*) retratar; (*describe*) pintar, describir; *Theat* (*character*) representar

portrayal [pɔ:ˈtreɪəl] *n* (*description*) descripción *f*, representación *f;* (*by actor*) interpretación *f*

Portugal [ˈpɔ:tjʊgəl] *n* Portugal

Portuguese [pɔ:tjʊˈgi:z] **1** *adj* portugués(esa), luso(a) ❏ **P. man-of-war** medusa *f*
2 *n* (**a**) (*person*) portugués(esa) *m,f* (**b**) (*language*) portugués *m*

POS [pi:əʊˈes] *n Com* (*abbr* **point of sale**) punto *m* de venta

pos (*abbr* **positive**) positivo(a)

pose [pəʊz] **1** *vt* (*problem, question*) plantear; (*threat*) representar
2 *vi* (**a**) (*for painting, photograph*) posar (**b**) *Pej* (*behave affectedly*) presumir, hacer pose (**c**) **to p. as** hacerse pasar por; **he posed as a doctor** se hizo pasar por médico
3 *n* (**a**) (*position, stance*) postura *f*, actitud *f* (**b**) *Pej* (*affectation*) pose *f*

poser¹ [ˈpəʊzər] *n Br Fam Pej* (*person*) presumido(a) *m,f*

poser² [ˈpəʊzər] *n* (*problem*) problema *m*; (*difficult question*) pregunta *f* difícil

posh [pɒʃ] *Br Fam* **1** *adj* (*hotel, restaurant etc*) elegante, de lujo; (*person*) *Esp* pijo(a), *Méx* fresa, *RP* (con)cheto(a), *Ven* sifrino(a); (*accent*) afectado(a)
2 *adv* **to talk p.** hablar con acento *Esp* pijo or *Méx* como una fresa or *RP* como un cocheto

position [pəˈzɪʃən] **1** *n* (**a**) (*place*) posición *f;* (*location*) situación *f;* *Sport* posición; **from this/that p.** desde aquí/ allí; *Sport* **what p. does she play?** ¿de qué juega? (**b**) (*right place*) sitio *m*, lugar *m*; **to be in/out of p.** estar en su sitio/ fuera de lugar; **to hold sth in p.** sujetar algo; **to put sth into p.** colocar algo (**c**) (*posture, stance*) posición *f*, postura *f;* **in a comfortable p.** en una postura cómoda; **in a horizontal/vertical p.** en posición horizontal/vertical (**d**) (*on scale, in competition*) posición *f*, lugar *m*; (*rank*) rango *m*; **a woman of her p.** una mujer de su categoría social; **in first/last p.** en primer/último lugar (**e**) (*situation*) lugar *m*, situación *f;* **put yourself in my p.** ponte en mi lugar; **the economic/political p.** la situación económica/política; **to be in an awkward p.** encontrarse en una situación delicada; **to be in a p. to do sth** estar en condiciones de hacer algo (**f**) (*opinion*) postura *f;* **you know my p. on this matter** ya sabes lo que opino sobre este tema (**g**) (*job*) puesto *m*, empleo *m*; **a p. of responsibility** un puesto de responsabilidad; **to apply for the p. of cook** solicitar el puesto de cocinero
2 *vt* (*put in place*) colocar; (*troops*) situar; **to p. oneself** ponerse en posición

positive [ˈpɒzɪtɪv] *adj* (**a**) (*affirmative*) positivo(a); (*criticism*) constructivo(a); *Math Ling Elec* positivo(a); (*person*) dinámico(a); (*sign*) favorable; (*proof*) incontrovertible; (*refusal*) categórico(a); *Med* **the tests were p.** las pruebas resultaron positivas (**b**) (*sure, certain*) seguro(a); **to be p. about sth** estar seguro(a) de algo (**c**) *Fam* (*absolute*) auténtico(a), verdadero(a); **it was a p. disaster** fue un auténtico desastre

positively [ˈpɒzɪtɪvlɪ] *adv* (**a**) (*answer*) en forma positiva; (*think*) positivamente; (*talk*) con convicción (**b**) *Fam* (*absolutely*) realmente, verdaderamente; **the food was p. revolting** la comida daba auténtico asco

posse [ˈpɒsɪ] *n* (*to catch criminal*) partida *f* or cuadrilla *f* (de persecución); *Fig* (*group*) banda *f*, cuadrilla *f*

possess [pəˈzes] *vt* (**a**) (*own*) poseer; **everything she possessed** todo cuanto tenía (**b**) (*take over*) apoderarse de; **what possessed him to buy it?** ¿cómo se le ocurrió comprarlo?

possessed [pəˈzest] *adj* poseído(a), endemoniado(a)

possession [pəˈzeʃən] *n* (**a**) (*ownership*) posesión *f;* *Sport* **to have p. of the ball** tener el balón or (*in soccer*) la pelota; **to have sth in one's p.** tener algo (en su poder); *Jur* **to take p. of sth** tomar posesión de algo (**b**) (*personal property*) posesión *f;* **her prized p.** su posesión más estimada; **it was his only p.** era lo único que tenía (**c**) **possessions** bienes *mpl* (**d**) (*by evil spirit*) posesión *f*

possessive [pəˈzesɪv] **1** *adj* posesivo(a); **to be p. about sth/with sb** ser posesivo(a) con algo/algn
2 *n Ling* posesivo *m*

possessor [pəˈzesər] *n* poseedor(a) *m,f*

possibility [pɒsɪˈbɪlɪtɪ] *n* (**a**) (*likelihood*) posibilidad *f;* **it's a p.** es posible; **it's within the realms of p.** queda dentro de lo posible; **there's a p. that they will accept** existe posibilidad or es posible que acepten (**b**) **possibilities** (*potential*) potencial *m sing;* **to have p.** ser prometedor(a)

possible [ˈpɒsɪbəl] **1** *adj* posible; **as much as p.** todo lo posible; **as often as p.** cuanto más mejor; **as soon as p.** cuanto antes; **if at all p.** a ser posible; **it's p. that they'll**

come es posible que vengan; **it's p. to go there** es posible *or* se puede ir allí; **to make sth p.** posibilitar algo

2 *n* **he's a p. for the job** es un candidato para el puesto

possibly ['pɒsɪblɪ] *adv* (**a**) *(perhaps)* posiblemente; **will you go? — p.** ¿irás? — puede que sí (**b**) *(for emphasis)* **as well as I p. can** lo mejor que pueda; **I can't p. come** no puedo venir de ninguna manera

post¹ [pəʊst] **1** *n (of wood)* estaca *f*, poste *m*; *Ftb (goalpost)* poste; *Fig* **to go from pillar to p.** ir de la Ceca a la Meca; *Br Slang* **to be pipped at the p.** perder por un pelo □ **starting/finishing p.** línea *f* de salida/llegada

2 *vt (fix)* fijar; **'post no bills'** *(notice)* 'prohibido fijar carteles'

post² [pəʊst] **1** *n* (**a**) *(position, job)* puesto *m*, cargo *m*; **to take up one's p.** ocupar el puesto (**b**) *Mil* puesto *m* □ **frontier p.** puesto *m* fronterizo; **last p.** toque *m* de retreta (**c**) *US* **trading p.** factoría *f*

2 *vt* (**a**) *Mil* enviar, destinar (**b**) *(send)* enviar, destinar

post³ [pəʊst] *Br* **1** *n (mail)* correo *m*; **by p.** por correo; **by return p.** a vuelta de correo; **by separate p.** por correo aparte; **is there any p.?** ¿hay cartas?; **to catch/miss the p.** alcanzar/no alcanzar el correo; **to come first/last p.** venir con el primer/último reparto □ **p. office** oficina *f* de correos; **P. Office Box** apartado *m* de correos; **P. Office Savings Bank** Caja *f* Postal de Ahorros; **p. office worker** empleado(a) *m,f* de correos

2 *vt (letter)* echar al correo; **to p. sth to sb** mandar algo por correo a algn; *Fig* **to keep sb posted about sth** tener a algn al tanto de algo

post- [pəʊst] *pref* post-, pos-

postage ['pəʊstɪdʒ] *n* franqueo *m*, porte *m*; **p. paid** franco de porte □ **p. and packing** gastos *mpl* de envío; **p. stamp** sello *m* (de correos), *Am* estampilla *f*

postal ['pəʊstəl] *adj* postal, de correos □ **p. district** distrito *m* postal; *Br* **p. order** giro *m* postal; **p. vote** voto *m* por correo

postbag ['pəʊstbæg] *n Br (mail)* cartas *fpl*, correspondencia *f*

postbox ['pəʊstbɒks] *n Br* buzón *m*

postcard ['pəʊstkɑːd] *n* tarjeta *f* postal

postcode ['pəʊstkəʊd] *n Br* código *m* postal

postdate [pəʊst'deɪt] *vt* poner fecha adelantada a

poster ['pəʊstər] *n* cartel *m*, póster *m*, *Am* afiche *m*

poste restante [pəʊstrɪ'stænt] *n Br* lista *f* de correos, *Am* poste *m* restante

posterior [pɒ'stɪərɪər] **1** *n Hum* trasero *m*, pompis *m*

2 *adj* posterior

posterity [pɒ'sterɪtɪ] *n* posteridad *f*

post-free [pəʊst'friː] *Br* **1** *adj* porte pagado

2 *adv* a porte pagado

postgraduate [pəʊst'grædjʊɪt] **1** *n* postgraduado(a) *m,f*, posgraduado(a) *m,f*

2 *adj* de postgraduado *or* posgraduado

posthaste [pəʊst'heɪst] *adv* a toda prisa

posthumous ['pɒstjʊməs] *adj* póstumo(a)

posthumously ['pɒstjʊməslɪ] *adv* póstumamente, después de la muerte

posting ['pəʊstɪŋ] *n* (**a**) *Mil* destino *m* (**b**) *Comptr* destino *m*

Post-it® ['pəʊstɪt] *n* **P. (note)** post-it® *m*

postman ['pəʊstmən] *n Br (pl* **postmen**) cartero *m*

postmark ['pəʊstmɑːk] **1** *n* matasellos *m inv*

2 *vt* timbrar, matasellar

postmaster ['pəʊstmɑːstər] *n* administrador *m* de correos □ *Br* **P. General** Director(a) *m,f* General de Correos

postmistress ['pəʊstmɪstrɪs] *n* administradora *f* de correos

post-modernism [pəʊst'mɒdənɪzəm] *n* posmodernismo *m*

post-modernist [pəʊst'mɒdənɪst] *adj & n* posmoderno(a) *(m,f)*

postmortem [pəʊst'mɔːtəm] *n* autopsia *f*

postnatal [pəʊst'neɪtəl] *adj* postnatal, (de) postparto

post-operative [pəʊst'ɒpərətɪv] *adj Med* pos(t)operatorio(a)

post-paid *adj & adv US see* **post-free**

postpone [pəʊst'pəʊn, pəs'pəʊn] *vt* aplazar, posponer

postponement [pəʊst'pəʊnmənt] *n* aplazamiento *m*

postscript ['pəʊsskrɪpt] *n* postdata *f*, posdata *f*

post-traumatic stress disorder ['pəʊsttrɔː'mætɪk'stresdɪsɔːdər] *n Med* síndrome *m* de estrés postraumático

postulate ['pɒstjʊleɪt] *vt* postular

posture ['pɒstʃər] **1** *n* postura *f*; *(affected)* pose *f*

2 *vi* adoptar una postura; *(affected)* adoptar una pose

postwar ['pəʊstwɔːr] *adj* de la postguerra *or* posguerra; **the p. period** la postguerra, la posguerra

posy ['pəʊzɪ] *n* ramillete *m*

pot [pɒt] **1** *n (container)* tarro *m*, pote *m*; *(for cooking)* olla *f*, puchero *m*; *(for tea)* tetera *f*; *(for coffee)* cafetera *f*; *(for flowers)* maceta *f*, tiesto *m*; *(ornament)* cacharro *m*; **pots and pans** batería *f* (de cocina); **to take a p. shot at sb** tirar *or* disparar al azar contra algn; *Fam* **to go to p.** irse al garete *or Am* al diablo; *Fam* **to have pots of money** estar forrado(a) □ *Culin* **p. roast** estofado *m or Andes Méx* ahogado *m* de carne; **p. shot** tiro *m* al azar

2 *vt (pt & pp* **potted**) (**a**) *(meat etc)* conservar en tarro; *(plant)* poner en maceta *or* tiesto (**b**) *(ball) (in billiards)* meter en la tronera; *(in golf)* meter en el hoyo

potable ['pəʊtəbəl] *adj* potable

potash ['pɒtæʃ] *n Chem* potasa *f*

potassium [pə'tæsɪəm] *n Chem* potasio *m*

potato [pə'teɪtəʊ] *n (pl* **potatoes**) *Esp* patata *f*, *Am* papa *f*; *Slang* **hot p.** patata caliente □ **jacket p.** patata *f* cocida *or* asada con piel; **mashed p.** puré *m* de patatas; **p. crisps**, *US* **p. chips** *Esp* patatas *fpl or Am* papas *fpl* fritas (de bolsa); **sweet p.** boniato *m*

potbellied ['pɒtbelɪd] *adj (fat)* barrigón(ona), *(malnourished)* de vientre hinchado

potency ['pəʊtənsɪ] *n* potencia *f*, fuerza *f*

potent ['pəʊtənt] *adj* potente, fuerte

potentate ['pəʊtənteɪt] *n* potentado *m*

potential [pə'tenʃəl] **1** *adj* potencial, posible

2 *n* (**a**) *(promise)* potencial *m*; **to have p.** ser prometedor(a); **to realize one's full p.** realizarse plenamente (**b**) *Elec Math* potencial *m*

potentially [pə'tenʃəlɪ] *adv* en potencia

pothole ['pɒthəʊl] *n Geol* cueva *f*; *(in road)* bache *m*

potholer ['pɒthəʊlər] *n Br Sport* espeleólogo(a) *m,f*

potholing ['pɒthəʊlɪŋ] *n Br Sport* espeleología *f*

potion ['pəʊʃən] *n* poción *f*, pócima *f*

potluck [pɒt'lʌk] *n Fam* **to take p.** conformarse con lo que haya

potpourri [pəʊ'pʊərɪ] *n (pl* **potpourris**) (**a**) *(of flowers)* pebete *m*; *(of music, poems, etc)* popurrí *m* (**b**) *Culin* olla *f* podrida

potted ['pɒtɪd] **1** *pt & pp see* **pot**

2 *adj (food)* en conserva; *(plant)* en maceta *or* tiesto; *Fam Fig* **a p. version** una versión resumida

potter¹ ['pɒtər] *n* alfarero(a) *m,f* □ **p.'s wheel** torno *m* de alfarero

potter² ['pɒtər] *vi Br* **to p. about** *or* **around** entretenerse

pottery ['pɒtərɪ] *n (craft, place)* alfarería *f; (objects)* cerámica *f*, loza *f* ❑ **p. mug** tazón *m* de barro

potty¹ ['pɒtɪ] *adj* (**pottier, pottiest**) *Br Fam* pirado(a), *Col* corrido(a), *CSur* rayado(a), *Méx* zafado(a); **to drive sb p.** volverle loco(a) a algn

potty² ['pɒtɪ] *n Fam* orinal *m*

potty-trained ['pɒtɪtreɪnd] *adj (child)* que ya no necesita llevar pañales

pouch [paʊtʃ] *n* **(a)** *(gen)* bolsa *f* pequeña; *(for ammunition)* morral *m*; *(for tobacco)* petaca *f* **(b)** *Zool* bolsa *f* abdominal

pouf(fe) [puːf] *n* puf *m*

poulterer ['pəʊltərər] *n Br* pollero(a) *m,f*

poultice ['pəʊltɪs] *n Med* cataplasma *f*, emplasto *m*

poultry ['pəʊltrɪ] *n (live)* aves *fpl* de corral; *(food)* pollos *mpl*, volatería *f* ❑ **p. farm** granja *f* avícola; **p. farmer** avicultor(a) *m,f*; **p. farming** avicultura *f*

pounce [paʊns] **1** *vi* **to p. on sb/sth** echarse encima de algn/algo
2 *n* salto *m*

pound¹ [paʊnd] **1** *vt (strike)* aporrear, machacar; **to p. at** *or* **on the door** golpear la puerta
2 *vi* **(a)** *(beat)* resonar; *(heart)* palpitar; *(waves)* romper **(b)** *(walk heavily)* andar con paso pesado

pound² [paʊnd] *n* **(a)** *(money)* libra *f* (esterlina) ❑ **p. note** billete *m* de una libra; **p. sign** *Br* símbolo *m* de la libra; *US* = el símbolo '#'; *(on telephone)* almohadilla *f*, numeral *m* **(b)** *(weight)* libra *f* (= 453,6g); **half a p.** media libra; **to sell sth by the p.** vender algo por libras

pound³ [paʊnd] *n (enclosure) (for dogs)* perrera *f*; *(for cars)* depósito *m* de coches

pounding ['paʊndɪŋ] *n (of heart)* palpitación *f*; *(of waves)* embate *m*; *Fam* **to give sb a p.** darle una paliza a algn

pour [pɔːr] **1** *vt (liquid)* echar, verter; *(spill)* derramar; **to p. money into a venture** invertir mucho dinero en un negocio; **to p. sb a drink** servirle una copa a algn; *Fig* **to p. cold water on a scheme** poner pegas a un proyecto; *Fig* **to p. scorn on sth** despreciar algo
2 *vi (liquid)* correr, fluir; *(spill)* derramarse; *(teapot)* echar; **it's pouring with rain** está lloviendo a cántaros; *Fam* **the sweat was pouring off him** sudaba la gota gorda

pour out *vt (liquid)* echar, verter; *(spill)* derramar; **to p. sb out a drink, p. out a drink for sb** servirle una copa a algn; *Fig* **to p. one's heart out to sb** desahogarse con algn

pouring ['pɔːrɪŋ] *adj (rain)* torrencial; *(custard etc)* para echar; **p. consistency** consistencia *f* líquida

pout¹ [paʊt] **1** *vi* hacer pucheros, poner mala cara
2 *n* puchero *m*, mala cara *f*

pout² [paʊt] *n (fish)* faneca *f*

poverty ['pɒvətɪ] *n* pobreza *f*; *Fig (of ideas)* falta *f*, carencia *f*; **extreme p.** miseria *f*; **to live in p.** vivir en la miseria

poverty-stricken ['pɒvətɪstrɪkən] *adj* necesitado(a); **to be p.-s.** vivir en la miseria

POW [piːəʊ'dʌbəljuː] *n (abbr* **prisoner of war**) prisionero(a) *m,f* de guerra

powder ['paʊdər] **1** *n* polvo *m*; **to reduce sth to p.** pulverizar algo, reducir algo a polvo ❑ **p. compact** polvera *f*; **p. keg** polvorín *m*; **p. puff** borla *f*, **p. room** baño *m* or *Esp* servicios *mpl* or *CSur* toilette *m* de señoras; **talcum p.** polvos *mpl* de talco
2 *vt* **(a)** *(reduce to powder)* pulverizar, reducir a polvo **(b)** *(put powder on)* **to p. one's nose** poner polvos en la cara; *Euph* ir a los servicios de señora or al tocador

powdered ['paʊdəd] *adj (milk)* en polvo

powdery ['paʊdərɪ] *adj (like powder)* polvoriento(a); *(powdered)* en polvo

power ['paʊər] **1** *n* **(a)** *(force, strength)* fuerza *f*; *(energy)* energía *f*; **electric/nuclear p.** energía eléctrica/nuclear; *Elec* **to cut off the p.** cortar la corriente ❑ **p. base** bastión *f* de popularidad; **p. cut** corte *m* de corriente or del fluido eléctrico; **p. plant** central *f* or *Andes RP* usina *f* eléctrica; **p. point** enchufe *m*, toma *f* (de corriente) or *Am* de contacto; **p. station** central *f* or *Andes RP* usina *f* eléctrica; *Aut* **p. steering** *Esp* dirección *f* asistida or *Am* hidráulica, *Esp* servodirección *f* **(b)** *(ability)* poder *m*, capacidad *f*; *(faculty)* facultad *f*; *Fig (impact)* poder; **to do everything in one's p. to achieve sth** hacer todo lo posible por conseguir algo; **powers of persuasion** poder de persuasión; **powers of resistance** poder or capacidad de resistencia; **the p. of speech** la facultad del habla; *Fig* el poder del habla; *Fam* **it did him a p. of good** le hizo mucho bien **(c)** *(authority)* poder *m*, autoridad *f*; *(nation)* potencia *f*; *Jur Pol* poder; *(influence)* influencia *f*; *(right)* derecho *m*; **the powers of darkness** las fuerzas del mal; **the great powers** las grandes potencias; **the p. of veto** el derecho de veto; *Pol* **to be in p.** estar en or tener el poder; *Pol* **to come into p., rise to p.** subir al poder; **to have p. over sb** tener influencia sobre algn; **to have sb in one's p.** tener a algn en su poder; *Fig* **the powers that be** las autoridades ❑ *Jur* **p. of attorney** poder *m*, procuración *f* **(d)** *Tech* potencia *f*, fuerza *f*; *(performance, output)* rendimiento *m* ❑ **p. drill** taladradora *f* mecánica; **p. saw** sierra *f* mecánica **(e)** *Math* potencia *f*; **two to the p. of four** dos elevado a la cuarta potencia
2 *vt (aircraft)* propulsar, impulsar; **powered by jet** impulsado(a) por motor a reacción; **to be powered by electricity** funcionar con electricidad

powerboat ['paʊəbəʊt] *n Naut* motora *f*, lancha *f* a motor

power-driven ['paʊədrɪvən] *adj Tech* mecánico(a); *Elec* eléctrico(a)

powerful ['paʊəfʊl] *adj (strong) (person)* fuerte, fornido(a); *(influential) (person, country)* poderoso(a); *(remedy)* eficaz; *(engine, machine)* potente; *(emotion)* fuerte; *(speech)* conmovedor(a), emocionante

powerfully ['paʊəfʊlɪ] *adv (with great strength)* con fuerza; *(argue)* convincentemente; *(speak)* de forma conmovedora

powerhouse ['paʊəhaʊs] *n Elec* central *f* eléctrica; *Fig (person)* persona *f* dinámica; *Fig (thing)* fuerza *f* motriz

powerless ['paʊəlɪs] *adj* impotente, ineficaz; **I was p. to help** no pude hacer nada para ayudar

powwow ['paʊwaʊ] *n Fam* plática *f*, conferencia *f*

pox [pɒks] *n Med* viruela *f*; *Fam* **the p.** la sífilis

poxy ['pɒksɪ] *adj* (**poxier, poxiest**) *Br Slang* pésimo(a), malísimo(a)

pp **(a)** *(abbr* **pages**) págs., pp. **(b)** *Br Com (on behalf of)* p.p.

PR [piː'ɑːr] *n (abbr* **public relations**) relaciones *fpl* públicas

pr **(a)** *(abbr* **pair**) par *m* **(b)** *(abbr* **price**) precio *m*

practicability [præktɪkə'bɪlɪtɪ] *n* factibilidad *f*

practicable ['præktɪkəbəl] *adj* factible, practicable

practical ['præktɪkəl] **1** *adj (gen)* práctico(a); *(useful)* útil; *(sensible)* sensato(a), adecuado(a); *(person)* práctico(a), realista; **for all p. purposes** en la práctica
2 *n (lesson)* clase *f* práctica

practicality [præktɪ'kælɪtɪ] *n (of suggestion, plan)* factibilidad *f*; **practicalities** detalles *mpl* prácticos

practically ['præktɪklɪ] *adv* **(a)** *(in practice)* en la práctica; **p. speaking** hablando de la práctica **(b)** *(almost)* casi; **I p. did it** por poco lo hago; **it's p. impossible** es casi imposible

practice ['præktɪs] **1** *n* **(a)** *(custom, habit)* costumbre *f*; **it's their p. to ask for references** acostumbran a or suelen

pedir informes; **it's the usual p.** es la costumbre; **sharp p.** trampas *fpl*; **to make a p.** of doing sth tener la costumbre de hacer algo (**b**) *(exercise)* práctica *f*, ejercicios *mpl*; *Sport* entrenamiento *m*; *Mus* ensayo *m*, práctica *f*; **it takes years of p.** requiere años de práctica *or* de entrenamiento; **to be out of p.** no estar en forma; **to keep in p.** mantenerse en forma; *Prov* **p. makes perfect** se aprende a base de práctica □ **choir p.** ensayo *m* coral; **piano p.** *(scales)* ejercicios *mpl* en el piano; *(studies)* estudios *mpl* del piano; *Sport* **p. match** partido *m* de entrenamiento (**c**) *(way of doing sth)* práctica *f*; *Ind (technique)* técnica *f*, métodos *mpl*; **in p.** en la práctica; **to put sth into p.** poner algo en práctica (**d**) *(exercise of profession)* ejercicio *m*; *(place) (of doctors)* consultorio *m*, consulta *f*; *(of lawyers)* bufete *m*, gabinete *m*; *(clients) (of doctors)* pacientes *mpl*; *(of lawyers)* clientela *f*; *Med* **private p.** consulta privada; **she's no longer in p.** ya no practica *or* ejerce; **to be in p.** *(doctor)* ejercer la medicina; *(lawyer)* ejercer la abogacía; **to set up in p. as a doctor** establecerse como médico
2 *vt & vi US see* **practise**

practise ['præktɪs] **1** *vt* (**a**) *(gen)* practicar; *(language, virtue)* practicar; *(method)* seguir; *(principle)* poner en práctica; *Mus Theat* ensayar; *(piano)* estudiar; **to p. one's Spanish on sb** practicar el español con algn; *Fig* **to p. what one preaches** predicar con el ejemplo (**b**) *(profession)* ejercer; **to p. medicine/law** ejercer la medicina/la abogacía
2 *vi* (**a**) *(gen)* practicar; *Sport* entrenar; *Mus Theat* ensayar (**b**) *(doctor)* practicar; *(lawyer)* ejercer

practised, *US* **practiced** ['præktɪst] *adj (skilled)* experto(a)

practising, *US* **practicing** ['præktɪsɪŋ] *adj (doctor etc)* que ejerce; *(Christian etc)* practicante

practitioner [præk'tɪʃənər] *n Br Med* **general p.** médico(a) *m,f* de cabecera; **medical p.** médico(a) *m,f*

pragmatic [præg'mætɪk] *adj* pragmático(a)

pragmatics [præg'mætɪks] *n* pragmática *f*

pragmatism ['prægmətɪzəm] *n* pragmatismo *m*

pragmatist ['prægmətɪst] *n* pragmatista *mf*

Prague [prɑːg] *n* Praga

prairie ['preərɪ] *n (gen)* pradera *f*; *US* llanura *f*, pampa *f* □ *Zool* **p. dog** perro *m* de las praderas

praise [preɪz] **1** *n* alabanza *f*, elogio *m*, loa *f*; **I have nothing but p. for what she has done** sólo tengo elogios para lo que ha hecho; **in p. of sth/sb** en alabanza de algo/algn; **p. be to God!** ¡alabado sea Dios!; *Fig* **to sing the praises of sth/sb** alabar *or* elogiar algo/a algn
2 *vt* alabar, elogiar; **to p. God** alabar a Dios; *Fig* **to p. sb to the skies** poner a algn por las nubes

praiseworthy ['preɪzwɜːðɪ] *adj* loable, digno(a) de elogio

praline ['prɑːliːn] *n US Culin* praliné *m*

pram [præm] *n Br* cochecito *m* de niño

prance [prɑːns] *vi (horse)* hacer cabriolas, encabritarse; *(person)* **to p. about** ir pegando brincos; **to p. in/out** entrar/salir dando brincos

prang [præŋ] *Br Slang* **1** *n (bombing)* bombardeo *m*; *(accident)* accidente *m*
2 *vt (bomb)* bombardear; *(crash)* estrellar

prank [præŋk] *n (piece of mischief)* travesura *f*; *(joke)* broma *f*; **to play a p. on sb** gastar una broma a algn

prat [præt] *n Br Slang* imbécil *mf*

prate [preɪt] *vi* decir tonterías

prattle ['prætəl] **1** *vi* charlar, parlotear
2 *n* charla *f*, parloteo *m*

prawn [prɔːn] *n Zool* gamba *f*, *Am* camarón *m*

pray [preɪ] *vi Rel* rezar, orar; **to p. to God that sth might happen** rogar a Dios para que pase algo; *Fam* **he's past praying for** es un caso perdido; *Fam* **we're praying for good weather** deseamos que haga buen tiempo

prayer [preər] *n Rel* rezo *m*, oración *f*; *(entreaty)* súplica *f*, ruego *m*; **morning prayers** *(in church)* maitines *mpl*; **the Lord's P.** el Padrenuestro; **to say one's prayers** rezar, orar; *Fig* **his prayers were answered** sus oraciones fueron escuchadas □ **evening prayers** vísperas *fpl*; **p. book** devocionario *m*, misal *m*; **p. mat** = esterilla que utilizan los musulmanes para el rezo; **p. meeting** reunión *f* para orar juntos

pre- [priː] *pref* pre-, ante-; **pre-1960** antes de 1960

preach [priːtʃ] **1** *vt Rel (gospel)* predicar; *(sermon)* dar, hacer
2 *vi Rel* predicar; *Fig* **to p. to sb** sermonear a algn

preacher ['priːtʃər] *n Rel (sermon giver)* predicador(a) *m,f*; *US (minister)* pastor *m*

preamble [priː'æmbəl] *n* preámbulo *m*

prearrange [priːə'reɪndʒ] *vt* arreglar de antemano

precarious [prɪ'keərɪəs] *adj (unstable)* precario(a); *(dangerous)* peligroso(a)

precariously [prɪ'keərɪəslɪ] *adv* precariamente; **p. balanced** *(object, situation)* en equilibrio precario

precaution [prɪ'kɔːʃən] *n* precaución *f*; **as a p. against illness** por precaución contra la enfermedad; **to take precautions** *(gen)* tomar precauciones; *(in sex)* usar contraceptivo; **to take the p. of doing sth** tomar la precaución de hacer algo

precautionary [prɪ'kɔːʃənərɪ] *adj* preventivo(a)

precede [prɪ'siːd] *vt* preceder; **the speech was preceded by an introduction** el discurso estuvo precedido por una introducción

precedence ['presɪdəns] *n* preferencia *f*, prioridad *f*; **in order of p.** por orden de preferencia; **to take p. over sth/sb** tener prioridad sobre algo/algn

precedent ['presɪdənt] *n* precedente *m*; **to create** *or* **set a p.** sentar un precedente; **without p.** sin precedente

preceding [prɪ'siːdɪŋ] *adj* precedente, anterior; **the week p. the accident** la semana anterior al accidente

precept ['priːsept] *n* precepto *m*

precinct ['priːsɪŋkt] *n (enclosure)* recinto *m*; *US (administrative, police division)* distrito *m*; *(police station)* comisaría *f* (de policía) □ **pedestrian/shopping p.** zona *f* peatonal/comercial

precious ['preʃəs] **1** *adj (valuable)* precioso(a); *(treasured)* precioso(a), querido(a); *Iron* maldito(a); **p. memories** gratos recuerdos *mpl*; **p. stones** piedras *fpl* preciosas; *Fam* **you and your p. car!** ¡tú y tu tan querido coche!
2 *n (term of endearment)* precioso(a) *m,f*, cariño *m*; **yes, my p.** sí, mi vida
3 *adv Fam* **p. little/few** muy poco/pocos

precipice ['presɪpɪs] *n* precipicio *m*; *Fig* **to be living on the edge of a p.** vivir al borde del precipicio

precipitate [prɪ'sɪpɪteɪt] **1** *vt (hasten)* precipitar, provocar; *Chem* precipitar; *Fig* arrojar
2 *adj* precipitado(a)
3 [prɪ'sɪpɪtɪt] *n Chem* precipitado *m*

precipitation [prɪsɪpɪ'teɪʃən] *n* precipitación *f*

precipitous [prɪ'sɪpɪtəs] *adj* (**a**) *(steep)* escarpado(a) (**b**) *(hasty)* precipitado(a)

précis ['preɪsiː] **1** *n (pl précis* ['preɪsiːz]) resumen *m*
2 *vt* resumir, sintetizar

precise [prɪ'saɪs] *adj* (**a**) *(exact)* preciso(a), exacto(a); **an hour, 55 minutes to be p.** una hora, 55 minutos para ser precisos; **at that p. moment** en aquel preciso *or* mismo momento; **be p.!** ¡sé preciso(a)!, ¡concreta! (**b**) *(meticulous)* meticuloso(a); *Pej* quisquilloso(a)

precisely [prɪˈsaɪslɪ] *adv (exactly)* precisamente, exactamente; *(with precision)* con precisión; **it's p. six o'clock** son las seis en punto; **p.!** ¡eso es!, ¡exacto!

precision [prɪˈsɪʒən] *n (exactness)* precisión *f*, exactitud *f*; **lack of p.** imprecisión *f* ❑ *Mil* **p. bombing** bombardeo *m* de precisión; **p. instrument** instrumento *m* de precisión

preclude [prɪˈkluːd] *vt (exclude)* excluir; *(avoid)* evitar; *(prevent)* impedir; **it precludes us from going** nos impide que vayamos; **to p. any misunderstanding** para evitar todo malentendido

precocious [prɪˈkəʊʃəs] *adj* precoz

precociousness [prɪˈkəʊʃəsnɪs] *n*, **precocity** [prɪˈkɒsɪtɪ] *n* precocidad *f*

preconceived [priːkənˈsiːvd] *adj* preconcebido(a)

preconception [priːkənˈsepʃən] *n (idea)* idea *f* preconcebida; *(prejudice)* prejuicio *m*

precondition [priːkənˈdɪʃən] *n* condición *f* previa

precook [priːˈkʊk] *vt* precocinar

precursor [prɪˈkɜːsər] *n* precursor(a) *m,f*

predate [priːˈdeɪt] *vt* (**a**) *(precede)* preceder, ser anterior a (**b**) *(put earlier date on)* poner fecha anterior a, antedatar

predator [ˈpredətər] *n Zool* depredador *m*, animal *m* de rapiña

predatory [ˈpredətərɪ] *adj Zool* predador(a), de rapiña; *Fig (person)* depredador(a)

predecease [priːdɪˈsiːs] *vt* morir antes que

predecessor [ˈpriːdɪsesər] *n (gen)* predecesor(a) *m,f*, antecesor(a) *m,f*; *(ancestor)* antepasado(a) *m,f*

predestination [priːdestɪˈneɪʃən] *n* predestinación *f*

predestine [priːˈdestɪn] *vt* predestinar

predetermination [priːdɪtɜːmɪˈneɪʃən] *n* predeterminación *f*

predetermine [priːdɪˈtɜːmɪn] *vt* predeterminar

predicament [prɪˈdɪkəmənt] *n* apuro *m*, aprieto *m*; **to be in a p.** *(difficult situation)* estar en un apuro; *(dilemma)* estar en un dilema

predicate [ˈpredɪkeɪt] **1** *vt* (**a**) *(state)* afirmar (**b**) *(base)* basar; **to be predicated upon sth** basarse en algo
   2 [ˈpredɪkɪt] *n Ling* predicado *m*

predict [prɪˈdɪkt] *vt* predecir, pronosticar

predictable [prɪˈdɪktəbəl] *adj* previsible; **she's very p.** actúa siempre de forma previsible

predictably [prɪˈdɪktəblɪ] *adv* como era de esperar

prediction [prɪˈdɪkʃən] *n* predicción *f*, pronóstico *m*

predispose [priːdɪˈspəʊz] *vt* predisponer; **to be predisposed to doing sth** *(conditioned)* estar predispuesto(a) a hacer algo; *(prone)* ser propenso(a) a hacer algo

predisposition [priːdɪspəˈzɪʃən] *n* predisposición *f*, propensión *f* (**to, towards** a)

predominance [prɪˈdɒmɪnəns] *n* predominio *m*

predominant [prɪˈdɒmɪnənt] *adj* predominante, prevalente

predominantly [prɪˈdɒmɪnəntlɪ] *adv (mostly)* en su mayoría

predominate [prɪˈdɒmɪneɪt] *vi* predominar

pre-eminence [prɪˈemɪnəns] *n* preeminencia *f*

pre-eminent [prɪˈemɪnənt] *adj* preeminente

pre-empt [prɪˈempt] *vt* adelantarse a

pre-emptive [prɪˈemptɪv] *adj Fin* **p. bid** licitación *f* or oferta *f* preferente; *Mil* **p. strike** ataque *m* preventivo

preen [priːn] *vt (feathers)* arreglar con el pico; **to p.**

oneself *(bird)* arreglarse las plumas; *Fig (person)* pavonearse

pre-establish [priːɪˈstæblɪʃ] *vt* establecer de antemano

pre-established [priːɪˈstæblɪʃt] *adj* preestablecido(a)

prefab [ˈpriːfæb] *n Fam (house)* casa *f* prefabricada

prefabricated [priːˈfæbrɪkeɪtɪd] *adj* prefabricado(a)

preface [ˈprefɪs] **1** *n* prólogo *m*, prefacio *m*
   2 *vt* prologar

prefect [ˈpriːfekt] *n Br Educ* monitor(a) *m,f*

prefer [prɪˈfɜːr] *vt* (**a**) *(pt & pp* **preferred**) preferir; **he prefers swimming to playing tennis** prefiere nadar a jugar al tenis; **I p. milk to tea** prefiero la leche al té, me gusta más la leche que el té; **she would p. us to come tomorrow** preferiría que viniéramos mañana; **we p. to stay at home** preferimos quedarnos en casa (**b**) *Jur* presentar; **to p. charges against sb** acusar a algn

preferable [ˈprefərəbəl] *adj* preferible (**to** a)

preferably [ˈprefərəblɪ] *adv* preferentemente, de preferencia

preference [ˈprefərəns] *n (preferred choice)* preferencia *f*; *(priority)* prioridad *f*; **in order of p.** en orden de preferencia; **to give p. to sth** dar prioridad a algo; **to have a p. for sth** preferir algo; **what's your p.?** ¿cuál prefieres?

preferential [prefəˈrenʃəl] *adj* preferente

preferred [prɪˈfɜːd] *adj* preferido(a), favorito(a); *US Fin* **p. stock** acciones *fpl* preferentes *or* privilegiadas

prefigure [priːˈfɪɡər] *vt* prefigurar

prefix [ˈpriːfɪks] *n Ling* prefijo *m*

pregnancy [ˈpreɡnənsɪ] *n* embarazo *m* ❑ **p. test** prueba *f* del embarazo

pregnant [ˈpreɡnənt] *adj (human)* embarazado(a); *(animal)* preñado(a); **to be three months p.** estar embarazada de tres meses; *Fig* **a p. pause** una pausa significativa

preheat [priːˈhiːt] *vt* precalentar

prehistoric(al) [priːhɪˈstɒrɪk(əl)] *adj* prehistórico(a)

prehistory [priːˈhɪstərɪ] *n* prehistoria *f*

prejudge [priːˈdʒʌdʒ] *vt (situation)* prejuzgar; *(person)* juzgar de antemano

prejudice [ˈpredʒʊdɪs] **1** *n* (**a**) *(bias)* prejuicio *m*; **to have a p. against sth** estar predispuesto(a) contra algo (**b**) *(harm)* perjuicio *m*; *Jur* **without p.** sin detrimento de sus propios intereses
   2 *vt* (**a**) *(bias)* predisponer (**b**) *(harm)* perjudicar

prejudiced [ˈpredʒʊdɪst] *adj* parcial; **to be p. against/in favour of sb/sth** estar predispuesto(a) contra/a favor de algn/algo

prejudicial [predʒʊˈdɪʃəl] *adj* perjudicial

prelate [ˈprelɪt] *n Rel* prelado *m*

preliminary [prɪˈlɪmɪnərɪ] **1** *adj (exam, remark)* preliminar; *Sport (round)* eliminatorio(a)
   2 *n* preliminar *m*; **preliminaries** preliminares *mpl*

prelude [ˈpreljuːd] *n* preludio *m*; **a p. to sth** un preludio de algo

premarital [priːˈmærɪtəl] *adj* prematrimonial

premature [preməˈtjʊər, ˈpremətjʊər] *adj* prematuro(a); **you're being a bit p.** te adelantas un poco

prematurely [ˈpremətjʊəlɪ] *adv* antes de tiempo

premeditate [prɪˈmedɪteɪt] *vt (crime)* premeditar; *(action)* calcular

premenstrual [priːˈmenstrʊəl] *adj Med* **p. tension** tensión *f* premenstrual

premier [ˈpremjər] **1** *n Pol* primer(a) ministro(a) *m,f*
   2 *adj* primer, primero(a)

premiere [ˈpremɪeər] n Cin estreno m

premise [ˈpremɪs] n premisa f

premises [ˈpremɪsɪz] npl local m sing; **business p.** local comercial; **licensed p.** = local autorizado para la venta de bebidas alcohólicas; **on/off the p.** en el/fuera del local

premium [ˈpriːmɪəm] n **(a)** Com Fin Ind prima f; **to be at a p.** estar sobre la par; Fig estar muy solicitado(a) or cotizado(a); **to put a p. on sth** dar un gran valor a algo ▫ **p. bonds** bonos mpl cotizados sobre la par **(b)** US (fuel) gasolina f súper

premium-rate [ˈpriːmɪəmˈreɪt] adj Tel (call) de tarifa superior

premonition [premaˈnɪʃən] n presentimiento m, premonición f

prenatal [priːˈneɪtəl] adj prenatal

prenuptial [ˈpriːˈnʌpʃəl] adj prenupcial; **p. agreement** acuerdo m prenupcial

preoccupation [priːɒkjʊˈpeɪʃən] n preocupación f

preoccupied [priːˈɒkjʊpaɪd] adj preocupado(a); **to be p. with sth** preocuparse por algo

preoccupy [priːˈɒkjʊpaɪ] vt (pt & pp **preoccupied**) preocupar

prep [prep] Br Fam **(a)** (abbr **preparation**) deberes mpl **(b)** (abbr **preparatory school**) Br = colegio privado para alumnos de entre 7 y 13 años; US = escuela privada de enseñanza secundaria y preparación para estudios superiores

prepaid [priːˈpeɪd] **1** pt & pp see **prepay**
2 adj porte pagado

preparation [prepaˈreɪʃən] n **(a)** (action) preparación f; **in p. for sth** en preparación para algo **(b)** (plan) preparativo m **(c)** Chem preparado m **(d)** Fam Educ deberes mpl

preparatory [prɪˈpærətərɪ] adj preparatorio(a), preliminar; **p. to doing sth** como preparativo para hacer algo ▫ Educ **p. school** Br = colegio privado para alumnos de entre 7 y 13 años; US = escuela privada de enseñanza secundaria y preparación para estudios superiores

prepare [prɪˈpeər] **1** vt **(a)** (gen) preparar; (document) redactar; (attack) montar; **to p. sb for sth** preparar a algn para algo; **to p. the way for talks** preparar el terreno para conversaciones; **to p. to do sth** prepararse or Am alistarse para hacer algo
2 vi prepararse, Am alistarse (**for** para)

prepared [prɪˈpeəd] adj **(a)** (ready) listo(a), preparado(a); **we're all p.** estamos todos listos **(b)** (willing) dispuesto(a); **to be p. to do sth** estar dispuesto(a) a hacer algo

prepay [priːˈpeɪ] vt (pt & pp **prepaid**) pagar por adelantado; **to send sth carriage prepaid** mandar algo a porte pagado

prepayment [priːˈpeɪmənt] n pago m por adelantado

preponderance [prɪˈpɒndərəns] n preponderancia f

preponderant [prɪˈpɒndərənt] adj preponderante

preposition [prepaˈzɪʃən] n Ling preposición f

prepositional [prepaˈzɪʃənəl] adj preposicional

prepossessing [priːpəˈzesɪŋ] adj agradable, atractivo(a)

preposterous [prɪˈpɒstərəs] adj absurdo(a), ridículo(a)

preppy, preppie [ˈprepɪ] adj US Fam Esp pijo(a), Méx fresa, RP (con)cheto(a)

preprogrammed [priːˈprəʊɡræmd] adj Comptr preprogramado(a)

prequel [ˈpriːkwəl] n = película o libro que desarrolla una historia o se refiere a eventos que preceden a otros contenidos en una obra ya existente

prerecord [priːrɪˈkɔːd] vt pregrabar, grabar de antemano

prerequisite [priːˈrekwɪzɪt] n condición f previa, requisito m

prerogative [prɪˈrɒɡətɪv] n prerrogativa f, privilegio m

Pres (abbr **President**) Presidente m, Pres

presage [ˈpresɪdʒ] Literary **1** n presagio m
2 vt presagiar

Presbyterian [prezbɪˈtɪərɪən] adj & n Rel presbiteriano(a) (m,f)

presbytery [ˈprezbɪt(ə)rɪ] n presbiterio m

preschool [priːˈskuːl] adj preescolar

preschooler [ˈpriːˈskuːlər] n US niño(a) m,f en edad preescolar

prescribe [prɪˈskraɪb] vt **(a)** (set down) prescribir, ordenar; **in the prescribed way** de la forma prescrita **(b)** Med recetar; Fig (recommend) recomendar

prescription [prɪˈskrɪpʃən] n Med receta f (médica); **it's available only on p.** se vende sólo con receta médica; **to make up a p.** preparar una receta

prescriptive [prɪˈskrɪptɪv] adj legal

preselect [ˈpriːsəˈlekt] vt (tracks, channels) preseleccionar

presence [ˈprezəns] n (gen) presencia f; (attendance) asistencia f; **don't mention it in her p.** no hables de ello delante de ella; **in the p. of** en presencia de; **to make one's p. felt** destacar, hacerse sentir; Fig **p. of mind** presencia f de ánimo, aplomo m, sangre f fría

present¹ [ˈprezənt] **1** adj **(a)** (in attendance) presente; **those p.** los presentes; **to be p. at** estar presente en, asistir a **(b)** (current) actual; **at the p. time** actualmente; **her p. address** su domicilio actual **(c)** Ling **p. participle** participio m de presente or activo; **p. perfect** pretérito m perfecto; **the p. tense** el (tiempo) presente
2 n (time) presente m, actualidad f; **at p.** actualmente; **for the p.** de momento, por ahora; **up to the p.** hasta ahora

present² [prɪˈzent] **1** vt **(a)** (give) (as gift) regalar; (formally) obsequiar; (make presentation) entregar, hacer la presentación de; **to p. sb with sth** regalar algo a algn, obsequiar a algn con algo **(b)** (offer) (cheque, report etc) presentar; (provide) (opportunity) ofrecer; (problems etc) plantear **(c)** (introduce) (person) presentar; **may I p. my brother** le presento a mi hermano; **to p. oneself** presentarse **(d)** Rad TV (programme) presentar
2 [ˈprezənt] n (gift) regalo m; (formal) obsequio m; **to give sb a p.** hacer un regalo a algn; **to make sb a p. of sth** regalar algo a algn

presentable [prɪˈzentəbəl] adj presentable, arreglado(a); **to make oneself p.** arreglarse

presentation [prezənˈteɪʃən] n **(a)** (act of giving) presentación f; **on p. of the ticket** al presentar or entregar la entrada; **to make the p.** hacer la presentación ▫ **p. ceremony** ceremonia f de entrega **(b)** Rad TV Theat representación f

present-day [ˈprezəntdeɪ] adj actual, de hoy en día; **p.-d. Britain** la Gran Bretaña de hoy en día

presenter [prɪˈzentər] n Rad locutor(a) m,f; TV presentador(a) m,f

presentiment [prɪˈzentɪmənt] n presentimiento m

presently [ˈprezəntlɪ] adv **(a)** (soon) dentro de poco **(b)** US (now) ahora

preservation [prezəˈveɪʃən] n **(a)** (protection) conservación f, preservación f ▫ Br **p. order** orden f de conservación (de un monumento o edificio de valor histórico-artístico) **(b)** Culin conservación f

preservative [prɪˈzɜːvətɪv] n Culin conservante m

preserve [prɪˈzɜːv] **1** vt **(a)** (keep) mantener, conservar; **to p. one's dignity/sense of humour** mantener la dignidad/

el sentido del humor (**b**) *Culin* conservar, guardar *or* poner en conserva

2 *n* (**a**) *(hunting)* coto *m*, vedado *m*; *Fig* **to trespass on sb's p.** meterse en terreno ajeno (**b**) *Culin* conserva *f*

preshrunk [priː'ʃrʌŋk] *adj* ya lavado(a)

preside [prɪ'zaɪd] *vi* presidir; **to p. at** *or* **over a meeting** presidir una reunión

presidency ['prezɪdənsɪ] *n Pol* presidencia *f*; *US Com* dirección *f*

president ['prezɪdənt] *n Pol* presidente(a) *m,f*; *US Com* director(a) *m,f*, gerente *mf*

presidential [prezɪ'denʃəl] *adj Pol* presidencial

press [pres] **1** *vt* (**a**) *(push down)* *(button)* apretar, presionar, pulsar; *(trigger)* presionar; *(keys on typewriter)* pulsar; *(squeeze)* apretar; *(fruit)* exprimir, estrujar; *(grapes)* pisar; *(flowers)* prensar; **he pressed his lips to hers** la besó en la boca (**b**) *(iron)* planchar (a vapor) (**c**) *(urge)* presionar, instar; *(insist on)* insistir en; **to p. a point** recalcar un punto; **to p. home an advantage** aprovecharse de una ventaja; **to p. sb to do sth** acosar a algn para que haga algo (**d**) *Jur* **to p. charges against sb** demandar a algn

2 *vi* (**a**) *(push)* apretar; **p. hard** aprieta fuerte; **to p. against sb/sth** apretarse contra algn/algo; **to p. (down) on sth** hacer presión sobre algo (**b**) *(crowd)* apiñarse; *(hurry)* apresurarse; **the crowd pressed towards the stage** el público se apresuró hacia el escenario (**c**) *(urge)* apremiar, insistir en; **time presses** el tiempo apremia; **to p. for an answer** exigir una respuesta

3 *n* (**a**) *(pressure)* presión *f*; **to give sth a p.** presionar *or* apretar algo; *(trousers etc)* planchar algo ◻ **p. stud** botón *m* de presión (**b**) *(machine)* prensa *f*; *Tech* **hydraulic p.** prensa hidráulica ◻ **oil/grape p.** prensa *f* de uvas/aceite; **trouser p.** prensa *f* para pantalones (**c**) *(printing)* **ready for p.** listo(a) para la impresión; **to go to p.** entrar en prensa ◻ **rotary/offset p.** rotativa *f*/offset *f* (**d**) *(newspapers)* prensa *f*; **the p.** la prensa, los periódicos; **freedom of the p.** libertad *f* de (la) prensa; **to get a good/bad p.** tener buena/mala prensa ◻ **p. agency** oficina *f* de prensa; *US* **p. clipping** recorte *m* de prensa; **p. conference** conferencia *f or* rueda *f* de (la) prensa; *Br* **p. cutting** recorte *m* de prensa; **p. gallery** tribuna *f* de prensa; **p. kit** carpeta *f or* dossier *m* de prensa; **p. officer** jefe(a) *m,f* de prensa; **p. secretary** secretario(a) *m,f* de prensa

press ahead *vi* **to p. ahead with sth** seguir adelante con algo

press on *vi* seguir adelante; **p. on!** ¡adelante!

pressed [prest] *adj* (**a**) *Culin* embutido(a); **p. chicken** embutido *m* de pollo (**b**) **to be (hard) p. for** andar escaso(a) de; **I'd be hard p. to do it** me costaría mucho hacerlo

press-gang ['presgæŋ] *vt Fam* **to p.-g. sb into doing sth** obligar a algn a hacer algo

pressing ['presɪŋ] *adj* apremiante, urgente

pressman ['presmən] *n Br* (*pl* **pressmen**) periodista *m*

pressure ['preʃər] *n* (**a**) *Phys Tech Elec* presión *f*; *(weight)* peso *m*; *Med Meteor* **high/low p.** altas/bajas presiones *fpl*; **to put p. on sth** hacer presión sobre algo ◻ **blood p.** tensión *f* arterial; *Med* **to have high/low blood p.** tener la tensión alta/baja; *Tech* **p. chamber** cámara *f* de presión; *Culin* **p. cooker** olla *f* a presión; *Tech* **p. gauge** manómetro *m*; **p. suit** traje *m* espacial (**b**) *Fig* presión *f*; **the pressures of work** las exigencias del trabajo; **to bring p. (to bear) on sb** ejercer presión sobre algn; **to work under p.** trabajar bajo presión

pressure-cook ['preʃəkʊk] *vt Culin* cocer en la olla a presión

pressurize ['preʃəraɪz] *vt* presurizar; *Fig* apremiar,

presionar; *Av* **pressurized cabin** cabina *f* presurizada; *Fig* **to p. sb into doing sth** ejercer presión sobre algn para que haga algo

prestige [pre'stiːʒ] *n* prestigio *m*

prestigious [pre'stɪdʒəs] *adj* prestigioso(a)

presumably [prɪ'zjuːməblɪ] *adv* es presumible *or* de suponer que, se supone que; **p. he's innocent** se supone que es inocente; **p. they'll come** se espera que vengan

presume [prɪ'zjuːm] **1** *vt* *(suppose)* suponer, imaginarse, presumir; **I p. that they will phone** supongo *or* me imagino que llamarán; **missing, presumed dead** desaparecido(a), probablemente muerto(a); **we p. so/not** suponemos que sí/no

2 *vi* (**a**) *(suppose)* suponer (**b**) *(rely)* **to p. on sb's generosity** abusar de la generosidad de algn

presumption [prɪ'zʌmpʃən] *n* (**a**) *(supposition)* suposición *f*, presunción *f* (**b**) *(conceit, boldness)* osadía *f*, presunción *f*

presumptuous [prɪ'zʌmptjʊəs] *adj* presuntuoso(a)

presuppose [priːsə'pəʊz] *vt* presuponer

presupposition [priːsʌpə'zɪʃən] *n* presuposición *f*

pretence [prɪ'tens] *n* (**a**) *(deception)* fingimiento *m*, simulacro *m*; **it's all a p.** es todo fingido; **to make a p. of doing sth** fingir hacer algo (**b**) *(pretext)* pretexto *m*; *Jur* **false pretences** estafa *f* sing, fraude *m* sing; **to obtain sth by false pretences** conseguir algo mediante estafa; **under the p. of friendship** so pretexto de amistad (**c**) *(claim)* pretensión *f*

pretend [prɪ'tend] **1** *vt* (**a**) *(feign)* fingir, simular, aparentar; **he pretended he couldn't understand us** fingía no entendernos; **she's pretending to be asleep** finge estar dormida (**b**) *(claim)* pretender; **I don't p. to be an authority on the subject** no pretendo ser experto en el tema

2 *vi* *(feign)* fingir; **stop pretending!** ¡déjate de mentiras!

3 *adj Fam* fingido(a), de mentirijillas

pretense [prɪ'tens] *n US see* **pretence**

pretension [prɪ'tenʃən] *n* (**a**) *(claim)* pretensión *f* (**b**) *(showiness)* pretensiones *fpl*, presunción *f*

pretentious [prɪ'tenʃəs] *adj* *(showy)* presumido(a), ostentoso(a), presuntuoso(a)

preterite, *US* **preterit** ['pretərɪt] *n Ling* pretérito *m*

pretext ['priːtekst] *n* pretexto *m*; **on** *or* **under the p. of doing sth** so pretexto de hacer algo

pretty ['prɪtɪ] **1** *adj* (**prettier, prettiest**) *(person)* bonito(a), guapo(a); *(thing)* bonito(a), mono(a); **it isn't a p. sight** no es nada bonito; *Fam* **it cost a p. penny** costó un dineral

2 *adv Fam* bastante; **p. easy** bastante fácil; **p. much the same** más o menos lo mismo; **p. well finished** casi terminado(a)

pretzel ['pretsəl] *n Culin* galleta *f* salada

prevail [prɪ'veɪl] *vi* (**a**) *(continue to exist)* predominar, regir; **the customs which prevailed** las costumbres que regían (**b**) *(win through)* prevalecer (**c**) *(persuade)* persuadir; **to p. upon** *or* **on sb to do sth** persuadir *or* convencer a algn para que haga algo

prevailing [prɪ'veɪlɪŋ] *adj* *(wind)* predominante; *(opinion)* general, común, predominante; *(condition, fashion)* actual

prevalent ['prevələnt] *adj* *(gen)* predominante, general; *(illness)* extendido(a)

prevaricate [prɪ'værɪkeɪt] *vi* andar con rodeos

prevarication [prɪværɪ'keɪʃən] *n* *(gen)* evasivas *fpl*; *Jur* prevaricación *f*

prevent [prɪ'vent] *vt* *(gen)* impedir; *(accident)* evitar; *(illness)* prevenir; **to p. sb from doing sth** impedir a algn hacer algo; **to p. sth from happening** evitar que pase algo

preventable [prɪ'ventəbəl] *adj* evitable

prevention [prɪ'venʃən] *n* prevención *f*; **p. of accidents** precauciones *fpl or* medidas *fpl* preventivas contra los accidentes; **Society for the P. of Cruelty to Animals/ Children** Sociedad *f* Protectora de Animales/de Niños; *Prov* **p. is better than cure** más vale prevenir que curar

preventive [prɪ'ventɪv] *adj* preventivo(a); **p. medicine** medicina *f* preventiva

preview ['priːvjuː] **1** *n (of film, exhibition etc)* preestreno *m*; *Fig* **to give sb a p. of sth** permitir a algn ver algo de antemano
2 *vt (film, exhibition etc)* ver en preestreno; *Fig* ver de antemano

previous ['priːvɪəs] **1** *adj* anterior, previo(a); **a p. engagement** un compromiso anterior; **on a p. occasion** en otra ocasión; **the p. afternoon** la tarde anterior ❑ *Jur* **p. conviction** antecedente *m* penal; **p. experience** conocimientos *mpl* previos
2 *adv* **p. to going** antes de ir

previously ['priːvɪəslɪ] *adv* anteriormente, previamente

prevue ['priːvjuː] *n & vt US see* **preview**

prewar ['priːwɔːr] *adj* de antes de la guerra; **the p. period** la preguerra

prey [preɪ] **1** *n* presa *f*; *Fig* presa, víctima *f*; **bird of p.** ave *f* de rapiña; *Fig* **to fall p. to temptation** caer en la tentación
2 *vi* cazar, alimentarse; **to p. on animals** alimentarse de animales; *Fig* **it's been preying on my mind** me ha estado dando vueltas por la cabeza

price [praɪs] **1** *n (value)* precio *m*, valor *m*; *(valuation)* valor; **fixed/cash p.** precio fijo/al contado; **high/low prices** precios *mpl* altos/bajos; **not at any p.** por nada del mundo; **peace at any p.** la paz a cualquier precio; **to go up/down in p.** subir/bajar de precio; **to pay a high p. for sth** pagar algo muy caro; **what p. is that coat?** ¿cuánto cuesta el abrigo?; *Fig* **the p. of fame/success** el precio de la fama/del éxito ❑ **p. control** control *m* de precios; **p. freeze** congelación *f* de precios; **p. index** índice *m* de precios; **p. limit** tope *m*, precio *m* tope; **p. list** lista *f* de precios; **p. reduction** descuento *m*, rebaja *f*; **p. tag** etiqueta *f*; **p. war** guerra *f* de precios
2 *vt (put price on)* poner un precio a; *(value)* poner un precio a, valorar, tasar; *(ask price of)* preguntar el precio de; **it is priced at $10** vale 10 dólares; **to be priced too high/ low** tener una valoración demasiado alta/baja; *Com* **to p. oneself out of the market** perder clientela por poner precios muy altos

price-fixing ['praɪs'fɪksɪŋ] *n Com* fijación *f* de precios

priceless ['praɪslɪs] *adj (invaluable)* que no tiene precio, inestimable; *Fam (very funny)* graciosísimo(a), divertidísimo(a)

pricey ['praɪsɪ] *adj* **(pricier, priciest)** *Fam* caro(a)

prick [prɪk] **1** *vt* **(a)** *(with pin etc)* picar; **to p. one's finger on sth** pincharse el dedo con algo; *Fig* **her conscience is pricking her** le remuerde la conciencia **(b)** **to p. (up)** levantar; *Fig* **to p. up one's ears** aguzar el oído
2 *n* **(a)** *(with pin etc)* pinchazo *m*; *Fig* **pricks of conscience** remordimientos *mpl* **(b)** *Slang (penis) Esp* polla *f*, *Am* verga *f*, *Chile* pico *m*, *Chile* penca *f*, *Méx* pito *m*, *RP* pija *f*, *Ven* pinga *f*; *Slang Offens (obnoxious person) Esp* gilipollas *mf inv*, *Am* pendejo(a) *m,f*, *RP* forro *m*

prickle ['prɪkəl] **1** *n (on plant, animal)* espina *f*; *(spike)* pincho *m*; *(sensation)* picor *m*, comezón *m*
2 *vt & vi* pinchar, picar

prickly ['prɪklɪ] *adj* **(pricklier, prickliest)** espinoso(a), lleno(a) de pinchos; *(sensation)* de picor, de hormigueo; *Fig (touchy)* enojadizo(a) ❑ *Med* **p. heat** sarpullido *m* por causa del calor; *Bot* **p. pear** higo *m* chumbo, *Am* tuna *f*

pricy ['praɪsɪ] *adj see* **pricey**

pride [praɪd] **1** *n (gen)* orgullo *m*; *(self-respect)* amor *m* propio; *(arrogance)* soberbia *f*, orgullo *m*; **false p.** vanidad *f*; **he has no p.** no tiene amor propio; **to take a p. in sth** enorgullecerse de algo; *Fig* **he's the family's p. and joy** es el orgullo de la familia; *Fig* **to take p. of place** tener el lugar de honor
2 *vt* **to p. oneself on** *or* **upon doing sth** enorgullecerse *or* estar orgulloso(a) de hacer algo

priest [priːst] *n* sacerdote *m*, cura *m*

priestess ['priːstɪs] *n* sacerdotisa *f*

priesthood ['priːsthʊd] *n (clergy)* clero *m*; *(body of priests)* sacerdocio *m*; **to enter the p.** hacerse *or* ordenarse sacerdote

priestly ['priːstlɪ] *adj* **(priestlier, priestliest)** sacerdotal

prig [prɪg] *n* gazmoño(a) *m,f*, mojigato(a) *m,f*

priggish ['prɪgɪʃ] *adj* gazmoño(a), mojigato(a)

prim [prɪm] *adj* **(primmer, primmest)** **p. (and proper)** remilgado(a)

primacy ['praɪməsɪ] *n* primacía *f*

prima donna [priːmə'dɒnə] *n (pl* **prima donnas)** diva *f*

prim(a)eval [praɪ'miːvəl] *adj* primitivo(a); **p. forest** selva *f* virgen

prima facie [praɪmə'feɪʃɪ] **1** *adj Jur* **to have a p. f. case** tener razón a primera vista
2 *adv* a primera vista

primarily [praɪ'merɪlɪ] *adv* en primer lugar, ante todo, principalmente

primary ['praɪmərɪ] **1** *adj* **(a)** *(main, chief)* fundamental, principal; **of p. importance** primordial, de suma importancia **(b)** *(basic)* primario(a); **p. colour** color *m* primario; **p. education/school** enseñanza *f*/escuela *f* primaria; **p. school teacher** maestro(a) *m,f* (de escuela)
2 *n Pol* elección *f* primaria

primate¹ ['praɪmeɪt] *n Rel* primado *m*

primate² ['praɪmeɪt] *n Zool* primate *m*

prime [praɪm] **1** *adj* **(a)** *(main, chief)* principal, primer, primero(a); *(major)* primordial, de suma importancia ❑ **P. Minister** primer(a) ministro(a) *m,f*; **p. time** *(on TV)* franja *f* (horaria) de máxima audiencia **(b)** *(first-rate)* de primera; **in p. condition** en perfecto estado; **p. meat** carne *f* de primera (calidad) **(c)** *Com* **p. cost** coste *m* de producción **(d)** *Math* primo(a); **p. number** número *m* primo
2 *n* **p. (of life)** flor *f* de la vida; **he has passed his p.** ya no está en sus mejores años; **to be in the p. of life** *or* **in one's p.** estar en la flor de la vida
3 *vt (pump, engine)* cebar; *(surface)* imprimar, preparar; *Fig (prepare)* enseñar, preparar; *Fig* **they were primed about how to answer** les enseñaron cómo tenían que contestar; *Fam* **he was well primed** *(drunk)* estaba medio borracho

primer¹ ['praɪmər] *n (textbook)* libro *m or* texto *m* elemental ❑ **history p.** texto *m* de introducción a la historia

primer² ['praɪmər] *n (paint)* imprimación *f*

primitive ['prɪmɪtɪv] **1** *adj (language, culture)* primitivo(a); *(method, tool)* rudimentario(a), básico(a)
2 *n Art (artist)* primitivista *mf*; *(work)* obra *f* primitivista

primly ['prɪmlɪ] *adv* con remilgo

primrose ['prɪmrəʊz] **1** *n Bot* primavera *f*
2 *adj* **p. (yellow)** (de color) amarillo claro

primula ['prɪmjʊlə] *n Bot* prímula *f*

Primus® ['praɪməs] *n* infiernillo *m*, camping-gas *m inv*, *Am* primus *m inv*

prince [prɪns] *n* príncipe *m*; **P. Charming** Príncipe Azul; **p. consort/regent** príncipe consorte/regente; *Fig* **P. of Darkness** Satanás *m*

princess [prɪnˈses] n princesa f

principal [ˈprɪnsɪpəl] **1** adj principal

2 n (**a**) Educ director(a) m,f; Theat (in play) protagonista mf principal ❏ BrTheat **p. boy** primera figura f (**b**) Fin capital m, principal m

principality [prɪnsɪˈpælɪtɪ] n principado m

principle [ˈprɪnsɪpəl] n (gen) principio m; (law) ley f; **a man of principles** un hombre de principios; **in p.** en principio; **it's against my principles to do that** va en contra de mis principios hacer eso; **on p.** por principio; **to have high principles** tener principios

principled [ˈprɪnsɪpəld] adj (person, behaviour) ejemplar, de grandes principios

print [prɪnt] **1** vt (**a**) (book etc) imprimir; (publish) publicar; Fig grabar; **printed matter** impresos mpl (**b**) (write) escribir con letra de imprenta (**c**) Tex (fabric) estampar (**d**) Phot **to p. a negative** sacar copias de un negativo

2 n (**a**) (mark) (of finger, foot) huella f; (of type) impresión f, marca f; **thumb p.** huella del pulgar (**b**) Typ letra f; **in small/large p.** con letra pequeña/grande; **to be in/out of p.** estar en venta/agotado(a) ❏ **p. run** tirada f; Am tiraje m (**c**) Tex estampado m ❏ **p. dress/skirt** vestido m estampado/falda f estampada (**d**) Art grabado m (**e**) Phot prueba f, copia f; **to make prints from a negative** hacer copias de un negativo

print out vt Comptr imprimir

printed [ˈprɪntɪd] adj impreso(a) ❏ Elec **p. circuit** circuito m impreso

printer [ˈprɪntər] n (person) impresor(a) m,f; (machine) máquina f impresora; **p.'s error** error m de imprenta

printing [ˈprɪntɪŋ] n (**a**) (industry) imprenta f; (process) impresión f; (print run) tirada f ❏ **p. press** prensa f; **p. works** imprenta f sing (**b**) (writing) letras fpl de imprenta

print-out [ˈprɪntaʊt] n Comptr impresión f

prior¹ [ˈpraɪər] adj previo(a), anterior; **p. to leaving** antes de salir; **to have a p. claim** tener prioridad (**to** sobre); **without p. warning** sin previo aviso

prior² [ˈpraɪər] n Rel prior m

prioritize [praɪˈɒrɪtaɪz] vt dar prioridad a

priority [praɪˈɒrɪtɪ] n prioridad f; **to have** or **take p. over sth** tener prioridad sobre algo; Fam **to get one's priorities right** saber lo que más le importa a uno en la vida

priory [ˈpraɪərɪ] n Rel priorato m

prise [praɪz] vt **to p. sth open/off** abrir/levantar algo con palanca

prism [ˈprɪzəm] n Geom Tech prisma f ❏ **p. binoculars** prismáticos mpl

prison [ˈprɪzən] n cárcel f, prisión f; **to be in p.** estar en la cárcel; **to be sent to p. for 10 years** ser condenado(a) a 10 años de cárcel; **to put sb in p. for 5 years** condenar a algn a 5 años de cárcel ❏ **p. camp** campamento m para prisioneros; **p. officer** carcelero(a) m,f

prisoner [ˈprɪzənər] n preso(a) m,f; Mil prisionero(a) m,f; **to take/hold sb p.** tomar preso/detener a algn ❏ **p. of war** prisionero(a) m,f de guerra

prissy [ˈprɪsɪ] adj Fam remilgado(a)

pristine [ˈprɪstaɪn, ˈprɪstiːn] adj prístino(a)

privacy [ˈpraɪvəsɪ, ˈprɪvəsɪ] n intimidad f, vida f privada, privacidad f; **in the p. of one's own home** en la intimidad del hogar; **one's right to p.** su derecho a la intimidad

private [ˈpraɪvɪt] **1** adj (not public) privado(a); (individual) particular; (personal) personal; (classes) particular; (school) de pago; (clinic, property) privado(a); (letter, conversation) confidencial; (bank account) personal; **in p.** en privado; **it's my p. opinion that ...** por mi parte pienso que ...; **it will be a p. celebration** se celebrará en la intimidad; **one's p. life**

la vida privada de uno; **'P.'** (notice) (on road) 'carretera privada'; (on gate) 'propiedad privada'; (on envelope) 'confidencial'; **to keep sth p.** no divulgar algo ❏ **p. citizen** particular mf; **p. detective**, Fam **p. eye** detective mf privado(a); **p. income** fortuna f personal; **p. investigator** detective mf privado(a); Tel **p. line** línea f privada; Pol **p. member's bill** = proyecto de ley propuesto por un diputado independiente; **p. school** escuela f privada; **p. secretary** secretario(a) m,f particular

2 n Mil soldado m raso

privately [ˈpraɪvɪtlɪ] adv (not publicly) en privado; (personally) personalmente; (in secret) en secreto; (discreetly) en la intimidad

privation [praɪˈveɪʃən] n (hardship) privación f; (poverty) estrechez f, privaciones fpl; **to suffer p.** pasar apuros

privatization [praɪvɪtaɪˈzeɪʃən] n privatización f

privatize [ˈpraɪvɪtaɪz] vt privatizar

privet [ˈprɪvɪt] n Bot alheña f

privilege [ˈprɪvɪlɪdʒ] **1** n privilegio m; Pol **parliamentary p.** inmunidad f parlamentaria; **to have the p. of doing sth** tener el honor or el privilegio de hacer algo

2 vt **to be privileged to do sth** gozar del honor or del privilegio de hacer algo

privileged [ˈprɪvɪlɪdʒd] adj privilegiado(a); **the p. few** unos cuantos privilegiados, la élite

privy [ˈprɪvɪ] **1** adj (privier, priviest) (**a**) (private) privado(a); Br **P. Council/Councillor** Consejo m/Consejero m Privado (**b**) **to be p. to sth** estar enterado(a) de algo · **2** n Fam (toilet) retrete m

prize¹ [praɪz] **1** n premio m; **to win first p.** ganar el primer premio; **he's won first p.** (in lottery) le ha tocado el gordo

2 adj (first-class) de primera (categoría or clase), selecto(a); Fam **a p. idiot** un tonto de remate ❏ **p. draw** sorteo m con premio; Box **p. fight** combate m (de boxeo) profesional

3 vt (value) apreciar, valorar

prize² [praɪz] vt US see **prise**

prize-giving [ˈpraɪzɡɪvɪŋ] n distribución f de premios

prizewinner [ˈpraɪzwɪnər] n premiado(a) m,f

prizewinning [ˈpraɪzwɪnɪŋ] adj premiado(a)

pro¹ [prəʊ] n pro m; **the pros and cons of an issue** los pros y los contras de una cuestión

pro² [prəʊ] n (abbr professional) Fam profesional mf, Méx profesionista mf

pro- [prəʊ] pref a favor de, pro-; **they're pro-Common Market** están a favor del Mercado Común

proactive [prəʊˈæktɪv] adj **to be p.** tomar la iniciativa

probability [prɒbəˈbɪlɪtɪ] n probabilidad f; **in all p. they will write** lo más probable es que escriban

probable [ˈprɒbəbəl] adj probable

probably [ˈprɒbəblɪ] adv probablemente; **he'll p. phone** es probable que llame

probate [ˈprəʊbɪt, ˈprəʊbeɪt] n Jur legalización f de un testamento

probation [prəˈbeɪʃən] n (in employment) período m de prueba; Jur libertad f condicional; Jur **to be on p.** estar en libertad condicional; **to be on two months' p.** (at work) trabajar dos meses de prueba ❏ **p. officer** = encargado(a) oficial de vigilar a los que están en libertad condicional

probationary [prəˈbeɪʃənərɪ] adj de prueba; **p. period** (in employment) período m de prueba; Jur período m de libertad condicional

probationer [prəˈbeɪʃənər] n (in employment) empleado(a) m,f a prueba; Jur persona f en libertad condicional

probe [prəʊb] **1** n (**a**) Med sonda f (**b**) (investigation) investigación *f*, sondeo *m* (**c**) *Astronaut* sonda *f* □ **space p.** sonda *f* espacial

2 *vt* (**a**) *Med* sondar (**b**) *(investigate)* investigar, sondear (**c**) *Astronaut* sondar, explorar

probe into *vt* investigar

probity ['prəʊbɪtɪ] *n* probidad *f*

problem ['prɒbləm] *n* problema *m*; **it poses many problems for us** nos crea muchos problemas; **she has a drink p.** tiene tendencia al alcoholismo; **the unemployment p.** el problema del desempleo; **we had no p. getting there** llegamos sin problemas; *Fam* **no p.!** ¡desde luego! □ **p. child** niño(a) *m,f* difícil; **p. family** familia *f* inadaptada; *Press* **p. page** consultorio *m* sentimental

problematic(al) [prɒblə'mætɪk(əl)] *adj* problemáti-co(a); **it's p.** hay problemas, tiene sus problemas

problem-solving ['prɒbləmsɒlvɪŋ] **1** *n* resolución *f* de problemas

2 *adj* **p.-s. skills** habilidades *fpl* para la resolución de problemas

procedure [prə'si:dʒər] *n* (*gen*) procedimiento *m*; *(legal, business)* gestión *f*, trámite *m*; **the normal p. is as follows** se suele proceder de la siguiente manera; **what's the p.?** ¿cómo se suele proceder?

proceed [prə'si:d] *vi* (**a**) *(go on)* seguir, avanzar, proceder; **to p. to do sth** empezar a *or* ponerse a hacer algo; **to p. to the next matter** pasar a la siguiente cuestión; **to p. with caution** avanzar con cuidado; **to p. with sth** seguir con algo; **we're not sure how to p.** no sabemos cómo proceder (**b**) *Jur* **to p. against sb** proceder contra algn

proceeding [prə'si:dɪŋ] *n* (**a**) *(way of acting)* proceder *m* (**b**) **proceedings** *(of meeting)* actas *fpl*; *(measures)* medidas *fpl*; *Jur* proceso *m sing*; **to take legal p. against sb** proceder contra algn

proceeds ['prəʊsi:dz] *npl* beneficios *mpl*, ganancias *fpl*

process¹ ['prəʊses] **1** *n* (**a**) *(working out)* proceso *m*; *(method)* método *m*, sistema *m*; **chemical/natural p.** proceso químico/natural; *Metal* **the Bessemer p.** el proceso de Bessemer; **they were in the p. of moving** estaban en vías de mudarse (**b**) *Jur* proceso *m*

2 *vt (information)* tramitar; *(food)* tratar; *Phot (negative)* revelar; *Comptr* procesar □ **processed cheese** *or US* **p. cheese** queso *m* fundido

process² [prə'ses] *vi (in procession)* desfilar

processing ['prəʊsesɪŋ] *n* *(of information)* trámites *mpl*; *(of food)* tratamiento *m*; *Phot (of negative)* revelado *m*; *Comptr* tratamiento *m* □ *Comptr* **p. speed** velocidad *f* de proceso

procession [prə'seʃən] *n* *(of people, floats)* desfile *m*; *Rel* procesión *f*

processor ['prəʊsesər] *n Comptr* procesador *m*

pro-choice ['prəʊtʃɔɪs] *adj* = en favor del derecho de la mujer a decidir en materia de aborto

proclaim [prə'kleɪm] *vt (announce)* proclamar, declarar; **to p. sb king/queen** proclamar rey/reina a algn; **to p. war/peace** declarar la guerra/paz

proclamation [prɒklə'meɪʃən] *n* proclamación *f*

proclivity [prə'klɪvɪtɪ] *n* inclinación *f*, propensión *f* (**for** para)

procrastinate [prəʊ'kræstɪneɪt] *vi* aplazar una decisión

procrastination [prəʊkræstɪ'neɪʃən] *n* dilación *f*

procreate ['prəʊkrɪeɪt] *vt & vi* procrear

procreation [prəʊkrɪ'eɪʃən] *n* procreación *f*

procure [prə'kjʊər] **1** *vt* (**a**) *(obtain)* conseguir, procurar, lograr; **to p. sth for sb** conseguir algo para algn (**b**) *(for prostitution)* llevar a la prostitución

2 *vi (for prostitution)* alcahuetear

procurement [prə'kjʊəmənt] *n* obtención *f*

prod [prɒd] **1** *vt (pt & pp* **prodded)** *(with finger, stick etc)* golpear, pinchar; *(push)* empujar; *Fig* empujar; **to p. sb in the ribs** darle a algn en las costillas; *Fig* **she needs prodding** necesita un estímulo; *Fig* **to p. sb into doing sth** estimular a algn para que haga algo

2 *n (with finger, stick)* golpecito *m*, pinchazo *m*; *(push)* empuje *m*; **to give sb a p.** empujar a algn; *Fig* **he needs a p.** le hace falta un empujón

prodigal ['prɒdɪgəl] *adj* pródigo(a)

prodigious [prə'dɪdʒəs] *adj (wonderful)* prodigioso(a); *(huge)* enorme

prodigy ['prɒdɪdʒɪ] *n* prodigio *m* □ **child p.** niño(a) *m,f* prodigio

produce [prə'dju:s] **1** *vt* (**a**) *(gen)* producir; *Ind* fabricar; *Press* editar; *Theat* dirigir; *Rad TV* realizar; *Cin* producir; *(give birth to)* dar a luz a; **oil producing country** país *m* productor de petróleo (**b**) *(show)* enseñar, presentar; *(bring out)* sacar; **she produced a sweet from her pocket** se sacó un caramelo del bolsillo (**c**) *(cause)* causar, ocasionar

2 ['prɒdju:s] *n Agr* productos *mpl*; **foreign p.** productos del extranjero; **p. of Spain** producto *m* de España

producer [prə'dju:sər] *n (gen)* productor(a) *m,f*; *Ind* fabricante *mf*; *Theat* director(a) *m,f* de escena; *Rad TV* realizador(a) *m,f*; *Cin* productor(a) *m,f*

product ['prɒdʌkt] *n (gen)* producto *m*; *Fig* producto *m*, fruto *m*, resultado *m*; **oil products** productos derivados del petróleo; *Com* **p. development** desarrollo *m* del producto

production [prə'dʌkʃən] *n* (**a**) *(gen)* producción *f*; *Ind* fabricación *f*; *Theat* representación *f*; *Rad TV* realización *f*; *Cin* producción *f*; **to put sth into p.** lanzar algo a la producción; **to take sth out of p.** retirar algo de la producción □ **mass p.** fabricación *f* en serie; **p. costs** costos *mpl* or *Esp* costes *mpl* de producción; **p. line** cadena *f* de producción; **p. manager** jefe(a) *m,f* de producción (**b**) *(showing)* presentación *f*; **on p. of one's passport** al enseñar el pasaporte

productive [prə'dʌktɪv] *adj Agr* productivo(a), fértil; *Fig* **a p. meeting** una reunión positiva *or* productiva

productivity [prɒdʌk'tɪvɪtɪ] *n* productividad *f*; **p. agreement** acuerdo *m* de productividad; **p. bonus** bono *m* de productividad

Prof *(abbr* **Professor)** *Br* catedrático(a) *m,f*

profane [prə'feɪn] **1** *adj (secular)* profano(a); *(irreverent)* sacrílego(a); *(language)* blasfemo(a)

2 *vt* profanar

profanity [prə'fænɪtɪ] *n* blasfemia *f*

profess [prə'fes] *vt (faith)* profesar; *(opinion)* proclamar, declarar; *(claim)* pretender; **I don't p. to be an authority on the matter** no pretendo ser experto en el tema

professed [prə'fest] *adj (Christian etc)* profeso(a); *(acknowledged)* declarado(a); *(supposed)* pretendido(a), supuesto(a)

profession [prə'feʃən] *n* (**a**) *(occupation)* profesión *f*; **by p.** de profesión; **the medical/teaching p.** los médicos/el profesorado; **the professions** las profesiones (**b**) *(declaration)* declaración *f*, afirmación *f*; **p. of faith** profesión *f* de fe

professional [prə'feʃənəl] **1** *adj* (**a**) *(gen)* profesional; *(soldier)* de profesión; **p. footballer/singer** futbolista *mf*/ cantante *mf* profesional; **to seek p. advice** buscar un consejo profesional; **to turn** *or* **go p.** hacerse profesional *or Méx* profesionista (**b**) *(polished) (work)* de gran calidad; *(person)* perito(a); **her work is very p.** su trabajo es de una gran calidad

2 *n* profesional *mf*, *Méx* profesionista *mf*

professionalism [prə'feʃənəlɪzəm] *n* profesionalismo *m*

professionally [prə'feʃənəlɪ] *adv* profesionalmente; **he's p. qualified** tiene un título profesional

professor [prə'fesər] *n Univ Br* catedrático(a) *m,f; US* profesor(a) *m,f*

proffer ['prɒfər] *vt Fml (gift etc)* ofrecer; *(thanks)* dar

proficiency [prə'fɪʃənsɪ] *n (in language)* capacidad *f; (in skill)* habilidad *f,* pericia *f*

proficient [prə'fɪʃənt] *adj (in language)* experto(a); *(in skill)* hábil, perito(a)

profile ['prəʊfaɪl] *n* **(a)** *(of face)* perfil *m;* **in p.** de perfil; *Fig* **to keep a low p.** procurar pasar desapercibido(a) **(b)** *Press* reseña *f* biográfica

profit ['prɒfɪt] **1** *n* **(a)** *Com* beneficio *m,* ganancia *f;* **gross/ net p.** beneficio bruto/neto; **to make a p. on sth** sacar beneficios de algo; **to sell sth at a p.** vender algo con un margen de ganancias ❑ **p. and loss account** cuenta *f* de ganancias y pérdidas; **p. margin** margen *m* de beneficio **(b)** *Fml (benefit)* provecho *m;* **to turn sth to p.** sacar provecho de algo
  2 *vi Com* ganar; *Fig* sacar provecho; **to p. from sth** aprovecharse de algo

profitability [prɒfɪtə'bɪlɪtɪ] *n* rentabilidad *f*

profitable ['prɒfɪtəbəl] *adj* **(a)** *Com* rentable **(b)** *Fig (worthwhile)* provechoso(a), positivo(a)

profitably ['prɒfɪtəblɪ] *adv* **(a)** *Com* con rentabilidad **(b)** *(worthwhile)* con provecho

profiteer [prɒfɪ'tɪər] **1** *n* especulador(a) *m,f*
  2 *vi* obtener beneficios excesivos

profit-making ['prɒfɪtmeɪkɪŋ] *adj (business)* rentable; *(charity)* con fines lucrativos; **non-p.-m.** sin fines lucrativos

profit-sharing ['prɒfɪtʃɑːrɪŋ] *n (by company)* reparto *m* de los beneficios

profligate ['prɒflɪgɪt] *adj Fml (immoral)* disoluto(a), libertino(a); *(wasteful)* despilfarrador(a)

profound [prə'faʊnd] *adj* profundo(a), grave, serio(a)

profundity [prə'fʌndɪtɪ] *n* profundidad *f*

profuse [prə'fjuːs] *adj* profuso(a), abundante

profusely [prə'fjuːslɪ] *adv* con profusión, abundantemente; **to apologize p.** disculparse efusivamente; **to sweat p.** sudar mucho

profusion [prə'fjuːʒən] *n* profusión *f,* abundancia *f*

progenitor [prəʊ'dʒenɪtər] *n Fml (ancestor)* antepasado(a) *m,f,* progenitor(a) *m,f; (forerunner)* precursor(a) *m,f*

progeny ['prɒdʒɪnɪ] *n Fml* progenie *f,* prole *f,* descendencia *f*

prognosis [prɒg'nəʊsɪs] *n (pl* **prognoses***)* Med pronóstico *m; Fig (prediction)* augurio *m*

prognosticate [prɒg'nɒstɪkeɪt] *vt Fml* pronosticar

program ['prəʊgræm] *Comptr* **1** *n* programa *m*
  2 *vi & vt (pp & pt* **programmed***)* programar

programmable [prəʊ'græməbəl] *adj* programable; **p. calculator** calculadora *f* programable

programme, *US* **program** ['prəʊgræm] **1** *n (gen)* programa *m; (plan)* plan *m;* **p. of activities** programa de actividades; **what's the p. for today?** ¿qué plan tenemos para hoy?
  2 *vt (plan)* planear, planificar; **to p. the central heating** regular la calefacción central

programmer, *US* **programer** ['prəʊgræmər] *n* programador(a) *m,f*

progress ['prəʊgres] **1** *n (advance)* progreso *m,* avance *m; (development)* desarrollo *m; Med* mejora *f;* **the p. of events** el curso de los acontecimientos; **to make good p.** hacer muchos progresos, avanzar; *Med* mejorar; **work in p.** trabajo *m* en curso ❑ **p. report** informe *m or Am*

reporte *m* sobre la marcha (del trabajo/de los estudios)
  2 [prəʊ'gres] *vi (advance)* avanzar; *(develop)* desarrollar; *(improve)* mejorar, hacer progresos, progresar; *Med* mejorar; **as the meeting progressed** a medida que avanzaba la reunión

progression [prəʊ'greʃən] *n (advance, development)* progresión *f,* avance *m; (series)* serie *f*

progressive [prəʊ'gresɪv] **1** *adj* **(a)** *(increasing)* progresivo(a) **(b)** *Pol* progresista
  2 *n Pol* progresista *mf*

progressively [prəʊ'gresɪvlɪ] *adv* progresivamente, poco a poco, de forma progresiva

prohibit [prə'hɪbɪt] *vt* prohibir; **'Smoking Prohibited'** 'Prohibido Fumar'; **to p. sb from doing sth** prohibir a algn hacer algo; **we were prohibited from entering** se nos prohibió entrar

prohibition [prəʊɪ'bɪʃən] *n* prohibición *f; US Hist* **P.** la Prohibición

prohibitive [prə'hɪbɪtɪv] *adj* prohibitivo(a)

project ['prɒdʒekt] **1** *n* **(a)** *(undertaking, plan)* proyecto *m; Educ (study)* trabajo *m,* estudio *m; Com* **p. manager** jefe(a) *m,f* de proyecto **(b)** *US (housing)* = urbanización con viviendas de protección oficial
  2 [prə'dʒekt] *vt* proyectar, planear
  3 *vi (stick out)* resaltar, sobresalir

projected [prə'dʒektɪd] *adj* proyectado(a)

projectile [prə'dʒektaɪl] *n Fml* proyectil *m*

projection [prə'dʒekʃən] *n* **(a)** *Fml (overhang etc)* resalto *m,* saliente *m* **(b)** *Cin* proyección *f* **(c)** *(forecast)* proyección *f*

projectionist [prə'dʒekʃənɪst] *n Cin* operador(a) *m,f* de cine

projector [prə'dʒektər] *n Cin* proyector *m*

prolapse ['prəʊlæps, prəʊ'læps] *n Med* prolapso *m*

proletarian [prəʊlɪ'teərɪən] *adj* proletario(a)

proletariat [prəʊlɪ'teərɪət] *n* proletariado *m*

pro-life [prəʊ'laɪf] *adj* pro vida, antiabortista

proliferate [prə'lɪfəreɪt] *vi* proliferar

proliferation [prəlɪfə'reɪʃən] *n* proliferación *f*

prolific [prə'lɪfɪk] *adj* prolífico(a)

prolix ['prəʊlɪks, prəʊ'lɪks] *adj Fml* prolijo(a)

prologue, *US* **prolog** ['prəʊlɒg] *n* prólogo *m*

prolong [prə'lɒŋ] *vt* alargar, extender, prolongar

prolongation [prəʊlɒŋ'geɪʃən] *n* extensión *f,* alargamiento *m,* prolongación *f*

prolonged [prə'lɒŋd] *adj* prolongado(a)

prom [prɒm] *n (abbr* **promenade***) Fam* **(a)** *Br (seafront)* paseo *m* marítimo **(b)** *Br (concert)* = concierto sinfónico en que parte del público está de pie **(c)** *US (school dance)* baile *m* de fin de curso

promenade [prɒmə'nɑːd] **1** *n* **(a)** *Br (at seaside)* paseo *m* marítimo ❑ *Naut* **p. deck** cubierta *f* de paseo **(b)** *Br* **p. concert** = concierto sinfónico en que parte del público está de pie **(c)** *US (school dance)* baile *m* de fin de curso
  2 *vi* pasearse

prominence ['prɒmɪnəns] *n (noticeable)* prominencia *f; Fig (importance)* importancia *f*

prominent ['prɒmɪnənt] *adj (standing out)* saliente, prominente; *Fig (important)* importante, destacado(a); *(famous)* famoso(a), eminente; **to play a p. part in sth** tener *or* desempeñar un papel importante en algo

prominently ['prɒmɪnəntlɪ] *adv (standing out)* muy a la vista; **to figure p. in sth** destacar en algo

promiscuity [prɒmɪ'skjuːɪtɪ] *n* promiscuidad *f*

promiscuous [prə'mɪskjʊəs] *adj* promiscuo(a)

promise ['prɒmɪs] **1** *n* (**a**) *(pledge)* promesa *f*; **to break/ keep a p.** faltar a/cumplir una promesa; **to make sb a p.** prometer algo a algn (**b**) *(expectation)* promesa *f*; **there's p. of an agreement** hay esperanzas de que se llegará a un acuerdo; **to show p.** ser prometedor(a)
  2 *vt (pledge)* prometer; **he promises to come** *or* **that he will come** promete que vendrá; **I'll do it, I p. you** lo haré, te lo prometo; **to p. sth to sb** prometer (dar) algo a algn; *Fig* **to p. sb the earth** prometer la luna a algn
  3 *vi* (**a**) *(pledge)* prometer; **I p.** te lo prometo (**b**) *(augur)* prometer, augurar; **it promises to be interesting** promete ser interesante

promising ['prɒmɪsɪŋ] *adj* prometedor(a)

promontory ['prɒmən tərɪ] *n* promontorio *m*

promote [prə'məʊt] *vt* (**a**) *(in rank)* promover, ascender; *Br (in league)* hacer subir; *Br* **our team has been promoted to the first division** nuestro equipo ha subido a primera división (**b**) *Com (product)* lanzar, promocionar (**c**) *(ideas etc)* fomentar

promoter [prə'məʊtər] *n* *(gen)* promotor(a) *m,f*; *Com* patrocinador(a) *m,f*

promotion [prə'məʊʃən] *n* (**a**) *(in rank)* promoción *f*, ascenso *m*; **to get p.** ser ascendido(a) (**b**) *Com (of product)* promoción *f* (**c**) *(of arts, ideas etc)* fomento *m*

promotional [prə'məʊʃənəl] *adj (literature, campaign)* promocional

prompt [prɒmpt] **1** *adj (quick)* rápido(a); *(punctual)* puntual; **to be p.** ser puntual
  2 *adv* en punto; **at 2 o'clock p.** a las 2 en punto
  3 *vt* (**a**) *(motivate)* instar, incitar; **to p. sb to do sth** instar a algn a hacer algo (**b**) *(actor)* apuntar; *(speaker)* alentar
  4 *n Comptr (short phrase)* mensaje *m* (al usuario)

prompter ['prɒmptər] *n Theat* apuntador(a) *m,f*

prompting ['prɒmptɪŋ] *n (persuasion)* persuasión *f*, insistencia *f*; **to do sth at sb's p.** acceder a hacer algo ante la insistencia de algn; **the promptings of his conscience** los dictados de su conciencia

promptly ['prɒmptlɪ] *adv (quickly)* rápidamente; *(punctually)* puntualmente, en punto

prone [prəʊn] *adj* (**a**) *(inclined)* propenso(a); **to be p. to sth/to do sth** ser propenso(a) a algo/a hacer algo (**b**) *Fml (face down)* boca abajo

prong [prɒŋ] *n* punta *f*, diente *m*

pronoun ['prəʊnaʊn] *n Ling* pronombre *m*

pronounce [prə'naʊns] **1** *vt* (**a**) *Ling* pronunciar (**b**) *Fml (declare)* declarar; **he was pronounced fit for work** le declararon hábil para trabajar; *Jur* **to p. sentence** dictar sentencia, pronunciar un fallo
  2 *vi Fml* **to p. on sth** opinar sobre algo

pronounced [prə'naʊnst] *adj* marcado(a)

pronouncement [prə'naʊnsmənt] *n Fml* declaración *f*

pronto ['prɒntəʊ] *adv Fam* enseguida, ya

pronunciation [prənʌnsɪ'eɪʃən] *n* pronunciación *f*

proof [pruːf] **1** *n* (**a**) *(evidence)* prueba *f*; *Math* comprobación *f*; *(test)* prueba *f*; **as p. of** como prueba de; **give me p.** dame pruebas; **p. of identity** documentos *mpl* de identidad; *Fig* **the p. of the pudding is in the eating** el movimiento se demuestra caminando *or Esp* andando (**b**) *Phot Typ* prueba *f*
  2 *adj* (**a**) *(secure)* resistente a, a prueba de; **p. against water** impermeable (**b**) *(of alcohol)* graduación *f*; **this rum is 70 degrees p.** este ron tiene 70 grados
  3 *vt* impermeabilizar

proofread ['pruːfriːd] *vt & vi (pt & pp* **proofread** ['pruːfred]) corregir pruebas de imprenta

proofreader ['pruːfriːdər] *n* corrector(a) *m,f* de pruebas (de imprenta)

prop[1] [prɒp] **1** *n (support)* puntal *m*; *Fig* apoyo *m*, sostén *m*
  2 *vt (pt & pp* **propped**) *(support)* apoyar; *Fig* apoyar, sostener; **to p. a bicycle/ladder against a wall** apoyar una bicicleta/escalera contra la pared

prop up *vt* apuntalar, apoyar; *Fig* fortalecer; **to p. up a wall** apuntalar una pared; *Fin* **to p. up the pound** reforzar la libra; *Fig* **to p. up a business** poner un negocio a flote

prop[2] [prɒp] *n Theat (abbr* **property**) *Fam* accesorio *m*

propaganda [prɒpə'gændə] *n Pej* propaganda *f*

propagate ['prɒpəgeɪt] *Fml* **1** *vt* propagar
  2 *vi* propagarse

propagation [prɒpə'geɪʃən] *n Fml* propagación *f*

propane ['prəʊpeɪn] *n Chem* propano *m*

propel [prə'pel] *vt (pt & pp* **propelled**) propulsar, impulsar; **to p. sb along** impulsar a algn; **propelled by electricity** propulsado(a) por electricidad

propellant, propellent [prə'pelənt] *n (for rocket)* propulsante *m*, combustible *m*; *(for aerosol)* propelente *m*

propeller [prə'pelər] *n* hélice *f*

propelling pencil [prəpelɪŋ'pensəl] *n* portaminas *m inv*

propensity [prə'pensɪtɪ] *n Fml* propensión *f*

proper ['prɒpər] **1** *adj* (**a**) *(appropriate)* adecuado(a); *(correct)* correcto(a); **p. clothing** ropa adecuada; **prim and p.** remilgado(a); **the p. answer** la respuesta correcta; **the p. way to do sth** la manera correcta de proceder; **the p. time** el momento oportuno (**b**) *(real)* real, auténtico(a); *(actual, exact)* propiamente dicho(a); **he isn't a p. doctor** no es médico de verdad; **he's a p. gentleman** es un caballero de pies a cabeza; **in the p. sense of the word** en el sentido estricto de la palabra; **outside the city p.** fuera de la ciudad propiamente dicha (**c**) *(characteristic)* propio(a); **customs p. to the region** costumbres propias a la región (**d**) *Ling* propio(a) ❑ **p. name, p. noun** nombre *m* propio
  2 *adv Br Fam* realmente, de verdad; **p. poorly** malito(a) de verdad

properly ['prɒpəlɪ] *adv* (**a**) *(appropriately, suitably, correctly)* bien, correctamente; **it wasn't p. closed** no estaba bien cerrado(a); **she refused, quite p.** se negó, y con razón; **to speak p.** hablar correctamente (**b**) *(decently)* correctamente; **he wasn't p. dressed** no iba correctamente vestido

property ['prɒpətɪ] *n* (**a**) *(quality)* propiedad *f*; **medicinal properties** propiedades medicinales (**b**) *(possession)* propiedad *f*, posesión *f*; **it's our p.** es de nuestra propiedad, nos pertenece; **lost p.** objetos *mpl* perdidos *or* extraviados; **personal p.** bienes *mpl*; **public p.** dominio *m* público (**c**) *(land, building)* propiedad *f*; *(estate)* finca *f*; **p. developer** promotor(a) *m,f* de construcciones; **p. manager** accesorista *mf*

prophecy ['prɒfɪsɪ] *n* profecía *f*

prophesy ['prɒfɪsaɪ] *vt (pt & pp* **prophesied**) *(predict)* predecir; *Rel* profetizar

prophet ['prɒfɪt] *n* profeta *mf*

prophetic [prə'fetɪk] *adj* profético(a)

prophylactic [prɒfɪ'læktɪk] *adj & n* profiláctico(a) *(m)*

propitiate [prə'pɪʃɪeɪt] *vt Fml* propiciar

propitious [prə'pɪʃəs] *adj Fml* propicio(a), favorable

proportion [prə'pɔːʃən] **1** *n* (**a**) *(ratio)* proporción *f*; *(part, quantity)* parte *f*; **in equal proportions** en partes iguales; **in p. to** *or* **with** en proporción a; **the p. of men to women** la proporción entre hombres y mujeres; **to be out of (all) p.** ser desproporcionado(a); **to keep a sense of p.** guardar

el sentido de la justa medida (**b**) **proportions** *(dimensions)* dimensiones *fpl*
  2 *vt* proporcionar

proportional [prə'pɔːʃənəl] *adj* proporcional (**to** a), en proporción (**to** con) ❑ *Pol* **p. representation** representación *f* proporcional

proportionate [prə'pɔːʃənɪt] *adj* proporcionado(a), proporcional

proposal [prə'pəʊzəl] *n (offer)* propuesta *f*, oferta *f*; *(suggestion)* sugerencia *f*; **p. of marriage** propuesta de matrimonio

propose [prə'pəʊz] **1** *vt* (**a**) *(offer)* proponer; *(suggest)* sugerir; **to p. a toast to sb** proponer un brindis por algn; **to p. marriage to sb** hacer una propuesta de matrimonio a algn (**b**) *Fml (plan, intend)* pretender, pensar; **what do you p. to do?** ¿qué piensas hacer?
  2 *vi* declararse; **to p. to sb** pedir la mano a algn, declararse a algn

proposer [prə'pəʊzər] *n* proponente *mf*, autor(a) *m,f* de la proposición

proposition [prɒpə'zɪʃən] **1** *n* (**a**) *(offer)* proposición *f*, propuesta *f*; **to make sb a p.** hacer una propuesta a algn (**b**) *Math* proposición *f* (**c**) *(business)* trato *m*, negocio *m*; **a paying p.** un negocio rentable
  2 *vt* hacer proposiciones (deshonestas) a

propound [prə'paʊnd] *vt Fml* exponer, plantear

proprietary [prə'praɪətərɪ] *adj Fml* patentado(a)

proprietor [prə'praɪətər] *n* propietario(a) *m,f*, dueño(a) *m,f*

propriety [prə'praɪətɪ] *n* (**a**) *(decency)* decoro *m*, decencia *f*; *(suitability)* conveniencia *f* (**b**) **proprieties** cánones *mpl* sociales, conveniencias *fpl*

propulsion [prə'pʌlʃən] *n* propulsión *f* ❑ **jet p.** propulsión *f* a chorro *or* por reacción

pro rata ['prəʊ'rɑːtə] **1** *adj* prorrateado(a)
  2 *adv* de forma prorrateada

prosaic [prəʊ'zeɪɪk] *adj* prosaico(a)

proscribe [prəʊ'skraɪb] *vt Fml* proscribir

prose [prəʊz] *n* (**a**) *Lit* prosa *f* ❑ **p. writer** prosista *mf* (**b**) *Educ (translation)* texto *m* para traducir

prosecute ['prɒsɪkjuːt] *vt Jur* procesar, entablar una acción judicial contra

prosecuting attorney ['prɒsɪkjuːtɪŋə'tɜːnɪ] *n US* fiscal *m*

prosecution [prɒsɪ'kjuːʃən] *n* (**a**) *Jur (action)* proceso *m*, juicio *m*; the **p.** *(person)* la parte acusadora ❑ **counsel for the p.** fiscal *mf*; **witness for the p.** testigo *mf* de cargo (**b**) *(carrying out)* realización *f*

prosecutor ['prɒsɪkjuːtər] *n Jur* acusador(a) *m,f*

prospect ['prɒspekt] **1** *n* (**a**) *(outlook)* perspectiva *f*; *(chance, hope)* esperanza *f*, probabilidad *f*; **future prospects** perspectivas para el futuro; **there's little p. of that happening** hay pocas probabilidades de que eso ocurra; **the job has prospects** es un trabajo con porvenir
  2 [prə'spekt] *vt* explorar
  3 *vi* **to p. for gold/oil** buscar oro/petróleo

prospective [prə'spektɪv] *adj (future)* futuro(a); *(possible)* eventual, probable

prospector [prə'spektər] *n* explorador(a) *m,f*, prospector(a) *m,f* ❑ **gold p.** buscador(a) *m,f* del oro

prospectus [prə'spektəs] *n* prospecto *m*

prosper ['prɒspər] *vi* prosperar

prosperity [prɒ'sperɪtɪ] *n* prosperidad *f*

prosperous ['prɒspərəs] *adj* próspero(a)

prostate ['prɒsteɪt] *n* próstata *f*

prosthetic [prɒs'θetɪk] *adj* artificial; **p. limb** prótesis *f*

prostitute ['prɒstɪtjuːt] **1** *n* prostituta *f*, puta *f* ❑ **male p.** puto *m*
  2 *vt* **to p. oneself** prostituirse

prostitution [prɒstɪ'tjuːʃən] *n* prostitución *f*

prostrate ['prɒstreɪt] **1** *adj (face down)* boca abajo, postrado(a); *Fig (powerless, exhausted)* abatido(a), postrado(a); **p. with grief** desconsolado(a)
  2 [prɒ'streɪt] *vt* **to p. oneself** postrarse

prostration [prɒs'treɪʃən] *n* postración *f*

protagonist [prəʊ'tægənɪst] *n* protagonista *mf*

protect [prə'tekt] *vt (gen)* proteger; *(interests etc)* salvaguardar; **to p. sb from/against sth** proteger a algn de/contra algo

protection [prə'tekʃən] *n* protección *f*, amparo *m*; **to be under sb's p.** estar protegido(a) *or* amparado(a) por algn ❑ **p. racket** chantaje *m*

protectionism [prə'tekʃənɪzəm] *n* proteccionismo *m*

protective [prə'tektɪv] *adj* protector(a); **p. clothing** ropa *f* de protección

protector [prə'tektər] *n (person)* protector(a) *m,f*; *(thing)* protector *m*

protégé(e) ['prəʊteʒeɪ] *n* protegido(a) *m,f*

protein ['prəʊtiːn] *n* proteína *f*

protest ['prəʊtest] **1** *n (gen)* protesta *f*; *(complaint)* queja *f*; **to make a p.** about sth protestar por algo; **under p.** bajo protesta ❑ **p. march** manifestación *f*, marcha *f* de protesta
  2 [prə'test] *vt* protestar de; **to p. one's innocence** protestar de su inocencia; **to p. that ...** protestar manifestando *or* diciendo que ...; *US* **to p. sth** protestar en contra de algo
  3 *vi Br* protestar; **to p. about sth** protestar por algo

Protestant ['prɒtɪstənt] *adj & n Rel* protestante *(mf)*

Protestantism ['prɒtɪstəntɪzəm] *n Rel* protestantismo *m*

protestation [prɒtes'teɪʃən] *n Fml* (**a**) *(protest)* protesta *f* (**b**) *(declaration)* declaración *f*

protester [prə'testər] *n* manifestante *mf*

protocol ['prəʊtəkɒl] *n* protocolo *m*

proton ['prəʊtɒn] *n Phys* protón *m*

prototype ['prəʊtətaɪp] *n* prototipo *m*

protracted [prə'træktɪd] *adj* prolongado(a), largo(a)

protractor [prə'træktər] *n Geom* transportador *m*

protrude [prə'truːd] *vi Fml* salir, sobresalir

protruding [prə'truːdɪŋ] *adj* saliente, sobresaliente, prominente; **p. eyes** ojos *mpl* saltones; **p. teeth** dientes *mpl* prominentes

protuberance [prə'tjuːbərəns] *n Fml* protuberancia *f*, saliente *m*

proud [praʊd] *adj* (**a**) *(gen)* orgulloso(a); *(arrogant)* soberbio(a); **a p. moment** un momento glorioso; **I'm p. to introduce ...** tengo el honor de presentar a ...; **to be p. of sth** estar orgulloso(a) de algo, enorgullecerse *or* ufanarse de algo; *Fam* **to do sb p.** tratar a algn a cuerpo de rey (**b**) *Literary (sticking out)* saliente, sobresaliente

proudly ['praʊdlɪ] *adv (gen)* orgullosamente, con orgullo; *(arrogantly)* soberbiamente, con soberbia

prove [pruːv] *vt (pt* **proved**; *pp* **proved** *or* **proven**) (**a**) *(give evidence of)* probar, demostrar; *Math* comprobar; **history proved him right** la historia le dio la razón; **the exception proves the rule** la excepción confirma la regla; **to p. oneself** dar pruebas de valor; **to p. sb's innocence** demostrar la inocencia de algn (**b**) *(turn out)* resultar; **it proved to be disastrous** resultó ser desastroso(a)

proven ['pruːvən] **1** *pp see* **prove**
  2 *adj* probado(a), demostrado(a); **this is not p.** esto está por comprobar

provenance ['prɒvənəns] *n Fml* procedencia *f*, origen *m*

proverb ['prɒvɜ:b] *n* refrán *m*, proverbio *m*

proverbial [prə'vɜ:bɪəl] *adj* proverbial

provide [prə'vaɪd] **1** *vt (gen)* proporcionar, facilitar; *(supplies)* suministrar, proveer; **provided with** provisto(a) de; **the firm will p. you with a car** la empresa te facilitará *or* dará un coche; **to p. oneself with sth** proveerse de algo; **to p. sb with food/water** suministrar comida/agua a algn

2 *vi* (**a**) *(make provision)* proveer; **God will p.** Dios proveerá; **to p. against misfortune** tomar medidas contra cualquier desgracia; **to p. for sb** mantener a algn; **to p. for the future** ahorrar para el futuro (**b**) *Jur* estipular; **the law provides that ...** la ley estipula que ...

provided [prə'vaɪdɪd] *conj* **p. (that)** con tal de que, a condición de que, siempre que

providence ['prɒvɪdəns] *n* providencia *f*

providential [prɒvɪ'denʃəl] *adj* providencial

provider [prə'vaɪdər] *n* proveedor(a) *m,f*, abastecedor(a) *m,f*

providing [prə'vaɪdɪŋ] *conj see* **provided**

province ['prɒvɪns] *n* (**a**) *(region)* provincia *f*; **to live in the provinces** vivir en provincias (**b**) *Fig (field of knowledge etc)* campo *m*, competencia *f*; **that's not my p.** no es de mi competencia

provincial [prə'vɪnʃəl] **1** *adj* provincial; *Pej* provinciano(a), pueblerino(a)

2 *n Pej (person)* provinciano(a) *m,f*

provision [prə'vɪʒən] *n* (**a**) *(supplying)* provisión *f*; **to make p. for sb** atender las necesidades de algn; **to make p. for the future** ahorrar para el futuro (**b**) *(supply)* suministro *m*; *(food)* **provisions** provisiones *fpl*, víveres *mpl* (**c**) *(condition)* disposición *f*; **there is no p. for this in the agreement** esto no está previsto en el acuerdo; **with the p. that they sell it** con tal de que lo vendan

provisional [prə'vɪʒənəl] *adj* provisional, *Am* provisorio(a)

provisionally [prə'vɪʒənəlɪ] *adv* provisionalmente

proviso [prə'vaɪzəʊ] *n (pl* **provisos** *or US* **provisoes)** **with the p.** that con tal de que, a condición de que, siempre que

provocation [prɒvə'keɪʃən] *n* provocación *f*; **at the slightest p.** a la más mínima provocación; **to act under p.** reaccionar ante una provocación

provocative [prə'vɒkətɪv] *adj* provocador(a), provocativo(a)

provocatively [prə'vɒkətɪvlɪ] *adv* de una forma provocadora *or* provocativa

provoke [prə'vəʊk] *vt* provocar; **he gets angry when provoked** se *esp Esp* enfada *or esp Am* enoja cuando lo provocan; **to p. sb to do sth** provocar a algn a que haga algo

provoking [prə'vəʊkɪŋ] *adj* provocador(a), que provoca

provost ['prɒvəst] *n* (**a**) *Scot* alcalde *m* (**b**) *Br Univ* rector *m*

prow [praʊ] *n* proa *f*

prowess ['praʊɪs] *n Fml* habilidad *f*, capacidad *f*

prowl [praʊl] **1** *n* merodeo *m*; **to be on the p.** merodear, rondar

2 *vi* merodear; *Fam* **to p. about** *or* **around** rondar

prowler ['praʊlər] *n Fam* merodeador *m*

proximity [prɒk'sɪmɪtɪ] *n Fml* proximidad *f*; **in p. to, in the p. of** cerca de

proxy ['prɒksɪ] *n Jur (power)* poderes *mpl*; *(person)* apoderado(a) *m,f*, mandatario(a) *m,f*; **by p.** por poderes

Prozac® ['prəʊzæk] *n* Prozac® *m*

prs *(abbr* **pairs)** pares *mpl*

prude [pru:d] *n* gazmoño(a) *m,f*, mojigato(a) *m,f*

prudence ['pru:dəns] *n Fml* prudencia *f*

prudent ['pru:dənt] *adj Fml* prudente

prudish ['pru:dɪʃ] *adj* remilgado(a)

prune¹ [pru:n] *n* ciruela *f* pasa

prune² [pru:n] *vt Hortic* podar; *Fig (text etc)* acortar, expurgar ❑ **pruning knife** podera *f*

prurient ['prʊərɪənt] *adj Fml* lascivo(a)

Prussia ['prʌʃə] *n* Prusia

Prussian ['prʌʃən] *adj & n* prusiano(a) *(m,f)*

pry [praɪ] *vi (pt & pp* **pried)** curiosear, husmear; **to p. into sb's affairs** meterse en asuntos ajenos

prying ['praɪɪŋ] *adj* entrometido(a), husmeador(a)

PS, ps [pi:'es] *(abbr* **postscript)** posdata *f*, P.S., P.D.

psalm [sɑ:m] *n Rel* salmo *m*

pseud [sju:d] *n Br Fam* pretencioso(a) *m,f*

pseudo- ['sju:dəʊ] *pref* pseudo-, seudo-

pseudonym ['sju:dənɪm] *n* pseudónimo *m*, seudónimo *m*

psoriasis [sə'raɪəsɪs] *n* soriasis *f*

PST [pi:es'ti:] *n US (abbr* **Pacific Standard Time)** = hora oficial de la costa del Pacífico en Estados Unidos

psyche ['saɪkɪ] *n* psique *f*, psiquis *f*

psychedelic [saɪkɪ'delɪk] *adj* psicodélico(a); sicodélico(a)

psychiatric [saɪkɪ'ætrɪk] *adj* psiquiátrico(a), siquiátrico(a)

psychiatrist [saɪ'kaɪətrɪst] *n* psiquiatra *mf*, siquiatra *mf*

psychiatry [saɪ'kaɪətrɪ] *n* psiquiatría *f*, siquiatría *f*

psychic ['saɪkɪk] **1** *adj* psíquico(a), síquico(a); *Fam* **you must be p.!** ¡cómo lo adivinaste!

2 *n (medium)* médium *mf*

psycho ['saɪkəʊ] *n Fam (pl* **psychos)** psicópata *mf*

psychoanalyse [saɪkəʊ'ænəlaɪz] *vt* psicoanalizar, sicoanalizar

psychoanalysis ['saɪkəʊə'nælɪsɪs] *n* psicoanálisis *f*, sicoanálisis *f*

psychoanalyst ['saɪkəʊ'ænəlɪst] *n* psicoanalista *mf*, sicoanalista *mf*

psychoanalyze ['saɪkəʊ'ænəlaɪz] *vi US see* **psychoanalyse**

psycholinguistics ['saɪkəʊlɪŋ'gwɪstɪks] *n* psicolingüística *f*

psychological ['saɪkə'lɒdʒɪkəl] *adj* psicológico(a), sicológico(a); **p. warfare** guerra *f* psicológica

psychologically ['saɪkə'lɒdʒɪklɪ] *adv* psicológicamente, sicológicamente

psychologist [saɪ'kɒlədʒɪst] *n* psicólogo(a) *m,f*, sicólogo(a) *m,f*

psychology [saɪ'kɒlədʒɪ] *n* psicología *f*, sicología *f*

psychometric ['saɪkə'metrɪk] *adj* **p. test** prueba *f* psicométrica *or* sicométrica

psychopath ['saɪkəʊpæθ] *n* psicópata *mf*, sicópata *mf*

psychopathic ['saɪkəʊ'pæθɪk] *adj* psicopático(a), sicopático(a)

psychosis [saɪ'kəʊsɪs] *n (pl* **psychoses** [saɪ'kəʊsi:z]) psicosis *f inv*, sicosis *f inv*

psychosomatic ['saɪkəʊsə'mætɪk] *adj* psicosomático(a), sicosomático(a)

psychotherapist ['saɪkəʊ'θerəpɪst] *n* psicoterapeuta *mf*, sicoterapeuta *mf*

psychotherapy [ˈsaɪkəʊˈθerəpɪ] *n* psicoterapia *f*, sicoterapia *f*

psychotic [saɪˈkɒtɪk] *adj & n* psicótico(a) *(m,f)*, sicótico(a) *(m,f)*

PT [piːˈtiː] *n (abbr* **physical training***)* educación *f* física

pt (**a**) *(also* **Pt**) *(abbr* **part***)* parte *f* (**b**) *(pl* **pts***) (abbr* **pint***)* pinta *f* (**c**) *(pl* **pts***) (abbr* **point***)* punto *m*

PTA [piːtiːˈeɪ] *n Educ (abbr* **Parent-Teacher Association***)* Asociación *f* de Padres de Familia y Profesores

ptarmigan [ˈtɑːmɪgən] *n Orn* perdiz *f* nival

Pte *Mil (abbr* **Private***)* soldado *m* raso

PTO, pto [piːtiːˈəʊ] *(abbr* **please turn over***)* sigue

pub [pʌb] *n Br Fam* bar *m*, pub *m*, taberna *f*

pub-crawl [ˈpʌbkrɔːl] *n Br Fam* **to go on a p.-c.** ir de tascas

puberty [ˈpjuːbətɪ] *n* pubertad *f*

pubescent [pjuːˈbesənt] *adj & n* pubescente *(mf)*

pubic [ˈpjuːbɪk] *adj* púbico(a) ❑ **p. hair** vello *m* púbico

pubis [ˈpjuːbɪs] *n Anat* pubis *m*

public [ˈpʌblɪk] **1** *adj* público(a); **in the p. interest** en interés del estado; **it's p. knowledge** es del dominio público; **to be in the p. eye** ser objeto del interés público; *Com* **to go p.** constituirse en sociedad anónima; **to make sth p.** hacer público algo ❑ **p. company** empresa *f* pública; *Br* **p. convenience** servicios *mpl or Esp* aseos *mpl*; **p. holiday** día *m* festivo *or Am* feriado; *Br* **p. house** pub *m*, taberna *f*; **p. opinion** opinión *f* pública; **p. ownership** titularidad *f* estatal; **p. relations** relaciones *fpl* públicas; **p. school** *Br* colegio *m* privado; *US* colegio *m* público; **p. sector** sector *m* estatal *or* público; **p. speaking** declamación *f*; **p. spirit** civismo *m*; **p. transport** transporte *m* público; *Com* **p. utility** (empresa *f* de) servicio *m* público

2 the p. *n* el público; **in p.** en público; **the British p.** los británicos

public-address system [pʌblɪkəˈdressɪstəm] *n* megafonía *f*, sistema *m* de altavoces

publican [ˈpʌblɪkən] *n Br* patrón(ona) *m,f* de un pub, tabernero(a) *m,f*

publication [pʌblɪˈkeɪʃən] *n* publicación *f* ❑ **p. date** fecha *f* de publicación

publicity [pʌbˈlɪsɪtɪ] *n* publicidad *f*

publicity-seeking [pʌbˈlɪsɪtɪˈsiːkɪŋ] *adj* en busca de publicidad

publicize [ˈpʌblɪsaɪz] *vt (make public)* divulgar, hacer público(a), dar a conocer; *(advertise)* promocionar, hacer publicidad para

publicly [ˈpʌblɪklɪ] *adv* públicamente; **p. owned** de titularidad pública

public-spirited [pʌblɪkˈspɪrɪtɪd] *adj* de espíritu cívico

publish [ˈpʌblɪʃ] *vt* publicar, editar; **published weekly** semanal; **just published** última novedad, de reciente publicación

publisher [ˈpʌblɪʃər] *n (person)* editor(a) *m,f*; *(firm)* (casa *f*) editorial *f*

publishing [ˈpʌblɪʃɪŋ] *n (business)* industria *f* editorial; **she works in p.** trabaja en una editorial ❑ **p. company** *or* **house** casa *f* editorial

puce [pjuːs] *adj* de color pardo rojizo

pucker [ˈpʌkər] **1** *vt (lips, brow)* fruncir, arrugar

2 *vi (lips, brow)* fruncirse, arrugarse; *Sew* fruncir

pudding [ˈpʊdɪŋ] *n Culin* budín *m*, pudín *m*; *Fam (dessert)* postre *m*; **what's for p.?** ¿qué hay de postre? ❑ **black p.** morcilla *f*; **Christmas p.** = pudín a base de frutos secos típico de Navidad; **p. basin** cuenco *m*; **rice p.** arroz *m* con leche; **steamed p.** budín *m*

puddle [ˈpʌdəl] *n* charco *m*

puerile [ˈpjʊəraɪl] *adj* pueril

Puerto Rican [pwɜːtəʊˈriːkən] *adj & n* puertorriqueño(a) *(m,f)*, portorriqueño(a) *(m,f)*

Puerto Rico [pwɜːtəʊˈriːkəʊ] *n* Puerto Rico

puff [pʌf] **1** *n* (**a**) *(of wind)* soplo *m*, racha *f*; *(of smoke)* bocanada *f*, *Esp* calada *f*, *Am* pitada *f*; **to take a p. on a cigarette** dar una calada a un cigarrillo; *Fam* **to be out of p.** quedarse *or* estar sin aliento (**b**) *(powder)* borla *f* (**c**) *Culin* **cream p.** petisú *m*; **p. pastry** pasta *f* de hojaldre

2 *vi (person)* jadear, resoplar; *(train)* echar humo *or* vapor; **to p. on a cigarette** dar chupadas *or Esp* caladas *or Am* pitadas a un cigarrillo

3 *vt* dar una calada a

puff up *vi* hincharse; *Fig* **to be puffed up with pride** hincharse de orgullo

Puffa jacket® [ˈpʌfəˈdʒækɪt] *n* chaqueta *f* de rapero

puffin [ˈpʌfɪn] *n Orn* frailecillo *m* (común)

puffy [ˈpʌfɪ] *adj* (**puffier, puffiest**) hinchado(a), inflado(a)

pug [pʌg] *n Zool* doguillo *m*

pugnacious [pʌgˈneɪʃəs] *adj* pugnaz, agresivo(a)

pug-nosed [ˈpʌgnəʊzd] *adj* de nariz chata

puke [ˈpjuːk] *vi Fam* devolver, vomitar

pull [pʊl] **1** *n* (**a**) *(tug)* tirón *m*, *Am salvo RP* jalón *m*; **to give sth a p.** dar un tirón *or Am salvo RP* jalón a algo (**b**) *Tech (of engine)* tracción *f* (**c**) *Fig (attraction)* atracción *f*; *(influence)* enchufe *m*, influencia *f*; **the p. of the big city** la atracción de la gran ciudad; **to have p. with sb** tener influencia sobre algn (**d**) *(journey)* trecho *m*; **a long p.** una tirada; **it was a long p. to the top** nos costó llegar a la cumbre (**e**) *(of bell)* cuerda *f* (**f**) *Typ* galerada *f*, primera prueba *f*

2 *vt (tug)* dar un tirón a; *Med* **to p. a muscle** sufrir un tirón en un músculo; **to p. the trigger of a gun** apretar el gatillo de una pistola; **to p. sth to pieces** hacer algo pedazos; *Fig* poner algo por los suelos; **to p. a face** hacer una mueca; *Fig* **to p. strings** tocar teclas; *Fig* **to p. sb's leg** tomar el pelo a algn; *Fam* **p. the other one!** ¡no me vengas con ésas!, *Esp* ¡a otro perro con ese hueso!, *Méx* ¡no mames!; *Fam* **to p. a fast one on sb** hacer una jugada a algn (**b**) *(draw)* tirar, arrastrar; **to p. sth open/shut** abrir/cerrar algo de un tirón *or Am salvo RP* jalón; **p. your chair up to the fire** acércate la silla al fuego; **to p. a heavy object** arrastrar un objeto pesado; *Fig* **to p. one's weight** hacer su parte del trabajo; *Fig* **to p. the wool over sb's eyes** engañar a algn (**c**) *(draw out)* sacar; **to p. a gun on sb** amenazar a algn con pistola (**d**) *Culin* **to p. a chicken** desplumar un pollo (**e**) *Fam (people)* atraer; **the new exhibition pulled in the punters** la nueva exposición atrajo mucha gente

3 *vi* (**a**) *(drag)* tirar, *Am salvo RP* jalar; **the car pulls to the right** el coche *or Am* carro *or RP* auto tira hacia la derecha; **to p. on one's pipe** dar chupadas *or Esp* caladas *or Am* pitadas a la pipa (**b**) *(move)* **to p. in/out** entrar en/salir de; **to p. alongside sb** acercarse a algn

pull apart *vt (gen)* desmontar; *(separate)* separar; *(break)* hacer pedazos; *Fig (criticize)* hacer pedazos

pull away 1 *vt* apartar, separar

2 *vi (car)* arrancar; *(train)* salir de la estación; *(ship)* desatracar

pull back 1 *vt* tirar hacia atrás

2 *vi* contenerse; *Mil* retirarse

pull down *vt (building)* derribar; *Fig (depress)* deprimir, abatir

pull in 1 *vt* (**a**) *(crowds)* atraer; *Fam (money)* aportar (**b**) *Fam (arrest)* detener

2 *vi* entrar; *(train)* entrar en la estación; *(stop)* parar

pull off 1 vt Fam (carry out) llevar a cabo; **to p. sth off** llevar algo a cabo
  2 vi (vehicle) salir, arrancar
pull out 1 vt (withdraw) retirarse
  2 vi Aut **to p. out to overtake** salir para adelantar
pull over vi hacerse a un lado
pull through vi reponerse, restablecerse
pull together 1 vt **to p. oneself together** calmarse, serenarse, tranquilizarse
  2 vi (cooperate) tirar en conjunto
pull up 1 vt (**a**) (lift up) levantar, quitar, Am sacar; (uproot) arrancar, quitar, Am sacar; **to p. up one's socks** subirse los calcetines; Fig espabilarse; Fig **to p. up one's roots** desarraigarse (**b**) (draw close) acercar (**c**) (scold) regañar
  2 vi (stop) pararse, detenerse
pull-down menu ['pʊldaʊn'menjuː] n Comptr menú m desplegable
pullet ['pʊlɪt] n pollo m
pulley ['pʊlɪ] n polea f
Pullman® ['pʊlmən] n coche-cama m
pull-out ['pʊlaʊt] **1** n Press (supplement) suplemento m
  2 adj (magazine) separable; (leaf of table etc) extensible
pullover ['pʊləʊvər] n suéter m, Esp jersey m, Col saco m, RP pulóver m
pulmonary ['pʌlmənərɪ] adj pulmonar
pulp [pʌlp] **1** n (of paper, wood) pasta f, pulpa f; (of fruit) pulpa f; Fam Fig (book etc) basura f; **to crush sth to a p.** hacer algo papilla
  2 vt reducir a pulpa
pulpit ['pʊlpɪt] n púlpito m
pulsate [pʌl'seɪt] vi vibrar, palpitar
pulse¹ [pʌls] n Anat pulso m; (of radio) pulsación f; Fig (rhythm) compás m; **to take sb's p.** tomar el pulso a algn
pulse² [pʌls] n Bot Culin legumbre f
pulverize ['pʌlvəraɪz] vt pulverizar
puma ['pjuːmə] n puma m
pumice (stone) ['pʌmɪs (stəʊn)] n piedra f pómez
pummel ['pʌməl] vt (pt & pp pummelled, US pummeled) aporrear
pump¹ [pʌmp] **1** n bomba f ❑ **gasoline p.** bomba f (de gasolina); **stomach p.** bomba f estomacal
  2 vt bombear; **the heart pumps blood** el corazón bombea la sangre; **to p. air into a tyre** inflar un neumático con una bomba; **to p. sth in/out** meter/sacar algo con una bomba; Fam Fig **to p. money into a venture** invertir dinero en una empresa; Fam Fig **to p. sb. for information** sonsacar información a algn
pump out vt (churn out) producir; (empty) vaciar
pump up vt (tyre) inflar
pump² [pʌmp] n (for ballet) zapatilla f de ballet; (for tennis) zapatilla f de tenis; Br (for beach) playera f
pumpkin ['pʌmpkɪn] n calabaza f, Andes RP zapallo m, Col Carib ahuyama f
pun [pʌn] n juego m de palabras, retruécano m
Punch [pʌntʃ] n **P. and Judy show** teatro m de títeres
punch¹ [pʌntʃ] **1** n (for making holes) perforadora f, taladro m; (in tickets) máquina f de picar billetes; (in leather etc) punzón m
  2 vt (make hole) perforar; (in ticket) picar; (in leather) punzar
punch² [pʌntʃ] **1** n (**a**) (blow) puñetazo m; (in boxing) pegada f; Fig **he doesn't pull any punches** no tiene pelos en la lengua (**b**) Fig (force) fuerza f, empuje m; **it lacks p.** le falta fuerza ❑ **p. line** remate m (de un chiste)
  2 vt (with fist) dar un puñetazo a

punch³ [pʌntʃ] n (drink) ponche m
punchbag ['pʌntʃbæg] n saco m (de boxeo)
punchball ['pʌntʃbɔːl] n (**a**) Br (equipment) punching-ball m (**b**) US (game) = versión simplificada del béisbol que se juega con una pelota de tenis y sin bate
punchbowl ['pʌntʃbəʊl] n ponchera f
punch-drunk [pʌntʃ'drʌŋk] adj aturdido(a), grogui
punching bag ['pʌntʃɪŋbæg] n US Box saco m de arena
punch-up ['pʌntʃʌp] n Fam riña f, pelea f
punchy ['pʌntʃɪ] adj Fam con garra
punctilious [pʌŋk'tɪlɪəs] adj Fml puntilloso(a), quisquilloso(a)
punctual ['pʌŋktjʊəl] adj puntual; **the train was p.** el tren llegó a la hora
punctuality [pʌŋktjʊ'ælɪtɪ] n puntualidad f
punctually ['pʌŋktjʊəlɪ] adv puntualmente, en punto
punctuate ['pʌŋktjʊeɪt] vt Ling puntuar; Fig **to p. a speech with anecdotes** salpicar un discurso con anécdotas
punctuation [pʌŋktjʊ'eɪʃən] n Ling puntuación f ❑ **p. mark** signo m de puntuación
puncture ['pʌŋktʃər] **1** n (in tyre etc) pinchazo m, Guat Méx ponchadura f; Aut **I've got a p.** se me ha pinchado or Guat Méx ponchado una rueda
  2 vt (tyre) pinchar, Guat Méx ponchar **to p. the skin** hacer una punción en la piel
  3 vi pincharse
pundit ['pʌndɪt] n Fam experto(a) m,f
pungency ['pʌndʒənsɪ] n (of smell) acritud f; (of taste) sabor m fuerte or picante; Fig (of remark) mordacidad f
pungent ['pʌndʒənt] adj (smell) acre; (taste) fuerte, picante; Fig (remark) mordaz
punish ['pʌnɪʃ] vt castigar; **to p. sb for doing sth** castigar a algn por haber hecho algo
punishable ['pʌnɪʃəbəl] adj castigable, punible; Jur delictivo(a)
punishment ['pʌnɪʃmənt] n castigo m; **to make the p. fit the crime** adecuar el castigo al crimen; Fig **the team took a lot of p.** el equipo sufrió una paliza ❑ **capital p.** pena f de muerte; **corporal p.** castigo m físico
punitive ['pjuːnɪtɪv] adj de castigo, punitivo(a)
punk [pʌŋk] n Fam (**a**) (person) punk m,f ❑ **p. music** música f punk (**b**) US (contemptible person) desgraciado(a) m,f
punnet ['pʌnɪt] n cestita f
punt¹ [pʌnt] **1** n (boat) batea f
  2 vt dirigir con percha
  3 vi ir en batea
punt² [pʌnt] vi Br Fam (bet) apostar
punter ['pʌntər] n Br Fam (**a**) (gambler) jugador(a) m,f, apostante m,f (**b**) (customer) cliente(a) m,f
puny ['pjuːnɪ] adj (punier, puniest) enclenque, endeble
pup [pʌp] n cachorro(a) m,f
pupil¹ ['pjuːpəl] n Educ alumno(a) m,f
pupil² ['pjuːpəl] n Anat pupila f
puppet ['pʌpɪt] n títere m, marioneta f; Fig títere ❑ Fig **p. government** gobierno m títere; **p. show** teatro m de títeres or de marionetas
puppy ['pʌpɪ] n (young dog) cachorro(a) m,f ❑ Br Fam **p. fat** gordura f infantil; Fam **p. love** amor m adolescente
purchase ['pɜːtʃɪs] **1** n (**a**) Com compra f, adquisición f ❑ **p. price** precio m de compra; **p. tax** impuesto m sobre la venta (**b**) (hold) agarre m, asidero m; **to get a p. on sth** agarrar algo bien

2 *vt Com Fml* comprar, adquirir; **purchasing power** poder *m* adquisitivo

purchaser ['pɜːtʃɪsər] *n* comprador(a) *m,f*

pure [pjʊər] *adj* puro(a); **it was p. chance** fue pura casualidad; **p. and simple** puro(a) y simple ❑ **p. new wool** pura lana *f* virgen; **p. science** ciencia *f* pura

purebred [pjʊə'bred] **1** *adj* de pura sangre, de raza
2 ['pjʊəbred] *n* animal *m* (de) pura sangre *or* de raza

purée ['pjʊəreɪ] **1** *n Culin* puré *m*; **apple p.** puré de manzana; **tomato p.** tomate *m* concentrado
2 *vt* pasar por el pasapurés, machacar

purely ['pjʊəlɪ] *adv* simplemente, sencillamente; **p. and simply** pura y simplemente; **p. for economic reasons** por motivos económicos más

purgative ['pɜːgətɪv] *adj & n Med* purgante *(m)*

purgatory ['pɜːgətərɪ] *n Rel & Fig* purgatorio *m*

purge [pɜːdʒ] **1** *n Med Pol* purga *f*
2 *vt Med* purgar; *Pol* purgar, depurar; *Fig (of thoughts etc)* librar (**of** de)

purify ['pjʊərɪfaɪ] *vt (pt & pp **purified**)* purificar

purist ['pjʊərɪst] *n* purista *mf*

puritan ['pjʊərɪtən] *n* puritano(a) *m,f*

puritanical [pjʊərɪ'tænɪkəl] *adj* puritano(a)

purity ['pjʊərɪtɪ] *n* pureza *f*

purl [pɜːl] **1** *n* punto *m* del revés
2 *vt* hacer punto del revés

purple ['pɜːpəl] **1** *n (colour)* color *m* morado, púrpura *f*
2 *adj* morado(a), purpúreo(a); **to go** *or* **turn p. (in the face)** ponerse morado(a)

purport ['pɜːpɔːt] **1** *n Fml* sentido *m*, significado *m*
2 [pɜː'pɔːt] *vi Fml* pretender; **to p. to be sth** pretender ser algo

purportedly [pə'pɔːtɪdlɪ] *adv Fml* supuestamente

purpose ['pɜːpəs] *n* (**a**) *(aim, intention)* propósito *m*, intención *f*; **on p.** a propósito; **to have a p. in life** tener una meta *or* un objetivo en la vida; **to have a sense of p.** ser firme en los propósitos; **what's the p. of your visit?** ¿con qué fin vienes a vernos? (**b**) *(use)* uso *m*, utilidad *f*; **for all practical purposes, to all intents and purposes** en la práctica; **for general purposes** para todos los usos; **it serves no useful p.** no sirve para nada; **to turn sth to good p.** aprovechar algo

purpose-built [pɜːpəs'bɪlt] *adj* construido(a) *or* hecho(a) a la medida

purposeful ['pɜːpəsfʊl] *adj (resolute)* decidido(a), resoluto(a); *(intentional)* intencionado(a)

purposely ['pɜːpəslɪ] *adv* a propósito, adrede

purr [pɜːr] **1** *n (of cat)* ronroneo *m*; *(of engine)* zumbido *m*
2 *vi (cat)* ronronear; *(engine)* zumbar

purse [pɜːs] **1** *n* (**a**) *Br (wallet)* monedero *m*; *Fig* **to hold the p. strings** administrar el dinero; *Prov* **you can't make a silk p. out of a sow's ear** no se puede pedir peras al olmo (**b**) *US (handbag) Esp* bolso *m*, *Col CSur* cartera *f*, *Méx* bolsa *f* (**c**) *(prize money)* premio *m* en metálico *f*
2 *vt* **to p. one's lips** apretarse los labios

purser ['pɜːsər] *n Naut* contador(a) *m,f*

pursue [pə'sjuː] *vt Fml* (**a**) *(criminal etc)* perseguir; *(person, animal)* seguir (**b**) *(pleasure, happiness)* buscar (**b**) *(carry out)* llevar a cabo; *(studies)* dedicarse a, seguir; *(profession, career)* ejercer

pursuer [pə'sjuːər] *n Fml* perseguidor(a) *m,f*

pursuit [pə'sjuːt] *n* (**a**) *(of criminal)* persecución *f*; *(of animal)* caza *f*; *(of pleasure, happiness)* busca *f*, búsqueda *f*; **in hot p. (of sb)** pisando los talones (a algn); **in p. of fame** en busca de la fama (**b**) *(occupation)* ocupación *f*, trabajo *m*; **leisure p.** pasatiempo *m*

purveyor [pə'veɪər] *n Com Fml* proveedor(a) *m,f*

pus [pʌs] *n* pus *m*

push [pʊʃ] **1** *n* (**a**) *(shove)* empujón *m* , *CAm Méx* aventón *m*; **to give sth/sb a p.** empujar algo/a algn, dar un empujón *or Am* aventón a algo/algn; *Fam* **at a p.** en caso de necesidad; *Br Fam* **to give sb the p.** *(employee)* poner a algn de patitas en la calle; *(lover)* dejar a algn (**b**) *Fig (drive)* empuje *m*, dinamismo *m*
2 *vt* (**a**) *(shove)* empujar; *(bell, button etc)* pulsar, apretar; **to p. one's finger into a hole** meter el dedo en un agujero; **to p. one's way through the crowd** abrirse paso a empujones entre la multitud; **to p. the door open/shut** abrir/cerrar la puerta empujándola; *Fam* **she's pushing forty** ronda los cuarenta (**b**) *Fig (pressurize)* instar, presionar; *(harass)* apremiar; **don't p. me too far!** ¡no te pases conmigo!; **to p. oneself too far** exigirse demasiado; **to p. sb for payment** apremiar a algn a pagar; **to p. sb into doing sth** empujar a algn a hacer algo, *Am* incitar a algn para que haga algo; *Fam* **to be (hard) pushed for time/money** estar apurado(a) *or RP* corto(a) de tiempo (**c**) *Com Fam (product)* promover, promocionar; *(trade)* fomentar; **to p. drugs** pasar *or* vender *or RP* transar droga; **to p. sales** hacer una campaña de venta
3 *vi (shove)* empujar; **'push'** *(on door)* 'empujar'; *(on bell, button etc)* 'pulse'; **to p. through the crowd** abrirse paso a empujones entre la multitud

push about, push around *vt Fam (bully)* intimidar

push ahead *vi* progresar, avanzar; **to p. ahead with sth** progresar con algo

push aside *vt (object)* apartar; *Fig (person)* hacer caso omiso de

push in 1 *vt* empujar
2 *vi (interrupt)* entrometerse, colarse

push off *vi (in boat)* desatracar; *Fam (leave)* marcharse; **p. off!** ¡lárgate!

push on *vi (continue)* seguir adelante

push over *vt (knock over)* volcar

push through *vt* abrirse paso *or* camino por *or* entre

push-bike ['pʊʃbaɪk] *n* bicicleta *f*

push-button ['pʊʃbʌtən] *adj* con botón de mando

pushchair ['pʊʃtʃeər] *n Br* sillita *f* (de ruedas)

pusher ['pʊʃər] *n Fam (of drugs)* camello *m*, *Am* dealer *m*

pushover ['pʊʃəʊvər] *n Fam* **it's a p.** está chupado; **she's a p.** es un ligue fácil

push-up ['pʊʃʌp] *n US (exercise)* flexión *f* de brazos

pushy ['pʊʃɪ] *adj* (**pushier, pushiest**) *Fam* agresivo(a), insistente

puss [pʊs] *n Fam* gatito *m*, minino *m*; **p., p.!** ¡miz, miz!

pussy ['pʊsɪ] *n Fam* **p. (cat)** gatito *m*, minino *m*; **p. willow** sauce *m* blanco

pussyfoot ['pʊsɪfʊt] *vi Fam* **to p. around** *or* **about** andarse con rodeos

pustule ['pʌstjuːl] *n* pústula *f*

put [pʊt] **1** *vt (pt & pp **put**)* (**a**) *(gen)* poner; *(place)* colocar, fijar; *(add)* echar, añadir; *(insert)* meter, introducir; *(when packing)* coger; **have you p. in any ties?** ¿has cogido corbatas?; **not to know where to p. oneself** no saber dónde ponerse *or* esconderse; **to p. the ball into the net** meter la pelota en la red; **to p. a bone out of joint** dislocarse un hueso; **to p. a child to bed** acostar a un niño; **to p. a coin into a slot** meter una moneda en una ranura; **to p. a picture up on the wall** colgar *or* fijar un cuadro en la pared; **to p. a stop to sth** prohibir algo, poner término a algo; **to p. an animal out of its misery** rematar un animal; **to p. money on a horse** jugarse dinero en un caballo; **to p. one's arms around sb** abrazar a algn; **to p. one's energy into sth** concentrarse en (hacer) algo; **to p. one's head on sb's shoulder** recostar or apoyar la cabeza en el hombro de algn; **to p. one's head round the door** asomarse por detrás de la puerta; **to p. one's pen through sth** tachar algo; **to p. one thing before another** anteponer una cosa a otra; **to p. salt in food** echar or añadir sal a la comida; **to p. sb on the train/plane** dejar a algn en el tren/el avión, acompañar a algn al tren/al avión; **to p. sb's mind al ease** tranquilizar a algn; **to p. sb/sth to the test** poner a algn/algo a la prueba; **to p. sb to a lot of trouble** ocasionar a algn muchas molestias; **to p. sth in the dustbin** echar or tirar algo a la basura; **to p. sth on the table** poner algo en la mesa; **to p. sth to good use** hacer buen uso de algo; **to p. the blame on sb** echar la culpa a algn; **to p. the finishing touches to sth** dar los últimos toques a algo; Fig **to p. one's foot in it** meter la pata (**b**) (ask, present) presentar, exponer; **to p. a proposal to a committee** someter una propuesta a una comisión; **to p. a question to sb** hacer una pregunta a algn; Jur **to p. one's case before the jury** exponer su caso al jurado (**c**) (express) expresar, decir; **as you p. it** como tú lo dices; **to. p. it bluntly** hablando sin rodeos; **to p. it mildly** por decirlo de alguna manera; **to p. sth into Spanish** traducir algo al español; **to p. sth into words** expresar algo en palabras; **to p. sth simply** explicar algo de manera sencilla (**d**) (estimate) calcular; **I'd p. his age at thirty** yo le echaría treinta años; **they p. the price at $50** calcularon que costaría unas 50 dólares (**e**) Com **to p. a product on the market** lanzar un producto al mercado (**f**) Fin (money) ingresar, poner; (invest) invertir; **to p. money into a bank account** Esp ingresar or Am depositar dinero en una cuenta (**g**) Sport **to p. the shot** lanzar el peso

  2 vi Naut **to p. into port** hacer escala en un puerto; **to p. to sea** zarpar

  3 adv **to be hard p. to do sth** costarle mucho hacer algo; **to stay p.** quedarse quieto(a)

put about vt (rumour etc) hacer correr; **she p. it about that ...** hizo correr la voz de que ...

put across vt (**a**) (idea etc) comunicar (**b**) Fam **to p. one across on sb** engañar a algn

put aside vt (**a**) (save) (money) ahorrar; (time) reservar; (food) guardar, poner a un lado (**b**) Fig (forget) dejar de lado

put away vt (**a**) (tidy away) guardar en su sitio, recoger (**b**) Fam (lock up) encerrar; (in prison) meter en la cárcel (**c**) Fam (eat) zamparse (**d**) (save money) ahorrar

put back vt (**a**) (postpone) aplazar (**b**) **to p. the clock back** retrasar la hora; Fig volver atrás (**c**) Fam (drink) beberse

put by vt (save) (money) ahorrar

put down 1 vt (**a**) (set down) dejar; **I couldn't p. the book down** leí el libro de un tirón (**b**) (suppress) sofocar; (humiliate) humillar; (criticize) criticar (**c**) (animal) rematar (**d**) (write down) apuntar; **p. it down in writing** ponlo por escrito; **to p. one's name down on a list** apuntarse en una lista

  2 vi (plane) aterrizar

put down for vt (donation) anotar, apuntar; (register) inscribir; **p. us down for $10** apuntanos por 10 dólares; **to p. one's name down for a course** inscribirse en un curso; **to p. a child down for a school** matricular a un niño en un colegio

put down to vt (attribute) achacar, atribuir; **to p. sth down to inexperience** atribuir algo a la falta de experiencia

put forward vt (theory) exponer; (proposal, suggestion) hacer; **to p. one's name forward for sth** presentarse or ofrecerse como candidato(a) para algo

put in 1 vt (**a**) (install) instalar (**b**) Agr (seeds) sembrar (**c**) (complaint, request) hacer, presentar; Jur (petition) presentar; Fig **to p. in a good word for sb** hablar a favor de algn (**d**) Pol (candidate) elegir (**e**) (spend time) pasar; **to p. in one's time reading** pasar el tiempo leyendo; **to p. in overtime** trabajar or hacer horas extraordinarias

  2 vi (**a**) Naut hacer escala (**at** en) (**b**) (apply) solicitar; **to p. in for a post** solicitar un puesto

put off vt (**a**) (postpone) aplazar; Fig **he kept putting off a decision** no logró decidirse (**b**) (dissuade) disuadir; **don't be p. off** no te desanimes; **to p. sb off (doing) sth** quitarle or Am sacarle a algn las ganas de (hacer) algo; **the smell puts me off eating** el olor me quita las ganas de comer; **to p. sb off with an excuse** quitarse a algn de encima con una excusa

put on vt (**a**) (clothes) poner, ponerse; **to p. clothes on sb** ponerle ropa a algn; **to p. on one's clothes** vestirse (**b**) Theat (show) montar; (concert) presentar (**c**) (increase) aumentar; (add to) añadir; **to p. on weight** aumentar de peso, engordar (**d**) (provide) poner; **to p. on an extra bus/train service** poner un servicio suplementario de autobuses/de trenes (**e**) (switch on) (radio, central heating) poner; (light) encender, Am prender; (water, gas) abrir; **to p. the kettle on** poner el agua a calentar; Aut **to p. on the brakes/handbrake** frenar/poner el freno de mano (**f**) (pretend) fingir; **to p. on a straight face** poner cara de serio(a); **he's just putting it on** está disimulando (**g**) (inform) informar; **to p. sb on to sth** informar a algn sobre algo (**h**) US Fam (tease) **you're putting me on!** ¡me estás tomando el pelo or vacilando!

put out 1 vt (**a**) (switch off) apagar (**b**) (place outside) sacar; **to p. the cat out** sacar el gato; **to p. clothes** or **washing out to dry** tender la ropa a secar (**c**) (extend) (arm) extender; (tongue) sacar; (hand) tender; **to p. one's head out of a window** asomarse por una ventana (**d**) Med dislocar (**e**) (publish) (periodical) publicar, editar; (spread) (rumour) hacer correr, hacer circular (**f**) (extinguish) apagar (**g**) (annoy) molestar; (inconvenience) incordiar; **I hope I'm not putting you out** espero que no te moleste (**h**) (anger) enfadar, enojar; **to be p. out by sb/sth** enfadarse or enojarse con algn/por algo

  2 vi Naut **to p. out to sea** hacerse a la mar

put over vt Fam comunicar

put through vt (**a**) (push through) hacer aceptar, forzar; (law) hacer aprobar (**b**) Tel (connect) poner; **p. me through to Pat, please** póngame con Pat, por favor (**c**) (unpleasant experience) hacer pasar por

put together vt (**a**) (join) unir, reunir, juntar; **all of them p. together** todos(as) juntos(as); Fig **to p. two and two together** atar cabos (**b**) (assemble) armar, montar

put up 1 vt (**a**) (raise) levantar, subir; (flag) izar; (shelves, picture) colocar; (curtains) colgar; (building) construir; (umbrella) abrir; (tent) armar; **to p. one's hair up** recogerse el pelo; **p. your hands up!** ¡manos arriba! (**b**) (prices) subir, aumentar (**c**) (offer) ofrecer; **to p. sth up for sale** poner algo a la venta; Pol **to p. sb up as a candidate** presentar a algn como candidato(a); **to p. up a reward for sth** ofrecer una recompensa por algo (**d**) (accommodate) alojar, hospedar (**e**) (resistance) luchar; **to p. up a fight** resistirse, ofrecer resistencia

  2 vi (stay) alojarse, hospedarse

put upon vt (exploit) explotar; **to p. upon sb** explotar a algn; **to be p. upon** dejarse pisotear

put up to vt **to p. sb up to sth** incitar a algn a hacer algo

put up with vt (tolerate) aguantar, soportar; **to p. up with sth/sb** aguantar algo/a algn

putative ['pjuːtətɪv] adj Fml presunto(a), supuesto(a); Jur (father) putativo(a)

put-down ['pʊtdaʊn] *n Fam* desaire *m*

put-on ['pʊtɒn] **1** *n Fam* **is that one of your put-ons?** ¿me estás tomando el pelo *or Esp Carib Méx* vacilando? **2** *adj* fingido(a), simulado(a)

putrefy ['pjuːtrɪfaɪ] *vi* (*pp & pt* **putrefied**) *Fml* podrir, pudrir

putrid ['pjuːtrɪd] *adj Fml* podrido(a)

putsch [pʊtʃ] *n* golpe *m* de estado

putt [pʌt] *Golf* **1** *n* putt *m*, golpe *m* con el putt(er) **2** *vt & vi* golpear con el putt(er), patear

putter ['pʌtər] *n Golf* putter *m*

putting ['pʌtɪŋ] *n Golf* minigolf *m* ❑ **p. green** *Br* minigolf *m*; *(part of golf course)* = terreno para practicar el putt

putty ['pʌtɪ] *n* masilla *f*; *Fig* **to be p. in sb's hands** ser como barro en las manos de algn

put-up ['pʊtʌp] *adj Fam* **a p.-up job** una estafa, un montaje

puzzle ['pʌzəl] **1** *n (game)* puzzle *m*; *(crossword)* crucigrama *m*; *(jigsaw)* rompecabezas *m inv*; *Fig (mystery)* misterio *m*, enigma *m*; *(riddle)* acertijo *m*; **it's a p. to me how/why ...** no entiendo cómo/por qué ... **2** *vt* dejar perplejo(a); **her letter puzzled us** su carta nos dejó perplejos; **to be puzzled about sth** no entender algo; **to p. sth out** lograr entender algo **3** *vi* **to p. about sth** dar vueltas a algo (en la cabeza)

puzzle out *vt* resolver; **to p. out a problem** resolver un problema

puzzle over *vt* **to p. over sth** dar vueltas a algo (en la cabeza)

puzzled ['pʌzəld] *adj* perplejo(a); **a p. expression** una cara de perplejidad

puzzlement ['pʌzəlmənt] *n* perplejidad *f*

puzzling ['pʌzəlɪŋ] *adj* extraño(a), curioso(a)

PVC [piːviːˈsiː] *n (abbr* **polyvinyl chloride**) cloruro *m* de polivinilo, PVC *m*

Pvt *US Mil (abbr* **Private**) soldado *m* raso

PW [piːˈdʌbəljuː] *Br (abbr* **Policewoman**) mujer *f* policía

pygmy ['pɪgmɪ] *n* pigmeo(a) *m,f*; *Fig* enano(a) *m,f*

pyjamas [pəˈdʒɑːməz] *npl* pijama *m*, *Am* piyama *m or f*.

pylon ['paɪlən] *n* (**a**) *Elec* poste *m*, torre *f* (de conducción eléctrica) (**b**) *Archit* pilón *m*, pilar *m*

pyramid ['pɪrəmɪd] *n* pirámide *f*

pyre [paɪər] *n* hoguera *f*, pira *f*

Pyrenees [pɪrəˈniːz] *npl* **the P.** los Pirineos

Pyrex® ['paɪreks] *n* pírex® *m*

pyromaniac [paɪərəʊˈmeɪnɪæk] *n* pirómano(a) *m,f*

pyrotechnics [paɪərəʊˈtekniks] *n* (**a**) *(gen)* pirotecnia *f* (**b**) *pl (fireworks)* fuegos *mpl* artificiales

python ['paɪθən] *n* pitón *m*

Q

Q, q [kju:] *n (the letter)* Q, q *f*

Qatar [kæ'tɑ:r] *n* Qatar

Qatari [kæ'tɑ:rɪ] **1** *n* persona *f* de Qatar
 2 *adj* de Qatar

QC [kju:'si:] *n Br Jur (abbr* **Queen's Counsel***)* abogado(a) *m,f* del Estado

QED [kju:i:'di:] *Math (abbr* **quod erat demonstrandum***)* (which was to be proved), lo que había que demostrar

qt *(abbr* **quart(s)***)* cuarto(s) *m(pl)* de galón

Q-tip® ['kju:tɪp] *n US* bastoncillo *m* (de algodón)

qty *Com (abbr* **quantity***)* cantidad *f*

quack [kwæk] **1** *n* **(a)** *(of duck)* graznido *m* **(b)** *Fam (doctor)* curandero(a) *m,f*
 2 *vi* graznar

quad [kwɒd] *n Fam* **(a)** *Br (of school, university)* patio *m* interior **(b)** *(quadruplet)* cuatrillizo(a) *m,f* **(c)** **q. bike** moto *f* de rally *(con cuatro ruedas gruesas)*

quadrangle ['kwɒdræŋgəl] *n* **(a)** *Geom* cuadrángulo *m* **(b)** *(courtyard)* patio *m* interior

quadrant ['kwɒdrənt] *n* cuadrante *m*

quadraphonic [kwɒdrə'fɒnɪk] *adj* cuadrafónico(a)

quadratic [kwɒ'drætɪk] *adj Math* cuadrático(a); **q. equation** ecuación *f* de segundo grado

quadrilateral [kwɒdrɪ'lætərəl] *adj & n* cuadrilátero *(m)*

quadriplegic [kwɒdrɪ'pli:dʒɪk] *adj & n* tetrapléjico(a) *(m,f)*

quadruped ['kwɒdrʊped] *n Fml* cuadrúpedo *m*

quadruple ['kwɒdrʊpəl, kwɒ'dru:pəl] **1** *n* cuádruplo *m*
 2 *adj* cuádruple
 3 *vt* cuadruplicar
 4 *vi* cuadruplicarse

quadruplet ['kwɒdrʊplɪt, kwɒ'dru:plɪt] *n* cuatrillizo(a) *m,f*

quadruplicate [kwɒ'dru:plɪkɪt] **1** *adj* cuadruplicado(a)
 2 *n* cuadruplicado *m*; **in q.** por cuadruplicado
 3 [kwɒ'dru:plɪkeɪt] *vt* cuadruplicar

quaff [kwɒf, kwɑ:f] *vt* beber a grandes tragos

quagmire ['kwægmaɪər, 'kwɒgmaɪər] *n* **(a)** *(land)* cenagal *m* **(b)** *Fig (embarrassing situation)* atolladero *m*

quail¹ [kweɪl] *n Orn* codorniz *f*

quail² [kweɪl] *vi Fig* encogerse, empequeñecerse; **he quailed at the sight of the sword** al ver la espada se encogió

quaint [kweɪnt] *adj (picturesque)* pintoresco(a); *(original)* singular; *(odd)* extraño(a), raro(a); **q. idea** idea *f* singular; **q. style** estilo *m* original

quake [kweɪk] **1** *vi (with fear)* temblar; **to q. at the knees** temblarle a uno las piernas
 2 *n Fam* temblor *m* de tierra

Quaker ['kweɪkər] *n Rel* cuáquero(a) *m,f*

Quakerism ['kweɪkərɪzəm] *n Rel* cuaquerismo *m*

qualification [kwɒlɪfɪ'keɪʃən] *n* **(a)** *(ability)* aptitud *f*; **to have/not to have the qualifications to ...** estar/no estar capacitado(a) para ... **(b)** *(requirement)* requisito *m*; **she has the right qualifications for the job** es la persona idónea para el puesto **(c)** *(diploma etc)* título *m* **(d)** *(reservation)* reserva *f*; **to accept without q.** aceptar sin reserva **(e)** *(restriction)* limitación *f* **(f)** *(act of qualifying)* **even after q. Bill found it difficult to get a job** a Bill le costó encontrar trabajo incluso despúes de haberse graduado

qualified ['kwɒlɪfaɪd] *adj* **(a)** *(competent)* capacitado(a); *(having diploma)* titulado(a); **to be q. to do sth** estar capacitado(a) para hacer algo; **q. teacher** profesor *m* titulado **(b)** *(modified)* restringido(a), limitado(a); **q. approval** aprobación *f* condicional

qualifier ['kwɒlɪfaɪər] *n* **(a)** *(person, team)* clasificado(a) *m,f*; *(match)* partido *m* de clasificación, eliminatoria *f* **(b)** *Ling* calificador *m*, modificador *m*

qualify ['kwɒlɪfaɪ] **1** *vt (pt & pp* **qualified***)* **(a)** *(make eligible, entitle)* capacitar, habilitar; **the letter qualified him for membership** la carta le dio derecho a hacerse socio **(b)** *(modify) (report)* modificar; *(declaration)* matizar; *Ling* calificar; **the adjective qualifies the noun** el adjetivo califica al sustantivo; **would you like to q. what you've just said?** ¿le importaría puntualizar lo que acaba de decir?
 2 *vi* **(a)** *(obtain diplomas etc)* **to q. as** sacar el título de; **she qualified as a doctor** obtuvo el título de médico; **when did you q.?** ¿cuándo terminaste la carrera? **(b)** *(in competition)* quedar clasificado(a)

qualifying ['kwɒlɪfaɪɪŋ] *adj (round, exam)* eliminatorio(a)

qualitative ['kwɒlɪtətɪv, 'kwɒlɪteɪtɪv] *adj* cualitativo(a)

qualitatively ['kwɒlɪtətɪvlɪ] *adv* cualitativamente

quality ['kwɒlɪtɪ] *n* **(a)** *(degree of excellence)* calidad *f*; **of good q.** de buena calidad; **of poor q.** de poca calidad; *Com* **q. goods** géneros *mpl* de calidad ❑ **q. control** control *m* de calidad; *Br* **q. newspapers** prensa *f* no sensacionalista; **q. time** = tiempo que uno reserva para disfrutar de la pareja, la familia, los amigos, etc., y alejarse de las preocupaciones laborales y domésticas **(b)** *(attribute)* cualidad *f*; **he has many good qualities** tiene muchas cualidades buenas

qualm [kwɑ:m] *n* **(a)** *(scruple)* escrúpulo *m*; **to have no qualms about doing sth** no tener escrúpulos en hacer algo **(b)** *(doubt)* duda *f*; *(worry)* inquietud *f*, ansia *f*; **he has qualms about whether he's doing his work properly** está intranquilo porque no sabe si da la talla con su trabajo

quandary ['kwɒndərɪ, 'kwɒndrɪ] n *(dilemma)* dilema m; *(difficulty)* apuro m; **to be in a q.** estar en un dilema

quango ['kwæŋgəʊ] n *(pl* **quangos**) *Br Pol* = organismo público semiindependiente

quanta ['kwɒntə] *npl see* **quantum**

quantifiable [kwɒntɪ'faɪəbəl] adj cuantificable; **a q. amount** una cantidad cuantificable

quantify ['kwɒntɪfaɪ] vt cuantificar

quantitative ['kwɒntɪtətɪv, 'kwɒntɪteɪtɪv] adj cuantitativo(a)

quantity ['kwɒntɪtɪ] n **(a)** *(amount)* cantidad f; **a small/large q. of ...** una pequeña/gran cantidad de ...; **in great quantities** en grandes cantidades, en abundancia; **unknown q.** incógnita f **(b)** *Math* cantidad f

quantum ['kwɒntəm] n *(pl* **quanta**) **(a)** *Phys* quantum m; **q. theory** teoría f de los quanta **(b)** *(amount) Fml* cantidad f

quarantine ['kwɒrəntiːn] **1** n cuarentena f; **to be in q.** estar en cuarentena

2 vt poner en cuarentena

quarrel ['kwɒrəl] **1** n **(a)** *(argument)* riña f, pelea f; **to have a big q.** pelearse; **to pick a q.** meterse con algn, buscar camorra (con algn) **(b)** *(disagreement)* desacuerdo m; **I have no q. with her** no tengo queja de ella, no tengo nada contra ella

2 vi *(pt & pp* **quarrelled,** *US* **quarreled)* **(a)** *(argue)* pelearse, reñir **(b)** **to q. with sth** discutir algo, poner algo en duda; **she quarrelled with their decision** les discutió su decisión

quarrelsome ['kwɒrəlsəm] adj camorrista, pendenciero(a)

quarry¹ ['kwɒrɪ] *Min* **1** n cantera f

2 vt *(pt & pp* **quarried)** extraer, sacar

quarry² ['kwɒrɪ] n presa f; *Fig* persona f acorralada; **the hunter's dog looked for the q.** el perro del cazador buscaba la presa

quart [kwɔːt] n *(measurement)* cuarto m de galón *(Br = 1,13 litros; US = 0,94 litros)*

quarter ['kwɔːtər] **1** n **(a)** *(fraction)* cuarto m, cuarta parte f; **a q. of a century** un cuarto de siglo; **a q. of an hour** un cuarto de hora; **a q. of a cake** la cuarta parte de un pastel; **what's a q. of sixteen?** ¿cuál es la cuarta parte de dieciséis? ❏ *US Can Mus* **q. note** negra f **(b)** *(telling the time)* **it's a q. to three,** *US* **it's a q. of three** son las tres menos cuarto; **it's a q. past** *or US* **after three** son las tres y cuarto **(c)** *(three months)* trimestre m; **he pays the gas bill every q.** paga la cuenta del gas por trimestres **(d)** *Br (weight)* cuarto m de libra *(= 113,4g)*; **a q. of tea** un cuarto de libra de té **(e)** *US (coin)* cuarto m (de dólar), veinticinco centavos mpl **(f)** *(district)* barrio m; **the Latin Q.** el barrio latino; **the old q.** el casco antiguo **(g)** *(area, people)* **there was criticism from all quarters** todos lo criticaron **(h)** *(of moon)* cuarto m; **the first q.** cuarto creciente; **the last q.** cuarto menguante **(i)** *Fig (mercy)* **they gave no q. to the enemy** no dieron cuartel al enemigo **(j)** **quarters** *(lodgings)* alojamiento m *sing; Mil* **officers' q.** residencia f *sing* de oficiales; **married q.** viviendas fpl del ejército; **at close q.** muy cerca

2 vt **(a)** *(cut into quarters)* dividir en cuartos; *(reduce)* reducir a la cuarta parte **(b)** *(accommodate)* alojar **(c)** *Hist (body)* descuartizar

quarterback ['kwɔːtəbæk] n *US Sport* quarterback m *(en fútbol americano, jugador que dirige el ataque),* mariscal m de campo

quarterdeck ['kwɔːtədek] n *Naut* alcázar m

quarterfinal ['kwɔːtəfaɪnəl] n *Sport* cuarto m de final

quarterfinalist ['kwɔːtəfaɪnəlɪst] n *Sport* participante mf en el cuarto de final

quarterlight ['kwɔːtəlaɪt] n *Br Aut* ventanilla f trasera

quarterly ['kwɔːtəlɪ] **1** adj trimestral

2 n publicación f trimestral

3 adv trimestralmente, cada tres meses

quartermaster ['kwɔːtəmaːstər] n **(a)** *Mil* oficial m de intendencia **(b)** *Naut* cabo m de la Marina

quartet(te) [kwɔː'tet] n *Mus* cuarteto m

quarto ['kwɔːtəʊ] **1** adj *(paper size)* en cuarto

2 n *(pl* **quartos**) *(book)* libro m en cuarto

quartz [kwɔːts] n *Min* cuarzo m; **q. watch** reloj m de cuarzo

quash [kwɒʃ] vt **(a)** *Jur (sentence)* anular, invalidar **(b)** *(uprising)* aplastar, sofocar

quasi ['kwaːzɪ, 'kweɪzaɪ] adv casi; *Jur* **q. contract** cuasicontrato m

quatrain ['kwɒtreɪn] n *Lit* cuarteto m

quaver ['kweɪvər] **1** n **(a)** *Mus (note)* corchea f; *(sound)* trémolo m **(b)** *(trembling)* temblor m

2 vi *(sound)* temblar; **his voice quavered** su voz temblaba

quavering ['kweɪvərɪŋ] adj tembloroso(a), trémulo(a); **voice** voz f temblorosa *or* trémula

quay [kiː] n *Naut* muelle m

quayside ['kiːsaɪd] n *Naut* muelle m

queasiness ['kwiːzɪnɪs] n náuseas fpl

queasy ['kwiːzɪ] adj **(queasier, queasiest)** mareado(a); **to feel q.** *(ill)* sentirse mal, tener náuseas; *(worried)* estar preocupado(a)

Quebec [kwɪ'bek] n *(provincia f de)* Quebec; *(city)* Quebec *(capital)*

Quechua ['ketʃwə] n *(person)* quechua mf; *(language)* quechua m

queen [kwiːn] n **(a)** *(of country)* reina f; **the Q. Mother** la reina madre **(b)** *Cards Chess* dama f, reina f **(c)** *Ent* reina f **(d)** *Offens* loca f, marica m

queenly ['kwiːnlɪ] adj **(queenlier, queenliest)** regio(a), de reina

queer [kwɪər] **1** adj **(a)** *(strange)* extraño(a), raro(a); **a q. looking lad** un chico de aspecto raro **(b)** *Fam (mad)* loco(a) **(c)** *Fam (unwell)* mareado(a); **to feel q.** no encontrarse bien **(d)** *Offens* marica, maricón **(e)** *Br Fam* **in q. street** estar con la soga *or Esp* el agua al cuello

2 n *Slang Pej* marica m, maricón m

3 vt *Fam* **to q. sb's pitch** fastidiar los planes de algn

quell [kwel] vt reprimir, sofocar, frenar; **to q. a rebellion** reprimir *or* sofocar una rebelión

quench [kwentʃ] vt **(a)** *(thirst)* saciar **(b)** *(fire)* apagar

querulous ['kwerʊləs, 'kwerjʊləs] adj *Fml* quejumbroso(a); **a q. old lady** una vieja quejumbrosa

query ['kwɪərɪ] **1** n **(a)** *(question)* pregunta f **(b)** *Ling* signo m de interrogación **(c)** *Comptr* **q. language** languaje m de consulta (estructurado)

2 vt *(pt & pp* **queried)** *(ask)* preguntar; *(have doubts about)* poner en duda

quest [kwest] **1** n *Literary* búsqueda f, busca f; **to go in q. of sth** ir en búsqueda *or Esp* busca de algo

2 vi buscar

question ['kwestʃən] **1** n **(a)** *(interrogative)* pregunta f; **questions and answers** preguntas y respuestas; **to ask sb a q.** hacer una pregunta a algn; **without q.** sin rechistar; **he did it without q.** lo hizo sin rechistar; *Hum* **to pop the q.** declararse ❏ **q. mark** *Ling* signo m de interrogación; *Fig* interrogante m; *Ling* **q. tag** coletilla f **(b)** *(problem, issue, matter)* asunto m, cuestión f, problema m; **it's a q. of** se trata de; **it's a q. of two hours** es cuestión de dos horas; **it's all a q. of time** con el tiempo se arreglará; **that's the q.**

he aquí el problema; **the Northern Ireland q.** el problema de Irlanda del Norte; **the q. of overtime** el asunto de las horas extras (**c**) *(criticism, doubt)* en duda; **beyond q.** fuera de duda; **in q.** en duda; **open to q.** dudoso(a); **to bring sth into q.** hacer reflexionar sobre algo; **to call sth into q.** poner algo en duda (**d**) *(suggestion, possibility)* posibilidad *f*; **out of the q.** imposible, impensable; **that's out of the q.** ¡ni hablar¡; **there is no q. of recovering the money** now ya no hay posibilidad alguna de recuperar el dinero (**e**) *Sch (exam)* pregunta *f*, problema *m*

2 *vt* (**a**) *(ask questions)* hacer preguntas; *(interrogate)* interrogar; **he questioned the boy** le hizo preguntas al niño; **they are being questioned about the theft** están interrogándoles sobre el robo (**b**) *(query)* poner en duda, dudar de

questionable ['kwestʃənəbəl] *adj (doubtful)* dudoso(a); *(debatable)* discutible; **of q. taste** de gusto dudoso; **it's q. whether he's right** eso de que tenga razón es discutible

questioner ['kwestʃənər] *n* interrogador(a) *m,f*

questioning ['kwestʃənɪŋ] *adj* inquisitivo(a); **a q. look** una mirada inquisitiva

questionnaire ['kwestʃə'neər] *n* cuestionario *m*

queue [kju:] *Br* **1** *n* (**a**) *Br (line)* cola *f*; **to jump the q.** colarse (**b**) *Comptr* cola *f*
2 *vi Br* **to q. (up)** hacer cola; **they queued up for the bus** hicieron cola para el autobús

queue-jumper ['kju:dʒʌmpər] *n Br Fam* = persona que se cuela

quibble ['kwɪbəl] **1** *n* pega *f*, objeción *f*
2 *vi* poner pegas (**with** a); *Fam* buscarle tres pies al gato

quibbler ['kwɪbələr] *n* polemista *mf*, porfiador(a) *m,f*

quiche [ki:ʃ] *n* quiche *m or f*

quick [kwɪk] **1** *adj* (**a**) *(fast)* rápido(a); **a q. look** un vistazo; **a q. reply** una respuesta pronta; **a q. sale** una venta inmediata; **a q. snack** un tentempié, un bocado; **as q. as lightning** *or* **a flash** como un rayo *or* una bala *or* una centella; **be q.!** ¡rápido!, ¡date prisa!, *Am* ¡apúrate!; **it's quicker by plane** se llega antes en avión; *Mil* **q. march!** ¡de frente!; **the quickest way** el camino más corto; **to have a q. lunch** tomar un bocado a la hora de comer; *Fam* **to have a q. one** tomar una copita (**b**) *(clever)* espabilado(a), listo(a); *(wit)* agudo(a); **a q. child** un niño espabilado *or* despierto (**c**) *(hasty)* genuido(a), irritable; **he's q. to take offence** se enfada por nada; **she has a q. temper** tiene un genio vivo; **to be q. to anger** tener mal genio
2 *n* **to cut sb to the q.** herir a algn en lo vivo

quick-acting ['kwɪkæktɪŋ] *adj* de acción rápida

quick-change ['kwɪktʃeɪndʒ] *adj Theat* **q.-c. artist** transformista *mf*

quicken ['kwɪkən] **1** *vt* (**a**) *(speed up)* acelerar; **to q. one's pace** acelerar el paso (**b**) *(stimulate)* estimular
2 *vi* (**a**) *(speed up)* acelerarse (**b**) *(become stronger)* acrecentarse, aumentarse

quickening ['kwɪkənɪŋ] *n Med* movimientos *mpl* del feto

quickie ['kwɪkɪ] *n Fam* **to have a q.** *(drink)* tomar una copa rápida

quicklime ['kwɪklaɪm] *n* cal *f* viva

quickly ['kwɪklɪ] *adv* rápido, rápidamente, de prisa

quickness ['kwɪknɪs] *n* (**a**) *(speed)* rapidez *f*, velocidad *f* (**b**) *(of wit)* agudeza *f*, viveza *f*

quicksand ['kwɪksænd] *n* arenas *fpl* movedizas

quicksilver ['kwɪksɪlvər] *n* mercurio *m*

quick-tempered [kwɪk'tempəd] *adj* irascible, de genio vivo

quick-witted [kwɪk'wɪtɪd] *adj* agudo(a), listo(a)

quid[1] [kwɪd] *n Br Slang* libra *f* (esterlina); **five q.** cinco libras

quid[2] [kwɪd] *n* mascada *f* de tabaco ·

quiescent [kwɪ'esənt] *adj Literary* inactivo(a), pasivo(a)

quiet ['kwaɪət] **1** *n* (**a**) *(silence)* silencio *m* (**b**) *(calm)* tranquilidad *f*, sosiego *m* (**c**) *(secretly) Fam* **to do sth on the q.** hacer algo a escondidas *or Esp* a la chita callando
2 *adj* (**a**) *(silent)* silencioso(a); *(town, street)* tranquilo(a); **a q. engine** un motor silencioso; **a q. voice** una voz suave; **keep q.¡** ¡silencio¡; **q. footsteps** pasos *mpl* silenciosos (**b**) *(peaceful, calm)* tranquilo(a); **she leads a very q. life** lleva una vida muy tranquila (**c**) *Com Fin* apagado(a); **business is q. today** hoy hay poco negocio; **the market was q.** el mercado estaba apagado (**d**) *(unobtrusive)* callado(a); **a q. man** un hombre reservado; **of a q. disposition** de carácter reservado (**e**) *(secret)* confidencial; **I'd like a q. word with him** quiero hablarle en privado; **keep (it) q.!** ¡no se lo digas a nadie¡ (**f**) *(without fuss, tranquil)* tranquilo(a); **a q. supper** una cena sencilla; **it was a q. wedding** la boda se celebró en la intimidad (**g**) *(not showy) (clothes)* sobrio(a), poco llamativo(a); *(colours)* suave, apagado(a)
3 *vt US* silenciar, calmar; **I quieted the children (down)** calmé a los niños
4 *vi US* calmarse

quieten ['kwaɪətən] **1** *vt* *(silence)* callar; *(calm)* tranquilizar, calmar
2 *vi (silence)* callarse; *(calm)* calmarse, tranquilizarse

quieten down *Br* **1** *vi* calmar
2 *vi* calmarse

quietism ['kwaɪətɪzəm] *n Rel* quietismo *m*

quietist ['kwaɪətɪst] *n Rel* quietista *mf*

quietly ['kwaɪətlɪ] *adv* (**a**) *(silently, not noisily)* silenciosamente; *(not loudly)* bajo; **he spoke q.** habló en voz baja (**b**) *(calmly)* tranquilamente (**c**) *(discreetly)* discretamente, con discreción (**d**) *(simply)* sencillamente

quietness ['kwaɪətnɪs] *n* (**a**) *(silence)* silencio *m* (**b**) *(calm)* tranquilidad *f*, sosiego *m*

quiff [kwɪf] *n Br (of hair)* copete *m*

quill [kwɪl] *n* (**a**) *(feather, pen)* pluma *f* (**b**) *(of porcupine)* púa *f*

quilt [kwɪlt] **1** *n* edredón *m*
2 *vt* acolchar; **quilted jacket** chaqueta *f* acolchada

quin [kwɪn] *n* quintillizo(a) *m,f*

quince [kwɪns] *n Bot Culin* membrillo *m*; **q. jelly** carne *f* de membrillo

quinine ['kwɪni:n, *US* 'kwaɪnaɪn] *n* quinina *f*

quintessence [kwɪn'tesəns] *n Fml* quintaesencia *f*

quintessential [kwɪntɪ'senʃəl] *adj* fundamental

quintet(te) [kwɪn'tet] *n Mus* quinteto *m*

quintuple ['kwɪntjʊpəl, kwɪn'tju:pəl] **1** *adj* quíntuplo(a)
2 *n* quíntuplo *m*
3 *vt* quintuplicar

quintuplet ['kwɪntjʊplɪt, kwɪn'tju:plɪt] *n* quintillizo(a) *m,f*

quip [kwɪp] **1** *n (remark)* salida *f*, ocurrencia *f*; *(joke)* chiste *m*
2 *vi* bromear

quire [kwaɪər] *n* mano *f* de papel

quirk [kwɜ:k] *n* (**a**) *(peculiarity)* manía *f*, rareza *f* (**b**) *(of fate)* vicisitud *f*, avatar *m*

quirky ['kwɜ:kɪ] *adj* (**quirkier, quirkiest**) raro(a)

quisling ['kwɪzlɪŋ] *n* colaboracionista *mf*, traidor(a) *m,f*

quit [kwɪt] **1** *vt* (*pt & pp* **quitted** *or esp US* **quit**) (**a**) *(leave)* dejar, abandonar; **to q. one's job** dejar el trabajo; *US* **he's q. school** ha dejado los estudios (**b**) *(stop)* **q. making that noise!** ¡deja de hacer ese ruido! (**c**) *Comptr* salir de
2 *vi* (**a**) *(go)* irse, marcharse; *(give up)* dimitir (**b**) *(cease)* dejar de hacer algo (**c**) *Comptr* salir

3 *adj* **quits** iguales; **let's call it q.** dejémoslo estar; **to be q. estar en paces**

quite [kwaɪt] *adv* (**a**) *(entirely)* del todo, totalmente; **I q. agree** estoy totalmente de acuerdo; **I q. understand** te entiendo perfectamente; **she hasn't q. recovered** no se ha recuperado del todo; **she's q. right** tiene toda la razón (**b**) *(fairly, rather)* bastante; **it's q. warm** hace bastante calor; **q. a few** bastantes; **q. a while** un buen rato; **q. often** con bastante frecuencia; **she's q. a good artist** es bastante buena como artista; **that's q. enough!** ¡ya basta!, ¡ya está bien! (**c**) *(exceptional)* excepcional; **he's q. a gentleman** está hecho un señor; **she's q. a character** es un tipo original; **to be q. something** ser increíble; **you've got q. a voice** tienes una voz excepcional (**d**) *(exactly)* exactamente; **I'm not q. sure** no estoy exactamente seguro; **it isn't q. what I wanted** no es exactamente lo que quería; **q. (so)!** ¡en efecto!, ¡exacto!

quiver¹ [ˈkwɪvər] **1** *n (trembling) (of lips, voice)* temblor *m*; *(of eyelids)* parpadeo *m*; *(shiver)* estremecimiento *m*
2 *vi* temblar, estremecerse

quiver² [ˈkwɪvər] *n* aljaba *f*, carcaj *m*

quivering [ˈkwɪvərɪŋ] *adj* tembloroso(a)

quixotic [kwɪkˈsɒtɪk] *adj* quijotesco(a)

quiz [kwɪz] **1** *n (pl* **quizzes**) (**a**) *Rad TV (competition)* concurso *m* (**b**) *US (test)* examen *m*, control *m*
2 *vt (pt & pp* **quizzed**) hacer preguntas

quizmaster [ˈkwɪzmɑːstər] *n* moderador *m*

quizzical [ˈkwɪzɪkəl] *adj* (**a**) *(bemused)* burlón(ona); **a q. smile** una sonrisa burlona (**b**) *(enquiring)* curioso(a); **a q. glance** una mirada llena de curiosidad

quoin [kɔɪn] *n Archit* piedra *f* angular

quoit [kɔɪt] *n* herrón *m*, aro *m*; **quoits** *(game)* juego *m* de los aros

quorum [ˈkwɔːrəm] *n* quórum *m*

quota [ˈkwəʊtə] *n* (**a**) *(proportional share)* cuota *f*, parte *f* (**b**) *(prescribed amount, number)* cupo *m*

quotable [ˈkwəʊtəbəl] *adj (remark, writer, book)* que se presta a ser citado

quotation [kwəʊˈteɪʃən] *n* (**a**) *Lit* cita *f*; **q. marks** comillas *fpl* (**b**) *(Stock Exchange)* cotización *f*

quote [kwəʊt] **1** *vt* (**a**) *(cite)* citar; **can I q. you?** ¿puedo repetir tus mismas palabras? (**b**) *Com* **to q. a price** dar un presupuesto (**c**) *(Stock Exchange)* cotizar
2 *n* (**a**) *Lit* cita *f* (**b**) *Com* presupuesto *m*

quotidian [kwəʊˈtɪdɪən] *adj Fml* cotidiano(a)

quotient [ˈkwəʊʃənt] *n* (**a**) *Math* cociente *m* (**b**) *(degree)* grado *m*, coeficiente *m*; **intelligence q.** coeficiente *m* intelectual

qv [kjuːˈviː] *Fml (abbr* **quod vide**) véase, v.

R

R, r [ɑːr] *n (the letter)* R, r *f; Fam Fig* **the three Rs** = lectura, escritura y aritmética

R (**a**) *(abbr* **Rex***)* rey *m* (**b**) *(abbr* **Regina***)* reina *f* (**c**) *US Pol (abbr* **Republican***)* republicano(a) (**d**) *US Cin (abbr* **restricted***)* = no recomendado(a) para menores

r *(abbr* **right***)* derecho(a), dcho(a)

RA [ɑːr'eɪ] *n Br* (**a**) *(abbr* **Royal Academy (of Arts)***)* Real Academia *f* (de las Artes) (**b**) *(abbr* **Royal Academician***)* miembro *mf* de la Real Academia

rabbi ['ræbaɪ] *n Rel* rabí *m*, rabino *m*

rabbit ['ræbɪt] **1** *n* (**a**) *Zool* conejo(a) *m,f* ❑ **r. hole** madriguera *f*; **r. hutch** conejera *f*
2 *vi Fam* enrollarse

rabble ['ræbəl] *n* multitud *m*, muchedumbre *f; Pej* **the r.** la chusma, el populacho

rabble-rouser ['ræbəlraʊzər] *n Pej* demagogo(a) *m,f*, agitador(a) *m,f*

rabble-rousing ['ræbəlraʊzɪŋ] *Pej* **1** *adj (speech etc)* demagógico(a)
2 *n (incitement)* demagogía *f*, agitación *f*

rabid ['ræbɪd, 'reɪbɪd] *adj* (**a**) *Med* rabioso(a) (**b**) *Fig (person)* furioso(a); *(supporter)* fanático(a)

rabies ['reɪbiːz] *n Med* rabia *f*

RAC [ɑːreɪ'siː] *n Br (abbr* **Royal Automobile Club***)* = organización británica de ayuda al automovilista, *Esp* RACE *m, Arg* ACA *m*

raccoon [rə'kuːn] *n Zool* mapache *m*

race¹ [reɪs] **1** *n* (**a**) *Sport* carrera *f*; **long-distance r.** carrera de larga distancia; **to run a r.** participar en una carrera; *Fig* **r. against time** carrera contra reloj ❑ *Fig* **arms r.** carrera *f* de armamentos; **r. meeting** carreras *fpl* (de caballos) (**b**) *(in sea, river)* corriente *f* fuerte (**c**) *Br* **the races** las carreras (de caballos)
2 *vt* (**a**) *(compete with)* competir con; **I'll r. you!** ¡te echo una carrera! (**b**) *(car, horse)* hacer correr (**c**) *(engine)* acelerar
3 *vi (go quickly)* correr; *(pulse)* acelerarse

race² [reɪs] *n (people)* raza *f*; **the human r.** la raza humana ❑ **r. relations** relaciones *fpl* raciales; **r. riots** disturbios *mpl* raciales

racecourse ['reɪskɔːs] *n Br Sport* hipódromo *m*

racehorse ['reɪshɔːs] *n Sport* caballo *m* de carreras

racer ['reɪsər] *n Sport* (**a**) *(person)* corredor(a) *m,f* (**b**) *(bicycle)* bicicleta *f* de carreras; *(car)* coche *m* de carreras

racetrack ['reɪstræk] *n Sport* (**a**) *(for cars, people, bikes)* pista *f* (**b**) *US (for horses)* hipódromo *m*

racial ['reɪʃəl] *adj* racial; **r. prejudice** prejuicio *m* racial

racialism ['reɪʃəlɪzəm] *n Br* racismo *m*

racialist ['reɪʃəlɪst] *adj & n Br* racista *(mf)*

racially ['reɪʃəlɪ] *adv* racialmente; **r. prejudiced** con prejuicios raciales

racing ['reɪsɪŋ] **1** *n Sport* carreras *fpl* ❑ **horse r.** carreras *fpl* de caballos
2 *adj* de carreras; **r. bike** moto *f* de carreras; **r. car** coche *m or Am* carro *m or CSur* auto *m* de carreras

racism ['reɪsɪzəm] *n* racismo *m*

racist ['reɪsɪst] *adj & n* racista *(mf)*

rack [ræk] **1** *n* (**a**) *(shelf)* estante *m*; *(for clothes)* percha *f*, perchero *m* ❑ **luggage r.** portaequipajes *m inv*; **plate r.** escurreplatos *m inv; Aut* **roof r.** baca *f* (**b**) *Hist (for torture)* potro *m; Fig* **on the r.** angustiado(a); *Fam* **to go to r. and ruin** venirse abajo (**c**) *Tech* **r. and pinion** engranaje *m* de cremallera y piñón ❑ *Rail* **r. railway** (ferrocarril *m* de) cremallera *m*
2 *vt Literary (torment)* atormentar; *Fam Fig* **to r. one's brains** devanarse los sesos

racket¹ ['rækɪt] *n* (**a**) *(din)* ruido *m*, alboroto *m, Esp* jaleo *m*; **to kick up a r.** armar alboroto *or Esp* jaleo (**b**) *(swindle)* timo *m*, estafa *f, (shady business)* chanchullo *m*

racket² ['rækɪt] *n Sport* raqueta *f*

racketeer [rækə'tɪər] *n* estafador(a) *m,f*, timador(a) *m,f*

racketeering [rækə'tɪərɪŋ] *n* crimen *m* organizado

raconteur [rækɒn'tɜːr] *n* anecdotista *mf*

racquet ['rækɪt] *n see* **racket²**

racquetball ['rækɪtbɔːl] *n US Sport* = juego parecido al frontón

racy ['reɪsɪ] *adj* (**racier, raciest**) *(lively)* vivo(a); *(risqué)* atrevido(a)

RADA ['rɑːdə] *n Br (abbr* **Royal Acadamy of Dramatic Art***)* Real Academia *f* de las Artes Dramáticas

radar ['reɪdɑːr] *n* radar *m* ❑ **r. operator** operador(a) *m,f* de radar; **r. screen** pantalla *f* de radar

radial ['reɪdɪəl] **1** *adj* radial
2 *n Aut* neumático *m or Col Méx* llanta *f or Arg* goma *f* (de cubierta) radial

radiance ['reɪdɪəns] *n* resplandor *m*

radiant ['reɪdɪənt] *adj (gen)* radiante, resplandeciente

radiate ['reɪdɪeɪt] **1** *vt (gen)* irradiar; *Fig* **she radiated happiness** rebosaba de alegría
2 *vi Phys* irradiar, emitir radiaciones

radiation [reɪdɪ'eɪʃən] *n* radiación *f*

radiator ['reɪdɪeɪtər] *n* radiador *m*

radical ['rædɪkəl] **1** *adj* radical
2 *n* (**a**) *(person)* radical *mf* (**b**) *Chem Math* radical *m*

radicalism ['rædɪkəlɪzəm] *n* radicalismo *m*

radii ['reɪdɪaɪ] *npl see* **radius**

radio ['reɪdɪəʊ] **1** n (pl **radios**) radio f; **on the r.** en or por la radio □ **r. ham** radioaficionado(a) m,f; **r. station** emisora f (de radio)
2 vt **to r. sb** enviar un mensaje a algn por radio
radioactive [reɪdɪəʊ'æktɪv] adj radiactivo(a), radioactivo(a)
radioactivity [reɪdɪəʊæk'tɪvɪtɪ] n radiactividad f, radioactividad f
radiocarbon [reɪdɪəʊ'kɑːbən] n Chem radiocarbón m
radio-controlled [reɪdɪəʊkən'trəʊld] adj teledirigido(a)
radiograph ['reɪdɪəʊɡrɑːf] n radiografía f
radiographer [reɪdɪ'ɒɡrəfər] n radiógrafo(a) m,f
radiography [reɪdɪ'ɒɡrəfɪ] n radiografía f
radiologist [reɪdɪ'ɒlədʒɪst] n radiólogo(a) m,f
radiology [reɪdɪ'ɒlədʒɪ] n radiología f
radiotherapist [reɪdɪəʊ'θerəpɪst] n radioterapeuta mf
radiotherapy [reɪdɪəʊ'θerəpɪ] n radioterapia f
radish ['rædɪʃ] n Bot rábano m
radium ['reɪdɪəm] n Chem radio m □ **r. therapy** radioterapia f
radius ['reɪdɪəs] n (pl **radii** or **radiuses**) Anat Geom radio m; **within a r. of** en un radio de
radon ['reɪdɒn] n Chem radón m
RAF [ɑːreɪ'ef, Fam ræf] n Br (abbr **Royal Air Force**) fuerzas fpl aéreas británicas
raffia ['ræfɪə] n Bot rafia f
raffish ['ræfɪʃ] adj pícaro(a)
raffle ['ræfəl] **1** n sorteo m, rifa f
2 vt sortear, rifar
raft¹ [rɑːft] n balsa f
raft² [rɑːft] n Fam montón m, cantidad f; **a r. of things** cantidad de cosas
rafter ['rɑːftər] n Archit viga f, par m
rag¹ [ræɡ] n (a) (torn piece) harapo m, andrajo m; **in rags** harapiento(a); Fig **from rags to riches** de la pobreza a la riqueza □ **r. doll** muñeca f de trapo (b) (for cleaning) trapo m; Br Fam Fig **it was like a red r. to a bull** era una provocación descarada (c) Fam **rags** (clothes) trapos mpl; **the r. trade** (el ramo de) la confección (d) Fam (newspaper) periodicucho m
rag² [ræɡ] Br Old-fashioned **1** n (prank) broma f pesada; Univ función f benéfica
2 vt (pt & pp **ragged**) gastar bromas a
ragamuffin ['ræɡəmʌfɪn] n golfillo(a) m,f, pilluelo(a) m,f
rag-and-bone [ræɡən'bəʊn] adj Br **r.-a.-b. man** trapero m
ragbag ['ræɡbæɡ] n Fam mezcla f, barullo m
rage [reɪdʒ] **1** n (fury) rabia f, cólera f; Fam Fig (craze) moda; **it's all the r.** hace furor
2 vi (a) (person) rabiar, estar furioso(a) (b) Fig (storm, sea) rugir; (wind) bramar
ragged ['ræɡɪd] adj (a) (clothes) hecho(a) jirones (b) (person) harapiento(a), andrajoso(a); Fam Fig **to run sb r.** dejar hecho(a) polvo a algn (c) (edge) dentado(a), mellado(a) (d) Fig (uneven) desigual
raging ['reɪdʒɪŋ] adj (a) (angry) furioso(a) (b) Fig (sea) embravecido(a) (c) (storm) violento(a); (intense) feroz, tremendo(a)
raglan ['ræɡlən] n abrigo m raglán □ **r. sleeve** manga f raglán
ragtime ['ræɡtaɪm] n Mus ragtime m
ragwort ['ræɡwɜːt] n Bot azuzón m, hierba f de Santiago
raid [reɪd] **1** n (a) Mil incursión f, raid m □ **air r.** ataque m

aéreo (b) (police) redada f (c) (robbery etc) atraco m
2 vt (a) Mil (place) asaltar, hacer una incursión en (b) (police) hacer una redada en (c) (rob) asaltar, atracar; Fam **to r. the larder** vaciar la despensa
raider ['reɪdər] n (a) (invader) invasor(a) m,f (b) (thief) ladrón(ona) m,f
rail¹ [reɪl] n (a) (of stairway, balcony, bridge) baranda f, Esp barandilla f □ **curtain r.** barra f de cortina; **towel r.** toallero m (b) Rail riel m, carril f; **by r.** (mail) por ferrocarril; (travel) en tren; Fam Fig **to go off the rails** irse por el mal camino □ **r. strike** huelga f de ferroviarios
rail in vt (animals, people) encerrar, cercar
rail off vt (land) encerrar, cercar
rail² [reɪl] vi Literary despotricar (**against** contra)
railcar ['reɪlkɑːr] n US vagón m
railcard ['reɪlkɑːd] n Br Rail = tarjeta para obtener billetes de tren con descuento
railing ['reɪlɪŋ] n (usu pl) verja f
railroad ['reɪlrəʊd] **1** n US (red f de) ferrocarril m □ **r. track** vía f férrea
2 vt Fam **to r. sb into sth** presionar a algn para que haga algo
railway ['reɪlweɪ] n Br (red f de) ferrocarril m □ **r. carriage** vagón m; **r. line, r. track** vía f férrea; **r. station** estación f de ferrocarril
railwayman ['reɪlweɪmən] n (pl **railwaymen**) Br Can ferroviario m
rain [reɪn] **1** n lluvia f; Fig (of bullets, insults) lluvia f; **the rains** (season) las lluvias; **in the r.** bajo la lluvia; Fam **come r. or shine** pase lo que pase; Fam Fig **as right as r.** fresco(a) como una rosa, sano(a) como una manzana
2 vt Fam **it's raining cats and dogs** llueve a cántaros
3 vi llover; **it's raining** llueve; Prov **it never rains but it pours** las desgracias nunca vienen solas
rain down vi Fig (criticisms etc) caer encima, llover
rain off vt Sport interrumpir or cancelar por la lluvia
rainbow ['reɪnbəʊ] n arco m iris □ Pol **r. coalition** = coalición de partidos minoritarios
raincoat ['reɪnkəʊt] n impermeable m
raindrop ['reɪndrɒp] n gota f de lluvia
rainfall ['reɪnfɔːl] n (falling of rain) precipitación f; (amount) pluviosidad f
rainforest ['reɪnfɒrɪst] n selva f tropical
rainproof ['reɪnpruːf] adj impermeable
rainstorm ['reɪnstɔːm] n aguacero m
rainwater ['reɪnwɔːtər] n agua f de lluvia
rainy ['reɪnɪ] adj (**rainier, rainiest**) lluvioso(a); **a r. day** un día de lluvia; Fig **to save** or **keep sth for a r. day** guardar algo para los tiempos difíciles
raise [reɪz] **1** n US (pay increase) aumento m (de sueldo)
2 vt (a) (gen) levantar; (glass) brindar; (voice) levantar, subir; (building, statue) erguir; Fig (embargo, restriction etc) levantar; Fig **to r. an eyebrow** hacer un gesto de desaprobación; Fam **to r. the roof** armar un follón (b) (increase) aumentar; Cards subir; **I'll r. you ten** igualo y subo diez (c) (money, help) reunir (d) (problem, subject) plantear (e) (crops, animals, children) criar (f) Rad comunicar con (g) (smile, laugh) provocar (h) (standards) mejorar
raised [reɪzd] adj (a) (elevated) (ground, platform) elevado(a) (b) (embossed) con relieve
raisin ['reɪzən] n pasa f
raison d'être [reɪzɒn'detrə] n Fml razón f de ser
rake¹ [reɪk] **1** n (a) (garden tool) rastrillo m (b) (for fire) hurgón m

2 vt (**a**) (leaves) rastrillar (**b**) (fire) hurgar (**c**) (with gunfire) barrer (**d**) (search for) escudriñar, registrar, hurgar

rake in vt Fam forrarse; **he's raking it in** se está forrando or Méx llenando de lana

rake over vt (topic, question) insistir en

rake up vt (**a**) (people) reunir (**b**) (bring up) sacar a luz; **to r. up the past** desenterrar el pasado

rake² [reɪk] n (dissolute man) calavera m, libertino m

rake³ [reɪk] n Theat (stage) inclinación f

raked [reɪkt] adj Theat (stage) inclinado(a)

rake-off ['reɪkɒf] n Slang tajada f, comisión f

rakish¹ ['reɪkɪʃ] adj (dissolute) libertino(a)

rakish² ['reɪkɪʃ] adj (jaunty) desenvuelto(a)

rally ['rælɪ] **1** n (**a**) (gathering) reunión f; Pol mitin m; **peace r.** manifestación f pacifista (**b**) Aut rallye m (**c**) Ten pelota f, jugada f
2 vt (pt & pp rallied) (support, troops) reunir
3 vi (after setback) reponerse, recuperarse

rally round vi unirse, formar una piña

RAM [ræm] n Comptr (abbr **random access memory**) memoria f de acceso aleatorio, RAM

ram [ræm] **1** n (**a**) Zool carnero m ❑ Mil **battering r.** ariete m (**b**) Tech maza f
2 vt (pt & pp rammed) (**a**) (drive into place) hincar, clavar; (cram) embutir; Fam **to r. sth down sb's throat** machacar algo a algn; Fam **to r. sth home** demostrar algo, hacer algo patente (**b**) (crash into) chocar con, darse contra

Ramadan [ræmə'dæn] n Rel ramadán m

ramble ['ræmbəl] **1** n (walk) paseo m, caminata f
2 vi (**a**) (walk) pasear, hacer una excursión a pie (**b**) Fig (digress) divagar (**c**) (plant) trepar

rambler ['ræmblər] n (**a**) (person) excursionista mf (**b**) Bot rosal m trepador

rambling ['ræmblɪŋ] **1** adj (**a**) (speech, writing) confuso(a), enmarañado(a); (incoherent) incoherente (**b**) (house) laberíntico(a), lleno(a) de recovecos (**c**) Bot trepador(a)
2 (**a**) (walking) **to go r.** ir de excursión, hacer senderismo (**b**) **ramblings** (digressions) divagaciones fpl

ramification [ræmɪfɪ'keɪʃən] n ramificación f

ramp [ræmp] n (**a**) (sloping surface) rampa f (**b**) Av (movable stairway) escalerilla f; Aut **hydraulic r.** elevador m hidráulico

rampage [ræm'peɪdʒ] **1** n destrozos mpl; **to be** or **go on the r.** comportarse violentamente, provocar destrozos
2 vi **to r. about** comportarse como un loco

rampant ['ræmpənt] adj desenfrenado(a), incontrolado(a); **corruption is r.** la corrupción está muy extendida

rampart ['ræmpɑːt] n Archit muralla f

ram-raiding ['ræm'reɪdɪŋ] n Br alunizaje m, = robo en una tienda embistiendo contra el escaparate con un vehículo

ramrod ['ræmrɒd] **1** n Tech baqueta f
2 adj tieso(a), derecho(a)

ramshackle ['ræmʃækəl] adj destartalado(a)

ran [ræn] pt see **run**

ranch [rɑːntʃ] n US rancho m, hacienda f

rancher ['rɑːntʃər] n US ranchero(a) m,f, haciendado(a) m,f

rancid ['rænsɪd] adj rancio(a)

rancorous ['ræŋkərəs] adj Fml rencoroso(a)

rancour, US **rancor** ['ræŋkər] n Fml rencor m

random ['rændəm] **1** n **at r.** al azar
2 adj fortuito(a), arbitrario(a); Comptr **r. access memory** memoria f de acceso aleatorio; **r. selection** selección f hecha al azar; **r. shot** bala f perdida

randy ['rændɪ] adj (**randier**, **randiest**) Br Fam caliente, Esp Méx cachondo(a)

rang [ræŋ] pt see **ring**

range [reɪndʒ] **1** n (**a**) (of mountains) cordillera f, sierra f (**b**) US (open land) pradera f, dehesa f (**c**) (choice, diversity) gama f, surtido m, variedad f; (of products) gama f ❑ **price r.** escala f de precios (**d**) Mus registro m (**e**) Mil firing **r.** campo m de tiro (**f**) (of bullet, gun) alcance m, distancia f máxima; **at close r.** de cerca; **long-/short-r. nuclear missiles** misiles mpl nucleares de largo/corto alcance (**g**) (capacity, extent) campo m; **r. of vision** campo de visión (**h**) (vehicles) autonomía f (**i**) Culin cocina f de carbón
2 vi (**a**) (extend) extenderse (**to** hasta) (**b**) (vary) variar, oscilar; **prices r. from five to twenty dollars** los precios oscilan entre cinco y veinte dólares
3 vt (**a**) (encompass) abarcar, comprender; (join together) reunir, unir (**b**) Literary (animals, people) vagar por, recorrer

rangefinder ['reɪndʒfaɪndər] n Mil Phot telémetro m

ranger ['reɪndʒər] n (**a**) (forest) **r.** guardabosques mf inv (**b**) US (mounted policeman) policía m montado (**c**) US Mil comando m

Rangoon [ræŋ'guːn] n Rangún m

rangy ['reɪndʒɪ] adj (**rangier**, **rangiest**) (**a**) (long-legged) larguirucho(a) (**b**) (spacious) amplio(a)

rank¹ [ræŋk] **1** n (**a**) Mil (row) fila f; **the ranks** los soldados rasos; **to break ranks** romper filas; **to rise from the ranks** ser ascendido(a) a oficial ❑ Pol **the r. and file** las bases (del partido) (**b**) (position in army) graduación f; (in society) rango m, categoría f; **to pull r.** abusar de su autoridad; **what r. is he?** ¿qué graduación tiene? (**c**) Br (taxi) **r.** parada f de taxis
2 vt (classify) clasificar, catalogar
3 vi (figure) estar, figurar; **to r. above/below sb** ser superior/inferior a algn; **to r. with** estar al mismo nivel que

rank² [ræŋk] adj Fml (**a**) (vegetation) exuberante (**b**) (foul-smelling) fétido(a) (**c**) (thorough) total, absoluto(a), completo(a); (injustice) flagrante

ranking ['ræŋkɪŋ] **1** n (position) clasificación f, ranking m; **the world r.** el ranking mundial
2 adj US (senior) de mayor rango

rankle ['ræŋkəl] vi **to r. with sb** dolerle or escocerle a algn

ransack ['rænsæk] vt (**a**) (plunder) saquear (**b**) (rummage in) registrar

ransom ['rænsəm] **1** n rescate m; **to hold sb to r.** pedir rescate por algn; Fig poner a algn entre la espada y la pared
2 vt (free) rescatar

rant [rænt] vi (shout) vociferar; Fam **to r. and rave** pegar gritos

rap [ræp] **1** n (**a**) (sharp blow) golpe m seco; (on door) golpecito m (**b**) (reprimand) amonestación f, reprimenda f; Fam **to take the r.** pagar el pato; US Fam **r. sheet** ficha f con los antecedentes penales (**c**) Mus rap m
2 vt & vi (pt & pp rapped) (**a**) (knock) golpear; Fig **to r. sb over the knuckles** echar Esp un rapapolvo or Méx un buen regaño or RP un buen reto a algn
3 vi (**a**) **to r. at the door** llamar a la puerta (**b**) US Fam (chat) charlar, CAm Méx platicar

rap out vt (order, question etc) gritar

rapacious [rə'peɪʃəs] adj Fml (greedy) rapaz; (voracious) voraz

rape¹ [reɪp] Jur **1** n violación f
2 vt violar

rape² [reɪp] n Bot colza f

rape³ [reɪp] n (skins and stalks of grapes) orujo m

rapeseed ['reɪpsiːd] n Bot semilla f de colza ❑ **r. oil** aceite m de colza

rapid ['ræpɪd] **1** adj rápido(a)
2 rapids npl (in river) rápidos mpl

rapidity [rə'pɪdɪtɪ] *n* rapidez *f*

rapidly ['ræpɪdlɪ] *adv* rápidamente

rapier ['reɪpɪər] *n* estoque *m*

rapist ['reɪpɪst] *n* violador(a) *m,f*

rapper ['ræpər] *n* rapero(a) *m,f*

rapport [ræ'pɔːr] *n* compenetración *f,* entendimiento *m*; **to have a good r.** compenetrarse bien

rapt [ræpt] *adj (distracted)* absorto(a); *(daydreaming)* ensimismado(a); *(attention)* profundo(a)

rapture ['ræptʃər] *n* éxtasis *m,* arrobamiento *m*; **to go into raptures over sth** extasiarse ante algo

rapturous ['ræptʃərəs] *adj Literary (with ecstasy)* extático(a), arrobado(a); *(with enthusiasm)* muy entusiasta; *(welcome)* caluroso(a)

rare[1] [reər] *adj* (**a**) *(uncommon)* raro(a), poco común; *(exceptional)* excepcional (**b**) *(atmosphere)* enrarecido(a) (**c**) *Fam* estupendo(a)

rare[2] [reər] *adj Culin (steak)* poco hecho(a)

rarebit ['reəbɪt] *n Culin* tostada *f* de queso

rarefied ['reərɪfaɪd] *adj* enrarecido(a)

rarely ['reəlɪ] *adv* raramente, raras veces

raring ['reərɪŋ] *adj Fam* ansioso(a), con ganas; *Fam* **to be r. to do sth** morirse de ganas de hacer algo

rarity ['reərɪtɪ] *n* rareza *f*

rascal ['rɑːskəl] *n* (**a**) *(naughty child)* pillo(a) *m,f,* granuja *mf* (**b**) *Old-fashioned or Hum (scoundrel)* bribón(ona) *m,f*

rash[1] [ræʃ] *n* (**a**) *Med* erupción *f* cutánea, sarpullido *m* (**b**) *(spate)* racha *f*

rash[2] [ræʃ] *adj (reckless)* impetuoso(a); *(words, actions)* precipitado(a), imprudente

rasher ['ræʃər] *n Br Culin* loncha *f*

rashly ['ræʃlɪ] *adv* sin reflexionar, a la ligera

rashness ['ræʃnɪs] *n (recklessness)* impetuosidad *f,* *(of words, actions)* precipitación *f,* imprudencia *f*

rasp [rɑːsp] **1** *n* (**a**) *Tech* escofina *f* (**b**) *(grating noise)* chirrido *m*
  2 *vt Tech* raspar, escofinar; *Fig* **to r. out** decir con voz áspera

raspberry ['rɑːzbərɪ] *n Bot* (**a**) *(fruit)* frambuesa *f* (**b**) *(plant)* frambueso *m* (**c**) *Fam* pedorreta *f*; **to blow a r. at sb** *(jeer)* hacer pedorretas a algn

rasping ['rɑːspɪŋ] *adj (sound)* chirriante; *(voice)* áspero(a)

Rastafarian [ræstə'feərɪən], *Fam* **Rasta** ['ræstə] *adj & n* rastafari *(mf)*

rat [ræt] *n* (**a**) *Zool* rata *f, Fig* **to smell a r.** olerse algo raro; *Fam Fig* **to look like a drowned r.** estar hecho(a) una sopa ❏ **r. poison** raticida *m* (**b**) *Fam (scoundrel)* canalla *m* (**c**) *US Fam (informer)* soplón(ona) *m,f, Esp* chivato(a) *m,f*
  2 *vi (pt & pp* **ratted**) (**a**) *(hunt rats)* cazar ratas (**b**) *Fam (inform)* **to r. on sb** chivarse de algn, denunciar a algn (**c**) *Fam (break promise)* romper

ratchet ['rætʃɪt] *n Tech* trinquete *m* ❏ **r. wheel** rueda *f* de trinquete

rate [reɪt] **1** *n* (**a**) *(ratio)* índice *m,* tasa *f; Fam Fig* **at any r.** *(at least)* al menos, por lo menos; *(anyway)* en todo caso; *Fam Fig* **at this r.** si continuamos así, si las cosas siguen así ❏ **birth r.** tasa *f* de natalidad; **growth r.** índice *m* de crecimiento (**b**) *(cost)* precio *m,* tarifa *f;* **hourly r.** precio por hora ❏ **postal r.** tarifa *f* postal; *Fin* **r. of exchange/interest** tipo *m* de cambio/interés (**c**) **at the r. of** *(speed)* a la velocidad *f* de; *(quantity)* a razón de ❏ *Med* **pulse r.** frecuencia *f* del pulso (**d**) *(quality)* categoría *f,* cualidad *f;* **first/second r.** de primera/segunda categoría (**e**) *Br Formerly* **rates** impuestos *mpl* municipales
  2 *vt* (**a**) *(estimate)* estimar (**b**) *(evaluate)* tasar (**c**) *(consider)*

considerar; **how did you r. the film?** ¿qué te pareció la película?

rateable ['reɪtəbəl] *adj Br* **r. value** valor *m* catastral

ratepayer ['reɪtpeɪər] *n Br Formerly* contribuyente *mf (de impuestos municipales)*

rather ['rɑːðər] **1** *adv* (**a**) *(quite)* más bien, bastante; *(very much so)* muy; **he's r. good-looking** es muy guapo; **it's r. cold** hace bastante frío; **we r. fancy going** nos apetece ir (**b**) *(more accurately)* mejor dicho; **r. than** *(instead of)* en vez de; *(more than)* más que; **r. them than me!** ¡ellos, no yo! (**c**) *(preference)* **she would r. stay here** prefiere quedarse aquí
  2 [rɑː'ðɜːr] *interj Old-fashioned Fam* ¡por supuesto!, ¡cómo no!; **do you like it? — r.!** ¿te gusta? — ¡ya lo creo! *or* ¡por supuesto!

ratification [rætɪfɪ'keɪʃən] *n Fml* ratificación *f*

ratify ['rætɪfaɪ] *vt (pt & pp* **ratified**) *Fml* ratificar

rating ['reɪtɪŋ] *n* (**a**) *(valuation)* tasación *f; (score)* valoración *f* (**b**) *TV* **(programme) ratings** índice *m sing* de audiencia (**c**) *Br Naut* marinero *m* sin graduación

ratio ['reɪʃɪəʊ] *n (pl* **ratios**) razón *f,* proporción *f,* relación *f;* **in direct r. to** en razón directa con; **in the r. of** a razón de

ration ['ræʃən, *US* 'reɪʃən] **1** *n* (**a**) *(allowance)* ración *f,* porción *f;* **to be on rations** sufrir racionamientos ❏ **r. book** cartilla *f* de racionamiento (**b**) **rations** víveres *mpl*
  2 *vt* racionar

rational ['ræʃənəl] *adj* racional, lógico(a)

rationale [ræʃə'nɑːl] *n* base *f,* razón *f* fundamental

rationalist ['ræʃənəlɪst] *n* racionalista *mf*

rationality [ræʃə'nælɪtɪ] *n* racionalidad *f*

rationalization [ræʃənəlaɪ'zeɪʃən] *n* racionalización *f*

rationalize ['ræʃənəlaɪz] *vt* racionalizar

rationing ['ræʃənɪŋ] *n* racionamiento *m*

ratted ['rætɪd] *adj Fam (drunk)* ciego(a)

rattle ['rætəl] **1** *n* (**a**) *(noise of train, cart)* traqueteo *m; (of metal)* repiqueteo *m; (of glass)* tintineo *m* (**b**) *(toy)* sonajero *m; (instrument)* matraca *f* (**c**) *(of death)* estertor *m*
  2 *vt* (**a**) *(keys, chains)* agitar, hacer sonar (**b**) *Fam (unsettle)* crispar, poner nervioso(a); **to get sb rattled** poner nervioso(a) a algn
  3 *vi (gen)* sonar; *(metal)* repiquetear; *(glass)* tintinear

rattle away *vi see* **rattle on**

rattle off *vt (person)* recitar *or* decir a toda prisa

rattle on *vi* parlotear, *Esp* cascar

rattle through *vt (work etc)* terminar rápidamente

rattler ['rætlər] *n US Fam* serpiente *f* de cascabel

rattlesnake ['rætəlsneɪk] *n Zool* serpiente *f* de cascabel

ratty ['rætɪ] *adj* (**rattier, rattiest**) *Br Fam* malhumorado(a)

raucous ['rɔːkəs] *adj (hoarse)* ronco(a); *(shrill)* estridente, chillón(ona)

raunchy ['rɔːntʃɪ] *adj* (**raunchier, raunchiest**) *Fam* lascivo(a)

ravage ['rævɪdʒ] *Fml* **1** *n* **ravages** estragos *mpl*
  2 *vt* asolar, devastar, destrozar

rave [reɪv] **1** *vi* (**a**) *(be delirious)* delirar (**b**) *(be angry)* enfurecerse (**at** con) (**c**) *(speak enthusiastically)* entusiasmarse (**about** por); **to r. about sth** poner algo por las nubes
  2 *n* (**a**) *MusTheat* **r. review** crítica *f* muy favorable (**b**) *Fam (trend)* moda *f*
  3 *adj Fam (fashionable)* de moda, enrollado(a)

raven ['reɪvən] *n Orn* cuervo *m;* **r.-haired** de pelo negro como el azabache

ravenous ['rævənəs] *adj* voraz; **I'm r.** tengo un hambre que no veo

raver ['reɪvər] n Br Fam juerguista mf

rave-up ['reɪvʌp] n Br Fam juerga f, farra f, Am pachanga f

ravine [rə'viːn] n Geog barranco m

raving ['reɪvɪŋ] n (a) (delirium) delirio m; Fam r. mad loco(a) de atar (b) (rambling talk) divagaciones fpl

ravish ['rævɪʃ] vt (a) Old-fashioned (rape) violar (b) (plunder) saquear (c) Literary encantar, cautivar

ravishing ['rævɪʃɪŋ] adj (person) encantador(a), cautivador(a)

raw [rɔː] **1** adj (a) (uncooked) crudo(a) (b) (not processed) bruto(a); (pure) puro(a) □ r. material materia f prima (c) (emotions) instintivo(a), primario(a) (d) (weather) crudo(a), frío(a) (e) (unfair) injusto(a); r. deal trato m injusto (f) (wound) abierto(a); r. flesh carne viva (g) US (inexperienced) novato(a), inexperto(a), bisoño(a); Mil r. recruits novatos mpl (h) (frank) franco(a) (i) (uncivilized) tosco(a)
2 n (a) (tender spot) carne f viva; to touch sb on the r. herir a algn en lo vivo (b) in the r. Fam (naked) en cueros, en pelotas

rawness ['rɔːnɪs] n (a) (of food, weather) crudeza f (b) US (lack of experience) falta f de experiencia

ray¹ [reɪ] n (of light etc) rayo m; Fig r. of hope resquicio m de esperanza

ray² [reɪ] n (fish) raya f

ray³ [reɪ] n Mus (note) re m

rayon ['reɪɒn] n Tex rayón m

raze [reɪz] vt arrasar; to r. a building to the ground arrasar un edificio

razor ['reɪzər] n (wet) navaja f de afeitar; (electric) máquinilla f de afeitar □ r. blade hoja f de afeitar

razorbill ['reɪzəbɪl] n Orn alca f común

razor-sharp [reɪzə'ʃɑːp] adj (knife etc) muy afilado(a); Fig (mind) perspicaz

razor-shell ['reɪzəʃel] n (fish) navaja f

razzle ['ræzəl] n Fam juerga f; to go out on the r. ir de marcha, irse de juerga

razzmatazz [ræzmə'tæz] n Fam jaleo m

RC [ɑː'siː] adj & n (abbr Roman Catholic) católico(a) (m,f)

R & D [ɑːrən'diː] n Com (abbr research and development) I+D, investigación f y desarrollo

Rd (abbr Road) calle f, c/

RDA [ɑːdiː'eɪ] n (abbr recommended daily allowance) cantidad f diaria recomendada

RE [ɑːr'iː] n Br Sch (abbr religious education) educación f religiosa

re [riː] prep Com respecto a, con referencia a

reach [riːtʃ] **1** vt (a) (arrive at) llegar a, alcanzar; (grab) alcanzar; (agreement) llegar a; Sport to r. the finals llegar a la final (b) (contact) comunicarse, localizar; where can I r. you? ¿dónde te puedo localizar?
2 vi (arrive at) llegar, alcanzar; (grab) alcanzar; he can't r. no llega; to r. for sth intentar coger algo; to r. out extender la mano
3 n (a) (range) alcance m; out of r. fuera del alcance; within r. al alcance; within easy r. muy cerca (b) Box (extension) extensión f del brazo (c) reaches (on a river) recta f sing

reachable ['riːtʃəbəl] adj (place) accesible; (goal, objective) asequible, alcanzable

react [rɪ'ækt] vi reaccionar

reaction [rɪ'ækʃən] n reacción f

reactionary [rɪ'ækʃənərɪ] adj & n reaccionario(a) (m,f)

reactivate [rɪ'æktɪveɪt] vt reactivar

reactive [rɪ'æktɪv] adj Chem reactivo(a)

reactor [rɪ'æktər] n Phys reactor m

read [riːd] **1** n Fam lectura f; to have a quiet r. pasar un rato tranquilo leyendo
2 vt (pt & pp read [red]) (a) (book, newspaper etc) leer; (poem) recitar (b) (decipher) descifrar (c) (understand) entender; (interpret) interpretar; it can be r. both ways se puede interpretar de las dos maneras; to r. sb's lips leer los labios de algn; Fig to r. between the lines leer entre líneas; Fig to r. sb's mind adivinar el pensamiento a algn; Fam do you r. me? ¿me entiendes?; Rad ¿me recibe? (d) Typ (proofs) corregir, Am revisar (e) Br Univ (subject) estudiar
3 vi (a) (dial) marcar (b) (signpost, text) decir, poner; the sign r. 'No Parking' el letrero decía 'Prohibido Aparcar'

read into vt (interpret) interpretar erróneamente; don't r. too much into this book no busques mensaje en este libro porque no lo hay

read out vt leer en voz alta

read up vt (subject) investigar (on -), buscar datos (on sobre)

readable ['riːdəbəl] adj (a) (interesting) interesante, que vale la pena leerse (b) (legible) legible

reader ['riːdər] n (a) (of books, newspapers etc) lector(a) m,f; she's a keen r. lee mucho (b) (book) libro m de lectura; a Russian r. un libro de lectura en ruso (c) Br Univ = profesor entre el rango de catedrático y el de profesor titular (d) (microfilm) lector m

readership ['riːdəʃɪp] n (a) Press lectores mpl (b) Br Univ = cargo entre el rango de catedrático y el de profesor titular

readily ['redɪlɪ] adv (a) (easily) fácilmente, libremente; r. available disponible en el acto (b) (willingly) de buena gana

readiness ['redɪnɪs] n (a) (preparedness) preparación f (b) (availability) disponibilidad f (c) (swiftness) rapidez f (d) (willingness) buena disposición f

reading ['riːdɪŋ] **1** n (a) (gen) lectura f; poetry r. recital m de poesía; the novel makes excellent r. es un libro excelente (b) (of gas meter etc) lectura f (c) Fig interpretación f; my r. of the situation is that ... según yo veo la situación ... (d) (of laws, bills) presentación f
2 adj de lectura □ r. glasses gafas fpl de lectura; r. lamp. lámpara f de leer; r. matter material m escrito, bibliografía f; r. room sala f de lectura

readjust [riːə'dʒʌst] vt (gen) reajustar; (adapt oneself) readaptarse

readjustment [riːə'dʒʌstmənt] n (gen) reajuste m; (adopting) readaptación f

readme file ['riːdmiː'faɪl] n Comptr (documento m) léeme m

readmit [riːəd'mɪt] vt readmitir (to en)

read-only ['riːd'əʊnlɪ] adj Comptr r. file archivo m de sólo lectura; r. memory memoria f de sólo lectura

readvertise [riː'ædvətaɪz] vt to r. a post volver a anunciar una oferta de empleo

ready ['redɪ] **1** adj (a) (prepared) listo(a), preparado(a); lunch is r.! ¡a comer!; Av r. for take-off preparado(a) para el despegue; Sport r., steady, go! ¡preparados, listos, ya!; r. when you are! ¡cuando quieras!; we're r. for bed nos vamos a la cama (b) (about to) a punto; r. to a punto de (c) (quick, convenient) a mano; (smile) fácil; to be r. with advice tener siempre un consejo a punto □ r. cash dinero m en efectivo (d) (willing) dispuesto(a) a
2 readies npl Br Fam (cash) pasta f sing
3 vt (pt & pp readied) (a) (make ready) preparar; the consignment will be readied el envío estará listo (b) Fml (person) prepararse

ready-cooked [redɪ'kʊkt] adj precocinado(a); r.-c. chickens pollos mpl asados para llevar

ready-made [redɪ'meɪd] *adj* confeccionado(a); hecho(a); **r.-m. clothes** ropa hecha

ready-to-wear ['redɪtə'weər] *adj* de confección

reaffirm [riːə'fɜːm] *vt* reafirmar

real [rɪəl] **1** *adj* (**a**) *(not imaginary)* real, verdadero(a); **in r. life** en la vida real; *Fam* **for r.** de veras; **this time it's for r.** esta vez va de veras; **is he for r.?** ¿qué le pasa a éste?, *Esp* ¿de qué va éste? (**b**) *(genuine)* auténtico(a), legítimo(a); **he's a r. friend** es un auténtico amigo; **r. leather** piel legítima; *Fam* **it's the r. McCoy, it's the r. thing** es el auténtico/la auténtica (**c**) *US Com* **r. estate** bienes *mpl* inmuebles; **r. estate agent** agente *m* inmobiliario

2 *adv US Fam (very)* **r. pleased** verdaderamente contento(a)

realign [riːə'laɪn] *vt* reordenar, restructurar

realignment [riːə'laɪnmənt] *n* restructuración *f*

realism ['rɪəlɪzəm] *n* realismo *m*

realist ['rɪəlɪst] *n* realista *mf*

realistic ['rɪəlɪstɪk] *adj* realista

reality [rɪ'ælɪtɪ] *n* realidad *f*; **in r.** en realidad; **r. TV** la televisión de los reality-shows

realizable [rɪə'laɪzəbəl] *adj* realizable

realization [rɪəlaɪ'zeɪʃən] *n* (**a**) *(understanding)* comprensión *f* (**b**) *(fulfilment)* realización *f* (**c**) *Com* realización *f*, venta *f*

realize ['rɪəlaɪz] *vt* (**a**) *(become aware of)* darse cuenta de; **I didn't r. that ...** no me di cuenta de que ... (**b**) *Fml (fulfil)* realizarse, hacerse realidad; **to r. one's full potential** realizarse (**c**) *Com (assets)* realizar, vender, convertir en efectivo (**d**) *Art Lit* realizar

real-life ['rɪəllaɪf] *adj* de la vida real; **his r.-l. wife** su mujer en la vida real

really ['rɪəlɪ] *adv* (**a**) *(truly)* verdaderamente, realmente; **it's r. sad** es verdaderamente triste; **you r. shouldn't have done it** no deberías haberlo hecho, de verdad (**b**) *(sure)* de verdad; **r.?** ¿de veras?; **r.!** ¡no me digas!

realm [relm] *n Fml* (**a**) *(kingdom)* reino *m* (**b**) *Fig (field)* terreno *m*, esfera *f*, mundo *m*

realtor ['rɪəltər] *n US* agente *mf* inmobiliario(a)

realty ['rɪəltɪ] *n US* bienes *mpl* inmuebles

ream [riːm] *n Fam* (**a**) *(of paper)* resma *f* (**b**) *Fig* **reams** *(writings)* montones *mpl*, gran cantidad *f sing*

reanimate [riː'ænɪmeɪt] *vt* reanimar, resucitar, dar nueva vida a

reap [riːp] *vt Agr* cosechar, recoger; *Fig* **to r. the benefits** llevarse los beneficios

reaper ['riːpər] *n* (**a**) *(person)* segador(a) *m,f* (**b**) *(machine)* segadora *f* □ **r. and binder** segadora *f* agavilladora

reappear [riːə'pɪər] *vi* reaparecer

reappearance [riːə'pɪərəns] *n* reaparición *f*

reapply [riːə'plaɪ] *vi (for job)* volver a presentar solicitud *or* presentarse

reappraisal [riːə'preɪzəl] *n Fml* revaluación *f*

reappraise [riːə'preɪz] *vt Fml* revaluar

rear[1] [rɪər] **1** *n* (**a**) *(back part)* parte *f* de atrás, parte *f* posterior; **in the r.** *Mil* en la retaguardia; **to bring up the r.** cerrar la marcha (**b**) *Aut* parte *f* de atrás (**c**) *Fam (buttocks)* trasero *m*

2 *adj* posterior, trasero(a) □ *Naut* **r. admiral** contralmirante *m*; **r. entrance** puerta *f* de atrás; *Aut* **r. wheel** rueda *f* trasera

rear[2] [rɪər] **1** *vt* (**a**) *(breed, raise)* criar (**b**) *(build)* erigir; *(lift up)* levantar, alzar; *(head)* levantar; *Fig* **corruption reared its ugly head** la corrupción hizo acto de presencia

2 *vi (horse)* **to r. up** encabritarse

rearguard ['rɪəgɑːd] *n Mil* retaguardia *f*; *Fig* **r. action** última tentativa *f*

rearm [riː'ɑːm] *Mil* **1** *vt* rearmar

2 *vi* rearmarse

rearmament [riː'ɑːməmənt] *n* rearme *m*

rearmost ['rɪəməʊst] *adj (nearest to the back)* último(a)

rearrange [riːə'reɪndʒ] *vt* (**a**) *(furniture)* colocar de otra manera (**b**) *(fix new date)* fijar otra fecha

rearrangement [riːə'reɪndʒmənt] *n* reorganización *f*, ajuste *m*

rear-view ['rɪəvjuː] *adj* **r.-v. mirror** (espejo *m*) retrovisor *m*

reason ['riːzən] **1** *n* (**a**) *(cause)* motivo *m*, razón *f*; **all the more r. why** razón de más; **for no r.** sin razón; **for reasons best known to him** por razones sólo conocidas por él; **for some r.** por algún motivo; **for this r.** por esta razón; **he has r. to think that ...** tiene motivos para pensar que ...; *Fml* **by r. of** en virtud de (**b**) *(good sense)* sentido *m* común, razón *f*; **it stands to r.** es lógico; **to listen to r.** atender a razones, *Am* atender razones; **to lose one's r.** perder la razón; **to see r.** ver la razón; **within r.** dentro de lo razonable

2 *vi* (**a**) *(be reasonable)* razonar; **to r. with sb** convencer a algn (**b**) *(argue, work out)* razonar, llegar a la conclusión

reason out *vt* solucionar con lógica

reasonable ['riːzənəbəl] *adj* (**a**) *(fair)* razonable, moderado(a) (**b**) *(sensible)* razonable, sensato(a) (**c**) *(average)* regular, pasable

reasonably ['riːzənəblɪ] *adv* (**a**) *(fairly)* bastante; **it was r. cheap** era bastante barato(a) (**b**) *(sensibly)* sensatamente

reasoning ['riːzənɪŋ] *n* razonamiento *m*; **by your r.** según tus cálculos

reassemble [riːə'sembəl] **1** *vt (machine etc)* volver a montar

2 *vi (people, group)* reunirse, volverse a juntar

reassert [riːə'sɜːt] *vt (authority)* reafirmar, volver a imponer; **her distrust of men reasserted itself** se reafirmó su desconfianza de los hombres

reassess [riːə'ses] *vt* (**a**) *(policy, situation)* replantearse (**b**) *Fin (tax)* revisar; *(property)* volver a tasar

reassign [riːə'saɪn] *vt (employee)* destinar (**to** a); *(work, project)* reasignar (**to** a)

reassurance [riːə'ʃʊərəns] *n (comfort)* consuelo *m*; *(words of comfort)* palabras *fpl* tranquilizadoras

reassure [riːə'ʃʊər] *vt* (**a**) *(comfort)* tranquilizar (**b**) *(restore confidence)* dar confianza a

reassuring [riːə'ʃʊərɪŋ] *adj* consolador(a), tranquilizador(a); **it's r. (to me) to know that ...** me tranquiliza saber que ...

reawaken [riːə'weɪkən] **1** *vt (feelings etc)* volver a despertar

2 *vi (from sleep)* despertar de nuevo

rebate ['riːbeɪt] *n Fin* (**a**) *(repayment)* devolución *f*, reembolso *m* □ **tax r.** devolución *f* fiscal (**b**) *(discount)* descuento *m*; rebaja *f*

rebel ['rebəl] **1** *adj & n* rebelde *(mf)*

2 [rɪ'bel] *vi* rebelarse, sublevarse (**against** contra)

rebellion [rɪ'beljən] *n* rebelión *f*, sublevación *f*

rebellious [rɪ'beljəs] *adj* rebelde

rebirth [riː'bɜːθ] *n* renacimiento *m*

reboot [riː'buːt] *vt & vi Comptr* reinicializar

reborn [riː'bɔːn] *adj* **to be r.** volver a nacer

rebound **1** ['riːbaʊnd] *n (of ball)* rebote *m*; *Fig* **to do sth on the r.** hacer algo de rebote; *Fig* **to marry on the r.** casarse por despecho

2 [rɪ'baʊnd] *vi (ball)* rebotar; *Fig (action)* repercutir

rebuff [rɪ'bʌf] **1** n rechazo m, desaire m; **to suffer a r.** verse rechazado(a)
2 vt rechazar, desairar

rebuild [riː'bɪld] vt (pt & pp **rebuilt**) reconstruir

rebuke [rɪ'bjuːk] **1** n reproche m, reprensión f
2 vt reprochar, reprender

rebut [rɪ'bʌt] vt (pt & pp **rebutted**) refutar

rebuttal [rɪ'bʌtəl] n Fml refutación f

recalcitrant [rɪ'kælsɪtrənt] adj Fml recalcitrante, obstinado(a)

recall [rɪ'kɔːl] **1** n (a) (soldiers) llamada f (b) (revocation) revocación f, anulación f (c) (memory) memoria f; **beyond** or **past r.** sepultado(a) para siempre; **total r.** gran capacidad de memoria
2 vt (a) (soldiers, products etc) hacer volver (b) (withdraw) retirar (c) (remember) acordarse, recordar; **as I r.** tal como yo lo recuerdo

recant [rɪ'kænt] vi Fml retractarse

recap [riː'kæp] Fam **1** vt & vi (pt & pp **recapped**) recapitular, resumir; **to r.** en resumen
2 ['riːkæp] n recapitulación f, resumen m

recapitulate [riːkə'pɪtjʊleɪt] vt & vi Fml recapitular, resumir

recapitulation [riːkəpɪtjʊ'leɪʃən] n Fml recapitulación f, resumen m

recapture [riː'kæptʃər] **1** n (of person) nueva detención f; (of place) reconquista f
2 vt (a) (person) volver a capturar; (place) reconquistar (b) Fig (memory, feeling) hacer revivir, recuperar

recast [riː'kɑːst] vt (pt & pp **recast**) (a) (redo) rehacer (b) (metal) refundir (c) Theat (play) cambiar el reparto; (actor, actress) dar otro papel a; **they r. the part of Grimbling** dieron el papel de Grimbling a otro actor

recd Com Fin (abbr **received**) recibido(a)

recede [rɪ'siːd] vi (withdraw) retroceder, retirarse; (fade) desvanecerse

receipt [rɪ'siːt] **1** n (a) (act) recepción f, recibo m; **to acknowledge r. of sth** acusar recibo de algo (b) Com (paper) recibo m; **to ask for a r.** pedir un recibo (c) **receipts** (takings) recaudación f sing
2 vt Com dar un recibo por

receive [rɪ'siːv] vt (a) (gen) recibir (b) Jur (stolen goods) ocultar (c) (welcome) acoger, recibir; **well/badly received** bien/mal acogido(a); Rel **to r. sb into the Church** recibir a algn en el seno de la Iglesia (d) TV Rad (transmission) captar, recibir (e) (in club) aceptar

received [rɪ'siːvd] adj (idea, opinion) común, aceptado(a); **r. pronunciation** pronunciación f estándar (del inglés)

receiver [rɪ'siːvər] n (a) (person) receptor(a) m,f, recibidor(a) m,f; (of letter) destinatario(a) m,f (b) Jur (of stolen goods) perista mf (c) Br Jur **official r.** síndico m (d) Tel auricular m, RP Ven tubo m; **to lift/put down the r.** descolgar/colgar el teléfono (e) Rad receptor m

receivership [rɪ'siːvəʃɪp] n Fin **to go into r.** declararse en quiebra

receiving [rɪ'siːvɪŋ] n Jur (stolen goods) encubrimiento m; Fig **to be on the r. end** ser la víctima or el blanco

recent ['riːsənt] adj reciente; **in r. years** en los últimos años

recently ['riːsəntlɪ] adv hace poco, recientemente

receptacle [rɪ'septəkəl] n receptáculo m, recipiente m

reception [rɪ'sepʃən] n (a) (welcome) recibimiento m, acogida f □ Br **r. centre** centro m de acogida; **r. room** sala f de recepción (b) (party) recepción f □ **wedding r.** banquete m de boda or Andes matrimonio or RP casamiento (c) (in hotel) **r. (desk)** recepción f (d) Rad TV recepción f

receptionist [rɪ'sepʃənɪst] n recepcionista mf

receptive [rɪ'septɪv] adj receptivo(a)

receptor [rɪ'septər] n receptor m

recess ['riːses, rɪ'ses] **1** n (a) (in a wall) hueco m (b) (remote place) lugar m apartado (c) (secret place) escondrijo m, recoveco m; Fig **the recesses of the mind** los recovecos de la mente (d) (rest period) descanso m; US Educ recreo m; Parl período m de vacaciones
2 [rɪ'ses] vi Parl suspender la sesión

recession [rɪ'seʃən] n Econ recesión f

recharge [riː'tʃɑːdʒ] vt Aut (battery) recargar; Fig **to r. one's batteries** recargar las baterías or pilas

rechargeable [riː'tʃɑːdʒəbəl] adj recargable

recherché [rə'ʃeəʃeɪ] adj rebuscado(a)

recidivism [rɪ'sɪdɪvɪzəm] n reincidencia f

recidivist [rɪ'sɪdɪvɪst] adj & n reincidente (mf)

recipe ['resɪpɪ] n (a) Culin receta f (b) Fig (formula) fórmula f; (secret) secreto m

recipient [rɪ'sɪpɪənt] n (a) (person) receptor(a) m,f (b) (of letter) destinatario(a) m,f

reciprocal [rɪ'sɪprəkəl] adj recíproco(a), mutuo(a)

reciprocate [rɪ'sɪprəkeɪt] vt & vi (gen) corresponder; (favour etc) devolver

recital [rɪ'saɪtəl] n recital m

recitation [resɪ'teɪʃən] n recitación f

recite [rɪ'saɪt] vt & vi recitar

reckless ['reklɪs] adj (unwise) imprudente; (fearless) temerario(a)

recklessness ['reklɪsnɪs] n (unwise) imprudencia f; (fearless) temeridad f

reckon ['rekən] vt & vi (a) (calculate) calcular; (count) contar (b) Fam (think) creer; (consider) considerar; **he reckons he's an expert on the subject** se considera un experto en el tema

reckon in vt tomar en cuenta, incluir

reckon on vt contar con

reckon up vt calcular, sumar

reckon with vt tener en cuenta; Fig **he's a man to be reckoned with** es un hombre muy poderoso

reckon without vt no contar con

reckoner ['rekənər] n **ready r.** tabla f de cálculo

reckoning ['rekənɪŋ] n cálculo m, cuenta f; **by my r. ...** según mis cálculos ...; **to be out in one's r.** equivocarse en las cuentas; Fig **day of r.** día m del juicio final

reclaim [rɪ'kleɪm] vt (a) (recover) recuperar; (demand back) reclamar (b) (waste products) recidir, tratar (c) (marshland, desert etc) convertir

reclamation [reklə'meɪʃən] n (a) (act of reclaiming) reclamación f (b) (waste products) reciclaje m (c) (marshland, desert etc) conversión f en tierra cultivable

recline [rɪ'klaɪn] vi recostarse, reclinarse

reclining [rɪ'klaɪnɪŋ] adj recostado(a), reclinado(a); **r. seat** asiento m con respaldo reclinable

recluse [rɪ'kluːs] n recluso(a) m,f

reclusive [rɪ'kluːsɪv] adj Fml recluso(a)

recognition [rekəg'nɪʃən] n (gen) reconocimiento m; (appreciation) apreciación f; (acceptance) aceptación f; **in r. of** en reconocimiento de; **the town has changed beyond all r.** el pueblo ha cambiado tanto que ahora es irreconocible

recognizable [rekəg'naɪzəbəl] adj reconocible

recognize ['rekəgnaɪz] vt reconocer

recognized ['rekəgnaɪzd] adj (approved) aprobado(a)

recoil ['riːkɔɪl] **1** n (of gun) culatazo m; (of cannon) retroceso m; (of spring) aflojamiento m

2 [rɪ'kɔɪl] vi (**a**) (gun) dar un culatazo; (cannon) retroceder; (spring) aflojarse (**b**) Fig (in fear) asustarse; (with disgust) disgustarse, sentir repugnancia por (**c**) Fig (rebound) repercutir

recollect [rekə'lekt] vt Fml acordarse de, recordar

recollection [rekə'lekʃən] n recuerdo m; **to the best of my r.** que yo recuerde

recommence [riːkə'mens] vt & vi recomenzar, empezar de nuevo

recommend [rekə'mend] vt recomendar; **he has little to r. him** poca cosa tiene a su favor; **not to be recommended** poco aconsejable or recomendable

recommendation [rekəmen'deɪʃən] n recomendación f

recompense ['rekəmpens] **1** n recompensa f; Jur (for damage) indemnización f

2 vt recompensar (**for** por); Jur indemnizar

reconcilable [rekən'saɪləbəl] adj (people) reconciliable; (opinions, accounts) conciliable

reconcile ['rekənsaɪl] vt (two people) reconciliar; (two ideas) conciliar; **to become reconciled** reconciliarse; **to r. oneself to** resignarse a, conformarse con

reconciliation [rekənsɪlɪ'eɪʃən] n (of two people) reconciliación f; (of two ideas) conciliación f

recondite [rɪ'kɒndaɪt, 'rekəndaɪt] adj Fml recóndito(a)

recondition [riːkən'dɪʃən] vt (engine) revisar, reparar

reconditioned [riːkən'dɪʃənd] adj (TV, washing machine) reparado(a)

reconnaissance [rɪ'kɒnɪsəns] n Mil reconocimiento m, exploración f

reconnoitre, US **reconnoiter** [rekə'nɔɪtər] vt Mil reconocer, explorar

reconquer [riː'kɒŋkər] vt reconquistar

reconquest [riː'kɒŋkwest] n reconquista f

reconsider [riːkən'sɪdər] vt reconsiderar, considerar de nuevo

reconsideration [riːkənsɪdə'reɪʃən] n reconsideración f, revisión f

reconstitute [riː'kɒnstɪtjuːt] vt (group, movement etc) reconstituir, reorganizar

reconstruct [riːkən'strʌkt] vt reconstruir

reconstruction [riːkən'strʌkʃən] n reconstrucción f

record ['rekɔːd] **1** n (**a**) (account) relación f; (of meeting) actas fpl; **for the r.** para que quede constancia; **off the r.** confidencialmente; **to go on r.** declarar públicamente; **to keep a r. of sth** anotar algo; **to put** or **set the r. straight** dejar las cosas claras (**b**) (document) documento m; **official r.** boletín m oficial; **r. of attendance** registro m de asistencia; **public records** archivos mpl (**c**) (case history) Univ expediente m académico; Med historial m médico; **police r.** antecedentes mpl penales; **to have a r.** (criminal) tener antecedentes (**d**) Mus disco m; **to cut/make a r.** grabar un disco ❏ **r. library** discoteca f; **r. player** tocadiscos m inv (**e**) Sport récord m; **to break a r.** batir un récord; **to hold the r.** tener el récord (**f**) Comptr registro m

2 [rɪ'kɔːd] vt (**a**) (relate) hacer constar; (note down) apuntar, anotar (**b**) (track, voice) grabar (**c**) (thermometer etc) marcar, registrar

record-breaking ['rekɔːdbreɪkɪŋ] adj que bate todos los récords

recorded [re'kɔːdɪd] adj (message) grabado(a); Br **r. delivery** correo m certificado

recorder [re'kɔːdər] (**a**) (person) registrador(a) m,f,

archivero(a) m,f; Jur magistrado(a) m,f municipal (**b**) Mus flauta f (**c**) **tape r.** magnetofón m

record-holder ['rekɔːdhəʊldər] n plusmarquista mf

recording [re'kɔːdɪŋ] n (**a**) (writing down) consignación f (**b**) (registering) registro m; **r. studio** estudio m de grabación ❏ **tape r.** grabación f

recount [rɪ'kaʊnt] vt (**a**) (tell) contar, relatar (**b**) (count again) volver a contar

re-count [riː'kaʊnt] **1** vi Pol hacer un recuento

2 ['riːkaʊnt] n Pol recuento m

recoup [rɪ'kuːp] vt (recover) recuperar; (losses) resarcirse de, recuperar

recourse [rɪ'kɔːs] n recurso m; **to have r. to** recurrir a

recover [rɪ'kʌvər] **1** vt (items, time) & Comptr recuperar; (consciousness, composure) recobrar

2 vi (from illness, setback etc) reponerse, recuperarse, restablecerse

re-cover [riː'kʌvər] vt (book) forrar de nuevo; (furniture) tapizar de nuevo

recoverable [rɪ'kʌvərəbəl] adj recuperable

recovery [rɪ'kʌvərɪ] n (**a**) (retrieval) recuperación f (**b**) (improvement) restablecimiento m, recuperación f

re-create [riːkrɪ'eɪt] vt recrear

recreation [rekrɪ'eɪʃən] n (**a**) (leisure) ocio m, esparcimiento m (**b**) Educ (playtime) recreo m ❏ **r. ground** terreno m de juegos

re-creation [riːkrɪ'eɪʃən] n recreación f

recreational [rekrɪ'eɪʃənəl] adj recreativo(a) ❏ **r. drug** = droga de consumo esporádico y por diversión; US Can **r. vehicle** autocaravana f, casa f caravana

recriminate [rɪ'krɪmɪneɪt] vt recriminar, reprochar

recrimination [rɪkrɪmɪ'neɪʃən] n recriminación f, reproche m

recriminatory [rɪ'krɪmɪnətərɪ] adj recriminatorio(a)

recruit [rɪ'kruːt] **1** n (**a**) Mil recluta m (**b**) (new member) miembro mf or socio(a) m,f nuevo(a)

2 vt (soldiers) reclutar, alistar; (members) admitir; (workers) contratar

recruitment [rɪ'kruːtmənt] n (of soldiers) reclutamiento m; (of employees) contratación f

recta ['rektə] npl see rectum

rectangle ['rektæŋgəl] n Geom rectángulo m

rectangular [rekt'æŋɡjʊlər] adj Geom rectangular

rectifiable [rektɪ'faɪəbəl] adj rectificable

rectify ['rektɪfaɪ] vt (pt & pp rectified) rectificar, corregir

rectitude ['rektɪtjuːd] n Fml rectitud f

rector ['rektər] n (**a**) Rel párroco m (**b**) Scot Educ director(a) m,f

rectory ['rektərɪ] n rectoría f

rectum ['rektəm] n (pl rectums or recta) Anat recto m

recumbent [rɪ'kʌmbənt] adj Literary recostado(a); **r. statue** estatua f yacente

recuperate [rɪ'kuːpəreɪt] vi Fml reponerse, restablecerse, recuperarse

recuperation [rɪkuːpə'reɪʃən] n restablecimiento m, recuperación f

recur [rɪ'kɜːr] vi (pt & pp recurred) reproducirse, repetirse

recurrence [rɪ'kʌrəns] n repetición f, reaparición f

recurrent [rɪ'kʌrənt] adj recurrente

recurring [rɪ'kɜːrɪŋ] adj periódico(a); **two point six r.** dos coma seis periódico

recycle [riː'saɪkəl] vt reciclar

recycling [riː'saɪklɪŋ] n reciclaje m **r. plant** planta f de reciclaje

red [red] **1** *adj* (**redder, reddest**) *(colour)* rojo(a); **as r. as a beetroot** *(person)* más rojo(a) que un tomate *or Méx* jitomate; **r. alert** alerta *f* roja; **r. flag** bandera *f* roja; **r. light** *(road signal)* semáforo *m* en rojo; **r. wine** vino *m* tinto; **to go r.** ponerse colorado(a); **to have r. hair** ser pelirrojo(a); *Fig* **r. herring** truco *m* para despistar; *Fam* **to roll out the r. carpet for sb** recibir a algn con todos los honores ❑ **R. Cross** Cruz *f* Roja; **R. Indian** piel roja *mf*; **R. Riding Hood** Caperucita *f* Roja; **the R. Sea** el Mar Rojo; **r. tape** papeleo *m*, trámites *mpl*
2 *n* (**a**) *(colour)* rojo *m*; *Fin* **to be in the r.** estar en descubierto *or* en números rojos; **to make sb see r.** poner negro(a) a algn (**b**) *Pol* rojo(a) *m,f*

red-blooded [red'blʌdɪd] *adj* **a r. male** un macho de pelo en pecho

redbreast ['redbrest] *n Orn* petirrojo *m*

redbrick ['redbrɪk] *adj* provincial ❑ **r. university** universidad *f* de provincias construida a finales del siglo diecinueve

redcurrant [red'kʌrənt] *n Bot* grosella *f* roja

redden ['redən] **1** *vi (person)* enrojecerse, ponerse colorado(a)
2 *vt (make red)* teñir de rojo

reddish ['redɪʃ] *adj* rojizo(a)

redecorate [riː'dekəreɪt] *vt* repintar, renovar la decoración de

redeem [rɪ'diːm] *vt* (**a**) *(regain)* recobrar, rescatar, recuperar; *(from pawn)* desempeñar; *(voucher etc)* canjear (**b**) *(pay off debt)* amortizar, cancelar (**c**) *(fulfil an obligation)* cumplir (**d**) *(compensate)* compensar, salvar (**e**) *Rel* redimir

redeemable [rɪ'diːməbəl] *adj* (**a**) *(exchanged)* canjeable; *(from pawn)* redimible (**b**) *(debt)* amortizable

redeemer [rɪ'diːmər] *n (saviour)* redentor(a) *m,f*; *Rel* **the R.** el Redentor

redeeming [rɪ'diːmɪŋ] *adj* compensatorio(a); **his only r. feature** lo único que le salva

redemption [rɪ'dempʃən] *n Fml* (**a**) *(of debt)* reembolso *m*, amortización *f* (**b**) *Rel* redención *f*, salvación *f*; **beyond r.** irredimible

redeploy [riːdɪ'plɔɪ] *vt Mil* transferir

red-eye ['redaɪ] *n* (**a**) *Phot* ojos *mpl* rojos (**b**) *US Fam (whisky)* whisky *m* de poca calidad

red-handed [red'hændɪd] *adj* flagrante; **to catch sb r.-h.** *Esp* coger *or Am* agarrar a algn en flagrante delito *or* con las manos en la masa

redhead ['redhed] *n* pelirrojo(a) *m,f*

red-hot [red'hɒt] *adj* (**a**) *(turned red)* al rojo vivo, candente; **r.-h. news** noticia(s) *f(pl)* de última hora (**b**) *Fam (passionate)* fervoroso(a), ardiente

redial ['riːdaɪəl] *Tel* **1** *n* **r. (feature)** (botón *m* de) rellamada *f*
2 [riː'daɪəl] *vt (number)* volver a marcar *or Andes RP* discar
3 *vi* volver a marcar *or Andes RP* discar (el número)

redid [riː'dɪd] *pt see* **redo**

redirect [riːdɪ'rekt] *vt* (**a**) *(alter)* redistribuir; **the government will r. funds to pension schemes** el gobierno destinará nuevos fondos a los planes de jubilación (**b**) *(forward)* remitir a la nueva dirección

rediscover [riːdɪs'kʌvər] *vt* redescubrir

redistribute [riː'dɪstrɪbjuːt] *vt* redistribuir

redistribution [riːdɪstrɪ'bjuːʃən] *n* redistribución *f*

red-letter [red'letər] *adj* **r.-l. day** día *m* memorable

red-light [red'laɪt] *adj Fam* **r.-l. district** barrio *m* chino, barrios *mpl* bajos

redo [riː'duː] *vt (pt* **redid**, *pp* **redone**) rehacer

redolent ['redələnt] *adj* **to be r. of** *(smell of)* oler a; *(be suggestive of)* tener reminiscencias de

redone [riː'dʌn] *pp see* **redo**

redouble [riː'dʌbəl] *vt* redoblar, incrementar; **to r. one's efforts** redoblar los esfuerzos

redoubt [rɪ'daʊt] *n Fml* (**a**) *(haven)* refugio *m*, amparo *m* (**b**) *(stronghold)* reducto *m*, fortaleza *f*

redraft [riː'drɑːft] *vt* redactar de nuevo, reescribir

redress [rɪ'dres] *Fml* **1** *n* reparación *f*; *Fig* desagravio *m*; **to seek r.** exigir reparación
2 *vt (grievance, wrong)* reparar; *Fig* **to r. the balance** equilibrar la balanza

redshank ['redʃæŋk] *n Orn* archibebe *m* común

redskin ['redskɪn] *n* piel roja *mf*

reduce [rɪ'djuːs] *vt* (**a**) *(make less)* reducir; **to r. output** disminuir la producción (**b**) *Mil (demote)* degradar; **to r. an officer to the ranks** degradar a un oficial (**c**) *Culin* espesar, trabar; **to r. a sauce** trabar una salsa (**d**) *Med* recomponer; **to r. a fracture** recomponer una fractura (**e**) *(force)* forzar; **to r. sb to tears** hacer llorar a algn; **he was reduced to borrowing money** se vio en la necesidad de pedir dinero prestado

reduced [rɪ'djuːst] *adj* reducido(a)

reduction [rɪ'dʌkʃən] *n (made smaller)* reducción *f*; *Com (cut)* descuento *m*, rebaja *f*; *(simplification)* simplificación *f*

reductive [rɪ'dʌktɪv] *adj* reductor(a)

redundancy [rɪ'dʌndənsɪ] *n* (**a**) *(superfluousness)* redundancia *f* (**b**) *Br Ind* despido *m*; **r. pay** indemnización *f* por despido

redundant [rɪ'dʌndənt] *adj* (**a**) *(superfluous)* redundante, superfluo(a) (**b**) *Br Ind* **to be made r.** perder el empleo; **to make sb r.** despedir a algn

reduplicate [rɪ'djuːplɪkeɪt] *vt* reduplicar

reduplication [rɪdjuːplɪ'keɪʃən] *n* reduplicación *f*

redwing ['redwɪŋ] *n Orn* zorzal *m* alirrojo

redwood ['redwʊd] *n Bot* secuoya *f*

reed [riːd] *n* (**a**) *Bot* caña *f* (**b**) *Mus* caramillo *m*; **r. instruments** instrumentos *mpl* de lengüeta

reeducate [riː'edjʊkeɪt] *vt* reeducar

reedy ['riːdɪ] *adj* (**reedier, reediest**) (**a**) *(place)* lleno(a) de cañas (**b**) *(sound)* aflautado(a), agudo(a)

reef [riːf] *n* (**a**) *(coral, rock)* arrecife *m*; **coral r.** arrecife de coral (**b**) *Naut (of sail)* rizo *m*; **r. knot** nudo *m* de rizo

reefer ['riːfər] *n* (**a**) **r. jacket** chaquetón *m* cruzado de lana (**b**) *Slang (drugs)* porro *m*

reek [riːk] **1** *n* tufo *m*, mal olor *m*
2 *vi* apestar; **he reeks of garlic** huele a ajo que apesta

reel [riːl] **1** *n* (**a**) *(spool)* bobina *f*, carrete *m*; *Br* **cotton r.** carrete de hilo; *Cin* **to change reels** cambiar de bobina (**b**) *Scot Mus* danza *f* tradicional
2 *vi (stagger)* tambalearse; **my head was reeling** la cabeza me daba vueltas

▸ **reel off** *vt* soltar, recitar; **to r. off a list of insults** soltar una retahíla de insultos; **to r. off a poem** recitar un poema de un tirón

re-elect [riːɪ'lekt] *vt* reelegir

re-election [riːɪ'lekʃən] *n* reelección *f*

re-enact [riːɪ'nækt] *vt (crime, battle)* reconstruir

re-enter [riː'entər] **1** *vt* (**a**) *(enter again)* volver a entrar (**b**) *(write again)* volver a apuntar
2 *vi* **to re-e. for an exam** presentarse a un examen por segunda vez

re-entry [riː'entrɪ] *n* vuelta *f*, reingreso *m*

re-establish [riːɪ'stæblɪʃ] *vt* restablecer

re-examine [riːɪgˈzæmɪn] *vt* examinar de nuevo

ref [ref] *n* (**a**) *Sport Fam* (*abbr* **referee**) árbitro(a) *m,f* (**b**) *Com* (*abbr* **reference**) referencia *f*, ref.

refectory [rɪˈfektərɪ] *n* refectorio *m*, cantina *f*

refer [rɪˈfɜːr] **1** *vt* (*pt & pp* **referred**) mandar, enviar; **I was referred to a specialist** me enviaron a un especialista; **they referred me to the manager** me mandaron hablar con el gerente; **to r. a matter to a tribunal** remitir un asunto a un tribunal
2 *vi* (**a**) (*allude*) referirse, aludir; **are you referring to me?** ¿te refieres a mí?; **the article refers to ...** el artículo hace referencia a ... (**b**) (*consult*) consultar; **to r. to one's notes** consultar los apuntes

referee [refəˈriː] **1** *n* (**a**) *Sport* árbitro(a) *m,f* (**b**) *Br* (*for job application*) garante *mf*
2 *vt Sport* arbitrar

reference [ˈrefərəns] *n* (**a**) (*mention*) referencia *f*, mención *f*; **there's no r. to it** no se hace mención de ello; **they want to keep it for future r.** quieren guardarlo para futuras referencias; **with r. to** referente a, con referencia a (**b**) (*in a book*) referencia *f*, nota *f*; **r. mark** llamada *f* (**c**) (*information*) de consulta □ **r. book** libro *m* de consulta; **r. library** biblioteca *f* de consulta (**d**) *Br* (*from employer*) informe *m*, referencia *f*

referendum [refəˈrendəm] *n* (*pl* **referendums** *or* **referenda** [refəˈrendə]) *Pol* referéndum *m*; **to have a r. on a matter** convocar un referéndum sobre un asunto

refill [ˈriːfɪl] **1** *n* (**a**) (*replacement*) recambio *m*; carga *f* (**b**) *Fam* otra copa *f*
2 [riːˈfɪl] *vt* (*bottle*) rellenar; (*pen, lighter*) recargar

refillable [riːˈfɪləbəl] *adj* recargable

refine [rɪˈfaɪn] *vt* refinar

refined [rɪˈfaɪnd] *adj* (**a**) (*purified, developed*) refinado(a) (**b**) (*genteel*) fino(a), delicado(a)

refinement [rɪˈfaɪnmənt] *n* refinamiento *m*

refiner [rɪˈfaɪnər] *n* refinador(a) *m,f*

refinery [rɪˈfaɪnərɪ] *n* refinería *f*

refining [rɪˈfaɪnɪŋ] *n* refinado *m*, refinación *f*

refit [ˈriːfɪt] **1** *n* reacondicionamiento *m*
2 [riːˈfɪt] *vt* (*pt & pp* **refitted**) reacondicionar

reflation [riːˈfleɪʃən] *n Econ* reflación *f*

reflect [rɪˈflekt] **1** *vt* (*light, sound, attitude*) reflejar; **does it r. your opinion?** ¿refleja tu opinión?; **her face was reflected in the mirror** su cara se reflejó en el espejo
2 *vi* (**a**) (*think*) reflexionar; **to r. upon sth** reflexionar *or* meditar sobre algo (**b**) **to r. well/badly on** dejar en buen/mal lugar a

reflected [rɪˈflektɪd] *adj* reflejado(a)

reflection [rɪˈflekʃən] *n* (**a**) (*indication, mirror image*) reflejo *m* (**b**) (*thought*) reflexión *f*; **on r.** pensándolo bien (**c**) (*criticism*) crítica *f*; **the fact that you're unemployed is no r. on you** el que no tengas trabajo no dice nada en contra tuya

reflective [rɪˈflektɪv] *adj* (**a**) (*surface*) reflectante (**b**) (*person*) reflexivo(a)

reflector [rɪˈflektər] *n* (**a**) *Astron* reflector *m* (**b**) (*on vehicle*) catafaro *m*

reflex [ˈriːfleks] *n* reflejo *m* □ **r. action** acto *m* reflejo; *Phot* **r. camera** cámara *f* réflex

reflexive [rɪˈfleksɪv] *adj Ling* reflexivo(a); **r. verb** verbo *m* reflexivo

reforestation [riːfɒrɪˈsteɪʃən] *n* reforestación *f*, repoblación *f* forestal

reform [rɪˈfɔːm] **1** *n* reforma *f*
2 *vt* reformar; **he is a reformed character** se ha reformado

re-form [ˈriːˈfɔːm] *vi* (*organization, pop group*) volver a unirse

reformat [ˈriːˈfɔːmæt] (*pt & pp* **reformatted**) *vt Comptr* (*disk*) volver a formatear

reformation [refəˈmeɪʃən] *n* reforma *f*

reformatory [rɪˈfɔːmətərɪ] *n* reformatorio *m*

reformer [rɪˈfɔːmər] *n* reformador(a) *m,f*

reformist [rɪˈfɔːmɪst] *adj & n* reformista (*mf*)

refraction [rɪˈfrækʃən] *n Phys* refracción *f*

refractory [rɪˈfræktərɪ] *adj* (*person*) refractario(a)

refrain [rɪˈfreɪn] **1** *n Mus* estribillo *m*; *Fig* lema *m*
2 *vi* abstenerse (**from** de); **please r. from smoking** se ruega no fumar

re-freeze [riːˈfriːz] *vt* volver a congelar

refresh [rɪˈfreʃ] *vt* refrescar; **to r. one's memory** refrescar la memoria; **to r. oneself** refrescarse

refresher [rɪˈfreʃər] *n* **r. course** cursillo *m* de reciclaje

refreshing [rɪˈfreʃɪŋ] *adj* refrescante; **a r. change** un cambio muy agradable

refreshment [rɪˈfreʃmənt] *n* refresco *m*

refrigerated [rɪˈfrɪdʒəreɪtɪd] *adj* refrigerado(a)

refrigeration [rɪfrɪdʒəˈreɪʃən] *n* refrigeración *f*

refrigerator [rɪˈfrɪdʒəreɪtər] *n* nevera *f*, *Esp* frigorífico *m*, *RP* heladera *f*, *Méx* refrigerador *m*

refuel [riːˈfjuːəl] **1** *vt* (*pt & pp* **refuelled**, *US* **refueled**) repostar combustible a
2 *vi* repostar; **to stop to r.** hacer escala para repostar

refuelling [riːˈfjuːəlɪŋ] *n* repostaje *m*; **r. plane/ship** avión *m*/barco *m* nodriza; **r. stop** escala *f* técnica *or* de repostaje

refuge [ˈrefjuːdʒ] *n* (*shelter*) refugio *m*, cobijo *m*; **to seek r.** buscar refugio; **to take r.** refugiarse

refugee [refjuˈdʒiː] *n Pol* refugiado(a) *m,f* **r. camp** campo *m* de refugiados

refund [ˈriːfʌnd] **1** *n* reembolso *m*, devolución *f*; **to demand a r.** exigir un reembolso
2 [riːˈfʌnd] *vt* reembolsar, devolver

refundable [riːˈfʌndəbəl] *adj* reembolsable

refurbish [riːˈfɜːbɪʃ] *vt Fml* (*building*) redecorar

refusal [rɪˈfjuːzəl] *n* negativa *f*; **to have first r. on sth** tener la primera opción en algo; **to meet with a r.** ser rechazado(a)

refuse¹ [rɪˈfjuːz] **1** *vt* (**a**) (*reject an offer*) rechazar; **he refused my offer of a lift** no aceptó mi ofrecimiento de que le llevara en coche (**b**) (*deny*) negar; **to r. sb sth** negar algo a algn; **to r. permission** negar el permiso; **we refused to do it** nos negamos a hacerlo
2 *vi* negarse; **they asked me but I refused** me lo pidieron pero dije que no

refuse² [ˈrefjuːs] *n* basura *f*; **r. bin** cubo *m* de la basura; **r. collector** basurero *m*; **r. dump** vertedero *m* de basuras

refutation [refjuˈteɪʃən] *n* refutación *f*, rebatimiento *m*

refute [rɪˈfjuːt] *vt* refutar, rebatir

regain [rɪˈgeɪn] *vt* (**a**) (*recover*) recuperar, recobrar; **to r. consciousness** volver en sí; **to r. possession of** recuperar la propiedad de; **to r. one's composure** serenarse (**b**) (*reach again*) llegar de nuevo

regal [ˈriːgəl] *adj* regio(a)

regale [rɪˈgeɪl] *vt* agasajar; **they regaled us with presents** nos agasajaron con regalos

regalia [rɪˈgeɪlɪə] *npl* galas *fpl*, adornos *mpl*; **in full r.** luciendo todas sus galas

regard [rɪˈgɑːd] **1** *n* (**a**) (*concern*) consideración *f*, respeto *m*; **to have r. for sb's feelings** respetar los sentimientos de algn; **with** *or* **in r. to** respecto a; **without r. to** indiferente a (**b**) *(esteem)* estima *f*, respeto *m*; **to hold sb in high r.** tener a algn en gran estima (**c**) **regards** *(good wishes)* saludos *mpl*, *CAm Col Ecuad* saludes *fpl*; **give him my r.** dale recuerdos de mi parte; **as r.** *(regarding)* respecto a

2 *vt (consider)* considerar, juzgar; **I r. it as my duty** lo considero mi deber

regarding [rɪˈɡɑːdɪŋ] *prep* respecto a; **r. our future ...** respecto a nuestro futuro ...

regardless [rɪˈɡɑːdlɪs] **1** *prep* a pesar de, sin tener en cuenta; **r. of the expense** cueste lo que cueste; **r. of the outcome** pase lo que pase

2 *adv* a todo coste; **to carry on r.** seguir a todo coste

regatta [rɪˈɡætə] *n Naut* regata *f*

regd *Com (abbr* **registered (trademark))** registrado(a); *(letter)* certificado(a)

regency [ˈriːdʒənsɪ] *n* regencia *f*

regenerate [rɪˈdʒenəreɪt] **1** *vt* regenerar, reproducir

2 *vi* regenerarse

regeneration [rɪdʒenəˈreɪʃən] *n* regeneración *f*

regent [ˈriːdʒənt] *n* regente *mf*

reggae [ˈreɡeɪ] *n Mus* reggae *m*

regime [reɪˈʒiːm] *n Pol* régimen *m*; **the present r.** el régimen actual

regiment [ˈredʒɪmənt] **1** *n Mil* regimiento *m*; *Fig* **a r. of people** una multitud

2 [ˈredʒɪmənt] *vt Mil* regimentar

regimental [redʒɪˈmentəl] *adj Mil* del regimiento

regimentals [redʒɪˈmentəlz] *npl Mil* uniforme *m sing* militar

regimentation [redʒɪmenˈteɪʃən] *n* reglamentación *f*

region [ˈriːdʒən] *n* (**a**) *(of country, body)* región *f* (**b**) **in the r. of** *(approximately)* aproximadamente

regional [ˈriːdʒənəl] *adj* regional

regionalism [ˈriːdʒənəlɪzəm] *n* regionalismo *m*

register [ˈredʒɪstər] **1** *n* (**a**) *(list)* registro *m*, lista *f*; **to call the r.** pasar lista; **r. of births, marriage and deaths** registro civil; **r. of voters** censo *m* electoral; *Br* **r. office** registro *m* civil (**b**) *US Com* contador *m*; **cash r.** caja *f* registradora (**c**) *Mus* registro *m* (**d**) *Ling* registro *m*

2 *vt* (**a**) *(record)* registrar; **to r. the birth of a child** inscribir el nacimiento de un niño *m* (**b**) *(letter, parcel)* certificar; *(luggage)* facturar (**c**) *(show)* marcar; **his face registered fear** en su rostro se reflejaba el miedo; **the thermometer registered forty degrees centigrade** el termómetro marcaba los cuarenta grados

3 *vi* (**a**) *(enter one's name)* inscribirse, registrarse; *Univ* matricularse (**b**) *Fam* fijarse, sonarse; **his name didn't r. with me** su nombre no me sonaba

registered [ˈredʒɪstəd] *adj* certificado(a)' □ *Br* **r. letter** carta *f* certificada; **r. nurse** enfermera *f* titulada; **r. trademark** marca *f* registrada; *Comptr* **r. user** usuario(a) *m,f* registrado(a)

registrar [redʒɪˈstrɑːr, ˈredʒɪstrɑːr] *n* (**a**) *(record keeper)* registrador(a) *m,f* (**b**) *Br (hospital doctor)* interno(a) *m,f* (**c**) *Univ* secretario(a) *m,f* general

registration [redʒɪˈstreɪʃən] *n* (**a**) *(enrolment)* inscripción *f*; *Univ* matrícula *f* (**b**) *(of trademark)* registro *m* (**c**) *Aut* registro *m* □ *Br* **r. number** matrícula *f*

registry [ˈredʒɪstrɪ] *n* registro *m* □ *Br* **r. office** registro *m* civil; **to get married in a r. office** casarse por lo civil

regress [rɪˈɡres] *vi Fml* retroceder

regression [rɪˈɡreʃən] *n Fml* retroceso *m*, regresión *f*

regressive [rɪˈɡresɪv] *adj Fml* regresivo(a)

regret [rɪˈɡret] **1** *n* (**a**) *(remorse)* remordimiento *m*; *(sadness)* pesar *m* (**b**) **regrets** *(excuses)* excusas *fpl*; **to**

send one's r. excusarse; **to have no r.** *(remorse)* no arrepentirse de nada

2 *vt (pt & pp* **regretted)** arrepentirse de, lamentar; **she regrets having gone** se arrepiente de haberse ido; **I r. to tell you that ...** *(in letter)* lamento decirle que ...

regretful [rɪˈɡretfʊl] *adj* arrepentido(a); **to be r. about sth** arrepentirse de algo

regrettable [rɪˈɡretəbəl] *adj* lamentable

regrettably [rɪˈɡretəblɪ] *adv* lamentablemente; **r. we were late** desgraciadamente llegamos tarde

regroup [riːˈɡruːp] **1** *vt* reagrupar

2 *vi* reagruparse

regular [ˈreɡjʊlər] **1** *adj* (**a**) *(unvarying)* regular; **as r. as clockwork** con una regularidad cronométrica; **at r. intervals** a intervalos regulares (**b**) *(usual)* usual, normal; **do you want it in the large or r. size?** lo quiere tamaño familiar o tamaño normal?; **r. customer** *(in shop)* cliente *mf* habitual; *(of bar)* asiduo(a) *m,f* (**c**) *(permanent)* permanente; **a r. job** un trabajo permanente (**d**) *(frequent)* frecuente; **the IRA carried out r. bombings** el IRA llevó a cabo frecuentes atentados con bombas (**e**) *(even)* regular; **r. features** facciones *fpl* regulares (**f**) *Ling* regular; **r. verb** verbo *m* regular (**g**) *Mil* **r. army** tropas *fpl* regulares (**h**) *US Fam* **a r. guy** *Esp* un tío legal, *Am* un tipo derecho

2 *n* (**a**) *(customer)* cliente *mf* habitual, asiduo(a) *m,f* (**b**) *Mil* militar *m* de carrera (**c**) *US (fuel)* súper *f*

regularity [reɡjʊˈlærɪtɪ] *n* regularidad *f*

regularize [ˈreɡjʊləraɪz] *vt* regularizar, normalizar

regularly [ˈreɡjʊləlɪ] *adv* regularmente, con regularidad

regulate [ˈreɡjʊleɪt] *vt* (**a**) *(control)* regular (**b**) *(make rules)* reglamentar

regulation [reɡjʊˈleɪʃən] **1** *n* (**a**) *(control)* regulación *f*, reglamentación *f* (**b**) *(rule)* regla *f*

2 *adj* reglamentario(a)

regulator [ˈreɡjʊleɪtər] *n* regulador(a) *m,f*

regulatory [reɡjʊˈleɪtərɪ] *adj* regulador(a)

regurgitate [rɪˈɡɜːdʒɪteɪt] *vt* regurgitar, devolver; *Fig* repetir maquinalmente

rehab [ˈriːhæb] *n Fam* rehabilitación *f*; **r. centre** centro *m* de rehabilitación

rehabilitate [riːəˈbɪlɪteɪt] *vt* (**a**) *(readapt)* rehabilitar, reeducar (**b**) *(building etc)* rehabilitar, renovar

rehabilitation [riːəbɪlɪˈteɪʃən] *n* (**a**) *(restore)* rehabilitación *f* (**b**) *(reeducation)* rehabilitación *f*, reeducación *f* □ **r. centre** centro *m* de reeducación

rehash [ˈriːhæʃ] **1** *n* refrito *m*, refundición *f*

2 [riːˈhæʃ] *vt* refundir

rehearsal [rɪˈhɜːsəl] *n* ensayo *m* □ **dress r.** ensayo general

rehearse [rɪˈhɜːs] *vt & vi Theat* ensayar

reheat [riːˈhiːt] *vt* recalentar

rehouse [riːˈhaʊz] *vt* dar una nueva vivienda a

reign [reɪn] **1** *n* reinado *m*

2 *vi* reinar; *Fig* **chaos reigned** reinaba el caos

reigning [ˈreɪnɪŋ] *adj* actual; **r. champion** campeón *m* actual

reimburse [riːɪmˈbɜːs] *vt Fml* reembolsar

reimbursement [riːɪmˈbɜːsmənt] *n Fml* reembolso *m*, pago *m*

rein [reɪn] *n* (**a**) *(for horse)* rienda *f*; *Fig* **he gave free r. to his emotions** dio rienda suelta a sus emociones; *Fig* **to keep sb on a tight r.** atar corto a algn (**b**) **reins** *(for child)* andadores *mpl*

reincarnation [riːɪnkɑːˈneɪʃən] *n* reencarnación *f*

reindeer [ˈreɪndɪər] *n Zool (pl* **reindeer** *or* **reindeers)** reno *m*

reinforce [riːɪnˈfɔːs] vt (strengthen) reforzar; (support) apoyar; Constr **reinforced concrete** hormigón m or Am concreto m armado

reinforcement [riːɪnˈfɔːsmənt] n (a) (of wall, structure) refuerzo m (b) Mil **reinforcements** refuerzos mpl

reinstate [riːɪnˈsteɪt] vt Fml (to job) reincorporar; (restore) restaurar

reinstatement [riːɪnˈsteɪtmənt] n Fml (to job) reincorporación f, reintegración f; (restoration) restauración f

reintegrate [riːˈɪntɪgreɪt] vt reintegrar; (into society) reinsertar

reintegration [riːɪntəˈgreɪʃən] n reintegración f; (into society) reinserción f (social)

reinvest [riːɪnˈvest] vt reinvertir

reissue [riːˈɪʃuː] **1** vt (book, record) reeditar; (stamp) volver a emitir

2 n (book, record) nueva edición f; (stamp) nueva emisión f

reiterate [riːˈɪtəreɪt] vt & vi Fml reiterar

reiteration [riːɪtəˈreɪʃən] n Fml reiteración f

reject 1 [ˈriːdʒekt] **1** n (a) (person) desecho m (b) Com **rejects** artículos mpl defectuosos

2 [rɪˈdʒekt] vt (offer, proposal) rechazar

rejection [rɪˈdʒekʃən] n rechazo m; **to meet with r.** ser rechazado(a)

rejoice [rɪˈdʒɔɪs] vi alegrarse, regocijarse (**at, over** de)

rejoicing [rɪˈdʒɔɪsɪŋ] n alegría f, regocijo m; **the r. lasted a week** las fiestas duraron una semana

rejoin[1] [riːˈdʒɔɪn] vt (a) (join again) volver a juntar (b) (meet again) reencontrar

rejoin[2] [rɪˈdʒɔɪn] vt Fml replicar

rejoinder [rɪˈdʒɔɪndər] n Fml réplica f

rejuvenate [rɪˈdʒuːvɪneɪt] vt (a) (regenerate) rejuvenecer (b) (revitalize) revitalizar

rejuvenation [rɪdʒuːvɪˈneɪʃən] n (a) (regeneration) rejuvenecimiento m (b) (revitalization) revitalización f

rekindle [riːˈkɪndəl] vt Fml volver a encender; Fig reanimar, reavivar

relapse [rɪˈlæps] **1** n (a) Med recaída f; **to have a r.** sufrir una recaída (b) Fml reincidencia f

2 vi (a) Med recaer (b) Fml reincidir, recaer; **to r. into crime** reincidir en el delito

relate [rɪˈleɪt] **1** vt (a) (connect) relacionar; **to r. two ideas** relacionar dos ideas (b) (tell) contar, relatar

2 vi relacionarse; **I can't r. to him** no estamos en la misma onda; **to r. to sb** llevarse bien con algn

related [rɪˈleɪtɪd] adj (a) (linked) relacionado(a) (**to** con); **it is thought that this illness is r. to excess exposure to the sun** se cree que esta enfermedad guarda relación con la excesiva exposición al sol (b) **to be r. to sb** (of the same family) ser pariente de algn (c) (of same origin) de la misma familia: **these languages are r.** estas lenguas son de la misma familia

relation [rɪˈleɪʃən] n (a) (link) relación f; **business relations** relaciones fpl comerciales; **in** or **with r. to** con relación a, respecto a; **it bears no r. to what we said** no tiene nada que ver con lo que dijimos □ **public relations** relaciones fpl públicas (b) (family) pariente(a) m,f; **she's a r. of mine** es pariente mía

relational [rɪˈleɪʃənəl] adj Comptr **r. database** base f de datos relacional

relationship [rɪˈleɪʃənʃɪp] n (a) (link) relación f; **what is the r. between reading and writing?** ¿qué relación hay entre la lectura y la escritura? (b) (between people) relaciones fpl; **to have a good/bad r. with sb** llevarse bien/mal con algn

relative [ˈrelətɪv] **1** n pariente(a) m,f; **a distant r.** un pariente lejano

2 adj (a) (not absolute) relativo(a); **everything is r.** todo es relativo (b) Ling **r. pronoun** pronombre m relativo; **r. clause** oración f de relativo

relatively [ˈrelətɪvli] adv relativamente, bastante; **they're r. poor** son bastante pobres

relativism [ˈrelətɪvɪzəm] n Philos relativismo m

relativity [reləˈtɪvɪti] n relatividad f; Phys **the theory of r.** la teoría de la relatividad

relax [rɪˈlæks] **1** vt (a) (calm) relajar (b) (loosen) aflojar (c) (rules) suavizar

2 vi relajarse; **r.!** ¡tranquilízate!

relaxation [riːlækˈseɪʃən] n (a) (rest) descanso m, relajación f; **methods of r.** métodos mpl de relajación; **r. period** período m de descanso (b) (of rules etc) relajación f, aflojamiento m (c) (pastime) distracción f; **it's my favourite r.** es mi distracción predilecta

relaxed [rɪˈlækst] adj (calm) relajado(a); (peaceful) tranquilo(a); **a r. atmosphere** un ambiente desenfadado

relaxing [rɪˈlæksɪŋ] adj relajante; **a r. holiday** unas vacaciones relajantes

relay [ˈriːleɪ] **1** n (a) (of workers) relevo m; Sport **r. (race)** carrera f de relevos; **100 metres r.** los 100 metros relevos; **to work in relays** trabajar por relevos (b) Elec relé m, repetidor m (c) Rad TV (broadcast) retransmisión f □ **r. station** estación f repetidora

2 [rɪˈleɪ] vt (a) (pass on) difundir, divulgar (b) Rad TV retransmitir

release [rɪˈliːs] **1** n (a) (setting free) liberación f, puesta f en libertad; (of gas) escape m (b) Com puesta f en venta (c) Cin estreno m; **on general r.** en todos los cines (d) Mus (record) emisión f (e) Press comunicado m □ **press r.** comunicado m de prensa

2 vt (a) (set free) liberar, poner en libertad; (gas) despedir; (feelings) desahogar, descargar; **to r. sb from an obligation** librar a algn de una obligación (b) Com poner en venta (c) Cin estrenar (d) Mus (record) sacar (e) (let go) soltar; **to r. the handbrake** soltar el freno de mano; Phot **to r. the shutter** disparar (f) (publish) publicar

relegate [ˈrelɪgeɪt] vt (a) (consign) relegar (b) Br Ftb **to be relegated** descender or bajar a una división inferior

relegation [relɪˈgeɪʃən] n (a) (of person, issue) relegación f (b) Br Ftb descenso m

relent [rɪˈlent] vi Fml ceder, aplacarse

relentless [rɪˈlentlɪs] adj implacable, despiadado(a), cruel

relentlessly [rɪˈlentlɪsli] adv implacablemente; **it rained r.** llovió sin cesar

relevance [ˈreləvəns] n relación f, pertinencia f

relevant [ˈreləvənt] adj pertinente (**to** a); **it is not r.** no viene al caso; **the r. details** los detalles pertinentes

reliability [rɪlaɪəˈbɪlɪti] n (a) (of employee) responsabilidad f (b) (of thing, information) fiabilidad f, Am confiabilidad

reliable [rɪˈlaɪəbəl] adj (a) (employee) responsable; **he's a r. worker** es un trabajador muy serio; **she's very r.** es muy de fiar (b) (thing) fiable, Am confiable; **a r. source** una fuente fidedigna

reliably [rɪˈlaɪəbli] adv de buena fuente; **to be r. informed that** saber de buena fuente que

reliance [rɪˈlaɪəns] n dependencia f

reliant [rɪˈlaɪənt] adj **to be r. on** depender de

relic [ˈrelɪk] n (a) Rel reliquia f (b) (reminder of past) vestigio m; recuerdo m (c) **relics** (human remains) restos mpl mortales, despojos mpl

relief [rɪ'liːf] n **(a)** *(alleviation)* alivio m; **to breathe a sigh of r.** dar un suspiro de alivio; **to bring r. from pain** aliviar el dolor; **what a r.!** ¡qué alivio! **(b)** *(aid)* auxilio m, ayuda f ▫ **r. fund** fondo m de asistencia a los necesitados **(c)** *(substitute)* relevo m **(d)** Art relieve m; **in r.** en relieve **(e)** Geog relieve m ▫ **r. map** mapa m en relieve **(f)** *(of city)* liberación f

relieve [rɪ'liːv] vt **(a)** *(ease)* aliviar; *(pain)* mitigar; *(monotony)* romper; **to r. sb of an obligation** librar a algn de una obligación **(b)** *(substitute)* relevar, sustituir **(c)** *(city)* liberar; Euph **to r. oneself** hacer sus necesidades; Euph **to r. sb of sth** coger algo a algn

relieved [rɪ'liːvd] adj aliviado(a), tranquilizado(a); **I'm r. to hear it** me tranquiliza oírlo

religion [rɪ'lɪdʒən] n religión f

religious [rɪ'lɪdʒəs] adj religioso(a)

religiously [rɪ'lɪdʒəslɪ] adv religiosamente; Fig **to do sth r.** hacer algo sin faltar nunca or religiosamente

relinquish [rɪ'lɪŋkwɪʃ] vt Fml renunciar a; **to r. one's hold on sth** soltar algo

relish ['relɪʃ] **1** n **(a)** Fml *(enjoyment)* gusto m, deleite m; **to do sth with great r.** deleitarse haciendo algo **(b)** Culin condimento m
2 vt agradar, gustar; **I don't r. the idea** no me agrada la idea

relive [riː'lɪv] vt revivir

reload [riː'ləʊd] **1** vt *(gun, camera)* volver a cargar
2 vi volver a cargar el arma, recargar

relocate [riːləʊ'keɪt] vt Fml trasladar

relocation [riːləʊ'keɪʃən] n Fml traslado m

reluctance [rɪ'lʌktəns] n desgana f

reluctant [rɪ'lʌktənt] adj reacio(a); **to be r. to do sth** no estar dispuesto(a) a hacer algo; **we were r. to explain** nos resistíamos a dar explicaciones

reluctantly [rɪ'lʌktəntlɪ] adv de mala gana, a regañadientes

rely [rɪ'laɪ] vi *(pt & pp relied)* contar **(on** con), confiar **(on** en); **r. on me** confía en mí; **they relied on the money he sent** contaban con el dinero que les mandaba

remain [rɪ'meɪn] **1** vi **(a)** *(stay)* permanecer, quedarse; **he remained at home** se quedó en casa; **they remained seated** permanecieron sentados(as); **to r. silent** permanecer silencioso(a) **(b)** *(be left)* quedar; **it remains to be seen** está por ver; **only one remains** sólo queda uno **(c)** *(in letters)* **I r.,** yours faithfully le saluda atentamente
2 n **remains** *(of building)* restos mpl; *(of earlier civilization)* vestigios mpl; **human r.** restos mortales

remainder [rɪ'meɪndər] **1** n **(a)** *(rest)* resto m; **the r. of the year** el resto del año **(b)** Math resto m
2 vt Com saldar

remaindered [rɪ'meɪndəːd] adj **r. books** libros mpl de saldo

remaining [rɪ'meɪnɪŋ] adj restante

remake ['riːmeɪk] **1** n Cin nueva versión f
2 [riː'meɪk] vt *(pt & pp remade)* hacer de nuevo

remand [rɪ'mɑːnd] **1** vt Jur remitir; **remanded in custody** en prevención; **remanded on bail** bajo fianza
2 n detención f; **on r.** detenido(a)

remark [rɪ'mɑːk] **1** n comentario m, observación f; **to pass a r. about sth** hacer una observación sobre algo
2 vt comentar, observar

remarkable [rɪ'mɑːkəbəl] adj **(a)** *(extraordinary)* extraordinario(a) **(b)** *(strange)* curioso(a), singular

remarkably [rɪ'mɑːkəblɪ] adv extraordinariamente

remarry [riː'mærɪ] vi volver a casarse

remedial [rɪ'miːdɪəl] adj Fml reparador(a); Educ **r. classes** clases fpl para niños atrasados; **r. exercises** ejercicios mpl correctivos

remedy ['remɪdɪ] **1** n Fml remedio m; **household r.** remedio casero; **r. for a cold** remedio contra un catarro
2 vt *(pt & pp remedied)* remediar

remember [rɪ'membər] **1** vt **(a)** *(recall)* acordarse de, recordar; **do you r. doing it?** ¿recuerdas haberlo hecho?; **I can't r. his name** no me acuerdo de su nombre **(b)** *(commemorate)* conmemorar; *(dead)* recordar **(c)** *(send good wishes)* dar recuerdos; **r. me to her** dale recuerdos de mi parte
2 vi acordarse, recordar; **as far as I r.** que yo recuerde

remembrance [rɪ'membrəns] n Fml **(a)** *(reminiscence)* recuerdo m **(b)** *(act)* conmemoración f; **in r. of** para conmemorar ▫ Br **R. Day** or **Sunday** día m en que se conmemora el armisticio de 1918

remind [rɪ'maɪnd] vt recordar; **r. me to do it** recuérdame que lo haga; **she reminds me of your sister** me recuerda a tu hermana; **that reminds me** ahora que me acuerdo

reminder [rɪ'maɪndər] n recordatorio m, aviso m; **to act as a r.** recordar, servir de recordatorio

reminisce [remɪ'nɪs] vi Fml rememorar; **to r. about the past** rememorar el pasado

reminiscence [remɪ'nɪsəns] n Fml memorias fpl

reminiscent [remɪ'nɪsənt] adj Fml nostálgico(a); **to be r. of** recordar

remiss [rɪ'mɪs] adj **(a)** *(lacking energy)* remiso(a) **(b)** *(negligent)* negligente, descuidado(a)

remission [rɪ'mɪʃən] n **(a)** *(of sins)* remisión f **(b)** **to be in r.** *(of disease)* haber remitido **(c)** Jur reducción f de la pena

remit [rɪ'mɪt] **1** vt *(pt & pp remitted)* Fml **(a)** *(pardon)* perdonar, remitir **(b)** *(send)* enviar, remitir **(c)** Jur referir a otro tribunal
2 ['riːmɪt] n informe m, órdenes fpl

remittance [rɪ'mɪtəns] n **(a)** *(sending)* envío m **(b)** *(payment)* giro m, pago m

remnant ['remnənt] n resto m; Fig *(trace)* vestigio m; **remnants of cloth** retales mpl

remold ['riːməʊld] n US see remould

remonstrance [rɪ'mɒnstrəns] n Fml *(complaint)* queja f; *(protest)* protesta f

remonstrate ['remənstreɪt] vi Fml protestar **(about** sth por algo); **to r. with sb** quejarse a algn

remorse [rɪ'mɔːs] n Fml remordimiento m; **to feel r. about sth** sentir remordimientos por algo

remorseful [rɪ'mɔːsfʊl] adj Fml lleno(a) de remordimiento

remorseless [rɪ'mɔːslɪs] adj despiadado(a), implacable

remortgage [riː'mɔːgɪdʒ] vt *(house, property)* volver a hipotecar

remote [rɪ'məʊt] adj **(a)** *(far away)* remoto(a); **r. country** país m remoto ▫ **r. control** mando m a distancia **(b)** *(isolated)* aislado(a), apartado(a), remoto(a); **r. spot** lugar m apartado **(c)** *(unlikely)* improbable; **not the remotest chance** ni la más mínima posibilidad **(d)** *(distant)* distante; **r. person** persona f reservada

remote-controlled [rɪməʊtkən'trəʊld] adj teledirigido(a), por control remoto

remotely [rɪ'məʊtlɪ] adv **(a)** *(vaguely)* vagamente **(b)** *(distantly)* aisladamente

remoteness [rɪ'məʊtnɪs] n **(a)** *(distance)* lejanía f **(b)** *(improbability)* improbabilidad f

remould ['ri:məʊld] n Aut neumático m recauchutado, Col Méx llanta f or Arg goma f recauchutada

remount [ri:'maʊnt] vt & vi (a) (bicycle) volver a subir (b) (photo) volver a enmarcar

removable [rɪ'mu:vəbəl] adj (a) (movable) móvil, movible (b) (detachable) que se puede quitar; **r. covers** fundas fpl de quita y pon

removal [rɪ'mu:vəl] n (a) (moving house) mudanza f, traslado m; **r. expenses** gastos mpl de traslado; **r. van** camión m de mudanzas (b) (getting rid of) eliminación f

remove [rɪ'mu:v] **1** vt (a) (move) quitar, retirar, Am sacar; **to r. an obstacle** eliminar un obstáculo; **to r. one's coat/hat** quitarse el abrigo/el sombrero; **to r. one's make-up** desmaquillarse; **to r. one's name from a list** tachar su nombre de una lista (b) (dismiss) despedir; **to r. sb from his/her post** despedir a algn
2 adj Fml **at one r. from** relacionado(a) con

removed [rɪ'mu:vd] adj (a) **far r. from** muy diferente de, ajeno(a) a (b) **cousin once r.** primo(a) m,f segundo(a)

remover [rɪ'mu:vər] n **make-up r.** desmaquillador m; **nail varnish r.** quitaesmalte m; **paint r.** quitapinturas m inv; **stain r.** quitamanchas m inv

remunerate [rɪ'mju:nəreɪt] vt Fml remunerar

remuneration [rɪmju:nə'reɪʃən] n Fml remuneración f

remunerative [rɪ'mju:nərətɪv] adj Fml remunerativo(a)

renaissance [rə'neɪsəns] **1** n renacimiento m; **the R.** el Renacimiento
2 adj renacentista

renal ['ri:nəl] adj renal

rename [ri:'neɪm] vt renombrar

rend [rend] vt (pt & pp rent) (tear) desgarrar, rasgar; (noise) invadir, irrumpir

render ['rendər] vt (a) (give) dar, prestar; **for services rendered** por los servicios prestados; **to r. homage to sb** rendir homenaje a algn (b) (make) hacer (c) Com presentar; **to r. an account** presentar una factura (d) (translate) traducir; **rendered into Spanish** traducido(a) al castellano (e) (plaster) enlucir

rendering ['rendərɪŋ] n (a) (performance) interpretación f (b) (translation) traducción f

rendezvous ['rɒndɪvu:] **1** n (pl rendezvous ['rɒndɪvu:z]) (a) (meeting) cita f; **to have a r. with sb** tener una cita con algn (b) (place) lugar m de reunión
2 vi reunirse

rendition [ren'dɪʃən] n interpretación f

renegade ['renɪgeɪd] n renegado(a) m,f

renege [rɪ'ni:g, rɪ'neɪg] vi Fml (a) **to r. on** (break) faltar a; **he reneged on his promise** faltó a su promesa (b) Cards renunciar

renew [rɪ'nju:] vt (passport, contract) renovar; (talks, activity) reanudar; **to r. talks** reanudar las conversaciones; **with renewed vigour** con nuevas fuerzas

renewable [rɪ'nju:əbəl] adj renovable

renewal [rɪ'nju:əl] n (of passport, contract) renovación f; (of talks, activity) reanudación f

rennet ['renɪt] n cuajo m

renounce [rɪ'naʊns] vt Fml renunciar

renouncement [rɪ'naʊnsmənt] n Fml renuncia f

renovate ['renəveɪt] vt restaurar

renovation [renə'veɪʃən] n restauración f

renown [rɪ'naʊn] n renombre m, fama f

renowned [rɪ'naʊnd] adj renombrado(a), célebre, famoso(a)

rent¹ [rent] **1** n (a) (of building, car, TV) alquiler m; **flat for r. se alquila piso; how much r. do you pay?** ¿cuánto pagas de alquiler?; **r. rebate** devolución f de alquiler (b) (of land) arriendo m
2 pt & pp see rend
3 vt (a) (building, car, TV) alquilar, Méx rentar (b) (land) arrendar

rent out vt alquilar

rent² [rent] pt & pp see rend

rentable ['rentəbəl] adj (a) (house etc) alquilable (b) (land) arrendable

rental ['rentəl] **1** n (a) (of house etc) alquiler m (b) (of land) arriendo m
2 adj de alquiler; **r. company** compañía f de alquileres

rented ['rentɪd] adj (house etc) alquilado(a), de alquiler (b) (land) arrendado(a)

rent-free [rent'fri:] **1** adj exento(a) de alquiler, gratuito(a)
2 adv sin pagar alquiler, gratis

renunciation [rɪnʌnsɪ'eɪʃən] n Fml renuncia f

reopen [ri:'əʊpən] **1** vt (frontier, investigation) reabrir; (talks) reanudar; Fig **to r. old wounds** abrir viejas heridas
2 vi (shop, theatre) volver a abrir; **school reopens on the 21st of August** las clases se reanudan el 21 de agosto

reorder [ri:'ɔ:dər] vt Com pedir de nuevo, hacer un nuevo pedido de

reorganization [ri:ɔ:gənaɪ'zeɪʃən] n reorganización f

reorganize [ri:'ɔ:gənaɪz] vt reorganizar; **to r. oneself** reorganizarse

reorient [ri:'ɔ:rɪent] vt reorientar; **to r. oneself** orientarse de nuevo

rep [rep] Fam (a) Com representante mf (b) Theat teatro m de repertorio

repackage [ri:'pækɪdʒ] vt (goods) reempaquetar, reembalar; Fig (renew image of) renovar la imagen de

repaid [ri:'peɪd] pt & pp see repay

repaint [ri:'peɪnt] vt repintar

repair [rɪ'peər] **1** n reparación f, arreglo m; **in good/bad r.** en buen/mal estado; **to be beyond r.** no tener arreglo; **to be under r.** estar en reparación
2 vt (a) (gen) arreglar; (car) reparar; (clothes) remendar; **to take sth to be repaired** llevar algo a arreglar (b) (make amends) reparar

repairable [rɪ'peərəbəl] adj reparable

repairman [rɪ'peəmæn] n (pl repairmen) técnico m

reparation [repə'reɪʃən] n (a) (amends) reparación f (b) **reparations** (compensation) indemnización f sing

repartee [repɑ:'ti:] n respuesta f ingeniosa, réplica f aguda

repast [rɪ'pɑ:st] n Literary colación f, comida f

repatriate [ri:'pætrɪeɪt] vt repatriar

repatriation [ri:pætrɪ'eɪʃən] n repatriación f

repay [ri:'peɪ] vt (pt & pp repaid) devolver; **to r. a debt** liquidar una deuda; **to r. a kindness** devolver un favor

repayable [ri:'peɪəbəl] adj pagadero(a), reembolsable

repayment [ri:'peɪmənt] n pago m, reembolso m, devolución f

repeal [rɪ'pi:l] Jur **1** n revocación f, abrogación f
2 vt revocar, abrogar

repeat [rɪ'pi:t] **1** vt repetir; **don't r. this to anyone** no se lo digas a nadie; Com **an offer that can't be repeated** una oferta única; **to r. oneself** repetirse
2 vi Fam (food) repetir
3 n (repetition) repetición f; TV reposición f; Cin reestreno m

repeated [rɪ'pi:tɪd] adj repetido(a)

repeatedly [rɪˈpiːtɪdlɪ] *adv* repetidas veces

repeater [rɪˈpiːtər] *n (firearm)* arma *f* de repetición

repel [rɪˈpel] *vt (pt & pp* **repelled**) (**a**) *(fight off)* repeler, rechazar (**b**) *(disgust)* repugnar, repeler (**c**) *Tech* repeler

repellent [rɪˈpelənt] **1** *adj* repelente; **water-r.** impermeable
  2 *n* (**insect**) **r.** loción *f* or spray *m* anti-insectos

repent [rɪˈpent] *vt & vi* arrepentirse (de)

repentance [rɪˈpentəns] *n* arrepentimiento *m*

repentant [rɪˈpentənt] *adj* arrepentido(a)

repercussion [riːpəˈkʌʃən] *n* repercusión *f*

repertoire [ˈrepətwɑːr] *n* repertorio *m*; **she has a great r. of songs** tiene un extenso repertorio de canciones

repertory [ˈrepətərɪ] *n Theat* teatro *m* de repertorio

repetition [repɪˈtɪʃən] *n* repetición *f*

repetitious [repɪˈtɪʃəs] *adj* repetitivo(a)

repetitive [rɪˈpetɪtɪv] *adj* reiterativo(a), lleno(a) de repeticiones; *(work)* monótono(a); *(rhythm)* machacón(ona)

rephrase [riːˈfreɪz] *vt* decir de otra manera

replace [rɪˈpleɪs] *vt* (**a**) *(put back)* volver a poner en su sitio; *Tel* **r. the receiver** cuelgue el teléfono (**b**) *(substitute)* sustituir, reemplazar; **to r. a broken glass** reemplazar un vaso roto; **to r. one thing for another** sustituir una cosa por otra

replacement [rɪˈpleɪsmənt] *n* (**a**) *(putting back)* sustitución *f*, substitución *f*, reemplazo *m* (**b**) *(person)* sustituto(a) *m,f*, substituto(a) *m,f* (**c**) *(part)* pieza *f* de recambio

replay [ˈriːpleɪ] *n Sport* repetición *f*; *TV* (**action**) **r.** repetición de una secuencia

replenish [rɪˈplenɪʃ] *vt* (**a**) *(fill up)* rellenar (**with** con) (**b**) *(stock up)* abastecer (**with** de); **to r. stocks** reponer las existencias

replete [rɪˈpliːt] *adj Fml* repleto(a)

replica [ˈreplɪkə] *n* réplica *f*, copia *f*

replicate [ˈreplɪkeɪt] *vt* reproducir

reply [rɪˈplaɪ] **1** *n* respuesta *f*, contestación *f*; *Com* **in r. to your letter** en respuesta a su carta; **what was his r.?** ¿cuál fue su respuesta?
  2 *vi* (*pt & pp* **replied**) responder, contestar; **to r. to a letter** contestar una carta

report [rɪˈpɔːt] **1** *n* (**a**) *(account)* informe *m*, *Andes CAm Méx Ven* reporte *m*; **medical r.** parte *m* médico; **monthly r.** informe mensual; *Br* **school r.**, *US* **r. card** boletín *m* de evaluación, *RP* carné *m* de notas *or* calificaciones; **weather r.** boletín *m* del tiempo (**b**) *(piece of news)* noticia *f* (**c**) *Press Rad TV* reportaje *m* (**on** sobre) (**d**) *(rumour)* rumor *m*, voz *f*; **there are reports that ...** corre el rumor de que ... (**e**) *Fml (of gun)* estampido *m*, detonación *f*
  2 *vt* (**a**) *(record)* informar, comunicar; **it is reported that ...** se dice que ...; **they reported that everything was going well** informaron de que todo iba bien (**b**) *(tell)* dar parte de, denunciar; **to r. an accident/a theft to the police** dar parte a la policía de un accidente/denunciar un robo a la policía (**c**) *Press* hacer un reportaje sobre (**d**) *(complain)* denunciar, acusar; **she reported him to her teacher** se quejó de él a su profesor
  3 *vi* (**a**) *(give account)* hacer un informe (**b**) *Press* informar, *CAm Méx* reportar (**c**) *(present oneself)* presentarse; **to r. for work** presentarse al trabajo; **to r. sick** coger la baja por enfermedad

reported [rɪˈpɔːtɪd] *adj Ling* **r. speech** estilo *m* indirecto

reportedly [rɪˈpɔːtɪdlɪ] *adv Fml* según se dice

reporter [rɪˈpɔːtər] *n* periodista *mf*, reportero(a) *m,f*

repose [rɪˈpəʊz] **1** *n* reposo *m*
  2 *vt & vi* reposar, descansar

repository [rɪˈpɒzɪtərɪ] *n* (**a**) *(place)* depósito *m*; **furniture r.** guardamuebles *m inv* (**b**) *(person)* depositario(a) *m,f* (**c**) *(source)* fuente *f*, mina *f*

repossess [riːpəˈzes] *vt* recuperar, volver a tomar posesión

repossession [riːpəˈzeʃən] *n* recuperación *f*

reprehensible [reprɪˈhensəbəl] *adj* reprensible, censurable

represent [reprɪˈzent] *vt* representar; **she represented France in the Olympic Games** representó a Francia en los Juegos Olímpicos; **what does that symbol r.?** ¿qué representa ese símbolo?

representation [reprɪzenˈteɪʃən] *n* (**a**) *(gen)* representación *f* □ *Pol* **proportional r.** representación *f* proporcional (**b**) *Fml* **representations** queja *f sing*; **to make r. to sb about sth** protestar a algn por algo

representative [reprɪˈzentətɪv] **1** *adj* representativo(a), típico(a), característico(a); **to be r. of** reflejar
  2 *n* (**a**) *(of company, on committee)* representante *mf* (**b**) *US Pol* representante *mf*, diputado(a) *m,f*; **House of Representatives** Cámara *f* de Representantes

repress [rɪˈpres] *vt* reprimir, contener

repressed [rɪˈprest] *adj* reprimido(a)

repression [rɪˈpreʃən] *n* represión *f*

repressive [rɪˈpresɪv] *adj* represivo(a); **r. measures** medidas represivas

reprieve [rɪˈpriːv] **1** *n* (**a**) *Jur* suspensión *f* de la ejecución de sentencia; *(pardon)* indulto *m* (**b**) *Fig* alivio *m*, respiro *m*; **I've been given a month's r.** me lo han aplazado un mes
  2 *vt* (**a**) *Jur* suspender la ejecución de sentencia; *(pardon)* indultar (**b**) *(give temporary relief)* aliviar temporalmente (**c**) *(postpone)* aplazar

reprimand [ˈreprɪmɑːnd] **1** *n* reprimenda *f*, reprensión *f*
  2 *vt* reprender

reprint [ˈriːprɪnt] **1** *n* reimpresión *f*, reedición *f*
  2 [riːˈprɪnt] *vt* reimprimir

reprisal [rɪˈpraɪzəl] *n* represalia *f*; **there were no reprisals** no hubo represalias

reproach [rɪˈprəʊtʃ] **1** *n Fml* reproche *m*; **a look of r.** una mirada de reproche; **above** *or* **beyond r.** sin tacha, intachable
  2 *vt* reprochar; **to r. oneself for sth** reprocharse algo

reproachful [rɪˈprəʊtʃfʊl] *adj* reprochador(a), reprobador(a)

reprobate [ˈreprəʊbeɪt] *adj & n* réprobo(a) *(m,f)*, libertino(a) *(m,f)*

reprocess [riːˈprəʊses] *vt* reprocesar, volver a tratar

reproduce [riːprəˈdjuːs] **1** *vt* reproducir
  2 *vi* reproducirse, multiplicarse

reproduction [riːprəˈdʌkʃən] *n* reproducción *f* □ **r. furniture** reproducciones *fpl* de muebles antiguos

reproductive [riːprəˈdʌktɪv] *adj* reproductor(a); **r. organs** órganos *mpl* reproductores

reproof [rɪˈpruːf] *n Fml* reprobación *f*, censura *f*

reprove [rɪˈpruːv] *vt Fml* reprobar, censurar

reproving [rɪˈpruːvɪŋ] *adj Fml* reprobatorio(a)

reptile [ˈreptaɪl] *n Zool* reptil *m*

reptilian [repˈtɪlɪən] *adj also Fig* de reptil

republic [rɪˈpʌblɪk] *n* república *f*

republican [rɪˈpʌblɪkən] *adj & n* republicano(a) *(m,f)*; *US Pol* **R. Party** Partido *m* Republicano

republicanism [rɪˈpʌblɪkənɪzəm] *n* republicanismo *m*

repudiate [rɪ'pju:dɪeɪt] *vt Fml* (**a**) *(reject)* rechazar (**b**) *(disown)* repudiar (**c**) *(refuse to acknowledge)* negarse a reconocer

repudiation [rɪpju:dɪ'eɪʃən] *n* (**a**) *(rejection)* rechazo *m* (**b**) *(disowning)* repudio *m*, repudiación *f* (**c**) *(refusal to acknowledge)* repudio *m*, repudiación *f*

repugnance [rɪ'pʌgnəns] *n* repugnancia *f*, repulsión *f*, aversión *f*

repugnant [rɪ'pʌgnənt] *adj* repugnante, repulsivo(a)

repulse [rɪ'pʌls] *vt* (**a**) *(repel)* rechazar (**b**) *(cause to retreat)* hacer retroceder a

repulsion [rɪ'pʌlʃən] *n* (**a**) *(revulsion)* repulsión *f*, repugnancia *f* (**b**) *(rejection)* rechazo *m*

repulsive [rɪ'pʌlsɪv] *adj* repulsivo(a)

reputable ['repjʊtəbəl] *adj (company etc)* acreditado(a); *(person, institution)* de buena reputación; *(person, products)* de toda confianza

reputably ['repjʊtəblɪ] *adv* acreditadamente

reputation [repjʊ'teɪʃən] *n* reputación *f*, fama *f*; **to have a good r.** tener buena reputación; **to have a r. for being a heavy drinker** tener fama de borracho(a)

repute [rɪ'pju:t] *n Fml* reputación *f*, fama *f*; **a singer of r.** un cantante famoso; **to hold in r.** tener en gran estima

reputed [rɪ'pju:tɪd] *adj* (**a**) *(supposed)* supuesto(a); **the r. offender** el supuesto delincuente (**b**) *(considered as)* considerado(a) como; **she is r. to be the best cook in the village** se la considera la mejor cocinera del pueblo

reputedly [rɪ'pju:tɪdlɪ] *adv* según se dice, supuestamente

request [rɪ'kwest] **1** *n* petición *f*, solicitud *f*; *Am* pedido *m*; **at her r.** a petición suya; **available on r.** disponible a petición de los interesados; **to make a r. for sth** hacer una petición *or Am* un pedido (de algo) ❑ *Aut* **r. stop** parada *f* discrecional

2 *vt* pedir, solicitar; *Fml* **Mr and Mrs Walton r. the pleasure of your company at their daughter's wedding** los Señores Walton tienen el honor de invitarles a la boda de su hija; *Fml* **you are requested not to smoke** se ruega no fumar

requiem ['rekwɪəm] *n Rel* réquiem *m* ❑ **r. mass** misa *f* de réquiem

require [rɪ'kwaɪər] *vt* (**a**) *(need)* necesitar, requerir; **what do you r.?** ¿qué necesitas?; **when required** cuando haga falta, en caso de necesidad (**b**) *(demand)* requerir, exigir, pedir; **it's a job which requires great patience** es un trabajo que exige mucha paciencia; **we are required by law to wear seat belts** la ley nos obliga a llevar cinturones de seguridad

required [rɪ'kwaɪəd] *adj* necesario(a), requerido(a); **the r. number of words** el número prescrito de palabras

requirement [rɪ'kwaɪəmənt] *n* (**a**) *(need)* necesidad *f* (**b**) *(demand)* requisito *m*; **to meet all the requirements** satisfacer todos los requisitos

requisite ['rekwɪzɪt] *Fml* **1** *adj* requerido(a), indispensable; *(decided beforehand)* prescrito(a)

2 *n* requisito *m* ❑ **sports requisites** equipo *m sing* para deporte; **travel requisites** artículos *mpl* de viaje

requisition [rekwɪ'zɪʃən] **1** *n* requisición *f*, requisa *f*

2 *vt* requisar

reran [ri:'ræn] *pt see* **rerun**

reredos ['rɪədɒs] *n* retablo *m*

rerelease ['ri:rɪ'li:s] **1** *n* (movie) reestreno *m*; (record) relanzamiento *m*

2 *vt* (movie) reestrenar; (record) relanzar

rerun [ri:'rʌn] **1** *vt* (*pt* **reran**; *pp* **rerun**) *Cin* reestrenar; *TV Theat* reponer

2 ['ri:rʌn] *n Cin* reestreno *m*; *TV Theat* reposición *f*

resale ['ri:seɪl, ri:'seɪl] *n* reventa *f*

resat [ri:'sæt] *pt & pp see* **resit**

rescind [rɪ'sɪnd] *vt Fml Jur (contract)* rescindir; *(law)* abrogar, revocar

rescue ['reskju:] **1** *n* rescate *m*; **to go to sb's r.** acudir en auxilio de algn ❑ **r. team** equipo *m* de rescate

2 *vt* rescatar, salvar

rescuer ['reskjʊər] *n* rescatador(a) *m,f*, salvador(a) *m,f*

research [rɪ'sɜ:tʃ] **1** *n* investigación *f*; **to do r. on a subject** investigar un tema ❑ **r. work** trabajo *m* de investigación

2 *vt* investigar; **to r. a book** documentarse para escribir un libro; **well researched** bien documentado(a)

3 *vi* investigar; **to r. into smoking habits** investigar los hábitos de los fumadores

researcher [rɪ'sɜ:tʃər] *n* investigador(a) *m,f*

resemblance [rɪ'zembləns] *n* parecido *m*, semejanza *f*; **it bears no r. to cheese** no se parece en absoluto al queso

resemble [rɪ'zembəl] *vt* parecerse a; **she resembles her mother** se parece a su madre

resent [rɪ'zent] *vt* resentirse, ofenderse por, tomar a mal; **he resented my being there** mi presencia le molestó; **I r. your attitude** tu actitud me ofende

resentful [rɪ'zentfʊl] *adj* resentido(a), ofendido(a)

resentment [rɪ'zentmənt] *n* resentimiento *m*; **to feel r. towards sb** guardar rencor a algn

reservation [rezə'veɪʃən] *n* (**a**) *(booking)* reserva, *Am* reservación *f*; **to make a r.** hacer la reserva (**b**) *(misgiving)* reserva *f*; **with reservations** con ciertas reservas (**c**) *(land)* reserva *f*; **Indian r.** reserva *f* india

reserve [rɪ'zɜ:v] **1** *n* (**a**) *(gen)* reserva *f*; **reserves of food** reservas de alimentos; **to keep sth in r.** guardar algo de reserva ❑ **game r.** coto *m* de caza; **natural r.** parque *m* natural (**b**) *Sport* reserva *mf*, suplente *mf* (**c**) *Mil* **reserves** reservas *fpl*

2 *vt* reservar; **to r. one's judgement on sth** reservarse la opinión sobre algo; **to r. one's strength** ahorrar fuerzas; **to r. seats** reservar plazas; **to r. sth for later** guardar algo para después

reserved [rɪ'zɜ:vd] *adj* reservado(a); **all rights r.** reservados todos los derechos

reservist [rɪ'zɜ:vɪst] *n Mil* reservista *mf*

reservoir ['rezəvwɑ:r] *n* (**a**) *(artificial lake)* embalse *m*, pantano *m* (**b**) *(large supply)* reserva *f*, acumulación *f*

reset [ri:'set] (*pt & pp* **reset**) *vt (watch)* ajustar; *(counter)* poner a cero; *Med (bone)* colocar en su sitio; *Comptr* **r. button** *or* **switch** botón *m* para reinicializar

reshape [ri:'ʃeɪp] *vt* rehacer; *Fig* reorganizar

reshuffle [ri:'ʃʌfəl] **1** *n Pol* reorganización *f*, remodelación *f*; **cabinet r.** reorganización del gabinete

2 *vt* (**a**) *Pol* reorganizar (**b**) *Cards* volver a barajar

reside [rɪ'zaɪd] *vi Fml* (**a**) *(live)* residir; **to r. in London** residir en Londres (**b**) *(be)* hallar; **power resides in the unions** los sindicatos tienen mucho poder

residence ['rezɪdəns] *n Fml (home)* residencia *f*; *(address)* domicilio *m*; *(period of time)* permanencia *f*; **to take up r.** fijar residencia ❑ *Br Univ* **hall of r.** residencia *f*

resident ['rezɪdənt] **1** *n* residente *mf*; *US Med* = médico que ha cumplido la residencia y prosigue con su especialización

2 *adj* residente; **to be r. in a town** residir en una ciudad ❑ **r. population** población *f* fija

residential [rezɪ'denʃəl] *adj* residencial; **r. area** barrio *m* residencial

residual [rɪ'zɪdjʊəl] *adj* residual

residue ['rezɪdjuː] n residuo m

resign [rɪ'zaɪn] **1** vt **(a)** (give up) dimitir; **he resigned from the committee** dimitió de la comisión **(b)** (accept sth unpleasant) resignarse a; **to r. oneself to sth** resignarse a algo.
2 vi dimitir, presentar la dimisión

resignation [rezɪg'neɪʃən] n **(a)** (from a job) dimisión f; **to hand in one's r.** presentar la dimisión **(b)** (surrender) resignación f

resigned [rɪ'zaɪnd] adj resignado(a); **he's r. to his fate** está resignado con su suerte

resilience [rɪ'zɪlɪəns] n **(a)** (strength) resistencia f **(b)** (flexibility) elasticidad f

resilient [rɪ'zɪlɪənt] adj **(a)** (strong) resistente, fuerte **(b)** (flexible) elástico(a)

resin ['rezɪn] n resina f

resist [rɪ'zɪst] vt **(a)** (not yield to) resistir; **I couldn't r. eating another chocolate** no pude resistir a la tentación de comer otro bombón **(b)** (oppose) oponerse; **to r. change** oponerse a los cambios

resistance [rɪ'zɪstəns] n resistencia f; **he offered no r.** no ofreció resistencia; **her r. to illness is low** tiene poca resistencia a las enfermedades; **to take the line of least r.** optar por la solución más fácil

resistant [rɪ'zɪstənt] adj resistente

resistor [rɪ'zɪstər] n Elec reóstato m

resit [riː'sɪt] vt (pt & pp resat) (exam) volver a presentarse a

resolute ['rezəluːt] adj resuelto(a), decidido(a)

resolutely ['rezəluːtlɪ] adv resueltamente, con firmeza

resolution [rezə'luːʃən] n resolución f, decisión f, determinación f; **she showed a great deal of r.** se mostró muy decidida; **to make/pass a r.** tomar/aprobar una resolución

resolve [rɪ'zɒlv] **1** n resolución f
2 vt resolver
3 vi resolverse; **to r. to do sth** resolverse a hacer algo

resonance ['rezənəns] n resonancia f

resonant ['rezənənt] adj resonante

resonate ['rezəneɪt] vi resonar

resort [rɪ'zɔːt] **1** n **(a)** (place) lugar m de vacaciones □ **seaside r.** lugar m de veraneo; **ski r.** estación f de esquí; **tourist r.** centro m turístico **(b)** (recourse) recurso m; **as a last r.** como último recurso
2 vi recurrir; **to r. to violence** recurrir a la violencia

resound [rɪ'zaʊnd] vi resonar; Fig tener resonancia

resounding [rɪ'zaʊndɪŋ] adj (of sound) resonante; (very great) impresionante; **a r. failure** un fracaso total; **a r. success** un éxito rotundo

resource [rɪ'sɔːs] n recurso m; **natural resources** recursos naturales; **to be left to one's own resources** tener que apañárselas por cuenta propia

resourceful [rɪ'sɔːsfʊl] adj ingenioso(a), despabilado(a)

respect [rɪ'spekt] **1** n **(a)** (deference) respeto m; **lack of r.** falta f de respeto; **to pay one's respects to sb** presentar sus respetos a algn; **to show r. for sb** respetar a algn **(b)** (relation, reference) respecto m; **in that r.** a ese respecto; **with r. to** con referencia a
2 vt respetar; **she was respected as a teacher** estaba bien considerada como profesora; **to r. sb's opinion** respetar la opinión de algn

respectability [rɪspektə'bɪlɪtɪ] n respetabilidad f

respectable [rɪ'spektəbəl] adj respetable; **to put on some r. clothes** ponerse ropa decente

respectably [rɪ'spektəblɪ] adv de forma respetable; **r. dressed** vestido(a) con decoro

respected [rɪ'spektɪd] adj respetado(a)

respectful [rɪ'spektfʊl] adj respetuoso(a)

respectfully [rɪ'spektfʊlɪ] adv respetuosamente, con respeto

respective [rɪ'spektɪv] adj respectivo(a)

respectively [rɪ'spektɪvlɪ] adv respectivamente

respiration [respə'reɪʃən] n respiración f

respiratory [rɪ'respərətərɪ] adj respiratorio(a)

respite ['respaɪt] n Fml **(a)** (rest) respiro m, tregua f; **I haven't had a moment's r.** no he tenido ni un momento de respiro **(b)** (postponement) plazo m

resplendent [rɪ'splendənt] adj resplandeciente; **to be r.** resplandecer

respond [rɪ'spɒnd] vi **(a)** (reply) responder, contestar **(b)** (react favourably) responder; Med **to r. to treatment** responder al tratamiento

respondent [rɪ'spɒndənt] n **(a)** Jur demandado(a) m,f **(b)** (of questionnaire) encuestado(a) m,f

response [rɪ'spɒns] n **(a)** (reply) respuesta f, contestación f; **in r. to** en respuesta a **(b)** (reaction) reacción f; **r. time** (of emergency services) tiempo m de respuesta

responsibility [rɪspɒnsə'bɪlɪtɪ] n responsabilidad f; **opening the shop is your r.** te corresponde a ti abrir la tienda; **to accept r.** asumir la responsabilidad; **to hold a position of r.** ocupar un puesto de responsabilidad

responsible [rɪ'spɒnsəbəl] adj responsable; **to be r. for one's actions** hacerse responsable de sus acciones; **to be r. to sb** tener que dar cuentas a algn, estar bajo las ordenes de algn

responsive [rɪ'spɒnsɪv] adj sensible (to a); Med **he was r. to treatment** respondió bien al tratamiento

responsiveness [rɪ'spɒnsɪvnɪs] n sensibilidad f

rest[1] [rest] **1** n **(a)** (break, repose) descanso m, reposo m; **I need a r.** necesito descansar; **to have a good r.** descansar bien; Fml **to lay sb to r.** enterrar a algn □ **r. cure** cura f de reposo; **r. home** Med casa f de reposo; (for old people) asilo m de ancianos; US **r. room** baño m, Esp servicios mpl, CSur toilette m **(b)** (peace) tranquilidad f, sosiego m; **at r.** (person) tranquilo(a); (object) inmóvil; **I shan't have any r. until they phone** no me quedaré tranquilo hasta que no llamen; **to set sb's mind at r.** tranquilizar a algn **(c)** (support) apoyo m, soporte m **(d)** Mus pausa f
2 vt **(a)** (cause to repose) descansar; **to r. one's legs** descansar las piernas **(b)** (lean) apoyar; **to r. a ladder against a wall** apoyar una escalera contra una pared
3 vi **(a)** (relax) descansar; **she's resting** está descansando; **to be resting** (actor) estar sin trabajo **(b)** (be calm) estar tranquilo(a), quedarse tranquilo(a); **I won't r. until I've finished it** no me quedaré tranquilo hasta que no lo termine **(c)** Jur **the case rests on ...** el pleito se basa en ... **(d)** Fml (be buried) descansar; **may he r. in peace** que descanse en paz

rest[2] [rest] **1** n (remainder) **the r.** el resto, lo demás; **I'll tell you the r. tomorrow** mañana te contaré el resto; **the r. of the day** el resto del día; **the r. of the girls** las demás chicas; **the r. of us** los demás
2 vi quedar; **it doesn't r. with me** no depende de mí; **it rests with him to decide** le corresponde a él decidir; **r. assured that** tenga la seguridad de que; **there the matter rests** allí queda el asunto

restaurant ['restərɒnt] n restaurante m □ Rail **r. car** coche m restaurante

restaurateur [restərə'tɜːr] n Fml dueño(a) m,f de un restaurante

restful ['restfʊl] adj descansado(a), tranquilo(a); **a r. holiday** unas vacaciones tranquilas

restitution [restɪ'tjuːʃən] *n Fml* restitución *f*; **to make r.** restituir

restive ['restɪv] *adj* inquieto(a), nervioso(a)

restless ['restlɪs] *adj* agitado(a), inquieto(a), intranquilo(a); **to have a r. night** pasar una noche agitada

restlessness ['restlɪsnɪs] *n* agitación *f*, inquietud *f*

restoration [restə'reɪʃən] *n* (a) *(giving back)* devolución *f*, restitución *f* (b) *Hist* **the R.** la Restauración (c) *(repairing)* restauración *f*

restorative [rɪ'stɒrətɪv] *adj & n* reconstituyente *(m)*

restore [rɪ'stɔːr] *vt* (a) *(give back)* devolver, restituir; **to r. sth to its owner** devolver algo a su dueño (b) *(re-establish)* restablecer; **to r. order** restablecer el orden; **to r. the monarchy** restaurar la monarquía (c) *(repair)* restaurar

restorer [rɪ'stɔːrər] *n* (a) *Art* restaurador(a) *m,f* (b) **hair r.** tónico *m* capilar

restrain [rɪ'streɪn] *vt* contener, controlar; **to r. one's anger** reprimir la cólera; **to r. oneself** contenerse

restrained [rɪ'streɪnd] *adj* (a) *(emotion)* contenido(a) (b) *(person)* sereno(a), dueño(a) de sí mismo(a)

restraint [rɪ'streɪnt] *n* (a) *(restriction)* restricción *f*; *(hindrance)* traba *f* (b) *(moderation)* moderación *f*; **to act with r.** actuar con moderación; **to show r./a lack of r.** saber/no saber dominarse

restrict [rɪ'strɪkt] *vt* restringir, limitar; **to r. oneself to two glasses of wine a day** limitarse a dos vasos de vino al día

restricted [rɪ'strɪktɪd] *adj* (a) *(access, opportunities)* restringido(a), limitado(a); *Aut* **r. area** zona *f* de velocidad limitada; **r. document** documento *m* secreto (b) *US (movie)* no recomendado(a) para menores

restriction [rɪ'strɪkʃən] *n* restricción *f*, limitación *f*

restrictive [rɪ'strɪktɪv] *adj* restrictivo(a); *Ind* **r. practices** prácticas *fpl* restrictivas de producción

restructure [riː'strʌktʃər] *vt* reestructurar

restructuring [riː'strʌktʃərɪŋ] *n Ind* reestructuración *f*, reconversión

result [rɪ'zʌlt] **1** *n* (a) *(outcome)* resultado *m*; *Pol* **election results** resultados *mpl* de las elecciones; **without r.** *(no consequence)* sin resultado; *(unsuccessful)* sin éxito (b) *(consequence)* consecuencia *f*; **as a r. of** como consecuencia de; **with the r. that ...** así es que ...
2 *vi* resultar; **to r. from** resultar de; **to r. in** causar; **it resulted in victory** acabó siendo una victoria

resultant [rɪ'sʌltənt] *adj* resultante

resume [rɪ'zjuːm] **1** *vt* *(journey, work, negotiations)* reanudar; *(control)* reasumir; *(conversation)* seguir; **to r. one's seat** volver a sentarse
2 *vi* recomenzar, comenzar de nuevo; continuar; **we will r. at ten o'clock** seguiremos a las diez

résumé ['rezjʊmeɪ] *n* (a) *(summary)* resumen *m* (b) *(CV)* currículum (vitae) *m*

resumption [rɪ'zʌmpʃən] *n* reanudación *f*, continuación *f*; **on r. of work** al reanudarse el trabajo

resurface [riː'sɜːfɪs] **1** *vt* *(roads)* rehacer el firme de
2 *vi* (a) *(submarine)* volver a salir a la superficie (b) *Fig* resurgir, surgir de nuevo

resurgence [rɪ'sɜːdʒəns] *n* resurgimiento *m*

resurgent [rɪ'sɜːdʒənt] *adj* renaciente

resurrect [rezə'rekt] *vt* resucitar; **to r. old customs** resucitar las viejas costumbres

resurrection [rezə'rekʃən] *n* resurrección *f*; *Rel* **the R.** la Resurrección

resuscitate [rɪ'sʌsɪteɪt] *vt Med* reanimar, resucitar

resuscitation [rɪsʌsɪ'teɪʃən] *n Med* reanimación *f*, resucitación *f*

retail ['riːteɪl] *Com* **1** *n* venta *f* al por menor, *Am* menoreo *m*
❑ **r. outlet** punto *m* de venta; **r. price** precio *m* de venta al público
2 *vt* vender al por menor *or* al detalle
3 *vi* venderse al por menor *or* al detalle; **it retails at ten dollars** se vende a diez dólares
4 *adv* al por menor, al detalle

retailer ['riːteɪlər] *n Com* detallista *mf*

retain [rɪ'teɪn] *vt* (a) *(keep temperature)* conservar; *(personal effects)* guardar, quedarse con; **to r. control of sth** mantener el control sobre algo (b) *(hold) (water etc)* retener (c) *(remember)* recordar, acordarse de, retener; **I can't r. names** no se me quedan los nombres en la memoria (d) *Jur* **to r. the services of a lawyer** contratar a un abogado

retainer [rɪ'teɪnər] *n* (a) *(payment)* anticipo *m* sobre los honorarios (b) *(servant)* criado(a) *m,f*

retake ['riːteɪk] **1** *n Cin (of a scene)* nueva toma *f*
2 [riː'teɪk] *vt* *(pt retook; pp retaken* [riː'teɪkən]*)* (a) *Mil* volver a tomar *or* capturar (b) *Cin* volver a rodar *or* tomar (c) *(exam)* presentarse a examen de recuperación

retaliate [rɪ'tælɪeɪt] *vi* tomar represalias (**against** contra), vengarse (**against** de)

retaliation [rɪtælɪ'eɪʃən] *n* represalias *fpl*, venganza *f*; **in r.** como represalia, para vengarse

retaliatory [rɪ'tælɪətərɪ] *adj* como *or* en represalia

retard ['riːtɑːd] **1** *n US Fam* retrasado(a) *m,f*
2 [rɪ'tɑːd] *vt* retardar, retrasar

retardant [rɪ'tɑːdənt] **1** *n* retardador *m*
2 *adj* retardador(a), retardante

retarded [rɪ'tɑːdɪd] *adj* atrasado(a); **the mentally r.** los atrasados mentales

retch [retʃ] *vi* tener náuseas, vomitar

retell [riː'tel] *vt (pt & pp retold)* volver a contar

retention [rɪ'tenʃən] *n* retención *f*

retentive [rɪ'tentɪv] *adj* retentivo(a); **to have a r. memory** tener buena memoria

rethink ['riːθɪŋk] **1** *n Fam* **to have a r. about sth** volver a reflexionar sobre algo
2 [riː'θɪŋk] *vt (pt & pp rethought* [riː'θɔːt]*)* volver a considerar, repensar

reticence ['retɪsəns] *n* reticencia *f*, reserva *f*

reticent ['retɪsənt] *adj* reticente, reservado(a)

retina ['retɪnə] *n Anat* retina *f*

retinue ['retɪnjuː] *n* séquito *m*

retire [rɪ'taɪər] **1** *vt* jubilar
2 *vi* (a) *(stop working)* jubilarse (b) *Fml (withdraw)* retirarse; **to r. for the night** irse a la cama, acostarse; **to r. to one's room** retirarse a su aposento

retired [rɪ'taɪəd] *adj* jubilado(a)

retiree [rɪtaɪə'riː] *n US* jubilado(a) *m,f*

retirement [rɪ'taɪəmənt] *n* jubilación *f* ❑ **r. age** edad *f* de jubilarse; *US* **r. plan** plan *m* de jubilación

retiring [rɪ'taɪərɪŋ] *adj* (a) *(reserved)* reservado(a) (b) *(leaving)* saliente; **the r. chairwoman** la presidenta saliente

retold [riː'təʊld] *pt & pp see* **retell**

retook [riː'tʊk] *pt see* **retake** II

retort¹ [rɪ'tɔːt] **1** *n (reply)* réplica *f*
2 *vi* replicar

retort² [rɪ'tɔːt] *n Chem* retorta *f*

retouch [riː'tʌtʃ] *vt Art Phot* retocar

retrace [rɪ'treɪs] *vt (go back over)* volver; *(recall)* reconstruir, reconstituir; **to r. one's steps** volver sobre sus pasos

retract [rɪ'trækt] **1** *vt* (**a**) *(draw in)* retraer, encoger; *Av (landing gear)* replegar (**b**) *Fml (withdraw) (promise)* retractar, retirar
2 *vi* (**a**) *(draw in)* retraerse, encoger; *Av (landing gear)* replegarse (**b**) *Fml (withdraw)* retractarse

retractable [rɪ'træktəbəl] *adj (gen)* retractable, retráctil; *Av (landing gear)* replegable

retraction [rɪtræk'ʃən] *n (of promise, statement etc)* retractación *f; Av (landing gear)* retracción *f*

retrain [ri:'treɪn] **1** *vt (employee)* reciclar
2 *vi (employee)* reciclarse

retread ['ri:tred] **1** *n Aut* neumático *m* recauchutado, *Col Méx* llanta *f or Arg* goma *f* recauchutada
2 [ri:'tred] *vt* recauchutar

retreat [rɪ'tri:t] **1** *n* (**a**) *Mil* retirada *f;* **to beat a hasty r.** irse corriendo (**b**) *(shelter)* refugio *m* (**c**) *Rel* retiro *m*
2 *vi* retirarse; *(danger)* refugiarse (**from** de); *(renege)* renegar; **they retreated to a warmer climate** se refugiaron en un clima más cálido

retrench [rɪ'trentʃ] *Fml* **1** *vt (expenses)* reducir
2 *vi* economizar, hacer ahorros

retrial [ri:'traɪəl] *n Jur* nuevo juicio *m*, revisión *f* del caso

retribution [retrɪ'bju:ʃən] *n* justo castigo *m*, merecido *m*

retrieval [rɪ'tri:vəl] *n* recuperación *f;* **beyond r.** irreparable ❑ *Comptr* **information r. system** sistema *m* para la recuperación de datos

retrieve [rɪ'tri:v] *vt* (**a**) *(recover)* recuperar, recobrar; *(hunting)* cobrar; *Comptr (data)* recoger (**b**) *(rescue)* salvar (**c**) *Ten* devolver

retriever [rɪ'tri:vər] *n Zool* perro *m* cazador

retro ['retrəʊ] *adj* retro

retroactive [retrəʊ'æktɪv] *adj Fml* retroactivo(a); **r. pay rise** aumento *m* de sueldo con efecto retroactivo

retrograde ['retrəʊgreɪd] *adj* retrógrado(a); **r. step** paso *m* hacia atrás

retrospect ['retrəʊspekt] *n* **in r.** retrospectivamente

retrospective [retrəʊ'spektɪv] **1** *adj* retrospectivo(a)
2 *n Art* exposición *f* retrospectiva

retrospectively [retrə'spektɪvlɪ] *adv* retrospectivamente

retry [ri:'traɪ] **1** *vt Jur* volver a procesar a
2 *vi Comptr* reintentar

return [rɪ'tɜːn] **1** *n* (**a**) *(coming or going back)* regreso *m*, vuelta *f;* **by r. of post** a vuelta de correo; **in r. for** a cambio de; **many happy returns!** ¡felicidades!, ¡feliz cumpleaños!; **on her r.** a su regreso; *Pol* **r. to office** reelección *f;* **the r. to school** la vuelta al colegio; **to pay sb a r. visit** devolver la visita a algn ❑ *Sport* **r. match** partido *m* de vuelta; *Br* **r. (ticket)** *Esp* billete *m or Am* boleto *m or Am* pasaje *m* de ida y vuelta (**b**) *(giving back)* devolución *f; Com* **on sale or r.** *(goods)* en depósito ❑ *Pol* **election returns** resultados *mpl* de la elección; **income tax r.** declaración *f* de impuestos (**c**) *Com (profit)* beneficio *m*, ganancia *f;* **to bring a good r.** dar mucho beneficio (**d**) *Fin (interest)* interés *m*
2 *vt* (**a**) *(give back)* devolver; *(on letter)* **'r. to sender'** 'devuélvase al remitente'; **to r. a favour/sb's love** corresponder a un favor/al amor de algn (**b**) *Br Pol* elegir (**as** como); **to r. sb to office** reelegir a algn (**c**) *Jur* pronunciar; **to r. a verdict** pronunciar un veredicto; **they returned a verdict of guilty** le declararon culpable
3 *vi* (**a**) *(come or go back)* volver, regresar; **they have returned** están de vuelta; **to r. home** volver a casa; **to r. to work** reanudar el trabajo (**b**) *(reappear)* reaparecer

returnable [rɪ'tɜːnəbəl] *adj (bottle)* recuperable, retornable

reunification [ri:ju:nɪfɪ'keɪʃən] *n* reunificación *f*

reunion [ri:'ju:njən] *n* reencuentro *m*, reunión *m*

reunite [ri:ju:'naɪt] **1** *vt* reunir; **to be reunited (with sb)** reencontrarse *or* volver a reunirse (con algn)
2 *vi* reunirse

reusable [re:'ju:zəbəl] *adj* reutilizable

reuse [ri:'ju:z] *vt* volver a utilizar, reutilizar

Rev. *(abbr* **Reverend)** Reverendo *m*, R., Rev., Revdo.

rev [rev] *Fam* **1** *n Aut* revolución *f* ❑ **r. counter** cuentarrevoluciones *m inv*
2 *vt (pt & pp* **revved) to r. (up)** acelerar el motor

revalue [ri:'vælju:] *vt, US* **revaluate** [ri:'væljʊeɪt] *vt* revalorizar

revamp [ri:'væmp] *vt* modernizar, renovar

Revd *(abbr* **Reverend)** Reverendo *m*, R., Rev., Revdo.

reveal [rɪ'vi:l] *vt* (**a**) *(make known) (secret, emotions)* revelar (**b**) *(show)* dejar ver

revealing [rɪ'vi:lɪŋ] *adj* revelador(a)

reveille [rɪ'vælɪ] *n Mil* diana *f;* **to sound the r.** tocar diana

revel ['revəl] *vi (pt & pp* **revelled**, *US* **reveled)** disfrutar (**in** con); **to r. in doing sth** gozar muchísimo haciendo algo

revelation [revə'leɪʃən] *n* revelación *f;* **it came as a r. to me** me sorprendió muchísimo; *Rel* **the book of Revelations** el Apocalipsis

reveller, *US* **reveler** ['revələr] *n* juerguista *mf*

revelry ['revəlrɪ] *n* jarana *f*, juerga *f*

revenge [rɪ'vendʒ] **1** *n* venganza *f;* **he did it in r.** lo hizo para vengarse; **to take r. on sb for sth** vengarse de algo en algn
2 *vt* vengar; **to be revenged** vengarse

revengeful [rɪ'vendʒfʊl] *adj* vengativo(a)

revenue ['revɪnju:] *n* renta *f* ❑ **Inland R.** Hacienda *f;* **public r.** rentas públicas

reverberate [rɪ'vɜːbəreɪt] *vi* (**a**) *(sound)* reverberar, resonar (**b**) *(ideas, news etc)* resonar, repercutir

reverberation [rɪvɜːbə'reɪʃən] *n* (**a**) *(sound)* resonancia *f*, reverberación *f* (**b**) *(ideas, news etc)* resonancia *f*, repercusión *f*

revere [rɪ'vɪər] *vt Fml* reverenciar

reverence ['revərəns] *n* reverencia *f*

reverend ['revərənd] *adj Rel* reverendo(a) ❑ **R. Mother** reverenda madre *m*

reverent ['revərənt] *adj* reverente

reverently ['revərəntlɪ] *adv* con reverencia

reverie ['revərɪ] *n* ensueño *m*

reversal [rɪ'vɜːsəl] *n* (**a**) *(of an order)* inversión *f* (**b**) *(change)* cambio *m* total; **r. of fortune** revés *m* de fortuna (**c**) *Jur (of a sentence)* revocación *f*

reverse [rɪ'vɜːs] **1** *adj* inverso(a); **in r. order** en orden inverso; **the r. side** el revés
2 *n* (**a**) *(opposite)* **the r.** lo contrario; **quite the r.** todo lo contrario (**b**) *(other side) (of cloth)* revés *m; (of coin)* cruz *f; (of medal)* reverso *m; (of page)* dorso *m* (**c**) *Aut* **r. gear** marcha *f* atrás; **to go into r.** poner marcha atrás
3 *vt* (**a**) *(invert) (order)* invertir (**b**) *(turn round)* volver al revés; *(picture)* dar la vuelta a (**c**) *(change)* cambiar totalmente; **to r. one's policy** cambiar radicalmente de política (**d**) *Jur (a sentence)* revocar, anular (**e**) *Br Tel* **to r. the charges** poner una conferencia a cobro revertido
4 *vi Aut* dar marcha atrás; **to r. into a parking space** dar marcha atrás para aparcar

reversible [rɪ'vɜːsəbəl] *adj* (**a**) *(garment, cloth)* reversible (**b**) *Jur (decision)* revocable

reversion [rɪ'vɜːʃən] *n* reversión *f*

revert [rɪ'vɜ:t] *vi* (**a**) *Fml* volver (**to** a); **they reverted to the original agreement** volvieron al primer acuerdo (**b**) *Jur (property)* revertir

review [rɪ'vju:] **1** *n* (**a**) *(examination)* examen *m*, análisis *m*; **to come under r.** ser examinado(a) (**b**) *Mil* revista *f* (**c**) *Press (article)* crítica *f*, reseña *f* □ **r. copy** ejemplar *m* para la prensa (**d**) *Press (magazine)* revista *f*
2 *vt* (**a**) *(examine)* examinar, analizar (**b**) *Mil* **to r. the troops** pasar revista a las tropas (**c**) *Press (book etc)* hacer una crítica de (**d**) *US (revise)* repasar

reviewer [rɪ'vju:ər] *n* crítico(a) *m,f*

revile [rɪ'vaɪl] *vt Fml* injuriar, insultar

revise [rɪ'vaɪz] **1** *vt* (**a**) *(text, policy, offer)* revisar; **to r. one's opinion** modificar su opinión (**b**) *Br (for exam) (subject, notes)* repasar (**c**) *Typ (proofs)* corregir; *(text)* refundir
2 *vt Br (for exam)* repasar (**for** para)

revision [rɪ'vɪʒən] *n* (**a**) *(of text)* revisión *f* (**b**) *Br (for exam)* repaso *m* (**c**) *Typ (proofs)* corrección *f*; *(text)* refundición *f*

revisionism [rɪ'vɪʒənɪzəm] *n Pol* revisionismo *m*

revisionist [rɪ'vɪʒənɪst] *n* revisionista *mf*

revisit [rɪ'vɪzɪt] *vt* volver a visitar

revitalize [ri:'vaɪtəlaɪz] *vt* revivificar

revival [rɪ'vaɪvəl] *n* (**a**) *(of interest)* renacimiento *m*; *(of old customs)* restablecimiento *m*; *(of a fashion)* reaparición *f*; *(of the economy)* reactivación *f*; *(of a country)* resurgimiento *m* □ **religious r.** despertar *m* religioso (**b**) *Theat* reestreno *m*, reposición *f* (**c**) *Med* reanimación *f*, resucitación *f*

revive [rɪ'vaɪv] **1** *vt* (**a**) *(interest)* renovar; *(a law)* restablecer; *(a fashion)* resucitar; *(the economy)* reactivar; *(conversation)* reanimar; *(hopes)* despertar (**b**) *Theat (a play)* reestrenar, reponer (**c**) *Med* reanimar, resucitar
2 *vi* (**a**) *(interest, hopes)* renacer; *(feelings)* resucitar (**b**) *Med* volver en sí

revoke [rɪ'vəʊk] **1** *vt (a law)* revocar; *(permission)* suspender
2 *vi Cards* renunciar

revolt [rɪ'vəʊlt] **1** *n* rebelión *f*, sublevación *f*; **to rise in r.** sublevarse, levantarse
2 *vi* rebelarse, sublevarse (**against** contra)
3 *vt* repugnar, dar asco a; **tripe revolts me** comer callos me da asco

revolting [rɪ'vəʊltɪŋ] *adj* (**a**) *(in revolt)* rebelde (**b**) *(disgusting)* repugnante, asqueroso(a)

revolution [revə'lu:ʃən] *n* (**a**) *(uprising)* revolución *f* (**b**) *Tech (of wheel)* revolución *f*; *(of planet)* rotación *f*; **40 revolutions per minute** 40 revoluciones por minuto

revolutionary [revə'lu:ʃənərɪ] *adj & n* revolucionario(a) *(m,f)*

revolutionize [revə'lu:ʃənaɪz] *vt* revolucionar

revolve [rɪ'vɒlv] **1** *vi* girar; **to r. around a planet** girar alrededor de un planeta; *Fig* **to r. around** girar en torno a, centrarse en
2 *vt* hacer girar

revolver [rɪ'vɒlvər] *n* revólver *m*

revolving [rɪ'vɒlvɪŋ] *adj* giratorio(a) □ **r. door** puerta *f* giratoria

revue [rɪ'vju:] *n Theat* revista *f*

revulsion [rɪ'vʌlʃən] *n* repulsión *f*, repugnancia *f*

reward [rɪ'wɔ:d] **1** *n* recompensa *f*; **as a r. for** en recompensa a *or* por
2 *vt* recompensar, premiar

rewarding [rɪ'wɔ:dɪŋ] *adj* provechoso(a), gratificador(a)

rewind [ri:'waɪnd] *(pt & pp* **rewound**) *vt (tape, film)* rebobinar

rewire [ri:'waɪər] *vt* **to r. a house** poner nueva instalación eléctrica a una casa

reword [ri:'wɜ:d] *vt* expresar con otras palabras

rework [ri:'wɜ:k] *vt (idea, text)* rehacer, reelaborar

rewound [ri:'waʊnd] *pt & pp see* **rewind**

rewrite [ri:'raɪt] *vt (pt* **rewrote** [ri:'rəʊt]; *pp* **rewritten** [ri:'rɪtən]) volver a escribir, escribir de nuevo

Reykjavik ['reɪkjəvi:k] *n* Reikiavik

rh [ɑ:r'eɪtʃ] (**a**) *(abbr* **right hand**) mano *f* derecha (**b**) *Med* (*abbr* **rhesus**) rhesus *m*

rhapsodic(al) [ræp'sɒdɪk(əl)] *adj (prose, description)* enardecido(a)

rhapsodize ['ræpsədaɪz] *vi Fml* entusiasmar; **to r. over** *or* **about** hablar con entusiasmo de

rhapsody ['ræpsədɪ] *n Mus* rapsodia *f*; *Fig* **to go into rhapsodies over sth** entusiasmarse con algo

rheostat ['rɪəstæt] *n Elec* reóstato *m*

rhesus ['ri:səs] *n* (**a**) *Biol* rhesus *m* □ **r. factor** factor *m* Rhesus; **R. positive/negative** Rhesus positivo/negativo (**b**) *Zool* **r. monkey** macaco *m* de la India

rhetoric ['retərɪk] *n* retórica *f*

rhetorical [rɪ'tɒrɪkəl] *adj* retórico(a); **r. question** pregunta *f* sin respuesta

rheumatic [ru:'mætɪk] *adj & n* reumático(a) *(m,f)* □ **r. fever** fiebre *f* reumática

rheumatism ['ru:mətɪzəm] *n Med* reuma *m*, reumatismo *m*

rheumatoid ['ru:mətɔɪd] *adj* **r. arthritis** reuma *m* articular

Rhine [raɪn] *n* **the R.** el Rin

rhinestone ['raɪnstəʊn] *n* piedra *f* falsa, diamante *m* de imitación

rhino ['raɪnəʊ] *(pl* **rhinos**) *n Fam* rinoceronte *m*

rhinoceros [raɪ'nɒsərəs] *n (pl* **rhinoceroses**) *Zool* rinoceronte *m*

rhizome ['raɪzəʊm] *n Bot* rizoma *m*

Rhodes [rəʊdz] *n* Rodas

rhododendron [rəʊdə'dendrən] *n Bot* rododendro *m*

rhomboid ['rɒmbɔɪd] *n* romboide *m*

rhombus ['rɒmbəs] *n (pl* **rhombuses**) *Geom* rombo *m*

Rhone [rəʊn] *n* **the R.** el Ródano

rhubarb ['ru:bɑ:b] *n Bot* ruibarbo *m*

rhyme [raɪm] **1** *n* (**a**) *(verse, poem)* rima *f*; *Fig* **without r. or reason** sin ton ni son (**b**) *(poetry)* poesía *f*, versos *mpl* □ **nursery r.** poesía *f* *or* canción *f* infantil
2 *vt & vi* rimar

rhythm ['rɪðəm] *n* ritmo *m* □ *Med* **r. method** método *m* Ogino

rhythmic(al) ['rɪðmɪk(əl)] *adj* rítmico(a)

rib¹ [rɪb] *n* (**a**) *Anat* costilla *f* □ **r. cage** caja *f* torácica (**b**) *Knit* canalé *m* (**c**) *(of umbrella)* varilla *f* (**d**) *Bot* nervio *m*

rib² [rɪb] *vt Fam* burlarse de; **to r. sb** tomar el pelo a algn, burlarse de algn

ribald ['rɪbəld] *adj (humour, joke)* verde, obsceno(a); *(language)* procaz

ribbed [rɪbd] *adj Knit* de canalé, acanalado(a)

ribbing ['rɪbɪŋ] *n* (**a**) *(on pullover)* cordoncillos *mpl* (**b**) *Fam (teasing)* tomadura *f* de pelo

ribbon ['rɪbən] *n* cinta *f*; *(in hair, clothes etc)* lazo *m*; **torn to ribbons** hecho(a) jirones □ **r. development** urbanización *f* lineal

riboflavin [raɪbəʊ'fleɪvɪn] *n* riboflavina *f*

rice [raɪs] *n* arroz *m* □ **brown r.** arroz *m* integral; **r. field** arrozal *m*; **r. grower** arrocero(a) *m,f*; **r. paper** papel *m* de arroz; *Culin* **r. pudding** arroz *m* con leche

rich [rɪtʃ] **1** *adj (wealthy)* rico(a); *(sumptuous)* suntuoso(a); *(food)* rico(a); *(heavy)* fuerte, pesado(a); *(wine)* generoso(a); *(soil)* fértil; *(harvest)* abundante; *(voice)* sonoro(a); *(colour)* vivo(a); *(perfume)* fuerte; **a r. family** una familia adinerada; **r. in minerals** rico(a) en minerales; **to grow r.** hacerse rico(a), enriquecerse
  2 the r. *npl* los ricos

riches ['rɪtʃɪz] *npl* riquezas *fpl*

richly ['rɪtʃlɪ] *adv (wealthily)* ricamente; *(sumptuously)* suntuosamente; **r. deserved** bien merecido(a)

richness ['rɪtʃnɪs] *n* riqueza *f*; *(sumptuousness)* suntuosidad *f*; *(of soil)* fertilidad *f*; *(abundance)* abundancia *f*; *(of voice)* sonoridad *f*; *(of colour)* viveza *f*

Richter Scale ['rɪktə'skeɪl] *n* escala *f* de Richter

rick¹ [rɪk] *n Agr* (hay) **r.** almiar *m*

rick² [rɪk] *vt esp Br Fam* torcer

rickets ['rɪkɪts] *n Med* raquitismo *m*

rickety ['rɪkətɪ] *adj (chair etc)* cojo(a); *(car)* desvencijado(a)

ricochet ['rɪkəʃeɪ] **1** *n* rebote *m*
  2 *vi (pt & pp* **ricoche(t)ted** ['rɪkəʃeɪd]) rebotar

rid [rɪd] *vt (pt & pp* **rid**) librar; **to get r. of sth** deshacerse de algo; **to r. oneself of** librarse de

riddance ['rɪdəns] *n* liberación *f*, *Fam* **good r. (to bad rubbish)!** *(when sb has left)* ¡ya era hora!

ridden ['rɪdən] *pp see* **ride**

riddle¹ ['rɪdəl] *n* **(a)** *(puzzle)* acertijo *m*, adivinanza *f* **(b)** *(mystery)* enigma *m*

riddle² ['rɪdəl] **1** *vt (with bullets)* acribillar; **riddled with bullets** acribillado(a) a balazos
  2 *n (sieve)* criba *f*

ride [raɪd] **1** *n* paseo *m*, vuelta *f*; **a short bus r.** un corto trayecto en autobús; **to give a child a r. on one's back** llevar a un niño a cuestas; **to give sb a r.** *(in car)* llevar a algn (en coche), *CAm Méx* dar aventón *or Cuba* botella a algn; *Fam* **to take sb for a r.** tomar el pelo a algn ❑ **horse r.** paseo *m* a caballo; **train r.** excursión *f* en tren
  2 *vt (pt* **rode**; *pp* **ridden**) **(a)** *(bicycle)* montar; *(horse)* montar; *US* **to r. the bus/train** viajar en autobús/tren; **can you r. a bike?** ¿sabes *Esp* montar *or Am* andar en bici?; **he rode his horse into town** fue al pueblo a caballo **(b)** *(travel over) US* recorrer, cruzar, atravesar
  3 *vi* **(a)** *(on horse)* montar a caballo; **can you r.?** ¿sabes *Esp* montar *or Am* andar a caballo?; **(b)** *(travel) (in bus, train etc)* viajar; *Fig* **our whole future is riding on it** nuestro futuro depende de ello **(c)** *Naut* flotar; **to r. at anchor** estar anclado(a) *or* fondeado(a); *Fam* **let it r.** déjalo correr

ride out *vt* sobrevivir; **to r. out the storm** capear el temporal

ride up *vi (sweater etc)* subirse

rider ['raɪdər] *n* **(a)** *(of horse)* jinete *m*, amazona *f*; *(of bicycle)* ciclista *mf*; *(of moped, motorbike)* motociclista *mf*, motorista *mf* **(b)** *Jur* cláusula *f* adicional

ridge [rɪdʒ] *n (crest of a hill)* cresta *f*; *(hillock)* loma *f*; *Agr (between furrows)* caballón *m*; *(of roof)* caballete *m*; *Anat (of nose)* caballete *m*; *Meteor* **r. of high pressure** línea *f* de alta presión. ,

ridicule ['rɪdɪkjuːl] **1** *n* burla *f*; **to expose sb to r.** poner a algn en ridículo
  2 *vt* burlarse de, poner en ridículo, ridiculizar

ridiculous [rɪ'dɪkjʊləs] *adj* ridículo(a); **to look r.** parecer ridículo(a)

ridiculously [rɪ'dɪkjʊləslɪ] *adv* **(a)** *(stupidly)* ridículamente; **he was r. dressed** iba vestido de forma ridícula **(b)** *Fam (very)* muy; **it was r. cheap** era baratísimo

ridiculousness [rɪ'dɪkjʊləsnɪs] *n* ridiculez *f*, lo ridículo

riding ['raɪdɪŋ] *n* equitación *f* ❑ **r. breeches/habit** pantalones *mpl*/traje *m* de montar; **r. school** escuela *f* hípica; **r. stables** picadero *m*

rife [raɪf] *adj Fml* abundante; **rumour is r. that ...** corre la voz de que ...; **to be r. with** abundar en, estar lleno(a) de

riffraff ['rɪfræf] *n Fam* chusma *f*, gentuza *f*

rifle¹ ['raɪfəl] *n* fusil *m*, rifle *m* ❑ **r. range** campo *m* de tiro

rifle² ['raɪfəl] **1** *vt* saquear, desvalijar; *(pockets)* vaciar
  2 *vi (search)* echar un vistazo (**through** a)

rift [rɪft] *n* **(a)** *(crack)* grieta *f*, fisura *f*, *Geol (fault)* falla *f* **(b)** *Fig (in friendship)* ruptura *f*; *Pol (in party)* escisión *f*, *(quarrel)* desavenencia *f*

rig [rɪg] **1** *n* **(a)** *Naut* aparejo *m* **(b)** **(oil) r.** *(onshore)* torre *f* de perforación; *(offshore)* plataforma *f* petrolífera **(c)** *(dress)* atuendo *m*
  2 *vt (pt & pp* **rigged**) **(a)** *Naut (boat)* aparejar **(b)** *(manipulate)* amañar; **to r. an election** amañar unas elecciones; *Box* **the fight was rigged** hubo tongo en el combate ,

rig out *vt Fam* vestir, ataviar

rig up *vt* improvisar, *Esp* apañar; **they rigged up a shelter** improvisaron un refugio

rigging ['rɪgɪŋ] *n Naut* aparejo *m*, jarcia *f*

right [raɪt] **1** *adj* **(a)** *(not left)* derecho(a); **I'd give my r. arm to do that** daría una mano por hacerlo; **the r. hand** la mano derecha **(b)** *(correct)* correcto(a), bueno(a); **all r.** de acuerdo; **r.?** *Esp* ¿vale?, *Méx* ¿órale?, *RP* ¿está bien?; **that's r.** eso es; **the r. answer** la respuesta correcta; **the r. word** la palabra justa; **to stay on the r. side of sb** no llevarle la contraria a algn; *Fam* **she's not r. in the head** no está bien de la cabeza **(c)** *(true)* cierto(a), verdad; **is that r.?** ¿es cierto?; **to be r.** tener razón **(d)** *(suitable)* adecuado(a); **the r. time** el momento oportuno **(e)** *(proper)* apropiado(a) **(f)** *Fam (healthy)* bien; **I don't feel r.** no me encuentro bien; **to feel as r. as rain** encontrarse de maravilla, *RP* sentirse perfecto **(g)** *(exact)* exacto(a); **have you got the r. time?** ¿tiene la hora exacta? **(h)** *Br Fam (complete)* auténtico(a), verdadero(a), completo(a); **it's a r. muddle** es un auténtico lío **(i)** *(in order)* en orden, ordenado(a) **(j)** *Geom* **r. angle** ángulo recto
  2 *n* **(a)** *(right side)* derecha *f*; *Aut* **keep to the r.** circulen por la derecha **(b)** *(right hand)* mano *f* derecha **(c)** *Pol* **the R.** la derecha **(d)** *(lawful claim)* derecho *m*; **in one's own r.** por derecho propio; **r. of way** *(across land)* derecho *m* de paso; *(on roads)* prioridad *f*; **to be within one's rights** estar en su derecho; **what r. have you to do that?** ¿con qué derecho haces eso? ❑ **civil rights** derechos *mpl* civiles; **women's rights** derechos *mpl* de la mujer **(e)** **r. and wrong** el bien y el mal
  3 *adv* **(a)** *(correctly)* bien; **do it r.** hazlo bien; **if I remember r.** si mal no recuerdo; **it's just r.** es justo lo que hace falta; **it serves you r.** lo tienes bien merecido; **nothing is going r.** todo sale mal; **to treat sb r.** tratar bien a algn **(b)** *(immediately)* inmediatamente; **I'll be r. back** en seguida vuelvo; **I'll be r. over** en seguida estoy ahí; **r. after lunch** justo después de comer; **r. away** en seguida, inmediatamente, *CAm Méx* ahorita, *Chile* al tiro **(c)** *(to the right)* a la derecha, *Mil* **eyes r.!** ¡vista a la derecha!; **r. and left** a diestro y siniestro; **to turn r.** girar a la derecha **(d)** *(precisely)* directamente, derecho; **go r. on** sigue recto; **r. at the front** delante de todo; **r. at the top** en todo lo alto; **r. in the middle** en pleno centro; **r. to the end** hasta el final **(e)** *Rel* **the R. Reverend** el reverendísimo
  4 *vt* **(a)** *(correct)* corregir; **to r. a wrong** enmendar un error **(b)** *Naut (put straight)* enderezar; **it righted itself** se enderezó

right-angled ['raɪtæŋgəld] *adj (triangle)* rectángulo(a); *(corner, bend)* en ángulo recto

right-click ['raɪtklɪk] *Comptr* **1** *vt* hacer clic con el botón derecho en

2 *vi* hacer clic con el botón derecho (**on** en)

righteous ['raɪtʃəs] *adj (upright)* recto(a); *(honest)* honrado(a)

righteousness ['raɪtʃəsnɪs] *n* rectitud *f*, honradez *f*

rightful ['raɪtfʊl] *adj* legítimo(a)

right-hand ['raɪthænd] *adj* derecho(a); *Aut* **r.-h. drive** conducción por la derecha; **r.-h. side** lado derecho; *Fam* **r.- h. man** brazo derecho

right-handed [raɪt'hændɪd] *adj (person)* que usa la mano derecha; *(tool)* para la mano derecha

rightist ['raɪtɪst] *Pol* **1** *adj* de derechas, derechista
2 *n* derechista *mf*

rightly ['raɪtlɪ] *adv* debidamente; **and r. so** y con razón; **r. or wrongly** con razón o sin ella

right-minded [raɪt'maɪndɪd] *adj* recto(a), honrado(a)

rightness ['raɪtnɪs] *n* (**a**) *(accuracy)* exactitud *f* (**b**) *(honesty)* rectitud *f*, honradez *f* (**c**) *(fairness)* justicia *f*

right-to-life ['raɪttə'laɪf] *adj* antiaborto *inv*, pro vida *inv*

right-wing ['raɪtwɪŋ] *adj Pol* de derechas, derechista

right-winger [raɪt'wɪŋər] *n Pol* derechista *mf*

rigid ['rɪdʒɪd] *adj* rígido(a), inflexible; **r. discipline** disciplina rigurosa; **to have r. ideas** tener unas ideas muy fijas

rigidity [rɪ'dʒɪdɪtɪ] *n* rigidez *f*, inflexibilidad *f*

rigidly ['rɪdʒɪdlɪ] *adv* rígidamente

rigmarole ['rɪgmərəʊl] *n Fam* galimatías *m inv*; **form filling is a r.** rellenar formularios es un rollo

rigor ['rɪgər] *n US see* **rigour**

rigor mortis ['rɪgə'mɔːtɪs] *n Med* rigidez *f* cadavérica, rigor *m* mortis

rigorous ['rɪgərəs] *adj* riguroso(a)

rigorously ['rɪgərəslɪ] *adv* rigurosamente, severamente

rigour ['rɪgər] *n* rigor *m*, severidad *f*

rig-out ['rɪgaʊt] *n Br Fam* atuendo *m*

rile [raɪl] *vt Fam* fastidiar, irritar, *Am* enojar; **her shouting riles me** sus gritos me ponen nervioso(a)

rim [rɪm] *n (edge)* borde *m*; *(of wheel)* llanta *f*; *(of spectacles)* montura *f*

rime¹ [raɪm] *n Lit* escarcha *f*

rime² [raɪm] *n see* **rhyme**

rind [raɪnd] *n (de fruta, queso)* corteza *f*

ring¹ [rɪŋ] **1** *n* (**a**) *(sound of bell)* toque *m*, repique *m*, tañido *m*; *(of doorbell)* timbre *m*; *(of alarm clock)* timbre *m*; **there was a r. at the door** llamaron a la puerta; *Fig* **it has a nice r. about it** suena bien (**b**) *Br Tel (call)* llamada *f*; **to give sb a r.** dar un telefonazo *or RP* tubazo a algn

2 *vt (pt* **rang**; *pp* **rung**) (**a**) *(bell)* tocar; *Fig* **it rings a bell** me suena; *Fig* **to r. true** parecer verdad (**b**) *Br Tel* llamar por teléfono, telefonear, *RP* hablar a

3 *vi* (**a**) *(bell etc)* sonar; **the telephone rang** sonó el teléfono (**b**) *(ears)* zumbar (**c**) *(call)* llamar; **to r. for sb** llamar a algn; **to r. for the lift** llamar el ascensor

ring back *vt Br Tel* volver a llamar

ring in *vi Br Tel* llamar (al lugar de trabajo)

ring off *vi Br Tel* colgar

ring out *vi* resonar

ring up *vt* (**a**) *Fam Tel* llamar (por teléfono a), telefonear a, *RP* hablar a (**b**) *(on a cash register)* teclear las cifras

ring² [rɪŋ] **1** *n* (**a**) *(metal hoop)* aro *m* ❑ **curtain r.** anilla *f*; **key r.** llavero *m*; **napkin r.** servilletero *m*; **r. binder** archivador *m or* carpeta *f* de anillas, *RP* bibliorato *m* (**b**) *(for finger)* anillo *m*, sortija *f* ❑ **diamond r.** sortija *f* de diamantes; **r. finger** dedo *m* anular (**c**) *(circle)* círculo *m*;

dark rings under the eyes ojeras *fpl*; *Fig* **to run rings round sb** dar cien vueltas a algn ❑ *Br Aut* **r. road** carretera *f* de circunvalación, ronda *f* (**d**) *(in gymnastics)* **rings** anillas *fpl* (**e**) *(group) (of people)* corro *m*, grupo *m*; *(of spies)* red *f*; *(of thieves)* banda *f*; **to stand in a r.** hacer un corro (**f**) *(arena etc)* pista *f*; *Box* ring *m*, cuadrilátero *m*; *(for bullfights)* ruedo *m* ❑ **circus r.** pista *f* del circo

2 *vt (pt & pp* **ringed**) (**a**) *(bird, animal)* anillar (**b**) *(surround)* rodear

ring-fence ['rɪŋ'fens] **1** *n (round field)* cerca *f (que rodea una propiedad)*
2 *vt Fin* proteger

ringing ['rɪŋɪŋ] *n (of bell)* toque *m*, repique *m*, tañido *m*; *(of doorbell)* toque *m* de timbre; *(in ears)* zumbido *m*; *Br Tel* **r. tone** señal *f* de llamada

ringleader ['rɪŋliːdər] *n* cabecilla *mf*

ringlet ['rɪŋlɪt] *n* tirabuzón *m*, rizo *m*

ringmaster ['rɪŋmɑːstər] *n* maestro *m* de ceremonias

ringside ['rɪŋsaɪd] **1** *n* primera fila *f*
2 *adj* de primera fila

ringworm ['rɪŋwɜːm] *n Med* tiña *f*

rink [rɪŋk] *n Sport* pista *f* ❑ **ice (skating) r.** pista *f* de hielo; **roller skating r.** pista *f* de patinaje

rinse [rɪns] **1** *n* (**a**) *(clean, wash)* enjuague *m*, *Esp* aclarado *m* (**b**) *(hair tint)* reflejo *m*; **blue r.** reflejos *mpl* azules

2 *vt* (**a**) *(gen)* enjuagar, *Esp* aclarar; **to r. out one's mouth** enjuagarse la boca (**b**) **to r. one's hair** *(tint)* dar reflejos a su pelo

riot ['raɪət] **1** *n* (**a**) *(uprising)* disturbio *m*, motín *m*; **to run r.** desmandarse; *Fam* **to read the r. act to sb** poner los puntos sobre las íes a algn, *Esp* leerle la cartilla a algn ❑ **race riots** disturbios *mpl* raciales; **r. police** policía *f* antidisturbios (**b**) *Fig* profusión *f*; **a r. of colour** una profusión de colores

2 *vi* amotinarse

rioter ['raɪətər] *n* amotinado(a) *m,f*

riotous ['raɪətəs] *adj* (**a**) *(behaviour)* descontrolado(a) (**b**) *(noisy)* ruidoso(a), bullicioso(a) (**c**) *(unrestrained)* desenfrenado(a); **a r. success** un éxito clamoroso; **r. living** vida desenfrenada

RIP [ɑːraɪ'piː] *(abbr* **requiescat** *or* **resquiescant in pace)** (rest in peace), en paz descanse, E.P.D.

rip [rɪp] **1** *n (tear)* rasgón *m*, desgarrón *m*

2 *vt (pt & pp* **ripped**) rasgar, desgarrar; **to r. a letter open** abrir un sobre desgarrándolo; **to r. one's trousers** hacerse un siete en el pantalón

3 *vi* (**a**) *(cloth, paper)* rasgarse (**b**) *Fam* **to let r.** reventar de cólera; **let it r.!** ¡dale al gas!

rip off *vt* (**a**) *(buttons etc)* arrancar (**b**) *Fam* **to r. sb off** clavar *or Esp* timar a algn

rip up *vt* hacer pedazos de

ripcord ['rɪpkɔːd] *n (of parachute)* cuerda *f* de apertura

ripe [raɪp] *adj* (**a**) *(fruit)* maduro(a); *Fam (language)* verde; **a r. old age** una edad avanzada (**b**) *(ready)* preparado(a), listo(a); **the time is r.** es el momento oportuno

ripen ['raɪpən] *vt & vi* madurar

ripeness ['raɪpnɪs] *n* madurez *f*

rip-off ['rɪpɒf] *n Fam* timo *m*, *Col RP* cagada *f*; **it's been a real r.-o.** nos han timado *or Esp* clavado de verdad

riposte [rɪ'pɒst] *Literary* **1** *n (reply)* respuesta *f* aguda
2 *vi* responder, replicar

ripper ['rɪpər] *n Fam* destripador(a) *m,f*; **Jack the R.** Jack el Destripador

ripple ['rɪpəl] **1** *n* (**a**) *(on water)* onda *f*; *(fabric etc)* onda *f*, ondulación *f* (**b**) *(sound)* murmullo *m* (**c**) *(bodily sensation)* estremecimiento *m*

2 *vt (water)* ondular, rizar

3 *vi* (**a**) *(water)* ondularse, rizarse (**b**) *(stream)* murmurar (**c**) *(applause)* extenderse

rise [raɪz] **1** *n* (**a**) *(of slope, hill)* cuesta *f,* subida *f* (**b**) *(of waters)* crecida *f* (**c**) *(in status)* subida *f*; **his r. to fame** se hizo famoso en un abrir y cerrar de ojos; **the r. to power** el ascenso al poder (**d**) *(in prices, temperature)* subida *f; (of wages)* aumento *m*; **to be on the r.** estar subiendo (**e**) *(in sound)* aumento *m* (**f**) **to give r. to** ocasionar, provocar, dar lugar a

2 *vi (pt rose; pp risen)* (**a**) *(mountain, land)* elevarse (**b**) *(waters)* crecer; *(in level)* subir; *(river)* nacer; *(tide)* subir; *(wind)* levantarse (**c**) *(sun, moon)* salir (**d**) *(from death)* resucitar (**e**) *(voice)* alzarse, levantarse (**f**) *(in rank)* ascender (**g**) *(prices, temperature)* subir; *(wages)* aumentar (**h**) *Theat (curtain)* subir (**i**) *Culin (dough)* leudarse, fermentar; *(in oven)* subir (**j**) *(from bed)* levantarse (**k**) *(stand up)* levantarse, ponerse de pie, *Am* pararse; *Fig (city, building)* erguirse, levantarse (**l**) *(meeting, court)* levantarse; **the court rises at three** la sesión se levanta a las tres (**m**) *(feelings, emotions)* crecer, aumentar (**n**) **to r. to a challenge** aceptar un reto; **to r. to the occasion** ponerse a la altura de las circunstancias

rise above *vi (be unaffected by)* estar por encima de

rise up *vi* (**a**) *(feelings)* crecer, aumentar (**b**) *(rebel)* rebelarse, sublevarse

risen ['rɪzən] *pp see* **rise**

riser ['raɪzər] *n* (**a**) **early r.** madrugador(a) *m,f* (**b**) *Tech (chair)* respaldo *m; (step)* contrahuella *f*

risible ['rɪzɪbəl] *adj Fml* ridículo(a)

rising ['raɪzɪŋ] **1** *adj* (**a**) *(sun)* naciente; *(tide)* creciente □ *Br Constr* **r. damp** humedad *f (que asciende por las paredes)* (**b**) *(prices)* creciente, en aumento (**c**) *(generation)* nuevo(a) (**d**) *(age)* cercano(a); **John is r. five** John va para los cinco años

2 *n* (**a**) *(of sun)* salida *f* (**b**) *(rebellion)* levantamiento *m*

risk [rɪsk] **1** *n* riesgo *m*; **at r.** en peligro; **at your own r.** por su cuenta y riesgo; **it's not worth the r.** no merece la pena arriesgarse; **to take risks** arriesgarse

2 *vt* arriesgar, arriesgarse; **I'll r. it** correré el riesgo; **to r. everything** jugarse el todo por el todo; **to r. failure** exponerse al fracaso; *Fam* **to r. one's neck** jugarse el tipo

risky ['rɪskɪ] *adj* (**rɪskɪer, rɪskɪest**) arriesgado(a), peligroso(a)

risotto [rɪs'zɒtəʊ] *n (pl* **risottos**) *Culin* risotto *m*

risqué ['rɪskeɪ] *adj* atrevido(a); *(joke)* picante

rissole ['rɪsəʊl] *n* = pequeña masa frita, generalmente redonda, de carne o verduras

rite [raɪt] *n* rito *m*; *Rel* **the last rites** los últimos sacramentos, la extremaunción

ritual ['rɪtjʊəl] *adj & n* ritual *(m)*

ritualistic [rɪtjʊə'lɪstɪk] *adj (following a pattern)* ritual; *Rel* ritualista

ritzy ['rɪtsɪ] *adj* (**ritzier, ritziest**) *Fam* lujoso(a), de película

rival ['raɪvəl] **1** *adj & n* rival *(m,f)*, competidor(a) *(m,f)*

2 *vt (pt & pp* **rivalled,** *US* **rivaled**) *(compete with)* rivalizar con, competir con; *(match)* alcanzar

rivalry ['raɪvəlrɪ] *n* rivalidad *f*, competencia *f*

river ['rɪvər] *n* río *m*; **down/up r.** río abajo/arriba; **r. traffic** navegación *f* fluvial; *Fig* **rivers of blood** ríos de sangre

river-bank ['rɪvəbæŋk] *n* orilla *f*, ribera *f*

river-bed ['rɪvəbed] *n* lecho *m*

riverside ['rɪvəsaɪd] *n* orilla *f*, ribera *f*; **r. restaurant** restaurante *m* al lado del río

rivet ['rɪvɪt] **1** *n Tech* remache *m*, roblón *m*

2 *vt Tech* remachar, roblonar; *Fig* fascinar, cautivar

riveting ['rɪvɪtɪŋ] *adj Fig* fascinante

rly *(abbr* **railway**) ferrocarril *m*, FC

RM [ɑːr'em] *Br Naut (abbr* **Royal Marines**) = infantería real de marina

rm *(abbr* **room**) habitación *f*, Hab

RN [ɑːr'en] (**a**) *US (abbr* **registered nurse**) enfermera *f* diplomada (**b**) *Br Mil (abbr* **Royal Navy**) Armada *f* Real

RNA [ɑːren'eɪ] *n Biol (abbr* **ribonucleic acid**) ARN *m*, ácido *m* ribonucleico

RNIB [ɑːrenaɪ'biː] *n Br (abbr* **Royal National Institute for the Blind**) = asociación británica de ayuda a los ciegos, *Esp* ONCE *f*

roach[1] [rəʊtʃ] *n (fish)* pardilla *f*

roach[2] [rəʊtʃ] *n* (**a**) *US Fam (cockroach)* cucaracha *f, Chile* barata *f* (**b**) *Slang (drugs) (filter)* colilla *f* de porro

road [rəʊd] *n* (**a**) *(in general)* carretera *f*; **A r.** carretera nacional; **B r.** carretera secundaria; **main r.** carretera principal; **r. accident** accidente *m* de tráfico; **'r. up'** 'obras'; *Fam* **my car is off the r.** tengo el coche averiado; *Fam Fig* **to have one for the r.** tomar la espuela *or* la última copa □ **r. haulage** transporte *m* por carretera; *Fam* **r. hog** conductor(a) *m,f* temerario(a), loco(a) *m,f* del volante; **r. safety** seguridad *f* vial *or* en carretera; **r. sign** señal *f* de tráfico; **r. works** obras *fpl* (**b**) *(in town)* calle *f*; **Peterloo R.** la calle Peterloo; **to cross the r.** cruzar la calle (**c**) *(way)* camino *m*; *Fig* **on the r. to recovery** en vías de recuperación; *Fam* **get out of my r.!** ¡quítate de en medio!

roadblock ['rəʊdblɒk] *n* control *m* policial

roadhog ['rəʊdhɒg] *n Aut Fam* dominguero(a) *m,f*

roadhouse ['rəʊdhaʊs] *n Old-fashioned* bar *m* de carretera

roadroller ['rəʊdrəʊlər] *n* apisonadora *f*

roadside ['rəʊdsaɪd] *n* borde *m* de la carretera; **r. restaurant/café** restaurante *m*/cafetería *m* de carretera

road-test ['rəʊdtest] *vt (car)* probar en carretera

roadway ['rəʊdweɪ] *n* calzada *f*

roadworthy ['rəʊdwɜːðɪ] *adj Aut (vehicle)* en buen estado

roam [rəʊm] **1** *vt* vagar por, rondar

2 *vi* vagar, errar

roaming ['rəʊmɪŋ] *adj* vagabundo(a), errante

roan [rəʊn] *n Zool* caballo *m* ruano

roar [rɔːr] **1** *n (of lion)* rugido *m*; *(of bull, sea, wind)* bramido *m*; *(of crowd)* clamor *m*

2 *vi (lion, crowd)* rugir; *(bull, sea, wind)* bramar; *(crowd)* clamar; *Fig* **to r. with laughter** reírse a carcajadas

roaring ['rɔːrɪŋ] *adj (lion)* rugiente; *(fire)* espectacular; *Fam Fig* **a r. success** un éxito clamoroso; *Fam Fig* **to do a r. trade** hacer un negocio redondo

roast [rəʊst] **1** *adj (meat)* asado(a); **r. beef** rosbif *m*

2 *n Culin* asado *m*

3 *vt (meat)* asar; *(coffee)* tostar, torrefactar; *(nuts, beans, fruits)* tostar

4 *vi* asarse; *Fam Fig* **I'm roasting** me aso de calor

roasted ['rəʊstɪd] *adj Culin (coffee)* tostado(a), torrefacto(a); *(nuts, beans, fruit)* tostado(a)

roasting ['rəʊstɪŋ] **1** *adj* abrasador(a)

2 *n* (**a**) *(of meat)* asado *m; (of coffee)* tostado *m*, torrefacción *f; (of nuts, beans, fruit)* tostado *m* (**b**) *Fam Fig* bronca *f*; **to give sb a r.** echar una regañina *or Esp* bronca a algn

rob [rɒb] *vt (pt & pp* **robbed**) robar; **to r. a bank** atracar un banco; *Fam* **we were robbed!** ¡nos robaron el partido!

robber ['rɒbər] *n* ladrón(ona) *m,f*; **bank r.** atracador(a) *m,f*

robbery ['rɒbərɪ] *n* robo *m*; **to commit a r.** cometer un robo ❑ **armed r.** robo *m* a mano armada

robe [rəʊb] **1** *n* (**a**) *(ceremonial)* toga *f* (**b**) *esp US (dressing gown)* bata *f* ❑ **bath r.** albornoz *m*
2 *vi Fml* vestir; **robed in red** vestido(a) de rojo

robin ['rɒbɪn] *n Orn* petirrojo *m*; **R. Hood** Robín *m* de los bosques

robinia [rə'bɪnɪə] *n Bot* acacia *f* falsa, robinia *f*

robot ['rəʊbɒt] *n* robot *m*

robotic [rəʊ'bɒtɪk] *adj* robótico(a)

robotics [rəʊ'bɒtɪks] *n sing* robótica *f*

robust [rəʊ'bʌst] *adj (strong, sturdy)* robusto(a); *(strong, energetic)* fuerte

rock [rɒk] **1** *n* (**a**) *(substance, large stone)* roca *f*; **the R. (of Gibraltar)** el Peñón (de Gibraltar); *Fig* **r. solid** sólido como una roca; *Fig* **to be on the rocks** *(marriage etc)* estar a punto de fracasar; *Fam Fig* **whisky on the rocks** whisky *m* con hielo ❑ **r. face** vertiente *f* rocosa; **r. garden** jardín *m* de rocas; **r. salmon** *(fish)* lija *f* (**b**) *US (stone)* piedra *f* (**c**) *Br* **stick of r.** *(sweet)* barra *f* de caramelo (**d**) *Mus* rock *m*, música *f* rock; **r. and roll** rock and roll *m*; **r. concert** concierto *m* de rock
2 *vt* (**a**) *(chair)* mecer; *(baby)* acunar (**b**) *(shake)* sacudir, hacer temblar; *Fig* **to r. the boat** crear problemas
3 *vi* (**a**) *(move to and fro)* mecerse, balancearse (**b**) *(shake)* temblar, vibrar

rock-bottom [rɒk'bɒtəm] *adj* bajísimo(a); **r.-b. prices** precios *mpl* regalados

rock-climber ['rɒkklaɪmər] escalador(a) *m,f*, alpinista *mf*

rock-climbing ['rɒkklaɪmɪŋ] *n* escalada *f*, alpinismo *m*

rocker ['rɒkər] *n* (**a**) *Aut* **r. arm** balancín *m* (**b**) *(rocking-chair)* mecedora *f* (**c**) *Mus* roquero(a) *m,f* (**d**) *Fam* **to be off one's r.** estar mal de la cabeza, *Esp* estar majara

rockery ['rɒkərɪ] *n* jardín *m* de rocas

rocket ['rɒkɪt] **1** *n* cohete *m*; *Fam Fig* **to give sb a r.** echar una regañina *or Esp* bronca a algn ❑ **r. launcher** lanzacohetes *m inv*
2 *vi Fam (prices)* aumentar enormemente; *Fig* **to r. to fame** hacerse famoso(a) de la noche a la mañana

rockfall ['rɒkfɔːl] *n* desprendimiento *m* (de piedras)

rock-hard ['rɒkhɑːd] *adj* (muy) duro(a)

Rockies ['rɒkɪz] *npl* (Montañas *fpl*) Rocosas *fpl or Am* Rocallosas *fpl*

rocking-chair ['rɒkɪŋtʃeər] *n* mecedora *f*

rocking-horse ['rɒkɪŋhɔːs] *n* caballito *m* de balancín

rock'n'roll [rɒkən'rəʊl] *n Mus* rock and roll *m*

rock-solid ['rɒk'sɒlɪd] *adj (support)* sólido(a) como una piedra

rocky ['rɒkɪ] *adj* (**rockier, rockiest**) rocoso(a); *Fam Fig (unsteady)* bamboleante; **the R. Mountains** las Montañas Rocosas *or Am* Rocallosas; *Fam Fig* **a r. government** un gobierno débil

rod [rɒd] *n* (**a**) *(of metal)* barra *f*; *(stick)* vara *f* ❑ **fishing r.** caña *f* de pescar (**b**) *(symbol of authority)* vara *f*; *Fig* **to rule with a r. of iron** mandar con mano de hierro

rode [rəʊd] *pt see* **ride**

rodent ['rəʊdənt] *n Zool* roedor *m*

rodeo ['rəʊdɪəʊ] *n* (*pl* **rodeos**) rodeo *m*

roe[1] [rəʊ] *n* (*pl* **roe** *or* **roes**) *Zool* **r. (deer)** corzo(a) *m,f*

roe[2] [rəʊ] *n* (*pl* **roe**) *(fish eggs)* hueva *f*

roebuck ['rəʊbʌk] *n Zool* corzo *m*

roger ['rɒdʒər] *interj Rad* ¡recibido!

rogue [rəʊg] *n Pej* (**a**) *(dishonest)* granuja *m*, pícaro *m*;

(criminal) delincuente *mf* ❑ **r. state** estado *m* delincuente *or* canalla (**b**) *(loner)* solitario(a) *m,f* ❑ **r. elephant** elefante *m* solitario

roguish ['rəʊgɪʃ] *adj Pej* pícaro(a), pillo(a)

role, rôle [rəʊl] *n* (**a**) *Cin Theat* papel *m*; **leading r.** papel principal; **supporting r.** papel secundario (**b**) *(in life)* papel *m*, función *f*; **to play a r.** desempeñar un papel

role-playing ['rəʊlpleɪŋ] *n* imitación *f*

roll [rəʊl] **1** *n* (**a**) *(of paper, cloth, film)* rollo *m*; *Fam (of fat, flesh)* *Esp* michelín *m*, *Méx* llanta *f*, *RP* rollo *m*; **r. of banknotes** fajo *m* de billetes; **toilet r.** rollo de papel higiénico (**b**) *Culin* **(bread) r.** bollo *m*, *Méx* bolillo *m* ❑ **ham r.** bocadillo *m* de jamón; **sausage r.** salchicha *f* empanada; **swiss r.** brazo *m* de gitano (**c**) *(list of names)* lista *f*, nómina *f*; *(register)* registro *m*; **to call the r.** pasar lista ❑ **electoral r.** censo *m*; **r. of honour** lista *f* de honor; *Jur* **to strike sb off the rolls** tachar a algn de la lista (**d**) *(ship etc)* balanceo *m* (**e**) *(of drum)* redoble *m*; *(of thunder)* fragor *m*
2 *vt* (**a**) *(ball)* hacer rodar; **to r. one's eyes** poner los ojos en blanco; **to r. one's r's** pronunciar fuerte las erres (**b**) *(cigarette)* liar (**c**) *(move)* mover (**d**) *(push)* empujar (**e**) *(flatten)* allanar
3 *vi* (**a**) *(ball, marble)* rodar; *Fig* **to keep the ball rolling** mantener la conversación; *Fam* **they were rolling in the aisles** se tronchaban de risa; *Fam* **to be rolling in money** nadar en la abundancia, *Esp* estar montado(a) en el dólar (**b**) *(animal)* revolcarse (**c**) *Naut (ship)* balancearse (**d**) *(drum)* redoblar; *(thunder)* retumbar; *(cannon)* tronar

roll about, roll around *vi* ir de acá para allá

roll along 1 *vt* hacer rodar por
2 *vi Fam* rodar; **things are rolling along nicely** todo anda muy bien

roll back *vt* (**a**) *(enemy)* hacer retroceder (**b**) *US (prices)* bajar, reducir

roll by *vi (years, months)* pasar

roll down *vt (blinds etc)* bajar; *(sleeves)* bajarse

roll in *vi Fam* (**a**) *(arrive)* llegar, presentarse (**b**) *(money)* llegar a raudales

roll on *vi* (**a**) *(gen)* seguir rodando (**b**) *Fam (time)* pasar; *Br* **r. on the holidays!** ¡que vengan las vacaciones!

roll over 1 *vt* derribar
2 *vi* dar una vuelta; **she rolled over on her side** se puso de costado

roll up 1 *vt* enrollar; *(blinds)* subir; **to r. up one's sleeves** (ar)remangarse
2 *vi* (**a**) *(map, carpet, paper)* enrollarse (**b**) *Fam (arrive)* llegar, presentarse

roll-call ['rəʊlkɔːl] *n* el acto de pasar lista

rolled [rəʊld] *adj* **r. gold** metal *m* laminado en oro; **r. oats** copos *mpl* de avena

rolled-up ['rəʊldʌp] *adj (umbrella, newspaper)* arrollado(a); *(clothes)* (ar)remangado(a)

roller ['rəʊlər] *n* (**a**) *Tech* rodillo *m* ❑ **r. blind** persiana *f* enrollable; **r. blades** patines *mpl* en línea; **r. coaster** montaña *f* rusa; **r. skate** patín *m* de ruedas; **r. skating** patinaje *m* sobre ruedas; **r. towel** toalla *f* de rodillo (**b**) *(large wave)* ola *f* grande (**c**) *usu pl (for hair)* rulo *m*, *Chile* tubo *m*, *RP* rulero *m*

roller-blading ['rəʊləbleɪdɪŋ] *n* **to go r.** patinar *(con patines en línea)*

roller-skate ['rəʊləskeɪt] *vi* patinar sobre ruedas

rolling ['rəʊlɪŋ] **1** *adj* (**a**) *(stone)* rodante, que rueda; *Fig* **a r. stone** un(a) vagabundo(a); *Prov* **a r. stone gathers no moss** piedra movediza nunca moho la cobija ❑ *Rail* **r. stock** material *m* rodante (**b**) *Fam Fig* rico(a); **he's rolling in money** *or* **in it** está forrado (**c**) *(countryside)* ondulado(a)

2 *n* rodamiento *m*; *(of ground)* apisonamiento *m* ❏ **r. pin** rodillo *m* (de cocina)

roll-neck(ed) ['rəʊlnek(t)] *adj* **r.-n. sweater** jersey *m* con cuello cisne

roll-on ['rəʊlɒn] *n* faja *f* elástica

roll-over ['rəʊləʊvər] *n (in UK national lottery)* **r. (jackpot)** bote *m* acumulado; **r. week** = semana en la que hay bote acumulado

rolltop ['rəʊltɒp] *adj (desk)* de tapa corrediza

roly-poly ['rəʊlɪ'pəʊlɪ] *n* **(a)** *Culin* **r.-p. (pudding)** = dulce compuesto de mermelada y masa pastelera enrollada **(b)** *Fam* gordinflón(ona) *m,f*

ROM [rɒm] *n Comptr (abbr* **read only memory)** memoria *f* sólo de lectura, ROM *f*

Roman ['rəʊmən] *adj & n* romano(a) *(m,f)* ❏ **R. alphabet** alfabeto *m* romano; **R. Catholic** católico(a) *m,f* (romano(a)); **R. Catholicism** catolicismo *m*; **R. law** ley *f* romana; **R. numerals** números *mpl* romanos; **R. nose** nariz *f* aguileña

Romance [rəʊ'mæns] *adj Ling* románico(a), romance; **R. languages** lenguas románicas

romance [rəʊ'mæns] **1** *n* **(a)** *(tale)* novela *f* romántica; *(medieval)* libro *m* de caballerías, romance *m* **(b)** *Mus* romanza *f* **(c)** *(love affair)* idilio *m*, aventura *f* amorosa, romance *m* **(d)** *(romantic quality)* lo romántico
2 *vi* fantasear

Romanesque [rəʊmə'nesk] *Archit* **1** *adj* románico(a)
2 *n* románico *m*, arte *m* románico

Romania [rəʊ'meɪnɪə] *n see* **Rumania**

Romanian [rəʊ'meɪnɪən] **1** *n* **(a)** *(person)* rumano(a) *m,f* **(b)** *(language)* rumano *m*
2 *adj* rumano(a)

romantic [rəʊ'mæntɪk] *adj & n* romántico(a) *(m,f)*

romantically [rə'mæntɪklɪ] *adv* de manera romántica; **to be r. involved with sb** tener un romance con algn

romanticism [rəʊ'mæntɪsɪzəm] *n* romanticismo *m*

romanticize [rəʊ'mæntɪsaɪz] *vi* fantasear

Romany ['rɒmənɪ, 'rəʊmənɪ] **1** *adj & n* gitano(a) *(m,f)*
2 *n (language)* lengua *f* de los gitanos; *(in Spain)* caló *m*

Rome [rəʊm] *n* Roma; *Prov* **all roads lead to R.** todos los caminos llevan a Roma; *Prov* **R. was not built in a day** no se ganó Zamora en una hora; *Prov* **when in R. do as the Romans do** cuando a Roma fueres, haz lo que vieres

romp [rɒmp] **1** *n* jugueteo *m*
2 *vi* juguetear; *Fam* retozar; *Fam* **to r. home** ganar con facilidad

romp through *vt* hacer con facilidad

rompers ['rɒmpəz] *npl* pelele *m sing*

roof [ru:f] **1** *n (pl* **roofs** [ru:fs, 'ru:vz]) **(a)** *Archit* tejado *m*; **flat r.** azotea *f*; **tiled r.** tejado *m*; *Fig* **to have a r. over one's head** tener donde cobijarse; *Fam Fig* **they can't live under the same r.** no pueden vivir bajo el mismo techo; *Fam Fig* **to go through the r.** *(prices)* estar por las nubes; *(with anger)* subirse por las paredes; *Fam Fig* **to hit the r.** enfadarse ❏ **r. garden** jardín *m* en la azotea **(b)** *Aut* techo *m* ❏ **r. rack** baca *f* **(c)** *(of mouth)* cielo *m*
2 *vt* techar

roofing ['ru:fɪŋ] *n Constr* materiales *mpl* usados para techar

roofless ['ru:flɪs] *adj* sin tejado

rooftop ['ru:ftɒp] *n* tejado *m*; *Fig* **to shout from the rooftops** divulgar a los cuatro vientos

rook [rʊk] **1** *n* **(a)** *Orn* grajo *m* **(b)** *Chess* torre *f*
2 *vt Fam (swindle)* estafar, timar

rookery ['rʊkərɪ] *n Orn* colonia *f* de grajos

rookie ['rʊkɪ] *n US Fam* **(a)** *Mil* recluta *m*, quinto *m* **(b)** *(novice)* novato(a) *m,f*

room [ru:m] **1** *n* **(a)** *(in house)* habitación *f*, cuarto *m*; *(in hotel)* habitación *f*; *(bedroom)* dormitorio *m*, *Am* cuarto *m*, *CAm Col Méx* recámara *f*; **r. and board** pensión *f* completa; **single r.** habitación individual ❏ **r. service** servicio *m* de habitación **(b)** *(space)* espacio *m*, sitio *m*, *Am* lugar *m*, *Andes* campo *m*; **make r. for me** hazme sitio; *Fig* **r. for improvement** posibilidades *fpl* de mejora
2 *vi US* alojarse; **to r. with sb** compartir la habitación *or* piso *or* casa con algn

roomful ['ru:mfʊl] *n* **a r. of people** una habitación llena de gente

rooming house ['ru:mɪŋhaʊs] *n US* casa *f* de huéspedes, pensión *f*

roommate ['ru:mmeɪt] *n* compañero(a) *m,f* de habitación

roomy ['ru:mɪ] *adj* (**roomier, roomiest**) amplio(a), espacioso(a)

roost [ru:st] **1** *n* palo *m*, percha *f*; **(hen) r.** gallinero *m*; *Fig* **to come home to r.** volverse en contra de uno; *Fig* **to rule the r.** llevar la batuta
2 *vi* posarse

rooster ['ru:stər] *n esp US Orn* gallo *m*

root[1] [ru:t] **1** *n* **(a)** *(plant, teeth, hair)* raíz *f*; *Bot* **r. crops** tubérculos *mpl*; **to take r.** echar raíces; **to pull up by the roots** arrancar de raíz; *Fig* **to put down roots in a country** establecerse en un país ❏ *US* **r. beer** = bebida gaseosa sin alcohol elaborada con extractos de plantas **(b)** *Math* raíz *f*; **square r.** raíz *f* cuadrada **(c)** *Fig* raíz *f*, origen *m*
2 *vt* arraigar; *Fig* **rooted to the spot** paralizado(a)
3 *vi Bot* echar raíces, arraigar

root out, root up *vt (plant)* desarraigar, arrancar de raíz

root[2] [ru:t] *vi (search)* buscar; **to r. about** *or* **around for sth** hurgar en busca de algo

root[3] [ru:t] *vi Fam* animar; **to r. for a team** animar a un equipo

rope [rəʊp] **1** *n* **(a)** *(small)* cuerda *f*; *(big)* soga *f*; *Naut* cabo *m*; **to give sb enough** *or* **plenty of r.** dar rienda suelta a algn **(b)** **ropes** *Box* cuerdas *fpl*; *(way)* truco *m sing*; *Fam Fig* **to have sb on the r.** tener a algn contra las cuerdas; *Fam Fig* **to know the r.** estar al tanto; *Fam Fig* **to learn the r.** ponerse al tanto; *Fam Fig* **to show sb the r.** poner a algn al tanto
2 *vt (package)* atar; *(climbers)* encordar

rope in *vt Fam (press-gang)* hacer participar; **we were roped in to going to the communion** no pudimos escaparnos de ir a la comunión

rope off *vt (cordon off)* acordonar

rop(e)y ['rəʊpɪ] *adj* (**ropier, ropiest**) *Fam* **(a)** *(bad quality)* de mala calidad, de pacotilla **(b)** *(ill)* pachucho(a), *Am* flojo(a)

rosary ['rəʊzərɪ] *n Rel* rosario *m*; **to say the r.** rezar el rosario

rose[1] [rəʊz] *pt see* **rise**

rose[2] [rəʊz] *n* **(a)** *Bot* rosa *f*; *Fam Fig* **life is no bed of roses** la vida no es un camino de rosas; *Prov* **there is no r. without a thorn** no hay rosa sin espina ❏ **dog r.** gavanza *f*; **r. bed** rosaleda *f*; **r. bush** rosal *m*; *Archit* **r. window** rosetón *m* **(b)** *(colour)* rosa *m*; *Fig* **that holiday put the roses back into his cheeks** esas vacaciones le han devuelto el buen color **(c)** *(of watering can)* alcachofa *f*

rosé ['rəʊzeɪ] *n* (vino *m*) rosado *m*

rosebud ['rəʊzbʌd] *n Bot* capullo *m* de rosa

rose-coloured, *US* **rose-colored** ['rəʊzkʌləd] *adj* rosa; *Fam Fig* **to see everything through r.-c. spectacles** verlo todo de color rosa

rosehip ['rəʊzhɪp] *n* escaramujo *m*

rosemary ['rəʊsmərɪ] *n Bot* romero *m*

rosette [rəʊ'zet] *n* (**a**) *(of ribbons)* escarapela *f* (**b**) *Archit* florón *m*

rose-water ['rəʊzwɔːtər] *n* agua *f* de rosas

rosewood ['rəʊzwʊd] *n Bot* palisandro *m*

roster ['rɒstər] *n* lista *f*

rostrum ['rɒstrəm] *n (pl* **rostrums** *or* **rostra** ['rɒstrə]) tribuna *f*

rosy ['rəʊzɪ] *adj* (**rosier, rosiest**) (**a**) *(complexion)* sonrosado(a) (**b**) *Fig (future)* prometedor(a), optimista

rot [rɒt] **1** *n* (**a**) *(decay)* putrefacción *f; Fig* **when the r. sets in** cuando las cosas empiezan a decaer ◻ **dry r.** putrefacción *f* de la madera (**b**) *Br Fam (nonsense)* sandeces *fpl, Am* pendejadas *fpl*
  2 *vt (pt & pp* **rotted**) pudrir

rot away *vi* pudrirse, descomponerse

rota ['rəʊtə] *n Br* lista *f*

rotary ['rəʊtərɪ] **1** *n US (roundabout)* rotonda *f*
  2 *adj* rotatorio(a), giratorio(a) ◻ *Typ* **r. press** rotativa *f*

rotate [rəʊ'teɪt] **1** *vt* (**a**) *(revolve)* hacer girar, hacer *or* dar vueltas a (**b**) *(jobs, crops)* alternarse
  2 *vi* (**a**) *(revolve)* girar, dar vueltas (**b**) *(jobs, crops)* alternarse

rotating [rəʊ'teɪtɪŋ] *adj* (**a**) *(turning)* giratorio(a) (**b**) *Agr* alternativo(a)

rotation [rəʊ'teɪʃən] *n* (**a**) *(circular movement)* rotación *f* (**b**) *Agr* **crop r.** rotación *f* de cultivos; **in r.** *(work)* por turno *or* turnos

rote [rəʊt] *n* rutina *f;* **to learn sth by r.** aprender algo de memoria

rotor ['rəʊtər] *n Tech* rotor *m*

rotten ['rɒtən] *adj* (**a**) *(decayed)* podrido(a); *(tooth)* cariado(a), picado(a); *(eggs)* podrido(a) (**b**) *Fam (quality, situation, luck)* malísimo(a), pésimo(a); *(health)* enfermo(a); *Fam* **I feel r.** me encuentro *Esp* fatal *or Am* pésimo; *Fam* **I feel r. about it** me sabe muy mal

rotter ['rɒtər] *n Br Fam Old-fashioned* sinvergüenza *mf*

rotund [rəʊ'tʌnd] *adj Literary* (**a**) *(rounded)* redondo(a) (**b**) *(plump)* regordete, corpulento(a) (**c**) *(bombastic)* rimbombante

rotunda [rəʊ'tʌndə] *n Archit* rotonda *f*

rouble ['ruːbəl] *n Fin* rublo *m*

rouge [ruːʒ] **1** *n* colorete *m*
  2 *vt* poner colorete a, pintar

rough [rʌf] **1** *adj* (**a**) *(surface, skin)* áspero(a); *(terrain)* accidentado(a); *(road)* desigual; *(sea)* agitado(a); *(weather)* tempestuoso(a), borrascoso(a) (**b**) *(rude, ill-mannered)* tosco(a), rudo(a), grosero(a); *(violent)* violento(a) (**c**) *(voice)* bronco(a) (**d**) *(wine)* áspero(a), agrio(a) (**e**) *(bad)* malo(a); **to have a r. time of it** pasarlo mal; *Fam* **to feel r.** encontrarse fatal (**f**) *(approximate)* aproximado(a); **a r. guess/idea** un cálculo aproximado/una idea aproximada (**g**) *(plan etc)* preliminar ◻ **r. draft** borrador *m;* **r. sketch** esbozo *m,* boceto *m* (**h**) *(hard, severe)* duro(a), severo(a); **r. justice** justicia *f* sumaria
  2 *adv* duramente; **to play r.** jugar duro; *Fam Fig* **to sleep r.** dormir a la intemperie *or Esp* al raso
  3 *n* (**a**) *Fam (person)* matón *m,* duro *m* (**b**) *Golf* hierba *f* alta, rough *m* (**c**) *Fig (bad times)* lo malo; **to take the r. with the smooth** estar a las duras y a las maduras, *Am* estar para las buenas y las malas
  4 *vt Fam* **to r. it** nos las arreglamos *or Esp* apañamos como pudimos

rough out *vt* esbozar

rough up *vt Fam* **to r. sb up** darle una paliza a algn

roughage ['rʌfɪdʒ] *n (substance)* fibra *f; (food)* alimentos *mpl* ricos en fibra

rough-and-ready [rʌfən'redɪ] *adj (makeshift)* improvisado(a); *(person)* campechano(a)

rough-and-tumble [rʌfən'tʌmbəl] *n (fight)* pelea *f; Fig* **the r.-a.-t. of life** los altibajos de la vida

roughcast ['rʌfkɑːst] *n Constr* mortero *m* grueso

roughen ['rʌfən] *vt* poner áspero(a)

roughhewn ['rʌfhjuːn] *adj (stone, wood)* desbastado(a)

roughly ['rʌflɪ] *adv* (**a**) *(crudely)* toscamente (**b**) *(clumsily)* torpemente (**c**) *(not gently)* bruscamente; **to treat sb r.** maltratar a algn (**d**) *(approximately)* aproximadamente, más o menos

roughneck ['rʌfnek] *n Fam* (**a**) *(tough)* matón *m,* duro *m* (**b**) *Ind* trabajador *m* en un pozo petrolífero

roughness ['rʌfnɪs] *n* (**a**) *(of surface, skin)* aspereza *f; (of terrain, road)* desigualdad *f; (of sea)* agitación *f* (**b**) *(of weather)* inclemencia *f* (**c**) *(of manner)* brusquedad *f; (impoliteness)* falta *f* de educación (**d**) *(violence)* violencia *f*

roughshod ['rʌfʃɒd] *adv* **to ride r. over sb's feelings** ignorar las opiniones de algn

rough-spoken [rʌf'spəʊkən] *adj (rude)* malhablado(a)

roulette [ruː'let] *n* ruleta *f* ◻ **Russian r.** ruleta *f* rusa

round [raʊnd] **1** *adj* redondo(a); **in r. figures** en números redondos; **to have r. shoulders** tener las espaldas cargadas ◻ **r. table** mesa *m* redonda; **r. trip** viaje *m* de ida y vuelta
  2 *n* (**a**) *(circle)* círculo *m* (**b**) *(series)* serie *f,* sucesión *f,* tanda *f; (session)* ronda *f;* **r. of talks** ronda de negociaciones (**c**) *Mil (ammunition)* cartucho *m; (salvo)* salva *f* (**d**) *(slice)* rebanada *f* (de pan); **a r. of toast** unas tostadas (**e**) *(of drinks)* ronda *f, Am* vuelta *f* (**f**) *(delivery)* reparto *m* (**g**) *(routine)* rutina *f;* **the daily r.** la rutina cotidiana (**h**) *(game) Golf* partido *m; Cards* partida *f* (**i**) *Box* round *m* (**j**) *(stage in competition)* vuelta *f,* eliminatoria *f* (**k**) **rounds** *(of doctor)* visita *f* sing; *(of salesman)* recorrido *m* sing
  3 *adv* a la redonda; **all year r.** durante todo el año; **to invite sb r.** invitar a algn a casa
  4 *prep* alrededor de; **r. here** por aquí; **r. the clock** día y noche; **r. the corner** a la vuelta de la esquina; **r. the garden** alrededor del jardín
  5 *vt (turn)* dar la vuelta a; **to r. a corner** dar la vuelta a una esquina

round off *vt* acabar, concluir

round on *vt (attack)* atacar

round up *vt* (**a**) *(cattle)* acorralar, rodear; *(people)* reunir (**b**) *(figures)* redondear al alta

roundabout ['raʊndəbaʊt] **1** *n Br* (**a**) *(at fairground)* tiovivo *m,* carrusel *m, RP* calesita *f* (**b**) *Aut* plaza *f* circular, rotonda *f, Esp* glorieta *f*
  2 *adj* indirecto(a); **r. phrase** rodeo *m,* circunloquio *m;* **could you explain it in a less r. way?** ¿podría explicarlo sin tantos rodeos?

rounded ['raʊndɪd] *adj* redondeado(a)

rounders ['raʊndəz] *n Br Sport* = juego parecido al béisbol

roundly ['raʊndlɪ] *adv* completamente, totalmente

round-shouldered [raʊnd'ʃəʊldəd] *adj* cargado(a) de espaldas

roundsman ['raʊndzmən] *n (pl* **roundsmen**) repartidor *m*

round-the-clock [raʊndðə'klɒk] *adj (service)* de veinticuatro horas

round-trip ['raʊnd'trɪp] *adj US (ticket)* de ida y vuelta

round-up ['raʊndʌp] n (a) (of cattle) rodeo m; (of suspects) redada f (b) (summary) resumen m

rouse [raʊz] vt (a) to r. sb (from sleep) despertar a algn; (from torpor) animar a algn (b) (provoke) (interest, suspicion) despertar, suscitar

rousing ['raʊzɪŋ] adj (cheer) entusiasta; (applause) caluroso(a); (speech, song) conmovedor(a)

rout¹ [raʊt] 1 n (a) (defeat) derrota f completa (b) (flight) desbandada f
   2 vt (a) (defeat) derrotar (b) (put to flight) poner en fuga

rout² [raʊt] vt (a) (person) hacer salir; (burrow) escarbar (b) (locate) localizar

route [ruːt] 1 n (a) (of traveller) ruta f; (of bus) línea f, recorrido m; Av ruta (aérea); Naut rumbo m, derrota f; Fig camino m □ r. **map** mapa m de carreteras; Mil r. **march** marcha f de entrenamiento (b) US R. carretera f nacional
   2 vt encaminar, mandar

router ['ruːtər] n Comptr router m, direccionador m

routine [ruː'tiːn] 1 n (a) (habit) rutina f (b) Theat número m; to go through a r. ensayar un número; Fam don't give me that oppressed female r.! ¡no me vengas con eso de las mujeres oprimidas!
   2 adj (a) (normal) habitual (b) (dull) rutinario(a), aburrido(a)

routinely [ruː'tiːnlɪ] adv habitualmente

rove [raʊv] vt & vi Literary errar

roving ['raʊvɪŋ] adj errante; r. **reporter** enviado(a) m,f especial; Fam to have a r. **eye** ser un ligón or una ligona

row¹ [raʊ] n fila f, hilera f; Fig **three times in a r.** tres veces seguidas □ US r. **house** casa f adosada

row² [raʊ] 1 n (trip in a rowing boat) paseo m en bote
   2 vt & vi remar

row³ [raʊ] 1 n (a) (quarrel) pelea f, bronca f, riña f; (industrial) disputa f (b) (noise, disturbance) jaleo m; (protest) escándalo m
   2 vi pelearse, reñir

rowan ['raʊən, 'raʊn] n Bot r. **tree** serbal m silvestre

rowboat ['raʊbaʊt] n US bote m de remos

rowdiness ['raʊdɪnɪs] n (noise) ruido m; (disorder) alboroto m

rowdy ['raʊdɪ] 1 adj (rowdier, rowdiest) (a) (noisy) ruidoso(a); (disorderly) alborotador(a) (b) (quarrelsome) camorrista, pendenciero(a)
   2 n camorrista mf, pendenciero(a) m,f

rower ['raʊər] n remero(a) m,f

rowing ['raʊɪŋ] n Sport remo m □ esp Br r. **boat** barco m a remo

rowlock ['raʊlɒk] n Naut tolete m, escálamo m

royal ['rɔɪəl] 1 adj real; a r. **welcome** una acogida muy calurosa; r. **blue** azul marino; the R. **Family** la Familia Real □ Cards r. **flush** escalera f real
   2 the **Royals** npl los miembros de la Familia Real

royalist ['rɔɪəlɪst] adj & n monárquico(a) (m,f)

royally ['rɔɪəlɪ] adv Fig magníficamente; Fam Fig **they get on r.** se llevan estupendamente bien

royalty ['rɔɪəltɪ] n (a) (rank) realeza f (b) (royal persons) miembro(s) m(pl) de la Familia Real (c) **royalties** derechos mpl de autor, royalties mpl

RP [ɑː'piː] n Ling (abbr **received pronunciation**) pronunciación f estándar (del inglés)

rpm [ɑːpiː'em] (abbr **revolutions per minute**) revoluciones fpl por minuto, r.p.m

R & R [ɑːrən'ɑːr] n Mil (abbr **rest and recreation**) permiso m

RRP [ɑːrɑː'piː] n Com (abbr **recommended retail price**) precio m recomendado de venta al público

RSVP [ɑːresviː'piː] (abbr répondez s'il vous plaît) se ruega contestación, S. R. C.

Rt Hon Dr Pol (abbr **(the) Right Honourable**) su Señoría

Rt Rev(d) Rel (abbr **Right Reverend**) muy Reverendo(a)

rub [rʌb] 1 n frotamiento m, fricción f; (touch) roce m; **give it a r.** frótalo un poco; Fig **there's the r.** ahí está el quid or el problema; Fig **to r. shoulders with sb** codearse con algn
   2 vt (pt & pp **rubbed**) (a) (hands, surface) frotar; (hard) restregar; **to r. one's hands together** frotarse las manos (b) (massage) friccionar
   3 vi rozar (**against** contra)

rub along vi Fam (a) (manage) defenderse, Esp apañarse (b) (get on well) llevarse bien

rub away vt quitar frotando; (erase) borrar

rub down vt frotar, friccionar; (horse) almohazar; (surface) raspar

rub in vt (a) (cream etc) frotar con; Fig **to r. sb's nose in it** echar en cara a algn algo (b) Fam insistir

rub off 1 vt quitar frotando; (erase) borrar
   2 vi (stain) quitarse frotando, borrarse; Fig **to r. off on sb** influir en algn

rub on vt (cream etc) frotar con

rub out vt (a) (erase) borrar (b) US Fam (murder) acabar con, Esp cepillarse a

rub up vt limpiar, sacar brillo a; Fam Fig **to r. sb up the wrong way** fastidiar a algn

rubber¹ ['rʌbər] n (a) (substance) (finished product) goma f, Am hule m; (raw material) caucho m □ r. **band** goma f; Fam r. **cheque** cheque m sin fondos; r. **industry** industria f del caucho; r. **plant** gomero m; r. **stamp** tampón m (b) Br (eraser) goma f de borrar; **blackboard r.** borrador m (c) Slang (contraceptive) goma f, Méx impermeable m, RP forro m

rubber² ['rʌbər] (a) Bridge rubber m (b) Sport = serie de juegos o partidos en cualquier deporte

rubberized ['rʌbəraɪzd] adj cauchutado(a)

rubber-stamp [rʌbə'stæmp] vt Fig (approve) dar el visto bueno a

rubbery ['rʌbərɪ] adj (meat) correoso(a); **it feels r.** parece de goma (al tacto)

rubbing ['rʌbɪŋ] n (scrubbing etc) frotamiento m; (friction) fricción f

rubbish ['rʌbɪʃ] n (a) (refuse) basura f □ r. **bin** cubo m or Am bote m de la basura; r. **collection** recogida f de la basura; r. **dump** vertedero m (b) Fam (worthless thing) birria f, porquería f; **the film was r.** la película fue una birria (c) Fam (nonsense) tonterías fpl; **don't talk r.!** ¡no digas tonterías!

rubbishy ['rʌbɪʃɪ] adj Fam de pésima calidad, Esp cutre

rubble ['rʌbəl] n escombros mpl

rubella [ruː'belə] n Med rubéola f

rubicund ['ruːbɪkənd] adj rubicundo(a)

ruble ['ruːbəl] n US Fin see **rouble**

rubric ['ruːbrɪk] n rúbrica f

ruby ['ruːbɪ] n rubí m □ r. **ring** sortija f de rubíes

ruck¹ [rʌk] n (rugby) melé f espontánea; Fig canalla f

ruck² [rʌk] 1 n (clothing, material) arruga f
   2 vi to r. up arrugarse

ruck³ [rʌk] n Slang pelea f

rucksack ['rʌksæk] n mochila f

ructions ['rʌkʃənz] npl Fam jaleo m sing, follón m sing; **there will be r.** se armará la gorda

rudder ['rʌdər] n Av Naut timón m

rudderless ['rʌdəlɪs] adj sin timón

ruddy ['rʌdɪ] adj (**ruddier, ruddiest**) (**a**) (complexion) rojizo(a), colorado(a) (**b**) Br Old-fashioned Fam (damned) maldito(a), condenado(a)

rude [ruːd] adj (**a**) (impolite) maleducado(a), descortés; (foul-mouthed) grosero(a); **don't be r. to your mother** no le faltes al respeto a tu madre (**b**) Literary (primitive) tosco(a) (**c**) Literary (sudden) brusco(a); **a r. awakening** un despertar repentino

rudeness ['ruːdnɪs] n (**a**) (impoliteness) falta f de educación, descortesía f; (offensiveness) grosería f (**b**) (roughness) tosquedad f (**c**) (suddenness) brusquedad f

rudimentary [ruːdɪ'mentərɪ] adj Fml rudimentario(a)

rudiments ['ruːdɪmənts] npl rudimentos mpl

rue¹ [ruː] n Bot ruda f

rue² [ruː] vt arrepentirse de, lamentar

rueful ['ruːfʊl] adj (**a**) (regretful) arrepentido(a) (**b**) (sad) triste

ruff¹ [rʌf] n (**a**) (on animal, bird) collarín m (**b**) (starched collar) gorguera f

ruff² [rʌf] n Cards fallo m

ruffian ['rʌfɪən] n Old-fashioned rufián m

ruffle ['rʌfəl] **1** n usu pl (on blouse, shirt) chorrera f; (on cuffs) volante m

2 vt (**a**) (disturb) agitar; (wind) levantar (**b**) (feathers) erizar; (hair) despeinar (**c**) Fig (annoy) hacer perder la calma a

ruffled ['rʌfəld] adj (**a**) (hair) alborotado(a); (clothes) en desorden (**b**) (perturbed) perturbado(a); **she never gets r.** nunca se altera (**c**) (with a ruff) (blouse, shirt) con chorrera; (cuffs) con volante

rug [rʌg] n alfombra f, alfombrilla f □ **travelling r.** manta f de viaje

rugby ['rʌgbɪ] n Sport rugby m; **r. league** rugby a trece; **r. union** rugby a quince

rugby-tackle ['rʌgbɪ'tækəl] vt **to r.-t. sb** hacer un placaje a algn, atrapar a algn por las piernas, Am tacklear algn

rugged ['rʌgɪd] adj (**a**) (terrain) accidentado(a), desigual (**b**) (features) duro(a) (**c**) (character) robusto(a), fuerte; (manner) tosco(a)

rugger ['rʌgər] n Fam rugby m

ruin ['ruːɪn] **1** n ruina f; **to fall into r.** caer en la ruina; **ruins** ruinas fpl, restos mpl; **in ruins** en ruinas

2 vt arruinar; (spoil) estropear

ruination [ruːɪ'neɪʃən] n ruina f, perdición f

ruined ['ruːɪnd] adj (**a**) (building, city) en ruinas (**b**) (career, reputation, health) arruinado(a); (clothes) estropeado(a)

ruinous ['ruːɪnəs] adj ruinoso(a)

ruinously ['ruːɪnəslɪ] adv **r. expensive** carísimo(a)

rule [ruːl] **1** n (**a**) (law) regla f, norma f; **rules and regulations** reglamento m; Ind **to work to r.** hacer una huelga de celo; Fig **by r. of thumb** a ojo de buen cubero (**b**) (government) dominio m, mando m; (of monarch) reinado m; **majority r.** gobierno de la mayoría; **r. of law** imperio m de la ley (**c**) (ruler) regla f (graduada)

2 vt & vi (**a**) (govern) mandar, gobernar; (monarch) reinar (**b**) (decide) decidir; (decree) decretar (**c**) (draw) tirar, trazar

rule out vt descartar, excluir

ruled [ruːld] adj rayado(a)

ruler ['ruːlər] n (**a**) (of country) gobernante mf (**b**) (for measuring) regla f

ruling ['ruːlɪŋ] **1** adj (in charge) dirigente; Fig (predominant) predominante, principal; **the r. party** el partido en el poder

2 n Jur fallo m; **to give a r. on** pronunciar un fallo sobre

rum [rʌm] **1** n (drink) ron m

2 adj Br Fam (odd) extraño(a)

Rumania [ruː'meɪnɪə] n Rumania

Rumanian [ruː'meɪnɪən] **1** adj rumano(a)

2 n (person) rumano(a) m,f; (language) rumano m

rumble ['rʌmbəl] **1** n (**a**) (of thunder, gunfire) rugido m, retumbo m (**b**) (of stomach) borborigmo m

2 vi (**a**) (thunder, guns) retumbar; **to r. past** (vehicle) pasar ruidosamente (**b**) (stomach) hacer ruidos (**c**) (drone) perorar; **the lecturer rumbled on** el conferenciante siguió con el rollo

3 vt Br Fam (see through) descubrir (el juego a), Esp pillar; **we've been rumbled** nos han pillado or Esp cogido or Am agarrado

rumbling ['rʌmblɪŋ] n (**a**) (of thunder, gunfire) rugido m, retumbo m (**b**) (of stomach) borborigmo m (**c**) **rumblings** (of danger, dissatisfaction) señales mpl, signos mpl; **there were r. about a strike** se mascaba una huelga

rumbustious [rʌm'bʌstjəs] adj Br bullicioso(a)

ruminant ['ruːmɪnənt] **1** n Zool rumiante m

2 adj (**a**) Zool rumiante (**b**) Fml (thoughtful) rumiante

ruminate ['ruːmɪneɪt] vi (**a**) Zool (chew) rumiar (**b**) Fig (ponder) rumiar; **to r. on a matter** meditar sobre un asunto

rumination [ruːmɪ'neɪʃən] n reflexión f, meditación f

ruminative ['ruːmɪnətɪv] adj Literary pensativo(a); **it was a r. period in his life** fue un período de reflexión en su vida

rummage ['rʌmɪdʒ] **1** n búsqueda f; **to have a r. about** rebuscar □ US **r. sale** venta f de artículos usados

2 vt revolver; **to r. through a drawer** revolver en un cajón

rummy ['rʌmɪ] n Cards rummy m

rumour, US rumor ['ruːmər] **1** n rumor m; **r. has it that ...** se dice que ..., corre el rumor de que ...

2 vt rumorear

rump [rʌmp] n (**a**) (of animal) ancas fpl; (quadruped) grupa f; Fam Hum (of person) trasero m □ **r. steak** filete m de lomo (**b**) **rumps** (die-hards) incondicionales mpl, irreductibles mpl

rumple ['rʌmpəl] vt Fam (crease) arrugar; **to r. sb's hair** despeinar a algn

rumpus ['rʌmpəs] n Fam jaleo m, bronca f, Esp follón m; **to kick up a r.** armar un jaleo or una bronca or Esp un follón; US **r. room** cuarto m de juegos

run [rʌn] **1** n (**a**) (act of running) carrera f; **to be on the r.** (fugitive) haberse fugado; **to break into a r.** echar a correr; **to go for a r.** hacer footing; **to make a r. for it** salir corriendo or Esp por piernas; **to score a r.** (in cricket) marcar una carrera; Fig **in the long r.** a largo plazo; Fig **to have a good r. for one's money** sacarle jugo al dinero □ trial r. prueba f (**b**) (trip) paseo m, vuelta f; **a ten minute r.** un viajecito de diez minutos (**c**) (sequence) serie f; **to have a r. of bad luck** tener una mala racha (**d**) (track) pista f □ **ski r.** pista f de esquí (**e**) (demand) gran demanda f (**f**) (use) uso m; **to give sb the r. of a house** poner una casa a disposición de algn (**g**) Typ (of book) tirada f (**h**) Cards escalera f (**i**) (in stocking) carrera f

2 vt (pt **ran**; pp **run**) (**a**) (gen) correr, recorrer; **to r. a race** correr or participar en una carrera; **to r. errands** hacer recados or Am mandados (**b**) (drive) llevar; **to r. sb to the airport** llevar a algn al aeropuerto, dar CAm Méx aventón or Cuba botella a algn hasta el aeropuerto (**c**) (house, business, etc) llevar; (company) dirigir; (organize) organizar, montar; **to r. one's own life** ser dueño de sí mismo (**d**) (pass) pasar; **to r. one's fingers through one's hair** pasarse la mano por el pelo (**e**) (operate) (machine, engine) hacer funcionar; Comptr (program) ejecutar; **it's a cheap car to r.** es un coche económico; **they r. trains every hour** hay un servicio de trenes cada hora; *Comptr* **to r. a program** pasar un programa (**f**) *Press* publicar; **to r. articles on drug addiction** publicar artículos sobre la drogadicción (**g**) *(temperature)* tener

3 *vi* (**a**) *(person)* correr; **to r. for a train** correr para alcanzar *or Esp* coger un tren; *Fam* **r. for it!** ¡corre! (**b**) *(colour)* desteñirse (**c**) *(flow) (water, river)* correr; *(drip)* gotear; **to leave the tap running** *Esp* dejar el grifo abierto, dejar la *Chile Col Méx* llave *or Carib Col Méx* pluma *or RP* canilla abierta; **to r. dry** secarse; *Fam* **your nose is running** te moquea *or RP* chorrea la nariz, tienes mocos (**d**) *(operate) (bus, train)* circular; **to leave an engine running** dejar un motor en marcha; **trains r. every two hours** hay trenes cada dos horas (**e**) *Naut* navegar; **to r. aground/ ashore** encallar/embarrancar (**f**) *Pol* participar, presentarse; **to r. for president** presentarse como candidato a la presidencia (**g**) *(story)* decir; **so the story runs** según lo que se dice (**h**) *(range)* oscilar; **prices r. from ten to fifty dollars** los precios oscilan entre diez y cincuenta dólares (**i**) *(quantity)* abastecer; **we're running low on** *or* **short of milk** nos queda poca leche (**j**) *(traits)* venir de; **shyness runs in the family** la timidez le viene de familia (**k**) *Cin Theat* estar en cartel (**l**) *(last)* durar (**m**) *(stocking)* hacerse una carrera

run about *vi* correr por todas partes

run across *vt* (**a**) *(bridge)* cruzar corriendo (**b**) *(meet)* tropezar con

run away *vi* escaparse, fugarse; *(horse)* desbocarse; *Fig* **don't r. away with the idea that** no te vayas a creer que

run down 1 *vt* (**a**) *(stairs)* bajar corriendo (**b**) *(knock down)* atropellar; *(hit)* pillar; **she was r. down by a car** la atropelló *or* pilló un coche (**c**) *(criticize)* criticar
2 *vi* (**a**) *(battery)* acabarse, agotarse; *(watch)* pararse

run in *vt* (**a**) *(arrest)* detener (**b**) *Aut* rodar

run into *vt* (**a**) *(enter)* entrar corriendo en (**b**) *(river)* desembocar en (**c**) *(people, problems)* tropezar con (**d**) *(crash into)* chocar contra (**e**) *(amount to)* sumar, alcanzar

run off 1 *vt* (**a**) *Typ (copies)* tirar (**b**) **to r. off the mains/ batteries** *(radio etc)* funcionar con electricidad/pilas
2 *vi* escaparse; **to r. off with sth** llevarse algo

run on 1 *vt Typ* enlazar
2 *vi* (**a**) *(function)* funcionar con (**b**) *(continue)* continuar (**c**) *Fam* hablar sin parar

run out *vi* (**a**) *(exit)* salir corriendo (**b**) *(finish)* acabarse, agotarse; *(stocks)* agotarse; *(contract)* vencer; **to r. out of** quedarse sin

run over 1 *vt* (**a**) *(knock down)* atropellar; *(hit)* pillar (**b**) *(rehearse)* ensayar
2 *vi* *(overflow)* rebosar; *(spill)* derramarse

run through *vt* (**a**) *(cross)* atravesar corriendo; *(river)* pasar por (**b**) *(read quickly)* echar un vistazo a (**c**) *(rehearse)* ensayar (**d**) *(fortune)* despilfarrar

run up 1 *vi* (**a**) *(ascend)* subir corriendo; *(arrive)* llegar corriendo (**b**) *(difficulties)* tropezar con
2 *vt* (**a**) *(flag)* izar (**b**) *(debts)* acumular (**c**) *Sew* hacer rápidamente

runabout ['rʌnəbaʊt] *n Fam* coche *m or Am* carro *m or CSur* auto *m* pequeño ❑ *Rail* **r. (ticket)** billete *m* kilométrico

run-around ['rʌnəraʊnd] *n Fam* **to give sb the r.-a.** enredar a algn

runaway ['rʌnəweɪ] **1** *n* fugitivo(a) *m,f*
2 *adj (person)* huido(a), fugitivo(a); *(horse)* desbocado(a); *(vehicle)* incontrolado(a); *(inflation)* galopante; *(success, victory)* aplastante; *(leader)* indiscutible

rundown ['rʌndaʊn] *n Fam* informe *m* detallado, *CAm Méx* reporte *m*; **to give sb a r.** poner a algn al corriente

run-down [rʌn'daʊn] *adj* (**a**) *(exhausted)* agotado(a) (**b**) *(dilapidated)* ruinoso(a); *(inefficient)* de capa caída, en declive

rung¹ [rʌŋ] *pp see* ring

rung² [rʌŋ] *n (of ladder)* escalón *m*, peldaño *m*; *Fig* escalón *m*

run-in ['rʌnɪn] *n Fam* **to have a r.-in with sb** tener una pelea *or* una riña con algn

runner ['rʌnər] *n* (**a**) *(athlete)* corredor(a) *m,f* (**b**) *(horse)* caballo *m* de carreras (**c**) *(messenger)* mensajero(a) *m,f*, recadero(a) *m,f* (**d**) *Tech* carro *m*; *(of skate)* cuchilla *f* (**e**) *(on table)* tapete *m* (**f**) *(carpet)* alfombra *f* de escalera *or* pasillo (**g**) *Br Bot* **r. bean** judía *f* verde, *Bol RP* chaucha *f*, *Chile* poroto *m* verde, *Col* habichuela *f*, *Méx* ejote *m*

runner-up [rʌnər'ʌp] *n* (*pl* **runners-up**) *Sport* subcampeón(ona) *m,f*; *(in competition)* ganador(a) *m,f* del segundo premio

running ['rʌnɪŋ] **1** *n* (**a**) *Sport* atletismo *m*; *(race)* carrera *f*; **long-distance r.** carreras de fondo; *Fig* **to be in the r. for sth** tener posibilidades de ganar *or* conseguir algo (**b**) *(management)* dirección *f*, organización *f* (**c**) *(of machine)* funcionamiento *m*
2 *adj* (**a**) *Sport* de carreras ❑ *Aut* **r. board** estribo *m*; *Rad TV* **r. commentary** comentario *m* en directo; **r. costs** costos *mpl or Esp* costes *mpl* de mantenimiento; *US Pol* **r. mate** candidato *m* a la vicepresidencia; *Med* **r. sore** llaga *f* supurante; **r. track** pista *f*; **r. water** agua *f* corriente (**b**) *(consecutive)* seguido(a); **three weeks r.** tres semanas seguidas (**c**) *Aut* funcionamiento *m*; **in good r. order** en buen estado; **r. in** en rodaje

runny ['rʌnɪ] *adj* (**runnier, runniest**) (**a**) *(soft)* blando(a); *(egg)* crudo(a); *(liquid)* líquido(a); *(melted)* derretido(a) (**b**) *(nose)* que moquea

run-off ['rʌnɒf] *n* (*pl* **run-offs**) *(contest)* partido *m* de desempate; *(race)* carrera *f* de desempate

run-of-the-mill [rʌnəvðə'mɪl] *adj* corriente y moliente

runproof ['rʌnpruːf] *adj (stockings)* indesmallable

runt [rʌnt] *n Fam* enano(a) *m,f*

run-through ['rʌnθruː] *n* ensayo *m*

run-up ['rʌnʌp] *n* (**a**) *(elections)* preliminares *mpl* (**b**) *Sport* carrera *f*

runway ['rʌnweɪ] *n* (**a**) *Av* pista *f* (de aterrizaje y despegue *or Am* decolaje) (**b**) *Sport (in long jump, pole vault)* pista *f* de aceleración (**c**) *US (at fashion show)* pasarela *f*

rupee [ruː'piː] *n Fin* rupia *f*

rupture ['rʌptʃər] **1** *n* (**a**) *Med* hernia *f* (**b**) *Fig* ruptura *f*
2 *vt* (**a**) *Med* **to r. oneself** hacerse una hernia, herniarse (**b**) *(break)* romper

rural ['rʊərəl] *adj* rural

ruse [ruːz] *n* ardid *m*, astucia *f*

rush¹ [rʌʃ] *n Bot* junco *m* ❑ **r. matting** estera *f* de juncos

rush² [rʌʃ] **1** *n* (**a**) *(hurry)* prisa *f*, *Am* apuro *m*; *(hustle and bustle)* ajetreo *m*; **it's a r. job** es urgente; **there's no r.** no corre prisa, *Am* no hay apuro; **they made a r. for the exit** se precipitaron hacia la salida ❑ **r. hour** hora *f Esp* punta *or Am* pico (**b**) *(demand)* demanda *f*; **there's a r. on sugar** hay una gran demanda de azúcar (**c**) *(of wind)* ráfaga *f* (**d**) *(of water)* torrente *m* (**e**) *Mil* ataque *m* (**f**) *Cin* **rushes** primeras pruebas *fpl*
2 *vt* (**a**) *(do hastily) (job)* hacer de prisa; *(hurry) (person)* meter prisa a, apresurar; **don't r. me!** ¡no me metas prisa!, *Am* ¡no me apures!; **to r. a meal** comer de prisa; **to be rushed off one's feet** tener un día muy ajetreado (**b**) *(hasten)* darse prisa; **to r. sb to hospital** llevar a algn urgentemente al hospital (**c**) *(attack)* abalanzarse sobre; *Mil* tomar por asalto

3 *vi* (**a**) *(act overhastily)* precipitarse (**b**) *(hurry)* apresurarse, *Am* apurarse; **don't r. at it** no te precipites; *Fig* **the blood rushed to her cheeks** se puso colorada

rush about *vi* correr de un lado a otro

rush in *vi* entrar precipitadamente

rush into *vt* entrar precipitadamente en; *Fig* **to r. into sth** hacer algo sin pensarlo bien

rush off *vi* irse corriendo

rush out *vt* salir precipitadamente

rush through *vt* hacer de prisa; *(piece of business)* despachar rápidamente

rusk [rʌsk] *n* galleta *f* dura para niños

russet ['rʌsɪt] **1** *adj* rojizo(a)
 2 *n (colour)* color *m* rojizo

Russia ['rʌʃə] *n* Rusia

Russian ['rʌʃən] **1** *adj* ruso(a)
 2 *n* (**a**) *(person)* ruso(a) *m,f* (**b**) *(language)* ruso *m*

rust [rʌst] **1** *n* (**a**) *(action)* oxidación *f*; *(substance)* orín *m*, herrumbre *f* (**b**) *(colour)* color *m* de orín, pardo *m* rojizo (**c**) *Bot* roya *f*
 2 *vt* oxidar
 3 *vi* oxidarse

rustic ['rʌstɪk] *adj* rústico(a), campestre

rusticate ['rʌstɪkeɪt] *vt Br Univ (student)* expulsar temporalmente

rustle ['rʌsəl] **1** *n (of paper, leaves)* crujido *m*
 2 *vt (papers etc)* hacer crujir
 3 *vi* (**a**) *(leaves)* crujir (**b**) *US (steal cattle)* robar ganado

rustle up *vt Fam (food)* preparar en un momento

rustler ['rʌslər] *n US (cattle thief)* ladrón *m* de ganado, cuatrero *m*

rustling ['rʌslɪŋ] *n* (**a**) *(of paper, leaves)* crujido *m* (**b**) *US (cattle theft)* robo *m* de ganado

rustproof ['rʌstpruːf] *adj* inoxidable

rusty ['rʌstɪ] *adj* (**rustier, rustiest**) oxidado(a); *Fam Fig* **my French is a bit r.** tengo el francés un poco oxidado

rut [rʌt] *n* (**a**) *(furrow)* surco *m*; *(groove)* ranura *f* (**b**) *Fig* **to be in a r.** ser esclavo de la rutina; **to get out of a r.** salir de la rutina (**c**) *Zool* celo *m*

ruthless ['ruːθlɪs] *adj (cruel)* cruel, despiadado(a); *(merciless)* implacable

ruthlessness ['ruːθlɪsnɪs] *n* crueldad *f*, implacabilidad *f*

rutted ['rʌtɪd] *adj (surface)* surcado(a), con ranuras

RV [ɑːˈviː] *n US (abbr* **recreational vehicle**) autocaravana *f*, casa *f* or coche *m* caravana

Rwanda [rʊˈændə] *n* (**a**) *(country)* Ruanda (**b**) *(language)* ruandés *m*

Rwandan [rʊˈændən] *adj & n* ruandés(esa) *(m,f)*

S

S, s [es] *n (the letter)* S, s *f*

S (**a**) *(abbr* **Saint**) San *m*, Santo *m*, S., Sto.; Santa *f*, Sta. (**b**) *(on clothes etc) (abbr* **small (size)**) (talla *f*) pequeña (**c**) *(abbr* **South**) Sur, S

s *(abbr* **single**) soltero(a)

SA *(abbr* **South Africa**) Sudáfrica

Sabbath ['sæbəθ] *n (Jewish)* sábado *m; (Christian)* domingo *m*

sabbatical [sə'bætɪkəl] *adj* sabático(a)

saber ['seɪbər] *n US see* **sabre**

sable ['seɪbəl] **1** *n (animal, fur)* marta *f* cebellina
  2 *adj (colour)* negro(a)

sabotage ['sæbətɑːʒ] **1** *n* sabotaje *m*
  2 *vt (machinery, plan)* sabotear

saboteur [sæbə'tɜːr] *n* saboteador(a) *m,f*

sabre ['seɪbər] *n* sable *m*

sac [sæk] *n Anat Biol* bolsa *f*

saccharin ['sækərɪn] *n* sacarina *f*

saccharine ['sækərɪn] *adj Pej (smile, film)* empalagoso(a)

sachet ['sæʃeɪ] *n* bolsita *f*, sobrecito *m*

sack [sæk] **1** *n* (**a**) *(bag)* saco *m* (**b**) *Br Fam (dismissal)* **to get the s.** ser despedido(a); *Fam* **to give sb the s.** despedir a algn, echar del trabajo a algn, poner de patitas en la calle a algn (**c**) *Fam (bed)* **to hit the s.** irse al sobre
  2 *vt* (**a**) *Br Fam (dismiss from job)* despedir, echar (**b**) *Mil* saquear

sackcloth ['sækklɒθ] *n Tex* arpillera *f; Rel* **in s. and ashes** en túnica de penitente

sacking ['sækɪŋ] *n* (**a**) *Tex* arpillera *f* (**b**) *(dismissal)* despido *m* (**c**) *(of city)* saqueo *m*

sacra ['sækrə] *npl see* **sacrum**

sacrament ['sækrəmənt] *n Rel* sacramento *m;* **to receive the S.** comulgar

sacred ['seɪkrɪd] *adj* sagrado(a), sacro(a); **nothing is s. any more** ya no se respeta nada; *Fig* **s. to** dedicado(a) a □ **s. cow** vaca *f* sagrada; **s. music** música *f* religiosa

sacredness ['seɪkrɪdnɪs] *n* carácter *m* sagrado, santidad *f*

sacrifice ['sækrɪfaɪs] **1** *n* (**a**) *(act, offering)* sacrificio *m* (**b**) *(in baseball)* sacrificio *m*
  2 *vt* sacrificar

sacrificial [sækrɪ'fɪʃəl] *adj* de sacrificio □ **s. lamb** chivo *m* expiatorio

sacrilege ['sækrɪlɪdʒ] *n* sacrilegio *m*

sacrilegious [sækrɪ'lɪdʒəs] *adj* sacrílego(a)

sacristan ['sækrɪstən] *n* sacristán(ana) *m,f*

sacristy ['sækrɪstɪ] *n Rel* sacristía *f*

sacrosanct ['sækrəʊsæŋkt] *adj* sacrosanto(a)

sacrum ['sækrəm] *n (pl* **sacra**) *Anat* sacro *m*

SAD [sæd] *n Med (abbr* **Seasonal Affective Disorder**) trastorno *m* afectivo estacional

sad [sæd] *adj* (**sadder, saddest**) (**a**) *(unhappy)* triste; **how s.!** ¡qué pena! (**b**) *(deplorable)* lamentable (**c**) *(colour)* apagado(a)

sadden ['sædən] *vt* entristecer

saddle ['sædəl] **1** *n (for horse)* silla *f* (de montar); *(of bicycle, motorbike)* sillín *m; Fam* **to be in the s.** llevar las riendas
  2 *vt (horse)* ensillar

saddlebag ['sædəlbæg] *n* alforja *f*

saddler ['sædlər] *n* guarnicionero(a) *m,f*

saddlery ['sædlərɪ] *n (equipment)* guarniciones *fpl; (workshop)* guarnicionería *f*

sadism ['seɪdɪzəm] *n* sadismo *m*

sadist ['seɪdɪst] *n* sádico(a) *m,f*

sadistic [sə'dɪstɪk] *adj* sádico(a)

sadly ['sædlɪ] *adv (to reply, smile)* tristemente; **you're s. mistaken** estás muy equivocado(a); **he is s. missed** lo echamos mucho de menos, *Am* lo extrañamos mucho; **s., this is so** así es, por desgracia

sadness ['sædnɪs] *n* tristeza *f*

sadomasochism [seɪdəʊ'mæsəkɪzəm] *n* sadomasoquismo *m*

sadomasochist [seɪdəʊ'mæsəkɪst] *n* sadomasoquista *mf*

SAE [eseɪ'iː] *n Br (abbr* **stamped addressed envelope**) = sobre franqueado con la dirección del remitente

safari [sə'fɑːrɪ] *n* safari *m;* **on s.** de safari □ **s. park** safari *m*, reserva *f*

safe [seɪf] **1** *adj* (**a**) *(unharmed)* ileso(a); *(out of danger)* a salvo, fuera de peligro; **s. and sound** sano(a) y salvo(a); **s. from** a salvo de (**b**) *(not dangerous)* inofensivo(a), inocuo(a) (**c**) *(secure, sure)* seguro(a); **it is s. to say that ...** se puede decir con seguridad que ...; **to be on the s. side** para mayor seguridad □ *Fam* **s. house** piso *m* franco; *Med* **s. period** período *m* de seguridad; **s. sex** sexo *m* seguro *or* sin riesgo (**d**) *(cautious)* prudente
  2 *n (for money etc)* caja *f* fuerte *or* de caudales *or* de seguridad □ **meat s.** fresquera *f*

safe-breaker ['seɪfbreɪkər] *n* ladrón(ona) *m,f* de cajas fuertes

safe-conduct [seɪf'kɒndəkt] *n* salvoconducto *m*

safe-cracker ['seɪfkrækər] *n see* **safe-breaker**

safe-deposit [seɪfdɪ'pɒzɪt] *n* **s.-d. (box)** cámara *f* blindada *or* acorazada

safeguard ['seɪfgɑːd] **1** *n (protection)* salvaguarda *f*, protección *f*; *(guarantee)* garantía *f*
2 *vt* proteger, salvaguardar

safekeeping [seɪf'kiːpɪŋ] *n* custodia *f*; **to be in s.** estar a buen recaudo

safely ['seɪflɪ] *adv* **(a)** *(certainly)* con toda seguridad **(b)** *(without mishap)* sin accidentes *or* contratiempos *or* percance; **to arrive s.** llegar a buen puerto

safety ['seɪftɪ] *n* seguridad *f*; **s. first!** ¡seguridad ante todo! ❑ **road s.** seguridad *f* vial; *Aut Av* **s. belt** cinturón *m* de seguridad; **s. catch** seguro *m*; **s. device** dispositivo *m* de seguridad; *US* **s. island** isleta *f* para peatones; *Min* **s. lamp** lámpara *f* de seguridad; **s. measures** medidas *fpl* de seguridad; **s. net** red *f* de protección *or* de seguridad; **s. pin** imperdible *m*, *Am* alfiler *m* de gancho, *CAm Méx* seguro *m*; **s. valve** válvula *f* de seguridad

saffron ['sæfrən] **1** *n Bot Culin* azafrán *m*
2 *adj (colour)* de color azafrán

sag [sæg] *vi (pt & pp sagged)* **(a)** *(roof)* hundirse; *(wall)* pandear; *(wood, iron)* combarse; *(flesh)* colgar **(b)** *Fig (spirits)* flaquear

saga ['sɑːgə] *n Lit* saga *f*

sagacious [sə'geɪʃəs] *adj* sagaz, perspicaz

sagacity [sə'gæsɪtɪ] *n* sagacidad *f*

sage¹ [seɪdʒ] **1** *adj (wise)* sabio(a)
2 *n (wise person)* sabio(a) *m,f*

sage² [seɪdʒ] *n Bot* salvia *f*; **s. green** verde salvia, verdigris

sagging ['sægɪŋ] **1** *adj (roof)* hundido(a); *(wall)* pandeado(a); *(wood, iron)* combado(a)
2 *n (of roof)* hundimiento *m*; *(of wall)* pandeo *m*; *(of wood, iron)* comba *f*

saggy ['sægɪ] *adj (mattress)* hundido(a); *(bottom)* fláccido(a), fofo(a); *(breasts)* caído(a)

Sagittarius [sædʒɪ'teərɪəs] *n Astrol Astron* Sagitario *m*

sago ['seɪgəʊ] *n Bot* sagú *m*

Sahara [sə'hɑːrə] *n* **the S.** el Sahara

Saharan [sə'hɑːrən] *adj* saharaui, sahariano(a)

said [sed] **1** *pt & pp see* **say**
2 *adj (aforementioned)* dicho(a), antes citado(a) *or* mencionado(a)

sail [seɪl] **1** *n* **(a)** *(canvas)* vela *f*; **to set s.** zarpar; *Fam* **to take the wind out of sb's sails** bajarle los humos a algn **(b)** *(trip)* paseo *m* en barco; *(journey)* viaje *m* en barco **(c)** *(of windmill)* aspa *f* **(d)** *(on boat)* velero *m*
2 *vt* navegar; *(ship)* gobernar; **to s. the Atlantic** cruzar el Atlántico en barco
3 *vi* **(a)** *(gen)* ir en barco **(b)** *(set sail)* zarpar

sail through *vt Fam* **you'll s. through the exam** te resultará muy fácil el examen

sailboat ['seɪlbəʊt] *n US* velero *m*

sailcloth ['seɪlklɒθ] *n Tex* lona *f*

sailing ['seɪlɪŋ] *n* navegación *f*; *(yachting)* vela *f*; *Fam* **it's all plain s.** es todo coser y cantar ❑ *Br* **s. boat** *or* **ship** velero *m*, barco *m* de vela

sailor ['seɪlər] *n* marinero *m*; *Fam* **to be a bad s.** marearse fácilmente

saint [seɪnt] *n* santo(a) *m,f*; *(before all masculine names except those beginning* **Do** *or* **To***)* San; *(before feminine names)* Santa; **S. Dominic** Santo Domingo; **S. Helen** Santa Elena; **S. John** San Juan; **S. Thomas** Santo Tomás ❑ **All Saints' Day** Día *m* de Todos los Santos; **s.'s day** santo *m*, onomástica *f*

sainthood ['seɪnthʊd] *n* santidad *f*

saintliness ['seɪntlɪnɪs] *n* santidad *f*

saintly ['seɪntlɪ] *adj* (**saintlier**, **saintliest**) santo(a)

sake [seɪk] *n* bien *m*; **for old times' sake** por los viejos tiempos; **for the s. of** por (el bien de); **for your own s.** por tu propio bien; **to talk for the s. of talking** hablar por hablar; *Fam* **for goodness' s.!** ¡por el amor de Dios!

salable ['seɪləbəl] *adj US see* **saleable**

salacious [sə'leɪʃəs] *adj* salaz

salad ['sæləd] *n Culin* ensalada *f* ❑ **fruit s.** macedonia *f* de frutas; **potato s.** ensaladilla *f* (rusa); **s. bar** *(in restaurant)* mostrador *m* de ensaladas; **s. bowl** ensaladera *f*; *Br* **s. cream** salsa *f* tipo mahonesa; *Fig* **s. days** años *mpl* de juventud; **s. dressing** aderezo *m*, *Esp* aliño *m*

salamander [sælə'mændər] *n* salamandra *f*

salami [sə'lɑːmɪ] *n Culin* salami *m*, *Am* salame *m*

salaried ['sælərɪd] *adj* asalariado(a)

salary ['sælərɪ] *n* salario *m*, sueldo *m*

sale [seɪl] *n* **(a)** *(gen)* venta *f*; **for** *or* **on s.** en venta; **to put sth up for s.** poner algo a la venta ❑ **sales department** departamento *m* comercial *or* de ventas; **sales manager** jefe(a) *m,f* de ventas, director(a) *m,f* comercial **(b)** *(at bargain prices)* liquidación *f*, saldo *m*, rebajas *fpl* ❑ **s. price** precio *m* rebajado **(c)** *(auction)* subasta *f*

saleable ['seɪləbəl] *adj* vendible

saleroom ['seɪlruːm] *n (auction room)* sala *f* de subastas

salesclerk ['seɪlzklɑːk] *n US* dependiente(a) *m,f*

salesgirl ['seɪlzgɜːl] *n* dependienta *f*

salesman ['seɪlzmən] *n (pl* **salesmen***)* **(a)** *(gen)* vendedor *m*; *(in shop)* dependiente *m* **(b)** *(commercial traveller)* representante *m*

salesmanship ['seɪlzmənʃɪp] *n* habilidad *f* para vender

salesperson ['seɪlzpɜːsən] *n (for company)* comercial *mf*, vendedor(a) *m,f*; *(in shop)* dependiente(a) *m,f*, vendedor(a) *m,f*

salesroom ['seɪlzruːm] *n US see* **saleroom**

saleswoman ['seɪlzwʊmən] *n (pl* **saleswomen** ['seɪlzwɪmɪn]*)* **(a)** *(gen)* vendedora *f*; *(in shop)* dependienta *f* **(b)** *(commercial traveller)* representante *f*

salient ['seɪlɪənt] *adj* **(a)** *(angle etc)* saliente, saledizo(a) **(b)** *Fig (feature)* sobresaliente, destacado(a)

saline ['seɪlaɪn] *adj* salino(a)

saliva [sə'laɪvə] *n* saliva *f*

salivary ['sælɪvərɪ] *adj* salival, salivar

salivate ['sælɪveɪt] *vi* salivar, segregar saliva; *Fig* **he was salivating** se le hacía la boca agua

sallow ['sæləʊ] *adj* cetrino(a)

sallowness ['sæləʊnɪs] *n* color *m* cetrino, palidez *f*

sally ['sælɪ] **1** *n* **(a)** *Mil* salida *f* **(b)** *(remark)* agudeza *f*, réplica *f*
2 *vi* **(a)** *Mil (also* **s. forth***)* hacer una salida **(b)** *(gen)* salir a buen paso, emprender la marcha

salmon ['sæmən] **1** *n* salmón *m* ❑ **s. trout** trucha *f* asalmonada, reo *m*
2 *adj* de color salmón

salmonella [sælmə'nelə] *n Biol Med* salmonela *f*; *(food poisoning)* salmonelosis *f*

salon ['sælɒn] *n* salón *m* ❑ **beauty s.** salón *m* *or* instituto *m* de belleza; **hairdressing s.** peluquería *f*

saloon [sə'luːn] *n* **(a)** *(public room)* salón *m*, sala *f*; *(on ship)* cámara *f* **(b)** *US (bar)* taberna *f*, bar *m*; *Br* **s. (bar)** bar *m* de lujo **(c)** *Br (car)* turismo *m*

saloonkeeper [sə'luːnkiːpər] *n US* tabernero(a) *m,f*

salopettes [sælə'pets] *npl Sport* pantalón *m sing* de esquí

salsify ['sælsɪfɪ] *n Bot* salsifí *m*

salt [sɔːlt] **1** *n* **(a)** *(substance)* sal *f*; *Fig* **the s. of the earth** la sal de la tierra; *Fig* **to take sth with a pinch of s.** creer algo con reservas; *Fig* **to be worth one's s.** merecer el pan que se come ❑ **s. industry** industria *f* salinera; **s. mine** mina *f* de sal, salina *f*; *US* **s. shaker** salero *m* **(b) salts** sales *fpl* ❑ **bath s.** sales *fpl* de baño; **Epsom s., liver s.** sal *f sing* de la Higuera, epsornita *f sing*; **smelling s.** sales *fpl* aromáticas

2 *adj (food, water)* salado(a) ❑ **s. beef** cecina *f*; **s. pork** tocino *m*

3 *vt* **(a)** *(cure)* salar, conservar en sal **(b)** *(add salt to)* echar sal a, sazonar con sal

salt away *vt Fam (money)* ahorrar

saltcellar ['sɔːltselər] *n* salero *m*

salt-free ['sɔːltfriː] *adj* sin sal

saltiness ['sɔːltɪnɪs] *n (of water)* salubridad *f*; *(of sea)* salinidad *f*; *(of food)* sabor *m* salado

saltpetre, *US* **saltpeter** [sɔːlt'piːtər] *n* salitre *m*

saltwater ['sɔːltwɔːtər] *adj* de mar, de agua salada; **s. fish** pez *m* de agua salada

salty ['sɔːltɪ] *adj* (**saltier, saltiest**) salado(a)

salubrious [sə'luːbrɪəs] *adj* salubre, sano(a)

salutary ['sæljʊtərɪ] *adj* **(a)** *(climate etc)* saludable **(b)** *(experience)* beneficioso(a); *(warning)* útil

salute [sə'luːt] **1** *n Mil (greeting)* saludo *m*

2 *vt* **(a)** *Mil* saludar; **to s. the flag** jurar bandera **(b)** *Fig (applaud)* aplaudir, aclamar

3 *vi Mil* saludar

Salvador(i)an [sælvə'dɔːr(ɪ)ən] *adj & n* salvadoreño(a) *(m,f)*

salvage ['sælvɪdʒ] **1** *n* **(a)** *(recovery)* salvamento *m*, rescate *m*; **s. team** equipo *m* de rescate **(b)** *(objects recovered)* objetos *mpl* recuperados, material *m* rescatado **(c)** *Jur* derecho *m* de salvamento

2 *vt (from ship etc)* salvar, rescatar

salvation [sæl'veɪʃən] *n* salvación *f* ❑ **S. Army** Ejército *m* de Salvación

salve [sælv, *US* sæv] **1** *n* pomada *f*, ungüento *m*, bálsamo *m* ❑ **lip s.** crema *f or* barra *f* protectora de labios

2 *vt* curar (con pomada); *Fig* **to s. one's conscience** aliviarse la conciencia

salver ['sælvər] *n (gen)* salvilla *f*; *(of silver)* bandeja *f* (de plata)

salvo ['sælvəʊ] *n (pl* **salvos** *or* **salvoes)** *(of guns, applause)* salva *f*

SAM [sæm] *n Mil (abbr* **surface-to-air missile)** misil *m* tierra-aire

Samaritan [sə'mærɪtən] *n Rel* samaritano(a) *m,f*; **the Samaritans** los Samaritanos, *Esp* el teléfono de la Esperanza

samba ['sæmbə] *n (dance)* samba *f*

same [seɪm] **1** *adj* mismo(a), igual, idéntico(a); **at that very s. moment** en ese mismísimo momento; **at the s. time** *(simultaneously)* al mismo tiempo, a la vez; *(however)* sin embargo, aun así; **in the s. way** del mismo modo; **it amounts to the s. thing** viene a ser lo mismo; **it's the s. old story** es la misma historia de siempre; **the two cars are the s.** los dos coches son iguales

2 *pron* **the s.** el mismo/la misma/lo mismo; **is that Harry Browne? — the very s.!** *(on phone)* ¿es usted Harry Browne? — ¡el mismísimo!; **I would do the s. again** volvería a hacer lo mismo; *Com* **we will ship s. tomorrow** lo enviaremos mañana; *Fam* **the s. here** lo mismo digo yo; *Fam* **the s. to you!** ¡igualmente!

3 *adv* del mismo modo, igual; **all the s., just the s.** sin embargo, aun así; **it's all the s. to me** (a mí) me da igual *or* lo mismo

same-day ['seɪmdeɪ] *adj Com* **s.-d. delivery** entrega *f* en el día

sameness ['seɪmnɪs] *n (identical nature)* identidad *f*, igualdad *f* **(b)** *(monotony)* monotonía *f*

sample ['sɑːmpəl] **1** *n* muestra *f* ❑ *Med* **blood s.** muestra *f* de sangre; **s. copy** ejemplar *m* de muestra

2 *vt (wines)* catar, probar; *(dish)* probar

sampler ['sɑːmplər] *n* **(a)** *(person)* catador(a) *m,f*, probador(a) *m,f* **(b)** *Sew* dechado *m*

sampling ['sɑːmplɪŋ] *n Mus* sampleado *m*

sanatorium [sænə'tɔːrɪəm] *n (pl* **sanatoriums** *or* **sanatoria** [sænə'tɔːrɪə]) sanatorio *m*

sancta ['sæŋktə] *npl see* **sanctum**

sanctify ['sæŋktɪfaɪ] *vt (pt & pp* **sanctified**) santificar, consagrar

sanctimonious [sæŋktɪ'məʊnɪəs] *adj* beato(a), santurrón(ona), mojigato(a)

sanctimoniousness [sæŋktɪ'məʊnɪəsnɪs] *n*, **sanctimony** ['sæŋktɪməʊnɪ] *n* beatería *f*, santurronería *f*, mojigatería *f*

sanction ['sæŋkʃən] **1** *n* **(a)** *(authorization)* autorización *f*, permiso *m* **(b)** *(penalty)* sanción *f* **(c)** *Pol* **sanctions** sanciones *fpl*

2 *vt (law etc)* sancionar, autorizar

sanctity ['sæŋktɪtɪ] *n (sacredness)* santidad *f*, carácter *m* sagrado; *(of marriage)* inviolabilidad *f*

sanctuary ['sæŋktjʊərɪ] *n* **(a)** *Rel* santuario *m* **(b)** *Pol* asilo *m*; **to take s.** refugiarse **(c)** *(for birds, animals)* reserva *f*

sanctum ['sæŋktəm] *n (pl* **sanctums** *or* **sancta**) *Fam* **the inner s.** el sanctasanctórum

sand [sænd] **1** *n* **(a)** *(gen)* arena *f* ❑ **s. castle** castillo *m* de arena; **s. dune** duna *f*; **s. pie** flan *m* de arena; *Golf* **s. trap** búnker *m* **(b)** **sands** *(beach)* playa *f sing*

2 *vt* **to s. (down)** lijar

sandal ['sændəl] *n* sandalia *f*, *Andes CAm* ojota *f*, *Méx* guarache *m*

sandalwood ['sændəlwʊd] *n Bot* sándalo *m*

sandbag ['sændbæg] **1** *n* saco *m* terrero, *RP* bolsa *f* de arena

2 *vt (pt & pp* **sandbagged**) proteger con sacos terreros

sandbank ['sændbæŋk] *n* banco *m* de arena

sandblast ['sændblɑːst] **1** *n* chorro *m* de arena

2 *vt* limpiar con chorro de arena

sandbox ['sændbɒks] *n US* recinto *m* de arena

sandboy ['sændbɔɪ] *n Br* **as happy as a s.** como un niño con zapatos nuevos

sander ['sændər] *n (tool)* lijadora *f*

sandman ['sændmæn] *n (pl* **sandmen**) = ser imaginario que trae el sueño a los niños

sandpaper ['sændpeɪpər] **1** *n* papel *m* de lija

2 *vt* lijar

sandpit ['sændpɪt] *n* **(a)** *Min* cantera *f* de arena **(b)** *(in playground etc)* arenal *m*

sandstone ['sændstəʊn] *n Geol* arenisca *f*

sandstorm ['sændstɔːm] *n* tempestad *f* de arena

sandwich ['sænwɪdʒ, 'sænwɪtʃ] **1** *n (sliced bread)* sandwich *m*, emparedado *m*; *(bread roll) Esp* bocadillo *m*, *Am* sándwich *m*, *CSur* sándwiche *m*, *Col* sánduche *m*, *Méx* torta *f*; **double-decker s.** sandwich de dos pisos ❑ *Educ* **s. course** curso *m* teórico-práctico

2 *vt* intercalar; **it was sandwiched between two lorries** quedó encajonado entre dos camiones

sandy ['sændɪ] *adj* (**sandier, sandiest**) **(a)** *(earth, beach)* arenoso(a) **(b)** *(hair)* rubio rojizo

sane [seɪn] *adj (person)* cuerdo(a); *(judgement)* sensato(a); *(mind)* sano(a); **perfectly s.** en su sano juicio

sang [sæŋ] *pt see* **sing**

sang-froid [sɒŋ'frwɑ:] *n* sangre *f* fría

sanguine ['sæŋgwɪn] **1** *adj* (**a**) *(optimistic)* optimista (**b**) *(colour)* sanguino(a)
2 *n (pencil)* sanguina *f*

sanitarium [sænɪ'teərɪəm] *n* (*pl* **sanitariums** *or* **sanitaria** [sænɪ'teərɪə]) *US* sanatorio *m*

sanitary ['sænɪtərɪ] *adj* sanitario(a), de sanidad; *(hygienic)* higiénico(a) □ **s. inspector** inspector(a) *m,f* de sanidad; *Br* **s. towel,** *US* **s. napkin** compresa *f, Am* toalla *f* higiénica

sanitation [sænɪ'teɪʃən] *n* sanidad *f* (pública); *(hygiene)* higiene *f; (plumbing)* sistema *m* de saneamiento

sanitize ['sænɪtaɪz] *vt US* esterilizar

sanity ['sænɪtɪ] *n (judgement)* cordura *f,* juicio *m; (good sense)* sensatez *f*

sank [sæŋk] *pt see* **sink**

Sanskrit ['sænskrɪt] **1** *adj* sánscrito(a)
2 *n (language)* sánscrito *m*

Santa Claus [sæntə'klɔːz] *n* Papá Noel *m,* San Nicolás *m*

sap¹ [sæp] *n Bot* savia *f*

sap² [sæp] **1** *Mil* zapa *f*
2 *vt* zapar; *(undermine)* minar; *Fig* debilitar, agotar

sapling ['sæplɪŋ] *n* (**a**) *Bot* árbol *m* joven (**b**) *Fig (youth)* jovenzuelo *m,* zagal *m*

sapper ['sæpər] *n Mil* zapador *m*

sapphire ['sæfaɪər] *n Min* zafiro *m*

sarcasm ['sɑːkæzəm] *n* sarcasmo *m,* sorna *f*

sarcastic [sɑː'kæstɪk] *adj (person, remark)* sarcástico(a)

sarcastically [sɑː'kæstɪklɪ] *adv* sarcásticamente

sarcophagus [sɑː'kɒfəgəs] *n* (*pl* **sarcophaguses** *or* **sarcophagi** [sɑː'kɒfəgaɪ]) sarcófago *m*

sardine [sɑː'diːn] *n (fish)* sardina *f, Fig* **packed in like sardines** como sardinas en lata

Sardinia [sɑː'dɪnɪə] *n* Cerdeña

Sardinian [sɑː'dɪnɪən] **1** *adj* sardo(a)
2 *n* (**a**) *(person)* sardo(a) *m,f* (**b**) *(language)* sardo *m*

sardonic [sɑː'dɒnɪk] *adj* sardónico(a)

sardonically [sɑː'dɒnɪklɪ] *adv* sardónicamente

sarge [sɑːdʒ] *n Mil Fam (abbr* **sergeant)** sargento *mf*

sari ['sɑːrɪ] *n (garment)* sari *m*

sartorial [sɑː'tɔːrɪəl] *adj* (**a**) *(dress)* de sastre; **s. elegance** elegancia *f* en el vestir (**b**) *Anat* sartorio(a)

sartorius [sɑː'tɔːrɪəs] *n* (*pl* **sartorii** [sɑː'tɔːrɪaɪ]) *Anat* sartorio *m*

SAS [eseɪ'es] *n Br Mil (abbr* **Special Air Service)** = comando de operaciones especiales del ejército británico

SASE [eseɪes'iː] *n US (abbr* **self-addressed stamped envelope)** = sobre franqueado con la dirección del remitente

sash¹ [sæʃ] *n (waistband etc)* faja *f*

sash² [sæʃ] *n* marco *m* de ventana □ **s. window** ventana *f* de guillotina

Sassenach ['sæsənæx] *n Scot Pej* inglés(esa) *m,f*

sassy ['sæsɪ] *adj* **(sassier, sassiest)** *US Fam* descarado(a), fresco(a)

SAT [sæt] *n* (**a**) *Br (abbr* **standard assessment task)** = tarea de la que se examina a un alumno para determinar si ha alcanzado el nivel de conocimientos correspondiente a su edad (**b**) *US (abbr* **scholastic aptitude test)** = examen que realizan al final de la enseñanza secundaria los alumnos que quieren ir a la universidad

Sat *(abbr* **Saturday)** sábado *m,* sáb.

sat [sæt] *pt & pp see* **sit**

Satan ['seɪtən] *n* Satán *m,* Satanás *m*

satanic [sə'tænɪk] *adj* satánico(a)

Satanist ['seɪtənɪst] *n* practicante *mf* del satanismo

satchel ['sætʃəl] *n* cartera *f* de colegial

sate [seɪt] *vt Fml* saciar

satellite ['sætəlaɪt] *n* satélite *m* □ *TV* **s. broadcasting** transmisión *f* por satélite; *TV* **s. dish** antena *f* parabólica; *Pol* **s. state** país *m* satélite

satiate ['seɪʃɪeɪt] *vt* saciar

satin ['sætɪn] *n Tex* satén *m; (paint)* **s. finish** acabado *m* satinado

satire ['sætaɪər] *n* sátira *f*

satirical [sə'tɪrɪkəl] *adj* satírico(a)

satirist ['sætərɪst] *n* escritor(a) *m,f* satírico(a)

satirize ['sætɪraɪz] *vt* satirizar

satisfaction [sætɪs'fækʃən] *n* satisfacción *f;* **to express one's s.** expresar su satisfacción

satisfactorily [sætɪs'fæktrɪlɪ] *adv* satisfactoriamente

satisfactory [sætɪs'fæktərɪ] **1** *adj* satisfactorio(a)
2 *n Sch Univ* suficiente *m,* aprobado *m*

satisfied ['sætɪsfaɪd] *adj* satisfecho(a)

satisfy ['sætɪsfaɪ] *vt (pt & pp* **satisfied)** (**a**) *(make happy)* satisfacer (**b**) *(fulfil)* cumplir con, satisfacer; **to s. the requirements** cumplir los requisitos (**c**) *(convince)* convencer (**d**) *(debt)* liquidar

satisfying ['sætɪsfaɪŋ] *adj* (**a**) *(gen)* satisfactorio(a), substancioso(a), sustancioso(a); *(pleasing)* agradable (**b**) *(meal)* completo(a)

saturate ['sætʃəreɪt] *vt* saturar; *Fam* empapar (**with** de)

saturation [sætʃə'reɪʃən] *n* saturación *f* □ *Mil* **s. bombing** bombardeo *m* intensivo

Saturday ['sætədɪ] *n* sábado *m;* **every other S.** un sábado sí y otro no, cada dos sábados; **every S.** todos los sábados; **last S.** el sábado pasado; **next S.** el próximo sábado, el sábado que viene; **on S.** el sábado; **on S. morning/afternoon** *or* **evening/night** el sábado por la mañana/tarde *or* noche; **on Saturdays** los sábados; **S.'s paper** el periódico del sábado; **the following S.** el sábado siguiente; **the S. after next, a week on S.,** **S. week** este sábado en ocho; **the S. before last** el sábado anterior; *TV* **the S. film** la película del sábado; **this S.** este sábado

Saturn ['sætɜːn] *n Astron* Saturno *m*

satyr ['sætər] *n Myth* sátiro *m*

sauce [sɔːs] *n* (**a**) *Culin* salsa *f* □ **s. boat,** *US* **s. dish** salsera *f;* **white s.** salsa *f* bechamel (**b**) *Br Fam (impudence)* descaro *m,* frescura *f*

saucepan ['sɔːspən] *n* cazo *m,* cacerola *f; (large)* olla *f*

saucer ['sɔːsər] *n* platillo *m* □ *Fam* **flying s.** platillo *m* volante

saucy ['sɔːsɪ] *adj* **(saucier, sauciest)** *Fam (impudent)* descarado(a), fresco(a)

Saudi ['saʊdɪ] **1** *n (person)* saudí *mf; Fam (country)* Arabia Saudí
2 *adj* saudí

Saudi Arabia [saʊdɪə'reɪbɪə] *n* Arabia *f* Saudita *or* Saudí

Saudi Arabian [saʊdɪə'reɪbɪən] *adj & n* saudita *(mf),* saudí *(mf)*

sauna ['sɔːnə] *n* sauna *f, Am* sauna *m or f*

saunter ['sɔːntər] **1** *n* paseo *m*
2 *vi* pasearse

sausage ['sɒsɪdʒ] *n (uncooked)* salchicha *f; (cured)* salchichón *m; (spicy)* chorizo *m,* embutido *m,* salami *m* □ *US* **blood s.** morcilla *f; Fam* **s. dog** perro *m* salchicha; **s.**

meat carne *f* de embutido; *Br* **s. roll** empanada *f* de carne

sauté ['səʊteɪ] *Culin* **1** *adj* salteado(a)
  2 *vt* (*pt & pp* **sautéed**) saltear

savage ['sævɪdʒ] **1** *adj* (**a**) *(ferocious)* feroz; *(cruel)* cruel; *(violent)* salvaje, violento(a) (**b**) *(primitive)* salvaje, primitivo(a)
  2 *n (primitive person)* salvaje *mf*
  3 *vt* (**a**) *(attack) (animal)* embestir; *Fig (person)* atacar violentamente (**b**) *(criticize)* desacreditar

savageness ['sævɪdʒnɪs] *n*, **savagery** ['sævɪdʒrɪ] *n* (**a**) *(ferocity)* ferocidad *f*; *(cruelty)* crueldad *f*; *(violence)* violencia *f*; *(cruel act)* salvajada *f* (**b**) *(primitive state)* salvajismo *m*

savanna(h) [sə'vænə] *n Geol* sabana *f*

save [seɪv] **1** *vt* (**a**) *(rescue)* salvar, rescatar (**from** de); *Rel* salvar; **God s. the Queen!** ¡Dios guarde a la Reina!; *Fig* **to s. face** salvar las apariencias; *Fig* **to s. the day** salvar la situación (**b**) *(gen) (put by)* guardar; *(money)* ahorrar; *Comptr* guardar, salvar; *(food)* almacenar; *(stamps)* coleccionar; **s. me a seat** guárdame un asiento (**c**) *(avoid spending) (money, energy)* ahorrar; *(time)* ahorrar, ahorrarse, ganar; **it saved him a lot of trouble** le evitó muchos problemas; **that way we'll s. ourselves an hour/$5** así nos ahorramos una hora/5 dólares
  2 *vi* (**a**) **to s. (up)** ahorrar (**b**) *(economize)* **to s. on food/gas/paper** ahorrar comida/gas/papel
  3 *n Ftb* parada *f*
  4 *prep Old-fashioned* salvo, excepto

saver ['seɪvər] *n* ahorrador(a) *m,f RP* ahorrista *mf*

saving ['seɪvɪŋ] **1** *n* (**a**) *(of time, money)* ahorro *m*, economía *f*; **to make savings** hacer economías, economizar (**b**) **savings** ahorros *mpl*; **to live off one's s.** vivir de sus ahorros ▫ **s. account** cuenta *f* de ahorros; **s. bank** caja *f* de ahorros; *US* **s. and loan association** caja *f* de ahorros
  2 *adj* **it's his only s. grace** es el único mérito que tiene

saviour, *US* **savior** ['seɪvjər] *n* salvador(a) *m,f*; *Rel* **Our S.** El Salvador

savoir-faire [sævwɑː'feər] *n* tacto *m*, don *m* de gentes

savour, *US* **savor** ['seɪvər] **1** *n* sabor *m*, gusto *m*
  2 *vi* saborear

savoury, *US* **savory** ['seɪvərɪ] **1** *adj (tasty)* sabroso(a); *(salted)* salado(a); *(spicy)* picante
  2 *n Br* entremés *m* salado, tapa *f*, canapé *m*

savvy ['sævɪ] *Fam* **1** *n (gen)* entendederas *fpl*, sentido *m* común; *(political)* habilidad *f*
  2 *vt* comprender, entender; captar

saw[1] [sɔː] **1** *n (tool)* sierra *f*, serrucho *m* ▫ **mechanical s.** sierra *f* mecánica
  2 *vt & vi* (*pt* **sawed**; *pp* **sawed** or **sawn**) serrar, aserrar

saw up *vt* serrar (**into** en), aserrar (**into** en); cortar (**into** en)

saw[2] [sɔː] *pt see* **see**[1]

sawdust ['sɔːdʌst] *n* serrín *m*, aserrín *m*

sawed-off shotgun ['sɔːdɒf'ʃɒtɡʌn] *n US* escopeta *f* de cañones recortados, recortada *f*

sawhorse ['sɔːhɔːs] *n* burro *m*, caballete *m*

sawmill ['sɔːmɪl] *n* aserradero *m*, serrería *f*

sawn [sɔːn] *pp see* **saw**[1]

sawn-off ['sɔːnɒf] *adj* recortado(a); **s.-o. shotgun** escopeta *f* de cañones recortados, recortada *f*

sax [sæks] *n Mus Fam* saxo *m*

Saxon ['sæksən] *adj & n* sajón(ona) *(m,f)*

saxophone ['sæksəfəʊn] *n Mus* saxofón *m*

saxophonist [sæk'sɒfənɪst] *n* saxofonista *mf*, saxo *mf*

say [seɪ] **1** *vt* (*pt & pp* **said**) (**a**) *(gen)* decir; *(express)* expresar; *(affirm)* afirmar, declarar; **as they s.** como se suele decir; **it goes without saying that ...** por supuesto que ..., huelga decir que ...; **it is said that ..., they s. that ...** dicen que ..., se dice que ...; **it's easier said than done** es más fácil decirlo que hacerlo; **no sooner said than done** dicho y hecho; **not to s.** incluso; **that is to s.** es decir; **there's no saying** es imposible de decir; **to s. the least** como mínimo; **to s. to oneself** decir para sí; **to s. yes/no** decir que sí/no; **to s. yes/no to an offer** aceptar/rechazar una oferta; **when all is said and done** al fin y al cabo; *Fam* **I s.!** ¡oiga!, ¡oye!; *Fam* **you don't s.!** ¡no me digas! (**b**) *(dictionary, notice etc)* decir, rezar; *(clock, thermometer etc)* decir, marcar; **what does the sign s.?** ¿qué pone en el letrero? (**c**) *(think)* pensar, opinar; **what do you s. to that?** ¿qué piensas de eso?, ¿qué te parece eso? (**d**) *(suppose)* suponer, poner; **(let's) s.** pongamos o por ejemplo; **it costs about $10** digamos que cuesta unas 10 dólares; **shall we s. Friday then?** ¿quedamos el viernes, pues?
  2 *n (gen)* opinión *f*; **I have no s. in the matter** no tengo ni voz ni voto en el asunto; **let him have his s.** déjele hablar; **to have one's s.** dar su opinión

saying ['seɪŋ] *n* refrán *m*, dicho *m*, proverbio *m*; **as the s. goes** como dice el refrán

say-so ['seɪsəʊ] *n Fam* (**a**) *(assertion)* afirmaciones *fpl* (**b**) *(approval)* aprobación *f*, visto *m* bueno

s/c *(abbr* **self-contained***)* con acceso independiente

scab [skæb] *n* (**a**) *Med* costra *f*, postilla *f* (**b**) *Fam Pej (blackleg)* esquirol *mf*, *Am* rompehuelgas *mf inv*, *RP* carnero *m*

scabbard ['skæbəd] *n* vaina *f* ▫ **s. fish** pez *m* cinto

scabby ['skæbɪ] *adj* (**scabbier, scabbiest**) *Med* costroso(a), lleno(a) de costras

scabies ['skeɪbiːz] *n inv Med* sarna *f*

scabrous ['skeɪbrəs] *adj* escabroso(a)

scad [skæd] *n (fish)* jurel *m*

scaffold ['skæfəld] *n* (**a**) *Constr* andamio *m* (**b**) *(for execution)* patíbulo *m*, cadalso *m*

scaffolding ['skæfəldɪŋ] *n Constr* andamio *n*, andamiaje *m*

scalawag [skæləwæg] *n US see* **scallywag**

scald [skɔːld] **1** *n* escaldadura *f*
  2 *vt* (**a**) *(skin etc)* escaldar (**b**) *(liquid)* calentar (**c**) *(sterilize)* esterilizar

scalding ['skɔːldɪŋ] *adj* **to be s. (hot)** estar ardiendo, escaldar

scale[1] [skeɪl] **1** *n* (**a**) *(of fish, reptile)* escama *f* (**b**) *(on skin)* escama *f*; *(on teeth)* sarro *m*; *(on ship, boiler)* incrustaciones *fpl*
  2 *vt* (**a**) *(fish)* escamar, quitar las escamas a (**b**) *(teeth)* quitar el sarro a, limpiar; *(ship, boiler)* desincrustar, limpiar

scale[2] [skeɪl] **1** *n* (**a**) *(gen)* escala *f*; **on a large s.** a gran escala; **sliding s.** escala móvil; **to s.** a escala ▫ **s. drawing** dibujo *m* (hecho) a escala; **s. model** maqueta *f* (**b**) *(of accident, disaster)* alcance *m* (**c**) *Mus* escala *f*
  2 *vt (mountain, wall)* escalar

scale down *vt (gen)* reducir proporcionalmente; *(drawing, map)* reducir a escala; *(production)* reducir, bajar

scale up *vt (gen)* aumentar proporcionalmente; *(drawing, map)* aumentar a escala; *(production)* aumentar, incrementar

scales [skeɪlz] *npl* (**pair** or **set of**) **s.** *(for shop, kitchen)* balanza *f sing*; *(for bathroom)* báscula *f sing*; *Astrol* **the S.** Libra *f sing*; *Fig* **to tip the s. in sb's favour** inclinar la balanza a favor de algn ▫ **letter s.** pesacartas *m inv*

scallion ['skæljən] *n* cebolleta *f*

scallop ['skɒləp] **1** n (**a**) *(mollusc)* vieira f, concha f de peregrino (**b**) *(shell)* concha f de peregrino, venera f (**c**) *Sew* festón m
   2 vt (**a**) *Culin* guisar al gratén (**b**) *Sew* festonear

scallywag ['skælɪwæg] n *Fam* granuja mf

scalp [skælp] **1** n *Anat* cuero m cabelludo; *Fig* cabeza f
   2 vt (**a**) *(in war)* arrancar el cuero cabelludo a (**b**) *Fam (tickets)* revender

scalpel ['skælpəl] n *Med* bisturí m; *(for dissection)* escalpelo m

scaly ['skeɪlɪ] adj (**scalier, scaliest**) escamoso(a)

scam [skæm] n *Slang* timo m, estafa f

scamp [skæmp] n *(child)* diablillo m, pilluelo(a) m,f; *(adult)* granuja mf, pícaro(a) m,f

scamper ['skæmpər] vi corretear

scampi ['skæmpɪ] n *Culin* cigalas fpl empanadas or rebozadas

scan [skæn] **1** vt *(pt & pp* **scanned**) (**a**) *(scrutinize)* escrutar, escudriñar; *(horizon)* otear (**b**) *(glance at)* ojear, echar un vistazo a (**c**) *(radar)* explorar (**d**) *Comptr* escanear
   2 vi *(poetry)* estar bien medido
   3 n *Med (gen)* exploración f ultrasónica; *(in gynaecology etc)* ecografía f

scandal ['skændəl] n (**a**) *(gen)* escándalo m; **political s.** escándalo político; **what a s.!** ¡qué vergüenza! (**b**) *(gossip)* chismorreo m, *Esp* cotilleo m

scandalize ['skændəlaɪz] vt escandalizar

scandalous ['skændələs] adj escandaloso(a), vergonzoso(a)

Scandinavia [skændɪ'neɪvɪə] n Escandinavia

Scandinavian [skændɪ'neɪvɪən] adj & n escandinavo(a) (m,f)

scanner ['skænər] n *Comptr Med* escáner m

scant [skænt] adj escaso(a)

scantily ['skæntɪlɪ] adv escasamente; **to be s. clad** or **dressed** ir ligero(a) de ropa

scanty ['skæntɪ] adj (**scantier, scantiest**) *(gen)* escaso(a); *(meal)* parco(a), insuficiente; *(clothes)* ligero(a)

scapegoat ['skeɪpɡəʊt] n cabeza f de turco, chivo m expiatorio

scar [skɑːr] **1** n cicatriz f, *Fig* cicatriz f, huella f
   2 vt *(pt & pp* **scarred**) marcar con una cicatriz; *Fig* **to s. sb for life** marcar a algn para toda la vida
   3 vi dejar una cicatriz

scarce [skeəs] adj *(in short supply)* escaso(a); *(rare)* raro(a); **to be s.** faltar, escasear; *Fam* **to make oneself s.** esfumarse, largarse

scarcely ['skeəslɪ] adv apenas; **I can s. believe it** me cuesta creerlo; **s. ever** casi nunca; **she s. spoke** apenas habló

scarceness ['skeəsnɪs] n, **scarcity** ['skeəsɪtɪ] n escasez f; *(shortage)* escasez f, falta f; *(rarity)* rareza f

scare [skeər] **1** n *(fright)* susto m; *(widespread alarm)* pánico m, alarma f; **to cause a s.** sembrar el pánico; **what a s. you gave me!** ¡qué susto me pegaste! ☐ **bomb s.** amenaza f de bomba; **polio s.** temor m a una epidemia de polio
   2 vt asustar, espantar; *Fam* **to be scared out of one's wits** sufrir un susto mortal
   3 vi asustarse

scare away, scare off vt ahuyentar, espantar

scarecrow ['skeəkrəʊ] n espantapájaros m inv, espantajo m

scared [skeəd] adj asustado(a); **to be s.** estar asustado(a); **to be s. of** tener miedo de; **to be s. stiff, to be s. to death** estar muerto(a) de miedo

scaremonger ['skeəmʌŋɡər] n alarmista mf

scaremongering ['skeəmʌŋɡərɪŋ] n alarmismo m

scarf [skɑːf] n (*pl* **scarfs** or **scarves**) *(long, woollen)* bufanda f; *(square)* pañuelo m; *(silk)* fular m

scarlet ['skɑːlɪt] **1** n escarlata f
   2 adj escarlata ☐ *Med* **s. fever** escarlatina f; *Pej* **s. woman** mujer f de la calle

scarp [skɑːp] n escarpa f, pendiente f

scarper ['skɑːpər] vi *Br Slang* largarse, abrirse

SCART [skɑːt] n *Elec* euroconector m; **S. cable** cable m (de) euroconector; **S. plug** enchufe m (de) euroconector; **S. socket** entrada f de euroconector

scarves [skɑːvz] npl see **scarf**

scary ['skeərɪ] adj (**scarier, scariest**) *Fam* espantoso(a), pavoroso(a); *(film)* de miedo or terror

scathing ['skeɪðɪŋ] adj mordaz, cáustico(a); **to be s. about** criticar duramente

scatological [skætə'lɒdʒɪkəl] adj escatológico(a)

scatter ['skætər] **1** vt (**a**) *(spread)* *(papers etc)* esparcir, desparramar; *(seeds)* sembrar a voleo (**b**) *(disperse)* dispersar
   2 vi *(crowd, flock)* dispersarse

scatterbrain ['skætəbreɪn] n *Fam* cabeza f de chorlito

scatterbrained ['skætəbreɪnd] adj *Fam* ligero(a) de cascos; *(forgetful)* despistado(a), olvidadizo(a)

scattered ['skætəd] adj esparcido(a), disperso(a); **s. population** población f diseminada; *Meteor* **s. showers** chubascos mpl aislados; **s. villages** pueblos mpl dispersos

scattering ['skætərɪŋ] n **a s. of** unos(as) pocos(as), unos(as) cuantos(as)

scatty ['skætɪ] adj (**scattier, scattiest**) *Br Fam* see **scatterbrained**

scavenge ['skævɪndʒ] **1** vi *(search)* rebuscar; **to s. through the dustbin** remover la basura en busca de algo
   2 vt *(find among rubbish)* encontrar en la basura

scavenger ['skævɪndʒər] n (**a**) *(person)* rebuscador(a) m,f, trapero m (**b**) *(animal)* animal m carroñero

scenario [sɪ'nɑːrɪəʊ] n (*pl* **scenarios**) *Theat* argumento m; *Cin* guión m

scene [siːn] n (**a**) *Theat Cin TV* escena f; **behind the scenes** entre bastidores; **the current political s.** el panorama político actual (**b**) *(place)* lugar m, escenario m; **a change of s.** un cambio de aires; **the s. of the crime** el lugar del crimen; **to appear on the s.** aparecer en escena; **to disappear from the s.** desaparecer de escena; *Fam* **it's not my s.** no me gusta mucho, *Esp* no me va nada ☐ **s. shifter** tramoyista mf (**c**) *(view)* panorama m, vista f (**d**) *(fuss)* escena f, escándalo m; *(quarrel)* riña f, pelea f; **to make a s.** hacer una escena, armar un escándalo

scenery ['siːnərɪ] n (**a**) *(landscape)* paisaje m (**b**) *Theat (on stage)* decorado m

scenic ['siːnɪk] adj *(picturesque)* pintoresco(a) ☐ **s. railway** *(miniature train)* tren m de recreo; *(roller coaster)* montaña f rusa; **s. route** ruta f panorámica

scent [sent] **1** n (**a**) *(smell)* olor m; *(of food)* aroma m (**b**) *(perfume)* perfume m (**c**) *(in hunting)* rastro m, pista f; *Fig* **to lose the s.** perder la pista
   2 vt (**a**) *(add perfume to)* perfumar (**b**) *(smell)* olfatear; *Fig* presentir

scepter ['septər] n *US* see **sceptre**

sceptic ['skeptɪk] n escéptico(a) m,f

sceptical ['skeptɪkəl] adj escéptico(a)

scepticism ['skeptɪsɪzəm] n escepticismo m

sceptre ['septər] n cetro m

sch *(abbr* **school)** escuela f, esc.

schedule ['skedʒʊəl, Br 'ʃedju:l] **1** n (a) *(plan, agenda)* programa m; *(timetable)* horario m; **according to s.** según lo previsto; **on s.** a la hora (prevista); **to be behind s.** llevar retraso, ir atrasado(a) (b) *(list)* lista f; *(inventory)* inventario m
  2 vt *(plan)* programar, fijar

scheduled ['skedʒʊəld, Br 'ʃedju:ld] adj previsto(a), fijo(a); **at the s. time** a la hora prevista; Av **s. flight** vuelo regular

schematic [ski:'mætɪk, skɪ'mætɪk] adj esquemático(a)

scheme [ski:m] **1** n (a) *(plan)* plan m, programa m; *(project)* proyecto m; *(idea)* idea f ❑ **colour s.** combinación f de colores (b) *(plot)* intriga f, conspiración f; *(trick)* ardid m, estratagema f, truco m
  2 vi *(plot)* tramar, intrigar, conspirar (**against** contra)

schemer ['ski:mər] n intrigante mf, maquinador(a) m,f

scheming ['ski:mɪŋ] **1** adj intrigante, maquinador(a)
  2 n intrigas fpl, maquinaciones fpl

schism ['sɪzəm] n cisma m

schizophrenia [skɪtsəʊ'fri:nɪə] n esquizofrenia f

schizophrenic [skɪtsəʊ'frenɪk] adj & n esquizofrénico(a) (m,f)

schlep [ʃlep] vt *(pt & pp* **schlepped)** Slang *(drag)* arrastrar

schmaltz [ʃmɔ:lts] n Fam sentimentalismo m

schnapps [ʃnæps] n aguardiente m alemán

scholar ['skɒlər] n (a) *(learned person)* erudito(a) m,f; *(specialist)* especialista mf, experto(a) m,f; **Greek s.** helenista mf; **Latin s.** latinista mf (b) *(pupil)* alumno(a) m,f; *(scholarship holder)* becario(a) m,f

scholarly ['skɒləlɪ] adj erudito(a)

scholarship ['skɒləʃɪp] n (a) *(learning)* erudición f (b) *(award, grant)* beca f ❑ **s. holder** becario(a) m,f

scholastic [skə'læstɪk] adj (a) *(year)* escolar; *(profession)* docente (b) Hist escolástico(a)

school¹ [sku:l] **1** n (a) *(gen)* escuela f, colegio m; **to leave s.** terminar or dejar la escuela ❑ **comprehensive s.** instituto m (de enseñanza media or de educación secundaria); **convent s.** colegio m de monjas; **drama s.** academia f de arte dramático; **driving s.** autoescuela f; **grammar s., high s.** instituto m (de enseñanza, media or de educación secundaria); **language s.** academia f or escuela f de idiomas; **night s.** escuela f nocturna; **nursery s.** jardín m de infancia, parvulario m; **primary s.** escuela f primaria; **public s.** Br colegio m privado, US instituto m; **s. age** edad f escolar; **s. board** *(of school, district)* consejo m escolar; **s. bus** autobús m escolar; **s. holidays** vacaciones fpl escolares; **s. year** año m escolar; **secondary s.** *(gen)* escuela f secundaria; *(private)* colegio m; *(state)* instituto m (de enseñanza media or de educación secundaria); **summer s.** cursos mpl de verano (b) *(pupils)* alumnado m, alumnos mpl (c) US *(college, university)* universidad f (d) *(university department)* facultad f; **law s.** facultad de derecho; **s. of medicine** facultad de medicina (e) *(group of artists etc)* escuela f; **s. of thought** corriente f de opinión f; **the Cubist s.** la escuela cubista
  2 vt (a) *(teach)* enseñar; *(train)* educar, formar; **to s. sb in sth** enseñar algo a algn (b) *(discipline)* disciplinar; **to s. one's temper** controlar el mal genio or humor

school² [sku:l] n *(of fish)* banco m

schoolbag ['sku:lbæg] n cartera f

schoolbook ['sku:lbʊk] n libro m de texto

schoolboy ['sku:lbɔɪ] n alumno m, colegial m

schoolchild ['sku:ltʃaɪld] n *(pl* **schoolchildren** ['sku:l-tʃɪldrən]) alumno(a) m,f

schooldays ['sku:ldeɪz] npl años mpl de colegio, tiempos mpl de colegio

schoolfellow ['sku:lfeləʊ] n compañero(a) m,f de clase

schoolgirl ['sku:lgɜ:l] n alumna f, colegiala f

schooling ['sku:lɪŋ] n educación f, estudios mpl

schoolmaster ['sku:lmɑ:stər] n profesor m; *(in primary school)* maestro m

schoolmate ['sku:lmeɪt] n see **schoolfellow**

schoolmistress ['sku:lmɪstrɪs] n profesora f; *(in primary school)* maestra f

schoolroom ['sku:lru:m] n aula f, clase f

schoolteacher ['sku:lti:tʃər] n profesor(a) m,f; *(in primary school)* maestro(a) m,f

schoolyard ['sku:ljɑ:d] n patio m de recreo

schooner ['sku:nər] n (a) Naut goleta f (b) *(for sherry)* copa f; US Austral *(for beer)* jarra f

sciatica [saɪ'ætɪkə] n Med ciática f

science ['saɪəns] n ciencia f; *(school subject)* ciencias fpl ❑ **natural s.** ciencias fpl naturales; **s. fiction** ciencia-ficción f

scientific [saɪən'tɪfɪk] adj científico(a)

scientifically [saɪən'tɪfɪklɪ] adv científicamente

scientist ['saɪəntɪst] n científico(a) m,f

sci-fi ['saɪfaɪ] n Fam *(abbr* **science fiction)** ciencia f ficción

scimitar ['sɪmɪtər] n cimitarra f

scintillate ['sɪntɪleɪt] vi *(sparkle)* centellear, destellar; Fig brillar

scintillating ['sɪntɪleɪtɪŋ] adj brillante

scissors ['sɪzəz] npl tijeras fpl; **a pair of s.** unas tijeras

sclerosis [sklɪə'rəʊsɪs] n Med esclerosis f; **multiple s.** esclerosis f en placas

scoff¹ [skɒf] vi *(mock)* mofarse (**at** de), burlarse (**at** de)

scoff² [skɒf] vt Br Fam *(eat fast)* tragarse, zamparse

scoffing ['skɒfɪŋ] n mofa f, burla f

scold [skəʊld] vt regañar, reñir

scolding ['skəʊldɪŋ] n regañina f, reprimenda f

scone [skəʊn, skɒn] n Culin bollo m, pastelito m

scoop [sku:p] **1** n (a) *(for flour)* pala f; *(for ice cream)* cucharón m; *(amount)* palada f, cucharada f (b) Fin Slang golpe m financiero (c) Press exclusiva f
  2 vt (a) Fin Slang *(benefit)* forrarse de (b) Press Fam **to s. the other newspapers** pisar una noticia a los otros periódicos

scoop out vt *(flour etc)* sacar con pala; *(water) (from boat)* achicar

scoop up vt recoger

scoot [sku:t] vi Fam **to s.** (**off** or **away)** salir disparado(a)

scooter ['sku:tər] n *(child's)* patinete m, patineta f; *(adult's)* escúter m, Vespa® f

scope [skəʊp] n (a) *(range)* alcance m; *(of book, undertaking)* ámbito m; *(ability)* competencia f (b) *(freedom)* libertad f; *(opportunity)* oportunidad f; **to give sb full s.** dar campo libre or carta blanca a algn

scorch [skɔ:tʃ] **1** n quemadura f
  2 vt *(burn)* quemar; *(singe)* chamuscar

scorcher ['skɔ:tʃər] n Fam día m abrasador

scorching ['skɔ:tʃɪŋ] adj abrasador(a)

score [skɔ:r] **1** n (a) Sport tanteo m; Cards Golf puntuación f; *(result)* resultado m, marcador m; **to keep the s.** seguir el marcador; **what's the s.?** ¿cómo van?; Fig **to know the s.** estar al tanto (b) *(notch)* muesca f (c) *(account)* cuenta f (d) *(reason)* **on that s.** por lo que se refiere a eso, a ese respecto (e) *(twenty)* veintena f; Fam **scores of** montones de (f) Mus *(of opera)* partitura f; *(of film)* música f
  2 vt (a) *(goal)* marcar; *(points)* ganar; **to s. a victory**

conseguir una victoria (**b**) *(notch) (wood)* hacer una muesca en; *(paper)* rayar

3 *vi* (**a**) *Sport* marcar un tanto; *Ftb* marcar un gol; *(keep the score)* llevar el marcador (**b**) *(have success)* tener éxito (**with** con); *Slang* ligar (**with** con); *Slang (obtain drugs)* conseguir *or Esp* pillar droga

score out *vt (word etc)* tachar

scoreboard ['skɔːbɔːd] *n* marcador *m*, tanteador *m*

scorecard ['skɔːkɑːd] *n Golf* tarjeta *f*

scorekeeper ['skɔːkiːpər] *n* encargado(a) *m,f* del marcador

score-line ['skɔːlaɪn] *n Sport* marcador *m*

scorer ['skɔːrər] *n* (**a**) *(goal striker)* goleador *m* (**b**) *(scorekeeper)* encargado(a) *m,f* del marcador

scoring ['skɔːrɪŋ] *n* (**a**) *(of goals, tries)* **to open the s.** abrir el marcador (**b**) *(orchestration)* orquestación *f*

scorn [skɔːn] **1** *n* desprecio *m*, desdén *m*
2 *vt* despreciar, desdeñar, menospreciar

scornful ['skɔːnfʊl] *adj* desdeñoso(a)

Scorpio ['skɔːpɪəʊ] *n Astrol Astron* Escorpión *m*

scorpion ['skɔːpɪən] *n Zool* alacrán *m*, escorpión *m* □ **s. fish** cabracho *m*

Scot [skɒt] *n* escocés(esa) *m,f*

Scotch [skɒtʃ] **1** *adj* escocés(esa) □ *Culin* **S. broth** potaje *m* de cordero, cebada y verduras; **S. egg** huevo *m* envuelto con carne de salchicha; *US* **S. tape®** cinta *f* adhesiva, *Esp* celo® *m*, *CAm Méx* Durex® *m*
2 *n (whisky)* whisky *m* escocés, scotch *m*

scotch [skɒtʃ] *vt (plot etc)* frustrar, hacer fracasar; *(rumour)* sofocar

scot-free [skɒt'friː] *adj* impune

Scotland ['skɒtlənd] *n* Escocia; **S. Yard** = sede de la policía londinense

Scots [skɒts] **1** *adj* escocés(esa)
2 *n* (**a**) *(language)* escocés *m* (**b**) *pl* **the S.** los escoceses

Scotsman ['skɒtsmən] *n (pl* **Scotsmen**) escocés *m*

Scotswoman ['skɒtswʊmən] *n (pl* **Scotswomen** ['skɒtswɪmɪn]) escocesa *f*

Scottish ['skɒtɪʃ] **1** *adj* escocés(esa)
2 *n (language)* escocés *m*

scoundrel ['skaʊndrəl] *n* sinvergüenza *mf*, canalla *m*

scour¹ [skaʊər] *vt (clean) (pots etc)* fregar, restregar

scour² [skaʊər] *vt (search) (countryside)* recorrer; *(building)* registrar

scourer [skaʊərər] *n*, **scouring pad** ['skaʊrɪŋpæd] *n* estropajo *m*

scourge [skɜːdʒ] *Fig* **1** *n* azote *m*
2 *vt* azotar

scout [skaʊt] **1** *n Mil* explorador(a) *m,f*; **boy s.** boy-scout *m*; *Mil* **s. plane** avión *m* explorador; *Sport Cin* **talent s.** cazatalentos *m inv*
2 *vi Mil* reconocer el terreno; **to s. around for sth** andar en busca de algo

scouting ['skaʊtɪŋ] *n* (**a**) *(activities)* actividades *fpl* de los exploradores *or* los scouts (**b**) *(boy scout movement)* escultismo *m*

scoutmaster ['skaʊtmɑːstər] *n* jefe *m* de los exploradores *or* los scouts

scowl [skaʊl] **1** *vi* fruncir el ceño; **to s. at sb** mirar a algn con ceño
2 *n* ceño *m*

scrabble ['skræbəl] **1** *vi* escarbar; *Fig* **to s. around for sth** revolver todo para encontrar algo
2 *n* **S.®** *(game)* Scrabble® *m*

scrag [skræg] **1** *n* pescuezo *m*
2 *vt* retorcer el pescuezo

scraggly ['skræglɪ] *adj* (**scragglier, scraggliest**) (**a**) *(beard etc)* descuidado(a) (**b**) *(rock)* mellado(a)

scraggy ['skrægɪ] *adj* (**scraggier, scraggiest**) delgado(a), flacucho(a)

scram [skræm] *vi Fam* largarse

scramble ['skræmbəl] **1** *vi* **to s. for seats** pelearse por encontrar asiento; **to s. into one's clothes** vestirse rápidamente; **to s. up a tree** trepar a un árbol
2 *vt* (**a**) *Culin* revolver; **scrambled eggs** huevos *mpl* revueltos (**b**) *Rad Tel (message)* cifrar; *(broadcast)* interferir, perturbar
3 *n* (**a**) *(climb)* subida *f*, trepa *f*; *(struggle)* lucha *f*, pelea *f* (**b**) *Sport* carrera *f* de motocross

scrambling ['skræmblɪŋ] *n Sport* (**motorcycle**) **s.** motocross *m*

scrap¹ [skræp] **1** *n* (**a**) *(small piece)* trozo *m*, trocito *m*, pedazo *m*; *(of conversation)* fragmento *m*; *(newspaper cutting)* recorte *m*; **s. (metal)** chatarra *f*; **there isn't a s. of truth in it** no tiene ni un ápice de verdad □ **s. dealer** *or* **merchant** chatarrero(a) *m,f*; **s. paper** papel *m* de borrador; **s. yard** *(gen)* parque *m* de chatarra; *(for cars)* cementerio *m* de coches (**b**) **scraps** *(gen)* restos *mpl*; *(of food)* sobras *fpl*
2 *vt (pt & pp* **scrapped**) *(discard)* desechar; *(cars etc)* convertir en chatarra; *Fig (idea)* descartar

scrap² [skræp] *Fam* **1** *n* pelea *f*
2 *vi (pt & pp* **scrapped**) pelearse (**with** con)

scrapbook ['skræpbʊk] *n* álbum *m* de recortes

scrape [skreɪp] **1** *vt (paint, wood)* raspar; *(vegetables)* rascar; *(graze) (knee etc)* arañarse, hacerse un rasguño; *Fig* **to s. together** reunir a duras penas; *Fig* **to s. a living** vivir muy apretado(a), ganar lo justo para vivir; *Fig* **to s. the bottom of the barrel** tocar fondo
2 *vi (make noise)* chirriar; *(rub)* rozar; **to s. against the wall** pasar rozando la pared
3 *n* (**a**) *(act)* raspado *m*; *(noise)* chirrido *m*; *(mark)* arañazo *m*, rasguño *m* (**b**) *Fam (trouble)* lío *m*, apuro *m*, aprieto *m*

scrape along, scrape by *vi Fam* ir tirando

scrape away, scrape off *vt* quitar raspando

scrape through *vi Fam (exam)* aprobar por los pelos *or* de chiripa

scraper ['skreɪpər] *n* (**a**) *(tool)* rasqueta *f*, rascador *m* (**b**) *(for shoes)* limpiabarros *m inv*

scrapheap ['skræphiːp] *n (rubbish pile)* montón *m* de desechos; *(dump)* vertedero *m*

scrappy ['skræpɪ] *adj* (**scrappier, scrappiest**) *(report, speech)* deshilvanado(a); *(conversation)* fragmentario(a); *(knowledge)* superficial; *(meal)* pobre, hecho(a) con sobras

scratch [skrætʃ] **1** *n* (**a**) *(mark) (on skin)* arañazo *m*, rasguño *m*; *(on paintwork)* arañazo *m*; *(on record, photo)* raya *f*; **to escape without a s.** salir ileso(a) □ *US* **s. pad** bloc *m* de notas; *Med* **s. test** cutirreacción *f* (**b**) *(noise)* chirrido *m* (**c**) *Fig* **to be** *or* **come up to s.** estar a la altura de las circunstancias, dar la talla; *Fig* **to start from s.** partir de cero
2 *adj (meal, team)* improvisado(a)
3 *vt* (**a**) *(with fingernail, claw)* arañar, rasguñar; *(paintwork, furniture)* rayar; *(initials on a tree)* grabar; *Fig* **to s. the surface of** tocar por encima (**b**) *(to relieve itching)* rascarse; *Fam* **you s. my back and I'll s. yours** hoy por ti y mañana por mí (**c**) *Sport (cancel)* cancelar, suspender
4 *vi* (**a**) *(cat etc)* arañar, rasguñar; *(pen)* raspear (**b**) *(to relieve itching)* rascarse (**c**) *US Fam* **to s. for oneself** buscarse la vida

scratch out *vt* tachar, borrar, retirar

scratchcard ['skrætʃkɑːd] *n* tarjeta *f* de rasca y gana, boleto *m* de lotería instantánea, *Am* raspadito *m*; *Arg* raspadita *f*

scratchy ['skrætʃɪ] *adj* (**scratchier, scratchiest**) *(pen)* que raspea; *(sound)* que chirria; *(fabric)* que pica; *(record)* rayado(a)

scrawl [skrɔ:l] **1** *n* garabatos *mpl*
2 *vt (message etc)* garabatear, garrapatear
3 *vi* garabatear, hacer garabatos

scrawny ['skrɔ:nɪ] *adj* (**scrawnier, scrawniest**) flaco(a), flacucho(a)

scream [skri:m] **1** *n (of pain, fear)* grito *m*, chillido *m*, alarido *m*; **screams of laughter** carcajadas *fpl*; **to let out a s.** soltar un grito; *Fam* **it was a s.** fue para morirse de risa *or Esp* para mondarse; *Fam* **she's a s.** es divertidísima, es la monda
2 *vt (insults etc)* gritar, vociferar; *Fam* **to s. the place down** desgañitarse
3 *vi* gritar, chillar; **to s. at sb** pegar gritos a algn; **to s. for help** pedir socorro a gritos; **to s. with laughter** partirse *or* troncharse de risa

scree [skri:] *n Geol* pedregal *m*

screech [skri:tʃ] **1** *n (of person)* chillido *m*; *(of tyres, brakes)* chirrido *m*
2 *vt* gritar, decir a gritos, vocear
3 *vi (person)* chillar; *(tyres, brakes)* chirriar

screed [skri:d] *n Fam (long speech etc)* rollo *m*; **to write screeds** escribir mucho

screen [skri:n] **1** *n* (a) *(movable partition)* biombo *m* □ **fire s.** pantalla *f* (b) *Fig* cortina *f*; **to act as a s.** servir de tapadera □ **smoke s.** cortina *f* de humo (c) *Cin TV Comptr* pantalla *f*; **the small s.** la pequeña pantalla □ *Comptr* **s. shot** pantallazo *m*, captura *f* de pantalla; **s. test** prueba *f*; **s. writer** guionista *mf*
2 *vt* (**a**) *(protect)* proteger (**from** de); *(conceal)* tapar, ocultar (**from** de) (**b**) *(sieve) (coal etc)* cribar, tamizar; *Fig (candidates for a job)* seleccionar; *Fam* pasar por el tamiz (**c**) *(show) (film)* proyectar; *(for first time)* estrenar (**d**) *Med* examinar; **to s. sb for an illness** hacer una exploración a algn

screening ['skri:nɪŋ] *n* (a) *(of candidates)* selección *f* (b) *(of film)* proyección *f*; *(for first time)* estreno *m* (c) *Med (of patient)* exploración *f*

screenplay ['skri:npleɪ] *n Cin* guión *m*

screensaver ['skri:nseɪvər] *n Comptr* salvapantallas *m*

screw [skru:] **1** *n* (a) *(for fixing)* tornillo *m*; *Fam* **he has a s. loose** le falta un tornillo; *Fam* **to put the screws on sb** apretarle los tornillos a algn (b) *Av Naut (propeller)* hélice *f* (c) *Slang (prison guard)* carcelero(a) *m,f*
2 *vt* (**a**) *(gen)* atornillar; **to s. sth down** *or* **in** *or* **on** fijar algo con tornillos; *Fam* **he's got his head screwed on (the right way)** tiene la cabeza bien sentada (**b**) *Slang* **to s. money out of sb** desplumar a algn (**c**) *Vulg (have sex with) Esp* follar, *Am* coger; **s. you!** *Esp* ¡que te den por culo!, *Méx* ¡vete a la chingada!, *RP* ¡ándate a la puta que te parió!

screw up *vt* (**a**) *(piece of paper)* arrugar; *(one's face)* torcer; *Fig* **to s. up one's courage** armarse de valor (**b**) *Slang (spoil, ruin)* joder, jorobar, fastidiar; **now he's really screwed things up** ahora lo ha jodido de verdad (**c**) *Fam* ponerse nervioso(a); **she's all screwed up** está muy nerviosa

screwball ['skru:bɔ:l] *adj & n US Slang* chalado(a) *(m,f)*, excéntrico(a) *(m,f)*

screwdriver ['skru:draɪvər] *n* (**a**) *(tool)* destornillador *m*, *Am* desatornillador *m* (**b**) *(cocktail)* vodka *m* con naranja

screwed-up ['skru:d'ʌp] *adj Fam* trastornado(a), hecho(a) polvo

screw-top(ped) ['skru:tɒp(t)] *adj* de tapón a rosca

screwy ['skru:ɪ] *adj* (**screwier, screwiest**) *US Fam (thinking etc)* retorcido(a)

scribble ['skrɪbəl] **1** *n* garabatos *mpl*
2 *vt (message etc)* garabatear, garrapatear
3 *vi* garabatear, hacer garabatos

scribbler ['skrɪblər] *n Pej (author)* escritorzuelo(a) *m,f*

scribbling ['skrɪblɪŋ] *n* garabatos *mpl* □ **s. pad** bloc *m* de notas

scribe [skraɪb] *n* escribiente *mf*, amanuense *mf*; *(in Bible)* escriba *m*

scrimmage ['skrɪmɪdʒ] *n* escaramuza *f*, refriega *f*

scrimp [skrɪmp] *vi* ahorrar, hacer economías; **to s. and save** apretarse el cinturón

script [skrɪpt] *n* (**a**) *(writing)* escritura *f*; *(handwriting)* letra *f*; *Typ* letra *f* cursiva (**b**) *(in exam)* escrito *m*, examen *m* (**c**) *Cin* guión *m* □ **s. girl** scriptgirl *f* (**d**) *Jur (document)* escritura *f*

scriptural ['skrɪptʃərəl] *adj* bíblico(a)

Scripture ['skrɪptʃər] *n Rel* **Holy S.** Sagrada Escritura *f*

scriptwriter ['skrɪptraɪtər] *n* guionista *mf*

scroll [skrəʊl] *n* rollo *m* de pergamino

scroll down *vi Comptr* bajar el cursor

scroll through *vt Comptr* bajar, recorrer

scroll up *vi Comptr* subir el cursor

scrooge [skru:dʒ] *n Fam (miser)* tacaño(a) *m,f*, avaro(a) *m,f*, agarrado(a) *m,f*, roña *mf*

scrotum ['skrəʊtəm] *n (pl* **scrotums** *or* **scrota** ['skrəʊtə]*) Anat* escroto *m*

scrounge [skraʊndʒ] *Fam* **1** *vi* **to s. off sb** vivir a costa de algn, *Esp Méx* vivir de algn por la gorra
2 *vt* **to s. sth from** *or* **off sb** gorrear *or Esp Méx* gorronear *or RP* garronear algo a algn
3 *n* **to be on the s.** andar gorreando *or Esp Méx* gorroneando *or RP* garroneando

scrounger ['skraʊndʒər] *n Fam* gorrero(a) *m,f*, *Esp Méx* gorrón(ona) *m,f*, *RP* garronero(a) *m,f*

scrub¹ [skrʌb] *n (undergrowth)* maleza *f*

scrub² [skrʌb] **1** *vt (pt & pp* **scrubbed**) (**a**) *(clean) (floor, dishes)* fregar; *(clothes)* lavar; **s. the tables clean** limpia bien las mesas (**b**) *Fam (cancel)* cancelar
2 *n (act of cleaning)* fregado *m*, lavado *m*; **to give sth a good s.** limpiar algo a fondo

scrub off *vt (dirt, stain)* quitar frotando

scrub up *vi (surgeon)* lavarse (las manos)

scrubber ['skrʌbər] *n Br Slang* fulana *f*, golfa *f*, furcia *f*

scrubbing ['skrʌbɪŋ] *n* fregado *m*, lavado *m* □ **s. brush** *(gen)* estregadera *f*; *(for horses)* bruza *f*

scrubland ['skrʌblænd] *n* monte *m* bajo, matorral *m*

scruff¹ [skrʌf] *n* pescuezo *m*, cogote *m*

scruff² [skrʌf] *n Fam (untidy person)* desaliñado(a) *m,f*, zarrapastroso(a) *m,f*, desaseado(a) *m,f*

scruffy ['skrʌfɪ] *adj* (**scruffier, scruffiest**) *Fam* desaliñado(a), zarrapastroso(a), desaseado(a)

scrum [skrʌm] *n Rugby (abbr* **scrummage**) *Esp* melé *f*, *Am* scrum *f*; *Fam* **what a s. to get on the train!** ¡vaya apretujones para subir al tren! □ **s. half** *Esp* medio (de) melé *mf*, *Am* medio scrum *mf*

scrummage ['skrʌmɪdʒ] *n Rugby Esp* melé *f*, *Am* scrum *f*

scrumptious ['skrʌmpʃəs] *adj Fam* delicioso(a), de rechupete

scrunch [skrʌntʃ] *vt (crush)* aplastar; *(crumple) (also* **s. up**) estrujar

scruple ['skru:pəl] *n* escrúpulo *m*

scrupulous ['skru:pjʊləs] *adj* escrupuloso(a)

scrupulously ['skru:pjʊləslɪ] *adv* escrupulosamente; **s.**

clean de lo más limpio(a), impecable; **s. honest/careful** sumamente honrado(a)/cuidadoso(a)

scrupulousness ['skruːpjʊləsnɪs] *n* escrupulosidad *f*

scrutineer [skruːtɪ'nɪər] *n (of votes)* escrutador(a) *m,f*

scrutinize ['skruːtɪnaɪz] *vt* **(a)** *(document etc)* escudriñar, examinar a fondo **(b)** *(votes)* escrutar, hacer el escrutinio de; *(re-count)* hacer el recuento de

scrutiny ['skruːtɪnɪ] *n* **(a)** *(of document)* examen *m* profundo, escrutinio *m* **(b)** *(of votes)* escrutinio *m*; *(re-count)* recuento *m*

scuba ['skjuːbə] *n* **s. diving** buceo *m* con botellas de oxígeno

scuff [skʌf] **1** *vt (the floor)* rayar; *(one's feet)* arrastrar
2 *n.* **mark** raya *f*

scuffle ['skʌfəl] **1** *n* refriega *f,* riña *f,* pelea *f*
2 *vi* reñirse, pelearse **(with** con)

scull [skʌl] **1** *n* remo *m* corto
2 *vi* remar

scullery ['skʌlərɪ] *n Br* fregadero *m,* trascocina *f;* **s. maid** fregona *f*

sculpt [skʌlpt] *vt & vi* esculpir

sculptor ['skʌlptər] *n* escultor *m*

sculptress ['skʌlptrɪs] *n* escultora *f*

sculpture ['skʌlptʃər] **1** *n* escultura *f*
2 *vt & vi* esculpir

scum [skʌm] *n* **(a)** *(on liquid)* espuma *f,* telilla *f; (on pond)* verdín *m* **(b)** *Fig* escoria *f*

scumbag ['skʌmbæg] *n very Fam (person)* cerdo(a) *m,f,* mamón(ona) *m,f*

scupper ['skʌpər] *vt* **(a)** *(ship)* barrenar, hundir deliberadamente **(b)** *Br Fam (plan etc)* sabotear, desbaratar, frustrar

scurf [skɜːf] *n (dandruff)* caspa *f*

scurrilous ['skʌrɪləs] *adj (abusive)* difamatorio(a), calumnioso(a); *(coarse)* grosero(a)

scurry ['skʌrɪ] *vi (pt & pp scurried) (run)* correr, corretear; *(hurry)* apresurarse; **to s. away** *or* **off** escabullirse

scurvy ['skɜːvɪ] *n Med* escorbuto *m*

scuttle¹ ['skʌtəl] *n* **coal s.** cubo *m* del carbón

scuttle² ['skʌtəl] *vt* **(a)** *(ship)* barrenar, hundir deliberadamente **(b)** *Fam (plan etc)* sabotear, desbaratar, frustrar

scuttle³ ['skʌtəl] *vi (run)* corretear; **to s. away** *or* **off** escabullirse

scythe [saɪð] **1** *n* guadaña *f*
2 *vt* guadañar, segar (con guadaña)

SDI [esdiː'aɪ] *n Mil (abbr* **Strategic Defence Initiative**) Iniciativa *f* para la Defensa Estratégica

SE *(abbr* **South-East**) sudeste, SE

sea [siː] *n* mar *m* or *f;* **at s.** en el mar; **by the s.** a orillas del mar; **choppy s.** mar picado; **out at s.** en alta mar; **rough s.** marejada *f;* **stormy s.** mar gruesa; **to go by s.** ir en barco; *(person)* **to go to s.** hacerse marinero; *(ship, crew)* **to put to s.** zarpar; *Fig* **a s. of faces** un mar de caras; *Fig* **to be all at s.** estar totalmente desorientado(a), estar perdido(a) □ **s. anemone** anémona *f* de mar; **s. bass** lubina *f;* **s. bream** besugo *m;* **s. breeze** brisa *f* marina; *Fig* **s. change** metamorfosis *f; Zool* **s. cow** manatí *m; Fig* **s. legs** equilibrio *m; Fam* **to find one's legs** acostumbrarse al mar, no marearse; **s. level** nivel *m* del mar; *Zool* **s. lion** león *m* marino; **s. trout** trucha *f* de mar, reo *m;* **s. water** agua *f* de mar

seabed ['siːbed] *n* fondo *m* del mar *or* marino

seabird ['siːbɜːd] *n* ave *f* marina

seaboard ['siːbɔːd] *n US* costa *f,* litoral *m*

seaborne ['siːbɔːn] *adj* marítimo(a)

seafarer ['siːfeərər] *n* marinero *m*

seafaring ['siːfeərɪŋ] *adj* marinero(a)

seafood ['siːfuːd] *n* mariscos *mpl;* **s. restaurant** marisquería *f*

seafront ['siːfrʌnt] *n* paseo *m* marítimo

seagoing ['siːgəʊɪŋ] *adj* de alta mar

sea-green [siː'griːn] *adj* verdemar

seagull ['siːgʌl] *n* gaviota *f*

sea-horse ['siːhɔːs] *n* caballito *m* de mar, hipocampo *m*

seal¹ [siːl] *n Zool* foca *f*

seal² [siːl] **1** *n* **(a)** *(official stamp) (on document)* sello *m;* **wax s.** sello de lacre; *Fig* **to give one's s. of approval to sth, to set one's s. to sth** aprobar algo, dar el visto bueno a algo **(b)** *(airtight closure)* cierre *m* hermético; *(on bottle)* precinto *m*
2 *vt* **(a)** *(document) (with official stamp)* sellar; *(with wax)* lacrar, sellar con lacre; *(bottle)* precintar **(b)** *(close)* cerrar; *(make airtight)* cerrar herméticamente; *Culin (meat)* encerrar el sabor de; **my lips are sealed** seré como una tumba **(c)** *(determine)* decidir, determinar; **this sealed his fate** esto decidió su destino

seal in *vt (flavour etc)* encerrar

seal off *vt (close) (pipe etc)* cerrar; *(block entry to) (street, area)* acordonar, cerrar el acceso a

seal up *vt (parcel, letter)* precintar, cerrar con precinto; *(crack, window)* tapar (completamente); *(jar)* cerrar herméticamente

sea-lane ['siːleɪn] *n* vía *f* or ruta *f* marítima

sealing ['siːlɪŋ] *n* **s. wax** lacre *m*

sealskin ['siːlskɪn] *n* piel *f* de foca

seam [siːm] *n* **(a)** *Sew* costura *f; Tech* juntura *f,* junta *f; Med* sutura *f;* **to come apart at the seams** descoserse; **to let out a s.** soltar una costura; *Fam* **to be bursting at the seams** *(person)* estar a punto de reventar; *(room)* rebosar de gente **(b)** *Geol Min* veta *f,* filón *m;* **coal s.** veta de carbón

seaman ['siːmən] *n (pl* **seamen**) marinero *m*

seamanship ['siːmənʃɪp] *n* náutica *f*

seamless ['siːmlɪs] *adj Sew* sin costura; *Tech* sin soldadura

seamstress ['semstrɪs] *n* costurera *f*

seamy ['siːmɪ] *adj (***seamier, seamiest**) *Fig* sórdido(a)

séance ['seɪɑːns] *n* sesión *f* de espiritismo

seaplane ['siːpleɪn] *n* hidroavión *m*

seaport ['siːpɔːt] *n* puerto *m* marítimo *or* de mar

sear [sɪər] *vt (skin)* quemar, abrasar; *Fig* **the image was seared on his memory** la imagen le quedó grabada a fuego en la memoria

search [sɜːtʃ] **1** *vt (records, files)* buscar en; *(building, suitcase, etc)* registrar; *(person)* cachear; *(one's conscience)* examinar; *Fam* **s. me!** ¡yo qué sé!
2 *vi* buscar **(for, after -**); **to s. through sb's pockets** registrar los bolsillos a algn; *Comptr* **s. and replace** buscar y reemplazar
3 *n (gen)* búsqueda *f; (of building etc)* registro *m; (of person)* cacheo *m;* **in s. of** en búsqueda *or Esp* busca de; *Comptr* **to do a s.** hacer una búsqueda □ *Comptr* **s. engine** motor *m* de búsqueda; **s. party** equipo *m* de salvamento; **s. warrant** orden *f* de registro

searcher ['sɜːtʃər] *n* buscador(a) *m,f*

searching ['sɜːtʃɪŋ] *adj (look)* penetrante; *(question)* agudo(a)

searchlight ['sɜːtʃlaɪt] *n* reflector *m,* proyector *m*

searing ['sɪərɪŋ] *adj (pain)* punzante; *(heat)* abrasador(a); *(criticism, indictment)* incisivo(a)

seascape ['siːskeɪp] *n* marina *f*

seashell ['siːʃel] *n* concha *f* marina

seashore ['siːʃɔːr] *n (shore)* costa *f,* litoral *m; (beach)* playa *f*

seasick ['siːsɪk] *adj* mareado(a); **to get s.** marearse

seasickness ['siːsɪknɪs] *n* mareo *m*

seaside ['siːsaɪd] *n* playa *f,* costa *f* ❏ **s. resort** lugar *m or* complejo *m* turístico de veraneo; **s. town** pueblo *m* costero, ciudad *f* costera

season¹ ['siːzən] *n (gen)* época *f; (spring, summer, etc)* estación *f; (for social activity, sport, etc)* temporada *f;* **at the height of the s.** en plena temporada; **'Season's Greetings'** 'Felices Pascuas'; **the busy s.** la temporada alta; **the dry/ rainy s.** la estación seca/de lluvias; **the football s.** la temporada de fútbol *or* futbolística; **the four seasons** las cuatro estaciones; **the off s.** la temporada baja; *(hunting)* **the open/close s.** la temporada de caza *or* de pesca/la veda; **the tourist s.** la temporada turística; **to be in s.** *(fruit)* estar en sazón; *(animal)* estar en celo ❏ *Rail Theat* **s. ticket** abono *m;* **s. ticket holder** abonado(a) *m,f*

season² ['siːzən] *vt (a) Culin* sazonar, condimentar **(b)** *(wood)* secar; *(wine)* madurar **(c)** *(person)* acostumbrar, avezar

seasonable ['siːzənəbəl] *adj (weather)* propio(a) de la estación; *(timely)* oportuno(a)

seasonal ['siːzənəl] *adj (activity)* estacional, temporal; **s. worker** temporero(a) *m,f*

seasoned ['siːzənd] *adj (a) Culin (food)* sazonado(a), condimentado(a); **a highly s. dish** un plato muy picante **(b)** *(wood)* seco(a); *(wine)* maduro(a) **(c)** *Fig (person)* experimentado(a), curtido(a), avezado(a)

seasoning ['siːzənɪŋ] *n* condimento *m,* aderezo *m*

seat [siːt] **1** *n (a) (gen)* asiento *m; (place)* plaza *f; Cin Theat* localidad *f; (ticket)* entrada *f; Cin Theat* **to book seats** reservar localidades; **to take a s.** sentarse ❏ *Aut Av* **s. belt** cinturón *m* de seguridad **(b)** *(of cycle)* sillín *m; (of toilet)* asiento *m; (of trousers)* fondillos *mpl; Fam (buttocks)* trasero *m,* pompis *m* **(c)** *(centre)* centro *m,* sede *f;* **s. of learning** centro de estudios **(d)** *Parl* escaño *m*

2 *vt (a) (child, guests, etc)* sentar; **please be seated** siéntese por favor; **to remain seated** quedarse sentado(a) **(b)** *(accommodate)* tener sitio para; *(theatre, hall, etc)* tener cabida para; **it will s. five hundred** tendrá un aforo para quinientas personas; **this table seats eight** esta mesa es para ocho personas

-seater ['siːtər] *suffix* **a two-s. car** un (coche) dos plazas; **a three-s. sofa** un sofá tres plazas

seating ['siːtɪŋ] *n (a) (capacity)* asientos *mpl;* **s. capacity** cabida *f,* aforo *m* **(b)** *(distribution)* distribución *f* de asientos

sea-urchin ['siːɜːtʃɪn] *n* erizo *m* de mar

sea-wall ['siːwɔːl] *n* rompeolas *m inv*

seaweed ['siːwiːd] *n* alga *f* (marina)

seaworthy ['siːwɜːðɪ] *adj (boat)* en condiciones de navegar

sebaceous [sɪ'beɪʃəs] *adj* sebáceo(a)

sec¹ [sek] *n Fam (abbr* **second**) segundo *m*

sec² *(abbr* **secretary**) secretario(a) *m,f*

secant ['siːkənt] *n Geom* secante *f*

secateurs [sekə'tɜːz] *npl* podadera *f sing*

secede [sɪ'siːd] *vi Pol* separarse **(from** de), independizarse **(from** de)

secession [sɪ'seʃən] *n Pol* secesión *f*

secluded [sɪ'kluːdɪd] *adj* aislado(a), retirado(a), apartado(a)

seclusion [sɪ'kluːʒən] *n* aislamiento *m,* retiro *m;* **in s.** aislado(a)

second¹ ['sekənd] **1** *adj* segundo(a); **every s. day** cada dos días; **it's s. nature to him** le viene de naturaleza; **it's the s. highest mountain in the world** es la segunda montaña más alta en el mundo; **on s. thought(s)** ... pensándolo bien ...; **s. teeth** segunda dentición *f;* **he's a s. Dr Crippen** parece otro Dr Crippen; **to be s. to none** no tener igual; **to have a s. helping of sth** repetir algo; **to have s. thoughts about sth** dudar de algo; **to marry for the s. time** casarse en segundas nupcias; **to play s. fiddle** ser segundón(ona) desempeñar un papel secundario; **to settle for s. best** conformarse con lo que hay; *Fig* **to get one's s. wind** despabilarse, espabilarse ❏ **s. class** segunda clase *f;* **s. cousin** primo(a) *m,f* segundo(a); **s. floor** *Br* segundo piso *m, US* primer piso *m;* **s. language** segunda lengua *f; Jur* **s. offence** reincidencia *f;* **s. opinion** segunda opinión *f; Ling* **s. person** segunda persona *f;* **s. sight** clarividencia *f*

2 *n (a) (in series, rank, etc)* segundo(a) *m,f;* **Charles the S.** Carlos Segundo; **the s. of October** *(date)* el dos de octubre **(b)** *Br Univ* **to obtain a s.** *(degree)* sacar un notable **(c)** *Aut (gear)* segunda *f;* **in s.** en segunda **(d)** *Com* **seconds** artículos *mpl* con tara *or* defectuosos

3 *vt (motion, proposal)* apoyar, secundar

4 *adv (in race, exam, etc)* segundo, en segundo lugar; **to come s.** terminar en segundo lugar; *Sport* **he came in s.** llegó segundo

second² ['sekənd] *n (time)* segundo *m;* **in a split s.** en un abrir y cerrar de ojos; *Fam* **I'll be back in a s.** enseguida vuelvo; *Fam* **just a s.!** ¡un momentito! ❏ **s. hand** segundero *m*

second³ [sɪ'kɒnd] *vt (officer, employee)* trasladar temporalmente

secondary ['sekəndərɪ] *adj* secundario(a) ❏ **s. education** educación *f* secundaria; **s. school** *(gen)* escuela *f* secundaria; *(private)* colegio *m; (state)* instituto *m* (de enseñanza media *or* de educación secundaria)

second-best [sekənd'best] **1** *adj* segundo(a), inferior

2 *adv* **to come off s.-b.** quedar en segundo lugar

second-class [sekənd'klɑːs] **1** *adj (mail)* de segunda (clase); *(goods)* de segunda categoría, de calidad inferior; **s.-c. citizen** ciudadano(a) *m,f* de segunda (clase)

2 *adv* **to travel s.-c.** viajar en segunda

second-degree ['sekəndɪgriː] *adj Med* de segundo grado; **s.-d. burns** quemaduras *fpl* de segundo grado

seconder ['sekəndər] *n* **the s. of a motion** la persona que secunda una moción

second-generation ['sekənddʒenə'reɪʃən] *adj (immigrant, computer)* de segunda generación

second-guess ['sekənd'ges] *vt* predecir, anticiparse a

second-hand ['sekəndhænd] **1** *adj (car, clothes, book)* usado(a), de segunda mano ❏ **s.-h. dealer** chamarilero(a) *m,f,* trapero(a) *m,f;* **s.-h. shop** rastrillo *m,* bazar *m,* rastro *m*

2 *adv* de segunda mano; **to buy sth s.-h.** comprar algo de segunda mano

second-in-command [sekəndɪnkə'mɑːnd] *n Mil* segundo *m* en jefe

secondly ['sekəndlɪ] *adv* en segundo lugar

secondment [sɪ'kɒndmənt] *n Br* traslado *m* temporal; **she's on s. to accounts** la han trasladado a contabilidad

second-rate ['sekəndreɪt] *adj* de segunda *or* baja categoría, de calidad inferior

secrecy ['siːkrəsɪ] *n (a) (gen)* secreto *m;* **in s.** en secreto **(b)** *(ability to keep secrets)* discreción *f,* reserva *f*

secret ['siːkrɪt] **1** *adj* secreto(a); **to keep sth s.** mantener algo en secreto; **s. ballot** votación *f* secreta ❏ **s. agent**

agente *mf* secreto(a), espía *mf*; **s. police** policía *f* secreta; **s. service** servicio *m* secreto

2 *n* secreto *m*; *Fig* clave *f*; **in s.** en secreto; **open s.** secreto a voces; **to be in on the s.** estar al tanto, estar en el ajo; **to keep a s.** guardar un secreto; **to let sb into a s.** revelar un secreto a algn, compartir un secreto con algn; **there's no s. about it** no tiene ningún misterio

secretarial [sekrɪ'teərɪəl] *adj* de secretario(a) □ **s. college** escuela *f* de secretariado; **s. studies** secretariado *m*

secretariat [sekrɪ'teərɪət] *n* secretaría *f*, secretariado *m*

secretary ['sekrətrɪ] *n* secretario(a) *m,f*; **general s.** secretario(a) *m,f* general; **private s.** secretario(a) *m,f* particular; **S. of State** *Br* ministro(a) *m,f* con cartera, *US* secretario(a) *m,f* de Estado, ministro(a) *m,f* de Asuntos Exteriores; *US* **S. of the Treasury** ministro(a) *m,f* de Hacienda

secretary-general [sekrətrɪ'dʒenərəl] *n* (*pl* **secretaries-general**) secretario *m* general

secrete [sɪ'kriːt] *vt* (**a**) *(emit) (liquid etc)* secretar, segregar (**b**) *(hide)* ocultar, esconder

secretion [sɪ'kriːʃən] *n* (**a**) *(of liquid)* secreción *f* (**b**) *(hiding)* ocultación *f*

secretive ['siːkrɪtɪv] *adj* sigiloso(a); *(quiet)* reservado(a), callado(a)

secretly ['siːkrɪtlɪ] *adv* en secreto, a escondidas

sect [sekt] *n* secta *f*

sectarian [sek'teərɪən] *adj & n* sectario(a) *(m,f)*

sectarianism [sek'teərɪənɪzəm] *n* sectarismo *m*

section ['sekʃən] **1** *n* (**a**) *(part)* sección *f*, parte *f*; *(of road, track)* tramo *m*; *(of law)* artículo *m*, apartado *m*; *(of newspaper)* sección *f*, página *f*; *(of population, community)* sector *m*; *(of orchestra)* sección *f*; *(department)* sección *f* (**b**) *(cut)* corte *m*, sección *f* □ *Med* **Caesarian s.** (operación *f* de) cesárea *f*; **cross s.** sección *f* transversal

2 *vt* cortar, seccionar

sectional ['sekʃənəl] *adj* (**a**) *(furniture)* desmontable (**b**) *(plan, diagram)* en corte (**c**) *(interest)* particular

sector ['sektər] *n* sector *m*; **the public s.** el sector público

secular ['sekjʊlər] *adj* *(school, teaching)* laico(a); *(music, art)* profano(a); *(priest)* seglar, secular

secularize ['sekjʊləraɪz] *vt* secularizar

secure [sɪ'kjʊər] **1** *adj* (**a**) *(safe, confident, certain)* seguro(a); **s. in the knowledge that** con la certeza de que; **to feel s.** sentirse seguro(a); **to have a s. job/future** tener un puesto seguro/el porvenir asegurado (**b**) *(firmly fastened) (knot etc)* seguro(a); *(window, door)* bien cerrado(a); *(steady) (ladder etc)* firme

2 *vt* (**a**) *(make safe) (future)* asegurar; **to s. oneself against sth** protegerse contra algo (**b**) *(fasten, fix) (rope, knot)* sujetar, fijar; *(object to floor)* afianzar; *(window, door)* asegurar, cerrar bien; *(animal, prisoner)* atar firmemente (**c**) *(obtain)* conseguir, obtener (**d**) *Fin (guarantee)* garantizar, avalar

secured [sɪ'kjʊəd] *adj (debt, loan)* garantizado(a)

securely [sɪ'kjʊəlɪ] *adv* (**a**) *(safely)* a buen recaudo (**b**) *(firmly)* firmemente; **the door was s. fastened** la puerta estaba firmemente cerrada

security [sɪ'kjʊərɪtɪ] *n* (**a**) *(safety, confidence)* seguridad *f*; **emotional s.** estabilidad *f* emocional; **job s.** seguridad en el empleo; **national s.** seguridad nacional; **social s.** seguridad social (**b**) *(from physical attack, spying, etc)* seguridad *f*; **s. was tight** se adoptaron fuertes medidas de seguridad □ **S. Council** Consejo *m* de Seguridad; **s. forces** fuerzas *fpl* de seguridad; **s. leak** fuga *f* (de información) (**c**) *Fin (guarantee)* fianza *f*, garantía *f*, aval *m*; *(guarantor)*

fiador(a) *m,f*; **to lend money on s.** prestar dinero sobre fianza; **to stand s. for sb** salir fiador de algn, garantizar a algn (**d**) *Fin* **securities** valores *mpl*, títulos *mpl*; **Government s.** valores del Estado

sedan [sɪ'dæn] *n* (**a**) *(also* **s. chair**) silla *f* de manos (**b**) *US Aut* turismo *m*

sedate [sɪ'deɪt] **1** *adj* sosegado(a), sereno(a), tranquilo(a)

2 *vt Med* administrar sedantes a, sedar

sedately [sɪ'deɪtlɪ] *adv* sosegadamente

sedation [sɪ'deɪʃən] *n Med* sedación *f*, administración *f* de sedantes

sedative ['sedətɪv] *adj & n* sedativo(a) *(m)*, sedante *(m)*, calmante *(m)*

sedentary ['sedəntərɪ] *adj* sedentario(a); **s. life** vida sedentaria

sediment ['sedɪmənt] *n (gen)* sedimento *m*; *(of wine)* poso *m*, hez *f*

sedition [sɪ'dɪʃən] *n* sedición *f*

seditious [sɪ'dɪʃəs] *adj* sedicioso(a)

seduce [sɪ'djuːs] *vt* seducir

seducer [sɪ'djuːsər] *n* seductor(a) *m,f*

seduction [sɪ'dʌkʃən] *n* seducción *f*

seductive [sɪ'dʌktɪv] *adj (person, idea)* seductor(a); *(smile, clothes)* provocativo(a); *(offer)* tentador(a)

seductively [sɪ'dʌktɪvlɪ] *adv* seductoramente

see[1] [siː] **1** *vt (pt* **saw;** *pp* **seen**) (**a**) *(gen)* ver; **I don't know what he sees in her** no sé qué ve en ella; **I'll s. what can be done** veré lo que se puede hacer; **it is worth seeing** merece la pena verlo; **that remains to be seen** eso queda por ver; **this handbag has seen better days** este bolso ha conocido mejores tiempos; **s. page 10** véase la página 10; **s. you (later)/soon/Monday!** ¡hasta luego/pronto/el lunes!; **we were glad to s. the back of him** nos alegramos de perderlo de vista; *Fig* **to s. the light** ver la luz; *Fam* **to s. red** ponerse negro(a) (de ira) (**b**) *(meet with)* ver, tener cita con; **the manager will s. you in just a moment** el jefe le verá en seguida; *(couple)* **they have been seeing each other for six months** hace seis meses que salen juntos (**c**) *(visit)* ver, visitar; **they s. a lot of each other** se ven muy a menudo; **to s. the sights/the world** recorrer la ciudad/el mundo (**d**) *(understand)* entender, ver; **I don't s. the joke** no le veo la gracia; **I don't s. why he can't go** no entiendo porqué no puede ir (**e**) *(imagine, visualize)* imaginarse, ver; **he sees himself as a second Caruso** se cree otro Caruso; **I can't s. her living abroad** no me la imagino viviendo en el extranjero; **you must be seeing things** ves visiones (**f**) *(ensure)* asegurarse de; procurar; **s. that the windows are securely fastened** asegúrese de que todas las ventanas estén bien cerradas; **s. that you arrive on time** procura llegar a la hora (**g**) *(accompany)* acompañar; **to s. sb home** acompañar a algn a casa

2 *vi* (**a**) *(gen)* ver; **go and s. if ...** vete a ver si ...; **let's s.** a ver, vamos a ver (**b**) *(understand)* entender, ver; **as far as I can s.** por lo visto, por lo que veo; **I s.** ya veo; **you s., he hasn't got a car** es que no tiene coche, ¿sabes?

see about *vt* (**a**) *(deal with)* ocuparse de, encargarse de (**b**) *(consider)* pensar

see in *vt* celebrar; **to s. in the New Year** celebrar el Año Nuevo

see into *vt (investigate)* investigar

see off *vt (say goodbye to)* despedirse de

see out *vt* (**a**) *(show out)* acompañar hasta la puerta (**b**) *(survive)* sobrevivir; **she will s. us all out** nos enterrará a todos

see over *vt (house etc)* visitar, recorrer

see through *vt* (**a**) *Fam (person)* calar, verle el plumero a

(b) *(help)* ayudar a salir de un apuro; **I'll s. you through** puedes contar con mi ayuda; **$20 should s. me through** con 20 dólares me las apaño **(c)** *(carry out)* llevar a cabo

see to *vt (deal with)* atender a, ocuparse de; **s. to it that dinner is served on time** procura que la cena se sirva a la hora

see² [si:] *n Rel* sede *f* □ **the Holy S.** la Santa Sede

seed [si:d] **1** *n* **(a)** *Bot (gen)* semilla *f; (for sowing)* simiente *f,* semilla *f; (of fruit)* pepita *f;* **to go** *or* **run to s.** *(plant)* granar; *Fig (person)* descuidarse, abandonarse, echarse a perder; *Fig* **to sow the seeds of discord** sembrar las semillas de la discordia □ **s. pearl** aljófar *m;* **s. potato** *Esp* patata *f or Am* papa *f* de siembra **(b)** *Ten (player)* cabeza *m f* de serie
2 *vt* **(a)** *(sow with seed) (lawn etc)* sembrar **(b)** *(grapes, raisins)* despepitar **(c)** *Ten (players)* preseleccionar; **seeded player** cabeza *m f* de serie
3 *vi (plants)* granar

seedbed ['si:dbed] *n* semillero *m*

seedcake ['si:dkeɪk] *n Culin* torta *f* de semillas aromáticas

seedless ['si:dlɪs] *adj* sin pepitas *or* semillas

seedling ['si:dlɪŋ] *n* plantón *m*

seedy ['si:dɪ] *adj* **(seedier, seediest)** *Fam* **(a)** *(run-down) (district, bar)* sórdido(a), *Esp* cutre; *(shabby) (clothes)* raído(a); *(appearance)* desaseado(a) **(b)** *(unwell)* malo(a), *Esp* pachucho(a); **to look s.** tener mala pinta

seeing ['si:ɪŋ] **1** *adj* vidente, que ve
2 *n* **s. is believing** ver para creer
3 *conj* **s. that** visto que, en vista de que, dado que

seeing-eye dog ['si:ɪŋaɪ'dɒɡ] *n US* perro *m* lazarillo *or* guía

seek [si:k] **1** *vt (pt & pp* **sought)** **(a)** *(look for)* buscar; **to s. employment/shelter** buscar empleo/cobijo; **to s. one's fortune** probar fortuna **(b)** *(ask for)* pedir, solicitar; *(post)* solicitar **(c)** *(try)* **to s. to do sth** procurar hacer algo
2 *vi* buscar

seek after *vt* buscar; **much sought after** *(person)* muy solicitado(a); *(thing)* muy cotizado(a)

seek out *vt (person)* buscar

seeker ['si:kər] *n* buscador(a) *m f* □ **status s.** trepa *m f,* arribista *m f*

seem [si:m] *vi* parecer; **he seems (to be) tired** parece cansado; **I s. to remember his name was Colin** creo recordar que su nombre era Colin; **it seems not** parece que no; **it seems to me that** me parece que; **she seems to have lost sth** parece que ha perdido algo; **so it seems** eso parece; **what seems to be the trouble?** ¿qué ocurre?, ¿qué pasa?

seeming ['si:mɪŋ] *adj* aparente, supuesto(a)

seemingly ['si:mɪŋlɪ] *adv* aparentemente, según parece, al parecer

seemly ['si:mlɪ] *adj* **(seemlier, seemliest)** *(behaviour)* correcto(a), decente

seen [si:n] *pp see* **see¹**

seep [si:p] *vi (ooze)* rezumarse; **to s. through/into/out** filtrarse *or* calarse *or* colarse por/en/de

seepage ['si:pɪdʒ] *n* filtración *f*

seer [sɪər] *n* vidente *m f*

seersucker ['sɪəsʌkər] *n Tex* vichy *m*

seesaw ['si:sɔ:] **1** *n* balancín *m,* subibaja *m* □ **s. movement** balanceo *m,* vaivén *m*
2 *vi* **(a)** *(on seesaw)* columpiarse, balancearse **(b)** *(prices, mood)* fluctuar

seethe [si:ð] *vi* bullir, hervir; *Fig (person)* **to s. with anger** estar furibundo(a), rabiar; *(place)* **to s. with people** estar a rebosar, ser (como) un hormiguero

see-through ['si:θru:] *adj* transparente

segment ['seɡmənt] *n (gen)* segmento *m; (of orange)* gajo *m*

segregate ['seɡrɪɡeɪt] *vt* segregar **(from** de)

segregation [seɡrɪ'ɡeɪʃən] *n* segregación *f*

Seine [seɪn, sen] *n* Sena

seismic ['saɪzmɪk] *adj* sísmico(a) □ **s. wave** onda *f* sísmica

seismograph ['saɪzməɡræf, 'saɪzməɡrɑ:f] *n* sismógrafo *m*

seismologist [saɪz'mɒlədʒɪst] *n* sismólogo(a) *m f*

seismology [saɪz'mɒlədʒɪ] *n* sismología *f*

seize [si:z] *vt (grab)* agarrar, asir, *Esp* coger; *(property, drugs)* incautar, embargar; *(newspaper, magazine)* secuestrar; *Mil (territory)* tomar, apoderarse de; *(hostages)* secuestrar; *(arrest)* detener; **to be seized with fear** estar sobrecogido(a) por el miedo; **to s. an opportunity** aprovechar una ocasión; *Pol* **to s. power** tomar el poder

seize on *vt (chance, offer)* valerse de, aprovechar; *(idea)* aferrarse a

seize up *vi* agarrotarse

seizure ['si:ʒər] *n* **(a)** *Jur (of property, drugs)* incautación *f,* embargo *m; (of newspaper, magazine)* secuestro *m; Mil (of territory)* toma *f; (of hostages)* secuestro *m; (arrest)* detención *f* **(b)** *Med* ataque *m* (de apoplejía)

seldom ['seldəm] *adv* rara vez, raramente; **I s. see you** te veo muy poco

select [sɪ'lekt] **1** *vt (thing)* escoger, elegir; *(team, player)* seleccionar
2 *adj (audience)* selecto(a), escogido(a); *(club, society)* selecto(a), exclusivo(a); *(fruit, wines)* selecto(a), de primera calidad; **a s. few** una minoría privilegiada □ *Br Parl* **s. committee** comisión *f* especial de investigación

selected [sɪ'lektɪd] *adj (gen)* selecto(a), escogido(a); *(team, player)* seleccionado(a); *Lit* **s. works** obras escogidas

selection [sɪ'lekʃən] *n (choosing)* elección *f; (people or things chosen)* selección *f; (range)* surtido *m* □ *Biol* **natural s.** selección *f* natural

selective [sɪ'lektɪv] *adj* selectivo(a)

selectively [sɪ'lektɪvlɪ] *adv* con un criterio selectivo

selectivity [sɪlek'tɪvɪtɪ] *n* selectividad *f*

selector [sɪ'lektər] *n* **(a)** *Sport* seleccionador(a) *m f* **(b)** *Tech* selector *m*

selenium [sɪ'li:nɪəm] *n Chem* selenio *m*

self [self] *n (pl* **selves)** uno(a) mismo(a), sí mismo(a); **his better s.** su lado bueno; **my other s.** mi otro yo; **she's her old s. again** es la misma de antes; *Psych* **the s.** el yo

self- [self] *pref* auto-

self-acting [self'æktɪŋ] *adj* automático(a)

self-addressed [selfə'drest] *adj* **s.-a. envelope** sobre *m* respuesta

self-adhesive [selfəd'hi:sɪv] *adj (label, envelope)* autoadhesivo(a), autoadherente

self-appointed [selfə'pɔɪntɪd] *adj* que se elige a sí mismo(a)

self-assurance [selfə'ʃʊərəns] *n* seguridad *f or* confianza *f* en sí mismo(a)

self-assured [selfə'ʃʊəd] *adj* seguro(a) de sí mismo(a)

self-awareness [selfə'weənɪs] *n* conocimiento *m* de sí mismo(a)

self-catering [self'keɪtərɪŋ] *adj (holiday, flat)* sin servicio de comida

self-centred, *US* **self-centered** [self'sentəd] *adj* egocéntrico(a)

self-cleaning [self'kli:nɪŋ] *adj* auto-limpiable

self-closing [self'kləʊzɪŋ] *adj* de cierre automático

self-confessed [selfkən'fest] *adj* confeso(a)

self-confidence [self'kɒnfɪdəns] *n* seguridad *f. or* confianza *f* en sí mismo(a)

self-confident [self'kɒnfɪdənt] *adj* seguro(a) de sí mismo(a)

self-congratulatory ['self'kəngrætjʊ'leɪtərɪ] *adj* de autosatisfacción

self-conscious [self'kɒnʃəs] *adj* cohibido(a), tímido(a)

self-consciously ['self'kɒnʃəslɪ] *adv (with embarrassment)* con inhibición, tímidamente; *(affectedly)* afectadamente, con afectación

self-contained [selfkən'teɪnd] *adj* (**a**) *(flat)* independiente, con entrada propia; *(person)* independiente (**b**) *(reserved) (person)* reservado(a), poco comunicativo(a)

self-contradictory ['selfkɒntrə'dɪktərɪ] *adj* contradictorio(a)

self-control [selfkən'trəʊl] *n* dominio *m* de sí mismo(a), autocontrol *m*

self-deception ['selfdɪ'sepʃən] *n* autoengaño *m*

self-defence, *US* **self-defense** [selfdɪ'fens] *n* defensa *f* personal, autodefensa *f*

self-denial [selfdɪ'naɪəl] *n* abnegación *f*

self-deprecating ['self'deprɪkeɪtɪŋ] *adj* **he's famous for his s.-d. humour** siempre se ríe de sí mismo

self-destructive ['selfdɪs'trʌktɪv] *adj* autodestructivo(a)

self-determination [selfdɪtɜːmɪ'neɪʃən] *n Pol* autodeterminación *f*, autonomía *f*

self-discipline [self'dɪsɪplɪn] *n* autodisciplina *f*

self-disciplined ['self'dɪsɪplɪnd] *adj* autodisciplinado(a)

self-doubt ['self'daʊt] *n* falta *f* de confianza (en sí mismo))

self-drive [self'draɪv] *adj* sin chófer

self-educated [self'edjʊkeɪtɪd] *adj* autodidacta

self-effacing [selfɪ'feɪsɪŋ] *adj* modesto(a), humilde

self-employed [selfɪm'plɔɪd] *adj (worker)* autónomo(a), que trabaja por cuenta propia

self-esteem [selfɪ'stiːm] *n* autoestima *f*, amor *m* propio

self-evident [self'evɪdənt] *adj* evidente, patente

self-explanatory [selfɪk'splænətərɪ] *adj* que se explica por sí mismo(a), evidente

self-expression ['selfɪk'spreʃən] *n* autoexpresión *f*

self-fulfilling ['selfʊl'fɪlɪŋ] *adj (prophecy, prediction)* que se autorrealiza

self-governing [self'gʌvənɪŋ] *adj* autónomo(a)

self-government [self'gʌvənmənt] *n* autonomía *f*, autogobierno *m*

self-help [self'help] *n* autoayuda *f*; **s.-h. group** grupo *m* de apoyo

self-image ['self'ɪmɪdʒ] *n* imagen *f* de sí mismo(a)

self-importance [selfɪm'pɔːtəns] *n* engreimiento *m*, presunción *f*

self-important [selfɪm'pɔːtənt] *adj* engreído(a), presumido(a)

self-improvement ['selfɪm'pruːvmənt] *n* autosuperación *f*

self-induced ['selfɪn'djuːst] *adj (hysteria, illness)* provocado(a) por uno mismo

self-indulgence [selfɪn'dʌldʒəns] *n* tendencia *f* a permitirse excesos, indulgencia *f* consigo mismo(a)

self-indulgent [selfɪn'dʌldʒənt] *adj* que se permite excesos, inmoderado(a)

self-inflicted ['selfɪn'flɪktɪd] *adj* autoinfligido(a)

self-interest [self'ɪntrɪst] *n* interés *m* propio, egoísmo *m*

selfish ['selfɪʃ] *adj* egoísta

selfishness ['selfɪʃnɪs] *n* egoísmo *m*

self-justification ['selfdʒʌstɪfɪ'keɪʃən] *n* autojustificación *f*

self-knowledge ['self'nɒlɪdʒ] *n* conocimiento *m* de sí mismo(a)

selfless ['selflɪs] *adj* desinteresado(a)

self-made ['selfmeɪd] *adj* **s.-m. man** hombre *m* que ha triunfado por sus propios esfuerzos, hombre *m* que se ha hecho a sí mismo

self-opinionated [selfə'pɪnjəneɪtɪd] *adj (stubborn)* testarudo(a), terco(a)

self-pity [self'pɪtɪ] *n* lástima *f* de sí mismo(a)

self-portrait [self'pɔːtreɪt] *n* autorretrato *m*

self-possessed [selfpə'zest] *adj* sereno(a), dueño(a) de sí mismo(a)

self-preservation [selfprezə'veɪʃən] *n* **(instinct of) s.-p.** instinto *m* de conservación

self-raising ['selfreɪzɪŋ] *adj Culin* **s.-r. flour** *Esp* harina *f* con levadura, *Am* harina *f* con polvos de hornear, *RP* harina *f* leudante

self-regulating [self'regjʊleɪtɪŋ] *adj Tech* autorregulador(a)

self-reliance [selfrɪ'laɪəns] *n* independencia *f*, autosuficiencia *f*

self-reliant [selfrɪ'laɪənt] *adj* independiente, autosuficiente

self-respect [selfrɪ'spekt] *n* amor *m* propio, dignidad *f*

self-respecting [selfrɪ'spektɪŋ] *adj* que tiene amor propio, que se respeta a sí mismo(a)

self-restraint [selfrɪ'streɪnt] *n* dominio *m* de sí mismo(a)

self-righteous [self'raɪtʃəs] *adj* farisaico(a), santurrón(ona), beato(a)

self-righteousness [self'raɪtʃəsnɪs] *n* fariseísmo *m*, santurronería *f*, beatería *f*

self-rising ['selfraɪzɪŋ] *adj US see* **self-raising**

self-rule [self'ruːl] *n see* **self-government**

selfsame ['selfseɪm] *adj* mismísimo(a)

self-satisfied [self'sætɪsfaɪd] *adj* satisfecho(a) de sí mismo(a), pagado(a) de sí

self-service [self'sɜːvɪs] **1** *n (in shop etc)* autoservicio *m* **2** *adj* de autoservicio

self-starter ['self'stɑːtər] *n (person)* persona *f* con iniciativa

self-styled ['selfstaɪld] *adj (president, king)* autoproclamado(a); *(philosopher, expert)* pretendido(a), sedicente

self-sufficiency [selfsə'fɪʃənsɪ] *n* autosuficiencia *f*

self-sufficient [selfsə'fɪʃənt] *adj* autosuficiente

self-supporting [selfsə'pɔːtɪŋ] *adj* económicamente independiente

self-taught [self'tɔːt] *adj* autodidacto(a)

sell [sel] **1** *vt (pt & pp* **sold)** (**a**) *(gen)* vender; **to know how to s. oneself** saber presentarse con ventaja; **to s. sth at a loss** vender algo con pérdida; *Fam* **to s. sb down the river** traicionar a algn (**b**) **to be sold on sth** entusiasmarse por algo; **he's not sold on it** no le convence

2 *vi* venderse; *Fig* **to s. like hot cakes** venderse como rosquillas

3 *n Com* **hard/soft s.** publicidad *f* agresiva/discreta

sell off *vt (property, stock)* liquidar

sell out 1 *vt* (**a**) **the concert is sold out** no quedan entradas *or Am* boletos para el concierto (**b**) *(betray)* vender, traicionar

   2 *vi* (**a**) **they have sold out of tickets** se han agotado las entradas *or Am* los boletos (**b**) *(betray belief)* venderse

sell up *vi* vender el negocio

sell-by date ['selbaɪdeɪt] *n Com* fecha *f* límite de venta

seller ['selər] *n* (**a**) *(person)* vendedor(a) *m,f* (**b**) *(product)* **to be a good s.** tener demanda, venderse bien

selling ['selɪŋ] *n* venta *f* □ **s. point** atractivo *m* comercial; **s. price** precio *m* de venta

sell-off ['selɒf] *n (of state-owned company)* privatización *f*

Sellotape® ['seləteɪp] *Br* **1** *n* cinta *f* adhesiva, *Esp* celo *m*, *CAm Méx* Durex® *m*

   2 *vt* pegar con cinta adhesiva *or Esp* celo *or CAm Méx* Durex®

sell-out ['selaʊt] *n* (**a**) lleno *m*; **the match was a s.-o.** se vendieron todas las entradas para el partido (**b**) *(act of disloyalty)* claudicación *f*, traición *f*

selves [selvz] *npl see* **self**

semantic [sɪ'mæntɪk] *adj* semántico(a)

semantics [sɪ'mæntɪks] *n* semántica *f*

semaphore ['seməfɔːr] *n Rail* semáforo *m*

semblance ['sembləns] *n* apariencia *f*; **there was some s. of truth in it** había algo de verdad en ello

semen ['siːmen] *n* semen *m*

semester [sɪ'mestər] *n* semestre *m*

semi ['semɪ] *n Fam* (**a**) *US (abbr* **semitrailer)** semirremolque *m* (**b**) *Br (abbr* **semidetached)** chalet *m or* chalé *m* adosado, casa *f* adosada

semi- ['semɪ, *US* 'semaɪ] *pref* semi-

semiautomatic ['semɪɔːtə'mætɪk] *adj* semiautomáti-co(a)

semibreve ['semɪbriːv] *n Mus* semibreve *f*

semicircle ['semɪsɜːkəl] *n* semicírculo *m*

semicircular [semɪ'sɜːkjʊlər] *adj* semicircular

semicolon [semɪ'kəʊlən] *n* punto *m* y coma

semiconductor [semɪkən'dʌktər] *n Elec* semiconductor *m*

semiconscious [semɪ'kɒnʃəs] *adj* semiconsciente

semidetached [semɪdɪ'tætʃt] **1** *adj (building)* adosado(a)

   2 *n* chalet *m or* chalé *m* adosado, casa *f* adosada

semifinal [semɪ'faɪnəl] *n* semifinal *f*

semifinalist [semɪ'faɪnəlɪst] *n Sport* semifinalista *mf*

seminal ['semɪnəl] *adj (very important)* trascendental

seminar ['semɪnɑːr] *n* seminario *m*, clase *f*

seminary ['semɪnərɪ] *n Rel* seminario *m*

semiofficial [semɪəʊ'fɪʃəl] *adj* semioficial

semiotics [semɪ'ɒtɪks] *n* semiótica *f*

semiprecious [semɪ'preʃəs] *adj Min* semiprecioso(a)

semiquaver ['semɪkweɪvər] *n Br Mus* semicorchea *f*

Semite ['siːmaɪt] *n* semita *mf*

Semitic [sɪ'mɪtɪk] *adj* semita, semítico(a)

semitone ['semɪtəʊn] *n Br Mus* semitono *m*

semitrailer ['semɪtreɪlər] *n US* semirremolque *m*

semolina [semə'liːnə] *n* sémola *f*

Sen (**a**) *(abbr* **Senator)** senador(a) *m,f* (**b**) *abbr see* **Snr**

senate ['senɪt] *n* (**a**) *Pol* senado *m* (**b**) *Univ* claustro *m*

senator ['senətər] *n* senador(a) *m,f*

send [send] **1** *vt (pt & pp* **sent)** (**a**) *(letter etc)* enviar, mandar; *(telex etc)* mandar, poner; *(radio signal)* transmitir;

(rocket, ball) lanzar; **he was sent to prison** lo mandaron a la cárcel; **it sent a shiver down my spine** me dio escalofríos; **s. her my regards** dale recuerdos de mi parte; **to s. sb to Coventry** hacerle el vacío a algn; **to s. sth flying** tirar algo; **to s. word to sb** avisar a algn; *Fam* **to s. sb packing** mandar a algn a paseo (**b**) *(cause to become)* volver; **the noise sent her mad** el ruido la volvió loca (**c**) *Slang (enrapture)* chiflar

   2 *vi* **to s. for sb** mandar llamar a algn; **to s. for sth** encargar *or* pedir algo

send away 1 *vt (dismiss)* despedir, despachar

   2 *vi* **to s. away for sth** escribir pidiendo algo

send back *vt (goods, meal, etc)* devolver; *(person)* hacer volver *or* regresar

send down *vt* (**a**) *(prices, temperature)* hacer bajar (**b**) *Br Univ* expulsar (**c**) *Fam (imprison) Esp* meter en chirona, *Andes Col RP* mandar en cana, *Méx* mandar al bote

send in *vt (application form etc)* mandar, enviar; *(troops, supplies)* enviar; *(visitor)* hacer pasar

send off 1 *vt* (**a**) *(letter etc)* enviar (por correo); *(goods)* despachar, mandar (**b**) *Ftb (player)* expulsar

   2 *vi* **to s. off for sth** escribir pidiendo algo

send on *vt* (**a**) *(letter)* reexpedir, hacer seguir; *(luggage) (ahead)* facturar; *(later)* enviar, mandar (más tarde) (**b**) *Sport (substitute)* sacar

send out 1 *vt* (**a**) *(person)* mandar salir, echar (**b**) *(leaflets, invitations)* enviar, mandar (**c**) *(emit) (smoke, light, heat)* emitir; *(radio signal)* emitir, dar

   2 *vi* **to s. out for sth** mandar traer algo

send round *vt* (**a**) *(deliver)* mandar a domicilio (**b**) *(circulate)* hacer circular

send up *vt* (**a**) *(person, luggage, meal)* hacer subir *or* montar; *(rocket etc)* lanzar; *(smoke, flames)* echar, arrojar; *(prices, temperature)* hacer subir (**b**) *Br Fam (make fun of) (person)* burlarse de; *(book etc)* satirizar (**c**) *Slang* meter en chirona *or* el talego

sender ['sendər] *n* remitente *mf*

sendoff ['sendɒf] *n Fam* despedida *f*

send-up ['sendʌp] *n Br Fam* parodia *f*

Senegal [senɪ'gɔːl] *n* Senegal

Senegalese [senɪgə'liːz] *adj & n* senegalés(esa) *(m,f)*

senile ['siːnaɪl] *adj* senil

senility [sɪ'nɪlɪtɪ] *n* senilidad *f*

senior ['siːnjər] **1** *adj* (**a**) *(in age)* mayor; **William Armstrong S.** William Armstrong padre □ **s. citizen** jubilado(a) *m,f*, persona *f* de la tercera edad; *US Sch* **s. high (school)** centro *m* de enseñanza secundaria (**b**) *(in position, rank)* superior; *(with longer service) Esp* más antiguo(a), de más antigüedad; *Mil* **s. officer** oficial *mf* de alta graduación; **s. partner** socio(a) *m,f* mayoritario(a); *Br* **the s. service** la marina

   2 *n* (**a**) *(in age)* mayor *mf*; **she's three years my s.** me lleva tres años (**b**) *Br Sch* mayor *mf*; *US Sch Univ* estudiante *mf* del último curso

seniority [siːnɪ'ɒrɪtɪ] *n* antigüedad *f*

sensation [sen'seɪʃən] *n* (**a**) *(feeling)* sensación *f* (**b**) *(great success)* sensación *f*, éxito *m*; **to be a s.** ser un éxito; **to cause a s.** causar sensación

sensational [sen'seɪʃənəl] *adj (marvellous)* sensacional; *(exaggerated) (headlines etc)* sensacionalista

sensationalism [sen'seɪʃənəlɪzəm] *n* sensacionalismo *m*

sense [sens] **1** *n* (**a**) *(faculty)* sentido *m*; **s. of hearing/ smell** sentido del oído/del olfato □ **s. organ** órgano *m* sensorial; **sixth s.** sexto sentido *m* (**b**) *(feeling)* sensación *f*; **s. of direction/duty/humour** sentido *m* de la orientación/

del deber/del humor; **to lose all s. of time** perder toda noción del tiempo **(c)** *(wisdom)* sentido *m* común, juicio *m*, sensatez *f*; **there's no s. in crying** ¿de qué sirve llorar?; **to make sb see s., to talk some s. into sb** hacer entrar en razón a algn ▫ **common s.** sentido *m* común **(d)** *(meaning)* *(gen)* sentido *m*; *(of word)* significado *m*; **I can't make (any) s. of it** no llego a comprenderlo; **in a s.** en cierto sentido, hasta cierto punto; **it doesn't make s.** no tiene sentido; **senses** juicio *m sing*; **to come to one's s.** recobrar el juicio; **to take leave of one's s.** perder el juicio

2 *vt* sentir, percibir, presentir

senseless ['senslɪs] *adj* **(a)** *(absurd)* insensato(a), absurdo(a) **(b)** *(unconscious)* sin conocimiento, inconsciente

sensibility [sensɪ'bɪlɪtɪ] *n* **(a)** *(of artist)* sensibilidad *f* **(b)** **sensibilities** susceptibilidad *f sing*, sensibilidad *f sing*

sensible ['sensɪbəl] *adj* **(a)** *(wise)* sensato(a) **(b)** *(reasonable) (decision)* razonable, prudente; *(choice)* acertado(a) **(c)** *(clothes, shoes)* práctico(a), cómodo(a) **(d)** *(difference)* apreciable, perceptible

sensibly ['sensɪblɪ] *adv* *(rationally)* sensatamente

sensitive ['sensɪtɪv] *adj* **(a)** *(emotionally)* sensible; *(touchy)* susceptible **(b)** *(skin, issue, etc)* delicado(a), sensible; *(document)* confidencial

sensitivity [sensɪ'tɪvɪtɪ] *n* **(a)** *(gen)* sensibilidad *f*; *(touchiness)* susceptibilidad *f* **(b)** *(of skin, issue, etc)* delicadeza *f*

sensitize ['sensɪtaɪz] *vt* sensibilizar

sensor ['sensər] *n Tech* sensor *m*, detector *m*

sensory ['sensərɪ] *adj* sensorial

sensual ['sensjʊəl] *adj* sensual

sensuality [sensjʊ'ælɪtɪ] *n* sensualidad *f*

sensuous ['sensjʊəs] *adj* sensual

sent [sent] *pt & pp see* **send**

sentence ['sentəns] **1** *n* **(a)** *Ling* oración *f*, frase *f* **(b)** *Jur* sentencia *f*, fallo *m*, condena *f*; **to pass s.** dictar sentencia; **to pass s. on sb** imponer una pena a algn ▫ **death s.** pena *f* de muerte; **life s.** cadena *f* perpetua

2 *vt Jur* condenar

sententious [sen'tenʃəs] *adj* sentencioso(a)

sentient ['sentɪənt] *adj* sensitivo(a), sensible

sentiment ['sentɪmənt] *n* **(a)** *(sentimentality)* sentimentalismo *m*, sensiblería *f* **(b)** *(feeling)* sentimiento *m* **(c)** *(opinion)* opinión *f*, parecer *m*, juicio *m*

sentimental [sentɪ'mentəl] *adj* sentimental ▫ **s. value** valor *m* sentimental

sentimentality [sentɪmen'tælɪtɪ] *n* sentimentalismo *m*, sensiblería *f*

sentimentally [sentɪ'mentəlɪ] *adv* sentimentalmente; **to be s. attached to sb** tener una relación sentimental con algn; **to be s. attached to sth** tener cariño a algo

sentry ['sentrɪ] *n Mil* centinela *m*; **to be on s. duty** estar de guardia ▫ **s. box** garita *f* de centinela; **s. post** puesto *m* de vigilancia

Seoul [səʊl] *n* Seúl

sepal ['sepəl] *n Bot* sépalo *m*

separable ['sepərəbəl] *adj* separable

separate 1 *vt (gen)* separar **(from** de); *(divide)* dividir **(into** en); *(distinguish)* distinguir; *Culin* **separated milk** leche desnatada; **she is separated from her husband** está *or* vive separada de su marido

2 *vi* separarse

3 ['sepərɪt] *adj (gen)* separado(a); *(apart)* apartado(a); *(different)* distinto(a), diferente; *(of organization)* independiente; *(of entrance)* particular; **to send sth under s. cover** mandar algo por separado

4 separates *npl (clothes)* piezas *fpl*

separately ['sepərətlɪ] *adv* por separado

separation [sepə'reɪʃən] *n* separación *f*

separatism ['sepərətɪzəm] *n* separatismo *m*

separatist ['sepərətɪst] *n* separatista *mf*

Sephardi [sɪ'fɑːdiː] *n* *(pl* **Sephardim** [sɪ'fɑːdɪm]) sefardí *mf*, sefardita *mf*

Sephardic [sɪ'fɑːdɪk] *adj* sefardí, sefardita

sepia ['siːpɪə] *adj & n* sepia *(f)*

sepsis ['sepsɪs] *n Med* sepsia *f*

Sept *(abbr* **September)** septiembre *m*, setiembre *m*, sept, sep

September [sep'tembər] *n* septiembre *m*, setiembre *m*; **in S.** en septiembre; **(on) the 7th of S.** el 7 de septiembre; *see also* **May**

septet [sep'tet] *n Mus* septeto *m*

septic ['septɪk] *adj Med* séptico(a); *(wound)* **to become s.** infectarse ▫ **s. tank** fosa *f* séptica

septicaemia, *US* **septicemia** [septɪ'siːmɪə] *n Med* septicemia *f*

sepulchre, *US* **sepulcher** ['sepəlkər] *n* sepulcro *m*

sequel ['siːkwəl] *n* secuela *f*

sequence ['siːkwəns] *n* **(a)** *(order)* secuencia *f*, orden *m*; *Ling (of tenses)* concordancia *f* **(b)** *(series)* secuencia *f*, serie *f*, sucesión *f*; *Cards* escala *f*; **dance s.** número *m* (de baile); *Cin* **film s.** secuencia

sequential [sɪ'kwenʃəl] *adj* secuencial

sequester [sɪ'kwestər] *vt* **(a)** *Jur (seize)* embargar, secuestrar **(b)** *(separate)* aislar

sequestrate ['sekwəstreɪt] *vt Jur* embargar

sequestration [siːkwe'streɪʃən] *n Jur (seizure)* embargo *m*, secuestro *m*

sequin ['siːkwɪn] *n* lentejuela *f*

sequoia [sɪ'kwɔɪə] *n Bot* secoya *f*, secuoya *f* ▫ **giant s.** secuoya *f* gigante

Serbia ['sɜːbɪə] *n* Serbia

Serb(ian) ['sɜːb(ɪən)] *adj & n* serbio(a) *(m,f)*

Serbo-Croat ['sɜːbəʊ'krəʊæt] *n (language)* serbocroata *m*

serenade [serɪ'neɪd] *Mus* **1** *n* serenata *f*

2 *vt* dar una serenata a

serene [sɪ'riːn] *adj* sereno(a), tranquilo(a)

serenely [sə'riːnlɪ] *adv* serenamente, con serenidad, con calma

serenity [sɪ'renɪtɪ] *n* serenidad *f*

serf [sɜːf] *n Hist* siervo(a) *m,f*

serge [sɜːdʒ] *n Tex* sarga *f*

sergeant ['sɑːdʒənt] *n Mil* sargento *m*; *(of police)* cabo *m* ▫ **s. major** sargento *m* mayor, brigada *m*

serial ['sɪərɪəl] **1** *n* **(a)** *Rad TV (gen)* serial *m*; *(soap opera)* radionovela *f*, telenovela *f* **(b)** *Press* novela *f* por entregas **(c)** **s. number** número *m* de serie

2 *adj* en serie; **s. killer** asesino(a) *m,f* en serie; *Comptr* **s. port** puerto *m* (en) serie

serialize ['sɪərɪəlaɪz] *vt* seriar

series ['sɪəriːz] *n inv (gen)* serie *f*; *(of books)* colección *f*; *(of concerts, lectures)* ciclo *m*

serious ['sɪərɪəs] *adj* **(a)** *(solemn)* serio(a); *(earnest)* serio(a), formal; **I am s.** hablo en serio; **he's s. about leaving the country** está decidido a salir del país; **she's s. about your brother** está enamorada de tu hermano; **you can't be s.!** no lo dirás en serio, ¿verdad?, es una broma, ¿no? **(b)** *(causing concern)* grave, serio(a); **s. damage/losses** daños/pérdidas importantes; **things are looking s.** la situación se está poniendo grave *or* seria

seriously ['sɪərɪəslɪ] *adv* (**a**) *(in earnest)* en serio; **don't take things so s.** no tome las cosas tan en serio; **s. though** bromas aparte (**b**) *(dangerously, severely)* gravemente, seriamente; **s. damaged** seriamente dañado(a); **s. wounded** herido(a) de gravedad

seriousness ['sɪərɪəsnɪs] *n* gravedad *f*, seriedad *f*; **in all s.** hablando en serio

sermon ['sɜːmən] *n* sermón *m*

serpent ['sɜːpənt] *n Zool & Literary* serpiente *f*

serrated [sɪ'reɪtɪd] *adj* dentado(a), serrado(a); **a knife with a s. edge** un cuchillo de sierra

serum ['sɪərəm] *n* (*pl* **serums** *or* **sera** ['sɪərə]) *Med* suero *m*

servant ['sɜːvənt] *n* (*domestic*) criado(a) *m,f*, sirviente(a) *m,f*; *Fig* servidor(a) *m,f* ◻ **civil s., public s.** funcionario(a) *m,f* del Estado

serve [sɜːv] **1** *vt* (**a**) *(work for)* servir (**b**) *(customer)* servir, atender; *(food, drink)* servir; **are you being served?** ¿le atienden?; **dinner is served** la cena está servida; *(on recipe)* **'serves four'** 'para cuatro personas'; *Rel* **to s. mass** ayudar en misa (**c**) *Ten* sacar, servir (**d**) *(be useful to)* servir, ser útil a; **if my memory serves me right** si no me falla la memoria, si mal no recuerdo; **it serves him right** bien merecido lo tiene (**e**) *(provide for)* **the area is served by both bus and underground** en la zona hay autobús y metro (**f**) *Jur* **to s. a summons on sb** entregar una citación a algn (**g**) *(complete, carry out)* cumplir, hacer; **to s. a prison sentence,** *Fam* **to s. time** cumplir una condena; **to s. one's apprenticeship** hacer el aprendizaje

2 *vi* (**a**) *(in household, army, etc)* servir; **to s. at table** servir la mesa; **to s. on a committee/jury** ser miembro de una comisión/un jurado (**b**) *Ten* sacar, servir (**c**) *(be useful)* servir (**as** de); **to s. as an example** servir de ejemplo

3 *n Ten* saque *m*

serve out, serve up *vt* *(food)* servir

server ['sɜːvər] *n* (**a**) *Rel (at mass)* monaguillo *m* (**b**) *Ten* jugador(ora) *m,f* al servicio (**c**) *(cutlery)* cubierto *m* de servir (**d**) *(tray)* bandeja *f*, salvilla *f* (**e**) *Comptr* servidor *m*

service ['sɜːvɪs] **1** *n* (**a**) *(provided by hotel, etc)* servicio *m*; **after-sales s.** servicio postventa *or* posventa; **at your s.!** ¡a sus órdenes!; **how can I be of s. to you?** ¿en qué puedo servirle?; **military s.** servicio militar; *(on bill)* **s. (charge) included** servicio incluido; **to die in active s.** morir en acto de servicio; **to do sb a s.** hacerle un favor a algn; **to see s.** prestar serivicio ◻ **s. area,** *Br* **services** *(on motorway)* área *f* de servicio; *Br* **s. flat** apartamento *m* con servicio; **s. industry** sector *m* de servicios; **s. road** vía *f* de acceso *or* de salida; *Aut* **s. station** estación *f* de servicio (**b**) *(department, system)* servicio *m*; **medical/social s.** servicios médicos/sociales; **National Health S.** Seguridad Social; **postal s.** servicio de correos; *Mil* **the Services** las Fuerzas Armadas; **the train/bus s. to Bristol** la línea de trenes/autobuses a Bristol ◻ **civil s.** administración *f* pública (**c**) *(maintenance)* revisión *f*, mantenimiento *m*; *(of car)* puesta *f* a punto (**d**) *Rel* oficio *m*, servicios *mpl*; *(mass)* misa *f*; **to hold a s.** celebrar un oficio; *(say mass)* celebrar misa (**e**) *Ten* saque *m*, servicio *m* ◻ **s. line** línea *f* de saque *or* de servicio (**f**) *(set of dishes)* juego *m*, servicio *m* ◻ **dinner s.** vajilla *f*; **tea s.** juego *m* de té

2 *vt* *(car, machine)* revisar

serviceable ['sɜːvɪsəbəl] *adj* (**a**) *(fit for use)* útil, utilizable, servible (**b**) *(practical)* práctico(a); *(durable)* duradero(a)

serviceman ['sɜːvɪsmən] *n* (*pl* **servicemen**) *Mil* militar *m*

servicewoman ['sɜːvɪswʊmən] *n* (*pl* **servicewomen** ['sɜːvɪswɪmɪn]) *Mil* militar *f*

serviette [sɜːvɪ'et] *n Br* servilleta *f* ◻ **s. ring** servilletero *m*

servile ['sɜːvaɪl] *adj* servil

servitude ['sɜːvɪtjuːd] *n* servidumbre *f*; **penal s.** trabajos *mpl* forzados

servo ['sɜːvəʊ] *n* (*pl* **servos**) *Fam* (*abbr* **servomechanism**) servosistema *m*, servomecanismo *m* ◻ **s. brakes** servofrenos *mpl*

servo-assisted ['sɜːvəʊəsɪstɪd] *adj* servoasistido(a); **s.-a. brakes** servofrenos *mpl*

servomechanism ['sɜːvəʊmekənɪzəm] *n* servosistema *m*, servomecanismo *m*

sesame ['sesəmɪ] *n Bot* sésamo *m*, ajonjolí *m*; **open s.!** ¡ábrete sésamo!

session ['seʃən] *n* (**a**) *(meeting)* sesión *f*, junta *f*, reunión *f*; *(sitting)* sesión *f*; **to be in s.** *(gen)* estar reunido(a); *(Parliament, court)* celebrar una sesión; **we're in for a long s.** tenemos para rato (**b**) *Sch Univ (academic year)* año *m or* curso *m* académico

set¹ [set] **1** *vt* (*pt & pp* **set**) (**a**) *(put, place)* poner, colocar; *(dog)* azuzar (**on** contra); *(trap)* tender (**for** para); **the novel to s. in Moscow** la novela se desarrolla en Moscú; **to s. fire to sth** prender fuego a algo; **to s. sb's mind at rest** tranquilizar a algn (**b**) *(fix) (date, time)* fijar, señalar; *(price)* fijar; *(record)* establecer; *(fashion)* imponer (**c**) *(adjust) (mechanism etc)* ajustar; *(bone)* encajar, componer; *(fix) (mechanism etc)* componer, arreglar; **she s. her alarm for six** puso el despertador para las seis; **to s. one's watch** poner el reloj en hora (**d**) *(arrange)* arreglar; **he s. the words to music** puso música a la letra; **I had my hair s.** me han peinado; **to s. the table** poner la mesa (**e**) *(assign) (exam, homework)* poner; *(example)* dar, poner; *(precedent)* sentar (**f**) *(cause to begin, do, etc)* poner; **it s. him thinking** le dio que pensar, le hizo reflexionar; *Naut* **to s. sail** zarpar; **to s. sb free** poner en libertad a algn; **to s. sth going** poner algo en marcha (**g**) *(mount) (diamond etc)* montar, engastar (**h**) *Typ (text)* componer

2 *vi* (**a**) *(sun, moon)* ponerse (**b**) *(jelly, jam)* cuajar; *(glue)* endurecerse; *(cement)* fraguarse, endurecerse; *(bone)* encajarse, componerse (**c**) *(begin)* **to s. to** ponerse a

3 *n* (**a**) *(in hairdressing)* marcado *m*; **shampoo and s.** lavar y marcar (**b**) *(stage) Cin* plató *m*; *Theat* escenario *m*; *(scenery)* decorado *m*

4 *adj* (**a**) *(fixed) (task, idea, purpose)* fijo(a); *(date, time)* señalado(a), determinado(a); *(opinion)* inflexible; *(smile)* rígido(a), forzado(a); *(gaze)* fijo(a); *(speech)* preparado(a); **s. lunch** menú del día; **s. phrase** frase hecha; **s. price** precio fijo; **to be dead s. against sth** oponerse rotundamente a algo; **to be s. in one's ways** tener unas costumbres muy arraigadas, ser reacio(a) al cambio; **to be s. on doing sth** estar empeñado(a) en hacer algo ◻ **s. square** cartabón *m*, escuadra *f* (**b**) *(ready)* listo(a); **on your marks, get s., go!** ¡preparados, listos, ya!

set about *vt* (**a**) *(begin)* empezar; **I don't know how to s. about it** no sé por dónde empezar (**b**) *(attack)* atacar, agredir

set against *vt* (**a**) **to s. one person against another** enemistar a dos personas (**b**) *(balance against)* comparar con

set aside *vt* (**a**) *(time, money)* guardar, reservar; *(differences)* dejar de lado (**b**) *(reject)* rechazar, desechar

set back *vt* (**a**) *(place at a distance)* apartar; **s. back from the road** apartado(a) de la carretera (**b**) *(delay)* retrasar; *(hinder)* entorpecer (**c**) *Fam (cost)* costar

set down *vt* (**a**) *(luggage etc)* poner, dejar (en el suelo); *Br (passengers)* dejar (**b**) *(write down)* poner por escrito

set forth *vi Literary* emprender marcha, partir

set in *vi* *(winter, rain)* comenzar; *(problems, complications)* aparecer, surgir; **panic s. in** cundió el pánico

set off 1 *vi* *(depart)* salir, marcharse, ponerse en camino

2 *vt* (**a**) *(bomb)* hacer estallar; *(burglar alarm)* hacer sonar *or* saltar; *(reaction)* desencadenar (**b**) *(enhance)* hacer resaltar

set out 1 vi (**a**) *(depart)* salir, marcharse, ponerse en camino; **to s. out for ...** partir hacia ... (**b**) *(intend)* **to s. out to do sth** intentar *or* proponerse hacer algo

 2 vt *(arrange, display) (goods)* disponer; *(present) (work)* presentar

set to vi ponerse a trabajar

set up 1 vt (**a**) *(position)* colocar; *(statue, barricades, camp)* levantar; *(assemble) (tent, stall, machinery)* montar (**b**) *(establish) (school, business)* establecer, crear; *Fam* montar; *(committee, inquiry)* constituir; **to s. oneself up as a photographer** establecerse como fotógrafo; **to s. sb up in business** ayudar a alguien a establecerse; **to s. up house** instalarse; **to s. up shop** montar una tienda; *Fam* **to be s. up for life** tener el porvenir asegurado; *Fam* **you've been s. up!** ¡te han timado!

 2 vi establecerse; **to s. up in business** establecerse

set upon vt *(attack)* abalanzarse sobre, atacar

set² [set] **1** n (**a**) *(series)* serie *f*; *(of brushes, golf clubs)* juego *m*; *(of dishes)* juego *m*, servicio *m*; *(of tools)* estuche *m*; *(of turbines etc)* equipo *m*, grupo *m*; *(of books, poems)* colección *f*; *(of teeth)* dentadura *f* ❑ **chess s.** juego *m* de ajedrez; **electric train s.** tren *m* eléctrico; **manicure s.** estuche *m* de manicura; **s. of cutlery** cubertería *f*; **s. of kitchen utensils** batería *f* de cocina; **s. of teeth** dentadura *f*; **tea s.** juego *m* de té (**b**) *(of people)* grupo *m*; *Pej (clique)* pandilla *f*, camarilla *f*; **the smart s.** la gente bien (**c**) *Math* conjunto *m* (**d**) *Ten* set *m* (**e**) *Elec* aparato *m* ❑ **TV s.** televisor *m* (**f**) **to make a dead s. at** *(attack)* emprenderla con; *(seduce)* proponerse ligar con

 2 vt *(pt & pp* **set***) (divide up)* dividir en grupos

setback ['setbæk] n revés *m*, contratiempo *m*

settee [se'tiː] n sofá *m*

setter ['setər] n *(dog)* (perro *m*) setter *m*

setting ['setɪŋ] n (**a**) *(background etc)* marco *m*; *(of novel, film)* escenario *m* (**b**) *(of jewel)* engaste *m*, montura *f* (**c**) *Tech (of controls, machine)* ajuste *m* (**d**) *Typ* composición *f* (**e**) **s. lotion** *(for hair)* fijador *m*

setting-up [setɪŋ'ʌp] n *(creation)* creación *f*, fundación *f*

settle ['setəl] **1** vt (**a**) *(place)* colocar, asentar (**b**) *(decide on)* decidir, acordar; *(date, price)* fijar; *(sort out) (problem)* resolver, solucionar; *(differences)* resolver, arreglar; **that settles it then** queda decidido entonces; *Jur* **to s. a case out of court** llegar a un acuerdo amistoso; **to s. one's affairs** poner los asuntos en orden; *Fam* **that settles it!** ¡se acabó! (**c**) *(pay) (debt)* pagar; *(account)* saldar, liquidar (**d**) *(calm) (nerves)* calmar; *(stomach)* asentar (**e**) *Fam (put an end to)* terminar, acabar con; **I'll soon s. him!** ¡ya me las pagará! (**f**) *(establish) (person)* instalar; *(colonize) (land)* colonizar, poblar

 2 vi (**a**) *(bird, insect)* posarse; *(dust)* depositarse; *(snow)* cuajar; *(sediment)* precipitarse; *(liquid)* asentarse, clarificarse; **a thick fog settled over the city** una densa niebla cayó sobre la ciudad; **to s. into an armchair** acomodarse en un sillón (**b**) *(put down roots)* afincarse, domiciliarse (**c**) *(weather)* serenarse, estabilizarse (**d**) *(child, nerves)* calmarse; *(situation)* normalizarse (**e**) *(pay)* pagar; *Jur* **to s. out of court** llegar a un acuerdo amistoso

settle down vi (**a**) *(put down roots)* afincarse, domiciliarse, instalarse; *(marry)* casarse; *(become more responsible)* sentar la cabeza (**b**) *(become accustomed)* acostumbrarse, adaptarse (**c**) *(begin)* **to s. down to work** ponerse a trabajar (**d**) *(child)* calmarse; *(situation)* normalizarse, volver a la normalidad

settle for vt conformarse con, contentarse con

settle in vi *(move in)* instalarse; *(become adapted)* acostumbrarse, adaptarse

settle into vt *(get used to)* acostumbrarse a, adaptarse a, hacerse a

settle on vt *(decide on)* decidirse por; *(choose)* escoger; *(agree on)* ponerse de acuerdo sobre

settle with vt *(pay debt to)* ajustar cuentas con

settled ['setəld] adj *(stable)* estable

settlement ['setəlmənt] n (**a**) *(agreement)* acuerdo *m*, solución *f*; **out-of-court s.** acuerdo amistoso (**b**) *(of debt)* pago *m*; *(of account)* liquidación *f* (**c**) *(dowry)* dote *m*; *(pension)* pensión *f*, venta *f* (**d**) *(colonization)* colonización *f*, población *f* (**e**) *(colony)* colonia *f*; *(village)* pueblo *m*, poblado *m*

settler ['setlə] n colono *m*, colonizador(a) *m,f*, poblador(a) *m,f*

set-to ['set'tuː] n *Fam (quarrel, fight)* riña *f*, pelea *f*

setup ['setəp] n *(system)* sistema *m*; *(situation)* situación *f*; *Slang* montaje *m*

seven ['sevən] **1** adj siete *inv*; **all s. of them left** se marcharon todos siete; **chapter/page s.** el capítulo/la página número siete; **it costs s. dollars** cuesta siete dólares; **it's s. minutes to five** son las cinco menos siete, faltan siete minutos para las cinco; **s. hundred** setecientos(as); **s. thousand** siete mil; **she is s. years old** tiene siete años; **they live at number s.** viven en el número siete

 2 n siete *m inv*; **a boy of s.** un niño de siete años; **come at s.** ven a las siete; **it's s. o'clock** son las siete; **s. and s. are fourteen** siete más siete son catorce; **the clock struck s.** dieron las siete; **the s. of hearts** el siete de corazones; **there were s. of us** éramos siete; **they are sold in sevens** se venden de siete en siete; **three out of s.** tres sobre siete; **we live at s. Carlton Street** vivimos en la calle Carlton, número siete

seventeen [sevən'tiːn] adj & n diecisiete *(m)*, diez y siete *(m)*; *see also* **seven**

seventeenth [sevən'tiːnθ] **1** adj decimoséptimo(a); **the s. century** el siglo diecisiete

 2 n *(in series)* decimoséptimo(a) *m,f*; *(fraction)* decimo-séptima parte *f*; **the s. of May** el diecisiete de mayo; *see also* **seventh**

seventh ['sevənθ] **1** adj séptimo(a); **Edward the s.** Eduardo séptimo; **he was the s. to arrive** fue el séptimo en llegar; **the s. century** el siglo siete; **the s. of October, October the s.** el siete de octubre; **to be in s. heaven** estar en la gloria, estar en el séptimo cielo; **to come s.** quedar en séptimo lugar; **we're leaving on the s.** nos marchamos el día siete; **your letter of the s.** su carta del día siete del corriente

 2 n (**a**) *(in series)* séptimo(a) *m,f* (**b**) *(fraction)* séptimo *m*, séptima parte *f*; **three sevenths** tres séptimos (**c**) *Mus* séptima *f*

seventieth ['sevəntɪθ] **1** adj septuagésimo(a)

 2 n (**a**) *(in series)* septuagésimo(a) *m,f* (**b**) *(fraction)* septuagésimo *m*, septuagésima parte *f*; *see also* **seventh**

seventy [sevəntɪ] **1** adj setenta *inv*; **about s. cars/ passengers** unos setenta coches/pasajeros; **he's about s. (years old)** anda por los setenta; **he will be s. (years old) tomorrow** mañana cumplirá los setenta años; **s. per cent of the staff** el setenta por ciento del personal

 2 n setenta *m inv*; **he must be in his seventies** debe andar por los setenta; **in the seventies** durante los (años) setenta; **the temperature was in the seventies** hacía más de setenta grados; **to be in one's early/late seventies** tener poco más de setenta/casi ochenta años; **to do s.** ir a setenta millas la hora

sever ['sevər] vt *(cut)* cortar; *Fig (relations, communications)* romper

several ['sevərəl] **1** adj (**a**) *(more than a few)* varios(as) (**b**) *(different)* distintos(as); *(separate)* respectivos(as)

 2 pron algunos(as)

severance ['sevərəns] *n (of relations etc)* ruptura *f* ❑ *Ind* **s. pay** indemnización *f* por despido

severe [sɪ'vɪər] *adj (gen)* severo(a); *(discipline, measures)* severo(a), riguroso(a), estricto(a); *(climate)* duro(a), riguroso(a); *(criticism, punishment)* severo(a); *(illness, loss)* grave, serio(a); *(blow)* duro(a), fuerte; *(pain)* agudo(a); *(style, architecture)* austero(a); **to be s. on sb** ser muy duro(a) con algn

severely [sə'vɪəlɪ] *adv (gen)* severamente; *(criticized, punished)* severamente, rigurosamente; *(ill)* gravemente

severity [sɪ'verɪtɪ] *n,* **severeness** [sɪ'vɪənɪs] *n* **(a)** *(harshness) (of person, punishment, criticism)* severidad *f*; *(of climate)* rigor *m* **(b)** *(of pain)* intensidad *f*; *(of illness)* gravedad *f* **(c)** *(austerity) (of style, architecture)* austeridad *f*, sobriedad *f*

Seville [sə'vɪl] *n* Sevilla

sew [səʊ] *vt & vi (pt* **sewed***; pp* **sewed** *or* **sewn***)* coser **(on a)**

sew up *vt (stitch together)* coser; *(mend)* remendar; *Fig* **it's all sewn up** ya está todo arreglado

sewage ['suːɪdʒ] *n* aguas *fpl* residuales ❑ **s. disposal** depuración *f* de aguas residuales; **s. farm** *or* **works** estación *f* depuradora; **s. system** alcantarillado *m*

sewer ['suːər] *n* alcantarilla *f*, cloaca *f*, albañal *m*; **main s.** colector *m*

sewerage ['suːərɪdʒ] *n* alcantarillado *m*

sewing ['səʊɪŋ] *n* costura *f* ❑ **s. machine** máquina *f* de coser

sewn [səʊn] *pp see* **sew**

sex [seks] *n* sexo *m*; **the fair s.** el bello sexo; **the opposite s.** el sexo opuesto; **the weaker s.** el sexo débil; **to have s. with sb** tener relaciones sexuales con algn; *Fam* hacer el amor *or* acostarse con algn ❑ **s. appeal** sex-appeal *m*; *Fam* gancho *m*; **s. change** cambio *m* de sexo; **s. education** educación *f* sexual; **s. maniac** obseso(a) *m,f* (sexual); **s. shop** sex-shop *m*; **s. symbol** símbolo *m* sexual, sex-symbol *m*

sexism ['seksɪzəm] *n* sexismo *m*

sexist ['seksɪst] *adj & n* sexista *(mf)*

sexless ['sekslɪs] *adj* asexual, asexuado(a)

sexologist [sek'sɒlədʒɪst] *n* sexólogo(a) *m,f*

sexology [sek'sɒlədʒɪ] *n* sexología *f*

sextet [seks'tet] *n Mus* sexteto *m*

sexton ['sekstən] *n Rel* sacristán *m*

sexual ['seksjʊəl] *adj* sexual ❑ **s. abuse** abusos *mpl* deshonestos, abuso *m* sexual; **s. discrimination** discriminación *f* sexual; **s. harassment** acoso *m* sexual

sexuality [seksjʊ'ælɪtɪ] *n* sexualidad *f*

sexually ['seksjʊəlɪ] *adv* sexualmente; **s. transmitted disease** enfermedad *f* de transmisión sexual

sexy ['seksɪ] *adj* **(sexier, sexiest)** *Fam* sexi, erótico(a)

Seychelles [seɪ'ʃel(z)] *npl* Seychelles *fpl*

Sgt *(abbr* **Sergeant)** Sargento *m*, Sarg

sh [ʃ] *interj* ¡chsss!, ¡shis(t)!

shabbiness ['ʃæbɪnɪs] *n* **(a)** *(of dress)* pobreza *f*, aspecto *m* lastimoso *or* harapiento; *(raggedness)* aspecto *m* desharrapado *or* andrajoso; *(of furniture etc)* aspecto *m* descuidado, mal aspecto *m* **(b)** *(of treatment)* mezquindad *f*

shabby ['ʃæbɪ] *adj* **(shabbier, shabbiest) (a)** *(garment)* raído(a), desharrapado(a); *(furniture)* de aspecto lastimoso; *(house)* desvencijado(a), destartalado(a); *(person)* pobremente vestido(a); *(in rags)* andrajoso(a), harapiento(a); *(unkempt)* desaseado(a) **(b)** *(treatment)* mezquino(a); **a s. trick** una mala pasada

shack [ʃæk] **1** *n* casucha *f*, *Esp* chabola *f*, *CSur Ven* rancho *m*
2 *vi Fam* **to s. up with sb** juntarse con algn

shackle ['ʃækəl] **1** *vt (prisoner)* poner grilletes a; *Fig (plan etc)* poner trabas a
2 shackles *npl* grilletes *mpl*, grillos *mpl*; *Fig* trabas *fpl*; **to cast** *or* **throw off one's s.** librarse de las ataduras *or* las trabas

shade [ʃeɪd] **1** *n* **(a)** *(shadow)* sombra *f*; **in the s.** a la sombra; *Fig* **to put sb in the s.** dejar a algn en la sombra, hacer sombra a algn **(b)** *(eyeshade)* visera *f*; *(lampshade)* pantalla *f*, *US (blind)* persiana *f* **(c)** *(of colour)* tono *m*, matiz *m*; *Fig (of opinion, meaning)* matiz *m*; *Fig* **of every s. and hue** de toda calaña **(d)** *(small amount)* poquito *m* **(e) shades** *Slang* gafas *fpl* *or Am* anteojos *mpl* de sol
2 *vt (from sun)* proteger contra el sol, resguardar

shade in *vt Art* sombrear

shading ['ʃeɪdɪŋ] *n Art* degradación *f*

shadow ['ʃædəʊ] **1** *n* **(a)** *(shade etc)* sombra *f*; *(darkness)* oscuridad *f*; *Art* sombreado *m*; **to cast a s.** hacer sombra, proyectar una sombra; *Fig* ensombrecer **(over -)**; *Fig* **she's a s. of her former self** es sólo una sombra de lo que fue; *Fam* **five o'clock s.** barba *f* de un día; *Fig* **without a s. of a doubt** sin lugar a dudas ❑ **eye s.** sombra *f* de ojos; *TV* **s. mask** máscara *f* perforada con ranuras; *Theat* **s. play** sombras *fpl* chinescas **(b)** *Br Parl* de la oposición; **the S. Cabinet** el gabinete de la oposición
2 *vt Fig (follow)* seguir la pista a

shadow-box ['ʃædəʊbɒks] *vi Fig* luchar contra molinos de viento

shadowy ['ʃædəʊɪ] *adj (dark)* oscuro(a); *(hazy)* vago(a), impreciso(a)

shady ['ʃeɪdɪ] *adj* **(shadier, shadiest) (a)** *(place)* a la sombra; *(tree)* que da sombra **(b)** *(suspicious) (person)* sospechoso(a); *(deal)* turbio(a)

shaft [ʃɑːft] *n* **(a)** *(of tool, golf club)* mango *m*; *(of lance)* asta *f*; *(of arrow)* astil *m*; *(of cart)* vara *f* **(b)** *Tech* eje *m* ❑ **drive s.** árbol *m* motor **(c)** *(of mine)* pozo *m*; *(of lift, elevator)* hueco *m* **(d)** *(beam) (of light)* rayo *m*

shag¹ [ʃæg] *n (shredded tobacco)* tabaco *m* picado

shag² [ʃæg] *n Orn* cormorán *m* moñudo

shag³ [ʃæg] *vt Br Vulg Esp* follar, *Am* cogerse a

shaggy ['ʃægɪ] *adj* **(shaggier, shaggiest)** *(hairy)* peludo(a); *(long-haired)* melenudo(a); *(hair, beard)* desgreñado(a), enmarañado(a); *Fam* **a s. dog story** un cuento chino

shah [ʃɑː] *n* cha *m*

shake [ʃeɪk] **1** *n* **(a)** *(gen)* sacudida *f*; **he denied it with a s. of the head** lo negó con un movimiento de la cabeza; *Fam* **in two shakes, in half a s.** en un santiamén **(b)** *Fam* **the shakes** *(trembling)* temblequera *f* *sing*; *(feverish)* tiritera *f* *sing*; **it gives me the s.** me hace temblar de miedo; *Fam* **it's no great s.** no es nada del otro jueves *or* mundo **(c)** *(milkshake)* batido *m*
2 *vt (pt* **shook***; pp* **shaken***) (carpet etc)* sacudir; *(bottle)* agitar; *(dice)* mover; *(building, table)* hacer temblar; **the news shook him** la noticia le conmocionó; **to s. hands with sb** estrechar *or* dar la mano a algn; **to s. one's head** negar con la cabeza; *Fam* **to s. a leg** darse prisa, *Am* apurarse
3 *vi (person, building)* temblar, estremecerse; **to s. with cold** tiritar de frío; **to s. with fear** temblar de miedo; **to s. with laughter** troncharse de risa

shake down *vt US Slang* **(a)** *(blackmail)* chantajear **(b)** *(search)* cachear

shake off *vt* **(a)** *(dust etc)* sacudirse **(b)** *Fig (bad habit)* librarse de; *(cough, cold)* quitarse *or Am* sacarse de encima; *(pursuer)* librarse de, dar esquinazo a

shake up *vt* **(a)** *(liquid in bottle)* agitar; *(pillow)* sacudir **(b)** *Fig (shock, stun)* conmocionar, trastornar **(c)** *Fig (reorganize)* reorganizar

shaken ['ʃeɪkən] *pp see* **shake**

Shakespearian [ʃeɪk'spɪərɪən] *adj* shakesperiano(a)

shake-up ['ʃeɪkʌp] *n Fig* reorganización *f*

shaky ['ʃeɪkɪ] *adj* (**shakier, shakiest**) *(hand, voice)* tembloroso(a); *(step)* inseguro(a); *(handwriting)* temblón(ona); *(table, ladder)* inestable; *(health)* débil; *(memory)* olvidadizo(a); *(argument)* sin fundamento; **his French is s.** su francés deja bastante que desear

shale [ʃeɪl] *n Geol* esquisto *m*

shall [ʃæl, *unstressed* ʃəl] *v aux* (**a**) *(used to form future tense) (first person only)* **I s.** *or* **I'll buy it tomorrow** lo compraré mañana; **I s. not** *or* **I shan't say anything about it** no diré nada al respecto; **we s.** *or* **we'll see them on Sunday** les veremos el domingo (**b**) *(used to form questions) (usu first person)* **s. I close the door?** ¿cierro la puerta?; **s. I mend it for you,?** ¿quieres que te lo repare?; **s. we go?** ¿nos, vamos? (**c**) *(emphatic, command, threat) (all persons)* **we s. overcome** venceremos; **you s. leave immediately** te irás enseguida

shallot [ʃə'lɒt] *n Bot* chalote *m*

shallow ['ʃæləʊ] **1** *adj (gen)* poco profundo(a); *Fig* superficial; **s. dish** plato llano
2 shallows *npl* bajío *m sing*, bajos *mpl*

shallowness ['ʃæləʊnɪs] *n (gen)* poca profundidad *f*, falta *f* de profundidad; *Fig* superficialidad *f*, falsa apariencia *f*

sham [ʃæm] **1** *adj (gen)* falso(a); *(illness etc)* fingido(a); *(jewellery)* de bisutería
2 *n* (**a**) *(pretence)* simulacro *m*, farsa *f*; **it's all a big s.** es un timo como una catedral (**b**) *(person)* fantasma *m*, fantoche *m*
3 *vt (pt & pp* **shammed**) fingir, simular
4 *vi* fingir, fingirse; *Fam* hacer el papipé; **she's just shamming** lo está fingiendo

shamble ['ʃæmbəl] *vi* **to s. along** andar arrastrando los pies, andar con paso pesado

shambles ['ʃæmbəlz] *n (chaos, mess)* confusión *f*, desorden *m*; **the performance was a s.** la función fue un desastre; *Fam* **what a s.!** ¡qué follón!

shambolic [ʃæm'bɒlɪk] *adj Fam* desastroso(a)

shame [ʃeɪm] **1** *n* (**a**) *(feeling of humiliation)* vergüenza *f*, *Am salvo RP* pena *f*; **s. on you!** ¡qué vergüenza!; **to bring s. on** deshonrar a; **to put to s.** *(disgrace)* deshonrar; *(surpass by far)* humillar, aplastar (**b**) *(pity)* pena *f*, lástima *f*; **what a s.!** ¡qué pena!, ¡qué lástima!
2 *vt* avergonzar, *Am salvo RP* apenar; *(disgrace)* deshonrar

shamefaced [ʃeɪm'feɪst] *adj* avergonzado(a), *Am salvo RP* apenado(a)

shameful ['ʃeɪmfʊl] *adj* vergonzoso(a); **how s.!** ¡qué vergüenza!

shameless ['ʃeɪmlɪs] *adj* desvergonzado(a); **he's about being it** no le da ninguna vergüenza *or Am salvo RP* pena hacerlo

shamelessness ['ʃeɪmlɪsnɪs] *n* desvergüenza *f*, descaro *m*

shammy ['ʃæmɪ] *n* **s. (leather)** gamuza *f*

shampoo [ʃæm'puː] **1** *n (pl* **shampoos**) champú *m*
2 *vt* lavar con champú; *(hair)* lavarse

shamrock ['ʃæmrɒk] *n Bot* trébol *m*

shandy ['ʃændɪ] *n Br* cerveza *f* con gaseosa, *Esp* clara *f*

shank [ʃæŋk] *n (of person)* espinilla *f*; *(of horse)* caña *f*; *(of lamb, beef)* pierna *f* (deshuesada)

shanty[1] ['ʃæntɪ] *n Mus* **(sea) s.** saloma *f*

shanty[2] ['ʃæntɪ] *n (dwelling)* casucha *f*, *Esp* chabola *f*, *CSur Ven* rancho *m*

shantytown ['ʃæntɪtaʊn] *n Esp* barrio *m* de chabolas,

Am barriada *f*, *Andes* pueblo *m* joven, *Arg Bol* villa *f* miseria, *Méx* ciudad *f* perdida

shape [ʃeɪp] **1** *n* (**a**) *(form, outline)* forma *f*; *(shadow)* silueta *m*, figura *f*; **in the s. of** en forma de; **to take s.** tomar forma; **what s. is it?** ¿qué forma tiene? (**b**) *(order, condition) (thing)* **in good/bad s.** en buen/mal estado; **he was in no s. to work** no estaba en condiciones de trabajar; **out of s.** en baja forma; *(health) (person)* **to be in good s.** estar en forma; **to get oneself into s.** ponerse en forma
2 *vt (gen)* dar forma a; *(clay)* modelar; *(stone)* tallar; *(character)* formar; *(future, destiny)* decidir, determinar; **star-shaped** con forma de estrella
3 *vi (also* **s. up**) tomar forma; **how's it shaping up?** ¿cómo evoluciona?; **to s. up well** *(events)* tomar buen cariz, prometer; *(person)* hacer progresos, prometer

shapeless ['ʃeɪplɪs] *adj* sin forma, informe

shapelessness ['ʃeɪplɪsnɪs] *n* falta *f* de forma

shapely ['ʃeɪplɪ] *adj* (**shapelier, shapeliest**) *(woman)* escultural

shape-up ['ʃeɪpʌp] *n* **s.-up classes** clases *fpl* de gimnasia *or* de puesta a punto

share ['ʃeər] **1** *n* (**a**) *(portion)* parte *f*; **to do one's s.** hacer su parte; *Fig* **the lion's s.** la parte del león; *Fam* **to go shares** compartir (**b**) *Fin* acción *f* ❑ **s. certificate** certificado *m* de acciones; **s. index** índice *m* de la Bolsa; **s. prices** cotizaciones *fpl*
2 *vt* (**a**) *(divide)* dividir (**b**) *(have in common)* compartir
3 *vi* compartir; **s. and s. alike** a partes iguales; **I s. in your sorrow** le acompaño en el sentimiento; **to s. in the profits** participar en los beneficios

share out *vt* repartir, distribuir

shareholder ['ʃeəhəʊldər] *n* accionista *mf*

shareholding ['ʃeəhəʊldɪŋ] *n Fin* participación *f* accionarial

share-out ['ʃeəraʊt] *n* reparto *m*

shark [ʃɑːk] *n* (**a**) *(fish)* tiburón *m* ❑ **blue s.** tintorera *f* (**b**) *Fam (swindler)* estafador(a) *m,f*, timador(a) *m,f* ❑ **loan s.** usurero(a) *m,f*

sharp [ʃɑːp] **1** *adj* (**a**) *(razor, knife)* afilado(a), *Am* filoso(a); *(needle, pencil)* puntiagudo(a) (**b**) *(angle)* agudo(a); *(features)* anguloso(a); *Aut (bend)* cerrado(a); *(slope)* empinado(a) (**c**) *(outline)* definido(a); *(photograph)* nítido(a); *(contrast)* marcado(a) (**d**) *(observant)* perspicaz; *(clever)* listo(a), inteligente; *(quick-witted)* (d)espabilado(a), avispado(a); *(cunning)* astuto(a); **s. practice** mañas *fpl*, manejos *mpl* (**e**) *(sudden)* brusco(a), repentino(a) (**f**) *(intense) (pain, cry)* agudo(a); *(wind)* penetrante; *(frost)* fuerte (**g**) *(taste) (sour)* acre; *(acidic)* ácido(a) (**h**) *(criticism)* mordaz; *(reprimand)* severo(a); *(temper)* arisco(a), violento(a); *(tone)* seco(a); *(tongue)* viperina(a) (**i**) *Mus* sostenido(a); **F s.** fa sostenido; *(out of tune)* desafinado(a)
2 *adv* (**a**) *(exactly)* **at 2 o'clock s.** a las dos en punto (**b**) *(quickly)* **look s.!** ¡rápido!, ¡muévete!; **to stop s.** pararse en seco
3 *n Mus* sostenido *m*

sharp-edged [ʃɑːp'edʒd] *adj* afilado(a)

sharpen ['ʃɑːpən] *vt* (**a**) *(knife)* afilar; *(pencil)* sacar punta a (**b**) *Fig (desire, intelligence)* agudizar; *(appetite)* abrir; **to s. one's wits** (d)espabilarse

sharpener ['ʃɑːpənər] *n (for knife)* afilador *m*; *(for pencil)* sacapuntas *m inv*

sharp-eyed [ʃɑːp'aɪd] *adj* con ojos de lince *or* de águila

sharply ['ʃɑːplɪ] *adv* (**a**) *(abruptly)* bruscamente, repentinamente (**b**) *(clearly)* claramente, marcadamente

sharpshooter ['ʃɑːpʃuːtər] *n Mil* tirador(a) *m,f* de primera *or* de élite

sharp-sighted [ʃɑːp'saɪtɪd] *adj* observador(a)

sharp-tongued [ʃɑːpˈtʌŋd] *adj* de lengua viperina

sharp-witted [ʃɑːpˈwɪtɪd] *adj* listo(a), avispado(a), perspicaz

shat [ʃæt] *pt & pp see* **shit**

shatter [ˈʃætər] **1** *vt (gen)* hacer añicos *or* pedazos, romper, despedazar; *(health)* destrozar, minar, quebrantar; *(nerves)* destrozar; *(hopes)* frustrar
2 *vi (gen)* hacerse añicos *or* pedazos, romperse, despedazarse; *(esp glass)* astillarse

shattered [ˈʃætəd] *adj Fam (shocked)* trastornado(a), pasmado(a); *(tired)* reventado(a)

shattering [ˈʃætərɪŋ] *adj (blow, defeat)* aplastante, contundente; *(news, experience)* terrible

shatterproof [ˈʃætəpruːf] *adj* inastillable

shave [ʃeɪv] **1** *n* afeitado *m*; **to have a s.** afeitarse; *Fig* **to have a close** *or* **narrow s.** escaparse *or* salvarse por los pelos
2 *vt (pt shaved; pp shaved or shaven* [ˈʃeɪvən]) *(person)* afeitar; *(wood)* cepillar; **to s. off one's beard** afeitarse la barba
3 *vi* afeitarse

shaver [ˈʃeɪvər] *n* **(electric) s.** máquina *f* de afeitar

shaving [ˈʃeɪvɪŋ] *n* **(a)** *(thin stip of wood)* viruta *f* **(b)** *(of the face)* afeitado *m* ▫ **s. brush** brocha *f* de afeitar; **s. cream** crema *f* de afeitar; **s. foam** espuma *f* de afeitar

shawl [ʃɔːl] *n (garment)* chal *m*, *Am* rebozo *m*

she [ʃiː] **1** *pers pron* ella; **it was s. who did it** fue ella quien lo hizo; **s. and I** ella y yo
2 *n* **is it a he or a s.?** *(animal)* ¿es macho o hembra?; *(baby)* ¿es niño o niña?

she- [ʃiː] *pref (of animal)* hembra; **s.-bear** osa *f*; **s.-cat** gata *f*

sheaf [ʃiːf] *n (pl sheaves)* *Agr* gavilla *f*; *(of arrows)* haz *m*; *(of papers, banknotes)* fajo *m*

shear [ʃɪər] *(pt sheared; pp shorn or sheared)* **1** *vt (sheep)* esquilar; *Fig* **to be shorn of sth** verse despojado(a) de algo, quedarse sin algo
2 *vi* **(a)** esquilar ovejas **(b)** *(break)* **to s. off** *or* **through** cortar

shearer [ˈʃɪərər] *n* esquilador(a) *m,f*

shearing [ˈʃɪərɪŋ] *n* esquileo *m*, esquila *f*

shears [ʃɪəz] *npl (gen)* tijeras *f* (grandes); *(for metal)* cizalla *f* sing; **a pair of s.** unas tijeras

shearwater [ˈʃɪəwɔːtər] *n Orn* pardela *f*

sheath [ʃiːθ] *n* **(a)** *(for sword)* vaina *f*; *(for knife, scissors)* funda *f*; *(for cable)* forro *m*, cubierta *f* ▫ **s. knife** cuchillo *m* de monte **(b)** *(contraceptive)* preservativo *m*, condón *m*

sheaves [ʃiːvz] *npl see* **sheaf**

shed¹ [ʃed] *n (in garden)* cobertizo *m*, tinglado *m*; *(workmen's hut)* barraca *f*; *(for cattle)* establo *m*; *(in factory)* nave *f*, *Andes Carib RP* galpón *m*

shed² [ʃed] *vt (pt & pp shed)* **(a)** *(get rid of) (clothes, leaves)* despojarse de; *(unwanted thing)* deshacerse de; **a lorry has s. its load on the motorway** un camión ha perdido su carga en la autopista; **the snake s. its skin** la serpiente mudó de piel; *Fam* **to s. a few pounds** perder unos kilos **(b)** *(pour forth) (blood, tears)* derramar; *Fig* **to s. light on** aclarar

sheen [ʃiːn] *n* brillo *m*, lustre *m*

sheep [ʃiːp] *n inv* oveja *f*; *Fig* **the black s. of the family** la oveja negra de la familia ▫ **s. farming** cría *f* de ovejas

sheep-dip [ˈʃiːpdɪp] *n* baño *m* desinfectante (para ovejas)

sheepdog [ˈʃiːpdɒg] *n* perro *m* pastor

sheepfold [ˈʃiːpfəʊld] *n* redil *m*, aprisco *m*

sheepish [ˈʃiːpɪʃ] *adj* tímido(a), avergonzado(a)

sheepishness [ˈʃiːpɪʃnɪs] *n* timidez *f*

sheepskin [ˈʃiːpskɪn] *n* piel *f* de carnero ▫ **s. jacket** pelliza *f*, zamarra *f*

sheer¹ [ʃɪər] *adj* **(a)** *(total, utter)* total, absoluto(a), puro(a); **in s. desperation** a la desesperada **(b)** *(cliff)* escarpado(a); *(drop)* vertical **(c)** *(transparent) (stockings, cloth)* fino(a)

sheer² [ʃɪər] *vi Naut* **to s. off** *or* **away** desviarse; *Fig* apartarse

sheet [ʃiːt] **1** *n* **(a)** *(on bed)* sábana *f*; **bottom s.** sábana bajera; **top s.** encimera *f*; *Fig* **as white as a s.** blanco como el papel **(b)** *(of paper)* hoja *f*; *(of tin, glass, plastic)* lámina *f*; *(of water, ice)* capa *f*; *(of flames, rain)* cortina *f* ▫ *Com* **balance s.** balance *m*; *Com* **order s.** hoja *f* de pedidos; *Comptr* **s. feeder** alimentador *m* de hojas sueltas; **s. lightning** relámpago *m*, fucilazo *m*; **s. metal** chapa *f* de metal; **s. music** partituras *fpl* sueltas
2 *vi (rain)* diluviar

sheetfeed [ˈʃiːtfiːd] *n Comptr* alimentador *m* de hojas sueltas

sheik(h) [ʃeɪk] *n* jeque *m*

shelf [ʃelf] *n (pl shelves)* **(a)** *(bookcase)* anaquel *m*, estante *m*; *(in cupboard)* tabla *f*, anaquel *m*; *(on wall)* estante *m*, repisa *f*; *(in oven)* parrilla *f*; **(set of) shelves** estantería *f*, *Fam* **to be left on the s.** quedarse para vestir santos ▫ *Com* **s. life** duración *f* **(b)** *(in rock)* promontorio *m*; *(underwater)* plataforma *f* ▫ **continental s.** plataforma *f* continental

shell [ʃel] **1** *n* **(a)** *(of egg, nut)* cáscara *f*; *(of pea)* vaina *f*; *(of tortoise, lobster, etc)* caparazón *m*; *(of snail, oyster, etc)* concha *f*; *Fig* **to come out of one's s.** salir del cascarón **(b)** *(of building)* armazón *m*, esqueleto *m*; *(of ship)* casco *m* **(c)** *Mil (mortar etc)* obús *m*, proyectil *m*; *(cartridge)* cartucho *m* ▫ *Med* **s. shock** neurosis *f* de guerra
2 *vt* **(a)** *(peas)* desvainar; *(nuts)* descascarar, pelar **(b)** *Mil* bombardear

shell out *vt Fam (money)* poner, *Esp* apoquinar

shellac [ʃəˈlæk, ˈʃelæk] *n (resin)* laca *f*; *(varnish)* barniz *m*

shellfire [ˈʃelfaɪər] *n Mil* bombardeo *m*

shellfish [ˈʃelfɪʃ] *n inv* marisco *m*, mariscos *mpl*

shelling [ˈʃelɪŋ] *n Mil* bombardeo *m*

shellproof [ˈʃelpruːf] *adj* a prueba de bombas

shell-shocked [ˈʃelʃɒkt] *adj Med* que padece neurosis de guerra

shelter [ˈʃeltər] **1** *n* **(a)** *(protection)* abrigo *m*, protección *f*, amparo *m*; **to take s.** refugiarse **(from** de) **(b)** *(gen) (place)* refugio *m*, cobijo *m*; *(for homeless etc)* asilo *m*; *(in mountain)* albergue *m* ▫ **air-raid s.** refugio *m* antiaéreo; **bus s.** marquesina *f*; **fallout s.** refugio *m* atómico
2 *vt (a) (protect)* abrigar, proteger, amparar **(b)** *(take into one's home)* esconder, dar refugio a
3 *vi* refugiarse, ponerse a cubierto; **to s. from the rain** abrigarse de la lluvia

sheltered [ˈʃeltəd] *adj (place)* abrigado(a), protegido(a); **to lead a s. life** vivir apartado(a) del mundo ▫ *Br* **s. housing** *or* **homes** viviendas *fpl* de protección oficial para la tercera edad

shelve [ʃelv] *vt* **(a)** *(place on shelf)* poner *or* ordenar en la estantería **(b)** *Fig (postpone)* dar carpetazo a, arrinconar

shelves [ʃelvz] *npl see* **shelf**

shelving [ˈʃelvɪŋ] *n* estanterías *fpl*

shepherd [ˈʃepəd] **1** *n* pastor *m* ▫ **s. boy** zagal *m*; *Culin* **s.'s pie** pastel *m* de carne picada con puré de papas
2 *vt Fig* **to s. sb in** hacer entrar a algn; **to s. sb out** acompañar a algn hasta la puerta

shepherdess [ˈʃepədɪs] *n* pastora *f*

sherbet [ˈʃɑːbət] *n* **(a)** *Br (sweet powder)* polvos *mpl* azucarados **(b)** *US (ice)* sorbete *m*

sheriff ['ʃerɪf] n US sheriff m; Br (in England and Wales) = representante de la Corona; Br (in Scotland) juez m de primera instancia

sherry ['ʃerɪ] n jerez m, vino m de jerez

Shetland ['ʃetlənd] n **the S. Isles, the Shetlands** las Islas Shetland ❑ **S. pony** poney m Shetland; **S. wool** lana f Shetland

shield [ʃiːld] **1** n (**a**) (of knight) escudo m; (of policeman) placa f (**b**) Tech (on machinery) blindaje m, pantalla f protectora
2 vt proteger (**from** de); **to s. one's eyes** taparse los ojos

shift [ʃɪft] **1** n (**a**) (change) cambio m; **a s. towards** un movimiento hacia; **there has been a s. in policy** ha habido un cambio de política ❑ US Aut (gear) **s.** cambio m de velocidades; (on typewriter) **s. key** tecla f de mayúsculas (**b**) (period of work, group of workers) turno m, tanda f; **she's on the 4 to 10 s.** está en el turno de 4 a 10; **to be on the day s.** hacer el turno de día; **to work (in) shifts** trabajar por turnos (**c**) (expedient) expediente m, recurso m; **to make s. with/without sth** conformarse con/arreglárselas sin algo
2 vt (change) cambiar; (move) cambiar de sitio, trasladar, desplazar; US Aut **to s. gears** cambiar de marcha; Fig **to s. one's ground** cambiar de táctica, adoptar una nueva postura
3 vi (**a**) (move) mover; (change place) cambiar de sitio; (cargo) desplazarse; (wind, opinion) cambiar; US Aut cambiar de marcha; **to s. over** or **up** apartarse, correrse; Fam **he won't s.** no se quiere mover; Fam **s.!** ¡quita or Am saca de en medio! (**b**) (manage) **to s. for oneself** arreglárselas

shiftless ['ʃɪftlɪs] n perezoso(a), vago(a)

shiftwork ['ʃɪftwɜːk] n trabajo m por turnos

shifty ['ʃɪftɪ] adj (shiftier, shiftiest) furtivo(a), disimulado(a), sospechoso(a); **s. look** mirada huidiza

Shiite ['ʃiːaɪt] n Rel chiíta mf

shillelagh [ʃə'leɪlɪ] n Ir cachiporra f

shilling ['ʃɪlɪŋ] n Fin chelín m

shillyshally ['ʃɪlɪʃælɪ] vi (pt & pp shillyshallied) Fam vacilar, titubear

shimmer ['ʃɪmər] **1** vi relucir, rielar; (shine) brillar
2 n luz f trémula, reflejo m trémulo; (shining) brillo m

shimmering ['ʃɪmərɪŋ] adj reluciente, brillante

shin [ʃɪn] **1** n Anat espinilla f, RP canilla f; Culin (of meat) jarrete m ❑ Sport **s. pad** espinillera f, RP canillera f
2 vi **to s. up a tree** trepar a un árbol

shinbone ['ʃɪnbəʊn] n Anat tibia f

shindy ['ʃɪndɪ] n Fam lío m, jaleo m; **to kick up a s.** armar un lío or jaleo

shine [ʃaɪn] **1** vi (pt & pp shone) (**a**) (sun, light) brillar; (polished metal) relucir; Fig **his face shone with happiness** su cara irradiaba felicidad (**b**) Fig (excel) sobresalir (**at** en)
2 vt (**a**) (light, lamp) dirigir; **s. the light over there** dirige la luz hacia allá (**b**) (pt & pp shined) (polish) sacar brillo a; (shoes) limpiar, lustrar
3 n brillo m, lustre m; **to give one's shoes a s.** limpiarse or lustrarse los zapatos; **to give sth a s.** sacar brillo a algo; Fig **come rain or (come) s.** pase lo que pase; Fam **to take a s. to sb** tomarle cariño a algn

shiner ['ʃaɪnər] n Fam ojo m morado or Esp a la funerala

shingle ['ʃɪŋgəl] n (**a**) (pebbles) guijarros mpl (**b**) (roof tile) tablilla f (**c**) US Fam (name plate) placa f

shingles ['ʃɪŋgəlz] npl Med herpes m

shining ['ʃaɪnɪŋ] adj (**a**) (light, metal, eyes) brillante, reluciente; (face) radiante; (hair) lustroso(a) (**b**) Fig (outstanding) destacado(a), ilustre, magnífico(a)

shinty ['ʃɪntɪ] n Sport hockey m (escocés) sobre hierba

shiny ['ʃaɪnɪ] adj (shinier, shiniest) (**a**) (bright) brillante (**b**) (worn) (clothes) sobado(a)

ship [ʃɪp] **1** n barco m, buque m, navio m; **on board s.** a bordo; **to abandon s.** abandonar or evacuar el barco; **the s.'s company** la tripulación; Fig **when my s. comes in** or **home** cuando lleguen las vacas gordas ❑ **hospital s.** buque m hospital; **merchant s.** buque m mercante; **passenger s.** buque m de pasajeros
2 vt (pt & pp shipped) (**a**) (take on board) embarcar, traer a bordo; **to s. oars** desarmar los remos (**b**) (transport) transportar (en barco); (send) (gen) enviar, mandar

ship off vt Fam despachar

shipboard ['ʃɪpbɔːd] n **a s. encounter** un encuentro a bordo; **on s.** a bordo

shipbuilder ['ʃɪpbɪldər] n constructor(a) m,f de buques

shipbuilding ['ʃɪpbɪldɪŋ] n construcción f naval

shipload ['ʃɪpləʊd] n cargamento m, carga f

shipmate ['ʃɪpmeɪt] n compañero(a) m,f de tripulación

shipment ['ʃɪpmənt] n (**a**) (act) embarque m, transporte m (**b**) (load) consignación f, envío m, remesa f

shipowner ['ʃɪpəʊnər] n armador(a) m,f, naviero(a) m,f

shipper ['ʃɪpər] n (person) cargador(a) m,f; (company) compañía f naviera

shipping ['ʃɪpɪŋ] n (**a**) (ships) barcos mpl, buques mpl; (fleet) flota f ❑ **s. lane** via f de navegación (**b**) (loading) embarque m; (transporting) transporte m (en barco); (sending) envío m ❑ **s. agent** agente mf marítimo(a); **s. company** or **line** compañía f naviera

shipshape ['ʃɪpʃeɪp] adj & adv en perfecto orden

shipwreck ['ʃɪprek] **1** n naufragio m
2 vt **to be shipwrecked** naufragar

shipyard ['ʃɪpjɑːd] n astillero m

shire [ʃaɪər] n Br condado m ❑ **s. horse** percherón(ona) m,f, caballo m de tiro

shirk [ʃɜːk] **1** vt (duty) esquivar; (problem) eludir
2 vi gandulear, hacer el vago

shirker ['ʃɜːkər] n gandul(ula) m,f, vago(a) m,f, Méx flojo(a) m,f, RP vagoneta m,f

shirt [ʃɜːt] n camisa f; Fig **to put one's s. on a horse** apostarse hasta el último real a un caballo; Fam **a stuffed s.** un pedante; Fam **keep your s. on!** ¡no te sulfures!

shirtsleeves ['ʃɜːtsliːvz] npl **to be in (one's) s.** estar en mangas de camisa

shirt-tail ['ʃɜːtteɪl] n faldón m de la camisa

shirtwaister ['ʃɜːtweɪstər] n, US **shirtwaist** ['ʃɜːtweɪst] n vestido m camisero

shirty ['ʃɜːtɪ] adj (shirtier, shirtiest) Br Slang **to get s.** mosquearse

shit [ʃɪt] Vulg **1** n mierda f; Slang **in the s.** jodido(a)
2 interj ¡mierda!, RP ¡la puta!
3 vi (pt & pp shit or shat) cagar

shitless ['ʃɪtlɪs] adj Vulg **to scare sb s.** hacer cagarse de miedo a algn, Esp acojonar a algn, Méx sacar un pedo a algn, RP hacer que algn se cague hasta las patas; **to be scared s.** estar cagado(a) de miedo, Esp estar acojonado(a)

shitty ['ʃɪtɪ] adj (shittier, shittiest) Vulg **a s. book** una porquería de libro; **what a s. thing to do!** ¡qué putada!

shiver ['ʃɪvər] **1** vi (with cold) tiritar; (with fear) temblar, estremecerse
2 n (with cold) escalofrío m, tiritón m; (with fear) escalofrío m; **it sent shivers down my spine** me dio escalofríos; **that sort of talk gives me the shivers** esa manera de hablar me da horror

shivery ['ʃɪvərɪ] adj (with cold) estremecido(a); (feverish) destemplado(a); (sensitive to the cold) friolero(a)

shoal [ʃəʊl] *n (of fish)* banco *m*

shock [ʃɒk] **1** *n* **(a)** *(jolt)* choque *m*, sacudida *f*, golpe *m*; **electric s.** descarga *f* eléctrica ❏ *Aut* **s. absorber** amortiguador *m*; *Mil* **s. tactics** táctica *f* sing de choque; *Mil* **s. troops** tropas *fpl* de choque *or* de asalto; **s. wave** onda *f* expansiva **(b)** *(upset)* conmoción *f*, golpe *m*; *(scare)* susto *m*; **it was a great s. to us** fue un golpe duro para nosotros; **the s. killed him** murió del susto; **what a s. you gave me!** ¡qué susto me has dado! **(c)** *Med* shock *m*, choque *m*; **in a state of s.** en estado de shock ❏ **s. therapy** tratamiento *m* de electrochoque

2 *vt (upset)* conmover, conmocionar; *(startle)* sobresaltar, asustar; *(scandalize)* escandalizar

shocked [ʃɒkt] *adj (startled)* conmocionado(a), impactado(a); *(scandalized)* escandalizado(a)

shocker [ʃɒkər] *n (news, event) (surprising)* bombazo *m*, escándalo *m*; *(very bad)* desastre *m*

shockheaded [ʃɒkhedɪd] *adj* greñudo(a), melenudo(a)

shocking [ʃɒkɪŋ] *adj* **(a)** *(causing horror)* espantoso(a), horroroso(a); *Fam (very bad)* malísimo(a), horroroso(a); **what s. weather!** ¡qué tiempo más feo! **(b)** *(disgraceful)* escandaloso(a), vergonzoso(a), chocante **(c)** *(garish)* **s. pink** rosa chillón

shockingly [ʃɒkɪŋlɪ] *adv Fam* la mar de, super; **s. expensive** super caro(a)

shockproof [ʃɒkpruːf] *adj (watch etc)* a prueba de choques

shod [ʃɒd] *pt & pp see* **shoe**

shoddy [ʃɒdɪ] *adj* (**shoddier, shoddiest**) *(goods)* de pacotilla; *(work)* chapucero(a)

shoe [ʃuː] **1** *n* **(a)** *(gen)* zapato *m*; *(for horse)* herradura *f*; **to put on one's shoes** ponerse los zapatos; *Fig* **I wouldn't like to be in her shoes** no me gustaría estar en su lugar ❏ *Aut* **brake s.** zapata *f*; *Com* **s. industry** industria *f* del calzado; **s. leather** cuero *m* para zapatos; **s. polish** betún *m*; **s. repair (shop)** remiendo *m* de zapatos, rápido *m*; **s. shop** *US* **s. store** zapatería *f*, tienda *f* de calzado **(b)** *Com* **shoes** calzado *m* sing

2 *vt (pt & pp shod) (horse)* herrar; *Literary* **he was shod in sandals** calzaba sandalias

shoebrush [ʃuːbrʌʃ] *n* cepillo *m* para los zapatos

shoehorn [ʃuːhɔːn] *n* calzador *m*

shoelace [ʃuːleɪs] *n* cordón *m* (de zapato)

shoemaker [ʃuːmeɪkər] *n* zapatero(a) *m,f*

shoeshine [ʃuːʃaɪn] *n* limpieza *f* de zapatos ❏ **s. boy** limpiabotas *m inv*

shoestring [ʃuːstrɪŋ] *n US* cordón *m* (de zapato); *Fig* **on a s.** *Esp* con cuatro perras, *Am* con poca plata

shoetree [ʃuːtriː] *n* horma *f*

shone [ʃɒn] *pt & pp see* **shine**

shoo [ʃuː] **1** *interj* ¡fuera!, ¡zape!

2 *vt* **to s. (away)** *(birds, animals)* espantar, ahuyentar

shook [ʃʊk] *pt see* **shake**

shoot [ʃuːt] **1** *n* **(a)** *Bot* brote *m*, retoño *m*, renuevo *m*; *(of vine)* sarmiento *m* **(b)** *Br (hunting party)* cacería *f*; *(shooting contest)* concurso *m* de tiro al blanco **(c)** *(game preserve)* coto *m* de caza

2 *vt (pt & pp shot)* **(a)** *(fire on)* pegar un tiro a; *(wound)* herir (de bala); *(kill)* matar; *(execute)* fusilar; *(hunt)* cazar; **he was shot in the head** una bala le alcanzó la cabeza; **to s. dead** matar a tiros; *Fam* **you'll get shot if you do that!** ¡te matarán si haces eso! **(b)** *(missile)* lanzar; *(bullet, arrow)* disparar; *(glance)* lanzar; *(kick) (ball)* disparar; *Ftb (goal)* marcar; *US* **to s. craps** jugar a los dados; **to s. questions at sb** bombardear a algn a preguntas **(c)** *(film)* rodar, filmar; *Phot (subject)* fotografiar, sacar una foto de; *(photograph)*

sacar **(d)** *(pass through) (rapids)* salvar; *(traffic lights)* saltarse **(e)** *Slang (heroin etc)* pincharse, *Esp* chutarse

3 *vi* **(a)** *(with gun, bow)* disparar (**at sb** sobre algn); **to s. at a target** tirar al blanco; *Ftb* **to s. at the goal** tirar a puerta, chutar **(b)** *(move rapidly)* **to s. past** *or* **by** pasar volando *or* como un rayo **(c)** *Bot* brotar

4 *interj US Fam* ¡miércoles!, ¡mecachis!, *Méx* ¡chin!

shoot down *vt (person)* matar de un tiro *or* a tiros; *(aircraft)* derribar

shoot off *vi Fam* salir disparado(a)

shoot out 1 *vi (rush out) (person)* salir disparado(a); *(water)* brotar; *(flames)* salir

2 *vt* **to s. it out** resolverlo a tiros

shoot up *vi* **(a)** *(flames)* salir; *(water)* brotar **(b)** *(prices)* dispararse, subir de repente **(c)** *(hands)* alzarse rápidamente **(d)** *(child, plant)* crecer rápidamente; *(new buildings)* construirse de la noche a la mañana **(e)** *Fam (inject drugs)* pincharse, *Esp* chutarse

shooting [ʃuːtɪŋ] **1** *n* **(a)** *(shots)* disparos *mpl*, tiros *mpl*; *(murder)* asesinato *m*; *(execution)* fusilamiento *m*; *(hunting)* caza *f*; *Fam* **the whole s. match** todo el tinglado ❏ **s. gallery** barraca *f or* caseta *f* de tiro al blanco; **s. match** tiroteo *m*; **s. star** estrella *f* fugaz; **s. stick** bastón *m* asiento **(b)** *(of film)* rodaje *m*, filmación *f*

2 *adj (pain)* punzante

shoot-out [ʃuːtaʊt] *n* tiroteo *m*

shop [ʃɒp] **1** *n* **(a)** *(gen)* tienda *f*; *(large store)* almacén *m*; *(business)* comercio *m*, negocio *m*; **to keep s.** tener una tienda; **to set up s.** poner *or* abrir una tienda; **to talk s.** hablar del trabajo; *Fam* **all over the s.** por todas partes ❏ **fish s.** pescadería *f*; **grocer's s.** tienda *f* de ultramarinos; **s. assistant** dependiente(a) *m,f*, **s. window** escaparate *m*, *Am* vidriera *f*, *Chile Col Méx* vitrina *f* **(b)** *(workshop)* taller *m*; **assembly s.** taller de montaje ❏ **s. floor** *(place)* planta *f*, *(workers)* personal *m* obrero, obreros *mpl*, operarios *mpl*; **s. steward** delegado(a) *m,f* sindical; **to work on the s. floor** trabajar en producción

2 *vi (pt & pp shopped)* hacer compras; **to go shopping** ir de compras; **to s. for** buscar

3 *vt Br Fam (betray) Esp* chivarse de, *Col* sapear, *Méx* soplar, *RP* mandar al frente

shop around *vi* comparar precios; **to s. around for bargains** ir de tienda en tienda en busca de gangas

shopaholic [ʃɒpəhɒlɪk] *n Fam* consumista *mf*

shopgirl [ʃɒpgɜːl] *n* dependienta *f*

shopkeeper [ʃɒpkiːpər] *n* tendero(a) *m,f*

shoplift [ʃɒplɪft] *vt & vi* robar en las tiendas

shoplifter [ʃɒplɪftər] *n* mechero(a) *m,f*, ratero(a) *m,f*

shoplifting [ʃɒplɪftɪŋ] *n* ratería *f*, hurto *m*

shopper [ʃɒpər] *n* comprador(a) *m,f*

shopping [ʃɒpɪŋ] *n (activity)* compra *f*, *Am* compras *fpl*; *(purchases)* compras *fpl*; **to do the s.** hacer las compras *or Esp* la compra ❏ **s. bag/basket** bolsa *f*/cesta *f* de la compra; *US* **s. cart** carrito *m*; **s. centre** centro *m* comercial; **s. channel** canal *m* de compras, teletienda *f*; *US* **s. mall** parque *m* comercial; **s. precinct** centro *m* comercial; *Br* **s. trolley** carrito *m*

shopsoiled [ʃɒpsɔɪld] *adj*, *US* **shopworn** [ʃɒpwɔːn] *adj* deteriorado(a), desgastado(a)

shore¹ [ʃɔːr] *n* **(a)** *(of sea, lake)* orilla *f*, *US (beach)* playa *f*; *(coast)* costa *f*; **on s.** en tierra; *(passengers)* **to go on s.** desembarcar ❏ *Naut* **s. leave** permiso *m* para bajar a tierra **(b)** *Shores Fig* país *m* sing; **his native s.** su tierra natal

shore² [ʃɔːr] *vt* **to s. (up)** *(building, tunnel)* apuntalar; *Fig (company, prices)* apoyar, sostener, consolidar

shoreline [ʃɔːlaɪn] *n* orilla *f*

shorn [ʃɔːn] *pp see* **shear**

short [ʃɔːt] **1** *adj* (**a**) *(gen)* corto(a); *(not tall)* bajo(a), *Méx* chaparro(a), *RP* petiso(a); **at s. notice** con poca antelación; **in a s. while** dentro de un rato; **in the s. term** a corto plazo; *Fam* **to make s. work of sth** despachar algo rápidamente ❏ *Elec* **s. circuit** cortocircuito *m*; **s. cut** atajo *m*; *Br* **s. list** lista *f* de seleccionados; *US* **s. order** comida *f* rápida; **s. story** cuento *m*; *US Cin* **s. subject** cortometraje *m*; *Br Ind* **s. time** jornada *f* reducida; *Rad* **s. wave** onda *f* corta (**b**) *(brief)* corto(a), breve; **'Bob' is s. for 'Robert'** 'Bob' es el diminutivo de 'Robert'; **for s.** para abreviar; **in s.** en pocas palabras (**c**) *(insufficient)* **she's a bit s. of cash** anda bastante mal de dinero; **to be s. of breath** faltarle a uno la respiración; **to be s. of food** andar escaso(a) de comida; **to be s. on experience** tener poca experiencia; **to give s. weight** no dar el peso exacto; **water is in s. supply** hay escasez de agua (**d**) *(brusque, curt)* brusco(a), seco(a), corto(a); **to be s. with sb** mostrarse seco(a) con algn; **to have a s. temper** tener mal genio

2 *adv* (**a**) *(abruptly)* **to pull up s.** pararse en seco (**b**) *(less than expected)* **to cut s.** *(holiday)* interrumpir; *(meeting)* suspender; **to go s. of food** pasarse sin comida, pasar hambre; **we're running s. of coffee** se nos está acabando el café; *Fig* **to sell sb s.** engañar a algn (**c**) *(except)* **s. of** excepto, menos

3 *n* (**a**) *Cin* cortometraje *m* (**b**) *Elec* cortocircuito *m* (**c**) *Br Fam (drink)* bebida *f* corta, copa *f*

4 *vt Elec* provocar un cortocircuito en

5 *vi* **to s. (out)** tener un cortocircuito

shortage [ʃɔːtɪdʒ] *n* falta *f*, escasez *f*, carencia *f*, carestía *f*; **manpower s.** falta de mano de obra

shortbread [ʃɔːtbred] *n Culin* mantecada *f*

shortcake [ʃɔːtkeɪk] *n Culin* (**a**) *Br* = especie de galleta elaborada con mantequilla, mantecada *f* (**b**) *US* = bizcocho que generalmente lleva fruta y nata batida

short-change [ʃɔːtʃeɪndʒ] *vt Fam* **to s.-c. sb** no devolver el cambio completo a algn; *Slang* timar a algn

short-circuit [ʃɔːtsɜːkɪt] *Elec* **1** *vt* provocar un corto-circuito en

2 *vi* tener un cortocircuito

shortcomings [ʃɔːtkʌmɪŋz] *npl* defectos *mpl*, puntos *mpl* flacos

shortcrust [ʃɔːtkrʌst] *n Culin* **s. pastry** pasta *f* brisa, pasta *f* medio hojaldrada

shorten [ʃɔːtən] *vt (skirt, visit)* acortar; *(word)* abreviar; *(text)* resumir; *(rations)* reducir

shortening [ʃɔːtənɪŋ] *n Culin (butter)* mantequilla *f*, *(lard)* manteca *f*

shortfall [ʃɔːtfɔːl] *n Com* déficit *m*

short-haired [ʃɔːtheəd] *adj* de pelo corto

shorthand [ʃɔːthænd] *n* taquigrafía *f*; **to take sth down in s.** escribir algo taquigráficamente ❏ **s. typing** taqui-mecanografía *f*; **s. typist** taquimecanógrafo(a) *m,f*, *Fam* taquimeca *mf*

short-handed [ʃɔːthændɪd] *adj* falto(a) de mano de obra

short-haul [ʃɔːthɔːl] *adj* de corto recorrido

short-list [ʃɔːtlɪst] *vt* seleccionar, poner en la lista de seleccionados

short-lived [ʃɔːtlɪvd] *adv* efímero(a)

shortly [ʃɔːtlɪ] *adv (soon)* dentro de poco; **s. after** poco después

short-range [ʃɔːtreɪndʒ] *adj Mil* de corto alcance

shorts [ʃɔːts] *npl* (**a**) *(short trousers)* pantalones *mpl* cortos, shorts *mpl*; **a pair of s.** un pantalón corto (**b**) *US (underpants)* calzoncillos *mpl*

short-sighted [ʃɔːtsaɪtɪd] *adj (person)* miope, corto(a) de vista; *Fig (plan etc)* corto(a) de vista

short-sightedness [ʃɔːtsaɪtɪdnɪs] *n* miopía *f*; *Fig* falta *f* de perspicacia

short-sleeved [ʃɔːtsliːvd] *adj* de manga corta

short-staffed [ʃɔːtstɑːft] *adj* escaso(a) de personal

short-stay [ʃɔːtsteɪ] *adj (car park)* para estancias breves

shortstop [ʃɔːtstɒp] *n US Sport* = jugador que intenta interceptar bolas entre la segunda y tercera base

short-tempered [ʃɔːttempəd] *adj* de mal genio, de genio vivo

short-term [ʃɔːttɜːm] *adj* a corto plazo; **s. contract** contrato *m* temporal

short-wave [ʃɔːtweɪv] *adj Rad* de onda corta

short-winded [ʃɔːtwɪndɪd] *adj* corto(a) de resuello

shorty [ʃɔːtɪ] *n Fam* retaco(a) *m,f*, canijo(a) *m,f*, *Méx* retacón(ona) *m,f*

shot¹ [ʃɒt] *n* (**a**) *(act, sound)* tiro *m*, disparo *m*, balazo *m*; **exchange of shots** tiroteo *m*; **to fire a s. at sb** disparar sobre algn; **warning s.** disparo al aire; **without firing a s.** sin pegar un tiro; *Fig* **long s.** posibilidad *f* remota; *Fig* **not by a long s.** ni mucho menos (**b**) *(projectile)* bala *f*, *(pellets)* perdigones *mpl*; *Fig* **he was off like a s.** salió disparado ❏ *Athlet* **s. put** lanzamiento *m* de peso *or Am* de bala (**c**) *(person)* tirador(a) *m,f* ❏ *Fam* **big s.** pez *m* gordo; **crack s.** tirador *m* de élite (**d**) *Sport (in soccer)* tiro *m* (a gol), chut *m*; *(in golf, billiards)* golpe *m* (**e**) *(attempt)* tentativa *f*, intento *m*; *(in game)* **it's your s.** te toca a ti; **to have a s.** probar; **to have a s. at sth** intentar hacer algo; *Fig* **a s. in the dark** un intento a ciegas (**f**) *(injection)* inyección *f*; *Fam* pinchazo *m* ❏ **polio s.** vacuna *f* contra la polio (**g**) *(drink)* trago *m* (**h**) *Phot* foto *f*; *Cin* toma *f*; **location shots** exteriores *mpl*

shot² [ʃɒt] **1** *pt & pp see* **shoot**

2 *adj Br Fam* **to get s. of sth/sb** quitarse *or Am* sacarse algo/a algn de encima

shotgun [ʃɒtɡʌn] *n* escopeta *f*; *Fam* **it was a s. wedding** se casaron a la fuerza *or Esp* de penalty *or RP* de apuro

should [ʃʊd, *unstressed* ʃəd] *v aux* (**a**) *(duty, advisability)* deber; **all employees s. wear helmets** todos los empleados deben llevar casco; **he s. have been an architect** debería haber sido arquitecto; **you s. see the dentist** deberías ir (a ver) al dentista (**b**) *(probability)* deber de; **he s. have finished work by now** ya debe de haber acabado el trabajo; **it s. be fine tomorrow** seguramente hará buen tiempo mañana; **this s. be interesting** esto promete ser interesante (**c**) *(conditional use)* **if anything strange s. happen** si pasara algo raro; **s. you wish to attend** si desea asistir (**d**) *(tentative statement)* **I s. like to ask a question** quisiera hacer una pregunta; **I s. like to have met your grandfather** me hubiera gustado conocer a tu abuelo; **I s. think so** me imagino que sí (**e**) *(surprise)* **who s. I meet but Charlie!** ¡imagínate mi sorpresa al encontrarme con Charlie!

shoulder [ʃəʊldər] **1** *n* (**a**) *Anat* hombro *m*; **s. to s.** hombro con hombro; **to carry sth on one's s.** llevar algo a hombros; **to shrug one's shoulders** encogerse de hombros; *Fig* **to cry on sb's s.** desahogarse con algn; *Fig* **to give sb the cold s.** volver la espalda *or* dar de lado a algn; *Fig* **to look over sb's s.** tener vigilado a algn; *Fig* **to rub shoulders with sb** codearse con algn ❏ **s. bag** bolso *m* (de bandolera); *Anat* **s. blade** omóplato *m*; **s. pad** hombrera *f*; **s. strap** *(of garment)* tirante *m*, *CSur* bretel *m*; *(of bag)* correa *f* (**b**) *Culin (of meat)* paletilla *f* (**c**) *(of hill)* lomo *m*; *(along road)* arcén *m*, *Méx* acotamiento *m*, *RP* banquina *f* ❏ *Br* **hard s.**, *US* **s.** arcén *m*; **soft s.** escalón *m* lateral

2 *vt* (**a**) *Fig (responsibilities)* cargar con (**b**) *(push)* **to s. one's way through** abrirse paso a codazos

shoulder-high [ʃəʊldəhaɪ] *adj* a hombros

shoulder-length [ˈʃəʊldələŋθ] *adj* (que llega) hasta los hombros

shout [ʃaʊt] **1** *n* grito *m*; **shouts of laughter** carcajadas *fpl*; *Fam* **give me a s. when you're ready** avísame cuando estés listo
2 *vt* gritar
3 *vi* gritar, chillar; **to s. at sb** gritar a algn; **to s. for help** pedir socorro a gritos

shout down *vt (person)* abuchear

shouting [ˈʃaʊtɪŋ] *n* gritos *mpl*, vocerío *m*

shove [ʃʌv] **1** *n Fam* empujón *m*; **to give sth a s.** dar un empujón a *or* empujar algo
2 *vt* empujar; **to s. sth into one's pocket** meterse algo en el bolsillo (a empellones)
3 *vi* empujar; *(jostle)* dar empellones

shove off *vi Fam* largarse

shove up *vi Fam* correrse

shovel [ˈʃʌvəl] **1** *n* pala *f*; **mechanical s.** pala mecánica, excavadora *f*
2 *vt (pt & pp* **shovelled**, *US* **shoveled**) echar a paladas; **to s. snow off the path** quitar *or Am* sacar la nieve del camino a paladas *or* con la pala; *Fam* **to s. food into one's mouth** zamparse la comida

shovelful [ˈʃʌvəlfʊl] *n* palada *f*, paletada *f*

show [ʃəʊ] **1** *vt (pt* **showed**; *pp* **shown** *or* **showed**) **(a)** *(exhibit) (ticket etc)* mostrar, enseñar; *(painting etc)* exponer; *(film, slides)* poner, pasar, proyectar; *(latest plans etc)* presentar **(b)** *(display, reveal)* demostrar, mostrar; **to s. the dirt** dejar ver la suciedad; **to s. kindness to sb** mostrarse amable con algn; **to s. oneself to be a coward** comportarse como un cobarde; **to s. signs of life** dar señales de vida; *Fam* **she'll never s. her face here again** nunca más aparecerá por aquí **(c)** *(teach)* enseñar, mostrar; *(explain)* explicar; **s. me how to do it** enséñame cómo se hace; *Fam* **I'll s. him!** ¡se va a enterar! **(d)** *(indicate)* indicar; *(temperature etc)* marcar, indicar; *(profit etc)* registrar; *(way)* indicar, enseñar; **as shown below** según se ve abajo; **the clock showed 4 o'clock** el reloj marcaba las 4 **(e)** *(prove)* demostrar, probar; **it only goes to s. that ...** demuestra claramente que ...; **time will s.** el tiempo lo dirá; *Fam* **it just goes to s.!** ¡hay que ver! **(f)** *(conduct)* llevar, conducir; **she was shown round the factory** la llevaron a visitar la fábrica; **to s. sb in** hacer pasar a algn; **to s. sb to the door** acompañar a algn hasta la puerta
2 *vi* **(a)** *(be visible)* verse, notarse; **the stain doesn't s.** no se nota *or* no se ve la mancha **(b)** *(appear)* aparecer **(c)** *Cin* dar, poner, proyectar; **what's showing at the Roxy?** ¿qué ponen en el Roxy?
3 *n* **(a)** *(display)* demostración *f*; **s. of hands** votación *f* a mano alzada ❑ **s. house** casa *f* piloto **(b)** *(outward appearance)* apariencia *f*; **for s.** por pura comedia; **to make a s. of** hacer gala *or* alarde de **(c)** *(exhibition)* exposición *f*; **to be on s.** estar expuesto(a) ❑ **agricultural s.** feria *f* del campo; **boat s.** salón *m* náutico; **fashion s.** desfile *m or* pase *m* de modelos; **flower s.** exposición *f* de flores; **horse s.** concurso *m* hípico; **motor s.** salón *m* del automóvil **(d)** *Theat (entertainment)* espectáculo *m*; *(performance)* función *f*; *Rad TV* programa *m*; *Fig (jolly)* **good s.!** ¡muy bien!, ¡bien hecho!; *Fig* **to put up a good/poor s.** hacer un buen/pobre papel; *Fig* **to steal the s.** llevarse la palma; *Fam* **to give the s. away** descubrir el pastel ❑ **s. business** el mundo del espectáculo; *Fam* **s. stopper** plato *m* fuerte **(e)** *(organization)* negocio *m*, empresa *f*; *Fam* **tinglado** *m*; **the grandfather runs the whole s.** el abuelo es el que lo lleva todo

show off 1 *vt* **(a)** *(highlight)* hacer resaltar **(b)** *Fam (flaunt)* hacer alarde de
2 *vi* alardear, fanfarronear

show up 1 *vt* **(a)** *(visitor etc)* hacer pasar **(b)** *(reveal)* revelar, sacar a luz; *(highlight)* hacer resaltar *or* destacar **(c)** *Fam (embarrass)* avergonzar, hacer pasar vergüenza, dejar en ridículo
2 *vi* **(a)** *(stand out)* resaltar, destacarse **(b)** *Fam (arrive, appear)* acudir, presentarse, aparecer

showbiz [ˈʃəʊbɪz] *n Fam* la farándula, el mundo del espectáculo

showcase [ˈʃəʊkeɪs] *n* vitrina *f*

showdown [ˈʃəʊdaʊn] *n* enfrentamiento *m*, confrontación *f*; **to have a s. with sb** enfrentarse con algn

shower [ˈʃaʊər] **1** *n* **(a)** *(of rain)* chubasco *m*, chaparrón *m*, aguacero *m*; **scattered showers** chubascos aislados **(b)** *Fig (of stones, blows, insults)* lluvia *f* **(c)** *(for washing)* ducha *f*, *Col Méx Ven* regadera *f*; **to have** *or* **take a s.** ducharse, tomar *or* darse una ducha ❑ **s. cap** gorro *m* de baño **(d)** *US Fam* **s. (party)** fiesta *f* de obsequio
2 *vt* **(a)** *(sprinkle)* espolvorear; *(spray)* rociar **(b)** *Fig* colmar, inundar; **to s. gifts/praise on** *or* **upon sb** colmar a algn de regalos/elogios; **we were showered with invitations** nos llovieron invitaciones
3 *vi* ducharse, tomar *or* darse una ducha

showerproof [ˈʃaʊəpruːf] *adj* impermeable

showery [ˈʃaʊərɪ] *adj* lluvioso(a)

showgirl [ˈʃəʊgɜːl] *n* corista *f*

showground [ˈʃəʊgraʊnd] *n* real *m*, recinto *m* ferial

showing [ˈʃəʊɪŋ] *n (gen)* exposición *f*; *(of film)* proyección *f*

showjumper [ˈʃəʊdʒʌmpər] *n Equit* jinete *m*

showjumping [ˈʃəʊdʒʌmpɪŋ] *n Equit (gen)* hípica *f*; *(event)* concurso *m* hípico

showman [ˈʃəʊmən] *n (pl* **showmen**) **(a)** *(entertainment manager)* empresario *m* (de espectáculos) **(b)** *(skilled performer)* actor *m* de primera, showman *m*

showmanship [ˈʃəʊmənʃɪp] *n* talento *m* para el teatro, teatralidad *f*

shown [ʃəʊn] *pp see* **show**

show-off [ˈʃəʊɒf] *n Fam* fanfarrón(ona) *m,f*, *Esp* fantasma *mf*

showpiece [ˈʃəʊpiːs] *n (in exhibition etc)* obra *f* maestra; *Fig (at school etc)* modelo *f*

showplace [ˈʃəʊpleɪs] *n* lugar *m* de interés turístico

showroom [ˈʃəʊruːm] *n Com* exposición *f*, *Art* galería *f*, sala *f* de exposiciones

showy [ˈʃəʊɪ] *adj* (**showier**, **showiest**) *Fam* llamativo(a), chillón(ona); *(person)* ostentoso(a)

shrank [ʃræŋk] *pt see* **shrink**

shrapnel [ˈʃræpnəl] *n Mil* metralla *f*

shred [ʃred] **1** *n (gen)* triza *f*; *(of cloth)* jirón *m*; *(of paper)* tira *f*; *Fig* chispa *f*; **in shreds** hecho(a) trizas *or* jirones; **to tear sth to shreds** hacer algo trizas; *Fig* **without a s. of evidence** sin la más mínima prueba
2 *vt (pt & pp* **shredded**) *(paper)* hacer trizas, triturar; *(vegetables)* rallar

shredder [ˈʃredər] *n (for waste paper)* trituradora *f*, *(for vegetables)* rallador *m*

shrew [ʃruː] *n* **(a)** *Zool* musaraña *f* **(b)** *Fig (woman)* arpía *f*, bruja *f*, fiera *f*

shrewd [ʃruːd] *adj (gen)* astuto(a); *(clear-sighted)* perspicaz; *(wise)* sabio(a); *(witty)* atinado(a); *(clever)* listo(a); *(of decision)* acertado(a); **to make a s. guess** hacer una suposición razonable

shrewdness [ˈʃruːdnɪs] *n (gen)* astucia *f*; *(clear-sightedness)* perspicacia *f*; *(wisdom)* juicio *m*; *(wit)* tino *m*

shriek [ʃriːk] **1** *n* chillido *m*, grito *m* agudo; **shrieks of laughter** carcajadas *fpl*

2 *vi* chillar, gritar; **to s. with laughter** reírse a mandíbula batiente

shrift [ʃrɪft] *n Fam* **to give sb short s.** despachar a algn sin rodeos, mandar a algn a paseo

shrike [ʃraɪk] *n Orn* alcaudón *m*

shrill [ʃrɪl] *adj (voice)* chillón(ona), agudo(a); *(sound)* agudo(a), estridente

shrimp [ʃrɪmp] **1** *n* (**a**) *Br (small crustacean)* camarón *m*, quisquilla *f; US (prawn)* gamba *f* (**b**) *Fam (person)* enano(a) *m,f,* renacuajo *m, Méx* chaparrito(a) *m,f, RP* retacón(ona) *m,f*
2 *vi* pescar camarones

shrine [ʃraɪn] *n Rel (tomb)* sepulcro *m; (relic case)* relicario *m; (chapel)* capilla *f; (in remote place)* ermita *f; (holy place)* lugar *m* santo *or* sagrado, santuario *m*

shrink [ʃrɪŋk] **1** *vt (pt* **shrank***; pp* **shrunk)** *(material, clothes)* encoger
2 *vi* (**a**) *(clothes)* encoger(se) (**b**) *(savings etc)* disminuir (**c**) *Fig* **to s. (back** *or* **away)** retroceder, echarse atrás; **to s. from doing sth** no tener valor para hacer algo
3 *n* (**a**) *(shrinkage)* encogimiento *m* (**b**) *Fam (psychiatrist)* loquero(a) *m,f*

shrinkage [ˈʃrɪŋkɪdʒ] *n* (**a**) *(of cloth)* encogimiento *m; (of metal)* contracción *f* (**b**) *(of savings etc)* disminución *f,* reducción *f*

shrinking [ˈʃrɪŋkɪŋ] *adj Fam* **s. violet** persona *f* tímida

shrink-wrapped [ˈʃrɪŋkræpt] *adj Com* envuelto(a) en plástico

shrivel [ˈʃrɪvəl] **1** *vt (pt & pp* **shrivelled,** *US* **shriveled)** **to s. (up)** *(plant)* marchitar, secar; *(skin)* arrugar
2 *vi (gen)* encogerse; *(plant)* marchitarse, secarse; *(skin)* arrugarse

shroud [ʃraʊd] **1** *n* (**a**) *Rel* mortaja *f,* sudario *m* (**b**) *Fig (of mist, secrecy)* velo *m*
2 *vt Fig* envolver

Shrove Tuesday [ʃrəʊvˈtjuːzdɪ] *n* martes *m* de carnaval

shrub [ʃrʌb] *n* arbusto *m*

shrubbery [ˈʃrʌbərɪ] *n* arbustos *mpl*

shrug [ʃrʌg] **1** *vt (pt & pp* **shrugged)** encoger; **to s. one's shoulders** encogerse de hombros
2 *vi* encogerse de hombros
3 *n* encogimiento *m* de hombros

shrug off *vt* no hacer caso de, quitar importancia a

shrunk [ʃrʌŋk] *pp see* **shrink**

shrunken [ˈʃrʌŋkən] *adj (body)* encogido(a)

shudder [ˈʃʌdər] **1** *n* (**a**) *(shiver)* escalofrío *m,* estremecimiento *m; Fam* **it gives me the shudders** me pone los pelos de punta (**b**) *(of engine, machinery)* vibración *f,* sacudida *f*
2 *vi* (**a**) *(person)* estremecerse, temblar (**with** de); **I s. to think of it** sólo pensarlo me dan escalofríos (**b**) *(machinery)* vibrar, dar sacudidas

shuffle [ˈʃʌfəl] **1** *vt* (**a**) *(drag)* arrastrar (**b**) *(papers etc)* revolver; *(cards)* barajar
2 *vi* (**a**) *(walk)* andar arrastrando los pies (**b**) *Cards* barajar
3 *n* (**a**) *(dragging)* arrastre *m;* **to walk with a s.** andar arrastrando los pies (**b**) *Cards* **to give the cards a s.** barajar las cartas

shun [ʃʌn] *vt (pt & pp* **shunned)** *(person)* evitar, esquivar; *(responsibility, publicity)* rehuir

shunt [ʃʌnt] *vt Rail* cambiar de vía; *Elec* derivar; *Fig* desviar

shunting [ˈʃʌntɪŋ] *n Rail* maniobras *fpl* ❑ **s. yard** estación *f* de maniobras

shush [ʃʊʃ] **1** *interj* ¡chis!, ¡chitón!
2 *vt* callar, hacer callar

shut [ʃʌt] **1** *vt (pt & pp* **shut)** cerrar; **to s. one's finger in the door** pillarse el dedo en la puerta; *Fig* **to s. the door on sth/sb** negarse a pensar en algo/algn; *Fam* **s. your mouth!** ¡cierra el pico!
2 *vi* cerrarse
3 *adj* cerrado(a)

shut away *vt (imprison)* encerrar

shut down 1 *vt (factory)* cerrar; *(machinery)* desconectar, apagar
2 *vi (factory)* cerrarse

shut in *vt* encerrar

shut off *vt* (**a**) *(switch off) (gas, water, etc)* cortar, cerrar; *(machinery)* cerrar, desconectar, apagar (**b**) *(street, area)* aislar (**from** de)

shut out *vt* (**a**) *(leave outside)* dejar fuera; *(put outside)* sacar, echar a la calle; *(lock out)* cerrar la puerta a (**b**) *(exclude)* excluir (**c**) *(light, view)* tapar

shut up 1 *vt* (**a**) *(close)* cerrar (**b**) *(enclose, imprison)* encerrar (**c**) *Fam (silence)* callar, hacer callar
2 *vi Fam (keep quiet)* callarse; **s. up!** ¡cállate!

shutdown [ˈʃʌtdaʊn] *n* cierre *m*

shuteye [ˈʃʌtaɪ] *n Fam* cabezada *f,* siesta *f;* **to get some s.** echar una cabezadilla

shut-in [ˈʃʌtˈɪn] *adj* encerrado(a)

shut-off [ˈʃʌtɒf] *n (device)* válvula *f* de cierre; *Elec* interruptor *m*

shutter [ˈʃʌtər] *n* (**a**) *(on window)* contraventana *f,* postigo *m; Fig* **to put up the shutters** echar el cierre (**b**) *Phot* obturador *m*

shuttered [ˈʃʌtəd] *adj* con las contraventanas cerradas

shuttle [ˈʃʌtəl] **1** *n* (**a**) *(in weaving)* lanzadera *f* (**b**) *Av* puente *m* aéreo ❑ **s. service** servicio *m* regular; *Astronaut* **(space) s.** transbordador *m* espacial
2 *vt* trasladar, transportar; *Fam* **to s. sb about** mandar a algn de acá para allá
3 *vi* ir y venir

shuttlecock [ˈʃʌtəlkɒk] *n (badminton)* volante *m*

shy[1] [ʃaɪ] **1** *adj* **(shyer, shyest** *or* **shier, shiest)** *(timid)* tímido(a); *(reserved)* reservado(a); *(cautious)* receloso(a); **don't be s.** no tengas vergüenza; **to be s. of doing sth** no atreverse a hacer algo; **to fight s. of sth** rehuir *or* esquivar algo
2 *vi (pt & pp* **shied)** *(horse)* espantarse (**at** de); *Fig* **to s. away from sth** huir de algo; *Fig* **to s. away from doing sth** negarse a hacer algo

shy[2] [ʃaɪ] *vt (pt & pp* **shied)** *(throw)* tirar, lanzar

shyness [ˈʃaɪnɪs] *n* timidez *f,* vergüenza *f*

shyster [ˈʃaɪstər] *n US (gen)* estafador(a) *m,f,* timador(a) *m,f; Fam (lawyer)* picapleitos *mf inv, Am* abogado(a) *m,f* buscapleitos

Siamese [saɪəˈmiːz] *adj & n* (**a**) *(person)* siamés(esa) *(m,f);* **S. cat** gato siamés; **S. twins** hermanos siameses (**b**) *(Thai)* tailandés(esa) *(m,f)*

Siberia [saɪˈbɪərɪə] *n* Siberia

Siberian [saɪˈbɪərɪən] *adj & n* siberiano(a) *(m,f)*

sibilant [ˈsɪbɪlənt] *adj & n Ling* sibilante *(f)*

sibling [ˈsɪblɪŋ] *n Fml (brother)* hermano *m; (sister)* hermana *f*

sic [sɪk] *adv* sic

Sicilian [sɪˈsɪlɪən] *adj & n* siciliano(a) *(m,f)*

Sicily [ˈsɪsɪlɪ] *n* Sicilia

sick [sɪk] **1** *adj* (**a**) *(ill)* enfermo(a); **to be off s.** estar ausente por enfermedad; **to go s.** darse de baja por enfermedad ❑ **s. leave** baja *f* por enfermedad; **s. list** lista *f* de enfermos; **s. pay** subsidio *m* de enfermedad (**b**) *(about to* *vomit)* mareado(a); **s. headache** jaqueca *f*, migraña *f*; **to be s.** vomitar, devolver; **to feel s.** estar mareado(a), tener náuseas **(c)** *Fam (fed up)* harto(a); **it (really) makes me s.** me revienta; **to be s. (and tired) of sth/sb** estar (más que) harto(a) de algo/algn **(d)** *Fam (mind, joke)* morboso(a); **s. humour** humor negro

  2 the s. *npl* los enfermos

  3 *vt & vi Br Fam* **to s. up** vomitar, devolver

sickbay ['sɪkbeɪ] *n* enfermería *f*

sickbed ['sɪkbed] *n* lecho *m* de enfermo

sicken ['sɪkən] **1** *vt (make ill)* poner enfermo(a); *(revolt, disgust)* dar asco a; **his attitude sickens me** su actitud me pone enfermo(a)

  2 *vi (fall ill)* caer *or* ponerse enfermo(a), enfermar; *Br* **to be sickening for something** estar empezando a ponerse enfermo

sickening ['sɪkənɪŋ] *adj* **(a)** *(nauseating)* nauseabundo(a); *(revolting, disgusting)* repugnante, asqueroso(a); *(horrifying)* escalofriante **(b)** *(annoying)* irritante, exasperante

sickle ['sɪkəl] *n Agr* hoz *f*; *Pol* **the hammer and s.** la hoz y el martillo

sickly ['sɪklɪ] *adj* **(sicklier, sickliest)** **(a)** *(person)* enfermizo(a); *(pale)* pálido(a), paliducho(a) **(b)** *(smell, taste)* empalagoso(a) **(c)** *(smile, affectation)* forzado(a)

sickness ['sɪknɪs] *n* **(a)** *(illness)* enfermedad *f* ❑ *Br* **s. benefit** subsidio *m* de enfermedad **(b)** *(nausea)* náuseas *fpl*, ganas *fpl* de vomitar

sickroom ['sɪkru:m] *n* enfermería *f*

side [saɪd] **1** *n* **(a)** *(gen)* lado *m*; *(of coin etc)* cara *f*; *(of mountain, hill)* ladera *f*, falda *f*; **by the s. of** junto a; **on the heavy s.** más bien pesado(a); **to put sth on one s. for sb** guardar algo para algn; *Fig* **(in order) to be on the safe s.** para estar seguro(a), para mayor seguridad; *Fig* **to keep on the right s. of sb** tratar de llevarse bien con algn; *Fig* **to make a bit of money on the s.** ganar algún dinero extra; *TV Fam* **the other s.** el otro canal **(b)** *(of body)* lado *m*, costado *m*; *(of animal)* ijar *m*, ijada *f*; **a s. of bacon** una lonja de tocino; **by my s.** a mi lado; **s. by s.** juntos, uno al lado de otro; *Fam* **to split one's sides laughing** troncharse de risa **(c)** *(edge)* borde *m*; *(of lake, river)* orilla *f* **(d)** *Fig (aspect)* aspecto *m*, faceta *f*, lado *m*; **to look on the bright s.** ver el lado bueno de las cosas **(e)** *Sport (team)* equipo *m*; *Pol (party)* partido *m*; **on his mother's s.** por parte de madre; **she's on our s.** está de nuestro lado; **to take sides with sb** ponerse de parte de algn,· unirse a algn ❑ **s. dish** acompañamiento *m*, guarnición *f*; **s. door** puerta *f* lateral; **s. effect** efecto *m* secundario; **s. entrance** entrada *f* lateral; **s. street** calle *f* lateral; **s. view** (vista *f* de) perfil *m*

  2 *vi (in argument)* **to s. with sb** ponerse de parte de algn

sideboard ['saɪdbɔ:d] *n Furn* aparador *m*

sideboards ['saɪdbɔ:dz] *npl*, *US* **sideburns** ['saɪdbɜ:nz] *npl* patillas *fpl*

sidecar ['saɪdkɑ:r] *n Aut* sidecar *m*

sidekick ['saɪdkɪk] *n US Fam* compinche *m*, amigote *m*, colega *mf*

sidelight ['saɪdlaɪt] *n Aut* luz *f* lateral, piloto *m*

sideline ['saɪdlaɪn] *n* **(a)** *Sport* línea *f* de banda; *Fig* **to sit on the sidelines** quedarse en el banquillo **(b)** *Com (product)* línea *f* suplementaria; *(business)* negocio *m* suplementario; *(job)* empleo *m* suplementario

sidelong ['saɪdlɒŋ] **1** *adj (glance etc)* de reojo, de soslayo

  2 *adv* de lado

sidereal [saɪ'dɪərɪəl] *adj Astron* sideral, sidéreo(a)

side-saddle ['saɪdsædəl] **1** *n* silla *f* de amazona

  2 *adv* **to ride s.-s.** montar a la amazona

sideshow ['saɪdʃəʊ] *n (at fairground)* atracción *f* secundaria

side-splitting ['saɪdsplɪtɪŋ] *adj Fam* desternillante, divertidísimo(a)

sidestep ['saɪdstep] **1** *vt (pt & pp* **sidestepped)** *(question, issue)* eludir, esquivar

  2 *vi Box* dar un quiebro, fintar

sideswipe ['saɪdswaɪp] *n* **to take a s. at sth/sb** meterse de pasada con algo/algn

sidetrack ['saɪdtræk] *vt Fig (person)* despistar; *(issue)* dejar de lado

sidewalk ['saɪdwɔ:k] *n US* acera *f*, *CAm Méx* banqueta *f*, *CSur* vereda *f*; **s. cafe** café *m* con terraza

sideways ['saɪdweɪz] **1** *adj (step, movement)* lateral; *(glance, look)* de reojo, de soslayo

  2 *adv (gen)* de lado; **to step s.** dar un paso hacia un lado

siding ['saɪdɪŋ] *n* **(a)** *Rail* apartadero *m*, vía *f* muerta **(b)** *US Constr* tabiques *mpl* pluviales

sidle ['saɪdəl] *vi* **to s. up to sb** acercarse furtivamente *or* sigilosamente a algn

siege [si:dʒ] *n* sitio *m*, cerco *m*; **to lay s. to** sitiar, poner sitio a, cercar; **to raise the s.** levantar el sitio

sienna [sɪ'enə] *n Art* (tierra *f* de) siena *f*

Sierra Leone [sɪeərəlɪ'əʊn(ɪ)] *n* Sierra Leona

siesta [sɪ'estə] *n* siesta *f*; **to have a s.** echar *or* dormir la siesta

sieve [sɪv] **1** *n (fine)* tamiz *m*; *(coarse)* criba *f*; *Fam* **to have a memory like a s.** tener muy mala memoria

  2 *vt (fine)* tamizar, pasar por el tamiz; *(coarse)* cribar

sift [sɪft] *vt* **(a)** *(sieve)* tamizar, cribar; *Fig* **to s. through** examinar cuidadosamente **(b)** *(sprinkle)* espolvorear

sifter ['sɪftər] *n* **(a)** *(sieve)* tamiz *m* **(b)** *(sprinkler)* espolvoreador *m*

sigh [saɪ] **1** *n (of person)* suspiro *m*; *(of wind)* susurro *m*, gemido *m*; **to breathe** *or* **heave a s. of relief** dar un suspiro de alivio

  2 *vi (person)* suspirar; *(wind)* susurrar, gemir

sight [saɪt] **1** *n* **(a)** *(faculty)* vista *f*; **at first s.** a primera vista; **he faints at the s. of blood** se desmaya cuando ve sangre; **it was love at first s.** fue un flechazo, fue amor a primera vista; **to catch s. of sth/sb** divisar algo/a algn; **to know sb by s.** conocer a algn de vista; **to lose s. of sth/sb** perder algo/a algn de vista; *Fig* **I hate the s. of him** no puedo ni verlo ❑ **long s.** presbicia *f*; **second s.** intuición *f*; **short s.** miopía *f* **(b)** *(range of vision)* vista *f*; **to be within s.** estar a la vista; **to come into s.** aparecer; **to keep out of s.** no dejarse ver, esconderse; **to shoot at** *or* **on s.** disparar a matar; *Slang* **out of s.** alucinante; *Prov* **out of s., out of mind** ojos que no ven, corazón que no siente **(c)** *(spectacle)* espectáculo *m*; **it's a s. for sore eyes** da gusto verlo; **it was a sorry s.** fue un triste espectáculo; *Fam* **what a s. you look!** ¡qué pinta tienes! **(d)** *(on gun)* mira *f*; **to take s.** apuntar; *Fig* **to set one's sights on sth** tener la mira puesta en algo; *Fig* **to set one's sights too high** apuntar demasiado alto, ser demasiado ambicioso(a) **(e)** *Fam (a great deal)* **a s. more expensive** muchísimo más caro(a); **not by a long s.** ni mucho menos **(f)** **sights** *(tourist attractions)* monumentos *mpl*; **to see the s. of the city** visitar la ciudad, hacer un recorrido turístico de la ciudad

  2 *vt (bird, animal)* observar, ver; *(person)* ver; *(land)* divisar

sighted ['saɪtɪd] *adj* vidente, de vista normal; **the partially s.** los que tienen problemas de vista

sighting ['saɪtɪŋ] *n* observación *f*

sightless ['saɪtlɪs] *adj* ciego(a), invidente

sightly ['saɪtlɪ] *adj* **(sightlier, sightliest)** atractivo(a)

sight-read ['saɪtri:d] *vt & vi Mus* repentizar

sight-reading ['saɪtri:dɪŋ] *n Mus* repentización *f*

sightseeing ['saɪtsiːɪŋ] *n* turismo *m*, visita *f* turística; **to go s.** hacer turismo, visitar la ciudad

sightseer ['saɪtsɪər] *n* turista *mf*

sign [saɪn] **1** *n* (**a**) *(symbol)* signo *m*, símbolo *m*; *Math* **plus/minus s.** signo de más/de menos; *Astrol* **the signs of the zodiac** los signos del zodíaco (**b**) *(gesture)* gesto *m*, seña *f*; *(signal)* señal *f*; **to make a s. to sb** hacer una señal a algn; **to make the s. of the Cross** hacer la señal de la cruz ❑ **s. language** lenguaje *m* por señas; **to use s. language** hablar por señas (**c**) *(indication)* señal *f*, muestra *f*; *(proof)* prueba *f*; *(trace)* rastro *m*, huella *f*; **as a s. of** como muestra de; **it's a sure s. of** es un claro indicio de; **there was no s. of him anywhere** no se le veía por ninguna parte; **to show signs of life** dar señales de vida (**d**) *(notice)* anuncio *m*, aviso *m*; *(board)* letrero *m*; *(over shop)* rótulo *m*; **there's a s. which says 'keep out'** hay un letrero que dice 'prohibida la entrada' ❑ **neon s.** rótulo *m* de neón; **road s.** *(giving warnings etc)* señal *f* de tráfico; *(showing route)* indicador *m* de carretera

2 *vt* (**a**) *(letter, document)* firmar; **to s. one's name** firmar (**b**) *Ftb (player)* fichar

3 *vi (with name)* firmar

sign away *vt* ceder

sign in *vi (in factory)* fichar, *Am* marcar tarjeta; *(in hotel)* registrarse

sign off *vi Rad TV* despedirse, cerrar el programa

sign on 1 *vt (worker)* contratar; *Ftb (player)* fichar

2 *vi (worker)* firmar un contrato; *Ftb (player)* fichar (**for** por); *(student)* matricularse; *Br Fam (unemployed person)* registrarse para recibir el seguro de desempleo, *Esp* apuntarse al paro

sign out 1 *vt* **to s. sth out** *(book, equipment)* registrar or consignar el préstamo de algo

2 *vi* firmar a la salida

sign over *vt* ceder

sign up 1 *vt (soldier)* reclutar; *(worker)* contratar; *Ftb (player)* fichar

2 *vi (soldier)* alistarse; *(worker)* firmar un contrato; *Ftb (player)* fichar (**with** por)

signal ['sɪgnəl] **1** *n* (**a**) *(gen)* señal *f*; *Rad TV* sintonía *f*; *US Tel* **busy s.** señal de ocupado; **to give the alarm s.** dar la señal de alarma ❑ *Rail* **s. box** garita *f* de señales; *Aut* **traffic signals** señales *mpl* de tráfico

2 *vt* (*pt & pp* **signalled**, *US* **signaled**) (**a**) *(transmit)* (*message*) transmitir or comunicar por señales (**b**) *(indicate)* (*direction etc)* indicar (**c**) *(signify)* señalar; **it signalled the end of an era** señaló el fin de toda una época

3 *vi (with hands)* hacer señales; *(in car)* señalar, poner el intermitente

signalman ['sɪgnəlmən] *n* (*pl* **signalmen**) *Rail* guardavía *m*

signatory ['sɪgnətərɪ] *n* firmante *mf*, signatario(a) *m,f*

signature ['sɪgnɪtʃər] *n* (*name*) firma *f*; *Rad TV* **s. tune** sintonía *f*

signboard ['saɪnbɔːd] *n* (*sign*) letrero *m*; *(hoarding)* cartelera *f*; *(noticeboard)* tablón *m* de anuncios

signet ['sɪgnɪt] *n* sello *m* ❑ **s. ring** (anillo *m* de) sello *m*

significance [sɪg'nɪfɪkəns] *n (meaning)* significado *m*; *(importance)* importancia *f*; **it's of no s.** carece de importancia

significant [sɪg'nɪfɪkənt] *adj (meaningful)* significativo(a); *(important)* importante, considerable; **s. other** media naranja *f*

significantly [sɪg'nɪfɪkəntlɪ] *adv (markedly)* sensiblemente; **s. enough, they are both women** es importante destacar que ambas son mujeres

signify ['sɪgnɪfaɪ] *vt* (*pt & pp* **signified**) (**a**) *(mean)* significar; *(denote)* señalar, indicar (**b**) *(show, make known)* indicar, mostrar

signpost ['saɪnpəʊst] *Aut* **1** *n* poste *m* indicador

2 *vt (route etc)* señalizar

signwriter ['saɪnraɪtər] *n* rotulista *mf*

Sikh [siːk] *adj & n* sij *(mf)*

silage ['saɪlɪdʒ] *n Agr* ensilado *m*, ensilaje *m*

silence ['saɪləns] **1** *n* silencio *m*; **deadly s.** silencio sepulcral; **in s.** en silencio; **to break s.** romper el silencio; *Prov* **s. is golden** el silencio es oro

2 *vt (person)* acallar, hacer callar; *(protests)* apagar; *(engine)* silenciar

silencer ['saɪlənsər] *n* silenciador *m*

silent ['saɪlənt] *adj (gen)* silencioso(a); *(not talkative)* callado(a); *(film, letter)* mudo(a); **the s. majority** la mayoría silenciosa; **to be s.** callarse; **to keep** *or* **remain s.** guardar silencio

silently ['saɪləntlɪ] *adv* silenciosamente, en silencio

silhouette [sɪluːˈet] **1** *n* silueta *f*

2 *vt* **to be silhouetted against** recortarse *or* perfilarse en *or* sobre

silica ['sɪlɪkə] *n Chem* sílice *f*

silicon ['sɪlɪkən] *n Chem* silicio *m* ❑ *Comptr* **s. chip** chip *m* (de silicio)

silicone ['sɪlɪkəʊn] *n Chem* silicona *f*

silicosis [sɪlɪˈkəʊsɪs] *n Med* silicosis *f*

silk [sɪlk] **1** *n* seda *f*; **raw s.** seda cruda; *Fig* **to be of the same s.** ser del mismo paño

2 *adj (shirt etc)* de seda; **the s. industry** la industria sedera

silken ['sɪlkən] *adj Fig* sedoso(a)

silk-screen ['sɪlkskriːn] *n* **s.-s. printing** serigrafía *f*

silkworm ['sɪlkwɜːm] *n* gusano *m* de seda

silky ['sɪlkɪ] *adj* (**silkier, silkiest**) *(cloth)* sedoso(a); *(voice etc)* suave

sill [sɪl] *n (of window)* alféizar *m*, antepecho *m*; *(of car)* faldón *m* trasero

silliness ['sɪlɪnɪs] *n* (**a**) *(quality)* estupidez *f*, necedad *f* (**b**) *(act)* tontería *f*, bobada *f*

silly ['sɪlɪ] *adj* (**sillier, silliest**) *(stupid)* tonto(a), bobo(a), necio(a); *(absurd)* absurdo(a); *(ridiculous)* ridículo(a); **to do sth s.** hacer una tontería; **to make sb look s.** poner a algn en ridículo; *Fam* **to drink oneself s.** agarrar una trompa de órdago

silo ['saɪləʊ] *n* (*pl* **silos**) *Agr Mil* silo *m*

silt [sɪlt] *n* cieno *m*, légamo *m*

silt up *vi* obstruirse con cieno *or* sedimentos

silting ['sɪltɪŋ] *n* sedimentación *f*

silver ['sɪlvər] **1** *n* (**a**) *(metal)* plata *f*; **sterling s.** plata de ley (**b**) *Br (coins)* monedas *fpl* (de plata) (**c**) *(tableware, articles)* plata *f*, vajilla *f* de plata

2 *adj* de plata; *Prov* **every cloud has a s. lining** no hay mal que por bien no venga ❑ **s. foil** papel *m* de plata; *(tinfoil)* papel *m* de aluminio; **s. jubilee** vigésimo quinto aniversario *m*, bodas *fpl* de plata; **s. medal** medalla *f* de plata; *Br* **s. paper** papel *m* de plata; **s. plate** *(coating)* plateado *m*; *(articles)* vajilla *f* plateada; **s. wedding** bodas *fpl* de plata

silver-plated [sɪlvəˈpleɪtɪd] *adj* plateado(a), con un baño de plata

silversmith ['sɪlvəsmɪθ] *n* platero(a) *m,f*

silverware ['sɪlvəweər] *n* plata *f*, vajilla *f* de plata

silvery ['sɪlvərɪ] *adj* (**a**) *(colour, material)* plateado(a) (**b**) *(sound)* argentino(a)

SIM [sɪm] n (abbr **subscriber identity module**) S. **card** (in mobile phone) tarjeta f SIM

similar ['sɪmɪlər] adj parecido(a), semejante, similar (**to** a); **s. in size** de tamaño parecido; **to be very s.** parecerse mucho ❑ Geom **s. triangle** triángulo m semejante

similarity [sɪmɪ'lærɪtɪ] n semejanza f, parecido m

similarly ['sɪmɪləlɪ] adv (**a**) (as well) igualmente (**b**) (likewise) del mismo modo, asimismo

simile ['sɪmɪlɪ] n Lit símil m

simmer ['sɪmər] **1** vt cocer or hervir a fuego lento
    2 vi cocerse or hervir a fuego lento

simmer down vi Fam calmarse, tranquilizarse

simper ['sɪmpər] **1** n sonrisa f afectada
    2 vi sonreír con afectación

simpering ['sɪmpərɪŋ] **1** adj afectado(a), melindroso(a)
    2 n melindres mpl

simple ['sɪmpəl] adj (**a**) (easy, straightforward) fácil, sencillo(a); (not complicated) sencillo(a), simple; **it's a question of money pure and s.** es pura y simplemente una cuestión de dinero ❑ Fin **s. interest** interés m simple (**b**) (plain, unsophisticated) sencillo(a); (natural) natural; **to be a s. soul** ser un alma de Dios (**c**) (foolish, backward) simple, tonto(a); (naïve) ingenuo(a), inocente; (dim) corto(a) de alcances, de pocas luces

simple-minded [sɪmpəl'maɪndɪd] adj simple, tonto(a), necio(a)

simpleton ['sɪmpəltən] n simplón(ona) m,f, inocentón(ona) m,f, papanatas mf

simplicity [sɪm'plɪsɪtɪ] n (**a**) (lack of sophistication) sencillez f, naturalidad f (**b**) (foolishness) simpleza f; (naïveté) ingenuidad f (**c**) (incomplexity) sencillez f

simplification [sɪmplɪfɪ'keɪʃən] n simplificación f

simplify ['sɪmplɪfaɪ] vt (pt & pp **simplified**) simplificar

simplistic [sɪm'plɪstɪk] adj simplista

simply ['sɪmplɪ] adv (**a**) (plainly, modestly) simplemente, sencillamente (**b**) (only) simplemente, solamente, sólo; (just, merely) meramente (**c**) (really) francamente, realmente

simulate ['sɪmjʊleɪt] vt (gen) simular; (object, noise) imitar

simulated ['sɪmjʊleɪtɪd] adj (flight) simulado(a); (leather etc) de imitación

simulation [sɪmjʊ'leɪʃən] n simulación f, simulacro m

simulator ['sɪmjʊleɪtər] n simulador m; Av **flight s.** simulador de vuelo

simultaneous [sɪməl'teɪnɪəs] adj simultáneo(a); Math **s. equations** sistema m de ecuaciones

simultaneously [sɪməl'teɪnɪəslɪ] adv simultáneamente, a la vez

sin¹ [sɪn] **1** n pecado m; **mortal s.** pecado mortal; Fig **it would be a s. to waste it** sería un crimen desperdiciarlo; Fam **as ugly as s.** más feo(a) que un pecado
    2 vi pecar

sin² [saɪn] Math (abbr **sine**) seno m, sen

since [sɪns] **1** adv desde entonces; **ever s.** desde entonces; **I have not seen him s.** no lo he vuelto a ver desde entonces; **long s.** hace mucho tiempo; (subsequently) **it has s. come out that ...** desde entonces se ha sabido que ...
    2 prep desde; **she has been living here s. 1975** vive aquí desde 1975
    3 conj (**a**) (time) desde que; **he hasn't worked s. he left school** está en paro desde que dejó el colegio; **how long is it s. you last saw him?** ¿cuánto tiempo hace desde que lo viste por última vez? (**b**) (because, as) ya que, puesto que; **s. he is unwell** ya que está enfermo

sincere [sɪn'sɪər] adj sincero(a)

sincerely [sɪn'sɪəlɪ] adv sinceramente; (in letter) **Yours s.** (le saluda) atentamente

sincerity [sɪn'serɪtɪ] n sinceridad f; **in all s.** con toda sinceridad

sinecure ['saɪnɪkjʊər] n sinecura f

sinew ['sɪnjuː] n (tendon) tendón m; (in meat) nervio m

sinewy ['sɪnjʊɪ] adj nervudo(a)

sinful ['sɪnfʊl] adj (person) pecador(a); (act, thought) pecaminoso(a); Fig (waste etc) escandaloso(a)

sing [sɪŋ] **1** vt (pt **sang**; pp **sung**) cantar; **to s. a baby to sleep** arrullar a un niño; Fig **to s. the praises of sth/sb** alabar algo/a algn
    2 vi (person, bird) cantar; (kettle, bullets) silbar; (insect, ears) zumbar; **can you s.?** ¿sabes cantar?

sing out vi (**a**) (sing loudly) cantar fuerte (**b**) Fam (shout) gritar

Singapore [sɪŋə'pɔːr] n Singapur

Singaporean [sɪŋə'pɔːrɪən] adj & n singapurense (mf)

singe [sɪndʒ] vt chamuscar

singer ['sɪŋər] n cantante mf; (in choir) cantor(a) m,f

singing ['sɪŋɪŋ] **1** n (art) canto m, cantar m; (songs) canciones fpl; (of kettle) silbido m; (in ears) zumbido m
    2 adj **s. lessons** lecciones de canto; **he has a fine s. voice** tiene buena voz

single ['sɪŋgəl] **1** adj (**a**) (solitary, individual) solo(a); **every s. day** todos los días; **there wasn't a s. ticket left** no quedó ni una sola entrada (**b**) (only one) único(a), sencillo(a); **in s. figures** por debajo del diez; **in s. file** en fila india (**c**) (not double) individual, sencillo(a) ❑ Br Culin **s. cream** Esp nata f or Am crema f líquida; **s. bed/room** cama f/habitación f individual; Br Rail **s. ticket** billete m or Am boleto m sencillo or de ida (**d**) (unmarried) soltero(a)
    2 n (**a**) Br Rail Esp billete m or Am boleto m sencillo or de ida (**b**) (record) disco m sencillo, single m (**c**) singles Sport individuales mpl (**d**) singles **bar/holiday** bar m/vacaciones fpl para solteros

single out vt (choose) escoger, seleccionar; (distinguish) distinguir, destacar, resaltar

single-breasted [sɪŋgəl'brestɪd] adj (suit, jacket) recto(a), sin cruzar

single-decker [sɪŋgəl'dekər] n autobús m de un solo piso

single-handed [sɪŋgəl'hændɪd] adj & adv sin ayuda, solo(a)

single-minded [sɪŋgəl'maɪndɪd] adj resuelto(a)

singleness ['sɪŋgəlnɪs] n **s. of purpose** resolución f, ahínco m

single-sex school ['sɪŋgəl'seks'skuːl] n (for girls) colegio m para niñas; (for boys) colegio m para niños

singlet ['sɪŋglɪt] n Br (vest) camiseta f (de tirantes or CSur breteles)

singly ['sɪŋglɪ] adv (individually) por separado; (one by one) uno por uno

sing-song ['sɪŋsɒŋ] **1** adj (voice, tone) cantarín(ina)
    2 n (**a**) (voice, tone) sonsonete m (**b**) (singing session) concierto m improvisado

singular ['sɪŋgjʊlər] **1** adj (**a**) Ling singular (**b**) Fml (outstanding) extraordinario(a), excepcional; **a woman of s. beauty** una mujer de excepcional belleza (**c**) Fml (unique, unusual) único(a), extraño(a), particular
    2 n Ling singular m; **in the s.** en singular

singularly ['sɪŋgjʊləlɪ] adv extraordinariamente, excepcionalmente

Sinhalese [sɪnə'liːz] **1** n (**a**) (person) cingalés(esa) m,f (**b**) (language) cingalés m
    2 adj cingalés(esa)

sinister ['sınıstər] *adj* siniestro(a)

sink¹ [sıŋk] *n (in kitchen)* fregadero *m*

sink² [sıŋk] **1** *vt (pt* **sank**; *pp* **sunk**) **(a)** *(ship)* hundir, echar a pique; *Fig (hopes, plans)* acabar con; *Fig* **to be sunk in thought** estar abstraído(a); **we sank our differences** hicimos las paces; *Fam* **we're sunk!** ¡estamos perdidos! **(b)** *(shaft, hole)* cavar, excavar; *(well)* abrir; *(post, pipe)* hincar; *(knife)* clavar, hundir; *(teeth)* hincar **(into** en) **(c)** *(invest)* invertir **(into** en) **(d)** *Br Fam (drink) Esp* soplarse, *Am* tomarse **(e)** *Sport Slang (golf, snooker)* meter

2 *vi* **(a)** *(ship, etc)* hundirse, irse a pique; *Fig* **to leave sb to s. or swim** abandonar a algn a su suerte; *Fig* **to s. into oblivion** caer en el olvido **(b)** *(land, building) (subside)* hundirse; **Venice is slowly sinking** Venecia se hunde lentamente; *Fig* **his hopes sank** sus esperanzas se vinieron abajo; *Fig* **my heart sank** se me cayó el alma a los pies **(c)** *(sun)* ponerse, bajar **(d)** *(figures, prices)* bajar **(e)** *(slump)* dejarse caer; **to s. back into an armchair** arrellanarse en un sillón; **to s. to one's knees** hincarse de rodillas

sink in *vi (penetrate)* penetrar; *Fig (words)* causar impresión; **it hasn't sunk in yet** todavía no ha hecho impacto

sinker ['sıŋkər] *n Fishing* plomo *m*

sinking ['sıŋkıŋ] *n (of ship)* hundimiento *m*

sinner ['sınər] *n* pecador(a) *m,f*

sinuous ['sınjʊəs] *adj* sinuoso(a)

sinus ['saınəs] *n Anat* seno *m*

sinusitis [saınə'saıtıs] *n* sinusitis *f inv*

sip [sıp] **1** *n* sorbo *m*
2 *vt (pt & pp* **sipped)** sorber, beber a sorbos

siphon ['saıfən] *n* sifón *m*

siphon off *vt (liquid)* sacar con sifón; *Fig (funds, traffic)* desviar

sir [sɜːr] *n Fml* señor *m*; **yes, s.!** sí, señor; *Mil* **s.!** ¡a sus órdenes!; *(in letter)* **Dear Sir** muy señor mío, estimado señor; *(title)* sir; **S. Walter Raleigh** Sir Walter Raleigh

sire [saıər] **1** *vt (beget)* ser padre de, engendrar
2 *n (animals)* macho *m*

siren ['saıərən] *n Myth* sirena *f*

sirloin ['sɜːlɔın] *n Culin* solomillo *m*

sisal ['saızəl] *n (plant)* pita *f*; *(material)* sisal *m*

sissy ['sısı] *n Fam (coward)* miedica *mf*

sister ['sıstər] **1** *n* **(a)** *(relation)* hermana *f* **(b)** *Br Med* enfermera *f* jefe **(c)** *Rel* hermana *f*, monja *f*; *(before name)* sor; **s. Maria** Sor Maria
2 *adj* **s. nation** nación *f* hermana; **s. ship** barco *m* gemelo

sisterhood ['sıstəhʊd] *n* hermandad *f*

sister-in-law ['sıstərınlɔː] *n (pl* **sisters-in-law)** cuñada *f*

sisterly ['sıstəlı] *adj* de hermana

sit [sıt] **1** *vt (pt & pp* **sat)** **(a)** *(child etc)* sentar **(in, on** en) **(b)** *(hall etc)* tener cabida para **(c)** *Br (exam)* presentarse a
2 *vi* **(a)** *(action)* sentarse; *(to dog)* **s.!** ¡siéntate! **(b)** *(be seated)* estar sentado(a); **to be sitting at table** estar sentado(a) a la mesa; *Fig* **to be sitting pretty** estar en una situación ventajosa; *Fig* **to s. tight** mantenerse en sus trece **(c)** *(object) (lie, rest)* yacer; *(be situated)* ubicarse, estar, hallarse; *(person) (remain)* quedarse; **he sits there all day** se pasa todo el día allí sentado **(d)** *(pose)* posar **(e)** *(be a member)* ser miembro; **to s. on a jury** ser miembro de un jurado **(f)** *Pol (represent)* representar **(g)** *(assembly)* reunirse, estar reunido(a) **(h)** *Fam (babysit)* cuidar niños, hacer de canguro

bout, sit around *vi* holgazanear, hacer el vago

sit back *vi (in chair)* recostarse; *Fig* **he just sat back and did nothing** no levantó ni un dedo para ayudar

sit down 1 *vt* sentar; **he sat himself down** se sentó
2 *vi* sentarse; **please s. down** siéntese por favor

sit in on *vt* asistir a sin participar

sit on *vt Fam* **(a)** *(keep secret)* ocultar, callar; *(delay dealing with)* dejar dormir, aplazar **(b)** *(person) (silence)* hacer callar; *(repress)* hacer la vida difícil a

sit out *vt (endure)* aguantar hasta el final

sit through *vt (as a spectator etc)* aguantar

sit up 1 *vt (baby etc)* sentar
2 *vi* **(a)** *(straight)* ponerse derecho(a); *(in bed)* incorporarse; *Fig* **to s. up and take notice** prestar atención **(b)** *(stay up late)* quedarse levantado(a), no acostarse; **to s. up waiting for sb** quedarse esperando a algn

sitcom ['sıtkɒm] *n TV* telecomedia *f* (de situación)

sit-down ['sıtdaʊn] **1** *adj* **s.-d. meal** comida *f* servida en la mesa
2 *n* **(a)** *(protest)* sentada *f* **(b)** *Fam* breve reposo *m*

site [saıt] **1** *n* **(a)** *(area)* terreno *m*, lugar *m* ❑ **building s.** solar *m*; *(under construction)* obra *f*; **camp s.** camping *m*; **caravan s.** camping *m* de caravanas **(b)** *(location)* situación *f*, emplazamiento *m*; **nuclear testing s.** zona *f* de pruebas nucleares
2 *vt (building etc)* situar, ubicar

sit-in ['sıtın] *n Fam (demonstration)* sentada *f*; *(strike)* huelga *f* de brazos caídos

siting ['saıtıŋ] *n* emplazamiento *m*, ubicación *f*

sitter ['sıtər] *n* **(a)** *Art* modelo *mf* **(b)** *(baby)* **s.** *Esp* canguro *mf*, *Am* babysitter *mf* **(c)** *Sport (easy chance)* ocasión *f* fácil

sitting ['sıtıŋ] **1** *n* **(a)** *(of committee, for portrait)* sesión *f*; *(in canteen)* turno *m*
2 *adj* **(a)** *(seated)* sentado(a) ❑ *Pol* **s. member** miembro *m* activo; **s. room** sala *f* de estar, salón *m*, living *m*; **s. tenant** inquilino(a) *m,f* con derecho a propiedad **(b)** *Fam Fig* **s. duck** blanco *m* facilísimo

situate ['sıtjʊeıt] *vt Fml* situar, ubicar

situated ['sıtjʊeıtıd] *adj (building etc)* situado(a), ubicado(a); *Fam* **how are you s. for money?** ¿cómo andas de dinero?

situation [sıtjʊ'eıʃən] *n* **(a)** *(location)* situación *f*, ubicación *f* **(b)** *(circumstances etc)* situación *f*; **the current economic s.** la situación económica actual ❑ **s. comedy** *(on TV)* telecomedia *f* (de situación) **(c)** *(job, position)* empleo *m*, puesto *m*; *(in newspaper)* **'situations vacant'** 'ofertas de trabajo', 'bolsa de trabajo'

sit-up ['sıtʌp] *n (exercise)* abdominal *m*

six [sıks] **1** *adj* seis *inv*
2 *n* seis *m inv*; *Fam Fig* **it's s. of one and half a dozen of the other** viene a ser lo mismo, da lo mismo, da igual; *Fam Fig* **to be at sixes and sevens** estar confuso(a), estar hecho(a) un lío; *see also* **seven**

six-pack ['sıkspæk] *n Com (of beer etc)* caja *f* de seis botellas *or* latas

sixpence ['sıkspəns] *n Br Formerly (coin)* moneda *f* de seis peniques

sixteen [sıks'tiːn] *adj & n* dieciséis *(m) inv*, diez y seis *(m) inv*; *see also* **seven**

sixteenth [sıks'tiːnθ] **1** *adj* decimosexto(a)
2 *n* **(a)** *(in series)* decimosexto(a) *m,f* **(b)** *(fraction)* dieciseisavo *m*, decimosexta parte *f* ❑ *US Mus* **s. note** semicorchea *f*; *see also* **seventh**

sixth [sıksθ] **1** *adj* sexto(a); **s. sense** sexto sentido; *Br Educ* **s. form** = últimos dos cursos del bachillerato previos a los estudios superiores; *Br Educ* **s. former** = estudiante de los dos últimos cursos del bachillerato

2 *n* **(a)** *(in series)* sexto(a) *m,f* **(b)** *(fraction)* sexto *m*, sexta parte *f*; *see also* **seventh**

sixtieth ['sɪkstɪəθ] **1** *adj* sexagésimo(a)

2 *n* **(a)** *(in series)* sexagésimo(a) *m,f* **(b)** *(fraction)* sesentavo *m*, sexagésima parte *f*; *see also* **seventh**

sixty ['sɪkstɪ] **1** *adj* sesenta *inv*

2 *n* sesenta *m inv*; *see also* **seventy** *and* **seven**

sixty-fourth note ['sɪkstɪ'fɔːθnəʊt] *n US Mus* semifusa *f*

size[1] [saɪz] *n (gen)* tamaño *m*; *(of garment)* talla *f*; *(of shoes)* número *m*; *(of person)* talla *f*, estatura *f*; *(scope)* alcance *m*; *(magnitude)* magnitud *f*; **life s.** tamaño natural; **she's a size ten** gasta la talla diez; **try it on for s.** pruébatelo para ver la talla que necesitas; **what s. do you take?** *(garment)* ¿qué talla tienes?; *(shoes)* ¿qué número calzas?; **what s. is the kitchen?** ¿de qué tamaño es la cocina?; **to cut sth to s.** cortar algo al tamaño que se necesita; *Fig* **to cut sb down to s.** bajar los humos a algn; *Fig* **that's about the s. of it** es más o menos así

size up *vt (person)* juzgar; *(situation, problem)* evaluar

size[2] [saɪz] **1** *n (for paper, textiles)* cola *f*, apresto *m*

2 *vt (paper, textiles)* encolar, aprestar

siz(e)able ['saɪzəbəl] *adj (estate, building, etc)* (bastante) grande; *(sum)* considerable; *(problem)* importante

sizzle ['sɪzəl] **1** *n* chisporroteo *m*

2 *vi* chisporrotear

skate[1] [skeɪt] **1** *n* patín *m*; *Fam* **get your skates on!** ¡date prisa!

2 *vi* patinar; *Fig* **to s. on thin ice** pisar un terreno peligroso

skate over, skate around *vt Fig (problem, difficulty)* evitar

skate[2] [skeɪt] *n (fish)* raya *f*

skateboard ['skeɪtbɔːd] *n* skateboard *m*, *Esp* monopatín *m*

skater ['skeɪtər] *n* patinador(a) *m,f*

skating ['skeɪtɪŋ] *n* patinaje *m*; **ice/roller s.** patinaje sobre hielo/sobre ruedas ◻ **s. rink** pista *f* de patinaje

skedaddle [skɪ'dædəl] *vi Fam* esfumarse, largarse

skeletal ['skelɪtəl] *adj Fml* esquelético(a)

skeleton ['skelɪtən] **1** *n* **(a)** *(of person, animal)* esqueleto *m* **(b)** *(of building, ship)* armazón *m*, estructura *f* **(c)** *(outline, plan)* esquema *m*, bosquejo *m*

2 *adj (staff, service)* reducido(a), limitado(a) ◻ **s. key** llave *f* maestra

skeptic ['skeptɪk] *n US see* **sceptic**

skeptical ['skeptɪkəl] *adj US see* **sceptical**

skepticism ['skeptɪsɪzəm] *n US see* **scepticism**

sketch [sketʃ] **1** *n* **(a)** *(rough drawing)* croquis *m*; *(preliminary drawing)* bosquejo *m*, esbozo *m*; *(drawing)* dibujo *m*; *(outline)* esquema *m*; *(rough draft)* boceto *m*, borrador *m*; *Lit* **character s.** breve descripción *f* de un personaje **(b)** *Theat TV* sketch *m*

2 *vt (draw)* dibujar; *(rough drawing)* hacer un croquis de; *(preliminary drawing)* bosquejar, esbozar

3 *vi (draw)* dibujar

sketch in *vt (details)* dibujar; *Fig* dar un resumen de

sketch-book ['sketʃbʊk] *n*, **sketch-pad** ['sketʃpæd] *n* bloc *m* de dibujo

sketchy ['sketʃɪ] *adj* **(sketchier, sketchiest)** *(incomplete)* incompleto(a); *(not detailed)* sin detalles; *(vague)* vago(a), impreciso(a)

skewed [skju:d] *adj (distorted)* sesgado(a)

skewer ['skjʊər] **1** *n Culin* pincho *m*, broqueta *f*, brocheta *f*

2 *vt (pieces of meat etc)* ensartar (en un pincho)

ski [ski:] **1** *n (equipment)* esquí *m*

2 *adj* de esquí, de esquiar ◻ **s. boots** botas *fpl* de esquiar; **s. instructor** monitor(a) *m,f* de esquí; **s. jump** *(action)* salto *m* con esquís; *(course)* pista *f* de salto; **s. lift** telesquí *m*; *(with seats)* telesilla *f*; **s. pants** pantalón *m sing* de esquiar; **s. resort** estación *f* de esquí *or* esquiar; **s. run** pista *f* de esquí; **s. stick** palo *m* de esquiar

3 *vi* esquiar; **to go skiing** ir a esquiar; **to s. down** bajar esquiando

skid [skɪd] **1** *n* **(a)** *Aut* patinazo *m*, derrapaje *m*, resbalón *m* **(b)** *US Fam* **s. row** barrio *m* bajo

2 *vi* (*pt & pp* **skidded**) *Aut* patinar, derrapar; **the truck skidded to a halt** el camión fue patinando hasta que se paró

skidmark ['skɪdmɑːk] *n* marca *f* de neumáticos

skier ['ski:ər] *n* esquiador(a) *m,f*

skiff [skɪf] *n Naut* esquife *m*

skiing ['ski:ɪŋ] *n* esquí *m*; **s. holiday** vacaciones de esquí

skilful, *US* **skillful** ['skɪlfʊl] *adj* hábil, diestro(a); *Fam* mañoso(a)

skilfully, *US* **skillfully** *adv* hábilmente, con destreza

skill [skɪl] *n* **(a)** *(ability)* habilidad *f*, destreza *f*; *(talent)* talento *m*, don *m* **(b)** *(technique)* técnica *f*, arte *m*, especialidad *f*

skilled [skɪld] *adj* **(a)** *(able, dextrous)* hábil, diestro(a); *(expert)* experto(a) **(b)** *(specialized)* *(worker)* cualificado(a), especializado(a); *(work)* especializado(a), de especialista

skim [skɪm] **1** *vt* (*pt & pp* **skimmed**) **(a)** *(soup)* espumar; **to s. the cream off the milk** *Esp* quitar la nata *or Am* sacar la crema a la leche ◻ **skimmed** *or US* **s. milk** leche *f* descremada *or* desnatada **(b)** *(brush against)* rozar; **to s. the ground** rozar el suelo; *(bird, plane)* volar a ras de suelo; **to s. stones** hacer cabrillas con piedrecitas

2 *vi* **to s. across the water/ground** pasar rozando el agua/suelo; *Fig* **to s. through a book** hojear un libro

skimp [skɪmp] **1** *vt (food, material)* escatimar

2 *vi* **to s. on food/material** escatimar comida/tela

skimpily ['skɪmpɪlɪ] *adv* **s. dressed** ligeramente vestido(a)

skimpy ['skɪmpɪ] *adj* **(skimpier, skimpiest)** *(dress)* ligero(a); *(meal)* escaso(a), pobre

skin [skɪn] **1** *n* **(a)** *(of person)* piel *f*; *(of face)* cutis *m*; *(complexion)* tez *f*; *Fig* **to be all s. and bone** estar en los huesos; *Fig* **to escape by the s. of one's teeth** librarse por los pelos; *Fig* **to get under one's s.** irritarle a uno; *Fig* **to have a thick/thin s.** ser poco sensible/muy susceptible; *Fam* **it's no s. off my nose** a mí me *Esp* trae *or Am* tiene sin cuidado; *Fam* **to save one's own s.** salvar el pellejo ◻ **s. cancer** cáncer *m* de piel; **s. cream** crema *f* de belleza; *Med* **s. disease** enfermedad *f* de la piel, dermatosis *f*; *Med* **s. graft** injerto *m* cutáneo *or* de piel; *Med* **s. test** prueba *f* cutánea, cutirreacción *f* **(b)** *(of animal)* piel *f*, pellejo *m*; *(pelt)* piel *f*; *(hide)* cuero *m* (curtido) **(c)** *Bot (of fruit)* piel *f*; *(hard)* cáscara *f*, corteza *f*; *(soft)* piel *f*; *(peeling)* monda *f*, mondadura *f* **(d)** *(of sausage)* pellejo *m* **(e)** *(on paint)* telilla *f*, capa *f* fina; *(on milk, custard)* nata *f*

2 *vt* (*pt & pp* **skinned**) **(a)** *(animal, fish)* despellejar, desollar; *(fruit, vegetable)* pelar **(b)** *(graze)* arañar, rascar; **to s. one's elbow/knee** hacerse un rasguño en el codo/la rodilla

skin-deep [skɪn'di:p] *adj* superficial

skin-diver ['skɪndaɪvər] *n* buceador(a) *m,f*, submarinista *mf*

skin-diving ['skɪndaɪvɪŋ] *n* buceo *m*, submarinismo *m*

skinflint ['skɪnflɪnt] *n Fam* tacaño(a) *m,f*

skinful ['skɪnfʊl] *n Fam* **to have had a s.** estar como una cuba

skinhead ['skɪnhed] *n Fam* cabeza *mf* rapada

skinny ['skɪnɪ] *adj* (**skinnier, skinniest**) *Fam* flaco(a), enjuto(a), delgaducho(a)

skint [skɪnt] *adj Br Fam* **to be s.** estar sin un centavo *or Esp* duro

skin-tight ['skɪntaɪt] *adj (clothing)* muy ajustado(a)

skip¹ [skɪp] **1** *n (jump)* salto *m*, brinco *m*
2 *vi (pt & pp* **skipped**) *(jump)* saltar, brincar; *(with rope)* saltar a la cuerda *or Esp* comba; *Fig* saltar; *Fig* **to s. over sth** saltarse algo
3 *vt Fig (page, meal, class)* saltarse; *Fam* **s. it!** ¡déjalo!

skip² [skɪp] *n Br Constr (container)* contenedor *m*, container *m*

skipper ['skɪpər] **1** *n Naut Fam* patrón *m*, capitán(ana) *m,f; Sport Fam* capitán(ana) *m,f*
2 *vt* capitanear

skipping ['skɪpɪŋ] *n* **she likes s.** le gusta saltar a la cuerda *or Esp* comba ❑ *Br* **s. rope** *Esp* comba *f, Am* cuerda *f* de saltar

skirmish ['skɜːmɪʃ] *n Mil* escaramuza *f; (fight)* pelea *f*, refriega *f*, trifulca *f; (argument)* escaramuza *f*, discusión *f*

skirt [skɜːt] **1** *n* (**a**) *(garment)* falda *f, CSur* pollera *f;* **straight/pleated s.** falda *or CSur* pollera recta/plisada (**b**) *(machinery guard)* cubierta *f*
2 *vt (town, hill, etc)* rodear; *(lake, coast)* bordear

skirt round, *US* **skirt around** *vt (problem, difficulty)* esquivar, eludir

skirting ['skɜːtɪŋ] *Br n Br* **s. (board)** zócalo *m*, rodapié *m*

skit [skɪt] *n Lit* sátira *f*, parodia *f; Theat* sketch *m* satírico

skittish ['skɪtɪʃ] *adj (capricious)* caprichoso(a), frívolo(a); *(animal)* excitable

skittle ['skɪtəl] *n* (**a**) *(pin)* bolo *m* (**b**) **skittles** *(game)* (juego *m* de) bolos *mpl*, boliche *m* ❑ **s. alley** bolera *f*, boliche *m*

skive [skaɪv] *vi Br Fam* zafarse, *Esp* escaquearse

skiver ['skaɪvər] *n Br Fam* holgazán(ana) *m,f*, gandul(ula) *m,f, Méx* flojo(a) *m,f*

skulduggery, *US* **skullduggery** [skʌl'dʌgərɪ] *n* tejemanejes *mpl*

skulk [skʌlk] *vi (hide)* esconderse; *(prowl)* merodear; *(lie in wait)* estar al acecho

skull [skʌl] *n* (**a**) *Anat* cráneo *m; Fam* calavera *f; (picture, sign)* **s. and crossbones** calavera *f* (**b**) *Fam* coco *m*

skullcap ['skʌlkæp] *n* casquete *m; (of priest)* solideo *m*

skunk [skʌŋk] *n Zool* mofeta *f*

sky [skaɪ] *n* cielo *m*, firmamento *m;* **in the s.** en el cielo; *Fam Fig* **the s.'s the limit!** ¡todo es posible! ❑ **s. blue** azul *m* celeste

sky-blue ['skaɪblu:] *adj (colour)* celeste

sky-diver ['skaɪdaɪvər] *n* paracaidista *mf*

sky-diving ['skaɪdaɪvɪŋ] *n* paracaidismo *m*

sky-high [skaɪ'haɪ] *adv* por las nubes; **to blow sth s.-h.** hacer volar algo por los aires

skylark ['skaɪlɑːk] *n Orn* alondra *f*

skylight ['skaɪlaɪt] *n* tragaluz *m*, claraboya *f*

skyline ['skaɪlaɪn] *n (horizon)* horizonte *m; (of city)* perfil *m*

skyscraper ['skaɪskreɪpər] *n* rascacielos *m inv*

slab [slæb] *n (of stone)* losa *f; (of chocolate)* tableta *f; (of cake)* trozo *m*

slack [slæk] **1** *adj* (**a**) *(not taut)* flojo(a) (**b**) *(lax, careless)* descuidado(a), negligente; *(lazy)* perezoso(a), vago(a) (**c**) *(market)* flojo(a); **the s. season** la temporada baja; **business is s.** hay poco trabajo
2 *n* (**a**) *(in rope)* parte *f* floja; **to take up the s.** tensar la cuerda ❑ *Min* cisco *m*
3 *vi Fam* gandulear, holgazanear

slacken ['slækən] **1** *vt* (**a**) *(rope)* aflojar; *(reins)* soltar (**b**) *(speed)* reducir, disminuir; *(one's pace)* reducir, aminorar
2 *vi* (**a**) *(rope)* aflojarse; *(wind)* amainar (**b**) *(trade)* aflojar, flaquear

slacken off *vi (speed, intensity)* reducirse, disminuirse

slacker ['slækər] *n Fam* vago(a) *m,f*, tirado(a) *m,f, Méx* flojo(a) *m,f*

slackness ['slæknɪs] *n* (**a**) *(of rope)* flojedad *f* (**b**) *(laxness, carelessness)* descuido *m*, negligencia *f; (laziness)* pereza *f*, gandulería *f* (**c**) *(of trade)* inactividad *f*, estancamiento *m*

slacks [slæks] *npl Old-fashioned (trousers)* pantalones *mpl*, pantalón *m*

slag [slæg] *n Br* (**a**) *Min* escoria *f* ❑ **s. heap** escorial *m* (**b**) *Slang (woman)* fulana *f, Esp* cualquiera *f, Col* aviona *f, Méx* piruja *f, RP* reventada *f*

slag off *vt (pt & pp* **slagged**) *Br Fam* criticar, *Esp* poner a parir *or* como un trapo, *Méx* viborear

slain [sleɪn] *Literary* **1** *pp see* **slay**
2 the s. *npl* los caídos

slake [sleɪk] *vt (one's thirst)* apagar, aplacar; **slaked lime** cal *f* apagada *or* muerta

slalom ['slɑːləm] *n Sport* slalom *m*

slam [slæm] **1** *n* (**a**) *(of lid etc)* golpe *m; (of door)* portazo *m* (**b**) *Bridge* slam *m;* **grand s.** gran slam
2 *vt (pt & pp* **slammed**) *(a) (bang)* cerrar de golpe; *Aut* **to s. on the brakes** dar un frenazo; **to s. sth down on the table** arrojar algo sobre la mesa; **to s. the door** dar un portazo; **to s. the door in sb's face** dar con la puerta en las narices de algn (**b**) *Fig (criticize, slate)* criticar, poner verde a, *Méx* viborear, *RP* verdulear
3 *vi (lid, door, etc)* cerrarse de golpe

slam-dunk ['slæm'dʌŋk] *n (in basketball)* mate *m*

slander ['slɑːndər] **1** *n (smear)* difamación *f; Jur (defamation)* calumnia *f*
2 *vt* difamar; *Jur* calumniar

slanderer ['slɑːndərər] *n* difamador(a) *m,f; Jur* calumniador(a) *m,f*

slanderous ['slɑːndərəs] *adj* difamatorio(a); *Jur* calumnioso(a)

slang [slæŋ] **1** *n* argot *m*, jerga *f;* **'butt' is s. for cigarette** en argot 'pitillo' quiere decir cigarillo
2 *vt Fam (insult)* criticar, poner verde a, *Méx* viborear, *RP* verdulear; *Br Fam* **slanging match** intercambio *m* de insultos

slangy ['slæŋɪ] *adj* (**slangier, slangiest**) muy coloquial, con mucho argot

slant [slɑːnt] **1** *n* (**a**) *(gen)* inclinación *f; (slope)* pendiente *f*, declive *m* (**b**) *Fig (turn)* giro *m; (point of view)* punto *m* de vista
2 *vt* (**a**) *(gen)* inclinar (**b**) *Fig (problem etc)* enfocar subjetivamente
3 *vi* inclinarse

slanting ['slɑːntɪŋ] *adj* inclinado(a)

slap [slæp] **1** *n (gen)* palmada *f; (smack)* cachete *m; (in face)* bofetada *f*, bofetón *m; Fig* desaire *m;* **s. on the wrist** tirón *m* de orejas
2 *adv Fam* de lleno; **he ran s. into the fence** dio de lleno contra la valla; **s. in the middle of …** justo en medio de …
3 *vt (pt & pp* **slapped**) *(gen)* pegar con la mano; *(hit in face)* abofetear, dar una bofetada a; **to s. sb on the back** dar a algn una palmada en la espalda; **to s. sth down on the table** arrojar algo sobre la mesa; *Fam* **to s. paint on a wall** dar un poco de pintura a una pared

slap around *vt* pegar

slap-bang ['slæpbæŋ] *adv Fam* (**a**) *(violently)* violentamente, con fuerza (**b**) *(exactly)* justo, exactamente; **s.-b. in the middle** justo en medio

slapdash ['slæp'dæʃ] *adj Fam (careless)* descuidado(a); *(work)* chapucero(a)

slap-happy ['slæp'hæpɪ] *adj Fam (carefree)* despreocupado(a)

slapstick ['slæpstɪk] *n* bufonadas *fpl*, payasadas *fpl*

slap-up ['slæpʌp] *adj Br Fam* **s.-up meal** comilona *f*, banquete *m*

slash [slæʃ] **1** *n* (a) *(with sword)* tajo *m*; *(with knife)* cuchillada *f*; *(with razor)* navajazo *m*; *(with whip)* latigazo *m* (b) *Br Vulg* **to have** *or* **go for a s.** mear (c) *Typ Fam* barra *f* oblicua
2 *vt* (a) *(with knife)* acuchillar; *(with sword etc)* dar un tajo a; *(with whip)* azotar (b) *Fig (prices, wages)* rebajar, reducir; *Com* **'prices slashed'** 'precios de remate'

slat [slæt] *n* tablilla *f*, listón *m*

slate [sleɪt] **1** *n* (a) *(stone)* pizarra *f*; **s. quarry** pizarral *m*; *Fig* **to wipe the s. clean** hacer borrón y cuenta nueva (b) *Fam* cuenta *f*
2 *vt* (a) *(roof)* empizarrar (b) *Br Fam (criticize)* vapulear, *Esp* poner por los suelos, *Méx* viborear, *RP* dejar por el piso

slaughter ['slɔːtər] **1** *n* *(of animals)* matanza *f*; *(of people)* carnicería *f*, matanza *f*
2 *vt (animals)* matar, sacrificar; *(people)* matar brutalmente; *(in large numbers)* masacrar, exterminar; *Fam Fig (thrash, defeat)* dar una paliza a; **United got slaughtered** le dieron una paliza al United

slaughterhouse ['slɔːtəhaʊs] *n* matadero *m*

Slav [slɑːv] *adj & n* eslavo(a) *(m,f)*

slave [sleɪv] **1** *n* esclavo(a) *m,f*; *Fig* **s. to fashion** esclavo(a) de la moda ❑ *Fam* **s. driver** negrero(a) *m,f*, tirano(a) *m,f*; **s. labour** *US* **s. labor** *(work)* trabajo *m* de negros; *(people)* esclavos *mpl*; **s. trade** trata *f* de esclavos
2 *vi (slog)* **to s. (away) at sth** trabajar como un negro en algo

slaver ['slævər] *vi* babear

slavery ['sleɪvərɪ] *n* esclavitud *f*

Slavic ['slɑːvɪk] *adj* eslavo(a)

slavish ['sleɪvɪʃ] *adj (servile)* esclavo(a), servil; *Fig* ciego(a)

slavishly ['sleɪvɪʃlɪ] *adv (with obedience)* servilmente; *(blindly)* ciegamente

Slavonic [slə'vɒnɪk] *adj* eslavo(a)

slay [sleɪ] *vt (pt* **slew** *; pp* **slain)** *Literary (kill)* matar, asesinar

sleaze [sliːz] *n Fam* corrupción *f*

sleazy ['sliːzɪ] *adj (sleazier, sleaziest) Fam (place, bar, hotel) Esp* cutre, *Col* corroncho(a), *Méx* gacho(a), *RP* groncho(a); *(government, politician)* corrupto(a); *(affair, reputation)* escandaloso(a) y sórdido(a)

sled [sled] **1** *n US* trineo *m*
2 *vi* ir en trineo

sledge [sledʒ] **1** *n* (a) *Br* trineo *m* (b) *Fam (tool)* almádana *f*
2 *vi* ir en trineo

sledgehammer ['sledʒhæmər] *n (tool)* almádana *f*

sleek [sliːk] *adj (hair)* liso(a), lustroso(a); *(appearance)* impecable, elegante; *(manner)* meloso(a)

sleep [sliːp] **1** *n* (a) *(gen)* sueño *m*; **to have a short s.** echar una siesta; **to get off to s.** conciliar el sueño; **to go to s.** dormirse; *Fig* **she didn't lose any s. over it** no perdió el sueño por ello; *Fam* **to drop off to s.** quedarse dormido(a); *Fam* **to put a patient to s.** dormir a un paciente; *Euph* **to put an animal to s.** sacrificar un animal; *Fig* **to send sb to s.** hacer dormir a algn (b) **to go to s.** *(go numb)* entumecerse; *Fam* **my foot has gone to s.** se me ha dormido el pie
2 *vt (pt & pp* **slept)** (a) *(gen)* dormir; **I haven't slept a wink all night** no he pegado ojo en toda la noche; **to s. the**

hours away pasar las horas durmiendo (b) *(accommodate)* **the cottage sleeps six** el chalet tiene camas para seis personas
3 *vi* dormir; **to s. soundly** dormir profundamente; *Fig* **to s. on sth** consultar algo con la almohada; *Fam* **to s. like a log** *or* **top** dormir como un lirón *or* como un tronco; *Fam* **to s. rough** dormir al aire libre

sleep around *vi Fam* acostarse con cualquiera

sleep in *vi Br (oversleep)* quedarse dormido(a), no levantarse a tiempo; *(have a lie-in)* quedarse en la cama

sleep off *vt Fam* **to s. it off** dormir la mona

sleep out *vi* dormir al aire libre; **it was so warm we decided to s. out** hacía tan buen tiempo que decidimos dormir al raso

sleep through *vt* **to s. through the alarm** no oír el despertador

sleep together *vi (couple)* dormir juntos

sleep with *vt Fam* **to s. with sb** acostarse con algn

sleeper ['sliːpər] *n* (a) *(person)* durmiente *mf*; **to be a heavy/light s.** tener el sueño pesado/ligero (b) *Br (on railway track)* traviesa *f* (c) *Rail (coach)* coche-cama *m*; *(berth)* litera *f*

sleepily ['sliːpɪlɪ] *adv* soñolientamente; **'yes,' he replied s.** 'sí,' contestó medio dormido

sleepiness ['sliːpɪnɪs] *n* somnolencia *f*

sleeping ['sliːpɪŋ] *adj* durmiente, dormido(a) ❑ **s. bag** saco *m* de dormir, *Col Méx* sleeping *m* (bag), *RP* bolsa *f* de dormir; **S. Beauty** la Bella durmiente; *Rail* **s. car** coche-cama *m*; *Br Com* **s. partner** socio(a) *m,f* comanditario(a); **s. pill** somnífero *m*; **s. quarters** dormitorio *m*; *Med* **s. sickness** encefalitis *f* letárgica, enfermedad *f* del sueño

sleepless ['sliːplɪs] *adj* **to have a s. night** pasar la noche en blanco

sleeplessness ['sliːplɪsnɪs] *n* insomnio *m*

sleepwalk ['sliːpwɔːk] *vi* caminar dormido(a) *or* sonámbulo(a)

sleepwalker ['sliːpwɔːkər] *n* sonámbulo(a) *m,f*

sleepwalking ['sliːpwɔːkɪŋ] *n* sonambulismo *m*

sleepy ['sliːpɪ] *adj (sleepier, sleepiest)* soñoliento(a); **to be** *or* **feel s.** tener sueño; **to make sb s.** dar sueño a algn; **it makes me s.** me da sueño

sleepyhead ['sliːpɪhed] *n Fam* dormilón(ona) *m,f*

sleet [sliːt] **1** *n* aguanieve *f*, cellisca *f*
2 *v impers* **it's sleeting** cae aguanieve

sleeve [sliːv] *n (of garment)* manga *f*; *(of record)* funda *f*; *Fig* **to have something up one's s.** guardar una carta en la manga

sleeveless ['sliːvlɪs] *adj (garment)* sin mangas

sleigh [sleɪ] *n* trineo *m* ❑ **s. bell** cascabel *m*

sleight [slaɪt] *n* **s. of hand** prestidigitación *f*, juego *m* de manos

slender ['slendər] *adj* (a) *(thin, slim) (person)* delgado(a), esbelto(a); *(wineglass)* delgado(a), fino(a) (b) *Fig (slight, poor) (hope, chance)* ligero(a); *(income)* escaso(a); **by a s. majority** por una escasa mayoría; **of s. means** de recursos escasos

slept [slept] *pt & pp see* **sleep**

sleuth [sluːθ] *n Fam* detective *m*, sabueso *m*

slew [sluː] *pt & pp see* **slay**

slice [slaɪs] **1** *n* (a) *(of bread)* rebanada *f*; *(of ham)* lonja *f*, loncha *f*; *(of beef etc)* tajada *f*; *(of salami, cucumber, lemon)* rodaja *f*; *(of melon)* raja *f*; *(of cake)* porción *f*, trozo *m*; *Fig (of population etc)* parte *f*; *(proportion)* proporción *f* (b) *(utensil)* pala *f*, paleta *f*
2 *vt (food)* cortar a rebanadas *or* tajos *or* rodajas; *(divide)*

partir; **sliced bread** pan de molde, *RP* pan lactal en rebanadas

  3 *vi Sport* dar efecto a la pelota

slice off *vt* cortar

slice through *vt* cortar, partir

slice up *vt* cortar a rebanadas *or* tajos *or* rodajas

slick [slɪk] **1** *adj* (**a**) *(programme, show)* ingenioso(a), logrado(a) (**b**) *(skilful)* hábil, mañoso(a); **a s. answer** una respuesta fácil (**c**) *Pej (glib)* despabilado(a); **a s. salesman** un vendedor con mucha labia; **he's a very s. dresser** siempre va hecho un maniquí

  2 *n* (**oil**) **s.** marea *f* negra

slick back, slick down *vt* alisar; **to s. back** *or* **down one's hair** alisarse el pelo

slicker ['slɪkər] *n Fam Pej* (**city**) **s.** tío(a) *m,f*, chulo(a) *m,f*

slide [slaɪd] **1** *n* (**a**) *(act)* deslizamiento *m*, desliz *m*; *(slip)* resbalón *m* (**b**) *Fin (drop)* baja *f*; **a s. in share prices** una baja en las cotizaciones (**c**) *(in playground)* tobogán *m* (**d**) *Phot* diapositiva *f* □ **s. projector** proyector *m* de diapositivas; **s. show** exposición *f* de diapositivas (**e**) *(of microscope)* platina *f*, portaobjetos *m inv* (**f**) *Math* **s. rule** regla *f* de cálculo (**g**) *Mus (on instrument)* vara *f*, corredera *f* (**h**) *Br (for hair)* pasador *m*

  2 *vt (pt & pp* **slid**) deslizar; *(furniture)* correr

  3 *vi (gen)* deslizarse; *(slip)* resbalar; **to s. down a drainpipe** deslizarse por un tubo de desagüe; *Fig* **to let things s.** dejar que las cosas vayan a peor

sliding ['slaɪdɪŋ] *adj (door, window)* corredizo(a) □ *Fin* **s. scale** escala *f* móvil

slight [slaɪt] **1** *adj* (**a**) *(small)* pequeño(a), ligero(a); **I haven't got the slightest idea** no tengo la menor idea; **not in the slightest** en absoluto; **to a s. extent** hasta cierto punto; **to take offence at the slightest thing** ofenderse por nada (**b**) *(person, build) (small)* menudo(a); *(slim)* delgado(a); *(weak-looking)* delicado(a) (**c**) *(trivial)* leve, insignificante; **a s. wound** una herida leve

  2 *n (affront)* desaire *m*

  3 *vt* (**a**) *(scorn)* despreciar, menospreciar (**b**) *(snub, insult)* desairar, ofender, insultar

slighting ['slaɪtɪŋ] *adj* (**a**) *(scornful)* despreciativo(a), menospreciativo(a) (**b**) *(offensive)* ofensivo(a)

slightly ['slaɪtlɪ] *adv* (**a**) *(a little)* un poco, ligeramente, algo (**b**) *(person)* **s. built** *(small)* menudo(a); *(slim)* delgado(a)

slily ['slaɪlɪ] *adv see* **slyly**

slim [slɪm] **1** *adj* (**slimmer, slimmest**) (**a**) *(person, build)* delgado(a); *(slender)* esbelto(a) (**b**) *Fig (resources, profits)* escaso(a); *(hopes, chances)* remoto(a); *(evidence)* insuficiente

  2 *vi (pt & pp* **slimmed**) adelgazar, hacer régimen

slim down *vt Fig* reducir

slime [slaɪm] *n (mud etc)* lodo *m*, cieno *m*; *(of snail)* baba *f*

slimline ['slɪmlaɪn] *adj (dishwasher, diary, calculator)* extraplano(a)

slimmer ['slɪmər] *n* persona *f* a régimen

slimming ['slɪmɪŋ] **1** *adj (diet, pills)* para adelgazar; *(food)* que no engorda

  2 *n (process)* adelgazamiento *m*

slimy ['slaɪmɪ] *adj* (**slimier, slimiest**) (**a**) *(muddy)* lodoso(a); *(snail)* baboso(a); *(sticky)* viscoso(a) (**b**) *Fig (person)* falso(a), zalamero(a)

sling [slɪŋ] **1** *n* (**a**) *(catapult)* honda *f*; *(child's)* tirador *m* (**b**) *Med* cabestrillo *m*

  2 *vt (pt & pp* **slung**) (**a**) *(throw)* lanzar, arrojar, tirar; *Br Fam* **to s. one's hook** largarse (**b**) *(suspend)* colgar (**from** de)

sling out *vt Fam (throw away)* tirar, *Am* botar; *(person)* echar

slink [slɪŋk] *vi (pt & pp* **slunk**) desplazarse sigilosamente; **to s. away** *or* **off** escabullirse

slinky ['slɪŋkɪ] *adj* (**slinkier, slinkiest**) *Fam* (**a**) *(garment)* ceñido(a), muy ajustado(a) al cuerpo (**b**) *(movement)* sensual, provocativo(a)

slip [slɪp] **1** *n* (**a**) *(slide)* resbalón *m*; *(fall)* caída *f*; *(trip)* traspiés *m inv*, tropezón *m*, paso *m* en falso; *Fam Fig* **to give sb the s.** dar esquinazo a algn (**b**) *(mistake)* error *m*, equivocación *f*; *(moral)* desliz *m*; **a s. of the pen** *or* **tongue** un lapsus; *Prov* **there's many a s. twixt cup and lip** del dicho al hecho hay mucho trecho (**c**) *(underskirt)* combinación *f*; *(petticoat)* enaguas *fpl* □ *(pillow)* **s.** funda *f* (**d**) *(of paper)* papelito *m*, trocito *m* de papel □ **sales s.** resguardo *m* (**e**) *Fam* menudencia *f*; **a s. of a boy/girl** un chiquillo/una chiquilla

  2 *vi (pt & pp* **slipped**) (**a**) *(slide)* resbalar; *Aut (clutch)* patinar; **it slipped from his hand** se le fue de la mano; **my foot slipped** me resbaló el pie; *Fig* **then everything slipped into place** entonces todo quedó claro; *Fig* **to let an opportunity s.** dejar escapar una oportunidad (**b**) *(move quickly)* ir de prisa, escabullirse; **to s. round to the baker's** ir un momento a la panadería (**c**) *(decline) (standards etc)* decaer, empeorar; *Fam* **you're slipping** estás perdiendo facultades

  3 *vt* (**a**) *(slide)* pasar, dar a escondidas; *Fam* **he slipped me a fiver** me puso en la mano un billete de cinco libras (**b**) *(miss) Knit* **to s. a stitch** dejar escapar un punto (**c**) *(overlook, forget)* pasar por alto; **it must have slipped his notice** le habrá pasado desapercibido; **it slipped my memory** se me fue de la memoria (**d**) *(escape from)* soltarse de; **the dog slipped its leash** el perro se soltó de la correa (**e**) *Med* dislocarse; **to have a slipped disc** tener una vértebra dislocada

slip away *vi* (**a**) *(time, years)* pasar volando (**b**) *(person)* escabullirse

slip by *vi (time, years)* pasar volando

slip off *vt (clothes)* quitarse, *Am* sacarse

slip on *vt (clothes)* ponerse rápidamente

slip out *vi* (**a**) *(leave)* salir, escabullirse (**b**) *Fig* **the secret slipped out** se le escapó el secreto

slip up *vi Fam (make a mistake)* equivocarse; *(blunder)* cometer un desliz, meter la pata

slipknot ['slɪpnɒt] *n* nudo *m* corredizo

slip-on ['slɪpɒn] *adj (shoes)* sin cordones

slipper ['slɪpər] *n* (**a**) *(shoe)* zapatilla *f* (**b**) *Tech (of brake)* zapata *f*, patín *m*

slippery ['slɪpərɪ] *adj* (**a**) *(surface)* resbaladizo(a); *(viscous)* escurridizo(a); *Fig* **to be on a s. slope** estar en un callejón sin salida (**b**) *Fig (person)* astuto(a), que no es de fiar

slippy ['slɪpɪ] *adj* resbaladizo(a), escurridizo(a)

slip-road ['slɪprəʊd] *n Br (on motorway)* vía *f* de acceso

slipshod ['slɪpʃɒd] *adj (careless)* descuidado(a); *(work)* chapucero(a)

slipstream ['slɪpstriːm] *n* estela *f*

slip-up ['slɪpʌp] *n Fam (mistake)* error *m*; *(blunder)* desliz *m*, metedura *f* de pata

slipway ['slɪpweɪ] *n Naut* grada *f*

slit [slɪt] **1** *n (opening)* abertura *f*, hendidura *f*; *(cut)* corte *m*, raja *f*

  2 *vt (pt & pp* **slit**) cortar, hender, rajar; **to s. open an envelope** rasgar un sobre

slither ['slɪðər] *vi (snake etc)* deslizarse

slithery ['slɪðərɪ] *adj (surface)* resbaladizo(a)

sliver ['slɪvər] *n (of wood, glass)* astilla *f*; *(of ham)* loncha *f* or tajada *f* fina

slob [slɒb] n Fam (untidy person) cerdo(a) m,f; (lazy person) dejado(a) m,f, tirado(a) m,f

slobber ['slɒbər] vi (dribble) babear; Fig **to s. over sb** hacerle la pamema a algn

sloe [sləʊ] n Bot (**a**) (shrub) endrino m (**b**) (fruit) endrina f ▫ **s. gin** licor m de endrinas

slog [slɒg] **1** n Fam paliza f; **it was a hard s. back to base camp** les costó un montón volver al campamento base
   2 vi (pt & pp **slogged**) (**a**) Fam (work hard) trabajar como un/una negro(a), Esp dar el callo; **to s. away (at sth)** trabajar como una bestia (en algo) (**b**) (walk) caminar or avanzar trabajosamente; **to s. up a hill** subir una cuesta a duras penas
   3 vt (hit) (ball, opponent) golpear fuerte

slogan ['sləʊgən] n slogan m, eslogan m, lema m

slogger ['slɒgər] n Fam (hard worker) currante mf; trabajador(a) m,f

sloop [slu:p] n Naut balandro m

slop [slɒp] **1** vi (pt & pp **slopped**) **to s. (over)** derramarse, verterse; **to s. about** chapotear
   2 vt derramar, verter
   3 n (**a**) **slops** (liquid food) gachas fpl, aguachirle m sing; (left-over food) bazofia f; (dirty water) lavazas fpl, agua f sing sucia; (dregs of tea) posos mpl de té (**b**) Lit Cin (slush) novela f or película f sentimentaloide

slope [sləʊp] **1** n (incline) cuesta f, pendiente f; (up) subida f; (down) bajada f, declive m; (of mountain) ladera f, falda f, vertiente f; (of roof) vertiente f; **steep s.** cuesta empinada; **the southern slopes** la vertiente sur
   2 vi inclinarse; **to s. up/down** subir/bajar en pendiente; **the gardens s. down to the sea** los jardines bajan hasta el mar

slope off vi Br Fam largarse

sloping ['sləʊpɪŋ] adj (ground) en pendiente, inclinado(a); (roof, handwriting) inclinado(a); **s. shoulders** hombros caídos

sloppily ['slɒpɪ] adv (**a**) (carelessly) de modo descuidado; **s. done** hecho(a) a la ligera or a la buena de Dios; **s. dressed** vestido(a) de cualquier manera (**b**) (slushy) de modo empalagoso or sentimentaloide

sloppy ['slɒpɪ] adj (**sloppier, sloppiest**) Fam (**a**) (careless) descuidado(a); (slipshod) chapucero(a); (appearance, dress) desaliñado(a), dejado(a) (**b**) (slushy) empalagoso(a), sentimentaloide (**c**) (loose) (garment) muy ancho(a); Fam **s. joe** jersey muy ancho

slosh [slɒʃ] vt Fam (splash) echar; **to s. paint on a wall** dar pintura a una pared a brochazos

slosh about vi chapotear

sloshed [slɒʃt] adj Fam **to get s.** agarrar una trompa

slot [slɒt] **1** n (**a**) (for coin) ranura f; (groove) muesca f; (opening) abertura f, rendija f ▫ **s. machine** (for gambling) (máquina f) tragaperras m inv; (vending machine) distribuidor m automático; **s. meter** contador m (**b**) Fig (in timetable) hueco m; Rad TV espacio m
   2 vt (pt & pp **slotted**) (place) meter, colocar; (put in) introducir; **s. piece X into piece Y** encaja la pieza X con la pieza Y; Fig **to s. a new song into the programme** incluir una nueva canción en el programa
   3 vi **to s. in** or **together** encajar

sloth [sləʊθ] n (**a**) Fml (laziness, idleness) pereza f, indolencia f (**b**) Zool (oso m) perezoso m

slothful ['sləʊθfʊl] adj (indolent) perezoso(a)

slouch [slaʊtʃ] **1** vi andar or sentarse con los hombros caídos; **don't s.!** ¡ponte derecho!; **to s. in an armchair** repantigarse en un sillón
   2 n Fam vago(a); **he's no s. when it comes to doing the housework** no tienes que decirle dos veces que haga la limpieza

Slovak ['sləʊvæk] **1** n (**a**) (person) eslovaco(a) m,f (**b**) (language) eslovaco m
   2 adj eslovaco(a)

Slovakia [sləʊ'vækɪə] n Eslovaquia

Slovakian [sləʊ'vækɪən] adj & n eslovaco(a) (m,f)

Slovene ['sləʊviːn], **Slovenian** [sləʊ'viːnɪən] **1** n (**a**) (person) esloveno(a) m,f (**b**) (language) esloveno m
   2 adj esloveno(a)

Slovenia [sləʊ'viːnɪə] n Eslovenia

slovenly ['slʌvənlɪ] adj (careless) descuidado(a), dejado(a); (scruffy) desaliñado(a), desaseado(a); (inefficient) chapucero(a)

slow [sləʊ] **1** adj (**a**) (gen) lento(a); Culin **in a s. oven** a fuego lento; Cin **in s. motion** a cámara lenta, al ralentí; **it's s. going** avanzamos muy lentamente; **s. recovery** recuperación lenta; **to be s. to do sth** tardar en hacer algo (**b**) (clock) atrasado(a); **my watch is ten minutes s.** mi reloj va atrasado diez minutos (**c**) (performance etc) aburrido(a), pesado(a) (**d**) (person) (stupid) lento(a), torpe, corto(a) de alcances; **he's a s. learner** le cuesta aprender; Fig **he's a bit s. on the uptake** or **off the mark** le cuesta entender las cosas, es un poco lento de reflejos
   2 adv despacio, lentamente; Ind **to go s.** trabajar a ritmo lento, hacer una huelga de celo
   3 vt (car, machine) reducir la marcha de; (progress, production) retrasar, retardar
   4 vi **to s. down** or **up** (gen) ir más despacio; (in car) reducir la velocidad; (when walking) aminorar el paso

slowcoach ['sləʊkəʊtʃ] n Br Fam tortuga f

slowish ['sləʊɪʃ] adj algo lento(a)

slowly ['sləʊlɪ] adv despacio, lentamente; **s. but surely** lento pero seguro

slow-moving ['sləʊ'muːvɪŋ] adj (person, car, queue, river) lento(a); (film, plot) lento(a)

slowness ['sləʊnɪs] n (**a**) (gen) lentitud f (**b**) (stupidity) torpeza f (**c**) (dullness) pesadez f

slowpoke ['sləʊpəʊk] n US Fam see **slowcoach**

slow-witted [sləʊ'wɪtɪd] adj lento(a), torpe, corto(a) de alcances

slowworm ['sləʊwɜːm] n Zool lución m

sludge [slʌdʒ] n (**a**) (mud) fango m, cieno m, lodo m; (sediment) sedimento m, residuos mpl (**b**) (sewage) aguas fpl residuales

slug [slʌg] **1** n (**a**) Zool babosa f (**b**) US Fam (bullet) posta f (**c**) Fam (blow) porrazo m (**d**) US Fam (shot) traguito m; **a s. of whisky** un traguito de whisky
   2 vt (pt & pp **slugged**) Fam (hit) aporrear, pegar un porrazo a

sluggish ['slʌgɪʃ] adj (**a**) (slow-moving) (river, engine) lento(a); Com (market, trade) flojo(a), inactivo(a) (**b**) (lazy) perezoso(a), holgazán(ana); Med (liver) perezoso(a)

sluggishness ['slʌgɪʃnɪs] n (**a**) (slowness) lentitud f; Com inactividad f (**b**) (laziness) pereza f

sluice [sluːs] **1** n (waterway) canal m; (valve) compuerta f
   2 vt **to s. sth down** lavar algo a chorro, regar algo

sluicegate ['sluːsgeɪt] n esclusa f

slum [slʌm] **1** n (district) barrio m bajo; (on outskirts) arrabal m, suburbio m; (house) tugurio m
   2 vt & vi (pt & pp **slummed**) Fam **to s. (it)** vivir con muy poco dinero; (for amusement) vivir en la miseria

slumber ['slʌmbər] Literary **1** n (sleep) sueño m; (deep sleep) sopor m ▫ US **s. party** fiesta f nocturna de adolescentes
   2 vi dormir

slummy ['slʌmɪ] adj (**slummier, slummiest**) Fam (run-down) sórdido(a)

slump [slʌmp] **1** *n* (**a**) *(drop in production, sales, etc)* baja *f* or caída *f* repentina, bajón *m* (**b**) *(economic depression)* crisis *f* económica, depresión *f* económica; **the 1929 s.** el crac de 1929; *Fig* **there was a s. in staff morale** se hundió la moral del personal

2 *vi* (**a**) *(production, sales, demand)* bajar or caer de repente; *(prices)* desplomarse, hundirse; *(the economy)* hundirse; *Fig (morale)* desplomarse (**b**) *(fall)* caer; **to s. into an armchair** derrumbarse en un sillón; **he slumped to the floor** se desplomó en el suelo, cayó desmayado al suelo; **she was slumped over the steering wheel** su cuerpo yacía encima del volante

slung [slʌŋ] *pt & pp see* **sling**

slunk [slʌŋk] *pt & pp see* **slink**

slur [slɜ:r] **1** *n* (**a**) *(stigma)* mancha *f*; *(slanderous remark)* calumnia *f*, difamación *f*; *(insult)* afrenta *f*; **to cast a s. on sb's reputation** manchar la reputación de algn (**b**) *Mus (symbol)* ligado *m*

2 *vt (pt & pp* **slurred)** (**a**) *(word)* pronunciar mal, comerse, tragarse (**b**) *Mus (note)* ligar

slurp [slɜ:p] **1** *vt & vi Fam (beer, soup, etc)* sorber or beber ruidosamente

2 *n (drinking noise)* = ruido que se hace al beber

slush [slʌʃ] *n* (**a**) *(melting snow)* aguanieve *f*, nieve *f* derretida; *(mud)* lodo *m*, fango *m* (**b**) *Fam (oversentimental novel, film, etc)* sentimentalismo *m*, sensiblería *f* (**c**) *US Fam* **s. fund** fondos *mpl* para sobornos

slushy [slʌʃi] *adj* (**slushier, slushiest**) (**a**) *(snow)* medio derretido(a); *(muddy)* lodoso(a), fangoso(a) (**b**) *Fam (novel, film, etc)* sentimentaloide, sensiblero(a)

slut [slʌt] *n Offens* (**a**) *(dirty, untidy woman)* marrana *f*, *Esp* guarra *f* (**b**) *(whore)* ramera *f*, fulana *f*

sly [slaɪ] **1** *adj* (**slyer, slyest** or **slier, sliest**) (**a**) *(cunning)* astuto(a), ladino(a), taimado(a) (**b**) *(secretive)* furtivo(a) (**c**) *(mischievous)* travieso(a) (**d**) *(underhand)* malicioso(a); **he's a s. old devil** es muy zorro

2 *n* **to do sth on the s.** hacer algo a hurtadillas or a escondidas

slyboots [slaɪbu:ts] *n inv Fam* zorro(a) *m,f*

slyly, slily [slaɪlɪ] *adv* (**a**) *(cunningly)* con astucia, astutamente (**b**) *(secretively)* furtivamente (**c**) *(underhandedly)* con malicia, maliciosamente

S & M [esən'em], **S/M** [es'em] *n (abbr* **sado-masochism)** SM, sado *m*

smack¹ [smæk] **1** *n* (**a**) *(slap)* bofetada *f*, tortazo *m*, cachete *m*; **to give a child a s.** dar una bofetada a un niño (**b**) *(sharp sound)* ruido *m* sonoro

2 *vt* (**a**) *(slap)* dar una bofetada a, abofetear; **I'll s. your bottom!** ¡te pegaré en el trasero! (**b**) *(hit)* golpear; *Fig* **to s. one's lips** relamerse

3 *adv Fam* directamente; **he ran s. into the wall** dio de lleno contra la pared; **s. (bang) in the middle** justo en medio

smack² [smæk] *vi Fig (be reminiscent)* **to s. of** oler a

smack³ [smæk] *n Naut* barca *f* de pesca

smack⁴ [smæk] *n Slang (drug)* heroína *f*, caballo *m*

smacker [smækər] *n Fam* (**a**) *(kiss)* besazo *m*, besuqueo *m* (**b**) *Br (pound)* libra *f*; *US (dollar)* dólar *m*

small [smɔ:l] **1** *adj* (**a**) *(gen)* pequeño(a), chico(a); **a s. table** una mesita; **a s. present** un regalito; **very s.** pequeñito(a); **in s. letters** en minúsculas; **in the s. hours** a altas horas de la noche; **in a s. voice** con la boca pequeña; **this skirt is too s.** esta falda es pequeña; **to cut sth up s.** cortar algo en trocitos; **to have a s. appetite** no ser de mucho comer; *Fig* **it's a s. world** el mundo es un pañuelo; *Fig* **it's s. wonder that ...** no me sorprende nada que ... ❏ **s. ads** pequeños anuncios *mpl*, anuncios *mpl* por palabras; **s. arms** armas *fpl* portátiles; *Fig* **s. print** letra *f* pequeña; *Fig* **s. screen** pequeña pantalla *f* (**b**) *(in height)* bajo(a), pequeño(a) (**c**) *(young)* jóven, pequeño(a) (**d**) *(scant)* escaso(a); *(meal)* ligero(a); *(sum)* pequeño(a), modesto(a) ❏ **s. change** cambio *m*, suelto *m*, *Am* vuelto *m* (**e**) *(unimportant, minor)* sin importancia, insignificante; **s. businessmen** pequeños comerciantes; *Fig* **to feel** or **look s.** sentirse humillado(a) ❏ *Fig* **s. fry** gente *f* de poca monta; **s. talk** charla *f* or *CAm Méx* plática *f* insustancial (**f**) *(increase, improvement)* ligero(a), mínimo(a)

2 *n* (**a**) **s. of the back** región *f* lumbar (**b**) **smalls** *Br Fam (underwear)* paños *mpl* menores, ropa *f* sing interior

smallholder [smɔ:lhəʊldər] *n Br* minifundista *mf*

smallholding [smɔ:lhəʊldɪŋ] *n Br* parcela *f*, granja *f* pequeña, minifundio *m*

smallish [smɔ:lɪʃ] *adj* más bien pequeño(a)

small-minded [smɔ:l'maɪndɪd] *adj (narrowminded)* de miras estrechas; *(petty)* mezquino(a)

smallness [smɔ:lnɪs] *n (size)* pequeñez *f*; *(scantiness)* escasez *f*

smallpox [smɔ:lpɒks] *n Med* viruela *f*

small-scale [smɔ:lskeɪl] *adj* en pequeña escala

small-time [smɔ:ltaɪm] *adj Fam* de poca categoría or monta; **a s.-t. crook** un delincuente menor

small-town [smɔ:ltaʊn] *adj* provinciano(a), pueblerino(a)

smarmy [smɑ:mɪ] *adj* (**smarmier, smarmiest**) *Fam* zalamero(a), cobista

smart [smɑ:t] **1** *adj* (**a**) *(elegant)* elegante; *(chic)* fino(a), de buen tono; **the s. set** la gente bien; **how s. you look!** ¡qué elegante vas! (**b**) *(clever, bright)* listo(a), inteligente; *(sharp)* listo(a), espabilado(a), despabilado(a); **he thinks he's very s.** se las da de listo ❏ *Fam* **s. alec(k)** sabelotodo *mf*, *Esp* listillo(a) *m,f*, *Méx RP* vivo(a) *m,f*; **s. bomb** bomba *f* teledirigida; **s. card** tarjeta *f* inteligente (**c**) *(quick) (action)* rápido(a); *(pace)* ligero(a); *Fam* **look s. about it!** ¡date prisa!

2 *vi* (**a**) *(sting) (eyes, graze)* picar, escocer; *(wound)* dar punzadas (**b**) *Fig* sufrir, dolerse; **he smarted from the injustice of her remarks** la injusticia de sus comentarios le hirió en lo más vivo

smarten [smɑ:tən] *vt* **to s. (up)** *(person, house)* arreglar; *Fam* **to s. up one's ideas** espabilarse; **to s. oneself (up)** arreglarse

smartly [smɑ:tlɪ] *adv* (**a**) *(elegantly)* elegantemente, con elegancia (**b**) *(cleverly)* inteligentemente (**c**) *(quickly)* rápidamente

smartness [smɑ:tnɪs] *n* (**a**) *(elegance)* elegancia *f*, buen tono *m* (**b**) *(cleverness)* inteligencia *f*

smarty-pants [smɑ:tɪpænts] *n inv Fam* sabelotodo *mf*, *Esp* listillo(a) *m,f*, *Méx RP* vivo(a) *m,f*

smash [smæʃ] **1** *n* (**a**) *(breaking)* rotura *f*; *(loud noise)* estrépito *m*, estruendo *m*; *Aut (collision)* choque *m* violento, colisión *f* ❏ *Fig* **s. hit** exitazo *m* (**b**) *Fin* quiebra *f* (**c**) *Ten* smash *m*, mate *m*

2 *vt* (**a**) *(break)* romper; *(shatter)* hacer pedazos or añicos; *(crush)* aplastar; *(car)* estrellar (**into** contra) (**b**) *(ruin)* arruinar; *(destroy)* destrozar; *(defeat)* vencer, derrotar; **a drugs ring has been smashed** se ha desarticulado una red de narcotraficantes (**c**) *Sport (record)* batir, superar (**d**) *Ten* **to s. the ball** dar un mate

3 *vi (break)* romperse; *(shatter)* hacerse pedazos or añicos; *(crash)* estrellar (**into** contra)

smash down *vt (knock down)* tirar abajo, derribar

smash in *vt (door)* forzar; *Br Fam* **to s. sb's face in** romperle or partirle la cara a algn

smash up *vt Fam (car)* hacer pedazos; *(place)* destrozar, destruir

smash-and-grab [smæʃən'græb] *n* **s.-a.-g. raid** robo *m* relámpago

smashed [smæʃt] *adj Fam (drunk)* como una cuba, *Esp RP* mamado(a), *Col* caído(a) (de la perra), *Méx* ahogado(a); *(on drugs)* colocado(a), *Col* trabado(a), *RP* falopeado(a)

smasher ['smæʃər] *n Fam* tío(a) *m,f* bueno(a); **to be a s.** estar como un tren

smashing ['smæʃɪŋ] *adj Br Fam* genial, *Méx* padre, *RP* bárbaro(a); **to have a s. time** pasarlo genial

smash-up ['smæʃʌp] *n Aut (collision)* choque *m* violento, colisión *f; (accident)* accidente *m*

smattering ['smætərɪŋ] *n* nociones *fpl;* **Brian had a s. of French** Brian hablaba un poquito de francés

smear [smɪər] **1** *n* (**a**) *(stain, smudge)* mancha *f* ▫ *Med* **s. (test)** frotis *f* del cuello del útero (**b**) *Fig (defamation)* calumnia *f* ▫ **s. campaign** campaña *f* de difamación

 2 *vt* (**a**) *(spread) (butter, ointment)* untar; *(grease, paint)* embadurnar (**b**) *(make dirty)* manchar; *(writing, ink)* borrar (**c**) *Fig (defame)* calumniar, difamar

 3 *vi (ink, paint)* correrse

smell [smel] **1** *n* (**a**) *(sense)* olfato *m* (**b**) *(odour)* olor *m; (perfume)* perfume *m,* aroma *m;* **it has a funny s.** huele raro; **there was a s. of burning** olía a quemado (**c**) *(action)* olfateo *m;* **have a s. of this flower** huele esta flor

 2 *vt (pt & pp* **smelled** *or* **smelt)** oler; *Fig* **I can s. a rat** aquí hay gato encerrado; *Fig* **to s. danger** olfatear el peligro

 3 *vi* oler (a); *(stink)* apestar; **it smells good/bad/stuffy/ like lavender** huele bien/mal/a cerrado/a lavanda; **his breath smelt of whisky** su aliento olía a whisky

smell out *vt (dog etc)* husmear; *Fam* apestar; **that cheese is smelling the house out** aquel queso está apestando la casa

smelling salts ['smelɪŋsɒlts] *npl* sales *fpl* aromáticas

smelly ['smelɪ] *adj* **(smellier, smelliest)** *Fam* maloliente, apestoso(a); *(stinking)* hediondo(a)

smelt¹ [smelt] *pt & pp see* **smell**

smelt² [smelt] *vt (ore)* fundir

smelting ['smeltɪŋ] *adj* **s. works** fundición *f*

smile [smaɪl] **1** *n* sonrisa *f;* **he was all smiles** no paraba de sonreír; **'hello,' she said with a s.** 'hola,' dijo sonriente; **to give sb a s.** sonreír a algn; **to wipe the s. off sb's face** quitarle a algn las ganas de sonreír

 2 *vi* sonreír; **to s. at sb** sonreír a algn; **to s. at sth** reírse de algo; *Fig* **fortune smiled on them** la fortuna les sonrió; *Fam* **keep smiling!** ¡ánimo!

smiling ['smaɪlɪŋ] *adj* sonriente, risueño(a)

smirk [smɜːk] **1** *n (conceited)* sonrisa *f* satisfecha; *(foolish)* sonrisa *f* boba

 2 *vi (conceitedly)* sonreír con satisfacción; *(foolishly)* sonreír bobamente

smite [smaɪt] *vt (pt* **smote**; *pp* **smitten)** *Literary* (**a**) *(hit)* golpear, pegar (**b**) *(punish)* castigar

smith [smɪθ] *n* herrero *m*

smithereens [smɪðə'riːnz] *npl Fam* añicos *mpl;* **to smash sth to s.** hacer algo añicos *or* trizas

smithy ['smɪðɪ] *n (forge)* herrería *f*

smitten ['smɪtən] **1** *pp see* **smite**

 2 *adj* **to be s. with flu** estar aquejado(a) de gripe; **to be s. with fear** estar lleno(a) de miedo; **to be s. with remorse** remorderle a uno la conciencia; *Fam (besotted)* **to be s. with sb** estar enamorado(a) de algn

smock [smɒk] *n (blouse)* camisa *f,* blusón *m; (worn in pregnancy)* blusón *m* de premamá; *(overall)* bata *f,* guarda-polvo *m*

smocking ['smɒkɪŋ] *n Sew (gen)* adorno *m* con frunces

smog [smɒg] *n Meteor* niebla *f* tóxica, smog *m*

smoke [sməʊk] **1** *n* (**a**) *(from fire)* humo *m;* **to go up in s.** quemarse, ser destruido(a) por un incendio; *Fig* irse en humo, quedar en agua de borrajas; *Prov* **there's no s. without fire** cuando el río suena, agua lleva ▫ **s. bomb** bomba *f* fumígena *or* de humo; **s. screen** cortina *f* de humo; **s. signal** señal *f* de humo (**b**) *Fam (cigarette)* cigarrillo *m,* cigarro *m,* pitillo *m; Fam (gen)* tabaco *m;* **to have a s.** fumarse un pitillo (**c**) *Br Slang* **the (Big) S.** Londres

 2 *vi (chimney, fire, etc)* humear, echar humo (**b**) *(person) (tobacco)* fumar; **do you s.?** ¿fumas?; **do you mind if I s.?** ¿te molesta que fume?

 3 *vt* (**a**) *(tobacco)* fumar; **to s. a pipe** fumar en pipa (**b**) *(fish, meat)* ahumar

smoke out *vt (insects)* ahuyentar con humo; *(people)* desalojar con bombas fumígenas

smoked [sməʊkt] *adj* ahumado(a)

smokeless ['sməʊklɪs] *adj* sin humo; **s. fuel** combustible sin humo; **s. zone** zona libre de humos

smoker ['sməʊkər] *n* (**a**) *(person)* fumador(a) *m,f;* **s.'s cough** tos *f* de fumador; **to be a heavy s.** fumar mucho (**b**) *Rail (carriage)* vagón *m* de fumadores

smokestack ['sməʊkstæk] *n* chimenea *f*

smoking ['sməʊkɪŋ] **1** *adj* humeante, que echa humo

 2 *n* fumar; **'no s.'** 'prohibido fumar' ▫ *Rail* **s. compartment,** *US* **s. car** vagón *m* de fumadores; **s. jacket** batín *m*

smoky ['sməʊkɪ] *adj* **(smokier, smokiest)** (**a**) *(chimney, fire)* humeante, que echa humo; *(room)* lleno(a) de humo; *(atmosphere)* cargado(a) (de humo); *(food)* ahumado(a) (**b**) *(colour)* ahumado(a); **s. blue** azul ahumado

smolder ['sməʊldər] *vi US see* **smoulder**

smooch [smuːtʃ] *vi Fam* (**a**) *(kiss, cuddle)* besuquearse (**b**) *(dance)* bailar a lo agarrado

smooth [smuːð] **1** *adj* (**a**) *(texture, surface)* liso(a); *(skin)* suave; *(road)* llano(a), uniforme; *(sea)* tranquilo(a), en calma (**b**) *(without lumps)* sin grumos (**c**) *(beer, wine)* suave (**d**) *(flowing)* fluido(a) (**e**) *(troublefree) (journey, flight)* tranquilo(a); *(take-off, landing)* suave; *(take-over, transition)* sin problemas (**f**) *Pej (slick, ingratiating)* zalamero(a), meloso(a); **he's a s. operator** *(in business)* es un tipo muy hábil; *(in love)* es un ligón de profesión; **to be a s. talker** tener un pico de oro

 2 *vt* (**a**) *(hair)* alisar; *(surface)* alisar, igualar; *Fig* **to s. the path** *or* **way for sb** preparar el terreno para algn (**b**) *(plane down)* limar (**c**) *(polish)* pulir

smooth away *vt (wrinkles)* quitar, hacer desaparecer; *Fig (doubts, fears)* calmar

smooth back *vt (hair)* alisar

smooth down *vt (hair)* alisar; *(surface)* alisar, igualar

smooth out *vt (creases)* alisar; *Fig (difficulties)* allanar; *(problems)* resolver

smooth over *vt Fig* limar; **to s. things over** limar asperezas

smoothie ['smuːðɪ] *n Fam* tipo *m* zalamero, pelota *mf*

smoothly ['smuːðlɪ] *adv* tranquilamente, correcta-mente; **everything is running s.** todo va sobre ruedas

smoothness ['smuːðnɪs] *n* (**a**) *(softness)* suavidad *f; (flatness)* llaneza *f,* lisura *f,* uniformidad *f* (**b**) *(peacefulness)* tranquilidad *f* (**c**) *(flattery etc)* zalamería *f*

smooth-running [smuːð'rʌnɪŋ] *adj (engine, machine)* suave; *(business, organization)* que funciona bien

smooth-talking ['smuːðtɔːkɪŋ] *adj* zalamero(a)

smote [sməʊt] *pt see* **smite**

smother ['smʌðər] **1** *vt* (**a**) *(asphyxiate)* asfixiar; *(suffocate)* sofocar (**b**) *(cover)* cubrir (**with** de); **to s. sb with kisses** colmar a algn de besos

 2 *vi (asphyxiate)* asfixiarse, ahogarse

smoulder ['sməʊldər] *vi (fire)* arder sin llama; *Fig (passions)* arder; **smouldering hatred** odio latente

SMS [esem'es] *n (abbr* **short message service)** *(service)* SMS *m; (message)* mensaje *m* SMS *or* de texto

smudge [smʌdʒ] **1** *n (stain)* mancha *f; (of ink)* borrón *m*
  2 *vt* manchar; *(piece of writing)* emborronar
  3 *vi (ink, paint)* correrse

smudgy ['smʌdʒɪ] *adj* **(smudgier, smudgiest)** *(stain)* manchado(a); *(piece of writing)* emborronado(a)

smug [smʌg] *adj* **(smugger, smuggest)** *(self-satisfied)* engreído(a), satisfecho(a)

smuggle ['smʌgəl] *vt (goods)* pasar de contrabando; **to s. sth in/out** pasar/sacar algo de contrabando; **to s. sth through customs** pasar algo de contrabando por la aduana

smuggler ['smʌgələr] *n* contrabandista *mf*

smuggling ['smʌgəlɪŋ] *n* contrabando *m*

smugly ['smʌglɪ] *adv* con engreimiento

smugness ['smʌgnɪs] *n* engreimiento *m*

smut [smʌt] *n* **(a)** *(flake of soot)* hollín *m*, carbonilla *f; (stain)* mancha *f* de hollín, tizón *m* **(b)** *Fam (crude talk)* obscenidades *fpl; (dirty jokes)* chistes *mpl* verdes; *(pornography)* pornografía *f*

smutty ['smʌtɪ] *adj* **(smuttier, smuttiest) (a)** *(dirty)* manchado(a), sucio(a); *(of smut)* tiznado(a) **(b)** *Fam (crude)* obsceno(a); *(joke)* verde; *(book, film, etc)* pornográfico(a)

snack [snæk] *n* bocado *m*, tentempié *m*, *Méx* botana *f* ⬜ **s. bar** cafetería *f*, bar *m*

snag [snæg] **1** *n* **(a)** *(of tree)* tocón *m*, gancho *m; (of tooth)* raigón *m* **(b)** *(pulled thread)* enganchón *m*, desgarrón *m*, rasgón *m*, siete *m* **(c)** *(difficulty)* pega *f*, problema *m*, dificultad *f;* **that's the s.** ahí esta la pega; **to come up against a s.** encontrarse con una pega
  2 *vt (pt & pp* **snagged)** *(catch) (clothing)* enganchar

snail [sneɪl] *n Zool* caracol *m;* **at a s.'s pace** a paso de tortuga ⬜ *Fam* **s. mail** correo *m* caracol, correo *m* tradicional

snake [sneɪk] **1** *n (big)* serpiente *f; (small)* culebra *f; (game)* **snakes and ladders** (el juego de) la oca; *Fig* **a s. in the grass** un traidor ⬜ **s. charmer** encantador(a) *m,f* de serpientes
  2 *vi Fig* serpentear

snakebite ['sneɪkbaɪt] *n* mordedura *f* de serpiente

snakeskin ['sneɪkskɪn] *n* piel *f* de serpiente

snaky ['sneɪkɪ] *adj* **(snakier, snakiest)** *(winding)* tortuoso(a), sinuoso(a)

snap [snæp] **1** *n* **(a)** *(sharp noise)* ruido *m* seco; *(of branch, fingers)* chasquido *m* **(b)** *(bite)* mordisco *m* **(c)** *Phot (foto f)* instantánea *f* **(d)** *Cards* guerra *f*
  2 *adj (sudden)* repentino(a); *(unexpected)* inesperado(a); **a s. decision** una decisión instantánea
  3 *vt (pt & pp* **snapped) (a)** *(break) (branch etc)* partir (en dos), romper **(b)** *(make sharp noise with)* **to s. one's fingers** chasquear los dedos; **to s. sth shut** cerrar algo de golpe; *Fig* **to s. one's fingers at sb** burlarse de algn **(c)** *Phot* sacar una foto de
  4 *vi* **(a)** *(break)* romperse **(b)** *(make sharp noise)* hacer un ruido seco; *(whip)* chasquear; *(lid etc)* **to s. shut** cerrarse de golpe **(c)** *(dog)* amenazar; *Fig* ladrar; **to s. at sb** intentar morder a algn; *Fam (person)* regañar a algn; *Fam* **there's no need to s.!** ¡no hace falta morder!
  5 *interj Br (on seeing two identical things)* ¡toma!

snap off 1 *vt (branch etc)* separar; *Fam* **to s. sb's head off** echarle un rapapolvo a algn
  2 *vi (branch etc)* separarse, desprenderse

snap out 1 *vt (order etc)* gritar, decir con brusquedad

  2 *vi Fam* **s. out of it!** *(forget it)* ¡olvídalo!; *(cheer up)* ¡anímate!

snap up *vt Fam* **to s. up a bargain** conseguir *or* llevarse una ganga

snapdragon ['snæpdrægən] *n Bot* dragón *m*

snappy ['snæpɪ] *adj* **(snappier, snappiest)** *Fam* **(a)** *(quick)* rápido(a); **look s.!, make it s.!** ¡date prisa! **(b)** *(stylish)* elegante; **to be a s. dresser** vestirse con elegancia **(c)** *(short-tempered)* irritable, irascible

snapshot ['snæpʃɒt] *n Phot (foto f)* instantánea *f*

snare [sneər] **1** *n (hunting)* lazo *m*, trampa *f*, cepo *m; Fig* trampa *f*
  2 *vt (animal)* coger con lazo, cazar con trampa; *Fig (person)* hacer caer en la trampa, engañar

snarl¹ [snɑːl] **1** *n (growl)* gruñido *m*
  2 *vi (dog, person)* gruñir; **to s. at sb** decirle algo a algn gruñendo

snarl² [snɑːl] **1** *n (in wool)* maraña *f*, enredo *m; (of traffic)* atasco *m*, embotellamiento *m*
  2 *vt* **to s. (up)** *(wool)* enmarañar; *(traffic)* atascar; *(plans)* enredar
  3 *vi (traffic)* **to s. up** atascarse

snarl-up ['snɑːlʌp] *n (gen)* enredo *m*, maraña *f; (in traffic)* atasco *m*

snatch [snætʃ] **1** *n* **(a)** *(grabbing)* arrebatamiento *m;* **to make a s. at sth** intentar arrebatar *or* agarrar algo **(b)** *Fam (theft)* robo *m*, hurto *m* ⬜ **s. bag** tirón *m;* **wages s.** robo *m* de la nómina de una empresa **(c)** *(fragment)* trocito *m*, fragmento *m*
  2 *vt* **(a)** *(grab)* arrebatar; *Fig* **to s. an opportunity** aprovechar una ocasión; *Fig* **to s. a meal** comer sobre la marcha; *Fig* **to s. some sleep** echar una cabecita **(b)** *Fam (steal)* robar; *(kidnap)* secuestrar
  3 *vi* **don't s.!** ¡no me lo quites así!; **to s. at sth** intentar agarrar algo

snatch up *vt* agarrar rápidamente

snazzy ['snæzɪ] *adj* **(snazzier, snazziest)** *Fam (trendy, stylish)* elegante; *(flashy)* vistoso(a), llamativo(a)

sneak [sniːk] **1** *n Fam (split) Esp* chivato(a) *m,f, Méx* hocicón(ona) *m,f, RP* buchón(ona) *m,f* ⬜ **s. preview** estreno *m* preliminar; **s. thief** ladronzuelo(a) *m,f*, ratero(a) *m,f*
  2 *vt (pt & pp* **sneaked,** *US* **snuck) to s. sth out of a place** sacar algo de un lugar a escondidas; **to s. a look at sth** mirar algo furtivamente *or* de reojo
  3 *vi* **(a)** *(gen)* moverse, ir; **to s. about** moverse sigilosamente; **to s. away** *or* **off** escabullirse; **to s. in/out** entrar/salir a hurtadillas; **to s. off with sth** llevarse algo furtivamente; **to s. past sb** pasar desapercibido(a) delante de algn; **to s. up on sb** sorprender a algn **(b)** *(tell tales)* chivarse **(on** de)

sneakers ['sniːkəz] *npl US* zapatillas *fpl* de deporte, playeras *fpl*

sneaking ['sniːkɪŋ] *adj* **(a)** *(secret)* secreto(a); **I have a s. admiration for him** en el fondo le admiro **(b)** *(slight)* ligero(a); **to have a s. feeling that ...** tener la sensación de que ...

sneaky ['sniːkɪ] *adj* **(sneakier, sneakiest)** *(sly)* solapado(a); *(splitter)* soplón(ona)

sneer [snɪər] **1** *n* **(a)** *(expression)* cara *f* de desprecio; *(smirk)* risa *f* burlona **(b)** *(remark)* comentario *m* desdeñoso *or* sarcástico
  2 *vi* **to s. at sth/sb** *(mock)* burlarse *or* mofarse de algo/algn; *(scorn)* desdeñar *or* despreciar algo/a algn

sneering ['snɪərɪŋ] *adj* *(mocking)* burlón(ona); *(scornful)* desdeñoso(a), despreciativo(a); *(sarcastic)* sarcástico(a), socarrón(ona)

sneeze [sni:z] **1** n estornudo m
2 vi estornudar; *Fam Fig* **it's not to be sneezed at** no es de despreciar

snicker ['snɪkər] *US* **1** n risilla f burlona
2 vi burlarse, reírse

snide [snaɪd] adj *Fam (trick etc)* bajo(a), vil; *(remark)* sarcástico(a)

sniff [snɪf] **1** n *(act of inhaling)* aspiración f, inhalación f; *(by dog)* husmeo m, olfateo m; **to take a s. at sth** olfatear algo
2 vt *(flower etc)* oler; *(suspiciously)* husmear, olfatear; *(snuff, smelling salts)* aspirar, inhalar; *(glue)* esnifar
3 vi aspirar por la nariz, sorber; **to s. at sth** *(person)* oler algo; *(dog)* husmear or olfatear algo; *Br Fam Fig* **it's not to be sniffed at** no es de despreciar

sniff out vt *Fig (secret, plot)* descubrir husmeando

sniffer dog ['snɪfədɒg] n perro m antidroga

sniffle ['snɪfəl] **1** n resfriado m; **to have the sniffles** estar resfriado(a)
2 vi *(due to head cold)* sorberse los mocos; *(on weeping)* lloriquear, gimotear

sniffy ['snɪfɪ] adj *Fam (disdainful)* desdeñoso(a); **to be s. about sth** tratar algo con desprecio

snifter ['snɪftər] n **(a)** *Fam* copa f, trago m; **to have a s.** echarse un trago **(b)** *US (brandy glass)* copa f de coñac

snigger ['snɪgər] **1** n *(snicker)* risa f disimulada, risilla f
2 vi reír disimuladamente; **to s. at sth** burlarse or mofarse de algo

sniggering ['snɪgərɪŋ] n risas fpl disimuladas, risillas fpl

snip [snɪp] **1** n **(a)** *(cut)* tijeretada f, tijeretazo m; *(action, noise)* tijereteo m; *(small piece)* recorte m **(b)** *Br Fam (bargain)* Esp chollo m, Am regalo m; **we got the car for a s.** el coche nos salió tirado de precio
2 vt *(pt & pp snipped)* tijeretear; **to s. sth off** cortar algo con tijeras

snipe [snaɪp] **1** n *Orn* agachadiza f
2 vi **(a)** *(sneer, dig)* criticar **(b)** *(shoot at)* disparar **(at** sobre); **to s. at sb** disparar sobre algn desde un escondite

sniper ['snaɪpər] n *Mil* francotirador(a) m,f

snippet ['snɪpɪt] n *(of cloth, paper)* trocito m, recorte m; *(of conversation, information)* fragmento m; **snippets of news** noticias fpl breves

snitch [snɪtʃ] *Fam* **1** vt *(steal)* birlar, afanar
2 vi *(tell tales)* **to s. on sb** Esp chivarse de algn, Col sapear or Mex soplar or RP botonear a algn

snivel ['snɪvəl] vi *(pt & pp snivelled, US* sniveled) lloriquear

snivelling, *US* **sniveling** ['snɪvəlɪŋ] **1** adj llorón(ona)
2 n lloriqueo m

snob [snɒb] n esnob mf, snob mf

snobbery ['snɒbərɪ] n esnobismo m, snobismo m

snobbish ['snɒbɪʃ] adj esnob, snob

snobby ['snɒbɪ] adj **(snobbier, snobbiest)** esnob, snob

snog [snɒg] *Br Fam* **1** n **to have a s.** besuquearse
2 vi *(pt & pp snogged)* besuquearse

snooker ['snuːkər] **1** n snooker m, billar m ruso
2 vt *Br Fam* poner en aprietos; **to be snookered** estar con el agua al cuello

snoop [snuːp] **1** n *(nosey person)* fisgón(ona) m,f; *(meddler)* entrometido(a) m,f; **to have a s. around** fisgonear
2 vi fisgonear; *(meddle)* entrometerse

snooper ['snuːpər] n *(nosey person)* fisgón(ona) m,f; *(meddler)* entrometido(a) m,f

snooty ['snuːtɪ] adj **(snootier, snootiest)** *Fam* altivo(a), presumido(a), esnob, snob

snooze [snuːz] **1** n *Fam* cabezada f, siestita f; **to have a s.**

echar una cabezada or una siestita ▫ **s. button** *(on alarm clock)* = botón para la función de dormitar
2 vi dormitar, echar una cabezada

snore [snɔːr] **1** n ronquido m
2 vi roncar

snoring ['snɔːrɪŋ] n ronquidos mpl

snorkel ['snɔːkəl] **1** n *(of swimmer)* tubo m de respiración; *(of submarine)* esnórquel m
2 vi *(pt & pp snorkelled, US* snorkeled) bucear con tubo de respiración

snorkelling, *US* **snorkeling** ['snɔːkəlɪŋ] n **to go s.** bucear con tubo de respiración

snort [snɔːt] **1** n *(horse)* resoplido m; *(person)* resoplido m, bufido m
2 vi *(horse)* resoplar; *(person) (with rage etc)* resoplar, bufar

snorter ['snɔːtər] n *Fam (drink)* trago m, copa f, chupito m; *Fig* **a s. of a problem** un problema de órdago

snot [snɒt] n *Fam* mocos mpl

snotty ['snɒtɪ] adj **(snottier, snottiest)** *Fam* **(a)** *(nose)* mocoso(a) **(b)** *(snooty)* altivo(a), presumido(a), esnob, snob

snotty-nosed ['snɒtɪ'nəʊzd] adj *Fam* **(a)** *(child)* mocoso(a) **(b)** *(arrogant)* creído(a), petulante

snout [snaʊt] n **(a)** *(of animal)* morro m, hocico m; *Fam Fig (person's nose)* morro m, napias fpl **(b)** *(gun, bottle, etc)* morro m

snow [snəʊ] **1** n **(a)** *Meteor* nieve f ▫ **s. line** límite m de las nieves perpetuas; **s. report** informe m sobre el estado de la nieve; **s. shower** nevada f **(b)** *(on TV screen)* nieve f, lluvia f **(c)** *Slang (cocaine)* cocaína f, nieve f, Col perica f, RP blanca f
2 v impers nevar; **it's snowing** está nevando
3 vt **to be snowed in** or **up** quedar aislado(a) or bloqueado(a) por la nieve; *Fig* **to be snowed under with work** estar agobiado(a) de trabajo

snowball ['snəʊbɔːl] **1** n bola f de nieve
2 vi *Fig* aumentar rápidamente

snow-blind ['snəʊblaɪnd] adj cegado(a) por la nieve

snow-blindness ['snəʊblaɪndnɪs] n ceguera f de la nieve

snowboarding ['snəʊbɔːdɪŋ] n snowboard m; **to go s.** hacer snowboard

snowbound ['snəʊbaʊnd] adj aislado(a) or bloqueado(a) por la nieve

snowcapped ['snəʊkæpt] adj cubierto(a) de nieve

snow-covered ['snəʊkʌvəd] adj cubierto(a) de nieve, nevado(a)

snowdrift ['snəʊdrɪft] n ventisquero m

snowdrop ['snəʊdrɒp] n *Bot* campanilla f de invierno

snowfall ['snəʊfɔːl] n nevada f

snowflake ['snəʊfleɪk] n copo m de nieve

snowman ['snəʊmæn] n *(pl* snowmen) figura f or muñeco m de nieve; **the abominable s.** el abominable hombre de las nieves

snowmobile ['snəʊməbiːl] n moto f para la nieve

snowplough, *US* **snowplow** ['snəʊplaʊ] n quitanieves m inv

snowshoe ['snəʊʃuː] n raqueta f (de nieve)

snowstorm ['snəʊstɔːm] n *(blizzard)* nevasca f, ventisca f, tormenta f de nieve

snowsuit ['snəʊsuːt] n traje m de esquiar

Snow White [snəʊ'waɪt] n Blancanieves f

snow-white [snəʊ'waɪt] adj blanco(a) como la nieve, níveo(a)

snowy ['snəʊɪ] adj **(snowier, snowiest)** **(a)** *(mountain)* nevado(a); *(region, climate)* de mucha nieve, nevoso(a); *(day)* de nieve; *(season)* de nieves; **it was very s. yesterday** ayer nevó mucho (**b**) *(white)* blanco(a) como la nieve, níveo(a)

Snr *(abbr* **senior)**

snub [snʌb] **1** *n (of person)* desaire *m; (of offer)* rechazo *m*
2 *vt (pt & pp* **snubbed)** *(person)* desairar; *(offer)* rechazar; **to be snubbed** sufrir un desaire
3 *adj* respingón(ona); **s. nose** nariz chata *or* respingona

snub-nosed ['snʌbnəʊzd] *adj* de nariz chata *or* respingona

snuck [snʌk] *US pt & pp see* **sneak**

snuff¹ [snʌf] *n* rapé *m;* **a pinch of s.** un pellizco de rapé; **to take s.** tomar rapé

snuff² [snʌf] *vt* apagar; *Br Fam* **to s. it** estirar la pata, liar el petate

snuff out *vt (rebellion)* sofocar

snuffbox ['snʌfbɒks] *n* caja *f* de rapé, tabaquera *f*

snuffle ['snʌfəl] **1** *n* catarro *m;* **to have the snuffles** estar resfriado(a) *or* acatarrado(a)
2 *vi (due to head cold)* sorberse los mocos; *(on weeping)* gimotear

snug [snʌg] **1** *adj* (**snugger, snuggest**) (**a**) *(cosy)* cómodo(a); *(cosy and warm)* calentito(a) (**b**) *(tight-fitting)* ajustado(a), ceñido(a)
2 *n Br (in pub)* saloncito *m*

snuggle ['snʌgəl] *vi* **to s. down** *or* **up in bed** acurrucarse en la cama; **to s. up to sb** arrimarse a algn

snugly ['snʌglɪ] *adv* cómodamente; **to fit s.** *(clothes)* quedar ajustado(a); *(object in box etc)* caber perfectamente, encajar

so [səʊ] **1** *adv* (**a**) *(to such an extent)* tanto; **he was so tired that ...** estaba tan cansado que ...; **it's so long since ...** hace tanto tiempo que ...; **please be so kind as to ...** tenga la bondad de ...; **she isn't so clever as her sister** no es tan lista como su hermana; *Fam* **so long!** ¡hasta luego!, ¡hasta pronto! (**b**) *(degree)* tanto; **a week or so** una semana más o menos; **he earns so much per hour** gana tanto por hora; **I haven't so much as a farthing** no tengo ni un real; **so many books** tantos libros; **so much money** tanto dinero; **twenty or so** una veintena; **we didn't get so much as a reply** ni siquiera nos contestaron; **we loved her so (much)** la queríamos tanto; *Fam* **he's ever so handsome** ¡es tan guapo!; *Fam* **what's so funny?** ¿qué pasa?, ¿de qué te ríes?; *Iron* **so much for his promises then!** ¡eso valen sus promesas!; *Iron* **so much for that** ¿qué le vamos a hacer? (**c**) *(thus, in this way)* así, de esta manera, de este modo; **and so on, and so forth** y así sucesivamente, etcétera; **he is right and so are you** él tiene razón y tú también; **how so?** ¿cómo es eso?; **if so** en este caso, de ser así; **I'm afraid so** me temo que sí; **I suppose so** me imagino que sí; **I think/hope so** creo/espero que sí; **I told you so** ya te lo dije; **it so happens that ...** da la casualidad de que ...; **press the button so** aprieta el botón así; **she likes everything to be just so** le gusta tener todo en orden; **so be it!** ¡así sea!; **so far** hasta aquí *or* allí *or* ahora; **so far as I know** que yo sepa; **so it is!** ¡así es!; **so it seems** según parece; **so they say** según dicen; **stand just so** ponte así; **you're late! — so I am!** ¡llegas tarde! — ¡tienes razón!
2 *conj* (**a**) *(expresses result)* así que, por lo tanto; **so you like England, do you?** ¿así que te gusta Inglaterra, pues?; **the child was feverish, so she called the doctor** el niño tenía fiebre, así que llamó al médico; *Fam* **so what?** ¿y qué? (**b**) *(expresses purpose)* para que; **he left his job so (that) he could concentrate on his studies** dejó el trabajo para dedicarse plenamente a los estudios; **I'll put the key here so (that) everyone can see it** pongo la llave aquí para que todos la vean; **they left early so as to arrive on time/so as not to miss the meeting** se marcharon antes para llegar a tiempo/para no perderse la reunión

soak [səʊk] **1** *vt (washing, food)* poner en remojo, remojar; *(cotton, wool)* empapar (**in** en), mojar (**in** en)
2 *vi (washing, food)* estar en remojo; **to leave sth to s.** dejar algo en remojo; **to s. through** penetrar
3 *n Fam (drunkard)* **an old s.** un borracho perdido

soak in *vi* penetrar; *Fig* **it hasn't soaked in yet** todavía no lo creo

soak up *vt* absorber

soaked [səʊkt] *adj* (**a**) *(person)* empapado(a), calado(a); **s. to the skin** calado(a) hasta los huesos; **we got s.** nos quedamos empapados (**b**) *(food)* macerado(a) **a cake s. in sherry** un pastel emborrachado con jerez

soaking ['səʊkɪŋ] **1** *n* remojo *m;* **to give sth a s.** poner algo en remojo; **to get a s.** empaparse
2 *adj (object)* completamente mojado(a); *(person)* empapado(a), calado(a) hasta los huesos

so-and-so ['səʊənsəʊ] *n Fam* fulano(a) *m,f;* **Mr So-a.-so** Don Fulano (de tal); *Pej* **an old so-a.-so** un viejo imbécil, un tío cabrón

soap [səʊp] **1** *n* (**a**) *(for washing)* jabón *m* ❑ **bar of s.** pastilla *f* de jabón; **s. dish** jabonera *f;* **s. flakes** jabón *m* en escamas; **s. powder** jabón *m* en polvo (**b**) **s. opera** *TV* telenovela *f; Rad* radionovela *f*
2 *vt* enjabonar, jabonar

soapbox ['səʊpbɒks] *n* tribuna *f* improvisada

soapsuds ['səʊpsʌds] *npl* jabonaduras *fpl*, espuma *f sing*

soapy ['səʊpɪ] *adj* (**soapier, soapiest**) *(water)* jabonoso(a); *(hands)* cubierto(a) de jabón; *(taste, smell)* jabonoso(a), parecido(a) al jabón

soar [sɔːr] *vi* (**a**) *(bird, plane)* remontar el vuelo; *(hover, glide)* planear (**b**) *Fig (skyscraper)* elevarse, encumbrarse; *(hopes, prices)* aumentar, crecer; *(music)* subir

soaring ['sɔːrɪŋ] *adj* (**a**) *(bird, plane)* que planea (**b**) *Fig (skyscraper)* altísimo(a); *(prices)* en alza; *(hopes, prices)* en aumento

sob [sɒb] **1** *n* sollozo *m; Fam Iron* **s. story** tragedia, drama
2 *vi (pt & pp* **sobbed)** sollozar
3 *vt Fig* **to s. one's heart out** llorar a lágrima viva

s.o.b. [esəʊˈbiː] *n US Fam (abbr* **son of a bitch)** hijo(a) *m,f* de su madre

sobbing ['sɒbɪŋ] *n* sollozos *mpl*

sober ['səʊbər] *adj* (**a**) *(not drunk)* sobrio(a) (**b**) *(moderate)* moderado(a) sobrio(a) (**c**) *(sensible)* sensato(a); *(serious)* serio(a) (**d**) *(colour)* discreto(a)

sober up *vi* by the next day he had sobered up al día siguiente se le había pasado la borrachera
2 *vt* quitar *or Am* sacar la borrachera a

sobering ['səʊbərɪŋ] *adj* moderador(a); **it had a s. effect on him** lo hizo entrar en razón, le dio que pensar

soberly ['səʊbəlɪ] *adv* con moderación, con sobriedad

sober-minded [səʊbəˈmaɪndɪd] *adj* sensato(a)

sobriety [səʊˈbraɪətɪ] *n Fml* (**a**) *(being sober)* sobriedad *f* (**b**) *(moderation)* moderación *f* (**c**) *(good sense)* sensatez *f; (seriousness)* seriedad *f*

Soc [sɒk] *(abbr* **society)** sociedad *f*, S

so-called ['səʊkɔːld] *adj* supuesto(a), llamado(a); **all these so-c. experts** estos así llamados expertos

soccer ['sɒkər] *n* fútbol *m* ❑ **s. match** partido *m* de fútbol; **s. player** futbolista *mf*, jugador(a) *m,f* de fútbol

sociable ['səʊʃəbəl] *adj (gregarious)* sociable, tratable; *(friendly)* amistoso(a), simpático(a)

social ['səʊʃəl] **1** *adj* (**a**) *(gen)* social; **to have a good s. life** hacer buena vida social ❑ **s. class** clase *f* social; **s. climber** arribista *mf; Press* **s. column** ecos *mpl* de sociedad; *Pol* **S. Democrat** socialdemócrata *mf; Pol* **S. Democratic**

socialdemócrata; **s. exclusion** exclusión f social; US **s. insurance** seguro m social; **s. outcast** marginado(a) m,f; **s. sciences** ciencias fpl sociales; **s. security** seguro m or seguridad f social; **s. studies** (ciencias fpl) sociales fpl; **s. welfare** asistencia f social; **s. work** asistencia f or trabajo m social; **s. worker** asistente(a) m,f social, trabajador(a) m,f social; **the s. services** los servicios sociales (**b**) (gregarious) sociable
  2 n (do) acto m social, reunion f
socialism ['səʊʃəlɪzəm] n socialismo m
socialist ['səʊʃəlɪst] adj & n Pol socialista (mf)
socialistic [səʊʃə'lɪstɪk] adj Pol socialista
socialite ['səʊʃəlaɪt] n vividor(a) m,f, mundano(a) m,f
socialization [səʊʃəlaɪ'zeɪʃən] n socialización f
socialize ['səʊʃəlaɪz] **1** vi (at party etc) circular, alternar, mezclarse con la gente; **he's good at socializing** tiene mucho don de gentes
  2 vt socializar
socially ['səʊʃəlɪ] adv socialmente; **s. deprived** marginado(a); **we don't see each other s.** no hacemos vida social en común
society [sə'saɪətɪ] **1** n (**a**) (social community) sociedad f; **the consumer s.** la sociedad de consumo; **to be a danger to s.** ser un peligro para la sociedad (**b**) (upper social circle) (**high**) **s.** la alta sociedad (**c**) (organization, club) sociedad f, asociación f □ **building s.** banco m hipotecario; **film s.** club m de cine, cineclub m (**d**) (company, companionship) compañía f
  2 adj de sociedad □ **s. column** ecos mpl de sociedad; **s. wedding** boda f de sociedad
socio- ['səʊsɪəʊ, 'səʊʃɪəʊ] pref socio-; **sociobiology** sociobiología f
socioeconomic [səʊsɪəʊiːkə'nɒmɪk] adj socioeconómico(a)
sociolinguistics ['səʊsɪəʊlɪŋ'gwɪstɪks] n sociolingüística f
sociological [səʊsɪə'lɒdʒɪkəl] adj sociológico(a)
sociologist [səʊsɪ'ɒlədʒɪst] n sociólogo(a) m,f
sociology [səʊsɪ'ɒlədʒɪ] n sociología f
sociopolitical ['səʊsɪəʊpə'lɪtɪkəl] adj sociopolítico(a)
sock¹ [sɒk] n calcetín m; Br Fam **put a s. in it!** ¡cierra el pico!; Br Fam **to pull one's socks up** hacer un esfuerzo
sock² [sɒk] Fam **1** n (blow) puñetazo m, tortazo m
  2 vt pegar, zurrar; **she socked him one** le pegó un tortazo; Fam Fig **s. it to them!** ¡a por ellos!, ¡dales caña!
socket ['sɒkɪt] n (**a**) (of eye) cuenca f; (of joint) glena f (**b**) Elec (power point) enchufe m, toma f de corriente (**c**) Tech **s. wrench** llave f de tubo
sod¹ [sɒd] n Fml (piece of turf) tepe m, terrón m; Fam **the old s.** su tierra natal, el terruño
sod² [sɒd] esp Br Slang **1** n (**a**) (obnoxious person) mamón(ona) m,f, Méx mamila mf, RP choto(a) m,f; (wretch) desgraciado(a) m,f; **the lazy s.!** ¡qué tipo más vago!; **the poor s. has got no family** el pobre no tiene familia (**b**) (nothing) **I've done s. all today** hoy no he pegado ni golpe (**c**) (annoying thing, task) plomazo m, Esp jodienda f, Esp coñazo m
  2 vt Vulg **s. it!** Esp ¡joder!, Méx ¡chin!, RP ¡la puta!; **s. you!** ¡vete a la mierda!
soda ['səʊdə] n (**a**) Chem sosa f; **baking s.** bicarbonato m sódico or de sosa; **caustic s.** sosa caústica (**b**) (mineral water) **s. (water)** (agua f de) seltz m, soda f; **a whisky and s.** un whisky con sifón or soda □ **s. syphon** sifón m (**c**) US (sweet fizzy drink) gaseosa f □ **s. fountain** puesto m de helados y refrescos, Carib Chile Col Méx fuente f de soda
sodden ['sɒdən] adj empapado(a)

sodding ['sɒdɪŋ] adj Br Vulg maldito(a), Esp puñetero(a), Méx pinche
sodium ['səʊdɪəm] n Chem sodio m □ **s. bicarbonate** bicarbonato m sódico or de sosa
sodomize ['sɒdəmaɪz] vt sodomizar
sodomy ['sɒdəmɪ] n sodomía f
sofa ['səʊfə] n sofá m; **s. bed** sofá cama
soft [sɒft] adj (**a**) (not hard) blando(a); (spongy) esponjoso(a); (bed) mullido(a); (flabby) fofo(a) □ **s. currency** moneda f débil; Br **s. furnishings,** US **s. goods** = artículos y materiales de decoración del tipo cortinas, cojines, alfombras, etc; **s. toy** muñeco m de peluche (**b**) (smooth) (skin, colour, etc) suave; (hair) suave, liso(a) (**c**) (not harsh) (light, music, etc) suave; (breeze, steps) ligero(a) □ **s. focus** difuminado m; Mus **s. pedal** sordina f (**d**) (weak) débil; (lenient) poco severo(a) □ **s. sell** venta f basada en la persuasión (**e**) (consonant, sound) suave; (voice) bajo(a) □ **s. palate** velo m del paladar (**f**) (foolish) tonto(a), lelo(a); **to be a s. touch** ser fácil de engañar; **to be s. in the head** ser tonto(a) del culo (**g**) (sentimental) sensiblero(a), sentimentaloide; **to have a s. spot for sb** tener debilidad por algn (**h**) (easy) (life etc) fácil □ **s. job** chollo m (**i**) (drink) no alcohólico(a) □ **s. drinks** refrescos mpl (**j**) (less harmful) blando(a) □ **s. drugs** drogas fpl blandas; **s. porn** porno m blando (**k**) Comptr **s. copy** copia f en formato electrónico; **s. return** retorno m automático
softball ['sɒftbɔːl] n = juego parecido al béisbol jugado en un campo más pequeño y con una pelota más blanda
soft-boiled ['sɒftbɔɪld] adj (egg) pasado(a) por agua
soft-core ['sɒftkɔːr] adj (pornography) blando(a)
soften ['sɒfən] **1** vt (leather, heart) ablandar; (skin) suavizar; (light) atenuar; (voice) bajar; Fig (blow) amortiguar
  2 vi (leather, heart) ablandarse; (skin) suavizarse; (light) atenuarse
soften up vt Fam (person) ablandar
softener ['sɒfənər] n (for water) suavizador m □ **fabric s.** suavizante m
soft-hearted [sɒft'hɑːtɪd] adj tierno(a), compasivo(a), bondadoso(a)
softie ['sɒftɪ] n Fam blandengue mf
softly ['sɒftlɪ] adv (gently) suavemente; (quietly) silenciosamente, suavemente; **to tread s.** pisar con cuidado
softly-softly [sɒftlɪ'sɒftlɪ] adj (manner, approach) cauteloso(a)
softness ['sɒftnɪs] n (**a**) (gen) blandura f (**b**) (of hair, colours) suavidad f (**c**) (weakness) debilidad f (**d**) (foolishness) estupidez f
soft-pedal [sɒft'pedəl] vt (pt & pp soft-pedalled, US soft-pedaled) Fig minimizar la importancia de
soft-soap [sɒft'səʊp] vt Fam dar jabón a, dar coba a
soft-spoken [sɒft'spəʊkən] adj de voz dulce or baja
software ['sɒftweər] n Comptr software m □ **s. engineer** ingeniero(a) m,f de programas; **s. package** paquete m de software
softy ['sɒftɪ] n Fam see **softie**
soggy ['sɒgɪ] adj (soggier, soggiest) (gen) empapado(a), saturado(a); (bread) pastoso(a), gomoso(a)
soil [sɔɪl] **1** n (earth) tierra f; Fig (land) tierra f; **on British s.** en suelo británico; **my native s.** mi tierra or país natal
  2 vt (dirty) ensuciar; (stain) manchar; Fig (reputation) manchar
soiled [sɔɪld] adj (dirty) sucio(a); (stained) manchado(a); **s. linen** ropa sucia
soirée ['swɑːreɪ] n Fml sarao m, velada f

solace ['sɒlɪs] n Fml consuelo m

solar ['səʊlər] adj solar ❑ **s. energy** energía f solar; Anat **s. plexus** plexo m solar; **s. power** energía f solar

solarium [səʊ'leərɪəm] n (pl **solariums** or **solaria** [səʊ'leərɪə]) solario m, solarium m

solar-powered ['səʊlə'paʊəd] adj por energía solar, alimentado(a) por energía solar

sold [səʊld] pt & pp see **sell**

solder ['sɒldər] **1** n soldadura f
   2 vt soldar

soldering ['sɒldərɪŋ] adj **s. iron** soldador m

soldier ['səʊldʒər] **1** n soldado m; (military man) militar m; **old s.** veterano m, excombatiente m; **toy s.** soldadito de plomo
   2 vi servir como soldado

soldier on vi Fig seguir adelante a pesar de todo, continuar contra viento y marea

sole[1] [səʊl] **1** n (foot) planta f; (shoe, sock) suela f; **half s.** media suela
   2 vt (shoes) poner suela a

sole[2] [səʊl] n (fish) lenguado m

sole[3] [səʊl] adj (a) (only, single) único(a) (b) (exclusive) exclusivo(a)

solecism ['sɒləsɪzəm] n Fml solecismo m

solely ['səʊllɪ] adv (a) (only) únicamente, solamente (b) (exclusively) exclusivamente

solemn ['sɒləm] adj (ceremony) solemne; (expression) serio(a)

solemnity [sə'lemnɪtɪ] n solemnidad f

solemnize ['sɒləmnaɪz] vt solemnizar; (marriage) celebrar

sol-fa [sɒl'fɑː] n Mus solfa f

solicit [sə'lɪsɪt] **1** vt (request) solicitar, pedir
   2 vi (prostitute) buscar clientes, abordar a los clientes

soliciting [sə'lɪsɪtɪŋ] n (by prostitutes) ejercicio m de la prostitución en las calles

solicitor [sə'lɪsɪtər] n Jur ≃ abogado que hace las veces de notario para contratos de compraventa y testamentos o que actúa de procurador en los juzgados ❑ **S. General** Br procurador(a) m,f de la Corona, US subsecretario(a) m,f de Justicia

solicitous [sə'lɪsɪtəs] adj Fml (a) (attentive) solícito(a) (**towards** con), atento(a) (**about, for** a) (b) (eager) deseoso(a) (**to** de)

solicitude [sə'lɪsɪtjuːd] n (a) (attention) solicitud f, atención f (b) (concern) preocupación f (c) (anxiety) ansiedad f

solid ['sɒlɪd] **1** adj (a) (not liquid) sólido(a); (firm) firme; **s. food** alimentos sólidos; **s. fuel** combustible sólido (b) (not hollow) macizo(a) (c) (pure) (metal) puro(a), macizo(a) (d) (dense) (fog, jungle) denso(a), espeso(a); (of strong material) (building etc) fuerte, resistente; **a man of s. build** un hombre fornido or bien plantado; **a s. mass** una masa compacta; **the streets were packed s.** las calles estaban abarrotadas de gente; Fig **we waited for two s. hours** esperamos (durante) dos horas enteras (e) (reliable) sólido(a), consistente; **he's a good s. worker** es un trabajador serio or de fiar (f) (unanimous) unánime; **s. support** apoyo unánime; **we're s. in our resolve** nos mantenemos firmes en nuestra resolución (g) Geom **s. angle** ángulo m sólido; **s. geometry** geometría f del espacio
   2 n (a) Chem sólido m (b) (usu pl) (food) (alimento m) sólido m (c) Geom sólido m

solidarity [sɒlɪ'dærɪtɪ] n solidaridad f

solidify [sə'lɪdɪfaɪ] vi (pt & pp **solidified**) solidificarse

solidity [sə'lɪdɪtɪ] n solidez f

solidly ['sɒlɪdlɪ] adv (gen) sólidamente; (house etc) **s. built** de construcción sólida; **to work s.** trabajar sin descanso; **they voted s. in favour of the agreement** votaron unánimemente a favor del acuerdo

solid-state [sɒlɪd'steɪt] adj Elec de estado sólido, transistorizado(a)

soliloquy [sə'lɪləkwɪ] n soliloquio m

solitaire ['sɒlɪteər] n solitario m

solitary ['sɒlɪtərɪ] adj (a) (alone) solitario(a); (secluded) retirado(a), apartado(a); **to be in s. confinement** estar incomunicado(a) (b) (sole, only) solo(a), único(a); **not a s. soul** ni un alma

solitude ['sɒlɪtjuːd] n soledad f

solo ['səʊləʊ] **1** n (pl **solos**) (a) Mus solo m; **a violin s.** un solo para violín (b) Cards solitario m
   2 adj (a) Mus **for s. violin** para violín solo (b) Av **s. flight** vuelo m en solitario
   3 adv solo, a solas; **to fly s.** volar en solitario

soloist ['səʊləʊɪst] n Mus solista mf

Solomon Islands ['sɒləmən'aɪləndz] npl **the S.** las Islas Salomón

solstice ['sɒlstɪs] n solsticio m

soluble ['sɒljubəl] adj soluble

solution [sə'luːʃən] n solución f

solve [sɒlv] vt resolver, solucionar

solvency ['sɒlvənsɪ] n solvencia f

solvent ['sɒlvənt] adj & n solvente (m)

Somali [sə'mɑːlɪ] adj & n somalí (mf)

Somalia [sə'mɑːlɪə] n Somalia

sombre, US **somber** ['sɒmbər] adj (dark) sombrío(a); (gloomy) umbrío(a), lúgubre; (pessimistic) pesimista; (melancholy) melancólico(a); **a s. prospect** una perspectiva sombría

sombrero [sɒm'breərəʊ] n (pl **sombreros**) sombrero m de ala ancha

some [sʌm] **1** adj (a) (with plural nouns) unos(as), algunos(as); (several) varios(as); (a few) unos(as) cuantos(as) or pocos(as); **did she bring s. flowers?** ¿trajo flores?; **there were s. roses** había unas or algunas rosas; **who wants s. more peas?** ¿quién quiere más guisantes? (b) (with singular nouns) algún, alguna; (a little) algo de, un poco de; **if you need s. help** si necesitas (alguna) ayuda; **there's s. wine left** queda un poco de vino; **try to get s. rest** intenta descansar un poco; **would you like s. coffee?** ¿quiere café? (c) (certain, but not all) cierto(a), alguno(a); **in s. ways** en cierto modo or sentido; **s. days I stay at home** hay días que me quedo en casa; **to s. extent** hasta cierto punto; **s. people say that ...** algunos dicen que ..., hay quien dice que ... (d) (unknown, unspecified) algún, alguna; **for s. reason or other** por una razón o por otra; **in s. book or other** en algún libro que otro; **s. day** algún día, un día de éstos; **s. day next week** algún día de la semana que viene; **s. other time** otra vez, otro día (e) (quite a lot of) bastante; **after s. time** pasado algún tiempo; **it's s. distance away** queda bastante lejos; **s. years ago** hace algunos años; **that was s. film!** (quite a) esto sí que fue una buena película; **the wound will take s. time to heal** la herida tardará bastante en cicatrizarse; Iron **s. friend you are!** ¡valiente amigo eres tú!
   2 pron (a) (people) algunos(as), unos(as); (certain, but not all) algunos, algunas personas; **s. go by bus and s. by train** unos van en autobús y otros en tren; **s. of my friends** algunos de mis amigos (b) (objects) algunos(as); (a few) unos(as) cuantos(as); (a little) algo, un poco; (certain ones)

ciertos(as), algunos(as); **have s.!** ¡tomal; **I agree with s. of what you say** estoy de acuerdo en parte con lo que dices; **s. more wine? — no thanks, I've got s.** ¿quiere más vino? — gracias, ya tengo; **would you like to take s. with you?** *(a few)* ¿quieres llevarte unos cuantos?; *(a little)* ¿quieres llevarte un poco?

3 *adv (approximately, about)* aproximadamente; **s. fifty people** unas cincuenta personas; **s. seventy miles away** a unas setenta millas de aquí

somebody ['sʌmbədɪ] **1** *pron* alguien; **s. is knocking at the door** alguien está llamando a la puerta; **s. else** otro(a), otra persona; **s. or other** alguien, no sé quién
2 *n* to be (a) s. ser todo un personaje; **he thinks he's (a) s.** se cree alguien

somehow ['sʌmhaʊ] *adv* **(a)** *(in some way)* de algún modo, de una u otra manera; **I'll manage s.** me las apañaré como sea **(b)** *(for some reason)* por alguna razón; **I never liked her s.** no sé por qué, pero nunca me cayó bien

someone ['sʌmwʌn] *pron & n see* **somebody**

someplace ['sʌmpleɪs] *adv US see* **somewhere**

somersault ['sʌməsɔːlt] **1** *n (by acrobat etc)* salto *m* mortal; *(by child)* voltereta *f; (by car)* vuelta *f* de campana, vuelco *m*
2 *vi (acrobat etc)* dar un salto mortal; *(child)* dar una voltereta; *(car)* dar una vuelta de campana

something ['sʌmθɪŋ] **1** *pron & n* **(a)** *(a bit, a bit of)* algo; **has it s. to do with the hold-up?** ¿tiene algo que ver con el atraco?; **it came as s. of a surprise to us** nos pilló un poco por sorpresa; **she's s. of an artist** tiene algo de artista; **s. to eat/drink** algo de comer/beber; **would you like s. to drink?** ¿quieres tomar algo? **(b)** *(unidentified)* algo; **are you drunk or s.?** ¿estás borracho o qué?; **s. must be done** hay que hacer algo; **s. or other** algo, alguna cosa; **s. tells me he's lying** no sé por qué, pero me parece que miente; **s. went wrong** algo falló; **she has a certain s.** tiene un no sé qué; **there's s. in what you say** hay algo de verdad en lo que dices; **you've got s. there** eso puede ser interesante **(c)** *(ill-defined)* algo; **is s. the matter?** ¿le pasa algo?; **she's called Jane s. or other** se llama Jane no sé qué más; **s. else** otra cosa; **s. nice** algo bonito; **s. of the kind** algo por el estilo **(d)** *(impressive)* algo; **it was really s.!** *US* **it was s. else!** ¡fue algo extraordinario!
2 *adv* **it cost s. like $10** costó unas 10 dólares; **now that's s. like it!** ¡eso sí que es!; *Fam* **the pain is s. shocking** duele una barbaridad

sometime ['sʌmtaɪm] **1** *adv* algún día; **s. last week** un día de la semana pasada; **s. next year** durante el año que viene; **s. or other** tarde o temprano; **s. soon** un día de éstos
2 *adj (former)* antiguo(a), ex

sometimes ['sʌmtaɪmz] *adv* a veces, de vez en cuando

somewhat ['sʌmwɒt] *adv Fml* algo, un tanto

somewhere ['sʌmweər] *adv* **(a)** *(in some place)* en alguna parte; *(to some place)* a alguna parte; **s. else** *(some other place)* en otra parte; *(to some other place)* a alguna parte; **s. in Australia** en algún lugar de Australia; **I read s. that ...** leí en alguna parte que ...; **s. near Oxford** cerca de Oxford; **s. or other** no sé dónde; *Fam* **now we're getting s.** ya empezamos a hacer progresos, ya empieza a marchar la cosa **(b)** *(approximately)* más o menos, alrededor; **it cost s. in the region of $70** costó unas 70 dólares más o menos; **she's s. in her forties** tendrá unos cuarenta y pico años

somnambulism [sɒm'næmbjʊlɪzəm] *n* sonambulismo *m*

somnambulist [sɒm'næmbjʊlɪst] *n* sonámbulo(a) *m,f*

somnolence ['sɒmnələns] *n* somnolencia *f*

somnolent ['sɒmnələnt] *adj* somnoliento(a), soñoliento(a)

son [sʌn] *n* hijo *m*; **eldest/youngest s.** hijo mayor/menor; *US Offens* **s. of a bitch** hijo de perra, *Méx* hijo de la chingada

sonar ['səʊnɑːr] *n Tech* sonar *m*

sonata [sə'nɑːtə] *n Mus* sonata *f*

son et lumière [sɒneɪ'luːmɪeər] *n* espectáculo *m* de luz y sonido

song [sɒŋ] *n (gen)* canción *f; (of bird)* canto *m*; **give us a s.!** ¡cántanos algo!; **to burst into s.** ponerse a cantar; *Br Fam* **there's no need to make a s. and dance about it** no es para tanto; *Fam* **we bought it for a s.** lo compramos regalado

songbird ['sɒŋbɜːd] *n* pájaro *m* cantor

songbook ['sɒŋbʊk] *n* cancionero *m*

songwriter ['sɒŋraɪtər] *n* compositor(a) *m,f* (de canciones)

sonic ['sɒnɪk] *adj* sónico(a) ❑ **s. boom** estampido *m* sónico; **s. depth finder** sonda *f* acústica

son-in-law ['sʌnɪnlɔː] *n (pl* **sons-in-law**) yerno *m*, hijo *m* político

sonnet ['sɒnɪt] *n* soneto *m*

sonny ['sʌnɪ] *n Fam* hijo *m*, hijito *m*

sonorous ['sɒnərəs] *adj* sonoro(a)

soon [suːn] *adv* **(a)** *(within a short time)* pronto, dentro de poco; *(quickly)* rápidamente; **it will s. be Friday** falta poco para el viernes; **see you s.!** ¡hasta pronto!; **she s. changed her mind** cambió rápidamente de idea; **s. after midnight** poco después de medianoche; **s. afterwards** poco después; **write to me s.** escríbeme pronto **(b)** **as s. as** en cuanto; **as s. as possible** cuanto antes, lo más pronto posible **(c)** *(early)* temprano, pronto; **are you leaving so s.?** ¿ya te vas?; **it's still too s. to tell** todavía es demasiado pronto para saber; **how s. will it be ready?** ¿cuándo estará listo?; **we arrived too s.** llegamos demasiado temprano; *Fig* **don't speak too s.** no cantes victoria **(d)** *(expresses preference)* **I would just as s. stay at home** prefiero *or* preferiría quedarme en casa; **I would as s. not see him now** prefiero *or* preferiría no verlo ahora mismo **(e)** *(expresses indifference)* **I would (just) as s. read as watch TV** tanto me da leer como mirar la tele

sooner ['suːnər] *adv* **(a)** *(earlier)* más temprano; **s. or later** tarde o temprano; **the s. the better** cuanto antes mejor **(b)** *(immediately after)* **no s. had he finished than he fainted** nada más acabar se desmayó; **no s. had she left than the telephone began to ring** apenas se había ido cuando empezó a sonar el teléfono; **no s. said than done** dicho y hecho **(c)** *(rather)* **I would s. do it alone** prefiero *or* preferiría hacerlo yo solo; **I would s. not go by train** prefiero *or* preferiría no ir en tren; *Fam* **I'd s. die!** ¡antes morir!, ¡antes la muerte!; *Fam* **s. you than me!** ¡no me das ninguna envidia!

soot [sʊt] *n* hollín *m*

soothe [suːð] *vt (calm)* calmar, tranquilizar; *(quieten)* acallar; *(anger)* aplacar; *(pain)* aliviar, calmar

soother ['suːðər] *n* chupete *m*

soothing ['suːðɪŋ] *adj (ointment, medicine)* calmante, sedante; *(bath)* relajante; *(tone, words)* calmante, tranquilizador(a)

soothsayer ['suːθseɪər] *n* adivino(a) *m,f*

sooty ['sʊtɪ] *adj (sootier, sootiest) (dirty)* cubierto(a) de hollín; *(black)* negro(a) como el hollín

sop [sɒp] *n* **(a)** *Fig (concession)* concesión *f*, favor *m; (bribe)* soborno *m*; **the bonus was intended as a s. to the workers** la prima fue ideada para apaciguar a los obreros **(b)** **sops** *(food)* sopa *f* sing

sop up *vt* absorber

sophisticated [sə'fɪstɪkeɪtɪd] *adj* sofisticado(a)

sophistication [səfɪstɪ'keɪʃən] n sofisticación f

sophistry ['sɒfɪstrɪ] n (art) sofistería f; (argument) sofisma m

sophomore ['sɒfəmɔ:r] n US estudiante mf de segundo año

soporific [sɒpə'rɪfɪk] **1** adj soporífero(a), soporífico(a) **2** n soporífero m

sopping ['sɒpɪŋ] adj Fam **s. (wet)** como una sopa

soppy ['sɒpɪ] adj (**soppier, soppiest**) Fam sentimentaloide

soprano [sə'prɑ:nəʊ] n (pl **sopranos**) Mus soprano mf, triple mf □ **s. clef** clave f de do; **s. voice** voz f de soprano

sorbet ['sɔ:bɪt] n Culin sorbete m

sorcerer ['sɔ:sərər] n brujo m, hechicero m

sorceress ['sɔ:sərɪs] n bruja f, hechicera f

sorcery ['sɔ:sərɪ] n brujería f, hechicería f

sordid ['sɔ:dɪd] adj sórdido(a)

sordidness ['sɔ:dɪdnɪs] n sordidez f

sore [sɔ:r] **1** adj (**a**) Med (aching) dolorido(a); (painful) doloroso(a); (inflamed) inflamado(a); **my eyes are s.** me pican los ojos; **to have a s. throat** tener dolor de garganta; **to have s. feet** tener los pies doloridos; Fig **it's a s. point** es un asunto delicado or espinoso (**b**) Fam (angry) molesto(a), esp Esp enfadado(a), esp Am enojado(a); **to feel s. about sth** estar resentido(a) por algo
  2 n Med llaga f, úlcera f □ **cold s.** herpes m labial, Esp calentura f, Méx fuego m

sorely ['sɔ:lɪ] adv (greatly) enormemente; **she will be s. missed** se la echará muchísimo de menos, Am se la extrañará muchísimo

soreness ['sɔ:nɪs] n dolor m

sorority [sə'rɒrɪtɪ] n US Univ = asociación femenina de estudiantes que suele funcionar como club social

sorrel¹ ['sɒrəl] n Zool alazán m

sorrel² ['sɒrəl] n Bot acedera f

sorrow ['sɒrəʊ] n pena f, pesar m, dolor m, tristeza f; **much to my s.** con gran pesar mío; Fam **to drown one's sorrows** ahogar las penas

sorrowful ['sɒrəʊfʊl] adj afligido(a), apenado(a), triste

sorry ['sɒrɪ] **1** adj (**sorrier, sorriest**) (**a**) (pity) lleno(a) de lástima; **to feel s. for sb** compadecer a algn; **I feel very s. for her** me da mucha pena; **to feel s. for oneself** compadecerse de uno mismo (**b**) (pitiful, wretched) triste, lamentable; **a s. sight** un triste espectáculo; **in a s. state** en un estado lamentable (**c**) (regretful) **to be s. about sth** sentir or lamentar algo; **I'm late** siento haber llegado tarde; **I'm very s. you couldn't come** siento de verdad que no hayas podido venir; **you'll be s.!** ¡te arrepentirás!
  2 interj (**a**) (apology) ¡perdón!, ¡perdone!, ¡disculpe! (**b**) Br (for repetition) ¿perdón?, ¿cómo?

sort [sɔ:t] **1** n (**a**) (kind) clase f, género m, tipo m, suerte f; (make, brand) marca f; **all sorts of cakes** toda clase de pasteles; **it's a s. of teapot** es una especie de tetera; **nothing of the s.!** ¡en absoluto!, ¡ni pensarlo!; **something of the s.** algo por el estilo (**b**) Fam (person) tipo m; **he's a strange s.** es un tipo raro; **I know his s.** conozco el paño; **it takes all sorts to make a world** de todo hay en la viña del Señor (**c**) of a s., of sorts de alguna clase; **he is a musician of a s.** tiene algo de músico; **there's an office of sorts** hay una especie de despacho (**d**) **s. of** un poco, en cierto modo; **did you like the film? — s. of** ¿te gustó la película? — en cierto modo; **it's s. of blue** es azulado; **it's s. of round** es más bien redondo; **I'm s. of lost** estoy como perdido; **I s. of expected it** en cierto modo me lo esperaba (**e**) **out of sorts** (unwell) pachucho(a); (moody) de mal humor
  2 vt (classify) ordenar, clasificar; Comptr ordenar

sort out vt (**a**) (classify) clasificar; (put in order) ordenar; **to s. out the good from the bad** separar lo bueno de lo malo (**b**) (problem, difficulty) arreglar, solucionar (**c**) Fam **to s. sb out** ajustar cuentas con algn

sortie ['sɔ:tɪ] n Av Mil salida f

sorting ['sɔ:tɪŋ] n clasificación f □ (in post office) **s. office** sala f de batalla

SOS [esəʊ'es] n S.O.S. m

so-so ['səʊsəʊ] adv Fam así así, de aquella manera, regular

soufflé ['su:fleɪ] n Culin soufflé m

sought [sɔ:t] pt & pp see **seek**

sought-after ['sɔ:tɑ:ftər] adj (person) solicitado(a); (object) codiciado(a)

soul [səʊl] n (**a**) (inner being) alma f, espíritu m, ánimo m; **it lacks s.** le falta ánimo; **the life and s. of the party** el alma de la fiesta □ **s. mate** compañero(a) m,f del alma (**b**) Rel alma f; **All Souls' Day** día de los Difuntos; **bless my s.!** ¡Dios mío!; **God rest his s.** que Dios le tenga en su gloria (**c**) (person) alma f, persona f; **not a s.** ni un alma; **he's a good s.** es muy buena persona; **poor s.!** ¡pobrecito! (**d**) (personification) ejemplo m: **she's the s. of discretion** es la discreción personificada (**e**) Mus música f soul

soul-destroying ['səʊldɪstrɔɪŋ] adj (boring) tedioso(a), monótono(a); (demoralizing) desmoralizador(a), degradante

soulful ['səʊlfʊl] adj conmovedor(a), emotivo(a)

soulless ['səʊllɪs] adj (person) inhumano(a), desalmado(a); (place) impersonal

soul-searching ['səʊlsɜ:tʃɪŋ] n examen m de conciencia

soul-stirring ['səʊlstɜ:rɪŋ] adj conmovedor(a)

sound¹ [saʊnd] **1** n (gen) sonido m; (noise) ruido m; **stereophonic s.** sonido estereofónico; **to the s. of the accordion** al son del acordeón; Fig **I don't like the s. of it** no me gusta nada la idea □ **s. archives** fonoteca f sing; **s. barrier** barrera f del sonido; **s. bite** frase f lapidaria (en medios de comunicación); Comptr **s. card** tarjeta f de sonido; **s. effects** efectos mpl sonoros; **s. engineer** ingeniero(a) m,f del sonido; **s. wave** onda f sonora
  2 vt (**a**) (trumpet, bell, alarm) tocar, hacer sonar; **to s. the alarm** dar la señal de alarma; **to s. the retreat** tocar a retirada (**b**) (pronounce) pronunciar (**c**) Med (chest etc) auscultar
  3 vi (**a**) (trumpet, bell, alarm) sonar, resonar (**b**) (give an impression) sonar, parecer; **he sounds German to me** yo diría que es alemán; **how does it s. to you?** ¿qué te parece?; **it sounds as if the match will be postponed** parece que el partido será aplazado; **it sounds empty** suena a vacío; **it sounds interesting** parece interesante; **it sounds like an ambulance** suena como una ambulancia; **it sounds like Mozart** me suena a Mozart; **she sounded upset** parecía disgustada

sound off vi Fam hablar a gritos; **to s. off about** (boast) jactarse de; (complain) quejarse de

sound² [saʊnd] **1** adj (**a**) (healthy) sano(a); (in good condition) en buen estado; **of s. mind** en su sano juicio; **safe and s.** sano(a) y salvo(a) (**b**) (safe, dependable) seguro(a); (correct) acertado(a); (logical) lógico(a), razonable; **a s. investment** una inversión segura; **a s. piece of advice** un buen consejo (**c**) (basis etc) sólido(a), fuerte, robusto(a) (**d**) (thorough) (defeat etc) rotundo(a); (examination etc) a fondo (**e**) (sleep) profundo(a)
  2 adv **to be s. asleep** estar profundamente dormido(a)

sound³ [saʊnd] vt Naut Med sondar

sound out vt (person) sondear

sound⁴ [saʊnd] n Geog estrecho m, brazo m de mar

sounding¹ [ˈsaʊndɪŋ] *adj (resonant)* resonante ❑ **s. board** caja *f* de resonancia

sounding² [ˈsaʊndɪŋ] *n Naut* sondeo *m* ❑ **s. balloon** globo *m* sonda

soundless [ˈsaʊndlɪs] *adj* silencioso(a)

soundly [ˈsaʊndlɪ] *adv* (**a**) *(solidly)* sólidamente (**b**) *(logically)* razonablemente (**c**) *(thoroughly)* **to sleep s.** dormir profundamente; **to thrash sb s.** dar a algn una buena paliza

soundproof [ˈsaʊndpruːf] **1** *adj* insonorizado(a), a prueba de sonidos
2 *vt* insonorizar

soundproofing [ˈsaʊndpruːfɪŋ] *n* (**a**) *(action)* insonorización *f* (**b**) *(material)* aislante *m* acústico

soundtrack [ˈsaʊndtræk] *n* banda *f* sonora

soup [suːp] *n* sopa *f*; *(thin, clear)* caldo *m*, consomé *m*; *Fam* **in the s.** en un apuro *or* aprieto ❑ **s. dish** plato *m* sopero; **s. kitchen** comedor *m* popular, olla *f* común; **s. spoon** cuchara *f* sopera

souped-up [ˈsuːptʌp] *adj Aut Slang* trucado(a)

sour [saʊər] *adj* (**a**) *(fruit)* agrio(a), ácido(a); *(milk)* cortado(a); *(butter)* rancio(a); *(wine)* agrio(a); **to go** *or* **turn s.** *(milk)* cortarse; *(wine)* agriarse; *Fig (situation)* empeorar; *Fam Fig* **s. grapes!** ¡te aguantas! ❑ **s. cream** *Esp* nata *f* agria, *Am* crema *f* de leche agria (**b**) *Fig (person)* amargado(a)

source [sɔːs] *n (of river)* fuente *f*, nacimiento *m*; *Fig (origin)* fuente *f*, origen *m*; *(of information)* fuente *f*; *Med (of infection)* foco *m*; **according to reliable sources** según fuentes fidedignas; **what was the s. of the information?** ¿de dónde procedía la información?

sourly [ˈsaʊəlɪ] *adv* agriamente, con amargura

sourness [ˈsaʊənɪs] *n* (**a**) *(of fruit)* acidez *f*, agrura *f*; *(of milk)* agrura *f* (**b**) *Fig (of person)* amargura *f*, acritud *f*

sourpuss [ˈsaʊəpʊs] *n Fam* amargado(a) *m,f*

souse [saʊs] *vt* (**a**) *Culin (fish)* escabechar; *(meat)* adobar (**b**) *(soak)* empapar, mojar; *(plunge)* sumergir; **to s. oneself with water** empaparse de agua (**c**) *Slang (make drunk)* **to get soused** coger una trompa

south [saʊθ] **1** *n* sur *m*; **in the s. of England** en el sur de Inglaterra, en **the s. of York** al sur de York
2 *adj* del sur; **s. wind** viento del sur ❑ **S. Africa** Sudáfrica; **S. African** sudafricano(a) *(m,f)*; **S. China Sea** Mar *m* de la China Meridional; **S. Dakota** Dakota del Sur; **S. Pole** Polo *m* Sur; **S. West Africa** Namibia; **the S. Seas** los mares del Sur
3 *adv (location)* al sur; *(direction)* hacia el sur; **s. of the border** al sur de la frontera; **to travel s.** viajar hacia el sur

southbound [ˈsaʊθbaʊnd] *adj* con rumbo al sur

southeast [saʊθˈiːst] **1** *n* sudeste *m*
2 *adj* (del) sudeste
3 *adv (location)* al sudeste; *(direction)* hacia el sudeste

southeasterly [saʊθˈiːstəlɪ] *adj (wind)* del sudeste

southeastern [saʊθˈiːstən] *adj (region)* del sudeste

southerly [ˈsʌðəlɪ] *adj (direction)* hacia el sur; *(point, aspect)* al sur; *(wind)* del sur

southern [ˈsʌðən] *adj* del sur, meridional, austral; **in s. Spain** en el sur de España; **s. accent** acento del sur; **S. Europe** Europa del Sur; **the s. hemisphere** el hemisferio sur *or* meridional

southerner [ˈsʌðənər] *n* habitante *mf* del sur, sureño(a) *m,f*

southward [ˈsaʊθwəd] *adj & adv Naut* hacia el sur, en dirección sur

southwards [ˈsaʊθwədz] *adv* hacia el sur

southwest [saʊθˈwest] **1** *n* suroeste *m*
2 *adj* suroeste
3 *adv (location)* al suroeste; *(direction)* hacia el suroeste

southwestern [saʊθˈwestən] *adj* del suroeste

souvenir [suːvəˈnɪər] *n* recuerdo *m*

sou'wester [saʊˈwestər] *n* sueste *m*

sovereign [ˈsɒvrɪn] **1** *n* (**a**) *(monarch)* soberano(a) *m,f* (**b**) *(coin)* soberano *m*
2 *adj* (**a**) *(self-governing)* soberano(a) (**b**) *(supreme)* soberano(a), supremo(a)

sovereignty [ˈsɒvrəntɪ] *n* soberanía *f*

Soviet [ˈsəʊvɪet] **1** *n (person)* soviético(a) *m,f*
2 *adj Formerly* soviético(a) ❑ **S. Russia** Rusia Soviética; **the S. Union** la Unión Soviética

soviet [ˈsəʊvɪet] *n Formerly (government council)* soviet *m*

sow¹ [səʊ] *vt* (*pt* **sowed**; *pp* **sowed** *or* **sown**) *(seeds)* sembrar

sow² [saʊ] *n Zool* cerda *f*, puerca *f*, *Am* chancha *f*

sower [ˈsəʊər] *n (person)* sembrador(a) *m,f*; *(machine)* sembradora *f*

sowing [ˈsəʊɪŋ] *n* siembra *f*

sown [səʊn] *pp see* **sow¹**

soy [sɔɪ] *n esp US* soja *f* ❑ **s. sauce** salsa *f* de soja

soya [ˈsɔɪə] *n Br* soja *f*

sozzled [ˈsɒzəld] *adj Fam* **to be s.** estar trompa; **to get s.** agarrarse una trompa

spa [spaː] *n* balneario *m* ❑ **s. resort** estación *f* balnearia

space [speɪs] **1** *n* (**a**) *(gen)* espacio *m*; **the conquest of s.** la conquista del espacio; **to gaze** *or* **stare into s.** mirar al vacío, tener la mirada perdida; **to travel through s.** viajar por el espacio; **to vanish into s.** desaparecer en el espacio ❑ **outer s.** el espacio exterior; **s. age** era *f* espacial; **s. agency** agencia *f* espacial; **s. capsule** cápsula *f* espacial; **s. flight** vuelo *m* espacial; **s. lab** laboratorio *m* espacial; **s. probe** sonda *f* espacial; **s. program(me)** programa *m* de vuelos espaciales; **s. shuttle** transbordador *m* espacial; **s. station** estación *f* espacial; **s. travel** viajes *mpl* por el espacio (**b**) *(room)* sitio *m*, lugar *m*, espacio *m*; **there isn't enough s. for all of them** no caben todos; **to clear a s. for sth** hacer sitio para algo; **to take up a lot of s.** ocupar mucho sitio; **in a confined s.** en un espacio cerrado; **they sell newspaper advertising s.** venden espacio publicitario en los periódicos (**c**) *(gap, empty place)* espacio *m*, hueco *m*; **blank s.** espacio en blanco; **he loves the wide open spaces** le encanta el campo abierto; **I'm looking for a parking s.** estoy buscando un lugar donde estacionar *or Esp* aparcar ❑ **s. bar** *(on keyboard)* barra *f* espaciadora (**d**) *(in time)* espacio *m*; **in a short s. of time** en un corto espacio; **in the s. of half an hour** en el espacio de media hora
2 *vt (also* **s. out**) espaciar, separar

space-age [ˈspeɪseɪdʒ] *adj* de la era espacial

spacecraft [ˈspeɪskrɑːft] *n inv* nave *f* espacial, astronave *f*

spaced out [speɪstˈaʊt] *adj Slang* colocado(a), flipado(a)

spaceman [ˈspeɪsmən] *n (pl* **spacemen**) astronauta *m*, cosmonauta *m*

space-saving [ˈspeɪsseɪvɪŋ] *adj* que ahorra *or* permite ahorrar espacio

spaceship [ˈspeɪsʃɪp] *n* nave *f* espacial

spacing [ˈspeɪsɪŋ] *n Typ* espacio *m*; **double s.** doble espacio

spacious [ˈspeɪʃəs] *adj* espacioso(a), amplio(a), de gran extensión

spade¹ [speɪd] *n (for digging)* pala *f*; *Fig* **to call a s. a s.** llamar al pan pan y al vino vino

spade² [speɪd] n Cards (international pack) pica f; (Spanish pack) espada f; **the ace of spades** el as de picas or Esp de espadas

spaghetti [spə'getɪ] n (gen) espaguetis mpl; (vermicelli) fideos mpl

Spain [speɪn] n España

spam [spæm] Comptr **1** n correo m basura
2 vt enviar correo basura a
3 vi enviar correo basura

span [spæn] **1** n (a) (of wing) envergadura f; (of hand) palmo m; (of arch, bridge) luz f, ojo m; (of road) tramo m (b) (of time) lapso m, espacio m; **life s.** duración de vida
2 vt (pt & pp spanned) (a) (bridge etc) extenderse sobre, atravesar, cruzar (b) (life etc) abarcar

spangle ['spæŋgəl] n lentejuela f

Spanglish ['spæŋglɪʃ] n spanglish m

Spaniard ['spænjəd] n español(ola) m,f

spaniel ['spænjəl] n (dog) perro m de aguas ▫ **cocker s.** cócker m

Spanish ['spænɪʃ] **1** adj español(ola); **the S. Armada** la Armada Invencible; **the S. Embassy** la Embajada de España ▫ **S. America** Hispanoamérica; **S. fly** cantárida f; **S. guitar** guitarra f clásica
2 n (a) (person) **the S.** los españoles (b) (language) español m, castellano m

Spanish-American [spænɪʃə'merɪkən] adj hispano-americano(a); **the S.-A. War** la Guerra de Cuba

Spanish-speaking ['spænɪʃspi:kɪŋ] adj de habla española, hispanohablante

spank [spæŋk] vt zurrar, pegar, dar azotes a

spanking¹ ['spæŋkɪŋ] n zurra f, azotaina f

spanking² ['spæŋkɪŋ] Fam **1** adj (lively) vivaz
2 adv **s. clean** limpísimo(a); **s. new** completamente nuevo(a), flamante

spanner ['spænər] n Br llave f plana (herramienta); Fam **to put** or **throw a s. in the works** fastidiar el asunto ▫ **box s.** llave f de tubo

spar¹ [spɑ:r] n Naut palo m, verga f

spar² [spɑ:r] vi (pt & pp sparred) (a) Box entrenarse (b) (argue) discutir

spar³ [spɑ:r] n Min esparto m

spare [speər] **1** vt (a) (do without) prescindir de, pasar sin; **can you s. five minutes?** ¿tienes cinco minutos?; **can you s. me ten?** ¿me puedes dar diez?; **I can't s. the time** no tengo tiempo; **there's none to s.** no sobra nada; **we can't s. her today** hoy no podemos prescindir de ella (b) (begrudge) escatimar; **they spared no effort** no escatimaron esfuerzos; **to s. no expense** no reparar en gastos; Prov **s. the rod and spoil the child** escatima la vara y malcriarás al niño (c) (show mercy to) perdonar; **to s. sb's feelings** procurar no herir los sentimientos de algn (d) (save) ahorrar; **s. me the details** ahórrate los detalles
2 adj (a) (left over) sobrante, que sobra; (surplus) de sobra, de más; (available) disponible; **a s. moment** un momento libre; **have you got any s. leaflets?** ¿te sobra algún folleto?; **there's some fish going s.** queda algo de pescado ▫ **s. bed** cama f supletoria; Fin **s. capital** fondos mpl disponibles; Aut **s. part** (pieza f de) recambio m or repuesto m; **s. room** cuarto m de los invitados; Aut **s. tyre** rueda f de repuesto or RP auxilio, Méx llanta f de refacción; Br Fam (on body) michelines mpl, Méx llantas fpl, RP rollos mpl; Aut **s. wheel** rueda f de repuesto or RP auxilio, Méx llanta f de refacción (b) (thin, emaciated) enjuto(a) (c) Br Slang (angry) **to go s.** cabrearse
3 n Aut (spare part) (pieza f de) recambio m or repuesto m; (tyre) rueda f de repuesto or RP de auxilio, Méx llanta f de refacción

sparerib [speə'rɪb] n Culin costilla f de cerdo

sparing ['speərɪŋ] adj (frugal) frugal; (economical) económico(a); **to be s. with food** racionar la comida; **to be s. with praise** escatimar elogios; **to be s. with words** ser parco(a) en palabras

sparingly ['speərɪŋlɪ] adv en poca cantidad

spark [spɑ:k] **1** n (a) (electrical, from fire) chispa f; Br Fam **bright s.** listillo(a) m,f ▫ Aut **s. plug** bujía f (b) Fig (glimmer, trace) chispa f, pizca f
2 vi echar chispas

spark off vt provocar, desatar

sparking ['spɑ:kɪŋ] adj Aut **s. plug** bujía f

sparkle ['spɑ:kəl] **1** n (a) (of diamond, glass) centelleo m, destello m, brillo m; (of eyes) brillo m (b) Fig (liveliness) viveza f; (wit) brillo m; **she lacks s.** le falta brillo
2 vi (a) (diamond, glass) centellear, destellar, brillar; (eyes) brillar, chispear; (firework) echar chispas, chispear (b) Fig (person) brillar, lucirse; (conversation) brillar

sparkler ['spɑ:klər] n (firework) bengala f (b) Fam (gem) brillante m

sparkling ['spɑ:klɪŋ] adj (a) (diamond, glass) centelleante, brillante; (eyes) brillante, chispeante; **s. clean** limpio(a) como un espejo ▫ **s. wine** vino m espumoso (b) Fig (person, conversation) brillante, chispeante

sparring ['spɑ:rɪŋ] n Box **s. partner** sparring m, compañero m de entrenamiento

sparrow ['spærəʊ] n Orn gorrión m ▫ **house s.** gorrión m común; **rock s.** gorrión m chillón; **Spanish s.** gorrión m moruno

sparrowhawk ['spærəʊhɔ:k] n Orn gavilán m

sparse [spɑ:s] adj (thin) escaso(a); (scattered) espaciado(a), disperso(a); (hair) ralo(a); **s. vegetation** vegetación escasa

Spartan ['spɑ:tən] adj & n espartano(a) (m,f)

spasm ['spæzəm] n (a) Med espasmo m; (of coughing) acceso m (b) (of anger, activity) arrebato m, acceso m; **in spasms** a rachas

spasmodic [spæz'mɒdɪk] adj (a) Med espasmódico(a) (b) (irregular) irregular, intermitente

spasmodically [spæz'mɒdɪklɪ] adv Fig de forma irregular, a rachas, de vez en cuando

spastic ['spæstɪk] adj & n (a) Med espástico(a) (m,f) (b) Slang Pej inútil (mf), patoso(a) (m,f)

spat¹ [spæt] pt & pp see **spit¹**

spat² [spæt] n polaina f

spate [speɪt] n (a) (of letters) avalancha f; (of words) torrente m; (of accidents) racha f (b) Br (river) **to be in full s.** estar crecido(a)

spatial ['speɪʃəl] adj espacial, del espacio

spatter ['spætər] vt (splash) salpicar (**with** de); (sprinkle) rociar (**with** de)

spatula ['spætjʊlə] n espátula f

spawn [spɔ:n] **1** n (a) (of fish, frogs) huevas fpl, freza f (b) Bot **mushroom s.** micelio m del hongo
2 vi (fish, frogs) frezar
3 vt Fig Pej engendrar, producir

speak [spi:k] **1** vt (pt spoke; pp spoken) (a) (utter) decir; **to s. one's mind** hablar claro or sin rodeos; **to s. the truth** decir la verdad (b) (language) hablar; **'English spoken'** 'se habla inglés'
2. vi (a) (gen) hablar, esp Am conversar, Méx platicar; **generally speaking** en términos generales; **I don't know him to s. to** sólo lo conozco de vista; **I'll s. to my boss about it** (discuss) lo hablaré con mi jefe; (mention) se lo diré al jefe; **legally speaking** desde el punto de vista legal; **roughly speaking** a grandes rasgos; **she has no savings**

to s. of no tiene ahorros que digamos; **so to s.** por así decirlo; **speaking of ...** a propósito de ...; **to be nothing to s. of** no ser nada especial; **to s. to sb** hablar con algn (**b**) *(make a speech)* pronunciar un discurso; *(take the floor)* tomar la palabra; **she spoke on cookery** habló de cocina (**c**) *Tel* hablar; **Browne speaking!** Browne al habla; **I'd like to s. to Mr Bow** póngame con el Sr. Bow, por favor; **speaking!** ¡al habla!; **who's speaking, please?** ¿de parte de quién?

speak for *vt (person, group)* hablar en nombre de; *(motion)* hablar en favor de; **it speaks for itself** es evidente, habla por sí solo; *Fam* **s. for yourself!** ¡eso lo dirás tú!

speak out *vi (give opinion)* hablar claro *or* sin rodeos; **to s. out against sth** denunciar algo

speak up *vi* hablar más fuerte; *Fig* **to s. up for sb** intervenir a favor de algn

speakeasy ['spi:ki:zɪ] *n US Fam* taberna *f* clandestina

speaker ['spi:kər] *n* (**a**) *(person) (in conversation, on radio)* interlocutor(a) *m,f*; *(at meeting)* orador(a) *m,f*; *(at conference)* conferenciante *mf*, orador(a) *m,f*, *Am* conferencista *mf*; **he's a good s.** es buen orador (**b**) *(of language)* hablante *mf*; **Spanish s.** hispanohablante *mf* (**c**) *Br Parl* **the S.** el Presidente de la Cámara de los Comunes; *US* **the S. of the House** el Presidente de la Cámara de los Representantes; *(form of address)* **Mr S.** Señor Presidente (**d**) *(loudspeaker)* altavoz *m*, *Am* altoparlante *m*, *Am* parlante *m*, *Méx* bocina *f*

speaking ['spi:kɪŋ] **1** *adj* hablante; *Theat* **a s. part** un papel hablado; **we are not on s. terms** no nos hablamos □ *Br Tel* **s. clock** información *f* horaria

2 *n (skill, art)* oratoria *f*; **plain s.** franqueza *f*

spear [spɪər] *n (gen)* lanza *f*, *(javelin)* jabalina *f*, *(harpoon)* arpón *m*

spearhead ['spɪəhed] **1** *n* punta *f* de lanza

2 *vt (attack etc)* encabezar

spearmint ['spɪəmɪnt] *n Bot* menta *f* verde

spec [spek] *n Fam* **on s.** sin garantías; **we went to the cinema on s.** fuimos al cine sin saber si quedarían entradas

special ['speʃəl] **1** *adj (gen)* especial; *(specific)* específico(a), particular; *(exceptional)* extraordinario(a); **nothing s.** nada del otro mundo; **what's so s. about him?** ¿qué tiene él de particular? □ **s. agent** agente *mf* secreto(a); *Br* **the S. Branch** el Servicio de Seguridad del Estado; **s. delivery** envío *m* urgente; **s. edition** edición *f* or número *m* especial; *Cin* **s. effects** efectos *mpl* especiales; *Com* **s. offer** oferta *f* (especial); *Pol* **s. powers** poderes *mpl* extraordinarios

2 *n* (**a**) *(train)* tren *m* especial (**b**) *Rad TV* programa *m* especial; *Press (newspaper edition)* número *m* especial; *(on menu)* **today's s.** plato *m* del día

specialist ['speʃəlɪst] *n* especialista *mf*; **to become an electronics s.** especializarse en la electrónica

speciality [speʃɪ'ælɪtɪ] *n* especialidad *f*

specialization [speʃəlaɪ'zeɪʃən] *n (of study)* especialidad *f*; *(act)* especialización *f*

specialize ['speʃəlaɪz] *vi* especializarse (**in** en)

specially ['speʃəlɪ] *adv (specifically)* especialmente; *(on purpose)* expresamente, a propósito

specialty ['speʃəltɪ] *n US see* **speciality**

species ['spi:ʃi:z] *n (pl* species) *Biol* especie *f*

specific [spɪ'sɪfɪk] **1** *adj (gen)* específico(a); *(definite)* concreto(a); *(precise, exact)* preciso(a); *(clear in meaning)* explícito(a); **for a s. reason** por una razón concreta; **to be s.** concretar □ **s. gravity** peso *m* específico

2 *n* (**a**) *Med (drug)* específico *m* (**b**) **specifics** datos *mpl* (concretos)

specifically [spɪ'sɪfɪklɪ] *adv* (**a**) *(exactly)* específicamente, concretamente; *(expressly)* expresamente (**b**) *(namely)* en concreto

specification [spesɪfɪ'keɪʃən] *n* (**a**) *(gen)* especificación *f* (**b**) *(plan)* plan *m* detallado; *(proposal)* propuesta *f* detallada (**c**) **specifications** datos *mpl* específicos

specify ['spesɪfaɪ] *vt (pt & pp* specified) especificar, precisar, concretar

specimen ['spesɪmɪn] *n (sample)* muestra *f*, espécimen *m*; *(example)* ejemplar *m*; **blood s.** muestra de sangre; **s. copy** ejemplar de muestra; **s. signature** muestra de firma; **urine/tissue s.** espécimen de orina/tejido; *Fam* **he's a strange s.** es un bicho raro

specious ['spi:ʃəs] *adj* engañoso(a), especioso(a)

speck [spek] *n (of dust, soot)* mota *f*; *(stain)* manchita *f*; *(small trace)* pizca *f*; *(dot)* punto *m* negro

speckled ['spekəld] *adj* moteado(a), con puntitos

specs [speks] *npl Fam (spectacles)* gafas *fpl*

spectacle ['spektəkəl] *n* (**a**) *(display)* espectáculo *m*; **to make a s. of oneself** hacer el ridículo, ponerse en ridículo (**b**) **spectacles** *(glasses)* gafas *fpl*, *Am* lentes *fpl*, *Am* anteojos *mpl*; *Fig* **to see everything through rose-tinted spectacles** verlo todo de color rosa □ **s. case** estuche *m* de gafas

spectacular [spek'tækjʊlər] **1** *adj* espectacular, impresionante

2 *n Cin TV* (gran) espectáculo *m*, superproducción *f*

spectacularly [spek'tækjʊləlɪ] *adj* espectacularmente, de forma espectacular; **to fail s.** fracasar estrepitosamente

spectator [spek'teɪtər] *n* espectador(a) *m,f*; **the spectators** el público □ **s. sport** deporte *m* espectáculo, deporte *m* de masas

spectre, *US* **specter** ['spektər] *n* espectro *m*, fantasma *m*

spectrum ['spektrəm] *n (pl* spectra ['spektrə]) (**a**) *Phys* espectro *m* (**b**) *(range)* espectro *m*, gama *f*

speculate ['spekjʊleɪt] *vi (gen)* especular (**on** *or* **about** sobre)

speculation [spekjʊ'leɪʃən] *n* especulación *f*

speculative ['spekjʊlətɪv] *adj* especulativo(a)

speculator ['spekjʊleɪtər] *n Fin* especulador(a) *m,f*

sped [sped] *pt & pp see* **speed**

speech [spi:tʃ] *n* (**a**) *(faculty)* habla *f*; *(pronunciation)* pronunciación *f*; **freedom of s.** libertad de expresión □ **s. defect** defecto *m* del habla; **s. therapist** foniatra *mf*, logopeda *mf*; **s. therapy** terapia *f* de la palabra (**b**) *(address)* discurso *m*; *(talk)* charla *f*; *(lecture)* conferencia *f*; **to give** *or* **make a s.** pronunciar un discurso (**on** sobre); *Br Sch* **s. day** día *m* del reparto de premios (**c**) *Ling* oración *f*; **direct/ indirect s.** oración directa/indirecta; **part of s.** parte *f* de la oración

speechless ['spi:tʃlɪs] *adj* mudo(a), boquiabierto(a)

speechwriter ['spi:tʃraɪtər] *n* redactor(a) *m,f* de discursos

speed [spi:d] **1** *n* (**a**) *(rate of movement)* velocidad *f*; *(quickness, rapidity)* rapidez *f*; *(haste)* prisa *f*; **at a s. of ...** a una velocidad de ...; **at top s.** a toda velocidad, a toda marcha; **to pick up** *or* **gather s.** cobrar *or* ganar *or Esp* coger velocidad □ *Fam* **s. cop** policía *mf* de tráfico *(en carretera)*; **s. dating** speed dating *m*, citas *fpl* rápidas; **s. dialling** marcado *m* rápido; **s. limit** velocidad *f* máxima; **s. trap** control *m* policial de velocidad, foto-radar *m* (**b**) *(on bicycle)* velocidad *f* (**c**) *Phot (of film)* velocidad *f*; *(aperture)* abertura *f* (**d**) *(drug) Slang* anfeta *f*

2 *vi* (**a**) *(pt & pp* sped) *(person) (go fast)* ir corriendo, ir a toda prisa; *(hurry)* apresurarse, darse prisa; *(car etc)* **to s.**

along ir a toda velocidad; **to s. past** pasar volando (**b**) *(pt & pp* **speeded**) *Jur (exceed speed limit)* conducir con exceso de velocidad

speed up 1 *vt (pt & pp* **speeded up**) *(process, matter)* acelerar; *(person)* apresurar

  2 *vi (person)* darse prisa, apresurarse, *Am* apurarse

speedboat ['spiːdbəʊt] *n* lancha *f* rápida

speedily ['spiːdɪlɪ] *adv (quickly)* rápidamente, con toda prisa; *(promptly)* con la mayor prontitud

speeding ['spiːdɪŋ] *n Aut* exceso *m* de velocidad

speedometer [spɪ'dɒmɪtər] *n Aut* velocímetro *m*

speedway ['spiːdweɪ] *n Sport* (**a**) *(racing)* carreras *fpl* de moto (**b**) *(track)* pista *f* de carreras

speedy ['spiːdɪ] *adj* (**speedier, speediest**) *(quick)* veloz, rápido(a); *(prompt)* pronto(a)

spell¹ [spel] **1** *vt (pt & pp* **spelt** *or* **spelled**) (**a**) *(write)* escribir correctamente; *(letter by letter)* deletrear; **b-o-x spells 'box'** 'box' se deletrea b-o-x; **how do you s. it?** ¿cómo se escribe *or* deletrea? (**b**) *Fig (denote)* significar, representar; *(foretell)* presagiar; **this news spells disaster for the country** esta noticia representa un desastre para el país

  2 *vi* saber escribir correctamente; **she can't s.** (siempre) hace faltas de ortografía

spell out *vt Fig* explicar con detalle

spell² [spel] *n (magical)* hechizo *m*, encanto *m*; **to cast a s. on sb** hechizar a algn

spell³ [spel] *n* (**a**) *(period)* temporada *f*, período *m*; *(short period)* rato *m*, racha *f*; *(rest)* descanso *m*; *Meteor* **cold s.** ola *f* or racha de frío; **he's going through a good/bad s.** está pasando una buena/mala época or racha (**b**) *(shift)* turno *m*

spellbinding ['spelbaɪndɪŋ] *adj* cautivador(a), fascinante

spellbound ['spelbaʊnd] *adj* hechizado(a), embelesado(a)

spell-checker ['speltʃekər] *n Comptr* corrector *m* ortográfico

spelling ['spelɪŋ] *n* ortografía *f* □ **s. bee** concurso *m* de ortografía; **s. mistake** falta *f* de ortografía

spelt [spelt] *pt & pp see* **spell**¹

spelunking [spe'lʌŋkɪŋ] *n* espeleología *f*

spend [spend] *vt (pt & pp* **spent**) (**a**) *(money)* gastar (**on** en); *Br Fam* **to s. a penny** hacer pipí (**b**) *(time)* pasar; **we spent Christmas in Scotland** pasamos las Navidades en Escocia (**c**) *(devote) (time)* dedicar; **s. more time on your homework** dedica más tiempo a tus deberes

spender ['spendər] *n* **to be a high/low s.** gastar mucho/poco

spending ['spendɪŋ] *n* gasto *m*, gastos *mpl*; **public s.** gasto público □ **s. cuts** recortes *mpl* en el presupuesto; **s. money** dinero *m* de bolsillo; **s. power** poder *m* adquisitivo

spendthrift ['spendθrɪft] *adj & n* derrochador(a) *(m,f)*, despilfarrador(a) *(m,f)*, manirroto(a) *(m,f)*

spent [spent] **1** *pt & pp see* **spend**

  2 *adj* gastado(a); **s. bullet** bala muerta; *(person)* **to be a s. force** estar quemado(a)

sperm [spɜːm] *n (pl* **sperms** *or* **sperm**) *Biol* esperma *mf* □ *Med* **s. bank** banco *m* de esperma; *Zool* **s. whale** cachalote *m*

spermicide ['spɜːmɪsaɪd] *n Med* espermicida *m*

spew [spjuː] **1** *vt* (**a**) **to s. (up)** vomitar, devolver (**b**) **to s. (out)** *(flames etc)* vomitar, arrojar

  2 *vi* **to s. (up)** vomitar, devolver

sphere [sfɪər] *n (gen)* esfera *f*; **in the s. of politics,** en el mundo de la política; **it's outside my s.** no es de mi

competencia; **s. of activity/influence** esfera de actividad/influencia

spheric(al) ['sferɪk(əl)] *adj* esférico(a)

sphincter ['sfɪŋktər] *n Anat* esfínter *m*

sphinx [sfɪŋks] *n (pl* **sphinxes** *or* **sphinges** ['sfɪndʒiːz]) esfinge *f*

spice [spaɪs] **1** *n* (**a**) *Culin* especia *f*, **mixed spice(s)** especias mixtas (**b**) *Fig* sazón *m*, sal *f*; *Prov* **variety is the s. of life** en la variedad está el gusto

  2 *vt* (**a**) *Culin* sazonar, condimentar (**b**) *(story etc)* **to s. (up)** echar salsa a

spick [spɪk] *n US very Fam* = término ofensivo para referirse a un latino

spic(k)-and-span [spɪkən'spæn] *adj (very clean)* limpísimo(a); *(like new)* flamante; *(neat)* pulcro(a); *(well-groomed)* acicalado(a)

spicy ['spaɪsɪ] *adj* (**spicier, spiciest**) (**a**) *Culin* sazonado(a), condimentado(a); *(hot)* picante (**b**) *Fig (story etc)* picante

spider ['spaɪdər] *n* araña *f* □ *Br* **s.'s** *or US* **s. web** telaraña *f*; **s. plant** cinta *f*

spiel [ʃpiːl] *n Fam* rollo *m*

spigot ['spɪgət] *n* (**a**) *(stopper)* espita *f*, bitoque *m* (**b**) *US (tap) Esp* grifo *m*, *Chile Col Méx* llave *f*, *RP* canilla *f*

spike¹ [spaɪk] *n* (**a**) *(sharp point)* punta *f*; *(metal rod)* pincho *m*; *(stake)* estaca *f*; *(on railing)* barrote *m*; *Sport (on shoes)* clavo *m* (**b**) *Sport* **spikes** zapatillas *fpl* con clavos

spike² [spaɪk] *n Bot* espiga *f*

spiky ['spaɪkɪ] *adj* (**spikier, spikiest**) *(gen)* puntiagudo(a); *(hedgehog)* erizado(a); *(hairstyle)* de punta

spill [spɪl] **1** *vt (pt & pp* **spilled** *or* **spilt**) *(liquid)* derramar; *(pour)* verter; *(knock over)* volcar; *Fam* **to s. the beans** *Esp* descubrir el pastel, *Am* destapar la olla

  2 *vi (liquid)* derramarse, verterse

  3 *n (spilling)* derrame *m*; *Fam* **to take a s.** caerse, medir el suelo

spill out *vi (crowd)* salir en tropel

spill over *vi* salirse, desbordarse

spillage ['spɪlɪdʒ] *n* derrame *m*

spilt [spɪlt] *pt & pp see* **spill**

spin [spɪn] **1** *vt (pt & pp* **spun**) (**a**) *(turn) (wheel etc)* hacer girar, dar vueltas a; *(washing)* centrifugar; **to s. a coin for sth** echar algo a cara o cruz *or Chile Col* cara o sello *or Méx* águila o sol *or RP* cara o seca (**b**) *(cotton, wool, etc)* hilar; *(spider's web)* tejer; *Fam* **to s. sb a yarn** pegarle un rollo a algn

  2 *vi* (**a**) *(wheel etc)* girar, dar vueltas; *Av (dive)* caer en barrena; *Aut (slide)* patinar; **my head was spinning** la cabeza me daba vueltas; **to send sth spinning** echar algo a rodar; **to s. round and round** dar vueltas y más vueltas (**b**) *(cotton, wool, etc)* hilar

  3 *n* (**a**) *(turn)* vuelta *f*, giro *m*, revolución *f*; *(of spin-dryer)* **long/short s.** centrifugado *m* largo/corto; **to give sth a s.** hacer girar algo; *Br Fam* **to be in a flat s.** estar hecho un lío (**b**) *Sport* efecto *m*; **to put s. on the ball** dar efecto a la pelota (**c**) *Pol (on news story)* sesgo *m*; **s. doctor** asesor(a) *m,f* político(a) *(para dar buena prensa a un partido o político)* (**d**) *Av* barrena *f*; *Aut* patinazo *m*; **to go into a s.** *Av* caer en barrena; *Aut* patinar (**e**) *Fam (ride)* vuelta *f*, paseo *m* (en coche *or* en moto); **to go for a s.** dar una vuelta

spin out *vt Fam (holiday, speech)* alargar, prolongar; *(time, money)* estirar

spinach ['spɪnɪtʃ] *n* espinacas *fpl*

spinal ['spaɪnəl] *adj Anat* espinal, vertebral □ **s. column** columna *f* vertebral; **s. cord** médula *f* espinal

spindle ['spɪndəl] *n* (**a**) *(for spinning)* huso *m* (**b**) *Tech (axle)* eje *m*; *(of lathe)* mandril *m*

spindly ['spɪndlɪ] *adj* (**spindlier, spindliest**) *Fam (long-bodied)* larguirucho(a); *(long-legged)* zanquilargo(a), zanquivano(a)

spin-dry [spɪn'draɪ] *vt* centrifugar

spin-dryer [spɪn'draɪər] *n* secador *m* centrífugo

spine [spaɪn] *n* (**a**) *Anat* columna *f* vertebral, espina *f* dorsal, espinazo *m*; *(of book)* lomo *m* (**b**) *Zool (of hedgehog etc)* púa *f*; *Bot* espina *f*

spine-chilling ['spaɪntʃɪlɪŋ] *adj* horripilante, escalofriante

spineless ['spaɪnlɪs] *adj* (**a**) *(invertebrate)* invertebrado(a) (**b**) *Fig (weak)* débil, sin carácter

spinet ['spɪnɪt] *n Mus* espineta *f*

spinner ['spɪnər] *n* (**a**) *(of cotton, wool, etc)* hilandero(a) *m,f* (**b**) *Fishing* cuchara *f*

spinney ['spɪnɪ] *n* bosquecillo *m*, soto *m*

spinning ['spɪnɪŋ] *n* (**a**) *(of cotton, wool, etc) (act)* hilado *m*; *(art)* hilandería ❑ **s. machine** máquina *f* de hilar; **s. wheel** rueca *f*, torno *m* de hilar (**b**) *(toy)* **s. top** peonza *f*, trompo *m*

spin-off ['spɪnɒf] *n (by-product)* derivado *m*, producto *m* secundario; *Fig* efecto *m* secundario

spinster ['spɪnstər] *n* soltera *f*; *Pej* **she's an old s.** es una vieja solterona

spiny ['spaɪnɪ] *adj* (**spinier, spiniest**) espinoso(a)

spiral ['spaɪrəl] **1** *n Geom* espiral *f*
2 *adj* espiral, en espiral ❑ **s. staircase** escalera *f* de caracol
3 *vi* (*pt & pp* **spiralled**, *US* **spiraled**) moverse en espiral; **spiralling prices** precios en alza vertiginosa; **to s. up/down** subir/bajar en espiral

spire [spaɪər] *n Archit* aguja *f*

spirit¹ ['spɪrɪt] *n* (**a**) *(soul)* espíritu *m*, alma *f*; *(ghost)* fantasma *m*; **evil s.** espíritu maligno ❑ *Rel* **the Holy S.** el Espíritu Santo (**b**) *(person)* ser *m*, alma *f* (**c**) *(attitude)* espíritu *m*; *(mood)* humor *m*; **community s.** civismo *m*; **team s.** espíritu de equipo; **to enter into the s. of sth** meterse en el ambiente de algo; *Fam* **that's the s.!** ¡eso es!, ¡así me gusta! (**d**) *(courage)* valor *m*; *(liveliness)* ánimo *m*, energía *f*; *(vitality)* vitalidad *f*, vigor *m*; *(strength)* fuerza *f*; **she lacks s.** le falta carácter; **to break sb's s.** quebrar la voluntad de algn; **to show s.** dar muestras de valor (**e**) *(intention)* espíritu *m*, sentido *m*; **to take sth in the right s.** tomar algo a bien (**f**) **spirits** *(mood)* humor *m sing*, moral *f sing*; **to be in good s.** estar de buen humor; **to be in high/low s.** estar muy animado(a)/desanimado(a); **to raise sb's s.** subirle la moral a algn

spirit away, spirit off *vt* llevarse como por arte de magia

spirit² ['spɪrɪt] *n* (**a**) *Chem* alcohol *m* ❑ **s. lamp** lámpara *f* de alcohol; *Constr* **s. level** nivel *m* de aire (**b**) **spirits** *(alcoholic drink)* licores *m*, alcohol *m sing*

spirited ['spɪrɪtɪd] *adj (person)* animado(a); *(horse)* fogoso(a); *(attack, reply)* enérgico(a), vigoroso(a); *(person, attempt)* valiente; *Mus* **to give a s. performance** tocar con brío

spiritual ['spɪrɪtjʊəl] **1** *adj* espiritual
2 *n Mus* (**Negro**) **s.** espiritual *m* negro

spiritualism ['spɪrɪtjʊəlɪzəm] *n* espiritismo *m*

spiritualist ['spɪrɪtjʊəlɪst] *adj & n* espiritista *(mf)*

spirituality [spɪrɪtjʊ'ælɪtɪ] *n* espiritualidad *f*

spiritually ['spɪrɪtjʊəlɪ] *adv* espiritualmente

spit¹ [spɪt] **1** *vt* (*pt & pp* **spat**, *US* **spit**) escupir
2 *vi* escupir (**at a**; **in** *or* **on** en); *(fire)* chisporrotear; **it's spitting (with rain)** chispea, caen gotas; *Fam* **he's the spitting image of his father** es el vivo retrato de su padre, es clavado a su padre
3 *n (saliva)* saliva *f*, esputo *m*; *Fam* **s. and polish** pulcritud *f*, limpieza *f*

spit out *vt* escupir; *Br Fam* **s. it out!** ¡suéltalo ya!

spit² [spɪt] *n* (**a**) *Culin* asador *m*, espetón *m* (**b**) *Geog (of sand)* banco *m*; *(of land)* punta *f*, lengua *f*

spite [spaɪt] **1** *n* (**a**) *(ill will)* rencor *m*, ojeriza *f*; **out of s.** por despecho (**b**) *(despite)* **in s. of** a pesar de, pese a; **in s. of being shy** a pesar de ser tímido(a); **in s. of everything** a pesar de todo; **in s. of the fact that** a pesar de que, pese a que
2 *vt (annoy)* fastidiar

spiteful ['spaɪtfʊl] *adj (person)* rencoroso(a); *(remark)* malévolo(a); *(tongue)* viperino(a)

spitefully ['spaɪtfʊlɪ] *adv* con rencor, por despecho

spitefulness ['spaɪtfʊlnɪs] *n* rencor *m*, despecho *m*

spittle ['spɪtəl] *n* saliva *f*, baba *f*

spittoon [spɪ'tuːn] *n* escupidera *f*

splash [splæʃ] **1** *vt* salpicar, rociar (**with** de); **he splashed coffee on his suit** se manchó el traje de café; **to s. sb with water** salpicar a algn de agua; *Fig* **the news was splashed across the front page** la noticia salió en grandes titulares de primera plana
2 *vi* (**a**) *(in water)* **to s. (about)** chapotear (**b**) *(water, mud, etc)* esparcirse, rociarse
3 *n* (**a**) *(noise)* chapoteo *m*, chapaleo *m* (**b**) *(spray)* salpicadura *f*, rociada *f*; *Fig (of colour, light)* mancha *f*; *Fam* **to make a s.** causar sensación
4 *interj* ¡plaf!

splash down *vi Astronaut* amerizar

splash out *vi Fam* derrochar dinero (**on** en), tirar la casa por la ventana

splashdown ['splæʃdaʊn] *n Astronaut* amerizaje *m*, amaraje *m*

splatter ['splætər] **1** *n* salpicadura *f*
2 *vt* **to s. sb with mud** salpicar a algn de barro

spleen [spliːn] *n* (**a**) *Anat* bazo *m* (**b**) *Fml Fig (anger)* cólera *f*, ira *f*; **to vent one's s.** descargar cólera (**on** en)

splendid ['splendɪd] *adj (excellent)* estupendo(a), maravilloso(a); *(magnificent)* espléndido(a), magnífico(a)

splendour, *US* **splendor** ['splendər] *n* esplendor *m*

splice [splaɪs] *vt (rope)* empalmar; *Cin* montar; *Br Fam* **to get spliced** pasar por la vicaría, casarse

splicer ['splaɪsər] *n Cin* máquina *f* de montaje, montadora *f*

spliff [splɪf] *n Fam* porro *m*, canuto *m*

splint [splɪnt] *n Med* tablilla *f*; **to be in splints** estar entablillado(a)

splinter ['splɪntər] **1** *n (of wood)* astilla *f*; *(of bone, stone, metal)* esquirla *f*, *(of glass)* fragmento *m* ❑ *Pol* **s. group** grupo *m* disidente, facción *f*
2 *vi* (**a**) *(wood, metal, etc)* astillarse, hacerse astillas (**b**) *Pol (party)* escindirse
3 *vt (wood, metal, etc)* astillar, hacer astillas

split [splɪt] **1** *n* (**a**) *(crack)* grieta *f*, hendidura *f*; *(tear)* desgarrón *m*, rasgón *m*; *Fig (division)* división *f*, ruptura *f*, cisma *m*; *Pol* escisión *f* (**b**) *(in gymnastics)* **to do the splits** abrir las piernas en cruz, despatarrarse (**c**) *Culin* **banana s.** = postre de plátano con helado, banana split *m*; **cream/jam s.** = pastelito con relleno de nata/mermelada
2 *adj (gen)* partido(a), hendido(a); *(party)* dividido(a); **in a s. second** en una fracción de segundo ❑ **s. ends** *(in hair)* puntas *fpl* rotas; *Culin* **s. peas** guisantes *mpl or Méx* chícharos *mpl* secos partidos, *Am* arvejas *fpl* secas partidas; *Psych* **s. personality** doble personalidad *f*
3 *vt* (*pt & pp* **split**) (**a**) *(crack, break)* agrietar, hender; *(cut)* partir; *(tear)* rajar, desgarrar; *Phys (atom)* desintegrar; **to s. one's head open** romperse *or* partirse la crisma; *Fig* **to s. hairs** rizar el rizo, buscarle tres pies al gato; *Fig* **to s. one's sides laughing** partirse de risa (**b**) *(divide)* dividir *(c)* *(share*

out) repartir, dividir; *Fam* **to s. the difference** partir la diferencia **(d)** *Pol (party)* escindir

4 *vi* **(a)** *(crack, break)* agrietarse, henderse; *(into two parts)* partirse; *(garment)* rajarse, desgarrarse **(b)** *(divide)* dividirse **(c)** *Pol (party)* escindirse **(d)** *Br Fam (tell tales)* soplar, chivarse; **to s. on sb** chivarse de algn **(e)** *Slang (leave)* abrirse, *Esp RP* pirarse, *Méx RP* rajarse

split off 1 *vt* separar

2 *vi* separarse, desprenderse

split up 1 *vt (break up)* partir; *(separate, divide up)* dividir; *(share out)* repartir

2 *vi (crowd, meeting)* dispersarse; *(couple)* separarse

split-second ['splɪtsekənd] *adj (decision)* instantáneo(a); *(timing)* al milímetro

splitting ['splɪtɪŋ] *adj (headache)* terrible, muy fuerte

splodge [splɒdʒ] *n Fam,* **splotch** [splɒtʃ] *n Fam* mancha *f,* borrón *m*

splurge [splɜːdʒ] *vt Fam* despilfarrar el dinero **(on** en)

splutter ['splʌtər] *vi* **(a)** *(person)* balbucear, farfullar **(b)** *(candle, fat)* chisporrotear; *(engine)* petardear, renquear

spoil [spɔɪl] **1** *vt (pt & pp* **spoiled** *or* **spoilt) (a)** *(ruin)* estropear, echar a perder; **it will s. your appetite** se quitará el apetito; **to s. sb's fun** aguarle la fiesta a algn **(b)** *(allow everything)* mimar, consentir; *(treat generously)* mimar; **to be spoilt for choice** tener demasiadas cosas para elegir

2 *vi (food)* estropearse, echarse a perder

3 spoils *npl Fml* botín *m sing*

spoil for *vt* buscar; **to be spoiling for a fight** buscar camorra

spoilsport ['spɔɪlspɔːt] *n Fam* aguafiestas *mf inv*

spoilt [spɔɪlt] **1** *vt pt & pp see* **spoil**

2 *adj* **(a)** *(food, merchandise)* estropeado(a) **(b)** *(child)* mimado(a), consentido(a)

spoke¹ [spəʊk] *pt see* **speak**

spoke² [spəʊk] *n (of wheel)* radio *m,* rayo *m; Br Fam* **to put a s. in sb's wheel** poner trabas a algn

spoken ['spəʊkən] *pp see* **speak**

spokesman ['spəʊksmən] *n (pl* **spokesmen)** portavoz *m*

spokesperson ['spəʊkspɜːsən] *n* portavoz *mf*

spokeswoman ['spəʊkswʊmən] *n (pl* **spokeswomen** ['spəʊkswɪmɪn]) portavoz *f*

sponge [spʌndʒ] **1** *n (gen)* esponja *f; Fig* **to throw in the s.** arrojar la toalla ❑ *Br* **s. bag** bolsa *f* de aseo, neceser *m; Br Culin* **s. cake** bizcocho *m*

2 *vt (wash)* limpiar *or* lavar *or* fregar con esponja; **to s. a stain off** *or* **out** quitar una mancha con una esponja

3 *vi Fam (scrounge) Esp Méx* vivir de gorra, *RP* vivir de arriba

sponge down *vt* limpiar *or* lavar *or* fregar con esponja

sponge off, sponge on *vt* vivir a costa de

sponger ['spʌndʒər] *n Fam* gorrero(a) *m,f, Esp Méx* gorrón(ona) *m,f, RP* garronero(a) *m,f*

spongy ['spʌndʒɪ] *adj* (**spongier, spongiest**) esponjoso(a)

sponsor ['spɒnsər] **1** *vt (gen)* patrocinar; *Fin* avalar, garantizar; *Rel* apadrinar; *(support)* respaldar, apoyar

2 *n (gen)* patrocinador(a) *m,f; Fin* avalador(a) *m,f,* garante *mf; Rel* padrino(a) *m,f*

sponsorship ['spɒnsəʃɪp] *n (gen)* patrocinio *m; (support)* respaldo *m,* apoyo *m;* **s. deal** *(of athlete, team)* contrato *m* con un patrocinador

spontaneity [spɒntə'neɪtɪ] *n* espontaneidad *f*

spontaneous [spɒn'teɪnɪəs] *adj* espontáneo(a)

spoof [spuːf] *n Fam* **(a)** *(parody)* parodia *f,* burla *f* **(b)** *(hoax)* engaño *m,* broma *f*

spook [spuːk] *n Fam (ghost)* fantasma *m*

spooky ['spuːkɪ] *adj* (**spookier, spookiest**) *Fam* espeluznante, horripilante, escalofriante

spool [spuːl] *n Phot Sew* bobina *f,* carrete *m*

spoon [spuːn] **1** *n (gen)* cuchara *f; (small)* cucharilla *f,* cucharita *f;* **coffee s.** cucharilla de café; **dessert s.** cuchara de postre; **soup s.** cuchara sopera; *Fig* **to be born with a silver s. in one's mouth** nacer con un pan bajo el brazo

2 *vt (gen)* sacar con cuchara; *(serve)* servir con cuchara

spoonerism ['spuːnərɪzəm] *n* trastocamiento *m* de letras, juego *m* de palabras

spoon-feed ['spuːnfiːd] *vt (pt & pp* **spoon-fed)** *(baby)* dar de comer, con cuchara a; *Fig (pupil)* dar la lección masticada a; *(spoil)* mimar

spoonful ['spuːnfʊl] *n (pl* **spoonfuls** *or* **spoonsful)** *n* cucharada *f*

sporadic [spə'rædɪk] *adj* esporádico(a), intermitente

spore [spɔːr] *n Biol* espora *f*

sporran ['spɒrən] *n Scot* = escarcela que se lleva encima de la falda escocesa

sport [spɔːt] *n* **(a)** *(activity)* deporte *m;* **to be good at s.** ser buen deportista **(b)** *Fam (person)* **to be a (good) s.** *Esp* ser un(a) tío(a) grande, *Am* ser buena gente; **to be a bad s.** *(bad loser)* ser mal perdedor, *Esp* tener mal perder

2 *vt (display)* lucir

sporting ['spɔːtɪŋ] *adj* **(a)** *(of sport)* deportivo(a); **s. event** acontecimiento deportivo **(b)** *(generous)* caballeroso(a), justo(a), deportivo(a)

sports [spɔːts] **1** *npl* deportes *mpl,* deporte *m sing;* **winter s.** deportes de invierno

2 *adj* deportivo(a), de sport ❑ **s. car** coche *m or Am* carro *m* deportivo; **s. day** día *m* dedicado a los deportes; **s. ground** terreno *m* de deportes; *Br* **s. jacket** chaqueta *f or Am* saco *m* (de) sport; *US* **s. lottery** quinielas *fpl*

sportsman ['spɔːtsmən] *n (pl* **sportsmen)** deportista *m*

sportsmanlike ['spɔːtsmənlaɪk] *adj (attitude, gesture)* caballeroso(a), deportivo(a)

sportsmanship ['spɔːtsmənʃɪp] *n* espíritu *m* deportivo, deportividad *f*

sportswear ['spɔːtsweər] *n (for sport)* ropa *f* de deporte; *(casual clothes)* ropa *f* (de) sport

sportswoman ['spɔːtswʊmən] *n (pl* **sportswomen** ['spɔːtswɪmɪn]) deportista *f*

sporty ['spɔːtɪ] *adj* (**sportier, sportiest**) *Fam* deportivo(a), aficionado(a) a los deportes

spot [spɒt] **1** *n* **(a)** *(dot)* punto *m; (on fabric)* lunar *m;* **to have spots before one's eyes** ver manchas; *Fam* **to knock spots off sb** *(defeat)* vencer fácilmente a algn; *(surpass)* dejar atrás a algn **(b)** *(mark, stain)* mancha *f* **(c)** *Med* grano *m* **(d)** *(place)* sitio *m,* lugar *m;* **a quiet s.** un lugar tranquilo ❑ **accident black s.** punto *m* negro; **night s.** centro *m* de vida nocturna; **(e)** *(there)* **on the s.** allí, presente; **to decide sth on the s.** decidir algo en el acto ❑ **s. check** comprobación *f* al instante, chequeo *m or* reconocimiento *m* rápido **(f)** *(point on the body)* punto *m;* **tender s.** punto sensible; *Fig* **weak s.** punto débil *or* flaco; *Fig* **to have a soft s. for sb** tener una debilidad por algn **(g)** *(trouble)* lío *m,* apuro *m,* aprieto *m;* **to be in a tight s.** estar en un apuro *or* aprieto; **to put sb on the s.** poner a algn en un aprieto **(h)** *Br Fam (small amount)* poquito *m,* poquitín *m;* **a s. of bother** unos problemillas, un pequeño disgusto **(i)** *Rad TV Theat (in show)* espacio *m; (advertisement)* spot *m* (publicitario), anuncio *m* **(j)** *Fam (spotlight)* foco *m*

2 *vt (pt & pp* **spotted)** *(notice)* darse cuenta de, notar; *(see)* ver; *(recognize)* reconocer; *(find)* encontrar; *(catch out)* pillar; **to s. the winner** elegir el ganador

spotless ['spɒtlɪs] *adj (very clean)* limpísimo(a); *(well-groomed)* impecable; *Fig (reputation, character)* intachable

spotlight ['spɒtlaɪt] *n (beam)* foco *m*; *Theat* proyector *m*, foco *m*; *(light)* luz *f* de foco; *Aut* faro *m* auxiliar; *Fig* **to be in the s.** ser objeto de la atención pública, ser el blanco de las miradas

spot-on [spɒt'ɒn] *adj Fam* perfecto(a), exacto(a)

spotted ['spɒtɪd] *adj (with dots)* con puntos; *(fabric)* con lunares; *(speckled)* moteado(a); *(stained)* manchado(a)

spotter ['spɒtər] *n* observador(a) *m,f* ❑ **train s.** aficionado(a) *m,f* a trenes; *Av Mil* **s. plane** avión *m* de reconocimiento

spotty ['spɒtɪ] *adj* (**spottier, spottiest**) *Pej* con granos

spot-welding ['spɒtweldɪŋ] *n* soldadura *f* por puntos

spouse [spaʊs] *n* cónyuge *mf*

spout [spaʊt] **1** *n (of jug)* pico *m*; *(of teapot)* pitorro *m*; *(of roof gutter)* canalón *m*; *(of fountain)* surtidor *m*; *(jet of water)* chorro *m*; *Fam* **our plans are up the s.** se han fastidiado nuestros planes; *Fam* **Richard's really up the s. now** Richard se ha metido en un buen apuro
2 *vt* (**a**) *(liquid)* echar, arrojar (**b**) *Fam (verse)* declamar; *(nonsense)* soltar
3 *vi* (**a**) *(liquid)* brotar, salir a chorros (**b**) *Fam (verse etc)* declamar

sprain [spreɪn] *Med* **1** *n* torcedura *f*
2 *vt* torcer; **to s. one's ankle/wrist** torcerse el tobillo/la muñeca

sprang [spræŋ] *pt see* **spring²**

sprat [spræt] *n (fish)* espadín *m*

sprawl [sprɔːl] **1** *vi* (**a**) *(sit, lie)* tumbarse, echarse, repantigarse, repanchingarse (**b**) *(city, plant) (stretch out)* extenderse
2 *n (of city)* extensión *f*; **the urban s.** el crecimiento urbano descontrolado

sprawling ['sprɔːlɪŋ] *adj* (**a**) *(person)* tumbado(a) (**b**) *(city)* de crecimiento descontrolado

spray¹ [spreɪ] **1** *n* (**a**) *(of water)* rociada *f*; *(from sea)* espuma *f*; *(from aerosol, atomizer)* pulverización *f* (**b**) *(aerosol)* spray *m*; *(atomizer)* atomizador *m*, vaporizador *m*; *(for garden)* pulverizador *m* ❑ **s. can** aerosol *m*; **s. gun** pistola *f* pulverizadora, pulverizador *m*; **s. paint** pintura *f* spray
2 *vt (water)* rociar, regar; *(perfume)* atomizar, vaporizar; *(insecticide)* pulverizar; *(crops)* fumigar; *Fig* **to s. sb with bullets** rociar a algn de balas

spray² [spreɪ] *n (of flowers)* ramita *f*

sprayer ['spreɪər] *n* pulverizador *m*

spread [spred] **1** *n* (**a**) *(gen)* extensión *f*; *(of ideas)* difusión *f*, diseminación *f*, propalación *f*; *(of disease, fire)* propagación *f*; *(of nuclear weapons)* proliferación *f*; *(of terrorism)* aumento *m* (**b**) *(scope)* extensión *f*, envergadura *f*; *(range)* gama *f* (**c**) *(of wings, sails)* envergadura *f*; *Fam* **middle-age s.** la curva de la felicidad (**d**) *Culin (for bread)* pasta *f*; **cheese s.** queso para untar (**e**) *Fam (large meal)* banquetazo *m*; comilona *f* (**f**) *Press* **full-page s.** plana *f* entera; **two-page s.** doble página *f*
2 *vt* (*pt & pp* **spread**) (**a**) *(unfold)* desplegar; *(lay out)* extender, tender; *Fig* **to s. one's wings** desplegar las alas (**b**) *(butter etc)* untar, extender (**c**) *(paint, glue)* extender, repartir (**d**) *(news, ideas)* difundir; *(rumour)* hacer correr; *(disease, fire)* propagar; *(panic, terror)* sembrar
3 *vi* (**a**) *(stretch out)* extenderse; *(open out, unfold)* desplegarse (**b**) *(paint, glue)* extenderse (**c**) *(news, ideas)* difundirse, diseminarse, propalarse; *(rumour)* correr; *(disease, fire)* propagarse; **the news s. like wildfire** la noticia corrió como la pólvora

spread out 1 *vt* (**a**) *(unfold)* desplegar; *(lay out)* extender,

tender; *(scatter)* esparcir (**b**) *(payments, visits, etc)* repartir, distribuir
2 *vi (stretch out)* extenderse; *(widen)* ensancharse

spread-eagled [spred'iːgəld] *adj* con los brazos y piernas abiertos, despatarrado(a)

spreadsheet ['spredʃiːt] *n Comptr* hoja *f* de cálculo

spree [spriː] *n* juerga *f*, jarana *f*, parranda *f*; **to go on a s.** ir de juerga; **to go on a shopping s.** ir a la compra loca

sprig [sprɪɡ] *n* ramita *f*, ramito *m*

sprightly ['spraɪtlɪ] *adj* (**sprightlier, sprightliest**) *(nimble)* ágil; *(energetic)* enérgico(a); *(lively)* animado(a)

spring¹ [sprɪŋ] **1** *n (season)* primavera *f*; **in s.** en la primavera
2 *adj* primaveral ❑ *Hortic* **s. cabbage** col *f* rizada; *Hortic* **s. onion** cebolleta *f*; *Culin* **s. roll** rollo *m* de primavera; **s. tide** marea *f* viva

spring² [sprɪŋ] **1** *n* (**a**) *(of water)* manantial *m*, fuente *f*; **hot springs** aguas *fpl* termales (**b**) *Tech (of watch, lock, etc)* resorte *m*; *(of mattress, seat)* muelle *m*; *Aut* ballesta *f*
2 *vi* (*pt* sprang; *pp* sprung) (**a**) *(jump)* saltar; **he sprang to his feet** se levantó de un salto; **nothing springs to mind** no se me ocurre nada; **the lid sprang open** la tapa se abrió de golpe (**b**) *(appear)* aparecer (de repente); **where did you s. from?** ¿de dónde has salido tú?
3 *vt* (**a**) *(boat, pipe)* **to s. a leak** hacer agua (**b**) *Fam (set free)* soltar (**c**) *Fig (news, surprise)* espetar; **he sprang the news on me** me espetó la noticia

spring up *vi* aparecer; *(plants)* brotar; *(buildings)* elevarse, levantarse; *(friendship)* nacer; *(problems)* surgir

springboard ['sprɪŋbɔːd] *n* trampolín *m*

spring-clean [sprɪŋ'kliːn] *vt* limpiar a fondo, hacer una limpieza general de

spring-cleaning [sprɪŋ'kliːnɪŋ] *n* limpieza *f* a fondo, limpieza *f* general

spring-like ['sprɪŋlaɪk] *adj* primaveral

springtime ['sprɪŋtaɪm] *n* primavera *f*

springy ['sprɪŋɪ] *adj* (**springier, springiest**) *(bouncy)* elástico(a); *Fig (step)* ligero(a)

sprinkle ['sprɪŋkəl] *vt (with water)* rociar, salpicar (**with** de); *(with sugar, flour)* espolvorear (**with** de)

sprinkler ['sprɪŋklər] *n* (**a**) *(water)* aspersor *m* (**b**) *(for sugar)* espolvoreador *m* de azúcar

sprinkling ['sprɪŋklɪŋ] *n Fig* pizca *f*; **there was a s. of rain** cayeron unas gotas

sprint [sprɪnt] **1** *n Sport* sprint *m*, esprint *m*; *(dash)* carrera *f* corta
2 *vi Sport* sprintar, esprintar; *(dash)* correr a toda velocidad

sprinter ['sprɪntər] *n Sport* sprinter *mf*, esprínter *mf*

sprocket ['sprɒkɪt] *n Tech* diente *m* de engranaje ❑ **s. wheel** rueda *f* dentada

sprout [spraʊt] **1** *vt* echar; **he's sprouting a beard** le está saliendo barba
2 *vi (bud)* brotar; *(branch)* echar brotes; *Fig* crecer rápidamente
3 *n Bot (shoot)* brote *m*, retoño *m* ❑ **(Brussels) sprouts** coles *fpl* or *CSur* repollitos *mpl* de Bruselas

spruce¹ [spruːs] *n inv Bot* picea *f* ❑ **Norway s.** picea *f* de Noruega, abeto *m* rojo

spruce² [spruːs] *adj (neat)* pulcro(a), acicalado(a); *(smart)* apuesto(a)

spruce up *vt* arreglar, acicalar

sprung [sprʌŋ] **1** *pp see* **spring²**
2 *adj* de muelles

spry [spraɪ] *adj* (**sprier, spriest**) *(nimble)* ágil; *(active)* activo(a); *(energetic)* enérgico(a); *(lively)* vivaz, animado(a)

spud [spʌd] *n Br Fam Esp* patata *f, Am* papa *f*

spun [spʌn] **1** *pt & pp see* **spin**
2 *adj* **s. silk** seda *f* hilada

spunk [spʌŋk] *n* **(a)** *Fam (courage)* valor *m* **(b)** *Br Slang Vulg (semen)* leche *f*

spunky ['spʌŋkɪ] *adj* (**spunkier, spunkiest**) *Fam* valiente

spur [spɜːr] **1** *n* **(a)** *(of horserider)* espuela *f; Zool (of cock)* espolón *m* **(b)** *Fig (stimulus)* aguijón *m*, espuela *f*; **on the s. of the moment** sin pensarlo; *Fig* **to win one's spurs** dar pruebas de su valor **(c)** *Geog* espolón *m*, estribación *f*
2 *vt* *(pt & pp* **spurred**) **(a)** *(horse)* espolear, picar con las espuelas **(b)** *Fig (stimulate)* estimular, incitar, aguijonear

spurious ['spjʊərɪəs] *adj* falso(a), espurio(a)

spurn [spɜːn] *vt Fml (disdain)* desdeñar, despreciar; *(reject)* rechazar

spurt [spɜːt] **1** *n* **(a)** *(of liquid)* chorro *m* **(b)** *Fig (of activity, effort, emotion)* racha *f*, ataque *m*; *(effort)* esfuerzo *m*; *Sport* **final s.** esfuerzo final
2 *vi* **(a)** *(liquid)* chorrear, salir a chorro **(b)** *(make an effort)* hacer un último esfuerzo, esforzarse; *(accelerate)* acelerar; *Sport* **to s. ahead** acelerar, esprintar

sputter ['spʌtər] *vi (candle, fat, fire)* chisporrotear; *(engine)* petardear, renquear

sputum ['spjuːtəm] *n (pl* **sputa** ['spjuːtə]*) Med* esputo *m*

spy [spaɪ] **1** *n* espía *mf* ❑ **police s.** confidente *mf*, soplón(ona) *m,f*, chivato(a) *m,f*; **s. ring** red *f* de espionaje
2 *vt (pt & pp* **spied**) *Fml (see)* divisar
3 *vi* espiar (**on** a)

spy out *vt* **(a)** *(investigate)* espiar, investigar **(b)** *(land)* reconocer, explorar

spyglass ['spaɪglɑːs] *n* catalejo *m*

spyhole ['spaɪhəʊl] *n* mirilla *f*

spying ['spaɪɪŋ] *n* espionaje *m*

Sq *(abbr* **Square**) Plaza *f*, Pza., Plza

sq *(abbr* **square**) cuadrado(a)

squabble ['skwɒbəl] **1** *n* riña *f*, disputa *f*, pelea *f*
2 *vi* reñir, disputar, pelearse (**over** por; **about** sobre)

squabbling ['skwɒbəlɪŋ] *n* riñas *fpl*, disputas *fpl*, peleas *fpl*

squad [skwɒd] *n Mil* pelotón *m*; *(of police)* brigada *f*; *Sport* equipo *m* ❑ **drugs s.** brigada *f* antidroga; **firing s.** pelotón *m* de fusilamiento *or* ejecución; **flying s.** brigada *f* móvil; **s. car** coche *m* patrulla

squadron ['skwɒdrən] *n Mil* escuadrón *m; Av* escuadrilla *f; Naut* escuadra *f*; **s. leader** comandante de escuadrilla

squalid ['skwɒlɪd] *adj (very dirty)* sucio(a), mugriento(a), asqueroso(a); *(poor)* miserable; *(sordid)* sórdido(a); *(motive)* vil

squall¹ [skwɔːl] *n (wind)* ráfaga *f*, *(storm)* chubasco *m*, tormenta *f*

squall² [skwɔːl] *vi* chillar, berrear

squalor ['skwɒlər] *n (dirtiness)* suciedad *f*, mugre *f*, *(poverty)* miseria *f*

squander ['skwɒndər] *vt (money)* malgastar, derrochar, despilfarrar; *(inheritance)* dilapidar; *(time)* desperdiciar

square [skweər] **1** *n* **(a)** *(shape)* cuadrado *m*, cuadro *m*; *(on fabric)* cuadro *m*; *(on chessboard, crossword, graph paper)* casilla *f; Fig* **we're back to s. one!** ¡volvemos a partir desde cero! **(b)** *(in town)* plaza *f; (in barracks)* patio *m; US (block of houses)* manzana *f* **(c)** *Math* cuadrado *m*; **9 is the s. of 3** 9 es el cuadrado de 3 **(d)** *Fam (old-fashioned person)* carroza *mf*, *(conservative)* carca *mf*
2 *adj* **(a)** *(in shape)* cuadrado(a); *(forming right angle)* en ángulo recto; *Fam* **a s. peg in a round hole** gallina en

corral ajeno ❑ *Typ* **s. brackets** corchetes *mpl*; **s. dance** baile *m* de figuras **(b)** *Math* cuadrado(a) ❑ **s. metre** metro *m* cuadrado; **s. root** raíz *f* cuadrada **(c)** *Fam (fair)* justo(a), equitativo(a); *(honest)* honesto(a); **to be s. with sb** ser franco(a) con algn; **to get a s. deal** recibir un trato justo; **to get s. with sb** ajustar cuentas con algn **(d)** **a s. meal** una buena comida, una comida decente **(e)** *(old-fashioned)* carroza; *(conservative)* carca
3 *adv (straight)* justamente, exactamente; **s. in the middle of** justo en medio de; **s. on the chin** de lleno en la barbilla
4 *vt* **(a)** *(make square)* cuadrar; **to s. one's shoulders** ponerse derecho(a), sacar el pecho **(b)** *Math* cuadrar, elevar al cuadrado; **3 squared is 9** 3 al cuadrado es 9 **(c)** *(settle)* arreglar, ajustar; **to s. matters** arreglar las cosas
5 *vi (agree)* cuadrar, concordar (**with** con)

square up *vi* **(a)** *(fighters)* ponerse en guardia; *Fig* **to s. up to a problem** hacer frente a un problema **(b)** *Fam (settle)* **to s. things up with sb** ajustar *or* saldar cuentas con algn

squared ['skweəd] *adj (paper)* cuadriculado(a)

squarely ['skweəlɪ] *adv (directly, straight)* directamente, de lleno

squash¹ [skwɒʃ] **1** *n* **(a)** *(crush)* aplastamiento *m*; *(in crowd)* apiñamiento *m*, agolpamiento *m*, apretujón *m* **(b)** *Br Culin (drink) Esp* zumo *m*, *Am* jugo *m* ❑ **orange s.** naranjada *f*, zumo *m* de naranja
2 *vt* **(a)** *(crush, flatten)* aplastar, esparruchar, chafar **(b)** *Fig (argument, objection)* echar por tierra, dar al traste con; *(person)* apabullar, callar
3 *vi (crush)* aplastarse, espachurrarse, chafarse

squash² [skwɒʃ] *n Sport* squash *m* ❑ **s. court** pista *f* de squash

squash³ [skwɒʃ] *n US Bot* calabaza *f*

squashy ['skwɒʃɪ] *adj* (**squashier, squashiest**) blando(a), fofo(a), esponjoso(a)

squat [skwɒt] **1** *adj* **(a)** *(person)* rechoncho(a), achaparrado(a) **(b)** *(building)* muy bajo(a)
2 *vi (pt & pp* **squatted**) **(a)** *(crouch)* agacharse, sentarse en cuclillas **(b)** *(in building)* ocupar ilegalmente
3 *n Br (action)* ocupación *f* ilegal; *(building)* edificio *m* ocupado ilegalmente

squatter ['skwɒtər] *n* ocupante *mf* ilegal

squaw [skwɔː] *n* india *f* norteamericana, piel roja *f*

squawk [skwɔːk] **1** *n* graznido *m*, chillido *m*
2 *vi* graznar, chillar

squeak [skwiːk] **1** *n* **(a)** *(of mouse)* chillido *m*; *(of hinge, wheel)* chirrido *m*, rechinamiento *m*; *(of shoes)* crujido *m*; *Fam* **there wasn't a s. out of him** no dijo ni pío
2 *vi (mouse)* chillar; *(hinge, wheel)* chirriar, rechinar; *(shoes)* crujir

squeaky ['skwiːkɪ] *adj* (**squeakier, squeakiest**) *(gen)* chirriante; *(voice)* chillón(ona) ; *(shoes)* que crujen

squeal [skwiːl] **1** *n (gen)* chirrido *m*; *(of animal, person)* chillido *m*
2 *vi* **(a)** *(gen)* chirriar; *(animal, person)* chillar **(b)** *Fam (inform)* cantar, chivarse; **to s. on sb** dar el soplo sobre algn, *Col* sapear *or Méx* soplar *or RP* botonear a algn
3 *vt* decir chillando

squeamish ['skwiːmɪʃ] *adj* muy sensible, remilgado(a), delicado(a); **to be s. about sth** tener horror a algo

squeeze [skwiːz] **1** *vt (gen)* apretar; *(lemon, orange)* exprimir; *(sponge)* estrujar; **he squeezed her hand** le apretó la mano; **to s. paste out of a tube** sacar pasta de un tubo; **to s. sth into one's pocket** meter algo atropelladamente en el bolsillo; **can you s. me in before midday?** ¿me podrá ver antes del mediodía?
2 *vi* **to s. in/out** meterse/salir apenas *or* con dificultad; **to s. through a crowd** abrirse paso entre una muchedumbre

con dificultad; *Fam* **s. up a bit!** ¡hazme sitio!, ¡córrete un poco!
  3 *n* (**a**) *(pressure)* estrujón *m*, presión *f*; **a s. of lemon** unas gotas de limón (**b**) *(of hand)* apretón *m*; *(hug)* abrazo *m*; *(crowd, crush)* apiñamiento *m*, agolpamiento *m*, apretujón *m*; **it was a tight s. for us** íbamos como sardinas en lata ❑ *Fin* **credit s.** reducción *f* de créditos

squeezer ['skwiːzər] *n* exprimidor *m*; **lemon s.** exprimelimones *m inv*

squelch [skweltʃ] *vi* chapotear; **to s. through the mud** ir chapoteando por el lodo

squib [skwɪb] *n* petardo *m*; *Fam* **it was a damp s.** fue un chasco

squid [skwɪd] *n Zool* calamar *m*; *(small)* chipirón *m*

squidgy ['skwɪdʒɪ] *adj* (**squidgier, squidgiest**) blando(a) y húmedo(a)

squiffy ['skwɪfɪ] *adj* (**squiffier, squiffiest**) *Br Fam* achispado(a), alegre

squiggle ['skwɪɡəl] **1** *n* garabato *m*
  2 *vi* garabatear, hacer garabatos

squiggly ['skwɪɡlɪ] *adj* (**squigglier, squiggliest**) ondulante, serpenteante

squint [skwɪnt] **1** *n* (**a**) *Med* bizquera *f*; **to have a s.** ser bizco(a) (**b**) *Fig (quick look)* vistazo *m*, ojeada *f*; *Fam* **let's have a s.** déjame echarle un vistazo
  2 *vi Med* bizquear, ser bizco(a) (**b**) *(in sunlight etc)* entrecerrar los ojos; **to s. at sth** *(glance)* echar un vistazo a algo; *(with eyes half-closed)* mirar algo con los ojos entrecerrados

squire [skwaɪər] *n (landowner)* terrateniente *m*, hacendado *m*

squirm [skwɜːm] *vi (wriggle)* retorcerse; *Fig (feel embarrassed)* sentirse incómodo(a)

squirrel ['skwɪrəl] *n* ardilla *f*

squirt [skwɜːt] **1** *n* (**a**) *(of liquid)* chorro *m* (**b**) *Offens (person)* mequetrefe *mf*
  2 *vt (liquid)* lanzar a chorro
  3 *vi (liquid)* **to s. out** salir a chorros

squishy ['skwɪʃɪ] *adj* (**squishier, squishiest**) *(fruit, mess)* blando(a) y húmedo(a); *(sound)* de chapoteo

Sr (**a**) *abbr see* **Snr** (**b**) *Rel (abbr* **Sister**) Hermana *f*, Hna

Sri Lanka [sriː'læŋkə] *n* Sri Lanka

SRN [esaːr'en] *n Br (abbr* **State Registered Nurse**) enfermera *f* titulada

SS (**a**) *(abbr* **Saints**) Santos *mpl*, Santas *fpl*, Stos, Stas (**b**) [es'es] *steamship* buque *m* de vapor, vapor *m*

St (**a**) *(abbr* **Saint**) San *m*, Santo *m*, Santa *f*, Sto, Sta (**b**) *(abbr* **Street**) calle *f*, c/

st *Br (abbr* **stone**) = peso que equivale a 6,348 kg

stab [stæb] **1** *n (with knife)* puñalada *f*, navajazo *m*; *(of pain)* punzada *f*; *Fam Fig* **to have a s. at doing sth** intentar hacer algo
  2 *vt (pt & pp* **stabbed**) apuñalar, acuchillar; *Fig* **to s. sb in the back** apuñalar a algn por la espalda

stabbing ['stæbɪŋ] **1** *adj (pain)* punzante
  2 *n* puñaladas *fpl*

stability [stə'bɪlɪtɪ] *n* estabilidad *f*

stabilize ['steɪbɪlaɪz] **1** *vt* estabilizar
  2 *vi* estabilizarse

stabilizer ['steɪbɪlaɪzər] *n Tech* estabilizador *m*

stable¹ ['steɪbəl] *adj (unchanging)* estable, constante; *(secure)* fijo(a), sujeto(a), estable

stable² ['steɪbəl] **1** *n (building)* cuadra *f*, caballeriza *f*, establo *m*; *Fig* **to close the s. door after the horse has bolted** a buenas horas, mangas verdes

2 *vt (put in stable)* encerrar en una cuadra; *(keep in stable)* guardar en una cuadra

stack [stæk] **1** *n* (**a**) *(pile)* montón *m*; *Fam* **he's got stacks of money** está forrado (**b**) *(haystack)* almiar *m* (**c**) *(chimneystack)* (cañon *m* de) chimenea *f*
  2 *vt (pile up)* amontonar, apilar; *Fig* **the cards** *or* **odds are stacked against us** todo está en contra nuestra

stadium ['steɪdɪəm] *n (pl* **stadiums** *or* **stadia** ['steɪdɪə]) estadio *m*

staff [staːf] **1** *n* (**a**) *(personnel)* personal *m*, empleados *mpl*; *Mil* estado *m* mayor; **on the s.** en plantilla ❑ **editorial s.** redactores *mpl*, redacción *f*; **s. entrance** entrada *f* del personal; **s. meeting** reunión *f* de profesores, claustro *m*; **s. nurse** enfermera *f* cualificada; **teaching s.** cuerpo *m* docente, profesorado *m* (**b**) *(stick)* bastón *m*; *(of shepherd)* cayado *m*; *Rel* báculo *m*; *(flagpole)* asta *f*; *Fig* **the s. of life** el báculo de la vida (**c**) *Mus (pl* **staves**) pentagrama *m*
  2 *vt* proveer de personal

staffer ['staːfər] *n Fam* empleado(a) *m,f*

staffroom ['staːfruːm] *n* sala *f* de profesores

stag [stæg] *n Zool* ciervo *m*, venado *m* ❑ *Ent* **s. beetle** ciervo *m* volante; *Fam* **s. party** *or* **night** despedida *f* de soltero

stage [steɪdʒ] **1** *n* (**a**) *(platform)* plataforma *f*, estrado *m*, tablado *m* (**b**) *(in theatre)* escenario *m*, escena *f*; *(theatre)* teatro *m*; **to go on s.** salir al escenario; **to go on the s.** hacerse actor/actriz ❑ **s. directions** acotaciones *fpl*; **s. door** entrada *f* de artistas; **s. fright** miedo *m* escénico; **s. manager** director(a) *m,f* de escena; **s. name** nombre *m* artístico; **s. whisper** aparte *m* (**c**) *(section, period, phase) (of development)* etapa *f*, fase *f*; *(of journey)* etapa *f*, jornada *f*; *(of road, pipeline)* tramo *m*; *(of rocket)* piso *m*, etapa *f*; **at this s. of the negotiations** a estas alturas de las negociaciones; **by** *or* **in stages** por etapas; **it's in its early stages** está aún en pañales (**d**) *Fam (stagecoach)* diligencia *f*
  2 *vt* (**a**) *Theat (play)* poner en escena, montar, representar (**b**) *(demonstration, welcome) (arrange)* organizar; *(carry out)* llevar a cabo, efectuar

stagecoach ['steɪdʒkəʊtʃ] *n* diligencia *f*

stagehand ['steɪdʒhænd] *n* tramoyista *mf*

stage-manage ['steɪdʒ'mænɪdʒ] *vt Theat* dirigir; *Fig (event, demonstration)* orquestar

stage-struck ['steɪdʒstrʌk] *adj* apasionado(a) por el teatro

stag(e)y ['steɪdʒɪ] *adj* (**stagier, stagiest**) *Pej* teatral, histriónico(a)

stagger ['stæɡər] **1** *vi* tambalearse; **to s. along** ir tambaleándose, ir dando tumbos; **to s. to one's feet** levantarse tambaleante
  2 *vt* (**a**) *(amaze)* asombrar (**b**) *(hours, work)* escalonar

staggering ['stæɡərɪŋ] *adj* asombroso(a), pasmoso(a)

stagnant ['stæɡnənt] *adj (water)* estancado(a); *Fig* paralizado(a), inactivo(a), anquilosado(a)

stagnate [stæɡ'neɪt] *vi* estancarse, quedarse *or* estar estancado(a)

stagnation [stæɡ'neɪʃən] *n* estancamiento *m*; *Fig* estancamiento *m*, paralización *f*

staid [steɪd] *adj (person)* conservador(a), tradicionalista; *(manner, clothes)* serio(a), formal

stain [steɪn] **1** *n* (**a**) *(gen)* mancha *f*; **blood s.** mancha de sangre ❑ **s. remover** quitamanchas *m inv* (**b**) *(dye)* tinte *m*, tintura *f*
  2 *vt* (**a**) *(gen)* manchar (**b**) *(dye)* teñir
  3 *vi* mancharse

stained [steɪnd] *adj* manchado(a) ❑ **s. glass** vidrio *m* de colores; **s. glass window** vidriera *f* de colores

stainless ['steɪnlɪs] *adj (gen)* inmaculado(a); *(steel)* inoxidable

stair [steər] *n* (**a**) *(single step)* escalón *m*, peldaño *m* (**b**) **stairs** escalera *f sing*

staircase ['steəkeɪs] *n* escalera *f*; **spiral s.** escalera de caracol

stake¹ [steɪk] **1** *n (stick)* estaca *f*, palo *m*; *(for plant)* rodrigón *m*; *(post)* poste *m*; *Hist* **to be burnt at the s.** morir en la hoguera
2 *vt* **to s. (out)** cercar *or* señalar con estacas

stake² [steɪk] **1** *n* (**a**) *(bet)* puesta *f*, apuesta *f*; **the issue at s.** el tema en cuestión; **to be at s.** *(at risk)* estar en juego; *(in danger)* estar en peligro (**b**) *(investment)* interés *m*; **he has a s. in the company** tiene intereses en la compañía
2 *vt (bet)* apostar; *(invest)* invertir; **to s. a claim to sth** reivindicar algo; **to s. one's life on sth** jugarse la vida en algo

stakeout ['steɪkaʊt] *n* **to be on s.** montar vigilancia

stalactite ['stæləktaɪt] *n* estalactita *f*

stalagmite ['stæləgmaɪt] *n* estalagmita *f*

stale [steɪl] *adj* (**a**) *(food)* pasado(a); *(bread)* duro(a) (**b**) *(air)* viciado(a); **s. smell** olor a cerrado (**c**) *(person)* agotado(a), gastado(a), quemado(a)

stalemate ['steɪlmeɪt] *n Chess* tablas *fpl*; *Fig* punto *m* muerto; *Fig* **to reach s.** llegar a un punto muerto, estancarse

staleness ['steɪlnɪs] *n* (**a**) *(of food)* rancidez *f*; *(of bread)* dureza *f* (**b**) *(of air)* lo viciado (**c**) *(of person)* agotamiento *m*

stalk¹ [stɔːk] *n Bot (of plant)* tallo *m*; *(of fruit)* rabo *m*; *(of cabbage)* troncho *m*

stalk² [stɔːk] **1** *vt (hunter)* cazar al acecho; *(animal)* acechar; *(detective etc)* seguir los pasos de
2 *vi (walk)* andar con paso majestuoso; **he stalked out of the room** salió airado de la habitación

stalker ['stɔːkər] *n* = persona que sigue o vigila obsesivamente a otra

stall¹ [stɔːl] **1** *n* (**a**) *(in market)* puesto *m*, tenderete *m*; *(at fair)* caseta *f* ❑ **newspaper s.** quiosco *m* de periódicos (**b**) *Agr (stable)* establo *m*; *(stable compartment)* casilla *f* de establo; *(manger)* pesebre *m* (**c**) *(in church)* coro *m* (**d**) *Br Cin Theat* **stalls** platea *f sing*
2 *vt Aut (engine)* parar, *Esp* calar
3 *vi Aut (engine)* pararse, *Esp* calarse; *Av (plane)* perder velocidad

stall² [stɔːl] *vi* andar con rodeos, dar largas al asunto, contestar con evasivas

stallholder ['stɔːlhəʊldər] *n* dueño(a) *m,f* de un puesto, *Am* puestero(a) *m,f*

stallion ['stæljən] *n Zool* semental *m*, garañón *m*

stalwart ['stɔːlwət] **1** *adj* (**a**) *(sturdy)* fuerte, robusto(a), fornido(a) (**b**) *(loyal)* leal, fiel
2 *n* partidario(a) *m,f* incondicional *or* leal

stamen ['steɪmen] *n Bot* estambre *m*

stamina ['stæmɪnə] *n (energy)* energía *f*, vigor *m*; *(endurance)* aguante *m*, resistencia *f*

stammer ['stæmər] **1** *n* tartamudeo *m*; **she has a s.** tartamudea
2 *vi* tartamudear
3 *vt* decir tartamudeando

stammering ['stæmərɪŋ] **1** *adj* tartamudeante
2 *n* tartamudez *f*

stamp [stæmp] **1** *n* (**a**) *(postage stamp)* sello *m*, *Am* estampilla *f*, *CAm Méx* timbre *m*; *(fiscal)* póliza *f*, timbre *m* ❑ **s. album** álbum *m* de sellos; **s. collector** coleccionista *mf* de sellos, filatelista *mf*; **s.** *Br* **duty** *or* *US* **tax** impuesto *m* del timbre, póliza *f*; **s. machine** distribuidora *f* automática de

sellos; **trading s.** cupón *m* (**b**) *(rubber stamp)* sello *m* de goma, tampón *m*; *(mark, seal)* sello *m*, tampón *m*; *(for metals)* cuño *m* (**c**) *(with foot)* patada *f*; *(in dancing)* zapateo *m*
2 *vt* (**a**) *(letter) (with postage stamp)* sellar, poner el sello a; **stamped addressed envelope** sobre franqueado (**b**) *(passport, document) (with rubber stamp)* sellar, marcar con sello; *(money)* acuñar (**c**) **to s. one's feet** patear, patalear; *(in dancing)* zapatear
3 *vi* patear, patalear; **to s. on sb's foot** pisarle *or* pisotearle el pie a algn

stamp out *vt* (**a**) *(fire)* apagar con los pies (**b**) *Fig (racism, violence)* acabar con; *(rebellion, epidemic)* sofocar

stampede [stæm'piːd] **1** *n* estampida *f*, desbandada *f*, espantada *f*; *Fig (rush)* desbandada *f*; **there was a sudden s. for the door** todos se precipitaron hacia la puerta
2 *vi* huir *or* salir en estampida, desbandarse; *Fig (rush)* precipitarse
3 *vt* provocar una estampida en

stance [stæns] *n* postura *f*; *Fig* postura *f*, actitud *f*

stand [stænd] **1** *n* (**a**) *(position)* posición *f*, postura *f*; *Mil* **to make a s. against the enemy** resistir al enemigo; *Fig* **to take a s. on a matter** adoptar una postura hacia una cuestión (**b**) *(of lamp, sculpture)* pie *m*, pedestal *m* ❑ **coat s.** perchero *m*; **music s.** atril *m* (**c**) *(market stall)* puesto *m*, tenderete *m*; *(at fair)* caseta *f*; *(at exhibition)* stand *m*, pabellón *m* ❑ **newspaper s.** quiosco *m* (**d**) *(at stadium)* **stand(s)** gradas *fpl*, *Esp* graderío *m* (**e**) *US Jur (witness box)* estrado *m*; **to take the s.** subir al estrado
2 *vt (pt & pp* **stood)** (**a**) *(place)* poner, colocar (**b**) *(withstand, tolerate)* aguantar, soportar; **to s. one's ground** mantenerse firme, seguir en sus trece; *Fam* **I can't s. him** no lo aguanto, no lo puedo tragar, no lo puedo ver (**c**) *Fam (invite)* invitar; **to s. sb a drink** invitar a algn a una copa
3 *vi* (**a**) *(be upright)* estar de pie *or Am* parado(a); *(get up)* ponerse de pie, levantarse, *Am* pararse; *(remain upright)* quedarse de pie *or Am* parado(a); **she could scarcely s.** apenas se tenía de pie; *Fig* **to s. fast** mantenerse firme; *Fig* **to s. on one's own two feet** apañárselas sólo; *Fam* **just stood there** se quedó allí mirando; *Fam* **s. still!** ¡estáte quieto!, ¡no te muevas! (**b**) *(measure)* medir; **the tower stands seventy feet high** la torre tiene setenta pies de alto; **the thermometer stood at 40 degrees** el termómetro marcaba 40 grados (**c**) *(be situated) (castle, village, etc)* estar, encontrarse (**d**) *(remain unchanged)* permanecer; **leave the dough to s. for half an hour** deja reposar la masa una media hora (**e**) *(remain valid) (decision, arrangement)* seguir en pie, seguir vigente (**f**) *(be, be placed)* estar; **as things s.** tal como están las cosas; **he stands to lose a lot of money** puede que pierda mucho dinero; **it stands to reason** es lógico; **we would like to know where we s.** nos gustaría saber a qué atenernos (**g**) *Pol* presentarse

stand back *vi (be set back)* estar apartado(a); *(allowing sb to pass)* abrir paso

stand by 1 *vi* (**a**) *(do nothing)* quedarse sin hacer nada (**b**) *(be ready for action)* estar preparado(a) *or* listo(a); *Av* **s. by for take-off!** ¡preparados para el despegue *or Am* decolaje!
2 *vt (person)* apoyar, respaldar; *(promise)* cumplir con; *(decision)* atenerse a; **I s. by what I said** me atengo a lo dicho

stand down *vi Fig (withdraw)* retirarse

stand for *vt* (**a**) *(mean)* significar; **BR stands for British Rail** BR son las siglas de la British Rail (**b**) *(represent)* representar; *Pol* **we have always stood for freedom** nosotros siempre hemos defendido la libertad (**c**) *(tolerate)* tolerar, aguantar

stand in *vi (substitute)* sustituir (**for** -)

stand out *vi (building, mountain, etc)* destacarse **(against** contra)*; Fig (person, qualities)* destacar, sobresalir; *Fam* **it stands out a mile!** ¡salta a la vista!

stand to *vi Mil* estar en estado de alerta

stand up 1 *vi (get up)* ponerse de pie, levantarse, *Am* pararse; *(be standing)* estar de pie; *Fig* **it will s. up to wear and tear** es muy resistente; *Fig* **this will not s. up in court** esto no convencerá a ningún tribunal; *Fig* **to s. up for oneself** defenderse solo(a); *Fig* **to s. up for sb** defender algn; *Fig* **to s. up to sb** hacer frente a algn
2 *vt Fam* **to s. sb up** dejar plantado(a) a algn

stand-alone ['stændələʊn] *adj Comptr* independiente, autónomo(a)

standard ['stændəd] **1** *n* **(a)** *(level, degree)* nivel *m*; **of a high/low s.** de alto/bajo nivel; **s. of living** nivel de vida **(b)** *(criterion, principle)* criterio *m*, valor *m* **(c)** *(norm)* norma *f*, regla *f*, estándar *m*; **to be up to/below s.** satisfacer/no satisfacer los requisitos **(d)** *(flag)* estandarte *m*, bandera *f*; *Naut* pabellón *m* **(e)** *(measure)* patrón *m*; *Fin* **the gold s.** el patrón oro
2 *adj* normal, estándar, corriente, común; **it is now s. practice** se ha impuesto ya como norma ▫ **s. English** inglés *m* normativo; **s. lamp** lámpara *f* de pie; **s. model** modelo *m* estándar; **s. size** tamaño *m* normal; **s. time** hora *f* oficial

standard-bearer ['stændədbeərər] *n Mil* abanderado *m*

standardization [stændədaɪ'zeɪʃən] *n* normalización *f*, estandarización *f*, estandardización *f*

standardize ['stændədaɪz] *vt* normalizar, estandarizar, estandardizar

standby ['stændbaɪ] *n* **(a)** *(thing)* recurso *m* **(b)** *(person)* suplente *mf*, sustituto(a) *m,f*; **to be on s.** *Mil (troops)* estar de retén; *Av (passenger)* estar en la lista de espera ▫ *Av* **s. ticket** billete *m or Am* boleto *m* de lista de espera

stand-in ['stændɪn] *n* suplente *mf*, sustituto(a) *m,f* **(for** de)*; Cin* doble *mf*

standing ['stændɪŋ] **1** *adj* **(a)** *(not sitting)* de pie; *(upright)* derecho(a), recto(a), vertical; **s. ovation** ovación *f* calurosa; **there was s. room only** no quedaban asientos; *Fig* **he left everyone else s.** dejó atrás a los demás **(b)** *Sport* **s. start** salida *f* parada **(c)** *(committee, body)* permanente; *(rule)* fijo(a); *(invitation)* abierto(a); *Fin* **s. order** pago fijo
2 *n* **(a)** *(social position)* rango *m*, categoría *f*, estatus *m*, standing *m*; *(importance)* importancia *f*; *(reputation)* reputación *f*, fama *f*; **of high s.** de mucha categoría, de alto standing **(b)** *(duration)* duración *f*; *(in job)* antigüedad *f*

stand-off ['stændɒf] *n* **(a)** *(deadlock)* punto *m* muerto **(b)** *US Sport (tie)* empate *m*

stand-offish [stænd'ɒfɪʃ] *adj Fam* estirado(a), altivo(a)

stand-offishness [stænd'ɒfɪʃnɪs] *n Fam* altivez *f*, distancia *f*, reserva *f*

standpipe ['stændpaɪp] *n* tubo *m* vertical

standpoint ['stændpɔɪnt] *n* punto *m* de vista; **from our s.** desde nuestro punto de vista

standstill ['stændstɪl] *n* **at a s.** *(car, traffic)* parado(a); *(industry, business)* paralizado(a); **to come to a s.** *(car, traffic)* pararse; *(industry, business)* paralizarse

stand-up ['stændʌp] **1** *n (comedy)* = humorismo que consiste en salir solo al escenario con un micrófono y contar chistes
2 *adj* **(a)** *(comedian)* de micrófono, = que basa su actuación en contar chistes al público solo desde el escenario **(b)** *(passionate)* **a s. argument** una violenta discusión; **a s. fight** una batalla campal, una pelea salvaje **(c)** *US (decent, honest)* decente

stank [stæŋk] *pt see* **stink**

stanza ['stænzə] *n* estrofa *f*

staple¹ ['steɪpəl] **1** *n* grapa *f*, *Chile* corchete *m*, *Col* gancho *m*, *RP* ganchito *m*
2 *vt* grapar, *Am* engrapar, *Chile* corchetear, *RP* abrochar

staple² ['steɪpəl] **1** *adj (food, diet)* básico(a); *(product)* de primera necesidad
2 *n (food)* alimento *m* básico; *(product)* artículo *m* de primera necesidad

stapler ['steɪplər] *n* grapadora *f*, *Am* engrapadora *f*, *Chile* corchetera *f*, *RP* abrochadora *f*

star [stɑ:r] **1** *n* **(a)** *Astrol Astron* estrella *f*; **shooting s.** estrella fugaz; **5-s. hotel** hotel *m* de 5 estrellas; *Br* **4-s. petrol** gasolina *f or RP* nafta *f* súper; *Fig* **to thank one's lucky stars** dar gracias al cielo; *Fig* **to see stars** ver estrellas; *Fam* **what do the stars say?** ¿qué dice el horóscopo? ▫ *US* **the Stars and Stripes** la bandera de las barras y estrellas **(b)** *(person)* estrella *f*, astro *m* ▫ **film s.** estrella *f* de cine
2 *adj* estelar ▫ **s. attraction** atracción *f* estelar; **s. part** papel *m* estelar; **s. turn** atracción estelar
3 *vt Cin* presentar como estrella a, tener como protagonista
4 *vi Cin* actuar en papel principal, protagonizar

starboard ['stɑ:bəd] *n Naut* estribor *m*

starch [stɑ:tʃ] **1** *n (for laundry)* almidón *m*; *(in rice)* almidón *m*; *(in potatoes etc)* fécula *f*
2 *vt (laundry)* almidonar

starchy ['stɑ:tʃɪ] *adj* **(starchier, starchiest)** *(food)* feculento(a); *Fig (person)* rígido(a), estirado(a)

stardom ['stɑ:dəm] *n* estrellato *m*; **to rise to s.** convertirse en estrella, alcanzar el estrellato

stare [steər] **1** *n* mirada *f* fija
2 *vi* mirar fijamente **(at** a), mirar de hito en hito **(at** a), clavar los ojos *or* la vista **(at** en); **to s. into space** mirar al vacío; **to s. one in the face** saltar a la vista

starfish ['stɑ:fɪʃ] *n Zool* estrella *f* de mar

staring ['steərɪŋ] *adj* **he had s. eyes** tenía la mirada fija

stark [stɑ:k] **1** *adj (landscape)* desolado(a), desierto(a); *(décor, colour)* austero(a); *(realism, truth)* escueto(a), sin adornos, desnudo(a); **s. poverty** la miseria
2 *adv* completamente; **s. naked** completamente desnudo(a); *Fam* **s. raving** *or* **staring mad** loco(a) de remate *or* de atar

starkers ['stɑ:kəz] *adj Br Fam* en cueros, en pelotas

starlet ['stɑ:lɪt] *n (young actress)* actriz *f* incipiente

starlight ['stɑ:laɪt] *n* luz *f* de las estrellas

starling ['stɑ:lɪŋ] *n Orn* estornino *m*

starlit ['stɑ:lɪt] *adj* iluminado(a) por las estrellas

starry ['stɑ:rɪ] *adj* **(starrier, starriest)** estrellado(a), sembrado(a) de estrellas

starry-eyed [stɑ:rɪ'aɪd] *adj (idealistic)* idealista, ilusionado(a); *(in love)* enamorado(a)

start [stɑ:t] **1** *n* **(a)** *(beginning)* principio *m*, comienzo *m*, inicio *m*; *(of race)* salida *f*; **at the s.** al principio; **false s.** salida nula; **for a s.** para empezar; **from the s.** desde el principio; **to get off to a good s.** empezar con buen pie; **to give sb a s. in life** ayudar a algn a establecerse; **to make an early s.** ponerse en camino *or* marcha a primera hora; **to make a fresh s. in life** comenzar una nueva vida, volver a empezar **(b)** *(advantage)* ventaja *f*; **I'll give you a five minute s.** te daré cinco minutos de ventaja **(c)** *(fright, jump)* susto *m*, sobresalto *m*; **to give sb a s.** dar un susto a algn; **to wake up with a s.** despertarse sobresaltado(a); **to work by fits and starts** trabajar a trompicones
2 *vt* **(a)** *(begin)* empezar, comenzar; *(conversation)* entablar; **to s. doing** *or* **to do sth** empezar a hacer algo; **to s. negotiations** iniciar negociaciones **(b)** *(cause, give rise to)* causar, provocar; **to s. a fashion** lanzar una moda **(c)**

(found) fundar, establecer; **to s. a business** montar un negocio (**d**) *(set in motion)* arrancar, poner en marcha

3 *vi* (**a**) *(begin)* empezar, comenzar; *(on journey)* ponerse en camino; *(car, engine)* arrancar, ponerse en marcha; **he started by welcoming everyone** empezó por dar la bienvenida a todos; **starting from Monday** a partir del lunes; **to s. at the beginning** empezar desde el principio; **to s. with ...** *(firstly)* para empezar ..., en primer lugar ...; *(at the beginning)* al principio ... (**b**) *(in fright)* asustarse, sobresaltarse

start back *vi* emprender el viaje de regreso

start off 1 *vi* (**a**) *(begin)* empezar, comenzar; **to s. off by/with** empezar por/con (**b**) *(leave)* salir, partir, ponerse en camino

2 *vt* (**a**) *(cause) (dispute, war, etc)* causar, provocar; **don't s. her off!** ¡no le des cuerda! (**b**) *(help to start) (person)* **his father started him off in the shoe business** su padre le dio el primer empujón en el comercio del calzado

start out *vi* (*begin)* empezar, comenzar; *(on journey)* salir, partir, ponerse en camino

start over *vi US* volver a empezar

start up 1 *vt (car, engine)* arrancar

2 *vi (car)* arrancar; *(orchestra etc)* empezar a tocar

starter ['stɑːtər] *n* (**a**) *Sport (official)* juez *mf* de salida; *(competitor)* competidor(a) *m,f*, participante *mf*; *Fam (child)* **to be a late s.** ser tardío(a) en el desarrollo (**b**) *Aut (motor)* motor *m* de arranque (**c**) *Culin Fam* primer plato *m*, entrada *f*; *Fig* **for starters** para empezar

starting ['stɑːtɪŋ] *n* comienzo *m*, inicio *m* □ **s. block** taco *m* de salida; *Aut* **s. handle** manivela *f* de arranque; **s. point** punto *m* de partida; *Sport* **s. post** línea *f* de salida; *Fin* **s. price** precio *m* inicial

startle ['stɑːtəl] *vt* asustar, sobresaltar

startling ['stɑːtlɪŋ] *adj* (**a**) *(frightening)* alarmante, sobrecogedor(a) (**b**) *(astonishing) (news, discovery)* asombroso(a), sorprendente; *(coincidence)* extraordinario(a) (**c**) *(eye-catching)* llamativo(a)

start-up ['stɑːtʌp] *n Com* puesta *f* en marcha; **s. costs** gastos *mpl* de puesta en marcha

starvation [stɑːˈveɪʃən] *n* hambre *f*, inanición *f*; **to die of s.** morir de inanición □ **s. diet** régimen *m* de hambre; **s. wages** sueldos *mpl* miserables

starve [stɑːv] **1** *vt* privar de comida, hacer pasar hambre a; **to s. sb to death** hacer morir de hambre a algn, matar de hambre a algn; *Fig* **he was starved of affection** fue privado de cariño

2 *vi (suffer from hunger)* pasar hambre; **to s. to death** morirse de hambre

starving ['stɑːvɪŋ] *adj* hambriento(a), muerto(a) de hambre; *Fam* **I'm s.!** estoy muerto de hambre, tengo un hambre que no veo

stash [stæʃ] *vt Fam* **to s. sth away** esconder algo, guardar algo en un lugar seguro

state [steɪt] **1** *n* (**a**) *(gen)* estado *m*; **s. of emergency** estado de emergencia; **s. of mind** estado de ánimo; **the s. of the nation** el estado de la nación; **to be in no fit s. to do sth** no estar en condiciones de hacer algo; **what a s. of affairs!** ¡qué lío!; *Fam* **to get into a s. about sth** afligirse por algo (**b**) *Pol* estado *m*; *US* **Secretary of S.** ministro(a) *m,f* de Asuntos *or Am* Relaciones Exteriores; *Br* **Secretary of S. for Education** ministro(a) *m,f* de Educación; *US* **the States** los estados Unidos; *US* **the S. Department** el Ministerio de Asuntos *or Am* Relaciones Exteriores (**c**) *(of deceased)* **to lie in s.** estar de cuerpo presente

2 *adj* (**a**) *Pol* estatal, del estado □ **s. capitalism** capitalismo *m* de estado; **s. education** enseñanza *f* pública; *US* **s. highway** carretera *f* nacional; **s. owner-**

ship propiedad *f* del Estado; **s. secret** secreto *m* de Estado; **s. sector** sector *m* estatal *or* público (**b**) *(ceremonial) (apartment, banquet, coach)* de gala; **s. occasion** ocasión *f* solemne; **s. visit** visita *f* oficial

3 *vt* declarar, afirmar; *(case, claim)* exponer; *(problem)* plantear; *(time, place)* fijar; **as stated above** como queda indicado arriba; **to s. one's opinion** dar su opinión

stated ['steɪtɪd] *adj* indicado(a), señalado(a); **at the s. time** a la hora indicada *or* señalada

stateless ['steɪtlɪs] *adj* apátrida

stately ['steɪtlɪ] *adj* (**statelier, stateliest**) majestuoso(a), imponente □ **s. home** casa *f* solariega

statement ['steɪtmənt] *n* (**a**) *(gen)* declaración *f*, afirmación *f*; **official s.** comunicado *m*; *Jur* **to make a s.** prestar declaración (**b**) *Fin* estado *m* de cuenta; **monthly s.** balance *m* mensual

state-of-the-art [steɪtəvðɑːt] *adj* de vanguardia; **s. technology** tecnología *f* punta

state-owned ['steɪtˈəʊnd] *adj* público(a), estatal

stateroom ['steɪtruːm] *n Naut* camarote *m*

state-run ['steɪtrʌn] *adj* estatal

statesman ['steɪtsmən] *n* (*pl* **statesmen**) estadista *m*, hombre *m* de Estado

statesman-like ['steɪtsmənlaɪk] *adj* propio(a) de un estadista

statesmanship ['steɪtsmənʃɪp] *n (skill)* habilidad *f* política; *(activity)* arte *m* de gobernar

static ['stætɪk] **1** *adj* estático(a); **s. electricity** electricidad *f* estática

2 *n (on radio, TV)* interferencias *fpl*

station ['steɪʃən] **1** *n* (**a**) *Rail* estación *f* de ferrocarril; *Rel* **the Stations of the Cross** el Viacrucis □ **bus s.** estación *or* terminal *f* de autobuses; **fire s.** cuartel *m* de bomberos; **petrol** *or* **filling** *or US* **gas s.** gasolinera *f*, estación *f* de servicio; **police s.** comisaría *f*; **power s.** central *f*; **radio s.** emisora *f*; **service s.** área *f* de servicio; *Austral* **sheep s.** granja *f* de ovejas; *US Aut* **s. wagon** break *m*, rubia *f*, camioneta *f*; **weather s.** estación *f* meteorológica (**b**) *(post, position)* puesto *m*, lugar *m*; *Mil* **action stations!** ¡zafarrancho de combate! □ *US* **s. house** *(of police)* comisaría *f* (**c**) *(social standing)* rango *m*; **to have ideas above one's s.** dárselas de importante

2 *vt (place)* colocar; *Mil (troops)* apostar, estacionar

stationary ['steɪʃənrɪ] *adj (not moving)* inmóvil, parado(a); *(unchanging)* estacionario(a), fijo(a)

stationer ['steɪʃənər] *n* papelero(a) *m,f*; **s.'s (shop)** papelería *f*

stationery ['steɪsənrɪ] *n (paper)* papel *m* de escribir; *(pens, ink, etc)* artículos *mpl* de escritorio

stationmaster ['steɪʃənmɑːstər] *n Rail* jefe *m* de estación

statistic [stəˈtɪstɪk] *n* estadística *f*

statistical [stəˈtɪstɪkəl] *adj* estadístico(a)

statistician [stætɪˈstɪʃən] *n* estadístico(a) *m,f*

statistics [stəˈtɪstɪks] *npl (science)* estadística *f sing*; *(data)* estadísticas *fpl*

statue ['stætjuː] *n* estatua *f*

statuesque [stætjʊˈesk] *adj* escultural

statuette [stætjʊˈet] *n* figurilla *f*

stature ['stætʃər] *n (size)* estatura *f*, talla *f*; *Fig* estatus *m*, rango *m*, categoría *f*

status ['steɪtəs] *n* estado *m*, condición *f* □ **legal s.** validez *f*; **marital s.** estado *m* civil; **social s.** posición *f* social, estatus *m*; **s. symbol** signo *m* de prestigio; **s. quo** status quo *m*

statute ['stætjuːt] n estatuto m, decreto m, ley f; **in accordance with the statutes** según los estatutos ❑ **s. book** código m de leyes

statutory ['stætjʊtərɪ] adj (gen) reglamentario(a); (offence) establecido(a) por la ley; (right) legal; (holiday) oficial

staunch¹ [stɔːntʃ] adj fiel, leal; **s. supporter** partidario acérrimo

staunch² [stɔːntʃ] vt (blood) restañar

stave [steɪv] **1** n (a) (of barrel) duela f (b) Mus pentagrama m **2** vt (pt & pp **stove**) desfondar (**in** -)

stave off vt (pt & pp **staved off**) (repel) (attack, crisis) rechazar; (avoid) evitar; (delay) aplazar, diferir

staves [steɪvz] npl see **staff**

stay¹ [steɪ] **1** n Esp Méx estancia f, Am estadía f; **a three-week s.** una Esp Méx estancia or Am estadía de tres semanas; Jur **s. of execution** aplazamiento m de sentencia **2** vi (a) (remain) quedarse, permanecer; **if it stays sunny** si el tiempo sigue soleado; **s. away from the river** no te acerques al río; (**it's here to s.** ya forma parte de nuestras vidas; **to s. at home** quedarse en casa; **why don't you s. to dinner?** ¿por qué no te quedas a cenar?; **you s. out of this!** ¡tú no te metas en esto! (**b**) (reside temporarily) alojarse, hospedarse; **she's staying with us for a few days** ha venido a pasar unos días con nosotros (**c**) (resist) **staying power** resistencia f, aguante m **3** vt resistir; **to s. the course** terminar la carrera; Fig aguantar hasta el final

stay in vi quedarse en casa, no salir

stay on vi quedarse, permanecer

stay out vi quedarse fuera; **to s. out all night** no volver a casa en toda la noche; **the strikers have decided to s. out** los huelguistas han decidido no volver al trabajo

stay up vi no acostarse; **to s. up late** acostarse tarde

stay² [steɪ] n Naut (guy rope) estay m, viento m

stay³ [steɪ] n (a) (Archit (prop) sostén m, soporte m (**b**) (in corset) ballena f

stay-at-home ['steɪəthəʊm] **1** adj casero(a), hogareño(a) **2** n persona f casera or hogareña

stayer ['steɪər] n Sport caballo m or yegua f de fondo; Fig persona f de mucha resistencia

stead [sted] n in sb's s. en lugar de algn; **to stand sb in good s.** resultar muy útil a algn

steadfast ['stedfəst, 'stedfɑːst] adj firme, resuelto(a)

steadfastness ['stedfəstnɪs] n firmeza f, resolución f

steadily ['stedɪlɪ] adv (grow, improve) constantemente; (walk) con paso seguro, decididamente; (gaze) fijamente; (rain, work) sin parar; **the situation is getting s. worse** la situación se vuelve cada vez peor

steadiness ['stedɪnɪs] n (of gait, hand) firmeza f; (of prices) estabilidad f; (of demand) constancia f; (of character) formalidad f

steady ['stedɪ] **1** adj (**steadier, steadiest**) (gen) firme, seguro(a); (gaze) fijo(a); (table) estable, equilibrado(a); (prices) estable; (demand, speed) constante; (heartbeat, pace) regular; (worker, student) aplicado(a); **she is making s. progress** hace progresos continuos; **s. downpour** lluvia continua; **s. boyfriend** novio; **s. job** empleo fijo **2** adv **s. (on)!** ¡despacio!, ¡quieto!; Fam **go s. on the brandy** cuidado con el coñac; Fam **they're going s.** son novios **3** n Fam novio(a) m,f **4** vt (table etc) estabilizar, equilibrar; (nervous person) calmar, tranquilizar; **this herb tea will s. your nerves** esta infusión de hierbas te calmará los nervios **5** vi (market, prices) estabilizarse

steak [steɪk] n (beef) filete m, bistec m, RP bife m; (of fish) filete m ❑ **rump s.** filete m de cadera; **s. and kidney pie** empanada f de carne con riñones; **s. house** parrilla f, RP churrasquería f; **stewing s.** carne f de vaca or Am res para estofar

steal [stiːl] (pt **stole**; pp **stolen**) **1** vt robar, hurtar; **to s. a glance at sth** echar una mirada furtiva a algo; **to s. a kiss** robar un beso; **to s. a march on sb** anticiparse a algn; **to s. the show** acaparar la atención de todos, llevarse todos los aplausos **2** vi (a) (rob) robar, hurtar; **children often s.** los niños roban a menudo (**b**) (move quietly) moverse con sigilo; **to s. away** escabullirse, marcharse a hurtadillas; **to s. into a room** colarse en una habitación; **to s. up on sb** acercarse sigilosamente a algn, sorprender a algn

stealing ['stiːlɪŋ] n robo m

stealth [stelθ] n cautela f, sigilo m ❑ **s. bomber** avión m or bombardero m invisible

stealthily ['stelθɪlɪ] adv a hurtadillas, furtivamente

stealthy ['stelθɪ] adj (**stealthier, stealthiest**) sigiloso(a), furtivo(a)

steam [stiːm] **1** n vapor m; Naut **full s. ahead!** ¡avante toda!; **to get up s.** dar presión; Fam **to let off s.** desfogarse, desahogarse; Fam **to run out of s.** quedar agotado(a), quemarse; Fam **under one's own s.** por sus propios medios ❑ **s. bath** baño m de vapor; **s. engine** máquina f de vapor; **s. iron** plancha f de vapor **2** vt Culin cocer al vapor; **to s. open a letter** abrir una carta al vapor **3** vi (give off steam) echar vapor; (bowl of soup etc) humear; **the ship steamed into port** el buque entró en el puerto echando vapor

steam up vi (window, spectacles) empañarse; Fam **to get steamed up about sth** sulfurarse or enfadarse por algo

steamer ['stiːmər] n (a) Naut vapor m, buque m de vapor (**b**) Culin olla f a vapor

steamroller ['stiːmrəʊlər] **1** n apisonadora f **2** vt Fig forzar; **to s. sb into doing sth** forzar or obligar a algn a hacer algo

steamship ['stiːmʃɪp] n Naut vapor m, buque m de vapor

steamy ['stiːmɪ] adj (**steamier, steamiest**) lleno(a) de vapor

steel [stiːl] **1** n acero m ❑ **stainless s.** acero m inoxidable; Mus **s. band** = conjunto de percusión del Caribe; **s. industry** industria f siderúrgica; **s. mill** fundición f de acero, altos hornos mpl, acería f, acerería f; **s. wool** estropajo m de acero **2** vt Fig endurecer; **to s. one's heart** endurecerse; **to s. oneself to do sth** armarse de valor para hacer algo; **to s. oneself against sth** hacer frente a algo

steelworks ['stiːlwɜːks] npl fundición f sing de acero, acería f sing, acerería f sing

steep¹ [stiːp] adj (hill, slope, climb) empinado(a), escarpado(a), abrupto(a); Fig (price) excesivo(a), exorbitante, desmedido(a); (increase) excesivo(a); Fam **that's a bit s.!** ¡eso es demasiado!

steep² [stiːp] vt (washing) remojar; (comida) poner en remojo; Fig **a city steeped in history** una ciudad empapada de historia

steeple ['stiːpəl] n (spire) aguja f, chapitel m

steeplechase ['stiːpəltʃeɪs] n Sport carrera f de obstáculos

steeplejack ['stiːpəldʒæk] n reparador(a) m,f de chimeneas or torres or campanarios

steer¹ [stɪər] **1** vt (gen) dirigir, guiar; (car) conducir, Am manejar; (ship) gobernar; (conversation etc) llevar **2** vi (car) conducir, Am manejar; **to s. for sth** dirigirse hacia algo; Fig **to s. clear of sth** evitar algo

steer² [stɪər] *n* buey *m*

steering ['stɪərɪŋ] *n Aut* dirección *f* ◻ *Aut* **assisted s.** dirección *f* asistida; *Aut* **s. column** columna *f* or árbol *m* de dirección; *Pol* **s. committee** comité *m* directivo, comisión *f* directiva; *Aut* **s. wheel** volante *m, Andes* timón *m*

stem [stem] **1** *n* (**a**) *(of plant)* tallo *m*; *(of glass)* pie *m*; *(of pipe)* tubo *m*, cañón *m* (**b**) *Ling (of word)* raíz *f*, lema *m*
2 *vi* **to s. from** ser el resultado de, derivarse de
3 *vt (blood)* restañar; *(flood, attack)* contener, detener; **to s. the tide of inflation** poner freno a la inflación

stench [stentʃ] *n* hedor *m*, peste *f*

stencil ['stensəl] **1** *n* (**a**) *(for artwork etc)* plantilla *f* (**b**) *(for typing)* cliché *m*
2 *vt (pt & pp* **stencilled***, US* **stenciled)** estarcir

stenographer [stə'nɒɡrəfər] *n US* taquígrafo(a) *m,f*

stenography [ste'nɒɡrəfɪ] *n* taquigrafía *f*

step [step] **1** *n* (**a**) *(gen)* paso *m*; *(sound)* paso *m*, pisada *f*; **it's quite a s. to the station** hay una buena caminata desde aquí hasta la estación; **s. by s.** paso a paso, poco a poco; **to keep in s.** *(walking)* llevar el paso; *(dancing)* llevar el compás *or* ritmo; *Fig* **to watch one's s.** ir con cuidado (**b**) *(measure)* medida *f*, paso *m*; *(formality)* gestión *f*, trámite *m*; **it was a s. in the right direction** fue un paso acertado; **to take steps to control sth** tomar medidas para controlar algo (**c**) *(stair)* peldaño *m*, escalón *m*; *(of vehicle)* estribo *m* (**d**) **steps** *(outdoor)* escalinata *f*; *(indoor)* escalera *f*; *(in stadium)* gradas *fpl*, graderío *m*, tribunas *fpl*; *(of plane)* escalerilla *f* ◻ *Br* **folding steps, pair of steps** escalera *f* *sing* de tijera (**e**) *US Mus* tono *m*
2 *vi (pt & pp* **stepped)** dar un paso; **s. this way, please** haga el favor de pasar por aquí; **to s. aside** hacerse a un lado, apartarse; **to s. on sb's foot** pisar *or* pisotear el pie a algn; **to s. over sth** pasar por encima de algo; *Fam* **s. on it!** ¡date prisa!, *Am* ¡apúrate!; *US Aut Fam* **s. on the gas!** ¡dale al gas!, ¡pisa a fondo!

step back *vi* **to s. back from a situation** enfocar una situación con más objetividad

step down *vi* renunciar; **to s. down from office** renunciar al cargo

step forward *vi* ofrecerse

step in *vi* intervenir

step out *vi* apretar el paso

step up *vt (production, efforts)* aumentar

stepbrother ['stepbrʌðər] *n* hermanastro *m*, medio hermano *m*

step-by-step ['stepbaɪ'step] *adj (guide, explanation)* paso a paso; *(approach)* progresivo(a), gradual

stepchild ['steptʃaɪld] *n (pl* **stepchildren** ['steptʃɪldrən]) hijastro(a) *m,f*

stepdaughter ['stepdɔːtər] *n* hijastra *f*

stepfather ['stepfɑːðər] *n* padrastro *m*

stepladder ['steplædər] *n* escalera *f* de tijera

stepmother ['stepmʌðər] *n* madrastra *f*

step-parent ['steppeərənt] *n (man)* padrastro *m*; *(woman)* madrastra *f*; **step-parents** padrastros *mpl*

steppe [step] *n Geog* estepa *f*

stepping-stone ['stepɪŋstəʊn] *n* pasadera *f*; *Fig* trampolín *m*

stepsister ['stepsɪstər] *n* hermanastra *f*, media hermana *f*

stepson ['stepsʌn] *n* hijastro *m*

stereo ['sterɪəʊ] **1** *n (pl* **stereos)** *(system)* equipo *m* estereofónico; *(sound)* estéreo *m*; **in s.** en estéreo
2 *adj* estereofónico(a)

stereophonic [sterɪə'fɒnɪk] *adj* estereofónico(a)

stereotype ['sterɪətaɪp] *n* estereotipo *m*

stereotyped ['sterɪətaɪpt] *adj* estereotipado(a)

stereotypical [sterɪə'tɪpɪkəl] *adj* estereotipado(a)

sterile ['steraɪl] *adj* (**a**) *(barren)* estéril (**b**) *(germ-free)* esterilizado(a)

sterility [ste'rɪlɪtɪ] *n* esterilidad *f*

sterilization [sterɪlaɪ'zeɪʃən] *n* esterilización *f*

sterilize ['sterɪlaɪz] *vt* esterilizar

sterilizer ['sterɪlaɪzər] *n* esterilizador *m*

sterling ['stɜːlɪŋ] **1** *n* la libra esterlina ◻ **s. silver** plata *f* de ley; **the pound s.** la libra esterlina
2 *adj (person, quality)* excelente, de buena calidad

stern¹ [stɜːn] *adj (severe)* severo(a), austero(a); *(hard)* duro(a); **s. resolve** resolución firme

stern² [stɜːn] *n Naut* popa *f*

sternum ['stɜːnəm] *n (pl* **sternums** *or* **sterna** ['stɜːnə]) *Anat* esternón *m*

steroid ['sterɔɪd] *n* esteroide *m*

stethoscope ['steθəskəʊp] *n Med* estetoscopio *m*

stetson ['stetsən] *n* sombrero *m* tejano

stevedore ['stiːvɪdɔːr] *n* estibador *m*

stew [stjuː] **1** *n Culin* guisado *m*, estofado *m*, cocido *m*; *Fig* **to be in a s.** estar hecho(a) un lío
2 *vt (meat)* guisar, estofar; *(fruit)* cocer, hacer una compota de; **stewed apple** manzana en compota; *Fam* **I let her s. in her own juice before helping her to sort it out** la dejé sufrir un poco antes de acudir en su ayuda

steward ['stjʊəd] *n (on estate)* administrador *m*; *(on ship)* camarero *m*; *(on plane)* auxiliar *m* de vuelo; *(butler)* mayordomo *m* ◻ *Ind* **shop s.** enlace *mf* sindical

stewardess ['stjʊədɪs] *n (on ship)* camarera *f*; *(on plane)* azafata *f, Am* aeromoza *f*;

stewed [stjuːd] *adj* **this tea is s.** este té ha reposado demasiado; **s. beef** carne *f* de vaca guisada; **s. fruit** compota *f*

Sth *(abbr* **South)** Sur, S

stick¹ [stɪk] *n* (**a**) *(piece of wood)* trozo *m* de madera, madera *f*; *(twig)* ramita *f*; *(for hitting)* palo *m*; *(walking stick)* bastón *m*; *(for plants)* rodrigón *m*, tutor *m*; *Mus (conductor's baton)* batuta *f*; *(of rhubarb)* tallo *m*; *(of celery)* rama *f*; *(of dynamite)* cartucho *m*; *Pol Fig* **s. policy** política del palo y tente tieso; *Fig* **to be in a cleft s.** estar entre la espada y la pared; *Fig* **to get hold of the wrong end of the s.** coger el rábano por las hojas ◻ *Ent* **s. insect** fasmo *m*, insecto *m* palo (**b**) **sticks** *(for fire)* astillas *fpl*, leña *f* sing; *Fam* **a few s. of furniture** unos cuantos muebles; *Fam* **to live in the s.** vivir en el quinto infierno *or Esp* pino (**c**) *Br Fam (criticism)* **to give sb s. for sth** poner verde a algn por algo (**d**) *US Aut* **s. shift** *(system)* palanca *f* de cambio manual

stick² [stɪk] **1** *vt (pt & pp* **stuck)** (**a**) *(push)* meter; *(knife, bayonet)* clavar, hincar; **I've stuck the needle in my finger** me he pinchado el dedo con la aguja; **he stuck his head out of the window** asomó la cabeza por la ventana (**b**) *Fam (put)* poner, meter; *(place)* colocar; *Fam* **she's always sticking her nose into other people's business** siempre anda metiendo la nariz en asuntos ajenos; *Fam* **s. it in your pocket** métetelo en el bolsillo; *Fam* **to get stuck into sth** meterse de lleno *or* de cabeza en algo; *Fam* **she's stuck at home all day** está metida en casa todo el día (**c**) *(attach with glue etc)* pegar; **to s. photos in an album** pegar fotos en un álbum (**d**) *Fam (tolerate)* soportar, aguantar; **I can't s. her** no la puedo tragar
2 *vi* (**a**) *(fix, become attached)* pegarse; **the rice has stuck to the pan** el arroz se ha quedado pegado a la cacerola; **these labels don't s. very well** estas etiquetas no pegan muy bien; **they can't make the charges s.** no pueden acusarle de nada (**b**) *(become fixed) (window, drawer)* estar

atrancado(a), atrancarse; *(machine part)* encasquillarse; *(car in mud)* estar atascado(a), atascarse; **the phrase stuck in my mind** la frase se me quedó grabada en la memoria

stick around *vi Fam* quedarse

stick at *vt* (a) *(persevere with)* perseverar en, seguir con (b) *Fam (stop)* **he will s. at nothing to get his own way** no se para en barras *or* ante nada para salirse con la suya

stick by *vt (friend)* apoyar, ser fiel a; *(promise)* cumplir con

stick out 1 *vi* (a) *(project, protrude)* salir, sobresalir; *(be noticeable)* resaltar, destacarse (b) *(be very obvious)* ser obvio(a) *or* evidente; *Fam* **it sticks out a mile** *or* **like a sore thumb** se ve a la legua
2 *vt* (a) *(tongue, hand)* sacar; *Fig* **to s. one's neck out** jugarse el tipo (b) *(difficult situation)* aguantar hasta el final

stick out for *vt* empeñarse en conseguir

stick to *vt (principles)* atenerse a; *(promise)* cumplir con; *(plans)* seguir con; **to s. to one's guns** mantenerse en sus trece

stick together *vi* mantenerse unidos, no separarse

stick up 1 *vi (project, protrude)* salir, sobresalir; *(hair)* ponerse de punta, erizarse
2 *vt* (a) *(poster)* fijar (b) *(raise) (hand etc)* levantar; *Fam* **s. 'em up!** ¡arriba las manos! (c) *US Fam (rob) (bank etc)* atracar

stick up for *vt (person, rights)* defender

stick with *vt (activity, idea)* seguir con

sticker ['stɪkər] *n* (a) *(label)* etiqueta *f* adhesiva; *(with slogan, for charity, etc)* pegatina *f* (b) *Fam (determined person)* persona *f* tenaz

stickiness ['stɪkɪnɪs] *n* pegajosidad *f*, lo pegajoso; *Fam (of situation)* dificultad *f*

sticking-plaster ['stɪkɪŋ'plɑːstər] *n Br (to cover wound) Esp* tirita® *f, Am* curita *m or f; (to keep bandage in place)* esparadrapo *m*

sticking-point ['stɪkɪŋ'pɔɪnt] *n* escollo *m*

stick-in-the-mud ['stɪkɪnðəmʌd] *n Fam* persona *f* chapada a la antigua, carroza *mf*

stickleback ['stɪkəlbæk] *n (fish)* espinoso *m*, espinosillo *m*

stickler ['stɪklər] *n* persona *f* quisquillosa; **to be a s. for detail** ser muy detallista, dar mucha importancia a los detalles

stick-on ['stɪkɒn] *adj* adhesivo(a)

stick-up ['stɪkʌp] *n US Fam* atraco *m*, asalto *m*, robo *m* a mano armada

sticky ['stɪkɪ] *adj* (**stickier, stickiest**) *(gen)* pegajoso(a); *(label)* engomado(a); *(weather)* bochornoso(a); *Fam (situation)* difícil, violento(a); *Br Fam* **to be on a s. wicket** estar en un aprieto; *Fam* **to come to a s. end** acabar mal; *Fam* **to have s. fingers** tener los dedos largos

stiff [stɪf] **1** *adj* (a) *(gen)* rígido(a), tieso(a); *(card, collar, lock)* duro(a); *(paste)* espeso(a); *(joint)* entumecido(a); *(machine part)* encasquillado(a), atascado(a); **to feel s.** tener agujetas; **to have a s. neck** tener tortícolis; *Fig* **to be as s. as a board** estar más tieso(a) que un palo *or* una tabla (b) *Fig (climb, test)* difícil, duro(a); *(breeze)* fuerte; *(punishment, sentence)* severo(a); *(resistance)* tenaz; *(price)* excesivo(a); *(drink)* fuerte, cargado(a); *(person, manner) (unnatural)* estirado(a); *(unyielding)* inflexible; *Fig* **to keep a s. upper lip** poner a mal tiempo buena cara; *Fam* **that's a bit s.!** ¡eso es demasiado!
2 *adv Fam* **to be bored s.** aburrirse como una ostra; *Fam* **to be scared s.** estar muerto(a) de miedo
3 *n US Fam (corpse)* fiambre *m*

stiffen ['stɪfən] **1** *vt (card, fabric)* reforzar; *(collar)* almi-

donar; *(paste)* endurecer; *Fig (resistance, morale)* fortalecer
2 *vi (person)* ponerse rígido(a) *or* tieso(a); *(joints)* entumecerse; *Fig (resistance, morale)* fortalecerse

stiffly ['stɪflɪ] *adv (move, turn)* rígidamente; *(smile, greet, bow)* fríamente, con frialdad

stiff-necked [stɪf'nekt] *adj (stubborn)* terco(a), testarudo(a)

stiffness ['stɪfnɪs] *n* rigidez *f*

stifle ['staɪfəl] **1** *vt (gen)* ahogar, sofocar; *(rebellion, opposition)* reprimir, sofocar; *(sound)* amortiguar, sofocar; *(yawn)* reprimir
2 *vi* ahogarse, sofocarse

stifling ['staɪflɪŋ] *adj* sofocante, agobiante

stigma ['stɪgmə] *n* estigma *m*

stigmatize ['stɪgmətaɪz] *vt* estigmatizar

stile [staɪl] *n* = escalones para pasar por encima de una valla

stiletto [stɪ'letəʊ] *n (pl* **stilettos**) *(dagger)* estilete *m; (shoe)* zapato *m* de tacón *or Am* taco de aguja ❑ **s. heel** tacón *m or Am* taco *m* de aguja

still¹ [stɪl] **1** *adv* (a) *(up to this time)* todavía, aún; **I can s. remember it** todavía lo recuerdo, aún lo recuerdo; **they're s. discussing the weather** siguen hablando del tiempo (b) *(with comp adj & adv) (even)* aún; **s. colder** aún más frío(a), más frío(a) todavía (c) *(nonetheless)* de todas formas, aún así; **he is s. your son** a pesar de todo, sigue siendo tu hijo (d) *(however)* sin embargo; **s., there's nothing we can do** en fin, nada podemos hacer (e) *(motionless)* **keep s.!** ¡estáte quieto!; **to stand s.** no moverse
2 *adj (quiet, calm)* tranquilo(a); *(peaceful)* sosegado(a); *(silent)* silencioso(a); *(motionless)* quieto(a), inmóvil; *(wine)* no espumoso(a); *(orange juice)* sin gas; *Prov* **s. waters run deep** del agua mansa me guarde Dios, (que de la brava me guardaré yo)
3 *n* (a) *Literary* tranquilidad *f*, silencio *m* (b) *Cin* vista *f* fija, fotograma *m* ❑ *Art* **s. life** bodegón *m*, naturaleza *f* muerta
4 *vt (fears etc)* calmar, acallar

still² [stɪl] *n (apparatus)* alambique *m; (place)* destilería *f*

stillbirth ['stɪlbɜːθ] *n* mortinato(a) *m,f*

stillborn ['stɪlbɔːn] *adj* mortinato(a), nacido(a) muerto(a)

stillness ['stɪlnɪs] *n* calma *f*, quietud *f*, tranquilidad *f; (silence)* silencio *m*

stilt [stɪlt] *n* zanco *m*

stilted ['stɪltɪd] *adj* afectado(a)

stimulant ['stɪmjʊlənt] *n* estimulante *m*

stimulate ['stɪmjʊleɪt] *vt* estimular; **to s. sb to do sth** animar *or* alentar a algn para que haga algo

stimulating ['stɪmjʊleɪtɪŋ] *adj* estimulante

stimulation [stɪmjʊ'leɪʃən] *n (stimulus)* estímulo *m; (act)* estimulación *f; (state)* excitación *f*

stimulus ['stɪmjʊləs] *n (pl* **stimuli** ['stɪmjʊlaɪ]) estímulo *m; Fig* incentivo *m*

sting [stɪŋ] **1** *n (of bee, wasp) (organ)* aguijón *m; (wound)* picadura *f; (burning sensation)* escozor *m*, picazón *m; Fig (of remorse)* punzada *f; Fig (of remark)* sarcasmo *m; Fig* **the proposal had a s. in its tail** la propuesta traía cola; *Fig* **to take the s. out of sth** quitar el hierro a algo
2 *vt (pt & pp* **stung**) *(insect, nettle)* picar; *Fig (conscience)* remorder; *Fig (remark)* herir en lo vivo *or* lo más hondo; *Fam (overcharge etc)* **they stung him for $10** le clavaron 10 dólares
3 *vi* picar

stinginess ['stɪndʒɪnɪs] *n* tacañería *f*

stinging ['stɪŋɪŋ] *adj (pain)* punzante; *(remark, criticism)* hiriente, despiadado(a); **s. nettle** ortiga *f*

stingray ['stɪŋreɪ] n pastinaca f (pez)

stingy ['stɪndʒɪ] adj (**stingier, stingiest**) (person) taca-ño(a), roñoso(a); (amount, meal) escaso(a); **to be s. with food** escatimar la comida

stink [stɪŋk] **1** n peste f, hedor m; Fam **to kick up a s. about sth** armar un escándalo por algo ❑ **s. bomb** bomba f fétida

2 vi (pt stank; pp stunk) apestar, heder (**of** a); **he stinks of garlic** apesta a ajo; Fam **to s. to high heaven** oler a rayos; Fam Fig **the whole idea stinks to me** a mí me parece una pésima idea

stinker ['stɪŋkər] n Fam (person) canalla mf; (difficult task) **this problem is a real s.** este problema es un verdadero quebradero de cabeza

stinking ['stɪŋkɪŋ] **1** adj (smelly) apestoso(a); (unpleasant) asqueroso(a); Fam **to have a s. cold** tener un catarro asqueroso

2 adv Fam **he's s. rich** está podrido de dinero, Méx tiene un chorro de lana

stint [stɪnt] **1** n (period of work etc) período m, temporada f; (shift) turno m, tanda f; **he did a two-year s. in the navy** sirvió durante dos anos en la Marina

2 vt escatimar; **don't s. on the cheese!** ¡no escatimes el queso!; **to s. oneself** privarse (**of** de)

stipend ['staɪpend] n estipendio m, remuneración f, salario m

stipple ['stɪpəl] vt puntear

stipulate ['stɪpjʊleɪt] vt estipular

stipulation [stɪpjʊ'leɪʃən] n estipulación f, condición f

stir [stɜːr] **1** n (**a**) (action) **to give sth a s.** remover algo (**b**) (excitement) **it caused a great s.** causó un gran revuelo

2 vt (pt & pp stirred) (**a**) (liquid, mixture) remover, revolver (**b**) (move) mover, agitar; **the wind stirred the leaves** el viento movía las hojas (**c**) Fig (curiosity, interest) despertar, excitar; (anger) provocar; (imagination) avivar, estimular; **to s. sb to do sth** incitar a algn a hacer algo; Fam **come on, s. yourself!** ¡anda, muévete!, ¡mueve el trasero!

3 vi (move) moverse; **she didn't s. from her seat** no dejó su asiento ni un momento

stir up vt (**a**) (dust, mud, etc) remover (**b**) Fig (memories, curiosity) despertar; (passions) excitar; (anger) provocar; (revolt) fomentar; **to s. up trouble** provocar un escán-dalo; Fam **she's always trying to s. things up** siempre anda con ganas de liar las cosas

stir-fry ['stɜːfraɪ] Culin **1** n = salteado de (carne y) verduras típico de la cocina china

2 vt saltear, rehogar a fuego vivo

stirrer ['stɜːrər] n Fam liante mf

stirring ['stɜːrɪŋ] adj conmovedor(a)

stirrup ['stɪrəp] n estribo m

stitch [stɪtʃ] **1** n (**a**) Sew puntada f; Knit punto m; Med punto m de sutura; Fam **he hadn't a s. on** estaba en cueros or en pelotas; Fam **we were in stitches** nos tronchábamos de risa; Prov **a s. in time saves nine** un remiendo a tiempo ahorra ciento (**b**) (sharp pain) punzada f

2 vt Sew coser (**on** a); Med suturar

stoat [stəʊt] n Zool armiño m

stock [stɒk] **1** n (**a**) (supply) reserva f, Com (goods) existencias fpl, stock m; (selection) surtido m; **surplus s.** excedentes mpl; **it's out of s.** está agotado(a); **to have sth in s.** tener existencias de algo, tener algo en stock; Fig **to take s. of the situation** evaluar la situación (**b**) Fin (company's capital) capital m social; **stocks and shares** acciones fpl, valores mpl ❑ **Government s.** papel m del Estado; **S. Exchange** Bolsa f de valores; **s. market** bolsa f, mercado m bursátil; **s. options** opciones fpl sobre acciones (**c**) Agr (livestock) ganado m ❑ **s. farming** ganadería f (**d**)

Culin caldo m ❑ **s. cube** cubito m or pastilla f de caldo (**e**) (descent, family) linaje m, estirpe f; **to be of good s.** ser de buena cepa or familia (**f**) Bot alhelí m

2 adj (**a**) (goods, size) corriente, normal, de serie (**b**) (argument, excuse, response) de siempre; (greeting, speech) consabido(a); (phrase, theme) trillado(a), gastado(a), muy visto(a)

3 vt (**a**) (shop) (have in stock) tener existencias de, tener en el almacén; **we don't s. wine** no tenemos or no tocamos vino (**b**) (shop, library) (provide) abastecer, surtir (**with** de); (cupboard) (fill up) llenar (**with** de); (river, pond) repoblar, poblar (**with** de)

stock up vi abastecerse (**on, with** de)

stockade [stɒ'keɪd] n empalizada f, estacada f

stockbreeder ['stɒkbriːdər] n ganadero(a) m,f

stockbreeding ['stɒkbriːdɪŋ] n ganadería f, cría f de ganado

stockbroker ['stɒkbrəʊkər] n corredor(a) m,f de Bolsa, bolsista mf

stockholder ['stɒkhəʊldər] n US accionista mf

Stockholm ['stɒkhəʊm] n Estocolmo

stocking ['stɒkɪŋ] n media f; **a pair of stockings** unas medias, un par de medias ❑ **body s.** malla f; Knit **s. stitch** punto m de media

stockist ['stɒkɪst] n almacenista mf, proveedor(a) m,f, distribuidor(a) m,f

stockpile ['stɒkpaɪl] **1** n reservas fpl

2 vt (gen) almacenar; (accumulate) acumular

stockpot ['stɒkpɒt] n olla f, marmita f

stockroom ['stɒkruːm] n almacén m, depósito m

stocks [stɒks] npl (**a**) Hist (as punishment) cepo m sing (**b**) Naut grada f sing de construcción, astillero m sing; **to be on the stocks** estar en construcción or astilleros

stock-still [stɒk'stɪl] adv immovil

stocktaking ['stɒkteɪkɪŋ] n Com inventario m, balance m

stocky ['stɒkɪ] adj (**stockier, stockiest**) (squat) chapa-rro(a); (heavily built) robusto(a), fornido(a)

stockyard ['stɒkjɑːd] n Agr corral m de ganado

stodge [stɒdʒ] n Fam comida f indigesta, mazacote m

stodgy ['stɒdʒɪ] adj (**stodgier, stodgiest**) (food) indiges-to(a); Fig (book, person) pesado(a)

stoic ['stəʊɪk] n estoico(a) m,f

stoical ['stəʊɪkəl] adj estoico(a)

stoicism ['stəʊɪsɪzəm] n estoicismo m

stoke [stəʊk] vt (**a**) (poke) atizar, avivar (**b**) **to s. (up)** (feed) alimentar

stoker ['stəʊkər] n Naut fogonero m

stole[1] [stəʊl] pt see steal

stole[2] [stəʊl] n estola f

stolen ['stəʊlən] pp see steal

stolid ['stɒlɪd] adj imperturbable, impasible

stomach ['stʌmək] **1** n Anat estómago m; **on an empty s.** en ayunas; Fig **it turns my s.** me revuelve el estómago ❑ **s. ache** dolor m de estómago; Med **s. pump** bomba f estomacal; **s. upset** trastorno m gástrico

2 vt Fig aguantar, soportar, tragar

stomp [stɒmp] vi **to s. about** pisar muy fuerte

stone [stəʊn] **1** n (**a**) (material, piece of rock) piedra f; (on grave) lápida f; Fig **at a s.'s throw** a tiro de piedra; Fig **to leave no s. unturned** no dejar piedra por mover, revolver Roma con Santiago (**b**) Med cálculo m, piedra f (**c**) (of fruit) hueso m, RP carozo m (**d**) (weight) = 6.348 kg; **she weighs 9 s.** pesa 57 kilos

2 adj de piedra, pétreo(a); **the S. Age** la Edad de Piedra

3 *vt* (**a**) *(person)* apedrear (**b**) *(fruit)* deshuesar

stone-cold [stəʊnˈkəʊld] *adj* helado(a)

stoned [stəʊnd] *adj Slang (drugged)* colocado(a), flipado(a), puesto(a); *(drunk)* trompa

stone-dead [stəʊnˈded] *adj Fam* tieso(a), muerto(a)

stone-deaf [stəʊnˈdef] *adj* sordo(a) como una tapia

stonemason [ˈstəʊnmeɪsən] *n* albañil *m*

stonewall [stəʊnˈwɔːl] *vi (gen)* andarse con evasivas; *Sport* jugar a la defensiva; *Parl* practicar el obstruccionismo

stoneware [ˈstəʊnweər] *n* (cerámica *f* de) gres *m*

stonework [ˈstəʊnwɜːk] *n* mampostería *f*

stony [ˈstəʊnɪ] *adj* (**stonier**, **stoniest**) *(ground, beach)* pedregoso(a); *Fig (look, silence)* frío(a), glacial; *Fig* **s. heart** corazón de piedra

stony-broke [stəʊnɪˈbrəʊk] *adj Fam* **to be s.-b.** estar sin blanca

stony-faced [ˈstəʊnɪˈfeɪst] *adj* impertérrito(a), impasible

stood [stʊd] *pt & pp see* **stand**

stooge [stuːdʒ] *n Theat* comparsa *mf*; *Fam* títere *m*, pelele *m*

stool [stuːl] *n* (**a**) *(seat)* taburete *m*, banqueta *f*, banquillo *m*; *Fig* **to fall between two stools** quedarse entre dos aguas ❏ *Fam* **s. pigeon** chivato(a) *m,f*, soplón(ona) *m,f* (**b**) *Med (faeces)* deposición *f*, heces *fpl*

stoop [stuːp] **1** *n* espaldas *fpl* encorvadas; **to walk with a s.** andar encorvado(a)
2 *vi* (**a**) *(have a stoop)* andar encorvado(a), ser cargado(a) de espaldas (**b**) *(bend)* **to s. (down)** inclinarse, agacharse (**c**) *Fig* **to s.** rebajarse a; **to s. to sth/to doing sth** rebajarse a algo/a hacer algo; **he wouldn't s. so low** a ese punto no llegaría

stop [stɒp] **1** *n* (**a**) *(halt)* parada *f*, alto *m*; **to come to a s.** pararse, hacer un alto; **to put a s. to sth** poner fin *or* término a algo ❏ *Aut* **s. sign** stop *m* (**b**) *(break)* pausa *f*, descanso *m*; *Av (for refuelling etc)* escala *f*; *(overnight stay)* estancia *f* (**c**) *(stopping place) (for bus, tram)* parada *f* ❏ **request s.** parada *f* discrecional (**d**) *(punctuation mark)* punto *m*; *(in telegram)* stop *m* (**e**) *Mus (on organ)* registro *m*; *Fig* **to pull out all the stops** tocar todos los registros
2 *vt* (*pt & pp* **stopped**) (**a**) *(gen)* parar; *(moving vehicle)* parar, detener; *(production)* parar, paralizar; *(gas, water supply)* cortar; *(conversation)* interrumpir; *(pain, abuse, etc)* poner fin *or* término a, acabar con; **s. thief!** ¡al ladrón!; *Fam* **he stopped a bullet** recibió un balazo (**b**) *(suspend) (payments, holidays)* suspender; *(cheque)* anular, cancelar, invalidar; **they stopped $20 from his wages** le retuvieron 20 dólares del sueldo (**c**) *(prevent)* evitar; **she stopped smoking** dejó de fumar; **s. it!** ¡basta ya! (**d**) *(prevent)* evitar; **to s. sb from doing sth** impedir a algn hacer algo; **to s. sth from happening** evitar que algo ocurra; **what's stopping you?** ¿por qué no lo haces?, ¿qué te retiene? (**e**) *(block) (hole, gap)* tapar, taponar; *(tooth)* empastar; *(flow of blood)* restañar
3 *vi* (**a**) *(person, moving vehicle)* pararse, detenerse; **he stopped to clean his shoe** se detuvo para limpiarse el zapato; **my watch has stopped** se me ha parado el reloj; **s.!** ¡pare!, ¡alto!; **to s. at nothing to do sth** no pararse en barras para hacer algo, no tener miramientos para hacer algo; **to s. dead** *or* **short** pararse en seco (**b**) *(cease)* acabarse, terminar; **the rain has stopped** ha dejado de llover; **without stopping** sin parar, sin cesar (**c**) *Fam (stay)* quedarse; **he's stopping at his aunt's** se aloja en casa de su tía; **why don't you s. for dinner?** ¿por qué no te quedas a cenar?

stop by *vi Fam* visitar; **I'll s. by this evening** pasaré esta tarde

stop in *vi Br Fam* quedarse en casa, no salir

stop off *vi* pararse un rato; **we stopped off in Rome on our way home** pasamos por Roma en el viaje de casa

stop over *vi* (**a**) *Av (for refuelling etc)* hacer escala (**b**) *Br (spend the night)* pasar la noche

stop up 1 *vt (block up) (hole)* tapar, taponar
2 *vi Br (stay up)* quedarse levantado(a)

stopcock [ˈstɒpkɒk] *n* llave *f* de paso

stopgap [ˈstɒpgæp] *n (thing)* recurso *m*, medida *f* provisional; *(person)* sustituto(a) *m,f*

stoplight [ˈstɒplaɪt] *n US Aut* semáforo *m*

stopover [ˈstɒpəʊvər] *n (gen)* parada *f*; *Av* escala *f*

stoppage [ˈstɒpɪdʒ] *n* (**a**) *(of game)* suspensión *f*; *(of work)* paro *m*, suspensión *f*; *(strike)* huelga *f*; *(of payments, leave)* suspensión *f*; *(deduction)* deducción *f* (**b**) *(blockage) (of pipe etc)* obstrucción *f*

stopper [ˈstɒpər] *n* tapón *m*

stop-press [stɒpˈpres] *n Press* **s. (news)** noticias *fpl* de última hora

stopwatch [ˈstɒpwɒtʃ] *n* cronómetro *m*

storage [ˈstɔːrɪdʒ] *n* almacenaje *m*, almacenamiento *m*; **to put sth into s.** poner algo en almacén *or* en depósito ❏ **s. battery** acumulador *m*; **s. charges** (gastos *mpl* de) almacenaje *m*; **s. heater** placa *f* acumuladora; **s. space** sitio *m* para guardar los trastos; **s. unit** armario *m*

store [stɔːr] **1** *n* (**a**) *(stock)* provisión *f*, reserva *f*; *Fig (of wisdom, knowledge)* reserva *f*; **there's a big surprise in s. for them** les espera *or Esp* aguarda una gran sorpresa; **to set great s. by sth** valorar algo mucho (**b**) **stores** *(provisions)* provisiones *fpl*, víveres *mpl*; *Mil* pertrechos *mpl* (**c**) *(warehouse)* almacén *m*, depósito *m* (**d**) *esp US (shop)* tienda *f* ❏ **department s.** grandes almacenes *mpl*, *Am* grandes tiendas *fpl*
2 *vt* (**a**) *(put in storage etc) (furniture, computer data)* almacenar; *(keep)* guardar (**b**) **to s. (up)** *(amass, keep in reserve)* acumular

storehouse [ˈstɔːhaʊs] *n* almacén *m*, depósito *m*; *Fig (of information)* mina *f*

storekeeper [ˈstɔːkiːpər] *n US (shopkeeper)* tendero(a) *m,f*

storeroom [ˈstɔːruːm] *n* despensa *f*

storey [ˈstɔːrɪ] *n* piso *m*; **a ten-s. building** un edificio de 10 pisos; **multi-s. carpark** parking de varios pisos

stork [stɔːk] *n Orn* cigüeña *f*

storm [stɔːm] **1** *n* (**a**) *(thunderstorm)* tormenta *f*; *(at sea)* tempestad *f*, temporal *m*; *(with wind)* borrasca *f*; *Fig (uproar)* escándalo *m*, revuelo *m*; *Fig* **a s. in a teacup** una tempestad en un vaso de agua ❏ **s. cloud** nubarrón *m*; **s. door** doble puerta *f*, contrapuerta *f* (**b**) *Fig (of missiles)* lluvia *f*; *(of insults, protests)* torrente *m*, lluvia *f*; **a s. of applause** una salva de aplausos; *Fig* **she has taken New York by s.** ha cautivado a todo Nueva York; *Mil* **to take a city by s.** tomar una ciudad por asalto ❏ *Mil* **s. troops** tropas *fpl* de asalto
2 *vt Mil* asaltar, tomar por asalto
3 *vi (with rage)* echar pestes, vociferar; **she stormed out** salió echando pestes

stormy [ˈstɔːmɪ] *adj* (**stormier**, **stormiest**) *(weather)* tormentoso(a); *Fig (meeting, discussion)* acalorado(a); *Fig (relationship)* borrascoso(a), de muchos altibajos, tempestuoso(a)

story[1] [ˈstɔːrɪ] *n (gen)* historia *f*; *(tale)* cuento *m*, relato *m*; *(account)* relato *m*, relación *f*; *(in newspaper)* artículo *m*; *(plot)* argumento *m*, trama *f*; *(joke)* chiste *m*; *(rumour)* rumor *m*; *(lie)* mentira *f*, cuento *m*; **but that's another s.** pero eso es otro cantar; **it's a long s.** sería largo de contar; **it's always the same old s.** es la historia de siempre; **so the s. goes** según cuenta la historia; **to cut a long s. short**

en resumidas cuentas, en pocas palabras ❏ **love s.** historia
f de amor; *Lit* **short s.** novela *f* corta; **tall s.** cuento *m*
chino

story² ['stɔːrɪ] *n US see* **storey**

storybook ['stɔːrɪbʊk] *n* libro *m* de cuentos

storyline ['stɔːrɪlaɪn] *n (of book, play, movie)* argumento *m*

storyteller ['stɔːrɪtelər] *n* cuentista *mf*

stout [staʊt] **1** *adj* (a) *(fat) (person)* gordo(a), corpulen-
to(a), robusto(a) (b) *(strong) (shoes, walking stick, etc)* fuerte,
sólido(a) (c) *(brave) (person, resistance)* valiente; *(determined)* firme, resuelto(a); **with a s. heart** valientemente,
resueltamente
  2 *n (beer)* cerveza *f* negra

stout-hearted [staʊt'hɑːtɪd] *adj* valiente, resuelto(a)

stoutly ['staʊtlɪ] *adv* resueltamente

stove¹ [stəʊv] *n* (a) *(for heating)* estufa *f* ❏ **oil s.** estufa *f* de
petróleo (b) *(cooker)* cocina *f*, *Col Méx Ven* estufa *f*

stove² [stəʊv] *pt & pp see* **stave**

stow [stəʊ] *vt* (a) *Naut (cargo)* estibar, arrumar (b) *(put
away)* guardar

stow away *vi (on ship, plane)* viajar de polizón

stowaway ['stəʊəweɪ] *n* polizón *mf*

straddle ['strædəl] *vt* (a) *(horse etc)* sentarse a horcajadas
sobre (b) *(combine, encompass)* abarcar

strafe [streɪf, strɑːf] *vt* bombardear

straggle ['strægəl] *vi* (a) *(lag behind)* rezagarse (b) *(spread
untidily)* desparramarse

straggler ['stræglər] *n* rezagado(a) *m,f*

straggling ['stræglɪŋ] *adj* (a) *(of town, houses)* disperso(a),
esparcido(a) (b) *(of plant)* desparramado(a) (b) *(of hair)*
desordenado(a)

straggly ['stræglɪ] *adj* (**stragglier, straggliest**) desorde-
nado(a)

straight [streɪt] **1** *adj* (a) *(not bent)* recto(a), derecho(a); *(of
line, skirt)* recto(a); *(of hair)* liso(a); **as s. as a die** derecho(a)
como una vela ❏ **s. angle** ángulo *m* recto; *Sew* **s. edge**
recta *f*; **s. face** cara *f* seria; **to keep a s. face** contener la risa
(b) *(successive)* seguido(a); **I work eight hours s.** trabajo
ocho horas seguidas (c) *(honest) (person)* honrado(a), de
confianza; *(answer)* sincero(a), claro(a); *(refusal, rejection)*
categórico(a), rotundo(a); **let's get things s.** hablemos
claro (d) *Theat (part, play)* serio(a) (e) *(alcoholic drink)*
solo(a), sin mezcla (f) *(tidy)* arreglado(a), en orden; **to be
all s.** estar en orden; **to put things s.** poner las cosas en
orden (g) *Slang (conventional)* carca (h) *Slang (heterosexual)*
heterosexual
  2 *adv* (a) *(in a straight line)* en línea recta; **sit up s.!** ¡ponte
derecho!; *Fam (criminal)* **to go s.** dejar el oficio (b) *(directly)*
directamente, derecho; **keep s. ahead** sigue todo recto;
she walked s. in entró sin llamar (c) *(immediately)* en
seguida; **I'll come s. back** en seguida vuelvo; **s. away** en
seguida; **s. off** en el acto, sin pensarlo (d) *(frankly)*
francamente, con franqueza; **tell him s. (out)** díselo sin
rodeos
  3 *n* (a) *(straight line)* línea *f* recta; *Fig* **to keep to the s. and
narrow** ir por el buen camino (b) *Br Sport* recta *f*; **the
home s.** la recta final (c) *Cards* escalera *f*, escalerilla *f*

straightaway [streɪtə'weɪ] *adv* en seguida, inmediatamente, *Méx* ahorita, *Andes RP* al tiro

straighten ['streɪtən] *vt* (a) *(sth bent)* enderezar, poner
derecho(a); *(tie, picture)* poner bien; *(hair)* estirar; **s. your
shoulders** ponte derecho *or* recto (b) **to s. (up)** *(tidy)*
ordenar, arreglar

straighten out **1** *vt (problem)* resolver; *(one's affairs)*
arreglar
  2 *vi* resolverse, arreglarse

straighten up **1** *vt* (a) *(make erect)* enderezar, poner
derecho(a) (b) *(tidy)* ordenar, arreglar
  2 *vi* ponerse derecho(a)

straightforward [streɪt'fɔːwəd] *adj* (a) *(honest)* honra-
do(a); *(sincere)* sincero(a), franco(a) (b) *Br (simple)*
sencillo(a), simple

strain¹ [streɪn] **1** *vt* (a) *(stretch) (rope etc)* estirar, tensar; *Fig*
crear tensiones *or* tirantez en (b) *Med (muscle, back)*
torcer(se); *(eyes, voice)* forzar; *(heart)* cansar; **to s. one's
ears** aguzar el oído (c) *(filter) (liquid)* filtrar; *(vegetables, tea)*
colar, pasar por (un) colador
  2 *vi (pull)* tirar (**at** de); *Fig (strive)* **to s. to do sth** esforzarse
por hacer algo
  3 *n* (a) *(on rope etc)* tensión *f*; *Phys (on metal etc)*
deformación *f* (b) *Fig (gen)* tensión *f*; *(of atmosphere)*
tensión *f*, tirantez *f*; *(effort)* esfuerzo *m*; *(exhaustion)*
agotamiento *m*; **mental s.** tensión nerviosa; **to be under
a lot of s.** estar sometido(a) a muchas tensiones; **it put a
great s. on her** le exigió un gran esfuerzo (c) *Med (on
muscle)* torcedura *f*, torsión *f* (d) *Mus* **strains** son *m sing*,
compás *m sing*

strain² [streɪn] *n* (a) *(race, breed)* raza *f*; *(descent)* linaje *m*,
cepa *f* (b) *(streak)* vena *f*; **a s. of madness** una vena de loco

strained [streɪnd] **1** *pt & pp see* **strain¹**
  2 *adj* (a) *(muscle)* torcido(a); *(eyes)* cansado(a); *(voice,
performance)* forzado(a) (b) *(atmosphere, relationship)*
tenso(a), tirante

strainer ['streɪnər] *n Culin* colador *m*

strait [streɪt] *n* (a) *(gen pl) Geog* estrecho *m*; **the S. of
Gibraltar** el estrecho de Gibraltar (b) *(gen pl) (difficulty)*
aprieto *m*; **in dire** *or* **desperate straits** en un gran aprieto

straitjacket ['streɪtdʒækɪt] *n* camisa *f* de fuerza

strait-laced [streɪt'leɪst] *adj* puritano(a), remilgado(a),
mojigato(a)

strand¹ [strænd] *vt* (a) *Naut (ship)* varar; **to be stranded**
quedar varado(a) *or* encallado(a) (b) *Fig (person)*
abandonar; *(without money, friends, transport)* **to leave
stranded** dejar en la estacada, dejar plantado(a)

strand² [strænd] *n (of thread)* hebra *f*, hilo *m*; *(of rope)*
ramal *m*; *(of hair)* pelo *m*; *(of pearls)* sarta *f*

strange [streɪndʒ] *adj* (a) *(unknown)* desconocido(a);
(unfamiliar) nuevo(a); **s. to the job** nuevo(a) en el oficio
(b) *(odd, bizarre)* raro(a), extraño(a); **she felt a bit s. at first**
al principio se sentía un poco desplazada; **s. to say** aunque
parezca extraño

strangely ['streɪndʒlɪ] *adv* extrañamente, de forma
extraña; **s. enough** aunque parezca extraño

strangeness ['streɪndʒnɪs] *n (oddness)* rareza *f*, extrañeza *f*

stranger ['streɪndʒər] *n (unknown person)* extraño(a) *m,f*,
desconocido(a) *m,f*; *(outsider)* forastero(a) *m,f*

strangle ['stræŋgəl] *vt* estrangular

stranglehold ['stræŋgəlhəʊld] *n* llave *f* al cuello; **to have
a s. on sb** tener a algn por el cuello; *Fig* tener a algn entre la
espada y la pared

strangler ['stræŋglər] *n* estrangulador(a) *m,f*

strangulation [stræŋgjʊ'leɪʃən] *n* estrangulación *f*

strap [stræp] **1** *n (of leather)* correa *f*, tira *f*; *(on shoulder bag)*
bandolera *f*; *(on dress)* tirante *m*, *CSur* bretel *m*; *(as
punishment)* **to give sb the s.** azotar a algn con una correa
  2 *vt (pt & pp* **strapped**) atar *or* sujetar con correa; *(in car,
plane)* **to s. oneself in** ponerse el cinturón de seguridad

straphanger ['stræphæŋər] *n Fam* pasajero(a) *m,f* que va
de pie

strapless ['stræplɪs] *adj* sin tirantes *or* CSur breteles

strapping ['stræpɪŋ] *adj Fam* fornido(a), robusto(a)

Strasbourg ['stræzbɜːg] *n* Estrasburgo

strata ['strɑːtə] *npl see* **stratum**

strategic [strə'tiːdʒɪk] **1** *adj* estratégico(a)
   2 strategics *n Mil* estrategia *f*

strategically [strə'tiːdʒɪklɪ] *adv* estratégicamente

strategist ['strætɪdʒɪst] *n* estratega *mf*

strategy ['strætɪdʒɪ] *n* estrategia *f*

stratification [strætɪfɪ'keɪʃən] *n* estratificación *f*

stratify ['strætɪfaɪ] *vt* (*pt & pp* **stratified**) estratificar

stratosphere ['strætəsfɪər] *n* estratosfera *f*

stratum ['strɑːtəm] *n* (*pl* **stratums** *or* **strata**) *Geol* estrato *m*; *Fig* estrato *m*, nivel *m*

straw [strɔː] *n* (**a**) *Agr* paja *f*; **s. hat** sombrero *m* de paja; *Fig* **to clutch** *or* **grasp at straws** agarrarse a un clavo ardiente; *Fam* **that's the last s.!** ¡eso ya es el colmo!, ¡lo que faltaba para el duro! ❑ **s. man** hombre *m* de paja (**b**) *(for drinking)* paja *f*, pajita *f*, *Méx* popote *m*

strawberry ['strɔːbərɪ] *n* fresa *f*, *CSur* frutilla *f* ❑ **s. jam** mermelada *f* de fresa *or CSur* frutilla; **s. mark** antojo *m*; **s. tree** madroño *m*

straw-coloured, *US* **straw-colored** ['strɔːkʌləd] *adj* pajizo(a), de color de paja

stray [streɪ] **1** *vi (from path etc)* desviarse; *(get lost)* extraviarse, perderse; **to let one's thoughts s.** dejar correr los pensamientos; **to s. from the point** divagar
   2 *n (gen)* animal *m* extraviado
   3 *adj (haphazard)* perdido(a), extraviado(a); *(bullet)* perdido(a); *(animal)* callejero(a)

streak [striːk] **1** *n* (**a**) *(line)* raya *f*, lista *f*; *(in minerals)* veta *f* ❑ **s. of lightning** rayo *m* (**b**) *(in hair)* mecha *f*, mechón *m*, reflejo *m* (**c**) *Fig (of genius, madness)* vena *f*, *Fig (of luck)* racha *f*; **he has a mean s. in him** tiene un lado mezquino
   2 *vt* rayar (**with** de); **his hair is streaked with grey** tiene mechones grises
   3 *vi* (**a**) **to s. past** pasar como un rayo (**b**) *Fam (run naked)* correr desnudo(a) por un lugar público

streaker ['striːkər] *n Fam* persona *f* que corre desnuda por un lugar público

streaky ['striːkɪ] *adj* (**streakier, streakiest**) (**a**) *(hair)* con mechas *or* mechones (**b**) *(bacon)* entreverado(a)

stream [striːm] **1** *n* (**a**) *(brook)* arroyo *m*, riachuelo *m*; *(river)* río *m* (**b**) *(current)* corriente *f*; **to go with/against the s.** ir con la corriente/a contracorriente (**c**) *(of water, air)* flujo *m*; *(of lava, tears)* torrente *m*; *(of blood)* chorro *m*; *(of light)* raudal *m*; *Tech* **to come on s.** entrar en servicio (**d**) *Fig (of abuse, excuses)* torrente *m*, sarta *f*; *(of tourists, immigrants)* oleada *f*; *(of cars, lorries)* desfile *m* continuo, caravana *f* ❑ *Lit* **s. of consciousness** monólogo *m* interior (**e**) *Br Sch* = cada una de las divisiones del alumnado en grupos por niveles de aptitud
   2 *vt* (**a**) *(liquid)* derramar, hacer correr (**b**) *Br Sch* **to s. pupils** dividir en grupos a los alumnos según su capacidad
   3 *vi* (**a**) *(liquid)* correr, manar, chorrear; **her eyes were streaming with tears** lloraba a lágrima viva (**b**) *Fig (people, vehicles)* desfilar; **to s. in/out/past** entrar/salir/pasar a raudales *or* en tropel (**c**) *(wave) (hair, banner)* ondear, flotar

streamer ['striːmər] *n (paper ribbon)* serpentina *f*

streaming ['striːmɪŋ] **1** *adj Fam* **a s. cold** un catarro muy fuerte
   2 *n Br Sch (of pupils)* = sistema de división del alumnado en grupos por niveles de aptitud

streamline ['striːmlaɪn] **1** *n (contour)* línea *f* aerodinámica
   2 *vt* (**a**) *(car)* aerodinamizar (**b**) *(system, method)* racionalizar

street [striːt] *n* calle *f*; **one-way s.** calle de sentido único; *Mil* **s. fighting** combates callejeros; **s. lighting** alumbrado público; **the back streets** las callejuelas; *Fig* los barrios bajos; **the man in the s.** el hombre de la calle; **to be on the streets** estar sin vivienda; **to walk the streets** *(person in gen)* callejear; *(prostitute)* hacer la carrera, trabajar las calles; *Fam* **that's right up my s.** eso es lo mío, *Esp* eso es lo que me va ❑ **s. map, s. plan** (plano *m*) callejero *m*; **s. sweeper** *(person)* barrendero(a) *m,f*; *(machine)* barredora *f*; **s. theatre** teatro *m* callejero *or* ambulante

streetcar ['striːtkɑːr] *n US* tranvía *m*

streetlamp ['striːtlæmp] *n*, **streetlight** ['striːtlaɪt] *n* farol *m*

streetwalker ['striːtwɔːkər] *n* prostituta *f* callejera

streetwise ['striːtwaɪz] *adj* espabilado(a), *RP* canchero(a)

strength [streŋθ] *n* (**a**) *(gen)* fuerza *f*; *(of nail, rope, etc)* resistencia *f*; *(of currency)* valor *m*, poder *m*; *(of argument, evidence)* fuerza *f*, validez *f*; *(of emotion, conviction, colour)* intensidad *f*; *(of alcohol)* graduación *f*; *(of light, sound)* potencia *f*; **by sheer s.** a viva fuerza (**b**) *(power)* poder *m*, potencia *f*; **on the s. of** a base de, en base a, fundándose en; **to go from s. to s.** ir ganando fuerzas (**c**) *(ability)* punto *m* fuerte (**d**) *(of character, mind)* entereza *f*, fuerza *f*; **to recover one's s.** recobrar las fuerzas, reponerse (**e**) *(workers, soldiers)* fuerza *f* numérica, número *m*; **in s.** en gran número; **to be at/below full s.** tener/no tener completo el cupo

strengthen ['streŋθən] **1** *vt* (**a**) *(gen)* reforzar; *(muscle, character)* fortalecer; *(economy etc)* reforzar, fortalecer; *(friendship)* consolidar (**b**) *(intensify)* intensificar
   2 *vi* (**a**) *(gen) (economy etc)* reforzarse, fortalecerse; *(friendship)* consolidarse, reforzarse (**b**) *(intensify)* intensificarse

strenuous ['strenjʊəs] *adj* (**a**) *(energetic) (gen)* enérgico(a); *(effort, life)* intenso(a); *(opposition)* firme, tenaz (**b**) *(exhausting) (occupation, game)* cansado(a), fatigoso(a), *Andes RP* cansador(a)

strenuously ['strenjʊəslɪ] *adv* enérgicamente

stress [stres] **1** *n* (**a**) *Tech* tensión *f* (**b**) *Med* tensión *f* (nerviosa), estrés *m* (**c**) *(emphasis)* hincapié *m*, énfasis *m*; **to lay great s. on sth** hacer hincapié en algo (**d**) *(on word)* acento *m*
   2 *vt* (**a**) *(emphasize)* recalcar, subrayar (**b**) *(word)* acentuar

stressed-out ['strest'aʊt] *adj Fam* agobiado(a), estresado(a)

stressful ['stresfʊl] *adj* estresante

stretch [stretʃ] **1** *vt* (**a**) *(extend) (elastic)* estirar; *(shoes)* ensanchar; *(arm, hand)* alargar; *(wings)* desplegar, extender; **to s. one's legs** estirar las piernas (**b**) *Fig (elaborate, expand)* forzar
   2 *vi* (**a**) *(elastic)* estirarse; *(fabric)* dar de sí; *(shoes)* ensancharse, dar de sí; *Fig (money)* llegar
   3 *n* (**a**) *(elasticity)* elasticidad *f*; **by no s. of the imagination** de ningún modo; *Fig* **to go at full s.** ir a todo gas *or* a toda mecha (**b**) *(length)* trecho *m*, tramo *m* (**c**) *(expanse) (of land)* extensión *f*; *(of time)* período *m*, tiempo *m*, intervalo *m* ❑ *Sport* **home s.** recta *f* final (**d**) *Fig (extent)* **at a s.** de un tirón

stretch out 1 *vt* (**a**) *(extend) (arm, hand)* alargar; *(legs)* estirar (**b**) *Fig (make long)* alargar, estirar
   2 *vi* (**a**) *(person)* estirarse; *(lie down)* tumbarse (**b**) *(countryside, years, etc)* extenderse

stretcher ['stretʃər] *n* camilla *f*

stretcher-bearer ['stretʃəbeərər] *n* camillero(a) *m,f*

stretchmarks ['stretʃmɑːks] *npl* estrías *fpl*

stretchsuit ['stretʃsuːt] *n (for baby)* pijama *m*

stretchy ['stretʃɪ] *adj* (**stretchier, stretchiest**) elástico(a)

strew [stru:] *vt* (*pt* **strewed**; *pp* **strewed** *or* **strewn** [stru:n]) esparcir, desparramar

stricken ['strɪkən] *adj (with grief)* afligido(a), acongojado(a); *(with illness)* aquejado(a); *(by disaster etc)* afectado(a), damnificado(a); *(damaged)* dañado(a), destrozado(a); **to be s. with remorse** remorderle a uno la conciencia

strict [strɪkt] *adj* (**a**) *(severe)* severo(a), estricto(a); *(discipline)* riguroso(a) (**b**) *(precise)* estricto(a), exacto(a), preciso(a) (**c**) *(absolute)* absoluto(a); **in the strictest confidence** en el más absoluto secreto

strictly ['strɪktlɪ] *adv* (**a**) *(severely)* severamente, estrictamente (**b**) *(categorically)* terminantemente (**c**) *(precisely)* estrictamente, exactamente; **s. speaking** en sentido estricto (**d**) *(exclusively)* exclusivamente, sólo

strictness ['strɪktnɪs] *n* (**a**) *(severity)* severidad *f* (**b**) *(precision)* exactitud *f*, precisión *f*

stride [straɪd] **1** *n* zancada *f*, trancada *f*, tranco *m*; *Fig (progress)* progresos *mpl*; *Fig* **to get into one's s.** agarrar *or Esp* coger el ritmo; *Fig* **to take sth in one's s.** tomarse las cosas con calma

2 *vi* (*pt* **strode**; *pp* **stridden** ['strɪdən]) **to s. (along)** andar a zancadas

3 *vt* cruzar de una zancada

strident ['straɪdənt] *adj (voice, sound)* estridente; *(protest etc)* fuerte

strife [straɪf] *n* conflictos *mpl*, luchas *fpl*; **industrial s.** conflictos laborales

strike [straɪk] **1** *vt* (*pt & pp* **struck**) (**a**) *(hit)* pegar, golpear; **to s. a blow** pegar un golpe (**at** a); *Fig* **to s. a blow for sth** romper una lanza en defensa de algo; *Prov* **s. while the iron is hot** al hierro caliente batir de repente (**b**) *(knock against, collide with)* dar *or* chocar contra; *(car)* atropellar; *(bullet, lightning)* alcanzar; **she struck her head against the door** dio con la cabeza contra la puerta; **the church tower was struck by lightning** cayó un rayo en el campanario; *Fig* **to s. the eye** saltar a la vista (**c**) *(coin, medal)* acuñar (**d**) *(match)* encender (**e**) *(pose, attitude)* adoptar (**f**) *(bargain, deal)* cerrar; *(balance)* encontrar (**g**) *(of clock)* dar, tocar; **the clock struck three** el reloj dio las tres (**h**) *(oil, gold)* descubrir, encontrar; *Fam* **to s. it lucky / rich** tener suerte/hacerse rico(a) (**i**) *(impress)* impresionar; **it strikes me ...** me parece ...; *Fam* **I'm not struck with the idea** esta idea no me va (**j**) (*pp* **struck** *or* **stricken**) *(render)* **to be struck dumb** quedarse mudo(a); **to s. sb dead** matar a algn

2 *vi* (*pt & pp* **struck**) (**a**) *Mil (attack)* atacar; *(disaster, misfortune)* sobrevenir; *(disease)* atacar, golpear; **then disaster struck** entonces sobrevino el desastre; **to s. home** dar en el blanco (**b**) *(clock)* dar la hora; **midnight struck** dieron las doce (**c**) *(workers)* declararse en *or* hacer huelga; **to s. for higher wages** ir a la huelga para conseguir un aumento de sueldo

3 *n* (**a**) *(by workers, students)* huelga *f*; **to be on s.** estar en huelga; **to call a s.** convocar una huelga □ **hunger s.** huelga *f* de hambre; **lightning s.** huelga *f* salvaje; **sit-down s.** sentada *f*; **s. fund** caja *f* de resistencia; **s. pay** subsidio *m* de huelga (**b**) *(of oil, gold)* hallazgo *m*, descubrimiento *m* (**c**) *(blow)* golpe *m*; *Fig* **lucky s.** golpe de suerte (**d**) *Sport (shot)* golpe *m*; *(in bowling)* bolada *f*; *(in baseball)* strike *m* (**e**) *Mil* ataque *m*; **air s.** ataque aéreo

strike back *vi (gen)* devolver el golpe; *Mil* contraatacar

strike down *vt (disease)* fulminar, abatir; **she was struck down in her prime** murió en la flor de la vida

strike off *vt (name from list)* tachar; *(doctor, lawyer)* suspender, no permitir que ejerza

strike out 1 *vt* (**a**) *(delete)* tachar (**b**) *(in baseball)* eliminar *(por cometer tres strikes)*, *Am* ponchar

2 *vi* (**a**) *(hit out)* **to s. out at sb** arremeter a *or* contra algn (**b**) *(set off)* ponerse en camino *or* dirigirse (**for** hacia); *(in business)* **to s. out on one's own** volar con sus propias alas (**c**) *(in baseball)* quedar eliminado(a) *(por cometer tres strikes)*, *Am* poncharse

strike up 1 *vt* (**a**) *(friendship)* trabar, entablar; *(conversation)* entablar, iniciar (**b**) *(tune)* empezar a tocar

2 *vi (band)* empezar a tocar

strikebound ['straɪkbaʊnd] *adj* paralizado(a) por la huelga

strikebreaker ['straɪkbreɪkər] *n* esquirol *mf*, rompehuelgas *mf inv*

striker ['straɪkər] *n* (**a**) *(worker)* huelguista *mf* (**b**) *Fam (in soccer)* marcador(a) *m,f*

striking ['straɪkɪŋ] *adj* (**a**) *(eye-catching)* llamativo(a); *(noticeable)* notable, sorprendente; *(impressive)* impresionante (**b**) *(on strike)* en huelga

string [strɪŋ] **1** *n* (**a**) *(cord)* cuerda *f*, cordel *m*; *(lace)* cordón *m*; *(of puppet)* hilo *m*; *Fig* **to pull strings for sb** enchufar a algn; *Fig* **with no strings attached** sin (ningún) compromiso (**b**) *(of garlic, onions)* ristra *f*; *Comptr* cadena *f*; *(of events)* cadena *f*, sucesión *f*; *(of lies)* sarta *f*; *(of insults)* retahíla *f* □ **s. bean** *Esp* judía *f* verde, *Bol RP* chaucha *f*, *Chile* poroto *m* verde, *Carib Col* habichuela *f*, *Méx* ejote *m* (**c**) *(of racket, guitar)* cuerda *f*; *Mus* **the strings** los instrumentos de cuerda □ *Mus* **s. orchestra** *Fam* **s. band** orquesta *f* de cuerdas; *Mus* **s. quartet** cuarteto *m* de cuerdas

2 *vt* (*pt & pp* **strung**) (**a**) *(beads)* ensartar, enhebrar (**b**) *(racket, guitar)* encordar (**c**) *(beans)* quitar la hebra a

string along *Fam* **1** *vi (agree)* seguir la corriente (**with** a)

2 *vt* tomar el pelo a

stringed [strɪŋd] *adj (instrument)* de cuerda

stringent ['strɪndʒənt] *adj* severo(a), estricto(a), riguroso(a)

string-pulling ['strɪŋpʊlɪŋ] *n Fam* enchufismo *m*

stringy ['strɪŋɪ] *adj* (**stringier, stringiest**) fibroso(a), hebroso(a)

strip¹ [strɪp] **1** *vt* (*pt & pp* **stripped**) (**a**) *(person)* desnudar; *(bed)* deshacer *(room)* vaciar; *(wallpaper, paint)* quitar, *Am* sacar; **to s. sb of sth** *(rank, honour)* despojar a algn de algo (**b**) *Tech* **to s. (down)** *(engine)* desmontar; *(ship)* desaparejar

2 *vi* *(undress)* desnudarse; *(perform striptease)* hacer un striptease

3 *n* striptease *m*; **s. club** club de striptease

strip off 1 *vt* quitar, *Am* sacar

2 *vi (undress)* desnudarse

strip² [strɪp] *n (of paper, leather)* tira *f*; *(of land)* franja *f*; *(of metal)* fleje *m*; *Fam* **to tear sb off a s.** echar una bronca a algn □ *Av* **landing s.** pista *f* de aterrizaje; **s. cartoon** historieta *f*; **s. lighting** alumbrado *m* fluorescente

stripe [straɪp] **1** *n (gen)* raya *f*, lista *f*; *Mil* galón *m*

2 *vt* pintar *or* dibujar a rayas

striped [straɪpt] *adj* rayado(a), a rayas

stripling ['strɪplɪŋ] *n* mozalbete *m*

stripper ['strɪpər] *n* (**a**) *(striptease artist)* persona *f* que hace striptease (**b**) *(for paint)* quitapinturas *m inv*

strip-search ['strɪpsɜːtʃ] **1** *n* registro *m* integral

2 *vt* **to s.-s. sb** someter a algn a un registro integral

striptease ['strɪptiːz] *n* striptease *m*

strive [straɪv] *vi* (*pt* **strove**; *pp* **striven** ['strɪvən]) esforzarse, procurar; **to s. for** *or* **after sth** esforzarse por conseguir algo

strobe [strəʊb] *n* estroboscopio *m* □ **s. lighting** luces *fpl* estroboscópicas

strode [strəʊd] *pt see* **stride**

stroke [strəʊk] **1** *n* (**a**) *(blow)* golpe *m*; *Fig (feat)* **a s. of**

genius una genialidad; **a s. of luck** un golpe de suerte (**b**) *Sport (in cricket, golf)* golpe *m*, jugada *f*; *(in billiards)* tacada *f*; *(in rowing)* remada *f*; *Swimming* brazada *f*; *(style)* estilo *m*; **butterfly s.** estilo mariposa; *Fig* **to put sb off his s.** distraer a algn (**c**) *(of bell)* campanada *f* (**d**) *(of piston)* carrera *f*; *(of engine)* tiempo *m* (**e**) *(of pen)* trazo *m*; *(of brush)* pincelada *f* (**f**) *(caress)* caricia *f* (**g**) *Med* apoplejía *f*, derrame *m* cerebral; **to have a s.** tener una apoplejía (**h**) *Fam (bit)* **I haven't done a s.** no he dado golpe
2 *vt* acariciar

stroll [strəʊl] 1 *vi* dar un paseo *or* una vuelta, pasear
2 *n* paseo *m*, vuelta *f*

stroller ['strəʊlər] *n US* cochecito *m*

strong [strɒŋ] 1 *adj* (**a**) *(gen)* fuerte; *(person)* fuerte, fornido(a), robusto(a); **to be as s. as an ox** ser fuerte como un toro ❑ **s. point** punto *m* fuerte (**b**) *(durable)* sólido(a), resistente (**c**) *(firm, resolute)* firme, profundo(a); *(of supporter)* acérrimo(a); *(protest)* fuerte, enérgico(a) (**d**) *(intense) (colour)* fuerte, intenso(a), vivo(a); *(smell, food, drink)* fuerte; *(light)* brillante; *(resemblance, accent)* fuerte, marcado(a); *Fam* **that scene was really s. meat** esa escena era muy fuerte (**e**) *(incontestable)* poderoso(a), convincente (**f**) *(team etc)* **to be 20 s.** contar con 20 miembros (**g**) *(severe)* severo(a); *(drastic)* drástico(a) (**h**) *Fin Com (of currency etc)* fuerte, en alza
2 *adv* fuerte; **to be going s.** *(business)* ir fuerte *or* en auge; *(elderly person)* conservarse bien

strong-arm ['strɒŋɑːm] *adj* de mano dura

strongbox ['strɒŋbɒks] *n* caja *f* fuerte

stronghold ['strɒŋhəʊld] *n Mil* fortaleza *f*; *Fig* baluarte *m*

strongly ['strɒŋlɪ] *adv (gen)* fuertemente; **a s. worded letter** una carta en tono fuerte; **he feels very s. about it** sus opiniones al respecto son muy contundentes

strongman ['strɒŋmæn] *n (in circus)* forzudo *m*; *Fig (dictator)* dictador *m*

strong-minded [strɒŋ'maɪndɪd] *adj* resuelto(a), decidido(a)

strongroom ['strɒŋruːm] *n* cámara *f* acorazada

strong-willed [strɒŋ'wɪld] *adj* decidido(a), obstinado(a)

strontium ['strɒntɪəm] *n Chem* estroncio *m*

stroppy ['strɒpɪ] *adj* (**stroppier, stroppiest**) *Br Fam* negro(a), de mala uva

strove [strəʊv] *pt see* strive

struck [strʌk] *pt & pp see* strike

structural ['strʌktʃərəl] *adj (gen)* estructural; **s. engineer** ingeniero(a) *m,f* de estructuras; *(in building)* **s. fault** fallo *m* de armazón

structuralism ['strʌktʃərəlɪzəm] *n* estructuralismo *m*

structuralist ['strʌktʃərəlɪst] *adj & n* estructuralista *(mf)*

structure ['strʌktʃər] 1 *n* (**a**) *(organization, composition)* estructura *f* (**b**) *(constructed thing)* construcción *f*; *(building)* edificio *m*
2 *vt (argument, novel)* estructurar

structured ['strʌktʃəd] *adj* estructurado(a) *Comptr* **s. query language** lenguaje *m* estructurado de consulta

struggle ['strʌgəl] 1 *vi (gen)* luchar; *(physically)* forcejear; **to s. to achieve sth** esforzarse por conseguir algo; **to s. to one's feet** levantarse con dificultad
2 *n (gen)* lucha *f*, *(physical fight)* pelea *f*, forcejeo *m*, forcejeo *m*; **it's a real s. to make ends meet** nos cuesta Dios y ayuda llegar a fin de mes; **without a s.** sin oponer resistencia

strum [strʌm] *vt (pt & pp* strummed*) (guitar)* rasguear

strung [strʌŋ] *pt & pp see* string

strung-out ['strʌŋ'aʊt] *adj Fam (tense)* tenso(a), agobiado(a); *(addicted)* enganchado(a) (**on** a)

strut [strʌt] 1 *vi (pt & pp* strutted*)* pavonearse; **to s. about the room** andar pavoneándose por la habitación
2 *n Archit* puntal *m*, riostra *f*

strychnine ['strɪkniːn] *n Chem* estricnina *f*

stub [stʌb] 1 *n* (**a**) *(of cigarette)* colilla *f* (**b**) *(of pencil, candle)* cabo *m* (**c**) *(of cheque)* matriz *f*
2 *vt (pt & pp* stubbed*)* (**a**) *(strike)* golpear (**b**) *(cigarette)* **to s. (out)** apagar

stubble ['stʌbəl] *n (in field)* rastrojo *m*; *(on chin)* barba *f* incipiente *or* mal afeitada

stubbly ['stʌblɪ] *adj* (**stubblier, stubbliest**) *(beard)* de unos días; *(chin)* con pelillos

stubborn ['stʌbən] *adj* (**a**) *(person, animal)* terco(a), testarudo(a), obstinado(a) (**b**) *(stain)* difícil (**c**) *(illness)* rebelde (**d**) *(refusal)* rotundo(a)

stubbornness ['stʌbənnɪs] *n (gen)* terquedad *f*, testarudez *f*

stubby ['stʌbɪ] *adj* (**stubbier, stubbiest**) rechoncho(a)

stucco ['stʌkəʊ] *n (pl* stuccos *or* stuccoes*)* estuco *m*

stuck [stʌk] 1 *pt & pp see* stick[2]
2 *adj* (**a**) *(jammed, immobile)* atascado(a); **to get s.** atascarse; **to be s. at home** estar metido(a) en casa sin poder salir; *Fam* **to be s. with sth/sb** tener que cargar con algo/algn (**b**) *Fam (without)* **to be s. for cash** *Esp* estar sin blanca, *Am* andar sin plata; **to be s. for something to say/ do** no saber qué decir/hacer

stuck-up [stʌk'ʌp] *adj Fam* creído(a), orgulloso(a)

stud[1] [stʌd] 1 *n* (**a**) *(fastener)* automático *m*, corchete *m*; *(for decoration)* tachón *m* ❑ *Br* **press s.** *(cierre m)* automático *m* (**b**) *(on soccer, rugby boots) Esp* taco *m*, *RP* tapón *m* (**c**) *(earring) Esp* pendiente *m*, *Am* arete *m*
2 *vt (pt & pp* studded*) (decorate)* tachonar (**with** de); *Fig (dot, cover)* salpicar (**with** de)

stud[2] [stʌd] *n* semental *m* ❑ **s. (farm)** cuadra *f*, caballeriza *f*

student ['stjuːdənt] *n Univ* estudiante *mf*, universitario(a) *m,f*; *Sch* alumno(a) *m,f*; *(researcher)* investigador(a) *m,f*; **part-time s.** estudiante a tiempo parcial ❑ **s. teacher** profesor(a) *m,f* en prácticas

studied ['stʌdɪd] *adj (gen)* pensado(a), estudiado(a); *(insult, indifference)* premeditado(a), calculado(a); *(style etc)* afectado(a)

studio ['stjuːdɪəʊ] *n (pl* studios*) TV Cin* estudio *m*; *(artist's)* estudio *m*, taller *m* ❑ **s. (apartment** *or Br* **flat)** estudio *m*; *TV* **s. audience** público *m* (invitado); **s. couch** sofá cama *m*

studious ['stjuːdɪəs] *adj (a) (devoted to study)* estudioso(a), aplicado(a) (**b**) *(thoughtful)* atento(a), solícito(a)

studiously ['stjuːdɪəslɪ] *adv* cuidadosamente, deliberadamente

study ['stʌdɪ] 1 *vt (pt & pp* studied*) (gen)* estudiar; *(university subject)* estudiar, cursar; *(facts etc)* examinar, investigar; *(behaviour, the stars)* observar
2 *vi* estudiar; *Fml* cursar estudios; **to s. for an exam** preparar un examen; **to s. hard** estudiar mucho; **to s. to be a doctor** estudiar para médico
3 *n* (**a**) *(gen)* estudio *m*; *(of facts, text, etc)* investigación *f*, estudio *m*; **s. group** grupo *m* de trabajo; **to make a s. of sth** investigar algo (**b**) *(room)* despacho *m*, estudio *m*

stuff [stʌf] 1 *vt* (**a**) *(fill) (container)* llenar (**with** de); *(cushion, doll)* rellenar (**with** con *or* de); *Culin* rellenar (**with** con *or* de); *(animal for display)* disecar (**b**) *(cram)* meter a la fuerza, atiborrar (**with** de); *Fam* **to s. oneself** atiborrarse; *Br Slang Offens* **he can s. his money!** ¡que se meta el dinero por el culo! (**c**) *Offens (have sex)* joder; *Br* **get stuffed!** ¡vete a hacer puñetas!; *Br* **s. him!** ¡que se joda! (**d**) *Slang (thrash)* dar una paliza a
2 *n* (**a**) *Fam (material, substance)* materia *f*, material *m*; **he**

certainly knows his s. sabe lo que se hace; **that's the s.!** ¡así es!, ¡así me gusta!; **to be hot s.** *(sexy)* estar bueno(a); **to do one's s.** hacer lo suyo **(b)** *Fam (things, possessions, equipment)* cosas *fpl; Fam* trastos *mpl,* cachivaches *mpl;* **put all your s. away** guarda tus cosas **(c)** *(cloth, fabric)* tela *f,* paño *m,* género *m*

stuffed [stʌft] *adj* **(a)** *(pepper, mushroom)* relleno(a); *Culin* **s. tomatoes** tomates rellenos ❑ *Sew* **s. toy** muñeco *m* de peluche; *Fam* **s. shirt** persona *f* envarada *or* estirada **(b)** *(nose)* **s. (up)** tapado(a)

stuffing [stʌfɪŋ] *n* relleno *m*

stuffy [stʌfɪ] *adj* **(stuffier, stuffiest)** **(a)** *(room)* mal ventilado(a); *(atmosphere)* cargado(a); **it's s. in here** aquí dentro huele a cerrado **(b)** *(pompous)* pomposo(a), estirado(a); *(narrow-minded)* de miras estrechas; *(strait-laced)* remilgado(a) **(c)** *(nose)* tapado(a)

stultify [stʌltɪfaɪ] *vt (pt & pp* **stultified)** anular, aniquilar

stumble [stʌmbəl] **1** *vi* tropezar, dar un traspié; *Fig* **to s. across** *or* **on** *or* **upon** tropezar *or* dar con
2 *n (trip, blunder)* tropezón *m,* traspié *m*

stumbling [stʌmblɪŋ] *n* **s. block** escollo *m,* tropiezo *m*

stump [stʌmp] **1** *n* **(a)** *(of pencil, candle)* cabo *m* **(b)** *(of tree)* tocón *m; (of arm, leg)* muñón *m,* chueca *f* **(c)** *(in cricket)* estaca *f,* palo *m* **(d)** *US* **to go on the s.** hacer una campaña electoral
. **2** *vt* **(a)** *(puzzle)* confundir; **to be stumped** estar perplejo(a) *or* confuso(a) **(b)** *(in cricket) (dismiss)* poner fuera de juego
3 *vi (walk heavily)* pisar fuerte

stump up *vi Br Fam* poner dinero, *Esp* apoquinar

stumpy [stʌmpɪ] *adj* **(stumpier, stumpiest)** rechoncho(a), achaparrado(a)

stun [stʌn] *vt (pt & pp* **stunned)** *(blow)* aturdir, atontar; *Fig (news etc)* sorprender

stung [stʌŋ] *pt & pp see* **sting**

stunk [stʌŋk] *pt & pp see* **stink**

stunner [stʌnər] *n Fam (woman)* mujer *f* fenomenal; *(thing)* cosa *f* alucinante

stunning [stʌnɪŋ] *adj (blow)* aturdidor(a); *(news)* alucinante; *Fam (woman, outfit)* imponente, fenomenal

stunt¹ [stʌnt] *vt (growth)* atrofiar

stunt² [stʌnt] *n* **(a)** *Av* acrobacia *f,* maniobra *f* peligrosa **(b)** *(trick)* truco *m* ❑ **publicity s.** truco *m* publicitario **(c)** *Cin* escena *f* peligrosa ❑ **s. man** doble *m*

stunted [stʌntɪd] *adj (tree etc)* enano(a), mal desarrollado(a) ❑ **s. growth** atrofia *f*

stupefaction [stju:pɪˈfækʃən] *n* estupefacción *f*

stupefy [stju:pɪfaɪ] *vt (pt & pp* **stupefied)** *(alcohol, drugs)* atontar, aletargar; *Fig (news etc)* dejar estupefacto(a) *or* pasmado(a)

stupendous [stju:ˈpendəs] *adj (wonderful)* estupendo(a), fabuloso(a); *(enormous)* tremendo(a), formidable; *(unusual)* extraordinario(a)

stupid [stju:pɪd] **1** *adj* tonto(a), imbécil; **how s. of me!** ¡mira que soy tonto!; **don't be s.!** ¡no seas tonto!
2 *n Fam* **I'm only joking, s.!** ¡lo digo en broma, tonto!

stupidity [stju:ˈpɪdɪtɪ] *n* estupidez *f*

stupidly [stju:pɪdlɪ] *adv* tontamente

stupor [stju:pər] *n* estupor *m*

sturdiness [stɜ:dɪnɪs] *n* robustez *f,* fuerza *f; Fig* energía *f,* vigor *m*

sturdy [stɜ:dɪ] *adj* **(sturdier, sturdiest)** *(child, table, material)* robusto(a), fuerte; *(opposition, resistance)* enérgico(a), vigoroso(a)

sturgeon [stɜ:dʒən] *n (fish)* esturión *m*

stutter [stʌtər] **1** *vi* tartamudear
2 *vt* decir tartamudeando
3 *n* tartamudeo *m*

stutterer [stʌtərər] *n* tartamudo(a) *m,f*

sty [staɪ] *n (pen)* pocilga *f*

sty(e) [staɪ] *n (pl* **sties** *or* **styes)** *Med* orzuelo *m*

style [staɪl] **1** *n* **(a)** *(gen)* estilo *m; (of dress; suit)* modelo *m; (hairstyle)* peinado *m;* **in the s. of** al estilo de **(b)** *(fashion)* moda *f;* **in s.** de moda; **it's the latest s.** es lo que se lleva **(c)** *(elegance)* estilo *m,* elegancia *f,* clase *f;* **to live in s.** vivir a lo grande
2 *vt (hair)* marcar

styli [staɪlaɪ] *npl see* **stylus**

styling [staɪlɪŋ] *n* diseño *m* ❑ **s. gel** gel *m* moldeador; **s. mousse** espuma *f* (moldeadora)

stylish [staɪlɪʃ] *adj (elegant)* fino(a), elegante; *(fashionable)* a la moda, de última moda

stylist [staɪlɪst] *n (hairdresser)* estilista *mf,* peluquero(a) *m,f*

stylistic [staɪˈlɪstɪk] *adj (device)* estilístico(a)

stylized [staɪlaɪzd] *adj* estilizado(a)

stylus [staɪləs] *n (pl* **styluses** *or* **styli)** **(a)** *(of record player)* aguja *f* **(b)** *(writing instrument)* estilo *m*

stymie [staɪmɪ] *vt Fam* frustrar; *Golf* interferir

Styrofoam® [staɪrəfəʊm] *n esp US* espuma *f* de poliestireno

suave [swɑ:v] *adj* amable, afable; *Pej* zalamero(a)

sub [sʌb] **1** *n Fam* **(a)** *(abbr* **submarine)** submarino *m* **(b)** *Sport (abbr* **substitute)** sustituto(a) *m,f* **(c)** *Press (abbr* **subeditor)** redactor(a) *m,f* **(d)** *(abbr* **subscription)** subscripción *f,* suscripción *f* **(e)** *Br Fam (advance payment)* anticipo *m*
2 *vt (pt & pp* **subbed)** *Press* corregir
3 *vi (in job)* hacer una suplencia; **to s. for sb** sustituir a algn

sub- [sʌb] *pref* sub-

subaltern [sʌbəltən] *n Br Mil* alférez *m*

subcommittee [sʌbkəmɪtɪ] *n* subcomisión *f,* subcomité *m*

subconscious [sʌbˈkɒnʃəs] **1** *adj* subconsciente
2 the s. *n* el subconsciente

subcontinent [sʌbˈkɒntɪnənt] *n* subcontinente *m*

subcontract [sʌbˈkɒntrækt] **1** *n* subcontrato *m*
2 [sʌbkənˈtrækt] *vt* subcontratar

subcontractor [sʌbkənˈtræktər] *n* subcontratista *mf*

subculture [sʌbkʌltʃər] *n* subcultura *f*

subdivide [sʌbdɪˈvaɪd] *vt* subdividir **(into** en**)**

subdue [səbˈdju:] *vt* **(a)** *(nation, people)* someter, sojuzgar **(b)** *(feelings, passions)* dominar, contener **(c)** *(sound, colour, light)* atenuar, suavizar

subdued [səbˈdju:d] *adj* **(a)** *(person, emotion)* callado(a), apagado(a) **(b)** *(voice, tone)* bajo(a) **(c)** *(light)* tenue; *(colour)* apagado(a)

subedit [sʌbˈedɪt] *vt (article, story)* corregir

subeditor [sʌbˈedɪtər] *n* redactor(a) *m,f*

subhead(ing) [sʌbhed(ɪŋ)] *n* subtítulo *m*

subhuman [sʌbˈhju:mən] *adj* infrahumano(a)

subject [sʌbdʒɪkt] **1** *n* **(a)** *(citizen)* súbdito *m* **(b)** *(theme, topic)* tema *m;* **to change the s.** cambiar de tema; **while we are on the s. of holidays ...** ya que hablamos de vacaciones ... ❑ **s. matter** tema *m,* materia *f; (contents)* contenido *m* **(c)** *Sch Univ* asignatura *f* **(d)** *Ling* sujeto *m*
2 *adj* **s. to** *(law, tax)* sujeto(a) a; *(charge, fine)* expuesto(a) a; *(changes, delays)* susceptible de; *(illness)* propenso(a) a;

(conditional upon) previo(a); **s. to government approval** previa aprobación gubernamental

3 [sə'dʒekt] *vt* someter; **to s. to torture** someter a tortura, torturar

subjective [səb'dʒektɪv] *adj* subjetivo(a)

subjectivity [sʌbdʒek'tɪvɪtɪ] *n* subjetividad *f*

sub judice [sʌb'dʒuːdɪsɪ] *adj Jur* pendiente de resolución

subjugate ['sʌbdʒʊgeɪt] *vt* sojuzgar, subyugar

subjunctive [səb'dʒʌŋktɪv] *Ling* **1** *adj* subjuntivo(a)
2 *n* subjuntivo *m*

sublet [sʌb'let] *vt & vi* (*pt & pp* **sublet**) realquilar, subaquilar, subarrendar

sublieutenant [sʌbləf'tenənt] *n Br Naut* alférez *m* de navío; *Mil* subteniente *m*

sublimate ['sʌblɪmeɪt] *vt* sublimar

sublime [sə'blaɪm] **1** *adj* (**a**) *(beauty etc)* sublime (**b**) *Iron (indifference, ignorance)* sumo(a), total
2 *n* **the s.** lo sublime

subliminal [sʌb'lɪmɪnəl] *adj* subliminal

sub-machine-gun [sʌbmə'ʃiːngʌn] *n* ametralladora *f*, metralleta *f*

submarine ['sʌbməriːn] *n Naut* submarino *m*

submerge [səb'mɜːdʒ] **1** *vt (plunge)* sumergir, hundir (**in** en); *(flood)* inundar; *Fig* **submerged in ...** sumido(a) en ...
2 *vi (submarine, diver)* sumergirse

submersion [səb'mɜːʃən] *n* sumersión *f*

submission [səb'mɪʃən] *n* (**a**) *(yielding)* sumisión *f*; **to starve into s.** reducir por hambre (**b**) *(of documents)* presentación *f* (**c**) *(report)* ponencia *f*, informe *m*

submissive [səb'mɪsɪv] *adj* sumiso(a), resignado(a)

submit [səb'mɪt] **1** *vt* (*pt & pp* **submitted**) (**a**) *(present) (application, proposal, claim)* presentar (**b**) *(subject) (person)* someter (**to** a) (**c**) *Jur* alegar
2 *vi (surrender)* rendirse, ceder

subnormal [sʌb'nɔːməl] *adj* subnormal

subordinate [sə'bɔːdɪnɪt] **1** *adj* subordinado(a); *Ling* **s. clause** oración subordinada
2 *n* subordinado(a) *m,f*
3 [sə'bɔːdɪneɪt] *vt* subordinar (**to** a)

subordination [səbɔːdɪ'neɪʃən] *n* subordinación *f*

subplot ['sʌbplɒt] *n Lit* argumento *m* secundario

subpoena [səb'piːnə] *Jur* **1** *n* citación *f*
2 *vt* citar

subprogram ['sʌbprəʊgræm] *n Comptr* subprograma *m*

subscribe [səb'skraɪb] *vi (newspaper, magazine)* subscribirse, suscribirse, abonarse (**to** a); *(opinion, theory)* estar de acuerdo (**to** con)

subscriber [səb'skraɪbər] *n (to newspaper, magazine)* subscriptor(a) *m,f*, suscriptor(a) *m,f*, abonado(a) *m,f*; *Tel* abonado(a) *m,f*

subscript ['sʌbskrɪpt] *n Typ* subíndice *m*; **s. 'a'** 'a' escrita como subíndice

subscription [səb'skrɪpʃən] *n (to newspaper, magazine)* subscripción *f*, suscripción *f*, abono *m*; *(to club)* cuota *f*; *(to opinion, theory)* adhesión *f*; **to take out a s.** suscribirse (**to** a)

subsection ['sʌbsekʃən] *n* apartado *m*

subsequent ['sʌbsɪkwənt] *adj* subsiguiente; **s. to** posterior a

subsequently ['sʌbsɪkwəntlɪ] *adv* posteriormente

subservient [səb'sɜːvɪənt] *adj* servil

subset ['sʌbset] *n* subconjunto *m*

subside [səb'saɪd] *vi (land, building)* hundirse; *(floodwater)* bajar, descender; *(storm, wind)* amainar; *Fig (anger)* calmarse, amainar

subsidence [səb'saɪdəns] *n (of land, building)* hundimiento *m*; *(of floodwater)* bajada *f*, descenso *m*; *(of storm, wind)* amaine *m*; *Fig (of anger)* apaciguamiento *m*

subsidiarity [sʌbsɪdɪ'ærɪtɪ] *n* subsidiariedad *f*

subsidiary [sʌb'sɪdɪərɪ] **1** *adj (role, interest)* secundario(a); *(troops)* subsidiario(a)
2 *n Com* sucursal *f*, filial *f*

subsidize ['sʌbsɪdaɪz] *vt (gen)* subvencionar; *(exports)* primar

subsidy ['sʌbsɪdɪ] *n* subvención *f*, subsidio *m* ❑ **export s.** prima *f*; **housing s.** subsidio *m* de vivienda

subsist [səb'sɪst] *vi* subsistir; **to s. on ...** subsistir a base de ...

subsistence [səb'sɪstəns] *n (existence)* subsistencia *f*, existencia *f*; *(sustenance)* sustento *m*, subsistencia *f* ❑ *Br* **s. allowance** *(advance payment)* anticipo *m*; *(for expenses)* dietas *mpl*; **s. wage** sueldo *m* miserable *or* muy bajo

subsoil ['sʌbsɔɪl] *n* subsuelo *m*

substance ['sʌbstəns] *n* (**a**) *(material)* substancia *f*, sustancia *f*, materia *f* ❑ *Fml* **s. abuse** abuso *m* de narcóticos (**b**) *(solid worth)* substancia *f*, solidez *f*; *(essence, gist)* esencia *f*; **an argument of little s.** un argumento que carece de substancia (**c**) *(wealth)* riqueza *f*; **a woman of s.** una mujer acaudalada

substandard [sʌb'stændəd] *adj* inferior (a la media)

substantial [səb'stænʃəl] *adj* (**a**) *(solid)* sólido(a) (**b**) *(considerable) (sum, loss, etc)* importante; *(difference, improvement)* substancial, notable; *(meal)* abundante

substantially [səb'stænʃəlɪ] *adv* (**a**) *(solidly)* sólidamente; **a s. built house** una casa muy sólida (**b**) *(considerably)* notablemente (**c**) *(essentially)* esencialmente; *(to a large extent)* en gran parte

substantiate [səb'stænʃɪeɪt] *vt (claim)* justificar

substantive ['sʌbstəntɪv] *n Ling* substantivo *m*, sustantivo *m*

substitute ['sʌbstɪtjuːt] **1** *vt* substituir, sustituir; **to s. X for Y** sustituir X por Y
2 *vi* sustituir, suplir (**for** a)
3 *n (person)* sustituto(a) *m,f*, suplente *mf*; *(thing)* sucedáneo *m*; **a coffee s.** un sucedáneo del café ❑ *US Ir* **s. teacher** profesor(a) *m,f* suplente

substitution [sʌbstɪ'tjuːʃən] *n* (**a**) *(gen)* substitución *f*, sustitución *f* (**b**) *(in job)* suplencia *f*

substratum [sʌb'strɑːtəm] *n (pl* **substrata** [sʌb'strɑːtə]) substrato *m*, subsuelo *m*

subsume [sʌb'sjuːm] *vt Fml* englobar, incluir

subterfuge ['sʌbtəfjuːdʒ] *n* subterfugio *m*

subterranean [sʌbtə'reɪnɪən] *adj* subterráneo(a)

subtitle ['sʌbtaɪtəl] *Cin* **1** *n* subtítulo *m*
2 *vt* subtitular, poner subtítulos a

subtitled ['sʌbtaɪtəld] *adj (film)* subtitulado(a)

subtle ['sʌtəl] *adj (colour, difference)* sutil; *(perfume, taste)* delicado(a); *(remark, analysis)* ingenioso(a), agudo(a); *(irony, joke)* fino(a)

subtlety ['sʌtəltɪ] *n (of colour, difference)* sutileza *f*; *(of perfume, taste)* delicadeza *f*, *(of remark, analysis)* ingeniosidad *f*, agudeza *f*; *(of irony, joke)* finura *f*

subtly ['sʌtlɪ] *adv* sútilmente, con sutileza

subtotal [sʌb'təʊtəl] *n* subtotal *m*

subtract [səb'trækt] *vt Math* restar; **to s. 3 from 10** restar 3 de 10

subtraction [səb'trækʃən] *n Math* resta *f*

subtropical [sʌb'trɒpɪkəl] *adj* subtropical

suburb ['sʌbɜːb] *n* barrio *m* periférico *or* residencial; **the suburbs** las afueras

suburban [sə'bɜːbən] *adj* suburbano(a) ❑ **s. train** tren *m* de cercanías

suburbia [sə'bɜːbɪə] *n* barrios *mpl* periféricos *or* satélites

subversion [səb'vɜːʃən] *n* subversión *f*

subversive [səb'vɜːsɪv] *adj & n* subversivo(a) *(m,f)*

subvert [səb'vɜːt] *vt (values)* subvertir; *(government)* derribar, derrocar

subway ['sʌbweɪ] *n* **(a)** *Br (underpass)* paso *m* subterráneo **(b)** *US (underground railway)* metro *m*, *RP* subte *m*

sub-zero [sʌb'zɪərəʊ] *adj* bajo cero

succeed [sək'siːd] **1** *vi* **(a)** *(be successful) (person)* tener éxito; *(plan, attempt)* salir bien; **to s. in doing sth** conseguir *or* lograr hacer algo; **to s. in life** triunfar en la vida **(b)** *(follow after)* suceder; **to s. to** *(throne, fortune)* suceder a, heredar
 2 *vt (monarch, son)* suceder a

succeeding [sək'siːdɪŋ] *adj* subsiguiente, sucesivo(a)

success [sək'ses] *n* éxito *m*; **he had no s.** no le salió bien; **it was a great s.** fue todo un éxito; **to make a s. of sth** triunfar en algo; **to meet with s.** tener éxito

successful [sək'sesfʊl] *adj (gen)* que tiene éxito, de éxito; *(application, plan)* logrado(a), acertado(a); *(business, businessman)* próspero(a); *(marriage)* feliz; **s. candidate** *Pol* candidato(a) elegido(a); *Sch* alumno(a) aprobado(a); **to be s. in doing sth** conseguir *or* lograr hacer algo

successfully [sək'sesfəlɪ] *adv* con éxito

succession [sək'seʃən] *n* **(a)** *(series)* sucesión *f*, serie *f*; **for three years in s.** durante tres años consecutivos; **in s.** sucesivamente **(b)** *(to post, throne)* sucesión *f*

successive [sək'sesɪv] *adj* sucesivo(a), consecutivo(a); **for five s. months** durante cinco meses seguidos

successor [sək'sesər] *n* sucesor(a) *m,f*

succinct [sək'sɪŋkt] *adj* sucinto(a)

succulent ['sʌkjʊlənt] **1** *adj (juicy, tasty)* suculento(a)
 2 *n Bot* planta *f* carnosa

succumb [sə'kʌm] *vi* sucumbir **(to** a)

such [sʌtʃ] **1** *adj* **(a)** *(of that sort)* tal, semejante, parecido(a); **artists s. as Monet and Renoir** artistas como Monet y Renoir; **at s. and s. a time** a tal hora; **in s. a case** en tal caso; **in s. a way that** de tal manera que; **I said no s. thing** no dije nada por el estilo; **s. is life!** ¡así es la vida!; **there's no s. thing** no existe tal cosa; **he comes from Salford or some s. place** es de Salford o de un sitio parecido *or* así **(b)** *(so much, so great)* tanto(a); **he's always in s. a hurry ...** siempre anda con tanta prisa ...; **she was in s. pain** sufría tanto; **s. a lot of books** tantos libros; **with s. courage** con tanto valor
 2 *adv (so very)* tan; **it's s. a long time** hace tanto tiempo; **she's s. a clever woman** es una mujer tan inteligente; **we had s. good weather** hizo un tiempo tan bueno

suchlike ['sʌtʃlaɪk] **1** *adj* tal, semejante; **football, rugby and s. sports** fútbol, rugby y otros deportes por el estilo
 2 *n (things)* cosas *fpl* por el estilo; *(people)* gente *f* por el estilo

suck [sʌk] **1** *vt (vacuum cleaner, pump)* aspirar; *(person) (liquid)* sorber; *(lollipop, blood, etc)* chupar; *(baby) (at breast)* mamar; **to s. one's thumb** chuparse el dedo
 2 *vi (person)* chupar, dar chupadas; *(baby)* mamar
 3 *n (on lollipop, thumb, etc)* chupada *f*

suck down *vt (whirlpool, mud)* tragar

suck in *vt (whirlpool, mud)* tragar; *(vacuum cleaner, pump)* aspirar

suck up 1 *vt (dust etc)* aspirar
 2 *vi Fam* **to s. up to sb** *Esp* hacer la pelota a *or Col* pasar el cepillo a *or Méx* lambisconear a *or RP* chuparle las medias a algn

sucker ['sʌkər] *n* **(a)** *Zool* ventosa *f*; *Bot* chupón *m* **(b)** *Fam (mug, pushover)* primo(a) *m,f*, bobo(a) *m,f*; **he's a s. for blondes** no puede resistir a las rubias

suckle ['sʌkəl] **1** *vt (mother)* amamantar, dar el pecho a
 2 *vi (child)* mamar

suckling ['sʌklɪŋ] *adj (child)* lactante

sucrose ['sjuːkrəʊz] *n* sacarosa *f*

suction ['sʌkʃən] *n (stick together)* succión *f*; *(water, air, etc)* aspiración *f* ❑ **s. pump** bomba *f* de aspiración

Sudan [suː'dɑːn, suː'dæn] *n* the S. (el) Sudán

Sudanese [suːdə'niːz] **1** *adj* sudanés(esa)
 2 *n inv* **(a)** *(person)* sudanés(esa) *m,f*; **the S.** los sudaneses **(b)** *(language)* sudanés *m*

sudden ['sʌdən] *adj* **(a)** *(hurried)* súbito(a), repentino(a) **(b)** *(unexpected)* imprevisto(a), inesperado(a) **(c)** *(abrupt)* brusco(a); **all of a s.** de repente, de pronto, de golpe ❑ **s. bend** viraje *m*

suddenly ['sʌdənlɪ] *adv* de repente, de pronto

suddenness ['sʌdənnɪs] *n (rapidity)* lo súbito, lo repentino; *(unexpectedness)* lo imprevisto, lo inesperado; *(abruptness)* brusquedad *f*

suds [sʌdz] *npl* espuma *f* de jabón, jabonaduras *fpl*

sue [suː, sjuː] **1** *vt Jur (person, organization)* demandar, presentar una demanda contra, llevar a juicio; **to s. sb for damages** demandar a algn por daños y perjuicios
 2 *vi* presentar una demanda, entablar acción judicial; **to s. for divorce** solicitar el divorcio

suede [sweɪd] **1** *n* ante *m*, gamuza *f*; *(for gloves)* cabritilla *f*
 2 *adj* de ante *or* gamuza; *(gloves)* de cabritilla

suet ['suːɪt] *n Culin* sebo *m*

suffer ['sʌfər] **1** *vt* **(a)** *(pain, injury)* sufrir **(b)** *(hardship, defeat, setback)* sufrir, padecer, experimentar **(c)** *(bear, tolerate)* aguantar, soportar; **he doesn't s. fools gladly** no aguanta a los imbéciles
 2 *vi* sufrir; **to s. from** sufrir de, padecer de, adolecer de; **she was suffering from shock** sufría los efectos de un shock; **they were suffering from the effects of the smoke** se resentían del humo; **your health/work will s.** perjudicará a tu salud/trabajo

sufferance ['sʌfərəns] *n* tolerancia *f*; *(forbearance)* resistencia *f*; **on s.** por tolerancia

sufferer ['sʌfərər] *n Med* enfermo(a) *m,f*; **arthritis sufferers** los artríticos

suffering ['sʌfərɪŋ] *n (affliction)* sufrimiento *m*; *(pain, torment)* dolor *m*

suffice [sə'faɪs] *Fml* **1** *vt* that should s. us con eso nos será suficiente
 2 *vi* bastar, ser suficiente

sufficiency [sə'fɪʃənsɪ] *n Fml* cantidad *f* suficiente

sufficient [sə'fɪʃənt] *adj* suficiente, bastante; **two kilos will be s.** con dos kilos basta

sufficiently [sə'fɪʃəntlɪ] *adv* suficientemente, bastante; **the food isn't s. hot** la comida no está lo suficientemente caliente

suffix ['sʌfɪks] *n Ling* sufijo *m*

suffocate ['sʌfəkeɪt] **1** *vt* asfixiar, ahogar
 2 *vi* asfixiarse, ahogarse

suffocating ['sʌfəkeɪtɪŋ] *adj (heat)* sofocante, agobiante; *(atmosphere)* bochornoso(a)

suffocation [sʌfə'keɪʃən] *n* asfixia *f*, ahogo *m*

suffrage ['sʌfrɪdʒ] *n* sufragio *m*

suffragette [sʌfrə'dʒet] *n Hist* sufragista *mf*

suffuse [sə'fjuːz] *vt Literary* bañar, cubrir; **suffused with light** bañado(a) de luz

sugar ['ʃʊgər] **1** *n* **(a)** *(food)* azúcar *m or f* ❑ **brown s.**

azúcar *f* morena; **caster s.** azúcar *m* extrafino; *Bot* **s. beet** remolacha *f* (azucarera), *Méx* betabel *m* (azucarero); **s. bowl** azucarero *m*; **s. candy** azúcar *m* cande; **s. cane** caña *f* de azúcar; *Fam* **s. daddy** amante *m* viejo y rico; **s. loaf** pan *m* de azúcar; **s. lump** terrón *m* de azúcar; **s. plantation** plantación *f* de azúcar; **s. refinery** refinería *f* de azúcar; **s. tongs** tenacillas *fpl* para el azúcar (**b**) *Fam (darling)* querido(a) *m,f*, cariño *m*
  2 *interj Br Fam* ¡ostras!
  3 *vt* azucarar, echar azúcar a; *Fig* **to s. the pill** dorar la píldora

sugar-coated [ʃʊɡə'kəʊtɪd] *adj* azucarado(a)

sugar-free [ʃʊɡə'fri:] *adj* sin azúcar

sugary ['ʃʊɡərɪ] *adj* (**a**) *(like sugar)* azucarado(a); *(sweet)* dulce (**b**) *Fig (insincere)* meloso(a), almibarado(a); *(oversentimental)* sentimentaloide

suggest [sə'dʒest] *vt* (**a**) *(propose)* sugerir, proponer; **I s. that we leave at once** sugiero que nos vayamos en seguida (**b**) *(advise, recommend)* aconsejar; **he suggested we looked** *or* **should look for alternative accommodation** nos aconsejó que buscáramos otro alojamiento (**c**) *(evoke)* evocar, sugerir; **what does the poem s. to you?** ¿qué te sugiere el poema? (**d**) *(indicate, imply)* indicar; **this suggests that he came alone** esto hace pensar que vino solo; **what are you trying to s.?** ¿qué insinúas?

suggestible [sə'dʒestɪbəl] *adj* sugestionable

suggestion [se'dʒestʃən] *n* (**a**) *(proposal)* sugerencia *f*; *(insinuation)* insinuación *f*; **his s. was that ...** él proponía que ...; **to make a s.** hacer una sugerencia (**b**) *(hint, trace)* sombra *f*, traza *f*; *(small amount)* pizca *f*

suggestive [sə'dʒestɪv] *adj* (**a**) *(gen)* sugestivo(a); **to be s. of sth** evocar algo (**b**) *(indecent, remark)* indecente, subido(a) de tono; *(gesture, look)* provocativo(a), provocador(a)

suicidal [sju:ɪ'saɪdəl] *adj* suicida; **s. tendencies** tendencias suicidas

suicide ['sju:ɪsaɪd] *n* suicidio *m*; **to commit s.** suicidarse; *Fam* **it would be s. to do that** sería una locura hacer eso ❑ **s. bombing** atentado *m* suicida con bomba

suit [su:t, sju:t] **1** *n* (**a**) *(man's)* traje *m*, *Andes RP* terno *m*; *(woman's)* traje *m* de chaqueta ❑ **bathing s.** bañador *m*, traje *m* de baño; **s. of armour** armadura *f* (**b**) *Jur (lawsuit)* pleito *m*; **to bring** *or* **file a s. against sb** entablar un pleito contra algn (**c**) *Cards* palo *m*; **to follow s.** arrastrar; *Fig (copy)* seguir el ejemplo
  2 *vt* (**a**) *(be convenient, acceptable)* convenir a, venir bien a; *Fam* **that suits me fine** me viene de perlas (**b**) *(be right, appropriate)* ir bien a, sentar bien a; **red really suits you** el rojo te favorece mucho; **they are well suited to each other** están hechos el uno para el otro (**c**) *(adapt)* adaptar a, ajustar a; **she suited her speech to her audience** ajustó su discurso al público (**d**) *(please)* agradar, satisfacer; **s. yourself!** ¡como quieras!; **you can't s. everybody** es imposible satisfacer a todos

suitability [sju:tə'bɪlɪtɪ] *n (convenience)* conveniencia *f*; *(aptness)* idoneidad *f*

suitable ['sju:təbəl] *adj (convenient)* conveniente; *(appropriate)* apropiado(a), adecuado(a); *(apt)* apto(a); **the most s. woman for the job** la mujer más indicada para el puesto; *TV* **this programme is not s. for children** este programa no es apto para niños

suitably ['su:təblɪ] *adv (correctly)* correctamente, como es debido; *(properly)* apropiadamente, adecuadamente

suitcase ['su:tkeɪs] *n* maleta *f*, *RP* valija *f*

suite [swi:t] *n* (**a**) *(of furniture)* juego *m*, mobiliario *m* ❑ **dining-room s.** (juego *m* de) comedor *m*; **three-piece s.** tresillo *m* (**b**) *(of hotel rooms)* suite *f* (**c**) *Mus* suite *f*

suitor ['sju:tər] *n* (**a**) *(wooer)* pretendiente *m* (**b**) *Jur* demandante *mf*

sulfate ['sʌlfeɪt] *n US see* **sulphate**

sulfide ['sʌlfaɪd] *n US see* **sulphide**

sulfur ['sʌlfər] *n US see* **sulphur**

sulfuric [sʌl'fjʊərɪk] *adj US see* **sulphuric**

sulk [sʌlk] **1** *vi* enfurruñarse, tener murria, estar de mal humor
  2 *n* mal humor *m*, murria *f*; **to have the sulks** enfurruñarse, poner morros

sulky ['sʌlkɪ] *adj* (**sulkier, sulkiest**) malhumorado(a), resentido(a)

sullen ['sʌlən] *adj (moody, surly)* hosco(a), arisco(a), huraño(a); *(sky)* plomizo(a)

sullenness ['sʌlənnɪs] *n* malhumor *m*, murria *f*

sully ['sʌlɪ] *vt* (*pt & pp* **sullied**) ensuciar; *Fig* manchar, mancillar

sulphate ['sʌlfeɪt] *n* sulfato *m* ❑ **copper s.** sulfato *m* de cobre

sulphide ['sʌlfaɪd] *n* sulfuro *m*

sulphur ['sʌlfər] *n* azufre *m*

sulphuric [sʌl'fjʊərɪk] *adj* sulfúrico(a) ❑ **s. acid** ácido *m* sulfúrico

sultan ['sʌltən] *n* sultán *m*

sultana [sʌl'tɑ:nə] *n* (**a**) *(wife of sultan)* sultana *f* (**b**) *esp Br (raisin)* pasa *f* sultana

sultanate ['sʌltəneɪt] *n* sultanato *m*

sultry ['sʌltrɪ] *adj* (**sultrier, sultriest**) (**a**) *(muggy)* bochornoso(a), sofocante (**b**) *(seductive)* sensual

sum [sʌm] *n* (**a**) *(arithmetic problem)* suma *f*, adición *f*; **sums** aritmética *f*, cálculo *m*; *Fam* **to be good at sums** estar fuerte en aritmética (**b**) *(amount of money)* suma *f*, cantidad *f*; **lump s.** suma *f* global, cantidad *f* global; *(total amount)* suma *f*, total *m*; *(of money, invoice)* importe *m*, monto *m*; **s. total** suma *f* total, total *m*; *Fig* **in s.** en suma, en resumen

sum up 1 *vt* (*pt & pp* **summed**) (**a**) *(summarize, encapsulate)* resumir, hacer un resumen de (**b**) *(size up)* evaluar (en el acto)
  2 *vi* resumir; **to s. up ...** en resumidas cuentas, ..., en resumen, ...

summarily ['sʌmerɪlɪ] *adv* sumariamente

summarize ['sʌmeraɪz] *vt* resumir

summary ['sʌmərɪ] **1** *n* resumen *m* ❑ *Rad TV* **news s.** resumen *m* de las noticias
  2 *adj (trial, dismissal, etc)* sumario(a)

summer ['sʌmər] **1** *n* verano *m*; **in s.** en verano ❑ **Indian s.** veranillo *m* de San Martín
  2 *adj (holiday, clothes)* de verano; *(weather, atmosphere)* veraniego(a); *(resort)* de veraneo ❑ **s. camp** colonia *f* de vacaciones; *Br* **s. school** escuela *f* de verano; **S. Time** hora *f* de verano

summerhouse ['sʌməhaʊs] *n* cenador *m*, glorieta *f*

summertime ['sʌmətaɪm] *n* verano *m*

summery ['sʌmərɪ] *adj* veraniego(a)

summing-up [sʌmɪŋ'ʌp] *n Jur* resumen *m*

summit ['sʌmɪt] *n* (**a**) *(of mountain)* cima *f*, cumbre *f* (**b**) *Pol* cumbre *f*

summon ['sʌmən] *vt* (**a**) *(meeting)* convocar (**b**) *(servant)* llamar; *(doctor, police)* llamar; *(aid, reinforcements)* pedir (**c**) *Jur (person)* citar, emplazar

summon up *vt (resources, help)* reunir, conseguir; **to s. up one's courage** *or* **strength** armarse de valor

summons ['sʌmənz] **1** *n* (**a**) *(call)* llamada *f*, llamamiento

m (**b**) *Jur* citación *f* judicial, emplazamiento *m*
2 *vt Jur* citar, emplazar

sump [sʌmp] *n* (**a**) *Aut* cárter *m* (**b**) *Min* sumidero *m*; *(cesspool)* letrina *f*

sumptuous ['sʌmptjʊəs] *adj* suntuoso(a)

sumptuousness ['sʌmptjʊəsnɪs] *n* suntuosidad *f*

Sun *(abbr* **Sunday)** dom.

sun [sʌn] **1** *n* sol *m*; **in the s.** al sol; **you've caught the s.** te ha cogido el sol ❑ *Br* **s. blind** *(awning)* toldo *m*; *(Venetian blind)* persiana *f*; **s. block** bloqueador *m* solar; **s. deck** cubierta *f* superior; *Br* **s. lounge** *US* **s. parlor** solana *f*
2 *vt (pt & pp* **sunned) to s. oneself** tomar el sol

sun-baked ['sʌnbeɪkt] *adj (parched)* quemado(a) por el sol; *(brick)* secado(a) al sol

sunbathe ['sʌnbeɪð] *vi* tomar el sol

sunbathing ['sʌnbeɪðɪŋ] *n* baños *mpl* de sol

sunbeam ['sʌnbiːm] *n* rayo *m* de sol

sunbed ['sʌnbed] *n* tumbona *f*

sunburn ['sʌnbɜːn] *n (burn)* quemadura *f* de sol; *(tan)* bronceado *m*

sunburnt ['sʌnbɜːnt] *adj (burnt)* quemado(a) por el sol; *(tanned)* bronceado(a)

sundae ['sʌndeɪ, 'sʌndɪ] *n Culin* helado *m* con fruta y nueces

Sunday ['sʌndɪ] *n* domingo *m inv*; **Easter S.** Domingo de Resurrección; **Palm S.** Domingo de Ramos; **S. newspaper** periódico del domingo; **S. school** catequesis; *Fig* **to be dressed in one's S. best** llevar el traje de los domingos, ir endomingado(a); *see also* **Saturday**

sundial ['sʌndaɪəl] *n* reloj *m* de sol

sundown ['sʌndaʊn] *n US* anochecer *m*; **at s.** al anochecer

sun-drenched ['sʌndrentʃt] *adj* bañado(a) por el sol

sun-dried ['sʌndraɪd] *adj* secado(a) al sol; **s. tomatoes** tomates *mpl or Méx* jitomates *mpl* secos

sundry ['sʌndrɪ] **1** *adj (various)* diversos(as), varios(as); *Fam* **all and s.** todos sin excepción, todo quisque
2 sundries *npl Com (miscellaneous goods)* artículos *mpl* diversos; *(expenses)* gastos *mpl* diversos

sunflower ['sʌnflaʊər] *n Bot* girasol *m*

sung [sʌŋ] *pp see* **sing**

sunglasses ['sʌnglɑːsɪz] *npl* gafas *fpl* de sol, *Am* anteojos *mpl* de sol

sunhat ['sʌnhæt] *n* pamela *f*, sombrero *m* de ala ancha

sunk [sʌŋk] *pp see* **sink**

sunken ['sʌŋkən] *adj* hundido(a)

sunlamp ['sʌnlæmp] *n* lámpara *f* solar, lámpara *f* de rayos ultravioletas

sunlight ['sʌnlaɪt] *n (sunshine)* sol *m*, luz *f* del sol; **in the s.** al sol

sunlit ['sʌnlɪt] *adj* iluminado(a) por el sol

sunny ['sʌnɪ] *adj* **(sunnier, sunniest)** (**a**) *(day)* de sol; *(place, room)* soleado(a); **it is s.** hace sol (**b**) *Fig (smile, disposition)* alegre; *(future)* risueño(a)

sunray ['sʌnreɪ] *n* rayo *m* de sol

sunrise ['sʌnraɪz] *n (sun-up)* salida *f* del sol; *(dawn)* alba *m*, amanecer *m* ❑ *Econ* **s. industry** industria *f* de tecnología punta

sunroof ['sʌnruːf] *n* (**a**) *Aut* techo *m* solar (**b**) *(on building)* azotea *f*

sunset ['sʌnset] *n (sundown)* puesta *f* del sol; *(twilight)* crepúsculo *m*, anochecer *m*

sunshade ['sʌnʃeɪd] *n (parasol)* sombrilla *f*; *(awning)* toldo *m*

sunshine ['sʌnʃaɪn] *n* sol *m*, luz *f* del sol; *Meteor* **hours of s.** horas *fpl* de sol *or* de insolación

sunspot ['sʌnspɒt] *n* (**a**) *Astron* mancha *f* solar (**b**) *Fam* lugar *m* de veraneo con mucho sol

sunstroke ['sʌnstrəʊk] *n* insolación *f*

suntan ['sʌntæn] *n* bronceado *m* ❑ **s. oil** *or* **lotion** (aceite *m*) bronceador *m*

sun-tanned ['sʌntænd] *adj* bronceado(a)

suntrap ['sʌntræp] *n* lugar *m* muy soleado

sun-up ['sʌnʌp] *n US (sunrise)* salida *f* de sol; *(dawn)* alba *m*, amanecer *m*

sup [sʌp] *vt (pt & pp* **supped)** beber a sorbos; *Fam* **s. up!** bébetelo de una vez

super ['suːpər] **1** *adj Fam* genial, *Méx* padre, *RP* bárbaro(a);
2 *n* (**a**) *(gasoline)* súper *f* (**b**) *US (of apartment building)* portero(a) *m,f*

super- ['suːpər] *pref* super-, sobre-

superabundant [suːpərə'bʌndənt] *adj* superabundante

superannuated [suːpər'ænjʊeɪtɪd] *adj Fml* antiguado(a)

superannuation [suːpərænjʊ'eɪʃən] *n Br* jubilación *f*, pensión *f*

superb [sʊ'pɜːb] *adj* espléndido(a), estupendo(a), magnífico(a)

supercharged ['suːpətʃɑːdʒd] *adj Aut* sobrealimentado(a)

supercharger ['suːpətʃɑːdʒər] *n Aut* sobrealimentador *m*, compresor *m* de sobrealimentación

supercilious [suːpə'sɪlɪəs] *adj (condescension)* altanero(a); *(disdainful)* desdeñoso(a)

superciliousness [suːpə'sɪlɪəsnɪs] *n (condescending)* altanería *f*; *(disdain)* desdén *m*

superconductor [suːpəkən'dʌktər] *n Phys* superconductor *m*

super-duper ['suːpə'duːpər] *adj Fam* genial, *Esp* superguay, *Am* salvo *RP* cheverísimo(a), *Méx* padrísimo(a), *RP* regenial

superficial [suːpə'fɪʃəl] *adj* superficial

superficiality [suːpəfɪʃɪ'ælɪtɪ] *n* superficialidad *f*

superfluous [suː'pɜːfluəs] *adj* superfluo(a), sobrante; **to be s.** sobrar

superhuman [suːpə'hjuːmən] *adj* sobrehumano(a)

superimpose [suːpərɪm'pəʊz] *vt* sobreponer, superponer **(on** en)

superintendent [suːpərɪn'tendənt] *n (supervisor)* director(a) *m,f*; *US (of apartment building)* portero(a) *m,f*; **police s.** subjefe(a) *m,f* de policía

superior [suː'pɪərɪər] **1** *adj* (**a**) *(gen)* superior **(to** a) (**b**) *(haughty)* presumido(a), altanero(a)
2 *n (senior)* superior(a) *m,f*; *Rel* **Mother S.** madre *f* superiora

superiority [suːpɪərɪ'ɒrɪtɪ] *n* superioridad *f*; **s. complex** complejo *m* de superioridad

superlative [suː'pɜːlətɪv] **1** *adj (superb, excellent, outstanding)* superlativo(a), supremo(a), sumo(a)
2 *n Ling* superlativo *m*; *Fig* **to speak in superlatives** deshacerse en elogios

superman ['suːpəmæn] *n (pl* **supermen)** superhombre *m*

supermarket ['suːpəmɑːkɪt] *n* supermercado *m*

supernatural [suːpə'nætʃərəl] **1** *adj* sobrenatural
2 the s. *n* lo sobrenatural

superpower ['suːpəpaʊər] *n Pol* superpotencia *f*

supersede [suːpə'siːd] *vt Fml* suplantar

supersonic [suːpə'sɒnɪk] *adj* supersónico(a)

superstar ['suːpəstɑːr] *n* superestrella *f*

superstition [suːpə'stɪʃən] *n* superstición *f*

superstitious [suːpə'stɪʃəs] *adj* supersticioso(a)

superstore ['suːpəstɔːr] *n Com* hipermercado *m*, gran superficie *f*

superstructure ['suːpəstrʌktʃər] *n* superestructura *f*

supertanker ['suːpətæŋkər] *n* superpetrolero *m*

supertax ['suːpətæks] *n* impuesto *m* adicional

supervise ['suːpəvaɪz] *vt* (a) *(watch over)* vigilar (b) *(superintend)* inspeccionar (c) *(run)* supervisar.

supervision [suːpə'vɪʒən] *n* supervisión *f*; **under adult s.** bajo la supervisión de un adulto

supervisor ['suːpəvaɪzər] *n* supervisor(a) *m,f*

supervisory [suːpə'vaɪzərɪ] *adj* de supervisión

superwoman ['suːpəwʊmən] *n* (*pl* **superwomen** ['suːpəwɪmɪn]) supermujer *f*

supine ['suːpaɪn] *adj* supino(a)

supper ['sʌpər] *n* cena *f*; **to have s.** cenar; **we had fish for s.** cenamos pescado

supper-time ['sʌpətaɪm] *n* hora *f* de cenar

supplant [sə'plɑːnt] *vt* suplantar, reemplazar

supple ['sʌpəl] *adj* flexible

supplement ['sʌplɪmənt] **1** *n* (*gen*) suplemento *m* **2** ['sʌplɪment] *vt* complementar

supplementary [sʌplɪ'mentərɪ] *adj* suplementario(a), adicional

suppleness ['sʌpəlnɪs] *n* flexibilidad *f*

supplicant ['sʌplɪkənt] *n Fml* suplicante *mf*

supplication [sʌplɪ'keɪʃən] *n* súplica *f*

supplier [sə'plaɪər] *n* (*gen*) suministrador(a) *m,f*; *Com* proveedor(a) *m,f*, abastecedor(a) *m,f*

supply [sə'plaɪ] **1** *n* (a) *(provision)* suministro *m*; *Com* provisión *f*, abastecimiento *m*; *(stock)* surtido *m*, existencias *fpl*; **salt is in short s.** hay escasez de sal; **s. and demand** oferta *f* y demanda ❑ **s. ship** buque *m* de abastecimiento; *Br* **s. teacher** profesor(a) *m,f* suplente (b) **supplies** *(food)* provisiones *fpl*, víveres *mpl*; *Mil* pertrechos *mpl*; **office s.** material *m* sing para oficina

2 *vt* (*pt & pp* **supplied**) (a) *(provide)* suministrar, proveer, abastecer; *(electricity, water, arms)* suministrar (b) *Mil* (*with provisions*) aprovisionar (c) *(information, proof)* facilitar, provisionar (d) *Com* surtir

support [sə'pɔːt] **1** *n* (a) *Constr Tech* soporte *m*, apoyo *m* (b) *Fig (moral)* apoyo *m*, respaldo *m*; *(allegiance, backing)* **to give** *or* **lend one's s. to** sth apoyar *or* respaldar algo (c) *(sustenance)* sustento *m*; **fishing is their sole means of s.** se sustentan únicamente con la pesca; *Jur* **without visible means of s.** sin oficio ni beneficio (d) *(financial assistance, funding)* ayuda *f* económica (e) *Sport* afición *f*

2 *vt* (a) *Constr Tech (weight, roof, etc)* sostener (b) *(physical)* sostener; **her legs can't s. the weight** no le sostienen las piernas (c) *Fig (back)* apoyar, respaldar; *(proposal, plan)* apoyar, estar de acuerdo con; *(corroborate, substantiate) (theory, evidence)* confirmar, respaldar (d) *Sport (team)* seguir (e) *(sustain, keep)* mantener; *(feed)* alimentar; **to s. oneself** ganarse la vida

supporter [sə'pɔːtər] *n Pol* partidario(a) *m,f*; *Sport* seguidor(a) *m,f*, *(fan)* hincha *mf*, forofo(a) *m,f*; **supporters** la afición; **supporters' club** peña *f* deportiva

supporting [sə'pɔːtɪŋ] *adj Cin Theat* secundario(a)

supportive [sə'pɔːtɪv] *adj (helpful)* que ayuda; *(understanding)* comprensivo(a)

suppose [sə'pəʊz] *vt* (a) (*gen*) suponer; **let us s. that ...** supongamos que ...; **s. she's right** ¿y si tiene razón? (b) *(presume, guess)* suponer, creer; **I don't s. she'll phone now** no creo que llame ahora; **I don't s. you know where she is?** ¿no sabrías por casualidad dónde se encuentra?; **I s. he's very tired** supongo que estará muy cansado; **I s. not/ so** supongo que no/sí; **it's supposed to be the best restaurant in town** dicen que es el mejor restaurante de la ciudad; **she is supposed to be an expert on the subject** se supone que es una experta en el tema; **what do you s. it means?** ¿qué significado tendrá?; **you're not supposed to smoke in here** no está permitido fumar aquí dentro; **you're supposed to be in bed** deberías estar acostado *or* en 'la cama ya (c) *(when making a suggestion or proposal)* **s. we change the subject?** ¿qué tal si cambiamos de tema?; **s. we leave now?** ¿y si nos fuéramos ya?

supposed [sə'pəʊzd] *adj* supuesto(a)

supposedly [sə'pəʊzɪdlɪ] *adv* según cabe suponer, aparentemente

supposition [sʌpə'zɪʃən] *n* suposición *f*

suppository [sə'pɒzɪtərɪ] *n Med* supositorio *m*

suppress [sə'pres] *vt (gen)* suprimir; *(feelings, laugh, etc)* contener, reprimir; *(news, truth)* callar, ocultar; *(revolt)* sofocar, reprimir

suppression [sə'preʃən] *n (gen)* supresión *f*; *(of feelings, revolt)* represión *f*; *(of facts, truth)* ocultación *f*

suppressor [sə'presər] *n Elec* supresor *m*; *Rad* antiparásito *m*

suppurate ['sʌpjʊreɪt] *vi Med* supurar

suppuration [sʌpjʊ'reɪʃən] *n Med* supuración *f*

supra- [suːprə] *pref* supra; **suprarenal** suprarrenal

supranational [suːprə'næʃənəl] *adj* supranacional

supremacy [sʊ'preməsɪ] *n* supremacía *f*

supreme [sʊ'priːm] *adj (gen)* supremo(a); **with s. indifference** con suma indiferencia ❑ *Mil* **s. commander** jefe *m* supremo; *US Jur* **s. court** tribunal *m* supremo, *Am* corte *f* suprema

supremely [suː'priːmlɪ] *adv* sumamente, totalmente

supremo [sʊ'priːməʊ] *n* (*pl* **supremos**) *Br Fam* mandamás *mf*, *Esp* jefazo(a) *m,f*

Supt *(abbr* **Superintendent***)* Subjefe(a) *m,f* de Policía

surcharge ['sɜːtʃɑːdʒ] *n* recargo *m*

sure [ʃʊər] **1** *adj* (a) *(positive, certain)* seguro(a), cierto(a); **be s. not to ...** ten cuidado de no ...; **be s. to ...** no te olvides de ...; **I'm not s. why ...** no sé muy bien por qué ...; **I'm s. (that) ...** estoy seguro de que ...; **it's almost s. to be fine** seguramente hará buen tiempo; **make s. that it's ready** asegúrate de que esté listo; **to be s. of sth** asegurarse de algo *(safe, reliable)* seguro(a); **it's the surest way of winning** es la manera más segura de ganar (c) *(confident)* seguro(a); **to be s. of oneself** estar seguro(a) de sí mismo(a) (d) *US Fam (of course)* **s. thing!** ¡claro!, ¡por supuesto!

2 *adv* (a) *(of course)* claro; **will you come with me? — s.!** ¿me acompañarás? — ¡claro que sí! (b) *US (really)* **he s. is handsome!** ¡qué guapo es!; **it s. was cold** ¡vaya frío que hacía! (c) *(for certain, certainly)* seguro; **as s. as fate** tan cierto como dos y dos son cuatro; **as s. as I'm standing here** palabra de honor; **tomorrow for s.** mañana sin falta (d) *(in agreement)* claro; **s. enough** efectivamente

sure-fire ['ʃʊəfaɪər] *adj US Fam* seguro(a), de éxito seguro

sure-footed [ʃʊə'fʊtɪd] *adj* de pie firme

surely ['ʃʊəlɪ] *adv* (a) *(without a doubt)* seguramente, sin duda; **s. not!** ¡no puede ser!; **s. you don't mean it!** ¡no lo dices en serio! (b) *(in a sure manner)* con seguridad; **slowly but s.** lentamente pero con seguridad

surety ['ʃʊərɪtɪ] *n Jur* (a) *(sum)* fianza *f*, garantía *f* (b) *(guarantor)* fiador(a) *m,f,* garante *mf;* **to stand s. for sb** ser fiador de algn

surf [sɜːf] **1** *n (waves)* oleaje *m; (foam)* espuma *f*
2 *vi Sport* hacer surf
3 *Comptr* **to s. the Net** navegar por Internet

surface ['sɜːfɪs] **1** *n (gen)* superficie *f; (of road)* firme *m; Fig* **on the s. it seems a good idea** a primera vista parece una buena idea
2 *adj* superficial; **s. area** área *f* de la superficie; **s. route/transport** ruta *f*/transporte *m* de superficie; **by s. mail** por vía terrestre *or* marítima
3 *vt (road)* revestir
4 *vi (submarine etc)* salir a la superficie, emerger; *Fig (person)* asomarse, dejarse ver

surface-to-air [sɜːfɪstʊ'eər] *adj* **s.-to-a. missile** misil *m* tierra-aire

surfboard ['sɜːfbɔːd] *n Sport* plancha *f or* tabla *f* de surf

surfeit ['sɜːfɪt] *n Fml* exceso *m*

surfer ['sɜːfər] *n Sport* surfista *mf*

surfing ['sɜːfɪŋ] *n Sport* surf *m*

surge [sɜːdʒ] **1** *n* (**a**) *(growth)* alza *f,* aumento *m* (**b**) *(of sea)* oleada *f,* oleaje *m,* marejada *f; Fig (of sympathy)* oleada *f; Fig (of anger, energy)* arranque *m;* **a s. of people** una oleada de gente
2 *vi (sea)* levantarse, encresparse; *(people)* avanzar a manadas

surgeon ['sɜːdʒən] *n* cirujano(a) *m,f* ❑ **dental s.** odontólogo(a) *m,f,* dentista *mf;* **veterinary s.** veterinario(a) *m,f*

surgery ['sɜːdʒərɪ] *n* (**a**) *(operation)* cirujía *f* ❑ **plastic s.** cirugía *f* estética (**b**) *Br (consulting room)* consultorio *m* ❑ **s. hours** horas *fpl* de consulta (**c**) *US (operating theatre)* quirófano *m,* sala *f* de operaciones

surgical ['sɜːdʒɪkəl] *adj* quirúrgico(a) ❑ **s. spirit** alcohol *m* de 90; *Mil* **s. strike** ataque *m* controlado *(de objetivos específicos)*

surly ['sɜːlɪ] *adj* (**surlier, surliest**) *(bad-tempered)* hosco(a), malhumorado(a), arisco(a); *(rude)* maleducado(a)

surmise [sɜː'maɪz] **1** *n* conjetura *f,* suposición *f*
2 *vt* conjeturar, suponer

surmount [sɜː'maʊnt] *vt* superar, vencer

surmountable [sɜː'maʊntəbəl] *adj* superable

surname ['sɜːneɪm] *n* apellido *m*

surpass [sɜː'pɑːs] *vt* superar, sobrepasar

surplice ['sɜːplɪs] *n Rel* sobrepelliz *f*

surplus ['sɜːpləs] **1** *n (of goods)* excedente *m,* sobrante *m; (of budget)* superávit *m*
2 *adj* excedente, sobrante; **sale of s. stock** liquidación de saldos

surprise [sə'praɪz] **1** *n* sorpresa *f;* **what a s.!** ¡vaya sorpresa!; **much to my s.** con gran sorpresa por mi parte; **to take sb by s.** *Esp* coger *or Am* agarrar a algn por sorpresa
2 *adj (visit, result)* inesperado(a); **s. attack** ataque sorpresa; **s. party** fiesta sorpresa
3 *vt* (**a**) *(astonish)* sorprender, extrañar; **I should not be surprised if it rained** no me extrañaría que lloviese (**b**) *(catch unawares)* sorprender

surprising [sə'praɪzɪŋ] *adj* sorprendente

surprisingly [sə'praɪzɪŋlɪ] *adv* sorprendentemente, de modo sorprendente; **s. enough, she stayed** para sorpresa de todos, se quedó

surreal [sə'rɪəl] *adj* surrealista

surrealism [sə'rɪəlɪzəm] *n Art* surrealismo *m*

surrealist [sə'rɪəlɪst] *adj & n Art* surrealista *(mf)*

surrealistic [sərɪə'lɪstɪk] *adj* surrealista

surrender [sə'rendər] **1** *n Mil (capitulate)* rendición *f; (of weapons)* entrega *f; Ins* rescate *m;* **s. value** valor de rescate
2 *vt Mil (weapons, town)* rendir, entregar (**to** a); *(right, privilege)* ceder, renunciar a
3 *vi (give in)* rendirse, entregarse

surreptitious [sʌrəp'tɪʃəs] *adj* subrepticio(a), furtivo(a)

surrogacy ['sʌrəgəsɪ] *n Med* alquiler *m* de úteros

surrogate ['sʌrəgɪt] *n Fml* sustituto(a) *m,f* ❑ **s. mother** madre *f* alquilada *or* de alquiler

surround [sə'raʊnd] **1** *n* marco *m,* borde *m*
2 *vt* rodear; **surrounded by trees** rodeado(a) de árboles

surrounding [sə'raʊndɪŋ] **1** *adj* circundante; **in the s. countryside** en el campo alrededor
2 surroundings *npl (of place)* alrededores *mpl,* cercanías *fpl; (environment)* entorno *m sing*

surtax ['sɜːtæks] *n* recargo *m*

surveillance [sɜː'veɪləns] *n* vigilancia *f;* **under s.** bajo vigilancia

survey ['sɜːveɪ] **1** *n* (**a**) *(of building, land)* inspección *f,* reconocimiento *m; (in topography)* medición *f* (**b**) *(of prices, trends, etc)* estudio *m,* encuesta *f; (report)* informe *m;* **to carry out a s.** hacer una encuesta; **a s. of public opinion** un sondeo de la opinión pública (**c**) *(overall view)* vista *f* de conjunto, panorama *m*
2 [sɜː'veɪ] *vt* (**a**) *(building)* inspeccionar; *(land)* hacer un reconocimiento de; *(in topography)* medir (**b**) *(prices, trends, etc)* estudiar, hacer una encuesta sobre (**c**) *(look at)* contemplar; *(give overall view of)* repasar

surveying [sɜː'veɪɪŋ] *n* agrimensura *f,* topografía *f*

surveyor [sɜː'veɪər] *n* agrimensor(a) *m,f,* topógrafo(a) *m,f* ❑ **quantity s.** aparejador(a) *m,f*

survival [sə'vaɪvəl] *n* (**a**) *(continued existence)* supervivencia *f* ❑ **s. kit** equipo *m* para emergencias (**b**) *(relic)* reliquia *f,* vestigio *m*

survive [sə'vaɪv] **1** *vi (gen)* sobrevivir; *(remain)* perdurar, quedar; **my pay is barely enough to s. on** mi salario apenas me llega para ir tirando; **only two paintings survived** sólo quedaron dos cuadros
2 *vt* sobrevivir a

survivor [sə'vaɪvər] *n* superviviente *mf,* sobreviviente *mf*

susceptibility [səseptə'bɪlɪtɪ] *n* (**a**) *(to attack)* susceptibilidad *f; (to illness)* propensión *f; (to beauty, flattery)* sensibilidad *f* (**b**) **susceptibilities** *(sensibilities)* sentimientos *mpl,* susceptibilidad *f sing*

susceptible [sə'septəbəl] *adj (to attack)* susceptible (**to** a); *(to illness)* propenso(a) (**to** a); *(to beauty, flattery)* sensible (**to** a); **s. to suggestion** sugestionable

sushi ['suːʃɪ] *n* sushi *m*

suspect ['sʌspekt] **1** *adj (dubious)* sospechoso(a)
2 *n* sospechoso(a) *m,f*
3 [sə'spekt] *vt* (**a**) *(person)* sospechar (**of** de); *(plot, motives)* recelar de; **he is suspected of being a terrorist** se sospecha de terrorismo (**b**) *(think likely)* imaginar, creer; **a suspected case of typhoid** un caso no confirmado de la fiebre tifoidea; **I suspected as much** me lo imaginaba

suspend [sə'spend] *vt* suspender; *(pupil)* expulsar

suspended [sə'spendɪd] *adj* (**a**) *(gen)* suspendido(a) ❑ **s. animation** muerte *f* aparente; *Jur* **s. sentence** condena *f* condicional (**b**) *Sport (player)* sancionado(a) (**c**) *(pupil)* expulsado(a)

suspender [sə'spendər] *n* (**a**) *Br (for stocking, sock)* liga *f* ❑ **s. belt** liguero *m* (**b**) *US* **suspenders** *(for trousers)* tirantes *mpl*

suspense [sə'spens] *n (anticipation)* incertidumbre *f; Cin Theat* suspense *m, Am* suspenso *m;* **to keep sb in s.**

mantener a algn en la incertidumbre; *Fam* **the s. is killing me** la duda *or* la incertidumbre no me deja vivir

suspension [sə'spenʃən] *n* (**a**) *(postponement)* suspensión *f* (**b**) *Sport (of player)* sanción *f* (**c**) *(of pupil, employee)* expulsión *f* (**d**) *(of car)* suspensión *f* (**e**) *Tech* **s. bridge** puente *m* colgante

suspicion [sə'spiʃən] *n* (**a**) *(gen)* sospecha *f*; *(mistrust)* recelo *m*, desconfianza *f*; *(doubt)* duda *f*; **I have my suspicions about his loyalty** dudo de su lealtad; **to arouse s.** despertar sospechas; **to arrest sb on s.** detener a algn como sospechoso(a); **to be above s.** estar por encima de toda sospecha; **to be under s.** estar bajo sospecha (**b**) *(slight trace)* pizca *f*, poco *m*; **a s. of garlic** una pizca de ajo

suspicious [sə'spiʃəs] *adj* (**a**) *(arousing suspicion)* sospechoso(a); *Fam* **he's a s. looking customer** es un tipo sospechoso; **it looks s. to me** me da mala espina (**b**) *(distrustful, wary)* receloso(a), desconfiado(a); **to be s. of sb** desconfiar de algn

suspiciously [sə'spiʃəsli] *adv* (**a**) *(behave)* de modo sospechoso; **it sounds s. like a case of murder** tiene todo el aspecto de ser un caso de asesinato (**b**) *(glance etc)* con recelo

suss [sʌs] *vt Br Fam* **to s. out** calar; **I can't s. out how it works** no consigo enterarme de cómo funciona; **I sussed him out straight away** le calé en seguida

sustain [sə'stein] *vt* (**a**) *(weight)* sostener (**b**) *(nourish)* sustentar (**c**) *(pretence, conversation, etc)* sostener, mantener (**d**) *Mus (note)* sostener (**e**) *Jur* admitir; **objection sustained** se admite la protesta (**f**) *(injury, loss, etc)* sufrir; *(wound)* recibir

sustainable [sə'steinəbl] *adj* sostenible; **s. development** desarrollo *m* sostenible

sustained [sə'steind] *adj (effort)* sostenido(a); *(applause)* prolongado(a); *Mus (note)* sostenido(a)

sustenance ['sʌstənəns] *n* sustento *m* ❏ **means of s.** medios *mpl* de subsistencia

suture ['su:tʃər] *n Med* sutura *f*

SUV [esju:'vi:] *n (abbr* **sport-utility vehicle)** todoterreno *m*

svelte [svelt] *adj* esbelto(a)

SW (**a**) *(abbr* **short wave)** onda *f* corta, OC *f* (**b**) *(abbr* **South-West)** Sudoeste, SO

swab [swɒb] **1** *n Med (cotton wool)* algodón *m*, tapón *m*; *(for specimen)* frotis *m*
2 *vt (pt & pp* **swabbed)** (**a**) *Med (wound)* limpiar (**b**) *Naut (deck)* limpiar, fregar

swag [swæg] *n Fam* botín *m*

swagger ['swægər] **1** *n* contoneo *m*, pavoneo *m*
2 *vi* contonearse, pavonearse

swaggering ['swægəriŋ] *adj* fachendoso(a), farolero(a)

swallow¹ ['swɒləʊ] **1** *n (of drink, food)* trago *m*
2 *vt* (**a**) *(gulp) (drink, food)* tragar (**b**) *Fig (believe)* tragarse; **to s. the bait** tragar el anzuelo; *(choke back)* **to s. one's pride** tragarse el orgullo; **to one's words** desdecirse de sus palabras
3 *vi* tragar; *Fig* **to s. hard** tragar saliva

swallow up *vt Fig* (**a**) *(of sea, darkness, crowd)* tragar, engullir (**b**) *(eat up)* consumir, absorber

swallow² ['swɒləʊ] *n Orn* golondrina *f* ❏ *Swimming* **s. dive** salto *m* del ángel

swam [swæm] *pt see* **swim**

swamp [swɒmp] **1** *n* pantano *m*, ciénaga *f* ❏ *Med* **s. fever** paludismo *m*
2 *vt* (**a**) *(land)* inundar, anegar; *(boat)* hundir (**b**) *Fig* inundar (**with, by** de); **we were swamped by letters** recibimos una avalancha de cartas (**c**) *Fig* agobiar, abrumar (**with, by** de)

swampy ['swɒmpi] *adj* (**swampier, swampiest**) pantanoso(a)

swan [swɒn] **1** *n Orn* cisne *m* ❏ **Bewick's s.** cisne *m* chico *or* de Bewick; **mute s.** cisne *m* vulgar
2 *vi Fam* **to s. around** pavonearse; **to s. around doing nothing** hacer el vago; **we s. off to Grimsby every weekend** nos escapamos a Grimsby todos los fines de semana

swank [swæŋk] *Fam* **1** *n* (**a**) *(arrogance, ostentation)* fanfarronada *f*, farol *m* (**b**) *(person)* fanfarrón(ona) *m,f*, fardón(ona) *m,f*
2 *adj (swish)* de lujo
3 *vi (show off)* fanfarronear; *(posturing)* farolear, fardar, darse tono

swanky ['swæŋki] *adj* (**swankier, swankiest**) *Fam (person)* fanfarrón(ona); *(posh) Esp* pijo(a), *Méx* fresa; *(restaurant, car, etc)* de lujo

swan-song ['swɒnsɒŋ] *n Fig* canto *m* del cisne

swap [swɒp] **1** *n Fam (exchange)* canje *m*, trueque *m*, cambalache *m*; **to do a s.** hacer un intercambio
2 *vt (pt & pp* **swapped)** (**a**) *(exchange, substitute)* canjear, cambiar (**b**) *(exchange)* cambiar; **to s. places with sb** cambiarse de sitio con algn
3 *vi* hacer un intercambio

swap round, swap over *vt (switch)* cambiar; **I swapped them round when he wasn't looking** los cambié de sitio cuando no miraba

swarm [swɔ:m] **1** *n (of bees)* enjambre *m*; *(of people)* enjambre *m*, multitud *f*
2 *vi (bees)* enjambrar; **Neath was swarming with tourists** Neath estaba lleno de turistas

swarthy ['swɔ:ði] *adj* (**swarthier, swarthiest**) moreno(a), atezado(a)

swashbuckling ['swɒʃbʌkliŋ] *adj* bravucón(ona)

swastika ['swɒstikə] *n* esvástica *f*, cruz *f* gamada

SWAT [swɒt] *n US (abbr* **Special Weapons and Tactics)** = unidad armada de la policía especializada en intervenciones peligrosas, *Esp* GEO *m*

swat [swɒt] **1** *vt (pt & pp* **swatted)** *(flies)* aplastar
2 *n* **to take a s. at sth** aplastar algo

swathe [sweið] **1** *n Agr (of cloth, land)* faja *f*, banda *f*
2 *vt (bind up)* envolver, vendar

swatter ['swɒtər] *n* matamoscas *m inv*

sway [swei] **1** *n* (**a**) *(movement)* balanceo *m*, vaivén *m*, movimiento *m* (**b**) *(power, influence)* dominio *m*, influencia *f* (**over** sobre); **to hold s. over sb** dominar a algn
2 *vi* (**a**) *(swing)* balancearse, mecerse (**b**) *(totter)* tambalearse
3 *vt Fig (influence, persuade)* convencer

swear [sweər] **1** *vt (pt* **swore**; *pp* **sworn)** *(vow)* jurar; **I s. (that) I did not do it** juro que no lo hice; **to s. an oath** prestar juramento, jurar; **to s. sb to secrecy** hacer jurar a algn que guardará el secreto; **to s. to do sth** jurar hacer algo; *Fig* **I could have sworn I heard footsteps** juraría que oí pasos
2 *vi* (**a**) *(formally, solemnly)* jurar, prestar juramento; **to s. on the Bible** jurar sobre la Biblia; **I couldn't s. to it** no lo juraría (**b**) *(curse)* soltar tacos, decir palabrotas; *(blaspheme)* jurar, blasfemar; **to s. at sb** echar pestes contra algn; **to s. like a trooper** jurar como un carretero

swear by *vt Fam (rely on)* tener una fe absoluta en

swear in *vt Jur (witness)* tomar juramento a; **to be sworn in** *(witness)* prestar juramento; *(official)* jurar el cargo

swearing ['sweəriŋ] *n* palabrotas *fpl*; **s. is naughty** decir palabrotas es de mala educación

swear-word ['sweəwɜ:d] *n* palabrota *f*, *Esp* taco *m*

sweat [swet] **1** *n (perspiration)* sudor *m*; *Fam (hard work)* trabajo *m* pesado; **to be dripping with s.** estar empapado(a) en sudor; *Fig* **by the s. of one's brow** con el sudor de su frente; *Fam* **no s.!** ¡no hay problema!; *Fam* **to be in a cold s.** tener canguelo; *Fam* **to get into a s. about sth** apurarse por algo; *Fam Fig* **this job's a real s.** este trabajo es una auténtica paliza ❏ **s. gland** glándula *f* sudorípara

2 *vi (perspire)* sudar; *Fig (work hard)* sudar la gota gorda

3 *vt Fig* sudar; **to s. blood** sudar sangre *or* tinta, sudar la gota gorda; *Fam* **to s. it out** aguantar

sweatband ['swetbænd] *n Sport* **(a)** *(around forehead)* venda *f*, banda *f* **(b)** *(around wrist)* muñequera *f*

sweated ['swetɪd] *adj* **s. labour** trabajo *m* mal pagado

sweater ['swetər] *n* suéter *m*, *Esp* jersey *m*, *Col* saco *m*, *RP* pulóver *m*

sweatshirt ['swetʃɜːt] *n* sudadera *f*, *Col RP* buzo *m*

sweatshop ['swetʃɒp] *n* = fábrica *or* taller donde se explota al obrero

sweaty ['swetɪ] *adj* **(sweatier, sweatiest)** sudoroso(a), sudado(a); **s. smell** olor *m* a sudor

Swede [swiːd] *n (person)* sueco(a) *m,f*

swede [swiːd] *n esp Br Bot* nabo *m* sueco

Sweden ['swiːdən] *n* Suecia *f*

Swedish ['swiːdɪʃ] **1** *adj* sueco(a)

2 *n* **(a)** *(language)* sueco *m* **(b)** *pl* **the S.** los suecos

sweep [swiːp] **1** *n* **(a)** *(with broom)* barrido *m*, *Am* barrida *f*; **it needs a s.** hay que barrerlo; *Fig* **to make a clean s. of things** barrer con todo, hacer tabla rasa; *Fig* **to s. the board** llevarse todos los premios **(b)** *(movement of arm)* movimiento *m or* gesto *m* amplio **(c)** *(range)* abanico *m* **(d)** *(of river, road)* curva *f* **(e)** *(stretch, extent)* extensión *f* **(f)** *(person)* **(chimney) s.** deshollinador(a) *m,f* **(g)** *(police)* redada *f*

2 *vt (pt & pp* **swept)** **(a)** *(floor etc)* barrer; *(chimney)* deshollinar; *Fig* **to s. sth under the carpet** ocultar algo **(b)** *(searchlight, telescope)* recorrer; *(minefield)* rastrear; *(wind, waves)* barrer, azotar **(c)** *(spread throughout)* extenderse, recorrer; **it's a craze which is sweeping the country** es una moda que hace furor en todo el país **(d)** *(remove at a stroke)* arrastrar, llevarse; **he was swept overboard** fue arrastrado al mar; *Fig* **she swept him off his feet** le hizo perder la cabeza

3 *vi* **(a)** *(with broom)* barrer **(b)** *(move quickly)* desplazarse rápidamente; **to s. in/out/past** entrar/salir/pasar rápidamente **(c)** *(road, river, etc)* extenderse

sweep aside *vt* apartar bruscamente; *Fig (suggestion)* descartar; *(objections)* rechazar

sweep away *vt* **(a)** *(dust, rubbish)* barrer **(b)** *(storm)* arrastrar, llevarse

sweep up 1 *vi* barrer, limpiar

2 *vt (room)* barrer; *(dust, rubbish)* recoger

sweeper ['swiːpər] *n* **(a)** *(person)* barrendero(a) *m,f*; *(machine)* barredora *f* **(b)** *Ftb* defensa *m* escoba, líbero *m*

sweeping ['swiːpɪŋ] *adj* **(a)** *(broad, huge)* amplio(a); **a s. statement** una declaración demasiado general **(b)** *(victory)* aplastante, arrollador(a) **(c)** *(far-reaching) (reforms, changes, etc)* radical

sweepstake ['swiːpsteɪk] *n* lotería *f*

sweet [swiːt] **1** *adj* **(a)** *(taste)* dulce; *(containing sugar)* azucarado(a); *(wine, cider)* dulce; **as s. as honey** dulce como la miel; **to have a s. tooth** ser goloso(a) ❏ *Bot* **s. basil** albahaca *f*; *Bot* **s. chestnut** castaño *m* dulce; *Bot* **s. pea** guisante *m or Am* arveja *f or Méx* chícharo *f* de olor; *Bot* **s. pepper** pimiento *m* morrón; *Bot* **s. potato** batata *f*, *Esp Cuba Urug* boniato *m*, *CAm Méx* camote *m*; *Br* **s. shop** confitería *f*, bombonería *f*; *Bot* **s. william** minutisa *f* **(b)** *(pleasant)* agradable; *(smell)* fragante; *(sound)* melodioso(a), suave; **s. nothings** susurros *mpl* amorosos; **'home s. home'** 'hogar, dulce hogar' **(c)** *(person, animal)* encanta-

dor(a), simpático(a); **what a s. little girl!** ¡qué monada!; **to go one's own s. way** actuar a su antojo

2 *n* **(a)** *Br (confectionery)* caramelo *m*, golosina *f*; *(chocolate)* bombón *m* **(b)** *Br (dessert)* postre *m* **(c)** *Fam (darling etc)* cariño *m*, cielo *m*, amor *m*

sweet-and-sour ['swiːtənsaʊər] *adj Culin* agridulce

sweetbreads ['swiːtbredz] *npl* mollejas *fpl*, lechecillas *fpl*

sweetcorn ['swiːtkɔːn] *n* maíz *m* tierno, *Andes RP* choclo *m*, *Méx* elote *m*

sweeten ['swiːtən] *vt* **(a)** *(tea, coffee)* azucarar **(b)** *Fig (temper)* aplacar, calmar; **to s. the pill** dorar la píldora

sweeten up *vt (person)* ablandar

sweetener ['swiːtənər] *n* dulcificante *m*, edulcorante *m*

sweetheart ['swiːthɑːt] *n* **(a)** *(boyfriend)* novio *m*; *(girlfriend)* novia *f* **(b)** *(dear, love)* cariño *m*, amor *m*

sweetie ['swiːtɪ] *n* **(a)** *Br (baby-talk)* caramelo *m*, golosina *f* **(b)** *Fam (darling)* cariño *mf*; **isn't she a s.!** ¡es un ángel!

sweetly ['swiːtlɪ] *adv* dulcemente, con dulzura

sweetness ['swiːtnɪs] *n* *(gen)* dulzura *f*; *(of smell)* fragancia *f*; *(of sound)* suavidad *f*; *(of character)* dulzura *f*, simpatía *f*; **now it's all s. and light between them** ahora hay perfecta armonía entre ellos

sweet-talk ['swiːttɔːk] *vt Fam* **to s. sb into doing sth** convencer a algn con halagos de que haga algo

sweet-tempered [swiːt'tempəd] *adj* amable, simpático(a)

sweet-toothed [swiːt'tuːθt] *adj* goloso(a)

swell [swel] **1** *n (of sea)* marejada *f*, oleaje *m*

2 *adj US Fam (excellent)* genial, *Méx* padre, *RP* bárbaro(a)

3 *vi (pt* **swelled**; *pp* **swollen)** *(part of body)* hincharse; *(river)* subir, crecer; *(sea)* levantarse; *(sales)* crecer, aumentar; *Fig* **to s. with pride** hincharse de orgullo

4 *vt (sales etc)* aumentar

swell up *vi* hincharse

swelling ['swelɪŋ] *n (gen)* bulto *m*, hinchazón *m*; *Med* tumefacción *f*

swelter ['sweltər] *vi* ahogarse de calor

sweltering ['sweltərɪŋ] *adj* agobiante, sofocante

swept [swept] *pt & pp see* **sweep**

sweptback ['sweptbæk] *adj (wing)* en flecha

swerve [swɜːv] **1** *n* **(a)** *(by car)* viraje *m or* desvío *m* brusco **(b)** *Sport (by player)* regate *m*; *(ball)* efecto *m*

2 *vi* **(a)** *(car)* dar un viraje brusco, desviarse bruscamente; **the taxi swerved to the right** el taxi viró bruscamente a la derecha **(b)** *Sport (player)* dar un regate, regatear; *(ball)* llevar efecto

3 *vt Sport (ball)* tirar *or* lanzar con efecto

swift [swɪft] **1** *adj* **(a)** *(runner, horse)* rápido(a), veloz **(b)** *(reaction, reply)* pronto(a), rápido(a)

2 *n Orn* vencejo *m* común

swift-footed [swɪft'fʊtɪd] *adj* rápido(a)

swiftly ['swɪftlɪ] *adv (speedily)* rápidamente, velozmente; *(promptly)* pronto, rápidamente

swiftness ['swɪftnɪs] *n (a) (speed)* rapidez *f*, velocidad *f* **(b)** *(promptness)* prontitud *f*, rapidez *f*

swig [swɪg] *Fam* **1** *n* trago *m*

2 *vt (pt & pp* **swigged)** *Esp* pimplar, *Am* tomar

swill [swɪl] **1** *n (food) (for pigs)* sobras *fpl* para los cerdos *or* puercos *or Am* chanchos; *Pej (for people)* bazofia *f*, *Esp* bodrio *m*

2 *vi Fam (drink) Esp* tragar, *Am* tomar

swill out *vt (rinse)* enjuagar, *Esp* aclarar

swim [swɪm] **1** *vi (pt* **swam**; *pp* **swum)** nadar; **to go swimming** ir a nadar, ir a bañarse; *Fig* **to s. with the tide**

seguir la corriente; *Fam* **my head is swimming** la cabeza me da vueltas

2 *vt (river, the Channel)* pasar *or* cruzar a nado; **he can't s. a stroke** no sabe nadar en absoluto; **to s. the butterfly** nadar estilo mariposa

3 *n* baño *m*; **to go for a** *or* **have a s.** ir a nadar *or* bañarse; *Fam* **to be in the s.** estar al tanto *or* al corriente

swimmer ['swɪmər] *n* nadador(a) *m,f*

swimming ['swɪmɪŋ] *n* natación *f* ❑ *Br* **s. baths** piscina *f* *sing or Méx* alberca *f sing or RP* pileta *f sing* cubierta; **s. cap** gorro *m* de baño; **s. costume** traje *m* de baño, bañador *m*; **s. pool** piscina *f*, *Méx* alberca *f*, *RP* pileta *f*; **s. trunks** traje *m* de baño, *Esp* bañador *m*, *RP* malla *f*

swimmingly ['swɪmɪŋlɪ] *adv* a las mil maravillas

swimsuit ['swɪmsuːt] *n* traje *m* de baño, *Esp* bañador *m*, *RP* malla *f*

swimwear ['swɪmweər] *n* moda *f* de baño

swindle ['swɪndəl] **1** *n (fiddle)* estafa *f*; *(con)* timo *m*; **what a s.!** ¡vaya timo!

2 *vt* estafar, timar; **to s. sb out of sth** estafar algo a algn

swindler ['swɪndələr] *n* estafador(a) *m,f*, timador(a) *m,f*

swine [swaɪn] *n* **(a)** *(pl* **swine)** *(pig)* cerdo *m*, puerco *m*, *Am* chancho *m* ❑ **s. fever** peste *f* porcina **(b)** *(pl* **swines)** *Fam (person)* canalla *mf*, cochino(a) *m,f*, marrano(a) *m,f*; **you s.!** ¡canalla!

swing [swɪŋ] **1** *n* **(a)** *(movement)* balanceo *m*, vaivén *m*; *(of pendulum)* oscilación *f*; *Fig (shift in votes etc)* cambio *m* brusco, giro *m*, viraje *m* ❑ **s. bridge** puente *m* giratorio; **s. door** puerta *f* giratoria **(b)** *Box Golf (swipe)* swing *m*; **to take a s. at sb** asestar un golpe a algn **(c)** *(plaything)* columpio *m*; *Fig* **it's a case of swings and roundabouts** lo que se pierde acá se gana allá **(d)** *(rhythm)* ritmo *m*; *(jazz style)* swing *m*; **to be in full s.** estar en plena marcha; **to go with a s.** ir sobre ruedas; *Fig* **to get into the s. of things** agarrar *or Esp* coger el ritmo de las cosas

2 *vi (pt & pp* **swung)** **(a)** *(move to and fro)* balancearse; *(pendulum, hanging object)* oscilar; *(arms, legs)* menearse; *(child on swing)* columpiarse; *(door)* **to s. open/shut** abrirse/cerrarse de golpe; *Fam* **he'll s. for this** le ahorcarán por eso **(b)** *(turn, change direction)* girar, cambiar de dirección *or* sentido; **he swung round** dio media vuelta; *Pol* **the country has swung to the left** el país ha virado a la izquierda; **to s. into action** ponerse en marcha **(c)** *(aim at, try to hit)* **to s. at** intentar golpear

3 *vt* **(a)** *(cause to move to and fro)* balancear; *(arms, legs)* menear; *(child on swing)* columpiar, balancear; **he swung his racket at the ball** intentó golpear la pelota con su raqueta; **she swung an axe at the tree** asestó un hachazo al árbol; *Fam* **to s. the lead** no dar golpe **(b)** *(turn)* hacer girar; **she swung the sack onto her back** se echó el saco a los hombros; *Fig* **they are hoping to s. the voters in their favour** esperan atraer el favor de los votantes; *Fam Fig* **there isn't room to s. a cat in here** aquí no hay sitio para nada; **to s. a deal** hacer un buen negocio; *Fam* **he swung it so that we could have a day off** lo arregló para que nos diesen un día de fiesta

swingeing ['swɪndʒɪŋ] *adj Br* aplastante, abrumador(a)

swipe [swaɪp] **1** *n* golpe *m*; **to take a s. at sb** asestar un golpe a algn

2 *vt* **(a)** *(hit)* golpear, pegar, dar un tortazo a **(b)** *Fam (steal)* afanar, birlar, *Méx* bajar

3 *vi (swipe, lunge)* **to s. at sb** asestar un golpe a algn

swirl [swɜːl] **1** *n (gen)* remolino *m*; *(of cream, smoke)* voluta *f*, *(of skirts)* vuelo *m*

2 *vi (whirl)* arremolinarse; *(person)* girar, dar vueltas

swish [swɪʃ] **1** *n (of water)* susurro *m*; *(of whip, cane)* silbido *m*, chasquido *m*; *(of skirt, silk)* frufrú *m*, crujido *m*

2 *adj Fam (smart)* muy elegante, elegantón(ona)

3 *vt (whip, cane)* chasquear; *(skirt)* hacer crujir; *(tail)* menear, sacudir

4 *vi (water)* susurrar; *(whip, cane)* dar un chasquido; *(skirt)* crujir

Swiss [swɪs] **1** *adj* suizo(a); **the S. Guard** la Guardia Suiza ❑ *Br Culin* **s. roll** brazo *m* de gitano

2 *n inv (person)* suizo(a) *m,f*; **the S.** los suizos

switch [swɪtʃ] **1** *n* **(a)** *Elec* interruptor *m*, botón *m*, llave *f* **(b)** *(changeover)* cambio *m* repentino; *(exchange, swap)* canje *m*, trueque *m* **(c)** *(stick)* vara *f*; *(whip)* látigo *m*; *(riding whip)* fusta *f* **(d)** *(hairpiece)* trenza *f* postiza **(e)** *US Rail (points)* agujas *fpl*

2 *vt* **(a)** *(plans, jobs, direction)* cambiar de **(b)** *(allegiance, support)* cambiar **(to** por); *(attention, conversation)* desviar **(to** hacia); **they've switched production to their Glasgow plant** han trasladado la producción a la fábrica de Glasgow **(c)** *Elec* poner; **s. the heater to 'low'** pon la estufa al mínimo **(d)** *Rail (train)* desviar, cambiar de vía

▸ **switch off 1** *vt (light, radio, TV, etc)* apagar; *(electrical current)* cortar; *Aut (engine)* parar

2 *vi (light, radio, TV)* apagar; *Aut (engine)* parar; *Fam (person)* distraerse

▸ **switch on 1** *vt (appliance, heating)* encender, *Am* prender

2 *vi (appliance, heating)* encenderse, *Am* prenderse

▸ **switch over** *vi* cambiar; **s. over to BBC1** cambiar a la BBC 1; **they switched over to gas last year** lo cambiaron todo a gas el año pasado

switchback ['swɪtʃbæk] *n* carretera *f* con muchos cambios de rasante

switchboard ['swɪtʃbɔːd] *n Tel* centralita *f*, *Am* conmutador *m* ❑ **s. operator** telefonista *mf*

switcher ['swɪtʃər] *n US TV Cin (machine)* mezclador *m* de imagen

switch-hitter ['swɪtʃhɪtər] *n US* **(a)** *(in baseball)* bateador(a) *m,f* ambidextro(a) **(b)** *very Fam (bisexual)* bisexual *mf*, *RP* bi *mf*

Switzerland ['swɪtsələnd] *n* Suiza

swivel ['swɪvəl] **1** *n Tech* eslabón *m* giratorio ❑ **s. chair** silla *f* giratoria

2 *vi (pt & pp* **swivelled,** *US* **sviveled)** girarse

3 *vt (head)* girar

swizz [swɪz] *n Br Fam* timo *m*, estafa *f*

swollen ['swəʊlən] **1** *pp see* **swell**

2 *adj (ankle, face)* hinchado(a); *(river, lake)* crecido(a); **he's got such a s. head** es tan engreído; **to have s. glands** tener los ganglios inflamados

swoon [swuːn] *Literary* **1** *n* desmayo *m*

2 *vi* desmayarse

swoop [swuːp] **1** *n* **(a)** *(of bird)* calada *f*; *(of plane)* descenso *m* en *Esp* picado *or Am* picada; *Fig* **at one fell s.** de un golpe **(b)** *(by police)* redada *f*

2 *vi* **(a)** **to s. down** *(bird)* abalanzarse **(on** sobre); *(plane)* bajar en *Esp* picado *or Am* picada **(b)** *(police)* hacer una redada

swop [swɒp] *vt see* **swap**

sword [sɔːd] *n* espada *f*; *Fig* **to cross swords with sb** reñirse con algn, habérselas con algn ❑ *Mus* **s. dance** danza *f* de las espadas

swordfish ['sɔːdfɪʃ] *n* pez *m* espada

swore [swɔːr] *pt see* **swear**

sworn [swɔːn] **1** *pp see* **swear**

2 *adj* jurado(a)

swot [swɒt] *Br Fam* **1** *n Esp* empollón(ona) *m,f*, *Méx* matado(a) *m,f*, *RP* traga *mf*

2 *vi (pt & pp* **swotted)** *(study hard)* matarse estudiando, *Esp* empollar, *RP* tragar **(for** para)

swum [swʌm] *pp see* **swim**

swung [swʌŋ] *pt & pp* **swing**

sycamore ['sɪkəmɔːr] *n* (**a**) *Br (maple)* plátano *m* falso, sicomoro *m* (**b**) *US (plane tree)* plátano *m*

sycophant ['sɪkəfənt] *n* adulador(a) *m,f,* pelota *mf*

sycophantic [sɪkə'fæntɪk] *adj* adulador(a)

syllabic [sɪ'læbɪk] *adj* silábico(a)

syllable ['sɪləbəl] *n Ling* sílaba *f*

syllabus ['sɪləbəs] *n* (*pl* **syllabuses** *or* **syllabi** ['sɪləbaɪ]) *Sch Univ* programa *m* de estudios

syllogism ['sɪlədʒɪzəm] *n* silogismo *m*

sylph [sɪlf] *n* sílfide *f*

sylphlike ['sɪlflaɪk] *adj* de sílfide

symbiosis [sɪmbɪ'əʊsɪs] *n* simbiosis *f*

symbiotic [sɪmbɪ'ɒtɪk] *adj* simbiótico(a)

symbol ['sɪmbəl] *n* símbolo *m*

symbolic [sɪm'bɒlɪk] *adj* simbólico(a)

symbolism ['sɪmbəlɪzəm] *n* simbolismo *m*

symbolist ['sɪmbəlɪst] *adj & n Art* simbolista *(mf)*

symbolize ['sɪmbəlaɪz] *vt* simbolizar

symmetrical [sɪ'metrɪkəl] *adj* simétrico(a)

symmetry ['sɪmɪtrɪ] *n* simetría *f*

sympathetic [sɪmpə'θetɪk] *adj* (**a**) *(showing pity, compassion)* compasivo(a) (**b**) *(understanding)* comprensivo(a); *(kind)* amable; **to be s. to a cause** simpatizar con una causa ❑ **s. strike** huelga *f* por solidaridad

sympathetically [sɪmpə'θetɪklɪ] *adv* (**a**) *(showing pity)* compasivamente (**b**) *(understanding)* comprensivamente; *(kindly)* amablemente

sympathize ['sɪmpəθaɪz] *vi* (**a**) *(show pity, compassion)* compadecerse (**with** de); *(express condolences)* dar el pésame (**b**) *(understand)* comprender; **I s. with your point of view** comprendo tu punto de vista

sympathizer ['sɪmpəθaɪzər] *n Pol* simpatizante *mf*

sympathy ['sɪmpəθɪ] *n* (**a**) *(pity, compassion)* compasión *f*, lástima *f* (**b**) *(condolences)* condolencia *f*, pésame *m*; **letter** *or* **message of s.** pésame *m*; **she has my deepest s.** le compadezco; **to express one's s.** dar el pésame; **you won't get any s. from him** él no mostrará ninguna compasión por ti (**c**) *(understanding)* comprensión *f*; **to strike in s.** declararse en huelga por solidaridad

symphonic [sɪm'fɒnɪk] *adj* sinfónico(a)

symphony ['sɪmfənɪ] *n* sinfonía *f* ❑ **s. orchestra** orquesta *f* sinfónica

symposium [sɪm'pəʊzɪəm] *n* (*pl* **symposiums** *or* **simposia** [sɪm'pəʊzɪə]) simposio *m*, conferencia *f*, coloquio *m*

symptom ['sɪmptəm] *n* síntoma *m*; *Fig* síntoma *m*, señal *f*, indicio *m*; **to show symptoms of** dar señales de

symptomatic [sɪmptə'mætɪk] *adj* sintomático(a) (**of** de)

synagogue ['sɪnəgɒg] *n Rel* sinagoga *f*

sync(h) [sɪŋk] *n Fam* sincronización *f*; **to be in/out of s. with ...** estar/no estar en sintonía con ...

synchromesh ['sɪŋkrəʊmeʃ] *n Aut* sincronizador *m*, cambio *m* sincronizado de velocidades

synchronization [sɪŋkrənaɪ'zeɪʃən] *n* sincronización *f*

synchronize ['sɪŋkrənaɪz] *vt* sincronizar

synchronizer ['sɪŋkrənaɪzər] *n* sincronizador *m*

syncopated ['sɪŋkəpeɪtɪd] *adj Mus* sincopado(a)

syncopation [sɪŋkə'peɪʃən] *n Mus* síncopa *f*

syndicate 1 *n (gen)* corporación *f*, empresa *f* ❑ **crime s.** sindicato *m* del crimen; **newspaper s.** sindicato *m* periodístico

    2 ['sɪndɪkeɪt] *vt (workers, newspaper article)* sindicar

syndrome ['sɪndrəʊm] *n Med* síndrome *m*

synergy ['sɪnədʒɪ] *n* sinergia *f*

synod ['sɪnəd] *n Rel* sínodo *m*

synonym ['sɪnənɪm] *n Ling* sinónimo *m*

synonymous [sɪ'nɒnɪməs] *adj* sinónimo(a) (**with** de)

synopsis [sɪ'nɒpsɪs] *n* (*pl* **synopses** [sɪ'nɒpsiːz]) sinopsis *f inv*, resumen *m*

synoptic [sɪ'nɒptɪk] *adj* sinóptico(a)

syntax ['sɪntæks] *n Ling* sintaxis *f inv* ❑ *Comptr* **s. error** error *m* de sintaxis

synthesis ['sɪnθɪsɪs] *n* (*pl* **syntheses** ['sɪnθɪsiːz]) síntesis *f inv*

synthesize ['sɪnθɪsaɪz] *vt* sintetizar

synthesizer ['sɪnθɪsaɪzər] *n Mus* sintetizador *m*

synthetic [sɪn'θetɪk] **1** *adj* sintético(a)

    2 *n* sintético *m*

syphilis ['sɪfɪlɪs] *n Med* sífilis *f*

syphon ['saɪfən] *n see* **siphon**

Syria ['sɪrɪə] *n* Siria

Syrian ['sɪrɪən] *adj & n* sirio(a) *(m,f)*

syringe [sɪ'rɪndʒ] **1** *n* jeringa *f*, jeringuilla *f*

    2 *vt Med* jeringar, inyectar

syrup ['sɪrəp] *n* jarabe *m*, almíbar *m* ❑ **cough s.** jarabe *m* para la tos; **golden s.** melaza *f*

syrupy ['sɪrəpɪ] *adj* almibarado(a)

system ['sɪstəm] *n* sistema *m*; *Fig* **it was a shock to her s.** fue un golpe muy duro para ella; *Fig* **to get sth out of one's s.** desahogarse de algo; *Fam* **the s.** el sistema, el orden establecido ❑ **digestive s.** aparato *m* digestivo; **metric s.** sistema *m* métrico; **nervous s.** sistema *m* nervioso; **solar s.** sistema *m* solar; *Comptr* **s. disk** disco *m* de sistema; *Comptr* **s. error** error *m* del sistema; *Comptr* **systems analysis** análisis *m* de sistemas; **systems analyst** analista *mf* de sistemas

systematic [sɪstɪ'mætɪk] *adj* sistemático(a), metódico(a)

T, t [tiː] *n (the letter)* T, t *f*; *Fig* **it suits me to a T** me viene de perlas, me sienta como anillo al dedo

t *(abbr* **ton(s), tonne(s))** tonelada(s) *f(pl)* (métrica(s)), t

TA [tiːˈeɪ] *n Br (abbr* **Territorial Army)** voluntarios *mpl* de la segunda reserva

ta [tɑː] *interj Br Fam* gracias

tab¹ [tæb] *n* (**a**) *(of garment)* presilla *f*; *(flap)* lengüeta *f*; *(label)* etiqueta *f*; *Fam* **to keep tabs on sb** vigilar a algn (**b**) *US Fam (bill)* cuenta *f*

tab² [tæb] *n Fam* tabulador *m*

tabby [ˈtæbɪ] *n* **t. (cat)** gato(a) *m,f* atigrado(a)

tabernacle [ˈtæbənækəl] *n Rel* tabernáculo *m*

table [ˈteɪbəl] **1** *n* (**a**) *Furn* mesa *f*; **at t.** en la mesa; **to clear the t.** quitar la mesa; **to lay** *or* **set the t.** poner la mesa; *Fig* **to turn the tables on sb** volverle las tornas a algn □ **t. lamp** lámpara *f* de mesa; **t. linen** mantelería *f*; **t. mat** salvamanteles *m inv*; *Sport* **t. tennis** ping-pong® *m*, tenis *m* de mesa; **t. wine** vino *m* de mesa (**b**) *(of figures)* tabla *f*, cuadro *m* □ *Math* **multiplication t.** tabla *f* de multiplicar; **t. of contents** índice *m* de materias

  2 *vt* presentar; **to t. a motion** *Br (present)* someter a discusión una moción; *US (postpone)* posponer la discusión de una moción

tableau [ˈtæbləʊ] *n (pl* **tableaux)** cuadro *m* viviente

tablecloth [ˈteɪbəlklɒθ] *n* mantel *m*

tableland [ˈteɪbəllænd] *n Geog* meseta *f*

tablespoon [ˈteɪbəlspuːn] *n* cucharón *m*

tablespoonful [ˈteɪbəlspuːnfʊl] *n* cucharada *f* grande

tablet [ˈtæblɪt] *n* (**a**) *Med* tableta *f*, comprimido *m*, pastilla *f* (**b**) *(of stone)* lápida *f* (**c**) *(of soap)* pastilla *f*; *(of chocolate)* tableta *f* (**d**) *US (of writing paper)* bloc *m*

tableware [ˈteɪbəlweər] *n* vajilla *f*

tabloid [ˈtæblɔɪd] *n Press* periódico *m* de pequeño formato; *Pej* periódico *m* de poca categoría □ **t. press** prensa *f* sensacionalista

taboo [təˈbuː] *adj & n (pl* **taboos)** tabú *(m)*

tabular [ˈtæbjʊlər] *adj* tabular

tabulate [ˈtæbjʊleɪt] *vt (figures)* disponer en listas *or* tablas; *(results)* clasificar

tabulator [ˈtæbjʊleɪtər] *n* tabulador *m*

tacit [ˈtæsɪt] *adj* tácito(a); **a t. understanding** un acuerdo tácito

tacitly [ˈtæsɪtlɪ] *adv* tácitamente

taciturn [ˈtæsɪtɜːn] *adj* taciturno(a)

taciturnity [tæsɪˈtɜːnɪtɪ] *n* taciturnidad *f*

tack [tæk] **1** *n* (**a**) *(small nail)* tachuela *f*; *Fig* **to get down to brass tacks** ir al grano (**b**) *Sew* hilván *m* (**c**) *Naut* amura *f*;

(distance) bordada *f*; **to make a t.** dar una bordada; *Fig* **on the right/wrong t.** encaminado(a)/desencaminado(a); *Fig* **to change t.** cambiar de rumbo

  2 *vt* (**a**) *(to nail)* clavar; **to t. sth down** clavar algo con tachuelas (**b**) *Sew* hilvanar (**c**) *(add)* añadir; **t. this on to the end of the letter** adjunta esto al final de la carta

  3 *vi Naut* virar de bordo

tacking [ˈtækɪŋ] *n Sew* hilvanado *m*; **to take out the t.** quitar los hilvanes

tackle [ˈtækəl] **1** *n* (**a**) *(equipment)* aparejos *mpl*, trastos *mpl* □ **fishing t.** aparejos *mpl* de pescar (**b**) *Naut* aparejo *m* (**c**) *Sport (challenge) (in soccer, hockey)* entrada *f*; *(in rugby, American football)* placaje *m*, *Am* tackle *m* (**d**) *Sport (position in American football)* tackle *m*

  2 *vt* (**a**) *(deal with) (task)* emprender; *(problem)* abordar; *(grapple with)* agarrar (**b**) *(in soccer, hockey)* entrar a; *(in rugby, American football)* hacer un placaje a, *Am* tacklear

tacky [ˈtækɪ] *adj* (**tackier, tackiest**) (**a**) *(sticky)* pegajoso(a) (**b**) *Fam (tasteless)* chabacano(a), ordinario(a), *Esp* hortera, *Méx* gacho(a), *RP* mersa

tact [tækt] *n* tacto *m*, diplomacia *f*

tactful [ˈtæktfʊl] *adj* diplomático(a), discreto(a)

tactic [ˈtæktɪk] *n* táctica *f*; **tactics** táctica *f sing*

tactical [ˈtæktɪkəl] *adj* táctico(a); **a person of great t. skill** un(a) gran estratega

tactician [tækˈtɪʃən] *n* táctico(a) *m,f*

tactile [ˈtæktaɪl] *adj* táctil

tactless [ˈtæktlɪs] *adj (person)* falto de tacto, poco diplomático(a); *(question)* indiscreto(a)

tactlessly [ˈtæktlɪslɪ] *adv* sin tacto

tad [tæd] *n US Fam* **a t. short** un poquitín *or Esp* pelín *or Am* chiquitín corto

tadpole [ˈtædpəʊl] *n Zool* renacuajo *m*

Tadzhikistan, Tajikistan [tɑːdʒɪkɪˈstɑːn] *n* Tayikistán

taffeta [ˈtæfɪtə] *n Tex* tafetán *m*

tag¹ [tæg] **1** *n* (**a**) *(label)* etiqueta *f* □ *Ling* **t. question** cláusula *f* final interrogativa (**b**) *(saying)* coletilla *f*

  2 *vt (pt & pp* **tagged)** (**a**) *(label)* etiquetar (**b**) *(attach)* añadir, incluir; **you could t. this sentence on to the first paragraph** podrías añadir esta frase al final del primer párrafo

tag along *vi Fam* pegarse; **to t. along** *or* **on behind** ir a la zaga

tag² [tæg] *n (game)* marro *m*

Tagus [ˈteɪgəs] *n* **the T.** el Tajo

Tahiti [təˈhiːtɪ] *n* Tahití

Tahitian [təˈhiːʃən] *adj & n* tahitiano(a) *(m,f)*

tail [teɪl] **1** *n* (**a**) *(of animal)* cola *f*, rabo *m*; *Fig* **to turn t.** huir;

Fig **with his t. between his legs** con el rabo entre las piernas (**b**) *(last or rear part)* cola *f*; *Fig* **there's a car on my t.** un coche me está pisando los talones ❑ **t. end** cola *f*; *Av* **t. unit** plano *m* de cola (**c**) *(of shirt)* faldón *m*; **to wear tails** ir de frac ❑ **t. coat** frac *m* (**d**) *Slang (spy)* detective *mf* (**e**) **tails** *(of coin)* cruz *f sing*, *Chile Col* sello *m sing*, *Méx* sol *m sing*, *RP* ceca *f sing*

   2 *vt* (**a**) *Slang (follow)* perseguir, seguir de cerca (**b**) *Culin (fruit)* quitar los rabos a

tail away, tail off *vi (sound)* desvanecerse

tailback ['teɪlbæk] *n Aut* caravana *f*

tailboard ['teɪlbɔːd], **tailgate** ['teɪlgeɪt] *n Aut* puerta *f* trasera

tailless ['teɪllɪs] *adj* rabón(ona)

tail-light ['teɪllaɪt] *n US Aut* luz *f* trasera

tailor ['teɪlər] **1** *n* sastre *m*; **t.'s (shop)** sastrería *f* ❑ **t.'s chalk** jaboncillo *m* de sastre

   2 *vt (suit)* confeccionar; *Fig* adaptar

tailor-made [teɪlə'meɪd] *adj* hecho(a) a medida; **it was t.-m. for her** estaba hecho a su medida; **t.-m. suit** traje sastre *or* a medida

tailplane ['teɪlpleɪn] *n Av* plano *m* de cola

tailspin ['teɪlspɪn] *n Av* barrena *f*; *Fig* **to go into a t.** entrar en barrena

tailwind ['teɪlwɪnd] *n Av Naut* viento *m* de cola

taint [teɪnt] *vt* contaminar; *Fig* corromper

tainted ['teɪntɪd] *adj* contaminado(a); *(reputation)* manchado(a)

Taiwan [taɪ'wɑːn] *n* Taiwan

Taiwanese [taɪwə'niːz] *adj & n* taiwanés(esa) *(m,f)*

take [teɪk] **1** *vt (pt* took, *pp* taken) (**a**) *(gen)* tomar, *Esp* coger; **t. it or leave it** cógelo o déjalo; *Mil* **to t. a city** tomar una ciudad; **to t. an opportunity** aprovechar una oportunidad; *Chess* **to t. a piece** comer una pieza; **to t. hold of sth** agarrar algo; **to t. sb by the hand** tomar *or Esp* coger a algn de la mano; **to t. sb in one's arms** tomar *or Esp* coger en brazos a algn; **to t. sth from one's pocket** sacarse algo del bolsillo (**b**) *(accept, receive)* tomar, aceptar; **not to t. no for an answer** no estar dispuesto(a) a aceptar una negativa; **she took the news very well/badly** se tomó la noticia muy bien/mal; **to t. all the responsibility** aceptar *or* asumir toda la responsabilidad; **to t. legal advice** consultar a un abogado; *(earn)* **to t. so much per week** recaudar tanto por semana; **what will you t. for it?** ¿cuánto pide por ello? (**c**) *(have)* darse; **t. your time!** ¡tómate tu tiempo!; **to t. a bath** bañarse; **to t. a holiday** tomarse unas vacaciones; **to t. a walk** dar un paseo; **to t. care** cuidar; **to t. it easy** asustarse; **to t. it easy** tomárselo con calma (**d**) *(contain, hold)* **his car takes six people** caben seis personas en su coche (**e**) *(win)* ganar; *(prize)* llevarse; *Cards* **to t. a trick** ganar una baza (**f**) *(occupy)* ocupar; **is this seat taken?** ¿está ocupado este asiento? (**g**) *(subtract)* quitar; **t. six from ten** resta seis a diez (**h**) *(make, produce, develop)* tomar; **to t. a decision** tomar una decisión; **to t. a liking/dislike to sb** tomar cariño/ antipatía a algn; **to t. a photograph** hacer *or* sacar una fotografía; **to t. effect** surtir efecto; **to t. notes** tomar notas (**i**) *(eat, drink)* tomar; **to t. drugs** drogarse (**j**) *(in school, university, etc)* **she's taking (a degree in)** law estudia derecho; **she's taking us for geography** ella nos da clase de geografía; **to t. an examination (in ...)** examinarse (de ...) (**k**) *(accompany)* llevar; **t. us to the station** llévanos a la estación; **they took me home** me acompañaron a casa (**l**) *(travel by)* tomar, *Esp* coger; **he took the corner too quickly** tomó la curva demasiado rápido; **t. the first road on the left** tome *or Esp* coja la primera a la izquierda; **to t. the bus/the train** tomar *or Esp*

coger el autobús/el tren (**m**) *(rent)* alquilar, *Méx* rentar (**n**) *(endure)* soportar, aguantar; **I can't t. any more** no aguanto más (**o**) *(consider)* considerar; **he takes it all very seriously** se lo toma muy en serio; **t. the Basque country for example** tomemos por ejemplo el País Vasco (**p**) *(assume)* **I t. it that ...** supongo que ...; **I took him for an Englishman** le tomé por un inglés; **what do you t. me for?** ¿por quién me tomas? (**q**) *(require)* requerir; **that will t. some explaining** costará trabajo explicar eso; **it takes an hour to walk there** se tarda una hora en ir andando hasta allí; **it took four men to hold him** hicieron falta cuatro hombres para sujetarle; **the journey takes five days** el viaje dura cinco días; **what size do you t.?** *(in clothes)* ¿cuál es su talla?; *(in shoes)* ¿qué número calza? (**r**) *(passive)* **to be taken ill** enfermar, ponerse enfermo(a) (**s**) *Ling (preposition)* regir

   2 *vi* prender; **the fire has taken** ha prendido fuego

   3 *n Cin* toma *f*

take after *vt* parecerse a; **she doesn't t. after her father** no se parece en nada a su padre

take apart *vt (machine)* desmontar; *Fig (criticize)* poner a la altura del betún

take away *vt* (**a**) *(carry off)* llevarse consigo; *Br* **food to t. away** comida para llevar (a casa) (**b**) **to t. sth away from sb** quitarle *or Am* sacarle algo a algn (**c**) *Math* restar; **to t. three away from five** restar tres de cinco

take back *vt* (**a**) *(give back)* devolver; *(receive back)* recuperar; *Fig* **that takes me back!** ¡esto me recuerda los viejos tiempos! (**b**) *(withdraw)* retractarse de (**c**) *(re-employ)* readmitir

take down *vt* (**a**) *(lower)* bajar (**b**) *(demolish)* derribar, demoler, desmontar (**c**) *(write)* apuntar; **to t. down notes** tomar apuntes *or* notas

take in *vt* (**a**) *(lodge)* alojar, recibir en casa; **to t. in lodgers** tener una casa de huéspedes (**b**) *Sew* meter; **to t. in a dress at the waist** meter la cintura a un vestido (**c**) *(include)* abarcar, comprender, incluir (**d**) *(understand)* entender; **to t. in the situation** comprender la situación (**e**) *(deceive)* engañar, embaucar (**f**) *(boat)* **to t. in water** hacer agua

take off 1 *vt* (**a**) *(gen)* quitar, quitarse, *Am* sacarse; **he took off his jacket** se quitó *or Am* sacó la chaqueta; **not to t. one's eyes off sth** no apartar la vista de algo; *Med* **they took his leg off** le amputaron la pierna; **to t. off one's clothes** desnudarse (**b**) *(lead or carry away)* llevarse; **to t. oneself off** marcharse, irse (**c**) *(deduct)* descontar; **they took off 10% of the price** rebajaron el precio en un 10% (**d**) *(imitate)* hacer burla de, remedar, imitar

   2 *vi Av* despegar, *Am* decolar

take on *vt* (**a**) *(undertake)* coger, encargarse de; **she took on the responsibility** asumió la responsabilidad (**b**) *(acquire)* tomar (**c**) *(employ)* contratar (**d**) *(compete with, challenge)* competir con, aceptar el reto de

take out *vt* (**a**) *(remove)* sacar, quitar; **to t. a child out for a walk** sacar a pasear a un niño; **to t. out a tooth** sacar *or* extraer una muela (**b**) *(invite)* **he's taking me out to dinner** me ha invitado a cenar (en un restaurante) (**c**) *(obtain)* obtener; **to t. out an insurance policy** hacerse un seguro (**d**) **the heat takes it out of me** el calor me agota; **to t. it out on sb** desquitarse con algn

take over 1 *vt* (**a**) *Com Pol* tomar posesión de; *(responsibility)* encargarse de; **the rebels took over the country** los rebeldes se apoderaron del país (**b**) *(convey)* transportar

   2 *vi* **to t. over from sb** relevar a algn

take to *vt (become fond of)* tomar *or Esp* coger cariño a; *Fig* **to t. to drink/drugs** darse a la bebida/a las drogas; *Fig* **to t. to one's heels** huir, fugarse

take up 1 *vt* **(a)** *(from ground)* levantar algo; *(upstairs)* subir algo **(b)** *Sew* acortar **(c)** *(accept)* aceptar; *(adopt)* adoptar **(d)** *(start doing)* dedicarse a; *(sport)* empezar a practicar **(e)** *(occupy)* ocupar; **he's very taken up with her** no piensa más que en ella; **to t. up all one's attention** absorber la atención de uno; **to t. up too much room** ocupar demasiado sitio
2 *vi* **to t. up with sb** trabar amistad con algn

takeaway ['teɪkəweɪ] *Br* **1** *n (food)* comida *f* para llevar; *(restaurant)* restaurante *m* que vende comidas para llevar
2 *adj (food)* para llevar (a casa)

take-home pay ['teɪkhəʊmpeɪ] *n Fin* sueldo *m* neto

taken ['teɪkən] **1** *pp see* **take**
2 *adj Fam* cogido(a); **we're very t. with the idea** nos atrae mucho la idea

takeoff ['teɪkɒf] *n* **(a)** *Av* despegue *m, Am* decolaje *m* **(b)** *(imitation)* burla *f,* remedo *m,* imitación *f*

takeout ['teɪkaʊt] *US* **1** *n (food)* comida *f* para llevar
2 *adj (food)* para llevar (a casa)

takeover ['teɪkəʊvər] *n* toma *f* de posesión; *Com (of company)* absorción *f,* adquisición *f* □ **military t.** golpe *m* de estado; *Fin* **t. bid** oferta *f* pública de adquisición, OPA *f*

taker ['teɪkər] *n (purchaser)* comprador(a) *m,f, (of lease)* arrendatario(a) *m,f*

takings ['teɪkɪŋz] *npl Com* caja *f sing,* recaudación *f sing*

talc [tælk] *n* talco *m*

talcum powder ['tælkəmpaʊdər] *n* polvos *mpl* de talco

tale [teɪl] *n* cuento *m*; **old wives' tales** cuentos de viejas; **to tell tales** contar chismes *or* cuentos

talent ['tælənt] *n (ability)* talento *m,* dotes *mpl; Art* **exhibition of local t.** exposición *f* de las obras de artistas locales; **to have a t. for sth** tener talento para algo □ *Cin* **t. scout** cazador(a) *m,f* de talentos

talented ['tæləntɪd] *adj* dotado(a), con talento

talisman ['tælɪzmən] *n (pl* **talismans**) talismán *m*

talk [tɔːk] **1** *vi* **(a)** *(speak)* hablar; **talking of that ...** a propósito de eso ...; **to learn to t.** aprender a hablar; **to t. big** fanfarronear, farolear; *Fig* **to t. through one's hat** decir tonterías; *Fam* **now you're talking!** ¡eso sí que me interesa!; *Fam* **t. about luck!** ¡vaya suerte! **(b)** *(converse)* hablar, conversar, *Méx* platicar; *(gossip)* chismorrear; **people will t.** la gente hablará; **to be talked about** ser algn la comidilla de todos; **to t. about the weather** hablar del tiempo
2 *vt* hablar; **to t. business** hablar de negocios; **to t. nonsense** decir tonterías; **to t. sense** hablar con sentido común; **to t. shop** hablar del trabajo
3 *n* **(a)** *(conversation)* conversación *f,* charla *f, CAm Méx* plática *f; Rad TV* coloquio *m,* entrevista *f;* **to have a t. with sb** hablar con algn □ *Rad TV* **t. show** programa *m* de entrevistas **(b)** *(words)* palabras *fpl;* **he's all t.** no hace más que hablar **(c)** *(rumour)* rumor *m,* voz *f; (gossip)* chismes *mpl,* habladurías *fpl;* **it's the t. of the town** es la comidilla de la ciudad; **there's some t. of his returning** corre la voz de que va a regresar **(d)** *(lecture)* conferencia *f,* charla *f;* **to give a t. on sth** dar una charla sobre algo

talk down 1 *vt Av* **to t. a plane down** dirigir un aterrizaje por radio
2 *vi* **to t. down to sb** hablar a algn con desprecio

talk into *vt* **to t. sb into sth** convencer a algn para hacer algo

talk out of *vt* **to t. sb out of sth** disuadir a algn de hacer algo

talk over *vt* discutir; **I have to t. it over with my friend** tengo que discutirlo con mi amigo

talk round *vt* **(a)** *Br* **to t. sb round** convencer a algn **(b)**

to t. round a subject no ir al grano, andarse con rodeos

talkative ['tɔːkətɪv] *adj* hablador(a), locuaz; *Pej* charlatán(ana), parlanchín(ina)

talkativeness ['tɔːkətɪvnɪs] *n* locuacidad *f*

talker ['tɔːkər] *n* hablador(a) *m,f; Pej* parlanchín(ina) *m,f,* charlatán(ana) *m,f*

talking ['tɔːkɪŋ] *n (conversation)* conversación *f; (chatter)* cháchara *f;* **no t. please!** ¡silencio, por favor!; **to do all the t.** ser el único que habla □ **t. book** audiolibro *m,* = cinta grabada con la lectura de un libro; **t. point** tema *m* de conversación

talking-to ['tɔːkɪŋtuː] *n (pl* **talking-tos**) *Fam* sermón *m, Esp* bronca *f;* **to give sb a t.-to** cantar las cuarenta a algn

tall [tɔːl] *adj* alto(a); **a tree ten metres t.** un árbol de diez metros (de alto); **how t. are you?** ¿cuánto mides?; **she's getting t.** está creciendo; *Fig* **that's a t. order** eso es mucho pedir; *Fig* **that's a t. story** ¡vaya cuento!

tallboy ['tɔːlbɔɪ] *n Furn* cómoda *f* alta

tallness ['tɔːlnɪs] *n* altura *f*

tallow ['tæləʊ] *n* sebo *m*

tally ['tælɪ] **1** *vi (pt & pp* **tallied**) *(correspond)* **they don't t.** no concuerdan; **to t. with sth** corresponder *or* concordar con algo
2 *n Com* anotación *f,* apunte *m;* **to keep a t. of goods** llevar la cuenta de las mercancías

talon ['tælən] *n* garra *f*

tamarind ['tæmərɪnd] *n* tamarindo *m*

tambourine [tæmbə'riːn] *n Mus* pandereta *f*

tame [teɪm] **1** *adj (animal)* domado(a), domesticado(a); *(by nature)* manso(a); *(person)* dócil, sumiso(a) **(b)** *(style)* insípido(a), soso(a)
2 *vt* domesticar, domar

tamer ['teɪmər] *n* domador(a) *m,f*

tamper ['tæmpər] *vi* **to t. with** *(machinery)* estropear; *(text)* adulterar; *(records, an entry)* falsificar; *(lock)* intentar forzar

tampon ['tæmpɒn] *n* tampón *m*

tan¹ [tæn] **1** *n (colour)* marrón *m* claro; *(of skin)* bronceado *m;* **to get a t.** ponerse moreno(a), broncearse
2 *adj (colour)* marrón claro; *(from sun)* bronceado(a)
3 *vt (pt & pp* **tanned**) **(a)** *(leather)* curtir; *Fam Fig* **to t. sb's hide** dar una paliza a algn **(b)** *(skin)* broncear, tostar
4 *vi* broncearse, ponerse moreno(a)

tan² *(abbr* **tangent)** tangente *f,* tang

tandem ['tændəm] *n* tándem *m*

tang [tæŋ] *n (taste)* sabor *m* fuerte; *(smell)* olor *m* fuerte

tangent ['tændʒənt] *n* tangente *f; Fig* **to go** *or* **fly off at a t.** salirse por la tangente

tangerine [tændʒə'riːn] *n Bot* clementina *f*

tangible ['tændʒəbəl] *adj* tangible; **t. assets** bienes *mpl* materiales

tangibly ['tændʒɪblɪ] *adv* de manera tangible *or* palpable

Tangier(s) [tæn'dʒɪə(z)] *n* Tánger *m*

tangle ['tæŋgəl] **1** *n (of thread)* maraña *f,* enredo *m; Fig* embrollo *m,* lío *m; Fig* **to be in a t.** estar hecho(a) un lío; *Fig* **to get into a t.** enredarse
2 *vt (threads)* enmarañar, enredar; *Fig* embrollar; **to get tangled up** enredarse, liarse

tangle with *vt* **to t. with sb** meterse con algn

tango ['tæŋgəʊ] **1** *n (pl* **tangos**) *(dance)* tango *m*
2 *vi* bailar el tango; *Fam* **it takes two to t.** tiene que haber sido cosa de dos

tangy ['tæŋɪ] *adj* **(tangier, tangiest)** *(taste)* ligeramente ácido(a); *(smell)* penetrante

tank [tæŋk] *n* (**a**) *(container)* depósito *m*, tanque *m*; **to fill (up) the t.** llenar el depósito ❑ *Br* **petrol** *or US* **gas t.** depósito *m* de gasolina (**b**) *Mil* tanque *m*, carro *m* de combate

tank up 1 *vi Aut* llenar el depósito

  2 *vt Fam* **to get tanked up** agarrarse un pedo, *Méx* ponerse una peda

tankard ['tæŋkəd] *n* bock *m*

tanker ['tæŋkər] *n Naut* tanque *m*, barco *m* cisterna; *(for oil)* petrolero *m*; *Aut* camión *m* cisterna

tanned [tænd] *pt & pp see* **tan**

tanner ['tænər] *n* curtidor(a) *m,f*

tannery ['tænərɪ] *n* curtiduría *f*, tenería *f*

tannin ['tænɪn] *n Chem* tanino *m*

tanning ['tænɪŋ] *n* (**a**) *(of hide)* curtido *m* (**b**) *(of skin)* bronceado *m* (**c**) *Fig (thrashing)* paliza *f*, zurra *f*

tantalize ['tæntəlaɪz] *vt* atormentar (con una esperanza falsa)

tantalizing ['tæntəlaɪzɪŋ] *adj* atormentador(a)

tantamount ['tæntəmaʊnt] *adj* **t. to** equivalente a; **that's t. to a refusal** eso equivale a una negativa

tantrum ['tæntrəm] *n* rabieta *f*; **to fly into a t.** agarrar *or Esp* coger una rabieta

Tanzania [tænzə'nɪə] *n* Tanzania

Tanzanian [tænzə'nɪən] *adj & n* tanzano(a) *(m,f)*

tap[1] [tæp] **1** *vt* (*pt & pp* **tapped**) *(knock)* golpear ligeramente; *(with hand)* dar una palmadita a

  2 *vi* **to t. at** *or* **on the door** llamar suavemente a la puerta

  3 *n* golpecito *m*; **there was a t. at the door** llamaron suavemente a la puerta ❑ **t. dancing** claqué *m*

tap[2] [tæp] **1** *n Br (for water) Esp* grifo *m*, *Chile Col Méx* llave *f*, *RP* canilla *f*; *(of barrel)* espita *f*; *Fig Fin* **funds on t.** fondos *mpl* disponibles ❑ **t. water** agua *f* del *Esp* grifo *or Chile Col Méx* de la llave *or RP* de la canilla

  2 *vt* (*pt & pp* **tapped**) (**a**) *(barrel)* agujerear; *(tree)* sangrar; *(wine, beer)* tirar, sacar del barril; *Fig Com* **to t. new markets** explotar nuevos mercados; *Fam* **to t. sb for a loan** sablear a algn (**b**) *Tel (phone)* interceptar

tape [teɪp] **1** *n* (**a**) *(gen)* cinta *f* ❑ *Sport* **(finishing) t.** cinta *f* de llegada; **insulating t.** cinta *f* aislante; *Fam* **red t.** papeleo *m*; **sticky t.** cinta *f* adhesiva; **t. measure** cinta *f* métrica (**b**) *(for recording)* cinta *f* magnetofónica ❑ **t. recorder** magnetofón *m*, magnetófono *m*; **t. recording** grabación *f*

  2 *vt* (**a**) *(stick with tape)* pegar con cinta adhesiva; *Fig* **I've got him taped** le tengo calado (**b**) *(record)* grabar en cinta

taper ['teɪpər] **1** *vt (make narrow)* estrechar; *(to a point)* afilar

  2 *vi* estrecharse; *(to a point)* afilarse

  3 *n* vela *f*

taper off *vi* ir disminuyendo

tape-record ['teɪprɪkɔːd] *vt* grabar (en cinta)

tapestry ['tæpɪstrɪ] *n* tapiz *m*

tapeworm ['teɪpwɜːm] *n Ent* tenia *f*, solitaria *f*

tapioca [tæpɪ'əʊkə] *n* tapioca *f*

tapped [tæpt] *pt & pp see* **tap**[1] & **tap**[2]

tapping[1] ['tæpɪŋ] *n (knocking)* golpecitos *mpl*

tapping[2] ['tæpɪŋ] *n* (**a**) *(of barrel)* apertura *f*; *(of tree)* sangría *f*; *(of resources)* explotación *f* (**b**) *Tel* interceptación *f*

tar [tɑːr] **1** *n* alquitrán *m*, brea *f*

  2 *vt* (*pt & pp* **tarred**) *(road)* alquitranar; *(boat)* embrear; *Fig* **they are tarred with the same brush** están cortados por el mismo patrón

tarantula [tə'ræntjʊlə] *n* tarántula *f*

tardy ['tɑːdɪ] *adj (tardier, tardiest) Fml* tardío(a)

target ['tɑːgɪt] *n* (**a**) *(object aimed at)* blanco *m*; **he was a t. for blackmailers** fue el blanco de los chantajistas; **to hit the t.** dar en el blanco ❑ *TV Rad* **t. audience** audiencia *f* a la que está orientada la emisión; **t. language** *(in translating)* lengua *f* de destino *or* llegada; **t. market** mercado *m* objeto *or* objetivo; **t. practice** tiro *m* al blanco (**b**) *(purpose)* fin *m*, meta *f*; **his t. was to raise $1,000** su objetivo era reunir 1.000 dólares

tariff ['tærɪf] *n* tarifa *f*, arancel *m*; *(in hotel etc)* lista *f* de precios

Tarmac® ['tɑːmæk] **1** *n* (**a**) *(substance)* alquitrán *m* (**b**) *Av* pista *f* de aterrizaje/despegue

  2 *vt* alquitranar

tarnish ['tɑːnɪʃ] **1** *vt* empañar; *Fig (sb's honour)* manchar, empañar

  2 *vi* empañarse, perder brillo

tarot ['tærəʊ] *n* tarot *m*

tarpaulin [tɑː'pɔːlɪn] *n Tex* lona *f*

tarragon ['tærəgən] *n Bot* estragón *m*

tarred [tɑːd] *pt & pp see* **tar**

tart[1] [tɑːt] *n Br Culin* tarta *f*

tart[2] [tɑːt] *adj (taste)* ácido(a), agrio(a); *Fig (answer)* acre, mordaz

tart[3] [tɑːt] *Fam* **1** *n* fulana *f*, *Esp* furcia *f* *Méx* piruja *f*, *RP* reventada *f*

  2 *vt Br* **to t. oneself up** emperifollarse

tartan ['tɑːtən] *n* tartán *m*

Tartar ['tɑːtər] **1** *adj* tártaro(a)

  2 *n* tártaro(a) *m,f*; *Fig* persona *f* intratable; **he's a t.** es una fiera

tartar ['tɑːtər] *n Chem* tártaro *m*

tartar(e) sauce ['tɑːtə'sɔːs] *n* salsa *f* tártara

tartaric [tɑː'tærɪk] *adj Chem* tártrico(a), tartárico(a)

tartness ['tɑːtnɪs] *n (of taste)* acidez *f*; *Fig (of remark)* acritud *f*

tarty ['tɑːtɪ] *adj* (**tartier, tartiest**) *Fam (clothes)* de fulana

task [tɑːsk] *n* tarea *f*, labor *f*; **to carry out a t.** llevar a cabo una tarea; **to take sb to t.** reprender a algn ❑ *Mil* **t. force** destacamento *m* de fuerzas

taskmaster ['tɑːskmɑːstər] *n* **a hard t.** un auténtico tirano

Tasmania [tæz'meɪnɪə] *n* Tasmania

Tasmanian [tæz'meɪnɪən] *adj & n* tasmanio(a) *(m,f)*

Tasman Sea [tæzmən'siː] *n* the **T. S.** el Mar de Tasmania

tassel ['tæsəl] *n* borla *f*

taste [teɪst] **1** *n* (**a**) *(sense)* gusto *m*; *(flavour)* sabor *m*, gusto *m*; **it has a burnt t.** sabe a quemado; **it has no t.** no tiene sabor (**b**) *(sample) (of food)* bocado *m*; *(of drink)* trago *m*, sorbo *m*; **to give sb a t. of his own medicine** pagar a algn con la misma moneda (**c**) *(liking)* afición *f*; **everyone to his t.** sobre gustos no hay nada escrito; **to have a t. for sth** gustarle a uno algo (**d**) *(choice)* gusto *m*; **it's in bad t.** es de mal gusto; **to have (good) t.** tener (buen) gusto

  2 *vt* (**a**) *(sample)* probar, catar; **t. this wine** prueba este vino (**b**) *(experience)* experimentar, conocer

  3 *vi* **to t. of sth** saber a algo; **what does it t. like?** ¿a qué sabe?

tasteful ['teɪstfʊl] *adj* de buen gusto

tastefully ['teɪstfəlɪ] *adv* con buen gusto

tasteless ['teɪstlɪs] *adj* (**a**) *(food)* insípido(a), soso(a) (**b**) *(in bad taste)* de mal gusto

taster ['teɪstər] *n* catador(a) *m,f*

tastiness ['teɪstɪnɪs] *n* buen sabor *m*

tasting ['teɪstɪŋ] *n* degustación *f*

tasty ['teɪstɪ] *adj* (**tastier, tastiest**) sabroso(a)

tat [tæt] *n Fam* porquería *f*

ta-ta [tæ'tɑː] *interj Br Fam* ¡chao!, *Am* ¡chau!

tattered ['tætəd] *adj* hecho(a) jirones, andrajoso(a)

tatters ['tætəz] *npl* andrajos *mpl*, jirones *mpl*; **in t.** hecho(a) jirones

tattle ['tætəl] **1** *vi* parlotear; *(gossip)* chismorrear, *Am* chismear, *Col Méx* chismosear
2 *n (empty talk)* parloteo *m*, cháchara *f*; *(gossip)* chismes *mpl*, habladurías *fpl*

tattletale ['tætəlteɪl] *n US (person)* acusica *mf*, *Esp* chivato(a) *m,f*

tattoo¹ [tæ'tuː] *n Mil* retreta *f*

tattoo² [tæ'tuː] **1** *vt* tatuar
2 *n (pl* **tattoos**) *(mark)* tatuaje *m*

tatty ['tætɪ] *adj* (**tattier, tattiest**) *Br* en mal estado; *(material, clothing)* raído(a); *(décor)* deslustrado(a)

taught [tɔːt] *pt & pp see* **teach**

taunt [tɔːnt] **1** *vt* **to t. sb with sth** echar algo en cara a algn
2 *n* pulla *f*, puyazo *m*

taunting ['tɔːntɪŋ] **1** *adj (tone)* sarcástico(a), burlón(ona)
2 *n* sarcasmo *m*

Taurus ['tɔːrəs] *n Astrol Astron* Tauro *m*

taut [tɔːt] *adj* tenso(a), tirante; **to make sth t.** tensar algo

tauten ['tɔːtən] **1** *vt* tensar
2 *vi* tensarse

tautness ['tɔːtnɪs] *n* tensión *f*

tautology ['tɔːtnɪs] *n* tensión *f*

tavern ['tævən] *n* taberna *f*

tawdry ['tɔːdrɪ] *adj* (**tawdrier, tawdriest**) hortera, de oropel; *(motive)* indigno(a)

tawny ['tɔːnɪ] *adj* (**tawnier, tawniest**) leonado(a), rojizo(a)

tax [tæks] **1** *n* contribución *f*, impuesto *m*, tasa *f*; **how much t. do you pay?** ¿cuánto pagas de impuestos? ⬜ **t. avoidance** elusión *f* fiscal; **t. break** ventaja *f* fiscal; **t. collector** recaudador(a) *m,f* (de impuestos); **t. cut** reducción *f* fiscal; **t. evasion** fraude *m or* evasión *f* fiscal; **t. return** declaración *f* de renta
2 *vt* (**a**) *(person)* imponer contribuciones a; *(thing)* gravar (**b**) *(patience etc)* poner a prueba (**c**) **to t. sb about sth** acusar a algn acerca de algo

taxable ['tæksəbəl] *adj* imponible

taxation [tæk'seɪʃən] *n* (**a**) *(taxes)* impuestos *mpl*, cargas *fpl* fiscales (**b**) *(act of taxing)* imposición *f* de contribuciones

tax-deductible [tæksdɪ'dʌktɪbəl] *adj* desgravable

tax-free ['tæks'friː] **1** *adj* libre de impuestos
2 *adv* sin pagar impuestos

taxi ['tæksɪ] **1** *n* (*pl* **taxis** *or* **taxies**) taxi *m* ⬜ **t. driver** taxista *mf*; **t.** *Br* **rank** *or US* **stand** parada *f* de taxis
2 *vi* (*pt & pp* **taxied**) *(aircraft)* rodar por la pista

taxidermist ['tæksɪdɜːmɪst] *n* taxidermista *mf*

taxidermy ['tæksɪdɜːmɪ] *n* taxidermia *f*

taximeter ['tæksɪmiːtər] *n* taxímetro *m*

taxing ['tæksɪŋ] *adj* exigente

taxpayer ['tækspeɪər] *n* contribuyente *mf*

TB, tb [tiː'biː] *n (abbr* **tuberculosis**) tuberculosis *f*

tbsp *(abbr* **tablespoonful**) cucharada *f* grande

tea [tiː] *n* (**a**) *(plant, drink)* té *m* ⬜ **t. bag** bolsita *f* de té; **t. break** descanso *m*; **t. caddy** cajita *f* para el té; *Br* **t. cloth** paño *m* (de cocina); **t. cosy** cubretetera *f*; **t. leaf** hoja *f* de té; *Bot* **t. rose** rosa *f* de té; **t. service** *or* **set** juego *m* de té; *Br* **t. towel** paño *m* (de cocina) (**b**) *(snack)* merienda *f*; **to give a t. party** dar una merienda ⬜ *Br* **(high) t.** *(meal)* merienda-cena *f*

teach [tiːtʃ] **1** *vt (pt & pp* **taught**) enseñar; *(subject)* dar clases de; **she teaches French** da clases de francés; *US* **she teaches school** se dedica a la enseñanza; **to t. sb (how) to do sth** enseñar a algn a hacer algo; *Fam* **that will t. him** eso le servirá de lección; *Fam* **to t. sb a thing or two** despabilar a algn
2 *vi* dedicarse a la enseñanza, dar clases

teacher ['tiːtʃər] *n* profesor(a) *m,f*; *(in primary school)* maestro(a) *m,f*; **the teachers** el profesorado

teaching ['tiːtʃɪŋ] *n* (**a**) *(profession, action)* enseñanza *f*; **t. profession** la enseñanza; **t. staff** profesorado *m*; **to go in for t.** dedicarse a la enseñanza (**b**) **teachings** enseñanzas *fpl*, doctrina *f sing*; **the teachings of the Church** la doctrina de la Iglesia

teacup ['tiːkʌp] *n* taza *f* de té

teak [tiːk] *n Bot* teca *f*

teal [tiːl] *n (pl* **teals** *or* **teal**) *Orn* cerceta *f* común

team [tiːm] **1** *n* equipo *m*; *(of oxen)* yunta *f* ⬜ **t. player** buen(a) trabajador(a) *m,f* en equipo
2 *vi* **to t. up with sb** juntarse con algn

team-mate ['tiːmmeɪt] *n* compañero(a) *m,f* de equipo

teamster ['tiːmstər] *n US* camionero(a) *m,f*

teamwork ['tiːmwɜːk] *n* trabajo *m* en equipo

teapot ['tiːpɒt] *n* tetera *f*

tear¹ [tɪər] *n* lágrima *f*; **to be in tears** estar llorando; **to burst into tears** ponerse a llorar ⬜ **t. gas** gas *m* lacrimógeno

tear² [teər] **1** *vt (pt* **tore**; *pp* **torn**) (**a**) *(rip)* rasgar; **to t. a hole in sth** hacer un agujero *or* un desgarrón en algo; *Fig* **to be torn between two courses of action** vacilar entre dos maneras de actuar (**b**) *(snatch)* **to t. sth out of sb's hands** arrancarle algo de las manos a algn
2 *vi* (**a**) *(cloth)* rasgarse (**b**) *Aut* **to t. along** ir a toda velocidad
3 *n* desgarrón *m*, rasgón *m*; **wear and t.** desgaste *m*

tear away *vt* **to t. sb away from his work** arrancar a algn de su trabajo

tear down *vt (pull down)* derribar, arrancar; *(demolish)* derribar, demoler

tear off 1 *vt* arrancar
2 *vi* irse a toda prisa

tear out *vt* arrancar

tear up *vt* (**a**) *(document, photo)* romper, rasgar (**b**) *(plant, floorboards)* arrancar

tearaway ['teərəweɪ] *n Br* alborotador(a) *m,f*, *Esp* elemento(a) *m,f*

teardrop ['tɪədrɒp] *n* lágrima *f*

tearful ['tɪəfʊl] *adj* lloroso(a), lacrimoso(a)

tearfully ['tɪəfəlɪ] *adv* llorando, con lágrimas en los ojos

tearing ['teərɪŋ] **1** *n* **t. off** *or* **out** arranque *m*
2 *adj* **to be in a t. hurry** tener muchísima prisa, *Am* tener muchísimo apuro

tearjerker ['tɪədʒɜːkər] *n Fam* **to be a real t.** *(movie, book)* ser lacrimógeno(a)

tearoom ['tiːruːm] *n Br see* **teashop**

tear-stained ['tɪəsteɪnd] *adj* manchado(a) de lágrimas

tease [tiːz] **1** *vt* tomar el pelo a, burlarse de
2 *n (person)* bromista *mf*

teaser ['tiːzər] *n (puzzle)* rompecabezas *m inv*

teashop ['tiːʃɒp] *n Br* salón *m* de té

teasing ['tiːzɪŋ] **1** *adj (person)* burlón(ona)
2 *n* burlas *fpl*; **she was tired of his t.** estaba cansada de que le tomara el pelo

teaspoon ['tiːspuːn] *n* cucharilla *f*

teaspoonful ['ti:spu:nfʊl] *n* cucharadita *f*

teat [ti:t] *n (of animal)* teta *f*; *(of bottle)* tetina *f*

teatime ['ti:taɪm] *n esp Br (in afternoon)* hora *f* del té; *(in evening)* hora *f* de la cena *or* de cenar

techie ['tekɪ] *n Fam Comptr (person)* experto(a) *m,f* en informática

technical ['teknɪkəl] *adj* técnico(a) ◻ *Br Educ* **t. college** instituto *m* de formación profesional; **t. term** tecnicismo *m*

technicality [teknɪ'kælɪtɪ] *n* detalle *m* técnico

technically ['teknɪklɪ] *adv* (**a**) *(in technical terms)* técnicamente (**b**) *(in theory)* estrictamente hablando

technician [tek'nɪʃən] *n* técnico(a) *m,f*

technique [tek'ni:k] *n* técnica *f*

technocrat ['teknəkræt] *n* tecnócrata *mf*

technological [teknə'lɒdʒɪkəl] *adj* tecnológico(a)

technologist [tek'nɒlədʒɪst] *n* tecnólogo(a) *m,f*

technology [tek'nɒlədʒɪ] *n* tecnología *f*

teddy ['tedɪ] *n* (**a**) *(toy)* **t. (bear)** osito *m* de peluche (**b**) *(underwear)* body *m*

tedious ['ti:dɪəs] *adj* tedioso(a), aburrido(a), pesado(a)

tedium ['ti:dɪəm] *n* tedio *m*, aburrimiento *m*, pesadez *f*

tee [ti:] **1** *n Golf* tee *m*
2 *vi* **to t. off** dar el primer golpe

teem [ti:m] *vi* abundar, rebosar; **teeming with wildlife** rebosante de vida salvaje; *Fam* **it was teeming down** llovía a cántaros

teenage ['ti:neɪdʒ] *adj* adolescente

teenager ['ti:neɪdʒər] *n* adolescente *mf*

teens [ti:nʒ] *npl* adolescencia *f sing*; **she's in her early t.** tendrá trece o catorce años

teen(s)y ['ti:n(z)ɪ] *adj* (**teen(s)ier**, **teen(s)iest**), **teen(s)y-ween(s)y** ['ti:n(z)ɪ'wi:n(z)ɪ] *adj* (**teen(s)y-ween(s)ier**, **teen(s)y-ween(s)iest**) *Fam* chiquitín(ina), *Esp* pequeñín(ina)

teenybopper ['ti:nɪbɒpər] *n Fam* = quinceañera seguidora de la música pop y sus modas

tee-shirt ['ti:ʃɜ:t] *n* camiseta *f*, *Chile* polera *f*, *RP* remera *f*

teeter ['ti:tər] *vi* balancearse

teeth [ti:θ] *npl see* **tooth**

teethe [ti:ð] *vi* echar los dientes

teething ['ti:ðɪŋ] *n* dentición *f* ◻ **t. ring** chupador *m*; *Fig* **t. troubles** dificultades *fpl* iniciales

teetotal [ti:'təʊtəl] *adj* abstemio(a)

teetotalism [ti:'təʊtəlɪzəm] *n* abstinencia *f* de bebidas alcohólicas

teetotaller, *US* **teetotaler** [ti:'təʊtələr] *n* abstemio(a) *m,f*

TEFL [ti:i:ef'el, 'tefəl] *n* (*abbr* **Teaching (of) English as a Foreign Language**) enseñanza *f* del inglés como idioma extranjero

Teh(e)ran [teə'rɑ:n] *n* Teherán

tel (*abbr* **telephone (number)**) (número *m* de) teléfono *m*, tel

telecommunications ['telɪkəmju:nɪ'keɪʃənz] *n* telecomunicación *f*

telecommute ['telɪkəmju:t] *vi* teletrabajar

telecommuting ['telɪkə'mju:tɪŋ] *n* teletrabajo *m*

teleconference [telɪ'kɒnfərəns] *n* teleconferencia *f*

teleconferencing ['telɪ'kɒnfərənsɪŋ] *n* teleconferencias *fpl*

telegenic [telɪ'dʒenɪk] *adj* telegénico(a)

telegram ['telɪgræm] *n* telegrama *m*

telegraph ['telɪgræf, 'telɪgrɑ:f] **1** *n* telégrafo *m* ◻ **t. operator** telegrafista *mf*; **t. pole** poste *m* telegráfico
2 *vt & vi* telegrafiar

telegraphic [telɪ'græfɪk] *adj* telegráfico(a)

telegraphist [tɪ'legrəfɪst] *n* telegrafista *mf*

telegraphy [tɪ'legrəfɪ] *n* telegrafía *f*

telemarketing [telɪ'mɑ:kɪtɪŋ] *n Com* telemarketing *m*, ventas *fpl* por teléfono

telepathic [telɪ'pæθɪk] *adj Psych* telepático(a)

telepathy [tɪ'lepəθɪ] *n Psych* telepatía *f*

telephone ['telɪfəʊn] **1** *n* teléfono *m*; **are you on the t.?** ¿tiene teléfono?; *(speaking)* **he's on the t.** está al aparato; **you're wanted on the t.** le llaman por teléfono ◻ *Com* **t. banking** telebanca *f*, banca *f* telefónica; **t. booth, t. box** cabina *f* (telefónica); **t. call** llamada *f* telefónica, *Am* llamado *m* telefónico; **t. directory** guía *f* telefónica, *Am* directorio *m* de teléfonos; **t. exchange** central *f* telefónica; **t. number** número *m* de teléfono; *US* **t. operator** telefonista *mf*
2 *vt* telefonear, llamar por teléfono
3 *vi* telefonear, hacer una llamada telefónica

telephonist [tɪ'lefənɪst] *n Br* telefonista *mf*

telephoto ['telɪfəʊtəʊ] *adj Phot* **t. lens** teleobjetivo *m*

teleprinter ['telɪprɪntər] *n* teletipo *m*

telesales [telɪ'seɪlz] *npl Com* televentas *fpl*, ventas *fpl* por teléfono

telescope ['telɪskəʊp] **1** *n Astron* telescopio *m*
2 *vi* plegarse (como un catalejo)
3 *vt* plegar; **to t. two things together** empotrar una cosa en otra

telescopic [telɪ'skɒpɪk] *adj* telescópico(a); *(umbrella)* plegable

teleshopping ['telɪʃɒpɪŋ] *n Com* telecompra *f*

teletext ['telɪtekst] *n TV* teletexto *m*

televangelist [telɪ'vændʒəlɪst] *n* predicador *m* evangelista televisivo

televise ['telɪvaɪz] *vt* televisar

television ['telɪvɪʒən] *n* televisión *f*; **colour t.** televisión en color; **it's on (the) t. tomorrow** lo van a poner en la televisión mañana ◻ **t. play** obra *f* televisada; **t. programme** programa *m* de televisión; **t. screen** pantalla *f* de televisión; **t. (set)** televisor *m*, aparato *m* de televisión

teleworking ['telɪwɜ:kɪŋ] *n* teletrabajo *m inv*

telex ['teleks] **1** *n* télex *m*
2 *vt* enviar por télex

tell [tel] **1** *vt* (*pt & pp* **told**) (**a**) *(say)* decir; *(relate)* contar, relatar, narrar; *(inform)* comunicar, informar; **can you t. me the way to the hospital?** puede indicarme como se va al hospital; **I have been told that ...** me han dicho que ...; **I'll t. you what happened** le contaré lo que sucedió; **I shall t. him the truth** le diré la verdad; **I told you so!** ¡ya te lo dije!; **t. me when they arrive** avísame cuando lleguen; **to t. lies** mentir; **to t. sb about sth** contarle algo a algn; *Fam* **I t. you what ...** mira, pues ...; *Fam* **t. me another!** ¡cuéntaselo a tu abuela!; *Fam* **you're telling me!** ¡a mí me lo vas a contar! (**b**) *(assure)* asegurar; **he'll be furious, I (can) t. you!** ¡se va a poner furioso, te lo garantizo!; **it's not so easy, let me t. you** le aseguro que no es tan fácil (**c**) *(order)* mandar; **do as you're told** haz lo que te dicen; **to t. sb to do sth** decir a algn que haga algo (**d**) *(distinguish)* distinguir; **I can't t. them apart** no puedo distinguirlos; **to know how to t. the time** saber decir la hora; **to t. right from wrong** discernir lo que está bien de lo que está mal; **you can t. him by his voice** se le reconoce por la voz; **you can t. she is intelligent** se nota que es inteligente; **you can't t. her from her sister** es imposible distinguirla de su hermana (**e**) *(count)* contar; **all told** en total, todo incluido

2 *vi* **(a)** *(reveal)* reflejar, notarse; **his face told of suffering** su rostro reflejaba el sufrimiento **(b)** *(know)* **who can t.?** ¿quién sabe?; **you never can t.** nunca se sabe **(c)** *(have effect)* notarse; **it's beginning to t.** se empieza a notar; **these drugs t. on one** el efecto de estas drogas se hace sentir

tell off *vt Fam* regañar, reñir

tell on *vt Fam* chivarse de, *Méx* soplar a, *RP* botonear a

teller ['telər] *n* **(a)** *(cashier)* cajero(a) *m,f* **(b)** *Pol* escrutador(a) *m,f* **(c)** *(of story)* narrador(a) *m,f*

telling ['telɪŋ] **1** *adj (action)* eficaz; *(blow, argument)* contundente
2 *n* **(a)** *(of story)* narración *f*, relato *m*; *(of secret)* divulgación *f* **(b)** *(knowing)* **there's no t.** no se sabe

telling-off [telɪŋ'ɒf] *n Fam* reprimenda *f*, *Esp* bronca *f*, *Méx* jalada *f*, *RP* rezongo *m*; **to give sb a t.-o.** echar una reprimenda *or Esp* bronca a algn, dar *Méx* una jalada *or RP* un rezongo a algn

telltale ['telteɪl] *n* acusica *mf*, *Esp* chivato(a) *m,f* □ **t. signs** señales *fpl* reveladoras

telly ['telɪ] *n Br Fam* **the t.** la tele

temerity [tɪ'merɪtɪ] *n* temeridad *f*, audacia *f*

temp¹ [temp] *n (abbr* **temporary)** *Fam* trabajador(a) *m,f* temporal

temp² *(abbr* **temperature)** temperatura *f*, temp

temper ['tempər] **1** *n* **(a)** *(mood)* humor *m*; **to be in a foul t.** estar muy *Esp* enfadado(a) *or Am* enojado(a); **to keep one's t.** no perder la calma; **to lose one's t.** perder los estribos **(b)** *(temperament)* temperamento *m*, carácter *m*; **to have a bad t.** tener (mal) genio *or* carácter **(c)** *Metal* temple *m*
2 *vt Metal* templar; *Fig* suavizar

temperament ['tempərəmənt] *n* temperamento *m*

temperamental [tempərə'mentəl] *adj* temperamental

temperance ['tempərəns] *n (restraint)* moderación *f*; *(from alcohol)* abstinencia *f*

temperate ['tempərɪt] *adj* **(a)** *(language, criticism)* moderado(a) **(b)** *(climate)* templado(a)

temperature ['temprɪtʃər] *n* temperatura *f*; **to have a t.** tener fiebre

tempered ['tempəd] *adj (steel)* templado(a)

tempest ['tempɪst] *n* tempestad *f*

tempestuous [tem'pestjʊəs] *adj* tempestuoso(a)

template ['templɪt] *n (gen)* & *Comptr* plantilla *f*

temple¹ ['tempəl] *n Archit* templo *m*

temple² ['tempəl] *n Anat* sien *f*

tempo ['tempəʊ] *n (pl* **tempos** *or* **tempi** ['tempiː]) *Mus* tempo *m*

temporal ['tempərəl] *adj* **(a)** *Rel* temporal, seglar **(b)** *Anat Ling* temporal

temporarily [tempə'rerɪlɪ] *adv* temporalmente, *Am* temporariamente

temporary ['tempərərɪ] *adj* temporal, provisional, *Am* temporario(a); *(setback, improvement)* momentáneo(a), pasajero(a); *(teacher)* suplente

temporize ['tempəraɪz] *vi* contemporizar, intentar ganar tiempo

tempt [tempt] *vt* tentar; **I am tempted to accept** estoy tentado(a) de aceptar; **to t. providence** tentar la suerte; **to t. sb to do sth** incitar a algn a hacer algo

temptation [temp'teɪʃən] *n* tentación *f*

tempter ['temptər] *n* tentador(a) *m,f*

tempting ['temptɪŋ] *adj (offer)* tentador(a), apetecible; *(food)* apetitoso(a)

temptress ['tem(p)trɪs] *n Literary* seductora *f*, mujer *f* fatal

ten [ten] **1** *adj* diez *inv*; **t. workers** una decena de trabajadores
2 *n* diez *m inv*; *Fam* **t. to one he finds out!** ¡a que se entera!; *see also* **seven**

tenable ['tenəbəl] *adj (opinion)* sostenible

tenacious [tɪ'neɪʃəs] *adj* tenaz, firme

tenacity [tɪ'næsɪtɪ] *n* tenacidad *f*

tenancy ['tenənsɪ] *n (of house)* alquiler *m*; *(of land)* arrendamiento *m*

tenant ['tenənt] *n (of house)* inquilino(a) *m,f*; *(of farm)* arrendatario(a) *m,f*

tench [tentʃ] *n (fish)* tenca *f*

tend¹ [tend] *vi (be inclined)* tender, tener tendencia **(to** a); **I t. to agree with you** me inclino a compartir tu opinión; **wool tends to shrink** la lana suele encoger

tend² [tend] *vt (care for)* cuidar, ocuparse de

tendency ['tendənsɪ] *n* tendencia *f*

tendentious [ten'denʃəs] *adj* tendencioso(a)

tender¹ ['tendər] *adj (affectionate)* cariñoso(a); *(sensitive, compassionate)* compasivo(a); *(fragile)* frágil, delicado(a); *(meat)* tierno(a); **t. to the touch** suave al tacto; *Fig* **of t. years** de tierna edad

tender² ['tendər] **1** *vt (offer)* ofrecer; *(in payment)* **please t. the exact fare** por favor, tenga preparado el precio exacto; **to t. one's resignation** presentar la dimisión
2 *vi Com* **to t. for** sacar a concurso
3 *n* **(a)** *Com* oferta *f*, propuesta *f*, licitación *f*; **to invite tenders for a piece of work** sacar un trabajo *or* una obra a concurso **(b)** *(money)* **legal t.** moneda *f* de curso legal

tender³ ['tendər] *n Naut* barco *m* avituallador; *Rail* ténder *m*

tenderhearted [tendə'hɑːtɪd] *adj (compassionate)* compasivo(a); *(gentle)* bondadoso(a)

tenderloin ['tendəlɔɪn] *n Culin* filete *m*

tenderly ['tendəlɪ] *adv (affectionately)* cariñosamente, afectuosamente

tenderness ['tendənɪs] *n* ternura *f*

tendon ['tendən] *n Anat* tendón *m*

tendril ['tendrɪl] *n Bot* zarcillo *m*

tenement ['tenɪmənt] *n* bloque *m* de apartamentos

tenet ['tenɪt] *n* principio *m*, dogma *m*

tenfold ['tenfəʊld] **1** *adj* **a t. increase** un aumento por diez
2 *adv* diez veces

tenner ['tenər] *n Fam* **(a)** *Br (ten-pound note)* billete *m* de diez libras **(b)** *US (ten-dollar note)* billete *m* de diez dólares

tennis ['tenɪs] *n* tenis *m*; **to play t.** jugar al tenis □ **t. ball** pelota *f* de tenis; **t. court** pista *f* de tenis; *Med* **t. elbow** codo *m* de tenista; **t. player** jugador(a) *m,f* de tenis, tenista *mf*; **t. racket** *or* **racquet** raqueta *f* de tenis; **t. shoe** zapatilla *f* de tenis

tenor ['tenər] *n* **(a)** *Mus* tenor *m* **(b)** *(content, sense)* contenido *m*, sentido *m* general **(c)** *(of events)* curso *m*, marcha *f*

tense¹ [tens] **1** *adj* tenso(a)
2 *vt* **to t. (up)** poner en tensión

tense² [tens] *n Ling* tiempo *m*

tension ['tenʃən] *n* tensión *f*; *Elec* **high t. circuit** circuito *m* de alta tensión

tent [tent] *n* tienda *f* de campaña, *Am* carpa *f*; **to pitch a t.** armar *or* montar una tienda de campaña *or Am* carpa □ **t. peg** estaca *f*

tentacle ['tentəkəl] n tentáculo m

tentative ['tentətɪv] adj (a) (not definite) de prueba, provisional; **a t. scheme** un plan experimental (b) (hesitant) indeciso(a)

tentatively ['tentətɪvlɪ] adv a modo de prueba, provisionalmente; (hesitantly) con reservas, con indecisión

tenterhooks ['tentəhʊks] npl Fig ascuas fpl; **to be on t.** estar sobre ascuas; **to keep sb on t.** tener a algn sobre ascuas

tenth [tenθ] **1** adj décimo(a)
  2 n (a) (in series) décimo(a) m,f (b) (fraction) décimo m; see also **seventh**

tenuous ['tenjʊəs] adj (connection) tenue; (argument) poco convincente, flojo(a)

tenure ['tenjʊər] n (a) (of office) ocupación f, ejercicio m (b) Jur tenencia f (c) (of property) arrendamiento m

tepid ['tepɪd] adj tibio(a)

term [tɜːm] **1** n (a) (limit) término m, límite m; (for payment) plazo m (b) (period) período m, duración f; Educ trimestre m; Jur período m de sesiones; **during his t. of office** durante su mandato; **in the long/short t.** a largo/corto plazo ❑ US Univ **t. paper** trabajo m de fin de trimestre (c) (word, expression) término m, expresión f; **legal t.** término jurídico; **that is a contradiction in terms** esos son términos contradictorios (d) Math término m; Fig **in terms of money** en cuanto al dinero (e) **terms** (conditions) condiciones fpl, términos mpl; Com **easy t.** facilidades fpl de pago; Com **inclusive t.** precio m todo incluido; Com **t. of payment** condiciones de pago; **to come to t. with sth** aceptar algo; **to dictate t.** imponer condiciones (f) **terms** (relationship) relaciones fpl; **to be on good/bad t. with sb** mantener buenas/malas relaciones con algn; **we are on the best of t.** somos muy amigos
  2 vt (call) calificar de

terminal ['tɜːmɪnəl] **1** adj Med terminal; **t. cancer** cáncer incurable
  2 n (a) (of battery) polo m (b) (rail, bus, air) terminal f (c) Comptr terminal m

terminally ['tɜːmɪnəlɪ] adv **to be t. ill** estar en la fase terminal de una enfermedad; **t. ill patient** enfermo(a) m,f terminal

terminate ['tɜːmɪneɪt] **1** vt terminar, poner fin a; Med **to t. a pregnancy** abortar, interrumpir el embarazo
  2 vi terminarse, concluirse

termination [tɜːmɪ'neɪʃən] n (a) (end) terminación f, fin m; Med **t. of pregnancy** aborto m provocado, interrupción f del embarazo (b) Ling terminación f, desinencia f

terminology [tɜːmɪ'nɒlədʒɪ] n terminología f

terminus ['tɜːmɪnəs] n (pl **terminuses** or **termini** ['tɜːmɪnaɪ]) término m

termite ['tɜːmaɪt] n termita f, termes m inv

tern [tɜːn] n Orn **black t.** fumarel m común; **common t.** charrán m común

terrace ['terəs] **1** n (a) Agr bancal m (b) Br (of houses) hilera f de casas adosadas (c) (patio) terraza f (d) Br Ftb **the terraces** las gradas
  2 vt Agr (hillside) disponer en bancales

terraced ['terəst] adj Br **t. house** casa f adosada

terracotta [terə'kɒtə] n terracota f

terrain [tə'reɪn] n terreno m

terrapin ['terəpɪn] n Zool tortuga f acuática

terrestrial [tə'restrɪəl] adj terrestre

terrible ['terəbəl] adj terrible, espantoso(a); Fig **I feel t.** me encuentro muy mal or Esp fatal; Fam **a t. meal** una comida horrible

terribly ['terɪblɪ] adv terriblemente; Fam **I am t. grateful to you** te estoy muy agradecido

terrier ['terɪər] n Zool terrier m

terrific [tə'rɪfɪk] adj (a) (excellent) fabuloso(a), bárbaro(a); **to have a t. time** pasarlo en grande (b) (extreme) tremendo(a); **a t. heat** un calor insoportable; **at a t. speed** a una velocidad vertiginosa

terrifically [tə'rɪfɪklɪ] adv Fam (very) **she's t. clever** es un genio

terrify ['terɪfaɪ] vt (pt & pp **terrified**) aterrar, aterrorizar; **to be terrified of sth** tener pánico a algo; **to t. sb out of their wits** darle un susto de mil demonios a algn

terrifying ['terɪfaɪɪŋ] adj aterrador(a), espantoso(a) ·

territorial [terɪ'tɔːrɪəl] adj territorial; **t. waters** aguas fpl territoriales

territory ['terɪtərɪ] n territorio m

terror ['terər] n (fear) terror m, espanto m; **to be in t. of one's life** temer por la vida; Fam (person) **that child is a t.** es un niño terrible

terrorism ['terərɪzəm] n terrorismo m

terrorist ['terərɪst] adj & n terrorista (mf)

terrorize ['terəraɪz] vt aterrorizar

terror-stricken ['terəstrɪkən] adj, **terror-struck** ['terəstrʌk] adj muerto(a) de miedo

terry ['terɪ] n Tex **t. (towelling** or US **cloth)** toalla f de rizo

terse [tɜːs] adj (curt) lacónico(a)

terseness ['tɜːsnɪs] n (curtness) laconismo m

Tertiary ['tɜːʃərɪ] adj (a) (era) terciario(a) (b) Br **t. education** enseñanza f superior

TESL [tiːiːes'el, 'tesəl] n (abbr **Teaching (of) English as a Second Language**) enseñanza f del inglés como segunda lengua

TESOL ['tiːsəl] n (abbr **Teaching of English to Speakers of Other Languages**) enseñanza f del inglés a hablantes de otras lenguas

test [test] **1** vt (gen) probar, someter a una prueba; (analyze) analizar; Med (blood, urine) hacer un análisis de; (new drug) experimentar; **to t. sb in algebra** examinar a algn de álgebra; **to t. sb's ability** comprobar la capacidad de algn
  2 n prueba f, examen m, test m; **to do tests** hacer pruebas; **to put to the t.** poner a prueba; **to stand the t.** pasar la prueba; Fig **acid t.** prueba del fuego; Fig **it was a t. of her patience** puso a prueba su paciencia ❑ Med **blood t.** análisis m inv de sangre; Aut **driving t.** examen m de Esp conducir or Am manejar; Jur **t. case** juicio m que hace jurisprudencia; Sport **t. match** partido m internacional; Av **t. pilot** piloto m de pruebas; **t. tube** probeta f, tubo m de ensayo; **t.-tube baby** niño m probeta

testament ['testəmənt] n testamento m ❑ **Old/New T.** Antiguo/Nuevo Testamento

test-drive ['testdraɪv] vt Aut probar en carretera

testicle ['testɪkəl] n testículo m

testify ['testɪfaɪ] **1** vt (pt & pp **testified**) Jur atestiguar, declarar; **to t. sth under oath** declarar algo bajo juramento; **to t. that ...** declarar que ...
  2 vi **to t. in sb's favour/against sb** declarar a favor/en contra de algn; Fig **to t. to sth** atestiguar algo

testily ['testɪlɪ] adv en tono irritado

testimonial [testɪ'məʊnɪəl] n (carta f de) recomendación f

testimony ['testɪmənɪ] n Jur testimonio m, declaración f; **to bear t. to sth** atestiguar algo

testing ['testɪŋ] adj **a t. time** una época difícil ❑ **t. ground** zona f de pruebas

testis ['testɪs] n (pl **testes** ['testiːz]) testículo m

testosterone [tes'tɒstərəʊn] n Biol testosterona f

thighbone ['θaɪbəʊn] *n Anat* fémur *m*

thimble ['θɪmbəl] *n* dedal *m*

thimbleful ['θɪmbəlfʊl] *n (of cognac etc)* dedo *m*

thin [θɪn] **1** *adj* (**thinner, thinnest**) (**a**) *(not thick)* delgado(a), fino(a); *(person)* delgado(a), flaco(a); **a t. slice** una loncha fina; **t.-lipped** de labios finos; **to get thinner** adelgazar (**b**) *(not thick or dense) (hair, vegetation)* ralo(a); *(liquid)* claro(a), poco denso(a); *(population)* escaso(a) (**c**) *Fig (voice)* endeble, débil; **a t. excuse** un pobre pretexto; **to have a t. time of it** pasarlo mal
2 *adv* **to cut t.** cortar en rebanadas finas; **to spread the paint t.** pintar con capas finas
3 *vt (pt & pp* **thinned**) **to t. (down)** *(person)* adelgazar; *(paint)* diluir; **to t. (out)** *(wood)* aclarar; *(plants)* entresacar
4 *vi* adelgazar; *(diminish)* disminuir (en espesor); **his hair is thinning** está perdiendo pelo

thine [ðaɪn] *Literary & Rel* **1** *adj* tu
2 *pron* tuyo

thing [θɪŋ] *n* (**a**) *(object)* cosa *f*; **that's the very t. for me** eso es exactamente lo que (me) hace falta; **what's that t.?** ¿qué es eso *or Esp* ese chisme *or CAm Carib Col* esa vaina? (**b**) *Fam (person)* **poor little t.!** ¡pobrecito!; **you lucky t.!** ¡vaya suerte que tienes! (**c**) *(situation, fashion, progress, etc)* cosas *fpl*; **as things are** tal como están las cosas; **first t. in the morning** a primera hora de la mañana; **for another t.** por otra parte; **for one t.** en primer lugar; **he expects great things of the new treatment** espera mucho del nuevo tratamiento; **I'd like to go, but the t. is ...** me gustaría ir, pero resulta que ...; **it's just one of those things** son cosas que pasan; **it's not the (done) t.** eso no se hace; **the latest t. in hats** lo último en sombreros; **things are going badly** las cosas van mal; **what with one t. and another** entre unas cosas y otras; *Fig* **to know a t. or two** conocer el percal (**d**) **things** *Fam (clothing)* ropa *f sing*; *(possessions)* cosas *fpl*; **to pack up one's t.** hacer las maletas; **to put one's t. away** ordenar las cosas; **to wash up the tea** *or* **dinner t.** fregar los platos

thingamajig ['θɪŋəmədʒɪɡ] *n Fam*, **thingumabob** ['θɪŋəməbɒb] *n Fam*, **thingummy** ['θɪŋəmɪ] *n Fam* chisme *m*

think [θɪŋk] **1** *vt (pt & pp* **thought**) (**a**) *(believe, consider)* pensar, creer; **I hardly t. it likely** me parece poco probable; **I t. so/not** creo que sí/no; **they are thought to be rich** pasan por ricos (**b**) *(have as opinion)* opinar, pensar; **I don't t. much of the idea** no me hace mucha gracia la idea; **she thought nothing of getting up at six a.m.** se levantaba a las seis de la madrugada y tan tranquila; **t. nothing of it** no tiene importancia; **what do you t.?** ¿a ti qué te parece?; **what do you t. of the house?** ¿qué opinas de la casa? (**c**) *(imagine)* imaginar; **I thought as much** yo me lo imaginaba; **to t. that it cost only a pound** y pensar que costó sólo una libra; **who would have thought it?** ¿quién lo hubiera dicho or imaginado?
2 *vi* (**a**) *(cogitate)* pensar (**of, about** en); **give me time to t.** dame tiempo para reflexionar; **his name was ..., let me t.** se llamaba ..., vamos a ver; **I didn't t. of telling her** no se me ocurrió decírselo; **she thinks of everything** piensa en todo; **to t. ahead** prevenir; *Fam* **to t. big** tener grandes proyectos (para el futuro); **to t. well** *or* **highly of sb** apreciar a algn (**b**) *(imagine)* imaginar; **just t.!** ¡imagínate!; **t. of what could happen** imagina lo que podría pasar (**c**) *(remember)* **I can't t. of her name** no recuerdo su nombre
3 *n* **to have a quiet t. about sth** pensar algo con calma; *Fam* **you've got another t. coming!** ¡no te hagas ilusiones!

think back *vi* **to t. back to when ...** recordar cuando ..., acordarse de cuando ...

think out *vt (matter)* examinar, meditar; *(plan)* elaborar; **a carefully thought-out answer** una respuesta razonada; **to t. things out for oneself** juzgar las cosas por uno mismo

think over *vt* reflexionar, pensar (detenidamente); **we'll have to t. it over** lo tendremos que pensar

think up *vt* imaginar, idear; *Fam* **what have you been thinking up?** ¿qué estás tramando?

thinker ['θɪŋkər] *n* pensador(a) *m,f*

thinking ['θɪŋkɪŋ] **1** *n* pensamiento *m*; **I'll have to do some t.** lo tendré que pensar; **to my way of t.** a mi parecer
2 *adj* racional; **to put on one's t. cap** reflexionar

think-tank ['θɪŋktæŋk] *n Fam* grupo *m* de expertos

thinly ['θɪnlɪ] *adv* poco, ligeramente; *(spread)* con capas finas; **t. populated** poco poblado(a)

thinned [θɪnd] *pt & pp see* **thin**

thinner ['θɪnər] *n* disolvente *m*

thinness ['θɪnnɪs] *n (of person)* delgadez *f*, flaqueza *f*; *(of liquid)* fluidez *f*

third [θɜːd] **1** *adj* tercero(a); *(before masculine singular noun)* tercer; **George the t.** Jorge III, Jorge Tercero; **(on) the t. of March** el tres de marzo ❑ **the T. World** el Tercer Mundo; *Ins* **t. party insurance** seguro *m* a terceros; *Jur* **t. person** tercero(a) *m,f*
2 *n* (**a**) *(in series)* tercero(a) *m,f* (**b**) *(fraction)* tercio *m*, tercera parte *f*; **a t. of the inhabitants** la tercera parte de los habitantes; *see also* **seventh** (**c**) *Mus* tercera *f* (**d**) *Aut* tercera (velocidad) *f*

third-class ['θɜːdklɑːs] *adj* de tercera clase

thirdly ['θɜːdlɪ] *adv* en tercer lugar

third-rate ['θɜːdreɪt] *adj* de calidad inferior

third-world ['θɜːd'wɜːld] *adj* del tercer mundo, tercer-mundista

thirst [θɜːst] *n* sed *f*; *Fig* afán *m*; **to quench one's t.** apagar la sed; *Fig* **the t. for knowledge** la sed de saber

thirsting ['θɜːstɪŋ] *adj Fig* sediento(a) (**for** de)

thirsty ['θɜːstɪ] *adj* (**thirstier, thirstiest**) sediento(a); **to be t.** tener sed

thirteen [θɜː'tiːn] *adj & n* trece *(m); see also* **seven**

thirteenth [θɜː'tiːnθ] **1** *adj* decimotercero(a); **(on) the t. of May** el trece de mayo
2 *n* (**a**) *(in series)* decimotercero(a) *m,f* (**b**) *(fraction)* decimotercera parte *f*; *see also* **seventh**

thirtieth ['θɜːtɪɪθ] **1** *adj* trigésimo(a); **(on) the t. of June** el treinta de junio
2 *n* (**a**) *(in series)* trigésimo(a) *m,f* (**b**) *(fraction)* trigésima parte *f*; *see also* **seventh**

thirty ['θɜːtɪ] *adj & n* treinta *(m)*; **t.-one** treinta y uno; **about t. people** una treintena de personas; *see also* **seven**

this [ðɪs] **1** *(pl* **these**) *dem pron* (**a**) *(indefinite)* esto; **do you want t. or that?** ¿quieres esto o aquello?; **it was like t.** fue así; **the thing is t.** lo que pasa es esto; **what good is t.?** ¿para qué sirve esto? (**b**) *(place)* **t. is where we met** fue aquí donde nos conocimos (**c**) *(time)* **it should have come before t.** debería haber llegado ya (**d**) *(specific person or thing)* éste *m*, ésta *f*; **I prefer these to those** me gustan más éstos que aquéllos; *(introduction)* **t. is Mr Alvarez** le presento al Sr. Alvarez; *Tel* **t. is Julia (speaking)** soy Julia
2 *dem adj (pl* **these**) *(masculine)* este; *(feminine)* esta; **t. book/these books** este libro/estos libros
3 *adv* **he got t. far** llegó hasta aquí; **t. high** así de alto

thistle ['θɪsəl] *n Bot* cardo *m*

thistledown ['θɪsəldaʊn] *n* vilano *m* de cardo

thither ['ðɪðər] *adv* **to run hither and t.** correr de un lado para otro

thong [θɒŋ] *n* (**a**) *(for fastening)* correa *f* (**b**) *(underwear)* tanga *m* (**c**) *Austral US (sandal)* chancleta *f*, chancla *f*

thorax ['θɔːræks] *n (pl* **thoraxes** *or* **thoraces** ['θɔːrəsiːz]) *Anat* tórax *m*

thorn [θɔːn] n espina f; Fig **to be a t. in sb's flesh** ser una espina clavada

thorny ['θɔːnɪ] adj (**thornier, thorniest**) espinoso(a)

thorough ['θʌrə] adj (**a**) (careful) minucioso(a); (work) concienzudo(a); (knowledge) profundo(a); **to carry out a t. enquiry into a matter** investigar a fondo un asunto; **to give a room a t. cleaning** limpiar una habitación a fondo (**b**) (utter) total; Fam **a t. scoundrel** un sinvergüenza redomado

thoroughbred ['θʌrəbred] **1** adj (horse) de pura sangre; (dog) de raza
2 n (horse) pura sangre mf; (dog) perro(a) m,f de raza

thoroughfare ['θʌrəfeər] n (road) carretera f; (street) calle f; **public t.** vía f pública

thoroughgoing ['θʌrəgəʊɪŋ] adj (**a**) (careful) minucioso(a) (**b**) (absolute) completo(a), total; (stupidity) profundo(a) (**c**) (firm) (supporter) acérrimo(a)

thoroughly ['θʌrəlɪ] adv (**a**) (carefully) a fondo (**b**) (wholly) completamente; **I t. enjoyed myself** me lo pasé en grande

thoroughness ['θʌrənɪs] n minuciosidad f, perfección f

those [ðəʊz] **1** dem pron pl ésos(as); (remote) aquéllos(as); (with rel) los, las
2 dem adj pl esos(as); (remote) aquellos(as); see **that**

thou [ðaʊ] pron Literary & Rel tú

though [ðəʊ] **1** conj aunque; **strange t. it may seem** por (muy) extraño que parezca; **we shall have to do it, even t. it's going to be difficult** tendremos que hacerlo, aunque resulte difícil; **as t.** como si; **he spoke as t. we were right** hablaba como si tuviéramos razón; **it looks as t. he's gone** parece que se ha ido
2 adv a pesar de todo, sin embargo; **we had a good time, t.** sin embargo, lo pasamos bien

thought [θɔːt] **1** pt & pp see **think**
2 n (**a**) (act of thinking) pensamiento m; **gloomy thoughts** pensamientos sombríos; **I didn't give it another t.** no volví a pensar en ello; **the mere t. of it** nada más pensarlo; **what a tempting t.!** ¡qué idea más tentadora!; **what a t.!** ¡qué horror!; Fam **a penny for your thoughts** ¿en qué estás pensando? (**b**) (reflection) reflexión f, consideración f; **after much t.** después de pensarlo mucho; **lack of t.** irreflexión f; **lost in t.** ensimismado(a); **on second thoughts** si bien se mira (**c**) (intention) intención f, propósito m; **it's the t. that counts** lo que cuenta es la intención; **with the t. of talking to him** con la intención de hablar con él

thoughtful ['θɔːtfʊl] adj (pensive) pensativo(a), meditabundo(a); (careful) sensato(a), prudente; (considerate) atento(a); **he was t. enough to let me know** tuvo la amabilidad de avisarme

thoughtfully ['θɔːtfəlɪ] adv pensativamente; (carefully) prudentemente; (considerately) con consideración, atentamente

thoughtfulness ['θɔːtfʊlnɪs] n meditación f; (carefulness) prudencia f; (consideration) consideración f

thoughtless ['θɔːtlɪs] adj (person) desconsiderado(a), poco atento(a); (action) irreflexivo(a)

thoughtlessness ['θɔːtlɪsnɪs] n (of person) falta f de consideración; (in action) irreflexión f

thought-out ['θɔːt'aʊt] adj **well/poorly t.-o.** (plan, scheme) bien/mal meditado(a)

thought-provoking ['θɔːtprəvəʊkɪŋ] adj intelectualmente estimulante

thousand ['θaʊzənd] **1** adj mil; **a t. men** mil hombres; **about a t. men** un millar de hombres; **a t. years** un milenio
2 n mil m, millar m; **he's one in a t.** es un hombre entre mil; **thousands of people** miles or millares de personas

thousandth ['θaʊzənθ] **1** adj milésimo(a)
2 n (**a**) (in series) milésimo(a) m,f (**b**) (fraction) milésima parte f

thrash [θræʃ] **1** vt dar una paliza a
2 vi to t. **about** or **around** agitarse, revolverse

thrash out vt (matter) discutir a fondo

thread [θred] **1** n (**a**) (of cotton, nylon) hilo m; **length of t.** hebra f; Fig **to hang by a t.** pender de un hilo (**b**) Fig (of argument etc) hilo m; **to lose the t. (of the story)** perder el hilo (de la historia) (**c**) (of screw) rosca f, filete m
2 vt (**a**) (needle) enhebrar; (beads) ensartar (**b**) to t. **one's way** abrirse paso, colarse (**through** por)

threadbare ['θredbeər] adj (clothes etc) raído(a); (argument) trillado(a)

threat [θret] n amenaza f; **to be under the t. of sth** estar amenazado(a) de algo; Fig **there is a t. of rain** amenaza lluvia

threaten ['θretən] **1** vt amenazar; **to t. to do sth** amenazar con hacer algo
2 vi **a storm is threatening** amenaza tormenta

threatening ['θretənɪŋ] adj amenazador(a)

threateningly ['θretənɪŋlɪ] adv (act) de modo amenazador; (speak) en tono amenazador

three [θriː] adj & n tres (m); **to come in t. by t.** or **t. at a time** entrar de tres en tres; see also **seven**

three-act ['θriːækt] adj (play) en tres actos

three-cornered ['θriːkɔːnəd] adj triangular □ **t.-c. hat** sombrero m de tres picos, tricornio m

three-course meal ['θriːkɔːs'miːl] n comida f de tres platos

three-dimensional [θriːdɪ'menʃənəl] adj tridimensional

threefold ['θriːfəʊld] **1** adj triple
2 adv tres veces; **the population has increased t.** la población se ha triplicado

three-four ['θriːfɔːr] adj Mus **t.-f. time** compás m de tres por cuatro

three-legged ['θriːlegɪd] adj de tres patas

three-piece ['θriːpiːs] adj **t.-p. suit** traje m de tres piezas; **t.-p. suite** tresillo m

three-ply ['θriːplaɪ] adj Tex de tres hebras

three-point ['θriːpɔɪnt] adj Aut **t.-p. turn** cambio m de sentido

three-quarter [θriː'kwɔːtər] adj (de) tres cuartos; **t.-q. length coat** abrigo m tres cuartos

three-quarters [θriː'kwɔːtəz] **1** pron (amount) tres cuartos mpl, tres cuartas fpl partes
2 adv **t.-q. full/finished** lleno(a)/terminado(a) en sus tres cuartas partes

threesome ['θriːsəm] n grupo m de tres personas; **we went in a t.** fuimos los tres juntos

three-wheeler [θriː'wiːlər] n Aut coche m de tres ruedas; (bicycle) triciclo m

thresh [θreʃ] vt Agr trillar

thresher ['θreʃər] n (implement) trillo m; (machine) trilladora f

threshold ['θreʃəʊld] n umbral m; Fig **to be on the t. of a new discovery** estar a las puertas de un nuevo descubrimiento

threw [θruː] pt see **throw**

thrice [θraɪs] adv Literary tres veces

thrift [θrɪft] n, **thriftiness** ['θrɪftɪnɪs] n economía f, frugalidad f

thrifty ['θrɪftɪ] *adj* (**thriftier, thriftiest**) económico(a), ahorrador(a)

thrill [θrɪl] **1** *n* (**a**) *(excitement)* emoción *f*, ilusión *f*; **what a t.!** ¡qué emoción! (**b**) *(quiver)* estremecimiento *m*

2 *vt* (**a**) *(excite)* emocionar; *(audience)* electrizar; **I am thrilled about the trip** estoy muy ilusionado con el viaje (**b**) *(make tremble)* estremecer

3 *vi* *(be excited)* emocionarse; *(tremble)* estremecerse

thriller ['θrɪlər] *n* *(novel)* novela *f* de *Esp* suspense *or Am* suspenso, thriller *m*; *(film)* película *f* de *Esp* suspense *or Am* suspenso, thriller *m*

thrilling ['θrɪlɪŋ] *adj* emocionante, apasionante; **how t.!** ¡qué emocionante!

thrive [θraɪv] *vi* (*pt* **thrived** *or* **throve**; *pp* **thrived** *or* **thriven** ['θrɪvən]) (**a**) *(person)* rebosar de salud; *(plant)* crecer bien (**b**) *Fig (business)* prosperar, medrar; **he thrives on it** le viene de maravilla; **to t. on other people's misfortunes** sacar provecho de las desgracias de otros

thriving ['θraɪvɪŋ] *adj* (**a**) *(plant)* lozano(a) (**b**) *Fig (person, business)* próspero(a), floreciente

throat [θrəʊt] *n* garganta *f*; **to clear one's t.** aclararse la voz; **to have a lump in one's t.** tener un nudo en la garganta; **to have a sore t.** tener dolor de garganta; *Fig* **to jump down sb's t.** echar una bronca a algn

throaty ['θrəʊtɪ] *adj* (**throatier, throatiest**) gutural

throb [θrɒb] **1** *n* *(of heart)* latido *m*, pulsación *f*; *(of machine)* zumbido *m*

2 *vi* (*pt & pp* **throbbed**) *(heart)* latir, palpitar; *(machine)* zumbar; **my head is throbbing** me va a estallar la cabeza

throbbing ['θrɒbɪŋ] *n* *(of heart)* latido *m*, palpitación *f*; *(of motor)* zumbido *m*; *(of wound)* punzada *f*

throes [θrəʊz] *npl* **to be in one's death t.** estar agonizando; *Fig* **we're in the t. of a revolution** estamos en plena revolución

thrombosis [θrɒm'bəʊsɪs] *npl Med* trombosis *f sing* ▫ **coronary t.** infarto *m sing* de miocardio

throne [θrəʊn] *n* trono *m*; **to come to the t.** subir al trono

throng [θrɒŋ] **1** *n* multitud *f*, gentío *m*

2 *vi* *(pack together)* apiñarse; **people thronged into the house** la gente entraba en tropel en la casa

3 *vt* atestar; **a street thronged with people** una calle llena de gente

throttle ['θrɒtəl] **1** *n* *(of engine)* **t. (valve)** válvula *f* reguladora; **to open (up) the t.** acelerar

2 *vt (person)* estrangular, ahogar

throttle back *vt (engine)* desacelerar

throttling ['θrɒtlɪŋ] *n* *(of person)* estrangulación *f*, estrangulamiento *m*

through [θruː] **1** *prep* (**a**) *(place)* a través de, por; **to look t. the window** mirar por la ventana; **to pass t. a city** pasar por una ciudad; **to talk t. one's nose** hablar con la nariz; *Fig* **to go t. sb's pockets** registrar los bolsillos de algn; *Fam* **he's been t. it** ha pasado lo suyo (**b**) *(time)* a lo largo de; **all t. his life** durante toda su vida; *US* **Monday t. Friday** de lunes a viernes (**c**) *(expressing progress)* **he's t. his examination** ha aprobado el examen; **I'm half-way t. this book** he leído la mitad de este libro (**d**) *(by means of)* por, mediante; **I learnt of it t. Jack** me enteré por Jack; **to send sth t. the post** enviar algo por correo (**e**) *(because of)* a *or* por causa de; **absent t. illness** ausente por enfermedad; **t. fear/ignorance** por miedo/ignorancia; **t. your stupidity, we got lost** por tu estupidez, nos perdimos

2 *adj* **t. ticket** billete *m* directo; **a t. train** un tren directo; **t. traffic** tránsito *m*

3 *adv* (**a**) *(from one side to the other)* de un lado a otro; **the**

water poured t. el agua entraba *or* salía a raudales; **to let sb t.** dejar pasar a algn; **wet t.** calado(a) hasta los huesos; *Fig* **socialist t. and t.** socialista a ultranza (**b**) *(to or at an end)* **I'm t. with him** he terminado con él; **to see sth t.** llevar algo a cabo (**c**) *(directly)* **the train runs t. to Paris** el tren va directo hasta París (**d**) *Tel* **to get t. to sb** comunicar con algn; **you're t.** hablen

throughout [θruː'aʊt] **1** *prep* (por) todo(a); **t. the country** por todo el país; **t. the year** durante todo el año

2 *adv* *(place)* en todas partes; *(time)* todo el tiempo; **central heating t.** calefacción central en todas las habitaciones

throughput ['θruːpʊt] *n* rendimiento *m*

throughway ['θruːweɪ] *n US* autopista *f*

throve [θrəʊv] *pt see* **thrive**

throw [θrəʊ] **1** *vt* (*pt* **threw**; *pp* **thrown**) (**a**) *(with hands)* *(in general)* tirar, *Am* aventar; *(ball, javelin)* lanzar; **to t. a sheet over sth** cubrir algo con una sábana (**b**) *(to the ground)* derribar, tumbar; *(rider)* desmontar (**c**) *(project) (image, shadow, voice)* proyectar; **to t. some light on a question** arrojar luz sobre un asunto; **to t. the blame on sb** echar la culpa a algn (**d**) *(have)* **to t. a fit** *(get angry)* ponerse hecho(a) una furia; **to t. a party** dar una fiesta (**e**) *(disconcert)* desconcertar

2 *n* tiro *m*, lanzamiento *m*; *(of dice)* lance *m*; *(in wrestling)* derribo *m*; **within a stone's t. of ...** a tiro de piedra de ...

throw about *vt (things)* esparcir; *(money)* derrochar; **to be thrown about** ser sacudido(a); **to t. one's arms about** agitar los brazos

throw away *vt (rubbish)* tirar, *Am* botar; *(time, money)* malgastar; *(opportunity)* perder, desaprovechar

throw down *vt* tirar (hacia abajo *or* al suelo); **to t. down a challenge** lanzar un desafío

throw in *vt* (**a**) *(into a place)* tirar; *Sport* sacar de banda; **he threw it in the river** lo tiró al río; *Cards* **to t. in one's hand** abandonar la partida; *Fig* **to t. in the towel** arrojar la toalla (**b**) *(include)* añadir; *(in deal)* incluir (gratis); *Fig* **to t. in one's lot with sb** compartir la suerte de algn

throw off *vt (person, thing)* deshacerse de; *(clothes)* quitarse; **to t. off a cold** curarse de un resfriado; **to t. the dogs off the scent** despistar a los perros

throw out *vt (rubbish)* tirar, *Am* botar; *(person)* echar, expulsar; *(legislation)* rechazar (**b**) **to t. out one's chest** sacar pecho (**c**) *(heat)* despedir, arrojar

throw up **1** *vt* (**a**) *(raise)* **to t. up one's hands** *(in horror, dismay)* echarse las manos a la cabeza (**b**) *Constr* construir rápidamente (**c**) *(abandon)* **to t. up one's job** dejar el trabajo

2 *vi* vomitar, devolver

throwaway ['θrəʊəweɪ] *adj* desechable; **t. cups/plates** tazas/platos desechables

throwback ['θrəʊbæk] *n* retroceso *m*

thrower ['θrəʊər] *n Sport* lanzador(a) *m,f*

throw-in ['θrəʊɪn] *n Sport* saque *m* de banda

thrown [θrəʊn] *pp see* **throw**

thru [θruː] *prep US see* **through**

thrush [θrʌʃ] *n Orn* tordo *m*, zorzal *m* ▫ **blue rock t.** roquero *m* solitario; **mistle t.** zorzal *m* charlo; **rock t.** roquero *m* rojo; **song t.** zorzal *m* común

thrust [θrʌst] **1** *vt* (*pt & pp* **thrust**) *(push)* empujar con fuerza; **he t. a letter into my hand** me puso una carta violentamente en la mano; **to t. oneself upon sb** pegarse a algn; **to t. one's way through the crowd** abrirse paso entre la multitud

2 *n* *(push)* empujón *m*; *(with sword)* estocada *f*; *Av Phys* empuje *m*; *Mil* ofensiva *f*

thruway ['θruːweɪ] *n US Aut* autopista *f*

thud [θʌd] **1** *n* ruido *m* sordo

  2 *vi (pt & pp* **thudded**) emitir un ruido sordo; **it thudded to the ground** cayó a tierra

thug [θʌg] *n (lout)* gamberro *m*, matón *m*; *(criminal)* gángster *m*

thumb [θʌm] **1** *n* pulgar *m*; **he's under his brother's t.** su hermano lo tiene metido en un puño; **to give sth the thumbs up/down** aprobar/desaprobar algo; *Fig* **to be all thumbs** ser un torpe *or* manazas ❑ **t. index** uñeros *mpl*

  2 *vt* **a well-thumbed book** un libro manoseado; *Fam* **to t. a ride** *or Br* **lift** hacer dedo, *CAm Méx Perú* pedir aventón

thumb through *vt (book)* hojear

thumb-index ['θʌmɪndeks] *vt (book)* poner uñeros a

thumbnail ['θʌmneɪl] *n* uña *f* del pulgar ❑ **t. sketch** *Art* croquis *m* en miniatura; *(description)* retrato *m* breve

thumbprint ['θʌmprɪnt] *n* huella *f* del pulgar

thumbtack ['θʌmtæk] *n US Esp* chincheta *f, Am* chinche *m*

thump [θʌmp] **1** *n* (**a**) *(sound)* ruido *m* sordo (**b**) *(blow)* golpazo *m*; *(with fist)* puñetazo *m*; *Fam* tortazo *m*, torta *f*

  2 *vt* golpear; *Fam* dar un tortazo a

  3 *vi* (**a**) **to t. on the table** golpear la mesa (**b**) *(heart)* latir ruidosamente

thumping ['θʌmpɪŋ] *adj Slang* **a t. great lorry** un enorme camionazo

thunder ['θʌndər] **1** *n* trueno *m*; **peals of t.** truenos *mpl*; **there's t. in the air** hace tiempo de tormenta; **t. of applause** estruendo *m* de aplausos

  2 *vi* tronar; *Fig* **to t. out threats** fulminar con amenazas

thunderbolt ['θʌndəbəʊlt] *n (lighting)* rayo *m*; *Fig (news)* bomba *f*

thunderclap ['θʌndəklæp] *n* trueno *m*

thundercloud ['θʌndəklaʊd] *n* nube *f* de tormenta; *Fig* nube negra

thundering ['θʌndərɪŋ] *adj* (**a**) *(sound)* atronador(a) (**b**) *Fig (success etc)* inmenso(a), fulminante; **to be in a t. rage** estar de un humor de perros

thunderous ['θʌndərəs] *adj Fig* ensordecedor(a); **t. applause** aplausos ensordecedores

thunderstorm ['θʌndəstɔːm] *n* tormenta *f*

thunderstruck ['θʌndəstrʌk] *adj* pasmado(a), atónito(a)

thundery ['θʌndərɪ] *adj (weather)* tormentoso(a), de tormenta

Thur, Thurs *(abbr* **Thursday)** jueves *m*, juev.

Thursday ['θɜːzdɪ] *n* jueves *m*; *see also* **Saturday**

thus [ðʌs] *adv* así, de esta manera; **and t. ...** así que ...; **you do it t.** lo haces así

thwart [θwɔːt] *vt* frustrar, desbaratar

thy [ðaɪ] *adj Literary & Rel* tu; **love t. neighbour** amarás al prójimo

thyme [taɪm] *n Bot* tomillo *m*

thyroid ['θaɪrɔɪd] **1** *adj* tiroideo(a)

  2 *n* **t. (gland)** (glándula *f*) tiroides *f inv*

thyself [ðaɪ'self] *pron Literary & Rel* tú mismo(a); **for t.** para ti mismo

tiara [tɪ'ɑːrə] *n Rel* tiara *f*; *(diadem)* diadema *f*

Tiber ['taɪbər] *n* **the T.** el Tíber

Tibet [tɪ'bet] *n* Tíbet

Tibetan [tɪ'betən] *adj & n* tibetano(a) *(m,f)*

tibia ['tɪbɪə] *n (pl* **tibias** *or* **tibiae** ['tɪbiːɪ]) *Anat* tibia *f*

tic [tɪk] *n* tic *m*

tick¹ [tɪk] **1** *n* (**a**) *(sound)* tic-tac *m* (**b**) *Br Fam (moment)*

momento *m*, instante *m*; **half a t.!** ¡un momentito!; **I'll do it in a t.** ahora mismo lo hago (**c**) *Br (mark)* marca *f*, señal *f*; **to put a t. against a name** hacer una marca al lado de un nombre

  2 *vi* hacer tic-tac

  3 *vt Br* marcar, señalar; **to t. an answer** señalar la respuesta correcta

tick off *vt* (**a**) *(mark)* marcar (**b**) *Br Fam (reprimand)* regañar, echar un rapapolvo a (**c**) *US Fam (irritate)* fastidiar, mosquear

tick over *vi Aut (engine)* funcionar al ralentí

tick² [tɪk] *n Ent* garrapata *f*

tick³ [tɪk] *n Br Fam (credit)* crédito *m*; **to buy sth on t.** comprar algo a crédito

ticker ['tɪkər] *n* (**a**) *Slang (heart)* corazón *m* (**b**) *(stock exchange)* **t. tape** cinta *f* de teletipo

ticket ['tɪkɪt] *n* (**a**) *(for train, plane, lottery)* billete *m*, *Am* boleto *m*, *esp Am* pasaje *m*; *(for theatre, cinema)* entrada *f*, *Col Méx* boleto *m* ❑ **t. collector** revisor(a) *m,f*; **t. office** taquilla *f*, *Am* boletería *f* (**b**) *(receipt)* recibo *m* (**c**) *(label)* etiqueta *f*, rótulo *m* (**d**) *Aut* multa *f*; **he got a t. for speeding** le pusieron una multa por exceso de velocidad (**e**) *Fam* **that's the t.** justo lo que necesitaba

ticking¹ ['tɪkɪŋ] *n (of clock)* tic-tac *m*

ticking² ['tɪkɪŋ] *n Tex* terliz *m*

ticking-off [tɪkɪŋ'ɒf] *n Fam* **to give sb a t.-o.** echar *Esp* un rapapolvo *or Am* un regaño a algn

tickle ['tɪkəl] **1** *vt* hacer cosquillas a; *Fam* **she was tickled pink with her new car** estaba feliz como unas pascuas con el coche nuevo; *Fam* **to t. sb's fancy** atraer *or Esp* apetecer *or Carib Col Méx* provocar *or Méx* antojársele a algn

  2 *vi* hacer cosquillas, picar; **this scarf tickles** esta bufanda pica

  3 *n* cosquillas *fpl*; **to have a t. in one's throat** tener la garganta irritada

tickling ['tɪklɪŋ] *n* cosquilleo *m*

ticklish ['tɪklɪʃ] *adj* (**a**) *(person)* **to be t.** tener cosquillas (**b**) *Fam (situation)* delicado(a), peliagudo(a), *Méx* pelón(ona)

tick-tock ['tɪktɒk] *n* tic-tac *m*

tic-tac-toe [tɪktæk'təʊ] *n US* tres en raya *m*

tidal ['taɪdəl] *adj* de la marea; **the river is t. as far as the lock** los efectos de la marea llegan hasta la esclusa ❑ **t. energy** energía *f* mareomotriz; **t. wave** ola *f* gigante

tidbit ['tɪdbɪt] *n US see* **titbit**

tiddler ['tɪdlər] *n Br Fam (fish)* pececito *m*; *(child)* renacuajo(a) *m,f*, *Méx* cosita *f*, *RP* piojo *m*

tiddly ['tɪdlɪ] *adj* (**tiddlier, tiddliest**) *Br Fam* trompa

tiddlywinks ['tɪdlɪwɪŋks] *n (game)* pulga *f*

tide [taɪd] **1** *n* (**a**) *(of sea)* marea *f*; **high/low t.** marea alta/baja (**b**) *Fig (of events)* marcha *f*, curso *m*; **the t. has turned** han cambiado las cosas; **the t. of opinion** la corriente de opinión; **to go against the t.** ir contra corriente

  2 *vt* **to t. over** echar un capote a; **thirty dollars will t. me over till the weekend** con treinta dólares me las arreglaré hasta el fin de semana

tidemark ['taɪdmɑːk] *n* línea *f* de la marea alta

tideway ['taɪdweɪ] *n* canal *m* de marea

tidied ['taɪdɪd] *pt & pp see* **tidy**

tidiness ['taɪdɪnɪs] *n (in good order)* orden *m*; *(of appearance)* pulcritud *f*, limpieza *f*

tidings ['taɪdɪŋz] *npl Literary* noticias *fpl*

tidy ['taɪdɪ] **1** *adj* (**tidier, tidiest**) (**a**) *(room)* ordenado(a); arreglado(a) (**b**) *(appearance)* arreglado(a), aseado(a);

(habits) ordenado(a), metódico(a) **(c)** *Fam* **it cost him a t. sum** le salió bastante caro

2 *vt (pt & pp* **tidied)** arreglar, poner en orden; **to t. away** poner en su sitio; **to t. oneself (up)** arreglarse

3 *vi* **to t. (up)** ordenar las cosas

tie [taɪ] **1** *vt (pt & pp* **tied) (a)** *(shoelaces etc)* atar; **to t. a knot** hacer un nudo; *Fig* **to be tied to one's family** estar muy atado(a) a la familia; *Fig* **to have one's hands tied** tener atadas las manos **(b)** *Mus* ligar

2 *vi Sport* empatar **(with** con)

3 *n* **(a)** *(bond)* lazo *m*, vínculo *m*; **blood ties** vínculos de sangre **(b)** *Fig (hindrance)* atadura *f*, traba *f*; **children can be a t.** los niños pueden ser una atadura **(c)** *(clothing)* corbata *f*; *(on invitation)* **black t.** de etiqueta ❑ **bow t.** pajarita *f* **(d)** *Mus* ligado *m* **(e)** *Sport (match)* partido *m*; *(draw)* empate *m*; *Br Ftb* **cup t.** partido *m* de copa **(f)** *US Rail* traviesa *f*

tie back *vt (hair)* recoger

tie down *vt* sujetar; *Fig* **to be tied down** no tener tiempo libre; *Fig* **to t. sb down to a promise** obligar a algn a cumplir una promesa

tie up *vt* **(a)** *(parcel, dog)* atar **(b)** *(wound)* vendar **(c)** *(deal)* concluir **(d)** *(bind up) (capital)* inmovilizar; **my money is tied up in shares** mi dinero está invertido en acciones; *Com* **we are tied up with another firm** estamos vinculados a otra empresa; *Fig* **just now I'm tied up** de momento estoy muy ocupado; *Fig* **to get tied up (in sth)** embrollarse (en algo)

tiebreaker ['taɪbreɪkər] *n Ten* tie-break *m*, muerte *f* súbita

tie-in ['taɪɪn] *n* **(a)** *(link)* relación *f* **(with** con) **(b) a film/ TV t.-in** = un producto a veces promocional relacionado con una nueva película o programa televisivo

tiepin ['taɪpɪn] *n* alfiler *m* de corbata

tier [tɪər] *n (of seats)* fila *f*, hilera *f*; *(in stadium)* grada *f*; **four-t. cake** pastel *m* de cuatro pisos

tie-up ['taɪʌp] *n* enlace *m*, vínculo *m*

TIFF [tɪf] *n Comptr (abbr* **Tagged Image File Format)** TIFF

tiff [tɪf] *n Fam* riña *f*, desavenencia *f*

tiger ['taɪgər] *n* tigre *m*

tight [taɪt] **1** *adj* **(a)** *(gen)* apretado(a), ajustado(a); *(clothing)* ajustado(a), ceñido(a); *(seal)* hermético(a); **my shoes are too t.** me aprietan los zapatos; **to keep a t. hold over sb** tener a algn muy controlado(a); *Fig* **to be in a t. corner** estar en un apuro **(b)** *(scarce)* escaso(a); **money is a bit t.** andamos escasos de dinero **(c)** *(mean)* agarrado(a), tacaño(a) **(d)** *Fam (drunk)* alegre, *Esp* piripi

2 *adv* estrechamente, firmemente; *(seal)* herméticamente; **hold t.** agárrate fuerte; **shut t.** bien cerrado(a); **to fit t.** ser muy ceñido(a); **to pull a rope t.** tensar *or* estirar una cuerda; **to screw a nut t.** apretar una tuerca lo más posible; **to sit t.** no moverse de su sitio

tighten ['taɪtən] **1** *vt (screw)* apretar, ajustar; *(rope)* tensar; *Fig* **to t. one's belt** apretarse el cinturón; *Fig* **to t. (up) restrictions** intensificar las restricciones

2 *vi (gen)* apretarse; *(cable)* tensarse

tightfisted [taɪt'fɪstɪd] *adj* tacaño(a)

tight-fitting [taɪt'fɪtɪŋ] *adj (garment)* ceñido(a); *(lid, cap)* hermético(a)

tightknit [taɪt'nɪt] *adj (community)* muy integrado(a)

tight-lipped [taɪt'lɪpt] *adj (secretive)* hermético(a), reservado(a); *(with anger)* con los labios apretados

tightly ['taɪtlɪ] *adv (hold, squeeze)* con fuerza; *(seal, close)* bien

tightness ['taɪtnɪs] *n (of cable)* tensión *f*, tirantez *f*; *(of clothes)* estrechez *f*

tightrope ['taɪtrəʊp] *n* cuerda *f* floja ❑ **t. walker** funámbulo *m,f*

tights [taɪts] *npl* **(a)** *(thin)* medias *fpl*, panties *mpl* **(b)** *(thick)* leotardos *mpl*, *Col* medias *fpl* veladas, *RP* cancanes *mpl*; *(of dancer)* mallas *fpl*

tigress ['taɪgrɪs] *n* tigresa *f*

tilde ['tɪldə] *n* tilde *f*

tile [taɪl] **1** *n (of roof)* teja *f*; *(glazed)* azulejo *m*; *(for paving, floor)* baldosa *f*

2 *vt (roof)* tejar; *(wall)* azulejar, revestir de azulejos, *Esp* alicatar; *(floor)* embaldosar

tiled [taɪld] *adj (roof)* de *or* con tejas; *(wall)* con azulejos, *Esp* alicatado(a); *(floor)* embaldosado(a)

tiling ['taɪlɪŋ] *n (of roof)* tejas *fpl*; *(on wall)* azulejos *mpl*; *(on floor)* embaldosado *m*, baldosas *fpl*

till¹ [tɪl] *n (for cash)* caja *f*; *Fig* **caught with one's hands in the t.** cogido(a) con las manos en la masa

till² [tɪl] *vt (field)* labrar, cultivar

till³ [tɪl] **1** *prep* hasta; **from morning t. night** de la mañana a la noche; **t. then** hasta entonces

2 *conj* hasta que; **I laughed t. I cried** reí hasta llorar; **I stayed t. it ended** me quedé hasta que terminó; **wait t. he comes** espera a que venga

tiller ['tɪlər] *n Naut* caña *f* del timón

tilt [tɪlt] **1** *n* **(a)** *(sloping position)* ladeo *m*, inclinación *f*; **to be at a t.** estar inclinado(a) **(b)** *(speed)* **(at) full t.** a toda velocidad

2 *vi* **to t. over** volcarse; **to t. (up)** inclinarse, ladearse

3 *vt* inclinar, ladear; **to t. one's chair back** balancearse sobre la silla

timber ['tɪmbər] *n (wood)* madera *f* de construcción; *(trees)* árboles *mpl*, bosque *m*; **(piece of) t.** viga *f*, madero *m*

timbered ['tɪmbəd] *adj (house)* enmaderado(a)

timberyard ['tɪmbəjɑːd] *n* depósito *m or* almacén *m* de madera

time [taɪm] **1** *n* **(a)** *(gen)* tiempo *m*; **all the t.** todo el tiempo; **as t. goes on** con el tiempo; **for a long t.** to come de aquí a mucho tiempo; **for some t. (past)** desde hace algún tiempo; **I haven't seen him for a long t.** hace mucho (tiempo) que no lo veo; **in a short t.** en poco tiempo; **in no t.** en un abrir y cerrar de ojos; **in t.** a tiempo; **in three weeks' t.** dentro de tres semanas; **it will take all your t. to ...** te costará trabajo...; **I've no t. for him** no tengo tiempo para él; **t.'s up!** ¡ya es la hora!; **to kill t.** matar el tiempo; **to lose** *or* **waste t.** perder el tiempo; **to make up for lost t.** recuperar el tiempo perdido; **to take one's t. over sth** hacer algo con calma; *Fig* **t. will tell** el tiempo dirá; *Fam* **to do t.** cumplir una condena ❑ **t. bomb** bomba *f* de relojería *or Am* tiempo; *Ind* **t. clock** reloj *m* registrador; **t. limit** límite *m* de tiempo; *(for payment, completion of task)* plazo *m*; *Rad* **t. signal** señal *f* horaria; **t. switch** interruptor *m* electrónico automático; **t. zone** huso *m* horario **(b)** *(period, age, era)* época *f*, tiempos *mpl*; **a sign of the times** un signo de los tiempos; **in our t.** en los tiempos en que vivimos; **in time(s) to come** en el futuro; **to be behind the times** tener ideas anticuadas **(c)** *(point in time)* momento *m*; **at a given t.** en un momento dado *or* determinado; **(at) any t. (you like)** cuando quiera; **at no t.** nunca; **at one t.** en otros tiempos; **at that t.** (en aquel) entonces; **at the present t.** actualmente, en la actualidad; **at the same t.** al mismo tiempo, a la vez; **at times** a veces; **by the t. that I got there it was over** cuando llegué ya se había acabado; **from t. to t.** de vez en cuando; **he may turn up at any t.** puede llegar en cualquier momento; **I was away at the t.** estaba ausente en aquel momento; **now's the t. to ...** ahora es el momento de ...; *Fig* **to die before one's t.** morir prematuramente **(d)** *(time of day)* hora *f*; **and about t. too!** ¡ya era hora!; **at dinner t.** a la hora de la cena; **a watch that keeps good t.** un reloj exacto; **Greenwich Mean T.** la hora de Greenwich; **in good**

t. con anticipación, temprano; **to arrive ahead of t./on t.** llegar con anticipación/puntualmente; **what's the t.?** ¿qué hora es?, *Am* ¿qué horas son?; **what t. do you** *Br* **make it** *or US* **have?** ¿qué hora tiene? (**e**) *(season)* **t. of the year** época *f* del año (**f**) *(age)* **at my t. of life** a mi edad (**g**) *(experience)* **to have a good/bad t.** pasarlo bien/mal; **to have a rough t. (of it)** pasarlo mal; **we had a marvellous t.** lo pasamos en grande (**h**) *(occasion)* vez *f*; **for weeks at a t.** durante semanas enteras; **four at a t.** cuatro a la vez; **four times as big** cuatro veces más grande; **next t.** la próxima vez; **several times over** varias veces; **three times running** tres veces seguidas; **t. and t. again, t. after t.** una y otra vez (**i**) *(in multiplication)* (multiplicado) por; **three times four is twelve** tres (multiplicado) por cuatro es igual a doce (**j**) *Mus (rhythm)* compás *m*; **in (strict) t.** a compás; **to beat t.** llevar el compás

2 *vt* (**a**) *(speech, programme)* calcular la duración de; *Sport (race)* cronometrar (**b**) *(choose the time of)* escoger *or* calcular el momento oportuno para; *(meeting)* fijar la hora de; **it is timed for three o'clock** debe comenzar a las tres; **to t. a blow** calcular un golpe; **you timed your arrival badly** escogiste mal momento para llegar

time-consuming ['taɪmkənsjuːmɪŋ] *adj* que ocupa *or* requiere mucho tiempo

time-honoured, *US* **time-honored** ['taɪmɒnəd] *adj* consagrado(a)

timekeeper ['taɪmkiːpər] *n Sport (person)* cronometrador(a) *m,f*; *(watch)* cronómetro *m*

timekeeping ['taɪmkiːpɪŋ] *n* (**a**) *Ind (in factory)* control *m* de puntualidad (**b**) *Br (punctuality)* puntualidad *f*; **good/poor t.** mucha/poca puntualidad

time-lag ['taɪmlæg] *n* intervalo *m*

timeless ['taɪmlɪs] *adj* eterno(a)

timely ['taɪmlɪ] *adj* (**timelier, timeliest**) oportuno(a)

time-out ['taɪmaʊt] *n Sport* tiempo *m* muerto; *Fig* descanso *m*

timepiece ['taɪmpiːs] *n* reloj *m*

timer ['taɪmər] *n (device)* temporizador *m*

time-saver ['taɪmseɪvər] *n* **the dishwasher is a great t.-s.** el lavavajillas (te) ahorra mucho tiempo

time-saving ['taɪmseɪvɪŋ] *adj (device, method)* que ahorra tiempo

timescale ['taɪmskeɪl] *n* plazo *m* (de tiempo)

timeserver ['taɪmsɜːvər] *n Pej* oportunista *mf*, chaquetero(a) *m,f*

time-share ['taɪmʃeər] *n* multipropiedad *f*, copropiedad *f*

timespan ['taɪmspæn] *n* plazo *m*

timetable ['taɪmteɪbəl] *n Educ Rail* horario *m*

time-wasting ['taɪmweɪstɪŋ] *n* pérdida *f* de tiempo

timework ['taɪmwɜːk] *n Ind* trabajo *m* por horas

timid ['tɪmɪd] *adj* tímido(a)

timidity [tɪ'mɪdɪtɪ] *n* timidez *f*

timidly ['tɪmɪdlɪ] *adv* con timidez

timing ['taɪmɪŋ] *n* (**a**) *(timeliness)* oportunidad *f*; *(coordination)* coordinación *f*; **your t. was wrong** no calculaste bien (**b**) *Sport* cronometraje *m* (**c**) *Tech* regulación *f*

timorous ['tɪmərəs] *adj* asustadizo(a), miedoso(a), timorato(a)

tin [tɪn] **1** *n* (**a**) *(metal)* estaño *m* □ **t. plate** hojalata *f*; *Mus* **t. whistle** flautín *m* (**b**) *(container)* lata *f*, *Am* tarro *m*; **baking t.** molde *m* (para pasteles); *Br* **biscuit t.** caja *f* para galletas

2 *adj (made of tin)* de estaño; *(of tinplate)* de hojalata; **t. soldiers** soldaditos *mpl* de plomo

3 *vt (pt & pp* **tinned***) Br (preserve in tins)* enlatar, conservar en lata; **tinned food** alimentos *mpl* enlatados, conservas *fpl*

tinder ['tɪndər] *n* yesca *f*

tinfoil ['tɪnfɔɪl] *n* papel *m* de estaño

ting-a-ling [tɪŋə'lɪŋ] *n (sound)* tilín *m*

tinge [tɪndʒ] **1** *n* tinte *m*, matiz *m*

2 *vt* teñir; **to t. sth with red** teñir algo de rojo; *Fig* **words tinged with sadness** palabras teñidas de tristeza

tingle ['tɪŋgəl] *vi (with emotion)* estremecerse; **her cheeks tingled** le ardían las mejillas; **my feet are tingling** siento un hormigueo en los pies

tingling ['tɪŋglɪŋ] *n* estremecimiento *m*; *(in feet etc)* hormigueo *m*

tinker ['tɪŋkər] **1** *n Pej* quinqui *mf*, gitano(a) *m,f*

2 *vi* **to t. about with sth** enredar con algo; **to t. with** *(mend)* arreglar; *(ruin)* estropear

tinkle ['tɪŋkəl] **1** *vi* tintinear

2 *vt* hacer tintinear

3 *n* tintineo *m*; *Br Fam* **to give sb a t.** *(on phone)* dar a algn un toque *or* telefonazo, *Méx* pegar a algn un grito

tinkling ['tɪŋklɪŋ] *n* tintineo *m*, tilín *m*

tinned [tɪnd] *pt & pp see* **tin**

tinnitus ['tɪnɪtəs] *n Med* zumbido *m* de oídos

tinny ['tɪnɪ] *adj* (**tinnier, tinniest**) *(sound)* metálico(a)

tin-opener ['tɪnəʊpənər] *n* abrelatas *m inv*

tinsel ['tɪnsəl] *n* oropel *m*

tint [tɪnt] **1** *n* tinte *m*, matiz *m*

2 *vt* teñir; **to t. one's hair** teñirse el pelo

tiny ['taɪnɪ] *adj* (**tinier, tiniest**) minúsculo(a), pequeñito(a); **a t. bit** un poquitín

tip¹ [tɪp] **1** *n (end)* punta *f*, extremidad *f*; *(of cigarette)* filtro *m*; **filter-t. cigarette** cigarrillo con filtro; **on the tips of one's toes** sobre las puntas de los pies; *Fig* **to have sth on the t. of one's tongue** tener algo en la punta de la lengua

2 *vt (pt & pp* **tipped***)* poner regatón *or* cantera a; **tipped cigarettes** cigarrillos *mpl* con filtro; **tipped with steel** con punta de acero

tip² [tɪp] **1** *n* (**a**) *(gratuity)* propina *f* (**b**) *(advice)* consejo *m*; **to take a t. from sb** seguir el consejo de algn (**c**) *Sport (racing)* pronóstico *m*

2 *vt (pt & pp* **tipped***)* (**a**) *(give money to)* dar una propina a (**b**) *Sport* pronosticar; **to t. a horse** pronosticar que un caballo ganará una carrera

tip off *vt (police)* pasar información a

tip³ [tɪp] **1** *n Br* **rubbish t.** basurero *m*, vertedero *m*

2 *vt (pt & pp* **tipped***)* ladear, inclinar; *(rubbish)* verter; **to t. sth onto the floor** tirar algo al suelo

3 *vi* **to t. (up)** ladearse; *(cart)* bascular

tip over 1 *vt* volcar

2 *vi* volcarse; *(boat)* zozobrar

tip-off ['tɪpɒf] *n* soplo *m*

tipped [tɪpt] *pt & pp see* **tip**

tipper lorry ['tɪpəlɒrɪ] *n Br* volquete *m*

tipping ['tɪpɪŋ] *n* vertido *m*; **'t. (of rubbish) prohibited'** 'prohibido verter basura'

tipple ['tɪpəl] *Fam* **1** *vi* empinar el codo, *Am* tomar

2. *n* bebida *f* alcohólica; **what's your t.?** ¿qué te gusta beber?

tippler ['tɪplər] *n Fam* bebedor(a) *m,f*, borrachín(ina) *m,f*

tipster ['tɪpstər] *n Sport* pronosticador(a) *m,f*

tipsy ['tɪpsɪ] *adj* (**tipsier, tipsiest**) achispado(a), piripi; **to get t.** achisparse

tiptoe ['tɪptəʊ] **1** *vi (pt & pp* **tiptoed***)* caminar *or Esp* andar

de puntillas; **to t. in/out** entrar/salir de puntillas
  2 *n* **on t.** de puntillas

tiptop ['tɪptɒp] *adj Fam* excelente, de primera

tip-up ['tɪpʌp] *adj (cart, lorry)* basculante; *(seat)* abatible

tirade [taɪ'reɪd] *n* diatriba *f*, invectiva *f*

Tirana [tɪ'rɑːnə] *n* Tirana

tire¹ [taɪər] *n US see* tyre

tire² [taɪər] **1** *vt* cansar; **to t. sb out** agotar a algn
  2 *vi* cansarse, fatigarse; **to t. of doing sth** cansarse de hacer algo

tired [taɪəd] *adj* cansado(a); **t. out** rendido(a); **to be t.** estar cansado(a); **to be t. of sth** estar harto(a) de algo

tiredness ['taɪədnɪs] *n* cansancio *m*, fatiga *f*

tireless ['taɪəlɪs] *adj* incansable, infatigable

tiresome ['taɪəsəm] *adj* pesado(a), aburrido(a)

tiring ['taɪərɪŋ] *adj* fatigoso(a), cansado(a), *Andes RP* cansador(a)

tiro ['taɪərəʊ] *n (pl* **tiros**) *see* tyro

tissue ['tɪʃuː, 'tɪsjuː] *n* **(a)** *Biol* tejido *m* **(b)** *Tex* tisú *m* ❏ **t. paper** papel *m* de seda **(c)** *(handkerchief)* pañuelo *m* de papel, kleenex® *m*; *Fig* **a t. of lies** una sarta de mentiras

tit¹ [tɪt] *n Orn* **coal t.** carbonero *m* garrapinos; **great t.** carbonero *m* común

tit² [tɪt] *n* **t. for tat** donde las dan las toman; **to give t. for tat** devolver la pelota

tit³ [tɪt] *n Slang (breast)* teta *f*, *Esp* pera *f*, *Méx* chichi *f*, *RP* lola *f*

titanic [taɪ'tænɪk] *adj* titánico(a)

titanium [taɪ'teɪnɪəm] *n Chem* titanio *m*

titbit ['tɪtbɪt] *n (snack)* tentempié *m*, refrigerio *m*

titillate ['tɪtɪleɪt] *vt* excitar

titillation [tɪtɪ'leɪʃən] *n* excitación *f*

titivate ['tɪtɪveɪt] *vt* emperifollar; **to t. oneself** emperifollarse

title ['taɪtəl] *n* **(a)** *(gen)* título *m* ❏ **t. page** portada *f*; *Theat* **t. role** papel *m* principal *(que da el título a la obra)* **(b)** *Jur* título *m*, derecho *m* ❏ **t. deed** título *m* or escritura *f* de propiedad

titled ['taɪtəld] *adj (person)* con título de nobleza, noble

titleholder ['taɪtlhəʊldər] *n Sport* campeón(ona) *m,f*

titter ['tɪtər] **1** *vi* reírse nerviosamente; *(foolishly)* reírse tontamente
  2 *n* risa *f* ahogada; *(foolish)* risilla *f* tonta

tittle-tattle ['tɪtəltætəl] *n* chismes *mpl*

titular ['tɪtjʊlər] *adj* titular

tizz [tɪz] *n Fam*, **tizzy** ['tɪzɪ] *n Fam* **to get into a t.** ponerse nervioso(a)

TLC [tiːel'siː] *n Fam (abbr* **tender loving care)** cariño *m*

TM *(abbr* **trademark)** marca *f* (de fábrica)

tn *US abbr see* **t**

TNT [tiːen'tiː] *n (abbr* **trinitrotoluene)** trinitrotolueno *m*, TNT

to [tuː, *unstressed before vowels* tʊ, *before consonants* tə] **1** *prep* **(a)** *(with place)* a; *(expressing direction)* hacia; **airlines to America** líneas aéreas con destino a América; **from town to town** de ciudad en ciudad; **he went to France/Japan** fue a Francia/al Japón; **I'm going to Mary's** voy a casa de Mary; **I am on my way to his house** voy hacia su casa; **it is thirty miles from London** está a treinta millas de Londres; **the road to London** la carretera a or *Esp* de Londres; **to the east** hacia el este; **to the right** a la derecha; **what school do you go to?** ¿a qué escuela vas?; *Fig* **the road to ruin** el camino de la ruina **(b)** *(time)* a; **from day to day** de día en día; **from morning to night** de la mañana a la

noche; **from two to four** de dos a cuatro; *Br* **it's ten to (six)** *Esp RP* son (las seis) menos diez, *Am salvo RP* faltan diez (para las seis) **(c)** *(as far as, until, down to)* hasta; **accurate to a millimetre** exacto(a) hasta el milímetro; **a year ago to the day** hace un año exactamente; **soaked to the skin** calado(a) hasta los huesos **(d)** *(with indirect object)* **he gave it to his cousin** se lo dio a su primo; **to drink to sb** brindar por algn; **what's that to you?** ¿qué te importa a ti? **(e)** *(towards a person)* con, para con; **he was very kind to me** se portó muy bien conmigo **(f)** *(of)* de; **heir to an estate** heredero *m* de una propiedad; **secretary to the manager** secretaria *f* del director **(g)** *(purpose, result)* **to come to sb's aid** acudir en auxilio de algn; **to everyone's surprise** para sorpresa de todos; **to this end** con este fin **(h)** *(according to)* **to all appearances** según todos los indicios; **to the best of my knowledge** que yo sepa **(i)** *(compared to)* **that's nothing to what I've seen** eso no es nada en comparación con lo que he visto yo **(j)** *(in proportion)* **one house to the square kilometre** una casa por kilómetro cuadrado; **six votes to four** seis votos contra cuatro; **to bet ten to one** apostar diez contra uno **(k)** *(about)* **that's all there is to it** no hay nada más que decir; **there's nothing to it** es facilísimo; **what did he say to my suggestion?** ¿qué contestó a mi sugerencia?; **what do you say to a holiday?** ¿qué te parece ir de vacaciones?

  2 *with infin* **(a)** *with simple infinitives* ***to*** *is not translated but is shown by the verb endings*; **to buy** comprar; **to come** venir; **to sell** vender **(b)** *(in order to)* para; *(with verbs of motion or purpose)* a, por; **he did it to help me** lo hizo para ayudarme; **he stopped to talk** se detuvo a hablar; **he strove to obtain it** se esforzó por conseguirlo; **he went to visit him** fue a visitarle **(c)** *various verbs followed by dependent infinitives take particular prepositions* (a, de, en, por, con, para, etc) *and others take no preposition; see the entry of the verb in question* **(d)** *(with adj and infin)* a, de; **difficult to do** difícil de hacer; **ready to listen** dispuesto(a) a escuchar; **to be good to eat** tener buen sabor; **too hot to drink** demasiado caliente para bebérselo **(e)** *(with infin used as noun)* **to lie is unwise** es imprudente mentir **(f)** *(with noun and infin)* **the first to complain** el primero en quejarse; **the only one to do it** el único en hacerlo; **this is the time to do it** éste es el momento de hacerlo; **to have a great deal to do** tener mucho que hacer **(g)** *(on doing sth)* **to look at her you wouldn't imagine that ...** al verla no te imaginarías que ... **(h)** *(expressing following action)* **he awoke to find the light still on** al despertarse encontró la lámpara todavía encendida **(i)** *(with verbs of ordering, wishing, etc)* **he asked me to do it** me pidió que lo hiciera; **I want him to do it** quiero que él lo haga **(j)** *(expressing obligation)* **fifty employees are to go** van a ser despedidos cincuenta empleados; **these are still to be done** éstos quedan por hacer; **to have to do sth** tener que hacer algo **(k)** *(replacing infin)* **go if you want to** váyase si quiere; **I didn't want to go, but I had to** no quería ir, pero no me quedaba más remedio
  3 *adv* **movement to and fro** vaivén *m*; **to come to** volver en sí; **to go to and fro** ir y venir; **to push the door to** ajustar la puerta

toad [təʊd] *n Zool* sapo *m*

toadstool ['təʊdstuːl] *n Esp* seta *f* venenosa, *Am* hongo *m* venenoso

toady ['təʊdɪ] **1** *n* cobista *mf*
  2 *vi* **to t. to sb** dar coba a algn

toast¹ [təʊst] **1** *n Culin* pan *m* tostado; **a slice** or **piece of t.** una tostada
  2 *vt* tostar

toast² [təʊst] **1** *n (drink)* brindis *m inv*; **to drink** or **give a t. to** brindar por
  2 *vt* brindar por

toaster ['təʊstər] n tostador m (de pan)

tobacco [tə'bækəʊ] n (pl **tobaccos** or **tobaccoes**) tabaco m ❑ t. **pouch** petaca f

tobacconist [tə'bækənɪst] n estanquero(a) m,f; Br t.'s **(shop)** estanco m, CSur quiosco m, Méx estanquillo m

Tobago [tə'beɪgəʊ] n Tobago

-to-be [tə'bi:] adj futuro(a); **bride-to-be** novia f; **mother-to-be** futura madre

toboggan [tə'bɒgən] **1** n tobogán m ❑ t. **run** pista f de tobogán
2 vi deslizarse en tobogán

today [tə'deɪ] **1** n hoy m; t.'s **paper** el periódico de hoy
2 adv hoy; (nowadays) hoy en día, actualmente; t. **week, a week t.** de hoy en ocho (días)

toddle ['tɒdəl] **1** vi (child) dar los primeros pasos; Fam **I must t. off** tengo que irme
2 n Fam paseíto m

toddler ['tɒdlər] n niño(a) m,f pequeño(a) (que empieza a andar); **the toddlers** los pequeñitos

toddy ['tɒdɪ] n (drink) ponche m

to-die-for [tə'daɪfɔ:r] adj Fam **it's t.** está que te mueres

to-do [tə'du:] n (pl **to-dos**) lío m, jaleo m; **what a to-do!** ¡menudo lío!

toe [təʊ] **1** n Anat dedo m del pie; **big t.** dedo gordo (del pie); Fig **to be on one's toes** estar alerta
2 vt (pt & pp **toed**) **to t. the line** conformarse, obedecer las órdenes

toecap ['təʊkæp] n puntera f

toehold ['təʊhəʊld] n (in climbing) punto m de apoyo; Fig **to gain a t. in the market** lograr introducirse en el mercado

toenail ['təʊneɪl] n uña f del dedo del pie

toffee ['tɒfɪ] n caramelo m; Br Fam **he can't sing for t.** no tiene ni idea de cantar

toffee-nosed ['tɒfɪnəʊzd] adj Br Slang engreído(a)

tofu ['təʊfu:] n Culin tofu m

together [tə'geðər] adv junto, juntos(as); **all t.** todos juntos; **the letter arrived t. with the book** la carta llegó junto con el libro; **to bring t.** reunir, juntar; **to go** or **belong t.** ir juntos

togetherness [tə'geðənɪs] n unidad f, unión f

togged up [tɒgd'ʌp] adj Fam **to get t. up** emperifollarse

toggle ['tɒgəl] n botón m de trenca ❑ Elec t. **switch** conmutador m de palanca

togs [tɒgz] npl Fam ropa f sing

toil [tɔɪl] **1** n trabajo m duro, esfuerzo m
2 vi afanarse, trabajar (duro); **to t. up a hill** subir penosamente una cuesta

toilet ['tɔɪlɪt] n **(a)** (lavatory) váter m, retrete m; (for public) baño(s) m(pl), Esp servicio(s) m(pl), CSur toilette f; **to go to the t.** ir al baño ❑ t. **paper** papel m higiénico or Chile confort; t. **roll** rollo m de papel higiénico or Chile comfort **(b)** (washing etc) aseo m (personal) ❑ t. **bag** or **case** neceser m; t. **soap** jabón m de tocador

toiletries ['tɔɪlɪtrɪz] npl artículos mpl de aseo

token ['təʊkən] **1** n **(a)** (sign) señal f, prueba f; **as a t. of respect** en señal de respeto; t. **of friendship** prueba de amistad **(b)** Tel ficha f; Com vale m ❑ **book/record t.** vale m para comprar libros/discos
2 adj (payment, strike) simbólico(a)

told [təʊld] pt & pp see **tell**

tolerable ['tɒlərəbəl] adj (pain) tolerable, soportable; (performance, effort) regular, tolerable

tolerance ['tɒlərəns] n tolerancia f

tolerant ['tɒlərənt] adj tolerante

tolerate ['tɒləreɪt] vt tolerar, soportar; **I can't t. noise** no aguanto or soporto el ruido

toleration [tɒlə'reɪʃən] n tolerancia f

toll¹ [təʊl] **1** vt (bell) tañer, doblar
2 vi **to t. for the dead** tocar a muertos

toll² [təʊl] n **(a)** Aut peaje m, Méx cuota f ❑ t. **bridge** puente m de peaje or Méx cuota; t. **road** carretera f de peaje or Méx cuota **(b)** (loss) pérdidas fpl; **rent takes a heavy t. of one's income** el alquiler supone una gran parte de los ingresos; **the death t. on the roads** el número de víctimas mortales en las carreteras

toll-free [təʊl'fri:] US **1** adj t. **number** (número m de) teléfono m gratuito
2 adv (call) gratuitamente

tolling ['təʊlɪŋ] n (of bell) doblar m, tañido m

Toltec ['tɒltek] adj & n Hist tolteca (mf)

Tom [tɒm] n Tomás; Fam **any T., Dick or Harry** todo hijo de vecino; Fam **Peeping T.** mirón m

tomahawk ['tɒməhɔ:k] n tomahawk m, hacha f de guerra

tomato [tə'mɑ:təʊ, US tə'meɪtəʊ] n (pl **tomatoes**) **(a)** (fruit) tomate m, Méx jitomate m ❑ Culin t. **ketchup** ketchup m; t. **plant** tomatera f; t. **sauce** salsa f de tomate or Méx jitomate **(b)** US Fam (beautiful woman) **she's a real t.** está buenísima

tomb [tu:m] n tumba f, sepulcro m

tombola [tɒm'bəʊlə] n Br tómbola f

tomboy ['tɒmbɔɪ] n chica f poco femenina

tombstone ['tu:mstəʊn] n lápida f sepulcral

tomcat ['tɒmkæt] n gato m (macho)

tome [təʊm] n Fml tomo m

tomfool [tɒm'fu:l] adj (plan etc) absurdo(a), ridículo(a)

tomfoolery [tɒm'fu:lərɪ] n tonterías fpl

Tommy gun ['tɒmɪgʌn] n Fam metralleta f

tomorrow [tə'mɒrəʊ] **1** n mañana m; **the day after t.** pasado mañana; t. **night** mañana por la noche
2 adv mañana; **see you t.!** ¡hasta mañana!; t. **week** mañana en ocho (días)

tom-tom ['tɒmtɒm] n tam-tam m

ton [tʌn] n tonelada f; **a 500 t. ship** un barco de 500 toneladas; Fam **we have tons of it** tenemos montones

tone [təʊn] **1** n **(a)** (sound) tono m; **in a gentle t.** en tono dulce; **to change one's t.** cambiar de tono; t. **of voice** tono de voz **(b)** (of colour) tono m, matiz m **(c)** (quality, class) clase f, tono m; **he's lowering the t. of the place** su presencia hace bajar el nivel del lugar **(d)** Fin tendencia f; **the t. of the market** la tendencia del mercado **(e)** Med tono m (muscular)
2 vi **to t. with sth** armonizar con algo

tone down vt atenuar, suavizar

tone-deaf ['təʊndef] adj **to be t.-d.** no tener oído

toneless ['təʊnlɪs] adj (voice) monótono(a)

toner ['təʊnər] n (for printer) tóner m

Tonga ['tɒŋgə, 'tɒŋə] n Tonga

Tongan ['tɒŋən] adj & n tongano(a) (m,f)

tongs [tɒŋz] npl (for sugar) tenacillas fpl; **(fire) t.** tenazas fpl; **curling t.** (for hair) tenacillas (de rizar)

tongue [tʌŋ] n **(a)** Anat lengua f; **to stick one's t. out at sb** sacar la lengua a algn; Fig **to hold one's t.** morderse la lengua; Fig **to say sth t. in cheek** decir algo con la boca pequeña ❑ Fig t. **twister** trabalenguas m inv **(b)** (language) lengua f, idioma m; **mother/native t.** lengua materna/nativa **(c)** (of shoe) lengüeta f; (of bell) badajo m

tongue-tied ['tʌŋtaɪd] adj mudo(a) (por la timidez); **she gets t.-t.** se le traba la lengua

tonic ['tɒnɪk] **1** n (**a**) Med tónico m (**b**) (drink) tónica f; **a gin and t.** un gintonic
2 adj tónico(a) ❑ Mus **t. sol-fa** solfeo m

tonight [tə'naɪt] adv & n esta noche

tonnage ['tʌnɪdʒ] n (of ship) tonelaje m

tonne [tʌn] n tonelada f (métrica)

tonsil ['tɒnsəl] n Anat amígdala f; **to have one's tonsils out** ser operado(a) de las amígdalas

tonsillectomy [tɒnsɪ'lektəmɪ] n Med amigdalotomía f

tonsillitis [tɒnsɪ'laɪtɪs] n Med amigdalitis f

too [tuː] adv (**a**) (besides) además, también; **it was very expensive t.** y además era muy caro (**b**) (also) también; **I shall go t.** yo iré también (**c**) (excessively) demasiado; **I know him all t. well** le conozco de sobra; **ten dollars t. much** diez dólares de más; **the work is t. much for me** es demasiado trabajo para mí; **t. frequently** con demasiada frecuencia; **t. much money** demasiado dinero; **t. old** demasiado viejo(a); Fam **he's not t. well** está pachucho

took [tʊk] pt see **take**

tool [tuːl] **1** n (**a**) (utensil) herramienta f, utensilio m; **farming/gardening tools** útiles mpl or herramientas de labranza/jardinería ❑ **t. shed** cobertizo m (para herramientas) (**b**) (person) instrumento m; **to make a t. of sb** servirse de algn
2 vt (metal, leather) labrar; (cover of book) estampar

toolbag ['tuːlbæg] n bolsa f de herramientas

toolbox ['tuːlbɒks] n also Comptr caja f de herramientas

tooling ['tuːlɪŋ] n (of metal) labrado m; (of cover, of book) estampación f

toolkit ['tuːlkɪt] n juego m de herramientas

toot [tuːt] **1** vt tocar
2 vi Aut tocar la bocina
3 n Aut bocinazo m; Mus toque m (de trompeta)

tooth [tuːθ] n (pl **teeth** [tiːθ]) (**a**) Anat diente m; (molar) muela f; **I had a t. out** me sacaron or extrajeron un diente or una muela; (**set of**) **false teeth** dentadura f postiza; (child) **to cut one's teeth** echar los dientes; Fig **to be sick to the teeth of sth** estar hasta la coronilla de algo; Fig **to fight t. and nail** luchar a brazo partido; Fig **to have a sweet t.** ser goloso(a); Fam **long in the t.** entrado(a) en años (**b**) (of saw) diente m; (of comb) púa f

toothache ['tuːθeɪk] n dolor m de muelas

toothbrush ['tuːθbrʌʃ] n cepillo m de dientes

toothless ['tuːθlɪs] adj sin dientes, desdentado(a)

toothpaste ['tuːθpeɪst] n pasta f dentífrica or de dientes, dentífrico m

toothpick ['tuːθpɪk] n mondadientes m inv

toothy ['tuːθɪ] adj (**toothier, toothiest**) **to give a t. smile** sonreír enseñando los dientes

top¹ [tɒp] **1** n (**a**) (upper part) parte f superior, parte de arriba, parta alta; (of hill) cumbre f, cima f; (of tree) copa f; **from t. to bottom** de arriba a abajo; **on t. of the tower** encima de la torre; **put them on t.** ponlos encima; Fig **from t. to toe** de pies a cabeza; Fig **on t. of it all he wanted ...** para colmo quería ...; Fig **on t. of the world** contento(a) y feliz; Fig **to come out on t.** salir ganando ❑ **t. hat** sombrero m de copa (**b**) (surface) superficie f; **to come to the t.** salir a la superficie (**c**) (head) cabeza f; **at the t. of the list** a la cabeza de la lista; Fig **to blow one's t.** salirse de sus casillas (**d**) (of bottle, container) tapa f, tapón m (**e**) (garment) (T-shirt) camiseta f, Chile polera f, Méx playera f, RP remera f, (blouse) blusa f, (of pyjamas, bikini) parte f de arriba (**f**) (best) lo mejor; **this one is the t. of the range** este es el mejor de su categoría (**g**) Aut directa f (**h**) Fig **at the t. of one's voice** a voz en cuello or en grito
2 adj (**a**) (part) superior, de arriba ❑ **the t. drawer** el cajón de arriba; **the t. floor** el último piso; **t. coat** (of paint) última mano f; (overcoat) abrigo m (**b**) (highest) extremo(a), máximo(a); Mus **the t. notes** las notas más altas ❑ Aut **t. gear** directa f (**c**) (best) primero(a), principal; **the t. people** la élite; Educ **to be t.** ser el primero de la clase; Fam **to be t. dog** ser un gallito
3 vt (pt & pp **topped**) (**a**) (cover) coronar, rematar; **to t. a cake with ...** cubrir una tarta con ...; Fam **and to t. it all ...** y para colmo ... (**b**) (tree) desmochar; **t. and tail the gooseberries** quite los rabillos a las grosellas (**c**) (lead) encabezar; Theat **to t. the bill** encabezar el reparto

top up vt llenar hasta el tope; Aut **to t. up the** Br **petrol** or US **gas tank** llenar el depósito (de gasolina)

top² [tɒp] n (toy) peonza f

topaz ['təʊpæz] n Min topacio m

top-heavy [tɒp'hevɪ] adj demasiado pesado(a) en la parte superior; Fig poco estable

topic ['tɒpɪk] n tema m

topical ['tɒpɪkəl] adj de actualidad; **t. conversation** conversación f sobre temas de actualidad

topless ['tɒplɪs] adj desnudo(a) de cintura para arriba; (bar) topless; **t. swimsuit** monobikini m, topless m

top-level ['tɒplevəl] adj de alto nivel

topmost ['tɒpməʊst] adj (el) más alto, (la) más alta

top-of-the-range ['tɒpəvðə'reɪndʒ], US **top-of-the-line** ['tɒpəvðə'laɪn] adj de gama alta; **it is our t.-of-t.-r. model** es el modelo más alto de la gama

topography [tə'pɒgrəfɪ] n topografía f

topped [tɒpt] pt & pp see **top¹**

topping ['tɒpɪŋ] n (for pizza) ingrediente m; **cake with cream t.** pastel m con Esp nata or Am crema de leche encima

topple ['tɒpəl] **1** vi (building) derribarse, venirse abajo; **to t.** (**over**) volcarse
2 vt volcar; Fig (government) derribar, derrocar

top-secret [tɒp'siːkrɪt] adj sumamente secreto(a)

topside ['tɒpsaɪd] n Culin (beef) redondo m

topsoil ['tɒpsɔɪl] n superficie f del suelo

topsy-turvy [tɒpsɪ'tɜːvɪ] adj & adv al revés; (in confusion) en desorden, patas arriba; **a t.-t. world** un mundo al revés

torch [tɔːtʃ] n (burning) antorcha f, tea f; Br (electric) linterna f

torchlight ['tɔːtʃlaɪt] n luz f de antorchas ❑ **t. procession** procesión f con antorchas

tore [tɔːr] pt see **tear²**

toreador ['tɒrɪədɔːr] n torero m

torment [tɔː'ment] **1** vt atormentar, torturar; Fig **tormented by hunger** atormentado(a) por el hambre
2 ['tɔːment] n tormento m, suplicio m

tormentor [tɔː'mentər] n atormentador(a) m,f

torn [tɔːn] pp see **tear²**

tornado [tɔː'neɪdəʊ] n (pl **tornados** or **tornadoes**) tornado m

torpedo [tɔː'piːdəʊ] **1** n (pl **torpedoes**) torpedo m; **t. boat** torpedero(a) m,f
2 vt (pt & pp **torpedoed**) torpedear

torpid ['tɔːpɪd] adj (sleepy) letárgico(a), somnoliento(a), aletargado(a); (sluggish) torpe

torpor ['tɔːpər] n letargo m; (sluggishness) torpeza f

torrent ['tɒrənt] n torrente m; **to rain in torrents** llover a cántaros; Fig **t. of abuse** torrente de insultos

torrential [tɒ'renʃəl] adj torrencial

torrid ['tɒrɪd] adj tórrido(a)

torso ['tɔːsəʊ] n (pl **torsos**) torso m

tortoise ['tɔːtəs] *n* tortuga *f* de tierra

tortoiseshell ['tɔːtəsʃel] **1** *n* carey *n*, concha *f*
  2 *adj* de carey

tortuous ['tɔːtjʊəs] *adj* tortuoso(a)

torture ['tɔːtʃər] **1** *vt* torturar, atormentar
  2 *n* tortura *f*, tormento *m*; *Fig* **it was sheer t.** fue un auténtico suplicio

Tory ['tɔːrɪ] *adj & n Br Pol* conservador(a) *(m,f)*; **the T. Party** el Partido Conservador

toss [tɒs] **1** *vt* **(a)** *(ball)* lanzar, tirar; *(rider)* derribar, desmontar; **he was tossed by a bull** fue embestido por un toro; **to t. a coin** echar a cara o cruz *or Chile Col* cara o sello *or Méx* águila o sol *or RP* cara o seca **(b)** *(throw about)* sacudir, agitar; **tossed by the waves** sacudido(a) por las olas; **to t. one's head** sacudir la cabeza
  2 *vi* **(a)** *(move)* **to t. about** agitarse; **to t. and turn in bed** dar vueltas en la cama **(b) to t. (up) for sth** *(with coin)* jugarse algo a cara o cruz *or Chile Col* cara o sello *or Méx* águila o sol *or RP* cara o seca
  3 *n* **(a)** *(of ball)* lanzamiento *m*; *(of coin)* sorteo *m* (a cara o cruz) **(b)** *(of head)* sacudida *f*, movimiento *m* brusco

toss off *vt* **(a)** *(drink)* beber de un trago **(b)** *(write)* escribir rápidamente

toss-up ['tɒsʌp] *n* **it's a t.-up whether we do it or not** quizá lo hagamos, quizá no; **to settle sth by a t.-up** decidir algo a cara o cruz *or Chile Col* cara o sello *or Méx* águila o sol *or RP* cara o seca

tot¹ [tɒt] *n* **(a)** *(child)* **(tiny) t.** nene(a) *m,f*, peque *mf* **(b)** *(of whisky etc)* trago *m*

tot² [tɒt] *Br* **1** *vt* *(pt & pp* **totted) to t. up** sumar
  2 *vi* **to t. up to** ascender a

total ['təʊtəl] **1** *n* total *m*; *(in bill)* importe *m* total; **grand t.** suma *f* total
  2 *adj* total, global; **a t. failure** un fracaso total; **they were in t. ignorance of it** lo ignoraban totalmente *or* por completo
  3 *vt* *(pt & pp* **totalled,** *US* **totaled)** sumar, hacer el total de
  4 *vi* **to t. up to** ascender a, sumar

totalitarian [təʊtælɪ'teərɪən] *adj* totalitario(a)

totalitarianism [təʊtælɪ'teərɪənɪzəm] *n* totalitarismo *m*

totality [təʊ'tælɪtɪ] *n* totalidad *f*

totalizator ['təʊtəlaɪzeɪtər] *n* totalizador *m*

totalled ['təʊtəld] *pt & pp see* **total**

totally ['təʊtəlɪ] *adv* totalmente, completamente

tote¹ [təʊt] **1** *vt Fam* acarrear
  2 *n US* **t. bag** petate *m*

tote² [təʊt] *n Fam* totalizador *m*

totem ['təʊtəm] *n* tótem *m*

totem pole ['təʊtəm'pəʊl] *n* tótem *m*

totted ['tɒtɪd] *pt & pp see* **tot²**

totter ['tɒtər] *vi* tambalearse; **to t. in** entrar tambaleándose

tottering ['tɒtərɪŋ] *adj* tambaleante; **a t. empire** un imperio a punto de caer; **t. steps** pasos titubeantes

toucan ['tuːkən] *n Orn* tucán *m*

touch [tʌtʃ] **1** *vt* **(a)** *(gen)* tocar; *(lightly)* rozar; **to t. sb on the shoulder** tocar a algn en el hombro; *Fig* **the law can't t. him** la ley no puede hacer nada contra él; *Br Fam* **t. wood!** ¡toca madera! **(b)** *(consume)* tocar; **I never t. wine** nunca bebo vino **(c)** *(equal)* igualar; **nobody can t. Frank as a comedian** Frank no tiene rival como cómico **(d)** *(move)* conmover, afectar; **I was touched by their kindness** me llegó al alma su amabilidad **(e)** *Fam* **to t. sb for a loan** dar un sablazo a algn
  2 *vi* tocarse; *(lightly)* rozarse; *(properties)* ser conti-

guos(as), tocar; *Fig* **it was t. and go whether we caught the train** estuvimos a punto de perder el tren
  3 *n* **(a)** *(gen)* toque *m*; *(light contact)* roce *m*; *(of typist)* pulsación *f*; *Mus* ejecución *f*; **I felt a t. on the arm** sentí que me tocaban en el brazo **(b)** *(sense of touch)* tacto *m*; **rough to the t.** áspero(a) al tacto **(c)** *(detail)* detalle *m*; **it was a nice t. of his** fue un detalle de su parte; **to add a few touches to a picture** retocar un cuadro; **to put the finishing t. to sth** dar el último toque a algo **(d)** *(ability)* **he's losing his t.** está perdiendo su habilidad **(e)** *(contact)* contacto *m*; **the personal t.** el contacto personal; **to be/get/keep in t. with sb** estar/ponerse/mantenerse en contacto con algn; **to be out of t. with sth** no estar al tanto de algo; **to get in t. with the police** avisar a la policía **(f)** *(small amount)* pizca *f*; **a t. of salt/garlic** una pizca de sal/ajo; **to have a t. of flu** estar ligeramente griposo(a); **with a t. of bitterness** con una nota de amargura **(g)** *Sport* **in t.** fuera de juego

touch down *vi* **(a)** *(plane)* aterrizar, tomar tierra **(b)** *Rugby* hacer un ensayo

touch off *vt* desencadenar, provocar

touch on *vt* **to t. on a subject** tocar un tema

touch up *vt* *(picture)* retocar

touchdown ['tʌtʃdaʊn] *n* **(a)** *(of plane)* aterrizaje *m*; *(of space capsule)* amerizaje *m* **(b)** *Rugby* ensayo *m*

touched [tʌtʃt] *adj* **(a)** *(moved)* emocionado(a), conmovido(a) **(b)** *Fam (crazy) Esp* tocado(a) del ala, *Am* zafado(a)

touchiness ['tʌtʃɪnɪs] *n* susceptibilidad *f*

touching ['tʌtʃɪŋ] **1** *adj* conmovedor(a), enternecedor(a)
  2 *prep* tocante a, respecto a

touchline ['tʌtʃlaɪn] *n Rugby* línea *f* de banda

touch-sensitive screen ['tʌtʃ'sensɪtɪv'skriːn] *n Comptr* pantalla *f* táctil

touchstone ['tʌtʃstəʊn] *n* piedra *f* de toque

touch-tone telephone ['tʌtʃtəʊn'teləfəʊn] *n* teléfono *m* de tonos *or* de marcado por tonos

touch-type ['tʌtʃtaɪp] *vi* mecanografiar (sin mirar el teclado)

touchy ['tʌtʃɪ] *adj* **(touchier, touchiest)** *Fam (person)* susceptible; *(subject)* delicado(a)

tough [tʌf] **1** *adj* *(material)* fuerte, resistente; *(test)* duro(a), difícil; *(competitor etc)* fuerte, resistente; *(criminal, meat)* duro(a); *(judgement, punishment)* severo(a); *(problem)* difícil; *Fam* **t. luck!** ¡mala suerte!
  2 *n (person)* matón *m*

toughen ['tʌfən] **1** *vt* endurecer
  2 *vi* endurecerse

toughness ['tʌfnɪs] *n (of material etc)* resistencia *f*; *(of test)* dureza *f*; *(of judgement, punishment)* severidad *f*; *(of problem, job)* dificultad *f*

toupee ['tuːpeɪ] *n* tupé *m*

tour [tʊər] **1** *n* **(a)** *(journey, holiday)* viaje *m*; **package t.** viaje organizado; **to do a t. of Europe** hacer un viaje por Europa □ **walking t.** excursión *f* a pie **(b)** *(of building, monument)* visita *f*; *(of city)* recorrido *m* turístico; *Ind* **t. of inspection** recorrido de inspección **(c)** *Sport Theat* gira *f*; **on t.** de gira
  2 *vt* **(a)** *(country)* recorrer, viajar por **(b)** *(building)* visitar **(c)** *Theat* **to t. the provinces** recorrer las provincias □ **t. company** compañía *f* que está de gira
  3 *vi* **(a)** *(travel)* estar de viaje **(b)** *Theat* estar de gira

tour de force [tʊədə'fɔːs] *n* hazaña *f*, proeza *f*

tourism ['tʊərɪzəm] *n* turismo *m*

tourist ['tʊərɪst] *n* turista *mf*; **the t. trade** la industria del turismo □ **t. agency** agencia *f* de viajes; **t. centre** centro *m* turístico; **t. class** clase *f* turista; **t. menu** menú *m* turístico

touristy ['tʊərɪstɪ] *adj Pej* demasiado turístico(a)

tournament ['tʊənəmənt] *n Sport* torneo *m*

tourniquet ['tʊənɪkeɪ] *n Med* torniquete *m*

tousle ['taʊzəl] *vt* despeinar

tousled ['taʊzəld] *adj (hair)* despeinado(a)

tout [taʊt] **1** *vt Com* tratar de vender; *(tickets)* revender
  2 *vi* salir a la caza y captura de compradores *or* clientes
  3 *n* **(a)** *Com* gancho *m* □ **ticket t.** revendedor(a) *m,f* de entradas **(b)** *Sport (in racing)* pronosticador(a) *m,f*

tow [taʊ] **1** *n* **(a)** *(pull)* **to take a ship/car in t.** remolcar un barco/un coche; **we can give you a t.** podemos remolcar su coche; *Fam* **he always has his family in t.** siempre va acompañado de su familia **(b)** *(vehicle towed)* vehículo *m* remolcado; *Naut* **a t. of barges** un convoy de barcazas
  2 *vt* remolcar; **his car was towed away** la grúa se llevó su coche

toward(s) [tə'wɔːdz], [tɔːdz] *prep* **(a)** *(direction)* hacia; **t. me** hacia mí **(b)** *(of time)* hacia, alrededor de; **t. noon** hacia mediodía; **t. the end of his life** hacia el fin de su vida **(c)** *(for)* hacia, (para) con; **he feels a great affection t. her** siente gran afecto hacia ella; **our duty t. others** nuestro deber para con los demás; **to save t. sth** ahorrar para algo; **what is your attitude t. religion?** ¿cuál es su actitud respecto a la religión?

towbar ['taʊbɑːr] *n Aut* barra *f* de remolque

towboat ['taʊbəʊt] *n Naut* remolcador *m*

towel ['taʊəl] **1** *n* toalla *f* □ **hand t.** toallita *f*; **t. rail** toallero *m*
  2 *vt (pt & pp* **towelled,** *US* **toweled) to t. dry** secar con una toalla

towelling ['taʊəlɪŋ] *n Tex* felpa *f*

tower ['taʊər] **1** *n* torre *f*; **(bell) t.** campanario *m*; *Fig* **he's a t. of strength** es un poderoso apoyo □ *Comptr* **t. system** torre *f*
  2 *vi* encumbrarse; **to t. over** *or* **above sth** dominar algo

towering ['taʊərɪŋ] *adj* grande, sobresaliente, altísimo(a)

towing ['təʊɪŋ] *n (act)* remolque *m*

towline ['təʊlaɪn] *n see* **towrope**

town [taʊn] *n* ciudad *f*; *(small town)* pueblo *m*, población *f*; **to go into t.** ir al centro; *Fam* **to go out on the t., to paint the t. red** ir de juerga; *Fam* **to go to t. over sth** gastar dinero a manos llenas en algo □ **t. council** ayuntamiento *m*; *Br* **t. councillor** concejal(a) *m,f*; **t. hall** ayuntamiento *m*; **t. planning** urbanismo *m*

townsfolk ['taʊnzfəʊk] *npl see* **townspeople**

township ['taʊnʃɪp] *n* **(a)** *(in US)* municipio *m* **(b)** *Formerly (in South Africa)* = área urbana reservada para la población negra

townsman ['taʊnzmən] *n (pl* **townsmen)** ciudadano *m*

townspeople ['taʊnzpiːpəl] *npl* ciudadanos *mpl*, conciudadanos *mpl*

townswoman ['taʊnzwʊmən] *n (pl* **townswomen** ['taʊnzwɪmɪn]) ciudadana *f*

towpath ['təʊpɑːθ] *n* camino *m* de sirga

towrope ['təʊrəʊp] *n* cable *m* de remolque

toxic ['tɒksɪk] *adj Med* tóxico(a)

toxicologist [tɒksɪ'kɒlədʒɪst] *n Med* toxicólogo(a) *m,f*

toxicology [tɒksɪ'kɒlədʒɪ] *n Med* toxicología *f*

toxin ['tɒksɪn] *n Med* toxina *f*

toy [tɔɪ] **1** *n* juguete *m* □ **t. car** coche de juguete; **t. trumpet** trompeta *f* de niño
  2 *vi* jugar; **to t. with an idea** acariciar una idea; **to t. with one's food** comer sin gana, juguetear con la comida; **to t. with sb's feelings** jugar con los sentimientos de algn

toyshop ['tɔɪʃɒp] *n* juguetería *f*

trace [treɪs] **1** *n* **(a)** *(sign)* indicio *m*, vestigio *m*, señal *f*; **there's no t. of it** no queda ningún vestigio de ello; **to disappear without a t.** desaparecer sin dejar huella □ *Chem* **t. element** oligoelemento *m* **(b)** *(tracks)* huella(s) *f(pl)*, rastro *m*
  2 *vt* **(a)** *(drawing)* calcar **(b)** *(plan)* trazar, bosquejar **(c)** *(track down, locate)* seguir la pista de; **he has been traced to Paris** le han seguido la pista hasta París; **he traced his family (back) to the Crusades** el origen de su familia se remonta a las Cruzadas; **I can't t. any reference to the accident** no encuentro ninguna mención del accidente; **to t. lost goods** encontrar *or* recobrar objetos perdidos

traceable ['treɪsəbəl] *adj* localizable

tracer ['treɪsər] *adj Mil* **t. bullet** bala *f* trazadora

tracery ['treɪsərɪ] *n Archit* **(window) t.** tracería *f*

trachea [trə'kiːə] *n (pl* **tracheae** [trə'kiːiː]) *Anat* tráquea *f*

tracheotomy [trækɪ'ɒtəmɪ] *n Med* traqueotomía *f*

tracing ['treɪsɪŋ] *n* calco *m* □ **t. paper** papel *m* de calco

track [træk] **1** *n* **(a)** *(mark, trail)* huellas *fpl*, pista *f*; **to follow in sb's tracks** seguir la pista a algn; **to keep/lose t. of sb** no perder/perder de vista a algn; **to throw sb off the t.** despistar a algn; *Fig* **to make tracks** largarse, marcharse **(b)** *(pathway)* camino *m*; **to be on the right/wrong t.** ir por el buen/mal camino; **to put sb on the right t.** encaminar a algn **(c)** *Sport* pista *f*; *(for motor racing)* autódromo *m*, circuito *m* □ **t. events** atletismo *m sing* en pista; **t. racing** carreras *fpl* en pista; **t. shoes** zapatillas *mpl* de atletismo; *Fig* **t. record** historial *m* **(d)** *Rail* vía *f*; **single t.** vía única; *Fig* **he has a one-t. mind** no piensa más que en eso **(e)** *(on record)* canción *f* **(f)** *(of tractor)* oruga *f* **(g)** *US Sch* = cada una de las divisiones del alumnado en grupos por niveles de aptitud
  2 *vt (follow, hunt)* rastrear, seguir la pista de; *(with radar)* seguir la trayectoria de

track down *vt (locate)* localizar, encontrar; *(investigate)* averiguar

tracked [trækt] *adj Aut* con orugas

tracker ['trækər] *n* **t. dog** perro *m* rastreador

tracking ['trækɪŋ] *n* **(a)** *(following) (of person, plane, satellite)* seguimiento *m* □ **t. device** dispositivo *m* de seguimiento; *Cin* **t. shot** travelling *m*; **t. station** *(for satellites)* estación *f* de seguimiento **(b)** *US Sch* = sistema de división del alumnado en grupos por niveles de aptitud **(c)** *Comptr* tracking *m*, espacio *m* entre palabras

tracksuit ['træksuːt] *n Esp* chándal *m*, *Méx* pants *mpl*, *RP* jogging *m*

tract¹ [trækt] *n (expanse)* extensión *f*

tract² [trækt] *n (treatise)* tratado *m*; *(pamphlet)* folleto *m*

tractability [træktə'bɪlɪtɪ] *n* docilidad *f*

tractable ['træktəbəl] *adj* dócil, tratable

traction ['trækʃən] *n* tracción *f* □ *Rail* **t. engine** locomotora *f* de tracción; *Rail* **t. wheels** ruedas *fpl* tractoras *or* de tracción

tractor ['træktər] *n* tractor *m*

trade [treɪd] **1** *n* **(a)** *(job)* oficio *m*; **he's a carpenter by t.** es carpintero de oficio; **to carry on a t.** ejercer un oficio **(b)** *(business)* industria *f*; **the building t.** (la industria de) la construcción **(c)** *Com* comercio *m*, negocios *mpl*; *US* **Department of T.** Ministerio *m* de Comercio; **foreign t.** comercio exterior; **it's good for t.** es bueno para los negocios; **the t. in diamonds** el comercio de diamantes; *Fam* **to do a roaring t.** vender muchísimo □ **t. deficit** déficit *m* comercial; **t. embargo** embargo *m* comercial; **t. name** nombre *m* comercial; **t. union** sindicato *m*; **t. unionism** sindicalismo *or* **t. unionist** sindicalista *mf* **(d)** **t. winds** vientos *mpl* alisios

2 *vi* comerciar (**in** en); *Fig* **to t. on sb's ignorance** aprovecharse de la ignorancia de algn
3 *vt* **to t. sth for sth** cambiar *or* trocar algo por algo
trade in *vt* dar como entrada; **I'm trading in my old car for a new one** el coche viejo me sirve de entrada para el nuevo

trademark ['treɪdmɑːk] *n* marca *f* (de fábrica); **registered t.** marca registrada

trade-off ['treɪdɒf] *n* **a t.-o. between speed and accuracy** un término medio *or* una solución a medio camino entre la velocidad y la precisión

trader ['treɪdər] *n* comerciante *mf*

tradesman ['treɪdzmən] *n* (*pl* **tradesmen**) comerciante *m*; *(shopkeeper)* tendero *m*

trading ['treɪdɪŋ] *n* comercio *m* ❑ *Br* **t. estate** zona *f* industrial

tradition [trə'dɪʃən] *n* tradición *f*

traditional [trə'dɪʃənəl] *adj* tradicional

traditionalist [trə'dɪʃənəlɪst] *adj & n* tradicionalista *(mf)*

traffic ['træfɪk] **1** *n* (**a**) *Aut* tráfico *m*, circulación *f*; **heavy t.** circulación densa ❑ *US* **t. circle** rotonda *f*, *Esp* glorieta *f*; *Fam* **t. cop** policía *mf or Esp* guardia *mf* de tráfico; **t. island** refugio *m*; **t. jam** atasco *m*, embotellamiento *m*; **t. lights** semáforos *mpl*; *Br* **t. warden** = agente que pone multa por estacionamiento indebido (**b**) *(trade)* tráfico *m*, comercio *m*; **t. in arms/drugs** tráfico de armas/narcóticos ❑ **white slave t.** trata *f* de blancas
2 *vi* (*pt & pp* **trafficked**) traficar; **to t. in drugs** traficar con droga

trafficator ['træfɪkeɪtər] *n Aut* intermitente *m*

trafficked ['træfɪkt] *pt & pp see* **traffic**

trafficker ['træfɪkər] *n* traficante *mf*

tragedy ['trædʒɪdɪ] *n* tragedia *f*; **the t. of it was ...** lo trágico fue que ...

tragic ['trædʒɪk] *adj* trágico(a) ❑ *Theat* **t. actor** actor *m* dramático

tragically ['trædʒɪklɪ] *adv* trágicamente

trail [treɪl] **1** *vt* (**a**) *(drag)* **to t. sth (along)** arrastrar algo (**b**) *(follow)* rastrear
2 *vi* (**a**) *(drag)* arrastrar; **to have sth trailing behind one** llevar algo arrastrando (**b**) *(linger)* **to t. (along)** rezagarse (**c**) *(plant)* trepar
3 *n* (**a**) *(track)* pista *f*, rastro *m*; **to pick up the t.** encontrar la pista (**b**) *(path)* senda *f*, camino *m* ❑ **t. bike** moto *f* de trial *or* motocross (**c**) *(of smoke)* estela *f*; *Fig* **to leave a t. of destruction** arrasar todo al pasar

trail away, trail off *vi (voice)* esfumarse, apagarse

trailblazer ['treɪlbleɪzər] *n* innovador(a) *m,f*, pionero(a) *m,f*

trailer ['treɪlər] *n* (**a**) *Aut* remolque *m* (**b**) *US Aut (caravan)* caravana *f*, roulotte *f* (**c**) *Cin* trailer *m*, avance *m*

trailing ['treɪlɪŋ] *adj (plant)* trepador(a)

train [treɪn] **1** *n* (**a**) *Rail* tren *m*; **to board the t.** subir al tren; **to change trains** cambiar de tren, hacer transbordo; **to travel by t.** viajar en tren ❑ **goods t.** mercancías *m inv*; **passenger t.** tren *m* de pasajeros (**b**) *(of vehicle)* convoy *m*; *(of mules)* recua *f*; *(of followers)* séquito *m*; *(of events)* serie *f*, sucesión *f* (**c**) *(of dress)* cola *f* (**d**) *Tech* **t. of gears** tren *m* de engranajes
2 *vt* (**a**) *(teach)* formar, capacitar, preparar; *Sport* entrenar; *(animal)* amaestrar; *(voice etc)* educar (**b**) *(plant)* guiar; **to t. a plant along a wall** hacer trepar una planta por una pared (**c**) *(gun)* apuntar (**on** a); *(camera)* enfocar (**on** a)
3 *vi (be taught)* formarse, prepararse; *(practise)* ejercitarse; *Sport* entrenarse; **he is training as a teacher/lawyer** está estudiando magisterio/derecho

trained [treɪnd] *adj* experto(a); *Hum* **her husband is very well t.!** ¡qué marido tan apañado tiene!

trainee [treɪ'niː] *n* empleado(a) *m,f* en prácticas; *(apprentice)* aprendiz(iza) *m,f*

trainer ['treɪnər] *n* (**a**) *Sport* entrenador(a) *m,f*; *(of dogs)* amaestrador(a) *m,f*; *(of lions, horses)* domador(a) *m,f* (**b**) *Br* **trainers** *(shoes)* zapatillas *mpl* de deporte

training ['treɪnɪŋ] *n* *(instruction)* formación *f*, capacitación *f*; *Sport* entrenamiento *m*; *(of animals)* amaestramiento *m*; *(of lions, horses)* doma *f*; **to go into t.** entrenarse; **vocational t.** formación profesional

traipse [treɪps] *vi Fam* andar, vagar; **to t. round the shops** ir de tienda en tienda

trait [treɪt] *n* rasgo *m*

traitor ['treɪtər] *n* traidor(a) *m,f*; **to turn t.** pasarse al enemigo

trajectory [trə'dʒektərɪ] *n* trayectoria *f*

tram [træm] *n*, **tramcar** ['træmkɑːr] *n Br* tranvía *m*

tramp [træmp] **1** *vi* (**a**) *(travel on foot)* caminar, viajar a pie (**b**) *(walk heavily)* andar *or* caminar con pasos pesados
2 *n* (**a**) *(person)* vagabundo(a) *m,f*; *US Pej* **she's a t.** es una fulana *or Méx* piruja *or RP* reventada (**b**) *(hike)* caminata *f* (**c**) *(sound)* ruido *m* de pasos pesados (**d**) *Naut* **t. (steamer)** vapor *m* volandero

trample ['træmpəl] **1** *vt* **to t. down the grass** hollar la hierba; **to t. sth underfoot** pisotear algo
2 *vi* **to t. on sth** pisotear *or* pisar algo; *Fig* **to t. on sb's feelings** herir los sentimientos de algn

trampoline ['træmpəliːn] *n Sport* trampolín *m*

trance [trɑːns] *n* trance *m*; **to go into a t.** entrar en trance

tranquil ['træŋkwɪl] *adj* tranquilo(a), sereno(a)

tranquillity, *US* **tranquility** [træŋ'kwɪlɪtɪ] *n* tranquilidad *f*, serenidad *f*

tranquillize, *US* **tranquilize** ['træŋkwɪlaɪz] *vt* tranquilizar, calmar

tranquillizer, *US* **tranquilizer** ['træŋkwɪlaɪzər] *n* tranquilizante *m*, calmante *m*

trans *(abbr* **translated)** traducido(a) (por), trad

transact [træn'zækt] *vt* negociar; **to t. business with sb** hacer un negocio con algn

transaction [træn'zækʃən] *n* *(procedure)* tramitación *f*; *(deal)* transacción *f*, operación *f* (comercial)

transalpine [trænz'ælpaɪn] *adj* transalpino(a), trasalpino(a)

transatlantic [trænzət'læntɪk] *adj* transatlántico(a), trasatlántico(a)

transcend [træn'send] *vt* estar por encima de, sobrepasar, rebasar; *Philos Rel* transcender, trascender

transcendental [trænsen'dentəl] *adj* transcendental, trascendental ❑ **t. meditation** meditación *f* trascendental

transcontinental [trænzkɒntɪ'nentəl] *adj* transcontinental, trascontinental

transcribe [træn'skraɪb] *vt* transcribir, trascribir

transcript ['trænskrɪpt] *n* (**a**) *(of speech, tapes)* transcripción *f* (**b**) *US Sch Univ* expediente *m* académico

transcription [træn'skrɪpʃən] *n* transcripción *f*

transept ['trænsept] *n Archit* crucero *m*

transfer [træns'fɜːr] **1** *vt* (*pt & pp* **transferred**) (**a**) *(employee, department, prisoner)* trasladar; *(funds)* transferir; *Jur* ceder, transferir; *Rail* transbordar, trasbordar; *Ftb* traspasar; **the t. a transferred charge call** una conferencia a cobro revertido (**b**) *(design)* calcar
2 ['trænsfɜːr] *n* (**a**) *(of employee, department, prisoner)* traslado *m*; *(of funds)* transferencia *f*; *Jur (of goods, rights)* cesión *f*, transferencia *f*; *Ftb* traspaso *m* ❑ *Comptr* **t. speed**

velocidad *f* de transmisión (**b**) *(picture, design)* calcomanía
f

transferable [træns'fɜːrəbəl] *adj* transferible, trasferible;
not **t.** intransferible, intrasferible

transferred [træns'fɜːd] *pt & pp see* **transfer** .

transfigure [træns'fɪɡər] *vt* transfigurar, trasfigurar

transfix [træns'fɪks] *vt (usu pass)* transfigurar, trasfigurar;
she was transfixed se quedó traspuesta; **transfixed with
horror** horrorizado(a)

transform [træns'fɔːm] *vt* transformar, trasformar

transformation [trænsfə'meɪʃən] *n* transformación *f*,
trasformación *f*

transformer [træns'fɔːmər] *n Elec* transformador *m*,
trasformador *m*

transfuse [træns'fjuːz] *vt* trasvasar; *Med* **to t. blood**
hacer una transfusión de sangre

transfusion [træns'fjuːʒən] *n Med* transfusión *f* (de
sangre)

transgress [trænz'ɡres] *vt* transgredir, trasgredir,
infringir

transgressor [trænz'ɡresər] *n* transgresor(a) *m,f*,
trasgresor(a) *m,f*

transience ['trænzɪəns] *n* transitoriedad *f*

transient ['trænzɪənt] **1** *adj* transitorio(a), pasajero(a)
2 transients *npl US (in hotel)* transeúntes *mpl*

transistor [træn'zɪstər] *n* transistor *m*

transit ['trænzɪt] *n* (**a**) *(passing)* tránsito *m*; **in t.** de
tránsito; **it was damaged in t.** ha sufrido daño durante el
viaje (**b**) *US (transport)* transporte *m*

transition [træn'zɪʃən] *n* transición *f* □ **t. period** período
m transitorio *or* de transición

transitional [træn'zɪʃənəl] *adj* de transición

transitive ['trænzɪtɪv] *adj* transitivo(a)

transitory ['trænzɪtərɪ] *adj* transitorio(a), pasajero(a)

translate [træns'leɪt] *vt* traducir; **it can't really be
translated** no tiene traducción exacta; **it's translated as
...** se traduce por ...; **translated from/into English**
traducido(a) del/al inglés

translation [træns'leɪʃən] *n* traducción *f*

translator [træns'leɪtər] *n* traductor(a) *m,f*

transliteration [trænzlɪtə'reɪʃən] *n* transcripción *f*,
trascripción *f*

translucent [trænz'luːsənt] *adj* translúcido(a), traslú-
cido(a)

transmissible [trænz'mɪsəbəl] *adj* transmisible, tras-
misible

transmission [trænz'mɪʃən] *n* transmisión *f*, trasmisión *f*

transmit [trænz'mɪt] *vt (pt & pp* **transmitted)** transmitir,
trasmitir

transmitter [trænz'mɪtər] *n Rad (set)* transmisor *m*; *Rad
TV (station)* emisora *f*

transom ['trænsəm] *n Constr* travesaño *m*, dintel *m*

transparency [træns'pærənsɪ] *n* (**a**) *(quality)* transparencia *f*, trasparencia *f* (**b**) *Phot* diapositiva *f*

transparent [træns'pærənt] *adj* transparente, trasparente

transpiration [trænspə'reɪʃən] *n* transpiración *f*,
traspiración *f*

transpire [træn'spaɪər] *vi* (**a**) *Bot* transpirar, traspirar (**b**)
Fam (happen) ocurrir; **his version of what transpired** su
versión de lo que ocurrió; **it transpired that ...** ocurrió
que ...

transplant [træns'plɑːnt] **1** *vt Hortic Med* transplantar,
trasplantar

2 ['trænsplɑːnt] *n Med* transplante *m*, trasplante *m* □ **heart
t.** transplante *m* de corazón

transport [træns'pɔːt] **1** *vt* transportar, trasportar

2 ['trænspɔːt] *n* transporte *m*, trasporte *m*; **have you got
t.?** ¿tienes coche? □ **Ministry of T.** Ministerio *m* de
Transportes; **t. aircraft** avión *m* de transporte; *Br* **t. café**
bar *m* de carretera; **t. ship** buque *m* de transport

transportation [trænspɔː'teɪʃən] *n* transporte *m*,
trasporte *m*

transporter [træns'pɔːtər] *n* transportador *m*, trasportador *m*

transpose [træns'pəʊz] *vt (gen)* transponer; *Mus*
transportar

transposition [trænspə'zɪʃən] *n* transposición *f*; *Mus*
transporte *m*

transsexual [træn(z)'seksjʊəl] *n* transexual *mf*

tran(s)ship [træn(s)'ʃɪp] *vt (pt & pp* **tran(s)shipped)**
transbordar

transversal [trænz'vɜːsəl] *adj*, **transverse** [trænz'vɜːs]
adj transversal, trasversal

transvestism [trænz'vestɪzəm] *n* travestismo *m*

transvestite [trænz'vestaɪt] *n* travestido(a) *m,f* travesti
mf

trap [træp] **1** *n* trampa *f*; **to set a t.** poner una trampa; *Fig*
to fall into the t. caer en la trampa; *Aut Fig* **speed t.**
control *m* de velocidad □ **t. door** *(gen)* trampilla *f*; *Theat*
escotillón *m*

2 *vt (pt & pp* **trapped)** coger en una trampa, atrapar;
trapped by flames cercado(a) por las llamas; *Fig* **to t. sb**
entrampar a algn

trapeze [trə'piːz] *n* trapecio *m* □ **t. artist** trapecista *mf*

trapped [træpt] *pt & pp see* **trap**

trapper ['træpər] *n* trampero(a) *m,f*

trappings ['træpɪŋz] *npl* parafernalia *f sing*

Trappist ['træpɪst] *adj & n Rel* trapense *(m)*

trash [træʃ] *n (inferior goods)* pacotilla *f*; *US (rubbish)*
basura *f*; *Fig* basura *f*; *Fig* **to talk a lot of t.** decir tonterías
□ *US* **t. can** cubo *m* de la basura

trashy ['træʃɪ] *adj* (**trashier, trashiest**) *Fam* de pacotilla,
Esp cutre, *Méx* gacho(a), *RP* groncho(a)

trauma ['trɔːmə] *n (pl* **traumas** *or* **traumata** ['trɔːmətə])
Med Psych trauma *m*

traumatic [trɔː'mætɪk] *adj* traumático(a)

traumatize ['trɔːmətaɪz] *vt* traumatizar

travel ['trævəl] **1** *vi (pt & pp* **travelled,** *US* **traveled)** (**a**) *(of
person, animal)* viajar; **he is travelling** está de viaje; **to t.
through** viajar por, recorrer (**b**) *(of sound, light, electricity)*
propagarse; **news travels fast round here** por aquí las
noticias vuelan

2 *vt* viajar por, recorrer; **distance travelled** distancia
recorrida

3 *n* viajes *mpl*; **I am fond of t.** me gusta viajar; **is he still
on his travels?** ¿todavía está de viaje? □ **t. agency, t.
bureau** agencia *f* de viajes

traveller, *US* **traveler** ['trævələr] *n* (**a**) *(gen)* viajero(a)
m,f □ *Br* **t.'s cheque,** *US* **t.'s check** cheque *m* de viaje (**b**)
(commercial) t. viajante *mf* (de comercio)

travelling, *US* **traveling** ['trævəlɪŋ] **1** *adj (salesman,
performer)* ambulante □ **t. crane** grúa *f* móvil

2 *n* viajes *mpl*, viajar *m*; **I'm fond of t.** me gusta viajar □ **t.
bag** bolsa *f* de viaje; **t. expenses** gastos *mpl* de viaje

travelogue, *US* **travelog** ['trævəlɒɡ] *n (film)* documental *m*; *(talk)* conferencia *f* sobre un viaje

travel-sick ['trævəlsɪk] *adj* **to be t.-s.** marearse

travel-sickness ['trævəlsɪknɪs] *n* mareo *m*

traverse ['trævɜːs, trə'vɜːs] **1** *vt* atravesar, cruzar, **2** *n* travesía *f*

travesty ['trævɪstɪ] **1** *n* farsa *f*, parodia *f* burda **2** *vt (pt & pp* **travestied**) parodiar

trawl [trɔːl] **1** *n* **t. (net)** red *f* barredera **2** *vt & vi* pescar con red barredera

trawler ['trɔːlər] *n (ship)* barco *m* arrastrero

trawling ['trɔːlɪŋ] *n* pesca *f* con red barredera

tray [treɪ] *n* (a) *(for food)* bandeja *f* ❑ **t. cloth** cubrebandeja *f* (**b**) *(for letters)* caja *f*, cesta *f* (para correspondencia); *Phot* cubeta *f*

treacherous ['tretʃərəs] *adj* (**a**) *(betraying) (person)* traidor(a); *(action)* traicionero(a) (**b**) *(dangerous)* peligroso(a)

treacherously ['tretʃərəslɪ] *adv* (**a**) *(betrayingly)* a traición (**b**) *(dangerously)* peligrosamente

treachery ['tretʃərɪ] *n* traición *f*

treacle ['triːkəl] *n Br* melaza *f*

tread [tred] **1** *vi (pt* **trod**; *pp* **trod** *or* **trodden**) pisar; **to t. in sth** meter el pie en algo; **to t. on sth** pisar algo; **you're treading on my foot** me estás pisando; *Fig* **to t. warily** andar con pies de plomo
2 *vt* (**a**) *(step on)* pisar; **to t. sth in** *or* **down** *or* **underfoot** pisotear algo (**b**) **to t. water** mantenerse a flote verticalmente
3 *n* (**a**) *(step)* paso *m*; *(sound)* ruido *m* de pasos (**b**) *(of stair)* escalón *m* (**c**) *(of tyre)* banda *f* de rodadura

treadle ['tredəl] *n* pedal *m* ❑ **t. sewing machine** máquina *f* de coser a pedales

treadmill ['tredmɪl] *n* rueda *f* de ardilla; *Fig* rutina *f*

treas *(abbr* **treasurer**) tesorero(a) *m,f*

treason ['triːzən] *n* traición *f*; **high t.** alta traición

treasonable ['triːzənəbəl] *adj* traicionero(a)

treasure ['treʒər] **1** *n* tesoro *m*; *Fig (child etc)* **she's a t.** es un cielo *or* un tesoro ❑ **t. hunt** caza *f* del tesoro
2 *vt (keep)* guardar como oro en paño; *(value)* apreciar muchísimo

treasurer ['treʒərər] *n* tesorero(a) *m,f*

treasure-trove ['treʒətrəʊv] *n Jur* tesoro *m* encontrado

treasury ['treʒərɪ] *n* tesoro *m*, tesorería *f*; **the T.** el Ministerio de Hacienda ❑ **T. bill** bono *m* del Tesoro

treat [triːt] **1** *n* (**a**) *(present)* regalo *m*; *(meal)* festín *m*, convite *m*; **it's my t.** invito yo (**b**) *(pleasure)* placer *m*; **to give oneself a t.** permitirse un lujo especial
2 *vt* (**a**) *(gen)* tratar; **to t. badly** maltratar (**b**) *(regard)* tomarse; **he treats it very seriously** se lo toma muy en serio; **to t. sth as a joke** tomar algo a broma (**c**) *(invite)* invitar; **he treated them to dinner** les invitó a cenar (**d**) *Med* tratar (**e**) *(subject)* tratar

treatise ['triːtɪz] *n* tratado *m*

treatment ['triːtmənt] *n* (**a**) *(of person)* trato *m*; **his t. of his friends** su forma de portarse con los amigos; **preferential t.** trato preferencial (**b**) *Med* tratamiento *m*; **patient undergoing t.** enfermo sometido a tratamiento; *Fam* **to give sb the t.** dar una paliza a algn (**c**) *(interpretation, handling)* tratamiento *m*; **the t. of this subject** el tratamiento de este tema

treaty ['triːtɪ] *n* (**a**) *(between nations)* tratado *m* (**b**) *(between persons)* acuerdo *m*, contrato *m*

treble ['trebəl] **1** *adj* (**a**) *(triple)* triple (**b**) *Mus* de tiple *or* soprano ❑ **t. clef** clave *f* de sol; **t. voice** voz *f* tiple *or* de soprano
2 *vt* triplicar
3 *vi* triplicarse

tree [triː] *n* árbol *m*; **apple/cherry t.** manzano *m*/cerezo

m; **to climb a t.** subirse a un árbol; *Fig* **at the top of the t.** en la cúspide ❑ *Bot* **t. of heaven** ailanto *m*, árbol *m* del cielo

treeless ['triːlɪs] *adj* sin árboles

treetop ['triːtɒp] *n* copa *f* de árbol

trefoil ['trefɔɪl] *n Bot* trébol *m*

trek [trek] **1** *n (journey)* viaje *m* (largo y difícil); *Fam (walk)* caminata *f*; *Fam* **it's quite a t.** hay un buen trecho
2 *vi (pt & pp* **trekked**) hacer un viaje largo y difícil; *Fam (walk)* ir caminando

trelliswork ['trelɪswɜːk] *n* enrejado *m*

tremble ['trembəl] **1** *vi* temblar, estremecerse
2 *n* temblor *m*; *(shiver)* estremecimiento *m*; *Br* **to be all of a t.** temblequear

trembling ['tremblɪŋ] **1** *adj* tembloroso(a); **t. all over** todo tembloroso(a)
2 *n* temblor *m*

tremendous [trɪ'mendəs] *adj (huge)* inmenso(a), enorme; *(success)* arrollador(a); *(shock, blow, mistake)* tremendo(a); *Fam (marvellous)* estupendo(a), fabuloso(a); *Fam* **to have a t. time** pasarlo bomba

tremendously [trɪ'mendəslɪ] *adv* inmensamente, enormemente; *Fam* **she does it t. well** lo hace a las mil maravillas

tremor ['tremər] *n* temblor *m*

tremulous ['tremjʊləs] *adj* (**a**) *(timid)* tímido(a) (**b**) *(trembling)* tembloroso(a)

trench [trentʃ] *n* (**a**) *(ditch)* zanja *f*; *Mil* trinchera *f* (**b**) **t. coat** trinchera *f*

trenchant ['trentʃənt] *adj (tone)* cáustico(a), mordaz

trend [trend] **1** *n (tendency)* tendencia *f*; *(fashion)* moda *f*
2 *vi* tender (**to, towards** hacia)

trendsetter ['trendsetər] *n* pionero(a) *m,f*

trendy ['trendɪ] *adj* (**trendier, trendiest**) *Br Fam (person)* moderno(a); *(clothes)* a la última

trepidation [trepɪ'deɪʃən] *n (anxiety)* turbación *f*, agitación *f*; *(trembling)* trepidación *f*

trespass ['trespəs] *vi* entrar sin autorización (en la propiedad de algn)

trespasser ['trespəsər] *n* intruso(a) *m,f*; **'trespassers will be prosecuted'** 'prohibida la entrada (bajo sanción)'

trestle ['tresəl] *n* caballete *m*

trial ['traɪəl] *n* (**a**) *Jur* proceso *m*, juicio *m*; **on t.** procesado(a); **to bring sb to t.** procesar a algn; **to stand t.** ser procesado(a) (**b**) *(test)* prueba *f*, ensayo *m*; **on t.** a prueba; **to do sth by t. and error** encontrar la forma de hacer algo probando diferentes posibilidades ❑ *Sport* **t. (game)** partido de selección; *Com* **t. order** pedido *m* de prueba; **t. run** ensayo *m* (**c**) **trials** *(competition)* concurso *m* *sing* (**d**) **trials** *(suffering)* aflicción *f sing*, sufrimiento *m sing*; *(nuisance)* molestia *f sing*; **t. and tribulations** tribulaciones *fpl*

triangle ['traɪæŋgəl] *n Geom* triángulo *m*

triangular [traɪ'æŋgjʊlər] *adj Geom* triangular

tribal ['traɪbəl] *adj* tribal

tribe [traɪb] *n* tribu *f*; *Fig* multitud *f*

tribesman ['traɪbzmən] *n (pl* **tribesmen**) miembro *m* de una tribu

tribulation [trɪbjʊ'leɪʃən] *n Fml* tribulación *f*

tribunal [traɪ'bjuːnəl] *n* tribunal *m*

tributary ['trɪbjʊtərɪ] **1** *n (river)* afluente *m*
2 *adj* tributario(a)

tribute ['trɪbjuːt] *n* (**a**) *(payment)* tributo *m* (**b**) *(mark of respect)* homenaje *m*; **floral tributes** *(to actress)* ramos *mpl* de flores; *(at funeral)* ramos *mpl* y coronas; **to pay t. to** rendir homenaje a

trice [traɪs] *n Fam* **in a t.** en un dos por tres, en un abrir y cerrar de ojos

triceps ['traɪseps] *n Anat* tríceps *m inv*

trick [trɪk] **1** *n* (a) *(ruse)* ardid *m*, artificio *m*; *(dishonest)* engaño *m*, estafa *f*; *(in question)* trampa *f*; **there's a t. in it** hay trampa (b) *(practical joke)* broma *f*; **dirty t.** faena *f*, trastada *f*, mala pasada *f*; **to play a t. on sb** gastarle una broma a algn; *(malicious)* jugar una mala pasada a algn; **you've been up to your old tricks** ya has vuelto a hacer de las tuyas (c) *(skill, knack)* truco *m*; **he knows all the tricks** conoce todas las triquiñuelas; **that'll do the t.!** ¡eso es exactamente lo que hace falta!; **the whole bag of tricks** todo el tinglado; **to get the t. of sth** cogerle el tranquillo a algo (d) *Cards* baza *f*; **to take a t.** ganar una baza

2 *vt* engañar, burlar; **to t. sb into doing sth** engañar a algn para que haga algo; **to t. sb out of sth** quitar *or Am* sacarle algo a algn a base de engaños; **we've been tricked!** ¡nos han timado!

trickery ['trɪkərɪ] *n* engaños *mpl*, trampas *fpl*; **piece of t.** trampa *f*, superchería *f*; **they got it by t.** lo consiguieron con trampas

trickle ['trɪkəl] **1** *vi* correr, discurrir; *(water)* gotear; *Fig (resources)* **to t. away** consumirse poco a poco

2 *n* hilo *m*, hilillo *m* ❏ *Elec* **t. charger** cargador *m* de régimen lento

trickster ['trɪkstər] *n (gen)* tramposo(a) *m,f*; *(swindler)* estafador(a) *m,f*

tricky ['trɪkɪ] *adj* (**trickier, trickiest**) *(person)* astuto(a), tramposo(a); *(situation, mechanism)* delicado(a)

tricolour, *US* **tricolor** ['trɪkələr, 'traɪkələr] *n* tricolor *f*; **the T.** la bandera tricolor

tricycle ['traɪsɪkəl] *n* triciclo *m*

trident ['traɪdənt] *n* tridente *m*

tried [traɪd] *pt & pp see* **try**

tried-and-tested ['traɪdən'testɪd] *adj* probado(a)

trier ['traɪər] *n Fam* **he's a t.** se esfuerza al máximo

trifle ['traɪfəl] **1** *n* (a) *(insignificant thing)* bagatela *f*, fruslería *f*; **he's a t. optimistic** es ligeramente optimista; **she worries over trifles** se preocupa por tonterías (b) *Br Culin* = postre de bizcocho, gelatina, frutas y crema

2 *vi* **to t. with** tomar a la ligera; **to t. with sb's affections** jugar con los sentimientos de algn

trifling ['traɪflɪŋ] *adj* insignificante, trivial; **of t. value** de un valor mínimo

trigger ['trɪgər] **1** *n (of gun)* gatillo *m*; *(of mechanism)* disparador *m*; *Fam* **to be t.-happy** estar siempre con el dedo en el gatillo

2 *vt* **to t. (off)** *(reaction)* desencadenar

trigonometry [trɪgə'nɒmɪtrɪ] *n Math* trigonometría *f*

trill [trɪl] **1** *n* (a) *Mus* trino *m* (b) *Ling* vibración *f* (c) *(of bird)* trino *m*, gorjeo *m*

2 *vi Mus* trinar

3 *vt* (a) *Mus* trinar (b) *Ling* vibrar

trillion ['trɪljən] *n* (a) *Br* trillón *m* (b) *US* billón *m*

trilogy ['trɪlədʒɪ] *n* trilogía *f*

trim [trɪm] **1** *adj* (**trimmer, trimmest**) *(neat)* aseado(a), arreglado(a); **to have a t. figure** tener buen tipo

2 *vt (pt & pp* **trimmed**) (a) *(cut)* recortar; *(hedge)* podar; *Fig (expenses)* disminuir (b) *(decorate)* adornar, guarnecer (**with** de); **trimmed with lace** adornado(a) con encajes

3 *n* (a) *(state)* orden *m*, estado *m*; *Naut* asiento *m*, estiba *f*; **to be in good t.** *(ship)* estar bien estibado(a) (b) *(cut)* recorte *m*; **to give sth a t.** recortar algo; **your hair needs a t.** tienes que cortarte las puntas

trimester ['traɪmestər] *n* trimestre *m*

trimming ['trɪmɪŋ] *n* (a) *(cut)* recorte *m*; *(of hedge)* poda *f*; *(of wood)* desbaste *m* (b) *(on clothes)* adorno *m* (c) *Culin* **trimmings** guarnición *f sing*; **dish with (the usual) t.** plato *m* guarnecido (de la manera habitual)

Trinidad ['trɪnɪdæd] *n* Trinidad ❏ **T. and Tobago** Trinidad y Tobago

Trinity ['trɪnɪtɪ] *n* **the (Holy) T.** La (Santísima) Trinidad ❏ **T. Sunday** fiesta *f* de la Trinidad

trinket ['trɪŋkɪt] *n* baratija *f*, abalorio *m*

trio ['triːəʊ] *n (pl* **trios**) trío *m*

trip [trɪp] **1** *n* (a) *(journey)* viaje *m*; *(excursion)* excursión *f*; **to go on a t.** ir de excursión (b) *Slang (on drugs)* viaje *m*; **to be on a t.** estar colocado(a); **to have a bad t.** reaccionar mal a una droga

2 *vi (pt & pp* **tripped**) (a) **to t. (up)** *(stumble)* tropezar (**over** con); *Fig (err)* equivocarse, cometer un error (b) **to t. along** ir con paso ligero

3 *vt* **to t. sb (up)** *(make stumble)* zancadillear a algn; *Fig (catch)* coger *or* pillar a algn

tripe [traɪp] *n* (a) *Culin* mondongo *m*, *Esp* callos *mpl*, *Chile* chunchules *mpl* (b) *Fam* bobadas *fpl*; *Fam* **it's a load of t.** son tonterías

triple ['trɪpəl] **1** *adj* triple ❏ *Mus* **t. time** compás *m* ternario

2 *vt* triplicar

3 *vi* triplicarse

triplet ['trɪplɪt] *n* trillizo(a) *m,f*

triplicate ['trɪplɪkɪt] **1** *adj* triplicado(a)

2 *n* triplicado *m*; **in t.** por triplicado

3 ['trɪplɪkeɪt] *vt* redactar por triplicado

tripod ['traɪpɒd] *n* trípode *m*

Tripoli ['trɪpəlɪ] *n* Trípoli

tripped [trɪpt] *pt & pp see* **trip**

tripper ['trɪpər] *n Br* excursionista *mf*, turista *mf*

triptych ['trɪptɪk] *n Art* tríptico *m*

tripwire ['trɪpwaɪər] *n* cable *m* trampa

trite [traɪt] *adj (sentiment)* banal; *(subject)* trillado(a)

triteness ['traɪtnɪs] *n* banalidad *f*

triumph ['traɪəmf] **1** *n (success)* triunfo *m*; *(joy)* júbilo *m*, alegría *f*

2 *vi* triunfar

triumphal [traɪ'ʌmfəl] *adj* triunfal ❏ **t. arch** arco *m* de triunfo

triumphalist [traɪ'ʌmfəlɪst] *adj* triunfalista

triumphant [traɪ'ʌmfənt] *adj* triunfante

triumphantly [traɪ'ʌmfəntlɪ] *adv (gen)* triunfalmente; *(speak)* en tono triunfal

trivet ['trɪvɪt] *n (on table)* salvamanteles *m inv* (de metal)

trivia ['trɪvɪə] *npl* futilidades *fpl*, trivialidades *fpl*

trivial ['trɪvɪəl] *adj* trivial, banal

triviality [trɪvɪ'ælɪtɪ] *n* trivialidad *f*; **to talk of trivialities** hablar de cosas triviales

trivialize ['trɪvɪəlaɪz] *vt* trivializar

trod [trɒd] *pt & pp see* **tread**

trodden ['trɒdən] *pp see* **tread**

Trojan ['trəʊdʒən] *adj* troyano(a) ❏ **T. Horse** caballo *m* de Troya

trolley ['trɒlɪ] *n Br (for food, luggage)* carrito *m* ❏ **t. bus** trolebús *m*; *US* **t. car** tranvía *m*

trombone [trɒm'bəʊn] *n* trombón *m*

trombonist [trɒm'bəʊnɪst] *n* trombonista *mf*

troop [truːp] **1** *n* (a) *(of people)* grupo *m* (b) *Mil (unit)* escuadrón *m* (de caballería); **troops** tropas *fpl* ❑ **t. train** tren *m* militar

2 *vi* **to t. in/out/off** entrar/salir/marcharse en tropel

trooper ['tru:pər] *n Mil (soldier)* soldado *m* de caballería; *US (policeman)* policía *mf*

trooping ['tru:pɪŋ] *n Br Mil* **t. the colour** = ceremonia en la que se rinde honores a la bandera de un regimiento

trophy ['trəʊfɪ] *n* trofeo *m*

tropic ['trɒpɪk] *n* trópico *m*; **the T. of Capricorn/Cancer** el Trópico de Capricornio/Cáncer

tropical ['trɒpɪkəl] *adj* tropical

trot [trɒt] **1** *vi (pt & pp* **trotted)** trotar, ir al trote; *Fam* **I'll just t. round to the shop** voy a salir un momento a la tienda

2 *n* trote *m*; **to break into a t.** empezar a trotar; **to go at a t.** ir al trote; *Fam* **they won six times on the t.** ganaron seis veces seguidas; *Fam* **to keep sb on the t.** no dejar a algn tranquilo(a) ni un momento

trot out *vt (names, list)* recitar de memoria; *(excuses)* sacar a relucir; *(for show)* hacer alarde de

Trotskyist ['trɒtskɪıst], **Trotskyite** ['trɒtskaɪt] *adj & n* trotskista *(mf)*

trotter ['trɒtər] *n* **(a)** *(horse)* trotón *m* **(b)** *Culin* **trotters** manos *fpl*; **sheep's/pig's t.** manos de oveja/cerdo

trouble ['trʌbəl] **1** *n* **(a)** *(affliction)* pena *f*, aflicción *f*; *(misfortune)* desgracia *f* **(b)** *(problems)* problemas *mpl*, dificultades *fpl*; **he's asking for t.** se está buscando problemas; **his troubles are over** ya se acabaron sus problemas; **money troubles** problemas económicos; **the t. is that ...** lo que pasa es que ...; **there was t. between his wife and his mother** entre su mujer y su madre había problemas; **to be in t.** estar en un lío o en un apuro; **to cause sb a lot of t.** dar mucha guerra a algn; **to get into t.** meterse en un lío; **to get sb out of t.** sacar a algn de un apuro; **to make t.** armar jaleo; *Fam Fig* **to get a girl into t.** dejar embarazada a una chica **(c)** *(effort)* esfuerzo *m*; **it's no t.** no es ninguna molestia; **it's not worth the t.** no merece la pena; **nothing is too much t. for him** no escatima esfuerzos; **to take the t. to do sth** molestarse en hacer algo **(d)** *Pol Ind (unrest, conflict)* conflicto *m*; **labour troubles** conflictos *mpl* laborales ❑ **t. spot** lugar *m* conflictivo **(e)** *Med* enfermedad *f*, mal *m*; **heart t.** enfermedad cardíaca; **to have eye/liver t.** padecer de los ojos/del hígado **(f)** *Aut* **engine t.** avería *f* del motor

2 *vt* **(a)** *(affect)* afligir, afectar; *(worry)* preocupar; **that doesn't t. him at all** eso le tiene sin cuidado; **to t. oneself about sth** preocuparse por algo **(b)** *(bother, disturb)* molestar, incomodar; **I'm sorry to t. you** perdone que le moleste; **I won't t. you with the details** no le cansaré con más detalles

3 *vi* molestarse; **don't t. to write** no se moleste en escribir

troubled ['trʌbəld] *adj (worried)* preocupado(a), inquieto(a); *(liquid)* turbio(a), revuelto(a); **to be t.** estar muy preocupado(a)

trouble-free ['trʌbəlfri:] *adj* sin problemas

troublemaker ['trʌbəlmeɪkər] *n* alborotador(a) *m,f*, provocador(a) *m,f*

troubleshooter ['trʌbəlʃu:tər] *n Ind* conciliador(a) *m,f*, mediador(a) *m,f*; *(mechanic)* especialista *mf* en diagnóstico de averías

troublesome ['trʌbəlsəm] *adj* molesto(a), fastidioso(a), pesado(a)

trough [trɒf] *n* **(a)** *(container)* **(drinking) t.** abrevadero *m*; **(feeding) t.** pesebre *m*; **(kneading) t.** artesa *f* **(b)** *Phys (of wave)* seno *m* **(c)** *Geog* depresión *f* **(d)** *Meteor* isobara *f* de mínima presión; *(area of low pressure)* zona *f* de baja presión, depresión *f*

trounce [traʊns] *vt* dar una paliza a

trouncing ['traʊnsɪŋ] *n* paliza *f*

troupe [tru:p] *n Theat* compañía *f*

trouser press ['traʊzə'pres] *n* prensa *f* para pantalones, percha *f* planchadora

trousers ['traʊzəz] *npl* pantalón *m sing*, pantalones *mpl*; **a pair of t.** unos pantalones; *Fig* **who wears the t. in their house?** ¿quién lleva los pantalones en su casa?

trouser suit ['traʊzə'su:t] *n* traje *m* de chaqueta y pantalón *(para mujer)*

trousseau ['tru:səʊ] *n* ajuar *m*

trout [traʊt] *n (pl* **trout** *or* **trouts)** trucha *f* ❑ **t. fishing** pesca *f* de truchas; **t. stream** río *m* truchero

trowel ['traʊəl] *n* **(a)** *(builder's)* palustre *m*; *Fig* **to lay it on with a t.** *(exaggerate)* recargar las tintas; *(flatter excessively)* dar coba **(b)** *Hortic* desplantador *m*

truancy ['tru:ənsɪ] *n* ausentismo *m or Esp* absentismo *m* escolar

truant ['tru:ənt] *n* niño(a) *m,f* que *Esp* hace novillos *or Col* capa clase *or Méx* se va de pinta *or RP* se hace la rabona; **to play t.** faltar a clase, *Esp* hacer novillos, *Col* capar clase, *Méx* irse de pinta, *RP* hacerse la rabona

truce [tru:s] *n* tregua *f*; **to call a t.** acordar una tregua

truck [trʌk] **1** *n* **(a)** *Br Rail* vagón *m* **(b)** *Aut* camión *m* ❑ **t. driver** camionero(a) *m,f*; **t. stop** bar *m* de carretera **(c)** *(handcart)* carretilla *f*; *(in mines)* vagoneta *f* **(d)** *US (produce)* productos *mpl*; **t. farm** explotación *f* agrícola; *US* **t. farmer** horticultor(ora) *m,f* **(e)** *Fam (dealings)* **I'll have no t. with him/it** no pienso tener nada que ver con él/ello

2 *vt (goods)* transportar en camión

3 *vi US (drive a truck) Esp* conducir *or Am* manejar un camión

trucker ['trʌkər] *n US* camionero(a) *m,f*

trucking ['trʌkɪŋ] *n US* camionaje *m*

truculence ['trʌkjʊləns] *n* violencia *f*, agresividad *f*, truculencia *f*

truculent ['trʌkjʊlənt] *adj* truculento(a), agresivo(a), violento(a)

trudge [trʌdʒ] *vi* caminar con dificultad; **we trudged up the hill** nos costó subir la colina

true [tru:] **1** *adj* **(truer, truest)** **(a)** *(factual)* verdadero(a); **it's t. that ...** es verdad *or* cierto que ...; **to come t.** cumplirse, realizarse **(b)** *(genuine)* verdadero(a), auténtico(a); **a t. friend** un amigo de verdad; **a t. Spaniard** un español auténtico **(c)** *(faithful)* fiel, leal; **to be t. to one's convictions/a promise** ser fiel a las propias convicciones / a una promesa; **to be** *or* **run t. to form** ser fiel a sí mismo(a) **(d)** *(accurate) (aim)* acertado(a); *(mechanism)* exacto(a) **(e)** *(level)* nivelado(a)

2 *n* **to be out of t.** *(wall)* no estar a plomo; *(surface)* no estar a nivel; *(beam)* estar alabeado(a); *(wheel)* estar descentrado(a)

3 *adv (of wheel)* **to run t.** estar bien centrado(a)

true-blue ['tru:'blu:] *adj Br* fiel, leal

true-life ['tru:'laɪf] *adj* verdadero(a), cierto(a)

truffle ['trʌfəl] *n* **(a)** *Bot* trufa *f* **(b)** *Br Culin* **(chocolate) t.** trufa *f* de chocolate

truism ['tru:ɪzəm] *n* truismo *m*

truly ['tru:lɪ] *adv* **(a)** *(really)* verdaderamente, de verdad; **I am t. grateful** se lo agradezco de verdad; **really and t.?** ¿de veras? **(b)** *(sincerely)* **yours t.** *(in letters)* atentamente; *Fam (myself)* este menda, un servidor

trump [trʌmp] **1** *n Cards* triunfo *m*; **what's trumps?** ¿qué pinta?; *Fig* **she always turns up trumps** siempre la favorece la suerte; *Fig* **to play one's t. card** jugar su carta maestra

2 *vt Cards* fallar

trump up *vt* **to t. up an excuse** inventar una excusa

trumped-up ['trʌmptʌp] *adj* inventado(a)

trumpet ['trʌmpɪt] **1** *n* trompeta *f*; **to blow one's own t.** cantar sus propias alabanzas
2 *vi* **(a)** *Mus* tocar la trompeta **(b)** *(elephant)* berrear, bramar, barritar

trumpeter ['trʌmpɪtər] *n* trompetista *mf*, trompeta *mf*

trumpeting ['trʌmpɪtɪŋ] *n* (of elephant) berrido *m*, bramido *m*

truncate [trʌŋ'keɪt] *vt* truncar

truncheon ['trʌntʃən] *n Br* porra *f* (de policía)

trundle ['trʌndəl] **1** *vt (cart)* empujar
2 *vi* rodar

trunk [trʌŋk] *n* **(a)** *(of tree, body)* tronco *m* **(b)** *(of elephant)* trompa *f* **(c)** *(case)* baúl *m* **(d)** *Br Tel* **t. call** llamada *f* or *Am* llamado *m* de larga distancia; *Aut* **t. road** carretera *f* principal **(e)** *US (of car)* maletero *m*, *CAm Méx* cajuela *f*, *RP* baúl *m*

trunks [trʌŋks] *npl* **(bathing) t.** traje *m sing* de baño, *Esp* bañador *m sing*, *RP* malla *f*

truss [trʌs] **1** *vt (tie)* atar
2 *n (of hay, straw)* haz *m*, lío *m* **(b)** *Constr* cuchillo *m* de armadura **(c)** *Med* braguero *m* **(d)** *(on plant)* racimo *m*

trust [trʌst] **1** *n* **(a)** *(belief, confidence)* confianza *f*; **breach of t.** abuso *m* de confianza; **position of t.** puesto *m* de responsabilidad; **to take sth on t.** creer algo a ojos cerrados **(b)** *Jur* fideicomiso *m* ❑ **t. deed** acta *f* de fideicomiso **(c)** *Com* **on t.** a crédito **(d)** *Fin* trust *m* ❑ **t. fund** fondo *m* en fideicomiso
2 *vt* **(a)** *(hope)* esperar; **I t. he will come** confío en que vendrá **(b)** *(rely upon)* confiar en, fiarse de; **he's not to be trusted** no es de fiar; **to t. sb with sth** confiar algo a algn **(c)** *Com (client)* dar crédito a
3 *vi* confiar **(in** de**); to t. in God** confiar en Dios; **to t. to luck** abandonarse al azar

trusted ['trʌstɪd] *adj (trustworthy)* de fiar, digno(a) de confianza; *(remedy)* probado(a)

trustee [trʌ'stiː] *n Jur* fideicomisario(a) *m,f*; *(in bankruptcy)* síndico *m*

trusteeship [trʌ'stiːʃɪp] *n Jur* cargo *m* de fideicomisario

trustful ['trʌstfʊl] *adj*, **trusting** ['trʌstɪŋ] *adj* confiado(a)

trustworthiness ['trʌstwɜːðɪnɪs] *n (of person)* honradez *f*, *Am* confiabilidad *f*; *(of source, information, data)* fiabilidad *f*, *Am* confiabilidad *f*

trustworthy ['trʌstwɜːðɪ] *adj (person)* fiable, de confianza, *Am* confiable; *(source)* fidedigno(a), fiable, *Am* confiable

trusty ['trʌstɪ] *adj* **(trustier, trustiest)** fiel, leal

truth [truːθ] *n* verdad *f*; **the honest t.** la pura verdad; **the t. is that ...** la verdad es que ...; **to tell the t.** decir la verdad; *Fam* **to tell sb a few home truths** decirle a algn cuatro verdades

truthful ['truːθfʊl] *adj (person)* veraz; *(testimony)* verídico(a)

truthfully ['truːθfʊlɪ] *adv* sinceramente, sin mentir; **tell me t.** dígame la verdad

truthfulness ['truːθfʊlnɪs] *n* veracidad *f*

try [traɪ] **1** *vt (pt & pp* **tried) (a)** *(attempt)* intentar; **to t. one's hand at (doing) sth** intentar (hacer) algo **(b)** *(test)* probar, ensayar, poner *or* someter a prueba; **to t. sb's patience** poner a prueba la paciencia de algn **(c)** *(taste)* probar; **have you tried alcohol-free beer?** ¿has probado la cerveza sin alcohol? **(d)** *Jur* juzgar; **his case is being tried at the High Court** el Tribunal Supremo está juzgando el caso
2 *vi* intentar; **he tried his hardest to save them** hizo todo lo posible para salvarles; **I shall t. again** volveré a intentarlo; **to t. for sth** intentar conseguir algo; **to t. to do sth, t. and do sth** tratar de *or* intentar hacer algo
3 *n* **(a)** *(attempt)* tentativa *f*, intento *m*; **it's worth a t.** vale la pena intentarlo; **to have a t. at doing sth** intentar hacer algo **(b)** *Sport* ensayo *m*

try on *vt* **(a)** *(dress)* probarse **(b)** *Fam* **to t. it on with sb** intentar engañar a algn

try out *vt* probar, ensayar; **t. it out on us first** pruébalo primero con nosotros, a ver qué pasa

trying ['traɪɪŋ] *adj (person)* molesto(a), pesado(a); **he's very t.** es pesadísimo; **to have a t. time** pasar un mal rato

tsar [zɑːr] *n* zar *m*

tsarina [zɑː'riːnə] *n* zarina *f*

tsetse fly ['tsetsɪflaɪ] *n* mosca *f* tsetsé

T-shirt ['tiːʃɜːt] *n* camiseta *f*, *Chile* polera *f*, *RP* remera *f*

tsp *(abbr* **teaspoonful)** cucharadita *f*

TTP [tiːtiː'piː] *n Comptr (abbr* **trusted third party)** *(for Internet transactions)* tercero *m* de confianza

tub [tʌb] *n* **(a)** *(for washing clothes)* tina *f* **(b)** *(bath)* bañera *f*, *Am* tina *f*, *Am* bañadera *f*

tuba ['tjuːbə] *n Mus* tuba *f*

tubby ['tʌbɪ] *adj* **(tubbier, tubbiest)** rechoncho(a)

tube [tjuːb] *n* **(a)** *(gen)* tubo *m*; *Anat* conducto *m*, trompa *f*; *(of bicycle)* **(inner) t.** cámara *f* (de aire) **(b)** *Br Fam (underground)* **the t.** el metro, *RP* el subte **(c)** *Fam (TV)* **the t.** la tele

tubeless ['tjuːblɪs] *adj* sin cámara

tuber ['tjuːbər] *n Bot* tubérculo *m*

tubercle ['tjuːbəkəl] *n* tubérculo *m*

tubercular [tjʊ'bɜːkjʊlər] *adj* tuberculoso(a)

tuberculin [tjʊ'bɜːkjʊlɪn] *n Med* tuberculina *f*

tuberculosis [tjʊbɜːkjʊ'ləʊsɪs] *n* tuberculosis *f*

tuberous ['tjuːbərəs] *adj Bot* tuberoso(a)

tubing ['tjuːbɪŋ] *n* tubería *f*; **(piece of) t.** (trozo *m* de) tubo *m*

tubular ['tjuːbjʊlər] *adj* tubular

tuck [tʌk] **1** *vt* **to t. in the bedclothes** remeter la ropa de la cama; **to t. one's shirt into one's trousers** meter la camisa por dentro (de los pantalones); **to t. sb up in bed** tapar a algn en la cama; **to t. sth away** esconder algo
2 *n* **(a)** *Sew* pliegue *m*; **to make** *or* **take a t. in a skirt** poner un pliegue a una falda **(b)** *Br Fam (food)* golosinas *fpl* ❑ **t. shop** = tienda que vende caramelos y patatas fritas (cerca de un colegio)

tuck in *vi Fam* manducar *or Esp Ven* papear sin cortarse; **t. in!** ¡come, come!

tuck into *vt* **to t. into a good meal** comer a dos carrillos

tuck-in ['tʌkɪn] *n Br Fam* comilona *f*

Tudor ['tjuːdər] *adj Hist* Tudor

Tue(s) *(abbr* **Tuesday)** martes *m*, mart

Tuesday ['tjuːzdɪ] *n* martes *m*; *see also* **Saturday**

tuft [tʌft] *n (of hair)* mechón *m*; *(of feathers)* copete *m*; *(of wool)* copo *m*, manojo *m*

tufted ['tʌftɪd] *adj Orn* copetudo(a)

tug [tʌg] **1** *vt (pt & pp* **tugged)** *(pull at)* tirar de; *(haul along)* arrastrar; *Naut* remolcar
2 *vi* **to t. at sth** tirar de algo
3 *n (pull)* tirón *m*, estirón *m*; **to give a good t.** tirar fuerte; **t. of war** *(game)* lucha *f* de la cuerda; *Fig* lucha encarnizada *y* prolongada **(b)** *Naut* remolcador *m*

tugboat ['tʌgbəʊt] *n* remolcador *m*

tugged [tʌgd] *pt & pp see* **tug**

tuition [tjuːˈɪʃən] n instruceión f, enseñanza f; **private t.** clases fpl particulares ❑ **t. fees** honorarios mpl

tulip [ˈtjuːlɪp] n Bot tulipán m ❑ **t. tree** tulipero m de Virginia

tulle [tjuːl] n Tex tul m

tum [tʌm] n (in children's language) tripita f, barriga f, Chile guata f

tumble [ˈtʌmbəl] **1** vi (person) caerse; (acrobat) dar volteretas; (building) hundirse, venirse abajo; **to t. downstairs** caer escaleras abajo; Fig **to t. into bed** echarse en la cama; Fig **to t. out of a car** bajar precipitadamente de un coche
2 vt volcar
3 n (a) (fall) caída f, revolcón m; **to take** or **have a t.** caerse (b) **t. dryer** secadora f

tumbledown [ˈtʌmbəldaʊn] adj (house) en ruinas, ruinoso(a)

tumbler [ˈtʌmblər] n vaso m

tummy [ˈtʌmɪ] n Fam tripa m, barriga f, Chile guata f; **to have (a) t. ache** tener dolor de tripa or barriga or Chile guata

tumour, US **tumor** [ˈtjuːmər] US [ˈtuːmər] n Med tumor m ❑ **brain t.** tumor m cerebral

tumult [ˈtjuːmʌlt] n tumulto m

tumultuous [tjuːˈmʌltjʊəs] adj tumultuoso(a)

tuna [ˈtjuːnə] US [ˈtuːnə] n (pl tuna or tunas) atún m, bonito m

tundra [ˈtʌndrə] n tundra f

tune [tjuːn] **1** n (a) (melody) melodía f; **to play a t.** tocar una melodía; Fig **to call the t.** imponer condiciones; Fig **to change one's t.** cambiar de tono; Fam Fig **expenses to the t. of $100** gastos por la friolera de 100 dólares (b) Mus tono m; **the piano is in/out of t.** el piano está afinado/desafinado; **to sing out of t.** desafinar; Fig (harmony) **to be in/out of t. with one's surroundings** entonar/desentonar con el ambiente
2 vt (a) Mus (instrument) afinar (b) Aut **to t. (up) the engine** poner a punto or reglar el motor
3 vi Rad TV **to t. in to a station/channel** sintonizar una emisora/cadena

tune up vi (orchestra) afinar los instrumentos

tuneful [ˈtjuːnfʊl] adj melodioso(a), armonioso(a)

tuneless [ˈtjuːnlɪs] adj disonante, poco melodioso(a)

tuner [ˈtjuːnər] (a) (of pianos) afinador(a) m,f (b) Rad TV (knob) sintonizador m

tune-up [ˈtjuːnʌp] n Aut (of engine) puesta f a punto, reglaje m

tungsten [ˈtʌŋstən] n Chem tungsteno m ❑ **t. steel** acero m al tunsgteno

tunic [ˈtjuːnɪk] n túnica f

tuning [ˈtjuːnɪŋ] n (a) Mus afinación f ❑ **t. fork** diapasón m (b) Rad TV **t. in** sintonización f

Tunis [ˈtjuːnɪs] n Túnez

Tunisia [tjuːˈnɪzɪə] n Túnez

Tunisian [tjuːˈnɪzɪən] adj & n tunecino(a) (m,f)

tunnel [ˈtʌnəl] **1** n túnel m; Min galería f; **to dig a t.** construir un túnel
2 vi (pt & pp tunnelled, US tunneled) **to t. through a mountain** abrir un túnel a través de una montaña

tunnelling, US **tunneling** [ˈtʌnəlɪŋ] n construcción f de un túnel or de túneles

tunny [ˈtʌnɪ] n Br (fish) atún m, bonito m

tupelo [ˈtjuːpɪləʊ] n (pl tupelos) Bot tupelo m negro

tuppence [ˈtʌpəns] n Br see twopence

Tupperware® [ˈtʌpəweər] n táper m, recipiente m hermético de plástico

turban [ˈtɜːbən] n turbante m

turbid [ˈtɜːbɪd] adj (liquid) turbio(a)

turbine [ˈtɜːbaɪn] n turbina f

turbojet [tɜːbəʊˈdʒet] n Tech turborreactor m; Av avión m turborreactor

turboprop [tɜːbəʊˈprɒp] n Tech turbopropulsor m

turbot [ˈtɜːbət] n (pl turbot or turbots) (fish) rodaballo m

turbulence [ˈtɜːbjʊləns] n turbulencia f

turbulent [ˈtɜːbjʊlənt] adj turbulento(a)

turd [tɜːd] n Fam (a) (excrement) cagada f, mierda f (b) (person) Esp gilipollas mf inv, Am pendejo(a) m,f, RP boludo(a) m,f

tureen [təˈriːn] n sopera f

turf [tɜːf] **1** n (pl turfs or turves) (a) (grass) césped m; (peat) turba f (b) Sport (horse racing) **the T.** el Turf ❑ Br **t. accountant** corredor(a) m,f de apuestas
2 vt cubrir con césped

turf out vt Br Fam **to t. sb out** poner a algn de patitas en la calle

Turk [tɜːk] n turco(a) m,f

Turkey [ˈtɜːkɪ] n Turquía

turkey [ˈtɜːkɪ] n (pl turkey or turkeys) Orn pavo m, Méx guajolote m ❑ **t. cock** pavo m, Méx guajolote m **t. hen** pava f

Turkish [ˈtɜːkɪʃ] **1** adj turco(a) ❑ **T. bath** baño m turco
2 n (language) turco m

Turkmenistan [tɜːkmenɪˈstɑːn] n Turkmenistán

turmeric [ˈtɜːmərɪk] n Bot cúrcuma f

turmoil [ˈtɜːmɔɪl] n confusión f, alboroto m; **mental t.** trastorno m mental; **to be in a t.** estar alborotado(a)

turn [tɜːn] **1** vt (a) (revolve) girar, hacer girar; **to t. a key in a lock** dar la vuelta a una llave en una cerradura (b) (turn over) volver la vuelta, volver una prenda del revés; **to t. a page** volver or pasar una página (c) (change direction of) **to t. one's head/gaze** volver la cabeza/mirada (towards hacia); Fig **success has turned his head** el éxito se le ha subido a la cabeza; Fig **without turning a hair** sin inmutarse (d) (deflect) desviar; **we couldn't t. him from his plan** no pudimos convencerle de que abandonara su plan (e) (pass) volver; **to t. the corner** doblar or Am voltear la esquina; Fig **he's turned forty** ha cumplido los cuarenta (años) (f) (change) cambiar, transformar (into en); **to t. a book into a film** adaptar un libro al cine; **to t. a house into flats** convertir una casa en pisos; **to t. a text into English** traducir un texto al inglés (g) (on lathe) tornear; Fig **a well-turned sentence** una frase elegante
2 vi (a) (revolve) girar, dar vueltas; Fig **everything turns on your answer** todo depende de tu respuesta; Fig **the talk turned on sport** la conversación giró en torno al deporte (b) (change direction) torcer, girar; (turn round) volverse, dar la vuelta; Fig (for help) acudir (to a); Mil **right t.!** ¡derecha!; **to t. to sb** volverse hacia algn; **to t. to the left** torcer a la izquierda; **to t. upside down** volcarse; Fig **I don't know which way to t.** no sé a quién acudir; Fig **to t. against sb** coger or tomar antipatía a algn; Fig **to t. on sb** volverse contra algn (c) (become) ponerse, volverse; **the milk has turned sour** la leche se ha cortado; **the situation is turning nasty** la situación se está poniendo fea; **to t. awkward** ponerse difícil; **to t. socialist** hacerse socialista; Fig **everything he touches turns to gold** convierte en oro todo lo que toca
3 n (a) (of wheel) vuelta f, revolución f; Culin **meat done to a t.** carne en su punto (b) (change of direction) cambio m de dirección; (in road) curva f, vuelta f; **sudden/sharp t.** curva brusca/cerrada; **to take a new t.** tomar otro sesgo;

to take a t. for the better empezar a mejorar; *Fig* at every
t. a cada paso (**c**) *(deed, action)* to do sb a good t. hacer un
favor a algn (**d**) *Med (fit)* ataque *m*; *Fig* you gave me quite
a t.! ¡vaya susto que me diste! (**e**) *(in game, queue)* turno *m*,
vez *f*; it's your t. te toca a ti; to take turns (at doing sth),
Br to take it in turns to do sth turnarse para hacer algo;
whose t. is it? ¿a quién le toca? (**f**) *Theat* número *m*; to do
a t. hacer un número (**g**) *(form)* t. of phrase giro *m* (**h**)
(inclination) t. of mind disposición *f*

turn aside 1 *vt* desviar, apartar
  2 *vi* desviarse

turn away 1 *vt (person)* rechazar
  2 *vi (look aside)* volver la cabeza

turn back 1 *vt (person)* hacer retroceder; *(clock)* retrasar;
(corner of page) doblar
  2 *vi* retroceder, volver(se) atrás

turn down *vt* (**a**) *(gas, radio, etc)* bajar (**b**) *(reject)*
rechazar (**c**) *(fold)* doblar; to t. down the bedclothes
abrir la cama

turn in 1 *vt* (**a**) *(person)* entregar a la policía (**b**) *(lost
property)* entregar; to t. in an essay entregar una
redacción *or* un trabajo (escrito)
  2 *vi Fam* acostarse

turn off 1 *vt (electricity)* desconectar; *(gas, light)* apagar;
(water) cerrar, parar
  2 *vi* desviarse (de la carretera)

turn on *vt (water, gas)* abrir; *(light, TV, engine)* encender,
Am prender; *Fam* it turns me on me chifla

turn out 1 *vt* (**a**) *(extinguish)* apagar, cerrar (**b**) *(eject)*
echar, expulsar; *(empty)* vaciar; *(room)* limpiar, arreglar;
Culin sacar del molde (**c**) *(produce)* producir, fabricar (**d**)
(person) well turned-out elegante, bien vestido(a) (**e**) *Mil*
to t. out the guard formar la guardia
  2 *vi* (**a**) *(attend)* asistir, aparecer; very few people turned
out for the meeting muy pocas personas asistieron a la
reunión (**b**) *(result)* salir; it turns out that ... resulta que ...;
the weather has turned out fine el tiempo ha mejorado;
things have turned out well las cosas han salido bien

turn over 1 *vt* (**a**) *(turn upside down)* poner al revés; *(page)*
dar la vuelta a; *Fig* to t. over an idea in one's mind darle
vueltas a una idea (**b**) *Com* hacer de caja; he turns over
$5,000 a week hace 5.000 dólares a la semana de caja (**c**)
(transfer) to t. sth over to sb entregar algo a algn
  2 *vi (animal, page)* volverse; to t. (right) over volcarse,
dar una vuelta de campana; *Fig* my stomach turned over
se me revolvió el estómago

turn round 1 *vt* volver, dar la vuelta a
  2 *vi (rotate)* girar, dar vueltas; *(about face)* darse la vuelta,
volverse; to t. round and round dar muchas vueltas

turn up 1 *vt* (**a**) *(collar)* levantar, alzar; *(skirt)* hacer un
dobladillo a; to t. up one's shirt sleeves arremangarse,
remangarse; turned-up nose nariz *f* respingona; *Fig* to t.
up one's nose at sth despreciar *or* desdeñar algo (**b**) *Elec
Rad TV* subir, poner más fuerte; t. the radio up sube la
radio (**c**) *Cards (ace, king)* sacar
  2 *vi* (**a**) *(appear)* aparecer; he turned up in Spain
apareció en España; *Fig* something is sure to t. up algo
pasará (**b**) *(arrive)* llegar, presentarse; he turned up too
late for the meeting llegó demasiado tarde para la
reunión (**c**) *(attend)* asistir, acudir; very few people
turned up asistieron muy pocas personas (**d**) *Cards* salir

turnaround ['tɜːnəraʊnd] *n* (**a**) *(in situation, opinion)*
vuelco *m*, giro *m* (**b**) *Com* t. time tiempo *m* de espera *(de
pedidos)*

turncoat ['tɜːnkəʊt] *n Esp* chaquetero(a) *m,f*, *Am*
oportunista *mf*, *RP* camaleón *m*

turning ['tɜːnɪŋ] **1** *adj* que da vueltas, giratorio(a)
  2 *n* (**a**) *(turnabout)* cambio *m* de dirección □ *Fig* t. point

punto *m* decisivo, momento *m* crítico (**b**) *(in road)* vuelta *f*,
recodo *m*; *(in town)* take the first t. on the right toma la
primera bocacalle a mano derecha

turnip ['tɜːnɪp] *n Bot* nabo *m*

turn-off ['tɜːnɒf] *n* (**a**) *(on road)* salida *f*, desviación *f* (**b**)
Fam it's a t. me corta el rollo

turn-on ['tɜːnɒn] *n Fam* it's a t. for her/him *(sexually)* le
vuelve loca/loco, *Esp* le pone a cien

turnout ['tɜːnaʊt] *n* asistencia *f*; there was a good/poor
t. asistió mucha/poca gente

turnover ['tɜːnəʊvər] *n* (**a**) *Com* facturación *f*, volumen *m*
de negocios; *(movement)* movimiento *m*; quick t. of goods
movimiento rápido de mercancías (**b**) *Culin* apple t.
empanada *f* de manzana

turnpike ['tɜːnpaɪk] *n US* autopista *f* de peaje

turnstile ['tɜːnstaɪl] *n* torniquete *m*

turntable ['tɜːnteɪbəl] *n* (**a**) *Rail* placa *f or* plataforma *f*
giratoria (**b**) *(for record)* plato *m* giratorio

turn-up ['tɜːnʌp] *n Br (of trousers)* vuelta *f*, *Fam Fig* what
a t.-up for the books! ¡vaya sorpresa!

turpentine ['tɜːpəntaɪn] *n* (esencia *f* de) trementina *f*,
aguarrás *m*

turquoise ['tɜːkwɔɪz] **1** *n (colour, stone)* turquesa *f*
  2 *adj* t. (blue) de color azul turquesa

turret ['tʌrɪt] *n* (**a**) *Archit* torrecilla *f* (**b**) *Mil (of tank)* torreta
f

turtle ['tɜːtəl] *n Zool (aquatic animal)* tortuga *f* (marina);
US (tortoise) tortuga *f*; *Naut Fig* to turn t. zozobrar □ t. soup
consomé *m* de tortuga

turtledove ['tɜːtəldʌv] *n Orn* tórtola *f*

turtleneck ['tɜːtəlnek] *n* cuello *m* alto; a t. sweater un
suéter *or Esp* un jersey de cuello alto

turves [tɜːvz] *npl see* turf

tusk [tʌsk] *n* colmillo *m*

tussle ['tʌsəl] **1** *vi* pelearse, luchar
  2 *n (fight)* pelea *f*, lucha *f*; *(commotion)* follón *m*; to have a
t. pelearse

tussock ['tʌsək] *n* mata *f*

tutor ['tjuːtər] **1** *n* (**a**) *Br Univ* tutor(a) *m,f* (**b**) *(personal
instructor)* (private) t. profesor(a) *m,f* particular
  2 *vt* to t. sb in English dar clases particulares de inglés a
algn

tutorial [tjuː'tɔːrɪəl] *n Br Univ* seminario *m*; *Comptr*
tutorial *f*

tutu ['tuːtuː] *n* tutú *m*

Tuvalu [tuːvəˈluː] *n* Tuvalu

tuxedo [tʌkˈsiːdəʊ] *n (pl* tuxedos) *US* smoking *m*

TV [tiːˈviː] *n (abbr* television) televisión *f*, TV

twaddle ['twɒdəl] *n Fam* tonterías *fpl*, bobadas *fpl*; stop
talking t.! ¡déjate de tonterías!

twang [twæŋ] **1** *n* (**a**) *(of instrument)* sonido *m* vibrante (**b**)
(quality) nasal t. gangueo *m*, voz *f* gangosa; to speak with
a t. ganguear
  2 *vt* to t. a guitar puntear una guitarra
  3 *vi Mus (string)* vibrar

tweak [twiːk] *vt* pellizcar; to t. sb's ears tirar de las orejas
a algn

twee [twiː] *adj Br* cursi; it's rather t. es un poco cursi

tweed [twiːd] *n Tex* cheviot *m*

tweet [twiːt] **1** *n* pío *m*, gorjeo *m*
  2 *vi* piar, gorjear

tweeter ['twiːtər] *n (loudspeaker)* altavoz *m* para los
sonidos agudos

tweezers ['twiːzəz] *npl* pinzas *fpl*

twelfth [twelfθ] **1** *adj* duodécimo(a); **(on) the t. of March** el doce de Marzo ▫ **T. Night** Noche *f* de Reyes

2 *n* (**a**) *(in series)* duodécimo(a) *m,f* (**b**) *(fraction)* duodécimo *m*, duodécima parte *f*; *see also* **seventh**

twelve [twelv] **1** *adj* doce; **t. o'clock** las doce

2 *n* doce *m*; *see also* **seven**

twentieth ['twentɪɪθ] **1** *adj* vigésimo(a); **(on) the t. of June** el veinte de Junio

2 *n* (**a**) *(in series)* vigésimo(a) *m,f* (**b**) *(fraction)* vigésimo *m*, vigésima parte *f*; *see also* **seventh**

twenty ['twentɪ] **1** *adj* veinte; **about t. people** una veintena de personas; **the t.-first of May** el veintiuno de mayo; **t.-one** veintiuno; *Med* **t.-t. vision** visión *f* normal; **t.-two** veintidós

2 *n* veinte *m*; **he's in his late twenties** tiene veintimuchos años; **in the early twenties** a principios de los años veinte; *see also* **seven**

twerp [twɜ:p] *n Fam* lerdo(a) *m,f*, *Esp* memo(a) *m,f*

twice [twaɪs] *adv* dos veces; **he's t. as old as I am** tiene el doble de años que yo; **in England it would cost t. as much** en Inglaterra costaría el doble; **to be t. as big as sth** ser el doble de grande que algo; **to do sth t. (over)** hacer algo dos veces; *Fam* **he didn't have to be asked t.** no se hizo de rogar

twiddle ['twɪdəl] **1** *vt* dar vueltas a, girar; **to t. one's moustache** mesarse el bigote; **to t. one's thumbs** estar mano sobre mano

2 *vi* **to t. with sth** juguetear con algo

twig[1] [twɪg] *n* ramilla *f*, ramita *f*

twig[2] [twɪg] **1** *vt (pt & pp* **twigged)** *Br Fam* comprender, caer en la cuenta de

2 *vi* comprender, caer en la cuenta

twilight ['twaɪlaɪt] *n* crepúsculo *m*; **in the t.** a media luz

twin [twɪn] **1** *n* gemelo(a) *m,f*, mellizo(a) *m,f*; **identical twins** gemelos idénticos ▫ **t. beds** camas *f* gemelas; **t. brother/sister** hermano gemelo/hermana gemela; **t.-engined aircraft** bimotor *m*

2 *vt (pt & pp* **twinned)** hermanar; **our town is twinned with one in Germany** nuestra ciudad está hermanada con una alemana

twine [twaɪn] **1** *n* bramante *m*

2 *vt* entretejer; **to t. sth round sth** enrollar algo alrededor de algo

3 *vi* **to t. round sth** enroscarse alrededor de algo

twinge [twɪndʒ] *n (of pain)* punzada *f*; *Fig* **t. of conscience** remordimiento *m*

twinkle ['twɪŋkəl] **1** *vi (stars)* centellear, parpadear; *(eyes)* brillar

2 *n (of stars)* centelleo *m*, parpadeo *m*; *(of eyes)* brillo *m*

twinkling ['twɪŋklɪŋ] *n (of stars)* centelleo *m*, parpadeo *m*; *Fig* **in the t. of an eye** en un abrir y cerrar de ojos

twinned [twɪnd] *pt & pp see* **twin**

twinset ['twɪnset] *n Br (matching garments)* conjunto *m*

twirl [twɜ:l] **1** *vt* (**a**) *(whirl)* girar rápidamente, hacer molinetes con (**b**) *(twist)* **to t. one's moustache** mesarse el bigote

2 *vi (spin)* girar rápidamente; *(dancer)* piruetear

3 *n* (**a**) *(movement)* giro *m* rápido; *(of dancer)* pirueta *f* (**b**) *(of smoke)* voluta *f*, espiral *f*

twist [twɪst] **1** *vt* (**a**) *(thread, rope)* retorcer; *(sense of something)* retorcer, tergiversar; **to t. off a lid** desenroscar una tapa; *Med* **to t. one's ankle** torcerse el tobillo; **to t. sb's arm** retorcerle el brazo a algn; **to t. sth round sth** enrollar algo alrededor de algo; **to t. together** entrelazar; *Fig* **she can t. him round her little finger** hace con él todo lo que quiere

2 *vi (smoke)* formar volutas; *(path)* serpentear; *(worm)* retorcerse

3 *n* (**a**) *(of yarn)* torzal *m*; **t. of hair** trenza *f*; **t. of paper** cucurucho *m* de papel (**b**) *(movement)* torsión *f*; *Med* torcedura *f*, esguince *m*; **to give sth a t.** torcer algo; *Fig* **to give a new t. to sth** dar un nuevo enfoque a algo (**c**) *(in road)* vuelta *f*, recodo *m*; **twists and turns** vueltas y más vueltas; *Br Fam* **to be round the t.** estar chiflado(a) (**d**) *(dance)* twist *m*

twisted ['twɪstɪd] *adj* torcido(a), retorcido(a)

twister ['twɪstər] *n* (**a**) *Br Fam (person)* estafador(a) *m,f* (**b**) *esp US (tornado)* tornado *m*

twisting ['twɪstɪŋ] **1** *adj (road, path)* que serpentea, que da vueltas

2 *n* torcedura *f*; *Fig (of facts)* tergiversación *f* deformación *f*

twit [twɪt] *n Br Fam* lerdo(a) *m,f*, *Esp* memo(a) *m,f*

twitch [twɪtʃ] **1** *vt* (**a**) *(pull)* dar un tirón a (**b**) *(hands)* crispar; *(animal)* **to t. its ears** mover nerviosamente las orejas

2 *vi* crisparse; **his face twitches** tiene un tic

3 *n* (**a**) *(movement)* tirón *m* (**b**) *(nervous)* tic *m* nervioso

twitter ['twɪtər] **1** *vi (bird)* gorjear

2 *n (of bird)* gorjeo *m*; *Fam* **to be in a t.** *or* **all of a t.** estar muy nervioso(a)

twittering ['twɪtərɪŋ] *n* gorjeo *m*

two [tu:] **1** *adj* dos *inv*; *Fig* **to be in** *or* **of t. minds about sth** estar indeciso(a) respecto a algo

2 *n (pl* **twos)** dos *m inv*; **the t. of us, we t.** nosotros dos; *Fig* **he and his brother are t. of a kind** él y su hermano son tal para cual; *Fig* **to put t. and t. together** atar *or* juntar cabos; *see also* **seven**

two-bit ['tu:'bɪt] *adj US Fam (insignificant)* de tres al cuarto, *RP* de morondanga

two-dimensional [tu:d(a)ɪ'menʃənəl] *adj* bidimensional; *Fig (character, film)* superficial, plano(a)

two-edged ['tu:edʒd] *adj* de doble filo

two-faced ['tu:feɪst] *adj* hipócrita

twofold ['tu:fəʊld] *adj* doble; **a t. rise** una subida del doble, una duplicación

two-legged ['tu:legɪd] *adj* bípedo(a)

two-party ['tu:pɑ:tɪ] *adj Pol* bipartidista

twopence ['tʌpəns] *n Br* dos peniques; *Fig* **I don't care t.** (no) me importa un bledo

two-piece ['tu:pi:s] **1** *adj* de dos piezas

2 *n (suit)* traje *m* de dos piezas

two-pin ['tu:pɪn] *adj (plug, socket)* de dos clavijas

two-ply ['tu:plaɪ] *adj (wool)* de dos hebras

two-seater ['tu:si:tər] *adj & n Aut* biplaza *(f)*

twosome ['tu:səm] *n* pareja *f*; **we went in a t.** fuimos los dos juntos

two-storey, *US* **two-story** ['tu:stɔ:rɪ] *adj* de dos pisos

two-stroke ['tu:strəʊk] *adj (engine)* de dos tiempos

two-time ['tu:taɪm] *vt Fam* **to t.-t. sb** engañar *or Esp* pegársela a algn

two-tone ['tu:təʊn] *adj* de dos colores

two-way ['tu:weɪ] *adj* (**a**) *(street)* de dos direcciones (**b**) *Rad* **t.-w. radio** aparato *m* emisor y receptor; *Elec* **t.-w. switch** conmutador *m* bidireccional

two-wheeler ['tu:wi:lər] *n Fam* bicicleta *f*

tycoon [taɪ'ku:n] *n* magnate *m*

type [taɪp] **1** *n* (**a**) *(kind)* tipo *m*, clase *f*; *(brand)* marca *f*; *(of car)* modelo *m*; **Gruyère-t. cheese** queso *m* tipo Gruyère; **he's a nasty t.** es un tipo antipático; **she's not my t.** no es mi tipo; **what t. of person is she?** ¿qué clase de persona

es? (**b**) *Typ* carácter *m*, tipo *m*; *(print)* caracteres *mpl*, tipos *mpl*; **in bold t.** en negrita; **in large/small t.** en caracteres grandes/pequeños
2 *vt (with typewriter)* escribir a máquina, mecanografiar; *(with word processor)* escribir *or* introducir en *Esp* el ordenador *or Am* la computadora
3 *vi* escribir a máquina

typecast ['taɪpkɑːst] *vt (pt & pp* **typecast**) encasillar

typeface ['taɪpfeɪs] *n* tipo *m* (de imprenta)

typescript ['taɪpskrɪpt] *n* texto *m* escrito a máquina *or* mecanografiado

typeset ['taɪpset] *vt (pt & pp* **typeset**) *Typ* componer

typesetter ['taɪpsetər] *n Typ* (**a**) *(person)* cajista *mf* (**b**) *(machine)* máquina *f* para componer tipos

typesetting ['taɪpsetɪŋ] *n Typ* composición *f* (tipográfica)

typewriter ['taɪpraɪtər] *n* máquina *f* de escribir

typewritten ['taɪprɪtən] *adj* escrito(a) a máquina, mecanografiado(a)

typhoid ['taɪfɔɪd] *n Med* **t.** (**fever**) fiebre *f* tifoidea

typhoon [taɪ'fuːn] *n* tifón *m*

typhus ['taɪfəs] *n Med* tifus *m*

typical ['tɪpɪkəl] *adj* típico(a); **that's t. of him** es muy típico de él

typify ['tɪpɪfaɪ] *vt (pt & pp* **typified**) tipificar, ser característico(a) de

typing ['taɪpɪŋ] *n (by typewriter)* mecanografía *f*; *(by word processor)* introducción *f* (de datos) en *Esp* el ordenador *or Am* la computadora ❑ **t. paper** papel *m* para escribir a máquina

typist ['taɪpɪst] *n* mecanógrafo(a) *m,f*

typographic(al) [taɪpə'græfɪk(əl)] *adj* tipográfico(a)

typography [taɪ'pɒɡrəfi] *n* tipografía *f*

tyrannical [tɪ'rænɪkəl] *adj* tiránico(a)

tyrannize ['tɪrənaɪz] *vt* tiranizar

tyrannous ['tɪrənəs] *adj see* **tyrannical**

tyranny ['tɪrənɪ] *n* tiranía *f*

tyrant ['taɪrənt] *n* tirano(a) *m,f*

tyre [taɪər] *n Br* neumático *m*, *Am* llanta *f*, *Arg* goma *f* ❑ **t. pressure** presión *f* de los neumáticos *or* de las ruedas

tyro ['taɪrəʊ] *n (pl* **tyros**) principiante *mf*

Tyrol [tɪ'rəʊl] *n* Tirol

Tyrolean [tɪrə'lɪən] *adj & n* tirolés(esa) *(m,f)*

U

U, u [juː] *n (the letter)* U, u *f*

UAE [juːerˈiː] *n (abbr* **United Arab Emirates)** Emiratos *mpl* Arabes Unidos, EAU *mpl*

ubiquitous [juːˈbɪkwɪtəs] *adj* ubicuo(a)

ubiquity [juːˈbɪkwɪtɪ] *n (gen)* ubicuidad *f; (of God)* omnipresencia *f*

udder [ˈʌdər] *n* ubre *f*

UEFA [juːˈerfə, juːˈiːfə] *n Sport (abbr* **Union of European Football Associations)** Unión *f* de Asociaciones Europeas de Fútbol, UEFA *f*

UFO, ufo [ˈjuːefˈəʊ, ˈjuːfəʊ] *(pl* **UFOs, ufos)** *n (abbr* **unidentified flying object)** objeto *m* volador no identificado, OVNI *m*, ovni *m*

Uganda [juːˈgændə] *n* Uganda

Ugandan [juːˈgændən] *adj & n* ugandés(esa) *(m,f)*

ugh [ʊx, ʊh, ʌh] *interj* ¡uf!, ¡puf!

ugliness [ˈʌɡlɪnɪs] *n* fealdad *f*

ugly [ˈʌɡlɪ] *adj* **(uglier, ugliest)** *(gen)* feo(a); *(incident, situation)* desagradable; **as u. as sin** más feo(a) que un pecado; **to grow u.** afearse; **to have an u. temper** tener mal genio; *Fig* **u. duckling** patito feo

UHF [juːertʃˈef] *n Rad TV (abbr* **ultra high frequency)** frecuencia *f* ultraalta, UHF *f*

uh-huh [ʌˈhʌ] *interj Fam* uh-h.! ¡ajá!

UK [juːˈkeɪ] *n (abbr* **United Kingdom)** Reino *m* Unido

Ukraine [ˈjuːkreɪn] *n* **the U.** Ucrania

Ukrainian [juːˈkreɪnɪən] **1** *adj* ucraniano(a), ucranio(a) **2** *n* **(a)** *(person)* ucraniano(a) *m,f* **(b)** *(language)* ucranio *m*

ukulele [juːkəˈleɪlɪ] *n* ukelele *m*

ulcer [ˈʌlsər] *n (outer)* llaga *f; (inner)* úlcera *f* ❑ **stomach u.** úlcera *f* de estómago

ulcerate [ˈʌlsəreɪt] **1** *vt* ulcerar **2** *vi* ulcerarse

ulna [ˈʌlnə] *n Anat* cúbito *m*

Ulster [ˈʌlstər] *n* el Ulster

ulterior [ʌlˈtɪərɪər] *adj* **(a)** *(hidden)* oculto(a) **(b)** *(further)* ulterior

ultimate [ˈʌltɪmɪt] **1** *adj* **(a)** *(final)* último(a); *(of aim)* final; *(of decision)* definitivo(a) **(b)** *(basic)* esencial, fundamental **2** **the u.** *n* el último grito, *Esp* el no va más

ultimately [ˈʌltɪmɪtlɪ] *adv* **(a)** *(finally)* finalmente **(b)** *(basically)* en el fondo

ultimatum [ʌltɪˈmeɪtəm] *n (pl* **ultimatums** *or* **ultimata** [ʌltɪˈmeɪtə])** ultimátum *m*

ultra- [ˈʌltrə] *pref* ultra-

ultramarine [ʌltrəməˈriːn] **1** *n* azul *m* ultramarino *or* de ultramar **2** *adj (from overseas)* ultramarino(a)

ultramodern [ʌltrəˈmɒdən] *adj* ultramoderno(a)

ultrasound [ˈʌltrəsaʊnd] *n* ultrasonido *m*

ultraviolet [ʌltrəˈvaɪəlɪt] *adj* ultravioleta

umbilical [ʌmˈbɪlɪkəl, ʌmbɪˈlaɪkəl] *adj* umbilical; **u. cord** cordón umbilical

umbrage [ˈʌmbrɪdʒ] *n* resentimiento *m*; **to take u. at sth** sentirse ofendido(a) por algo

umbrella [ʌmˈbrelə] *n* **(a)** *(device)* paraguas *m inv, Col* sombrilla *f* ❑ **beach u.** quitasol *m*, parasol *m*, sombrilla *f*; **u. stand** paragüero *m* **(b)** *Av Mil* cobertura *f* aérea **(c)** *Fig (protection)* manto *m*, protección *f; (patronage)* patrocinio *m* ❑ **u. organization** organismo *m* madre

umpire [ˈʌmpaɪər] **1** *n* árbitro *m* **2** *vt* arbitrar

umpteen [ʌmpˈtiːn] *adj Fam* muchísimos(as), la tira de; **u. guests** un montón de invitados

umpteenth [ʌmpˈtiːnθ] *adj* enésimo(a)

UN [juːˈen] *n (abbr* **United Nations (Organization))** (Organización *f* de las) Naciones *fpl* Unidas, ONU *f sing*

un- [ʌn] *pref* in-, des-, poco ..., sin ...; **unadvisable** desaconsejable, poco aconsejable; **unanswered** sin contestar

'un [ʌn] *pron Fam* **he's a bad 'un** es un tipo de mucho cuidado; **the little 'uns** los chiquitines, los peques

unabashed [ʌnəˈbæʃt] *adj* descarado(a); **to be u. (by** *or* **at)** no sentir vergüenza *or Am* pena (de *or* por)

unable [ʌnˈeɪbəl] *adj* incapaz; **I'm u. to attend the meeting** me es imposible asistir a la reunión; **to be u. to do sth/anything** no poder hacer algo/nada

unabridged [ʌnəˈbrɪdʒd] *adj* íntegro(a); **u. edition** edición íntegra

unacceptable [ʌnəkˈseptəbəl] *adj* inaceptable

unaccommodating [ʌnəˈkɒmədeɪtɪŋ] *adj (person)* poco sociable

unaccompanied [ʌnəˈkʌmpənɪd] *adj* **(a)** *(person)* solo(a), sin compañía **(b)** *Mus* sin acompañamiento

unaccomplished [ʌnəˈkʌmplɪʃt] *adj* **(a)** *(unfinished)* incompleto(a), sin acabar **(b)** *(mediocre)* mediocre

unaccountable [ʌnəˈkaʊntəbəl] *adj* inexplicable

unaccounted-for [ʌnəˈkaʊntɪdfɔːr] *adj* **to be u.-f.** faltar; **five passengers are still u.-f.** se desconoce aún el paradero de cinco pasajeros

unaccustomed [ʌnəˈkʌstəmd] *adj* desacostumbrado(a) **(to** a**)**; **he's u. to this climate** no está muy acostumbrado a este clima

unacquainted [ʌnəˈkweɪntɪd] *adj* **to be u. with** no

conocer, ignorar; **I'm u. with Shaw's plays** no conozco las obras de Shaw

unadventurous [ʌnəd'ventʃərəs] *adj* poco atrevido(a) *or* arriesgado(a)

unadvisable [ʌnəd'vaɪzəbəl] *adj* desaconsejable, poco aconsejable

unaffected [ʌnə'fektɪd] *adj* (**a**) *(unchanged)* no afectado(a) (**by** por) (**b**) *(indifferent)* indiferente (**by** a); **u. by his insults** inmutable ante sus insultos (**c**) *(natural) (person)* natural, afable, campechano(a); *(style)* llano(a), sin afectación

unafraid [ʌnə'freɪd] *adj* sin miedo (**of** a); **to be u. of sth/ sb** no tenerle miedo a algo/algn

unaided [ʌn'eɪdɪd] *adj* sin ayuda, solo(a)

unalterable [ʌn'ɔːltərəbəl] *adj* inalterable

unambiguous [ʌnæm'bɪɡjʊəs] *adj* inequívoco(a)

unambitious [ʌnæm'bɪʃəs] *adj* (**a**) *(person)* poco ambicioso(a), sin ambición (**b**) *(idea, project)* poco ambicioso(a), de corto alcance

unanimity [juːnə'nɪmɪtɪ] *n* unanimidad *f*

unanimous [juː'nænɪməs] *adj* unánime

unanimously [jʊ'nænɪməslɪ] *adv* unánimemente

unannounced [ʌnə'naʊnst] *adj* sin avisar; **she came in u.** *(without knocking)* entró sin llamar; *(without announcement)* entró sin ser anunciada

unanswerable [ʌn'ɑːnsərəbəl] *adj* (**a**) *(argument etc)* irrefutable (**b**) *(question)* sin respuesta (posible), que no tiene respuesta

unanswered [ʌn'ɑːnsəd] *adj* sin contestar

unappreciated [ʌnə'priːʃeɪtɪd] *adj* poco apreciado(a) *or* valorado(a)

unappreciative [ʌnə'priːʃɪətɪv] *adj* desagradecido(a); **to be u. of** no apreciar, no valorar

unapproachable [ʌnə'prəʊtʃəbəl] *adj* inabordable, inaccesible

unarmed [ʌn'ɑːmd] *adj* desarmado(a); **u. combat** lucha a cuerpo limpio

unashamed [ʌnə'ʃeɪmd] *adj* descarado(a); **he was completely u. about it** no le dio ninguna vergüenza *or Am* pena

unasked [ʌn'ɑːskt] *adv* (**a**) **u. (for)** *(unrequested)* no solicitado(a); *(spontaneous)* espontáneo(a) (**b**) *(not invited)* sin ser invitado(a); **she often helps quite u.** muchas veces ayuda sin que se lo pidan

unassailable [ʌnə'seɪləbəl] *adj* *(castle, position)* inexpugnable; *(argument, theory)* irrebatible

unassuming [ʌnə'sjuːmɪŋ] *adj* modesto(a), sin pretensiones

unattached [ʌnə'tætʃt] *adj* (**a**) *(independent)* libre, independiente; *(loose)* suelto(a) (**b**) *(not engaged or married)* soltero(a) y sin compromiso (**c**) *Jur (of property etc)* no embargado(a)

unattainable [ʌnə'teɪnəbəl] *adj* inalcanzable

unattended [ʌnə'tendɪd] *adj* (**a**) *(not looked after) (counter, desk)* desatendido(a); **to leave a child u.** dejar a un niño sin nadie que le vigile (**b**) *(alone)* solo(a)

unattractive [ʌnə'træktɪv] *adj* poco atractivo(a), feo(a)

unauthorized [ʌn'ɔːθəraɪzd] *adj* (**a**) *(person)* no autorizado(a); **'no entry to u. persons'** 'prohibido el paso a toda persona ajena a la empresa *or* a la obra' (**b**) *(trade etc)* ilícito(a), ilegal

unavailable [ʌnə'veɪləbəl] *adj* no disponible; **Mr X is u. today** el Sr. X no le puede atender hoy; **that brand is u. in supermarkets** esa marca no se vende en los supermercados

unavailing [ʌnə'veɪlɪŋ] *adj (effort)* inútil, vano(a)

unavoidable [ʌnə'vɔɪdəbəl] *adj (gen)* inevitable; *(accident)* fortuito(a)

unaware [ʌnə'weər] *adj* ignorante, inconsciente (**of** de); **to be u. of the danger** ser inconsciente del peligro; **to be u. of sth** ignorar algo

unawares [ʌnə'weəz] *adv* (**a**) *(unexpectedly)* desprevenido(a); **he caught me u.** me agarró *or Esp* cogió desprevenido (**b**) *(without knowing)* inconscientemente, sin darse cuenta; **she dropped it u.** se le cayó sin darse cuenta

unbalanced [ʌn'bælənst] *adj* desequilibrado(a)

unbearable [ʌn'beərəbəl] *adj* insoportable, inaguantable, intolerable

unbeatable [ʌn'biːtəbəl] *adj (team)* invencible, sin rival; *(price, quality)* inmejorable, inigualable

unbecoming [ʌnbɪ'kʌmɪŋ] *adj* (**a**) *(unsuitable)* poco apropiado(a), impropio(a) (**de** of); **u. of a gentleman** impropio de un caballero (**b**) *(unflattering)* poco favorecedor(a)

unbelievable [ʌnbɪ'liːvəbəl] *adj* increíble

unbend [ʌn'bend] **1** *vt (pt & pp* unbent [ʌn'bent]*) (fork, wire)* enderezar
2 *vi Fam Fig* relajarse

unbending [ʌn'bendɪŋ] *adj* inflexible

unbia(s)sed [ʌn'baɪəst] *adj* imparcial

unblinking [ʌn'blɪŋkɪŋ] *adj* sin pestañear; *Fig* imperturbable

unborn [ʌn'bɔːn] *adj* sin nacer, aún no nacido(a), nonato(a)

unbounded [ʌn'baʊndɪd] *adj* ilimitado(a); *Fig* desmedido(a)

unbreakable [ʌn'breɪkəbəl] *adj* irrompible; *Fig* inquebrantable

unbridled [ʌn'braɪdəld] *adj Fig* desenfrenado(a)

unbroken [ʌn'brəʊkən] *adj* (**a**) *(whole)* intacto(a), sin romper (**b**) *(uninterrupted)* ininterrumpido(a), continuo(a); **six hours of u. sleep** seis horas de sueño continuo (**c**) *(untamed)* sin domar (**d**) *(record)* sin batir or igualar

unburden [ʌn'bɜːdən] *vt* descargar; *Fig* **to u. one's heart to sb** desahogarse con algn, confiarse a algn

unbusinesslike [ʌn'bɪznɪslaɪk] *adj (lacking in method)* poco metódico(a), desorganizado(a); *(informal)* informal

unbutton [ʌn'bʌtən] *vt (a) (undo)* desabrochar (**b**) *Fam* **to u. oneself** relajarse

uncalled-for [ʌn'kɔːldfɔːr] *adj* (**a**) *(inappropriate)* inapropiado(a), insensato(a), fuera de lugar (**b**) *(unjustified)* inmerecido(a), injustificado(a) (**c**) *(unnecessary)* innecesario(a), superfluo(a)

uncannily [ʌn'kænɪlɪ] *adv* asombrosamente; **u. accurate** de una precisión asombrosa

uncanny [ʌn'kænɪ] *adj* misterioso(a), extraño(a)

uncaring [ʌn'keərɪŋ] *adj* indiferente

unceasing [ʌn'siːsɪŋ] *adj* incesante, continuo(a)

uncertain [ʌn'sɜːtən] *adj* (**a**) *(not certain)* incierto(a); *(doubtful)* dudoso(a); *(unspecified)* indeterminado(a); **I'm still u.** (as to) whether or not she is coming aún no sé con toda seguridad si viene ella o no; **in no u. terms** claramente, sin rodeos (**b**) *(not reliable)* inseguro(a) (**c**) *(changeable) (weather etc)* variable (**d**) *(hesitant)* indeciso(a)

uncertainty [ʌn'sɜːtəntɪ] *n* incertidumbre *f*, duda *f*

unchallenged [ʌn'tʃælɪndʒd] *adj (right etc)* indiscutido(a), incontestado(a)

unchangeable [ʌn'tʃeɪndʒəbəl] *adj* inmutable, inalterable

unchanged [ʌn'tʃeɪndʒd] *adj* igual, sin alteración; **it has remained u.** ha quedado igual

uncharacteristic [ʌnkærəktə'rɪstɪk] *adj* atípico(a), poco característico(a)

uncharitable [ʌn'tʃærɪtəbəl] *adj* cruel

uncharted [ʌn'tʃɑːtɪd] *adj* desconocido(a), inexplorado(a)

unchecked [ʌn'tʃekt] *adj* **(a)** *(not restrained)* desenfrenado(a); **u. advance** avance sin obstáculos **(b)** *(not examined)* no comprobado(a), sin comprobar

uncivil [ʌn'sɪvəl] *adj (impolite)* descortés

uncivilized [ʌn'sɪvɪlaɪzd] *adj (tribe)* incivilizado(a), salvaje; *(not cultured)* inculto(a); *Fig* **u. hour** hora intempestiva

unclaimed [ʌn'kleɪmd] *adj* sin reclamar

uncle ['ʌŋkəl] *n* tío *m* ❏ *US Fam* **U. Sam** el Tío Sam

unclean [ʌn'kliːn] *adj* sucio(a); *Rel* impuro(a)

unclear [ʌn'klɪər] *adj* poco claro(a), confuso(a)

uncoil [ʌn'kɔɪl] **1** *vt* desenrollar
2 *vi* desenrollarse

uncombed [ʌn'kəʊmd] *adj (hair)* despeinado(a)

uncomfortable [ʌn'kʌmftəbəl] *adj* **(a)** *(physically)* incómodo(a), poco confortable **(b)** *(awkward)* incómodo(a), molesto(a); **to feel u.** no estar a gusto, sentirse incómodo(a) **(c)** *(unpleasant)* desagradable; **to make things u. for sb** complicarle la vida a algn

uncommitted [ʌnkə'mɪtɪd] *adj* no comprometido(a)

uncommon [ʌn'kɒmən] *adj* **(a)** *(rare)* poco común *or* corriente, insólito(a); *(unusual)* extraordinario(a) **(b)** *(excessive)* excesivo(a), desmesurado(a)

uncommonly [ʌn'kɒmənlɪ] *adv* extraordinariamente; **not u.** con cierta frecuencia

uncommunicative [ʌnkə'mjuːnɪkətɪv] *adj* poco comunicativo(a), reservado(a), cerrado(a)

uncompromising [ʌn'kɒmprəmaɪzɪŋ] *adj* intransigente, inflexible; **u. honesty** sinceridad absoluta

unconcealed [ʌnkən'siːld] *adj* no dismulado(a), evidente

unconcerned [ʌnkən'sɜːnd] *adj* indiferente **(about** a)

unconditional [ʌnkən'dɪʃənəl] *adj* incondicional; **u. surrender** rendición *f* incondicional

unconditioned [ʌnkən'dɪʃənd] *adj* **(a)** *Psych* no condicionado(a); **u. reflex** reflejo espontáneo **(b)** *(unconditional)* incondicional

unconfirmed [ʌnkən'fɜːmd] *adj* no confirmado(a), sin confirmar

uncongenial [ʌnkən'dʒiːnɪəl] *adj (person)* antipático(a); *(work)* desagradable

unconnected [ʌnkə'nektɪd] *adj* no relacionado(a); **the two events are quite u.** los dos sucesos no guardan relación entre sí

unconscionable [ʌn'kɒnʃənəbəl] *adj* **(a)** *(unscrupulous)* sin escrúpulos **(b)** *(excessive)* excesivo(a), desmesurado(a)

unconscious [ʌn'kɒnʃəs] **1** *adj* **(a)** *Med* inconsciente; **she was u. for two hours** estuvo dos horas sin conocimiento; **to become u.** perder el conocimiento **(b)** *(unaware)* inconsciente **(of** de) **(c)** *(unintentional)* involuntario(a)
2 the u. *n Psych* el inconsciente

unconsciousness [ʌn'kɒnʃəsnɪs] *n Med* pérdida *f* del conocimiento, inconsciencia *f*

unconsidered [ʌnkən'sɪdəd] *adj (rash)* irreflexivo(a)

unconstitutional [ʌnkɒnstɪ'tjuːʃənəl] *adj* anticonstitucional, inconstitucional

uncontested [ʌnkən'testɪd] *adj* incontestado(a) ❏ *Pol* **u. seat** escaño *m* ganado sin oposición

uncontrollable [ʌnkən'trəʊləbəl] *adj (gen)* incontrolable; *(people)* ingobernable; *(desire)* irresistible; *(laughter)* incontenible

unconventional [ʌnkən'venʃənəl] *adj* poco convencional, original

unconvinced [ʌnkən'vɪnst] *adj* poco convencido(a), escéptico(a)

unconvincing [ʌnkən'vɪnsɪŋ] *adj* poco convincente

uncooked [ʌn'kʊkt] *adj* crudo(a)

uncooperative [ʌnkəʊ'ɒpərətɪv] *adj* poco cooperativo(a)

uncoordinated [ʌnkəʊ'ɔːdɪneɪtɪd] *adj* no coordinado(a), sin coordinar

uncork [ʌn'kɔːk] *vt* descorchar; *Fig* soltar, dar rienda suelta a

uncorrected [ʌnkə'rektɪd] *adj* sin corregir

uncountable [ʌn'kaʊntəbəl] *adj Ling* incontable

uncouple [ʌn'kʌpəl] *vt Rail* desenganchar, desacoplar, desconectar

uncouth [ʌn'kuːθ] *adj (rude)* grosero(a); *(rough)* tosco(a)

uncover [ʌn'kʌvər] *vt* **(a)** *(remove cover from)* destapar **(b)** *(discover) (plot etc)* revelar, descubrir

uncovered [ʌn'kʌvəd] *adj* destapado(a), al descubierto

unctuous ['ʌŋktjʊəs] *adj Pej* untuoso(a), empalagoso(a)

uncultivated [ʌn'kʌltɪveɪtɪd] *adj* **(a)** *(person)* inculto(a) **(b)** *Agr (land)* sin cultivar, baldío(a), yermo(a)

uncurbed [ʌn'kɜːbd] *adj (unchecked)* desenfrenado(a)

uncut [ʌn'kʌt] *adj* **(a)** *(grass etc)* sin cortar; *(book)* intonso(a) **(b)** *(gemstone)* sin tallar

undamaged [ʌn'dæmɪdʒd] *adj* **(a)** *(article etc)* sin desperfectos, en buen estado; *(person)* indemne, ileso(a) **(b)** *Fig (reputation etc)* intacto(a)

undated [ʌn'deɪtɪd] *adj* sin fecha

undaunted [ʌn'dɔːntɪd] *adj* firme, impávido(a) **(by** ante); **to be u. in one's resolve** ser firme en sus propósitos

undeceive [ʌndɪ'siːv] *vt Fml* desengañar

undecided [ʌndɪ'saɪdɪd] *adj* **(a)** *(person)* indeciso(a); **he is u. whether to go** no sabe si ir o no **(b)** *(issue)* pendiente; **that's still u.** eso está aún por decidir

undecipherable [ʌndɪ'saɪfərəbəl] *adj* indescifrable

undefeated [ʌndɪ'fiːtɪd] *adj* invicto(a)

undefended [ʌndɪ'fendɪd] *adj* indefenso(a); *Jur* **u. suit** pleito *m* sin defensa

undefined [ʌndɪ'faɪnd] *adj* indefinido(a), indeterminado(a)

undelivered [ʌndɪ'lɪvəd] *adj* sin entregar; **if u. please return to sender** en caso de ausencia devuélvase al remitente; **u. letter** carta devuelta

undemanding [ʌndɪ'mɑːndɪŋ] *adj (job)* fácil, que exige poco esfuerzo; *(person)* poco exigente

undemonstrative [ʌndɪ'mɒnstrətɪv] *adj* reservado(a)

undeniable [ʌndɪ'naɪəbəl] *adj* innegable, irrefutable

under ['ʌndər] **1** *prep* **(a)** *(below, beneath)* debajo de, bajo, *Am* abajo de; **u. the table** debajo de la mesa; **from u.** de debajo de; **u. the sun** bajo el sol **(b)** *(less than)* menos de; **he ran a mile in u. four minutes** corrió una milla en menos de cuatro minutos; **incomes u. $1,000** ingresos inferiores a 1.000 dólares; **u. age** menor de edad **(c)** *Mil (lower than)* de rango inferior a; **no one u. a captain** nadie de rango inferior a capitán **(d)** *(in the power of)* bajo; **u. Caesar** bajo César; **u. the doctor** en manos del médico **(e)** *(subject to, in)* bajo; **u. arrest** bajo arresto, detenido(a); **u. cover** a cubierto; **u. lock and key** bajo llave; **u. obligation to** en la obligación de; **u. repair** en reparación; **u. the circumstances** dadas las circunstancias; *Fig* **I was u. the impression that ...** tenía la impresión de que ... (**f**) *(according to)* según, conforme a; **u. his father's will** según el testamento de su padre; **u. the terms of the contract** según los términos del contrato (**g**) *(known by)* **he worked there u. a false name** trabajó allí bajo un nombre falso (**h**) *Astrol* bajo; **born u. Aries** nacido(a) bajo el signo de Aries

2 *adv* debajo, *Am* abajo; **to go u.** ir a pique; *Fam* **down u. a** o *en* Australia; *Fam* **he's one degree u. today** hoy no anda muy fino

under- ['ʌndər] *pref (below)* sub-, infra-; *(insufficiently)* insuficientemente

underachiever [ʌndərə'tʃiːvər] *n* = persona que rinde por debajo de sus posibilidades

under-age [ʌndər'eɪdʒ] *adj* **to be u.-a.** ser menor de edad; **u.-a. drinking** consumo *m* de alcohol por menores; **u.-a. sex** relaciones *fpl* sexuales entre menores

underarm ['ʌndərɑːm] **1** *adj* (**a**) *Sport (throw)* por debajo del hombro (**b**) *(below the arm)* axilar; **u. deodorant** desodorante para las axilas

2 *adv Sport* por debajo del hombro; **to bowl u.** *(in cricket)* lanzar la pelota por debajo

undercarriage ['ʌndəkærɪdʒ] *n Av* tren *m* de aterrizaje

undercharge [ʌndə'tʃɑːdʒ] *vt* cobrar de menos

underclass ['ʌndəklɑːs] *n* clase *f* marginal

underclothes ['ʌndəkləʊðz] *npl*, **underclothing** ['ʌndəkləʊðɪŋ] *n* ropa *f* sing interior

undercoat ['ʌndəkəʊt] *n (of paint)* primera mano *f*

undercook [ʌndə'kʊk] *vt* **to be undercooked** no estar lo suficientemente hecho(a)

undercover [ʌndə'kʌvər] **1** *adj* secreto(a), clandestino(a)

2 *adv* en la clandestinidad; **to go u.** pasar a la clandestinidad

undercurrent ['ʌndəkʌrənt] *n* (**a**) *(in sea)* corriente *f* submarina (**b**) *Fig* tendencia *f* oculta

undercut [ʌndə'kʌt] **1** *vt (pt & pp* **undercut**) *Com (competitor)* vender más barato que

2 ['ʌndəkʌt] *n Culin* filete *m* de solomillo

underdeveloped [ʌndədɪ'veləpt] *adj* (**a**) *(economy, country)* subdesarrollado(a) (**b**) *Phot* insuficientemente revelado(a)

underdevelopment [ʌndədɪ'veləpmənt] *n* subdesarrollo *m*

underdog ['ʌndədɒg] *n* desvalido(a) *m,f*, perdedor(a) *m,f*

underestimate [ʌndər'estɪmeɪt] **1** *vt* subestimar, infravalorar

2 [ʌndər'estɪmɪt] *n* infravaloración *f*, menosprecio *m*

underexposure [ʌndərɪk'spəʊʒər] *n Phot* subexposición *f*

underfed [ʌndə'fed] *adj* subalimentado(a), desnutrido(a)

underfoot [ʌndə'fʊt] *adv* debajo de los pies, en el suelo; **to trample sth u.** pisotear algo

underfunding [ʌndə'fʌndɪŋ] *n* escasez *f* de fondos

undergarment ['ʌndəgɑːmənt] *n* prenda *f* (de ropa) interior

undergo [ʌndə'gəʊ] *vt (pt* **underwent**; *pp* **undergone** [ʌndə'gɒn]) *(gen)* experimentar; *(change)* sufrir; *(test etc)* pasar por; **to u. an operation** someterse a una intervención quirúrgica

undergraduate [ʌndə'grædjʊɪt] *n* estudiante *mf* universitario(a)

underground ['ʌndəgraʊnd] **1** *adj* subterráneo(a); *Fig* clandestino(a); *Fig Cin Mus* underground; **the u. press** la prensa clandestina

2 [ʌndə'graʊnd] *adv* bajo tierra; *Fig* clandestinamente; *Fig* **to go u.** pasar a la clandestinidad; *Fig* **we had to work u.** tuvimos que trabajar en la clandestinidad

3 ['ʌndəgraʊnd] *n* (**a**) *(area, region)* subterráneo *m* (**b**) *Pol (gen)* movimiento *m* clandestino; *(during World War II)* resistencia *f* (**c**) *Br (transport)* **the u.** el metro, *RP* el subte

undergrowth ['ʌndəgrəʊθ] *n* maleza *f*

underhand ['ʌndəhænd] **1** *adj (method)* ilícito(a), poco limpio(a); *(person)* solapado(a), ladino(a); **u. affair** asunto turbio

2 *adv* bajo cuerda, ilícitamente

underlie [ʌndə'laɪ] *(pt* **underlay** [ʌndə'leɪ], *pp* **underlain** [ʌndə'leɪn]) *vt* subyacer tras *or* bajo

underline [ʌndə'laɪn] *vt* subrayar

underling ['ʌndəlɪŋ] *n Pej* mandado(a) *m,f*, subordinado(a) *m,f*

underlying [ʌndə'laɪŋ] *adj* (**a**) *(concealed)* subyacente (**b**) *(basic)* esencial, fundamental

undermanned [ʌndə'mænd] *adj* escaso(a) de personal; *Naut* con una tripulación insuficiente

undermentioned ['ʌndəmenʃənd] *adj* abajo citado(a) *or* mencionado(a)

undermine [ʌndə'maɪn] *vt* socavar, minar

underneath [ʌndə'niːθ] **1** *prep* debajo de, bajo

2 *adv* abajo, debajo

3 *adj* de abajo, inferior

4 *n* parte *f* inferior, fondo *m*

undernourished [ʌndə'nʌrɪʃt] *adj* desnutrido(a), subalimentado(a)

underpaid [ʌndə'peɪd] *adj* mal pagado(a); **we're u. and overworked** nos pagan mal y encima nos matan a trabajar

underpants ['ʌndəpænts] *npl* calzoncillos *mpl*, *Chile* fundillos *mpl*, *Col* pantaloncillos *mpl*, *Méx* calzones *mpl*, *Méx* chones *mpl*

underpass ['ʌndəpɑːs] *n* paso *m* subterráneo

underpin [ʌndə'pɪn] *(pt & pp* **underpinned**) *vt (support)* sustentar

underprivileged [ʌndə'prɪvɪlɪdʒd] **1** *adj* desvalido(a), marginado(a)

2 the u. *npl* los desvalidos

underrate [ʌndə'reɪt] *vt see* **undervalue**

under-secretary [ʌndə'sekrətrɪ] *n* (**a**) *(in UK)* viceministro(a) *m,f* (**b**) *(in US)* subsecretario(a) *m,f*

undersell [ʌndə'sel] *vt (pt & pp* **undersold**) (**a**) *(sell at low price)* malvender (**b**) *(undercut)* vender a menor precio que

undershirt ['ʌndəʃɜːt] *n US* camiseta *f*

underside ['ʌndəsaɪd] *n* parte *f* inferior

undersigned ['ʌndəsaɪnd] *adj & n* abajo firmante *(mf)*

undersized [ʌndə'saɪzd] *adj (thing)* demasiado pequeño(a), diminuto(a); *(person)* diminuto(a)

underskirt ['ʌndəskɜːt] *n* (**a**) *(petticoat)* enaguas *fpl*, *(modern sense)* combinación *f* (**b**) *(lining)* forro *m*

undersold [ʌndə'səʊld] *pt & pp see* **undersell**

understaffed [ʌndə'stɑːft] *adj* falto(a) de personal

understand [ʌndə'stænd] **1** *vt (pt & pp* **understood**) (**a**) *(comprehend)* entender, comprender; **I can't u. it** no logro entenderlo; **I u. French perfectly** entiendo perfectamente el francés; **that's easily understood** eso se comprende fácilmente; **to u. business** entender de negocios; *Fam* **do I make myself understood?** ¿me explico? (**b**) *(assume, believe)* entender; **am I to u. that ...?** ¿quiere eso decir que ...?; **she gave me to u. that ...** me dio a entender que ...

(**c**) *(hear)* tener entendido; **I u. he'll give his consent** tengo entendido que dará su aprobación (**d**) *(be compatible with)* **to u. one another** entenderse (**e**) *(take for granted) (word, meaning)* sobreentender

2 *vi* entender, comprender

understandable [ʌndəˈstændəbəl] *adj* comprensible

understandably [ʌndəˈstændəblɪ] *adv* comprensible-mente

understanding [ʌndəˈstændɪŋ] **1** *n* (**a**) *(intellectual grasp)* entendimiento *m*, comprensión *f*; **it's beyond u.** no hay forma de entenderlo (**b**) *(interpretation)* intepretación *f*; **it was my u. that he would pay the expenses** yo tenía entendido que los gastos correrían a su cargo (**c**) *(agreement)* acuerdo *m*; **to come to** *or* **reach an u.** llegar a un acuerdo (**d**) *(condition)* condición *f*; **on the u. that ...** a condición de que ...

2 *adj* comprensivo(a), compasivo(a)

understated [ʌndəˈsteɪtɪd] *adj (clothes, design)* discre-to(a)

understatement [ʌndəˈsteɪtmənt] *n* atenuación *f*, eufemismo *m*; **to say that the boy is rather clever is an u.** decir que el chico es bastante listo es quedarse corto

understood [ʌndəˈstʊd] **1** *pt & pp see* **understand**

2 *adj* (**a**) *(assumed)* entendido(a); **I wish it to be u. that ...** (quiero) que conste que ... (**b**) *(agreed on)* convenido(a) (**c**) *(implied)* sobreentendido(a), implícito(a)

understudy [ˈʌndəstʌdɪ] *n Theat* suplente *mf*

undertake [ʌndəˈteɪk] *vt (pt* **undertook**; *pp* **undertaken** [ʌndəˈteɪkən]) (**a**) *(take on) (responsibility)* asumir; *(task, job)* encargarse de (**b**) *(promise)* **to u. to do sth** comprometerse a hacer algo

undertaker [ˈʌndəteɪkər] *n* empresario(a) *m,f* de pompas fúnebres; **u.'s** funeraria *f*, pompas *fpl* fúnebres

undertaking [ʌndəˈteɪkɪŋ] *n* (**a**) *(responsibility)* respon-sabilidad *f*, carga *f*; *(task)* tarea *f*, empresa *f*; **large-scale u.** empresa a gran escala (**b**) *(guarantee)* garantía *f*; **I can give you no such u.** no puedo garantizárselo

undertone [ˈʌndətəʊn] *n* (**a**) *(low voice)* voz *f* baja; **in an u.** en voz baja (**b**) *Fig (suggestion)* fondo *m*, matiz *m*

undertook [ʌndəˈtʊk] *pp see* **undertake**

undertow [ˈʌndətəʊ] *n* resaca *f*

undervalue [ʌndəˈvælju:] *vt* subestimar, infravalorar

underwater [ʌndəˈwɔːtər] **1** *adj* submarino(a)

2 *adv* bajo el agua

underway [ʌndəˈweɪ] *adj* en marcha; **to get u.** ponerse en marcha

underwear [ˈʌndəweər] *n inv* ropa *f* interior

underweight [ʌndəˈweɪt] *adj* de peso insuficiente; **to be u.** *(gen)* pesar menos de lo debido; *(boxer, jockey)* no dar el peso

underwent [ʌndəˈwent] *pt see* **undergo**

underworld [ˈʌndəwɜːld] *n* (**a**) *(of criminals)* hampa *f*, bajos fondos *mpl* (**b**) *Myth* **the u.** el averno, el Hades

underwrite [ʌndəˈraɪt] *vt (pt* **underwrote**; *pp* **under-written**) (**a**) *Fin* suscribir (**b**) *(guarantee)* garantizar, avalar (**c**) *(insure)* asegurar

underwriter [ˈʌndəraɪtər] *n* (**a**) *Fin* suscriptor(a) *m,f* (**b**) *(insurer)* asegurador(a) *m,f*

underwritten [ʌndəˈrɪtən] *pp see* **underwrite**

underwrote [ʌndəˈrəʊt] *pt see* **underwrite**

undeserved [ʌndɪˈzɜːvd] *adj* inmerecido(a)

undeserving [ʌndɪˈzɜːvɪŋ] *adj (case etc)* de poco mérito, que no merece atención; **u. of** indigno(a) de

undesirable [ʌndɪˈzaɪrəbəl] *adj & n* indeseable *(mf)*

undetected [ʌndɪˈtektɪd] *adj (mistake etc)* pasado(a) por

alto, no detectado(a); **to pass u.** pasar desapercibido(a)

undetermined [ʌndɪˈtɜːmɪnd] *adj* indeterminado(a), indefinido(a)

undeterred [ʌndɪˈtɜːd] *adj* sin inmutarse; **u. by** sin arredrarse ante

undeveloped [ʌndɪˈveləpt] *adj (gen)* sin desarrollar; *(land)* sin explotar

undid [ʌnˈdɪd] *pt see* **undo**

undies [ˈʌndɪz] *npl Fam* bragas *fpl*

undigested [ʌndɪˈdʒestɪd] *adj* (**a**) *(food)* indigesto(a) (**b**) *Fig* mal digerido(a) *or* asimilado(a); **u. knowledge** conocimientos mal asimilados

undignified [ʌnˈdɪɡnɪfaɪd] *adj (person)* poco digno(a); *(attitude etc)* indecoroso(a), indigno(a)

undiluted [ʌndaɪˈluːtɪd] *adj* no diluido(a), sin diluir; *Fig* **to talk u. nonsense** decir disparates *or* chorradas

undiplomatic [ʌndɪpləˈmætɪk] *adj* poco diplomático(a)

undiscerning [ʌndɪˈsɜːnɪŋ] *adj* sin discernimiento

undischarged [ʌndɪsˈtʃɑːdʒd] *adj* (**a**) *(bankrupt)* no rehabilitado(a) (**b**) *(debt)* sin liquidar (**c**) *(duty)* no cumplido(a)

undisciplined [ʌnˈdɪsɪplɪnd] *adj* indisciplinado(a)

undisclosed [ʌndɪsˈkləʊzd] *adj* sin revelar

undiscovered [ʌndɪsˈkʌvəd] *adj* sin descubrir, desconoci-do(a)

undiscriminating [ʌndɪsˈkrɪmɪneɪtɪŋ] *adj* indiscrimi-nado(a), sin discriminación

undisguised [ʌndɪsˈɡaɪzd] *adj* no disimulado(a)

undisputed [ʌndɪsˈpjuːtɪd] *adj (unchallenged)* incon-testable; *(unquestionable)* indiscutible, incuestionable

undisturbed [ʌndɪsˈtɜːbd] *adj* (**a**) *(person)* tranquilo(a); **I wish to be left u.** que no me molesten (**b**) *(things)* sin tocar; **we left everything u.** dejamos las cosas tal como estaban

undivided [ʌndɪˈvaɪdɪd] *adj* (**a**) *(complete)* entero(a) (**b**) *(unanimous)* unánime; **to give one's u. attention** prestar toda la atención

undo [ʌnˈduː] *vt (pt* **undid**; *pp* **undone**) (**a**) *(unfasten) (knot)* desatar, deshacer; *(button)* desabrochar (**b**) *(destroy)* deshacer, destruir; *Prov* **what is done cannot be undone** a lo hecho pecho (**c**) *(put right)* enmendar; **to u. the damage** reparar el daño (**d**) *Comptr (command)* deshacer

undoing [ʌnˈduːɪŋ] *n* perdición *f*

undone[1] [ʌnˈdʌn] *adj (unfinished)* inacabado(a); **to leave some work u.** dejar trabajo sin hacer *or* acabar

undone[2] [ʌnˈdʌn] **1** *pp see* **undo**

2 *adj (unfastened) (knot etc)* deshecho(a); **to come u.** *(shoelace)* desatarse; *(button, blouse)* desabrocharse; *(neck-lace etc)* soltarse

undoubted [ʌnˈdaʊtɪd] *adj* indudable

undoubtedly [ʌnˈdaʊtɪdlɪ] *adv* indudablemente

undreamed [ʌnˈdriːmd] *adj*, **undreamt** [ʌnˈdremt] *adj* **u. (of)** nunca soñado(a), inimaginable

undress [ʌnˈdres] **1** *vt* desvestir, desnudar

2 *vi* desvestirse, desnudarse

undressed [ʌnˈdrest] *adj (naked)* desnudo(a); *(partially dressed)* medio vestido(a); **to get u.** desnudarse

undue [ʌnˈdjuː] (**a**) *adj (excessive)* excesivo(a); **with u. haste** con demasiada premura (**b**) *(improper)* indebido(a); **u. optimism** optimismo injustificado

undulate [ˈʌndjʊleɪt] **1** *vt* hacer ondear

2 *vi* ondular, ondear

undulating [ˈʌndjʊleɪtɪŋ] *adj* ondulante

undulation [ʌndjʊˈleɪʃən] *n* ondulación *f*

unduly [ʌnˈdjuːlɪ] *adv* excesivamente

undying [ʌnˈdaɪɪŋ] *adj* eterno(a)

unearned [ʌnˈɜːnd] *adj* (**a**) *(undeserved)* inmerecido(a) (**b**) *(wages etc)* no ganado(a) ❏ *Fin* **u. income** renta *f; Fin* **u. increment** plusvalía *f*

unearth [ʌnˈɜːθ] *vt* desenterrar; *Fig (information etc)* desenterrar, sacar a luz; *Fig (plot etc)* descubrir

unearthly [ʌnˈɜːθlɪ] *adj* (**a**) *(supernatural)* sobrenatural, de otro mundo; *(mysterious)* misterioso(a) (**b**) *(heavenly)* celestial (**c**) *Fam (outlandish)* espantoso(a); **u. din** ruido de mil demonios; **why do we have to get up at this u. hour?** ¿por qué nos tenemos que levantar a esta hora tan intempestiva?

unease [ʌnˈiːz] *n* inquietud *f*, desasosiego *m*

uneasiness [ʌnˈiːzmɪs] *n* (**a**) *(of person)* inquietud *f*, desasosiego *m* (**b**) *(of situation)* incomodidad *f*

uneasy [ʌnˈiːzɪ] *adj* (**a**) *(troubled, worried)* inquieto(a), preocupado(a); *(disturbing)* inquietante; **to be u. about sth** inquietarse *or* preocuparse por algo; **u. sleep** sueño *m* agitado (**b**) *(uncomfortable)* incómodo(a), molesto(a)

uneconomic(al) [ʌniːkəˈnɒmɪk(əl)] *adj* poco económico(a) *or* rentable

uneducated [ʌnˈedjʊkeɪtɪd] *adj* inculto(a), ignorante; **u. speech** habla popular

unemployed [ʌnɪmˈplɔɪd] **1** *adj* desempleado(a), *Esp* parado(a), *Am* desocupado(a); **to be u.** estar desempleado(a) *or Esp* en (el) paro *or Am* desocupado(a) **2 the u.** *npl* los desempleados, *Esp* los parados, *Am* los desocupados

unemployment [ʌnɪmˈplɔɪmənt] *n* desempleo *m, Esp* paro *m, Am* desocupación *f* ❏ **u. benefit,** *US* **u. compensation** subsidio *m* de desempleo, *Esp* paro *m, Am* subsidio *m* de desocupación

unending [ʌnˈendɪŋ] *adj* interminable, inacabable

unenthusiastic [ʌnɪnθjuːzɪˈæstɪk] *adj* poco entusiasta

unenviable [ʌnˈenvɪəbəl] *adj* poco *or* nada envidiable

unequal [ʌnˈiːkwəl] *adj* (**a**) *(not equal)* desigual; *(pulse)* irregular (**b**) *(inadequate)* poco apto(a); **to be u. to a task** no estar a la altura de una tarea

unequalled, *US* **unequaled** [ʌnˈiːkwəld] *adj* sin igual *or* par; **u. strength** fuerza *f* inigualable

unequivocal [ʌnɪˈkwɪvəkəl] *adj* inequívoco(a), claro(a)

UNESCO [juːˈneskəʊ] *n* (*abbr* **United Nations Educational, Scientific and Cultural Organization**) Organización *f* de las Naciones Unidas para la Educación, la Ciencia y la Cultura, UNESCO *f*

unethical [ʌnˈeθɪkəl] *adj* poco ético(a)

uneven [ʌnˈiːvən] *adj* (**a**) *(not level)* desigual; *(jagged, bumpy)* accidentado(a); **an u. road** una carretera con baches (**b**) *(variable)* variable, irregular (**c**) *(not fairly matched)* desigual

unevenness [ʌnˈiːvənnɪs] *n* (**a**) *(of surface, distribution)* desigualdad *f* (**b**) *(of progress etc)* irregularidad *f*

uneventful [ʌnɪˈventfʊl] *adj* sin acontecimientos; **an u. life** *(quiet)* una vida tranquila; *(routine)* una vida monótona *or* rutinaria

unexceptionable [ʌnɪkˈsepʃənəbəl] *adj* irreprochable, intachable

unexceptional [ʌnɪkˈsepʃənəl] *adj* ordinario(a), corriente

unexciting [ʌnɪkˈsaɪtɪŋ] *adj* *(monotonous)* monótono(a); *(uninteresting)* sin interés

unexpected [ʌnɪkˈspektɪd] *adj* *(unhoped for)* inesperado(a); *(event)* imprevisto(a)

unexplained [ʌnɪkˈspleɪnd] *adj* inexplicado(a); **his disappearance remains u.** su desaparición sigue siendo un enigma

unexplored [ʌnɪkˈsplɔːd] *adj* inexplorado(a)

unexposed [ʌnɪkˈspəʊzd] *adj* (**a**) *Phot (film)* virgen (**b**) *(crime)* no descubierto(a)

unexpurgated [ʌnˈekspəgeɪtɪd] *adj* no expurgado(a), íntegro(a)

unfailing [ʌnˈfeɪlɪŋ] *adj* *(gen)* indefectible; *(incessant)* constante; *(patience)* inagotable; *(humour)* inalterable; *(memory)* infalible

unfair [ʌnˈfeər] *adj* injusto(a); *Sport* sucio(a) ❏ *Com* **u. competition** competencia *f* desleal

unfairly [ʌnˈfeəlɪ] *adv* injustamente

unfairness [ʌnˈfeənɪs] *n* injusticia *f*

unfaithful [ʌnˈfeɪθfʊl] *adj* *(friend)* desleal; *(husband, wife)* infiel

unfaithfulness [ʌnˈfeɪθfʊlnɪs] *n* *(of friend)* deslealtad *f, (of husband, wife)* infidelidad *f*

unfamiliar [ʌnfəˈmɪljər] *adj* (**a**) *(unknown)* desconocido(a) (**b**) *(not conversant)* no familiarizado(a) (**with** con)

unfashionable [ʌnˈfæʃənəbəl] *adj* *(fashion etc)* pasado(a) de moda; *(ideas etc)* poco popular

unfasten [ʌnˈfɑːsən] *vt* *(knot)* desatar; *(clothing, belt)* desabrochar; *(door, window)* abrir

unfathomable [ʌnˈfæðəməbəl] *adj Fml* insondable

unfavourable, *US* **unfavorable** [ʌnˈfeɪvərəbəl] *adj* *(gen)* desfavorable; *(criticism)* adverso(a); *(winds)* contrario(a)

unfavourably, *US* **unfavorably** *adv* desfavorablemente

unfeeling [ʌnˈfiːlɪŋ] *adj* *(insensitive)* insensible; *(not sympathetic)* sin compasión

unfettered [ʌnˈfetəd] *adj* sin trabas

unfinished [ʌnˈfɪnɪʃt] *adj* inacabado(a), sin acabar, incompleto(a); **u. business** asunto(s) *mpl* pendiente(s)

unfit [ʌnˈfɪt] *adj* (**a**) *(not suitable) (thing)* inadecuado(a), impropio(a); *(person)* no apto(a) (**for** para), incapaz (**to** de) (**b**) *(incompetent)* incompetente (**c**) *(physically)* incapacitado(a), inútil; **to be u.** no estar en forma

unflagging [ʌnˈflægɪŋ] *adj* *(courage)* infatigable, incansable; *(interest)* constante

unflappable [ʌnˈflæpəbəl] *adj Fam* imperturbable, flemático(a)

unflattering [ʌnˈflætərɪŋ] *adj* poco halagüeño(a) *or* halagador(a)

unflinching [ʌnˈflɪntʃɪŋ] *adj* (**a**) *(determined)* resuelto(a) (**b**) *(fearless)* impávido(a)

unfold [ʌnˈfəʊld] **1** *vt* (**a**) *(paper etc)* desplegar; *(sheet)* desdoblar; *(newspaper)* abrir; *(map)* extender (**b**) *(outline)* exponer (**c**) *(reveal)* revelar; *(secret)* descubrir **2** *vi* (**a**) *(open up)* desplegarse, desdoblarse, abrirse; *(landscape)* extenderse (**b**) *(thoughts, plot)* desarrollarse (**c**) *(secret)* revelarse, descubrirse

unforeseeable [ʌnfɔːˈsiːəbəl] *adj* imprevisible

unforeseen [ʌnfɔːˈsiːn] *adj* imprevisto(a)

unforgettable [ʌnfəˈgetəbəl] *adj* inolvidable

unforgivable [ʌnfəˈgɪvəbəl] *adj* imperdonable

unforgiving [ʌnfəˈgɪvɪŋ] *adj* que no perdona, implacable

unforthcoming [ʌnfɔːθˈkʌmɪŋ] *adj* reservado(a)

unfortunate [ʌnˈfɔːtʃənɪt] *adj* *(person)* desgraciado(a), desafortunado(a); *(event)* desgraciado(a); *(remark)* desafortunado(a); **how u.!** ¡qué mala suerte!, ¡qué pena!

unfortunately [ʌnˈfɔːtʃənətlɪ] *adv* desgraciadamente, por desgracia

unfounded [ʌnˈfaʊndɪd] *adj* *(rumour)* infundado(a), sin fundamento; *(complaint)* injustificado(a)

unfreeze [ʌnˈfriːz] *vt* (*pt* **unfroze**; *pp* **unfrozen**) (**a**) *(thaw)* descongelar (**b**) *Fin Com (prices, wages)* descongelar; *(credit, account)* desbloquear

unfrequented [ʌnfrɪˈkwentɪd] *adj* poco frecuentado(a)

unfriendly [ʌnˈfrendlɪ] *adj* (**unfriendlier, unfriendliest**) antipático(a), poco amistoso(a), hostil

unfroze [ʌnˈfrəʊz] *pt*, **unfrozen** [ʌnˈfrəʊzən] *pp see* **unfreeze**

unfruitful [ʌnˈfruːtfʊl] *adj Fig* infructuoso(a)

unfulfilled [ʌnfʊlˈfɪld] *adj* (**a**) *(not carried out)* incumplido(a), frustrado(a) (**b**) *(not satisfied)* no satifecho(a), insatisfecho(a); *(ambition)* frustrado(a); *(dream)* irrealizado(a)

unfurl [ʌnˈfɜːl] **1** *vt (flag, sails)* desplegar
2 *vi* desplegarse

unfurnished [ʌnˈfɜːnɪʃt] *adj* sin amueblar

ungainly [ʌnˈgeɪnlɪ] *adj* (**ungainlier, ungainliest**) *(clumsy)* torpe; *(gait)* desgarbado(a)

ungodly [ʌnˈgɒdlɪ] *adj* (**ungodlier, ungodliest**) *(behaviour, language)* impío(a); *Fam Fig* **at an u. hour** a una hora intempestiva, a las tantas de la noche

ungovernable [ʌnˈgʌvənəbəl] *adj* (**a**) *Pol (people)* ingobernable (**b**) *(feelings)* incontrolable, incontenible, irreprimible

ungracious [ʌnˈgreɪʃəs] *adj* descortés, poco amable

ungrammatical [ʌngrəˈmætɪkəl] *adj* incorrecto(a) (gramaticalmente)

ungrateful [ʌnˈgreɪtfʊl] *adj (unthankful)* desagradecido(a); *(thankless)* ingrato(a)

ungrudging [ʌnˈgrʌdʒɪŋ] *adj (liberal)* generoso(a); *(of support)* incondicional

ungrudgingly [ʌnˈgrʌdʒɪŋlɪ] *adv* de buena gana

unguarded [ʌnˈgɑːdɪd] *adj* (**a**) *(unprotected)* indefenso(a), sin protección (**b**) *(imprudent)* desprevenido(a), descuidado(a), imprudente (**c**) *(frank)* franco(a)

unhampered [ʌnˈhæmpəd] *adj* libre (**by** de), sin estorbos

unhappily [ʌnˈhæpɪlɪ] *adv (unfortunately)* desgraciadamente; *(sadly)* tristemente

unhappiness [ʌnˈhæpɪnɪs] *n* (**a**) *(sadness)* tristeza *f* (**b**) *(wretchedness)* desdicha *f*, infelicidad *f*

unhappy [ʌnˈhæpɪ] *adj* (**unhappier, unhappiest**) (**a**) *(sad)* triste (**b**) *(wretched)* desdichado(a), desgraciado(a), infeliz; *(unfortunate)* desafortunado(a), poco afortunado(a)

unharmed [ʌnˈhɑːmd] *adj* ileso(a), indemne

UNHCR [juːeneɪtʃsiːˈɑːr] *n* (*abbr* **United Nations High Commission for Refugees**) Alto Comisionado *m* de las Naciones Unidas para los Refugiados, ACNUR *m*

unhealthy [ʌnˈhelθɪ] *adj* (**unhealthier, unhealthiest**) (**a**) *(ill)* enfermo(a), enfermizo(a) (**b**) *(unwholesome)* malsano(a), insalubre (**c**) *Fig* morboso(a), malsano(a)

unheard [ʌnˈhɜːd] *adj* (**a**) *(unheeded)* no oído(a); **her request went u.** su petición no fue atendida (**b**) **u. of** *(outrageous)* inaudito(a); *(without precedent)* sin precedente

unheeded [ʌnˈhiːdɪd] *adj* desatendido(a); **the warning went u.** nadie hizo caso de la advertencia

unhelpful [ʌnˈhelpfʊl] *adj (advice)* inútil; *(person)* poco servicial

unhesitating [ʌnˈhezɪteɪtɪŋ] *adj* (**a**) *(person)* resuelto(a), decidido(a) (**b**) *(reply)* inmediato(a)

unhesitatingly [ʌnˈhezɪteɪtɪŋlɪ] *adv* sin vacilar

unhindered [ʌnˈhɪndəd] **1** *adj* **he was u. by any doubts** no tuvo ninguna duda
2 *adv* **to work u.** trabajar sin estorbos

unhinged [ʌnˈhɪndʒd] *adj* (**a**) *(door)* desquiciado(a) (**b**) *Fig (mind)* trastornado(a), desquiciado(a)

unholy [ʌnˈhəʊlɪ] *adj* (**unholier, unholiest**) (**a**) *(place, subject)* profano(a); *(person)* impío(a) (**b**) *Fam* terrible; **an u. muddle** un lío endiablado; **an u. row** un escándalo de órdago

unhook [ʌnˈhʊk] *vt (from hook, nail, etc)* descolgar; *(clothing)* desabrochar

unhoped [ʌnˈhəʊpt] *adj* **u. for** inesperado(a)

UNHRC [juːeneɪtʃɑːˈsiː] *n* (*abbr* **United Nations Human Rights Commission**) Comisión *f* de Derechos Humanos de las Naciones Unidas, UNHRC *f*

unhurt [ʌnˈhɜːt] *adj* ileso(a), indemne

unhygienic [ʌnhaɪˈdʒiːnɪk] *adj* antihigiénico(a)

UNICEF [ˈjuːnɪsef] *n* (*abbr* **United Nations Children's Fund**) Fondo *m* de las Naciones Unidas para la Ayuda a la Infancia, UNICEF *f*

unicorn [ˈjuːnɪkɔːn] *n Myth* unicornio *m*

unidentified [ʌnaɪˈdentɪfaɪd] *adj* no identificado(a), sin identificar ❑ **u. flying object** objeto *m* volador no identificado, ovni *m*

unification [juːnɪfɪˈkeɪʃən] *n* unificación *f*

uniform [ˈjuːnɪfɔːm] **1** *adj* uniforme; *(temperature)* constante
2 *n* uniforme *m*; **in u.** de uniforme, uniformado(a)

uniformed [ˈjuːnɪfɔːmd] *adj* uniformado(a)

uniformity [juːnɪˈfɔːmɪtɪ] *n* uniformidad *f*

unify [ˈjuːnɪfaɪ] *vt* (*pt & pp* **unified**) unificar

unilateral [juːnɪˈlætərəl] *adj* unilateral

unimaginable [ʌnɪˈmædʒɪnəbəl] *adj* inimaginable

unimaginative [ʌnɪˈmædʒɪnɪtɪv] *adj* poco imaginativo(a), falto(a) de imaginación

unimpaired [ʌnɪmˈpeəd] *adj (unharmed)* intacto(a); *(health)* inalterado(a); *(strength)* no disminuido(a)

unimportant [ʌnɪmˈpɔːtənt] *adj* sin importancia, poco importante, insignificante

unimpressed [ʌnɪmˈprest] *adj* no impresionado(a)

unimpressive [ʌnɪmˈpresɪv] *adj* poco impresionante, mediocre

uninformed [ʌnɪnˈfɔːmd] *adj* mal informado(a), ignorante; *(opinion)* sin fundamento

uninhabitable [ʌnɪnˈhæbɪtəbəl] *adj* inhabitable

uninhabited [ʌnɪnˈhæbɪtɪd] *adj* desierto(a)

uninhibited [ʌnɪnˈhɪbɪtɪd] *adj* sin inhibiciones, desinhibido(a)

uninitiated [ʌnɪˈnɪʃɪeɪtɪd] *adj* lego(a), no iniciado(a), ignorante

uninspired [ʌnɪnˈspaɪəd] *adj (person)* falto(a) de inspiración; *(performance)* insulso(a), aburrido(a), poco inspirado(a)

uninspiring [ʌnɪnˈspaɪərɪŋ] *adj* que no inspira

unintelligent [ʌnɪnˈtelɪdʒənt] *adj* poco inteligente

unintelligible [ʌnɪnˈtelɪdʒəbəl] *adj* ininteligible, incomprensible

unintentional [ʌnɪnˈtenʃənəl] *adj* involuntario(a)

unintentionally [ʌnɪnˈtenʃənəlɪ] *adv* involuntariamente, sin querer; **I did it u.** lo hice sin querer

uninterested [ʌnˈɪntrɪstɪd] *adj* no interesado(a), indiferente

uninteresting [ʌnˈɪntrɪstɪŋ] *adj* poco interesante, sin interés

uninterrupted [ʌnɪntəˈrʌptɪd] *adj* ininterrumpido(a)

uninvited [ʌnɪnˈvaɪtɪd] *adj* (**a**) *(guest)* no invitado(a) (**b**) *(comment)* gratuito(a), no solicitado(a)

uninviting [ʌnɪn'vaɪtɪŋ] *adj (offer, appearance)* poco atractivo(a); *(food)* poco apetecible *or* apetitoso(a)

union ['juːnjən] **1** *n* **(a)** *(of countries)* unión *f*; *Fig (marriage)* enlace *m*; **to live in perfect u.** vivir en perfecta armonía **(b)** *(organization)* sindicato *m*; **the students' u.** el sindicato estudiantil; *Ind* **(trade) u.** sindicato *m* **(c)** *US* **the U.** los Estados Unidos ❑ **U. Jack** bandera *f* del Reino Unido, bandera *f* británica
   2 *adj* sindical, del sindicato

unionization [juːnjənaɪ'zeɪʃən] *n* sindicación *f*, sindicalización *f*

unionize ['juːnjənaɪz] **1** *vt* sindicalizar
   2 *vi* sindicalizarse

unique [juː'niːk] *adj (singular, peculiar)* único(a); *(extraordinary)* extraordinario(a)

unisex ['juːnɪseks] *adj* unisex

unison ['juːnɪsən] *n Mus* unisonancia *f*; *Fig (harmony)* armonía *f*; **in u.** al unísono

unit ['juːnɪt] *n* **(a)** *(subdivision)* unidad *f* ❑ **monetary u.** unidad *f* monetaria; **u. price** precio *m* por unidad; *Br Fin* **u. trust** sociedad *f* de inversiones **(b)** *Furn* módulo *m*, elemento *m* ❑ **kitchen u.** mueble *m* de cocina **(c)** *Math* unidad *f* **(d)** *Mil* unidad *f* **(e)** *Tech* grupo *m* ❑ *Comptr* **central processing u.** procesador *m* central; **generator u.** grupo *m* electrógeno; **stereo u.** equipo *m* estereofónico; *Comptr* **visual display u.** pantalla *f* **(f)** *(centre)* centro *m*; *(department)* servicio *m* ❑ *Med* **intensive care u.** unidad *f* de cuidados intensivos, unidad *f* de vigilancia intensiva; **research u.** centro *m* de investigaciones **(g)** *(team)* equipo *m*; *Cin TV* **film u.** equipo *m* de rodaje

unite [juː'naɪt] **1** *vt* **(a)** *(join)* unir **(b)** *(assemble)* reunir
   2 *vi* unirse, juntarse

united [juː'naɪtɪd] *adj* unido(a) ❑ **United Arab Emirates** Emiratos *mpl* Árabes Unidos; **U. Kingdom** Reino *m* Unido; **U. Nations** Naciones *fpl* Unidas; **U. States (of America)** Estados *mpl* Unidos (de América)

unity ['juːnɪtɪ] *n (union)* unidad *f*; *(harmony)* armonía *f*

Univ *(abbr* **University)** Universidad *f*, Univ *f*

universal [juːnɪ'vɜːsəl] *adj* universal; **u. remedy** panacea *f*

universe ['juːnɪvɜːs] *n* universo *m*

university [juːnɪ'vɜːsɪtɪ] **1** *n* universidad *f*
   2 *adj* universitario(a)

UNIX ['juːnɪks] *n Comptr (abbr* **Uniplexed Information and Computing System)** UNIX *m*

unjust [ʌn'dʒʌst] *adj (unfair)* injusto(a), *(unfounded)* sin fundamento, infundado(a)

unjustifiable [ʌndʒʌstɪ'faɪəbəl] *adj* injustificable

unjustified [ʌn'dʒʌstɪfaɪd] *adj* injustificado(a)

unkempt [ʌn'kempt] *adj (gen)* descuidado(a); *(hair)* despeinado(a); *(appearance)* desaliñado(a)

unkind [ʌn'kaɪnd] *adj (not nice)* poco amable, desconsiderado(a); *(cruel)* cruel; *(criticism)* despiadado(a)

unkindly [ʌn'kaɪndlɪ] *adv* con poca amabilidad, desconsideradamente

unkindness [ʌn'kaɪndnɪs] *n* falta *f* de amabilidad *or* consideración

unknowing [ʌn'nəʊɪŋ] *adj* **(a)** *(unaware)* inconsciente **(b)** *(ignorant)* ignorante

unknowingly [ʌn'nəʊɪŋlɪ] *adv* inconscientemente, sin darse cuenta

unknown [ʌn'nəʊn] **1** *adj* desconocido(a); **the u. soldier** el soldado desconocido ❑ *Math* **u. quantity** incógnita *f*
   2 the u. *n* lo desconocido

unlabelled [ʌn'leɪbəld] *adj* sin etiqueta

unlawful [ʌn'lɔːfʊl] *adj (not legal)* ilegal; *(not legitimate)* ilegítimo(a)

unleaded [ʌn'ledɪd] **1** *n* gasolina *f* or *RP* nafta *f* sin plomo
   2 *adj* **u.** *Br* **petrol** *or US* **gasoline** gasolina *f* or *RP* nafta *f* sin plomo

unleash [ʌn'liːʃ] *vt* **(a)** *(dog)* soltar **(b)** *Fig (release)* liberar, dar rienda suelta a; *(provoke)* provocar, desencadenar

unleavened [ʌn'levənd] *adj* ácimo, sin levadura ❑ **u. bread** pan *m* ácimo

unless [ʌn'les] *conj* a menos que, a no ser que

unlike [ʌn'laɪk] **1** *adj* diferente (a), distinto(a) (de); **she is not u. her sister** se parece bastante a su hermana; **that was very u. her** no es lo normal en ella
   2 *adv* a diferencia de; **he, u. his father, ...** a diferencia de su padre, él ...

unlikelihood [ʌn'laɪklɪhʊd] *n* improbabilidad *f*

unlikely [ʌn'laɪklɪ] *adj* **(unlikelier, unlikeliest)** **(a)** *(improbable)* poco probable; **it's not at all u. that ...** bien pudiera ser que ... **(b)** *(unusual, unexpected)* inverosímil; **in the u. event that she should want to come** suponiendo que quisiera venir, lo cual es mucho suponer

unlimited [ʌn'lɪmɪtɪd] *adj* ilimitado(a); **there were u. supplies of beer** había cerveza a granel

unlisted [ʌn'lɪstɪd] *adj* **(a)** *Fin* **u. company** compañía *f* que no cotiza en bolsa; **u. securities** títulos *mpl* no cotizados **(b)** *US (phone number)* que no figura en la guía (telefónica)

unlit [ʌn'lɪt] *adj (fire, cigarette, etc)* sin encender, *Am* sin prender; *(place)* sin luz, no iluminado(a)

unload [ʌn'ləʊd] **1** *vt (gen)* descargar; *Fig (get rid of)* deshacerse de; *(problems)* descargar (on en)
   2 *vi (lorry, ship)* descargar

unloading [ʌn'ləʊdɪŋ] *n* descarga *f* ❑ **u. bay** descargadero *m*

unlock [ʌn'lɒk] *vt* **(a)** *(door)* abrir (con llave) **(b)** *Fig (mystery)* resolver, revelar

unlooked-for [ʌn'lʊktfɔːr] *adj* inesperado(a)

unloved [ʌn'lʌvd] *adj* no amado(a)

unlovely [ʌn'lʌvlɪ] *adj* poco atractivo(a), nada agraciado(a)

unloving [ʌn'lʌvɪŋ] *adj* poco cariñoso(a)

unluckily [ʌn'lʌkɪlɪ] *adv* desafortunadamente, desgraciadamente, por desgracia

unlucky [ʌn'lʌkɪ] *adj* **(unluckier, unluckiest)** *(unfortunate)* desafortunado(a), desgraciado(a); **to be u.** *(person)* tener mala suerte; *(thing)* traer mala suerte

unmade [ʌn'meɪd] *adj (bed)* sin hacer

unmanageable [ʌn'mænɪdʒəbəl] *adj (people)* ingobernable; *(child, hair)* indomable; *(machine)* difícil de manejar, poco manejable

unmanly [ʌn'mænlɪ] *adj* poco viril, afeminado(a)

unmanned [ʌn'mænd] *adj (spacecraft etc)* no tripulado(a)

unmarked [ʌn'mɑːkt] *adj* **(a)** *(spotless)* en perfecto estado, como nuevo(a) **(b)** *(unidentified) (street)* sin letrero; *(grave)* sin lápida; *(police car)* camuflado(a) **(c)** *Br Ftb (player)* desmarcado(a)

unmarried [ʌn'mærɪd] *adj* soltero(a)

unmask [ʌn'mɑːsk] *vt* desenmascarar; *Fig (plot)* descubrir

unmatched [ʌn'mætʃt] *adj (unique)* sin par, incomparable

unmentionable [ʌn'menʃənəbəl] *adj* que no se debe mencionar, tabú

unmerciful [ʌn'mɜːsɪfʊl] *adj* despiadado(a), sin piedad

unmethodical [ʌnmɪ'θɒdɪkəl] *adj* poco metódico(a)

unmistak(e)able [ʌnmɪs'teɪkəbəl] *adj* inconfundible

unmistak(e)ably [ʌnmɪs'teɪkəblɪ] *adv* sin lugar a dudas

unmitigated [ʌn'mɪtɪgeɪtɪd] *adj* **(a)** *(absolute)* absoluto(a), total; *(liar)* rematado(a) **(b)** *(grief)* profundo(a)

unmolested [ʌnmə'lestɪd] *adv* tranquilamente, sin problemas

unmoved [ʌn'muːvd] *adj* impasible, indiferente; *(to pleas etc)* insensible (**by** a)

unmusical [ʌm'mjuːzɪkəl] *adj* **(a)** *(sound)* poco armonioso(a) **(b)** *(person)* *(untalented)* sin dotes para la música; *(unenthusiastic)* poco aficionado(a) a la música

unnamed [ʌn'neɪmd] *adj* no mencionado(a)

unnatural [ʌn'nætʃərəl] *adj* **(a)** *(against nature)* antinatural; *(abnormal)* anormal **(b)** *(affected)* afectado(a), poco natural

unnecessary [ʌn'nesɪsərɪ] *adj* innecesario(a), inútil; **it's u. to add that ...** sobra añadir que ...

unnerve [ʌn'nɜːv] *vt (disconcert)* desconcertar, turbar; *(frighten)* acobardar

unnerving [ʌn'nɜːvɪŋ] *adj* desconcertante

unnoticed [ʌn'nəʊtɪst] *adj* inadvertido(a), desapercibido(a); **to let sth pass u.** pasar algo por alto, no reparar en algo

unnumbered [ʌn'nʌmbəd] *adj* sin numerar

UNO ['juːnəʊ] *n (abbr* **United Nations Organization**) Organización *f* de las Naciones Unidas, ONU *f*

unobserved [ʌnɒb'zɜːvd] *adj* inadvertido(a), desapercibido(a)

unobtainable [ʌnəb'teɪnəbəl] *adj* inasequible, inalcanzable

unobtrusive [ʌnəb'truːsɪv] *adj* discreto(a)

unobtrusively [ʌnəb'truːsɪvlɪ] *adv* con discreción

unoccupied [ʌn'ɒkjʊpaɪd] *adj* **(a)** *(person)* desocupado(a) **(b)** *(house)* desocupado(a); *(region)* despoblado(a); *(seat)* libre; *Mil (territory)* no ocupado(a)

unofficial [ʌnə'fɪʃəl] *adj* extraoficial, no oficial

unofficially [ʌnə'fɪʃəlɪ] *adv* extraoficialmente

unopened [ʌn'əʊpənd] *adj* sin abrir

unorthodox [ʌn'ɔːθədɒks] *adj* **(a)** *(behaviour, technique, etc)* poco ortodoxo(a) **(b)** *Rel* heterodoxo(a)

unpack [ʌn'pæk] **1** *vt (boxes)* desembalar; *(suitcase)* deshacer, *Am* desempacar; *(objects)* desempaquetar, desenvolver
2 *vi* deshacer la(s) maleta(s), *Am* desempacar

unpaid [ʌn'peɪd] *adj* **(a)** *(bill, debt)* sin pagar, impagado(a) **(b)** *(work)* no retribuido(a), sin renumeración

unpalatable [ʌn'pælətəbəl] *adj (taste)* desagradable (al gusto); *Fig* desagradable, difícil de aceptar

unparalleled [ʌn'pærəleld] *adj* **(a)** *(in quality)* sin par, incomparable **(b)** *(without precedent)* sin precedente

unpardonable [ʌn'pɑːdənəbəl] *adj* imperdonable

unpatriotic [ʌnpætrɪ'ɒtɪk] *adj (person)* poco patriota; *(action)* antipatriótico(a)

unperturbed [ʌnpə'tɜːbd] *adj* impasible; **she carried on u.** continuó sin inmutarse; **u. by** no perturbado(a) por

unpick [ʌn'pɪk] *vt Sew* descoser

unplanned [ʌn'plænd] *adj* imprevisto(a), inesperado(a)

unplayable [ʌn'pleɪəbəl] *adj Sport (ball)* imposible de jugar

unpleasant [ʌn'plezənt] *adj* **(a)** *(nasty, not nice)* desagradable, molesto(a) **(b)** *(unfriendly)* antipático(a) (**to** con)

unpleasantness [ʌn'plezəntnɪs] *n* **(a)** *(nastiness)* carácter *m* desagradable, lo desagradable **(b)** *(ill-feeling)* disgusto *m*

unplug [ʌn'plʌg] *vt (pt & pp* **unplugged**) desenchufar

unplugged [ʌn'plʌgd] *adj Mus* desenchufado(a), acústico(a)

unpolished [ʌn'pɒlɪʃt] *adj* **(a)** *(gen)* sin brillo; *(shoes)* sin lustrar; *(diamond)* en bruto **(b)** *Fig (manner, style)* poco pulido(a)

unpolluted [ʌnpə'luːtɪd] *adj* no contaminado(a)

unpopular [ʌn'pɒpjʊlər] *adj* impopular; **to make oneself u.** ganarse la antipatía de todos

unpopularity [ʌnpɒpjʊ'lærɪtɪ] *n* impopularidad *f*

unprecedented [ʌn'presɪdəntɪd] *adj (without precedent)* sin precedente; *(unheard of)* inaudito(a)

unpredictable [ʌnprɪ'dɪktəbəl] *adj* imprevisible; **she's very u.** no se sabe nunca cómo reaccionará *or* cómo actuará

unprepared [ʌnprɪ'peəd] *adj* **(a)** *(speech etc)* improvisado(a); *(person)* desprevenido(a) **(b)** *(not ready)* no preparado(a); **I was u. for what happened** no esperaba lo que ocurrió; **she went into marriage u.** se casó sin saber en lo que se metía

unprepossessing [ʌnpriːpə'zesɪŋ] *adj* poco atractivo(a)

unpresentable [ʌnprɪ'zentəbəl] *adj* impresentable

unpretentious [ʌnprɪ'tenʃəs] *adj (simple)* modesto(a), sencillo(a); *(humble)* sin pretensiones

unprincipled [ʌn'prɪnsɪpəld] *adj* sin principios *or* escrúpulos

unprintable [ʌn'prɪntəbəl] *adj (book)* impublicable; *(word, comment)* que no se puede repetir

unproductive [ʌnprə'dʌktɪv] *adj (inefficient)* improductivo(a); *(fruitless)* infructuoso(a)

unprofessional [ʌnprə'feʃənəl] *adj (unethical)* poco profesional, no ético(a); *(substandard)* de aficionado(a)

unprofitable [ʌn'prɒfɪtəbəl] *adj (inefficient)* poco rentable; *(fruitless)* poco provechoso(a)

unpromising [ʌn'prɒmɪsɪŋ] *adj* poco prometedor(a)

unpronounceable [ʌnprə'naʊnsəbəl] *adj* impronunciable

unprotected [ʌnprə'tektɪd] *adj* indefenso(a), sin protección

unprovoked [ʌnprə'vəʊkt] *adj* no provocado(a); *(attack)* gratuito(a)

unpublishable [ʌn'pʌblɪʃəbəl] *adj* impublicable

unpublished [ʌn'pʌblɪʃt] *adj* inédito(a), no publicado(a)

unpunished [ʌn'pʌnɪʃt] *adj* sin castigar; *(crime)* impune; **to go u.** *(person)* no ser castigado(a); *(deed)* quedar impune

unputdownable [ʌnpʊt'daʊnəbəl] *adj Fam (book)* absorbente, que se lee de una sentada

unqualified [ʌn'kwɒlɪfaɪd] *adj* **(a)** *(without qualification)* sin título; *(incompetent)* incompetente; **I am u. to speak on the subject** no soy quién para hablar sobre este tema; **u. to vote** sin derecho a voto **(b)** *(unconditional)* incondicional; *(denial)* rotundo(a); *(endorsement)* sin reserva; *(success)* total

unquenchable [ʌn'kwentʃəbəl] *adj (thirst)* insaciable

unquestionable [ʌn'kwestʃənəbəl] *adj* indiscutible, incuestionable

unquestionably [ʌn'kwestʃənəblɪ] *adv* indiscutiblemente, indudablemente

unquestioned [ʌn'kwestʃənd] *adj (right etc)* indiscutido(a), incontrovertido(a); *(undoubted)* indudable

unquestioning [ʌn'kwestʃənɪŋ] *adj (gen)* incondicional; *(obedience)* ciego(a)

unquote [ʌn'kwəut] *vi* quote ... unquote se abren comillas ... se cierran comillas

unravel [ʌn'rævəl] **1** *vt (pt & pp* unravelled, *US* unraveled) **(a)** *(untangle)* desenredar, desenmarañar **(b)** *Fig (mystery)* desenmarañar, desembrollar
2 *vi* **(a)** *(become untangled)* desenredarse, desenmarañarse **(b)** *Fig (mystery)* desenmarañarse

unread [ʌn'red] *adj (book)* sin leer, no leído(a)

unreadable [ʌn'riːdəbəl] *adj* **(a)** *(handwriting)* ilegible **(b)** *(book)* imposible de leer

unreal [ʌn'rɪəl] *adj* irreal

unrealistic [ʌnrɪə'lɪstɪk] *adj* poco realista

unreasonable [ʌn'riːzənəbəl] *adj* poco razonable; *(demands)* desmedido(a); *(prices)* exorbitante; *(hour)* inoportuno(a)

unreasoning [ʌn'riːzənɪŋ] *adj* irracional

unrecognizable [ʌnrekəg'naɪzəbəl] *adj* irreconocible

unrecognized [ʌn'rekəgnaɪzd] *adj (talent, government, etc)* no reconocido(a); **to go u.** pasar sin ser reconocido(a)

unrecorded [ʌnrɪ'kɔːdɪd] *adj* **(a)** *(music)* no grabado(a), sin grabar **(b)** *(fact, comment)* no mencionado(a); *(not taken down)* no registrado(a), sin registrar

unrefined [ʌnrɪ'faɪnd] *adj* **(a)** *Ind* no refinado(a), sin refinar ❑ **u. sugar** azúcar *m* sin refinar **(b)** *(person)* tosco(a), poco fino(a), basto(a)

unrehearsed [ʌnrɪ'hɜːst] *adj (unprepared)* improvisado(a); *Theat (play)* sin ensayar

unrelated [ʌnrɪ'leɪtɪd] *adj* **(a)** *(not connected)* no relacionado(a), inconexo(a) **(b)** *(family)* sin parentesco; **Mr Hardy and Miss Miller are u.** entre el Sr. Hardy y la Srta. Miller no hay parentesco alguno

unrelenting [ʌnrɪ'lentɪŋ] *adj (behaviour)* implacable; *(struggle)* encarnizado(a)

unreliability [ʌnrɪlaɪə'bɪlɪtɪ] *n* **(a)** *(of person)* poca formalidad *f* **(b)** *(of information)* poca fiabilidad *f*; *(of weather)* inestabilidad *f*; *(of machine)* tendencia *f* a averiarse

unreliable [ʌnrɪ'laɪəbəl] *adj* **(a)** *(person)* que no es de fiar, de poca confianza; **my daily help is very u.** no se puede contar con mi asistenta **(b)** *(information)* que no es de fiar; *(machine)* poco seguro(a) *or* fiable; **their washing machine is u.** su lavadora es poco fiable

unrelieved [ʌnrɪ'liːvd] *adj* **(a)** *(pain)* no aliviado(a) **(b)** *(monotonous)* monótono(a); *(boredom)* total

unremitting [ʌnrɪ'mɪtɪŋ] *adj* **(a)** *(efforts etc)* incesante, continuo(a) **(b)** *(person)* incansable

unrepentant [ʌnrɪ'pentənt] *adj* impenitente

unreported [ʌnrɪ'pɔːtɪd] **1** *adj* **an u. incident / problem** un incidente/problema del que no se ha informado *or CAm Méx* reportado
2 *adv* **many crimes go u.** muchos delitos no se denuncian *or CAm Méx* reportan

unrepresentative [ʌnreprɪ'zentətɪv] *adj* no representativo(a)

unrepresented [ʌnreprɪ'sentɪd] *adj* no representado(a), sin representación

unrequited [ʌnrɪ'kwaɪtɪd] *adj* **u. love** amor no correspondido

unreserved [ʌnrɪ'zɜːvd] *adj* **(a)** *(praise, support)* sin reserva, incondicional **(b)** *(person, nature)* abierto(a) **(c)** *(seats)* libre, sin reservar

unreservedly [ʌnrɪ'zɜːvɪdlɪ] *adv* sin reserva

unresolved [ʌnrɪ'zɒlvd] *adj see* unsolved

unresponsive [ʌnrɪ'spɒnsɪv] *adj* insensible

unrest [ʌn'rest] *n (social etc)* malestar *m*; **political u.** desasosiego *m* de raíz política

unrewarded [ʌnrɪ'wɔːdɪd] *adj* sin recompensa; **my efforts were u.** mis esfuerzos no se vieron premiados

unrivalled, *US* **unrivaled** [ʌn'raɪvəld] *adj* único(a), sin par, sin rival

unroll [ʌn'rəul] **1** *vt* desenrollar
2 *vi* desenrollarse

unruffled [ʌn'rʌfəld] *adj Fig* tranquilo(a), sereno(a)

unruly [ʌn'ruːlɪ] *adj* (unrulier, unruliest) **(a)** *(child)* revoltoso(a), indisciplinado(a) **(b)** *(hair)* rebelde

unsaddle [ʌn'sædəl] *vt* desensillar

unsafe [ʌn'seɪf] *adj (dangerous)* peligroso(a); *(risky)* inseguro(a), arriesgado(a); **to feel u.** sentirse inseguro(a)

unsaid [ʌn'sed] *adj* sin decir; **it's better left u.** más vale no decir nada; **much was left u.** quedó mucho por decir

unsalaried [ʌn'sælərɪd] *adj* no remunerado(a)

unsalted [ʌn'sɔːltɪd] *adj* sin sal

unsanitary [ʌn'sænɪtərɪ] *adj* antihigiénico(a)

unsatisfactory [ʌnsætɪs'fæktərɪ] *adj* insatisfactorio(a); **it's most u.** deja mucho que desear

unsatisfied [ʌn'sætɪsfaɪd] *adj* insatisfecho(a)

unsatisfying [ʌn'sætɪsfaɪɪŋ] *adj* **(a)** *(job etc)* poco satisfactorio(a) **(b)** *(meal)* insuficiente

unsavoury, *US* **unsavory** [ʌn'seɪvərɪ] *adj* desagradable

unscathed [ʌn'skeɪðd] *adj* ileso(a), indemne

unscented [ʌn'sentɪd] *adj* sin perfume

unscientific [ʌnsaɪən'tɪfɪk] *adj* poco científico(a)

unscramble [ʌn'skræmbəl] *vt* descifrar

unscrew [ʌn'skruː] *vt* destornillar, desatornillar

unscrupulous [ʌn'skruːpjʊləs] *adj* sin escrúpulos

unseasonable [ʌn'siːzənəbəl] *adj (weather)* atípico(a), anormal

unseasoned [ʌn'siːzənd] *adj* **(a)** *(inexperienced)* inexperto(a), poco avezado(a) **(b)** *(green)* verde **(c)** *Culin* sin condimentar *or* sazonar

unseat [ʌn'siːt] *vt* **(a)** *Equit* derribar **(b)** *Parl (deputy etc)* quitarle el escaño a; *Pol (government)* derribar, derrocar

unseconded [ʌn'sekəndɪd] *adj (motion)* no apoyado(a)

unseemly [ʌn'siːmlɪ] *adj* impropio(a); **in an u. manner** sin decoro

unseen [ʌn'siːn] **1** *adj (invisible)* no visto(a), invisible; *(unnoticed)* inadvertido(a)
2 *n* **(a)** *Br Educ* texto *m* no trabajado en clase **(b)** **the u.** lo invisible

unselfconscious [ʌnself'kɒnʃəs] *adj* natural

unselfish [ʌn'selfɪʃ] *adj* desinteresado(a), generoso(a)

unserviceable [ʌn'sɜːvɪsəbəl] *adj* inservible, inútil

unsettle [ʌn'setəl] *vt* perturbar, inquietar

unsettled [ʌn'setəld] *adj* **(a)** *(person)* nervioso(a), intranquilo(a); *(situation)* inestable **(b)** *(weather)* variable, inestable **(c)** *(lifestyle etc)* agitado(a) **(d)** *(matter, question)* pendiente **(e)** *(debt)* pendiente **(f)** *(land)* sin colonizar

unshak(e)able [ʌn'ʃeɪkəbəl] *adj* firme, inquebrantable

unshaven [ʌn'ʃeɪvən] *adj* sin afeitar

unshrinkable [ʌn'ʃrɪŋkəbəl] *adj Tex* que no encoge

unsightly [ʌn'saɪtlɪ] *adj* feo(a), desagradable

unsigned [ʌn'saɪnd] *adj* sin firmar

unskilful, *US* **unskillful** [ʌn'skɪlfʊl] *adj* torpe, desmañado(a)

unskilled [ʌn'skɪld] *adj* **(a)** *(without skill) (worker)* no cualificado(a); *(work)* no especializado(a) (**b**) *(untalented)* inexperto(a); **he is quite u. at drawing** se le da bastante mal el dibujo

unsociable [ʌn'səʊʃəbəl] *adj* insociable, huraño(a)

unsold [ʌn'səʊld] *adj* no vendido(a), sin vender

unsolicited [ʌnsə'lɪsɪtɪd] *adj* no solicitado(a), voluntario(a); **he did it u.** lo hizo espontáneamente

unsolved [ʌn'sɒlvd] *adj* no resuelto(a), sin resolver

unsophisticated [ʌnsə'fɪstɪkeɪtɪd] *adj* (**a**) *(naïve)* ingenuo(a) (**b**) *(simple)* poco sofisticado(a), sencillo(a)

unsound [ʌn'saʊnd] *adj* (**a**) *(unstable)* inestable, débil; *Jur* **of u. mind** demente (**b**) *(fallacious)* falso(a), erróneo(a) (**c**) *(defective)* defectuoso(a); *(not firm)* poco sólido(a) (**d**) *Fin (investment)* poco seguro(a), especulativo(a)

unsparing [ʌn'speərɪŋ] *adj* pródigo(a); **u. in one's efforts** sin escatimar esfuerzos; **u. of praise** pródigo(a) en alabanzas

unspeakable [ʌn'spiːkəbəl] *adj* (**a**) *(pain)* indecible (**b**) *Fig (evil)* infando(a), atroz

unspecified [ʌn'spesɪfaɪd] *adj* indeterminado(a), sin especificar

unspoiled [ʌn'spɔɪld] *adj*, **unspoilt** [ʌn'spɔɪlt] *adj* *(unaltered)* intacto(a), conservado(a); *(not developed)* sin explotar

unspoken [ʌn'spəʊkən] *adj* (**a**) *(tacit)* tácito(a), implícito(a) (**b**) *(unuttered) (word)* sin pronunciar; *(feeling)* no expresado(a)

unstable [ʌn'steɪbəl] *adj* *(thing)* inestable, movedizo(a); *(person)* inestable, voluble, tornadizo(a)

unsteady [ʌn'stedɪ] *adj* (**a**) *(not firm)* inestable; *(table, chair)* cojo(a); *(hand, voice)* tembloroso(a); **to be u. on one's feet** tambalearse (**b**) *(varying)* variable; *(pulse)* irregular

unstinting [ʌn'stɪntɪŋ] *adj* pródigo(a) (**in** en, de); **to be u. in one's praise** no escatimar elogios

unstitch [ʌn'stɪtʃ] *vt* descoser; **to come unstitched** descoserse

unstressed [ʌn'strest] *adj* *Ling* átono(a)

unstuck [ʌn'stʌk] *adj* **to come u.** *(stamp, label)* despegarse, desengancharse; *Fig (person)* fracasar, darse un batacazo; *(plan)* fallar

unsubstantiated [ʌnsəb'stænʃɪeɪtɪd] *adj* *(accusation)* no probado(a), no demostrado(a); *(rumour)* infundado(a)

unsuccessful [ʌnsək'sesfʊl] *adj* (**a**) *(fruitless)* fracasado(a), fallido(a); *(useless)* vano(a), inútil (**b**) *(businessman etc)* fracasado(a); *(candidate)* derrotado(a), vencido(a); *(in exam)* suspendido(a); **to be u. at sth** no tener éxito con algo, fracasar en algo

unsuccessfully [ʌnsək'sesfəlɪ] *adv* sin éxito, infructuosamente, en vano

unsuitable [ʌn'suːtəbəl] *adj* (**a**) *(person)* no apto(a); **he's quite u. for the post** es la persona menos indicada para el puesto (**b**) *(thing)* impropio(a), inadecuado(a); *(remark)* inoportuno(a); *(time)* inconveniente, intempestivo(a); *Cin* **'u. for children'** 'no apto para menores'; **u. for the occasion** impropio(a) para la ocasión

unsuited [ʌn'suːtɪd] *adj* (**a**) *(inappropiate) (person)* no apto(a); *(thing)* impropio(a) (**to** para) (**b**) *(incompatible)* incompatible

unsupported [ʌnsə'pɔːtɪd] *adj* (**a**) *(statement)* infundado(a) (**b**) *(person)* sin apoyo, sin respaldo; **u. financially** sin apoyo financiero

unsure [ʌn'ʃʊər] *adj* poco seguro(a); **to be u. about sth** dudar de algo; **to be u. of oneself** carecer de confianza en sí mismo(a)

unsurpassed [ʌnsɜː'pɑːst] *adj* no superado(a)

unsuspected [ʌnsə'spektɪd] *adj* (**a**) *(not suspected)* insospechado(a) (**b**) *(unknown)* desconocido(a)

unsuspecting [ʌnsə'spektɪŋ] *adj* confiado(a); **he went in u.** entró sin sospechar nada

unsweetened [ʌn'swiːtənd] *adj* sin azúcar; *Ind* sin edulcorar

unswerving [ʌn'swɜːvɪŋ] *adj* firme, constante (**in** en)

unsympathetic [ʌnsɪmpə'θetɪk] *adj* *(unfeeling)* impasible, sin compasión; *(not understanding)* poco comprensivo(a); **she was totally u.** no fue nada comprensiva; **they were u. to my request** se mostraron indiferentes a mi petición

unsystematic [ʌnsɪstɪ'mætɪk] *adj* poco sistemático(a), poco metódico(a)

untainted [ʌn'teɪntɪd] *adj* (**a**) *(water etc)* no contaminado(a) (**b**) *Fig (reputation)* sin mancha; **u. by scandal** limpio(a) de escándalos

untamed [ʌn'teɪmd] *adj* *(animal)* salvaje

untangle [ʌn'tæŋgəl] *vt* desenredar, desenmarañar

untapped [ʌn'tæpt] *adj* *(mine etc)* sin explotar

untarnished [ʌn'tɑːnɪʃt] *adj* *(metal)* sin oxidar; *Fig* sin mancha

untaxed [ʌn'tækst] *adj* libre de impuestos

untempered [ʌn'tempəd] *adj* *Metal* sin templar

untenable [ʌn'tenəbəl] *adj* insostenible, indefendible

untested [ʌn'testɪd] *adj* (**a**) *(not tested)* no probado(a) (**b**) *(not proved)* sin comprobar

unthinkable [ʌn'θɪŋkəbəl] *adj* impensable,· inconcebible; **it's u. that ...** es impensable que … (+ *subj*)

untidiness [ʌn'taɪdɪnɪs] *n* *(gen)* desorden *m*; *(of appearance)* desaseo *m*, desaliño *m*

untidy [ʌn'taɪdɪ] *adj* (**untidier, untidiest**) *(room, person)* desordenado(a); *(hair)* despeinado(a); *(appearance)* desaseado(a), desaliñado(a)

untie [ʌn'taɪ] *vt* (**a**) *(unfasten)* desatar (**b**) *(set free)* soltar, desligar

until [ʌn'tɪl] **1** *conj* hasta que; **he won't come u. you invite him** no vendrá hasta que no le invites; **she worked u. she collapsed** trabajó hasta caerse; **u. she gets back** hasta que vuelva; **u. you told me** hasta que me lo dijiste **2** *prep* hasta; **u. after dinner** hasta después de cenar; **u. now** hasta ahora; **u. ten o'clock** hasta las diez; **not u. Monday** hasta el lunes no

untimely [ʌn'taɪmlɪ] **1** *adj* (**a**) *(premature)* prematuro(a); **to come to an u. end** morir antes de tiempo (**b**) *(inopportune)* inoportuno(a); *(hour)* intempestivo(a) **2** *adv* (**a**) *(early)* prematuramente (**b**) *(inopportunely)* inoportunamente, a deshora

untiring [ʌn'taɪərɪŋ] *adj* incansable, infatigable

untitled ['ʌn'taɪtəld] *adj* *(painting)* sin título

untold [ʌn'təʊld] *adj* (**a**) *(indescribable)* indecible, inefable (**b**) *Fig (incalculable) (loss)* incalculable; *(wealth)* fabuloso(a) (**c**) *(not told)* sin contar, nunca contado(a)

untouchable [ʌn'tʌtʃəbəl] *adj & n* intocable *(mf)*

untouched [ʌn'tʌtʃt] *adj* (**a**) *(not touched)* intacto(a) (**b**) *(unharmed)* ileso(a), indemne; *(not damaged)* intacto(a) (**c**) *(unaffected)* insensible (**by** a)

untoward [ʌntə'wɔːd, ʌn'təʊəd] *adj* (**a**) *(unfortunate)* desafortunado(a); **I hope nothing u. has happened** espero que no hayan tenido ningún contratiempo (**b**) *(adverse)* adverso(a)

untrained [ʌn'treɪnd] *adj* (**a**) *(unskilled)* sin preparación profesional; *(teacher)* sin título (**b**) *(inexpert)* inexperto(a) (**c**) *Sport* sin entrenar, desentrenado(a) (**d**) *(animal)* no amaestrado(a)

untransferable [ˌʌntrænsˈfɜːrəbəl] adj intransferible

untranslatable [ˌʌntrænsˈleɪtəbəl] adj intraducible

untried [ʌnˈtraɪd] adj (a) (not attempted) no probado(a); **to leave nothing u.** intentarlo or probarlo todo (b) Jur (person) no juzgado(a), sin juicio; (case) no visto(a)

untroubled [ʌnˈtrʌbəld] adj tranquilo(a), despreocupado(a); **to be u. (by)** no estar afectado(a) (por)

untrue [ʌnˈtruː] adj (a) (false) falso(a) (b) (unfaithful) infiel, desleal (c) (inexact) inexacto(a)

untrustworthy [ʌnˈtrʌstwɜːðɪ] adj (person) de poca confianza; **he's quite u.** no es de fiar en absoluto (b) (source) dudoso(a), no fidedigno(a)

untruth [ʌnˈtruːθ] n mentira f

untruthful [ʌnˈtruːθfʊl] adj (a) (person) mentiroso(a); **she was u. about her past** mintió sobre su pasado (b) (report) falso(a)

untuned [ʌnˈtjuːnd] adj Mus desafinado(a)

unusable [ʌnˈjuːzəbəl] adj inservible, inutilizable

unused [ʌnˈjuːzd] adj (a) (not used) (car) sin usar, nuevo(a); (flat etc) sin estrenar; (stamp) sin matar (b) (not in use) que no se utiliza (c) [ʌnˈjuːst] (unaccustomed) desacostumbrado(a) (to a); **I'm u. to this kind of life** no estoy acostumbrado a este tipo de vida

unusual [ʌnˈjuːʒʊəl] adj (rare) insólito(a), raro(a), poco común; (original) (original); (exceptional) excepcional; **it's u. for her to be so late** es raro que llegue tan tarde; **of u. interest** de excepcional interés; **that's u.!** ¡qué raro!

unusually [ʌnˈjuːʒʊəlɪ] adv excepcionalmente; **u. attentive** más atento(a) que de costumbre

unutterable [ʌnˈʌtərəbəl] adj indecible, inefable

unvarnished [ʌnˈvɑːnɪʃt] adj sin barnizar; Fig **the u. truth** la verdad desnuda

unvarying [ʌnˈveərɪŋ] adj invariable, constante

unveil [ʌnˈveɪl] vt (a) (uncover) descubrir (b) Fig (reveal) (plot) descubrir, desvelar; (secret) revelar

unventilated [ʌnˈventɪleɪtɪd] adj sin ventilación

unverifiable [ʌnˈverɪfaɪəbəl] adj que no puede verificarse

unvoiced [ʌnˈvɔɪst] adj (a) (untold) no expresado(a) (b) Ling sordo(a)

unwaged [ʌnˈweɪdʒd] Br **1** adj (not paid) no remunerado(a)
2 the u. npl (not paid) los no asalariados; (unemployed) los desempleados, Esp los parados, Am los desocupados

unwanted [ʌnˈwɒntɪd] adj (a) (gen) indeseado(a); (child) no deseado(a) (b) (superfluous) superfluo(a); **u. hair** vello m

unwarranted [ʌnˈwɒrəntɪd] adj (a) (gen) injustificado(a); (remark) gratuito(a); (interference) indebido(a) (b) (unauthorized) no autorizado(a)

unwary [ʌnˈweərɪ] adj imprudente, incauto(a)

unwashed [ʌnˈwɒʃt] adj sucio(a), sin lavar

unwavering [ʌnˈweɪvərɪŋ] adj (a) (undaunted) (loyalty) constante, firme; (courage) inquebrantable; **u. in one's resolve** firme en sus propósitos (b) (fixed) fijo(a)

unwelcome [ʌnˈwelkəm] adj (a) (visitor) molesto(a); **to make sb feel u.** hacer que algn se sienta incómodo(a) (b) (visit) inoportuno(a); Fig (news etc) desagradable

unwell [ʌnˈwel] adj malo(a), indispuesto(a)

unwholesome [ʌnˈhəʊlsəm] adj (a) (climate etc) insalubre (b) Fig (practice etc) depravado(a)

unwieldy [ʌnˈwiːldɪ] adj (tool) poco manejable; (object, system) aparatoso(a)

unwilling [ʌnˈwɪlɪŋ] adj no dispuesto(a); **to be u. to do sth** no estar dispuesto(a) a hacer algo

unwillingly [ʌnˈwɪlɪŋlɪ] adv de mala gana

unwillingness [ʌnˈwɪlɪŋnɪs] n desgana f

unwind [ʌnˈwaɪnd] (pt & pp unwound) **1** vt desenrollar
2 vi (a) (string, wool) desenrollarse (b) (relax) relajarse

unwise [ʌnˈwaɪz] adj imprudente, desaconsejable

unwitting [ʌnˈwɪtɪŋ] adj involuntario(a)

unworkable [ʌnˈwɜːkəbəl] adj (a) (not feasible) impracticable; (suggestion) irrealizable (b) (mine) inexplotable

unworldly [ʌnˈwɜːldlɪ] adj poco mundano(a), espiritual

unworthy [ʌnˈwɜːðɪ] adj no digno(a), indigno(a) (of de); **he is u. of my trust** no merece mi confianza; **u. conduct** conducta reprobable; **u. of notice** que no merece atención

unwound [ʌnˈwaʊnd] pt & pp see unwind

unwrap [ʌnˈræp] vt (pt & pp unwrapped) (gift) desenvolver; (package) deshacer, abrir

unwritten [ʌnˈrɪtən] adj (gen) no escrito(a); (agreement) verbal ❑ Jur **u. law** derecho m consuetudinario

unyielding [ʌnˈjiːldɪŋ] adj inflexible, rígido(a)

unzip [ʌnˈzɪp] vt (pt & pp unzipped) (clothes, bag) abrir la cremallera or Am el cierre de; (trousers) bajar la cremallera or Am el cierre de

up [ʌp] **1** prep (a) (movement) **to climb** or **go up the mountain** escalar la montaña; **to walk up and down the room** ir de un lado a otro de la habitación; **to walk up the street** ir calle arriba (b) (position) en lo alto de; **further up the street** más adelante (en la misma calle); **halfway up the ladder** a mitad de la escalera; **up a tree** en lo alto de un árbol

2 adv (a) (upwards) arriba, hacia arriba; **from $10 up** de 10 dólares para arriba; **halfway up** a medio camino; **hands up!** ¡arriba las manos!; **right up (to the top)** hasta arriba (del todo); **to go** or **come up** subir; **to look up** (from below) mirar hacia arriba; (raise one's eyes) levantar la mirada or la vista; **to stand up** ponerse en pie, levantarse; **to throw sth up into the air** lanzar algo al aire; **to walk up and down** ir de un lado para otro (b) (stationary) arriba; **face up** boca arriba; (on parcel) **'this side up'** 'este lado hacia arriba' (c) (in the sky) **the moon is up** ha salido la luna (d) (towards) hacia; **to come** or **go up to sb** acercarse a algn (e) (in, to) **he's up in Yorkshire** está en Yorkshire; **to go up north** ir al norte (f) (out of bed) **to get up** levantarse; **to stay up all night** no acostarse (g) (increased) **bread is up again** el pan ha subido otra vez; **he put up his offer** aumentó su oferta; **prices have gone up** los precios han subido (h) (agitated) **his blood was up** le hervía la sangre; **to be up in arms** poner el grito en el cielo (i) Jur (in court) **he was up before the magistrate** compareció ante el juez; **she was up for speeding** le inculparon por exceso de velocidad (j) (exposed) **it's up for discussion** se está discutiendo; **up for sale** en venta; Br **road up** (sign) carretera en obras (k) (taught) **she's well up in Latin** sabe mucho latín (l) Fam (happening) **something's up** pasa algo; **what's up?** (what's happening) ¿qué pasa?; US (as greeting) ¿qué (te) cuentas?; **what's up with you?** ¿qué pasa contigo? (m) **up with ...!** ¡viva ...! (n) **to be up against sth** enfrentarse con algo (o) **up to** (as far as, until) hasta; **I can spend up to $15** puedo gastar un máximo de 15 dólares; **up to here** hasta aquí; **up to now** hasta ahora, hasta la fecha (p) **to be up to** (depend on) depender de; **it's up to him to do it** le toca a él hacerlo; **it's up to you** depende de ti, la decisión está en tus manos (q) **to be up to** (be capable of) estar a la altura de; **I don't feel up to doing it today** hoy no me encuentro con fuerzas para hacerlo; **it's not up to much** no vale gran cosa; **she isn't up to the journey** no está en condiciones de hacer el viaje (r) **to be up to** (devise) traerse entre manos; **he's up to sth** está tramando algo; **she's up to no good** no puede estar haciendo nada bueno; **what are you up to?** ¿qué te traes entre manos? (**s**) *Slang Offens* **up yours** ¡métetelo por el culo!

3 *adj* (**a**) *(out of bed)* **up (and about)** levantado(a) (**b**) *(finished)* terminado(a); **his leave's up** se le ha acabado el permiso; **time's up** (ya) es la hora; *Fam* **the game's up!** ¡se acabó (la broma)! (**c**) *Rail (line)* de ascenso; *(train)* ascendente (**d**) *(escalator etc)* de subida

4 *vt (pt & pp* **upped**) *Fam* aumentar

5 *vi Fam* **to up and ...** agarrar *or Esp* coger y ...; **she upped and went** agarró *or Esp* cogió y se fue

6 *n* **ups and downs** altibajos *mpl*, vicisitudes *fpl*; **to be on the up and up** *Br* ir a mejor; *US Fam (honest)* ser *Esp* legal *or Am* recto(a)

up-and-coming [ˌʌpənˈkʌmɪŋ] *adj* que promete mucho; **an up-a.-c. lawyer** un abogado con futuro

upbeat [ˈʌpbiːt] *adj (optimistic)* optimista

upbraid [ʌpˈbreɪd] *vt* recriminar; **to u. sb for sth** recriminar algo a algn

upbringing [ˈʌpbrɪŋɪŋ] *n* educación *f*

update [ʌpˈdeɪt] **1** *vt* actualizar, poner al día
2 [ˈʌpdeɪt] *n* puesta *f* al día

upend [ʌpˈend] *vt (turn upside down)* poner boca abajo; *(knock over)* derribar

upfront [ˈʌpfrʌnt] *adj Fam* franco(a), sincero(a)

upgradable [ʌpˈgreɪdəbəl] *adj Comptr (hardware, system)* actualizable; *(memory)* ampliable

upgrade [ʌpˈgreɪd] **1** *vt* (**a**) *(promote)* ascender, subir de categoría (**b**) *(improve)* mejorar la calidad de (**c**) *Comptr (hardware, system)* actualizar; *(memory)* ampliar
2 [ˈʌpgreɪd] *n Comptr (of hardware, system)* actualización *f*; *(of memory)* ampliación *f*

upheaval [ʌpˈhiːvəl] *n* trastorno *m*, agitación *f*

upheld [ʌpˈheld] *pt & pp see* **uphold**

uphill [ˈʌphɪl] **1** *adj* ascendente; *Fig* arduo(a), duro(a)
2 *adv* cuesta arriba

uphold [ʌpˈhəʊld] *vt (pt & pp* **upheld**) (**a**) *(maintain)* sostener, mantener; **to u. the law** hacer respetar las leyes (**b**) *(support)* apoyar

upholster [ʌpˈhəʊlstər] *vt* tapizar

upholstery [ʌpˈhəʊlstəri] *n* (**a**) *(covering)* tapizado *m*, tapicería *f* (**b**) *(padding)* relleno *m* (**c**) *(trade)* tapicería *f*

upkeep [ˈʌpkiːp] *n* (**a**) *(maintenance)* mantenimiento *m*, conservación *f* (**b**) *(costs)* gastos *mpl* de mantenimiento

uplift [ʌpˈlɪft] **1** *vt* elevar; *Fig* inspirar
2 [ˈʌplɪft] *n Fig* edificación *f*

uplifting [ʌpˈlɪftɪŋ] *adj Fig* edificante

upload [ˈʌpləʊd] *vt Comptr* cargar, subir

up-market [ˈʌpmɑːkɪt] *adj* de calidad superior, de categoría

upon [əˈpɒn] *prep Fml* en, sobre; **once u. a time ...** érase una vez ...; **u. my word** (mi) palabra de honor

upper [ˈʌpər] **1** *adj* (**a**) *(position)* superior; **the u. jaw** la mandíbula superior; **u. storey** *or US* **story** piso de arriba; *Fig* **to get** *or* **have the u. hand** llevar ventaja, llevar la delantera ❑ *Typ* **u. case** mayúscula *f*; **U. Volta** Alto Volta; (**b**) *(in rank)* alto(a); **the u. class** la clase alta; *Pol* **the U. House** la Cámara Alta; *Fam* **the u. crust** la flor y nata
2 *n* (**a**) *(of shoe)* pala *f* (**b**) *Fam* **to be on one's uppers** estar sin blanca *or* un céntimo (**c**) *Slang (drugs)* anfeta *f*

upper-class [ˈʌpəklæs] *adj* de clase alta

upper-crust [ʌpəˈkrʌst] *adj Fam (person, accent)* de clase alta

uppermost [ˈʌpəməʊst] *adj* más alto(a); *Fig* predominante; *Fig* **it was u. in my mind** era lo que me preocupaba más

uppity [ˈʌpɪti] *adj Fam* creído(a), engreído(a); **to get u.** darse aires

upright [ˈʌpraɪt] **1** *adj* (**a**) *(vertical)* vertical; **u. piano** piano vertical (**b**) *(honest)* honrado(a), de honor
2 *adv* derecho, en posición vertical
3 *n* (**a**) *(stake)* montante *m*; *Ftb (post)* poste *m* (**b**) *(piano)* piano *m* vertical

uprising [ˈʌpraɪzɪŋ, ʌpˈraɪzɪŋ] *n* sublevación *f*, alzamiento *m*

uproar [ˈʌprɔːr] *n* tumulto *m*, alboroto *m*; **the town is in an u.** la ciudad está alborotada

uproarious [ʌpˈrɔːrɪəs] *adj (noisy)* escandaloso(a); *(funny)* divertidísimo(a)

uproot [ʌpˈruːt] *vt* desarraigar

upscale [ˈʌpskeɪl] *adj US (neighbourhood, restaurant)* elegante

upset [ʌpˈset] **1** *vt (pt & pp* **upset**) (**a**) *(overturn)* volcar; *(capsize)* hacer zozobrar; *(spill)* derramar (**b**) *(shock)* trastornar; *(worry)* preocupar; *(displease)* disgustar; **he is easily u.** se disgusta por nada (**c**) *(spoil)* desbaratar (**d**) *(make ill)* sentar mal; **spicy food upsets my stomach** las comidas picantes me sientan mal
2 [ˈʌpset] *n* (**a**) *(setback)* revés *m*, contratiempo *m*; **we had a bit of an u.** sufrimos un ligero contratiempo (**b**) *Sport (win)* victoria *f* inesperada (**c**) *(disorder etc)* trastorno *m*, disgusto *m*
3 [ˈʌpset] *adj* (**a**) *(overturned)* volcado(a) (**b**) *(shocked)* trastornado(a), alterado(a); *(displeased)* disgustado(a) (**c**) **to have an u. stomach** sentirse mal del estómago (**d**) *(spoiled)* desbaratado(a)

upsetting [ʌpˈsetɪŋ] *adj* preocupante, desconcertante

upshot [ˈʌpʃɒt] *n* resultado *m*; **what will be the u. of it all?** ¿cómo acabará todo?

upside [ˈʌpsaɪd] *n (top)* parte *f* superior

upside down [ˈʌpsaɪdˈdaʊn] **1** *adj al or* del revés
2 *adv* to hang u. d. *(person, animal)* colgar cabeza abajo; **to turn sth u. d.** poner algo del revés; *Fam Fig* **the house was u. d.** la casa estaba patas arriba

upstage [ʌpˈsteɪdʒ] **1** *adv & adj Theat* en el fondo del escenario
2 *vt Fam* eclipsar

upstairs 1 [ʌpˈsteəz] *adv* arriba; **she lives u.** vive en el piso de arriba; **to go u.** subir
2 [ˈʌpsteəz] *adj (apartment, bathroom)* de arriba

upstanding [ʌpˈstændɪŋ] *adj Fig* recto(a), honrado(a), ejemplar

upstart [ˈʌpstɑːt] *n* (**a**) *(newly risen)* advenedizo(a) *m,f* (**b**) *(arrogant)* impertinente *mf*

upstream [ʌpˈstriːm] *adv* río arriba, contra la corriente

upsurge [ˈʌpsɜːdʒ] *n* aumento *m*, subida *f*

upswing [ˈʌpswɪŋ] *n (improvement)* mejora *f*, alza *f*

uptake [ˈʌpteɪk] *n Fam* **to be quick on the u.** cogerlas al vuelo

uptight [ʌpˈtaɪt] *adj Fam* nervioso(a); **to get u.** agobiarse

up to date [ʌptəˈdeɪt] *adj (a) (current)* al día; **to be up to d. on sth** estar al tanto *or* al corriente de algo (**b**) *(modern)* moderno(a), a la moda

upturn [ˈʌptɜːn] *n (improvement)* mejora *f*

upturned [ʌpˈtɜːnd] *adj* **u. nose** nariz *f* respingona

upward [ˈʌpwəd] **1** *adj* ascendente, hacia arriba ❑ **u. mobility** ascenso *m* en la escala social; *Fin* **u. tendency** tendencia *f* al alza
2 *adv see* **upwards**

upward-compatible [ˈʌpwədkəmˈpætɪbəl] *adj Comptr* compatible con versiones posteriores

upwardly mobile ['ʌpwədlɪ'məʊbaɪl] *adj* = que va ascendiendo en la escala social

upwards ['ʌpwəd(z)] *adv* hacia arriba; **face u.** boca arriba; **from ten (years) u.** a partir de los diez años; **from $20 u.** de 20 dólares para arriba; *Fam* **u. of** algo más de

Urals ['jʊərəlz] *n pl* **the U.** los (Montes) Urales

uranium [jʊ'reɪnɪəm] *n Chem* uranio *m*

Uranus [jʊ'reɪnəs] *n Astron* Urano *m*

urban ['ɜːbən] *adj* urbano(a)

urbane [ɜː'beɪn] *adj* urbano(a), cortés

urbanization [ɜːbənaɪ'zeɪʃən] *n (process)* urbanización *f*

urbanize ['ɜːbənaɪz] *vt* urbanizar

urchin ['ɜːtʃɪn] *n* (a) *(child)* pilluelo(a) *m,f*, golfillo(a) *m,f*; (b) *Zool* **sea u.** erizo *m* de mar

urea [jʊ'rɪə] *n* urea *f*

urethra [jʊ'riːθrə] *n (pl* **urethras** *or* **urethrae** [jʊ'riːθriː]*)* *Anat* uretra *f*

urge [ɜːdʒ] **1** *vt* (a) *(incite)* incitar; *(press)* instar; *(plead)* exhortar; **she urged the soldiers to put down their arms** exhortó a los soldados a que dejaran las armas (b) *(advocate)* preconizar; *(insist on)* instar; **to u. that sth should be done** insistir en que se haga algo (c) **to u. sb on** *(incite)* darle cuerda a algn; *(encourage)* animar a algn
  2 *n* impulso *m*; **to feel an u. to do sth** sentir un vivo deseo de hacer algo

urgency ['ɜːdʒənsɪ] *n* urgencia *f*; **of great u.** muy urgente

urgent ['ɜːdʒənt] *adj (gen)* urgente; *(need, tone)* apremiante; **it is u. that I speak to her** me urge hablar con ella

urgently ['ɜːdʒəntlɪ] *adv* urgentemente

urinal [jʊ'raɪnəl, 'jʊərɪnəl] *n* (a) *(toilet)* urinario *m* (b) *(bowl)* orinal *m*

urinary ['jʊərɪnərɪ] *adj Anat* urinario(a)

urinate ['jʊərɪneɪt] *vi* orinar

urine ['jʊərɪn] *n* orina *f*

urn [ɜːn] *n* (a) *(decorative)* urna *f*; **burial u.** urna cineraria (b) **tea u.** tetera *f* grande

urology [jʊ'rɒlədʒɪ] *n Med* urología *f*

Ursa ['ɜːsə] *n Astron* Osa *f* ◻ **U. Major** Osa *f* Mayor; **U. Minor** Osa *f* Menor

Uruguay ['jʊərəgwaɪ] *n* Uruguay

Uruguayan [jʊərə'gwaɪən] *adj & n* uruguayo(a) *(m,f)*

US [juː'es] *n (abbr* **United States)** Estados *mpl* Unidos, EE.UU. *mpl*

us [ʌs] *pers pron* (a) *(as object)* nos; **give us some** danos algo; **he sees us** nos ve; **let's forget it** olvidémoslo; **let us in** déjanos entrar (b) *(after prep)* nosotros(as); **among us** entre nosotros; **both of us** nosotros dos; **come with us** ven con nosotros; **four of us** cuatro de nosotros; **he's one of us** es de los nuestros; **there are three of us** somos tres; **they are luckier than us** tienen más suerte que nosotros (c) *(after v to be)* nosotros(as); **she wouldn't believe it was us** no creía que fuéramos nosotros (d) *Br Fam (me)* me; **give us a kiss!** ¡dame un beso!; **let's have a look** déjame ver

USA [juːes'eɪ] *n* (a) *US (abbr* **United States Army)** Ejército *m* de los Estados Unidos (b) *(abbr* **United States of America)** Estados *mpl* Unidos de América, EE.UU. *mpl*

usable ['juːzəbəl] *adj* utilizable

USAF [juːeser'ef] *n (abbr* **United States Air Force)** Fuerzas *fpl* Aéreas de los Estados Unidos, USAF

usage ['juːsɪdʒ] *n* (a) *(use)* uso *m*, empleo *m* (b) *(habit, custom)* costumbre *f* (c) *Ling* uso *m*

use [juːz] **1** *vt* (a) *(gen)* emplear, utilizar, usar; **he used a pair of pliers to remove the nails** utilizó unos alicates

para sacar los clavos; **I u. it as a hammer** me sirve de martillo; **you can u. my name as a reference** puedes dar mi nombre si te piden referencias; **what is it used for?** ¿para qué sirve?; *Fam* **u. your head!** ¡piensa un poco!, ¡utiliza la cabeza! (b) *(apply)* emplear; **to u. every means** emplear todos los medios; **to u. force** hacer uso de la fuerza; **to u. one's influence** valerse de su influencia (c) *(consume)* consumir, gastar; **how much coffee have you used so far?** ¿cuánto café llevas gastado? (d) **to u. up** acabar; **it's all used up** está agotado, no queda nada; **to u. up the scraps** aprovechar los restos (e) *(take unfair advantage of)* aprovecharse de; **they are (just) using you** se aprovechan de ti (f) *Fam (need)* **I could u. a drink** no me vendría mal un trago
  2 *v aux (past tense only)* soler, acostumbrar; **I used to live in Scotland as a child** de pequeño viví en Escocia; **they didn't u. to play together** no solían jugar juntos; **things aren't what they used to be** las cosas han cambiado, ya no es como antes; **where did you u. to live?** ¿dónde vivías (antes)?
  3 [juːs] *n* (a) *(gen)* uso *m*, empleo *m*, utilización *f*; *(handling)* manejo *m*; **directions for u.** modo de empleo, instrucciones para el uso; **fit for u.** en buen estado; **for emergency u. only** utilícese sólo en caso de emergencia; *Pharm* **'for external u.'** 'para uso externo'; **in everyday u.** de uso corriente; **in u.** en uso; *(on lift)* **'not in u.'** 'no funciona'; **ready for u.** listo(a) para usar; **room with u. of kitchen** habitación con derecho a cocina; **to come into u.** empezar a utilizarse; **to make (good) u. of sth** aprovechar algo; **to put sth to good u.** sacar partido de algo (b) *(application)* aplicación *f* (c) *(usefulness)* utilidad *f*; **I have no further u. for it** ya no me sirve para nada; **it's no u.** es inútil, no vale la pena; **what's the u.?** ¿para qué?; **what's the u. of writing to her?** ¿de qué sirve escribirle?; *Fam* **it's no u. crying** no sirve de nada llorar (d) **of u.** útil; **to be of u.** servir; **can I be of any u. to you?** ¿puedo serle útil en algo?

use-by date ['juːzbaɪdeɪt] *n Com* fecha *f* de caducidad

used [juːzd] *adj* (a) *(second-hand)* usado(a), de segunda mano (b) [juːst] *(accustomed)* **to be u.** to estar acostumbrado(a) a; **to get u. to** acostumbrarse a

useful ['juːsfʊl] *adj (gen)* útil; *(practical)* práctico(a); **this is u. for storing things** esto va bien para guardar cosas; **to come in u.** venir bien; **to make oneself u.** ser útil, ayudar

usefulness ['juːsfʊlnɪs] *n* utilidad *f*

useless ['juːslɪs] *adj* (a) *(futile)* inútil; **it's u.** es inútil (b) *Fam (person)* inútil (**at** para); **I'm u. at that sort of thing** soy un negado para ese tipo de cosas; **she's quite u.** es un cero a la izquierda

user ['juːzər] *n* (a) *(of road, dictionary, computer)* usuario(a) *m,f*; **telephone users** los usuarios de teléfono ◻ *Comptr* **u. interface** interfaz *m or f* de usuario; *Comptr* **u. name** nombre *m* de usuario (b) *Fam (of drugs)* drogadicto(a) *m,f*

user-friendly [juːzə'frendlɪ] *adj (gen) & Comptr* de fácil manejo

usher ['ʌʃər] **1** *n* (a) *Cin Theat* acomodador(a) *m,f* (b) *(in court etc)* ujier *m*
  2 *vt* **to u. in** *Cin Theat* acomodar; *(at home)* hacer pasar; **to u. out** acompañar hasta la puerta

USM [juːes'em] *n* (a) *(abbr* **United States Mail)** = servicio estadounidense de correos (b) *(abbr* **United States Mint)** = organismo estadounidense encargado de la fabricación de billetes y monedas, *Esp* Fábrica *f* Nacional de Moneda y Timbre

USMC [juːesem'siː] *n* (abbr* **United States Marine Corps)** = cuerpo de infantería de marina de Estados Unidos

USN [juːes'en] *n (abbr* **United States Navy)** Armada *f* de los Estados Unidos, USN

USPHS [juːespiːeɪtʃ'es] *n (abbr* **United States Public Health Service**) = servicio de salud pública de los Estados Unidos

USS [juːes'es] *n (abbr* **United States Ship**) barco *m* de los Estados Unidos

USSR [juːeses'ɑːr] *n Formerly (abbr* **Union of Soviet Socialist Republics**) Unión *f* de Repúblicas Socialistas Soviéticas, URSS *f*

usual ['juːʒʊəl] **1** *adj* corriente, normal; **as u.** como siempre, como de costumbre; **at the u. hour** a la hora habitual; **earlier than u.** más pronto que de costumbre; **it's not u. for her to be late** no suele llegar tarde; **it's the u. practice** es lo normal; **the u. problems** los problemas de siempre; **the u. thing** lo de siempre

   2 *n* **the u.** lo habitual, lo usual; *Fam (drink etc)* lo de siempre; **out of the u.** fuera de lo común

usually ['juːʒʊəlɪ] *adv* normalmente; **she was more than u. polite** estuvo más amable de lo habitual; **what do you u. do on Sundays?** ¿qué sueles hacer los domingos?

usurer ['juːʒərər] *n* usurero(a) *m,f*

usurp [juː'zɜːp] *vt* usurpar

usurper [jʊ'zɜːpər] *n* usurpador(a) *m,f*

usury ['juːʒʊrɪ] *n* usura *f*

utensil [juː'tensəl] *n* utensilio *m* ❑ **kitchen utensils** batería *f* sing *or* utensilios *mpl* de cocina

uterus ['juːtərəs] *n (pl* **uteri** ['juːtəraɪ]) *Anat* útero *m*, matriz *f*

utilitarian [juːtɪlɪ'teərɪən] **1** *adj* **(a)** *Philos* utilitarista **(b)** *(useful)* utilitario(a)

   2 *n Philos* utilitarista *mf*

utility [juː'tɪlɪtɪ] *n* **(a)** *(usefulness)* utilidad *f* ❑ **u. goods** artículos *mpl* utilitarios; *Comptr* **u. program** utilidad *f;* **u. room** *(for storage)* trascocina *f; (for ironing)* cuarto *m* de planchar; **u. vehicle** utilitario *m* **(b) (public) u.** empresa *f* de servicio público **(c)** *US* **utilities** *(service charges)* servicio *m*

utilize ['juːtɪlaɪz] *vt* utilizar, servirse de

utmost ['ʌtməʊst] **1** *adj* sumo(a); **it is of the u. importance that ...** es de suma importancia que ... *(+ subj);* **the u. ends of the earth** los confines más remotos de la tierra; **with the u. ease** con suma facilidad

   2 *n* máximo *m;* **to do** *or* **try one's u.** hacer todo lo posible; **to the u.** al máximo, a más no poder

utopia [juː'təʊpɪə] *n* utopía *f*

utopian [juː'təʊpɪən] **1** *adj* utópico(a)

   2 *n* utopista *mf*

utter¹ ['ʌtər] *vt (words)* pronunciar; *(threat)* proferir; *(sigh)* dar; *(cry)* lanzar; **she didn't u. a word** no pronunció palabra, no dijo ni pío

utter² ['ʌtər] *adj* total, completo(a), absoluto(a); **he's an u. fool** es tonto de remate; **she's an u. stranger to me** no le conozco de nada; **that's u. nonsense!** ¡es pura tontería!; **u. bliss** la más completa felicidad

utterance ['ʌtərəns] *n* declaración *f*

utterly ['ʌtəlɪ] *adv* completamente, totalmente

U-turn ['juːtɜːn] *n* cambio *m* de sentido

UV [juː'viː] *adj Phys (abbr* **ultra-violet**) ultravioleta; **UV rays** rayos *mpl* ultravioleta

uvula ['juːvjʊlə] *n (pl* **uvulas** *or* **uvulae** ['juːvjʊliː]) *Anat* úvula *f*, campanilla *f*

uvular ['juːvjʊlər] *adj* uvular

Uzbekistan [ʊzbekɪ'stɑːn] *n* Uzbekistán

V

V, v [viː] *n (the letter)* V, v *f*

V *Elec (abbr* **volt(s)**) voltio(s) *m(pl)*,V

v (**a**) (*pl* **vv**) (*abbr* **verse**) verso *m*, v (**b**) (*also* **vs**) *Jur Sport* (*abbr* **versus**) contra (**c**) *Fam* (*abbr* **very**) muy (**d**) (*abbr* **vide**) (see), véase, vid

VA [viːˈeɪ] *n* (*abbr* **Veterans Administration**) = organismo estadounidense que se ocupa de los veteranos de guerra

vacancy [ˈveɪkənsɪ] *n* (**a**) (*job, post*) vacante *f*, puesto *m* vacante; **to fill a v.** ocupar un puesto; **'v. for a waiter'** 'se necesita camarero' (**b**) (*room in hotel*) habitación *f* libre; **'no vacancies** 'completo'

vacant [ˈveɪkənt] *adj* (**a**) (*empty*) vacío(a) (**b**) (*job, post*) vacante; **'situations v.'** 'ofertas de trabajo' (**c**) (*room, seat, hour*) libre (**d**) (*mind, expression*) vacío(a); **with a v. stare** con la mirada perdida

vacantly [ˈveɪkəntlɪ] *adv* (*absent-mindedly*) distraídamente

vacate [vəˈkeɪt] *vt* (**a**) (*post*) dejar, dejar vacante (**b**) (*flat etc*) desalojar, desocupar

vacation [vəˈkeɪʃən] **1** *n* (**a**) *Sch Univ* vacaciones *fpl*; **the long v.** las vacaciones de verano (**b**) *US* vacaciones *fpl*; **to be on v.** estar de vacaciones; **to take a v.** tomarse unas vacaciones **2** *vi US* pasar las vacaciones (**in, at** en)

vacationer [vəˈkeɪʃənər] *n US* turista *mf*; **summer v.** veraneante *mf*

vaccinate [ˈvæksɪneɪt] *vt Med* vacunar

vaccination [væksɪˈneɪʃən] *n Med* vacunación *f*

vaccine [ˈvæksiːn] *n Med* vacuna *f*

vacillate [ˈvæsɪleɪt] *vi* (**a**) (*hesitate*) vacilar, dudar (**b**) (*sway*) oscilar

vacillating [ˈvæsɪleɪtɪŋ] *adj* (**a**) (*hesitating*) vacilante, indeciso(a) (**b**) (*swaying*) oscilante

vacuous [ˈvækjʊəs] *adj* (**a**) (*empty*) vacío(a), vacuo(a) (**b**) (*mindless*) necio(a), tonto(a)

vacuum [ˈvækjʊəm] **1** *n Phys* vacío *m*; *Fig* **to leave a v.** dejar un vacío ❏ v. **brake** freno *m* de vacío; **v. cleaner** aspiradora *f*; **v. flask** termo *m* **2** *vt* limpiar con aspiradora; **to v. the living room** pasar la aspiradora por el salón

vacuum-packed [ˈvækjʊəmpækt] *adj* envasado(a) al vacío

vade mecum [vɑːdɪˈmeɪkʊm] *n* vademécum *m*

vagabond [ˈvægəbɒnd] *adj & n* vagabundo(a) *(m,f)*

vagary [ˈveɪgərɪ, vəˈgeərɪ] *n Fml* capricho *m*

vagina [vəˈdʒaɪnə] *n* (*pl* **vaginas** or **vaginae** [vəˈdʒaɪniː]) *Anat* vagina *f*

vaginal [vəˈdʒaɪnəl] *adj* vaginal

vagrancy [ˈveɪgrənsɪ] *n* vagabundeo *m*, vagabundería *f*

vagrant [ˈveɪgrənt] *adj & n* vagabundo(a) *(m,f)*

vague [veɪg] *adj* (*imprecise*) vago(a), impreciso(a); (*indistinct*) borroso(a); **I haven't the vaguest idea** no tengo la más mínima idea; **she was v. about it** no dio detalles

vaguely [ˈveɪglɪ] *adv* vagamente

vagueness [ˈveɪgnɪs] *n* (*gen*) vaguedad *f*, imprecisión *f*; (*of outline*) lo borroso

vain [veɪn] *adj* (**a**) (*proud*) vanidoso(a), presumido(a) (**b**) (*hopeless*) vano(a); **in v.** en vano

valance [ˈvæləns] *n* (*of bed*) cenefa *f*, doselera *f*

vale [veɪl] *n Literary* valle *m*; *Fig* **v. of tears** valle de lágrimas

valence [ˈveɪləns] *n US Chem see* **valency**

Valencia [vəˈlensɪə] *n* Valencia

Valencian [vəˈlensɪən] *adj & n* valenciano(a) *(m,f)*

valency [ˈveɪlənsɪ] *n Chem* valencia *f*

valentine [ˈvæləntaɪn] *n* (**a**) (*card*) = tarjeta que se manda el Día de los Enamorados (14 de febrero) (**b**) (*sweetheart*) novio(a) *m,f*

valerian [vəˈleərɪən] *n Bot* valeriana *f*

valet [ˈvælɪt, ˈvæleɪ] *n* ayuda *m* de cámara

valiant [ˈvæljənt] *adj* valiente

valid [ˈvælɪd] *adj* (*gen*) válido(a); (*ticket*) valedero(a); **no longer v.** caducado(a); (*ticket*) **v. for six months** valedero para seis meses

validate [ˈvælɪdeɪt] *vt* validar

validity [vəˈlɪdɪtɪ] *n* validez *f*

valise [væˈliːz] *n US* (*small suitcase*) maleta *f* de fin de semana

valley [ˈvælɪ] *n* valle *m*

valour, *US* **valor** [ˈvælər] *n* valor *m*, valentía *f*

valuable [ˈvæljʊəbəl] **1** *adj* valioso(a), de valor **2 valuables** *npl* objetos *mpl* de valor

valuation [væljʊˈeɪʃən] *n* (**a**) (*act*) valoración *f*, valuación *f* (**b**) (*price*) valor *m*

value [ˈvæljuː] **1** *n* (*gen*) valor *m*; **50 pence is good v.** 50 peniques es un buen precio; **of great/little v.** de gran/poco valor; **of no v.** sin valor; **to get good v. for money** sacarle jugo al dinero; **to increase in v.** aumentar en valor; **to the v. of** por el valor de; **traditional values** valores tradicionales ❏ **v. added tax** impuesto *m* sobre el valor añadido *or Am* agregado **2** *vt* (**a**) (*estimate value of*) valorar, tasar (**b**) (*appreciate*) valorar, estimar, apreciar

valued [ˈvæljuːd] *adj* (*friend*) estimado(a), apreciado(a); (*contribution*) valioso(a)

valueless [ˈvæljʊlɪs] *adj* sin valor

valuer [ˈvæljʊər] *n* tasador(a) *m,f*

valve [vælv] *n* (**a**) *Anat Tech* válvula *f* ❏ **safety v.** válvula *f* de seguridad (**b**) *Rad* lámpara *f* (**c**) *Bot Zool* valva *f* (**d**) *Mus* llave *f*

valvular ['vælvjʊlər] *adj* valvular

vamp¹ [væmp] *n Fam* vampiresa *f*

vamp² [væmp] *n* pala *f*, empella *f*

vampire ['væmpaɪər] *n* vampiro *m* ❑ *Zool* **v. bat** vampiro *m*

van [væn] *n* (**a**) *Aut* furgoneta *f*, camioneta *f* ❑ *Br* **breakdown v.** grúa *f*; **delivery v.** furgoneta *f* de reparto; **prison v.** coche *m* celular; **removal v.** camión *m* de mudanza (**b**) *Br Rail* furgón *m*

vandal ['vændəl] *n* (*hooligan*) vándalo(a) *m,f, Esp* gamberro(a) *m,f*

vandalism ['vændəlɪzəm] *n* vandalismo *m, Esp* gamberrismo *m*

vandalize ['vændəlaɪz] *vt* destruir, destrozar, hacer estragos en

vane [veɪn] *n* (**weather** or **wind**) **v.** veleta *f*

vanguard ['vængɑːd] *n* vanguardia *f*; **to be in the v. of** estar en la vanguardia de

vanilla [və'nɪlə] *n* vainilla *f*

vanish ['vænɪʃ] *vi* desaparecer, esfumarse; **to v. from sight** desaparecer de la vista; *Fig* **to v. into thin air** esfumarse

vanishing point ['vænɪʃɪŋpɔɪnt] *n* punto *m* de fuga

vanity ['vænɪti] *n* vanidad *f*; **out of sheer v.** por pura vanidad ❑ **v. bag, v. case** neceser *m*

vanquish ['væŋkwɪʃ] *vt Literary* vencer

vantage ['vɑːntɪdʒ] *n* ventaja *f*; **v. point** atalaya *f*; *Fig* posición *f* ventajosa or estratégica

Vanuatu [vænu:'ætu:] *n* Vanuatu

vapid ['væpɪd] *adj* insípido(a), soso(a)

vapor ['veɪpər] *n US see* **vapour**

vaporize ['veɪpəraɪz] **1** *vt* vaporizar
2 *vi* vaporizarse

vaporizer ['veɪpəraɪzər] *n* (*device*) vaporizador *m*; (*spray*) pulverizador *m*, atomizador *m*

vaporous ['veɪpərəs] *adj* vaporoso(a)

vapour ['veɪpər] *n* (*gen*) vapor *m*; (*on windowpane*) vaho *m* ❑ **v. trail** estela *f* de humo

variability [veərɪə'bɪlɪti] *n* variabilidad *f*

variable ['veərɪəbəl] *adj & n* variable (*f*)

variance ['veərɪəns] *n Fml* discrepancia *f*; **to be at v.** no concordar; **to be at v. with sb** estar en desacuerdo con algn

variant ['veərɪənt] *adj & n* variante (*f*)

variation [veərɪ'eɪʃən] *n* variación *f*

varicose ['værɪkəʊs] *adj Med* varicoso(a) ❑ **v. veins** varices *fpl*

varied ['veərɪd] *adj* variado(a), diverso(a)

variegated ['veərɪgeɪtɪd] *adj* abigarrado(a)

variety [və'raɪɪti] *n* (**a**) (*diversity*) variedad *f*, diversidad *f*; (*assortment*) surtido *m*; **for a v. of reasons** por razones diversas; **there is a wide v. of opinions** hay gran diversidad de opiniones; *Prov* **v. is the spice of life** en la variedad está el gusto (**b**) *Theat* variedades *fpl* ❑ **v. show** espectáculo *m* de variedades

various ['veərɪəs] *adj* (**a**) (*different*) diversos(as), varios(as); **the v. authorities on the subject** las distintas autoridades en el tema (**b**) (*several*) varios(as)

varnish ['vɑːnɪʃ] **1** *n* barniz *m* ❑ *Br* **nail v.** esmalte *m* de uñas
2 *vt* barnizar

vary ['veərɪ] *vi* (*pt & pp* **varied**) variar; **opinions v.** las opiniones varían; **prices v. from £2 to £4** los precios oscilan entre 2 y 4 libras; **to v. in size** variar de tamaño

varying ['veərɪɪŋ] *adj* diverso(a); **with v. degrees of success** con más o menos éxito

vascular ['væskjʊlər] *adj Anat Biol* vascular

vase [vɑːz, *US* veɪz] *n* florero *m*, jarrón *m*

vasectomy [væ'sektəmɪ] *n Med* vasectomía *f*

Vaseline® ['væsɪliːn] *n* vaselina *f*

vassal ['væsəl] *n Hist* vasallo(a) *m,f*

vast [vɑːst] *adj* (*area etc*) vasto(a), inmenso(a), enorme; (*majority*) abrumador(a); **v. sums of money** grandes cantidades de dinero

vastness ['vɑːstnɪs] *n* vastedad *f*, inmensidad *f*

VAT, Vat [viːeɪ'tiː, væt] *n* (*abbr* **value added tax**) impuesto *m* sobre el valor añadido, IVA *m*

vat [væt] *n* cuba *f*, tina *f*

Vatican ['vætɪkən] *n* **the V.** el Vaticano ❑ **V. City** Ciudad *f* del Vaticano

vaudeville ['vəʊdəvɪl, 'vɔːdəvɪl] *n Theat* vodevil *m*

vault¹ [vɔːlt] *n* (**a**) *Archit* bóveda *f* (**b**) (*cellar*) sótano *m*; (*for wine*) bodega *f* (**c**) (*tomb*) tumba *f* (**d**) (*of bank*) cámara *f* acorazada, *Am* bóveda *f* de seguridad

vault² [vɔːlt] **1** *vt & vi* saltar
2 *n* (*in gymnastics*) salto *m* ❑ **pole v.** salto *m* de pértiga

vaulting ['vɔːltɪŋ] *adj* (*in gymnastics*) **v. horse** potro *m*; *Sport* **v. pole** pértiga *f*

vaunt [vɔːnt] *vt Fml* jactarse de, hacer alarde de

VC [viː'siː] *n* (**a**) *Com* (*abbr* **Vice-Chairman**) Vicepresidente(a) *m,f* (**b**) *Br Mil* (*abbr* **Victoria Cross**) Cruz *f* de (la Reina) Victoria

VCR [viːsiː'ɑːr] *n* (*abbr* **video cassette recorder**) (aparato *m* de) vídeo *m* or *Am* video *m*

VD [viː'diː] *n Med* (*abbr* **venereal disease**) enfermedad *f* venérea

VDU [viːdiː'juː] *n Comptr* (*abbr* **visual display unit**) monitor *m*

veal [viːl] *n Culin* ternera *f*

vector ['vektər] *n Math* vector *m*

veer [vɪər] *vi* (*ship*) virar; (*car*) cambiar de dirección, girar; (*road*) torcer; *Fig* **to v. from one's course** desviarse de su camino; *Fig* **to v. round** cambiar de opinión

veg [vedʒ] *n* (*abbr* **vegetable(s)**) *Br Fam* verdura(s) *f(pl)*, hortaliza(s) *f(pl)*

vegan ['viːgən] *n* vegetariano(a) *m,f* estricto(a) (*que no come ningún producto de origen animal*)

vegeburger ['vedʒɪbɜːgər] *n* hamburguesa *f* vegetariana

vegetable ['vedʒtəbəl] *n* (*gen*) vegetal *m*; (*food*) verdura *f*, hortaliza *f*, legumbre *f*; **early vegetables** verduras tempranas ❑ **the v. kingdom** el reino vegetal; **v. garden** huerta *f*, huerto *m*

vegetarian [vedʒɪ'teərɪən] *adj & n* vegetariano(a) (*m,f*)

vegetarianism [vedʒɪ'teərɪənɪzəm] *n* vegetarianismo *m*

vegetate ['vedʒɪteɪt] *vi* vegetar

vegetation [vedʒɪ'teɪʃən] *n* vegetación *f*

vehemence ['viːɪməns] *n* vehemencia *f*

vehement ['viːɪmənt] *adj* vehemente

vehicle ['viːɪkəl] *n* (**a**) *Tech* vehículo *m* ❑ **armoured v.** vehículo *m* blindado; **motor v.** automóvil *m* (**b**) *Fig* vehículo *m*, medio *m*

vehicular [vɪ'hɪkjʊlər] *adj* de vehículos; **v. traffic** tránsito rodado

veil [veɪl] **1** *n* velo *m*; *Rel* **to take the v.** tomar el velo; *Fig* **to draw a v. over sth** correr un tupido velo sobre algo
2 *vt* (**a**) (*person*) cubrir con velo (**b**) (*truth, feelings*) velar, ocultar; **veiled reference** alusión velada

vein [veɪn] *n* (**a**) *Anat* vena *f* (**b**) *Bot* vena *f*, nervio *m* (**c**) *Geol Min* vena *f*, veta *f* (**d**) *(in wood, marble)* vena *f*, filón *m* (**e**) *Fig (mood)* vena *f*, humor *m*; **to be in v.** estar en vena

veined [veɪnd] *adj* veteado(a)

veiny ['veɪnɪ] *adj* (**veinier, veiniest**) venoso(a)

velar ['viːlər] *adj & n Ling* velar *(f)*

Velcro® ['velkrəʊ] *n* velcro® *m*

vellum ['veləm] *n* vitela *f* ❑ **v. paper** papel *m* vitela

velocity [vɪ'lɒsɪtɪ] *n* velocidad *f*

velodrome ['veləbdrəʊm] *n* velódromo *m*

velour(s) [və'lʊər] *n Tex* veludillo *m*

velum ['viːləm] *n Anat* velo *m* (del paladar)

velvet ['velvɪt] *n Tex* terciopelo *m*; **an iron hand in a v. glove** mano de hierro en guante de terciopelo

velveteen [velvɪ'tiːn] *n Tex* pana *f*

velvety ['velvɪtɪ] *adj* aterciopelado(a)

venal ['viːnəl] *adj* venal, sobornable

venality [vɪ'nælɪtɪ] *n* venalidad *f*

vend [vend] *vt Jur* vender

vendetta [ven'detə] *n* enemistad *f*, odio *m*

vending ['vendɪŋ] *n* **v. machine** máquina *f* expendedora

vendor ['vendɔːr] *n Jur* vendedor(a) *m,f*

veneer [vɪ'nɪər] **1** *n* (**a**) *(covering)* chapa *f* (**b**) *Fig* apariencia *f*
2 *vt* chapar, chapear

venerable ['venərəbəl] *adj* venerable

venerate ['venəreɪt] *vt* venerar

venereal [vɪ'nɪərɪəl] *adj Med* venéreo(a); **v. disease** enfermedad *f* venérea

Venetian [vɪ'niːʃən] *adj & n* veneciano(a) *(m,f)* ❑ **v. blind** persiana *f* graduable

Venezuela [venɪ'zweɪlə] *n* Venezuela

Venezuelan [venɪ'zweɪlən] *adj & n* venezolano(a) *(m,f)*

vengeance ['vendʒəns] *n* venganza *f*; **to take v. on sb** vengarse de algn; *Fam* **it was raining with a v.** llovía con ganas

vengeful ['vendʒfʊl] *adj* vengativo(a)

venial ['viːnɪəl] *adj* venial; **v. sin** pecado *m* venial

Venice ['venɪs] *n* Venecia

venison ['venɪsən] *n Culin* carne *f* de venado

venom ['venəm] *n* veneno *m*

venomous ['venəməs] *adj* venenoso(a); *Fig* **v. tongue** lengua *f* viperina

venous ['viːnəs] *adj Anat* venoso(a)

vent [vent] **1** *n* (**a**) *(opening)* abertura *f*, orificio *m*; *(grille)* rejilla *f* de ventilación; *Fig* **to give v. to one's feelings** desahogarse ❑ **air v.** respiradero *m* (**b**) *(of volcano)* chimenea *f*
2 *vt Fig (feelings)* descargar; **to v. one's anger on sb** desahogarse con algn

ventilate ['ventɪleɪt] *vt* ventilar, airear

ventilation [ventɪ'leɪʃən] *n* ventilación *f* ❑ *Min* **v. shaft** pozo *m* de ventilación

ventilator ['ventɪleɪtər] *n* ventilador *m*

ventricle ['ventrɪkəl] *n Anat* ventrículo *m*

ventriloquism [ven'trɪləkwɪzəm] *n*, **ventriloquy** [ven'trɪləkwɪ] *n* ventriloquia *f*

ventriloquist [ven'trɪləkwɪst] *n* ventrílocuo(a) *m,f*

venture ['ventʃər] **1** *vt* arriesgar, aventurar; **to v. an opinion** aventurar una opinión; **he didn't v. to ask** no se atrevió a preguntarlo; *Prov* **nothing ventured, nothing gained** quien no arriesga no cruza la mar

2 *vi* arriesgarse; **to v. out of doors** atreverse a salir

3 *n* empresa *f* arriesgada, aventura *f*; **business/joint v.** empresa comercial/colectiva; **it's a completely new v.** es algo completamente nuevo ❑ *Fin* **v. capital** capital *m* de riesgo

venue ['venjuː] *n* (**a**) *Jur* jurisdicción *f* (**b**) *(meeting place)* lugar *m* de reunión (**c**) *(for concert etc)* local *m*

Venus ['viːnəs] *n* (**a**) *Myth* Venus *f* (**b**) *Astron* Venus *m*

veracious [ve'reɪʃəs] *adj Fml* veraz, sincero(a)

veracity [ve'ræsɪtɪ] *n Fml* veracidad *f*

veranda(h) [və'rændə] *n* veranda *f*, terraza *f*

verb [vɜːb] *n Ling* verbo *m*

verbal ['vɜːbəl] *adj* verbal

verbalize ['vɜːbəlaɪz] *vt* verbalizar

verbally ['vɜːbəlɪ] *adv* verbalmente, de palabra

verbatim [və'beɪtɪm] **1** *adj* textual
2 *adv* palabra por palabra, textualmente

verbena [vɜː'biːnə] *n Bot* verbena *f*

verbiage ['vɜːbɪɪdʒ] *n* verborrea *f*, verbosidad *f*

verbose [vɜː'bəʊs] *adj* verboso(a), locuaz

verbosity [vɜː'bɒsɪtɪ] *n* verbosidad *f*

verdant ['vɜːdənt] *adj Literary* verde

verdict ['vɜːdɪkt] *n* (**a**) *Jur* veredicto *m*, fallo *m*; **to return a v. of guilty/not guilty** pronunciar un veredicto de culpabilidad/inocencia (**b**) *(opinion)* opinión *f*, juicio *m*; **give me your v. on it** dime lo que opinas de ello

verge [vɜːdʒ] **1** *n* (**a**) *(margin)* borde *m*, margen *m*; *Fig* on the **v. of** al borde de, a dos dedos de; *Fig* **to be on the v. of doing sth** estar a punto de hacer algo (**b**) *Br (of road)* arcén *m*
2 *vi* rayar (**on** en); **it verges on madness** raya en la locura; **she's verging on fifty** ronda los cincuenta años

verger ['vɜːdʒər] *n* sacristán *m (de la Iglesia anglicana)*

verifiable ['verɪfaɪəbəl] *adj* verificable

verification [verɪfɪ'keɪʃən] *n* verificación *f*, comprobación *f*

verify ['verɪfaɪ] *vt (pt & pp* **verified**) verificar, comprobar

verisimilitude [verɪsɪ'mɪlɪtjuːd] *n Fml* verosimilitud *f*

veritable ['verɪtəbəl] *adj* verdadero(a), auténtico(a)

verity ['verɪtɪ] *n Fml or Literary* verdad *f*

vermicelli [vɜːmɪ'selɪ] *npl Culin* fideos *mpl*

vermil(l)ion [və'mɪljən] **1** *n* bermellón *m*
2 *adj* bermejo(a)

vermin [vɜːmɪn] *npl* (**a**) *(animals)* bichos *mpl*, sabandijas *fpl* (**b**) *Fig* gentuza *f* sing, chusma *f* sing

verminous ['vɜːmɪnəs] *adj* lleno(a) de bichos

vermouth ['vɜːməθ] *n* vermú *m*, vermut *m*

vernacular [və'nækjʊlər] **1** *n* lengua *f* vernácula
2 *adj* vernáculo(a)

veronica [və'rɒnɪkə] *n Bot* verónica *f*

verruca [ve'ruːkə] *n Med* verruga *f (especialmente en las plantas de los pies)*

Versailles [veə'saɪ] *n* Versalles

versatile ['vɜːsətaɪl] *adj* (**a**) *(person)* polifacético(a); *(object)* dúctil, de múltiples aplicaciones (**b**) *Zool* versátil

versatility [vɜːsə'tɪlɪtɪ] *n* (**a**) *(of person)* carácter *m* polifacético; *(of object)* ductilidad *f*, variedad *f* de aplicaciones (**b**) *Zool* versatilidad *f*

verse [vɜːs] *n* (**a**) *(stanza)* estrofa *f* (**b**) *(poetry)* versos *mpl*, poesía *f*; **blank v.** verso blanco; **free v.** verso libre; **in v.** en verso (**c**) *(of song)* copla *f* (**d**) *(of Bible)* versículo *m*

versed [vɜːst] *adj* versado(a); **to be (well) v. in** ser (muy) versado(a) en

versification [vɜːsɪfɪ'keɪʃən] *n* versificación *f*

versify ['vɜːsɪfaɪ] *vi* (*pt & pp* **versified**) versificar

version ['vɜːʃən, 'vɜːʒən] *n* (**a**) *(gen)* versión *f*; **the uncut v. of the film** la versión íntegra de la película ❑ *Theat* **stage v.** adaptación *f* teatral (**b**) *Mus* interpretación *f* (**c**) *Aut* modelo *m*; **the economy v.** el modelo económico

verso ['vɜːsəʊ] *n* (*pl* **versos**) *Typ* reverso *m*

versus ['vɜːsəs] *prep Jur Sport* contra

vertebra ['vɜːtɪbrə] *n* (*pl* **vertebras** *or* **vertebrae** ['vɜːtɪbriː]) *Anat* vértebra *f*

vertebral ['vɜːtɪbrəl] *adj* vertebral

vertebrate ['vɜːtɪbreɪt, 'vɜːtɪbrɪt] *adj & n* vertebrado(a) *(m)*

vertex ['vɜːteks] *n* (*pl* **vertexes** *or* **vertices**) (**a**) *Anat Geom* vértice *m* (**b**) *Fig* cumbre *f*, cima *f*

vertical ['vɜːtɪkəl] *adj & n* vertical *(f)*

vertices ['vɜːtɪsiːz] *npl see* **vertex**

vertigo ['vɜːtɪgəʊ] *n Med* vértigo *m*

vervain ['vɜːveɪn] *n Bot* verbena *f*

verve [vɜːv] *n* vigor *m*, brío *m*, energía *f*

very ['verɪ] **1** *adv* (**a**) *(extremely)* muy; **it's v. kind of you** es muy amable de tu parte; **to be v. hungry** tener mucha hambre; **v. few** muy pocos(as), poquísimos(as); **v. little** muy poco; **v. much** mucho, muchísimo; **v. tall** muy alto(a), altísimo(a); **v. well** muy bien (**b**) *(emphatic)* **at the v. latest** a más tardar, como máximo; **at the v. least** como mínimo, por lo menos; **the v. best** el mejor de todos; **the v. first/last** el/la primero(a)/último(a) de todos; **the v. same day** el mismo día

2 *adj* (**a**) *(extreme)* de todo; **at the v. end** al final de todo (**b**) *(precise)* exacto(a), mismo(a); **at this v. moment** en este mismo momento; **her v. words** sus palabras exactas; **in the v. middle** justo en medio; *Fam* **it's the v. thing** es justo lo que hacía falta (**c**) *(mere)* **the v. thought of it!** ¡sólo con pensarlo!

vesicle ['vesɪkəl] *n Anat* vesícula *f*

vesicular [ve'sɪkjʊlər] *adj Anat* vesicular

vespers ['vespəz] *npl Rel* vísperas *fpl*

vessel ['vesəl] *n* (**a**) *(container)* vasija *f*, recipiente *m* (**b**) *Naut* buque *m*, nave *f*, navío *m* ❑ **cargo v.** buque *m* de carga (**c**) *Anat Bot* vaso *m* ❑ **blood v.** vaso *m* sanguíneo

vest [vest] **1** *n* (**a**) *Br (undershirt)* camiseta *f* (**b**) *US* chaleco *m*

2 *vt Jur* dar posesión a (**with** de), conferir a (**with** -); **to v. sb with rights** conferir derechos a algn

vestal ['vestəl] *adj* vestal ❑ **v. virgin** vestal *f*

vested ['vestɪd] *adj Jur Fin* absoluto(a), efectivo(a); **v. interests** derechos *mpl* adquiridos; *Fig* intereses *mpl* creados *or* personales; **to have a v. interest in a matter** tener intereses personales en un asunto

vestibule ['vestɪbjuːl] *n* (**a**) *(entrance hall)* vestíbulo *m*, entrada *f* (**b**) *Anat* vestíbulo *m*

vestige ['vestɪdʒ] *n* vestigio *m*, rastro *m*

vestigial [ves'tɪdʒɪəl] *adj* vestigial

vestment ['vestmənt] *n Rel* vestidura *f* sacerdotal

vestry ['vestrɪ] *n Rel* sacristía *f*

Vesuvius [vɪ'suːvɪəs] *n* Vesubio *m*

vet¹ [vet] **1** *n Fam* (*abbr* **veterinary surgeon**)

2 *vt* (*pt & pp* **vetted**) *Br* someter a investigación, examinar

vet² [vet] *n US Mil* (*abbr* **veteran**) excombatiente *mf*

vetch [vetʃ] *n Bot* arveja *f*

veteran ['vetərən] *n* (**a**) *(gen)* veterano(a) *m,f*; *Fig* **he's a v. photographer** es un fotógrafo experimentado ❑ *Br* **v. car** coche *m* de época *(construido antes de 1919)*; **v. soldier** soldado *m* veterano (**b**) *US Mil* **(war) v.** ex combatiente *mf*

veterinarian [vetərɪ'neərɪən] *n US* veterinario(a) *m,f*

veterinary ['vetərɪnərɪ] *adj* veterinario(a) ❑ **v. medicine**

veterinaria *f*; *Br* **v. surgeon** veterinario(a) *m,f*

veto ['viːtəʊ] **1** *n* (*pl* **vetoes**) veto *m*; **power** *or* **right of v.** derecho *m* de veto; **to impose a v. over sth** poner el veto a algo

2 *vt* (*pt & pp* **vetoed**) vetar; *(forbid)* vedar, prohibir

vetting ['vetɪŋ] *n Br* investigación *f*, examen *m*

vex [veks] *vt (annoy)* molestar, disgustar; *(anger) esp Esp* enfadar, *esp Am* enojar

vexation [vek'seɪʃən] *n* (**a**) *(annoyance)* disgusto *m*, vejación *f* (**b**) *(worry)* preocupación *f*

vexatious [vek'seɪʃəs] *adj* molesto(a)

vexed [vekst] *adj* (**a**) *(annoyed)* disgustado(a), molesto(a); **she was v. at the delay** le disgustó el retraso (**b**) *(worried)* inquieto(a) (**c**) *(debated)* controvertido(a)

VHF [viːeɪtʃ'ef] *Rad* (*abbr* **very high frequency**) frecuencia *f* muy alta, VHF

VHS [viːeɪtʃ'es] *n TV* (*abbr* **video home system**) VHS *m*

via ['vaɪə] *prep* por, vía; **they travelled v. Paris** viajaron vía París

viability [vaɪə'bɪlɪtɪ] *n* viabilidad *f*

viable ['vaɪəbəl] *adj* viable, factible, practicable

viaduct ['vaɪədʌkt] *n* viaducto *m*

vibes [vaɪbz] *npl* (*abbr* **vibrations**) *Fam* vibraciones *fpl*, *Esp* rollo *m*, *Am* onda *f*

vibrant ['vaɪbrənt] *adj* (**a**) *(sound)* vibrante (**b**) *Fig (personality)* vital, fuerte; *(city)* animado(a)

vibraphone ['vaɪbrəfəʊn] *n Mus* vibráfono *m*

vibrate [vaɪ'breɪt] *vi* vibrar (**with** de)

vibration [vaɪ'breɪʃən] *n* vibración *f*

vibrator [vaɪ'breɪtər] *n* vibrador *m*

vibratory ['vaɪbrətərɪ] *adj* vibratorio(a)

viburnum [vaɪ'bɜːnəm] *n Bot* viburno *m*

vicar ['vɪkər] *n* (**a**) *(in Church of England)* párroco *m* (**b**) *(in Roman Catholic Church)* vicario *m*; **the V. of Christ** el Vicario de Cristo ❑ **v. general** vicario *m* general

vicarage ['vɪkərɪdʒ] *n* casa *f* del párroco, vicaría *f*

vicarious [vɪ'keərɪəs] *adj (gen)* experimentado(a) por otro; *(punishment)* sufrido(a) por otro; **v. pleasure** placer *m* indirecto

vice¹ [vaɪs] *n* vicio *m* ❑ **v. squad** brigada *f* contra el vicio

vice² [vaɪs] *n Br (tool)* torno *m* *or* tornillo *m* de banco

vice³ [vaɪs] *pref* vice- ❑ *Mil* **v. admiral** vicealmirante *m*; *Br Univ* **v. chancellor** rector(a) *m,f*; **v.-presidency** vicepresidencia *f*; **v.-president** *(of country)* vicepresidente(a) *m,f*; *US Com (of company)* vicepresidente(a) *m,f*

vice-chairman [vaɪs'tʃeəmən] *n* (*pl* **vice-chairmen**) vicepresidente *m*

vice-chairwoman [vaɪs'tʃeəwʊmən] *n* (*pl* **vice-chairwomen** [vaɪs'tʃeəwɪmɪn]) vicepresidenta *f*

viceroy ['vaɪsərɔɪ] *n* virrey *m*

viceroyalty [vaɪs'rɔɪəltɪ] *n* virreinato *m*

vice versa [vaɪsɪ'vɜːsə] *adv* viceversa

vicinity [vɪ'sɪnɪtɪ] *n* (**a**) *(area)* vecindad *f*, inmediaciones *fpl*; **in the v. of** cerca de, en las inmediaciones de (**b**) *(nearness)* proximidad *f*

vicious ['vɪʃəs] *adj (violent)* virulento(a), violento(a); *(malicious)* malintencionado(a); *(cruel)* cruel, depravado(a), perverso(a); **to have a v. tongue** tener una lengua viperina ❑ **v. circle** círculo *m* vicioso

viciousness ['vɪʃəsnɪs] *n (violence)* virulencia *f*, violencia *f*; *(malice)* maldad *f*, mala intención *f*; *(cruelty)* crueldad *f*, depravación *f*, perversidad *f*

vicissitude [vɪ'sɪsɪtjuːd] *n* vicisitud *f*

victim ['vɪktɪm] n víctima f; **to be the v. of** ser víctima de; Fig **to fall v. to sb's charms** sucumbir ante los encantos de algn

victimization [vɪktɪmaɪ'zeɪʃən] n persecución f, trato m injusto

victimize ['vɪktɪmaɪz] vt (punish) perseguir, tomar como víctima; (retaliate against) tomar represalias contra

victor ['vɪktər] n vencedor(a) m,f, triunfador(a) m,f

Victorian [vɪk'tɔːrɪən] adj & n victoriano(a) (m,f)

Victoriana [vɪktɔːrɪ'ɑːnə] npl antigüedades fpl victorianas

victorious [vɪk'tɔːrɪəs] adj victorioso(a), vencedor(a); Sport **the v. team** el equipo ganador

victory ['vɪktərɪ] n victoria f, triunfo m; **a sweeping v.** una victoria aplastante; Fam **to pull off a v.** conseguir una victoria

victualler ['vɪtələr] n Br **licensed v.** (gen) vendedor(a) m,f autorizado(a) de bebidas alcohólicas; (pub owner) dueño m de un bar

victuals ['vɪtəlz] npl (food) víveres mpl, vituallas fpl; (provisions) provisiones fpl

video ['vɪdɪəʊ] n (pl **videos**) vídeo m, Am video m ▫ **v. camera** videocámara f; **v. cassette** videocasete f; **v. club** videoclub m; **v. frequency** videofrecuencia f; **v. game** videojuego m; **v. (cassette) recorder** vídeo m, Am video; **v. tape** videocinta f, cinta f de vídeo or Am video

videoconferencing ['vɪdɪəʊkɒnfrənsɪŋ] n videoconferencias fpl

videodisc ['vɪdɪəʊdɪsk] n videodisco m

videophone ['vɪdɪəfəʊn] n videoteléfono m

video-tape ['vɪdɪəʊteɪp] vt grabar (en vídeo or Am video)

vie [vaɪ] vi (pt & pp **vied**) competir, rivalizar (**against, with** con)

Vienna [vɪ'enə] n Viena

Viennese [vɪə'niːz] adj & n vienés(esa) (m,f)

Vietnam [vjet'næm] n Vietnam

Vietnamese [vjetnə'miːz] **1** adj vietnamita
2 n (a) (person) vietnamita mf; **the v.** los vietnamitas (b) (language) vietnamita m

view [vjuː] **1** n (a) (sight) vista f, panorama m; **a lovely v.** una vista preciosa; **in full v. of** a plena vista de; **to be on v.** estar a la vista; **to come into v.** aparecer; Fig **in v. of** en vista de; Fig **in v. of the fact that ...** dado que ... (b) (opinion) opinión f, parecer m; **in my v.** en mi opinión; **point of v.** punto de vista; **to take a dim** or **poor v. of sth** ver algo con malos ojos (c) (survey) visión f de conjunto, panorama m (d) (aim) fin m; **with a v. to doing sth** con la intención de hacer algo; **with this in v.** con este fin
2 vt (a) (look at) mirar; (house etc) visitar (b) (look on) contemplar, ver; (topic, problem) enfocar; **they v. his policies as a potential threat** consideran que su política es amenazadora

viewer ['vjuːər] n (a) TV telespectador(a) m,f, televidente mf (b) Phot visionador m

viewfinder ['vjuːfaɪndər] n Phot visor m

viewing ['vjuːɪŋ] n (a) (of movie, TV programme) **for home v.** para ver en casa; **this programme is essential v.** no se debe perder este programa (b) (of house) visita f

viewpoint ['vjuːpɔɪnt] n punto m de vista

vigil ['vɪdʒɪl] n (a) (watch) vigilia f, vela f; **all-night v.** vela nocturna; **to keep v.** velar (b) Rel vigilia f

vigilance ['vɪdʒɪləns] n vigilancia f

vigilant ['vɪdʒɪlənt] adj alerta

vigilante [vɪdʒɪ'læntɪ] n vigilante mf

vignette [vɪ'njet] n Phot viñeta f

vigorous ['vɪgərəs] adj vigoroso(a), enérgico(a)

vigour, US **vigor** ['vɪgər] n vigor m, fuerza f

Viking ['vaɪkɪŋ] adj & n vikingo (m)

vile [vaɪl] adj (a) (evil) vil, infame, despreciable (b) (disgusting) repugnante (c) Fam (awful) malísimo(a), horrible; **to be in a v. temper** estar de un humor de perros

vileness ['vaɪlnɪs] n vileza f

vilify ['vɪlɪfaɪ] vt (pt & pp **vilified**) denigrar, difamar

villa ['vɪlə] n (a) (country house) villa f, quinta f, casa f de campo (b) Br chalet m

village ['vɪlɪdʒ] n (small) pueblecito m, aldea f; (larger) pueblo m

villager ['vɪlɪdʒər] n aldeano(a) m,f

villain ['vɪlən] n (gen) villano(a) m,f, canalla m; Cin Theat malo(a) m,f

villainous ['vɪlənəs] adj (a) (evil) vil, infame (b) Fam (very bad) malísimo(a), horrible

villainy ['vɪlənɪ] n villanía f, vileza f, bajeza f

vim [vɪm] n Slang marcha f

vinaigrette [vɪneɪ'gret] n Culin **v. (sauce)** (salsa f) vinagreta f

vindicate ['vɪndɪkeɪt] vt (a) (actions etc) justificar, vindicar (b) (rights) reivindicar

vindication [vɪndɪ'keɪʃən] n (a) (justification) justificación f, vindicación f; **in v. of sth** para justificar algo (b) (claim) reivindicación f

vindicatory ['vɪndɪkeɪtərɪ] adj vindicatorio(a), vindicativo(a)

vindictive [vɪn'dɪktɪv] adj vindicativo(a), vengativo(a); **to feel v. towards sb** guardar rencor a algn

vindictively [vɪn'dɪktɪvlɪ] adv con venganza, con rencor

vine [vaɪn] n Bot (along ground) vid f; (climbing) parra f ▫ **v. grower** viticultor(a) m,f, viñador(a) m,f ▫ **v. growing** viticultura f; **v. leaf** hoja f de parra or de vid; **v. shoot** sarmiento m

vinegar ['vɪnɪgər] n vinagre m ▫ **v. bottle** vinagrera f

vine-growing ['vaɪngrəʊɪŋ] adj vitícola

vineyard ['vɪnjəd] n viña f, viñedo m

vintage ['vɪntɪdʒ] **1** n (a) (crop, year) cosecha f; **what v. is it?** ¿de qué cosecha es? (b) (season) vendimia f (c) (era) era f; **of Victorian v.** de la era victoriana
2 adj (a) (wine) añejo(a) (b) (classic) clásico(a); Aut **v. car** coche de época (construido entre 1919 y 1930)

vinyl ['vaɪnɪl] Chem n vinilo m

viola¹ [vɪ'əʊlə] n Mus viola f

viola² [vaɪ'əʊlə] n Bot viola f, violeta f

violate ['vaɪəleɪt] vt (a) (rape) violar (b) (break) infringir

violation [vaɪə'leɪʃən] n (a) (rape) violación f (b) (of law etc) infracción f

violator ['vaɪəleɪtər] n Jur violador(a) m,f

violence ['vaɪələns] n violencia f; **to resort to v.** recurrir a la violencia; Fig **to do v. to sth** perjudicar algo

violent ['vaɪələnt] adj (a) (place, person, death, film) violento(a); **to have a v. temper** ser de temperamento violento (b) (intense) intenso(a); profundo(a); **to take a v. dislike to sth** sentir una fuerte aversión por algo

violently ['vaɪələntlɪ] adv (a) (with violence) violentamente; **to behave v.** mostrarse violento(a) (b) (intensely) terriblemente; **to be v. ill** vomitar mucho

violet ['vaɪəlɪt] **1** n (a) Bot violeta f ▫ Fam **shrinking v.** persona f tímida (b) (colour) violeta m, violado m
2 adj violeta, violado(a)

violin [vaɪə'lɪn] n Mus violín m

violinist [vaɪə'lɪnɪst] n violinista mf, violín mf

VIP [ˌviːaɪˈpiː] *n Fam (abbr* **very important person)** personaje *m* muy importante; **VIP lounge** *(at airport etc)* sala *f* de personalidades; **VIP treatment** privilegios *mpl* especiales

viper [ˈvaɪpər] *n Zool* víbora *f*

virago [vɪˈrɑːgəʊ] *n (pl* **viragoes** *or* **viragos)** arpía *f*

viral [ˈvaɪrəl] *adj Med* viral, vírico(a)

virgin [ˈvɜːdʒɪn] **1** *n* virgen *f*; **the V. Mary** la Virgen María; **to be a v.** ser virgen
2 *adj* virgen ◻ **V. Islands** Islas *fpl* Vírgenes

virginal¹ [ˈvɜːdʒɪnəl] *adj* virginal

virginal² [ˈvɜːdʒɪnəl] *n Mus* virginal *m*

virginity [vəˈdʒɪnɪtɪ] *n* virginidad *f*

Virgo [ˈvɜːgəʊ] *n Astrol Astron* Virgo *m*

virile [ˈvɪraɪl] *adj* viril, varonil

virility [vɪˈrɪlɪtɪ] *n* virilidad *f*

virtual [ˈvɜːtʃʊəl] *adj* virtual ◻ *Comptr* **v. reality** realidad *f* virtual

virtually [ˈvɜːtʃʊəlɪ] *adv (in effect)* virtualmente, en la práctica; *(almost)* casi; **it's v. impossible** es prácticamente imposible

virtue [ˈvɜːtjuː, ˈvɜːtʃuː] *n* **(a)** *(gen)* virtud *f*; **by v. of** en virtud de; *Prov* **to make a v. of necessity** poner a mal tiempo buena cara **(b)** *(advantage)* ventaja *f*

virtuoso [vɜːtjʊˈəʊzəʊ] *n (pl* **virtuosos** *or* **virtuosi** [vɜːtjʊˈəʊsiː]) *Mus* virtuoso(a) *m,f*

virtuous [ˈvɜːtʃʊəs] *adj* virtuoso(a)

virulence [ˈvɪrʊləns] *n* virulencia *f*

virulent [ˈvɪrʊlənt] *adj* virulento(a)

virus [ˈvaɪrəs] *n (pl* **viruses)** *Med Comptr* virus *m inv* ◻ *Comptr* **v. check** detección *f* de virus; **v. infection** infección *f* viral *o* vírica

Vis, Visc (a) *(abbr* **Viscount)** Vizconde *m* **(b)** *(abbr* **Viscountess)** Vizcondesa *f*

visa [ˈviːzə] *n* visado *m*, *Am* visa *f*

vis-à-vis [viːzɑːˈviː] *prep* **(a)** *(regarding)* respecto a **(b)** *(opposite)* frente a, enfrente de

viscera [ˈvɪsərə] *npl Anat* vísceras *fpl*

visceral [ˈvɪsərəl] *adj* visceral

viscose [ˈvɪskəʊs] *n Tex* viscosa *f*

viscosity [vɪsˈkɒsɪtɪ] *n* viscosidad *f*

viscount [ˈvaɪkaʊnt] *n* vizconde *m*

viscountess [ˈvaɪkaʊntɪs] *n* vizcondesa *f*

viscous [ˈvɪskəs] *adj* viscoso(a)

vise [vaɪs] *n US see* **vice²**

visibility [vɪzɪˈbɪlɪtɪ] *n* visibilidad *f*; **poor v.** escasa visibilidad

visible [ˈvɪzɪbəl] *adj* visible

visibly [ˈvɪzɪblɪ] *adv* visiblemente

vision [ˈvɪʒən] *n* **(a)** *(faculty)* visión *f* **(b)** *(eyesight)* vista *f*; **to have good v.** tener buena vista **; *Fig* tunnel v.** estrechez *f* de miras **(c)** *(apparition)* visión *f*; **to see visions** ver visiones; *Fam* **I had visions of being left homeless** ya me veía sin casa **(d)** *(foresight)* visión *f*, clarividencia *f*; **a man of v.** un hombre con visión de futuro

visionary [ˈvɪʒənərɪ] *n* visionario(a) *m,f*

visit [ˈvɪzɪt] **1** *vt* **(a)** *(person)* visitar, hacer una visita a **(b)** *(place)* visitar, ir a; **we are visiting the town** estamos de visita en la ciudad
2 *n* visita *f*; **he's on a v. to France** se ha ido de viaje a Francia; **to pay sb a v.** ir a ver a algn; **official v.** visita oficial; *Fam* **flying v.** visita relámpago

visitation [vɪzɪˈteɪʃən] *n* **(a)** *(visit)* visita *f* oficial **(b)** *Rel* **the V.** la Visitación

visiting [ˈvɪzɪtɪŋ] *adj* **(a)** *(for visiting)* de visita ◻ *Br* **v. card** tarjeta *f* de visita; *Med* **v. hours** horas *fpl* de visita **(b)** *(guest)* visitante ◻ *Sport* **v. team** equipo *m* visitante; *Univ* **v. lecturer** profesor(a) *(m,f)* invitado(a)

visitor [ˈvɪzɪtər] *n* **(a)** *(guest)* invitado(a) *m,f*; **we've got visitors** tenemos visita **(b)** *(in hotel)* cliente(a) *m,f* **(c)** *(tourist)* turista *mf*, visitante *mf*; **visitors to our city** los visitantes de nuestra ciudad **(d)** *Br Med* **health v.** enfermera *f* visitante

visor [ˈvaɪzər] *n* visera *f*

vista [ˈvɪstə] *n* vista *f*, panorama *m*; *Fig* perspectiva *f*, horizonte *m*

visual [ˈvɪʒʊəl, ˈvɪzjʊəl] *adj* **(a)** *(gen)* visual ◻ *Educ* **v. aids** medios *mpl* visuales; **v. arts** artes *mpl* visuales **(b)** *(optical)* ocular

visualize [ˈvɪʒʊəlaɪz, ˈvɪzjʊəlaɪz] *vt* **(a)** *(imagine)* imaginar, imaginarse, plantearse **(b)** *(foresee)* prever

visually [ˈvɪʒʊəlɪ] *adv* visualmente; **the v. handicapped** las personas con discapacidades visuales

vital [ˈvaɪtəl] *adj* **(a)** *(gen)* vital ◻ *Med* **v. function** función *f* vital **(b)** *(lively)* vital, vivo(a), enérgico(a) **(c)** *(essential)* fundamental, indispensable; **of v. importance** de suma importancia **(d)** *(decisive)* decisivo(a), clave ◻ **v. statistics** *(data)* datos *mpl* demográficos; *Fam* medidas *fpl (del cuerpo de la mujer)*

vitalist [ˈvaɪtəlɪst] *adj & n* vitalista *(mf)*

vitality [vaɪˈtælɪtɪ] *n* vitalidad *f*

vitalize [ˈvaɪtəlaɪz] *vt* vitalizar

vitally [ˈvaɪtəlɪ] *adv* sumamente; **it's v. important** es de suma importancia

vitamin [ˈvɪtəmɪn, *US* ˈvaɪtəmɪn] *n* vitamina *f*; **with added vitamins** vitaminado(a) ◻ **v. B** vitamina *f* B; **v. content** contenido *m* vitamínico; **v. deficiency** avitaminosis *f inv*

vitiate [ˈvɪʃɪeɪt] *vt* viciar

vitreous [ˈvɪtrɪəs] *adj* vítreo(a)

vitriol [ˈvɪtrɪɒl] *n Chem* vitriolo *m*

vitriolic [vɪtrɪˈɒlɪk] *adj* **(a)** *Chem* vitriólico(a) **(b)** *Fig* virulento(a), mordaz

vituperative [vɪˈtjuːpərətɪv] *adj Fml* injurioso(a)

viva [ˈvaɪvə] *n Br Univ (abbr* **viva voce)** examen *m* oral

vivacious [vɪˈveɪʃəs] *adj* vivaz, animado(a)

vivaciousness [vɪˈveɪʃəsnɪs] *n*, **vivacity** [vɪˈvæsɪtɪ] *n* viveza *f*, vivacidad *f*

vivid [ˈvɪvɪd] *adj* **(a)** *(bright, lively)* vivo(a), intenso(a) **(b)** *(graphic)* gráfico(a), realista

vividly [ˈvɪvɪdlɪ] *adv (remember, describe)* vívidamente

vividness [ˈvɪvɪdnɪs] *n* viveza *f*

viviparous [vɪˈvɪpərəs] *adj Biol* vivíparo(a)

vivisection [vɪvɪˈsekʃən] *n* vivisección *f*

vixen [ˈvɪksən] *n* **(a)** *Zool* zorra *f* **(b)** *Fig* arpía *f*

viz [vɪz] *(abbr* **videlicet)** (namely), a saber, es decir

V-neck(ed) [ˈviːnek(t)] *adj* de (cuello de) pico

VOA [viːəʊˈeɪ] *n (abbr* **Voice of America)** = cadena de radio exterior estadounidense

vocabulary [vəˈkæbjʊlərɪ] *n* vocabulario *m*, léxico *m*

vocal [ˈvəʊkəl] *adj* **(a)** *(gen)* vocal ◻ *Anat* **v. cords** cuerdas *fpl* vocales **(b)** *(noisy)* ruidoso(a), chillón(ona)

vocalist [ˈvəʊkəlɪst] *n* cantante *mf*, vocalista *mf*

vocalize [ˈvəʊkəlaɪz] **1** *vt* vocalizar
2 *vi Ling* vocalizarse

vocation [vəʊˈkeɪʃən] *n* vocación *f*; **to miss one's v.** errar la vocación

vocational [vəʊ'keɪʃənəl] *adj* profesional; **v. guidance** orientación *f* profesional

vocative ['vɒkətɪv] *adj & n Ling* vocativo(a) *(m)*

vociferate [vəʊ'sɪfəreɪt] *vi* vociferar

vociferous [vəʊ'sɪfərəs] *adj* **(a)** *(vehement)* vociferador(a), vociferante **(b)** *(noisy)* ruidoso(a), clamoroso(a)

vociferously [vəʊ'sɪfərəslɪ] *adv* a gritos, a voces

vodka ['vɒdkə] *n* vodka *m or f*

vogue [vəʊg] *n* boga *f*, moda *f*; **to be in v.** estar de moda, estar en boga

voice [vɔɪs] **1** *n* **(a)** *(of person)* voz *f*; **in a loud/low v.** en voz alta/baja; **to lose one's v.** quedarse afónico(a); **to raise one's v.** levantar la voz; *Fig* **at the top of one's v.** a voz en grito; *Fig* **to give v. to an opinion** expresar una opinión ❑ *Comptr* **v. recognition** reconocimiento *m* de voz **(b)** *Ling* voz *f*
2 *vt* **(a)** *(express)* expresar **(b)** *Ling* sonorizar

voiced [vɔɪst] *adj Ling* sonoro(a)

voiceless ['vɔɪslɪs] *adj* **(a)** *(hoarse)* afónico(a) **(b)** *Ling* sordo(a)

voice-over [vɔɪs'əʊvər] *n Cin TV* voz *f* en off

void [vɔɪd] **1** *adj* **(a)** *(empty)* vacío(a); *(post)* vacante **(b)** *Jur* nulo(a), inválido(a); **to make a contract v.** anular un contrato
2 *n* vacío *m*

vol (a) *(pl* **vols)** *(abbr* **volume)** tomo *m*, t.; **a 3 v. edition** una edición en tres tomos **(b)** *(abbr* **volume)** volumen *m*, cantidad *f*, vol

volatile ['vɒlətaɪl] *adj* volátil

volcanic [vɒl'kænɪk] *adj* volcánico(a)

volcano [vɒl'keɪnəʊ] *n (pl* **volcanos** *or* **volcanoes)** volcán *m*

volcanology [vɒlkə'nɒlədʒɪ] *n* vulcanología *f*

vole [vəʊl] *n Zool* campañol *m*, ratón *m* campestre

volition [və'lɪʃən] *n Fml* volición *f*; **of** *or* **on one's own v.** por voluntad propia

volley ['vɒlɪ] **1** *n* **(a)** *(of shots)* descarga *f* **(b)** *Fig (of stones, insults)* lluvia *f* **(c)** *Ten* volea *f*
2 *vi Mil* lanzar una descarga
3 *vt Ten* volear

volleyball ['vɒlɪbɔːl] *n Sport* balonvolea *m*, voleibol *m*

volt [vəʊlt] *n Elec* voltio *m*

voltage ['vəʊltɪdʒ] *n Elec* voltaje *m*

volte-face [vɒlt'fɑːs] *n inv Literary* cambio *m* de opinión

voltmeter ['vəʊltmiːtər] *n* voltímetro *m*

volubility [vɒljʊ'bɪlɪtɪ] *n* locuacidad *f*

voluble ['vɒljʊbəl] *adj* locuaz, hablador(a)

volume ['vɒljuːm] *n* **(a)** *Phys* volumen *m* **(b)** *(amount)* volumen *m*, cantidad *f* **(c)** *Rad TV* volumen *m*; **to turn up/down the v.** subir/bajar el volumen **(d)** *(book)* volumen *m*, tomo *m*; *Fig* **to speak volumes** decirlo todo

voluminous [və'luːmɪnəs] *adj* voluminoso(a)

voluntarily [vɒlʌn'teərɪlɪ] *adv* voluntariamente

voluntary ['vɒləntərɪ] *adj* voluntario(a) ❑ **v. organization** organización *f* benéfica; **v. work** obras *fpl* benéficas; **v. worker** voluntario(a) *mf*

volunteer [vɒlən'tɪər] **1** *n* voluntario(a) *m,f* ❑ *Mil* **v. army** ejército *m* de voluntarios
2 *vt (help etc)* ofrecer; **to v. information** facilitar datos
3 *vi* ofrecerse (voluntariamente) **(for** para); *Mil* alistarse como voluntario(a); **she volunteered to do the washing up** se ofreció para lavar los platos

voluptuous [və'lʌptjʊəs] *adj* voluptuoso(a)

voluptuousness [və'lʌptjʊəsnɪs] *n* voluptuosidad *f*

vomit ['vɒmɪt] **1** *vt & vi* vomitar, devolver
2 *n* vómito *m*

voodoo ['vuːduː] *n (pl* **voodoos)** vudú *m*

voracious [vɒ'reɪʃəs] *adj* voraz

voraciousness [vɒ'reɪʃəsnɪs] *n,* **voracity** [vɒ'ræsɪtɪ] *n* voracidad *f*

vortex ['vɔːteks] *n (pl* **vortexes** *or* **vortices** ['vɔːtɪsiːz]) vórtice *m*; *Fig* vorágine *f*

votary ['vəʊtərɪ] *n* **(a)** *Rel* devoto(a) *m,f* **(b)** *(adherent)* partidario(a) *m,f*

vote [vəʊt] **1** *n* **(a)** *(choice)* voto *m*; **by a majority v.** por mayoría de votos **(b)** *(voting)* votación *f*; **to take a v. on sth** someter algo a votación; **v. of censure** voto *m* de censura; **v. of confidence** voto de confianza; **write-in v.** votación por escrito **(c)** *(right to vote)* derecho *m* al voto *or* de votar
2 *vt* **(a)** *(in ballot)* votar; **they voted to adjourn the meeting** votaron que se suspendiera la reunión; **to v. sb into office** elegir a algn para un cargo **(b)** *(elect)* elegir; **she was voted president** fue elegida presidenta **(c)** *Fam* proponer
3 *vi (gen)* votar; **to v. by a show of hands** votar a mano alzada; **to v. Communist** votar comunista; **to v. for sb** votar por algn; **to v. on sth** someter algo a votación

voter ['vəʊtər] *n* votante *mf*

voting ['vəʊtɪŋ] *n* votación *f* ❑ **v. booth** cabina *f* electoral; **v. paper** papeleta *f*; **v. pattern** tendencia *f* del voto

votive ['vəʊtɪv] *adj Rel* votivo(a)

vouch [vaʊtʃ] **1** *vi* **to v. for sth/sb** responder de algo/por algn
2 *vt* asegurar, garantizar

voucher ['vaʊtʃər] *n* **(a)** *(document)* comprobante *m* **(b)** *Br* vale *m* ❑ **luncheon v.** vale *m* de comida

vow [vaʊ] **1** *n Rel* voto *m*; **v. of chastity** voto de castidad; **v. of poverty** voto de pobreza; **to take one's vows** pronunciar sus votos
2 *vt* jurar; **to v. obedience** jurar obediencia; **to v. that ...** jurar que ...

vowel ['vaʊəl] *n Ling* vocal *f*; **v. sound** sonido *m* vocálico

voyage ['vɔɪdʒ] *n (gen)* viaje *m*; *(by sea)* viaje en barco; *(crossing)* travesía *f*; **maiden v.** viaje inaugural; **to go on a v.** hacer un viaje en barco

voyager ['vɔɪdʒər] *n* viajero(a) *m,f*

voyeur [vɔɪ'jɜːr] *n* voyeur *mf*

VP *(abbr* **Vice President)** Vicepresidente(a) *m,f*

V-sign ['viːsaɪn] *n* **(a)** *(of victory)* señal *f* de la victoria **(b)** *Br (as insult)* corte *m* de mangas

VSO [viːes'əʊ] *n Br (abbr* **Voluntary Service Overseas)**

VTOL [viːtiːəʊ'el] *n Av (abbr* **vertical take-off and landing (aircraft))** despegue *m* y aterrizaje vertical

VTR [viːtiː'ɑːr] *n (abbr* **video tape recorder)** (aparato *m* de) vídeo *m or Am* video *m*

vulcanize ['vʌlkənaɪz] *vt Tech* vulcanizar

vulcanology [vʌlkə'nɒlədʒɪ] *n see* **volcanology**

vulgar ['vʌlgər] *adj* **(a)** *(coarse)* vulgar, ordinario(a), grosero(a); *(in poor taste)* de mal gusto; **don't be v.!** ¡no seas grosero! **(b)** *Ling* vulgar; **v. Latin** latín vulgar **(c)** *Math* **v. fraction** fracción *f* común

vulgarism ['vʌlgərɪzəm] *n Ling* vulgarismo *m*

vulgarity [vʌl'gærɪtɪ] *n (coarseness)* vulgaridad *f*, ordinariez *f*, grosería *f*; *(poor taste)* mal gusto *m*

vulgarize ['vʌlgəraɪz] *vt* **(a)** *(debase)* degradar **(b)** *(popularize)* vulgarizar

vulnerability [vʌlnərə'bɪlɪtɪ] *n* vulnerabilidad *f*

vulnerable ['vʌlnərəbəl] *adj* vulnerable

vulture ['vʌltʃər] *n Orn* buitre *m* ❑ **bearded v.** quebrantahuesos *m inv*

vulva ['vʌlvə] *n (pl* **vulvas** *or* **vulvae** ['vʌlviː]) *Anat* vulva *f*

W, w [ˈdʌbəljuː] *n (the letter)* W, w *f*

W (**a**) *(abbr* **West)** Oeste, O (**b**) *Elec (abbr* **Watt(s))** vatio(s) *m(pl)*, W

wacky [ˈwæki] *adj* (**wackier, wackiest**) *US Fam (person)* chiflado(a), chalado(a); *(thing)* absurdo(a)

wad [wɒd] **1** *n (of paper)* taco *m*; *(of cotton wool)* bolita *f*; *Med* tapón *m*; *(of banknotes)* fajo *m*
  2 *vt (pt & pp* **wadded)** rellenar, acolchar

wadding [ˈwɒdɪŋ] *n* relleno *m*

waddle [ˈwɒdəl] *vi* caminar *or Esp* andar como un pato

wade [weɪd] *vi* caminar en el agua; **to w. across a river** vadear un río

wade through *vt (water)* caminar por; *Fig* **I'm wading through the book** me cuesta mucho terminar el libro

wader [ˈweɪdər] *n* (**a**) *Orn* ave *f* zancuda (**b**) **waders** botas *fpl* de pescador

wafer [ˈweɪfər] *n Culin* barquillo *m*; *Rel* hostia *f*; *(for sealing)* oblea *f*

wafer-thin [ˈweɪfəθɪn] *adj* (**a**) *(slice)* muy fino(a); **to cut sth w.-t.** cortar algo en lonchas muy finas (**b**) *Fig (majority)* escasísimo(a)

waffle¹ [ˈwɒfəl] *n Culin Esp* gofre *m*, *Am* wafle *m*

waffle² [ˈwɒfəl] *Br Fam* **1** *vi* meter mucha paja; **to w. on** parlotear
  2 *n* paja *f*, *Am* palabrerío *m*

waft [wɑːft, wɒft] **1** *vt (sound, smell)* llevar por el aire
  2 *vi (sound, scent)* flotar (por *o* en el aire)

wag¹ [wæg] **1** *vt (pt & pp* **wagged)** *(tail, finger)* menear
  2 *vi (tail)* menearse; *Fam* **tongues will w.** van a chismorrear
  3 *n* meneo *m*; **with a w. of its tail** meneando la cola

wag² [wæg] *n Fam (wit)* bromista *mf*, guasón(ona) *m,f*

wage [weɪdʒ] **1** *n (also* **wages)** salario *m*, sueldo *m*; **basic/minimum w.** salario base/mínimo □ **w. claim** reivindicación *f* salarial; **w. earner** asalariado(a) *m,f*
  2 *vt (campaign)* realizar (**against** contra); **to w. war** hacer la guerra (**on** a)

wage-packet [ˈweɪdʒpækɪt] *n* sueldo *m*

wager [ˈweɪdʒər] *Fml* **1** *n* apuesta *f*
  2 *vt* apostar

waggish [ˈwægɪʃ] *adj* burlón(ona), bromista

waggle [ˈwægəl] **1** *vt (ears etc)* menear
  2 *vi* menearse

wa(g)gon [ˈwægən] *n (horse-drawn)* carro *m*; *(lorry)* camión *m*, furgón *m*; *Br Rail* vagón *m*; **covered w.** carromato *m*; **goods w.** vagón de mercancías; *Fam* **to go on the w.** dejar la bebida

wagtail [ˈwægteɪl] *n Orn* lavandera *f* □ **grey w.** lavandera *f* cascadeña; **white w.** lavandera *f* blanca

waif [weɪf] *n* niño(a) *m,f* desamparado(a)

wail [weɪl] **1** *n* (**a**) *(of sorrow)* lamento *m*, gemido *m*, plañido *m* (**b**) *(of siren)* aullido *m*
  2 *vi* (**a**) *(person)* lamentar, gemir, plañir (**b**) *(siren)* aullar, ulular

wailing [ˈweɪlɪŋ] **1** *adj* gemidor(a)
  2 *n* lamentaciones *fpl*, gemidos *mpl* □ **W. Wall** Muro *m* de *Esp* las Lamentaciones *or Am* los Lamentos

waist [weɪst] *n Anat* cintura *f*; *Sew* talle *m*

waistband [ˈweɪstbænd] *n* cinturilla *f*

waistcoat [ˈweɪstkəʊt] *n Br* chaleco *m*

waistline [ˈweɪstlaɪn] *n Anat* cintura *f*; *Sew* talle *m*

wait [weɪt] **1** *n* espera *f*; *(delay)* demora *f*; **to lie in w.** estar al acecho; **we had a long w.** tuvimos que esperar mucho tiempo
  2 *vt* (**a**) *(wait for)* esperar; **to wait one's turn** esperar su turno (**b**) *US (serve at)* **to w. table(s)** servir mesas
  3 *vi* (**a**) *(in general)* esperar, aguardar; **I can't w. to see her** me muero de ganas de verla; **let's w. and see** esperemos a ver qué pasa; **repairs while you w.** reparaciones en el acto; **to keep sb waiting** hacer esperar a algn; **to w. for sth** esperar algo; **w. a moment!** ¡un momento! (**b**) *Br (serve)* **to w. at table** servir mesas

wait about, wait around *vi* esperar, perder el tiempo

wait on *vt* servir; **to w. on sb hand and foot** tratar a algn a cuerpo de rey

wait up *vi Br* **to w. up for sb** esperar a algn levantado(a)

waiter [ˈweɪtər] *n* camarero *m*, *Andes RP* mozo *m*, *Chile Ven* mesonero *m*, *Col Guat Méx Salv* mesero *m*

waiting [ˈweɪtɪŋ] *n* espera *f*; *Br Aut* **no w.** *(sign)* prohibido aparcar; **to play a w. game** esperar el momento oportuno □ **w. list** lista *f* de espera; **w. room** sala *f* de espera

waitress [ˈweɪtrɪs] *n* camarera *f*, *Andes RP* moza *f*, *Chile Ven* mesonera *f*, *Col Guat Méx Salv* mesera *f*

waive [weɪv] *vt Fml (demand, rights)* abdicar, renunciar a; *(rule)* no aplicar

wake¹ [weɪk] **1** *vt (pt* **woke**; *pp* **woken) to w. sb (up)** despertar a algn
  2 *vi* **w. (up)** despertar(se); *Fig* **to w. up to the truth** darse cuenta de la verdad; *Fig* **w. up!** ¡despierta!, ¡despabílate!
  3 *n Ir (for dead)* velatorio *m*, *Am* velorio *m*

wake² [weɪk] *n (in water)* estela *f*; *Fig* **in the w. of the storm** tras la tormenta; *Fig* **to leave chaos in one's w.** dejar una estela de caos

wakeful [ˈweɪkfʊl] *adj* (**a**) *(sleepless)* desvelado(a); **to have a w. night** pasar la noche en blanco (**b**) *Fml (alert)* vigilante, alerta

waken ['weɪkən] *vt Literary* despertar

wakey ['weɪkɪ] *interj Fam* **w.!, w.!** ¡despierta!, ¡arriba!

waking ['weɪkɪŋ] *adj* de vigilia, sin dormir; **w. hours** horas *fpl* que uno pasa despierto, horas *fpl* de vigilia

Wales [weɪlz] *n* (el país de) Gales; **the Prince of W.** el príncipe de Gales

walk [wɔːk] **1** *n* (**a**) *(long)* caminata *m*; *(short)* paseo *m*; **it's an hour's w.** está a una hora de camino; **to go for a w.** dar un paseo, pasear; **to slow down to a w.** aflojar el paso; **to take the dog for a w.** sacar a pasear al perro (**b**) *(gait)* modo *m* de caminar *or* andar, andares *mpl* (**c**) *(avenue)* paseo *m* (**d**) *(sphere)* **people from all walks of life** gente *f* de toda condición

2 *vt* (**a**) *(cover on foot)* caminar, *Esp* andar; **to w. it** ir a pie; *Fam* ganar fácil; **to w. the streets** callejear; *Euph (prostitute)* hacer la carrera; **we walked her home** la acompañamos a casa (**b**) *(dog)* pasear; *(horse)* llevar al paso; **he walked me off my feet** me agotó a fuerza de pasear

3 *vi* (**a**) *(move on foot)* caminar, *Esp* andar; *US* **w. (sign)** = señal que autoriza a los peatones a cruzar (**b**) *(go on foot)* ir caminando *or Esp* andando, ir a pie; **I had to w. home** tuve que volver a casa a pie

walk about *vi* ir y venir, pasear

walk across 1 *vt* atravesar
2 *vi* acercarse; **to w. across to sb** abordar a algn

walk away *vi* irse (caminando *or Esp* andando); *Fig* **she walked away from the crash** salió ilesa del choque; *Fig* **to w. away with a prize** llevarse un premio

walk down *vt (stairs)* bajar; *(street)* bajar por

walk into *vt* (**a**) *(place)* entrar en; *Fig (trap)* caer en (**b**) *(bump into)* tropezar con (**c**) *Fig* **to w. into a job** encontrar un trabajo sin esfuerzo alguno

walk off *vi (steal, win easily)* **to w. off with sth** llevarse algo

walk on *vi Theat* salir a escena

walk out *vi* salir; *Ind* declararse en huelga; **to w. out of a meeting** abandonar una reunión en señal de protesta; **to w. out on sb** abandonar a algn

walk over 1 *vt Fam* **to w. all over sb** tratar a algn a patadas
2 *vi* acercarse; **to w. over to sb** abordar a algn

walk up 1 *vt (stairs)* subir; *(street)* subir por
2 *vi* acercarse; **to w. up to sb** abordar a algn; **to w. up and down** andar *or* pasear de un lado para otro

walkabout ['wɔːkəbaʊt] *n (by Queen, President, etc)* paseo *m* informal entre la gente

walker ['wɔːkər] *n* paseante *mf*; *Sport* marchador(a) *m,f*; **he's a fast w.** anda deprisa

walkie-talkie [wɔːkɪ'tɔːkɪ] *n Rad* walkie-talkie *m*

walk-in cupboard ['wɔːkɪn'kʌbəd] *n (for clothes)* armario *m* vestidor; *(for food)* despensa *f*

walking ['wɔːkɪŋ] **1** *n* **I like w.** me gusta caminar *or Esp* andar
2 *adj* **at w. pace** a paso de marcha; *Fam Fig* **he's a w. encyclopaedia** es una enciclopedia ambulante ❏ **w. boots** botas *fpl* de senderismo; **w. stick** bastón *m*; **w. tour** excursión *f* a pie

Walkman® ['wɔːkmən] *n (pl* **Walkmans)** walkman® *m*

walk-on ['wɔːkɒn] *adj Theat* **w.-o. part** papel *m* de figurante *or* comparsa

walkout ['wɔːkaʊt] *n Ind* huelga *f*

walkover ['wɔːkəʊvər] *n* triunfo *m* fácil; **it was a w.** fue un paseo *or* pan comido

walk-up ['wɔːkʌp] *n US* casa *m* sin ascensor

walkway ['wɔːkweɪ] *n esp US* paso *m* de peatones

wall [wɔːl] *n* (**a**) *(freestanding, exterior)* muro *m*; **the Berlin W.** el muro de Berlín; *Fig* **a w. of flame** una cortina de llamas; *Fig* **a w. of silence** un muro de silencio; *Fig* **to form a human w.** formar una pared humana; *Com* quebrar; *Fig* **to have one's back to the w.** estar entre la espada y la pared; *Fam Fig* **it's driving me up the w.** me está volviendo loco ❏ **cavity w.** muro *m* doble; **city w.** muralla *f*; **garden w.** tapia *f*; **sea w.** dique *m* (**b**) *(interior)* pared *f*; **partition w.** tabique *m*; **party w.** pared medianera; *Fam Fig* **I'm banging my head against a brick w.** es para darse contra las paredes ❏ **w. lamp** aplique *m*; **w. map** mapa *m* mural; **w. unit** módulo *m* de estantería (**c**) *(of cave, rock)* pared *f* (**d**) *Anat* **abdominal w.** pared *f* abdominal (**e**) *Ftb* barrera *f*

wall in *vt* tapiar, cercar con tapia

wall off *vt* amurallar, aislar *or* separar con pared

wall up *vt* tapiar; *(door, fireplace)* condenar

wallaby ['wɒləbɪ] *n (pl* **wallaby** *or* **wallabies)** *Zool* ualabí *m*

walled [wɔːld] *adj (city)* amurallado(a); *(garden)* cercado(a) con tapia

wallet ['wɒlɪt] *n* cartera *f*

wallflower ['wɔːlflaʊər] *n* (**a**) *Bot* alhelí *m* (**b**) *(person) Fam* **to be a w.** ser un invitado de piedra

Walloon [wɒ'luːn] **1** *adj* valón(ona)
2 *n (person)* valón(ona) *m,f*; *(language)* valón *m*

wallop ['wɒləp] *Fam* **1** *n* tortazo *m*, golpetazo *m*, *Méx* madrazo *m*
2 *vt* (**a**) *(hit)* pegar fuerte (**b**) *(defeat)* dar una paliza a

walloping ['wɒləpɪŋ] *n Fam (beating, defeat)* paliza *f*

wallow ['wɒləʊ] *vi (animal)* revolcarse (**en** in); **to w. in the mud** revolcarse en el lodo; *Fig* **to w. in self-pity** sumirse en la lástima de sí mismo(a)

wallpaper ['wɔːlpeɪpər] **1** *n (on walls)* papel *m* pintado; *Comptr* papel *m* tapiz
2 *vt (decorate)* empapelar

wall-to-wall [wɔːltə'wɔːl] *adj* **w.-to-w. carpeting** *Esp* moqueta *f*, *Am* alfombra *f*

wally [wɒːli] *n Br Fam* idiota *mf*, inútil *mf*

walnut ['wɔːlnʌt] *n Bot (fruit)* nuez *f*; *(tree, wood)* nogal *m* ❏ **black walnut** nogal *m* negro; **common w.** nogal *m*

walrus ['wɔːlrəs] *n Zool* morsa *f*

waltz [wɔːls] *Mus* **1** *n* vals *m*
2 *vi* valsar; *Fam Fig* **to w. in/out** entrar/salir con desenvoltura; *Fam Fig* **to w. off with sth** llevarse algo como si tal cosa

WAN [wæn] *n Comptr (abbr* **wide area network)** red *f* de área extensa

wan [wɒn] *adj* (**wanner, wannest)** *(face)* pálido(a); *(look, smile)* apagado(a); *(light)* macilento(a)

wand [wɒnd] *n* **(magic) w.** varita *f* (mágica)

wander ['wɒndər] **1** *n* paseo *m*, vuelta *f*; **to go for a w.** dar una vuelta
2 *vt* **to w. the streets** vagar por las calles
3 *vi* (**a**) *(aimlessly)* vagar, errar; **to w. about** deambular; **to w. in/out** entrar/salir sin prisas; **to w. off on one's own** apartarse para estar solo(a) (**b**) *(stray)* desviarse, apartarse; *(mind)* divagar; **his glance wandered round the room** recorrió el cuarto con la mirada; **to let one's thoughts w.** dejar vagar la imaginación

wanderer ['wɒndərər] *n* andariego(a) *m,f*; *(traveller)* viajero(a) *m,f*; *(nomad)* nómada *mf*

wandering ['wɒndərɪŋ] **1** *adj* errante, errabundo(a); *(tribe)* nómada; *(minstrel)* ambulante; *(speech)* divagador(a) ❏ *Bot* **w. Jew** tradescantia *f*

2 wanderings *npl* **(a)** *(travels)* andanzas *fpl*, viajes *mpl* **(b)** *(of mind, speech)* divagaciones *fpl*

wane [weɪn] **1** *vi (moon)* menguar; *Fig (strength, influence)* menguar, decrecer; *(interest)* decaer, decrecer; *(light)* mermar

2 *n* **to be on the w.** *(moon, strength)* estar menguando; *(power)* estar en decadencia

wangle ['wæŋgəl] *vt Fam* agenciarse; **she'll w. it somehow** se las amañará de algún modo; **to w. a free ticket** pillar una invitación

waning ['weɪnɪŋ] *adj (moon)* menguante; *Fig* decadente, decreciente

wank [wæŋk] *Br Slang* **1** *n* paja *f*

2 *vi* hacerse una *or Am* la paja

wanker ['wæŋkər] *n Br Slang Esp* gilipollas *mf inv, Am* pendejo(a) *m,f, RP* pelotudo(a) *m,f*

want [wɒnt] **1** *n* **(a)** *(lack)* falta *f*, carencia *f*; **for w. of anything better to do** a falta de algo mejor que hacer; **it wasn't for w. of trying** no fue por falta de esfuerzos **(b)** *(poverty)* indigencia *f*, miseria *f*

2 *vt* **(a)** *(desire)* querer, desear; **do you w. a cigarette?** ¿quieres un pitillo?; **I know when I'm not wanted** sé cuando estoy de más; **it's just what I w.** es exactamente lo que quiero; **she wants a bike for her birthday** pide *or* quiere una bicicleta para su cumpleaños; **what more do you w.?** ¿qué más quieres? **(b)** *(wish)* **I don't w.** to no quiero; **I don't w. you making a noise** no quiero que hagas ruido; **to w. to do sth** querer/desear hacer algo; **you can say what you w.** puedes decir lo que quieras **(c)** *Fam (need)* necesitar; **he wants a good talking-to** no le vendría mal un fuerte rapapolvo; **the grass wants cutting** hace falta cortar el césped **(d)** *(seek)* buscar; **'cook wanted'** 'se necesita cocinero(a)'; **he is wanted by the police** le busca la policía; **you're wanted on the phone** te llaman al teléfono

want for *vt* carecer de; **they w. for nothing** lo tienen todo

want out *vi Fam* querer dejarlo; **he'd had enough and wanted out** estaba harto y quería dejarlo

wanted ['wɒntɪd] *adj* **(a)** *(necessary)* necesario(a) **(b)** *(by police)* buscado(a)

wanting ['wɒntɪŋ] *adj* **(a)** *(missing)* **to be w.** faltar; **she is w. in tact** le falta tacto **(b)** *(deficient, short)* deficiente (**in** en); **he was found w.** no daba la talla

wanton ['wɒntən] *adj* **(a)** *(motiveless)* sin motivo, sin sentido; **w. cruelty** crueldad *f* inmotivada *or* gratuita **(b)** *(person) (unrestrained)* desenfrenado(a); *(licentious)* lascivo(a)

WAP [wæp] *n Comptr (abbr* **Wireless Application Protocol)** WAP *m* **W. phone** teléfono *m* WAP

war [wɔːr] *n* guerra *f*; **between the wars** en el período de entreguerras; **to be at w.** estar en guerra (**with** con); **to go to w.** emprender la guerra (**over** por); *Fig* **to declare/wage w.** declarar/hacer la guerra; *Hum* **you seem to have been in the wars** te noto bastante maltrecho ❑ **cold w.** guerra *f* fría; **w. criminal** criminal *mf* de guerra; **w. games** *Mil* ejercicios *mpl* de simulacro de combate; *(games)* juegos *mpl* de estrategia militar; **w. memorial** monumento *m* a los caídos; **w. of nerves** guerra *f* de nervios

warble ['wɔːbəl] **1** *n* gorjeo *m*

2 *vi* gorjear

warbler ['wɔːblər] *n Orn* pájaro *m* cantor, ave *f* cantora ❑ **reed w.** carricero *m* común; **willow w.** mosquitero *m* musical; **wood w.** mosquitero *m* silbador

warbling ['wɔːblɪŋ] *n* gorjeo *m*, trinos *mpl*

ward [wɔːd] *n* **(a)** *(of hospital)* sala *f* **(b)** *Jur* pupilo(a) *m,f* ❑ **w. of court** pupilo(a) *m,f* bajo tutela judicial **(c)** *Br Pol* distrito *m* electoral

ward off *vt (blow)* parar, desviar; *(attack)* rechazar; *(danger)* evitar; *(illness)* prevenir

warden ['wɔːdən] *n (of residence)* guardián(ana) *m,f*, encargado(a) *m,f*; *US (of prison)* director(a) *m,f*, alcaide(esa) *m,f* ❑ **game w.** guarda *mf* de caza; *Br* **traffic w.** guardia *m* urbano

warder ['wɔːdər] *n Br* carcelero(a) *m,f*

wardrobe ['wɔːdrəʊb] *n* **(a)** *Furn* armario *m*, ropero *m* **(b)** *(clothes)* guardarropa *m*; **she has a large w.** tiene un vestuario muy amplio **(c)** *Theat* vestuario *m*

wardroom ['wɔːdruːm] *n Naut* cámara *f* de oficiales

wardship ['wɔːdʃɪp] *n Jur* tutela *f*

warehouse ['weəhaʊs] *n* almacén *m*, depósito *m*

wares [weəz] *npl* mercancías *fpl*

warfare ['wɔːfeər] *n* guerra *f*; **germ w.** guerra bacteriológica; *Fig* **class w.** lucha *f* de clases

warhead ['wɔːhed] *n* **(nuclear) w.** cabeza *f* or ojiva *f* nuclear

warhorse ['wɔːhɔːs] *n Fig* **an old w.** un(a) veterano(a)

warlike ['wɔːlaɪk] *adj* belicoso(a), guerrero(a)

warlord ['wɔːlɔːd] *n* señor *m* de la guerra

warm [wɔːm] **1** *adj* **(a)** *(water)* tibio(a), templado(a); *(hands)* caliente; *(wind, climate)* cálido(a); **a w. day** un día caluroso *or* de calor; **I am w.** *(disagreeably)* tengo calor, *(rather than cold)* ya he entrado en calor; **it is (very) w. today** hoy hace (mucho) calor; **keep w.** abrígate; **this coffee is only w.** este café está templado; **to get w.** calentarse; **to keep sth w.** mantener algo caliente; **w. clothing** ropa de abrigo; *Fig (riddles)* **you're getting w.** ¡caliente, caliente! **(b)** *(welcome, applause)* cálido(a)

2 *n Fam* **to sit in the w.** sentarse al calor

3 *vt* calentar; *Fig* alegrar; **to w. one's hands** calentarse las manos

4 *vi* calentarse; *Fig* **to w. to an idea** (empezar a) entusiasmarse con una idea; **to w. to sb** cogerle simpatía a algn

warm up 1 *vt* **(a)** *(room, engine)* calentar; *(soup)* (re)calentar; *(person)* hacer entrar en calor **(b)** *Fig (audience etc)* animar

2 *vi* **(a)** *(room, engine)* calentarse; *(food)* (re)calentarse; *(person)* entrar en calor **(b)** *(athlete)* hacer ejercicios de calentamiento; *(performer)* ambientarse **(c)** *Fig (audience, party)* animarse

warm-blooded [wɔːm'blʌdɪd] *adj* de sangre caliente

warm-hearted [wɔːm'hɑːtɪd] *adj* afectuoso(a), bondadoso(a)

warmly ['wɔːmlɪ] *adv Fig* calurosamente; *(thank)* con efusión; *(recommend)* con entusiasmo

warmonger ['wɔːmʌŋgər] *n* belicista *mf*

warmth [wɔːmθ] *n (heat)* calor *m*; *Fig* cordialidad *f*

warm-up ['wɔːmʌp] *n Sport* (ejercicios *mpl* de) calentamiento *m*; **a w.-up match** un partido de preparación

warn [wɔːn] *vt* avisar (**of** de), advertir, prevenir (**about** sobre; **against** contra); **he warned me not to go** *or* **against going** me advirtió que no fuera; **the policeman warned me for speeding** el policía me amonestó por exceso de velocidad; **to w. sb that** advertir a algn que, prevenir a algn de que; **you've been warned!** ¡estás avisado!

warn away, warn off *vt* avisar

warning ['wɔːnɪŋ] **1** *adj (glance, shot)* de advertencia, de aviso; *(letter)* admonitorio(a) ❑ *Aut* **w. light** piloto *m*; **w. sign** *(of illness)* síntoma *m*

2 *n* **(a)** *(of danger)* advertencia *f*, aviso *m*; *Meteor* **gale w.** aviso de vientos fuertes; **let this be a w. to you** que esto te sirva de escarmiento **(b)** *(replacing punishment)* amonestación f (**c**) (notice) aviso m; **to give sb fair w.** avisar a algn debidamente; **without w.** sin previo aviso

warp [wɔ:p] **1** n (a) (also **warping**) (of wood) alabeo m (**b**) Tex urdimbre f
 2 vt (**a**) (wood) alabear, combar (**b**) Fig (mind) pervertir, torcer
 3 vi alabearse, combarse

war-paint ['wɔ:peɪnt] n pintura f de guerra

warpath ['wɔ:pɑ:θ] n Fam **to be on the w.** estar con ganas de guerra

warped [wɔ:pt] adj (**a**) (wood) alabeado(a), combado(a) (**b**) (mind, sense of humour) retorcido(a)

warplane ['wɔ:pleɪn] n avión m de combate

warrant ['wɒrənt] **1** n (**a**) Jur mandamiento m or orden f judicial; **there is a w. out for his arrest** se ha ordenado su detención □ **death w.** sentencia f de muerte; **search w.** mandamiento m or orden f de registro; Mil **w. officer** suboficial m (**b**) (authorization note) cédula f; Com bono m, vale m; **w. for payment** libramiento m, orden f de pago □ **travel w.** vale m de viaje
 2 vt (**a**) (justify) justificar (**b**) (guarantee) garantizar; **I w. you** se lo aseguro

warranty ['wɒrəntɪ] n Com garantía f

warren ['wɒrən] n zona f de conejeras; Fig laberinto m

warring ['wɔ:rɪŋ] adj (nations) en guerra; **the w. factions** las facciones opuestas

warrior ['wɒrɪər] n guerrero(a) m,f

Warsaw ['wɔ:sɔ:] n Varsovia

warship ['wɔ:ʃɪp] n buque m or barco m de guerra

wart [wɔ:t] n Med verruga f; Fam **warts and all** con todas sus imperfecciones

wart-hog ['wɔ:thɒg] n jabalí m verrugoso

wartime ['wɔ:taɪm] **1** n tiempos mpl de guerra
 2 adj **w.** economía f de guerra

wary ['weərɪ] adj (**warier**, **wariest**) cauteloso(a), precavido(a), prudente; **to be w. of doing sth** temer or dudar en hacer algo; **to be w. of sth/sb** tener cuidado con algo/ algn recelar de algo/algn

was [wɒz] pt see **be**

wash [wɒʃ] **1** n (**a**) (person) lavado m; (of clothes) lavado m, Esp colada f; **to give sth a w.** lavar algo; **to have a w.** lavarse; Fig **it will all come out in the w.** todo saldrá bien (**b**) (of ship) estela f; (of water) remolinos mpl; (sound) chapoteo m (**c**) (of paint) capa f
 2 vt (**a**) (gen) lavar; (dishes) fregar; **to w. oneself** lavarse; **to w. one's hair** lavarse la cabeza (**b**) (sea, river) llevar; **to w. sth ashore** echar algo a la playa; **he was washed overboard** un golpe de mar le arrojó por la borda
 3 vi (**a**) (person) lavarse; **this material doesn't w. well** esta tela no se lava bien; Fam **that (story) won't wash** eso no colará (**b**) (lap) batir; **the waves washed against the ship** las olas bañaban el navío

wash away vt (of sea) llevarse; (traces) borrar; **he was washed away by the current** fue arrastrado por la corriente

wash down vt (wall etc) lavar; (food) rociar

wash off vi lavarse

wash out 1 vt (bottle) enjuagar; (shirt) dar un lavado rápido a
 2 vi salir, quitarse lavando

wash up 1 vt (**a**) Br (washing-up) fregar (**b**) (of sea) arrojar a la playa (**c**) Fam **to be (all) washed up** estar acabado(a)
 2 vi (**a**) Br fregar los platos (**b**) US (have a wash) lavarse

washable ['wɒʃəbəl] adj lavable

washbasin ['wɒʃbeɪsən] n lavabo m, Am lavamanos m inv

washbowl ['wɒʃbəʊl] n US palangana f, barreño m

washcloth ['wɒʃklɒθ] n US manopla f

washed-out [wɒʃt'aʊt] (**a**) (colours) descolorido(a), desteñido(a) (**b**) Fig (tired) sin energías, agotado(a); (complexion) pálido(a)

washer ['wɒʃər] n (**a**) (machine) lavadora f (**b**) Tech (bolt) arandela f; (on tap) junta f

washer-up [wɒʃər'ʌp] n (pl **washers-up**) Fam friegaplatos mf inv

wash(-)hand basin ['wɒʃhænd'beɪsən] n lavabo m, Am lavamanos m inv

washing ['wɒʃɪŋ] n (action) lavado m; (of clothes) lavado, colada f; **are there w. facilities?** (personal) ¿hay lavabos?; (for clothes) ¿hay lavadero?; **bring in the w.** recoge la ropa tendida; (dirty) **w.** ropa f sucia or para lavar; **to do the w.** hacer la colada □ **w. line** tendedero m; **w. machine** lavadora f, RP lavarropas m inv; **w. powder** detergente m; **w. soda** sosa f

washing-up [wɒʃɪŋ'ʌp] n Br (**a**) (action) fregado m; **to do the w.-up** fregar los platos □ **w.-up bowl** palangana f, Esp barreño m; **w.-up liquid** detergente m para vajillas (**b**) (dishes) platos mpl (para fregar)

washout ['wɒʃaʊt] n Fam fracaso m

washroom ['wɒʃru:m] n US lavabo m, baño m, Esp servicios mpl, CSur toilette f

washstand ['wɒʃstænd] n lavabo m

WASP [wɒsp] n (abbr **white Anglo-Saxon Protestant**) WASP mf, = persona de raza blanca, origen anglosajón y protestante

wasp [wɒsp] n avispa f □ **wasps' nest** avispero m

waspish ['wɒspɪʃ] adj (temperament) irritable, enojadizo(a), irascible; (comment) punzante

wastage ['weɪstɪdʒ] n pérdidas fpl, merma f

waste [weɪst] **1** adj (**a**) (unwanted) desechado(a); **w. food** restos mpl de comida; Ind **w. products** productos mpl de desecho (**b**) (ground) baldío(a), yermo(a); **w. ground** terreno m baldío
 2 n (**a**) (unnecessary use) desperdicio m; (of resources, effort) derroche m; (of money) despilfarro m, derroche m; (of time) pérdida f; **it's a w. of money** es tirar el dinero; **to go to w.** desperdiciarse, echarse a perder (**b**) (left-overs) desperdicios mpl, desechos mpl, (rubbish) basura f □ **radio-active w.** desechos radioactivos; **w. disposal unit** trituradora f (de desperdicios); **w. pipe** tubo m de desagüe (**c**) (usu pl) yermo m; **the Arctic wastes** los desiertos árticos
 3 vt (squander) desperdiciar, malgastar; (resources) derrochar; (money) despilfarrar, malgastar; (time, chance) desperdiciar, perder; Fig **kindness is wasted on her** ser amable con ella es una pérdida de tiempo; Prov **w. not, want not** quien guarda halla

waste away vi consumirse, demacrarse

wastebasket ['weɪstbɑ:skɪt] n esp US papelera f, cesto m de los papeles, Arg Méx cesto m, Méx bote m

wasted ['weɪstɪd] adj (life) desperdiciado(a); (body) atrofiado(a)

wasteful ['weɪstfʊl] adj (person) despilfarrador(a), pródigo(a); (habits, use) pródigo(a)

wastefulness ['weɪstfʊlnɪs] n despilfarro m, prodigalidad f

wasteland ['weɪstlænd] n baldío m, yermo m

wastepaper [weɪst'peɪpər] n papeles mpl usados or viejos □ **w. basket** papelera f, Arg Méx cesto m, Méx bote m

waster ['weɪstər] n Fam vago(a) m,f

wasting ['weɪstɪŋ] adj Med **w. disease** enfermedad f que debilita

wastrel ['weɪstrəl] *n (spendthrift)* manirroto(a) *m,f; (good-for-nothing)* perdido *m*

watch [wɒtʃ] **1** *n* (**a**) *(look-out)* vigilancia *f;* **to be on the w.** estar al acecho (**for** de); **to keep a close w. on sth/sb** vigilar algo/a algn muy atentamente; **to keep w.** vigilar (**over** a) (**b**) *Mil (period, body)* guardia *f; (individual)* centinela *m; Naut (period, body)* guardia *f; (individual)* vigía *m;* **to be on w., keep w.** estar de guardia (**c**) *Hist* (**night**) **w.** ronda *f* (**d**) *(timepiece)* reloj *m;* **digital/wrist w.** reloj digital/de pulsera ❑ **w. chain** leontina *f*
  2 *vt* (**a**) *(observe)* mirar, observar; **to w. sb do sth** mirar a algn hacer algo; **to w. television/a match** mirar la televisión/un partido (**b**) *(keep an eye on)* vigilar, observar; *(with suspicion)* acechar; **w. the noticeboard/the time** estén atentos al tablón de anuncios/al reloj (**c**) *(be careful of)* tener cuidado con; **w. it!** ¡ojo!, ¡cuidado!; **w. what you say** fíjate en *or* ten cuidado con lo que dices; **w. you don't fall** ten cuidado de no caerte; **w. your head!** ¡cuidado con la cabeza!; *Fig* **to w. one's step** ir con pies de plomo
  3 *vi (look)* mirar, observar

watch out for *vt* tener cuidado con; **w. out!** ¡ojo!; **w. out for the traps** cuidado *or* ojo con las trampas

watch over *vt* vigilar; **to w. over sb's interests** velar por los intereses de algn

watchband ['wɒtʃbænd] *n US see* **watchstrap**

watchdog ['wɒtʃdɒg] *n* perro *m* guardián; *Fig* guardián(ana) *m,f*

watcher ['wɒtʃər] *n* observador(a) *m,f,* espectador(a) *m,f*

watchful ['wɒtʃfʊl] *adj* vigilante, atento(a)

watchfulness ['wɒtʃfʊlnɪs] *n* vigilancia *f*

watchmaker ['wɒtʃmeɪkər] *n* relojero(a) *m,f*

watchman ['wɒtʃmən] *n (pl* **watchmen**) vigilante *m;* **night w.** *(of factory, site)* vigilante nocturno; *(on Spanish street)* sereno *m*

watchstrap ['wɒtʃstræp] *n* correa *f* (de reloj)

watchtower ['wɒtʃtaʊər] *n* atalaya *f*

watchword ['wɒtʃwɜːd] *n* (**a**) *(password)* contraseña *f* (**b**) *(motto)* lema *m*

water ['wɔːtər] **1** *n* (**a**) *(liquid, element)* agua *f;* **drinking/running w.** agua potable/corriente; **hard/soft w.** agua dura/blanda; **salt/fresh w.** agua salada/dulce; **the road is under w.** la carretera está inundada; *Fig* **the theory doesn't hold w.** la teoría cae por su base; *Fig* **to get into hot w.** meterse en un buen lío; *Fig* **to spend money like w.** gastar dinero como agua ❑ **hot w. bottle** bolsa *f* de agua caliente; **w. bottle** cantimplora *f;* **w. closet** wáter *m,* retrete *m;* **w. cooler** refrigerador *m* del agua; *Sport* **w. jump** ría *f;* **w. lily** nenúfar *m;* **w. main** conducción *f* de aguas; **w. pipe** cañería *f;* **w. pistol** pistola *f* de agua; **w. polo** water polo *m;* **w. power** fuerza *f* hidráulica; *Br* **w. rates** tarifa *f* del agua; **w. softener** acondicionador *m* de agua; **w. tank** depósito *m* de agua; **w. wings** flotadores *mpl* (**b**) *(of river, sea)* agua *f;* **coastal/territorial waters** aguas costeras/jurisdiccionales; *Naut* **high/low w.** marea *f* alta/baja; *Fig* **it's all w. under the bridge** ha llovido mucho desde entonces; *Fig* **to get into deep w.** meterse en camisa de once varas; *Fig* **to keep one's head above w.** mantenerse a flote ❑ **w. rat** rata *f* de agua; **w. sports** deportes *mpl* acuáticos (**c**) *(urine)* **to pass w.** orinar; *Med* **difficulty in passing w.** retención *f* de orina (**d**) *Med* **w. on the brain** hidrocefalia *f;* **w. on the knee** derrame *m* sinovial
  2 *vt* (**a**) *(plants, river)* regar (**b**) *(horses)* abrevar

water down 1 *vt (drink)* aguar; *Fig* **a watered-down version** una versión atenuada
  2 *vi (eyes)* lagrimear, llorar; **my mouth watered** se me hizo la boca agua

water-bed ['wɔːtəbed] *n* colchón *m* de agua

watercolour, *US* **watercolor** ['wɔːtəkʌlə] *n Art* acuarela *f*

water-cooled ['wɔːtəkuːld] *adj Tech* refrigerado(a) por agua

watercourse ['wɔːtəkɔːs] *n* lecho *m,* cauce *m,* canal *m*

watercress ['wɔːtəkres] *n* berro *m*

waterfall ['wɔːtəfɔːl] *n* cascada *f,* salto *m* de agua, catarata *f*

waterfowl ['wɔːtəfaʊl] *n* ave *f* acuática

waterfront ['wɔːtəfrʌnt] *n (shore)* orilla *f* del agua; *(promenade)* paseo *m* marítimo; *(harbour)* puerto *m*

waterhole ['wɔːtəhəʊl] *n* charca *f*

watering ['wɔːtərɪŋ] *n* (**a**) *(of plants)* riego *m;* **w. can** regadera *f* (**b**) *(of drink)* **w. (down)** dilución *f; Fig* atenuación *f* ❑ *(for cattle)* **w. place** abrevadero *m*

watering hole ['wɔːtərɪŋ'həʊl] *n (for animals)* bebedero *m; Fam (bar)* bar *m*

waterline ['wɔːtəlaɪn] *n Naut* línea *f* de flotación

waterlogged ['wɔːtəlɒgd] *adj (land, wood)* empapado(a), anegado(a)

watermark ['wɔːtəmɑːk] *n* filigrana *f*

watermelon ['wɔːtəmelən] *n* sandía *f*

watermill ['wɔːtəmɪl] *n* molino *m* de agua

waterproof ['wɔːtəpruːf] **1** *adj (material)* impermeable; *(watch)* sumergible
  2 *n (coat)* impermeable *m*
  3 *vt* impermeabilizar

water-resistant ['wɔːtərɪsɪstənt] *adj (watch)* sumergible; *(fabric)* impermeable

watershed ['wɔːtəʃed] *n Geog* línea *f* divisoria de aguas; *Fig* coyuntura *f* crítica, punto *m* decisivo

waterside ['wɔːtəsaɪd] *n* ribera *f*

water-ski ['wɔːtəskiː] *Sport* **1** *n* esquí *m* acuático
  2 *vi (pt & pp* **water-skied** *or* **water-ski'd**) hacer esquí acuático

water-skiing ['wɔːtəskiːɪŋ] *n Sport* esquí *m* acuático

watertight ['wɔːtətaɪt] *adj (waterproof)* estanco(a), hermético(a); *Fig* irrefutable

waterway ['wɔːtəweɪ] *n* vía *f* fluvial; **inland w.** canal *m* (navegable)

water-wheel ['wɔːtəwiːl] *n Ind* rueda *f* hidráulica; *(mill)* molino *m*

waterworks ['wɔːtəwɜːks] *npl* (**a**) *(for treating water)* central *f sing* de abastecimiento de agua (**b**) *Br Med Fam Euph* aparato *m sing* urinario (**c**) *Fam* **to turn on the w.** empezar a llorar

watery ['wɔːtərɪ] *adj* (**a**) *(like water)* acuoso(a); *(soup)* aguado(a); *(coffee)* flojo(a) (**b**) *(eyes)* lacrimoso(a) (**c**) *(pale)* pálido(a)

watt [wɒt] *n Elec* vatio *m*

wattage ['wɒtɪdʒ] *n* potencia *f* en vatios

wave [weɪv] **1** *n* (**a**) *(at sea)* ola *f* (**b**) *(in hair)* onda *f* (**c**) *Rad Phys* onda *f* ❑ **medium/short w.** onda *f* media/corta; **shock waves** *(of explosion)* onda *f sing* expansiva; *Fig* conmoción *f sing,* repercusión *f sing* (**d**) *Fig (of anger, strikes, attackers)* oleada *f; (of protest, crime)* ola *f,* oleada *f* (**e**) *(fashion)* **the new w.** la nueva ola (**f**) *(gesture)* saludo *m* con la mano
  2 *vt* (**a**) *(shake)* agitar; *(brandish)* blandir; *(help, objection)* **to w. aside** rechazar, desechar; **to w. goodbye to sb** despedirse de algn con la mano; **to w. one's arms (about)** agitar los brazos (**b**) *(hair)* ondular, marcar
  3 *vi* (**a**) *(shake arm)* agitar el brazo; **she waved (to me)** *(greeting)* me saludó con la mano; *(goodbye)* se despidió (de

mí) con la mano; *(signal)* me hizo señas *or* señales con la mano **(b)** *(flag)* ondear; *(corn)* ondular **(c)** *(shake)* agitarse **(d)** *(hair)* ondular

waveband ['weɪvbænd] *n Rad* banda *f* (sonora)

wavelength ['weɪvleŋθ] *n Rad* longitud *f* de onda; *Fam* we're not on the same w. no estamos en la misma onda

waver ['weɪvər] *vi (hesitate)* vacilar, oscilar **(between** entre); *(voice)* temblar; *(courage)* flaquear, vacilar

wavering ['weɪvərɪŋ] *adj (person)* indeciso(a), vacilante; *(voice)* tembloroso(a)

wavy ['weɪvɪ] *adj* **(wavier, waviest)** *(hair, line)* ondulado(a)

wax¹ [wæks] **1** *n* cera *f*; *(in ear)* cerumen *m* **2** *vt* **(a)** *(polish)* encerar **(b)** *Fam (record)* grabar

wax² [wæks] *vi* **(a)** *(moon)* crecer **(b)** *Fml* ponerse; **to w. lyrical** entusiasmarse, exaltarse

waxen ['wæksən] *adj Literary* de cera; *Fig (complexion)* céreo(a)

waxwing ['wækswɪŋ] *n Orn* ampelis *m* europeo

waxwork ['wækswɜːk] *n* **w. (dummy)** figura *f* de cera; **waxworks** museo *m* de cera

waxy ['wæksɪ] *adj* **(waxier, waxiest)** céreo(a)

way [weɪ] **1** *n* **(a)** *(route)* camino *m*; **a letter/another baby is on the w.** una carta/otro niño está en camino; **he made his own w. back (home)** volvió solo (a casa); **I know my w. about** conozco estos parajes; **I must be on my w.** es hora de irme; **on the w.** en el camino, de paso; **on the w. here** de camino para aquí; **out of the w.** apartado(a), remoto(a); **the bank is on your w.** el banco te pilla de camino; **the river wound its w. along the valley** el río serpenteaba por el valle; **to ask the w.** preguntar el camino; **to force one's w. in** entrar a la fuerza; **to go by w. of Burgos** ir vía Burgos; **to go the long w. round** ir por el camino más largo; **to go the wrong w.** errar el camino; **to lose one's w.** perderse; **to make one's w. through the crowd** abrirse camino entre la multitud; **to push one's w. through** abrirse paso a empujones; **which is the w. to the station?** ¿por dónde se va a la estación?; *Fig* **is there a w. round the problem?** ¿hay un modo de soslayar el problema?; *Fig* **reforms are on the w.** se avecinan reformas; *Fig* **she went out of her w. to help** se desvivió para ayudar; *Fig* **to go one's own w.** ir a lo suyo; *Fig* **to make one's w. (in the world)** abrirse camino (en el mundo); *Fig* **to see one's w. (clear) to doing sth** ver la forma *or* la manera de hacer algo; *Fig* **to work one's w. up** ascender a fuerza de trabajo; *Fig* **we went our separate ways** seguiremos cada cual por nuestro camino; *Fam Fig* **to talk one's w. out of trouble** salir del apuro a base de labia; *Fam Fig* **to pay one's w.** *(person)* pagar su parte; *(firm)* ser solvente; *Fam Fig* **we drank our w. through three bottles** nos liquidamos tres botellas **(b)** *(with adv)* **I can't find my w. out** no encuentro la salida; **I stopped off on the w. back** hice escala en el viaje de regreso; **I stopped on the w. out** me detuve al salir; **on the w. up/down** en la subida/bajada; **she's on the w. back** está regresando; **there's no w. through** el paso está cerrado; **to be on the w. up** ir subiendo; **w. in** entrada *f*; **w. out** salida *f*; *Fig* **the easy w. out** la solución fácil; *Fig* **to look for a w. out** buscar una salida; *Fig* **waistcoats are on the w. out** los chalecos van camino de desaparecer **(c)** *(road)* vía *f*, camino *m*; **across** *or* **over the w.** enfrente **(from** de); **the Appian W.** la Vía Apia; *Rel* **the W. of the Cross** el viacrucis; *Fig* **the parting of the ways** el momento de separarse **(d)** *(space, path)* paso *m*; **(get) out of the** *or* **my w.!** ¡quítate de en medio!; **I kept out of the w.** me mantuve a distancia; **right of w.** derecho *m* de paso; *Jur* servidumbre *f* de paso; *Aut* prioridad *f*; **there's a wall in the w.** hay un muro de por medio; **to get out of the w. of sth** dejarle paso a algo,

apartarse de algo; **to give w.** *(collapse)* ceder, hundirse; *(yield)* ceder **(to** a); *Br Aut* ceder el paso; **to keep out of sb's w.** evitar encontrarse con algn; **to push sb out of the w.** apartar a algn a empujones; **to put obstacles in sb's w.** ponerle obstáculos en el camino a algn; **you're in the w.** estás estorbando; *Fig* **as soon as the elections are out of the w.** en cuanto terminen las elecciones; *Fig* **to get sth/sb out of the w.** desembarazarse de algo/algn; *Fig* **to stand in the w.** ser un obstáculo **(e)** *(direction)* dirección *f*; **a three-w. discussion** una discusión trilateral; **come this w.** venga por aquí; **I'll be down your w. tomorrow** estaré en su barrio mañana; **if the opportunity comes my w.** si se me presenta la oportunidad; **which w. did he go?** ¿por dónde se fue?; **that w.** por allá; **the other w. round** al revés; **to be the right/wrong w. up** estar cabeza arriba/abajo; **to split sth three ways** dividir algo en tres partes iguales; *Fig* **it's the other w. round** es al contrario; *Fig* **to look the other w.** hacer la vista gorda ❑ **one-w. street** calle *f* de sentido único **(f)** *(distance)* distancia *f*; **a long w. off** lejos; **it's a long w.** es un largo camino; **we've a long w. to go** nos queda un gran trecho por recorrer; *Fig* **he'll go a long w.** llegará lejos; *Fig* **I'm with you all the w.** estoy totalmente de acuerdo contigo; *Fig* **that went a long w. towards reassuring her** eso contribuyó en gran medida a tranquilizarla; *Fig* **the soup went a long w.** la sopa cundió mucho; *Fig* **we've come a long w.** hemos hecho grandes progresos; *Fig Fam* **you're w. out** andas muy desacertado **(g)** *(motion, progress)* **to be under w.** *Naut* estar en marcha; *(work)* estar en marcha, avanzar; *(meeting, match)* haber empezado; **the building is well under w.** la construcción ya está bastante avanzada; **to get under w.** *Naut* zarpar; *(travellers, work)* ponerse en marcha; *(meeting, match)* empezar **(h)** *(means, method)* método *m*, manera *f*, camino *m*; **do it any w. you like** hazlo del modo que quieras; **have it your own w.** como tú quieras; **I'll do it my w.** lo haré a mi manera; **there are many ways of doing it** hay muchas maneras de hacerlo; **ways and means** medios *mpl*; **to get one's own w.** salirse con la suya **(i)** *(manner)* modo *m*, manera *f*, forma *f*; **can I help in any w.?** ¿puedo ayudar de alguna manera?; **I feel the same w.** yo opino lo mismo; **in a friendly w.** de modo amistoso; **in a small w.** en plan modesto; **one w. or another** de un modo o de otro; **strikes have become a w. of life** las huelgas son ya una costumbre; **that's the w. it is** así es; **that's the w.!** ¡eso es!; **the French w. of life** el estilo de vida francés; **the w. he spoke** el modo en que habló; **the w. things are going** tal como van las cosas; **there's no w. I can accept it** me es imposible aceptarlo; **to do things in a big w.** hacer las cosas a lo grande; **to my w. of thinking** a mi modo de ver; **you're going about it the wrong w.** vas por camino equivocado; *Fam* **no w.!** ¡ni hablar!, ¡de ninguna manera! **(j)** *(talent)* don *m*; **she has a w. with children** tiene un don para los niños **(k)** *(respect)* aspecto *m*; **by w. of introduction/of an experiment** a modo de introducción/de experimento; **either w. you lose** en cualquier caso pierdes; **in a w.** en cierto sentido *or* modo; **in many ways** desde muchos puntos de vista; **in some ways** en algunos aspectos; **it doesn't matter to me one w. or the other** me da exactamente igual; **she is in no w. to blame** no es culpable de ninguna manera; **there are no two ways about it** no tiene vuelta de hoja; **what is there in the w. of refreshment?** ¿qué hay como refrigerio?; **you can't have it both ways** no se puede repicar e ir en la procesión ❑ *(racing)* **each w. bet** apuesta *f* a colocado **(l)** *(custom)* hábito *m*, costumbre *f*; **it's always the w.** siempre es así; **to be set in one's ways** tener costumbres arraigadas; **to get out of the w. of doing sth** perder la costumbre de hacer algo; **to mend one's ways** enmendarse **(m)** *(state)* estado *m*; **leave it the w. it is** déjalo tal como está; **the car is in a bad w.** el coche está en mal estado; **the patient is in a bad w.** el enfermo está bastante mal; *Euph* **to be in the family w.** estar en estado **(n)** *(course)* **by the w.** a propósito, por cierto, dicho sea de paso; **in the w. of business** en el curso de los negocios; **that is by the w.** eso no viene *or* no hace al caso

2 *adv Fam* mucho, muy; **I'm w. behind with my work** estoy atrasadísimo en mi trabajo; **it was w. off target** no alcanzó ni con mucho el blanco; **w. back in 1940** allá en 1940; **w. past the church** mucho más allá de la iglesia

wayfarer ['weɪfeərər] *n* caminante *mf*, viajero(a) *m,f*

waylay [weɪ'leɪ] *vt (pt & pp* **waylaid)** **(a)** *(attack)* atacar por sorpresa **(b)** *Fig (intercept)* salirle al paso a, abordar

way-out [weɪ'aʊt] *adj Fam* estrafalario(a), exagerado(a), supermoderno(a)

wayside ['weɪsaɪd] *n* borde *m or* lado *m* del camino; **a w. inn** una posada de camino; *Fig* **to fall by the w.** quedarse en el camino

wayward ['weɪwəd] *adj (non-conformist)* rebelde; *(capricious)* caprichoso(a); *(shot, aim)* desviado(a)

WC, wc [dʌbljuː'siː] *n (abbr* **water closet)** wáter *m*, WC

we [wiː] *pers pron* nosotros(as); **we went in** (nosotros(as)) entramos; **here we are** aquí estamos; **we English** nosotros los ingleses

weak [wiːk] *adj (structure, body)* débil, endeble; *(character, government)* débil; *(argument, excuse)* pobre, poco convincente; *(joke, team, piece of work)* flojo(a); *(tea)* flojo(a); **I know your w. spot** conozco tu punto flaco; **to be w. at French** estar flojo(a) en francés; **to grow w.** debilitarse, desfallecer

weaken ['wiːkən] **1** *vt* debilitar; *(argument)* quitar fuerza a **2** *vi* **(a)** *(person)* debilitarse, desfallecer; *(structure, resistance, opponent)* flaquear **(b)** *(concede ground)* ceder, aflojar

weak-kneed [wiːk'niːd] *adj Fig* medroso(a), pusilánime

weakling ['wiːklɪŋ] *n (physical, moral)* débil *mf*; *(physical)* debilucho *m*, alfeñique *m*

weakly ['wiːklɪ] *adv* débilmente

weakness ['wiːknɪs] *n* **(a)** *(in strength)* debilidad *f*, flaqueza *f* **(b)** *(character flaw)* flaqueza *f*, punto *m* flaco; **to have a w. for sth/sb** tener una debilidad por algo/algn

weak-willed [wiːk'wɪld] *adj* de poca voluntad

weal [wiːl] *n Med* cardenal *m*, equimosis *f inv*

wealth [welθ] *n* riqueza *f*; *Fig* abundancia *f*; **a w. of detail** una profusión de detalles

wealthy ['welθɪ] *adj* (**wealthier, wealthiest**) rico(a), adinerado(a), acaudalado(a); **the w.** los ricos

wean [wiːn] *vt (child)* destetar; *Fig* **to w. sb from a habit** desacostumbrar (gradualmente) a algn de un hábito

weapon ['wepən] *n* arma *f*

wear [weər] **1** *vt (pt* **wore**; *pp* **worn) (a)** *(clothes)* llevar (puesto(a)), vestir; *(shoes)* calzar; **he usually wears a suit** suele usar traje; **he wears glasses** lleva gafas; **he wears his hair long** lleva el pelo largo; **to w. black** vestirse de negro; *(mourning)* ir de luto; **what shall I w.?** ¿qué me voy a poner? **(b)** *(erode)* desgastar; **he walked so far that he wore a hole in his shoes** caminó tanto que se le agujerearon los zapatos **(c)** *Fam (tolerate)* tolerar, aceptar; **he won't w. it** no lo soportará

2 *vi (gen)* llevarse, aguantar; **these shoes are wearing well** estos zapatos están dando buen resultado; *(garment)* **to w. into holes** agujerearse con el uso; **to w. (thin/ smooth)** desgastarse (con el roce); *Fig* **my patience is wearing thin** se me está acabando la paciencia; *Fig* **she is wearing well** se conserva bien

3 *n* **(a)** *(clothing)* ropa *f* □ **evening w.** traje *m* de noche; **leisure w.** ropa *f* de sport **(b)** *(use) (clothes)* uso *m*; **for everyday w.** para todos los días; **I got a lot of w. out of it** me duró mucho; **it will stand hard w.** es muy resistente **(c)** *(deterioration)* desgaste *m*; **normal w. and tear** desgaste *m or* deterioro *m* natural; **to be the worse for w.** *(object)* estar deteriorado(a); *Fig (person)* estar desmejorado(a); **I feel the worse for w.** me siento maltrecho

wear away 1 *vt (stone etc)* erosionar, desgastar; *(inscription)* borrar
2 *vi (stone etc)* erosionarse, desgastarse; *(inscription)* borrarse

wear down 1 *vt (heels)* desgastar; *Fig* **to w. sb down** vencer la resistencia de algn
2 *vi* desgastarse

wear off *vi (effect, pain)* pasar, desaparecer; **the novelty has worn off** ha dejado de ser una novedad

wear on *vi (time)* transcurrir, pasar; **the day wore on** avanzaba el día

wear out 1 *vt* gastar, desgastar; *Fig* agotar, rendir; **to w. oneself out** agotarse
2 *vi* gastarse, desgastarse

wearable ['weərəbəl] *adj (clothes, shoes)* llevable

wearily ['wɪərɪlɪ] *adv* con cansancio, cansadamente

weariness ['wɪərɪnɪs] *n* cansancio *m*, fatiga *f*

wearing ['weərɪŋ] *adj* **(a)** *(tiring)* cansado(a), agotador(a), *Andes, RP* cansador(a) **(b)** *Fig (tiresome)* pesado(a)

wearisome ['wɪərɪsəm] *adj* **(a)** *(tiring)* cansado(a), fatigoso(a), *Andes, RP* cansador(a) **(b)** *(tedious)* pesado(a), fatigoso(a)

weary ['wɪərɪ] **1** *adj* (**wearier, weariest**) **(a)** *(tired)* cansado(a), fatigado(a) **(b)** *(fed up)* cansado(a), harto(a); **to grow w. of doing sth** cansarse de hacer algo
2 *vt (pt & pp* **wearied)** cansar
3 *vi* cansarse (**of** de)

weasel ['wiːzəl] *n (pl* **weasels** *or* **weasel)** *Zool* comadreja *f*

weather ['weðər] **1** *n* tiempo *m*; **bad w.** mal tiempo; **in hot w.** en tiempo caluroso; **in this w.** con el tiempo que hace; **the w. is fine** hace buen tiempo; **w. permitting** si el tiempo no lo impide; **what's the w. like?** ¿qué tiempo hace?; *Fig* **he made heavy w. of it** le costó mucho trabajo hacerlo; *Fig* **to feel under the w.** no encontrarse bien □ **w. centre** servicio *m* meteorológico; **w. chart, w. map** mapa *m* meteorológico; **w. forecast, w. report** parte *m* meteorológico; **w. vane** veleta *f*

2 *vt* **(a)** *(wood)* curar; *Geol* **weathered rocks** rocas erosionadas **(b)** *Fig (crisis)* aguantar; *Naut Fig* **to w. the storm** capear el temporal

3 *vi (rock)* desgastarse; *(building)* adquirir la pátina del tiempo

weather-beaten ['weðəbiːtən] *adj (person)* curtido(a); *(building)* deteriorado(a) por los agentes naturales

weathercock ['weðəkɒk] *n* veleta *f*

weatherfish ['weðəfɪʃ] *n (fish)* lomo *m* de lago

weatherman ['weðəmæn] *n (pl* **weathermen)** hombre *m* del tiempo

weatherproof ['weðəpruːf] *adj (house)* impermeabilizado(a); *(clothing)* impermeable

weave [wiːv] **1** *n* tejido *m*

2 *vt (pt* **wove**; *pp* **woven) (a)** *Tex* tejer **(b)** *(intertwine)* entretejer, tejer; *(wicker)* trenzar **(c)** *(intrigues)* tramar, urdir, tejer; **to w. a spell** echar un conjuro (**on** a)

3 *vi* **(a)** *(person, road)* zigzaguear; **the car wove in and out of the traffic** el coche se abría paso por entre el tráfico **(b)** *Fam* **get weaving!** ¡espabílate!

weaver ['wiːvər] n tejedor(a) m,f

weaving ['wiːvɪŋ] n tejido m

web [web] n (a) **(spider's) w.** telaraña f (**b**) Fig (intrigue) red f, organización f; (tangle) embrollo m (**c**) (of duck, frog) membrana f interdigital m (**d**) Comptr **the W.** la Web; **w. page** página f web; **w. site** sitio m Web

webbed [webd] adj Orn palmeado(a); **w. foot** pata f palmeada

webbing ['webɪŋ] n Furn (entramado m de) tiras fpl de cáñamo

webcam ['webkæm] n cámara f web

web-footed [web'fʊtɪd] adj Orn palmípedo(a)

weblog ['weblɒg] n Comptr weblog m, bitácora f

Wed (abbr **Wednesday**) miércoles m, miérc.

wed [wed] vt (pt & pp **wed** or **wedded**) casarse con

wedded ['wedɪd] adj (**a**) (married) casado(a); **w. bliss** felicidad f conyugal (**b**) Fig **to be w. to an idea** aferrarse or estar aferrado(a) a una idea

wedding ['wedɪŋ] n boda f, Andes matrimonio m, RP casamiento m; **to have a church w.** casarse por la iglesia ❑ **w. breakfast** banquete m nupcial; **w. cake** tarta f nupcial, Andes torta f de matrimonio, RP torta f de casamiento; **w. day** día m de la boda or Andes del matrimonio or RP del casamiento; **w. dress** traje m or vestido m de novia; **w. present** regalo m de boda; **w. ring** alianza f, anillo m de boda or Andes matrimonio or RP casamiento

wedge [wedʒ] **1** n (**a**) (for door, wheel) cuña f, calzo m; (for table leg) calce m; (for splitting) cuña; Fig **it's the thin end of the w.** éste es sólo el primer paso (**b**) (of cake, cheese) trozo m grande

2 vt (wheel, leg of chair, etc) calzar; (object) **to be wedged tight** estar completamente atrancado(a) or trabado(a); **to w. a door open** mantener abierta una puerta mediante una cuña

wedlock ['wedlɒk] n Jur matrimonio m; **to be born out of w.** nacer fuera del matrimonio

Wednesday ['wenzdɪ] n miércoles m; see also **Saturday**

wee[1] [wiː] adj esp Scot pequeñito(a), chiquito(a); **a w. bit** un poquitín; **a w. bit heavy** un poco pesado(a)

wee[2] [wiː] Br Fam **1** n pipí m; **to go for a w.** (ir a) hacer pipí; Fam **to do a w.** (urinate) hacer pis or pipí

2 vi hacer pipí

weed [wiːd] **1** n (**a**) Bot mala hierba f (**b**) Slang (marijuana) hierba f, maría f (**c**) Pej (person) debilucho(a) m,f, canijo(a) m,f

2 vt (a) (garden) desherbar, escardar (**b**) Fig **to w. out** eliminar, suprimir

3 vi escardar

weeding ['wiːdɪŋ] n escarda f

weedkiller ['wiːdkɪlər] n herbicida m

weedy ['wiːdɪ] adj (**weedier, weediest**) Pej debilucho(a), desmirriado(a)

week [wiːk] n semana f; **a w. (ago) today/yesterday** hoy hace/ayer hizo una semana; **a w. today** de hoy en ocho días; **in a w.'s time** dentro de una semana; **in/during the w.** entre semana; **last/next w.** la semana pasada/que viene; **once a w.** una vez a la or por semana; **the w. after next** no la semana que viene sino la otra; **w. in, w. out** semana tras semana ❑ Rel **Holy W.** Semana f Santa

weekday ['wiːkdeɪ] n día m laborable; **on a w.** entre semana

weekend [wiːk'end] n fin m de semana; Br **at** or US **on the w.** (once) (durante) el fin de semana; (regularly) los fines de semana

weekly ['wiːklɪ] **1** adj semanal

2 adv semanalmente; **twice w.** dos veces por semana

3 Press semanario m

weeknight ['wiːknaɪt] n noche f de entre semana

weep [wiːp] **1** vi (pt & pp **wept**) llorar; **to w. for sb** llorar a algn; **to w. with joy** llorar de alegría

2 vt (tears) derramar

3 n **to have a good w.** llorar a lágrima viva; **to have a little w.** llorar un poco

weeping ['wiːpɪŋ] **1** adj lloroso(a); Bot **w. willow** sauce m llorón

2 n llanto m

weepy ['wiːpɪ] adj (**weepier, weepiest**) Fam (book, film, ending) lacrimógeno(a), Chile cebollero(a); **to be w.** (person) estar lloroso(a)

weevil ['wiːvɪl] n Ent gorgojo m

wee-wee ['wiːwiː] n & vi see **wee**[2]

weft [weft] n Tex trama f

weigh [weɪ] **1** vt (**a**) (gen) pesar (**b**) Fig (consider) ponderar, sopesar; **he weighs his words** pondera sus palabras; **to w. one thing against another** contraponer una cosa a otra (**c**) Naut **to w. anchor** levar anclas

2 vi (**a**) (gen) pesar; (responsibilities) pesar (**upon** sobre); **it doesn't w. anything** no pesa; **it weighs three kilos** pesa tres kilos; Fig **it is weighing on his conscience** pesa sobre su conciencia; Fig **time weighs heavily on his hands** se le hace largo el tiempo; Fam **it weighs a ton** pesa una tonelada (**b**) Fig (influence) influir; **his age weighed heavily in his favour** su edad influyó mucho a favor suyo

weigh down vt sobrecargar (**with** de); **she was weighed down with parcels** iba muy cargada de paquetes

weigh in vi (**a**) Sport pesarse (**b**) Fam (join in) intervenir

weigh out vt (food etc) pesar

weigh up vt (consider) (thing, matter) evaluar, ponderar; (person) formar una opinión sobre; **she soon had him weighed up** no tardó en calarle; **to w. up the pros and cons** sopesar los pros y los contras

weighbridge ['weɪbrɪdʒ] n báscula f de puente

weigh-in ['weɪɪn] n Sport pesaje m

weight [weɪt] **1** n (**a**) (of person, object) peso m; **feel the w. of this** sopesa esto; **to lose w.** perder peso, adelgazar; **to put on w.** ganar peso, engordar; **to sell sth by w.** vender algo a peso; **weights and measures** pesos y medidas; Fig **it's worth its w. in gold** vale su peso en oro; Fam Fig **to pull one's w.** poner de su parte; Fam Fig **to throw one's w. about** hacer sentir su autoridad or su fuerza (**b**) (for scales, of clock) pesa f (**c**) Fig (influence) peso m; **this adds w. to the case** esto le da peso al argumento; **to carry w.** (opinion, argument) tener peso; (person) pesar, tener influencia (**d**) Fig (burden) peso m, carga f; **that's a w. off my mind** eso me quita or Am saca un peso de encima

2 vt poner peso en; (net) lastrar; **to w. sth down** sujetar algo con pesos

weighting ['weɪtɪŋ] n Br (on salary) suplemento m de salario

weightless ['weɪtlɪs] adj ingrávido(a)

weightlessness ['weɪtlɪsnɪs] n ingravidez f

weightlifter ['weɪtlɪftər] n Sport levantador(a) m,f de pesos, halterófilo(a) m,f

weightlifting ['weɪtlɪftɪŋ] n Sport halterofilia f, levantamiento m de pesos

weightwatcher ['weɪtwɒtʃər] n persona f a dieta

weighty ['weɪtɪ] adj (**weightier, weightiest**) pesado(a); Fig (problem, matter) importante, grave; (argument) de peso

weir [wɪər] n presa f

weird [wɪəd] adj raro(a), extraño(a)

weirdness ['wɪədnɪs] n rareza f

weirdo ['wɪədəʊ] *n* (*pl* **weirdos**) *Fam* tipo(a) *m,f* raro(a)

welcome ['welkəm] **1** *adj* (*person*) bienvenido(a); *(news)* grato(a); *(change)* oportuno(a); **the money would be most w.** el dinero me vendría muy bien; **to make sb w.** acoger a algn calurosamente; **w. home!** ¡bienvenido a casa!; **you're w.!** ¡no hay de qué!; **you're w. to stay** puede quedarse con toda confianza

2 *n* (*greeting*) bienvenida *f*, acogida *f*

3 *vt* (*gen*) acoger, recibir; *(more formally)* darle la bienvenida a; *(news)* acoger con agrado; *(decision)* aplaudir; **I would w. the opportunity** agradecería la oportunidad

welcoming ['welkəmɪŋ] *adj* (*speech*) de bienvenida; *(smile)* acogedor(a)

weld [weld] *vt* soldar

welder ['weldər] *n* soldador *m*

welding ['weldɪŋ] *n* soldadura *f* □ **spot w.** soldadura *f* por puntos

welfare ['welfeər] *n* (**a**) *(well-being)* bienestar *m*; *(public)* salud *f* □ **animal/child w.** protección *f* de animales/de menores; **w. work** (trabajos *mpl* de) asistencia *f* social; **w. worker** asistente *mf* social (**b**) *US (social security)* **w. (payments)** (prestaciones *fpl* de la) seguridad *f* social

well¹ [wel] *n* (**a**) *(for water, oil)* pozo *m* □ **oil w.** pozo *m* de petróleo (**b**) *(of staircase)* caja *f*; *(of lift)* hueco *m* (**c**) *(of court, hall)* hemiciclo *m*

well up *vi* brotar; **tears welled up in his eyes** se le llenaron los ojos de lágrimas

well² [wel] **1** *adj* (**a**) *(healthy)* bien; **are you keeping w.?** estás bien de salud?; **he's not w.** no se encuentra bien; **(I'm) very w., thank you** (estoy) muy bien, gracias; **I don't feel w.** no me siento bien; **to get w.** reponerse; **you look w.** tienes buena cara (**b**) *(satisfactory, fortunate)* **all is w.** todo va bien; **if that's the case, w. and good** si es así, bien está; **it's just as w.** menos mal; **just as w. you stayed** menos mal que te quedaste; **that's all very w. but ...** todo eso está muy bien, pero ...; **you're w. rid of him** menos mal que te has librado de él; *Prov* **all's w. that ends w.** bien está lo que bien acaba (**c**) *(advisable)* recomendable; **it is as w. to remember that** conviene recordar que; **it might/would be as w. to consult him** quizás convenga/estaría bien consultarle

2 *adv* (*better, best*) (**a**) *(properly, successfully)* bien; **he has done w. (for himself)** ha prosperado; **the business is doing *or* going w.** el negocio marcha bien; **they get on very w. (together)** se entienden muy bien; **to do sth w.** hacer algo bien; **she did w. in the exam** el examen le fue bien; **w. done!** ¡bien hecho!, ¡muy bien!, ¡bravo! (**b**) *(favourably, kindly)* bien; **he speaks w. of you** habla bien de ti; **it was in bad taste but he took it w.** fue de mal gusto pero lo tomó a bien (**c**) *(thoroughly)* bien; **I know him w.** le conozco bien; **I know it only too w.** lo sé de sobra; *Culin* **w. done** muy hecho(a) (**d**) *(much, by a big margin)* bien; **he's w. over thirty** tiene treinta años bien cumplidos; **it's pretty w. finished** está casi terminado; **it's w. worth a visit** vale la pena visitarlo; **w. after six o'clock** mucho después de las seis; **w. in advance** muy por adelantado; **w. over a hundred** mucho más de cien; *Fam* **he'll damn *or* jolly w. have to go!** ¡mal que bien tendrá que ir! (**e**) *(easily, with good reason)* bien; **he couldn't very w. say no** difícilmente podía decir que no; **I may w. do that** bien puedo hacer eso; **it may w. rain** es muy posible que llueva; **you might as w. admit it** más vale que lo confieses (**f**) **as w.** también; **as w. as** así como, lo mismo que; **bring the baby as w.** traiga al niño también; **children as w. as adults** tanto niños como adultos; **he is clever as w. as good-looking** además de guapo es inteligente

3 *interj* (**a**) *(surprise)* ¡bueno!, ¡vaya!; **w. I never!** ¡no me digas!; **w., w.!** ¡vaya, vaya! (**b**) *(agreement, interrogation,*

resignation) bueno; **very w.** bueno, muy bien; **w.?** ¿y bien?, ¿qué?; **w., all right** bueno, está bien; **w., what now?** ¿bueno, y ahora qué? (**c**) *(doubt)* bueno, pues; **w., I don't know** pues no sé (**d**) *(resumption)* bueno, pues (bien); **w., as I was saying** bueno *or* pues (bien), como iba diciendo (**e**) *(consequence)* (bueno) pues; **I'm tired — w., go to bed** estoy cansando — (bueno) pues, acuéstate

well-adjusted [welə'dʒʌstɪd] *adj (person)* equilibrado(a)

well-attended [welə'tendɪd] *adj* muy concurrido(a); **the meeting was w.** a la reunión acudió *or* asistió mucha gente

well-balanced ['welbælənst] *adj (diet, person)* equilibrado(a)

well-behaved ['welbeheɪvd] *adj (child)* formal, educado(a)

well-being ['welbiːɪŋ] *n* bienestar *m*

well-bred ['welbred] *adj (person)* (bien) educado(a)

well-built ['welbɪlt] *adj (building etc)* de construcción sólida; *(person)* fornido(a)

well-chosen [wel'tʃəʊzən] *adj (remarks)* acertado(a)

well-disposed [weldɪ'spəʊzd] *adj* bien dispuesto(a) **(towards** hacia)

well-done ['weldʌn] *adj* bien hecho(a); *(steak etc)* bien pasado(a)

well-dressed [wel'drest] *adj* elegante; **to be w.-d.** ir bien vestido(a)

well-earned ['welɜːnd] *adj* (bien) merecido(a)

well-educated [wel'edʊkeɪtɪd] *adj* culto(a), instruido(a)

well-fed [wel'fed] *adj* bien alimentado(a)

well-founded ['welfaʊndɪd] *adj (suspicion)* bien fundado(a)

well-heeled ['welhiːld] *adj Fam* ricachón(ona), forrado(a)

wellies ['welɪz] *npl Br Fam*, **wellingtons** ['welɪŋtənz] *npl* botas *fpl* de agua *or* goma *or Méx Ven* caucho

well-informed ['welɪnfɔːmd] *adj* bien informado(a) (**on** acerca de)

well-intentioned [welɪn'tenʃənd] *adj* bienintencionado(a)

well-judged ['weldʒʌdʒd] *adj* bien calculado(a)

well-kept [wel'kept] *adj (garden)* cuidado(a); *(secret)* bien guardado(a)

well-known [welnəʊn] *adj* (bien) conocido(a)

well-made ['welmeɪd] *adj* bien hecho(a)

well-mannered ['welmænəd] *adj* educado(a), cortés, formal

well-meaning [wel'miːnɪŋ] *adj* bien intencionado(a)

well-meant ['welment] *adj* bienintencionado(a)

well-nigh ['welnaɪ] *adv* casi

well-off [wel'ɒf] *adj* (**a**) *(rich)* acomodado(a), rico(a), pudiente (**b**) *Fam Fig (fortunate)* **you don't know when you're w.-o.** no te das cuenta de la suerte que tienes

well-paid [wel'peɪd] *adj* bien pagado(a)

well-read [wel'red] *adj* leído(a), = que ha leído mucho

well-spoken [wel'spəʊkən] *adj* con acento culto

well-timed [wel'taɪmd] *adj* oportuno(a)

well-to-do [weltə'duː] *adj* acomodado(a); **the w.-to-do** la gente pudiente

well-versed [wel'vɜːst] *adj* **to be w.-v. in sth** estar muy ducho(a) *or* versado(a) en algo

well-wisher ['welwɪʃər] *n* admirador(a) *m,f*, partidario(a) *m,f*

well-worn ['welwɔːn] *adj (clothes etc)* gastado(a), raído(a); *(path)* trillado(a); *Fig (theme, phrase)* gastado(a), trillado(a)

well-written [wel'rɪtən] *adj* bien escrito(a)

Welsh [welʃ] **1** *adj* galés(esa) ❑ *Furn* **W. dresser** aparador *m*; *Culin* **W. rarebit** tostada *f* con queso fundido
2 *n* **(a)** *(language)* galés *m* **(b)** *pl* **the W.** los galeses

Welshman ['welʃmən] *n (pl* **Welshmen**) galés *m*

Welshwoman ['welʃwumən] *n (pl* **Welshwomen** ['welʃwɪmɪn]) galesa *f*

welt [welt] **1** *n* **(a)** *(of shoe)* vira *f* **(b)** *Sew* ribete *m* **(c)** *(weal)* cardenal *m*, verdugón *m*
2 *vt (shoe)* poner una vira a; *Fam Fig* pegar, dar una hostia a

welter ['weltər] *n Fml* mezcla *f* confusa, mescolanza *f*

welterweight ['welterweɪt] *n Box (category, boxer)* (peso *m*) wélter *m*

wench [wentʃ] *n Old-fashioned or Hum* moza *f*, mozuela *f*

wend [wend] *vt Literary* **to w. one's way** dirigir sus pasos **(towards** hacia)

went [went] *pt see* **go**

wept [wept] *pt & pp see* **weep**

were [wɜːr, *unstressed* wər] *pt see* **be**

werewolf ['wɪəwulf] *n (pl* **werewolves** ['wɪəwulvz]) hombre *m* lobo

west [west] **1** *n* oeste *m*, occidente *m*; **in** *or* **to the w.** al oeste; **the Far W.** el Lejano Oeste; *Pol* **the W.** los países occidentales
2 *adj* del oeste, occidental; **the w. coast** la costa occidental; **the W. Indies** las Antillas; **w. wind** viento *m* del oeste; **W. Indian** antillano(a)
3 *adv* al oeste, hacia el oeste; **it faces w.** da al oeste; *Fam Fig (be ruined)* **to go w.** desgraciarse, estropearse

westbound ['westbaund] *adj (traffic etc)* en dirección al oeste

westerly ['westəlɪ] *adj (wind)* del oeste; **in a w. position** orientado(a) hacia el oeste; **in a w. direction** en dirección al oeste

western ['westən] **1** *adj* del oeste, occidental; **W. Europe** Europa Occidental; **in W. France** en el oeste de Francia
2 *n Cin* western *m*

westernized ['westənaɪzd] *adj* occidentalizado(a)

westward ['westwəd] *adj* **in a w. direction** hacia el oeste

westwards ['westwədz] *adv* hacia el oeste

wet [wet] **1** *adj* **(wetter, wettest)** **(a)** *(damp)* húmedo(a); *(soaked)* mojado(a); *(paint, ink)* fresco(a); **I got (my feet) w.** me mojé (los pies); **'w. paint'** 'recién pintado'; **w. through**, **soaking w.** *(person)* calado(a) hasta los huesos; *(thing)* empapado(a) ❑ **w. suit** traje *m* isotérmico **(b)** *(rainy)* lluvioso(a); **it has been very w.** ha llovido mucho; **the w. season** la época de las lluvias **(c)** *Br Fam (person)* apocado(a), soso(a) ❑ **w. blanket** aguafiestas *mf inv*
2 *n* **(a)** *(rain)* lluvia *f*; *(damp)* humedad *f* **(b)** *Br Fam (person)* apocado(a) *m,f*
3 *vt (pt & pp* **wet)** mojar, humedecer; **to w. oneself** orinarse; **to w. the bed** mojar, orinarse en la cama

wetness ['wetnɪs] *n* humedad *f*

whack [wæk] **1** *vt (person)* dar un porrazo *or Méx* madrazo a; *(ball)* golpear fuertemente; *US Fam (murder)* liquidar, *Esp* cepillarse, *Esp* cargarse
2 *n* **(a)** *(blow)* porrazo *m*, *Méx* madrazo *m* **(b)** *Fam (share)* parte *f*, porción *f*

whacked [wækt] *adj Fam* agotado(a)

whacking ['wækɪŋ] *adj Fam* **a w. great car** un coche grandísimo

whale [weɪl] *n (pl* **whale** *or* **whales)** *Zool* ballena *f*; *Fam* **we had a w. of a time** nos lo pasamos pipa *or* en grande

whalebone ['weɪlbəun] *n* (barba *f* de) ballena *f*

whaler ['weɪlər] *n (person)* ballenero *m,f*; *(ship)* ballenero *m*

whaling ['weɪlɪŋ] *n* caza *f* de ballenas; **the w. industry** la industria ballenera

wharf [wɔːf] *n (pl* **wharfs** *or* **wharves** [wɔːvz]) muelle *m*, embarcadero *m*

wharfage ['wɔːfɪdʒ] *n* muellaje *m*

what [wɒt, *unstressed* wət] **1** *adj* **(a)** *(direct question)* qué; **w. (sort of) bird is that?** ¿qué tipo de ave es ésa?; **w. good is that?** ¿para qué sirve eso?; **w. time is it?** ¿qué hora es? **(b)** *(indirect question)* qué; **ask him w. size he takes** pregúntale qué talla usa **(c)** *(all the)* **he gave me w. money he had** me dio (todo) el dinero que tenía; **she lost w. little she had** perdió lo poco que tenía
2 *pron* **(a)** *(direct question)* qué; **w. are you talking about?** ¿de qué estás hablando?; **w. about me?** ¿y yo?; **w. about going tomorrow?** ¿qué te parece si vamos mañana?; **w. about the money you owe me?** ¿qué hay del dinero que me debes?; **w. can I do for you?** ¿en qué puedo servirle?; **w. did it cost?** ¿cuánto costó?; **w. did you do that for?** ¿por qué hiciste eso?; **w. (did you say)?** ¿cómo?; **w. does he look like?** ¿qué aspecto tiene?; **w. does it sound like?** ¿cómo suena?; **w. do you take me for?** ¿por quién me tomas?; **w. if it rains?** ¿y si llueve?; **w. is happening?** ¿qué pasa?; **w. is it?** *(definition)* ¿qué es?; *(what's the matter)* ¿qué hay?; **w. is your surname?** ¿cuál es su apellido?; **w.'s it called?** ¿cómo se llama?; **w.'s the French for 'cat'?** ¿cómo se dice'cat'en francés?; **w.'s this for?** ¿para qué sirve esto?; **w. was the film like?** ¿qué tal la película?; *Fam* **so w.?**, **w. about it?**, **w. of it?** ¿y qué?; *Fam* **w. d'you know!** ¡mira por dónde! **(b)** *(relative)* qué; **he asked me w. I thought** me preguntó lo que pensaba; **I didn't know w. to say** no sabía qué decir; **I wonder w. will happen** me pregunto qué va a pasar; *Fam* **books, journals and w. have you** libros, revistas y tal; *Fam* **he knows w.'s w.** sabe lo que se hace; **(and) w.'s more** y además; **come w. may** pase lo que pase; **guess w.!** ¿sabes qué?; **it's just w. I need** es exactamente lo que necesito; **w. with the heat and the noise, I couldn't sleep** entre el calor y el ruido no pude dormir; *Fam* **I'll tell you w.** pues, mira; *Fam* **to give sb w. for** darle a algn su merecido
3 *interj* qué; **w. a goal!** ¡qué *or* vaya golazo!; **w. a lovely picture!** ¡qué cuadro más bonito!; **w. weather!** ¡qué tiempo!; **w., no coffee!** ¡cómo que no hay café!

what-d'ye-call-her ['wɒtjəkɔːlər] *n Fam (person)* fulanita *f*, menganita *f*

what-d'ye-call-him ['wɒtjəkɔːlɪm] *n Fam (person)* fulanito *m*, menganito *m*

what-d'ye-call-it ['wɒtjəkɔːlɪt] *n Fam (thing)* chisme *m*, *CAm Carib Col* vaina *f*, *RP* coso *m*

whatever [wɒt'evər, *unstressed* wət'evər] **1** *adj* **(a)** *(any)* cualquiera que; **at w. time you like** a la hora que quieras; **of w. colour** no importa de qué color **(b)** *(with negative)* **nothing w.** nada en absoluto; **with no interest w.** sin interés alguno
2 *pron* **(a)** *(anything, all that)* (todo) lo que; **do w. you like** haz lo que quieras; **w. I have is yours** todo lo que tengo es tuyo **(b)** *(no matter what)* **don't tell him w. you do** no se te ocurra decírselo bajo ningún concepto; **w. (else) you find** cualquier (otra) cosa que encuentres; **he goes out w. the weather** sale haga el tiempo que haga
3 *interr* **w. happened?** ¿qué (diablos) pasó?

whatnot ['wɒtnɒt] *n* **(a)** *Fam* **...and w.** ...y cosas así, ...y cosas por el estilo **(b)** *Furn* rinconera *f*

what's-her-name ['wɒtsəneɪm], **what's-his-**

name ['wɒtsɪzneɪm], **what's-its-name** ['wɒtsɪts-neɪm] n Fam see **what-d'ye-call-her/him/it**

whatsoever [wɒtsəʊ'evər] adj en absoluto; **nothing w.** nada en absoluto

wheat [wiːt] n trigo m ❑ **w. germ** germen m de trigo

wheatfield ['wiːtfiːld] n trigal m

wheedle ['wiːdəl] vt engatusar; **to w. sb into doing sth** engatusar a algn para que haga algo; **to w. sth out of sb** sonsacar algo a algn halagándole

wheel [wiːl] **1** n rueda f; **the big w.** la noria; Aut **the front wheels** las ruedas delanteras; **to be at the w.** Aut ir al volante; Naut llevar el timón; Fig **the wheels of government** la maquinaria del gobierno; Fig **there are wheels within wheels** es más complicado de lo que parece
2 vt (bicycle) empujar
3 vi (**a**) (bird) revolotear (**b**) (person) **to w. round** girar sobre los talones (**c**) Mil dar la vuelta; **right w.!** ¡vuelta a la derecha!

wheelbarrow ['wiːlbærəʊ] n carretilla f

wheelbase ['wiːlbeɪs] n Aut distancia f entre ejes

wheelchair ['wiːltʃeər] n silla f de ruedas

wheeling ['wiːlɪŋ] n **w. and dealing** negocios mpl sucios, maquinaciones fpl

wheeze [wiːz] **1** vi respirar con dificultad, resollar
2 n respiración f dificultosa or sibilante, resuello m

wheezy ['wiːzɪ] adj (**wheezier, wheeziest**) (person) asmático(a); (breathing) sibilante

whelk [welk] n Zool buccino m

when [wen] **1** adv (**a**) (direct question) cuándo; **from or since w.?** ¿desde cuándo?; **w. did he arrive?** ¿cuándo llegó? (**b**) (indirect question) cuándo; **tell me w. to go** dime cuándo he de irme; (while pouring) **say w.** me dirás basta (**c**) (on which) cuando, en que; **one day w. I'm passing through** un día cuando esté de paso; **the days w. I work** los días en que trabajo
2 conj (**a**) (with time) cuando; **I'll tell you w. she comes** se lo diré cuando llegue; **it will look good w. painted** tendrá buen aspecto cuando esté pintado; **it was raining w. I got up** llovía cuando me levanté; **w. he saw her he stopped** al verla se detuvo; **w. he was a boy ...** de niño ..., cuando era pequeño ... (**b**) (whenever) cuando; **we have fun w. he comes** nos divertimos mucho cuando viene (**c**) (given that, if) cuando, si; **you should stay in bed w. you've got the flu** deberías quedarte en la cama cuando tienes la gripe (**d**) (although) aunque; **he withdrew w. he might have won** se retiró aunque podía haber ganado

whence [wens] adv Fml or Literary (**a**) (from where) de dónde (**b**) Fig por lo cual

whenever [wen'evər] **1** conj (when) cuando; (every time) siempre que; **come w. you like** venga cuando quiera; **w. I see it** I think of you siempre que lo veo, pienso en ti
2 adv **Monday, Tuesday or w.** lunes, martes o cuando sea; **w. that might be** sea cuando sea

where [weər] adv (**a**) (direct question) dónde; (direction) adónde; **w. are you going?** ¿adónde vas?; **w. did we go wrong?** ¿en qué nos equivocamos?; **w. do we begin?** ¿por dónde empezamos?; **w. do you come from?** ¿de dónde es usted?; **w. is the exit?** ¿dónde está la salida?; **w. to?** ¿adónde? (**b**) (indirect question) dónde; (direction) adónde; **tell me w. you went** dime adónde fuiste (**c**) (at, in which) donde, en que; (direction) adonde, a donde; **I'll stay w. I am** me quedaré donde estoy; **that's (just) w. you're wrong** en eso se equivoca usted; **the house w. I was born** la casa donde or en que nací; **go w. you like** ve donde quieras (**d**) (when) cuando; **w. safety is involved** cuando se trata de seguridad

whereabouts 1 [weərə'baʊts] adv (por) dónde; **w. do you live?** ¿por dónde vives?
2 ['weərəbaʊts] n paradero m; **his w. are unknown** se desconoce su paradero

whereas [weər'æz] conj (**a**) (but, while) mientras que; **she is tall w. her sister is short** ella es alta mientras que su hermana es baja (**b**) Jur considerando que

whereby [weə'baɪ] adv Fml por el/la/lo cual; **the means w.** el medio por el cual

wherefore ['weəfɔːr] n Fml see **why 2**

whereupon [weərə'pɒn] conj Fml con lo cual, después de lo cual

wherever [weər'evər] **1** conj dondequiera que; **I'll find him w. he is** le encontraré dondequiera que esté; **I try to help w. possible** procuro ayudar donde sea posible; **sit w. you like** siéntate donde quieras; **Zafra, w. that might be** Zafra, quién sabe dónde está
2 adv (**a**) (direct question) adónde; (emphatic) **w. did you go?** ¿adónde diablos fuiste? (**b**) (somewhere) **Burgos, Avila or w.** Burgos, Avila o donde sea

wherewithal ['weəwɪðɔːl] n Fam pelas fpl; **we don't have the w. to go on holiday this year** no tenemos dinero para ir de vacaciones este año

whet [wet] vt (pt & pp **whetted**) (**a**) **to w. sb's appetite** despertar or abrir el apetito a algn (**b**) (tool, blade) afilar

whether ['weðər] conj (**a**) (if) si; **I don't know w. it is true** no sé si es verdad; **I doubt w. he'll win** dudo que gane; **it depends on w. he comes (or not)** depende de si viene (o no) (**b**) (in comparison) **w. by accident or design** fuera por accidente o a propósito; **w. he comes or not** venga o no

whew [hjuː] interj (**a**) (relief, fatigue) ¡uf! (**b**) (astonishment) ¡hala!

whey [weɪ] n suero m

which [wɪtʃ] **1** adj (**a**) (direct question) qué; **w. colour do you prefer?** ¿qué color prefieres?; **w. one?** ¿cuál?; **w. ones?** ¿cuáles?; **w. shops did you go to?** ¿a qué tiendas fuiste?; **w. way?** ¿por dónde? (**b**) (indirect question) qué; **tell me w. dress you like** dime qué vestido te gusta (**c**) (in relative constructions) el/la cual, los/las cuales; **by w. time** y para entonces; **in w. case** en cuyo caso
2 pron (**a**) (direct question) cuál, cuáles; **w. is the faster road?** ¿cuál es la carretera más rápida?; **w. of the cars did you buy?** ¿qué coche compraste?; **w. of you is going?** ¿cuál de Esp vosotros or Am ustedes va? (**b**) (indirect question) cuál, cuáles; **I can't tell w. is w.** no distingo cuál es cuál; **I don't know w. (one) I'd rather have** no sé cuál prefiero (**c**) (defining relative) que; (after preposition) que, el/la cual, los/las cuales, el/la que, los/las que; **here are the books w. I have read** aquí están los libros que he leído; **the accident w. I told you about** el accidente de que te hablé; **the car in w. he was travelling** el coche en (el) que viajaba; **the countries through w. we passed** los países por donde pasamos; **the match w. we went to** el partido a que asistimos; **this is the one (w.) I like** éste es el que me gusta, ésta es la que me gusta (**d**) (non-defining relative) el/la cual, los/las cuales; **I played three sets, all of w. I lost** jugué tres sets, todos los cuales perdí; **six pears, half of w. are ripe** seis peras, de las cuales la mitad están maduras (**e**) (referring to a clause) lo cual, lo que; **he won, w. made me very happy** ganó, lo cual or lo que me alegró mucho

whichever [wɪtʃ'evər] **1** adj el/la que, cualquiera que; **I'll take w. books you don't want** tomaré los libros que no quieras; **w. system you choose** cualquiera que sea el sistema que elijas; **w. way you go** por dondequiera que vayas
2 pron el que, la que; **take w. suits you best** tome el que le convenga más

whiff [wɪf] *n* (**a**) *(quick smell)* olor *m* pasajero, vaharada *f*; *(of air, smoke)* bocanada *f*; **I caught a w. of gas** percibí de repente un olor de gas (**b**) *Fam (bad smell)* tufo *m*

while [waɪl] **1** *n* (**a**) *(length of time)* rato *m*, tiempo *m*; **after a w.** al rato, al poco tiempo; **all the w.** *(constantly)* a cada rato; *(without stopping)* todo el tiempo; **I'll be a good w.** tardaré un buen rato; **in a little w.** dentro de poco; **once in a w.** de vez en cuando; **stay a little w.** quédate un ratito (**b**) *(compensation)* pena *f*, recompensa *f*; **it's not worth your w. staying** no merece la pena que te quedes; **it's worth w. going** vale la pena ir; *Fam* **I'll make it worth your w.** te recompensaré bien

 2 *vt (spend)* **to w. away the time (doing sth)** pasar el rato (haciendo algo)

 3 *conj* (**a**) *(time)* mientras; **he fell asleep w. driving** se durmió mientras conducía; **w. he was here** mientras estuvo aquí (**b**) *(although)* aunque; **w. I understand your fears, I don't share them** aunque comprendo tus temores, no los comparto (**c**) *(whereas)* mientras que; **I like football, w. he prefers tennis** a mí me gusta el fútbol mientras que él prefiere el tenis

whilst [waɪlst] *conj Br see* **while 3**

whim [wɪm] *n* capricho *m*, antojo *m*; **as the w. takes him** según se le antoja

whimper ['wɪmpər] **1** *n* gimoteo *m*, quejido *m*; *(of dog)* gemido *m*

 2 *vi* gimotear, lloriquear; *(dog)* gemir

whimsical ['wɪmsɪkəl] *adj (person, idea)* caprichoso(a); *(smile)* enigmático(a)

whine [waɪn] **1** *n* (**a**) *(of pain)* quejido *m*; *(of dog)* gemido *m* (**b**) *(of engine)* rechinamiento *m*

 2 *vi* (**a**) *(child)* gimotear, lloriquear; *(dog)* gemir; *(with pain)* dar quejidos (**b**) *(complain)* gimotear, quejarse (**c**) *(engine)* rechinar

whining ['waɪnɪŋ] **1** *adj (child)* quejica

 2 *n (of child)* gimoteo *m*; *(of dog)* gemidos *mpl*

whinny ['wɪnɪ] **1** *vi* relinchar

 2 *n* relincho *m*

whip [wɪp] **1** *n* (**a**) *(for punishment)* azote *m*; *(of lion tamer)* látigo *m*; *(for riding)* fusta *f*, *Br Fam Fig* **to get a fair crack of the w.** tener la misma oportunidad (**b**) *Br Parl (person)* = oficial encargado de la disciplina de un partido

 2 *vt (pt & pp whipped)* (**a**) *(as punishment)* azotar, fustigar; *(horse)* dar latigazos a (**b**) *Culin* batir; *whipped cream Esp* nata *f* montada, *Am* crema *f* batida (**c**) *Fam Fig (beat easily)* dar una paliza a (**d**) *Fam (steal)* afanar, *Esp* mangar

whip away *vt* arrebatar, coger bruscamente

whip off *vt (clothes etc)* quitarse, *Am* sacarse

whip out *vt* sacar de repente

whip up *vt (passions, enthusiasm)* avivar, excitar; *(help)* activar, fomentar

whiplash ['wɪplæʃ] *n* (**a**) *(thong)* tralla *f* (**b**) *(stroke)* latigazo *m*

whippet ['wɪpɪt] *n Zool* galgo *m* pequeño

whipping ['wɪpɪŋ] *n* azotes *mpl*; **to give sb a w.** *(punish)* azotar a algn; *Fam (defeat)* dar una soberana paliza a algn ❑ *Culin* **w. cream** *Esp* nata *f* para montar, *Am* crema *f* para batir; *Fig* **w. boy** cabeza *f* de turco

whip-round ['wɪpraʊnd] *n Fam* colecta *f*; **to have a w.-r.** hacer una colecta

whirl [wɜːl] **1** *n* giro *m*, vuelta *f*; *Fig* torbellino *m*; *Fig* **my thoughts/senses are in a w.** tengo los pensamientos/los sentidos trastornados; *Fig* **the social w.** la vida mundana; *Fam* **let's give it a w.** probemos suerte

 2 *vt* **to w. sth round** dar vueltas a *or* hacer girar algo

 3 *vi* **to w. along/past** ir/pasar como un relámpago; **to w. round** girar con rapidez; *(dust, leaves)* arremolinarse; **my**

head's whirling me está dando vueltas la cabeza

whirlpool ['wɜːlpuːl] *n* remolino *m*, vorágine *f*

whirlwind ['wɜːlwɪnd] *n* torbellino *m*, remolino *m*

whir(r) [wɜːr] **1** *n* zumbido *m*, runrún *m*

 2 *vi* zumbar, runrunear

whisk [wɪsk] **1** *n* (**a**) *(movement)* movimiento *m* brusco; **a w. of the tail** un coletazo (**b**) *Culin* batidor *m*; *(electric)* batidora *f*

 2 *vt* (**a**) *(animal)* sacudir *(la cola)* (**b**) *Culin (eggs etc)* batir

 3 *vi* **to w. past** pasar a toda velocidad

whisk away, whisk off *vt* quitar bruscamente, llevarse de repente; **he was whisked off to hospital** lo llevaron a toda prisa al hospital; **using its tail to w. away the flies** sacudiéndose las moscas con la cola

whisker ['wɪskər] *n* pelo *m* (de la barba); **whiskers** *(of person)* barbas *fpl*, patillas *fpl*; *(of cat)* bigotes *mpl*; *Fig* **to win by a w.** ganar por un pelo

whisky, *US Ir* **whiskey** ['wɪskɪ] *n* whisky *m*, güisqui *m*

whisper ['wɪspər] **1** *n* (**a**) *(of person, leaves)* susurro *m*; **to speak in a w.** hablar en voz baja, *Am* hablar despacio (**b**) *(rumour)* rumor *m*

 2 *vt* decir en voz baja; **a whispered conversation** una conversación en voz baja

 3 *vi* cuchichear, susurrar, hablar en voz baja; *Fig (leaves)* susurrar

whispering ['wɪspərɪŋ] *n* (**a**) *(of people, voices)* cuchicheo *m*; *(of leaves)* susurro *m*, murmullo *m* (**b**) *(rumours)* murmuración *f*

whist [wɪst] *n Cards* whist *m*

whistle ['wɪsəl] **1** *n* (**a**) *(instrument)* pito *m*, silbato *m*; **to blow a** *or* **the w.** pitar; *Fig* **it broke as clean as a w.** se rompió limpiamente (**b**) *(sound)* silbido *m*, pitido *m*; **blast on a w.** pitido *m*, silbido *m*

 2 *vt (tune)* silbar

 3 *vi* (**a**) *(person, kettle, wind)* silbar; *(train)* pitar; **to w. (to) sb/a dog** llamar a algn/a un perro con un silbido (**b**) *(in protest)* silbar, pitar (**c**) *Fig (missile, train)* to w. past silbando (**d**) *Fam* **he can w. for his money** en lo que se refiere a su dinero, ya puede esperar sentado

whistle-blower ['wɪsəlbləʊər] *n (in company, government)* denunciante *mf* (de ilegalidades o corruptelas)

whistle-stop tour [wɪsəlstɒp'tʊər] *n Pol* = serie de visitas breves durante una campaña electoral

whistling ['wɪslɪŋ] *n* silbido(s) *m(pl)*

Whit [wɪt] **1** *adj* **W. Sunday/Monday** domingo *m*/lunes *m* de pentecostés

 2 *n Fam* pentecostés *m*; **at W.** en pentecostés

whit [wɪt] *n Fam* pizca *f*; **not a w.** ni un ápice, ni pizca

white [waɪt] **1** *adj* blanco(a); **a w. man** un hombre blanco; **to go w.** *(face)* palidecer, ponerse pálido(a); *(hair)* encanecer; **w. bread** pan blanco; **w. coffee** café *m* con leche; **w. hair** pelo *m* blanco *or* cano; *Fig* **as w. as a sheet** pálido(a) como la muerte; **as w. as snow** más blanco(a) que la nieve; *Fig* **to have a w. wedding** casarse por la iglesia ❑ **a w. Christmas** una Navidad con nieve; **the W. House** la Casa Blanca; **w. elephant** elefante *m* blanco; **w. heat** incandescencia *f*; **w. horses** *(in sea)* palomas *fpl*; **a w. lie** una mentira piadosa; *Parl* **w. paper** libro *m* blanco; *Bot* **w. poplar** álamo *m* blanco, chopo *m* blanco; *Culin* **w. sauce** bechamel *m*, *Col CSur* salsa *f* blanca; *Fam Pej* **w. trash** gentuza *f* blanca

 2 *n* (**a**) *(colour)* blanco *m*; **dressed in w.** vestido(a) de blanco (**b**) *(person)* blanco(a) *m,f* (**c**) *(of egg)* clara *f* (**d**) *Anat (of eye)* blanco *m* (**e**) **whites** ropa *f* sing blanca

whitebait ['waɪtbeɪt] *n* pescaditos *mpl* fritos

whitebeam ['waɪtbiːm] *n Bot* **common w.** mostajo *m*, mostellar *m*

white-collar ['waɪtkɒlər] *adj* **w.-c. worker** empleado(a) *m,f* administrativo(a) *or* de oficina

white-hot [waɪt'hɒt] *adj* candente, incandescente

whiten ['waɪtən] *vt* blanquear, blanquecer

whiteness ['waɪtnɪs] *n* blancura *f*

whitening ['waɪtənɪŋ] *n (for walls, shoes)* blanco *m* de España

whitewash ['waɪtwɒʃ] **1** *n* **(a)** *(paint)* lechada *f*, cal *f* **(b)** *Fig (cover-up)* encubrimiento *m* **(c)** *Fig (defeat)* paliza *f*
2 *vt* **(a)** *(wall)* enjalbegar, encalar, blanquear **(b)** *Fig (matter)* encubrir

whither ['wɪðər] *adv Literary* ¿adónde?

whiting ['waɪtɪŋ] *n inv (fish)* pescadilla *f*

whitish ['waɪtɪʃ] *adj* blanquecino(a)

Whitsun(tide) ['wɪtsən(taɪd)] *n Rel* pentecostés *m*

whittle ['wɪtəl] *vt* cortar en pedazos; **to w. away at** roer; *Fig* **to w. down** cercenar; *(expenses, list)* reducir poco a poco

whizz [wɪz] **1** *n Fam (expert)* genio *m* **(at de); w. kid** joven *mf* prodigio
2 *vi (bullet)* zumbar, silbar; *(person, car)* ir corriendo, ir zumbando; *(arrow)* rehilar; **to w. past** pasar zumbando; **he whizzed through the work** hizo el trabajo a toda velocidad

WHO [dʌbəlju:eɪtʃ'əʊ] *n (abbr* **World Health Organization)** Organización *f* Mundial de la Salud, OMS

who [hu:] *pron* **(a)** *(direct question)* quién, quiénes; **w. are they?** ¿quiénes son?; **w. is it?** ¿quién es?; *Fam* **w. did you meet?** ¿a quién encontraste?; *Fam* **w. is the book for?** ¿para quién es el libro?; **(b)** *(indirect question)* quién; **I don't know w. did it** no sé quién lo hizo; **to know w.'s w.** saber quién es quién; **w. should it be but Maria!** no podía ser otra (más) que María **(c)** *(defining relative)* que; **those w. don't know** los que no saben; *Fam* **the man w. I saw** el hombre que *or* a quien vi **(d)** *(nondefining relative)* quien, quienes, el/la cual, los/las cuales; **Elena's mother, w. is very rich ...** la madre de Elena, la cual es muy rica ... **(e)** **'Who's W.'** 'Quién es Quién'

whoa [wəʊ] *interj* ¡so!

whodun(n)it [hu:'dʌnɪt] *n Fam (book)* novela *f* de *Esp* suspense *or Am* suspenso; *(film)* película *f* de *Esp* suspense *or Am* suspenso *(centrada en la resolución de un caso de asesinato)*

whoever [hu:'evər] *pron* **(a)** *(anyone that)* quienquiera que; **whoever finds it may keep it** quienquiera que lo encuentre, puede quedarse con ello; **give it to w. you like** dáselo a quien quieras; **w. said that is a fool** el que dijo eso es un tonto; **w. you are** quienquiera que seas **(b)** *(direct question)* **w. told you that?** *(surprised)* ¿pero quién te dijo eso?; *(annoyed)* ¿quién (diablos) te dijo eso?

whole [həʊl] **1** *adj* **(a)** *(entire)* entero(a), íntegro(a); **a w. week** una semana entera; **he took the w. lot** se los llevó todos; **the w. truth** toda la verdad; **the w. world** el mundo entero; *Fig* **a w. lot of things** muchas *or* muchísimas cosas; *US Mus* **w. note** semibreve *f*, *Am* redonda *f* **(b)** *(in one piece)* intacto(a), sano(a); **there was not a glass left w.** no quedó un vaso sano **(c)** *Math* entero(a); **a w. number** un número entero
2 *n* **(a)** *(single unit)* todo *m*, conjunto *m*; **as a w.** en su totalidad, en conjunto; **the parts form a w.** las partes forman un conjunto **(b)** *(all)* totalidad *f*; **the w. of London** todo Londres; **the w. of the school** la escuela entera **(c)** **on the w.** en general, en conjunto

wholefood ['həʊlfu:d] *n* alimento(s) *m(pl)* integral(es) □ **w. shop** tienda *f* de dietética

wholehearted [həʊl'hɑ:tɪd] *adj (enthusiastic)* entusiasta; *(sincere)* sincero(a); *(unreserved)* incondicional; **my w. support** mi apoyo absoluto

wholeheartedly [həʊl'hɑ:tɪdlɪ] *adv* con entusiasmo, sinceramente, de todo corazón, sin reservas; **I agree w.** estoy totalmente de acuerdo

wholemeal ['həʊlmi:l] *adj Br* integral □ **w. bread** pan *m* integral

wholesale ['həʊlseɪl] *Com* **1** *n* venta *f* al por mayor, *Am* mayoreo *m*
2 *adj* al por mayor; *Fig* total, general; *Fig* **the w. destruction of plant life in the region** la destrucción absoluta de la vida vegetal de la región
3 *adv* al por mayor; *Fig* de modo general, en su totalidad; **the prisoners were massacred w.** los prisioneros fueron aniquilados por completo

wholesaler ['həʊlseɪlər] *n* mayorista *mf*

wholesome ['həʊlsəm] *adj (food)* sano(a); *Fig* sano(a), saludable

wholewheat ['həʊlwi:t] *adj esp US* integral

wholly ['həʊlɪ] *adv* enteramente, completamente

whom [hu:m] *pron Fml* **(a)** *(direct question) (accusative)* a quién; **w. did you see?** ¿a quién viste?; *(after preposition)* of *or* from **w.?** ¿de quién?; **to w. are you referring?** ¿a quién te refieres? **(b)** *rel (accusative)* que, a quien, a quienes; **those w. I have seen** los que he visto **(c)** *rel (after preposition)* quien, quienes, el/la cual, los/las cuales; **my brothers, both of w. are miners** mis hermanos, que son mineros los dos

whoop [wu:p] **1** *n* grito *m* de alegría
2 *vi* gritar de alegría; *Fam* **to w. it up** pasárselo en grande

whoopee [wʊ'pi:] *interj* ¡yupi!, ¡yuju!

whooping cough ['hu:pɪŋkɒf] *n Med* tos *f* ferina

whoops [wʊps] *interj* ¡ay!, ¡up lá!

whopper ['wɒpər] *n Fam* **(a)** *(big thing)* cosa *f* descomunal; *(of fish)* **what a w.!** ¡qué pez más gigante! **(b)** *(lie)* trola *f*, bola *f*

whopping ['wɒpɪŋ] *adj Fam* enorme, descomunal; **a w. great dinner** una cena impresionante

whore [hɔ:r] *n Offens* puta *f*

whose [hu:z] *pron* **(a)** *(direct question)* de quién, de quiénes; **w. are these gloves?** ¿de quién son estos guantes?; **w. car should we go in?** ¿en qué coche vamos a ir?; **w. daughter are you?** ¿de quién es usted hija?; **w. is this?** ¿a quién pertenece esto? **(b)** *(indirect question)* de quién, de quiénes; **I don't know w. these coats are** no sé de quién son estos abrigos **(c)** *rel* cuyo(s), cuya(s); **the man w. children we saw** el hombre a cuyos hijos vimos

why [waɪ] **1** *adv* por qué; *(for what purpose)* para qué; **I don't know w. he did it** no sé por qué lo hizo; **that is w. I didn't come** por eso no vine; **there's no reason w. you shouldn't go** no hay motivo para que no vayas; **w. not go to bed?** ¿por qué no te acuestas?; **w. (on earth) did you do that?** ¿por qué (demonios) hiciste eso?; **w. worry?** ¿por qué preocuparse?
2 *n Fam* porqué *m*; **the whys and wherefores** el porqué y el cómo
3 *interj* **(a)** *(fancy that!)* ¡toma!, ¡vaya!; **w., it's David!** ¡sí es David! **(b)** *(protest, assertion)* sí, vamos; **w. it's quite simple!** ¡si es muy sencillo!; **w., of course!** ¡vaya que sí!, ¡por supuesto que sí!

wick [wɪk] *n* mecha *f*; *Br Fam Fig* **to get on sb's w.** tocarle las narices a algn

wicked ['wɪkɪd] *adj* **(a)** *(person)* malvado(a), malo(a); *(action)* malo(a), perverso(a); **a w. grin** una sonrisa traviesa **(b)** *Fam* malísimo(a); *(temper)* terrible; *(waste)* vergonzoso(a); *(weather)* feo(a), horrible

wickedly ['wɪkɪdlɪ] *adv* **(a)** *(behave)* malvadamente, perversamente **(b)** *Fam* **w. expensive** terriblemente caro(a)

wickedness ['wɪkɪdnɪs] *n* maldad *f*

wicker ['wɪkər] **1** *n* mimbre
  2 *adj* de mimbre; **w. chair** silla *f* de mimbre

wickerwork ['wɪkəwɜːk] *n (material)* mimbre *m*; *(art)* cestería *f*; *(articles)* artículos *mpl* de mimbre

wicket ['wɪkɪt] *n* **(a)** *(in cricket) (stumps)* palos *mpl*; *(pitch)* terreno *m*; *Br Fig* **to be on a sticky w.** encontrarse en apuros **(b) w. gate** postigo *m*, portillo *m*

wicketkeeper ['wɪkɪtkiːpər] *n (in cricket)* cátcher *m*

wide [waɪd] **1** *adj* **(a)** *(road, trousers)* ancho(a); *(eyes)* muy abiertos; *(gap, interval)* grande; *(measure)* **it is ten metres w.** tiene diez metros de ancho; **the curtain is too w. for the window** la cortina es demasiado ancha para la ventana **(b)** *(area)* amplio(a), extenso(a); *(knowledge, experience, repercussions)* amplio(a), extenso(a); *(coverage, range, support)* extenso(a); **a w. variety** una gran variedad; **to win by a w. margin** ganar por un amplio margen; **w. interests** intereses muy diversos **(c)** *(off target)* desviado(a); *Ftb* **the shot was w.** el tiro salió desviado; **to be w. of the mark** no dar en el blanco; *Fig* no acertar
  2 *adv* **from far and w.** de todas partes; *(at dentist)* **open w.!** ¡abra bien la boca!; **to open one's eyes w.** abrir los ojos de par en par; *Ftb* **to shoot w.** chutar el balón muy desviado; *Aut* **to take the bend w.** tomar la curva abierta; **w. apart** muy separados(as); **w. awake** completamente despierto(a); *Fig* despabilado(a); **w. open** *(door, eyes, mouth)* abierto(a) de par en par; *(spaces)* muy abiertos(as); **with mouth w. open** boquiabierto(a)

wide-angle ['waɪdæŋgəl] *adj Phot* **w.-a. lens** objetivo *m* gran angular

wide-eyed [waɪd'aɪd] *adj* con los ojos muy abiertos

widely ['waɪdlɪ] *adv (travel, scatter)* extensamente; *(believed, available)* generalmente; **he is w. known** es muy conocido; **her books are w. read** su obra es muy leída

widen ['waɪdən] **1** *vt (road, hole, etc)* ensanchar; *(interests)* ampliar, extender
  2 *vi* ensancharse; *Fig* **the gap has widened** las diferencias han aumentado

wide-ranging ['waɪdreɪndʒɪŋ] *adj (interests)* múltiples, muy diversos(as); *(discussion)* amplio(a); *(survey, study)* de gran alcance

widespread ['waɪdspred] *adj (unrest, belief)* general; *(damage)* extenso(a); **to become w.** generalizarse

widow ['wɪdəʊ] *n* viuda *f*

widowed ['wɪdəʊd] *adj* enviudado(a); **to be w.** enviudar

widower ['wɪdəʊər] *n* viudo *m*

widowhood ['wɪdəʊhʊd] *n* viudez *f*

width [wɪdθ] *n* **(a)** *(gen)* extensión *f*, anchura *f* **(b)** *(of material)* ancho *m*

wield [wiːld] *vt (weapon, pen)* manejar; *(weapon)* blandir; *Fig (power)* ejercer

wife [waɪf] *n (pl wives)* mujer *f*, esposa *f* □ *Fig* **old wives' tale** cuento *m* de viejas

wig [wɪg] *n* peluca *f*

wigging ['wɪgɪŋ] *n Br Fam* **to give sb a w.** echar un rapapolvo a algn

wiggle ['wɪgəl] **1** *vt (finger etc)* menear; **to w. (one's) hips** contonearse
  2 *vi* menearse

wiggly ['wɪglɪ] *adj* **(wigglier, wiggliest)** ondulado(a)

Wight [waɪt] *n* **Isle of W.** Isla *f* de Wight

wigwam ['wɪgwæm] *n US* tienda *f* india, tepe *m*

wild [waɪld] **1** *adj* **(a)** *(animal, tribe)* salvaje; *(bull)* bravo(a); **w. beast** fiera *f*; **w. goose** ganso *m* salvaje; *Fig* **w. horses wouldn't drag me there** no iría ni por todo el oro del mundo □ *Fig* **w. goose chase** búsqueda *f* inútil **(b)** *(plant)* silvestre, salvaje **(c)** *(landscape)* agreste, salvaje; *(wind)* furioso(a), borrascoso(a); **a w. night** una noche tormentosa; **the W. West** el Salvaje Oeste **(d)** *(temperament, behaviour)* alocado(a), desordenado(a); *(appearance)* desordenado(a); *(passions, imagination, dance)* desenfrenado(a); *(laughter, enthusiasm)* loco(a); *(applause)* fervoroso(a); *(thoughts)* extravagante, loco(a); *Fam Fig* **she is w. party** una fiesta bárbara; *Sport* **a w. shot** un tiro incontrolado; **to make a w. guess** adivinar al azar; **w. with joy/jealousy** loco(a) de alegría/celos; *Fam Fig* **she is w. about him/about tennis** está loca por él/por el tenis **(e)** *Br Fam Fig (angry)* furioso(a); **it makes me w.** me exaspera; **to be w.** estar furioso(a) **(with** contra) **(f)** *Cards Comptr* **w. card** comodín *m*
  2 *adv (garden)* **to grow w.** ser silvestre; **to run w.** *(animal)* vivir en su estado natural; *(garden)* volver al estado silvestre; *Fig (children)* desmandarse; *Fig (hooligans)* portarse como salvajes
  3 *n (animals)* **in the w.** en el estado salvaje *or* natural; **the wild (of Africa)** las regiones salvajes (de África); *Fig* **to live out in the wilds** vivir en el campo

wildcat ['waɪldkæt] *n (pl* **wildcat** *or* **wildcats)** *Zool* gato(a) *m,f* montes □ *Ind* **w. strike** huelga *f* salvaje

wildebeest ['wɪldɪbiːst] *n* ñu *m*

wilderness ['wɪldənɪs] *n* desierto *m*, yermo *m*

wildfire ['waɪldfaɪər] *n* **to spread like w.** correr como la pólvora

wildfowl ['waɪldfaʊl] *npl Orn* aves *fpl* de caza

wildlife ['waɪldlaɪf] *n* fauna *f* □ **w. park** safari *m*

wildly ['waɪldlɪ] *adv* **(a)** *(rush round, gesticulate)* como un(a) loco(a), frenéticamente; *(applaud)* fervorosamente; *(shoot)* sin apuntar; *(hit out)* a tontas y a locas **(b) w. enthusiastic** loco(a) de entusiasmo; **w. exaggerated** exageradísimo(a); **w. inaccurate** sumamente inexacto(a)

wildness ['waɪldnɪs] *n* **(a)** *(of animal)* estado *m* salvaje; *(plants)* estado *m* silvestre **(b)** *(of landscape)* aspecto *m* agreste *or* salvaje **(c)** *(of wind)* furia *f* **(d)** *(of temperament, passions)* locura *f*, desenfreno *m*; *(of behaviour)* desórdenes *mpl*; *(of appearance)* desorden *m*; *(of ideas)* extravagancia *f*

wiles [waɪlz] *npl (tricks)* artimañas *fpl*, artificios *mpl*; *(cunning)* astucia *f*

wilful, *US* **wilfull** ['wɪlfʊl] *adj* **(a)** *(stubborn)* voluntarioso(a); **a w. child** un niño terco **(b)** *Jur* premeditado(a)

wilfully, *US* **willfully** ['wɪlfʊlɪ] *adv* **(a)** *(stubbornly)* voluntariosamente, tercamente **(b)** *esp Jur (deliberately)* premeditadamente; **on the day in question, you did w. and maliciously plan the bombing** en el día de la fecha, planeó con premeditación y alevosía la colocación de la bomba

will[1] [wɪl] **1** *n* **(a)** *(resolve, determination)* voluntad *f*; **against my w.** contra mi voluntad, a pesar mío; **an iron w.** una voluntad de hierro; **good/ill w.** buena/mala voluntad; **of my own free w.** por mi propia voluntad; **the w. to live** la voluntad de vivir; **with the best w. in the world** con la mejor voluntad del mundo; *Prov* **where there's a w. there's a way** querer es poder **(b)** *Jur (testament)* testamento *m*; **he left me the house in his w.** me dejó *or* legó la casa; **last w. and testament** última disposición *f or* voluntad *f*; **to make one's w.** hacer testamento
  2 *vt* desear; **fate willed that …** el destino quiso que …

will[2] [wɪl] *v aux (pt* **would)** **(a)** *(future) (esp 2nd & 3rd person)* **don't forget, w. you!** ¡que no se te olvide, eh!; **I'll starve — no, you won't!** voy a morir de hambre — ¡qué va!; **she w. not** *or* **she won't do it** no lo hará; **they w. come, they'll come** vendrán; **w. he be there? — yes, he w.** ¿estará allí? — sí, (estará); **you'll tell him, won't you?**

se lo dirás, ¿verdad? (**b**) *(command)* **you w. be here at eleven!** ¡estarás aquí a las once! (**c**) *(future perfect)* **they w.** *or* **they'll have finished by tomorrow** habrán terminado para mañana (**d**) *(willingness)* **be quiet, w. you! — no, I won't!** ¿quiere callarse? — no quiero; *(marriage ceremony)* **I w.** sí, quiero; **I won't have it!** ¡no lo permito!; **the car won't start** no arranca el coche; **w. you have a drink? — yes, I w.** ¿quiere tomar algo? — sí, por favor; **won't you sit down?** ¿quiere sentarse? (**e**) *(custom)* **accidents w. happen** siempre habrá accidentes; **he w. play for hours** suele jugar durante horas y horas (**f**) *(persistence)* **he w. have it that ...** se obstina en creer que ...; **if you w. go out without a coat ...** si te empeñas en salir sin abrigo ... (**g**) *(probability)* **he'll be on holiday now** ahora estará de vacaciones (**h**) *(ability)* **the car w. do a hundred miles per hour** el coche puede alcanzar cien millas por hora; **the lift w. hold ten people** en el ascensor caben diez personas

willie ['wɪlɪ] *n Br Fam* pito *m*, pilila *f*

willies ['wɪlɪz] *npl Fam* susto *m sing*; **that man gives me the w.** ese hombre me pone la piel de gallina; **to put the w. up sb** poner los pelos de punta a algn

willing ['wɪlɪŋ] *adj (obliging)* servicial, complaciente; **God w.** si Dios quiere; **I'm willing w. to do it** lo haré con mucho gusto; **there were plenty of w. hands** no faltaban personas dispuestas a ayudar; **to be w. to do sth** estar dispuesto(a) a hacer algo; **to show w.** dar pruebas de buena voluntad

willingly ['wɪlɪŋlɪ] *adv* de buena gana, de (buen) grado; **I would w. pay but ...** pagaría de buena gana pero ...

willingness ['wɪlɪŋnɪs] *n* buena voluntad *f*; **his w. to help** su buena disposición para ayudar

will-o'-the-wisp [wɪləðə'wɪsp] *n* fuego *m* fatuo

willow ['wɪləʊ] *n Bot* **w. (tree)** sauce *m* □ **crack w.** mimbrera *f*; **goat w.** sauce *m* cabruno; **white w.** sauce *m* blanco

willowy ['wɪləʊɪ] *adj* esbelto(a)

willpower ['wɪlpaʊər] *n* (fuerza *f* de) voluntad *f*; **she lacks w.** tiene poca voluntad

willy-nilly [wɪlɪ'nɪlɪ] *adv* de grado o por fuerza

wilt [wɪlt] *vi (plant)* marchitarse

wily ['waɪlɪ] *adj* (**wilier**, **wiliest**) astuto(a), zorro(a)

WIMP [wɪmp] *Comptr n* (*abbr* **windows, icons, menus and pointing device** *or* **pointer**) **W. (interface)** interfaz *f* WIMP

wimp [wɪmp] *n Fam (physically)* debilucho(a) *m,f*; *(lacking character)* blandengue *mf*

win [wɪn] **1** *n* victoria *f*; **to have a w. (on the pools)** ganar (en las quinielas)
2 *vt* (*pt & pp* **won**) (**a**) *(gen)* ganar; *(prize)* ganar, llevarse; *(victory)* conseguir, ganar; **to w. a place in the team** conseguir un puesto en el equipo; **to w. sth from sb** ganarle algo a algn; **to w. the pools** ganar en las quinielas (**b**) *Fig (sympathy)* ganarse, granjearse; *(friendship)* granjearse; *(praise)* cosechar, atraerse; **to w. friends** granjearse amistades; **to w. sb's love** *or* **heart** conquistar a algn
3 *vi* ganar; *Fam* **you can't w.!** ¡no hay manera de hacerlo bien!

win back *vt (land etc)* reconquistar; *(money)* recuperar

win over *vt* ganar; *(to cause, idea)* atraer (**to** a, hacia); *(voters)* ganarse, arrastrar

win through *vi* conseguir triunfar

wince [wɪns] **1** *vi* tener un rictus de dolor
2 *n* mueca *f* or rictus *m* de dolor

winch [wɪntʃ] **1** *n* cigüeña *f*, torno *m*, cabrestante *m*
2 *vt* **to w. sth up** levantar algo con un torno

wind¹ [wɪnd] **1** *n* (**a**) *(air current)* viento *m*; **high winds** vientos fuertes; **into the w.** contra el viento; **north w.** viento del norte; **to sail close to the w.** *Naut* navegar de bolina; *Fig* jugar con una situación peligrosa; *Naut* **to sail /** **run before the w.** navegar viento en popa; *Fig* **there's something in the w.** algo flota en el aire; **to get w. of sth** olerse algo; *Fig (curb)* **to take the w. out of sb's sails** pararle los pies a algn; *Fig* **to throw caution to the w.** dejar de lado la prudencia; *Fam Fig* **to get the w. up** ponerse nervioso(a); *Prov* **it's an ill w. (that blows nobody any good)** no hay mal que por bien no venga □ **w. energy** energía *f* eólica; **w. farm** parque *m* eólico, central *f* eólica; **w. tunnel** túnel *m* aerodinámico (**b**) *(breath)* aliento *m*; **to get one's second w.** recobrar el aliento (**c**) *Med* flato *m*, flatulencia *f*; **to have w.** tener gases; *Euph* **to break w.** ventosear (**d**) *Mus* **w. instrument** instrumento *m* de viento
2 *vt* cortar la respiración a; **to be winded** quedarse sin aliento

wind² [waɪnd] **1** *vt* (*pt & pp* **wound**) (**a**) *(onto a reel)* arrollar, devanar; **to w. a bandage round one's finger** envolverse el dedo con una venda; **to w. wool (up) into a ball** ovillar lana (**b**) *(film, tape)* **to w. on/back** avanzar/rebobinar (**c**) *(in fishing)* **to w. in the line** cobrar el sedal (**d**) *(clock)* dar cuerda a (**e**) *(handle, winch)* dar vueltas a
2 *vi (road, river)* serpentear; *(snake)* enroscarse (**around** alrededor de)
3 *n (of road, river)* recodo *m*, vuelta *f*

wind down 1 *vt Aut (window)* bajar
2 *vi* (**a**) *(clock)* quedarse sin cuerda (**b**) *Fam (relax)* relajarse

wind up 1 *vt* (**a**) *(roll up)* devanar, enrollar (**b**) *(close)* *(business etc)* cerrar, liquidar; *(session, debate)* clausurar (**c**) *(clock)* dar cuerda a (**d**) *Fam* **to be all wound up** estar nerviosísimo(a)
2 *vi* (**a**) *(meeting)* terminar; *(speaker)* acabar el discurso (**b**) *Fam (end up)* acabar; **you'll w. up in hospital** acabarás en el hospital

windbag ['wɪndbæg] *n Fam* charlatán(ana) *m,f*

windbreak ['wɪndbreɪk] *n* abrigo *m*, abrigadero *m*

winder ['waɪndər] *n (of watch)* corona *f*

windfall ['wɪndfɔːl] *n (fruit)* fruta *f* caída; *Fig* ganancia *f* inesperada *or* caída del cielo

winding ['waɪndɪŋ] *adj (road, river)* sinuoso(a), tortuoso(a); *(staircase)* de caracol

windlass ['wɪndləs] *n Tech* torno *m*

windmill ['wɪndmɪl] *n* molino *m* (de viento)

window ['wɪndəʊ] *n (of house)* & *Comptr* ventana *f*; *(of vehicle, of ticket office, in post office)* ventanilla *f*; *Rail* **a w. seat** un asiento junto a la ventanilla; *(shop)* **w.** escaparate *m*, *Am* vidriera *f*, *Chile Col Méx* vitrina *f*; **to clean the windows** limpiar los cristales; **to lean out of the window** asomarse a la ventana □ *Archit* **stained-glass w.** vidriera *f*; **w. box** jardinera *f*; **w. cleaner** limpiacristales *mf inv*; **w. dresser** escaparatista *mf*; **w. dressing** decoración *f* de escaparates; *Fig* fachada *f*, apariencias *fpl*; **w. frame** marco *m* de ventana

windowpane ['wɪndəʊpeɪn] *n* vidrio *m* *or Esp* cristal *m* (de ventana)

window-shopping ['wɪndəʊʃɒpɪŋ] *n* **to go w.-s.** ir a mirar escaparates

windowsill ['wɪndəʊsɪl] *n* alféizar *m*, antepecho *m*

windpipe ['wɪndpaɪp] *n Anat* tráquea *f*

windscreen ['wɪndskriːn] *n, US* **windshield** ['wɪndʃiːld] *n Aut* parabrisas *m inv* □ **w. washer** lavaparabrisas *m inv*; **w. wiper** limpiaparabrisas *m inv*

windsock ['wɪndsɒk] *n Av* manga *f*, cataviento *m*

windsurfing ['wɪndsɜːfɪŋ] *n* **to go w.** ir a hacer windsurf *or* tabla a vela

windswept ['wɪndswept] *adj (landscape)* azotado(a) por el viento; *(person, hair)* despeinado(a) (por el viento)

windward ['wɪndwəd] **1** *adj Naut* de barlovento; **the W. Islands** las Islas de Barlovento
2 *n* barlovento *m*; **to w.** a barlovento

windy ['wɪndɪ] *adj* (**windier, windiest**) (**a**) *(day, weather)* ventoso(a); *(place)* expuesto(a) al viento; **it is very w. today** hoy hace mucho viento (**b**) *Fam Fig* miedoso(a), cagón(ona); **he got w.** le entró canguelo *or* mieditis

wine [waɪn] **1** *n* vino *m*; **red w.** vino tinto; **table w.** vino de mesa; **w.-producing region** región *f* vitícola ❏ **w. cellar** bodega *f*; **w. list** lista *f* de vinos; **w. merchant** vinatero(a) *m,f*; **w. tasting** cata *f* de vinos; **w. vinegar** vinagre *m* de vino
2 *vt Fam Fig* **to w. and dine sb** agasajar a algn, tratar a algn por todo lo alto

wineglass ['waɪnɡlɑːs] *n* copa *f* (para vino)

wineskin ['waɪnskɪn] *n* odre *m*

wing [wɪŋ] **1** *n* (**a**) *(of bird, plane)* ala *f*; **to take w.** alzar el vuelo; *Fig* **to clip sb's wings** cortarle las alas a algn; *Fig* **to take sb under one's w.** tomar a algn bajo su protección ❏ *Br Av* **w. commander** teniente *m* coronel; **w. tip** punta *f* del ala (**b**) *(of building)* ala *f* (**c**) *Br Aut* aleta *f* ❏ **w. mirror** retrovisor *m* externo (**d**) *(of armchair)* oreja *f* (**e**) **wings** *Theat* (**in the**) **w.** (entre) bastidores *mpl*; *Fig* **to wait in the w.** esperar la entrada en escena (**f**) *Ftb* banda *f*; **to dribble down the right w.** driblar por la banda derecha (**g**) *Pol* ala *f*; **the left w.** el ala izquierda, la izquierda (**h**) **w. nut** *(for bolt)* tuerca *f* mariposa
2 *vt* **to w. its way** ir volando

winger ['wɪŋər] *n Ftb* extremo *m*

wingspan ['wɪŋspæn] *n (of bird, plane)* envergadura *f*

wink [wɪŋk] **1** *n* guiño *m*; **to give sb a w.** hacerle un guiño a algn; *Fig* **as quick as a w.** en un abrir y cerrar de ojos; *Fig* **to tip sb the w.** darle el soplo a algn; *Fam Fig* **a nod is as good as a w.** a buen entendedor con pocas palabras basta; *Fam Fig* **I didn't get a w. (of sleep)** no pegué ojo; *Fam Fig* **to have forty winks** echar una siestecita *or* una cabezada
2 *vi* (**a**) *(person)* guiñar el ojo (**b**) *(light)* titil(e)ar, parpadear

winker ['wɪŋkər] *n Br Aut* intermitente *m*

winking ['wɪŋkɪŋ] *adj* pestañeante

winkle ['wɪŋkəl] **1** *n Zool* bígaro *m*, bigarro *m*
2 *vt Br Fam* **to w. sth out of sb** sacar *or* sonsacar algo a algn

winner ['wɪnər] *n* ganador(a) *m,f*, vencedor(a) *m,f*; *Fam Fig* **this product is a w.** este producto será un gran éxito

winning ['wɪnɪŋ] *adj (person, team)* ganador(a), vencedor(a); *(number, ticket)* premiado(a); *(stroke, goal)* decisivo(a); *(ways, smile)* atractivo(a) ❏ **w. post** meta *f*

winnings ['wɪnɪŋz] *npl* ganancias *fpl*

winnow ['wɪnəʊ] *vt Agr* aventar

wino ['waɪnəʊ] *(pl* **winos***) n Fam (alcoholic)* borracho(a) *m,f*

winsome ['wɪnsəm] *adj* encantador(a), atractivo(a)

winter ['wɪntər] **1** *n* invierno *m*; **in w. (time)** en invierno
2 *adj* de invierno, invernal; **w. clothes** ropa *f* de invierno ❏ **w. sports** deportes *mpl* de invierno
3 *vi* pasar el invierno, invernar

wintertime ['wɪntətaɪm] *n* invierno *m*

wint(e)ry ['wɪnt(ə)rɪ] *adj* (**wintrier, wintriest**) *(scene, weather)* invernal, de invierno

wipe [waɪp] **1** *vt* limpiar, enjugar; **to w. one's brow** enjugarse la frente; **to w. one's feet/nose** limpiarse los pies/las narices; **to w. sth (dry/clean)** enjugar/limpiar algo; **to w. the dishes** enjugar los platos; *Fam Fig (defeat)* **to w. the floor with sb** cascarle una paliza a algn
2 *n* limpión *m*; **to give sth a w.** darle un limpión a algo

wipe away *vt (tear)* enjugar

wipe down *vt (walls)* rascar

wipe off *vt* quitar frotando; **to w. sth off the blackboard/the tape** borrar algo de la pizarra/de la cinta; *Fam Fig* **to w. the smile off sb's face** quitarle a algn las ganas de reír

wipe out *vt* (**a**) *(erase)* borrar; *Fig* **to w. out the memory of sth** borrar algo de la memoria (**b**) *(illness)* erradicar, extirpar (**c**) *(destroy) (army)* aniquilar; *(species, population)* exterminar

wipe up *vt* limpiar

wiper ['waɪpər] *n Aut* limpiaparabrisas *m inv*; **w. blade** goma *f* del limpiaparabrisas

wire [waɪər] **1** *n* (**a**) *(in general)* alambre *m*; *Elec* cable *m*; *Tel* hilo *m*; *Fig* **she's a live w.** tiene muchísima energía ❏ **barbed w.** alambre *m* de espino *or* de púas; *Mil* **barbed w. entanglement** *or* **fence** alambrada *f*; **w. brush** cepillo *m* metálico; **w. cutters** cortaalambres *m inv*, cizalla *f sing*; **w. netting** red *f* de alambre, tela *f* metálica; *(on window)* alambrera *f*; **w. wool** estropajo *m* metálico (**b**) *US (telegram)* telegrama *m*, cable(grama) *m*
2 *vt* (**a**) *(tie)* atar con alambre (**b**) *Elec* **to w. (up) a house** poner *or* instalar el cableado de una casa; **to w. (up) an appliance to the mains** conectar un aparato a la toma eléctrica; **wired for sound** sonorizado(a) (**c**) *(telegram etc)* poner un telegrama a, enviar por telegrama

wireless ['waɪəlɪs] **1** *n Old-fashioned* (**a**) *(system)* radiofonía *f*, radio *f* ❏ **w. operator** radiotelegrafista *mf* (**b**) **w. (set)** (aparato *m* de) radio *f*; **I heard it on the w.** lo oí por la radio
2 *adj Comptr* wireless, inalámbrico(a)

wiretap ['waɪətæp] *US* **1** *n* escucha *f* telefónica
2 *vt* intervenir

wiretapping ['waɪətæpɪŋ] *n US* intervención *f* de teléfonos

wiring ['waɪərɪŋ] *n Elec (network)* cableado *m*; *(action)* instalación *f* del cableado ❏ **w. diagram** esquema *m* del cableado

wiry ['waɪərɪ] *adj* (**wirier, wiriest**) *(hair)* estropajoso(a); *(person)* nervudo(a)

wisdom ['wɪzdəm] *n* (**a**) *(learning)* sabiduría *f*, saber *m* (**b**) *(good sense) (of person)* cordura *f*, (buen) juicio *m*; *(of action)* prudencia *f*, lo prudente (**c**) **w. tooth** muela *f* del juicio

wise [waɪz] *adj* (**a**) *(learned)* sabio(a); **a w. man** un sabio; *(Bible)* **the Three W. Men** los Reyes Magos ❏ *US Fam* **w. guy** sabelotodo *mf* (**b**) *(knowledgeable)* sabio(a), entendido(a); *Fig* **it's easy to be w. after the event** todo el mundo es listo después de visto; *Fam Fig* **I'm none the wiser** sigo sin entender; *Fam Fig* **I've got w. to him** ya le he calado; *Fam Fig* **nobody will be any the wiser** nadie se dará cuenta; *Fam Fig* **to put sb w.** poner a algn al tanto (**to, about** de) (**c**) *(sensible) (advice)* sabio(a), cuerdo(a); *(remark)* juicioso(a); *(decision, move)* atinado(a), acertado(a); **it would be w. to keep quiet** sería prudente callarse; **you were very w.** obraste con acierto *or* con mucho tino

wise up *vi Fam* (**a**) *(realise)* darse cuenta (**b**) *(accept)* aceptar; **w. up!** ¡para que lo sepas!, ¡a ver si te enteras!

wisecrack ['waɪzkræk] *Fam* **1** *n* salida *f*, chiste *m*
2 *vi* chancear, bromear

wisely ['waɪzlɪ] *adv* (**a**) *(with wisdom)* sabiamente (**b**) *(with prudence)* juiciosamente, prudentemente

wish [wɪʃ] **1** *n* (**a**) *(desire)* deseo *m* (**for** de); **according to/against his wishes** según/contra sus deseos; **I haven't the slightest w. to go** no tengo el menor deseo de ir; **to**

make a w. pedir un deseo **(b) wishes** deseos *mpl*; *(greeting)* **best w.** felicitaciones *fpl*; **give your mother my best w.** salude a su madre de mi parte; **with best w. for the future** con mis/nuestros mejores deseos para el futuro; *(end of letter)* **with best w., Peter** saludos (cordiales) de Peter

2 *vt* **(a)** *(want)* querer, desear; **I w. he would hurry up** estoy deseando que se dé prisa; **I w. I could stay longer** me gustaría poder quedarme más tiempo; **I w. that I were in your place** quisiera estar en tu lugar; **I w. you had told me!** ¡ojalá me lo hubieras dicho!; **to w. to do sth** querer *or* desear hacer algo **(b)** *(foist)* desear; **to w. sth onto sb** endosarle algo a algn; **I wouldn't w. it on anyone** no desearía que lo sufriera nadie **(c)** *(desire)* desear; **to w. sb goodnight** darle las buenas noches a algn; **to w. sb well** *or* **luck** *or* **all the best** desearle a algn mucha suerte

3 *vi* **(a)** *(with wishbone etc)* pedir un deseo **(b)** *(want)* desear; **as you w.** como quieras; **do as you w.** haga lo que quiera; **I have everything I could w. for** tengo todo cuanto pudiera desear; **to w. for sth** desear algo

wishbone ['wɪʃbəʊn] *n Anat Orn* espoleta *f*

wishful ['wɪʃfʊl] *adj* **it's w. thinking** es hacerse ilusiones

wishy-washy ['wɪʃɪwɒʃɪ] *adj Fam (person)* soso(a), insípido(a), sin carácter; *(ideas)* borroso(a)

wisp [wɪsp] *n (of straw)* brizna *f; (of wool, hair)* mechón *m; (of smoke)* voluta *f; Fig* **a mere w. of a girl** una chica menudita

wispy ['wɪspɪ] *adj* **(wispier, wispiest)** tenue, delgado(a)

wistful ['wɪstfʊl] *adj* melancólico(a), nostálgico(a), pensativo(a)

wit [wɪt] *n* **(a)** *(intelligence) (often pl)* inteligencia *f; (ingenuity)* ingenio *m;* **a battle of wits** una pugna de inteligencias; **she didn't have the w. to say no** no tuvo suficiente inteligencia *or* presencia de ánimo para decir que no; *Fig* **to be at one's wits' end** estar para volverse loco(a); *Fam Fig* **to have one's wits about one** ser *or* estar despabilado(a) **(b)** *(humour)* ingenio *m*, agudeza *f*, chispa *f* **(c)** *(person)* chistoso(a) *m,f*, persona *f* salada

witch [wɪtʃ] *n* bruja *f* □ **w. doctor** hechicero *m*

witchcraft ['wɪtʃkrɑ:ft] *n* brujería *f*, hechicería *f*

witch-hunt ['wɪtʃhʌnt] *n Pol* caza *f* de brujas

with [wɪð, wɪθ] *prep* **(a)** *(in possession of)* con; **a room w. a bath/w. no bath** un cuarto con baño/sin baño; **do you have any money w. you?** traes dinero?; **the man w. the glasses** el hombre de las gafas **(b)** *(accompanying)* con; **he went w. me/you** fue conmigo/contigo; **to leave a child w. sb** dejar a un niño al cuidado de algn; *Naut* **to sail w. the wind** navegar con el viento; *Fam* **w. (sugar) or without (sugar)?** ¿azúcar? **(c)** *(including)* con; **I have six w. this one** con éste tengo seis; **it cost 40 euros w. wine** costó 40 euros vino incluido **(d)** *(despite)* con; **w. all his faults, I admire him** le admiro con todos sus defectos **(e)** *(given)* con; **w. your help/permission** con su ayuda/ permiso; **w. your intelligence it will be easy** dada su inteligencia será fácil **(f)** *Fig (on the side of)* con; **we're all w. you** todos estamos contigo **(g)** *(contact, relationship)* con; **he's w. Lloyd's** trabaja para Lloyd's; **it has nothing to do w. politics** no tiene nada que ver con la política; **she is popular w. her colleagues** es popular entre sus colegas; **to deal/mix w. sb** tratar/asociarse con algn **(h)** *(against)* con; **at war w. France** en guerra con Francia; **to fight/ compete w. sb** pelearse/competir con algn **(i)** *(regarding)* con; **I had trouble w. the clutch** tuve problemas con el embrague; **w. him, money is everything** para él, todo es cuestión de dinero **(j)** *(manner)* con, de; **to fill a vase w. water** llenar un jarrón de agua; **w. difficulty** con dificultad; **w. one gulp** de un trago; **w. tears in her eyes** con los ojos llenos de lágrimas **(k)** *(instrument)* con; **it is**

made w. butter está hecho con mantequilla; **they cut the bread w. a knife** cortaron el pan con un cuchillo **(l)** *(circumstances)* con; **I can't phone w. my boss here** no puedo telefonear estando mi jefe aquí; **to sleep w. the window open** dormir con la ventana abierta **(m)** *(because of)* de; **she put on weight w. so much eating** engordó de tanto comer; **to be paralysed w. fear** estar paralizado(a) de miedo **(n)** *(after)* con; **w. experience** con la experiencia; **w. that, he went out** con lo cual salió; **w. these words he left** dicho esto, se marchó **(o)** *(from)* de, con; **to break w. sb** romper con algn; **to part company w. sb** separarse de algn **(p)** *(according to)* con, según; **it varies w. the season** varía con la temporada **(q)** *(expressions)* **down w. the president!** ¡abajo el presidente!; **on w. the show!** ¡que siga el espectáculo!; **to hell w. the neighbours!** ¡al diablo con los vecinos!

withdraw [wɪð'drɔ:] **1** *vt (pt* **withdrew***; pp* **withdrawn)** **(a)** *(gen)* retirar, sacar; **to w. money from the bank** retirar *or* sacar dinero del banco **(b)** *(go back on)* retirar; *(statement, accusation)* retractarse de; *(plan)* renunciar a; *Jur (demand)* renunciar a, apartarse de

2 *vi* **(a)** *(move back)* retirarse, apartarse; *(from room)* retirarse; *Mil* replegarse, retirarse **(b)** *(drop out)* renunciar; *Sport* **to w. from a competition** retirarse de un concurso

withdrawal [wɪð'drɔ:əl] *n* retirada *f; (of statement, accusation)* retractación *f; (of complaint, plan, candidate)* renuncia *f; Sport* retirada *f* □ **w. method** *Fam* marcha *f* atrás; *Med* **w. symptoms** síndrome *m* de abstinencia

withdrawn [wɪð'drɔ:n] **1** *pp see* **withdraw**
2 *adj (person)* introvertido(a), cerrado(a)

withdrew [wɪð'dru:] *pt see* **withdraw**

wither ['wɪðər] **1** *vt (plant)* marchitar
2 *vi* marchitarse

withered ['wɪðəd] *adj (plant)* marchito(a); *Fig (person)* **old and w.** viejo(a) y ajado(a)

withering ['wɪðərɪŋ] *adj (look)* fulminante; *(criticism)* mordaz

withhold [wɪð'həʊld] *vt (pt & pp* **withheld** [wɪð'held]) *(money)* retener; *(decision)* aplazar; *(consent)* negar; *(information)* ocultar

within [wɪ'ðɪn] **1** *prep* **(a)** *(inside)* dentro de; **w. the city limits** dentro de los límites de la ciudad **(b)** *(distance, range)* **accurate to w. a centimetre** exacto(a) con una diferencia de un centímetro; **it is w. walking distance** se puede ir caminando *or Esp* andando; **situated w. five kilometres of the town** situado(a) a menos de cinco kilómetros de la ciudad; **w. a radius of ten miles** en un radio de diez millas; **w. sight of the sea** con vistas al mar; *Fig* **w. an inch of death** a dos dedos de la muerte **(c)** *(time)* **they arrived w. a few days of each other** llegaron con pocos días de diferencia; **w. the hour** dentro de una hora; **w. the next five years** durante los cinco años que vienen

2 *adv* dentro; **enquire w.** razón aquí; **from w.** desde dentro

with-it ['wɪðɪt] *adj Fam* **a w.-it hairstyle** un peinado a la última moda; **she is very w.-it** tiene ideas muy modernas; **to get w.-it** ponerse de moda

without [wɪ'ðaʊt] **1** *prep* sin; **he did it w. my knowing** lo hizo sin que lo supiera yo *or* sin saberlo yo; **the house is not w. charm** la casa no deja de tener su encanto; **to go out w. a coat** salir sin abrigo; **w. money or luggage** sin dinero ni equipaje; *Fig* **to do** *or* **go w. sth** *(voluntarily)* prescindir de algo; *(forcibly)* pasarse sin algo, arreglárselas sin algo

2 *adv Literary* fuera, desde fuera; **w. the city walls** extramuros

withstand [wɪð'stænd] *vt (pt & pp* **withstood)** *(gen)* resistir a; *(pain)* aguantar, soportar

witness ['wɪtnɪs] **1** n (**a**) (person) testigo mf; **John will be my w.** pongo por testigo a John; **to call sb as a w.** citar a algn como testigo; Jur **w. for the prosecution/for the defence** testigo de cargo/de descargo ❑ Jur **w. box**, US **w. stand** barra f de los testigos (**b**) (evidence) testimonio m; **to bear w. to sth** dar fe de or atestiguar algo (**c**) Rel **Jehovah's W.** testigo mf de Jehová

2 vt (**a**) (see) presenciar; **was the crash witnessed by anybody?** ¿hay testigos del accidente? (**b**) Fig (notice) notar (**c**) Jur **to w. a document** firmar un documento como testigo

witter ['wɪtər] vi parlotear; **to w. on about sth** insistir en un tema

witticism ['wɪtɪsɪzəm] n agudeza f, ocurrencia f, salida f

wittily ['wɪtɪlɪ] adv ingeniosamente, con gracia

wittiness ['wɪtɪnɪs] n agudeza f, ingenio m

witty ['wɪtɪ] adj (**wittier, wittiest**) (person) ingenioso(a), salado(a); (remark) agudo(a); (speech) gracioso(a)

wives [waɪvz] npl see **wife**

wizard ['wɪzəd] n hechicero m, mago m; Fam **a financial w.** un lince de los negocios

wizardry ['wɪzədrɪ] n hechicería f, magia f; Fam genio m

wizened ['wɪzənd] adj (face) arrugado(a); (withered) marchito(a)

wk (abbr **week**) semana, sem

wobble ['wɒbəl] **1** vi (table) cojear, tambalearse; (ladder, bicycle) titubear; (jelly) temblar; (needle) oscilar; (wheel) trepidar (**b**) (sway) bambolearse, tambalearse

2 n (**a**) (table) tambaleo m; (ladder, bicycle) titubeo m; (jelly) temblor m; (needle) oscilación f; Aut **wheel w.** trepidación f de las ruedas (**b**) (swaying) bamboleo m

wobbly ['wɒblɪ] adj (**wobblier, wobbliest**) (table) tambaleante, cojo(a); (ladder, bicycle) titubeante, poco firme; (jelly) temblón(ona); **my legs feel w.** tengo las piernas débiles

woe [wəʊ] n (**a**) Literary infortunio m, mal m; **a tale of w.** una retahíla de desgracias; **w. betide you if I catch you!** ¡ay de ti si te cojo! (**b**) **woes** penas fpl, desgracias fpl

woebegone ['wəʊbɪgɒn] adj desconsolado(a), cariacontecido(a)

woeful ['wəʊfʊl] adj (**a**) (person) afligido(a), apenado(a) (**b**) (sight) triste, penoso(a); **w. ignorance** una ignorancia lamentable

woefully ['wəʊfʊlɪ] adv tristemente, lamentablemente

wok [wɒk] n wok m, = sartén china con forma de cuenco

woke [wəʊk] pt see **wake¹**

woken ['wəʊkən] pp see **wake¹**

wolf [wʊlf] **1** n (pl **wolves**) (**a**) Zool lobo m; Fig **a w. in sheep's clothing** un lobo con piel de cordero; Fig **to cry w.** gritar '¡al lobo!'; Fig **to keep the w. from the door** no pasar hambre ❑ Fig **lone w.** lobo m solitario; **w. cub** lobato m, lobezno m (**b**) Fam seductor m, tenorio m ❑ **w. whistle** silbido m de admiración

2 vt **to w. (down) one's food** zampar(se) la comida

wolfhound ['wʊlfhaʊnd] n perro m lobo

wolfish ['wʊlfɪʃ] adj lobuno(a)

wolves [wʊlvz] npl see **wolf**

woman ['wʊmən] n (pl **women**) mujer f; **old w.** vieja f, anciana f; **women's magazine** revista f femenina; **women's libber** feminista mf; **women's liberation movement**, Fam **women's lib** movimiento m feminista; **women's rights** derechos mpl de la mujer; **young w.** joven f

womanhood ['wʊmənhʊd] n (adulthood) edad f de mujer; **to reach w.** hacerse mujer

womanizer ['wʊmənaɪzər] n mujeriego m

womanly ['wʊmənlɪ] adj femenino(a)

womb [wuːm] n Anat matriz f, útero m

women ['wɪmɪn] npl see **woman**

won [wʌn] pt & pp see **win**

wonder ['wʌndər] **1** n (**a**) (miracle) maravilla f, milagro m; **a nine-day w.** un prodigio efímero; **no w. he hasn't come** no es de extrañar que no haya venido; Fig **to do** or **work wonders** hacer maravillas; Fam **it's a w. he hasn't lost it** es un milagro que no lo haya perdido (**b**) (amazement) admiración f, asombro m; **they gazed at it in w.** lo contemplaban asombrados

2 adj **w. drug** remedio m milagroso, panacea f

3 vt (**a**) (be surprised) sorprenderse; **I don't w. that he is angry** no me extraña que esté enfadado (**b**) (ask oneself) preguntarse; **I w. why** ¿por qué será?

4 vi (**a**) (marvel) maravillarse; **to w. at sth** admirarse de algo; Fam **he'll be in the bar I shouldn't w.** me imagino que estará en el bar (**b**) (reflect) pensar; **it makes you w.** te da en qué pensar; **I was wondering about going to Spain** pensaba en la posibilidad de ir a España; **why do you ask?** **— just wondered** ¿por qué preguntaste? — por pura curiosidad

wonderful ['wʌndəfʊl] adj maravilloso(a), estupendo(a); **we had a w. time** lo pasamos de maravilla or en grande

wonderfully ['wʌndəfʊlɪ] adv maravillosamente, de maravilla

wonderland ['wʌndəlænd] n mundo m maravilloso; **Alice in W.** Alicia en el País de las Maravillas

wonderment ['wʌndəmənt] n admiración f

wont [wəʊnt] **1** adj Fml acostumbrado(a); **to be w. to** soler

2 n costumbre f; **it is his wont to ...** tiene la costumbre de ...

woo [wuː] vt (pt & pp **wooed**) Literary (court) cortejar; Fig buscar el favor de; (voters) solicitar el apoyo de

wood [wʊd] n (**a**) (forest) (often pl) bosque m; Fig **we're not out of the w. yet** todavía no estamos a salvo; Fig **you can't see the w. for the trees** los árboles no dejan ver el bosque (**b**) (material) madera f; (for fire) leña f; **sherry from the w.** jerez m de barril; Fam Fig **touch w.!** ¡toca madera! ❑ **w. pulp** pulpa f de madera; **w. shavings** virutas fpl (**c**) Golf palo m de madera (**d**) Sport (bowling) bola f

woodcarver ['wʊdkɑːvər] n tallista mf

woodcarving ['wʊdkɑːvɪŋ] n (**a**) (craft) tallado m en madera (**b**) (object) talla f en madera

woodcock ['wʊdkɒk] n Orn becada f, chochaperdiz f

woodcut ['wʊdkʌt] n grabado m en madera

woodcutter ['wʊdkʌtər] n leñador(a) m,f

wooded ['wʊdɪd] adj arbolado(a)

wooden ['wʊdən] adj (**a**) (of wood) de madera; **w. spoon/leg** cuchara f/pata f de palo; Br Sport Fam **to win the w. spoon** ser el colista (**b**) Fig (expression, style) rígido(a); (movement) tieso(a); (acting) sin expresión

woodland ['wʊdlənd] n bosque m, monte m, arbolado m

woodlouse ['wʊdlaʊs] n (pl **woodlice** ['wʊdlaɪs]) Ent cochinilla f

woodpecker ['wʊdpekər] n Orn pico m, pájaro m carpintero ❑ **great spotted w.** pico m picapinos; **green w.** pito m real; **lesser-spotted w.** pico m menor

wood-pigeon ['wʊdpɪdʒən] n Orn paloma f torcaz

woodpile ['wʊdpaɪl] n montón m de leña

woodshed ['wʊdʃed] n leñera f

woodwind ['wʊdwɪnd] *n Mus* **w. (instruments)** instrumentos *mpl* de viento de madera

woodwork ['wʊdwɜːk] *n* (**a**) *(craft)* carpintería *f* (**b**) *(of building)* maderaje *m*, maderamen *m*

woodworm ['wʊdwɜːm] *n* carcoma *f*; **it has w.** está carcomido

woody ['wʊdɪ] *adj* (**woodier, woodiest**) (**a**) *(area)* arbolado(a) (**b**) *(texture)* leñoso(a)

woof [wʊf] *interj (of dog)* ¡guau!

wool [wʊl] **1** *n Tex* lana *f*; **ball of w.** ovillo *m* de lana; *Fig* **to pull the w. over sb's eyes** embaucar *or Esp* dar el pego a algn; *Fam Fig* **a dyed-in-the-w. communist** un(a) comunista fanático(a) *or* acérrimo(a) ❏ **steel w.** fibra *f* metálica
  2 *adj* de lana

woollen, *US* **woolen** ['wʊlən] **1** *adj* (**a**) *(cloth, dress)* de lana (**b**) *Com* lanero(a)
  2 woollens *npl* géneros *mpl* de lana *or* de punto

woolly, *US* **wooly** ['wʊlɪ] *adj* (**woollier, woolliest**, *US* **woolier, wooliest**) (**a**) *(made of wool)* de lana, lanudo(a) (**b**) *Fig (unclear)* confuso(a); *(outline)* borroso(a); *(sound)* impreciso(a)
  2 woollies *npl Fam* ropa *f sing* de lana

word [wɜːd] **1** *n* (**a**) *(spoken)* palabra *f*; **in other words ...** es decir ..., o sea ...; **she didn't say a w.** no dijo ni una palabra *or* ni pío; **without a w.** sin decir palabra, sin chistar; **words failed me** me quedé sin habla; *Fig* **a w. of advice** un consejo; *Fig* **a w. of warning** una advertencia; *Fig* **don't put words in my mouth** no me atribuyas cosas que no he dicho; *Fig* **he's too stupid for words** es de lo más estúpido que hay; *Fig* **I'd like a w. with you** quiero hablar contigo un momento; *Fig* **it's the last w. in cameras** es el grito en cámaras; *Fig* **she didn't have a good w. (to say) for him** no dijo absolutamente nada en su favor; *Fig* **she didn't say it in so many words** no lo dijo de modo explícito; *Fig* **to get a w. in (edgeways)** meter baza; *Fig* **to have words with sb** tener unas palabras con algn; *Fam Fig* **to put in a good w. for sb** interceder por algn (**b**) *(written)* palabra *f*, vocablo *m*, voz *f*; **in the words of the poet ...** como dice el poeta ...; **the words of a song** la letra de una canción; *Fig* **w. for w.** palabra por palabra ❏ *Comptr* **w. processing** procesamiento *m* de textos; *Comptr* **w. processor** procesador *m* de textos (**c**) *Fig (message)* mensaje *m*, recado *m*; **by w. of mouth** de palabra; **is there any w. from him?** ¿hay noticias de él?; **he left w. that he was going away** dejó dicho que se marchaba; **to send w.** mandar recado; **w. came that ...** llegó noticia de que ... (**d**) *(rumour)* voz *f*, rumor *m*; **w. is going round that ...** corre la voz de que ... (**e**) *Fig (promise, assurance)* palabra *f*; **he's a man of his w.** es hombre de palabra; **I give my w. that ...** doy mi palabra que ...; **to keep** *or* **be as good as one's w.** cumplir su palabra; **w. of honour!** ¡palabra de honor! (**f**) *Fig (command)* orden *f*; **just say the w.** sus deseos son órdenes
  2 *vt (express)* expresar, formular; **a badly worded letter** una carta mal redactada

wording ['wɜːdɪŋ] *n* términos *mpl*, expresión *f*; **I changed the w. slightly** cambié algunas palabras

word-of-mouth [wɜːdəv'maʊθ] *adj* boca a boca; **w. advertising** publicidad *f* boca a boca

word-perfect [wɜːd'pɜːfɪkt] *adj* **to be w.-p.** *(actor)* saber su papel; *(text, speech)* ser correcto(a) hasta la última palabra

wordplay ['wɜːdpleɪ] *n* juego *m* de palabras

wordy ['wɜːdɪ] *adj* (**wordier, wordiest**) prolijo(a), verboso(a)

wore [wɔːr] *pt see* **wear**

work [wɜːk] **1** *n* (**a**) *(gen)* trabajo *m*; **a day's w.** el trabajo de un día; **he was hard at w.** trabajaba con ahínco; **his w. in the field of physics** su labor en el campo de la física; **it's hard w.** cuesta trabajo; **'Men at W.'** 'Obras'; **to be at w.** estar trabajando; **to set to w.** ponerse a trabajar; **we have our w. cut out to finish it** nos va a costar trabajo terminarlo; *Fam* **to make short w. of sth** despachar algo deprisa (**b**) *(employment)* trabajo *m*, empleo *m*; **a day off w.** un día de asueto; **to be off w.** estar ausente en el trabajo; **to be out of w.** no tener trabajo; **to go to w.** ir al trabajo (**c**) *(action)* obra *f*; **keep up the good w.!** ¡que siga así!; *Fig* **the forces at w.** los elementos en juego; *Fam* **nice w.!** ¡muy bien!, ¡bravo! (**d**) *(product)* trabajo *m*, obra *f*; **a piece of w.** un trabajo, una labor; **a w. of art/fiction** una obra de arte/de ficción; **crochet w.** labor *f* de ganchillo; **it's all my own w.** es obra de mi propia mano (**e**) **works** obras *fpl*; **public w.** obras (públicas); **road w.** obras (de carretera) (**f**) **works** *(machinery)* mecanismo *m sing*; *Fam Fig* **to give sb the (full) w.** *(treat well)* tratar a algn a lo grande; *(beat, scold)* sacudirle el polvo a algn (**g**) **works** *(factory)* fábrica *f*, *Am* planta *f*

  2 *vt* (**a**) *(drive)* hacer trabajar; **he works his men very hard** hace trabajar muchísimo a sus empleados; **to w. oneself to death** matarse trabajando; **to w. one's way through college** costearse los estudios trabajando; **to w. one's way up** subir/bajar a duras penas; *Fig* **to w. one's way up in a firm** lograr ascender en una empresa (**b**) *(machine)* manejar; *(mechanism)* accionar; *(plan)* realizar; **how do you w. this lighter?** ¿cómo haces funcionar este mechero?; **it is worked by electricity** funciona con electricidad (**c**) *(miracles, changes)* operar, hacer; *Fam* **how can we w. it (so that we don't pay)** ¿cómo podemos arreglárnoslas (para no pagar)? (**d**) *Agr (land)* cultivar; *Min (mine)* explotar (**e**) *(wood, metal, etc)* trabajar, labrar; *Culin* **w. the butter into the flour** mézclese la mantequilla con la harina

  3 *vi* (**a**) *(gen)* trabajar (**on, at** en); **down to w.!** ¡a trabajar!, ¡manos a la obra!; **he's working on the car** está reparando el coche; **my wife goes out to w.** mi mujer trabaja fuera de casa; **to w. as a gardener** trabajar de jardinero; **to w. hard/harder** trabajar mucho/más; *Fam Fig* **to w. like a Trojan** trabajar como un negro; **to w. on a case** investigar un caso; *Ind* **to w. to rule** estar en huelga de celo; *Fam* **I'm working on it** estoy en ello (**b**) *(machine)* funcionar, marchar; **it works on gas** funciona con gas; **the light isn't working** la luz no funciona (**c**) *(drug)* surtir efecto; *(system)* funcionar bien; *(plan, trick)* tener éxito, salir bien; **that idea won't w.** esa idea no es factible (**d**) *(operate)* obrar; **it will w. against you** redundará en contra de ti; **to w. loose** soltarse, aflojarse; **to w. through** penetrar (**to** hasta); **we have no data to w. on** no tenemos datos en que basarnos; **we w. on the principle that ...** nos guiamos por el principio de que ...; **we're working towards a solution** nos vamos aproximando poco a poco a una solución; *Fig* **it works both ways** es un arma de dos filos

work off *vt (fat)* quitarse trabajando; *(energy)* consumir trabajando; *(anger)* desahogar

work out **1** *vt* (**a**) *(plan)* idear, elaborar; *(itinerary)* planear; *(details)* desarrollar; **I've got it all worked out** lo tengo todo perfectamente planeado (**b**) *(problem)* resolver, solucionar; *(solution)* encontrar; *(amount)* calcular; **I can't w. out how he did it** no me explico cómo lo hizo; **w. out how much I owe you** calcule cuánto te debo
  2 *vi* (**a**) *(problem)* resolverse; **things didn't w. out for her** las cosas no le salieron bien (**b**) *(calculation)* salir; **it works out at 5 each** sale a 5 cada uno (**c**) *Sport* hacer ejercicio

work up **1** *vt* (**a**) *(develop)* desarrollar; **I'm working up an appetite** se me está abriendo el apetito (**b**) *(excite)* exaltar, acalorar; **to get worked up** excitarse, exaltarse; **to w. up enthusiasm** entusiasmarse (**for** con; **por**)

2 *vi* **to w. up to sth** preparar el terreno para algo

workable ['wɜːkəbəl] *adj* factible, viable

workaday ['wɜːkədeɪ] *adj* rutinario(a)

workaholic [wɜːkə'hɒlɪk] *n Fam* adicto(a) *m,f* al trabajo

work-basket ['wɜːkbaːskɪt] *n Sew* costurero *m*

workbench ['wɜːkbentʃ] *n* banco *m* de trabajo

worker ['wɜːkər] *n (gen)* trabajador(a) *m,f; (manual)* obrero(a) *m,f*; **he's a good/fast w.** trabaja bien/con rapidez; *Pol* **the workers** los obreros, los trabajadores □ *Ent* **w. bee** (abeja *f*) obrera *f*

workforce ['wɜːkfɔːs] *n* mano *f* de obra

work-in ['wɜːkɪn] *n* encierro *m* en la fábrica

working ['wɜːkɪŋ] **1** *adj* **(a)** *(population, partner, capital)* activo(a) □ **w. class** clase *f* obrera; **w. man** obrero *m*; **w. party** grupo *m* de trabajo **(b)** *(clothes, surface, conditions)* de trabajo; *(week, hours)* laborable □ **w. day** *(not rest day)* día *m* laborable; *(number of hours)* jornada *f* laboral; **w. lunch** comida *m* de negocios **(c)** *(machine)* **it is in w. order** funciona; **the w. parts of a machine** las piezas móviles de una máquina □ **w. model** modelo *m* que funciona **(d)** *(majority)* suficiente; **w. knowledge** conocimientos *mlp* básicos □ **w. agreement** acuerdo *m* provisional'

2 *n* **(a)** *(of machine)* funcionamiento *m* **(b) workings** *(mechanics)* funcionamiento *m sing*; *Min (of pit)* explotación *f sing*

workload ['wɜːkləʊd] *n* cantidad *f* de trabajo

workman ['wɜːkmən] *n (pl* **workmen)** *(gen)* trabajador *m*; *(manual)* obrero *m*

workmanlike ['wɜːkmənlaɪk] *adj* hábil, concienzudo(a), bien hecho(a)

workmanship ['wɜːkmənʃɪp] *n (appearance)* ejecución *f*, hechura *f; (skill)* habilidad *f*, arte *m*; **a fine piece of w.** un trabajo primoroso

workmate ['wɜːkmeɪt] *n Br* compañero(a) *m,f* de trabajo

work out ['wɜːkaʊt] *n Sport* entrenamiento *m*; **to have a w.-o.** hacer ejercicio

workplace ['wɜːkpleɪs] *n* lugar *m* de trabajo

workroom ['wɜːkruːm] *n* sala *f* de trabajo

work-sharing ['wɜːkʃeərɪŋ] *n* repartición *f* del trabajo

worksheet ['wɜːkʃiːt] *n Ind* plan *m* de trabajo

workshop ['wɜːkʃɒp] *n* taller *m*

workshy ['wɜːkʃaɪ] *adj* gandul(ula), holgazán(ana)

workstation ['wɜːksteɪʃən] *n Comptr* estación *f* de trabajo

worktop ['wɜːktɒp] *n* encimera *f*

work-to-rule [wɜːktə'ruːl] *n Ind* huelga *f* de celo

world [wɜːld] *n* **(a)** *(gen)* mundo *m*; **all over the w.** en todo el mundo; **the best in the w.** el mejor del mundo; **to see the w.** ver mundo; *Fig* **he would give the w. to know** daría lo que fuera por saberlo; *Fig* **it will do you the w. of good** te hará un provecho enorme; *Fig* **there is a w. of difference between A and B, and A and B are worlds apart** hay un mundo de diferencia entre A y B; *Fig* **to come down in the w.** venir a menos; *Fig* **to come up in the w.** prosperar, medrar; *Fig* **to feel on top of the w.** *(health)* estar como una rosa; *(morale)* sentirse fenomenal; *Fig* **to think the w. of sb** querer mucho *or* adorar a algn; *Fam Fig* **his house is out of this w.** tiene una casa que es un sueño *or* una maravilla; *Fam Fig* **I wouldn't hurt her for the w.** no la heriría por nada del mundo; *Fam Fig* **it's a small w.** el mundo es un pañuelo; *Fam Fig* **it's not the end of the w.** el mundo no va a hundirse por esto □ **the Third W.** el Tercer Mundo; *Fin* **the W. Bank** el Banco Mundial; *Ftb* **the W. Cup** el Mundial; **w. music** música *f* étnica; **w. power** potencia *f* mundial; **w. record** récord *m* mundial; **W. Series** = final a

siete partidos entre los dos campeones de las ligas de béisbol en Estados Unidos; **w. war** guerra *f* mundial **(b)** *(life)* mundo *m*, vida *f; Fig* **in this w.** en esta vida; *Fig* **the next w.** el otro mundo; *Fig* **to be dead to the w.** estar profundamente dormido(a) **(c)** *(sphere)* mundo *m*; **the animal w.** el reino animal; **the business/theatre w.** el mundo comercial/del teatro; *Fam Fig* **he is** *or* **lives in a w. of his own** vive ajeno a las cosas de este mundo

world-class ['wɜːldklɑːs] *adj* de categoría mundial

world-famous ['wɜːldfeɪməs] *adj* de fama mundial

worldliness ['wɜːldlɪnɪs] *n* mundanería *f*

worldly ['wɜːldlɪ] *adj* mundano(a); **w. goods** bienes *mpl* materiales

world-weary ['wɜːldwɪːrɪ] *adj* hastiado(a) del mundo

worldwide ['wɜːldwaɪd] *adj* mundial, universal; *Comptr* **the W. Web** la Web

worm [wɜːm] **1** *n* **(a)** *Zool* gusano *m; Fig* **w.'s eye view** vista *f* a ras de tierra; *Fam Fig* **the w. has turned** se me/le ha agotado la paciencia; *Fam* **you w.!** ¡vil gusano! □ **(earth) w.** lombriz *f* **(b)** *Med* **worms** lombrices *fpl* **(c)** *(of screw)* tornillo *m* sin fin □ **w. gear** engranaje *m* de tornillo sin fin

2 *vt* sacar; **to w. a secret out of sb** sonsacarle un secreto a algn; *Fam Fig* **to w. one's way into a group** colarse en un grupo

worm-eaten ['wɜːmiːtən] *adj (wood)* carcomido(a); *(fruit)* agusanado(a)

wormwood ['wɜːmwʊd] *n Bot* ajenjo *m*

worn [wɔːn] **1** *pp see* **wear**
2 *adj* gastado(a), usado(a)

worn-out ['wɔːnaʊt] *adj (thing)* gastado(a), estropeado(a); *(person)* rendido(a), agotado(a)

worried ['wʌrɪd] *adj* inquieto(a), preocupado(a); **to get w.** inquietarse

worrier ['wʌrɪər] *n* **to be a w.** ser propenso(a) a preocuparse

worry ['wʌrɪ] **1** *vt (pt & pp* **worried) (a)** *(make anxious)* preocupar, inquietar; **it doesn't w. me** me tiene sin cuidado; *Fam* **don't w. your head about it** no te preocupes en absoluto por eso **(b)** *(pester)* molestar **(c)** *(dog)* perseguir, atacar

2 *vi* preocuparse, inquietarse (**about, over** por); **don't w.** no te preocupes, no importa; **there's no need to w.** no hay por qué inquietarse

3 *n (state)* inquietud *f*, intranquilidad *f; (cause)* preocupación *f*; **financial worries** problemas *mpl* económicos; **that's the least of my worries** eso es lo que menos me preocupa

worrying ['wʌrɪŋ] *adj* inquietante, preocupante; *Fam* **he's the w. sort** es de los que se inquietan por nada

worse [wɜːs] **1** *adj (comp of* **bad)** peor; **I have seen w.** he visto casos peores; **in a w. condition than before** en peor condición que antes; **if/he gets w. and w.** va de mal en peor; **to get w.** empeorar; **to make matters w.** para colmo de desgracias; *Fig* **he's none the w. for the experience** la experiencia no le ha perjudicado; *Fam* **so much** *or* **all the w. for him** tanto peor para él; *Fam* **w. luck!** mala suerte; *Fam Fig* **to be the w. for drink** estar bebido(a) *or* borracho(a)

2 **the w.** *n* lo peor; **a change for the w.** un empeoramiento; *Fig* **to take a turn for the w.** empeorar

3 *adv (comp of* **badly)** peor; **he is behaving w. than ever/ w. and w.** se está portando peor que nunca/cada vez peor; **I am w. off than before** *(in health)* me encuentro peor que antes; *(financially)* ando peor de dinero que antes; **I don't think any the w. of her for that** no la estimo en menos por eso

worship ['wɜːʃip] **1** vt (pt & pp **worshipped**, US **worshiped**) Rel adorar, venerar; Fig **he worships money** rinde culto al dinero

2 n (**a**) Rel adoración f, culto m; Fig adoración f, veneración f (**b**) Rel (ceremony) culto m ▫ **place of w.** templo m (**c**) Br (address) **his W. the Mayor** el señor alcalde; Jur **yes, your W.** sí, su señoría

worshipper ['wɜːʃipər] n adorador(a) m,f, devoto(a) m,f

worst [wɜːst] **1** adj (superl of **bad**) peor; **his w. mistake** su error más grave; **the w. part about it is that ...** lo peor es que ...; **the w. two pupils in the class** los dos peores alumnos de la clase

2 n (**a**) (person) el/la peor, los/las peores (**b**) (impersonal) lo peor; **the w. of the storm is over** ya ha pasado lo peor de la tormenta; Fig **let him do his w.** que haga todo lo que quiera

3 adv (superl of **badly**) peor; **the w. dressed man** el hombre peor vestido; **the w. off** (gen) los más perjudicados; (financially) los más pobres; Fig **to come off w.** llevarse la peor parte

worst-case scenario ['wɜːstkeɪsɪ'nɑːrɪəʊ] (pl **worst-case scenarios**) n **this is a w.-c. s.** esto es lo que ocurriría en el peor de los casos

worsted ['wʊstɪd] n Tex estambre m

worth [wɜːθ] **1** adj (**a**) (of the value of) que vale, con un valor de; **a house w. $250,000** una casa que vale 250.000 dólares; **it's w. the money** (before buying) vale lo que piden; (after buying) vale lo que costó; Fam Fig **it's more than my job is w.** me jugaría o arriesgaría mi empleo; Fam Fig **she's w. a fortune** está forrada (**b**) (deserving of) lo que merece, merecedor(a) de; **a book w. reading** un libro que merece la pena leer; **for what it's w.** por si sirve de algo; **it's w. a visit** vale la pena visitarlo; **it's w. the trouble** or **it's w. your while** or **it's w. it** vale o merece la pena; **it's w. thinking about/mentioning** es digno de consideración/ mención

2 n (**a**) (in money) valor m; **five dollars' w. of gasoline** gasolina por valor de cinco dólares, cinco dólares de gasolina; Fam Fig **to get one's money's w.** sacarle jugo al dinero (**b**) (of person) valía f

worthiness ['wɜːðɪnɪs] n mérito m

worthless ['wɜːθlɪs] adj (gen) sin valor; (effort) inútil; (person) despreciable

worthlessness ['wɜːθlɪsnɪs] n falta f de valor

worthwhile [wɜːθ'waɪl] adj valioso(a), útil, que vale la pena; **the journey was w.** el viaje merecía la pena

worthy ['wɜːðɪ] **1** adj (**worthier**, **worthiest**) (**a**) (deserving) digno(a) (**of** de), merecedor(a) (**of** de); (winner, cause) justo(a); **it is w. of attention** es digno de atención; **there is no museum w. of the name** no hay museo que merezca ese nombre; **a w. opponent** un adversario digno de respeto (**b**) (distinguished) benemérito(a); (citizen) respetable, honorable; (effort, motives) loable; (action) meritorio(a)

2 n Hum prócer m

would [wʊd, unstressed wəd] v aux (**a**) (conditional) **I w.** or **I'd go if I had time** iría si tuviera tiempo; **he w.** or **he'd have won but for that** habría ganado si no hubiera sido por eso; **we w. if we could** lo haríamos si pudiéramos (**b**) (reported speech) **he said that he w.** or **he'd come** dijo que vendría (**c**) (willingness) **the car wouldn't start** el coche no arrancaba; **they asked him to come but he wouldn't** le invitaron a venir pero no quiso; **w. you do me a favour?** ¿quiere hacerme un favor? (**d**) (wishing) **he w.** or **he'd like to know why** quisiera saber por qué; **I'd rather go home** preferiría ir a casa; **w. you like a cigarette?** ¿quiere un pitillo?; Literary **w. that I could** ojalá que pudiera (**e**) (custom) **we w.** or **we'd go for walks** solíamos dar un

paseo (**f**) (persistence) **try as I w.** por mucho que lo intentara; **well, if you w. eat so many apples ...** pues si te empeñaste en comer tantas manzanas ... (**g**) (conjecture) **it w. have been about three weeks ago** debe haber sido hace unas tres semanas; **w. this be your cousin?** ¿será éste su primo? (**h**) (expectation) **so it w. appear** según parece

would-be ['wʊdbiː] adj en potencia; **a w.-be politician** un aspirante a político; **the w.-be assassin** el asesino fracasado; Pej **a w.-be poet** un supuesto poeta

wound[1] [waʊnd] pt & pp see **wind**[2]

wound[2] [wuːnd] **1** n herida f; Fig **he left licking his wounds** se fue con el rabo entre las piernas; Fig **to rub salt into the w., he said ...** para hacer más daño todavía, dijo ...

2 vt herir

wounded ['wuːndɪd] adj herido(a)

wounding ['wuːndɪŋ] adj hiriente

wove [wəʊv] pt see **weave**

woven ['wəʊvən] pp see **weave**

wow [waʊ] Fam **1** n éxito m sensacional; **it was a w.** fue sensacional

2 vt (spectators etc) encandilar

3 interj ¡hala!, RP ¡uau!

WP [dʌbljuː'piː] Comptr (**a**) (abbr **word processing**) procesamiento m de textos (**b**) (abbr **word processor**) procesador m de textos

WPC [dʌbljuːpiː'siː] n Br (abbr **Woman Police Constable**) agente f de policía

wpm [dʌbljuːpiː'em] Com (abbr **words per minute**) pulsaciones fpl por minuto, p.p.m

wrangle ['ræŋgəl] **1** n disputa f, altercado m

2 vi disputar (**over** acerca de, por), reñir (**over** acerca de, por)

wrap [ræp] **1** vt (pt & pp **wrapped**) (**a**) (parcel etc) **to w. (up)** envolver; **he wrapped his arms around her** la estrechó entre sus brazos; **he wrapped his scarf round his neck** se abrigó con la bufanda; Fig **wrapped in mystery** rodeado(a) en el misterio; Fig **wrapped up in one's work/one's thoughts/oneself** absorto(a) en su trabajo/en sus pensamientos/en sí mismo(a); Fam **we soon wrapped up the deal** no tardamos nada en concluir el negocio

2 vi (snake, rope) **to w. round sth** enrollarse or enroscarse en algo; Fam **w. up well** abrígate (**b**) (be quiet) callarse; Fam **w. up!** ¡cierra el pico!

3 n (shawl) chal m; (cape) capa f; (housecoat) bata f; Fam Fig **to keep sth under wraps** mantener algo secreto(a)

wraparound ['ræpəraʊnd] **1** n (**a**) (skirt) falda f or RP pollera f cruzada (**b**) Comptr contorneo m

2 adj (skirt) cruzado(a)

wrapper ['ræpər] n (of sweet) envoltorio m; (of book) sobrecubierta f

wrapping ['ræpɪŋ] n envoltura f, envoltorio m ▫ **w. paper** papel m de envolver

wreath [riːθ] n (pl **wreaths** [riːðz, riːθs]) (of flowers) corona f ▫ **laurel w.** corona f de laurel

wreathe [riːð] vt enguirnaldar, coronar; Fig **wreathed in mist** envuelto(a) en niebla

wreck [rek] **1** n (**a**) Naut naufragio m; (ship) barco m naufragado o hundido (**b**) (of car, plane) restos mpl; (of building) ruinas fpl; **the car was a complete w.** el coche quedó completamente destrozado; Fam **he drives an old w.** conduce un cacharro (**c**) Fig (person) ruina f; **I'm a nervous w.** tengo los nervios destrozados

2 vt (**a**) Naut (ship) hacer naufragar (**b**) (car, plane) destrozar, estropear (**c**) Fig (health, career) arruinar; (life, marriage) destrozar; (hopes, plans) dar al traste con

wreckage ['rekɪdʒ] n (of ship, car, plane) restos mpl; (of building) ruinas fpl

wrecked ['rekt] adj (a) (ship) naufragado(a); (sailor) náufrago(a) (b) (car, plane) destrozado(a); (building) destruido(a) (c) Fig (life, career) arruinado(a); (hopes) arruinado(a); (plans) estropeado(a)

wrecker ['rekər] n US (a) (of building) demoledor(a) m,f (b) Aut w. (truck) grúa f

wren [ren] n Orn chochín m

wrench [rentʃ] 1 n (a) (pull) tirón m, arranque m; to give sth a w. darle un tirón brusco a algo (b) Med torcedura f (c) Fig separación f dolorosa; it will be a w. for me to leave me costará trabajo irme (d) (tool) (monkey) w. llave f inglesa
2 vt (pull) to w. oneself free soltarse de un tirón; to w. sth off sb/out of sb's hands arrebatarle algo a algn/de las manos de algn; to w. sth off/out/open quitar/arrancar/ abrir algo de un tirón

wrest [rest] vt to w. sth from sb arrebatarle or arrancarle algo a algn

wrestle ['resəl] vi Sport luchar

wrestler ['reslər] n Sport luchador(a) m,f

wrestling ['reslɪŋ] n Sport lucha f ◻ all-in w. lucha libre; w. match combate m de lucha

wretch [retʃ] n (a) (poor) w. pobre diablo m, desgraciado(a) m,f (b) (child) pillo(a) m,f, pícaro(a) m,f; you little w.! ¡granuja!, ¡tunante!

wretched ['retʃɪd] adj (a) (unhappy) desdichado(a), abatido(a); I felt w. about it dio mucha pena (b) (pitiful, unfortunate) desgraciado(a), desdichado(a); (conditions) miserable, lamentable; Fam (bad, poor) horrible, malísimo(a); what w. weather! ¡qué tiempo más feo or espantoso! (c) (ill) indispuesto(a); I feel w. me encuentro fatal (d) (contemptible) miserable, despreciable (e) Fam (damned) maldito(a), condenado(a); that w. boy ese maldito chiquillo

wretchedness ['retʃɪdnɪs] n (a) (unhappiness, misfortune) desdicha f, desgracia f (b) (of conditions) miseria f

wriggle ['rɪgəl] 1 vt (gen) menear; Fam Fig how did he w. his way in? ¿cómo logró introducirse?
2 vi to w. (about) (worm) serpentear, retorcerse; (restless child) moverse or revolverse nerviosamente; to w. free escapar deslizándose; Fam Fig to w. out of a tight spot/ obligation librarse habilmente de un apuro/una obligación

wriggly ['rɪglɪ] adj (wrigglier, wriggliest) sinuoso(a)

wring [rɪŋ] vt (pt & pp wrung) (a) (clothes) escurrir; (hands) retorcer; to w. the neck of a chicken retorcerle el pescuezo a un pollo; Fam I'll w. his neck if I catch him si lo pillo lo mato or le retuerzo el pescuezo (b) Fig (extract) arrancar, sacar; to w. money/a secret out of sb arrancarle dinero/un secreto a algn

wringer ['rɪŋər] n escurridor m; Fam to put sb through the w. hacer pasar un mal trago a algn

wringing ['rɪŋɪŋ] adj to be w. wet (garment) estar empapado(a); (person) estar calado(a) hasta los huesos

wrinkle ['rɪŋkəl] 1 n arruga f
2 vt arrugar
3 vi arrugarse

wrinkled ['rɪŋkəld] adj arrugado(a)

wrist [rɪst] n muñeca f

wristwatch ['rɪstwɒtʃ] n reloj m de pulsera

writ [rɪt] n Jur mandamiento m or orden f judicial, auto m; to issue a w. against sb llevar a algn a juicio; to serve a w. on sb entregar una orden a algn

write [raɪt] 1 vt (pt wrote; pp written) (gen) escribir;

(article) redactar; (cheque) extender; US to w. sb escribir a algn; Fig his guilt is written all over his face lleva la culpabilidad escrita or impresa en la cara
2 vi escribir (about sobre); he writes es escritor; Press to w. for a paper colaborar en un periódico; to w. (in) for sth escribir pidiendo algo; we w. (to each other) regularly nos escribimos or nos carteamos con regularidad; w. to this address diríjase a la dirección siguiente; Fam Fig it's nothing to w. home about no es nada del otro mundo

▸ **write away** vi to w. away for sth pedir algo por escrito

▸ **write back** vi contestar

▸ **write down** vt (gen) poner por escrito; (note) apuntar, anotar

▸ **write in 1** vt (a) (name, answer) escribir (b) US Pol = en las elecciones, votar por un candidato que no aparece en la papeleta escribiendo su nombre
2 vi escribir; many listeners wrote in to complain muchos oyentes escribieron quejándose

▸ **write off 1** vt (debt) condonar (person) dar por acabado(a); Fam (car) cargarse, Méx dar en la madre, RP hacer bolsa
2 vi escribir; to w. off for sth pedir algo por escrito

▸ **write out** vt (cheque) extender; (instructions, recipe) escribir, copiar; to w. sth out neatly pasar algo a limpio; w. your name out in full escríbase su nombre completo

▸ **write up** vt (notes, thesis) redactar; (diary, journal) poner al día

write-off ['raɪtɒf] n ruina f; the car's a w.-o. el coche está hecho una ruina

write-protected ['raɪtprə'tektɪd] adj Comptr protegido(a) contra escritura

writer ['raɪtər] n (a) (by profession) escritor(a) m,f; (of book, letter) autor(a) m,f (b) (of handwriting) to be a good/ bad w. tener buena/mala letra

write-up ['raɪtʌp] n reportaje m; Cin Theat crítica f, reseña f

writhe [raɪð] vi retorcerse

writing ['raɪtɪŋ] n (a) (script) escritura f; (handwriting) letra f; I can't read his w. no entiendo su letra; (to put sth) in w. (poner algo) por escrito; Fig the w. on the wall los malos presagios (b) writings escritos mpl (c) (action) escritura f ◻ w. desk escritorio m (d) (profession) profesión f de escritor, trabajo m literario

written ['rɪtən] 1 pp see write
2 adj escrito(a); w. consent consentimiento m por escrito; w. exam examen m escrito

wrong [rɒŋ] 1 adj (a) (erroneous) incorrecto(a), erróneo(a), equivocado(a); Mus a w. note una nota falsa; I got the w. train me equivoqué de tren; my watch is w. mi reloj anda mal; Tel sorry, I've got the w. number lo siento, lo he confundido de número; the lamp is in the w. place la lámpara está mal colocada; to drive on the w. side of the road conducir or Am manejar por el lado contrario de la carretera; to go the w. way equivocarse de camino; Fam the cake has gone down the w. way se me ha atragantado el pastel; Fam Fig you're going the w. way about it lo estás haciendo mal (b) (unsuitable) impropio(a) inadecuado(a); (time) inoportuno(a); he's the w. man for the job no es la persona apropiada para el puesto; to say the w. thing decir algo inoportuno; Fig to be on the w. side of forty tener cuarenta años bien cumplidos; Fam Fig to get out of bed on the w. side levantarse con el pie izquierdo (c) (not right) (person) equivocado(a); I was w. about that boy me equivoqué con ese chico; to be w. no tener razón, estar equivocado(a); you're not all w. no andas muy descaminado; you're w. in thinking that ... te equivocas si piensas que ... (**d**) *(immoral etc)* malo(a); **it is w. to steal** robar está mal; **it was w. of him to say that** hizo mal en decir eso; **there's nothing w. in that** no hay nada malo en eso; **what's w. with smoking?** ¿qué tiene de malo fumar? (**e**) *(amiss)* **is anything w.?** ¿pasa algo?; **something's w. (somewhere)** hay algo que no está bien; **there's something w. with the car** se ha averiado el coche; **what's w.?** ¿qué hay?; **what's w. with you?** ¿qué te pasa?, ¿qué tienes?

2 *adv* mal, incorrectamente; **everything has gone w.** todo ha salido mal; **to get it w.** equivocarse, no acertar; **to get the answer w.** contestar mal; *Math* equivocarse en el cálculo; **you can't go w.** no tiene pérdida; **you won't go far w. if ...** no andarás muy descaminado si ...; *Fam Fig* **don't get me w.** no me comprendas mal; *Fam* **to go w.** *(mistake)* equivocarse; *(on road)* equivocarse de camino; *(machinery, watch)* estropearse; *(plan)* fallar, fracasar; *Fam Fig* **you've got it w.** te equivocas, lo entiendes mal; *Fam* **you're doing it (all) w.** lo estás haciendo (muy) mal

3 *n* (**a**) *(evil, bad action)* mal *m*; **to know right from w.** saber distinguir entre el bien y el mal; **you did w. to hit him** hiciste mal en pegarle; *Fam Fig* **two wrongs do not make a right** no se subsana un error cometiendo otro (**b**) *(injustice)* injusticia *f*; *(offence)* agravio *m*; **the rights and wrongs of a matter** lo justo y lo injusto de un asunto; **to right a w.** deshacer un entuerto (**c**) **to be in the w.** *(to*

blame) tener la culpa; *(mistaken)* no tener razón

4 *vt (treat unfairly)* ser injusto(a) con; *(judge unfairly)* juzgar mal; *(offend)* agraviar

wrongdoer ['rɒŋduːər] *n* malhechor(a) *m,f*

wrongdoing ['rɒŋduːɪŋ] *n* maldad *f*

wrongful ['rɒŋfʊl] *adj* injusto(a), ilegal; **w. dismissal** despido *m* improcedente

wrongly ['rɒŋlɪ] *adv* (**a**) *(incorrectly)* incorrectamente, mal; **w. worded** mal expresado(a) (**b**) *(mistakenly)* equivocadamente, erróneamente, sin razón; **rightly or w.** por fas o por nefas (**c**) *(unjustly)* injustamente

wrote [rəʊt] *pt see* **write**

wrung [rʌŋ] *pt & pp see* **wring**

wry [raɪ] *adj* (**wrier, wriest** *or* **wryer, wryest**) sardónico(a), irónico(a)

WTO ['dʌbəljuːtiːˈeʊ] *n (abbr* **World Trade Organization**) OMC *f*

WWF [dʌbəljuːdʌbəljuːˈef] *n (abbr* **World Wildlife Fund, Worldwide Fund for Nature**) Fondo *m* mundial para la naturaleza

WWW *n (abbr* **Worldwide Web**) WWW *f*

WYSIWYG ['wɪzɪwɪg] *n Comptr (abbr* **what you see is what you get**) WYSIWYG, = se imprime lo que ves

X

X, x [eks] *n (the letter)* X, x *f*; **Mr X** el Sr. X; *Br Formerly* **X certificate** para mayores de 18 años

xenon ['zenɒn] *n Chem* xenón *m*

xenophobia [zenə'fəʊbɪə] *n* xenofobia *f*

xenophobic [zenə'fəʊbɪk] *adj* xenófobo(a)

xerography [zɪ'rɒɡrəfɪ] *n* xerografía *f*

Xerox® ['zɪərɒks] **1** *n* xerocopia *f*
  2 *vt* xerocopiar

XL [eks'el] *(abbr extra large (size))* (talla *f*) muy grande

Xmas ['eksməs, 'krɪsməs] *n (abbr Christmas)* Navidad *f*

X-ray ['eksreɪ] **1** *n* **(a)** *(beam)* rayo *m* X; **X-r. therapy** radioterapia *f* **(b)** *(picture)* radiografía *f*; **to have an X-r.** hacerse una radiografía
  2 *vt* radiografiar

xylophone ['zaɪləfəʊn] *n* xilófono *m*

xylophonist [zaɪ'lɒfənɪst] *n* xilofonista *mf*

Y

Y, y [waɪ] *n (the letter)* Y, y *f*

yacht [jɒt] *n* yate *m*; **y. club** club *m* náutico; **y. race** regata *f*

yachting ['jɒtɪŋ] *n Sport* navegación *f* a vela; *(competition)* regatas *fpl*

yachtsman ['jɒtsmən] *n (pl* **yachtsmen**) tripulante *m* de yates, deportista *m* de vela, balandrista *m*

yachtswoman ['jɒtswʊmən] *n (pl* **yachtswomen** ['jɒtswɪmɪn]) tripulante *f* de yates, deportista *f* de vela, balandrista *f*

yak [jæk] *n Zool* yac *m*, yak *m*

yam [jæm] *n Bot* **(a)** *(vegetable)* ñame *m* **(b)** *US (sweet potato)* batata *f*, *Esp* boniato *m*, *Am* camote *m*

Yank [jæŋk] *n Br Pej* yanqui *mf*

yank [jæŋk] *Fam* **1** *vt* tirar; *(tooth)* arrancar
2 *n* tirón *m*; **give it a y.** dale un tirón

Yankee ['jæŋkɪ] *Fam* **1** *n* **(a)** *Br (person from the USA)* yanqui *mf*, gringo(a) *m,f* **(b)** *US (person from north-eastern USA)* = estadounidense procedente del nordeste del país
2 *adj Br* yanqui, gringo(a)

yap [jæp] **1** *vi (pt & pp* **yapped**) **(a)** *(dog)* aullar **(b)** *Fam (of person)* darle al pico *or* a la sinhueso
2 *n* aullido *m*

yard¹ [jɑːd] *n* **(a)** *(measure)* yarda *f* (=0.914 metros) **(b)** *Naut* verga *f*

yard² [jɑːd] *n* **(of house)** patio *m*; **(of farm)** corral *m*; **(of school)** patio de recreo; *US (garden)* jardín *m*; **back y.** patio *m*; **builder's y.** depósito *m* de materiales; *Rail* **goods y.** depósito *m* de mercancías

yardage ['jɑːdɪdʒ] *n* medida *f* en yardas

yardarm ['jɑːdɑːm] *n Naut* penol *m*

yardstick ['jɑːdstɪk] *n* vara *f* que mide una yarda; *Fig* criterio *m*, norma *f*

yarn [jɑːn] *n* **(a)** *Sew* hilo *m*, hilado *m* **(b)** *(story)* historia *f*, cuento *m*; *(lie)* **to spin a y.** inventarse *or* contar una historia

yawl [jɔːl] *n Naut* yola *f*

yawn [jɔːn] **1** *vi* bostezar
2 *n* bostezo *m*; *Fig* aburrimiento *m*

yawning ['jɔːnɪŋ] *adj (gap)* profundo(a)

yaws [jɔːz] *n Med* pián *m*, frambesia *f*

yd *(pl* **yds**) *(abbr* **yard**) yarda *f*

ye [jiː, *unstressed* jɪ] *pers pron Literary* vos

yea [jeɪ] *adv & n Archaic or Literary* sí *m*

yeah [jeə] *adv Fam* sí

year [jɪər] *n* **(a)** *(period of time)* año *m*; **all y. round** durante todo el año; **a y. ago last March** en marzo hizo un año; **I haven't seen you for (donkey's) years** hace siglos que no te veo; **last y.** el año pasado; **next y.** el próximo año, el año

que viene; **the New Y.** el Año nuevo; **y. in, y. out, y. after y.** año tras año ❑ **calendar y.** año *m* civil; **financial y.** año *m* económico; **leap y.** año *m* bisiesto; **light y.** año *m* luz; **New Y.'s Day** el día de Año nuevo; **New Y.'s Eve** Noche *f* vieja; **school y.** año *m* escolar **(b)** *(age)* año *m*; **he's getting on in years** va para viejo; **I'm ten years old** tengo diez años; *Fam Fig* **to put years on sb** echarle años a algn **(c)** *Educ* curso *m*; **first-y. student** estudiante de primero; **she's in my y.** es de mi curso

yearbook ['jɪəbʊk] *n* boletín *m or* revista *f* anual, anuario *m*

yearling ['jɪəlɪŋ] *adj & n* añal *(m)* ❑ **y. (colt)** potro *m* de un año

yearly ['jɪəlɪ] **1** *adj* anual
2 *adv* anualmente, cada año

yearn [jɜːn] *vi* anhelar, añorar; **to y. for sth** anhelar algo

yearning ['jɜːnɪŋ] *n* anhelo *m*, ansia *f* (**for** de)

yeast [jiːst] *n Culin* levadura *f*

yell [jel] **1** *vi* gritar, aullar
2 *vt (insults etc)* gritar
3 *n* grito *m*, alarido *m*

yellow ['jeləʊ] **1** *adj* amarillo(a); *Press (press)* sensacionalista; *Fam Fig (cowardly)* cobarde ❑ **y. fever** fiebre *f* amarilla; *Tel* **the Y. Pages**® las páginas amarillas
2 *n* amarillo *m*
3 *vi* volverse amarillo(a)

yellowhammer ['jeləʊhæmər] *n Orn* escribano *m* cerillo

yellowish ['jeləʊɪʃ] *adj* amarillento(a)

yelp [jelp] **1** *vi* gañir, aullar
2 *n* gañido *m*, aullido *m*

Yemen ['jemən] *n* (the) Y. (el) Yemen

Yemeni ['jemənɪ] *adj & n* yemení *(mf)*, yemenita *(mf)*

Yen [jen] *n inv Fin* yen *m*

yen [jen] *n (desire)* deseo *m*, ganas *fpl*

yeoman ['jəʊmən] *n (pl* **yeomen**) *Br Mil* **Y. of the Guard** alabardero *m* de la Casa Real británica

yes [jes] **1** *adv* **(a)** *(affirmation)* sí; **to answer y. or no** responder sí o no; **you said y.** dijiste que sí **(b)** *(interrogation) (to sb waiting to speak)* ¿sí?; *(answering phone)* ¿sí?, *Esp* ¿diga?, *Am* ¿aló?, *Carib RP* ¿oigo?, *Méx* ¿bueno?, *RP* ¿hola? **(c)** *(answering a summons)* **y.!** ¡voy!
2 *n (affirmation)* sí *m*

yes-man ['jesmæn] *n (pl* **yes-men** ['jesmen]) cobista *m*, pelota *m*

yesterday ['jestədeɪ] *adv & n* ayer *m*; **the day before y.** anteayer; **y. morning** ayer por la mañana; **y. week** ayer hizo una semana

yesteryear ['jestəjɪər] *adv Literary* **(of)** y. (de) antaño

yet [jet] **1** *adv* **(a)** *(so far)* aún no, todavía no; **as y.** hasta ahora; **I haven't decided y.** aún no lo he decidido; *(in a question)* **has he arrived y.?** ¿ha venido ya? **(b)** *(even)* más; **y. again** otra vez; **y. more** todavía más, más aún; **y. more flowers** más flores aún **(c)** *(eventually)* todavía, aún; **he'll win y.** todavía puede ganar **2** *conj* sin embargo; **y. I like him** sin embargo, me gusta

yeti ['jetɪ] *n* yeti *m*

yew [ju:] *n Bot* tejo *m*

Yiddish ['jɪdɪʃ] **1** *adj* judeoalemán(ana) **2** *n (language)* dialecto *m* judeoalemán, yiddish *m*

yield [ji:ld] **1** *n* **(a)** *(gen)* rendimiento *m*, producción *f* **(b)** *Agr* cosecha *f* **(c)** *Fin* beneficio *m*, rédito *m* ❏ **net y.** rédito *m* **2** *vt (results, interest)* producir; *(crop)* dar; *(money)* rendir **3** *vi* **(a)** *(surrender)* rendirse, ceder **(b)** *(break)* hundirse, ceder **(c)** *US Aut* **'y.'** 'ceder el paso'

yielding ['ji:ldɪŋ] *adj* **(a)** *(flexible)* blando(a), flexible **(b)** *(person)* complaciente

yippee [jɪ'pi:] *interj Fam* ¡yupi!

YMCA [waɪemsi:'eɪ] *n (abbr* **Young Men's Christian Association)** albergue *m* para jóvenes hombres

yob(bo) ['jɒb(əʊ)] *n (pl* **yob(bo)s)** *Br Fam* vándalo *m*, *Esp* gamberro *m*, *Perú RP* patotero *m*

yodel ['jəʊdəl] *vi (pt & pp* **yodelled,** *US* **yodeled)** cantar a la tirolesa *or* al estilo tirolés

yoga ['jəʊgə] *n* yoga *m*

yog(h)urt ['jɒgət] *n* yogur *m*

yoke [jəʊk] **1** *n* **(a)** *(cross-piece)* yugo *m*; *Fig* yugo *m* **(b)** *(pair of oxen)* yunta *f* **(c)** *(Sew* canesú *m* **2** *vt (oxen)* uncir; *Fig* unir

yokel ['jəʊkəl] *n Pej* palurdo(a) *m,f*, *Esp* paleto(a) *m,f*

yolk [jəʊk] *n* yema *f*

yon [jɒn] *adj Literary (sing)* aquel, aquella; *(pl)* aquellos(as)

yonder ['jɒndər] **1** *adj Literary (sing)* aquel, aquella; *(pl)* aquellos(as) **2** *adv* más allá

yonks [jɒŋks] *npl Br Fam* **I haven't done that for y.** hace un montón de tiempo que no hago eso; **y. ago** hace la tira *or Méx* un chorro *or RP* un toco (de tiempo)

you [ju:, *unstressed* jʊ] *pers pron* **(a)** *(subject) (usually omitted in Spanish, except for contrast) (singular)* tú, *esp RP* vos, *Fml* usted; *(plural) Esp* vosotros(as), *Am or Fml* ustedes; **y. seem happy** *(singular)* pareces feliz, *Fml* parece feliz; *(plural) Esp* parecéis felices, *Am or Fml* parecen felices **(b)** *(direct object) (singular)* te, *Fml* lo(la); *(plural) Esp* os, *Am or Fml* los(las); **they hate y.** *(singular)* te odian, *Fml* lo odian; *(plural) Esp* os odian, *Am or Fml* los odian; **(c)** *(indirect object) (singular)* te, *Fml* le; *(plural) Esp* os, *Am or Fml* les; **I gave y. the book** *(singular)* te di el libro, *Fml* le di el libro; *(plural) Esp* os di el libro, *Am or Fml* les di el libro **(d)** *(after preposition) (singular)* ti, *Fml* usted; *(plural) Esp* vosotros(as), *Am or Fml* ustedes; **with you** *(singular)* contigo, *Fml* con usted; *(plural) Esp* con vosotros, *Am or Fml* con ustedes **(e)** *(impers use)* **y. never know** nunca se sabe; **alcohol makes you drunk** el alcohol emborracha

young [jʌŋ] **1** *adj (age)* joven; *(sister, brother, etc)* pequeño(a); *Fig* **the night is still y.** la noche es joven; *Fam* **I'm not as y. as I was** los años no pasan en balde; *Fam* **you are only y. once** sólo se vive una vez ❏ **y. lady** señorita *f*; *(fiancée)* prometida *f*; **y. man** joven *m*; *(fiancé)* prometido *m* **2** *n* **(a)** *(people)* **the y.** los jóvenes, la juventud **(b)** *(animals)* crías *fpl*

youngster ['jʌŋstər] *n* muchacho(a) *m,f*, joven *mf*; **the youngsters** los chicos

your [jɔ:, *unstressed* jə] *poss adj* **(a)** *(of one person)* tu, *Fml* su; **y. house** tu casa, *Fml* su casa; **y. books** tus libros, *Fml* sus libros **(b)** *(of more than one person) Esp* vuestro(a), *Am or Fml* su; **y. house** *Esp* vuestra casa, *Am or Fml* su casa; **y. books** *Esp* vuestros libros, *Am or Fml* sus libros **(c)** *(impers use)* **the house is on y. right** la casa queda a la derecha; **they clean y. shoes for you** te limpian los zapatos; **you get y. ticket first** primero se compra el billete; *Fam* **y. average Spaniard** el español medio; **y. typical feminist** la típica feminista **(d)** *(formal address)* **Y. Highness** Su Alteza; **Y. Majesty** Su Majestad

yours [jɔ:z] *poss pron* **(a)** *(of one person) (singular)* tuyo(a), *Fml* suyo(a); *(plural)* tuyos(as), *Fml* suyos(as); **this book is y.** este libro es tuyo, *Fml* este libro es suyo; **these books are y.** estos libros son tuyos, *Fml* estos libros son suyos; **is this y.?** ¿es el tuyo?, *Fml* ¿es la tuya? **(b)** *(of more than one person) (singular) Esp* vuestro(a), *Am or Fml* suyo(a); *(plural) Esp* vuestros(as), *Am or Fml* suyos(as); **this book is y.** *Esp* este libro es vuestro, *Am or Fml* este libro es suyo; **these books are y.** *Esp* estos libros son vuestros, *Am or Fml* estos libros son suyos **(c)** *(in letters)* **y. faithfully** le(s) saluda atentamente; **y. sincerely** reciba un cordial saludo de

yourself [jɔ:'self, *unstressed* jə'self] *(pl* **yourselves** [jɔ:'selvz])* **1** *pers pron (sing)* tú mismo(a), *Fml* usted mismo(a); *(pl) Esp* vosotros(as) mismos(as), *Am or Fml* ustedes mismos(as); **by y.** (tú) solo(a), *Fml* (usted) solo(a); **by yourselves** *Esp* vosotros(as) solos(as), *Am or Fml* ustedes solos(as); **do it y.** hazlo tú, *Fml* hágalo usted; **do it yourselves** *Esp* hacedlo vosotros(as), *Am or Fml* háganlo ustedes **2** *reflexive pron (reflexive)* te, *Fml* se; *(plural) Esp* os, *Am or Fml* se; **have you hurt y.?** ¿te has hecho daño?, *Fml* ¿se ha hecho daño?; **have you hurt yourselves?** *Esp* ¿os habéis hecho daño?, *Am or Fml* ¿se han hecho daño?; **enjoy y.!** ¡diviértete!, ¡que te diviertas!(*Fml* ¡diviértase!, ¡que se divierta!; **enjoy yourselves** *Esp* ¡divertíos!, ¡que os divertáis!, *Am or Fml* ¡diviértanse!, ¡que se diviertan!

youth [ju:θ] *n* **(a)** *(period of life)* juventud *f* **(b)** *(young man)* joven *m* **(c)** *(young people)* juventud *f* ❏ **y. club** club *m* juvenil; **y. hostel** albergue *m* juvenil

youthful ['ju:θfʊl] *adj* juvenil, joven

youthfulness ['ju:θfʊlnɪs] *n* juventud *f*

yowl [jaʊl] **1** *n* aullido *m* **2** *vi* aullar

yo-yo ['jəʊjəʊ] *n* yoyo *m*, yoyó *m*

yr *(pl* **yrs) (a)** *(abbr* **year)** año *m*, A **(b)** *(abbr* **your)** tu, su

Yucatan [ju:kə'tæn] *n* Yucatán *m*

Yucatecan ['ju:kə'tekən] *adj* yucateco(a)

yucca ['jʌkə] *n Bot* yuca *f*

yucky ['jʌkɪ] *adj* **(yuckier, yuckiest)** *Fam* asqueroso(a)

Yugoslav ['ju:gəʊslɑ:v] *adj & n* yugoslavo(a) *(m,f)*

Yugoslavia [ju:gəʊ'slɑ:vɪə] *n* Yugoslavia

Yugoslavian [ju:gəʊ'slɑ:vɪən] *adj & n* yugoslavo(a) *(m,f)*

Yuletide ['ju:ltaɪd] *n Fml* Navidades *fpl*

yummy ['jʌmɪ] *adj* **(yummier, yummiest)** *Fam* rico(a)

yuppie ['jʌpɪ] *n* yupi *mf*; **a y. restaurant** un restaurante de yupis; *Fam* **y. flu** la gripe *or Am* gripa del yupi *(encefalomielitis miálgica)*

YWCA [waɪdʌbəlju:si:'eɪ] *n (abbr* **Young Women's Christian Association)** albergue *m* para jóvenes mujeres

Z

Z, z [zed, *US* zi:] *n (the letter)* Z, z *f*
Zaire [zɑːˈɪər] *n Formerly* Zaire
Zairean [zɑːˈɪərɪən] *adj & n Formerly* zaireño(a) *(mf)*
Zambezi [zæmˈbiːzɪ] *n* Zambeze
Zambia [ˈzæmbɪə] *n* Zambia
Zambian [ˈzæmbɪən] *adj & n* zambiano(a) *(m,f)*
zany [ˈzeɪnɪ] *adj* (**zanier, zaniest**) *Fam* (**a**) *(mad) Esp* chiflado(a), *Am* zafado(a), *RP* rayado(a) (**b**) *(eccentric)* estrafalario(a), extravagante
zap [zæp] **1** *interj* ¡zas¡
  2 *vt Slang* (*pt & pp* **zapped**) (**a**) *(hit)* pegar (**b**) *Fam (kill)* cargarse (**c**) *(do quickly)* hacer rápidamente
zapper [ˈzæpər] *n Fam (TV remote control)* mando *m* a distancia, telemando *m*
zeal [ziːl] *n (fanatical)* celo *m* excesivo; *(enthusiasm)* entusiasmo *m*
zealot [ˈzelət] *n* fanático(a) *m,f*
zealous [ˈzeləs] *adj (fanatical)* celoso(a); *(enthusiastic)* entusiasta
zebra [ˈziːbrə, ˈzebrə] *n Zool* cebra *f* ❑ *Br* **z. crossing** paso *m* cebra *or* de peatones
zebu [ˈziːbuː] *n Zool* cebú *m*
zed [zed] *n, US* **zee** [ziː] *n* zeta *f*
Zen [zen] *n* Zen *m*
zenith [ˈzenɪθ] *n Astron* cenit *m*; *Fig* apogeo *m*
zephyr [ˈzefər] *n* céfiro *m*
zeppelin [ˈzepəlɪn] *n Av* zepelín *m*
zero [ˈzɪərəʊ] **1** *n* (*pl* **zeros** *or* **zeroes**) cero *m*; **two degrees below z.** dos grados bajo cero ❑ **z. hour** hora *f* cero; **z. tolerance** tolerancia *f* cero, inflexibilidad *f* absoluta
  2 *vi* (*pt & pp* **zeroed**) *Mil* **to z. in on** apuntar hacia; *Fig (problem)* centrarse en
zest [zest] *n* (**a**) *(eagerness)* brío *m*, entusiasmo *m* (**b**) *(wit)* gracia *f* (**c**) *Culin* cáscara *f*, corteza *f*
zigzag [ˈzɪgzæg] **1** *n* zigzag *m*
  2 *vi* (*pt & pp* **zigzagged**) zigzaguear
zilch [zɪltʃ] *n US Slang* nada, nada de nada
Zimbabwe [zɪmˈbɑːbweɪ] *n* Zimbabue
Zimbabwean [zɪmˈbɑːbweɪən] *adj & n* zimbabuense *(m,f)*, zimbabuo(a) *(m,f)*

zinc [zɪŋk] *n Chem* cinc *m*, zinc *m*
Zion [ˈzaɪən] *n* Sión *m*
Zionism [ˈzaɪənɪzəm] *n* sionismo *m*
Zionist [ˈzaɪənɪst] *adj & n* sionista *(mf)*
zip [zɪp] **1** *n* (**a**) *Br Sew* **z. (fastener)** cremallera *f*, *Am* cierre *m* (**b**) *Fam* brío *m*, energía *f* (**c**) *US* **z. code** código *m* postal (**d**) *Comptr* **Zip® disk** disco *m* Zip®; **z. file** archivo *m* zip
  2 (*pt & pp* **zipped**) *vt* **to z. sth up/shut** cerrar *or* unir *or* subir la cremallera de algo
zip by *vi* pasar como un rayo
zip up *vt (clothes, bag)* cerrar la cremallera *or Am* el cierre de; **z. me up, please** súbeme la cremallera, por favor
zipper [ˈzɪpər] *n US* cremallera *f*, *Am* cierre *m*
zippy [ˈzɪpɪ] *adj* (**zippier, zippiest**) *Fam* brioso(a), vivaz
zircon [ˈzɜːkɒn] *n Min* circón *m*
zirconium [zɜːˈkəʊnɪəm] *n Chem* circonio *m*
zither [ˈzɪðər] *n Mus* cítara *f*
zodiac [ˈzəʊdɪæk] *n Astrol* zodiaco *m*, zodíaco *m*
zombie [ˈzɒmbɪ] *n* zombie *f*
zone [zəʊn] **1** *n* zona *f* ❑ *US* **postal z.** distrito *m* postal; **time z.** huso *m* horario
  2 *vt* dividir en zonas
zoning [ˈzəʊnɪŋ] *n* división *f* en zonas
zonked [zɒŋkt] *adj Fam* (**a**) *(exhausted)* reventado(a), molido(a) (**b**) *(drugged)* colocado(a), *Col* trabado(a), *Méx* pingo(a), *RP* fálopeado(a) (**c**) *(drunk)* mamado(a)
zoo [zuː] *n* (*pl* **zoos**) zoo *m*
zoological [zəʊəˈlɒdʒɪkəl] *adj* zoológico(a); **z. garden** parque *m* zoológico
zoologist [zəʊˈɒlədʒɪst] *n* zoólogo(a) *m,f*
zoology [zəʊˈɒlədʒɪ] *n* zoología *f*
zoom [zuːm] **1** *n* (**a**) *(buzz)* zumbido *m* (**b**) *Phot* **z. lens** zoom *m*, teleobjetivo *m*
  2 *vi* (**a**) *(buzz)* zumbar (**b**) *(rush)* **to z. past** pasar volando
zoom in *vi (camera)* acercarse rápidamente
zoom out *vi (camera)* alejarse rápidamente
zucchini [zuːˈkiːnɪ] *n* (*pl* **zucchini** *or* **zucchinis**) *US* calabacín *m*
Zulu [ˈzuːluː] *adj & n* zulú *(mf)*

Spanish Grammar

Contents

Contents

GLOSSARY OF GRAMMATICAL TERMS

ABSTRACT NOUN
An abstract noun is one that refers not to a concrete physical object or a person or animal but to a quality or a concept.
Examples of abstract nouns are *happiness, life, length*.

ACTIVE
The active form of a verb is the basic form as in *I remember her*. It contrasts with the passive form of the verb as in *she will be remembered*.

ADJECTIVAL NOUN
An adjectival noun is an adjective used as a noun. For example, the adjective *young* is used as a noun in *the young at heart*.

ADJECTIVE
An adjective is a describing word telling us what something or someone is like (e.g., *a **small** house, the **Royal** Family, an **interesting** pastime*).

ADVERB
Adverbs are normally used with a verb to add extra information by indicating **how** the action is done (adverbs of manner), or **when, where** and **to what extent** the action is done (adverbs of time, place and degree). Adverbs may also be used with an adjective or another adverb (e.g., *a **very** attractive girl, surprisingly well*).

AGREEMENT
In Spanish, words such as adjectives, articles and pronouns are said to agree in number and gender with the noun or pronoun they refer to. This means that their form changes according to the **number** of the noun (singular or plural) and its **gender** (masculine or feminine).

APPOSITION
A word or a phrase is said to be in apposition to another when it is placed directly after it without any joining word (e.g., *Mr. Jones, **our bank manager**, rang today*).

ARTICLE
See DEFINITE ARTICLE and INDEFINITE ARTICLE.

AUGMENTATIVE
An augmentative is an ending added to a noun to indicate largeness or awkwardness, e.g., *un hombr**ón**, una mujer**ona***.

AUXILIARY
Auxiliary verbs are used to form compound tenses of other verbs, eg **have** in *I **have** seen* or **will** in *she **will** go*. The main auxiliary verbs in Spanish are **haber, estar** and **ser**.

CARDINAL
Cardinal numbers are numbers such as *one, two, ten, fourteen*, as opposed to **ordinal** numbers (e.g., *first, second*).

CLAUSE
A clause is a group of words that contains at least a **subject** and a **verb**: *he said* is a clause. A clause often contains more than this basic information, eg *he said this to her yesterday*. Sentences can be made up of several clauses, e.g., *he said / he'd call me / if he were free*. See SENTENCE.

COLLECTIVE
A collective noun is one that refers to a group of people or things but that is singular in form. Examples of collective nouns are *flock* and *fleet*.

COLLOQUIAL
Colloquial language is the sort of language that can be used in everyday informal conversation but is avoided in formal writing such as legal contracts, etc.

COMPARATIVE
The comparative forms of adjectives and adverbs are used to compare two or more things, persons or actions. In English, *more ... than, -er than, less ... than* and *as ... as* are used for comparison.

COMPOUND
Compound tenses are verb tenses consisting of more than one element. In Spanish, the compound tenses of a verb are formed by using the **auxiliary** verb with the **present** or **past participle**: *estoy hablando, han llegado*.

COMPOUND NOUNS
Compound nouns are nouns made up of two or more separate words. English examples are *goalkeeper* or *dinner party*. Spanish compound nouns are normally linked by *de*, e.g., *un muro **de** piedra*.

CONDITIONAL
The conditional **mood** is used to describe what someone would do, or to say

Glossary of grammatical terms

what would happen if a condition were fulfilled (e.g., *I* **would come** *if I was well; the chair* **would have broken** *if he had sat on it*). It is also used to express "future in the past", e.g., *he said he* **would come**.

CONJUGATION
The conjugation of a verb is the set of different forms taken in the particular **tenses** and **moods** of that verb.

CONJUNCTION
Conjunctions are linking words (e.g., *and, but, or*). They may be coordinating or subordinating. Coordinating conjunctions are words like *y, o, pero*; subordinating conjunctions are words like *que, si, aunque*.

DEFINITE ARTICLE
The definite article is *the* in English and *el, la, los, las* in Spanish.

DEMONSTRATIVE
Demonstrative adjectives (e.g., *this, that, these*) and pronouns (e.g., *this one, that one*) are used to point out a particular person or thing.

DIMINUTIVE
A diminutive is an ending added to a noun (or occasionally to an adjective) to indicate smallness or a favorable or unfavorable attitude on the part of the speaker, e.g., *mesita, hijito*.

DIRECT OBJECT
A direct object is a noun or a pronoun that in English follows a verb without any linking preposition, e.g., *I met a friend*. Note that in English the preposition before an **indirect object** is often omitted, e.g., *I sent* **him** *a present* – *him* is equivalent to *to him* – *a present* is the direct object.

ENDING
The ending of a verb is determined by the **person** (1st/2nd/3rd) and **number** (singular/plural) of its subject.

EXCLAMATION
Exclamations are words or phrases used to express surprise, annoyance etc (e.g., *what!, wow!, how lucky!, what a nice day!*). Exclamations in Spanish begin with an upside-down exclamation mark, e.g., *¡caramba!*

FEMININE
See GENDER.

GENDER
The gender of a noun indicates whether the noun is **masculine** or **feminine**. In Spanish, the gender of a noun is not always determined by the sex of what it refers to, eg *la víctima* (*the victim*) is a feminine noun, even when it refers to a man.

IDIOMATIC
Idiomatic expressions (or idioms) are expressions that cannot normally be translated word for word. For example, *it's raining cats and dogs* is translated by *está lloviendo a cántaros*.

IMPERATIVE
The imperative **mood** is used for giving orders (e.g., *stop!, don't go!*) or for making suggestions (e.g., *let's go*).

INDEFINITE
Indefinite pronouns are words that do not refer to a definite person or thing (e.g., *each, someone*).

INDEFINITE ARTICLE
The indefinite article is *a* in English and *un, una* in Spanish.

INDICATIVE
The indicative **mood** is normally used in making statements or asking questions, as in *I like, he came, we are trying*. It contrasts with the **subjunctive**, **conditional** and **imperative**.

INDIRECT OBJECT
An indirect object is a pronoun or noun which follows a verb sometimes with a linking preposition (usually *to*), e.g., *I spoke to* **my friend/him**, *she gave* **him** *a kiss*.

INFINITIVE
The infinitive is the form of the verb as found in dictionaries. Thus *to eat, to finish, to take* are infinitives. In Spanish, all infinitives end in **-r**: *tomar, beber, vivir*.

INTERROGATIVE
Interrogative words are used to ask a question. They may be used in a direct question (**when** *will you arrive?*) or an indirect question (*I don't know* **when** *he'll arrive*). See QUESTION.

MASCULINE
See GENDER.

MOOD
Mood is the name given to each of the four main areas within which a verb is conjugated. See INDICATIVE, SUBJUNCTIVE, CONDITIONAL, IMPERATIVE.

NEUTER
There are no neuter nouns in Spanish. Only the definite article *lo*, the pronoun *ello*

and the demonstrative pronouns *esto, eso* and *aquello* have a neuter form. The article *lo* is used with adjectives, eg *lo bueno* (that which is good, the good thing), and the demonstratives are used to refer to an entire situation, e.g., *no acepto eso* (I don't accept that).

NOUN
A noun is a word that refers to living creatures, things, places or abstract ideas, e.g., *postman, cat, shop, passport, life*.

NUMBER
The number of a noun indicates whether the noun is **singular** or **plural**. A singular noun refers to one single thing or person (e.g., *boy, train*) and a plural noun to several (e.g., *boys, trains*).

OBJECT
See DIRECT OBJECT, INDIRECT OBJECT.

ORDINAL
Ordinal numbers are numbers such as *first, second, third, fourth*, etc., as opposed to **cardinal** numbers (e.g., *one, three*).

PASSIVE
A verb is used in the passive when the subject of the verb does not perform the action but is subjected to it. In English, the passive is formed by using a part of the verb *to be* or *to get* and the past participle of the verb, e.g., *he **was rewarded**/ he **got beaten up***.

PAST PARTICIPLE
The past participle of a verb is the form that is used after *to have* in English to form the perfect tense, e.g., *I have **eaten**, I have **said**, you have **tried***.

PERSON
In any tense, there are three persons in the singular (1st: *I*..., 2nd: *you*..., 3rd: *he/she/it*...), and three in the plural (1st: *we*..., 2nd: *you*..., 3rd: *they*...). See also ENDING.

PERSONAL PRONOUNS
Personal pronouns are used to stand for a noun. In English they are words like *I, you, he/she/it, we, they* or *me, you, him/her/it, us, them*.

PLURAL
See NUMBER.

POSSESSIVE
Possessives are used to indicate possession or ownership. They are words like *my/mine, your/yours, our/ours*.

PREPOSITION
Prepositions are words that indicate relationships in space and time, such as *with, in, to, at*. They are normally followed by a noun or a pronoun.

PRESENT PARTICIPLE
The present participle is the verb form that ends in **-ing** in English (**-ndo** in Spanish).

PROGRESSIVE
The progressive tenses are formed in English by the verb *to be* and the **present participle**, e.g., *I am speaking, he was writing*. In Spanish it is formed by *estar* and the **present participle**, e.g., *estoy hablando, estaba escribiendo*.

PRONOUN
A pronoun is a word that stands for a noun. The main categories of pronouns are:
- **Personal pronouns** (e.g., *you, him, us*)
- **Possessive pronouns** (e.g., *mine, yours, his*)
- **Reflexive pronouns** (e.g., *myself, himself*)
- **Interrogative pronouns** (e.g., *who?, what?, which?*)
- **Relative pronouns** (e.g., *who, which, that*)
- **Demonstrative pronouns** (e.g., *this, that, these*)
- **Indefinite pronouns** (e.g., *something, none*)

QUESTION
There are two question forms: **direct** questions stand on their own and require a question mark at the end (e.g., *when will he come?*); **indirect** questions are introduced by a clause and require no question mark (e.g., *I wonder **when he will come***). Direct questions begin in Spanish with an upside-down question mark, e.g., *¿qué haces?*

REFLEXIVE
Reflexive verbs 'reflect' the action back onto the subject (e.g., *I dressed myself*). They are always found with a reflexive pronoun and are more common in Spanish than in English. Verbs are often used reflexively in Spanish where English would use the **passive**.

SENTENCE
A sentence is a group of words made up of one or more clauses (see CLAUSE). The end of a sentence is indicated by a punctuation mark (usually a period, a question mark or an exclamation mark).

Glossary of grammatical terms

SINGULAR   See NUMBER.

STEM   See VERB STEM.

SUBJECT   The subject of a verb is the **noun** or **pronoun** that performs the action. In the sentences *the train left early* and *she bought a record*, *the train* and *she* are the subjects.

SUBJUNCTIVE   The subjunctive is a verb form that is rarely used in English (e.g., *if I* **were** *you, God* **save** *the Queen*). It is very much more common in Spanish.

SUPERLATIVE   The superlative is the form of an **adjective** or an **adverb** which, in English, is marked by *the most ..., the -est* or *the least ...*

TENSE   Verbs are used in tenses, which indicate when an action takes place, e.g., in the present, the past, the future.

VERB   A verb is a 'doing' word that usually describes an action (e.g., *to sing, to work, to watch*). Some verbs describe a state (e.g., *to be, to have, to hope*).

VERB STEM   The stem of a verb is its 'basic unit' to which the various **endings** are added. To find the stem of a Spanish verb remove **-ar**, **-er** or **-ir** from the infinitive. The stem of *hablar* is **habl**, of *beber*, **beb**, of *vivir*, **viv**.

VOICE   The two voices of a verb are its **active** and **passive** forms.

Part One
FUNCTIONS

1. REFERRING TO THINGS: THE NOUN

The word 'thing' is used here not just to refer to objects – books, houses, cars, etc., also known as *inanimate* nouns – but also to people and animals – *animate* nouns – and to what are known as *abstract* nouns. Abstract nouns refer not to things that you can touch or see, but only to ideas that you can think about – justice, peace, democracy and so on.

A. USES OF THE DEFINITE AND INDEFINITE ARTICLES

For the formation of the definite and indefinite articles, see page 67.

There is a considerable degree of agreement between Spanish and English as to when a noun is used with a definite or an indefinite article. However, some important differences also occur.

The traditional terms 'definite article' ('the' in English) and 'indefinite article' ('a', 'an' in English) are to some extent misleading, since it is not necessarily the case that the definite article refers to a specific object (or idea) and the indefinite article does not. For example, in the sentences:

> **la casa es vieja**
> the house is old

and:

> **hemos comprado una casa en el campo**
> we have bought a house in the country

both nouns refer to a specific house.

Moreover, there are in fact *three* different cases to consider:

> cases where the noun is used with a definite article
> cases where the noun is used with an indefinite article
> cases where the noun is used with no article at all

As you will see later, *truly* indefinite nouns are in fact used without any article in Spanish.

a) Nouns that are used to represent *all* of the thing or things they are referring to – *all* butter, *all* wine, *all* Spaniards and the like – are preceded by the definite article in Spanish:

> **me gusta la cerveza, pero no me gusta el vino**
> I like beer (all beer, beer in general), but I don't like wine (wine in general)

> **los españoles beben mucho vino**
> Spaniards (all Spaniards) drink a lot of wine

If the noun is used with an adjective or an adjectival phrase, it will still take the definite article if it refers to all of the thing or things indicated by the noun plus the adjective or phrase:

> **no me gusta el vino tinto**
> I don't like red wine

Here **el vino tinto** does not represent all wine, but it does stand for all red wine.

> **los granjeros del sur de España cultivan muchas frutas**
> farmers in the south of Spain grow a lot of fruit

This refers to all farmers in the south of Spain.

b) Abstract nouns take the definite article in Spanish, since they also refer to the idea as a whole:

> **la justicia es necesaria para que la democracia sobreviva**
> justice is necessary if democracy is to survive

> **la inflación está subiendo**
> inflation is going up

If the abstract noun is used with an adjective, then in some cases it can take the indefinite article:

> **me miró con una curiosidad creciente**
> he looked at me with growing curiosity

c) Names of languages take the definite article:

> **el español es muy interesante, pero no me gusta el francés**
> Spanish is very interesting, but I don't like French

However, no article is used after **en, de** and the verbs **hablar** and **estudiar**:

> **¿hablas español?**
> do you speak Spanish?

> **el libro está escrito en español**
> the book is written in Spanish

(7)

Referring to things: the noun

Again, if a particular example of the language is being referred to rather than the language as a whole, the indefinite article is used:

John habla un español excelente
John speaks excellent Spanish (i.e., the particular Spanish that he speaks is excellent)

d) Names of academic subjects follow the same pattern as in **c)**:

no me gustan las matemáticas, prefiero la física
I don't like math, I prefer physics

but no article is necessary in the following cases:

he comprado un libro de química
I've bought a chemistry book

estudia matemáticas
he is studying mathematics

es licenciado en física
he has a degree in physics

e) Names of illnesses and diseases usually take the definite article, unless the idea of 'a case of' is clearly meant, in which case no article is used:

¿tiene algo contra la laringitis?
do you have anything for laryngitis?

but:

tengo laringitis
I have laryngitis

f) In general physical descriptions, names of parts of the body take the definite article:

tiene el pelo castaño y los ojos verdes
she has brown hair and green eyes

However, if the description highlights how one person's eyes, etc., are different from everyone else's, the indefinite article is used:

tiene unos ojos azules que nadie puede resistir
she has blue eyes which no-one can resist

When the part of the body is the subject of the verb, the possessive adjective is normally used:

sus ojos son azules como el mar
her eyes are blue like the sea

g) Where English uses the possessive adjective, Spanish uses the definite article (sometimes

together with the indirect object pronouns for greater precision) to indicate possession in relation to parts of the body and items of clothing:

levantó la cabeza
he lifted his head

me duele la cabeza
my head is sore

su madre le lavó la cara
his mother washed his face

se puso la chaqueta y salió
he put on his jacket and went out

h) For reasons of style the definite article is frequently omitted in lists of words, even where you might expect it to appear:

necesitarás entusiasmo e interés
you will need enthusiasm and interest

B. CASES IN WHICH NO ARTICLE IS USED

a) In general, no article is used with the noun if:

the noun does not refer either to the thing as a whole or to a specific example of the thing in question:

me llamó ladrón
he called me a thief

the noun refers to an indefinite amount or number of the thing(s) in question:

no bebo cerveza
I don't drink beer

b) No article is used with general statements of profession or occupation, political or religious conviction, and the like:

mi padre es médico y mi tía es enfermera
my father is a doctor and my aunt is a nurse

ella es católica; él es comunista
she is a Catholic; he is a communist

However, if the noun is made more precise by being used with an adjective, then the indefinite article is used:

su padre es un cirujano conocido
his father is a well known surgeon

Not all surgeons are famous.

c) Frequently (though not always) when a noun is

dependent on a negative or a question, no article is used:

¿tienes carro? – no, no tengo carro
have you got a car? – no, I don't have a car

Again, this is not a reference to any particular car. If you did wish to refer to a particular car, you would use the indefinite article:

¿tienes un carro rojo?
do you have a red car?

d) When the noun is used with one of a small number of adjectives the article is omitted. These are **otro** (other), and **tal, semejante** and **parecido** (all meaning 'such'), and **cierto** (certain, some):

¿me das otro libro, por favor?
would you give me another book, please? (i.e., any other *undefined* book)

semejante situación nunca se había producido antes
such a situation had never arisen before (a situation of this general kind)

estoy de acuerdo contigo hasta cierto punto
I agree with you up to a point (an *undefined* point)

e) No article is used after **qué** and **vaya** in exclamations:

¡qué lástima!
what a shame!

¡vaya sorpresa!
what a surprise!

¡vaya paliza!
what a bore!

Note that any adjective used in such an exclamation is usually preceded by **tan** or **más**:

¡qué día más magnífico!
what a magnificent day!

This **más** is not considered comparative (see page 18), and does not become **mejor** or **peor** when used with **bueno** or **malo**:

¡qué idea más buena!
what a good idea!

f) No article is used after **como** in expressions such as the following:

te hablo como amigo
I'm speaking to you as a friend

I am speaking to you not as a particular friend, but as any friend would.

mándenos diez cajas como pedido de prueba
send us ten boxes as a trial order

Compare this with the following:

ya hemos recibido un pedido de prueba de esa empresa
we have already received a trial order from this firm

This is a reference to a specific trial order.

g) The article is not used when expressing indefinite quantities:

¿tienes mantequilla?
do you have (any) butter?

no quiero vino, siempre bebo cerveza
I don't want (any) wine, I always drink beer

Compare this with **la cerveza** in A.a). above, which meant 'all beer, beer in general'.

buen número de personas no querían aceptar eso
a good number of people did not want to accept this

parte/buena parte/gran parte del dinero se invirtió en el proyecto
part/a good part/a large part of the money was invested in the project

tengo cantidad/infinidad de preguntas que hacerte
I've got loads/masses of questions to ask you

h) The article is omitted with nouns in apposition:

vive en Bogotá, capital de Colombia
he lives in Bogotá, the capital of Colombia

C. NAMES OF PERSONS, COUNTRIES, ETC.

A proper noun is invariably the name of a person, country, continent, organization or the like. Most proper nouns, including virtually all feminine names of countries, are used without any article in Spanish (see page 67 for a list of names of countries that do take the article):

Alemania es un país mucho más rico que España
Germany is a much richer country than Spain

However, the article is used in the following cases:

a) When a person's name is preceded by a title of some kind:

el señor Carballo no estaba
señor Carballo wasn't in

el general Olmeda ya se había marchado
General Olmeda had already left

The exceptions to this are:

– the titles **don** and **doña**
– when the title is used in direct address
– foreign titles

¿qué piensa de esto, señor Carballo?
what do you think of this, señor Carballo?

Lord Byron era un poeta inglés muy conocido
Lord Byron was a very famous English poet

b) When the noun is used with an adjective:

el pobre Juan no sabía qué hacer
poor Juan didn't know what to do

esto ha ocurrido muchas veces en la historia de la América hispana
this has happened many times in the history of Hispanic America

However, **Gran Bretaña** and **Estados Unidos** have come to be regarded as proper nouns in their own right, so that the definite articles are no longer used in these cases:

Gran Bretaña votó en contra de la propuesta
Great Britain voted against the proposal

c) Acronyms

An acronym is a name consisting of the initial letters of a series of words. Known as **siglas**, these are very widely used in Spanish. With the exception of certain names of political parties, **siglas** always take the definite article, and their gender is determined by the gender of the first noun in their expanded form.

A few common acronyms:

la UE	la Unión Europea	the EU
la OTAN	la Organización del Tratado del Atlántico Norte	NATO
la RAE	la Real Academia Española	Institution in charge of the Spanish language
la CEPAL	la Comisión Económica para América Latina	Economic Commission for Latin America and the Caribbean
la ONU	la Organización de las Naciones Unidas	United Nations
el TLCAN	el Tratado de Libre Comercio de América del Norte	NAFTA (North American Free Trade Agreement)

México es miembro de la ONU
Mexico is a member of the UN

España sigue siendo miembro de la OTAN
Spain is still a member of NATO

Even those acronyms that are not names of organizations take the definite article:

la EEB	la Encefalopatía Espongiforme Bovina	BSE
el IVA	el Impuesto sobre el Valor Agregado	value added tax
el PVP	el Precio de Venta al Público	retail price

el comercio de productos cárnicos se ha visto gravemente afectado por la EEB
the trade in meat products has been hard hit by BSE

D. THE NEUTER ARTICLE *lo*

1. Abstract nouns

The neuter article **lo** is used almost exclusively with adjectives and adverbs. When used with an adjective, **lo** transforms the adjective into the corresponding abstract noun. For example **lo bueno** means 'that which is good.' The translation of such 'nouns' varies according to their context:

lo esencial es que todos estemos de acuerdo
the essential thing is for all of us to agree

lo verdaderamente importante es que
todos lo acepten
what's really important is for everyone to
accept it

lo más absurdo es que él no sabía nada
the most absurd part of it is that he knew
nothing

2. Meaning 'how'

lo + adjective expresses the idea of 'how' in
constructions such as the following. Note that in
these constructions the adjective agrees with the
noun it describes:

no me había dado cuenta de lo caros que
son
I hadn't realized how expensive they are

If there is no noun, the uninflected form of the
adjective is used:

¿no ves lo práctico que es?
can't you see how practical it is?

E. USING A VERB AS A NOUN

A verbal noun is a verb used as the subject or
object of another verb. In Spanish the *infinitive* is
used to express the verbal noun, whereas in
English we use the present participle. When used
as the subject of a verb, the infinitive is sometimes
preceded by the definite article **el**, though it is
more common without:

fumar es peligroso para la salud
smoking is dangerous for your health

detesto tener que hacer esto
I hate having to do this

⚠ Under *no* circumstances can a present
participle be used as a verbal noun in
Spanish as it is in English. Note in particular
that the infinitive is the *only* form of the verb
that can come after a preposition in Spanish:

tomó un café antes de salir
he had a coffee before leaving

se sintió mejor después de dormir un rato
he felt better after sleeping a while

F. SITUATING SOMETHING IN PLACE OR TIME: DEMONSTRATIVES

This function is carried out in Spanish by the
demonstrative adjectives and pronouns (see page
68). The difference between the three
demonstrative adjectives in Spanish is as follows:

1. Used to denote place

este	refers to something that is close to the speaker
ese	refers to something that is close to the listener
aquel	refers to something that is remote from both speaker and listener

¿me das ese libro?
will you give me that book? (i.e., the one near
you)

tomo esta caja
I'll take this box (i.e., this one I'm holding,
pointing to, etc.)

aquellas flores son muy hermosas
those flowers are very beautiful (i.e., those
over there)

2. Used to denote time

este is used, as in English, if the *noun* refers to
present time:

esta semana fuimos a la playa
we went to the beach this week

Both **ese** and **aquel** can be used to refer to past
time with little difference in meaning, though
aquel may suggest that the action is more
remote:

en esa época no se permitían los partidos
políticos
at that time political parties were not allowed

en aquella época la población de la Ciudad
de México era de sólo un millón de personas
at that time the population of Mexico City was
only one million

3. 'those who,' 'those of'

Note that 'those who' is expressed in Spanish as
los que or **las que**. The actual demonstratives are
not used:

los que piensan eso se equivocan
those who think that are wrong

Likewise, 'that of,' 'those of' are expressed as **el de,
la de, los de, las de. el** takes the same
contractions as it does when it is used as a definite
article – ie **a + el** becomes **al** and **de + el**
becomes **del** (see page 67):

preferimos las mercancías de Vds. a las de
sus competidores
we prefer your products to those of your
competitors

prefiero el carro de Luis al de Paco
I prefer Luis's car to Paco's (to that of Paco)

4. The demonstrative pronouns

For the formation of the demonstrative pronouns, see page 68.

The demonstrative pronouns denote time and place in the same way as the demonstrative adjectives. Note, however, the use of **aquél** and **éste** to express the idea of 'the former' and 'the latter':

éste es más difícil que aquél
the latter is more difficult than the former

The neuter demonstrative pronouns **esto, eso** and **aquello** are used to represent an unknown object, a general situation, an entire idea.

⚠ They can *never* be used to represent a specific noun whose identity is known to the speaker:

¿qué es esto?
what's this? (unknown object)

no puedo aceptar esto
I can't accept this (this situation)

Compare this with:

no puedo aceptar esta situación
I can't accept this situation

G. LINKING NOUNS

For a list of coordinating conjunctions, see page 96.

1. *y* and *o*

The simplest way of linking nouns is by using the conjunctions **y** (and) and **o** (or). Note that **y** is replaced by **e** if the pronunciation of the next word begins with the vowel **i**. It is the pronunciation that is important, not the way the noun is spelled:

padres e hijos
parents and children

Likewise, **o** is replaced by **u** if the next word begins with the sound **o**:

siete u ocho
seven or eight

In Spanish journalism, **o** is frequently written **ó** between numbers to avoid confusion with the number **0**:

60 ó 70
60 or 70

2. Expressing 'both'

a) 'both' + plural noun

When 'both' is followed by a *single* plural noun, **los dos** or **las dos** is used, depending on the gender of the noun. In more formal Spanish, the adjective **ambos** may be used:

los dos hermanos vinieron/ambos hermanos vinieron
both brothers came

comí las dos tartas/comí ambas tartas
I ate both cakes

⚠ Neither *los/las dos* nor *ambos* may be used to express the idea of 'both ... and ...' in Spanish.

b) 'both' + two adjectives

'both' used to link two adjectives referring to the same noun is **a la vez**:

encuentro este libro a la vez divertido e interesante
I find this book both entertaining and interesting

c) 'both' + two nouns or pronouns

By far the commonest way of expressing 'both ... and ...' linking two dissimilar things in Spanish is **tanto ... como ....** Since **tanto** is used as an adverb in this construction, it never changes, no matter what the number or gender of the nouns involved:

tanto tú como yo queremos resolver este problema
both you and I want to solve this problem

2. RELATIONSHIPS BETWEEN THINGS

A. PREPOSITIONS

The commonest way of expressing relationships between nouns is by the use of prepositions. For a detailed list of both simple and compound prepositions and their uses, see pages 71-76. However, the following deserve special mention:

1. *por* and *para*

As well as having a variety of other meanings, both **por** and **para** can be used to express the ideas of 'for' and 'by' in Spanish. Their uses in these meanings can be summarized as follows:

a) Meaning 'for'

(i) In a general sense, it can be said that **por** refers to *causes*, whereas **para** refers to *aims* or *objectives*.

The following short examples, both of which mean 'I am doing it for my brother,' may clarify the difference:

> **lo hago por mi hermano**

Here the emphasis is on what *caused* the speaker to decide to do what he is doing. He is doing it because his brother asked for it to be done, or because his brother needed help in some way.

> **lo hago para mi hermano**

para here indicates that the action is being done in order to secure some advantage for the brother in the future.

Likewise, the question **¿por qué hiciste esto?** asks for an explanation of what caused the action to be done, whereas the question **¿para qué hiciste esto?** asks for an explanation of the future objectives.

Here are some other examples showing the distinction between **por** and **para** (note that, although the basic ideas remain unchanged, 'for' is not always the best translation in English):

> **lo hizo por necesidad**
> he did it out of necessity

> **cometió el error por cansancio**
> he made the mistake through tiredness

> **lo dejaron para otro día**
> they left it for another day

> **estamos estudiando para un examen**
> we're studying for an exam

(ii) If there is any idea of an exchange, **por** is always used:

> **pagué diez mil dólares por este carro**
> I paid ten thousand dollars for this car

> **voy a cambiar mi viejo coche por otro más moderno**
> I am going to exchange my old car for a more modern one

(iii) To express the idea of 'as regards,' 'as far as it concerns,' use **para**:

> **este libro es demasiado difícil para mí**
> this book is too difficult for me

> **tal situación sería inaceptable para México**
> such a situation would be unacceptable for Mexico

b) Meaning 'by'

(i) When introducing the person or thing by whom an action was carried out (when using the passive mood), **por** is always used:

> **el edificio fue inaugurado por el rey Juan Carlos**
> the building was inaugurated by King Juan Carlos

(ii) When 'by' refers to a future deadline, **para** is used:

> **necesitamos las mercancías para finales de octubre**
> we need the goods by the end of October

2. *a* and *en*

Basically **a** indicates motion *toward* a thing or place, whereas **en** indicates position *in* or *on* a thing or place. The difference is usually clear in English, but problems can arise when translating the preposition 'at.' If 'at' indicates position *in* or *on*, **en** must be used:

> **Juan está en casa**
> Juan is at home

> **vi esta computadora en la feria de muestras**
> I saw this computer at the exhibition

3. *antes de, delante de, ante*

a) **antes de** usually refers to time:

> **llegamos antes de medianoche**
> we arrived before midnight

Colloquially, it may also refer to place, though the idea of 'before you arrive at ...' is usually involved:

> **la iglesia está antes del cruce**
> the church is before the junction

b) **delante de** refers to physical position:

> **el buzón está delante de Correos**
> the mailbox is in front of the Post Office

c) **ante** refers to mental position, and is usually used with abstract nouns. It expresses roughly the

(13)

same idea as the English expressions 'in the presence of,' '(when) faced with' and the like:

> **el gobierno no sabía cómo reaccionar ante este problema**
> the government did not know how to react when faced with this problem

There are a few set expressions where **ante** may refer to physical position, but these are very limited and often refer to legal contexts:

> **compareció ante el juez**
> he appeared before the judge

B. POSSESSION

For the formation of the possessive adjectives and pronouns, see page 68.

The weak forms of the possessive adjectives, which are *by far* the commonest, are placed before the noun. The strong forms go after the noun.

1. **The weak possessive adjectives**
   ⚠ It is important to note that, like any other adjective, the possessive adjective agrees in gender and number with the noun it describes. The 'owner' of the things described is irrelevant from this point of view:

   > **¿dónde están nuestras maletas?**
   > where are our suitcases?

   nuestras is in the feminine plural form because **maletas** is feminine plural. The owners ('we') could be either male or female.

   > **los chicos hablaban con su abuelo**
   > the boys were speaking with their grandfather

   > **las chicas ayudaban a su madre**
   > the girls were helping their mother

   su is singular because both **abuelo** and **madre** are singular. The fact that there were a number of boys or girls does not alter this in any way.

2. **The strong possessive adjectives**
   In contemporary Spanish, the strong forms of the possessive adjectives are for all practical purposes restricted to forms of direct address, or to expressing the idea 'of mine,' 'of yours,' etc.:

   > **esto no es posible, amigo mío**
   > this is not possible, my friend

   > **unos amigos míos vinieron a verme**
   > some friends of mine came to see me

3. **The possessive pronouns**
   The possessive pronouns take the definite article unless they are used with the verb **ser**:

   > **¿quieres el mío?**
   > do you want mine?

   > **esta radio no es tuya, es nuestra**
   > this radio isn't yours, it's ours

   > **su casa es mucho más grande que la mía**
   > his house is much bigger than mine

4. **Cases where confusion might arise**
   On occasions, confusion may arise with the use of the adjective **su** and the pronoun **suyo**. These forms can mean 'his,' 'her(s),' 'your(s)' (singular), 'their(s),' 'your(s)' (plural). In most cases the context will make it clear which meaning is involved. However, if confusion is likely to arise, the following forms can be used instead:

his	**de él**
her(s)	**de ella**
your(s) (singular)	**de Vd.**
their(s)	**de ellos, de ellas**
your(s) (plural)	**de Vds.**

   > **María no ha perdido su propia maleta, ha perdido la de ellos**
   > María has not lost her own suitcase, she has lost *theirs*

   > **¿es de ella este libro?**
   > is this book hers?

5. **Possession in general**
   There is no equivalent of the English 'apostrophe s' in Spanish. Possession is expressed in various ways, the most common being the use of the preposition **de**. The order in which the nouns are expressed is the exact opposite of English:

   > **el amigo de mi padre**
   > my father's friend

   Note that **de** + **el** becomes **del**:

   > **el primo del amigo del profesor**
   > the teacher's friend's cousin

6. **Expressing 'whose'**
   'whose' in a question is **¿de quién?**

   > **¿de quién es este lápiz?**
   > whose is this pencil?

   In an adjectival clause, 'whose' is expressed by the adjective **cuyo**, which agrees with the thing owned:

el hombre cuya ventana rompieron está furioso
the man whose window they broke is furious

la mujer cuyos hijos se fueron
the woman whose children went away

7. **The verb *pertenecer***

Possession of objects can sometimes be expressed by the use of the verb **pertenecer** (to belong). However, this is rather formal and is much less common than the use of **de**:

¿a quién pertenece esto? – pertenece al profesor
whose is this? – it's the teacher's

The more common meaning of **pertenecer** is 'belong' in the sense of 'be a member of':

pertenece al partido socialista
he belongs to the socialist party

8. **With parts of the body and items of clothing**

⚠ When used as the object of a verb, parts of the body and items of clothing take the definite article, not the possessive adjective as in English. The 'owner' is often indicated by means of the indirect object pronoun:

su madre le lavó la cara
his mother washed his face

se quemó la mano
he burned his hand (i.e., his own hand)

C. COMPOUND NOUNS

A compound noun consists of a group of nouns that go together to express a more complex idea, e.g., kitchen table, bedroom carpet.

a) Using **de**

In Spanish, the elements of a compound noun are usually joined by a preposition, which will in most cases be **de**:

una pared de piedra
a stone wall

un portavoz del Ministerio de Energía
an energy department spokesman

Note that the order in which the nouns are expressed is again the opposite of English, and that the gender of the compound noun in Spanish is based on the gender of the first noun:

un sombrero de paja viejo
an old straw hat (**viejo** agrees with **sombrero** and not with **paja**)

b) Other compounds

In recent years a number of compound nouns have appeared in Spanish that do not have a preposition of any kind. The two nouns simply appear side by side, or are joined by a hyphen. Such nouns take the gender of the first noun, and are also made plural by making the first noun plural:

un coche-bomba	**coches-bomba**
a car bomb	car bombs
la fecha límite	**fechas límite**
the closing date	closing dates
un retrato robot	**retratos robot**
a composite sketch	composite sketches

You should beware of inventing your own compound nouns of this type. Use only those you know for certain to exist. Otherwise always use the construction with **de** as described above.

3. DESCRIBING THINGS

A. AUGMENTATIVES AND DIMINUTIVES

For the formation of augmentatives and diminutives, see page 69.

A particular characteristic of Spanish is to suggest a different view of something by adding either an augmentative or a diminutive to the end of the noun.

Both augmentatives and diminutives can have a merely physical meaning, or they can introduce a more subjective point of view.

Both augmentatives and diminutives require a certain amount of care in Spanish, and the learner should beware of inventing his own at random. Use only those whose connotations you know about.

▪ Diminutives

Diminutives are widely used in spoken Spanish, though they are much less common in formal written Spanish, and would frequently be out of place there. They may simply express size, but they more often suggest a favorable/unfavorable attitude of the speaker toward what he is describing. There is often no simple translation for a diminutive used in this way.

Describing things

a) Size

> **un momentito, por favor**
> just a moment, please

> **había una mesita en el rincón**
> there was a small table in the corner

b) Favorable attitude
This is expressed primarily by the diminutive **-ito**, which is the commonest of all the diminutives:

> **me miraba con la carita cubierta de lágrimas**
> he looked at me with his face covered in tears

> **'hola', me dijo con su vocecita encantadora**
> 'hello,' she said in her charming little voice

c) Unfavourable attitude
This is expressed by the diminutive **-ucho** which is comparatively rare:

> **pasamos por dos o tres aldeúchas sin interés**
> we passed through two or three uninteresting little villages

▪ Augmentatives

Augmentatives indicate mostly size, though sometimes the idea of clumsiness or even ugliness may also be implied:

> **llegó un hombrón y se puso a trabajar**
> a big fellow arrived and started to work

> **un hombrote, un hombrazo, un hombracho**
> a big brute of a fellow

> **una mujerona**
> a big strong woman

Some augmentatives and diminutives have now become words in their own right and no longer have any of the connotations mentioned above:

el sillón	armchair
la tesina	dissertation
el gatillo	trigger

B. THE ADJECTIVE

1. Agreement
For the formation of the feminine and plural of adjectives, see page 70.

All adjectives in Spanish must agree both in gender and number with the noun they are describing: .

> **las paredes eran blancas, y el suelo era blanco también**
> the walls were white, and the floor was white as well

If a single adjective refers to a mixture of masculine and feminine nouns, it takes the màsculine form:

> **las paredes y el suelo eran blancos**
> the walls and the floor were white

If a plural noun is followed by two or more adjectives and each adjective refers to only one of the things mentioned in the noun, each adjective may take the singular form:

> **los partidos socialista y comunista votaron en contra de la ley**
> the socialist and communist parties voted against the bill (there is only one socialist party and one communist party)

2. Lists of adjectives
A number of adjectives may be used to describe the same noun, as in English. Those adjectives considered most important should be placed closest to the noun. This will usually result in an order of adjectives in Spanish that is the exact opposite of English:

> **un diputado socialista español conocido**
> a well-known Spanish socialist MP

> **la política agraria común europea**
> the European common agricultural policy

3. Choice of position
Although most adjectives usually follow the noun (see pages 69-70), they can be placed in front of the noun for emphasis. This option is widely used in contemporary written Spanish, though it is less common in spoken Spanish:

> **este equipo da una fiel reproducción del sonido original**
> this equipment gives a faithful reproduction of the original sound

This is very much a question of style, and should be used with caution unless you have seen or heard the particular example you wish to use.

C. THE INDEFINITE ADJECTIVES
For the forms of **alguno** and **cualquiera** see pages 69-70.

1. 'some'

In the singular, the adjective **alguno** means 'some' in the sense of 'some ... or other':

> **compró el libro en alguna librería**
> he bought the book in some bookstore (or other)

In the plural it simply means 'some.' In this case it can be replaced without change of meaning by the appropriate form of **unos/unas**:

> **vinieron algunos/unos hombres y se pusieron a trabajar**
> some men turned up and started to work

2. 'any'

Both the adjective **alguno** and the adjective **cualquiera** can be translated into English as 'any,' and the difference between the two is often difficult for the English-speaking learner to grasp.

alguno in this sense appears mostly in questions, and is used to find out whether a specific thing or group of things actually exists.
cualquiera, on the other hand, refers in a completely indefinite way to things which are known to exist. It expresses much the same idea as the English phrases 'any at all,' 'any whatsoever.'

Compare the following:

> **¿hay alguna librería por aquí?**
> are there any bookstores around here?

This question is asked to see if any bookstores exist: i.e., are there any actual bookstores? (Note that *in a question* **alguno** is almost always used in the *singular* in Spanish, even when a plural would normally be used in English).

> **puedes encontrar este libro en cualquier librería**
> you can find this book in any bookstore

i.e., you can buy it in any bookstore whatsoever. This statement assumes that there are indeed bookstores.

In other cases, the logic of the statement will require one adjective to be used rather than the other:

> **cualquier mecánico podría hacer eso**
> any mechanic could do that

i.e., any mechanic at all. **algún** would not make any sense in this context.

Note that very often English 'any' is not translated into Spanish:

> **¿tiene mantequilla?**
> do you have any butter?

> **no tenemos plátanos**
> we don't have any bananas

The order of 'indefiniteness' in Spanish is as follows:

alguna librería	some bookstore (or other)
algunas/unas librerías	some bookstores
cualquier librería	any bookstore whatsoever
librerías	bookstores

D. VARYING THE FORCE OF AN ADJECTIVE

1. Diminutives and augmentatives

It is possible to add diminutives, and in a small number of cases augmentatives, to certain adjectives. The connotations involved are as for nouns. This feature requires special care. Use only those you know to exist and about which you feel confident:

> **el agua está calentita hoy**
> the water is nice and warm today

> **¡qué tontita eres!**
> how silly you are!

> **el niño está muy grandón**
> the child is very big (for his age)

2. Adverbs

A whole range of adverbs can be used to vary the force of an adjective. For the formation of adverbs, see page 78. A list of adverbs of degree can be found on page 80.

Any adjective modified by an adverb in this way *must* go after the noun, even if the simple form normally precedes the noun:

> **me dió un libro sumamente interesante**
> he gave me an extremely interesting book

⚠ It is essential to remember that adverbs are invariable, in other words, they *never* change their form, no matter what the gender or number of the adjective they modify.

3. Increasing the force of the adjective

> **encuentro todo esto muy aburrido**
> I find all of this very boring

muy cannot be used on its own. If there is no adjective to follow it, it is replaced by **mucho**. In this case **mucho** is used as an adverb and never changes its form:

> ¿encontraste interesante la revista? – sí, mucho
> did you find the magazine interesting? – yes, very

> este libro es sumamente (or extremamente or extremadamente) interesante
> this book is extremely interesting

4. **Decreasing the force of the adjective**

The adverb **poco** is used to lessen or even *negate* the force of an adjective:

> me parece poco probable que venga
> it seems unlikely to me that he will come

⚠ *poco* must not be confused with *un poco*, which means 'a little.' *la sopa está poco caliente* (the soup is not very hot) is clearly not the same as *la sopa está un poco caliente* (the soup is a little hot).

E. COMPARING THINGS: THE COMPARATIVE AND THE SUPERLATIVE

THE COMPARATIVE

For the formation of comparatives, see pages 70-71.

▪ Simple comparison

a) The comparison of equality (one thing is as good, as interesting, etc., as another)

If the comparison is based on an adjective, it is expressed by **tan** + adjective + **como**:

> Juan es tan alto como su hermana
> Juan is as tall as his sister

> Luisa no es tan trabajadora como su hermana
> Luisa isn't as hard-working as her sister

If the comparison is based on a noun (i.e., it is one of quantity – 'as much as,' 'as many as'), it is expressed by **tanto** + noun + **como**. tanto is used as an adjective here and therefore agrees with the noun:

> yo tengo tantos discos como tú
> I have as many records as you

b) The comparison of superiority (one thing is better, longer, etc., than another)

When the comparison is based on an adjective, the construction **más** + adjective + **que** is used (see pages 70-71 for irregular comparatives):

> María es más inteligente que su hermano
> María is smarter than her brother

If the comparison is one of quantity, the construction **más** + noun + **que** is used:

> ellos tienen más dinero que nosotros
> they have more money than us

If the comparison is made with a specific number or amount, **de** is used instead of **que**:

> vinieron más de cien personas
> more than one hundred people came

> esperamos más de media hora
> we waited for over half an hour

c) The comparison of inferiority (one thing is less good, less interesting than another)

The comparison of inferiority is expressed by **menos**. It follows the same patterns as the comparison of superiority:

> esta revista es menos interesante que aquélla
> this magazine is less interesting than that one

> tú haces menos errores que yo
> you make fewer mistakes than me

> pagué menos de mil pesos
> I paid less than a thousand pesos

d) Note that, whereas English uses the terms 'ever' and 'anyone' in a comparison, Spanish uses the corresponding *negative* terms:

> la situación es más grave que nunca
> the situation is more serious than ever

> él sabe más que nadie
> he knows more than anyone

Other indefinite comparisons are usually expressed by using the adjective **cualquiera** (see page 70):

> Isabel es más inteligente que cualquier otro estudiante
> Isabel is more intelligent than any other student

▪ Comparison with a clause

When the comparison is being made not with a noun but with a clause, **que** is replaced by more complex forms.

a) Comparison based on an adjective

When the comparison is based on an adjective, the clause is introduced by **de lo que**:

la situación es más compleja de lo que piensas
the situation is more complex than you think

el problema era más difícil de lo que habían dicho
the problem was more difficult than they had said

b) Comparison based on a noun (i.e., comparison of quantity)

In this case, the appropriate form of **del que, de la que, de los que, de las que** is used. The form chosen must agree in gender and number with the noun:

vinieron más personas de las que esperábamos
more people came than we expected

surgieron más problemas de los que habíamos previsto
more problems arose than we had foreseen

The **los** in **de los que** agrees with **problemas**, which is masculine.

gasté más dinero del que ahorré
I spent more money than I saved

The **el** in **del que** agrees with **dinero**.

▪ Other phrases of comparison

a) 'more and more' is expressed in Spanish by the phrase **cada vez más**:

encuentro su comportamiento cada vez más extraño
I find his behavior more and more odd

vez may be replaced by another word indicating time without the idea of 'more and more' being lost:

la situación se pone cada día más grave
the situation is becoming more and more serious every day

'less and less' is **cada vez menos**:

encuentro sus explicaciones cada vez menos verosímiles
I find his explanations less and less plausible

b) 'the more/less ... the more/less ...' is expressed by **cuanto** + comparative ... **tanto** + comparative ... If used with an adjective or adverb **cuanto** is invariable, but agrees in comparisons of quantity (i.e., with nouns).

In all cases the **tanto** can be omitted, and it is in fact more common to omit it:

cuanto más fáciles son los ejercicios, más le gustan
the easier the exercises are, the more he likes them

cuanto más dinero tiene, más quiere
the more money he has, the more he wants

cuantos menos problemas tengamos, más contento estaré
the fewer problems we have, the happier I'll be

c) 'all the more' + adjective + 'because' is expressed in Spanish as **tanto** + comparative + **cuanto que**. This construction is limited to very formal Spanish:

esto es tanto más importante cuanto que nos queda poco tiempo
this is all the more important because we don't have much time

THE SUPERLATIVE

For the formation of superlatives, see page 71.

▪ The relative superlative

a) The relative superlative is used to express one thing's superiority over all others of its kind:

el español es la asignatura más interesante de las que estudio
Spanish is the most interesting subject I study

Luisa se puso su mejor traje
Luisa put on her best suit

b) The scope of the superlative

The preposition **de** is used to introduce the scope of the superlative, whereas in English we use 'in':

es el hombre más rico de la ciudad
he's the richest man in town

Estados Unidos es el país más poderoso del mundo
The United States is the most powerful country in the world

c) Order of superlatives
A descending order of superlatives ('the second oldest man,' 'the third richest woman') is expressed as follows:

el segundo hombre más viejo
the second oldest man

la tercera mujer más rica
the third richest woman

▪ The absolute superlative

It is important to distinguish clearly in Spanish between the relative superlative used to compare one thing with others, and the absolute superlative that refers only to one thing without reference to others (for the formation of the absolute superlative see page 71):

eso es rarísimo
that's most unusual

No comparison is involved here – the statement is simply that something is *very* unusual.

The absolute superlative can also be expressed by one of the adverbs of intensity:

encuentro esto sumamente interesante
I find this most interesting

F. ADJECTIVAL PHRASES

Spanish, like English, can use a wide range of adjectival phrases to describe a noun. Such phrases are often the only way to translate certain compound adjectives into Spanish. They consist mostly of nouns introduced by the preposition **de** though other prepositions do occur:

un hombre de dos metros de altura
a man two meters tall

una mujer de pelo rubio y ojos azules
a fair-haired, blue-eyed woman

refugiados sin casa ni dinero
homeless, penniless refugees

G. ADJECTIVAL CLAUSES

Adjectival clauses are used to describe things. The thing being described is referred to as the 'antecedent.' Like all clauses, an adjectival clause *must* contain a verb.

▪ The relative pronoun

For the formation of the relative pronouns, see page 76.

⚠ Unlike English, *all* adjectival clauses in Spanish must be introduced by a relative pronoun. Failure to use a relative pronoun will result in a failure to communicate successfully with your listener or reader.

1. The relative pronoun *que*
In most cases, the simple relative pronoun **que** can be used:

los hombres que están charlando son peruanos
the men who are chatting are Peruvian

¿viste la película que pusieron ayer?
did you see the film (that/which) they put on yesterday?

2. Adjectival clauses with prepositions

⚠ Note that a preposition can *never* appear at the end of an adjectival clause in Spanish. Such a construction is meaningless to a Spanish-speaking person. Any preposition *must* be placed before the relative pronoun:

los muchachos con quienes jugaba se han marchado
the boys he was playing with (with whom he was playing) have gone away

la carta en que leí esto por primera vez está en la mesa
the letter I read this in for the first time (the letter in which I read this ...) is on the table

If the antecedent is a *person*, **que** may not be used. It is usually replaced by **quien** (or plural **quienes**), though the appropriate forms of **el que** or **el cual** are also sometimes used:

el hombre con quien hablaba es mi tío
the man I was speaking with is my uncle

los turistas a quienes vendí mi carro
the tourists I sold my car to

If the antecedent is a *thing*, the following rules apply:

a) If the relative pronoun is preceded by a compound preposition (i.e., one consisting of more than one word, e.g., **detrás de**), one of the compound forms of the relative pronoun must be used. You must choose the form of **el que** or **el cual** which agrees in number and gender with the antecedent:

la casa detrás de la cual se encuentra el lago
the house behind which the lake is to be found

el árbol debajo del cual nos besamos por primera vez
the tree under which we first kissed

Since the **el que** and **el cual** forms are in fact forms of the definite article followed by **que** or **cual**, the usual contractions occur (see page 67):

el edificio delante del cual esperábamos
the building we were waiting in front of

preferimos tu nuevo carro al que tenías antes
we prefer your new car to the one you had before

b) After the simple prepositions **de, en, con**, etc., **que** may be used, though in more formal Spanish the compound forms are often preferred:

la casa en que vivimos es muy vieja
the house we live in is very old

3. *lo que, lo cual*
If the antecedent is not an identifiable thing or things but refers instead to an entire situation or an idea, then the neuter forms **lo que** or **lo cual** *must* be used. They are interchangeable:

Juan insistió en acompañarnos, lo que no me gustó nada
Juan insisted on coming with us, which did not please me at all

What displeased you was not Juan, but the fact that he insisted on coming along.

María se negó a hacerlo, lo que no entiendo
María refused to do it, which I don't understand

Again, it is not María that you do not understand, but the fact that she refused to do it.

▪ Adjectival clauses with an indefinite or negative antecedent

An adjectival clause has an indefinite antecedent if the noun being described refers to something (object/person/idea) which may or may not exist.

The antecedent is negative if the noun being described refers to something that does not exist.

⚠ In both these cases, the verb in the adjectival clause *must* be put into the subjunctive.

For the formation of the subjunctive see pages 85-87. Use the present or the imperfect subjunctive, depending on which is more logical in the context.

1. **Indefinite antecedents**

busco a alguien que hable español
I am looking for someone who can speak Spanish

This person may not exist – you may not find him or her.

Compare this with **busco a un hombre que habla español**, where the use of the indicative **habla** indicates that you know a specific gentleman who in fact speaks Spanish, but you just cannot find him at the moment.

los que no quieran participar pueden irse ahora
those who don't wish to take part can leave now

There is no way of telling how many people will not want to take part. In fact everyone might want to take part.

This construction is frequently used with adjectival clauses that refer to the future:

los que no lleguen a tiempo no podrán entrar
those who don't arrive on time will not be allowed in

Obviously, everyone might arrive on time.

In formal Spanish, **quien** is used on its own as an indefinite relative pronoun meaning 'someone (who),' 'anyone (who).' It can be either the subject or the object of the adjectival clause:

busco quien me ayude
I am looking for someone to help me (who can help me)

quien diga eso no entiende nada
anyone who says that understands nothing

2. **Negative antecedents**
no hay nadie que sepa hacerlo
there is no one who knows how to do it

no tengo ningún libro que te valga
I haven't got any books that would be any use to you

no conozco ningún país donde permitan eso
I don't know any country where they allow that

4. REFERRING TO ACTIONS: THE VERB

The word 'actions' is used here not just to refer to actions as they are normally understood. It also includes mental activities such as 'thinking,' 'considering' and the like, as well as states such as 'being,' 'seeming,' 'appearing' and so on.

A. WHO IS PERFORMING THE ACTION?: THE SUBJECT

1. **The subject pronoun**
   For the subject pronouns, see page 76.

a) Cases where the subject pronoun is not stated

   In English, the subject of the verb is either explicitly stated – 'my friend went back to Spain yesterday' – or it is replaced by a pronoun – 'he went back to Spain yesterday'.

   However, the ending of the verb in Spanish usually makes it clear who the subject is – for example **hablo** can only mean 'I speak,' **hablamos** can only mean 'we speak.' Consequently, it is also possible in Spanish to use the verb on its own without a subject pronoun:

   ¿qué piensas de todo esto?
   what do you think of all this?

   iremos a la playa mañana
   we'll go to the beach tomorrow

   This is in fact more common than using the subject pronoun with the verb. However, **Vd.** and **Vds.** are used more frequently than other pronouns. This is to avoid confusion with, for example, **él, ella** and **ellos, ellas** since the verb endings are the same.

   ¿por qué estudia Vd. español?
   why are you studying Spanish?

   Note that the subject pronoun is also not used in constructions such as the following:

   los escoceses preferimos la cerveza
   we Scots prefer beer

   los españoles bebéis mucho vino
   you Spaniards drink a lot of wine

b) Use of the subject pronouns

   However, the subject pronouns *are* expressed (1) for emphasis or (2) where obvious confusions would arise:

   ¿qué piensas tú de todo esto?
   what do *you* think of all this?

   él salió al cine, pero ella se quedó en casa
   he went out to the cinema, but she stayed at home

   If the pronouns were not expressed here, it would not be clear who did what.

   Remember that **nosotros, vosotros** and **ellos** have feminine forms that must be used if only girls or women are involved:

   María y Carmen, ¿qué pensáis vosotras de esto?
   María and Carmen, what do you think of this?

   Note also the difference between Spanish and English in constructions such as the following:

   ¿quién es? – soy yo/somos nosotros
   who is it? – it's me/it's us

   soy yo quien quiere hacerlo
   it's me who wants to do it

   As can be seen, the verb **ser** agrees here with its expressed subject.

c) *ello*

   ello is a *neuter* pronoun in Spanish and can *never* be used to refer to a specific object. It is used to refer to an entire idea or situation. Its use as a genuine subject is rare and is mainly restricted to a few constructions in formal Spanish:

   todo ello me parece extraño
   all of that seems very strange to me

   ello here refers to a situation which has just been described.

   por ello decidió no continuar
   he therefore decided not to continue

d) Emphasizing the subject pronoun

   The subject pronouns are emphasized by using the appropriate form of the adjective **mismo**:

   lo hice yo mismo
   I did it myself

   A woman saying this would obviously say **lo hice yo misma**.

me lo dijeron ellos mismos
they told me so themselves

e) *tú* and *usted*

Traditionally, **tú** has been reserved for close friends and relatives, and children, **usted** being used in any more formal situation. However, there is little.doubt that the use of **tú** has increased dramatically in Spanish-speaking countries in recent years, and any young person going to Spanish-speaking countries can confidently expect to be automatically addressed as **tú** by people of his or her own age, and should also respond using **tú**.

Even the not-so-young will find themselves addressed as **tú** by people they have never spoken to before. However, a certain amount of caution is still required. When addressing an older person or someone in authority for the first time, **usted** is recommended. In general, you should take your lead from the Spanish-speaker you are talking to. If everyone is using **tú**, it would be silly (and unfriendly) to persist with **usted**.

⚠ In some areas of Central America, Colombia, Bolivia and the River Plate (Argentina and Uruguay), the pronoun **vos** is used as an even more informal alternative to **tú**.

2. The indefinite subject
In colloquial English, the indefinite subject is expressed as 'you' and less frequently as 'they.' In more formal spoken and written English, it is expressed as 'one.' In Spanish it can be expressed in the following ways:

a) Use of *tú*

In colloquial Spanish the **tú** forms of the verb can also be used to express an indefinite subject:

bajas por esta calle y tomas la primera a la izquierda
you go down this street and you take the first left

Like its English equivalent, this is not a reference to the person addressed, but is a truly indefinite subject.

In formal spoken and in written Spanish, however, this construction would be out of place. Two alternative constructions are available, as follows.

b) Reflexive use of the verb

se dice que los precios en Bolivia son muy bajos
they say that prices are low in Bolivia

se cree que habrá menos turistas este año
they think there will be fewer tourists this year

c) The use of *uno* or *la gente*

uno no puede por menos de reírse
one cannot help laughing

la gente no cree todo lo que dice el gobierno
people don't believe everything the government says

Either **uno** or **la gente** is obligatory if the verb itself is used reflexively:

a la larga uno se acostumbra a todo
you can get used to anything in the long run

3. Agreement of subject and verb
The verb in Spanish *must* agree in number and person with the subject.

⚠ Remember in particular that nouns such as *la gente, el gobierno* and phrases such as *todo el mundo* are grammatically *singular*. They may be logical plurals (i.e., they refer to a number of people), but they are singular nouns and *must* take a singular verb:

la gente no quiere que el gobierno haga eso
people don't want the government to do that

todo el mundo lo sabe
everyone knows it

la mayoría and **la mayor parte** (both meaning 'the majority,' 'most') take a singular verb. However, if they are followed by a second plural noun, the verb is usually plural:

la mayoría votó en contra de la propuesta
the majority voted against the proposal

la mayoría de los diputados votaron en contra de la propuesta
most of the legislators voted against the proposal

On the other hand, there are a small number of plural nouns which are perceived as referring to a singular object, and which are regularly followed by a singular verb:

Estados Unidos ha expresado su desacuerdo con esta decisión
the United States has expressed its disagreement with this decision

Referring to actions: the verb

Estados Unidos is treated here simply as the name of a country. This also occurs with the name of the trade union **Comisiones Obreras**:

> **Comisiones Obreras se opuso a la política del gobierno**
> Comisiones Obreras opposed the government's policy

However, if the article were used, the verb would indeed be plural:

> **los Estados Unidos no están de acuerdo**
> the United States is not in agreement

Note also that if the verb **ser** is followed by a plural noun, it is itself plural, even if its apparent subject is singular:

> **el problema son los elevados precios del petróleo**
> the problem is the high prices of petrol

B. TO WHOM IS THE ACTION BEING DONE?: THE OBJECT

1. Direct and indirect objects

If the action of a verb applies *directly* to a person or thing, that person or thing is the *direct object* of the verb.

If the action does not apply directly, but the idea of 'to someone or something' or 'for someone or something' is involved (even if this idea is not explicitly expressed) then the person or thing is the *indirect object* of the verb.

A verb can have both a direct and an indirect object at the same time:

> **le escribí una carta a mi hermano**
> I wrote a letter to my brother

In this sentence **carta** is the direct object since it is the letter which is written, and **hermano** is the indirect object since it is the brother that the letter is written *to*.

a) 'to' or 'for'

This can sometimes be confusing for an English-speaking learner of Spanish because the difference between direct and indirect objects is not always clear in English, whereas it must *always* be clearly signaled in Spanish. Take the following examples:

> I gave the dog to my brother
> I gave the dog a bone

In the first sentence, 'the dog' is the direct object of the verb 'give', since the dog is what you actually gave, and 'brother' is the indirect object, since you gave the dog *to* your brother.

In the second sentence, 'the dog' is no longer the direct object, since here you are not giving the dog at all. What you are giving is 'a bone', and 'bone' is now the direct object. You gave the bone *to* the dog, so 'the dog' is now the *indirect* object. Although 'the dog' has changed from being the direct to the indirect object, there is nothing in the words used in English to indicate this change.

This is not the case in Spanish. An indirect object is *always* clearly marked in Spanish by being preceded by the preposition **a**. Consequently the Spanish translation of the sentences given above is:

> **le di el perro a mi hermano**
> **le di un hueso al perro**

(For the use of the pronoun **le** here, see page 25.) As can be seen, if both nouns are expressly stated in Spanish (as opposed to being replaced by pronouns), the direct object precedes the indirect object.

b) 'from'

Unlike English, Spanish uses an indirect object to indicate the person 'from' whom something is taken, stolen, bought or hidden:

> **le compré la casa a mi padre**
> I bought the house from my father

> **le robó el dinero a su madre**
> he stole the money from his mother

> **trataron de ocultar la verdad al profesor**
> they tried to hide the truth from the teacher

2. The personal *a*

> If the direct object of a verb is a particular person or a particular group of people, it is *essential* to precede it in Spanish by the preposition *a*.

> It must be clearly understood that this *a* does not transform the direct object into an indirect object. This *a* is not translated in English:

> **veo a mi hermano**
> I can see my brother

> **encontré a mi padre**
> I met my father

If the direct object is a person but is not a *particular* person, the **a** is not used:

(24)

buscamos un médico
we are looking for a doctor

Not a particular doctor, but any doctor at all.

The personal **a** is also used with certain pronouns referring to people, even though these may not always refer to specific people:

conozco a alguien que puede ayudarte
I know someone who can help you

no veo a nadie
I can't see anyone

The personal **a** is also used with animals if it is a specific animal which is being referred to:

llevé a mi perro a dar un paseo
I took my dog for a walk

3. The object pronouns

The function of a pronoun is to stand for a noun. For example, in the sentence 'John wanted the book, so I gave it to him,' 'it' stands for 'the book,' and 'him' stands for 'John.' For the forms of the object pronouns, see page 76.

a) Direct and indirect object pronouns

⚠ The direct object pronoun can only stand for the direct object of a verb as explained above. If there is **any** idea of 'to' or 'for,' the indirect object pronoun **must** be used in Spanish, even though the words 'to' or 'for' may not actually be used in the equivalent English expression.

This does not apply with verbs of motion – for example **ir a** – or where the idea of 'to' or 'for' is contained in the verb – for example **buscar**, meaning 'to look for' (for a list of such verbs, see page 92):

le di el dinero
I gave him/her the money (I gave the money to him/her)

les ofreció diez mil dólares
he offered them ten thousand dollars (he offered ten thousand dollars to them)

le mandé una carta ayer
I sent her a letter yesterday (I sent a letter to her)

In both spoken and written Spanish, the third person indirect object pronoun is almost always used even when the indirect object is explicitly stated:

le di el libro a mi amigo
I gave the book to my friend

él se lo dio a su hermano
he gave it to his brother

b) **lo** and **le** as direct object pronouns

Strictly speaking, **lo** is used as the direct object referring to a man or boy (a masculine *person*), or a masculine *thing*:

¿ves a mi hermano? – sí, sí, lo veo
can you see my brother? – yes, yes, I can see him

¿ves el libro? – sí, sí, lo veo
can you see the book? – yes, yes, I can see it

However, in spoken and in written Spanish, **le** is often used instead of **lo**, especially in Spain. However, it is only considered grammatically acceptable when referring to a man or boy. This is known as **leísmo** (the use of **le** for **lo**):

¿ves a mi hermano? – sí, sí, le veo
can you see my brother? – yes, yes, I can see him

4. The neuter pronoun **lo**

The neuter pronoun **lo** can never refer to an identifiable person or thing. It refers only to a whole idea or situation:

¿sabes que ha llegado Juan? – sí, ya lo sé
do you know that Juan has arrived? – yes, I do (I know it)

What you know is that 'Juan has arrived.' **lo** in this sense often translates 'so' in English:

tú mismo me lo dijiste
you told me so yourself

lo can also be used after either of the verbs 'to be' (**ser** and **estar**). In this case it usually refers back to the last adjective, though in the case of **ser** it can also refer back to a noun.

Remember that **lo** *never* changes its form, no matter what the gender or number of the adjective or noun to which it refers:

ellos están cansados, y nosotros lo estamos también
they are tired, and so are we

lo here refers back to **cansados**.

su padre es médico, y el mío lo es también
his father is a doctor, and so is mine

lo here refers back to the noun **médico**.

5. The strong object pronouns

For the forms of the strong object pronouns, see page 76. The strong pronouns are used after prepositions:

> **¿este dinero es para mí? – no, es para ellos**
> is this money for me? – no, it's for them

The strong pronouns are also used with the preposition **a** to lend emphasis to direct or indirect pronouns which are stated in the same sentence:

> **me dio el libro a mí, no a ti**
> he gave the book to *me*, not to you

> **te veo a ti, pero no la veo a ella**
> I can see you, but I can't see her

This emphasis can be further heightened by placing the strong pronoun before the verb:

> **a mí no me gusta nada**
> *I* don't like it at all

C. EMPHASISING THE ACTION

In English all verb tenses have two forms – the standard form ('I read') and the progressive form ('I am reading'). As well as this, the present and past tenses have an emphatic form ('I do read,' 'I did read'), which is used to give special emphasis to the verb, or to ask questions. In Spanish, only the standard and progressive forms of the verb are available.
If you wish to emphasize the verb, other constructions must be used, for example:

> **sí que te creo; te aseguro que te creo**
> I *do* believe you

> **ella sí que no vendrá; seguro que ella no vendrá**
> she definitely won't come

Occasionally an action is emphasized by using first the infinitive and then the appropriate part of the verb:

> **¿tú bebes? – beber no bebo, pero fumo mucho**
> do you drink? – I don't drink, but I smoke a lot

D. NEGATING THE ACTION

1. Simple negation

In simple negation, **no** is placed in front of the verb:

> **no leo muchas revistas, no me gustan**
> I don't read many magazines, I don't like them

> **no lo vi porque no vino**
> I didn't see him because he didn't come

2. Compound negation

With compound negatives, two possibilities are usually available:

a) **no** is placed before the verb and the other negative is placed after the verb. In most cases this construction is preferred:

> **no conozco a nadie aquí**
> I don't know anyone here

> **no sabe nada**
> he doesn't know anything

Note that this does *not* constitute a double negative as in English. This applies even when the second negative is in a different clause:

> **no quiero que hables con nadie**
> I don't want you to speak to anyone

> **no es necesario que hagas nada**
> it isn't necessary for you to do anything

b) **no** is omitted and the negative is placed before the verb on its own. This construction is usually confined to uses of **nadie** as subject of the verb, and to **tampoco, nunca** and **jamás**:

> **nadie sabe adónde ha ido**
> no-one knows where he has gone

> **Luisa nunca llega a tiempo**
> Luisa never arrives on time

> **a mí tampoco me gusta**
> I don't like it either

⚠ Note that *también no* is not used in Spanish.

3. Other negatives

The phrases **estar sin** + infinitive and **estar por** + infinitive negate the action in a way that can suggest that it has *not yet* been done:

> **la puerta todavía está sin reparar**
> the door hasn't been repaired yet

> **este problema todavía está por resolver**
> this problem has still to be solved

estar can be replaced by **quedar**:

> **queda mucho trabajo por hacer**
> there's still a lot of work to do

4. Negatives after prepositions

Note that the prepositions **sin** and **antes de** are

followed by negatives whereas in English they are followed by the corresponding positive term:

salió sin hablar con nadie
he went out without speaking to anyone

decidió comer algo antes de hacer nada más
he decided to eat something before doing anything else

5. More than one negative
A number of negatives may be used together in Spanish as in English. In English, however, only the first term is negative. In Spanish, *all* terms are negative:

nadie sabe nunca nada
no one ever knows anything

no hablo nunca con nadie
I never speak to anyone

6. Emphasizing the negative *(nouns)*
With nouns, the negative can be emphasized by using the negative adjective **ninguno** (see page 69). **ninguno** is seldom used in the plural:

no me queda ningún dinero
I have no money left

For added emphasis, the appropriate form of **alguno** may be placed *after* the noun:

no tiene miedo alguno
he's not the least bit afraid

In colloquial Spanish, **nada de** can also be used before the noun:

no me queda nada de dinero
I have no money left at all

The order of 'negativeness' in Spanish is:

no tengo miedo	I'm not afraid
no tengo ningún miedo	I'm not at all afraid
no tengo miedo alguno/no tengo nada de miedo	I'm not the slightest bit afraid

Note also the following:

no tengo ni idea/ no tengo ni la menor idea/no tengo la más mínima idea	I haven't the slightest idea

7. Emphasizing the negative *(adjectives)*
In the case of an adjective, the negative can be

emphasized by placing **nada** before the adjective. **nada** is invariable:

no encuentro sus libros nada interesantes
I don't find his/her books at all interesting

8. Emphasizing the negative *(verbs)*
nada can also be used as an emphatic negative rather than meaning 'nothing,' though this construction is seldom used if the verb takes a direct object:

la película no me gustó nada
I didn't like the film at all

no he dormido nada
I haven't slept at all

If the verb has an object, a phrase such as **en absoluto** may be used:

no entiendo esto en absoluto
I don't understand this at all

Note that, on its own, **en absoluto** means 'not at all':

¿me crees? – en absoluto
do you believe me? – not at all

E. ASKING QUESTIONS
As is the case with negations, questions are formed using the standard or progressive forms of the verb, as appropriate.

1. Simple questions
Simple questions do not begin with an interrogative word. They can have the subject after the verb as in English.

¿está aquí tu hermano?
is your brother here?

However, they can sometimes be identical in form to statements, though this tends to suggest that the speaker expects the answer **sí**. In this case, the fact that they are questions is conveyed to the listener by the speaker's tone of voice:

¿el agua está fría?
is the water cold?

The idea of 'isn't it?', etc., is expressed in Spanish by **¿no es verdad?**, **¿verdad?**, or more colloquially, simply **¿no?** These expressions are all invariable:

tú le diste el dinero, ¿verdad?
you gave him the money, didn't you?

te gusta hablar español, ¿no?
you like speaking Spanish, don't you?

éste está mejor, ¿no es verdad?
this one's better, isn't it?

2. Interrogative pronouns and adjectives

⚠️ A preposition can *never* be placed at the end of a question in Spanish. Any preposition present must be placed in front of the interrogative pronoun or adjective. A Spanish speaker will not connect a preposition placed anywhere else in the question with the interrogative word, and will consequently not understand the question:

¿a quién le diste el dinero?
who did you give the money to? (to whom did you give the money?)

¿con quién fuiste al cine?
who did you go to the cinema with?

Note that **cuál** is an interrogative pronoun. If the noun is expressed, **cuál** must be followed by **de**:

¿cuál de los carros prefieres?
which of the cars do you prefer?

¿cuál te gustó más?
which did you like best?

qué is used (1) as an indefinite interrogative pronoun or (2) as an interrogative adjective immediately in front of a noun:

¿qué quieres?
what do you want?

¿qué libro te gustó más?
which book did you like most?

Note that **qué** is invariable.

3. Indirect questions

Indirect questions are introduced either by the conjunction **si** (whether), or by an interrogative pronoun or adjective. The tenses used are identical to those used in English:

me preguntó si había visto la película
he asked me if I had seen the film

no sé cuál de los carros prefiero
I don't know which of the cars I prefer

Again, any preposition *must* precede the pronoun or adjective:

se negó a decirme con quién había salido
he refused to tell me who he had gone out with

F. REFLEXIVE USES OF THE VERB
1. The reflexive pronouns

A verb is used reflexively if the subject of the verb performs the action on himself/herself/itself. The verb is made reflexive in Spanish by using it with the appropriate form of the reflexive pronoun (see page 76).

In English, a number of verbs can be used either with or without the reflexive pronoun without changing their meaning. For example, there is no real difference between 'I wash' and 'I wash myself,' between 'he shaves' and 'he shaves himself.' This freedom to choose is not available in Spanish. If a particular action is perceived as reflexive, the reflexive forms of the verb *must* be used.

The number of actions perceived as reflexive is much greater in Spanish than in English:

se levantó, se lavó, se vistió y salió
he got up, washed, got dressed and went out

The indirect reflexive pronouns express the idea of 'for oneself':

se compró un disco
he bought himself an album

⚠️ The reflexive pronouns are also essential with actions done to parts of one's own body or one's own clothes. Where English would use the possessive adjective, the noun is preceded by the *definite article* in Spanish:

se rompió la pierna
he broke his leg

se puso la chaqueta
he put on his jacket

2. The prefix *auto-*

In contemporary Spanish a number of reflexive verbs also have the prefix **auto-** (meaning 'self') joined to them to emphasize the reflexive nature of the action. However, such verbs should be used with care. Use only those you have seen and know to exist:

se autoexcluyeron
they opted out (they excluded themselves)

estos grupos se autoubican en la izquierda
these groups claim to be (place themselves) on the left

This prefix is also found in a large number of nouns: **autodominio** (self-control), **autocrítica** (self-criticism), etc.

3. Reciprocal action

A verb can be used reflexively not only to express the idea of doing an action to oneself, but also to express the idea of doing the action 'to each other.' In such cases the verb is invariably plural:

> **nos encontramos en la calle**
> we met in the street

> **nos vemos mañana**
> see you tomorrow (we'll see each other tomorrow)

If the verb is itself reflexive, the reciprocal action may be indicated by the use of **uno a otro**, though this also may be omitted if the context makes it clear that reciprocal action is involved.

> **se felicitaron uno a otro**
> they congratulated each other

If the verb takes a preposition before its object, this preposition will replace the **a** of **uno a otro**:

> **se despidieron uno de otro**
> they said goodbye to each other

se despidieron would simply mean 'they said goodbye.'

In very formal language, **uno a otro** can be replaced by the adverbs **mutuamente** or **recíprocamente**:

> **se ayudan mutuamente**
> they help each other

4. Other meanings

A number of verbs can be used reflexively in Spanish with little or no true reflexive meaning, and with very little difference in meaning from the nonreflexive forms. The commonest of these are:

caer, caerse	to fall
morir, morirse	to die

Others change their meanings in largely unpredictable ways:

comer	to eat	**comerse**	to eat up
dormir	to sleep	**dormirse**	to go to sleep
ir	to go	**irse**	to go away
llevar	to carry	**llevarse**	to take away
quedar	to remain, to be left	**quedarse**	to stay

G. GIVING COMMANDS

For the formation of the imperative, see page 87. For the position of pronouns with imperatives, see page 77.

It is important to remember that the imperative proper is used only for positive commands addressed either to **tú** or **vosotros/vosotras**. In *all* other cases (positive commands addressed to **Vd.** and **Vds.**, and *all* negative commands) the appropriate form of the subjunctive is used:

> **no leas esa revista, lee ésta**
> don't read that magazine, read this one

> **tenéis que escribir la carta en español, no la escribáis en inglés**
> you have to write the letter in Spanish, don't write it in English

> **vengan mañana, no vengan hoy**
> come tomorrow, don't come today

The subjunctive is also used for third person imperatives, which are usually preceded by **que**:

> **¡que lo hagan ellos mismos!**
> let them do it themselves!

First person imperatives (i.e., 'we') may be formed either by the subjunctive, or by **vamos a** followed by the infinitive. The use of the subjunctive implies a more committed attitude to the action in question:

> **vamos a ver**
> let's see

> **vamos a empezar**
> let's start

> **hagamos eso ahora mismo**
> let's do it right now

H. THE PASSIVE

1. *ser* plus the past participle

The passive is formed in Spanish by **ser** plus the past participle. It must be borne clearly in mind that the passive is used exclusively to express an *action*. If you are not referring to an action but are describing a state, then **estar** is used.

In this construction the past participle *always* agrees with the subject, i.e., with the thing or person to whom the action was done:

> **el palacio fue construido en el siglo XV**
> the palace was built in the 15th century

This is a reference to the castle actually being built. Compare also the following:

la ventana fue rota por la explosión
the window was shattered by the explosion

cuando entré en la sala vi que la ventana estaba rota
when I went into the room I saw that the window was broken

The first of these sentences refers to an action that occurred at a precise moment in time. The second describes a state. The corresponding action took place some time before you entered the room – you are now describing the *state* the window was in when you entered the room.

⚠️ ***ser* + past participle cannot be used to express the idea of 'to' or 'for' as the equivalent construction can in English – there is no direct Spanish equivalent of 'I was given a book' (a book was given *to* me). If you have to express such an idea in Spanish, a different construction must be used (see below).**

2. **Use of the reflexive**
An alternative method of expressing the passive in Spanish is to put the verb into the reflexive form. This is not a way of 'avoiding' the passive. On the contrary, this construction is interpreted as a genuine passive by Spanish-speakers. On hearing the sentence:

el palacio se construyó en 1495
the palace was built in 1495

no Spanish-speaker believes, even for the merest fraction of a second, that the palace actually built itself.

se dice con frecuencia que España es un país atrasado
it is often said that Spain is an underdeveloped country

las mercancías pueden mandarse por vía aérea
the goods can be sent by air freight

This construction can be used to express the idea of 'to' or 'for' by combining it with the appropriate form of the indirect object pronoun. However, this is very formal, and the construction using the third person plural of the active form would normally be preferred:

se me concedió un libro como premio/me concedieron un libro como premio
I was given a book as a prize

3. **Use of the active forms of the verb**
Although by no means rare, the passive forms are rather less used in Spanish than in English. It is always possible to use the active forms of the verb instead, and indeed this construction is necessary in certain circumstances. For example, 'I was given a book by the teacher' must be expressed in Spanish as **el profesor me dio un libro**.

el vendedor me ofreció un descuento del diez por ciento
I was offered a ten percent discount by the salesman

If no agent is expressed, the third person plural form of the verb is used:

construyeron la central hace dos años
the power station was built two years ago

suprimirán todos los derechos de aduana
all customs duties will be abolished

5. SITUATING ACTIONS IN TIME

A. EXPRESSING TIME THROUGH VERBAL PHRASES

Verbal phrases of time are extremely useful in that they can be applied to any time, present, past or future, without any change in their form.

1. **Preposition + infinitive**

a) Prepositions of time + infinitive
Most verbal phrases of time are formed by a preposition of time followed by a verb in the infinitive. This construction is most often used when the subject of the infinitive is the same as the subject of the main verb of the sentence:

tomé un café antes de salir
I had a coffee before leaving

después de terminar mis deberes, escucharé la radio
after finishing my homework, I'll listen to the radio

In rather literary style, it is possible for the infinitive to have a different subject from the main verb, but this subject must be placed *after* the infinitive:

me cambié de ropa antes de llegar mis amigos
I changed before my friends arrived

b) **al** + infinitive

This is a very useful construction in Spanish, though it is more common in the written than in the spoken language. The closest English equivalent is 'on' + present participle. It expresses simultaneous actions in present, future or past time. It may even take its own subject which can be different from that of the main verb in the sentence:

al entrar vieron a los otros salir

when they came in (on coming in) they saw the others leaving

al aparecer el cantante, el público aplaudió

when the singer appeared, the audience applauded

This construction can also have a causal meaning:

al tratarse de una emergencia, llamamos a un médico

since it was an emergency, we called a doctor

2. **Preposition + past participle**

In literary Spanish, both **después de** and **una vez** can be used with the past participle to form a phrase of time, though this construction is never used in the spoken language. The past participle agrees with the subject of the phrase:

después de terminadas las clases, volvimos a casa

after classes had finished we returned home

pagaremos la factura una vez entregadas las mercancías

we will pay the invoice once the goods have been delivered

B. EXPRESSING PRESENT TIME

1. **The use of the progressive forms of the present tense**

The progressive forms consist of the appropriate form of **estar** (see pages 41, 106-7) followed by the present participle of the verb (verbs other than **estar** may also be used, as explained below). The use of the progressive forms in Spanish is similar to their use in English, though they are less common in Spanish.

a) **estar** + present participle

The progressive forms present any action essentially as an *activity*. If something cannot be viewed as an activity, the progressive forms are not used in Spanish, for example:

me siento bien

I feel fine/I'm feeling fine

The progressive forms are used for an action which is seen as actually taking place:

no hagas tanto ruido, estoy escuchando la radio

don't make so much noise, I'm listening to the radio (I'm listening to it right now)

They are also used when an activity was begun in the past and the speaker still feels involved in it, even though it may not actually be happening right now:

estoy escribiendo una tesis sobre la política chilena

I'm writing a thesis on Chilean politics

I may not be writing it at this very minute (in fact, I may not have worked on it for several weeks), but I've already started and it's one of my current activities.

Compare

no me interrumpas, estoy pensando

don't interrupt me, I'm thinking

and

pienso que tienes razón

I think you're right

In the first sentence, 'thinking' is seen as an activity, in the second it is not.

Unlike English, the progressive forms in Spanish cannot be used to express intentions or to refer to future time. In such cases the standard present must be used.

vamos a Venezuela la semana que viene

we are going to Venezuela next week

They are also rather less widely used in questions and negative statements than their English counterparts:

¿por qué me miras así?

why are you looking at me like that?

no estudio griego

I'm not studying Greek

However, they can be used in such constructions if the idea of activity is to be emphasized:

no está cantando, está gritando

he isn't singing, he's shouting

b) *ir* + present participle

ir emphasizes the gradual nature of an action, and also suggests its continuation into the future:

> **poco a poco nos vamos acostumbrando**
> we are slowly getting used to it (and will continue to do so)

> **la tasa de inflación va aumentando**
> the rate of inflation is rising (and will continue to rise)

c) *venir* + present participle

venir indicates that the action has continued from the past to the present. In fact, it points so clearly toward the past that it is often translated into English not by a present tense, but by a perfect tense:

> **las medidas que vienen adoptando son inútiles**
> the measures they have been adopting are pointless

> **los ejercicios que venimos haciendo no son interesantes**
> the exercises we've been doing aren't interesting

2. The general present

All other aspects of present time (repeated actions, general truths, and the like) are expressed by the standard forms of the present tense:

> **vamos a Costa Rica todos los años**
> we go to Costa Rica every year

> **la vida es dura**
> life is difficult

C. FUTURE TIME IN A MAIN CLAUSE

1. The committed and uncommitted future

Spanish differentiates between a committed future and an uncommitted future, and can also express a completed future. All of these variations on future time can also be expressed as futures in the past.

The committed future is expressed in Spanish by the *present* tense of the verb. The uncommitted future is expressed by the standard future tense. Note however that the present tense can only be used to refer to the future if there is some other word in the sentence that points clearly to future time or if the context clearly relates to the future.

The present tense can also be used to express a committed future in English (e.g., 'I'm leaving tomorrow,' 'the ship sails next Tuesday'), but its use is less widespread than it is in Spanish.

a) present and future tenses

It must be stressed that the difference between these two futures is in no way related to the action being referred to, or to its distance from the speaker in time. It is quite possible to use both futures in relation to the same action. What determines the speaker's choice is his level of commitment to the action named.

Compare the following:

> **lo hago mañana**
> **lo haré mañana**

Both of these mean 'I will do it tomorrow.' However, the first expresses a much more solid intention on the part of the speaker to actually do it.

The committed future is more common in the first person singular and plural ('I' and 'we'). However, it is also used with the third persons if the speaker is referring to an event about which he is absolutely certain:

> **los Reyes visitan Alemania la semana que viene**
> the King and Queen are visiting (will visit) Germany next week

> **el primer centenario de la caída del muro de Berlín se celebra en 2089**
> the centennial of the fall of the Berlin wall will take place in 2089

Both of these sentences could have been written using the future tense (**visitarán** and **celebrará**), but the speaker would in this way have indicated a certain remoteness from the event.

The present tense is also widely used in direct requests for immediate action:

> **¿me prestas veinte dólares?**
> will you lend me twenty dollars?

A less direct alternative is to use the verbs **poder** or **querer** followed by the infinitive:

> **¿puedes darme esas tijeras?**
> will you give me that pair of scissors?

> **¿quieres pasarme ese bolígrafo?**
> will you pass me that pen?

The use of the future tense in a request indicates that an immediate response is not being asked for:

> **¿me terminarás eso?**
> will you finish that for me? (at some point in the future)

b) *ir a* + infinitive

As in the English construction 'I am going to do that later,' a committed future can also be expressed in Spanish using **ir a** followed by the infinitive, though it is less common than its English equivalent:

> **voy a estudiar medicina en la universidad**
> I am going to study medicine at university

> **van a ver esa película mañana**
> they're going to see that film tomorrow

c) points to note

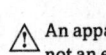 An apparent future in English is sometimes not an expression of future time, but of willingness or refusal. Such ideas are expressed by the verbs *querer, negarse* or similar in Spanish.

For example:

> **se niega a tomar el desayuno por la mañana**
> he won't eat his breakfast in the morning

> **no quiere aceptar las reglas**
> he won't accept the rules

2. The completed future

The completed future is used to relate one action in the future to another action. It indicates that the action in question will have been completed by the time the second action applies. In a main clause, the completed future is expressed by the future perfect tense (for formation see page 85):

> **ya lo habré hecho cuando vuelvas**
> I'll already have done it when you come back

> **si llegamos tarde, ya se habrá marchado**
> if we arrive late he'll already have gone

It can also be used to indicate that the action will have been completed before a particular moment in time:

> **lo habré terminado para el sábado**
> I will have finished it by Saturday

> **ya habrá llegado**
> he will already have arrived

3. Future in the past

The following sentence gives an example of future in the past:

> **me dijo que iba a Guatemala la semana siguiente**
> he told me he was going to Guatemala the following week

He said **voy a Guatemala**, referring to the future. However, he said this in the past, so this is a case of future in the past.

In a main clause, future in the past is expressed either by the imperfect (committed future) or by the conditional (uncommitted future). However, the conditional is considerably more common in this construction than the imperfect:

> **me explicó que lo haría después de volver de sus vacaciones**
> he told me he would do it when he came back from his vacation

The conditional perfect expresses completed future in the past:

> **me aseguró que habría terminado el trabajo antes de medianoche**
> he assured me that he would have finished the work by midnight

D. THE FUTURE IN SUBORDINATE CLAUSES OF TIME

A subordinate clause of time is a clause introduced by a word or phrase of time such as **cuando, así que, antes de que** and the like.

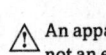 In a subordinate clause of time, future time is expressed by the appropriate tense of the subjunctive of the verb.

1. The future

The future is expressed by the present subjunctive. There is no distinction between a committed and an uncommitted future:

> **en cuanto llegue, se lo diré**
> as soon as he arrives, I will tell him

> **¿qué harás cuando termine tu contrato?**
> what will you do when your contract runs out?

Note that after the conjunctions **mientras** and **hasta que**, both meaning 'until,' the word **no** is sometimes placed before the verb in the subordinate clause. It must be kept in mind that this does *not* make the verb negative. It is simply a quirk of style and does not affect the verb in any way:

> **no podemos hacerlo mientra no nos autoricen**
> we can't do it until they authorize us

> **no podemos mandar las mercancías hasta que no nos manden el pedido**
> we can't send the goods until they send us the order

2. The completed future

In a subordinate clause of time, the completed future is expressed by the perfect subjunctive:

podrás salir cuando hayas terminado tus deberes
you will be able to go out when you've finished your homework

insisto en que te quedes hasta que lo hayas hecho
I insist that you stay until you have done it

3. Future in the past

In a subordinate clause of time, future in the past is expressed by the imperfect subjunctive:

me aseguró que lo haría en cuanto llegara
he assured me that he would do it as soon as he arrived

nos informaron que los mandarían tan pronto como fuese posible
they informed us they would send them as soon as possible

E. PAST TIME

Spanish distinguishes between four levels of past time. These are:

past related to the present	expressed by	the perfect tense
the past in progress	expressed by	the imperfect tense
the completed past	expressed by	the preterite tense
the more distant past	expressed by	the pluperfect tense

It must be emphasized that the tense you choose is not dependent in any sense on the action to which you are referring. It is not dependent on the nature of the action (i.e., whether it is a single action or a repeated action), nor on the duration of the action (whether it lasted one second or a century), nor on its position in time (whether it happened a minute ago or a thousand years ago).

The tense you choose is determined *entirely* by your subjective perception of the action, particularly as regards its relation to present time and its relation to other actions to which you also refer.

1. Past related to the present

The perfect tense is used to refer to a past action which, though completed, the speaker sees as somehow related to the present. The relationship seen between the past action and present time is often indicated by the presence of related verbs or adverbs referring to present time. There is no limit

to how long ago the action or series of actions may have taken place.

By and large, the uses of the perfect tense in Spanish and English coincide (but see 'SPECIAL CASES,' page 35):

he visitado muchos países europeos últimamente
I have visited many European countries recently

en los últimos diez años he aprendido diez idiomas extranjeros
in the last ten years I have learned ten foreign languages

2. The past in progress

The past in progress is expressed by the imperfect tense. An action will be expressed in the imperfect tense if what is uppermost in the speaker's mind is the fact that the action was in progress as opposed to having been completed. There is no limit to how short or long the action can be.

As a rule, the imperfect is used in Spanish where English would use the imperfect progressive forms ('I was talking,' 'he was writing,' etc.), or forms such as 'I used to talk,' and the like:

cuando era pequeño, iba todos los días a la piscina
when I was little, I went (used to go) to the swimming pool every day

mientras Pepe veía la televisión, Juan hacía sus deberes
while Pepe was watching TV, Juan was doing his homework

⚠ In particular, if one action is presented as occurring while another is already in progress, the action 'occurring' will be expressed by the preterite, and the action in progress by the imperfect:

mientras Juan llamaba a la puerta, el teléfono sonó
while Juan was knocking on the door, the telephone rang

Like the present tense, the imperfect also has a progressive form, formed by the imperfect of **estar** plus the present participle of the verb. This again presents the action primarily as an activity:

estábamos escuchando la radio cuando María entró
we were listening to the radio when María came in

Note that an apparent conditional in English is not always a genuine conditional. In a sentence such as 'he would always read his paper on the train,' the 'would' is used to highlight the fact that the action is seen extending over time. This is translated by the *imperfect* in Spanish:

> **siempre leía el periódico en el tren**
> he would always read his paper on the train

3. The completed past

The completed past indicates that the aspect of the action (or series of actions) most important for the speaker is the fact that it has been completed. Whether the action was a repeated one, or whether it lasted a great length of time is unimportant. If completion is being stressed, the preterite will be used:

> **hizo esto cada día durante casi diez años**
> he did this every day for almost ten years

> **viví en España durante más de veinte años**
> I lived in Spain for over twenty years

It should be possible from these examples to see that it is perfectly feasible in Spanish to use either the imperfect or the preterite to refer to the same action, depending on how your perception of the action changes. The following small narrative should illustrate the point:

> **Juan llamó a la puerta. Mientras llamaba a la puerta, el teléfono sonó. Mientras el teléfono sonaba, el bebé empezó a llorar.**
> Juan knocked at the door. While he was knocking at the door, the telephone rang. While the telephone was ringing, the baby started to cry.

4. Stylistic expressions of past time

a) Present for preterite
For reasons of style, past time is often expressed, particularly in written Spanish, by the present tense of the verb (the so-called historic present). This is used to lend a dramatic quality to a narrative. The historic present is also used in English, though to a lesser extent than in Spanish:

> **en el siglo XV sale Colón para América**
> in the fifteenth century Columbus set sail for America

It would also have been possible to use the present tense in English here.

b) Imperfect for preterite
Again in written Spanish, and once more for

reasons of style and dramatic effect, an action is sometimes expressed in the imperfect where a preterite would have been the everyday choice:

> **en 1975 moría Franco y comenzaba la transición a la democracia**
> in 1975 Franco died and the transition to democracy began

5. The more distant past

a) Pluperfect
The more distant past is expressed by the pluperfect. An action belongs to the more distant past if the speaker wishes to indicate that it was completed *before* another action in the past:

> **llegué a las tres, pero Juan ya se había marchado**
> I got there at three, but Juan had already gone

> **no podía salir porque había perdido su llave**
> he couldn't go out because he had lost his key

b) Past anterior
In very literary Spanish, the more distant past in a subordinate clause of time is sometimes expressed by the past anterior:

> **cuando hubimos terminado, nos marchamos**
> when we had finished, we left

The past anterior is not used in spoken Spanish, and would give a distinctly literary flavor in contemporary written Spanish. The pluperfect or the simple preterite are usually used instead.

F. SPECIAL CASES

1. Actions on the limits of present and past time

a) The future limit
Actions that are about to take place are expressed in Spanish by the present tense of **estar a punto de** or less commonly **estar para** followed by the infinitive:

> **estoy a punto de empezar**
> I'm just about to start

> **el tren está para salir**
> the train is just about to leave

The imperfect is used when this idea is expressed in the past:

> **estaba a punto de salir cuando Juan llegó**
> I was just about to go out when Juan arrived

b) The past limit

Actions that have just taken place are expressed by the present tense of **acabar de** followed by the infinitive:

> **acabamos de ver el programa**
> we have just seen the program

> **acaban de volver del cine**
> they've just come back from the movies

Again, the imperfect is used if this idea is expressed in the past:

> **acabábamos de poner la tele cuando entraron**
> we had just switched on the TV when they came in

2. Actions continuing from one time to another

An action that starts in the past and continues right up to the present (and may well continue into the future) is considered in Spanish to belong to present time, and is therefore expressed by the present tense.

a) Present tense + **desde (hace)**

The length of time involved is introduced by **desde** if a starting point is indicated, or by **desde hace** if a length of time is stated. This is in complete contrast with English which uses the perfect tense with 'for':

> **¿desde cuándo esperas aquí?**
> how long have you been waiting here?

> **espero aquí desde hace casi media hora**
> I've been waiting here for almost half an hour

> **estudio español desde 1996**
> I've been studying Spanish since 1996

> **estudio español desde hace dos años**
> I've been studying Spanish for two years

b) **hace** + present tense + **que**

Alternatively, the time span can be introduced by **hace** followed by a subordinate clause introduced by **que**:

> **hace media hora que espero aquí**
> I've been waiting here for half an hour

c) **llevar** + present participle

A further possibility is to use the present tense of the verb **llevar** followed by the present participle of the verb:

> **llevamos tres meses aprendiendo ruso**
> we've been learning Russian for three months

d) Continuing actions in the past

When these actions are expressed in the past, all the constructions given above are used in the imperfect (as opposed to the past perfect in English):

> **trabajaba desde hacía diez años como profesor**
> he had been working as a teacher for ten years

> **hacía veinte años que vivían en España**
> they'd been living in Spain for twenty years

> **llevaba quince minutos esperando**
> I had been waiting for fifteen minutes

6. DESCRIBING AN ACTION

A. THE ADVERB

For the formation of adverbs, see page 78.

⚠ It is essential to remember that adverbs are invariable – they never change their form whatever the circumstances in which they are used:

> **entraron lenta y silenciosamente**
> they came in slowly and quietly

> **tú trabajas mucho más rápidamente que yo**
> you work much more quickly than I do

1. Adverbial phrases

Rather than a simple adverb, Spanish very often uses adverbial phrases formed mostly with the nouns **manera** or **modo**:

> **esto nos afecta de una manera indirecta**
> this affects us indirectly

Noun/adjective combinations may also be used:

> **hablar en voz alta/en voz baja**
> to speak loudly/quietly

2. The use of adjectives

An attractive feature of Spanish is its ability to use adjectives with almost adverbial force. In this case the adjectives must agree with the *subject* of the verb:

> **vivieron felices durante muchos años**
> they lived happily for many years

> **le miramos atónitos**
> we looked at him in astonishment

B. VARYING THE FORCE OF AN ADVERB

1. Another adverb

As in English, one adverb may be used to vary the force of another:

lo hizo increíblemente bien
he did it unbelievably well

Adverbs of time and place can be emphasized by adding **mismo** after them. **mismo** is invariable in this usage:

aquí mismo, ahora mismo
right here, right now

2. Comparative and superlative

The comparative and superlative of adverbs are formed in exactly the same way as those of adjectives (see pages 70-71).

tú trabajas más rápidamente que yo
you work more quickly than I do

However, when a phrase of possibility is placed after a superlative, **lo** is always placed before **más** (this construction is rarely translated by a superlative in English):

lo hicimos lo más rápidamente posible
we did it as quickly as possible

---

7. RELATIONSHIPS BETWEEN ACTIONS

A. THE PRESENT PARTICIPLE

For the formation of the present participle, see page 84.

a) Expressing means

Only the present participle can be used in Spanish to express the idea of 'by doing,' 'by going' and the like. No other construction is available:

gané este dinero trabajando durante las vacaciones
I earned this money by working during the holidays

conseguí hacerlo dejando otras cosas para más tarde
I managed to do it by leaving other things till later

⚠ *por* followed by a present participle is not possible in Spanish. *por* followed by an infinitive does not express means, but *cause*, e.g.: *le sirvieron primero por ser cliente regular* (they served him first because he was a regular customer).

b) Expressing simultaneous action

The present participle is widely used to express an action taking place simultaneously with another:

entró corriendo
he rushed in (he came in running)

'está bien,' dijo sonriendo
'OK,' he said smiling

This construction is often the only way of expressing certain phrasal verbs of motion in English (see 'he rushed in' above):

pasó corriendo
he ran past

⚠ The present participle is invariable in Spanish, in other words it *never* changes its form, irrespective of the gender or number of the subject of the verb:

las chicas salieron corriendo
the girls rushed out

After a verb of perception (seeing, hearing, etc.), the present participle may be replaced by an infinitive. In fact this construction is, if anything, more common than the use of the present participle:

vi a mi hermano atravesando/atravesar la calle
I saw my brother crossing the street

c) Cause

A present participle can also express cause:

estando en Madrid, decidí visitar a mi amigo
since I was in Madrid, I decided to visit my friend

no sabiendo como continuar, decidió pedir ayuda
not knowing how to proceed, he decided to ask for help

d) Continuation

The present participle is used with the verbs **seguir** and (less frequently) **continuar** to express the continuation of an action:

siguió trabajando a pesar de todo
he went on working in spite of everything

continuaron repitiendo la misma cosa
they kept on repeating the same thing

B. INFINITIVE OR SUBORDINATE CLAUSE?

When two verbs are linked in Spanish, you must choose whether to put the second verb into the infinitive form (preceded or not by a preposition) or whether to put it into a subordinate clause introduced by **que**.

If the subject of both verbs is the same, in most cases you can use the simple infinitive. If the subjects are different, you must, with very few exceptions, put the second verb into a subordinate clause (and frequently also into the subjunctive). Compare:

1. Same subject

quiero hacerlo
I want to do it

I am not only the person 'wanting', I am also the person who wants 'to do' it. No one else is involved.

entré sin verle
I came in without seeing him

I came in, and *I* did not see him.

Spanish goes further in the use of this construction than English does:

creyó estar soñando
he thought he was dreaming

creemos poder hacerlo
we think we can do it

2. Different subjects

Compare the sentences given above with:

quiero que tú lo hagas
I want you to do it

There are two people involved here. *I* 'want,' but *you* are the person who is 'to do.'

entré sin que él me viera
I came in without him seeing me

I came in, but *he* did not see me.

3. Verbs where the infinitive may take a different subject

There are a small number of verbs with which the subject of a following infinitive may be different from that of the first verb (see page 92):

me dejaron entrar
they let me come in

4. Infinitives after prepositions

The most obvious exceptions to the general rule are phrases consisting of a preposition followed by an infinitive. In this case the infinitive may have a subject different from that of the main verb, but this subject is always placed *after* the infinitive:

quiero hacerlo antes de llegar los otros
I want to do it before the others arrive

However, such expressions are rather literary in style, and even in these cases Spanish-speakers will often prefer to use a subordinate clause:

quiero hacerlo antes de que lleguen los otros
I want to do it before the others arrive

C. THE INFINITIVE

1. verb + preposition + infinitive

A verb used in the infinitive after another verb can either appear on its own, or can be introduced by one of a wide range of prepositions. There are few truly useful rules for predicting which preposition is to be used, and in most cases the preposition required must simply be learned through observation and practice.

For a list of the prepositions required by some common verbs, see pages 91-92.

2. adjective + infinitive

It may be useful at this point to note the following very common construction in Spanish:

(indirect object +) verb + adjective + infinitive

The indirect object may be a pronoun or a noun. The verb may be **ser, parecer, resultar** or similar. A wide range of adjectives is available and any verb can be used in the infinitive after the adjective:

me es difícil creer lo que estás diciendo
it's difficult for me to believe what you're saying

nos parece absurdo proponer tal cosa
it seems absurd to us to suggest such a thing

The same construction can be used with various verbs of 'considering,' but in this case there is no indirect object:

encuentro difícil aceptar esto
I find it difficult to accept this

consideramos poco aconsejable continuar así
we consider it inadvisable to continue in this way

3. **adjective + *de* + infinitive**
If the adjective is not part of an impersonal expression but relates to an identifiable thing or things already stated in the sentence, it is then followed by **de** + infinitive. The adjective agrees with the thing being described:

estos ejercicios son fáciles de hacer
these exercises are easy to do

encuentro este libro difícil de leer
I find this book difficult to read

4. ***que* + infinitive**
Note that **que** is placed before the infinitive in expressions such as the following:

tengo una factura que pagar
I've got a bill to pay

nos queda mucho trabajo que hacer
we still have lots of work to do

D. THE SUBORDINATE CLAUSE: INDICATIVE OR SUBJUNCTIVE?

The verb in a subordinate clause will be either in the indicative or in the subjunctive. Since the subjunctive has relatively few uses in English, this can be a difficult concept for the learner of Spanish to grasp.

However, the subjunctive is very widely used in Spanish, and there is really little point in learning 'ways to avoid the subjunctive.' The best approach is to try to understand what the indicative and the subjunctive are used to express.

In general terms the indicative is used to introduce actions the speaker *believes* to be clear and material statements of fact. The subjunctive, on the other hand, is used if the speaker feels that the statements are untrue, or if he feels unable in some way to guarantee that they will prove to be true, or if, rather than simply stating them, he is expressing an emotional reaction to them. This can be due to a variety of reasons:

− he doubts, disbelieves or denies the statements;
− the actions have not yet taken place: they belong to the future and therefore cannot be guaranteed;
− the actions are expressed as conditions that are not or cannot be fulfilled;
− the actions are introduced by a statement of emotion.

It is important to realize that there is no single set of rules for the use of the subjunctive in Spanish. For example, different rules apply when referring to future time than when expressing a condition or expressing emotion, and so on. Each case must be dealt with independently.

In general, however, *any* impersonal expression that does not introduce a straightforward statement of fact will be followed by the subjunctive:

es posible/probable/una pena que esté allí
it's possible/probable/a shame that he'll be there

E. INDIRECT OR REPORTED SPEECH

The indicative is used exclusively for statements and questions in indirect speech in Spanish, since the speaker is simply relating actions that he presents as having actually taken place. The tenses used in Spanish correspond exactly to those used in English.

⚠ Contrary to English usage, *all* indirect statements must be introduced by *que* in Spanish. Omission of the *que* would be confusing for your Spanish-speaking listener:

dijo que vendría más tarde
he said (that) he would come later

me explicó que ya lo habían hecho
he explained to me that they had already done it

le contesté que no sería posible
I told him in reply that it wouldn't be possible

8. SOME SPECIAL VERBS

A. TO BE

1. ***ser* and *estar***
There are two verbs 'to be' in Spanish, **ser** and **estar**. In general terms it can be said that:

ser is used to *define* things.
estar is used to describe characteristics that could change without affecting the essential definition of the thing.

It is not necessarily the case that **ser** describes permanent characteristics and **estar** does not. The question of *definition* is much more important in deciding which verb to use.

Some special verbs

The uses of these verbs can be divided into three categories:

> cases where **ser** is obligatory;
> cases where **estar** is obligatory;
> cases where either is possible.

These can be summarized as follows:

a) Cases where **ser** is obligatory

(i) **When the verb 'to be' is followed by a noun, *ser* must be used, since a noun always provides at least a partial definition of the object in question**

Typical examples would include professions, nationality or origin, names, statements of possession, materials from which something is made, expressions of time and almost all impersonal expressions:

> **mi padre es minero**
> my father is a miner

In Spanish, your occupation is considered to be at least part of your 'definition.' The fact that your father may lose his job one day and no longer be a miner (or that it may even be a temporary job) does not alter this in any way.

> **no somos portugueses, somos españoles**
> we are not Portuguese, we are Spaniards

> **Bolivia es un país interesante**
> Bolivia is an interesting country

Note that **es** goes with the noun **país** and not the adjective **interesante**. Your interest in Bolivia may diminish later, but it will continue to be a country.

> **este carro es de mi madre**
> this car is my mother's

> **la mesa es de madera**
> the table is made of wood

> **¿qué hora es? – son las dos de la tarde**
> what time is it? – it's two in the afternoon

> **es necesario hacerlo ahora mismo**
> it's necessary to do it right now

(ii) **ser** + adjectives describing defining characteristics

> **yo creo que el español es muy fácil de aprender**
> I think that Spanish is easy to learn

The fact that others might disagree, or that you might later change your mind, is irrelevant. For the time being 'easy' is part of your definition of Spanish.

Note that color and size are usually considered to be defining characteristics in Spanish:

> **la plaza de toros es muy grande**
> the bull ring is very large

> **las paredes eran blancas**
> the walls were white

They may be painted a different color later, but for the time being 'being white' is part of their definition.

If the color is not seen as a defining characteristic, a different construction (and in some cases a different adjective) is likely to be used:

> **tenía los ojos enrojecidos**
> his eyes were red

(iii) **ser** is used with the past participle to express the passive in Spanish (for an explanation of the passive, see pages 29-30):

> **la cosecha fue destruida por las heladas**
> the crop was destroyed by the frosts

b) Cases where **estar** is obligatory

(i) **estar** must be used when referring to position, whether of persons or things, whether temporary or permanent. The position of an object, however permanent, is not seen as part of its definition in Spanish:

> **estuve en la playa ayer**
> I was at the beach yesterday

> **los pirineos están en la frontera entre España y Francia**
> the Pyrenees are on the frontier between Spain and France

They're likely to remain there for some time, but (in theory at least) the Pyrenees would still be the Pyrenees even if they turned up somewhere else.

Note that **estar** is used to express not only physical position, but also mental position and in fact position of any kind:

> **estamos a favor de las negociaciones**
> we are in favor of negotiations

> **estamos en contra de la política del gobierno**
> we are against the government's policy

el problema está en el precio
the problem is (lies) in the price

(ii) **estar** is used with the present participle of the verb to form the progressive forms in Spanish:

¿qué estás haciendo? – estoy leyendo una revista española
what are you doing? – I'm reading a Spanish magazine

estábamos escuchando la radio cuando Juan entró
we were listening to the radio when Juan came in

(iii) **estar** is typically used with adjectives to express moods and other temporary characteristics:

estoy furioso contigo
I'm furious with you

estoy muy cansado, he trabajado mucho hoy
I'm very tired, I've worked a lot today

'Being tired' is unlikely to be part of your definition. You will still be the same person when you have recovered your energy.

c) Cases where either is possible
When used with many other adjectives, either **ser** or **estar** may be possible. Which you choose will depend on the extent to which you feel that:

(i) the adjective defines the thing in question, for however short a time this definition might apply, in which case you will use **ser**:

María es muy guapa
María is very pretty

(ii) the adjective merely describes a characteristic of the thing in question, in which case you will use **estar**:

María está muy guapa hoy
María is looking very pretty today
Compare:

mi profesor es muy pesado
my teacher is very boring

estás muy pesado hoy
you're being a real bore today

eres tonto
you're silly

estás tonto
you're being silly

(iii) In a negative command with adjectives like **pesado** and **tonto**, however, only **ser** would be used:

no seas tonto
don't be silly

Since silliness is not seen here as a mood in Spanish, **estar** cannot be used. With adjectives of mood, however, **estar** would be used:

no estés furioso
don't be furious

d) Some special cases
A few adjectives actually have different meanings when used with **ser** and **estar**:

	ser	*estar*
bueno	good	well (in good health)
cansado	tiring	tired
consciente	aware	conscious (awake, not unconscious)
grave	serious	seriously ill
listo	clever	ready
malo	bad	ill (in poor health)
moreno	dark-haired	suntanned
pesado	heavy (thing)	boring (person)
rico	rich	cute (child), nice (food)
seguro	sure (thing) safe (thing)	sure, certain (person)
verde	green	unripe

Other changes are more subtle. Compare **ser viejo** (to be old) with **estar viejo** (to look older than you are), **ser pequeño** (to be small) with **estar pequeño** (to be small for your age).

Note that, when referring to happiness, Spanish-speakers invariably say **estar contento**, but both **ser feliz** and **estar feliz** are possible, depending on whether it refers to a defining characteristic or a mood.

2. *encontrarse, hallarse, verse, quedar*
encontrarse and **hallarse** can sometimes replace **estar**:

el lago se encuentra detrás de la casa
the lake is behind the house

no me encuentro bien hoy
I don't feel well today

Both **verse** and **quedar** can replace **ser** when used with a past participle. **verse** is almost always used in preference to **ser** with **obligado**:

Some special verbs

el gobierno se vio obligado a retirar su propuesta
the government was forced to withdraw its proposal

la casa quedó completamente destruida
the house was completely destroyed

3. *haber*

'there is'and 'there are'are expressed in Spanish by **hay. hay** is in fact the third person singular of the present tense of **haber** – **ha** – with the obsolete word **y** (there) tagged on at the end:

hay mucha gente en la playa
there are lots of people on the beach

It is important to realize that this is in fact part of the verb **haber** since the standard parts of **haber** are used in all other tenses and constructions:

había por lo menos cincuenta personas en la habitación
there were at least fifty people in the room

Note that the singular form is always used, even when referring to a plural noun (**personas**). Note also the following infinitive construction:

debe haber otra manera de abordar el problema
there must be another way of approaching the problem

'there must be' is *never* **debe ser** or **debe estar**, which mean 'it must be.' However, in the following construction the appropriate forms of **ser** and **estar** are indeed used:

¿cuántos sois? – somos siete
how many of you are there? – there are seven of us

estábamos cinco en la cocina
there were five of us in the kitchen

4. *deber*

'is to,' 'was to'and the like, indicating that something is due to happen or was supposed to happen, are translated by the present or imperfect of **deber**:

el trabajo debía empezar el día cinco
work was to begin on the fifth

la factura debe pagarse a la entrega de las mercancías
the invoice is to be paid on delivery of the goods

5. **General weather conditions**

Most descriptions of general weather conditions are made using the verbs **hacer** and **haber**:

¿qué tiempo hace?	what's the weather like?
hace frío/calor	it's cold/warm
hace buen/mal tiempo	the weather is fine/bad
hace mucho sol	it's very sunny
hace/hay mucho viento	it's very windy
hay neblina	it's misty
había luna	the moon was shining

Since Spanish uses nouns here as opposed to the English adjectives, the idea of 'very' is expressed by the appropriate form of **mucho** (or any other appropriate adjective or adjectival clause):

hace mucho calor
it's very hot

está haciendo un frío que pela
it's bitterly cold

Some weather conditions are expressed simply by a verb:

llueve, está lloviendo	it's raining
nieva, está nevando	it's snowing
hiela, está helando	it's freezing
tronaba, estaba tronando	there was a lot of thunder

6. **Personal descriptions**

Many personal descriptions are made using the verb **tener**:

tengo hambre/sed	I'm hungry/thirsty
tiene sueño/miedo	he's sleepy/afraid
tenemos frío/calor	we're cold/hot
tengo ganas de ir	I'm eager to go
hemos tenido suerte	we were lucky

Again, since Spanish uses nouns here, 'very' is expressed by **mucho** or a similar adjective:

tenemos mucho frío
we are very cold

B. TO BECOME

There is no single verb equivalent to 'to become' in Spanish. How you translate this idea will depend on its context:

a) 'become' with an adjective
With an adjective, 'become' is usually expressed by **hacerse, ponerse** or **volverse. ponerse**

indicates a temporary change, **volverse** indicates a longer-lasting one:

> **se puso furioso cuando oyó esta noticia**
> he became furious when he heard this piece of news

> **se hacía oscuro fuera**
> it was becoming dark outside

> **se volvió muy antipático**
> he became very unfriendly

b) 'become' with a noun
With a noun, 'become' is usually expressed by **hacerse** or **convertirse en**:

> **esta empresa se ha convertido en la más importante de Perú**
> this firm has become Peru's leading company

> **se hizo diputado a los 30 años de edad**
> he became an MP at the age of 30

If there is an idea of achievement, **llegar a ser** can also be used:

> **llegó a ser presidente a pesar de todas las dificultades**
> he became president despite all the difficulties

c) Other verbs
In many cases where the verb 'become' would be used in English, Spanish would choose a different approach altogether:

> **España ingresó en el Mercado Común en 1986**
> Spain became a member of the Common Market in 1986

C. TO HAVE

1. **tener** and **haber**

a) **tener**
tener expresses 'to have' in the sense of 'to possess':

> **¿tienes coche?**
> do you have a car?

> **¿cuánto dinero tienes?**
> how much money do you have?

contar con and **disponer de** are also often used to express 'to have,' less in the sense of 'to own' but 'to have at one's disposal':

> **España cuenta con nueve centrales nucleares**
> Spain has nine nuclear power stations

See also the following section.

b) *haber*
haber is used with the participle to form the compound tenses of verbs (see pages 84-87).

⚠ Note that in these constructions the past participle *never* changes its form, irrespective of the number and gender of either the subject or the object of the verb:

> **¿habéis visto la última película de Almodóvar?**
> have you seen Almodóvar's latest film?

visto is unaffected by the fact that **habéis** is plural (**vosotros**) or that **película** is feminine.

tener is sometimes used with the participle to express an idea similar to those of the compound tenses. This construction cannot be used unless the verb has an object, and the past participle agrees with the object of the verb:

> **ya tengo escritas las cartas**
> I have written the letters

The following two usages are particularly common:

> **tenemos pensado ir a jugar al tenis**
> we intend to go and play tennis

> **tengo entendido que ha sido un éxito**
> I understand it was a success

2. *hacer*
Note that phrases of the type 'to have a house built', 'to have the room painted,' etc., are expressed in Spanish using the verb **hacer**. The second verb goes into the infinitive, unlike English where the past participle is used:

> **se hicieron construir una casa en el campo**
> they had a house built in the country

> **haremos ejecutar su pedido cuanto antes**
> we will have your order carried out as soon as possible

D. TO KNOW

There are two verbs 'to know' in Spanish, **conocer** and **saber**. **Conocer** means to know in the sense of 'to be familiar with,' 'to be acquainted with.' **Saber** is to know in a mental or intellectual sense, to have learned or understood, to know something to be a fact. Compare the following:

Some special verbs

¿conoces la teoría de la relatividad?
do you know the theory of relativity?

Have you heard of the theory of relativity? You may be able to answer **sí** to this question without having any idea what the theory means.

¿te sabes la teoría de la relatividad?
do you know the theory of relativity?

Do you understand the theory of relativity? Could you explain it?

conocer is invariably used with people, countries and the like:

conozco muy bien a Pedro
I know Pedro very well

no conozco Cuba
I don't know Cuba (I've never been there)

saber is invariably used with noun clauses:

sé lo que estás pensando
I know what you're thinking

no sé cómo ocurrió esto
I don't know how this happened

E. ACTIONS CONSIDERED IMPERSONAL IN SPANISH

A number of commonly expressed actions take a personal subject in English, but are expressed by an impersonal construction in Spanish. As a result, what is considered to be the object of the verb in English becomes the subject of the Spanish verb, and it is with this subject that the verb agrees. The subject of the English verb is then expressed by an indirect object in Spanish.

The commonest of these verbs are:

verb	meaning	used to translate
faltar	to be absent	not to have enough of, to need, to be left
gustar	to please	to like
parecer	to seem	to think
quedar	to remain	to have ... left
sobrar	to exist in greater amounts than required	to have too much of, to have ... left

a) *faltar*

me faltan diez dólares
I'm ten dollars short

faltan dos horas
there are two hours left

hacer falta is also used with the same meaning:

me hace falta más tiempo
I need more time

b) *gustar*

⚠ It must always be remembered that *gustar* does not actually mean 'to like,' it means 'to please.' Consequently the English object becomes the Spanish subject, and the English subject becomes the Spanish indirect object. *gustar* agrees in number with the thing 'liked':

a Juan no le gustan estos caramelos
Juan does not like these sweets (literally, the sweets are not pleasing to Juan)

nos gusta mucho la tortilla española
we like Spanish omelette very much

Although forms such as **gusto** or **gustamos** do occur, they are relatively infrequent. If you are tempted to use one of these forms, make sure you have not misunderstood how to use **gustar**.

If 'like' does not include the idea of 'please,' **gustar** is not used:

quisiera más información sobre este hotel
I would like more information about this hotel

It is not that this information would be pleasing to you (it might in fact be unpleasant). You are simply asking for information.

c) *parecer*

¿qué te parece mi nuevo carro? – me parece estupendo
what do you think of my new car? – I think it's great

esa idea me parece ridícula
I find that idea ridiculous

d) *quedar*

¿cuánto dinero te queda?
how much money do you have left?

nos quedaban dos horas
we had two hours left

e) *sobrar*

aquí sobran jefes y faltan guerreros
there are too many chiefs here and not enough Indians

me sobran veinte euros
I have twenty euros left

nos sobra tiempo
we've got loads of time

Note also the phrase:

basta y sobra, *Am* **alcanza y sobra**
there's more than enough

9. COMMUNICATING IN SPANISH

A. BELIEF/DISBELIEF/DOUBT/DENIAL

Statements of belief in the positive, however vague, are followed by the verb in the indicative *irrespective of whether the statement is actually true in fact.* The fact that the statement is presented as being true is sufficient to require the indicative:

tenía la impresión de que ya te habías marchado
I was under the impression you'd already left

The fact that you're still here is irrelevant.

supongo que vendrá
I suppose he'll come

creo que tienes razón
I think you're right

Note that Spanish uses **que** in expressions such as the following:

creo que sí **creo que no**
I think so I don't think so

1. Direct questions

In the case of a direct question, either the indicative or the subjunctive may be used. The subjunctive expresses actual doubt on the part of the speaker. If the speaker is simply unsure, the indicative is used. In usage the indicative is more common in this construction than the subjunctive.

¿crees que Juan vendrá mañana?
do you think that Juan will come tomorrow?

¿crees que Juan venga?
do you think that Juan will come? (I suspect he won't)

2. Verbs of belief in the negative, or verbs of doubting or denying in the affirmative

If a verb of belief is used in the negative, or if a verb of doubting or denying is used in the affirmative, the verb in the subordinate clause is in the subjunctive:

no creo que sea justo decir eso
I don't think it's fair to say that

dudo que consiga hacerlo
I doubt that he'll manage to do it

niego absolutamente que sea así
I absolutely deny that this is the case

It is important to differentiate between statements of opinion and indirect speech. In the latter the indicative is *always* used whether the introductory verb is positive or negative:

yo no digo que el Gobierno tenga razón
I'm not saying that the Government is right

yo no dije que Juan había llegado
I didn't say that Juan had arrived

The first of these is a statement of opinion. The second is a narrative of events that happened (or did not happen) in the past.

3. Verbs of doubting or denying in the negative

If a verb of doubting or denying is used in the negative, either the subjunctive or the indicative may be used. The indicative is used if the speaker is very positive about what is being said:

no dudo que tengas/tienes razón

The use of **tengas** implies something like 'I don't doubt that you might be right,' whereas the use of **tienes** means 'I am quite sure that you are right.'

no niego que sea/es posible hacerlo
I don't deny that it might be/is possible to do it

B. CONDITIONS

Conditions in Spanish can be divided into two large groups, each of which requires a different use of the verb:

Type	*Definition*	*Verb*
open-ended conditions	those that may or may not be fulfilled, those whose outcome has not yet been decided	indicative

Communicating in Spanish

unfulfilled conditions	those presented as unfulfilled, those that the speaker believes not to be the case or not to have been carried out	subjunctive

You must be clear which kind of condition you are dealing with, since the rules for expressing the different kinds of conditions are markedly different from each other.

— If the condition is perceived as open-ended in the sense that it may or may not be fulfilled, the indicative is used (with one exception — see open-ended conditions of future time below):

> **si llueve mañana, iré al cine**
> if it rains tomorrow, I'll go to the cinema

— If the condition is perceived as genuinely unreal in the sense that it has not been or cannot be fulfilled, the subjunctive is used in the **si** clause:

> **si fuera rico, no trabajaría**
> if I was rich, I wouldn't work

Do not confuse conditions with the conditional tenses. The *tenses* used in Spanish are in all cases identical to English. The differences between the two languages relate to the uses of the indicative and the subjunctive.

1. Open-ended conditions

Open-ended conditions in Spanish can relate to present, future or past time. They are expressed as follows:

a) Present time

Open-ended conditions relating to present time are expressed in Spanish by the present indicative. The verb in the main clause is usually in the present indicative or sometimes in the imperative:

> **si quieres evitar más problemas, cállate**
> if you want to avoid further problems, keep quiet

i.e., if you want to avoid problems *now*. You may choose either to avoid the problems or not.

> **si no te gusta éste, puedes tomar otro**
> if you don't like this one, you can take another

You may in fact like this one, in which case you won't take another.

b) Future time

Conditions relating to future time are by definition open-ended since their outcome cannot yet be known. Future conditions are expressed in Spanish by the present indicative. The verb in the main clause is usually future (committed or uncommitted):

> **si vuelves borracho, te mato**
> if you come home drunk I'll kill you

> **si no lo termino a tiempo, no podré salir**
> if I don't finish in time, I won't be able to go out

> **si lo haces, te doy mil dólares**
> if you do it, I'll give you a thousand dollars

⚠ However, an open-ended condition of future time *may* take the imperfect subjunctive if the speaker wishes to present it as a more remote possibility. The conditional is then used in the main clause:

> **si hicieras eso, los otros se enfadarían**
> if you were to do that, the others would be annoyed

This is a more remote condition than:

> **si haces eso, los otros se enfadarán**
> if you do that the others will be annoyed

but both refer to future time.

c) Past time

Open-ended conditions relating to past time take the same tense of the verb as in English:

> **si no ha hecho sus deberes, no podrá salir**
> if he hasn't done his homework, he won't be able to go out

He may indeed have done it. You are expressing this condition precisely because you are unsure. The condition may indeed have been fulfilled.

> **si lo utilizó, sabrá como funciona**
> if he used it, he'll know how it works

You are unable to say for certain whether he used it or not.

> **si no llovía, ¿por qué estás mojado?**
> if it wasn't raining, why are you wet?

2. Unfulfilled conditions

Unfulfilled conditions relate only to present time and past time.

a) Present time

Unfulfilled conditions relating to present time are expressed in Spanish by the imperfect subjunctive. Either form of the imperfect subjunctive may be used. The verb in the main clause is usually, though not always, in the conditional:

si Juan estuviera aquí, hablaría con él
if Juan was here I'd speak to him

i.e., if he was here *now*. You would not be saying this unless you believed that he was *not* there. The fact that he might be there is irrelevant. In your opinion this is an unfulfilled condition.

si tuviera dinero, iría a España
if I had money, I'd go to Spain

si fuera más barato, lo compraríamos
if it was cheaper, we'd buy it

Again, you are only saying this because you do not believe you have enough money.

b) The completed past
Unfulfilled conditions relating to the completed past are expressed in Spanish by the pluperfect subjunctive (either the **hubiera** or the **hubiese** forms). They are unfulfilled in that they refer to events which did not in fact take place. The verb in the main clause is usually in the conditional perfect or less commonly in the pluperfect subjunctive (**hubiera** forms):

si lo hubiéramos sabido, habríamos venido
if we had known, we would have come

We didn't know, so we didn't come.

si hubieras llegado a tiempo, lo habrías visto
if you'd arrived on time, you'd have seen him

3. **como + present subjunctive**
In colloquial Spanish, **como** + present subjunctive is frequently used to express a condition of future time. The subjunctive is *always* used in this construction even though the condition is open-ended:

como llegues tarde me enfado
if you arrive late I'll be angry

como is not interchangeable with **si** in all cases. If you are unsure, it is always safer to use **si**.

4. **de + infinitive**
In formal written Spanish, a condition is sometimes expressed by the preposition **de** followed by the infinitive:

de continuar así, suspenderá el examen
if he goes on like this, he'll fail the exam

For past time the perfect infinitive is used:

de haberlo sabido, no habría venido
if I had known I wouldn't have come

5. Negative conditions
Any condition can be made negative by simply placing **no** before the verb in the conditional clause or by using some other negative:

si no haces tus deberes, no podrás salir
if you don't do your homework, you won't be able to go out

However, negative conditions can also be expressed either by **a menos que** or more formally by **a no ser que**. Both mean 'unless,' and are always followed by the appropriate tense of the subjunctive:

saldremos mañana a menos que llueva/a no ser que llueva
we'll go out tomorrow unless it rains

6. **Conditions introduced by conditional conjunctions**
Conditional clauses introduced by conditional conjunctions always have their verb in the subjunctive. The most common of these conjunctions are:

en caso de que	if
a condición de que	on condition that, provided that
con tal (de) que	so long as, as long as
siempre que	so long as, as long as

en caso de que venga, se lo diré
if he comes, I'll tell him

puedes salir con tal que prometas volver antes de medianoche
you can go out so long as you promise to be home by midnight

los compraremos a condición de que sean baratos
we'll buy them provided they're cheap

7. **Points to note**
Not all conditions are introduced in English by 'if.' Other forms are sometimes used. This choice is not available in Spanish. If you are translating, you must use **si** (or the **de** + infinitive construction) no matter what the form of the English condition:

had I known, I would have told you
si lo hubiera sabido/de haberlo sabido, te lo habría dicho

were this the case, I would agree with you
si fuera así/de ser así, estaría de acuerdo contigo

If **si** means 'whenever,' it introduces a clause of time and only the indicatives are used:

si tenía mucho que hacer, nunca salía antes de las nueve

if I had a lot to do, I never went out before nine

If **si** means 'whether,' it introduces an indirect question and again the indicative is used:

me preguntó si lo haría
he asked me if (i.e., whether) I would do it

no sé si vendrá
I don't know if he'll come

C. CONTRADICTING A PREVIOUS STATEMENT

1. *pero and sino*

The idea of 'but' is expressed by two words in Spanish, **pero** and **sino**. **sino** is used to introduce a statement that contradicts a previous one. **pero** *cannot* be used in such situations:

la casa es grande pero no cuesta mucho
the house is big but it doesn't cost a lot

el libro no es verde, sino rojo
the book isn't green, but red

mi padre no es médico, sino profesor
my father isn't a doctor, but a teacher

If the contradiction is contained in a clause, **sino que** is used:

no se come, sino que se bebe
you don't eat it, you drink it

If the intention is not to contradict, but to emphasise a following affirmation, **pero sí** is used:

no conozco España, pero sí conozco Portugal
I don't know Spain, but I do know Portugal

no es moderno, pero sí interesante
it isn't modern, but it is interesting

2. *no es que, no porque*

Both of these expressions are followed by a verb in the subjunctive:

no es que no tenga confianza en ti
it's not that I don't trust you

lo hace, no porque quiera hacerlo, sino porque no tiene más remedio
he does it not because he wants to, but because he has no choice

D. DISCOUNTING A DIFFICULTY

1. 'despite'

The simplest way of discounting a difficulty is to use the compound preposition **a pesar de** followed by the noun. In written Spanish, **pese a** is sometimes used instead of **a pesar de**:

decidió continuar a pesar de las dificultades
he decided to continue in spite of the difficulties

2. 'although'

The idea of 'although' can be expressed either by **aunque** or **a pesar de que**. In written Spanish **si bien** is a fairly frequent alternative to **aunque**, though it is little used in the spoken language.

aunque may be followed by either the indicative or the subjunctive, depending on the speaker's perception of the difficulty. The indicative suggests a real difficulty, whereas the subjunctive implies a potential difficulty:

no se ha puesto el abrigo aunque hace mucho frío
he hasn't put on his coat even though it's very cold

continuaremos aunque haya problemas
we'll continue even though there may be problems

a pesar de que is used mostly with reference to present and past time and is therefore usually followed by the indicative:

lo hizo a pesar de que nadie estaba de acuerdo con él
he did it even though nobody agreed with him

si bien is always followed by the indicative:

se cambiará la ley, si bien hay mucha oposición
the law will be changed although there is a lot of opposition

In written Spanish, **con** + infinitive is sometimes used to express the idea of 'although,' though this is not a common usage:

con ser pobres, viven bien
although they're poor, they live well

3. **'however'/'no matter how' + adjective or adverb + verb**

This idea is expressed as follows in Spanish: **por** + adjective/adverb + **que** + verb in the subjunctive:

> **las compraremos, por caras que sean**
> we'll buy them, however expensive they are (might be)

> **no dejaré de hacerlo, por difícil que parezca**
> I won't fail to do it, no matter how difficult it might seem

> **por bien que lo haga, no lo aceptaré**
> however well she does it, I won't accept it

4. **'whatever,' 'however,' 'wherever' etc + verb**

There are two ways of expressing this idea in Spanish:

a) verb in the subjunctive + relative + verb in the subjunctive. The same verb is repeated in this construction:

> **lo compraremos, cueste lo que cueste**
> we'll buy it, whatever it costs

> **no quiero verlo, sea quien sea**
> I don't want to see him, whoever he is (might be)

> **lo encontraremos, esté donde esté**
> we'll find him, wherever he is (might be)

b) indefinite pronoun or adjective + **que** + verb in the subjunctive. The indefinite pronouns and adjectives are formed by adding **-quiera** to the end of the corresponding relative (there is no equivalent form for **lo que**):

> **no quiero verle, quienquiera que sea**
> I don't want to see him, whoever he is (might be)

> **lo encontraremos, dondequiera que esté**
> we'll find him, wherever he is (might be)

If the pronoun or adjective is to be made plural, it is the part before the **-quiera** which becomes plural while **-quiera** itself remains unchanged:

> **no quiero verlos, quienesquiera que sean**
> I don't want to see them, whoever they are

E. EMOTION/FEAR/HOPE/REGRET

1. Emotion

a) One subject
An expression of emotion where there is only one subject is followed by the verb in the infinitive:

> **estamos muy contentos de veros**
> we are very pleased to see you

We are pleased, and we see you – there is only one subject.

> **espero poder hablar con él mañana**
> I hope to be able to speak to him tomorrow

b) More than one subject
However, if more than one subject is involved, the expression of emotion is followed by a verb in the subjunctive. The range of emotions goes from approval to disapproval, pleasure to anger and the like:

> **me alegra que pienses así**
> I'm glad you feel that way

> **le molestó que no estuviéramos de acuerdo con él**
> it annoyed him that we did not agree with him

The expression of emotion may be implicit in an impersonal construction:

> **es triste/lógico/natural/una pena que sea así**
> it's sad/logical/natural/a shame that it should be like this

All of these expressions imply an emotional reaction (however implicit) on the speaker's part rather than a straightforward statement of fact.

Note that the verb is in the subjunctive only if it belongs to a clause introduced by **que** that is *directly* dependent on the expression of emotion. If the clause is introduced by **porque** or if it is dependent on some other verb, the subjunctive is not used:

> **estaba triste porque todos lo habían abandonado**
> he was sad because everyone had left him

> **se puso furioso al ver que nadie lo escuchaba**
> he became furious when he saw that no one was listening to him

In this case the clause is dependent on the verb **ver**, not on the expression of emotion.

2. Fear

a) to fear something/be afraid of something
The simplest way to express fear is to use a phrase such as **tener miedo a**, or less commonly the verb **temer**. Note that the preposition used with **tener**

miedo can be either **a** or **de** (as opposed to only 'of' in 'to be afraid of' in English):

> **tengo miedo a los perros**
> I'm afraid of dogs

In colloquial Spanish, the phrase **dar miedo** may also be used. However, the object of the English verb becomes the subject of the Spanish verb, and the subject of the English verb becomes the indirect object of the Spanish verb (as with **gustar**, page 44):

> **me dan miedo las arañas**
> I'm afraid of spiders

b) 'to fear' + verb

The rules for one or more subjects mentioned earlier (see section E.1) also apply here:

> **me da miedo salir por la noche**
> I am afraid of going out at night

> **temo que surjan problemas imprevistos**
> I'm afraid that unforeseen problems might crop up

Note that the expression 'I'm afraid' is often used in English to introduce statements of fact or possibility where there is no real suggestion of any fear. **Temer** may also be used in this way in Spanish (it is frequently used reflexively in this context).

In this case **temerse** may be followed by either the indicative or the subjunctive. The indicative is used for a statement of fact. The subjunctive suggests the possibility that something may have happened:

> **me temo que lo ha/haya perdido**
> I'm afraid he's lost it/he may have lost it

c) Other expressions

Other expressions indicating genuine fear are also followed by the subjunctive:

> **se escondió por miedo a que se burlasen de él**
> he hid for fear that they would laugh at him

3. Hope

a) to hope for something

This is expressed simply by **esperar**. The idea of 'for' is included in the verb, so that no preposition is used:

> **esperábamos una respuesta más positiva**
> we were hoping for a more positive reply

b) 'to hope' + verb

'to hope' is again usually expressed in this context by the verb **esperar**. With this meaning **esperar** may take either the indicative or the subjunctive (**esperar** meaning 'to wait' is *always* followed by the subjunctive).

When followed by the indicative **esperar** expresses eagerness. When followed by the subjunctive it expresses genuine hope. Compare the following:

> **espero que vendrá** (indicative)
> I hope he'll come

I'm counting on him coming. I'll be disappointed/annoyed if he doesn't come.

> **espero que tengas éxito** (subjunctive)
> I hope you succeed

This is genuine hope, and does not have the connotations of 'counting on' mentioned above.

c) Impersonal expressions

Impersonal expressions of hope are followed by the subjunctive:

> **hay pocas esperanzas de que venga**
> there's little hope that he'll come

> **mi ilusión es que un día se resuelva el problema**
> my hope is that one day the problem will be solved

d) *ojalá*

In spoken Spanish **ojalá** is frequently used to introduce an expression of hope. **ojalá** is invariable and never changes its form. It is always followed by the subjunctive:

> **ojalá no llueva mañana**
> I hope it doesn't rain tomorrow

> **ojalá venga**
> I hope he comes

4. Regret

a) Apologizing for something

The simplest statements of apology are of course **perdón, perdone** (an imperative) and **lo siento**. They are different in that **perdón** and **perdone** are both requests for forgiveness, whereas **lo siento** is a direct expression of regret:

> **¡ay, perdona! no te vi**
> oh, sorry! I didn't see you

In this case the **tú** form of the imperative (**perdona**) is used.

> **lo siento, pero no será posible terminarlo hoy**
> sorry, but it won't be possible to finish it today

When the thing or action regretted is explicitly stated, the **lo** of **lo siento** is no longer used. The idea of 'for' is included in the verb and is not explicitly stated in Spanish:

> **sentimos la molestia**
> we are sorry/apologize for the inconvenience

In more formal Spanish, **lamentar** is often used in preference to **sentir**:

> **lamentamos la molestia que les hemos causado**
> we regret the inconvenience we have caused

b) 'to regret' + verb

If there is only one subject, the infinitive is used, otherwise a clause with the verb in the subjunctive is required:

> **sentimos tener que molestarlo**
> we are sorry to have to bother you

> **sentimos mucho que no hayas podido hacerlo**
> we are very sorry that you were not able to do it

Again, the clause must be directly dependent on the verb expressing regret. If it is dependent on any other verb, the indicative will be used:

> **lamentamos informarles que ya no están disponibles**
> we are sorry to inform you that they are no longer available

The clause here is dependent on **informar** and not on **lamentamos**.

F. INTENTIONS AND OBJECTIVES

1. Statements of intention

Simple statements of intention are expressed using the verb **pensar** or the phrase **tener la intención de**, both followed by the infinitive. In spoken Spanish, the construction **tener pensado** + infinitive is also widely used.

> **pensamos ir en coche/tenemos la intención de ir en coche**
> we intend to go by car

> **tengo pensado salir esta noche**
> I intend to go out this evening

2. Statement of objectives

a) One subject

If only one person is involved, objectives are usually expressed by the preposition **para** followed by the infinitive. More formal alternatives are **a fin de, con el fin de, con la intención de, con el objetivo de** or **con la finalidad de**, all followed by the infinitive:

> **lo hice para ganar un poco de dinero**
> I did it to earn a little money

> **me dirijo a Vds. con el objetivo de pedir información**
> I am writing to you to ask for information

After verbs of motion, intention is usually expressed by the preposition **a** followed by the infinitive, though **para** is also possible:

> **vine aquí a hablar contigo**
> I came here to speak to you

Other verbs are followed by different prepositions (see pages 93-95):

> **luchaban por mejorar sus condiciones de vida**
> they were fighting to improve their living conditions

b) *Two different subjects*

If more than one subject is involved, **para que** followed by the subjunctive is necessary. A straightforward infinitive will be wrong in Spanish:

> **les ayudamos para que pudieran acabarlo pronto**
> we helped them so that they could get it done sooner

The more formal alternatives given earlier can also be used followed by **que** and the subjunctive:

> **me voy, a fin de que puedan empezar inmediatamente**
> I'm going, so that they can start immediately

G. OBLIGATION

1. General obligation

A number of constructions exist in Spanish to express obligation on a very general level. The commonest of these are:

> **hay que** + infinitive
> **es preciso** + infinitive
> **es necesario** + infinitive

The degree of obligation can be heightened as follows:

es esencial + infinitive
es imprescindible + infinitive

These expressions are not addressed to any one person in particular. They simply express a general obligation.

hay que tener cuidado
you (i.e., one) must be careful

¿hay que ser miembro para poder jugar aquí?
do I/you have to be a member to play here?

hay que verificarlo
it'll have to be checked

será necesario verificarlo con él
it will be necessary to check it with him

2. **Personal obligation**
More personal kinds of obligation (i.e., those affecting particular people or groups of people) are expressed using the verb **deber** + infinitive or the verb **tener** followed by **que** + infinitive:

tendrás que trabajar mucho
you'll have to work hard

tengo que terminarlo cuanto antes
I have to finish it as soon as possible

debemos salir a las ocho en punto
we must leave at eight on the dot

The sense of obligation can be heightened by using one of the phrases given in section **1.** (with the exception of **hay que**) followed by **que** and a verb in the subjunctive:

es imprescindible que lo hagas ahora mismo
you absolutely must do it right now

Note that 'have to' in English does not always denote an obligation. For example, in the phrase 'I had to laugh,' you were not, of course, obliged to laugh. This simply means that you could not stop yourself from laughing. This idea is expressed in Spanish as follows:

no pudimos por menos de reír
we had to laugh/could not help laughing

3. **Moral obligation**
Moral obligation is expressed in Spanish by the conditional (or less frequently the imperfect) of **deber** followed by the infinitive. This is usually expressed in English by 'should' or 'ought to':

deberíamos ir a verle
we should go and see him

This is not an obligation in the sense that we are being *forced* to go and see him, but we feel that it is our 'duty.'

⚠ **The use of 'should' in English to express moral obligation can *never* be translated into Spanish by the conditional. For example, *haría* can never express the idea of 'I ought to do.' Only *debería hacer* will convey this idea succesfully.**

To put this idea into the past, use the perfect infinitive after the conditional of **deber**:

deberíamos haberlo hecho antes
we should have done it sooner

no deberías haber bebido tanto
you shouldn't have drunk so much

4. **Obliging someone to do something**
This idea is usually expressed by **obligar** or **forzar** + **a** + infinitive. Alternatively, **hacer** + infinitive can be used. The subject of the infinitive will be different from that of **obligar**:

me obligaron a salir   **me hizo levantar-**
they forced me to leave   **me temprano**
                            he made me get up
                            early

When expressing the idea of 'being obliged to do something,' **verse** is almost always used in preference to **ser**:

me vi obligado a devolverlo
I was obliged to give it back

H. PROBABILITY/IMPROBABILITY

The adverb **probablemente** (like all adverbs) has no effect on whether the verb is in the indicative or the subjunctive:

probablemente vendrá mañana
he'll probably come tomorrow

However, any impersonal expression of either probability or improbability is followed by a subordinate clause with its verb in the subjunctive:

es probable que salga por la tarde
I'll probably go out this evening (it's probable that I'll go out ...)

es improbable que vuelva
he's unlikely to come back (it's improbable that he'll come back)

me parece increíble que consiga hacerlo
I find it unlikely that he'll manage to do it

tenemos que aceptar la probabilidad de que esto ocurra
we must accept the likelihood that this will happen

I. PERMISSION/PREVENTION/ PROHIBITION

1. General permission and prohibition

The most general forms of permission and prohibition are expressed using the verb **poder**:

¿puedo pasar?
may I come in?

¿se puede aparcar por aquí?
can you (i.e., one) park around here?

no puedes pasar ahora
you may not come in just now

The prohibition corresponding to **se puede** is **se prohíbe, está prohibido** or simply **prohibido**. These are found mostly in official signs:

prohibido/se prohíbe pisar el césped
please do not walk on the grass

This can be emphasized as follows:

queda terminantemente prohibido cruzar la vía
crossing the line is strictly forbidden

2. Personal permission, prevention and prohibition

The commonest verbs of permitting, preventing and prohibiting belong to the group that may be followed by an infinitive with a different subject (see page 92). This usually avoids the need for a subordinate clause:

me dejaron entrar pero me impidieron verlo
they let me go in but they prevented me from seeing him

nos prohibieron fumar
they did not allow us to smoke

Note the very common phrase:

¿me permite?
may I?

In many cases a straightforward imperative may be used:

no digas tacos
don't use bad words

J. POSSIBILITY/IMPOSSIBILITY

1. In a personal sense

a) *poder* and related verbs

The simplest way of expressing possibility is to use the verb **poder**:

no podré venir mañana
I won't be able to come tomorrow

no habríamos podido hacerlo sin ti
we wouldn't have been able to do it without you

The verbs **conseguir** and **lograr** are used with the same meaning (of these **conseguir** is the more common):

no conseguimos llegar a tiempo
we didn't manage to arrive on time

logramos evitar un conflicto
we managed to avoid a conflict

A further alternative is to use the impersonal expression **ser (im)posible**. The person for whom the action is (im)possible becomes the indirect object:

no me será posible venir
I won't be able (it won't be possible for me) to come

nos fue imposible resolver el problema
we couldn't solve the problem

resultar is sometimes used instead of **ser**:

me resultó imposible hacer lo que quería
I could not do what he wanted

b) *saber*

Note that 'to be able' in the sense of 'to know how to' rather than 'to be capable of' is expressed in Spanish by **saber** rather than **poder**:

¿sabes tocar la guitarra?
can you play the guitar?

sí, pero no sé tocar el piano
yes, but I can't play the piano

This is a skill rather than a physical ability.

c) Verbs of perception

'to be able' with verbs of perception (seeing, hearing and the like) is not usually expressed in Spanish unless you wish to suggest that there is some kind of obstacle involved:

¿me oyes?
can you hear me?

no podía verlo por la niebla
I couldn't see him because of the fog

2. In a general sense

a) *quizá, quizás, tal vez*
Possibility in a more general sense (i.e., not 'being able to do something,' but the possibility that something might happen or not) can be expressed by one of the adverbs **quizás, quizá** or **tal vez**. **quizás** and **quizá** are more widely used.

These may be followed by either the indicative or the subjunctive, depending on your view of how likely it is that the thing will in fact happen. The indicative expresses a greater degree of confidence than the subjunctive:

quizás venga mañana, no sé
(subjunctive)
he may come tomorrow, I don't know

tal vez tienes razón (indicative)
you may be right

b) Verbal forms
poder can also be used to express a general possibility:

puede haber cambios importantes dentro de poco
there may be important changes soon

This idea can also be expressed by the impersonal expressions **es posible que** and **puede que** followed by the appropriate form of the subjunctive:

es posible que venga mañana
he may come tomorrow

puede que no sea verdad
it may not be true

In fact, any impersonal expression of possibility or chance is followed by the subjunctive:

existe la posibilidad de que surjan problemas
there is the possibility that problems will crop up

Note the following expression:

parece mentira que esto haya ocurrido
it seems impossible that this should have happened

K. REQUESTS AND COMMANDS

1. Direct requests

a) Informal requests
Spanish speakers are usually more direct in their requests than the average English speaker, who tends to use polite formulas such as 'would you ... '. A straightforward question is more likely in Spanish:

¿me pasas esa revista?
would you pass me that magazine?

¿me prestas diez dólares?
would you lend me ten dollars?

Alternatively, for a slightly less direct request ('could you' in English), the appropriate form of **poder** + infinitive can be used:

¿puedes abrir la ventana?
could you open the window?

¿podría decirme qué hora es?
could you tell me the time, please?

The expression **hacer el favor de** + infinitive is also used if a little more formality is required:

¿me hace el favor de cerrar la ventana?
would you be so kind as to close the window, please

b) Formal requests
There are much more formal ways of introducing a request, particularly in written Spanish. The most common of these are the expressions **tenga(n) la bondad de** + infinitive and **le(s) ruego que** followed by the verb in the subjunctive:

tenga la bondad de cerrar la puerta
be so kind as to close the door

In the very formal Spanish of a business letter, the **que** is sometimes omitted after **le(s) ruego**. This usage should not be imitated in contexts other than business correspondence:

les rogamos nos manden dos cajas
please send us two boxes

c) Ultraformal requests
In very formal Spanish, the old-fashioned form **sírvase** can still be found. This is in fact an imperative. If addressed to more than one person, **sírvanse** is used instead. This construction is restricted to business correspondence and official signs:

sírvanse mandarnos más información
please send us more information

2. **Indirect requests**

Since there are always at least two subjects involved in an indirect request, the verb is always followed by a subordinate clause with its verb in the subjunctive.

The most common verb used to introduce an indirect request is **pedir**. In more formal Spanish, **rogar** is again sometimes used in preference to **pedir**:

> **le pedí que se callara**
> I asked him to be quiet

> **nos rogaron que les ayudáramos**
> they asked us to help them

⚠ It is essential not to confuse *pedir* and *preguntar*. *preguntar* means 'to ask a question,' and is used to introduce an indirect question. It does not involve the idea of a request.

More intense requests can be expressed by verbs such as **suplicar**:

> **me suplicó que no revelara su secreto**
> he pleaded with me not to reveal his secret

3. **Indirect commands**

For direct commands (the imperative) see pages 29, 54, 87.

There are always at least two subjects involved in an indirect command. Normally, this means a subordinate clause with the verb in the subjunctive:

> **me dijo que lo hiciera inmediatamente**
> he told me to do it immediately

> **insistimos en que nos lo devuelvan ahora mismo**
> we insist that you give it back to us right now

However, the verbs **mandar** and **ordenar** belong to the small group of verbs that can be used with a direct infinitive (see page 92):

> **me mandó salir del edificio**
> he ordered me to leave the building

L. SUPPOSITION

1. **Future tense**

Apart from the usual verbs of supposition (for example **suponer**), the simplest way of expressing supposition in Spanish is to use the future tense for a supposition in the present, and a conditional for a supposition in the past. A similar construction exists in English, though it is less used than its Spanish equivalent:

> **supongo que vendrá**
> I imagine he'll come

> **¿qué hora es? – serán las once**
> what time is it? – it must be about eleven (it'll be about eleven)

> **la casa estará por aquí**
> the house must be around here somewhere (will be around here somewhere)

> **serían las cinco más o menos cuando llegó**
> it must have been about five (it would be about five) when he arrived

2. **deber de + infinitive**

Supposition can also be expressed by the verb **deber** followed by **de** and the infinitive. Do not confuse this with **deber** followed by a direct infinitive, which expresses an obligation.

> **debes de estar cansado después de tanto trabajo**
> you must be tired after so much work

⚠ Note that the Spanish verb *asumir* does *not* mean 'to assume' in the sense of 'to suppose,' but in the sense of 'to take on' as in 'to assume power.' If you need to translate 'assume' in the sense of 'suppose,' either use *suponer* or one of the constructions explained above.

M. THANKS

1. **Simple expressions of thanks**

a) *gracias* and related terms

The simplest expression of thanks is, of course, **gracias**. Since thanking someone always involves the idea of an exchange (you thank someone in exchange for what they have given you, or done for you), the preposition used with **gracias** is always **por**:

> **muchas gracias por el regalo**
> thanks a lot for the present

> **me dio las gracias por el regalo**
> he thanked me for the present

A verb used after **gracias** may be put into either the present or the perfect infinitive:

> **gracias por ayudarme/haberme ayudado**
> thanks for helping me

Likewise, any noun or adjective expressing thanks or gratitude is followed by **por**:

queremos expresar nuestro reconocimiento por todo
we want to express our gratitude for everything

b) *agradecer*

In more formal Spanish, **gracias** is almost always replaced by the appropriate form of the verb **agradecer**. **agradecer** is an exception to what has been said above in that the idea of 'for' is contained within the verb:

 agradecer is not followed by any kind of preposition in Spanish:

les agradecemos su cooperación en este asunto
we thank you for your cooperation in this matter

nos agradecieron nuestra ayuda
they thanked us for our help

2. Subordinate clauses

The verb in a subordinate clause following an expression of gratitude goes into the subjunctive. The commonest occurrences of such expressions are the following:

agradeceremos mucho que nos ayuden
agradeceríamos mucho que nos ayudasen

Both of these are Spanish equivalents of 'we would be grateful if you could help us.' Either may be used on any occasion, despite the difference in tenses. Note the idea of 'could' is not expressed in Spanish.

 Note that, unlike English, Spanish does not consider this kind of expression to be a condition, so no *si* clause is used.

In the very formal Spanish of commercial correspondence, the **que** may be omitted from this expression. This should not be imitated in contexts other than business correspondence:

agradeceremos nos manden diez cajas
we would be grateful if you could send us ten boxes

N. WISHES/DESIRES/PREFERENCES

1. One subject

If only one subject is involved, a straightforward infinitive is used:

quiero hablar contigo
I want to speak to you

preferiría salir ahora
I would prefer to leave now

valdría más empezar enseguida
it would be better to start right away

The expression of a wish can always be 'softened' in Spanish by using the imperfect subjunctive of **querer**:

quisiéramos comer ahora
we'd like to eat now

2. Two subjects

In this case the verb of wishing must be followed by a subordinate clause with its verb in the subjunctive:

quiero que lo hagan ellos mismos
I want them to do it themselves

me gustaría que Vds. empezaran enseguida
I would like you to start right away

hubiera preferido que escogieras otra cosa
I would have preferred you to choose something else

10. NUMBERS AND NUMBER-RELATED FUNCTIONS

A. NUMBERS

1. The cardinal numbers

For the forms of the cardinal numbers, see page 97.

Note that, though most numbers are invariable (i.e., they never change their form), there are feminine forms of **uno** and of all the hundreds between 200 and 900 inclusive. It is a very common error not to make the hundreds agree:

me costó quinientas libras
it cost me five hundred pounds

uno also agrees in compound numbers:

veintiuna ovejas
twenty-one sheep

Note that 'one' is not expressed in expressions such as the following:

¿qué carro prefieres? – el rojo
which car do you prefer? – the red one

No article is used with **cien** or **mil**, or with the adjective **medio**:

cien mil soldados
one hundred thousand soldiers

esperamos media hora
we waited for half an hour

Note that both **millón** and **billón** are nouns and *must* be followed by **de**:

el gobierno invertirá diez millones de dólares
the government will invest ten million dollars

un billón in Spanish means one million million. Nevertheless, in Mexico, **un billón** means one thousand million.

2. The ordinal numbers
For the formation of the ordinal numbers, see page 98.

These are seldom used beyond **décimo**, being usually replaced by the cardinal numbers:

vivo en el tercer piso
I live on the third floor

but

en el siglo veinte
in the twentieth century

en la página treinta y dos
on page thirty-two

3. Approximate numbers
An approximate number can be made from any multiple of ten by dropping the final vowel and adding the ending **-ena**, though such numbers are in fact very rare beyond forty:

una veintena de muchachos
about twenty boys

Some other numbers also formed with this ending have become words in their own right:

| **una docena** | a dozen |
| **una quincena** | a fortnight (two weeks) |

The approximate numbers corresponding to **ciento** and **mil** are **centenar** and **millar**, though **cientos** and **miles** may also be used:

vinieron millares de hinchas
thousands of fans turned up

Approximate numbers can also be expressed by a variety of terms such as **en torno a, alrededor de, aproximadamente, más o menos**, or the plural article **unos** (**a eso de** is limited to expressions of time):

había aproximadamente cincuenta personas en la sala
there were about fifty people in the room

llegaron unos diez hombres
about ten men arrived

cuesta unos dos mil pesos
it costs about two thousand pesos

Note also the following:

se lo dije hasta veinte veces
I told him as many as twenty times

por lo menos doscientos
at least two hundred

cuarenta y tantos
forty odd

unos pocos, unos cuantos
a few

4. Fractions and decimals
a) Fractions
Note that, when used with another number, the phrase **y medio** comes after the *noun* and not after the number as in English:

dos horas y media
two and a half hours

This also applies in the case of the nouns **millón** and **billón**:

seis millones y medio de turistas británicos
six and a half million British tourists

b) Decimals
Spanish speakers use a comma to indicate a decimal fraction, and not a point as in English:

dos coma siete por ciento (2,7 por 100)
two point seven percent

In colloquial Spanish, the word **coma** is often replaced by **con**:

cinco con cuatro millones (5,4 millones)
five point four million

Numbers and number-related functions

B. TIME

1. There are several words in Spanish for 'time.' They all have different meanings and must not be confused:

la hora	time on the clock
la época	a period of time of unspecified duration but not measured by the clock
el tiempo	time in general
la vez	an occasion

quizás podríamos vernos a una hora conveniente
perhaps we could meet at a convenient time

siempre hay muchos turistas en esta época del año
there are always lots of tourists at this time of year

pasó mucho tiempo en Panamá
he spent a long time in Panama

ya te lo he dicho por lo menos diez veces
I've already told you at least ten times

Note also the following:

de una vez por todas
once and for all

a la tercera va la vencida (Spanish proverb)
third time's the charm

2. **Time on the clock**

Time on the clock is expressed as follows:

¿qué hora es? what time is it?	**son las tres** it's three o'clock
es la una it's one o'clock	**son las diez** it's ten o'clock

The feminine definite articles are used because the word understood but not expressed is **hora** or **horas**.

Time after the hour is expressed as follows:

son las tres y cinco	it's five past three
son las siete y cuarto	it's a quarter past seven
son las ocho y veinticinco	it's twenty-five past eight
son las once y media	it's half past eleven

Time to the hour:

es la una menos diez	it's ten to one
son las cuatro menos cuarto	it's a quarter to four

'at' is expressed by **a**:

a mediodía	at noon
a medianoche	at midnight
a las seis y diez	at ten past six

Note also:

a las diez en punto	at ten o'clock on the dot
a eso de las ocho	at around eight o'clock
a las tres y pico	just after three
¿qué hora tienes?	what time do you reckon/think it is?
tengo las ocho	I reckon it's eight o'clock
daban las diez	it was striking ten o'clock

For the purposes of specifying time, the Spanish day is divided into more sections than its English equivalent:

la madrugada	from midnight till dawn
la mañana	from dawn till noon
el mediodía	from noon till early afternoon
la tarde	from early afternoon till dark
la noche	from nightfall till midnight

madrugada can be replaced by **mañana**. The use of **madrugada** emphasises the fact that the speaker considers the time in question to be very early (or very late) from his point of view:

me levanté/me acosté a las dos de la madrugada
I got up/went to bed at two in the morning

a las tres de la madrugada	at three in the morning
a las diez de la mañana	at ten in the morning
a la una del mediodía	at one in the afternoon
a las cinco de la tarde	at five in the evening

a las diez de la noche at ten in the
evening

The twenty-four hour clock is also used in timetables and official announcements, though it is not used conversationally:

a las quince treinta y cinco at fifteen thirty-five

If no specific time of day is mentioned, broad time of day is expressed using the preposition **por**:

salieron por or *(Mex)* **en la mañana**
they went out in the morning

volveremos por or *(Mex)* **en la tarde**
we'll come back in the afternoon

Note also the following:

anoche	last night
ayer	yesterday
antes de ayer/ anteayer	the day before yesterday
mañana	tomorrow
pasado mañana	the day after tomorrow
ayer por or *(Mex)* en la mañana	yesterday morning
mañana por or *(Mex)* la noche	tomorrow evening
dos veces por hora	twice an hour
ochenta kilómetros por hora	eighty kilometers an hour

3. Days of the week

For a list of days, months and seasons, see page 98.

Days of the week are written with a small letter. 'on' is expressed simply by the definite article. No preposition is used:

fuimos al cine el sábado
we went to the cinema on Saturday

vamos a la playa los domingos
we go to the beach on Sundays

el lunes por la mañana
on Monday morning

los lunes por la mañana
(on) Monday mornings

Note also:

el miércoles pasado **el sábado que viene**
last Wednesday   next Saturday

dos veces al día   **cinco veces a la**
twice a day   **semana**
five times a week

mil pesos por semana
a thousand pesos per week

4. The date

The months are written with a small letter. 'the first' may be expressed as **el primero** or **el uno**. All other dates are expressed only by the appropriate cardinal number (i.e., three, four, etc., not third, fourth, etc.).

'on' is expressed simply by the definite article, or by placing **el día** in front of the number. The only exception is in the heading to a letter, where no article is used:

¿a cuántos estamos hoy?/¿a qué día del mes estamos?/¿qué día es hoy?
what date is it today?

hoy estamos a dos
today is the second

llegaremos el 12 de febrero
we will arrive on February 12

salieron el día 9
they left on the 9th

In a full date, both the month and the year are introduced by **de**:

el quince de octubre de mil novecientos ochenta y ocho
the fifteenth of October nineteen eighty-eight

Note also:

el siglo veinte   **el siglo dieciocho**
the twentieth century   the eighteenth century

en los años treinta **la España de los**
in the thirties   **años ochenta**
the Spain of the eighties

a principios/   at the beginning of
primeros de enero   January

a mediados de   in the middle of
marzo   March

a finales/fines de   at the end of October
octubre

en lo que va de año **a lo largo del año**
this year so far   throughout the year

dos veces al mes	cuatro veces al año
twice a month	four times a year

5. The seasons
The names of the seasons are preceded by a definite article unless used with **en**:

la primavera es muy agradable en México
spring is very pleasant in Mexico

iremos a Uruguay en otoño
we're going to Uruguay in the fall

6. Age
Age is expressed as follows:

¿cuántos años tienes?	¿qué edad tiene
how old are you?	**tu hermano?**
	what age is your brother?

tengo diecisiete años
I'm seventeen

Note also the following:

ronda los cuarenta	hoy cumplo veinte años
he's pushing forty	I'm twenty today

la juventud	la tercera edad
youth, young people	senior citizens, seniors

7. Some useful expressions of time

hoy en día, hoy día	nowadays
hoy por hoy	nowadays
en la actualidad	nowadays
a corto/medio/largo plazo	in the short/medium/long term
hace diez años	ten years ago
diez años antes	ten years earlier
a partir de ahora	from now on
de aquí/hoy en adelante	from now on
en el futuro	in the future
en el porvenir	in the future
en lo sucesivo *(Fml)*	in the future
en lo venidero *(Fml)*	in the future
en los años venideros	in the years to come
al día siguiente	the following day
la próxima semana	next week
la semana siguiente	the next week
la semana anterior	the previous week

C. PRICES/MEASUREMENTS/ PERCENTAGES

1. Prices
Rate in prices is expressed by the definite article:

este vino cuesta tres euros el litro
this wine costs three euros a liter

lo vendían a seis dólares el kilo
they were selling it at six dollars a kilo

Note also:

¿cuánto cuestan/valen las manzanas?/¿a cómo se venden las manzanas?
how much are the apples?

2. Measurements
Measurements may be expressed using either the adjective or the noun relating to the measurement in question (length, height, breadth, etc.):

¿cuál es la altura del muro?
how high is the wall?

el muro tiene dos metros de alto/altura
the wall is two meters high

la calle tiene cien metros de largo/ longitud
the street is one hundred meters long

Note that in the following construction the adjective agrees:

una calle de cien metros de larga
a street one hundred meters long

Note also:

¿cuánto pesas?	¿cuánto mides?
how much do you weigh?	how tall are you?

mide casi dos metros
he's almost two meters tall

tiene una superficie de cien metros cuadrados
it has a surface area of one hundred square meters

tiene una capacidad de dos metros cúbicos
it has a capacity of two cubic meters

Distance is always indicated by the preposition **a**:

¿a qué distancia está la playa? – a unos cinco kilómetros
how far away is the beach? – about five kilometers

3. Percentages
Percentages in Spanish are invariably preceded by either a definite or an indefinite article. There is no difference in meaning:

la inflación ha aumentado en un diez por ciento
inflation has gone up ten percent

el treinta por ciento de las personas entrevistadas no contestó
thirty percent of those interviewed did not give an answer

Percentages are usually written in Spanish as **5 por 100** and the like. **100 por 100** is almost invariably pronounced **cien por cien**.

The amount by which a percentage increases or decreases is indicated in Spanish by the preposition **en**. The commonest verbs used in this connection are:

Increase:

aumentar, incrementar, crecer, subir

Decrease:

caer, bajar, reducir(se)

hemos reducido nuestros precios en un 15 por 100
we have reduced our prices by 15 percent

If a percentage is not involved, normally no preposition is used:

las acciones han bajado un par de pesos
shares have come down by a few pesos

---

11. SENTENCE STRUCTURE

Sentence structure is not the same as word order. Sentence structure concerns the place occupied by the different *component parts* of the sentence, rather than *individual words*. Any of these component parts can consist of a number of words. For example, in a sentence such as the following:

el padre del amigo de mi hermano trabaja en la Cuidad de México
my brother's friend's father works in Mexico City

the words **el padre del amigo de mi hermano** all go together to form the subject of the verb **trabaja**. The verb itself occupies the second *place* in the sentence, although it is the eighth *word*.

The most important elements of any sentence are the verb, the subject of the verb (i.e., who or what is carrying out the action of the verb), and the object or

complement. A transitive verb takes an object, an intransitive verb may be followed by a complement. There are other elements – adverbs, prepositional phrases, etc. – but these are less important and are not dealt with here.

1. **English sentence structure**
    Sentence structure is very predictable in English. Most English sentences follow the order subject – verb – object/complement, e.g.:

subject	verb	object/complement
the boys	watch	television (object)
Spanish	is	easy (complement)

    The only consistent exception to this order in English is found in questions, where the order verb – subject – object/complement is more common:

verb	subject	object/complement
is	Spanish	easy

2. **Spanish sentence structure**
    Sentence structure is *very* much more flexible in Spanish than it is in English. This is not to suggest that the order subject – verb – object/complement is in any sense uncommon in Spanish. On the contrary, it is probably the commonest pattern in spoken Spanish, and is also commonly used in questions. Nonetheless, it is nowhere near as dominant in Spanish as it is in English, and a Spanish speaker will happily place the verb before the subject, and on occasions will even place the object before the verb.

    There are few rules governing sentence structure in Spanish, but in general it could be said that:

    –   the closer any element of the sentence is to the beginning of the sentence, the more emphasis it receives, the first position in the sentence being obviously the most emphatic;
    –   it is unusual for the verb not to occupy the first or second *position* in the sentence (see the difference between position and word order given above).

    The choice made by a Spanish speaker may be based on reasons of emphasis, but more often it will have to do with the rhythm of the sentence. Rhythms are not something which can be taught. A feeling for such rhythms can be obtained only through exposure to large amounts of genuine spoken Spanish.

3. **Examples of different sentence structures**
    a) subject – verb

        mi hermano está estudiando inglés
        my brother is studying English

¿el carro está en el garaje?
is the car in the garage?

b) verb – subject

llegaron dos tíos y se pusieron a trabajar
two fellows came along and started to work

me lo dijo una vez mi padre
my father told me so once

c) object – verb – subject

el cuadro lo pintó un amigo mío
one of my friends painted the picture

la moto la compramos Juan y yo
Juan and I bought the motorbike

Note that when the object is placed before the verb, the corresponding object pronoun *must* also be placed before the verb.

d) use of first position for emphasis

a mí no me gusta nada
I don't like it at all

tal decisión no la apoyaremos nunca
we will never support such a decision

a ella no la puede ver
he can't stand her

4. Punctuation

Punctuation in Spanish is largely identical to English. Remember, however, that the upside-down question marks and exclamation marks are written at the beginning of the question and of the exclamation respectively. This is not necessarily at the beginning of the sentence:

¿qué quieres tomar?
what will you have?

y éste, ¿cuánto cuesta?
and how much does this one cost?

estuviste anoche en la discoteca, ¿verdad?
you were at the club last night, weren't you?

el público gritó '¡olé!'
the crowd shouted 'olé!'

Part II
FORMS

1. ACCENTUATION

Written accents in Spanish relate primarily to *spoken* stress. If you know how a word is pronounced, you can tell by applying a few simple rules if it requires a written accent, and, if so, where the accent should be written.

1. **Syllables**

   In order to know when and where to write an accent it is important to understand what is meant by a syllable. A syllable is a group of letters within a word at least one of which *must* be a vowel. If there is no vowel, there is no syllable. In many cases, the number of syllables in a word is the same as the number of vowels:

   ca-sa (two syllables)   **con-cen-tra-da** (four syllables)

   If there are one or more consonants between each vowel, as in the examples just given, the division into syllables is quite straightforward. However, the situation is slightly more complex if two or more vowels are written together.

   Vowels in Spanish are divided into strong and weak vowels.

   the strong vowels are: A, E and O
   the weak vowels are: I and U

   The rules regarding whether or not two or more vowels written together form one or more syllables are as follows:

a) When two strong vowels appear together they belong to two distinct syllables:

   pa-se-ar (three syllables)
   pe-or (two syllables)

b) When a strong and weak vowel appear together and there is no written accent on any of the weak vowels, they form only one syllable, and the strong vowel takes the stress:

   fue*r*-te (two syllables)
   vie-jo (two syllables)
   an-cia-no (three syllables)

   If one of the weak vowels is accentuated, it forms a separate syllable:

   ha-cí-a (three syllables)
   pú-a (two syllables)

c) When two or more weak vowels appear together they form only one syllable and the stress falls on the second vowel:

   viu-da (two syllables)
   fui (one syllable)

   These rules apply to *pronunciation* only, and are unaffected by the way a word is written. For example, the **o** and first **i** of **prohibir** belong to the same syllable, despite the fact that there is a written (but completely unpronounced) **h** between them. The **e** and **u** of **rehusar** belong to the same syllable for the same reason.

2. **Spoken stress**

   All words in Spanish have one main stressed vowel, and it is the position of this stressed vowel in the word which determines whether or not there is a written accent. The rules for spoken stress are as follows:

a) The stress falls naturally on the second to the last syllable of the word when:

   – the word ends in a vowel
     lla-mo, re-ba-ño, ve-o, va-rio, re-ci-bie-ra
   – the word ends in **-n** or **-s**
     can-tan, li-bros, jo-ven

b) The stress falls naturally on the last syllable when the word ends in a consonant other than **-n** and **-s**:
     can-tar, ciu-dad, no-mi-nal

3. **Primary use of the written accent**

   The written accent is mainly used in Spanish to show deviations from the rules for natural spoken stress given above. The pronunciation of the vowel on which the accent is written is not otherwise affected.

   If the stress falls where the rules say it should fall, there is no written accent. If it does not, a written accent is placed over the vowel actually carrying the stress. This accounts for the overwhelming majority of cases of written accents in Spanish.

   The general rules are, therefore:

   – If a word ending in a vowel, **-n** or **-s** is *not* stressed on the second last syllable, a written accent is placed on the vowel that is in fact stressed:

   menú, región, inglés

Accentuation

– If a word ending in a consonant other than **-n** or **-s** is not stressed on the last syllable, a written accent is placed on the vowel that is in fact stressed:

césped, **fá**cil

More specifically, it can be seen that:

– Any word stressed on the third to the last syllable carries an accent on the stressed vowel irrespective of its ending:

música, **ré**gimen

– Any word ending in a stressed vowel carries an accent on that vowel:

café, rubí

– In any combination of a weak vowel and a strong vowel where the weak vowel carries the stress, this weak vowel will have a written accent:

quer*í*a, vac*í*o

Further examples:

stress in 'natural' position (no accent)		stress out of position (written accent)	
varias	several	var**í**as	you vary
cont**í**nuo	continuous	contin**ú**o	I continue
am**a**r	to love	**á**mbar	amber
fabr**i**ca	he manufactures	f**á**brica	factory

Remember again that what counts is pronunciation and not spelling. The written accent on **prohíbo** or **rehúso** is explained by the fact that the weak vowel in the spoken syllables **oi** and **eu** is stressed.

Note also that written accents may have to be omitted from or added to plural forms:

región regiones joven jóvenes

4. Secondary uses of the written accent

Other uses of the written accent are:

– to differentiate between two words with the same spelling:

el (the)	– **él** (he)	**si** (if)	– **sí** (yes)
tu (your)	– **tú** (you)	**de** (of)	– **dé** (give)
mi (my)	– **mí** (me)		

– to identify the interrogative and exclamatory forms of certain pronouns and adverbs:

donde – **¿dónde?**	**quien** – **¿quién?**
where – where?	who – who?

– to differentiate the pronoun forms from the adjectival forms of the demonstratives (the pronouns are written with an accent):

este – **éste**	**aquella** – **aquélla**
this – this one	that – that one

Since the neuter pronouns cannot be confused with any other forms, no accent is required:

esto	**eso**	**aquello**
this (one)	that (one)	that (one)

5. The dieresis

A dieresis is only ever written over the letter **u** in Spanish, in which case it appears as **ü**. The dieresis occurs only in the combinations **güe** and **güi**, and indicates that the **ü** is to be pronounced as a separate vowel. If no dieresis is present, the **u** is not pronounced:

la cigüeña	the stork
la vergüenza	shame
la lingüística	linguistics
el piragüismo	canoeing

Compare these with words such as **la guerra, la guirnalda** and the like, where the **u** is not pronounced.

Note that a dieresis must sometimes be added or indeed omitted in certain forms of certain verbs, to ensure that the pronunciation of the verb is correctly reflected in the spelling, e.g.:

averiguo (*indicative*: I find out)
averigüe (*subjunctive*)

avergonzarse (*infinitive*: to be ashamed)
me avergüenzo (*first person singular*)

arguyo (*first person singular*)
argüir (*infinitive*: to argue)

2.
GENDER

In Spanish all nouns are either *masculine* or *feminine*. There is no equivalent of the English neuter gender for nouns.

All words used with any noun (adjectives, articles, etc.) take the same gender as the noun.

1. Gender by ending

The gender of a noun can often be deduced from its ending:

a) Most nouns ending in **-o** are masculine:

el libro	**el dinero**	**el piano**
the book	the money	the piano

There are a few common exceptions:

la radio	**la mano**
the radio	the hand

b) Most nouns ending in **-a** are feminine:

la aduana	**la casa**	**la mañana**
the Customs	the house	the morning

Some common exceptions to this:

el día	**el mapa**	**el idioma**	**el clima**
the day	the map	the language	the climate

Also, most nouns ending in **-ema** and a few ending in **-ama** are masculine:

el problema	**el sistema**	**el lema**
the problem	the system	the slogan

el programa	**el drama**	**el telegrama**
the program	the drama	the telegram

c) Almost all nouns ending in **-d** are feminine:

la ciudad	**la vid**	**la juventud**
the city	the vine	youth

la pared	**la dificultad**
the wall	the difficulty

d) Almost all nouns ending in **-ión** are feminine:

la nación	**la región**
the nation	the region

There are a few common exceptions:

el camión	**el avión**
the truck	the plane

2. Gender by meaning

a) People and animals

When referring to people and animals, often, though not always, the meaning of the noun decides its gender, eg:

el hombre	**la mujer**	**la vaca**
the man	the woman	the cow

However, there are some exceptions to the above, for example **la víctima** is the Spanish for a victim of either sex.

b) Some nouns are going through a period of transition:

el juez is the Spanish for 'judge' in general, but, as more women judges are appointed in Spanish-speaking countries, you will now hear and read both **la juez** and **la jueza**.

Such alternative forms can coexist for some time. For example, Mrs. Thatcher was referred to in the Spanish press as **la Primer Ministro** and **la Primera Ministra**.

c) Words with both genders

There are many words ending in **-ista**, which can be either masculine or feminine, according to the gender of the person referred to:

el socialista, la socialista
the socialist

el periodista, la periodista
the journalist

⚠ There is no separate 'masculine' form of these nouns – all the masculine forms end in **-ista**, like the feminines.

d) Nouns with corresponding forms for both genders

Some nouns may have both genders, depending on the gender of the person described:

el camarero	**la camarera**
the waiter	the waitress

el niño	**la niña**
the boy	the girl

Sometimes, a more substantial change of spelling is required:

el emperador	**la emperatriz**
the emperor	the empress

el actor	**la actriz**
the actor	the actress

e) Nouns with different meanings for different genders

Some nouns may appear with either gender, but their meanings change:

el policía	**la policía**
the policeman	the police force

el guía	**la guía**
the guide (*person*)	the guidebook

el capital	la capital
capital (*money*)	the capital city

el cura	la cura
the parish priest	the cure

el pendiente	la pendiente
the earring	the slope

el moral	la moral
the mulberry bush	ethics

3. THE NOUN – PLURAL OF NOUNS

1. Formation
The plural of Spanish nouns is formed as follows:

a) Adding **-s** to nouns ending in an unstressed vowel:

los libros	las reglas
the books	the rulers

b) Most nouns ending in a stressed vowel add **-es**:

el rubí	los rubíes
the ruby	the rubies

but some common nouns only add **-s**:

los cafés	las mamás	los papás
the cafes	the moms	the dads

c) Adding **-es** to nouns ending in a consonant other than **-es**:

los señores	las tempestades
the men	the storms

d) Nouns already ending in **-s**
If the last syllable is stressed, add **-es**:

el inglés	los ingleses
the Englishman	(the) Englishmen

However, if the last syllable is not stressed, the word does not change:

el lunes	los lunes
Monday	Mondays

e) Some nouns require a spelling change in the plural. Where nouns end in **-z**, this changes to **-ces**:

la actriz	las actrices
the actress	the actresses

f) Changes in written accent
Most singular nouns having a written accent on the last syllable lose this accent in the plural as it is no longer necessary:

la nación	las naciones
the nation	the nations

The few nouns ending in **-n** and stressed on the second to the last syllable in the singular need a written accent in the plural:

el joven	los jóvenes
the young man	the young men
el crimen	los crímenes
the crime	the crimes

g) There are two plurals in Spanish that actually change their accentuation from the singular to the plural form:

el carácter	los caracteres
the character	the characters
el régimen	los regímenes
the regime	the regimes

h) In the case of acronyms, plural forms are indicated by doubling the initials:

EE.UU.	Estados Unidos (USA)
CC.OO.	Comisiones Obreras (Trade Union)
FF.AA.	Fuerzas Armadas (Armed Forces)

i) Most English words used in Spanish form the plural by adding **-s**:

el camping	los campings
el póster	los pósters
el cómic	los cómics

However, some English words long established in Spanish for a long time have also adopted a Spanish plural:

el club	los clubes
el bar	los bares
el superman	los supermanes

2. Special use of the masculine plural
The masculine plural form is frequently used to indicate both genders:

mis padres	los Reyes	mis tíos
my parents	the King and Queen	my aunt and uncle

4.
THE ARTICLES

1. The definite article
a) The standard form
The definite article has both a masculine and a feminine form, each of which can also be put into the plural:

	masculine	feminine
singular	**el**	**la**
plural	**los**	**las**

el señor
the man

la chica
the girl

los señores
the men

las chicas
the girls

b) A special feminine form
Note that the form of the feminine definite article used immediately before nouns that begin with a stressed **a-** or **ha-** is **el** and not **la**:

el agua
the water

el hambre
hunger

This change does not affect the *gender* of the noun. Other words accompanying the noun continue to take the feminine form:

el agua está fría
the water is cold

c) Contraction of the definite article
The masculine definite article joins together with the prepositions **a** and **de** to give the following forms:

a + el al   **de + el del**

fui al cine
I went to the movies

la casa del profesor
the teacher's house

This does not happen if the **el** is part of a title in capital letters:

escribí a El Diario
I wrote to El Diario

However, feminines and plurals *never* contract.

d) Countries whose names are preceded by the definite article
The names of the following countries are preceded by the appropriate form of the definite article:

el Brasil	Brazil
la Argentina	Argentina
la India	India
el Japón	Japan
el Perú	Peru
el Uruguay	Uruguay

2. The indefinite article
a) The standard form
The indefinite article has both a masculine and a feminine form. Unlike English, both of these can also be put into the plural.

	masculine	feminine
singular	**un**	**una**
plural	**unos**	**unas**

un hombre
a man

una cantidad
a quantity

b) A special feminine form
Note that the form of the feminine indefinite article used immediately before nouns which begin with a stressed **a-** or **ha-** is **un**:

un hacha
an axe

un ala
a wing

This change does not affect the *gender* of the noun. Other words accompanying the noun continue to take the feminine form:

construyeron un ala nueva
they built a new wing

c) The plural forms are used:
- with nouns that exist only in the plural or are normally used in the plural

- to express the idea of 'some,' 'a few'

Otherwise, they are not required:

compré unos pantalones
I bought a pair of pants

tengo un libro	**tengo unos libros**	**tengo libros**
I have a book	I have some books	I have books

5. THE DEMONSTRATIVES

1. **The demonstrative adjectives**

   The demonstrative adjectives in Spanish are **este** (this) and **ese** and **aquel** (both meaning 'that'). Their forms are as follows:

	masculine	feminine
singular	este	esta
plural	estos	estas
singular	ese	esa
plural	esos	esas
singular	aquel	aquella
plural	aquellos	aquellas

   The demonstrative adjectives are placed *before* the noun:

   > **este mes**   **ese sillón aquella bicicleta**
   > this month   that armchair   that bike

   See pages 11-12 for their uses.

2. **The demonstrative pronouns**

   The demonstrative pronouns are identical to the demonstrative adjectives with the single exception that they carry a written accent on the stressed vowel:

   > **éste, éstos, ésta, éstas**
   > **ése, ésos, ésa, ésas**
   > **aquél, aquéllos, aquélla, aquéllas**

   There is also a neuter form that is *not* written with an accent:

   > **esto, eso, aquello**

   See page 12 for the uses of the demonstrative pronouns.

6. THE POSSESSIVE ADJECTIVES AND PRONOUNS

1. **The weak possessive adjectives**

   The weak possessive adjectives are placed before the noun. Their forms are as follows:

	masc. sing	fem. sing.	masc. plural	fem. plural
my	mi	mi	mis	mis
your	tu	tu	tus	tus
his/her/ its/your	su	su	sus	sus
our	nuestro	nuestra	nuestros	nuestras
your	vuestro	vuestra	vuestros	vuestras
their/ your	su	su	sus	sus

mi cuchillo my knife   **mi cuchara** my spoon

mis cuchillos my knives   **mis cucharas** my spoons

tu pañuelo your handkerchief   **tu chaqueta** your jacket

tus pañuelos your handkerchiefs   **tus chaquetas** your jackets

su saco his/her/your sack   **su maleta** his/her/your suitcase

sus sacos his/her/your sack   **sus maletas** his/her/your suitcases

nuestro piso our apartment   **nuestra casa** our house

nuestros pisos our apartments   **nuestras casas** our houses

vuestro coche your car   **vuestra casa** your house

vuestros coches your cars   **vuestras casas** your houses

su saco your/their sack   **su maleta** your/their suitcase

sus sacos your/their sacks   **sus maletas** your/their suitcases

For a fuller treatment of **su** and **sus**, see page 14.

2. **The strong possessive adjectives and pronouns**

   The strong possessive adjectives and the possessive pronouns are identical in form. They are as follows:

masc. sing.	fem. sing.	masc. plural	fem. plural
mío	mía	míos	mías
tuyo	tuya	tuyos	tuyas
suyo	suya	suyos	suyas
nuestro	nuestra	nuestros	nuestras
vuestro	vuestra	vuestros	vuestras
suyo	suya	suyos	suyas

See page 14 for an explanation of the use of these forms.

7. AUGMENTATIVES AND DIMINUTIVES

1. The augmentatives

a) The following suffixes are added to nouns, adjectives, participles and adverbs as augmentatives (see pages 15-16):

masculine	-ón	-azo	-acho	-ote
feminine	-ona	-aza	-acha	-ota

b) Any vowel at the end of the original word is dropped.

un muchachazo	**un hombrote**
a big boy	a big man

2. The diminutives

a) The following suffixes are added to nouns, adjectives, participles and adverbs as diminutives (see pages 15-16):

-ito	longer forms:	-cito, -ecito
-illo	longer forms:	-cillo, -ecillo
-uelo	longer forms:	-zuelo, -ezuelo
-in	(no longer forms)	
-ucho	(no longer forms)	

All of these endings can be made feminine by changing the **-o** to **-a** (**-in** becomes **-ina**).

b) When the word ends in a vowel, this is dropped:

Ana	→	**Anita**
señora	→	**señorita**

c) Of the longer forms, **-cito**, **-cillo** and **-zuelo** are used with words of more than one syllable that end in **-n** or **-r**:

salón	→	**saloncito**
calor	→	**calorcito**

d) The forms **-ecito**, **-ecillo** and **-ezuelo** are used with words of one syllable:

flor	→	**florecita, florecilla,** *(RP)* **florcita**
pez	→	**pececito, pececillo**

Note that spelling changes (**z** to **c**) may be necessary.

They are also used with words of two syllables when the first syllable is **-ie** or **-ue**. The final vowel is dropped:

pueblo	→	**pueblecito,** *(Am)* **pueblito**
nieto	→	**nietecito,** *(Am)* **nietito**

e) Written accents are dropped from the ending of the original word when a suffix is added:

salón	→	**saloncito**

A written accent is added to the weak vowel of the suffix when the original word ends in an accentuated vowel:

mamá	→	**mamaíta,** *(Mex)* **mamacita,** *(RP)* **mamita**

8. THE ADJECTIVE

1. Shortened form of adjectives

a) Certain adjectives drop the **-o** from the masculine singular immediately before the noun:

alguno	¿hay *algún camión por aquí?* are there any buses around here?
ninguno	no veo *ningún* tren I don't see any trains
bueno	un *buen* vino a good wine
malo	el *mal* tiempo the bad weather
primero	el *primer* día del año the first day of the year
tercero	el *tercer* edificio the third building

Note that **ninguno** and **alguno** require a written accent when shortened in this way.

b) **grande** is shortened to **gran** before both masculine and feminine singular nouns:

un gran señor	**una gran señora**
a great man	a great lady

When **grande** refers to physical size, it usually comes after the noun, in which case it is not shortened:

un coche grande	**una cocina grande**
a large car	a large kitchen

The adjective

c) **cualquiera** becomes **cualquier** before both masculine and feminine singular nouns:

cualquier libro	**cualquier casa**
any book	any house

The plural of this adjective is **cualesquiera**. It is seldom used.

d) **santo** becomes **san** before saints' names, except those beginning with either **Do-** or **To-**:

San Pablo	**San Pedro**
Santo Domingo	**Santo Tomás**

2. Forming the feminine of adjectives

a) Adjectives ending in **-o** change to **-a**:

un vuelo corto	**una estancia corta**
a short flight	a short stay

b) Adjectives ending in other vowels or consonants (other than those in sections c and d) have the same form for both masculine and feminine:

un coche verde	**una hoja verde**
a green car	a green leaf

un problema fundamental	**una dificultad fundamental**
a fundamental problem	a fundamental difficulty

c) Those ending in **-án**, **-és**, **-ín**, **-ón**, and **-or** add **-a**:

un niño hablador	**una mujer habladora**
a talkative boy	a talkative woman

The exceptions are the comparative adjectives ending in **-or**, see page 71:

una idea mejor
a better idea

Note also that those ending in **-án**, **-és**, **-ín**, and **-ón** lose their accent in the feminine:

una muchacha muy holgazana
a very lazy girl

d) Adjectives indicating nationality or where someone or something comes from add **-a** if they end in a consonant. Any written accent is also lost:

un hotel escocés	**una pensión escocesa**
a Scottish hotel	a Scottish boarding house

un vino andaluz	**una sopa andaluza**
an Andalusian wine	an Andalusian soup

e) Adjectives ending in **-ícola** and **-ista** have the same form for both masculine and feminine:

un país agrícola	**una región vinícola**
an agricultural country	a wine-growing region

el partido comunista	**la ideología socialista**
the communist party	socialist ideology

⚠ Note that there is no separate 'masculine' form for these adjectives. The masculine forms end in **-ista** and **-ícola** like the feminines.

3. The plural of adjectives

Adjectives follow the same rules as nouns for the formation of the plural (see page 66):

estos libros son viejos y sucios
these books are old and dirty

unas personas amables
some friendly people

The same spelling and accentuation changes also occur:

feliz – felices	**holgazán – holgazanes**

---

9. THE COMPARATIVE

See pages 18-20 for uses of the comparative.

1. The standard forms

To form the comparative in Spanish, simply place the word **más** (more), or **menos** (less) before the adjective:

más barato	**más caro**
cheaper	more expensive

menos guapo	**menos feo**
less handsome	less ugly

2. Irregular comparatives

There are six irregular comparatives:

bueno	(good)	→	**mejor**	(better)
grande	(big)	→	**mayor**	(bigger)*
malo	(bad)	→	**peor**	(worse)
mucho	(a lot)	→	**más**	(more)
pequeño	(small)	→	**menor**	(smaller)*
poco	(a little)	→	**menos**	(less)

A number of other adjectives are considered to

belong to this group, although their comparative meaning has to some extent been lost:

superior (superior)
inferior (inferior)
anterior (previous)
posterior (rear, subsequent)

* **más grande** and **más pequeño** exist, but refer rather to physical size. **mayor** and **menor** refer more to the relative importance of the object or person, or to age.

When referring to age, **mayor** is often treated in spoken Spanish as a simple adjective meaning 'old,' 'grown up' and is sometimes itself put into the comparative:

mi hermano más mayor
my older brother

Although fairly widespread, this usage is regarded as ungrammatical and should certainly not be imitated in formal written Spanish.

superior and **inferior** are widely used with numbers, amounts, quantities etc:

el paro es superior a tres millones
unemployment is in excess of three million

los beneficios son inferiores a los del año pasado
profits are down on last year's

10. THE SUPERLATIVE

1. The relative superlative

The relative superlative is identical in form to the comparative:

Juan es el estudiante más insolente de la clase
Juan is the most insolent student in class

este libro es el más caro
this book is the most expensive

es la peor película que jamás he visto
it's the worst film I've ever seen

2. The absolute superlative

The absolute superlative is formed by adding the ending **-ísimo** to the adjective. If the adjective already ends in a vowel, this is dropped:

alto	**altísimo**
importante	**importantísimo**
fácil	**facilísimo**

When a vowel is dropped from the adjective, spelling changes may be necessary to ensure that the pronunciation of the absolute superlative is properly reflected in the spelling of the word:

rico	**riquísimo**
feliz	**felicísimo**
largo	**larguísimo**

Like any other adjective, the relative superlative agrees with the noun described:

estás guapísima hoy, María
you're looking extremely pretty today, María

estos libros son carísimos
these books are very expensive

11. PREPOSITIONS

A

to	destination	**voy a la escuela/a casa** I am going to school/home
		¿adónde fuiste? where did you go?
at/in	place	**llega a Madrid mañana** he arrives in Madrid tomorrow
at/on	time	**comemos a la una** we eat at one o'clock
		se fue a los quince años he left at the age of fifteen
		al día siguiente murió he died (on) the next day
at/on	place where	**torcieron a la izquierda** they turned to the left
		sentarse a la mesa to sit down at the table
on	means of transport	**a pie, a caballo** on foot, on horseback
at	cost	**los vendían a diez pesos cada uno** they were selling them at ten pesos each
away from	place/time	**a los dos días volvió** he came back two days later
		la casa se sitúa a cien metros de aquí the house is a hundred meters from here
a	frequency	**dos veces al día** twice a day

Prepositions

in	opinion	**a mi ver, a mi juicio, a mis ojos** in my opinion, in my view				

in	opinion	**a mi ver, a mi juicio, a mis ojos** in my opinion, in my view
purpose	verbs of motion	**fui a comprar pan** I went to buy bread
personal *a*	see page 58	**he visto a Juan** I saw Juan

ANTE

before	in the presence of	**lo llevaron ante el rey** they brought him before the king
before	in the face of	**ante tanto trabajo huyó** in the face of so much work he fled

BAJO

under-(neath)	place	**construyeron un túnel bajo el mar** they built a tunnel under the sea
	figuratively	**bajo el reinado de Felipe II** under the reign of Philip II

CON

with	association	**se fueron con su primo** they left with their cousin
	means	**lo cortó con las tijeras** she cut it with the scissors
to		**hablaba con su amigo** he was talking to his friend
toward	figuratively	**no seas cruel conmigo** don't be cruel to me

In this last meaning, **con** is sometimes preceded by **para**:

era muy amable para con todos
he was very kind to everyone

CONTRA

against	position	**se apoyaba contra la pared** he was leaning against the wall
	opposition	**los rebeldes luchaban contra el gobierno** the rebels were fighting against the government

In this last meaning, the compound preposition **en contra de** is often preferred:

votaron en contra de la ley
they voted against the bill

DE

of	possession	**es el coche de mi hermana** it's my sister's car
	material	**el vestido es de lana** the dress is made of wool
	contents	**un paquete de cigarrillos** a packet of cigarettes
(for)	purpose	**una cuchara de café** a coffee spoon
from	place	**es de Londres** he comes from London
		va de Montevideo a Buenos Aires he goes from Montevideo to Buenos Aires
	time	**de año en año vienen aquí** they come here year after year
		cenamos de diez a once we had dinner from ten to eleven
		se fueron de pequeños they left as little children
	number	**el peso es de cien kilos** the weight is one hundred kilos
		el total era de mil dólares the total was a thousand dollars
	cost	**un coche de cinco mil libras** a car costing five thousand pounds
with	descriptions	**la muchacha de los ojos azules** the girl with the blue eyes **el señor de la barba** the man with the beard **¡el bobo del niño!** the silly boy!
to form adjectival phrases		**la comida de siempre** the usual food **la parte de fuera** the outside part
to form compound prepositions		**además de, alrededor de** etc. See page 75.

DESDE

from	place	**lo vi llegar desde mi ventana** I saw him arrive from my window
from/since	time	**toca la guitarra desde niño** he has been playing the guitar since he was a boy

with **hasta**				figuratively	**muestra hostilidad hacia el jefe**
from ... to/	time	**desde las dos hasta las cuatro**			he shows hostility to the boss
till		from two o'clock till four			
from ... to	place	**desde Madrid hasta Barcelona**	*about*	time	**llegaron hacia las tres**
		from Madrid to Barcelona			they arrived about three o'clock

EN

in/at/on	position	**paró en la puerta**
		he stopped in the doorway
		quedarse en casa
		to stay at home
		la computadora está en la mesa
		the computer is on the table
		los vimos en la Feria de Muestras
		we saw them at the Exhibition
	opinion	**en mi opinión sería imprudente**
		in my opinion it would be unwise
into	numbers	**lo dividió en tres partes**
		he divided it into three
within	time	**no lo he visto en quince días**
		I haven't seen him in a fortnight
by	increase/ decrease	**los precios han aumentado en un diez por ciento**
		the prices have gone up by ten per cent
phrases		**en balde,** in vain **en vano**
		en seguida immediately
		en absoluto absolutely not

ENTRE

between	**entre la puerta y la pared**
	between the door and the wall
	entre tú y yo
	between you and me
among	**lo encontré entre tus papeles**
	I found it among your papers
together	**lo hicimos entre todos**
	we did it together

HACIA

toward	place	**fue corriendo hacia su padre**
		he ran toward his father

HASTA

until	time	**esto continuó hasta el siglo veinte**
		this continued until the 20th century
up to	number	**vinieron hasta cien personas**
		as many as a hundred people turned up
as far as	place	**te acompaño hasta tu casa**
		I'll walk you home
even	figuratively	**hasta los niños quieren acompañarnos**
		even the children want to come with us

INCLUSO

even	**incluso mi padre está de acuerdo**
	even my father agrees

MEDIANTE

by means of	**lo consiguió mediante mucho trabajo**
	he achieved it by hard work

PARA

in order to	purpose	**salió para lavar el coche**
		he went out to wash the car
		compró una navaja para cortar la cuerda
		she bought a penknife to cut the rope
		estudió para cura
		he studied to become a priest
for	in the direction of	**se fueron para Estados Unidos**
		they left for the USA
by	time by which	**quiero ese trabajo para mañana**
		I want that work by tomorrow
		para entonces ya me habré marchado
		I'll have gone away by then

Prepositions

for	as concerns	**el cálculo no es difícil para ella** the calculation isn't difficult for her	*per/by*	rate/ sequence	**cincuenta kilómetros por hora** fifty kilometers per hour
for	concession	**para ser español, habla muy bien inglés** for a Spaniard, he speaks very good English	*out of/by/ through*	cause	**por no estudiar no aprobó el examen** he failed the exam through not having studied
to		**siempre murmuraba para sí** she was always muttering to herself	*for the sake of/ through*		**por amor lo siguió a Colombia** she followed him to Colombia out of love
with **estar**	on the point of	**estábamos todos para salir** we were all ready to go out	*times*	multiplica- tion	**dos por dos son cuatro** two times two is four
			for	to get	**voy a por hielo** I am going to get some ice
idioms		**bastante ... para** enough ... to/for **demasiado ... para** too much ... to/for **suficiente ... para** enough ... to/for **cuesta demasiado para mí** it's too expensive for me	*idioms*	tomar ... por	**¿me tomas por idiota?** do you take me for a fool?
				pasar por	**pasa por buen conductor** he is considered a good driver
				estar por	**los platos están por lavar** the dishes still have to be washed

POR

				estoy por salir I'm about to leave
by	agent	**el reparo fue terminado por el jefe** the repair was finished by the boss		

SEGÚN

for	time during	**habló por dos minutos** he spoke for two minutes	*according to*	**según él, es peligroso** according to him, it's dangerous
		ocurrió el robo el domingo por la noche the robbery took place on Sunday night		**los precios varían según la época del año** the prices vary according to the time of year
out (of)		**lo echó por la ventana** she threw it out (of) the window		

SIN

through		**pasaron por Valencia** they went through Valencia	*without*	**continuaremos sin su ayuda** we will go on without your help
about	place	**rodaron por las cercanías** they roamed about the neighborhood		**sin saber** without knowing
		vive por aquí he lives around here		

SOBRE

by/through	means	**por mí se informaron sobre el desastre** they found out about the disaster through me	*on/over*	place	**las tazas están sobre la mesa** the cups are on the table
		por avión, por teléfono by air, by telephone			**el avión voló sobre las montañas** the plane flew over the mountains
in exchange for		**vendió el coche por cien libras** he sold the car for a hundred pounds	*around*	time	**vendrá sobre las siete** he will come around seven o'clock

on/about	concerning	**he leído un artículo sobre la guerra** I read an article about the war

TRAS

after	time	**tras una reunión de tres horas** after a three hour meeting
	succession	**uno tras otro** one after the other

COMPOUND PREPOSITIONS

acerca de	about/concerning	**el jefe me habló acerca del empleado** the boss spoke to me about the employee
a causa de	because of	**no salimos a causa de la tormenta** we are not going out because of the storm
a favor de	in favor of/for	**¿estás a favor de la energía nuclear?** are you in favor of nuclear energy?
a fuerza de	by dint of	**consiguió terminar a fuerza de trabajar noche y día** he managed to get finished by dint of working both night and day
a pesar de	in spite of	**salieron a pesar de la lluvia** they went out in spite of the rain
a lo largo de	along	**hay flores a lo largo del río** there are flowers all along the riverside
	throughout	**a lo largo del mes de agosto** throughout the month of August
a través de	across/through	**la luz entra a través de la ventana** the light comes in through the window
además de	besides/as well as	**compré pan además de mantequilla** I bought bread as well as butter
alrededor de	about/around	**gana alrededor de veinte dólares al día** he earns around twenty dollars a day

		las casas están situadas alrededor de la iglesia the houses are situated around the church
antes de	before (time)	**antes de entrar dejen salir** let people off before getting on
cerca de	near	**la casa está cerca del colegio** the house is near the school
	around	**tiene cerca de mil ovejas** he has nearly a thousand sheep
debajo de	under	**se pararon debajo del árbol** they stopped under the tree
delante de	in front of	**el coche se detuvo delante del hotel** the car stopped in front of the hotel
dentro de	inside	**encontró un regalo dentro del paquete** she found a gift inside the parcel
después de	after	**salió después de terminar su trabajo** he went out after finishing his work
		después de las dos after two o'clock
		después de todo after all
detrás de	behind	**el bar se encuentra detrás del mercado** the bar is behind the market
en lugar de/en vez de	instead of	**en lugar de telefonear, les escribió** instead of calling, he wrote to them
en medio de	in the midst of	**paró en medio de tocar la sonata** he stopped in the midst of playing the sonata
encima de	on (top of)	**colocó el vaso encima de la mesa** she put the glass on the table
enfrente de	opposite	**la iglesia está enfrente del Ayuntamiento** the church is opposite the Town Hall
fuera de	apart from	**fuera de los de al lado, no conozco a nadie** apart from the next-door neighbors, I don't know anyone

Relative pronouns

	outside	**la granja está situada fuera de la aldea**	
		the farm is outside the village	
lejos de	far from	**la iglesia no está lejos de la escuela**	
		the church is not far from the school	
		lejos de acatar la ley	
		far from respecting the law	
por medio de	by (means of)	**consiguió obtener el dinero por medio de un embuste**	
		he managed to get the money by means of trickery	

12. RELATIVE PRONOUNS

For a detailed explanation of the use of relative pronouns, see pages 20-21.

1. Simple relative pronouns
a) **que** (who, whom, which, that)
que relates to either persons or things, singular or plural. Note that it is invariable.
b) **quien/quienes** (who, whom, that)
quien (singular), **quienes** (plural) relate exclusively to people and are normally used after prepositions.

2. Compound relative pronouns
The compound relative pronouns have separate forms for masculine singular and plural, and feminine singular and plural. They also have a neuter form.

a) **el que** (who, whom, which, that)

	masculine	feminine	neuter
singular	**el que**	**la que**	**lo que**
plural	**los que**	**las que**	

b) **el cual** (who, whom, which, that)

	masculine	feminine	neuter
singular	**el cual**	**la cual**	**lo cual**
plural	**los cuales**	**las cuales**	

13. PRONOUNS

1. Subject pronouns

	singular	plural
1st person	**yo** (I)	**nosotros, nosotras** (we)
2nd person	**tú** (you)	**vosotros, vosotras** (you)
3rd person	**él** (he, it)	**ellos** (they)
	ella (she, it)	**ellas** (they)
	ello (it)	
	usted (you)	**ustedes** (you)

usted and **ustedes** are commonly abbreviated to **Vd.** and **Vds.** (or occasionally to **Ud.** and **Uds.**). They are followed by the *third* person forms of the verb. For the difference between **Vd.** and **tú**, see page 23. For the use of **ello** see pages 22-23.

2. Weak object pronouns
For the use of the weak object pronouns, see pages 25-26.

a) Direct object pronouns

		singular	plural
1st person		**me** (me)	**nos** (us)
2nd person		**te** (you)	**os** (you)
3rd person		**lo** (him, you)	**los** (them, you)
		la (her, it, you)	**las** (them, you)
		lo (it)	**los** (them)

b) Indirect object pronouns

	singular	plural
1st person	**me** (to me)	**nos** (to us)
2nd person	**te** (to you)	**os** (to you)
3rd person	**le** (to him/her/ it/you)	**les** (to them/you)

c) Reflexive pronouns (myself, etc.)

	singular	plural
1st person	**me**	**nos**
2nd person	**te**	**os**
3rd person	**se**	**se**

3. Strong object pronouns
For the use of the strong object pronouns, see page 26.

	singular	plural
1st person	**mí**	**nosotros, nosotras**
2nd person	**ti**	**vosotros, vosotras**
3rd person	**él, ella, ello Vd.**	**ellos, ellas Vds.**
(reflexive)	**sí**	**sí**

mí, **ti** and **sí** combine with **con** to give the following forms:

conmigo	with me
contigo	with you
consigo	with himself/ herself/yourself/ themselves/ yourselves

4. Position of the pronouns

The weak object pronouns normally come before the verb. In the compound tenses they are placed before the auxiliary verb:

él lo hizo	**yo lo he visto**
he did it	I saw him
nos hemos levantado	**Vd. se despierta**
we got up	you wake up

In the following three cases the pronouns come after the verb and are joined to it:

a) when the verb is in the infinitive:

quiero verla	**salió después de hacerlo**
I want to see her	he went out after doing it

However, if the infinitive immediately follows another verb, the pronoun may precede the first verb:

querían encontrarnos	they wanted to meet us
OR **nos querían encontrar**	

b) when the verb is in the present participle:

estoy pintándolo	**estaba cantándola**
I am painting it	he was singing it

Again, in the case of a progressive form of the verb, the pronoun may precede the first verb:

están llevándolo	they are carrying it
OR **lo están llevando**	

c) when giving a positive command:

¡déjalo!	**¡date prisa!**
leave it!	hurry up!
¡quédese aquí!	**¡espéreme!**
stay here!	wait for me!

However, the pronoun precedes the verb in a negative command:

¡no lo hagas!	**¡no te muevas!**
don't do it!	don't move!

5. Changes in accentuation and spelling

a) Accents

Note that when more than one pronoun is added to an infinitive, a present participle or an imperative, a written accent is usually required on

the original verb to indicate spoken stress if this has moved to the third to the last syllable (see page 64):

¿quieres pasarme el vino?	**¿quieres pasármelo?**
will you pass me the wine?	will you pass me it?
está explicándome la lección	**está explicándomela**
he is explaining the lesson to me	he is explaining it to me
dame el libro	**dámelo**
give me the book	give me it
ponga el libro en la mesa	**póngalo en la mesa**
put the book on the table	put it on the table
dígame	
hello (on the phone)	

b) Changes in spelling

When **-se** is joined to the verb, any final **s** of the verb ending is dropped:

vendámoselo
let's sell it to him

The final **s** of the first person plural is dropped before the reflexive pronoun **nos**:

sentémonos
let's sit down

The **d** of the second person plural imperative is dropped before the reflexive pronoun **os**:

sentaos, por favor
have a seat, please

With third conjugation verbs, an accent is then required on the **i**:

vestíos
get dressed

The only exception is the verb **ir**, where the **d** of the imperative is in fact retained:

idos
go away

6. Order of pronouns

When two or more pronouns are being used together they come in the following order:

a) The reflexive **se** must always come first:

se me ha ocurrido	**se le olvidó**	**rápida** quick **rápidamente** quickly	
it occurred to me	he forgot		

b) When a direct and an indirect object pronoun are both being used, the indirect comes first:

me lo dio   **nos la mostraron**
he gave me it   they showed it to us

c) If there are both a third person direct object pronoun (**lo, la, le, los, las, les**) and a third person indirect object pronoun (**le, les**), the indirect **le** and **les** are both replaced by **se** before the direct object pronoun:

se la vendieron   **se los mandó (a**
(a ella)   **Vd.)**
they sold it to her   he sent them to you

The addition of **a él, a ella, a Vd.** or **a Vds.** and the like can clarify to whom the **se** refers.

d) In those cases where the direct object pronouns **me, te, nos** or **os** are used with another indirect object pronoun, the direct object pronoun stands before the verb, and the indirect pronoun is replaced by **a** + the corresponding strong pronoun after the verb:

me mandaron a ti
they sent me to you

nos acercamos a ellos
we approached them

---

14. ADVERBS

Adverbs are used with verbs, adjectives and other adverbs. When used with a verb, they describe:

how an action is done	adverbs of manner
when an action is done	adverbs of time
where an action is done	adverbs of place
to what *degree* an action is done	adverbs of degree

1. Adverbs of manner

a) Most of these adverbs can be formed by adding **-mente** to the feminine singular form of the adjective:

lenta	slow	**lentamente**	slowly
extensa	wide	**extensamente**	widely

Accents appearing on the adjective are retained on the adverb:

lógica	logical	**lógicamente**	logically

b) When two or more adverbs are used to describe the same verb, only the last one takes **-mente**, but the initial ones retain the feminine form of the adjective:

caminaron nerviosa y rápidamente
they walked anxiously and fast

c) The following adverbs of manner do not have a form in **-mente**:

bien	well	**mal**	badly
adrede	on purpose	**así**	in this way
despacio	slowly	**deprisa**	quickly

caminaban despacio por el calor que hacía
they walked slowly because of the heat

tú has trabajado bien, Juanito
you've done a good job, Juanito

2. Adverbs of time

Most of these adverbs are not formed from adjectives. The commonest are:

ahora	now
anoche	last night
anteanoche	the night before last
anteayer/antes de ayer	the day before yesterday
antes	before
ayer	yesterday
después	after
entonces	then
hoy	today
luego	presently
mañana	tomorrow
nunca	never
pasado mañana	the day after tomorrow
primero	firstly
pronto	soon
prontísimo	very soon
siempre	always
tarde	late
tardísimo	very late
temprano	early
tempranísimo	very early
todavía	still/yet
ya	already/now/presently

Some common adverbial phrases of time:

a continuación	next
acto seguido	immediately after
algunas veces	sometimes

a menudo	often
a veces	sometimes
dentro de poco	soon
de vez en cuando	from time to time
en breve	soon
muchas veces	often
nunca más	never again
otra vez	again
pocas veces	rarely
rara vez	seldom
repetidas veces	again and again
una y otra vez	again and again

quiero empezar ahora, no espero hasta mañana
I want to start now, I'm not waiting until tomorrow

siempre va en tren hasta el centro, luego coge el autobús
she always takes the train downtown and then catches a bus

quedamos en vernos pasado mañana, no mañana
we agreed to meet the day after tomorrow, not tomorrow

Points to note

a) As well as meaning 'already,' **ya** is used in everyday speech to mean 'right away':

¡ya voy!
I'm coming right away!

There are times when **ya** has no clear translation into English as it is often used as a filler:

ya me lo decía yo
I thought so

In the negative **ya no** means 'no longer':

siempre iba a ver a su tía el sábado, pero ya no va
he always used to visit his aunt on Saturdays, but he no longer does

⚠ It should not be confused with *todavía no*, which means 'not yet':

todavía no han llegado
they haven't arrived yet

b) **luego** can also mean 'therefore':

pienso luego existo
I think therefore I am

c) **recientemente** is shortened to **recién** before past

participles. **recién** is invariable and does not change its form whatever the gender or number of the past participle:

una niña recién nacida
a newborn baby girl

los recién casados
the newlyweds

3. **Adverbs of place**
The commonest of these are:

abajo	down/below
ahí/allí	there
allá	over there
aquí/acá	here
arriba	up/above
cerca	near
debajo	below/beneath
delante	forward/in front
dentro	inside
detrás	behind/back
donde	where
encima	over/above/on
enfrente	opposite
fuera	outside
lejos	far

Some adverbial phrases:

en alguna parte	somewhere
en otra parte	somewhere else
en/por todas partes	everywhere

la aldea donde nací
the village where I was born

¿dónde está Juan? – está dentro
where's Juan? – he's inside

¿hay alguna tienda por aquí cerca?
is there a shop around here?

se me cayeron encima
they fell on me

Points to note

a) **aquí**, **allí** and **allá** express the same relationships as the demonstrative adjectives **este**, **ese** and **aquel** (see page 11):

aquí/acá	means 'here, near me'
allí/ahí	means 'there, near you'
allá	means 'there, far from both of us'

b) The forms **arriba**, **abajo**, **adelante** and **atrás** can be used immediately after a noun in adverbial phrases such as:

caminábamos calle abajo
we walked down the street

aquello sucedió años atrás
that event took place years later

adentro and **a través** also appear in set phrases:

mar adentro
(out) at sea

campo a través
cross country

4. **Adverbs of degree**
The commonest of these are:

algo	somewhat
apenas	hardly
bastante	fairly/rather/ enough
casi	almost
como	about
cuánto	how/how much
demasiado	too much
más	more
menos	less
mitad/medio	half
mucho	very much
muy	very much
nada	not at all
poco	little
qué	how
suficientemente	enough
tan	so/as
tanto	so much/as much
todo	entirely
un poco	a little

la casa es muy vieja pero es bastante grande
the house is very old but it is fairly big

me gusta mucho el pescado, pero no me gustan nada los calamares
I like fish very much, but I don't like squid at all

tiene casi tres años, todavía es demasiado pequeño para ir solo
he is almost three, still too little to go by himself

hoy se siente un poco mejor
he is feeling a little better today

Points to note

a) This use of **qué** is restricted to exclamations:

¡qué inteligente eres!
how clever you are!

b) **muy** is used with adjectives and adjectival phrases, and adverbs:

estoy muy cansado
I am very tired

me parece muy temprano
it seems very early to me

In a few exceptional cases, it can be used with a noun:

es muy amigo mío
he's a very good friend of mine

When used as an adverb, **mucho** goes with verbs, comparative adverbs, and comparative adjectives:

me gustó mucho
I liked it a lot
está mucho mejor
he's much better

c) When used as an adverb, **medio** never changes its form:

María estaba medio dormida
María was half asleep

d) Note the common construction with **suficientemente**:

no es lo suficientemente inteligente como para entender esto
he isn't clever enough to understand this

15. THE VERB

DIFFERENT CATEGORIES OF VERBS: THE CONJUGATIONS

There are three conjugations of verbs in Spanish. The infinitive of a verb indicates which conjugation it belongs to.

all verbs ending in **-ar** belong to the first conjugation

all verbs ending in **-er** belong to the second conjugation

all verbs ending in **-ir** belong to the third conjugation

Some verbs are irregular, and others have minor deviations from the rules. These will be treated separately.

Spanish has many 'radical changing verbs' where changes are made to the stressed vowel of the stem, although the endings of these verbs are perfectly normal. These verbs will be dealt with in a separate section.

All newly coined verbs automatically go into the first conjugation and adopt its endings and forms, e.g., **informatizar** (to computerize).

A. THE TENSES OF THE INDICATIVE – THE SIMPLE TENSES

Tenses may be either simple – consisting of one word only – or compound, where an auxiliary verb is used with a participle of the main verb.

1. THE PRESENT TENSE

The stem for the present tense of the verb is found by removing the endings **-ar**, **-er** or **-ir** from the infinitive. The present tense itself is then formed by adding the following endings to the stem:

1st conjugation	-o, -as, -a, -amos, -áis, -an
2nd conjugation	-o, -es, -e, -emos, -éis, -en
3rd conjugation	-o, -es, -e, -imos, -ís, -en

cant-ar	beb-er	recib-ir
canto	bebo	recibo
cantas	bebes	recibes
canta	bebe	recibe
cantamos	bebemos	recibimos
cantáis	bebéis	recibís
cantan	beben	reciben

a) Irregularities in the present tense

For **ser** and **estar**, and the irregular verbs **haber**, **dar**, **ir**, **tener** and **venir** see the Spanish Verbs section on pages 99-115. For radical changing verbs see pages 87-90.

b) First conjugation verbs ending in **-iar** and **-uar**

Most of these verbs have the spoken accent and also a written accent on the final **i** and **u** of the stem in all but the first and second persons plural:

enviar	continuar
envío	continúo
envías	continúas
envía	continúa
enviamos	continuamos
enviáis	continuáis
envían	continúan

The commonest exceptions are the verbs **cambiar** (to change) and **averiguar** (to ascertain).

c) Second conjugation verbs ending in **-ecer**

The ending of the first person singular is **-ezco**.

All other forms are regular:

| parecer | parezco, pareces ... |
| crecer | crezco, creces ... |

d) Third conjugation verbs ending in **-uir**, and the verb **oír**

These verbs add **y** to the stem *unless* the stem is followed by a stressed **i**, i.e., in all but the first and second persons plural. Note that **oír** also has an irregular first person singular (see below):

construir	oír
construyo	oigo
construyes	oyes
construye	oye
construimos	oímos
construís	oís
construyen	oyen

e) Third conjugation verbs ending in **-ucir**

The ending of the first person singular is **-uzco**. All other forms are regular:

| conducir | conduzco, conduces ... |
| producir | produzco, produces ... |

f) Second and third conjugation verbs whose stem ends in **c** or **g**

Such verbs change the **c** to **z** and the **g** to **j** in the first person singular. All other forms are regular:

vencer	venzo, vences ...
esparcir	esparzo, esparces ...
escoger	escojo, escoges ...
rugir	rujo, ruges ...

g) Third conjugation verbs whose stem ends in **qu** or **gu**

Such verbs change the **qu** to **c** and the **gu** to **g** in the first person singular. All other forms are regular:

| delinquir | delinco, delinques ... |
| distinguir | distingo, distingues ... |

h) Third conjugation verbs whose infinitive ends in **-güir**

These verbs drop the dieresis except in the first and second persons plural:

| argüir | arguyo, arguyes, arguye, argüimos, argüís, arguyen |

i) Verbs with an irregular first person singular

The following verbs have largely unpredictable irregularities in the first person singular:

The verb

caber	to fit	quepo
caer	to fall	caigo
conocer	to know	conozco
decir	to say	digo
estar	to be	estoy
hacer	to do/make	hago
ir	to go	voy
oír	to hear	oigo
saber	to know	sé
salir	to go out/leave	salgo
ser	to be	soy
tener	to have	tengo
traer	to bring	traigo
valer	to be worth	valgo
venir	to come	vengo

Any compound form of these verbs shares the same irregularities.

contradecir	to contradict	contradigo
obtener	to obtain	obtengo

Note that **satisfacer** behaves in the same way as **hacer**:

satisfacer	to satisfy	satisfago

2. THE FUTURE TENSE
The future tense of all conjugations is formed by adding the following endings to the infinitive of the verb, irrespective of its conjugation:

-é, -ás, -á, -emos, -éis, -án

cantaré	beberé	recibiré
cantarás	beberás	recibirás
cantará	beberá	recibirá
cantaremos	beberemos	recibiremos
cantaréis	beberéis	recibiréis
cantarán	beberán	recibirán

Irregularities in the future tense

A number of verbs add these endings to an irregular stem:

caber	to fit	cabré
decir	to say	diré
haber	to have	habré
hacer	to do/make	haré
poder	to be able	podré
poner	to put	pondré
querer	to want	querré
saber	to know	sabré
salir	to go out/leave	saldré
tener	to have	tendré
valer	to be worth	valdré
venir	to come	vendré

Again, any compounds share the same irregularities:

deshacer	to undo	desharé
convenir	to agree/suit	convendré

3. THE IMPERFECT TENSE

The imperfect tense is formed by adding the following endings to the stem of the infinitive:

1st conjugation	-aba, -abas, -aba, -ábamos, -abais, -aban
2nd &3rd conjugations	-ía, -ías, -ía, -íamos, -íais, -ían

cantaba	bebía	recibía
cantabas	bebías	recibías
cantaba	bebía	recibía
cantábamos	bebíamos	recibíamos
cantabais	bebías	recibíais
cantaban	bebían	recibían

Irregularities in the imperfect tense

There are only three irregular imperfects in Spanish:

ser	ir	ver
era	iba	veía
eras	ibas	veías
era	iba	veía
éramos	íbamos	veíamos
erais	ibais	veíais
eran	iban	veían

4. THE PRETERITE TENSE
The preterite is formed by adding the following endings to the stem of the infinitive:

1st conjugation	-é, -aste, -ó, -amos, -asteis, -aron
2nd &3rd conjugations	-í, -iste, -ió, -imos, -isteis, -ieron

canté	bebí	recibí
cantaste	bebiste	recibiste
cantó	bebió	recibió
cantamos	bebimos	recibimos
cantasteis	bebisteis	recibisteis
cantaron	bebieron	recibieron

Irregularities in the preterite tense

a) The so-called **pretérito grave**
This group comprises a sizable number of mostly second and third conjugation verbs that all add the following endings to irregular stems:

-e, -iste, -o, -imos, -isteis, -ieron

Note in particular that the first and third person singular endings are not stressed (the term **grave** in **pretérito grave** means 'stressed on the *second to the last* syllable').

If the stem itself ends in **j**, the third person plural ending is shortened to **-eron**.

andar	anduve, anduviste, anduvo, anduvimos, anduvisteis, anduvieron
caber	cupe, cupiste, cupo, cupimos, cupisteis, cupieron
decir	dije, dijiste, dijo, dijimos, dijisteis, dijeron
estar	estuve, estuviste, estuvo, estuvimos, estuvisteis, estuvieron
haber	hube, hubiste, hubo, hubimos, hubisteis, hubieron
hacer	hice, hiciste, hizo, hicimos, hicisteis, hicieron
poder	pude, pudiste, pudo, pudimos, pudisteis, pudieron
poner	puse, pusiste, puso, pusimos, pusisteis, pusieron
querer	quise, quisiste, quiso, quisimos, quisisteis, quisieron
tener	tuve, tuviste, tuvo, tuvimos, tuvisteis, tuvieron
traer	traje, trajiste, trajo, trajimos, trajisteis, trajeron
saber	supe, supiste, supo, supimos, supisteis, supieron
venir	vine, viniste, vino, vinimos, vinisteis, vinieron

All compounds of these verbs share the same irregularities:

contraer	contraje ...
componer	compuse ...

This group also comprises all verbs ending in -**ucir**, with the exception of **lucir**, which is regular. Their stem for the preterite ends in **uj**:

producir	produje, produjiste, produjo, produjimos, produjisteis, produjeron

b) Other verbs

The following verbs are also irregular:

dar	di, diste, dio, dimos, disteis, dieron

ir	fui, fuiste, fue, fuimos, fuisteis, fueron
ser	fui, fuiste, fue, fuimos, fuisteis, fueron
ver	vi, viste, vio, vimos, visteis, vieron

As can be seen, the preterites of **ir** and **ser** are identical. However, the context always indicates clearly which one is involved.

c) Spelling changes

First conjugation verbs whose stems end in **c** or **g** change these to **qu** and **gu** in the first person singular of the preterite. All other forms are regular:

explicar	expliqué, explicaste ...
llegar	llegué, llegaste ...

Verbs ending in **-aer**, **-eer**, **-oer** and **-uir**

In these verbs, the **i** of the third person singular and plural ending changes to **y**. All other forms are regular:

caer	cayó	cayeron
construir	construyó	construyeron
leer	leyó	leyeron
roer	royó	royeron

oír also belongs to this group:

oír	oyó	oyeron

Third conjugation verbs ending in -**güir** drop the dieresis in the third persons singular and plural:

arguir	argüí, argüiste, arguyó, argüimos, argüisteis, arguyeron

Second and third conjugation verbs whose stems end in **ñ** drop the **i** from the third person singular and plural endings:

gruñir	gruñó	gruñeron
tañer	tañó	tañeron

5. THE CONDITIONAL

The conditional is formed for all conjugations by adding the following endings to the infinitive of the verb:

-ía, -ías, -ía, -íamos, -íais, -ían

cantaría	bebería	recibiría
cantarías	beberías	recibirías

cantaría	bebería	recibiría
cantaríamos	beberíamos	recibiríamos
cantaríais	beberíais	recibiríais
cantarían	beberían	recibirían

Irregularities in the conditional

Any verb with an irregular stem in the future uses the same stem for the formation of the conditional (see page 82):

hacer	haría
venir	vendría

and so on.

B. COMPOUND TENSES

Compound tenses are formed by using an auxiliary verb with either the present or the past participle.

1. THE PRESENT PARTICIPLE

a) The regular forms

The present participle is formed by adding the following endings to the stem of the infinitive:

1st conjugation	-ando
2nd & 3rd conjugations	-iendo

b) Irregular present participles

Verbs ending in **-aer**, **-eer**, **-oer** and **-uir**, and the verb **oír**.

In these verbs the **i** of the ending is changed to **y**:

caer	cayendo
construir	construyendo
creer	creyendo
oír	oyendo
roer	royendo

Verbs ending in **-güir** drop the dieresis in the present participle:

argüir	arguyendo

Second and third conjugation verbs whose stems end in **ñ** drop the **i** from the ending:

gruñir	gruñendo
tañer	tañendo

Third conjugation radical changing verbs of groups 3, 4 and 5 also have irregular present participles (see pages 89-90):

dormir	durmiendo
pedir	pidiendo
sentir	sintiendo

2. THE PAST PARTICIPLE

a) The regular forms

To form the past participle of a regular verb remove the infinitive ending and add:

1st conjugation	-ado	cantado
2nd & 3rd conjugations	-ido	bebido, recibido

b) Irregular past participles

Some verbs have irregular past participles. The most common are:

abrir	to open	**abierto**	opened
cubrir	to cover	**cubierto**	covered
decir	to say	**dicho**	said
escribir	to write	**escrito**	written
hacer	to make/to do	**hecho**	made/done
morir	to die	**muerto**	dead
poner	to put	**puesto**	put
resolver	to solve	**resuelto**	solved
ver	to see	**visto**	seen
volver	to return	**vuelto**	returned

Compounds of these verbs have the same irregularities in their past participles, eg:

descubrir	to discover	**descubierto**	discovered
describir	to describe	**descrito**	described

The verb **satisfacer** behaves in the same way as **hacer**:

satisfacer	to satisfy	**satisfecho**	satisfied

3. THE PROGRESSIVE FORMS OF THE TENSES

A progressive form of any tense can be formed by using **estar** (or one of an associated group of verbs) with the present participle. For the full conjugation of **estar**, see pages 106-7:

estamos trabajando
we are working

yo estaba estudiando cuando Juan entró
I was studying when Juan came in

For a full discussion of the progressive tenses, see pages 31-32.

4. THE PERFECT TENSE

The compound past tenses are formed with the appropriate tense of the verb **haber** together with the past participle of the verb. For the full conjugation of **haber**, see pages 100-1.

The perfect tense is formed by using the present tense of **haber** with the past participle of the main verb:

he cantado	he bebido	he recibido
has cantado	has bebido	has recibido
ha cantado	ha bebido	ha recibido
hemos cantado	hemos bebido	hemos recibido
habéis cantado	habéis bebido	habéis recibido
han cantado	han bebido	han recibido

5. THE PLUPERFECT TENSE

The pluperfect tense is formed by using the imperfect of **haber** with the past participle of the main verb:

había cantado	había bebido	había recibido
habías cantado	habías bebido	habías recibido
había cantado	había bebido	había recibido
habíamos cantado	habíamos bebido	habíamos recibido
habíais cantado	habíais bebido	habíais recibido
habían cantado	habían bebido	habían recibido

6. THE FUTURE PERFECT TENSE

The future perfect tense is formed by using the future of **haber** with the past participle of the main verb:

habré cantado	habré bebido	habré recibido
habrás cantado	habrás bebido	habrás recibido
habrá cantado	habrá bebido	habrá recibido
habremos cantado	habremos bebido	habremos recibido
habréis cantado	habréis bebido	habréis recibido
habrán cantado	habrán bebido	habrán recibido

7. THE PAST ANTERIOR TENSE

The past anterior tense is formed by using the preterite of **haber** with the past participle of the main verb:

hube cantado	hube bebido	hube recibido
hubiste cantado	hubiste bebido	hubiste recibido
hubo cantado	hubo bebido	hubo recibido
hubimos cantado	hubimos bebido	hubimos recibido
hubisteis cantado	hubisteis bebido	hubisteis recibido

hubieron cantado	hubieron bebido	hubieron recibido

8. THE CONDITIONAL PERFECT

The conditional perfect is formed by using the conditional of **haber** with the past participle of the main verb:

habría cantado	habría bebido	habría recibido
habrías cantado	habrías bebido	habrías recibido
habría cantado	habría bebido	habría recibido
habríamos cantado	habríamos bebido	habríamos recibido
habríais cantado	habríais bebido	habríais recibido
habrían cantado	habrían bebido	habrían recibido

C. THE TENSES OF THE SUBJUNCTIVE MOOD

1. THE PRESENT SUBJUNCTIVE

With the exception of a few irregular verbs (**estar, ser, ir, dar**) the stem for the present subjunctive of a verb is found by removing the **-o** from the ending of the first person singular of the present tense. The subjunctive is then formed by adding the following endings to that stem.

1st conjugation	-e, -es, -e, -emos, -éis, -en
2nd & 3rd conjugations	-a, -as, -a, -amos, -áis, -an

cant-o	beb-o	recib-o
cante	beba	reciba
cantes	bebas	recibas
cante	beba	reciba
cantemos	bebamos	recibamos
cantéis	bebáis	recibáis
canten	beban	reciban

Irregularities in the present subjunctive:
(For radical changing verbs see pages 87-90.)

a) Verbs in *-iar* and *-uar*

Such verbs have the same pattern of accentuation in the subjunctive as they do in the indicative, i.e., a written accent on the **i** or **u** of the stem in all but the first and second persons plural:

enviar	envíe, envíes, envíe, enviemos, enviéis, envíen
continuar	continúe, continúes, continúe, continuemos, continuéis, continúen

The verb

b) Irregular stems

Since the stem of the subjunctive is based on the first person singular of the indicative, any irregularities there appear throughout the present subjunctive, for example:

infinitive	1st pers pres	subjunctive
decir	digo	diga, digas, diga, digamos, digáis, digan
coger	cojo	coja, cojas, coja, cojamos, cojáis, cojan
parecer	parezco	parezca, parezcas, parezca, parezcamos, parezcáis, parezcan
poner	pongo	ponga, pongas, ponga, pongamos, pongáis, pongan
vencer	venzo	venza, venzas, venza, venzamos, venzáis, venzan

c) Spelling changes

buscar	busque, busques, busque, busquemos, busquéis, busquen
llegar	llegue, llegues, llegue, lleguemos, lleguéis, lleguen

First conjugation verbs ending in **-guar** require a dieresis throughout the present subjunctive.

averiguar	averigüe, averigües, averigüe, averigüemos, averigüéis, averigüen

2. THE IMPERFECT SUBJUNCTIVE

The stem for the imperfect subjunctive is found by removing the ending **-ron** from the third person plural of the preterite of the verb. The imperfect subjunctive has two possible forms, formed by adding the following endings to that stem:

1st conjugation	-ara, -aras, -ara, -áramos, -arais, -aran
	-ase, -ases, -ase, -ásemos, -aseis, -asen
2nd & 3rd conjugations	-iera, -ieras, -iera, -iéramos, -ierais, -ieran
	-iese, -ieses, -iese, -iésemos, -ieseis, -iesen

cantara/cantase	bebiera/bebiese
cantaras/cantases	bebieras/bebieses
cantara/cantase	bebiera/bebiese
cantáramos/cantásemos	bebiéramos/bebiésemos
cantarais/cantaseis	bebierais/bebieseis
cantaran/cantasen	bebieran/bebiesen

recibiera/recibiese
recibieras/recibieses
recibiera/recibiese
recibiéramos/recibiésemos
recibierais/recibieseis
recibieran/recibiesen

In general, the first form of each pair is more common in spoken Spanish.

Verbs whose preterites are irregular display the same irregularity in the imperfect subjunctive:

infinitive	preterite	imperfect subjunctive
decir	dijeron	dijera/dijese
tener	tuvieron	tuviera/tuviese
venir	vinieron	viniera/viniese

Compounds of these verbs display the same irregularities:

convenir	conviniera/conviniese
obtener	obtuviera/obtuviese

3. THE PERFECT SUBJUNCTIVE

The perfect tense of the subjunctive is formed by using the present subjunctive of **haber** with the past participle of the main verb:

haya cantado	haya bebido	haya recibido
hayas cantado	hayas bebido	hayas recibido
haya cantado	haya bebido	haya recibido
hayamos cantado	hayamos bebido	hayamos recibido
hayáis cantado	hayáis bebido	hayáis recibido
hayan cantado	hayan bebido	hayan recibido

4. THE PLUPERFECT SUBJUNCTIVE

The pluperfect of the subjunctive is formed by using the imperfect subjunctive of **haber** with the past participle of the main verb:

hubiera cantado	hubiera bebido	hubiera recibido
hubieras cantado	hubieras bebido	hubieras recibido
hubiera cantado	hubiera bebido	hubiera recibido
hubiéramos cantado	hubiéramos bebido	hubiéramos recibido
hubierais cantado	hubierais bebido	hubierais recibido
hubieran cantado	hubieran bebido	hubieran recibido
hubiese cantado	hubiese bebido	hubiese recibido
hubieses cantado	hubieses bebido	hubieses recibido
hubiese cantado	hubiese bebido	hubiese recibido
hubiésemos cantado	hubiésemos bebido	hubiésemos recibido
hubieseis cantado	hubieseis bebido	hubieseis recibido
hubiesen cantado	hubiesen bebido	hubiesen recibido

5. THE IMPERATIVE

A separate imperative form exists only for the **tú** and **vosotros** forms of the verb, and is used *only* in positive commands (the form **vos** also has a corresponding imperative, but it is less used and will not be included here). The imperative is formed as follows:

tú	Remove the **s** from the second person singular of the present indicative of the verb. This applies for all conjugations.
vosotros	First and second conjugations: remove the **áis/éis** from the second person plural of the present indicative of the verb and replace it with **ad/ed**.
	Third conjugation: remove the **ís** from the second person plural of the present indicative of the verb and replace it with **id**.

hablar	habla	hablad
comer	come	comed
escribir	escribe	escribid

Note that, since the **tú** form is based on the second person singular of the verb, any radical changes will also be present in the singular, but not in the plural (**vosotros**) form of the imperative:

cerrar	cierra	cerrad
torcer	tuerce	torced
pedir	pide	pedid

There are a number of irregular imperatives in the **tú** form:

decir	di	decid
hacer	haz	haced
ir	ve	id
poner	pon	poned
salir	sal	salid
ser	sé	sed (also irregular in plural)
tener	ten	tened
valer	val	valed
venir	ven	venid

ustedes	The formal imperative with **usted**, and the plural **ustedes** (which is used instead of **vosotros** in Latin America, even in informal contexts) are formed regularly from the third person of the present subjunctive. The subjunctive is also used for the **nosotros** (i.e., 'let's') imperative. See page 29 for details.

D. THE RADICAL CHANGING VERBS

Some verbs have spelling changes to their stem when the latter is stressed. The endings are not affected unless the verb itself is irregular.

1. **e** changes to **ie** (first and second conjugations only)

The commonest of these verbs are:

acertar	to guess correctly
alentar	to encourage
apretar	to squeeze
ascender	to go up, come to
atender	to attend to
aterrar	to terrify
atravesar	to cross
calentar	to heat
cerrar	to close
comenzar	to begin
concertar	to agree to
condescender	to condescend
confesar	to confess
defender	to defend
desalentar	to discourage
desatender	to disregard
descender	to come down
desconcertar	to disconcert
despertar	to waken
desplegar	to unfold
discernir	to discern
empezar	to begin

The verb

encender	to light, switch on
encerrar	to enclose
encomendar	to entrust
entender	to understand
enterrar	to bury
extender	to extend
fregar	to scrub
gobernar	to govern
helar	to freeze
manifestar	to show
merendar	to have tea
negar	to deny
nevar	to snow
pensar	to think
perder	to lose
quebrar	to break
recomendar	to recommend
regar	to irrigate
reventar	to burst
sembrar	to sow
sentarse	to sit
sosegar	to calm
temblar	to tremble
* tener	to have
tender	to stretch out
tentar	to attempt
tropezar	to stumble
verter	to pour

The change occurs in the present indicative and the present subjunctive only, wherever the **e** is stressed, i.e., the three persons of the singular and the third person plural:

PRESENT INDICATIVE	PRESENT SUBJUNCTIVE
atravieso	atraviese
atraviesas	atravieses
atraviesa	atraviese
atravesamos	atravesemos
atravesáis	atraveséis
atraviesan	atraviesen

Note that if the stressed **e** is the first letter in the word, it changes to **ye** and not **ie**:

errar to wander   **yerro, yerras, yerra, erramos, erráis, yerran**

* **tener** has an irregular first person singular: **tengo**

The subjunctive of **tener** is based on this irregular first person singular:

tenga, tengas, tenga, tengamos, tengáis, tengan

2. o changes to **ue** (first and second conjugations only)

The commonest verbs in this group are:

absolver	to absolve
acordarse	to remember
acostarse	to go to bed
almorzar	to lunch
apostar	to bet
aprobar	to approve
avergonzarse	to be ashamed
cocer	to cook
colarse	to slip in
colgar	to hang
comprobar	to check
concordar	to agree
conmover	to move
consolar	to console
contar	to count, tell
costar	to cost
demostrar	to demonstrate
desaprobar	to disapprove
descolgar	to take down
descontar	to deduct
desenvolverse	to get by
despoblar	to depopulate
devolver	to give back
disolver	to dissolve
doler	to hurt
encontrar	to meet, find
envolver	to wrap
esforzarse	to endeavor
forzar	to force
holgar	to be idle
* jugar	to play
llover	to rain
moler	to grind
morder	to bite
mostrar	to show
mover	to move
** oler	to smell
probar	to try, taste
promover	to promote
recordar	to remember
renovar	to renew
resolver	to resolve
resollar	to wheeze
resonar	to resound
revolver	to stir
rodar	to prowl
rogar	to beg
soldar	to weld
soler	to be in the habit of
soltar	to let go
sonar	to ring, sound
soñar	to dream
torcer	to twist, turn
tostar	to toast
trocar	to exchange
tronar	to thunder
volar	to fly

volcar	to tip over
volver	to return

The pattern of change is identical to that of group 1:

PRESENT INDICATIVE	PRESENT SUBJUNCTIVE
vuelvo	**vuelva**
vuelves	**vuelvas**
vuelve	**vuelva**
volvemos	**volvamos**
volvéis	**volváis**
vuelven	**vuelvan**

* **jugar**: the **u** changes to **ue** when stressed: **juego**.

** **oler**: **h** is added to all forms where the change occurs: **huele**, etc.

3. e changes to **ie** and **i** (third conjugation only)

The commonest verbs in this group are:

adherir	to join
*adquirir	to acquire
advertir	to notice
arrepentirse	to repent
asentir	to agree
conferir	to confer
consentir	to agree
convertir	to convert
digerir	to digest
divertir	to amuse
** erguir	to raise
herir	to wound
hervir	to boil
inferir	to infer
* inquirir	to inquire into
invertir	to invest
mentir	to tell lies
pervertir	to pervert
preferir	to prefer
presentir	to foresee
proferir	to utter
referir	to refer
requerir	to require
resentirse	to resent
sentir	to feel
subvertir	to subvert
sugerir	to suggest
transferir	to transfer
*** venir	to come

When stressed, **e** changes to **ie** in the present indicative, present subjunctive, and imperative singular.

Also, unstressed **e** changes to **i** in:
- the 1st and 2nd persons plural of the present subjunctive
- the present participle

- the 3rd persons singular and plural of the preterite
- all of the imperfect subjunctive:

PRESENT	PRETERITE
siento	**sentí**
sientes	**sentiste**
siente	**sintió**
sentimos	**sentimos**
sentís	**sentisteis**
sienten	**sintieron**

PRESENT SUBJUNCTIVE	IMPERFECT SUBJUNCTIVE
sienta	**sintiera/ sintiese**
sientas	**sintieras/ sintieses**
sienta	**sintiera/ sintiese**
sintamos	**sintiéramos/ sintiésemos**
sintáis	**sintierais/ sintieseis**
sientan	**sintieran/ sintiesen**

IMPERATIVE	PRESENT PARTICIPLE
siente	**sintiendo**

* In the case of **adquirir** and **inquirir** it is the **i** of the stem that changes to **ie**.

** When stressed, the **e** of **erguir** changes to **ye** and not **ie**:

> **yergo, yergues, yergue, erguimos, erguís, yerguen**

*** **venir** has an irregular first person singular: **vengo**

The subjunctive of **venir** is based on this irregular first person singular:

> **venga, vengas, venga, vengamos, vengáis, vengan**

4. e changes to **i** (third conjugation only)
The commonest verbs in this group are:

colegir	to collect
competir	to compete
concebir	to design
conseguir	to manage
corregir	to correct
derretir	to melt
despedir	to sack
elegir	to elect
expedir	to dispatch

The verb

gemir	to groan
impedir	to prevent
invertir	to invest
medir	to measure
pedir	to ask for
perseguir	to persecute
proseguir	to continue
regir	to govern
rendir	to yield
repetir	to repeat
seguir	to follow
servir	to serve
vestir	to dress

When stressed, **e** changes to **i** in the present indicative, present subjunctive, and imperative singular.

Also, unstressed **e** changes to **i** in:
– the 1st and 2nd persons plural of the present subjunctive
– the present participle
– the 3rd persons singular and plural of the preterite
– all of the imperfect subjunctive:

PRESENT	PRETERITE
pido	pedí
pides	pediste
pide	pidió
pedimos	pedimos
pedís	pedisteis
piden	pidieron

PRESENT SUBJUNCTIVE	IMPERFECT SUBJUNCTIVE
pida	pidiera/pidiese
pidas	pidieras/ pidieses
pida	pidiera/pidiese
pidamos	pidiéramos/ pidiésemos
pidáis	pidierais/ pidieseis
pidan	pidieran/ pidiesen

IMPERATIVE	PRESENT PARTICIPLE
pide	pidiendo

Verbs in this group that end in **-eír** and **-eñir** make an additional change: if the ending begins with an unstressed **i**, this **i** is dropped if it comes immediately after the **ñ** or **i** of the stem. This occurs only in the present participle, the third persons singular and plural of the preterite, and in the imperfect subjunctive.

The commonest verbs in this group are:

ceñir	to fit closely	**desteñir**	to fade
freír	to fry	**reír**	to laugh
reñir	to scold	**sonreír**	to smile
teñir	to dye		

reír	ceñir
riendo	ciñendo
rió	ciñó
rieron	ciñeron

5. **o** changes to **ue** and **u** (third conjugation only)
The pattern of changes is identical to that of group 3 above. In other words:

When stressed, **o** changes to **ue** in the present indicative, present subjunctive, and imperative singular.

Unstressed **o** changes to **u** in:
– the 1st and 2nd persons plural of the present subjunctive
– the present participle
– the 3rd persons singular and plural of the preterite
– all of the imperfect subjunctive.

The commonest verbs in this group are

dormir	to sleep	**morir**	to die

and their compounds.

PRESENT	PRETERITE
duermo	dormí
duermes	dormiste
duerme	durmió
dormimos	dormimos
dormís	dormisteis
duermen	durmieron

PRESENT SUBJUNCTIVE	IMPERFECT SUBJUNCTIVE
duerma	durmiera/ durmiese
duermas	durmieras/ durmieses
duerma	durmiera/ durmiese
durmamos	durmiéramos/ durmiésemos
durmáis	durmierais/ durmieseis
duerman	durmieran/ durmiesen

IMPERATIVE	PRESENT PARTICIPLE
duerme	durmiendo

16. VERBS AND THEIR OBJECTS

A number of verbs in Spanish cannot be used without a specific preposition if their object is expressed.

1. Verbs taking *a* before an object

acercarse a	to approach
aproximarse a	to approach
asistir a	to attend
asomarse a	to lean out of
dar a	to look out onto
faltar a	not to fulfill/keep
jugar a	to play (*game*)
llegar a	to arrive at/in
oler a	to smell of
oponerse a	to oppose
parecerse a	to resemble
renunciar a	to give up
resistir a	to resist
saber a	to taste of
sobrevivir a	to outlive

faltó a su promesa
he didn't keep his promise

la ventana de mi cuarto daba a un matadero
the window of my room looked out onto a slaughterhouse

la pequeña se parece a su padre
the little girl looks like her father

2. Verbs taking *de* before an object

abusar de	to misuse
acordarse de	to remember
apoderarse de	to seize
asombrarse de	to wonder at
burlarse de	to make fun of
cambiar de	to change
carecer de	to lack
compadecerse de	to take pity on
depender de	to depend on
desconfiar de	to distrust
despedirse de	to say goodbye to
disfrutar de	to enjoy
dudar de	to doubt
enamorarse de	to fall in love with
enterarse de	to find out
gozar de	to enjoy
maravillarse de	to wonder at
mudar de	to change
ocuparse de	to attend to
olvidarse de	to forget
pasar de	to exceed
prescindir de	to do without

reírse de	to make fun of
responder de	to answer for
saber de	to know of
salir de	to leave (*a place*)
servirse de	to use
sospechar de	to distrust
tirar de	to pull
tratarse de	to be about
variar de	to change
vengarse de	to take revenge for/on

se trata de mi primo
it's about my cousin

afortunadamente gozamos de buena salud
fortunately we enjoy good health

dudar can be used with the direct object **lo** in cases like:

lo dudo	**no lo dude Vd.**
I doubt it	don't you doubt it

Otherwise it takes **de**:

dudo de su testimonio
I doubt his testimony

3. Verbs taking *con* before an object

acabar con	to put an end to
casarse con	to marry
contar con	to rely on
dar con	to come across
divertirse con	to be amused by
encontrarse con	to meet
hablar con	to talk to
portarse con	to behave toward
soñar con	to dream about

¡acabemos con estas mentiras!
let's put an end to these lies!

cuento contigo
I'm counting on you

4. Verbs taking *en* before an object

consentir en	to agree to
consistir en	to consist of
convenir en	to agree to
entrar en	to enter/go into
fijarse en	to look at
ingresar en	to enter
penetrar en	to penetrate
* pensar en	to think about
reparar en	to notice

consintió en ello
he agreed to it

¡fíjate en aquel edificio!
just look at that building!

* do not confuse **pensar en** with **pensar de** which means 'to have an opinion of.'

pensaba en sus vacaciones en España
she was thinking about her holidays in Spain

¿qué piensas de esta idea?
what do you think of this idea?

5. **Verbs taking *por* before an object**

asomarse por	to lean out of
felicitar por	to congratulate on
interesarse por	to take an interest in
preguntar por	to ask about

el cura preguntó por mi tía, que está enferma
the priest asked about my aunt who is ill

6. **Verbs that take no preposition before the object in Spanish though they do in English**

agradecer	to be grateful for
aguantar	to put up with
aprobar	to approve of
aprovechar	to take advantage of
buscar	to look for
cuidar	to take care of
escuchar	to listen to
esperar	to wait for
lamentar	to be sorry about
mirar	to look at
pagar	to pay for
recordar	to remind of
regalar	to make a present of
rumiar	to ponder over
sentir	to be sorry about
soportar	to put up with

aprovecharon la ocasión para felicitar a Juan
they took advantage of the opportunity to congratulate Juan

le agradezco mucho el regalo
thank you very much for the gift

¿cuánto pagaste por la casa?
how much did you pay for the house?

17. VERBS FOLLOWED BY AN INFINITIVE

1. **Verbs followed immediately by the infinitive**
The direct infinitive is used after the following verbs, though they may also be followed by a clause with its verb in the subjunctive:

a) Verbs of making, advising, ordering, preventing and permitting

aconsejar	to advise to
amenazar	to threaten to
conceder	to concede to
dejar	to let/allow to
hacer	to make
impedir	to prevent from
mandar	to command/order to
ordenar	to command/order to
permitir	to permit/allow to
prohibir	to prohibit from/ forbid to

mis padres no me dejan poner la radio después de medianoche
my parents don't allow me to have the radio on after midnight

me mandó salir
he ordered me to leave

b) Verbs of the senses: **sentir, ver** and **oír**

oír	to hear
sentir	to feel
ver	to see

no te vi llegar
I didn't see you come in

lo oí roncar
I heard him snoring

c) Impersonal verbs, where the verb used in the infinitive is the subject of the impersonal verb

alegrarse	me alegra verte de nuevo
	I am happy to see you again
gustar	nos gusta mucho pasear en el campo
	we love walking in the country
hacer falta	te hace falta estudiar
	you need to study

olvidarse	se me olvidó ir al banco I forgot to go to the bank	debemos pagar la cuenta ahora we must pay the bill now
parecer	¿te parece bien salir ahora? do you think it's a good idea to leave now?	nuestro equipo consiguió ganar el partido our team managed to win the match
convenir	no me conviene partir mañana it doesn't suit me to leave tomorrow	el niño resultó ser el hijo del rey the boy turned out to be the king's son solemos merendar en el bosque los domingos we usually go for a picnic in the woods on Sundays

d) After the following verbs when the subject is the same as that of the infinitive

acordar	to agree to
ansiar	to long to
concertar	to agree to
confesar	to confess to
conseguir	to succeed in -ing, manage to
creer	to believe
deber	to have to
decidir	to decide to
decir	to say, tell
descuidar	to neglect to
desear	to wish/want to
esperar	to hope/expect to
evitar	to avoid -ing
figurarse	to suppose, imagine
fingir	to pretend to
imaginar	to imagine -ing
intentar	to try to
lograr	to succeed in -ing, to manage to
merecer	to merit -ing
necesitar	to need to
negar	to deny -ing
ofrecer	to offer to
olvidar	to forget to
osar	to dare to
parecer	to appear to
pedir	to ask to
pensar	to intend to
poder	to be able to
preferir	to prefer to
presumir	to presume to
pretender	to try/claim to
procurar	to endeavor to
prometer	to promise to
querer	to wish to
recordar	to remember to
resistir	to resist -ing
resolver	to resolve to
resultar	to turn out to (be)
saber	to know how to
sentir	to regret to/-ing
soler	to be accustomed to -ing
temer	to be afraid to

2. Verbs followed by a + infinitive

The verbs given below take the preposition **a** before a following infinitive. In most cases the idea of 'in order to' is involved.

a) Verbs of motion

acercarse a	to come forward to
acudir a	to come to
adelantar a	to overtake
andar a	to go to
apresurarse a	to hurry to
bajar a	to go down to
correr a	to run to
dirigirse a	to head for
entrar a	to go in to
enviar a	to send to
ir a	to go to
lanzarse a	to rush to
mandar a	to send to
precipitarse a	to rush to
salir a	to go out to
sentarse a	to sit down to
subir a	to go up to
traer a	to bring to
venir a	to come to
volver a	to do ... again

el mecánico se acercó a hablar conmigo
the mechanic came forward to speak to me

la chica se apresuró a hacer las camas
the maid rushed off to make the beds

el jefe mandó al chico a recoger las cartas
the boss sent the boy to pick up the mail

volveré a llamarte mañana
I'll call you again tomorrow

b) Verbs of forcing, compelling, inviting

animar a	to encourage to
conducir a	to lead to
convidar a	to invite to
empujar a	to push into
excitar a	to excite to

Verbs followed by an infinitive

exhortar a	to exhort to
forzar a	to force to
impulsar a	to impel to
incitar a	to incite to
inducir a	to induce to
invitar a	to invite to
llamar a	to call to
llevar a	to bring/lead to
obligar a	to oblige to
persuadir a	to persuade to

animaron a la niña a montar al caballo
they encouraged the little girl to get on the horse

el dueño forzó al camarero a limpiar los platos
the owner forced the waiter to clean the plates

me invitó a pasar el fin de semana
he invited me to spend the weekend

c) Verbs of beginning

comenzar a	to begin to
echarse a	to start -ing
empezar a	to begin to
ponerse a	to begin to, set about -ing
romper a	to break into, do suddenly

el bebé se echó a llorar
the baby burst into tears

todos los alumnos se pusieron a trabajar
all the pupils started to work

d) Verbs used reflexively to mean deciding or refusing

decidirse a	to decide to
negarse a	to refuse to
resolverse a	to resolve to

el niño se negó a comer
the little boy refused to eat

e) The following miscellaneous verbs

acostumbrarse a	to get used to -ing
aguardar a	to wait to
alcanzar a	to manage to
aprender a	to learn to
arriesgarse a	to risk -ing
aspirar a	to aspire to
atreverse a	to dare to
autorizar a	to authorize to
aventurarse a	to venture to
ayudar a	to help to
comprometerse a	to promise to
condenar a	to condemn to

contribuir a	to contribute to -ing
dedicarse a	to devote oneself to
detenerse a	to stop to
disponerse a	to get ready to
enseñar a	to teach to
entregarse a	to devote oneself to
exponerse a	to expose oneself to
habituarse a	to get used to -ing
limitarse a	to limit oneself to -ing
ofrecerse a	to offer oneself to
oponerse a	to object to -ing
prepararse a	to prepare to
pararse a	to stop to
quedarse a	to stay and
renunciar a	to give up -ing
resignarse a	to resign oneself to -ing
tender a	to tend to

los chicos no se arriesgaron a cruzar el río
the boys didn't dare cross the river

después del accidente, Juan se dedicó a cuidar de su mujer
after the accident, Juan devoted himself to taking care of his wife

se detuvo a hablar conmigo
he stopped to speak to me

3. **Verbs followed by *de* + infinitive**
In these cases **de** is required before a following infinitive:

a) Verbs of stopping or abandoning an action

abstenerse de	to abstain from -ing
acabar de	to finish -ing, have just
cansarse de	to become tired of -ing
cesar de	to cease -ing
dejar de	to stop -ing
desistir de	to desist from -ing
disuadir de	to dissuade from -ing
excusar de	to excuse from -ing
fatigarse de	to grow tired of -ing
guardarse de	to take care not to
hartarse de	to grow tired of -ing
librarse de	to escape from -ing
parar de	to stop -ing
saciarse de	to grow tired of -ing
terminar de	to finish -ing

When **dejar de** is used in the negative, it expresses the idea of 'not to fail to':

no dejes de devolverme los discos la semana que viene
make sure you give me back the records next week

b) Also the following verbs

acordarse de	to remember to
acusar de	to accuse of -ing
alegrarse de	to be glad to
arrepentirse de	to repent of -ing
avergonzarse de	to be ashamed of -ing
consolarse de	to console oneself for -ing
cuidar de	to be careful to
desconfiar de	to mistrust
desesperar de	to despair of -ing
dispensar de	to excuse from -ing
encargarse de	to undertake to, see to -ing
jactarse de	to boast of -ing
maravillarse de	to marvel at
olvidarse de	to forget to
no poder por menos de	not to be able to help -ing
tratar de	to try to
tratarse de	to be a question of

yo me encargo de hacer eso
I'll see to doing that

el joven se olvidó de acudir a la cita
the young man forgot to keep his appointment

se trata de trabajar más
it's a question of working more

no pude por menos de reírme
I couldn't help laughing

4. Verbs followed by *en* + infinitive

complacerse en	to take pleasure in -ing
consentir en	to consent to
consistir en	to consist in -ing
convenir en	to agree to
dudar en	to hesitate to
empeñarse en	to insist on -ing
entretenerse en	to amuse oneself in -ing
esforzarse en	to try hard to
hacer bien en	to do well/right to
hacer mal en	to do badly/wrong in
insistir en	to insist on -ing
interesarse en	to be interested in -ing
obstinarse en	to be determined to
pensar en	to think of -ing
persistir en	to persist in -ing

quedar en	to agree to
soñar en	to have in mind to
tardar en	to take (a long) time to
vacilar en	to hesitate to

la niña se esforzaba en montar en bicicleta
the little girl was trying hard to ride the bicycle

haces bien en ayudar a tu madre
you do well to help your mother

los amigos quedaron en verse a los ocho
the friends agreed to meet at eight o'clock

el tren tardó treinta minutos en llegar
the train took thirty minutes to come

5. Verbs followed by *con* + infinitive

amenazar con	to threaten to
contentarse con	to content oneself with -ing
soñar con	to dream of

el hombre de negocios soñaba con ir a Río de Janeiro
the businessman dreamed of going off to Rio

6. Verbs followed by *por* + infinitive

a) Verbs of beginning and ending, with the sense of English 'by'

acabar por	to end up by -ing
comenzar por	to begin by -ing
empezar por	to begin by -ing

acabó por comprarse el traje azul
she ended up buying the blue suit

b) Verbs of longing/trying to, etc.

esforzarse por	to make an effort to
luchar por	to struggle to
morirse por	to be dying to
rabiar por	to be dying to

la niña se moría por abrir los paquetes
the little girl was dying to open the packages

18. CONJUNCTIONS

1. Simple conjunctions

Simple conjunctions consist of one word only. The commonest are:

aunque	although
como	as (reason)

Conjunctions

conforme	as (in proportion as)		para que	in order that
conque	so, so then		por lo que	for which reason
cuando	when		por si	in case
e	and		puesto que	since
* mas	but		salvo que	except that
mientras	while		siempre que	whenever, so long as
ni	neither/nor		sino que	but
o	or		tan pronto como	as soon as
pero	but		ya que	since
porque	because			
pues	since, so			
que	that, for (because)			
según	according to			
si	if, whether			
sino	but			
siquiera	if only			
u	or			
y	and			

* **mas** is old-fashioned nowadays, the everyday word for 'but' being **pero**.

me fui al cine porque creía que ya no venías
I went to the theater because I thought you weren't coming

sabremos pronto si hemos ganado el premio
we'll soon know whether we've won the prize

se puso triste cuando se murió su perro
he became sad when his dog died

no grites tanto, que ya te oigo
don't shout so much, I can hear you

2. Compound conjunctions

These conjunctions consist of two or more words, the last one usually being **que**:

a condición de que	on condition that
a fin de que	so that
a medida que	as
a menos que	unless
a no ser que	unless
antes de que	before
a pesar de que	despite
así que	so (that)
con tal (de) que	provided that
de manera que	so (that)
de modo que	so (that)
desde que	since
después de que	after
en caso de que	in case
hasta que	until
luego que	as soon as
mientras	while
mientras que	whereas

vamos a preparar la comida por si vienen pronto
let's get the meal ready in case they come soon

los niños jugaban mientras su madre se ocupaba de la casa
the children played while their mother took care of the house

llevo el paraguas por si llueve
I'll take my umbrella in case it rains

⚠ Note that whereas *puesto que* and *ya que* refer to cause, *desde que* refers *only* to time in Spanish:

todo marcha bien desde que él llegó
everything has been fine since he arrived

puesto que las mercancías ya no están disponibles
since the merchandise is no longer available

3. Coordinating conjunctions

Coordinating conjunctions come in pairs and are used to link two closely associated ideas:

apenas ... (cuando)	hardly ... when
bien ... bien	either ... or
o ... o	either ... or
o bien ... o bien	either ... or
ni ... ni	neither ... nor
no sólo ... sino también	not only ... but also
que ... o que	whether ... or
ya ... ya	sometimes ... sometimes
tanto ... como	both ... and
no ... sino	not ... but
no ... pero sí	not ... but

ni los sindicatos ni los empresarios están contentos
neither the unions nor the employers are happy

tanto tú como yo
both you and I

19. NUMBERS

1. THE CARDINAL NUMBERS

0	cero	10	diez
1	uno, una	11	once
2	dos	12	doce
3	tres	13	trece
4	cuatro	14	catorce
5	cinco	15	quince
6	seis	16	dieciséis
7	siete	17	diecisiete
8	ocho	18	dieciocho
9	nueve	19	diecinueve
20	veinte	21	veintiuno
22	veintidós	23	veintitrés
24	veinticuatro	25	veinticinco
26	veintiséis	27	veintisiete
28	veintiocho	29	veintinueve
30	treinta	31	treinta y uno/una
40	cuarenta	42	cuarenta y dos
50	cincuenta	53	cincuenta y tres
60	sesenta	64	sesenta y cuatro
70	setenta	75	setenta y cinco
80	ochenta	86	ochenta y seis
90	noventa	97	noventa y siete
100	ciento	101	ciento uno/una
105	ciento cinco	115	ciento quince
120	ciento veinte	123	ciento veintitrés
150	ciento cincuenta	176	ciento setenta y seis
200	doscientos/as	202	doscientos dos
300	trescientos/as	317	trescientos diecisiete
400	cuatrocientos/as	428	cuatrocientos veintiocho
500	quinientos/as	539	quinientos treinta y nueve
600	seiscientos/as	645	seiscientos cuarenta y cinco
700	setecientos/as	754	setecientos cincuenta y cuatro
800	ochocientos/as	863	ochocientos sesenta y tres
900	novecientos/as	971	novecientos setenta y uno/una

1,000	mil	2,000	dos mil
3,000	tres mil	4,000	cuatro mil
5,000	cinco mil	6,000	seis mil
7,000	siete mil	8,000	ocho mil
9,000	nueve mil	10,000	diez mil

200,000	doscientos mil
300,000	trescientos mil
600,000	seiscientos mil
1,000,000	un millón
2,000,000	dos millones

a) Alternative forms
There are alternative forms for 16 to 19 written as three separate words:

diez y seis, diez y siete, etc.

b) Shortened forms of certain numbers

uno is shortened to **un** when followed by a noun or adjective + noun:

treinta y un meses
thirty-one months
doscientos un días
two hundred and one days

ciento is shortened to **cien** when followed by (1) a noun, (2) an adjective + noun, (3) the numeral **mil**:

cien panes
a hundred loaves
cien mil hojas
a hundred thousand leaves

cien millones de euros
a hundred million euros
cien buenos días
a hundred good days

c) Agreement
Cardinal numbers are invariable except for the plural hundreds and numbers ending in **-uno**:

doscientas personas
two hundred people
quinientas cincuenta libras
five hundred and fifty pounds

Days, months and seasons

veintiuna páginas
twenty-one pages
ciento una cosas
a hundred and one things

d) Accents
Written accents are necessary for some of the twenties:

22 **veintidós**   23 **veintitrés**   26 **veintiséis**

also: **veintiún años**   twenty-one years

e) Counting by hundreds stops at 900:

| 1966 | **mil novecientos sesenta y seis** nineteen hundred and sixty-six |
| 1200 euros | **mil doscientos euros** twelve hundred euros |

2. THE ORDINAL NUMBERS

primero	first	**sexto**	sixth
segundo	second	**séptimo**	seventh
tercero	third	**octavo**	eighth
cuarto	fourth	**noveno**	ninth
quinto	fifth	**décimo**	tenth

a) Ordinals are adjectives and as such agree with their noun:

la segunda esquina
the second corner
la séptima semana
the seventh week

b) **primero** and **tercero** are shortened to **primer** and **tercer** before a masculine singular noun:

el primer tren
the first train
el tercer coche
the third car

c) Ordinals are rarely used beyond the tenth, when cardinals are used instead:

el siglo once
the eleventh century
Luis XIV – Luis catorce
Louis XIV – Louis the fourteenth

20. DAYS, MONTHS AND SEASONS

The names of the days of the week, the months and the seasons are written with small letters in Spanish.

Days of the week

el lunes	Monday
el martes	Tuesday
el miércoles	Wednesday
el jueves	Thursday
el viernes	Friday
el sábado	Saturday
el domingo	Sunday

Months

enero	January
febrero	February
marzo	March
abril	April
mayo	May
junio	June
julio	July
agosto	August
se(p)tiembre	September
octubre	October
noviembre	November
diciembre	December

These are the seasons in the Northern hemisphere. Bear in mind that they are the opposite in the Southern Hemisphere.

Seasons

primavera	spring
verano	summer
otoño	autumn, fall
invierno	winter

Spanish Verbs

This guide to Spanish verbs opens with the three regular conjugations (verbs ending in "**-ar**", "**-er**" and "**-ir**"), followed by the two most common auxiliary verbs: **haber**, which is used to form the perfect tenses, and **ser**, which is used to form the passive. These five verbs are given in full.

These are followed by a list of Spanish irregular verbs, numbered 3–76. A number refers you to these tables after irregular verbs in the main part of the dictionary.

The first person of each tense is always shown, even if it is regular. Of the other forms, only those which are irregular are given. An *etc* after a form indicates that the other forms of that tense use the same irregular stem, e.g. the future of **decir** is **yo diré** *etc*, i.e.: **yo diré, tú dirás, él dirá, nosotros diremos, vosotros diréis, ellos dirán**.

When the first person of a tense is the only irregular form, then it is not followed by *etc*, e.g. the present indicative of **placer** is **yo plazco** (irregular), but the other forms (**tú places, él place, nosotros placemos, vosotros placéis, ellos placen**) are regular and are thus not shown.

For the imperative, only the **tú** form is shown. The vosotros form is derived from the infinitive by replacing the final "**-r**" with a "**-d**". The other forms of the imperative (**usted, nosotros, ustedes**) are the same as the present subjunctive.

In Latin America the **vosotros** forms are rarely used, and the **ustedes** forms are used instead, even in informal contexts. In the imperative, the plural form is therefore not the "**-d**" form but instead the same as the third person plural of the present subjunctive, e.g. the plural imperatives of **ser** and **decir** are **sean** and **digan**.

	INDICATIVE				CONDITIONAL
	Present	Imperfect	Preterite	Future	Present
Regular "-ar": amar					
	yo amo	yo amaba	yo amé	yo amaré	yo amaría
	tú amas	tú amabas	tú amaste	tú amarás	tú amarías
	él ama	él amaba	él amó	él amará	él amaría
	nosotros amamos	nosotros amábamos	nosotros amamos	nosotros amaremos	nosotros amaríamos
	vosotros amáis	vosotros amabais	vosotros amasteis	vosotros amaréis	vosotros amaríais
	ellos aman	ellos amaban	ellos amaron	ellos amarán	ellos amarían
Regular "-er": temer					
	yo temo	yo temía	yo temí	yo temeré	yo temería
	tú temes	tú temías	tú temiste	tú temerás	tú temerías
	él teme	él temía	él temió	él temerá	él temería
	nosotros tememos	nosotros temíamos	nosotros temimos	nosotros temeremos	nosotros temeríamos
	vosotros teméis	vosotros temíais	vosotros temisteis	vosotros temeréis	vosotros temeríais
	ellos temen	ellos temían	ellos temieron	ellos temerán	ellos temerían
Regular "-ir": partir					
	yo parto	yo partía	yo partí	yo partiré	yo partiría
	tú partes	tú partías	tú partiste	tú partirás	tú partirías
	él parte	él partía	él partió	él partirá	él partiría
	nosotros partimos	nosotros partíamos	nosotros partimos	nosotros partiremos	nosotros partiríamos
	vosotros partís	vosotros partíais	vosotros partisteis	vosotros partiréis	vosotros partiríais
	ellos parten	ellos partían	ellos partieron	ellos partirán	ellos partirían
[1] haber					
	yo he	yo había	yo hube	yo habré	yo habría
	tú has	tú habías	tú hubiste	tú habrás	tú habrías
	él ha	él había	él hubo	él habrá	él habría
	nosotros hemos	nosotros habíamos	nosotros hubimos	nosotros habremos	nosotros habríamos
	vosotros habéis	vosotros habíais	vosotros hubisteis	vosotros habréis	vosotros habríais
	ellos han	ellos habían	ellos hubieron	ellos habrán	ellos habrían
[2] ser					
	yo soy	yo era	yo fui	yo seré	yo sería
	tú eres	tú eras	tú fuiste	tú serás	tú serías
	él es	él era	él fue	él será	él sería
	nosotros somos	nosotros éramos	nosotros fuimos	nosotros seremos	nosotros seríamos
	vosotros sois	vosotros erais	vosotros fuisteis	vosotros seréis	vosotros seríais
	ellos son	ellos eran	ellos fueron	ellos serán	ellos serían
[3] acertar					
	yo acierto	yo acertaba	yo acerté	yo acertaré	yo acertaría
	tú aciertas				
	él acierta				
	ellos aciertan				
[4] actuar					
	yo actúo	yo actuaba	yo actué	yo actuaré	yo actuaría
	tú actúas				
	él actúa				
	ellos actúan				
[5] adquirir					
	yo adquiero	yo adquiría	yo adquirí	yo adquiriré	yo adquiriría
	tú adquieres				
	él adquiere				
	ellos adquieren				
[6] agorar					
	yo agüero	yo agoraba	yo agoré	yo agoraré	yo agoraría
	tú agüeras				
	él agüera				
	ellos agüeran				

SUBJUNCTIVE		IMPERATIVE	PARTICIPLE	
Present	Imperfect		Present	Past

yo ame	yo amara *or* amase		amando	amado
tú ames	tú amaras *or* amases	ama (tú)		
él ame	él amara *or* amase	ame (usted)		
nosotros amemos	nosotros amáramos *or* amásemos	amemos (nosotros)		
vosotros améis	vosotros amarais *or* amaseis	amad (vosotros)		
		amen (ustedes)		
ellos amen	ellos amaran *or* amasen			

yo tema	yo temiera *or* temiese		temiendo	temido
tú temas	tú temieras *or* temieses	teme (tú)		
él tema	él temiera *or* temiese	tema (usted)		
nosotros temamos	nosotros temiéramos *or* temiésemos	temamos (nosotros)		
vosotros temáis	vosotros temierais *or* temieseis	temed (vosotros)		
		teman (ustedes)		
ellos teman	ellos temieran *or* temiesen			

yo parta	yo partiera *or* partiese		partiendo	partido
tú partas	tú partieras *or* partieses	parte (tú)		
él parta	él partiera *or* partiese	parta (usted)		
nosotros partamos	nosotros partiéramos *or* partiésemos	partamos (nosotros)		
vosotros partáis	vosotros partierais *or* partieseis	partid (vosotros)		
		partan (ustedes)		
ellos partan	ellos partieran *or* partiesen			

yo haya	yo hubiera *or* hubiese		habiendo	habido
tú hayas	tú hubieras *or* hubieses	he (tú)		
él haya	él hubiera *or* hubiese	haya (usted)		
nosotros hayamos	nosotros hubiéramos *or* hubiésemos	hayamos (nosotros)		
vosotros hayáis	vosotros hubierais *or* hubieseis	habed (vosotros)		
		hayan (ustedes)		
ellos hayan	ellos hubieran *or* hubiesen			

yo sea	yo fuera *or* fuese		siendo	sido
tú seas	tú fueras *or* fueses	sé (tú)		
él sea	él fuera *or* fuese	sea (usted)		
nosotros seamos	nosotros fuéramos *or* fuésemos	seamos (nosotros)		
vosotros seáis	vosotros fuerais *or* fueseis	sed (vosotros)		
		sean (ustedes)		
ellos sean	ellos fueran *or* fuesen			

yo acierte	yo acertara *or* acertase	acierta (tú)	acertando	acertado
tú aciertes				
el acierte				
ellos acierten				

yo actúe	yo actuara *or* actuase	actúa (tú)	actuando	actuado
tú actúes				
él actúe				
ellos actúen				

yo adquiera	yo adquiriera *or* adquiriese	adquiere (tú)	adquiriendo	adquirido
tú adquieras				
él adquiera				
ellos adquieran				

yo agüere	yo agorara *or* agorase	agüera (tú)	agorando	agorado
tú agüeres				
él agüere				
ellos agüeren				

	INDICATIVE Present	Imperfect	Preterite	Future	CONDITIONAL Present
[7] andar	yo ando	yo andaba	yo anduve tú anduviste él anduvo nosotros anduvimos vosotros anduvisteis ellos anduvieron	yo andaré	yo andaría
[8] argüir	yo arguyo tú arguyes él arguye ellos arguyen	yo argüía	yo argüí él arguyó ellos arguyeron	yo argüiré	yo argüiría
[9] asir	yo asgo	yo asía	yo así	yo asiré	yo asiría
[10] avergonzar	yo avergüenzo tú avergüenzas él avergüenza ellos avergüenzan	yo avergonzaba	yo avergoncé	yo avergonzaré	yo avergonzaría
[11] averiguar	yo averiguo	yo averiguaba	yo averigüé	yo averiguaré	yo averiguaría
[12] caber	yo quepo	yo cabía	yo cupe tú cupiste él cupo nosotros cupimos vosotros cupisteis ellos cupieron	yo cabré *etc*	yo cabría *etc*
[13] caer	yo caigo	yo caía	yo caí tú caíste él cayó nosotros caímos vosotros caísteis ellos cayeron	yo caeré	yo caería
[14] cazar	yo cazo	yo cazaba	yo cacé	yo cazaré	yo cazaría
[15] cocer	yo cuezo tú cueces él cuece ellos cuecen	yo cocía	yo cocí	yo coceré	yo cocería
[16] colgar	yo cuelgo tú cuelgas él cuelga ellos cuelgan	yo colgaba	yo colgué	yo colgaré	yo colgaría
[17] comenzar	yo comienzo tú comienzas él comienza ellos comienzan	yo comenzaba	yo comencé	yo comenzaré	yo comenzaría

SUBJUNCTIVE		IMPERATIVE	PARTICIPLE	
Present	Imperfect		Present	Past
yo ande	yo anduviera *or* anduviese *etc*	anda (tú)	andando	andado
yo arguya *etc*	yo arguyera *or* arguyese *etc*	arguye (tú)	arguyendo	argüido
yo asga *etc*	yo asiera *or* asiese	ase (tú)	asiendo	asido
yo avergüence tú avergüences él avergüence nosotros avergoncemos vosotros avergoncéis ellos avergüencen	yo avergonzara *or* avergonzase	avergüenza (tú)	avergonzando	avergonzado
yo averigüe *etc*	yo averiguara *or* averiguase	averigua (tú)	averiguando	averiguado
yo quepa *etc*	yo cupiera *or* cupiese *etc*	cabe (tú)	cabiendo	cabido
yo caiga *etc*	yo cayera *or* cayese *etc*	cae (tú)	cayendo	caído
yo cace *etc*	yo cazara *or* cazase	caza (tú)	cazando	cazado
yo cueza tú cuezas él cueza nosotros cozamos vosotros cozáis ellos cuezan	yo cociera *or* cociese	cuece (tú)	cociendo	cocido
yo cuelgue tú cuelgues él cuelgue nosotros colguemos vosotros colguéis ellos cuelguen	yo colgara *or* colgase	cuelga (tú)	colgando	colgado
yo comience tú comiences él comience nosotros comencemos vosotros comencéis ellos comiencen	yo comenzara *or* comenzase	comienza (tú)	comenzando	comenzado

	INDICATIVE Present	Imperfect	Preterite	Future	CONDITIONAL Present
[18]	**conducir**				
	yo conduzco	yo conducía	yo conduje	yo conduciré	yo conduciría
			tú condujiste		
			él condujo		
			nosotros condujimos		
			vosotros condujisteis		
			ellos condujeron		
[19]	**conocer**				
	yo conozco	yo conocía	yo conocí	yo conoceré	yo conocería
[20]	**dar**				
	yo doy	yo daba	yo di	yo daré	yo daría
			tú diste		
			él dio		
			nosotros dimos		
			vosotros disteis		
			ellos dieron		
[21]	**decir**				
	yo digo	yo decía	yo dije	yo diré *etc*	yo diría *etc*
	tú dices		tú dijiste		
	él dice		él dijo		
			nosotros dijimos		
			vosotros dijisteis		
	ellos dicen		ellos dijeron		
[22]	**delinquir**				
	yo delinco	yo delinquía	yo delinquí	yo delinquiré	yo delinquiría
[23]	**desosar**				
	yo deshueso	yo desosaba	yo desosé	yo desosaré	yo desosaría
	tú deshuesas				
	él deshuesa				
	ellos deshuesan				
[24]	**dirigir**				
	yo dirijo	yo dirigía	yo dirigí	yo dirigiré	yo dirigiría
[25]	**discernir**				
	yo discierno	yo discernía	yo discerní	yo discerniré	yo discerniría
	tú disciernes				
	él discierne				
	ellos disciernen				
[26]	**distinguir**				
	yo distingo	yo distinguía	yo distinguí	yo distinguiré	yo distinguiría
[27]	**dormir**				
	yo duermo	yo dormía	yo dormí	yo dormiré	yo dormiría
	tú duermes				
	él duerme		él durmió		
	ellos duermen		ellos durmieron		
[28]	**erguir**				
	yo irgo *or* yergo	yo erguía	yo erguí	yo erguiré	yo erguiría
	tú irgues *or* yergues				
	él irgue *or* yergue		él irguió		
	nosotros erguimos				
	vosotros erguís				
	ellos irguen *or* yerguen		ellos irguieron		

SUBJUNCTIVE		IMPERATIVE	PARTICIPLE	
Present	Imperfect		Present	Past
yo conduzca *etc*	yo condujera *or* condujese *etc*	conduce (tú)	conduciendo	conducido
yo conozca *etc*	yo conociera *or* conociese	conoce (tú)	conociendo	conocido
yo dé él dé	yo diera *or* diese *etc*	da (tú)	dando	dado
yo diga *etc*	yo dijera *or* dijese *etc*	di (tú)	diciendo	dicho
yo delinca *etc*	yo delinquiera *or* delinquiese	delinque (tú)	delinquiendo	delinquido
yo deshuese tú deshueses él deshuese ellos deshuesen	yo desosara *or* desosase	deshuesa (tú)	desosando	desosado
yo dirija *etc*	yo dirigiera *or* dirigiese	dirige (tú)	dirigiendo	dirigido
yo discierna tú disciernas él discierna ellos disciernan	yo discerniera *or* discerniese	discierne (tú)	discerniendo	discernido
yo distinga *etc*	yo distinguiera *or* distinguiese	distingue (tú)	distinguiendo	distinguido
yo duerma tú duermas él duerma nosotros durmamos vosotros durmáis ellos duerman	yo durmiera *or* durmiese *etc*	duerme (tú)	durmiendo	dormido
yo irga *or* yerga tú irgas *or* yergas él irga *or* yerga nosotros irgamos vosotros irgáis ellos irgan *or* yergan	yo irguiera *or* irguiese	irgue *or* yergue (tú)	irguiendo	erguido

	INDICATIVE				CONDITIONAL
	Present	Imperfect	Preterite	Future	Present
[29]	**errar**				
	yo yerro	yo erraba	yo erré	yo erraré	yo erraría
	tú yerras				
	él yerra				
	ellos yerran				
[30]	**estar**				
	yo estoy	yo estaba	yo estuve	yo estaré	yo estaría
	tú estás		tú estuviste		
	él está		él estuvo		
			nosotros estuvimos		
			vosotros estuvisteis		
	ellos están		ellos estuvieron		
[31]	**forzar**				
	yo fuerzo	yo forzaba	yo forcé	yo forzaré	yo forzaría
	tú fuerzas				
	él fuerza				
	ellos fuerzan				
[32]	**guiar**				
	yo guío	yo guiaba	yo guié	yo guiaré	yo guiaría
	tú guías				
	él guía				
	ellos guían				
[33]	**hacer**				
	yo hago	yo hacía	yo hice	yo haré *etc*	yo haría *etc*
			tú hiciste		
			él hizo		
			nosotros hicimos		
			vosotros hicisteis		
			ellos hicieron		
[34]	**huir**				
	yo huyo	yo huía	yo huí	yo huiré	yo huiría
	tú huyes				
	él huye		él huyó		
	ellos huyen		ellos huyeron		
[35]	**ir**				
	yo voy	yo iba *etc*	yo fui	yo iré	yo iría
	tú vas		tú fuiste		
	él va		él fue		
	nosotros vamos		nosotros fuimos		
	vosotros vais		vosotros fuisteis		
	ellos van		ellos fueron		
[36]	**jugar**				
	yo juego	yo jugaba	yo jugué	yo jugaré	yo jugaría
	tú juegas				
	él juega				
	ellos juegan				
[37]	**leer**				
	yo leo	yo leía	yo leí	yo leeré	yo leería
			tú leíste		
			él leyó		
			nosotros leímos		
			vosotros leísteis		
			ellos leyeron		

| SUBJUNCTIVE | | IMPERATIVE | PARTICIPLE | |
Present	Imperfect		Present	Past
yo yerre tú yerres él yerre ellos yerren	yo errara *or* errase	yerra (tú)	errando	errado
yo esté tú estés él esté ellos estén	yo estuviera *or* estuviese *etc*	está (tú)	estando	estado
yo fuerce tú fuerces él fuerce nosotros forcemos vosotros forcéis ellos fuercen	yo forzara *or* forzase	fuerza (tú)	forzando	forzado
yo guíe tú guíes él guíe ellos guíen	yo guiara *or* guiase	guía (tú)	guiando	guiado
yo haga *etc*	yo hiciera *or* hiciese *etc*	haz (tú)	haciendo	hecho
yo huya *etc*	yo huyera *or* huyese *etc*	huye (tú)	huyendo	huido
yo vaya *etc*	yo fuera *or* fuese *etc*	ve (tú)	yendo	ido
yo juegue tú juegues él juegue nosotros juguemos vosotros juguéis ellos jueguen	yo jugara *or* jugase	juega (tú)	jugando	jugado
yo lea	yo leyera *or* leyese *etc*	lee (tú)	leyendo	leído

	INDICATIVE Present	Imperfect	Preterite	Future	CONDITIONAL Present
[38]	**llegar** yo llego	yo llegaba	yo llegué	yo llegaré	yo llegaría
[39]	**lucir** yo luzco	yo lucía	yo lucí	yo luciré	yo luciría
[40]	**mecer** yo mezo	yo mecía	yo mecí	yo meceré	yo mecería
[41]	**mover** yo muevo tú mueves él mueve ellos mueven	yo movía	yo moví	yo moveré	yo movería
[42]	**nacer** yo nazco	yo nacía	yo nací	yo naceré	yo nacería
[43]	**negar** yo niego tú niegas él niega ellos niegan	yo negaba	yo negué	yo negaré	yo negaría
[44]	**oír** yo oigo tú oyes él oye ellos oyen	yo oía	yo oí él oyó ellos oyeron	yo oiré	yo oiría
[45]	**oler** yo huelo tú hueles él huele ellos huelen	yo olía	yo olí	yo oleré	yo olería
[46]	**parecer** yo parezco	yo parecía	yo parecí	yo pareceré	yo parecería
[47]	**pedir** yo pido tú pides él pide ellos piden	yo pedía	yo pedí él pidió ellos pidieron	yo pediré	yo pediría
[48]	**placer** yo plazco	yo placía	yo plací él plació *or* plugo ellos placieron *or* pluguieron	yo placeré	yo placería
[49]	**poder** yo puedo tú puedes él puede ellos pueden	yo podía	yo pude tú pudiste él pudo nosotros pudimos vosotros pudisteis ellos pudieron	yo podré *etc*	yo podría *etc*

SUBJUNCTIVE		IMPERATIVE	PARTICIPLE	
Present	Imperfect		Present	Past
yo llegue *etc*	yo llegara *or* llegase	llega (tú)	llegando	llegado
yo luzca *etc*	yo luciera *or* luciese	luce (tú)	luciendo	lucido
yo meza *etc*	yo meciera *or* meciese	mece (tú)	meciendo	mecido
yo mueva tú muevas él mueva ellos muevan	yo moviera *or* moviese	mueve (tú)	moviendo	movido
yo nazca *etc*	yo naciera *or* naciese	nace (tú)	naciendo	nacido
yo niegue tú niegues él niegue nosotros neguemos vosotros neguéis ellos nieguen	yo negara *or* negase	niega (tú)	negando	negado
yo oiga *etc*	yo oyera *or* oyese *etc*	oye (tú)	oyendo	oído
yo huela tú huelas él huela ellos huelan	yo oliera *or* oliese	huele (tú)	oliendo	olido
yo parezca *etc*	yo pareciera *or* pareciese	parece (tú)	pareciendo	parecido
yo pida *etc*	yo pidiera *or* pidiese *etc*	pide (tú)	pidiendo	pedido
yo plazca tú plazcas él plazca *or* plegue nosotros plazcamos vosotros plazcáis ellos plazcan	yo placiera *or* placiese él placiera *or* placiese, pluguiera *or* pluguiese ellos placieran *or* placiesen	place (tú)	placiendo	placido
yo pueda tú puedas él pueda ellos puedan	yo pudiera *or* pudiese *etc*	puede (tú)	pudiendo	podido

	INDICATIVE Present	Imperfect	Preterite	Future	CONDITIONAL Present
[50]	**poner**				
	yo pongo	yo ponía	yo puse	yo pondré *etc*	yo pondría *etc*
			tú pusiste		
			él puso		
			nosotros pusimos		
			vosotros pusisteis		
			ellos pusieron		
[51]	**predecir**				
	yo predigo	yo predecía	yo predije	yo prediciré *or* prediré *etc*	yo prediciría *or* prediría *etc*
	tú predices		tú predijiste		
	él predice		él predijo		
			nosotros predijimos		
			vosotros predijisteis		
	ellos predicen		ellos predijeron		
[52]	**proteger**				
	yo protejo	yo protegía	yo protegí	yo protegeré	yo protegería
[53]	**querer**				
	yo quiero	yo quería	yo quise	yo querré *etc*	yo querría *etc*
	tú quieres		tú quisiste		
	él quiere		él quiso		
			nosotros quisimos		
			vosotros quisisteis		
	ellos quieren		ellos quisieron		
[54]	**raer**				
	yo rao, raigo *or* rayo	yo raía	yo raí	yo raeré	yo raería
			tú raíste		
			él rayó		
			nosotros raímos		
			vosotros raísteis		
			ellos rayeron		
[55]	**regir**				
	yo rijo	yo regía	yo regí	yo regiré	yo regiría
	tú riges				
	él rige		él rigió		
	ellos rigen		ellos rigieron		
[56]	**reír**				
	yo río	yo reía	yo reí	yo reiré	yo reiría
	tú ríes				
	él ríe		él rió		
	ellos ríen		ellos rieron		
[57]	**roer**				
	yo roo, roigo *or* royo	yo roía	yo roí	yo roeré	yo roería
			él royó		
			ellos royeron		
[58]	**saber**				
	yo sé	yo sabía	yo supe	yo sabré *etc*	yo sabría *etc*
			tú supiste		
			él supo		
			nosotros supimos		
			vosotros supisteis		
			ellos supieron		
[59]	**sacar**				
	yo saco	yo sacaba	yo saqué	yo sacaré	yo sacaría

| SUBJUNCTIVE | | IMPERATIVE | PARTICIPLE | |
Present	Imperfect		Present	Past
yo ponga *etc*	yo pusiera *or* pusiese *etc*	pon (tú)	poniendo	puesto
yo prediga *etc*	yo predijera *or* predijese *etc*	predice (tú)	prediciendo	predicho
yo proteja *etc*	yo protegiera *or* protegiese	protege (tú)	protegiendo	protegido
yo quiera tú quieras él quiera ellos quieran	yo quisiera *or* quisiese *etc*	quiere (tú)	queriendo	querido
yo raa, raiga *or* raya *etc*	yo rayera *or* rayese *etc*	rae (tú)	rayendo	raído
yo rija *etc*	yo rigiera *or* rigiese *etc*	rige (tú)	rigiendo	regido
yo ría tú rías él ría nosotros riamos vosotros riáis ellos rían	yo riera *or* riese *etc*	ríe (tú)	riendo	reído
yo roa, roiga *or* roya *etc*	yo royera *or* royese *etc*	roe (tú)	royendo	roído
yo sepa *etc*	yo supiera *or* supiese *etc*	sabe (tú)	sabiendo	sabido
yo saque *etc*	yo sacara *or* sacase	saca (tú)	sacando	sacado

	INDICATIVE Present	Imperfect	Preterite	Future	CONDITIONAL Present
[60]	**salir**				
	yo salgo	yo salía	yo salí	yo saldré *etc*	yo saldría *etc*
[61]	**seguir**				
	yo sigo	yo seguía	yo seguí	yo seguiré	yo seguiría
	tú sigues				
	él sigue		él siguió		
	ellos siguen		ellos siguieron		
[62]	**sentir**				
	yo siento	yo sentía	yo sentí	yo sentiré	yo sentiría
	tú sientes				
	él siente		él sintió		
	ellos sienten		ellos sintieron		
[63]	**sonar**				
	yo sueno	yo sonaba	yo soné	yo sonaré	yo sonaría
	tú suenas				
	él suena				
	ellos suenan				
[64]	**tender**				
	yo tiendo	yo tendía	yo tendí	yo tenderé	yo tendería
	tú tiendes				
	él tiende				
	ellos tienden				
[65]	**tener**				
	yo tengo	yo tenía	yo tuve	yo tendré *etc*	yo tendría *etc*
	tú tienes		tú tuviste		
	él tiene		él tuvo		
			nosotros tuvimos		
			vosotros tuvisteis		
	ellos tienen		ellos tuvieron		
[66]	**traer**				
	yo traigo	yo traía	yo traje	yo traeré	yo traería
			tú trajiste		
			él trajo		
			nosotros trajimos		
			vosotros trajisteis		
			ellos trajeron		
[67]	**trocar**				
	yo trueco	yo trocaba	yo troqué	yo trocaré	yo trocaría
	tú truecas				
	él trueca				
	ellos truecan				
[68]	**valer**				
	yo valgo	yo valía	yo valí	yo valdré *etc*	yo valdría *etc*
[69]	**venir**				
	yo vengo	yo venía	yo vine	yo vendré *etc*	yo vendría *etc*
	tú vienes		tú viniste		
	él viene		él vino		
			nosotros vinimos		
			vosotros vinisteis		
	ellos vienen		ellos vinieron		
[70]	**ver**				
	yo veo	yo veía *etc*	yo vi	yo veré	yo vería
[71]	**yacer**				
	yo yazco, yazgo	yo yacía	yo yací	yo yaceré	yo yacería
	or yago				
[72]	**zurcir**				
	yo zurzo	yo zurcía	yo zurcí	yo zurciré	yo zurciría

| SUBJUNCTIVE | | IMPERATIVE | PARTICIPLE | |
Present	Imperfect		Present	Past
yo salga *etc*	yo saliera *or* saliese	sal (tú)	saliendo	salido
yo siga *etc*	yo siguiera *or* siguiese *etc*	sigue (tú)	siguiendo	seguido
yo sienta tú sientas él sienta nosotros sintamos vosotros sintáis ellos sientan	yo sintiera *or* sintiese *etc*	siente (tú)	sintiendo	sentido
yo suene tú suenes él suene ellos suenen	yo sonara *or* sonase	suena (tú)	sonando	sonado
yo tienda tú tiendas él tienda ellos tiendan	yo tendiera *or* tendiese	tiende (tú)	tendiendo	tendido
yo tenga *etc*	yo tuviera *or* tuviese *etc*	ten (tú)	teniendo	tenido
yo traiga *etc*	yo trajera *or* trajese *etc*	trae (tú)	trayendo	traído
yo trueque tú trueques él trueque ellos truequen	yo trocara *or* trocase	troca (tú)	trocando	trocado
yo valga *etc*	yo valiera *or* valiese	vale (tú)	valiendo	valido
yo venga *etc*	yo viniera *or* viniese *etc*	ven (tú)	viniendo	venido
yo vea *etc*	yo viera *or* viese	ve (tú)	viendo	visto
yo yazca, yazga *or* yaga *etc*	yo yaciera *or* yaciese	yace *or* yaz (tú)	yaciendo	yacido
yo zurza *etc*	yo zurciera *or* zurciese	zurce (tú)	zurciendo	zurcido

	INDICATIVE Present	Imperfect	Preterite	Future	CONDITIONAL Present
[73]	**abolir**				
	(not used)	yo abolía	yo abolí	yo aboliré	yo aboliría
	(not used)				
	(not used)				
	nosotros abolimos				
	vosotros abolís				
	(not used)				
[74]	**balbucir**				
	(not used)	yo balbucía	yo balbucí	yo balbuciré	yo balbuciría
	tú balbuces				
[75]	**desolar**				
	(not used)	yo desolaba	yo desolé	yo desolaré	yo desolaría
	(not used)				
	(not used)				
	(not used)				
	nosotros desolamos				
	vosotros desoláis				
	(not used)				
[76]	**soler**				
	yo suelo	yo solía	yo solí	*(not used)*	*(not used)*
	tú sueles				
	él suele				
	ellos suelen				

SUBJUNCTIVE		IMPERATIVE	PARTICIPLE	
Present	Imperfect		Present	Past
(not used)	yo aboliera *o* aboliese	*(not used)* abolid (vosotros)	aboliendo	abolido
(not used)	yo balbuciera *o* balbuciese	balbuce (tú) balbucid (vosotros)	balbuciendo	balbucido
(not used)	yo desolara *o* desolase	*(not used)* desolad (vosotros)	desolando	desolado
yo suela tú suelas el suela ellos suelan	yo soliera *o* soliese	*(not used)*	soliendo	solido

Español-Inglés
Spanish-English

A

A (*pl* **Aes**) *nf*, **a** (*pl* **aes**) [a] *nf* (*la letra*) A, a

A (*abrev de* **amperio**) A

a *prep véase tamb* **al** (**a**) (*dirección*) to; **caer al suelo** to fall to o onto the floor; **girar a la izquierda** to turn (to the) left; **ir a Colombia** to go to Colombia; **ir al cine** to go to the cinema; **llegar a Valencia** to arrive in o reach Valencia; **subir a un tren/al autobús** to get on a train/the bus; **vete a casa** go home (**b**) (*distancia*) away; **a cien kilómetros de aquí** a hundred kilometres (away) from here (**c**) (*posición*) at, on; **a la derecha** on the right; **a la entrada** at the entrance; **a la orilla del mar** by the sea; **a lo lejos** in the distance; **a mi lado** at o by my side, next to me; **a orillas del Támesis** on the banks of the Thames; **al lado de** at the side of, next to, beside; **al norte/sur de** to the north/south of; **al sol** in the sun; **sentarse a la mesa** to sit down at (the) table (**d**) (*tiempo*) at; **a la mañana** (on) the following morning; **a la semana** per week; **a los sesenta años** at the age of sixty; **a los tres meses/la media hora** three months/half an hour later; **a los tres meses de su llegada** three months after his arrival; **a tiempo** in time; **al final** in the end; **al principio** at first (**e**) (*manera*) **a ciegas** blindly; **a la carta** à la carte; **a la francesa** (in the) French fashion o style; **a lápiz** in pencil; **a mano** by hand; **escrito a mano/máquina** handwritten/typewritten; **hecho a mano/máquina** hand-made/machine-made; **a oscuras** in the dark; **a pie** on foot; **a su manera** in his/her own way; **olla a presión** pressure cooker (**f**) (*cantidad*) **a cientos** in hundreds, by the hundred; (*medida*) **a noventa kilómetros por hora** at ninety kilometres an hour; (*precio*) **¿a cuánto están las cerezas?** — three euros a kilo; **ganar cuatro a dos** to win four two (**g**) (*complemento directo*) **vi a tu madre/al rey** I saw your mother/the king; **saludé a tu tía** I said hello to your aunt (**h**) (*complemento indirecto*) (*destinatario*) to; **díselo a Javier** tell Javier; **te lo di a ti** I gave it to you; (*procedencia*) from; **se lo compré al representante** I bought it from the sales representative (**i**) (*finalidad*) **fueron a ayudarle** they went to help him; **vino a vernos** he came to see us; *Fam* **ir a por vino** to go and get some wine (**j**) (*verbo + a + infin*) to; **aprender a nadar** to learn (how) to swim; **negarse a salir** to refuse to come out (**k**) (*nombre + a + infin*) **sueldo a convenir** salary to be agreed; **total a pagar** total amount payable (**l**) (*condicional*) **a decir verdad** to tell (you) the truth; **a no ser por ...** if it were not for ... (**m**) (*desafío*) **¿a que no lo haces?** I bet you don't do it! (**n**) (*exclamaciones imperativas*) **¡a comer!** lunch/dinner etc. is ready!; **¡a dormir!** bedtime!; **a ver** let's see; **¡a ver!, ¿qué pasa aquí?** all right, what's going on here?

AA 1 *nmpl* (*abrev de* **Alcohólicos Anónimos**) AA

2 *nfpl* (*abrev de* **Aerolíneas Argentinas**) = Argentinian state airline

abacería *nf* grocery store, *Br* grocer's (shop)

abacero, -a *nm,f* grocer

ábaco *nm* abacus

abad *nm Rel* abbot

abadejo *nm* (*pez*) pollack

abadesa *nf Rel* abbess

abadía *nf Rel* (**a**) (*edificio*) abbey (**b**) (*dignidad*) abbacy

abajeño, -a *Am* **1** *adj* lowland, coastal

2 *nm,f* lowlander, coastal dweller

abajo 1 *adv* (**a**) (*posición*) below, down; (*en una casa*) downstairs; **ahí a.** down there; **aquí a.** down here; **a. del todo** right at the bottom; **el piso de a.** (*apartamento*) the flat downstairs; (*planta*) the floor below; **¿la de arriba o la de a.?** the top one or the bottom one?; **la parte de a.** the bottom (part); **más a.** further down (**b**) (*dirección*) down, downward; **calle a.** down the street; **cuesta a.** downhill; **echar algo a.** to knock sth down; **hacia a.** down, downwards; **ven aquí a.** come down here; (*en una casa*) come downstairs; **venirse a.** (*caer*) to fall down; *Fig* (*proyecto*) to fall through

2 *interj* **¡a. la censura!** down with censorship!

abalanzarse [14] *vpr* to rush forward, spring forward; **a. hacia** to rush towards; **a. sobre** to rush at, pounce on

abalear *vt Andes CAm Ven* to shoot o fire at

abalorio *nm* (**a**) (*cuenta de vidrio*) glass bead (**b**) (*adorno de poco valor*) trinket

abanderado, -a 1 *pp de* **abanderar**

2 *nm,f* (**a**) (*portaestandarte*) standard bearer (**b**) *Fig* leader, champion

abanderar *vt Náut* to register

abandonado, -a 1 *pp de* **abandonar**

2 *adj* (**a**) (*lugar*) abandoned, deserted; **sentirse a.** to feel abandoned (**b**) (*descuidado*) neglected; **el jardín está a.** the garden hasn't been looked after (**c**) (*desaseado*) untidy, unkempt

abandonar 1 *vt* (**a**) (*lugar*) to leave, quit; (*persona*) to abandon; (*actividad*) to give up, withdraw from; (*traicionar*) to desert; **a. el barco** to abandon ship; **a. la carrera** to drop out; **me ha abandonado la suerte** luck has forsaken me (**b**) (*renunciar*) to relinquish, renounce (**c**) (*descuidar*) to neglect; **abandonó sus obligaciones** he neglected his duties (**d**) *Dep* to withdraw from

2 abandonarse *vpr* (**a**) (*ceder*) to give way, give in; **a. a la bebida** to overindulge in drinking (**b**) (*descuidarse*) to neglect one's appearance, let oneself go

abandono *nm* (**a**) (*acción*) abandoning, desertion ❑ *Jur* **a. de hogar** desertion (*of family, spouse*) (**b**) (*actividad, idea*) giving up (**c**) (*descuido*) neglect, lack of care; **estado de a.**

abandoned state (**d**) *(dejadez)* apathy, carelessness, laziness (**e**) *Dep* withdrawal; **ganar por a.** to win by default (**f**) *Náut* abandonment

abanicar [59] **1** *vt* to fan
2 abanicarse *vpr* to fan oneself

abanico *nm* (**a**) *(para abanicarse)* fan; **en (forma de) a.** fan-shaped (**b**) *(gama)* range; **un amplio a. de posibilidades** a wide range of possibilities

abaniqueo *nm* fanning

abarajar *vt RP Fam* to catch in flight

abaratamiento *nm* reduction in price

abaratar 1 *vt* to cut o reduce the price of
2 abaratarse *vpr (artículos)* to become cheaper, come down in price; *(precios)* to come down

abarca *nf (prenda)* sandal

abarcar [59] *vt* (**a**) *(con los brazos)* to get one's arms round (**b**) *(englobar)* to cover, embrace; **el libro abarca varios temas** the book covers several topics; *Prov* **quien mucho abarca poco aprieta** do not bite off more than you can chew (**c**) *(ver)* to be able to see, have a view of; **desde aquí se abarca todo el valle** you can see the whole valley from here; **hasta donde abarca la vista** as far as the eye can see

abaritonado, -a *adj Mús* baritone

abarquillar 1 *vt (madera)* to warp
2 abarquillarse *vpr* to warp

abarrancarse *vpr Fig* to get bogged down, get stuck (**en** in)

abarrotado, -a 1 *pp de* **abarrotar**
2 *adj* packed (**de** with), crammed (**de** with); **a. de gente** (jam-)packed, very crowded

abarrotar *vt* (**a**) *(llenar)* to pack, cram, fill up (**de** with); **el público abarrotaba la sala** the room was packed (with people) (**b**) *CAm Méx (acaparar)* to buy up

abarrotería *nf CAm Méx* grocery store, *Br* grocer's shop

abarrotero, -a *nm,f CAm Méx* grocer

abarrotes *nmpl Andes CAm Méx* groceries

abastecedor, -a 1 *adj* supplying, providing
2 *nm,f* supplier, purveyor

abastecer [46] **1** *vt* to supply, provide
2 abastecerse *vpr* to stock up (**de** o **con** with), lay in supplies (**de** o **con** of); **a. de víveres** to get in supplies

abastecimiento *nm (acción)* supplying; **a. de agua** water supply

abasto *nm* (**a**) *(provisión)* supply; *Fam* **es que no doy a.** I just can't cope, I can't keep up (**b**) **abastos** *(víveres)* provisions, supplies; **mercado de a.** wholesale food market

abate *nm Rel* father, abbé

abatible *adj* folding, collapsible; **asiento a.** folding seat

abatido, -a 1 *pp de* **abatir**
2 *adj* (**a**) *(deprimido)* depressed, downhearted (**b**) *(caído)* fallen, drooping (**c**) *(despreciable)* despicable, low

abatimiento *nm* depression, dejection

abatir 1 *vt* (**a**) *(derribar)* to knock down, pull down; *(árbol)* to cut down (**b**) *(matar)* to kill; *(herir)* to wound; *(a tiros)* to shoot down (**c**) *(desanimar)* to depress, dishearten (**d**) *Fml (bajar)* to lower, take down
2 abatirse *vpr* (**a**) *(ave, avión)* to swoop (**sobre** down on), dive (**sobre** down on); *Fig* **la desgracia se abatió sobre la familia** misfortune fell upon the family (**b**) *(desanimarse)* to lose heart, become depressed

abdicación *nf* abdication

abdicar [59] *vt & vi* to abdicate; **abdicó (la corona) en su hijo** she abdicated (from the throne) in favour of her son; *Fig* **a. de una ideología** to give up an ideology

abdomen *nm Anat* abdomen

abdominal 1 *adj Anat* abdominal
2 abdominales *nmpl (ejercicios)* sit-ups

abecé *nm* (**a**) *(alfabeto)* ABC, alphabet (**b**) *Fig (principio)* basics *pl*, rudiments *pl*

abecedario *nm* (**a**) *(alfabeto)* alphabet (**b**) *(libro)* spelling book

abedul *nm Bot* birch ❑ **a. pubescente** downy birch

abeja *nf* (**a**) *Ent* bee ❑ **a. reina** queen bee (**b**) *Fig (persona)* busy bee

abejón *nm Ent* (**a**) *(zángano)* drone (**b**) *(abejorro)* bumblebee

abejorro *nm* (**a**) *Ent (abeja)* bumblebee; *(coleóptero)* cockchafer (**b**) *Fig (persona)* bore, nuisance

aberración *nf* aberration

aberrante *adj* aberrant

abertura *nf* (**a**) *(hueco)* opening, gap; *(grieta)* crack, slit (**b**) *Geog (entre montañas)* pass; *(ensenada)* cove, creek (**c**) *Cost* vent (**d**) *Fot* aperture

abetal *nm* fir plantation

abeto *nm* fir (tree) ❑ **a. rojo** spruce

abicharse *vpr CSur (fruta)* to go maggoty

abiertamente *adv* openly

abierto, -a 1 *pp de* **abrir**
2 *adj* (**a**) *(puerta, boca, tienda)* open; **campo a.** open country; **a. de par en par** wide open; **una ciudad abierta al mar** a seaward-looking city; **guerra abierta** open war; **herida abierta** open o gaping wound; *Fig* **con los brazos abiertos** with open arms; *Fig* **quedarse con la boca abierta** to be left speechless; *Fig* **ver el cielo a.** to see a way out (**b**) *(grifo)* (turned) on; **dejar el grifo a.** to leave the tap running (**c**) *Fig (persona) (sincero)* open, frank; *(comprensivo)* open-minded (**d**) *Ling (vocal)* open

abigarrado, -a *adj* (**a**) *(multicolor)* gaudy (**b**) *(mezclado)* jumbled, mixed up; **un discurso a.** a disjointed speech

abisal *adj* **fosa a.** ocean trough; **pez a.** abyssal fish

Abisinia *n Antes* Abyssinia

abisinio, -a *adj & nm,f Antes* Abyssinian

abismal *adj* abysmal; *Fig* **una diferencia a.** a world of a difference

abismar 1 *vt Fml* **a. a algn en la desesperación** to plunge sb into despair
2 abismarse *vpr* (**a**) **a. en** *(lectura)* to become engrossed in (**b**) *Andes RP (asombrarse)* to be amazed (**c**) *Carib (arruinarse)* to be ruined

abismo *nm* abyss; *Fig* **al borde del a.** on the brink of ruin; *Fig* **entre ellos media un a.** they are worlds apart

Abiyán *n* Abidjan

abjuración *nf* abjuration

abjurar *vt & vi* to abjure, forswear

ablación *nf Med (de tejido, órgano)* excision, surgical removal ❑ **a. del clítoris** female circumcision

ablandamiento *nm* softening

ablandar 1 *vt* (**a**) *(gen)* to soften (**b**) *Fig (calmar)* to soothe, appease; *Fig* **a. a algn** to soften sb up
2 ablandarse *vpr* (**a**) *(gen)* to soften (up), go soft o softer (**b**) *Fig (persona)* to mellow

ablativo *nm Ling* ablative (case)

ablución *nf Rel* ablution

abnegación *nf* abnegation, self denial

abnegado, -a *adj* selfless, self-sacrificing

abnegarse [43] *vpr* to deny oneself

abobado, -a *adj* (**a**) *(tonto)* stupid, silly (**b**) *(pasmado)* bewildered

abocado, -a *adj* (**a**) estar *o* verse **a. a** to be heading for; **está a. al fracaso** it is doomed to failure (**b**) *(vino)* medium dry

abocar [59] *vi* **a. en un fracaso** to end in failure

abochornado, -a 1 *pp de* **abochornar**
2 *adj Fig* ashamed, embarrassed

abochornar 1 *vt* (**a**) *(avergonzar)* to shame, embarrass (**b**) *(acalorar)* to make flushed
2 abochornarse *vpr* (**a**) *(avergonzarse)* to become embarrassed; *(estar avergonzado)* to be ashamed (**b**) *(planta)* to wilt

abofetear *vt* to slap

abogacía *nf* legal profession

abogado, -a *nm,f* (**a**) *Jur* lawyer, *US* attorney; **ejercer de a.** to practise law, be a lawyer ◻ **a. de oficio** legal aid lawyer; **a. defensor** counsel for the defense; **a. del diablo** devil's advocate; **a. del Estado** public prosecutor, *US* attorney general; **a. laboralista** labour lawyer (**b**) *Fig (defensor)* advocate, champion

abogar [38] *vt* to plead; **a. a favor de** to plead for, defend; **a. por algo** to advocate *o* champion sth

abolengo *nm* ancestry, lineage; **de rancio a.** of ancient lineage

abolición *nf* abolition

abolicionismo *nm* abolitionism

abolicionista *adj & nmf* abolitionist

abolir [73] *vt* to abolish

abollado, -a 1 *pp de* **abollar**
2 *adj* dented

abolladura *nf (hundimiento)* dent; *(bollo)* bump

abollar 1 *vt* to dent
2 abollarse *vpr* to get dented

abombado, -a 1 *pp de* **abombar**
2 *adj* (**a**) *(hacia fuera)* buckled (**b**) *Andes RP Fam (aturdido)* dopey

abombar 1 *vt* to buckle (outwards)
2 abombarse *vpr* (**a**) *(pared)* to buckle (outwards) (**b**) *Am (estropearse)* to spoil, go off (**c**) *Andes RP Fam (aturdirse)* to be dazed

abominable *adj* abominable; **el a. hombre de las nieves** the abominable snowman

abominación *nf* abomination

abominar *vt & vi* **a. (de)** to abominate, loathe

abonable *adj Fin* payable

abonado, -a 1 *pp de* **abonar**
2 *adj* (**a**) *Fin (pagado)* paid; **a. en cuenta** credited (**b**) *Agr (tierra)* fertilized, manured
3 *nm,f* (**a**) *Ferroc Teat* season ticket holder (**b**) *(al teléfono, a revista)* subscriber

abonar 1 *vt* (**a**) *Fml (pagar)* to pay (for); **a. al contado** to pay cash (**b**) *(avalar)* to vouch for, guarantee; **le abona su reputación** his reputation speaks for itself (**c**) *(subscribir)* to subscribe (**d**) *Agr (tierra)* to manure, fertilize
2 abonarse *vpr* (**a**) *(a una revista)* to subscribe (**a** to) (**b**) *Ferroc Teat* to buy a season ticket

abonero, -a *nm,f Méx* hawker, street trader

abono *nm* (**a**) *(a revista etc)* subscription; *Ferroc Teat* season ticket (**b**) *(pago)* payment; *(depósito)* deposit (**c**) *Agr (producto)* fertilizer; *(estiércol)* manure; *(acción)* fertilizing (**d**) *Méx (plazo)* instalment

abordable *adj (persona)* approachable; *(lugar)* accessible; *(asunto)* manageable

abordaje *nm Náut (choque)* collision, fouling; *(ataque)* boarding; **¡al a.!** stand by to board!

abordar *vt* (**a**) *Náut (chocar)* to run foul of, collide with;

(atacar) to board (**b**) *Fig* to approach; **a. a algn** to approach sb; **a. un asunto** to tackle a subject

aborigen 1 *adj* native, indigenous; *(en Australia)* aboriginal
2 *nmf* native; *(en Australia)* aborigine

aborrecer [46] *vt* (**a**) *(odiar)* to detest, hate, loathe (**b**) *(las crías)* to abandon

aborrecible *adj* detestable, loathesome

aborrecimiento *nm* hate, hatred, loathing

aborregado, -a 1 *pp de* **aborregarse**
2 *adj* (**a**) *(cielo)* covered with fleecy clouds (**b**) *Fam (persona)* mindless, sheeplike

aborregarse [38] *vpr* (**a**) *(cielo)* to become covered with fleecy clouds (**b**) *Fam (persona)* to become sheeplike, follow the crowd

abortar 1 *vi* (**a**) *(involuntariamente)* to miscarry, have a miscarriage; *(intencionadamente)* to abort, have an abortion (**b**) *Fig (fracasar)* to fail, miscarry
2 *vt* (**a**) *Med (feto)* to abort (**b**) *Av (despegue)* to abort

abortista *nmf* abortionist

abortivo, -a 1 *adj* abortive
2 *nm* abortifacient

aborto *nm* (**a**) *(espontáneo)* miscarriage; *(provocado)* abortion (**b**) *Ofens (persona)* freak, ugly person; *(cosa)* abortion

abotargado, -a 1 *pp de* **abotargarse**
2 *adj* swollen

abotargamiento *nm* swelling

abotargarse [38] *vpr* to swell up

abotinado, -a *adj* **zapato a.** ankle boot

abotonar 1 *vt (ropa)* to button (up)
2 abotonarse *vpr* (**a**) *(persona)* to do one's buttons up (**b**) *(ropa)* to button (up)

abovedado, -a 1 *pp de* **abovedar**
2 *adj Arquit* vaulted, arched

abovedar *vt Arquit* to vault, arch

abra *nf* (**a**) *Geog (bahía)* cove, inlet; *(desfiladero)* gorge, mountain pass (**b**) *Geol (grieta)* fissure (**c**) *Col (de puerta)* leaf; *(de ventana)* pane (**d**) *RP (en bosque)* clearing

abracadabra *nm* abracadabra

abrasado, -a 1 *pp de* **abrasar**
2 *adj* burnt; **morir a.** to be burnt to death

abrasador, -a *adj* burning, scorching; *Fig* **pasión abrasadora** consuming passion

abrasar 1 *vt & vi* to burn, scorch; **este café abrasa** this coffee is scalding hot
2 abrasarse *vpr* to burn; *Fig* **a. de calor** to be sweltering; *Fig* **a. de sed** to be parched

abrasión *nf* abrasion

abrasivo, -a *adj & nm* abrasive

abrazadera *nf Téc* clamp, brace

abrazar [14] **1** *vt* to embrace, hug; *Fig (doctrina, causa)* to embrace
2 abrazarse *vpr* **a. a** *o* **con algn** to embrace sb; **se abrazaron** they embraced each other

abrazo *nm* embrace, hug; **dar un a. a algn** to embrace sb; *(en carta)* **un a.** *o* **abrazos** with best wishes from; *(más íntimo)* love

abrebotellas *nm inv* bottle opener

abrecartas *nm inv* letter-opener, paperknife

abrelatas *nm inv Br* tin opener, *US* can opener

abrevadero *nm* drinking trough

abrevar *vt (animales)* to water, give water to

abreviación *nf (de texto)* abridgement

abreviado, -a 1 *pp de* **abreviar**
2 *adj* shortened; *(texto)* abridged; *(palabra)* abbreviated; *(explicación)* brief

abreviar 1 *vt* to shorten; *(texto)* to abridge; *(palabra)* to abbreviate; *(discurso, estancia)* to cut short; **a. los trámites** to speed up the formalities
2 *vi* to be quick o brief; **para a.** to cut a long story short

abreviatura *nf* abbreviation

abridor *nm* (a) *(de latas, botellas) Br* (tin) opener, *US* (can) opener (b) *(pendiente)* sleeper

abrigado, -a 1 *pp de* **abrigar**
2 *adj* (a) *(lugar)* sheltered, protected (b) *(persona)* wrapped up; **ir muy a.** to be well wrapped up

abrigador, -a *nm,f Méx Jur* accessory (after the fact)

abrigar [38] **1** *vt* (a) *(contra el frío)* to wrap up, keep warm; **abriga al niño** wrap the child up well; **esta chaqueta abriga mucho** this cardigan is very warm (b) *(proteger)* to protect, shelter (c) *Fig (esperanza)* to foster, cherish (d) *(duda, sospecha)* to have, harbour, *US* harbor
2 abrigarse *vpr* (a) *(protegerse)* to shelter, take shelter (b) *(con ropa)* to wrap oneself up

abrigo *nm* (a) *(prenda)* coat, overcoat; **ropa de a.** warm clothes *pl* (b) *(refugio)* shelter; **al a. de** protected o sheltered from; **al a. de la ley** under the protection of the law (c) *Esp Fam* **es un tipo de a.** *(de cuidado)* he's an ugly character; **hace un sol de a.** *(tremendo)* it's roasting hot

abril *nm* April; **una muchacha de quince abriles** a girl of fifteen summers; *Prov* **en a., aguas mil** (March winds and) April showers bring forth May flowers; *véase tamb* **noviembre**

abrileño, -a *adj* April; **tiempo a.** April weather

abrillantador, -a 1 *nm* (a) *(producto)* polish ◻ **a. de muebles** furniture polish (b) *(instrumento)* polishing tool
2 *nm,f (persona)* polisher

abrillantar *vt* (a) *(pulir)* to polish, burnish, make shine (b) *Fig (embellecer)* to embellish

abrir *(pp* **abierto) 1** *vt* (a) *(puerta, boca, tienda)* to open; **¡abrid paso!** make way!; **a. un agujero** to make a hole; **a. un túnel** to dig a tunnel; **a. una cremallera** to undo a zip; *Fig* **a. la mano** to relax standards; *Fig* **en un a. y cerrar de ojos** in the twinkling of an eye; *Fam* **abrirle la cabeza a algn** to smash sb's head in; *Fam* **no abrió la boca** he didn't say a word (b) *(gas, luz)* to switch on, turn on; **abre el grifo** turn the tap on (c) *(empezar) (campaña)* to head; *(manifestación)* to lead; *(baile)* to open; *(negocio)* to open, set up, start up; *Jur* **a. un expediente** to start proceedings; *Mil* **a. fuego** to open fire *(apetito)* to whet (d) *Inform* to open
2 abrirse *vpr* (a) *(gen)* to open; *(extenderse)* to spread out, unfold; *Fig* **a. paso en la vida** to make one's way in life (b) *(dar)* to open (**a** onto), look (**a** onto) (c) *(sincerarse)* to open out; **a. a algn** to confide in sb (d) *Fam (largarse)* to clear off, be off; **¡me abro!** I'm off!

abrochadora *nf RP (para papeles)* stapler

abrochar *vt* (a) *(botones, cremallera)* to do up; *(camisa)* to button (up); *(cinturón)* to fasten (b) *RP (papeles)* to staple

abrogación *nf Jur* abrogation, repeal

abrogar [38] *vt Jur* to abrogate

abrojal *nm* thistle patch

abrojo *nm* (a) *Bot* thistle (b) *Náut* **abrojos** reef *sing*

abroncar [59] *vt Fam* (a) *(reñir)* to tear a strip off, give a dressing-down to (b) *(abuchear)* to boo, heckle

abrótano *nm Bot* southernwood

abrumado, -a 1 *pp de* **abrumar**
2 *adj* overwhelmed; **a. de trabajo** snowed under with work

abrumador, -a *adj* overwhelming, crushing; **mayoría abrumadora** overwhelming majority

abrumar 1 *vt* to overwhelm, crush; **tantos problemas me abruman** all these problems are getting on top of me; *Fig* **le abrumó con sus atenciones** his attentions made her feel uncomfortable
2 abrumarse *vpr Meteor* to become misty

abrupto, -a *adj* (a) *(pendiente)* steep; *(terreno)* rugged (b) *(brusco)* abrupt, sudden

ABS *nm (abrev de* **antilock braking system)** ABS; **frenos A.** antilock brakes

absceso *nm Med* abscess

abscisa *nf Mat* x-axis

absenta *nf* absinthe

absentismo *nm Esp (de trabajadores)* absenteeism; *(de terrateniente)* absentee landlordism

ábside *nm Arquit* apse

absolución *nf* (a) *Rel* absolution (b) *Jur* acquittal

absolutamente *adv* absolutely, completely; **a. nada** nothing at all

absolutismo *nm* absolutism

absolutista *adj & nmf* absolutist

absoluto, -a *adj* absolute; **en a.** not at all, by no means; **nada en a.** nothing at all; **lo a.** the absolute

absolutorio, -a *adj Jur* **sentencia absolutoria** verdict of not guilty

absolver [41] *(pp* **absuelto)** *vt* (a) *Rel* to absolve (b) *Jur* to acquit

absorbencia *nf* absorbency

absorbente 1 *adj* (a) *(papel)* absorbent (b) *Fig (trabajo)* absorbing, engrossing; *(exigente)* demanding; *(persona)* domineering
2 *nm* absorbent

absorber *vt* (a) *(líquidos)* to absorb, soak up (b) *Fig (conocimientos)* to absorb; *(consumir)* to use up; *(cautivar)* to captivate; **la lectura le absorbe por completo** he gets completely absorbed in his reading

absorción *nf* absorption

absorto, -a *adj* (a) *(ensimismado)* absorbed, engrossed (en in); **estar a. en sus pensamientos** to be lost in thought (b) *(pasmado)* amazed, bewildered

abstemio, -a 1 *adj* teetotal, abstemious; **es a.** he's a teetotaller
2 *nm,f* teetotaller

abstención *nf* abstention

abstencionismo *nm* abstentionism

abstencionista *adj & nmf* abstentionist

abstenerse [65] *vpr* to abstain (**de** from), refrain (**de** from); **a. de votar** to abstain (from voting); **en la duda a.** when in doubt, don't

abstinencia *nf* abstinence; *(de drogas)* withdrawal; **síndrome de a.** withdrawal symptoms *pl*

abstracción *nf* (a) *(gen)* abstraction (b) *(concentración mental)* concentration; **tiene gran capacidad de a.** he has great powers of concentration

abstracto, -a *adj* abstract; **en a.** in the abstract

abstraer [66] **1** *vt* to abstract
2 *vi* to think in the abstract
2 abstraerse *vpr* (a) *(ensimismarse)* to become lost in thought; *(concentrarse)* to engross oneself (**en** in) (b) *(prescindir)* **a. de** to leave aside

abstraído, -a 1 *pp de* **abstraer**
2 *adj* (a) *(ensimismado)* absorbed, engrossed (b) *(distraído)* absentminded

abstruso, -a *adj* abstruse

absuelto, -a 1 *pp de* **absolver**
  2 *adj* **(a)** *Rel* absolved **(b)** *Jur* acquitted

absurdidad *nf* absurdity

absurdo, -a 1 *adj* absurd; **lo a.** sería irse ahora it would be crazy for us to leave now; **¡no seas a.!** don't be ridiculous!; **¡qué a.!** how absurd!
  2 *nm* absurdity, absurd thing; **eso es un a.** that's absurd!

abubilla *nf Orn* hoopoe

abuchear *vt* to boo, jeer at

abucheo *nm* booing, jeering

Abu Dabi *n* Abu Dhabi

abuela *nf* **(a)** *(pariente)* grandmother, *Fam* grandma, granny; *Fam* **¡cuéntaselo a tu a.!** pull the other one!; *Fam* **éramos pocos y parió la a.** as if that wasn't enough, that was all we needed; *Fam* **no tiene a.** he is not afraid of blowing his own trumpet; *Fam* **¡tu a.!** rubbish! **(b)** *Fig* old woman

abuelo *nm* **(a)** *(pariente)* grandfather, *Fam* grandad, grandpa **(b) abuelos** grandparents; *Fig (antepasados)* ancestors **(c)** *Fig* old man

abuhardillado, -a *adj* **techo a.** sloping o slanted roof

abulense 1 *adj* of o from Avila
  2 *nmf* person from Avila

abulia *nf* apathy, lack of willpower

abúlico, -a *adj* apathetic, lacking in willpower

abultado, -a 1 *pp de* **abultar**
  2 *adj (paquete, bulto)* bulky, big

abultamiento *nm* **(a)** *(bulto)* bulkiness **(b)** *(agrandamiento)* increase (in size) **(c)** *(hinchazón)* swelling

abultar 1 *vt* **(a)** *(agrandar)* to enlarge, increase **(b)** *Fig* to exaggerate
  2 *vi* to be bulky; **abulta mucho** it takes up a lot of space

abundamiento *nm Fml* **a mayor a.** furthermore

abundancia *nf* abundance, plenty; **en a.** in abundance; *Fig* **nadar en la a.** to be rolling in money

abundante *adj* abundant, plentiful

abundar *vi* **(a)** *(ser abundante)* to abound, be plentiful; **abundan las ciruelas** there are plenty of plums; **en Noruega abunda la madera** Norway is rich in timber **(b) a. en** *(tener en abundancia)* to abound in, be full of; **la región abunda en recursos naturales** the region is rich in natural resources **(c) a. en** *(insistir)* to insist on; *(estar de acuerdo con)* to share, support

abur *interj Fam* cheerio!, see you!

aburguesado, -a 1 *pp de* **aburguesarse**
  2 *adj* bourgeois

aburguesamiento *nm* process of becoming bourgeois

aburguesarse *vpr* to become bourgeois

aburrido, -a 1 *pp de* **aburrir**
  2 *adj* **(a)** *(que aburre)* boring, tedious; *(monótono)* dull, dreary; **¡qué a.!** how boring!; **ser a.** to be boring **(b)** *(harto, fastidiado)* bored; **a. de** tired of, fed up with; **a. de esperar** tired of waiting; **estar a.** to be bored

aburrimiento *nm* boredom; **¡qué a.!** how boring!, what a bore!; *(cosa, persona)* **ser un a.** to be a bore

aburrir 1 *vt* to bore; *(cansar)* to tire
  2 aburrirse *vpr* to get bored; **a. como una ostra** to be bored stiff

abusado, -a *Méx Fam* **1** *adj* smart, sharp
  2 *interj* look out!

abusar *vi* **(a)** *(propasarse)* to go too far; **a. de** *(situación, persona)* to take (unfair) advantage of; *(poder)* to abuse, misuse; *(salud, amabilidad)* to abuse; *Jur* **a. de un niño/una**

mujer to molest a child/woman; **¡sin a.!** don't push it too far! **(b)** *(usar demasiado)* to overindulge **(de** in**)**, overuse; **a. de la bebida** to drink too much o to excess

abusivo, -a *adj* excessive, exorbitant; **precio a.** exorbitant price; **trato a.** ill-treatment

abuso *nm* **(a)** *(uso excesivo)* abuse, misuse □ **a. de confianza** betrayal of trust, breach of faith; **a. de poder** abuse of power; *Jur* **abusos deshonestos** indecent assault *sing* **(b)** *(injusticia)* injustice; **¡es un a.!** this is most unfair!

abusón, -ona *Esp Fam* **1** *adj (fresco)* shameless; *(gorrón)* sponging, scrounging; *(injusto)* unfair, abusive
  2 *nm,f (gorrón)* sponger, scrounger; *(injusto)* unfair person

abyección *nf* abjection, wretchedness

abyecto, -a *adj* abject, wretched

a. C. *(abrev de* **antes de Cristo***)* BC

a/c *Com (abrev de* **a cuenta***)* on account

acá *adv* **(a)** *(lugar)* here, over here; **a. y allá** here and there; **de a. para allá** to and fro, up and down; **más a.** nearer; **¡ven a.!** come here! **(b)** *(tiempo)* **de entonces a.** since then; **de un tiempo a.** lately

acabado, -a 1 *pp de* **acabar**
  2 *adj* **(a)** *(terminado)* finished, complete **(b)** *Fig (gastado)* worn-out, spent; **está a. como político** as a politician he's finished; **una persona acabada** a has-been
  3 *nm Téc* finish

acabar 1 *vt* to finish (off); *(completar)* to complete
  2 *vi* **(a)** to finish, end; **acaba en punta** it has a pointed end; **a. bien** to have a happy ending; **a. con algo** *(terminarlo)* to finish sth; *(romperlo)* to break sth; **acabarás conmigo** you'll be the end of me; **a. de ...** to have just ...; **no acaba de convencerme** I'm not quite convinced; **a. mal** to end badly; *Fam* **¡acabáramos!** now I get it!, you could have said so before!; *Fam* **para a. de arreglarlo** to cap it all **(b)** **(a. + ger, a. + por + inf)** to end up; **acabaron casándose** o **por casarse** they ended up getting married
  2 acabarse *vpr* **(a)** to finish, end, come to an end, stop; **acábate la leche** drink up your milk; **se (nos) acabó la gasolina** we ran out of petrol; *Fam* **¡se acabó!** that's that!; *Fam* **se acabó lo que se daba** that's it! **(b)** *(morir)* to die

acabóse *nm Fam* **eres el a.** you're the limit; **esto es el a.** this is the end

acacia *nf Bot* acacia

academia *nf* **(a)** *(sociedad)* academy; **A. de Bellas Artes** Royal Academy of Arts; **la Real A. Española** the Spanish Academy **(b)** *(centro de enseñanza)* school, academy □ **a. de idiomas** language school; **a. militar** military academy

academicismo *nm* academicism

académico, -a 1 *adj* academic; *Univ* **estudios académicos** university studies
  2 *nm,f* academician, member of an academy

acaecer [46] *vi* to happen, occur

acallar *vt (protestas, rebeldes)* to silence; *(rumores)* to put an end to

acalorado, -a 1 *pp de* **acalorar**
  2 *adj* **(a)** *(por calor)* hot; *(cara)* flushed **(b)** *Fig (excitado)* worked up, excited; *(debate etc)* heated, angry

acaloramiento *nm* **(a)** *(calor)* heat **(b)** *Fig* heat, passion

acalorar 1 *vt* **(a)** *(dar calor)* to warm up, heat up **(b)** *Fig* to excite; *(pasiones)* to arouse, inflame
  2 acalorarse *vpr* **(a)** *(sentir calor)* to get warm o hot **(b)** *Fig (persona)* to get excited o worked up; *(debate etc)* to become heated

acampada *nf* camping; **zona de a.** camp site

acampanado, -a *adj* bell-shaped; *(prenda)* flared

acampar *vi* to camp

acanalado, -a *adj (gen)* grooved; *Arquit* fluted; *Tricot* ribbed

acanaladura *nf (gen)* groove; *Arquit* fluting

acantilado, -a 1 *adj (costa)* steep, sheer; *(fondo del mar)* shelving; *(rocoso)* rocky, craggy
2 *nm* cliff

acanto *nm Bot* acanthus

acantonamiento *nm Mil (acción)* billeting; *(lugar)* billet

acantonar *vt Mil (tropas)* to billet, quarter (**en** in)

acaparador, -a 1 *adj* hoarding; *(tendencia)* monopolizing
2 *nm,f* hoarder; *(monopolizador)* monopolizer

acaparamiento *nm* hoarding; *Fig* monopolizing

acaparar *vt* (**a**) *(productos)* to hoard; *(el mercado)* to corner (**b**) *Fig* to monopolize, keep for oneself; **acaparó la atención de todos** he commanded the attention of everyone

acápite *nm Am* paragraph

acaracolado, -a *adj* spiral-shaped; *(pelo)* very curly

acaramelado, -a 1 *pp de* **acaramelar**
2 *adj* (**a**) *(color)* caramel-coloured, *US* caramel-colored (**b**) *Fig (pareja)* lovey-dovey, starry-eyed; *(voz)* syrupy, sugary

acaramelar 1 *vt* to coat with caramel
2 acaramelarse *vpr Fig* to become lovey-dovey o starry-eyed

acariciador, -a *adj* caressing; *Fig* **una voz acariciadora** a sensuous voice

acariciar 1 *vt* (**a**) *(persona)* to caress; *(pelo, animal)* to stroke (**b**) *Fig (esperanza, sueño)* to cherish; *(idea)* to have in mind
2 acariciarse *vpr* to caress each other; **a. el bigote** to stroke one's moustache

ácaro *nm* mite

acarrear *vt* (**a**) *(transportar)* to carry, transport (**b**) *Fig (conllevar)* to cause, bring, give rise to

acarreo *nm* transport, carriage; **gastos de a.** transport costs, haulage

acartonado, -a 1 *pp de* **acartonarse**
2 *adj* (**a**) *(piel)* wizened, shrivelled up (**b**) *(estilo, personaje)* wooden

acartonarse *vpr (piel)* to become wizened, shrivel up

acaso *adv* perhaps, maybe; **¿a. no te lo dijo?** didn't she tell you?; **a. podamos verlo** perhaps we will see him; **no es torpe, si a. inseguro** he's not dull, if anything insecure; **por si a.** just in case; **si a. viene ...** if he should come ...

acatamiento *nm (de la ley)* observance; *(persona)* respect

acatar *vt* (**a**) *(leyes, normas)* to observe, comply with; *(persona)* to respect (**b**) *CAm (oir)* to hear

acatarrado, -a 1 *pp de* **acatarrarse**
2 *adj* **estar a.** to have a cold

acatarrarse *vpr* to catch a cold

acaudalado, -a 1 *pp de* **acaudalar**
2 *adj* rich, wealthy, well-off

acaudalar *vt* to accumulate, amass

acaudillar *vt* to lead

acceder *vi* (**a**) *(consentir)* **a. a** to agree to, accede to, consent to (**b**) *(tener acceso)* **a. a la universidad** to gain admittance to o enter university; **a. al poder** to accede to power, take office; **a. al trono** to accede o succeed to the throne

accesibilidad *nf* accessibility

accesible *adj* accessible; *(persona)* approachable

accésit *nm inv (mención)* honourable mention; *(premio)* consolation prize

acceso *nm* (**a**) *(a edificio, Internet, persona)* access; *(a página Web)* hit; **'prohibido el a.'** 'no admittance'; *Univ* **prueba de a.** entrance examination ❑ *Inform* **a. aleatorio** random access (**b**) *(a carretera, ciudad)* approach, access; **los accesos a Barcelona** the approaches to Barcelona; **carretera de a.** approach road; **vía de a.** slip road (**c**) *Med (de tos)* fit; *(de fiebre)* attack, bout; *Fig* fit, outburst

accesorio, -a 1 *adj* accessory; *(gastos)* incidental
2 *nm* accesory, extra

accidentado, -a 1 *pp de* **accidentarse**
2 *adj* (**a**) *(persona)* injured (**b**) *(lleno de incidentes)* eventful; *(vida)* troubled, stormy (**c**) *(terreno)* uneven, bumpy, hilly
3 *nm,f* casualty, accident victim

accidental *adj* accidental; **un encuentro a.** a chance meeting

accidentarse *vpr* to have an accident

accidente *nm* (**a**) *(suceso)* accident; **por a.** by accident, accidentally; **sufrir un a.** to have an accident ❑ **a. aéreo** plane crash; **a. de carretera** o **circulación** road o traffic accident; **a. ferroviario** rail accident; **a. de trabajo** industrial accident (**b**) *Geog (del terreno)* unevenness, irregularity ❑ **a. geográfico** geographical feature

acción *nf* (**a**) *(gen)* action; *(acto)* act, deed; **poner en a.** to put into action; **ponerse en a.** to go into action ❑ *Rel* **a. de gracias** thanksgiving; *Mil* **a. de guerra** act of war; **buena a.** good deed; **campo de a.** field of action; **hombre de a.** man of action; **película de a.** adventure movie o *Br* film; *Tec* **radio de a.** operating range (**b**) *Jur* action, lawsuit; **ejercitar una a. contra algn** to bring an action against sb (**c**) *Fin (bolsa)* share; **acciones** *esp Br* shares, *esp US* stock; **acciones en cartera** *Br* own shares held, *US* Treasury stock; **acciones ordinarias** equity shares, *Br* ordinary shares, *US* common stock

accionamiento *nm* starting, activation

accionar 1 *vt (máquina)* to drive, activate, work
2 *vi* to gesticulate

accionariado *nm Fin esp Br* shareholders, *esp US* stockholders

accionista *nmf Fin esp Br* shareholder, *esp US* stockholder

Accra *n* Accra

acebo *nm Bot (hoja)* holly; *(árbol)* holly tree

acechanza *nf véase* **acecho**

acechar *vt* (**a**) *(vigilar)* to watch, spy on; *(esperar)* to lie in wait for; *(animal)* to stalk (**b**) *(amenazar)* to threaten; **un grave peligro nos acecha** great danger is looming (up)

acecho *nm* watching; **estar al a. de** *(vigilar)* to be on the watch for; *(esperar)* to lie in wait for

acecinar 1 *vt (carne)* to cure, salt
2 acecinarse *vpr Fig (persona)* to become thin and wizened

acedera *nf Bot* sorrel

acedía[1] *nf* (**a**) *(acidez)* sourness, acidity (**b**) *Med* heartburn (**c**) *Fig (desabrimiento)* sourness, unpleasantness

acedía[2] *nf (pez)* dab

acéfalo, -a *adj Zool* acephalous; *Fig (sociedad, partido)* leaderless

aceitar *vt* to oil

aceite *nm* oil ❑ **a. esencial** essential oil; **a. de girasol** sunflower/corn/olive oil; **a. vegetal** vegetable oil; *Fig* **balsa de a.** millpond; **mancha de a.** *(en el mar)* oil slick

aceitera *nf* (**a**) *Culin* oil bottle; **aceiteras** *sing* oil and vinegar set (**b**) *Aut* oil can

aceitero, -a 1 *adj* oil; **la industria aceitera** the oil industry
2 *nm,f* oil merchant

aceitoso, -a *adj* oily; *(grasiento)* greasy

aceituna *nf* olive ❑ **a. rellena** stuffed olive

aceitunado, -a *adj* olive, olive-coloured; **de tez aceitunada** olive-skinned

aceitunero, -a *nm,f* **(a)** *(recolector)* olive picker *o* harvester **(b)** *(vendedor)* olive seller

aceituno *nm Bot* olive tree

aceleración *nf Fís* acceleration

acelerado, -a 1 *pp de* **acelerar**
2 *adj* accelerated, fast, quick; *Fís* **movimiento a.** accelerated motion

acelerador, -a 1 *adj* accelerating
2 *nm Aut* accelerator; **pisar el a.** to step on the accelerator

aceleramiento *nm véase* **aceleración**

acelerar 1 *vt* to accelerate; *Fig* to speed up; **a. el paso** to quicken one's pace
2 acelerarse *vpr Fig (apresurarse)* to hasten, hurry up

acelerón *nm* sudden acceleration; *Aut* **dar un a.** to step on the accelerator, put one's foot down

acelga *nf Bot* chard

acémila *nf* **(a)** *Zool (mula)* mule; *(bestia de carga)* pack horse **(b)** *Fig (persona torpe)* clumsy idiot

acendrado, -a 1 *pp de* **acendrar**
2 *adj* pure, unblemished

acendrar *vt* to purify

acento *nm* **(a)** *Ling (gráfico)* accent; *(tónico)* stress ❑ **a. ortográfico** (written) accent **(b)** *Fig (énfasis)* stress, emphasis; **poner el a. en algo** to stress *o* emphasise sth **(c)** *(tono)* accent; **a. vasco** Basque accent

acentuación *nf* accentuation

acentuado, -a 1 *pp de* **acentuar**
2 *adj* **(a)** *Ling (con acento gráfico)* accented; *(con acento tónico)* stressed **(b)** *Fig (marcado)* strong, marked

acentuar [4] **1** *vt* **(a)** *(al escribir)* to accent; *(al hablar)* to stress **(b)** *Fig* to emphasize, stress, accentuate
2 acentuarse *vpr Fig* to become more pronounced *o* noticeable *o* marked

aceña *nf* watermill

acepción *nf* **(a)** *(de palabra)* meaning, sense; **en su más amplia a.** in the broadest sense of the word **(b)** *(preferencia)* preference; **sin a. de personas** without respect of persons

aceptabilidad *nf* acceptability

aceptable *adj* acceptable

aceptación *nf* **(a)** *(aprobación)* acceptance **(b)** *(éxito)* success; **tener poca a.** to have little success, not to be popular

aceptar *vt* to accept

acequia *nf* irrigation ditch *o* channel

acera *nf Br* pavement, *US* sidewalk; *Fam* **ser de la a. de enfrente** to be one of them, be queer

acerado, -a 1 *pp de* **acerar**
2 *adj* **(a)** *Metal* steel, steely **(b)** *Fig (mordaz)* cutting, sharp

acerar *vt* **(a)** *(recubrir de acero)* to steel **(b)** *(convertir en acero)* to turn into steel **(c)** *Fig (fortalecer)* to strengthen

acerbo, -a *adj* **(a)** *(sabor)* sour, bitter **(b)** *Fig (tono)* harsh, bitter; *(dolor)* cruel, harsh

acerca *adv* **a. de** about, on

acercamiento *nm* **(a)** *(acción)* bringing together, coming together **(b)** *Fig (de enemigos)* bringing together, reconciliation; *Pol (entre naciones, partidos)* rapprochement; **se produjo un a. entre los dos** the two of them came closer together

acercar [59] **1** *vt* to bring near *o* nearer, bring (over), draw up; *Fig* to bring together; **acerca un poco la tele** could you move the TV a bit closer?; **¿me acercas la sal?** can you pass me the salt?; **¿te acerco a casa?** can I give you a *Br* lift *o US* ride home?
2 acercarse *vpr* **(a)** *(aproximarse)* to come closer, approach; **a. a algn** to go up to sb, come up to sb **(b)** *(ir)* to go; **acércate a la farmacia** go to the chemist's; *(venir)* **Pilar se acercó a vernos** Pilar dropped in to see us

acería *nf* steelworks *sing*, steel mill

acerico *nm Cost* pincushion

acero *nm* **(a)** *(metal)* steel; *Fig* **tener nervios de a.** to have nerves of steel ❑ **a. inoxidable** stainless steel **(b)** *Fig (espada)* sword, steel

acérrimo, -a *adj (partidario)* staunch, steadfast, earnest; *(enemigo)* bitter

acertado, -a 1 *pp de* **acertar**
2 *adj* **(a)** *(opinión, solución)* right, correct; *(comentario)* fitting; *(idea, decisión)* clever; *(color)* well-chosen; **la palabra acertada** the exact word **(b)** *(conveniente)* suitable, wise; **no estuviste muy a. al decir eso** it wasn't very wise of you to say that

acertante 1 *adj* winning
2 *nmf (ganador)* winner; *(de problemas)* solver

acertar [3] **1** *vt* to get right; *(adivinar)* to guess correctly; **a. el tiro** to hit the mark; **a. las quinielas** to win the pools; **acertó tres preguntas** she got three questions right
2 *vi* **(a)** *(al contestar)* to guess correctly, be right; **acertó con la calle que buscaba** she found the street she was looking for; **has acertado** you are right **(b)** *(suceder)* **a. a** to happen to; **acertó a pasar por allí un hombre** a man happened to pass nearby

acertijo *nm* riddle

acervo *nm Jur* common property ❑ *Pol* **a. comunitario** acquis communautaire; **a. cultural** cultural tradition *o* heritage; **a. familiar** family property; **a. popular** cultural tradition *o* heritage

acetato *nm Quím* acetate

acético, -a *adj Quím* acetic

acetileno *nm Quím* acetylene

acetona *nf Quím* acetone

achacable *adj* attributable (**a** to)

achacar [59] *vt (atribuir)* to attribute

achacoso, -a *adj* ailing, unwell

achampañado, -a *adj (vino)* champagne-style

achantar *Fam* **1** *vt* to put the wind up; **a ese no le achanta nada** nothing gets him scared
2 achantarse *vpr* to get the wind up; **no se achanta ante nada** she doesn't get frightened by anything

achaparrado, -a *adj* squat, stocky

achaque *nm* ailment, complaint; **achaques propios de la vejez** old age complaints

acharolado, -a *adj* varnished

achatado, -a 1 *pp de* **achatar**
2 *adj* flattened

achatamiento *nm* flattening

achatar *vt* to flatten

achicado, -a *adj* childish

achicar [59] **1** *vt* **(a)** *(amilanar)* to intimidate **(b)** *(encoger)* to reduce, make smaller **(c)** *(mina)* to drain; *(barco)* to bale out
2 achicarse *vpr* **(a)** *(amilanarse)* to lose heart **(b)** *(encogerse)* to get smaller

achicharradero *nm Fam* oven, furnace; **esta habitación es un a.** this room is like an oven

achicharrado, -a 1 *pp de* **achicharrar**
2 *adj (quemado)* burnt to a crisp; *(acalorado)* boiling (hot)

achicharrante *adj* burning, scorching, searing, sweltering

achicharrar 1 *vt* (**a**) *(quemar)* to burn, scorch; *Fam* **hace un sol que achicharra** it's roasting (**b**) *(importunar)* to bother, pester; **a. a preguntas** to plague with questions (**c**) *Andes (aplastar, estrujar)* to squash
2 achicharrarse *vpr (quemarse)* to roast

achicoria *nf Bot* chicory

achinado, -a *adj* (**a**) *(persona)* oriental-looking; *(ojos)* slanting (**b**) *RP (aindiado)* Indian-looking

achispado, -a *adj Fam* tipsy

achispar 1 *vt (emborrachar)* to make tipsy
2 achisparse *vpr (emborracharse)* to get tipsy o tight

acholado, -a *adj* (**a**) *Bol Chile Perú Pey (mestizo) (físicamente)* Indian-looking, mestizo; *(culturalmente)* = who has adopted Indian ways (**b**) *Ecuad (avergonzado)* ashamed, red in the face

acholar 1 *vt Bol Chile Perú* to embarrass, make blush
2 acholarse *vpr* (**a**) *Bol Chile Perú Fam Pey (acriollarse)* to go native (**b**) *Ecuad (avergonzarse)* to be ashamed (**c**) *Bol Chile Perú (atemorizarse)* to get scared; *(acobardarse)* to get cold feet

achuchado, -a 1 *pp de* achuchar
2 *adj Esp Fam* tough, difficult

achuchar *vt* (**a**) *(en ataque)* to set on; *(atosigar)* to set against (**b**) *(estrujar)* to crush, squeeze

achucharrar 1 *vt Col Hond* to crush, squash
2 achucharrarse *vpr* (**a**) *Méx (desanimarse)* to be disheartened, be discouraged (**b**) *Col Méx (quemarse) (carne)* to burn o get burnt; *(planta)* to wither (in the sun)

achuchón *nm* (**a**) *(empujón)* push, shove (**b**) *(indisposición)* indisposition (**c**) *Fam (pareja)* **darse achuchones** to pet

achucutar 1 *vt (humillar)* to shame, humiliate; *(abatir)* to depress, discourage
2 achucutarse *vpr (humillarse)* to be ashamed; *(abatirse)* to become depressed o discouraged

achulado, -a *adj Esp Fam* cocky

achunchar *Andes* **1** *vt (asustar)* to frighten, scare; *(avergonzar)* to shame
2 achuncharse *vpr (asustarse)* to get scared; *(avergonzarse)* to feel ashamed

achurar *vt RP Fam* (**a**) *(acuchillar)* to stab to death (**b**) *(animal)* to disembowel

achuras *nfpl Perú RP* (dish of) offal

aciago, -a *adj* ill-fated, fateful; **un día a.** a fateful day

acíbar *nm (planta)* aloe; *(jugo)* aloes *pl; Fig* bitterness, sorrow

acicalado, -a 1 *pp de* acicalar
2 *adj* well-dressed, smart

acicalamiento *nm* smartening up

acicalar 1 *vt (persona, habitación)* to smarten up
2 acicalarse *vpr* to dress up, smarten up

acicate *nm* (**a**) *(espuela)* spur (**b**) *Fig (aliciente)* spur, incentive, stimulus

acidez *nf* (**a**) *(de sabor)* sharpness, sourness (**b**) *Quím* acidity □ *Med* **a. de estómago** heartburn

acidificar [59] *vt* to acidify

ácido, -a 1 *adj (sabor)* sharp, tart, acidic; *Quím* acidic; *Fig (tono)* harsh
2 *nm Quím* acid □ **a. acético/clorhídrico/sulfúrico** acetic/hydrochloric/sulphuric acid

acierto *nm* (**a**) *(a pregunta)* correct guess, right answer; *(idea, decisión)* good choice o idea (**b**) *(tino)* wisdom, good judgement; **con gran a.** very wisely (**c**) *(éxito)* success

ácimo, -a *adj* unleavened; **pan á.** unleavened bread

acimut *nm Astron* azimuth

aclamación *nf* acclamation, acclaim

aclamar *vt* to acclaim

aclaración *nf* explanation; **exijo una a.** I demand an explanation

aclarado *nm Esp* rinsing, rinse

aclarar 1 *vt* (**a**) *(color, pelo)* to lighten, make lighter (**b**) *(líquido)* to thin (down) (**c**) *Esp (enjuagar)* to rinse (**d**) *(explicar)* to clarify, explain; **quiero a. una cosa** I'd like to make something clear
2 *v impers (el tiempo)* to clear (up)
2 aclararse *vpr* (**a**) *(entender)* to understand; **es que no me aclaro** I don't really know what's going on; *Fam* **¡a ver si te aclaras!** *(explícate)* explain yourself!; *(decídete)* make up your mind! (**b**) *(el tiempo)* to clear (up); *Fig* **a. la voz** to clear one's throat

aclaratorio, -a *adj* explanatory

aclimatable *adj* able to become acclimatized o *US* acclimated

aclimatación *nf* acclimatization, *US* acclimation

aclimatar 1 *vt* to acclimatize, *US* acclimate (**a** to)
2 aclimatarse *vpr* to become acclimatized o *US* acclimated (**a** to); *Fig* **a. a algo** to get used to sth

acné *nf Med* acne

ACNUR [ak'nur] *nf* (*abrev de* **Alta Comisaría de las Naciones Unidas para los Refugiados**) UNHCR

acobardar 1 *vt* to frighten, unnerve
2 acobardarse *vpr* to become frightened, lose one's nerve, shrink back (**ante** from)

acodado, -a *adj* (**a**) *(cañería)* elbowed (**b**) *(apoyado)* leaning (on one's elbows)

acodar 1 *vt* (**a**) *(doblar)* to bend (**b**) *Bot* to layer
2 acodarse *vpr* to lean on one's elbows

acodo *nm* (**a**) *Bot* layering (**b**) *Constr (moldura)* frame

acogedor, -a *adj (persona)* friendly, welcoming; *(lugar)* cosy, warm

acoger [52] **1** *vt* (**a**) *(recibir)* to receive; *(a invitado)* to welcome; **le acogieron con los brazos abiertos** they welcomed him with open arms (**b**) *(admitir)* to admit, accept; **a. a un huérfano/refugiado** to take in an orphan/refugee (**c**) *(guarecer)* to shelter, protect
2 acogerse *vpr* (**a**) *(protegerse)* to take refuge; *Fig* **a. a** to take refuge in (**b**) **a. a** *(promesa, amnistía)* to avail oneself of; **a. a la ley** to have recourse to the law

acogida *nf* reception, welcome; **dar a. a algn** to welcome sb

acogido, -a 1 *pp de* acoger
2 *nm,f (en asilo, orfanato)* inmate, resident

acogotar *vt* (**a**) *(matar)* to kill (with a blow on the neck) (**b**) *(derribar)* to knock down (**c**) *Fig (acobardar)* to frighten, intimidate

acojonado, -a *Esp Vulg* **1** *pp de* acojonar
2 *adj* (**a**) *(asustado)* shit-scared (**b**) *(asombrado)* gobsmacked

acojonante *adj Esp muy Fam (impresionante)* damn fine, *Br* bloody incredible

acojonar *Esp muy Fam* **1** *vt* (**a**) *(asustar)* **a. a algn** to scare the crap out of sb (**b**) *(impresionar)* to gobsmack
2 acojonarse *vpr* **me acojoné y no se lo dije** I crapped out of telling her

acojone *nm*, **acojono** *nm Esp muy Fam* **me entró un a. terrible** I started crapping myself

acolchado, -a 1 *pp de* acolchar
2 *adj (pared, puerta)* padded; *(prenda)* quilted
3 *nm Arg (para cama)* bedspread

acolchar *vt (rellenar)* to pad; *(prenda)* to quilt

acólito *nm* (**a**) *Rel* acolyte; *(monaguillo)* altar boy (**b**) *Fig (ayudante)* acolyte; *Irón* minion

acollarar *vt CSur (unir)* to tie together

acomedido, -a *adj Andes CAm Méx* accommodating, obliging

acomedirse [47] *vpr Andes CAm Méx* to offer to help, volunteer

acometer *vt* (**a**) *(emprender)* to undertake; **a. una tarea** to undertake a task (**b**) *(atacar)* to attack (**c**) *(afectar súbitamente)* to be seized by; **le acometió la tos** he had a coughing fit; **le acometió la risa** she burst out laughing

acometida *nf* (**a**) *(ataque)* attack (**b**) *Elec (conexión)* connection

acomodación *nf* (**a**) *(colocación conveniente)* arrangement; **la a. de los invitados al banquete** the seating arrangements for the banquet (**b**) *(vivienda)* preparation (**c**) *(adaptación)* adaptation; **la a. de los hechos a la realidad** the adaptation of theory to practice

acomodadizo, -a *adj* accommodating, easy-going

acomodado, -a 1 *pp de* **acomodar**
2 *adj* (**a**) *(ordenado, colocado)* arranged (**b**) *(adaptado)* applied, adapted (**c**) *(rico)* well-off, well-to-do (**d**) *(comodón)* comfort-loving (**e**) *(precio)* moderate, reasonable (**f**) *(conveniente)* suitable

acomodador, -a *nm,f (hombre)* usher; *(mujer)* usherette

acomodar 1 *vt* (**a**) *(colocar)* to arrange; **a. los paquetes en el maletero** to fit the parcels into the *Br* boot o *US* trunk (**b**) *(aplicar)* to apply, adapt; **se podría a. este ejemplo a otros casos** this example is applicable in other cases (**c**) *(alojar)* to lodge, accommodate (**d**) *(proporcionar empleo a)* to provide with a job, find a job for (**e**) *(en un cine, teatro)* to find a place for; **nos acomodó en la segunda fila** he found us a seat in the second row (**f**) *(conciliar)* to reconcile
2 acomodarse *vpr* (**a**) *(instalarse)* to make oneself comfortable; **se acomodó en el sillón** he settled down in the armchair (**b**) *(adaptarse)* to adapt oneself; **se acomoda a todo** he adapts to everything

acomodaticio, -a *adj* accommodating, easy-going

acomodo *nm* (**a**) *(trabajo)* job (**b**) *(alojamiento)* accommodation

acompañado, -a 1 *pp de* **acompañar**
2 *adj* accompanied; **bien/mal a.** in good/bad company

acompañamiento *nm* (**a**) *(gen)* accompaniment (**b**) *(comitiva)* retinue, escort (**c**) *Mús* accompaniment

acompañanta *nf* (female) companion; *Mús* (female) accompanist

acompañante 1 *adj* accompanying
2 *nmf* companion, escort; *Mús* accompanist

acompañar 1 *vt* (**a**) *(persona)* to accompany, go with; **le acompañó hasta la puerta** she saw him to the door; **me acompañó al médico** he came with me to see the doctor; **¿te acompaño a casa?** can I walk you home?; *Fml* **le acompaño en el sentimiento** my condolences (**b**) *Mús* to accompany (**c**) *(adjuntar)* to enclose
2 acompañarse *vpr Mús* to accompany oneself (**a** on)

acompasado, -a 1 *pp de* **acompasar**
2 *adj* (**a**) *(ruido, movimiento)* rhythmic (**b**) *(paso)* slow, measured; *(habla)* slow, deliberate

acompasar *vt* (**a**) *Mús* to mark the time of, mark the rhythm of (**b**) *Fig (ajustar)* to keep in time, adjust

acomplejado, -a 1 *pp de* **acomplejar**
2 *adj* with a complex; **estar a.** to have a complex (**por** about)
3 *nm,f* person with a complex; **es un a.** he has a complex

acomplejar 1 *vt* to give a complex; *Fam* **me acomplejas**

con tantos conocimientos I feel so ignorant in your company
2 acomplejarse *vpr* **a. por** to develop a complex about

Aconcagua *nm* **el A.** Aconcagua

acondicionado, -a 1 *pp de* **acondicionar**
2 *adj (preparado)* equipped, fitted-out; **el piso no está a.** the flat is not fit to be lived in

acondicionador *nm* conditioner; **a. de aire** air conditioner

acondicionamiento *nm* conditioning, setting up, fitting up; *(mejoramiento)* improvement

acondicionar *vt* to prepare, set up, fit up; *(mejorar)* to improve; **a. la red ferroviaria/viaria** to improve the railway/road network

aconfesional *adj* secular

acongojado, -a 1 *pp de* **acongojar**
2 *adj* distressed, afflicted, anguished

acongojar 1 *vt* to grieve, make suffer
2 acongojarse *vpr* to be grieved, be distressed

aconsejable *adj* advisable

aconsejar 1 *vt* to advise; **necesito que me aconsejes** I need your advice
2 aconsejarse *vpr* to seek advice

acontecer [46] *vi* to happen, take place

acontecimiento *nm* event, happening

acopiar *vt* to gather, collect

acopio *nm* (**a**) *(acción)* storing (**b**) *(cosa)* store, stock; **hacer a. de** to store up

acoplable *adj* adjustable, adaptable

acoplado *nm CSur* trailer

acoplador *nm* coupler, adapter

acopladura *nf*, **acoplamiento** *nm* (**a**) *Téc (acción)* coupling connection; *(junta)* joint (**b**) *Astronáut* docking

acoplar 1 *vt* (**a**) *(juntar)* to fit (together), join, adjust (**b**) *Téc (conectar)* to couple, connect, join (**c**) *(animales)* to mate, pair
2 acoplarse *vpr* (**a**) *(piezas)* to fit together (**b**) *(animales)* to mate (**c**) *Astronáut* to dock

acoquinamiento *nm Fam* fear, loss of nerve

acoquinar *Fam* **1** *vt* to frighten, intimidate
2 acoquinarse *vpr* to get frightened, lose one's nerve

acorazado, -a 1 *pp de* **acorazar**
2 *adj (blindado)* armoured, *US* armored, armour-plated, *US* armorplated
3 *nm Náut (barco)* battleship

acorazar [14] **1** *vt (blindar)* to armour, *US* armor, armour-plate, *US* armor-plate
2 acorazarse *vpr (endurecerse)* to steel oneself, harden oneself (**contra** against)

acorazonado, -a *adj* heart-shaped

acorchar 1 *vt* to cover with cork
2 acorcharse *vpr* (**a**) *(material)* to become cork-like (**b**) *(miembro)* to go numb

acordado, -a 1 *pp de* **acordar**
2 *adj* agreed; **en el plazo a.** within the agreed period; **según lo a.** as agreed

acordar [63] **1** *vt* (**a**) *(ponerse de acuerdo en)* to agree (on); **a. hacer algo** to agree to do sth (**b**) *Am (otorgar)* to award
2 acordarse *vpr* to remember; **no me acuerdo** I can't remember; **¿te acuerdas de Iñaki?** do you remember Iñaki?

acorde 1 *adj* in agreement
2 *nm Mús* chord; **a los acordes del himno nacional** to the tune of the National Anthem

acordeón *nm* (**a**) *Mús* accordion (**b**) *Col Méx Fam (en examen)* crib

acordeonista *nmf* accordionist

acordonado, -a 1 *pp de* **acordonar**
2 *adj* cordoned off, sealed off

acordonar *vt* (**a**) *(zona)* to cordon off, seal off (**b**) *(atar con cordones)* to lace up

acorralamiento *nm* cornering

acorralar *vt* to corner; **a. a un animal** to put an animal at bay

acortar 1 *vt* to shorten, make shorter; **a. distancias** to cut down the distance
2 acortarse *vpr Fig* to be shy

acosamiento *nm* harassment

acosar *vt (perseguir)* to chase, pursue; *(hostigar)* to harass; **a. a algn a preguntas** to bombard sb with questions

acoso *nm (persecución)* chase, pursuit; *(hostigamiento)* harassment □ **a. sexual** sexual harassment

acostado, -a 1 *pp de* **acostar**
2 *adj (en la cama)* in bed; *(tumbado)* lying down

acostar [63] **1** *vt* to put to bed
2 acostarse *vpr* (**a**) *(irse a la cama)* to go to bed; **hora de a.** bedtime; **voy a acostarme un ratito** I'm going to lie down for a while (**b**) *Fam* **a. con algn** to sleep with sb, go to bed with sb

acostumbrado, -a 1 *pp de* **acostumbrar**
2 *adj* (**a**) *(habitual)* usual, customary; **es lo a.** it is the custom (**b**) *(habituado)* used, accustomed; **a. al frío** used to the cold

acostumbrar 1 *vt* (**a**) *(habituar)* to accustom (**a** to); **hay que acostumbrarlos desde el principio** you must get them used to it from the start (**b**) *(soler)* to be in the habit of; **acostumbra salir por las tardes** she usually goes out in the evenings
2 acostumbrarse *vpr* (**a**) *(habituarse)* to become accustomed (**a** to), get used (**a** to); **pronto te acostumbrarás** you'll soon get used to it (**b**) *(uso impers)* to be usual; **ya no se acostumbra** it is no longer usual

acotación *nf* (**a**) *(en un escrito)* (marginal) note; *Teat* stage direction (**b**) *(en un mapa)* elevation mark

acotado, -a 1 *pp de* **acotar**
2 *adj* (**a**) *(terreno)* enclosed (**b**) *(escrito)* annotated

acotamiento *nm* (**a**) *(de terreno)* enclosing, demarcation (**b**) *Méx (arcén) Br* hard shoulder, *US* shoulder

acotar *vt* (**a**) *(área)* to enclose, demarcate; *Fig (tema)* to delimit (**b**) *(poner notas)* to add notes to; *(texto)* to annotate (**c**) *Geog (mapa)* to mark with elevations

acotejar *vt Andes Carib* to arrange

ácrata *adj & nmf* anarchist

acre¹ *adj* (**a**) *(sabor)* sour, bitter; *(olor)* acrid (**b**) *Fig (palabras)* bitter, harsh; *(crítica)* biting

acre² *nm (medida)* acre

acrecentamiento *nm* increase, growth

acrecentar [3] **1** *vt* to increase
2 acrecentarse *vpr* to increase, grow

acreditación *nf* accreditation

acreditado, -a 1 *pp de* **acreditar**
2 *adj* (**a**) *(prestigioso)* reputable, prestigious (**b**) *(embajador, representante)* accredited

acreditar 1 *vt* (**a**) *(dar fama a)* to give credit to, be a credit to, add to the reputation of (**b**) *(probar)* to prove; **este documento le acredita como único heredero** this document proves him to be the sole heir (**c**) *(embajador)* to accredit (**d**) *Fin (abonar en cuenta)* to credit
2 acreditarse *vpr* to make one's name, gain a reputation

acreditativo, -a *adj* which proves, which gives proof

acreedor, -a 1 *adj* deserving; **a. a un premio** worthy of a prize
2 *nm,f Com* creditor

acribillar *vt* (**a**) *(con agujeros)* to riddle, pepper; **a. a algn a balazos** to riddle sb with bullets (**b**) *Fig* to pester, harass; **a. a algn a preguntas** to bombard sb with questions

acrílico, -a *adj* acrylic

acrimonia *nf véase* **acritud**

acriollarse *vpr Am* to adopt local ways

acrisolar *vt* (**a**) *Metal* to purify; *Fig* to perfect (**b**) *Fig (probar)* to prove, show

acristalado, -a 1 *pp de* **acristalar**
2 *adj (terraza, galería)* glazed

acristalar *vt* to glaze

acritud *nf* (**a**) *(al gusto)* sourness, bitterness; *(al olfato)* acridness (**b**) *(de dolor)* intensity, sharpness (**c**) *Fig (mordacidad)* acrimony

acrobacia *nf* (**a**) *(en circo)* acrobatics *sing*; *Fig* **hacer acrobacias con las cifras** to massage the figures (**b**) *(de avión)* aerobatic manoeuvre

acróbata *nmf* acrobat

acrobático, -a *adj* acrobatic

acromático, -a *adj* achromatic

acromatismo *nm* achromatism

acrónimo *nm Ling* acronym

acrópolis *nf inv* acropolis

acta *nf* (**a**) *(de junta, reunión)* minutes *pl*, record; *(publicadas)* transactions *pl*; **levantar a.** to draw up the minutes (**b**) *(certificado)* certificate, official document □ **a. notarial** affidavit (**c**) **actas** minutes, record *sing*; *(publicadas)* transactions

actitud *nf (disposición)* attitude; *(postura)* position; **en a. de ataque** ready to attack

activación *nf* (**a**) *Téc* activation (**b**) *Fig (avivamiento)* livening up, quickening

activar *vt* (**a**) *Téc* to activate (**b**) *Fig (avivar)* to liven up, quicken

actividad *nf* activity

activismo *nm Pol* activism

activista *nmf Pol* activist

activo, -a 1 *adj* (**a**) *(persona, principio)* active; *(veneno)* fast-acting; *(población)* working; **volcán a.** active volcano; **en a.** on active service (**b**) *Ling* active
2 *nm Fin* asset, assets *pl* □ **a. disponible** liquid assets *pl*; **a. financiero** financial assets; **a. y pasivo** assets and liabilities

acto *nm* (**a**) *(acción)* act, action; **a. seguido** immediately afterwards; **en a. de servicio** in action; **en el a.** at once; **hacer a. de presencia** to put in an appearance; **'se hacen llaves en el a.'** 'keys cut while you wait' □ **a. reflejo** reflex action; **a. sexual** sexual intercourse (**b**) *(ceremonia)* ceremony □ **a. de inauguración** opening ceremony **a. electoral** election rally; **actos culturales** cultural events; **salón de actos** assembly hall (**c**) *Teat* act; **comedia en tres actos** three-act play (**d**) *Rel* Act; **Actos de los Apóstoles** Acts of the Apostles

actor, -a 1 *adj Jur* **parte actora** prosecution
2 *nm Cin Teat* actor □ **a. de cine** movie *o Br* film actor

actriz *nf Cin Teat* actress □ **a. de cine** movie *o Br* film actress

actuación *nf* (**a**) *Cin Teat Dep* performance (**b**) *(intervención)* intervention, action

actual 1 *adj* current, present; *(al día)* up-to-date; **en las circunstancias actuales** under the present circumstances; **un tema muy a.** a very topical subject

2 *nm Fml* this month; **el 28 del a.** the 28th of this month

actualidad *nf* (**a**) *(situación)* current situation; **en la a.** *(momento presente)* at the present time, nowadays; **estar de a.** *(ser de interés)* to be topical; **poner algo de a.** to make sth topical; **la a. política** the current political situation (**b**) *(noticia)* news *sing;* **la a. informativa** the news; **la a. deportiva** the sports news; **ser a.** to be making the news (**c**) *(vigencia)* relevance to modern society; **sus libros siguen teniendo gran a.** her books are still very relevant today

actualización *nf* (**a**) *(puesta al día)* updating, bringing up to date (**b**) *Filos* actualization

actualizar [14] *vt* (**a**) *(poner al día)* to update, bring up to date (**b**) *Filos* to actualize (**c**) *Inform (software, hardware)* to upgrade

actualmente *adv (hoy en día)* nowadays, these days; *(ahora)* at the moment, at present

actuar [4] **1** *vt* to actuate, work
  2 *vi* (**a**) *(obrar, producir efecto)* to act; **a. como** *o* **de** to act as; **actuó como debía** he did what he had to do (**b**) *Cin Teat* to perform, act

actuario *nm Jur* clerk (of the court); *Fin* actuary

acuarela *nf Arte* watercolour, *US* watercolor

acuarelista *nmf* watercolourist, *US* watercolorist

Acuario *nm Astrol Astron* Aquarius

acuario *nm (de peces)* aquarium

acuartelamiento *nm Mil* (**a**) *(alojamiento)* quartering (**b**) *(retención)* confinement to barracks (**c**) *(lugar)* barracks (for confinement)

acuartelar *vt Mil* (**a**) *(alojar)* to quarter, billet (**b**) *(retener)* to confine to barracks

acuático, -a *adj* aquatic, water; **ave acuática** aquatic bird

acuatinta *nf Arte* aquatint

acuchillar *vt* (**a**) *(herir, matar)* to knife, stab (**b**) *Cost (hacer aberturas)* to slash (**c**) *Carp* to plane (down)

acuciante *adj* urgent, pressing; **necesidad a.** urgent need

acuciar *vt* to urge on; **acuciado por la necesidad** urged on by necessity

acuclillarse *vpr* to squat (down)

acudir *vi* (**a**) *(ir)* to go; *(venir)* to come, arrive; **acudió puntualmente a la cita** he arrived punctually for the meeting (**b**) *(sobrevenir)* to come back; **aquellos recuerdos acudían a su memoria** those memories kept coming back to him (**c**) *(ir en ayuda)* to help, come forward; **pidió ayuda pero nadie acudió** she asked for help, but nobody came forward (**d**) *(recurrir)* to resort; **acudiré al gobernador** I'll see the governor (about it), I'll take this matter to the governor; **no sé dónde a.** I don't know where to turn

acueducto *nm* aqueduct

acuerdo *nm* agreement; **¡de a.!** all right!, O.K.!; **de a. con** in accordance with; **de común a.** by common consent; **estar de a. en algo/en hacer algo** to agree on sth/to do sth; **llegar a un a.** to come to an agreement; **ponerse de a.** to agree □ **a. comercial** commercial agreement; **a. marco** framework agreement

acuicultura *nf* aquaculture

acuidad *nf Fml* acuity, sharpness

acuífero *nm Geol* aquifer

acuilmarse *vpr CAm Méx* to falter, lose one's nerve

acullá *adv* (over) there, yonder; **aquí, allá y a.** here, there and yonder

acumulable *adj* accumulable; *Com* **intereses acumulables** accumulable interest *sing*

acumulación *nf* accumulation

acumulador, -a 1 *adj* accumulative
  2 *nm Elec* accumulator, storage battery

acumular 1 *vt* to accumulate; **a. datos** to gather data; **a. dinero** to amass money
  2 acumularse *vpr* to accumulate, pile up, build up

acumulativo, -a *adj* accumulative

acunar *vt* to rock

acuñación *nf* striking, minting

acuñar *vt* (**a**) *(monedas)* to strike, mint, coin; *Fig* **a. una frase** to coin a phrase (**b**) *(poner cuñas)* to wedge

acuosidad *nf* (**a**) *(gen)* wateriness (**b**) *(jugosidad)* juiciness

acuoso, -a *adj* (**a**) *(gen)* watery (**b**) *(jugoso)* juicy; **un buen melocotón a.** a nice juicy peach

acupuntor, -a *nm,f* acupuncturist

acupuntura *nf Med* acupuncture

acurrucarse [59] *vpr* to curl up, snuggle up

acusación *nf* (**a**) *(inculpación)* accusation (**b**) *Jur* charge; **la a. particular** the private prosecutor; **acta de a.** indictment

acusado, -a 1 *pp de* **acusar**
  2 *adj* (**a**) *(inculpado)* accused; **a. de asesinato** charged with murder (**b**) *Fig (marcado)* marked, noticeable
  3 *nm,f* accused, defendant

acusador, -a 1 *adj* accusing
  2 *nm,f* accuser

acusar 1 *vt* (**a**) *(inculpar)* to accuse (**de** of); *Jur* to charge (**de** with) (**b**) *(delatar)* **todo parece acusarla** all evidence seems to point to her; *Fig* **esta máquina acusa cualquier cambio de temperatura** this machine is susceptible to any slight change in temperature; *Fig* **se acusa la falta de organización** the lack of organization is evident; *Fig* **su cara acusaba el cansancio** his face showed his exhaustion (**c**) *(recibir)* to take; **a. los golpes** to take the blows (**d**) *Com* **a. recibo** to acknowledge receipt
  2 acusarse *vpr* (**a**) *(confesar)* to confess (**b**) *(acentuarse)* to become more pronounced

acusativo *nm Ling* accusative

acusatorio, -a *adj* accusatory

acuse *nm Com* **a. de recibo** acknowledgment of receipt

acusica *adj & nmf*, **acusón, -ona** *adj & nm,f Fam* telltale

acústica *nf* acoustics *sing*

acústico, -a *adj* acoustic

adagio *nm* (**a**) *(proverbio)* proverb (**b**) *Mús* adagio

adalid *nm* (**a**) *(caudillo)* leader (**b**) *(guía)* champion

adamascado, -a *adj* damask

Adán *nm* Adam

adán *nm Fam* untidy *o* slovenly person

adaptable *adj* adaptable

adaptación *nf* adaptation

adaptado, -a 1 *pp de* **adaptar**
  2 *adj* adapted

adaptador *nm Elec* adapter

adaptar 1 *vt* (**a**) *(modificar)* to adapt; **un modelo adaptado a condiciones desérticas** a model adapted to suit desert conditions (**b**) *(libro, obra de teatro)* to adapt (**a** for)
  2 adaptarse *vpr* to adjust (**a** to); **no se ha adaptado al clima local** he hasn't adjusted *o* got used to the local climate; **se adaptó fácilmente a trabajar en equipo** she quickly adjusted to teamwork

adarga *nf* shield

adarme *nm* jot, whit, scrap; **por adarmes** in dribs and drabs

Addis Abeba *n* Addis Ababa

adecentar 1 *vt* to tidy (up), clean (up)
2 adecentarse *vpr* to tidy oneself up

adecuación *nf* adaptation

adecuado, -a 1 *pp de* **adecuar**
2 *adj* appropriate, suitable, fitting

adecuar *vt* to adapt, make suitable

adefesio *nm* (**a**) *(persona)* freak (**b**) *(cosa)* monstrosity (**c**) *Fam (disparate)* nonsense

a. de J.C. *(abrev de* **antes de Jesucristo**) BC

Adelaida *n* Adelaide

adelantado, -a 1 *pp de* **adelantar**
2 *adj* (**a**) *(aventajado)* advanced; *(desarrollado)* developed; *(precoz)* precocious (**b**) *(antes de tiempo)* early; **pagar por a.** to pay in advance (**c**) *(reloj)* fast (**d**) *(atrevido)* bold, forward

adelantamiento *nm Aut* overtaking; **hacer un a.** to overtake

adelantar 1 *vt* (**a**) *(mover hacia adelante)* to move o bring forward; *Fig* to advance; *Dep (pelota)* to pass forward; **a. tres puestos** to go up three places (**b**) *(reloj)* to put forward (**c**) *(pasar delante)* to pass; *Aut* to overtake; **adelantó un coche rojo** he overtook a red car (**d**) *(acelerar)* to speed up, accelerate (**e**) *(dinero)* to pay in advance, advance; **a. a algn el sueldo** to advance sb's pay (**f**) *Fig (aventajar)* to overtake; **le adelantó en matemáticas** he overtook him in maths
2 *vi* (**a**) *(avanzar)* to advance; **así adelantamos más** it's quicker this way (**b**) *(progresar)* to make progress; **ha adelantado bastante** she's been doing very well (**c**) *(ganar)* to gain, get; **con eso no adelantas nada** that's a waste of time (**d**) *(reloj)* to be fast
2 adelantarse *vpr* (**a**) *(ir delante)* to go ahead; **adelántate y compra las entradas** go ahead and get the tickets; **se adelantó a su tiempo** he was ahead of his time (**b**) *(llegar temprano)* to be early; **el verano se ha adelantado** we are having an early summer (**c**) *(anticiparse)* to get ahead (**a** of); **se me adelantó a pagar** I was going to pay, but he beat me to it; *Fig* **no nos adelantemos a los acontecimientos** let's not jump the gun, we'll cross that bridge when we come to it (**d**) *(aproximarse)* to go o come forward; **se adelantó a saludarla** he went forward to greet her (**e**) *(reloj)* to gain, be fast

adelante 1 *adv* forward, ahead; **de ahora en a.** from now on; **de aquí en a.** from here on; **llevar a. un plan** to carry out a plan; **más a.** *(lugar)* further on; *(tiempo)* later; **sacó a sus hijos a.** he gave his children all they needed; **seguir a.** to keep going, carry on; *Fig* **van saliendo a.** they're managing
2 *interj (pase)* come in!; *(siga)* go ahead!, carry on!

adelanto *nm* (**a**) *(técnico)* advance; **los adelantos de la ciencia** the progress of science (**b**) *(tiempo)* **este reloj lleva diez minutos de a.** this watch is ten minutes fast; **le lleva media hora de a.** he has half an hour's lead over her (**c**) *Com (de dinero)* advance payment

adelfa *nf Bot* oleander, rosebay

adelgazamiento *nm* slimming ❏ **cura de a.** slimming cure, diet

adelgazante *adj* slimming

adelgazar [14] **1** *vt (persona)* to make thin, slim; *(cosa)* to make slim
2 *vi (enflaquecer)* to slim, lose weight; **ha adelgazado mucho** he's lost a lot of weight

además *nm* (**a**) *(movimiento)* movement; *(gesto)* gesture; **en a. de** with the intention of, as if about to; **hacer a. de** to look as if one is about to (**b**) **ademanes** manners

además *adv* besides, in addition; **a. de él** besides him; *(también)* also, as well; **a., no lo he visto nunca**

furthermore, I've never seen him; **llegó cansado, y a., enfermo** he arrived tired and ill to boot

adentrarse *vpr* (**a**) *(penetrar)* to penetrate deep, enter deep (**en** into) (**b**) *Fig (profundizar)* to go deeply into, study thoroughly

adentro 1 *adv* (**a**) *(dentro)* inside; **venid a.** come inside (**b**) *(hacia o en el interior)* **mar a.** out to sea; **no te vayas muy a.** don't go too far in; **tierra a.** inland
2 adentros *nmpl* **decir algo para sus a.** to say sth to oneself

adepto, -a 1 *adj* who follows, who supports
2 *nm,f* follower, supporter

aderezar [14] **1** *vt* (**a**) *Culin (comida)* to season; *(ensalada)* to dress; *(bebida)* to mix (**b**) *(preparar)* to get ready, prepare (**c**) *Fig (adornar)* *(persona)* to make beautiful; *(cosa)* to embellish
2 aderezarse *vpr (arreglarse)* to dress up, get ready

aderezo *nm* (**a**) *Culin (de comida)* seasoning; *(de ensalada)* dressing (**b**) *(preparación)* preparation, disposition (**c**) *(joyas)* set of jewellery (**d**) *(arreos)* harness, trappings *pl*

adeudar 1 *vt* (**a**) *(deber)* to owe, have a debt of (**b**) *Com (en cuenta)* to charge, debit; **a. una cuenta** to charge an account
2 adeudarse *vpr (contraer deudas)* to get into debt

adeudo *nm* (**a**) *(deuda)* debt (**b**) *Com* debit, charge

a D. g. *(abrev de* **a Dios gracias**) thanks be to God

adherencia *nf* (**a**) *(adhesión)* adherence; *(pegajosidad)* adhesion, sticking (**b**) *Aut* roadholding

adherente 1 *adj* adherent
2 *nm* (**a**) *(requisito)* requisite (**b**) *(adhesivo)* adhesive

adherir [62] **1** *vt* to stick on
2 *vi* to stick (**a** to)
2 adherirse *vpr Fig* **a. a** to adhere to, follow

adhesión *nf* adhesion, adherence; *Fig (apoyo)* support; *Fig (a una doctrina)* adherence to a doctrine; *Fig* **contaba con la a. de todos** he had everyone's support

adhesivo, -a *adj & nm* adhesive

ad hoc *adj* ad hoc

adicción *nf* addiction; **crear a.** to be addictive

adición *nf* (**a**) *(suma)* addition (**b**) *RP (cuenta) Br* bill, *US* check

adicional *adj* additional

adicionar *vt* to add; *Mat* to add up

adictivo, -a *adj* addictive

adicto, -a 1 *adj* (**a**) *(a droga, hábito)* addicted (**a** to) (**b**) *(partidario)* **a.** in favour of; **no soy muy a. a las reformas propuestas** I'm not greatly enamoured of the proposed reforms
2 *nm,f* (**a**) *(a droga, hábito)* addict; **un a. a la heroína/al tabaco** a heroin/nicotine addict (**b**) *(partidario)* supporter; **los adictos al régimen** the supporters of the regime

adiestrado, -a 1 *pp de* **adiestrar**
2 *adj* (**a**) *(animal)* trained, instructed (**b**) *(en heráldica)* dexterwise

adiestrador, -a *nm,f* trainer; **a. de perros** dog handler

adiestramiento *nm* training, instruction

adiestrar 1 *vt* to train, instruct
2 adiestrarse *vpr* to train onself

adinerado, -a 1 *adj* wealthy, rich
2 *nm,f* rich person

adiós 1 *interj* goodbye; *Fam* bye-bye; *(al cruzarse con algn)* hello; *Fam* **¡a. las vacaciones!** that's my holidays finished!
2 *nm* goodbye; **decir a. con la mano** to wave goodbye; *Fam Fig* **decir a. a algo** to say goodbye to sth

adiposidad *nf* fattiness

adiposo, -a *adj Anat* fatty

aditamento *nm (añadidura)* added piece, addition; *(complemento)* accessory

aditivo, -a *adj & nm* additive

adivinación *nf* (**a**) *(conjetura)* guessing; **a. del pensamiento** mind-reading (**b**) *(predicción)* divination, forecast

adivinador, -a *nm,f* fortune-teller

adivinanza *nf* riddle, puzzle

adivinar *vt* (**a**) *(acertar)* to guess; **a. el pensamiento a algn** to read sb's mind (**b**) *(presagiar)* to foretell, forecast

adivinatorio, -a *adj* divinatory

adivino, -a *nm,f* fortune-teller

adjetivación *nf Ling* adjectival use

adjetival *adj Ling* adjectival

adjetivar *vt* (**a**) *Ling* to use adjectivally *o* as an adjective (**b**) *Fig (calificar)* to label, describe

adjetivo, -a 1 *adj* adjectival, adjective
2 *nm* adjective

adjudicación *nf* (**a**) *(concesión)* award, awarding (**b**) *(en subasta)* sale

adjudicar [59] **1** *vt* (**a**) *(premio)* to award (**b**) *(vender)* to sell, knock down; **¡adjudicado!** sold!
2 adjudicarse *vpr (apropiarse)* to appropriate, take over

adjudicatario, -a *nm,f* (**a**) *(premiado)* awardee (**b**) *(comprador)* buyer, successful bidder

adjuntar *vt* to enclose, attach; *(en carta)* **adjunto una muestra** please find enclosed sample

adjunto, -a 1 *pp de* **adjuntar**
2 *adj* (**a**) *(en carta)* enclosed; *Inform (archivo)* attached; **rellenar el cupón a.** fill in the enclosed form (**b**) *Educ* assistant; **profesor a.** assistant teacher
3 *nm,f Educ* assistant teacher

adlátere *nm* henchman, follower

adm., admón., *(abrev de* **administración**) administration

administración *nf* (**a**) *(gobierno)* **la A.** *Br* the Government, *US* the Administration ◻ *Pol* **a. central** central government; **a. pública** public administration (**b**) *(de empresa)* administration, management ◻ **consejo de a.** board of directors (**c**) *(cargo)* post of administrator; post of manager (**d**) *(despacho)* administrator's office, manager's office (**e**) *(oficina)* (branch) office ◻ **A. de Hacienda** (local) tax office; **a. local** local government; *Esp* **a. de lotería** lottery office

administrador, -a 1 *adj* administrating
2 *nm,f (de empresa)* manager; *(de bienes, fincas)* administrator
3 *nm Inform* **a. de archivos** file manager

administrar 1 *vt* (**a**) *(empresa, finca)* to manage, run; *(casa)* to run; *(país)* to govern, run; *(recursos)* to manage **a. justicia** to administer justice. (**b**) *Fml (dar)* to give; **le administró un antibiótico** he gave him an antibiotic
2 administrarse *vpr* to manage one's own finances

administrativo, -a 1 *adj* administrative
2 *nm,f* (**a**) *(funcionario)* official (**b**) *(de empresa, banco)* office worker

admirable *adj* admirable

admiración *nf* admiration; **causar a.** to impress; **sentir a. por** to admire

admirador, -a 1 *adj* admiring
2 *nm,f* admirer

admirar 1 *vt* (**a**) *(personaje, obra de arte)* to admire (**b**) *(sorprender)* to amaze, surprise, astound, astonish; **me**

admira su valor I am amazed by his courage; **quedarse admirado** to be astonished
2 admirarse *vpr* to be amazed, be astonished

admirativo, -a *adj* admiring

admisibilidad *nf* admissibility

admisible *adj* admissible, acceptable

admisión *nf* (**a**) *(de persona)* admission; **'reservado el derecho de a.'** 'the management reserves the right to refuse admission' (**b**) *(aceptación)* acceptance (**c**) *Téc* inlet, intake

admitir *vt* (**a**) *(dejar entrar)* to admit, let in (**b**) *(aceptar)* to admit, accept; **'no se admiten cheques'** 'no cheques accepted' (**c**) *(permitir)* to allow; **no admito este tipo de conversación** I will not tolerate this type of conversation; *Fig* **este libro admite varias lecturas** this book is open to various interpretations (**d**) *(reconocer)* to admit, acknowledge; **admito que fui demasiado lejos** I admit that I took things too far (**e**) *(haber lugar)* to hold; **admite hasta cien personas** there is room for up to a hundred people

admonición *nf* warning, reproof

admonitorio, -a *adj* warning

ADN *nm (abrev de* **ácido desoxirribonucleico**) DNA

adobado, -a 1 *pp de* **adobar**
2 *adj Culin* marinated

adobar *vt* (**a**) *Culin (carne, pescado)* to marinate (**b**) *(pieles)* to tan

adobe *nm* adobe

adobo *nm Culin* (**a**) *(acción)* marinating (**b**) *(salsa)* marinade

adocenado, -a 1 *pp de* **adocenarse**
2 *adj* common or garden, ordinary

adocenarse *vpr* to become commonplace

adoctrinamiento *nm* indoctrination

adoctrinar *vt* to indoctrinate

adolecer [46] *vi (sufrir)* to be ill; **adolecía de asma** he suffered from asthma; *Fig Fml* **adolece de excesivo barroquismo** it is far too baroque

adolescencia *nf* adolescence

adolescente *adj & nmf* adolescent

adonde *adv* where

adónde *adv interr* where (to)?

adondequiera *adv* wherever

adonis *nm inv* Adonis, handsome young man

adopción *nf* adoption; **país de a.** country of adoption

adoptar *vt* to adopt

adoptivo, -a *adj (hijo)* adopted, adoptive; *(padres)* adoptive; *Fig* **hijo a. de la ciudad** honorary citizen; *Fig* **país a.** country of adoption

adoquín *nm* cobble, paving stone

adoquinado, -a 1 *pp de* **adoquinar**
2 *adj* cobbled
3 *nm* cobbling, paving

adoquinar *vt* to cobble, pave

adorable *adj* adorable

adoración *nf* (**a**) *Rel* worship, adoration (**b**) *Fig* adoration, worshipping

adorador, -a 1 *adj* (**a**) *Rel* worshipping (**b**) *Fig* adoring
2 *nm,f* (**a**) *Rel* worshipper (**b**) *Fig* adorer, worshipper

adorar *vt* (**a**) *Rel* to worship (**b**) *Fig* to adore

adormecedor, -a *adj* sleep-inducing, soporific

adormecer [46] **1** *vt* (**a**) *(producir sueño)* to send to sleep, make sleepy (**b**) *Fig (acallar)* to quieten; *(calmar)* to soothe

2 adormecerse *vpr* (a) *(dormirse)* to doze off (b) *(miembro)* to go to sleep, go numb

adormecido, -a 1 *pp de* adormecer
2 *adj* sleepy, drowsy

adormecimiento *nm* (a) *(sueño)* drowsiness, sleepiness (b) *(de miembro)* numbness

adormidera *nf Bot* poppy

adormilado, -a *adj (dormido)* dozing; *(con sueño)* sleepy

adormilarse *vpr* to doze, drowse

adornar *vt* to adorn, decorate; *Fig* to embellish

adorno *nm (gen)* decoration, adornment; *Cost* trimming; **de a.** decorative

adosado, -a 1 *pp de* adosar
2 *adj Constr* semidetached

adosar *vt* to lean (**a** against)

adquirido, -a 1 *pp de* adquirir
2 *adj* acquired

adquirir [5] *vt* to acquire

adquisición *nf (gen)* acquisition; *(compra)* buy, purchase

adquisitivo, -a *adj* acquisitive

adrede *adv* deliberately, on purpose, purposely

adrenalina *nf* adrenalin

adriático, -a 1 *adj* Adriatic
2 *nm* **el (Mar) A.** the Adriatic (Sea)

adscribir *(pp* adscrito**) 1** *vt* (a) *(atribuir)* to ascribe (**a** to) (b) *(a un trabajo)* to appoint (**a** to)
2 adscribirse *vpr (afiliarse)* to affiliate (**a** to)

adscripción *nf* (a) *(atribución)* ascription (b) *(a un trabajo)* appointment

adscrito, -a 1 *pp de* adscribir
2 *adj* (a) *(atribuido)* ascribed (b) *(a un trabajo)* appointed

adsorbente *adj & nm Fís* adsorbent

adsorber *vt Fís* to adsorb

adsorción *nf Fís* adsorption

aduana *nf* customs *pl*; **el tabaco no paga a.** there's no duty on tobacco; **pasar por la a.** to go through customs ❑ **oficial de a.** customs officer

aduanero, -a 1 *adj* customs
2 *nm,f* customs officer

aducir [18] *vt* to adduce, allege

adueñarse *vpr* **a. de** to appropriate, seize; *Fig* **el terror se adueñó de ella** she was seized by terror

adulación *nf* adulation, flattery

adulador, -a 1 *adj* adulating, flattering
2 *nm,f* adulator, flatterer

adular *vt* to adulate, flatter, soft-soap

adulón, -ona 1 *adj* fawning, grovelling, *US* groveling
2 *nm,f* crawler, groveller, *US* groveler

adulteración *nf* adulteration

adulterar *vt* to adulterate

adulterio *nm* adultery

adúltero, -a 1 *adj* adulterous
2 *nm,f (hombre)* adulterer; *(mujer)* adulteress

adulto, -a *adj & nm,f* adult; **los adultos** grown-ups; **una persona adulta** an adult

adustez *nf* harshness, severity

adusto, -a *adj* harsh, stern, austere, severe

aduzco *indic pres véase* aducir

advenedizo, -a *adj & nm,f* parvenu, parvenue, upstart

advenimiento *nm (gen)* advent, coming; *(al trono)* accession

adventicio, -a *adj* accidental; *Biol* adventitious

adventismo *nm Rel* Adventism

adventista *adj & nmf Rel* Adventist

adverbial *adj Ling* adverbial

adverbio *nm Ling* adverb

adversario, -a 1 *adj* opposing; **el equipo a.** the opposing team
2 *nm,f* adversary, opponent

adversativo, -a *adj Ling* adversative

adversidad *nf* adversity, misfortune, setback

adverso, -a *adj* (a) *(condiciones)* adverse; **incluso en las condiciones más adversas** even in the worst o most adverse conditions (b) *(destino)* unkind; **la suerte le fue adversa** fate was unkind to him (c) *(viento)* unfavourable

advertencia *nf* warning; *(consejo)* piece of advice; **te voy a hacer una a.** mark my words

advertido, -a 1 *pp de* advertir
2 *adj* warned; *(informado)* informed; **estás o quedas a.** you've been warned

advertir [62] *vt* (a) *(prevenir, avisar)* to warn; **te lo había advertido** I told you; *Fam* **te advierto que él tampoco lo vio** mind you, he didn't see it either (b) *(darse cuenta)* to notice; **no advirtió su presencia** he didn't notice he was there

adviento *nm Rel* Advent

advocación *nf Rel* invocation; **bajo la a. de** under the protection of

adyacente *adj* adjacent

AEE *nf (abrev de* **Agencia Espacial Europea)** ESA

aéreo, -a *adj* (a) *(del aire)* aerial; **vista aérea** aerial view (b) *Av* air; **líneas aéreas** airlines; **tráfico a.** air traffic

aero- *pref* aero-; *Av* **aerobús** airbus

aerobic *nm*, **aeróbic** *nm* aerobics *sing*

aeróbico, -a *adj* aerobic

aerobio, -a *Biol* **1** *adj* aerobic
2 *nm* aerobe

aeroclub *nm* flying club

aerodeslizador *nm* hovercraft

aerodinámica *nf Fís* aerodynamics *sing*

aerodinámico, -a *adj Fís* aerodynamic; **de línea aerodinámica** streamlined

aeródromo *nm* aerodrome

aeroespacial *adj Av* aerospace

aerofagia *nf Med* aerophagia

aerofaro *nm* beacon

aerógrafo *nm Arte* airbrush

aerograma *nm* aerogram, aerogramme

aerolínea *nf* airline

aerolito *nm* aerolite

aeromodelismo *nm Br* aeroplane modelling, *US* airplane modeling

aeromodelista 1 *adj Br* aeroplane modelling, *US* airplane modeling
2 *nmf Br* aeroplane modeller, *US* airplane modeler

aeromodelo *nm* model aeroplane o *US* airplane

aeromozo, -a *nm,f Am* flight attendant

aeronauta *nmf* aeronaut

aeronáutica *nf* aeronautics *sing*

aeronáutico, -a *adj* aeronautic, aeronautical

aeronaval *adj Av Náut* air-sea

aeronave *nf* airship ❑ **a. espacial** spaceship

aeroplano *nm* aeroplane

aeropuerto *nm* airport

aerosol *nm Quím* aerosol

aerospacial *adj Av* aerospace

aerostática *nf Fís* aerostatics *sing*

aerostático, -a *adj Fís* aerostatic; **globo a.** hot-air balloon

aerostato *nm Fís* hot-air balloon

aerotaxi *nm* light aircraft *(for hire)*

aerotransportado, -a 1 *pp de* **aerotransportar**
2 *adj (tropas, polen)* airborne

aerotransportar *vt* to airlift

a/f *(abrev de* **a favor)** in favour *o US* favor

afabilidad *nf* affability

afable *adj* affable

afamado, -a 1 *pp de* **afamar**
2 *adj* famous, well-known

afamar 1 *vt* to make famous
2 afamarse *vpr* to become famous

afán *nm* **(a)** *(esfuerzo)* effort **(b)** *(celo)* zeal; *(interés)* keenness, eagerness; **con a.** keenly

afanador, -a *nm,f* **(a)** *Méx (empleado)* (office) cleaner **(b)** *Méx RP Fam (ladrón)* crook, thief

afanar 1 *vt Fam (robar)* to nick, pinch, swipe
2 afanarse *vpr (esforzarse)* to work with zeal; **a. por conseguir algo** to do one's best to achieve *o* obtain sth

afanoso, -a *adj* **(a)** *(persona)* keen, zealous, eager **(b)** *(tarea)* hard, tough, laborious

afarolarse *vpr Andes Cuba Fam (emocionarse)* to get worked up, get excited; *(enojarse)* to get angry

afasia *nf Med* aphasia

afásico, -a *adj & nm,f Med* aphasic

afear *vt* **(a)** *(persona)* to make ugly **(b)** *Fig (reprochar)* to reproach; **afearle a algn la conducta** to censure sb's behaviour

afección *nf* **(a)** *(enfermedad)* complaint, disease; **una a. de garganta** a throat complaint **(b)** *(afición)* fondness

afectación *nf* affectation

afectado, -a 1 *pp de* **afectar**
2 *adj* **(a)** *(gen)* affected; **la región afectada por la sequía** the area affected by (the) drought **(b)** *(fingido)* pretended, affected **(c)** *(emocionado)* affected, upset; **está muy a.** he's very upset **(d)** *(involucrado)* involved; **las personas afectadas** the people involved **(e)** *Med* **a. de hepatitis** suffering from hepatitis

afectar *vt* **(a)** *(gen)* to affect; **a. la voz** to talk in an affected way; **afectó indiferencia** she affected indifference; **le afectó mucho** she was deeply affected; **nos afecta a todos** it concerns all of us **(b)** *(dañar)* to damage; **le afectó a los ojos** it damaged his eyes

afectísimo, -a *adj Fml superl de* **afecto, -a**; *(en una carta)* **suyo a.** yours faithfully

afectividad *nf* affectivity

afectivo, -a *adj* **(a)** *(sensibilidad)* sensitive **(b)** *Psic* affective

afecto, -a 1 *adj* **(a)** *(aficionado)* fond **(a** of) **(b)** *Med* suffering **(de** from)
2 *nm* affection; *(en carta)* **con todo mi a.** with all my love; **tomarle a. a algn** to become fond of sb

afectuosamente *adv (en carta)* (yours) affectionately

afectuosidad *nf* affection

afectuoso, -a *adj* affectionate

afeitado *nm* **(a)** *(de persona)* shave, shaving **(b)** *Taur (de cuernos)* blunting

afeitadora *nf* razor, shaver

afeitar 1 *vt* **(a)** *(persona)* to shave **(b)** *Taur (toro)* to blunt the horns of
2 afeitarse *vpr* to shave

afeite *nm Anticuado* make-up

afelpado, -a *adj Tex* velvety

afeminación *nf* effeminacy

afeminado, -a 1 *pp de* **afeminar**
2 *adj* effeminate
3 *nm* effeminate man; *Fam* sissy

afeminamiento *nm* effeminacy

afeminar 1 *vt* to make effeminate
2 afeminarse *vpr* to become effeminate

aferrado, -a 1 *pp de* **aferrar**
2 *adj* **a. a** clinging to, clutching, holding on to; *Fig* **a. a sus ideas** sticking to his guns

aferramiento *nm (a idea, creencia)* clinging

aferrar 1 *vt* **(a)** *(agarrar)* to clutch, cling, grasp **(b)** *Náut (anclar)* to anchor, moor; **a. las velas** to furl the sails
2 aferrarse *vpr* to cling; **a. a una creencia** to cling to a belief

affmo., -a. *(abrev de* **afectísimo, -a)** *(en carta)* **suyo a.** *(si se desconoce el nombre del destinatario)* yours faithfully; *(si se conoce el nombre del destinatario)* yours sincerely

Afganistán *n* Afghanistan

afgano, -a *adj & nm,f* Afghan

AFI *nm Ling (abrev de* **Asociación Fonética Internacional)** IPA

afianzamiento *nm* **(a)** *(de construcción)* reinforcement **(b)** *(de ideas, relaciones)* consolidation

afianzar [14] **1** *vt* **(a)** *(construcción)* to reinforce **(b)** *(posición)* to make secure; **afianzó el pie en el escalón** he steadied his foot on the step **(c)** *(idea, relación)* to consolidate
2 afianzarse *vpr* **(a)** *(en lugar)* to steady oneself; **a. en una posición** *(en organización)* to establish oneself in a position **(b)** *(idea, creencia)* to take root; *(relación)* to become stronger *o* closer; **se afianzó en su opinión** he became more convinced of his opinion

afiche *nm Am* poster

afición *nf* **(a)** *(inclinación)* penchant, liking; **tiene a. por la música** he is fond of music **(b)** *(ahínco)* interest, zeal; **con a.** keenly **(c)** *Dep* **la a.** the fans *pl*

aficionado, -a 1 *pp de* **aficionar**
2 *adj* **(a)** *(interesado)* keen, fond; **ser a. a viajar** to be fond of travelling **(b)** *(no profesional)* amateur
3 *nm,f* **(a)** *(interesado)* enthusiast; **un a. a la música** a music lover **(b)** *(no profesional)* amateur

aficionar 1 *vt (interesar)* to interest, make fond of
2 aficionarse *vpr (interesarse)* to become fond **(a** of), take a liking **(a** to); **se aficionó al teatro** she became a theatre lover

afijo, -a *Ling* **1** *adj* affixed
2 *nm* affix

afilado, -a 1 *pp de* **afilar**
2 *adj (con filo)* sharp; *(con punta)* pointed; *Fig* **cara afilada** long, thin face
3 *nm* sharpening

afilador, -a 1 *adj* sharpening
2 *nm,f (persona)* knife-grinder
3 *nm (máquina)* sharpener

afilalápices *nm inv* pencil sharpener

afilamiento *nm Fig (de cara, nariz)* sharpness

afilar 1 *vt (cuchillo, lápiz)* to sharpen
2 *vi RP (flirtear)* to flirt
3 afilarse *vpr* to grow pointed *o* sharp

afiliación *nf* affiliation

afiliado, -a 1 *pp de* **afiliar**
2 *adj* affiliated, member
3 *nm,f* affiliate, member

afiliar 1 *vt* to affiliate, make a member
2 afiliarse *vpr* to affiliate, become a member

afiligranado, -a *adj Arte* filigreed; *Fig* delicate, dainty, fine

afín *adj* (a) *(semejante)* kindred, similar; *(relacionado)* related; **el alcohol y los productos afines** alcohol and related products; **gustos afines** similar tastes (b) *(próximo)* adjacent, next

afinación *nf* (a) *(gen)* polishing, refining (b) *(música, máquina)* tuning

afinador, -a *Mús* **1** *nm,f (persona)* tuner
2 *nm* tuning fork

afinar *vt* (a) *(gen)* to polish, perfect; *(puntería)* to sharpen (b) *(instrumento)* to tune (c) *(metales)* to refine

afincarse [59] *vpr* to settle down, establish oneself

afinidad *nf* affinity; *Quím* similarity

afirmación *nf* (a) *(aseveración)* statement, assertion (b) *(afianzamiento)* strengthening

afirmar 1 *vt* (a) *(aseverar)* to state, declare; **afirmó no saber nada** he said he knew nothing (about it) (b) *(afianzar)* to strengthen, reinforce
2 afirmarse *vpr* **a. en algo** to reaffirm sth

afirmativa *nf* affirmative answer

afirmativo, -a *adj* affirmative; **en caso a. ...** if the answer is yes ...

aflautado, -a *adj* flute-like

aflicción *nf* affliction, suffering, grief

afligido, -a 1 *pp de* **afligir**
2 *adj* afflicted, grieved, troubled

afligir [24] **1** *vt* to afflict, grieve, trouble
2 afligirse *vpr* to grieve, be distressed

aflojamiento *nm* loosening; *Fig* relaxation

aflojar 1 *vt (soltar)* to loosen; *Fig (esfuerzo)* to relax; *Fam* **a. la mosca** to fork out
2 *vi (disminuir)* to weaken, grow weak; **el calor ha aflojado un poco** the heat has let up a bit
2 aflojarse *vpr (soltarse)* to come o work loose; **se aflojó el tornillo** the screw came loose

afloramiento *nm Min* outcrop

aflorar *vi* (a) *Min* to crop out, outcrop (b) *Fig (asomar)* to come to the surface, appear

afluencia *nf* inflow, influx; **la a. de público** the flow of people

afluente 1 *adj (caudaloso)* flowing, inflowing; *(persona)* verbose, wordy
2 *nm Geog* tributary

afluir [34] *vi* to flow (a into)

aflujo *nm* afflux

afmo., -a. *(abrev de* **afectísimo, -a)** *(en carta)* **suyo a.** yours faithfully

afonía *nf Med* loss of voice, hoarseness

afónico, -a *adj* voiceless, hoarse; **estar a.** to have lost one's voice

aforar *vt Téc* to gauge

aforismo *nm* aphorism

aforístico, -a *adj* aphoristic

aforo *nm* (a) *(capacidad)* seating capacity (b) *(evaluación)* valuation, assessment

afortunadamente *adv* fortunately, luckily

afortunado, -a *adj* fortunate, lucky; *(dichoso)* happy;

Fig **una respuesta poco afortunada** a rather inappropriate answer; *Prov* **a. en el juego, desgraciado en amores** lucky at cards, unlucky in love

afrancesado, -a 1 *adj* (a) *(galicista)* pro-French, who has gone French (b) *Hist* supporting Napoleon
2 *nm,f Hist* (Spanish) supporter of Napoleon

afrancesamiento *nm* pro-French attitude, Frenchification

afrenta *nf Fml* affront, offense; **hacerle una a. a algn** to affront sb

afrentar *Fml* **1** *vt* to affront, offend
2 afrentarse *vpr* to be ashamed (**de** of)

afrentoso, -a *adj Fml* (a) *(que ofende)* offending, offensive (b) *(que avergüenza)* shameful, disgraceful

África *n* Africa

africada *nf Ling* affricate

africado, -a *adj Ling* affricative

africano, -a *adj & nm,f* African

afrikaans *nm (idioma)* Afrikaans

afrikáner *adj & nmf* Afrikaner

afro *adj Fam* afro

afroamericano, -a *adj & nm,f* Afro-American

afroasiático, -a *adj & nm,f* Afro-Asian

afrodisíaco, -a *adj & nm* aphrodisiac

afrontamiento *nm* confrontation

afrontar *vt* (a) *(hacer frente)* to confront, face; **a. las consecuencias** to face up to the consequences; **a. una situación** to face a situation (b) *Jur (carear)* to confront, bring face to face (c) *(poner enfrente)* to face

afrutado, -a *adj* fruity

afta *nf Med* aphtha

after hour(s) ['after 'awars] *nm inv Fam* = club which opens well after midnight and stays open into the following morning

aftoso, -a *adj Med* **fiebre aftosa** foot-and-mouth disease

afuera 1 *adv* outside; **la parte de a.** the outside; **más a.** further out; **salir a.** to come/go out
2 afueras *nfpl* outskirts; **vivían en las a. de Pamplona** they lived on the outskirts of Pamplona

afuereño, -a *nm,f Am* outsider

agachada *nf (acción)* squatting; *(ardid)* trick, ruse

agachadiza *nf Orn* snipe

agachar 1 *vt* to lower, bow
2 agacharse *vpr* (a) *(encogerse)* to cower; *(agazaparse)* to crouch (down), squat; *(protegerse)* to duck (down) (b) *Fam (aguantarse)* to put up with

agalla 1 *nf* (a) *(de pez)* gill (b) *Bot* gall, gallnut
2 agallas *nfpl* (a) *(valor)* guts, pluck *sing*; **tiene a.** she's got guts (b) *Carib (codicia)* greed

agalludo, -a *adj Carib Fam* (a) *(codicioso, avaro)* grasping (b) *(ruin, mezquino)* mean

ágape *nm* (a) *(banquete)* feast, banquet (b) *Hist* agape

agarrada *nf Fam* quarrel; **tener una a. con algn** to have a row with sb

agarraderas *nfpl Fam* **tener buenas a.** to be well connected, have the right friends

agarradero *nm* (a) *(asa)* handle (b) *Fam (excusa)* excuse

agarrado, -a 1 *pp de* **agarrar**
2 *adj Fam* stingy, tight; **baile a.** cheek-to-cheek dancing

agarrar 1 *vt* (a) *(con las manos)* to grasp, clutch, seize; **agárralo fuerte** hold it tight (b) *Esp Fam (pillar) (ladrón, enfermedad)* to catch; **a. una borrachera** to get drunk o pissed; **agarró un cabreo** he flew off the handle (c) *Am* *(tren, avión)* to get, take; **agarró el autobús** he took the bus **2** *vi* **(a)** *Esp (asir)* **a. de** to take hold of; **¡agarra de la cuerda!** grab the rope! **(b)** *(tinte)* to take **(c)** *(planta)* to take root **(d)** *(ruedas)* to grip **(e)** *Am (encaminarse)* **a. para** to head for; **agarró para la izquierda** he took a left **(f)** *Fam* **a. y hacer algo** to go and do sth; **agarró y se fue** she upped and went

2 agarrarse *vpr* **(a)** *(sujetarse)* **a. a** to hold on to, cling to, clutch; **agárrate bien** hold tight; **a. a** *o* **de algo** to hold on to sth; *Fig* **a. a un clavo ardiendo** to clutch at straws; *Fam* **se agarra a lo que sea para no trabajar** he seizes on any excuse to avoid work **(b)** *Culin (pegarse)* to stick **(c)** *Fam (pelearse)* to quarrel, fight

agarrón *nm Fam* **(a)** *(tirón)* pull, tug **(b)** *(agarrada)* fight, quarrel

agarrotado, -a 1 *pp de* **agarrotar 2** *adj* **(a)** *(apretado)* tight **(b)** *(músculo)* stiff **(c)** *(motor)* seized up

agarrotamiento *nm* **(a)** *(atadura)* tightening **(b)** *(rigidez)* stiffening **(c)** *(de máquina)* seizing up

agarrotar 1 *vt* **(a)** *(atar)* to tighten, tie up tightly **(b)** *(músculos)* to stiffen **(c)** *(estrangular)* to strangle; *(dar garrote)* to garotte **2 agarrotarse** *vpr* **(a)** *(entumecerse músculos)* to stiffen; *(perder sensibilidad)* to go numb **(b)** *(máquina)* to seize up

agasajar *vt (obsequiar)* to smother with attentions, treat well; *(dar agasajo)* to wine and dine

agasajo *nm* **(a)** *(acogida)* royal welcome; *(trato)* kindness **(b)** *(comida)* reception, banquet **(c)** *(regalo)* gift

ágata *nf Min* agate

agaucharse *vpr SAm* to adopt gaucho ways

agave *nf Bot* agave

agavillar *vt Agr* to bind, sheave

agazapado, -a *adj* crouching

agazapar 1 *vt* to grab (hold of) **2 agazaparse** *vpr (agacharse)* to crouch (down), squat; *(esconderse)* to hide

agencia *nf* agency; *(sucursal)* branch ❑ **a. bancaria** bank; *Esp* **a. inmobiliaria** *Br* estate agent's, *US* real estate office; **a. de publicidad** advertising agency; **a. de seguros** insurance company; **la A. Tributaria** *Br* ≃ the Inland Revenue, *US* ≃ the IRS; **a. de viajes** travel agency

agenciarse *vpr* **(a)** *(apañarse)* to manage, look after oneself; **agenciárselas** to manage; **ya me las agenciaré como pueda** I'll manage **(b)** *(proporcionarse)* to get oneself; **se ha agenciado un cochazo increíble** he's got himself a fantastic car

agenda *nf* diary; **a. del día** agenda ❑ **a. electrónica** electronic personal organizer

agente 1 *adj Ling* **complemento a.** agent **2** *nmf* agent ❑ **a. comercial** broker; **a. de inmigración** immigration officer; **a. inmobiliario** *Br* estate agent, *US* realtor; **a. de policía** *(hombre)* policeman; *(mujer)* policewoman; **a. secreto** secret agent; **a. de tráfico** *(hombre)* traffic policeman; *(mujer)* traffic policewoman **3** *nm* ❑ **a. provocador** agent provocateur; **agentes naturales** natural agents

agigantado, -a 1 *pp de* **agigantar 2** *adj* massive, huge; **a pasos agigantados** by leaps and bounds

agigantar 1 *vt* to enlarge; *Fig* to exaggerate **2 agigantarse** *vpr* to become huge

ágil *adj* agile

agilidad *nf* agility; **con a.** swiftly ❑ **a. mental** mental agility

agilipollado, -a *adj Esp Vulg* stupid, daft

agilización *nf* speeding up

agilizar [14] *vt* to make agile; *Fig* to speed up; **a. los trámites** to speed up the paperwork

agio *nm Econ* agio

agiotaje *nm Com* speculation

agiotista *nmf Com* speculator

agitación *nf* agitation; *Fig (inquietud)* excitement, restlessness; **a. política** political agitation

agitado, -a 1 *pp de* **agitar 2** *adj* **(a)** *(persona)* anxious **(b)** *(ajetreado)* hectic; **una vida muy agitada** a very hectic life **(c)** *(mar)* rough

agitador, -a 1 *nm,f (persona)* agitator **2** *nm Quím* agitator

agitanado, -a *adj* gypsy-like

agitar 1 *vt (botella)* to shake; *(pañuelo)* to wave; *Fig (multitudes)* to agitate; **'agítese antes de usarlo'** 'shake before use' **2 agitarse** *vpr* **(a)** *(moverse)* to move restlessly; *Fig (inquietarse)* to become agitated **(b)** *(mar)* to become rough

aglomeración *nf* **(a)** *(gen)* agglomeration **(b)** *(de gente)* crowd

aglomerado *nm* **(a)** *Constr* agglomerate **(b)** *(combustible)* briquette

aglomerante *nm* binding material

aglomerar 1 *vt (agrupar)* to agglomerate, amass **2 aglomerarse** *vpr* **(a)** *(agruparse)* to agglomerate, amass; **los coches se aglomeraban en la plaza** cars piled up in the square **(b)** *(gente)* to crowd, form a crowd

aglutinación *nf* agglutination

aglutinante 1 *adj* agglutinant, binding; *Ling* **lengua a.** agglutinative language **2** *nm* agglutinant

aglutinar 1 *vt* to agglutinate, bind; *Fig* to bring together **2 aglutinarse** *vpr* to agglutinate; *Fig* to come together

agnosticismo *nm* agnosticism

agnóstico, -a *adj & nm,f* agnostic

agobiado, -a 1 *pp de* **agobiar 2** *adj (doblado)* bent down, weighed down; *Fig* **a. de problemas** snowed under with problems; *Fig* **a. de trabajo** up to one's eyes in work

agobiador, -a *adj*, **agobiante** *adj (cansado)* backbreaking, exhausting; *(carga)* overwhelming; *(lugar)* claustrophobic; *(calor)* oppressive; *(persona)* tiresome, tiring

agobiar 1 *vt (doblar)* to bend down, weigh down; *Fig (abrumar)* to overwhelm, overburden; **me agobia la gran ciudad** the big city is too much for me **2 agobiarse** *vpr (angustiarse)* to worry too much; **enseguida se agobia por todo** he worries about everything

agobio *nm* burden, suffocation, oppression

agolparse *vpr* to crowd, throng; *Fig* **las lágrimas se agolpaban en sus ojos** tears welled up in his eyes

agonía *nf* **(a)** *(de moribundo)* dying breath, last gasp; **en su a.** on his deathbed; **tener una larga a.** to die after a long illness **(b)** *Fig (sufrimiento)* agony, grief, sorrow

agónico, -a *adj* dying, death; **estertores agónicos** death rattle; **estar en estado a.** to be about to die

agonizante 1 *adj* dying **2** *nmf* dying person

agonizar [14] *vi* **(a)** *(persona)* to be dying; **está agonizando** he could die any moment now **(b)** *Fig (extinguirse)* to fail, fade away

ágora *nm Hist* agora

agorafobia *nf Psic* agoraphobia

agorero, -a 1 *adj* ominous; *Fig* **ave agorera** bird of ill omen; *Fam* **¡qué a. eres!** what a jinx you are!
2 *nm,f* prophet of doom

agostar 1 *vt (secar)* to wither, parch; *Fig (debilitar)* to ruin
2 agostarse *vpr (campo)* to dry up; *(planta)* to wither, shrivel

agosto *nm* August; *Fam* **hacer su a.** to make a packet *o* pile; *véase tamb* **noviembre**

agotado, -a 1 *pp de* **agotar**
2 *adj* **(a)** *(cansado)* exhausted, worn out **(b)** *Com* sold out; *(existencias)* exhausted; *(libro)* out of print

agotador, -a *adj* exhausting

agotamiento *nm* exhaustion ⃞ **a. físico** physical strain; **a. nervioso** nervous exhaustion

agotar 1 *vt* **(a)** *(cansar)* to exhaust, tire out, wear out **(b)** *(acabar)* to exhaust, use up (completely)
2 agotarse *vpr* **(a)** *(acabarse)* to run out, be used up; *Com* to be sold out **(b)** *(persona)* to become exhausted *o* tired out

agraciado, -a 1 *pp de* **agraciar**
2 *adj* **(a)** *(hermoso)* beautiful, pretty; **poco a.** unattractive, plain **(b)** *(ganador)* winning
3 *nm,f* lucky winner

agraciar *vt* **(a)** *(embellecer)* to beautify, make more attractive **(b)** *Fml (conceder una gracia)* to reward with a favour

agradable *adj* pleasant, agreeable; **de sabor a.** pleasant tasting; **poco a.** unpleasant

agradar *vt* to please; **no me agrada** I don't like it

agradecer [46] *vt* **(a) a. algo a algn** *(dar las gracias)* to thank sb for sth; *(estar agradecido)* to be grateful to sb for sth; **te lo agradezco mucho** I am very grateful to you **(b)** *(uso impers)* to be welcome; **siempre se agradece un descanso** a rest is always welcome

agradecido, -a 1 *pp de* **agradecer**
2 *adj* grateful; **le estoy muy a.** I am very grateful to you; **le quedaría muy a. si ...** I should be very much obliged if ...

agradecimiento *nm* gratefulness, gratitude

agrado *nm* pleasure; **con a.** with pleasure; **no es de su a.** he doesn't like it, it isn't to his liking

agrandar 1 *vt* **(a)** *(ampliar)* to enlarge, make larger **(b)** *Fig (exagerar)* to exaggerate
2 agrandarse *vpr* **(a)** *(ampliarse)* to enlarge, become larger **(b)** *(acentuarse)* to become more intense

agrario, -a *adj* agrarian, land; **política agraria** agricultural policy

agrarismo *nm* agrarianism

agravamiento *nm* aggravation, worsening

agravante 1 *adj Jur* aggravating
2 *nm & f* added difficulty; *Jur* aggravating circumstance ⃞ **robo con a.** aggravated theft

agravar 1 *vt* to aggravate, worsen
2 agravarse *vpr* to worsen, get worse

agraviar *vt* to offend, insult

agravio *nm* offense, insult

agraz *nm* **(a)** *(uva)* unripe *o* sour grape; *(zumo)* sour grape juice; *Fig* **en a.** prematurely, before its time **(b)** *Fig (amargura)* bitterness; *(sinsabor)* unpleasantness

agredido, -a *nm,f* victim

agredir *vt* to attack

agregación *nf* **(a)** *(añadidura)* aggregation **(b)** *Educ* post of teacher

agregado, -a 1 *pp de* **agregar**
2 *adj Educ* **profesor a.** *(escuela)* secondary school teacher; *Univ* assistant teacher
3 *nm,f Pol* attaché; **a. cultural** cultural attaché

agregaduría *nf Pol* post of attaché; *(oficina)* office of the attaché

agregar [38] **1** *vt* **(a)** *(añadir)* to add; **a. un poco de agua** add a small amount of water **(b)** *(destinar)* to appoint
2 agregarse *vpr (añadirse a)* to join; **se agregó al grupo** she joined the group

agresión *nf* aggression, attack

agresividad *nf* aggressiveness

agresivo, -a *adj* aggressive

agresor, -a 1 *adj* attacking
2 *nm,f* aggressor, attacker

agreste *adj* **(a)** *(campesino)* country, rural **(b)** *(sin cultivar)* uncultivated, wild **(c)** *Fig (grosero)* coarse, uncouth

agriado, -a 1 *pp de* **agriar**
2 *adj* **(a)** *(agrio)* sour **(b)** *Fig (persona)* sour, embittered

agriar [32] **1** *vt* **(a)** *(vino)* to turn sour **(b)** *(persona)* to embitter
2 agriarse *vpr* to turn sour

agrícola *adj* agricultural

agricultor, -a *nm,f* farmer

agricultura *nf* agriculture; **dedicarse a la a.** to be a farmer, farm

agridulce *adj* bittersweet; *Culin* **cerdo a.** sweet and sour pork

agrietamiento *nm* cracking

agrietar 1 *vt (resquebrajar)* to crack; *(piel, labios)* to chap
2 agrietarse *vpr (resquebrajarse)* to crack; *(manos)* to get chapped

agrimensor, -a *nm,f* surveyor

agrimensura *nf* surveying

agringarse [38] *vpr Am* to behave like a gringo

agrio, -a 1 *adj* sour
2 agrios *nmpl* citrus fruits

agriparse *vpr Andes Méx* to catch the flu

agrisado, -a *adj* greyish

agro *nm* agriculture

agroalimentario, -a *adj* **sector a.** food-processing industry

agronomía *nf* agronomy

agronómico, -a *adj* agronomical, agronomic

agrónomo, -a 1 *adj* farming
2 *nm,f* **(ingeniero) a.** agronomist

agropecuario, -a *adj* farming, agricultural

agroturismo *nm* rural tourism

agrupación *nf* **(a)** *(asociación)* association, group **(b)** *(agrupamiento)* grouping

agrupamiento *nm* grouping

agrupar 1 *vt (congregar)* to group, put into groups
2 agruparse *vpr* **(a)** *(congregarse)* to group together, form a group **(b)** *(asociarse)* to associate

agua *nf* water; **aguas arriba** upstream; *Med (parturienta)* **ha roto aguas** her waters have broken; *Fig* **ahogarse en un vaso de a.** to make a mountain out of a molehill; *Fig* **está más claro que el a.** it's as clear as crystal; *Fig* **estar con el a. al cuello** to be up to one's neck in it; *Fig* **nos vino como a. de mayo** it was a godsend; *Fam* **nunca digas de este a. no beberé** never say never; *Fam* **se me hace la boca a.** it makes my mouth water; *Fam* **parecerse como dos gotas de a.** to be as alike as two peas in a pod ⃞ **a. bendita** holy water; **a. corriente** running water; **a. de colonia** (eau de) cologne; **a. destilada** distilled water; **a. de lluvia** rainwater; **a. de mar** seawater; **a. del grifo** tap water; **a. dulce** fresh water; **a. mineral sin gas** still mineral water; **a. mineral con gas** fizzy *o* sparkling mineral water; **a. oxigenada** (hydrogen) peroxide; **a. potable** drinking water; **a. salada** salt water; **aguas jurisdiccionales** territorial waters; *Fam* **aguas menores** pee *sing*; **aguas residuales** sewage *sing*; **aguas termales** thermal springs

aguacate *nm Bot (árbol)* avocado; *(fruto)* avocado (pear)

aguacero *nm* shower, downpour

aguachirle *nm Esp Fam* dishwater

aguada *nf Arte* gouache

aguado, -a 1 *pp de* aguar
2 *adj* wishy-washy, watered down; **leche aguada** watered-down milk

aguador, -a *nm,f* water carrier

aguafiestas *nmf inv* spoilsport, killjoy, wet blanket

aguafuerte *nm* **(a)** *Arte* etching; **grabar al a.** to etch **(b)** *Quím* nitric acid

aguamanil *nm (jarro)* water jug; *(palangana)* water bowl

aguamarina *nf Min* aquamarine

aguamiel *nm* **(a)** *Am (bebida)* water mixed with honey or cane syrup **(b)** *Carib Méx (jugo)* maguey juice

aguanieve *nf Meteor* sleet

aguanoso, -a *adj* **(a)** *(fruto)* watery **(b)** *(lugar)* waterlogged

aguantable *adj* bearable, tolerable

aguantaderas *nfpl Fam* patience *sing*

aguantar 1 *vt* **(a)** *(retener)* to hold, hold back; **aguanta la respiración** hold your breath **(b)** *(soportar)* to tolerate; **no lo aguanto más** I can't stand it any longer **(c)** *(sostener)* to support, hold; **aguanta esto** hold this
2 aguantarse *vpr* **(a)** *(contenerse)* to keep back; *(risa, lágrimas)* to hold back **(b)** *(resignarse)* to resign oneself; *Fam* **¡que se aguante!** that's his/her tough luck!

aguante *nm* patience, endurance; **tener mucho a.** *(ser paciente)* to be very patient; *(tener resistencia)* to be strong, have a lot of stamina

aguar [11] **1** *vt* to water down, add water to; *Fig* **a. la fiesta a algn** to spoil sb's fun
2 aguarse *vpr* to be flooded

aguardar 1 *vt* to wait for, await; **no sabía lo que le aguardaba** he didn't know what was in store for him
2 *vi* to wait

aguardentoso, -a *adj* which contains liquor

aguardiente *nm* liquor, brandy □ **a. de caña** rum

aguarrás *nm* turpentine

aguatero, -a *nm,f Am* water seller

aguazal *nm* puddle

agudeza *nf* **(a)** *(de vista, olfato)* keenness **(b)** *(viveza)* wit, wittiness **(c)** *(dicho ingenioso)* witticism, witty saying **(d)** *(de filo, punta)* sharpness **(e)** *(de sonido)* high pitch

agudización *nf,* **agudizamiento** *nm* **(a)** *(agravamiento)* worsening, aggravation **(b)** *(aumento)* increase, intensification

agudizar [14] **1** *vt* **(a)** *(afilar)* to sharpen (up) **(b)** *(sentido)* to make keener; *(mente)* to sharpen; **a. el ingenio** to sharpen one's wits **(c)** *(problema, crisis)* to exacerbate, make worse; **el frío agudizó el dolor** the cold made the pain worse
2 agudizarse *vpr* **(a)** *(problema, crisis)* to get worse **(b)** *(ingenio)* to get sharper

agudo, -a *adj* **(a)** *(filo, punta)* sharp **(b)** *(vista, olfato)* keen **(c)** *(crisis, problema, enfermedad)* serious, acute **(d)** *(dolor)* sharp **(e)** *(sonido)* treble, high; *(voz)* high-pitched **(f)** *(ingenioso)* witty; *(mordaz)* sharp **(g)** *Ling* oxytone **(h)** *Mat* acute

agüero *nm* omen, presage; *Fig* **pájaro de mal a.** bird of ill omen

aguerrido, -a *adj* hardened; **a. en la lucha** battle-hardened

aguijón *nm* **(a)** *Zool* sting **(b)** *Bot* thorn, prickle **(c)** *Fig (estímulo)* sting, spur **(d)** *(espuela)* spur

aguijonazo *nm (punzada)* sting; *Fig* goad

aguijonear *vt* **(a)** *(punzar)* to goad **(b)** *Fig (estimular)* to spur on

águila *nf* eagle; *Fig* **tener vista de á** to be eagle-eyed □ **á. imperial** Imperial eagle; **á. pescadora** osprey; **á. real** golden eagle

aguileño, -a *adj* aquiline; **nariz aguileña** aquiline nose

aguilera *nf* eyrie

aguilucho *nm Orn* **(a)** *(águila joven)* eaglet **(b)** *(ave rapaz)* harrier

aguinaldo *nm* **(a)** *(de navidad)* Christmas box **(b)** *(retribución)* bonus **(c)** *(villancico)* Christmas carol

aguja *nf* **(a)** *(de coser, jeringuilla)* needle; *Tricot* knitting needle; *(de ganchillo)* crochet hook; *(de reloj)* hand; *(de tocadiscos)* stylus; *Fig* **buscar una a. en un pajar** to look for a needle in a haystack □ **a. hipodérmica** hypodermic needle; **a. de punto** knitting needle **(b)** *(pez)* garfish **(c)** *Arquit (capitel)* spire, steeple **(d)** **de a.** *(vino)* slightly sparkling, *Espec* pétillant **(e)** *Culin* carne de agujas shoulder **(f)** *Ferroc Br* point, *US* switch

agujereado, -a 1 *pp de* agujerear
2 *adj* with holes, perforated

agujerear *vt* to make holes in, perforate

agujero *nm* hole; **lleno de agujeros** riddled with holes; *Fig* **la empresa tiene un a. de seis millones de euros** six million euros are missing from the company's books □ *Astron* **a. negro** black hole

agujetas *nfpl* stiffness *sing*; **tener a.** to be stiff

agur *interj Fam* bye!, see you!

agusanarse *vpr* to get maggoty *o* wormy

agustino, -a *adj & nm,f Rel* Augustinian

agutí *nm Zool* agouti

aguzar [14] *vt* **(a)** *(afilar)* to sharpen **(b)** *Fig (estimular)* to spur on, prick; **a. el oído** to prick up one's ears; **a. la vista** to look attentively; **la necesidad aguza el ingenio** necessity is the mother of invention

ah *interj* oh!

ahí *adv* **(a)** *(lugar determinado)* there; **a. está** there he/she/it is; **vete por a.** go that way; *Fig* **a. está el problema** that's the problem; *Fam* **a. es nada** not bad eh?; *Fam* **¡a. le duele!** you've hit the nail on the head; *Fam* **¡a. va!** my goodness! **(b)** *(lugar indeterminado)* **por a.** there, round there; **luego nos vamos a pasear por a.** then we can go out for a walk **(c)** *(aproximadamente)* **por a., por a.** more or less; **por a. va la cosa** that's not a bad guess **(d)** *(consecuencia)* **de a. se deduce que no es verdad** from which we deduce that it is not true

ahijado, -a 1 *pp de* ahijar
2 *nm,f* godchild; *(hombre)* godson; *(mujer)* goddaughter; **ahijados** godchildren

ahijar [32] **1** *vt* **(a)** *(niño)* to adopt **(b)** *Fig* to attribute, impute
2 ahijarse *vpr (niño)* to adopt

ahínco *nm* keenness, enthusiasm, eagerness; **con a.** enthusiastically, eagerly

ahíto, -a 1 *adj* **(a)** *(de comida)* full, stuffed **(b)** *Fig (harto)* fed up
2 *nm* indigestion

ahogado, -a 1 *pp de* ahogar

2 *adj* **(a)** *(en líquido)* drowned; **morir a.** to drown **(b)** *(asfixiado)* asphyxiated, suffocated; *Fig* **a. de tiempo** pushed for time; *Fig* **estar a. de dinero** to find it difficult to make ends meet; *Fig* **un grito a.** a muffled cry **(c)** *(lugar)* stuffy, close
3 *nm,f* drowned person

ahogar [38] **1** *vt* **(a)** *(en líquido)* to drown **(b)** *(asfixiar)* to asphyxiate, suffocate **(c)** *Fig (reprimir)* to stifle; **a. las lágrimas** to hold back one's tears; **a. las penas** to drown one's sorrows **(d)** *Fig (oprimir)* to oppress, afflict; **a. una rebelión** to put down a rebellion; **el trabajo nos ahoga** we're snowed under with work **(e)** *Aut (motor)* to flood **(f)** *Andes Méx Culin (guisar)* to stew
2 ahogarse *vpr* **(a)** *(en líquido)* to drown, be drowned; *Fig* **a. en un vaso de agua** to make a mountain out of a molehill **(b)** *(asfixiarse)* to suffocate; *Fig* **me ahogo de calor** I'm suffocating with this heat **(c)** *Aut (motor)* to be flooded

ahogo *nm* **(a)** *(al respirar)* breathing trouble, tightness of the chest **(b)** *Fig (congoja)* grief, sorrow, distress **(c)** *Fig (penuria)* financial difficulty

ahondar 1 *vt (profundizar)* to deepen, make deeper
2 *vi* to go deep; *Fig* **a. en un problema** to examine a problem in depth

ahora 1 *adv* **(a)** *(en este momento)* now; **a. mismo** right now; **a. o nunca** it's now or never; **a. que lo pienso** now that I come to think of it; **de a. en adelante** from now on; **por a.** for the time being **(b)** *(hace poco tiempo)* a while ago; **a. mismo acabo de enterarme** I've just heard about it **(c)** *(dentro de poco tiempo)* shortly; **a. voy** I'm coming; **a. vuelvo** I'll be back in a minute; **hasta a.** *(hasta el momento)* until now, so far; *(hasta luego)* see you later
2 *conj* **a. bien** *o* **que** but, however; **a. bien, ¿tú estás de acuerdo?** now then, do you agree?; **a mí me gusta, a. bien, ¿le gustará a ella?** I like it, but will she like it?

ahorcado, -a 1 *pp de* **ahorcar**
2 *adj* hanged
3 *nm,f* hanged person

ahorcamiento *nm* hanging

ahorcar [59] **1** *vt* to hang
2 ahorcarse *vpr* to hang oneself

ahorita *adv Am salvo RP Fam* (right) now; **a. voy** I'm just coming

ahormar *vt* **(a)** *(zapatos, ropa)* to shape, form **(b)** *Fig (carácter)* to mould, *US* mold

ahorquillado, -a *adj* forked

ahorrador, -a 1 *adj* thrifty
2 *nm,f* thrifty person

ahorrar 1 *vt (dinero)* to save, put aside; *Fig* **eso me ahorra tener que ir al centro** it'll save me going into town
2 ahorrarse *vpr* to save oneself; **a. trabajo** to save oneself work; **ahórrate los comentarios** keep your comments to yourself

ahorrativo, -a *adj* thrifty

ahorrista *nmf RP* saver

ahorro *nm* saving; **tener unos ahorros** to have a few savings; **un a. de energía** an energy saving

ahuecar [59] **1** *vt* **(a)** *(tronco)* to hollow out; **a. las manos** to cup one's hands; *Fam* **a. el ala** to clear off, beat it **(b)** *(almohada, cabello)* to fluff up; *(tierra)* to loosen **(c)** *(voz)* to deepen
2 ahuecarse *vpr Fam (engreírse)* to become conceited, give oneself airs

ahuevar 1 *vt* **(a)** *(forma)* to make egg-shaped **(b)** *(vino)* to clarify with egg white **(c)** *CAm Ecuad Perú Fam (volver tonto)* to stupefy
2 ahuevarse *vpr CAm, Ecuad, Perú Fam (atontarse)* **me ahuevé** I didn't know what to say

ahumado, -a 1 *pp de* **ahumar**
2 *adj* **(a)** *(pescado, jamón)* smoked; *(bacon)* smoky; **salmón a.** smoked salmon **(b)** *(cristal)* smoked
3 *nm (proceso)* smoking

ahumar [4] **1** *vt* **(a)** *(carne, pescado)* to smoke; **a. un cristal** to smoke a pane of glass **(b)** *(lugar)* to fill with smoke, smoke out
2 *vi (echar humo)* to smoke, give off smoke
2 ahumarse *vpr* **(a)** *(ennegrecerse)* to be blackened by smoke **(b)** *Culin* to acquire a smoky taste **(c)** *Fam (emborracharse)* to get drunk

ahuyentar *vt* to scare away, drive away; *Fig* **a. los malos pensamientos** to dismiss bad thoughts

AI *nf (abrev de* **Amnistía Internacional)** AI

AID *nf (abrev de* **Asociación Internacional de Desarrollo)** IDA

AIEA *nf (abrev de* **Agencia Internacional de Energía Atómica)** IAEA

ailanto *nm Bot* tree of heaven

aimara *adj & nmf* Aymara

aindiado, -a *adj Am* Indian-like

airado, -a 1 *pp de* **airar**
2 *adj* angry, irritated, furious

airar [32] **1** *vt (irritar)* to anger, irritate, make furious
2 airarse *vpr (irritarse)* to get angry

airbag ['erβaɣ, air'βaɣ] *(pl* **airbags)** *nm (en vehículo)* airbag

aire *nm* **(a)** air; **al a.** *(hacia arriba)* into the air; *(al descubierto)* uncovered; **al a. libre** in the open air; **cambiar de aires** to change one's surroundings; **en el a.** *(pendiente)* in the air; *Rad (en antena)* on the air; **hacerse a.** to fan oneself; **saltar por los aires** to blow up; **tomar el a.** to take the air, get some fresh air; **vivir del a.** to live on air □ **a. acondicionado** air conditioning **(b)** *(viento)* wind; *(corriente)* draught; **hace a.** it's windy **(c)** *Fig (aspecto)* air, appearance; **con a. cansado** looking tired **(d)** *Fig (parecido)* likeness; **a. de familia** family likeness **(e)** *Fig (gracia)* gracefulness **(f)** *(estilo)* style, manner, way; **dejar a algn a su a.** to let sb do what he/she wants **(g)** *Mús (canción)* air, tune **(h) aires** *Fig (vanidad)* conceit *sing*; **darse a.** to put on airs

aireación *nf* ventilation

aireado, -a *adj* airy

airear 1 *vt (ropa, habitación)* to air; *Fig (asunto)* to publicize
2 airearse *vpr* **(a)** *(pillar un resfriado)* to catch a cold **(b)** *(tomar el aire)* to get some fresh air

aireo *nm* airing; *Fig* publicizing

airoso, -a *adj* graceful, elegant; *Fig* **salir a. de una situación** to come out of a situation with flying colours

aislacionismo *nm* isolationism

aislacionista *adj & nmf* isolationist

aislado, -a 1 *pp de* **aislar**
2 *adj* **(a)** *(remoto)* isolated; *(incomunicado)* cut off **(b)** *Téc* insulated

aislador, -a *Téc* **1** *adj* insulating
2 *nm* insulator

aislamiento *nm* **(a)** *(de lugar, persona, virus)* isolation **(b)** *Téc* insulation

aislante *Téc* **1** *adj* insulating
2 *nm* insulator

aislar [32] **1** *vt* **(a)** *(persona, virus)* to isolate **(b)** *Téc* to insulate
2 aislarse *vpr* to isolate oneself **(de** from)

ajá *interj* good!

ajado, -a 1 *pp de* **ajar**

2 *adj* (**a**) *(ropa)* shabby (**b**) *(piel)* wizened

ajamonarse *vpr Fam (mujer)* to get plump

ajar 1 *vt* to wear out, spoil
   2 ajarse *vpr (piel)* to become wizened, wrinkle

ajardinado, -a *adj* landscaped

ajardinar *vt* to landscape, lay out with gardens

ajedrecista *nmf* chess player

ajedrez *nm* (**a**) *(juego)* chess (**b**) *(piezas y tablero)* chess set

ajedrezado, -a *adj Br* chequered, *US* checkered

ajenjo *nm* (**a**) *Bot* wormwood, absinth, absinthe (**b**) *(licor)* absinth, absinthe

ajeno, -a *adj* (**a**) *(de otro)* belonging to other people; *Dep* **jugar en campo a.** to play away from home; **por causas ajenas a nuestra voluntad** for reasons beyond our control; **vivir a costa ajena** to live off other people (**b**) *(distante)* detached; **a. a lo que estaba ocurriendo** unaware of what was happening; **a. al tema** outside the subject (**c**) *(impropio)* **a. a su manera de ser** unlike him (**d**) *(extraño)* '**prohibido el paso a toda persona ajena a la obra**' 'workers only'

ajetreado, -a *adj* (very) busy, hectic

ajetreo *nm* activity, hard work, bustle

ají (*pl* **ajís** *o* **ajíes**) *nm Andes RP (pimiento)* chilli (pepper); *(salsa)* = sauce made from oil, vinegar, garlic and chilli

ajiaco *nm Andes Carib* = chilli-based stew

ajillo *nm Culin* **al a.** fried with garlic

ajo *nm* garlic; *Fam* **estar en el a.** to be in on it ◻ **a. tierno** = green stalk of young garlic plant; **cabeza de a.** head of garlic; **diente de a.** clove of garlic

ajolote *nm Zool* axolotl

ajonjolí *nm Bot* sesame

ajotar *vt PRico* to urge on, incite

ajuar *nm (de novia)* trousseau; *(de niño)* layette; *(moblaje)* household furnishings *pl*; *(bienes)* property, goods *pl*

ajumarse *vpr Fam* to get drunk

ajuntar 1 *vt Fam* to be friends with; **¿me ajuntas?** will you be my friend?; **ya no te ajunto** I am not friends with you any more
   2 ajuntarse *vpr Fam (una pareja)* to live together, cohabit

ajustable *adj* adjustable; **sábana a.** fitted sheet

ajustado, -a 1 *pp de* ajustar
   2 *adj* (**a**) *(justo)* right, correct; **un precio a.** a reasonable price (**b**) *(ropa)* tight, clinging; **bien a.** well-fitting

ajustador, -a 1 *adj* adjusting, fitting
   2 *nm,f* fitter

ajustar 1 *vt* (**a**) *(pieza)* to fit; *(mecanismo)* to adjust; **a. dos piezas** to make two pieces fit (**b**) *(ceñir)* to tighten (**c**) *(concertar)* to settle, fix (**d**) *(acordar)* to agree, arrange (**e**) *Impr* to make up (**f**) *Com Fin (cuenta) (saldar)* to balance; *(liquidar)* to settle; *Fig* **ajustarle las cuentas a algn** to settle a score with sb
   2 ajustarse *vpr* to fit; **a. el cinturón** to tighten one's belt; *Fig (adaptarse)* **ajústate a lo que te han dicho** just do as you have been told

ajuste *nm* (**a**) *(de pieza)* fitting; *(de mecanismo)* adjustment ◻ *TV* **carta de a.** test card (**b**) *(de precio, cuenta)* settlement, fixing ◻ *Fig* **a. de cuentas** settling of scores (**c**) *Impr* make-up, composition

ajusticiado, -a 1 *pp de* ajusticiar
   2 *adj* **morir a.** to be executed
   3 *nm,f* executed person

ajusticiamiento *nm* execution

ajusticiar *vt* to execute

al *(contracción de* a & **el**) (**a**) *véase* **a** (**b**) *(+ infin)* **al parecer**

apparently; **al salir** on leaving; **está al caer** it's about to happen

Alá *nm* Allah

ala 1 *nf* (**a**) *(de ave, edificio, partido)* wing; *Fig* **cortarle las alas a algn** to clip sb's wings; *Fig* **dar alas a** to egg on, encourage; *Fig* **volar con sus propias alas** to stand on one's own two feet ◻ **a. delta** *(deporte)* hang-gliding; *(aparato)* hang-glider (**b**) *(de sombrero)* brim (**c**) *(de hélice)* blade
   2 *nmf Dep* winger, wing

alabanza *nf* (**a**) *(elogio)* praise (**b**) *(jactancia)* boasting, bragging

alabar 1 *vt (elogiar)* to praise
   2 alabarse *vpr (jactarse)* to boast, brag

alabardero *nm* halberdier

alabastro *nm* alabaster

alabear 1 *vt* to warp
   2 alabearse *vpr* to warp

alabeo *nm* warp, warping

alacena *nf* (food) cupboard

alacrán *nm Zool* scorpion

alado, -a *adj* (**a**) *(con alas)* winged (**b**) *Fig (veloz)* fast, quick

ALALC *nf Antes (abrev de* **Asociación Latinoamericana de Libre Comercio**) LAFTA

alambicado, -a 1 *pp de* alambicar
   2 *adj* (**a**) *Fig (escaso)* given sparingly (**b**) *Fig (rebuscado)* overcomplicated

alambicamiento *nm* (**a**) *(destilación)* distilling, distillation (**b**) *(sutileza)* affectation

alambicar [59] *vt* (**a**) *(líquidos)* to distil, *US* distill (**b**) *(examinar)* to scrutinize (**c**) *Fig (estilo, lenguaje)* to subtilize, overcomplicate (**d**) *Fig (ganancias)* to reduce to a minimum

alambique *nm* still

alambrada *nf*, **alambrado** *nm* wire fence

alambrar *vt* to fence with wire

alambre *nm* wire; *Fig* **estar como un a.** to be as thin as a rake ◻ **a. de púas** barbed wire

alambrera *nf (de ventana)* wire netting; *(para comida)* food safe

alambrista *nmf* tightrope walker

alameda *nf* (**a**) *(árboles)* poplar grove (**b**) *(paseo)* promenade, avenue, boulevard

álamo *nm Bot* poplar

alano, -a *adj & nm,f* (**a**) *Hist* Alan (**b**) *Zool* (**perro**) **a.** mastiff

alar *nm* eaves *pl*

alarde *nm* *(ostentación)* bragging, boasting, (vain) display; **hacer a. de** to flaunt, parade, show off

alardear *vi* to brag, boast, show off; **a. de rico** *o* **de riqueza** to flaunt one's wealth

alardeo *nm véase* **alarde**

alargado, -a 1 *pp de* alargar
   2 *adj* elongated, long

alargador *nm* extension lead *o* cable

alargamiento *nm* (**a**) *(en longitud)* lengthening (**b**) *(en tiempo)* prolongation, extension

alargar [38] **1** *vt* (**a**) *(en longitud)* to lengthen; *(estirar)* to stretch; **ella alargó la mano para cogerlo** she stretched out her hand to get it (**b**) *(en tiempo)* to prolong, extend; **alargaron su estancia en Madrid** they extended their stay in Madrid (**c**) *(dar)* to pass, hand over; **alárgame ese jersey** can you pass me that jumper?
   2 alargarse *vpr* (**a**) *(día, sombra)* to lengthen, get longer; **en verano los días se alargan** in summer the days get

longer; **la reunión se alargó hasta las dos** the meeting went on until two (**b**) *(excederse)* to be long-winded, go on (too long)

alarido *nm* screech, shriek, yell; **dar un a.** to howl

alarma *nf* (a) *(señal, preocupación)* alarm; **dar la a.** to give the alarm; **entonces sonó la a.** then the alarm went off □ **falsa a.** false alarm; **señal de a.** alarm (signal); **voz de a.** alarm (call) (**b**) *(dispositivo)* alarm

alarmante *adj* alarming

alarmar 1 *vt* to alarm
  2 alarmarse *vpr* to be alarmed

alarmismo *nm* alarmism

alarmista *nmf* alarmist

Alaska *n* Alaska

alavés, -esa 1 *adj* of o from Alava
  2 *nm,f* person from Alava

alazán, -ana *adj & nm,f* **(caballo) a.** chestnut

alba *nf* (a) *(amanecer)* dawn, daybreak; **al (rayar el) a.** at daybreak, at dawn (**b**) *Rel (prenda)* alb

albacea *nmf (hombre)* executor; *(mujer)* executrix

albaceteño, -a 1 *adj* of o from Albacete
  2 *nm,f* person from Albacete

albacora *nf (pez)* albacore, long-fin tunny

albahaca *nf Bot* basil

albanés, -esa *adj & nm,f* Albanian

Albania *n* Albania

albano, -a *adj & nm,f véase* **albanés, -esa**

albañal *nm* sewer, drain

albañil *nm* bricklayer; *(obrero)* building worker

albañilería *nf* (a) *(oficio)* bricklaying (**b**) *(obra)* **pared de a.** brick wall

albar *adj* white

albarán *nm Esp Com* delivery note, despatch note

albarda *nf* (a) *(arreos)* packsaddle (**b**) *CAm Méx (silla)* saddle

albardón *nm* (a) *Am* = raised land between lakes o beaches (**b**) *Méx* = type of saddle

albaricoque *nm Esp Bot* (a) *(fruta)* apricot (**b**) *(árbol)* apricot tree

albaricoquero *nm Esp Bot* apricot tree

albarrana *adj* **torre a.** watchtower

albatros *nm inv* albatross

albayalde *nm* white lead

albedrío *nm* will □ **libre a.** free will

alberca *nf* (a) *(depósito)* water tank (**b**) *Col Méx (piscina)* swimming pool

albergar [38] **1** *vt (alojar)* to house, accommodate; *Fig (sentimientos)* to cherish, harbour, *US* harbor
  2 albergarse *vpr (alojarse)* to stay

albergue *nm* (a) *(lugar)* hostel □ **a. juvenil** youth hostel (**b**) *(refugio)* shelter, refuge; **dar a.** to take in, put up

alberguista *nmf* youth hosteller

albero, -a 1 *adj (blanco)* white
  2 *nm (paño)* dishcloth

albinismo *nm* albinism

albino, -a *adj & nm,f* albino

Albión *n* Albion

albis: in albis *loc adv* left in the dark; **estar in a.** not to have the faintest idea; **me quedé in a.** my mind went blank

albo, -a *adj Literario* white

albóndiga *nf,* **albondiguilla** *nf* meatball

albor *nm* (a) *(blancura)* whiteness (**b**) **albores** beginning

sing; **en los a. de ...** at the dawn of ..., at the beginning of ...

alborada *nf* (a) *(alba)* dawn, daybreak (**b**) *Mús* dawn song (**c**) *Mil (diana)* reveille

alborear *v impers* to dawn

albornoz *nm (prenda)* bathrobe

alborotadizo, -a *adj* excitable

alborotado, -a 1 *pp de* **alborotar**
  2 *adj* (a) *(persona)* worked up, agitated, excited (**b**) *(desordenado)* untidy, messy

alborotador, -a 1 *adj* (a) *(rebelde)* rebellious, turbulent; *(ruidoso)* noisy, rowdy (**b**) *(mar)* rough, tempestuous
  2 *nm,f* troublemaker, agitator

alborotar 1 *vt* (a) *(agitar)* to stir up, agitate, work up (**b**) *(desordenar)* to make untidy, turn upside down (**c**) *(sublevar)* to incite to rebel
  2 *vi* (a) *(hacer jaleo)* to kick up a racket (**b**) *(causar desorden)* to cause disorder; **no alborotes más** stop it, behave yourself
  2 alborotarse *vpr* (a) *(persona)* to get excited o worked up (**b**) *(mar)* to get rough

alboroto 1 *nm* (a) *(jaleo)* din, racket, row (**b**) *(desorden)* disturbance, uproar (**c**) *(susto)* shock, alarm
  2 alborotos *nmpl CAm Culin* popcorn *sing*

alborozar [14] **1** *vt* to fill with joy, delight
  2 alborozarse *vpr* to be overjoyed

alborozo *nm* merriment, gaiety, joy

albricias 1 *nfpl (regalo)* present *sing*, gift *sing*
  2 *interj* great!, smashing!

albufera *nf Geog* lagoon, pool

álbum *nm* album

albumen *nm Bot* albumen

albúmina *nf Biol* albumin

albuminoide *adj Quím* albuminoid

albur *nm* chance; **los albures de la vida** the ups and downs of life

albura *nf Fml* whiteness

alburear *vi Méx Fam* to pun, make a pun

ALCA ['alka] *nf (abrev de* **Área de Libre Comercio de las Américas)** FTAA

alcachofa *nf* (a) *Bot* artichoke (**b**) *Esp (de tubo, regadera)* rose, sprinkler; *(de ducha)* shower head

alcahuete, -a *nm,f* lovers' go-between

alcahuetería *nf* **el antiguo oficio de la a.** the former calling of the go-between

alcalde *nm* mayor

alcaldesa *nf (que ejerce)* lady mayor, mayoress; *(mujer del alcalde)* mayoress

alcaldía *nf* (a) *(cargo)* mayorship; **fue durante la a. del Sr Reyes** it was when Sr Reyes was mayor (**b**) *(oficina)* mayoralty, mayor's office (**c**) *(territorio)* land under the jurisdiction of a mayor

alcalinidad *nf Quím* alkalinity

alcalino, -a *adj Quím* alkaline

alcaloide *nm Quím* alkaloid

alcance *nm* (a) *(de persona)* reach; **al a. de cualquiera** within everybody's reach; **al a. de la vista** in sight; **dar a. a** to catch up with; **fuera del a. de los niños** out of the reach of children; **no está a mi a.** I can't afford it (**b**) *(de arma, radio)* range (**c**) *Fig* scope, importance, significance; **de gran a.** far-reaching (**d**) **alcances** *(inteligencia)* intelligence *sing*; **persona de pocos a.** unintelligent person

alcancía *nf* (a) *(hucha)* money box (**b**) *Andes RP (para limosnas)* collecting box

alcanfor *nm* camphor

alcanforado, -a *adj* camphorated

alcanforero *nm Bot* camphor tree

alcantarilla *nf* sewer; *(boca)* drain

alcantarillado *nm* sewer system

alcantarillar *vt* to lay sewers in

alcanzar [14] **1** *vt* (**a**) *(gen)* to reach; *(tren, autobús)* to catch; *(persona)* to catch up with; **la piedra le alcanzó en la cabeza** the stone hit him on the head; **la producción alcanza 2.000 unidades diarias** production is up to 2,000 units a day (**b**) *(pasar)* to pass, hand over; **alcánzame el pan** pass me the bread (**c**) *(llegar a tener)* to attain, achieve, obtain; **alcanzó lo que tanto deseaba** he got what he was longing for (**d**) *(afectar)* to affect; **las consecuencias nos alcanzan a todos** its consequences affect us all (**e**) *(conseguir)* to manage; **a. a ver/comprender** to be able to see/understand
  2 *vi* (**a**) *(ser suficiente)* to be sufficient; **con un kilo no alcanza para todos** one kilo won't be enough for all of us; **me alcanzó para un mes** it lasted me a month (**b**) *(ser capaz)* to manage; **él alcanza a todo** he manages to do everything

alcaparra *nf Bot* (**a**) *(fruto)* caper (**b**) *(planta)* caper bush

alcaraván *nm Orn* stone curlew

alcaravea *nf* caraway

alcatraz *nm Orn* gannet

alcaucil *nm RP* artichoke

alcaudón *nm Orn* shrike

alcayata *nf* hook

alcazaba *nf Mil* fortress, citadel

alcázar *nm* (**a**) *(fortaleza)* fortress, citadel (**b**) *(castillo)* castle, palace

alce *nm Zool* elk, moose

alcista 1 *adj (bolsa)* rising, bullish; **tendencia a.** upward tendency
  2 *nmf (bolsa)* bull

alcoba *nf* bedroom; *Fig* **secretos de a.** intimacies

alcohol *nm* (**a**) *Quím* alcohol ❑ **a. metílico** *o* **desnaturalizado** methylated spirit; **a. de quemar** methylated spirits (**b**) *(bebida)* alcohol, spirits *pl*

alcoholemia *nf* blood alcohol level; **test de a.** *Br* Breathalyzer® test, *US* drunkometer test

alcohólico, -a *adj & nm,f* alcoholic ❑ **Alcohólicos Anónimos** Alcoholics Anonymous

alcoholímetro *nm Br* Breathalyzer®, *US* drunkometer

alcoholismo *nm* alcoholism

alcoholización *nf* alcoholization

alcoholizado, -a 1 *pp de* alcoholizar
  2 *adj & nm,f* alcoholic

alcoholizar [14] **1** *vt* to alcoholize
  2 alcoholizarse *vpr* to become an alcoholic

alcohómetro *nm Br* Breathalyzer®, *US* drunkometer

alcor *nm Geog* hill

alcornocal *nm* cork oak grove

alcornoque *nm* (**a**) *Bot* cork oak (**b**) *Fig (persona)* idiot, dimwit

alcotana *nf* pickaxe, *US* pickax

alcurnia *nf* lineage, ancestry; **de alta a.** of noble lineage

alcuza *nf* (**a**) *(para aceite)* oil bottle (**b**) *Andes (vinagreras)* cruet

alcuzcuz *nm Culin* couscous

aldaba *nf* (**a**) *(llamador)* door knocker (**b**) *(pestillo)* latch, bar, bolt (**c**) *Fig* **tener buenas aldabas** to know the right people

aldabilla *nf* latch, hook

aldabón *nm* large door knocker

aldabonazo *nm* (**a**) *(en puerta)* loud knock; *Fig* shock (**b**) *(advertencia)* warning

aldea *nf* small village, hamlet

aldeano, -a 1 *adj* (**a**) *(de aldea)* village (**b**) *Fig* rustic
  2 *nm,f* villager

ale *interj* come on!

aleación *nf* alloy

alear *vt (metales)* to alloy

aleatorio, -a *adj* fortuitous, chance, accidental

alebrestado, -a 1 *pp de* alebrestarse
  2 *adj* (**a**) *Méx (alborotado)* excited (**b**) *Col (nervioso)* nervous

alebrestarse *vpr* (**a**) *Méx (alborotarse, entusiasmarse)* to get excited (**b**) *Col (ponerse nervioso)* to get nervous

aleccionador, -a *adj (instructivo)* instructive; *(ejemplar)* exemplary

aleccionamiento *nm (instrucción)* instruction; *(adiestramiento)* training

aleccionar *vt (instruir)* to teach, instruct; *(adiestrar)* to train

aledaño, -a 1 *adj* adjoining, adjacent
  2 aledaños *nmpl* outskirts

alegación *nf* claim, plea, allegation

alegador, -a *adj Am* argumentative

alegar [38] **1** *vt (aducir)* to claim, allege, plea
  2 *vi Am* (**a**) *(quejarse)* to complain (**b**) *(discutir)* to argue

alegato *nm* (**a**) *(argumento)* claim, plea (**b**) *(razonamiento)* forceful statement (**c**) *Andes (disputa)* dispute, argument

alegoría *nf* allegory

alegórico, -a *adj* allegorical, allegoric

alegrar 1 *vt* (**a**) *(complacer)* to make happy *o* glad; **alegra que se lo hayas dicho** I am glad you told her (**b**) *(avivar)* to enliven, brighten up (**c**) *Euf (achispar)* to make tipsy
  2 alegrarse *vpr* (**a**) *(estar contento)* to be glad, be happy, be pleased; **me alegro de verte** I am pleased to see you; **me alegro por ti** I am happy for you (**b**) *Euf (achisparse)* to get merry

alegre *adj* (**a**) *(contento)* happy, glad, joyful; **es muy a.** she is a very happy person (**b**) *(color)* bright; *(música)* lively; *(habitación)* pleasant, cheerful (**c**) *Euf (achispado)* tipsy, merry (**d**) *Pey* **mujer de vida a.** loose woman (**e**) *Pey (irreflexivo)* thoughtless, irresponsible, rash

alegremente *adv* (**a**) *(con alegría)* happily, joyfully (**b**) *Pey (irreflexivamente)* blithely

alegría *nf* (**a**) *(felicidad)* joy, happiness; **saltar de a.** to jump with *o* for joy; **¡qué a.!** that's wonderful! (**b**) *Pey (irresponsabilidad)* thoughtlessness, irresponsibility, rashness (**c**) **alegrías** *Mús* = song and dance from Cádiz

alegro *adv & nm Mús* allegro

alegrón *nm Fam* pleasant surprise

alejado, -a 1 *pp de* alejar
  2 *adj* (**a**) *(lejano)* far away, remote (**b**) *(separado)* aloof, apart; **a. de su familia** aloof from his family

alejamiento *nm* (**a**) *(separación)* spacing out, separation (**b**) *(persona)* estrangement

Alejandría *n* Alexandria

alejandrino *adj & nm Lit* Alexandrine

alejar 1 *vt* to move further away, remove; *(separar)* to separate; *Fig* **aleja esos pensamientos** stop thinking like that; *Fig* **a. las dudas** to avert doubts
  2 alejarse *vpr* to go away, move away; **el coche se alejó**

the car drove off into the distance; **no te alejes de mí** keep close to me

alelado, -a 1 *pp de* **alelar**
2 *adj* (**a**) *(atontado)* in a daze; **estoy a. hoy** I'm just not with it today (**b**) *(sorprendido)* **quedarse a.** to be stunned, be left speechless

alelar *vt* to daze, stupefy

aleluya 1 *nm o nf* hallelujah, alleluia
2 *interj* hallelujah!

alemán, -ana 1 *adj* German
2 *nm,f (persona)* German
3 *nm (idioma)* German

Alemania *n* Germany ❑ *Antes* **A. del Este** East Germany; *Antes* **A. Occidental/Oriental** West/East Germany

alentado, -a 1 *pp de* **alentar**
2 *adj* (**a**) *Andes Méx Ven (recuperado)* better (**b**) *Chile (listo)* bright (**c**) *Chile (experimentado)* (sexually) experienced

alentador, -a *adj* encouraging; **un panorama poco a.** a rather black future

alentar [3] **1** (**a**) *vt (animar)* to encourage (**b**) *(albergar)* to harbour; **su corazón alienta los más bellos sentimientos** the most noble sentiments burn within his heart
2 alentarse *vpr Andes Méx Ven (recuperarse)* to recover, get better

alerce *nm Bot* larch

alergeno *nm*, **alérgeno** *nm Med* allergen

alergia *nf* allergy

alérgico, -a *adj* allergic

alero *nm* (**a**) *Arquit* eaves *pl* (**b**) *Aut (guardabarros)* wing

alerón *nm Av* aileron

alerta 1 *adv (vigilante)* alert
2 *nf (atención)* alert; **dar la (voz de) a.** to give the alert; **en estado de a.** on the alert
3 *adj* alert
4 *interj* look out!, watch out!

alertar 1 *vt* to alert (**de** to); **nos alertó del peligro** he alerted us to the danger
2 *vi* to be alert

aleta *nf* (**a**) *(de pez)* fin; *(de foca, de nadador)* flipper (**b**) *Av (alerón)* aileron (**c**) *Aut (guardabarros)* wing (**d**) *(de nariz)* ala, wing

aletargado, -a 1 *pp de* **aletargar**
2 *adj* lethargic; *(amodorrado)* drowsy

aletargamiento *nm* (**a**) *(letargo)* lethargy (**b**) *Fig (modorra)* drowsiness, sleepiness

aletargar [38] **1** *vt (amodorrar)* to make drowsy *o* sleepy
2 aletargarse *vpr (amodorrarse)* to become drowsy *o* sleepy

aletear *vi* (**a**) *(aves)* to flutter *o* flap its wings (**b**) *(con los brazos)* to wave *o* flap one's arms about

aleteo *nm* (**a**) *(de alas)* fluttering *o* flapping of wings (**b**) *(de brazos)* waving *o* flapping of the arms (**c**) *Fig (palpitación)* palpitation

alevín *nm* (**a**) *(pescadito)* fry, young fish (**b**) *Fig (principiante)* beginner

alevosía *nf* *(traición)* treachery; *(premeditación)* premeditation; **con a.** *(a traición)* treacherously; *(premeditadamente)* deliberately

alevoso, -a *adj (traidor)* treacherous; *(premeditado)* premeditated

alfa *nf (letra)* alpha; *Fig* **a. y omega** beginning and end, alpha and omega

alfabético, -a *adj* alphabetical, alphabetic

alfabetización *nf* teaching to read and write; **campaña de a.** literacy campaign

alfabetizar [14] *vt* (**a**) *(ordenar)* to alphabetize, arrange in alphabetical order (**b**) *(enseñar)* to teach to read and write

alfabeto *nm* (**a**) *(abecedario)* alphabet (**b**) *(código)* code ❑ **a. telegráfico** telegraphic code

alfaguara *nf* abundant spring

alfajor *nm* (**a**) *(de ajonjolí)* = crumbly shortbread, flavoured with sesame seeds (**b**) *(en Argentina)* = small sponge cake filled with creamy toffee

alfalfa *nf Bot* lucerne, alfalfa

alfanje *nm* (**a**) *(sable)* cutlass (**b**) *(pez)* swordfish

alfanumérico, -a *adj Inform* alphanumeric

alfar *nm* (**a**) *(taller)* pottery, potter's workshop (**b**) *(arcilla)* clay

alfarería *nf* (**a**) *(arte)* pottery (**b**) *(taller)* potter's workshop; *(tienda)* pottery shop

alfarero, -a *nm,f* potter

alféizar *nm Arquit* sill, windowsill

alfeñique *nm* (**a**) *(dulce)* almond flavoured sugar pastry (**b**) *Fig (persona)* weakling (**c**) *(remilgo)* primness, affectation

alférez *nmf Mil* second lieutenant

alfil *nm Ajedrez* bishop

alfiler *nm* (**a**) *Cost* pin; **sujetar con alfileres** to pin up; *Fam Fig* **no cabe ni un a.** it's crammed full (**b**) *(broche)* pin, brooch; *(del pelo)* clip; *(de corbata)* tiepin; *(de tender ropa)* peg

alfilerazo *nm* (**a**) *(punzada)* pinprick (**b**) *Fig (pulla)* taunt

alfiletero *nm* pin box, pin case

alfombra *nf* (**a**) *(grande)* carpet; *(pequeña)* rug ❑ **a. mágica** magic carpet (**b**) *(del baño)* bathmat

alfombrado, -a 1 *pp de* **alfombrar**
2 *adj* carpeted
3 *nm* carpeting

alfombrar *vt* to carpet

alfombrilla *nf* rug, mat; *Inform (para ratón)* mouse pad

alforja *nf* (**a**) *(para caballerías)* saddlebag; *(al hombro)* knapsack (**b**) *alforjas Fig* provisions

alga *nf Bot* alga; *(marina)* seaweed

algalia *nf Zool* civet

algarabía *nf* hubbub, hullabaloo

algarada *nf* (**a**) *(alboroto)* din, row, racket (**b**) *Mil (correría)* raid

algarroba *nf Bot* (**a**) *(planta)* vetch (**b**) *(fruto)* carob bean

algarrobal *nm* (**a**) *(de algarrobas)* vetch plantation (**b**) *(de algarrobos)* carob tree plantation

algarrobo *nm* carob tree

algazara *nf* din, row, racket

álgebra *nf* algebra

algebraico, -a *adj* algebraic, algebraical

álgido, -a *adj* (**a**) *Fig (culminante)* culminating, critical; **el punto a.** the height (**b**) *Fml (muy frío)* very cold, icy

algo 1 *pron indef* (**a**) *(alguna cosa)* something; *(en interrogativas)* anything; **a. así** something like that; **a. así como veinte** round about twenty; **de hacer a. te llamaría** if I decided to do anything, I'd give you a ring; **di a.** say something; **por a. será** there must be a reason for it; **¿te pasa a.?** is anything the matter?; **toma a.** have something to drink *o* eat; *Fam* **a. es a.** it's better than nothing, isn't it?; *Fam* **me va a dar a.** I'm going to go round the bend (**b**) *(cantidad pequeña)* a bit, a little; **a. de** some; **¿queda a. de pastel?** is there any cake left?
2 *adv (un poco)* quite, somewhat; **está a. mejor** she's feeling a bit better; **te queda a. grande** it's a bit too big for you

3 *nm Fam* **ella tiene a.** she has a certain something about her

algodón *nm Bot Tex* cotton; *Fam* **criado entre algodones** pampered ❏ *Farm* **a. hidrófilo** *Br* cotton wool, *US* absorbent cotton

algodonal *nm* cotton plantation *o* field

algodonero, -a 1 *adj* cotton; **la industria algodonera** the cotton industry
2 *nm Bot* cotton plant
3 *nm,f* cotton grower

algodonoso, -a *adj* cottony

algoritmo *nm Inform Mat* algorithm

alguacil *nm* (**a**) *(del ayuntamiento)* mayor's assistant; *(del juzgado)* bailiff (**b**) *Zool RP (libélula)* dragonfly

alguacilillo *nm Taur* = mounted official at bullfight

alguien *pron indef* (**a**) *(afirmativo)* somebody, someone; **a. ha robado mi paraguas** someone has stolen my umbrella; *Fig* **creerse a.** to think one is somebody; *Fig* **ser a.** to be somebody *o* important (**b**) *(interrogativo)* anybody, anyone; **¿has visto a a.?** have you seen anybody?

algún *adj (delante de nombres masculinos) véase* **alguno, -a**

alguno, -a 1 *adj* (**a**) *(delante del nombre) (afirmativo)* some; *(interrogativo)* any; **alguna que otra vez** now and then; **algunos días** some days; **salgo alguna (que otra) tarde** I go out the odd evening; **¿has tomado alguna medicina?** have you taken any medicine?; **¿le has visto alguna vez?** have you ever seen him? (**b**) *(después del nombre) (negativo)* **no vino persona alguna** nobody came
2 *pron indef* (**a**) *(persona)* someone, somebody; **a. dirá que ...** someone might say that ...; **a. que otro** someone (**b**) **algunos** some (people); **a. de o entre ellos** some of them

alhaja *nf* (**a**) *(joya)* jewel, gem (**b**) *Fig (objeto, persona)* gem, treasure; *Irón (persona)* **¡menuda a.!** he's a fine one!

alharaca *nf* fuss; **hacer alharacas** to make a lot of fuss and bother

alhelí *(pl* **alhelíes)** *nm Bot* wallflower, stock

alheña *nf* (**a**) *Bot (planta)* privet; *(flor)* privet blossom (**b**) *(polvo)* henna

alhucema *nf Bot* lavender

aliado, -a 1 *pp de* **aliar**
2 *adj* allied
3 *nm,f* ally; *Hist* **los Aliados** the Allies

alianza *nf* (**a**) *(pacto)* alliance (**b**) *(anillo)* wedding ring

aliar [32] **1** *vt* (**a**) *(naciones)* to ally (**b**) *(cualidades)* to combine
2 aliarse *vpr* to become allies, form an alliance

alias *adv & nm inv también Inform* alias

alicaído, -a *adj* (**a**) *(débil)* weak, feeble (**b**) *(deprimido)* down, depressed

alicantino, -a 1 *adj* of *o* from Alicante
2 *nm,f* person from Alicante

alicatado, -a *Esp* **1** *pp de* **alicatar**
2 *nm* tiling

alicatar *vt Esp* to tile

alicates *nmpl* pliers *pl*

aliciente *nm* (**a**) *(atractivo)* lure, charm (**b**) *(incentivo)* incentive, encouragement

alicorto, -a *adj* (**a**) *(de alas cortas)* with clipped wings (**b**) *Fig (sin aspiraciones)* without ambition

alícuota *adj* aliquot

alienación *nf Psic* alienation, derangement

alienado, -a 1 *pp de* **alienar**
2 *adj (loco)* insane, deranged
3 *nm,f (lunático)* lunatic

alienante *adj* alienating

alienar 1 *vt* to alienate
2 alienarse *vpr* to become alienated

alienígena *nmf* alien

alienígeno, -a *adj & nm,f* alien

alienista *nmf* alienist, psychiatrist

aliento *nm* (**a**) *(respiración)* breath; **cobrar a.** to get one's breath back; **sin a.** breathless (**b**) *Fig (ánimo)* encouragement, boost; **dar a. a** to encourage to

aligeramiento *nm* (**a**) *(carga)* lightening (**b**) *(paso)* quickening (**c**) *(dolor)* easing, soothing

aligerar *vt* (**a**) *(descargar)* to make lighter (**b**) *(acelerar)* to speed up; **a. el paso** to quicken one's pace; *Fam* **¡aligera!** hurry up! (**c**) *Fig (atenuar)* to relieve, soothe

alijo *nm* contraband; **un a. de drogas** a consignment of drugs

alimaña *nf Zool* vermin, pest

alimentación *nf* (**a**) *(acción)* feeding; *Téc* feed (**b**) *(comida)* food; **una a. basada en cereales** a diet based on cereals

alimentador, -a 1 *adj Téc* feeding ❏ *Inform* **a. de papel** paper feed
2 *nm* feeder

alimentar 1 *vt* (**a**) *(dar alimento)* to feed; *(servir de alimento)* to nourish; **el pescado alimenta mucho** fish is very nutritious; **la madre alimenta a su hijo** the mother feeds her son; **la fábrica alimenta a toda la comarca** the whole area owes its living to the factory (**b**) *Fig (alentar)* to encourage, foster; **a. pasiones** to feed passions (**c**) *Inform* to feed
2 alimentarse *vpr* **a. con** *o* **de** to live on

alimentario, -a *adj* food

alimenticio, -a *adj* nutritious; **productos alimenticios** food products, foodstuffs; **valor a.** nutritional value

alimento *nm* (**a**) *(comida)* food; *Fig* **el odio es el a. de las guerras** hate fuels war (**b**) *(valor nutritivo)* nutritional value; **tiene poco a.** it is not very nourishing

alimón : al alimón *loc adv Esp* together, in collaboration

alineación *nf* (**a**) *(colocación en línea)* alignment, lining up (**b**) *Dep (equipo)* line-up

alineado, -a 1 *pp de* **alinear**
2 *adj* aligned, lined-up; *Pol* **países no alineados** non-aligned countries

alineamiento *nm* alignment; *Pol* **política de no a.** non-alignment policy

alinear 1 *vt* (**a**) *(colocar en línea)* to align, line up (**b**) *Dep (formar equipo)* to line up (**c**) *Mil (formar)* to form up
2 alinearse *vpr* (**a**) *(colocarse en línea)* to line up (**b**) *Mil (formar)* to fall in (**c**) *Pol* to become aligned

aliñar *vt Culin* to season, flavour, *US* flavor; *(ensalada)* to dress

aliño *nm Culin* seasoning, dressing

alioli *nm Culin* garlic mayonnaise

alirón *interj* hooray!

alisar *vt* to smooth

alisios *adj & nmpl* **(vientos) alisios** trade winds

aliso *nm Bot* alder

alistamiento *nm Mil* recruitment, enlistment

alistar 1 *vt Mil* to recruit, enlist
2 alistarse *vpr Mil* to enlist, enrol, *US* enroll; **¡alístate!** join the army!

aliteración *nf Lit* alliteration

aliviadero *nm* spillway

aliviador, -a *adj* comforting, consoling

alivianar 1 *vt Am (ayudar)* to help out, give a hand to
2 aliviarse *vpr* (**a**) *Am (tranquilizarse)* to take it easy (**b**) *Méx (ser comprensivo)* **ya se aliviano y sí va a participar en la obra de teatro** he's come round and he will be taking part in the play; **se aliviana con el trabajo doméstico** he's cool about doing housework

aliviar 1 *vt* (**a**) *(aligerar)* to lighten, make lighter (**b**) *(calmar)* to soothe, relieve (**c**) *(consolar)* to comfort, console (**d**) *Fam (darse prisa)* to hurry
2 aliviarse *vpr (dolor)* to diminish, get better

alivio *nm* (**a**) *(mejoria)* relief (**b**) *(consuelo)* comfort, consolation (**c**) *Fam* **es un tipo de a.** a fine one, he is!; **un calor de a.** stifling heat

aljaba *nf (para flechas)* quiver

aljama *nf Hist* (**a**) *(barrio) (judio)* Jewish quarter; *(árabe)* Moorish quarter (**b**) *(sinagoga)* synagogue; *(mezquita)* mosque

aljibe *nm* cistern, tank

aljófar *nm (perla)* pearl; *(rocío)* dewdrop

allá *adv* (**a**) *(lugar alejado)* there, over there; **a. abajo/arriba** down/up there; **¡a. voy!** here I go!; **más a.** further on; **más a. de** beyond; **no tan a.** not that far; **el más a.** the beyond (**b**) *(tiempo)* back; **a. por los años veinte** back in the twenties (**c**) *(locuciones)* **a. cada uno** you have to decide for yourself; **a. se las componga** that's his problem, that's his tough luck; **a. tú** that's your problem; *Fam* **no muy a.** nothing special

allanamiento *nm* (**a**) *(aplanamiento)* levelling, flattening (**b**) *Fig (de dificultades)* smoothing-out (**c**) *Jur Esp* **a. de morada** unlawful entry

allanar 1 *vt* (**a**) *(aplanar)* to level, flatten (**b**) *Fig (dificultades)* to smooth out; **a. el terreno** to clear the way (**c**) *Jur* to break into
2 allanarse *vpr (acceder)* to agree, conform

allegado, -a 1 *pp de* **allegar**
2 *adj* close, related; **personas allegadas** close friends
3 *nm,f* close friend

allegar [38] **1** *vt* (**a**) *(reunir)* to gather, collect (**b**) *(acercar)* to bring closer
2 allegarse *vpr (acceder)* to agree, conform

allende *adv Fml* beyond; **a. los mares** overseas

allí *adv (lugar)* there, over there; *(tiempo)* then; **a. abajo/arriba** down/up there; **de a. para acá** back and forth; **hasta a. no tuvimos problemas** up until then we had no problems

alma *nf* soul; **como a. que lleva el diablo** in a flash; **con el a. destrozada** broken-hearted; **con toda el a.** wholeheartedly; **en cuerpo y a.** body and mind; **llegar al a. de algn** to touch o move sb; **no había ni un a.** there was not a soul; **no poder algn con su a.** to be absolutely exhausted; **parecer un a. en pena** to look like a ghost; **se le cayó el a. a los pies** her heart sank; **sentir algo en el a.** to be deeply sorry about o for sth; **ser el a. de la fiesta** to be the life and soul of the party; *Fig* **a. de Dios** good soul; *Fam* **almas gemelas** kindred spirits

almacén *nm* (**a**) *(local)* warehouse, storehouse; *(habitación)* storeroom (**b**) **(grandes) almacenes** *Com* department store *sing* (**c**) *Andes RP (de alimentos)* grocery store, *Br* grocer's (shop)

almacenaje *nm* (**a**) *(almacenamiento)* storage, warehousing (**b**) *Com (coste)* storage charge

almacenamiento *nm* (**a**) *(gen)* storage, warehousing (**b**) *(cosas almacenadas)* stock (**c**) *Inform* storage

almacenar *vt* (**a**) *(guardar)* to store, warehouse (**b**) *(acumular)* to store up, keep; **a. trastos** to keep junk

almacenero *nm* warehouseman, storekeeper

almacenista *nmf (vendedor)* wholesaler; *(propietario)* warehouse owner

almádena *nf Téc* sledgehammer

almadraba *nf* (**a**) *(pesca)* tunny fishing (**b**) *(lugar)* tunny-fishing ground (**c**) *(red)* tunny net

almanaque *nm* almanac, calendar

almazara *nf Ind* oilmill

almeja *nf Zool* clam

almena *nf* merlon; **almenas** battlements; **con almenas** castellated, battlemented

almendra *nf* (**a**) *Bot* almond ❑ **a. garapiñada** sugared almond (**b**) *(piedra)* pebble

almendrado, -a 1 *adj* almond-shaped
2 *nm* almond paste

almendral *nm* almond grove

almendro *nm* almond tree

almendruco *nm* unripe almond

almeriense 1 *adj* of o from Almeria
2 *nmf* person from Almeria

almiar *nm* haystack

almíbar *nm* syrup

almibarado, -a 1 *pp de* **almibarar**
2 *adj* (**a**) *(dulce)* syrupy (**b**) *Fig (meloso)* sugary, sweet

almibarar *vt (cubrir con almíbar)* to cover in syrup; *Fig* **a. las palabras** to use honeyed words

almidón *nm* starch

almidonado, -a 1 *pp de* **almidonar**
2 *adj* starched
3 *nm* starching

almidonar *vt* to starch

alminar *nm Arquit* minaret

almirantazgo *nm Mil* admiralty

almirante *nm Mil* admiral

almirez *nm* mortar

almizcle *nm* musk

almizcleño, -a *adj* musky

almizclero, -a 1 *adj* musky
2 *nm Zool* musk deer

almohada *nf* pillow; *Fam* **consultarlo con la a.** to sleep on it

almohade *adj & nmf Hist* Almohade

almohadilla *nf* (**a**) *(almohadón pequeño)* cushion (**b**) *RP (tampón)* inkpad

almohadillado, -a 1 *pp de* **almohadillar**
2 *adj* padded
3 *nm* padding

almohadillar *vt* (**a**) *(forrar)* to pad (**b**) *Arquit* to decorate with bolsters

almohadón *nm* large pillow, cushion

almoneda *nf* (**a**) *(subasta)* auction (**b**) *(venta a bajo precio)* clearance

almorávide *adj & nmf* Almoravid

almorrana *nf Med Fam* pile

almorzar [31] **1** *vi (al mediodía)* to have lunch; *(desayunar)* to have breakfast
2 *vt (al mediodía)* to have for lunch; *(desayunar)* to have for breakfast

Almte. *(abrev de* **Almirante***)* Adm

almuecín *nm*, **almuédano** *nm Rel* muezzin

almuerzo *nm* (**a**) *(al mediodía)* lunch ❑ **a. de trabajo** working lunch (**b**) *(desayuno)* breakfast (**c**) *(a media mañana)* mid-morning snack

aló *interj Andes Carib (al teléfono)* hello

alocado, -a *adj (distraído)* scatterbrained; *(irreflexivo)* thoughtless, rash

alocución *nf* speech, address

aloe *nm*, **áloe** *nm* (**a**) *Bot* aloe (**b**) *Med* aloes *sing*

alojamiento *nm* accommodation, lodging; **dar a.** to accommodate

alojar 1 *vt* (**a**) *(hospedar)* to accommodate, house, lodge (**b**) *(balsa)* to lodge
   2 alojarse *vpr (hospedarse)* to lodge, stay

alón *nm* plucked wing

alondra *nf Orn* skylark

alopatía *nf Med* allopathy

alopecia *nf Med* alopecia

alotropía *nf Quím* allotropy

alpaca[1] *nf Zool Tex* alpaca

alpaca[2] *nf Metal* alpaca, German silver

alpargata *nf* canvas sandal, espadrille

alpargatería *nf* (**a**) *(tienda)* espadrille shop (**b**) *(taller)* espadrille factory

Alpes *npl* **los A.** the Alps

alpestre *adj* Alpine; *Fig* mountainous, rough

alpinismo *nm* mountaineering, climbing

alpinista *nmf* mountaineer, climber

alpino, -a *adj* Alpine

alpiste *nm* (**a**) *Bot* birdseed, canary grass (**b**) *Fam (bebida)* booze; *(comida)* food

alquería *nf Esp* farmstead

alquilar *vt* to hire; *(pisos, casas)* to rent; **se alquila** *(en letrero)* to let

alquiler *nm* (**a**) *(acción)* hiring; *(de pisos, casas)* renting, letting ❑ **a. de coches** car hire; *Ind* **a. de equipo** *Br* plant hire, *US* plant leasing **de a.** *(pisos, casas)* to let, rented; *(coche)* for hire; *(televisión)* for rent (**b**) *(precio)* hire, rental; *(de pisos, casas)* rent

alquimia *nf* alchemy

alquimista *nmf* alchemist

alquitrán *nm* tar ❑ **a. de hulla** coal tar

alquitranado, -a 1 *pp de* **alquitranar**
   2 *adj* tarred, tarry
   3 *nm* (**a**) *(acción)* tarring (**b**) *(pavimento)* tarmac

alquitranar *vt* to tar

alrededor 1 *adv (lugar)* round, around; **a. de la mesa** round the table; *(aproximadamente)* **a. de las dos** around two o'clock; **a. de quince** about fifteen; **mira a.** look around
   2 alrededores *nmpl* surrounding area *sing*; **en los a. de Barcelona** in the area round Barcelona, just outside Barcelona

Alsacia *n* Alsace

alsaciano, -a *adj & nm,f* Alsatian

alt. *(abrev de* **altitud**) alt

alta *nf (ingreso)* admission; **dar de** o **el a.** *(a un empleado)* to register in the National Health System; *(a un enfermo)* to discharge from hospital; *Mil* to pass as fit; **darse de a.** *(socio)* to join; *(enfermo)* to discharge oneself; **solicitar el a.** to apply to be a member

altamente *adv* highly, extremely

altanería *nf* arrogance, haughtiness, conceit

altanero, -a *adj* arrogant, haughty, conceited

altar *nm Rel* altar; *Fig* **llevar a algn al a.** to lead sb down the aisle; *Fig* **poner en un a.** to put on a pedestal ❑ **a. mayor** high altar

altavoz *nm* loudspeaker

alterabilidad *nf* changeability

alterable *adj* changeable

alteración *nf* (**a**) *(cambio)* alteration (**b**) *(excitación)* uneasiness, agitation, restlessness (**c**) *(alboroto)* quarrel, row; **a. del orden público** disturbance of the peace

alterado, -a *adj* (**a**) *(cambiado)* altered, changed (**b**) *(perturbado)* upset; **los niños están muy alterados con la llegada de las vacaciones** the children are rather over-excited with the holidays coming up

alterar 1 *vt* (**a**) *(cambiar)* to alter, change (**b**) *(perturbar)* to upset; *(poner nervioso)* to agitate, make feel restless (**c**) *(dañar)* to spoil, make go bad
   2 alterarse *vpr* (**a**) *(cambiar)* to change (**b**) *(perturbarse)* to be upset, lose one's temper; **no se altera por nada** he never loses his temper (**c**) *(deteriorarse)* to spoil, go bad o off

altercado *nm* quarrel, argument

alternador *nm Elec* alternator

alternancia *nf* alternation

alternante *adj* alternating

alternar 1 *vt* to alternate
   2 *vi* (**a**) *(relacionarse)* to meet people, socialize; **le gusta a.** he's very sociable (**b**) *(con hombres)* to entertain; **(ella) alterna con hombres** she entertains men
   2 alternarse *vpr* to alternate

alternativa *nf* alternative, option, choice; **tomar una a.** to decide, choose

alternativo, -a *adj* alternative

alterne *nm Euf* **bar de a.** = bar where women encourage people to drink in return for a commission

alterno, -a *adj* alternate, alternating; **días alternos** alternate days

alteza *nf* Highness; **Su A. Real** His/Her Royal Highness

altibajos *nmpl Fig* **los a. de la vida** the ups and downs of life

altillo *nm* (**a**) *Arquit* attic (**b**) *Geog* hillock

altilocuente *adj* grandiloquent

altímetro *nm* altimeter

altiplanicie *nf.* **altiplano** *nm Geog* high plateau

altísimo, -a 1 *superl de* **alto, -a**
   2 *nm* **el A.** *Rel* the Almighty

altisonancia *nf* grandiloquence

altisonante *adj* grandiloquent, pompous

altitud *nf* altitude, height

altivez *nf,* **altiveza** *nf* arrogance, haughtiness, conceit

altivo, -a *adj* arrogant, haughty, conceited

alto[1] *nm* (**a**) *(interrupción)* stop, break; **hacer un a. en el trabajo** to take a short break from work (**b**) *Mil* halt; **¡a.!** halt; **¡a. el fuego!** cease fire!; **dar el a.** to order to halt; **un a. el fuego** a cease-fire

alto, -a[2] **1** *adj* (**a**) *(persona, árbol, edificio)* tall; *(montaña, techo, presión)* high; **mi hija es muy alta** my daughter is very tall; **tiene una casa de techos altos** she has a house with high ceilings; **un barco en alta mar** a ship on the high seas; *Fig* **pasar por a.** to overlook (**b**) *(elevado)* top, upper; **el A. Aragón** Upper Aragon; **en lo a.** at the top; **los pisos altos** the top floors (**c**) *(superior, avanzado)* **a altas horas de la noche** late at night; **alta sociedad** high society; **alta tecnología** high technology; **clase alta** upper class; **precio a.** high price (**d**) *(sonido) (fuerte)* loud; *(agudo)* high, sharp; **en voz alta** aloud, in a loud voice; **una nota alta** a high note
   2 *adv* (**a**) *(arriba)* high, high up; **no subas tan a.** don't go so far up; **sal con las manos en a.** come out with your hands up (**b**) *(fuerte)* loud, loudly; **pon la radio más alta** turn the radio up

3 *nm* (**a**) *(altura)* height; **¿cuánto mide de a.?** *(persona)* how tall is he?; *(cosa)* how high is it?; *Fig* **por todo lo a.** in a grand way; *Fig* **tirando por lo a.** at the most, at the outside (**b**) *(elevación)* hill (**c**) *Andes Méx RP (montón)* pile, heap (**d**) *CSur Perú* **altos** *(de casa)* upstairs *Br* flat *o US* apartment *(with its own front door)*

altoparlante *nm Am* loudspeaker

altozano *nm (elevación)* hillock, hill

altramuz *nm Bot* lupin

altruismo *nm* altruism

altruista 1 *adj* altruistic
2 *nmf* altruist

altura *nf* (**a**) *(cualidad, posición)* height; **a. del agua** depth of the water; **de diez metros de a.** ten metres high; **de poca a.** not very high (**b**) *(nivel)* level; **a la a. de la calle Ancha** at the junction with Calle Ancha; **a la a. del cine** by the cinema; **a la misma a.** on the same level; *Geog* on the same latitude; *Fig* **estar a la a. de las circunstancias** to rise to the occasion; *Fig* **no está a su a.** he does not measure up to him; *Fam* **quedar a la a. del betún** to make a very poor showing (**c**) *Fig (de sentimientos)* loftiness, nobleness (**d**) **alturas** *(cumbres)* heights; *Rel* heaven *sing*; *Fig* **a estas a.** by now; *Fig* **a estas a. ya no se puede cambiar nada** it's too late to change anything now

alubia *nf Culin* bean

alucinación *nf* hallucination

alucinado, -a 1 *pp de* **alucinar**
2 *adj Fam* staggered, *Br* gobsmacked

alucinador, -a *adj* hallucinatory

alucinamiento *nm* hallucination

alucinante *adj* (**a**) *(que provoca alucinaciones)* hallucinatory (**b**) *Argot (extraordinario)* brilliant, mind-blowing

alucinar 1 *vt Fig (cautivar)* to fascinate
2 *vi* (**a**) *(tener alucinaciones)* to hallucinate (**b**) *Argot* to be amazed, be spaced out

alucinógeno, -a 1 *adj* hallucinogenic
2 *nm* hallucinogen

alud *nm* avalanche

aludido, -a 1 *pp de* **aludir**
2 *adj* above-mentioned, in question; *Fig* **darse por a.** to take the hint

aludir *vi* **a. a** to allude to, mention

alumbrado, -a 1 *pp de* **alumbrar**
2 *adj* (**a**) *(iluminado)* lit, lighted (**b**) *Fam (alegre)* merry, tipsy
3 *nm* (**a**) *Elec* lighting □ **a. público** street lighting (**b**) *Aut* lights *pl*

alumbramiento *nm* (**a**) *Elec* lighting (**b**) *Med* childbirth

alumbrar 1 *vt* to light, give light to, illuminate; **alumbró el camino con una linterna** he lit the way with a torch; **las antorchas que alumbran la sala** the torches which light the hall
2 *vi* to give light; **alumbra muy poco** it doesn't give much light

alumbre *nm Quím* alum

alúmina *nf Quím Br* aluminium *o US* aluminum oxide

aluminio *nm Metal Br* aluminium, *US* aluminum

alumnado *nm Educ* (**a**) *(de colegio)* pupils *pl* (**b**) *Univ* student body

alumno, -a *nm,f* (**a**) *(de colegio)* pupil; **a. externo** day pupil; **a. interno** boarder (**b**) *Univ* student

alunado, -a *adj RP* annoyed, in a bad mood

alunizaje *nm* moon landing

alunizar [14] *vi* to land on the moon

alusión *nf* allusion, mention

alusivo, -a *adj* allusive (**a** to)

aluvial *adj* alluvial

aluvión *nm* alluvion, flood; *Fig* **un a. de preguntas** a barrage of questions

alveolar *adj Anat Ling* alveolar

alveolo *nm*, **alvéolo** *nm* (**a**) *Anat* alveolus (**b**) *(de panal)* cell

alverja *nf Am* pea

alza *nf* (**a**) *(de tiempo, temperatura)* rise; **en a.** rising; *(bolsa)* **jugar al a.** to bull the market; *Fig* **estar en a.** to be coming up (**b**) *Impr* underlay (**c**) *Mil* sight

alzacuello *nm* clerical collar

alzada *nf* (**a**) *(de un caballo)* height at the withers (**b**) *Jur (apelación)* appeal

alzado, -a 1 *pp de* **alzar**
2 *adj* (**a**) *(militar)* rebel (**b**) *(precio)* fixed; **a tanto a.** *(modo de pago)* in a single payment (**c**) *Andes RP Fam (salvaje)* wild (**d**) *Am Fam (en celo) Br* on heat, *US* in heat (**e**) *Am Fam (insolente)* insolent (**f**) *Col Fam (borracho)* drunk
3 *nm Arquit* elevation

alzamiento *nm* (**a**) *(aumento)* raising, increase (**b**) *(rebelión)* uprising

alzar [14] **1** *vt* (**a**) *(levantar)* to raise, lift; **a. el telón** to raise the curtain; **a. el vuelo** to take off; **a. la voz** to raise one's voice; **a. los ojos** to look up; **a. un edificio** to erect a building; *Náut* **a. velas** to hoist sail (**b**) *(quitar)* to remove, take off (**c**) *Impr* to gather (**d**) *(cosecha)* to get in, gather in
2 alzarse *vpr* (**a**) *(levantarse)* to get up, rise (**b**) *(sobresalir)* to stand out (**c**) *Pol (rebelarse)* to rise, rebel; **a. en armas** to rise (**d**) *(conseguir)* to obtain, achieve; **a. con la victoria** to win, be victorious (**e**) *Am (animal)* to run wild

Alzheimer *nm* **(enfermedad de) A.** Alzheimer's (disease)

AM *(abrev de* **amplitude modulation***)* AM

ama *nf (señora)* lady of the house; *(dueña)* owner □ **a. de casa** housewife; **a. de cría** wet nurse; **a. de llaves** housekeeper

amabilidad *nf* kindness; *Fml* **tenga la a. de esperar** would you be so kind as to wait

amable *adj* kind, nice; *Fml* **¿sería usted tan a. de seguirme?** would you be so kind as to follow me?

amado, -a 1 *pp de* **amar**
2 *adj* loved, beloved
3 *nm,f* sweetheart

amadrinar *vt* to be the godmother of

amaestrado, -a 1 *pp de* **amaestrar**
2 *adj* trained; *(domado)* tamed; **ratón a.** performing mouse

amaestrador, -a 1 *adj* training; *(domador)* taming
2 *nm,f (entrenador)* trainer; *(domador)* tamer

amaestramiento *nm* training; *(doma)* taming

amaestrar *vt (animal)* to train; *(domar)* to tame; **amaestró a su perro** he trained his dog

amagar [38] **1** *vt* (**a**) *(dar indicios de)* to show signs of; **amagaba una sonrisa** there was the hint of a smile on his lips (**b**) *(amenazar)* to threaten; **le amaga un gran peligro** he is threatened by great danger (**c**) *(fingir)* to dissemble, simulate; **a. una retirada** to simulate a retreat
2 *vi* (**a**) *(ser inminente)* to threaten, be imminent; **amagaba tormenta** a storm was threatening (**b**) *(enfermedad)* to show the first signs; **a. un ataque al corazón** to show symptoms of the onset of a heart attack

amago *nm* first sign, indication; **a. de infarto** onset of a heart attack

amainar *vi* (**a**) *(viento, tormenta)* to drop, die down (**b**) *Fig (apaciguarse)* to calm down

amalgama *nf* amalgam

amalgamación *nf* amalgamation

amalgamar *vt* to amalgamate

amamantamiento *nm* breast-feeding, suckling

amamantar *vt* to breast-feed, suckle

amancay *nm Andes* golden hurricane lily

amancebamiento *nm* cohabitation

amancebarse *vpr* to cohabit

amanecer [46] **1** *v impers* to dawn; **amanece temprano** day breaks early
   2 *vi* to be somewhere at daybreak; **amanecimos en Finlandia** we were in Finland at daybreak
   3 *nm* dawn, daybreak; **al a.** at dawn

amanerado, -a 1 *pp de* amanerar
   2 *adj* mannered, affected

amaneramiento *nm* affectation

amanerar 1 *vt (maneras)* to affect
   2 amanerarse *vpr* to become affected

amansadora *nf RP Fam* tedious wait

amansar 1 *vt* (**a**) *(animal)* to tame; **a. un caballo** to break in a horse; *Fig* **la música amansa a las fieras** music soothes the savage breast (**b**) *(persona)* to calm down; *(pasiones)* to calm
   2 amansarse *vpr (animal)* to become tame

amante 1 *adj* **es a. de su familia** he loves his family; **a. del arte** fond of art
   2 *nmf* lover

amanuense *nmf* scribe

amañado, -a 1 *pp de* amañar
   2 *adj* (**a**) *(hábil)* clever, skilful, *US* skillful (**b**) *(falso)* faked

amañar 1 *vt (falsear)* to fix, fiddle; **a. las cuentas** to cook the books; **a. las elecciones** to rig the elections; **a. una historia** to fabricate a story
   2 amañarse *vpr Fam (apañárselas)* **amañárselas** to manage; **siempre se las amaña para conseguir lo que quiere** he always manages to get his way

amaño *nm* trick, fiddle, scheme

amapola *nf Bot* poppy

amar 1 *vt* to love
   2 amarse *vpr* to love each other, be in love (with each other)

amaraje *nm* (**a**) *Náut* landing at sea (**b**) *Astronáut* splashdown

amaranto *nm Bot* amaranth

amarar *vi* (**a**) *Náut* to land at sea (**b**) *Astronáut* to splash down

amargado, -a 1 *pp de* amargar
   2 *adj Fig* embittered, bitter; *(resentido)* resentful; **ella está amargada** she feels very bitter; **una sonrisa amargada** a sour smile
   3 *nm,f* bitter person

amargar [38] **1** *vt* to make bitter; *Fig* to embitter, sour; **amargarle la existencia a algn** to make sb's life a misery; **aquello nos amargó la tarde** that ruined the whole evening
   2 *vi* to taste bitter
   3 amargarse *vpr Fig* to become embittered *o* bitter; **no te amargues por eso** don't let that make you bitter

amargo, -a 1 *adj* bitter
   2 *nm* bitterness

amargor *nm* bitterness

amargura *nf* bitterness, grief, sorrow, sadness

amariconado, -a *adj Fam (afeminado)* limp-wristed, *Br* poofy, *US* faggy

amarillear *vi* (**a**) *(volverse amarillo)* to yellow, go yellow (**b**) *(tirar a amarillo)* to be yellowish

amarillento, -a *adj* yellowish

amarillez *nf* yellowness

amarillismo *nm Prensa* sensationalism

amarillista *adj Prensa* sensationalist

amarillo, -a *adj & nm* yellow

amarilloso, -a *adj Col Méx Ven* yellowish

amaro *nm Bot* clary sage

amarra *nf* (**a**) *Náut* mooring rope; **soltar amarras** to cast off, let go (**b**) *Fig (lazo)* tie, binding; **soltarse las amarras** to break loose (**c**) **amarras** *Fam* connections

amarradero *nm Náut (argolla)* mooring ring; *(lugar)* mooring

amarraje *nm Náut* mooring charges *pl*

amarrar 1 *vt* (**a**) *Náut* to moor, tie up (**b**) *(atar)* to tie (up), bind
   2 amarrarse *vpr Am salvo RP (pelo)* to tie up; *(zapatos, cordones)* to tie

amarre *nm Náut* mooring

amarrete *adj Andes RP Fam* mean, stingy, tight

amartelado, -a 1 *pp de* amartelarse
   2 *adj* starry-eyed

amartelarse *vpr* to become very loving

amartillar *vt* (**a**) *(martillear)* to hammer (**b**) *(escopeta)* to cock

amasandería *nf Chile* baker's shop, bakery

amasar *vt* (**a**) *Culin (masa)* to knead (**b**) *Constr (yeso, cemento)* to mix (**c**) *Fig (dinero)* to amass (**d**) *Fam (urdir)* to cook up

amasiato *nm CAm Chile Méx* **vivir en a.** to live together

amasijo *nm* (**a**) *Culin (masa)* dough (**b**) *Constr (de yeso, cemento)* mixture (**c**) *Fam (mezcolanza)* hotch-potch, jumble

amasio, -a *nm,f CAm Méx (hombre)* common-law husband; *(mujer)* common-law wife

amateur [ama'ter] *(pl* **amateurs**) *adj & nmf* amateur

amatista *nf Min* amethyst

amatorio, -a *adj* love; **poesía amatoria** love poetry

amazacotado, -a *adj* (**a**) *(duro)* hard, tough; **arroz a.** stodgy rice (**b**) *(apretado)* crammed

amazona *nf* (**a**) *(jinete)* horsewoman (**b**) *Mit* Amazon

Amazonas *n* **el A.** the Amazon

Amazonia *nf* **la A.** the Amazon

amazónico, -a *adj* Amazonian

ambages *nmpl* **hablar sin a.** to go straight to the point; **ir** *o* **andarse con a.** to beat around the bush

ámbar *nm* amber

ambarino, -a *adj* amber

Amberes *n* Antwerp

ambición *nf* ambition

ambicionar *vt* to have as an ambition; **siempre ambicionó ser rico** he always wanted to be rich

ambicioso, -a 1 *adj* ambitious
   2 *nm,f* ambitious person

ambidextro, -a 1 *adj* ambidextrous
   2 *nm,f* ambidextrous person

ambientación *nf Lit Teat* setting

ambientador *nm (de aire)* air freshener

ambiental *adj* environmental

ambientar 1 *vt* (**a**) *(dar ambiente)* to give atmosphere to;

este café está muy bien **ambientado** this cafe has a very nice atmosphere (**b**) *Lit Teat (situar)* to set; **la obra está ambientada en la Edad Media** the play o the book is set in the Middle Ages

2 ambientarse *vpr (en nuevo trabajo, lugar)* to settle in

ambiente 1 *adj* environmental; **temperatura a.** room temperature

2 *nm* (**a**) *(medio)* atmosphere, environment, milieu; **cambiar de a.** to change one's surroundings; **el a. familiar** the family environment; **en este a. no hay quien trabaje** it is impossible to work in these conditions; **en este pueblo no hay a.** there is not much going on in this village (**b**) *Esp Fam* **el a.** *(homosexual)* the gay scene (**c**) *Andes RP (habitación)* room

ambigú (*pl* **ambigú** o **ambigúes**) *nm* buffet, buffet supper

ambigüedad *nf* ambiguity

ambiguo, -a *adj* ambiguous

ámbito *nm* (**a**) *(espacio)* space, sphere; **de a. local** local; **empresa de a. nacional** nationwide company; **en el a. de** within; **en el a. de esta provincia** within this county (**b**) *(ambiente)* atmosphere, environment

ambivalencia *nf* ambivalence

ambivalente *adj* ambivalent

ambos, -as *adj pl Fml* both; **por a. lados** on both sides

ambrosía *nf* ambrosia

ambulancia *nf* ambulance

ambulante *adj* travelling, *US* traveling, mobile

ambulatorio, -a 1 *adj* ambulatory
2 *nm* surgery, clinic

ameba *nf* amoeba, *US* ameba

amedrentar 1 *vt* to scare, frighten
2 amedrentarse *vpr* to get scared o frightened

amén[1] *nm Rel* amen; *Fam* **decir a. a todo** to agree with everything; *Fam* **en un decir a.** in the twinkling of an eye

amén[2] *adv* **a. de** *(excepto)* except for; *(además de)* in addition to

amenaza *nf* threat, menace ▭ **a. de bomba** bomb scare; **a. de muerte** death threat

amenazador, -a *adj*, **amenazante** *adj* threatening, menacing

amenazar [14] *vt* to threaten; **a. de muerte a algn** to threaten to kill sb; *Fig* **amenaza lluvia** it is threatening to rain

amenidad *nf* pleasantness, agreeableness

amenizar [14] *vt* to make (more) entertaining; **para a. la velada** to liven up the party

ameno, -a *adj* pleasant, enjoyable, entertaining

América *n* America ▭ **A. Central** Central America; **A. del Norte** North America; **A. del Sur** South America

americana *nf (prenda)* jacket

americanismo *nm Ling* Americanism

americanista *nmf* Americanist

americanización *nf* Americanization

americanizar [14] **1** *vt* to Americanize
2 americanizarse *vpr* to become Americanized, go American

americano, -a *adj & nm,f* American

amerindio, -a *adj & nm,f* Amerindian, American Indian

ameritado, -a 1 *pp de* ameritar
2 *adj Am* worthy

ameritar *vt Am* to deserve

amerizaje *nm véase* amaraje

amerizar [14] *vi véase* amarar

amestizado, -a *adj* like a half-breed

ametrallador, -a *adj* **fusil a.** automatic rifle

ametralladora *nf* machine gun

ametrallar *vt* to machine-gun

amianto *nm Min* asbestos

amigable *adj* amicable, friendly

amígdala *nf Anat* tonsil

amigdalitis *nf Med* tonsillitis

amigo, -a 1 *adj* (**a**) *(no enemigo)* friendly; **una mano amiga** a friendly hand; **son muy amigos** they are very good friends (**b**) *(aficionado)* fond (**de** of); **a. del buen vino** fond of good wine

2 *nm,f* (**a**) *(persona)* friend; **hacerse a. de** to make friends with; **hacerse amigos** to become friends; **un a. mío** a friend of mine (**b**) *(novio)* boyfriend; *(novia)* girlfriend; *(amante)* lover

amigote *nm Fam* pal, *Br* mate, *US* buddy

amiguete *nm Fam véase* amigote

amiguismo *nm* **hay mucho a.** there are always jobs for the boys

amilanamiento *nm* (**a**) *(miedo)* fear (**b**) *(desánimo)* discouragement; *(abatimiento)* depression

amilanar 1 *vt* (**a**) *(asustar)* to frighten, scare (**b**) *(desanimar)* to discourage, depress
2 amilanarse *vpr* (**a**) *(asustarse)* to be frightened (**b**) *(desanimarse)* to be discouraged, become depressed

aminoácido *nm Quím* amino acid

aminoración *nf* reduction, decrease, cut; **a. de la velocidad** slowing down

aminorar *vt* to reduce, decrease, cut; **a. el paso** to slow down

amistad *nf* (**a**) *(relación)* friendship; **trabar a. con** to make friends with (**b**) **amistades** *(amigos)* friends; **hacer nuevas a.** to make new friends

amistoso, -a *adj* friendly; **en plan a.** in a friendly way; *Dep* **partido a.** friendly match

amnesia *nf Med* amnesia, loss of memory

amnésico, -a 1 *adj* amnesic
2 *nm,f* amnesiac

amniocentesis *nf inv Med* amniocentesis

amniótico, -a *adj Med* amniotic; **líquido a.** amniotic fluid

amnistía *nf* amnesty ▭ **A. Internacional** Amnesty International

amnistiar [32] *vt* to amnesty, grant an amnesty to

amo *nm* (**a**) *(señor)* master; *Fig* **ser el a.** to be the boss; *Fam* **ser el a. del cotarro** to rule the roost (**b**) *(dueño)* owner

amoblar [63] *vt* to furnish

amodorrado, -a 1 *pp de* amodorrarse
2 *adj* sleepy, drowsy

amodorramiento *nm* sleepiness, drowsiness

amodorrarse *vpr (adormecerse)* to become sleepy o drowsy; *(dormirse)* to fall into a stupor

amojonamiento *nm* marking out

amojonar *vt* to mark out

amolado, -a 1 *pp de* amolar
2 *adj* sharpened, ground
3 *nm* sharpening, grinding

amolar [63] *vt* (**a**) *(afilar)* to sharpen, grind (**b**) *Fam (fastidiar)* to annoy, pester

amoldable *adj* adaptable; *Fig* **Juan es muy a.** Juan adapts to everything

amoldamiento *nm (adaptación)* adaptation

amoldar 1 *vt* to adapt, adjust
2 amoldarse *vpr* to adapt oneself; **ella no pudo a. a la nueva vida** she couldn't get used to the new lifestyle

amonestación *nf* (**a**) *(advertencia)* rebuke, reprimand, reprehension; *Dep (tarjeta)* warning (**b**) **amonestaciones** *Rel* banns

amonestar *vt* (**a**) *(advertir)* to rebuke, reprimand; *Dep* to warn (**b**) *Rel* to publish the banns of

amoniacal *adj Quím* ammoniacal

amoniaco *nm*, **amoníaco** *nm* ammonia

amontillado, -a *adj (vino)* pale dry, amontillado

amontonamiento *nm* (**a**) *(acción)* piling, heaping (**b**) *(montón)* pile, heap

amontonar 1 *vt* (**a**) *(apilar)* to pile up, heap up (**b**) *(reunir)* to collect, gather; **a. trastos** to keep junk
2 amontonarse *vpr (problemas, trabajo)* to pile up; *(gente)* to crowd together

amor *nm* (**a**) *(sentimiento)* love; *(con esmero)* loving care; **ella fue su gran a.** she was his great love; **hacer el a.** to make love; **por el a. de Dios** for God's sake; *Fig* **en cada puerto, un a.** a girl in every port; *Fam* **con** *o* **de mil amores** with pleasure; *Fam* **por a. al arte** for the love of it; *Prov* **a. con a. se paga** one good turn deserves another ▭ *Lit* **a. cortés** courtly love; **a. platónico** platonic love; **a. propio** self-esteem (**b**) **amores** *(persona)* loves; *(asuntos)* love affairs

amoral *adj* amoral

amoralidad *nf* amorality

amoratado, -a 1 *pp de* **amoratarse**
2 *adj* (**a**) *(de frío)* blue with cold (**b**) *(de un golpe)* black and blue; **con un ojo a.** with a black eye

amoratarse *vpr* (**a**) *(de frío)* to turn blue (**b**) *(de un golpe)* to turn black and blue

amorcillo *nm* Cupid

amordazar [14] *vt (perro)* to muzzle; *(persona)* to gag

amorfo, -a *adj* amorphous

amorío *nm* love affair, flirtation

amoroso, -a *adj* loving, affectionate

amortajamiento *nm* shrouding

amortajar *vt* to shroud, wrap in a shroud

amortiguación *nf (de un dolor)* alleviation, mitigation; *(de un golpe)* damping; *(de un ruido)* muffling; *(de una luz)* subduing

amortiguador, -a 1 *adj (de dolor)* alleviating, mitigating; *(de golpe)* damping, cushioning; *(de ruido)* muffling; *(de luz)* subduing
2 *nm Aut* shock absorber; *Téc* damper

amortiguamiento *nm véase* **amortiguación**

amortiguar [11] *vt (dolor)* to alleviate, mitigate; *(golpe)* to damp, cushion; *(ruido)* to muffle; *(luz)* to subdue

amortizable *adj Fin* redeemable

amortización *nf Fin* (**a**) *(reembolso)* redemption (**b**) *(depreciación)* amortization, depreciation, writing off

amortizar [14] *vt Fin* (**a**) *(reembolsar)* to redeem (**b**) *(depreciar)* to amortize, depreciate, write off; *Fam* **me costó caro, pero lo he amortizado** it was expensive, but I've got my money's worth out of it

amoscarse [59] *vpr Fam* to get angry

amostazarse [14] *vpr Andes CAm* to become embarrassed

amotinado, -a 1 *pp de* **amotinar**
2 *adj (insurrecto)* riotous, insurgent; *Mil* mutinous
3 *nm,f (insurrecto)* rioter, insurgent; *Mil* mutineer

amotinamiento *nm* riot, rioting; *(insurrección)* insurrection; *Mil* mutiny

amotinar 1 *vt* to incite to riot; *Mil* to incite to mutiny
2 amotinarse *vpr* to rise up, riot; *Mil* to mutiny

amovible *adj* detachable, removable

amparar 1 *vt* to protect; *(ayudar)* to help; *(favorecer)* to favour, *US* favor
2 ampararse *vpr* to use as protection; *(defenderse)* to take shelter; **se amparó en sus amigos** he sought the help of his friends

amparo *nm* protection, shelter; **al a. de** under the protection of

amperaje *nm Elec* amperage

amperímetro *nm Elec* ammeter

amperio *nm Elec* ampère, amp

ampliable *adj* enlargeable

ampliación *nf* enlargement, extension; *Constr* extension; *Fot* enlargement; *Fin* **a. de capital** increase in capital; **a. de estudios** furthering of studies

ampliadora *nf Fot* enlarger

ampliamente *adv* (**a**) *(con espacio)* easily; **aquí cabe todo a.** there's more than enough room for everything here (**b**) *(extensamente) (aceptado, admitido)* widely

ampliar [32] *vt* to enlarge extend; *Constr (casa, edificio)* to build an extension to; *Fot (fotografía)* to enlarge; *Fin (capital)* to increase; **a. una idea** to develop an idea

amplificación *nf* amplification

amplificador, -a 1 *adj* amplifying
2 *nm* amplifier

amplificar [59] *vt* to amplify

amplio, -a *adj* large, roomy, spacious; *(ancho)* wide, broad; **en el sentido más a. de la palabra** in the broadest sense of the word

amplitud *nf* (**a**) *(espaciosidad) (de sala, maletero)* roominess, spaciousness; *(de avenida)* wideness; *Fig* **de gran a.** far-reaching ▭ **a. de miras** broad-mindedness (**b**) *(espacio)* room, space (**c**) *Fís* amplitude

ampolla *nf* (**a**) *Med* blister (**b**) *(vasija)* flask, bottle (**c**) *(burbuja)* bubble

ampollarse *vpr* to blister; **se me han ampollado los pies** I've got blisters on my feet

ampulosidad *nf* pomposity, bombast

ampuloso, -a *adj* pompous, bombastic

amputación *nf* (**a**) *Med* amputation (**b**) *Fig (supresión)* cutting out

amputar *vt* (**a**) *Med* to amputate (**b**) *Fig (suprimir)* to cut out

Amsterdam *n* Amsterdam

amucharse *vpr Andes RP* to squeeze up, make room

amueblado, -a 1 *adj (apartamento)* furnished
2 *nm RP* room hired for sex

amueblar *vt* to furnish

amuermado, -a 1 *pp de* **amuermar**
2 *adj Esp Fam* (**a**) *(atontado)* dopy, dopey, groggy (**b**) *(deprimido)* down, depressed (**c**) *(aburrido)* bored

amuermar *vt Esp Fam* (**a**) *(atontar)* to make feel dopy *o* dopey *o* groggy (**b**) *(deprimir)* to depress (**c**) *(aburrir)* to bore

amulatado, -a *adj* like a mulatto

amuleto *nm* amulet ▭ **a. de la suerte** lucky charm

amurallado, -a 1 *pp de* **amurallar**
2 *adj* walled

amurallar *vt* to wall, fortify

anabaptismo *nm Rel* Anabaptism

anabaptista *adj & nmf Rel* Anabaptist

anabolismo *nm Biol* anabolism

anabolizante 1 *adj* anabolic
  2 *nm* anabolic steroid
anacarado, -a *adj* pearly
anacardo *nm Bot (árbol)* cashew tree; *(fruto)* cashew nut
anacoluto *nm Ling* anacoluthon
anaconda *nf Zool* anaconda
anacoreta *nmf* anchorite, anchoret
anacrónico, -a *adj* anachronistic, anachronic
anacronismo *nm* anachronism
ánade *nm Orn* duck
anaerobio, -a *Biol* **1** *adj* anaerobic
  2 *nm* anaerobe
anafe *nm* portable stove *o* cooker
anagrama *nm* anagram
anal *adj Anat* anal
anales *nmpl* annals
analfabetismo *nm* illiteracy
analfabeto, -a *nm,f* illiterate; *Fig* **es un a.** he is stupid
analgesia *nf Med* analgesia
analgésico, -a *adj & nm Med* analgesic
análisis *nm inv* analysis □ *Fin* **a. coste-beneficio** cost benefit analysis; **a. de mercado** market analysis; **a. de orina** urine analysis; **a. de sangre** blood test; **a. sintáctico** syntactic analysis
analista *nmf* analyst □ **a. de mercados** market analyst
analítico, -a *adj* analytical, analytic
analizable *adj* analyzable
analizador, -a 1 *adj* analyzing
  2 *nm Fis* analyzer
analizar [14] *vt* to analyze
analogía *nf* analogy
analógico, -a *adj* **(a)** *(análogo)* analogical **(b)** *Inform Tec* analogue, analog
análogo, -a *adj* analogous, similar
ananá *nm* , **ananás** *nm inv* pineapple
anaquel *nm* shelf
anaranjado, -a *adj & nm (color)* orange
anarco *nmf Fam* anarchist
anarcosindicalismo *nm Pol* anarchosyndicalism
anarcosindicalista *adj & nmf Pol* anarchosyndicalist
anarquía *nf* anarchy
anárquico, -a *adj* anarchical, anarchic
anarquismo *nm* anarchism
anarquista *adj & nmf* anarchist
anarquizante *adj* anarchist
anatema *nm* anathema; **lanzar anatemas** to curse
anatematizar [14] *vt* to anathematize; *Fig* to curse
anatomía *nf* anatomy
anatómico, -a *adj* anatomical, anatomic
anca *nf* haunch □ **ancas de rana** frogs' legs
ancestral *adj* ancestral
ancestro *nm* ancestor
ancho, -a 1 *adj* wide, broad; **a lo a.** breadthwise; **te está muy a.** it's too big for you; *Esp Fam* **quedarse tan a.** to behave as if nothing had happened
  2 *nm* **(a)** *(anchura)* width, breadth; **dos metros de a.** two metres wide; **¿qué a. tiene?** how wide is it? □ *Inform* **a. de banda** bandwidth **(b)** *Cost* width
  2 anchas *nfpl Fam* **a mis** *o* **tus a.** at ease, comfortable; **me sentí a mis a.** I felt comfortable *o* at home
anchoa *nf (pez)* anchovy

anchura *nf (ancho)* width, breadth; *Cost* **a. de cintura** waist measurement
anchuroso, -a *adj* wide, broad; *(espacioso)* spacious
ancianidad *nf* old age
anciano, -a 1 *adj* very old
  2 *nm,f* old person; **los ancianos** old people □ **residencia de ancianos** old people's home
ancla *nf Náut* anchor; **echar anclas** to drop anchor; **levar anclas** to weigh anchor
anclaje *nm* **(a)** *Náut* anchorage **(b)** *Constr Tec* anchor
anclar *vt & vi Náut Tec* to anchor
áncora *nf Náut Tec* anchor
anda *interj* **(a)** *(indica sorpresa)* gosh!; **¡a. la osa!** good grief! **(b)** *(por favor)* go on! **(c)** *(venga)* come on! **(d)** **¡a. ya!** *(negativa despectiva)* get away!, come off it!
andadas *nfpl Fam* old ways; **volver a las a.** to go back to one's old tricks
andaderas *nfpl* baby-walker *sing*
andador, -a 1 *adj (aficionado a andar)* fond of walking; *(rápido)* fast-walking
  2 *nm,f (bueno)* good walker; *(rápido)* fast walker
  3 *nm* baby-walker
andadura *nf* walking
ándale *interj CAm Méx Fam* come on!
Andalucía *n* Andalusia
andalucismo *nm* **(a)** *Ling* Andalusian word *o* expression **(b)** *Pol* Andalusian nationalism
andalusí *Hist* **1** *adj* Moorish
  2 *nmf* Moor, = of or related to the Arab empire of Al-Andalus in southern Spain 711—1492
andaluz, -a *adj & nm,f* Andalusian
andamiaje *nm Constr* scaffolding
andamio *nm Constr* scaffold
andana *nf* row, line
andanada *nf* **(a)** *(represión)* reprimand, rebuke **(b)** *Taur* covered stand **(c)** *Mil (descarga)* broadside **(d)** *(andana)* row, line
andante 1 *adj* **caballero a.** knight errant
  2 *nm Mús* andante
andanza *nf* adventure, happening
andar [7] **1** *vi* **(a)** *esp Esp (caminar)* to walk; *(venir)* to come; *(ir)* to go; **a. de puntillas** to tiptoe; *Fam* **¡andando!** let's go!, let's get a move on! **(b)** *(trasladarse algo)* to move; **este coche anda despacio** this car goes very slowly **(c)** *(funcionar)* to work, go, function; **este ascensor no anda** this lift is out of order; **esto no anda** this doesn't work **(d)** *Fam (estar)* to be; **anda por los cuarenta** he's about forty; **anda preocupada estos días** she's been rather worried lately; **anda siempre diciendo que ...** he's always saying that ...; **¿qué tal andamos de tiempo?** how are we off for time?; **tus calcetines deben a. por ahí** your socks must be there somewhere **(e)** *(obrar)* **anda con cuidado** take care, be careful; *Prov* **dime con quién andas y te diré quién eres** birds of a feather flock together; *Prov* **quien mal anda mal acaba** those who live by the sword die by the sword
  2 *vt (recorrer)* to walk; **a. diez kilómetros** to walk ten kilometres
  3 andarse *vpr* **ándate con cuidado** mind what you do, take good care of yourself; *Fig* **a. con rodeos, a. por las ramas** to beat about the bush
andares *nmpl* walk *sing*, gait *sing*
andariego, -a 1 *adj* **(a)** *(que anda)* fond of walking **(b)** *(que viaja)* fond of travelling
  2 *nm,f* **(a)** *(andador)* good walker **(b)** *(viajero)* person who likes travelling

andarín, -ina 1 *adj* good at walking
  2 *nm,f* good walker

andas *nfpl* portable platform *sing*; *Rel* **llevaban el santo en a.** they carried the saint on a float; *Fig* **llevar a algn en a.** to pamper sb

ándele *interj CAm Méx Fam* come on!

andén *nm Ferroc* platform

Andes *npl* Andes

andinismo *nm Am* mountaineering

andinista *nmf Am* mountaineer

andino, -a *adj & nm,f* Andean

Andorra *n* Andorra

andorrano, -a *adj & nm,f* Andorran

andrajo *nm* rag, tatter; **hecho un a.** in rags

andrajoso, -a *adj* ragged, tattered

androceo *nm Bot* androecium

andrógeno *nm Biol* androgen

andrógino, -a *Biol* **1** *adj* androgynous, androgyne
  2 *nm* androgyne

androide *nm* android

andurriales *nmpl Fam* out-of-the way place *sing*

anea *nf Bot Br* bulrush, *US* cattail

anécdota *nf* anecdote

anecdotario *nm* collection of anecdotes

anecdótico, -a *adj* anecdotic, anecdotal

anegación *nf* flooding

anegadizo, -a *adj* subject to flooding

anegamiento *nm véase* **anegación**

anegar [38] **1** *vt* to flood
  2 anegarse *vpr* to flood; *Fig* **a. en lágrimas** to fill with tears

anejo, -a 1 *adj* attached, joined (**a** to)
  2 *nm* annexe, *US* annex

anemia *nf Med* anaemia, *US* anemia

anémico, -a 1 *adj Med* anaemic, *US* anemic
  2 *nm,f Med* anaemia *o US* anemia sufferer

anemómetro *nm Fís* anemometer

anémona *nf,* **anemona** *nf,* **anemone** *nf* (**a**) *Bot* anemone (**b**) *Zool* **a. de mar** sea anemone

anestesia *nf Med* anaesthesia, *US* anesthesia □ **a. general** general anaesthesia/anaesthetic; **a. local** local anaesthesia/anaesthetic

anestesiar *vt Med* to anaesthetize, *US* anesthetize

anestésico, -a *adj & nm Med* anaesthetic, *US* anesthetic

anestesista *nmf Med* anaesthetist, *US* anesthesiologist

aneurisma *nm Med* aneurysm

anexar *vt* to annex

anexión *nf* annexation

anexionar *vt véase* **anexar**

anexionismo *nm Pol* annexationism, annexionism

anexionista *adj & nmf Pol* annexationist, annexionist

anexo, -a 1 *adj* attached, joined (**a** to)
  2 *nm* annexe, *US* annex

anfeta *nf Argot* amphetamine

anfetamina *nf Farm* amphetamine

anfibio, -a 1 *adj* amphibious
  2 *nm Zool* amphibian; **los anfibios** amphibia *pl*

anfibología *nf Ling* amphibology

anfiteatro *nm* (**a**) *(romano)* amphitheatre, *US* amphitheater (**b**) *Univ* lecture theatre *o US* theater (**c**) *(en teatro)* circle; *(en cine)* balcony

anfitrión, -ona *nm,f (hombre)* host; *(mujer)* hostess

ánfora *nf* amphora

angarillas *nfpl (carretilla)* handbarrow *sing*; *(camilla)* stretcher *sing*

ángel *nm* angel; *Fig* **es un á.** he behaves beautifully; *Fig* **tener á.** to have a something about one □ *Rel* **á. de la guarda** guardian angel; *Dep* **salto del á.** swallow dive

angélica *nf Bot* angelica

angelical *adj,* **angélico, -a** *adj* angelical, angelic

angelito *nm Fam* little angel; *Irón* **menudo a. estás tú hecho** you are a fine one!

angelote *nm* (**a**) *(niño)* chubby child (**b**) *(adulto)* good person

ángelus *nm inv Rel* Angelus

angina *nf Med* angina; **estar con anginas** to have a sore throat □ *Med* **a. de pecho** angina pectoris

anglicanismo *nm Rel* Anglicanism

anglicano, -a *adj & nm,f Rel* Anglican; **la Iglesia Anglicana** the Anglican Church, the Church of England

anglicismo *nm* Anglicism

anglo, -a 1 *adj* Anglian
  2 *nm,f* Angle, Anglian

angloamericano, -a *adj & nm,f* Anglo-American

anglófilo, -a *adj & nm,f* Anglophile

anglófobo, -a *adj & nm,f* Anglophobe

anglófono, -a 1 *adj* English-speaking
  2 *nm,f* English speaker

Anglonormando, -a *adj* **las Islas Anglonormandas** the Channel Islands

anglosajón, -ona *adj & nm,f* Anglo-Saxon

Angola *n* Angola

angoleño, -a *adj & nm,f* Angolan, Angolese

angora *nf* angora; **gato de a.** Angora cat; **lana de a.** angora wool

angosto, -a *adj Fml* narrow

angostura *nf* (**a**) *(estrechez)* narrowness (**b**) *Bot* angostura

ángstrom *(pl* **ángstroms)** *nm Fís* angstrom

anguila *nf (pez)* eel □ **a. de mar** conger eel

angula *nf (pez)* elver

angular *adj* angular; *Fot* **(objetivo) gran a.** wide-angle lens; *Arquit* **piedra a.** cornerstone

ángulo *nm* (**a**) *Geom* angle; **en á. con** at an angle to □ **á. agudo/obtuso/recto** acute/obtuse/right angle; *Aut* **á. muerto** blind spot; *Mil* **á. de tiro** elevation (**b**) *(esquina, rincón)* corner

anguloso, -a *adj* angular

angurria *nf Am* (**a**) *(hambre)* hunger (**b**) *(codicia, avidez)* greed

angustia *nf* (**a**) *(aflicción)* anxiety; **¡qué a.!** how distressing! (**b**) *(sensación física)* sickness, nausea

angustiado, -a 1 *pp de* **angustiar**
  2 *adj (afligido)* distressed; *(preocupado)* worried

angustiar 1 *vt (afligir)* to distress; *(preocupar)* to worry
  2 angustiarse *vpr (afligirse)* to become distressed; *(preocuparse)* to worry

angustioso, -a *adj (acongojante)* distressing; *(preocupado)* worrying

anhelante *adj* longing, yearning

anhelar *vt* to long for, yearn for; **anhelaba encontrarse con ella** he was longing to meet her

anhelo *nm* longing, yearning

anhídrido *nm Quím* anhydride

anidar 1 *vi Orn* to nest, make one's nest; *Fig* **la esperanza anidó en su corazón** hope filled his heart
2 *vt Fig* to shelter

anilina *nf Quím* aniline, anilin

anilla *nf* (**a**) *(aro)* ring (**b**) **anillas** *Dep* rings

anillado, -a 1 *pp de* **anillar**
2 *nm Orn* ringing

anillar *vt* (**a**) *(dar forma de anillo)* to make into a ring (**b**) *(sujetar con anillos)* to ring (**c**) *Orn (marcar)* to ring

anillo *nm* (**a**) *(aro)* ring; *Fig* **me viene como a. al dedo** it's just what I needed; *Fig Irón* **no se te van a caer los anillos por eso** doing that wouldn't be beneath you ❑ **a. de boda** wedding ring; **a. de prometida** engagement ring (**b**) *Astron* ring (**c**) *Arquit* annulet (**d**) *(de gusano)* annulus; *(de culebra)* coil

ánima *nf* (**a**) *Rel* soul ❑ **á. bendita** soul in Purgatory (**b**) *(de arma)* bore (**c**) **ánimas** *Rel* evening bell *sing*

animación *nf* (**a**) *(alegría)* liveliness; **dar a. a una fiesta** to liven a party up (**b**) *(bullicio)* hustle and bustle, activity; **hay gran a. en la plaza** there is a lot of bustle in the square

animadamente *adv* cheerfully

animado, -a 1 *pp de* **animar**
2 *adj* (**a**) *(entretenido)* lively, entertaining, jolly; **una película muy animada** a very entertaining movie *o Br* film (**b**) *(con buen ánimo)* cheerful, in high spirits

animador, -a 1 *adj* cheering, encouraging
2 *nm,f (en baile)* entertainer; *Dep* cheerleader

animadversión *nf* ill feeling, animosity

animal 1 *adj* (**a**) *(instintos, funciones)* animal; **el reino a.** the animal kingdom (**b**) *Fam (persona) (basto)* rough; *(necio)* ignorant; *(grosero)* rude, coarse
2 *nm* animal ❑ **a. de bellota** pig; **a. de carga** beast of burden; **a. de compañía** pet
3 *nmf Fam (persona) (basto)* rough person, brute; *(necio)* dunce; *(grosero)* rude person

animalada *nf Fam* **su comportamiento fue una auténtica a.** he behaved like a complete animal

animalidad *nf* animality

animar 1 *vt* (**a**) *(alentar)* to encourage (**b**) *(alegrar) (persona)* to cheer up; *(local, fiesta, reunión)* to liven up, brighten up
2 animarse *vpr* (**a**) *(persona)* to cheer up; *(cosas)* to brighten up (**b**) *(decidirse)* to make up one's mind; **¿te animas a venir?** do you feel like coming along, then?; **¡venga, anímate!** come on, say that you will!

anímico, -a *adj* **estado** *o* **state of mind**

animismo *nm Rel* animism

animista 1 *Rel adj* animistic
2 *Rel nmf* animist

ánimo *nm* (**a**) *(espíritu)* spirit; *(mente)* mind; *(alma)* soul; **no tenía en el á. sino una idea** he had only one idea in his mind ❑ **estado de á.** frame *o* state of mind (**b**) *(intención)* intention; **con á. de** with the intention of; **no estaba en mí á. ofenderle** it wasn't my intention to offend him; **sin á. de ofenderte** no offence intended (**c**) *(valor, coraje)* courage; **dar ánimos a** to encourage; **¡levanta ese á.!** cheer up!; **no tiene ánimos para nada** he's really in low spirits

animosidad *nf* animosity, ill feeling

animoso, -a *adj* cheerful, encouraged

aniñado, -a 1 *pp de* **aniñarse**
2 *adj* childlike; *Pey* childish

aniñarse *vpr* to grow *o* become childish

anión *nm Fís* anion

aniquilación *nf* annihilation, destruction

aniquilador, -a *adj* annihilating, destructive

aniquilamiento *nm véase* **aniquilación**

aniquilar *vt* to annihilate, destroy; **a. al enemigo** to wipe out the enemy

anís *nm* (**a**) *Bot (planta)* anise; *(grano)* aniseed; *Fam* **no ser grano de a.** to be no trifle (**b**) *(bebida)* anisette (**c**) *(confite)* aniseed ball

anisado, -a 1 *pp de* **anisar**
2 *adj* flavoured with aniseed

anisar *vt* to flavour with aniseed

anisete *nm* anisette

aniversario *nm* anniversary ❑ **a. de boda** wedding anniversary

Ankara *n* Ankara

ano *nm Anat* anus

anoche *adv (tarde)* last night; *(temprano)* yesterday evening; **antes de a.** the night before last

anochecer [46] **1** *v impers* to get dark; **cuando anochece** at nightfall, at dusk
2 *vi* to be somewhere at dusk; **anochecimos en Cuenca** we were in Cuenca at dusk
3 *nm* nightfall, dusk

anodino, -a *adj* (**a**) *Med* anodyne (**b**) *Fig (ineficaz)* inefficient; *(insubstancial)* insubstantial (**c**) *Fig (soso)* insipid, dull

ánodo *nm Fís* anode

anomalía *nf* anomaly

anómalo, -a *adj* anomalous

anonadado, -a *adj* astonished, bewildered

anonadamiento *nm* astonishment, bewilderment

anonadar *vt* (**a**) *(sorprender)* to astonish, bewilder (**b**) *(abatir)* to stun

anonimato *nm* anonimity; **permanecer en el a.** to remain anonymous *o* nameless

anónimo, -a 1 *adj* (**a**) *(desconocido)* anonymous (**b**) *Com (sociedad) Br* limited, *US* incorporated
2 *nm* (**a**) *(carta)* anonymous letter; *(obra)* anonymous work (**b**) *(anonimato)* anonimity

anorak *(pl* **anoraks**) *nm (prenda)* anorak

anorexia *nf Med* anorexia ❑ **a. nerviosa** anorexia nervosa

anoréxico, -a *adj & nm,f* anorexic

anormal 1 *adj* (**a**) *(anómalo)* abnormal (**b**) *(subnormal)* subnormal; *Fam (como insulto)* moronic (**c**) *Med* subnormal
2 *nmf (persona)* subnormal person; *Fam (como insulto)* moron

anormalidad *nf* abnormality

anotación *nf* (**a**) *(acotación)* annotation (**b**) *(apunte)* noting (**c**) *(nota)* note

anotar *vt* (**a**) *(acotar)* to annotate, add notes to (**b**) *(apuntar)* to take down, make a note of

anovulatorio *nm Farm* anovulatory

anquilosado, -a 1 *pp de* **anquilosar**
2 *adj* anchylosed, ankylosed; *Fig* paralysed; **costumbres anquilosadas** stagnated customs

anquilosamiento *nm* anchylosis, ankylosis; *Fig* stagnation, paralysis

anquilosar 1 *vt* to anchylose, ankylose
2 anquilosarse *vpr* to anchylose, ankylose; *Fig* to stagnate, be paralysed

anquilosis *nf* anchylosis, ankylosis

ánsar *nm Orn* goose

ansia *nf* (**a**) *(deseo)* longing, yearning; **a. de poder** longing for power (**b**) *(ansiedad)* anxiety; *(angustia)* anguish (**c**) *Med* sick feeling

ansiar [32] *vt* to long for, yearn for; **ansiaba volver a casa** he was longing to go back home

ansiedad *nf* anxiety; **con a.** anxiously; *Med* nervous tension

ansiolítico, -a *adj & nm Med* sedative, *Espec* anxiolytic

ansioso, -a *adj* **(a)** *(deseoso)* eager, longing **(b)** *(desasosegado)* anxious, worried **(c)** *(codicioso)* greedy, covetous

anta[1] *nf (alce) (europeo)* elk; *(americano)* moose

anta[2] *nf* **(a)** *(menhir)* menhir **(b)** *Arquit* anta

antagónico, -a *adj* antagonistic

antagonismo *nm* antagonism

antagonista 1 *adj* antagonistic
  2 *nmf* antagonist

antaño *adv* in the past, formerly

antártico, -a 1 *adj* Antarctic
  2 el A. *nm* the Antarctic Ocean

Antártida *n* Antarctica

ante[1] *nm* **(a)** *Zool* elk, moose **(b)** *(piel)* suede

ante[2] *prep* **(a)** *(delante de, en presencia de)* before, in the presence of; *Jur* **a. notario** in the presence of a notary; **a. todo** first of all **(b)** *(en comparación con)* compared with, next to **(c)** *(frente a) (hecho, circunstancia)* in the face of; **a. las circunstancias** under the circumstances; **a. tanta amabilidad** seeing how very kind he was

anteanoche *adv* the night before last

anteayer *adv* the day before yesterday

antebrazo *nm Anat* forearm

antecámara *nf* antechamber, anteroom

antecedente 1 *adj* antecedent, previous
  2 *nm* antecedent; **¿hay algún a. de esta enfermedad en su familia?** is there any history of this illness in your family?
  2 antecedentes *nmpl* **(a)** *(historial)* record *sing*; **tener malos a.** to have a bad record ❑ *Jur* **a. penales** criminal record *sing* **(b)** *Fig (persona)* **estar en a.** to be in the picture; **poner en a.** to put in the picture

anteceder *vt* to precede, go before

antecesor, -a *nm,f* **(a)** *(en un cargo)* predecessor **(b)** *(antepasado)* ancestor

antedatar *vt* to antedate

antedicho, -a 1 *adj* aforementioned, aforesaid
  2 *nm,f* person mentioned before

antediluviano, -a *adj* antediluvian; *Fig* as old as the hills

antefirma *nf Fml* title of the signatory

antelación *nf* precedence; **con a. a estos hechos** before these things happened; **con poca a.** at short notice; **con un mes de a.** a month beforehand, with a month's notice; *Fml* **con la debida a.** well in advance, in good time

antemano *adv* **de a.** beforehand, in advance

antena *nf* **(a)** *Rad TV* aerial, antenna ❑ **a. parabólica** satellite dish, parabolic aerial **(b)** *Zool Ent* antenna, feeler

anteojeras *nfpl Br* blinkers, *US* blinders

anteojo 1 *nm (telescopio)* telescope
  2 anteojos *nmpl* **(a)** *(prismáticos)* binoculars **(b)** *(quevedos)* pince-nez **(c)** *Am (gafas)* spectacles, glasses

antepasado, -a 1 *adj* previous, prior
  2 *nm,f* ancestor

antepecho *nm* **(a)** *(de ventana)* sill **(b)** *(pretil)* parapet, guardrail

antepenúltimo, -a *adj* antepenultimate; **el capítulo a.** the last chapter but two

anteponer [50] *(pp* **antepuesto)** *vt* to put *o* place in front

anteproyecto *nm* **(a)** *(gen)* preliminary plan, draft **(b)** *Jur* first draft, discussion document; **a. de ley** draft bill

antepuesto, -a 1 *pp de* **anteponer**
  2 *adj* placed in front

anterior 1 *adj* **(a)** *(previo)* previous, before; **el día a.** the day before **(b)** *(delantero)* anterior, fore, front; **parte a.** front part
  2 el a., la a. *nmf* the previous one

anterioridad *nf* **con a.** before; **con a. a** prior to, before

anteriormente *adv* previously, before

antes 1 *adv* **(a)** *(tiempo)* before, earlier; **'a. de entrar dejen salir'** 'let people off *o* out before boarding'; **cuanto a., lo a. posible** as soon as possible; **él llegó a.** he arrived first; **mucho a.** long before **(b)** *(antaño)* in the past; **a. llovía más** it used to rain more in the past **(c)** *(lugar)* in front, before; **a. de mí en la cola** in front of me in the queue; **a. del semáforo** before the traffic lights **(d)** *(preferencia)* **a. prefiero hacerlo yo** I'd rather do it myself
  2 conj a. (bien) on the contrary
  3 *adj* before; **la noche a.** the night before

antesala *nf* antechamber, anteroom; **hacer a.** to wait; *Fig* **en la a. de** on the verge of

antevíspera *nf* two days before

anti- *pref* anti-; **antimilitarismo** antimilitarism

antiabortista 1 *adj* anti-abortion, pro-life
  2 *nmf* anti-abortion *o* pro-life campaigner

antiácido, -a *adj & nm Med* antacid

antiadherente *adj* nonstick

antiaéreo, -a *adj* anti-aircraft

antialcohólico, -a 1 *adj* teetotal
  2 *nm,f* teetotaller

antiamericano, -a *adj* anti-American

antiarrugas *adj inv* anti-wrinkle

antiatómico, -a *adj* **refugio a.** fall-out shelter

antibalas *adj inv* bullet-proof

antibiótico, -a *adj & nm Med* antibiotic

antibloqueo 1 *adj inv* **frenos a.** anti-lock brakes
  2 *nm inv* anti-lock braking system

anticancerígeno *nm* cancer drug

anticarro *adj inv* antitank

anticaspa *adj* anti-dandruff; **champú a.** (anti-)dandruff shampoo

anticelulítico, -a *adj* anticellulite

antichoque *adj* shockproof

anticiclón *nm Meteor* anticyclone, high pressure area

anticipación *nf* bringing forward; **con a.** in advance; **con suficiente a.** in good time, enough in advance

anticipadamente *adv* in advance

anticipado, -a 1 *pp de* **anticipar**
  2 *adj* brought forward; *(temprano)* early; **elecciones anticipadas** early elections; **gracias anticipadas** thanks in advance; *Com* **por a.** in advance

anticipar 1 *vt (acontecimiento)* to bring forward; *(dinero)* to pay in advance; **no anticipemos acontecimientos** we'll cross that bridge when we come to it
  2 anticiparse *vpr* **(a)** *(adelantarse)* to beat to it; **iba a decírtelo, pero él se me anticipó** I was going to tell you, but he beat me to it **(b)** *(llegar antes)* to arrive early; **las lluvias se han anticipado este año** the rain has come earlier than expected this year; *Fig* **a. a su tiempo** to be ahead of one's time

anticipo *nm* **(a)** *(presagio)* foretaste **(b)** *Fin (adelanto)* advance; **pedir un a.** to ask for an advance (on one's wages) **(c)** *Fin (préstamo)* prepayment

anticlerical *adj & nmf* anticlerical
anticlericalismo *nm* anticlericalism
anticlinal *nm Geol* anticline
anticoagulante *adj & nm* anticoagulant
anticomunista *adj & nmf* anti-communist
anticoncepción *nf* contraception
anticonceptivo, -a *adj & nm* contraceptive
anticonformismo *nm* non-conformism
anticongelante *adj & nm (de radiador)* antifreeze; *(de parabrisas)* de-icer
anticonstitucional *adj* unconstitutional
anticorrosivo, -a 1 *adj* anticorrosive
2 *nm* anticorrosive substance
anticorrupción *adj inv* anticorruption
anticristo *nm Rel* Antichrist
anticuado, -a *adj* antiquated, old-fashioned, out-of-date
anticuario, -a *nm,f (conocedor)* antiquarian, antiquary; *(comerciante)* antique dealer
anticuerpo *nm Biol* antibody
antidemocrático, -a *adj Pol* undemocratic
antideportivo, -a *adj Dep* unsportsmanlike, unsporting
antidepresivo, -a 1 *adj* antidepressant
2 *nm* antidepressant (drug)
antideslizante 1 *adj (neumático)* anti-skid; *(suelo)* nonslip
2 *nm* anti-skid device
antideslumbrante *adj* anti-glare, anti-dazzle
antidetonante *adj* antiknock
antidisturbios 1 *adj inv* riot; **material a.** riot gear
2 *nmpl (policía)* riot police
antidoping [anti'ðopin] *adj Dep* doping; **prueba a.** doping test
antídoto *nm Farm* antidote
antidroga *adj* antidrug; **la lucha a.** the fight against drugs
antidumping [anti'ðumpin] *adj inv Econ (medidas, leyes)* antidumping
antiestético, -a *adj* ugly, unsightly
antifascista *nmf Pol* anti-fascist
antifaz *nm (prenda)* mask
antigás *adj* **careta a.** gas mask
antígeno, -a *Med* **1** *adj* antigenic
2 *nm* antigen
antiglobalización *nf* antiglobalization
antigripal 1 *adj* designed to combat flu
2 *nm* flu remedy
antigualla *nf (cosa)* old-fashioned thing; *(persona)* has-been
Antigua y Barbuda *n* Antigua and Barbuda
antigubernamental *adj* anti-government
antigüedad *nf* **(a)** *(periodo histórico)* antiquity, age; **en la a.** in olden days, in former times **(b)** *(en un empleo, cargo)* seniority **(c)** *(objeto)* antique; **tienda de antigüedades** antique shop
antiguo, -a 1 *adj* **(a)** *(viejo)* old; *(inmemorial)* ancient; **de a.** since ancient times; **un coche a.** an old car **(b)** *(pasado de moda)* old-fashioned; **a la antigua** in an old-fashioned way; **estar chapado a la antigua** to be an old fogey **(c)** *(en un empleo, cargo)* senior; **los socios más antiguos** the most senior members **(d)** *(anterior)* former; **a. alumno** ex-pupil, former pupil, *US* alumnus
2 los antiguos *nmpl* the ancients

antihéroe *nm* antihero
antihielo *nm* de-icer
antihigiénico, -a *adj* unhygienic, unhealthy
antihistamínico, -a *adj & nm Med* antihistamine
antiinflacionista *adj Econ* anti-inflationary
antiinflamatorio, -a 1 *adj* anti-inflammatory
2 *nm* anti-inflammatory drug
antillano, -a *adj & nm,f* West Indian
Antillas *npl* **las A.** the West Indies, the Antilles
antílope *nm* antelope
antimateria *nf Fís* antimatter
antimilitarismo *nm* antimilitarism
antimilitarista *adj & nmf* antimilitarist
antimisil *adj* antimissile
antimonio *nm Quím* antimony
antimonopolio *adj inv Econ* antitrust
antinatural *adj* unnatural, contrary to nature
antiniebla *adj inv* **faros a.** foglamps, *US* foglights
antinomia *nf* antinomy
antinómico, -a *adj* antinomic
antioxidante *Quím* **1** *adj (para alimentos)* antioxidant; *(para metales)* antirust
2 *nm (para alimentos)* antioxidant; *(para metales)* antirust substance
antipapa *nm Rel* antipope
antiparasitário, -a 1 *adj (para perro, gato)* **collar a.** flea collar; **pastillas antiparasitarias** worming tablets
2 *nm* **(a)** *(para perro, gato) (collar)* flea collar; *(pastilla)* worming tablet **(b)** *Tel* suppressor
antiparras *nfpl Esp Fam* specs, glasses
antipatía *nf* antipathy, dislike; **coger a.** to take a dislike to; **tener a.** to dislike
antipático, -a *adj* unfriendly, unkind, unpleasant, not nice; **Julio me es a.** I don't like Julio; **ser a.** to be unfriendly; **una persona antipática** an unpleasant person
antipatriótico, -a *adj* unpatriotic
antipirético, -a *adj & nm Med* antipyretic
antípodas *nfpl* Antipodes
antiquísimo, -a 1 *superl de* **antiguo, -a**
2 *adj* very old, ancient
antirrábico, -a *adj Farm* anti-rabies, anti-rabic
antirreflectante *adj* non-reflective
antirreglamentario, -a *adj* against the rules
antirrobo 1 *adj inv* antitheft; **alarma a.** burglar alarm
2 *nm (para coche)* antitheft device; *(para casa)* burglar alarm
antisemita 1 *adj* anti-Semitic
2 *nmf* anti-Semite
antisemítico, -a *adj* anti-Semitic
antisemitismo *nm* anti-Semitism
antiséptico, -a *adj & nm* antiseptic
antisocial *adj* antisocial
antitanque *adj inv* antitank
antítesis *nf inv* antithesis
antitetánico, -a *adj* anti-tetanus
antitético, -a *adj* antithetic, antithetical
antitoxina *nf* antitoxin
antivirus *nm inv Inform* antivirus system
antojadizo, -a *adj* capricious, fanciful, unpredictable
antojarse *vpr* **(a)** *(encapricharse)* to feel like, fancy; **cuando se me antoje** when I feel like it; **se le antojó un**

helado he fancied an ice cream (**b**) *(suponer)* to suppose; **se me antoja que no lo sabe** I have the feeling that he doesn't know

antojitos *nmpl Ecuad Méx* snacks, appetizers

antojo *nm* (**a**) *(capricho)* whim, fancy, caprice; *(de embarazada)* craving; **a su a.** in one's own way, as one pleases (**b**) *Anat* birthmark

antología *nf* anthology; *Fig* **de a.** remarkable, outstanding

antológico, -a *adj* anthological

antónimo, -a *Ling* **1** *adj* antonymous
   2 *nm* antonym

antonomasia *nf* antonomasia; **por a.** par excellence

antorcha *nf* (**a**) *(tea)* torch ◻ **a. olímpica** Olympic torch (**b**) *Fig (guía)* guiding light

antracita *nf Min* anthracite

ántrax *nm inv Med* anthrax

antro *nm (tugurio)* dump, hole; *Fig* **a. de perdición** den of vice

antropocéntrico, -a *adj* anthropocentric

antropocentrismo *nm* anthropocentrism

antropofagia *nf* anthropophagy

antropófago, -a **1** *adj* anthropophagic, anthro-pophagous
   2 *nm,f* anthrophagite

antropoide **1** *adj* anthropoid, anthropoidal
   2 *nmf* anthropoid

antropología *nf* anthropology

antropológico, -a *adj* anthropological

antropólogo, -a *nm,f* anthropologist

antropomórfico, -a *adj* anthropomorphic

antropomorfismo *nm* anthropomorphism

antropomorfo, -a *adj* anthropomorphous

anual *adj* annual; **ingresos anuales** yearly income

anualidad *nf* annual payment, annuity

anuario *nm* yearbook

anudadura *nf*, **anudamiento** *nm* (**a**) *(acción)* knotting, tying, fastening (**b**) *(nudo)* knot

anudar **1** *vt* (**a**) *(atar)* to knot, tie, fasten (**b**) *Fig (unir)* to join, bring together
   2 anudarse *vpr* to get into a knot; *Fig* **se le anudó la lengua** he became tonguetied

anuencia *nf* consent, approval

anuente *adj* consenting, consentient

anulable *adj* cancellable

anulación *nf* annulment, cancellation; *(de ley)* repeal; **a. de matrimonio** annulment of marriage

anular¹ **1** *adj* annular, ring-shaped; **dedo a.** ring finger
   2 *nm* ring finger

anular² **1** *vt* (**a**) *(matrimonio)* to annul; *Com (pedido)* to cancel; *Dep (gol)* to disallow; *Jur (ley)* to repeal; *(sentencia)* to quash; **a. el efecto de algo** to cancel out the effect of sth (**b**) *Fig (persona)* to deprive of authority
   2 anularse *vpr (persona)* to lose one's authority

anunciación *nf Rel* **la a. de la Virgen** the Annunciation

anunciador, -a, anunciante **1** *adj* (**a**) *(de noticia)* announcing, who announces (**b**) *(de publicidad)* advertising; **la empresa anunciadora** the advertiser
   2 *nm,f & nmf* (**a**) *(de noticia)* announcer (**b**) *(de publicidad)* advertiser

anunciar **1** *vt* (**a**) *(avisar)* to announce (**b**) *(dar publicidad)* to advertise
   2 anunciarse *vpr (darse publicidad)* to advertise oneself;

a. en un periódico to put an advert in a newspaper

anuncio *nm* (**a**) *(aviso)* announcement; **son un a. de primavera** they are a sign of spring (**b**) *(comercial)* advertisement, advert, ad; *(valla publicitaria)* Br hoarding, US billboard (**c**) *(cartel)* notice, poster; **pon un a. en la escuela** put a notice up in the school; **tablón de anuncios** Br noticeboard, US bulletin board

anverso *nm* (**a**) *(de moneda)* obverse (**b**) *(de página)* recto

anzuelo *nm Pesca* (fish) hook; *Fig* **echar el a. a** to try to hook; *Fig* **morder o picar el a.** to swallow the bait, take the hook

añadido, -a 1 *pp de* **añadir**
   2 *adj* added
   3 *nm* (**a**) *(postizo)* switch, hairpiece (**b**) *(cosa añadida)* addition, piece added on

añadidura *nf* addition, piece added on; **por a.** besides, on top of everything else

añadir *vt* to add (**a** to)

añagaza *nf* (**a**) *Caza* decoy, stool pigeon, lure (**b**) *Fig (artificio)* lure, trick

añal 1 *adj* (**a**) *(anual)* annual (**b**) *(animal)* year-old
   2 *nmf (animal)* yearling

añejar 1 *vt (envejecer)* to age; *(vino, queso)* to mature; *(jamón)* to cure
   2 añejarse *vpr* (**a**) *(mejorar)* to improve with age, mature (**b**) *(estropearse)* to deteriorate

añejo, -a *adj* (**a**) *(vino, queso)* mature; *(jamón)* cured (**b**) *(viejo)* old (**c**) *(estropeado)* stale

añicos *nmpl* bits; **hacer algo a.** to smash sth to pieces

añil 1 *adj* indigo, blue
   2 *nm* (**a**) *Bot* indigo plant (**b**) *(color)* indigo (**c**) *(para lavar)* blue

año *nm* (**a**) *(periodo de tiempo)* year; **el a. pasado** last year; **hace años** a long time ago, years ago; **los años cincuenta** the fifties; **todo el a.** all the year (round); **una vez al a.** once a year ◻ **a. bisiesto** leap year; *Educ* **a. escolar** school year; **a. fiscal** tax year, *Br* financial year, *US* fiscal year; **a. luz** light year; *Fig* **estar a años luz de** to be miles away from; **a. sabático** sabbatical (year) (**b**) **años** *(edad)* age *sing*; **¿cuántos a. tienes?** how old are you?; **tiene nueve a.** he's nine years old; **cumplió 18 a.** she was 18, she celebrated her 18th birthday; **en sus a. mozos** in his youth; **entrado en a.** getting on

añojo *nm (becerro)* yearling calf; *(cordero)* yearling lamb

añoranza *nf* longing, yearning, nostalgia; **sentir a. de su país** to be homesick

añorar 1 *vt* (**a**) *(pasado)* to long for, yearn for, miss (**b**) *(país)* to feel homesick for, miss (**c**) *(persona fallecida)* to mourn
   2 *vi* to pine

añoso, -a *adj* very old

aojar *vt* to cast the evil eye on

aorta *nf Anat* aorta

aovar *vi* to lay eggs

apabullamiento *nm* bewilderment, perplexity, confusion

apabullante *adj* overwhelming

apabullar *vt* (**a**) *Fam (aplastar)* to crush, flatten (**b**) *(dejar confuso)* to bewilder, perplex, confuse

apacentamiento *nm* pasturing, grazing

apacentar [3] **1** *vt* (**a**) *(ganado)* to put out to pasture, graze (**b**) *Fig (cuidar)* to take care of; *(alimentar)* to feed
   2 apacentarse *vpr (ganado)* to pasture, graze

apache *adj & nmf* Apache

apachurrar *vt* to squash, flatten

apacibilidad *nf* gentleness, mildness, calmness

apacible *adj* gentle, mild, calm

apaciguador, -a 1 *adj* pacifying
2 *nm,f* pacifier

apaciguamiento *nm* pacifying, appeasement

apaciguar [11] **1** *vt (calmar)* to pacify, appease
2 apaciguarse *vpr (calmarse)* to calm down; *(tormenta)* to abate

apadrinamiento *nm* (**a**) *(de bautizo)* function of godfather (**b**) *(de boda)* function of best man (**c**) *(de duelo)* function of second (**d**) *(mecenazgo)* sponsoring, patronage

apadrinar *vt* (**a**) *(bautizo)* to act as godfather to (**b**) *(boda)* to be best man for (**c**) *(duelo)* to act as second to (**d**) *(artista)* to sponsor

apagado, -a 1 *pp de* apagar
2 *adj* (**a**) *(luz etc)* out; **este cigarrillo está a.** this cigarette is out (**b**) *(color)* dull (**c**) *(voz)* sad; *(mirada)* expressionless, lifeless; *(carácter, persona)* spiritless

apagar [38] **1** *vt* (**a**) *(fuego)* to extinguish, put out (**b**) *(luz)* to turn out or off, put out; **apaga esa luz** turn off that light (**c**) *(desconectar)* to turn off, switch off; **apaga la tele** switch the telly off; *Inform* **a. equipo** *(en menú)* shut down (**d**) *(color)* to soften (**e**) *Fig (dolor)* to soothe; **la a. la sed** to quench one's thirst (**e**) *Esp Fam* **apaga y vámonos: si no quieren ayudarnos, ¡apaga y vámonos!** if they don't want to help us, let's not waste any more time over this
2 apagarse *vpr* (**a**) *(luz)* to go out; *(televisión)* to go off (**b**) *(morir)* to pass away

apagavelas *nm inv* candle snuffer

apagón *nm* power cut, blackout

apaisado, -a *adj* landscape

apalabrar *vt* (**a**) *(concertar)* to make a verbal agreement on; **apalabraron el precio por teléfono** they agreed the price over the phone (**b**) *(contratar)* to engage verbally

Apalaches *npl* **los (Montes) A.** the Appalachians

apalancado, -a 1 *pp de* apalancar
2 *adj Esp Argot* **se pasó la tarde a. delante de la tele** he spent the afternoon lounging in front of the telly

apalancamiento *nm Econ* leverage

apalancar [59] **1** *vt* (**a**) *(para abrir)* to lever up; **a. una puerta** to lever a door open (**b**) *(esconder)* to hide
2 apalancarse *vpr Esp Argot* to ensconce oneself, settle down; **se apalancaron delante de la tele** they settled down in front of the telly

apalanque *nm Esp Argot* laziness

apaleamiento *nm* beating, hitting, thrashing

apalear *vt* (**a**) *(pegar)* to beat, hit, thrash (**b**) *Agr (varear)* to thresh

apañado, -a 1 *pp de* apañar
2 *adj* (**a**) *(ordenado)* tidy; *(limpio)* clean; *(arreglado)* well-dressed, smart (**b**) *(hábil)* clever, skilful, *US* skillful; *(mañoso)* handy (**c**) *(adecuado)* smart and practical; **es un vestido muy a.** it's a very smart dress and you can wear it anywhere (**d**) *Fam* **estar a.** to be in for a surprise; *Fam* **pues sí que estamos apañados** now we're really done for, now we've had it

apañar 1 *vt* (**a**) *(ordenar)* to tidy; *(limpiar)* to clean; *(ataviar)* to smarten up (**b**) *(comprender, remendar)* to mend, fix (**c**) *(recoger)* to collect; *Fig (robar)* to clean out (**d**) *Andes CAm RP (proteger)* to shelter, conceal, protect
2 apañarse *vpr Esp Fam* **apañárselas** to manage; **ya me las apañaré solo** I'll manage on my own

apaño *nm* (**a**) *(arreglo)* tidying; *(limpieza)* cleaning; *(atavío)* smartening up (**b**) *(componenda, remiendo)* mend, repair; **no tiene a.** nothing can be done about it (**c**) *(habilidad)* skill (**d**) *Fam (lío amoroso)* (love) affair;

(persona) lover; **tener un a.** to have a bit on the side

apapachado, -a *adj Méx Fam* pampered, spoilt

apapachador, -a *adj Méx Fam* comforting

apapachar *vt Méx Fam (mimar)* to cuddle; *(consentir)* to spoil

apapachos *nmpl Méx Fam* cuddles

aparador *nm* (**a**) *(mueble)* sideboard, cupboard (**b**) *(escaparate)* shop window

aparato *nm* (**a**) *(máquina)* machine; *(electrodoméstico)* appliance; **a. para destilar el agua** water-distilling device ❏ *Anat* **a. circulatorio** circulatory system; **a. de radio** radio set; **a. de televisión** television set; **a. digestivo** digestive system; **a. reproductor** reproductive system; **a. respiratorio** respiratory system; **a. urinario** urinary tract; **aparatos eléctricos** domestic appliances; *Pol* **el a. del estado** the State apparatus (**b**) *Tel* telephone; **¿quién está al a.?** who's speaking? (**c**) *Av* plane (**d**) *(en gimnasia) (en competición, escuela)* piece of apparatus; *(en gimnasio privado)* exercise machine (**e**) *(ostentación)* pomp, ostentation; **con mucho a.** very pompously; **una tormenta con gran a. eléctrico** a storm with tremendous flashes of lightning

aparatosidad *nf* (**a**) *(pomposidad)* pomposity, ostentation, showiness, show (**b**) *(espectacularidad)* spectacularity

aparatoso, -a *adj* (**a**) *(pomposo)* pompous, ostentatious, showy (**b**) *(espectacular)* spectacular; **un accidente a.** a spectacular accident

aparcamiento *nm Esp* (**a**) *(acción)* parking; **maniobra de a.** parking manoeuvre (**b**) *(para un vehículo)* parking place (**c**) *(para muchos vehículos)* Br car park, *US* parking lot ❏ **a. subterráneo** underground car park

aparcar [59] *vt Esp* (**a**) *(vehículo)* to park; **'prohibido a.'** 'no parking' (**b**) *Fig (tema, cuestión)* to put on one side

aparcería *nf Agr* sharecropping

aparcero, -a *nm,f Agr* sharecropper

apareamiento *nm* (**a**) *(de cosas)* pairing off, matching up (**b**) *(de animales)* mating

aparear 1 *vt* (**a**) *(cosas)* to pair off, match up (**b**) *(animales)* to mate
2 aparearse *vpr (animales)* to mate

aparecer [46] **1** *vi* (**a**) *(ante la vista)* to appear; **no aparece en mi lista** he is not on my list (**b**) *(en el mercado)* to come out (**en onto**) (**c**) *(algo perdido)* to turn up; **¿apareció por fin el dinero?** did the money turn up in the end?; **rara vez aparece por aquí** he seldom shows his face round here
2 aparecerse *vpr* to appear; **se le apareció un ángel** an angel appeared to him

aparecido, -a 1 *pp de* aparecer
2 *nm,f* ghost

aparejado, -a 1 *pp de* aparejar
2 *adj* (**a**) *(adecuado)* suitable, fit (**b**) **ir a. con** to go along with; **llevar** *o* **traer a.** to entail

aparejador, -a *nm,f* (**a**) *Arquit* quantity surveyor; clerk of works (**b**) *Náut* rigger

aparejar *vt* (**a**) *(caballo)* to harness (**b**) *(aparear)* to pair off, match up (**c**) *Náut* to rig out (**d**) *(preparar)* to get ready, prepare

aparejo *nm* (**a**) *(equipo)* equipment, gear ❏ **a. de pesca** fishing tackle (**b**) *(arreos)* harness (**c**) *Náut* rigging (**d**) *Arquit* bond (**e**) *Téc (poleas)* block and tackle

aparentar 1 *vt* (**a**) *(simular)* to pretend, affect; **a. indiferencia** to pretend to be indifferent, affect indifference (**b**) *(tener aspecto)* to look; **no aparenta esa edad** she doesn't look that age
2 *vi* to show off

aparente *adj* (**a**) *(falso, supuesto)* apparent; **sin motivo a.** for no apparent reason (**b**) *(visible)* visible (**c**) *(vistoso)* showy

aparentemente *adv* apparently, seemingly; **a. fácil/inocente** apparently easy/innocent

aparición *nf* (**a**) *(de persona, cosa)* appearance, appearing (**b**) *(de ser sobrenatural)* apparition

apariencia *nf* appearance; **en a.** apparently; **según todas las apariencias** to all appearances; **tiene a. de bueno** he looks like a good person; *Fig* **guardar las apariencias** to keep up appearances

apartado, -a 1 *pp de* **apartar**
2 *adj (distante)* remote, isolated; **a. de la vida política** retired from political life; **mantente a. de él** keep away from him; **un lugar a.** a remote place
3 *nm* (**a**) *(párrafo)* section, paragraph (**b**) **a. de correos** Post Office Box

apartamento *nm esp Am (en edificio) Br* flat, *US* apartment; *Esp (más pequeño)* apartment

apartamiento *nm* (**a**) *(separación)* separation, putting aside (**b**) *(habitación)* room, lodging

apartar 1 *vt* (**a**) *(alejar)* to move away, remove; **aparta** move out of the way; **aparta eso de mi vista** take that away immediately; **a. (a algn) de un empujón** to push (sb) aside; **a. (algo) de una patada** to kick (sth) aside; **a. la mirada** to look away (**b**) *(separar)* to separate, put aside; **apártame la comida** keep my lunch for me; **apartó sus libros** she put her books aside
2 apartarse *vpr* (**a**) *(alejarse)* to move over, move away; **apártate de en medio** move out of the way; **apártate el pelo de la cara** move your hair out of your face (**b**) *(separarse)* to separate, withdraw; **no nos apartemos del tema** let's not get off the subject; **se apartó de todos** she cut herself off from everybody

aparte 1 *adv* (**a**) *(en otro lugar, a un lado)* aside, to one side; **envíalo a.** send it under separate cover; **eso hay que pagarlo a.** you have to pay for that separately (**b**) *(además)* besides; **a. de eso** besides that; *(con omisión de)* apart from; **eso a.** apart from that (**c**) *(por separado)* separately; **vino a.** it didn't come with the rest
2 *adj (especial)* special; *(diferente)* different, separate; **ella es algo a.** she is something special; **eso es capítulo a., eso es caso a.** that's completely different, that's another kettle of fish altogether
3 *nm* (**a**) *Teat* aside; *Fig* **ella se lo comentó en un a.** she called him aside and told him (**b**) *Ling* new paragraph; **punto y a.** full stop, new paragraph

apartheid [apar'χeiθ] *(pl* **apartheids***) nm Pol* apartheid

aparthotel *nm* = hotel with self-catering facilities

apasionado, -a 1 *pp de* **apasionar**
2 *adj* passionate, fervent, enthusiastic; **a. por la música** very fond of music

apasionamiento *nm* passion, enthusiasm; **hablar con a.** to speak passionately o with passion

apasionante *adj* exciting, fascinating

apasionar 1 *vt* to excite, thrill, fascinate; **le apasiona el jazz** he is mad about jazz
2 apasionarse *vpr* (**a**) *(entusiasmarse)* to get excited, become enthusiastic (**por, de** about); **se apasionó por ese trabajo** she got really involved in that job (**b**) *(enamorarse)* to fall head over heels in love (**por, de** with)

apatía *nf* apathy

apático, -a 1 *adj* apathetic
2 *nm,f* apathetic person

apátrida 1 *adj* stateless
2 *nmf* stateless person

apdo. *(abrev de* **apartado***)* P.O.B

apeadero *nm Ferroc* = minor train stop with no permanent buildings, *Br* halt

apear 1 *vt* (**a**) *(desmontar)* to take down; *(del caballo)* to help down (**de** from); *Fig* **a. el tratamiento** to drop sb's formal title (**b**) *(árbol)* to fell (**c**) *(caballo)* to hobble (**d**) *(finca)* to survey (**e**) *(vehículo)* to wedge, scotch (**f**) *Constr (apuntalar)* to prop up (**g**) *Fam (disuadir)* **a. a algn de** to talk sb out of (**h**) *CAm (reprender)* to tell off
2 apearse *vpr (de un autobús, tren)* to alight, get off; *(de un coche)* to get out; **se apeó en Jerez** he got off in Jerez; *Fig* **a. de sus ideas** to give up one's ideas; *Fam* **a. del burro** to back down

apechugar [38] *vi Fam* **a. con** *(aguantar)* to put up with; **a. con todo el trabajo** to shoulder all the work

apedrear *vt* (**a**) *(tirar piedras a)* to throw stones at (**b**) *(matar a pedradas)* to stone (to death)

apegarse [38] *vpr* to become devoted o attached (**a** to)

apego *nm* love, affection; **tomar a. a** to become attached to

apelable *adj Jur* appealable

apelación *nf* (**a**) *Jur* appeal; **interponer a.** to appeal; **recurso de a.** appeal (**b**) *Fig* help; **no tener a.** to be helpless

apelar *vi* (**a**) *Jur* to appeal; **a. de una sentencia** to appeal against a sentence (**b**) *Fig (recurrir)* **a. a** to resort to; **a. a la buena voluntad de algn** to appeal to sb's goodwill

apelativo *nm (nombre)* name; *Ling* form of address; **un a. cariñoso** a term of endearment

apellidar 1 *vt* to call
2 apellidarse *vpr* to have as a surname, be called

apellido *nm* surname, family name; **a. de soltera** maiden name; *Fig* **con nombre y apellidos** with all the details

apelmazado, -a *adj* heavy, stodgy

apelmazar [14] **1** *vt (amazacotar)* to compress, squeeze together
2 apelmazarse *vpr (amazacotarse)* to cake, go lumpy

apelotonar 1 *vt* (**a**) *(amontonar)* to pile up, put into a pile (**b**) *(hacer una pelota)* to roll into a ball
2 apelotonarse *vpr (gente)* to crowd together

apenar 1 *vt (entristecer)* to grieve, make sad
2 apenarse *vpr* (**a**) *(entristecerse)* to be grieved (**b**) *Am salvo RP (avergonzarse)* to be embarrassed

apenas *adv* (**a**) *(casi no)* hardly, scarcely; **a. come** he hardly eats anything; **a. si hay nieve** there is hardly any snow (**b**) *(tan pronto como)* as soon as; **a. llegó, sonó el teléfono** just as he arrived the phone rang, no sooner had he arrived than the phone rang

apencar [59] *vi Fam véase* **apechugar**

apéndice *nm* (**a**) *Anat* appendix (**b**) *Fig (persona)* lapdog

apendicitis *nf Med* appendicitis

Apeninos *nmpl* **los (Montes) A.** the Apennines

aperar *vt* (**a**) *Andes RP Ven (caballo)* to harness (**b**) *Ven (persona)* to equip

apercibimiento *nm* (**a**) *(preparación)* preparation (**b**) *Jur (advertencia)* warning

apercibir 1 *vt* (**a**) *(preparar)* to get ready, prepare (**b**) *(avisar)* to warn
2 apercibirse *vpr* (**a**) *(prepararse)* to get ready (**b**) *(percatarse)* to notice

apercollar [63] *vt Col* to hug tightly

apergaminado, -a 1 *pp de* **apergaminarse**
2 *adj (piel, papel)* parchment-like

apergaminarse *vpr (piel)* to become parchment-like

aperitivo, -a 1 *adj* appetizing
2 *nm (bebida)* apéritif; *(comida)* appetizer

apero *nm* tool ❑ **aperos de labranza** farming implements

aperrear 1 *vt (cansar)* to wear out, exhaust
 2 aperrearse *vpr Fig (emperrarse)* to insist

apertura *nf* **(a)** *(comienzo)* opening, beginning; **a. del curso** beginning of the academic year; **sesión de a.** opening session **(b)** *Pol (liberalización)* liberalization **(c)** *Fot* aperture

aperturismo *nm Pol* progressive policies
aperturista *adj & nmf Pol* progressive

apesadumbrado, -a 1 *pp de* **apesadumbrar**
 2 *adj* sad, distressed

apesadumbrar *vt* to sadden, distress, pain

apestado, -a 1 *pp de* **apestar**
 2 *adj* **(a)** *Med* plagueridden **(b)** *(olor)* foul, pestilential **(c)** *Fig* infested **(de** with)

apestar 1 *vi (oler mal)* to stink: **esta habitación apesta** this room stinks
 2 *vt* to infect with the plague

apestoso, -a *adj* stinking; **olor a.** foul smell

apetecer [46] *vi Esp* to feel like, fancy; **¿qué te apetece para cenar?** what would you like for supper?; **¿te apetece ir al cine?** do you fancy going to the cinema?

apetecible *adj* tempting, inviting

apetencia *nf* **(a)** *(apetito)* hunger, appetite **(b)** *Fig (deseo)* longing, craving, desire

apetito *nm* appetite; **abrir el a.** to whet one's appetite; **a. carnal** sexual appetite, desire

apetitoso, -a *adj* appetizing, tempting; *(comida)* delicious, tasty

apiadarse *vpr* to take pity **(de** on)

ápice *nm* **(a)** *(punta)* apex **(b)** *Fig (parte pequeña)* tiny piece; **ni un á.** not a bit; **no me gusta ni un á.** I don't like it at all

apícola *adj* **la industria a.** the beekeeping industry

apicultor, -a *nm,f* beekeeper, *Espec* apiculturist, apiarist

apicultura *nf* beekeeping, *Espec* apiculture

apilamiento *nm* piling up, heaping up

apilar 1 *vt* to pile up
 2 apilarse *vpr* to pile up; **se nos está apilando el trabajo** we've got a backlog of work building up

apilonar *vt Ven* to pile up, heap up

apiñado, -a 1 *pp de* **apiñar**
 2 *adj* **(a)** *(apretado)* crammed, packed **(b)** *(en forma de piña)* cone-shaped

apiñamiento *nm* cramming, packing

apiñar 1 *vt (apretar)* to cram, pack
 2 apiñarse *vpr (arremolinarse)* to crowd together

apio *nm Bot* celery

apisonadora *nf* roadroller, steamroller

apisonar *vt (carretera)* to roll

aplacamiento *nm* placation, calming

aplacar [59] **1** *vt* to placate, calm; **a. el hambre** to satisfy one's hunger
 2 aplacarse *vpr* to calm down

aplanamiento *nm* levelling, *US* leveling, smoothing

aplanar 1 *vt* **(a)** *(igualar)* to level, smooth, flatten **(b)** *Fig (deprimir)* to dishearten, depress
 2 aplanarse *vpr* **(a)** *(edificio)* to fall down **(b)** *Fig (persona)* to become disheartened o depressed

aplastamiento *nm* **(a)** *(por peso)* flattening, squashing **(b)** *Fig (emocional)* crushing

aplastante *adj* crushing, overwhelming; *Fig (en elecciones)* **triunfo a.** landslide victory

aplastar 1 *vt* **(a)** *(por el peso)* to flatten, squash; **el árbol aplastó el coche** the tree crushed the car **(b)** *Fig (vencer)* to crush, destroy
 2 aplastarse *vpr* to be crushed; **se aplastó contra la pared** it got smashed against the wall

aplatanado, -a *Esp Méx* **1** *pp de* **aplatanarse**
 2 *adj Fam* listless

aplatanarse *vpr Esp Méx Fam* to become listless

aplaudir 1 *vi (dar palmadas)* to clap, applaud
 2 *vt Fig (aprobar)* to applaud, approve

aplauso *nm* **(a)** *(ovación)* applause **(b)** *Fig (aprobación)* applause, praise

aplazamiento *nm* postponement, adjournment; *Fin (de un pago)* deferment

aplazar [14] *vt* **(a)** *(posponer)* to postpone, adjourn; *Fin (pago)* to defer **(b)** *RP (en examen)* to fail

aplicable *adj* applicable

aplicación *nf* **(a)** *(uso, utilidad)* application **(b)** *(adorno)* appliqué **(c)** *Inform* application

aplicado, -a 1 *pp de* **aplicar**
 2 *adj* **(a)** *(diligente)* studious, diligent, hard-working; **un alumno a.** a hardworking pupil **(b)** *(práctico)* applied; **ciencias aplicadas** applied sciences

aplicar 1 *vt* **(a)** *(técnica, pintura, teoría)* to apply **(b)** *(destinar)* to assign
 2 aplicarse *vpr* **(a)** *(esforzarse)* to apply oneself, work hard **(b)** *(usar)* to apply, be applicable; **puede a. en todos los casos** it can be applied in all cases

aplique *nm* **(a)** *(adorno)* appliqué **(b)** *(lámpara)* wall light, wall lamp

aplomar *vt* to plumb

aplomo *nm* aplomb, composure, self-assurance

apnea *nf* **(a)** *Med* apnoea; **a. del sueño** sleep apnoea **(b)** *Dep (buceo)* free diving

apocado, -a 1 *pp de* **apocar**
 2 *adj* **(a)** *(intimidado)* intimidated, frightened **(b)** *(tímido)* shy, timid

apocalipsis *nm inv* apocalypse

apocalíptico, -a *adj* apocalyptic

apocamiento *nm* timidity, lack of self-confidence

apocar [59] *vt* **(a)** *(intimidar)* to intimidate, frighten **(b)** *(humillar)* to humiliate, belittle

apocopar *vt Ling* to apocopate

apócope *nm Ling* apocope, apocopation

apócrifo, -a *adj* apocryphal

apodar *vt* to nickname

apoderado, -a 1 *pp de* **apoderar**
 2 *adj* authorized; *Jur* with power of attorney to
 3 *nm,f* **(a)** *Jur* agent, representative **(b)** *(de torero, deportista)* manager

apoderar 1 *vt* to authorize, empower; *Jur* to grant power of attorney to
 2 apoderarse *vpr* to take possession **(de** of), seize; *Fig* **miedo se apoderó de ella** she was seized by fear

apodo *nm* nickname

apófisis *nf Anat* apophysis

apogeo *nm* **(a)** *Astron* apogee **(b)** *Fig (punto culminante)* height, climax; **en pleno a. de** at the height of

apolillado, -a 1 *pp de* **apolillar**
 2 *adj* moth-eaten

apolillar 1 *vt* to eat, make holes in
 2 apolillarse *vpr* to get moth-eaten

apolíneo, -a *adj* Apollonian

apolítico, -a *adj* apolitical

apologético, -a *adj* apologetic

apología *nf* apology, defence, *US* defense

apologista *nmf* apologist

apoltronamiento *nm* laziness, idleness

apoltronarse *vpr* (**a**) *(vegetar)* to get lazy, get idle (**b**) *(sentarse)* to sit back, lounge

apoplejía *nf Med* apoplexy

apoplético, -a *adj & nm,f* apoplectic

apoquinar *vt Esp Fam* to cough up, fork out

aporrear *vt* to beat, hit, thrash; **a. la puerta** to bang the door; *Fam* **a. el piano** to bang (away) on the piano

aporreo *nm* beating, thrashing; *(de puerta)* banging; *Fam (de piano)* thumping

aportación *nf* contribution

aportar 1 *vt* (**a**) *(contribuir con)* to contribute; *Fig* **a. su granito de arena** to chip in one's small contribution (**b**) *(proporcionar)* to give, provide; **a. ideas** to offer some ideas
   2 *vi Náut* to reach port

aporte *nm* (**a**) *Geol* supply (**b**) *Fig (contribución)* contribution

aposentar 1 *vt* to house, lodge
   2 aposentarse *vpr* to stay, lodge

aposento *nm* (**a**) *(cuarto)* room (**b**) *(hospedaje)* lodgings *pl*; **tomar a. en** to put up at

aposición *nf Ling* apposition

apósito *nm Med* dressing

aposta *adv Esp* on purpose, intentionally

apostante 1 *adj* betting
   2 *nmf* better, bettor

apostar¹ [63] **1** *vt* to bet, stake; **a. a los caballos** to bet on horses; **te apuesto una cena a que no viene** I bet you a dinner that he won't come
   2 *vi* to bet; **aposté por tu caballo** I bet on your horse; **apuesto a que sí viene** I bet she will come
   2 apostarse *vpr* to bet; **me apuesto lo que quieras** I bet you anything

apostar² **1** *vt (situar)* to post, station
   2 apostarse *vpr* to post oneself, station oneself

apostasía *nf Rel* apostasy

apóstata *nmf* apostate

apostatar *vi* to apostatize

apostilla *nf* note; *Jur* apostille

apostillar *vt* to add notes to, annotate

apóstol *nm* (**a**) *Rel* apostle (**b**) *Fig (defensor)* apostle, champion

apostolado *nm* apostolate

apostólico, -a *adj* (**a**) *(de los apóstoles)* apostolic (**b**) *(del papa)* apostolic, papal; **bendición apostólica** papal blessing

apostrofar *vt Fig (reprender)* to reprimand, tell off

apóstrofe *nm & f Fig (reprimenda)* insult, offence, *US* offense

apóstrofo *nm Ling* apostrophe

apostura *nf* (**a**) *(garbo)* good bearing (**b**) *(apariencia)* appearance, look

apoteósico, -a *adj* enormous, tremendous; **un recibimiento a.** a mass welcome

apoteosis *nf inv* apotheosis; *(de un espectáculo)* **a. final** grand finale

apoyabrazos *nm inv* armrest

apoyacabezas *nm inv* headrest

apoyamuñecas *nm inv* wrist rest

apoyar 1 *vt* (**a**) *(inclinar)* to lean; **apoya la cabeza en la**

pared rest your head against the wall (**b**) *(basar)* to base, found (**c**) *(defender) (una causa)* to support; *(persona)* to back, second
   2 apoyarse *vpr* (**a**) *(sostenerse)* to lean; **apóyate en mi brazo** lean on my arm (**b**) *Fig (basarse)* to be based, rest; **su teoría se apoya en la investigación** his theory is based on research

apoyo *nm* (**a**) *(respaldo)* support ❑ **punto de a.** *Fís* fulcrum; *Fig (fundamento)* base (**b**) *Fig* support, backing, help

apreciable *adj* (**a**) *(perceptible)* appreciable, noticeable (**b**) *(estimable)* valuable, precious

apreciación *nf* appreciation

apreciar 1 *vt* (**a**) *(sentir aprecio)* to regard highly, hold in high esteem; **le aprecia mucho** she is very fond of him (**b**) *(reconocer el valor)* to appreciate; **a. el buen vino** to appreciate good wine (**c**) *(formar juicio)* to appraise, value (**d**) *(percibir)* to notice, see; **no puedo a. la diferencia** I can't really tell the difference
   2 apreciarse *vpr* to be noticeable; **se aprecia un cambio notable** a remarkable change can be seen

apreciativo, -a *adj* appreciative

aprecio *nm* regard, esteem; **sentir a. por algn** to be fond of sb

aprehender *vt* (**a**) *(atrapar) (persona)* to apprehend; *(alijo, mercancía)* to seize (**b**) *(entender)* to understand

aprehensión *nf* (**a**) *(de persona)* arrest, capture; *(de alijo, mercancía)* seizure (**b**) *(entendimiento)* comprehension, understanding

apremiante *adj* urgent, pressing

apremiar 1 *vt* (**a**) *(compeler)* to compel, urge, press (**b**) *(dar prisa)* to hurry (along) (**c**) *(oprimir)* to oppress
   2 *vi* to be urgent; **el tiempo apremia** we are running short of time

apremio *nm* (**a**) *(urgencia)* urgency; **por a. de trabajo** because of pressure of work (**b**) *Jur* writ

aprender *vt* to learn; **así aprenderás** that'll teach you

aprendiz, -a *nm,f* apprentice, trainee

aprendizaje *nm* (**a**) *(adquisición de conocimientos)* apprenticeship, traineeship (**b**) *Psic* learning; **técnicas de a.** learning techniques

aprensión *nf* apprehension; **sentir a.** to feel apprehensive

aprensivo, -a *adj & nm,f* apprehensive

apresamiento *nm* seizure, capture

apresar *vt* to seize, capture

aprestar 1 *vt* (**a**) *(preparar)* to prepare, get ready (**b**) *Tex* to size
   2 aprestarse *vpr (prepararse)* to get ready

apresto *nm* (**a**) *(preparación)* preparation (**b**) *(acción)* sizing; *(material)* size

apresurado, -a *adj* **1** *pp de* **apresurar**
   2 *adj* (**a**) *(persona)* in a hurry (**b**) *(cosa)* hurried

apresuramiento *nm* haste

apresurar 1 *vt* to accelerate, hurry up, speed up
   2 apresurarse *vpr* to hurry up; **se apresuró a salir** he hurried towards the door

apretado, -a 1 *pp de* **apretar**
   2 *adj* (**a**) *(ropa, nudo)* tight; **íbamos todos apretados en el coche** we were all squashed together in the car (**b**) *Fig (difícil)* tight, difficult; **una situación apretada** a tight spot (**c**) *(ocupado)* busy; **una jornada apretada** a busy day

apretar [3] **1** *vt* (**a**) *(nudo, tornillo)* to tighten; *(botón)* to press; **a. el gatillo** to pull the trigger; **a. el paso** to quicken one's pace; **me aprietan las botas** these boots are too tight for me **(b)** *(estrechar)* to squeeze, hug; **a. la mano a algn** to shake sb's hand; **la apretó contra sí** he hugged her **(c)** *Fig (acosar)* to pester; *(presionar)* to put pressure on

2 *vi* **(a)** *(aumentar)* to get worse, get stronger; **apretaba el calor** it got hotter and hotter **(b)** *(esforzarse)* to work hard; **tienes que a. más si quieres aprobar** you'll have to pull your socks up if you want to pass

3 apretarse *vpr (agolparse)* to crowd together; *(acercarse)* to squeeze up; *Fig* **a. el cinturón** to tighten one's belt

apretón *nm* **(a)** *(estrechamiento)* squeeze ❏ **a. de manos** handshake **(b) apretones** crush *sing*; **los a. del metro** the crush on the *Br* underground *o US* subway

apretujar 1 *vt* to squeeze, crush

2 apretujarse *vpr* to squeeze together, cram together

apretujón *nm Fam* squeeze, crowding, crush

aprieto *nm* tight spot, fix, jam; **poner a algn en un a.** to put sb in an awkward situation; **salir del a.** to get out of trouble

apriorismo *nm Filos* apriorism

apriorístico, -a *adj Filos* aprioristic

aprisa *adv* quickly

aprisco *nm* (sheep) fold

aprisionar *vt* **(a)** *(encarcelar)* to put in prison, imprison **(b)** *Fig (atrapar)* to trap

aprobación *nf* approval; **le dio su a.** he gave his consent, he approved it

aprobado, -a 1 *pp de* **aprobar**

2 *adj* approved

3 *nm Educ* pass, *Br* pass mark, *US* passing grade; **sacar un a.** to get a pass

aprobar [63] *vt* **(a)** *(proyecto, medida)* to approve **(b)** *(estar de acuerdo)* to approve of; **no apruebo su conducta** I do not approve of his behaviour **(c)** *Educ (examen)* to pass; *(estudiante)* to pass, give a pass to; **todos aprobaron el examen de francés** they all passed the French exam **(d)** *Pol (ley)* to pass

aprobatorio, -a *adj* approving, approbatory

apropiación *nf* **(a)** *(adecuación)* adaptation **(b)** *(robo)* appropriation ❏ *Jur* **a. indebida** theft

apropiado, -a 1 *pp de* **apropiar**

2 *adj* suitable, appropriate

apropiar 1 *vt* to adapt, make suitable

2 apropiarse *vpr* to appropriate, steal

aprovechable *adj* that can be used, usable, serviceable

aprovechado, -a 1 *pp de* **aprovechar**

2 *adj* **(a)** *(bien empleado)* well used *o* spent; **mal a.** wasted **(b)** *(espacio)* well-planned **(c)** *(alumno)* diligent, studious **(d)** *Fam Pey (egoísta)* selfish; *(sinvergüenza)* who sponges *o* scrounges; **es un tipo muy a.** he's a sponger *o* scrounger

aprovechamiento *nm* **(a)** *(uso)* use, exploitation; **a. de aguas residuales** use of sewage **(b)** *Educ* progress, improvement

aprovechar 1 *vt* **(a)** *(tiempo, dinero)* to make the most of; *(oferta, ocasión)* to take advantage of; *(conocimientos, experiencia)* to use, make use of; **Ana aprovechó el tiempo** Ana made good use of her time; **aprovechamos mucho la tarde** we've done lots of things this afternoon; **a. la ocasión** to seize the opportunity; *Pey* **aprovechó que era un pobre diablo para engañarlo** seeing that he was a poor devil he cheated him **(b)** *(lo inservible)* to put to good use

2 *vi* to be useful; *Fam* **¡que aproveche!** enjoy your meal!, bon appétit!

3 aprovecharse *vpr* to take advantage; **a. de algn** to take advantage of sb; **a. de algo** to make the most of sth

aprovisionamiento *nm* supply, suplying, provision

aprovisionar *vt* to supply, provide; **a. las tropas** to give supplies to the troops

aprox. *(abrev de* **aproximadamente)** approx

aproximación *nf* **(a)** *(en cálculo)* approximation; **por a.** by approximation; *Fam* **ni por a.** far from it **(b)** *(acercamiento)* bringing together; *(de países)* rapprochement **(c)** *(lotería)* consolation prize

aproximado, -a 1 *pp de* **aproximar**

2 *adj* approximate; **un cálculo a.** a rough estimate

aproximar 1 *vt* to bring *o* put nearer; **aproxima la silla un poco** draw your chair up a bit; **aquello las aproximó más** that made them feel closer together

2 aproximarse *vpr* **(a)** *(en el espacio)* to move nearer; **aproxímate más** come closer **(b)** *(en el tiempo)* to be near, be close; **se aproximan los exámenes** the exams are getting nearer

aproximativo, -a *adj* approximate, rough

aptitud *nf* ability, aptitude; **a. para la pintura** aptitude for painting; **prueba de a.** aptitude test

apto, -a *adj* **(a)** *(apropiado)* suitable, appropriate; *Cin* **a. para todos los públicos** *Br* ≃ U, *US* ≃ G; *Cin* **no a.** for adults only **(b)** *(capaz)* capable, able; **un trabajador a.** a capable worker **(c)** *(físicamente)* fit; **a. para el servicio** fit for (military) service

apuesta *nf* bet, wager

apuesto, -a *adj* good-looking; *(hombre)* handsome

apunarse *vpr Andes* to get altitude sickness

apuntado, -a 1 *pp de* **apuntar**

2 *adj* **(a)** *(anotado)* written down, taken down **(b)** *(terminado en punta)* pointed, sharp

apuntador, -a *nm,f Teat* prompter

apuntalamiento *nm* propping-up, shoring-up, underpinning

apuntalar *vt* to prop up, shore up, underpin

apuntar 1 *vt* **(a)** *(señalar)* to point at; **no apuntes con el dedo** don't point at people *o* things with your finger; **quisiera a. que ...** I'd like to point out that ... **(b)** *(arma)* to aim, point; *Mil* **¡apunten!** take aim! **(c)** *(anotar)* to note down, make a note of; **apúntalo en mi cuenta** put it on my account; **a. a algn en una lista** to put sb on a list **(d)** *(estar encaminado)* **a.** to be aimed at, be designed to; **estas medidas apuntan a mejorar la situación** these measures are aimed at improving the situation **(e)** *(indicar)* to indicate, suggest; **todo parece a. a ...** everything seems to point to ... **(f)** *Teat* to prompt; *Educ Fam* to whisper the answer **(a** to) **(g)** *Cost* to tack

2 *vi* **(a)** *(empezar a manifestarse)* to (begin to) show; **cuando apunta el día** when day breaks **(b)** *Teat* to prompt

3 apuntarse *vpr* **(a)** *(en una lista)* to put one's name down **(b)** *(matricularse)* to enrol, *US* enroll **(c)** *Fam (participar)* to take part **(a** in); **¿te apuntas?** are you game?

apunte *nm* **(a)** *(gen pl)* note; **tomar apuntes** to take notes **(b)** *(dibujo)* sketch; **sacar un a.** to do a sketch **(c)** *Teat (apuntador)* prompter; *(voz de apuntador)* prompt; *(impreso)* prompt book **(d)** *Naipes* stake

apuntillar *vt Taur* to finish off

apuñalamiento *nm* stabbing

apuñalar *vt* to stab

apurado, -a 1 *pp de* **apurar**

2 *adj* **(a)** *(terminado)* finished **(b)** *(preocupado)* worried; *(avergonzado)* embarrassed **(c)** *(necesitado)* in need; **a. de dinero** hard up for money; **a. de tiempo** in a hurry **(d)** *(difícil)* awkward, difficult; **una situación apurada** a tight spot, a jam

apurar 1 *vt* **(a)** *(terminar)* to finish off, end; *(agotar)* to wear out, exhaust; **a. una copa** to drain a glass; *Fig* **apurarle la**

paciencia a algn to exhaust sb's patience; *Fig* **si me apuras** if you insist; *Fam* if you twist my arm (**b**) *(preocupar)* to worry (**c**) *(apremiar)* to rush, hurry, pester; **no me apures** don't rush me, don't pester me
   2 apurarse *vpr Esp Méx (preocuparse)* to worry, get worried; **no te apures** don't worry

apuro *nm* (**a**) *(situación difícil)* tight spot, fix, jam; **estar** *o* **encontrarse en un a.** to be in a tight spot (**b**) *(escasez de dinero)* hardship; **pasar apuros** to be hard up (**c**) *(vergüenza)* embarrassment; **¡qué a.!** how embarrassing!

apurruñar *vt Ven Fam* (**a**) *(estrujar)* to scrunch up (**b**) *(abrazar)* to give a bear hug

aquejado, -a 1 *pp de* aquejar
   2 *adj* suffering (**de** from)

aquejar *vt* to afflict, affect; **le aqueja una grave enfermedad** he is suffering from a serious illness

aquel, -ella *adj dem* that; **a. niño** that boy; **aquellos, -as** those; **aquellas niñas** those girls

aquél, -élla 1 *pron dem m,f* (**a**) *(ese)* that one; *(nombrado antes)* the former; **coge a.** take that one; **vinieron Pedro y Manuel, a.** disfrazado de Tarzán Pedro and Manuel came, the former dressed up as Tarzan (**b**) **todo a. que** anyone who, whoever; **a. que hable** he who speaks (**c**) **aquéllos, -as** those; *(los anteriores)* the former; **llévate a.** take those
   2 *nm Fam* something; **ella tiene un a.** she's got something about her

aquelarre *nm* witches' sabbath

aquella *adj dem f véase* aquel, -ella

aquélla *pron dem f véase* aquél, -élla

aquello *pron dem neut* that, it; **a. parecía una casa de locos** it was sheer bedlam in that place; **¿le has hablado de a.?** have you spoken to him about it?; *Fam* **a. de que no hacían falta entradas era verdad** it was true that we didn't need (to get) tickets; *Fam* **por a. de que no se molestara** so that he wouldn't feel put out

aquellos, -as *adj dem pl véase* aquel, -ella

aquéllos, -as *pron dem m,fpl véase* aquél, -élla

aquerenciarse *vpr* **a. a** *(a un lugar)* to become fond of

aquí *adv* (**a**) *(lugar)* here; **a. arriba** up here; **a. está** here it is; **a. fuera** out here; **a. mismo** right here; **a. y allá** here and there; **de a. para allá** up and down, to and fro; **hasta a.** this far; **por a. por favor** this way please; **tiene que estar por a.** it must be around here somewhere; *Fig* **hasta a. podíamos llegar** that's the end of it; *Fam* **a. un amigo** thio is a friend (**b**) *(tiempo)* now; then; **a. empieza lo peor** here begins the worst; **de a. a poco** soon; **de a. en adelante** from now on; **hasta a.** up till now (**c**) *(consecuencia)* **de a. (que)** hence; **de a. que no te lo dijera** and that's why I didn't tell you

aquiescencia *nf* acquiescence

aquietar 1 *vt* to pacify, calm down
   2 aquietarse *vpr* to calm down

aquilatamiento *nm* (**a**) *(de oro, piedra preciosa)* assay (**b**) *Fig (evaluación)* assessment, evaluation

aquilatar *vt* (**a**) *(metales, piedras preciosas)* to assay (**b**) *Fig (evaluar)* to assess, evaluate

Aquiles *nm* Achilles

aquilino, -a *adj (nariz)* aquiline

ara *nf* altar; *(piedra)* altar stone; *Fml* **en aras de** for the sake of; **en aras de la paz** so as to keep the peace

árabe 1 *adj (de Arabia)* Arab, Arabian; *(lengua, literatura)* Arabic
   2 *nmf (persona)* Arab
   3 *nm (idioma)* Arabic

arabesco *nm* arabesque

Arabia *n* Arabia; **A. Saudí** *o* **Saudita** Saudi Arabia

arábigo, -a 1 *adj* Arabic, Arabian; **goma arábiga** gum arabic; **números arábigos** Arabic numerals
   2 *nm (idioma)* Arabic

arabismo *nm* Arabic expression

arabista *nmf* Arabist

arácnido *nm Zool* arachnid

arada *nf* (**a**) *(acción)* ploughing, *US* plowing (**b**) *(tierra)* ploughed *o US* plowed land

arado *nm* plough, *US* plow

arador *nm* ploughman, *US* plowman

Aragón *n* Aragon

aragonés, -esa *adj & nm,f* Aragonese

arameo, -a 1 *adj* Aramaean, Aramean
   2 *nm,f (persona)* Aramaean, Aramean
   3 *nm (idioma)* Aramaic

arancel *nm* tariff, customs duty

arancelario, -a *adj* tariff, duty; **derechos arancelarios** duties

arándano *nm* bilberry

arandela *nf* (**a**) *(anila) (de metal)* washer; *(de papel, plástico)* ring reinforcement (**b**) *CAm Méx (de camisa)* frills, ruffle

araña *nf* (**a**) *Zool* spider ❏ **tela de a.** spider's web (**b**) *(cangrejo)* **a. de mar** spider crab (**c**) *(pez)* weever (**d**) *Bot* love-in-a-mist (**e**) *(lámpara)* chandelier

arañar 1 *vt* (**a**) *(raspar)* to scratch (**b**) *Fig (reunir)* to scrape together
   2 arañarse *vpr* to scratch oneself

arañazo *nm* scratch

arar *vt Agr* to plough, *US* plow

araucano, -a *adj & nm,f* Araucanian

araucaria *nf Bot* araucaria, monkey puzzle tree

arbitraje *nm* (**a**) *(desacuerdo)* arbitration (**b**) *Dep* refereeing; *Ten* umpiring

arbitral *adj* of the referee; **sentencia a.** judgement by arbitration

arbitrar *vt* (**a**) *Jur* to arbitrate (**b**) *(obtener)* to contrive; *(reunir)* to collect; **a. fondos** to raise funds (**c**) *Dep* to referee, umpire

arbitrariedad *nf* (**a**) *(cualidad)* arbitrariness (**b**) *(acción)* arbitrary action

arbitrario, -a *adj* arbitrary

arbitrio *nm* (**a**) *(voluntad)* will; *(juicio)* judgement; **lo dejo a tu a.** I leave it to your discretion (**b**) *(medio)* mean (**c**) **arbitrios** taxes

árbitro, -a *nm,f* (**a**) *Jur* arbiter, arbitrator; *(mujer)* arbitress (**b**) *Dep* referee, umpire

árbol *nm* (**a**) *Bot* tree; *Fig* **los árboles no dejan ver el bosque** you can't see the wood for the trees ❏ **á. del amor** Judas tree; **á. del cielo** tree of Heaven; **á. frutal** fruit tree (**b**) *Téc* shaft (**c**) *Náut* mast (**d**) *(gráfico)* tree (diagram) ❏ **á. genealógico** family *o* genealogical tree

arbolado, -a 1 *pp de* arbolar
   2 *adj* (**a**) *(con árboles)* wooded, with trees (**b**) *(mar)* very high
   3 *nm* woodland

arboladura *nf Náut* masts and spars *pl*

arbolar 1 *vt* (**a**) *Náut* to mast (**b**) *(enarbolar)* to hoist; *(esgrimir)* to brandish
   2 arbolarse *vpr (las olas)* to rear up

arboleda *nf* wood, copse, spinney, grove

arbóreo, -a *adj* arboreal; **vegetación arbórea** trees *pl*

arborescente *adj* arborescent

arboricultor, -a *nm,f* arboriculturist

arboricultura *nf* arboriculture

arbotante *nm Arquit* flying buttress

arbustivo, -a *adj* bushlike

arbusto *nm* bush, shrub

arca *nf* (**a**) *(arcón)* chest (**b**) *(caja de caudales)* strongbox, safe □ **arcas públicas** Treasury *sing* (**c**) *Rel* **el A. de Noé** Noah's Ark

arcabucero *nm Hist* arquebusier

arcabuz *nm Hist* arquebus

arcada *nf* (**a**) *(conjunto de arcos)* arcade (**b**) *(de puente)* arch (**c**) *(náusea)* retching

arcaico, -a *adj* archaic

arcaísmo *nm* archaism

arcaizante *adj* archaistic

arcángel *nm* archangel

arcano, -a 1 *adj* arcane
  2 *nm* mystery

arce *nm* maple (tree) □ **a. menor** common o field maple; **a. real** Norway maple; **a. rojo** red maple

arcediano *nm* archdeacon

arcén *nm Esp Br* hard shoulder, *US* shoulder

archi- *pref* super-; **archiconocido** super-famous; **archisabido** extremely well-known

archidiácono *nm* archdeacon

archidiócesis *nf inv* archdiocese

archiduque, -esa *nm,f (hombre)* archduke; *(mujer)* archduchess

archipiélago *nm* archipelago

archivador, -a 1 *nm,f* archivist
  2 *nm* filing cabinet

archivar *vt* (**a**) *(ordenar)* to file (away) (**b**) *(arrinconar)* to shelve (**c**) *Inform* to file (**d**) *Fam (guardar)* to put (away)

archivero, -a *nm,f* archivist

archivo *nm* (**a**) *(lugar)* archive; **imágenes de a.** library pictures (**b**) *Inform* file (**c**) *(conjunto de documentos)* archives *pl* (**d**) *(archivador)* filing cabinet

archivolta *nf Arquit* archivolt

arcilla *nf* clay; **a. cocida** baked clay

arcilloso, -a *adj* clayey, clayish

arcipreste *nm Rel* archpriest

arco *nm* (**a**) *Mat* arc (**b**) *Arquit* arch □ **a. apuntado** lancet o pointed arch; **a. carpanel** three-centred arch; **a. de herradura** horseshoe arch; **a. de medio punto** semicircular arch; **a. de triunfo** triumphal arch; **a. tudor** four-centred o Tudor arch (**c**) *Mús (de violín)* bow (**d**) *Elec* arc □ **a. voltaico** electric arc (**e**) *Dep* bow □ **tiro con a.** archery (**f**) *Meteor* **a. iris** rainbow

arcón *nm Mueb* large chest

arder *vi* to burn; **a. completamente** to burn down; **la casa estaba ardiendo** the house was in flames; *Fig* **ardiendo de fiebre** burning with fever; *Fig* **a. de pasión** to burn with passion; *Fig* **a. en guerras** to be lashed by war; *Fam* **la cosa está que arde** things are getting pretty hot

ardid *nm* scheme, trick, plot

ardiente *adj* (**a**) *(encendido)* burning, scalding, boiling hot; **capilla a.** funeral o mortuary chapel (**b**) *Fig (intenso)* ardent, passionate; *(fervoroso, activo)* eager

ardilla *nf* squirrel

ardite *nm Fam* **me importa un a.** I couldn't give a damn

ardor *nm* (**a**) *(calor)* burning sensation, burn; *(calor)* heat □ *Med* **a. de estómago** heartburn (**b**) *Fig (ansia)* ardour, *US* ardor, fervour, *US* fervor; **con a.** passionately

ardoroso, -a *adj* (**a**) *(caliente)* burning, boiling hot (**b**) *Fig* ardent, passionate

arduo, -a *adj* arduous, very difficult, awkward

área *nf* (**a**) *(zona)* area, zone; **en esta á. de la ciudad** in this part of (the) town □ *Dep* **á. de castigo** penalty area; **á. de descanso** *(en carretera) Br* lay-by, *US* rest area; **á. metropolitana** metropolitan area; *Aut* **á. de servicio** service area (**b**) *(superficie)* area (**c**) *(medida)* are (100 square metres)

arena *nf* (**a**) *(de playa)* sand; **playa de a.** sandy beach □ **arenas movedizas** quicksand *sing* (**b**) *(de circo romano)* arena (**c**) *Taur (plaza)* bullring

arenal *nm* large extension of sand

arenga *nf* harangue; **pronunciar una a.** to harangue

arengar [38] *vt* to harangue

arenilla *nf* (**a**) *(polvo)* fine sand (**b**) **arenillas** *Med (del riñón)* stones

arenisca *nf* sandstone

arenoso, -a *adj* sandy

arenque *nm (pez)* herring □ *Culin* **a. ahumado** kipper, kippered herring

arete *nm Andes Méx (pendiente)* earring

argamasa *nf Constr* mortar

Argel *n* Algiers

Argelia *n* Algeria

argelino, -a *adj & nm,f* Algerian

argentado, -a *adj* (**a**) *(bañado de plata)* silver-plated (**b**) *Literario* silvery

argentífero, -a *adj* argentiferous

Argentina *n* Argentina

argentinismo *nm Ling* Argentinean expression

argentino, -a *adj & nm,f* Argentinean, Argentine

argolla *nf* (**a**) *(aro)* (large) ring (**b**) *Andes Méx (alianza)* wedding ring

argón *nm Quím* argon

argonauta *nm Mit* argonaut

argot *nm (popular)* slang; *(técnico)* jargon

argucia *nf* sophism, fallacy

argüir [8] *vt* (**a**) *(deducir)* to deduce, conclude (**b**) *(argumentar)* to argue (**c**) *(probar)* to prove, show

argumentación *nf* line of argument

argumentar *vt véase* **argüir**

argumento *nm* (**a**) *(razonamiento)* argument (**b**) *Lit Teat (trama)* plot

arguyo *indic pres véase* **argüir**

aria *nf Mús* aria

aridez *nf* (**a**) *(de terreno, clima)* aridity (**b**) *Fig (de libro, tema)* dryness

árido, -a 1 *adj* arid; *Fig* dry
  2 áridos *nmpl Com* dry goods

Aries *nm Astron Astrol* Aries

ariete *nm* (**a**) *Mil Hist* battering ram (**b**) *Ftb* centre forward

ario, -a *adj & nm,f* Aryan

arisco, -a *adj* (**a**) *(persona)* unfriendly, stand-offish; *(áspero)* surly, gruff (**b**) *(animal)* unfriendly

arista *nf* edge

aristocracia *nf* aristocracy

aristócrata *nmf* aristocrat

aristocrático, -a *adj* aristocratic

aristotélico, -a *adj Filos* Aristotelian

aritmética *nf* arithmetic

aritmético, -a *adj* arithmetical, arithmetic

arlequín *nm Lit* Harlequin

arlequinada *nf* (piece of) clowning o buffoonery

arma *nf* (**a**) *(instrumento)* weapon, arm; **alzarse en armas** to rise up in arms; **pasar por las armas** to execute; **presentar armas** to present arms; **rendir armas** to surrender; **tomar las armas** to take up arms; *Fig* **a. de doble filo** double-edged sword; *Fam* **ser de armas tomar** to be formidable o frightening ❏ **a. blanca** knife, blade, steel; **a. corta** small arm; **a. de artillería** artillery; **a. de fuego** firearm; **a. homicida** murder weapon; **a. nuclear** nuclear weapon; **licencia de armas** firearms licence (**b**) **armas** *Mil (profesión militar)* army *sing; (fuerzas militares)* military forces; *(empresa militar)* military combat *sing;* **hecho de a.** fact of arms

armada *nf* navy, naval forces *pl; Hist* **la A. Invencible** the Spanish Armada

armadillo *nm Zool* armadillo

armado, -a 1 *pp de* **armar**
  2 *adj* armed; **ir a.** to be armed

armador, -a *nm,f Náut* shipowner

armadura *nf* (**a**) *Hist* suit of armour o *US* armor (**b**) *(armazón)* frame; **a. de las gafas** spectacle frame (**c**) *Arquit* framework

armamentista *adj* arms; **la carrera a.** the arms race

armamento *nm* (**a**) *(acción)* armament, arming (**b**) **armamentos** *(armas)* armaments, arms

armar 1 *vt* (**a**) *(tropas, personas)* to arm (**b**) *(cargar) (arma de fuego)* to load; *(bayoneta)* to fix (**c**) *(montar)* to fit o put together, assemble; *(tienda)* to pitch; **está sin a.** it hasn't been put up yet (**d**) *(disponer, preparar)* to arrange, prepare (**e**) *Fam (organizar)* **¡ahora sí que la has armado!** you've really done it now!; **armaron un escándalo** they kicked up a fuss
  2 armarse *vpr* to arm oneself; **todos los habitantes se armaron** everybody prepared for war; *Fig* **a. de paciencia** to summon up one's patience; *Fig* **a. de valor** to pluck up courage; *Fig* **a. de papel y lápiz** to provide oneself with paper and pencil; *Fam* **se va a a. la de Dios es Cristo, se va a a. la gorda** there's going to be real trouble

armario *nm (para ropa)* wardrobe; *(de cocina)* cupboard ❏ **a. empotrado** built-in wardrobe o cupboard

armatoste *nm (cosa)* monstrosity; *(máquina)* useless contraption; *(persona)* useless great oaf

armazón *nf* o *nm (estructura)* framework, frame; *(de vehículo)* chassis; *(de edificio)* skeleton

Armenia *n* Armenia

armenio, -a 1 *adj & nm,f* Armenian
  2 *nm (idioma)* Armenian

armería *nf* (**a**) *(tienda)* gunsmith's (shop) (**b**) *(oficio)* gunsmith's craft (**c**) *(museo)* armoury, *US* armory, museum of arms

armero, -a *nm,f* armourer, *US* armorer; *(de armas de fuego)* gunsmith; *Mil* **(maestro) a.** armourer, *US* armorer

armiño *nm* ermine

armisticio *nm* armistice

armonía *nf* harmony

armónica *nf* harmonica, mouth organ

armónicamente *adv* in harmony, harmoniously

armónico, -a 1 *adj* harmonic
  2 *nm Mús* harmonic

armonio *nm Mús* harmonium

armonioso, -a *adj* harmonious

armonización *nf* harmonizing

armonizar [14] *vt & vi* to harmonize

ARN *nm (abrev de* **ácido ribonucleico)** RNA

arnés *nm* (**a**) *(armadura)* armour, *US* armor (**b**) **arneses** *(arreos)* harness *sing,* trappings

árnica *nf Bot* arnica; **tintura de á.** (tincture of) arnica

aro *nm* (**a**) *(círculo)* hoop, iron ring; *Fam* **entrar** o **pasar por el a.** to knuckle under (**b**) *(juego)* hoop (**c**) *Bot* cuckoopint (**d**) *Am (pendiente)* earring

aroma *nm* aroma, fragrance; *(de vino)* bouquet

aromaterapia *nf* aromatherapy

aromático, -a *adj* aromatic, fragrant

aromatización *nf* scenting, perfuming

aromatizador *nm* air freshener

aromatizar [14] *vt* to scent, perfume

arpa *nf* harp

arpegio *nm Mús* arpeggio

arpía *nf* (**a**) *Mit* harpy (**b**) *Fig (mujer)* harpy, old witch

arpillera *nf Tex* sackcloth, *Br* hessian, *US* burlap

arpista *nmf* harpist

arpón *nm* harpoon

arponear *vt* to harpoon

arponero, -a *nm,f* harpooner

arquear 1 *vt* (**a**) *(madera)* to warp; *(vara, fusta)* to flex (**b**) *(cejas, espalda)* to arch
  2 arquearse *vpr* (**a**) *(madera)* to warp (**b**) *(cejas, espalda)* to arch

arqueo *nm* (**a**) *(de cejas, espalda, lomo)* arching (**b**) *Com* checking, cashing up; **hacer el a.** to cash up (**c**) *Náut* registered tonnage

arqueolítico, -a *adj* Stone-Age

arqueología *nf* archaeology, *US* archeology

arqueológico, -a *adj* archaeological, *US* archeological

arqueólogo, -a *nm,f* archaeologist, *US* archeologist

arquería *nf Arquit* arcade

arquero, -a *nm,f* archer; *(hombre)* bowman

arqueta *nf Mueb* small chest

arquetípico, -a *adj* archetypal

arquetipo *nm* archetype

arquitecto, -a *nm,f* architect

arquitectónico, -a *adj* architectural, architectonic

arquitectura *nf* architecture

arquitrabe *nm Arquit* architrave

arquivolta *nf Arquit* archivolt

arrabal *nm* (**a**) *(suburbio)* suburb (**b**) **arrabales** *(afueras)* outskirts

arrabalero, -a *Esp Pey* **1** *adj* ill-bred
  2 *nm,f* ill-bred person

arracimarse *vpr* to bunch o cluster together

arraigado, -a 1 *pp de* **arraigar**
  2 *adj* deeply rooted

arraigar [38] **1** *vi* to take root
  2 arraigarse *vpr* to settle down

arraigo *nm (acción)* act of taking root; *Fig (raíces)* roots *pl;* **una tradición con mucho a.** a deeply-rooted tradition

arramblar 1 *vt* to cover with sand
  2 *vi Fam* **a. con algo** to make off with sth

arrancada *nf* jerk, jolt

arrancar [59] **1** *vt* (**a**) *(sacar de su sitio) (árbol)* to uproot; *(malas hierbas, flor)* to pull up; **a. de raíz** *(árbol)* to uproot; *Fig (eliminar una costumbre)* to wipe out (**b**) *(separar con fuerza)* to pull o tear off o out; **a. un diente/el pelo** to pull out a tooth/one's hair; **a. una etiqueta** to tear off a label; **me arrancó el libro de las manos** he wrenched the book from my hands; *Fig* **le arrancaron la confesión con**

torturas they extracted the confession from him by torture (**c**) *Aut (coche)* to start (**d**) *Inform* to start up, to boot (up)

2 *vi* (**a**) *Aut Téc* to start; **el coche no arranca** the car won't start (**b**) *(partir)* to set off, start out; *(barco)* to set sail (**c**) *(empezar)* to begin; **a. a correr** to break into a run; **a. a llorar/reír** to burst out crying/laughing; *Fig* **el problema arranca de años atrás** the problem goes back several years

3 arrancarse *vpr* **a. a hacer algo** to start doing something; *Fam* **¿y ahora te arrancas con eso?** why on earth didn't you tell me before?

arranchar *vt Andes CAm (arrebatar)* to seize, snatch

arranque *nm* (**a**) *Aut Téc* starting ❑ **motor de a.** starter motor (**b**) *(comienzo)* start ❑ **punto de a.** beginning (**c**) *Arquit* foot (**d**) *Fam (arrebato)* outburst, fit

arrapiezo *nm (niño)* whippersnapper, urchin

arrasar *vt* (**a**) *(edificio, zona)* to devastate, destroy (**b**) *(terreno)* to level, smooth

arrastrado, -a 1 *pp de* **arrastrar**

2 *adj Fam (miserable)* miserable, wretched

arrastrar 1 *vt* to pull (along), drag (along), haul; **arrástralo** pull it along; **a. los pies** to drag one's feet; **la corriente lo arrastró** the current swept him away; *Fig* **a. a las masas** to sway the crowds; *Fig* **dejarse a.** to get carried away

2 *vi* (**a**) *(por el suelo)* to trail (on the ground) (**b**) *Naipes* to lead

2 arrastrarse *vpr* to drag oneself, crawl; *Fig (humillarse)* to creep, crawl

arrastre *nm* (**a**) *(acarreo)* pulling, dragging; *Fam* **para el a.** *(persona)* on one's last legs; *(cosa)* done for; **(pesca de) a.** trawling (**b**) *Naipes* lead (**c**) *(telesquí)* drag lift

arrayán *nm Bot* myrtle

arre *interj* gee up!, giddy up!

arrea *interj Fam* goodness me!

arrear *Fam* **1** *vt* (**a**) *(azuzar)* to spur on; *(caballo)* to urge on; *(ganado)* to drive (**b**) *(apresurar)* to hurry up (**c**) *Fam (asestar)* to give; **a. una bofetada a algn** to slap sb in the face, give sb a slap in the face

2 *vi Fam* **salir arreando** to rush off

arrebatado, -a 1 *pp de* **arrebatar**

2 *adj* (**a**) *(precipitado)* rash, hasty (**b**) *(iracundo)* furious, enraged (**c**) *(impulsivo)* impulsive (**d**) *(ruborizado)* blushing, flushed (**e**) *Culin Fam (quemado)* burnt

arrebatador, -a *adj Fig* captivating, fascinating

arrebatar 1 *vt* (**a**) *(coger)* to snatch, seize; *Fig (cautivar)* to captivate, fascinate (**b**) *Ven (atropellar)* to run over, knock down

2 arrebatarse *vpr* (**a**) *(enfurecerse)* to become furious; *(exaltarse)* to get carried away (**b**) *Culin Fam (quemarse)* to burn

arrebato *nm*, **arrebatamiento** *nm* (**a**) *(arranque)* outburst, fit; **le dio un a. y dejó el trabajo** he suddenly upped and left his job (**b**) *(furor)* anger, fury, rage

arrebol *nm* (**a**) *(de las nubes)* red glow; *(de las mejillas)* ruddiness, redness (**b**) **arreboles** red clouds

arrebolar 1 *vt* (**a**) *(enrojecer)* to give a red glow to (**b**) *(persona)* to make ruddy

2 arrebolarse *vpr* (**a**) *(enrojecer)* to glow red (**b**) *(persona)* to blush

arrebujar 1 *vt* (**a**) *(arrugar)* to crumple up (**b**) *(envolver)* to wrap up

2 arrebujarse *vpr (envolverse)* to wrap oneself up

arrechar *CAm Col Méx Ven Vulg* **1** *vt* to make horny, turn on

2 arrecharse *vpr* to get horny

arrechucho *nm Fam* (**a**) *Med* temporary ailment (**b**) *(arranque)* sudden impulse, outburst, fit

arreciar *vi (empeorar)* to get worse; *(aumentar)* to get heavier *o* stronger

arrecife *nm* reef ❑ **a. de coral** coral reef

arredrar 1 *vt (asustar)* to frighten

2 arredrarse *vpr (asustarse)* to be frightened

arreglado, -a 1 *pp de* **arreglar**

2 *adj* (**a**) *(solucionado)* settled, fixed, sorted out; **lo de tu billete ya está a.** your ticket is all sorted out now (**b**) *(reparado)* repaired, fixed (**c**) *(ordenado)* tidy, arranged, neat (**d**) *(persona)* well-dressed, smart (**e**) *Fam* **¡estamos arreglados!** we're really done for!; *Irón* **¡vas a. si crees que él lo va a hacer!** you're in for a shock if you think he's going to do it!

arreglar 1 *vt* (**a**) *(gen)* to settle, fix up, sort out, arrange; **arreglaron los papeles para casarse** they got their papers in order so that they could get married; **yo lo arreglaré** I'll see to it (**b**) *(componer)* to repair, fix, mend; *(cabello)* to do; *(habitación)* to decorate; *(escrito)* to rearrange; *Mús (composición)* to arrange; *Cost (vestido)* to alter; **lo llevé a a.** I had it repaired; *Fig* **el tiempo lo arregla todo** time is a great healer (**c**) *(ordenar)* to tidy up, put in order; **a. la casa** to do the housework (**d**) *(niño)* to dress and smarten up, get ready (**e**) *Fam* to sort out; **yo le arreglaré** I'll teach him!

2 arreglarse *vpr* (**a**) *(acicalarse)* to get ready, dress up; *Fam* **a. de punta en blanco** to dress up to the nines (**b**) *Fam (apañarse)* to manage; **con este trozo me arreglo** this piece will do (for) me, I'll make do with this piece; **tendrás que arreglarte sin el coche** you'll have to get by without the car; **él siempre se las arregla para hacer lo que quiere** he always manages to get his way; **arréglatelas como puedas** *(haz lo que puedas)* do as best you can; *(allá tú)* that's your problem, not mine (**c**) *(resolverse)* to be solved; **todo se arreglará** things will be all right (in the end) (**d**) *(pactar)* to reach an agreement

arreglista *nmf Mús* arranger

arreglo *nm* (**a**) *(de una disputa)* settlement, arrangement (**b**) *(reparación)* repair, mend; *(modificación)* change, alteration; *(de una casa)* conversion, redecoration; **no tiene a.** it is beyond repair; *Fam* **¡tú no tienes a.!** you're hopeless! (**c**) *(limpieza)* cleaning, tidying (**d**) *Fml* **con a. a** in accordance with

arrejuntarse *vpr Fam* to cohabit, live together

arrellanarse *vpr* to sit back; **se arrellanó en el sillón** he settled back in the armchair

arremangar [38] **1** *vt (mangas etc)* to roll up

2 arremangarse *vpr* to roll one's sleeves/trouser legs up

arremeter *vi* to attack; **el toro arremetió contra él** the bull charged at him; *Fig* **arremetió contra la ley** he attacked the law

arremetida *nf* attack, assault

arremolinarse *vpr* to whirl about; *Fig (gente)* to crowd together, cram together

arrendador, -a 1 *adj* renting, leasing

2 *nm,f* lessor; *(hombre)* landlord; *(mujer)* landlady

arrendajo *nm Orn* jay

arrendamiento *nm* (**a**) *(alquiler)* renting, leasing (**b**) *(precio)* rent, lease

arrendar [3] *vt (piso)* to rent, lease; *(dar en arriendo)* to let on lease; *(tomar en arriendo)* to take on lease

arrendatario, -a 1 *adj* renting, leasing

2 *nm,f* leaseholder, lessee; *(inquilino)* tenant

arreo 1 *nm Am* herd, drove

2 arreos *nmpl* (**a**) *(de caballería)* harness *sing*, trappings (**b**) *(adornos)* adornments; *(cosas, bultos)* stuff *sing*, trappings

arrepanchigarse [38] *vpr Fam* to stretch out, sprawl

arrepentido, -a 1 *pp de* **arrepentirse**
2 *adj* regretful, repentant; **está a.** he's regretful (of having done it), he regrets it

arrepentimiento *nm* regret, repentance

arrepentirse [62] *vpr* to regret; **te arrepentirás** you'll regret it; **a. de sus pecados** to repent one's sins

arrestado, -a 1 *pp de* **arrestar**
2 *adj* arrested, detained, imprisoned

arrestar *vt* to arrest, detain; *(encarcelar)* to put in prison

arresto *nm* (a) *(detención)* arrest ❑ *Jur* **a. domiciliario** house arrest; **a. mayor** close arrest; **a. menor** open arrest (b) **arrestos** *(determinación)* daring *sing*; *Fam* guts

arriar [32] *vt (bandera)* to strike; *(velas)* to lower

arriate *nm* flower bed

arriba 1 *adv* up; *(encima)* on the top; **ahí a.** up there; **a. del todo** right on the top; **cuesta a.** uphill; **de a. abajo** from top to toe, from top to bottom; **desde a.** from above; **hacia a.** upwards; **la parte de a.** the top (part); **más a.** higher up, further up; **patas a.** upside down; **sueldos de un millón para a.** salaries from one million upwards; **ven aquí a.** come up here; **vive a.** he lives upstairs; *Fml* **véase más a.** see above; *Fig* **los de a.** the upper classes; *Fam* **mirar a algn de a. abajo** to look sb up and down
2 *interj* get up!, up you get!; **¡a. la República!** long live the Republic!; **¡a. las manos!** hands up!

arribada *nf Náut* arrival

arribar *vi Náut* to reach port, arrive

arribeño, -a *Am* **1** *adj* highland
2 *nm,f* highlander

arribismo *nm* arrivisme, social climbing

arribista 1 *adj* ambitious, self-seeking
2 *nmf* arriviste, parvenu, *pai* venue, social climber

arribo *nm Náut* arrival

arriendo *nm* lease; *(de un piso)* renting; **dar en a.** to let out on lease; **tomar en a.** to take on lease

arriero, -a *nm,f* muleteer

arriesgado, -a 1 *pp de* **arriesgar**
2 *adj* (a) *(peligroso)* risky, dangerous (b) *(persona)* fearless, daring

arriesgar [38] **1** *vt* to risk, endanger; **a. todo lo que uno tiene** to stake all one has got; **a. una hipótesis** to venture a theory; *Fam* **a. el pellejo** to risk one's neck
2 **arriesgarse** *vpr* to risk; **a. a fracasar** to risk failure; **se arriesga demasiado** he's taking too many risks

arrimadero *nm* (a) *(estribo)* support (b) *(de pared)* wainscot

arrimado, -a 1 *pp de* **arrimar**
2 *nm,f Col Méx Ven Fam* scrounger; **está de a. en mi casa** he's living off me

arrimar 1 *vt* (a) *(acercar)* to move closer, bring near o nearer; **arrímalo a la pared** move it up to the wall; *Fam* **a. el hombro** to lend a hand (b) *(arrinconar)* to put away
2 **arrimarse** *vpr* to move o get close, come near o nearer; **no te arrimes a la pared** keep away from the wall, don't lean against the wall; *Fig* **a. a algn** to seek sb's protection; *Fam* **a. al sol que más calienta** to get on the winning side

arrimo *nm (apoyo)* support, protection; *(ayuda)* help; **al a. de** under the protection of

arrinconado, -a 1 *pp de* **arrinconar**
2 *adj* put away, laid aside, forgotten; *(persona)* forsaken

arrinconar 1 *vt* (a) *(poner en un rincón)* to put in a corner (b) *(retirar del uso)* to put away, lay aside (c) *(acorralar)* to corner
2 **arrinconarse** *vpr (aislarse)* to isolate oneself

arriscado, -a *adj* (a) *(arriesgado)* risky, dangerous (b) *(con riscos)* craggy, cliffy

arrítmico, -a *adj* arrythmic

arroba *nf* (a) *Inform (símbolo)* at, @ sign (b) *(medida)* arroba; *(de peso)* 11.5 kg; *(de volumen)* variable liquid measure; *Fig* **por arrobas** by the score

arrobamiento *nm véase* **arrobo**

arrobar 1 *vt (embelesar)* to rapture, enthral, *US* enthrall, fascinate
2 **arrobarse** *vpr (embelesarse)* to go into raptures, be enthralled, be fascinated

arrobo *nm* rapture, enthralment, *US* enthrallment, fascination

arrocero, -a 1 *adj* rice; **la industria arrocera** the rice industry
2 *nm,f* rice grower

arrodillado, -a 1 *pp de* **arrodillar**
2 *adj* kneeling down, on one's knees; **estar a.** to be kneeling down

arrodillar 1 *vt* to force to kneel
2 **arrodillarse** *vpr* to kneel down

arrogación *nf Jur* arrogation

arrogancia *nf* (a) *(orgullo)* arrogance (b) *(gallardía)* gallantry, valour, *US* valor, bravery

arrogante *adj* (a) *(orgulloso)* arrogant (b) *(gallardo)* gallant, valiant, brave

arrogarse [38] *vpr* to arrogate

arrojadizo, -a *adj* for throwing; **arma arrojadiza** projectile, missile

arrojado, -a 1 *pp de* **arrojar**
2 *adj (osado)* fearless, bold, daring

arrojar 1 *vt* (a) *(tirar)* to throw, fling, hurl; **'prohibido a. basuras'** 'no dumping' (b) *(echar)* to throw out; **los arrojó de su casa** he threw them out of the house (c) *(humo)* to kick o belch out; *(lava)* to spew out; *Fig* **a. luz sobre** to shed light on (d) *Com* to produce; **a. un saldo positivo** to give a favourable balance
2 *vi Fam (vomitar)* to throw up, be sick
3 **arrojarse** *vpr (tirarse)* to throw oneself, fling oneself; **a. por la ventana** to throw oneself out of the window; **se arrojó sobre él** he jumped on him

arrojo *nm* fearlessness, daring, courage

arrollable *adj* rollable

arrollador, -a *adj Fig* irresistible, overwhelming; **un éxito a.** a resounding success; **una personalidad arrolladora** a captivating personality

arrollamiento *nm* (a) *(acción)* rolling, rolling up (b) *(atropello)* running over, knocking down (c) *Fig (aplastamiento)* crushing, routing (d) *(por agua, viento)* sweeping away, carrying off (e) *Elec* winding

arrollar 1 *vt* (a) *(enrollar)* to roll, roll up (b) *(atropellar)* to run over, knock down (c) *Fig (aplastar)* to crush, rout (d) *(agua, viento)* to sweep away, carry off
2 *vi (ganar todos los premios)* to sweep the board; *(vencer claramente)* to achieve a crushing victory

arropamiento *nm* wrapping up

arropar 1 *vt* to wrap up; **ella lo arropó en la cama** she tucked him up in bed
2 **arroparse** *vpr* to wrap oneself up

arrope *nm Culin* boiled must, grape syrup

arrostrar *vt (las consecuencias)* to face; *(peligro)* to brave

arroyo *nm* (a) *(corriente)* brook, stream (b) *(de calle)* gutter; *Fig* **sacar (a algn) del a.** to drag (sb) from the gutter; *Fig* **poner (a algn) en el a.** to chuck (sb) out (c) *Cuba (calzada)* road (surface), *US* pavement

arroz *nm* rice ❑ **a. blanco** boiled rice; **a. con leche** rice pudding; **a. integral** brown rice

arrozal *nm* rice field, rice plantation

arruga *nf* (**a**) *(piel)* wrinkle (**b**) *(ropa)* crease

arrugamiento *nm (piel)* wrinkling; *(ropa)* creasing

arrugar [38] **1** *vt (piel)* to wrinkle; *(ropa)* to crease; *(papel)* to crumple (up); *Fig* **a. el ceño** to frown
2 arrugarse *vpr* (**a**) *(piel)* to wrinkle; *(ropa)* to crease (**b**) *Fam (acobardarse)* to get the wind up

arruinado, -a 1 *pp de* **arruinar**
2 *adj* (**a**) *(empresa)* bankrupt, ruined (**b**) *(inservible)* ruined

arruinar 1 *vt* to bankrupt, ruin
2 arruinarse *vpr* to be bankrupt, be ruined

arrullar 1 *vt* (**a**) *Orn (paloma)* to coo at (**b**) *(bebé)* to lull
2 arrullarse *vpr* to bill and coo

arrullo *nm* (**a**) *Orn (de paloma)* cooing (**b**) *(nana)* lullaby (**c**) *(de enamorados)* billing and cooing

arrumaco *nm Fam* kissing, hugging; **hacerse arrumacos** to pet; **ir con arrumacos a algn** to flatter sb

arrumar 1 *vt Náut* to stow
2 arrumarse *vpr Náut* to cloud over

arrumbar 1 *vt* (**a**) *(desechar)* to put away, lay aside (**b**) *Fig (persona)* to neglect, ignore
2 *vi Náut* to set course (**hacia** for)

arsenal *nm* (**a**) *Náut* shipyard (**b**) *(de armas)* arsenal (**c**) *Fig (cúmulo)* store, storehouse; *(conjunto)* array

arsénico *nm Quím* arsenic

art. *(abrev de* **artículo***)* art

arte *nm & f* (**a**) *(creación estética)* art; **a. abstracto** abstract art; **el a. bizantino** Byzantine art; *Fig* **no tener ni a. ni parte en algo** to have nothing to do with sth; *Fam* **por a. de birlibirloque** as if by magic ❑ **artes plásticas** plastic arts; **bellas artes** fine arts (**b**) *(habilidad)* workmanship, skill ❑ **malas artes** deceit *sing* (**c**) *Pesca* **a. (de pesca)** fishing gear

artefacto *nm (aparato)* appliance, device ❑ **a. explosivo** explosive device, bomb

artejo *nm* (**a**) *Anat (nudillo)* knuckle (**b**) *Zool (de artrópodos)* article, segment

artemisa *nf Bot* artemisia

arteria *nf Anat* artery ❑ **a. carótida** carotid artery; **a. coronaria** coronary artery

artería *nf* craftiness, artfulness

arterial *adj Anat* arterial

arterio(e)sclerosis *nf Med* arteriosclerosis

artero, -a *adj* crafty, artful

artesa *nf* trough

artesanado *nm* craftsmen *pl*

artesanal *adj* handmade; **actividades artesanales** arts and crafts

artesanía *nf* (**a**) *(cualidad)* craftsmanship (**b**) *(obra)* crafts *pl* , handicrafts *pl* ❑ **objeto de a.** handmade object

artesano, -a 1 *adj* handmade
2 *nm,f (hombre)* craftsman; *(mujer)* craftswoman

artesiano, -a *adj* artesian; **pozo a.** artesian well

artesón *nm Arquit* (**a**) *(adorno)* coffer (**b**) *(artesonado)* coffered ceiling

artesonado, -a *Arquit* **1** *adj* coffered
2 *nm* coffered ceiling

ártico, -a 1 *adj* arctic; **el océano Á.** the Arctic Ocean
2 el Á. *nm* the Arctic

articulación *nf* (**a**) *Ling* articulation (**b**) *Anat* joint, articulation (**c**) *Téc* joint

articulado, -a 1 *pp de* **articular**
2 *adj* (**a**) *(lenguaje)* articulate (**b**) *(tren, muñeco)* articulated

3 *nm (de una ley, un reglamento)* articles *pl*

articular 1 *adj* articulated
2 *vt* to articulate

articulatorio, -a *adj* articulatory

articulista *nmf Prensa* writer of articles

artículo *nm* (**a**) *Ling* article ❑ **a. definido** *o* **determinado** definite article; **a. indefinido** *o* **indeterminado** indefinite article (**b**) *Prensa* article ❑ **a. de fondo** leading article (**c**) *(mercancía)* article, product; **artículos alimenticios** foodstuffs; **artículos de limpieza** cleaning products ❑ **a. de primera necesidad** basic commodity; *Fam* **hacer el a.** to plug sth (**d**) *Rel* article; **a. de fe** article of faith; *Fam* **como a. de fe** as if it were gospel truth

artífice *nmf* (**a**) *(artista)* artist (**b**) *(autor)* author; *Fig* **ella ha sido el a. del acuerdo** she is the architect of the agreement

artificial *adj* artificial; *Tex* **fibras artificiales** manmade *o* synthetic fibres; **una sonrisa a.** an artificial smile

artificiero, -a *nm,f* artificier, armourer, *US* armorer

artificio *nm* (**a**) *(mecanismo)* artifice ❑ **a. pirotécnico, fuego de a.** firework (**b**) *(habilidad, arte)* skill, dexterity (**c**) *(astucia)* artifice

artificioso, -a *adj* (**a**) *(habilidoso)* skilful, *US* skillful, dexterous (**b**) *(astuto)* crafty, artful

artillería *nf Mil* artillery ❑ **a. antiaérea** anti-aircraft guns *pl*

artillero *nm Mil* artilleryman

artilugio *nm* (**a**) *(aparato)* gadget, device (**b**) *(ardid)* trick, scheme

artimaña *nf* artifice, trick, ruse

artista *nmf* artist ❑ **a. de cine** movie *o Br* film star; **a. gráfico** graphic artist

artístico, -a *adj* artistic

artrítico, -a *adj Med* arthritic

artritis *nf Med* arthritis

artrópodo *nm Zool* arthropod

artrosis *nf Med* arthrosis

arveja *nf RP (guisante)* pea

Arz., Arzpo. *(abrev de* **Arzobispo***)* Abp

arzobispal *adj* archiepiscopal; **el palacio a.** the archbishop's palace

arzobispo *nm* archbishop

as *nm* (**a**) *(cartas)* ace; **a. de picas/tréboles** ace of spades/ clubs (**b**) *Fig* ace, star, wizard; **a. del volante** ace driver

asa *nf* handle

asadero, -a 1 *adj* (for) roasting
2 *nm Fig* oven

asado, -a 1 *pp de* **asar**
2 *adj Culin* roast, roasted; **pollo a.** roast chicken; *Fig* **a. de calor** roasting, boiling hot
3 *nm Culin* roast

asador *nm* (**a**) *(aparato)* roaster (**b**) *(restaurante)* grill, grillroom

asaduras *nfpl Culin* offal *sing*; *(de ave)* giblets

asaetar *vt* to shoot arrows at; *(herir)* to wound with arrows; *(matar)* to kill with arrows; *Fig* **a. a preguntas** to bombard with questions

asalariado, -a 1 *pp de* **asalariar**
2 *adj* salaried; **trabajador a.** wage earner, salaried worker
3 *nm,f* wage earner, salaried worker

asalariar *vt* to employ

asaltante 1 *adj* assaulting, attacking
2 *nmf* attacker; *(en un robo)* raider, robber

asaltar *vt* to assault, attack; *(para robar)* to raid, rob; *Fig*

le asaltaron las dudas he was filled with doubts

asalto *nm* (**a**) *(ataque)* assault, attack; *(con robo)* raid, robbery; **tomar por a.** to take by storm (**b**) *Box* round

asamblea *nf* assembly, meeting □ **a. general** general meeting

asambleario, -a *adj* **reunión asamblearia** full meeting; **decisión asamblearia** decision taken by a meeting

asambleísta *nmf* member of an assembly o meeting

asar **1** *vt* (**a**) *Culin* to roast; **a. a la parrilla** to grill (**b**) *Fig (molestar)* to annoy, pester
   2 asarse *vpr Fig* to be roasting, be boiling hot

asaz *adj Literario* (**a**) *(muy)* very (**b**) *(bastante)* rather, quite

asbesto *nm* asbestos

ascendencia *nf* (**a**) *(linaje)* ancestry, ancestors *pl*; **de a. judía** of Jewish descent (**b**) *(influencia)* ascendancy

ascendente **1** *adj* ascendant, ascending
   2 *nm* ascendant

ascender [64] **1** *vt* to promote; **le han ascendido a capitán** he's been promoted to captain
   2 *vi* (**a**) *(subir)* to ascend, move upward; *(temperatura, nivel)* to rise; **la cuenta asciende a mil pesos** the bill adds up to one thousand pesos (**b**) *(aumentar)* to increase (**c**) *(al trono)* to ascend; *(de categoría)* to be promoted; **a. a primera división** to be promoted to the first division

ascendiente **1** *nm* ascendancy, power
   2 *nmf (persona)* ancestor

ascensión *nf* (**a**) *(subida)* climb, climbing □ *Rel* **día de la A.** Ascension Day (**b**) *(al trono)* accession

ascensional *adj* ascendant, upward

ascenso *nm* promotion

ascensor *nm Br* lift, *US* elevator

ascensorista *nmf Br* lift attendant, *US* elevator attendant

asceta *nmf* ascetic

ascético, -a *adj* ascetic

ascetismo *nm* asceticism

ASCII ['asθi] *nm Inform (abrev de **American Standard Code for Information Interchange**)* ASCII

asco *nm* disgust, repugnance; **está hecho un a.** *(cosa)* it's filthy, it's a mess; *(persona)* he's very much under the weather; **me da a.** it makes me (feel) sick; **¡qué a.!** how disgusting o revolting!

ascua *nf* live coal; *Fig* **en** o **sobre ascuas** on tenterhooks; *Fam* **arrimar el a. a su sardina** to look after number one

aseado, -a **1** *pp de* **asear**
   2 *adj* clean, tidy, neat

asear **1** *vt* to clean, tidy up
   2 asearse *vpr* to wash, get washed

asechanza *nf (conspiración)* scheme; *(trampa)* trap

asediar *vt* to besiege, lay siege to; *Fig* **a. con preguntas** to besiege with questions

asedio *nm* siege; *Fig* **el a. de los periodistas** the harassment by journalists

asegurado, -a **1** *pp de* **asegurar**
   2 *adj* (**a**) *Seg* insured (**b**) *(indudable)* secure; **el éxito está a.** it's bound to be a success

asegurador, -a *Seg* **1** *adj* insuring, insurance
   2 *nm,f* insurer

asegurar **1** *vt* (**a**) *Seg* to insure (**b**) *(garantizar)* to assure, guarantee; **le aseguro que ...** I can assure you that ...; **me han asegurado que llega hoy** I've been promised that it'll arrive today (**c**) *(sujetar) (puerta)* to secure; *(cerrar)* to close tightly
   2 asegurarse *vpr* to make sure; **a. de cerrar el gas** to make sure that the gas is turned off

asemejar **1** *vt* to make alike, make similar
   2 asemejarse *vpr* to be similar, look alike; **a. a** to look like, be like

asenso *nm* assent, consent; **dar a.** to believe

asentaderas *nfpl Fam* bottom *sing*, buttocks

asentado, -a 1 *pp de* **asentar**
   2 *adj* (**a**) *(situado)* placed, situated (**b**) *(firme)* firm, secure; **un edificio mal a.** a building with bad foundations (**c**) *(establecido)* established, settled

asentamiento *nm* (**a**) *Mil* emplacement (**b**) *(poblado)* settlement

asentar [3] **1** *vt* (**a**) *(situar)* to place, situate, site; **a. un campamento** to set up camp; **a. los cimientos** to lay the foundations (**b**) *(asegurar)* to secure, make firm; **no está bien asentado** it's not steady
   2 asentarse *vpr* (**a**) *(situarse)* to be situated (**b**) *(persona)* to settle down, establish oneself (**c**) *(tierra)* to sink

asentimiento *nm* assent, consent

asentir [62] *vi* to assent, agree; **a. con la cabeza** to nod

aseo *nm* (**a**) *(acción)* cleaning, tidying up (**b**) *(limpieza)* cleanliness, tidiness □ **a. personal** personal cleanliness (**c**) *Esp* **(cuarto de) a.** bathroom; **aseos** *Br* toilets, *US* restroom

asepsia *nf* (**a**) *Med* asepsis (**b**) *Fig (frialdad)* coldness, coolness

aséptico, -a *adj* (**a**) *Med* aseptic (**b**) *Fig (frío)* cold, cool

asequible *adj* obtainable, accessible; **a. a todos** *(de comprar)* within everybody's reach; *(de entender)* easy to understand

aserción *nf* assertion, statement

aserradero *nm* sawmill

aserrado, -a 1 *pp de* **aserrar**
   2 *adj* serrated
   3 *nm* sawing

aserrar [3] *vt* to saw (up)

aserrín *nm* sawdust

aserruchar *vt CSur* to saw (up)

aserto *nm* assertion, statement

asesinar *vt* to murder, kill; *Pol (cometer magnicidio)* to assassinate

asesinato *nm* murder, killing; *(magnicidio)* assassination

asesino, -a 1 *adj* murderous; **el arma asesina** the murder weapon; *Fig* **una mirada asesina** a murderous look
   2 *nm,f* killer; *(hombre)* murderer; *(mujer)* murderess

asesor, -a 1 *adj* advisory
   2 *nm,f* adviser, advisor, consultant □ **a. financiero** financial adviser; **a. fiscal** tax advisor; **a. de imagen** image consultant

asesoramiento *nm* (**a**) *(acción)* advising (**b**) *(consejo)* advice

asesorar **1** *vt* (**a**) *(gen)* to advise, give (professional) advice to (**b**) *Com* to act as consultant to
   2 asesorarse *vpr* to consult; **asesórate bien antes de actuar** take good advice before you do anything

asesoría *nf* (**a**) *(cargo)* consultancy, consultantship (**b**) *(oficina)* consultant's office □ **a. fiscal** tax consultancy

asestar *vt* to deal; **a. un golpe a algn** to hit sb; **a. un puñetazo** to punch; **a. una patada** to kick; **a. una puñalada** to stab

aseveración *nf* asseveration, assertion

aseverar *vt* to asseverate, assert

asexuado, -a *adj*, **asexual** *adj* asexual

asfaltado, -a 1 *pp de* **asfaltar**
   2 *adj* asphalted

3 *nm* (**a**) *(acción)* asphalting (**b**) *(pavimento)* asphalted (road) surface, Tarmac

asfaltar *vt* to asphalt

asfáltico, -a *adj* containing asphalt

asfalto *nm* asphalt

asfixia *nf Med* suffocation, asphyxiation, asphyxia

asfixiado, -a 1 *pp de* **asfixiar**
2 *adj Fam* broke; **estar a.** to be broke

asfixiante *adj* suffocating, asphyxiating; **hace un calor a.** it's stifling

asfixiar 1 *vt* (**a**) *(ahogar)* to suffocate, asphyxiate (**b**) *(agobiar)* to stifle (**c**) *(económicamente)* to cripple
2 asfixiarse *vpr* to suffocate, asphyxiate; **¡aquí me asfixio!** *(de calor)* I'm suffocating in here!

asgo *indic pres véase* **asir**

así 1 *adv* (**a**) *(de este modo)* this way, like this; *(de ese modo)* that way, like that; **a las seis o a.** around six o'clock; **algo a.** something like this *o* that, something along these *o* those lines; **a. a.** so-so; **a. de grande/alto** this big/tall; **a. es** that's right; **a. es la vida** such is life; **a. fue** that's how it was; **a. se lo dije** I told him so; **¿cómo a.?** how come?; **diez años o a.** ten years more or less; **¿no es a.?** isn't that so *o* right?; **ponlo a.** put it this way; **y a. todo** and the same applies to all the rest; *Fam* **lo mismo le da a. que asá** she couldn't care less (**b**) *(tanto como)* as; **a. en casa como en la oficina** the same at home as in the office; **no puedo decidirlo a. como a.** I can't decide just like that (**c**) *(aunque)* **a. tenga que hacerlo yo mismo** even if I have to do it myself (**d**) *(a pesar de todo)* **y aun a.** and despite that; **y a. y todo no lo entiendo** even now I can't understand it (**e**) *(por tanto, de modo que)* **a. pues** therefore; **a. que no pude ir** that's why I couldn't go; *Fam* **¿a. que te has casado?** so you've got married, have you? (**f**) *(tan pronto como)* **a. que lo sepas llámame** as soon as you know give me a ring
2 *adj* **un marido a. es una joya** a husband like that is a gem

Asia *n* Asia ❑ **A. Menor** Asia Minor

asiático, -a *adj & nm,f* Asian

asidero *nm* (**a**) *(asa)* handle (**b**) *Fig (pretexto)* pretext, excuse

asiduidad *nf* assiduity; **con a.** frequently, regularly

asiduo, -a *adj* assiduous, regular

asiento *nm* (**a**) *(silla, butaca)* seat; **a. trasero** rear *o* back seat; **tome a.** take a seat (**b**) *(de vasija)* bottom (**c**) *(poso)* sediment (**d**) *Fin* entry, registry (**e**) *Com (contrato)* trading contract (**f**) *Arquit* settling

asignación *nf* (**a**) *(atribución)* assignment, allocation (**b**) *(nombramiento)* appointment, assignment (**c**) *(paga)* allocation, allowance; *(sueldo)* wage, salary

asignar *vt* (**a**) *(atribuir)* to assign, allot, allocate (**b**) *(nombrar)* to assign, appoint

asignatario, -a *nm,f Am Jur* beneficiary

asignatura *nf Educ* subject; **a. pendiente** failed subject

asilado, -a *nm,f* (**a**) *(pobre)* person who lives in a charity home (**b**) *Pol (refugiado)* refugee

asilar *vt* (**a**) *(recoger)* to take in, give shelter to (**b**) *Pol (dar refugio)* to grant *o* give political asylum to

asilo *nm* (**a**) *(hospicio)* home ❑ **a. de ancianos** old people's home (**b**) *Fig (protección)* protection, help, assistance; **dar a.** to shelter ❑ *Pol* **a. político** political asylum

asimetría *nf* asymmetry

asimétrico, -a *adj* asymmetrical, asymmetric

asimiento *nm* (**a**) *(acción)* grasping, seizing, holding (**b**) *(efecto)* attachment

asimilable *adj* assimilable

asimilación *nf* assimilation

asimilar 1 *vt* to assimilate
2 asimilarse *vpr* to assimilate, be assimilated

asimismo *adv* (**a**) *(también)* also, as well (**b**) *(de esta manera)* likewise; *(además)* moreover

asíncrono, -a *adj Inform* asynchronous

asir [9] **1** *vt (agarrar)* to take, grasp, seize, take hold of
2 *vi Bot (echar raíces)* to take root
3 asirse *vpr (agarrarse)* to get hold of one another; *Fig* **a. a una idea** to cling to an idea

asirio, -a *adj & nm,f Hist* Assyrian

asistencia *nf* (**a**) *(presencia)* attendance; **con la a. de** in the presence of; **falta de a. al trabajo** absence from work (**b**) *(público)* audience, public; **hubo mucha a.** there was a large audience (**c**) *(ayuda)* assistance, help, aid; **con la a. de** with the help of ❑ **a. médica** medical attention; **a. sanitaria** health care; **a. social** social work; **a. técnica** technical assistance

asistencial *adj Med* healthcare; **servicios asistenciales** healthcare services

asistenta *nf Esp* charlady, cleaning lady

asistente 1 *adj* attending; **el público a.** the audience
2 *nmf* (**a**) *(ayudante)* assistant, helper ❑ **a. social** social worker (**b**) **asistentes** public *sing*; **los a. al acto** the audience, the public

asistido, -a 1 *pp de* **asistir**
2 *adj* assisted; **a. por ordenador** computer-aided

asistir 1 *vt* to assist, help; **le asistió el médico de cabecera** he was treated *o* attended by his general practitioner; *Fml* **le asiste la razón** he's right
2 *vi* (**a**) *(acudir)* to attend, be present; **lleva un mes sin a. a clase** he hasn't been to school for a month (**b**) *(servir)* to work as a servant

asma *nf Med* asthma

asmático, -a *Med* **1** *adj* asthmatic
2 *nm,f* asthmatic person, person suffering from asthma

asno *nm* (**a**) *Zool* donkey, ass (**b**) *Fam (persona)* ass, idiot

asociación *nf* association ❑ **a. de consumidores** consumer association; **a. de ideas** association of ideas; **a. de vecinos** residents' association

asociacionismo *nm* associationism

asociado, -a 1 *pp de* **asociar**
2 *adj* associated, associate
3 *nm,f* associate, partner

asocial *adj* asocial

asociar 1 *vt* (**a**) *(relacionar)* to associate, link, connect; **a. ideas** to associate ideas (**b**) *Com* to take into partnership
2 asociarse *vpr* (**a**) *(relacionarse)* to be associated; **se asocia con el alcohol** it is associated with alcohol (**b**) *Com* to become partners; **a. con algn** to become sb's partner

asociativo, -a *adj* associative

asocio *nm Col* association

asolación *nf* devastation, destruction, razing

asolador, -a *adj* devastating, destructive

asolamiento *nm* devastation, destruction, razing

asolar [63] *vt* to devastate, destroy, raze

asoleada *nf Andes Méx RP* **darse una a.** to get a bit of sunshine

asolear 1 *vt* to put in the sun
2 asolearse *vpr* (**a**) *Andes Méx RP (tomar el sol)* to sunbathe (**b**) *CAm Méx (sufrir una insolación)* to get sunstroke

asomar 1 *vt* to show, put out, stick out; **asoma la cabeza por la ventana** put your head out of the window
2 *vi (empezar)* to appear; **ya asoma el día** day is breaking

3 asomarse vpr to lean out; (balcón) to come out; **a. a la ventana** to lean out of the window

asombrar 1 vt (sorprender) to surprise, amaze, astonish
2 asombrarse vpr (sorprenderse) to be astonished; **a. de algo** to be amazed at sth

asombro nm surprise, amazement, astonishment

asombroso, -a adj surprising, amazing, astonishing

asomo nm sign, trace, hint; **sin el menor a. de interés** without any interest at all

asonada nf Mil putsch

asonancia nf Lit assonance

asonante adj Lit assonant

asordar vt to deafen

asorocharse vpr Andes (a) (por la altitid) to suffer from altitude sickness (b) (ruborizarse) to blush

aspa nf (a) (de molino) arm; (de ventilador) blade; (armazón) arms pl (b) (cruz) X-shaped cross; **en forma de a.** X-shaped (c) RP (asta) horn

aspar vt (a) (crucificar) to crucify (b) Fig (fastidiar) to annoy, pester (c) Fam **¡que me aspen si ...!** I'll be damned if ...!

aspaviento nm fuss; **hacer aspavientos** to gesticulate and wave one's arms about

aspecto nm (a) (apariencia) look, appearance; **¿qué a. tenía?** what did he look like?; **tener a. de** to look like; **tiene muy buen a.** (persona) he's looking very well; (cosa) it looks very good (b) (de un asunto) aspect, side; **bajo este a.** from this angle; **en todos los aspectos** in every respect

aspereza nf roughness, coarseness, asperity; Fig **limar asperezas** to smooth things over

asperjar vt to sprinkle; Rel to sprinkle with holy water

áspero, -a adj rough, coarse, asperous; Fig (carácter) surly

asperón nm sandstone

aspersión nf sprinkling □ **riego por a.** spraying

aspersor nm sprinkler

áspid nm Zool asp

aspidistra nf Bot aspidistra

aspillera nf Mil loophole

aspiración nf (a) (de aire) (por una persona) inhalation, breathing in; **a. de aire** intake of air (b) Ling aspiration (c) Téc sucking in (d) **aspiraciones** (pretensión) aspiration sing, strong desire sing; **tiene pocas a. profesionales** he has few professional ambitions

aspirado, -a 1 pp de **aspirar**
2 adj Ling aspirated
3 n Ling aspirate

aspirador, -a 1 adj sucking; **bomba aspiradora** suction pump
2 nm,f vacuum cleaner, Br Hoover®

aspirante 1 adj **bomba a.** suction pump
2 nmf (para puesto de trabajo) candidate, applicant

aspirar 1 vt (a) (respirar) to inhale, breath in (b) Ling (sonido) to aspirate (c) Téc (absorber) to suck in, draw in
2 vi Fig (desear) to aspire; **a. a ser famoso** to aspire after fame

aspirina nf aspirin

asquear 1 vt to disgust, revolt, make sick
2 asquearse vpr to be disgusted o revolted

asquerosidad nf filthy o revolting thing; **¡que a.!** how revolting!

asqueroso, -a 1 adj (a) (que da asco) disgusting, revolting (b) (malo) mean
2 nm,f (a) (que da asco) disgusting o revolting person (b) (mala persona) mean person

asta nf (a) (de bandera) staff, pole; **a media a.** at half-mast (b) (cuerno) horn (c) (palo de la lanza) haft; (pica) lance, pike

astado, -a 1 adj horned
2 nm Taur bull

astenia nf Med asthenia

asténico, -a adj & nm,f Med asthenic

asterisco nm asterisk

asteroide adj & nm asteroid

astigmático, -a Med **1** adj astigmatic
2 nm,f astigmatic

astigmatismo nm Med astigmatism

astil nm (a) (mango) handle (b) (de flecha) shaft (c) (de balanza) arm, beam

astilla nf splinter, chip; Fig **hacer astillas** to smash to smithereens; Prov **de tal palo, tal a.** like father, like son

astillar vt to splinter

astillero nm shipyard, dockyard

astilloso, -a adj brittle, easily splintered

astracán nm astrakhan

astrágalo nm (a) Anat astragalus (b) Arquit astragal

astral adj astral; Astrol **carta a.** birth chart, individual horoscope

astringencia nf astringency

astringente adj & nm astringent

astringir [24] vt to astringe, constrict

astro nm star; Literario **el a. rey** the sun

astrofísica nf astrophysics sing

astrolabio nm Astron astrolabe

astrología nf astrology

astrológico, -a adj astrological

astrólogo, -a nm,f astrologer

astronauta nmf astronaut

astronáutica nf astronautics sing

astronave nf spacecraft, spaceship

astronomía nf astronomy

astronómico, -a adj (a) (de los astros) astronomical, astronomic (b) Fig (elevado) astronomical

astrónomo, -a nm,f astronomer

astroso, -a adj (a) (andrajoso) shabby, ragged, untidy (b) (desdichado) unfortunate

astucia nf astuteness, cunning, shrewdness

asturiano, -a adj & nm,f, **astur** adj & nmf Asturian

Asturias n Asturias; **Príncipe de A.** ≃ Prince of Wales

astuto, -a adj astute, cunning, shrewd

asueto nm short holiday

asumir vt to assume, take upon oneself; **a. el poder** to assume control

asunceno, -a, asunceño, a 1 adj of o from Asunción
2 nm,f person from Asunción

Asunción n Asunción

asunción nf assumption, taking on

asunto nm (a) (tema) (general) subject; (específico) matter; (de obra, libro) theme; **a. de faldas** affair with a woman; **el a. es que ...** the thing is that ...; **no es a. mío** it is nothing to do with me; **no es a. tuyo** mind your own business; **y a. concluido** and let that be the end of the matter (b) **asuntos** Pol affairs; **A. Exteriores** Foreign Affairs

asustadizo, -a adj easily frightened o scared

asustar 1 vt to frighten, scare
2 asustarse vpr to be frightened, be scared; **ella se asusta por todo** she's frightened of everything

atacante 1 *adj* attacking, assailing
   2 *nmf* attacker, assailant

atacar [59] *vt* (**a**) *(acometer)* to attack, assault, assail (**b**) *(dañar)* to attack, affect, damage; **atacó la cosecha** it attacked the crops; **le atacó a los pulmones** it attacked his lungs; *Fig* **atacarle los nervios a algn** to get on sb's nerves (**c**) *(combatir)* **todos atacaron sus ideas** everyone attacked his ideas

atado, -a 1 *pp de* atar
   2 *adj* (**a**) *(ligado)* tied, bound; **a. a un árbol** tied to a tree (**b**) *Fig (tímido)* timid, shy
   3 *nm* (**a**) *(legajo)* bundle (**b**) *Arg (cajetilla)* packet

atadura *nf* (**a**) *(acción)* tying, binding, fastening (**b**) *(cuerda)* binding, string, cord (**c**) *Fig (impedimento)* tie, hindrance

atajar 1 *vi* to take a shortcut (**por** across *o* through)
   2 *vt* (**a**) *(entorpecer el paso)* to halt, stop; **a. un incendio** to check the spread of a fire; **a. un mal de raíz** to kill sth at the root; **a. una manifestación** to check a demonstration; **Eva me atajó cuando salía** Eva stopped me as I was leaving (**b**) *(interrumpir)* to interrupt, cut short; **atajaron al orador** they interrupted the speaker

atajo *nm* (**a**) *(camino corto, medio rápido)* shortcut; *Fig* **echar por un a.** to take a shortcut, take the easiest way out (**b**) *Esp (grupo)* bunch; **sois un a. de sinvergüenzas** you're a bunch of rotters

atalaya *nf (torre)* watchtower, lookout; *(mirador)* vantage point

atañer *vi* to concern, have to do with; **en lo que atañe a este asunto** as far as this subject is concerned, with regard to this subject; **eso a ti no te atañe** that has nothing to do with you

ataque *nm* (**a**) *(acometida)* attack; assault ❑ **a. aéreo** air raid (**b**) *Med* fit; *Fig* **un a. de celos/odio** a fit of jealousy/hatred ❑ **a. al corazón** heart attack; **a. de nervios** fit of hysterics; **a. de pánico** panic attack; **a. de tos** fit of coughing

atar 1 *vt* (**a**) *(ligar)* to tie, bind; **átale los zapatos** do his shoes up; **átalo bien** fasten it tight; **a. de pies y manos** to bind hand and foot; *Fig* **a. cabos** to put two and two together; *Fam* **estar loco de a.** to be as mad as a hatter (**b**) *Fig* to bind, tie down; **a. corto a algn** to keep a tight rein on sb; **una profesión que ata mucho** a profession that ties one down a lot
   2 atarse *vpr Fig* to get tied up

atarazana *nf* shipyard, dockyard

atardecer [46] **1** *v impers* to get *o* grow dark
   2 *nm* evening, dusk

atareado, -a 1 *pp de* atarear
   2 *adj* busy, occupied

atarear 1 *vt* to keep busy, assign a task to
   2 atarearse *vpr* to be busy, work hard

atarugar [38] **1** *vt Fam* (**a**) *(llenar)* to stuff, pack, cram; **a. a algn con comida** to stuff sb with food (**b**) *Fig (hacer callar)* to shut up
   2 atarugarse *vpr* (**a**) *Fig (avergonzarse)* to feel confused *o* embarrassed; *(cortarse)* to stop short, become tongue-tied (**b**) *Fig (atragantarse)* to choke

atascar [59] **1** *vt* (**a**) *(bloquear)* to block (up), obstruct; **a. una cañería** to clog up a pipe (**b**) *Fig (obstaculizar)* to hamper, hinder
   2 atascarse *vpr* (**a**) *(bloquearse)* to become obstructed, become blocked; **se ha atascado el fregadero** the sink is blocked (**b**) *(coche, motor)* to get jammed, get stuck (**c**) *Fig (estancarse)* to get tangled up, get bogged down

atasco *nm* (**a**) *(acción)* obstruction, blockage (**b**) *(de tráfico)* traffic jam

ataúd *nm* coffin

ataviar [32] **1** *vt* (**a**) *(adornar)* to deck, adorn (**b**) *(arreglar)* to dress up
   2 ataviarse *vpr (arreglarse)* to dress oneself up, attire oneself

atávico, -a *adj* atavistic

atavío *nm* (**a**) *(adorno)* adornment (**b**) *(vestido)* dress, attire

atavismo *nm* atavism

ateísmo *nm* atheism

atemorizar [14] **1** *vt* to frighten, scare
   2 atemorizarse *vpr* to be frightened, be scared

atemperar 1 *vt* (**a**) *(moderar)* to moderate, temper (**b**) *(adaptar)* to adjust, accommodate (**a** to)
   2 atemperarse *vpr* (**a**) *(moderarse)* to moderate oneself, restrain oneself (**b**) *(ajustarse)* to adjust oneself, accommodate oneself

atemporal *adj* timeless

Atenas *n* Athens

atenazado, -a 1 *pp de* atenazar
   2 *adj Fig* gripped, tormented; **a. por el miedo** seized by fear

atenazar [14] *vt* (**a**) *(sujetar)* to gnash, clench (**b**) *Fig* to torture, torment; **el remordimiento lo atenazaba** he was tormented by remorse

atención 1 *nf* (**a**) *(interés)* attention; **al principio no me llamó la a.** at first I didn't notice anything unusual; **'a., carretera en obras'** 'danger, roadworks ahead'; **llamar la a.** to attract attention; **llamar la a. a algn** to tell sb off; **prestar a.** to pay attention (**a** to) (**b**) *(detalle)* nice thought; **en a. a** as a sign of respect for; **ha sido una a. por su parte** it was terribly kind of him (**c**) **atenciones** attentions; **tener muchas a. con algn** to smother sb with attentions
   2 *interj (cuidado)* watch out!

atender [64] **1** *vt* (**a**) *(diente)* to attend to; *(consejo, advertencia)* to heed, listen to; *(máquina)* to service; *(niño, inválido)* to look after, care for (**b**) *(escuchar)* to attend to, pay attention to
   2 *vi* (**a**) **a. a** to attend to, pay attention to (**b**) **a. por** to answer to the name of

ateneo *nm* athenaeum, *US* atheneum

atenerse [65] *vpr.* **a. a** *(regla)* to abide by; *(promesa)* to stand by; **atente a las consecuencias** bear the consequences in mind; **no sabe a qué a.** he doesn't know where he stands

ateniense *adj & nmf* Athenian

atentado *nm* attack, assault; **a. contra la vida de algn** attempt on sb's life ❑ **a. terrorista** terrorist attack

atentamente *adv* (**a**) *(con atención, cortesía)* attentively (**b**) *(en carta)* **le saluda a.** yours sincerely *o* faithfully

atentar 1 *vi* **a.** *o* **contra** to commit a crime against; **a. contra la vida de algn** to make an attempt on sb's life
   2 *vt (delito)* to attempt, commit

atento, -a 1 *pp de* atender
   2 *adj* (**a**) *(pendiente)* attentive, observant; **estar a. a los riesgos** to be mindful *o* aware of the risks (**b**) *(amable)* polite, thoughtful, considerate; **es muy a.** he is very considerate; *(en carta)* **su atenta (carta)** your esteemed letter (**c**) *Fml* **a. a** in view of, considering

atenuación *nf* attenuation, lessening; *Jur* extenuation

atenuante 1 *adj* attenuating; *Jur (circunstancias)* extenuating
   2 *nm Jur* extenuating circumstance

atenuar [4] *vt* (**a**) *(disminuir, suavizar)* to diminish; *(dolor)* to ease, alleviate; *(sonido, luz)* to attenuate; *Jur* to extenuate (**b**) *(importancia)* to lessen, diminish

ateo, -a 1 *adj* atheistic
2 *nm,f* atheist

aterciopelado, -a *adj* velvet, velvety; *Fig* **voz aterciopelada** sweet voice

aterido, -a 1 *pp de* **aterirse**
2 *adj* stiff with cold, numb

aterirse *vpr* to be stiff with cold, be numb

aterrado, -a *adj* terror-stricken

aterrador, -a *adj* terrifying, frightful

aterramiento *nm* fear, terror

aterrar¹ 1 *vt* to terrify, frighten
2 aterrarse *vpr* to be terrified *o* frightened, panic

aterrar² [27] 1 *vt* **(a)** *(derribar)* to pull down, demolish **(b)** *(cubrir con tierra)* to cover with earth
2 *vi Av* to land; *Náut* to stand inshore

aterrizaje *nm Av* landing ◻ **a. forzoso** forced landing; **a. violento** crash landing

aterrizar [14] *vi* **(a)** *Av* to land **(b)** *Fig* to show up, arrive

aterrorizar [14] 1 *vt* to terrify; *Mil Pol* to terrorize
2 aterrorizarse *vpr* to be terrified

atesoramiento *nm* hoarding, accumulation, storing up

atesorar *vt* **(a)** *(acumular)* to hoard, accumulate, store up **(b)** *Fig (cualidades, defectos)* to possess

atestación *nf* attestation, testimony

atestado¹ *nm Jur* affidavit, statement; **atestados** testimonials

atestado, -a² 1 *pp de* **atestar²**
2 *adj (abarrotado)* packed, crammed; **estaba a. de gente** it was full of people

atestar¹ *vt Jur (testificar)* to testify to

atestar² [27] 1 *vt (abarrotar)* to pack, cram, stuff **(de** with)
2 atestarse *vpr (de comida)* to stuff oneself

atestiguación *nf* attestation, testimony

atestiguar [11] *vt* **(a)** *Jur (testificar)* to testify to, bear witness to, give evidence of **(b)** *Fig* to vouch for

atezado, -a *adj* **(a)** *(por el sol)* tanned **(b)** *(negro)* black, blackened

atiborrar 1 *vt (abarrotar)* to fill, pack, stuff **(de** with)
2 atiborrarse *vpr Fam (de comida)* to stuff oneself

ático *nm (vivienda)* = attic *Br* flat *o US* apartment, usually with a roof terrace; *(desván)* attic

atigrado, -a *adj (tigre)* striped; *(gato)* tabby

atildado, -a 1 *pp de* **atildar**
2 *adj (elegante)* smart, neat, spruce

atildamiento *nm* **(a)** *(esmero)* elegance, tidiness **(b)** *Fig (censura)* censure

atildar 1 *vt* **(a)** *Tip* to mark with a tilde **(b)** *Fig (asear)* to tidy, clean up **(c)** *Fig (censurar)* to criticize, censure, find fault with
2 atildarse *vpr (asearse)* to titivate oneself, spruce oneself up

atinadamente *adv* correctly, sensibly; **según dijo a. as** he rightly said

atinado, -a 1 *pp de* **atinar**
2 *adj (correcto)* accurate, correct; *(pertinente)* pertinent; *(persona)* sensible; **una decisión a.** a wise decision

atinar *vi (acertar)* to guess right, be right, do the right thing; **a. a hacer algo** to succeed in doing sth; **a. al blanco** to hit the target; **atinó con la solución** he found the solution

atingencia *nf Arg CAm Chile Méx (relación)* connection, relation

atípico, -a *adj* atypical

atiplado, -a 1 *pp de* **atiplar**
2 *adj* high-pitched

atiplar 1 *vt (agudizar)* to raise the pitch of
2 atiplarse *vpr (voz)* to go squeaky

atisbar *vt* **(a)** *(observar)* to spy on, observe, watch **(b)** *Fig (vislumbrar)* to make out

atisbo *nm* **(a)** *(acción)* spying, watching **(b)** *Fig (indicios)* slight sign, inkling; **no hay el menor a. de esperanza** there's not the slightest hope

atizador *nm* poker

atizar [14] 1 *vt (fuego)* to poke, stoke; *(vela)* to snuff
2 *Fig (rebelión)* to stir up; *(pasiones)* to rouse, excite
3 atizarse *vpr Esp Fam (comer, beber)* to knock back; **se atizó toda una botella de vino** he knocked back a whole bottle of wine

atlántico, -a 1 *adj* Atlantic
2 *nm* **el (océano) A.** the Atlantic (Ocean)

atlas *nm inv* atlas; **los (montes) A.** the Atlas Mountains

atleta *nmf* athlete

atlético, -a *adj* athletic

atletismo *nm* athletics *sing*

atmósfera *nf* **(a)** *(capa gaseosa)* atmosphere **(b)** *Fig* atmosphere, sphere of influence

atmosférico, -a *adj* atmospheric, atmospherical

atole *nm*, **atol** *nm* **(a)** *CAm Méx (con maíz)* = thick hot drink made of corn meal **(b)** *Ven (con arroz, cebada)* = thick drink made with boiled rice, barley or sago and variously flavoured

atolladero *nm* **(a)** *(lugar fangoso)* morass, quagmire **(b)** *Fig (aprieto)* fix, jam, scrape; **estar en un a.** to be in a jam, tight spot; **sacar a algn de un a.** to get sb out of a fix; **salir del a.** to get out of a jam

atollarse *vpr* **(a)** *(atascarse)* to get stuck in the mud, get bogged down **(b)** *Fig (atrancarse)* to get into a fix *o* scrape

atolón *nm Geog* atoll

atolondrado, -a 1 *pp de* **atolondrar**
2 *adj* **(a)** *(desatinado)* scatterbrained, reckless, silly **(b)** *(aturdido)* stunned, bewildered

atolondramiento *nm* **(a)** *(desatino)* recklessness, silliness **(b)** *(aturdimiento)* confusion, bewilderment

atolondrar 1 *vt* to confuse, stun, bewilder
2 atolondrarse *vpr* to be confused, stunned, bewildered

atómico, -a *adj* atomic

atomización *nf* atomization, spraying

atomizador *nm* atomizer, spray

atomizar [14] *vt* to atomize, spray

átomo *nm* **(a)** *Quím* atom **(b)** *Fig (pizca)* atom, particle, speck; **ni un a. de** not a trace of

atonal *adj* atonal

atonalidad *nf Mús* atonality

atonía *nf (de mercado, economía)* sluggishness

atónito, -a *adj* amazed, astonished, nonplussed

átono, -a *adj* atonic, unstressed

atontadamente *adv* **(a)** *(tontamente)* foolishly, recklessly **(b)** *(de manera confusa)* in a stunned *o* bewildered way

atontado, -a 1 *pp de* **atontar**
2 *adj* **(a)** *(tonto)* silly, foolish **(b)** *(aturdido)* stunned, bewildered, amazed

atontamiento *nm* bewilderment

atontar 1 *vt (aturdir)* to stun, confuse, bewilder
2 atontarse *vpr (aturdirse)* to be *o* get confused *o* mixed-up *o* bewildered

atorar 1 *vt (embarrancar)* to obstruct, block, choke
2 atorarse *vpr (embarrancarse)* to get stuck in the mud

atormentar 1 *vt* (**a**) *(torturar)* to torture (**b**) *Fig (importunar)* to torment, harass; *(tentar)* to tantalize
  2 atormentarse *vpr (sufrir)* to torment oneself, suffer agonies

atornillar *vt* to screw on o up o down o together

atorrante *RP* **1** *adj* lazy
  2 *nmf* layabout

atortolarse *vpr* to fall in love

atosigador, -a 1 *adj* (**a**) *(venenoso)* poisonous (**b**) *Fig (apremio)* harassing, pressing
  2 *nm,f* (**a**) *(envenenador)* poisoner (**b**) *Fig (opresor)* oppressor, tormentor

atosigamiento *nm* (**a**) *(envenenamiento)* poisoning (**b**) *Fig (apremio)* harassment

atosigar [38] *vt* (**a**) *(envenenar)* to poison (**b**) *(preocupar)* to worry (**c**) *Fig (apremiar)* to harass, pester

atrabancar [59] **1** *vt* to rush o hurry over
  2 atrabancarse *vpr* to get into a jam

atrabiliario, -a 1 *adj* bad-tempered, moody
  2 *nm,f* bad-tempered person, moody person

atracadero *nf Náut* landing place, wharf, berth

atracador, -a *nm,f (de banco)* (bank) robber; *(en la calle)* attacker, mugger

atracar [59] **1** *vt* (**a**) *(robar)* to hold up, rob (**b**) *Fam (de comida)* to stuff, gorge
  2 *vi Náut* to come alongside, tie up
  3 atracarse *vpr (de comida)* to stuff oneself (**de** with), gorge oneself (**de** on)

atracción *nf* (**a**) *(física)* attraction (**b**) **atracciones** attractions, show *sing* ❑ **parque de a.** funfair

atraco *nm* hold-up, robbery ❑ *Jur* **a. a mano armada** armed robbery

atracón *nm Fam* (**a**) *(de comida)* binge, blowout; **darse un a. de algo** *(de comida)* to stuff one's face with sth; *(de películas, televisión)* to overdose on sth (**b**) *Ven (embotellamiento)* traffic jam

atractivamente *adv* attractively

atractivo, -a 1 *adj* attractive, charming, appealing,
  2 *nm* attraction, charm, appeal

atraer [66] *vt* (**a**) *(gen)* to attract; *(imaginación)* to appeal to; *(adhesión)* to win (**b**) *(cautivar)* to charm, captivate

atragantarse *vpr* to choke (**con** on), swallow the wrong way; **a. con un cacahuete** to choke on a peanut; *Fig* **ese chico se me atraganta** I can't stand that boy

atraigo *indic pres véase* **atraer**

atrancar [59] **1** *vt (puerta)* to bar, bolt
  2 *vi Fam (persona)* to stride along; *(en la lectura)* to read hastily
  3 atrancarse *vpr (encerrarse)* to lock oneself in

atrapar *vt* to seize, capture, catch

atraque *nm Náut* mooring place, berth; *(de nave espacial)* link-up

atrás 1 *adv* (**a**) *(lugar)* at the back, behind; **cuenta a.** countdown; **estar a.** to be behind o at the back; **ir hacia a.** to go backwards; **puerta de a.** back o rear door; *Fig* **volverse a.** to change one's mind (**b**) *(tiempo)* previously, in the past, ago; **un año a.** a year ago; **venir de muy a.** to go o date back a long time
  2 *interj* get back!

atrasado, -a 1 *pp de* **atrasar**
  2 *adj* (**a**) *(en el tiempo)* delayed; *(pago)* overdue; *(reloj)* slow; **andar a.** to be slow; *Prensa* **número a.** back number (**b**) *(país)* backward, underdeveloped; *(alumno)* backward

atrasar 1 *vt* to delay; *(reloj)* to put back
  2 *vi (reloj)* to lose, be slow

3 atrasarse *vpr* (**a**) *(demorarse)* to be late *Fig* **a. con los pagos** to fall into arrears (**b**) *(quedarse atrás)* to fall behind

atraso *nm* (**a**) *(demora)* delay; *(de reloj)* slowness; **llegar con media hora de a.** to arrive half an hour late (**b**) *(de país)* backwardness (**c**) **atrasos** *Fin* arrears

atravesado, -a 1 *pp de* **atravesar**
  2 *adj* (**a**) *(persona)* cross-eyed, squinting (**b**) *(animal)* mongrel, crossbred (**c**) *Fig (mal intencionado)* wicked, difficult, bloody-minded; **me tiene a.** he can't stand me

atravesar [3] **1** *vt* (**a**) *(cruzar)* to cross, cross over, go across, go over, pass through; *Fig* **a. una mala racha** to go through a bad patch (**b**) *(bala, navaja)* to pierce, go through (**c**) *(puente)* to cross, span, bridge (**d**) *(objeto)* to lay across, put across, put crosswise
  2 atravesarse *vpr* (**a**) *(estar atravesado)* to be across, be in the way (**b**) *Fig* to interrupt, butt in (**c**) *Fig (inmiscuirse)* to interfere, meddle (**d**) *Fig* **se me ha atravesado la vecina** I can't stand my neighbour

atrayente *adj* attractive

atreverse *vpr* to dare, venture; **a. a hacer algo** to dare to do sth; **a. con algn** to be cheeky o insolent to sb; **a. con algo** to take sth on; **¿te atreves?** are you game?

atrevido, -a 1 *pp de* **atreverse**
  2 *adj* (**a**) *(osado)* daring, bold (**b**) *(insolente)* insolent, impudent (**c**) *(indecoroso)* daring, risqué

atrevimiento *nm* (**a**) *(actitud)* daring, audacity (**b**) *(insolencia)* insolence, impudence, effrontery

atrezo *nm Teat Cin* props *pl*

atribución *nf* (**a**) *(acción)* attribution (**b**) *(poder)* power, authority

atribuible *adj* attributable

atribuir [34] **1** *vt* to attribute, ascribe
  2 atribuirse *vpr (poderes)* to assume

atribular 1 *vt* to afflict, distress, grieve
  2 atribularse *vpr* to suffer, be distressed, be grieved

atributivo, -a *adj* attributive

atributo *nm* attribute

atril *nm* lectern, bookrest; *Mús* music stand

atrincheramiento *nm* entrenchment

atrincherar 1 *vt* to entrench, dig a trench in o around
  2 atrincherarse *vpr* to entrench oneself

atrio *nm Hist* atrium, portico; *Arquit* entrance hall, porch

atrocidad *nf* (**a**) *(barbaridad)* atrocity, outrage (**b**) *(disparate)* silly remark, foolish thing

atrofia *nf Med* atrophy

atrofiar 1 *vt* (**a**) *(músculo, función orgánica)* to atrophy (**b**) *(deteriorar)* to weaken
  2 atrofiarse *vpr* (**a**) *(músculo, función orgánica)* to atrophy (**b**) *(deteriorarse)* to deteriorate, become atrophied

atronador, -a *adj* thundering, deafening

atronamiento *nm* (**a**) *(ruido)* thundering (**b**) *(aturdimiento)* daze, stunned state (**c**) *Fig (confusión)* bewilderment, confusion

atronar [63] *vt* (**a**) *(ensordecer)* to deafen (**b**) *(aturdir)* to stun, daze (**c**) *Fig (confundir)* to bewilder, confuse

atropellado, -a 1 *pp de* **atropellar**
  2 *adj* (**a**) *(persona)* hasty, impetuous, rash (**b**) *(comportamiento)* abrupt, brusque

atropellar 1 *vt* (**a**) *(sujeto: vehículo)* to run over; **lo atropelló un coche** he was knocked down o run over by a car (**b**) *Fig* to rush through, hurry over; *(sentimientos)* to outrage, hurt; *(derechos)* to disregard; *(inferior)* to bully, oppress
  2 *vi* **a. por** *(abrirse camino)* to push one's way through; *Fig (abusar)* to ride roughshod over

3 atropellarse *vpr Fig* to speak *o* act hastily, rush in
atropello *nm* (**a**) *(por vehículo)* running over (**b**) *Fig (abuso)* abuse, outrage
atroz *adj* (**a**) *(bárbaro)* atrocious, outrageous (**b**) *Fam (enorme)* enormous, huge, tremendous
atrozmente *adv* (**a**) *(cruelmente)* atrociously, outrageously (**b**) *Fam (como intensificador)* dreadfully, tremendously
ATS *nmf Esp Med (abrev de* **ayudante técnico sanitario**) qualified nurse
atte. *(abrev de* **atentamente**) Yours faithfully/sincerely
atuendo *nm* dress, attire
atufar 1 *vt Fig (irritar)* to vex, irritate
2 *vi (oler mal)* to stink
3 atufarse *vpr* (**a**) *(vino)* to turn sour (**b**) *Fig (enfadarse)* to get angry *o* annoyed (**c**) *Andes (aturdirse)* to become dazed *o* confused; **se atufó por los gases** he was overcome by the fumes
atún *nm (pez)* tunny, tuna
atunero, -a 1 *adj* tuna
2 *nm* tuna *o* tunny fisherman
aturdido, -a 1 *pp de* **aturdir**
2 *adj* (**a**) *(confundido)* stunned, dazed (**b**) *(atolondrado)* harebrained, reckless
aturdimiento *nm* (**a**) *(confusión)* confusion, bewilderment (**b**) *(atolondramiento)* thoughtlessness, recklessness
aturdir 1 *vt* (**a**) *(por un golpe)* to stun, daze; *(por un ruido)* to deafen; *(por una droga)* to stupefy (**b**) *Fig (atolondrar)* to stun, dumbfound; *(confundir)* to bewilder, confuse
2 aturdirse *vpr* (**a**) *(por golpe, noticia)* to be stunned (**b**) *Fig (atolondrarse)* to become confused *o* bewildered
aturrullar *Fam* **1** *vt (aturdir)* to confuse, bewilder
2 aturrullarse *vpr* to get confused *o* bewildered
atusar 1 *vt (pelo) (cortar)* to trim; *(peinar)* to comb, smooth down
2 atusarse *vpr* to overdress
audacia *nf* audacity, boldness, daring
audaz *adj* audacious, bold, daring
audible *adj* audible
audición *nf* (**a**) *(acción)* hearing; *Rad TV* reception (**b**) *Teat (prueba)* audition; **le hicieron una a.** they gave him an audition (**c**) *Mús (concierto)* concert
audiencia *nf* (**a**) *(recepción)* audience, hearing; *(entrevista)* formal interview (**b**) *Jur (tribunal)* high court (**c**) *(público)* audience
audífono *nm* hearing aid, deaf aid
audímetro *nm TV* audiometer, audience-monitoring device
audiometría *nf* audiometry
audiovisual *adj* audio-visual
auditar *vt* to audit
auditivo, -a 1 *adj* auditory; ear
2 *nm (auricular)* earpiece, receiver
auditor, -a *nm,f Fin* auditor
auditoría *nf* (**a**) *(proceso)* audit, auditing (**b**) *(empleo)* auditorship ☐ **a. externa/interna** external/internal audit
auditorio *nm* (**a**) *(público)* audience (**b**) *(sala)* auditorium, hall
auge *nm* (**a**) *(punto culminante)* peak, summit; *Com* boom, upsurge, upturn; *Fig* **estar en a.** to be thriving *o* booming (**b**) *Astron* apogee
auguración *nf* augury
augural *adj* augural

augurar *vt* to augur
augurio *nm* omen, sign
augusto, -a *adj* august, magnificent, majestic
aula *nf Educ* classroom; *Univ* lecture room ☐ **a. magna** great hall
aullador, -a *adj* howling, yelling
aullar [4] *vi* to howl, yell
aullido *nm* howl, yell
aumentar 1 *vt* to augment, increase, add to; *(precios)* to put up; *(producción)* to step up; *Fot* to enlarge; *Ópt* to magnify; *Rad (sonido)* to amplify
2 aumentarse *vpr* to increase, be on the increase; *(precios)* to go up, rise; *(valor)* to appreciate
aumentativo, -a *adj* augmentative
aumento *nm* increase, growth; *Fot* enlargement; *Ópt* magnification; *Rad* amplification; **a. de precios** rise in prices; **ir en a.** to be on the increase
aun *adv* even; **a. así** even so, even then; **a. cuando** even though; **a. más** even more
aún *adv* still, yet; **a. está aquí** he's still here; **ella no ha venido a.** she hasn't come yet
aunar [4] **1** *vt* to unite, join, combine
2 aunarse *vpr* to unite, combine
aunque *conj* although, though; *(enfático)* even if, even though; **a. no vengas** even if you don't come; **es severo a. justo** he's strict but fair
aúpa *interj Esp* up!, get up!
au pair [o'per] (*pl* **au pairs**) *nf* au pair
aupar [4] *vt* (**a**) *(levantar)* to help up (**b**) *Fig (alabar)* to praise
aura *nf* (**a**) *Literario (brisa)* gentle breeze (**b**) *Fig (aplauso)* applause, acclamation (**c**) *(halo)* aura
áureo, -a *adj* golden
aureola *nf* aureole, halo
aurícula *nf* auricle
auricular 1 *adj* auricular, of the ear
2 *nm* (**a**) *(dedo)* little finger (**b**) *Tel* earpiece, receiver (**c**) **auriculares** earphones, headphones
aurífero *adj* gold-bearing
aurora *nf* daybreak, dawn ☐ **a. boreal** *o* **borealis** aurora borealis, northern lights
auscultación *nf Med* sounding, auscultation
auscultar *vt Med* to sound (with a stethoscope)
ausencia *nf* absence
ausentarse *vpr* (**a**) *(faltar)* to absent oneself (**b**) *(irse)* to disappear, go missing
ausente 1 *adj* (**a**) *(no presente)* absent (**b**) *(distraído)* lost in thought
2 *nmf* (**a**) *(no presente)* absentee (**b**) *Jur* missing person
ausentismo *nm* absenteeism
auspiciar *vt (apoyar)* to back
auspicio *nm* auspice
austeridad *nf* (**a**) *(sobriedad)* austerity (**b**) *(severidad)* severity
austero, -a *adj* (**a**) *(sobrio)* austere (**b**) *(severo)* severe, stern
austral *adj* south, southern
Australia *n* Australia
australiano, -a *adj & nm,f* Australian
Austria *n* Austria
austríaco, -a *adj & nm,f*, **austriaco, -a** *adj & nm,f* Austrian
austro *nm Meteor* south wind

autarquía *nf Econ* autarky

autárquico, -a *adj* (**a**) *Econ* autarkic, self-sufficient (**b**) *Pol* autarchical

autenticación *nf* authentication; *(legalización)* legalization

autenticar [59] *vt* to authenticate; *(legalizar)* to authorize, legalize

autenticidad *nf* authenticity

auténtico, -a *adj* authentic, genuine

autentificar [59] *vt* to authenticate

autillo *nm Orn* scops owl

autismo *nm* autism

autista *nmf* autistic person

autístico, -a *adj* autistic

auto¹ *nm esp CSur* car

auto² *nm Jur* decree, writ; *(pleito)* **autos** papers, documents; *Fam* **estar en autos** to be in the know

autoabastecerse *vpr* to be self-sufficient (**de** in)

autoabastecimiento *nm* self-sufficiency

autoadhesivo, -a *adj* self-adhesive

autoafirmación *nf* assertiveness

autoalimentación *nf Inform* automatic paper feed

autoanálisis *nm* self-analysis

autoaprendizaje *nm* self-directed learning; **un libro de a.** a teach-yourself book

autoayuda *nf* self-help

autobiografía *nf* autobiography

autobiográfico, -a *adj* autobiographical

autobomba *nf* fire engine

autobombo *nm Fam* self-praise, blowing one's own trumpet

autobronceador *nm* self-tanning cream

autobús *nm* bus

autocamión *nm* truck, *Br* lorry

autocar *nm Esp Aut* bus, *Br* coach

autocensura *nf* self-censorship

autoclave *nf* (**a**) *Med* autoclave, sterilizer (**b**) *Culin* pressure cooker

autocomplacencia *nf* self-satisfaction

autocomplaciente *adj* self-satisfied

autocontrol *nm* self-control

autocracia *nf Pol* autocracy

autocrático, -a *adj Pol* autocratic

autocrítica *nf* self-criticism

autocrítico, -a *adj* self-critical

autóctono, -a *adj* indigenous, autochthonous

autodefensa *nf* self-defence, *US* self-defense

autodestrucción *nf* self-destruction

autodestruirse *vpr* to self-destruct

autodeterminación *nf Pol* self-determination

autodiagnóstico *nm Inform* self-test

autodidacta **1** *adj* self-taught
2 *nmf* self-taught person

autodirigido, -a *adj* guided

autodisciplina *nf* self-discipline

autodominio *nm* self-control

autoedición *nf Inform* desktop publishing

autoempleo *nm* self-employment

autoescuela *nf* driving school, school of motoring

autoestima *nf* self-esteem

autoestop *nm véase* **autostop**

autoestopista *nmf véase* **autostopista**

autofinanciación *nf Fin* self-financing

autogestión *nf* self-management

autogestionar **1** *vt* **autogestionan sus fondos** they manage their own finances
2 autogestionarse *vpr* (**a**) *(empresa)* to manage itself (**b**) *(región, país)* to govern itself

autogiro *nm Av* autogyro, helicopter

autogobierno *nm Pol* self-government

autógrafo, -a 1 *adj* autographic
2 *nm* autograph

autoinculparse *vpr* **a. de algo** to incriminate oneself of sth

autoinmune *adj Med* autoimmune

autómata *nm* automaton

automaticidad *nf* automaticity

automático, -a *adj* automatic

automatismo *nm* automatism

automatización *nf* automation

automatizar [14] *vt* to automate

automedicarse [59] *vpr* to self-administer medicine

automoción *nf (sector)* car industry

automotor, -a 1 *adj* self-propelled
2 *nm Ferroc* diesel train

automóvil *nm* car, *US* automobile

automovilismo *nm* motoring

automovilista *nmf* motorist

automovilístico, -a *adj* car; **accidente a.** car accident

autonomía *nf* autonomy, home rule

autonómico, -a *adj* autonomous, self-governing

autonomismo *nm Pol* autonomy movement

autonomista *adj & nmf Pol* autonomist

autónomo, -a *adj* autonomous, free

autopista *nf Br* motorway, *US* freeway **a. de peaje,** *Méx* **a. de cuota** *Br* toll motorway, *US* turnpike

autoproclamarse *vpr* to proclaim oneself

autopropulsado, -a *adj* self-propelled

autopropulsión *nf* self-propulsion

autopsia *nf* (**a**) *Med* autopsy, post mortem (**b**) *Fig* critical dissection

autor, -a *nm,f (gen)* writer; *(hombre)* author; *(mujer)* authoress; *Teat* manager; *(de crimen)* perpetrator

autoría *nf (de obra)* authorship; *(de crimen)* perpetration

autoridad *nf* authority

autoritariamente *adv* in an authoritarian way, dictatorially

autoritario, -a *adj* authoritarian

autoritarismo *nm* authoritarianism

autorización *nf* authorization

autorizado, -a 1 *pp de* **autorizar**
2 *adj* authoritative, official

autorizar [14] *vt* (**a**) *(dar permiso a)* to allow; *(en situaciones oficiales)* to authorize; *Jur* to legalize (**b**) *(aprobar)* to approve, give authority to

autorradio *nm o nf* car radio

autorretrato *nm* self-portrait

autoservicio *nm* (**a**) *(restaurante)* self-service restaurant (**b**) *(tienda)* supermarket

autostop *nm* hitch-hiking; **hacer a.** to hitch-hike

autostopista *nmf* hitch-hiker

autosuficiencia *nf* self-sufficiency

autosuficiente *adj* self-sufficient

autosugestión *nf* autosuggestion

autosugestionarse *vpr* to convince oneself (**de** of)

autovía *nf Br* dual carriageway, *US* divided highway

auxiliador, -a 1 *adj* helping
  2 *nm,f* helper

auxiliar 1 *adj & nmf* auxiliary, assistant ❑ **a. administrativo** administrative assistant; **a. de vuelo** flight attendant
  2 *vt* to help, assist; *(país)* to bring aid to; *(moribundo)* to attend

auxilio *nm* help, aid, assistance, relief ❑ **primeros auxilios** first aid *sing*

Av., Avda. *(abrev de* **Avenida)** Ave

a/v *(abrev de* **a vista)** at o on sight

aval *nm Com Fin* endorsement, guarantee ❑ **a. bancario** bank guarantee

avalancha *nf* avalanche

avalar *vt Com* to guarantee, endorse

avalista *nmf Com* guarantor

avance *nm* (**a**) *(acción)* advance (**b**) *Fin* advance payment; *Com (balance)* balancing; *(presupuesto)* estimate (**c**) *Cin* trailer ❑ *TV* **a. informativo** news preview, *US* news brief

avante *adv Náut* ahead, forward

avanzada *nf Mil* advance guard

avanzadilla *nf* advance party; *Mil* advance patrol

avanzado, -a 1 *pp de* **avanzar**
  2 *adj* advanced; **de avanzada edad** advanced in years

avanzar [14] **1** *vt* to advance, move forward; *Fin (dinero)* to advance; *(propuesta)* to put forward
  2 *vi* (**a**) *(moverse)* to advance, go forward (**b**) *(noche, invierno)* to draw in

avaricia *nf* avarice, meanness, miserliness; *Fam* **con a.** extremely; **es pelma con a.** he's terribly boring

avaricioso, -a 1 *adj* avaricious, miserly
  2 *nm,f* miser

avariento, -a *adj* avaricious, mean, miserly

avaro, -a 1 *adj* avaricious, mean, miserly
  2 *nm,f* miser

avasallador, -a *adj* overwhelming

avasallamiento *nm* subjection, subjugation, domination

avasallar 1 *vt* to subdue, subject
  2 **avasallarse** *vpr* to yield, accept domination

avatar *nm* (**a**) *(cambio)* change, transformation (**b**) **avatares** ups and downs

AVE *nm (abrev de* **alta velocidad española)** = Spanish high-speed train

ave *nf* bird; *Fig* **es un a. nocturna** he's a night owl ❑ **a. del Paraíso** bird of paradise; **a. de presa** bird of prey; **a. de rapiña** bird of prey; **aves de corral** poultry

avecinar 1 *vt* to bring close o up to
  2 **avecinarse** *vpr* to approach, come near

avecindarse *vpr* to settle, take up residence

avejentado, -a *adj (persona, cuero)* aged

avejentarse *vpr* to age (prematurely)

avellana *nf* hazelnut

avellano *nm Bot* hazelnut tree; *(madera)* hazel wood

avemaría *nf Rel* Ave Maria, Hail Mary; *Fam* **en un a.** in a jiffy; *Fam* **saber algo como el a.** to know sth backwards

avena *nf* oats *pl*

avenencia *nf* agreement, compromise

avengo *indic pres de* **avenir**

avenida *nf* (**a**) *(calle)* avenue (**b**) *(de río)* flood, spate

avenido, -a 1 *pp de* **avenir**
  2 *adj* **bien a.** in agreement, on good terms; **mal a.** in disagreement, on bad terms

avenimiento *nm* agreement, compromise; *(concilio)* harmony, understanding

avenir [69] **1** *vt* to reconcile, harmonize
  2 *vi* to happen
  3 **avenirse** *vpr (ponerse de acuerdo)* to come to an agreement; *(llevarse bien)* to be on good terms; **a. a hacer algo** to agree to do sth; **a. con algo** to come to terms with sth

aventajado, -a 1 *pp de* **aventajar**
  2 *adj* (**a**) *(ventajoso)* advantageous, favourable; *US* favorable (**b**) *(sobresaliente)* outstanding, exceptional; *(en cabeza)* in the lead

aventajar *vt* (**a**) *(estar por delante de)* to lead, be ahead o in front of; *(llegar aventajado)* to come ahead of (**b**) *(superar)* to surpass, outdo; **nadie le aventaja en compañerismo** nobody beats him for team spirit

aventar [3] *vt* (**a**) *Agr* to winnow (**b**) *(el viento)* to blow away; *(el fuego)* to blow (on), fan; **a. las cenizas** to cast ashes to the wind

aventura *nf* (**a**) *(suceso, empresa)* adventure; **novela de aventuras** adventure novel (**b**) *(riesgo)* risk, danger (**c**) *(relación amorosa)* (love) affair

aventurado, -a 1 *pp de* **aventurar**
  2 *adj (arriesgado)* risky, dangerous; **no sería demasiado a. afirmar que ...** it would not be going too far to state that ...

aventurar 1 *vt* (**a**) *(dinero, capital)* to risk, venture (**b**) **a. una opinión** to hazard an opinion
  2 **aventurarse** *vpr* to venture, dare

aventurero, -a 1 *adj* adventurous; **de espíritu a.** venturesome
  2 *nm,f (hombre)* adventurer; *(mujer)* adventuress

avergonzado, -a 1 *pp de* **avergonzar**
  2 *adj* ashamed, embarrassed

avergonzar [10] **1** *vt* to shame, put to shame; *(turbar)* to embarrass
  2 **avergonzarse** *vpr* to be ashamed (**de** of), be embarrassed

avería *nf* (**a**) *Com Náut (daño)* damage (**b**) *Téc (desperfecto)* failure, malfunction; **el viento ocasionó una a. en el transformador** the wind damaged the transformer; **en caso de a.** in case of breakdown (**c**) *Aut* breakdown; **tuvimos una a.** we had a breakdown in the car

averiado, -a 1 *pp de* **averiar**
  2 *adj* (**a**) *(máquina)* out of order; **está a.** it's out of order, it's not working, something is wrong with it (**b**) *Aut* broken down

averiar [32] **1** *vt* (**a**) *(dañar)* to damage, spoil (**b**) *Téc (estropear)* to cause to malfunction
  2 **averiarse** *vpr* (**a**) *(dañarse)* to get damaged (**b**) *(estropearse)* to malfunction, go wrong, fail (**c**) *Aut* to break down

averiguación *nf* investigation, inquiry

averiguar [11] **1** *vt* to investigate, inquire into, find out about, ascertain; **averigua su número de teléfono** find out his phone number
  2 *vi CAm Méx (discutir)* to argue

averno *nm Lit* Hades, the nether regions *pl*

averroísmo *nm Filos* Averroism

aversión *nf* aversion, loathing; **sentir a. por** to loathe

avestruz *nm* ostrich

avezado, -a *adj (acostumbrado)* used

aviación *nf* (**a**) *(navegación)* aviation ❑ **accidente de a.** plane crash; **a. civil** civil aviation (**b**) *Mil* air force

aviador, -a *nm,f* (**a**) *(piloto)* aviator, flier; *Mil (piloto)* air force pilot (**b**) *Méx Fam* = person listed as an employee in a government office and who is paid but who never comes to work

aviar [32] *vt* (**a**) *(preparar)* to prepare, get ready (**b**) *(arreglar)* to tidy; *(ordenar)* to put in order (**c**) *(proveer)* to supply, equip (**d**) *(apresurar)* to hurry up

avícola *adj* poultry

avicultor, -a *nm,f* poultry keeper

avicultura *nf* aviculture; *(de aves de corral)* poultry keeping

avidez *nf* avidity, eagerness

ávido, -a *adj* avid, eager; **á. de aventuras** hungry for adventure

avieso, -a *adj* evil, wicked, depraved

avinagrado, -a 1 *pp de* **avinagrar**
  2 *adj* vinegary, sour; *Fig* sour; **carácter a.** sour character

avinagrar 1 *vt* to turn sour, embitter
  2 avinagrarse *vpr* to turn sour; *Fig (carácter)* to become sour o bitter

avío *nm* (**a**) *(preparativo)* preparation, tidying; **el a. de la casa** household chores (**b**) *(de labrador, de pastor)* provisions *pl* (**c**) **avíos** *(utensilios)* gear *sing*, tackle *sing*, equipment *sing* (**d**) *Méx (préstamo)* agricultural loan

avión¹ *nm* plane, *Br* aeroplane, *US* airplane; **por a.** *(en carta)* airmail; **viajar en a.** to fly, go by plane ❑ **a. de carga** cargo plane; **a. a reacción** jet (plane)

avión² *nm Orn* house martin

avioneta *nf* light aircraft o plane

avisado, -a 1 *pp de* **avisar**
  2 *adj* (**a**) *(informado)* warned; **estás a.** you've been warned (**b**) *(sagaz)* shrewd; *(prudente)* wise, prudent

avisador, -a 1 *adj* warning
  2 *nm* (**a**) *Téc (alarma)* warning device, bell (**b**) *(persona)* messenger

avisar *vt* (**a**) *(informar)* to inform, notify, announce; **avísame cuando hayas acabado** let me know when you finish; **a. con un mes de antelación** to give a month's notice (**b**) *(advertir)* to warn; **avisamos a los conductores que ...** we warn motorists that ...; **ya te avisé** I warned you (**c**) *(mandar llamar)* to call for, to notify; **'avisamos grúa'** 'cars will be towed away'; **a. a la policía** to notify the police; **a. al médico** to send for the doctor

aviso *nm* (**a**) *(notificación)* notice; *(advertencia)* warning; *(nota)* note; **hasta nuevo a.** until further notice; **mandar a. de que** to inform that; **sin previo a.** without notice (**b**) **andar** o **estar sobre a.** to be on the alert, keep one's eyes open; **estar sobre a.** *(estar enterado)* to know what's going on, be in on it; *(ya haber avisado)* to have been warned; **poner sobre a.** to forewarn; **ya me han puesto sobre a.** I've been told (about it) (**c**) *Am (anuncio)* advertisement, advert

avispa *nf* wasp

avispado, -a 1 *pp de* **avispar**
  2 *adj Fam* quick-witted, quick on the uptake

avispar 1 *vt Chile* to frighten
  2 avisparse *vpr Fam* to wise up

avispero *nm* (**a**) *(conjunto de avispas)* swarm of wasps (**b**) *(nido)* wasps' nest (**c**) *Fig (atolladero)* tight spot, mess (**d**) *Med* carbuncle

avistar *vt* to see, sight

avitaminosis *nf Med* avitaminosis, vitamin deficiency

avituallamiento *nm* provisioning

avituallar *vt* to provision, supply with food

avivado, -a 1 *pp de* **avivar**
  2 *adj Fig* enlivened, quickened; *(pasión, enfado)* stirred, aroused

avivar 1 *vt* (**a**) *(fuego)* to stoke (up); *(color, luz)* to brighten; *(pasión, dolor)* to intensify (**b**) *Fig (sentimiento)* to rekindle; *(paso)* to quicken
  2 *vi Fam* **¡aviva!** hurry up!, move on!
  3 avivarse *vpr* to become brighter o livelier

avizor, -a *adj* **estar ojo a.** to be on the alert o on the lookout

avizorar *vt* to spy on, watch

avutarda *nf Orn* great bustard

axial *adj* axial

axila *nf* (**a**) *Anat* armpit, axilla (**b**) *Bot* axil

axilar *adj* axillar, axillary

axioma *nm* axiom

axiomático, -a *adj* axiomatic

ay 1 *interj (dolor)* ouch!; *(queja)* **¡ay de mí!** poor me!; *(amenaza)* **¡ay de ti como te coja!** I'll give it to you if I catch you!; *(sobresalto)* **¡ay! ¡qué susto!** God! what a fright!
  2 *nm (suspiro, queja)* aah!

aya *nf* governess

ayatola *nm*, **ayatolá** *nm* ayatollah

ayer 1 *adv* (**a**) *(el día anterior)* yesterday; **antes de a.** the day before yesterday; **a. por la mañana/por la tarde** yesterday morning/afternoon; **a. por la noche** last night; **parece que fue a.** it seems like yesterday (**b**) *(en tiempo pasado)* before, formerly
  2 *nm* past; **los recuerdos del a.** memories from the past

aymara *adj & nmf* Aymara

ayo *nm* tutor

ayote *nm Bot CAm (fruto)* gourd, pumpkin

ayuda *nf* (**a**) *(asistencia)* help, assistance; **con la a. de un bastón** with the aid of a walking stick; **ir en a. de algn** to come to sb's assistance; **prestar a.** to help ❑ **a. de cámara** valet; **a. humanitaria** humanitarian aid (**b**) *Med (lavativa)* enema

ayudante *nmf* assistant ❑ *Cin Teat* **a. de dirección** production assistant; *Esp Med* **a. técnico-sanitario** qualified nurse

ayudantía *nf* assistantship; *Mil* adjutancy

ayudar 1 *vt* to help, assist, aid; **¿en qué puedo ayudarle?** (how) can I help you?
  2 ayudarse *vpr* **a. de** o **con** to make use of

ayunar *vi* to fast

ayunas *nfpl* **en a.** *(sin comer)* without having eaten breakfast; *Fig* in the dark; **hay que tomarlo en a.** you have to take it on an empty stomach; **quedarse en a.** not to understand a thing

ayuno *nm* fasting, fast; **guardar a.** to fast

ayuntamiento *nm* (**a**) *(corporación)* town council, *US* city council (**b**) *(edificio)* town hall, *US* city hall (**c**) *Fml* **a. carnal** sexual intercourse

azabache *nm Min* jet; *Fig* **pelo negro como el a.** jet black hair, raven hair

azada *nf* hoe

azadón *nm* (wide) hoe

azafata *nf* (**a**) *(de avión)* air stewardess, *Br* air hostess (**b**) *(de congresos, exposiciones)* hostess ❑ **a. de tierra** ground stewardess

azafrán *nm Bot Culin* saffron

azafranado, -a *adj* saffron-coloured, *US* saffron-colored

azahar *nm Bot (del naranjo)* orange blossom; *(del limonero)* lemon blossom ❑ **agua de a.** orange-flower water

azalea *nf Bot* azalea

azar *nm* (a) *(casualidad)* chance; **al a.** at random; **por puro a.** by pure chance ❑ **juegos de a.** games of chance (b) *(desgracia)* misfortune, accident; **los azares de la vida** the ups and downs of life

azarado, -a 1 *pp de* azarar
  2 *adj* embarrassed

azaramiento *nm* embarrassment

azarar 1 *vt* to embarrass
  2 azararse *vpr* to be embarrassed

azaroso, -a *adj* hazardous, dangerous, risky

Azerbaiyán *n* Azerbaijan

azerbaiyano, -a *adj & nm,f* Azerbaijani

ázimo, -a *adj* pan á. unleavened bread

azimut *nm Astron* azimuth

azogar [38] *vt* to (coat with) quicksilver; *(espejo)* to silver

azogue *nm* mercury, quicksilver

azor *nm Orn* goshawk

azorado, -a 1 *pp de* azorar
  2 *adj* embarrassed

azoramiento *nm* embarrassment

azorar 1 *vt* to embarrass
  2 azorarse *vpr* to be embarrassed

Azores *nfpl* **las (Islas) A.** the Azores

azotado, -a 1 *pp de* azotar
  2 *adj* (a) *(con látigo)* whipped, flogged (b) *Fig* whipped, lashed

azotaina *nf Fam* spanking, smacking; **darle una a. a un niño** to spank a child

azotar 1 *vt* (a) *(con látigo)* to whip, flog (b) *(golpear)* to beat, beat down on (c) *Fig (peste, hambre)* to scourge
  2 azotarse *vpr* (a) *(persona)* to flog oneself (b) *Bol (lanzarse)* to throw oneself

azote *nm* (a) *(vara)* whip, scourge (b) *(golpe)* lash, stroke (of the whip); **diez azotes** ten lashes (c) *Fam* smacking, spanking (d) *Fig* scourge

azotea *nf* flat roof; *Fam* **estar mal de la a.** to have a screw loose, not be right in the head

azteca *adj & nmf* Aztec

azúcar *nm & f* sugar ❑ **a. blanquilla** white sugar; **a. cande, a. candi** sugar candy; **a. de caña** cane sugar; *Esp Méx* **a. glas** *Br* icing *o US* confectioner's sugar; **a. moreno** brown sugar; **terrón de a.** lump of sugar

azucarado, -a 1 *pp de* azucarar
  2 *adj* (a) *(con azúcar)* sugared, sweetened (b) *(como el azúcar)* sugar-like; *(dulce)* sweet (c) *Fig* sugary

azucarar 1 *vt* to sugar, put sugar in, sweeten
  2 azucararse *vpr Am* to crystallize

azucarera *nf* sugar factory

azucarero, -a 1 *adj* sugar; **la industria azucarera** the sugar industry
  2 *nm* sugar bowl

azucarillo *nm* sugar lump

azucena *nf Bot* white lily

azufrar *vt Quím* to sulphur, *US* sulfur, sulphurate, *US* sulfurate

azufre *nm Quím* sulphur, *US* sulfur

azufroso, -a *adj Quím* sulphurous, *US* sulfurous

azul *adj & nm* blue ❑ **a. celeste** light blue; **a. eléctrico** electric blue; **a. marino** navy blue; **a. turquesa** turquoise; **príncipe a.** Prince Charming; **sangre a.** blue blood

azulado, -a *adj* blue, bluish

azulejo *nm (glazed)* tile

azulete *nm (para la ropa)* blue

azulgrana *adj inv* (a) *(colores)* blue and scarlet (b) *Dep* relating to Barcelona Football Club

azuzar [14] *vt* (a) **a. los perros a algn** to set the dogs on sb (b) *Fam* to egg on, urge

B

B, b *Esp* [be, *Am* be('larɤa)] *nf (la letra)* B, b

baba *nf (de niño)* dribble; *(de adulto)* saliva, spittle; *(de animal)* saliva; *(de caracol)* slime; *Fig* **caérsele a uno la b.** to be delighted; *Fig* **se le cae la b. con su nieto** he dotes on his grandson; *Fam* **tener muy mala b.** to have a nasty streak

babear *vi* **(a)** *(niño)* to dribble; *(adulto, animal)* to slobber **(b)** *Fig* to drool

babel *nm & f* bedlam; **la casa está hecha una b.** the house is upside down; **la reunión se convirtió en un verdadero b.** the meeting became sheer bedlam

babero *nm* bib

Babia *n Fig* **estar en B.** to be daydreaming, have one's head in the clouds

babieca 1 *adj* silly, simple-minded
 2 *nmf* fool, simpleton

babilla *nf Zool* stifle

Babilonia *n Hist* Babylon

babilonio, -a *n adj & nm,f Hist* Babylonian

bable *nm Ling* Asturian dialect

babor *nm Náut* port, port side, larboard; **a b.** to port, on the port side; **¡tierra a b.!** land to port!

babosa *nf Zool* slug

babosada *nf CAm Méx Fam (disparate)* daft thing; **no digas babosadas** don't talk *Br* rubbish *o US* bull!

babosear *vt* to slobber over, drool over

baboseo *nm* slobbering, drooling

baboso, -a *adj* **(a)** *(niño)* dribbly; *(adulto)* slobbery **(b)** *Fam Fig* sloppy

babucha *nf* slipper

babuino *nm Zool* baboon

baca *nf Aut* roof rack

bacalao *nm (pez)* cod; *Esp Fam* **cortar el b.** to be the boss; *Fam* **¡te conozco b.!** you can't fool me

bacanal *nf* bacchanalia, orgy

bacará *nm*, **bacarrá** *nm Naipes* baccarat

bache *nm* **(a)** *(en la carretera)* pothole **(b)** *Av* air pocket **(c)** *Fig* bad patch; **pasar un b.** to go through a bad patch; **salir del b.** to recover from a bad patch **(d)** *Econ* slump, depression

bachiller *Antes* **1** *nmf* = pupil who has obtained the bachillerato
 2 *nm véase* **bachillerato**

bachillerato *nm* = academically orientated school course for pupils in the final years of secondary education

bacilo *nm Biol* bacillus

bacín *nm*, **bacinilla** *nf* chamberpot

---

bacon ['beikon] *nm Esp* bacon

bacteria *nf* bacterium, germ; **bacterias** bacteria

bacteriano, -a *adj* bacterial

bactericida 1 *adj* bactericidal, germ-killing
 2 *nm* bactericide, germicide

bacteriología *nf* bacteriology

bacteriológico, -a *adj* bacteriological

bacteriólogo, -a *nm,f* bacteriologist

báculo *nm* **(a)** *(bastón)* walking stick **(b)** *(de obispo)* crosier **(c)** *Fig* support, comfort; **ella fue el b. de su vejez** she was the staff of his old age

badajo *nm* clapper

badana *nf* sheepskin; *Esp Fig* **zurrarle la b. a algn** to give sb a good hiding

badén *nm* **(a)** *(cauce)* paved ford **(b)** *(zanja)* gully; *Aut* uneven road

badil *nm*, **badila** *nf (pala)* fire shovel; *(atizador)* poker

bádminton *nm* badminton

bafle *(pl* **bafles)**, **baffle** ['bɑfle] *(pl* **baffles)** *nm* loudspeaker

bagaje *nm* **(a)** *Mil* baggage **(b)** *Fig* experience, background; **b. intelectual** intellectual background

bagatela *nf* trifle; **no te enfades por una b.** don't get worked up over nothing

Bagdad *n* Baghdad

bagre *nm (pez)* catfish

bah *interj* bah!

Bahamas *npl* **las (Islas) B.** the Bahamas

bahameño, -a *adj & nm,f* Bahamian

bahía *nf* bay; **B. de Hudson** Hudson Bay

Bahrein *n* Bahrain

bailable *adj* dance, for dancing; **música b.** dance music, music that one can dance to

bailador, -a *nm,f (bailarín)* dancer; *(de flamenco)* Spanish folk dancer

bailaor, -a *nm,f* flamenco dancer

bailar 1 *vt* to dance; **b. la polca** to dance the polka
 2 *vi* **(a)** *(danzar)* to dance; **nadie la saca a b.** no one asks her to dance; **no me gusta b. agarrado** I don't like dancing cheek to cheek; *Fig* **b. al son que le tocan** to toe the line; *Fig* **le bailaban los ojos de alegría** her eyes sparkled with joy; *Fam* **otro que tal baila** they're two of a kind; *Fam* **¡que me quiten lo baila(d)o!** but at least I had a good time!; *Fam* **siempre me toca b. con la más fea** I always get the short straw **(b)** *(quedar grande)* to be too big; **esta falda me b.** this skirt is loose on me **(c)** *(moverse)* to wobble; **esta mesa b.** this table's wobbly

bailarín, -ina 1 *adj* dancing
  2 *nm,f* dancer; *(clásico)* ballet dancer

baile *nm* **(a)** *(danza)* dance; **la sardana es un b. catalán** the sardana is a Catalan dance; **¿me concede usted este b.?** may I have the pleasure of this dance? ❑ **b. clásico** ballet **(b)** *(fiesta popular)* dance; *(de etiqueta)* ball ❑ **b. de disfraces** masked ball, fancy dress ball; **b. de gala** gala ball **(c)** *Med* **b. de San Vito** Saint Vitus's dance

bailón, -ona *Fam* **1** *adj* fond of dancing
  2 *nm,f* bopper

bailongo *nm Fam* low-class dance, hop

bailotear *vi Fam* to dance, jig about

bailoteo *nm Fam* dancing, jigging about

baja *nf* **(a)** *(disminución)* drop, fall; **estar en b.** to be dropping o falling; **redondear el precio a la b.** to round the price down; **el precio del cacao sigue a la b.** the price of cocoa is continuing to fall, the slump in the price of cocoa is continuing; **tendencia a la b.** downward trend; *Fin* **jugar a la b.** to bear **(b)** *Mil* loss, casualty; **bajas de guerra** war losses; **dar a un soldado de b.** to discharge a soldier; **ser b.** to be reported missing **(c)** *(cese)* **dar de b. a algn** *(despedir)* *(de una empresa)* to lay sb off; *(de un club, de una sociedad)* to take away sb's membership; *(de un colegio profesional)* to strike sb off; **darse de b.** *(de un club)* to resign **(de** from), drop out **(de** of); *(en una suscripción)* tó cancel **(c)** *Esp (por enfermedad)* sick leave; **estar/darse de b.** to be on/take sick leave ❑ **b. incentivada** voluntary redundancy; **b. por maternidad** maternity leave

bajada *nf* **(a)** *(descenso)* descent; *(disminución)* decrease, reduction **(b)** *(camino por donde se baja)* way down, slope **(c)** *(taxi)* **b. de bandera** minimum fare

bajamar *nf* low tide, ebb-tide

bajante *nf* drainpipe

bajar 1 *vt* **(a)** *(descender)* to bring o get o take down; **baja la maleta del armario** take the suitcase down from the cupboard; *Teat* **b. el telón** to lower the curtain; **b. la categoría a algn** to demote sb; **b. las persianas** to let down the blinds; *Fig* **b. los humos a algn** to take sb down a peg or two **(b)** *(recorrer de arriba abajo)* to come o go down; **b. la escalera** to come o go downstairs **(c)** *(inclinar)* to lower; **b. la cabeza** to bow o lower one's head **(d)** *(disminuir)* *(volumen)* to turn down; *(voz)* to lower; *(precios etc)* to reduce, lower, cut; **¡baja esa maldita música!** turn that bloody music down!; **los mayoristas han bajado los precios** the wholesalers have cut prices **(e)** *Fam Inform* to download

  2 *vi* **(a)** *(ir de un lugar a otro más bajo)* to go o come down; **bajo en seguida** I'll be down in a minute **(b)** *(apearse) (de un tren, autobús, avión)* to get off; *(de una moto, bicicleta)* to get off; *(de un coche)* to get out **(de** of); **bajó del coche** he got out of the car **(c)** *(disminuir)* to fall, drop; **ha bajado el azúcar** sugar has come down in price; **han bajado las ventas** sales are down; **no bajará de tres horas** it will take at least three hours; **¡ojalá baje la temperatura!** let's hope the temperature drops!

  3 bajarse *vpr* **(a)** *(descender) (de árbol, escalera, silla)* to come o go down; **bájate de ahí** get down **(b)** *(apearse) (de un tren, autobús, avión)* to get off; *(de una moto, bicicleta)* to get off; *(de un coche)* to get out **(de** of); **se bajó de la bici** she got off the bike; **se bajó del coche** he got out of the car **(c)** *(inclinarse)* to bend over o down **(d)** *Fam Inform* to download

bajel *nm Literario & Náut* vessel, ship

bajera *nf* **(a)** *CAm Col Méx (tabaco)* low quality tobacco leaves **(b)** *RP (de cabalgadura)* saddle blanket

bajero, -a *adj* lower

bajeza *nf* **(a)** *(acción vil)* vile deed, base action **(b)** *(condición)* lowliness; **b. intelectual** lack of intelligence

bajial *nm Méx Perú* lowland

bajinis: por lo bajinis *loc adv Fam* on the sly; **hablar por lo b.** to speak quietly

bajío *nm* **(a)** *(banco de arena)* sandbank **(b)** *Am (terreno bajo)* lowland

bajista *Fin* **1** *adj* bearish; **tendencia b.** tendency to lower prices
  2 *nmf* bear

bajo, -a 1 *adj* **(a)** *(cosa, precio)* low; *(persona)* short; *(sonido)* faint, soft; *(voz)* low; **en voz baja** in a low voice; **un techo muy b.** a very low ceiling; **una mujer baja** a short o small woman **(b)** *(en lugar inferior)* **un piso b.** a lower floor *Br* flat o *US* apartment; *(en nivel inferior)* **de baja calidad** of poor quality; **la clase baja** the lower classes; *Fig* **tirando por lo b.** at a conservative guess **(c)** *(inclinado)* low; **con la cabeza baja** with bowed head **(d)** *(territorio, río)* lower; **el B. Aragón** lower Aragon **(e)** *Fig (vil)* base, contemptible
  2 *nm* **(a)** *Geog* lowland, depression **(b)** *Náut* sandbank **(c)** *Mús (cantante, voz, instrumento)* bass **(d)** **bajos** *(planta baja) Br* ground floor, *US* first floor; *(sótano)* basement *sing* **(e)** **bajos** *(de pantalones)* bottoms, *US* cuffs; *(de falda)* hem *sing*
  3 *adv* **(a)** *(en lugar inferior)* **volar b.** to fly low **(b)** *(en voz baja)* quietly, softly; **hablar b.** to speak quietly, whisper; *Fig* **por lo b.** in secret, on the sly
  4 *prep* **(a)** *(lugar)* under, underneath; **b. la lluvia** in the rain; **b. tierra** underground, buried **(b)** *Pol Hist* under; **b. Nerón/la República** under Nero/the Republic **(c)** *(temperatura)* below; **cinco grados b. cero** five degrees below zero **(d)** *(garantía, condición)* under; **b. fianza** on bail; **b. juramento** under oath; **b. pena de muerte** on pain of death

bajón *nm* **(a)** *Mús (instrumento)* bassoon; *(músico)* bassoonist **(b)** *(bajada)* sharp fall, decline **(c)** *Com Fin* slump **(d)** *(de salud)* relapse, deterioration; **ha sufrido un b.** she has taken a turn for the worse

bajorrelieve *nm Arte* bas-relief

bajura *nf* **pesca de b.** coastal fishing

bala 1 *nf* **(a)** *Mil* bullet; *Fig* **como una b.** like a shot ❑ **b. de cañón** cannonball; **b. de goma** rubber bullet; **b. perdida** stray bullet **(b)** *(de lana, algodón)* bale **(c)** *Col Méx Fam* **ni a b.** no way
  2 *nmf Fam (persona)* **b. perdida** oddball

balacear *vt Am* to shoot

balacera *nf Am* shoot-out

balada *nf Lit Mús* ballad

baladí *(pl* baladíes*) adj* trivial; **asunto b.** secondary matter, triviality

balalaika *nf Mús* balalaika

balance *nm* **(a)** *(vaivén)* to-and-fro, rocking **(b)** *Fin (operación contable)* balance; *(declaración)* balance sheet ❑ **b. consolidado** consolidated balance sheet **(c)** *(cálculo)* estimate; **el b. provisional de heridos** the provisional estimate of casualties; **hacer b. de una situación** to take stock of a situation

balancear 1 *vt* **(a)** *(poner en equilibrio)* to balance **(b)** *(mecer)* to rock
  2 balancearse *vpr* **(a)** *(en una mecedora)* to rock; *(en un columpio)* to swing **(b)** *(barco)* to roll

balanceo *nm* rocking, swinging, rolling

balancín *nm* **(a)** *(mecedora)* rocking-chair **(b)** *(de balanza)* balancing beam **(c)** *Téc Aut* rocker arm **(d)** *(circo)* balancing pole

balandra *nf Náut* sloop

balandro *nm Náut* yacht

balanza *nf* **(a)** *(aparato)* scales *pl*; *Fig* **estar en la b.** to be in the balance o in danger; **b. de precisión** precision balance (**b**) *Com Fin Pol* balance ❑ **b. comercial** balance of trade; **b. de pagos** balance of payments

balar *vi* to bleat, baa

balarrasa *nm Fam* (**a**) *(aguardiente)* strong brandy (**b**) *(persona)* madcap

balasto *nm* ballast

balaustrada *nf* balustrade, railing

balaustre *nm,* **balaústre** *nm* baluster

balay *nm Am (cesta)* wicker basket

balazo *nm* (**a**) *(disparo)* shot; **matar a algn de un b.** to shoot sb dead (**b**) *(herida)* bullet wound; **murió de un b.** she died of a bullet wound

balboa *nm Fin* standard monetary unit of Panama

balbucear *vi* (**a**) *(adulto)* to stutter, stammer (**b**) *(niño)* to babble

balbuceo *nm* (**a**) *(adulto)* stuttering, stammering (**b**) *(niño)* babbling

balbuciente *adj* (**a**) *(adulto)* stuttering, stammering (**b**) *(niño)* babbling

balbucir [74] *vi véase* **balbucear**

Balcanes *npl* **los B.** the Balkans

balcánico, -a *adj* Balkan; **la Península balcánica** the Balkan Peninsula

balcanización *nf Pol* balkanization

balcón *nm* (**a**) *(terraza)* balcony; **asomarse al b.** *(mirar a la calle)* to look over the balcony; *(salir)* to go out onto the balcony ❑ **b. corrido** row of balconies (**b**) *Fig (miranda)* vantage point

balconada *nf (balcón corrido)* long balcony *(running across building)*

balda *nf Esp* shelf

baldado, -a 1 *pp de* **baldar**
2 *adj* (**a**) *(impedido)* crippled (**b**) *Fam (cansado)* shattered

baldaquín *nm,* **baldaquino** *nm* canopy, baldachin

baldar 1 *vt* (**a**) *(lisiar)* to cripple, maim; **b. a algn a palos** to give sb a thorough beating (**b**) *Fam (cansar)* to wear out
2 baldarse *vpr Fam (cansarse)* to wear oneself out

balde 1 *nm* pail, bucket
2 de balde *loc adv (gratis)* free; **viajar de b.** to travel without paying; **trabajar de b.** to work without getting paid
3 en balde *loc adv (en vano)* in vain; **he venido en b.** I have come for nothing

baldear *vt Náut* (**a**) *(regar)* to wash, swill down (**b**) *(achicar)* to bale out

baldeo *nm* wash, washing, swilling down

baldío, -a 1 *adj* (**a**) *(tierra)* uncultivated, waste (**b**) *(vano)* vain, useless
2 nm (**a**) *(erial)* wasteland (**b**) *Méx RP (solar)* vacant lot

baldón *nm (deshonra)* shame; *(injuria)* insult, offence; **tu conducta es un b. para la familia** your behaviour is a disgrace to the family

baldosa *nf* (ceramic) floor tile; *(para pavimentar)* flagstone, paving stone

baldosín *nm* small tile

balear 1 *adj* Balearic
2 nmf person from the Balearic Islands

Baleares *npl* **las (Islas) B.** the Balearic Islands

baleárico, -a *adj & nm,f véase* **balear**

Bali *n* Bali

balido *nm* bleating, bleat

balín *nm* small bullet

balística *nf* ballistics *sing*

balístico, -a *adj* ballistic

baliza *nf* (**a**) *Náut* buoy (**b**) *Av* beacon

balizamiento *nm Náut* marker buoys; *Av* beacons; *Aut* warning lights *(for roadworks)*

balizar [14] *vt Náut* to mark out with buoys; *Av* to mark out with beacons; *Aut* to mark out with warning lights

ballena *nf* (**a**) *Zool* whale ❑ **b. azul** blue whale (**b**) *(de corsé)* whalebone, stay (**c**) *Fam* fat person, fatso

ballenero, -a 1 *adj* whaling; **industria ballenera** whaling industry
2 nm (**a**) *(persona)* whaler (**b**) *(barco)* whaler, whaling boat

ballesta *nf* (**a**) *Hist* crossbow (**b**) *Aut* spring

ballet [ba'le] *(pl* **ballets)** *nm* ballet

balneario, -a 1 *adj* health, thermal
2 nm spa, health resort

balompié *nm* soccer, *Br* football

balón *nm* (**a**) *Dep* ball; **b. de fútbol** soccer ball, *Br* football (**b**) *(recipiente)* cylinder; *(gases)* bag ❑ **b. de oxígeno** oxygen cylinder; *Fig* godsend, boost, shot in the arm

baloncestista *nmf* basketball player

baloncesto *nm* basketball

balonmano *nm* handball

balonvolea *nm* volleyball

balotaje *nm Am* run-off, = second round of voting

balsa *nf* (**a**) *(estanque, charca)* pond, pool; **como una b. de aceite** *(mar)* as calm as a millpond; *Fig* very quiet (**b**) *Náut* raft; **b. salvavidas** life raft

balsámico, -a *adj* balsamic; *Fig* soothing

bálsamo *nm* balsam, balm

balsero, -a *nm,f* = refugee fleeing Cuba on a raft

Báltico *nm* **el (Mar) B.** the Baltic (Sea)

baluarte *nm* (**a**) *(fortificación)* bulwark, bastion (**b**) *Fig* stronghold, bastion; **un b. de la democracia** a bastion of democracy

bamba *nf (baile)* = Cuban dance

bambalina *nf Teat* fly, flies *pl*

bambolearse *vpr (gen)* to swing; *(persona, árbol)* to sway; *(mesa, silla)* to wobble; *(barco)* to rock, roll

bamboleo *nm (gen)* swinging; *(persona, árbol)* swaying; *(mesa, silla)* wobbling, wobble; *(barco)* rocking, rolling

bambú *nm (pl* **bambúes** *o* **bambús**) bamboo

banal *adj* banal, trivial

banalidad *nf* triviality, banality

banalizar [14] *vt* to trivialize

banana *nf* banana

bananero, -a 1 *adj* banana
**2 nm (plantación)* banana plantation

banano *nm* (**a**) *(fruto)* banana (**b**) *(árbol)* banana tree

banca *nf* (**a**) *(asiento)* bench (**b**) *Com Fin (conjunto de bancos)* (the) banks; *(actividad)* banking ❑ **b. electrónica** electronic banking; **el sector de la b.** the banking sector; **nacionalización de la b.** nationalization of the banks (**c**) *(en juegos)* bank; **hacer saltar la b.** to break the bank

bancada *nf Andes RP* parliamentary group

bancario, -a *adj Com Fin* banking; **sistema b.** banking system

bancarrota *nf Fin* bankruptcy; **estar en b.** to be bankrupt

banco *nm* (**a**) *(asiento)* bench; *(de iglesia)* pew (**b**) *Téc* bench ❑ **b. de pruebas** test bench; *Fig* testing ground (**c**) *Com Fin* bank ❑ *Inform* **b. de datos** data bank; **b. de ojos** eye bank; **b. de sangre** blood bank; **B. Mundial** World Bank (**d**) *Náut* bank ❑ **b. de arena** sandbank (**e**) *(de peces)* shoal, school (**f**) *Geol (estrato)* layer

banda *nf* (**a**) *(faja, condecoración)* sash, band, ribbon ▫ **b. magnética** magnetic strip (**b**) *Ind* belt ▫ **b. transportadora** conveyor belt (**c**) *Mús* band (**d**) *Cin* **b. sonora** sound track (**e**) *(personas)* gang; *(de pájaros)* flock (**f**) *Rad* waveband ▫ *Tel* **b. ancha** broadband; **b. de frecuencias** frequency (band) (**g**) *Náut* side (**h**) *Bill* cushion (**i**) *Fin* **b. impositiva** tax band, tax bracket; **b. salarial** wage bracket, salary band

bandada *nf (de pájaros)* flock

bandazo *nm* lurch; **dar bandazos** to lurch

bandearse *vpr* to manage, cope; **sabe bandeárselas bien** he knows how to look after himself

bandeja *nf* tray; *Fig* **servir algo a algn en b.** to hand sth to sb on a plate

bandera *nf* flag; *Mil* **jurar b.** to swear allegiance to the flag; **la b. española** the Spanish flag; *Fam* **lleno hasta la b.** packed full; *Esp Fam* **de b.** fantastic, terrific; **una chica de b.** a real cracker ▫ **b. blanca** white flag

banderilla *nf* (**a**) *Taur* banderilla; *Fig* **clavar** *o* **plantar banderillas a algn** to slight *o* taunt sb (**b**) *Esp Culin* = savoury snack on a cocktail stick

banderillear *vt Taur* **b. al toro** to thrust banderillas into the bull's neck

banderillero *nm Taur* banderillero

banderín *nm* (**a**) *(bandera pequeña)* pennant, small flag (**b**) *Mil (soldado)* pennant bearer

banderita *nf* little flag; **el día de la b.** flag day

banderola *nf* banderole

bandidaje *nm* banditry

bandido *nm* bandit, outlaw; *Fam* crook

bando[1] *nm* (**a**) *Jur (edicto)* edict, proclamation (**b**) bandos banns

bando[2] *nm* (**a**) *(facción)* faction, side; **pasarse al otro b.** to go over to the other side, change allegiances; *Fam* **ser del b. contrario** to be gay (**b**) *(de peces)* shoal, school; *(de aves)* flock

bandolera[1] *nf (mujer)* woman bandit

bandolera[2] *nf (correa)* bandoleer, bandolier; **en b.** over one's shoulder

bandolerismo *nm* banditry

bandolero *nm* bandit, outlaw

bandurria *nf Mús* bandurria

Bangkok *n* Bangkok

Bangladesh [baŋglaˈðeʃ] *n* Bangladesh

Bangui *n* Bangui

banjo [ˈbanjo] *nm Mús* banjo

Banjul [banˈjul] *n* Banjul

banquero, -a *nm,f* banker

banqueta *nf* (**a**) *(banco)* bench, form (**b**) *(taburete)* stool

banquete *nm* banquet, feast; **b. de bodas** wedding reception *o* feast

banquetear *vt & vi* to banquet

banquillo *nm* (**a**) *Jur* dock; *Fig* **sentar a algn en el b. de los acusados** to have sb on the carpet (**b**) *Dep* bench

banquisa *nf* floe, ice field

bañadero *nm* = water hole used by animals

bañado, -a 1 *pp de* bañar
 2 *adj Fig* bathed; **b. en lágrimas/sangre/sudor** bathed in tears/blood/sweat
 3 *nm Bol RP* marshland, swamp

bañador *nm Esp (de mujer)* bathing *o* swimming costume; *(de hombre)* swimming trunks *pl*

bañar 1 *vt* (**a**) *(lavar)* to bath (**b**) *(cubrir)* to coat, cover; *Téc*

to dip; **b. de oro** to gild; **b. un pastel en chocolate** to cover a cake in chocolate (**c**) *Fml (dar el sol, la luz)* to bathe; **la luz de la luna bañaba la habitación** the room was bathed in moonlight

2 bañarse *vpr (limpiarse)* to have *o* take a bath; *(mar, piscina)* to go swimming, go for a swim, have a swim *o* a dip

bañera *nf (baño)* bath, bathtub

bañero, -a *nm,f* lifeguard

bañista *nmf* bather, swimmer

baño *nm* (**a**) *(gen)* bath; **tomar un b.** to have *o* take a bath; *Fig* **b. de sangre** bloodbath; *Fig* **b. de sol** sun-bath; *Esp Fig* **dar un b. a algn** to beat *o* outshine sb ▫ *Fot* **b. fijador** fixing bath; *Culin* **b. María** bain-marie; **b. turco** Turkish bath; **traje de b.** swimming costume (**b**) *(capa) (de pintura)* coat; *(de chocolate, almíbar)* coating, covering (**c**) *(cuarto de baño)* bathroom; *(lavabo) Br* toilet, *US* bathroom, washroom (**d**) **baños** *(balneario)* spa *sing*; *(aguas)* waters; **tomar los b.** to take the waters ▫ **b. medicinales** medicinal waters; **b. romanos** Roman baths

baptisterio *nm* (**a**) *(edificio)* baptistry (**b**) *(pila)* font

baquelita *nf Quím* Bakelite

baqueta *nf* (**a**) *(de fusil)* ramrod; *Fig* **tratar a algn a (la) b.** to treat sb badly, push sb around (**b**) **baquetas** *Mús* drumsticks

baqueteado, -a 1 *pp de* baquetear
 2 *adj* hardened

baquetear *vt (tratar mal)* to treat harshly *o* roughly; *(curtir)* to toughen, harden

baqueteo *nm* rough treatment

báquico, -a *adj* bacchic, bacchanalian

bar *nm* (**a**) *(lugar)* bar, snack bar, café (**b**) *Fis* bar

barahúnda *nf (ruido)* din, uproar; *(confusión)* chaos

baraja *nf* Naipes (**a**) *(conjunto) Br* pack *o US* deck (of cards); *Fig* **jugar con dos barajas** to play a double game (**b**) *Am (individual)* playing card

barajar *vt* (**a**) *Naipes* to shuffle; *(papeles)* to mix, jumble up; *Fig (nombres)* to juggle, play with; **b. nombres de posibles candidatos** to consider names of possible candidates (**b**) *Chile (detener) (golpe)* to parry (**c**) *RP (agarrar al vuelo)* to grab

baranda *nf* (**a**) *(listón)* handrail; *(valla) (al borde de algo)* rail; *(en escalera)* banister (**b**) *Bill* cushion

barandilla *nf Esp* (**a**) *(listón)* handrail (**b**) *(valla) (al borde de algo)* rail; *(en escalera)* banister

baratija *nf* trinket, knick-knack; **baratijas** junk *sing*

baratillo *nm* (**a**) *(cosas)* junk, second-hand goods *pl* (**b**) *(tienda)* junk shop, second-hand dealer's; *(mercadillo)* flea market

barato, -a 1 *adj* cheap; **sale más b. en tren** it's cheaper by train
 2 *adv* cheaply; **allí se come muy b.** you can eat very cheaply there

baratura *nf* cheapness, low price

baraúnda *nf véase* barahúnda

barba *nf* beard; **b. cerrada** thick beard; **barbas de chivo** goatee (beard); *Esp Fig* **cien por b.** a hundred a head; *Fig* **es un tipo con toda la b.** he's every inch a man; *Fig* **se rió en mis barbas** he laughed in my face

barbacana *nf* barbican

barbacoa *nf* barbecue

barbado, -a *adj* bearded

Barbados *n* Barbados

bárbaramente *adv* (**a**) *(de forma bárbara)* savagely, barbarously (**b**) *Fam* fantastically

barbaridad *nf* (**a**) *(crueldad)* cruelty, atrocity, outrage;

Fam **¡qué b.!** how terrible!, how awful! (**b**) *(disparate)* piece of nonsense; **no digas barbaridades** don't talk nonsense (**c**) *Fig* **una b.** a lot; **beber una b.** to drink like a fish; **costar una b.** to cost a fortune

barbarie *nf* (**a**) *(crueldad)* savagery, cruelty (**b**) *(falta de cultura)* ignorance

barbarismo *nm Ling* barbarism

bárbaro, -a 1 *adj* (**a**) *Hist* barbarian (**b**) *(cruel)* barbaric, barbarous (**c**) *(inculto, tosco)* rough, uncouth (**d**) *(temerario)* daring, bold (**e**) *Fam (enorme)* massive; **tener un hambre bárbara** to be ravenous *o* starving (**f**) *Fam (estupendo)* tremendous, terrific; **una cosa bárbara** something fantastic
 2 *nm,f Hist* barbarian
 3 *interj Fam* **¡b.!** great!, fantastic!

barbechar *vt Agr* to leave fallow

barbecho *nm Agr* fallow land; **dejar una tierra en b.** to leave a piece of land fallow

barbería *nf* barber's (shop)

barbero *nm* barber

barbilampiño 1 *adj* beardless, smooth-faced
 2 *nm* greenhorn, novice, inexperienced youth

barbilla *nf* chin

barbitúrico *nm* barbiturate

barbo *nm (pez)* barbel ❑ **b. de mar** red mullet

barbudo, -a *adj* bearded

barca *nf* small boat

barcarola *nf Mús* barcarole

barcaza *nf Náut* lighter

barcelonés, -esa 1 *adj* of *o* from Barcelona
 2 *nm,f* person from Barcelona

barco *nm* boat, ship, vessel ❑ **b. cisterna** tanker; **b. de pasajeros** liner; **b. de vapor** steamer; **b. de vela** sailing ship; **b. mercante** merchant ship

bardana *nf Bot* burdock

bardo *nm* bard, poet, minstrel

baremo *nm* (**a**) *Mat* ready reckoner (**b**) *(tarifas)* scale, table, list

bario *nm Quím* barium

barítono *nm Mús* baritone

barloventear *vi Náut* to ply windward, sail to windward

barlovento *nm Náut* windward; **Islas de B.** Windward Islands

barman (*pl* **barmans** *nm*) barman

barnacla *nf* **b. canadiense** Canada goose; **b. cariblanca** barnacle goose

barniz *nm* (**a**) *(en madera)* varnish; *(en cerámica)* glaze (**b**) *Fig* smattering; **tener un b. de cultura** to have a veneer of culture

barnizado, -a 1 *pp de* **barnizar**
 2 *adj (madera)* varnished; *(cerámica)* glazed
 3 *nm (madera)* coat of varnish, varnishing; *(cerámica)* glaze, glazing

barnizar [14] *vt (madera)* to varnish; *(cerámica)* to glaze

barométrico, -a *adj* barometric

barómetro *nm* barometer

barón *nm* (**a**) *(noble)* baron (**b**) *Pol Fam* top man, mandarin

baronesa *nf* baroness

baronía *nf* barony

barquero, -a *nm,f (hombre)* boatman; *(mujer)* boatwoman

barquilla *nf Av* gondola

barquillero, -a *nm,f* wafer seller

barquillo *nm (plano)* wafer; *(cono)* cone, *Br* cornet

barra *nf* (**a**) *(gen)* bar; *Fig* **no pararse en barras** to stop at nothing ❑ **b. de bicicleta** crossbar; **b. de hierro** iron bar; **b. de labios** lipstick; **b. de pan** French loaf, baguette; **b. libre** = unlimited drink for a fixed price (**b**) *Jur (del acusado)* dock; *(de testigo)* witness box; *(barandilla)* bar (**c**) *(mostrador)* bar ❑ **b. americana** = bar with hostesses. (**d**) *Dep* **b. fija** horizontal bar (**e**) *Andes RP Fam (amigos)* gang; ·*Dep* crowd ❑ **b. brava** = group of violent soccer supporters (**e**) *Inform* **b. de desplazamiento** scroll bar

barrabás *nm* scamp, rascal

barrabasada *nf Fam (travesura)* piece of mischief; *(mala pasada)* mean *o* low trick; **decir barrabasadas** to talk nonsense

barraca *nf* (**a**) *(caseta)* shack, hut (**b**) *(en Valencia y Murcia)* thatched farmhouse (**c**) *(puesto de feria)* stall, booth (**d**) *RP (tienda)* builders' merchant's (shop)

barracón *nm* prefab hut

barracuda *nf (pez)* barracuda

barranca *nf* (**a**) *(precipicio)* precipice; *(hondonada)* ravine; *(menos profunda)* gully (**b**) *RP (cuesta)* hill; **ir(se) b. abajo** to go downhill

barranco *nm (precipicio)* precipice; *(hondonada)* ravine; *(menos profunda)* gully

barranquismo *nm Dep* canyoning

barreduras *nfpl* sweepings, rubbish *sing*

barreminas *nm inv* minesweeper

barrena *nf* (**a**) *Téc (metal)* twist drill; *(madera)* bit; **b. de mano** gimlet (**b**) *Av* spin; **entrar en b.** to go into a spin

barrenar *vt* (**a**) *Téc* to drill; *(agujeros)* to bore (**b**) *Náut* to scuttle (**c**) *(desbaratar)* to frustrate, foil (**d**) *(infringir una ley)* to break, violate

barrendero, -a *nm,f* sweeper, street sweeper

barreno *nm* (**a**) *(taladro)* large drill (**b**) *(agujero)* bore, borehole; *Min* blasthole (**c**) *Min (carga explosiva)* charge

barreño *nm Esp* washing-up bowl

barrer *vt* (**a**) *(limpiar con escoba)* to sweep (**b**) *Fig (el viento)* to sweep away; *Fig* **b. con todo** to take everything away; *Fig* **b. para adentro** to look after number one

barrera *nf* (**a**) *(obstáculo)* barrier, fence; **b. del sonido** sound barrier; *Fig* barrier, obstacle; **poner barreras a algo** to hinder sth, impede sth (**b**) *Taur (valla)* fence; *(localidad)* first row of seats; *Fig* **ver los toros desde la b.** to sit on the fence

barretina *nf* = Catalan cap

barriada *nf (barrio)* neighbourhood, area; *Am* shanty town

barrica *nf* (medium-sized) barrel

barricada *nf* barricade; **levantar barricadas** to erect barricades

barrida *nf* **dar una b. a algo** to give sth a sweep

barrido *nm* (**a**) *(con escoba)* **dar un b. a algo** to give sth a sweep; *Fig* **servir** *o* **valer tanto para un b. como para un fregado** *(persona)* to be a jack-of-all-trades (**b**) *Inform Med* scan, scanning (**c**) *Cin* pan, panning

barriga *nf (vientre)* belly; *Fam* tummy; *Fam* **echar b.** to get a paunch, get fat; *Fam* **llenarse la b.** to gorge *o* stuff oneself; *Fam* **rascarse** *o* **tocarse la b.** to laze around, lounge about (**b**) *(de una vasija)* belly, bulge (**c**) *(comba de una pared)* bulge

barrigón, -ona *adj*, **barrigudo, -a** *adj* big-bellied, potbellied

barril *nm* barrel, keg; **cerveza de b.** draught beer

barrilete *nm* (**a**) *(barril)* small barrel (**b**) *(de revólver)* chamber (**c**) *Carp* clamp

barrillo *nm* pimple, spot

barrio *nm* area, district; **del b.** local; **el B. Gótico** the Gothic Quarter; *Esp Fam* **irse al otro b.** to kick the bucket; *Fam* **mandar a algn al otro b.** to do sb in □ **b. chino** Chinatown; *Esp* red-light district; **b. latino** Latin Quarter; **barrios bajos** slums

barriobajero, -a *adj* slummy, slum

barritar *vi (elefante)* to trumpet

barrizal *nm* mire, quagmire

barro *nm* (a) *(lodo)* mud (b) *(arcilla)* clay; **b. cocido** baked clay; **objetos de b.** earthenware *sing*; **un cacharro de b.** an earthenware pot, a ceramic pot (c) *Chile* **barros luco** = toasted beef and cheese sandwich

barroco, -a *adj* (a) *Arte* baroque (b) *Fig* ornate, extravagant

barroquismo *nm* (a) *Arte* baroque style (b) *Fig* extravagance

barroso, -a[1] *adj (con barro)* muddy

barroso, -a[2] *adj Med (con granos)* spotty

barrote *nm* bar; *(de silla, mesa)* crosspiece

barruntar *vt (sospechar)* to suspect; *(presentir)* to have a feeling, suspect; **barruntaba un desenlace trágico** I suspected a tragic outcome

barrunto *nm* (a) *(presentimiento)* feeling, presentiment; *(sospecha)* suspicion (b) *(señal, indicio)* sign, indication

bartola: a la bartola *loc adv Fam* carelessly; **tenderse** *o* **tumbarse a la b.** to laze around, idle away one's time

bártulos *nmpl Fam* things, stuff *sing*, bits and pieces; **liar los b.** to pack up one's things, pack one's bags *o* stuff

barullo *nm* *(alboroto)* row, din; *(confusión)* confusion, mess; **armar b.** to raise hell; **armarse un b.** to get into a muddle; *Fam* **a b.** lots of, loads of, tons of; **bombones a b.** chocolates galore; **había niños a b.** there were loads of children

basa *nf* base

basáltico, -a *adj* basaltic

basalto *nm* basalt

basamento *nm (de una columna)* base, plinth

basar 1 *vt* (a) *(asentar)* to put on a base (b) *Fig (argumentos)* to base (**en** on)
2 basarse *vpr* (a) *(una persona)* to base oneself (**en** on); **¿en qué te basas para decir eso?** what grounds do you have for saying that?; **me baso en lo que he visto** I'm going by what I have seen (b) *(una teoría)* to be based (**en** on)

basca *nf* (a) *(náusea)* nausea; **le produce bascas** it makes him feel sick; *Fam* **si me da la b.** if I feel like it (b) *Esp Argot* people, crowd

báscula *nf* scales *pl*; *(para camiones)* weighbridge, platform scale

basculante *adj* tilting; *(camión)* tip-up

bascular *vi (oscilar)* to tilt

base *nf* (a) *(gen)* base; *Fig* basis; **el arroz es la b. de su alimentación** rice forms the basis of their diet; **la b. de una estatua** the base of a statue; *Pol Fig* **la b. del partido** the rank and file of the party; *Fig* **su argumento carece de b.** her argument has no foundation □ **alimento b.** staple food *o* diet; **sueldo b.** minimum wage (b) *(principio, conocimiento)* basis, grounding; **este libro te dará una buena b. en astronomía** this book will give you a good grounding in astronomy; **si partimos de la b. de que ... si** if we start from the premise that ... (c) *Mil* base □ **b. aérea** air base; **b. de operaciones** field headquarters; **b. naval** naval base (d) *Inform* **b. de datos** database (e) **a b. de** by; **a b. de no hacer nada** by doing nothing; **comida a b. de verduras** vegetarian meal; *Esp Fam* **a b. de bien** extremely well

básico, -a *adj* (a) *(fundamental)* basic, essential (b) *Quím* basic

Basilea *n* Basel

basílica *nf* basilica

basilisco *nm Mit* basilisk; *Fig* **ponerse hecho un b.** to become furious

básquet *nm* , *Am* **básquetbol** *nm Dep* basketball

basquetbolista *nmf Am* basketball player

basset *nm* basset hound

bastante 1 *adj* (a) *(suficiente)* enough; **hay b. comida para todos** there's enough food for everyone; **no tengo b. dinero** I haven't got enough money; **¿tienes bastantes libros?** have you got enough books?; **ya tenemos bastantes problemas** we've got enough problems already (b) *(abundante)* quite a lot of; **b. gente** quite a lot of people; **b. tiempo** quite some time; **hace b. calor/frío** it's quite hot/cold; **tiene bastantes amigos** she's got quite a lot of friends
2 adv (a) *(suficiente)* enough; **con esto hay b.** that is enough; **no soy lo b. rico para ...** I am not rich enough to ... (b) *(un poco)* fairly, quite; **b. alto** quite tall; **b. bien** quite well; **me gusta b.** I quite like it; **vamos b. al cine** we go to the cinema quite often

bastar 1 *vi* to be sufficient *o* enough, suffice; **basta con tocarlo para que se abra** you only have to touch it and it opens; **basta con tres** three will be enough; **¡basta de tonterías!** enough of this nonsense!; *Fam* **me basta y me sobra** that's more than enough for me
2 bastarse *vpr* **b. a sí mismo** to be self-sufficient, rely only on oneself
3 *interj* **¡basta (ya)!** that's enough!, that will do!

bastardía *nf (calidad de bastardo)* bastardy; *Fig (bajeza)* baseness, meanness

bastardilla *nf Impr* **en b.** in italics

bastardillo, -a *adj Impr* italic

bastardo, -a 1 *adj* bastard; *Fig (despreciable)* base, mean
2 *nm,f* bastard

basteza *nf* coarseness

bastidor *nm* (a) *Constr Cost* frame (b) *Esp Aut* chassis (c) **bastidores** *Teat* wings; *Fig* **entre b.** behind the scenes

bastilla *nf Cost* hem

bastión *nm* bastion

basto[1] *nm Naipes (carta española)* ≃ club; **bastos** *(palo de la baraja)* ≃ clubs

basto, -a[2] *adj (cosa)* rough, coarse; *(persona)* rude, coarse, uncouth

bastón *nm* (a) *(para andar)* stick, walking stick (b) *(insignia)* baton; *Fig* **empuñar el b.** to take charge *o* command

bastonazo *nm* blow with a stick

bastoncillo *nm Anat (de la retina)* rod

bastonera *nf* umbrella stand

basura *nf (desperdicios)* rubbish, *US* trash, garbage; **tirar algo a la b.** to throw something away □ **cubo de la b.** dustbin, *US* trash can

basurero *nm* (a) *(persona)* *Br* dustman, refuse collector, *US* garbage collector (b) *(lugar)* *Br* rubbish dump, *US* garbage dump

bata *nf (para casa)* dressing gown; *(para el trabajo)* overall; *(de médico etc)* white coat, lab coat

batacazo *nm* (a) *(golpe)* crash, bang, bump; *Fig* **darse un b.** to come a cropper (b) *CSur Fam (triunfo)* surprise victory

batalla *nf* (a) *(lucha)* battle; **librar b.** to do *o* join battle; **presentar b.** to draw up in battle array; *Fam* **dar b.** to be a lot of trouble; **este niño da mucha b.** this child is a real handful □ **b. campal** pitched battle; **campo de b.**

battlefield (**b**) *Fam* **de b.** ordinary, everyday; **zapatos de b.** everyday shoes

batallador, -a 1 *adj* fighting, struggling
  2 *nm,f* fighter, struggler

batallar *vi* (**a**) *(reñir con armas)* to battle, wage war (**b**) *Fig (disputar)* to fight, quarrel; **tendré que b. con el jefe para que me aumente el sueldo** I'll have to battle with the boss to get him to give me a rise

batallón *nm* battalion; **b. de infantería** infantry battalion; *Fam Fig* **un b. de niños** a crowd of children

batata *nf Esp Arg Col Ven* sweet potato

bate *nm Dep* bat

batea *nf* tray

bateador, -a *nm,f (en béisbol)* batter; *(en críquet) (hombre)* batsman; *(mujer)* batswoman

batear 1 *vi* to bat; **es su turno para b.** it is his turn to bat
  2 *vt* to hit; **b. la pelota** to hit o bat the ball

batel *nm Náut* small boat

batería 1 *nf* (**a**) *Mil* battery; *Fig* **una b. de preguntas** a barrage of questions (**b**) *Elec* battery ❏ **b. solar** solar cell (**c**) *Teat* footlights *pl* (**d**) *Mús (de orquesta)* percussion; *(de conjunto)* drums *pl*; **toca la b.** he plays the drums (**e**) *(conjunto de cosas)* set ❏ **b. de cocina** pots and pans, set of pans (**f**) **aparcar en b.** to park at an angle to the *Br* pavement o *US* sidewalk
  2 *nmf* drummer; **el b. del conjunto es holandés** the group's drummer is Dutch

baterista *nmf Am* drummer

batiborrillo *nm*, **batiburrillo** *nm* jumble, mess

batida *nf* (**a**) *Caza* beat (**b**) *Mil* reconnaissance (**c**) *(de la policía)* raid

batido, -a 1 *pp de* batir
  2 *adj Culin* whipped
  3 *nm* milk shake

batidor, -a *nm,f* (**a**) *Mil (explorador)* scout (**b**) *Caza* beater

batidora *nf Culin (automática)* blender; *(manual)* whisk

batiente 1 *adj* banging; **reírse a mandíbula b.** to laugh one's head off
  2 *nm* (**a**) *(jamba)* jamb (**b**) *(hoja de puerta)* leaf

batín *nm* short dressing gown

batintín *nm* gong

batir 1 *vt* (**a**) *(gen)* to beat; *(metales)* to hammer; *(palmas)* to clap; *(alas)* to flap (**b**) *Culin (huevos)* to beat; *(nata, claras)* to whip (**c**) *Dep (marca, récord)* to break; **batió el récord mundial de los cien metros libres** she broke the world hundred metres freestyle record (**d**) *(derribar)* to break down; **b. una puerta** to break down a door (**e**) *(desmontar)* to take down (**f**) *(reconocer) Mil* to reconnoitre (**g**) *Caza* to beat
  2 batirse *vpr* to fight; **b. en duelo** to fight a duel; **b. en retirada** to beat a retreat

batiscafo *nm* bathyscaphe

batista *nf Tex* cambric, batiste

batracio, -a *adj & nm* batrachian

batuecas *nfpl Fam* **estar en las b.** to be daydreaming, have one's head in the clouds

baturro, -a *nm,f Fam* Aragonese peasant

batuta *nf Mús* baton; *Fig* **llevar la b.** to be in charge, be the boss

baúl *nm* (**a**) *(mueble)* trunk (**b**) *Arg Col (en vehículo) Br* boot, *US* trunk

bauprés *nm Náut* bowsprit

bautismal *adj* baptismal

bautismo *nm* baptism, christening ❏ *Fig* **b. de fuego**

baptism of fire; *Fig* **b. del aire** first flight, maiden flight; **fe de b.** certificate of baptism

bautista *adj & nmf Rel* Baptist

bautisterio *nm* baptistry

bautizar [14] *vt* (**a**) *Rel* to baptize, christen; **bautizaron al niño con el nombre de David** the child was christened David (**b**) *(poner nombre a)* to name; **b. una calle/un barco** to name a street/ship; **le bautizaron con el mote de 'El Alto'** he was nicknamed 'El Alto' (**c**) *Fam (mezclar con agua)* to water down

bautizo *nm Rel* baptism, christening; *(fiesta)* christening party

bauxita *nf Min* bauxite

bávaro, -a *adj & nm,f* Bavarian

Baviera *n* Bavaria

baya *nf* berry

bayeta *nf* (**a**) *Tex* flannel (**b**) *(paño)* floorcloth

bayo, -a 1 *adj (color)* whitish yellow
  2 *nm* (**a**) *(caballo)* bay (**b**) *(mariposa)* silkworm moth

bayoneta *nf* bayonet; **ataque a la b.** bayonet charge; **calar la b.** to fix bayonets

bayonetazo *nm (golpe)* bayonet thrust; *(herida)* bayonet wound

baza *nf Naipes* trick; *Fig* **meter b.** to interfere, butt in; **no me dejaron meter b.** they didn't let me get a word in edgeways

bazar *nm* bazaar

bazo *nm Anat* spleen

bazofia *nf (comida)* pigswill; *(libro, película)* **ser (una) b.** to be *Br* rubbish o *US* garbage

bazooka *nm* bazooka

Bco. *(abrev de* **banco)** bank

be *nf Esp* name of the letter B in Spanish; *Fig* **be por be** down to the last detail ❏ *Am* **be larga** b *(to distinguish from* v*)*

beata *nf* (**a**) *Rel* lay sister (**b**) *(beatificada)* woman who has been beatified (**c**) *(piadosa)* devout woman (**d**) *Fam Pey* prude, sanctimonious woman

beatería *nf* sanctimoniousness

beatificación *nf* beatification

beatificar [59] *vt* to beatify

beatífico, -a *adj* beatific

beatitud *nf* beatitude

beatnik ['bitnik] *(pl* **beatniks)** *nmf* beatnik

beato, -a 1 *adj* (**a**) *Rel (beatificado)* beatified; *(piadoso)* devout (**b**) *Pey* prudish, sanctimonious (**c**) *(feliz)* happy
  2 *nm* (**a**) *Rel* lay brother (**b**) *(beatificado)* man who has been beatified; *(piadoso)* devout person

bebe, -a *nm,f Andes RP Fam* baby

bebé *nm* baby ❏ **b. probeta** test-tube baby

bebedero *nm* (**a**) *(abrevadero)* drinking trough, water trough (**b**) *(vasija)* drinking dish (**c**) *(lugar)* watering place

bebedizo *nm Med* potion; *Lit* poisonous potion; *(de amor)* love potion

bebedor, -a 1 *adj (hard o heavy)* drinking
  2 *nm,f (hard o heavy)* drinker

beber 1 *vt (agua, vino)* to drink; **b. algo a grandes tragos** to gulp sth down; **b. algo de un trago** to drink sth down in one go; *Fig* **b. los vientos por algo** to long for sth, be dying for sth
  2 *vi (brindar)* to toast, drink to sb's health; **bebamos a o por la felicidad de los novios** let us drink to the happiness of the bride and groom; *Fig* **b. de o en buenas fuentes** to have reliable sources of information

bebercio *nm Esp Argot* **el b.** drink, booze; **dedicarse al b.** *(siempre)* to take to the bottle; *(alguna vez)* to drink, booze

bebible *adj* drinkable

bebida *nf* drink, beverage; **darse a la b.** to take to drink ❑ **bebidas alcohólicas** alcoholic drinks

bebido, -a 1 *pp de* **beber**
2 *adj (borracho)* drunk; *(entonado)* tipsy

beca *nf (del gobierno)* grant; *(de organización privada)* scholarship ❑ **b. de investigación** research grant/scholarship

becada *nf Orn* woodcock

becado, -a 1 *pp de* **becar**
2 *adj* **alumno b.** *(por el gobierno)* grant holder; *(por organización privada)* scholarship holder
3 *nm,f esp Am (del gobierno)* grant holder; *(de organización privada)* scholarship holder

becar [59] *vt (sujeto: gobierno)* to award a grant to; *(sujeto: organización privada)* to award a scholarship to

becario, -a *nm,f* **(a)** *(del gobierno)* grant holder; *(de organización privada)* scholarship holder **(b)** *(en prácticas)* = person on a work placement, *US* intern

becerrada *nf Taur* = bullfight with young bulls

becerro *nm* calf; *Fig* **b. de oro** golden calf

bechamel *adj* & *nf Culin* bechamel; **salsa b.** bechamel sauce, white sauce

becuadro *nm Mús* natural sign

bedel *nm Univ* beadle, head porter

beduino, -a *adj* & *nm,f* Bedouin

befo, -a *adj* thick-lipped

begonia *nf Bot* begonia

beicon *nm Esp* bacon

beige [beiʃ] *(pl* **beiges***) adj* & *nm* beige

Beijing [bei'jin] *n* Beijing

Beirut *n* Beirut

beis *adj inv* & *nm inv Esp* beige

béisbol *nm* baseball; **jugador de b.** baseball player

beisbolero, -a *nm,f* baseball player

beisbolista 1 *adj* baseball
2 *nmf* baseball player

bejuco *nm Bot* liana, reed

beldad *nf Fml o Hum (hermosura)* beauty; *(mujer bella)* beauty, belle; **su hija es una b.** your daughter is a real beauty

Belén *n* Bethlehem

belén *nm* **(a)** *Rel* nativity scene, crib **(b)** *Fig* mess, chaos; **armar un b.** to kick up a fuss o rumpus; **esta casa es un b.** it's bedlam in this house; **meterse en belenes** to get into difficulties

belfo, -a 1 *adj* thick-lipped
2 *nm* thick lip

belga *adj* & *nmf* Belgian

Bélgica *n* Belgium

Belgrado *n* Belgrade

Belice *n* Belize

belicense *adj* & *nmf*, **beliceño, -a** *adj* & *nm,f* Belizean

belicismo *nm* warmongering, bellicosity

belicista 1 *adj* belligerent, bellicose
2 *nmf* warmonger

bélico, -a *adj (de espíritu)* warlike, bellicose; *(preparativos etc)* war; **material b.** armaments *pl*

belicosidad *nf* bellicosity

belicoso, -a *adj (de guerra)* warlike, bellicose; *(pendenciero)* aggressive

beligerancia *nf* belligerency, belligerence; **política de no b.** policy of non-aggression

beligerante *adj* belligerent; **los países beligerantes** the countries at war

bellaco, -a 1 *adj* **(a)** *(persona)* villainous, wicked **(b)** *RP (caballo)* vicious
2 *nm,f* villain, scoundrel

belladona *nf Bot* belladonna, deadly nightshade

bellaquería *nf* wickedness, roguery

belleza *nf (gen)* beauty; **crema de b.** beauty cream; *(mujer)* **una b.** a beauty

bello, -a *adj* beautiful; *Educ* **bellas artes** (fine) arts; **el b. sexo** the fair sex; *Lit* **la bella durmiente** Sleeping Beauty

bellota *nf* acorn

bemba *nf Andes Carib Fam* thick lips *pl*

bemol 1 *adj Mús* flat; **si b.** B flat
2 *nm* **(a)** *Mús* flat **(b)** *Fam Fig* **esto tiene b.** this is a tough one

benceno *nm Quím* benzene

bencina *nf* benzine

bendecir [51] *vt* to bless; **b. la mesa** to say grace; **¡Dios te bendiga!** God bless you!

bendición *nf* **(a)** *(acción)* blessing; *(ceremonia)* Benediction; **es una b. de Dios** it's a godsend; **es una b. oírle** he's a joy to listen to; **¡qué b.!** how marvellous!; *Fam* **echar la b. a algn** to have done with sb ❑ **b. de la mesa** grace **(b)** **bendiciones** wedding *sing*; **echar las b. a** to join in marriage

bendito, -a 1 *pp de* **bendecir**
2 *adj* **(a)** *(alma)* blessed; **¡b. sea Dios!** *(liturgia)* thanks be to God!; *Fam* thank goodness!; *Fam* **esa bendita costumbre de fumar en la mesa** this damned habit of smoking at table **(b)** *(de pocos alcances)* simple, simple-minded
3 *nm,f* **(a)** *(santo)* saint; **dormir como un b.** to sleep like a baby **(b)** *(bonachón)* good sort, kind soul; *(tontorrón)* simple soul

benedictino, -a *adj* & *nm* Benedictine

benefactor, -a 1 *adj* beneficent
2 *nm,f* benefactor

beneficencia *nf* beneficence, charity; **organización de b.** charity organization, welfare organization

beneficiado, -a 1 *pp de* **beneficiar**
2 *adj* favoured, *US* favored; **salir b. de algo** to do well out of sth, profit from sth
3 *nm Rel* beneficiary

beneficiar 1 *vt* **(a)** *(hacer bien)* to benefit, favour, *US* favor; **esa decisión no beneficia a nadie** that decision benefits nobody **(b)** *Fin (acciones)* to sell below par **(c)** *Carib Chile (ganado)* to slaughter
2 beneficiarse *vpr* **(a)** *(favorecerse)* to benefit **(b)** *Com Fin* to profit; **b. de o con algo** to profit from o by sth **(c)** *Esp Vulg* **b. a algn** to have sb, *Br* have it away with sb

beneficiario, -a *nm,f* beneficiary

beneficio *nm* **(a)** *Com Fin* profit; **b. neto** net profit **(b)** *(bien)* benefit; **en b. de todos** in everyone's interest; **en b. propio** in one's own interest; **en b. tuyo/suyo** for your/his own good **(c)** *Teat* charity performance; **un concierto a b. del asilo de ancianos** a concert in aid of the old people's home **(d)** *Carib Chile (ganado)* slaughter

beneficioso, -a *adj* beneficial, useful, good

benéfico, -a *adj* charitable; **función benéfica** charity performance; **institución benéfica** charitable body, charity

Benelux *nm (abrev de* **België-Nederland-Luxembourg***)* **el B.** Benelux

Benemérita *nf Esp* **la B.** = the Spanish Civil Guard

benemérito, -a *adj Fml* worthy, meritous

beneplácito *nm Fml* approval, consent

benevolencia *nf* benevolence, kindness

benevolente *adj*, **benévolo, -a** *adj* benevolent, kind

Bengala *n* Bengal

bengala *nf* flare

bengalí 1 *adj* Bengali
  2 *nmf (persona)* Bengali
  3 *(idioma)* Bengali

benigno, -a *adj (persona)* gentle, benign, affable; *(clima)* mild

Benín *n* Benin

benjamín, -ina *nm,f* youngest child; **Rosa es la benjamina de la familia** Rosa is the baby of the family

benzol *nm Quím* benzol

beodo, -a *adj & nm,f* drunk

berberecho *nm Zool* (common) cockle

berberisco, -a *adj & nm,f* Berber

berbiquí *nm Téc* **b. y barrena** brace and bit

beréber *nmf*, **berebere** *nmf* Berber

berenjena *nf Br* aubergine, *US* eggplant

berenjenal *nm Br* aubergine o *US* eggplant bed; *Fam* **te has metido en un b.** you've got yourself into a fine mess

bergamota *nf* bergamot

bergante *nm* scoundrel, ruffian

bergantín *nm Náut* brig, brigantine

beriberi *nm Med* beriberi

berilo *nm Min* beryl

Berlín *n* Berlin

berlina *nf* (a) *(carruaje)* berlin ❑ **b. inglesa** mailcoach (b) *Aut* saloon

berlinés, -esa 1 *adj* of o from Berlin
  2 *nm,f* Berliner

bermejo, -a *adj* reddish, red

bermellón *nm* vermilion

bermudas 1 *nfpl* o *nmpl (prenda)* Bermuda shorts
  2 *nfpl* **las (Islas) B.** Bermuda *sing*

Berna *n* Bern

berrear *vi* (a) *(becerro)* to bellow, low (b) *Fam (gritar)* to howl, bawl (c) *Mús Fam* to sing off key, sing out of tune

berrido *nm* (a) **dar berridos/un b.** *(animal)* to bellow; *(niño)* to howl (b) *Fam (cantar mal)* **dar berridos** to screech

berrinche *nm Fam* rage, tantrum; *Esp* **coger** o *Am* **hacer un b.** to throw a tantrum

berro *nm* cress, watercress

berrocal *nm* rocky place

berza *nf* cabbage

berzal *nm* cabbage patch

berzas *nmf inv*, **berzotas** *nmf inv Esp Fam* idiot, halfwit

besamanos *nm inv* (a) *(recepción oficial)* royal audience (b) *(modo de saludar)* hand kissing

besamel *nf*, **besamela** *nf véase* **bechamel**

besar 1 *vt* to kiss; *Fig* **b. el suelo** to fall flat on one's face; *Fig* **fue llegar y b. el santo** it was as easy as pie, it was a piece of cake, it was a walkover
  2 besarse *vpr* (a) *(con los labios)* to kiss; **se besaron al despedirse** they kissed each other goodbye (b) *Fam (tropezar)* to bump heads; **se besaron al doblar la esquina** they bumped into each other as they turned the corner

beso *nm* kiss; *Fam* **comerse a algn a besos** to kiss sb passionately

bestia 1 *nf* beast, animal ❑ **b. de carga** beast of burden **b. negra** bête noire
  2 *nmf Fam Fig* brute, beast; **estar hecho un b.** to be as strong as a horse; **ser una mala b.** to be a nasty piece of work
  3 *adj Fig* brutish, boorish; **a lo b.** rudely, inconsiderately; **aquí te tratan a lo b.** they are really rude to you in here, they treat you like animals in here; **¡no seas b.!** *(grosero)* don't be rude!; *(exagerado)* don't exaggerate!

bestial *adj* (a) *(brutal)* animal, bestial (b) *Fam (enorme)* huge, tremendous; *(extraordinario)* fantastic, terrific, great; **esa película es b.** that movie o *Br* film is brilliant; **una comida b.** a huge meal

bestialidad *nf* (a) *(brutalidad)* bestiality, savagery (b) *Fam (estupidez)* stupidity; **decir bestialidades** to say horrible things (c) *Fam (cantidad grande)* **una b. de** tons of, stacks of

bestiario *nm Lit* bestiary

best-seller [bes'seler] *(pl* best-sellers) *nm* best-seller

besucón, -ona 1 *adj* fond of kissing
  2 *nm,f* person who is fond of kissing

besugo *nm* (a) *(pez)* sea bream (b) *Esp Pey (persona)* idiot, half-wit; **mantener** o **sostener un diálogo de besugos** to talk at cross purposes

besuquear *Fam* **1** *vt* to kiss, cover with kisses
  2 besuquearse *vpr* to smooch

besuqueo *nm Fam* smooching

beta *nf (letra griega)* beta; **rayos b.** beta rays

bético, -a *adj Hist* Andalusian

betún *nm* (a) *Quím* bitumen, asphalt (b) *(para el calzado)* shoe polish; *Fam* **quedar a la altura del b.** to give a poor show

bezo *nm* thick lip

bezudo, -a *adj* thick-lipped

Bhutan *n* Bhutan

bianual *adj* (a) *(dos veces al año)* biannual, twice-yearly (b) *(cada dos años)* biennial

biberón *nm* baby's bottle, feeding bottle

Biblia *nf* (a) *Rel* Bible; **la (Santa) B.** the (Holy) Bible; *Fam* **saber la B. en verso** to know everything, be very knowledgeable (b) **b.** *Argot (drogas)* book of cigarette papers

bíblico, -a *adj* biblical

bibliófilo, -a *nm,f* bibliophile, booklover

bibliografía *nf* bibliography

bibliográfico,a *adj* bibliographic, bibliographical

bibliógrafo, -a *nm,f* bibliographer

biblioteca *nf* (a) *(lugar, conjunto de libros)* library ❑ **b. ambulante** mobile library; **b. pública** public library (b) *Mueb* bookcase, bookshelves *pl*

bibliotecario, -a *nm,f* librarian

bicameral *adj Pol* bicameral, two-chamber

bicampeón, -ona *nm,f* two-times o twice champion

bicarbonato *nm Quím* bicarbonate ❑ **b. sódico** bicarbonate of soda

bicéfalo, -a *adj* bicephalous, two-headed

bicentenario *nm* bicentenary, *US* bicentennial

bíceps *nm inv Anat* biceps

bicha *nf* snake

bicharraco *nm Fam* (a) *(animal)* disgusting creature (b) *(persona mala)* nasty piece of work

biche *adj Col (fruta)* green, unripe

bichero *nm* boathook

bicho *nm* (**a**) *(insecto)* bug, creepy-crawly; *Fig* ¿qué b. te ha picado? *Br* what's up with you?, *US* what's eating you? (**b**) *(animal)* beast, animal; *Taur* bull (**c**) *Fam (persona)* odd character; **mal b.** nasty piece of work; **todo b. viviente** every living soul; **un b. raro** a weird person, an oddball

bichoco, -a *adj CSur (animal)* old, decrepit

bici *nf Fam* bike

bicicleta *nf* bicycle; **ir en b.** to go by bicycle; ¿**sabes montar en b.?** can you ride a bicycle? ❏ **b. de carreras** racing bicycle; **b. de montaña** mountain bike; **b. estática** exercise bike

bicicross *nm* cyclocross

bicoca *nf Fam Fig* bargain; **es una bicoca** it's a bargain

bicolor *adj* two-colour, two-tone; *Pol* **gobierno b.** two-party government

bicornio *nm* two-cornered hat

bidé *nm* bidet

bidimensional *adj* two-dimensional

bidón *nm* large can, drum; **b. de gasolina** oil drum

biela *nf Aut* connecting rod

bieldo *nm*, **bielda** *nf Agr* winnowing fork

Bielorrusia *n* Belarus

bielorruso, -a *adj & nm,f* Belorussian, Byelorussian

biempensante 1 *adj* right-thinking; **la sociedad b.** respectable society
2 *nmf* **los biempensantes** right-thinking o respectable people

bien¹ 1 *adv* (**a**) *(como es debido)* well, properly; **habla b. el italiano** she speaks Italian well; **hay que escribirlo b.** it must be written correctly; **hiciste b. en decírmelo** you were right to tell me; **las cosas le van b.** things are going well for him; **oler b.** to smell nice o lovely; *(comida)* to smell good; **portarse b.** to behave well; *Prov* **quien b. te quiere te hará llorar** you have to be cruel to be kind (**b**) *(excelente)* all right, O.K.; **¡b.!** good!, great!; **¡muy b.!** excellent, first class!; **pasarlo b.** to have a good time; **¡qué b.!** great!, fantastic! (**c**) *(con buena salud)* well; ¿**no te encuentras b.?** aren't you feeling well? (**d**) *(cómodamente)* well, comfortably; **viven b.** they're comfortably off (**e**) *(fácilmente)* easily; **b. podía haberme avisado** she might have let me know; **b. puede acabarlo en un día** he can easily finish it off in a day; **b. puedes permitirte el lujo de fumar puros** if anybody can afford to treat himself to cigars, you can; **b. puedo creer que ...** I can well believe that ... (**f**) *(con gusto)* really; *(de buena gana)* willingly, gladly; **b. lo pagaría si tuviera bastante dinero** I'd gladly pay for it if I had enough money; **b. me tomaría ahora una sopita de cebolla** I'd really love a bowl of onion soup right now (**g**) *(seguramente)* **b. se gastaron la mitad de la herencia en aquella casa** they must have spent half the inheritance on that house (**h**) *(muy, bastante)* very, quite; **b. es verdad que ...** it's quite clear that ...; **b. temprano** very early, nice and early; **dame un té b. caliente** I'd like a nice hot cup of tea; **la casa está b. lejos del pueblo** the house is a long way from the village (**i**) *(mucho)* lots of/a lot of, many; **b. de veces** lots of times (**j**) *(en interrogativas)* ¿**y b.?** and so?, what then? (**k**) *(estar + bien) (de dinero)* well-off; *(de salud)* well; **la abuela está muy b. de salud** grandmother is in really good health; *(cómodamente)* **aquí dentro se está muy b.** it's nice and cosy in here; *(es bueno)* **esta comida está b.** this meal is fine; *(prenda)* **esta falda te está b.** this skirt suits you; *(merecer)* **le está b. empleado que se le haya escapado el avión** I'm glad he missed the plane, it serves him right; **¡está b.!** *(de acuerdo!)* fine!, all right!; *(¡basta!)* that's enough!; **¡ya está b.!** that's (quite) enough!; *Fam (bonito, interesante)* **esa película francesa está muy b.** that French movie o *Br* film is very good; *Fam* **su novia** **está muy b.** his girlfriend is very nice; *Irón* **¡(pues) sí que estamos b.!** *(well)*, we are in a fine mess! (**l**) *(para)* **b.** to agree with; **no me ha sentado b. la fruta** the fruit has disagreed with me; **sus comentarios no se me sentaron b.** I didn't like his remarks (**m**) *Fml* **tener a b. de** to be so kind as to; **rogamos tenga a bien de ...** would you please ...?, we should be grateful if you would ... (**n**) **más b.** rather, a little; **es más b. tímida** she's on the shy side, she's a little shy
2 *conj* **ahora b.** now, now then; **b. ... o b. ...** either ... or ...; **b. en metro o b. en coche** either by *Br* tube o *US* subway or by car; **no b.** as soon as; **no b. llegó la policía, empezó el tiroteo** no sooner had the police arrived than the shooting began; **si b.** while, although, even if
3 *adj* well-to-do, well-off

bien² 1 *nm* (**a**) *(bondad)* good, good thing; **el b. y el mal** good and evil; **un hombre de b.** an upright o upstanding man; *Prov* **haz b. y no mires a quien** do well and dread no shame (**b**) *(bienestar, provecho)* benefit, advantage; **dedicó su vida al bien de los demás** she devoted her life to others; **por el b. de** for the good of, in the interest of; **lo hace por el b. de sus hijos** he does it for the sake of his children; **lo hicieron por tu b.** they did it for your own good
2 bienes *nmpl* goods ❏ **b. de equipo** *(maquinaria, instalaciones)* capital goods; *Jur* property; **b. gananciales** shared possessions; **b. inmuebles** real estate, *US* real property; **b. muebles** personal property; **b. públicos** public property

bienal 1 *adj* biennial
2 *nf* biennial (exhibition)

bienaventurado, -a 1 *adj* (**a**) *Rel* blessed (**b**) *(afortunado)* fortunate, happy
2 *nm,f* naïve person

bienaventuranza *nf* (**a**) *(felicidad)* happiness, bliss (**b**) *Rel* **las bienaventuranzas** the Beatitudes

bienestar *nm (personal)* well-being, contentment; *(comodidad)* ease, comfort

bienhablado, -a *adj* well-spoken

bienhechor, -a 1 *adj* beneficent, beneficial
2 *nm,f (hombre)* benefactor; *(mujer)* benefactress

bienintencionado, -a *adj* well-meaning, well-intentioned

bienio *nm* biennium, two-year period

biempensante *adj & nmf véase* **biempensante**

bienvenida *nf* welcome; **dar la b. a algn** to welcome sb

bienvenido, -a *adj* welcome

bies *nm inv Cost* bias; **al b.** on the bias

bifásico, -a *adj Elec* two-phase

bife *nm Andes RP* (**a**) *Culin* steak (**b**) *(bofetada)* slap

bífido, -a *adj Anat Bot* bifid

bífidus *nm inv* bifidus

bifocal *adj* bifocal

bifurcación *nf* bifurcation; *(de la carretera)* fork

bifurcado, -a *adj* forked

bifurcarse [59] *vpr* to fork, branch off

bigamia *nf* bigamy

bígamo, -a 1 *adj* bigamous
2 *nm,f* bigamist

bígaro *nm Zool* winkle

bigote *nm* (**a**) *(de persona)* moustache, *US* mustache; *(de gato)* whiskers *pl* (**b**) *Esp Fam* **de b.** *(enorme)* huge; *(sensacional)* tremendous, great, terrific; **una comida de b.** a fantastic meal

bigotera *nf (compás)* bow compass

bigotudo, -a *adj* with a large moustache, moustachioed

bigudí *nm* hair-curler, roller

bilateral *adj* bilateral; **acuerdo b.** bilateral agreement

bilbaíno, -a 1 *adj* of *o* from Bilbao
2 *nm,f* person from Bilbao

biliar *adj* biliary; *Med* **cálculo b.** bile stone

bilingüe *adj* bilingual

bilingüismo *nm* bilingualism

bilioso, -a *adj* bilious

bilis *nf* (a) *Med* bile (b) *Fig* bile, spleen; **descargar la b. contra algn** to vent one's spleen on sb; **esa actitud me exalta la b.** that attitude makes my blood boil

billar *nm* (a) *(juego)* billiards *sing*; **jugar al b.** to play billiards □ **b. americano** pool; **b. romano** pinball; **b. ruso** snooker (b) *(mesa)* billiard table (c) **billares** billiard room *sing*, pool room *sing*

billetaje *nm* tickets *pl*

billete *nm* (a) *(de banco)* Br note, US bill; **un b. de mil** a thousand euro/peso *etc* Br note *o* US bill (b) *Esp (de bus, avión etc)* ticket; **sacar un b.** to buy a ticket □ **b. abierto** open ticket; **b. de ida y vuelta** Br return (ticket), US round-trip ticket; *Ferroc* **b. kilométrico** = ticket to travel a set distance; **b. sencillo** *o* **de ida** Br single (ticket), US one-way ticket (c) *(de rifa, lotería)* ticket

billetera *nf*, **billetero** *nm* wallet, US billfold

billón *nm* billion, US trillion

bimensual *adj* twice-monthly, bi-monthly, fortnightly

bimestral *adj* every two months

bimestre 1 *adj véase* **bimestral**
2 *nm* period of two months

bimotor 1 *adj* twin-engine, twin-engined
2 *nm* twin-engined plane

binario, -a *adj* binary; *Mat* **sistema b.** binary system

bingo *nm* (a) *(juego)* bingo (b) *(sala)* bingo hall

binoculares *nmpl* field glasses, binoculars

binóculo *nm* pince-nez

binomio *nm Mat* binomial

biocombustible *nm* biofuel

biodegradable *adj* biodegradable

biodiversidad *nf* biodiversity

bioética *nf* bioethics *(sing)*

biofísica *nf* biophysics *(sing)*

biofísico, -a *adj* biophysical

biografía *nf* biography

biográfico, -a *adj* biographic, biographical

biógrafo, -a *nm,f* biographer

bioingeniería *nf* bioengineering

biología *nf* biology

biológico, -a *adj* biological

biólogo, -a *nm,f* biologist

biomasa *nf Biol* biomass

biombo *nm* (folding) screen

biopsia *nf Med* biopsy

bioquímica *nf* biochemistry

bioquímico, -a 1 *adj* biochemical
2 *nm,f* biochemist

biorritmo *nm* biorhythm

biosfera *nf* biosphere

biotecnología *nf* biotechnology

bioterrorismo *nm* bioterrorism

bióxido *nm Quím* dioxide □ **b. de carbono** carbon dioxide

bipartidismo *nm Pol* two-party system, bipartisanship

bipartito, -a *adj* bipartite

bípedo, -a *adj & nm,f* biped

biplano *nm* biplane

biplaza 1 *adj* **vehículo b.** two-seater
2 *nm* two-seater

bipolar *adj* bipolar

biquini *nm (prenda)* bikini

birlar *vt Fam* to pinch, *Br* nick; **me han birlado la cartera** my wallet's been pinched

birlibirloque *nm Esp* **por arte de b.** as if by magic

Birmania *n* Burma

birmano, -a *adj & nm,f* Burmese

birreactor *Av* **1** *adj* twin-jet
2 *nm* twin-jet plane

birreta *nf Rel* biretta

birrete *nm* cap, beret; *Rel* biretta; *Univ* mortarboard, academic cap

birria *nf Fam* **es una b.** it's a load of *Br* rubbish *o* US garbage

birrioso, -a *adj Fam (malo)* pathetic; *(escaso)* measly

biruji *nm Fam* chilly wind

bis 1 *adv* twice; **viven en el 34 b.** they live at 34 A
2 *nm* encore

bisabuela *nf* great-grandmother

bisabuelo *nm* great-grandfather; **bisabuelos** great-grandparents

bisagra *nf* hinge

bisar *vt* to give as an encore, repeat

bisbisar *vt*, **bisbisear** *vt* to mutter, mumble

bisbiseo *nm* muttering, mumbling

bisección *nf* bisection

bisector *adj Geom* bisecting

bisectriz *Geom* **1** *adj* bisecting
2 *nf* bisector, bisectrix

bisel *nm* bevel edge, bevel

biselar *vt* to bevel

bisemanal *adj* twice-weekly

bisexual *adj & nmf* bisexual

bisexualidad *nf* bisexuality

bisiesto *adj* **año b.** leap year

bisílabo, -a *adj* two-syllabled, disyllabic

bismuto *nm Quím* bismuth

bisnieto, -a *nm,f (niño)* great-grandson; *(niña)* great-granddaughter; **mis bisnietos** my great-grandchildren

bisojo, -a *adj* cross-eyed

bisonte *nm* bison, American buffalo

bisoñé *nm* toupee

bisoño, -a 1 *adj Mil* raw; *Fig* inexperienced, green
2 *nm,f Mil* raw recruit, US rookie; *Fig* greenhorn, novice

bistec *nm*, **bisté** *nm* steak

bisturí *nm* scalpel, surgical knife

bisutería *nf* imitation jewellery *o* US jewelry

bit *(pl* bits) *nm Inform* bit

bitácora *nf Náut* binnacle □ **cuaderno de b.** log-book

bíter *nm* bitters *pl*

bitoque *nm* (a) *(tapón)* spigot (b) *Am Med* cannula

bituminoso, -a *adj* bituminous

bivalente *adj Quím* bivalent

bivalvo, -a *adj* bivalve

bizantino, -a 1 *adj* (a) *Hist* Byzantine (b) *Fig* pointless; **discusiones bizantinas** hair-splitting arguments
2 *nm,f Hist* Byzantine

bizarría *nf* (a) *(valor)* gallantry, bravery (b) *(generosidad)* generosity

bizarro, -a *adj* (a) *(valiente)* gallant, brave (b) *(generoso)* generous

bizco, -a 1 *adj* cross-eyed; *Fig* **quedarse b.** to be dumbfounded *o* flabbergasted
2 *nm,f* cross-eyed person

bizcocho *nm* sponge cake *o* finger

biznieto, -a *nm,f véase* **bisnieto, -a**

bizquear *vi* to go cross-eyed

blanca *nf* (a) *Mús Br* minim, *US* half note (b) *Esp Fam* **estar** *o* **quedarse sin b.** to be flat broke

Blancanieves *nf Lit* Snow White

blanco, -a¹ 1 *adj* white; **más b. que la nieve** as white as snow; **tez blanca** fair complexion
2 *nm,f (hombre)* white man; *(mujer)* white woman; **los blancos** whites

blanco² ** *nm* (a) *(color)* white; **en b. y negro in black and white ◻ *Constr* **b. de España** whiting; *Anat* **b. de la uña** half-moon; *Anat* **b. del ojo** white of the eye (b) *(vacío)* blank; **dejó la hoja en b.** he left the page blank; **votos en b.** blank votes; *Fig* **pasar la noche en b.** to have a sleepless night; **quedarse en b.** to fail to understand (c) *(diana)* target; **dar en el b.** to hit the target *o* the bull's eye; **tirar al b.** to shoot at a target; **tiro al b.** target shooting; *Fig* **ser el b. de todas las miradas** to be the centre of attention

blancor *nm*, **blancura** *nf* whiteness

blancuzco, -a *adj Pey* whitish

blandengue *adj Pey* weak, soft, feeble

blandir *vt* to brandish

blando, -a *adj* (a) *(maleable)* soft; **un colchón b.** a soft mattress; **tiene las carnes muy blandas** he is flabby (b) *Fig (suave)* soft, gentle; **clima b.** mild climate; **es demasiado b. con sus hijos** he's too soft with the children; **una mirada blanda** a tender look

blanducho, -a *adj*, **blandujo, -a** *adj Fam* softish; *Pey (cuerpo)* flabby

blandura *nf* (a) *(calidad)* softness (b) *Fig (dulzura)* gentleness, tenderness; *(debilidad)* mildness, weakness

blanduzco, -a *adj Pey* softish

blanqueador, -a 1 *adj (que pone blanco)* whitening; *(con lejía)* whitewashing; **un producto b.** a whitening *o* bleaching agent
2 *nm,f* whitewasher

blanquear 1 *vt* (a) *(poner blanco)* to whiten; *(con lejía)* to bleach (b) *(con cal)* to whitewash (c) *Fig (dinero)* to launder
2 *vi* to turn white, be whitish

blanquecino, -a *adj* whitish

blanqueo *nm* (a) *(de ropa)* whitening; *(con lejía)* bleaching (b) *(con cal)* whitewashing; *Téc* blanching (c) *Fig (de dinero)* laundering

blasfemar *vi Rel* to blaspheme (**contra** against); *(decir palabrotas)* to curse, swear

blasfemia *nf Rel* blasphemy; *(palabrota)* curse

blasfemo, -a 1 *adj* blasphemous
2 *nm,f* blasphemer

blasón *nm* (a) *(escudo)* coat of arms (b) *(heráldica)* heraldry (c) *(divisa)* device (d) *Fig (gloria, honor)* glory, honour, *US* honor; **hacer b. de algo** to boast about sth

blasonar *vt* to emblazon
2 *vi Fig* to boast (**de** about)

blástula *nf Biol* blastula

blazer ['bleiser] *(pl* **blazers)** *nm* blazer

bledo *nm Bot* blite; *Fam* **me importa un b.** I couldn't give a damn, I couldn't care less

blenorragia *nf Med* blennorrhagia

blenorrea *nf Med* blennorrhoea, *US* blennorrhea

blindado, -a *adj* (a) *Mil* armoured, *US* armored, armour-plated, *US* armor-plated; *(antibalas)* bullet-proof; **coche b.** bullet-proof car; *(furgoneta)* security van; **puerta blindada** reinforced door, security door (b) *Téc* shielded

blindaje *nm* (a) *(de puerta)* armour-plating, *US* armor-plating; *(de vehículo)* armour, *US* armor (b) *Téc* shield

blindar *vt* (a) *(puerta, vehículo)* to armour, *US* armor (b) *Téc* to shield

bloc *nm* pad ◻ **b. de notas** notepad

blocaje *nm (en fútbol)* bodycheck

blocar [59] *vt Ftb* to block

blog [bloɣ] *(pl* **blogs)** *nm Inform* blog

blonda *nf* blond lace

blondo, -a *adj Literario* blond, blonde, fair

bloque *nm* (a) *(gen)* block; **un b. de cemento** a concrete block; **en b.** en bloc ◻ **b. de apartamentos** *Br* block of flats, *US* apartment block (b) *(manzana de casas)* block (c) *Pol* bloc; **el b. de países comunistas** the Communist Bloc countries

bloquear *vt* (a) *Mil* to blockade (b) *Com Fin (precios)* to freeze (c) *Téc* to jam, block (d) *Ftb (pelota)* to block (e) *Parl (ley, decreto)* to block (f) *(obstruir)* to block, obstruct; **la nieve bloqueó todas las vías de acceso al pueblo** the village was cut off by snow

bloqueo *nm* (a) *Mil* blockade; **forzar el b.** to run the blockade; **levantar un b.** to raise a blockade ◻ **b. naval** naval blockade (b) *Com Fin (precios)* freeze, freezing ◻ **b. económico** economic blockade (c) **b. mental** mental block

blues [blus] *nm inv Mús* blues *pl*

blusa *nf* blouse

blusón *nm* loose blouse, smock

boa *nf Zool* boa

boato *nm* show, ostentation

bobada *nf (acción)* silliness, fooling about; *(comentario)* nonsense, *Br* rubbish, *US* garbage; **decir bobadas** to talk nonsense; **¡no hagas bobadas!** don't be silly!

bobalicón, -ona *Fam* **1** *adj* simple, stupid
2 *nm,f* simpleton, idiot

bobear *vi (decir bobadas)* to talk nonsense; *(hacer bobadas)* to do silly things, fool about

bobería *nf véase* **bobada**

bóbilis: de bóbilis bóbilis *loc adv Esp Fam* (a) *(de balde)* free, for nothing (b) *(sin esfuerzo)* without lifting a finger

bobina *nf* (a) *(de película)* reel, spool; *(de hilo)* bobbin, reel, spool; *(de cinta magnética)* reel (b) *Elec* coil ◻ **b. de encendido** ignition coil

bobinado *nm Elec* winding, coiling

bobinar *vt* to wind

bobo, -a 1 *adj (tonto)* stupid, silly; *(ingenuo)* naïve, simple
2 *nm,f* fool, simpleton, dunce; **entre bobos anda el juego** they are all the same, they are all as bad as each other
3 *nm Teat* buffoon, jester

boca *nf* (a) *Anat* mouth; **b. abajo** face downward; **b. arriba** face upward; *Fig* **a b. llena** openly, straight out; *Fig* **a pedir de b.** in accordance with one's wishes; *Fig* **todo le salió a pedir de b.** everything turned out exactly as he had wished; *Fig* **andar de b. en b.** to be the talk of the town; *Fig* **b. de escorpión** evil tongue; *Fig* **decir algo con la b. chica**

to say one thing and mean another; *Fig* **hacer b.** to whet one's appetite; *Fig* **írsele la b. a algn** to be unable to keep one's mouth shut, let the cat out of the bag; *Fig* **meterse en la b. del lobo** to put one's head into the lion's mouth; *Fig* **quitarle a algn las palabras de la b.** to take the words right out of sb's mouth; *Fig* **tengo cinco bocas que mantener** I've got five mouths to feed; *Fam* **cerrarle la b. a algn** to shut sb up; *Fam* **con la b. abierta** open-mouthed, agape; *Fam* **no abrir la b., no decir esta b. es mía** not to open one's mouth, not to say a word; *Fam* **quedarse con la b. abierta** to be astounded o amazed; *Fam* **se le hizo la b. agua** his mouth watered; *Fam* **taparle la b. a algn** to shut sb up, keep sb quiet; *Fam* **¡cállate la b.!** shut up!; *Prov* **en b. cerrada no entran moscas** silence is golden; *Prov* **por la b. muere el pez** the least said the better ❏ **b. a b.** kiss of life, mouth-to-mouth resuscitation (**b**) *(entrada)* entrance; *Téc* opening, aperture; **b. del estómago** pit of the stomach; **la b. de un túnel** the mouth of a tunnel; **b. de incendios** fire hydrant; **b. de metro** *Br* tube o underground entrance, *US* subway entrance; **b. de riego** hydrant (**c**) *(vino)* bouquet, aroma

bocacalle *nf (calle secundaria)* side street; *(entrada)* entrance to a street, intersection

bocadillo *nm* (**a**) *(comida)* sandwich; **tomar un b.** to have a snack; **un b. de jamón/tortilla** a ham/omelette sandwich (**b**) *(de cómic, chiste)* balloon

bocado *nm* (**a**) *(mordisco)* mouthful; *(piscolabis)* bite to eat, snack, tidbit; **con el b. en la boca** having scarcely finished eating; **no he probado b. en todo el día** I haven't had a bite to eat all day; *Fam* **b. sin hueso** soft job, cushy number ❏ *Anat* **b. de Adán** Adam's apple (**b**) *(mordedura)* bite (**c**) *(freno del caballo)* bit

bocajarro: a bocajarro *loc adv* (**a**) *(disparar)* point-blank (**b**) *(decir)* straight out

bocamanga *nf* cuff, wristband

bocanada *nf* (**a**) *(de vino)* mouthful (**b**) *(de humo)* whiff, puff; **una b. de viento** a gust of wind

bocata *nm Esp Argot* sandwich

bocazas *nmf inv Fam* bigmouth, blabbermouth

bocel *nm Arquit* torus

bocera *nf* (**a**) *(comida)* = food left around the mouth after eating or drinking, moustache (**b**) *Med* cold sore

boceras *nmf inv Fam* bigmouth, blabbermouth

boceto *nm Arte* sketch, outline; *(de un trabajo escrito)* outline, plan

bocha *nf* (**a**) *(bola)* bowl (**b**) **bochas** *(juego)* bowls

bochar *vt RP Fam* (**a**) *(suspender)* to fail (**b**) *(rechazar)* to dismiss

bochinche *nm Fam* uproar, din, riot; **armar un b.** to kick up a row

bochinchero, -a *adj Am Fam* rowdy

bochorno *nm* (**a**) *(tiempo)* sultry o close weather; *(calor sofocante)* stifling heat; **hacer b.** to be sultry o close o muggy (**b**) *Fig (vergüenza)* shame, embarrassment (**c**) *(rubor)* blush, flush

bochornoso, -a *adj* (**a**) *(tiempo)* sultry, close, muggy, oppressive; *(calor)* stifling (**b**) *Fig (vergonzoso)* shameful, embarrassing

bocina *nf* (**a**) *Aut* horn; **tocar la b.** to blow o sound one's horn (**b**) *Mús* horn, trumpet (**c**) *(de gramófono)* horn

bocinazo *nm Aut* hoot, honk, toot

bocio *nm Med* goitre

bocón, -ona *Fam* **1** *adj* big-mouthed
   2 *nm,f* big-mouth, braggart

bocoy *nm (pl* bocoyes*)* large cask

boda *nf* wedding, marriage ❏ **bodas de diamante/oro/plata** diamond/gold/silver wedding *sing*; **lista de bodas** wedding list

bodega *nf* (**a**) *(en vivienda)* wine cellar; *(tienda)* wine shop (**b**) *Náut* hold (**c**) *Méx (almacén)* store (**d**) *CAm Carib (tienda de comestibles)* grocery store, *Br* grocer's (shop)

bodegón *nm* (**a**) *(restaurante)* cheap restaurant (**b**) *(taberna)* tavern (**c**) *Arte* still-life painting

bodeguero, -a *nm,f (propietario)* = owner of a wine cellar; *(encargado)* cellarman

bodoque 1 *nm* (**a**) *Cost* tuft (**b**) *Guat Méx (chichón)* bump, lump, swelling
   2 *nmf Fam* dimwit, dunce

bodorrio *nm Pey* wedding

bodrio *nm* (**a**) *Fam (comida)* slop, pigswill (**b**) *(basura)* **su última novela es un b.** his latest novel is *Br* rubbish o *US* trash; **¡vaya b. de película!** what a dreadful movie o *Br* film!

body ['boði] *(pl* bodies*)* *nm* bodystocking, leotard

BOE ['boe] *nm (abrev de* Boletín Oficial del Estado*)* Official Gazette

bóer *adj & nmf* Boer

bofe 1 *nm (pulmón)* lung, lights *pl*; *Fam Fig* **echar el b.** o **los bofes** *(trabajar mucho)* to work flat out, slog one's guts out; *(esforzarse mucho)* to go all out
   2 *adj Am (desagradable)* disagreeable, unpleasant

bofetada *nf* slap round the face; *Fig* blow; **dar una b. a algn** to slap sb's face; *Esp Fig* **darse de bofetadas por algo** to come to blows over sth; **esos colores se dan de bofetadas** those colours really clash; *Fig* **no tener (ni) media b.** to be a weakling, be weedy; *Fig* **¡qué b. le has dado al decir eso!** what you said was a real blow to him!

bofetón *nm* hard slap round the face

bofia *nf Esp Argot* **la b.** the fuzz, the cops *pl*, the law; **tiene jaleos con la b.** he's in trouble with the law

boga¹ *nf (pez) (de agua dulce)* bream; *(de mar)* bogue

boga² *nf* (**a**) *Náut* rowing (**b**) *Fig* **estar en b.** to be in fashion

bogar [38] *vi* (**a**) *(remar)* to row (**b**) *(navegar)* to sail

bogavante *nm* lobster

Bogotá *n* Bogota

bogotano, -a 1 *adj* of o from Bogota
   2 *nm,f* person from Bogota

bohemia *nf* Bohemia, Bohemian life

bohemio, -a *adj & nm,f* Bohemian

bohío *nm Carib* hut, cabin

boicot *(pl* boicots*)* *nm* boycott

boicotear *vt* to boycott

boicoteo *nm* boycott, boycotting

boina *nf* beret

boj *nm* (**a**) *(árbol)* box (**b**) *(madera)* boxwood

bojar 1 *vt (medir)* to measure; **b. una isla** to measure the perimeter of an island
   2 *vi (medir)* to measure; **la isla boja cuarenta kilómetros** the island has a perimeter of forty kilometres

bojote *nm Andes CAm Carib* bundle, package

bol *nm* bowl

bola *nf* (**a**) *(cuerpo esférico)* ball, sphere; *(canica)* marble; *Dep Fam* ball; *Fig* **dejar que ruede la b.** to let things take their course; **no dar pie con b.** to be unable to do anything right ❏ **b. de billar** billiard ball; **b. de cristal** crystal ball; **b. de nieve** snowball; *Téc* **cojinete de bolas** ball bearing; **queso de b.** Edam cheese (**b**) *Fam Fig (mentira)* fib, lie; **meter bolas** to tell fibs (**c**) *Bridge* slam (**d**) *muy Fam* **bolas** *(testículos)* balls (**e**) *Cuba Chile* **bolas** croquet

bolada *nf (lanzamiento)* throw; *Bill* stroke
bolardo *nm Náut* bollard
bolchevique *adj & nmf* Bolshevik
bolcheviquismo *nm,* **bolchevismo** *nm* Bolshevism
boldo *nm Bot* boldo
boleada *nf Méx* shine, polish
boleadoras *nfpl RP* bolas
bolear *vt* (a) *RP (cazar)* to bring down with bolas (b) *Méx (embetunar)* to polish
bolera *nf* bowling alley
bolero, -a¹ 1 *adj (mentiroso)* lying, fibbing
  2 *nm,f* liar, fibber
bolero, -a² 1 *nm,f Mús* bolero dancer
  2 *nm* (a) *Mús* bolero (b) *(chaquetilla)* bolero (c) *Méx (limpiabotas)* shoeshine, *Br* bootblack
boleta *nf* (a) *(para entrar)* (admission) ticket (b) *Cuba Méx RP (para votar)* ballot, voting slip (c) *CAm CSur (multa)* parking ticket (d) *Méx (de calificaciones) Br* (school) report, *US* report card
boletería *nf Am (de estación)* ticket office; *(de cine, teatro)* ticket office, box office
boletero, -a *nm,f Am* box office attendant
boletín *nm* (a) *(publicación)* journal, bulletin; **B. Oficial del Estado** Official Gazette, = daily state publication, giving details of legislation etc □ **b. de noticias** news bulletin; **b. informativo** news bulletin; **b. meteorológico** weather forecast (b) *(impreso)* form
boleto *nm* (a) *(de rifa, lotería)* ticket; *(de quinielas)* coupon (b) *Am (para medio de transporte)* ticket (c) *Col Méx (para espectáculo)* ticket □ **b. redondo** *Br* return (ticket), *US* round-trip (ticket)
boli *nm Esp Fam* ballpen, biro®
boliche *nm* (a) *(juego de bolos)* ten-pin bowling (b) *(en la petanca)* jack (c) *(lugar)* bowling alley (d) *(juguete)* cup-and-ball game (e) *CSur Fam (tienda)* small-town store; *(taberna)* cheap bar (f) *Arg (discoteca)* disco
bólido *nm* (a) *Astron* meteor, meteorite; *Fam* **ir como un b.** to go at a rate of knots, *Br* go like the clappers; **siempre vas como un b.** you're always in a mad rush (b) *Aut* racing car
bolígrafo *nm* ballpoint (pen), biro®
bolilla *nf RP (en sorteo)* numbered ball
bolillo *nm Cost* bobbin; **encaje de bolillos** bobbin lace
bolívar *nm Fin* bolivar
Bolivia *n* Bolivia
boliviano, -a 1 *adj* Bolivian
  2 *nm,f (persona)* Bolivian
  3 *nm Fin* boliviano
bollera *nf muy Fam* dyke
bollería *nf* bakery, baker's
bollo *nm* (a) *Culin* bun, bread roll; *Fig* **no está el horno para bollos** it's not the right time (b) *(abolladura)* dent (c) *Esp (chichón)* bump, swelling (d) *Esp (alboroto)* fuss, confusion
bolo 1 *nm* (a) *(pieza)* bowling pin (b) **bolos** *(juego)* (tenpin) bowling; **jugar a los b.** to bowl, go bowling
  2 *adj CAm Fam* sloshed
bolsa¹ *nf* (a) *(recipiente)* bag □ **b. de agua caliente** hot water bottle; *Av* **b. de aire** air pocket; **b. de aseo** toilet bag; **b. de deportes** sports bag; **b. de la compra** shopping bag; *Am* **b. de dormir** sleeping bag; **b. de papel** paper bag; **b. de plástico** *(en tiendas)* carrier o plastic bag; **b. de viaje** travel bag (b) *(de dinero)* purse; **¡la b. o la vida!** your money or your life! (c) *Anat (lacrimal)* sac; *(bajo los ojos)* bag (d) *Min* pocket (e) *(en prenda)* bag, pucker

bolsa² *nf Fin* Stock Exchange; **jugar a la b.** to play the market □ **agente de b.** stockbroker; **b. de trabajo** employment exchange, *Br* job centre
bolsear *vt CAm Méx* **b. a algn** *(robar)* to pick sb's pocket
bolsillo *nm* (a) *(en prenda)* pocket; **de b.** pocket, pocket-size; **diccionario de b.** pocket dictionary; **edición de b.** pocket edition; **libro de b.** paperback; *Fig* **meterse a algn en el b.** to win sb over; *Fig* **tener a algn en el b.** to have sb in one's pocket o eating out of one's hand (b) *(monedero)* purse, *US* pocketbook; **consultar con el b.** to check the state of one's finances; **lo pagó de su b.** he paid for it himself, he paid for it out of his own pocket; *Fam* **rascarse el b.** put one's hand in one's pocket, fork out
bolsín *nm Fin* local stock exchange, *US* curb market
bolsista *nmf* (a) *Fin* stockbroker (b) *CAm Méx (carterista)* pickpocket
bolsístico, -a *adj Fin* stock market; **actividad bolsística** activity on the stock market
bolso *nm* bag; *Esp (de mujer) Br* handbag, *US* purse
boludear *vi RP Fam (hacer tonterías)* to mess about o around
boludez *nf RP Fam* (a) *(acto, dicho)* **¡qué b.!** what a damn stupid thing to do/say! (b) *(cosa insignificante)* silly little thing
boludo, -a *RP Fam* 1 *adj* (a) *(estúpido)* damn stupid (b) *(perezoso)* bone idle
  2 *nm,f* (c) *(estúpido) Br* prat, *US* jerk (d) *(perezoso)* lazybones
bomba¹ *nf* (a) *Téc* pump □ **b. aspirante** suction pump; **b. de aire** air pump; **b. de incendios** *Br* fire engine, *US* fire truck; *Med* **b. gástrica** stomach pump; **b. lacrimógena** tear gas grenade (b) *Mús* slide
bomba² 1 *nf* (a) *Mil* bomb; *Fig* **a prueba de bombas** bombproof, shellproof; *Fig* **estar** o **ir echando bombas** to be furious; *Fig* **la noticia cayó como una b.** the news burst like a bombshell □ **b. atómica** atomic bomb; **b. de hidrógeno** hydrogen bomb; **b. de mano** hand grenade; **b. de neutrones** neutron bomb; **b. de relojería** time bomb; **b. fétida** stink bomb; **b. incendiaria** incendiary bomb (b) *(de lámpara)* glass lampshade, globe
  2 *adj Fam* **noticia b.** shattering piece of news
  3 *adv Esp Fam* **pasarlo b.** to have a great time o a whale of a time
bombacho, -a *adj* baggy, loose-fitting; **pantalón b.** knickerbockers *pl*
bombachos *nmpl* baggy *Br* trousers o *US* pants
bombardear *vt Mil* to bomb, shell, bombard; *Fís (átomo)* to bombard; *Fig* **b. a algn a preguntas** to bombard sb with questions
bombardeo *nm* (a) *Mil* bombing, bombardment □ **b. aéreo** air raid (b) *Fís* bombardment
bombardero, -a 1 *adj* bombing, bomber; **avión b.** bomber (plane); **lancha bombardera** gunboat
  2 *nm* (a) *Av* bomber (b) *Hist (soldado)* bombardier
bombazo *nm* bomb explosion o blast; *Fig* **menudo b. cuando se enteren** there'll be hell to pay when they find out
bombear *vt* to pump
bombeo *nm* (a) *(de líquido)* pumping; **estación de b.** pumping station (b) *(curvatura)* camber
bombero, -a *nm,f (hombre)* fireman; *(mujer)* firewoman; *US (ambos sexos)* firefighter □ **cuerpo de bomberos** *Br* fire brigade, *US* fire department; **parque de bomberos** fire station
bombilla *nf Esp Elec* (light) bulb
bombillo *nm CAm Carib Col Méx* light bulb

bombín nm (**a**) (sombrero) bowler hat (**b**) (para hinchar) pump (**c**) (de cerradura) cylinder

bombita nf RP light bulb

bombo nm (**a**) Mús bass drum; Fig **a b. y platillo(s)** with a great song and dance; **anunciar algo a b. y platillo(s)** to announce sth with much ballyhoo; Fam **dar b. a algn** to praise sb excessively; Fam **darse b.** to blow one's own trumpet; Fam **dejar a una chica con b.** to get a girl into trouble (**b**) (de sorteo) lottery drum (**c**) (de lavadora) drum

bombón nm (**a**) (de chocolate) chocolate; **de b.** chocolate-coated; **una caja de bombones** a box of chocolates (**b**) Fam (mujer) Br stunner, US tomato; **es un b.** she's Br a stunner o US a tomato

bombona nf (**a**) (garrafa) carafe; Quím carboy; **una b. de vino** a carafe of wine (**b**) (recipiente metálico) cylinder ❑ **b. de butano** butane gas cylinder

bombonera nf (**a**) (caja) chocolate box (**b**) Fig (lugar) small, cosy place o room o house

bombonería nf Br sweet shop, US candy store

bonachón, -ona 1 adj good-natured, easy-going
 2 nm,f kind o good-natured soul, easy-going person

bonaerense 1 adj o of o from Buenos Aires
 2 nmf person from Buenos Aires

bonancible adj (**a**) (tiempo) fair; (mar) calm (**b**) (persona) kind

bonanza nf (**a**) Náut (tiempo) fair weather; (mar) calm at sea (**b**) Fig (prosperidad) prosperity (**c**) Min bonanza

bondad nf (calidad de bueno) goodness; (amabilidad) kindness, generosity; Fml **tenga la b. de esperar** please be so kind as to wait

bondadoso, -a adj kind, good, good-natured

bonete nm Rel cap, biretta; Univ cap, mortar-board

bongó nm bongo, bongo drum

boniato nm Esp Cuba Urug sweet potato

bonificación nf (**a**) (mejora) improvement (**b**) Com (descuento) discount, allowance, rebate; Fin **b. fiscal** tax rebate

bonificar [59] vt Com to discount, allow

bonito, -a[1] adj pretty, nice

bonito[2] nm (pez) (Atlantic) bonito

Bonn n Bonn

bono nm (**a**) (vale) voucher (**b**) Fin bond, debenture; **bonos del tesoro** o **del Estado** Treasury bonds

bonobús nm Esp bus pass

bonsái nm bonsai

bonzo nm Rel bonze

boñiga nf cow dung

booleano, -a adj Mat Inform Boolean

boom [bum] (pl **booms**) nm boom; **el b. turístico** the tourist boom

boomerang nm boomerang

boqueada nf last breath; **dar la última b.** to breathe one's last

boquear vi to gasp; (en agonía) to breathe one's last; Fam Fig to be on one's last legs

boquera nf Med crack, cold sore

boquerón nm (pez) anchovy

boquete nm (paso angosto) narrow opening, small gap; (brecha) breach

boquiabierto, -a adj open-mouthed; **se quedó b. al oír la noticia** he was flabbergasted when he heard the news, he was stunned by the news

boquilla nf (**a**) (para fumar) cigarette holder; (de cigarrillo)

tip; (de pipa) mouthpiece; **decir algo de b.** to pay lip service to sth (**b**) Mús mouthpiece (**c**) (de manguera) nozzle

bórax nm inv Quím borax

Borbón n Hist Bourbon

borbónico, -a adj Hist Bourbon

borborigmo nm Med rumbling

borbotar vi, **borbotear** vi to bubble

borboteo nm bubbling

borbotón nm bubbling; Fig **hablar a borbotones** to gabble; Fig **salir a borbotones** to gush forth

borda nf (**a**) Náut (de barco) gunwale; **arrojar** o **echar por la b.** to throw overboard; Fig to renounce ❑ (**motor de**) **fuera de b.** outboard motor (**b**) Náut (de galera) mainsail

bordada nf Náut tack, board

bordado, -a 1 pp de **bordar**
 2 adj Cost embroidered
 3 nm embroidery

bordador, -a nm,f embroiderer

bordadura nf embroidery

bordar vt (**a**) Cost to embroider (**b**) Fig (ejecutar perfectamente) to do excellently; **el actor ha bordado su papel** the actor gave an excellent performance

borde[1] nm (de mesa, camino) edge; Cost hem, edge; (de vasija) rim, brim; **al b. de** on the brink of, on the verge of; **al b. del mar** at the seaside ❑ Av **b. de ataque/salida** leading/trailing edge

borde[2] Esp Fam **1** adj **ser muy b.** to be a real Br ratbag o US s.o.b.
 2 nmf Br ratbag, US s.o.b.

bordear vt (**a**) (ir por el borde) to go round the edge of, skirt (**b**) Fig (aproximarse) to border on, verge on; **bordeaba los cuarenta años** he was pushing forty (**c**) Náut to tack

bordillo nm Br kerb, US curb

bordo nm Náut board; **a b.** on board; **subir a b.** to go on board; **de alto b.** seagoing

bordón nm (**a**) (bastón) staff (**b**) (muletilla) pet phrase (**c**) Mús (cuerda) bass string (**d**) Impr omission

bordonear vi Mús (guitarra) to strum

boreal adj northern, boreal

borgoña nm (vino) Burgundy

bórico, -a adj Quím boric ❑ **ácido b.** boric acid

borla nf (**a**) Cost tassel (**b**) (para polvos) powder puff

borne nm Elec terminal

Borneo n Borneo

boro nm Quím boron

borona nf (**a**) (maíz) maize, US corn (**b**) (mijo) millet

borra nf (**a**) (para colchones) flock; Fig **meter b.** to pad (out) (**b**) (pelusa) fluff (**c**) (poso) sediment, dregs pl

borrachera nf (**a**) (embriaguez) drunkenness; **agarrar** o **coger** o **pillar una b.** to get drunk; Fam **se pilló una b. de órdago** he got drunk out of his skull (**b**) Fig (exaltación) ecstasy, rapture, enthusiasm

borrachín nm Fam soak, boozer

borracho, -a 1 adj (**a**) (bebido) drunk; **b. como una cuba, b. perdido** blind drunk; **estar b.** to be drunk; Fig **b. de poder/de felicidad** drunk with power/happiness (**b**) Culin (bizcocho) rum baba
 2 nm,f drunkard, drunk; **ser un b.** to be a drunkard

borrado nm Inform clearing

borrador nm (**a**) (escrito) rough copy, first draft (**b**) (croquis) rough o preliminary sketch (**c**) (goma de borrar) Br rubber, US eraser; (de la pizarra) Br board rubber o duster, US eraser

borradura *nf* crossing out, erasure

borraja *nf Bot* borage; *Fam Fig* **quedar en agua de borrajas** to come to nothing, fizzle o peter out

borrajear *vt (palabras)* to scribble; *(papel)* to doodle o scribble on

borrar 1 *vt* (**a**) *(con goma) Br* to rub out, *US* erase; *(tachar)* to cross out o off; **b. la pizarra** to clean the blackboard (**b**) *Inform* to erase, delete; **b. un archivo/documento** to erase a file/document (**c**) *Fig* to erase, wipe away
2 borrarse *vpr* (**a**) *(olvidarse)* to be erased; **se me borró de la memoria** I forgot all about it (**b**) *(darse de baja)* to drop out, withdraw; **me he borrado del club** I'm not a member of the club any more

borrasca *nf* (**a**) *Meteor (tormenta)* storm; *(chubasco)* squall; *(nieve)* flurry (**b**) *Fig (contratiempo)* hitch

borrascoso, -a *adj* (**a**) *Meteor (tormentoso)* stormy; *(viento)* gusty, squally (**b**) *Fig* stormy, tempestuous

borrego, -a *nm,f* (**a**) *(corderillo)* yearling lamb (**b**) *Fam Fig (persona)* ass, dimwit (**c**) *Fam (pelliza)* sheepskin coat

borrico *nm* (**a**) *Zool* ass, donkey (**b**) *Fam Fig* ass, dimwit

borrón *nm* (**a**) *(mancha de tinta)* blot, smudge; *Fig* **b. y cuenta nueva** let's wipe the slate clean, let's start afresh (**b**) *(escrito)* rough copy, rough draft (**c**) *(croquis)* rough o preliminary sketch (**d**) *Fig (imperfección, deshonor)* blemish

borronear *vt (palabras)* to scribble; *(en papel)* to doodle o scribble on

borroso, -a *adj (confuso, impreciso)* blurred, hazy, indistinct; **escritura borrosa** smudgy o illegible handwriting; **ideas borrosas** vague o hazy ideas; **veo b.** I can't see clearly, everything's blurred

boscaje *nm* (**a**) *(bosque pequeño)* thicket, grove, copse (**b**) *Arte (paisaje)* woodland scene

boscoso, -a *adj* wooded

Bósforo *nm* **el B.** the Bosphorus

Bosnia *n* Bosnia

bosnio, -a *adj & nm,f* Bosnian

bosque *nm* wood, forest

bosquejar *vt (dibujo)* to sketch, outline; *Fig (plan)* to draft, outline

bosquejo *nm (dibujo)* sketch, study; *Fig (plan)* draft, outline

bosquimano, -a *nm,f* Bushman

bossa-nova [bosa'noβa] *nf* bossa nova

bostezar [14] *vi* to yawn

bostezo *nm* yawn

bota *nf* (**a**) *(calzado)* boot; *Fig* **morir con las botas puestas** to die with one's boots on; *Fam* **ponerse las botas** to strike it rich, make a killing, feather one's nest; *Fam* **ponerse las botas comiendo** to stuff oneself ❑ **botas camperas** cowboy boots; **botas de montar** riding boots (**b**) *(de vino)* = small leather container for wine

botadero *nm Andes Ven (para basura) Br* rubbish tip o dump, *US* garbage dump

botador, -a *nm* (**a**) *Náut* boatpole (**b**) *Carp* nail puller, claw hammer (**c**) *Impr* shooting stick

botadura *nf Náut* launching (of a boat)

botafumeiro *nm Rel* incense burner, thurible, censer

botalón *nm Náut* boom

botana *nf Méx* snack

botánica *nf* botany

botánico, -a 1 *adj* botanical, botanic
2 *nm,f* botanist

botanista *nmf* botanist

botar 1 *vi* (**a**) *(saltar)* to jump; *(caballo)* to buck; *Fam* **está**

que bota she's hopping mad (**b**) *Esp (pelota)* to bounce, rebound
2 *vt* (**a**) *Náut (barco)* to launch (**b**) *Am salvo RP (tirar)* to throw away; *(derribar, volcar)* to knock over (**c**) *Fam (despedir)* to fire (**d**) *Esp (pelota)* to bounce (**e**) *Am salvo RP (malgastar)* to waste, squander

botarate 1 *adj* foolish
2 *nmf* madcap, fool

botarel *nm Arquit* flying buttress

bote¹ *nm* (**a**) *(acción de botar)* jump, bound; **dar botes** to jump up and down; **de un b.** with one leap (**b**) *(de pelota)* bounce, rebound (**c**) *(de caballo)* buck

bote² *nm (de cristal)* jar; *Esp (lata)* can, tin; *(para propinas)* = jar o box for tips; **leche de b.** tinned milk; *Esp Fam* **chupar del b.** to scrounge; **sólo quiere chupar del b.** he's just a hanger-on; *Esp Fam* **tener a algn (metido) en el b.** to have sb under one's thumb, have sb in the palm of one's hand ❑ **b. de humo** smoke bomb

bote³ *nm (lancha)* boat ❑ **b. salvavidas** lifeboat

bote⁴ *nm* **de b. en b.** packed, full to bursting

botella *nf* bottle

botellazo *nm* blow with a bottle

botellero *nm* wine rack

botellín *nm* small bottle

botellón *nm Esp Fam* = informal street gathering where young people meet to drink and socialize

botepronto *nm (rugby)* dropkick; *(football, tennis)* half volley; *Fam* **a b.** all of a sudden

botica *nf Anticuado (farmacia)* pharmacy, *Br* chemist's (shop), *US* drugstore; *Fam* **hay de todo como en b.** there's a bit of everything

boticario, -a *nm,f Anticuado* pharmacist, *Br* chemist, *US* druggist

botija *nf (vasija)* earthenware pitcher

botijo *nm* earthenware pitcher *(with spout and handle)*; *Fam Fig* **estar hecho un b.** to be like a barrel

botín¹ *nm (de un robo)* loot, booty

botín² *nm (calzado)* ankle boot, spat, legging

botiquín *nm* medicine chest o cabinet, first aid kit

boto *nm* boot

botón *nm* (**a**) *Cost* button; *Fig* **b. de muestra** sample (**b**) *Bot (capullo)* bud ❑ **b. de oro** buttercup (**c**) *Téc* button; **pulsar el b.** to press the button (**d**) *(tirador)* knob

botonadura *nf* buttons *pl*, set of buttons

botonear *vi RP Fam* **b. (a algn)** to squeal (on sb), snitch (on sb)

botones *nm inv (en un hotel)* bellboy, *US* bellhop; *(chico de recados)* messenger, errand boy

Botsuana *n* Botswana

botsuanés, -esa *adj & nm,f* Botswanan

Botswana *n* Botswana

botulismo *nm Med* botulism

boutique [bu'tik] *nf* boutique

bóveda *nf* (**a**) *Arquit* vault ❑ *Arquit* **b. de cañón** barrel vault; **b. celeste** vault of heaven; *Anat* **b. craneana** cranial cavity (**b**) *(cripta)* crypt

bóvido, -a *Zool* **1** *adj* bovid
2 bóvidos *nmpl* bovidae *pl*, bovines

bovino, -a 1 *adj* bovine
2 bóvinos *nmpl* bovines

box *nm* (**a**) *(de caballo)* stall (**b**) *(de coches)* pit; **entrar en boxes** to make a pit stop (**c**) *Am (boxeo)* boxing

boxeador *nm* boxer

boxear *vi* to box

boxeo *nm* boxing

bóxer (*pl* **bóxers**) *nm* (**a**) *Hist* Boxer (**b**) *(perro)* boxer

boya *nf* (**a**) *Náut* buoy (**b**) *Pesca (corcho)* float

boyante *adj* (**a**) *Náut* buoyant (**b**) *(próspero)* prosperous, thriving (**c**) *(feliz)* buoyant, happy (**d**) *Taur (toro)* easy to fight

boy scout [boxes'kaut] (*pl* **boy scouts**) *nm* boy scout

bozal *nm* muzzle

bozo *nm* (**a**) *(vello)* down, fuzz; *(moustache)* youthful moustache, fine hairs (**b**) *(parte exterior de la boca)* mouth, lips

bracear *vi* (**a**) *(mover los brazos)* to swing *o* wave one's arms about (**b**) *(nadar)* to swim (**c**) *(forcejear)* to struggle, wrestle

bracero *nm* (day) labourer, *US* (day) laborer

braga *nf Esp (usu pl) Br* knickers *pl*, *US* panties *pl*; *Fam* **estar hecho una b.** to be whacked; *Fam Fig* **pillar a algn en bragas** to catch sb out

braguero *nm* truss

bragueta *nf Br* flies *pl*, *US* zipper

braguetazo *nm Esp Fam* **dar el b.** to marry (into) money

braguetero *nm Fam* lecher

brahmán *nm Rel* Brahman, Brahmin

brahmánico, -a *adj Rel* Brahmanic, Brahminic

brahmanismo *nm Rel* Brahmanism, Brahminism

braille ['braile] *nm* braille

bramante *nm* hemp string *o* cord

bramar *vi* (**a**) *(toro, vaca)* to low, bellow; *(elefante)* to trumpet (**b**) *(persona) (de dolor)* to bawl, howl; *(de ira)* to roar, thunder (**c**) *(viento)* to howl, roar; *(mar)* to roar, thunder; *(trueno)* to rumble, roll

bramido *nm* (**a**) *(toro, vaca)* lowing, bellowing; *(elefante)* trumpeting (**b**) *(de dolor)* bawling, howling; *(de ira)* roaring, thundering (**c**) *(viento)* howling, roaring; *(mar)* roaring, thundering; *(trueno)* rumbling, rolling

brandy *nm* brandy

branquia *nf* gill, branchia

branquial *adj* branchial

brasa *nf* ember, red-hot coal; **chuletas a la b.** barbecued chops

brasear *vt* to barbecue

brasero *nm* brazier

brasier *nm Carib Col Méx* bra

Brasil *n* Brazil

brasileño, -a *adj & nm,f,* **brasilero, -a** *adj & nm,f* Brazilian

Brasilia *n* Brasilia

bravata *nf* (**a**) *(amenaza)* piece *o* act of bravado (**b**) *(fanfarronada)* boasting, bragging, showing off; **decir bravatas** to brag, boast, show off

braveza *nf* (**a**) *(bravura)* courage, bravery (**b**) *(de los elementos)* wildness, violence

bravío, -a 1 *adj* (**a**) *(salvaje)* wild, untamed; *(silvestre)* wild (**b**) *Fig (rústico)* uncouth, uneducated
 2 *nm (bravura)* wildness, ferocity

bravo, -a 1 *adj* (**a**) *(valiente)* brave, courageous (**b**) *(feroz)* fierce, ferocious; **un toro b.** a fighting bull (**c**) *(mar)* rough, stormy; *(terreno)* rugged; *(paisaje)* wild (**d**) *(carácter)* churlish, bad-tempered
 2 *interj* ¡**b.!** well done!, bravo!

bravucón, -ona 1 *adj* boastful, boasting
 2 *nm,f* boaster, braggart

bravuconada *nf* boast, brag

bravuconear *vi* to brag

bravuconería *nf* bravado

bravura *nf* (**a**) *(de los animales)* ferocity, fierceness (**b**) *(de las personas)* courage, bravery (**c**) *(de toro)* fighting spirit (**d**) *(balandronada)* boasting, bragging

braza *nf* (**a**) *Náut (medida)* fathom (**b**) *Esp Natación* breast stroke; **nadar a b.** to swim breast stroke

brazada *nf Natación* stroke

brazalete *nm* (**a**) *(insignia)* armband (**b**) *(pulsera)* bracelet

brazo *nm* (**a**) *Anat* arm; *Zool* foreleg; *(de sillón, tocadiscos, balanza)* arm; *(de río, candelabro)* branch; *(de árbol)* branch; *(de grúa)* boom, jib; *(de micrófono)* boom; *(de molino)* sail arm; **a b. partido** with bare fists; *Fig* tooth and nail; **en brazos** in one's arms; **ir del b.** to walk arm in arm; *Fig* **con los brazos abiertos** with open arms; *Fig* **con los brazos cruzados** lazily, doing nothing; *Fig* **no dar su b. a torcer** not to give in, stand firm; *Fig* **ser el b. derecho de algn** to be sb's right-hand man; *Fam* **estar hecho un b. de mar** to be dressed to kill □ *Culin* **b. de gitano** *Br* swiss roll, *US* jelly roll; *Geog* **b. de mar** inlet; **huelga de brazos caídos** go slow (**b**) *Fig (poder, esfuerzo)* power strength; **el b. de la ley** the long arm of the law (**c**) **brazos** *(trabajadores, ayuda)* hands; **siempre faltan b.** more hands are always needed

Brazzaville [bratsa'βil] *n* Brazzaville

brea *nf* (**a**) *(sustancia)* tar, pitch (**b**) *(tela)* tarpaulin

break [breik] (*pl* **breaks**) *nm Dep* **punto de b.** break point

brebaje *nm* concoction, brew

breca *nf (pez)* pandora

brecha *nf* (**a**) *(en muro, pared)* opening, break, gap; *Mil* breach; *Fig* **estar siempre en la b.** to be always at it (**b**) *(en la cabeza, en una ceja)* gash (**c**) *Fig* breach; **nada hace b. en él** nothing affects him

brécol *nm* brocoli, broccoli

brega *nf* (**a**) *(lucha)* struggle, fight (**b**) *(riña)* row, quarrel (**c**) *(trabajo duro)* hard work, toil; **andar a la b.** to slog away, toil away

bregar [38] **1** *vt (amasar)* to knead
 2 *vi* (**a**) *(luchar)* to struggle, fight (**b**) *(reñir)* to row, quarrel (**c**) *(trabajar con afán)* to slog away, toil away

breque *nm CAm (freno)* brake

Bretaña *nf* Brittany; **Gran B.** Great Britain

brete *nm* shackles *pl*, fetters *pl*; *Fig* **poner a algn en un b.** to put sb in a tight spot

bretel *nm CSur* strap; **sin breteles** *(vestido)* strapless

bretón, -ona 1 *adj* Breton
 2 *nm,f (persona)* Breton
 3 *nm (idioma)* Breton

breva *nf* (**a**) *(higo)* early fig; *Fam Fig* **de higos a brevas** once in a blue moon (**b**) *(puro)* flat cigar (**c**) *Esp Fig* ¡**no caerá esa b.!** no such luck!

breve 1 *adj* brief, short; **en b.** shortly, soon; **en breves palabras** in short; **hicieron una b. pausa** they paused briefly; **seré b.** I shall be brief
 2 *nm Rel* (papal) brief
 3 *nf Mús Ling* breve

brevedad *nf* briefness, brevity, shortness; **con b.** concisely, briefly; **con la mayor b. posible** as soon as possible

brevet *nm* (**a**) *Chile (de avión)* pilot's licence (**b**) *Bol Ecuad Perú (de automóvil) Br* driving licence, *US* driver's license (**c**) *RP (de velero)* sailing licence

breviario *nm* (**a**) *Rel* breviary (**b**) *(compendio)* compendium, summary

brezal *nm* heath, moor

brezo *nm Bot* heather

briago, -a *adj Méx Fam* plastered, blitzed

bribón, -ona 1 *adj* roguish, dishonest
 2 *nm,f* rogue, rascal

bribonada *nf* piece of mischief, rascally trick

bricolaje *nm Br* DIY, do-it-yourself, *US* home improvement

brida *nf* (a) *(rienda)* rein, bridle; **a toda b.** at full gallop (b) *Med* adhesion (c) *Téc* flange

bridge [britʃ] *nm Naipes* bridge; **jugar al b.** to play bridge

brigada 1 *nf* (a) *Mil* brigade ❑ **general de b.** brigadier, *US* brigadier general (b) *(de policías)* squad ❑ **b. antiterrorista** anti-terrorist squad; **b. móvil** flying squad (c) *(de trabajadores)* gang
 2 *nmf Mil* sergeant major

brigadier *nm* brigadier

brillante 1 *adj* (a) *(reluciente)* brilliant, sparkling (b) *Fig (excelente)* bright, brilliant; **un escritor b.** an outstanding writer
 2 *nm* diamond; **un collar de brillantes** a diamond necklace

brillantez *nf* (a) *(resplandor)* brilliance, brightness (b) *Fig (excelencia)* brilliance

brillantina *nf* brilliantine

brillar *vi* (a) *(resplandecer)* to shine; *(piedra preciosa, ojos etc)* to sparkle; *(estrella)* to twinkle, shine; *(sol, luna)* to shine; *(lentejuelas etc)* to glitter; *(metal pulido)* to gleam; *(seda)* to shimmer; *(luz muy fuerte)* to glare, sparkle; *(ascuas etc)* to glow (b) *Fig (destacar)* to stand out **b. por su ausencia** to be conspicuous by one's absence

brillo *nm* (a) *(resplandor)* shine; *(de las estrellas)* twinkling; *(del sol, de la luna)* brightness; *(de lentejuelas etc)* glittering; *(de los metales)* shine; *(de una superficie)* gloss, shine; *(del cabello, de una tela)* sheen; *(de un color)* brilliance; *(de una pantalla)* brightness; *(de los zapatos)* shine; **sacar b. a** to shine, polish (b) *Fig* brilliance, splendour, *US* splendor

brilloso, -a *adj Am* shining

brincar [59] *vi (dar saltos)* to jump, hop, skip, frolic; *(cordero)* to gambol

brinco *nm* jump, hop, skip; **de un b.** with a jump

brindar 1 *vi* to drink, toast, drink a toast; **brindemos por tu salud** let us drink to your health
 2 *vt* (a) *(ofrecer)* to offer, provide; **le agradezco la oportunidad que me brinda** I thank you for giving me this opportunity (b) *Taur* to dedicate (a to)
 3 brindarse *vpr* to offer (a to), volunteer (a to); **se brindó a invitarnos** he offered to pay for the meal

brindis *nm* (a) *(con bebida)* toast (b) *Taur* dedication (of the bull)

brío *nm* (a) *(pujanza)* energy, force; **lleno de b.** full of go (b) *(resolución)* determination (c) *(garbo, gallardía)* dash, spirit

brioche *nm* brioche

brioso, -a *adj* (a) *(enérgico)* energetic, vigorous (b) *(decidido)* determined, resolute (c) *(con garbo, gallardía)* dashing, spirited (d) *(caballo)* fiery, spirited

briqueta *nf* briquette, briquet

brisa *nf* breeze; **b. marina** sea breeze

brisca *nf Naipes* = Spanish card game

británico, -a 1 *adj* British; **las Islas Británicas** the British Isles
 2 *nm,f* British person, Briton; **los británicos** the British

brizna *nf* (a) *(de hierba)* blade; *(de hilo)* strand, thread (b) *(trozo)* bit

broca *nf* (a) *Téc (taladro)* drill, bit (b) *(clavo)* tack (c) *Cost* bobbin

brocado *nm Tex* brocade

brocal *nm* curb (of a well) .

brocearse *vpr Andes Arg Min* to become mined out

brocha *nf Arte Constr* paintbrush, brush; *(de afeitar)* shaving brush; *Constr* **pintor de b. gorda** painter and decorator; **bromas de b. gorda** crude o tasteless jokes

brochada *nf,* **brochazo** *nm* brush stroke; *Fig* **de un b.** at one stroke

broche *nm* (a) *(de prenda)* fastener, clasp, clip (b) *(joya)* brooch; *Fig* **cerrar con b. de oro** to finish with a flourish

brocheta *nf Culin* skewer

brócoli *nm* broccoli

bróculi *nm* broccoli

broma *nf* *(chiste)* joke; *(chanza)* trick, prank, lark; **bromas aparte** seriously (though); **¡déjate de bromas!** stop mucking around!, let's talk seriously now!; **echar** o **tomar algo a b.** not to take sth seriously, treat sth as a joke; **en b.** as a joke; **estar de b.** to be in a joking mood; **gastar bromas/una b. a algn** to play jokes/a joke on sb; **medio en b. medio en serio, entre bromas y veras** half jokingly; **¡ni en b.!** not on your life!; **¡15.000 pesos me costó la b.!** 15,000 pesos it cost me! ❑ **b. pesada** practical joke

bromato *nm Quím* bromate

bromear *vi* to joke

bromista 1 *adj* fond of joking o playing jokes
 2 *nmf* joker, prankster

bromo *nm Quím* bromine

bromuro *nm Quím* bromide

bronca *nf* (a) *(riña)* quarrel, row; **se armó una b. de miedo** an almighty row broke out (b) *(pelea)* scuffle, brawl, fight (c) *Esp (represión)* telling off, ticking off, dressing down; **el jefe le echó una b.** the boss told him off; **llevarse una b.** to get a ticking o telling off (d) *(abucheo)* jeering, booing, boos *pl* (e) *RP Fam (rabia)* **me da b.** it hacks me off

bronce *nm* bronze; *Fig* **ser de b.** to be as hard as nails, have a heart of stone; *Fam* **ligar b.** to sunbathe

bronceado, -a 1 *pp de* **broncear**
 2 *adj* (a) *(de color bronce)* bronze, bronze coloured o *US* colored (b) *(por el sol)* suntanned, tanned, sunburnt
 3 *nm (por el sol)* suntan, tan

bronceador, -a 1 *adj* tanning, suntan; **leche bronceadora** suntan cream o lotion
 2 *nm (crema)* suntan cream o lotion; *(aceite)* suntan oil

broncear 1 *vt (metal, estatua)* to bronze
 2 broncearse *vpr* to get a tan o a suntan

bronco, -a *adj* (a) *(superficie)* rough, coarse; *(metales)* brittle (b) *(sonido, voz)* harsh, raucous (c) *Fig (carácter)* rough, rude, surly

bronconeumonía *nf Med* bronchopneumonia

broncoscopio *nm* bronchoscope

bronquial *adj Anat* bronchial

bronquio *nm Anat* bronchus

bronquítico, -a *adj Med* bronchitic

bronquitis *nf inv Med* bronchitis

broqueta *nf véase* **brocheta**

brotar *vi* (a) *Bot (planta)* to sprout; *(sacar capullos)* to come into bud; *(sacar hojas)* to sprout, come into leaf (b) *(manar)* to spring, gush forth; *(río)* to rise (c) *(lágrimas)* to well up (d) *Med (erupción)* to break out (e) *Fig (nacer, manifestarse)* to appear, spring up

brote *nm* (a) *Bot (renuevo)* bud, shoot; *(acción de brotar)* budding (b) *(de agua)* gushing (c) *(de lágrimas)* welling up (d) *Med (de erupción)* outbreak, appearance (e) *Fig (epidémico, violento)* outbreak

broza *nf* (**a**) *(despojo de las plantas)* dead leaves o wood (**b**) *(desechos) Br* rubbish, *US* trash (**c**) *(maleza)* undergrowth, thicket (**d**) *Fig (paja)* padding

brucelosis *nf Med* brucellosis

bruces: de bruces *loc adv* face downwards; **se cayó de b.** he fell flat on his face

bruja *nf* (**a**) *(hechicera)* witch, sorceress (**b**) *Fam (mujer fea)* old hag o crone; *(arpía)* witch

brujería *nf* witchcraft, sorcery

brujo *nm* wizard, sorcerer; *(en una tribu primitiva)* witch doctor, medicine man

brújula *nf* compass; *Fig* **perder la b.** to lose one's bearings

bruma *nf (niebla)* mist; *(de calor)* (heat) haze

brumoso, -a *adj* misty, hazy

Brunei *n* Brunei

bruñido *nm* (**a**) *(acción)* polishing, burnishing (**b**) *(efecto)* polish, burnish

bruñir *vt* to polish, burnish

brusco, -a *adj* (**a**) *(persona)* brusque, abrupt (**b**) *(repentino)* sudden, sharp; **un descenso b. de temperatura** a sharp drop in temperature

Bruselas *n* Brussels

bruselense 1 *adj* of o from Brussels
2 *nmf* person from Brussels

brusquedad *nf* (**a**) *(de carácter)* brusqueness, abruptness (**b**) *(de superficie etc)* suddenness, abruptness

brutal *adj* (**a**) *(violento, cruel)* brutal, rough (**b**) *Fam (enorme)* huge, colossal, gigantic; **hubo una subida b. de precios** there was a tremendous rise in prices (**c**) *Fam (magnífico)* great, terrific, fantastic; **es una película b.** it's a terrific movie o *Br* film

brutalidad *nf* (**a**) *(crueldad)* brutality, savagery (**b**) *(acción cruel)* brutal o savage act

bruto, -a 1 *adj* (**a**) *(necio, incapaz)* stupid, thick (**b**) *(inculto)* ignorant, uneducated (**c**) *(tosco)* rough, coarse, uncouth (**d**) *(piedra preciosa)* rough, uncut; **un diamante en b.** an uncut diamond (**e**) *(sin refinar)* crude; **petróleo b.** crude oil (**f**) *Fin* gross; **90.000 pesos brutos** 90,000 pesos before tax (**g**) *(peso)* gross
2 *nm,f* (**a**) *(estúpido)* blockhead, brute (**b**) *(inculto)* ignoramus
3 *nm Zool* brute, beast

Bs.As. *(abrev de* **Buenos Aires**) Buenos Aires

bubónico, -a *adj Med* bubonic; **peste bubónica** bubonic plague

bucal *adj Anat* buccal, oral, of the mouth

bucanero *nm Hist* buccaneer

Bucarest *n* Bucharest

búcaro *nm* = vase o jar made of clay

buceador, -a *nm,f* diver

bucear *vi* (**a**) *(en agua)* to dive, swim under water (**b**) *b. en Fig* to investigate, explore, sound (out)

buceo *nm* (underwater) diving

buche *nm* (**a**) *Zool (de ave)* crop, craw; *(de animales)* maw; *Fig* **guardar algo en el b.** to keep quiet about sth (**b**) *Fam (estómago)* belly, stomach (**c**) *(de líquido)* mouthful

bucle *nm* curl, ringlet

bucólica *nf* bucolic, pastoral poem

bucólico, -a *adj* bucolic, pastoral

Buda *nm* Buddha

Budapest *n* Budapest

budín *nm* pudding

budismo *nm* Buddhism

budista *adj* Buddhist

buen *adj (delante de un nombre)* **¡b. viaje!** have a good trip!; **un b. trabajo** a good job; *Fig* **un b. día** all of a sudden; *véase tamb* **bueno, -a**

buenamente *adv* (**a**) *(fácilmente)* easily; **haz lo que b. puedas** just do what you can; **si b. puedes** if you possibly can (**b**) *(voluntariamente)* readily, willingly

buenaventura *nf* good fortune, good luck; **echar la b. a algn** to tell sb's fortune

buenazo, -a 1 *adj* good-natured
2 *nm,f* goodnatured person

bueno, -a 1 *adj* (**a**) *(gen)* good; **lo b.** the good thing; *Irón* **lo b. es que ...** the funny thing (about it) is that ...; **ser de buena familia** to be from a good family; **un buen alumno** a good pupil; **una buena madre** a good mother; **una buena película** a good movie o *Br* film (**b**) *(agradable)* nice, pleasant (**c**) *(amable)* *(con* ser**)** good, kind, good-natured; **es muy buena persona** she's a very kind soul; **ser más b. que el pan** to be as good as gold (**d**) *(sano)* *(con* estar**)** well, in good health (**e**) *(tiempo)* good; **hoy hace buen tiempo** the weather is good today; **mañana hará un día b.** it will be a nice day tomorrow (**f**) *(útil)* useful (**g**) *(conveniente)* good; **no es b. comer tanto** it's not good for you to eat so much; **sería b. que cambiáramos de coche este verano** it would be a good idea if we changed our car this summer (**h**) *(todavía servible)* usable; **esos zapatos son buenos aún** those shoes are still wearable (**i**) *(considerable)* considerable; **un buen número de** a good number of; **una buena cantidad** a considerable amount (**j**) *Irón* fine, real, proper; **¡en buen lío te has metido, chico!** that's a fine mess you've got yourself into, my boy! (**k**) *(grande)* good, big; **un buen trozo de pastel** a nice big piece of cake; **una buena paliza** a good hiding (**l**) *Fam (de gran atractivo físico)* gorgeous, sexy; **¡qué b. está!, ¡tío b.!** he's a bit of all right!; **¡tía buena!** she's a bit of all right! (**m**) **¡buenas!** *(saludos)* hello!; **buenas noches** good evening; **buenas tardes** good afternoon, good evening; **buenos días** good morning (**n**) *(locuciones)* **de buena gana** willingly; **de buenas a primeras** suddenly, all at once; **estar de buenas** to be in a good mood; **los buenos tiempos** the good old days; **por las buenas** willingly; **por las buenas o por las malas** willy-nilly; *Fam* **tirarse una buena vida** to lead a cushy life; *Irón* **¡buena la has hecho!** that's done it!; *Irón* **de los buenos** lovely, grand; **un susto de los buenos** a real fright; *Irón* **¡ésta sí que es buena!** that's a good one!; *Irón* **¡estamos buenos!** what a fine mess we're in!; *Irón* **¡estaría b.!** I should jolly well hope not!; *Irón* **librarse de una buena** to have a lucky o narrow escape; *Irón* **poner b. a algn** to criticize sb, *Br* slate sb
2 *nm, f* **los buenos** the good guys; **el b. de Carlos** good old Carlos
3 *interj* **¡b.! 1** *(sorpresa)* well! (**b**) *(bien, de acuerdo)* all right, OK

Buenos Aires *n* Buenos Aires

buey *nm* ox □ **b. marino** sea cow

búfalo, -a *nm,f* buffalo

bufanda *nf* scarf, muffler

bufar *vi* (**a**) *(toro)* to snort; *(gato)* to spit; *(caballo)* to neigh (**b**) *Fig (persona)* to be fuming; **el jefe está que bufa** the boss is hopping mad

bufé *nm* (**a**) *Culin* buffet □ **b. libre** self-service buffet meal (**b**) *(mueble)* sideboard

búfer *(pl* **búfers**) *nm Inform* buffer

bufete *nm* (**a**) *(mesa de escribir)* desk, writing table (**b**) *(despacho)* lawyer's office (**c**) *(clientela del abogado)* practice

buffer ['bafer] *(pl* **buffers**) *nm Inform* buffer

buffet *(pl* **buffets)** *nm véase* **bufé**

bufido *nm* **(a)** *(de toro)* snort; *(de gato)* spit; *(de caballo)* neigh **(b)** *Fig* outburst

bufo, -a 1 *adj* comic, clownish; **ópera bufa** comic opera
   2 *nm,f* clown, buffoon

bufón, -ona 1 *adj* comical, farcical
   2 *nm,f* clown, buffoon, jester

bufonada *nf* jest, piece of buffoonery; **bufonadas** clowning *sing,* buffoonery *sing*

bufonesco, -a *adj* comical, farcical

bug [buɣ] *(pl* **bugs)** *nm Inform* bug

buganvilla *nf* bougainvillea

buhardilla *nf* **(a)** *(desván)* attic, garret **(b)** *(ventana)* dormer window

búho *nm* owl ❏ **b. real** eagle owl

buhonería *nf (baratijas)* pedlar's *o* hawker's wares *pl*; *(oficio)* peddling, hawking

buhonero, -a *nm,f* pedlar, hawker

buitre *nm* **(a)** *Orn* vulture **(b)** *Fig (persona)* opportunist

buje *nm Téc* axle box, bushing

bujía *nf* **(a)** *(vela)* candle **(b)** *Aut* sparking plug, spark plug **(c)** *Fís* candlepower

bula *nf* **(a)** *Rel (documento)* papal bull **(b)** *Hist (sello de plomo)* bulla

bulbo *nm Anat Bot* bulb

bulboso, -a *adj* bulbous

buldog *nm* bulldog

buldózer *(pl* **buldozers)** *nm* bulldozer

bulerías *nfpl* = Andalusian song and dance, accompanied by clapping

bulevar *nm* boulevard

Bulgaria *n* Bulgaria

búlgaro, -a 1 *adj* Bulgarian
   2 *nm,f (persona)* Bulgarian
   3 *nm (idioma)* Bulgarian

bulimia *nf* bulimia

bulímico, -a *adj* bulimic

bulla *nf* **(a)** *(griterío)* racket, row, uproar **(b)** *(muchedumbre)* crowd, mob

bullanga *nf* tumult, racket

bullanguero, -a 1 *adj* noisy, riotous
   2 *nm,f* noisy person, troublemaker

bulldozer [bul'doθer] *(pl* **bulldozers)** *nm* bulldozer

bullicio *nm* **(a)** *(ruido)* din, hubbub, noise **(b)** *(movimiento y ruido)* bustle, hustle and bustle **(c)** *(tumulto)* uproar

bullicioso, -a *adj* **(a)** *(ruidoso)* noisy, rowdy **(b)** *(animado)* bustling, busy

bullir 1 *vi* **(a)** *(hervir)* to boil, bubble (up) **(b)** *Fig (sangre)* to boil **(c)** *Fig (de ira)* to seethe **(d)** *(pulular)* to swarm, teem **(e)** *(tener gran actividad)* to bustle about **(f)** *(moverse)* to move, stir
   2 bullirse *vpr (moverse)* to move, stir, budge

bulo *nm* hoax, rumour, *US* rumor, false report

bulto *nm* **(a)** *(volumen, tamaño)* size, volume, bulk; **hacer mucho b.** to be very bulky, take up a lot of space; *Fig* **a b.** roughly, broadly; **escoger a b.** to choose at random; *Fig* **de b.** important, obvious; **un error de b.** a serious mistake; *Fam* **escurrir el b.** to dodge, pass the buck **(b)** *(cuerpo que se distingue mal)* shape, form **(c)** *(fardo, maleta, caja)* bundle, piece of luggage, box **(d)** *Med (chichón)* bump, swelling **(e)** *Med (protuberancia)* lump **(f)** *CAm Col Méx Ven (carpatacio)* satchel, briefcase

bumerán *nm* boomerang

bungalow [bunga'lo] *(pl* **bungalows)** *nm* bungalow

búnker *nm* **(a)** *(refugio)* bunker **(b)** *Esp Fam Pol* **el b.** reactionaries *pl*, reactionary forces *pl*

buñuelo *nm* **(a)** *Culin* doughnut **(b)** *Fam (cosa mal hecha)* botch-up, bungle, mess

buque *nm* ship ❏ **b. de desembarco** landing craft; **b. de guerra** warship; **b. de pasajeros** liner, passenger ship; **b. escuela** training ship; **b. insignia** flagship

buqué *nm* bouquet

burbuja *nf* bubble; **hacer burbujas** to bubble, make bubbles ❏ **b. inmobiliaria** property bubble

burbujear *vi* to bubble

burbujeo *nm* bubbling

burdel *nm* brothel

Burdeos *n* Bordeaux

burdeos 1 *adj inv* maroon
   2 *nm inv* Bordeaux

burdo, -a *adj* **(a)** *(tosco)* coarse, rough; **paño b.** coarse cloth **(b)** *(grosero)* rude, rough **(c)** *(torpe)* clumsy

bureta *nf Quím* burette

búrger *(pl* **búrgers)**, *nm,* **burguer** ['burɣer] *(pl* **burguers)** *nm Fam* burger bar *o* restaurant

burgo *nm* hamlet

burgomaestre *nm* burgomaster, mayor

burgués, -a 1 *adj* bourgeois, middle-class
   2 *nm,f* bourgeois *o* middle-class person

burguesía *nf* bourgeoisie, middle class, middle classes *pl*

buril *nm* burin, engraver's chisel

burilar *vt* to engrave with a burin

Burkina Faso *n* Burkina-Faso

burla *nf* **(a)** *(mofa)* gibe, jeer, taunt; **hacer b. de algo** *o* **algn** to mock *o* make fun of sth *o* sb; *Fig* **b. burlando** quietly, on the quiet, without anyone noticing **(b)** *(broma)* joke; **en son de b.** in fun; **no te lo digo en son de b.** I'm not joking; **entre burlas y veras** half jokingly **(c)** *(engaño)* trick, hoax, deception

burladero *nm* **(a)** *Taur* refuge in bullring **(b)** *Aut* (traffic) island, *US* safety island

burlador *nm* Casanova, Don Juan, seducer

burlar 1 *vt* **(a)** *(engañar)* to deceive, trick, outwit **(b)** *(eludir)* to dodge, evade; **b. las leyes** to flout the law
   2 burlarse *vpr* **b. de** to make fun of, mock, ridicule, laugh at

burlesco, -a *adj* burlesque, comic, funny

burlete *nm Téc* draught *o US* draft excluder

burlón, -ona 1 *adj* mocking
   2 *nm,f* joker, wag

buró *nm* **(a)** *(escritorio)* bureau, desk **(b)** *Pol* executive committee **(c)** *Méx (mesa de noche)* bedside table

burocracia *nf* bureaucracy

burócrata *nmf* bureaucrat

burocrático, -a *adj* bureaucratic

burocratización *nf* bureaucratization

burocratizar [14] *vt* to bureaucratize

burrada *nf* **(a)** *(dicho necio)* stupid *o* foolish remark; **decir burradas** to talk nonsense **(b)** *(hecho necio)* stupid *o* foolish act **(c)** *Esp Fam* loads *pl*, lots *pl*; **¿cuánto trabajo tienes? —una b.** how much work have you got? — loads; **la película me gustó una b.** I really liked the movie *o Br* film; **una b. de gente** loads of people, tons of people; **vale una b.** it costs a fortune

burrito *nm CAm Méx* burrito

burro, -a 1 *adj* (**a**) *Fam (de pocos alcances)* stupid, dumb; **tu hermano es muy b.** your brother's a real dimwit (**b**) *Fam (tozudo)* stubborn; **ponerse b.** to dig one's heels in

2 *nm,f* (**a**) *Zool* donkey, ass; *Fam Fig* **apearse** *o* **bajarse del b.** to climb *o* back down; *Fam Fig* **no ver tres en un b.** to be as blind as a bat (**b**) *Fam (estúpido)* ass, dunce, dimwit, blockhead (**c**) *Fam (persona laboriosa)* drudge, plodder; **b. de carga** dogsbody, drudge

3 *nm Carp* sawhorse

bursátil *adj* stock-exchange, stock-market; **precios bursátiles** stock-exchange quotations

burundés, -esa *adj & nm,f* Burundian

Burundi *n* Burundi

bus *nm* bus

busca 1 *nf* (**a**) *(búsqueda)* search, hunt; **ir en b. de** to go in search of (**b**) *Caza* party of hunters, beating party (**c**) *(provecho)* perks *pl* , fringe benefits *pl*

2 *nm Esp (buscapersonas)* pager

buscador, -a 1 *nm,f (persona)* hunter; **b. de oro** gold prospector

2 *nm Inform (en Internet)* search engine

buscapersonas *nm inv (aparato)* bleeper, pager

buscapiés *nm inv* firecracker, jumping jack

buscapleitos *nmf inv* troublemaker

buscar [59] **1** *vt (gen)* to look *o* search for; **b. una llave perdida** to search for a lost key; **b. una palabra en el diccionario** to look up a word in the dictionary; **buscó su nombre en la lista** he looked for her name on the list; **está buscando empleo** she's looking for work *o* a job; **ir a b. algo** to go and get sth, fetch sth; **fue a buscarme a la estación** she picked me up at the station; *Fig* **b. ayuda** to seek *o* fetch help; *Fig* **b. camorra** to be looking for trouble *o* a fight; *Fig* **b. una aguja en un pajar** to look for a needle in a haystack; *Fig* **buscarle tres pies al gato** to split hairs,

complicate matters; *Fam Fig* **buscarle las cosquillas a algn** to annoy sb, rub sb up the wrong way

2 buscarse *vpr Fam* **b. la vida** to try and earn one's living, try and make one's way in life; *Fam* **buscársela** to ask for it, be looking for trouble; *Fam* **tú te lo has buscado** you asked for it

buscavidas *nmf inv Fam* (**a**) *(entrometido)* nosy person, *Br* nosy parker (**b**) *(ambicioso)* go-getter

buscón, -ona *nm,f (ladrón)* petty thief; *(estafador)* crook, swindler

buscona *nf (prostituta)* whore, streetwalker

buseta *nf Col CRica Ecuad Ven* minibus

búsqueda *nf* search, quest; *Inform* search

busto *nm* (**a**) *Anat (de mujer)* bust; *(de hombre)* chest (**b**) *Arte* bust

butaca *nf* (**a**) *(sillón)* armchair, easy chair (**b**) *Cin Teat* seat; **b. de platea** *o* **patio** *Br* seat in the stalls, *US* orchestra seat; **patio de butacas** *Br* stalls *pl*, *US* orchestra

Bután *n* Bhutan

butano *nm Quím* butane; **(gas) b.** butane gas; **bombona de (gas) b.** cylinder of butane gas

buten: de buten *loc adv Esp Argot* first rate, excellent, terrific

butifarra *nf* = Catalan sausage

buzo *nm* diver

buzón *nm* (**a**) post box, *Br* letter box, *US* mailbox; **echar una carta al b.** to post *o US* mail a letter (**b**) *Inform (de correo electrónico)* mailbox, e-mail address

buzoneo *nm* leafleting

bypass [bai'pas] *nm Med* heart bypass operation

byte *nm Inform* byte

C

C, c [θe] *nf (la letra)* C, c

C (**a**) *(abrev de* **Celsius**) C (**b**) *(abrev de* **centígrado**) C

C. *(abrev de* **capítulo**) ch

C., Ca *(abrev de* **compañía**) Co

c/ (**a**) *(abrev de* **calle**) St, Rd (**b**) *(abrev de* **cuenta**) a/c

ca *interj* not at all!, not a bit of it!

cabal 1 *adj* (**a**) *(exacto)* exact, precise; **2.000 pesos cabales** 2,000 pesos exactly (**b**) *(completo)* complete (**c**) *Fig* honest, upright; **un hombre c.** an upright man
2 cabales *nmpl Fam* **no estar algn en sus c.** to have a screw loose

cábala *nf* (**a**) *(doctrina)* cabala, cabbala (**b**) *(suposición)* **hacer cábalas sobre algo** to speculate about sth

cabalgada *nf Hist (tropa)* troop of riders; *(correría)* cavalry raid

cabalgadura *nf* (**a**) *(montura)* mount (**b**) *(de carga)* beast of burden

cabalgar [38] **1** *vi* to ride, go riding
2 *vt* (**a**) *(caballo)* to ride (**b**) *(semental)* to cover

cabalgata *nf Esp* cavalcade ❏ **la c. de los Reyes Magos** the procession of the Three Wise Men

cabalista *nmf* cabalist, cabbalist; *Fig (intrigante)* intriguer

cabalístico, -a *adj* cabalistic, cabbalistic; *Fig (oculto)* hidden

caballa *nf (pez)* mackerel

caballar *adj* horse; **ganado c.** horses *pl*

caballeresco, -a *adj* chivalric, chivalrous, knightly

caballería *nf* (**a**) *(cabalgadura)* mount, steed (**b**) *Mil* cavalry; **c. ligera** light cavalry (**c**) *Hist* chivalry, knighthood; *Lit* **libros de caballerías** novels of chivalry

caballeriza *nf* (**a**) *(cuadra)* stable (**b**) *(conjunto de caballos)* stud (**c**) *(personal)* grooms *pl*, stable hands *pl*

caballerizo *nm* groom, stableboy, stableman; *Hist* **c. mayor del rey** Master of the King's Horse

caballero *nm* (**a**) *(señor)* gentleman; **¿qué desea, c.?** can I help you, sir?; **ropa de c.** menswear (**b**) *Hist* knight, cavalier; **armar c. a algn** to knight sb

caballerosidad *nf* gentlemanliness, chivalry

caballeroso, -a *adj* gentlemanly, chivalrous; **una actitud poco caballerosa** an ungentlemanly attitude

caballete *nm* (**a**) *Téc (soporte)* trestle (**b**) *Anat (de la nariz)* bridge (**c**) *Arquit (de tejado)* ridge (**d**) *(de pintor)* easel

caballista *nmf* (**a**) *(jinete)* good rider (**b**) *(experto)* horse expert

caballito *nm* (**a**) *Zool* **c. de mar** sea-horse (**b**) *Ent* **c. del diablo** dragonfly (**c**) **caballitos** merry-go-round *sing*, *US* carousel *sing*

caballo *nm* (**a**) *Zool* horse; **a c.** on horseback; **montar a c.** to ride; *Fig* **a c. entre ...** halfway between ...; *Prov* **a c. regalado no le mires el dentado** don't look a gift horse in the mouth ❏ **c. de carreras** racehorse (**b**) *Téc* horsepower; **un (coche) dos caballos** a 2 CV (car) (**c**) *Ajedrez* knight (**d**) *Naipes* queen (**e**) *Argot (heroína)* junk, horse, scag, smack

caballuno, -a *adj* horsey, horse-like

cabalmente *adv* exactly

cabaña *nf* (**a**) *(choza)* hut, shack (**b**) *(ganado)* livestock (**c**) *RP (finca)* cattle ranch

cabaret *(pl* **cabarets**) *nm* cabaret, nightclub

cabe¹ *prep Literario* next to

cabe² *nm Fam Ftb* header

cabecear 1 *vi* (**a**) *(negar)* to shake one's head (**b**) *(dormirse)* to nod (**c**) *(inclinarse)* to bend, sway (**d**) *Náut* to pitch
2 *vt Ftb* to head

cabeceo *nm* (**a**) *(negación)* shake of the head (**b**) *(al dormirse)* nodding, nod (**c**) *(inclinación)* bending, swaying (**d**) *Náut* pitching

cabecera *nf* (**a**) *(de fila, mesa)* head; *(de cama)* top end; **estar a la c. de (la cama de) algn** to be at sb's bedside; **médico de c.** family doctor, GP (**b**) *Esp (de texto)* heading; *(de periódico)* masthead (**c**) *(de programa televisivo)* title sequence (**d**) *(de río)* source; *(de manifestación)* head

cabecilla *nmf* leader

cabellera *nf* (**a**) *(pelo)* (long) hair (**b**) *(de cometa)* tail

cabello *nm* (**a**) *(pelo)* hair (**b**) *Culin* **c. de ángel** = preserve made of strands of pumpkin in syrup (**c**) **cabellos** *(de maíz)* corn silk *sing*

cabelludo, -a *adj* hairy; **cuero c.** scalp

caber [12] *vi* (**a**) *(haber espacio para)* to fit, be (able to be) contained; **cabe en el rincón** it fits in the corner; **¿cabemos todos?** is there room for all of us?; **¿cuántas personas caben en este teatro?** what's the capacity of this theatre?; **en esta jarra caben tres litros** this jar holds three litres; **no cabe por la puerta** it won't go through the door; *Fig* **no cabe (la menor) duda de que ...** there is no doubt that ...; *Fig* **no c. en sí de gozo** to be beside oneself with joy; *Fig* **no cabe ni un alfiler** it is packed; *Fig* **no me cabe en la cabeza** I can't understand it (**b**) *(ser posible)* to be possible; **cabe la posibilidad de que ...** there is a possibility o chance that ...; **no está mal dentro de lo que cabe** it isn't bad, considering the circumstances (**c**) *Fml (corresponder)* **me cabe la satisfacción de anunciar ...** it gives me great pleasure to announce ...; **me cupo el honor de ...** I had the honour to o of ... (**d**) *Mat* to go; **doce entre cuatro caben a tres** four into twelve goes three (times)

cabestrillo *nm* sling; **con el brazo en c.** with her arm in a sling

cabestro *nm* (**a**) *(dogal)* halter (**b**) *(buey manso)* leading ox (for bulls)

cabeza 1 *nf* (**a**) *(de persona, animal, objeto)* head; **c. abajo** upside down; **c. arriba** the right way up; **dolor de c.** headache; **lavarse la c.** to wash one's hair; **volver la c.** to look round ▫ **c. de puente** bridgehead (**b**) *(persona)* head; **20.000 por c.** 20,000 a head *o* per person ▫ *Fig* **c. de turco** scapegoat (**c**) *(res)* head *inv*; **un rebaño de mil cabezas** a thousand head of sheep (**d**) *(posición)* **a la c. de** *(guiando)* at the head of; *(en primer lugar)* at the front *o* top of (**e**) *(expresiones)* **de c.** *(directamente)* headfirst; *Esp Fam* **andar/ ir de c.** *(muy atareado)* to be snowed under; **de pies a c.** from top *o* head to toe; *Fam* **calentarse la c. por** to get worked up about; *Fig* **estar mal de la c.** to be a mental case; *Fig* **irse la c.** to get dizzy; *Fig* **no tener ni pies ni c.** to be absurd *o* pointless; *Fig* **pasarle a algn por la c.** to occur to sb; *Fig* **perder la c.** *(sensatez)* to lose one's head; *Fig* **quitarle a algn una idea de la c.** to talk sb out of an idea; *Fig* **subirse algo a la c.** to go to one's head; *Fig* **tener mucha c.** to be very bright; *Fam Fig* **meterse algo en la c.** to get sth into one's head; *Fam Fig* **no levantar c.** not to recover, not get back to normal; *Fam Fig* **romperse la c.** *(golpearse)* to smash one's head; *(pensar)* to rack one's brains; *Fam Fig* **tengo la c. como un bombo** my head's splitting; *Esp Fam* **traer de c. a algn** to drive sb mad

2 *nmf Fam* **c. de chorlito** *o* **loca** scatterbrain; *Fam* **c. cuadrada** bigot; **c. de familia** head of the family; *Dep* **c. de serie** seed

cabezada *nf* (**a**) *(golpe)* butt, blow on the head (**b**) *(gesto)* nod; *Fam* **echar una c.** to have a snooze (**c**) *(correaje)* cavesson (**d**) *Náut* pitch, pitching (**e**) *Andes RP* saddlebow

cabezal *nm* (**a**) *Téc* head, headstock; *(de tocadiscos)* pickup (**b**) *(almohada)* bolster (**c**) *(vendaje)* compress (**d**) *Chile Méx (travesaño)* lintel

cabezazo *nm* (**a**) *(golpe dado)* butt (**b**) *(golpe recibido)* blow on the head (**c**) *Ftb* header

cabezón, -ona *adj Fam* (**a**) *(persona)* pigheaded (**b**) *(vino)* heady

cabezonada *nf Fam* pigheaded action

cabezonería *nf Fam* (**a**) *(cualidad)* pigheadedness (**b**) *(acción)* pigheaded action

cabezota *Fam* **1** *adj* pigheaded
2 *nmf* pigheaded person

cabezudo, -a 1 *adj (persona)* bigheaded
2 *nm (figura)* = carnival figure with a huge head

cabezuela *nf* (**a**) *(harina)* second grade flour (**b**) *Bot* flower head

cabida *nf* capacity; **dar c. a** to leave room for

cabildear *vi* to intrigue, scheme

cabildeo *nm* intriguing, scheming

cabildo *nm* (**a**) *(ayuntamiento)* town council (**b**) *Rel* chapter

cabina *nf* cabin, booth ▫ **c. electoral** polling *o* voting booth; *Cin* **c. de proyección** projection room; *Tel* **c. telefónica** phone box, *US* phone booth

cabinero, -a *nm,f Col* flight attendant

cabizbajo, -a *adj* crestfallen

cable *nm* (**a**) *Elec Inform (para conectar)* cable, lead; *(dentro de aparato)* wire; *Fam* **echarle un c. a algn** to give sb a hand (**b**) *(de fibra óptica)* cable; **televisión por c.** cable television; **c. de fibra óptica** *Br* fibre-optic *o US* fiber-optic cable

cableado, -a *Inform* **1** *adj* hardwired
2 *nm* wiring

cablegrafiar [32] *vt* to send a cable to, cable

cablegrama *nm* cablegram, cable

cablevisión *nf* cable television

Cabo *n* (**a**) **Ciudad del C.** Cape Town (**b**) **C. de Hornos** Cape Horn; **C. Verde** Cape Verde

cabo *nm* (**a**) *(extremo)* end, stub (**b**) *Fig (fin)* **al c.** finally; **al c. de dos horas/tres días** after two hours/three days; **al fin y al c.** after all; **de c. a rabo** from start to finish (**c**) *Náut* rope, line, cable; *Fig* **atar** *o* **juntar cabos** to put two and two together; *Fig* **no dejar ningún c. suelto** to leave no loose ends (**d**) *Mil* corporal; *(policía)* sergeant (**e**) *Geog* cape (**f**) **cabos** *(de caballo)* tail and mane *sing*

cabotaje *nm* (**a**) *Náut* coastal traffic, cabotage; **barco de c.** coaster (**b**) *RP* **vuelo de c.** *(en avión)* internal flight

caboverdiano, -a *adj & nm,f* Cape Verdean

cabra *nf* (**a**) *Zool* goat; *Fam* **estar como una c.** to be off one's head ▫ **c. montés** wild goat (**b**) *Carib Col (trampa)* trick

cabrales *nm inv* = type of blue cheese from Asturias

cabré *indic fut véase* **caber**

cabrear *Vulg* **1** *vt* to make angry; **estar cabreado** to be *Br* pissed off *o US* pissed
2 cabrearse *vpr* to get worked up; **ella se cabrea por cualquier cosa** she blows her top over everything

cabreo *nm Vulg* anger; **agarrar(se)** *o Esp* **coger un c.** to get really *Br* pissed off *o US* pissed; **¡tengo** *o* **llevo un c. encima!** I'm really pissed off!

cabrero, -a *nm,f* goatherd

cabrestante *nm Náut* capstan

cabria *nf Téc* gin

cabrilla *nf* (**a**) *(trípode)* sawhorse (**b**) **cabrillas** *(espuma)* white horses, whitecaps

cabrillear *vi* (**a**) *(olas)* to break into white horses (**b**) *(rielar)* to glisten

cabrío, -a *adj* goat-like, goatish

cabriola *nf (de caballo)* capriole; *(de niño)* caper, skip

cabriolé *nm Antes* cabriolet

cabritilla *nf* kid, kidskin

cabrito *nm* (**a**) *Zool* kid (**b**) *Fam Euf Br* basket, *US* son of a gun

cabro, -a *nm,f Chile Fam* kid

cabrón, -ona 1 *adj Vulg* (**a**) *(insulto)* **ser muy c.** to be a real bastard (**b**) *Méx (difícil)* **el examen estuvo bien c.** the exam was a bitch
2 *nm,f Vulg (hombre)* bastard; *(woman)* bitch
3 *nm* (**a**) *Zool* he-goat, billy goat (**b**) *Vulg (cornudo)* cuckold (**c**) *Méx Vulg (tipo)* guy

cabronada *nf Vulg* dirty trick; **hacer una c. a algn** to do the dirty on sb, play a dirty trick on sb

cabronazo *nm Ofens* bastard, fucker

cabujón *nm Min* cabochon

cabuya *nf* (**a**) *Bot* agave, pita (**b**) *CAm Col Ven* rope; **dar c.** *(atar)* to moor

caca *nf Fam* (**a**) *(excremento) Br* poo, *US* poop; **el niño (se) ha hecho c.** the baby did it in his pants; *Fig* **este libro es una c.** this book is crap (**b**) *(en lenguaje infantil)* poopoo; **no toques eso que es c.** don't touch that, it's dirty *o* nasty

cacahuate *nm CAm Méx Bot véase* **cacahuete**

cacahuero *nm Am* = owner of cacao plantations

cacahuete *nm Bot (fruto)* peanut; *(planta)* groundnut

cacalote *nm* (**a**) *CAm Méx (de maíz)* popcorn (**b**) *Méx Orn* crow

cacao *nm* (**a**) *Bot* cacao (**b**) *(polvo, bebida)* cocoa (**c**) *Esp (para labios)* lip salve (**d**) *Fam (lío)* mess, cockup; **tener un c. mental** to be confused *o US* screwed up

cacaotal *nm* cacao plantation

cacarear 1 *vi (gallina)* to cluck; *(gallo)* to crow

2 *vt Fig* to boast about; **su tan cacareado éxito** his much talked of success

cacareo *nm* (**a**) *(de gallina)* clucking; *(de gallo)* crowing (**b**) *Fig* boasting, bragging

cacatúa *nf* (**a**) *Orn* cockatoo (**b**) *Fig Pey (mujer)* ugly old woman

cacereño, -a 1 *adj* of o from Cáceres
2 *nm,f* person from Cáceres

cacería *nf* hunting, shooting, hunt, shoot

cacerola *nf* saucepan, casserole

cacha¹ 1 *nf* (**a**) *Fam (muslo)* thigh (**b**) *(de un arma)* butt
2 cachas *adj inv Esp* **estar c.** to be hunky, be a hunk

cacha² *nf Andes CAm (engaño)* trick, swindle

cachaco, -a 1 *adj* (**a**) *Col (de Bogotá)* of o from Bogotá (**b**) *Andes Ven* foppish
2 *nm,f Col (de Bogotá)* person from Bogotá
3 *nm Bol Perú Fam Pey (policía)* cop

cachada *nf* (**a**) *Am (cornada)* goring (**b**) *RP (burla)* taunt, jeer

cachalote *nm Zool* cachalot, sperm whale

cachar *vt* (**a**) *CAm Ecuad RP (burlarse de)* to tease (**b**) *Am (cornear)* to gore (**c**) *Am Fam (atrapar)* to catch (**d**) *Nic RP Fam (agarrar)* to grab (**e**) *CAm Fam (robar)* to swipe, pinch (**f**) *CSur Fam (entender)* to understand, get

cacharpas *nfpl Am* junk *sing*, useless objects

cacharrazo *nm Fam* thump

cacharrería *nf* pottery shop

cacharrero, -a *nm,f* pottery maker o dealer

cacharro *nm* (**a**) *(recipiente)* pot; **cacharros** *(de cocina)* pots and pans; **fregar los cacharros** to do the dishes (**b**) *Fam Pey (trasto)* piece of junk (**c**) *Fam Pey (coche)* banger

cachaza *nf* sluggishness, phlegm; **¡qué c. tienes!** how slow you are!

cachazudo, -a 1 *adj* (**a**) *(lento)* sluggish (**b**) *(flemático)* calm, placid
2 *nm,f* (**a**) *(lento) Br* slowcoach, *US* slowpoke (**b**) *(flemático)* phlegmatic person (**c**) *Cuba (paciente)* **es un c.** he's the soul of patience
3 *nm Cuba Méx (gusano)* tobacco worm

cache *adj Am* sloppy, slovenly

caché *(pl* **cachés)** *nm* (**a**) *(tarifa de artista)* fee (**b**) *(distinción)* cachet (**c**) *Inform* **(memoria) c.** cache memory

cachear *vt* to frisk, search

cachemir *nm*, **cachemira** *nf Tex* cashmere

Cachemira *n* Kashmir

cacheo *nm* frisk, frisking

cachet [ka'tʃe] *(pl* **cachets)** *nm véase* **caché**

cachetada *nf* slap

cachete *nm* (**a**) *(bofetada)* slap (**b**) *(moflete)* chubby cheek

cachetón, -ona *adj Fam* (**a**) *Am (carrilludo)* fat-faced, chubby cheeked (**b**) *Méx (despreocupado)* heartless, selfish

cachiporra *nf* (**a**) *Fam (garrote)* club, cudgel; *(de policía)* truncheon (**b**) *Cuba (ave)* blacknecked stilt

cachiporrazo *nm* clubbing, blow with a club

cachirulo *nm* thingamajig

cachirulos *nmpl Fam* thingamabob *sing*, thingummy *sing*

cachivache *nm Fam* thing, knick-knack, piece of junk

cacho¹ *nm Fam* (**a**) *(pedazo)* bit, piece (**b**) *Esp (como intensificador)* **¡qué c. de animal!** what a nasty piece of work!

cacho² *nm* (**a**) *Andes Ven (cuerno)* horn (**b**) *Andes Guat Ven (cuento)* story, tale (**c**) *Andes (cubilete)* dice cup (**d**) *RP* **c. de banana** hand of bananas

cachón, -ona 1 *adj CAm Col* big-horned
2 *nm,f* big-horned animal

cachondearse *vpr Esp Fam* **c. de** to make a fool out of, *Br* take the mickey out of; **se cachondea de todo** he takes everything as a joke

cachondeo *nm Esp Fam* laugh; **¡vaya c.!** what a laugh!

cachondo, -a *adj Fam* (**a**) *Esp Méx (excitado sexualmente)* hot, horny, *Br* randy (**b**) *Esp (divertido)* funny

cachorro, -a *nm,f* (**a**) *(de perro)* pup, puppy (**b**) *(de gato)* kitten (**c**) *(de otros animales)* cub, baby

cacique *nm* (**a**) *(jefe indio)* cacique (**b**) *(déspota)* despot, tyrant

caciquil *adj Pey* despotic

caciquismo *nm* (**a**) *Pol* caciquism (**b**) *Pey* despotism

caco *nm Fam* thief

cacofonía *nf* cacophony, dissonance

cacofónico, -a *adj* cacophonous, cacophonic

cacto *nm*, **cactus** *nm inv Bot* cactus *inv*

cacumen *nm Fam Fig* brains *pl*

cada *adj* (**a**) *(uso distributivo)* each; *(con números, frecuencia)* every; **nos deben mil a c. uno** they owe each of us a thousand; **c. dos por tres** every other minute; **cuatro de c. diez** four out of (every) ten **a c. paso** at every step; **c. día** every day **¿c. cuánto?** how often?; **a c. cual lo suyo** each to his own; **que c. cual se las apañe como pueda** it's every man for himself (**b**) *(valor progresivo)* **c. vez lo entiendo menos** it becomes harder and harder (for me) to understand; **c. vez más** more and more; **c. vez más tarde** later and later; **c.** *(valor enfático)* **¡te inventas c. historia!** you come up with some fine stories!

cadalso *nm (patíbulo)* scaffold; *(plataforma)* platform

cadáver *nm* (**a**) *(de persona)* corpse, (dead) body; **ingresar c.** to be dead on arrival (**b**) *(de animal)* body, carcass

cadavérico, -a *adj* cadaverous; **con palidez c.** deathly pale

cadejo *nm CAm Fam (animal fantástico)* = imaginary animal that comes out at night

cadena *nf* (**a**) *(de eslabones, piezas)* chain; *(correa de perro)* lead, leash; **tirar de la c. (del wáter)** to flush the toilet (**b**) *(de empresas)* chain; **una c. de cines/supermercados** a chain of cinemas/supermarkets (**c**) *(red de emisoras)* station; *(canal)* channel (**d**) *Ind* line; **trabajo en c.** assembly line work ❑ **c. de montaje** assembly line; **c. de producción** production line ❑ *Geog* **c. montañosa** mountain range (**f**) *Jur* **c. perpetua** life imprisonment (**g**) *Fig (serie)* chain; **reacción en c.** chain reaction ❑ **c. alimentaria** food chain (**h**) **cadenas** *Aut* tyre o *US* tire chains

cadencia *nf* cadence, rhythm; *Mús* cadenza

cadencioso, -a *adj* rhythmical

cadeneta *nf* (**a**) *Tricot* chain stitch (**b**) *(de papel)* paper chain

cadera *nf* hip; **con las manos en las caderas** hands on hips

cadete¹ *nmf* (**a**) *Mil* cadet (**b**) *Dep* = sports player aged 14-15

cadete², -a *nm,f RP (en trabajo)* office junior

Cádiz *n* Cadiz

cadmio *nm Quím* cadmium

caducado, -a *adj (carné, pasaporte)* expired, out-of-date; *(alimento, medicamento)* past its use-by date

caducar [59] *vi* to expire, lose validity

caducidad *nf* expiration, loss of validity, lapse; **fecha de c.** *(en alimentos)* ≃ sell-by date; *(en medicinas)* to be used before

caduco, -a *adj* (**a**) *(pasado)* expired, out-of-date, invalid; *(idea, moda)* outmoded (**b**) *Bot* **de hoja caduca** deciduous

caedizo *nm CAm Col Méx* overhang

caer [13] **1** *vi* (**a**) *(hacia abajo)* to fall; **c. de bruces** to fall flat on one's face; **c. de cabeza/de espaldas** to fall on one's head/back; **dejar c.** to drop; **la falda te cae por un lado** your skirt dips at one side; *Fig* **c. enfermo** *o* **en cama** to fall ill; *Fig* **c. en la tentación** to give in *o* yield to temptation; *Fig* **c. en manos de** to fall into the hands of; *Fig* **c. en un error** to make a mistake; *Fig* **está al c.** *(llegar)* he'll arrive any minute now; *(ocurrir)* it's on the way; *Fig* **¡qué bajo has caído!** I never thought you'd sink so low!; *Fam* **déjate c. alguna vez por casa** come round and see us sometime (**b**) *(fechas)* to fall; **su cumpleaños cae en sábado** his birthday falls on a Saturday (**c**) *(premio, lotería) (tocar)* to go; **el primer premio cayó en Granada** the first prize went to Granada; *Fig* **¡la que nos ha caído encima!** what a lovely situation to be in! (**d**) *(entender)* to understand, see; **no caigo en lo que me quieres decir** *Esp* I don't quite understand what you're getting at; **ya caigo** I get it (**e**) *(hallarse) Esp* to be; **cae por Salamanca** it is somewhere near Salamanca (**f**) *(sentar)* **c. bien** a to agree with; *(prenda)* to suit; **el pescado no me ha caído bien** the fish didn't agree with me; *Esp* **esa chaqueta te cae bien** that jacket suits you; *(persona)* **me cae bien/gorda** *o* **mal** I like/don't like her (**g**) *(perder) (en combate)* to surrender; *(cargo, posición)* to fall; **el gobierno ha caído** the government has fallen (**h**) *(abalanzarse)* to throw oneself (**sobre** on) (**i**) *(finalizar)* **al c. el día** in the evening; **al c. la noche** at nightfall

2 caerse *vpr* to fall (down); **me caí de la escalera** I fell off the ladder; **se te ha caído el pañuelo** you've dropped your handkerchief; *Fam* **no tener dónde c. muerto** not to have a penny to one's name; *Fam Fig* **caérsele a uno la cara de vergüenza** to die of shame

café *nm* (**a**) *Bot* coffee; **un grano de c.** a coffee bean (**b**) *(bebida)* coffee ❑ **c. con leche** white coffee; *Am* **c. negro** black coffee; *Andes Esp* **c. solo** black coffee; *Andes Ven* **c. tinto** black coffee (**c**) *(lugar)* café, coffee bar *o* shop

cafeína *nf* caffeine

cafetal *nm* coffee plantation

cafetera *nf* (**a**) *(para hacer café)* coffee-maker ❑ **c. exprés** expresso-coffee machine (**b**) *(para servir café)* coffeepot (**c**) *Fam (coche viejo)* old banger *o* crock; *(persona)* **estar como una c.** to be barmy *o* nuts

cafetería *nf* snack bar, coffee bar; *Ferroc* buffet car

cafetero, -a *adj* (**a**) *(de café)* coffee; **la producción cafetera** coffee production (**b**) *Fam (persona)* coffee-loving; **es muy c.** he loves coffee

cafeto *nm Bot* coffee bush

caficultor, -a *nm,f CAm Col Méx* coffee grower

cafre 1 *adj (persona)* brutal, barbarous
2 *nm,f (persona)* savage, beast

cagada *nf Vulg* (**a**) *(mierda)* shit (**b**) *Fig (error) Br* cock-up, *US* foul-up

cagado, -a 1 *pp de* **cagar**
2 *adj* (**a**) *Fam* **lleva los pantalones cagados** he's shit his pants (**b**) *Vulg (cobarde)* coward; **estar c.** to be shit-scared
3 *nm,f Vulg (cobarde)* shit, yellow belly

cagalera *nf Vulg* the runs *pl*; **darle a algn la** *o* **una c.** to be shit-scared

cagar [38] *Vulg* **1** *vi* to (have a) shit
2 *vt (estropear)* to ruin, spoil; **la has cagado comprándote este coche** you fucked up buying this car
3 cagarse *vpr* to shit oneself; **c. de miedo** to be shit-scared; **¡me cago en ...!** bloody ...!; **¡me cago en diez** *o* **la**

mar! damn it!; **¡me cago en la leche!** *Br* bleeding hell!, *US* goddamn it!

cagarruta *nf* sheep *o* goat dirt

cagón, -ona 1 *adj* (**a**) *Fam* loose-bowelled (**b**) *Vulg (cobarde)* yellow
2 *nmf Vulg* chicken

cagueta *Vulg* **1** *adj* yellow
2 *nmf* coward, chicken

caída *nf* (**a**) *(de persona, objeto)* fall; *(de pelo, diente)* loss; **c. de ojos** demure look ❑ **c. libre** free fall (**b**) *(del terreno)* slope (**c**) *(de precios)* drop (**d**) *(de tela)* body, hang (**e**) *Fig* downfall, collapse; *Hist* **la c. del Imperio Romano** the fall of the Roman Empire

caído, -a 1 *pp de* **caer**
2 *adj* (**a**) *(árbol, hoja)* fallen; *(hombros)* round, sloping; *(pechos)* saggy (**b**) *Fig* **c. del cielo** *(inesperado)* out of the blue; *(oportuno)* heavensent
3 los caídos *nmpl* the fallen *pl*

caigo *indic pres véase* **caer**

caimán *nm* caiman, cayman, alligator

Caín *nm* Cain; *Fig* evil person; *Fam* **pasar las de C.** to go through hell

Cairo *n* **El C.** Cairo

caja *nf* (**a**) *(gen)* box; *Fam Fig* **echar a algn con cajas destempladas** to send sb packing ❑ **c. de caudales** safe, strongbox; *Esp* **c. de cerillas** box of matches; **c. de colores** paintbox; *Elec* **c. de empalmes** junction box; **c. de herramientas** toolbox; **c. de música** music *o* musical box; **c. fuerte** strongroom; *Av* **c. negra** black box; **c. rápida** express checkout; **c. registradora** cash register; **c. torácica** chest cavity; *Fam TV* **la c. tonta** the box, *Br* the telly, *US* the boob tube (**b**) *(de embalaje)* crate, case; **una c. de cerveza** a crate of beer (**c**) *(féretro)* coffin, casket (**d**) *Fin (en una tienda)* cash desk; *(en un banco)* cashier's desk; **ayer robaron la c.** they robbed the till yesterday; **hacer mucha c.** to take a lot; **pague en c.** pay at the cash desk (**e**) *Impr* case ❑ **c. alta/baja** upper/lower case (**f**) *Aut (carrocería)* body ❑ **c. de cambios** gearbox (**g**) *Com (banco)* bank ❑ *Esp* **c. de ahorros** savings bank; **C. Postal de Ahorros** Post Office Savings Bank (**h**) *Anat* **c. craneana** cranium, skull (**i**) *Téc* housing, casing (**j**) *Mús (de piano)* case; *(de violín)* body (**k**) *Mil* **entrar en c.** to enlist, join up (**l**) *Perú (depósito)* water tank (**m**) *Chile (de un río)* dry riverbed

cajearse *vpr Méx Fam* **c. con** *(multa)* to be landed with

cajero, -a *nm,f* cashier ❑ **c. automático** cash point, cash dispenser

cajeta *nf* (**a**) *CAm Méx (dulce)* = toffee pudding made with caramelized milk (**b**) *PRico (turrón)* = type of nougat

cajetilla *nf (de cigarrillos)* packet, *US* pack

cajista *nmf Impr* typesetter

cajón *nm* (**a**) *(caja grande)* crate, box (**b**) *(en un mueble)* drawer; *Fig* **c. de sastre** jumble; *Fam* **de c.** obvious, self-evident (**c**) *(ataúd) Br* coffin, *US* casket (**d**) *Méx (de estacionamiento)* parking space *o* bay

cajonera *nf* chest of drawers

cal¹ *nf* lime; *Fig* **a. y canto** hermetically; *Fig* **de c. y canto** strong, tough; *Fam* **una de c. y otra de arena** six of one and half a dozen of the other ❑ **c. apagada** *o* **muerta** slaked lime; **c. viva** quicklime

cal² *(abrev de* **caloría(s))** cal

cala¹ *nf (de fruta)* sample piece

cala² *nf* (**a**) *(ensenada)* creek, cove, inlet (**b**) *Náut* hold

cala³ *nf Bot* arum

calabacín *nm*, *Méx* **calabacita** *nf Br* courgette, *US* zucchini

calabaza *nf* (**a**) *Bot* pumpkin, gourd (**b**) *Fam (persona)* dolt (**c**) *Fam Fig* **dar calabazas a algn** *(suspender)* to fail sb; *(a un pretendiente)* to turn sb down

calabazar *nm* gourd o pumpkin field

calabobos *nm inv Meteor* drizzle

calabozo *nm* (**a**) *(prisión)* jail, prison (**b**) *(celda)* cell

calada *nf Esp Fam (de cigarrillo)* drag, puff; *Argot (de porro)* hit, toke

caladero *nm* fishing grounds, fishery

calado, -a 1 *pp de* **calar**
2 *adj* soaked; **vengo calado** I'm soaked (to the skin)
3 *nm* (**a**) *Cost* openwork, embroidery (**b**) *Náut* draught, *US* draft (**c**) *(profundidad del mar)* depth

calador *nm Am (para grano)* grain sampler

calafate *nm* caulker

calafatear *vt Náut* to caulk

calamar *nm Zool* squid *inv*; *Culin* **calamares a la romana** squid fried in batter

calambre *nm* (**a**) *Elec (descarga)* electric shock; **ese cable da c.** that wire is live (**b**) *(espasmo)* cramp; **me dio un c. en la pierna** I got a cramp in my leg

calamidad *nf* (**a**) *(catástrofe)* calamity, disaster (**b**) *(persona)* dead loss, good-for-nothing

calamitoso, -a *adj* calamitous, disastrous

calandraca *adj RP Fam Pey* doddery

calandrado *nm Téc* calendering

calandrar *vt Téc* to calender

calandria¹ *nf Orn* calandra lark

calandria² *nf Téc (de lustrar)* calender; *(torno)* treadmill

calaña *nf Pey* (**a**) *(carácter)* nature, disposition; **una persona de mala c.** a bad sort (**b**) *(clase)* kind, stock; **no me gusta la gente de esa c.** I don't like that kind of people

calar 1 *vt* (**a**) *(mojar)* to soak, drench (**b**) *(agujerear)* to pierce, penetrate (**c**) *(sombrero)* to jam on (**d**) *Téc* to do fretwork on (**e**) *Cost* to do openwork on (**f**) *Mil (bayoneta)* to fix (**g**) *Fam (persona, asunto)* to see through, *Br* suss out; **¡te tengo calado!** I've got your number! (**h**) *Esp (motor)* to stall (**i**) *Am (grano)* to sample
2 *vi* (**a**) *Náut* to draw (**b**) *Fig (penetrar)* **c. en** to have an effect on; **tus consejos han calado hondo en ella** she has taken your advice to heart
3 calarse *vpr* (**a**) *(mojarse)* to get soaked (**b**) *(el sombrero)* to pull down (**c**) *Esp Aut (el motor)* to stop, stall

calavera 1 *nf* (**a**) *(hueso)* skull (**b**) *Méx Aut* tail light (**c**) *Méx (dulce)* sugar skull
2 *nm (hombre)* tearaway, madcap

calaverada *nf* madcap escapade

calcado, -a 1 *pp de* **calcar**
2 *adj* traced, copied; *Fig* **es c. a su padre** he's the spitting image of his father
3 *nm* tracing

calcamonía *nf Fam* transfer, *US* decal

calcar [59] *vt* (**a**) *(un dibujo)* to trace (**b**) *Fig (imitar)* to copy, imitate

calcáreo, -a *adj Geol* calcareous

calce *nm* (**a**) *(llanta)* rim (**b**) *(cuña)* wedge (**c**) *Guat Méx PRico Jur* footnote

calceta *nf* (**a**) *(prenda)* stocking (**b**) *Tricot* knitting; **hacer c.** to knit

calcetín *nm* sock

cálcico, -a *adj* calcium, calcic

calcificación *nf* calcification

calcificar [59] **1** *vt* to calcify
2 calcificarse *vpr* to calcify

calcinación *nf* calcination

calcinar *vt* to calcine; *Fig* to burn

calcio *nm Quím* calcium

calco *nm* (**a**) *(de un dibujo)* tracing (**b**) *(copia)* (carbon) copy (**c**) *Fig (imitación)* imitation, copy

calcomanía *nf* transfer, *US* decal

calcopirita *nf Min* chalcopyrite

calculable *adj* calculable

calculador, -a 1 *adj* calculating
2 *nm & f* calculator

calcular *vt* (**a**) *(cantidades)* to calculate, work out, figure (**b**) *(evaluar)* to estimate, work out; **calcula lo que necesitas** work out how much you need; **calculando por lo bajo** at the lowest estimate (**c**) *(suponer)* to think, suppose, figure, guess; **calculo que llegará tarde** I don't expect him until late

cálculo *nm* (**a**) *(operación)* calculation, estimate, figures *pl*; **según mis cálculos** by my reckoning; **si mis cálculos no fallan** if I am right ❑ **c. mental** mental arithmetic (**b**) *Med* stone, gallstone ❑ **c. biliar** bile stone; **c. renal** kidney stone (**c**) *Mat* calculus ❑ **regla de c.** slide rule

Calcuta *n* Calcutta

caldas *nfpl* thermal springs

caldeamiento *nm* heating, warming

caldear *vt* (**a**) *(una habitación)* to heat, warm (**b**) *Fig (excitar)* to heat o warm up; **sus palabras caldearon el ambiente** his words stirred up those present

caldera *nf* boiler; *(caldero)* cauldron; *Fam* **las calderas de Pedro Botero** Hell

calderada *nf* boilerful, cauldronful

caldería *nf* (**a**) *(oficio)* boilermaking (**b**) *(lugar)* boilermaker's shop

calderero, -a *nm,f* boilermaker

caldereta *nf Culin (de cordero)* lamb stew; *(de pescado)* fish stew

calderilla *nf Fin* small change

caldero *nm* (**a**) *(caldera)* small cauldron (**b**) *(contenido)* cauldronful

calderón *nm Mús* pause

caldillo *nm* liquid *(on plate of food)*

caldo *nm* (**a**) *Culin* stock, broth (**b**) *Biol* **c. de cultivo** culture medium; *Fig (terreno abonado)* breeding ground (**c**) **caldos** *(vino)* wines (**d**) *Méx (de caña)* sugarcane juice

caldoso, -a *adj* with a lot of stock

calé *adj & nm* gypsy

calefacción *nf* heating ❑ **c. central** central heating

calefactor, -a *nm* (**a**) *(persona)* heating engineer (**b**) *(máquina)* heater

calefón *nm CSur (calentador de agua)* water heater

caleidoscópico, -a *adj* kaleidoscopic

caleidoscopio *nm* kaleidoscope

calendario *nm* (**a**) *(sistema, objeto)* calendar ❑ **c. escolar/laboral** school/working year (**b**) *(programa)* schedule, programme

calendas *nfpl* calends; *Literario* **c. griegas** never

caléndula *nf Bot* calendula

calentador, -a 1 *adj* heating
2 *nm* heater; **c. de agua** water heater

calentamiento *nm* heating; **ejercicios de c.** warm-up exercises ❑ **c. global** global warming

calentar [3] **1** *vt* (**a**) *(agua, horno)* to heat; *(comida, habitación)* to warm up; *Dep* **c. los músculos** to tone up one's muscles; *Fig* **c. el asiento** *(no trabajar)* to warm the chair; *Fig* **c. los sesos** o **los cascos** *(importunar)* to get hot under the collar (**b**) *Fig (exaltar)* to heat up, inflame (**c**) *Fig (irritar)* to annoy (**d**) *Fam (pegar)* to tan, warm (**e**) *Fam (excitar)* to arouse (sexually), turn on

2 calentarse *vpr* (**a**) *(por calor) (persona)* to warm oneself, get warm; *(cosa)* to heat up (**b**) *Fig (exaltarse)* to get excited; **se calentaron los ánimos** people became very excited (**c**) *Fig (enfadarse)* to get heated o annoyed (**d**) *Fam (excitarse)* to get horny o *Br* randy

calentón, -ona *adj*, **calentorro, -a** *adj Fam* horny, randy

calentura *nf* (**a**) *(fiebre)* fever, temperature (**b**) *(herida)* cold sore; **me ha salido una c.** I've got a cold sore (**c**) *Chile (tisis)* tuberculosis, consumption (**d**) *Carib (planta)* = type of milkweed (**e**) *Carib (descomposición)* fermentation (**f**) *Col RP Fam (rabieta)* fit of anger, rage

calenturiento, -a *adj* feverish; **mente calenturienta** *(exaltada)* hothead; *(excitada)* dirty mind

calesa *nf Antes* calash, calèche

calibrado *nm* boring, gauging

calibrador *nm (para medir)* gauge; callipers *(de mordazas) pl*, *US* calipers *pl* ◻ **c. micrométrico** vernier calliper, calliper rule

calibrar *vt* (**a**) *Téc* to gauge, bore (**b**) *Fig (juzgar)* to judge, size up

calibre *nm* (**a**) *Téc* bore, gauge (**b**) *(de arma)* calibre (**c**) *Fig (importancia)* size, importance

caliche *nm Andes Quím* Chile saltpetre o nitre

calidad *nf* (**a**) *(de producto, servicio)* quality; **muebles de primera c.** top-quality furniture; **vino de c.** good-quality wine ◻ **c. de vida** quality of life (**b**) *(condición)* capacity; **en c. de profesor** as a 'teacher (**c**) *(clase)* kind, type; **las distintas calidades de tomates** the various types of tomatoes

cálido, -a *adj* warm; **una cálida acogida** a warm welcome

calidoscópico, -a *adj véase* **caleidoscópico, -a**

calidoscopio *nm véase* **caleidoscopio**

calientabraguetas *nf inv Vulg* prick teaser

calientaplatos *nm inv* hotplate

caliente *adj* (**a**) *(a alta temperatura)* hot; *(templado)* warm; **un baño/café c.** a hot bath/cup of coffee (**b**) *Fig (acalorado)* heated, spirited; **en c.** in the heat of the moment (**c**) *Fam (excitado)* horny, *Br* randy

califa *nm* caliph

califato *nm* caliphate

calificable *adj* qualifiable

calificación *nf* (**a**) *Educ (nota)* *Br* mark, *US* grade; **libro de calificaciones** *Br* (school) report, *US* report card (**b**) *Econ* rating

calificado, -a 1 *pp de* **calificar**
2 *adj* (**a**) *(prestigioso)* eminent, well-known (**b**) *(apto)* apt, suitable

calificador, -a *adj* examining

calificar [59] *vt* (**a**) *(denominar)* to describe, consider; **calificaron sus ideas de progresistas** his ideas were considered progressive; **le calificó de inmoral** he called him immoral (**b**) *Educ (examen, ejercicio)* to mark, grade (**c**) *Ling (palabra)* to qualify

calificativo, -a 1 *adj* qualifying; **adjetivo c.** qualifying adjective
2 *nm* epithet; **no encuentro calificativos** words fail me

californiano, -a *adj & nm,f* Californian

caligrafía *nf* calligraphy; **ejercicios de c.** handwriting exercises; **tiene una c. infantil** his handwriting looks childish

caligráfico, -a *adj* calligraphic

calígrafo, -a *nm,f* calligrapher

calima *nf* haze, mist

calimocho *nm Esp* = drink made with wine and Coca-Cola

calina *nf Meteor véase* **calima**

calipso *nm* calypso

cáliz *nm* (**a**) *Rel* chalice (**b**) *Bot* calyx (**c**) *Literario (copa)* cup

caliza *nf* limestone

calizo, -a *adj Geol* lime

callada *nf* silence; **dar la c. por respuesta** to ignore the other person's question o request

callado, -a 1 *pp de* **callar**
2 *adj* quiet, silent; **una persona muy callada** a very quiet o reserved person; *Fam* **más c. que un muerto** as quiet as a mouse; *Fam* **¡qué c. te lo tenías!** how quiet you've kept it!

callampa *nf Chile (seta)* mushroom

callampas *nfpl Chile* shanty town

callana *nf Andes RP* = flat earthenware pan

callar 1 *vi* (**a**) *(en silencio)* to be quiet, keep quiet, say nothing; **los que deberían hablar callan** those who ought to speak remain silent (**b**) *(dejar de hablar)* to stop talking, shut up; **¡callad!** be quiet!; *Fam* **¡calla! ¿de verdad?** don't tell me!, is that true?

2 *vt (esconder)* not to mention, keep to oneself; **ella calló su nombre** she kept quiet about her name

3 callarse *vpr* (**a**) *(no hablar)* to be quiet, say nothing; **se calló cuando le preguntaron** he didn't answer when (he was) asked (**b**) *(dejar de hablar)* to stop talking, be quiet; *Fam* **c. la boca** to clam up, shut up

calle *nf* (**a**) *(en población)* street, road; **c. de dirección única** one-way street; **doblar la c.** to turn the corner; *Fig* **dejar a algn en la c.** *(sin trabajo)* to fire sb; *(sin casa)* to leave sb homeless; *Fig* **echar** o **poner a algn (de patitas) en la c.** to throw o kick sb out; *Fig* **el hombre de la c.** the man in the street; *Fig (prostituta)* **hacer la c.** to walk the streets, solicit; *Fig* **llevar** o **traer a algn por la c. de la amargura** to give sb a tough time; *Fig* **quedarse en la c.** to be left jobless/homeless ◻ **c. mayor** high street, *US* main street; **c. peatonal** pedestrian precinct (**b**) *Esp Atlet Natación* lane

calleja *nf* narrow street

callejear *vi* to wander (about) the streets

callejeo *nm* wandering about

callejero, -a 1 *adj* **hace mucha vida callejera** he likes going out a lot; **disturbios callejeros** street riot **celebración callejera** celebration in the street; **gato c.** stray cat
2 *nm (mapa)* street directory

callejón *nm* back alley o street ◻ **c. sin salida** cul-de-sac, dead end; *Fig* **en un c. sin salida** at an impasse

callejuela *nf* narrow street, lane

callicida *nm* corn remover

callista *nmf* chiropodist

callo *nm* (**a**) *Med* callus, corn; *Fam* **darle al c.** to slog (**b**) *Fam (persona fea)* (ugly) sight (**c**) *Esp Culin* **callos** tripe *sing*

callosidad *nf* callosity, callus

calloso, -a *adj* callous

calma *nf* (**a**) *(sin ruido o movimiento)* calmness, tranquillity, *US* tranquility; **perder la c.** to lose one's patience; **todo está en c.** all is calm; **tómatelo con c.** take it easy (**b**) *(negocio)* slack period, lull (**c**) *(cachaza)* phlegm, slowness; **¡qué c. tienes!** how calm you are! (**d**) *Meteor* calm weather ◻ **c. chicha** dead calm

calmante 1 *adj* sedative, soothing
2 *nm Farm* painkiller, sedative, tranquillizer, *US* tranquilizer

calmar 1 *vt (persona)* to calm (down); *(dolor)* to soothe, relieve
2 *vi (estado)* to fall calm
3 calmarse *vpr* **(a)** *(persona)* to calm down **(b)** *(dolor, viento)* to abate, ease off
calmoso, -a *adj* calm, serene
caló *nm Esp (idioma)* = gypsy dialect
calor *nm* **(a)** *(temperatura alta)* heat; *(tibieza)* warmth; **al c. de** *(calentado por)* in the heat of; *Fig (amparado por)* under the wing of; **entrar en c.** to warm up; **hacer c.** to be hot; *(persona)* **tener c.** to be hot; *Fig* **el c. del hogar** the warmth of home **(b)** *Fig (afecto)* warmth, love; *(entusiamo)* ardour, *US* ardor, passion
caloría *nf* calorie, calory
calórico, -a *adj* caloric, calorific
calorífero, -a *adj* heat-producing
calorífico, -a *adj véase* **calórico, -a**
calostro *nm Biol* colostrum
calote *nm RP Fam* swindle, fraud
calumnia *nf (oral)* slander; *(escrita)* libel
calumniador, -a 1 *adj* slanderous
2 *nm,f* slanderer
calumniar *vt (oralmente)* to slander; *(por escrito)* to libel
caluroso, -a *adj* warm, hot; *Fig* **una calurosa acogida** a warm reception
calva *nf* **(a)** *(de la cabeza)* bald patch **(b)** *(claro)* clearing
calvario *nm* **(a)** *Rel* Calvary; *(Vía Crucis)* stations *pl* of the Cross **(b)** *Fig (sufrimiento)* ordeal, calvary
calvero *nm (claro)* clearing
calvicie *nf* baldness
calvinismo *nm Rel* Calvinism
calvinista *Rel* **1** *adj* Calvinist
2 *nmf* Calvinist
calvo, -a 1 *adj* **(a)** *(persona)* bald; **ni tanto ni tan c.** neither one extreme nor the other **(b)** *(terreno)* barren, bare
2 *nm* bald man
calza *nf* **(a)** *(cuña)* wedge, scotch **(b)** *Anticuado* stocking **(c)** *Col (empaste)* filling
calzada *nf* road, roadway, *US* pavement
calzado, -a 1 *pp de* **calzar**
2 *adj* **(a)** *(con zapatos)* wearing shoes; **c. por el mejor zapatero** shod by the best shoemaker **(b)** *Rel* calced, shod
3 *nm* shoes *pl*, footwear; **un buen c.** a good pair of shoes
calzador *nm* shoehorn
calzar [14] **1** *vt* **(a)** *(poner calzado)* to put shoes on; **viste y calza al niño** dress the child and put his shoes on **(b)** *(llevar calzado)* to wear; **¿qué número calza?** what size do you take?; *Fig* **el mismo que viste y calza** in person **(c)** *(hacer zapatos)* to make shoes for; **le calza el mejor zapatero** he has his shoes made by the best shoemaker **(d)** *(poner una cuña)* to wedge, scotch **(e)** *Col (muela)* to fill
2 calzarse *vpr* **c. los zapatos** to put on one's shoes
calzo *nm* **(a)** *(cuña)* wedge, scotch **(b)** **calzos** *(de caballo)* stockings
calzón *nm* **(a)** *Esp Dep* shorts **(b)** *Andes Méx RP (bragas)* panties, *Br* knickers; **calzones** panties, *Br* knickers **(c)** *Bol, Méx* **calzones** *(calzoncillos) Br* underpants, *US* shorts **(d)** *RP* **en calzones** *(en ropa interior)* in one's underwear **(e)** *Bol (guiso)* pork stew
calzonazos *nm inv Fam* henpecked husband
calzoncillos *nmpl Br* underpants, *US* shorts
calzonudo *nm Am Fam* henpecked husband
cama *nf* bed; **estar en** o **guardar c.** to be confined to bed; *(indefinidamente)* to be bedridden; **hacer la c.** to make the bed; **irse a la c.** to go to bed; **meterse en la c.** *(para dormir)* to go to bed; *(meterse dentro)* to get into bed; *Fam* **llevarse a algn a la c.** to get off with sb ◻ **c. doble/sencilla** double/ single bed; **c. turca** couch
camachuelo *nm Orn* bullfinch
camada *nf* **(a)** *(de pájaros)* brood; *(de animal)* litter **(b)** *(capa)* layer **(c)** *Fig (banda)* gang, band
camafeo *nm* cameo
camaleón *nm* **(a)** *Zool* chameleon **(b)** *PRico (ave)* falcon
camaleónico, -a *adj (persona)* chameleon-like
camalote *nm Am Bot* water hyacinth
cámara 1 *nf* **(a)** *(de un palacio, castillo)* room, chamber ◻ **c. acorazada** strongroom; **c. nupcial** bridal suite **(b)** *(persona)* **ayuda de c.** valet; **médico de c.** royal doctor **(c)** *(institución)* chamber ◻ **c. alta/baja** upper/lower house; **c. de comercio** chamber of commerce; **C. de los Diputados** *Br* ≃ House of Commons, *US* ≃ House of Representatives **(d)** *Cin Fot TV* camera; **a c. lenta** in slow motion ◻ **c. de vídeo** video camera; **c. digital** digital camera; **c. fotográfica** camera; **c. web** web camera, webcam **(e)** *Téc* chamber ◻ **c. de aire/gas** air/gas chamber; **c. frigorífica** cold-storage room **(f)** *Aut* inner tube **(g)** *Mús* chamber; **música de c.** chamber music
2 *nm,f (hombre)* cameraman; *(mujer)* camerawoman
camarada *nmf* **(a)** *(de trabajo)* colleague, fellow worker; *(de colegio)* schoolmate, schoolfellow **(b)** *Pol* comrade
camaradería *nf* camaraderie
camarera *nf* **(a)** *(de hotel)* chambermaid **(b)** *(sirvienta)* maid **(c)** *Hist (de una reina)* lady-in-waiting **(d)** *Am (azafata)* air hostess
camarero, -a *nm,f* **(a)** *(de bar, restaurante) (hombre)* waiter; *(mujer)* waitress; *(detrás de la barra) (hombre)* barman; *(mujer)* barmaid **(b)** *(de barco, avión) (hombre)* steward; *(mujer)* stewardess
camarilla *nf* clique; *Pol* pressure group, lobby
camarín *nm* small chapel
camarista *nmf* **(a)** *Arg (juez)* appeal court judge **(b)** *Méx (en hotel)* chamberperson; *(mujer)* chambermaid
camarón *nm* **(a)** *(marisco)* shrimp **(b)** *CAm Col (propina)* tip **(c)** *Perú (persona)* turncoat
camarote *nm Náut* cabin
camastro *nm* rickety old bed
cambado, -a *adj RP* bowlegged
cambalache *nm Fam* **(a)** *(trueque)* swap **(b)** *RP (tienda)* junk shop **(c)** *RP (gran desorden)* chaos
cambalachear *vt (fruslerías)* to swap, exchange
cambiante *adj (tiempo)* changeable; *(situación)* constantly changing, unstable
cambiar 1 *vt* **(a)** *(alterar, modificar)* to change; **eso no cambia nada** that doesn't make any difference; **han cambiado el horario de los trenes** the train schedules have been changed **(b)** *(cambiar de sitio)* to shift, move; **no cambies esos libros de sitio)** leave those books where they are **(c)** *(intercambiar)* to swap, exchange; **c. impresiones** to exchange views **(d)** *(dinero)* to change; **¿me puede c. mil pesos?** can you change a thousand pesos for me? **(e)** *(moneda extranjera)* to change, exchange
2 *vi* to change; **c. de casa** to move (house); **c. de idea** to change one's mind; **c. de táctica** to shift one's ground; **c. de trabajo** to get another job; *Aut* **c. de velocidad** to change gear
3 cambiarse *vpr* **(a)** *(de ropa)* to change (clothes) **(b)** *(de casa)* to move (house)
cambiazo *nm Fam* switch; **dar el c. (a algn)** to do a switch (on sb)
cambio *nm* **(a)** *(gen)* change, changing; **c. de planes/**

política change of plans/policy; **un c. en la opinión pública** a shift in public opinion ❑ **c. climático** *(calentamiento global)* climate change; **c. de impresiones** exchange of views; **c. de la guardia** changing of the guard; **c. de sentido** U-turn **(b)** *(dinero)* change; **me han dado mal el c.** they gave me the wrong change; **¿tienes c. de mil pesos?** have you got change for a thousand pesos? **(c)** *Fin (de acciones)* price, quotation; *(de divisas)* exchange ❑ **letra de c.** bill of exchange; **libre c.** free trade **(d)** *Aut* gear change ❑ **c. automático** automatic transmission; **caja de cambios** gearbox **(e)** *Fig* **a c. de** in exchange for, instead of **(f)** **en c.** however; **para él significa mucho, en c. para mí no significa nada** it means a lot to him but nothing to me

cambista *nmf* **(a)** *(de dinero)* money changer **(b)** *RP Ferroc Br* pointsman, *US* switchman

Camboya *n* Cambodia

camboyano, -a *adj & nm,f* Cambodian

cambur *nm Ven* **(a)** *(empleo)* job **(b)** *(empleado)* clerk **(c)** *(plátano)* banana

camelar *vt Fam* **(a)** *(convencer)* to cajole, blarney **(b)** *(galantear)* to flirt with **(c)** *Méx (observar)* to watch, observe

camelia *nf* camellia

camello, -a 1 *nm,f* camel
2 *nm Argot (traficante de drogas)* (drug) pusher, dope dealer

camellón *nm Col Méx (en avenida) Br* central reservation, *US* median (strip)

camelo *nm Fam* **(a)** *(engaño)* hoax; **¡vaya un c.!** what a sham! **(b)** *(bulo)* cock-and-bull story

camerino *nm Teat* dressing room

camero, -a *adj* **cama camera** small double bed

Camerún *n* Cameroon

camerunés, -esa *adj & nm,f* Cameroonian

camilla *nf* **(a)** *(para enfermos)* stretcher **(b)** *(mesa)* **(mesa) c.** = small round table under which a heater is placed

camillero, -a *nm,f* stretcher-bearer

caminante *nmf* walker

caminar 1 *vi* to walk
2 *vt* to cover, travel; **caminaron diez kilómetros** they walked for ten kilometres; **caminamos horas y horas** we walked for hours

caminata *nf* *(tiring)* long walk

caminero, -a *adj* **peón c.** roadman

camino *nm* **(a)** *(vía)* path, track; **ir c. de** to be going to; **ponerse en c.** to set off; *Fig* **c. de rosas** bed of roses; *Fig* **el c. del éxito** the road to success; *Fig* **ir por buen/mal c.** to be on the right/wrong track ❑ **c. de herradura** bridle path; *Astron* **el C. de Santiago** the Milky Way **(b)** *(ruta)* route, way; **a medio c.** half-way; **en el c. de casa al trabajo** on the way to work; **estar en c.** to be on the way; **nos coge o pilla de c.** it is on the way **(c)** *(medio, modo)* way; **abrir c.** to clear the way; **abrirse c.** to break through; *Fig* **ha abierto el c. para nuevas investigaciones** he's paved the way for new research; *Fig* **no es el c. para convencerla** that's not the (best) way to bring her over

camión *nm* truck, *Br* lorry; *Fam* **estar como un c.** to be gorgeous o a knockout ❑ **c. cisterna** tanker; **c. de la basura** dustcart, *US* garbage truck; **c. frigorífico** refrigerated truck o *Br* lorry; **c. de mudanzas** removal van

camionaje *nm* haulage, cartage

camionero, -a *nm,f Br* lorry driver, *US* trucker

camioneta *nf* van

camisa *nf* **(a)** *(prenda)* shirt; **en mangas de c.** in one's shirtsleeves; *Fig* **cambiar de c.** to change sides; *Fig* **dejar a algn sin c.** to leave sb penniless; *Fig* **jugarse hasta la c.** to

put one's shirt on sth; *Fam* **meterse en c. de once varas** to bite off more than one can chew; *Fam* **no llegarle a algn la c. al cuerpo** to be terrified ❑ **c. de dormir** nightdress, nightgown; **c. de fuerza** straitjacket **(b)** *Téc (de horno)* lining; *(de cilindro)* sleeve **(c)** *Zool (de serpiente)* slough **(d)** *(carpeta)* folder

camisería *nf* outfitter's (shop), shirt shop

camisero, -a 1 *adj* **blusa camisera** shirt blouse; **vestido c.** shirtwaister
2 *nm,f* outfitter, shirt maker

camiseta *nf* **(a)** *(de uso interior)* vest, *US* undershirt **(b)** *(de uso exterior)* T-shirt **(c)** *Dep* shirt; **sudar la c.** to sweat (for it)

camisola *nf* **(a)** *(prenda interior)* camisole **(b)** *Am (de mujer)* woman's blouse

camisón *nm* **(a)** *(para dormir)* nightdress, nightgown, nightie **(b)** *Andes Carib (blusa)* blouse

camomila *nf* camomile

camorra *nf Fam* trouble; *(riña)* fight; **buscar c.** to look for trouble

camorrista 1 *adj* quarrelsome, rowdy
2 *nmf* troublemaker

camote *nm* **(a)** *Andes CAm Méx (batata)* sweet potato; *(bulbo)* tuber, bulb **(b)** *Méx Fam (complicación)* mess; **meterse en un c.** to get into a mess o pickle; **tragar c.** to stammer **(c)** *Andes Fam (enamoramiento)* **estar c. por** o **de algn** to be madly in love with sb **(d)** *Perú Fam (novio)* lover, sweetheart **(e)** *Ecuad Méx (bobo, tonto)* fool

camotillo *nm* **(a)** *Andes (dulce)* = sweet made of mashed sweet potatoes **(b)** *Méx (madera)* = type of violet-coloured wood streaked with black **(c)** *CAm (cúrcuma)* turmeric

camp [kamp] *adj inv (estilo, moda)* retro

campal *adj* **batalla c.** pitched battle

campamento *nm* camp ❑ **c. base** base camp; **c. de trabajo** work camp; **c. de verano** summer camp

campana *nf* bell; **dar una vuelta de c.** to overturn; *Fig* **a toque de c.** to the sound of bells; *Fam* **tú has oído campanas y no sabes dónde** you haven't got a clue ❑ **c. de buzo** diving bell; **c. de cristal** bell jar o glass; **c. extractora (de humos)** extractor hood

campanada *nf* peal o ringing *(of a bell)*; *Fig* **dar la c.** to cause a sensation o a scandal

campanario *nm* belfry, bell tower

campanear 1 *vi* to ring the bells
2 campanearse *vpr* to sway, swagger

campaneo *nm* **(a)** *(de campanas)* peal o pealing *(of bells)* **(b)** *(contoneo)* sway, swagger

campanero, -a *nm,f* **(a)** *(persona que toca)* bell-ringer **(b)** *(constructor)* bell founder **(c)** *Ven (ave)* bellbird

campanilla *nf* **(a)** *(campana pequeña)* small bell; **tocar la c.** to ring the handbell; *Fam* **de campanillas** de luxe, topnotch **(b)** *Anat* uvula **(c)** *Bot* bell flower

campanillear *vi* to ring the bells

campanilleo *nm* ringing *(of bells)*

campante *adj Fam* **(a)** *(despreocupado)* cool, unconcerned; **se quedó tan c.** he didn't bat an eyelid **(b)** *(ufano)* proud, self-satisfied

campaña *nf* **(a)** *(actividad, empresa)* campaign ❑ *Pol* **c. electoral** election campaign; **c. publicitaria** advertising campaign **(b)** *Mil (expedición)* expedition; **de c.** field ❑ **misa de c.** open-air mass **(c)** *(campo)* country, countryside ❑ **tienda de c.** tent

campar *vi* to wander, roam; *Fam* **c. por sus respetos** to do as one pleases

campear *vi* **(a)** *(dejarse ver)* to be visible; **en lo alto campeaba una bandera** a flag could be seen at the top **(b)**

CSur (buscar) to search o scour the countryside

campechana *nf Cuba Méx (bebida)* cocktail

campechanía *nf* geniality, good-natured character

campechano, -a *adj (persona)* genial, good-natured

campeón, -ona *nm,f* champion

campeonato *nm* championship; *Fam* **de c.** great, brilliant; **un tonto de c.** an utter idiot

campera *nf (a) Esp* **camperas** *(botas)* cowboy boots **(b)** *RP (chaqueta)* jacket

campero, -a 1 *adj (a) (de campo)* country, rural; **(botas) camperas** cowboy boots **(b)** *CSur (persona)* = expert in agricultural matters
2 *nm Andes* Jeep®

campesinado *nm* peasantry, peasants *pl*

campesino, -a 1 *adj* country, rural
2 *nm,f (hombre)* countryman; *(mujer)* countrywoman

campestre *adj* country, rural

camping ['kampin] *(pl* **campings)** *nm* camping site; **hacer** o **ir de c.** to go camping □ **c. gas** portable gas stove

campiña *nf* countryside

campista *nmf* camper

campo *nm* **(a)** *(campiña)* country, countryside; **a c. raso** in the open air; **a c. traviesa** o **través** cross-country □ **casa de c.** country house **(b)** *Agr* field; **las faenas del c.** agricultural work; **trabaja (en) el c.** he works (on) the land **(c)** *Mil* field □ **c. de batalla** battlefield; **c. de concentración** concentration camp; **c. de pruebas** testing ground; **c. de tiro** shooting range **(d)** *Esp Dep* field □ **c. de fútbol** football pitch; **c. de golf** golf links, golf course; **c. deportivo** playing field; **c. de tenis** tennis court **(e)** *(espacio)* space; *Fig* **dejarle a algn el c. libre** to leave the field open for sb; **c. visual** visual field **(f)** *(ámbito)* field, scope; **en el c. de la psicología** in the field of psychology □ **trabajo de c.** fieldwork **(g)** *Elec Fís* field □ **c. magnético** magnetic field; *Fot* **profundidad de c.** depth of field

camposanto *nm* cemetery

campus *nm inv* campus

camuflado, -a *adj Mil* camouflaged; *(oculto)* hidden; **un coche c. de la policía** an unmarked police car

camuflaje *nm* camouflage, disguise

camuflar *vt* to camouflage, disguise

can *nm Literario Zool* dog

cana *nf* grey hair, white hair; *Fam* **echar una c.** o **una canita al aire** to let one's hair down

Canadá *n* Canada

canadiense *adj & nmf* Canadian

canal *nm* **(a)** *(artificial)* canal □ **c. de riego** irrigation channel **(b)** *(natural)* channel □ **C. de la Mancha** English Channel **(c)** *Elec TV* channel □ **c. de pago** subscription channel **(d)** *(de tejado)* gutter **(e)** *Anat* canal **(f)** *(res)* open carcass; **abrir (un animal) en c.** to slit (an animal) open **(g)** *Fig (vía)* channel; **por otros canales** through other channels

canaleta *nf Bol CSur* roof gutter

canalización *nf* **(a)** *(acción)* canalization **(b)** *(tuberías)* piping **(c)** *(de recursos, esfuerzos)* channelling, *US* channeling

canalizar [14] *vt* **(a)** *(agua)* to canalize; *(riego)* to channel **(b)** *(area)* to canalize **(c)** *(recursos, esfuerzos)* to channel

canalla *Pey* **1** *nm (bribón)* swine, rotter
2 *nf (chusma)* riffraff, mob

canallada *nf* dirty trick

canallesco, -a *adj Pey* rotten, despicable

canalón *nm* gutter

canalones *nmpl Culin* cannelloni

canapé *nm* **(a)** *(sofá)* couch, sofa **(b)** *Culin* canapé

canario, -a 1 *adj & nm,f* Canarian □ **Islas Canarias** Canary Islands, Canaries
2 *nm* **(a)** *Orn* canary **(b)** *Chile (silbato)* clay whistle

canasta *nf* **(a)** *(cesto)* basket; *RP Econ* **el precio de la c. familiar** the cost of the average week's shopping **(b)** *Naipes* canasta **(c)** *(en baloncesto)* basket

canastilla *nf* **(a)** *(cestito)* small basket **(b)** *(de un bebé)* layette

canasto 1 *nm (cesto)* big basket, hamper
2 canastos! *interj* good heavens!

cancán *nm* **(a)** *Mús* cancan **(b)** *(prenda)* frilly petticoat

cancanear *vi CAm Méx Fam (tartamudear)* to stammer

cancel *nm* **(a)** *(contrapuerta)* storm door **(b)** *(reja)* ironwork screen **(c)** *Guat Méx PRico (mampara)* folding screen

cancela *nf* wrought-iron gate

cancelación *nf* cancellation

cancelar *vt* to cancel

cáncer *nm* **(a)** *Med* cancer; **c. de pulmón/mama** lung/breast cancer **(b)** *Astrol Astron* Cancer

cancerbero, -a 1 *nm Mit* Cerberus
2 *nm,f Ftb* goalkeeper

canceriano, -a *adj & nm,f Am Astrol* Cancer

cancerígeno, -a *Med* **1** *adj* carcinogenic
2 *nm* carcinogen

cancerología *nf Med* oncology

cancerológico, -a *adj Med* oncological

cancerólogo, -a *nm,f Med* cancer specialist, oncologist

canceroso, -a *Med* **1** *adj* cancerous
2 *nm* patient suffering from cancer

cancha 1 *nf* **(a)** *Dep (de tenis, baloncesto)* court; *Am (de fútbol, rugby)* field; *Am (de golf)* course □ *Chile* **c. de aterrizaje** runway; *Am* **c. de carreras** racetrack **(b)** *Am (descampado)* open space, open ground **(c)** *RP Fig* **abrir** o **dar c. a algn** to give sb an advantage **(d)** *RP Fig* **estar uno en su c.** to be in one's element **(e)** *RP Fig* **tener c.** to have experience **(f)** *Andes PRico Fam (maíz) Br* toasted maize, *US* toasted corn
2 *interj Arg (para abrir paso)* out of the way!

canchero, -a 1 *adj RP Fam* savvy, streetwise
2 *nm,f (a) RP Fam (desenvuelto)* savvy o streetwise person **(b)** *Am (cuidador) (hombre)* groundsman; *(mujer)* groundswoman

canciller *nm* chancellor

cancillería *nf* chancellery, chancellory

canción *nf* song; *Fam* **ya estás otra vez con la misma c.** you're harping on the same old story again

cancionero *nm* **(a)** *Lit* collection of songs o poems **(b)** *Mús* songbook

candado *nm* padlock

candanga *adj Am Fam* **ser c.** *(situación)* to be nasty; *(persona)* to be a pain

candeal 1 *adj* **pan c.** white bread
2 *nm Am (bebida)* = drink made of milk, eggs and brandy

candela *nf (a) (vela)* candle; *Fam (lumbre)* light **(b)** *(fuego)* fire; *(llama)* flame **(c)** *Fís (unidad)* candle

candelabro *nm* candelabrum, candlestick

candelero *nm* candlestick; *Fig* **en el c.** at the top

candelilla *nf* **(a)** *(planta)* euphorbia **(b)** *Arg, Chile (fuego fatuo)* will-o'-the-wisp **(c)** *Am (luciérnaga)* firefly, glowworm **(d)** *Am (en costura)* hemstitch **(e)** *Cuba (insecto)* = insect which attacks leaves of tobacco plant

candente *adj* candescent, red-hot, white-hot; *Fig* **tema c.** pressing issue

candidato, -a *nm,f* candidate

candidatura *nf* (**a**) *(opción)* candidature, candidacy; **presentar su c.** to put forward one's candidature (**b**) *(lista)* list of candidates

candidez *nf* candour, *US* candor, ingenuousness

cándido, -a *adj* candid, ingenuous

candil *nm* (**a**) *(lámpara de aceite)* oil lamp (**b**) *Méx (candelabro)* chandelier

candilejas *nfpl Teat* footlights

candombe *nm*, **candomblé** *nm (danza)* = South American carnival dance of African origin

candor *nm* candour, *US* candor, innocence, pureness

candoroso, -a *adj* innocent, pure

canela *nf* cinnamon; *Fam* **ser c. fina** to be exquisite *o* excellent

canelo, -a 1 *adj* cinnamon
  2 *nm* cinnamon tree

canelón 1 *nm Guat Ven (rizo)* corkscrew curl
  2 canelones *nmpl Culin* cannelloni

canesú *(pl* canesús) *nm* bodice

cangilón *nm* (**a**) *(jarro)* pitcher; *(de molino)* bucket (**b**) *Am* cart track

cangrejo *nm (de mar)* crab; *(de río)* freshwater crayfish; *Fam* **avanzar como los cangrejos** to take one step forward and two steps back; *Fam* **rojo como un c.** as red as a lobster

canguelo *nm Argot* funk

canguro 1 *nm* kangaroo
  2 *nmf Esp Fam* babysitter

caníbal *adj & nmf* cannibal

canibalismo *nm* cannibalism

canica *nf* marble; **jugar a las canicas** to play marbles

caniche *nm* poodle

canícula *nf* dog days, midsummer heat

canicular *adj* **calor c.** blistering heat

canijo, -a *adj Fam* puny, weak

canilla *nf* (**a**) *Anat* shinbone; *(de ave)* wing bone (**b**) *Esp (carrete)* bobbin, reel (**c**) *RP (grifo) Br* tap, *US* faucet (**d**) *Méx (fuerza)* strength; **a c.** by force (**e**) *Perú (juego)* = type of dice game

canillera *nf Am* (**a**) *(espinillera)* shin pad (**b**) *(temblor de piernas)* **tenía c.** his legs were trembling *o* shaking

canillita *nm Am* newspaper boy

canino, -a 1 *adj* canine; *Fam* **tener un hambre canina** to be starving
  2 *nm (colmillo)* canine

canje *nm* exchange

canjeable *adj* exchangeable

canjear *vt* to exchange

cannabis *nm inv* cannabis

cano, -a *adj* white, grey, *US* gray; **de pelo c.** with white *o* grey hair

canoa *nf* (**a**) *Náut* canoe, small boat (**b**) *Am (cajón)* oblong shaped box; *(canal)* wooden *o* metal pipe

canódromo *nm* dog *o* greyhound track

canon *nm* (**a**) *(gen)* canon, norm; **como mandan los cánones** in accordance with the rules (**b**) *Mús Rel* canon (**c**) *Com* royalty

canónico, -a *adj* canonical; *Rel* **derecho c.** canon law

canónigo *nm (persona)* canon

canonización *nf* canonization

canonizar [14] *vt* to canonize

canoso, -a *adj* white-haired, grey-haired, *US* gray-haired; **pelo c.** white *o* grey hair

cansado, -a 1 *pp de* cansar
  2 *adj* (**a**) *(gen)* tired, weary; **estar c.** to be tired; **tiene la vista cansada** his eyes are tired (**b**) *(pesado)* boring, tiring; **un viaje c.** a tiring journey

cansador, -a *adj Andes RP* (**a**) *(que cansa)* tiring (**b**) *(que aburre)* boring

cansancio *nm* tiredness, weariness; *Fam* **estoy muerto de c.** I'm on my last legs

cansar 1 *vt* to tire, weary; **me cansa subir corriendo** running upstairs tires me out
  2 *vi* to be tiring; **después de un rato acaba por c.** after a while it gets boring; **siempre el mismo trabajo cansa** one gets tired of always doing the same job
  3 cansarse *vpr* to get tired; **c. enseguida** to get tired easily; **se cansó de esperar y se fue** he got fed up (with) waiting and left

cansino, -a *adj* weary, slow

cantábrico, -a *adj* Cantabrian; **Mar C.** Bay of Biscay

cántabro, -a *adj & nm,f* Cantabrian

cantada *nf Fam* blunder

cantado, -a 1 *pp de* cantar
  2 *adj Fam* **el resultado está c.** the result is a foregone conclusion

cantaleta *nf Am* harping on, nagging

cantamañanas *nm inv Fam* bullshitter

cantante 1 *adj* singing; **llevar la voz c.** to rule the roost
  2 *nmf* singer

cantaor, -a *nm,f* flamenco singer

cantar¹ 1 *vt Mús* to sing; *Fig* **c. las excelencias de** to sing the praises of; *Fig* **cantarle a algn las verdades** *o* **las cuarenta** to give sb a piece of one's mind
  2 *vi* (**a**) *Mús* to sing; **c. a dos voces** to sing a duet; *Fig* **en menos que canta un gallo** in a flash (**b**) *Argot (confesar)* to sing, spill the beans (**c**) *Esp Argot (oler mal)* to stink, whiff

cantar² *nm Literario* song; *Fam* **¡eso es otro c.!** that's a totally different thing! □ *Lit* **c. de gesta** chanson de geste; *Rel* **C. de los Cantares** Song of Songs, Song of Solomon

cantarín, -ina *adj* (**a**) *(persona)* fond of singing (**b**) *(voz)* sing-song

cántaro *nm (recipiente)* pitcher; *(contenido)* pitcherful; *Fig* **a cántaros** plenty, in buckets; *Fig* **llover a cántaros** to rain cats and dogs

cantata *nf Mús* cantata

cantautor, -a *nm,f* singer-songwriter

cante *nm* (**a**) *(canto)* singing □ **c. hondo, c. jondo** flamenco (**b**) *Esp Fig Fam* **dar el c.** *(llamar la atención)* to stick out a mile

cantera *nf* (**a**) *(de piedra)* quarry (**b**) *Fig Ftb* young players *pl*

cantería *nf* stone cutting; **puente de c.** bridge made of hewn stone

cantero *nm Cuba RP* flowerbed

cántico *nm Rel* canticle

cantidad 1 *nf* quantity, amount, sum; **en c.** a lot; **pagaron una c. astronómica por el rescate** they paid an astronomical amount for his release; *Fam* **había c. de gente** there were thousands of people; *Fam* **cantidades industriales** tons, loads
  2 *adv Esp Fam* a lot; **me gusta c.** I love it

cántiga *nf*, **cantiga** *nf Lit Mús* song, ballad

cantil *nm Am* edge of a cliff

cantilena *nf Lit Mús* cantilena, song; *Fam* **siempre estás con la misma c.** you're always going on about the same old story

cantimplora *nf* water bottle

cantina *nf* canteen, buffet

cantinela *nf véase* **cantilena**

cantinero, -a *nm,f* bar attendant

canto¹ *nm* (**a**) *Mús (arte)* singing; **estudia c.** he is studying singing (**b**) *(canción)* song; *Fig* **c. del cisne** swan-song ▫ **c. fúnebre** funeral chant (**c**) *Lit* canto

canto² *nm* (**a**) *(borde)* edge; **de c.** on its side; **ponlo de c.** put it sideways; **tiene cinco centímetros de c.** it is five centimetres thick; *Fam* **no me caí por el c. de un duro** I missed falling by the skin of my teeth (**b**) *(guijarro)* pebble, stone ▫ **c. rodado** *(grande)* boulder; *(pequeño)* pebble (**c**) *Fam* **al c.** for sure, straight away; **cada vez que nos vemos, bronca al c.** every time we meet we have a row

cantón *nm* canton

cantonal *adj* cantonal

cantonera *nf* corner piece

cantor, -a 1 *adj* singing; **los niños cantores de Viena** the Vienna Boys' Choir; **pájaro c.** songbird
2 *nm,f* singer

canturrear *vi* to hum, croon

canturreo *nm* humming, crooning

cánula *nf Téc* cannula

canutas *nfpl Esp Fam* **pasarlas c.** to have a hard time

canuto *nm* (**a**) *(tubo)* tube (**b**) *Bot* internode (**c**) *Argot (porro)* joint

caña *nf* (**a**) *(planta)* reed; *(tallo)* cane, stem ▫ **c. de azúcar** sugar cane (**b**) *(vaso)* tall slender glass (**c**) *Anat* bone marrow (**d**) *(de una bota)* leg; **botas de media c.** calf-length boots (**e**) *(de pescar)* rod (**f**) *Esp Fam (cerveza)* glass of draught *o US* draft beer (**g**) *Andes Cuba RP (aguardiente)* rum (**h**) *Fam* **dar** *o* **meter c. a algn** to do sb over; **dar** *o* **meter c.** *(coche)* to go at full speed

cañabrava *nf Cuba RP* = reed used for building roofs and walls

cañada *nf* (**a**) *(barranco)* gully, ravine (**b**) *(camino)* cattle track (**c**) *RP (arroyo)* stream (**d**) *Cuba (valle)* valley

cañadón *nm RP* narrow deep stream

cañamazo *nm* burlap

cáñamo *nm Bot* hemp; *(tela)* hempen cloth ▫ **c. indio** cannabis

cañamón *nm Bot* hemp seed

cañaveral *nm* cane plantation

cañería *nf* (piece of) piping

cañero, -a 1 *adj Esp Fam (música)* heavy
2 *nm,f Am (trabajador)* sugar plantation worker; *(propietario)* sugar plantation owner

cañero, -a 1 *adj Esp Fam (música)* heavy
2 *nm Méx (almacén)* sugar mill storeroom

cañí *adj & nmf Fam* gypsy

cañizal *nm,* **cañizar** *nm véase* **cañaveral**

cañizo *nm* cane wattle

caño *nm* (**a**) *(tubo)* tube (**b**) *(chorro)* spout (**c**) *Min (galería)* gallery (**d**) *Náut (canal)* navigation channel (**e**) *Arg (tubería)* pipe, piping

cañón *nm* (**a**) *(arma)* gun ▫ **c. antiaéreo** anti-aircraft gun (**b**) *Hist* cannon; *Fig* **al pie del c.** without yielding; *Fam* **estar c.** to be *o* look terrific (**c**) *(de fusil)* barrel; **escopeta de doble c.** double-barrelled rifle (**d**) *(tubo)* tube, pipe; **c. de estufa** stove flue (**e**) *Geog* canyon (**f**) *Teat TV* spotlight (**g**) *(de pluma)* barrel (**h**) *RP (dulce)* = pastry filled with cream or

runny toffee (**i**) *Col (tronco)* tree trunk (**j**) *Perú (sendero)* path (**k**) *Méx (paso estrecho)* defile

cañonazo *nm* (**a**) *(disparo)* gunshot; **salva de 21 cañonazos** 21-gun salute (**b**) *Ftb* strong shot

cañonear *vt* to shell

cañonero, -a *adj* armed; **(lancha) cañonera** gunboat

caoba *nf* (**a**) *Bot* mahogany (**b**) *CAm Chile (caño)* gutter (**c**) *Chile Nic (artesa)* trough

caolín *nm Min* kaolin

caos *nm* chaos

caótico, -a *adj* chaotic

Cap. *(abrev de* **capitán***)* Capt

cap. *(abrev de* **capítulo***)* ch

capa *nf* (**a**) *(prenda)* cloak, cape; *Fig* **de c. caída** lowspirited; **andar de c. caída** to have seen better days; *Fig* **defender a c. y espada** to fight tooth and nail; *Fam* **hacer de su c. un sayo** to do as one feels like (**b**) *(pretexto)* excuse; **so c. de** with the excuse that, under the pretext of (**c**) *(mano)* layer, coat; **una c. de pintura** a coat of paint; **una c. de polvo** a film of dust; *Culin* **una c. de chocolate** a coating of chocolate (**d**) *Geol (estrato)* stratum, layer ▫ **c. de ozono** ozone layer (**e**) *Fig (clase social)* class, stratum

capacete *nm* (**a**) *(de armadura)* casque (**b**) *Carib Méx (de automóvil)* *Br* bonnet, *US* hood

capacho *nm (cesto grande)* big basket

capacidad *nf* (**a**) *(cabida)* capacity; **con c. para 100 personas** with room for 100 people; **un depósito de 50 litros de c.** a 50-litre tank (**b**) *(aptitud)* capacity, ability; **no tiene c. para la música** he hasn't got an ear for music; **tiene una gran c. de trabajo** he's a very hard worker

capacitación *nf* training

capacitador, -a *Am* **1** *adj* **curso c.** training course
2 *nm,f* trainer

capacitar *vt* (**a**) *(instruir)* to train; **estar capacitado para ...** to be trained *o* qualified to ... (**b**) *(autorizar)* to authorize, license, make able; **no estoy capacitado para responder** I'm not able to answer

capar *vt* (**a**) *(castrar)* to castrate (**b**) *Andes Carib (podar)* to prune (**c**) *Col Fam* **c. clase** *(faltar)* to play *Br* truant *o US* hooky

caparazón *nm* (**a**) *(concha)* shell (**b**) *Fig (refugio)* cover, protection

capataz *nm,f (hombre)* foreman; *(mujer)* forewoman

capaz 1 *adj* (**a**) *(con capacidad)* capable, able; **Pedro no sería c. de una cosa así** Pedro wouldn't do something like that; **¿serías c.?** *(podrías)* could you?; *(te atreverías)* would you dare?; **si se entera es c. de despedirle** if he finds out he could quite easily sack him (**b**) *(eficiente)* efficient (**c**) *(con espacio)* with room (for); **un teatro c. para mil personas** a theatre which holds a thousand people
2 *adv Andes, RP Fam (tal vez)* maybe; **c. (que) viene Pedro** Pedro might come

capazo *nm* (**a**) *(cesto)* basket (**b**) *(de bebé)* Moses basket, *Br* carrycot

capcioso, -a *adj Pey* captious, artful; **pregunta c.** catch question

capea *nf Taur* amateur bullfight

capear *vt* (**a**) *(dificultad etc)* to dodge, shirk; *Fig* **c. el temporal** to weather the storm (**b**) *Taur* to make passes at with the cape

capella : a capella *loc adj & adv Mús* a cappella

capellán *nm Rel* chaplain

capellanía *nf Rel* chaplaincy

capelo *nm* (**a**) *(sombrero)* cardinal's hat (**b**) *(cargo)* cardinalship

caperuza *nf* (**a**) *(prenda)* hood (**b**) *(tapa)* cap; **la c. de una pluma** the cap of a pen

capia *nf Am* maize, *US* corn

capicúa 1 *adj* **número c.** reversible number; **palabra c.** palindrome
  2 *nm* palindrome

capilar 1 *adj* (**a**) *(del cabello)* hair; **loción c.** hair lotion (**b**) *Fís* capillary
  2 *nm* capillary

capilaridad *nf* capillarity

capilla *nf* (**a**) *(oratorio)* chapel; **estar en c.** *(condenado a muerte)* to be awaiting execution; *Fig (en ascuas)* to be like a cat on hot bricks ❑ **c. ardiente** funeral chapel (**b**) *Mús* choir

capirotada *nf Méx* = bread pudding with nuts and raisins

capirotazo *nm* flip, flick

capirote *nm* (**a**) *(prenda)* hood; *Fam* **tonto de c.** silly idiot (**b**) *(capirotazo)* flip, flick

capital 1 *adj* (**a**) *(primordial)* capital, main, chief; **de importancia c.** of capital importance; **pena c.** capital punishment (**b**) *(ciudad)* capital
  2 *nf* capital ❑ **c. de provincia** county town, *US* county seat
  3 *nm Com Fin* capital ❑ **c. activo** *o* **social** working *o* share capital; **c. circulante/fijo** working/fixed capital; **c. de riesgo** venture capital, risk capital; **c. inicial** capital

capitalismo *nm Econ* capitalism

capitalista *Econ* **1** *adj* capitalist, capitalistic
  2 *nmf* capitalist

capitalización *nf Econ Fin* capitalization

capitalizar [14] *vt Econ Fin* to capitalize

capitán, -ana *nmf* (**a**) *Mil* captain ❑ **c. general** field marshal, *US* general of the army (**b**) *Náut* captain, skipper ❑ **c. de corbeta** lieutenant-commander; **c. de fragata** commander; **c. general de la Armada** Admiral of the Fleet (**c**) *(jefe)* leader; **la capitana del grupo** the leader of the group (**d**) *Dep* captain

capitanear *vt* (**a**) *Mil Náut* to captain, command (**b**) *(dirigir)* to lead (**c**) *Dep (equipo)* to captain

capitanía *nf Mil* captaincy, captainship ❑ **c. general** *(cargo)* rank of field marshal; *(edificio)* military headquarters

capitel *nm Arquit* capital, chapiter

capitolio *nm* Capitol

capitoste *nm Pey* bigwig

capitulación *nf* agreement; *Mil* capitulation ❑ *Jur* **capitulaciones matrimoniales** marriage settlement

capitular¹ *adj* capitular; **sala c.** chapterhouse

capitular² *vi Mil* to capitulate, surrender; *(llegar a un acuerdo)* to reach an agreement

capítulo *nm* (**a**) *(de libro)* chapter (**b**) *Fig (tema)* subject; **dentro del c. de las innovaciones** among the innovations; *Fig* **eso ya es c. aparte** that's another story; *Fig* **llamar a algn a c.** to call sb to account

capo *nm (de la mafia)* mafia boss, capo

capó *nm Aut Br* bonnet, *US* hood

capón *nm* (**a**) *(pollo)* capon (**b**) *(golpe)* rap on the head with the knuckles

caporal *nm* (**a**) *Mil (cabo)* corporal (**b**) *Agr (capataz)* farm manager

capota *nf Aut Br* convertible roof, *US* convertible top

capote *nm* (**a**) *(prenda)* cape, cloak with sleeves; *Mil* greatcoat; *Fig* **pensar** *o* **decir para su c.** to think *o* tell oneself (**b**) *Taur* cape; *Fig* **echarle un c. a algn** to give sb a hand

capotear *vt Taur* to distract with the cape

capotera *nf Am* clothes hanger, clothes hook

capricho *nm* (**a**) *(antojo)* whim, caprice; **hacer algo por puro c.** to do sth because it takes one's fancy (**b**) *Mús* caprice, capriccio

caprichoso, -a 1 *adj* whimsical, fanciful; **formas caprichosas** fanciful forms
  2 *nm,f* whimsical person

capricorniano, -a *Am adj & nm,f Astrol* Capricorn

Capricornio *nm Astrol Astron* Capricorn

caprino, -a *adj* goat; **ganado c.** goats

cápsula *nf* (**a**) *(gen)* capsule (**b**) *(de botella)* top, cap

capsular *adj* capsular

Capt. (*abrev de* **Capitán**) Capt

captación *nf* (**a**) *(de ondas, de agua)* reception (**b**) *(comprensión)* understanding, comprehension (**c**) *(atracción)* fascination, captivation ❑ **c. de fondos** fundraising; *Pol* **c. de votos** winning of votes

captar *vt* (**a**) *(ondas, agua)* to receive, pick up (**b**) *(comprender)* to understand, grasp (**c**) *(interés, atención)* to attract, hold

captor, -a *nm,f* captor

captura *nf* capture

capturar *vt (criminal)* to capture; *(cazar, pescar)* to catch; *Mil* to seize

capucha *nf (prenda)* hood

capuchino, -a 1 *adj Rel* Capuchin
  2 *nm* (**a**) *Rel (monje)* Capuchin monk (**b**) *(café)* capuccino, white coffee (**c**) *Carib (cometa)* = small paper kite

capuchón *nm* (**a**) *(de prenda)* hood (**b**) *(de bolígrafo, pluma)* top, cap

capullo 1 *nm* (**a**) *Ent* cocoon (**b**) *Bot* bud; **en c.** budding (**c**) *Esp Vulg Anat (prepucio)* foreskin
  2 *nm,f Esp Ofens (persona despreciable)* jerk, *Br* dickhead

caqui 1 *adj (color)* khaki
  2 *nm Bot* persimmon

cara 1 *nf* (**a**) *(gen)* face; **c. a c.** face to face; **c. a la pared** facing the wall; **con c. de felicidad** with a happy expression; **poner buena c.** to look pleased; **poner c. de asco** to look disgusted; **poner mala c.** to pull a long face; **tener buena/mala c.** to look good/bad; **tener c. de** to look; **tenía c. de no haber dormido** he looked as if he hadn't had any sleep; **ella tiene c. de no estar a gusto** she looks unhappy; **tienes mala c. hoy** you look a bit off-colour today; **volver la c.** to look the other way; *Fig* **c. de circunstancias** serious look; *Fig* **dar la c.** to face the consequences (of one's acts); *Fig* **dar la c. por algn** to stand up for sb; *Fig* **(de) c. a las próximas elecciones** with a view to the forthcoming election; **decir algo a algn** *Esp* **a la cara** *o Am* **en a la c.** to say sth to sb's face; *Fig* **echarle a algn algo en c.** to reproach sb for sth; *Fig Esp* **plantar c. a algn** to face up to sb; *Fig* **verse las caras** to come face to face; *Fam* **c. de pocos amigos** unfriendly face; *Fam* **romperle la c. a algn** to smash sb's face in (**b**) *(lado)* side; *(de medalla, moneda)* right side; **c. o cruz** *o Andes Ven* **sello** *o RP* **ceca** heads or tails; **echar** *o* **jugar algo a c. o cruz** to toss (a coin) for sth; **la c. oculta de la luna** the dark side of the moon (**c**) *(de un edificio)* face (**d**) *Fam (desfachatez)* cheek, nerve; **¡qué c. (más dura) tienes!** what a cheek you've got!; *Esp* **tener más c. que espalda** to have a lot of cheek
  2 *nmf Fam (persona)* cheeky person

carabela *nf Náut* caravel

carabina *nf* (**a**) *(arma)* carbine, rifle (**b**) *Fam (acompañante)* chaperone; **ir de c.** *Br* to play gooseberry, *US* be like a fifth wheel

carabinero *nm* (**a**) customs officer (**b**) *Chile (policía)* armed policeman

cárabo *nm* tawny owl

Caracas *n* Caracas

caracol 1 *nm* (**a**) *Zool (de tierra)* snail; *(de mar)* winkle (**b**) *Anat (del oído)* cochlea (**c**) *(rizo de pelo)* kiss-curl (**d**) *Equit* caracole; **hacer caracoles** to caracole
  2 ¡caracoles! *interj* good heavens!

caracola *nf Zool* conch

caracolear *vi (caballo)* to prance about

carácter (*pl* **caracteres**) *nm* (**a**) *(temperamento)* character; **de gran** *o* **mucho c.** with a strong character; **tener buen/mal c.** to be good-natured/bad-tempered (**b**) *Fig (índole)* nature; **con c. de invitado** as a guest; **por razones de c. privado** for private reasons (**c**) *Impr (signo)* letter ❑ **c. de imprenta** type, typeface; **caracteres góticos** Gothic type

característica *nf* characteristic

característico, -a 1 *adj* characteristic
  2 *nm,f Teat (hombre)* character actor; *(mujer)* character actress

caracterización *nf* characterization

caracterizado, -a 1 *pp de* **caracterizar**
  2 *adj* (**a**) *(gen)* characterized, portrayed; **la figura del padre está muy bien caracterizada** the character of the father is very well portrayed (**b**) *(disfrazado)* disguised; **c. de Papá Noel** dressed up as Father Christmas

caracterizar [14] **1** *vt* to characterize, portray
  2 caracterizarse *vpr* (**a**) *(distinguirse)* to be characterized (**b**) *Teat* to portray

caracterología *nf* study of character *o* character type

caracterológico, -a *adj* character type

caracú (*pl* **caracús** *o* **caracúes**) *nm Andes RP Zool* bone marrow

caradura *nmf Fam* cheeky devil; **¡qué c. eres!** you're so cheeky!, you've got a nerve!

carajillo *nm Fam* coffee with a dash of brandy

carajo *Vulg* **1** *nm (pene)* prick
  2 *interj* shit!; **la fiesta se fue al c.** the party fell through; **¡vete al c.!** go to hell!

caramanchel *nm Arg Chile* snack bar

caramba *interj Fam* (**a**) *(sorpresa)* good grief! (**b**) *(enfado)* damn it!

carámbano *nm* icicle

carambola *nf Bill* cannon, *US* carom; *Fam* **por c.** by a fluke

caramelizar [14] *vt (bañar)* to cover with caramel

caramelo *nm* (**a**) *(dulce)* sweet, *US* candy (**b**) *(azúcar quemado)* caramel; *Culin* **a punto de c.** syrupy

carantoña *nf* (**a**) *(máscara)* ugly mask (**b**) *Pey (mujer)* mutton dressed as lamb (**c**) **carantoñas** caresses; **hacerle c. a algn** *(acariciar)* to fondle sb; *Fig (adular)* to butter sb up

carapacho *nm* (**a**) *(caparazón)* carapace (**b**) *Am Culin* = seafood dish cooked in the shell

caraqueño, -a 1 *adj* of *o* from Caracas
  2 *nm,f* person from Caracas

carátula *nf* (**a**) *(máscara)* mask; *Fig* **el mundo de la c.** theatre (**b**) *(cubierta)* cover (**c**) *Méx (de reloj)* dial, face

caravana *nf* (**a**) *(expedición)* caravan (**b**) *Aut (vehículo)* caravan (**c**) *Aut (atasco)* traffic jam; **había mucha c.** there was a long tailback

caravaning [kara'βanin] (*pl* **caravanings**) *nm* caravanning

caray *interj* God!, good heavens!; **¡este c. de chico me tiene harta!** this damned boy is trying my patience!

carbohidrato *nm* carbohydrate

carbón *nm* (**a**) *(gen)* coal; *Fam* **¡se acabó el c.!** that's that! ❑ **c. de leña** charcoal; **c. de piedra** coal; **c. mineral** coal; **c. vegetal** charcoal; **mina de c.** coal mine; **papel c.** carbon paper (**b**) *(para dibujar)* charcoal

carbonada *nf Am Culin* = meat vegetable and rice stew

carboncillo *nm* charcoal

carbonera *nf* coal cellar

carbonería *nf* coal merchant's

carbonero, -a 1 *adj* coal
  2 *nm* (**a**) *(persona)* coal merchant (**b**) *Orn* great tit

carbónico, -a *adj* carbonic; *Quím* **anhídrido c.** carbon dioxide; **agua carbónica** mineral water

carbonífero, -a *adj* carboniferous; *Geol Hist* **el periodo c.** the Carboniferous period

carbonilla *nf* (**a**) *(dibujo)* charcoal (**b**) *(ceniza)* coal dust; **c. de locomotora** locomotive soot

carbonización *nf* carbonization; *(combustión)* burning, charring

carbonizar [14] **1** *vt* to carbonize, burn, char; **morir carbonizado** to be burnt to death
  2 carbonizarse *vpr (gen)* to carbonize, burn, char

carbono *nm Quím* carbon ❑ **c. 14** carbon 14; **dióxido de c.** carbon dioxide

carbunco *nm Med* anthrax

carburación *nf* carburation

carburador *nm Aut Elec* carburettor, *US* carburetor

carburante *nm Aut Elec* fuel

carburar *vi* (**a**) *(quemar)* to carburet (**b**) *Fam (funcionar)* to work properly; **hoy no carburo** I just can't do anything right today

carburo *nm* carbide

carca *adj & nmf Fam* square, straight; *Pol* reactionary

carcaj *nm (de flechas)* quiver

carcajada *nf* guffaw; **reírse a carcajadas** to laugh one's head off; **soltar una c.** to burst out laughing

carcajearse *vpr* to laugh heartily; **me carcajeo yo de sus amenazas** his threats make me laugh

carcamal *nm, Méx RP* **carcamán** *nm Fam* old fogey

carcasa *nf (de CD, ordenador)* case; *(de máquina)* casing

cárcava *nf Geol* gully

cárcel *nf* (**a**) *(prisión)* prison, gaol, jail (**b**) *Téc* clamp

carcelario, -a *adj* (**a**) *(de cárcel)* prison, gaol, jail (**b**) *Téc* clamping

carcelero, -a *nm,f* gaoler, jailer, warder, *US* warden

carcinoma *nm Med* carcinoma, cancer

carcoma *nf* (**a**) *Ent* woodworm (**b**) *Fig (preocupación)* anguish, anxiety

carcomer 1 *vt (madera)* to eat away; *Fig (salud)* to undermine, eat away
  2 carcomerse *vpr* to be consumed (**de** with)

carcomido, -a *adj (madera)* wormeaten

carda *nf* (**a**) *(máquina)* card, carding machine, teasel (**b**) *(cardado)* carding

cardado *nm* (**a**) *Ind* carding (**b**) *(de pelo)* backcombing

cardamomo *nm* cardamom

cardán *nm* cardan joint

cardar *vt* (**a**) *(lana, algodón)* to card (**b**) *(pelo)* to backcomb

cardenal *nm* (**a**) *Rel* cardinal (**b**) *Med (hematoma)* bruise (**c**) *Chile (planta)* geranium

cardenalato *nm Rel* cardinalship

cardenalicio, -a *adj Rel* of *o* related to a cardinal; **colegio c.** college of cardinals

cárdeno, -a *adj* purple, violet

cardiaco, -a *adj & nm,f,* **cardíaco, -a** *adj & nm,f* **1** *adj* cardiac, heart; **ataque c.** heart attack
2 *nm,f* person with a heart condition

cárdigan *nm* cardigan

cardinal *adj* cardinal; **número c.** cardinal number

cardiografía *nf* cardiography

cardiograma *nm* electrocardiogram

cardiología *nf Med* cardiology

cardiólogo, -a *nm,f Med* cardiologist

cardiopatía *nf Med* heart condition *o* disease

cardiovascular *adj* cardiovascular

cardo *nm* (**a**) *Bot (comestible)* cardoon; *(con espinas)* thistle; **c. borriquero** cotton thistle (**b**) *Esp (persona) Fam* **ser un c. (borriquero)** to be an unsociable *o* harsh person; **ser un c.** to be very ugly

cardón *nm* (**a**) *Arg (cacto)* = type of giant cactus (**b**) *CRica Méx Perú (pita)* = type of agave cactus

cardumen *nm* (**a**) *(de peces)* school, shoal (**b**) *Andes RP Ven (abundancia) (de gente, insectos)* swarm

carear *vt* (**a**) *Jur (encarar)* to bring face to face (**b**) *(comparar)* to compare

carecer [46] *vi* to lack; **carezco de experiencia** I lack experience

carena *nf,* **carenado** *nm* (**a**) *Náut* careening (**b**) *Aut* streamlining

carenar *vt* (**a**) *Náut (un barco)* to careen (**b**) *Aut (un coche)* to streamline

carencia *nf* lack (**de** of)

carente *adj* lacking; **c. de interés** lacking interest

careo *nm Jur* confrontation

carero, -a *adj Fam* expensive, overpriced

carestía *nf* (**a**) *(falta)* lack, shortage (**b**) *Fin* high price *o* cost; **la c. de la vida** the high cost of living

careta *nf* mask; *Fig* **quitarle la c. a algn** to unmask sb ◻ **c. antigas** gas mask

carey (*pl* **careys**) *nm* (**a**) *Zool* sea turtle (**b**) *(concha)* tortoiseshell; **una montura de c.** a tortoiseshell frame

carezco *indic pres véase* **carecer**

carga *nf* (**a**) *(acción)* loading; *Fig* **c. afectiva** emotional content; *Fig* **ser un burro de c.** to be a dogsbody; *Fig* **volver a la c.** to go on and on about sth ◻ *Ferroc* **andén de c.** loading platform; *Náut* **buque de c.** freighter; *Aut* **zona de c. y descarga** loading and unloading bay (**b**) *(cosa cargada)* load; *Av Náut (de avión, barco)* cargo, freight ◻ **animal de c.** beast of burden; **c. máxima** maximum load (**c**) *Fin (gasto)* debit; *(peso)* burden, load ◻ **c. fiscal** tax charge (**d**) *(repuesto)* refill (**e**) *Mil* charge; **a paso de c.** at the double ◻ **c. explosiva** explosive charge (**f**) *Elec (de condensador)* charge; *(en circuito)* load (**g**) *Fig (obligación)* burden; **las cargas de un trabajo** the duties *o* responsibilities of a job

cargado, -a 1 *pp de* **cargar**
2 *adj* (**a**) *(gen)* loaded; **una pistola cargada** a loaded gun (**b**) *Fig* burdened; **c. de deudas** up to one's eyes in debt; **c. de razón** strongly convinced that one is right (**c**) *Elec* charged (**d**) *(bebida)* strong; **un café c.** a strong coffee (**e**) *(espeso)* dense, heavy; **atmósfera cargada** stuffy atmosphere

cargador, -a 1 *adj* loading
2 *nm,f* (**a**) *(persona)* loader; *(de muelle)* docker, stevedore (**b**) *(de alto horno)* stocker
3 *nm* (**a**) *(dispositivo)* charger (**b**) *(de bolígrafo)* filler

cargamento *nm* (**a**) *(carga)* load (**b**) *(de avión, barco)* cargo, freight

cargante *adj Fam* annoying

cargar [38] **1** *vt* (**a**) *(gen)* to load; **c. un mechero/una pluma** to fill a lighter/a pen; **le cargó el saco a la espalda** he put the sack on his back; *Fig* **c. las culpas a algn** to put the blame on sb; *Fam* **c. la mano** *o* **las tintas** to overdo it (**b**) *Fig (achacar)* to burden (**c**) *Com (cobrar)* to charge; **cárguelo a mi cuenta** charge it to my account (**d**) *(recargar)* to put too much; **ha cargado la habitación de cuadros** she's put too many paintings in the room (**e**) *Fot Mil* to load (**f**) *Elec (batería)* to charge (**g**) *Naipes* to trump (**h**) *Esp Fam (fastidiar)* to annoy; **su conversación me carga** I find her conversation very boring (**i**) *Inform* to load
2 *vi* (**a**) *Arquit (apoyarse)* to rest (**b**) *(recaer)* **c. sobre** to fall upon (**c**) *(llevar)* **c. con** to carry; **c. con la responsabilidad/con la culpa** to take the responsibility/the blame; **yo cargaré con la mochila** I'll carry the rucksack; *Fig* **c. con las consecuencias** to suffer the consequences (**d**) *Mil (contra el enemigo etc)* to charge
3 **cargarse** *vpr* (**a**) *(gen)* to load oneself; **c. de paciencia** to display as much patience as one has got; **c. de pastillas** to stuff oneself with pills; *Fam* **cargársela** to get into hot water; *Esp Fam* **te la vas a cargar** you're asking for trouble and you're going to get it (**b**) *Meteor* to become overcast (**c**) *Fam Educ* to fail (**d**) *Fam (estropear, destrozar)* to smash, ruin; **me he cargado la radio** I've broken the radio (**e**) *Fam (matar)* to kill; **se cargaron a cuatro** they bumped off four

cargazón *nf* (**a**) *Med (estómago, ojos)* heavy feeling (**b**) *Meteor* heavy cloud

cargo *nm* (**a**) *(puesto)* post, position; **alto c.** top job, high ranking position; **desempeñar** *o* **ocupar el c. de** to have a post as; **jurar el c.** to take an oath ◻ **c. público** public office (**b**) *(dirección, custodia)* charge; **correr** *o* **estar al c. de** to be in charge of; **hacerse c. de** to take charge of; **tener a su c.** to have in one's charge (**c**) *Fin (débito)* charge, debit; **con c. a mi cuenta** charged to my account (**d**) *Jur* charge, accusation ◻ **testigo de c.** witness for the prosecution (**e**) *(carga)* load, weight; *Fig* **hazte c. de mi situación** please try to understand my situation ◻ *Fig* **c. de conciencia** weight on one's conscience

cargosear *vt CSur* to pester

cargoso, -a *adj CSur* annoying

carguero, -a *nm* (**a**) *(avión)* transport plane, freighter (**b**) *(barco)* freighter

cariacontecido, -a *adj* crestfallen

cariar 1 *vt (dientes, huesos)* to cause to decay
2 cariarse *vpr* to decay

cariátide *nf Arquit* caryatid

caribe 1 *adj* Caribbean
2 *nm,f (persona)* Caribbean
3 *nm (idioma)* Carib

caribeño, -a 1 *adj* Caribbean
2 *nm,f* person from the Caribbean

caricato *nm* (**a**) *Teat* = comedian who imitates famous people (**b**) *Am (caricatura)* caricature

caricatura *nf* (**a**) *(dibujo)* caricature (**b**) *Méx (dibujos animados)* cartoon film

caricaturista *nmf* caricaturist

caricaturizar [14] *vt* to caricature

caricia *nf* caress, stroke

Caricom [kari'kom] *nm o nf (abrev de* **Comunidad (Económica) del Caribe**) Caricom

caridad *nf* charity ◻ **obra de c.** charitable deed

caries *nf inv Med* decay, caries

carilla *nf Impr* page, side of a piece of paper

carillón *nm Mús* carillon

carimbo *nm Am* branding iron

cariñena *nm (vino)* = sweet wine from Cariñena (Zaragoza)

cariño *nm* (a) *(amor)* affection, love; **coger** *o* **tomar c. a algo/algn** to grow fond of sth/sb; **con todo c.** *(en carta)* lots of love; **ella le tiene mucho c.** she's very fond of him; **lo ha hecho con todo el c.** he made it with loving care (b) *(querido)* darling; **ven c.** come here darling *o* dear (c) *CAm Chile (regalo)* gift, present (d) *RP* **càriños** *(en carta)* love

cariñoso, -a *adj* loving, affectionate

carioca *adj & nm,f* Brazilian

carisma *nm* charisma, charism

carismático, -a *adj* charismatic

caritativo, -a *adj* charitable

cariz *nm* aspect, look

carlinga *nf Av* (a) *(para piloto)* cockpit (b) *(para pasajeros)* cabin

carlismo *nm Hist* Carlism

carlista *adj & nmf Hist* Carlist

carmelita *adj & nmf Rel* Carmelite

carmesí *(pl* **carmesíes)** *adj & nm Literario* crimson

carmín 1 *adj & nm* **(de color) c.** carmine
　　2 *nm* **c. (de labios)** lipstick

carnada *nf* bait

carnal 1 *adj* (a) *(de carne)* fleshy, carnal (b) *(pariente)* first; **primo/tía c.** first cousin/aunt
　　2 *nm Méx Fam (amigo)* friend, *Br* mate, *US* buddy

carnaval *nm* carnival ❑ **martes de c.** Shrove Tuesday

carnavalesco, -a *adj* carnival; **ambiente c.** carnival atmosphere

carnaza *nf véase* **carnada**

carne *nf* (a) *Anat* flesh; *Fig* **en c. y hueso** in person; *Fig Fam* **de pocas carnes** thin; *Fam* **metido en carnes** plump; *Fam* **uno es de c. y hueso** one is only human ❑ *Fig* **c. de cañón** cannon fodder; **c. de gallina** goosepimples *pl;* **poner la c. de gallina a algn** to give sb the creeps; **c. viva** raw flesh (b) *(alimento)* meat; **no comer c.** he doesn't eat meat; *Fig* **echar toda la c. en el asador** to go in for everything ❑ **c. de cerdo** *o Andes* **chancho** pork; **c. de cordero** lamb; **c. de res** *Méx* beef; **c. de ternera** veal; **c. de vaca** beef; *Esp RP* **c. picada** *Br* mince, *US* mincemeat; **c. roja** red meat (c) *(de fruta)* pulp (d) *Filos Rel* **la c. y el espíritu** flesh and spirit

carné *(pl* **carnés)**, *nm,* **carnet** *(pl* **carnets)** *nm* card ❑ **c. de conducir** *o RP* **de conductor** *Br* driving licence, *US* driver's license; **c. de estudiante** student card; **c. de identidad** identity card; **c. de socio** membership card

carneada *nf Andes RP (acción)* slaughtering, butchering

carnear *vt* (a) *Andes RP (animal)* to slaughter (b) *Chile (engañar)* to deceive, take in

carnero *nm* (a) *Zool* ram (b) *Culin (carne)* mutton

carnicería *nf* (a) *(tienda)* butcher's (shop) (b) *Fig (masacre)* slaughter, bloodshed

carnicero, -a 1 *adj* (a) *(carnívoro)* carnivorous (b) *Fig (cruel)* bloodthirsty
　　2 *nm,f* (a) *(comerciante)* butcher (b) *Fam (médico)* sawbones

cárnico, -a *adj* meat; **productos cárnicos** meat products

carnitas *nfpl Méx* = small pieces of braised pork

carnívoro, -a 1 *adj* carnivorous
　　2 *nm,f* carnivore

carnoso, -a *adj* fleshy

caro, -a 1 *adj* (a) *(costoso)* expensive, dear (b) *Literario (querido)* dear

2 *adv* **costar** *o* **salir c.** to cost a lot; **pagar c.** to pay a high price; **vender c.** to sell at a high price

carolingio, -a *adj Hist* Carolingian, Carlovingian

carota *nmf Esp Fam* cheeky person

carótida *nf Anat* carotid

carozo *nm RP (de fruta, aceituna)* stone, *US* pit

carpa *nf* (a) *(pez)* carp ❑ *Dep* **salto de la c.** jack-knife (b) *(de circo)* big top, marquee, big tent (c) *Am (tienda de campaña)* tent

Cárpatos *npl* Carpathians

carpe *nm Bot* hornbeam

carpeta *nf también Inform* folder, file

carpetazo *nm* termination; **dar c. a un asunto** to shelve a matter

carpetovetónico, -a 1 *adj* Spanish through and through
　　2 *nm,f* Spanish chauvinist

carpintería *nf* (a) *(oficio)* carpentry ❑ **c. metálica** metalwork (b) *(taller)* carpenter's (shop)

carpintero, -a *nm,f* carpenter

carpir *vt Am* to weed, hoe

carraca *nf* (a) *(instrumento)* rattle (b) *Orn* roller (c) *Fam (coche viejo)* banger; *(persona)* decrepit old person

carrasca[1] *nf Bot* kermes oak

carrasca[2] *nf Am Mús* scraper

carrasco *nm Am* large forest, forest land

carraspear *vi* to clear one's throat

carraspeo *nm* clearing of the throat

carraspera *nf* hoarseness

carrera *nf* (a) *(acción)* run; **a la c.** in a hurry; **darse una c.** to hurry; **tomar c.** to take a run (b) *(trayecto)* route, ride (c) *Dep* race ❑ **c. contra reloj** race against the clock; **c. de caballos** horse race; **c. de coches** rally, meeting; **c. de relevos/de vallas** relay/hurdle race; **coche de carreras** racing car (d) *(estudios)* university education *o* training; **Claudia estudió** *o* **hizo la c. de abogado** Claudia studied law; **dar c. a algn** to pay for sb's studies (e) *(profesión)* career, profession; **hacer c. de** to succeed as; **hacer c. en la vida** to succeed in life; **c. diplomática** diplomatic career (f) *Euf (prostitución)* prostitution; **hacer la c.** to walk the streets (g) *(calle)* street, avenue (h) *(en medias) Br* ladder, *US* run (i) *Mil* **c. de armamentos** arms race

carrerilla *nf* run; **de c.** parrot fashion; **tomar** *o Esp* **coger c.** to take a run

carreta *nf* cart

carretada *nf* (a) *(carga)* cartload (b) *Fam (montón)* **una c.** heaps, loads

carrete *nm* (a) *(de hilo)* bobbin, reel; *(de película)* spool; *(de cable)* coil

carretera *nf* road ❑ **c. comarcal** minor road, *Br* ≃ B road; **c. de circunvalación** *Br* ≃ ring road, *US* ≃ beltway; *Méx* **c. de cuota** toll road; **c. nacional** *Br* ≃ A road, *US* ≃ state highway; **mapa** *o* **red de carreteras** road map *o* network

carretería *nf* (a) *(oficio)* cartwright's work (b) *(taller)* cartwright's shop

carretero *nm* (a) *(constructor)* cartwright (b) *(conductor)* carter, cart driver; *Fam* **blasfemar** *o* **jurar como un c.** to swear like a trooper

carretilla *nf* wheelbarrow; *Fam* **saber algo de c.** to know sth parrot fashion

carretón *nm* (a) *(carrito)* small cart (b) *CAm (de hilo)* bobbin

carricero *nm Orn* reed warbler

carril *nm* (a) *Ferroc* rail (b) *Aut* lane ❑ **c. bici** *Br* cycle lane, *US* bikeway; **c. bus** bus lane (c) *(surco)* furrow

carrillo *nm Anat* cheek; *Fam* **comer a dos carrillos** to devour, gobble up

carrito *nm* (**a**) *(para equipaje, de supermercado)* trolley, *US* cart (**b**) *Méx Ven* **carritos chocones** Dodgems®, bumper cars

carro *nm* (**a**) *(carreta)* cart; *Fam* **¡alto o para el c.!** hold your horses!; *Fam* **apéarse del c.** to give up *o* way (**b**) *Mil* tank ❏ **c. de combate** tank (**c**) *(de máquina de escribir)* carriage (**d**) *Am salvo RP (coche)* car

carrocería *nf Aut* body, bodywork

carromato *nm* caravan, covered cart

carroña *nf* carrion

carroñero, -a *adj (animal)* carrion-eating

carroza **1** *nf* (**a**) *(coche de caballos)* coach, carriage (**b**) *(de carnaval)* float
2 *nmf Fam* out-of-date person; **tu eres ya un c.** you're not that young any more
3 *adj Fam* old-fashioned, out-of-date

carruaje *nm* carriage, coach

carrusel *nm* (**a**) *(tiovivo)* merry-go-round, *US* carousel (**b**) *(de caballos)* dressage, display of horsemanship

carta *nf* (**a**) *(gen)* letter; **echar una c.** to *Br* post *o US* mail a letter; *Fig* **a c. cabal** through and through; *Fig* **tomar cartas en un asunto** to intervene in an affair ❏ **c. abierta** open letter; **c. certificada/urgente** registered/express letter; *Am* **c. de presentación/recomendación** *(para un tercero)* letter of introduction; *(con un currículum) Br* covering letter, *US* cover letter; **c. postal** postcard (**b**) *(minuta)* menu; **a la c.** à la carte ❏ **c. de vinos** wine list (**c**) *Naipes* card; **echar las cartas a algn** to tell sb's fortune; *Fig* **jugárselo todo a una c.** to put all one's eggs in one basket; *Fig* **no saber a qué c. quedarse** not to know what to do *o* think; *Fig* **poner las cartas sobre la mesa** to put *o* lay one's cards on the table, come clean (**d**) *Geog (mapa)* chart ❏ **c. de navegación** navigation chart (**e**) *Jur (documento)* chart ❏ **c. blanca** carte blanche; **dar c. blanca a algn** to give sb a free rein; **c. de naturaleza, c. de ciudadanía** naturalization papers **c. verde** green card (**f**) *TV* **c. de ajuste** *Br* test card, *US* test pattern

cartabón *nm* (**a**) *(regla)* set square, triangle (**b**) *Am (talla)* size

cartagenero, -a **1** *adj* of *o* from Cartagena
2 *nm,f* person from Cartagena

cartaginés, -esa *adj & nm,f Hist* Carthaginian

cartapacio *nm* (**a**) *(cuaderno)* writing pad, notebook (**b**) *(carpeta)* folder, file

cartearse *vpr* to correspond, exchange letters

cartel *nm* poster, bill; **esta obra lleva tres años en c.** this play's been running for three years; **pegar carteles** to put *o* stick up bills; **prohibido fijar carteles** post no bills; *Fig* **de c.** reputed; *Fig* **tener buen c.** to be popular

cártel *nm* cartel

cartelera *nf* hoarding, *US* billboard ❏ *Prensa* **c. de espectáculos** entertainments section *o* page

carteo *nm* correspondence, exchange of letters

cárter *(pl* **cárters** *o* **cárteres)** *nm* (**a**) *Téc* housing (**b**) *Aut* crankcase

cartera *nf* (**a**) *(de bolsillo)* wallet, *US* billfold (**b**) *(para documentos etc)* briefcase; *(de colegial)* satchel, schoolbag; *Fig* **tener algo en c.** to be planning sth (**c**) *Pol (ministerio)* portfolio; **ministro sin c.** minister without portfolio (**d**) *Com* portfolio ❏ **c. de pedidos** order book (**e**) *Andes RP (bolso) Br* handbag, *US* purse; **c. de valores** portfolio

carterista *nm* pickpocket

cartero, -a *nm,f (hombre) Br* postman, *US* mailman; *(mujer) Br* postwoman, *US* mailwoman

cartesianismo *nm Filos* Cartesianism

cartesiano, -a *adj & nm,f Filos* Cartesian

cartilaginoso, -a *adj* cartilaginous

cartílago *nm* cartilage

cartilla *nf* (**a**) *(libreta)* book ❏ **c. de ahorros** savings book; **c. militar** military record (**b**) *(libro)* first reader; *Fam* **cantarle** *o* **leerle la c. a algn** to tell sb off

cartografía *nf* cartography

cartográfico, -a *adj* cartographic, cartographical

cartógrafo, -a *nm,f* cartographer

cartomancia *nf* cartomancy

cartón *nm* (**a**) *(material)* card, cardboard ❏ **caja de c.** cardboard box; *Arte* **c. piedra** papier mâché (**b**) *(de cigarrillos)* carton (**c**) *Arte (dibujo)* sketch

cartoné *nm* **en c.** bound in boards

cartuchera *nf* cartridge holder *o* belt

cartucho *nm* (**a**) *(de arma)* cartridge; *Fig* **quemar el último c.** to play one's last card ❏ **c. de fogueo** blank cartridge (**b**) *(de papel)* paper bag, paper cone

cartuja *nf* charterhouse

cartujo, -a *nm,f* Carthusian; *Fam* **vivir como un c.** to live like a hermit

cartulina *nf* card

casa *nf* (**a**) *(edificio)* house; *(piso) Br* flat, *US* apartment; **buscar c.** to look for a place to live; **c. de pisos** *Br* block of flats, *US* apartment block; **en c. de un amigo** at a friend's house; **fuimos a c. de Daniel** we went to Daniel's; *Fig* **echar** *o* **tirar la c. por la ventana** to go all out, spare no expense; *Fig* **empezar la c. por el tejado** to put the cart before the horse; *Fam* **hacer la c.** to do the housework (**b**) *(hogar)* home; **de andar por c.** run-of-the-mill, ordinary; **vestido de andar por c.** dressed casually; **no paro en c.** I'm never at home; **no sale de c.** she never goes out; **pásate por c.** come round *o* over; **vete a c.** go home; *Fig* **como Pedro por su c.** as if he owned the place; *Fig* **llevar la c.** to run the household; *Fig* **ser muy de c.** to be home-loving; *Fam* **se me cae la c. encima** I can't stand being in the house; *Prov* **en c. del herrero cuchara de palo** the shoemaker's wife is always the worst shod (**c**) *(familia)* family; **un amigo de la c.** a friend of the family (**d**) *(linaje)* house; **la C. de los Austrias** the House of Hapsburg (**e**) *Com (empresa)* company, firm; **la política de esta c.** the company's policy *o* **c. matriz/principal** head/central office (**f**) **c. de altos** *Am salvo RP (edificio)* multistorey building; *CSur Perú (casa de arriba)* upstairs *Br* flat *o US* apartment; *Euf* **c. de citas** brothel, house of ill repute; **c. de huéspedes** boarding house; **c. de juego** gambling house; **c. de modas** fashion shop; **c. de socorro** first aid post

casaca *nf* (**a**) *Hist* long coat (**b**) *(chaqueta)* short coat

casación *nf Jur* cassation, annulment

casadero, -a *adj* of marrying age

casado, -a **1** *pp de* **casar**
2 *adj* married; **está c. con Adela** he's married to Adela
3 *nm,f* married person; **los recién casados** the newlyweds

casamentero, -a **1** *adj* matchmaking
2 *nm,f* matchmaker

casamiento *nm* (**a**) *(matrimonio)* marriage (**b**) *(boda)* wedding

casanova *nm* Casanova, ladies' man, rake

casar **1** *vt* (**a**) *(en matrimonio)* to marry; **ya ha casado a sus dos hijas** he's already married off his two daughters (**b**) *(encajar)* to join, fit (**c**) *Jur (derogar)* to annul, quash
2 *vi* to match, go *o* fit together
3 **casarse** *vpr* to marry, get married; **c. en segundas nupcias** to get married again; **c. por la iglesia/por lo civil**

to get married in church/in a registry office; *Fam* **se casaron de penalty** it was a shotgun wedding

cascabel *nm* bell; *Zool* **serpiente de c.** rattle-snake

cascada *nf* waterfall, cascade

cascado, -a 1 *pp de* **cascar**
  2 *adj Fig* (**a**) *Esp (persona)* worn-out, aged (**b**) *(voz)* harsh, hoarse

cascajo *nm* (**a**) *(cascote)* gravel, rubble (**b**) *(trozo)* fragment, shred (**c**) *Fig (persona)* **estar hecho un c.** to be a wreck

cascanueces *nm inv* nutcracker

cascar [59] **1** *vt* (**a**) *(romper)* to crack (**b**) *Fam (pegar)* to belt, thump; **te voy a c. como lo vuelvas a hacer** I'll belt you one if you do it again (**c**) *Esp Fam (dañar)* to harm; **el tabaco casca mucho** smoking does you a lot of harm; *Fam* **cascarla** to kick the bucket, snuff it
  2 *vi Esp* (**a**) *Fam (charlar)* to chat away (**b**) *Fam (morir)* to peg out; **se puso enfermo y cascó** he fell ill and died
  3 *cascarse vpr* (**a**) *(romperse)* to crack (**b**) *Esp (voz)* to become harsh o hoarse (**c**) *Esp Vulg (masturbarse)* **cascársela** to wank, *US* jerk off

cáscara 1 *nf* (**a**) *(de huevo, de nuez)* shell (**b**) *(de fruta)* skin, peel (**c**) *(de grano)* husk (**d**) *Fig Pol* **ser de (la) c. amarga** to be progressive (**e**) *Méx Fam* **echar una c.** *(un partido)* to have a game
  2 *interj* **¡cáscaras!** well, I never!

cascarilla *nf* husk

cascarón *nm* eggshell; *Fig* **recién salido del c.** wet behind the ears

cascarrabias *nmf inv Fam* short-tempered person

casco *nm* (**a**) *(para la cabeza)* **c. protector** o **de motorista** crash helmet (**b**) *(de caballería)* hoof (**c**) *Náut* hull (**d**) *(de ciudad)* ❏ **c. antiguo** old (part of) town; **c. urbano** city centre, central area (**e**) *(trozo)* broken piece, fragment (**f**) *(de metralla)* piece of shrapnel (**g**) *Esp Méx (envase)* empty bottle (**h**) *(de sombrero)* crown (**i**) **cascos** *(auriculares)* headphones; *(cabeza)* brains, head *sing*; **calentarse** o **romperse los c.** to rack one's brains; **ser alegre de c.** to be a scatterbrain (**j**) *Andes Cuba RP (gajo de fruta)* segment, piece (**k**) *Méx RP (en estancia, hacienda)* farmstead

cascote *nm* piece of rubble o debris; **cascotes** rubble *sing*

casería *nf Am* customers *pl*

caserío *nm* (**a**) *(pueblo)* hamlet, small village (**b**) *(casa)* country house

casero, -a 1 *adj* (**a**) *(hecho en casa)* home-made; **comida casera** home-made food (**b**) *(familiar)* family; **una velada casera** a family get-together (**c**) *(persona)* home-loving (**d**) *Dep Fam (árbitro)* favouring o *US* favoring the home team
  2 *nm,f* (**a**) *(dueño) (hombre)* landlord; *(mujer)* landlady (**b**) *(guarda)* keeper (**c**) *Andes Cuba (parroquiano)* customer, client

caserón *nm* big rambling house

caseta *nf* (**a**) *(barraca)* hut, booth (**b**) *(de feria, exposición)* stand, stall; *(de balneario, playa)* bathing hut, *US* bath house (**c**) *Dep* changing room

casete 1 *nm (magnetófono)* cassette player o recorder
  2 *nf (cinta)* cassette (tape)

cash-flow ['kaʃflou] *nm* cash flow

casi *adv* almost, nearly; **c. mil personas** almost one thousand people; **c. ni me acuerdo** I can hardly remember it; **c. nunca** hardly ever; **me fui c. sin comer** I left having eaten hardly anything; *Fam* **c., c.** just about; *Fam* **c. que** sort of, nearly; *Fam* **diez millones, ¡c. nada!** ten million, peanuts!

casilla *nf* (**a**) *(de casillero)* pigeonhole ❏ *Andes RP* **c. de correos** *CAm Carib Méx* **c. postal** PO Box (**b**) *(cuadro,*

cuadrícula) square (**c**) *Fig* **sacar a algn de sus casillas** to drive sb mad

casillero *nm* (**a**) *(de cartas etc)* pigeonholes *pl* (**b**) *Dep (marcador)* scoreboard

casino *nm* casino

caso *nm* (**a**) *(ocasión, evento)* case; **cuando llegue el c.** in due course; **el c. es que ...** the fact o thing is that ...; **el c. Mattei** the Mattei affair; **en c. contrario** otherwise; **en c. de necesidad** if need be; **en cualquier c.** in any case; **en el mejor/peor de los casos** at best/worst; **en este c.** in such a case; **en todo c.** in any case o instance; **en un c. extremo, en último c.** as a last resort; **hacer c. a** o **de algn** to pay attention to sb; **hacer c. omiso de** to take no notice of; **no venir al c.** to be beside the point; **para el c. tanto da** it doesn't make any difference; **pongamos por c.** let's say; **se daba el c. de que ...** it so happened that ...; *Med* **un c. de apendicitis** an appendicitis case ❏ **c. de conciencia** case of conscience; **c. de fuerza mayor** dire necessity (**b**) *(suceso)* event, happening; **dado el c. de que ...** in the event of ...; *Fam* **¡eres un c.!** you're a case! (**c**) *Ling* case

casona *nf* large house

casorio *nm Esp Fam* unwise marriage

caspa *nf* (**a**) *(en el pelo)* dandruff (**b**) *Esp* **la c.** *(famosos)* C-list celebs

Caspio *n* Caspian Sea

cáspita *interj* Anticuado *(sorpresa)* my word!; *(enojo)* dash it!

casposo, -a *adj* (**a**) *(con caspa)* covered in dandruff (**b**) *Esp Fam (música, película)* cheesy; **los famosos casposos** C-list celebs

casquería *nf (tienda)* = shop selling offal; *(productos)* offal; *Fam Fig* **en esa película sale demasiada c.** that movie is too gory

casquete *nm* (**a**) *(prenda)* skullcap (**b**) *Geom* **c. esférico** fragment of a sphere (**c**) *Geog* **c. polar** polar cap (**d**) *Vulg (polvo)* bang, screw; **echar un c.** to have a bang o a screw

casquillo *nm* (**a**) *(de cartucho)* case (**b**) *Téc* ferrule, tip (**c**) *CAm (herradura)* horseshoe

casquivano, -a *adj Fam* scatterbrained

cassette [ka'sete, ka'set] *nm & f véase* **casete**

casta *nf* (**a**) *(linaje)* lineage, descent; **de c.** of breeding, of good stock; *Prov* **de c. le viene al galgo** it runs in the family (**b**) *(animales)* breed; **de c.** thoroughbred, purebred (**c**) *(división social)* caste

castaña *nf* (**a**) *Bot* chestnut; *Fig* **sacarle a algn las castañas del fuego** to get sb out of trouble ❏ **c. pilonga** dried chestnut (**b**) *(moño)* bun (**c**) *Méx (barril pequeño)* keg (**d**) *Esp Fam (bofetada)* slap; *(golpe)* blow, punch; **se pegó una c. con el coche** he had a car crash; *Fam* **¡toma c.!** what do you think of that, then! (**e**) *Esp Fam (borrachera)* binge, skinful

castañar *nm* chestnut grove

castañazo *nm Fam* (**a**) *Aut* crash (**b**) *(golpe)* thump, whack

castañero, -a *nm,f* chestnut seller

castañeta *nf* snap of the fingers

castañetear 1 *vt (castañuelas)* to play castanets
  2 *vi (dientes)* to chatter

castañeteo *nm* (**a**) *(de castañuelas)* sound of castanets (**b**) *(de dientes)* chattering

castaño, -a 1 *adj* chestnut-brown; *(pelo)* brown, dark; **ojos castaños** brown eyes
  2 *nm* (**a**) *Bot* chestnut; *Fam* **eso pasa de c. oscuro** this is going a bit too far ❏ **c. de Indias** horse chestnut (tree) (**b**) *(madera)* chestnut

castañuela *nf* castanet; *Fam* **más contento que unas castañuelas** as happy as a sandboy

castellanismo *nm Ling* = word *o* expression common to the Castilian spoken in Castile

castellanizar [14] *vt Ling* to Hispanicize

castellano, -a 1 *adj* Castilian
  2 *nm,f (persona)* Castilian
  3 *nm (idioma)* Spanish, Castilian

castellanohablante 1 *adj* Spanish-speaking
  2 *nmf* Spanish speaker

castellanoparlante *adj & nmf véase* **castellanohablante**

casticismo *nm* love of tradition

castidad *nf* chastity

castigador, -a *Fam nm,f (hombre)* ladies' man; *(mujer)* man-eater

castigar [38] *vt* **(a)** *(imponer castigo a)* to punish, chastise **(b)** *(dañar)* to harm, ruin; **el viento castigó los árboles** the wind whipped the trees **(c)** *(afligir)* to afflict **(d)** *Jur* to penalize **(e)** *Dep* to punish, penalize **(f)** *Fam (enamorar)* to seduce

castigo *nm* **(a)** *(sanción)* punishment, chastisement; **c. ejemplar** exemplary punishment; **levantar un c.** to withdraw a punishment **(b)** *(daño)* torture, suffering **(c)** *Jur* penalty **(d)** *Dep* **área de c.** penalty area; **c. máximo** penalty

Castilla *n* Castile; *Fig* **¡ancha es C.!** it's a free country!

castillo *nm* castle; *Fig* **hacer** *o* **levantar castillos en el aire** to build castles in the sky □ **c. de fuegos artificiales** firework display

casting ['kastin] *(pl* **castings)** *nm Cin Teat* audition

castizo, -a *adj* pure, authentic; **madrileño c.** Madrilenian to the core

casto, -a *adj* chaste

castor *nm Zool* beaver

castración *nf* castration, gelding

castrado, -a 1 *pp de* **castrar**
  2 *adj* castrated, gelded
  3 *nm* eunuch

castrador, -a *adj* **una madre castradora** a strong *o* dominant mother

castrar *vt* to castrate, geld; *Fig (debilitar)* to mutilate

castrense *adj* military; **vida c.** military life

castrismo *nm Pol* Castroism

castrista *adj & nmf Pol* Castroist

casual 1 *adj* accidental, chance; **fue un encuentro c.** we/ they met by chance
  2 *nm Fam* chance; **por un c.** by any chance

casualidad *nf* chance, coincidence; **de** *o* **por c.** by chance; **dió la c. que ...** it so happened that ...; **¿tienes un lápiz, por c.?** do you happen to have a pencil?; **una c. increíble** an amazing coincidence

casualmente *adv* by chance

casucha *nf Pey* hovel, dump

casuística *nf* casuistry

casuístico, -a *adj* casuistic, casuistical

casulla *nf Rel* chasuble

cata *nf* **(a)** *(acción)* tasting **(b)** *(muestra)* taste, sample **(c)** *Col (secreto)* hidden *o* secret thing **(d)** *CSur (ave)* parakeet

cataclismo *nm* catastrophe; *Fig* cataclysm

catacumbas *nfpl Hist* catacombs

catador, -a *nm,f* taster; **c. de vinos** wine taster

catadura *nf Pey* looks *pl*

catafalco *nm* catafalque

catalán, -ana 1 *adj* Catalan, Catalonian

  2 *nm,f* Catalan, Catalonian
  3 *nm (idioma)* Catalan

catalanismo *nm* **(a)** *Ling* Catalanism, = Catalan word *o* expression used in Spanish **(b)** *Pol* Catalan nationalism

catalanista *Pol* **1** *adj* of *o* relating to Catalan nationalism
  2 *nmf* Catalan nationalist

catalejo *nm* telescope

catalepsia *nf* catalepsy

cataléptico, -a *adj & nm,f* cataleptic

catalítico, -a *adj Quím* catalytic

catalizador, -a 1 *adj* catalytic
  2 *nm* catalyst

catalizar [14] *vt* **(a)** *Quím* to catalyse **(b)** *Fig (atraer)* to act as a catalyst for

catalogación *nf* cataloguing

catalogar [38] *vt* **(a)** *(en catálogo)* to catalogue, *US* catalog **(b)** *(clasificar)* to classify

catálogo *nm* catalogue, *US* catalog

catalpa *nf Bot* catalpa, Indian bean tree

Cataluña *n* Catalonia

catamarán *nm* catamaran

cataplasma *nf* **(a)** *Farm* cataplasm, poultice **(b)** *Fam (pelmazo)* bore; **que c. eres** what a pain in the neck you are

cataplines *nmpl Fam (testículos)* nuts, *Br* goolies

catapulta *nf* catapult

catapultar *vt* to catapult

catar *vt (vino, comida)* to taste

catarata *nf* **(a)** *(de agua)* waterfall; **las cataratas del Niágara** Niagara Falls **(b)** *Med* cataract; **operar (a algn) de cataratas** to perform a cataract operation (on sb)

catarral *adj* catarrhal, cold

catarro *nm* (common) cold, catarrh

catarsis *nf* catharsis, katharsis

catártico, -a *adj* cathartic

catastral *adj* cadastral; **registro c.** land register

catastro *nm* cadastre, cadaster

catástrofe *nf* catastrophe □ **c. natural** natural disaster

catastrófico, -a *adj* catastrophic

catastrofismo *nm* scaremongering, alarmism

catastrofista *adj & nmf* alarmist

catavino *nm (recipiente)* wine taster

catavinos *nm inv (persona)* wine taster

catchup *(pl* **catchups)** *nm* ketchup, *US* catsup

cate *nm Fam* **(a)** *(golpe)* thump, whack **(b)** *Educ* failed subject, fail; **¿cuántos cates has sacado?** how many subjects did you fail?

catear *vt* **(a)** *Esp Fam (suspender)* to fail, *US* flunk; **he cateado** *o* **me han cateado la física** I failed *o US* flunked physics **(b)** *Andes RP (mina)* to prospect **(c)** *Am (casa)* to search

catecismo *nm Rel* catechism

cátedra *nf* **(a)** *Univ* professorship; *(de instituto)* post of head of a department □ **ex c.** ex cathedra; **sentar c.** to lay down the law **(b)** *Univ (departamento)* department; **la c. de historia** the history department

catedral *nf* cathedral; *Fam* **como una c.** huge

catedralicio, -a *adj* cathedral

catedrático, -a *nm,f Educ* **(a)** *Univ* professor **(b)** *(de instituto)* head of department

categoría *nf* category, class; **con/sin c.** with/without class; **una persona de c.** an important person □ **c. gramatical** part of speech

categórico, -a *adj* categoric; **un no c.** a flat refusal

catequesis *nf Rel* catechesis

catequista *nmf Rel* catechist, catechizer

catequizar [14] *vt Rel* to catechize

caterva *nf* host, multitude

catéter *nm Med* catheter

cateto¹ *nm Geom* cathetus, short side of a right-angled triangle

cateto, -a² *nm,f Pey* yokel, bumpkin

catinga *nf Am (olor) (persona)* body odour *o US* odor; *(animales o plantas)* stench, strong smell

catión *nm Fís* cation

catódico, -a *adj* cathodic, cathode

cátodo *nm Elec* cathode

catolicismo *nm Rel* Catholicism

católico, -a *adj & nm,f Rel* Catholic; *Fam* **no estar muy c.** *(persona)* not to feel well

catorce *inv* **1** *adj (cardinal)* fourteen; *(ordinal)* fourteenth **2** *nm* **(a)** *(número)* fourteen, fourteenth **(b)** *Fam (quiniela)* jackpot; *véase tamb* **ocho**

catorceavo, -a **1** *adj* fourteenth **2** *nm,f* fourteenth (part); *véase tamb* **octavo, -a**

catre *nm Fam* bed; *Vulg* **llevarse algn al c.** to lay sb

catrín, -ina *nm,f CAm Méx Fam* moneybags; *Br* toff

catsup *(pl* **catsups)** *nm Méx* ketchup, *US* catsup

caucásico, -a *adj & nm,f* Caucasian

Cáucaso *n* Caucasus

cauce *nm* **(a)** *(de un río)* bed **(b)** *Fig (canal)* channel; **cauces oficiales** official channels

caucho *nm* rubber

çaución *nf Jur* bail, guarantee

caudal¹ *nm* **(a)** *(de un río)* flow **(b)** *(riqueza)* wealth, riches *pl* **(c)** *Fig (abundancia)* plenty, abundance; **c. de conocimientos** wealth of (intellectual) knowledge

caudal² *adj* caudal; *(de pez)* **aleta c.** caudal fin

caudaloso, -a *adj* copious, heavy, abundant; **un río muy c.** a large river

caudillaje *nm* leadership

caudillo *nm* leader, head

causa *nf* **(a)** *(origen, objetivo)* cause, motive; **a** *o* **por c. de** because of; **c. común** common cause; **con conocimiento de c.** with full knowledge of the facts; **por tu c.** for your sake **(b)** *(ideal)* cause; **morir por una c.** to die for a cause **(c)** *Jur (caso)* case; *(juicio)* trial; **instruir una c.** to institute legal proceedings **(d)** *Andes (comida ligera)* light meal, snack **(e)** *Perú (guiso)* = dish of mashed potatoes mixed with cheese, olives, sweetcorn and lettuce, eaten cold

causal *adj* causal

causalidad *nf* causality

causante **1** *adj* causal, causing; **el hecho c. de la protesta** what caused the protest **2** *nm,f* person who causes; **el c. del malentendido** the one to blame for the misunderstanding

causar *vt* **(a)** *(gen)* to cause, bring about *o* on **(b)** *(hacer, dar)* to make, give; **me causa un gran placer** it gives me great pleasure; **me causó muy buena impresión** he made a good impression on me

causeo *nm Andes (comida ligera)* light meal, snack

causticidad *nf* causticity

cáustico, -a *adj* caustic

cautela *nf* caution, cautiousness

cautelar *adj* precautionary, preventive

cauteloso, -a **1** *adj* cautious, careful **2** *nm,f* cautious person

cauterización *nf Med* cauterization

cauterizar [14] *vt Med* to cauterize, fire; *Fig* to apply drastic measures to

cautivador, -a *adj* captivating

cautivar *vt* **(a)** *(apresar)* to capture, take prisoner **(b)** *Fig (fascinar)* to captivate, enchant

cautiverio *nm*, **cautividad** *nf* captivity; **vivir en c.** to live in captivity

cautivo, -a *adj & nm,f* captive

cauto, -a *adj* cautious, wary

cava¹ *nf (cavada)* digging

cava² *nf (bodega)* wine cellar **2** *nm (vino espumoso)* cava, champagne

cavar **1** *vt* to dig; *Fig* **c. uno su propia fosa** to dig one's own grave **2** *vi Fig (meditar)* to meditate **(en** on)

caverna *nf* **(a)** *(cueva)* cave, cavern; **hombre de las cavernas** caveman **(b)** *Anat* cavity

cavernícola **1** *adj* **(a)** *(de las cavernas)* cave dwelling; **hombre c.** caveman **(b)** *Fam (carca)* reactionary **2** *nm,f* **(a)** *(de las cavernas)* cave dweller **(b)** *Fam (carca)* reactionary

cavernoso, -a *adj* **(a)** *(con cavernas)* cavernous **(b)** *(voz, sonido)* deep, resounding; **voz cavernosa** deep and hollow voice

caviar *nf* caviar

cavidad *nf* cavity

cavilación *nf* pondering, musing

cavilar *vt* to ponder, brood over

caviloso, -a *adj* thoughtful, pensive

cayado *nm* **(a)** *(de pastor)* shepherd's crook **(b)** *(de obispo)* crosier, crozier **(c)** *Anat* **c. de la aorta** arch of the aorta

cayena *nf* cayenne pepper

cayo *nm Geog* key

cayuco *nm Am* = small flat-bottomed canoe

caza **1** *nf* **(a)** *(acción de cazar)* hunting; **ir de c.** to go hunting; **partida de c.** hunt *Fig* ❑ **c. de brujas** witch-hunt **(b)** *(animales)* game ❑ **c. furtiva** poaching; **c. mayor/ menor** big/small game **(c)** *Fig (persecución)* pursuit, chase; **andar a la c. de algo** to hunt for sth; **levantar la c.** to give the game away **2** *nm Av* fighter, fighter plane

cazabombardero *nm Av* fighter bomber

cazador, -a **1** *adj* hunting **2** *nm,f* hunter; **c. furtivo** poacher

cazadora *nf (prenda)* (waist-length) jacket

cazadotes *nm inv* fortune hunter

cazalla *nf* aniseed spirit

cazar [14] *vt* **(a)** *(animales)* to hunt; **fue a c. elefantes** he went elephant hunting **(b)** *(cobrar)* to catch, bag; **han cazado diez faisanes** they bagged ten pheasants; *Fam* **cazarlas al vuelo** to be quick on the uptake **(c)** *Fig (acosar)* to hunt *o* track down **(d)** *Fam (conseguir)* to catch, land; **c. un marido** to trap a husband

cazarrecompensas *nmf inv* bounty hunter

cazatalentos *nmf inv* head-hunter

cazatorpedero *nm Mil* (torpedo-boat) destroyer

cazo *nm* **(a)** *(cacerola)* saucepan **(b)** *(cucharón)* ladle

cazón *nm (pez)* dogfish

cazuela *nf* **(a)** *(recipiente)* casserole, saucepan **(b)** *Culin (guiso)* casserole, stew; **a la c.** stewed

cazurro, -a *adj* sullen, surly

cc *(abrev de* **centímetros cúbicos)** cc

c/c *(abrev de* **cuenta corriente)** c/a

CC. OO. *nfpl (abrev de* **Comisiones Obreras)** = Spanish left-wing trade union

CD 1 *nm (abrev de* **compact disc)** CD; **CD interactivo** interactive CD

2 (a) *(abrev de* **club deportivo)** *(en fútbol)* FC **(b)** *(abrev de* **cuerpo diplomático)** CD

CD-R *nm (abrev de* **compact disc recordable)** CD-R

CD-ROM ['θeðe'rrom] *(pl* **CD-ROMs)** *nm* CD-ROM

CD-RW *nm (abrev de* **compact disc rewritable)** CD-RW

CE *nf Antes (abrev de* **Comunidad Europea)** EC

ce *nf (la letra)* c; *Fig* **ce por ce** in great detail, with a fine-toothed comb; *Fig* **por ce o por be** for one reason or another

cebada *nf* barley

cebado, -a *adj (gordo)* huge

cebador *nm Téc* primer

cebadura *nf RP (de mate)* measure of maté

cebar 1 *vt* **(a)** *(animal)* to fatten; *Fam (persona)* **estar cebado** to be as fat as a pig **(b)** *(poner un cebo a)* to bait **(c)** *Téc (máquina, bomba)* to prime **(d)** *RP (mate)* to prepare, brew

2 cebarse *vpr* **c. en** *(ensañarse)* to be merciless with

cebiche *nm véase* **ceviche**

cebo *nm* bait

cebolla *nf* onion

cebolleta *nf* **(a)** *(especie)* chives *pl* **(b)** *(cebolla tierna)* Br spring onion, *US* scallion

cebollino *nm* **(a)** *(especie)* chive **(b)** *(cebolla)* Br spring onion, *US* scallion **(c)** *Fam (persona)* idiot, nitwit

cebra *nf* **(a)** *Zool* zebra **(b)** *Aut* **paso c.** zebra crossing, *US* crosswalk

ceca *nf* **(a)** *Hist* Royal Mint **(b)** *Fam Fig* **de la C. a la Meca** from pillar to post

cecear *vi* to lisp

ceceo *nm* lisp

cecina *nf* cured beef

cedazo *nm* sieve

ceder 1 *vt* **(a)** *(dar)* to cede, give, hand over; **c. una propiedad** to cede a property **(b)** *Aut* **c. el paso** to give way; **señal de 'ceda el paso'** 'give way' sign, *US* 'yield' sign **(c)** *Dep (pelota)* to pass (over)

2 (a) *(darse)* to yield, give way; **han cedido los cimientos** the foundations have given way **(b)** *(disminuir)* to diminish, slacken, go down **(c)** *(rendirse)* to give up, yield; **hay que saber c.** one has to make concessions at times

cedilla *nf (la letra)* cedilla

cedro *nm* cedar

cédula *nf* **(a)** *(documento)* document, certificate; **c. personal** identity card □ *Am* **c. de identidad** identity card **(b)** *Com Fin* bond, certificate, warrant

cefalalgia *nf Med* cephalalgia, headache

cefalea *nf Med* severe cephalalgia, migraine

cefalópodo *nm Zool* cephalopod

céfiro *nm Literario* zephyr

cegador, -a *adj* blinding

cegar [43] **1** *vt* **(a)** *(dejar ciego)* to blind; *Fig* **cegado por la ira** blind with rage **(b)** *(tapar)* to blind; *(puerta, ventana)* to wall up

2 cegarse *vpr Fig* to become blinded

cegato, -a *Fam* **1** *adj* short-sighted

2 *nm,f* short-sighted person

ceguera *nf* **(a)** *(invidencia)* blindness **(b)** *Fig (ofuscación)* blindness, short-sightedness

Ceilán *n Antes* Ceylon

ceilandés, -esa *adj & nm,f* Sinhalese

ceja *nf* **(a)** *Anat* eyebrow; **fruncir las cejas** to frown; *Fig* **se le ha metido entre c. y c.** she's got it into her head; *Fam* **quemarse las cejas** to burn the midnight oil **(b)** *Mús (del violín etc)* bridge

cejar *vi* to yield, give way; **c. en el empeño** to give up, slacken one's efforts

cejijunto, -a *adj* **(a)** *(persona)* with bushy eyebrows too close together **(b)** *(ceñudo)* frowning

cejilla *nf* capo

celada¹ *nf* trap, ambush

celada² *nf Hist (de armadura)* sallet, helmet

celador, -a *nm,f* attendant; *(de un colegio)* monitor; *(de una cárcel)* Br warder, *US* guard

celar¹ *vt* **(a)** *(la ley)* to observe closely, abide strictly by **(b)** *(vigilar)* to watch over, spy on

celar² *vt* to hide, conceal

celda *nf* **(a)** *(habitación)* cell □ **c. de castigo** punishment cell **(b)** *Inform* cell

celdilla *nf (beehive)* cell

celebérrimo, -a *adj* most famous, well-known

celebración *nf* **(a)** *(festejo)* celebration **(b)** *(cumplimiento, realización)* holding; **la c. del juicio tendrá lugar hoy** the trial will be held today

celebrante 1 *adj* celebrating

2 *nm Rel* celebrant *o* officiating priest

celebrar 1 *vt* **(a)** *(reunión)* to hold **(b)** *(festejar)* to celebrate **(c)** *(alabar)* to praise **(d)** *Rel (misa)* to celebrate **(e)** *(estar contento)* to be glad *o* happy; **celebro que todo saliera bien** I'm glad everything went well

2 *vi Rel (oficiar misa)* to celebrate mass

3 celebrarse *vpr* to take place, be held; **el partido se celebrará en Cádiz** the match will be held in Cadiz; **su cumpleaños se celebra el ocho de abril** his birthday falls on April 8th

célebre *adj (famoso)* famous, celebrated, well-known

celebridad *nf* **(a)** *(fama)* celebrity, fame **(b)** *(persona)* celebrity

celeridad *nf* celerity, swiftness, speed

celeste 1 *adj* **(a)** *(de cielo)* celestial **(b)** *(color)* sky-blue

2 *nm* sky blue

celestial *adj (del cielo, paraíso)* celestial, heavenly; *Fam* **ser algo música c.** to be heavenly music **(b)** *Fig (delicioso)* heavenly, delightful

celestina *nf* go-between

celibato *nm* celibacy

célibe *adj & nm,f* celibate

celo *nm* **(a)** *(esmero)* zeal, conscientiousness **(b)** *Biol (macho)* rut; *(hembra)* heat; **en c.** *(macho)* in rut; *(hembra)* Bron *o US* in heat **(c)** *celos* jealousy *sing*; **tener c. (de algo/algn)** to be jealous (of sth/sb)

celo® *nm Esp Fam Br* Sellotape®, *US* Scotch tape®

celofán *nm* cellophane

celosía *nf (reja)* lattice; *(ventana)* lattice window

celoso, -a *adj* **(a)** *(cuidadoso)* zealous, conscientious; **c. de su vida privada** protective of his private life **(b)** *(envidioso)* jealous

celta 1 *adj* Celtic

2 *nm,f* Celt

3 *nm (idioma)* Celtic

celtibérico, -a *adj & nm,f*, **celtíbero, -a** *adj & nm,f* Celtiberian

céltico, -a *adj* Celtic

célula *nf* cell; *Fig Pol* **c. comunista** comunist cell ❑ **c. fotoeléctrica** photoelectric cell, electric eye; **c. madre** stem cell, mother cell

celular *adj* (**a**) *Biol* cellular, cell (**b**) *(penitenciario)* jail; **coche c.** *Br* police van, *US* police wagon

celulitis *nf inv* cellulitis

celuloide *nm* (**a**) *(material)* celluloid (**b**) *Fig (cine)* cinema; **estrella del c.** movie *o Br* film star

celulosa *nf Quím* cellulose

cementación *nf* case-hardening

cementar *vt* to case-harden

cementerio *nm* cemetery, graveyard ❑ **c. de coches** scrapyard

cemento *nm* (**a**) *Constr* concrete, cement; **c. armado** reinforced concrete (**b**) *(de los dientes)* cement

cena *nf* supper; *(completa o formal)* dinner

cenáculo *nm* (**a**) *Hist* cenacle (**b**) *Fig (círculo social)* group

cenador *nm* bower, arbour, US arbor

cenagal *nm* (**a**) *(lugar cenagoso)* marsh, swamp (**b**) *Fig (apuro)* jam, tight spot

cenagoso, -a *adj* muddy, marshlike

cenar 1 *vi* to have supper *o* dinner
2 *vt* to have for supper *o* dinner; **¿qué cenamos hoy?** what is there for supper tonight?

cencerrada *nf Fam* = tin-pan serenade (given to a widow *o* widower who remarries)

cencerro *nm* cowbell; *Fam* **estar como un c.** to be nuts *o* crackers

cendal *nm Tex* silk stuff

cenefa *nf* (**a**) *(de ropa)* edging, trimming (**b**) *(de suelo, techo)* ornamental border, frieze

cenetista *Pol* **1** *adj* = of *o* related to the CNT (Confederación Nacional del Trabajo)
2 *nmf* member of the CNT

cenicero *nm* ashtray

Cenicienta *nf* **la C.** Cinderella

ceniciento, -a *adj* ashy, ashen

cenit *nm* zenith

cenital *adj* zenithal

ceniza *nf* (**a**) *(de cigarrillo, madera)* ash (**b**) **cenizas** *(restos mortales)* ashes

cenizo *nmf Fam* jinxed person; **ser un c.** to be jinxed

cenobio *nm* monastery

censar 1 *vt* (incluir en el censo) to register (in a census)
2 *vi* (hacer un censo) to take a census

censo *nm* (**a**) *(padrón)* census; **hacer un c.** to take a census ❑ *Esp* **c. electoral** electoral roll (**b**) *(tributo)* tax

censor *nm* (**a**) *(funcionario)* censor; *Esp Fin* **c. jurado de cuentas** auditor (**b**) *(crítico)* critic

censura *nf* (**a**) *(prohibición)* censorship; **pasar por la c.** to be censured (**b**) *(crítica)* censure, criticism; **digno de c.** censurable ❑ *Esp Com Fin* **c. de cuentas** audit, auditing

censurable *adj* censurable

censurar *vt* (**a**) *(libro, película)* to censor (**b**) *(condenar)* to censure, criticize

centauro *nm Mit* centaur

centavo, -a 1 *adj* hundredth
2 *nm* (**a**) *(número)* hundredth (part) (**b**) *Fin (moneda)* cent, centavo; *véase tamb* **octavo, -a**

centella *nf* (**a**) *(chispa)* spark; *(luz intermitente)* flash; *Fig* **rápido como una c.** (as) quick as a flash (**b**) *(rayo)* lightning

centelleante *adj* flashing, sparkling

centellear *vi* to flash, sparkle; **las estrellas**

centelleaban en el cielo the stars twinkled in the sky

centelleo *nm* flashing, sparkling

centena *nf*, **centenar** *nm* hundred; **a centenares** by the hundred

centenario, -a 1 *adj* hundred-year-old, more than a hundred years old; **una cifra centenaria** a three-figure sum
2 *nm,f* centenarian
3 *nm (aniversario)* centenary, hundredth anniversary

centeno *nm* rye

centesimal *adj* centesimal

centésimo, -a 1 *adj* hundredth; **la centésima parte** a hundredth
2 *nm,f (de una serie)* hundredth
3 *nm* (**a**) *(parte)* hundredth (**b**) *(moneda)* cent; *véase tamb* octavo, -a

centígrado, -a *adj* centigrade

centigramo *nm* centigram, centigramme

centilitro *nm* centilitre, *US* centiliter

centímetro *nm* centimetre, *US* centimeter

céntimo *nm* cent, centime; *Fam* **estar sin un c.** to be penniless

centinela *nm* (**a**) *Mil* sentry; **estar de c.** to stand sentry (**b**) *Fig (vigilante)* lookout, watch

centolla *nf*, **centollo** *nm* spider crab

centrado, -a 1 *pp de* centrar
2 *adj* (**a**) *(situado en el centro)* centred, *US* centered (**b**) *(equilibrado)* balanced; *(dedicado)* devoted (**en** to)

central 1 *adj* central
2 *nf* (**a**) *Elec* power station ❑ **c. eléctrica** power station; **c. nuclear** nuclear power station; **c. térmica** thermal power station (**b**) *(oficina principal)* head office; **c. de correos** central *o* main post office; **c. telefónica** telephone exchange (**c**) *Carib CAm (de azúcar)* sugar mill

centralismo *nm* centralism

centralista *adj & nmf* centralist, centralistic

centralita *nf Tel* switchboard

centralización *nf* centralization

centralizador, -a *adj* centralizing

centralizar [14] **1** *vt* to centralize
2 centralizarse *vpr* to become centralized

centrar 1 *vt* (**a**) *(colocar en el centro)* to centre, *US* center; **c. un cuadro** to centre a picture; *Fig* **c. un tema** to define a subject (**b**) *(esfuerzos, atención)* to concentrate, centre, *US* center; **centra su vida en la política** she dedicates herself to politics (**c**) *(basar)* to centre *o US* center around, base (**d**) *Dep* **c. el balón** to centre *o US* center the ball
2 *vi Dep* to centre, *US* center
3 centrarse *vpr* (**a**) *(tener como objeto)* to be centred *o US* centered *o* based; **la novela se centra en la vida del niño** the novel revolves around the child's life (**b**) *(concentrarse)* to concentrate (**en** on)

céntrico, -a *adj* centrally situated; *(de ciudad)* **zona céntrica** town *o* city centre, *US* downtown

centrifugado *nm (de ropa)* spin

centrifugadora *nf* (**a**) *(de ropa)* spin-dryer (**b**) *Téc* centrifuge

centrifugar [38] *vt* (**a**) *(ropa)* to spin-dry (**b**) *Téc* to centrifuge

centrífugo, -a *adj* centrifugal

centrípeto, -a *adj* centripetal

centrismo *nm Pol* centrism

centrista *Pol* **1** *adj* centre, *US* center; **partido c.** centre party
2 *nmf* centrist

centro nm (**a**) *(área, punto central)* middle, centre, US center; **c. de la ciudad** town o city centre, US downtown; **el c. de la Tierra** the centre of the Earth (**b**) *(establecimiento)* institution, centre, US center ▫ **c. benéfico** charitable organization; **c. cívico** community centre; **c. comercial** shopping centre o US mall; **c. cultural** cultural centre; **c. de acogida** *(para refugiados)* reception centre; *(para mujeres maltratadas)* (women's) refuge; **c. de cálculo** computer centre; **c. docente** o **de enseñanza** educational institution; **c. óptico** optic centre **c. sanitario** o **de salud** hospital, clinic (**c**) *Mat* centre, US center (**d**) *Dep* centre, US center ▫ **delantero c.** centre forward; **medio c.** centre half (**e**) *Pol* centre, US center; **partido de c.** centre party (**f**) *Méx (traje)* suit

centroafricano, -a adj central African

Centroamérica n Central America

centroamericano, -a adj & nm,f Central American

centrocampista nmf Ftb midfield player

centroderecha nm Pol centre o US center right

centroeuropeo, -a adj & nm,f Central European

centroizquierda nm Pol centre o US center left

centuplicar [59] **1** vt to centuplicate, multiply a hundredfold
2 centuplicarse vpr to be multiplied a hundredfold

céntuplo, -a adj & nm hundredfold, centuple

centuria nf century

centurión nm centurion

ceñido, -a 1 pp de **ceñir**
2 adj tight-fitting, clinging

ceñir [47] **1** vt (**a**) *(ajustar, apretar)* to take in (**b**) *(abrazar, rodear)* to embrace; **la ciñó con sus brazos** he embraced her tightly; **esa falda te ciñe demasiado** that skirt is too tight on you (**c**) *Literario (llevar ceñido)* to wear; **c. la espada** to gird the sword
2 ceñirse vpr (**a**) *(atenerse, limitarse)* to limit oneself, stick (a to); **c. al tema** to keep to the subject; **ciñéndonos a este caso en concreto** coming down to this particular case (**b**) *(prenda)* to cling (**a** to)

ceño nm scowl, frown; **con el c. fruncido** frowning

ceñudo, -a adj frowning

CEOE nf (*abrev de* **Confederación Española de Organizaciones Empresariales**) = Spanish employers' association, Br ≃ CBI

cepa nf (**a**) *Bot (de vid)* vine; *(tronco)* stump (**b**) *Fig (origen)* origin; **de pura c.** authentic, true; **vasco de pura c.** Basque through and through

CEPAL [θe'pal] nf (*abrev de* **Comisión Económica para América Latina**) ECL

cepillado, -a 1 pp de **cepillar**
2 adj (**a**) *(con cepillo)* brushed (**b**) *Carp* planed
3 nm (**a**) *(con cepillo)* brushing (**b**) *Carp* planing

cepillar 1 vt (**a**) *(con cepillo)* to brush (**b**) *Carp* to plane (down) (**c**) *Esp Col Fam (adular)* to butter up (**d**) *Fam (desplumar)* to fleece
2 cepillarse vpr (**a**) *(con cepillo)* to brush (**b**) *Fam (matar)* to do in; *Educ* to plough; *(acabar)* to finish; **se cepilló la tarta él solito** he gobbled up the whole cake himself (**c**) *Vulg (mujer)* to lay

cepillo nm (**a**) *(para limpiar)* brush ▫ **c. de dientes** toothbrush; **c. del pelo** hairbrush; **c. de uñas** nailbrush (**b**) *Carp* plane (**c**) *(para limosnas)* alms box

cepo nm (**a**) *(rama)* branch (**b**) *Caza* trap (**c**) *Aut* clamp (**d**) *Hist (tortura)* stocks pl (**e**) *(para limosnas)* alms box

ceporro nm (**a**) *(cepa)* log (**b**) *Fam* dimwit, blockhead; **dormir como un c.** to sleep like a log

cera nf (**a**) *(sustancia)* wax; *(de abeja)* beeswax; **blanco como la c.** as white as snow (**b**) *(del oído)* earwax, cerumen (**c**) *(para suelos, muebles)* wax, polish (**d**) *Andes Méx (vela)* candle

cerámica nf (**a**) *(arte)* ceramics sing, pottery (**b**) *(objeto)* piece of pottery

cerámico, -a adj ceramic

ceramista nmf ceramist, potter

cerbatana nf blowpipe

cerca¹ nf fence, wall

cerca² adv (**a**) *(en el espacio)* near, close; **ven más c.** come closer; **ya estamos c.** we are almost there (**b**) **c. de** *(casi)* nearly, around; **c. de cien personas** about a hundred people (**c**) **c. de** *(poco distante)* near, close; **el colegio está c. de mi casa** the school is near my house (**d**) **de c.** closely; **lo vi muy de c.** I saw it close up

cercado nm (**a**) *(lugar cerrado)* enclosure (**b**) *(cerca)* fence, wall (**c**) *Bol Perú (división territorial)* district, = provincial capital and surrounding towns

cercanía nf (**a**) *(proximidad)* proximity, nearness (**b**) **cercanías** outskirts, suburbs; **tren de c.** suburban train

cercano, -a adj near, nearby, close; **de un pueblo c.** from a neighbouring town o village ▫ **el C. Oriente** the Near East

cercar [59] vt (**a**) *(poner una cerca)* to fence, enclose (**b**) *(rodear)* to fence in, wall in, encircle (**c**) *Mil (sitiar)* to besiege, surround

cercenar vt (**a**) *(cortar)* to cut off, amputate (**b**) *Fig (disminuir)* to diminish, reduce, slash

cerceta nf Orn teal

cerciorar 1 vt to assure
2 cerciorarse vpr to make sure; **se cercioró de que no había nadie en la casa** he checked that the house was empty

cerco nm (**a**) *(marca)* circle, ring; **c. luminoso** circle of light (**b**) *Mil (sitio)* siege; **c. policíaco** police cordon; **poner c. (a una ciudad)** to besiege (a town) (**c**) *(marco)* frame (**d**) *Am (valla)* fence

cerda nf (**a**) *Zool* sow (**b**) *(pelo) (de cerdo)* bristle; *(de caballo)* horsehair; **cepillo de c.** bristle brush (**c**) *Vulg (mujer)* pig

cerdada nf Fam dirty trick; **hacerle una c. a algn** to do the dirty on sb

Cerdeña n Sardinia

cerdo nm (**a**) *Zool* pig (**b**) *(carne)* pork (**c**) *Fam Pey (hombre)* pig, Br arsehole, US asshole

cereal 1 adj cereal
2 nm cereal; **cereales** breakfast cereal sing

cerealero, -a Am **1** adj *(región)* cereal-growing; **producción cerealera** cereal production
2 nm,f cereal-grower

cerealista adj cereal, cereal-producing

cerebelo nm Anat cerebellum

cerebral adj (**a**) *(del cerebro)* cerebral, brain (**b**) *(frío, intelectual)* calculating

cerebro nm (**a**) *Anat* brain (**b**) *Fig (inteligencia)* brains pl; **ella es el c. de la organización** she's the brains of the organization ▫ **lavado de c.** brainwashing

ceremonia nf (**a**) *(acto)* ceremony ▫ **maestro de ceremonias** master of ceremonies (**b**) *(cumplido)* deference, ceremony; **con gran c.** with great pomp

ceremonial nm ceremonial

ceremonioso, -a adj ceremonious, formal; *Pey* pompous, stiff

céreo, -a adj wax, waxen

cerería nf chandler's shop

cereza *nf* (**a**) *(fruto)* cherry (**b**) *Am* husk of the coffee bean

cerezo *nm* cherry tree

cerilla *nf Esp* match

cerillero, -a *nm,f* match seller

cerillo *nm CAm Ecuad Méx* match

cerner [64], **1** *vt (harina)* to sift
   2 cernerse *vpr* (**a**) *(pájaro, avión)* to hover (**b**) *Fig* to loom, threaten

cernícalo *nm* (**a**) *Orn* kestrel (**b**) *Fig (persona)* blockhead, dolt

cernir [25] *vt & vpr véase* **cerner**

cero *nm* (**a**) *Mat* zero; **tres grados bajo c.** three degrees below zero (**b**) *(cifra)* nought, zero; **sacar un c. en literatura** to get a nought in literature; *Fig* **partir de c.** to start from scratch; *Fig* **ser un c. a la izquierda** to be useless o a good-for-nothing (**c**) *Dep* nil; **dos a c.** two nil (**d**) *(ninguno)* none; **sacó c. puntos** he didn't get any points at all

cerquillo *nm Am Br* fringe, *US* bangs

cerrado, -a 1 *pp de* **cerrar**
   2 *adj* (**a**) *(puerta, boca, tienda)* closed, shut; **a puerta cerrada** in camera; *Fig* **a ojos cerrados** with one's eyes closed (**b**) *Ling* **vocal cerrada** closed vowel (**c**) *(marcado) (acento)* broad; *(curva)* tight, sharp; *(ovación)* thunderous (**d**) *(barba)* bushy (**e**) *Fig (oculto)* hidden, obscure (**f**) *(persona) (introvertida)* uncommunicative, reserved; *(intransigente)* intransigent, uncompromising, unyielding; *Fam (torpe)* thick; **c. de mollera** thickheaded

cerradura *nf* lock; **c. antirrobo** antitheft lock

cerrajería *nf* (**a**) *(oficio)* locksmith's trade (**b**) *(taller)* locksmith's shop

cerrajero, -a *nm,f* locksmith

cerrar [3] **1** *vt (ventana, libro, tienda, ojos)* to shut, close; *(grifo, gas)* to turn off; *(luz)* to turn off, switch off; *(cremallera)* to fasten, zip (up); *(negocio, oficina)* to close down; *(cuenta)* to close; *(discusión)* to end, finish; *(compra)* to close, conclude; *(sobre)* to seal; *(agujero)* to plug; *(grieta)* to fill; *(puños)* to clench; *(en dominó)* to block; **c. con llave** to lock; **c. el paso a algn** to block sb's way; **c. la marcha** to bring up the rear; *Fam* **c. el pico** to shut one's trap
   2 *vi* (**a**) *(gen)* to close, shut (**b**) *Tricot* to cast off
   3 cerrarse *vpr* (**a**) *(al exterior)* to close, shut; **la puerta se cerró de golpe** the door slammed shut; *Fam* **c. en banda** to stick to one's guns (**b**) *(obstinarse)* to stand fast, persist (**en** in) (**c**) *Med (cicatrizar)* to close up, heal (**d**) *Aut* to close in (**e**) *Meteor* to cloud over

cerrazón *nf* (**a**) *(obstinación)* obstinacy (**b**) *(estupidez)* dimness, denseness; **c. mental** narrow-mindedness (**c**) *RP (niebla)* heavy mist

cerril *adj* (**a**) *(terreno)* rough (**b**) *(animal)* wild, untamed (**c**) *(persona) (tosca)* uncouth, coarse; *(obstinada)* pig-headed, headstrong

cerro *nm* hill; *Esp Fig* **irse por los cerros de Ubeda** to beat around the bush

cerrojazo *nm* **dar c. (a algo/algn)** to cut (sth/sb) short

cerrojo *nm* (**a**) *(para cerrar)* bolt; **echar** o **correr el c.** to bolt the door (**b**) *Ftb* blanket defence o *US* defense

certamen *nm* competition, contest

certero, -a *adj* (**a**) *(tiro, tirador)* accurate, good; **es un tirador muy c.** he's a crack shot (**b**) *(acertado)* accurate, certain

certeza *nf*, **certidumbre** *nf* certainty; **saber (algo) con c.** to be certain (of sth); **tener la c. de que ...** to be sure o certain that ...

certificación *nf* (**a**) *(confirmación)* certification (**b**) *(de un envío)* registration (**c**) *(documento)* certificate

certificado, -a 1 *pp de* **certificar**
   2 *adj* (**a**) *(documento)* certified (**b**) *(envío)* registered
   3 *nm* (**a**) *(gen)* certificate ❑ **c. médico** medical certificate (**b**) *(carta)* registered letter; *(paquete)* registered package

certificar [59] *vt* (**a**) *(gen)* to certify, guarantee (**b**) *(carta, paquete)* to register

cerúleo, -a *adj* cerulean, deep-blue

cerumen *nm* cerumen, earwax

cerval *adj* **miedo c.** terror, funk

cervantino, -a *adj* of o relating to Cervantes, Cervantine

cervato *nm Zool* fawn

cervecería *nf* (**a**) *(bar)* pub, bar (**b**) *(fábrica)* brewery

cervecero, -a 1 *adj* beer; **la producción cervecera** beer production
   2 *nm* brewer

cerveza *nf* beer, ale ❑ **c. de barril** draught beer; **c. dorada** o **ligera** lager; **c. negra** stout

cervical *adj Anat* cervical, neck

cérvido, -a *Zool* **1** *adj* cervid
   2 *nm* cervid

cerviz *nf* cervix, nape of the neck; *Fig* **ser duro de c.** to be pig-headed

cesación *nf* cessation, suspension

cesante 1 *adj* (**a**) *(destitución)* dismissed; *(ministro)* removed from office; *(embajador)* recalled (**b**) *CSur Méx (parado)* unemployed
   2 *nm,f* *(funcionario)* suspended official; *(parado)* unemployed worker

cesantear *vt Am* to make redundant

cesantía *nf* (**a**) *(destitución)* dismissal (**b**) *Chile CSur (desempleo)* unemployment

cesar *vi* (**a**) *(parar)* to stop, cease; **sin c.** incessantly (**b**) *(dejar un empleo)* to leave, quit; **c. en el cargo** to cease one's functions

cesárea *nf Med* Caesarean (section), *US* Cesarean (section)

cese *nm* (**a**) *(detención, paro)* cessation, suspension (**b**) *(despido)* dismissal; **dar el c. a algn** to dismiss sb

cesio *nm* caesium

cesión *nf* cession; **c. de tierras** assignment of land

cesionario, -a *nm,f* cessionary, assignee

cesionista *nmf* grantor, assignee

césped *nm* lawn, grass; **cortar el c.** to mow the lawn

cesta *nf* (**a**) *(canasta)* basket ❑ **c. de la compra** shopping basket, *US* shopping cart; **c. de Navidad** Christmas hamper (**b**) *Dep* pelota o jai-alai basket

cestería *nf* (**a**) *(material)* wickerwork, basketwork (**b**) *(fabricación)* basket making (**c**) *(tienda)* basket shop

cesto *nm* basket; **c. de los papeles** wastepaper basket

cesura *nf Lit* caesura

ceta *nf véase* **zeta**

cetáceo, -a *Zool* **1** *adj & nm* cetacean, whale
   2 cetáceos *nmpl* cetaceans

cetrería *nf* falconry, hawking

cetrino, -a *adj* (**a**) *(cara)* sallow (**b**) *Fig (melancólico)* melancholic

cetro *nm* sceptre, *US* scepter; *Literario* **empuñar el c.** to ascend the throne; *Fig* **ostentar el c.** to hold the lead

ceutí (*pl* **ceutíes**) **1** *adj* of o from Ceuta
   2 *nmf* person from Ceuta

ceviche *nm* ceviche, = raw fish marinated in lemon and garlic

cf. *abrev de* **confróntese**) cf

CFC *nmpl (abrev de* **clorofluorocarbonos)** CFC

cfr. *abrev véase* **cf.**

cg *(abrev de* **centigramo)** cg

Ch, ch [tʃe, θe'atʃe] *nf* = formerly fourth letter of the Spanish alphabet

chabacanería *nf* (**a**) *(acción, comentario)* **lo que hizo/dijo fue una c.** what he did/said was vulgar (**b**) *(cualidad)* vulgarity

chabacano, -a 1 *adj* vulgar
  2 *nm Méx* (**a**) *(fruto)* apricot (**b**) *(árbol)* apricot tree

chabola *nf Esp* shack; **barrio de chabolas** shanty town

chabolismo *nm Esp* shanty towns; **quieren acabar con el c.** they want to do away with shanty towns

chabolista *nmf Esp* shanty dweller

chacal *nm* jackal

chácara *nf* (**a**) *Am Anticuado (granja)* farm (**b**) *Col Pan Ven (para monedas)* purse

chacarera *nf* = Argentinian folk dance

chacarero, -a *nm,f Andes RP* peasant farmer, farm labourer, *US* farm laborer

chacha *nf Fam (niñera)* nanny, nursemaid; *(criada)* maid

chachachá *nm*, **cha-cha-chá** *nm Mús* cha-cha, cha-cha-cha

chachalaca *nf CAm Méx Fam* chatterbox

cháchara *nf* (**a**) *Fam (charla)* small talk, chinwag; **estar de c.** to have a yap (**b**) **chácharas** *(baratijas)* trinkets, junk *sing*

chacharear 1 *vi* (**a**) *Fam (charlar)* to chatter, gossip (**b**) *Méx (comerciar)* to deal in trinkets
  2 *vt Méx (comprar y vender)* to buy and sell

chachi *adj Esp Fam* great, terrific, fantastic; **lo pasamos c.** we had a ball

chacho, -a *Esp nm,f* (**a**) *Fam (muchacho)* boy, lad; *(muchacha)* girl, lass (**b**) *Fam (tratamiento) (muchacho)* pal, *Br* mate, *US* buddy; *(muchacha)* love, dear (**c**) *CAm (mellizo)* twin

chacina *nf* seasoned pork

chacinería *nf* pork butcher's (shop)

chacolí *nm* dry wine from the Basque Country

chacota *nf* joking, banter; **hacer c. de algo** to have a laugh about sth; **tomar algo a c.** to take sth as a joke

chacra *nf Andes RP* small farm *o* holding

Chad *nm* **el C.** Chad

chador *nm* chador

chafar 1 *vt* (**a**) *(aplastar)* to squash, crush, flatten (**b**) *(arrugar)* to crease, crumple (**c**) *Fam (plan, negocio)* to ruin, spoil (**d**) *Esp Fam (abatir)* to crush; *(desilusionar)* to disappoint
  2 chafarse *vpr* (**a**) *(aplastarse)* to be squashed *o* crushed *o* flattened (**b**) *(arrugarse)* to become creased *o* crumpled

chaflán *nm* chamfer; **la casa que hace c.** the house on the corner

chaguar [11] *vt Arg (clothes, sponge)* to wring out, squeeze

chaira *nf* (**a**) *(cuchilla de zapatero)* shoemaker's knife (**b**) *(acero de afilar)* (sharpening) steel (**c**) *(navaja)* jack-knife

chal *nm (prenda)* shawl

chala *nf* (**a**) *Andes RP (de mazorca) Br* maize husk, *US* corn husk (**b**) *Chile (sandalia)* leather sandal

chalado, -a *Fam* **1** *pp de* **chalar**
  2 *adj (chiflado)* crazy, nuts, crackers; *(enamorado)* **estar c. por algo/algn** to be crazy about sth/sb

chaladura *nf Fam (chifladura)* crazy idea; *(enamoramiento)* crazy love.

chalanear *vt Am (caballos)* to break (in)

chalar 1 *vt Fam* to drive crazy *o* round the bend
  2 chalarse *vpr Fam* to go mad *o* nuts; **c. por algo/algn** to be mad about sth/sb

chalé *(pl* **chalés)** *nm véase* **chalet**

chaleco *nm Br* waistcoat, *US* vest; *(de punto)* sleeveless pullover ❏ **c. antibalas** bullet-proof vest; *Am* **c. de fuerza** straitjacket; **c. salvavidas** life jacket

chalet *(pl* **chalets)** *nm (casa de campo)* country house *o* cottage; *(de lujo)* villa; *(en la montaña)* mountain chalet; *(en la ciudad)* house; *(individual)* detached house; *(adosado)* semi-detached house

chalina *nf* (**a**) *(corbata)* cravat (**b**) *Am (chal estrecho)* stole

chalón *nm Am* black shawl

chalote *nm* shallot

chalupa 1 *nf* (**a**) *Náut (lancha)* boat, launch (**b**) *Méx (torta de maíz)* = oval-shaped tortilla
  2 *adj Fam (chalado)* nuts; **estar c.** to be bonkers

chamaco, -a *nm,f Méx Fam (muchacho)* boy, lad; *(muchacha)* girl, lass

chamagoso, -a *adj Méx* (**a**) *(astroso)* grubby, shabby (**b**) *(cosa)* rough, cheap

chamal *nm Am* = cloak worn by Indians

chamán *nm* shaman

chamanismo *nm* shamanism

chamarilear *vi* to swap *o* deal in second-hand goods

chamarileo *nm* trading in second-hand goods

chamarilero, -a *nm,f*, **chamarillero, -a** *nm,f* second-hand *o* junk dealer

chamarra *nf (zamarra)* sheepskin jacket

chamarro *nm CAm* coarse woollen blanket

chamba¹ *nf* (**a**) *CAm Méx Perú Ven Fam (trabajo)* job (**b**) *Col, Ven (zanja)* ditch

chamba² *nf Fam* fluke, piece of luck, lucky break; **por c.** by a fluke

chambear *vi Méx* (**a**) *(feriar)* to swap, exchange, barter (**b**) *(trabajar)* to work for a pittance

chambelán *nm* chamberlain

chambergo *nm RP Hist* broad-brimmed hat

chambón, -ona *Fam* **1** *adj* (**a**) *(torpe)* clumsy (**b**) *(afortunado)* flukey, jammy
  2 *nm,f* (**a**) *(torpe)* clumsy person (**b**) *(suertudo)* lucky *o* jammy person

chambonada *nf*, **chamboneada** *nf Am Fam (chapuza)* botch, botched job

chambonear *vi Am Fam* to botch things up, bungle

chamiza *nf* (**a**) *(planta)* chamiso (**b**) *(leña)* brushwood

chamizo *nm* (**a**) *(leño, árbol)* half-burnt log *o* tree (**b**) *(choza)* thatched hut (**c**) *Pey (tugurio)* hovel, shack, shanty

chamorro, -a *adj* shorn, close-cropped

champa *nf CAm* palm leaf shack

champán *nm*, **champaña** *nm* champagne

champiñón *nm* mushroom

champola *nf* (**a**) *CAm Carib (refresco de guanábana)* soursop milkshake (**b**) *Chile (refresco de chirimoya)* = drink made from custard apple

champú *(pl* **champús** *o* **champúes)** *nm* shampoo ❏ **c. anticaspa** anti-dandruff shampoo

champurrado *nm Méx* (**a**) *(bebida)* = drink made from chocolate (**b**) *Fam (enredo)* hotch-potch, jumble, mess

chamuchina *nf Andes Cuba Hond* (**a**) *(populacho)* rabble, mob (**b**) *(niños)* gang of kids

chamullar *vi Vulg* (**a**) *(hablar)* to speak, talk (**b**) *(chapurrear)* to jabber; **sólo sé c. en francés** I only have a smattering of French

chamuscar [59] **1** *vt* **(a)** *(socarrar)* to singe, scorch **(b)** *Méx (vender barato)* to sell cheaply
2 chamuscarse *vpr (socarrarse)* to singe, scorch, get scorched

chamusquina *nf* singeing, scorching; *Fam* **esto me huele a c.** there's something fishy going on here

chancaca *nf* **(a)** *Am (masa)* syrup cake **(b)** *CAm (torta)* = maize cake with honey

chancar [59] *vt Andes* **(a)** *(triturar)* to crush, grind **(b)** *(maltratar)* to treat badly; *(golpear)* to beat

chance *nm o nf Am* opportunity, chance; **tener c. de hacer algo** to have the chance to do sth; **¿me das un chance?** can I have a go?

chancear 1 *vi (bromear)* to joke, horse around
2 chancearse *vpr (bromear)* to joke; **c. de** to make fun of

chancero, -a *adj* fond of joking

chanchada *nf Am Fam* dirty trick

chanchería *nf Am* pork butcher's (shop)

chancho, -a *Am* **1** *adj (sucio)* dirty, filthy
2 *nm,f* **(a)** *Zool* pig, hog □ **c. salvaje** boar **(b)** *(carne)* pork

chanchullero, -a *Fam* **1** *adj* crooked, bent, underhand
2 *nm,f* crook, racketeer

chanchullo *nm Fam* fiddle, wangle, racket; **meterse en chanchullos** to be on the fiddle

chancla *nf (sandalia)* backless sandal; *(para la playa)* flip-flop, *US* thong

chancleta *nf* **(a)** *(sandalia)* backless sandal; *(para la playa)* flip-flop, *US* thong **(b)** *Andes RP Fam* baby girl

chanclo *nm (zueco)* clog; *(de goma)* overshoe, galosh

chancro *nm Med* chancre

chándal *(pl* **chandals)** *nm Dep* track *o* jogging suit

chanfaina *nf Culin* offal stew; *(en Andalucía)* vegetable soup

changa *nf* **(a)** *Bol RP (trabajo temporal)* odd job **(b)** *Andes Cuba (chiste)* joke

changador *nm RP* porter

changarro *nm Méx (tienda)* small store; *(puesto)* stand

chango, -a 1 *adj* **(a)** *Carib (bromista)* playful, joking **(b)** *Chile (fastidioso)* tedious, annoying **(c)** *Méx PRico* **estar c.** to be cheap and plentiful
2 *nm,f* **(a)** *Carib (bromista)* joker, prankster **(b)** *Chile (fastidioso)* tedious person **(c)** *Arg Bol Méx (muchacho)* youngster
3 *nm* **(a)** *Méx (mono)* monkey **(b)** *Ven* **changos** *(harapos)* rags

changuear *Ven* **1** *vi (bromear)* to joke, jest
2 changuearse *vpr (bromear)* to joke, jest; **c. de** to make fun of

changüí *nm Fam* **(a)** *(engaño)* trick, hoax; **dar c. a algn** *(engañar)* to play a trick on sb; *(tomar el pelo)* to tease sb **(b)** *(novato)* novice, beginner

chanquete *nm (pez)* transparent goby

chantaje *nm* blackmail; **hacer c. a algn** to blackmail sb

chantajear *vt* to blackmail

chantajista *nmf* blackmailer

chantillí *nm* whipped cream

chantre *nm Rel* precentor, cantor

chanza *nf* joke; **de** *o* **en c.** jokingly, in fun; **estar de c.** to be joking

chao *interj Fam* so long!, bye!, ciao!

chapa *nf* **(a)** *(de metal)* sheet, plate; **c. ondulada** corrugated iron **(b)** *(de madera)* panel-board, sheet;

(enchapado) veneer; *(contrachapado)* plywood; **madera de 3 chapas** 3-ply wood **(c)** *(tapón)* bottle top, cap **(d)** *(ficha metálica)* metal tag, tally, token; *(medalla)* badge, disc; *Mil* **c. de identificación** identity disc; *Fam* **estar sin c.** to be penniless **(e)** *Fig (sentido común)* common sense; **hombre de c.** sensible man **(f)** *Col Cuba Méx (cerradura)* lock **(g)** *RP (de matrícula) Br* number plate, *US* license plate **(h)** **chapas** *(juego)* pitch-and-toss, *US* penny-pitching

chapado, -a 1 *pp de* **chapar**
2 *adj* **(a)** *(metal)* plated; **c. en oro** gold-plated **(b)** *(madera, mueble)* veneered, finished **(c)** *Fig* **c. a la antigua** old-fashioned **(d)** *Esp Fam (cerrado)* shut, closed

chapalear *vi* to splash about

chapapote *nm* oil sludge

chapar *vt* **(a)** *(metal)* to plate **(b)** *(madera, mueble)* to veneer, finish **(c)** *Esp Fam (cerrar)* to shut, close

chaparral *nm* thicket of kermes oaks

chaparro *nm (rechoncho)* short, stocky person

chaparrón *nm* **(a)** *Meteor* downpour, heavy shower; **ha caído un buen c.** there's been a heck of a downpour **(b)** *Fig (de preguntas etc)* shower, bombardment

chapela *nf* beret

chapero *nm Argot* male prostitute, *Br* rent boy

chapetón, -ona *Am* **1** *adj (torpe)* clumsy, awkward
2 *nm,f* **(a)** *(immigrante)* = recently-arrived European immigrant **(b)** *(torpe)* clumsy *o* awkward person
3 *nm (chaparrón)* downpour, heavy shower

chapín *CAm Méx* **1** *adj (guatemalteco)* Guatemalan
2 *nm (guatemalteco)* Guatemalan

chapista *nm,f* sheet metal worker; *Aut* panel beater

chapistería *nf* sheet metal work; *Aut* panel beating; **taller de c.** body repair shop

chapitel *nm Arquit* **(a)** *(de torre)* spire **(b)** *(de columna)* capital

chapó¹ *nm* = type of billiards

chapó² *interj Fam* well done!, bravo!

chapopote *nm Carib Méx* bitumen, pitch

chapotear *vi* to splash about, paddle

chapoteo *nm* splashing (about), paddling

chapucear *vt (hacer aprisa y mal)* to botch, bungle, make a mess of

chapucería *nf* **(a)** *(chapuza)* botched job, shoddy piece of work **(b)** *(tosquedad)* shoddiness **(c)** *(embuste)* lie

chapucero, -a 1 *adj (trabajo)* slapdash, shoddy, sloppy; *(persona)* bungling, clumsy
2 *nm,f* **(a)** *(frangollón)* botcher, bungler **(b)** *(embustero)* liar

chapulín *nm CAm Méx* **(a)** *(langosta)* locust **(b)** *(niño)* kid, child

chapurrear *vt* to speak badly *o* with difficulty; **sólo chapurreaba el francés** he spoke only a few words of French

chapurreo *nm* jabbering

chapuza *nf* **(a)** *(trabajo ocasional)* odd job **(b)** *(trabajo mal hecho)* botched job, shoddy piece of work

chapuzón *nm (zambullida)* duck, ducking, dive; *(baño corto)* dip; **darse un c.** to have a dip

chaqué *nm* morning coat

chaqueta *nf* jacket; **hay que ir de c.** suits must be worn; *Fig Pol* **cambiar de c.** to change sides; *Fam* **ser más vago que la c. de un guardia** to be bone idle □ **c. de punto** knitted cardigan; **c. de smoking** dinner jacket; **traje de c.** suit

chaquetear *vi Esp Fam Pol* to change sides, be a turncoat

chaquetero, -a *nm,f Esp Fam Pol* turncoat

chaquetilla *nf* short jacket ❏ *Taur* **c. torera** bull-fighter's jacket

chaquetón *nm (de lana)* heavy woollen jacket; *(trenca)* duffel jacket ❏ **c. tres cuartos** three-quarter length jacket

chaquira *nf Hist SAm* glass bead

charada *nf* charade

charamusca¹ *nf Méx* candy twist

charanga *nf* **(a)** *Mús Mil* brass band **(b)** *Fam (alboroto)* din, racket, hullabaloo **(c)** *Am (baile)* informal dance

charango *nm* = small South American guitar, often made from armadillo shell

charca *nf* pond, pool

charco *nm* puddle, pool; *Fam* **cruzar** *o* **pasar el c.** *(ir a América)* to cross the pond

charcón, -ona *Arg Bol* **1** *adj* thin, skinny
2 *nm,f* emaciated animal *o* person

charcutería *nf* pork butcher's (shop), delicatessen

charcutero, -a *nm,f* pork butcher

charla *nf (conversación)* talk, chat; *(conferencia)* talk, informal lecture *o* address

charlar *vi* to talk, chat

charlatán, -ana **1** *adj (parlanchín)* talkative; *(chismoso)* gossipy
2 *nm,f* **(a)** *(parlanchín)* chatterbox; *(chismoso)* gossip; *(bocazas)* charlatan, bigmouth **(b)** *(embaucador)* trickster, charmer

charlatanería *nf* **(a)** *(palabrería)* talkativeness, verbosity **(b)** *(de vendedor)* sales patter, spiel

charlestón *nm Mús* charleston

charlotada *nf* **(a)** *Taur* comic bullfight **(b)** *Fam (payasada)* clowning around, buffoonery

charlotear *vi Fam (parlotear)* to chatter, prattle, natter; *(charlar)* to chat

charloteo *nm Fam (parloteo)* prattling, nattering; *(charla)* chat

charnego, -a *nm,f Pey* = Spanish immigrant worker, often from southern Spain, who has settled in Catalonia

charnela *nf* hinge

charol *nm* **(a)** *(barniz)* varnish; *Fam* **darse c.** to blow one's trumpet, brag **(b)** *(piel)* patent leather ❏ **zapatos de c.** patent leather shoes **(c)** *Andes (bandeja)* tray

charolar *vt* to varnish

charquear *vt Andes RP (carne)* to dry, cure

charqui *nm Andes RP (carne)* dried beef, cured meat; *(fruta)* dried fruit

charquicán *nm Andes Arg* **(a)** *Culin (guiso)* = dried meat and vegetable stew **(b)** *Fig (barullo)* jumble, confusion

charrán *nm Orn* tern

charrasquear *vt Ecuad Pan Ven (instrumento)* to strum

charreada *nf Méx (espectáculo)* = display of horseriding skills by **charros** ≃ rodeo

charretera *nf Mil* epaulette

charro, -a **1** *adj* **(a)** *(recargado)* gaudy, showy **(b)** *Esp (salmantino)* Salamancan **(c)** *Méx (líder sindical)* = in league with the bosses
2 *nm,f* **(a)** *Esp (salmantino)* Salamancan **(b)** *Méx (jinete)* horseman; *(mujer)* horsewoman

chárter *adj inv* **(vuelo) c.** charter (flight)

chas *interj* crash!, wham!

chasca *nf* **(a)** *(leña menuda)* brushwood **(b)** *Andes (cabellera revuelta)* mop of hair, tangled hair; *(maraña)* tangle

chascar [59] **1** *vt (lengua)* to click; *(dedos)* to snap; *(látigo)* to crack; *(chocolate etc)* to crunch
2 *vi (ruido de madera etc)* to crack

chascarrillo *nm (chiste)* joke, funny story; *(historieta)* witty anecdote

chasco *nm* **(a)** *(broma)* trick, joke; **dar un c. a algn** to play a trick on sb **(b)** *(decepción)* disappointment; **llevarse un c.** to be disappointed; **¡menudo c. me llevé!** I was so disappointed!

chasis *nm inv* **(a)** *Aut* chassis; *Fam* **quedarse en el c.** to be reduced to skin and bone **(b)** *Fot* plate holder

chasquear¹ *vt* **(a)** *(gastar una broma)* to play a trick on **(b)** *(decepcionar)* to disappoint, let down **(c)** *(promesa)* to break, fail to keep

chasquear² **1** *vt (lengua)* to click; *(dedos)* to snap; *(látigo)* to crack; *(chocolate etc)* to crunch
2 *vi (madera etc)* to crack, crackle

chasqui *nm Am* messenger, courier

chasquido *nm (de la lengua)* click; *(de los dedos)* snap; *(de látigo, madera)* crack; *(de chocolate etc)* crunch

chat *(pl* **chats)** *nm Inform (charla)* chat; *(sala)* chat room

chata *nf* bedpan

chatarra *nf* *(escoria)* scrap (metal), scrap iron; *Fam* **este coche es una c.** this car is a heap of junk ❏ **parque de c.** scrap yard **(b)** *Fam (monedas)* small change **(c)** *Fam Pey (joyas)* gaudy jewellery *o US* jewelery

chatarrería *nf* scrapyard

chatarrero, -a *nm,f* scrap dealer *o* merchant

chatear *vi Esp Fam* to go out drinking, *US* barhop

chateo *nf Esp Fam* **ir de c.** to go out for a few drinks

chato, -a **1** *adj* **(a)** *(nariz)* snub; *(persona)* snub-nosed **(b)** *(objeto)* flat, flattened; *(barco)* flat, shallow; *(torre)* low, squat **(c)** *PRico RP Fam (sin ambiciones)* commonplace; **una vida chata** a humdrum existence
2 *nm Esp* (small) glass of wine; **tomar unos chatos** to have a few drinks
3 *nm,f* **(a)** *(persona)* snub-nosed person **(b)** *Fam (apelativo cariñoso)* dear, duckie, love; **¡muchas gracias, c.!** thanks a lot, love!

chau *interj Bol CSur Perú Fam* bye!, see you!

chaucha *nf* **(a)** *Bol RP (judía verde)* green bean **(b)** *Andes (papa)* early potato **(c)** *Andes RP (moneda)* coin of little value; **costar chauchas y palitos** to cost next to nothing

chauvinismo [tʃoβiˈnismo] *nm* chauvinism

chauvinista [tʃoβiˈnista] *adj & nmf* chauvinist

chaval, -a *nm,f Fam (chico)* boy, lad; *(chica)* girl, lass; *(joven)* kid, youngster; *Fam (apelativo)* pal, *Br* mate, *US* buddy

chaveta *nf* **(a)** *Téc (clavija)* key, cotter (pin); *Fam* **estar mal de la c.** to have a screw loose; *Fam* **perder la c.** to go off one's rocker; *Fam* **perder la c. por** to be crazy about **(b)** *Andes (navaja)* penknife

chavo **1** *nm,f Méx Fam (chico)* guy; *(chica)* girl
2 *nm Fam (dinero)* **no tener un c.** to be penniless

chayote *nm CAm Méx Bot (fruto y planta)* chayote

che 1 *nf (dígrafo)* = name of the digraph Ch in Spanish
2 *interj Am* **(a)** *(para llamar la atención)* hey!, listen! **(b)** *RP Fam (muletilla)* man, mate, you know, I mean; **no sabe lo que dice, c.** he doesn't know what he's saying, man

checa *nf* detention cell, cooler

checar [59] *vt Andes CAm Méx* to check; **chécalo bien** look at that!, check it out!

chechén, -ena *adj & nm,f* Chechen

Chechenia *n* Chechnya

checheno, -a *adj & nm,f* Chechen

checo, -a 1 *adj* Czech
2 *nm,f (persona)* Czech
3 *nm (idioma)* Czech

checoslovaco, -a *adj & nm,f Antes* Czechoslovakian, Czechoslovak

Checoslovaquia *n Antes* Czechoslovakia

chef [tʃef] *(pl* **chefs)** *nm* chef

chele *CAm* **1** *adj (rubio)* blond, blonde; *(de piel blanca)* fair-skinned
2 *nmf (rubio)* blond(e) person; *(de piel blanca)* fair-skinned person

cheli *nm Argot* = Spanish urban slang

chelín *nm* shilling

chelo *nm* cello

chenca *nf CAm* cigarette end *o* butt

chepa *nf Fam* hump

cheposo, -a, chepudo, -a *Fam* **1** *adj* hunchbacked
2 *nm,f* hunchback

cheque *nm Br* cheque, *US* check; **cobrar un c.** to cash a cheque; **extender un c.** to issue a cheque; **extender** *o* **hacer un c. a nombre de** to make out a cheque to ▢ **c. abierto** open cheque; **c. al portador** cheque payable to bearer; **c. cruzado** crossed cheque; **c. de viaje** *o* **viajero** traveller's cheque; **c. en blanco** blank cheque; **c. nominativo** cheque in favour of a specific person; **c. sin fondos** dud *o* bouncing cheque; **talonario de cheques** cheque book

chequear *vt (controlar, examinar)* to check; *(comprobar)* to check up on; *Aut (vehículo)* to service; *Med* to give a checkup to

chequeo *nm Med* checkup

chequera *nf Br* cheque book, *US* check book

chévere *adj Fam* **(a)** *Am salvo RP (estupendo)* great, fantastic **(b)** *Andes Carib (benévolo, indulgente)* really kind *o* nice **(c)** *Carib (petrimetre)* foppish, dandified **(d)** *Ven (valentón)* swaggering, cocky

cheviot *(pl* **cheviots)** *nm Tex* cheviot

chic *adj inv (elegante)* chic, elegant; *(de moda)* fashionable

chicano, -a *adj & nm,f* chicano

chicarrón, -ona *nm,f Fam (chico)* strapping lad; *(chica)* strapping lass

chicha[1] *nf Esp Fam* **(a)** *(para comer)* meat **(b)** *(de persona)* flesh; **tiene pocas chichas** *(está flaco)* he's as thin as a rake

chicha[2] *nf Am* **(a)** *(bebida alcohólica)* chicha, maize liquor; **c. de uva** = drink made from grape juice; *Fam* **de c. y nabo** insignificant; *Fam* **no ser ni c. ni limonada** to be a waste of space **(b)** *Fig (berrinche)* rage, bad temper

chicha[3] *adj inv Náut* **calma c.** dead calm

chícharo *nm CAm Méx* **(a)** *(guisante)* pea **(b)** *(garbanzo)* chickpea

chicharra *nf* **(a)** *Ent* cicada; *Fig* **cantaba la c.** it was boiling hot **(b)** *Méx Elec* buzzer, bell **(c)** *Fam (parlanchín)* chatterbox

chicharro *nm* **(a)** *(de cerdo)* pork crackling, fried pork rind **(b)** *(pez)* scad, horse mackerel

chicharrón *nm* **(a)** *(de cerdo)* pork crackling, fried pork rind; *Fam* **quedar hecho un c.** to be burnt to a cinder **(b)** *Fig (persona)* sunburnt person

chiche 1 *adj Andes RP (delicado)* fine, delicate
2 *nm* **(a)** *Andes RP Fam (juguete)* toy **(b)** *Andes RP (adorno)* delicate ornament **(c)** *CAm Méx muy Fam (pecho)* tit

chichear *vt & vi* to hiss

chicheme *nm CAm* = cold drink made from corn, milk and sugar

chicheo *nm* hissing

chichería *nf Am (bar)* chicha bar, tavern; *(tienda)* chicha shop

chichero, -a *nm,f Am* **(a)** *(vendedor)* chicha seller **(b)** *(fabricante)* chicha maker

chichón[1] *nm* bump, lump

chichón, -ona[2] *adj CAm* easy

chichonera *nf (gorro)* padded cap; *(casco)* helmet

chicle *nm* chewing gum

chico, -a 1 *adj* **(a)** *(pequeño)* small, little; **estos pantalones se me han quedado chicos** I've grown out of these trousers; *Fig* **dejar c. a algn** to make sb look small
2 *nm,f* **(a)** *(muchacho)* boy, lad; *(muchacha)* girl, lass; **el c. de los recados** the office boy; **es buena chica** she's a good girl; *Fam* **como c. con zapatos nuevos** like a kid with a new toy; *Cin Fam* **el c. de la película** the goody **(b)** *(para dirigirse a algn)* sonny, *Br* mate, *US* buddy; **mira, c., yo de ti me iría** listen mate, if I were you I'd go
3 *nf (criada)* maid

chicoria *nf* chicory

chicote, -a 1 *nm,f Fam (hombre)* fine lad; *(mujer)* fine lass
2 *nm* **(a)** *Fam (puro)* cigar **(b)** *Am (látigo)* whip **(c)** *CAm (serie, retahíla)* volley, stream

chifa *nm Andes* Chinese restaurant

chifla *nf (siseo)* hiss, hissing; *(silbido)* whistle, whistling

chiflado, -a *Fam* **1** *pp de* **chiflar**
2 *adj (loco)* mad, crazy, barmy, nuts, round the twist *o* bend; **estar c. con** *o* **por** to be mad *o* crazy about
3 *nm,f* nut, loony, headcase

chifladura *nf Fam* **(a)** *(locura)* madness, craziness **(b)** *(idea alocada)* barmy idea, madcap scheme **(c)** *(afición)* craze, mania; **su c. es el fútbol** he's mad on football

chiflar 1 *vt* **(a)** *(silbar)* to hiss (at), boo (at), whistle (at); *(pito)* to blow **(b)** *Fam (encantar, fascinar)* to enchant, entrance, fascinate, captivate; **esa canción me chifla** that song's fantastic; **nos chiflan los coches antiguos** we're mad on old cars
2 *vi (silbar)* to whistle
3 **chiflarse** *vpr Fam (volverse loco)* to go mad *o* round the bend; **c. por** to fall head over heels in love with

chiflido *nm* whistle, whistling

chigua *nf Am* large basket, hamper

chigüín *nm CAm* rachitic child

chihuahua *nm* chihuahua

chiíta *adj & nmf* Shiite

chilaba *nf (prenda)* jellaba, jellabah

chilango, -a *Méx Fam* **1** *adj* of *o* from Mexico City
2 *nm,f* person from Mexico City

chilca *nf Am Bot* boneset

Chile *n* Chile

chile *nm* **(a)** *Bot Culin CAm Méx* chilli (pepper) ▢ **c. molido** chili powder; **c. poblano** = large fresh chilli, similar to a green pepper **(b)** *CAm Fam (mentira)* lie

chileno, -a *adj & nm,f* Chilean

chilindrina *nf Fam* **(a)** *(cosilla)* trifle **(b)** *(anécdota)* anecdote, story; *(chiste)* joke; *(chanza)* joking, banter

chilindrón *nm* **(a)** *Culin* = sauce made from tomatoes and red peppers; **pollo al c.** = chicken in a tomato and red pepper sauce **(b)** *Naipes* = type of card game

chilla *nf Caza* decoy, bird call

chillar *vi* **(a)** *(persona)* to scream, shriek, shout, cry; *(cerdo)* to squeal; *(ratón)* to squeak; *(pájaro)* to squawk, screech; *(radio)* to blare; *(frenos)* to screech, squeal; *(puerta, ventana)* to creak, squeak; *Fam* **chillarle a algn** to give sb a dressing-down **(b)** *Fig (protestar)* to protest, complain; **¡no chilles!** stop moaning! **(c)** *(colores)* to be loud *o* gaudy, clash

chillería *nf* **(a)** *(griterío)* screaming, shrieking, yelling, howling **(b)** *(regaño)* dressing-down, telling-off, reprimand

chillido *nm (de persona)* scream, shriek, shout, cry; *(de cerdo)* squeal; *(de ratón)* squeak; *(de pájaro)* squawk; screech; *(de frenos)* screech, squeal; *(de puerta, ventana)* creaking, squeaking

chillón, -ona 1 *adj* **(a)** *(voz)* shrill, high-pitched; *(sonido)* harsh, strident, screechy **(b)** *(color)* loud, gaudy, shocking
  2 *nm,f* loud person

chilmole *nm Méx Culin* = tomato, onion, and pepper sauce

chilpayate, -a *nm,f Méx Fam* kid

chimbo *nm Am* = sweet made from egg yolk, syrup and almonds

chimenea *nf* **(a)** *(conducto, tubo)* chimney; *(de barco)* funnel, stack ❑ **c. de ventilación** air shaft **(b)** *(hogar abierto)* fireplace, hearth ❑ **c. (francesa)** fireplace with a mantelpiece **(c)** *Fam (cabeza)* nut, block; **no andar bien de la c.** to be off one's rocker

chimichurri *nm RP* = barbecue sauce made from garlic, parsley, oregano and vinegar

chimpancé *nm* chimpanzee

China *n* China

china¹ *nf* **(a)** *(piedra)* pebble, small stone; *Fam* **tocarle a uno la c.** to have bad luck, be left carrying the can **(b)** *Argot (droga)* deal **(c)** *Am Pey (india)* Indian woman **(d)** *RP (mujer del gaucho)* = gaucho's wife

china² *nf (porcelana)* china; *(vajilla)* china, chinaware

chinchar *Fam* **1** *vt (fastidiar)* to annoy, pester, bug; **eso es lo que más me chincha** that's what bugs me most of all
  2 chincharse *vpr (fastidiarse)* to grin and bear it, get on with it; **¡chínchate!, ¡para que te chinches!** so there!; **no me hizo caso, pues ahora, que se chinche** he didn't listen to me, so now he'll have to lump it

chincharrero *nm* flea pit, bug-infested place

chinche 1 *adj Fam* annoying
  2 *nf o nm (insecto)* bedbug; *Fam* **caer** *o* **morir como chinches** to drop *o* die like flies
  3 *nf Am (chincheta) Br* drawing pin, *US* thumbtack
  4 *nmf Fam (persona)* pest, pain

chincheta *nf Esp Br* drawing pin, *US* thumbtack

chinchilla *nf* chinchilla

chinchín *nm* **(a)** *(ruido)* chink, clash and tinkle; *Mús (orquesta)* tinny music; *(brindis)* toast, chin-chin; **¡c.!** cheers!, (to) your (good) health!; **hacer c. con las copas** to clink glasses **(b)** *CAm (sonajero)* baby's rattle

chinchón® *nm* aniseed liquor

chinchorro *nm* **(a)** *Méx (red)* dragnet **(b)** *(bote)* dinghy

chinchoso, -a *adj Fam Fig* wearisome, tiresome

chinchulines *nmpl Andes RP (plato)* = piece of sheep or cow intestine, plaited and then roasted

chinear *vt CAm* **(a)** *(niño)* to carry in one's arms, piggyback **(b)** *(mimar)* to pamper, spoil

chinela *nf (zapatilla)* slipper, mule; *(chanclo)* clog

chinero *nm Mueb* china cupboard *o* cabinet; *(alacena)* dresser

chinesco, -a *adj* Chinese; **sombras chinescas** shadow theatre *sing*

chinga *nf* **(a)** *CAm Ven (colilla)* cigar end **(b)** *Ven (borrachera)* drunkenness **(c)** *CAm Ven (en el juego)* = fee paid by gamblers **(d)** *Méx muy Fam (paliza)* **me dieron una c.** they kicked the shit out of me **(e)** *Méx muy Fam (trabajo duro)* **es una c.** it's a bitch of a job **(f)** *Méx muy Fam (fastidio)* pain in the *Br* arse *o US* ass

chingada *nf Méx Vulg Ofens* **hijo de la c.** son of a bitch; **¡vete a la c.!** bugger off!

chingadera *nf Méx Fam* **¡deja de hacer chingaderas!** stop mucking about!

chingado, -a *adj* **(a)** *Esp Méx muy Fam (estropeado)* bust, *Br* knackered **(b)** *Méx Vulg (como intensificador)* fucking

chingana *nf Am* **(a)** *(taberna)* tavern, bar, saloon; dance hall **(b)** *(fiesta)* wild party, rowdy celebration

chingar [38] **1** *vt* **(a)** *Esp Méx muy Fam (estropear)* to bust, *Br* knacker **(b)** *Esp Méx muy Fam* **c. a algn** *(molestar)* to get up sb's nose, piss sb off **(c)** *Esp Méx Vulg (copular con)* to screw, fuck; *Méx* **¡chinga tu madre!** fuck you! **(d)** *Méx muy Fam (beber)* to drink a lot of **(e)** *Méx muy Fam* **me chingaron en el examen** *(me suspendieron)* I flunked the exam **(f)** *Méx muy Fam* **chingarle a algn plata** *(estafarlo)* to screw sb out of some money
  2 *vi* **(a)** *Esp Méx Vulg (copular)* to screw, fuck **(b)** *Méx Fam (molestar)* **¡deja de c.!** stop pissing me off!
  3 chingarse *vpr Méx muy Fam* **(a)** *(estropearse)* to pack in, conk out **(b)** *(comerse)* to scoff, wolf down

chingo, -a 1 *adj* **(a)** *CAm (cuchillo)* blunt; *(animal)* tailless; *(vestido)* short **(b)** *CAm Ven (nariz)* snub
  2 chingos *nmpl CAm (ropa)* underwear *sing*

chingón, -ona *adj Méx muy Fam (muy bueno)* fantastic, great, *US* neat

chinita *nf* **(a)** *Am (criada)* maid **(b)** *Chile (animal) Br* ladybird, *US* ladybug

chino, -a 1 *adj* **(a)** *(de la China)* Chinese **(b)** *Am (mestizo)* of mixed ancestry
  2 *nm,f (persona)* Chinese person; *Fam* **un trabajo de chinos** a fiddly task *o* piece of work; *Fam* **engañar a algn como a un c.** to take sb for a ride
  3 *nm* **(a)** *(idioma)* Chinese; *Fam* **eso me suena c.** it's all Greek to me **(b)** *(colador)* sieve **(c)** *(piedra)* pebble, stone; **juego de los chinos** = guessing game in which pebbles *o* coins are hidden in clenched fists **(d)** *Méx* **chinos** *(rizos)* curls

chip *(pl* **chips)** *nm Inform* chip

chipa *nf Col* straw fruit basket

chipén *adj Fam* **de c.** great, terrific, fantastic

chipirón *nm (pez)* baby squid

Chipre *n* Cyprus

chipriota *adj & nmf* Cypriot

chiqueadores *nmpl Méx* = poultice for headaches

chiquear 1 *vt Cuba Méx* **(a)** *(mimar)* to pamper, spoil **(b)** *(adular)* to flatter
  2 chiquearse *vpr* **(a)** *CAm (pavonearse)* to seek flattery **(b)** *Am (contonearse)* to swagger along

chiquero *nm (corral)* stockyard; *(pocilga)* pigsty

chiquigüite 1 *adj Méx (abobado)* dim-witted, dumb
  2 *nm CAm (cesto)* basket without handles

chiquillada *nf (travesura)* childish prank; *(niñería)* childish thing; **hacer chiquilladas** to behave childishly

chiquillería *nf Fam* crowd of noisy kids *o* youngsters

chiquillo, -a *nm,f* kid, youngster; **portarse como un c.** to behave like a child

chiquitín, -ina 1 *adj (pequeño)* tiny, weeny
  2 *nm,f (niño)* tiny tot

chiquito, -a 1 *adj (pequeño)* tiny, weeny, very small
  2 *nm,f (niño)* tiny tot, kid; *Fam* **no andarse con chiquitas** not to beat about the bush
  3 *nm* **(a)** *Esp (de vino)* = small glass of wine **(b)** *RP Fam (instante)* minute; **espere un c.** wait a minute

chiribita *nf* **(a)** *(chispa)* spark; *Fam* **echar chiribitas** to be furious *o* hopping mad **(b)** **chiribitas** *Fam* spots before the eyes **(c)** *Bot* daisy

chiribitil *nm (desván)* attic, loft, garret; *(cuchitril)* tiny room, cubbyhole

chirigota *nf Fam* joke; **estar de c.** to be joking; **tomarse algo a c.** to take sth as a joke

chirimbolo *nm Fam* thing, thingummyjig, whatsit

chirimiri *nm* drizzle, fine misty rain

chirimoya *nf (fruto)* custard apple

chirimoyo *nm (árbol)* custard apple tree

chiringo *nm Méx* = small piece of sth

chiringuito *nm (en playa etc)* refreshment stall o stand; *(en carretera)* roadside o seaside snack bar; **montarse un c.** to set up a small business

chirinola *nf* (a) *(debate)* heated discussion; *(discusión)* quarrel, row (b) *(fruslería)* trifle; **estar de c.** to be in a good mood (c) *(juego)* skittles *pl* (d) *(conversación)* lengthy conversation

chiripa *nf* (a) *Bill* fluke, scratch, lucky stroke (b) *Fam Fig* **de** o **por c.** by a fluke, by chance; **cogió el tren por c.** it was sheer luck that he caught the train

chirivía *nf* (a) *Bot* parsnip (b) *Orn* wagtail

chirla *nf (pez)* small clam

chirle *adj Fam* insipid

chirlo *nm (herida)* gash, slash; *(cicatriz)* scar

chirola *nf* (a) *CAm Argot (cárcel)* clink, nick (b) *Arg (moneda)* = coin of little value

chirona *nf Esp Argot (cárcel)* clink, nick; **estar en c.** to be in the clink o nick, be inside

chirriar [32] *vi (sonar)* to screech; *(puerta, madera)* to creak; *(bisagra, muelles)* to squeak

chirriar *vi* [13] (a) *(gozne, puerta)* to creak; *(frenos)* to screech, squeal (b) *(pájaro)* to squawk, screech

chirrido *nm* (a) *(de gozne, puerta)* creak, creaking; *(de frenos)* screech, screeching, squeal, squealing (b) *(de pájaro)* squawk, squawking, screech, screeching

chirrión *nm Am (látigo)* leather whip

chirusa *nf*, **chiruza** *nf Am Fam* coarse o uncouth woman

chis *interj (¡silencio!)* sh!, ssh!, hush!

chischás *nm (de espada)* clash, clashing

chiscón *nm* hut, hovel

chisgarabís *nm Fam (entrometido)* busybody, meddler

chisme *nm* (a) *(habladuría)* piece of gossip; **chismes** gossip, tittle-tattle; **siempre andan con chismes** they're always gossiping (b) *Fam (trasto)* knick-knack; *(utensilio)* gadget; **chismes** *(cosas)* things, odds and ends; **tiene mil y un chismes eléctricos** she's got tons of electrical gadgets; **coge tus chismes y vete** pack your bags and go; *(dispositivo)* **hay que apretar este c.** you have to press this thing here

chismear *Am vi* to gossip

chismografía *nf Hum* gossip, gossiping

chismorrear *vi Fam* to gossip

chismorreo *nm Fam* gossip, gossiping

chismoso, -a 1 *adj (murmurador)* gossipy, gossiping
2 *nm,f (individuo)* gossip, gossipmonger

chispa 1 *nf* (a) *(de la lumbre)* spark; *Elec* spark, flash; *Fig* sparkle, glitter; *Fam* **echar chispas, estar uno que echa chispas** to be very annoyed (b) *Fam (pedacito, un poco)* bit, tiny amount; **ni c.** nothing at all; **una c. de coñac** a drop of brandy; **una c. de sal** a pinch of salt; *Fig* **no tiene ni c. de gracia** it's not a bit funny; *Fig* **no tienen ni c. de inteligencia** they haven't an ounce of intelligence (c) *Meteor (gota de lluvia)* drop, droplet; **caen chispas** it's spitting (d) *Fam (agudeza, gracia)* wit, sparkle; *(inteligencia)* intelligence; *(viveza)* liveliness; **ser una c.** to be very bright;

tener c. to be witty o funny, be a real live wire; **una película con c.** a brilliant movie o *Br* film (e) *Fam (borrachera)* drunkenness; **coger** o **pillar una c.** to ˙get sloshed; **¡menuda c. llevabas anoche!** you were well and truly canned last night! (f) *(mentira)* lie
2 *adj Méx (gracioso)* amusing

chispazo *nm* (a) *(de la lumbre)* spark; *Fig (brote)* **aquello fue el c. que originó el incidente** that was what sparked off the incident; *Fig* **c. de ingenio** flash of genius (b) *Fam (chisme, cotilleo)* piece of gossip

chispeante *adj* sparkling; *Fig* scintillating, brilliant

chispear *vi* (a) *(echar chispas)* to spark, throw out sparks; *Fig (relucir)* to sparkle (b) *Meteor (lloviznar)* to spit

chisporrotear *vi (fuego)* to spark, throw out sparks; *(leña)* to crackle; *(aceite)* to splutter, spit; *(carne)* to sizzle

chisporroteo *nm (del fuego)* sparking; *(de la leña)* crackling; *(del aceite)* spluttering, spitting; *(de la carne)* sizzling

chisquero *nm* pocket lighter

chist *interj* (a) *(¡silencio!)* sh!, ssh!, hush! (b) *(para llamar la atención)* psst!

chistar *vi* to speak; **no c.** not to say a word; **sin c.** without saying a word

chiste *nm* (a) *(cuento gracioso)* joke, funny story; **caer en el c.** to get the joke; **contar un c.** to tell a joke; *Irón* **tener c.** to be funny; **la cosa no tiene c.** it's no joke; **tomar algo a c.** to take sth as a joke □ **c. verde,** *Méx* **c. colorado** blue joke, dirty joke (b) *(dibujo humorístico)* cartoon

chistera *nf* (a) *(sombrero de copa)* top hat (b) *Dep (guante de mimbre) (en pelota)* basketwork glove (c) *(cesta de pescador)* fish basket, angler's basket

chistoso, -a 1 *adj (persona)* funny, witty, fond of joking; *(anécdota, suceso)* funny, amusing
2 *nm,f (bromista)* joker, comic, comedian

chistu *nm* Basque flute

chistulari *nm* Basque flute player

chita *nf* (a) *Anat* anklebone (b) *(juego)* jacks *pl*, knucklebones *pl*, quoits *pl* (c) *Esp Fam* **a la c. callando** *(en silencio)* quietly, unobtrusively; *(con disimulo)* secretly, stealthily

chitón *interj Fam (¡silencio!)* sh!, ssh!, hush!

chiva *nf* (a) *Am (perilla)* goatee beard (b) *CAm (manta)* woollen blanket (c) **chivas** *Méx (bártulos)* things, junk *sing*

chivar 1 *vt* (a) *Fam (molestar)* to annoy, pester (b) *Fam (acusar)* inform
2 chivarse *vpr* (a) *Esp Fam* to tell, *Br* split; **c. a la policía** to inform the police (b) *Am Vulg (fastidiarse)* to get cross

chivatazo *nm Esp Fam (soplo)* informing; *(advertencia)* tip-off; **dar el c.** to squeal, *Br* grass

chivatear *vi Fam Esp (soplonear)* to squeal, *Br* grass

chivato, -a 1 *nm,f Esp Fam (delator) Br* grass, *US* rat; *(acusica)* telltale
2 *nm* (a) *(dispositivo)* device, gadget (b) *Zool* kid, young goat (c) *Ven Fam (pez gordo)* big cheese

chivo, -a¹ *nm,f Zool* kid, young goat; *Fig* **c. expiatorio** scapegoat; *Fam* **estar como un c.** o **una chiva** to be mad

chivo² *nm Méx (salario)* day's wage

chivudo, -a *adj Arg Cuba Ven* bearded

choc *(pl* **chocs)** *nm Med* shock; **c. nervioso** nervous shock

chocante *adj* (a) *(persona)* funny, witty (b) *(cosa)* surprising, startling; *(raro)* strange; *(escandaloso)* shocking, offensive (c) *RP (indigno)* unworthy (d) *Am Fam (antipático)* **no la invitaron por c.** she wasn't invited because she's such a pain

chocar [59] **1** *vi* (a) *(topar)* to crash, collide; *Aut* **c. con** o

contra to crash into, run into, collide with; **chocaron dos autobuses** two buses collided, two buses crashed (into each other); *(pelota)* **c. contra** to hit, strike **(b)** *Mil* to clash, fight **(c)** *Fig (en discusión)* to clash, fall out

2 *vt* **(a)** *(gen)* to clink; *(la mano)* to shake; **vamos a chocar las copas y brindaremos por Juan** let's raise our glasses and toast Juan; *Fam* **¡chócala!, ¡choca esos cinco!** shake (on it)!, put it there! **(b)** *Fig (sorprender)* to surprise, startle; *(extrañar)* to shock; *(causar enfado)* to annoy; **me chocó que no me contestara** I was very surprised that he didn't reply

chocarrería *nf (chiste grosero)* coarse o dirty joke

chocarrero, -a *adj* coarse, vulgar

chochaperdiz *nf Orn* woodcock

chochear *vi* **(a)** *(de viejo)* to dodder, be senile **(b)** *(de cariño)* to be soft

chochera *nf*, **chochez** *nf* **(a)** *(vejez)* dotage, senility **(b)** *(sentimentalismo)* silliness, sentimentality

chochín *nm Orn* wren

chocho[1] *nm* **(a)** *(altramuz)* lupin **(b)** *Esp Méx Vulg (de mujer) Br* fanny, *US* beaver

chocho, -a[2] *adj* **(a)** *(senil)* doddering, senile; **viejo c.** old dodderer **(b)** *(sentimental)* soft, sentimental

choclo[1] *nm (chanclo) (de madera)* clog; *(de goma)* overshoe, galosh

choclo[2] *nm* **(a)** *Andes RP* corncob, ear of maize o *US* corn; *Fam* **¡qué c.!** what a drag! **(b)** *Culin* = stew made with tender maize **(c)** *Arg (percance)* mishap **(d)** *Méx (zapato)* = flat shoe worn by men; *Fam* **meter el c.** to put one's foot in it

choco, -a 1 *adj CAm Chile Méx (persona) (cojo)* one-legged; *(manco)* one-armed

2 *nm,f* **(a)** *Col (persona morena)* dark-skinned person **(b)** *CAm Chile Méx (tullido) (cojo)* one-legged person; *(manco)* one-armed person

3 *nm* **(a)** *(sepia)* cuttlefish **(b)** *Andes (perro)* spaniel **(c)** *Andes* **chocos** curls

chocolate *nm* **(a)** *Culin* chocolate; *(bebida)* drinking chocolate, cocoa ❑ **c. blanco** white chocolate; **c. con leche** milk chocolate; **tableta de c.** bar of chocolate; *Fam* **las cosas claras y el c. espeso** let's get things clear **(b)** *Esp Argot (drogas)* dope, hashish

chocolatera *nf* **(a)** *(recipiente)* chocolate pot **(b)** *Fam (trasto)* piece of junk; *(coche)* old banger

chocolatería *nf (fábrica)* chocolate factory; *(establecimiento)* = café serving drinking chocolate

chocolatero, -a 1 *adj* fond of chocolate, chocolate-loving

2 *(fabricante)* chocolate maker; *(vendedor)* chocolate vendor

chocolatina *nf (tableta)* bar of chocolate, chocolate bar; *(bombón)* chocolate

chófer *nmf Am*, **chofer** *nmf (gen)* driver; *(particular)* chauffeur; **coche de alquiler sin c.** self-drive hire car

cholla *nf* **(a)** *Fam (cabeza)* nut, block, head; *(inteligencia)* brains, grey matter **(b)** *CAm (llaga)* wound **(c)** *CAm (pereza)* laziness

chollar *vt CAm* **(a)** *(desollar)* to skin **(b)** *(mortificar)* to reprehend

chollo *nm Esp Fam* **(a)** *(sinecura)* cushy number, doddle **(b)** *(ganga)* bargain, snip

cholo, -a 1 *adj* **(a)** *Am (mestizo)* mestizo, half-caste **(b)** *Chile (cobarde)* cowardly **(c)** *Ven (querido)* dear, darling **(d)** *Ecuad (ordinario)* poor, common; **¡qué c.!** how common!

2 *nm,f* **(a)** *Am (mestizo)* half-caste, mestizo **(b)** *Am (indio)* = educated o westernized Indian **(c)** *Chile (cobarde)* coward

choloque *nm Am Bot* soapberry

chompa *nf Andes* jumper, pullover, jersey

chongo *nm Méx* **(a)** *(moño)* bun **(b)** **chongos** *Culin* = dessert made from milk curds served in syrup

chonta *nf CAm Perú* palm tree

chontal *nmf Am (inculto)* bumpkin, yokel, peasant

chop [ʃop] *(pl* **chops***) nm CSur (jarra)* beer mug *(cerveza)* (mug of) beer

chopera *nf* poplar grove

chopo[1] *nm* poplar ❑ **c. blanco** white poplar; **c. lombardo** Lombardy poplar; **c. negro** black poplar

chopo[2] *nm Mil Fam* gun; *Fig* **cargar con el c.** to join up

choque *nm* **(a)** *(gen)* impact; *Aut Ferroc etc* crash, smash, collision ❑ **c. de frente** head-on collision; **c. múltiple** pile-up **(b)** *Fig (contienda)* clash; *Mil* skirmish; **fuerzas de c.** shock troops; **policía de c.** riot police **(c)** *Med* shock

chorcha *nf* **(a)** *(cresta de ave)* crest **(b)** *Méx (grupo de gente alegre)* band, gang

chorizar [14] *Esp vt Fam* to pinch

chorizo *nm* **(a)** *Culin* chorizo, salami, = highly-seasoned pork sausage **(b)** *Esp Fam (ratero)* thief, pickpocket **(c)** *(en el circo)* balancing pole

chorlitejo *nm Orn* plover

chorlito *nm Orn* plover; *Fam Fig* **cabeza de c.** scatterbrain

chorra 1 *adj & nmf Vulg (tonto) Br* wally, *US* jerk; **hacer el c.** to act the fool

2 *nf* **(a)** *Fam (suerte)* luck; **¡qué c. tiene el tío ese!** how lucky can you get! **(b)** *Vulg (pene)* prick

chorrada *nf Esp Fam Br* rubbish, *US* garbage; **decir chorradas** to talk *Br* rubbish o *US* bull; **decir una c.** to say something stupid

chorrear 1 *vi* **(a)** *(salir a chorros)* to gush, spurt, spout; *Fam* **c. de sudor** to pour with sweat; *Fam* **tengo el abrigo que chorrea** my coat is dripping wet **(b)** *(gotear)* to drip, trickle **(c)** *Fam (suceder sin interrupción)* to flow

2 *vt Fam (reprender)* to tick off, give a dressing-down to

chorreo *nm* **(a)** *(en chorro)* gush, gushing, spurting, spouting **(b)** *(goteo)* dripping, trickle **(c)** *Fam (reprimenda)* ticking-off, dressing-down **(d)** *Fam Fig (gasto)* drain; **un c. de gastos** a drain on resources

chorrera *nf* **(a)** *(canalón)* gully, channel; *(señal de agua)* mark **(b)** *Cost* shirt frill **(c)** *Am (serie)* **una c. de** a string o stream of

chorretón *nm* **(a)** *(chorro)* spurt; **le caían chorretones de helado por la barbilla** he'd got ice cream all over his chin **(b)** *(mancha)* stain

chorrillo *nm Fig* steady flow o trickle

chorro *nm* **(a)** *(de agua etc)* jet, spurt; *(poca cantidad)* trickle; **salir a chorros** to gush forth **(b)** *Téc* jet, blast; **de propulsión a c.** jet propelled ❑ **avión a c.** jet plane; **c. de arena** sandblast; **c. de vapor** steam jet **(c)** *Fig* stream, flood, torrent; **a chorros** in plenty, in abundance, copiously; **hablar a chorros** *(atropelladamente)* to gabble; *(mucho)* to talk nineteen to the dozen; **llover a chorros** to pour down **(d)** *Am (grifo) Br* tap, *US* faucet **(e)** *RP Fam (ladrón)* thief

chotacabras *nm inv Orn* nightjar

chotear 1 *vt Fam* to make fun of

2 chotearse *vpr Fam* to joke; **c. de** to make fun of, scoff at

choteo *nm Fam* joking; **de c.** in fun; **tomarse algo a c.** to take sth as a joke

chotis *nm* schottische, = dance typical of Madrid

choto, -a *nm,f (cabrito)* kid, young goat; *(ternero)* sucking calf; *Fam* **estar como una chota** to be nuts

chova *nf Orn* **c. piquirroja** chough

chovinismo *nm* chauvinism

chovinista 1 *adj* chauvinistic
  2 *nmf* chauvinist
choza *nf* (**a**) *(cabaña)* hut (**b**) *Esp Fam (vivienda)* pad
christmas ['krismas] *nm inv* Christmas card
chubasco *nm* (**a**) *Meteor* heavy shower, downpour; **c. de nieve** brief snowstorm (**b**) *Fig (contratiempo)* setback; **aguantar el c.** to weather the storm
chubasquero *nm* raincoat
chúcaro, -a *adj Andes CAm RP (ganado)* wild, untamed
chucha *nf* (**a**) *Zool* bitch (**b**) *Arg Chile Vulg* cunt
chuchería *nf Fam* (**a**) *(fruslería)* trinket, knick-knack (**b**) *(bocado)* tidbit, snack; *(golosina)* sweet, *US* candy
chucho¹ *nm Fam* dog, mongrel
chucho² *nm RP* shiver
chucho³ *interj (al perro)* shoo!, scat!
chuchoca *nf SAm (para sazonar)* toasted maize
chuchumeco *nm PRico* (**a**) *(hombre mezquino)* contemptible fellow, rat (**b**) *(enano)* dwarf, runt
chuco, -a *adj Am (carne)* high, off
chucrut *nm* sauerkraut
chueca *nf* (**a**) *(de árbol)* stump (**b**) *Anat* ball and socket joint (**c**) *Dep* = game resembling hockey
chueco, -a *adj Am* (**a**) *(torcido)* crooked, bent, twisted (**b**) *(patizambo)* bow-legged, bandy-legged
chufa *nf Bot* chufa, groundnut; **horchata de c.** = milky drink made from **chufas**
chufla *nf Fam (broma)* joke; *(mofa)* taunt, jeer; **hacer c. de** to mock
chulada *nf Fam* (**a**) *(grosería)* coarse remark o act; *(desfachatez)* cheeky remark o act; *(mala jugada)* dirty trick (**b**) *(bravuconada)* brag, boast, swagger
chulapo, -a *nm,f,* **chulapón, -ona** *nm,f Fam* (**a**) *(hombre)* spiv, flash Harry, show-off; *(mujer)* flashy female (**b**) *(castizo)* = working-class person from Madrid
chulear *Fam* **1** *vt* (**a**) *(burlarse de)* to make fun of (**b**) *(robar)* to pinch, nick
  2 *vi (pavonearse)* to brag, swagger, throw one's weight about
  3 chulearse *vpr Fam* (**a**) *(burlarse)* **c. de** to make fun of (**b**) *(pavonearse)* to brag, swagger, throw one's weight about
chulería *nf Fam* (**a**) *(donaire)* charm, sparkle, wit (**b**) *(valentonería)* bragging, swaggering, bravado (**c**) *(vulgaridad)* coarseness, vulgarity (**d**) *(grosería)* coarse remark o behaviour; *(desfachatez)* cheeky remark o behaviour
chulesco, -a *adj Fam* (**a**) *(descarado)* cheeky, cocky (**b**) *(vulgar)* flashy, loud, brassy
chuleta *nf* (**a**) *Culin* chop, cutlet; **c. de cerdo** pork chop (**b**) *Fam (bofetada)* slap (**c**) *Esp Ven Educ Fam* crib (note), *US* trot (**d**) **chuletas** *Fam* whiskers, sideburns
chuletada *nf* barbecue
chulo, -a 1 *adj* (**a**) *Esp (descarado)* cocky; **ponerse c.** to get cocky (**b**) *Esp Méx Fam (bonito)* cool, *Br* top, *US* neat (**c**) *Esp Fam (lesionado)* **tengo la pata chula** I've done my leg in
  2 *nm,f* (**a**) *Esp (descarado)* cocky person (**b**) *(madrileño)* = lower-class native of 18th-19th century Madrid
  3 *nm Esp (proxeneta)* pimp
chumbe *nm* (**a**) *Col Ven (faja)* sash (**b**) *Andes Arg (sulfato)* zinc sulphide
chumbo, -a *adj* **higo c.** prickly pear
chumino *nm Esp muy Fam Br* fanny, *US* beaver
chunga *nf Esp Fam* joke, fun; **estar de c.** to be in a joking mood; **tomar algo a o en c.** to treat sth as a joke
chungo, -a *adj Fam (malo)* naff; *(sin valor)* worthless; **es un tío muy c.** he's a really nasty piece of work

chunguear 1 *vi Fam* to joke
  2 chunguearse *vpr Fam* to joke; **c. de** *(broma)* to joke about; *(mofa)* to make fun of
chupa *nf Esp (prenda)* short jacket; *Fam* **poner a algn como c. de dómine** to give sb a dressing-down, haul sb over the coals
chupa-chups® *nm inv Esp* lollipop *(spherical)*
chupacirios *nm Pey Fam* Holy Joe, Holy Willie
chupada *nf (a un piruli etc)* suck; *(a un cigarro)* puff, drag; *(en pipa)* pull, puff; **dar chupadas a un cigarro** to puff at a cigar
chupado, -a 1 *pp de* **chupar**
  2 *adj* (**a**) *(flaco)* skinny, bony, thin; **de cara chupada** gaunt, hollow-cheeked (**b**) *Argot* **está c.** it's dead easy
chupador *nm (para bebé)* teething ring
chupar 1 *vt* (**a**) *(gen)* to suck; *(un cigarro)* to puff at; *(beber a sorbos)* to sip; *Fam* **chuparle la sangre a algn** to bleed sb dry (**b**) *(lamer)* to lick (**c**) *(absorber)* to suck up, soak up, absorb (**d**) *Am (beber)* to booze on, tipple
  2 *vi Fam* (**a**) *(en deportes)* to hog the ball (**b**) *Am (beber)* to booze, tipple
  3 chuparse *vpr* (**a**) **c. el dedo** to suck one's thumb; **c. los dedos** to lick one's fingers; *Fam* **está para c. los dedos** it's really yummy; *Fam* **¡chúpate eso!** stick that in your pipe and smoke it! (**b**) *(consumirse)* to grow thin, waste away (**c**) *Esp Fam (aguantar)* to put up with; **nos chupamos toda la película** we sat through the whole film; **me chupé todo su viaje** I put up with all the details of his trip
chupatintas *nm inv Pey* penpusher, office drudge
chupete *nm (para bebé) Br* dummy, *US* pacifier
chupetear *vt* to suck at
chupeteo *nm* sucking
chupetón *nm* (**a**) *(con la lengua)* lick; *(con los labios)* suck; **dar un c. a algo** to lick sth (**b**) *Esp Fam (mordura en la piel)* lovebite, *US* hickey
chupi *adj Esp Fam* great, terrific, fantastic
chupinazo *nm* (**a**) *(cañonazo)* loud bang (**b**) *Ftb Fam* hard kick
chupito *nm* shot
chupón, -ona 1 *adj* (**a**) *(que chupa)* sucking (**b**) *Fam (gorrón)* sponging, scrounging
  2 *nm* (**a**) *Bot* sucker (**b**) *(piruli)* lollipop (**c**) *Méx Ven Br* dummy, *US* pacifier; *Andes CAm Méx (de biberón)* teat (**d**) *(desatrancador)* plunger
chupóptero, -a *nm,f Fam* sponger, scrounger
churrasco *nm* barbecued meat, barbecued steak
churrasquería *nf RP* steakhouse
churre *nm Fam* filth, grease
churrería *nf* fritter shop
churrero, -a *nm,f* (**a**) *(vendedor)* fritter maker, fritter seller (**b**) *Argot (afortunado)* lucky person
churrete *nm* dirty mark, grease spot
churria *nf Carib Col Guat* **churrias** diarrhoea *sing*, *US* diarrhea *sing*
churrigueresco, -a *adj* (**a**) *Arquit* churrigueresque, Spanish baroque (**b**) *Fig* excessively ornate, loud, flashy, tawdry
churro *nm* (**a**) *Culin* fritter, *US* cruller (**b**) *Fam (chapuza)* botch, mess, slapdash job (**c**) *Fam (chiripa)* fluke, piece of good luck
churruscar [59] **1** *vt* to burn
  2 churruscarse *vpr* to burn
churrusco *nm* piece of burnt toast
churumbel *nm Esp Fam* kid, child

chusco, -a¹ *adj (divertido)* funny, droll; *(gracioso)* witty

chusco² *nm* **(a)** *(mendrugo)* chunk of stale bread **(b)** *Mil Fam* ration bread

chusma *nf* rabble, mob, riffraff

chusmear *vi Am Fam* to gossip

chusmerío *nm RP* piece of gossip

chuspa *nf Andes RP* bag, pouch

chusquero *nm Mil Fam* ranker

chut *(pl* **chuts)** *nm Dep* shot, kick

chutar 1 *vi* **(a)** *Dep (a gol)* to shoot **(b)** *Esp Fam* to go well; **va que chuta** it's going really well; **¡y vas que chutas!** and then you're well away!

2 chutarse *vpr Esp (drogas) Argot* to fix, shoot up, mainline

chute *nm Esp Argot (drogas)* fix

chuza *nf Méx (en bolos)* strike

chuzo *nm (bastón)* metal-tipped stick; *Fam Fig* **caer chuzos de punta** to pour down, *Br* bucket down

CI *nm (abrev de* **cociente de inteligencia)** IQ

CIA ['θia] *nf (abrev de* **Central Intelligence Agency)** CIA

Cía., cía *(abrev de* **compañía)** Co

cianuro *nm Quim* cyanide

ciática *nf Med* sciatica

cibercafé *nm, Fam* **ciber** *nm* cybercafe

ciberdelito *nm Inform* cybercrime

ciberespacio *nm* cyberspace

cibernauta *nmf* Net user

cibernética *nf* cybernetics *sing*

cibernético, -a *adj* cybernetic

ciberokupa *nmf Inform* cybersquatter

ciberokupación *nm Inform* cybersquatting

cibersexo *nm* cybersex

cicatería *nf* stinginess, meanness

cicatero, -a 1 *adj* stingy, mean

2 *nm,f* miser

cicatriz *nf* scar

cicatrización *nf* healing

cicatrizante *adj* healing

cicatrizar [14] *v& vi* to heal

cicerone *nmf* guide, cicerone

ciclamen *nm* cyclamen

cíclico, -a *adj* cyclic, cyclical

ciclismo *nm* cycling

ciclista 1 *adj* cycle, cycling

2 *nmf* cyclist

ciclo *nm (gen)* cycle; *(de conferencias etc)* course, series □ **c. menstrual** menstrual cycle; **c. vital** life cycle

ciclocross *nm,* **ciclocrós** *nm* cyclo-cross

ciclomotor *nm* moped

ciclón *nm Meteor* cyclone; *Fig* **como un c.** like a whirlwind

cíclope *nm Mit* Cyclops

ciclópeo, -a *adj* gigantic, huge, massive

ciclostil *nm* cyclostyle, mimeograph

cicloturismo *nm* bicycle touring

cicloturista *nmf* = person on cycling holiday

ciclovía *nf Am (para bicicletas) Br* cycle lane, *US* bikeway

CICR *nm (abrev de* **Comité Internacional de la Cruz Roja)** IRCC

cicuta *nf* hemlock

cidra *nf (fruta)* citron

cidro *nm (árbol)* citron (tree)

ciego, -a 1 *adj* **(a)** *(persona)* blind; **a ciegas** blindly; *Fig* without a clue; **quedarse c.** to go blind; *Fig* **c. de cólera** blind with anger; *Fam* **ponerse c.** *Esp (bebiendo)* to get blind drunk; *Esp (drogas)* to get very stoned **(b)** *Constr* blocked up

2 *nm,f* blind person; **los ciegos** the blind *pl*

3 *nm* **(a)** *Anat* caecum **(b)** *Esp Fam (de droga)* trip; **tener/cogerse un c.** *(de alcohol)* to be/get blind drunk *o Br* pissed **(c)** *RP (en naipes)* = player who has no trump cards in their hand

cielo 1 *nm* **(a)** *(atmósfera)* sky; **a c. abierto** opencast, *US* opencut; *Fig* **venirse el c. abajo** *(llover)* to pour down; *(desmoralizarse)* to lose heart; *Fig* **ver el c. abierto** to see the way out *(of a difficulty)* **(b)** *Rel* heaven; *Fig* **bajado** *o* **caído del c.** *(oportuno)* heaven-sent; *(inesperado)* out of the blue; *Fig* **clamar al c.** to cry out to heaven; *Fig* **mover** *o* **remover c. y tierra** to move heaven and earth; *Fig* **ser un c.** to be an angel □ *Arquit* **c. raso** ceiling **(c)** *Anat (de la boca)* roof

2 *interj* **¡c. santo!** good heavens!

ciempiés *nm inv* centipede

cien *adj & nm inv* hundred; **c. libras** a *o* one hundred pounds; **es c. por c. cierto** it's one hundred per cent true; **éste es el que hace c.** this is the hundredth; *Fam* **ponerse a c.** to get worked up, be up to a hundred

ciénaga *nf* marsh, bog

ciencia *nf* **(a)** *(disciplina)* science; **hombre de c.** scientist; *Fig* **saber algo a c. cierta** to know something for certain □ *Lit Cin* **c. ficción** science fiction; **c. infusa** intuition; **ciencias empresariales** business studies; **ciencias exactas** mathematics; **ciencias ocultas** the occult *sing* **(b)** *(saber)* knowledge, erudition

cienmilésimo, -a *adj & nm,f,* **cienmillonésimo, -a** *adj & nm,f* hundred millionth

cieno *nm* mud, mire

cientificismo *nm* = over-emphasis on scientific ideas

científico, -a 1 *adj* scientific

2 *nm,f* scientist

cientista *nmf CSur* **c. social** sociologist

ciento *adj* hundred; **c. doce** a *o* one hundred and twelve; **por c.** per cent; **por cientos** by the hundred; *Fam* **c. y la madre** a crowd; *Fam* **dar c. y raya a algn** to run rings round sb

ciernes *nmpl* **en c.** *(en potencia)* in embryo *o* potential; **es un tenista en c.** he's got potential as a tennis player

cierre *nm* **(a)** *(acción)* closing, shutting; *(de fábrica)* shutdown; *Rad TV* close-down □ **c. patronal** lockout **(b)** *(mecanismo) (de bolso)* clasp; *(de una puerta, ventana)* catch; *(de una tienda)* shutter; *(prenda)* fastener □ *Aut* **c. centralizado** central locking; **c. de seguridad** safety lock **(c)** *Andes Méx RP (cremallera) Br* zip (fastener), *US* zipper; **c.** *Andes Méx* **relámpago** *o Chile* **eclair** *o Urug* **metálico** *Br* zip, *US* zipper

cierto, -a 1 *adj* **(a)** *(seguro)* sure, definite; *(verdadero)* right, true; **estar en lo c.** to be right; **lo c. es que** ... the fact is that ...; **por c.** by the way **(b)** *(algún)* certain; **ciertas personas** some people; **de cierta edad** elderly; **en ciertos casos** in certain *o* some cases

2 *adv* certainly

ciervo, -a *nm,f* deer; *(macho)* stag, hart; *(hembra)* doe, hind

cierzo *nm Meteor* north wind

cifra *nf* **(a)** *Mat (número)* figure, number **(b)** *(suma)* amount; **c. global** lump sum *o* **c. de negocios** turnover **(c)** *(código)* cipher, code; **en c.** in code; *Fig* mysteriously

cifrado, -a 1 *pp de* **cifrar**

2 *adj* **(a)** *(en cifra)* coded, in code **(b)** *Fig (ilusión, esperanza)* placed

cifrar 1 vt (a) *(mensaje)* to encode (b) *Fig (ilusión, esperanza)* to place
  2 cifrarse vpr to amount o come to
cigala nf Dublin Bay prawn, scampi
cigarra nf cicada
cigarrera nf *(estuche)* cigar case
cigarrero, -a nm,f *(persona)* street tobacco seller
cigarrillo nm cigarette ❑ **c. con filtro** filter(-tip) cigarette
cigarro nm (a) *(puro)* cigar (b) *(cigarrillo)* cigarette
cigoto nm Biol zygote
cigüeña nf (a) Orn stork (b) Téc crank
cigüeñal nm Téc crankshaft
cilantro nm coriander
cilicio nm Rel *(prenda)* hair shirt
cilindrada nf Aut Téc cylinder capacity
cilíndrico, -a adj cylindric, cylindrical
cilindro nm (a) *(figura)* cylinder (b) CAm Méx *(organillo)* barrel organ
cima nf summit; Fml **dar c. a algo** to crown sth
cimarrón, -a Am **1** adj (a) Zool wild animal (b) Hist **esclavo c.** runaway slave
  2 nm,f Am Hist runaway slave
címbalo nm cymbal
cimborio nm, **cimborrio** nm Arquit cupola
cimbra nf (a) Arquit soffit (b) Constr centring, US centering
cimbrear 1 vt (a) *(gen)* to make quiver; *(caña)* to waggle (b) Constr to erect a centring o US centering for an arch
  2 cimbrearse vpr to sway
cimbreo nm (a) *(balanceo)* waggle, quiver (b) *(al andar)* sway, swaying
cimentación nf Constr (a) *(acción)* laying of foundations (b) *(cimientos)* foundation, foundations pl
cimentar [3] vt Constr to lay the foundations of; Fig *(amistad, idea)* to strengthen, consolidate
cimero, -a adj *(alto)* topmost; Fig *(sobresaliente)* foremost, most outstanding
cimientos nmpl Constr foundations; **echar** o **poner los c.** to lay the foundations; Fig **desde los c.** from the very start
cinamomo nm cinnamon (tree)
cinc *(pl* **cines)** nm Metal zinc
cincel nm chisel
cincelado, -a 1 pp de **cincelar**
  2 adj chiselled, US chiseled
  3 nm chiselling, US chiseling
cincelar vt to chisel
cincha nf Equit girth, US cinch
cincho nm (a) *(cinturón)* belt (b) *(aro de hierro)* hoop (c) Am *(de caballo)* girth, cinch
cinco inv **1** adj *(cardinal)* five; *(ordinal)* fifth; **el té de las c.** five o'clock tea
  2 nm five; Fam **¡choca** o **vengan esos c.!** put it there!, give me five!; *véase tamb* **ocho**
cincuenta inv **1** adj *(cardinal)* fifty; *(ordinal)* fiftieth
  2 nm fifty; *véase tamb* **ochenta** y **ocho**
cincuentavo, -a 1 adj fiftieth; **cincuentava parte** fiftieth
  2 nm,f fiftieth; *véase tamb* **octavo, -a**
cincuentena nf fifty
cincuentenario nm fiftieth anniversary
cincuentón, -ona adj & nm,f Fam fifty-year-old
cine nm (a) *(local)* cinema, US movie theater; **ir al c.** to go to the cinema, US go to the movies ❑ **c. de estreno** first-

run cinema (b) *(arte)* cinema; **hacer c.** to make movies, Br make films; Fam **ser de c.** to be fabulous ❑ **c. mudo/sonoro** silent/talking movies o Br films pl; **estrella de c.** movie o Br film star
cineasta nmf movie o Br film director, movie o Br film maker
cineclub nm *(pl* **cineclubs** o **cineclubes)** small film society
cinéfilo, -a nm,f Br film lover, US moviegoer
cinegética nf hunting
cinegético, -a adj o related to hunting
cinema nm véase **cine**
cinemateca nf véase **filmoteca**
cinemática nf kinematics *sing*
cinematografía nf movie o Br film making, cinematography
cinematográfico, -a adj cinematographic; **la industria cinematográfica** the movie o Br film industry
cinematógrafo nm movie projector, Br film projector
cinerama® nm Cinerama®
cinética nf kinetics *sing*
cinético, -a adj kinetic
cingalés, -esa adj & nm,f Singhalese
cíngaro, -a adj & nm,f Tzigane, gypsy
cínico, -a 1 adj cynical
  2 nm,f cynic
cinismo nm cynicism
cinta nf (a) *(tira)* band, strip; *(para adornar)* ribbon; Cost braid, edging; **c. para (sujetar) el pelo** headband (b) Téc tape ❑ **c. adhesiva** adhesive o sticky tape; RP *(esparadrapo)* surgical tape; **c. aislante** insulating tape; **c. de ametralladora** loading belt; **c. magnética** magnetic tape; **c. magnetofónica** recording tape; **c. métrica** tape measure; **c. transportadora** conveyor belt (c) Cin film
cinto nm *(cinturón)* belt; *(de sable)* swordbelt
cintura nf waist; Fam **meter a algn en c.** to bring sb into line
cinturón nm belt; Fig **apretarse el c.** to tighten one's belt ❑ **c. de castidad/seguridad** chastity/safety belt · **c. industrial/verde** industrial/green belt; Dep **c. negro** black belt
cipe adj CAm **niño c.** sickly child
cipote 1 adj stupid
  2 nm (a) Ofens *(persona)* tit, cunt (b) Vulg *(pene)* prick, cock
ciprés nm cypress
circense adj circus
circo nm (a) *(espectáculo)* circus (b) Geog cirque
circuito nm Elec Dep circuit ❑ TV **c. cerrado de televisión** closed circuit television; Téc **corto c.** short circuit
circulación nf (a) *(gen)* circulation; **fuera de c.** out of circulation; Fin **poner en/retirar de la c.** to put into/withdraw from circulation ❑ Med **c. de la sangre** o **sanguínea** blood circulation (b) Aut *(tráfico)* traffic; **una carretera de mucha c.** a very busy road ❑ **c. rodada** vehicular traffic; **código de la c.** highway code
circulante adj Fin **capital c.** working capital
circular 1 adj & nf circular
  2 vi (a) *(moverse)* to circulate, move, pass; *(líquido)* to flow; *(trenes, autobuses)* to run; **circulan muchos coches por esta calle** there's a lot of traffic on this street; **¡circulen!** move along, please!; **hacer c.** *(documento)* to circulate; *(líquido)* to make flow; Fig *(rumor)* to spread; **hoy no circulan trenes** there are no trains running today; *(en*

letrero) **peatón circule por la** *o* **su izquierda** pedestrians keep to the left (**b**) *Aut (conducir)* to drive; **c. por la izquierda/derecha** to drive on the left/right

circulatorio, -a *adj* circulatory

círculo *nm* (**a**) *(gen)* circle ❑ *Fig* **c. vicioso** vicious circle (**b**) *(club)* circle, club

circuncidar *vt* to circumcise

circuncisión *nf* circumcision

circunciso, -a *adj* circumcised

circundante *adj* surrounding

circundar *vt* to surround, encircle

circunferencia *nf* circumference

circunflejo *adj* & *nm* *Ling* circumflex

circunloquio *nm* circumlocution; **déjate de circunloquios** stop beating about the bush

circunnavegar [38] *vt* to circumnavigate, sail round

circunscribir (*pp* **circunscrito**) **1** *vt* *Geom* to circumscribe

2 circunscribirse *vpr* *Fig* to confine *o* limit oneself

circunscripción *nf* district ❑ **c. electoral** constituency

circunscrito, -a 1 *pp de* **circunscribir**

2 *adj* circumscribed

circunspección *nf* circumspection, seriousness

circunspecto, -a *adj* circumspect, serious, grave

circunstancia *nf* circumstance; **en estas circunstancias ...** under the circumstances ...; **estar a la altura de las circunstancias** to rise to the occasion; *Fam* **poner cara de circunstancias** to look grave

circunstancial *adj* circumstancial; *Ling* **complemento c.** adverbial complement

circunvalación *nf* (**a**) *Hist* circumvallation (**b**) *Aut* **carretera de c.** *Br* ring road, *US* beltway; **línea de c.** *(de tren)* circular line; *(de autobús)* circular route

circunvalar *vt* to circumvallate, surround

circunvolución *nf* (**a**) *(vuelta)* circumvolution (**b**) *Anat (cerebral)* convolution

cirílico, -a *adj* *Ling* Cyrillic

cirio *nm* wax candle; *Fam* **armar un c.** to kick up a rumpus

cirro *nm* *Meteor* cirrus

cirrosis *nf* *Med* cirrhosis

cirrótico, -a *adj* *Med* cirrhotic; *Fam Fig* **estar c.** to be an alcoholic

cirrótico, -a *adj* cirrhotic

ciruela *nf* plum ❑ **c. claudia** greengage; **c. pasa** prune

ciruelo *nm* plum tree

cirugía *nf* surgery ❑ **c. estética** *o* **plástica** plastic surgery

cirujano, -a *nm,f* surgeon

ciscar [59] *vt* *Cuba Méx* to bother, distract

cisco *nm* (**a**) *(carbón)* charcoal (**b**) *Fam (trifulca)* row, rumpus; *Fam* **estoy hecho c.** I'm done for; *Fam* **hacer c. algo** to smash sth to pieces

Cisjordania *nf* the West Bank

cisma *nm* (**a**) *Rel* schism (**b**) *Pol* split

cismático, -a *adj* & *nm,f* schismatic

cisne *nm* swan

cisterna *nf* cistern, tank ❑ **buque** *o* **camión c.** tanker

cistitis *nf inv* *Med* cystitis

cita *nf* (**a**) *(convocatoria)* appointment; **en el congreso se dieron c. casi mil especialistas** almost a thousand experts attended the conference; **tener una c. con algn** to have arranged to meet sb (**b**) *(amorosa)* date ❑ **casa de citas** house of ill repute, brothel (**c**) *(mención)* quotation

citación *nf* *Jur* citation, summons *sing*

citado, -a 1 *pp de* **citar**

2 *adj* aforementioned

citar 1 *vt* (**a**) *(dar cita)* to arrange to meet, make an appointment with (**b**) *Jur* to summon; **c. a algn a juicio** to call sb as a witness (**c**) *(mencionar)* to quote; **cito de memoria** I'm quoting from memory; **para c. sólo un ejemplo** to give just one example

2 citarse *vpr* to arrange to meet, make a date (**con** with)

cítara *nf* zither, sitar

citología *nf* *Biol* cytology

citoplasma *nm* cytoplasm

cítrico, -a 1 *adj* citric, citrus

2 cítricos *nmpl* citrus fruits

ciudad *nf* town, city; **ir a la c.** to go to *o* into town; **la gran c.** the big city ❑ **c. dormitorio** dormitory suburb *o* town; **c. jardín** garden city; **c. satélite** satellite town; **c. universitaria** university campus

ciudadanía *nf* citizenship

ciudadano, -a 1 *adj* civic; **deberes ciudadanos** civic duties

2 *nm,f* citizen

ciudadela *nf* citadel, fortress

ciuredano, -a *nm,f* *Inform* netizen

civeta *nf* *Zool* civet

cívico, -a *adj* civic

civil 1 *adj* (**a**) *(no religioso)* civil; **matrimonio c.** civil marriage; **casarse por lo c.** to get married in a registry office (**b**) *Mil* civilian

2 *nm* *(no militar, no religioso)* civilian

civilización *nf* civilization

civilizado, -a 1 *pp de* **civilizar**

2 *adj* civilized

civilizador, -a 1 *adj* civilizing

2 *nm,f* civilizer

civilizar [14] **1** *vt* to civilize

2 civilizarse *vpr* to become civilized

civismo *nm* good citizenship, civility

cizalla *nf*, **cizallas** *nfpl* (**a**) *(herramienta)* metal shears *pl*, wire cutters *pl* (**b**) *Metal* metal clippings *pl* *o* cuttings *pl*

cizaña *nf* *Bot* bearded darnel; *Fig* **sembrar c.** to sow discord

cl *(abrev de* **centilitro(s))** cl

clamar *vt* to cry out for, clamour *o* *US* clamor 'for; **c. venganza** to cry out for revenge

clamor *nm* clamour, *US* clamor

clamoroso, -a *adj* clamorous; **un éxito c.** an overwhelming success

clan *nm* clan

clandestinidad *nf* secrecy; **en la c.** underground, in secrecy

clandestino, -a *adj* clandestine, underground, secret

claque *nf* *Fig Teat* claque

claqué *nm* tap dancing

claqueta *nf* clapperboard

clara *nf* (**a**) *(de huevo)* white (**b**) *Esp Fam (bebida)* shandy

claraboya *nf* *Arquit* skylight

claramente *adv* clearly

clarear 1 *vt* to light up; *(habitación)* to illuminate; *(color)* to make lighter

2 *vi* (**a**) *(amanecer)* to dawn (**b**) *Meteor (despejar)* to clear up (**c**) *Tex (transparentar)* to wear thin, become transparent

3 clarearse *vpr* to let the light through; *Fig (delatarse)* to give oneself away

clarete *adj & nm (vino)* claret

claridad *nf* (**a**) *(luz)* light, brightness (**b**) *(inteligibilidad)* clearness, clarity; **con c.** clearly

clarificación *nf* clarification

clarificador, -a 1 *adj* clarifying
  2 *nm,f* clarifier

clarificar [59] *vt* to clarify, clear up

clarín *nm* bugle; **toque de c.** bugle call

clarinete *nm* (**a**) *(instrumento)* clarinet (**b**) *(persona)* clarinettist

clarinetista *nmf* clarinettist

clarividencia *nf* (**a**) *(lucidez)* lucidity, clear thinking (**b**) *(percepción)* clairvoyance, far-sightedness

clarividente 1 *adj* (**a**) *(lúcido)* lucid (**b**) *(perceptivo)* clairvoyant, far-sighted
  2 *nmf (persona)* clairvoyant

claro, -a 1 *adj* (**a**) *(gen)* clear; **dejar algo c.** to make sth clear; **¿está c.?** is that clear?; *Fig* **más c. que el agua** as clear as daylight; *Fig* **mente clara** clear mind; *Fam* **a las claras** openly; *Esp Fam* **¡lo llevas c.!** you've got it coming to you! (**b**) *(bien iluminado)* bright, well-lit (**c**) *(líquido, salsa)* thin (**d**) *(color)* light
  2 *interj* of course!; **¡c. que no!** of course not!; **¡c. que sí!** certainly!
  3 *nm* (**a**) *(espacio)* gap, space; *(en un bosque)* clearing; **c. de luna** moonlight; **dejar un c.** to leave a gap (**b**) *Meteor* bright spell
  4 *adv* clearly; **¡habla c.!** make yourself clear!; *Fig* **no lo veo (nada) c.** I can't see it working

claroscuro *nm Arte* chiaroscuro

clase *nf* (**a**) *(grupo, distinción)* class; **tener c.** to have class ◻ **c. alta/media** upper/middle class; **c. obrera/dirigente** working/ruling class; **c. social** social class; **c. turista** tourist class; **clases pasivas** pensioners; **primera/segunda c.** first/second class (**b**) *Educ (curso)* class; **dar c. a algn** to teach sb ◻ **c. de conducir** *o Am* **manejar** driving lesson; **c. particular** private class *o* lesson (**c**) *Educ (aula)* classroom; *Univ* lecture hall (**d**) *(tipo)* kind, sort; **de buena c.** good quality; **de toda(s) clase(s)** of all kinds *o* sorts; **toda c. de ...** all kinds of ...

clasicismo *nm* classicism

clasicista 1 *adj* classicistic
  2 *nmf* classicist

clásico, -a 1 *adj* (**a**) *(de la Antigüedad)* classical; **música clásica** classical music (**b**) *(típico)* classic, typical; **es el ejemplo c.** that's the classic example (**c**) *(en el vestir)* classic
  2 *nm* classic
  3 clásicas *nfpl Ling* the classics

clasificación *nf* (**a**) *(gen)* classification; *Dep* league, table; *(de discos)* ≃ top twenty (**b**) *(distribución)* sorting (out)

clasificador, -a 1 *adj* classifying
  2 *nm,f* classifier
  3 *nm* filing cabinet

clasificar [59] **1** *vt* to classify, class; *(libros, cartas)* to sort (out)
  2 clasificarse *vpr* (**a**) *Dep* to qualify; **el equipo se clasificó para la final** the team qualified for the final (**b**) *Dep (llegar)* to come; **se clasificó segundo** he came (in) second

clasismo *nm* class-consciousness

clasista 1 *adj* class-conscious
  2 *nmf* class-conscious person

claudicación *nf* submission, yielding

claudicar [59] *vi* to yield, give in

claustro *nm* (**a**) *Arquit* cloister (**b**) *Rel Fig* monastic life (**c**) *Educ (profesores)* staff; *(junta)* staff meeting; *Univ* senate

claustrofobia *nf* claustrophobia

claustrofóbico, -a *adj* claustrophobic

cláusula *nf* clause

clausura *nf* (**a**) *(cierre)* closure, closing ◻ **ceremonia de c.** closing ceremony (**b**) *Rel* enclosure ◻ **monja de c.** enclosed nun

clausurar *vt (curso, conferencia)* to close; *(debate)* to end, conclude; *Jur (bar, local)* to close (down)

clavadista *nmf CAm Méx* diver

clavado, -a 1 *pp de* clavar
  2 *adj* (**a**) *(con clavos)* nail-studded, nailed (**b**) *(fijo)* firmly fixed; *Fig* **con la mirada clavada en ...** staring at ...; *Fam* **dejar a algn c.** to leave sb dumbfounded (**c**) *Fam (exacto)* **es c. a su padre** he's the spitting image of his father; **son las diez clavadas** it's ten o'clock sharp *o* on the dot

clavar 1 *vt* (**a**) *(gen)* to nail; *(clavo)* to bang *o* hammer in; *(estaca)* to drive; *Fig* **c. los ojos en ...** to rivet one's eyes on ... (**b**) *Fam (cobrar caro)* to sting *o* fleece
  2 clavarse *vpr* (**a**) *(gen)* to get; **c. un cuchillo** to thrust a knife in one's hand/body; **c. una astilla** to get a splinter in one's finger; **c. una espina** to prick oneself on a thorn (**b**) *Méx Fam (dedicarse intensamente)* **c. a estudiar** to study hard (**c**) *Méx Fam* **c. de algn** *(enamorarse)* to fall head over heels in love with sb (**d**) *RP Fam (estar confinado)* **c. en casa** to be stuck at home

clave 1 *nm* harpsichord
  2 *nf* (**a**) *(de un enigma)* key, clue; **la c. de su actitud** the key to her attitude (**b**) *(código)* key, cipher; **en c.** in code ◻ **c. de acceso** access code (**c**) *Mús (tono)* key; *(signo)* clef (**d**) *Arquit* keystone (**e**) *Inform* password
  3 *adj (importante)* important; **la palabra c.** the key word; **ocupa un puesto clave** he holds a top position

clavel *nm* carnation

clavellina *nf Bot* pink

clavetear *vt* to stud with nails

clavicordio *nm* clavichord

clavícula *nf Anat* clavicle, collarbone

clavija *nf* (**a**) *Téc* peg; *Fig* **apretarle las clavijas a algn** to tighten the screws on sb (**b**) *Elec Tel* plug

clavo *nm* (**a**) *(pieza metálica)* nail, stud; *Fig* **agarrarse a un c. ardiendo** to clutch at straws; *Fig* **dar en el c.** to hit the nail on the head; *Fig* **remachar el c.** to make matters worse; *Fam* **como un c.** very punctual; *Fam* **estar sin un c.** to be dead broke (**b**) *Bot* clove (**c**) *Vulg (pene)* prick, horn

claxon *nm Aut* horn, hooter; **tocar el c.** to sound the horn

clemencia *nf* mercy, clemency

clemente *adj* merciful, clement

clementina *nf Bot* clementine

cleptomanía *nf* kleptomania

cleptómano, -a *adj & nm,f* kleptomaniac

clerecía *nf* clergy

clerical 1 *adj* clerical
  2 *nmf* clericalist

clericalismo *nm* clericalism

clérigo *nm* priest

clero *nm* clergy

clic *(pl* **clics)** *nm Inform* click; **hacer c.** to click; **hacer doble c.** to double click

clicar [59] *Inform* **1** *vt* to click on
  2 *vi* to click

cliché *nm* (**a**) *Fot* negative (**b**) *Impr* plate (**c**) *(lugar común)* cliché

click (*pl* **clicks**) *nm véase* **clic**

cliente *nmf* customer, client

clientela *nf* customers *pl*, clients *pl*, clientele

clientelismo *nm Pol* = practice of giving preferential treatment to a particular interest group in exchange for its support

clima *nm* climate; *Fig* atmosphere; **en un c. de cordialidad** in a cordial atmosphere

climaterio *nm* climacteric

climático, -a *adj* climatic, climatical

climatización *nf* air conditioning

climatizado, -a 1 *pp de* **climatizar**
2 *adj* air-conditioned

climatizar [14] *vt* to air-condition

climatología *nf* climatology

climatológico, -a *adj* climatologic, climatological

clímax *nm inv* climax

clínica *nf* clinic

clínico, -a 1 *adj* clinical
2 *nm,f (persona)* clinician, physician

clip (*pl* **clips**) *nm (para papel)* clip; *(para pelo)* hair-grip, *US* bobby pin

clíper *nm Náut* clipper

clítoris *nm inv Anat* clitoris

cloaca *nf* sewer, drain

clon *nm* clone

clonación *nf* cloning

clonar *vt* to clone

clónico, -a 1 *adj* cloned
2 *nm Inform (computador)* clone

cloquear *vi* to cluck

cloqueo *nm* cluck, clucking

cloración *nf* chlorination

clorado, -a 1 *pp de* **clorar**
2 *adj* chlorinated
3 *nm* chlorination

clorar *vt* to chlorinate

clorato *nm Quím* chlorate

clorhídrico, -a *adj Quím* hydrochloric

clórico, -a *adj Quím* chloric

cloro *nm* (**a**) *Quím* chlorine (**b**) *CAm Chile Méx (lejía)* bleach

clorofila *nf* chlorophyll, *US* chlorophyl

clorofílico, -a *adj* chlorophyllous

cloroformo *nm* chloroform

cloruro *nm Quím* chloride ▫ **c. sódico** sodium chloride

clóset (*pl* **clósets**) *nm Am* fitted cupboard, *US* closet

club (*pl* **clubs** *o* **clubes**) *nm* club ▫ **c. de fans** fan club; **c. de fútbol** soccer *o Br* football club; **c. náutico** yacht club

clueca 1 *adj* broody
2 *nf* broody hen

cm (*abrev de* **centímetro(s)**) cm

Cnel. (*abrev de* **Coronel**) Col

CNT *nf* (*abrev de* **Confederación Nacional del Trabajo**) = Spanish anarchist trade union

coacción *nf* coercion

coaccionar *vt* to coerce, compel

coactivo, -a *adj* coercive, compelling

coadjutor, -a 1 *adj & nm,f* coadjutant
2 *nm Rel* coadjutor

coadyuvante *adj & nmf Fml* coadjutant

coadyuvar *vt Fml* to contribute, help

coagulación *nf* coagulation, clotting

coagulante 1 *adj* coagulative
2 *nm* coagulant, coagulator

coagular 1 *vt & vi (gen)* to coagulate; *(sangre)* to clot; *(leche)* to curdle
2 coagularse *vpr (gen)* to coagulate; *(sangre)* to clot; *(leche)* to curdle

coágulo *nm* coagulum, clot

coalición *nf* coalition

coaligar [38] **1** *vt* to ally, unite
2 coaligarse *vpr* to unite, join together

coartada *nf* alibi

coartar *vt* to hinder; *Fig* to restrict

coaseguro *nm Fin* coinsurance

coautor, -a *nm,f* coauthor

coaxial *adj* coaxial

coba *nf Esp Méx Fam* soft soap; **dar c. a algn** to soft-soap sb

cobalto *nm* cobalt ▫ **bomba de c.** cobalt bomb

cobarde 1 *adj* cowardly ·
2 *nmf* coward

cobardía *nf* cowardice

cobaya *nf*, **cobayo** *nm* guinea pig

cobertizo *nm* shed, shack

cobertor *nm* (**a**) *(colcha)* bedspread (**b**) *(manta)* blanket

cobertura *nf* cover ▫ **c. de seguros** insurance cover; **c. informativa** news *o* media coverage; **c. sanitaria** health cover

cobija *nf* (**a**) *Am (manta)* blanket (**b**) *PRico (techo)* = roof made from thatched palm leaves

cobijar 1 *vt (gen)* to shelter; *(fugitivo)* to harbour, *US* harbor
2 cobijarse *vpr* to take shelter

cobijo *nm (techo)* shelter; *Fig (protección)* protection, refuge

cobista *Fam* **1** *adj* soapy
2 *nmf* crawler, toady

cobra *nf Zool* cobra

cobrador, -a *nm,f* (**a**) *(de autobús etc) (hombre)* conductor; *(mujer)* conductress (**b**) *(de luz, agua etc)* collector

cobrar 1 *vt* (**a**) *(dinero)* to charge; *(cheque)* to cash; *(salario)* to earn; **cóbralo todo junto** put it all together; **¿cuánto cobras al mes?** how much do you earn a month?; **han venido a c. el alquiler** they've been to collect the rent; **me cobró mil pesos** he charged me a thousand pesos; *Com* **por c.** unpaid (**b**) *Irón* to get beaten *o* a slap; **¡vas a c.!** you'll cop a clout!, you're in for it! (**c**) *Caza* to retrieve (**d**) *Fig (adquirir)* to gain, get; **c. aliento** to get one's breath back; **c. ánimos** to take courage *o* heart; **c. importancia** to become important
2 cobrarse *vpr (dinero)* to take, collect; **cóbrese de aquí** take it out of this, please

cobre *nm* (**a**) *Metal* copper; *Fam* **batir el c.** to go hard at it (**b**) *Am (moneda)* copper cent; **no tener un c.** to be flat broke

cobrizo, -a *adj* copper, copper-coloured, *US* copper-colored, coppery

cobro *nm* (**a**) *(pago)* collecting; *(de cheque)* cashing; **el c. del gas** the gas payment; *Com* **presentar al c.** to hand in for payment; *Tel* **llamar a c. revertido a algn** *Br* to make a reverse-charge call to sb, *US* call sb collect (**b**) *Caza* retrieval

coca *nf* (**a**) *Bot* coca (**b**) *Argot (droga)* cocaine, coke

cocaína *nf* cocaine

cocainómano, -a *nm,f* cocaine addict, coke head

cocción *nf* cooking; *(en agua)* boiling; *(en horno)* baking

cóccix *nm inv* coccyx

cocear *vi* to kick

cocer [15] **1** *vt (comida)* to cook; *(hervir)* to boil; *(en horno)* to bake
2 *vi (hervir)* to boil
3 cocerse *vpr* (**a**) *(comida)* to cook; *(hervir)* to boil; *(en horno)* to bake (**b**) *Fam (de calor)* to roast, be boiling (**c**) *(tramarse)* to be afoot o going on, be cooking

cochambre *nf* filth, muck

cochambroso, -a *adj* filthy

coche *nm* (**a**) *Aut* car, *US* automobile; **fuimos en c.** we went by car ❑ **c. automático** automatic; **c. blindado** armoured car; **c. bomba** car bomb; **c. celular** police van; **c. de alquiler** hired car, *US* rented car; **c. de bomberos** fire engine, *US* fire truck; **c. de carreras** racing car; **c. de época** vintage car; **c. familiar** estate (car), *US* station wagon; **c. fúnebre** hearse (**b**) *Ferroc* carriage, coach ❑ **c. cama** sleeping car, *US* sleeper (**c**) *(de caballos)* coach, *Br* carriage, *US* car (**d**) *(de niño)* *Br* pram, *US* baby carriage

cochecito *nm (de niño)* *Br* pram, *US* baby carriage

cochera *nf Aut* (**a**) *(garaje)* garage (**b**) *(de autobuses, tranvías)* depot

cochero *nm* coachman

cochinada *nf Fam* filthy o dirty thing; *Fam Fig (obscenidad)* obscenity; **decir cochinadas** to say foul o obscene things; **hacer una c. (a algn)** to play a dirty trick (on sb)

cochinería *nf* (**a**) *(suciedad)* filthiness (**b**) *véase* **cochinada**

cochinilla¹ *nf* woodlouse

cochinilla² *nf Ent* cochineal

cochinillo *nm* sucking pig

cochino, -a 1 *adj* (**a**) *(sucio)* filthy, disgusting (**b**) *Fam (miserable)* *Br* bloody, *US* goddamn
2 *nm,f* (**a**) *(macho)* pig, swine; *(hembra)* sow (**b**) *Fam (persona)* filthy person, pig

cocido, -a 1 *pp de* **cocer**
2 *adj* (**a**) cooked, boiled (**b**) *Esp Fam (borracho)* *Br* pissed, *US* loaded
3 *nm Culin* stew

cociente *nm Mat* quotient ❑ **c. intelectual** IQ

cocina *nf* (**a**) *(arte)* cooking ❑ **c. casera** home cooking; **c. de mercado** food in season; **c. española** Spanish cooking o cuisine; **libro de c.** cookery book, *US* cookbook (**b**) *(habitación)* kitchen ❑ **utensilios de c.** kitchen utensils (**c**) *(aparato)* cooker, *US* stove ❑ **c. económica** stove; **c. eléctrica/de gas** electric/gas cooker

cocinar *vt & vi* to cook

cocinero, -a *nm,f* cook

cocinilla *nf* (small portable) cooker o *US* stove

cocker ['koker] (*pl* **cockers**) *nm* cocker (spaniel)

cocktail *nm véase* **cóctel**

coco¹ *nm (árbol)* coconut palm; *(fruta)* coconut

coco² *nm* (**a**) *Fam (fantasma)* bogeyman; **ser un c.** *(ser feo)* to be ugly; *(dar miedo)* to be frightening (**b**) *Argot (cabeza)* nut; **comer el c. a algn** to brainwash sb; **comerse el c.** to get worked up, rack one's brains

cococha *nf* barbel

cocodrilo *nm* crocodile

cocotal *nm* coconut grove

cocotero *nm* coconut palm

cóctel *nm* cocktail ❑ **c. Molotov** Molotov cocktail

coctelera *nf* cocktail shaker

coctelería *nf* cocktail bar

codazo *nm* (**a**) *(señal)* nudge with one's elbow (**b**) *(golpe)* blow with one's elbow; *Fig* **abrirse paso** o **camino a codazos** to elbow one's way through

codear 1 *vi* (**a**) *(empujar)* to elbow (**b**) *Andes (pedir con insistencia)* to keep on
2 codearse *vpr (relacionarse)* to rub shoulders (**con** with), hobnob (**con** with)

codeína *nf Farm* codeine

codera *nf* elbow patch

códice *nm Lit* codex

codicia *nf* greed, thirst

codiciable *adj* desirable

codiciado, -a 1 *pp de* **codiciar**
2 *adj* much desired, coveted

codiciar *vt* to covet, crave for

codicioso, -a 1 *adj* covetous, greedy
2 *nm,f* greedy person

codificación *nf* (**a**) *Jur* codification (**b**) *(de mensajes)* encoding

codificador, -a 1 *adj* (**a**) *Jur* codifying (**b**) *(de mensajes)* encoding
2 *nm,f* (**a**) *Jur* codifier (**b**) *(de mensajes)* encoder (**c**) *Inform* encoder

codificar [59] *vt (ley)* to codify; *(mensajes)* to encode

código *nm también Inform* code ❑ **c. civil/penal** civil/penal code; **c. genético** genetic code; **c. Morse** Morse code; **c. postal** *Br* post code, postal code, *US* zip code

codillo *nm* (**a**) *Anat* elbow (**b**) *Culin* shoulder (**c**) *Téc (de tubería)* elbow

codo *nm* (**a**) *Anat* elbow; **de codos** on one's elbows; *Fig* **c. a** o **con c.** side by side; *Fig* **desgastarse** o **romperse los codos** to study a lot, swot, cram; *Fam* **alzar** o **empinar el c.** to knock them back; *Fam* **hablar por los codos** to talk nonstop (**b**) *Téc (de tubería)* elbow

codorniz *nf Orn* quail

COE ['koe] *nm Dep (abrev de* **Comité Olímpico Español***)* Spanish Olympic Committee

coedición *nf* joint publication

coeditar *vt* to publish jointly

coeducación *nf* coeducation

coeficiente *nm* (**a**) *Mat* coefficient (**b**) *(grado)* degree, rate ❑ **c. de crecimiento** growth rate; **c. de inteligencia** intelligence quotient

coercer [40] *vt* to restrict, constrain

coerción *nf* coercion

coercitivo, -a *adj* coercive

coetáneo, -a *adj & nm,f* contemporary

coexistencia *nf* coexistence

coexistir *vi* to coexist

cofa *nf Náut* top ❑ **c. mayor** maintop

cofia *nf (prenda)* bonnet

cofrade *nm,f (gen)* member *(of brotherhood)*; *(hombre)* brother *(of brotherhood)*; *(mujer)* sister *(of brotherhood)*

cofradía *nf (hermandad)* brotherhood; *(asociación)* association

cofre *nm* (**a**) *(arca, baúl)* trunk, chest (**b**) *(para dinero, joyas)* box, casket

coger [52] **1** *vt* (**a**) *(asir)* to seize, take hold of; **coge esto un momento** hold this a second; *Fam* **cogió la puerta y se**

marchó he upped and left; *Fam* **no hay por donde cogerlo** he hasn't got a leg to stand on (**b**) *(tomar)* to take; **he cogido un buen sitio** I've got a very good place; *Fig* **no ha cogido un libro en su vida** he hasn't read a book in his life (**c**) *(tomar prestado)* to borrow; **te he cogido la pluma** I've borrowed your pen (**d**) *(pelota, ladrón, resfriado)* to catch; *Fig* **me cogió desprevenido** I was caught unawares (**e**) *Fig (entender)* to understand; **no cogí el chiste** I didn't get the joke (**f**) *(recoger)* to pick (up); *(fruta, flores)* to gather; *Tricot* **c. puntos** to pick up stitches (**g**) *(acento, costumbre)* to pick up; **coger miedo a** to become afraid of; *Fam* **c. una manía a algo** to get hooked on sth (**h**) *(velocidad, fuerza)* to gather (**i**) *(emisora, canal)* to pick up (**j**) *(transporte)* to take, catch (**k**) *(empleados, empleo)* to take on (**l**) *(atropellar)* to run over, knock down (**m**) *(espacio)* to take up (**n**) *Am Vulg* to fuck
  2 *vi* (**a**) *(plantas, colores)* to take (**b**) *(ir)* to go; **coge por la calle de la iglesia** take the church road (**c**) *Fam* **cogió y se fue** he upped and left; **cogió y se puso a chillar** he started to scream like mad (**d**) *Am Vulg (tener relaciones sexuales)* to screw, fuck; **c. con algn** to screw o fuck sb
  3 cogerse *vpr (pillarse)* to catch; *(agarrarse)* to hold, clutch; **cógete bien** hold tight; **ella se cogió de su brazo** she took his arm; *Fam* **se cogió un cabreo** he got very angry

cogestión *nf* copartnership

cogida *nf Taur* gore, goring

cogido, -a 1 *pp de* **coger**
  2 *adj (sujeto)* fixed; *(atrapado)* trapped, caught
  3 *nm* gather, pleat

cognición *nf* cognition

cognitivo, -a *adj* cognitive

cognoscitivo, -a *adj* cognitive

cogollo *nm* (**a**) *(de lechuga, col)* heart; *Fam* **hasta el c.** to the core (**b**) *(brote)* shoot (**c**) *Fig (la flor y la nata)* **el c.** the cream

cogorza *nf Fam* **agarrar** o **pillar una c.** to get blotto o smashed

cogotazo *nm Fam* blow on the back of the neck

cogote *nm Esp* nape o back of the neck

cohabitación *nf* cohabitation

cohabitar *vi* to live together, cohabit

cohecho *nm Fml Jur* bribery

coherencia *nf* coherence, coherency

coherente *adj* coherent

cohesión *nf* cohesion

cohesionar 1 *vt* to unite
  2 cohesionarse *vpr* to unite

cohete *nm* (**a**) rocket; *Fam* **como un c.** like a rocket □ **c. espacial** space rocket (**b**) *Méx (pistola)* pistol (**c**) *Méx (agujero)* blasting hole (**d**) *RP Fam* **al c.** *(en vano)* in vain

cohibición *nf* inhibition, restraint

cohibido, -a 1 *pp de* **cohibir**
  2 *adj* inhibited, restrained

cohibir 1 *vt* to inhibit, restrain
  2 cohibirse *vpr* to feel inhibited o embarrassed

COI ['koi] *nm Dep (abrev de* **Comité Olímpico Internacional)** IOC

coima *nf Andes RP* bribe

coincidencia *nf* coincidence; **dio la c. de que ...** it just so happened that ...; **en c. con** in agreement with

coincidente *adj* coincident, coinciding

coincidir *vi* (**a**) *(acordar)* to coincide; **nuestras ideas no coinciden** our ideas don't coincide o agree (**b**) *(encontrarse)* to meet; **coincidí con ella en Madrid** I was in Madrid at the same time as her

coito *nm* coitus, intercourse

cojear *vi (persona)* to limp, hobble; *(mueble)* to wobble; *Fig (ir mal)* to falter; *Fam* **c. del mismo pie** to have the same faults

cojera *nf* limp, lameness

cojín *nm* cushion

cojinete *nm Téc* bearing □ **c. de agujas/bolas** needle/ball bearing

cojo, -a 1 *adj (persona)* lame, limping; *(mueble)* wobbly; *Fig (defectuoso)* faulty, incomplete
  2 *nm,f* lame person

cojón *Esp Vulg* **1** *nm Anat* ball; **de cojones** *(estupendo)* *Br* bloody o *US* goddamn brilliant o good; *(pésimo)* *Br* bloody o *US* goddamn awful o bad; **ponérsele los cojones como corbata** to shit bricks; **por cojones** like it or not; **tener cojones** to have guts o balls
  2 *interj* fuck it!

cojonudo, -a *adj Esp Vulg Br* bloody o *US* goddamn brilliant o good

cojudear 1 *vi Andes Fam (hacer tonterías)* to piss about, muck about
  2 *vt (engañar)* to trick

cojudez *nf Andes muy Fam* **decir cojudeces** to talk a load of *Br* bloody o *US* goddamn nonsense

cojudo, -a *adj Andes muy Fam Br* bloody o *US* goddamn stupid

col *nf* cabbage □ **c. de Bruselas** Brussels sprout; **c. lombarda** red cabbage; **c. rizada** kale, collard

cola¹ *nf* (**a**) *Av Zool* tail; *(de vestido)* train; *(de chaqueta)* tail □ **c. de caballo** *Bot* horsetail; *(peinado)* ponytail (**b**) *Fam (pene)* *Br* willie, *US* peter (**c**) *(parte posterior)* **a la c.** at the back o rear □ *Ferroc* **vagón de c.** rear coach (**d**) *(fila)* *Br* queue, *US* line; **hacer c.** *Br* to queue (up), *US* stand in line; **ponerse en la c.** *Br* to get into the queue, *US* get in line; *Fam* **traer c.** to have consequences (**e**) *Am Fam (nalgas)* *Br* bum, *US* fanny (**f**) *Arg (de película)* trailer

cola² *nf* glue; *Fam* **no pega ni con c.** it doesn't match at all

colaboración *nf* (**a**) *(cooperación)* collaboration (**b**) *Prensa* contribution

colaboracionismo *nm Pol* collaboration

colaboracionista *Pol* **1** *adj* collaborating
  2 *nmf* collaborator

colaborador, -a 1 *adj* collaborating □ **c. externo** freelancer
  2 *nm,f* (**a**) *(compañero)* collaborator (**b**) *Prensa* contributor

colaborar *vi* (**a**) *(ayudar)* to collaborate, cooperate (**b**) *Prensa* to contribute

colación *nf* (**a**) *(refrigerio)* light meal, snack (**b**) *(cotejo)* collation; **sacar** o **traer algo a c.** to bring sth up (**c**) *Am (dulce)* *Br* sweet, *US* candy

colada *nf* (**a**) *Esp (lavado)* wash, laundry; **hacer la c.** to do the washing o laundry (**b**) *Esp (ropa limpia)* washing (**c**) *Metal* tapping (**d**) *Geol (volcánica)* outflow

coladera *nf* (**a**) *Am (colador)* colander (**b**) *Méx (alcantarilla)* sewer

colado, -a 1 *pp de* **colar**
  2 *adj* (**a**) *(líquido)* filtered, strained (**b**) *Fam (enamorado)* madly in love, head over heels (in love)

colador *nm (de té, café)* strainer; *(para comida, caldo)* colander, sieve; *Fig* **como un c.** full of holes, like a sieve; *Fam* **dejar como un c.** to riddle with bullets

coladura *nf Fam* clanger, slip-up

colágeno *nm* collagen

colapsar 1 *vt* to cause to collapse
  2 colapsarse *vpr* to break down, collapse

colapso *nm* (**a**) *Med* collapse (**b**) *(de tráfico)* traffic jam, hold-up

colar [63] **1** *vt* (**a**) *(líquido)* to strain, filter (**b**) *Fam (hacer pasar)* to pass, slip; *(moneda)* to pass off; *(hecho, historia)* to give

2 *vi Fam* to wash; **esto no colará** this won't wash

3 colarse *vpr* (**a**) *(escabullirse)* to slip in, gatecrash; *(en una cola)* to jump the *Br* queue *o US* line (**b**) *Fam (equivocarse)* to slip up, make a mistake; *(enamorarse)* **c. por algn** to fall for sb

colateral *adj* collateral

colcha *nf* bedspread

colchón *nm* mattress ▫ *Téc* **c. de aire** air cushion; **c. neumático** air mattress

colchonería *nf* mattress maker's (shop)

colchonero, -a *nm,f* mattress maker

colchoneta *nf Dep* small mattress

cole *nm Fam* school

colear 1 *vt* (**a**) *Col Méx Ven (res)* to throw down by the tail (**b**) *Chile (examen)* to fail (**c**) *Col Méx Fam (molestar)* to bug, *Br* nark

2 *vi* (**a**) *(animal)* to wag its tail (**b**) *(asunto, problema)* to drag on

3 colearse *vpr Arg Ven (patinar)* to skid

colección *nf* collection

coleccionable 1 *adj* collectable

2 *nm* = special supplement in serialized form

coleccionar *vt* to collect

coleccionismo *nm* collecting

coleccionista *nmf* collector

colecta *nf* collection

colectar *vt* to collect

colectivero *nm Arg* minibus driver

colectividad *nf* community; **en c.** communally

colectivismo *nm* collectivism

colectivización *nf* collectivization

colectivizar [14] *vt* to collectivize

colectivo, -a 1 *adj* collective

2 *nm* (**a**) *(asociación)* association, guild (**b**) *Ling* collective noun (**c**) *Arg Bol (autobús)* bus (**d**) *Andes (taxi)* collective taxi *(with a fixed rate and that travels a fixed route)*

colector *nm* (**a**) *(sumidero)* main sewer (**b**) *Téc* **c. de admisión/escape** inlet/exhaust manifold

colega *nmf* (**a**) *(compañero profesional)* colleague, *US* co-worker (**b**) *Esp Argot (amigo)* pal, *Br* mate, *US* buddy

colegiado, -a 1 *pp de* **colegiarse**

2 *adj* (**a**) *(afiliado)* collegiate (**b**) *(colectivo)* collective

3 *nm* collegian; *Dep* referee

colegial 1 *adj (escolar)* school; **vida c.** school life

2 *nm* schoolboy; **los colegiales** schoolchildren

colegiala *nf* schoolgirl

colegiarse *vpr* to join a professional association

colegiata *nf* collegiate church

colegiatura *nf* (**a**) *Andes CAm Méx (matrícula)* tuition fees *pl* (**b**) *Chile Col RP (afiliación)* = membership of a professional association

colegio *nm* (**a**) *(escuela)* school; **de vuelta al c.** back to school ▫ **c. privado** *o* **de pago** private school, *Br* public *o* independent school; **c. público** *Br* state school, *US* public school (**b**) *(asociación profesional)* association, college; **el c. de abogados** the Bar ▫ *Pol* **c. electoral** polling station (**c**) *Univ (residencia)* **c. mayor** *o* **universitario** hall of residence

colegir [55] *vt* to infer, deduce

coleóptero *nm* beetle

cólera¹ *nf* (**a**) *(ira)* anger, rage; **montar en c.** to fly into a temper (**b**) *(bilis)* bile

cólera² *nm Med* cholera

colérico, -a *adj* (**a**) *(encolerizado)* furious (**b**) *(carácter)* bad-tempered

colesterol *nm* cholesterol

coleta *nf* pigtail, ponytail; **cortarse la c.** *Taur* to retire from bullfighting; *Fig* to retire

coletazo *nm* (**a**) *(golpe de cola)* wag *o* swish of the tail; *Aut* **dar coletazos** to sway about (**b**) *Fig (manifestación última)* death throes *pl*, final tremor, stir

coletilla *nf* postscript, addition

coleto *nm (prenda)* doublet; *Fig* **echarse algo al c.** *(comer)* to eat sth right up; *(beber)* to drink sth down

colgado, -a 1 *pp de* **colgar**

2 *adj* (**a**) *(cuadro)* hanging; **un jamón c. del techo** a leg of ham hanging from the ceiling (**b**) *(ahorcado)* hung (**c**) *Fam Educ* **tener asignaturas colgadas** to still have subjects to pass (**d**) *Argot* **dejar a algn c.** to leave sb in the lurch (**e**) *Argot (drogado)* stoned, high

colgador *nm* (coat) hanger

colgadura *nf (gen pl)* hangings *pl*, *US* drapes *pl*

colgajo *nm* (**a**) *(de ropa)* rag, torn piece (**b**) *(de uva)* bunch (**c**) *Med (de piel)* flap, graft

colgante 1 *adj* hanging

2 *nm* (**a**) *Arquit (festón)* festoon (**b**) *(joya)* pendant

colgar [16] **1** *vt* (**a**) *(gen)* to hang (up); *(colada)* to hang (out) (**b**) *(ahorcar)* to hang (**c**) *Fam (suspender)* to fail; **me han colgado en matemáticas** I've failed maths (**d**) *(abandonar)* **c. los libros** to give up studying

2 *vi* (**a**) *(pender)* to hang (**de** from); **cuelga de un lado** it dips on one side; *Fig* **c. de un hilo** to hang by a thread (**b**) *Tel* to put down, hang up; **me han colgado** they've hung up on me; **¡no cuelgue!** hold on!, hold the line please

2 colgarse *vpr* (**a**) *(ahorcarse)* to hang oneself (**b**) *Inform (ordenador)* to crash

colibrí *nm* humming bird

cólico *nm* colic

coliflor *nf* cauliflower

coligar [38] **1** *vt* to ally, unite

2 coligarse *vpr* to unite, join together

colijo *indic pres véase* **colegir**

colilla *nf* (cigarette) end *o* butt

colimbo *nm Orn* diver

colina *nf* hill, slope

colindante *adj* adjoining, adjacent

colindar *vi* to be adjacent (**con** to)

colirio *nm Farm* eyewash, collyrium

coliseo *nm Arquit* coliseum, colosseum

colisión *nf* collision, crash, clash

colisionar *vi* to collide, crash, clash

colista *nmf Dep (persona, equipo)* last

colistero, -a *nm,f Inform Fam* list member

colitis *nf Med* colitis

collado *nm* (**a**) *(colina)* hill (**b**) *(paso entre montañas)* pass

collage [ko'laʃ] *nm Arte* collage

collar *nm* (**a**) *(adorno)* necklace (**b**) *(de perro)* collar (**c**) *Téc (abrazadera)* collar, ring

collarín *nm* surgical collar

collera *nf* (**a**) *(de arreos)* collar (**b**) *Am (pareja)* couple (**c**) *Arg Chile (animales)* pair (**d**) *Andes* **colleras** *(gemelos)* cufflinks

colmado, -a 1 *pp de* **colmar**

2 *adj* full, filled; **una cucharada colmada** a heaped tablespoonful
3 *nm* grocery store, *Br* grocer's (shop)

colmar *vt* (**a**) *(recipiente)* to fill (right up); *(vaso, copa)* to fill to the brim (**b**) *Fig* to shower, overwhelm; **nos colmaron de regalos** the showered us with gifts (**c**) *Fig (ambiciones)* to fulfil, satisfy

colmena *nf* beehive; *Fig* **c. humana** human hive

colmenar *nm* apiary

colmenero, -a *nm,f* beekeeper

colmillo *nm Anat* eye *o* canine tooth; *Zool (de carnívoro)* fang; *(de jabalí, elefante)* tusk; *Fig* **enseñar los colmillos** *(los animales)* to bare its teeth; *Fig* to show one's teeth

colmo *nm* height, summit; **el c. de la ineficacia** the height of inefficiency; **¡eso es el c.!** that's the last straw!; **para c. (de desgracias)** to top it all

colocación *nf* (**a**) *(acto)* positioning, collocation (**b**) *(situación)* situation, place (**c**) *Fin (de capital)* investment (**d**) *(empleo)* job, employment

colocado, -a 1 *pp de* colocar
2 *adj* (**a**) *(empleado)* employed; **estar muy bien c.** to have a very good job (**b**) *Argot (embriagado)* sozzled; *(drogado)* stoned, high

colocar [59] **1** *vt* (**a**) *(gen)* to place, put; *(alfombra)* to lay; *(cuadro)* to hang; *Mil (tropas)* to position (**b**) *Fin (invertir)* to invest (**c**) *(emplear)* to give work to (**d**) *Fam (casar)* to marry off; **ha colocado a todas sus hijas** he's married off all his daughters (**e**) *Fam (artículos defectuosos)* to fob off (**f**) *Argot (drogar)* to stone
2 colocarse *vpr* (**a**) *(situarse)* to put *o* install *o US* instal oneself (**b**) *(emplearse)* to take a job; **se ha colocado de secretaria** she's got a job as a secretary (**c**) *Dep (clasificarse)* to be; **se colocó en tercer lugar** he moved into third position *o* place (**d**) *Argot (embriagarse)* to get sozzled; *(drogarse)* to get stoned *o* high

colocón *nm Argot* high

colofón *nm* (**a**) *(apéndice)* colophon (**b**) *Fig (remate)* crowning, climax

coloidal *adj* colloidal

coloide *nm* colloid

Colombia *n* Colombia

colombianismo *nm* Colombian expression

colombiano, -a *adj & nm,f* Colombian

colombino, -a *adj* = of *o* relating to Christopher Columbus

Colombo *n* Colombo

colombofilia *nf* pigeon breeding

colombófilo, -a 1 *adj* pigeon-breeding
2 *nm,f* pigeon breeder

Colón *n (Cristóbal)* **C.** Christopher Columbus

colon *nm Anat* colon □ **c. irritable** irritable bowel syndrome

colón *nm Fin* = standard monetary unit of Costa Rica and El Salvador

colonia¹ *nf* (**a**) *Biol Pol* colony; **c. de veraneantes** colony *o* group of holiday-makers (**b**) *(gen pl) (campamento)* summer camp (**c**) *Méx (barrio)* district

colonia² *nf (agua de colonia)* cologne

coloniaje *nm Am Hist (período)* colonial period

colonial 1 *adj* (**a**) *Pol* colonial (**b**) *Com* imported
2 coloniales *nmpl* imported *o* overseas foodstuffs

colonialismo *nm* colonialism

colonialista *adj & nm,f* colonialist

colonización *nf* colonization

colonizador, -a 1 *adj* colonizing
2 *nm,f* colonizer, colonist

colonizar [14] *vt* to colonize

colono *nm* (**a**) *Agr* tenant farmer (**b**) *(habitante)* colonist, colonial, settler

coloquial *adj* colloquial

coloquialismo *nm* colloquialism

coloquio *nm* discussion, colloquium

color *nm* (**a**) *(que se ve)* colour, *US* color; **c. rojo** red; *Tex* **c. sólido** fast colour; **dar c. a** *(colorear)* to colour; *Fig (animar)* to liven up; **de c.** *(en colores)* in colour, coloured; *Euf (persona)* coloured; **de colores** multicoloured; *Cin Fot* **en color(es)** in colour; *Fig* **un discurso carece de c.** a boring speech; *Fig Pol* **sin distinción de credos ni colores** regardless of race *o* creed; *Fig (picante)* **subido de c.** risqué; *Fig* **verlo todo de c. de rosa** to see life through rose-coloured spectacles (**b**) *(colorido)* colour, *US* color (**c**) **colores** *(bandera)* colours, *US* colors, flag *sing*; *Dep (equipo)* team *sing*

coloración *nf* coloration, colouring, *US* coloring

colorado, -a 1 *adj* red; **ponerse c.** to blush
2 *nm* red

colorante 1 *adj* colouring, *US* coloring
2 *nm* colouring, *US* coloring, dye

colorear *vt* to colour, *US* color

colorete *nm* rouge

colorido *nm* colour, *US* color

colorín *nm* (**a**) *(color fuerte)* bright *o* vivid colour *o US* color; **y c. colorado, este cuento se ha acabado** and that's the end of the story (**b**) *Orn* goldfinch

colorismo *nm Arte* predominant use of colour *o US* color

colorista 1 *adj* colouristic, *US* coloristic
2 *nmf* colourist, *US* colorist

colosal *adj* (**a**) *(estatura, tamaño)* colossal (**b**) *Fig (extraordinario)* splendid, excellent

coloso *nm* colossus

columbrar *vt* (**a**) *(vislumbrar)* to see, make out (**b**) *Fig (conjeturar)* to guess

columna *nf* column □ *Anat* **c. vertebral** vertebral column, spinal column

columnata *nf* colonnade

columnista *nmf Prensa* columnist

columpiar 1 *vt (mecerse)* to push *(on a swing)*, swing
2 columpiarse *vpr* (**a**) *(mecerse)* to swing (**b**) *Fam (meter la pata)* to drop a clanger

columpio *nm* swing

colza *nf* rape, colza; **aceite de c.** rapeseed oil

coma¹ *nf* (**a**) *Ling Mús* comma; **sin faltar (ni) una c.** down to the last detail □ **punto y c.** semicolon (**b**) *Mat* point

coma² *nm Med* coma; **entrar en c.** to go into a coma

comadre *nf* (**a**) *(vecina)* neighbour, *US* neighbor; *(amiga)* friend (**b**) *Pey (chismosa)* gossip, gossipmonger (**c**) *(madrina)* godmother (**d**) *Fam (alcahueta)* gobetween

comadrear *vi* to gossip

comadreja *nf* weasel

comadreo *nm* gossip, gossiping, tittle-tattle

comadrería *nf* piece of gossip

comadrona *nf* midwife

comanche *adj & nmf* Comanche

comandancia *nf* (**a**) *(distrito, graduación)* command (**b**) *(local, edificio)* commander's headquarters (**c**) *(zona)* = area under a commander's jurisdiction

comandante *nm* (**a**) *Mil (oficial)* commander,

commanding officer; *(graduación)* ≃ major (**b**) *Av* pilot

comandar *vt Mil* to command

comandita *nf Com* (**sociedad en**) **c.** *Br* limited *o US* silent partnership; *Fam* **ir en c.** to go en masse

comanditar *vt Com* to enter as a *Br* sleeping *o US* silent partner

comanditario, -a *adj Br* sleeping, *US* silent; **sociedad comanditaria** *Br* limited *o US* silent partnership

comando *nm* (**a**) *Mil* commando ❑ **c. terrorista** terrorist cell (**b**) *Inform* command

comarca *nf* region, area

comarcal *adj* regional, local

comatoso, -a *adj Med* comatose; **en estado c.** in coma

comba *nf* (**a**) *(curvatura)* curve, bend (**b**) *Esp (juego)* skipping; *(cuerda) Br* skipping rope, *US* jump rope; **saltar a la c.** to skip, *US* jump rope

combadura *nf (de cuerda, cable)* bend, curve; *(de viga, pared)* sag, bulge

combar 1 *vt (curvar)* to bend
   2 combarse *vpr (curvarse)* to bend, curve; *(una pared)* to sag

combate *nm (lucha)* combat, struggle; *Box* fight; *Mil* battle; **dejar a alguien fuera de c.** to knock sb out; *(eliminado)* out of action; **librar c.** to wage battle

combatiente 1 *adj* fighting
   2 *nmf (persona)* fighter, combatant

combatir 1 *vt (luchar)* to fight; *Fig (oponerse a)* to combat
   2 *vi* to fight, struggle (**contra** against)

combatividad *nf* fighting spirit, aggressiveness

combativo, -a *adj* spirited, aggressive

combi *nm* (**a**) *Esp (frigorífico)* fridge-freezer (**b**) *Am (autobús)* minibus

combinación *nf* (**a**) *(unión, mezcla)* combination (**b**) *(prenda)* slip (**c**) *Fam* fiddle, wangle

combinado, -a 1 *pp de* **combinar**
   2 *adj* combined, mixed
   3 *nm (mezcla)* mixture; *(cóctel)* cocktail

combinar 1 *vt* (**a**) *(ingredientes, esfuerzos)* to combine (**b**) *(colores)* to put together
   2 *vi (colores)* to go together, match
   3 combinarse *vpr* to combine

combinatoria *nf Mat* combinatorial analysis

combo, -a *adj* bent, curved; *(pared)* sagging

combustible 1 *adj* combustible
   2 *nm* fuel

combustión *nf* combustion

comecocos *nm inv Argot (de tragaperras)* pac-man; *(asunto, libro etc)* soul-destroyer

comedero *nm* feeding trough, manger

comedia *nf Teat* comedy; *Fig (farsa)* sham, farce; *Fam* **hacer c.** to put on an act ❑ **c. de enredo** farce

comediante, -a *nm,f Teat (hombre)* actor; *(mujer)* actress; *Fig (farsante)* fraud

comedido, -a 1 *pp de* **comedirse**
   2 *adj* (**a**) *Esp (moderado)* self-restrained, moderate, reserved (**b**) *Am (servicial)* helpful, obliging, pleasing

comedimiento *nm* restraint, moderation

comediógrafo, -a *nm,f Teat* playwright, dramatist

comedirse [47] *vpr* (**a**) *Esp (moderarse)* to restrain oneself (**b**) *Am (ofrecerse)* to volunteer oneself

comedor, -a 1 *adj* big-eating; **es muy c.** he's a big eater
   2 *nm* (**a**) *(sala)* dining room; *(de fábrica)* canteen; *(de universidad)* refectory (**b**) *Mueb* dining-room suite

comensal *nmf* fellow diner, companion at table

comentar *vt (escribir)* to comment on; *(hablar, discutir)* to discuss, talk about

comentario *nm* (**a**) *(observación)* comment, remark; *Lit Rad TV (crítica)* commentary (**b**) **comentarios** *(murmuración)* gossip; **sin c.** no comment

comentarista *nmf Prensa Rad TV* commentator

comenzar [17] *vt & vi* to begin, start, commence; **comenzó a llover** it started raining *o* to rain; **comenzó diciendo que ...** he started by saying that ...

comer 1 *vt* (**a**) *(alimentos)* to eat; **c. paella** to have paella; *Fam* **sin comerlo ni beberlo** without having had anything to do with it (**b**) *Esp Méx (al mediodía)* to have for lunch; *esp Andes (a la noche)* to have for dinner (**c**) *(color)* to fade (**d**) *(corroer)* to corrode; *Fig* **me come la envidia** I'm green with envy (**e**) *Ajedrez* to take, capture (**f**) *Fig (gastar)* to eat away; *(combustible)* to use (up)
   2 *vi* (**a**) to eat; **dar de c. a algn** to feed sb; **echar de c. a los animales** to feed the animals; **¿has comido?** have you eaten yet?; **no tener qué c.** not to have enough to live on; *Fig* **c. a dos carrillos** to gulp down one's food (**b**) *Esp Méx (al mediodía)* to have lunch; *esp Andes (a la noche)* to have dinner
   3 comerse *vpr* (**a**) *(alimentos)* to eat; **c. las uñas** to bite one's nails; **¡cómetelo!** eat it up!; *Fig* **c. a algn a besos** to smother sb with kisses; *Fig* **c. a algn con los ojos** to be unable to take one's eyes off sb; *Fig* **c. algo con los ojos** to devour sth with one's eyes; *Fam* **¿eso con qué se come?** what the heck is that?; *Vulg* **esta tía está como para comérsela** I could really give her one (**b**) *Fig (saltarse)* to omit; *(párrafo)* to skip; *(palabra)* to swallow; **se come las palabras** he slurs his words (**c**) *(color)* to fade

comercial *adj* commercial, sales; **banco c.** commercial bank; **película c.** commercial movie *o Br* film; **tradado c.** trade agreement

comercialización *nf* commercialization, marketing

comercializar [14] *vt* to commercialize, market

comerciante 1 *adj* business-minded
   2 *nmf* merchant; *Pey* **ser (un) c.** to be a moneymaker

comerciar *vi (comprar y vender)* to trade, buy and sell; *(hacer negocios)* to do business

comercio *nm* (**a**) *(de productos)* commerce, trade ❑ **c. electrónico** e-commerce; **c. exterior/interior** foreign/ domestic trade; **c. justo** fair trade; **libre c.** free trade (**b**) *(tienda)* shop, store

comestible 1 *adj* edible, eatable
   2 comestibles *nmpl sing,* foodstuff(s); **tienda de comestibles** grocery store, *Br* grocer's (shop)

cometa 1 *nm Astron* comet
   2 *nf (juguete)* kite

cometer *vt (error, falta)* to make; *(delito, crimen)* to commit

cometido *nm* (**a**) *(tarea)* task, assignment; **desempeñar su c.** to carry out one's task (**b**) *(deber)* duty; **cumplir su c.** to do one's duty

comezón *nm* itch, itching; **sentir c.** to have an itch; *Fig* **sentía c. por replicar** I was itching to answer back

cómic *(pl* **cómics**) *nm Arte Lit* comic

comicial *adj* = of *o* relating to elections

comicidad *nf* comicalness, funniness

comicios *nmpl Pol* elections

cómico, -a 1 *adj* (**a**) *(divertido)* comical, comic, funny (**b**) *Teat* comedy; **actor c.** comedian
   2 *nm,f* comic; *(hombre)* comedian; *(mujer)* comedienne

comida *nf* (**a**) *(alimento)* food ❑ **c. basura** junk food (**b**) *(acción)* meal; **tres comidas al día** three meals a day ❑ **c. campestre** picnic (**c**) *(almuerzo, cena)* meal; *Esp Méx (al mediodía)* lunch

comidilla *nf Fam* talk; **esa pareja es la c. del barrio** that couple are the talk of the street

comido, -a 1 *pp de* **comer**
2 *adj* eaten; **c. por la polilla** motheaten; **se fueron comidos** they went after having had lunch

comienzo *nm* beginning, start; **a comienzos de** at the beginning of; **dar c. a algo** to begin *o* start sth; **en sus comienzos** in its early stages

comillas *nfpl* inverted commas; **entre c.** in inverted commas

comilón, -ona 1 *adj* greedy, gluttonous
2 *nm,f* big eater, glutton

comilona *nf Fam* big meal, feast

comino *nm Bot* cumin, cummin; *Fam* **me importa un c.** I don't give a damn (about it); *Fam* **no valer un c.** not to be worth tuppence

comisaría *nf* police station, *US* precinct

comisario *nm* (**a**) *(de policía) Br* superintendent, *US* captain (**b**) *(delegado)* commissioner, deputy, delegate ▫ **c. europeo** European Commissioner

comiscar [59] *vt & vi Fam* to nibble

comisión *nf* (**a**) *Com (retribución)* commission; **a** *o* **con c.** on a commission basis; **cobrar (una) c.** to get a commission (**por** *o* **sobre** on) ▫ **C. Europea** European Commission; **c. parlamentaria** parliamentary committee (**b**) *(comité)* committee; **c. permanente** standing commission (**c**) *Jur (perpetración)* perpetration, committing

comisionado, -a 1 *pp de* **comisionar**
2 *adj* commisioned
3 *nm,f* commissioner

comisionar *vt* to commission

comisionista *nmf* commission agent

comisura *nf Anat* corner, angle

comité *nm* committee ▫ **c. ejecutivo** executive committee; *Ind* **c. de empresa** works council

comitiva *nf* suite, retinue, procession

como 1 *adv* (**a**) *(modo, manera)* as; **blanco c. el marmol** as white as snow; **dilo c. quieras** say it however you like; **estás c. ausente** you are in another world; **habla c. su padre** he talks like his father; **me gusta c. cantas** I like the way you sing; **tanto c. eso no** not as much as that (**b**) *(en calidad de)* as; **c. presidente** as president; **lo compré c. recuerdo** I bought it as a souvenir (**c**) *(aproximadamente)* about; **c. a la mitad de camino** about halfway; **c. unos diez** about ten (**d**) *(según, conforme)* as; **c. decíamos ayer** as we were saying yesterday
2 *conj* (**a**) *Esp (si)* if; **c. no estudies vas a suspender** if you don't study hard, you'll fail (**b**) *(porque)* as, since; **c. no venías me marché** as you didn't come I left (**c**) *(modo, comparación)* as; **c. si nada** *o* **tal cosa** as if nothing had happened; *Fam* **c. si lo viera** I can imagine perfectly well (**d**) *(que)* **no vimos nada de tanta gente c. había** there were so many people that we couldn't see a thing (**e**) **c. quiera** *véase* **comoquiera**

cómo 1 *adv* (**a**) *(interrogativo)* how, what; **¿c. es grande/ancho?** how big/wide is it?; **¿c. estás?** how are you?; **¿c. ha dicho?** I beg your pardon?; **¿c. lo sabes?** how do you know?; *Esp (a cuanto)* **¿a c. están los tomates?** how much are the tomatoes?; *(por qué)* **¿c. fue que no viniste a la fiesta?** why didn't you come to the party?; *Fam* **¿c.? what?; *Fam* **¿c. es eso?, ¿c. así?** how come? (**b**) *(exclamativo)* how; **¡c. corre el tiempo!** how time flies!; **¡c. has crecido!** you've really grown a lot!; **¡c. no!** but of course!
2 *nm* **el c. y el porqué** the whys and wherefores

cómoda *nf Mueb* chest of drawers, commode

comodidad *nf* comfort, convenience; **con c.** comfortably

comodín *nm Naipes* joker; *Fig* excuse

cómodo, -a *adj* (**a**) *(confortable)* comfortable; **ponerse c.** to make oneself comfortable (**b**) *(útil)* handy, convenient

comodón, -ona *Fam* **1** *adj* comfort-loving
2 *nm,f* comfort lover

comodoro *nm Mil* commodore

comoquiera *adv* (**a**) *(de cualquier manera)* anyway, anyhow; **c. que sea** whatever way, one way or another (**b**) *(puesto que)* **c. que no estaba enterado** as he didn't know

Comores *nfpl* **las (Islas) C.** the Comoros (Islands)

compact [ˈkompak] *nm inv* compact disc, CD

compactación *nf Inform* compression; **c. de ficheros** file compression, zipping

compactar *vt* to compress

compact disk, compact disc [ˈkompakˈðis(k)] *(pl* **compact disks, discs**) *nm* compact disc

compacto, -a 1 *adj* compact, dense
2 *nm (disco)* compact disc, CD

compadecer [46] **1** *vt* to feel sorry for, pity
2 compadecerse *vpr* to have *o* take pity **(de** on)

compadraje *nm* conspiracy, plot

compadre *nm* (**a**) *(padrino)* godfather (**b**) *Am Fam (amigo, compañero)* friend, pal, *Br* mate

compadrear *vi* (**a**) *Am (ser amigos)* to be friends (**b**) *RP (jactarse)* to bluster, boast

compadreo *nm* friendship

compaginación *nf* (**a**) *(combinación)* reconciling (**b**) *Impr* page make-up

compaginar 1 *vt* (**a**) *(combinar)* to combine, make compatible, reconcile (**b**) *Impr* to make up
2 compaginarse *vpr* to be compatible, go together

compaña *nf Fam* company, friends

compañerismo *nm* companionship, comradeship, fellowship

compañero, -a *nm,f* (**a**) *(pareja, acompañante)* companion ▫ **c. de armas** comrade-in-arms; **c. de colegio** *o* **escuela** schoolmate; **c. de equipo** team-mate; **c. de habitación** roommate (**b**) *Fig (de zapato, guante etc)* other one

compañía *nf* (**a**) *(gen)* company; **malas compañías** bad company; **señora de c.** lady companion; **hacer c. a algn** to keep sb company; **en c. de** in the company of (**b**) *(empresa)* company ▫ **c. aérea** airline; **c. de seguros/de teatro** insurance/theatre company (**c**) *Mil* company

comparable *adj* comparable

comparación *nf* comparison; **en c.** comparatively; **en c. con** compared to; **sin c.** beyond compare

comparado, -a 1 *pp de* **comparar**
2 *adj* comparative

comparar *vt* to compare; *Fam* **¡no compares!** far from it!

comparativo, -a *adj & nm* comparative

comparecencia *nf Jur* appearance; **no c.** non-appearance

comparecer [46] *vi* (**a**) *Jur* to appear (**ante** before) (**b**) *(presentarse)* to show up

comparsa 1 *nf* (**a**) *Teat* extras *pl* (**b**) *(de carnaval)* = group of people in carnival dress, masquerade
2 *nm,f* walk-on, extra

compartimentar *vt* to compartmentalize

compartimento *nm*, **compartimiento** *nm* compartment ▫ *Téc* **c. estanco** watertight compartment;

Ferroc Náut **c. de primera/segunda clase** first-/second-class compartment

compartir *vt* **(a)** *(dividir)* to divide (up), share (out) **(b)** *(piso, opinión)* to share

compás *nm* **(a)** *Téc (instrumento)* (pair of) compasses **(b)** *Náut (brújula)* compass **(c)** *Mús (división)* time; *(intervalo)* beat; *(ritmo)* rhythm; **c. de espera** *Mús* bar rest; *Fig (pausa)* delay; **al c. (de la música)** in time (to the music); **llevar el c.** *(con la mano)* to beat time; *(bailando)* to keep time; **perder el c.** to lose the beat

compasión *nf* compassion, pity; **una persona sin c.** a merciless person; **tener c. de algn** to feel sorry for sb

compasivo, -a *adj* compassionate, sympathetic

compatibilidad *nf* compatibility

compatibilizar [14] *vt* to make compatible

compatible *adj también Inform* compatible

compatriota *nmf* compatriot; *(hombre)* fellow countryman; *(mujer)* fellow countrywoman

compay *(pl* **compays)** *nm Cuba Fam* friend, *Br* mate, *US* buddy

compeler *vt Fml* to compel, force

compendiar *vt* to abridge, summarize

compendio *nm* summary, résumé, synopsis

compenetración *nf* **(a)** *(persona)* mutual understanding **(b)** *Fís* interpenetration

compenetrado, -a *adj* **están muy compenetrados** they understand each other very well; **es un equipo muy c.** they work very well as a team

compenetrarse *vpr* **(a)** *(personas)* to understand each other *o* one another; **ella se compenetra muy bien con su papel** she identifies herself very well with her role **(b)** *Fís* to interpenetrate

compensación *nf* compensation, indemnity; **en c.** *(en pago)* in payment, as compensation; *(a cambio)* in exchange ❏ *Fin* **c. bancaria** clearing

compensador, -a 1 *adj* compensating
   2 *nm* compensator

compensar 1 *vt (pérdida, error)* to make up for; *(indemnizar)* to compensate (for), indemnify (against *o* for); *Téc* to balance, compensate; **le compensaron con dos millones** he got two million in compensation
   2 *vi* to be worthwhile; **este trabajo no me compensa** this job's not worth my time

competencia *nf* **(a)** *(rivalidad)* competition; *(a algn, producto)* **hacer la c.** to compete with *o* against ❏ *Com* **c. desleal** unfair competition **(b)** *(incumbencia)* field, scope, province; **eso no es de mi c.** that is outside my scope *o* not in my field **(c)** *(capacidad)* ability, competence, proficiency **(d)** *Am (deportiva)* competition

competente *adj* **(a)** *(adecuado)* appropriate **(b)** *(capaz)* competent, proficient **(c)** *Jur* competent

competer *vt (incumbir)* to come under the jurisdiction of; *(concerner)* to be in the field of; *(corresponder)* to be up to

competición *nf* competition, contest

competidor, -a 1 *adj* competing
   2 *nm,f* **(a)** *Com Dep* competitor **(b)** *(participante)* contestant, candidate **(c)** *(rival)* rival, opponent

competir [47] *vi* **(a)** *(concursar)* to compete **(con** with *o* against, **en** in, **por** for) **(b)** *(rivalizar)* to rival

competitividad *nf* competitiveness

competitivo, -a *adj* competitive

compilación *nf* **(a)** *(acción)* compiling **(b)** *(colección)* compilation

compilador, -a *nm,f* compiler

compilar *vt* to compile

compincharse *vpr* **c. para hacer algo** to plot to do sth

compinche *nmf* **(a)** *Fam (compañero)* chum, pal **(b)** *Pey (cómplice)* accomplice

complacencia *nf* **(a)** *(satisfacción)* satisfaction **(b)** *(indulgencia)* indulgence; **tener excesivas complacencias con** *o* **hacia algn** to be overindulgent towards sb

complacer [42] **1** *vt* **(a)** *(agradar)* to please; **¿en qué puedo complacerle?** what can I do for you?; *Fml* **me complace presentarles a ...** it gives me great pleasure to introduce to you ... **(b)** *(satisfacer)* to satisfy, gratify; *Fml* to oblige
   2 complacerse *vpr* **(a)** *(satisfacerse)* to delight **(en** in), take pleasure **(en** in) **(b)** *Fml* to take pleasure in, be pleased to

complacido, -a 1 *pp de* **complacer**
   2 *adj* pleased, satisfied

complaciente *adj* **(a)** *(agradable)* obliging, helpful **(b)** *Lit (marido)* complaisant

complejidad *nf* complexity

complejo, -a 1 *adj* complex ❏ **c. industrial** industrial park
   2 *nm Ind Psic* complex

complementar 1 *vt* to complement
   2 complementarse *vpr* to complement each other

complementario, -a *adj* complementary

complemento *nm* **(a)** *(gen)* complement ❏ **c. vitamínico** vitamin supplement; *Mil* **oficial de c.** reserve officer **(b)** *Ling* complement, object ❏ **c. directo/indirecto** direct/indirect object **(c)** *(perfección)* culmination, perfection

completamente *adv* completely

completar *vt (gen)* to complete; *(perfeccionar)* to round off; *(acabar)* to finish

completo, -a *adj* **(a)** *(terminado)* complete, completed; **por c.** completely; *(perfecto)* round, perfect; *(terminado)* finished **(b)** *(total)* full; **al c.** full up, full to capacity

complexión *nf Anat* build; **de c. fuerte** well-built

complicación *nf* complication; **buscarse complicaciones** to make life difficult for oneself

complicado, -a 1 *pp de* **complicar**
   2 *adj* **(a)** *(complejo)* complicated, complex **(b)** *(implicado)* involved **(c)** *(persona)* complex

complicar [59] **1** *vt* **(a)** *(gen)* to make complicated, complicate **(b)** *(involucrar)* to involve **(en** in)
   2 complicarse *vpr (gen)* to get complicated; **c. la vida** to make life difficult for oneself

cómplice *nmf* accomplice

complicidad *nf* complicity

complot *(pl* **complots)** *nm* conspiracy, plot

componenda *nf* shady deal; **hacer componendas** to scheme

componente 1 *adj* component, constituent
   2 *nm* **(a)** *(parte, pieza)* component, constituent; *(ingrediente)* ingredient **(b)** *(persona)* member **(c)** *Meteor* **viento de c. norte/sur** northerly/southerly wind

componer [50] *(pp* **compuesto) 1** *vt* **(a)** *(formar)* to compose, make up, form **(b)** *(reparar)* to mend, fix, repair; *Am (hueso)* to set **(c)** *(discusión etc)* to settle; *(ánimos etc)* to soothe **(d)** *(música, versos)* to compose **(e)** *Impr (texto, página)* to compose, set **(f)** *(adornar)* to decorate, adorn
   2 componerse *vpr* **(a)** *(consistir)* to be made up **(de** of), consist **(de** of) **(b)** *(engalanarse, arreglarse)* to dress up **(c)** *Fam* **componérselas** to manage; **¿cómo te las compondrás para hacerlo?** how will you manage to do it?

comportamiento *nm* behaviour, *US* behavior, conduct

comportar 1 *vt (implicar)* to entail, involve

2 comportarse *vpr (conducirse)* to behave; **c. mal** to misbehave; **saber c.** to know how to behave oneself

composición *nf* **(a)** *(gen)* composition; **hacer(se) una c. de lugar** *(decidirse)* to make a plan of action; *(formarse una idea)* to get a picture of a situation **(b)** *(acuerdo)* settlement; *(reconciliación)* reconciliation **(c)** *Impr* setting, composition

compositor, -a *nm,f* **(a)** *(de música)* composer **(b)** *RP (de caballos)* trainer **(c)** *Chile (de huesos)* bonesetter

compostelano, -a 1 *adj* of o from Santiago de Compostela
2 *nm,f* person from Santiago de Compostela

compostura *nf* **(a)** *(composición)* composition, arrangement **(b)** *(reparación)* mending, repair **(c)** *(moderación)* restraint, moderation **(d)** *(dignidad)* composure; **nunca pierde la c.** he never loses his composure **(d)** *(convenio)* agreement

compota *nf Culin* compote

compra *nf* purchase, buy; **la c. de un piso** the purchase of a *Br* flat o *US* apartment; **ir de c.** to go shopping ❑ **c. a crédito** credit purchase; **c. a plazos** *Br* hire purchase, *US* instalment buying

comprador, -a *nm,f* purchaser, buyer, shopper

comprar 1 *vt* **(a)** *(adquirir)* to buy; **cómprame uno** *(para mí)* buy me one, buy one for me; *(yo te lo vendo)* buy one from me **(b)** *Fig (sobornar)* to bribe, buy off
2 comprarse *vpr* to buy (for oneself); **me compré una bicicleta** I bought myself a bicycle

compraventa *nf Com* buying and selling, dealing; **contrato de c.** contract of sale

comprender 1 *vt* **(a)** *(entender)* to understand; **¿comprendes?** you see?; **c. mal** to misunderstand; **hacerse c.** to make oneself understood; **se comprende** it's understandable **(b)** *(contener)* to comprise, include; **viaje con todo comprendido** all-in o inclusive trip
2 comprenderse *vpr* to understand each other o one another

comprensible *adj* understandable

comprensión *nf* understanding

comprensivo, -a *adj* understanding

compresa *nf* **(a)** *(higiénica) Br* sanitary towel, *US* sanitary napkin **(b)** *Med (vendaje)* compress

compresibilidad *nf* compressibility

compresible *adj* compressible

compresión *nf también Inform* compression; **relación de c.** compression ratio

compresor, -a 1 *adj* compressing
2 *nm* compressor

comprimible *adj* compressible

comprimido, -a 1 *pp de* **comprimir**
2 *adj* compressed; **escopeta de aire c.** air rifle
3 *nm Farm* tablet

comprimir 1 *vt también Inform* to compress; *(gente)* to cram together
2 comprimirse *vpr* to get compressed; *(gente)* to squeeze

comprobable *adj* verifiable, provable

comprobación *nf* verification, check, checking

comprobante *nm* **(a)** *Com (recibo, justificante)* voucher, receipt **(b)** *Jur* document in proof

comprobar [63] *vt* **(a)** *(verificar)* to verify, check; *(demostrar)* to prove **(b)** *(confirmar)* to confirm; **compruébalo tú mismo** see o look for yourself

comprometedor, -a 1 *adj* **(a)** *(cosa)* compromising **(b)** *(persona)* troublemaking
2 *nm,f* troublemaker

comprometer 1 *vt* **(a)** *(arriesgar)* to endanger, risk, jeopardize; *(persona)* to compromise **(b)** *(empeñar)* to commit; *(obligar)* to compel, oblige, force **(c)** *(involucrar)* to involve **(d)** *(poner en un aprieto)* to embarrass
2 comprometerse *vpr* **(a)** *(gen)* to compromise oneself **(b)** *(obligarse)* to commit oneself; **c. a hacer algo** to undertake to do sth **(c)** *(involucrarse)* to involve oneself; **no te comprometas** don't get involved

comprometido, -a 1 *pp de* **comprometer**
2 *adj* **(a)** *(arriesgado)* in jeopardy; *(persona)* compromised **(b)** *(obligado)* obliged, compelled **(c)** *(involucrado)* involved **(d)** *(para casarse)* engaged **(e)** *(trabajo, situación)* delicate, difficult, awkward

compromisario, -a *adj & nm,f* representative

compromiso *nm* **(a)** *(obligación)* obligation, commitment; **libre de c.** without obligation; **por c.** out of a sense of duty; **ella siempre cumple sus compromisos** she always honours o fulfils her commitments **(b)** *(acuerdo)* agreement **(c)** *Fml (cita)* appointment; *(amorosa)* date; **c. matrimonial** engagement; **soltero y sin c.** single and unattached **(d)** *(situación difícil)* difficult situation; **poner a algn en un c.** to put sb in a difficult o embarrassing situation

compuerta *nf Téc* sluice, floodgate

compuesto, -a 1 *pp de* **componer**
2 *adj* **(a)** *(múltiple)* compound, composite; **palabra/sustancia compuesta** compound word/substance **(b)** *(elegante)* dressed up; *(arreglado)* tidy **(c)** *(comedido)* composed **(d)** *(reparado)* mended, repaired
3 *nm* compound

compulsa *nf* **(a)** *(cotejo)* collation, comparison **(b)** *Jur (documento)* certified true copy

compulsar *vt* **(a)** *(cotejar)* to collate **(b)** *Jur (hacer copia)* to make a certified true copy of

compulsión *nf* compulsion

compulsivo, -a *adj* compulsory

compunción *nf* *(arrepentimiento)* compunction; *(tristeza)* sorrow, sadness

compungido, -a 1 *pp de* **compungir**
2 *adj* *(arrepentido)* remorseful; *(triste)* sorrowful, sad

compungir [24] **1** *vt (entristecer)* to make sorry o sad
2 compungirse *vpr (arrepentirse)* to feel remorseful; *(entristecerse)* to feel sorry o sad

computable *adj* computable

computación *nf* computing

computacional *adj* computational, computer

computador *nm*, **computadora** *nf esp Am* computer

computar *vt* **(a)** *(calcular)* to compute, calculate **(b)** *Fml (conmutar)* to consider valid; **el primer año no se computa a efectos de antigüedad** the first year doesn't count for seniority

computarizar *vt*, **computerizar** [14] *vt* to computerize

cómputo *nm* computation, calculation

comulgante *nmf* communicant

comulgar [38] **1** *vi* **(a)** *Rel* to receive Holy Communion **(b)** *Fig* **c. con** *(compartir ideas etc)* to share; **no comulgo con esas teorías** I don't agree with these theories; *Fam* **c. con ruedas de molino** to be extremely gullible o credulous
2 *vt* to administer Holy Communion to

comulgatorio *nm Rel* communion rail

común *adj* **(a)** *(gen)* common; **bien c.** common good; **de c. acuerdo** by common consent; **hacer algo en c.** to do sth jointly; **poco c.** unusual; **por lo c.** generally **(b)** *(compartido)* shared, communal; **amigos comunes** mutual friends; **dormitorio/televisión c.** communal dormitory/television; **gastos comunes** shared expenses

2 *nm* (**a**) *(pueblo)* **el c.** the community; *(mayoría)* **el c. de la gente** the majority of people (**b**) *Br Pol* **los Comunes** the Commons

comuna *nf* (**a**) *(comunidad)* commune (**b**) *Am (municipio)* municipality; *(ayuntamiento)* town council

comunal *adj* (**a**) *(común)* communal (**b**) *Am (del municipio)* municipal

comunicable *adj* (**a**) *(transmitible)* communicable (**b**) *(comunicativo)* sociable

comunicación *nf* (**a**) *(gen)* communication; **estar/ ponerse en c. (con algn)** to be/get in touch (with sb); **vía de c.** thoroughfare (**b**) *(comunicado)* communication; *(oficial)* communiqué (**c**) *Tel* connection (**d**) *(unión)* link, connection (**e**) **comunicaciones** *(correos, transportes etc)* communications

comunicado, -a 1 *pp de* **comunicar**
2 *adj* served; **una zona bien comunicada** a well-served area; **dos ciudades bien comunicadas** two towns with good connections (between them)
3 *nm (parte)* communiqué; **c. de prensa** press release

comunicador, -a *nm,f* communicator

comunicante 1 *adj (que comunica)* communicating; **vasos comunicantes** communicating vessels
2 *nmf (informador)* informer

comunicar [59] **1** *vt* (**a**) *(gen)* to communicate; **comuníquenoslo lo antes posible** let us know as soon as possible (**b**) *(transmitir)* to convey (**c**) *(conectar)* to connect
2 *vi* (**a**) *(estar, ponerse en comunicación)* to communicate; *(por carta)* to correspond **c. con algn** to get in touch with sb (**b**) *(estar conectado)* to be linked, be connected (**c**) *EspTel Br* to be engaged, *US* be busy; **está comunicando** the line is *Br* engaged *o US* busy
3 comunicarse *vpr* (**a**) *(gen)* to communicate (**b**) *(transmitirse)* to be transmitted

comunicativo, -a *adj* communicative, sociable

comunidad *nf* community; **en c.** together ❑ *Pol* **c. autónoma** autonomous region, = largest administrative division in Spain, with its own Parliament and a number of devolved powers; *Jur* **c. de bienes** co-ownership; **c. de propietarios** owners' association

comunión *nf* (**a**) *(compenetración)* communion, fellowship (**b**) *(comunidad)* community (**c**) *Rel* Holy Communion

comunismo *nm Pol* communism

comunista *adj & nmf Pol* communist

comunitario, -a *adj* (**a**) *(de una comunidad)* community; **espíritu c.** community spirit (**b**) *(de la UE)* of the European Union, Community

con *prep* (**a**) *(gen)* with; *(instrumento, medio, modo)* with; **¿c. qué lo cortarás?** what will you cut it with?; **voy cómodo c. estas botas/este jersey** I'm comfortable in these boots/ this sweater (**b**) *(en compañía, juntamente)* with; **c. buena salud** in good health; **c. ese frío/niebla** in that cold/fog; **estar c. (la) gripe/(un) resfriado** to have the flu/a cold; **vine c. mi hermana** I came with my sister (**c**) *(contenido)* with; **una bolsa c. dinero** a bag of money (**d**) *(relación)* to; **habló c. todos** he spoke to everybody; **sé amable c. ella** be nice to her (**e**) *(con la condición)* as; **c. (sólo) que ...** as long as ...; **c. tal (de) que ...** provided that ...; **c. todo (y eso)** even so (**f**) *(con infinitivo)* **c. llamar ya quedarás bien** you'll make a good impression just by phoning (**g**) *(a pesar de)* in spite of; **c. ser tan caro no funciona bien** it doesn't work despite being expensive

conato *nm* (**a**) *(intento)* attempt; **hizo un c. de irse** he made an attempt to go (**b**) *(principio)* beginnings *pl*, start (**c**) *(tendencia)* tendency, inclination

concadenar *vt véase* **concatenar**

concatenación *nf* concatenation, linking

concatenar *vt* to concatenate, link together

concavidad *nf* concavity

cóncavo, -a *adj* concave

concebible *adj* conceivable, imaginable

concebir [47] **1** *vt* (**a**) *(plan, hijo)* to conceive; **no concibo cómo pudo hacerlo** I can't understand why he did it (**b**) *Fig (sentimiento)* to have, experience; **c. esperanzas** to build up one's hopes; **no le hagas c. esperanzas** don't raise his hopes
2 *vi (quedarse embarazada)* to become pregnant, conceive

conceder *vt* (**a**) *(gen)* to grant, concede; *(premio)* to award; **concédeme cinco minutos** give me five minutes; **c. demasiado valor a algo** to attach too much value to sth (**b**) *(admitir)* to admit, concede

concejal, -a *nm,f* town councillor

concejalía *nf* councillorship

concejo *nm* (town) council

concelebrar *vt Rel* to concelebrate

concentración *nf (gen)* concentration; *(de manifestantes)* gathering, rally ❑ **campo de c.** concentration camp; **c. parcelaria** (land) consolidation

concentrado, -a 1 *pp de* **concentrar**
2 *adj (gen)* concentrated; *(gente)* gathered
3 *nm* concentrate, extract

concentrar 1 *vt* to concentrate; **la manifestación concentró miles de personas** thousands of people turned up at the rally
2 concentrarse *vpr* to concentrate; **concéntrate en lo que haces** concentrate on what you're doing; **se concentraron más de un millón de personas** over a million people turned up

concéntrico, -a *adj* concentric

concepción *nf* conception

concepto *nm* (**a**) *(idea)* concept, conception, idea; **formarse un c. (de algo/algn)** to form an opinion (of sth/ sb) (**b**) *(opinión)* opinion, view; **tener buen/mal c. de** to have a good/bad opinion of (**c**) *(aspecto)* **bajo/por ningún c.** under no circumstances (**d**) *(en calidad de)* **en c. de** by way of (**e**) *Fin (apartado)* heading, section

conceptual *adj* conceptual

conceptualizar [14] *vt* to conceptualize

conceptuar [4] *vt* to deem, consider, think; **bien/mal conceptuado** well/badly considered

conceptuoso, -a *adj* high-sounding, sententious

concerniente *adj* concerning, regarding; *Fml* **en lo c. a** with regard to

concernir [25] *v impers* (**a**) *(afectar)* to concern, touch; **en lo que a mí/ti concierne** as far as I am/you are concerned; **en lo que concierne a** with regard *o* respect to (**b**) *(corresponder)* to be up to; **a ti te concierne decidir** it's up to you to decide

concertación *nf* settlement; *Ind* **c. social** = process of employer-trade union negotiations

concertado, -a 1 *pp de* **concertar**
2 *adj* (**a**) *(acordado)* arranged (**b**) *Esp (colegio)* state-assisted

concertar [3] **1** *vt* (**a**) *(actividad, acción)* to plan, co-ordinate; *(cita, entrevista)* to arrange; *(precio)* to agree on; *(acuerdo)* to reach; *(tratado)* to conclude (**b**) *Mús (voces)* to harmonize
2 *vi* (**a**) *(concordar)* to agree, tally (**b**) *Mús (armonizar)* to harmonize, be in tune
3 concertarse *vpr (ponerse de acuerdo)* to get together, reach an agreement

concertina *nf Mús* concertina

concertino *nm Mús* first violin

concertista *nmf* soloist

concesión *nf* (**a**) *(gen)* concession, granting; **hacer concesiones** to make concessions (**b**) *(de un premio)* awarding

concesionario, -a *adj* concessionary
  2 *nm,f Com* concessionaire, concessioner, licence *o US* license holder, licensee

concha *nf* (**a**) *Zool (caparazón)* shell; *(carey)* tortoiseshell (**b**) *Teat (del apuntador)* prompt box (**c**) *Andes RP Vulg* cunt

conchabar 1 *vt* (**a**) *(unir)* to blend (**b**) *CSur (contratar)* to hire
  2 conchabarse *vpr* (**a**) *(confabularse)* to gang up, scheme (**b**) *(emplearse como criado)* to offer one's services as a servant

concheto, -a *RP Fam* **1** *adj* posh
  2 *nm,f* rich kid

concho¹ *nm Andes (residuos)* residue; *(sobras de comida)* leftovers *pl*

concho² *interj Fam* fudge!, sugar!

conchudo, -a *adj* (**a**) *Andes Méx Ven Fam (desfachatado)* shameless; *(cómodo)* lazy (**b**) *Méx Ven Fam (oportunista)* **es muy c.** he always has an eye for the main chance, *Br* he's a chancer (**c**) *Perú RP muy Fam (persona despreciable)* **ser muy c.** to be a real jerk *o Br* dickhead

conciencia *nf* (**a**) *(conocimiento)* consciousness, awareness; **a c.** conscientiously; **en c.** in truth; **tener/tomar c. (de algo)** to be/become aware (of sth) (**b**) *(moral)* conscience; **con la c. tranquila** with a clear conscience; **me remuerde la conciencia** I have a guilty conscience

concienciar 1 *vt* to make aware (**de** of)
  2 concienciarse *vpr* to become aware (**de** of)

concienzudo, -a *adj* conscientious

concierto *nm* (**a**) *(acuerdo)* agreement; *Fig* concord, concert (**b**) *(disposición)* order; **sin orden ni c.** any old how (**c**) *Mús* concert; *(composición)* concerto

conciliábulo *nm* secret meeting

conciliación *nf* conciliation, reconciliation

conciliador, -a *adj* conciliating, conciliatory

conciliar¹ *vt* (**a**) *(ideas, grupos etc)* to conciliate, bring together; *(enemigos)* to reconcile, placate (**b**) **c. el sueño** to get to sleep

conciliar² *adj* conciliar

conciliatorio, -a *adj* conciliatory

concilio *nm Rel* council; **el C. de Trento** the Council of Trent

concisión *nf* concision, conciseness

conciso, -a *adj* concise, brief

concitar *vt* to stir up, incite; **concitó el odio del pueblo contra el gobierno** he incited the people's hatred for the government

conciudadano, -a *nm,f* fellow citizen

cónclave *nm*, **conclave** *nm* (**a**) *Rel* conclave (**b**) *Fig (reunión)* private meeting; **tener un c.** to sit in conclave

concluir [34] **1** *vt* (**a**) *(terminar)* to finish; *(negocio)* to close (**b**) *(deducir)* to conclude, infer
  2 *vi* to finish, end
  3 concluirse *vpr* to finish, end

conclusión *nf* (**a**) *(final)* conclusion, end; *(resultado)* result; **en c.** in conclusion (**b**) *(deducción)* conclusion; **llegar a una c.** to come to a conclusion

concluyente *adj* conclusive, decisive

concomerse *vpr* to be consumed, itch; **c. de impaciencia** to itch with impatience; **c. de envidia** to be green with envy

concomitancia *nf* concomitance

concomitante *adj* concomitant

concordancia *nf* concordance

concordante *adj* concordant

concordar [63] **1** *vt (concertar)* to bring into agreement; *Ling (palabras)* to make agree
  2 *vi (gen)* to agree; **esto no concuerda con lo que dijo ayer** this doesn't fit in with what he said yesterday

concordato *nm* concordat

concorde *adj* in agreement

concordia *nf* concord, harmony

concreción *nf* (**a**) *(concisión)* concision, conciseness (**b**) *Geol Med* concretion

concretamente *adv* (**a**) *(exactamente)* exactly; **no sé qué quiere c.** I don't know exactly what he wants (**b**) *(en particular)* in particular, specifically; **quiero ése c.** I want that one in particular

concretar 1 *vt* (**a**) *(precisar)* to specify, state explicitly; *(fijar)* to fix; **c. una fecha/una hora** to fix a date/a time (**b**) *(limitar)* to limit, direct; **concretemos nuestros esfuerzos en algo práctico** let's direct our efforts to practical objectives (**c**) *(resumir)* to sum up
  2 concretarse *vpr* (**a**) *(limitarse)* **c. a** to confine oneself *o* keep to (**b**) *(materializarse)* to become established *o* definite; **mis ideas empiezan a c.** my ideas are beginning to take shape

concretizar [14] *vt* to specify, state exactly

concreto, -a 1 *adj* (**a**) *(preciso, real)* concrete; **en c.** *(específicamente)* specifically; *(en resumen)* in brief, in short (**b**) *(particular)* particular; **buscaba un tipo de vestido c.** I was looking for a particular type of dress; **en el caso c. de ...** in the particular case of ...
  2 *nm Am* concrete

concubina *nf* concubine

concubinato *nm* concubinage

conculcar [59] *vt* to infringe, break; **este acto conculca los principios de la ley** this act violates all principles of law

concuñado, -a *nm,f (hombre)* husband of one's brother-in-law *o* sister-in-law; *(mujer)* sister *o* wife of one's brother-in-law *o* sister in law

concupiscencia *nf* concupiscence, lustfulness

concupiscente *adj* concupiscent, lustful

concurrencia *nf* (**a**) *(conjunción)* concurrence, conjunction (**b**) *(público)* attendance, audience; **divirtió a la c.** he kept the audience amused

concurrente 1 *adj* concurrent
  2 *nmf* person present; **los concurrentes** those present; *(público)* members of the audience

concurrido, -a 1 *pp de* **concurrir**
  2 *adj* (**a**) *(espectáculo)* well-attended, popular (**b**) *(calle, lugar público)* crowded, busy

concurrir *vi* (**a**) *(convergir) (gente)* to converge (**en** on), meet (**en** in); *Geom (líneas)* to cross, intersect; **todos concurrieron a la boda** everybody attended the wedding (**b**) *(coincidir)* to concur, coincide; **concurren unas circunstancias especiales** under very special circumstances (**c**) *(contribuir)* to contribute (**en** to) (**d**) *(concursar) (en concurso)* to compete; *(en elecciones, examen)* to be a candidate

concursante *nmf* (**a**) *(en un concurso)* contestant, competitor, participant (**b**) *(para un empleo)* candidate

concursar *vi* (**a**) *(competir)* to compete (**b**) *(para un empleo)* to be a candidate; *(para proyecto de trabajo)* to tender

concurso *nm* (**a**) *(competición)* competition; *(de belleza, deportiva)* contest; **fuera de c.** out of the running ☐ **c. radiofónico** radio quiz (programme) (**b**) *Fml (concurrencia)* concourse, help, collaboration; **con el c. de todos** with everyone's assistance (**c**) *(llamamiento)* tender; **presentar (una obra) a c.** to invite tenders (for a piece of work)

condado *nm* county

condal *adj* = of o relating to a count; **la Ciudad C.** Barcelona

conde *nm* count

condecoración *nf* decoration, medal

condecorar *vt* to decorate

condena *nf* (**a**) *(desaprobación)* condemnation, disapproval (**b**) *Jur (sentencia)* sentence, conviction; **cumplir la c.** to serve one's sentence

condenable *adj* condemnable, blameworthy

condenación *nf* condemnation; *Rel* damnation

condenadamente *adv Fam* darned

condenado, -a 1 *pp de* **condenar**
2 *adj* (**a**) *Jur* convicted; **c. a muerte** condemned to death (**b**) *Rel* damned (**c**) *Constr (cegado)* condemned (**d**) *(sin arreglo)* hopeless, doomed; **un plan c. al fracaso** a plan doomed to fail (**e**) *Fam (maldito)* damned
3 *nm,f* (**a**) *Jur* convicted person; *(a muerte)* condemned person; *Fam* **trabajar como un c.** to work like a horse (**b**) *Fam (miserable)* wretch

condenar 1 *vt* (**a**) *Jur* to convict, find guilty; **la condenaron a muerte** she was condemned to death (**b**) *(desaprobar)* to condemn (**c**) *(plan)* to doom (**d**) *Constr (puerta, ventana)* to block o wall off
2 condenarse *vpr Rel* to be damned

condenatorio, -a *adj* condemnatory

condensable *adj* condensable

condensación *nf* (**a**) *(acción)* condensing (**b**) *(efecto)* condensation

condensado, -a 1 *pp de* **condensar**
2 *adj* condensed; **leche condensada** condensed milk

condensador *nm Elec* condenser

condensar 1 *vt* to condense
2 condensarse *vpr* to condense

condesa *nf* countess

condescendencia *nf* (**a**) *(deferencia)* condescension (**b**) *(amabilidad)* affability

condescender [64] *vi* (**a**) *(dignarse)* to condescend (**b**) *(ceder)* to comply (with), consent (to)

condescendiente *adj* (**a**) *(transigente)* condescending (**b**) *(complaciente)* obliging, helpful

condestable *nm Hist* High Constable

condición *nf* (**a**) *(situación)* condition, state; **condiciones de salud** state of health; **en buenas/malas condiciones** in good/bad condition; **estar en condiciones de hacer algo** *(físicas)* to be fit to do sth; *(morales)* to be in a position to do sth (**b**) *(manera de ser)* nature, character; **de c. rebelde/bonachona** of a rebellious/an easy-going nature (**c**) *(índole)* status, position; **en su c. de director** in his capacity as director (**d**) *(circunstancia)* circumstance, condition; **condiciones de trabajo** working conditions; **con la c. de que ...** on condition that ...; **poner condiciones** to lay down conditions (**e**) *(aptitud)* aptitude, talent; **tener condiciones para la música** to have an aptitude o a talent for music

condicionado, -a 1 *pp de* **condicionar**
2 *adj* conditioned

condicional 1 *adj* conditional
2 *nm Ling* conditional

condicionamiento *nm* conditioning

condicionante *nm* determinant

condicionar *vt* to condition; **una cosa condiciona la otra** one thing determines the other

cóndilo *nm Anat* condyle

condimentación *nf Culin* seasoning, flavouring, *US* flavoring

condimentar *vt Culin* to season, flavour, *US* flavor

condimento *nm Culin* seasoning, flavouring, *US* flavoring

condiscípulo, -a *nm,f Educ* fellow pupil o student, schoolmate

condolencia *nf* condolence, sympathy

condolerse [41] *vpr* **c. (de)** to sympathize (with), feel pity (for), feel sorry (for)

condominio *nm* (**a**) *Jur* joint ownership (**b**) *Pol* condominium (**c**) *Am (edificio) Br* block of flats, *US* condominium

condón *nf* condom, rubber

condonación *nf* condonation, remission

condonar *vt (ofensa)* to condone; *(deuda)* to cancel, remit

cóndor *nm Orn* condor

conducción *nf* (**a**) *Esp Aut* driving (**b**) *Fís* conduction (**c**) *(transporte)* transportation; *(por tubería)* piping; *(por cable)* wiring (**d**) *(cañería)* pipe, intake

conducir [18] **1** *vt (coche, ganado)* to drive; *(líquido)* to convey; *(electricidad)* to carry, conduct; *(gente, ejército)* to lead; *(negocio)* to manage
2 *vi* (**a**) *Aut* to drive; **permiso de c.** driving licence, *US* driver's license (**b**) *(llevar)* to lead; **eso no conduce a nada** this leads nowhere
3 conducirse *vpr Fml* to conduct oneself, behave

conducta *nf* behaviour, *US* behavior, conduct; **mala c.** misbehaviour, misconduct

conductibilidad *nf*, **conductividad** *nf Elec* conductivity

conductismo *nm Psic* behaviourism, *US* behaviorism

conductividad *nf Fís* conductivity

conducto *nm* (**a**) *(tubería)* pipe (**b**) *Anat* duct, canal (**c**) *Fig (canal)* channel; **por conductos oficiales** through official channels

conductor, -a 1 *adj* conductive
2 *nm,f Aut* driver
3 *nm Elec* conductor; **no c.** non-conductor

conectado, -a *adj* (**a**) *Elec* connected (**a** to) (**b**) *Inform* on-line

conectar 1 *vt* (**a**) *(aparato, mecanismo) (con cables)* to connect (**b**) *(encender) (radio, calefacción)* to turn on, switch on
2 *vi* (**a**) *Rad TV* **c. con** to go over to (**b**) *(comunicar)* **c. con** to enter into a relationship with (**c**) *Fam (enterarse)* to be tuned in, understand

conectividad *nf Inform* connectivity

conector *nm (clavija, enchufe)* connector; *(cable)* cable, lead

coneja *nf Zool* doe; *Fam* **ser una c.** to breed like rabbits

conejar *nm* rabbit hutch

conejera *nf (doméstica)* rabbit hutch; *(en libertad)* rabbit warren o burrow; *Fig* **viven en una c.** they live in a right dive

conejero, -a 1 *adj* rabbit-hunting
2 *nm* rabbit breeder

conejillo *nm Zool* **c. de Indias** guinea pig
conejo *nm* (**a**) *Zool* rabbit (**b**) *Esp Vulg (coño)* pussy, *US* beaver
conexión *nf* (**a**) *Téc* connection; **estar en c. con** to be connected to (**b**) *Fig* relationship; **nuestra empresa tiene buenas conexiones** our company has good connections
conexo *adj* connected
confabulación *nf* conspiracy, plot
confabulador, -a *nm,f* conspirator, plotter
confabular 1 *vi* to confabulate, discuss
 2 confabularse *vpr* to conspire, plot
confección *nf* (**a**) *Cost* dressmaking, tailoring; *(ropa hecha)* off-the-peg clothes; **la industria de la c.** the clothing industry (**b**) *(realización)* making, making up
confeccionador, -a *nm,f* (**a**) *Cost* outfitter (**b**) *(realizador)* maker, author
confeccionar *vt (vestido, lista)* to make (up); *Culin (plato)* to cook
confeccionista *nmf Cost* outfitter
confederación *nf* confederation, confederacy
confederado, -a 1 *pp de* **confederar**
 2 *adj & nm,f* confederate
confederal *adj* confederative
confederar 1 *vt* to confederate
 2 confederarse *vpr* to confederate, become a confederation
conferencia *nf* (**a**) *(charla)* lecture, talk; **dar una c. (sobre algo)** to lecture (on sth), give a lecture (on sth) (**b**) *Pol* conference, meeting ❑ **c. de prensa** press conference (**c**) *Tel (llamada)* long-distance call; **poner una c. con Toledo** to make o place a call to Toledo
conferenciante *nmf* lecturer
conferenciar *vi* to confer (**sobre** on, **con** with)
conferencista *nmf Am* speaker
conferir [62] *vt Fml* (**a**) *(honor, privilegio)* to confer, bestow, award (**b**) *(dar)* to give; **las canas le conferían un aire digno** his white hair gave him an air of dignity
confesar [3] **1** *vt* to confess, admit; *(crimen)* to own up to; *Rel (pecados)* to confess; *(pecador)* hear the confession of; **¡confiésalo!** own up!
 2 *vi Jur (decir toda la verdad)* to own up; *Fam* **c. de plano** to admit everything
 3 confesarse *vpr* to confess; *Rel* to go to confession, make one's confession; **c. culpable** to admit one's guilt
confesión *nf* confession, admission; *Rel* confession
confesional *adj* denominational
confesionario *nm Rel* confessional
confeso, -a 1 *adj Jur* self-confessed
 2 *nmf Hist* converted Jew
confesonario *nm Rel véase* **confesionario**
confesor *nm* confessor
confeti *nm* confetti
confiabilidad *nf Am* reliability
confiable *adj Am* reliable
confiado, -a 1 *pp de* **confiar**
 2 *adj* (**a**) *(engreído)* self-satisfied; *(presumido)* conceited (**b**) *(crédulo)* gullible, unsuspecting
confianza *nf* (**a**) *(seguridad)* confidence; **con toda c.** in all confidence; **en c.** confidentially; **tener c. en uno mismo** to be self-confident; *Fml (cartas)* **en la c. de que ...** trusting that ... (**b**) *(fe)* trust; **de c.** *(fiable)* reliable; *(de responsabilidad)* trustworthy (**c**) *(presunción)* conceit (**d**) *(franqueza)* familiarity, intimacy; **estar en c.** to be among friends; **tener mucha c. con algn** to be on intimate terms

with sb; **tomarse (demasiadas) confianzas** to take liberties
confiar [32] **1** *vt (entregar)* to entrust; *(información, secreto)* to confide
 2 *vi (estar seguro de)* to be confident; *(tener fe)* to trust; **confío en ella** I trust her; **no confíes en su ayuda** don't count on his help
 3 confiarse *vpr* to confide (**en** o **a** in); **c. demasiado en algo** to be over-confident about sth
confidencia *nf* confidence, secret
confidencial *adj* confidential
confidencialidad *nf* confidentiality
confidente, -a *nm,f* (**a**) *(hombre)* confidant; *(mujer)* confidante (**b**) *(de la policía)* informer
configuración *nf* (**a**) configuration, shape; **la c. del terreno** the lie of the land (**b**) *Inform* configuration
configurar *vt* (**a**) to shape, form (**b**) *Inform* to configure
confín *nm* limit, boundary; **los confines del conocimiento** the limits of knowledge
confinamiento *nm* , **confinación** *nf* (**a**) *(de detenido)* confinement (**en** to) (**b**) *(de desterrado)* banishment (**a** o **en** to)
confinar *vt* (**a**) *(detener)* to confine (**en** to) (**b**) *(desterrar)* to banish (**a** o **en** to)
confinar 1 *vt Jur* to confine
 2 *vi (territorio)* **c. con** to border on
 3 confinarse *vpr* to shut oneself away o up
confirmación *nf* confirmation
confirmar *vt* to confirm; *Prov* **la excepción confirma la regla** the exception proves the rule
confirmatorio, -a *adj* confirmatory
confiscación *nf* confiscation
confiscar [59] *vt* to confiscate
confitado, -a 1 *pp de* **confitar**
 2 *adj* candied, glacé; **frutas confitadas** crystallized fruit
confitar *vt (fruta)* to candy; *(carne)* to preserve
confite *nm Br* sweet, *US* candy
confitería *nf* (**a**) *(tienda)* *Br* sweet shop, confectioner's (shop), *US* candy store (**b**) *RP (cafetería)* café
confitero, -a *nm,f* confectioner
confitura *nf* preserve, jam
conflagración *nf Fml* (**a**) *(fuego)* conflagration (**b**) *(guerra)* outbreak
conflictividad *nf* **c. laboral** labour o *US* labor disputes *pl* o unrest
conflictivo, -a *adj* delicate; **tiempos conflictivos** times of conflict; **un tema c.** a delicate o difficult subject
conflicto *nm* conflict ❑ **c. armado** armed conflict; **c. laboral** labour o *US* labor dispute
confluencia *nf* confluence
confluente *adj* confluent
confluir [34] *vi* to converge; *(ríos, caminos)* to meet, come together
conformación *nf* structure, shape
conformar 1 *vt (configurar)* to shape
 2 *vi (concordar)* to agree (**con** with); **de buen c.** easy going
 3 conformarse *vpr (contentarse)* to resign oneself, be content; **se conformó con una recompensa insignificante** he agreed to a small compensation
conforme 1 *adj* (**a**) *(satisfecho)* satisfied; **c.** agreed, all right; **no estoy c.** I don't agree (**b**) *(acorde)* **c. a** in accordance o keeping with; **c. a la realidad/sus necesidades** in accordance with reality/his needs
 2 *conj* (**a**) *(según, como)* as; **c. lo vi/lo oí** as I saw/heard it

(**b**) *(en cuanto)* as soon as; **ven c. te llame** como as soon as I call you (**c**) *(a medida que)* as; **la policía los detenía c. iban saliendo** the police were arresting them as they came out
3 *nm* approval, agreement

conformidad *nf* (**a**) *(aprobación)* approval, consent (**b**) *(resignación)* resignation (**c**) *(afinidad)* conformity; **en c. (con algo)** in conformity (with sth); **no c.** nonconformity

conformismo *nm* conformity

conformista *adj & nmf* conformist

confort *(pl* **conforts**) *nm* comfort; *(en anuncio)* **'todo c.'** 'all mod cons'

confortable *adj* comfortable

confortador, -a *adj,* **confortante** *adj* (**a**) *(que fortalece)* invigorating (**b**) *Fig (que consuela)* comforting; *(que anima)* cheering

confortar *vt* (**a**) *(fortalecer)* to invigorate (**b**) *Fig (consolar)* to comfort; *(animar)* to cheer

confraternar *vi* to fraternize

confraternidad *nf* brotherliness

confraternizar [14] *vi* to fraternize

confrontación *nf* (**a**) *(enfrentamiento)* confrontation (**b**) *(comparación)* comparison, collation

confrontar 1 *vt* (**a**) *(encarar)* to confront; *(carear)* to bring face to face (**b**) *(cotejar)* to compare, collate
2 *vi (lindar)* to border
3 confrontarse *vpr* **c. con** to face, confront

confundible *adj* **c. con** easily confused with o mistaken for

confundir 1 *vt* (**a**) *(equivocar)* to confuse (**con** with), mistake (**con** for); *(persona)* to mislead; **le confundió con su prima** he mistook her for his cousin (**b**) *(mezclar)* to mix (**c**) *(turbar)* to confound, embarrass; **me ha confundido su amabilidad** I'm overwhelmed by his kindness
2 confundirse *vpr* (**a**) *(equivocarse)* to be mistaken; *(teléfono)* **se ha confundido** you've got the wrong number (**b**) *(mezclarse)* to mingle; *(colores, formas)* to blend; **la casa se confunde con el paisaje** the house blends into the landscape; **se confundió entre el gentío** he disappeared into the crowd (**c**) *(turbarse)* to be confused o embarrassed

confusión *nf* (**a**) *(desorden)* confusion, chaos (**b**) *(equivocación)* confusion, mistake (**c**) *(turbación)* confusion, embarrassment

confusionismo *nm* confusion

confuso, -a *adj* (**a**) *(poco claro) (estilo)* confused, obscure; *(formas, recuerdos)* blurred, vague; *(ideas)* confused (**b**) *(mezclado)* mixed up (**c**) *(turbado)* confused, embarrassed

conga *nf Mús* conga

congelación *nf* (**a**) *(gen)* freezing (**b**) *Fin (de salarios, precios)* freeze (**c**) *Med* frostbite

congelado, -a 1 *pp de* **congelar**
2 *adj* frozen; *Med* frostbitten
3 congelados *nmpl* frozen food *sing*

congelador *nm* freezer

congelar 1 *vt (alimento, líquido)* to freeze; *Fin* **c. precios** to freeze prices; *Med* **un dedo congelado** a frostbitten finger
2 congelarse *vpr* (**a**) *(alimento, líquido)* to freeze; *Fam* **me estoy congelando** I'm freezing (**b**) *Med* to get frostbitten

congénere 1 *adj* congeneric, congenerous
2 *nm,f* (**a**) *Bot Zool* congener (**b**) *Pey* sort, kind

congeniar *vi* to get on (**con** with); **no congenia con su familia** he doesn't get on very well with his family

congénito, -a *adj* congenital, innate

congestión *nf* congestion ◻ *Med* **c. cerebral** stroke

congestionado, -a *adj (cara)* flushed; *(calle)* congested; *(nariz)* blocked

congestionar 1 *vt Aut Med* to congest
2 congestionarse *vpr* to become congested

conglomeración *nf* conglomeration

conglomerado, -a *pp de* **conglomerar**
2 *nm Geol Téc* conglomerate

conglomerar *vt* to conglomerate

Congo *nm* **el C.** *(río) Br* the (River) Congo, *US* the Congo (River); *(país)* (the) Congo

congoja *nf* (**a**) *(angustia)* anguish, distress (**b**) *(pena)* sorrow, grief

congoleño, -a *adj & nm,f,* **congolés, -esa** *adj & nm,f* Congolese

congraciar 1 *vt* to win over
2 congraciarse *vpr* to ingratiate oneself (**con** with)

congratulación *nf Fml* congratulation

congratular 1 *vt* to congratulate (**por** on)
2 congratularse *vpr* to congratulate oneself (**por** on)

congregación *nf (junta)* assembly; *Rel* congregation

congregante *nmf* member of the congregation

congregar [38] **1** *vt* to assemble, bring together
2 congregarse *vpr* to assemble, gather

congresista *nmf, Arg Chile* **congresal** *nmf* member of congress

congreso *nm* congress, conference. ◻ *Pol* **C. de los Diputados** Parliament, *US* Congress

congrio *nm (pez)* conger (eel)

congruencia *nf* (**a**) *(coherencia)* congruity (**b**) *Mat* congruence

congruente *adj,* **congruo, -a** *adj* (**a**) *(coherente)* coherent, suitable (**b**) *Mat* congruent

cónico, -a *adj* (**a**) *(en forma de cono)* conical (**b**) *Geom* conic

conífera *nf* conifer

conífero, -a *adj* coniferous

conjetura *nf* conjecture; **por c.** by guesswork

conjeturar *vt* to conjecture

conjugación *nf* conjugation

conjugar [38] *vt* to conjugate; *Fig (planes, opiniones)* to join, bring together

conjunción *nf Ling* conjunction

conjuntado, -a 1 *pp de* **conjuntar**
2 *adj* co-ordinated

conjuntar *vt* to co-ordinate

conjuntiva *nf Anat* conjunctiva

conjuntivitis *nf Med* conjunctivitis

conjuntivo, -a *adj* conjunctive

conjunto, -a 1 *adj* (**a**) *(combinado)* combined (**b**) *(compartido)* joint ◻ **base conjunta** joint base
2 *nm* (**a**) *(grupo)* collection, group; **un c. de poemas** a collection of poems (**b**) *(todo)* whole; **de c.** overall; **en c.** on the whole; **en su c.** as a whole (**c**) *(prenda)* outfit, ensemble (**d**) *Mús (clásico)* ensemble; *(pop)* group, band (**e**) *Mat* set ◻ **c. vacío** empty set (**f**) *Dep* team

conjura *nf,* **conjuración** *nf* conspiracy, plot

conjurado, -a 1 *pp de* **conjurar**
2 *adj* conspiring, plotting
3 *nm,f* conspirator, plotter

conjurar 1 *vt* (**a**) *(demonio, mal pensamiento)* to exorcise; *(peligro)* to stave off, ward off (**b**) *Literario (rogar)* to beseech
2 *vi* to conspire, plot
3 conjurarse *vpr* to conspire, plot

conjuro *nm* (**a**) *(exorcismo)* exorcism (**b**) *(encantamiento)* spell, incantation

conllevar vt (enfermedad) to put up with; (dolor) to bear

conmemoración nf commemoration

conmemorar vt to commemorate

conmemorativo, -a adj commemorative

conmensurable adj commensurable

conmigo pron pers with me; **Clara hablaba c.** Clara was talking to me

conminación nf threat

conminar vt to threaten, menace

conminativo, -a adj, **conminatorio, -a** adj threatening, menacing

conmiseración nf Fml commiseration, pity

conmoción nf commotion, shock ❏ Med **c. cerebral** concussion

conmocionar vt to shock; Med to concuss

conmovedor, -a adj moving, touching; **una película conmovedora** a moving film

conmover [41] **1** vt (persona) to touch, move; (objeto, casa) to shake
2 conmoverse vpr (a) (persona) to be touched o moved (b) (cosas) to be shaken

conmutabilidad nf commutability

conmutable adj commutable

conmutación nf commutation

conmutador nm (a) Elec switch (b) Am Tel switchboard

conmutar vt to exchange; Jur (castigo, sentencia) to commute; Elec (corriente) to commutate

conmutativo, -a adj commutative

connatural adj connatural, inherent

connivencia nf connivance, collusion

connotación nf connotation

connotar vt to connote

connubio nm Literario matrimony, marriage

cono nm cone

conocedor, -a adj & nm,f expert

conocer [19] **1** vt (a) (saber cosas acerca de) to know; **dar algo a c.** to make sth known; **darse a c.** to make oneself known; **no conozco bien este tema** I am not very familiar with this subject; Fam **c. algo al dedillo** o **palmo a palmo** to know something off by heart (b) (identificar) to recognize; **¿de qué o dónde me conoces?** where do you know me from?; **te he conocido por la voz** I recognized you by your voice (c) (a algn por primera vez) to meet; **c. a algn de vista** to know sb by sight; **¿conoces a Teresa?** have you met Teresa? (d) (visitar país, lugar) to get to know, visit for the first time; **no conozco Rusia** I haven't been to Russia yet
2 vi **c. de** (ser conocedor) to know about; Jur (caso) to hear
3 conocerse vpr (a) (a sí mismo) to know oneself (b) (dos personas) to know each other; (por primera vez) to meet; **se conocieron en el metro** they met on the Br tube o US subway (c) (uso impers) **se le conoce la felicidad en la cara** happiness shows in his face; Fam **se conoce que se enfadó** apparently he got angry

conocido, -a **1** pp de **conocer**
2 adj known; (famoso) well-known; **esa cara me es conocida** I've seen that face before; **me suena c.** it rings a bell
3 nm,f acquaintance; **es un c. suyo** he's an acquaintance of his

conocimiento nm (a) (saber) knowledge; **con c. de causa** with full knowledge of the facts; **tener c. de algo** to know about sth; **tiene pocos conocimientos de biología** he knows little about biology (b) (madurez) **tener c.** to have an understanding of (c) (conciencia) conciousness; **perder/**

recobrar el c. to lose/regain conciousness (d) (sentido común) common sense

conque conj so; **llegas tarde, c. date prisa** you're late, so hurry up

conquense **1** adj of o from Cuenca
2 nmf person from Cuenca

conquista nf conquest; (amorosa) **hacer una c.** to make a conquest

conquistador, -a **1** adj conquering
2 nm,f conqueror
3 nm (galán) lady-killer

conquistar vt Mil (país, ciudad) to conquer; Fig (puesto, título) to win; (a un hombre o una mujer) to win over

consabido, -a adj (a) (bien conocido) well-known (b) (usual) familiar, usual

consagración nf (a) Rel consecration (b) (de un artista, escritor) recognition; (de una costumbre) establishment

consagrado, -a **1** pp de **consagrar**
2 adj (a) Rel consecrated (b) (reconocido) recognized, time-honoured, US time-honored, established, hallowed

consagrar **1** vt (a) Rel (iglesia, pan y vino) to consecrate (b) (persona) (confirmar) to confirm; (palabra, expresión) to establish (c) (dedicar) to devote, consecrate
2 consagrarse vpr (a) (dedicarse) to devote oneself (a to), dedicate oneself (a to) (b) (lograr fama) to establish oneself

consanguíneo, -a **1** adj related by birth, Fml consanguineous; **hermano c.** half-brother
2 nm,f blood relation

consanguinidad nf blood relationship, Fml consanguinity

consciencia nf véase **conciencia**

consciente adj (a) (despierto) conscious, aware; **ser c. de algo** to be aware of sth (b) Med conscious; **estar c.** to be conscious (c) (responsable) reliable

consecución nf (a) (de un objetivo) achievement, attainment; (de un deseo) realization (b) (obtención) obtaining, obtainment

consecuencia nf (a) (resultado) consequence, result; **a o como c. de** as a consequence o result of; **atenerse a las consecuencias** to suffer the consequences; **en c.** therefore; **tener o traer (malas) consecuencias** to have (ill) effects (b) (coherencia) consistency

consecuente adj (a) (coherente) consistent; **c. con sus ideas** consistent with one's ideas (b) (siguiente) consequent

consecuentemente adv (a) (con coherencia) consistently (b) (por consiguiente) consequently, as a result

consecutivo, -a adj consecutive

conseguir [61] vt (a) (obtener) (cosa) to get, obtain; (objetivo) to achieve, attain (b) (lograr) to manage, succeed in; **conseguí terminar** I managed to finish

consejero, -a nm,f (a) (asesor) adviser (b) Pol councillor (c) Com member (of a board of directors) ❏ **c. delegado** chief executive, esp Br managing director, US chief executive officer

consejo nm (a) (recomendación) advice; **pedir c. (a algn)** to ask (sb) for advice; **te daré un c.** I'll give you a piece of advice (b) (junta) council; **celebrar c.** to hold council ❏ **c. de administración** board of directors; **C. de Europa** Council of Europe; **c. de guerra** court martial; **c. de ministros** cabinet; (reunión) cabinet meeting; **C. de Seguridad** Security Council

consenso nm (a) (consentimiento) assent, consent (b) (acuerdo) consensus

consensual adj consensual

consensuar [4] vt to approve by consensus

consentido, -a *pp de* **consentir** **2** *adj (mimado)* spoiled, spoilt **3** *nm,f* spoiled o spoilt child o person

consentimiento *nm* consent

consentir [62] **1** *vt* **(a)** *(tolerar)* to tolerate, allow, permit; **no consientas que haga eso** don't allow him to do that **(b)** *(mimar)* to spoil **(c)** *(aguantar peso, esfuerzo)* to bear, admit **2** *vi* **c. en algo/en hacer algo** to agree to sth/to do sth; **consiente en quedarse** he agrees to stay **3 consentirse** *vpr (debilitarse)* to be weakened

conserje *nm* porter; *(encargado) Br* caretaker, *US* superintendent

conserjería *nf* **(a)** *(lugar)* porter's lodge, *Br* caretaker's o *US* superintendent's office, reception **(b)** *(oficio)* job of porter, *Br* caretaker o *US* superintendent etc

conserva *nf* **(a)** *(en lata)* canned o *Br* tinned food **(b)** *(dulces)* preserves *pl*

conservación *nf* **(a)** *(de alimentos)* preservation; *(de costumbres, patrimonio)* conservation; **instinto de c.** survival instinct **(b)** *(mantenimiento)* maintenance, upkeep

conservador, -a **1** *adj & nm,f* conservative; *Pol* Conservative **2** *nm (de museo)* curator

conservadurismo *nm Pol* conservatism

conservante *nm* preservative

conservar **1** *vt* to conserve, preserve; *(mantener)* to keep up, maintain; *Culin* to preserve; **c. la salud** to keep healthy; **consérvalo** keep it, hold on to it **2 conservarse** *vpr* **(a)** *(mantener hábito, tradición)* to survive **(b)** *Fig* to age well; **Ana se conserva muy bien** Ana looks well for her age

conservatorio *nm Mús* conservatory, conservatoire, school of music

conservería *nf* canning industry

conservero, -a **1** *adj* canning **2** *nm,f* canner

considerable *adj* considerable, substantial, large

consideración *nf* **(a)** *(reflexión)* consideration, attention, **tomar algo en c.** to take sth into account **(b)** *(respeto)* regard; **con c.** *(con respeto)* respectfully; *(con cuidado)* carefully; **en c.** considering; **por c. a** out of consideration for **(c)** **de c.** important, considerable; **herido de c.** seriously injured

considerado, -a **1** *pp de* **considerar** **2** *adj* **(a)** *(apreciado)* highly regarded o thought of; **estar bien/mal c.** to be well/badly thought of **(b)** *(atento)* considerate, thoughtful

considerar *vt* **(a)** *(meditar)* to consider, think over; **c. los pros y los contras** to weigh up the pros and cons **(b)** *(juzgar)* to judge, regard, deem; **lo considero imposible** I think it's impossible **(c)** *(respetar)* to treat with consideration, respect

consigna *nf* **(a)** *Mil* orders *pl*, instructions *pl* **(b)** *(de estación, aeropuerto) Br* left-luggage office, *US* checkroom **(c)** *(señal, lema)* watchword; **'por la igualdad' era su c.** 'equality for all' was their watchword

consignación *nf* **(a)** *(asignación)* allocation **(b)** *Com (de mercancías)* consignment; *Náut* shipment

consignar *vt* **(a)** *(asignar)* to allocate; *(cantidad)* to assign **(b)** *Com (mercancía)* to consign, ship, dispatch **(c)** *(hacer constar)* to record; *(declaración)* to take down

consignatario, -a *nm,f* **(a)** *Com* consignee ❏ **c. de buques** shipbroker **(b)** *Jur (depositario)* trustee, mortgagee

consigo¹ *pron pers* **(a)** *(tercera persona)* with him/her; *(plural)* with them; **c. mismo** with himself/herself; **c. mismos** with themselves; *Fam Fig* **ella no las tenía todas**

c. she didn't rate her chances highly **(b)** *(usted)* with you; **c. mismo** with yourself

consigo² *indic pres véase* **conseguir**

consiguiente *adj* resulting, resultant, consequent; **por c.** therefore, consequently

consintiente *adj* consenting, agreeing

consistencia *nf* **(a)** *(de masa, crema, salsa)* consistency, firmness, solidness; *Culin* **tomar c.** to thicken **(b)** *Fig (de argumento)* soundness

consistente *adj* **(a)** *(firme)* firm, solid **(b)** *Fig (argumento)* sound **(c)** **c. en** consisting of

consistir *vi* to consist **(en** in, of**); el secreto consiste en tener paciencia** the secret lies in being patient

consistorial *adj* **casa c.** town o *US* city hall

consistorio *nm* **(a)** *Rel* consistory **(b)** *(ayuntamiento)* town o *US* city council

consocio, -a *nm,f* partner, associate

consola *nf* **(a)** *Mueb* console table **(b)** *(tablero de instrumentos)* console ❏ **c. de videojuegos** video console

consolación *nf* consolation, comfort ❏ **premio de c.** consolation prize

consolador, -a *adj* consoling, comforting

consolar [63] **1** *vt* to console, comfort **2 consolarse** *vpr* to console oneself, take comfort (**con** from)

consolidación *nf* consolidation

consolidar **1** *vt* to consolidate; *(deuda)* to fund **2 consolidarse** *vpr* to consolidate

consomé *nm* clear soup, consommé

consonancia *nf* **(a)** *Lit* consonance, rhyme **(b)** *Fig* harmony; **en c. con** in keeping with

consonante *adj & nf* consonant

consonántico, -a *adj* consonantal

consonar [63] *vi* **(a)** *Mús Lit* to harmonize, rhyme **(b)** *Fig* to agree, fit, be in harmony

consorcio *nm Com* consortium, association, partnership

consorte **1** *adj* **príncipe c.** prince consort **2** *nmf* **(a)** *(cónyuge)* partner, spouse **(b)** *Jur* **consortes** accomplices, joint partners

conspicuo, -a *adj* **(a)** *Literario* conspicuous, obvious **(b)** *(notable)* prominent, outstanding

conspiración *nf* conspiracy, plot

conspirador, -a *nm,f* conspirator, plotter

conspirar *vi (confabularse)* to conspire, plot

constancia *nf* **(a)** *(perseverancia)* constancy, perseverance; **hacer algo con c.** to persevere at sth **(b)** *(testimonio)* proof, evidence; **dejar c. de algo** *(registrar)* to put sth on record; *(probar)* to prove sth

constante **1** *adj* constant, steady; *(persona)* steadfast **2** *nf* constant, constant feature

constantemente *adv* constantly

constar *vi* **(a)** *(figurar)* to figure **(en** in**),** be included **(en** in**); c. en acta** to be on record; **hacer c.** *(decir)* to express; *(escribir)* to put down; *Fml* **para que así conste** for the record **(b)** *(ser evidente)* to be a fact; **me consta que ...** I am absolutely certain that ...; **que conste que ...** it's a fact that ... **(c)** *(consistir)* **c. de** to be made up of, consist of

constatación *nf* **(a)** *(observación)* confirmation **(b)** *(comprobación)* verification

constatar *vt* **(a)** *(observar)* to confirm **(b)** *(comprobar)* to check

constelación *nf Astron* constellation

constelado, -a *adj Fig* strewn (**de** with)

consternación *nf* consternation, dismay

consternado, -a *adj* dismayed, extremely upset

consternar *vt* to dismay

constipado, -a *Med* **1** *adj* **estar c.** to have a cold *o* a chill
2 *nm* cold, chill

constiparse *vpr* to catch a cold *o* a chill

constitución *nf* **(a)** *(naturaleza)* constitution; **tener una c. fuerte/débil** to have a strong/weak constitution **(b)** *Pol* constitution **(c)** *(creación)* creation, forming **(d)** *(composición)* composition, make-up

constitucional 1 *adj* constitutional
2 *nm Pol* constitutionalist

constitucionalidad *nf* constitutionality

constituir [34] **1** *vt* **(a)** *(formar)* to constitute, make up; **está constituido por cinco islas** it consists of five islands **(b)** *(ser)* to be, represent; **constituye un honor para mí** it is a great honour for me **(c)** *(fundar)* to constitute, set up **(d)** *(nombrar)* to appoint
2 constituirse *vpr* to set oneself up **(en** as)

constitutivo, -a *adj* constituent, component

constituyente *adj & nmf Pol* constituent

constreñimiento *nm* **(a)** *(obligación)* constraint, imposition **(b)** *(opresión)* restriction

constreñir [47] *vt* **(a)** *(forzar)* to compel, force **(b)** *(oprimir)* to restrict **(c)** *Med (arteria)* to constrict; *(estreñimiento)* to constipate

constricción *nf* constriction

construcción *nf* **(a)** *(acción)* construction; **la industria de la c.** the construction industry; **en (vías de) c.** under construction **(b)** *(edificio)* building

constructivo, -a *adj* constructive

constructor, -a 1 *adj* building, construction; **empresa constructora** builders *pl*, construction company
2 *nm,f* builder

construir [34] *vt* to construct, build

consuegra *nf* son-in-law's *o* daughter-in-law's mother

consuegro *nm* son-in-law's *o* daughter-in-law's father

consuelo *nm* consolation; **es un c.** that's comforting; **sin c.** inconsolably

consuetudinario, -a *adj* customary; **derecho c.** common law

cónsul *nmf* consul

consulado *nm* **(a)** *(oficina)* consulate **(b)** *(cargo)* consulship

consular *adj* consular

consulta *nf* **(a)** *(sobre un problema) (acción)* consultation; *(pregunta)* query, enquiry; **quería hacerte una c.** I need your advice ❑ **obra de c.** reference book **(b)** *Med Br* surgery, *US* office; **pasar c.** to see patients; **horas de c.** surgery hours **(c)** *Med (despacho)* consulting room

consultar *vt* to consult, seek advice **(con** from); *(en un libro)* to look up; *Fig* **consultarlo con la almohada** to sleep on it

consulting [kon'sultin] *nm* consultancy (firm)

consultivo, -a *adj* consultative, advisory

consultor, -a *nm,f* consultant; **c. (en administración) de empresas** management consultant

consultora *nf*, **consultoría** *nf* consultancy firm

consultorio *nm* **(a)** *(asesoría)* office, information office; *(de médico)* consulting room; *(en hospital)* outpatients' department **(b)** *Prensa* problem page, advice column ❑ **c. sentimental** *(en radio)* = phone-in where people get advice on their personal problems

consumación *nf* consummation, completion; *(de un crimen)* perpetration

consumado, -a 1 *pp de* **consumar**
2 *adj (perfecto)* consummate; **un bobo c.** a complete fool

consumar *vt* to complete, carry out; *(crimen)* to commit; *(matrimonio)* to consummate

consumibles *nmpl* consumables

consumición *nf* **(a)** *(acción)* consumption **(b)** *(bebida)* drink ❑ **c. mínima** basic charge

consumido, -a 1 *pp de* **consumir**
2 *adj* **(a)** *(gastado)* wasted, spent **(b)** *Fig (devorado)* **c. por los celos** consumed by jealousy

consumidor, -a 1 *adj* consuming; **países consumidores de café** coffee-drinking countries
2 *nm,f* consumer

consumir 1 *vt* **(a)** *(gastar)* to consume; *Fig* **me consumió esperar tanto** it got on my nerves waiting so long **(b)** *(destruir)* to destroy; **el fuego consumió el edificio** the fire destroyed the building
2 consumirse *vpr* **(a)** *(extinguirse)* to burn out; *Fig (persona)* to waste away **(b)** *(secarse)* to boil away **(c)** *Fig (por la pasión)* to be consumed *o* devoured

consumismo *nm* consumerism

consumo *nm* consumption ❑ **c. de drogas** drug-taking; **bienes de c.** consumer goods; **sociedad de c.** consumer society

consunción *nf Med* consumption

consuno *adv* **de c.** with one accord

consustancial *adj* **ser c. con** to be inseparable from

contabilidad *nf Com* **(a)** *(profesión)* accountancy **(b)** *(de empresa, sociedad)* accounting, book-keeping; **llevar la c.** to keep the books

contabilización *nf Com* entering

contabilizar [14] *vt Com* to enter in the books

contable 1 *adj* countable
2 *nmf Esp Com* accountant, book-keeper

contactar *vt* to contact, get in touch **(con** with)

contacto *nm* contact; *Aut* ignition; **entrar en c.** to make contact; **perder el c.** to lose touch; **ponerse en c.** to get in touch

contado, -a 1 *pp de* **contar**
2 *adj* **(a)** *(sumado)* counted; **tiene los días contados** his days are numbered **(b)** *(raro)* scarce; *(poco)* little; *(pocos)* few and far between; **contadas veces** very seldom **(c)** *Com* **pagar algo al c.** *(en un plazo)* to pay for sth all at once *o Br* on the nail; *(en metálico)* to pay for sth in cash, pay cash for sth

contador, -a 1 *nm,f* **(a)** *(narrador)* teller **(b)** *Am (contable)* accountant, book-keeper
2 *nm* meter ❑ **c. de agua** water meter

contaduría *nf* **(a)** *(oficio)* accountancy **(b)** *(oficina)* accountant's office ❑ *Am* **c. general** audit office

contagiar 1 *vt Med (enfermedad)* to transmit, pass on; *Fig* **me contagió la risa** their laughter was infectious
2 contagiarse *vpr* **(a)** *(enfermar)* to get infected, catch **(b)** *(transmitirse)* to be contagious

contagio *nm* **(a)** *Med* contagion, infection **(b)** *Fig* corruption, perversion

contagioso, -a *adj* **(a)** *Med* contagious, infectious **(b)** *Fam* catching; **risa contagiosa** infectious laugh

container *(pl* **containers)** *nm (para mercancías)* container

contaminación *nf* contamination; *(de la atmósfera)* pollution ❑ **c. acústica** noise pollution

contaminador, -a *adj* contaminating; *(de la atmósfera)* polluting

contaminante 1 *adj* polluting, contaminating
2 *nm* pollutant

contaminar 1 *vt* (**a**) *(envenenar)* to contaminate; *(aire, agua)* to pollute (**b**) *Fig (pervertir)* to contaminate, corrupt

2 contaminarse *vpr* to become contaminated (**con, de** with, by)

contante *adj* **dinero c. (y sonante)** hard *o* ready cash

contar [63] **1** *vt* (**a**) *(sumar)* to count; **cuenta los puntos** count how many points (**b**) *(considerar)* to consider, reckon (**c**) *(tener)* to have; **cuenta cincuenta años** he's fifty years old (**d**) *(narrar)* to relate, tell; **cuéntame un cuento** tell me a story; **habría mucho que c.** it's a long story; *Fam* **¡cuéntamelo a mí!** you're telling me!; *Fam* **¡cuéntaselo a tu abuela!** come off it! (**e**) *(incluir)* to count (in), include; **te cuento entre mis amigos** I consider you one of my friends (**f**) *(suponer)* to count (on), expect; **ella cuenta llegar allí a las doce** she expects to arrive there at twelve

2 *vi* (**a**) *(sumar)* to count (**b**) **c. con los dedos** to count on one's fingers; *(tener importancia)* to count; **ese partido no cuenta** that match doesn't count (**c**) **c. con algn** *(confiar en algn)* to count on; *(incluir a algn)* to count sb in; **cuenta con ello** you can count on it (**d**) *(tener presente)* **c. con** to take into account; **no había contado con eso** I hadn't allowed for that (**e**) *(tener)* **c. con** to have, be provided with; **cuenta con un dispositivo especial** it has got a special device

3 contarse *vpr* (**a**) *(incluirse)* to be counted; **estoy muy orgulloso de contarme entre sus amigos** I am very proud to number myself among her friends; **se cuentan por miles** there are thousands of them (**b**) *Fam* **¿qué te cuentas?** how's it going?

contemplación *nf* contemplation; *Fam* **no andarse con contemplaciones** to make no bones about it, come straight to the point

contemplar *vt* (**a**) *(paisaje, monumento)* to look at, contemplate (**b**) *(opción, posibilidad)* to contemplate, consider; **está contemplando presentar la dimisión** he is considering handing in his resignation; **la ley contempla varios supuestos** the law provides for *o* covers various cases; **esta propuesta no contempla los ingresos por publicidad** this proposal doesn't take into account income from advertising (**c**) *(consentir)* to spoil

contemplativo, -a *adj* contemplative

contemporaneidad *nf* contemporaneousness

contemporáneo, -a *adj & nm,f* contemporary

contemporizador, -a 1 *adj* compliant, compromising

2 *nm,f* conformist, middle-of-the-road person

contemporizar [14] *vi* to compromise, be compliant

contención *nf* (**a**) *(moderación)* moderation, control (**b**) *Constr* **muro de c.** retaining wall (**c**) *Jur* lawsuit

contencioso, -a 1 *adj* contentious; *Jur* litigious; **asunto c.** judicial matter

2 *nm Jur* legal action, case

contendedor, -a *nm,f* contender, antagonist

contender [64] *vi* (**a**) *(pelear)* to contend, fight (**b**) *(competir)* to contest

contendiente 1 *adj* contending, competing

2 *nmf* contender, contestant

contenedor *nm (recipiente grande)* container; *(para escombros)* Br skip, US Dumpster®; **c. de basura** trash container (with wheels); **c. de vidrio** bottle bank

contener [65] **1** *vt* (**a**) *(encerrar, llevar)* to contain, hold (**b**) *(reprimir)* to restrain, hold back; **no pudo c. la risa** he couldn't hold back his laughter

2 contenerse *vpr* to control oneself, hold (oneself) back

contenido, -a 1 *pp de* **contener**

2 *adj* (**a**) *(dentro de recipiente)* contained (**en** in) (**b**) *(persona)* reserved, circumspect

3 *nm* content, contents *pl*

contenta *nf* (**a**) *(agasajo)* good treatment *o* welcome (**b**) *Am Com* acknowledgement

contentadizo, -a *adj* easy to please

contentar 1 *vt* (**a**) *(satisfacer)* to please (**b**) *(alegrar)* to cheer up

2 contentarse *vpr* (**a**) *(conformarse)* to make do (**con** with), be satisfied (**con** with) (**b**) *(alegrarse)* to cheer up

contento, -a 1 *adj* happy, pleased (**con** with, **de** about)

2 *nm* happiness, contentment, joy

conteo *nm* counting-up

contera *nf* tip; *Fig* **echar la c.** to finish, end; *Fig* **por c.** to cap it all

contertulio, -a *nm,f* = member of a social group *o* gathering

contestable *adj* debatable

contestación *nf* (**a**) *(respuesta)* answer; **dar c.** to answer (**b**) *(oposición)* opposition (**c**) *Jur* plea

contestador *nm* **c. automático** answering machine

contestar 1 *vt* (**a**) *(responder)* to answer; **c. bien/mal** to give the right/wrong answer (**b**) *(oponerse a)* to contest, question (**c**) *Jur* to confirm

2 *vi (replicar)* to answer back

contestatario, -a 1 *adj* argumentative; *Fam* bolshie

2 *nm,f* attacker, dissenter

contexto *nm* context; *Fig* environment

contextual *adj* contextual

contextualizar [14] *vt (problema, situación)* to put into perspective *o* context

contextura *nf* (**a**) *(disposición)* texture (**b**) *(complexión de persona)* build

contienda *nf* contest, struggle, dispute

contigo *pron pers* with you; *Prov* **c. pan y cebolla** anything will do as long as we are together

contigüidad *nf* contiguity, closeness, nearness

contiguo, -a *adj* contiguous (**a** to), adjoining, adjacent (**a** to)

continencia *nf (en el sexo)* continence; *(en la gula)* moderation

continental *adj* continental

continente *nm* (**a**) *Geog* continent (**b**) *(recipiente)* container (**c**) *(compostura)* countenance; *(aspecto)* air

contingencia *nf* (**a**) *(probabilidad)* contingency, eventuality (**b**) *(riesgo)* risk, hazard

contingente 1 *adj (posible)* contingent, accidental

2 *nm* (**a**) *(grupo)* contingent (**b**) *Mil* contingent (**c**) *Com Fin* quota, share (**d**) *(contingencia)* contingency

continuación *nf* continuation, follow-up; **a c.** next; **tener c.** to be continued

continuador, -a 1 *adj* continuing

2 *nm,f* continuator

continuamente *adv* continuously

continuar [4] **1** *vt & vi* to continue, carry on (with); **ella continúa durmiendo** she's still asleep; **continúa en Francia** he's still in France; **continuará** to be continued; **continuaron su camino** they went on their way

2 continuarse *vpr* to continue, go on; **la carretera se continúa hasta el mar** the road runs all the way down to the sea

continuidad *nf* continuity

continuo, -a 1 *adj* (**a**) *(seguido)* continuous, endless ❑ **línea continua** *(en dibujo etc)* unbroken line; *Aut* solid white line (**b**) *(reiterado)* continual, constant

2 *nm* continuum; **un c. de gente** a constant flow of people

contonearse *vpr* to swing one's hips

contoneo *nm* swinging of the hips, hip-swinging

contorno *nm* (**a**) *(perfil)* outline; *(perímetro)* perimeter; **el c. de la figura** the shape of the figure (**b**) *(de moneda)* rim, edge (**c**) *(alrededores)* surroundings *pl* , environment; *(territorio)* region, district

contorsión *nf* contortion

contorsionarse *vpr* to contort o twist oneself, writhe

contorsionista *nmf* contorsionist

contra 1 *prep* against; **debemos luchar c. ellos** we must fight them; **en c. de lo que se esperaba** contrary to expectations; **hablar en c. de** to criticize; **opinar en c.** to disagree
  2 *nm* **los pros y los contras** the pros and cons
  3 *nf Fam* drawback, snag; **llevar la c. a algn** to disagree with sb

contraalmirante *nm Mil* rear admiral

contraatacar [59] *vi* to counterattack

contraataque *nm* counterattack

contrabajo *nm Mús (instrumento)* double bass; *(voz)* low bass

contrabandista *nmf* smuggler; **c. de armas** gunrunner

contrabando *nm* (**a**) *(acción)* smuggling; **c. de armas** gunrunning; **pasar algo de c.** to smuggle sth in (**b**) *(mercancías)* smuggled goods *pl*; **un reloj de c.** a contraband watch

contracción *nf* contraction

contracepción *nf* contraception

contraceptivo, -a *adj* contraceptive

contrachapado *nm* plywood

contracorriente *nf* crosscurrent; **ir a c.** to go against the tide

contráctil *adj* contractile

contractual *adj* contractual

contractura *nf (muscular)* cramp

contracultura *nf* counterculture

contradanza *nf* country dance

contradecir [51] *(pp* **contradicho)** **1** *vt* (**a**) *(decir lo contrario)* to contradict; **siempre me contradices** you're always contradicting me (**b**) *(estar en oposición)* to run against, disagree with; **sus actos contradicen sus palabras** he says one thing and does another
  2 contradecirse *vpr* to contradict oneself; *(decir cosas contradictorias)* to be inconsistent

contradicción *nf* contradiction; **el espíritu de la c.** contrariness

contradictorio, -a *adj* contradictory

contraer [66] **1** *vt* (**a**) *(encoger)* to contract, tighten (up) (**b**) *(enfermedad)* to catch (**c**) *(deuda)* to contract; *(hábito)* to pick up; **c. matrimonio con algn** to marry sb
  2 contraerse *vpr* (**a**) *(encogerse)* to contract, tighten (**b**) *Am (concentrarse)* to apply oneself (**a** to)

contraespionaje *nm* counterespionage

contrafuerte *nm* (**a**) *Arquit* buttress (**b**) *(en calzado)* stiffener (**c**) *(de montaña)* foothill

contrahecho, -a *adj* hunchbacked, deformed

contraindicación *nf Med* contraindication; **'contraindicaciones, ninguna,'** 'it can be used safely by anyone'

contraindicado, -a *adj* **está c. beber alcohol durante el embarazo** alcohol should be avoided during pregnancy

contraindicar [59] *vt Med* to advise against

contralmirante *nm Mil véase* **contraalmirante**

contralor, -a *nm,f Am* comptroller ❑ **C. General** Comptroller General

contraloría *nf Am (oficina)* comptroller's office

contralto *nmf Mús* contralto

contraluz *nm* view against the light; **a c.** against the light

contramaestre *nm* (**a**) *Náut* warrant officer (**b**) *(capataz)* foreman

contramano : a contramano *loc adv* the wrong way o direction

contraofensiva *nf Mil* counteroffensive

contraoferta *nf* counter offer

contraorden *nf* countermand

contrapartida *nf* (**a**) *Com Fin* balancing entry (**b**) *Fig* compensation

contrapelo : a contrapelo *loc adv* the wrong way; *Fig* the wrong way, against the grain; **acariciar un gato a c.** to stroke a cat the wrong way

contrapesar *vt* (**a**) *(equilibrar)* to counterbalance, counterpoise (**b**) *Fig (compensar)* to offset, balance

contrapeso *nm* counterweight

contraponer [50] *(pp* **contrapuesto)** **1** *vt* (**a**) *(oponer)* to set in opposition (**a** to), set up (**a** against); *(encarar)* to set against (**b**) *Fig (contrastar)* to contrast
  2 contraponerse *vpr (oponerse)* to be opposed

contraportada *nf* back page

contraposición *nf (oposición)* clash, conflict; *(contraste)* contrast; **estar en c.** to clash

contraproducente *adj* counterproductive; **tener un resultado c.** to have a boomerang effect

contrapuerta *nf* storm door, double door

contrapuesto, -a 1 *pp de* **contraponer**
  2 *adj (en oposición)* clashing, conflicting; *(en contraste)* contrasting

contrapuntear *vi* (**a**) *Andes RP Ven (versos)* = to compete in a poetry improvising contest (**b**) *Carib RP (rivalizar)* to compete, contend

contrapunto *nm* (**a**) *Mús* counterpoint (**b**) *Andes RP Ven (de versos)* poetry improvisation contest

contrariado, -a *adj* upset

contrariamente *adv* **c. a ...** contrary to ...

contrariar [32] *vt* (**a**) *(oponerse)* to oppose, go against; **lo dice por contrariarme** he says that just to be awkward (**b**) *(disgustar)* to upset; **por no contrariarte** so as not to upset you (**c**) *(obstaculizar)* to obstruct, hinder

contrariedad *nf* (**a**) *(oposición)* opposition (**b**) *(disgusto)* annoyance; **hacer un gesto de c.** to look annoyed (**c**) *(contratiempo)* obstacle, setback, hitch

contrario, -a 1 *adj* (**a**) *(opuesto)* contrary, opposite; **al c.** on the contrary; **de lo c.** otherwise; **en dirección contraria** in the wrong direction; **llevar la contraria** to be contrary; **no llevarle la contraria a algn** to humour sb; **por el c.** on the contrary; **todo lo c.** quite the opposite (**b**) *(perjudicial)* contrary (**a** to), harmful (**a** to); **c. a nuestros intereses** not in our interests
  2 *nm,f* opponent, rival

contrarreembolso *nm* cash on delivery

Contrarreforma *nf Hist* Counter-Reformation

contrarreloj 1 *adj inv Dep* **etapa c.** time trial
  2 *nf inv Dep* time trial; *Fig* **trabajar a c.** to work against the clock

contrarrembolso *nm* cash on delivery

contrarréplica *nf* reply; **en su c., el ministro dijo que ...** the minister countered that ...

contrarrestar *vt* (**a**) *(hacer frente)* to resist, oppose;

(compensar) to offset, counteract (**b**) *(pelota)* to return

contrarrevolución *nf* counter-revolution

contrarrevolucionario, -a *adj & nm,f* counterrevolutionary

contrasentido *nm* (**a**) *(gen)* contradiction; *(disparate)* piece of nonsense (**b**) *(mala interpretación)* misinterpretation

contraseña *nf (consigna)* secret mark; *Mil* password, watchword; *Inform* password

contrastar 1 *vt* (**a**) *(oponer)* to contrast (**con** with) (**b**) *(pesos, medidas)* to check (**c**) *(oro, plata)* to hallmark
  2 *vi (oponerse)* to contrast (**con** with), be in contrast (**a** to)

contraste *nm* (**a**) *(oposición)* contrast (**b**) *(de pesos y medidas)* verification, inspection (**c**) *(en oro, plata)* hallmark

contrata *nf* contract

contratación *nf* (**a**) *(pedidos)* total orders *pl* , volume of business (**b**) *(contrato)* hiring

contratante *nmf* contracting party

contratar *vt (servicio, mercancía)* to sign a contract for; *(empleado)* to hire, engage; *(deportista)* to sign up; *(arriendo)* to take on

contraterrorismo *nm* counterterrorism

contratiempo *nm* (**a**) *(contariedad)* setback, hitch; *(accidente)* mishap (**b**) *Mús* **a c.** off beat; *Fig* in the off beat

contratista *nmf* contractor ❑ *Constr* **c. de obras** building contractor

contrato *nm* contract ❑ **c. basura** short-term contract *(with poor conditions)*; **c. de alquiler** lease, leasing agreement; **c. de trabajo** work contract; **c. temporal** temporary *o* short-term contract

contravención *nf Jur* contravention, infringement, violation

contraveneno *nm* antidote

contravenir [69] *vt Jur* to contravene, infringe, violate

contraventana *nf* shutter

contrayente 1 *adj* contracting
  2 *nmf (en un matrimonio)* contracting party

contribución *nf* (**a**) *(aporte)* contribution (**b**) *Fin (impuesto)* tax, rates *pl* ❑ **c. territorial** land tax; **c. urbana** = tax for local services, *Br* ≃ council tax

contribuir [34] **1** *vt* to contribute (**a** to, **para** towards)
  2 *vi* (**a**) *(aportar)* to contribute; *Fig* **c. al éxito de algo** to contribute to the success of sth (**b**) *Fin (pagar impuestos)* to pay taxes

contribuyente *Fin* **1** *adj* taxpaying
  2 *nmf* taxpayer

contrición *nf* contrition; **hacer un acto de c.** to repent

contrincante *nmf* rival, opponent

contristar 1 *vt (afligir)* to make sad
  2 contristarse *vpr (afligirse)* to become sad, grieve

contrito, -a *adj* contrite

control *nm* (**a**) *(dominio, mando)* control; **bajo c.** under control; **bajo el c. de** under the supervision of; **c. de (la) natalidad** birth control; **ejercer** *o* **llevar el c.** to be in control ❑ **c. a distancia** *o* **remoto** remote control; **c. antidoping** dope *o* drugs test; **c. de calidad** quality control; **c. de natalidad** birth control (**b**) *(lugar)* checkpoint ❑ **c. de pasaportes** passport inspection *o* check; *Aut* **c. policial** roadblock

controlador, -a 1 *adj* control; **ficha controladora** control chart
  2 *nm,f Av* **c. (aéreo)** air traffic controller

controlar 1 *vt* (**a**) *(gen)* to control (**b**) *(comprobar)* to check; *Com Fin* to audit
  2 controlarse *vpr (moderarse)* to control oneself

controversia *nf* controversy, argument

controvertido, -a *adj* controversial

controvertir [62] **1** *vt* to dispute, argue about
  2 *vi* to argue

contubernio *nm* *Pey* (**a**) *(cohabitación ilícita)* cohabitation (**b**) *(confabulación)* conspiracy, clique

contumacia *nf* (**a**) *(obstinación)* obstinacy; *(desobediencia)* insubordination (**b**) *Jur* contumacy

contumaz *adj* (**a**) *(obstinado)* obstinate; *(desobediente)* insubordinate (**b**) *Jur* contumacious

contundencia *nf* (**a**) *(fuerza)* force, energy (**b**) *Fig (convicción)* conviction, force; **me convenció con la c. de sus argumentos** I was convinced by the weight of her argument

contundente *adj* (**a**) *(arma)* blunt (**b**) *Fig (convincente)* forceful, convincing; **un argumento c.** a convincing *o* weighty argument

conturbación *nf* anxiety, dismay, perturbation

conturbado, -a 1 *pp de* conturbar
  2 *adj* anxious, dismayed, perturbed

conturbar 1 *vt* to trouble, dismay, perturb
  2 conturbarse *vpr* to be troubled, be dismayed, become perturbed

contusión *nf* contusion, bruise

contusionar *vt* to contuse, bruise

conuco *nm Carib* small farm

convalecencia *nf* convalescence

convalecer [46] *vi* to convalesce (**de** after), recover (**de** from)

convaleciente *adj & nmf* convalescent

convalidación *nf Educ* validation; *(documento)* ratification

convalidar *vt* to validate; *(documento)* to ratify

convección *nf Fís* convection

convecino, -a 1 *adj* neighbouring, *US* neighboring
  2 *nm,f* neighbour, *US* neighbor

convector *nm* convector

convencer [40] **1** *vt* to convince, persuade; **c. a algn de algo** to convince sb of *o* about sth; **dejarse c.** to let oneself be persuaded; **no me convence la idea** I'm not sold on the idea
  2 convencerse *vpr* to be convinced, become convinced; **me convencí de mi error** I realized my mistake

convencimiento *nm* conviction, certainty; **llegar al c. de que ...** to be convinced that ...

convención *nf* (**a**) *Pol (pacto)* convention, treaty (**b**) *(asamblea)* convention, congress (**c**) *(conformidad)* convention

convencional *adj* conventional

convencionalismo *nm* conventionalism, conventionality

convenible *adj* (**a**) *(conveniente)* suitable, fitting; *(precio)* fair, reasonable (**b**) *(persona)* accommodating

convenido, -a 1 *pp de* convenir
  2 *adj* agreed, arranged, set

conveniencia *nf* (**a**) *(utilidad)* usefulness; *(oportunidad)* suitability, advisability (**b**) *(provecho)* convenience (**c**) *(convenio)* agreement ❑ **conveniencias sociales** proprieties

conveniente *adj* (**a**) *(útil)* useful; *(oportuno)* suitable, convenient; *(aconsejable)* advisable; **creo c. avisarle** I feel I should warn him; **en el momento c.** at the right time (**b**) *(precio)* good, fair

convenio *nm* agreement, treaty, convenant ❑ *Ind* **c.**

colectivo collective agreement; **c. laboral** labour agreement

convenir [69] *vt & vi* **(a)** *(acordar)* to agree; **c. en** to agree on; **c. una fecha** to agree on a date; **sueldo a c.** salary negotiable **(b)** *(ser oportuno)* to suit, be good for; **conviene recordar que ...** it's as well to remember that ...; **te conviene descansar** you need a rest

conventillero, -a *nm,f Andes RP Fam Pey (persona)* gossip

convento *nm Rel (de monjas)* convent; *(de monjes)* monastery

conventual *adj Rel* conventual

convergencia *nf* convergence

convergente *adj* convergent, converging, concurring

converger [52] *vi,* **convergir** [6] *vi* to converge, meet

conversación *nf* conversation, talk; **dar c.** to keep sb chatting; *Fig* **dejar caer una cosa en la c.** to bring sth up in conversation; *Fig* **trabar c. con algn** to get into conversation with sb ❑ **c. de paz** peace talks

conversada *nf Am Fam* chat

conversador, -a 1 *adj* talkative
2 *nm,f* **(a)** *(hablador)* conversationalist, talker **(b)** *Am (charlatán)* gabber

conversar *vi* to converse, talk

conversión *nf* conversion

converso, -a 1 *adj* converted
2 *nm,f* convert

conversón, -ona *adj CAm* talkative

convertibilidad *nf* convertibility

convertible 1 *adj* convertible
2 *nm* convertible

convertir [25] **1** *vt* **(a)** *(transformar)* to change, convert **(b)** *Rel* to convert; **c. a algn al cristianismo** to convert sb to Christianity
2 convertirse *vpr* **(a) c. en** to turn into, become; **se convirtió en una escritora famosa** she became a famous writer **(b)** *Rel* to be converted **(a** to)

convexidad *nf* convexity

convexo, -a *adj* convex

convicción *nf* conviction; **mis convicciones no me permiten hacer eso** it's against my beliefs to do that; **tengo la c. de que ...** I firmly believe that ...

convicto, -a *adj* guilty, convicted

convidado, -a 1 *pp de* **convidar**
2 *adj* invited
3 *nm,f* guest; *Fig* **como un c. de piedra** silent as the grave

convidar 1 *vt* **(a)** *(invitar)* to invite; **nos convidó a una copa** he offered us a drink **(b)** *Fig (incitar)* to inspire, prompt
2 convidarse *vpr Fam* to invite oneself; **se convidó por la cara** he invited himself along

convincente *adj* convincing

convite *nm* **(a)** *(fiesta)* party; *(comida)* dinner, lunch **(b)** *(invitación)* invitation

convivencia *nf* life together; *Fig* coexistence; **la c. se hizo imposible** living together became impossible

convivir *vi* to live together; **saber c.** to give and take; *Fig* to coexist **(con** with)

convocar [59] *vt* to convoke, call together, summon; **c. oposiciones** to hold competitive examinations; **c. una reunión** to call a meeting

convocatoria *nf* **(a)** *(citación)* convocation, summons *sing,* call (to a meeting) ❑ **c. de huelga** strike call, call for strike action **(b)** *Educ* examination; **c. de setiembre** second sitting (in September)

convoy *nm* **(a)** *Aut Náut (escolta)* convoy **(b)** *Ferroc* train

convoyar *vt* to convoy, guard, escort

convulsión *nf Med* convulsion; *Fig* upheaval

convulsionar *vt Med* to convulse

convulsivo, -a *adj* convulsive

convulso, -a *adj* convulsed **(de** with)

conyugal *adj* conjugal ❑ **vida c.** married life

cónyuge *nmf* spouse, partner; *(marido)* husband; *(mujer)* wife; **cónyuges** married couple *sing,* husband and wife

coña *nf Esp Vulg* **(a)** *(guasa)* joking, larking about; **estar de c.** to have a joke; **ser la c.** to be the limit; **tomar algo a c.** to take sth as a joke **(b)** *(molestia)* nuisance

coñac *(pl* coñacs) *nm* brandy, cognac

coñazo *nm Esp Vulg* pain, drag; **dar el c.** to be a real pain

coño *esp Esp* **1** *nm Anat Vulg* cunt; **estar en el quinto c.** to be miles away
2 *interj Vulg (sorpresa)* well, fuck me!; *(disgusto, enfado)* for fuck's sake!; **¡qué c. quieres!** what the hell do you want!

coop. *(abrev de* **cooperativa)** co-op

cooperación *nf* co-operation

cooperador, -a *adj* co-operative

cooperante 1 *adj* co-operating
2 *nmf* (overseas) volunteer worker

cooperar *vi* to co-operate **(a, en** in, **con** with); **c. a un fin** to have a common aim

cooperativismo *nm* co-operative movement

cooperativo, -a 1 *adj* co-operative
2 *nf* co-operative ❑ **c. agrícola** farmers' co-operative

coordenada *nf* co-ordinate

coordenado, -a 1 *pp de* **coordenar**
2 *adj* co-ordinated

coordinación *nf* co-ordination

coordinador, -a 1 *adj* co-ordinating
2 *nm,f* co-ordinator

coordinadora *nf (comité)* co-ordinating committee; **c. general** joint committee

coordinar *vt* to co-ordinate; **c. los esfuerzos** to combine forces

copa *nf* **(a)** *(vaso)* glass; *(alcohol)* **irse de copas** to go out drinking; **llevar una c. de más** to have one too many; **tomar una c.** to have a drink ❑ **sombrero de c.** top hat **(b)** *(del árbol)* top **(c)** *Dep (campeonato, trofeo)* cup; **la c. mundial** the world cup **(d)** **copas** *Naipes (baraja española)* hearts

copar *vt* to take; **los puestos están todos copados** the jobs are all taken up

copartícipe *adj & nmf (socio)* partner; *(colaborador)* collaborator; *(copropietario)* joint owner, co-owner

copear *vi* to drink; *(ir de copas)* to go drinking

Copenhague *n* Copenhagen

copeo *nm* drinking; **ir de c.** to go out drinking

copete *nm* **(a)** *(de pelo)* tuft; *(penacho)* crest; *(de caballo)* forelock; *(de helado)* top **(b)** *Fig (altanería)* pride, haughtiness **(c)** *Fig* **de alto c.** high-class

copia *nf* **(a)** *(reproducción)* copy; **sacar una c.** to make a copy ❑ *Inform* **c. de seguridad** backup; **papel de c.** copy paper **(b)** *(persona)* image **(c)** *Cin* print; **c. diaria** rushes *pl* **(d)** *Literario (abundancia)* abundance

copiador, -a *adj* copying

copiadora *nf* photocopier

copiar *vt* **(a)** *(gen) también Inform* to copy **(b)** *(escribir)* to copy, take down **(c)** *(imitar)* to copy, imitate **(d)** *Educ* to cheat; **la pillaron copiando** she was caught cheating

copiloto *nm Av* copilot; *Aut* co-driver

copión, -ona *nm,f Fam* cheat, cheater; *(imitador)* copycat

copiosidad *nf* abundance

copioso, -a *adj* abundant, copious, plentiful; **copiosas lluvias** heavy rain *sing*

copista *nmf* copyist

copla *nf* **(a)** *(verso, estrofa)* verse, couplet; *Fam* **andar en coplas** to be the talk of the town; *Fam* **la misma c.** the same old story **(b) coplas** *(canciones)* folk songs, popular songs

copo¹ *nm* **(a)** *(gen)* flake; *(de nieve)* snowflake; *(de algodón)* ball *(of cotton)*; **copos de avena** rolled oats **(b)** *RP (nubes)* bank of clouds **(c)** *Col Ven (de árbol)* treetop

copo² *nm (pesca)* catch *(of fish)*

copón *nm Esp Fam* **se armó un lío del c.** there was a great mess

coproducción *nf* co-production, joint production

copropiedad *nf* co-ownership, joint ownership

copropietario, -a *adj & nm,f* co-owner, joint owner

coprotagonista *nmf* co-star

coprotagonizar [14] *vt* to co-star in

copudo, -a *adj* bushy, thick

cópula *nf* **(a)** *(coito)* copulation, intercourse **(b)** *Ling* conjunction

copulación *nf (gen) & Ling* copulation

copular *vi* to copulate **(con** with)

copulativo, -a *adj* copulative

copyright [kopi'rrait] *(pl* **copyrights)** *nm* copyright

coque *nm Min* coke

coquetear *vi* to flirt **(con** with)

coqueteo *nm* flirtation

coquetería *nf* coquetry, flirtation

coqueto, -a 1 *adj* flirtatious
2 *nm,f* **(a)** *(mujer)* coquette, flirt; *(hombre)* flirt **(b)** *Mueb (tocador)* dressing table

coquetón, -ona *adj (mujer)* coquette, flirty; *(hombre)* flirtatious

coraje *nm* **(a)** *(valor)* toughness, courage; **echar c.** to take courage **(b)** *(ira)* anger, annoyance; **dar c. a** to infuriate; **¡qué c.!** how maddening!

corajudo, -a *adj* **(a)** *(valiente)* tough, brave **(b)** *(irritable)* quick-tempered

coral¹ *nm Zool* coral; **corales** coral necklace *sing*

coral² 1 *adj* choral
2 *nm Mús* choral, chorale

coralina *nf Bot* coralline

coralino, -a *adj* coral

corambre *nf* hides *pl*, skins *pl*

Corán *nm Rel* Koran

coránico, -a *adj Rel* Koranic

coraza *nf* **(a)** *(armadura)* armour, *US* armor, cuirass; *Fig* armour, *US* armor, protection **(b)** *Zool (caparazón)* shell

corazón *nm* **(a)** *Anat* heart; **estar enfermo** *o* **padecer del c.** to have heart trouble; *Fig* **abrir algn su c.** to open one's heart; *Fig* **con el c. en un puño** with one's heart in one's mouth; *Fig* **de (todo) c.** in all sincerity; *Fig* **hablar con el c. en la mano** to wear one's heart on one's sleeve; *Fig* **romper el c. a algn** to break sb's heart; *Fig* **tener buen c.** to be kindhearted **(b)** *(parte central)* heart, core; *(de fruta)* core; **en el c. de la ciudad** in the heart of the city **(c)** *(apelativo cariñoso)* darling, sweetheart **(d) corazones** *Naipes* hearts

corazonada *nf* **(a)** *(presentimiento)* hunch, feeling; **tuve la c. de que ...** something told me that ... **(b)** *(impulso)* impulse

corbata *nf* **(a)** *(indumentaria)* tie, *US* necktie; **con c.** wearing a tie **(b)** *(en bandera)* sash, tassel **(c)** *Arg (pañuelo)* bandanna, bandana, scarf

corbatín *nm CAm Carib Col* bow tie

corbeta *nf Náut* corvette

Córcega *n* Corsica

corcel *nm Literario* steed, charger

corchea *nf Mús Br* quaver, *US* eighth note

corchero, -a *adj* cork; **industria corchera** cork industry

corchete *nm* **(a)** *Cost (gafete)* hook and eye, snap fastener **(b)** *Impr* square bracket

corcho *nm* **(a)** *(gen)* cork; *(corteza)* cork bark **(b)** *(tapón)* cork **(c)** *(pesca)* float **(d)** *(flotador)* float

córcholis *interj (sorpresa)* goodness me!, *US* gee!

corcova *nf Anat (joroba)* hunchback, hump

corcovado, -a 1 *adj* hunchbacked
2 *nm,f* hunchback

corcovear *vi (a) Am (refunfuñar)* to grumble; *(indignarse)* to get upset **(b)** *Méx (tener miedo)* to be afraid

corcovo *nm* prance

cordada *nf* = roped party of mountaineers

cordaje *nm* **(a)** *(cuerdas)* ropes *pl*, cordage **(b)** *Náut* rigging

cordel *nm* rope, cord; **a c.** in a straight line

cordelería *nf* **(a)** *(oficio)* ropemaking **(b)** *Náut* rigging

cordelero, -a *nm,f* ropemaker

cordero, -a 1 *nm,f* lamb; *Fig* **ser un c.** to be as meek as a lamb
2 *nm* lambskin

cordial 1 *adj* **(a)** *(afable)* cordial, warm, friendly **(b)** *Farm (tonificante)* cordial, stimulating
2 *nm Farm* cordial

cordialidad *nf* cordiality, warmth, friendliness

cordillera *nf* mountain chain *o* range

Córdoba *n* Cordoba

cordobán *nm* cordovan (leather)

cordobés, -esa *adj & nm,f* Cordoban

cordón *nm* **(a)** *(gen)* rope, string; *(de zapatos)* shoelace, shoestring; *Elec* flex; *(hebra)* **lana de 3 cordones** 3-ply wool ❑ **c. sanitario** cordon sanitaire; *Anat* **c. umbilical** umbilical cord **(b)** *(cadena humana)* cordon ❑ **c. policial** police cordon **(c)** *CSur Cuba (de la vereda)* Br kerb, *US* curb

cordoncillo *nm (cordón pequeño)* cord; *Cost* braid, piping

cordura *nf* sound judgement, good sense; **con c.** sensibly, prudently, wisely

Corea *n* Korea

corea *nf Med* Saint Vitus's dance

coreano, -a 1 *adj & nm,f* Korean
2 *nm (idioma)* Korean

corear *vt* **(a)** *(cantar a coro)* to sing in chorus **(b)** *Fig (opinión)* to echo **(c)** *(aclamar)* to applaud

coreografía *nf* choreography

coreográfico, -a *adj* choreographic

coreógrafo, -a *nm,f* choreographer

corista *nf Teat* chorus girl

coriza *nf Med* coryza

cormorán *nm Orn* **c. (grande)** cormorant

cornada *nf Taur* goring; **dar cornadas a** to gore

cornamenta *nf* **(a)** *(gen)* horns *pl*; *(del ciervo)* antlers *pl* **(b)** *Fam Ofens (del marido)* cuckold's horns *pl*

córnea *nf Anat* cornea

cornear *vt* to gore

corneja *nf Orn* crow

cornejo *nm Bot* dogwood

córneo, -a *adj* horn-like, corneous

córner (*pl* **córners**) *nm Ftb* corner, corner (kick); **sacar un c.** to take a corner

corneta 1 *nf Mús (instrumento)* bugle; **c. de llaves** cornet
2 *nm Mil (persona)* bugler

cornetín *nm Mús* (**a**) *(instrumento)* cornet (**b**) *(persona)* cornet player

cornisa *nf* (**a**) *Arquit* cornice (**b**) *Geog* **la C. Cantábrica** the Cantabrian Coast

corno *nm Mús* horn; **c. inglés** cor anglais, English horn

cornucopia *nf* cornucopia, horn of plenty

cornudo, -a 1 *adj* (**a**) *(animal)* horned, antlered (**b**) *Fam Ofens (marido)* cuckolded
2 *nm (marido)* cuckold

coro *nm* (**a**) *Mús* choir (**b**) *Teat* chorus; *Fig* **a c.** all together; *Fig* **hacer c.** to join in the chorus

corola *nf Bot* corolla

corolario *nm* corollary

corona *nf* (**a**) *(de monarca)* crown; **mensaje de la c.** King's o Queen's speech (**b**) *(aureola)* halo (**c**) *(de ramas, flores)* wreath, garland ▫ **c. funeraria** funeral wreath (**d**) *Anat* crown (of the head); *(del diente)* crown (**e**) *(moneda)* crown

coronación *nf* (**a**) *(acto)* coronation (**b**) *Fig (culminación)* crowning

coronamiento *nm* (**a**) *(culminación)* crowning (**b**) *Arquit* crown

coronar 1 *vt* (**a**) *(poner una corona a)* to crown; *Literario* **la sierra está coronada de nieve** the mountains are capped with snow (**b**) *Fig (culminar)* to culminate, crown; **c. la cima** to reach the summit
2 coronarse *vpr (en el parto)* to crown; **el niño se corona** the baby's head is showing

coronario, -a *adj Med* coronary; **insuficiencia coronaria** cardiac arrest

coronel *nm Mil* colonel

coronilla *nf Anat* crown of the head; *Fam* **andar de c.** to run around in circles; *Fam* **estar hasta la c.** to be fed up (**de** with)

corpachón *nm* big body, big frame

corpiño *nm* (**a**) *(de vestido, top)* bodice (**b**) *Arg (sostén)* bra

corporación *nf* corporation; **c. metropolitana** city corporation; *Com Fin* company, association

corporal 1 *adj* corporal, body; **castigo c.** corporal punishment
2 *nm (lienzo)* corporal, corporale

corporativismo *nm Pol* = self-interested behaviour, especially of professional groups

corporativo, -a *adj* corporative; **asociación corporativa** syndicate

corpóreo, -a *adj* bodily, physical

corpulencia *nf* corpulence, stoutness

corpulento, -a *adj* corpulent, stocky, stout

corpus (*pl inv o* **corpora** *nm* (**a**) *(conjunto)* corpus (**b**) *Rel* **C. Corpus Christi**

corpúsculo *nm Biol* corpuscle

corral *nm* (**a**) *(gen)* yard; *(de granja)* farmyard, *US* corral; *(de casa)* courtyard (**b**) *(para niños)* playpen

correa *nf* (**a**) *(tira)* strap; *(de reloj)* watchstrap; *(de pantalón)* belt; *(de perro)* lead, *US* leash (**b**) *Téc* belt; **c. sin fin** conveyor belt (**c**) *(elasticidad)* elasticity, stretch; *Fig* **tiene mucha c.** he can take a joke

correaje *nm* belts *pl*, straps *pl*

corrección *nf* (**a**) *(rectificación)* correction, adjustment ▫ *Tip* **c. de pruebas** proofreading (**b**) *(cortesía)* courtesy, correctness, politeness; **tratar a la gente con c.** to be polite (**c**) *(reprimenda)* rebuke; *(castigo)* punishment

correccional *adj & nm* reformatory

correctamente *adv* (**a**) *(sin errores)* correctly, accurately (**b**) *(con educación)* correctly, politely, properly

correctivo, -a *adj & nm* corrective

correcto, -a *adj* (**a**) *(sin errores)* correct, accurate, good (**b**) *(rasgos)* regular; **facciones correctas** regular o even features (**c**) *(cortés)* polite, courteous (**con** to); *(conducta)* proper; *(ropa)* suitable

corrector, -a 1 *adj* corrective
2 *nm,f Impr* **c. de estilo** copy editor; **c. de pruebas** proofreader
3 *nm Inform* **c. ortográfico** spellchecker

corredera *nf* (**a**) *(ranura)* runner; **puerta c.** sliding door (**b**) *Arg Fam* **la c.** *(diarrea)* the runs

corredero, -a *adj* sliding

corredizo, -a *adj* sliding; **nudo c.** slipknot

corredor, -a 1 *adj* running; *Orn* **ave corredora** flightless bird
2 *nm,f* (**a**) *Dep* runner (**b**) *Fin* **c. de bolsa** stockbroker; **c. de fincas** land agent

correduría *nf Com* **c. de seguros** *(oficina)* insurance broker's

corregible *adj* which can be corrected, rectifiable

corregir [55] **1** *vt* (**a**) *(gen)* to correct, rectify (**b**) *Impr (pruebas etc)* to read (**c**) *(reprender)* to scold, reprimand, tell off (**d**) *Educ (ejercicios)* to mark
2 corregirse *vpr (persona)* to mend one's ways; *(defecto)* to right itself

correlación *nf* correlation

correlacionar *vt* to correlate

correlativo, -a *adj & nm* correlative

correligionario, -a *nm,f (en política, ideología)* = person of the same ideological persuasion; *(en religión)* fellow believer; **Churchill y sus correligionarios** Churchill and his fellow conservatives

correntoso, -a *adj Andes RP* fast-flowing, torrential

correo *nm* (**a**) *(sistema, cartas)* *Br* post, *US* mail; **a vuelta de c.** by return (of post); **echar al c.** to post; **por c.** by post ▫ **c. aéreo** airmail; *Inform* **c. basura** junk mail, spam; **c. caracol** snail mail; **c. certificado** registered post; **c. de voz** voice mail; *Inform* **c. electrónico** electronic mail; **(tren) c.** mail train (**b**) *Esp* **correos** *(edificio)* post office *sing*; **lista de c.** poste restante (**c**) *(persona)* courier; *Mil* dispatch rider

correoso, -a *adj* (**a**) *(flexible)* flexible, leathery (**b**) *Fig (difícil de masticar)* tough, leathery

correr 1 *vi* (**a**) *(gen)* to run; **echar a c.** to start running; **se fue corriendo** he ran off o away (**b**) *(ir deprisa)* to rush, hurry; **no corras, habla más despacio** don't rush yourself, speak slower (**c**) *(coche)* to go fast; *(conductor)* to drive fast; *(caballo)* to race, run (**d**) *(tiempo)* to pass, go by; **el mes/año que corre** the current month/year (**e**) *(noticia)* to circulate, spread; **la noticia corrió como la pólvora** the news spread like wildfire (**f**) *(río)* to run, flow; *(camino etc)* to run; **la carretera corre entre las montañas** the road winds through the mountains (**g**) *(viento)* to blow (**h**) *(sueldo)* to be payable (**i**) *(encargarse)* **c. con los gastos** to foot the bill; **corre a mi cargo** I'll take care of it (**j**) **c. prisa** to be urgent (**k**) *Am Fam (ser válido)* to be in use (**l**) *Méx Ven (funcionar)* to be running; **hoy no corren los trenes** the trains aren't running today
2 *vt* (**a**) *(distancia)* to cover; *(país etc)* to travel through; **c.**

mundo to globetrot (**b**) *(echar)* to close; *(cortina)* to draw; **c. el cerrojo** to bolt the door/gate (**c**) *(mover)* to pull up, draw up (**d**) *(arriesgarse)* to run (**e**) *(aventura etc)* to have; **corrimos un gran peligro** we were in great danger (**f**) *(noticia etc)* to spread; **c. la voz** to pass it on (**g**) *Fam* **correrla** to live it up (**h**) **dejar c. algo** to let sth pass (**i**) *Am (echar)* to let off, fire

3 correrse *vpr* (**a**) *(persona)* to move over; *(objeto)* to shift, slide (**b**) *(color, tinta)* to run; **se corre al lavarlo** it runs in the wash (**c**) *(avergonzarse)* to blush, go red (**d**) *Fam (juerga)* to go on; **se corrieron una juerga monumental** they went on a real bender (**e**) *Andes Esp Argot (tener orgasmo)* to come (**f**) *Cuba Guat Méx (escaparse)* to run away, escape

correría *nf* (**a**) *(incursión)* raid, foray (**b**) **correrías** *(andanzas)* travels

correspondencia *nf* (**a**) *(gen)* correspondence; **esta palabra no tiene c. en español** there's no translation for this word in Spanish (**b**) *(comunicación)* communication; *Ferroc (enlace)* connection (**c**) *(cartas)* correspondence, mail; **mantener c. con algn** to correspond with sb

corresponder 1 *vi* (**a**) *(gen)* to correspond (**a** to, **con** with), tally (**con** with) (**b**) *(ser apropiado)* to be suitable *o* be right; *(color, mueble)* to match, go (**con** with); *Fig* **no corresponde con lo que esperaba** it doesn't come up to my expectations (**c**) *(incumbir)* to concern, be incumbent upon; **esta tarea te corresponde a ti** it's your job to do this (**d**) *(tocar, pertenecer)* to be one's due; **me dieron lo que me correspondía** they gave me my share (**e**) *(devolver)* to return, reciprocate; *(favor)* to repay; **amor no correspondido** unrequited love; **c. a la amabilidad de algn** to repay sb's kindness (**f**) *Ferroc* to connect (**con** with)

2 corresponderse *vpr* (**a**) *(ajustarse)* to correspond, agree; *(armonizar)* to be in harmony (**con** with) (**b**) *(apreciarse)* to have mutual affection; *(amarse)* to love one another, love each other (**c**) *(cifras)* to tally

correspondiente *adj* (**a**) *(que corresponde)* corresponding (**a** to) (**b**) *(apropiado)* appropriate; *(oportuno)* convenient (**c**) *(respectivo)* own; **cada uno con su c. etiqueta** each one with its own label

corresponsal *nmf Prensa* correspondent

corresponsalía *nf Prensa* post of correspondent

corretaje *nm Fin* brokerage (fee)

corretear 1 *vi* (**a**) *(correr)* to run about (**b**) *Fam (vagar)* to hang about
2 *vt* (**a**) *Andes (perseguir)* to chase (**b**) *CAm (ahuyentar)* to scare *o* ward off

correteo *nm* running about, hustle and bustle

correveidile *nmf inv Fig* (**a**) *(chismoso)* gossip (**b**) *(alcahuete)* go-between

corrida *nf* (**a**) *(paso rápido)* run, dash, race; **de c.** *(rápidamente)* in a flash; *(de memoria)* from memory, by heart (**b**) *Taur (fiesta)* **c. (de toros)** bullfight

corrido, -a 1 *pp de* **correr**
2 *adj* (**a**) *(peso)* heavy; **un kilo c.** over a kilo, a good kilo (**b**) *(cortina)* drawn (**c**) *(continuo)* continuous; **balcón c.** full balcony; **seto c.** unbroken hedge (**d**) *Fig (avergonzado)* abashed; **dejar c.** to embarrass; **quedarse c.** to feel embarrassed (**e**) *Fam (experimentado)* **hombre/mujer c.** man/woman of the world (**f**) **de c.** without stopping; **recitar de c.** to reel off; **traducir de c.** to translate at *o* on sight (**g**) *Am (completo)* full, complete
3 *nm Méx* ballad

corriente 1 *adj* (**a**) *(común)* ordinary, average, run-of-the-mill; **es c. ver ...** you often see ...; **lo más c. es ...** the usual thing is ...; **salirse de lo c.** to be out of the ordinary; **un vestido c.** an ordinary dress (**b**) *(agua)* running (**c**) *(mes, año)* current, present; **el diez del c.** the tenth of this month (**d**) *Fin (cuenta)* current; *(moneda)* valid (**e**) *(al día)* **al c.** up to

date; **estar al c.** to be in the know; **poner algn al c. (de algo)** to fill sb in (on sth); **ponerse al c.** to get up to date; **tener a algn al c.** to keep sb informed
2 *nf* (**a**) *(de río)* current, stream, flow; **c. abajo** downstream; **c. arriba** upstream; **ir** *o* **navegar contra c.** to swim against the tide; *Fig* to go against the tide; *Fig* **dejarse llevar por la c.** to follow the herd; *Fig* **seguir la c. a** to follow the crowd; *Fam* **seguirle** *o* **llevarle la c. a algn** to humour sb □ *Elec* **c. alterna** alternating current; *Elec* **c. eléctrica** (electric) current; *Geog* **c. del Golfo** Gulf Stream; **c. sanguínea** bloodstream (**b**) *(de aire)* draught, *US* draft (**c**) *(tendencia)* trend; **corrientes del arte** trends in art

corrientemente *adv* usually, normally

corrijo *indic pres véase* **corregir**

corrillo *nm* small group of people talking, clique

corrimiento *nm Geol* slipping, sliding □ **c. de tierras** landslide

corro *nm* (**a**) *(de personas)* circle, ring; *Fig* **hacer c. aparte** to form a small circle; *Fig* **hacerle c. a algn** to gather round sb (**b**) *(juego infantil)* ring-a-ring-a-roses

corroboración *nf* corroboration

corroborar *vt* to corroborate

corroborativo, -a *adj* corroborative

corroer [57] **1** *vt* (**a**) *(degastar)* to corrode; *Geol* to erode (**b**) *Fig (minar)* to corrode, eat away *o* up; **la envidia le corroe el alma** he is consumed with envy
2 corroerse *vpr* (**a**) *(desgastarse)* to become corroded (**b**) *Fig* to be eaten up (**de** with)

corromper 1 *vt* (**a**) *(pudrir)* to turn bad, rot (**b**) *(pervertir)* to corrupt, pervert (**c**) *(sobornar)* to bribe (**d**) *(estropear)* to spoil; **la falta de lectura corroe el lenguaje** not reading enough can impoverish one's language
2 corromperse *vpr* (**a**) *(pudrirse)* to go bad, rot (**b**) *(pervertirse)* to become corrupted

corrosión *nf* corrosion, rust; *Geol* erosion

corrosivo, -a *adj* (**a**) *(sustancia)* corrosive (**b**) *Fig (mordaz)* caustic

corrupción *nf* (**a**) *(putrefacción)* rot, decay (**b**) *Fig* corruption, degradation; *(soborno)* bribe; *(perversión)* seduction □ *Jur* **c. de menores** corruption of minors

corruptela *nf* corruption, sharp practice

corrupto, -a *adj* corrupt; **un juez c.** a corrupt judge

corruptor, -a 1 *adj* corrupting
2 *nm,f* corrupter, perverter

corrusco *nm Fam* crust of stale bread

corsario, -a 1 *adj* privateer
2 *nm* corsair, privateer

corsé *nm (prenda)* corset

corsetería *nf* ladies' underwear shop

corso, -a *adj & nm,f* Corsican

corta *nf* tree felling

cortacésped *nm & f* lawnmower

cortacircuitos *nm inv Elec* circuit breaker

cortado, -a 1 *pp de* **cortar**
2 *adj* (**a**) *(troceado)* cut (up); *(en lonchas)* sliced (**b**) *(leche)* sour (**c**) *(labios)* chapped (**d**) *Fig (estilo)* concise, clipped (**e**) *Fam (aturdido)* dumbfounded; **quedarse c.** to be speechless *o* lost for words
3 *nm* = small coffee with a dash of milk

cortador, -a 1 *adj* cutting
2 *nm* cutter

cortadura *nf* (**a**) *(corte)* cut (**b**) *Geog (paso)* gorge (**c**) **cortaduras** *(recortes)* cuttings, clippings

cortafuego *nm*, **cortafuegos** *nm inv* (**a**) *(en monte)* firebreak (**b**) *(en edificio)* fire wall (**c**) *Inform* firewall

cortante *adj* cutting, sharp; *Fig (viento)* biting, bitter; *Fig (estilo)* incisive, acrid, cutting

cortapapeles *nm inv* paperknife; *Téc* guillotine

cortapisa *nf Fig* restriction, limitation, condition; **sin cortapisas** with no strings attached

cortaplumas *nm inv* penknife

cortar 1 *vt* (a) *(gen)* to cut; *(pelo)* to cut, trim; *(pastel)* to cut (up); *(carne)* to carve; *(árbol)* to cut down; *Cost (vestido)* to cut out; **c. por la mitad** to cut in half, split down the middle; *Fam Fig* **c. con un amigo** to split up with a friend (b) *(piel)* to chap, crack (c) *Naipes* to cut (d) *(detener, interrumpir)* to cut off, interrupt; **nos han cortado el teléfono** our telephone has been disconnected; *Fig* **c. algo de raíz** to nip sth in the bud; *Fam* **c. algo por lo sano** to take drastic measures (e) *(bloquear)* to block; **la nieve nos cortó el paso** we were cut off by the snow (f) *(suprimir)* to cut out; *Cin (película)* to cut (g) *(viento, frío)* to chill, bite; **un viento que corta** a biting wind (h) *Fig (dividir)* to divide, split; **el río corta el valle en dos** the river cuts through the valley (i) *(avergonzar)* **hablar en público me corta mucho** I get tongue-tied speaking in public (j) *Culin (mayonesa etc)* to curdle (k) *Inform* to cut

2 *vi (destacarse)* to stand out

3 cortarse *vpr* (a) *(herirse)* to cut oneself; **c. el pelo** *(uno mismo)* to cut one's hair; *(por otro)* to have one's hair cut (b) *(piel)* to become chapped (c) *(leche)* to curdle; *(mayonesa)* to separate, curdle (d) *Tel* to be cut off; **se cortó la comunicación** we were cut off (e) *Fam (aturdirse)* to get confused *o* tongue-tied (f) *Vulg* **cortársela** to cut one's dick off (g) *Andes RP (separarse)* to be left behind (h) *Chile (caballo)* to catch a chill

cortaúñas *nm inv* nail clippers *pl*

corte¹ *nm* (a) *(gen)* cut; **c. de pelo** haircut; **me he hecho un c. en la mano** I cut my hand (b) *Esp (filo)* edge (c) *(sección)* section; **c. transversal** cross section (d) *Cost* cut; **este vestido tiene un c. elegante** this dress has an elegant cut □ **c. y confección** dressmaking (e) *(de libro)* edge (f) *(tela para vestido)* length (g) *(pausa)* break □ **c. publicitario** commercial break (h) *Fam (respuesta brusca)* rebuff; **dar un c. a algn** to cut sb dead; **¡jo, qué c.!** what a blow! (i) *Vulg* **hacer un c. de mangas a algn** ≃ to give sb the finger

corte² *nf* (a) *(de reyes)* court; *Fig Hum (séquito)* retinue; **hacer la c. a** to court (b) *Esp* **Cortes** (Spanish) Parliament *sing* (c) *Am Jur (tribunal)* court

cortedad *nf* (a) *(pequeñez)* shortness, smallness (b) *Fig (timidez)* shyness, timidity (c) *Fig (falta)* lack; **c. de ánimo** lack of courage

cortejar *vt* to court

cortejo *nm* (a) *(galanteo)* courting (b) *(comitiva)* entourage, retinue □ **c. fúnebre** funeral cortège (c) *Fig (secuela)* sequel, aftermath

cortés *(pl* **corteses)** *adj* courteous, polite; *Prov* **lo c. no quita lo valiente** you can be polite but firm at the same time

cortesana *nf (prostituta)* courtesan

cortesano, -a 1 *adj (modales)* courtly; **la vida cortesana** life at court

2 *nm,f (personaje de la corte)* courtier

cortesía *nf* (a) *(educación)* courtesy, politeness; **acto de c.** politeness; **la c. pide que ...** etiquette demands that ... □ **visita de c.** courtesy call (b) *(en cartas)* formal ending (c) *(reverencia)* bow, curtsy

cortésmente *adv* courteously, politely

córtex *nm inv Anat* cortex

corteza *nf* (a) *(de árbol)* bark; *(de fruta)* peel, skin; *(de queso)* rind; *(de pan)* crust (b) *Fig (apariencia)* outside, outward appearance

corticoide *nm* corticoid

cortijero, -a *nm,f* Andalusian farmer

cortijo *nm* Andalusian farm *o* farmhouse

cortina *nf* curtain, screen; **c. de tienda** tent flap; **correr las cortinas** to draw the curtains □ *Mil Fig* **c. de fuego** barrage; *Fig* **c. de humo** smoke screen

cortinaje *nm* drapery

cortinilla *nf* small lace curtain

cortisona *nf Med* cortisone

corto, -a 1 *adj* (a) *(distancia)* short; **novela corta** short story; *Fam* **c. de alcances** not very bright, dim; *Fam* **c. de miras** narrow-minded □ **c. de vista** short-sighted; *Aut* **luz corta** dipped headlights *pl* (b) *(tiempo)* short, brief; **el viaje se hizo c.** the journey went by quickly; *Fig* **a la corta o a la larga** sooner or later (c) *(escaso)* scant, meagre; *Fam* **quedarse c.** *(calcular mal)* to underestimate; *(no decir todo)* to hold something back (d) *Fam (tonto)* thick, dim (e) *(apocado)* timid, shy

2 *nm Cin* short (film); *Am* **cortos** *(avances)* trailer

cortocircuito *nm Elec* short circuit

cortometraje *nm Cin* short (movie *o Br* film)

coruñés, -esa 1 *adj* of *o* from La Coruña

2 *nm,f* person from La Coruña

corvadura *nf* curvature, curve

corvejón *nm (de caballo)* hock

corvina *nf (pez)* meagre

corvo, -a *adj* curved, bent; **nariz corva** hooked nose

corzo, -a *nm,f Zool (macho)* roe buck; *(hembra)* roe deer

cosa¹ *nf* (a) *(gen)* thing; **mete tus cosas en el cajón** put your things in the drawer; **tengo que decirte una c.** I've got something to tell you; **tal como están las cosas** as things stand (b) *(asunto)* matter, business; **cosas de negocios** business matters; **eso es c. tuya** that's your business *o* affair; **eso es otra c.** that's different (c) *(frase negativa)* nothing, not anything; **no he visto c. igual** I've never seen anything like it (d) *(tiempo)* **c. de** about; **es c. de unas horas** it'll take a couple of hours (e) *(manía)* hang-up; **cada uno tiene sus cosas** we've all got our hang-ups (f) *(locuciones)* **como si tal c.** just like that; **son cosas de la vida** that's life; **decir cuatro cosas** to tell a few home truths; **no sea c. que ...** make sure that ...; **no ser gran c.** not to be important, not be up to much; **no valer gran c.** not to be worth much; **ser c. hecha** to be no sooner said than done; **ser poquita c.** not to be much

cosa² *conj Am* so that

cosaco, -a *adj & nm* Cossack; *Fam* **beber como un c.** to drink like a fish

coscarse [59] *vpr Fam* (a) *(darse cuenta de)* to notice, realize (b) *(entender)* to understand

coscorrón *nm* knock *o* blow on the head

cosecha *nf* (a) *Agr* harvest, crop; **de c. propia** homegrown; *Fig* of one's own invention; **hacer la c.** to harvest (b) *(tiempo)* harvest time (c) *(año del vino)* vintage

cosechadora *nf Téc* combine harvester

cosechar *vt* (a) to harvest, gather (in); **se cosecha en setiembre** harvest time is in September (b) *(cultivar)* to grow (c) *Fig (recoger)* to reap, harvest; **c. disgustos** to build up trouble (for oneself)

cosechero, -a *nm,f* harvester, grower

coseno *nm Mat* cosine

coser *vt* (a) *(con hilo)* to sew; **te he cosido el botón** I've sewn the button on for you; *Fam* **es c. y cantar** it's plain sailing, it's a piece of cake (b) *Med* to stitch up (c) *(grapar)* to staple (together) (d) *Fig (atravesar)* **c. a balazos** to riddle with bullets

cosido, -a 1 *pp de* **coser**
2 *adj* sewn-on
3 *nm* (**a**) *(con hilo)* sewing (**b**) *Med* stitching

cosmética *nf* cosmetics *pl*

cosmético, -a *adj & nm* cosmetic

cósmico, -a *adj* cosmic

cosmogonía *nf* cosmogony

cosmografía *nf* cosmography

cosmográfico, -a *adj* cosmographic, cosmographical

cosmología *nf* cosmology

cosmológico, -a *adj* cosmologic, cosmological

cosmonauta *nmf* cosmonaut

cosmopolita *adj & nmf* cosmopolitan

cosmos *nm inv* cosmos

cosmovisión *nf* world view

coso *nm* (**a**) *(cercado)* arena, enclosure; *Taur Literario* bullring (**b**) *(carcoma)* woodworm

cosquillas *nfpl* tickles, tickling *sing*; **hacer c. a algn** to tickle sb; **tener c.** to be ticklish; *Fam* **buscarle las c. a algn** to annoy sb

cosquillear *vt* to tickle; **me cosquillea la idea de ...** I've been toying with the idea of ...

cosquilleo *nm* tickling

costa[1] *nf Geog (litoral)* coast, coastline; *(playa)* beach, seaside, *US* shore; **veraneamos en la c.** we spend our summer holidays at the seaside ❏ **C. de Marfil** Ivory Coast

costa[2] *nf* (**a**) *(coste) Fin* cost, price; **a c. de** at the expense of; **a c. de muchos esfuerzos** by dint of great effort; **a toda c.** at all costs, at any price; **vive a c. mía** he lives off me (**b**) **costas** *Jur (gastos)* costs; **pagar las c.** to pay costs

costado *nm (lado)* side; **de c.** sideways; *Fig* **por los cuatro costados** on all sides; *Fig* **es catalana por los cuatro costados** she's Catalan through and through

costal *nm* sack

costalada *nf*, **costalazo** *nm* fall (on one's back); **darse una c.** to fall on one's back

costanero, -a *adj* (**a**) *(inclinado)* sloping (**b**) *Náut (costero)* coastal

costanilla *nf* steep street

costar [63] *vi* (**a**) *Fin Com* to cost; **c. barato** to be cheap; **c. caro** to be expensive, cost a lot; **¿cuánto cuesta?** how much is it?; *Fam* **cuesta un ojo de la cara** it costs an arm and a leg (**b**) *Fig* **c. caro algo a algn** to pay dearly for sth; **c. trabajo** o **mucho** to be hard; **cueste lo que cueste** at any cost; **le costó la vida** it cost him his life; **me cuesta hablar francés** I find it difficult to speak French

Costa Rica *n* Costa Rica

costarricense *adj & nmf*, **costarriqueño, -a** *adj & nm,f* Costa Rican

coste *nm Esp* cost, price, expense; **a precio de c.** (at) cost price ❏ **c. de la vida** cost of living

costear[1] 1 *vt* to afford, pay for; **c. los gastos** to foot the bill
2 costearse *vpr* **c. algo** to pay for sth oneself

costear[2] *vt Náut* to coast

costero, -a *adj* coastal, coast; **ciudad costera** seaside town

costilla *nf* (**a**) *Anat* rib (**b**) *Culin* cutlet

costillar *nm Anat* ribs *pl*

costo[1] *nm* cost, price ❏ **c. unitario** unit cost

costo[2] *nm Esp Argot (hachís)* dope, shit, stuff

costoso, -a *adj* (**a**) *(caro)* costly, expensive (**b**) *(difícil)* hard; **es un trabajo c.** it's hard work

costra *nf* crust; *Med* scab

costumbre *nf* (**a**) *(hábito)* habit; **como de c.** as usual; **la fuerza de la c.** force of habit; **tenía la c. de madrugar** he used to get up early (**b**) *(tradición)* custom; **es una c. china** it's a Chinese custom (**c**) **costumbres** *(personales)* manner *sing*, ways; *(de pueblo)* customs

costumbrismo *nm Arte Lit* folk literature

costumbrista 1 *adj (novela)* about local customs o traditions
2 *nmf* writer of folk literature

costura *nf* (**a**) *(cosido)* sewing; **cesto de la c.** needlework basket (**b**) *(confección)* dressmaking ❏ **alta c.** haute couture (**c**) *(línea de puntadas)* seam; **medias sin c.** seamless stockings

costurera *nf* seamstress

costurero *nm* sewing basket

costurón *nm* (**a**) *(cosido)* untidy seam (**b**) *Med (cicatriz)* noticeable scar

cota[1] *nf Geog* height above sea level; *Fig* **la delincuencia ha alcanzado cotas muy elevadas** delinquency has increased alarmingly

cota[2] *nf Hist* tabard ❏ **c. de malla** coat of mail

cotarro *nm Fam* noisy gathering; **dirigir el c., ser el amo del c.** to be (the) boss, run the show

cotejable *adj* comparable

cotejar *vt* to check, compare

cotejo *nm* check, comparison

cotidianidad *nf* *(vida cotidiana)* everyday life; *(frecuencia)* commonness

cotidiano, -a *adj* daily; **vida cotidiana** everyday life; **ser algo c.** to be an everyday occurrence

cotilla *nmf Esp Fam* busybody, gossip

cotillear *vi Esp Fam* to gossip (**de** about)

cotilleo *nm Esp Fam* gossip, gossiping

cotillón *nm* = party on New Year's Eve or 5th of January

cotizable *adj Fin* quotable; **acciones cotizables en bolsa** stock market shares

cotización *nf* (**a**) *Fin* (market) price, quotation ❏ **c. de cierre** closing price; **c. del día** current price; **c. máxima** high (**b**) *(cuota)* membership fees *pl*, subscription

cotizar [14] 1 *vt* (**a**) *Fin* to quote, price (**b**) *(pagar cuota)* to pay *(a subscription)*
2 cotizarse *vpr* (**a**) *Com Fin* **c. a** to sell at; **¿a cuánto se cotizan las acciones?** what are the shares selling at? (**b**) *Fig* to be valued, be in demand

coto *nm* (**a**) *(vedado)* enclosure, reserve ❏ **c. de caza** game preserve (**b**) *(límite)* **poner c. a** to put a stop to

cotón *nm Am (prenda)* work shirt

cotona *nf* (**a**) *Am (camisa)* cotton shirt (**b**) *Méx (chaqueta)* chamois leather jacket

cotorra *nf* (**a**) *Orn* parrot (**b**) *Fig (persona)* chatterbox; **hablar como una c.** to be a chatterbox

cotorrear *vi* to chatter, prattle

cotorreo *nm* chatter, prattle

covacha *nf* hovel

coxis *nm inv* coccyx

coyote *nm* (**a**) *(animal)* coyote (**b**) *Méx Fam (intermediario)* fixer, middleman

coyotear *vi Méx Fam* to wheel and deal

coyuntura *nf* (**a**) *Anat (articulación)* articulation, joint (**b**) *Fig (circunstancia)* moment, juncture; **c. crítica** turning point; *Econ* **la c. económica** the economic situation

coyuntural *adj* temporary, provisional

coz *nf* kick; **dar una c.** to kick; *Fig* **tratar a algn a coces** to treat sb like dirt

C.P. *(abrev de* **código postal***) Br* postcode, *US* zip code

CPI *nf (abrev de* **Corte Penal Internacional***)* ICC

cps *Inform (abrev de* **caracteres por segundo***)* cps

CPU *nf Inform (abrev de* **Central Processing Unit***)* CPU

crac *(pl* **cracs***) nm* **(a)** *(onomatopeya)* crack, snap; **la silla hizo crac y me quedé sentado en el suelo** the chair went 'crack' and I ended up (sitting) on the floor **(b)** *Fin* bankruptcy, crash; *Hist* **el c. de la bolsa neoyorquina** the Wall Street crash

crack [krak] *(pl* **cracks***) nm* **(a)** *(estrella)* star, superstar **(b)** *Fin* crash **(c)** *(droga)* crack

cracker *(pl* **crackers***) nmf Fam Inform* cracker

craneal *adj,* **craneano, -a** *adj* cranial, skull

cráneo *nm Anat* cranium, skull; *Fam* **romperle el c. a algn** to smash sb's head in

crápula *Literario* **1** *nf (vida licenciosa)* debauchery
2 *nm (persona)* reprobate

craso, -a *adj Literario* **(a)** *(person)* fat, gross **(b)** *Fig (error)* gross, crass

cráter *nm* crater

creación *nf* creation

creador, -a 1 *adj* creative
2 *nm,f* creator

crear 1 *vt (gen)* to create, make; *(inventar)* to invent; *(gobierno)* to set up; *(escuela, institución)* to found; **c. amistades** to make friends; **c. problemas** to create problems
2 crearse *vpr* to make; **te creas muchos problemas** you make life difficult for yourself

creatividad *nf* creativity

creativo, -a *adj* creative

crecer [46] **1** *vi* **(a)** *(persona, planta)* to grow; **¡cómo has crecido!** how you've grown!; **dejar c. la barba** to grow a beard **(b)** *(incrementar)* to increase; **crecen los días** the days are getting longer; **c. en importancia** to become more important **(c)** *Tricot (puntos)* to add, increase **(b)** *(río, marea)* to rise; *(luna)* to wax **(c)** *(aumentar)* to spread; **crece el malestar** discontent is spreading
2 crecerse *vpr* to become conceited; **c. ante los problemas** to thrive on problems

creces *nfpl* increase (in volume) *sing; Fig* **con c.** fully, in full; **devolver con c.** to return with interest; **lo pagarás con c.** you'll more than pay for this

crecida *nf* flood, spate

crecido, -a 1 *pp de* **crecer**
2 *adj* **(a)** *(persona)* grown, grown-up **(b)** *(número)* big, large **(c)** *(río)* in flood *o* spate **(d)** *Fig* vain, conceited

creciente 1 *adj (interés)* growing, increasing; *(precios)* rising; *(luna)* crescent
2 *nf (de río)* flood, spate

crecimiento *nm (desarrollo)* growth, increase; *(subida)* rise

credencial 1 *adj* credential; **cartas credenciales** credentials
2 *nf* **(a)** *(de acceso a un lugar)* pass; **credenciales (diplomáticas)** credentials **(b)** *Arg Chile Méx (carné)* card

credibilidad *nf* credibility

crediticio, -a *adj Fin* credit; **restricción crediticia** credit squeeze

crédito *nm* **(a)** *(confianza)* credit, belief, credence; **dar c. a** to believe (in), credit **(b)** *(fama)* reputation, standing; **persona digna de c.** reliable person **(c)** *Com Fin* credit; **a c.** on credit **(d)** *(préstamo)* loan; **c. bancario** bank loan; **c. blando** soft loan; **c. oficial** official credit; **c. personal** personal loan

credo *nm* **(a)** *Rel* Creed **(b)** *Mús* Credo **(c)** *Fig (creencias)* creed, credo

credulidad *nf* credulity, gullibility

crédulo, -a *adj* credulous, gullible

creencia *nf* belief; **creencias religiosas** religious beliefs

creer [37] **1** *vt* **(a)** *(admitir)* to believe; **hay que verlo para creerlo** it has to be seen to be believed **(b)** *(estimar, opinar)* to think; **creo que no** I don't think so; **creo que sí** I think so; **creo que te equivocas** I think you are mistaken
2 *vi (tener fe)* to believe; **c. en** to believe in; **no creo en las brujas** I don't believe in witches; **no cree, es ateo** he's not a believer, he's an atheist
3 creerse *vpr* **(a)** *(estar convencido)* to consider oneself to be; **¿qué te has creído?** what *o* who do you think you are?; **se creen muy inteligentes** they think they are very intelligent **(b)** *(aceptar)* to believe; **todo te lo crees** you'll swallow anything

creíble *adj* credible, believable

creído, -a 1 *pp de* **creer**
2 *adj* arrogant, vain; *Fam* **ser un c.** to be full of oneself

crema 1 *nf* **(a)** *Culin (de leche)* cream; *(natillas)* custard; **c. de champiñones** cream of mushroom soup **(b)** *(ungüento)* cream; *(betún)* shoe polish ❏ **c. de afeitar/de broncear** shaving/suntan cream; **c. hidratante** moisturizing cream **(c)** *Fig* **la c.** *(lo mejor)* the cream; **ella se codea con la c. de la ciudad** she rubs shoulders with the top people in the city
2 *adj* cream, cream coloured *o US* colored

cremación *nf* cremation

cremallera *nf* **(a)** *(de vestido) Br* zip (fastener), *US* zipper; *Fam* **echar la c.** to shut one's mouth **(b)** *Téc* rack ❏ **ferrocarril de c.** rack *o* cog railway

crematístico, -a *adj* financial

crematorio, -a *nm* **(horno) c.** crematorium

cremoso, -a *adj* creamy; **queso c.** full fat cheese

crepe *nf Culin* crêpe, pancake

crepé *nm* **(a)** *Tex* crepe **(b)** *(suela)* crêpe

crepitar *vi* to crackle

crepuscular *adj* twilight; **luz c.** twilight

crepúsculo *nm* twilight

crescendo [kre'ʃendo] *nm* crescendo; **in c.** growing

crespo, -a *adj* **(a)** *(pelo)* frizzy **(b)** *(irritado)* angry **(c)** *(estilo)* obscure

crespón *nm Tex* crepe

cresta *nf* **(a)** *Orn* crest; *(de gallo)* comb; *Fig* **dar a algn en la c.** to deflate sb **(b)** *Geog (de montaña)* crest, summit **(c)** *(de ola)* crest **(d)** *(cabello)* toupee .

Creta *n* Crete

creta *nf* chalk, chalky lime

cretino, -a 1 *adj* stupid, cretinous
2 *nm,f* cretin

cretona *nf Tex* cretonne

creyente *nmf* believer

crezco *indic pres véase* **crecer**

cría *nf* **(a)** *(de animales)* breeding, raising; **c. de cerdos** pig breeding **(b)** *(cachorro)* young; **la gata tuvo siete crías** the cat had seven kittens **(c)** *(camada)* brood, litter

criada *nf* maid, servant

criadero *nm* **(a)** *(de plantas)* nursery ❏ *Zool* **c. de ostras** oyster bed **(b)** *Min* seam

criadilla *nf* **(a)** *Culin* bull's testicle **(b)** *Bot* potato, tuber **(c)** *(trufa)* **c. de tierra** truffle

criado, -a 1 *pp de* **criar**
2 *adj (animal)* reared, raised; *(persona)* bred, brought up; **niño mal criado** spoilt child
3 *nm,f* servant

criador, -a 1 *adj* producing

2 *nm,f (de animales)* breeder; *(de vinos)* grower

crianza *nf (de animales)* breeding; *(lactancia)* nursing; **vinos de c.** vintage wines

criar [32] **1** *vt* (**a**) *(animales)* to breed, raise, rear; *(niños)* to bring up, rear, care for; **me crió mi abuela** my grandmother brought me up; *Prov* **Dios los cría y ellos se juntan** birds of a feather flock together (**b**) *(nutrir, amamantar)* to nurse; **crió a sus niños a pecho** she breast-fed her children (**c**) *(producir)* to have, grow; **esta tierra cría buenos melones** this is good soil for melons; **los perros crían pulgas** dogs have flees (**d**) *(vino)* to make, mature

2 *vi (engendrar)* to give birth; **las ovejas crían en primavera** sheeps lamb in spring

3 criarse *vpr* (**a**) *(crecer)* to grow; *(formarse)* to be brought up (**b**) *(producirse)* to grow; **aquí no se cría trigo** wheat isn't grown here

criatura *nf* (**a**) *(ser)* (living) creature (**b**) *(crío)* baby, child; *Fig* **a sus veinte años aún se comporta como una c.** even though he's twenty he still behaves like a child

criba *nf* (**a**) *(tamiz)* sieve; *Fig* **estar como una c.** to be riddled with holes (**b**) *Fig (sistema de selección)* screening; **pasar por la c.** to screen; *Fam Educ* **hacer una c.** to fail many students

cribado *nm SAm* = type of embroidery

cribar *vt* (**a**) *(colar)* to sieve, sift (**b**) *Fig (candidatos)* to screen

cric *(pl crics) nm Aut* jack

crimen *nm (asesinato)* murder; *(delito)* crime ⃞ **c. de guerra** war crime; **c. organizado** organized crime

criminal 1 *adj* (**a**) *(gen)* criminal (**b**) *Fam (malísimo)* awful, appalling, criminal

2 *nmf (malhechor)* criminal

criminalidad *nf* criminality, guilt ⃞ **índice de c.** crime rate

criminalista *nmf* (**a**) *Jur (abogado)* criminal lawyer (**b**) *(estudioso)* criminologist

criminalizar [14] *vt* to criminalize

criminología *nf* criminology

criminólogo, -a *nm,f* criminologist

crin *nf,* **crines** *nfpl* mane *sing*

crío, -a 1 *adj* young, babyish
2 *nm Fam* kid

criogenia *nf* cryogenics *(sing)*

criollo, -a *adj & nm,f* Creole

crioterapia *nf* cryotherapy

cripta *nf* crypt

críptico, -a *adj* cryptic

criptografía *nf* cryptography, coding

críquet *nm Dep* cricket

crisálida *nf Ent* chrysalis

crisantemo *nm Bot* chrysanthemum

crisis *nf inv* (**a**) *(ataque)* fit, attack ⃞ **c. de asma** asthma attack; **c. de llanto** fit of tears; **c. nerviosa** nervous breakdown (**b**) *(dificultad)* crisis ⃞ *Pol* **c. de gobierno** cabinet crisis; **c. económica** recession; **c. energética** energy crisis; **c. financiera** financial crisis (**c**) *(escasez)* shortage

crisma 1 *nm Rel* chrism, holy oil
2 *nf Fam* nut, *Br* bonce; **se rompió la c.** he split his head open

crisol *nm* crucible; *Fig* melting pot

crispación *nf* tenseness, contraction

crispado, -a *adj* tense

crispar *vt (causar contracción)* to tense; *Fig* **eso me crispa los nervios** that sets my nerves on edge, that gets on my nerves; *Fam* **c. a algn** to annoy sb intensely

cristal *nm* (**a**) *(vidrio fino)* crystal ⃞ **c. de cuarzo** quartz crystal; **c. de roca** rock crystal; **c. líquido** liquid crystal (**b**) *Esp (vidrio)* glass ⃞ **botella de c.** glass bottle; **copa de c.** wine glass; **vaso de c.** drinking glass (**c**) *(de gafas)* lense (**d**) *Esp (de ventana)* (window) pane (**e**) **cristales** (broken) glass; **ella se cortó el pie con unos c.** she cut her foot on some broken glass (**f**) *Am (vaso)* glass

cristalera *nf (puerta)* French window; *(ventana)* large window

cristalería *nf* (**a**) *(fábrica)* glassworks *sing* (**b**) *(tienda)* glassware shop (**c**) *(conjunto)* glassware; *(vasos)* glasses *pl*

cristalero, -a *nm,f* glazier

cristalino, -a 1 *adj* transparent, clear
2 *nm* crystalline lens

cristalización *nf* (**a**) *Quím* crystallization (**b**) *Fig* consolidation

cristalizar [14] *vi* (**a**) *Quím* to crystallize (**b**) *Fig* to crystallize, take shape

cristianar *vt Fam* to christen, baptize

cristiandad *nf* Christendom

cristianismo *nm* Christianity

cristianización *nf* Christianization, conversion to Christianity

cristianizar [14] *vt* to convert to Christianity

cristiano, -a 1 *adj* (**a**) *Rel* Christian (**b**) *Fam (vino)* watered

2 *nm Fam* (**a**) *(persona)* person; **cualquier c.** anybody; **ni un c.** not a soul (**b**) *(lenguaje)* plain language; **hablar en c.** *(hablar claro)* to speak plainly; *(hablar español)* to speak Spanish (**c**) *CAm (bonachón)* good-natured person

3 *nm,f Rel* Christian

Cristo *nm Rel* Christ; *Fam* **armar un c.** to kick up a big fuss; *Fam* **donde C. dio las tres voces** in the middle of nowhere; *Fam* **ni C.** nobody; *Fam* **poner a algn hecho un C.** to have a real go at sb

criterio *nm* (**a**) *(pauta)* criterion, yardstick; **c. estrecho** narrow viewpoint; **persona de amplios criterios** broad-minded person (**b**) *(discernimiento)* discernment, discrimination; **lo dejo a tu c.** I leave it to your discretion; **tener buen c.** to have sound judgement (**c**) *(opinión)* opinion, point of view; **cambiar de c.** to change one's mind

crítica *nf* (**a**) *(juicio)* criticism (**b**) *Prensa (reseña)* review, write-up; **escribir una c.** to write a review; **tener buena c.** to get good reviews ⃞ **c. teatral** theatre column (**c**) *(conjunto de críticos)* critics (**d**) *(censura)* criticism; **ser dado a las críticas** to be very critical

criticable *adj* censurable, open to criticism

criticar [59] **1** *vt* to criticize
2 *vi (murmurar)* to gossip

crítico, -a 1 *adj* critical
2 *nm,f* critic

criticón, -ona *Fam* **1** *adj* fault-finding, hypercritical
2 *nm,f* fault-finder

Croacia *n* Croatia

croar *vi* to croak

croata 1 *adj* Croatian
2 *nmf* Croat, Croatian

crocante *nm Culin* almond brittle

croché *nm* crochet

croissant [krwa'san] *(pl croissants) nm Culin* croissant

croissantería [krwasante'ria] *nf* = shop selling filled croissants

crol *nm Natación* crawl

cromado 1 *pp de* **cromar**
2 *adj* chrome
3 *nm* chroming

Cromañón *nm* Cro-Magnon

cromar *vt* to chrome

cromático, -a *adj* chromatic

cromatismo *nm* colouring, *US* coloring

cromo *nm* (**a**) *(metal)* chromium, chrome (**b**) *Esp (cromolitografía)* picture card, transfer; *Fam* **ir hecho un c.** to look a real sight

cromosoma *nm Biol* chromosome

cromosómico, -a *adj* chromosomal

crónica *nf* (**a**) *(gen)* account, chronicle (**b**) *Hist* chronicle (**c**) *Prensa* column, feature, article ❑ **c. de sucesos** news page *o* column (**d**) *Rad* programme, feature

crónico, -a *adj* chronic; *Fig* deeply rooted

cronista *nmf Prensa* feature writer, columnist; *(periodista)* journalist ❑ **c. de radio** radio commentator

cronología *nf* chronology

cronológico, -a *adj* chronological

cronometraje *nm* timing

cronometrar *vt* to time

cronómetro *nm Dep* stopwatch

cróquet (*pl* **cróquets**) *nm Dep* croquet

croqueta *nf Culin* croquette ❑ **c. de carne** meat rissole; **c. de pescado** fishcake

croquis *nm inv* sketch

cross *nm inv Dep (carrera)* cross-country race; *(deporte)* cross-country (running)

cruasán *nm* croissant

cruce *nm* (**a**) *(gen)* crossing; *Aut* crossroads (**b**) *(mezcla)* cross; *(de razas)* crossbreeding (**c**) *Tel* crossed line; **hay un c. de líneas** the lines are crossed

crucero *nm* (**a**) *Arquit* transept (**b**) *Náut* cruise; *(barco)* cruiser

crucial *adj* crucial, critical

crucificado, -a 1 *pp de* **crucificar**
2 *adj* crucified

crucificar [59] *vt* to crucify; *Fig* to torture

crucifijo *nm* crucifix

crucifixión *nf* crucifixion

crucigrama *nm* crossword (puzzle)

cruda *nf Guat Méx Fam* drunkenness

crudeza *nf* (**a**) *(dureza)* harshness (**b**) *(rudeza)* crudeness, coarseness (**c**) *(de alimento)* rawness, unripeness (**d**) **crudezas** undigested food *sing*

crudo, -a 1 *adj* (**a**) *(natural)* raw; **este pollo está c.** the chicken is underdone; *Tec* **seda cruda** raw silk; *Fam Fig* **lo veo muy c.** it doesn't look too good, I don't hold out much hope (**b**) *(clima)* harsh (**c**) *Fig (fuerte)* crude, coarse (**d**) *(color)* natural, unbleached (**e**) *Méx Guat (resaca)* hung over
2 *nm (petróleo)* oil

cruel *adj (persona)* cruel; *(inclemente)* harsh, severe

crueldad *nf* cruelty; *Fig* **la c. del clima** the severity of the climate

cruento, -a *adj* bloody, gory

crujido *nm (de puerta)* creak, creaking; *(de patatas fritas)* crunching; *(de hojas, papel)* rustle, rustling; *(de dientes)* grinding

crujiente *adj (alimentos)* crunchy; *(seda)* rustling

crujir *vi (puerta)* to creak; *(patatas fritas)* to crunch; *(hojas, papel)* to rustle; *(dientes)* to grind

crupier *nm* croupier

crustáceo *nm Zool* crustacean

cruz *nf* (**a**) *(gen)* cross; **con los brazos en c.** with outstretched arms; *Fig* **hacer c. y raya** to swear never again ❑ **c. gamada** swastika; **C. Roja** Red Cross (**b**) *Fig (carga)* burden, cross (**c**) *(de moneda)* tails *pl*; **¿cara o c.?** heads or tails?

cruzada *nf* (**a**) *Hist* crusade (**b**) *(campaña)* campaign

cruzado, -a 1 *pp de* **cruzar**
2 *adj* (**a**) *(gen)* crossed; **con los brazos cruzados** arms folded; *Com* **cheque c./no cruzado** crossed/open cheque; *Fig* **estar de brazos cruzados** to be doing nothing (**b**) *Cost (abrigo, chaqueta)* double-breasted (**c**) *(atravesado)* **había un camión c. en la carretera** a lorry was blocking the road (**d**) *(animal, planta)* crossbred
3 *nm Hist* crusader

cruzar [14] **1** *vt* (**a**) *(gen)* to cross; *Geom (línea)* to intersect; **c. a nado** to swim across; **c. apuestas** to make bets; **c. los brazos** to fold one's arms; **c. un río** to cross a river; **cruzarle la cara a algn** to slap sb's face (**b**) *(poner atravesado)* **c. algo con una raya** to draw a line across *o* through sth (**c**) *(palabras, miradas)* to exchange (**d**) *(animal, planta)* to cross, crossbreed
2 *vi (atravesar)* to cross; **los coches cruzaban en todas direcciones** cars were crossing in all directions
3 **cruzarse** *vpr* (**a**) *(juntarse)* to meet; **c. con algn** to pass sb; **c. de brazos** to fold one's arms; *Fig* to sit back and do nothing; *Fig* **c. en el camino de algn** to cross sb's path

CSIC [θe'sik] *nm (abrev de* **Consejo Superior de Investigaciones Científicas)** = Spanish council for scientific research

cta. *Com (abrev de* **cuenta)** a/c

cta. cte. *Com (abrev de* **cuenta corriente)** c/a

Cte. *Mil (abrev de* **comandante)** Maj

cte. *(abrev de* **corriente)** of the present month *o* year

CTI [sete'i] *nm Am (abrev de* **centro de tratamiento intensivo)** ICU

ctra. *(abrev de* **carretera)** rd

cts. *(abrev de* **céntimos)** cents

c/u *(abrev de* **cada uno)** per item

cuaderna *nf Náut* frame

cuadernillo *nm* booklet

cuaderno *nm (libreta)* notebook; *Educ* exercise book ❑ *Náut* **c. de bitácora** logbook

cuadra *nf* (**a**) *Agr (establo)* stable (**b**) *Am (manzana)* block *(of houses)*

cuadrado, -a 1 *pp de* **cuadrar**
2 *adj* (**a**) *Geom* square (**b**) *(complexión física)* broad, stocky; *Vulg* **tenerlos cuadrados** to have the balls to do it (**c**) *Fig (mente)* rigid; **tener una mente cuadrada** to have a one-track mind
3 *nm Geom Mat* square; **elevar (un número) al c.** to square (a number)

cuadragésimo, -a 1 *adj* fortieth
2 *nm,f (de una serie)* fortieth
3 *nm* fortieth; *véase tamb* **octavo, -a**

cuadrangular *adj* quadrangular

cuadrángulo *nm* quadrangle

cuadrante *nm* (**a**) *Náut Mat (instrumento)* quadrant (**b**) *(reloj de sol)* sundial (**c**) *(cojín)* square pillow

cuadrar 1 *vt Mat* to square
2 *vi* (**a**) *(coincidir)* to square, agree *(con* with); *(sumas, cifras)* to tally (**b**) *Fig (convenir)* to suit
3 **cuadrarse** *vpr* (**a**) *(soldado)* to stand at attention (**b**) *Fig (mantenerse firme)* to dig one's heels in

cuadratura *nf Mat* quadrature; **la c. del círculo** squaring the circle

cuadrícula *nf* squares *pl* , crisscross pattern ❑ **papel de c.** squared paper

cuadriculado, -a *adj* squared; *Fam Fig* **ser muy c.** *(rígido)* to have a very rigid mentality

cuadricular¹ *adj* squared

cuadricular² *vt* to square, divide into squares

cuadrilátero 1 *adj* quadrilateral, four-sided

2 *nm Box* ring

cuadrilla *nf (equipo)* gang, team; *Mil* squad; *Taur* bullfighter's team

cuadro *nm* **(a)** *Geom* square; **tela a cuadros** checked cloth **(b)** *Arquit Tec* frame **(c)** *Arte* painting, picture; **un c. falso** a fake **(d)** *Teat* scene **(e)** *Lit* description, picture; **c. de la vida rural** picture of country life **(f)** *(bancal)* bed, patch, plot **(g)** *Elec Tec* panel ❑ **c. de distribución** switchboard; **c. de mandos** control panel **(h)** *(gráfico)* chart, graph **(i)** *(personal)* staff; *Mil* cadre ❑ **c. de dirigentes** leaders *pl*; **c. facultativo** medical staff **(j)** *Am (matadero)* slaughterhouse

cuadrúpedo, -a *adj & nm* quadruped

cuádruple *adj* quadruple, fourfold

cuadruplicar [59] *vt* to quadruple

cuajada *nf Culin* curd

cuajado, -a 1 *pp de* **cuajar**

2 *adj* **(a)** *(leche)* curdled; *(sangre)* clotted; *(huevo)* set **(b)** *(lleno)* full, filled; **c. de** filled with; **c. de peligros** fraught with danger

cuajar 1 *vt* **(a)** *(leche)* to curdle; *(sangre)* to clot; *(huevo)* to set **(b)** *(llenar)* to fill **(de** with)

2 *vi* **(a)** *(nieve)* to lie **(b)** *Fig (tener éxito)* to be a success, be well received; *(idea)* to catch on; **la idea no cuajó** the idea didn't get off the ground; **su estilo no cuajó** his style wasn't liked

cuajo *nm* **(a)** *(cuajadura)* rennet **(b)** *Fam (cachaza)* calmness, phlegm; **tener mucho c.** to be phlegmatic **(c)** **arrancar algo de c.** to tear sth out by the roots

cual *pron (precedido de artículo)* **(a)** *(persona)* who, whom; **inventado por un español, el c. se llamaba ...** invented by a Spaniard, who was called ... **(b)** *(cosa)* which; **la casa, la c. se construyó el año pasado** the house, which was built last year; **me levanté tarde, con lo c. perdí el tren** I got up late, which meant I missed the train; **tuvieron una avería, lo c. les retrasó mucho** they broke down, which meant they were delayed a long time **(c)** *Literario (valor adverbial)* like; **el agua brillaba c. un espejo** the water sparkled like a mirror; **c. si** as if

cuál *pron* **(a)** *(interrogativo)* what?; *(en concreto, especificando)* which (one)?; **¿c. es tu nombre?** what's your name?; **¿c. quieres?** which one do you want? **(b)** *(en oraciones distributivas)* **c. más, c. menos, todos ayudaron** everybody did what they could to help; **a c. más** equally; **a c. más deprisa** each as fast as the other

cualidad *nf* **(a)** *(de persona)* quality, attribute, trait **(b)** *(de cosa)* quality

cualificación *nf* degree of skill *(of a worker)*; **debemos mejorar la c. de los obreros** we have to get a more highly skilled workforce

cualificado, -a 1 *pp de* **cualificar**

2 *adj (obrero)* skilled

cualificar [59] **1** *vt* to qualify

2 cualificarse *vpr* to become qualified, complete one's training

cualitativo, -a *adj* qualitative

cualquier *adj indef* any; **en c. momento** at any moment *o* time; **c. cosa vale** anything will do

cualquiera *(pl* **cualesquiera)** **1** *adj indef* **(a)** *(indefinido)* any; **una dificultad c.** any difficulty **(b)** *(corriente)* ordinary; **no compres uno c.** don't buy any old one; **no es un plato c.** it's no ordinary dish

2 *pron indef* anybody; **c. te lo puede decir** anybody can tell you; **¡c. lo sabe!** who knows?; **¡c. lo come!** nobody could eat that!; **c. que sea** whatever it is; **c. que sea la hora** no matter what time it is

3 *nmf Fig Pey* **ser un c.** to be a nobody; **es una c.** she's a hussy

cuan *adv* as ... as; **tendido c. largo era** lying flat out

cuán *adv interr* how; **¡c. agradable sería!** how lovely it would be!; **c. pronto ocurrió** as soon as it happened

cuando 1 *adv (de tiempo)* when; **c. más** *o* **mucho** at the most; **c. menos** at least; **de c. en c., de vez en c.** from time to time; **el martes es c. surgirán los problemas** the problems will start on Tuesday

2 *conj* **(a)** *(temporal)* when; **c. quieras** whenever you want; **c. vengas** when you come **(b)** *(condicional) (si)* since, if; **c. tú lo dices** if you say so **(c)** *(concesiva) (aunque)* **(aun)** c. even if; **aun c. lo supiera no te lo diría** even if I knew I wouldn't tell you **(d)** *(causal) (puesto que)* **c. tú lo dices, será verdad** if you say so, then it must be true

3 *prep* during, at the time of; **c. la guerra** during the war; **c. niño** as a child; *(yo)* when I was a child

cuándo 1 *adv interr* when?; **¿de c. acá?** since when?; **¿para c. lo quieres?** when do you want it for?

2 *nm* when; **debes especificar el cómo y el c.** you must make clear how and when

cuantía *nf (suma)* quantity, amount; *(dimensión)* extent; **de mayor c.** important; **de menor c.** insignificant

cuántica *nf* quantum mechanics *(sing)*

cuántico, -a *adj* quantum; **mecánica/teoría cuántica** quantum mechanics/theory

cuantificable *adj* quantifiable

cuantificar [59] *vt* to quantify, measure

cuantioso, -a *adj (cantidad)* substantial, considerable; *(número)* numerous

cuantitativo, -a *adj* quantitative

cuanto¹ *nm Fís* quantum; **teoría de los cuantos** quantum theory

cuanto, -a² **1** *adj rel* all that, whatever, whoever; **gasta c. dinero gana** he spends every penny he earns

2 *pron rel* as much as; **coma c. quiera** eat as much as you want; **regala todo c. tiene** he gives away everthing he's got

3 *pron indef pl* **unos cuantos** a few

4 *adv* **(a)** *(tiempo)* **c. antes** as soon as possible; **en c.** when; **en c. termine** as soon as *o* when I finish **(b)** *(cantidad)* **c. más ... más** the more ... the more; **c. más lo miro, más me gusta** the more I look at it the more I like it **(c)** *(por lo que corresponde a)* **c. a, en c. a** with respect to, regarding **(d)** *(causal)* **por c.** given that, since

cuánto, -a 1 *adj & pron interr* how many?, how much?; **¿cuántas veces?** how many times?; **¿c. es?** how much is it?; **¿cuántos alumnos sois?** how many are there in your class?; **¿cuántos sois?** how many of you are there?

2 *adv* how, how much; **¡cuánta gente hay!** what a lot of people there are!; **¡c. me gusta!** I really like it!; **¡c. has escrito!** what a lot you've written!

cuáquero, -a *adj & nm,f Rel* Quaker

cuarenta 1 *adj inv (cardinal)* forty; *(ordinal)* fortieth

2 *nm inv* forty; *Fam* **cantarle a algn las c.** to give sb a piece of one's mind; *véase tamb* **ochenta** *y* **ocho**

cuarentavo, -a 1 *adj* fortieth; **cuarentava parte** fortieth

2 *nm (parte)* fortieth; *véase tamb* **octavo, -a**

cuarentena *nf* **(a)** *(cuarenta unidades)* forty, about forty (**b**) *Med* quarantine; *Fig* **poner a algn en c.** to send sb to Coventry

cuarentón, -ona 1 *adj (persona)* forty-year-old
2 *nm,f* person in his/her forties

cuaresma *nf Rel* Lent

cuartear 1 *vt* (**a**) *(carne)* to quarter (**b**) *(rajar)* to crack, split
2 cuartearse *vpr* (**a**) *(rajarse)* to crack, split (**b**) *Méx (acobardarse)* to chicken out; *(desdecirse)* to go back on one's word

cuartel *nm Mil* barracks *pl*; **vida de c.** army life; *Fig* **no dar c.** to show no mercy ❑ **c. de invierno** winter quarters *pl*; **c. general** headquarters

cuartelada *nf*, **cuartelazo** *nm Mil* military uprising, revolt

cuartelero, -a *adj* barrack, barracks

cuartelillo *nm Mil* post, station

cuartería *nf Cuba Chile R Dom* block *(of houses)*

cuarterón *nm* (**a**) *(medida)* quarter pound (**b**) *(de puerta o ventana)* panel

cuarteto *nm Mús* quartet

cuartilla *nf* (**a**) *(hoja)* sheet of paper (**b**) **cuartillas** *Tip* copy

cuarto, -a 1 *adj* fourth; **cuarta fila** fourth row
2 *nm,f (de una serie)* fourth
3 *nm* (**a**) *(parte)* fourth; **abrigo tres cuartos** three-quarter length coat; *Fam* **de tres al c.** worthless; *véase tamb* **octavo, -a** (**b**) *(de hora)* quarter; **las tres y c.** quarter *Br* past *o US* after three; **he esperado tres cuartos de hora** I've been waiting for three quarters of an hour ❑ **c. creciente** first quarter; **c. menguante** last quarter (**c**) *(de carne)* joint ❑ **c. delantero** shoulder; **c. trasero** hindquarter (**d**) *Dep* **cuartos de final** quarter finals (**e**) *(habitación)* room ❑ **c. de baño** bathroom; **c. de estar** living room; *Fot* **c. oscuro** *(para revelar fotografía)* darkroom; *RP (en elecciones)* voting booth; **c. trasero** junk room (**f**) **cuartos** *Fam* dough, money; **cuatro cuartos** very little money; **estar sin un c.** to be broke *o* skint

cuartucho *nm Fam* hovel, cramped room

cuarzo *nm Min* quartz

cuate, -a *adj & nm,f* (**a**) *Méx CAm Ecuad (mellizo)* twin; *Fig* very similar, alike (**b**) *CAm Méx (compinche)* pal, *Br* mate, *US* buddy

cuatrero, -a 1 *adj* (**a**) *CAm (traidor)* treacherous (**b**) *Méx (que dice disparates)* preposterous
2 *nm,f (ladrón de caballos)* rustler, horse thief

cuatrillizo, -a *nm,f* quadruplet

cuatrimestral *adj* (**a**) *(en frecuencia)* four-monthly (**b**) *(en duración)* four-month, lasting four months; *Educ* **asignatura c.** = four-month course in a given subject

cuatrimestre *nm* (period of) four months

cuatrimotor *nm Av* four-engined plane

cuatro 1 *adj inv (cardinal)* fourth; *(ordinal)* fourth; **a las c.** at four o'clock
2 *nm inv* (**a**) *(número)* four (**b**) *Fam (unos cuantos)* a few; **cayeron c. gotas** it rained a little bit; **decir c. cosas** to say a few things; **más de c.** several; **a más de c. les gustaría estar en tu lugar** I know quite a few people who'd like to be in your position; *Méx Fam* **meter las c.** *(meter la pata)* to (really) put one's foot in it; *véase tamb* **ocho**

cuatrocientos, -as *adj & nm* four hundred

Cuba *n* Cuba

cuba *nf* cask, barrel; *Fam* **estar como una c.** to be (as) drunk as a lord

cubalibre *nm* rum *o* gin and coke

cubano, -a *adj & nm,f* Cuban

cubata *nm Fam véase* **cubalibre**

cubertería *nf* cutlery

cubeta *nf* (**a**) *(cubo)* bucket, pail; *(en laboratorio)* tank, dish (**b**) *(del barómetro)* bulb

cúbico, -a *adj* cubic

cubículo *nm* cubicle

cubierta *nf* (**a**) *(gen)* cover, covering (**b**) *Aut (capó) Br* bonnet, *US* hood (**c**) *(neumático)* tyre, *US* tire (**d**) *Arquit* roof ❑ **c. de lona** tarpaulin, canvas (**e**) *Av Náut* deck

cubierto, -a 1 *pp de* **cubrir**
2 *adj* (**a**) *(gen)* covered; *(cielo)* overcast; *Fam* **tener las espaldas cubiertas** to be well-heeled (**b**) *(plaza, vacante)* filled
3 *nm* (**a**) *(en la mesa)* place setting; **a diez euros el c.** ten euros per head; **precio del c.** cover charge (**b**) *(techumbre etc)* cover; **estar a c.** to be under cover; **ponerse a c.** to take cover (**c**) **cubiertos** cutlery *sing*

cubil *nm* lair

cubilete *nm* (**a**) *(de dados)* dicebox; *(juego)* cup (**b**) *Culin (flanero)* mould, *US* mold

cubismo *nm Arte* cubism

cubista *adj & nmf Arte* cubist

cubitera *nf* ice bucket

cubito *nm* little cube ❑ **c. de hielo** ice cube

cúbito *nm Anat* ulna

cubo *nm* (**a**) *(balde, recipiente)* bucket ❑ **c. de la basura** *Br* rubbish bin, *US* garbage can (**b**) *Geom Mat* cube; **elevar al c.** to cube (**b**) *Aut (de rueda)* hub

cubrecama *nm* bedspread

cubrir *(pp* **cubierto**) **1** *vt* (**a**) *(gen)* to cover; **el agua le cubría hasta la cintura** the water came up to his waist; **una fina capa de polvo cubría la mesa** the table was covered in a thin layer of dust (**b**) *Arquit (edificio)* to put a roof on (**c**) *(ocultar)* to hide; **la niebla cubría el valle** the valley was veiled in mist (**d**) *(sentimiento)* to hide (**e**) *(llenar)* to fill; **c. de besos** to smother with kisses; **c. una plaza** *o* **una vacante** to fill a vacancy (**f**) *(satisfacer)* to meet; **c. gastos** to cover expenses; **c. las necesidades** to cover *o* meet one's needs; **c. una deuda** to meet a debt (**g**) *(recorrer)* to cover; *(distancia)* to travel (**h**) *Prensa (suceso, noticia)* to cover (**i**) *Zool (montar)* to mate with
2 cubrirse *vpr (ponerse sombrero)* to put one's hat on; *(revestirse)* to cover oneself (**con** with) (**c**) *Fig (protegerse)* to cover oneself (**de** against) (**d**) *Meteor (cielo)* to become overcast (**e**) *(vacante)* to be filled

cuca *nf* (**a**) *Chile Orn* = type of heron (**b**) *Col Ven Vulg* pussy, *Br* fanny

cucaña *nf (juego)* greasy pole

cucaracha *nf Ent* cockroach

cuchara *nf* (**a**) spoon; **c. de palo** wooden spoon; *Fig* **meter algo a algn con c.** to drum sth into sb; *Fam* **meter c.** to butt in (**b**) *Am (de albañil)* trowel

cucharada *nf* spoonful; **c. rasa/colmada** level/heaped spoonful

cucharilla *nf* teaspoon ❑ **c. de café** coffee spoon

cucharón *nm* ladle

cuchichear *vi* to whisper

cuchicheo *nm* whispering

cuchilla *nf* (**a**) *(hoja)* blade ❑ **c. de afeitar** razor blade (**b**) *Andes Carib (cortaplumas)* penknife (**c**) *Am (cumbre)* ridge, crest

cuchillada *nf*, **cuchillazo** *nm* cut, stab, knife wound; **ayer hubo cuchilladas en el puerto** there was a stabbing down at the port last night

cuchillo *nm* (a) *(gen)* knife ❑ **c. de monte** hunting knife; **c. de pan** breadknife; **c. de trinchar** carving knife (b) *Arquit* support

cuchipanda *nf Fam* spree, meal; **salir de c.** to go out on the town

cuchitril *nm* (a) *(establo)* pigsty (b) *Fam (cuartucho)* hovel, hole

cucho, -a *adj* (a) *CAm (jorobado)* hunchbacked (b) *Méx (desnarigado)* small-nosed

cuchufleta *nf Fam* joke

cuchumbo *nm CAm* (a) *(embudo)* funnel (b) *(cubeta)* bucket

cuclillas: en cuclillas *loc adv* squatting, crouching; **ponerse en c.** to squat *o* crouch down

cuclillo *nm Orn* cuckoo

cuco, -a 1 *adj Fam* (a) *(mono)* cute (b) *Esp (astuto)* shrewd, crafty
2 *nm* (a) *Orn* cuckoo (b) *(pesca)* red gurnard

cucú *nm* (a) *(canto)* cuckoo (b) *(reloj)* cuckoo clock

cucurucho *nm* (a) *(envoltorio)* paper cone (b) *(helado)* cone, cornet (c) *(capirote)* pointed hood (d) *Am (prenda)* hooded garment

cuelgue *nm Fam* (a) *(por drogas)* high (b) *(enamoramiento)* **tener un c. con** *o* **por algn** to be crazy about sb, be hooked on sb

cuello *nm* (a) *Anat (garganta)* neck; **cortar el c. a algn** to slit sb's throat; *Fig* **con el agua hasta el c.** in a tight spot; *Fig* **estar metido hasta el c.** to be up to one's neck in it; *Fam* **me apuesto el c.** I'd put my shirt on it (b) *(de ropa)* collar; **jersey de c. redondo** crew-necked jumper; **c. de pajarita** bow tie; *Fam* **hablar para el c. de su camisa** to mutter to oneself (c) *(de botella)* neck

cuenca *nf* (a) *Geog* basin; **la c. del río** the river basin (b) *Anat (de los ojos)* socket (c) *Min* **c. minera** coalfield

cuenco *nm* (a) *(vasija)* earthenware bowl (b) *(concavidad)* hollow; **c. de la mano** hollow of the hand

cuenta *nf* (a) *(cálculo)* count, counting; **hacer cuentas** to do sums; **sacar cuentas** to work out; *Fam* **hacer la c. de la vieja** to count on one's fingers ❑ **c. atrás** countdown (b) *Com (factura)* bill; **la c. del teléfono** the telephone bill; **pasar la c.** to send the bill; **por c. de la casa** on the house (c) *Fin (en banco)* account ❑ **c. al descubierto** overdrawn account; **c. bancaria** bank account; **c. corriente** *Br* current account, *US* checking account; **c. de inversión** investment account (d) *(de collar, rosario)* bead (e) *Inform* account (f) *(locuciones)* **ajustar cuentas** to settle up; **caer en la c.** to realize; **dar c.** to report; **dar cuentas a** to inform *o* answer to; **beber más de la c.** to have one too many; **darse c.** to realize; **en resumidas cuentas** in short; **pedir cuentas** to ask for an explanation; **tener en c.** to take into account; **trabajar por c. propia** to be self-employed; **traer c.** to be worthwhile

cuentagotas *nm inv Med* dropper

cuentakilómetros *nm inv (distancia) Br* ≃ mileometer, *US* ≃ odometer; *(velocidad)* speedometer

cuentarrevoluciones *nm inv* rev counter

cuentista 1 *adj (exagerado)* overdramatic
2 (a) *nmf (narrador)* storyteller (b) *(cotilla)* gossip (c) *(exagerado)* overdramatic person

cuento *nm (gen)* story, tale; *Lit* short story; **contar un c.** to tell a story; *Fig* **hacer el c. de la lechera** to count one's chickens before they are hatched; *Fig* **eso no viene a c.** that's beside the point; *Fig* **traer algo a c.** to mention sth, bring sth up; *Fam* **¡déjate de cuentos!** get on with it!; *Fam* **es el c. de nunca acabar** it just drags on and on; *Fam* **ir a algn con el c.** to tell tales to sb; *Fam* **tiene más c. que**

Calleja he's always making such a fuss; *Fam* **vivir del c.** to live by one's wits ❑ **c. chino** tall story; **c. de hadas** *(narración)* fairy story; *(sensacional)* cock-and-bull story

cuerda *nf* (a) *(cordel)* string, rope; *Fig* **bailar en la c. floja** to be hanging from a thread; *Fig* **aflojar la c.** to ease up; *Fig* **apretar la c.** to tighten up; *Fig* **bajo c.** dishonestly ❑ **c. de la ropa** clothes-line; **c. de presos** chain gang; **c. floja** tightrope (b) *Mús* string; *(voz)* voice ❑ *Anat* **cuerdas vocales** vocal cords (c) *(del reloj)* spring; **dar c. a un reloj** to wind up a watch; *Fig* **parece que le hayan dado c.** he seems to have been encouraged to talk; *Fam Fig* **se me acabó la c.** I've nothing left to say; *(estar cansado)* I'm exhausted (d) *Geom* chord

cuerdo, -a 1 *adj (acto)* prudent, sensible; *(persona)* sane; **no está c.** he is not in his right mind
2 *nm,f* sane person

cuereada *nf Ven* beating

cuerna *nf* (a) *(cornamenta)* antlers *pl*, horns *pl* (b) *(de caza)* hunting horn

cuerno *nm* (a) *(gen)* horn; *(de ciervo)* antler; *Fig* **me huele a c. quemado** I think there is something fishy going on; *Fam* **mandar a algn al c.** to send sb packing; *Fam* **mandar algo al c.** to pack sth in; *Fam* **romperse los cuernos** to break one's back; *Fam Fig* **poner cuernos a algn** to be unfaithful to sb; *Vulg* **¡vete al c.!** get lost! (b) *Mil* wing (c) *Mús* horn

cuero *nm* (a) *(pellejo de animal)* skin, hide; *(material)* leather; **chaqueta de c.** leather jacket (b) *(persona)* skin; *Fam* **en cueros (vivos)** (stark) naked; *Fam* **quedarse en cueros** to strip off ❑ *Anat* **c. cabelludo** scalp (c) *(odre)* wineskin (d) *Ftb (balón)* ball (e) *Am (correa)* whip (f) *Ecuad Ven Pey (mujer) Br* bird, *US* broad

cuerpo *nm* (a) *Anat (ser)* body; *(constitución)* build; *(figura)* figure; *(tronco)* trunk; **a c. descubierto** defenceless; **de c. entero** full-length; **echar el c. atrás** to lean back; **lucha a c.** hand-to-hand combat; *Fig* **hombre de c. entero** man of integrity; *Fig* **entregarse en c. y alma** to give one's all; *Fig* **tomar c.** to take shape; *Fig* **vivir a c. de rey** to live like a king; *Euf* **hacer de c.** to relieve oneself ❑ *Jur* **c. del delito** evidence; *Mat* **c. geométrico** regular solid; **cuerpos celestes** heavenly bodies (b) *(cadáver)* corpse; **de c. presente** lying in state (c) *(parte)* section, part; *(parte principal)* main part, main body; **armario de tres cuerpos** wardrobe in three sections; **c. superior** upper section; **el c. del libro** the main body of the book (d) *(grosor)* body, thickness (e) *(grupo)* body, corps, force ❑ **c. de baile** corps de ballet; **c. de bomberos** fire brigade; **c. de policía** police force; **c. de sanidad** medical corps; **c. diplomático** diplomatic corps

cuervo *nm Orn* raven; *Prov* **cría cuervos (y te sacarán los ojos)** = you bring up your children/befriend someone only to see them turn on you

cuesta 1 *nf* slope; **c. abajo** downhill; **c. arriba** uphill; *Fig* **ir c. abajo** to be declining; *Fig* **se me hace c. arriba** I find it an uphill struggle ❑ **la c. de enero** the January squeeze
2 a cuestas *loc adv* on one's back *o* shoulders

cuestación *nf* charity collection; **hacer una c.** to raise money for charity

cuestión *nf* (a) *(asunto)* matter, question, problem; **c. candente** burning question; **es c. de vida o muerte** it's a matter of life or death; **en c. de unas horas** in just a few hours; **no es c. de enfadarse** it's nothing to get angry about; **una c. jurídica** a legal matter (b) *(pregunta)* question (c) *(discusión)* quarrel, argument

cuestionable *adj* questionable, debatable

cuestionar *vt* to question, debate

cuestionario *nm* questionnaire

cuete 1 *adj Méx Fam (borracho) Br* pissed, *US* loaded **2** *nm* (**a**) *Am (nave espacial)* (space) rocket (**b**) *Am* **cuetes** *(fuegos artificiales)* fireworks (**c**) *Méx RP Fam (borrachera)* **estar en c.** *Br* to be pissed, *US* be loaded (**d**) *RP Fam (pedo)* (loud) fart (**e**) *Chile Fam (puñetazo)* **le dio un c. en la boca** he socked him one in the mouth (**f**) *Perú Fam (pistola)* shooter, *US* piece
 3 al cuete *loc adv RP Fam (inútilmente)* for nothing

cueva *nf* cave; *Fig* **c. de ladrones** den of thieves

cuévano *nm* pannier

cuezo *indic pres véase* **cocer**

cuico *nm Méx Fam* cop

cuidado, -a 1 *pp de* **cuidar**
 2 *adj* looked after; **un jardín muy c.** a well cared for garden
 3 *nm* (**a**) *(esmero)* care; **con c.** carefully; **de c.** *(enfermo)* very ill; *(peligroso)* dangerous, suspicious; **estar al c. de** *(cosa)* to be in charge of; *(persona)* to look after; **ir** *o* **andarse con c.** to go carefully; **me trae sin c.** I don't care; **tener c.** to be careful (**b**) *Fam Med* **cuidados intensivos** intensive care (unit) *sing* (**c**) *(recelo)* worry; **siente c. por la herida** he's concerned about the injury
 4 *interj* look out!, watch out!; **¡c. con el perro!** beware of the dog!; **¡c. con lo que dices!** watch what you say!; **¡c. con los niños!** mind the children!

cuidador, -a *nm,f (de anciano)* carer; *(de niño)* childminder; **el c. de los monos** the person who looks after the monkeys

cuidadoso, -a *adj* (**a**) *(atento)* careful (**b**) *(celoso)* cautious

cuidar 1 *vt* to care for, look after; **c. de que** to make sure that; **c. de que todo salga bien** to make sure that everything goes alright; **c. los detalles** to pay attention to details; **c. una herida** to dress a wound
 2 cuidarse *vpr* (**a**) *(conservarse)* to look after oneself, take care of oneself; **cuídate** look after yourself (**b**) *(preocuparse)* **c. de** to worry about, mind; **no se cuida de la opinión de la gente** he doesn't care what people think; **c. de que** to make sure that, be careful to

cuita¹ *nf* worry, trouble

cuita² *nf CAm* excrement

cuja *nf Am (cama)* bed

culamen *nm Vulg* fat arse *o US* ass

culata *nf* (**a**) *(de arma)* butt (**b**) *Aut* cylinder head (**c**) *(de animales)* haunch, hindquarters *pl*

culatazo *nf (de arma)* recoil, kick

culebra *nf (serpiente)* snake

culebrear *vi (zigzaguear)* to zigzag; *(río)* to meander, wind

culebrilla *nf* (**a**) *(de cometa)* zigzag (**b**) *Med* ringworm

culebrina *nf* forked lightning

culebrón *nm Esp Fam* television serial, soap

culero *nm Arg* leather belt

culinario, -a *adj* culinary, cooking; **arte c.** cuisine

culminación *nf* culmination

culminante *adj (punto)* highest; *(momento)* culminating

culminar *vi* (**a**) *(perfeccionarse)* to reach a peak *o* its highest point (**b**) *Fig (acabar)* to end, culminate (**con, en** in)

culo *nm* (**a**) *Fam o Vulg Anat (nalgas) Br* bum, *US* butt; *Fam (ano) Br* arsehole, *US* asshole; **caer de c.** to fall flat on one's backside *o Br* bum; *Fig* **con el c. al aire** in a fix, in a tight spot; *Fig* **ir de c.** *(estar muy ocupado)* to be rushed off one's feet; *Fig* **ser c. de mal asiento** to be a fidget; *Vulg* **lamer el c. a algn** to lick sb's *Br* arse *o US* ass; *Ofens* **¡métetelo por el c.!** stick it up your *Br* arse *o US* ass!; *Fig* **mojarse el c.** to

come down off the fence; *Esp Ofens* **¡vete tomar por el c.!**, **¡que te den por c.!** fuck off! (**b**) *Fam (de recipiente)* bottom; **queda** *o* **hay un c.** there is a little bit left in the bottom

culón, -ona *adj Fam* big-bottomed

culpa *nf* (**a**) *(error)* fault; **fue c. mía** it was my fault; **por tu c.** because of you (**b**) *(responsabilidad)* blame; **cargar a algn con la c.** to lay the blame on sb; **echar la c. a algn** to blame sb; **sentimiento de c.** guilty feeling

culpabilidad *nf* guilt, culpability

culpabilizar [14] **1** *vt* to blame
 2 culpabilizarse *vpr* to accept the blame (**de** for)

culpable 1 *adj* guilty; *Jur* **declararse c.** to plead guilty
 2 *nmf* offender, culprit; **yo no soy el c.** I'm not to blame

culpar 1 *vt* to blame; **c. a algn de un delito** to accuse sb of an offence; **no se puede c. a nadie** nobody is to blame
 2 culparse *vpr* to blame oneself, take the blame

cultamente *adv* in a refined *o* elegant manner

cultivable *adj* cultivable, arable

cultivado, -a 1 *pp de* **cultivar**
 2 *adj* (**a**) *Agr* cultivated, tilled (**b**) *(con cultura)* cultured, refined

cultivador, -a *nm,f* grower

cultivar *vt* (**a**) *Agr* to cultivate, farm (**b**) *Fig (amistad)* to cultivate (**c**) *(ejercitar)* to work at, practise, *US* practice, improve; **c. la memoria** to improve one's memory (**d**) *Biol (producir)* to culture

cultivo *nm* (**a**) *(labranza)* farming, cultivation; **dedicarse al c. de** to grow; **poner en c.** to cultivate (**b**) *(cultivo)* crop; **c. de maíz** crop of corn (**c**) *Biol* culture; **c. de tejidos** tissue culture (**d**) *Fig (desarrollo)* development, growth

culto, -a 1 *adj (persona)* cultured, educated; *(estilo)* refined
 2 *nm* (**a**) *(devoción)* worship; **c. dominical** Sunday worship (**b**) *(religión)* cult

cultura *nf* (**a**) *(culture)*; **la c. prerromana** Pre-Roman culture; **una mujer de c.** an educated woman (**b**) *(sabiduría)* learning, knowledge ☐ **c. general** general knowledge

cultural *adj* cultural

culturismo *nm* body-building

culturista *nmf* body-builder

culturizar [14] *vt* to educate

cumbia *nf* = Colombian dance

cumbre *nf* (**a**) *(de montaña)* summit, top (**b**) *Fig (culminación)* pinnacle; **alcanzar la c.** to reach the top; *Pol* **(conferencia) c.** summit (conference)

cumiche *nm CAm* baby (of the family)

cumpleaños *nm inv* birthday; **¡feliz c.!** happy birthday!; **fiesta de c.** birthday party

cumplido, -a 1 *pp de* **cumplir**
 2 *adj* (**a**) *(orden)* carried out; *(promesa)* kept; *(deber, profecía)* fulfilled; **misión cumplida** mission accomplished; **plazo c.** expiry date; **trabajo c.** finished work (**b**) *(abundante)* large; **un almuerzo muy c.** a big lunch (**c**) *(perfecto)* accomplished; **un c. caballero** a perfect gentleman (**d**) *(cortés)* polite, well-bred
 3 *nm (cortesía)* compliment; **cambiar cumplidos con algn** to exchange pleasantries with sb; **por c.** out of courtesy

cumplidor, -a *adj* reliable, dependable

cumplimentar *vt* (**a**) *(felicitar)* to congratulate (**b**) *(cumplir)* to fulfil, *US* fulfill, carry out

cumplimiento *nm* (**a**) *(observación)* fulfilment, *US* fulfillment; **c. de la ley** observance of the law (**b**) *(cumplido)* courtesy, politeness

cumplir 1 *vt* (**a**) *(realizar)* to carry out, fulfil, *US* fulfill; **c.**

un deseo to fulfil a wish; **c. una orden** to carry out an order; *Jur* **c. una pena** to serve a sentence; **c. una promesa** to keep a promise (**b**) *(respetar)* **c. con algn** to keep one's promise to sb; **c. con el deber** to do one's duty; **c. con la ley** to abide by the law (**c**) *(años)* to be; **al c. los sesenta** when he o she turned sixty; **ayer cumplí veinte años** I was twenty (years old) yesterday; **¡que cumplas muchos años!** many happy returns!

2 *vi* (**a**) *(cumplimentar)* to be polite; **lo hice por c.** I was just being polite (**b**) *(plazo)* to expire, end (**c**) *(satisfacer)* to do one's duty

3 cumplirse *vpr* (**a**) *(realizarse)* to be fulfilled, come true; **se cumplió su deseo** his wish came true (**b**) *(años)* to be; **hoy se cumple la fecha de ...** today is the anniversary of ...

cúmulo *nm* (**a**) *(sinnúmero)* pile, load; **un c. de problemas** a load of problems (**b**) *Fig (conjunto)* accumulation; **este chico es un c. de cualidades** that boy's got it all (**c**) *Meteor* cumulus

cuna *nf* (**a**) *(camita)* cradle, cot ◻ **canción de c.** lullaby (**b**) *Fig (origen)* cradle, beginning; **c. de la civilización** cradle of civilization (**c**) *(estirpe)* stock; **de humilde c.** of humble birth (**d**) *(lugar de nacimiento)* birthplace

cunda *nm Cuba Méx* wag

cundir *vi* (**a**) *Esp (dar de sí)* to go far o a long way; **me cunde mucho el trabajo** o **el tiempo** I seem to get a lot done (**b**) *(extenderse)* to spread; **cundió el pánico** panic spread; **cundió la voz de que ...** rumour had it that ...

cuneta *nf (zanja)* ditch; *(de la carretera)* verge

cuña *nf* (**a**) *(taco)* wedge; **hacer c.** to be wedged in; *Fig* **meter c.** to stir up trouble (**b**) *CAm Aut* two-seater (car) (**c**) *Andes RP Fam (enchufe)* **tener c.** to have friends in high places

cuñado, -a *nm,f (hombre)* brother-in-law; *(mujer)* sister-in-law

cuño *nm* (**a**) *(troquel)* die, stamp (**b**) *(sello)* stamp, mark; **tener el c.** to bear the mark; *Fig* **de nuevo c.** newly-coined

cuota *nf* (**a**) *(porción)* quota, share ◻ **c. de pantalla** audience share (**b**) *(contribución)* membership fees *pl*, dues *pl*

cupé *nm Aut* coupé

cupiera *subj imperf véase* **caber**

cuplé *nm Mús* = popular lyric song

cupletista *nf* music-hall singer

cupo *nm* (**a**) *(cuota)* quota (**b**) *Mil* contingent; **excedente de c.** exempt from military service (**c**) *Méx Fam (cárcel)* prison

cupón *nm Com (vale)* coupon, voucher; *Com* trading stamp; *Fam* **c. de los ciegos** lottery for the blind

cúpula *nf Arquit* dome, cupola

cura 1 *nm Rel* priest ◻ **c. párroco** parish priest

2 *nf Med* cure, healing; **hacer las primeras curas** to give first aid; *Fig* **no tiene c.** there's no cure (for it)

curaca *nm Hist* = chief of an adminstrative region of the Inca empire

curación *nf (cura)* cure, treatment; *(de herida)* healing; **c. milagrosa** miracle cure; **pronta c.** speedy recovery

curado, -a 1 *pp de* **curar**

2 *adj* (**a**) *(sanado)* cured; *(herida)* healed (**b**) *(carne, pescado)* cured, salted; *(piel)* tanned

curandero, -a *nm,f* quack

curar *vt* (**a**) *(sanar)* to cure; *(herida)* to dress; *(enfermedad)* to treat; **c. con medicamentos** to treat with medication; *Fig* **c. un mal** to right a wrong (**b**) *(piel)* to tan; *(carne, pescado)* to cure; *(madera)* to season

2 *vi* (**a**) *(recuperarse)* to recover, get well (**b**) *(herida)* to heal (up)

3 curarse *vpr (sanar)* to recover, get well; *(herida)* to heal up

curare *nm* curare

curasao *nm* curaçao

curativo, -a *adj* curative; **poder c.** healing power

curato *nm Rel* (**a**) *(cargo)* curacy (**b**) *(parroquia)* parish

curazao [kura'sao] *nm* curaçao

curca *nf Am (joroba)* hump

curco, -a *adj Am (jorobado)* hunchbacked

curda *nf Fam Esp RP* drunkenness; **agarrar** o *Esp* **coger una c.** to get plastered

curdo, -a 1 *adj* Kurdish

2 *nm,f (persona)* Kurd

3 *nm (lengua)* Kurdish

curia *nf* (**a**) *Rel* curia (**b**) *Jur* Bar

curiosear 1 *vt & vi (fisgar)* to pry into; *(visitar)* to look round

2 *vi (en asuntos ajenos)* to pry

curiosidad *nf* (**a**) *(indiscreción)* curiosity, inquisitiveness; **despertar la c. de algn** to arouse sb's curiosity; **tener c. de** to be curious about (**b**) *(objeto raro)* curiosity (**c**) *(aseo)* care, cleanliness

curioso, -a 1 *adj* (**a**) *(indiscreto)* curious, inquisitive (**b**) *(extraño)* strange, odd; **lo c. es que ...** the strange thing is that ... (**c**) *(ordenado)* neat, tidy

2 *nm,f* (**a**) *(mirón)* onlooker (**b**) *Pey (chismoso)* nosey-parker, busybody

curita *nf Am Br* (sticking) plaster, *US* Band-aid®

currante *nmf Esp Argot* worker

currar *vi Esp Argot* to graft, grind, slave

curre *nm Esp Argot* work

currelar *vi Esp Argot véase* **currar**

currículo *nm véase* **currículum**

currículum (*pl* **curricula**) *nm* **c. vitae** curriculum vitae, *Br* CV, *US* résumé

curro *nm Esp Argot* work

currutaco, -a *adj Andes Guat Ven* plump

curry (*pl* **currys**) *nm Culin* curry

cursado, -a 1 *pp de* **cursar**

2 *adj* (**a**) *(cartas)* dispatched (**b**) *(versado)* experienced

cursar *vt* (**a**) *(enviar)* to send, dispatch; *(orden)* to give (**b**) *(tramitar)* to make, submit *(an application)* (**c**) *(estudiar)* to study

cursi 1 *adj (vestido, canción)* tacky, *Br* naff; *(modales, persona)* affected

2 *nmf* affected o showy person

cursilada *nf* **ser una c.** *(acto, comportamiento)* to be affected; *(comentario)* to be stupid o *Br* naff; *(decoración, objeto)* to be tacky

cursilería *nf* (**a**) *(cualidad)* tackiness, *Br* naffness (**b**) *(cosa cursi)* tacky object

cursillista *nmf* participant, student *(on a course)*

cursillo *nm* short course, training course ◻ **c. de conferencias** course of lectures; **c. de reciclaje** refresher course

cursivo, -a *adj* **letra cursiva** italics *pl*

curso *nm* (**a**) *(dirección)* course; **el c. de los acontecimientos** the course of events; *Fig* **año** o **mes en c.** current year o month; *Fig* **dar c. a** *(tramitar)* to deal with; *Fig (dar libertad)* to give free rein to; *Fig* **dejar que las cosas sigan su c.** to let things take their course; *Fig* **en el c. de ...** during the course of ...; *Fig* **estar en c.** to be under way (**b**) *(del río)* flow, current (**c**) *Educ (académico)* academic o school year; **estamos en el mismo c.** we are in the same year o class; **exámenes de fin de c.** final exams, finals; **mis compañeros de c.** my classmates **(d)** *Educ (asignatura)* course, subject; **c. de filosofía** philosophy course **(e)** *Fin* **moneda de c. legal** legal tender

cursor *nm Téc* slide; *Inform* cursor

curtido, -a 1 *pp de* **curtir**
2 *adj* **(a)** *(rostro)* tanned, sunburnt; *(cuero)* tanned **(b)** *Fig (avezado)* hardened
3 *nm (piel)* tanning

curtidor, -a *nm,f* tanner

curtiduría *nf* tannery

curtir 1 *vt* **(a)** *(piel)* to tan; **el sol y el viento curten la piel** sun and wind tan the skin **(b)** *Fig (avezar)* to harden, toughen
2 curtirse *vpr* **(a)** *(piel)* to get tanned **(b)** *Fig (avezarse)* to become hardened

curva *nf* **(a)** *(gen)* curve; **trazar una c.** to draw a curve; *Fam* **¡vaya curvas tiene esa mujer!** what a body that woman's got! **(b)** *(en carretera)* bend ❑ **c. cerrada** sharp bend **(c)** *(gráfico)* curve, graph

curvar *vt (gen)* to curve; *(espalda)* to arch

curvatura *nf* curvature

curvilíneo, -a *adj* **(a)** *Geom* curvilinear, curvilineal **(b)** *Fam (cuerpo de mujer)* curvaceous, shapely

curvo, -a *adj (objeto)* curved; *(doblado)* crooked, bent

cusca *nf Pey Méx* flirty tart

cuscurro *nm Culin* crust of bread

cuscús *nm Culin* couscous

cúspide *nf* **(a)** *Geog* summit, peak **(b)** *Geom* apex **(c)** *Fig (culminación)* peak

custodia *nf* **(a)** *(vigiliancia)* custody, care; **bajo c.** in custody; **encargar a algn la c. de algo** to give sb custody of sth **(b)** *Rel* monstrance

custodiar *vt (proteger)* to keep, take care of, look after; *(vigilar)* to guard, watch over

custodio *nm* custodian, guardian, keeper

cutáneo, -a *adj* cutaneous, skin; *Med* **enfermedad cutánea** skin disease; *Med* **erupción cutánea** rash

cúter *(pl* **cúteres** *o* **cúter)** *nm (cuchilla)* Stanley knife®

cutícula *nf* cuticle

cutis *nm* complexion, skin

cutre *adj Esp Fam* **(a)** *(de bajo precio, calidad)* cheap and nasty **(b)** *(sórdido)* shabby, dingy **(c)** *(tacaño)* tight, stingy

cutrería *nf,* **cutrez** *nf Esp Fam* shabbiness, dinginess; **este hotel es una c.** this hotel is a dump; **me regaló una c.** he gave me a cheap and nasty present

cuy *nm Andes RP Zool* guinea pig

cuyo, -a *pron rel & pos* whose, of which; **en c. caso** in which case; **la familia en cuya casa nos quedamos** the family in whose house we stayed; **la señora, c. hijo es tu amigo, vive aquí** the lady, whose son is your friend, lives here

CV *(abrev de* **caballos de vapor)** HP

D

D, d [de] *nf (la letra)* D, d

D. *(abrev de* **don)** Mr

Da *(abrev de* **doña)** Mrs, Miss

dable *adj* possible, feasible, practicable

dabuten *adj Esp Argot* great, terrific

Dacca *n* Dacca

dactilar *adj* digital; **huellas dactilares** fingerprints

dactilografía *nf* typing, typewriting

dactilógrafo, -a *nm,f* typist

dadá *nm,* **dadaísmo** *nm Arte* Dada, Dadaism

dadaísta *adj & nmf Arte* Dadaist

dádiva *nf (regalo)* gift, present; *(donativo)* donation; *(compensación)* sop

dadivoso, -a 1 *adj* generous

2 *nm,f* generous person

dado, -a¹ 1 *pp de* **dar**

2 *adj* **(a)** *(concreto, determinado)* given; **dada su edad** in view of his age; **en un caso d.** in a given case; **en un momento d.** at a given moment, at a certain point **(b)** *(aficionado a)* **ser d. a** to be keen on, be fond of; **sus padres son muy dados a viajar** his parents are very fond of travelling **(c)** *(en vista de)* **d. que** as, since, in view of, given that; **d. que tienes fiebre, mejor que te quedes en casa** since you've got a temperature, you'd better stay at home **(d)** *Fam* **ir d.** to be heading for trouble; **con el nuevo jefe vamos dados** we're in for it with this new boss

dado² ** *nm* **(a) *(para juegos)* die, dice *pl;* **echar los dados** to throw the dice; *Fig* **cargar los dados** to load the dice **(b)** *Téc* block **(c)** *Arquit* dado

dador, -a *nm,f* **(a)** *(gen)* donor **(b)** *(de carta)* bearer; *(de letra de cambio etc)* drawer

daga *nf* dagger

daguerrotipo *nm Fot* daguerreotype

Dakar *n* Dakar

Dakota *n* Dakota; **D. del Norte** North Dakota; **D. del Sur** South Dakota

dalai-lama *nm* Dalai Lama

dale *interj* **¡d.! ¡otra vez con lo mismo!** there you go again!; **¡y dale!** there he/she goes again!; **seguir dale que dale con algo, seguir dale que te pego con algo** to keep on and on doing sth

dalia *nf Bot* dahlia

dálmata 1 *adj* Dalmatian

2 *nm* Dalmatian (dog)

daltoniano, -a 1 *adj* colour-blind, *US* color-blind

2 *nm,f* person who is colour-blind *o US* color-blind

daltónico, -a 1 *adj* colour-blind, *US* color-blind

2 *nm,f* person with colour, *US* color blindness

daltonismo *nm* colour *o US* color blindness

dama *nf* **(a)** *(señora)* lady □ **d. de honor** *(de reina)* lady-in-waiting; *(de novia)* bridesmaid; **primera d.** *Teat* leading lady; *Pol* first lady **(b)** *Ajedrez Naipes* queen; *(damas)* king **(c)** **damas** *(juego)* Br draughts *sing*, *US* checkers *sing;* **tablero de d.** Br draughtboard, *US* checkerboard

damajuana *nf* demijohn

Damasco *n* Damascus

damasco *nm* **(a)** *Tex* damask **(b)** *Andes RP Bot (albaricoque)* apricot

damasquinado *nm Téc* damascene

damasquinar *vt* to damascene, damask

damisela *nf Hist & Irón* damsel, young lady

damnificado, -a 1 *pp de* **damnificar**

2 *adj (person)* injured; *(cosa)* damaged

3 *nm,f* victim, injured person; **los damnificados por el incendio** the victims of the fire

damnificar [59] *vt (person)* to injure, harm; *(cosa)* to damage

Damocles *nm* Damocles; *Fig* **la espada de D.** the sword of Damocles

dandi *nm,* **dandy** *nm* dandy

danés, -esa 1 *adj* Danish

2 *nm,f (persona)* Dane

3 *nm* **(a)** *(idioma)* Danish **(b)** *(perro)* **gran d.** Great Dane

dantesco, -a *adj Fig* Dantesque, horrific

Danubio *nm* **el D.** the Danube

danza *nf* **(a)** *(gen)* dancing; *(baile)* dance; **d. guerrera** war dance; **la d. de la muerte** the dance of death; *Fig* **está siempre en d.** she's always on the go □ **d. del vientre** belly dance **(b)** *Fig (negocio sucio)* shady business *o* deal; *(lío)* mess **(c)** *Fam (jaleo)* rumpus, row; **armar una d.** to make a scene

danzante 1 *adj* dancing

2 *nmf* **(a)** *(que baila)* dancer **(b)** *Fam (vivaracho)* enterprising person; *(entrometido)* busybody, meddler; *(casquivano)* scatterbrain, featherbrain

danzar [14] **1** *vt* to dance

2 *vi* **(a)** *(bailar)* to dance **(con** with) **(b)** *Fam (entrometerse)* to meddle, interfere **(en** with, in)

danzarín, -ina *nm,f (profesional)* dancer

dañado, -a 1 *pp de* **dañar**

2 *adj* **(a)** *(estropeado)* damaged, spoiled **(b)** *(malo)* wicked, evil

dañar 1 *vt (cosa)* to damage; *(persona)* to hurt, harm; *(estropear)* to spoil; **dañará su reputación** it will damage her reputation

2 dañarse *vpr* (**a**) *(cosa)* to get damaged; *(persona)* to get hurt, be harmed (**b**) *(comestibles)* to rot, go bad o off

dañino, -a *adj* harmful, damaging (**para** to); **animales dañinos** pests, vermin *sing*

daño *nm (a cosa)* damage; *(a persona)* hurt, harm, injury; *(perjuicio)* wrong; **hacer d. a** *(a cosa)* to damage; *(a persona)* to harm; **hacerse d.** to hurt oneself; **se hizo d. en la pierna** he hurt his leg; **los daños ocasionados por la inundación** the damage caused by the flooding; **no hace d.** *(indoloro)* it doesn't hurt, it isn't painful; *(inofensivo)* it's harmless, it does no harm ❑ *Jur* **daños y perjuicios** (legal) damages

dañoso, -a *adj* harmful

dar [20] **1** *vt* (**a**) *(gen)* to give; *(entregar) (paquete, carta etc)* to deliver, hand over; *(pan, sal etc)* to pass, hand; *(recado, recuerdos)* to pass on, give; *(noticia)* to tell, announce, report; *(consejos)* to give; *(naipes)* to deal; *(pintura, cera)* to apply, put on; *(olor)* to give off; *(gas, luz)* to turn on; **d. brillo a los zapatos** to polish one's shoes; **d. clase** to teach; *(universidad)* to lecture; **d. la enhorabuena** to congratulate (**por** on); **d. la mano a algn** to shake hands with sb; **d. las gracias por algo** to say thank you for sth; *Fml* to give thanks for sth; **d. los buenos días/las buenas noches a algn** to wish sb good morning/good evening, say hello to sb; **d. lugar a** to give rise to; **d. muestras de alegría/tristeza** to look happy/sad; **d. palmadas** to clap; **d. parte de** to report; **d. razón** to give an account (**de** of); **d. un grito** to let out a cry; **d. un paseo** to go for a walk o stroll; **d. un paso** to take a step; **d. una puñalada a algn** to stab sb; **d. voces** *(gritar)* to shout; *(correr la voz)* to let it be known; **me da asco/miedo/lástima** o **pena** it makes me feel sick/afraid/sad, it disgusts/frightens/saddens me; **me da lo mismo, lo mismo da, me da igual** it's all the same to me; **me da no sé qué** it gives me a strange feeling; **no d. una** not to get anything right; **nos da mucho gusto verlo/oírlo** we are very pleased to see/hear it; **¿qué más da?** what does it matter?, it makes no difference (**b**) *(reloj)* to strike; **el reloj de la catedral dio las 4** the cathedral clock struck 4; **ya han dado las 9** it's gone 9 (o'clock) (**c**) *(película)* to show, screen; *(obra de teatro)* to perform, put on; *(obra musical)* to play, perform; *(concierto)* to hold, put on; *(fiesta)* to throw, give; **¿qué dan en el Roxy?** what's on at the Roxy? (**d**) *(producir) (cosecha)* to produce, yield; *(fruto, flores)* to bear; *(beneficio, interés)* to give, yield (**e**) *(pegar)* to hit; **¡dale fuerte!** hit him hard!, let him have it! (**f**) **d. a conocer** *(persona)* to introduce, present; *(noticia)* to release; **d. a entender que ...** to give to understand that ..., imply that ... (**g**) *Fam (tener el hábito)* **darle a la botella** to be (too) fond of the bottle

2 *vi* (**a**) *(ataque, risa)* **darle a algn un ataque de tos/risa** to have a coughing fit/an attack of the giggles (**b**) **d. a** *(ventana, habitación)* to look out onto, overlook; *(puerta)* to open onto, lead to (**c**) **d. con** *(persona)* to meet, come across, bump into; *(cosa)* to find, discover; **d. con los huesos en la cárcel** to end o land up in jail; **d. consigo en el suelo** to collapse; **dio con la moto contra el muro** he crashed the motorbike into the wall (**d**) *(suministrar)* to give; **d. de beber/comer a algn** to give sb something to drink/eat; **d. de comer al bebé/gato/perro** to feed the baby/cat/dog; **d. de espaldas** to turn one's back on; **d. de palos a algn** to beat sb (up) (**e**) *(ropa)* **d. de sí** to stretch, give (**f**) *(pegar)* **d. a algn en la cabeza** to hit sb on the head; **el sol me daba en la cara** the sun was shining in my face (**g**) *(acertar)* **d. con** o **en una solución** to hit upon o find a solution; *Fig* **d. en el clavo** to hit the nail on the head (**h**) *(ser suficiente)* **d. para** to be enough o sufficient for; **el presupuesto no da para más** the budget will not stretch any further (**i**) *(empeñarse)* **darle a uno por hacer algo** to take it into one's head to do sth; **ahora le ha dado por ahí** that's his latest fad; **le dio por la pintura** he took up painting (**j**) *(considerar)* **d. por** to assume, consider; **lo dieron por**

muerto he was assumed dead, he was given up for dead; **d. por hecho** o **concluido un asunto** to consider a matter closed (**k**) **d. que hablar** to set people talking; **d. que hacer** to make work, give trouble; **el suceso dio que pensar** the incident gave people food for thought

3 darse *vpr* (**a**) *(entregarse)* to give in, surrender (**b**) *(suceder)* to happen, occur; **luego se dio un caso extraño** then something strange happened (**c**) *(crecer) (planta etc)* to grow; *(hallarse)* to be found, exist; **las setas se dan muy bien en este bosque** there are lots of mushrooms in this wood; **no se dan mucho los pinos en esta zona** few pine trees are to be found (growing) in this region (**d**) *(consagrarse)* **d. a** to devote oneself o give oneself over to; *Pey* to take to, abandon oneself to; **se dio a la bebida** he took to drink; **d. a conocer** to make oneself known (**e**) *(golpearse)* **d. con** o **contra** to bump o crash into (**f**) *(considerarse)* **d. por** to consider oneself; **d. por aludido** to take the hint; *(sentirse ofendido)* to take sth personally; **d. por satisfecho** to feel satisfied; **d. por vencido** to give in, surrender (**g**) *(resultar)* **se le da bien/mal el francés** she's good/bad at French; **se me dan fatal las matemáticas** I'm hopeless at maths (**h**) *(importar)* **tanto te da suspender** he couldn't care less about failing (the exam); *Fam* **¿qué se me da?** why should I care? (**i**) *(presumir)* **dárselas de** to pose as, fancy oneself as; **no te las des de inocente** stop acting innocent; **se las da de experto en el tema** he thinks he's an expert on the subject

dardo *nm (flecha)* dart, arrow; *Fig* caustic remark

dársena *nf Náut* dock

darvinismo *nm* Darwinism

darvinista *adj & nmf* Darwinist

data *nf* (**a**) *(fecha)* date (**b**) *Com* item

datación *nf (de restos arqueológicos)* dating

datar 1 *vt* to date, put a date on

2 *vi* **d. de** to date back to o from; **esa costumbre data del siglo doce** that custom dates back to the twelfth century

dátil *nm* (**a**) *Bot (fruto)* date ❑ **d. de mar** date shell (**b**) **dátiles** *Fam (dedos)* fingers

datilera *nf Bot (árbol)* date palm

dativo, -a *adj & nm Ling* dative; **en d.** in the dative

dato *nm* (**a**) fact, datum, piece of information; **por falta de datos** because of lack of information ❑ **datos estadísticos** statistical data *usu sing*; **datos personales** personal details (**b**) **datos** *Inform* data

dcha. *(abrev de* **derecha***)* right

d. de J.C. *(abrev de* **después de Jesucristo***)* AD

de¹ *nf* = name of the letter D in Spanish

de² *prep* (**a**) *(pertenencia)* of, 's, s'; **el coche/hermano de Elvira** Elvira's car/brother; **el padre de la niña** the girl's father; **el padre de las niñas** the girls' father; **el título de la novela** the title of the novel (**b**) *(procedencia)* from; **de Lugo a Monforte** from Lugo to Monforte; **esta carta viene de tu oficina** this letter is from your office; **soy de Almería** I am from Almería (**c**) *(descripción)* **el niño de ojos azules** the boy with blue eyes; **la señora del vestido rojo** the lady in the red dress; **un reloj de oro** a gold watch; **un vaso de plástico** a plastic cup (**d**) *(contenido)* of; **un saco de patatas** a sack of potatoes (**e**) *(uso)* **gafas de sol** sunglasses; **goma de borrar** rubber, *US* eraser (**f**) *(oficio)* by, as; **es arquitecto de profesión** he's an architect by profession; **hace de secretaria** she's working as a secretary (**g**) *(precio)* at; **la de cincuenta pesos** the one at fifty pesos, the fifty peso one; **patatas de sesenta centavos el kilo** potatoes at sixty cents a kilo (**h**) *(medida)* **una avenida de quince kilómetros** an avenue fifteen kilometres long; **una botella de litro** a litre bottle (**i**) *(con superlativo)* in; **el más**

largo de España the longest in Spain; **el mejor del mundo** the best in the world (**j**) *(tiempo)* **a las tres de la tarde** at three in the afternoon; **de día** by day; **de lunes a jueves** from Monday to Thursday; **de noche** at night (**k**) *(causa)* with, because of; **llorar de alegría** to cry with joy; **morir de hambre** to die of hunger (**l**) *(condicional)* **de haber llegado antes** if he had arrived before; **de no ser así** if that wasn't o weren't so, if that wasn't o weren't the case; **de ser cierto** if it was o were true (**m**) *(en expresiones de queja, lástima etc)* **¡ay de mí!** poor me!; **¡el desagraciado de mi hijo!** oh my poor son!

dé *subj pres véase* **dar**

deambular *vi* to saunter, stroll, wander

deambulatorio *nm Arquit* ambulatory

deán *nm* dean

debacle *nf* disaster, downfall

debajo *adv* underneath, below; **el mío es el de d.** mine is the one below; **está d. de la mesa** it's under the table; **por d. de lo normal** below normal; **salió por d. del coche** he came out from under the car

debate *nm* debate, discussion ❑ **d. parlamentario** parliamentary debate

debatir 1 *vt* to debate
2 debatirse *vpr* to struggle; **d. entre la vida y la muerte** to fight for one's life

debe *nm Com* debit, debit side

deber¹ *nm* (**a**) *(obligación)* duty, obligation; **cumplir con su d.** to do one's duty (**b**) **deberes** *Educ* homework *sing*; **hacer los d.** to do one's homework

deber² **1** *vt* (**a**) *(adeudar)* to owe; **me debes cien pesos** you owe me a hundred pesos (**b**) /(**d.** + *infinitivo) (en presente y futuro)* to have to, must; **debe comer** he must eat; **debe irse ahora** she has to leave now; **deberás estar allí a las ocho** you have to be there at eight (o'clock); **no debes salir con este tiempo** you mustn't go out in this weather (**c**) /(**d.** + *infinitivo) (en condicional)* should, ought to; **debería haber ido ayer** I should have gone yesterday; **deberías visitar a tus padres** you ought to visit your parents; **no deberías haber ido** you shouldn't have gone (**d**) /(**d.** + *infinitivo) (en pretérito)* should have, ought to have; **debiste decírmelo** you ought to have told me; **debía hacerlo pero no tuve tiempo** I should have done it, but I didn't have time; **debía hacerlo porque así me lo ordenaron** I had to do it because I was ordered to; **no debiste hacerlo** you shouldn't have done it
2 *v aux (probabilidad)* **d. de** must; **deben de estar fuera** they must be out; **ha debido de caerse** he must have fallen over; **no deben de estar en casa** they can't be at home; **no debió de encontrarlo** he can't have found it
3 deberse *vpr* (**a**) *(ser consecuencia de)* to be due to; **¿a qué se debe esta actitud?** what is the reason for this attitude?; **esto se debe a la falta de agua** this is because of the water shortage (**b**) *(dedicarse)* **se debe a la patria** he has an obligation to his country; **ella se debe a su trabajo** she must put her work first

debidamente *adv* duly, properly

debido, -a 1 *pp de* **deber²**
2 *adj* (**a**) *(justo)* due; **a su d. tiempo** in due course; **con el d. respeto** with due respect (**b**) *(conveniente)* right; **a la temperatura debida** at the right temperature (**c**) *(adecuado)* proper; **más de lo d.** too much; **tomaron las debidas precauciones** they took the proper precautions (**d**) *(requerido)* **como es d.** properly; **como es d.** eat properly; **espero que le reciban como es d.** I hope they will welcome him as they ought to (**e**) *(a causa de)* **d. a** because of, owing to, due to; **d. a que** because of the fact that; **d. al mal tiempo** because of the bad weather

débil 1 *adj* (**a**) *(flojo)* weak, feeble; **tiene el pulso d.** his

pulse is weak (**b**) *(poco perceptible)* faint; **un ruido d.** a faint noise; **una luz d.** a dim light (**c**) *(vocal, sílaba)* weak
2 *nmf* weak person; **d. mental** mentally retarded person; **los económicamente débiles** the poor

debilidad *nf* weakness, feebleness; *Fig* **tener d. por** *(persona)* to have a soft spot for; *(cosa)* to have a weakness for; *Fig* **tiene d. por el teatro** he is really keen on the theatre

debilitación *nf* weakening

debilitador, -a *adj* weakening, debilitating

debilitamiento *nm véase* **debilitación**

debilitar 1 *vt* to weaken, debilitate
2 debilitarse *vpr* to weaken, grow weak

debilucho, -a *Pey* **1** *adj* weak, frail, delicate
2 *nm,f* weakling

debitar *vt* to debit

débito *nm* (**a**) *(deuda)* debt (**b**) *(debe)* debit

debocar [59] *vi Arg Bol* to vomit

debut (*pl* **debuts**) *nm* début, debut

debutante 1 *nmf (actor, actriz)* person who gives his/her first public performance
2 *nf (en sociedad)* debutante

debutar *vi* to make one's début o debut

década *nf* decade

decadencia *nf* decadence, decline, decay

decadente *adj & nmf* decadent

decaedro *nm Mat* decahedron

decaer [13] *vi* to decay, decline, deteriorate; **está decayendo el comercio** business is falling off; **su ánimo no decae a pesar de la enfermedad** she doesn't lose heart in spite of her illness; **su entusiasmo no decae** his enthusiasm never flags; **su salud ha decaído** his health has deteriorated; **tarde o temprano todos los imperios decaen** all empires decay sooner or later

decágono *nm* decagon

decaído, -a 1 *pp de* **decaer**
2 *adj* (**a**) *(débil)* weak (**b**) *(desmoralizado)* depressed, downhearted

decaimiento *nm* (**a**) *(decadencia)* decline, decay (**b**) *(debilidad)* weakness, weakening (**c**) *(desaliento)* gloominess, low spirits *pl*

decalitro *nm* decalitre, *US* decaliter

decálogo *nm* decalogue

decámetro *nm* decametre, *US* decameter

decanato *nm* (**a**) *(cargo)* deanship (**b**) *(despacho del decano)* deanery

decano, -a *nm,f* (**a**) *Univ* dean (**b**) *(miembro más antiguo)* senior member; *(hombre)* doyen; *(mujer)* doyenne

decantación *nf* decanting

decantar¹ 1 *vt Literario (alabar)* to praise, extol
2 decantarse *vpr (inclinarse por)* to lean towards; *Fig* to show a preference for

decantar² *vt (verter)* to decant

decapar *vt* to strip the paint from

decapitación *nf* beheading, decapitation

decapitar *vt* to behead, decapitate

decasílabo, -a 1 *adj* decasyllabic
2 *nm* decasyllable

decatlón *nm* decathlon

deceleración *nf* deceleration

decelerar *vi* to decelerate, slow down

decena *nf* (about) ten; **una d. de veces** (about) ten times; **por decenas** in tens

decencia *nf* (**a**) *(decoro)* decency; **con d.** decently (**b**) *(honradez)* honesty

decenio *nm* decade

decente *adj* (**a**) *(honrado)* honest, respectable; **un hombre d.** a respectable man (**b**) *(decoroso)* decent, modest (**c**) *(limpio)* clean, tidy

decepción *nf* disappointment, disenchantment

decepcionante *adj* disappointing

decepcionar *vt* to disappoint

deceso *nm Fml* decease, passing

dechado *nm* model, example; **ser un d. de virtudes** to be a paragon of virtue

decibellio *nm*, *Am* **decibel** *nm Fís* decibel

decididamente *adv* (**a**) *(resueltamente)* resolutely (**b**) *(definitivamente)* definitely

decidido, -a 1 *pp de* decidir
   2 *adj* determined, resolute

decidir 1 *vt* (**a**) *(determinar)* to decide; *(asunto)* to settle; **decidieron suspender la reunión** they decided to cancel the meeting (**b**) *(resolver)* to resolve (**c**) *(convencer, persuadir)* to decide, persuade; **su madre la decidió a dejar de fumar** his mother persuaded him to stop smoking
   2 *vi* to decide, choose; **d. entre dos cosas** to choose between two things
   3 decidirse *vpr* to make up one's mind; **d. a hacer algo** to make up one's mind to do sth; **d. por algo** to decide on sth

decigramo *nm* decigram

decilitro *nm* decilitre, *US* deciliter

décima *nf* (**a**) *Mat* tenth, tenth part (**b**) *(en un termómetro)* tenth of a degree; **tener décimas** to have a slight temperature (**c**) *Lit* ten-line stanza

decimal 1 *adj* decimal; **el sistema métrico d.** the metric system
   2 *nm (número)* decimal

decímetro *nm* decimetre, *US* decimeter

décimo, -a 1 *adj* tenth; **décima parte** tenth
   2 *nm,f (de una serie)* tenth
   3 *nm* (**a**) *(parte)* tenth; *véase tamb* **octavo, -a** (**b**) *(billete de lotería)* tenth part of a lottery ticket (**c**) *Am (moneda)* ten cent coin

decimoctavo, -a 1 *adj* eighteenth; **decimoctava parte** eighteenth
   2 *nm,f (de una serie)* eighteenth
   3 *nm (parte)* eighteenth; *véase tamb* **octavo, -a**

decimocuarto, -a 1 *adj* fourteenth; **decimocuarta parte** fourteenth
   2 *nm,f (de una serie)* fourteenth
   3 *nm (parte)* fourteenth; *véase tamb* **octavo, -a**

decimonónico, -a *adj* nineteenth-century

decimonoveno, -a 1 *adj* nineteenth; **decimonovena parte** nineteenth
   2 *nm,f (de una serie)* nineteenth
   3 *nm (parte)* nineteenth; *véase tamb* **octavo, -a**

decimoquinto, -a 1 *adj* fifteenth; **decimoquinta parte** fifteenth
   2 *nm,f (de una serie)* fifteenth
   3 *nm (parte)* fifteenth; *véase tamb* **octavo, -a**

decimoséptimo, -a 1 *adj* seventeenth; **decimoséptima parte** seventeenth
   2 *nm,f (de una serie)* seventeenth
   3 *nm (parte)* seventeenth; *véase tamb* **octavo, -a**

decimosexto, -a 1 *adj* sixteenth; **decimosexta parte** sixteenth
   2 *nm,f (de una serie)* sixteenth
   3 *nm (parte)* sixteenth; *véase tamb* **octavo, -a**

decimotercero, -a 1 *adj* thirteenth; **decimotercera parte** thirteenth
   2 *nm,f (de una serie)* thirteenth
   3 *nm (parte)* thirteenth; *véase tamb* **octavo, -a**

decir[1] *nm* saying; *Fam* **es un d.** it's just a saying

decir[2] [21] *(pp* dicho*)* **1** *vt* (**a**) *(gen)* to say; **¿cómo se dice 'papaya' en inglés?** how do you say 'papaya' in English?; **dice que no quiere venir** he says he doesn't want to come; **se dice que ...** they say that ...; **d. el padrenuestro** to say the Lord's Prayer (**b**) *(contar)* to tell; **d. una mentira/la verdad** to tell a lie/the truth (**c**) *(llamar)* to call; **le dicen la casa del diablo** it's known as the devil's house; **se llama Enrique pero le dicen Quique** his name's Enrique, but he's called Quique (for short) (**d**) *(opinar)* to think; **¿qué me dices del nuevo jefe?** what do you think of the new boss? (**e**) *(denotar)* to tell, show; **su actitud dice mal de su educación** his behaviour doesn't say much for his upbringing; **su cara dice que está mintiendo** you can tell from his face that he's lying (**f**) *(sugerir)* to mean; **los juegos electrónicos no me dicen nada** I'm not the least bit interested in electronic games; **¿qué te dice el cuadro?** what does the picture mean to you?; **su última película no me dice nada** I'm not too impressed by her latest film (**g**) *querer* **d.** to mean; **no quise d. eso** I didn't mean to say that; **¿qué quieres d.?** what do you mean? (**h**) *(locuciones)* **¿cómo diría yo?** how shall I put it?; **como quien dice, como si dijéramos** as it were, so to speak; **d. por d.** to speak for the sake of speaking; **dicho de otro modo** in other words; **dicho y hecho** no sooner said than done; **digamos** let's say; **digo yo** in my opinion; **dímelo a mí** you're telling me!; **el qué dirán** what people say; **es d.** that is (to say); **Juan es lo que se dice un imbécil** Juan is what you would call an idiot; **ni que d. tiene** needless to say; **¡no me digas!** really!; **o mejor dicho** or rather; **por así decirlo** so to speak; *Esp* **¡y que lo digas!** you bet!
   2 decirse *vpr* to tell oneself; **sé lo que me digo** I know what I am saying

decisión *nf* (**a**) *(resolución)* decision; **tomar una d.** to take *o* make a decision (**b**) *(firmeza de carácter)* determination, resolution; **con d.** decisively

decisivo, -a *adj* decisive; **de forma decisiva** definitely

decisorio, -a *adj* decision-making

declamación *nf* (**a**) *(acción)* recitation (**b**) *(arte)* declamation

declamar *vt & vi* to declaim, recite

declamatorio, -a *adj* declamatory

declaración *nf* (**a**) *(gen)* declaration; *(afirmación)* statement; **d. de amor** declaration of love; **d. de quiebra** declaration of bankruptcy; **d. de renta** tax declaration *o* return; **hacer una d.** to make a statement; **negarse a hacer declaraciones** to refuse to comment (**b**) *Jur* **prestar d.** to give evidence (**c**) *Bridge* bid

declaradamente *adv* openly

declarado, -a 1 *pp de* declarar
   2 *adj* open, professed; **enemigo d.** sworn enemy

declarante 1 *adj* declaring, who declares
   2 *nmf Jur* witness

declarar 1 *vt* (**a**) *(gen)* to declare; *(afirmar)* to state; **el presidente declaró que ...** the president stated that ...; **fue declarado vencedor** he was declared (the) winner (**b**) *Jur* **d. culpable/inocente a algn** to find sb guilty/not guilty (**c**) *Bridge* to bid
   2 *vi* (**a**) *(manifestar)* to declare (**b**) *Jur* to testify
   3 declararse *vpr* (**a**) *(manifestarse)* to declare oneself; *(a un chico, una chica)* to declare one's love (**a** for); **d. a favor/en contra de** to declare oneself in favour of/against; **d. en huelga** to go on strike; **d. en quiebra** to go into

bankruptcy, become bankrupt (**b**) *(epidemia, guerra, incendio)* to start, break out (**c**) *Jur* **d.** **culpable** to plead guilty

declaratorio, -a *adj* declaratory

declinación *nf* (**a**) *(caída)* decline, decay (**b**) *Ling* declension (**c**) *Astron* declination

declinar 1 *vi* (**a**) *(decaer)* to decline, decay (**b**) *(disminuir)* to diminish, lessen; *(fiebre)* to abate, diminish (**c**) *(terminar)* **al d. el día** when the day draws to a close
2 *vt* (**a**) *(rechazar)* to decline (**b**) *Ling* to decline

declive *nm* (**a**) *(del terreno)* incline, slope (**b**) *(decadencia)* decline

decolaje *nm Am* take-off

decolar *vi Am* to take off

decoloración *nf (de pelo)* bleaching; *(pérdida de color)* fading

decolorante *nm* bleaching agent

decolorar 1 *vt* to bleach; **d. el pelo** to bleach one's hair
2 decolorarse *vpr* to fade; **d. el pelo** to bleach one's hair

decomisar *vt* to confiscate, seize

decomiso *nm* (**a**) *(artículos, bienes)* confiscated article o goods *pl* (**b**) *(acción)* confiscation, seizure

decoración *nf* (**a**) *(acción)* decoration; **d. de escaparates** window dressing (**b**) *Teat* scenery, set

decorado *nm Teat* scenery, set

decorador, -a 1 *adj* decorating
2 *nm,f* (**a**) *(persona)* decorator; **d. de escaparates** window dresser; **pintor d.** painter and decorator, interior designer (**b**) *Teat* set designer

decorar *vt* to decorate, adorn; **d. una casa** to decorate a house

decorativo, -a *adj* decorative, ornamental; **ser o estar de figura decorativa** to be there for decorative purposes only

decoro *nm* (**a**) *(respeto)* dignity, decorum; **el d. de la profesión** the dignity of the profession (**b**) *(dignidad)* decency; **vivir con d.** to live decently (**c**) *(pudor)* modesty, decency; **hablar con d.** to speak decorously; **sin d.** indecently

decoroso, -a *adj* (**a**) *(correcto)* proper, seemly, decorous (**b**) *(digno)* decent, respectable; **un trabajo d.** a respectable job; **un sueldo d.** a decent salary (**c**) *(decente)* decent, modest; **un vestido d.** a decent dress

decrecer [46] *vi* to decrease, diminish; **las aguas decrecieron** the waters subsided; **los días decrecen** the days are getting shorter; **decrece el interés por el fútbol** interest in football is declining

decreciente *adj* decreasing, diminishing, declining

decrecimiento *nm* decrease

decrépito, -a *adj* decrepit

decrepitud *nf* decrepitude

decretar *vt* to decree, ordain

decreto *nm* decree, order ❑ **d. ley** government decree

decúbito *nm* horizontal position; **estar en d. prono/ supino** to be lying face down/up, be lying prone/supine

decurso *nm Fml* **en el d. de los años** over the years

dedal *nm* thimble

dédalo *nm* labyrinth

dedicación *nf* (**a**) *(entrega)* dedication, devotion; **su d. a la familia/al partido** his devotion to his family/to the party (**b**) *Rel (consagración)* dedication, consecration

dedicar [59] **1** *vt (gen)* to dedicate; *(tiempo, esfuerzos)* to devote (**a** to); **dedicó al público unas palabras de agradecimiento** he addressed a few words of thanks to the audience

2 dedicarse *vpr (consagrarse)* to devote o dedicate oneself to; **¿a qué se dedica?** what do you do for a living?; **los fines de semana ella se dedica a la pesca** at weekends she spends her time fishing

dedicatoria *nf* dedication, inscription

dedicatorio, -a *adj* dedicatory

dedil *nm* fingerstall

dedillo *nm* **cumplir las instrucciones al d.** to carry out instructions to the letter; **saber algo al d.** to have sth at one's fingertips, know sth very well

dedo *nm Anat (de la mano)* finger; *(del pie)* toe; **meterse los dedos en la nariz** to pick one's nose; *Fig* **a dos dedos de** only an inch away from; *Fig* **elegir a algn a d.** to hand-pick sb; *Fam* **hacer d.** to hitchhike; *Fig* **no mover un d.** not to lift a finger; *Fig* **no tener dos dedos de frente** to be as thick as two short planks; *Fig* **poner el d. en la llaga** to touch on a sore spot; *Fam Esp* **cogerse o pillarse los dedos** to get caught in the act; *Fam Fig* **está para chuparse los dedos** it's delicious o mouthwatering; *Fam Fig* **no se chupa el d.** he wasn't born yesterday ❑ **d. anular** third finger, ring finger; **d. corazón** middle finger; **d. gordo** *(de la mano)* thumb; *(del pie)* big toe **d. índice** index finger; **d. meñique** little finger; **d. del pie** toe; **d. pulgar** *(de la mano)* thumb; *(del pie)* big toe

deducción *nf* deduction

deducible *adj* (**a**) *(idea)* deducible, inferable (**b**) *Com* deductible

deducir [18] **1** *vt* (**a**) *(inferir)* to deduce, infer (**b**) *Com* to deduct, subtract
2 deducirse *vpr* to follow; **de aquí se deduce que ...** from this it follows that ...

deductivo, -a *adj* deductive

defecación *nf* defecation

defecar [59] *vt* to defecate

defección *nf* defection, desertion

defectivo, -a *adj* defective; *Ling* **verbo d.** defective verb

defecto *nm* (**a**) *(físico)* defect, fault; **d. de pronunciación** speech defect (**b**) *(moral)* fault, shortcoming; **en d. de** for lack of, for want of

defectuoso, -a *adj* defective, faulty

defender [64] **1** *vt* (**a**) *(país, ideas)* to defend (**contra** against, **de** from) (**b**) *(proteger)* to protect; **d. del frío** to protect from the cold (**c**) *(opinión, afirmación)* to defend, uphold; *(persona)* to stand up for (**d**) *Jur* to defend; **d. una causa** to argue a case
2 defenderse *vpr* (**a**) *(protegerse)* to defend oneself (**b**) *Fam (espabilarse)* to get by, manage; **se defiende bastante bien en francés** he can get by quite well in French

defendible *adj* defensible, justifiable

defendido, -a 1 *pp de* **defender**
2 *nm,f Jur* defendant

defenestración *nf* defenestration

defenestrar *vt* to throw out of a window

defensa 1 *nf* (**a**) *(protección)* defence, *US* defense; **en d. propia, en legítima d.** in self-defence; **salir en d. de algn** to come out in defence of sb ❑ **d. personal** self-defence (**b**) *Méx Aut (parachoques) Br* bumper, *US* fender
2 *nm Dep* defender, back

defensiva *nf* defensive; **estar/ponerse a la d.** to be/go on the defensive

defensivo, -a *adj* defensive

defensor, -a 1 *adj* defending; *Jur* **abogado d.** counsel for the defence
2 *nm,f* defender; *Jur* counsel for the defence ❑ *Esp* **d. del pueblo** ombudsman

defeño, -a *nm,f Méx* = person from the DF *(Mexico City)*

deferencia *nf* deference; **en** *o* **por d. a** in deference to

deferente *adj* deferential

deferir [62] **1** *vi* to defer to
  2 *vt Jur* to delegate (**a** to), transfer (**a** to)

deficiencia *nf* (**a**) *(defecto)* defect, deficiency, shortcoming; **las deficiencias del servicio** the shortcomings of the service (**b**) *(insuficiencia)* lack; **d. mental** mental deficiency; **la d. de medios** the lack of means

deficiente 1 *adj* (**a**) *(defectuoso)* deficient, faulty; **un trabajo d.** a shoddy piece of work (**b**) *(insuficiente)* insufficient, lacking; **una iluminación d.** poor lighting
  2 *nmf* **d. mental** mentally retarded person

déficit *(pl* **déficits)** *nm* (**a**) *Com Fin* deficit ❑ **d. comercial** trade deficit; **d. presupuestario** budget deficit; **d. público** public deficit (**b**) *Fig* shortage

deficitario, -a *adj* showing a deficit; **balance d.** balance showing a deficit

definible *adj* definable

definición *nf* (definition); **por d.** by definition

definido, -a 1 *pp de* **definir**
  2 *adj* definite, defined; *Ling* **artículo d.** definite article

definir 1 *vt* to define
  2 definirse *vpr* to make oneself clear

definitivamente *adv* (**a**) *(para siempre)* for good, once and for all (**b**) *(finalmente)* finally; **la boda será d. el catorce** the wedding will finally be held on the fourteenth

definitivo, -a *adj* definitive, final; **en definitiva** finally, in short; **en definitiva, no hay motivo de alarma** in short, there is nothing to worry about

deflación *nf Econ* deflation

deflacionista *adj Econ* deflationary

deflagración *nf* deflagration

deflagrar *vi* to deflagrate

deflector *nm Téc* baffle, deflector

deforestación *nf* deforestation

deforestar *vt* to deforest

deformación *nf* deformation

deformar 1 *vt* (gen) to deform, put out of shape; *(cara)* to disfigure; *Fig* **d. la realidad/la verdad/una imagen** to distort reality/the truth/a picture
  2 deformarse *vpr* to go out of shape, become distorted

deforme *adj (persona, miembro)* deformed; *(imagen)* distorted; *(objetos)* misshapen

deformidad *nf* (**a**) *(malformación)* deformity, malformation (**b**) *(error)* fault, shortcoming

defraudación *nf* (**a**) *(decepción)* disillusionment (**b**) *(fraude)* fraud ❑ **d. fiscal** tax evasion

defraudado, -a 1 *pp de* **defraudar**
  2 *adj* disillusioned

defraudador, -a 1 *adj* (**a**) *(decepcionante)* disillusioning (**b**) *(engañoso)* deceiving, cheating
  2 *nm,f* person who commits fraud ❑ **d. fiscal** tax evader

defraudar *vt* (**a**) *(decepcionar)* to disillusion; *(esperanzas)* to dash; **tu comportamiento me ha defraudado** I am disappointed with your behaviour (**b**) *(cometer fraude)* to defraud, cheat; **d. a Hacienda** to evade taxes

defunción *nf Fml* decease, demise

degeneración *nf* degeneration

degenerado, -a 1 *pp de* **degenerar**
  2 *adj & nm,f* degenerate

degenerar *vi* to degenerate

degenerativo, -a *adj* degenerative

deglución *nf* swallow, swallowing

deglutir *vt & vi* to swallow

degollación *nf* (**a**) *(decapitación)* beheading, execution (**b**) *(matanza)* slaughter, massacre

degolladero *nm* slaughterhouse

degolladura *nf* cut in the throat

degollar [63] *vt* (**a**) *(cortar la garganta a)* to cut *o* slit the throat of; *(decapitar)* to behead (**b**) *Fig (arruinar)* to ruin, spoil

degollina *nf Esp Fam* slaughter, massacre

degradable *adj* degradable

degradación *nf* (**a**) *(de moral, naturaleza)* degradation (**b**) *Mil* demotion

degradante *adj* degrading, humiliating

degradar 1 *vt* (**a**) *(humillar)* to degrade, humiliate (**b**) *Mil* to demote
  2 degradarse *vpr* to degrade *o* demean oneself

degüello *nm (degolladura)* throat cutting; *(decapitación)* beheading

degustación *nf* tasting; **d. de vinos** wine tasting

degustar *vt* to taste, try, sample

dehesa *nf* pasture, meadow

deidad *nf* deity

deificación *nf* deification

deificar [59] *vt* to deify

deísmo *nm* deism

deísta 1 *adj* deistic
  2 *nmf* deist

dejadez *nf* (**a**) *(abandono de sí mismo)* slovenliness, neglect (**b**) *(descuido general)* negligence, carelessness (**c**) *(pereza)* laziness, apathy

dejado, -a 1 *pp de* **dejar**
  2 *adj* (**a**) *(descuidado)* untidy, slovenly (**b**) *(negligente)* negligent, careless (**c**) *(perezoso)* lazy, apathetic (**d**) *Fam* **d. de la mano de Dios** godforsaken
  3 *nm,f* untidy *o* slovenly person

dejante *adv Am* (**a**) *(además de)* in addition to (**b**) *(no obstante)* nevertheless

dejar 1 *vt* (**a**) *(colocar)* to put, leave; **deja el vaso donde estaba** put the glass back where it was; **dejó las llaves sobre la mesa** he left the keys on the table (**b**) *(abandonar)* to leave; **d. algo por imposible** to give sth up; **d. plantado a algn** to stand sb up; **dejé el tabaco y la bebida** I gave up smoking and drinking; **dejó a su familia** he abandoned his family; **dejó la casa a las diez** he left home at ten (**c**) *(omitir)* to leave out, omit; **déjalo** forget it (**d**) *(legar)* to leave; **su abuela le dejó una fortuna** her grandmother left her a fortune (**e**) *(ceder)* to give, leave, hand over; **me dejó su silla cuando se fue** he gave me his seat when he left (**f**) *(producir)* to produce, leave; **el fuego deja ceniza** fire leaves ashes; **el negocio le deja grandes beneficios** he gets good profits from his business (**g**) *(causar un efecto)* to make; **déjame en paz** *o* **tranquilo** leave me alone; **d. preocupado** to worry; **d. sorprendido** to surprise; **d. triste** to make sad; *Fig* **d. frío** to leave cold (**h**) *(permitir)* to let, allow; **d. caer** to drop; **d. el paso libre** to get out of the way; **d. entrar/salir** to let in/out; **me dejaron salir antes** they let me leave early; **no dejan fumar aquí** smoking is not allowed here (**i**) *Esp (prestar)* to lend; **me dejó el libro** she lent me the book (**j**) *(esperar)* to wait; **deja que se le pase el enfado** wait until he's cooled down (**k**) *(aplazar)* to put off; **dejaron el viaje para el verano** they put the trip off until the summer (**l**) *(cesar)* to stop (**de** -), give up (**de** -); **dejé de verle en verano** I stopped seeing him in the summer; **dejó de fumar el año pasado** he gave up smoking last year; **no puedo d. de extrañarme** I can't get used to the idea

2 *v aux* (**a**) *(no d. de + infinitivo)* not to fail to; **no deja de venir a clase ni un día** he never misses a class; **ella no deja de llamarme** she's always phoning me up; **no deja de ser extraño que ...** it is still surprising that ...; **no dejaré de tenerlo en cuenta** I'll keep it in mind (**b**) *(d. + participio)* **d. dicho** to leave word *o* a message; **d. algo escrito** to put sth into writing; **dejó dicho que le despertaran** he asked to be woken up

3 dejarse *vpr* (**a**) *(permitir)* to let *o* allow oneself; **d. engañar** to let oneself be deceived; **no te dejes insultar así** don't let yourself be insulted like that (**b**) *(olvidar)* to forget; **me he dejado las llaves dentro** I've left the keys inside; **te has dejado tres líneas sin copiar** you've forgotten to copy three lines (**c**) *(abandonarse)* to neglect oneself, let oneself go (**d**) *(locuciones)* **d. barba** to grow a beard; **d. caer en un sillón** to flop into an armchair; **d. caer por casa de algn** to drop in on sb; **d. llevar por algn** to be influenced by sb; **d. llevar por algo** to get carried away by sth; **d. ver** to be seen; **se deja sentir el frío/verano** one can feel the cold/that summer is here

deje *nm* slight accent

del *(contracción de* de + el*) véase* de²

delación *nf* denunciation, accusation, revelation

delantal *nm* (**a**) *(mandil)* apron (**b**) *RP (bata)* white coat

delante *adv* (**a**) *(en primer lugar, en la parte delantera)* in front; *(enfrente)* opposite; **el de d.** the one in front; **la entrada de d.** the front entrance; **mi hermana es la que está d.** my sister is the one in front (**b**) **d. de** in front of, ahead of; **d. de mí** in front of me; **d. de tus ojos** before your eyes; **nos encontramos d. de la estación** we met outside the station (**c**) **por d.** in front; **se entra por d.** the entrance is at the front; **se lo lleva todo por d.** he destroys everything in his path; **tiene toda la vida por d.** he has his whole life ahead of him

delantera *nf* (**a**) *(parte frontal)* front (part) (**b**) *(ventaja)* lead; **coger** *o* **tomar la d.** to get ahead, take the lead; **llevar la d.** to be in the lead (**c**) *Ftb* forward line, forwards *pl* (**d**) **delanteras** *Vulg (tetas)* tits

delantero, -a 1 *adj* front; **parte delantera** front part; **rueda d.** front wheel
　2 *nm* (**a**) *Ftb (jugador)* forward ❑ **d. centro** centre forward (**b**) *Cost* front

delatar *vt* (**a**) *(denunciar)* to denounce, inform on *o* against (**b**) *Fig* to give away; **sus ojos le delataron** his eyes gave him away

delator, -a 1 *adj* (**a**) *(denunciante)* who informs, who denounces (**b**) *Fig* which gives away, that reveals; **tenía una sonrisa delatora en sus labios** his smile was a giveaway
　2 *nm,f (informador)* informer

delco *nm* *Esp Aut* distributor

deleble *adj* which can be erased *o* rubbed out easily

delectación *nf* delight, delectation

delegación *nf* (**a**) *(acto, delegados)* delegation (**b**) *(oficina)* local office, branch

delegado, -a 1 *pp de* delegar
　2 *adj* delegated
　3 *nm,f* (**a**) *(representante)* delegate; **d. de Hacienda** chief tax inspector (**b**) *Esp Com* representative

delegar [38] *vt* to delegate; **d. poderes en algn** to delegate powers to sb

deleitar 1 *vt* to delight
　2 deleitarse *vpr* **d. con** *o* **en** to delight in, take delight in

deleite *nm* delight, pleasure

deleitoso, -a *adj* delightful, enjoyable

deletéreo, -a *adj* poisonous, deadly

deletrear *vt* to spell (out)

deletreo *nm* spelling (out)

deleznable *adj* (**a**) *(resbaladizo)* slippery (**b**) *(que se rompe fácilmente)* fragile; **arcilla d.** crumbly clay (**c**) *(poco duradero)* ephemeral (**d**) *(inconsistente)* weak

delfín¹ *nm Zool* dolphin

delfín² *nm Hist* dauphin

delgadez *nf* (**a**) *(flacura)* thinness (**b**) *(esbeltez)* slenderness

delgado, -a *adj* (**a**) *(flaco)* thin (**b**) *(esbelto)* slender, slim

delgaducho, -a *adj Pey* skinny

deliberación *nf* deliberation

deliberado, -a 1 *pp de* deliberar
　2 *adj* deliberate, intentional

deliberar *vi* to deliberate (on), consider

deliberativo, -a *adj* deliberative

delicadeza *nf* (**a**) *(finura)* delicacy, daintiness (**b**) *(tacto)* tactfulness; **falta de d.** tactlessness, bad manners *pl*; **es una falta de d. no levantarse para saludar** it's bad manners not to stand up when greeting sb; **tuvo la d. de no mencionar el tema** he was tactful enough not to mention the subject (**c**) *(fragilidad)* fragility

delicado, -a *adj* (**a**) *(fino)* delicate, dainty; *(exquisito)* exquisite; **un gusto d.** a refined taste (**b**) *(difícil)* delicate, difficult; **un trabajo d.** a tricky job; **una situación delicada** a delicate situation (**c**) *(enfermizo)* delicate, frail (**d**) *(difícil de contentar)* fussy, hard to please (**e**) *(cortés)* refined, polite (**f**) *(muy sensible)* hypersensitive (**g**) *(frágil)* fragile

delicia *nf* delight; **esta tarta es una d.** this pie is delightful; **hacer las delicias de algn** to delight sb

delicioso, -a *adj* delightful, charming; **una comida deliciosa** a delicious meal

delictivo, -a *adj* criminal, punishable; **conducta delictiva** criminal conduct

delicuescencia *nf* deliquescence

delimitación *nf* delimitation, demarcation

delimitar *vt* to delimit, mark the boundaries of

delincuencia *nf* delinquency ❑ **d. juvenil** juvenile delinquency

delincuente *adj & nmf* delinquent ❑ **d. habitual** habitual offender

delineación *nf* delineation, outlining

delineante *nmf* *(hombre)* *Br* draughtsman, *US* draftsman; *(mujer)* *Br* draughtswoman, *US* draftswoman

delinear *vt* to delineate, outline

delinquir [22] *vi* to break the law, commit an offence *o US* offense

delirante *adj* delirious, frenzied

delirar *vi* to be delirious, rave; *Fig* to talk nonsense

delirio *nm* (**a**) *(por fiebre, borrachera)* delirium; **delirios de grandeza** delusions of grandeur (**b**) *Fig (disparate)* nonsense (**c**) *Fam* **¡fue el d.!** it was really great!

delírium tremens *nm inv Med* delirium tremens

delito *nm* crime, offence, *US* offense; **lo cogieron en flagrante d.** he was caught red-handed *o* in the act ❑ **d. ecológico** ecological crime; **d. fiscal** tax offence; **d. informático** computer crime

delta 1 *nm Geog* delta
　2 *nf (letra griega)* delta

demacrado, -a 1 *pp de* demacrarse
　2 *adj* emaciated

demacrarse *vpr* to become emaciated

demagogia *nf* demagogy

demagógico, -a *adj* demagogic, demagogical

demagogo, -a *nm,f* demagogue

demanda *nf* (**a**) *(petición)* request, demand (**b**) *(pregunta)* inquiry (**c**) *(búsqueda)* search; **en d. de** asking for (**d**) *Jur* lawsuit; **presentar una d. contra algn** to take legal action against sb (**e**) *Com* demand; **la ley de la oferta y la d.** the law of supply and demand

demandado, -a 1 *pp de* **demandar**
2 *nm,f Jur* defendant

demandante *nmf Jur* claimant

demandar *vt* (**a**) *Jur* to sue (**b**) *(pedir, rogar)* to request

demarcación *nf* (**a**) *(señalización)* demarcation (**b**) *(terreno)* district, zone

demarcar [59] *vt* to demarcate

demás 1 *adj & pron* the rest (of); **la d. gente** the rest of the people; **lo d., ya lo sabes** you already know the rest; **los d. se fueron antes** the rest left earlier; **por lo d.** otherwise, apart from that; **estoy cansado pero, por lo d., me encuentro bien** I am tired, but, apart from that, I am all right; **todo lo d.** everything else
2 *adv* **por d.** in vain, uselessly; **es por d. difícil** it's much too difficult; **está por d. que le llames** there's no point in calling her; **y d.** etcetera; **me levanté, me lavé, me vestí y d.** I got up, had a wash, got dressed, and so on

demasía *nf* (**a**) *(exceso)* excess, surplus; **en d.** excessively; **bebe en d.** he drinks too much (**b**) *(abuso)* offence, outrage (**c**) *(descaro)* insolence; *(atrevimiento)* audacity

demasiado, -a 1 *adj (singular)* too much; *(plural)* too many; **hay demasiada comida** there is too much food; **quieres demasiadas cosas** you want too many things
2 *adv* too (much); **es d. grande/caro** it is too big/dear; **fumas/trabajas d.** you smoke/work too much

demencia *nf* dementia, insanity, madness ❑ **d. senil** senile dementia

demencial *adj Fam* chaotic

demente 1 *adj* insane, mad
2 *nmf* mental patient; *Ofens* lunatic

demérito *nm* demerit, fault

democracia *nf* democracy ❑ *Pol* **d. popular** people's democracy

demócrata 1 *adj* democratic
2 *nmf* democrat

democratacristiano, -a *adj & nm,f Pol* Christian Democrat

democrático, -a *adj* democratic

democratización *nf* democratization

democratizador, -a *adj* democratizing; **proceso d.** process of democratization

democratizar [14] *vt* to democratize

democristiano, -a *adj & nm,f Pol* Christian Democrat

demografía *nf* demography

demográfico, -a *adj* demographic; **crecimiento d.** population increase o growth

demoledor, -a *adj* (**a**) *(huracán, críticas)* devastating (**b**) *(argumento)* overwhelming, crushing

demoler [41] *vt* to demolish, pull down

demolición *nf* demolition

demoniaco, -a *adj* demoniac, demoniacal

demonio *nm* devil, demon; *Fig* **llevarse (a algn) el d.** o **todos los demonios** to get furious; *Fig* **ponerse como un d.** to get really angry; *Fig* **ser un d.** to be a real devil; *Fam* **¿cómo demonios ...?** how the hell ...?; *Fam* **¡demonio(s)!** hell!, damn!; *Fam* **¡d. de niño!** you little devil!; *Fam* **¿dónde demonios ...?** where the hell ...?; *Fam* **el d. de tu hermano** your devil of a brother; *Fam* **hace un frío de mil demonios** it's perishing; *Fam* **¡qué demonio(s)!** damn it!; *Fam* **¿quién demonios ...?** who the hell ...?; *Fam* **saber/oler a demonios** to taste/smell horrible o foul

demonología *nf* demonology

demontre *interj* damn it!

demora *nf* delay; **sin d.** without delay

demorar 1 *vt (aplazar)* to delay, hold up; **la tormenta demoró la llegada del avión** the plane was held up by the storm
2 demorarse *vpr* (**a**) *(retrasarse)* to be delayed, be held up; **la conferencia se demoró más de lo previsto** the lecture started later than expected (**b**) *(detenerse)* to stay, linger on (**c**) *esp Am (tardar)* to be late

demostrable *adj* demonstrable

demostración *nf* (**a**) *(gen)* demonstration; **hacer una d. de cómo funciona una máquina** to demonstrate how a machine works; **una d. atlética** an athletic display; **una d. de fuerza** a show of strength (**b**) *Mat* proof

demostrar [63] *vt* (**a**) *(mostrar)* to show, demonstrate; **eso demuestra que no entiendas bien el inglés** that shows that you don't understand English very well (**b**) *(probar)* to prove; **ha demostrado su valor en tales circunstancias** he has proved his courage in these circumstances (**c**) *Mat* to prove

demostrativo, -a *adj & nm Ling* demonstrative

demudado, -a 1 *pp de* **demudar**
2 *adj (pálido)* pale; *(alterado)* upset

demudar 1 *vt (color de la cara)* to alter, change
2 demudarse *vpr (persona, rostro)* to change one's expression o colour

denario *nm Hist* denarius

dendrita *nf Biol Min* dendrite

denegación *nf (desestimación)* refusal, denial ❑ *Jur* **d. de demanda** dismissal

denegar [43] *vt (desestimar)* to refuse; *(negar)* to deny; *Jur* **d. una demanda** to dismiss a claim

dengue *nm* fastidiousness, fussiness; **hacer dengues** to be fussy o finicky

denigración *nf* denigration, defamation

denigrante *adj* denigrating, disparaging

denigrar *vt* to denigrate, disparage, run down

denominación *nf* (**a**) *(nombre)* name; *(vinos)* **'d. de origen'** 'appellation d'origine' (**b**) *(confesión religiosa)* denomination

denominado, -a 1 *pp de* **denominar**
2 *adj* named, designated; **el candidato d.** the candidate appointed

denominador, -a 1 *adj* denominative ❑ *Mat & Fig* **d. común** common denominator
2 *nm Mat* denominator ❑ **mínimo común d.** lowest common denominator

denominar *vt* to name, designate

denominativo, -a *adj Ling* denominative

denostar [63] *vt* to insult

denotar *vt* to denote, indicate

densidad *nf* density, thickness; **d. de población** population density

densificar [59] *vt* to make dense, densify, thicken

denso, -a *adj* dense, thick

dentado, -a 1 *pp de* **dentar**
2 *adj* toothed; **cuchillo d.** knife with a serrated edge; *Bot* **hoja dentada** dentate leaf; **rueda dentada** cog wheel

dentadura *nf* teeth, set of teeth; **tiene una d. preciosa** she has beautiful teeth ❑ **d. postiza** false teeth *pl*, dentures *pl*

dental *adj* dental

dentar [3] **1** *vi* to teethe, cut teeth
  2 *vt* to serrate

dentellada *nf* (**a**) *(mordisco)* bite (**b**) *(señal)* toothmark

dentellar *vi* to chatter; **dentellaba de frío** his teeth were chattering with cold

dentellear *vt* to nibble at

dentera *nf* **dar d. a algn** to set sb's teeth on edge; *Fig* to make sb green with envy

dentición *nf* (**a**) *(proceso)* teething (**b**) *(conjunto)* teeth

dentífrico, -a 1 *adj* tooth; **pasta dentífrica** tooth-paste
  2 *nm* toothpaste

dentista *nmf* dentist; **ir al d.** to go to the dentist's

dentistería *nf CAm Col Ecuad Ven (consultorio)* dental surgery; *(estudios)* dentistry

dentón, -ona 1 *adj* toothy, buck-toothed
  2 *nm,f* toothy o buck-toothed person

dentro *adv* (**a**) *(en el interior)* inside; **aquí d.** in here; **el regalo está d.** the present is inside; **muy d.** deep inside; **por d.** inside; **es verde por d.** it's green (on the) inside; **por d. está triste** deep down (inside) he feels sad; **vamos d. (de la casa)** let's go indoors (**b**) *(tiempo)* **d. de lo posible** as far as possible; **d. de lo que cabe** under the circumstances; **d. de poco** shortly, soon; **d. de un mes** in a month's time

dentudo, -a *adj* & *nm,f* véase **dentón, -ona**

denuesto *nm* insult

denuncia *nf* (**a**) *(acusación)* accusation; *(condena)* denunciation (**b**) *Jur (documento)* report; **presentar una d.** to report, lodge a complaint, bring an action

denunciable *adj* which may be reported

denunciante *nmf Jur* = person who reports a crime

denunciar *vt* (**a**) *(delito)* to report (**a** to) (**b**) *(condenar)* to denounce (**c**) *Fig (indicar)* to indicate; **el retraso denuncia la falta de planificación** the delay points to a lack of planning

deontología *nf* deontology

deontológico, -a *adj* **código d.** code of ethics

D. E. P. *(abrev de* **descanse en paz***)* RIP

deparar *vt* to give, afford; **el viaje me deparó un placer inesperado** the journey brought me unexpected pleasure; **nunca se sabe lo que nos depara el destino** we never know what fate has in store for us

departamental *adj* departmental

departamento *nm* (**a**) *(división territorial)* province, district (**b**) *(de un organismo)* department, section (**c**) *Educ* department; **d. de lenguas extranjeras** modern languages department (**d**) *Ferroc* compartment (**e**) *(de un objeto)* compartment, section (**f**) *Arg (apartamento) Br* flat, *US* apartment

departir *vi Fml* to talk, converse

depauperado, -a *adj* impoverished

dependencia *nf* (**a**) *(de una persona, país)* dependence, dependency (**b**) **dependencias** rooms, outbuildings

depender *vi* to depend (**de** on); **depende de ti** it is up to you; **depende del tiempo (que haga)** it depends on the weather; **dependo de mis padres** I am dependent on my parents; **en lo que de mí depende** as far as I am concerned

dependiente, -a 1 *adj* dependent (**de** on)
  2 *nm,f Br* shop assistant, *US* sales clerk

depilación *nf* depilation; **d. a la cera** waxing

depiladora *nf* ladies' shaver, hair remover

depilar 1 *vt* to depilate, remove the hair from; *(cejas)* to pluck
  2 depilarse *vpr* to depilate

depilatorio, -a *adj* & *nm* depilatory; **crema depilatoria** hair-remover, hair-removing cream

deplorable *adj* deplorable, regrettable

deplorar *vt* to deplore, regret deeply, lament

deponente *Ling* **1** *adj* deponent
  2 *nm* deponent verb

deponer [50] *(pp* depuesto*)* *vt* (**a**) *(dejar)* to abandon; **al final depuso su actitud hostil** in the end he set aside his hostility; **d. las armas** to lay down one's arms (**b**) *(destituir)* to remove from office; *(líder)* to depose (**c**) *Jur* to testify about, give evidence about (**d**) *(defecar)* to defecate (**e**) *CAm Méx (vomitar)* to vomit

deportación *nf* deportation

deportado, -a 1 *pp de* deportar
  2 *adj* deported
  3 *nm,f* deportee, deported person

deportar *vt* to deport

deporte *nm* sport; **campo de deportes** sports ground; **hacer algo por d.** to do sth as a hobby; **hacer d.** to practise sports; **¿practicas algún d.?** do you go in for any sport?, do you take part in sports? ▫ **deportes de invierno** winter sports

deportista 1 *adj* sporty, keen on sport
  2 *nmf (hombre)* sportsman; *(mujer)* sportswoman

deportividad *nf* sportsmanship

deportivo, -a 1 *adj* (**a**) *(de deportes)* sports; **club d.** sports club; **chaqueta deportiva** sports jacket (**b**) *(imparcial)* sporting, sportsmanlike
  2 *nm Aut* sports car

deposición *nf* (**a**) *(de un oficial)* removal from office; *(líder)* deposition (**b**) *Jur* testimony, deposition, evidence (**c**) *Fml (evacuación de vientre)* defecation

depositante *nmf Fin* depositor

depositar 1 *vt* (**a**) *Fin* to deposit (**b**) *(colocar)* to place, put; *Fig* **ha depositado en mí toda su confianza** she has placed all her trust in me (**c**) *(almacenar)* to store
  2 depositarse *vpr (posos, polvo)* to settle

depositaría *nf* depository

depositario, -a 1 *nm,f* (**a**) *(de dinero)* depositary, trustee (**b**) *(de un secreto etc)* repository (**c**) *(de mercancías)* depositary
  2 *nm (tesorero)* treasurer, cashier

depósito *nm* (**a**) *Fin (bancario)* deposit (**b**) *(lugar)* dump; *(almacén)* store, warehouse, depot ▫ **d. de basuras** rubbish tip o dump; **d. de cadáveres** mortuary, *US* morgue; **d. de chatarra** scrapyard; **d. de objetos perdidos** lost property office, *US* lost-and-found department (**c**) *(contenedor)* tank ▫ **d. de agua** water tank; **d. de gasolina** *Br* petrol tank, *US* gas tank (**d**) *(sedimento)* deposit, sediment (**e**) *Mil* depot **d. legal** = copy of a publication legally required to be sent to the authorities

depravación *nf* depravity, depravation

depravado, -a 1 *pp de* depravar
  2 *adj* depraved
  3 *nm,f* depraved person, degenerate

depravar 1 *vt* to deprave, corrupt
  2 depravarse *vpr* to become depraved

depre *nf Fam* downer, depression

depreciación *nf Fin* depreciation; **la d. de la moneda** currency depreciation

depreciar 1 *vt* to decrease o reduce the value of
  2 depreciarse *vpr* to depreciate, lose value

depredación *nf* (**a**) *(entre animales)* hunting, preying on (**b**) *Fig (daño)* depredation, pillaging

depredador, -a 1 *adj* pillaging, plundering
2 *nm,f* pillager, plunderer

depredar *vt* to pillage, plunder

depresión *nf* depression; **d. económica** economic depression; *Hist* **los años de la d.** the years of the Depression ❑ *Meteor* **d. atmosférica** atmospheric depression; *Med* **d. nerviosa** nervous breakdown

depresivo, -a *adj* depressing; *Med* depressive

depresor, -a 1 *adj* depressing
2 *nm Med* depressor

deprimente *adj* depressing

deprimido, -a 1 *pp de* **deprimir**
2 *adj* depressed

deprimir 1 *vt* to depress
2 deprimirse *vpr* to get depressed

deprisa *adv* quickly

depuesto, -a *pp de* **deponer**

depuración *nf* (**a**) *(del agua)* purification, depuration; *(de la sangre)* cleansing (**b**) *Fig* purge, purging

depurado, -a 1 *pp de* **depurar**
2 *adj (estilo)* refined, polished; *(diseño, líneas)* sleek, elegant

depurador, -a 1 *adj* purifying;
2 *nm (sustancia)* depurative; *(máquina, aparato)* purifier

depurar *vt* (**a**) *(purificar) (agua)* to purify, depurate; *(sangre)* to cleanse (**b**) *Pol (partido)* to purge (**c**) *(perfeccionar)* to perfect, refine

depurativo, -a *adj & nm Med* depurative

derby (*pl* **derbys**) *nm (en hípica)* derby; *(en fútbol)* (local) derby

derecha 1 *nf* (**a**) *(mano)* right hand (**b**) *(lugar)* right, right-hand side; **a la d.** to o on the right, on the right-hand side (**c**) *Pol* **la d.** the right, the right wing; **ser de** *Esp* **derechas** o *Am* **d.** to be right-wing
2 *interj Mil* **¡d.!** right turn

derechazo *nm Box* right

derechista 1 *adj* right-wing, rightist
2 *nmf* right-winger, rightist

derecho, -a 1 *adj* (**a**) *(de la derecha)* right; **el ojo d.** the right eye (**b**) *(recto)* upright, straight; **ponte d.** stand up straight; *Esp Fig* **no hacer nada a derechas** to do nothing right; *Fig* **un hombre hecho y d.** a real man
2 *nm* (**a**) *Jur (conjunto de leyes)* law; **estudiar d.** to study law ❑ **d. administrativo** administrative law; **d. civil** civil law; **d. internacional** international law; **d. mercantil** commercial law; **d. penal** criminal law; **d. político** constitutional law (**b**) *(privilegio)* right, claim; **con d. a** with the right to; **dar d.** to entitle; **de d.** by right; **derechos civiles/humanos** civil/human rights; **el d. al voto** the right to vote; **estar en su d.** to be within one's rights; **no hay d.** it's not fair; **'reservados todos los derechos'** 'all rights reserved', 'copyright'; **tener d. a** to be entitled to, have the right to (**c**) *(de una tela)* right side; **¿cuál es el d. y cuál es el revés?** which is the right side and which the wrong side? (**d**) *Com* **derechos** duties, taxes ❑ **d. de admisión** right *sing* to refuse admission; **d. de aduana** customs duties; **d. de autor** royalties; **d. de matrícula** registration o enrolment fees; **d. de sucesión** death duties
3 *adv* straight, directly; **andar d.** to walk straight; **fue d. a la puerta** he went straight to the door; **siga todo d.** to go straight on

deriva *nf Náut* drift; **a la d.** adrift; **ir a la d.** to drift

derivación *nf* (**a**) *Ling* derivation (**b**) *(de una carretera)* turn-off, diversion (**c**) *Elec* shunt

derivada *nf Mat* derivative

derivado, -a 1 *pp de* **derivar**
2 *adj* derived, derivative
3 *nm* (**a**) *Ling* derivative (**b**) *Quím* derivative, by-product

derivar 1 *vt* (**a**) *(cambiar la dirección)* to direct, divert; **derivó la conversación hacia otro tema** he steered the conversation on to a different subject (**b**) *Elec* to shunt
2 *vi* (**a**) *(cambiar de dirección)* to drift; **después, sus gustos derivaron hacia el cine** later, his tastes inclined towards the cinema; **la reunión derivó hacia otros derroteros** the meeting drifted on to other matters (**b**) *(proceder)* to spring, arise; **su amistad deriva de intereses comunes** their friendship stems from common interests (**c**) *Náut* to drift (**d**) *Ling* to be derived (**de** from), derive (**de** from); **'ventanal' deriva de 'ventana'** 'ventanal' is derived from 'ventana'
3 derivarse *vpr* (**a**) *(proceder)* to result o stem (**de** from) (**b**) *Ling* to be derived (**de** from)

derivativo, -a *adj & nm* derivative

dermatitis *nm inv Med* dermatitis

dermatología *nf Med* dermatology

dermatológico, -a *adj Med* dermatological

dermatólogo, -a *nm,f Med* dermatologist

dermatosis *nf inv Med* dermatosis

dérmico, -a *adj* dermal, dermic, skin

dermis *nf inv* dermis, derm

dermoprotector, -a *adj* skin-protecting; **crema dermoprotectora** skin cream

derogable *adj Jur* repealable

derogación *nf* repeal, abolition

derogar [38] *vt* (**a**) *Jur* to repeal, abolish, annul (**b**) *(contrato)* to rescind, cancel

derogatorio, -a *adj* repealing, abolishing, annulling

derramamiento *nm* spilling, overflowing; **d. de sangre** bloodshed

derramar 1 *vt* to spill, pour; **d. lágrimas/sangre** to shed tears/blood
2 derramarse *vpr* (**a**) *(líquido)* to spill; **la leche se derramó sobre la mesa** the milk spilt all over the table (**b**) *(desparramarse)* to scatter; **los rebeldes se derramaron por la ciudad** the rebels scattered throughout the city

derrame *nm* (**a**) *(gen)* spilling; *(de sangre)* shedding (**b**) *(pérdida)* leak, leakage (**c**) *Med* discharge ❑ **d. cerebral** brain haemorrhage (**d**) *Arquit (de puerta, ventana)* splay

derrapar *vi Aut* to skid

derrape *nm Aut* skid

derredor *nm* **al** o **en d. de** round, around

derrengar [43] **1** *vt* (**a**) *(deslomar)* to break sb's back (**b**) *Fig (cansar)* to wear out; **estoy derrengado** I'm shattered
2 derrengarse *vpr* to wear oneself out

derretido, -a 1 *pp de* **derretir**
2 *adj* (**a**) *(fundido)* melted; **mantequilla derretida** melted butter; **plomo d.** molten lead (**b**) *Fam Fig* **está d. por ella** he's madly in love with her

derretimiento *nm* (**a**) *(acción)* melting; *(de la nieve)* thawing (**b**) *Fam Fig* intense love, burning passion

derretir [47] **1** *vt* (**a**) *(gen)* to melt (down); *(hielo, nieve)* to thaw (**b**) *(derrochar)* to squander, waste
2 derretirse *vpr* (**a**) *(metal)* to melt; *(hielo, nieve)* to thaw; *Fam Fig* **d. de amor** to burn with love (**b**) *(inquietarse)* to fret, worry

derribar *vt* (**a**) *(demoler)* to pull down, knock down; **d. una casa** to demolish a house; **el viento derribó muchos árboles** the wind blew down a lot of trees (**b**) *(hacer caer) (persona)* to knock down o over; *(avión)* to shoot down;

derribó tres aviones enemigos he shot down three enemy planes (**c**) *Fig (destituir) (cargo)* to remove o oust from office; *(gobierno)* to overthrow, bring down

derribo *nm* (**a**) *(de edificio)* demolition; *(de avión, jugador)* bringing down; **materiales de d.** rubble (**b**) *(lugar)* demolition site

derrocamiento *nm* (**a**) *Pol* overthrow, toppling (**b**) *(edificio)* demolition

derrocar [59] *vt* (**a**) *(rey)* to overthrow; *(gobierno)* to bring down; *(ministro)* to oust from office, topple (**b**) *(edificio)* to demolish, pull down

derrochador, -a 1 *adj* spendthrift, wasteful, squandering
2 *nm,f* spendthrift, wasteful person, squanderer

derrochar *vt* (**a**) *(dinero)* to waste, squander (**b**) *(rebosar)* to be full of; **d. salud/simpatía** to be full of health/good humour

derroche *nm* (**a**) *(gasto)* waste, squandering (**b**) *(abundancia)* profusion, abundance (**c**) *(energía)* burst

derrota *nf* (**a**) *(fracaso)* defeat, failure, setback (**b**) *Náut (rumbo)* (ship's) course

derrotado, -a 1 *pp de* **derrotar**
2 *adj* (**a**) *(vencido)* defeated (**b**) *(andrajoso)* in tatters, ragged (**c**) *Argot (acabado)* knackered

derrotar *vt* to defeat, beat; **nuestro equipo derrotó al equipo local** our team beat the local team

derrotero *nm* (**a**) *Náut* sailing directions *pl* (**b**) *Fig* path, course o plan of action (**c**) *Náut (libro de navegación)* book of charts

derrotismo *nm* defeatism

derrotista *adj & nmf* defeatist

derruido, -a 1 *pp de* **derruir**
2 *adj* in ruins

derruir [34] *vt* to demolish, knock down, pull down

derrumbamiento *nm* (**a**) *(demolición)* demolition (**b**) *(caída)* collapse, falling down; *(techo)* caving in (**c**) *Fig (gobierno, civilización)* collapse

derrumbar 1 *vt* (**a**) *(edificio)* to demolish, knock down, pull down (**b**) *(despeñar)* to throw, hurl down (**c**) *(hundir)* to ruin, destroy
2 derrumbarse *vpr* (**a**) *(edificio)* to collapse, fall down; *(techo)* to fall in, cave in (**b**) *(precipitarse)* to hurl o fling oneself headlong (**por** down) (**c**) *Fig* to collapse; **sus esperanzas se derrumbaron** her hopes were shattered

derrumbe *nm* collapse

derviche *nm Rel* dervish

desabastecer [46] *vt* **d. a algn de** to leave sb short of

desabastecido, -a 1 *pp de* **desabastecer**
2 *adj* short of, out of

desaborido, -a 1 *adj* (**a**) *(comida)* tasteless, insipid (**b**) *Fig (persona)* dull
2 *nm,f Fig* dull person

desabotonar *vt* to unbutton

desabrido, -a *adj* (**a**) *(comida)* tasteless, insipid (**b**) *(tiempo)* unpleasant (**c**) *Esp (hosco) (persona)* surly; *(tono)* harsh (**d**) *Am (soso) (persona)* wet, bland, dull

desabrigado, -a 1 *pp de* **desabrigar**
2 *adj* (**a**) *(lugar)* open, exposed (**b**) *(persona)* **ir muy d.** to be lightly clad (**c**) *Fig* unprotected, defenceless, *US* defenseless

desabrigar [38] **1** *vt* (*ropa*) to take off o remove
2 desabrigarse *vpr (sacar ropa)* to take off some of one's clothes; *(en la cama)* to throw off one's bedclothes

desabrochar 1 *vt* to undo, unfasten
2 desabrocharse *vpr* (**a**) *(persona)* to undo, unfasten;

desabróchate la camisa undo your shirt (**b**) *(prenda)* to come undone o unfastened

desacatar *vt (falta de respeto)* to show no respect towards; *(orden)* to disobey, not observe

desacato *nm* lack of respect, disrespect (**a** for); *Jur* **d. al tribunal** contempt of court

desacertado, -a 1 *pp de* **desacertar**
2 *adj (inadecuado)* inappropriate, unwise; *(inoportuno)* untimely; *(erróneo)* wrong, mistaken; **un regalo d.** a badly chosen present; **una observación desacertada** a tactless remark

desacertar [3] *vi* (**a**) *(fallar)* to be wrong, be mistaken (**b**) *(falta de tacto)* to lack tact, be tactless

desacierto *nm (error)* mistake, error; *(mala selección)* bad choice; **fue un d. hacer este comentario** it was an unfortunate remark to make

desaconsejado, -a 1 *pp de* **desaconsejar**
2 *adj* ill-advised

desaconsejar *vt* to advise against; **le desaconsejaron los viajes largos** they advised him against long journeys

desacoplar *vt Téc* to uncouple; *Elec* to disconnect

desacorde *adj* (**a**) *Mús* discordant (**b**) *(opiniones)* conflicting; **opiniones desacordes** conflicting opinions

desacostumbrado, -a 1 *pp de* **desacostumbrar**
2 *adj* unusual, uncommon

desacostumbrar 1 *vt* **d. a algn de hacer algo** to break sb of the habit of doing sth; **estoy desacostumbrado** I've lost the habit
2 desacostumbrarse *vpr* to get out of the habit, give up

desacreditar 1 *vt* to discredit, bring into discredit, run down, disparage
2 desacreditarse *vpr* to become discredited

desactivado, -a *adj (bomba, explosivo)* defused; *(mecanismo, alarma)* disconnected

desactivar *vt (bomba, explosivo)* to defuse; *(mecanismo, alarma)* to disconnect; *Inform* to disable, deactivate

desacuerdo *nm* disagreement; **estar en d. con** to be in disagreement o at variance with

desafecto, -a 1 *adj* disaffected, opposed
2 *nm* lack of affection, coldness

desafiante *adj* challenging, defiant

desafiar [32] *vt* to challenge, defy; **te desafío, ¿a que no lo haces?** I dare you to do it

desafinado, -a 1 *pp de* **desafinar**
2 *adj Mús* out of tune

desafinar 1 *vi (gen)* to be out of tune; *(canción)* to sing out of tune; *(instrumento)* to play out of tune
2 *vt* to put out of tune
3 desafinarse *vpr* to go out of tune

desafío *nm* (**a**) *(reto)* challenge (**b**) *(duelo)* duel

desaforadamente *adv (desmedidamente)* excessively; *(escandalosamente)* outrageously

desaforado, -a *adj* (**a**) *(desmedido)* huge, enormous; **gritos desaforados** terrible cries (**b**) *(escandaloso)* outrageous; *(persona)* loud, rowdy

desafortunado, -a *adj* unlucky, unfortunate

desafuero *nm* (**a**) *Jur* violation o infringement of the laws (**b**) *(abuso)* outrage, excess

desagradable *adj* unpleasant, disagreeable

desagradar *vi* to displease; **me desagrada su conducta** I don't like his behaviour

desagradecer [46] *vt* to be ungrateful for, show ingratitude for

desagradecido, -a 1 *pp de* **desagradecer**
2 *adj* ungrateful
3 *nm,f* ungrateful person

desagradecimiento *nm* ingratitude, ungratefulness

desagrado *nm* displeasure; **con d.** reluctantly

desagraviar *vt* (**a**) *(excusarse)* to make amends for (**b**) *(compensar)* to indemnify, compensate

desagravio *nm* **en señal de d.** (in order) to make amends

desaguar [11] **1** *vt (vaciar)* to drain

2 *vi* (**a**) *(vaciarse)* to drain (off); *(el baño)* to empty (**b**) *(desembocar)* to flow, drain (**en** into); **el Ebro desagua en el Mediterráneo** the Ebro flows into the Mediterranean

desagüe *nm (vaciado)* drain, outlet; *(cañería)* waste pipe, drainpipe; *Aut* **d. del radiador** radiator overflow pipe

desaguisado, -a **1** *adj (contra ley)* illegal, unlawful; *(contra razón)* outrageous

2 *nm* (**a**) *(delito)* offence, *US* offense; *(agravio)* outrage (**b**) *Fam (destrozo)* damage; *(fechoría)* mischief

desahogado, -a **1** *pp de* **desahogar**

2 *adj* (**a**) *(espacioso)* spacious, roomy (**b**) *(acomodado)* well-off, well-to-do (**c**) *Fig (descarado)* cheeky, insolent

desahogar [38] **1** *vt (dolor)* to relieve; *(desfogar)* to vent, pour out

2 desahogarse *vpr* (**a**) *(desfogarse)* to let off steam (**b**) *(confiarse)* to open one's heart (**con** to) (**c**) *(descargarse)* to get something off one's chest

desahogo *nm* (**a**) *(alivio)* relief; **le sirve de d.** it helps him let off steam (**b**) *(descanso)* relaxation (**c**) *(holgura económica)* comfort, ease; **vivir con d.** to live comfortably

desahuciado, -a **1** *pp de* **desahuciar**

2 *adj* (**a**) *(enfermo)* hopeless (**b**) *(inquilino)* evicted

desahuciar *vt* (**a**) *(desalojar)* to evict (**b**) *(quitar toda esperanza)* to deprive of all hope; **d. a un enfermo** to give up all hope for a patient

desahucio *nm* eviction

desairado, -a **1** *pp de* **desairar**

2 *adj* (**a**) *(sin éxito)* unsuccessful; *(sin gracia)* awkward; *(humillado)* spurned; **quedar d.** to come off badly, create a bad impression; **una situación desairada** an awkward situation (**b**) *(desgarbado)* unattractive

desairar *vt* to slight, snub, spurn; **acepté su regalo para no desairarla** I accepted her present so as not to offend her

desaire *nm* slight, rebuff; **hacerle un d. a algn** to snub sb

desajustar **1** *vt* (**a**) *(aparato, motor, máquina)* to put out of kilter; *(pieza, tuerca)* to loosen (**b**) *Fig* **d. los planes de algn** to upset sb's plans

2 desajustarse *vpr (aparato, motor, máquina)* to go out of kilter; *(pieza, tuerca)* to come loose

desajuste *nm* (**a**) *(máquinas) (mal funcionamiento)* maladjustment; *(avería)* breakdown (**b**) *(desconcierto)* disorder; *(desequilibrio)* imbalance; **d. económico** economic imbalance; **un d. de horarios** clashing timetables

desalado, -a¹ **1** *pp de* **desalar¹**

2 *adj Culin* desalted; **bacalao d.** desalted cod

desalado, -a² **1** *pp de* **desalar²**

2 *(apresurado)* hasty; **fue d. a la comisaría** he rushed to the police station

desalar¹ *vt Culin* to remove the salt from, desalt

desalar² **1** *vt (aves)* to clip the wings of

2 desalarse *vpr (apresurarse)* to rush; *Fig* **se desalaba por llegar** he longed to arrive

desalentador, -a *adj* discouraging, disheartening

desalentar [3] **1** *vt* to leave *o* put out of breath; *Fig* to discourage, dishearten

2 desalentarse *vpr* to get discouraged, lose heart

desaliento *nm (desánimo)* discouragement; *(abatimiento)* dismay

desalinear **1** *vt* to put out of line

2 desalinearse *vpr* to get *o* go out of line

desalinizar [14] *vt* to desalinate

desaliñado, -a **1** *pp de* **desaliñar**

2 *adj* scruffy, untidy, down-at-heel

desaliñar *vt* to make scruffy *o* untidy

desaliño *nm* scruffiness, untidiness

desalmado, -a **1** *adj* (**a**) *(malo)* wicked (**b**) *(cruel)* cruel, heartless

2 *nm,f* (**a**) *(malo)* wicked person (**b**) *(cruel)* cruel *o* heartless person

desalojamiento *nm* (**a**) *(expulsión) (inquilino)* eviction; *(personas)* dislodging, removal; *(lugar)* evacuation, clearing (**b**) *(abandono)* abandonment

desalojar **1** *vt* (**a**) *(inquilino)* to evict; *(personas)* to remove, dislodge; *(lugar)* to clear, evacuate; **la policía desalojó el teatro** the police cleared the theatre (**b**) *(abandonar)* to move out of, abandon; **d. una casa** to vacate a house

2 *vi* to move house, move out

desalojo *nm véase* **desalojamiento**

desalquilado, -a *adj* vacant, unrented

desalquilarse *vpr (local, inmueble)* to become vacant

desamarrar *vt Náut (barco)* to unmoor, cast off; *(desatar)* to untie

desambientado, -a *adj* (**a**) *(persona)* out of place; *(desorientado)* disoriented (**b**) *(lugar)* lacking in atmosphere

desamor *nm (desafecto)* lack of affection, coldness; *(indiferencia)* indifference; *(antipatía)* dislike

desamortizable *adj* alienable

desamortización *nf* alienation, disentailment

desamortizar [14] *vt* to alienate, disentail

desamparado, -a **1** *pp de* **desamparar**

2 *adj (persona)* helpless, unprotected; *(lugar)* abandoned, forsaken

3 *nm,f* helpless *o* abandoned person

desamparar *vt* (**a**) *(persona)* to abandon, desert (**b**) *Jur* to renounce, relinquish

desamparo *nm* helplessness; **en d.** deserted, abandoned

desamueblado, -a **1** *pp de* **desamueblar**

2 *adj* unfurnished

desamueblar *vt* to remove *o* clear the furniture from

desandar [7] *vi* to go back over, retrace; **d. lo andado** to retrace one's steps

desangelado, -a *adj (casa, habitación)* drab; *(acto, celebración)* dull, uninspiring

desangramiento *nm* bleeding

desangrar **1** *vt* (**a**) *(sangrar)* to bleed (**b**) *(desaguar)* to drain (**c**) *Fig (empobrecer)* to bleed white

2 desangrarse *vpr* to lose (a lot of) blood

desanidar **1** *vi* to leave the nest

2 *vt Fig* to oust (**de** from)

desanimado, -a **1** *pp de* **desanimar**

2 *adj* (**a**) *(persona)* downhearted, dejected, discouraged (**b**) *(fiesta etc)* dull, lifeless

desanimar **1** *vt* to discourage, dishearten, depress

2 desanimarse *vpr* to lose heart, get depressed *o* discouraged

desánimo *nm (desaliento)* discouragement, dejection; *(depresión)* depression

desanudar *vt* (**a**) *(nudo)* to untie; *(paquete, corbata)* to undo (**b**) *Fig (desenmarañar)* to straighten *o* sort out

desapacible *adj (gen)* unpleasant, disagreeable; *(sonido)* harsh, discordant, jarring; *(tiempo)* nasty, unpleasant

desaparecer [46] **1** *vi* to disappear; **hacer d.** to cause to disappear, hide; *Fam Fig* **d. del mapa** to vanish off the face of the earth
2 *vt Am (persona)* = to detain extrajudicially during political repression and possibly kill

desaparecido, -a 1 *pp de* desaparecer
2 *adj* missing
3 *nm,f* missing person; **hay tres desaparecidos** there are three people missing

desaparición *nf* disappearance

desapasionadamente *adv* dispassionately, objectively, impartially

desapasionado, -a *adj* dispassionate, objective, impartial

desapego *nm* indifference, lack of affection

desapercibido, -a *adj* (**a**) *(inadvertido)* unnoticed; **pasar d.** to go unnoticed (**b**) *(desprevenido)* unprepared

desaplicado, -a 1 *adj* slack, lazy
2 *nm,f* lazybones *sing*, slacker

desapolillarse *vpr Fam Fig* to shake off the cobwebs

desaprensión *nf* unscrupulousness

desaprensivo, -a 1 *adj* unscrupulous
2 *nm,f* unscrupulous person

desapretar [3] **1** *vt* to loosen, make loose
2 desapretarse *vpr* to become loose

desaprobación *nf* disapproval

desaprobador, -a *adj* disapproving

desaprobar [63] *vt* (**a**) *(no aprobar)* to disapprove of (**b**) *(rechazar)* to reject; *(censurar)* to oppose

desaprovechado, -a 1 *pp de* desaprovechar
2 *adj* (**a**) *(desperdiciado)* wasted (**b**) *(persona) (lento)* slow; *(poco trabajador)* unproductive; **un estudiante d.** a student who could do better

desaprovechamiento *nm (de tiempo, ocasión, talento)* waste; *(de espacio, recursos, terreno)* failure to exploit fully

desaprovechar *vt* (**a**) *(tiempo, ocasión, talento)* to waste (**b**) *(espacio, recursos, terreno)* to underuse, fail to exploit fully

desarbolar *vt (nave)* to dismast

desarmable *adj* that can be taken to pieces, collapsible

desarmador *nm Méx* screwdriver

desarmar *vt* (**a**) *(desmontar)* to dismantle, take to pieces; **d. un motor** to strip down an engine (**b**) *Mil Pol* to disarm (**c**) *Fig* to disarm

desarme *nm* (**a**) *Mil Pol* disarmament ▫ **d. nuclear** nuclear disarmament (**b**) *(de una máquina)* dismantling

desarraigado, -a 1 *pp de* desarraigar
2 *adj* (**a**) *(árbol)* uprooted (**b**) *Fig (persona)* rootless, without roots, uprooted

desarraigar [38] *vt* (**a**) *(árbol, persona)* to uproot (**b**) *Fig (vicio)* to break the habit of
2 desarraigarse *vpr* (**a**) *(árbol etc)* to become uprooted (**b**) *Fig (persona)* to lift up one's roots

desarraigo *nm* (**a**) *(árbol, persona)* uprooting (**b**) *Fig (vicio)* breaking of a habit

desarrapado, -a *adj & nm,f véase* desharrapado, -a

desarreglado, -a 1 *pp de* desarreglar
2 *adj* (**a**) *(habitación)* untidy (**b**) *(persona)* untidy, slovenly

desarreglar *vt* (**a**) *(desordenar)* to untidy, make untidy, mess up; **los niños han desarreglado las camas** the children have untidied the beds; **te han desarreglado todo el peinado** they've messed your hair up (**b**) *(estropear)* to spoil, upset; **has desarreglado mis planes** you've upset my plans

desarreglo *nm (desorden)* disorder, mess; *(desorganización)* confusion

desarrollado, -a 1 *pp de* desarrollar
2 *adj* developed; **país d.** developed country

desarrollador, -a *nm,f Inform* developer; **d. de software** software developer

desarrollar 1 *vt* (**a**) *(gen)* to develop, evolve, expand; **d. el crecimiento** to promote growth; **d. la industria de un país** to develop a country's industry (**b**) *(desplegar)* to show; **d. un mapa** to unfold a map; *Fig* **d. una gran inteligencia** to show great intelligence (**c**) *Mat (ecuación)* to expand; *(problema)* to work out (**d**) *(explicar)* to expound; *(teoría)* to explain
2 desarrollarse *vpr* (**a**) *(crecer)* to develop; *(incrementar)* to grow (**b**) *(tener lugar)* to take place; **el concierto se desarrolló sin incidencias** the concert went off without incident; **la acción se desarrolla en la India** the story is set in India

desarrollismo *nm* = policy of development at all costs

desarrollo *nm* (**a**) *(desenvolvimiento, crecimiento)* development; *(incremento)* growth; **índice de d.** growth rate; **industria en pleno d.** flourishing industry; **países en vías de d.** developing countries ▫ **d. sostenible** sustainable development (**b**) *Mat (de ecuación)* expansion; *(de problema)* working out

desarropar 1 *vt (prendas)* to take off *o* remove
2 desarroparse *vpr (en la cama)* to throw off one's bed-clothes

desarrugar [38] *vt* to smooth out; *(ropa)* to remove the creases from; **desarruga el entrecejo** stop frowning ·

desarticulación *nf* (**a**) *Med* dislocation (**b**) *Fig (descoyuntar)* breaking up; **la d. de un comando terrorista** the smashing of a terrorist command group

desarticulado, -a 1 *pp de* desarticular
2 *adj* disjointed

desarticular *vt* (**a**) *Med* to dislocate (**b**) *(piezas)* to take to pieces (**c**) *Fig (descoyuntar)* to break up; *Pol* to smash; **d. un complot** to foil a plot

desaseado, -a 1 *adj* untidy, scruffy, unkempt
2 *nm,f* untidy person, scruff

desaseo *nm* untidiness, scruffiness, dirtiness

desasir [9] **1** *vt* to release, let go
2 desasirse *vpr* to get loose; **d. de** to free *o* rid oneself of

desasistido, -a *adj* **dejar a algn d.** to leave sb unattended (to)

desasnar *vt Fam* to teach good manners to, civilize

desasosegado, -a 1 *pp de* desasosegar
2 *adj* restless, anxious

desasosegar [43] **1** *vt (intranquilizar)* to make restless *o* uneasy; *(inquietar)* to disturb
2 desasosegarse *vpr* to become uneasy *o* restless

desasosiego *nm* restlessness, anxiety, uneasiness

desastrado, -a 1 *adj* (**a**) *(desaseado)* untidy, scruffy (**b**) *(sucio)* dirty
2 *nm,f* scruffy person

desastre *nm* (**a**) *(hecho)* disaster; **la excursión fue un d.** the outing was a disaster; **¡que d.!** what a mess! (**b**) *(persona)* disaster; **tu hermano es un d.** your brother's just hopeless; **un d. de persona** a dead loss, a hopeless case

desastroso, -a *adj* disastrous

desatado, -a 1 *pp de* desatar
2 *adj* (**a**) *(atadura, animal)* loose (**b**) *Fig (temperamento)* wild; *(pasiones)* uncontrolled

desatar 1 *vt* (**a**) *(nudo, lazo)* to untie; *(paquete)* to undo (**b**) *Fig (la lengua)* to loosen; *(pasiones)* to unleash

2 desatarse *vpr* (**a**) *(nudo, lazo)* to come undone; **d. los zapatos** to undo one's shoes; **el perro se desató** the dog broke loose; **por fin se le desató la lengua** he finally began to talk (**b**) *Fig (desencadenarse)* to break loose, explode; **se desató la tormenta** the storm broke; **su cólera se desató** she exploded with anger

desatascador *nm* (sink) plunger

desatascar [59] *vt (tubería)* to unblock, clear

desatención *nf* (**a**) *(falta de atención)* lack of attention; *(distracción)* neglect (**b**) *(descortesía)* impoliteness, discourtesy

desatender [64] *vt* to neglect, not pay attention to; **dejar a un cliente desatendido** to leave a customer unattended (to)

desatento, -a *adj* (**a**) *(distraído)* inattentive; *(descuidado)* careless (**b**) *(descortés)* impolite, discourteous

desatinado, -a 1 *pp de* **desatinar**
2 *adj* (**a**) *(tonto)* silly, foolish (**b**) *(imprudente)* rash, reckless
3 *nm,f (persona)* fool

desatinar 1 *vi (acto)* to act foolishly; *(hablando)* to talk nonsense
2 *vt* to exasperate, bewilder

desatino *nm* (**a**) *(disparate)* silly thing; *(hablando)* foolish remark; **cometer desatinos** to act foolishly; **decir desatinos** to talk nonsense (**b**) *(equivocación)* blunder, mistake

desatornillador *nm Andes CAm* screwdriver

desatornillar *vt* to unscrew

desatracar [59] *vi Náut* to cast off, unmoor

desatrancar [59] *vt* (**a**) *(tubería)* to unblock, clear (**b**) *(puerta)* to unbolt, unbar

desautorización *nf* (**a**) *(gen)* refusal to give permission *o* authority (**b**) *(de manifestación, huelga)* banning (**c**) *(desmentir)* denial (**d**) *(desacreditar)* discrediting

desautorizado, -a 1 *pp de* **desautorizar**
2 *adj* (**a**) *(gen)* unauthorized (**b**) *(manifestación, huelga)* banned, forbidden (**c**) *(desmentir)* denied (**d**) *(desacreditar)* discredited

desautorizar [14] *vt* (**a**) *(gen)* to disallow, declare unauthorized (**b**) *(manifestación, huelga)* to ban, forbid (**c**) *(desmentir)* to deny (**d**) *(desacreditar)* to discredit

desavenencia *nf* (**a**) *(desacuerdo)* disagreement, discord (**b**) *(riña)* quarrel, row

desavenido, -a 1 *pp de* **desavenir**
2 *adj* (**a**) *(desunido)* in disagreement (**b**) *(enemistado)* on bad terms

desavenir [69] **1** *vt* to cause to quarrel
2 desavenirse *vpr* to quarrel; **d. con algn** to fall out with sb, have a difference of opinion with sb

desaventajado, -a *adj* (**a**) *(persona)* at a disadvantage (**b**) *(situación)* disadvantageous, unfavourable

desayunar 1 *vi* to have breakfast; *Fml* to breakfast; **ya he desayunado** I have already had breakfast
2 *vt* to have for breakfast; **ayer desayuné café y tostadas** yesterday, I had coffee and toast for breakfast
3 desayunarse *vpr* (**a**) *(tomar desayuno)* to have breakfast (**b**) *Fig (enterarse)* to hear about sth for the first time; **¿no sabías que Pepe se había casado? — ahora me desayuno** didn't you know that Pepe had got married? — that's the first I've heard of it

desayuno *nm* breakfast

desazón *nf* (**a**) *(de gusto)* lack of flavour, tastelessness (**b**) *Med* discomfort (**c**) *Fig* anxiety, uneasiness

desazonado, -a 1 *pp de* **desazonar**
2 *adj* (**a**) *(gusto)* without flavour, tasteless (**b**) *Med* feeling unwell (**c**) *Fig* anxious, uneasy

desazonar 1 *vt* (**a**) *(gusto)* to make tasteless (**b**) *Fig* to cause anxiety to, worry
2 desazonarse *vpr Med* to feel unwell *o* off-colour *o US* off-color

desbancar [59] *vt* (**a**) *(en el juego)* to take the bank from (**b**) *Fig (suplantar)* to supplant, replace, oust

desbandada *nf, RP* **desbande** *nm* scattering; **a la d.** in great disorder; **hubo una d. general** everyone scattered

desbandarse *vpr* to scatter, disperse; **todos sus hijos se desbandaron después de su divorcio** all their children went their own way after their divorce

desbarajustar *vt (desordenar)* to throw into confusion *o* disorder; *(trastocar)* to upset

desbarajuste *nm* confusion, disorder; **hay tal d. que no encuentro tu libro** everything's in such a mess that I can't find your book

desbaratado, -a 1 *pp de* **desbaratar**
2 *adj* ruined, wrecked

desbaratamiento *nm* spoiling, wrecking

desbaratar *vt* (**a**) *(romper)* to spoil, ruin, wreck; **su llegada desbarató mis planes** his arrival messed up my plans (**b**) *Mil* to rout, throw into confusion

desbarrar *vi Esp (hablar)* to talk nonsense; *(hacer)* to do silly things

desbastar *vt* (**a**) *Carp (madera)* to rough plane; *Min (piedra, mineral)* to smooth down (**b**) *Fig (educar)* to refine

desbloquear *vt* (**a**) *(un sitio)* to lift the blockade on (**b**) *Econ (créditos, precios)* to unfreeze

desbloqueo *nm* (**a**) *(de un sitio)* lifting of the blockade (**b**) *Econ (de créditos, precios)* unfreezing

desbocado, -a 1 *pp de* **desbocarse**
2 *adj* (**a**) *(caballo)* runaway (**b**) *(inflación, tasa de desempleo)* soaring, rampant

desbocarse [59] *vpr* (**a**) *(caballo)* to bolt, run away (**b**) *(inflación, tasa de desempleo)* to soar, get out of control

desbordamiento *nm* (**a**) *(de río)* overflowing (**b**) *(de rabia, alegría)* outburst, outbreak, explosion

desbordante *adj* overflowing, bursting

desbordar 1 *vt* (**a**) *(cauce, ribera)* to overflow; **el agua desbordó el cauce del río** the water overflowed the banks of the river (**b**) *(sobrepasar)* to go beyond, surpass; **su actitud desborda mi comprensión** his attitude is beyond my comprehension
2 *vi* to overflow (**de** with), burst (**de** with)
3 desbordarse *vpr* (**a**) *(río)* to flood, burst its banks; *(bañera)* to overflow; **el café se está desbordando de la cafetera** the coffeepot is overflowing (**b**) *Fig* to burst; **su corazón se desborda de alegría** her heart is bursting with joy

desbravar 1 *vt (animal)* to tame; *(caballo)* to break in
2 desbravarse *vpr (animal)* to become tame; *(caballo)* to be broken in

desbrozar [14] *vt (área)* to clear of weeds *o* undergrowth; *(camino)* to clear

desbrozo *nm* clearing of weeds *o* undergrowth

descabalar *vt* to leave incomplete

descabalgar [38] *vi Equit* to dismount

descabellado, -a *adj* crazy, wild; **una idea descabellada** a crazy idea

descabezar [14] **1** *vt* (**a**) *(persona)* to behead, decapitate (**b**) *(planta, árbol)* to top (**c**) **d. un sueño** to take a nap
2 descabezarse *vpr Fam* to rack one's brains

descacharrante *adj Fam* hilarious

descacharrar *vt Fam (romper)* to break; *(estropear)* to ruin, mess up

descafeinado, -a *adj* (**a**) *(café)* decaffeinated (**b**) *Hum* watered-down, diluted

descafeinar [32] *vt* to decaffeinate

descalabrado, -a 1 *pp de* **descalabrar**
 2 *adj* (**a**) *(herido en la cabeza)* with a head injury, wounded in the head (**b**) *Fig* damaged, injured

descalabrar *vt* (**a**) *(herir en la cabeza)* to wound in the head (**b**) *Fig* to damage, harm

descalabro *nm* setback, misfortune

descalcificación *nf Med* decalcification

descalcificar [59] **1** *vt* to decalcify
 2 descalcificarse *vpr* to become decalcified

descalificación *nf* disqualification

descalificar [59] *vt* to disqualify

descalzar [14] **1** *vt (zapatos)* to take off
 2 descalzarse *vpr* to take one's shoes off

descalzo, -a 1 *adj* (**a**) barefoot, barefooted; **ir d.** to go barefoot (**b**) *Rel* barefoot
 2 *nm,f Rel (hombre)* barefoot monk; *(mujer)* barefoot nun

descamación *nf Med* desquamation, flaking; *(pelarse)* peeling

descamarse *vpr Med* to desquamate, flake off; *(pelarse)* to peel off

descambiar *vt Com* to exchange

descaminado, -a 1 *pp de* **descaminar**
 2 *adj* **andar** o **ir d.** *(equivocado)* to be on the wrong track; *(caminante, excursionista)* to be heading in the wrong direction

descaminar 1 *vt* (**a**) *(malas compañías)* to lead astray (**b**) *(guía)* **los desencaminó** he took them the wrong way
 2 descaminarse *vpr* (**a**) *(por malas compañías)* to go astray (**b**) *(en una excursión)* to go the wrong way

descamisado, -a 1 *adj* (**a**) *(sin camisa)* without a shirt, shirtless (**b**) *Fig* wretched, poor
 2 *nm* (**a**) *(pobre)* wretch, poor person (**b**) **descamisados** *(en Argentina)* supporters of Perón

descampado, -a 1 *adj* open, without trees o buildings
 2 *nm* open space, open field; **en d.** in the open country

descansado, -a 1 *pp de* **descansar**
 2 *adj* (**a**) *(persona)* rested; **estar d.** to be rested (**b**) *(tranquilo)* restful; **una vida descansada** a peaceful life

descansar 1 *vi* (**a**) *(gen)* to rest, have a rest; *(corto tiempo)* to take a break; **necesito d. un rato** I need to have a little rest (**b**) *(dormir)* to sleep; **hasta mañana y que descanses** good night and sleep well; *Euf* **que en paz descanse** may he o she rest in peace (**c**) *(confiar)* to trust (**sobre** in), confide (**sobre** on) (**d**) *Arquit (apoyarse)* to rest (**sobre** on), be supported (**sobre** by); *(basarse)* to be based (**sobre** on) (**e**) *Agr* to lie fallow
 2 *vt* to rest; **descansa los pies sobre el cojín** rest your feet on the cushion; *Mil* **¡descansen armas!** order arms!

descansillo *nm Arquit* landing

descanso *nm* (**a**) *(reposo)* rest, break; **me voy a tomar un día de d.** I'm going to take a day off; **sin d.** without a break (**b**) *Cin Teat* interval; *Dep* half-time, interval (**c**) *(alivio)* relief; **¡qué d.!** what a relief! (**d**) *(rellano)* landing (**e**) *Mil* **¡d.!** at ease!

descapotable *adj & nm Aut* convertible

descaradamente *adv* impudently, shamelessly

descarado, -a 1 *adj* *(insolente)* cheeky, insolent; *(desvergonzado)* shameless; **es un robo d.** it's an absolute rip-off
 2 *nm,f* cheeky person, scoundrel

descarga *nf* (**a**) *(de mercancías)* unloading (**b**) *Elec* shock
 ❑ **d. eléctrica** electric shock (**c**) *(arma)* firing, discharge; **d. cerrada** volley

descargadero *nm* wharf, unloading dock

descargador, -a *nm,f* **d. de muelle** docker, stevedore

descargar [38] **1** *vt* (**a**) *(mercancías, barco)* to unload (**b**) *Fig (aliviar)* to relieve (**de** of) (**c**) *Elec* to discharge; **d. la batería** to run down the battery (**d**) *(arma) (disparar)* to fire; *(vaciar)* to unload; *(golpe)* to deal; **descargó un golpe sobre el árbitro** he dealt the referee a blow (**e**) *Jur (absolver)* to absolve (**de** of), acquit (**de** of) (**f**) *Inform* to download
 2 *vi Meteor (nubes)* to burst
 3 descargarse *vpr* (**a**) *(de responsabilidad)* to free oneself (**b**) *Jur (excusa)* to clear oneself (**c**) *Elec (batería)* to go flat

descargo *nm* (**a**) *(gen)* unloading (**b**) *Com* credit (**c**) *Jur* discharge, acquittal; **en su d.** in his defence; **testigo de d.** witness for the defence

descarnado, -a 1 *pp de* **descarnar**
 2 *adj* (**a**) *(delgado)* lean (**b**) *Fig* harsh, unadorned; **hizo una descripción descarnada del accidente** he gave a straightforward description of the accident

descarnar *vt* (**a**) *(hueso)* to strip the flesh from (**b**) *Fig* to lay bare

descaro *nm* cheek, impudence, nerve; **tuvo el d. de llamarme por teléfono** he had the nerve to phone me; **¡qué d.!** what a cheek!

descarriado, -a 1 *pp de* **descarriar**
 2 *adj (animal)* stray; *Fig* **ser la oveja descarriada** to be the lost sheep

descarriar [32] **1** *vt* to lead astray, put on the wrong road
 2 descarriarse *vpr* to go astray, lose one's way

descarrilamiento *nm Ferroc* derailment

descarrilar *vi Ferroc* to run off the rails, go off the rails, be derailed

descartable *Am* **1** *adj (pañal, jeringuilla, envase)* disposable
 2 *nm (pañal)* disposable
 3 *nf (jeringuilla)* disposable

descartar 1 *vt* to discard, reject, rule out; **esto queda descartado** this is out
 2 descartarse *vpr Naipes* to discard, throw away

descarte *nm* rejection, casting aside; *Naipes* cards thrown away

descascarillarse *vpr* to chip, peel, flake off

descastado, -a 1 *adj* ungrateful
 2 *nm,f* ungrateful person

descatalogar *vt (libro, disco)* **lo han descatalogado** they've dropped it from their catalogue

descendencia *nf* descendants *pl* , offspring; **morir sin d.** to die without issue

descendente *adj* descending, downward

descender [64] **1** *vt* (**a**) *(valor, temperatura, nivel)* to fall, drop (**b**) *(bajar)* to descend
 2 *vi* (**a**) *(valor, temperatura, nivel)* to fall, drop (**b**) *(de vehículo)* **d. de un avión** to get off a plane; **d. de un coche** to get out of a car

descendiente *nm,f* descendant, offspring

descendimiento *nm* descent, taking down, lowering

descenso *nm* (**a**) *(de una altura)* descent; *(en la temperatura)* fall, drop (**b**) *Fig* lowering, decline (**c**) *Dep* relegation

descentrado, -a 1 *pp de* **descentrar**
 2 *adj* (**a**) *(geométricamente)* off-centre, off-beam (**b**) *Fig* all-at-sea, disorientated

descentralización *nf* decentralization

descentralizar [14] *vt* to decentralize

descentrar *vt* (**a**) *(geométricamente)* to knock off centre (**b**) *(desconcentrar)* to distract

desceñir [47] *vt (cinturón)* to loosen

descepar *vt (cepa)* to uproot; *(plantas)* to pull up by the roots

descerebrado, -a *Esp Andes RP Fam* **1** *adj* moronic, brainless
2 *nm,f* moron, halfwit

descerrajar *vt* (**a**) *(la cerradura)* to force, break open (**b**) *Fam (tiro)* to fire

descifrable *adj* decipherable; *(letra)* legible

desciframiento *nm* deciphering, decoding

descifrar *vt* (**a**) *(mensaje)* to decipher, decode (**b**) *(misterio)* to solve; *(motivos, causas)* to figure out

desclasificar [59] *vt* to declassify

desclavar *vt* to remove the nails from; **d. un cuadro** to take down a picture

descoagulante *adj* decoagulating

descoagularse *vpr* to decoagulate

descocado, -a **1** *pp de* **descocarse**
2 *adj Fam* brazen, cheeky

descocarse [59] *vpr* to get brazen *o* cheeky

descoco *nm Fam* cheek, boldness

descodificador *nm* decoder

descodificar [59] *vt* to decode

descojonado, -a **1** *pp de* **descojonarse**
2 *adj Vulg* (**a**) *(de risa)* **estábamos descojonados de risa** we pissed ourselves laughing (**b**) *(cansado)* knackered

descojonante *adj Vulg* bloody funny; **una película d.** a bloody funny film

descojonarse *vpr Vulg* to piss oneself laughing

descojono *nm*, **descojone** *nm muy Fam* **ser un d.** to be a scream, make one wet oneself

descolgar [16] **1** *vt (cuadro, cortinas)* to take down; **d. el teléfono** to pick up the telephone; **el teléfono está descolgado** the telephone is off the hook
2 **descolgarse** *vpr* (**a**) *(bajar)* to let oneself down, slide down (**b**) *Fam* to appear suddenly *o* unexpectedly, turn up (**c**) *Fam (decir)* to come out with

descollante *adj* outstanding

descollar [63] *vi* to stand out; **la iglesia descuella sobre las casas del pueblo** the church towers above the houses in the village; *Fig* **descuella por su inteligencia** her intelligence makes her stand out

descolocar [59] *vt* (**a**) *(objeto)* to put out of place; **no descoloques los papeles** don't disturb the papers (**b**) *Ind* to lay off

descolonización *nf* decolonization

descolonizar [14] *vt* to decolonize

descoloramiento *nm (desteñir)* fading; *(perder color)* discolouration, *US* discoloration

descolorar *vt (desteñir)* to fade; *(perder color)* to discolour, *US* discolor

descolorido, -a *adj (desteñido)* faded; *(que pierde color)* discoloured, *US* discolored

descombrar *vt* to clear of debris

descomedido, -a **1** *pp de* **descomedirse**
2 *adj Esp Fml* (**a**) *(descortés)* rude, insolent (**b**) *(desproporcionado)* excessive, disproportionate

descomedimiento *Esp Fml nm* rudeness, insolence

descomedirse [47] *vpr Esp Fml* to be rude *o* disrespectful

descompasado, -a *adj* **llevaban un ritmo d.** they weren't playing in time

descompensar *vt* to unbalance

descomponer [50] (*pp* **descompuesto**) **1** *vt* (**a**) *(corromper)* to rot, decompose (**b**) *(separar)* to break down; *Mat* to split up (**c**) *Téc* to put out of order (**d**) *(desordenar)* to disturb, unsettle, upset (**e**) *Fís* to resolve; **d. una fuerza** to resolve a force (**f**) *Mat* to factorize
2 **descomponerse** *vpr (turbarse)* to become upset; *(perder la paciencia)* to lose one's temper, lose control

descomposición *nf* (**a**) *(putrefacción)* decomposition, rotting, decay (**b**) *(separación)* separation, analysis; *Téc* breakdown (**c**) *Esp Fam (diarrea)* looseness of the bowels, diarrhoea, *US* diarrhea (**d**) *Mat* factorizing

descompostura *nf* (**a**) *(desaliño)* slovenliness, untidiness (**b**) *(falta de pudor)* insolence, lack of respect, rudeness (**c**) *Méx RP (avería)* breakdown

descompresión *nf también Inform* decompression

descompresor *nm Téc* decompressor

descomprimir *vt* to decompress, depressurize

descompuesto, -a **1** *pp de* **descomponer**
2 *adj* (**a**) *(putrefacto)* rotten, decomposed, decayed (**b**) *Méx RP (estropeado)* out of order, broken down (**c**) *(encolerizado)* furious (**d**) **estar d.** to have diarrhoea *o US* diarrhea (**e**) *Fig (inmodesto)* brazen (**f**) *Andes CAm PRico (borracho)* drunk

descomunal *adj* huge, massive

desconcentrar **1** *vt* to distract
2 **desconcentrarse** *vpr* to get distracted

desconcertado, -a **1** *pp de* **desconcertar**
2 *adj* disconcerted; **estar d.** to be disconcerted *o* thrown

desconcertante *adj* disconcerting

desconcertar [3] **1** *vt* to disconcert; **su respuesta lo desconcertó** her answer threw him
2 **desconcertarse** *vpr* to be thrown *o* bewildered

desconchado, -a **1** *pp de* **desconchar**
2 *adj (pintura, yeso)* peeling, flaking; *(loza)* chipped

desconchar *vt* to strip off
2 **desconcharse** *vpr* to flake off, chip

desconchinflar *Méx Fam* **1** *vt* to wreck, bust
2 **desconchinflarse** *vpr* to pack up, *Br* pack in

desconchón *nm (acción)* flaking, chipping, peeling; *(marca)* bare patch, chip

desconcierto *nm* disorder, chaos, confusion, bewilderment; **sembrar el d.** cause confusion

desconectado, -a **1** *pp de* **desconectar**
2 *adj* disconnected, cut off

desconectar *vt* to disconnect, cut off, switch off, unplug

desconexión *nf* disconnection

desconfiado, -a **1** *pp de* **desconfiar**
2 *adj* distrustful, wary, suspicious
3 *nm,f* suspicious *o* wary person

desconfianza *nf* distrust, mistrust, suspicion

desconfiar [32] *vi* to distrust (**de** -), mistrust (**de** -), be suspicious (**de** of)

descongelar *vt (nevera)* to defrost; *(créditos)* to unfreeze; *(comida)* to thaw out

descongestión *nf (gen)* relieving of congestion; *(de la nariz)* clearing

descongestionar *vt (gen)* to relieve of congestion; *(nariz)* to clear

desconocedor, -a *adj* unaware (**de** of)

desconocer [19] *vt* (**a**) *(no saber)* not to know, be unaware of; **desconozco su paradero** I don't know where he is (**b**) *(no reconocer)* not to recognize; *(fingir)* to ignore, pretend not to know; **me desconoció** he ignored me (**c**) *(rechazar)* to disown

desconocido, -a 1 *pp de* **desconocer**
  2 *adj* unknown, unfamiliar; *Fig (irreconocible)* unrecognizable; **Alan estaba d.** Alan was unrecognizable; **lo d.** the unknown; **una persona desconocida** a stranger
  3 *nm,f* stranger

desconocimiento *nm* ignorance, lack of knowledge

desconsideración *nf* lack of consideration, inconsideration, thoughtlessness

desconsiderado, -a 1 *pp de* **desconsiderar**
  2 *adj* inconsiderate, thoughtless, rash
  3 *nm,f* inconsiderate *o* thoughtless *o* rash person

desconsolado, -a 1 *pp de* **desconsolar**
  2 *adj* disconsolate, grief-stricken, dejected

desconsolar [63] **1** *vt* to distress, grieve
  2 desconsolarse *vpr* to be distressed *o* full of grief

desconsuelo *nm* grief, sorrow

descontado, -a 1 *pp de* **descontar**
  2 *adj Fam* **dar por d.** to take for granted; **por d.** needless to say, of course

descontaminación *nf* decontamination

descontaminar *vt* to decontaminate

descontar [63] *vt* **(a)** *(rebajar)* to discount, deduct; *(no incluir)* to leave out, disregard; **descontando los gastos** excluding expenses **(b)** *Dep (añadir)* to add on; **el árbitro descontó las perdidas de tiempo** the referee added on time for stoppages

descontentadizo, -a *adj* hard to please, fussy

descontentar *vt* to make unhappy *o* dissatisfied

descontento, -a 1 *adj* discontented, unhappy, dissatisfied
  2 *nm* discontent, dissatisfaction

descontrol *nm Fam* lack of control; **había un d. total** it was absolute chaos

descontrolado, -a 1 *pp de* **descontrolarse**
  2 *adj* uncontrolled, haywire; **estar d.** to be out of control

descontrolarse *vpr* to lose control

desconvocar [59] *vt* to call off, cancel

descorazonador, -a *adj* disheartening

descorazonar 1 *vt* to dishearten, discourage
  2 descorazonarse *vpr* to lose heart, become discouraged

descorchador *nm* corkscrew

descorchar *vt* to uncork

descorche *nm* uncorking

descornar [63] **1** *vt* to remove the horns from
  2 descornarse *vpr Esp Fam* **(a)** *(pensar)* to *Br* rack *o US* cudgel one's brains **(b)** *(trabajar)* to slave (away), toil

descorrer 1 *vt (gen)* to draw back; *(cortina)* to open; **d. el cerrojo** to unbolt the door
  2 *vi (escurrir)* to drip, trickle

descortés *(pl* **descorteses)** *adj* rude, impolite, discourteous

descortesía *nf* discourtesy, rudeness, impoliteness

descortezar [14] *vt* **(a)** *(árbol)* to bark, remove the bark from **(b)** *Culin* to peel, remove the crust from

descoser 1 *vt Cost* to unstitch, unpick
  2 descoserse *vpr (a) Cost* to come unstitched; *Fig* to start to speak **(b)** *Fam Fig* to fart

descosido *nm* **(a)** *(roto)* open seam; *Fam* **como un d.** like mad, wildly **(b)** *Fig (persona)* babbler

descoyuntar *vt Med (hueso)* to dislocate; *Fam* **estoy descoyuntado** I am dead beat

descrédito *nm* disrepute, discredit; **caer en d.** to fall into disrepute

descreído, -a *adj* disbelieving, unbelieving
  2 *nm,f* disbeliever, unbeliever

descreimiento *nm* disbelief

descremado, -a 1 *pp de* **descremar**
  2 *adj* skimmed; **leche descremada** skim *o* skimmed milk; **yogur d.** low-fat yoghurt

descremar *vt (leche)* to skim

describir *(pp* **descrito)** *vt* **(a)** *(explicar)* to describe **(b)** *(trazar)* to trace

descripción *nf* description, describing, tracing

descriptible *adj* describable

descriptivo, -a *adj* descriptive

descrito, -a 1 *pp de* **describir**
  2 *adj* described

descruzar [14] *vt (piernas)* to uncross; *(brazos)* to unfold

descuajaringar [38] **1** *vt Fam* to pull *o* take to pieces; *Fig* **estoy descuajaringado** I am on my last legs
  2 descuajaringarse *vpr Fam* **d. de risa** to crack up, fall about laughing

descuartizamiento *nm (de persona)* quartering; *(de cosas)* carving up, cutting into pieces

descuartizar [14] *vt (persona)* to quarter; *(cosas)* to cut up, cut into pieces; *Fam Fig (personas, opiniones)* to pull to pieces, tear apart

descubierta *nf Mil* reconnaissance, reconnoitring, scouting

descubierto, -a 1 *pp de* **descubrir**
  2 *adj* **(a)** *(sin cubierta)* open, uncovered; **a cara** *o* **a cuerpo d.** openly; **a cielo d.** in the open; *(sin sombrero)* bareheaded **(b)** *(encontrado)* discovered
  3 *nm* **(a)** *Fin* overdraft; **estar al d.** to be overdrawn, be in the red **(b)** **dormir al d.** to sleep out in the open; **poner al d.** to uncover, expose, bring out into the open; **quedar en d.** to be exposed, come out into the open

descubridor, -a *nm,f* discoverer

descubrimiento *nm* discovery

descubrir *(pp* **descubierto) 1** *vt* **(a)** *(gen)* to discover; *(conspiración)* to uncover; *(petróleo)* to find; *(remedio)* to discover **(b)** *(enterarse)* to find out about, discover **(c)** *(delatar)* to give away; **no me descubras a la policía** don't tell the police about me **(d)** *(divisar)* to make out, see **(e)** *(destapar)* to uncover; **el rey descubrió una placa comemorativa** the king unveiled a commemorative plaque
  2 descubrirse *vpr* **(a)** *(quitarse el sombrero)* to take off one's hat **(b)** *Box* to lower one's guard

descuento *nm Com* discount, reduction, deduction; **con d.** at a discount

descuidado, -a 1 *pp de* **descuidar**
  2 *adj* **(a)** *(desaseado)* untidy, neglected **(b)** *(negligente)* careless, negligent **(c)** *(desprevenido)* off one's guard

descuidar 1 *vt* to neglect, overlook
  2 *vi* to be careless; **descuida, voy yo** don't worry, I'll go; **descuide usted** don't worry, have no fear
  3 descuidarse *vpr* to be careless; **como te descuides, llegarás tarde** if you don't watch out, you'll be late

descuidero *nm* pickpocket

descuido *nm* **(a)** *(falta de cuidado)* negligence, carelessness, neglect **(b)** *(distracción)* oversight, slip, mistake **(c)** **al d.** casually, nonchalantly; **por d.** inadvertently, by mistake

desde *adv* **(a)** *(tiempo)* since; **d. ahora** from now on; **¿d. cuándo?** since when?; **d. el lunes** since Monday; **d. entonces** since then, from then on; **d. hace un año** for a year; **d. siempre** always **(b)** *(lugar)* from; **d. aquí** from here; **d. arriba/abajo** from above/below; **d. mi casa hasta la**

tuya hay una buena tirada it's a bit of a way from my house to yours (**c**) **d. luego** *(como coletilla)* well, really!; **d. luego no se puede confiar en nadie hoy en día** really, you can't trust anyone these days (**d**) **d. luego** *(como respuesta)* of course; **¿me puedes prestar tu coche?** — **d. luego** can you lend me your car? — yes, of course

desdecir [51] *(pp* **desdicho)** **1** *vi* **d. de** *(desmerecer)* to be unworthy of; *(no cuadrar con)* not to go with, clash with
2 desdecirse *vpr* to go back on one's word

desdén *nm* disdain, contempt, scorn

desdentado, -a 1 *adj* toothless
2 *nm Zool* edentate

desdeñable *adj* (**a**) *(despreciable)* contemptible, despicable (**b**) *(sin importancia)* negligible, insignificant; **su fortuna no es nada d.** he has a considerable fortune

desdeñar 1 *vt* (**a**) *(despreciar)* to disdain, scorn (**b**) *(rechazar)* to turn down (**c**) *(no tener en cuenta)* to ignore
2 desdeñarse *vpr* to disdain to, not deign to

desdeñoso, -a *adj* disdainful, scornful, contemptuous

desdibujado, -a 1 *pp de* **desdibujar**
2 *adj* blurred, faint, shadowy

desdibujar 1 *vt* to blur
2 desdibujarse *vpr* to become blurred *o* faint

desdicha *nf* misfortune, adversity, misery; **por d.** unfortunately; **para colmo de desdichas** to top it all

desdichadamente *adv* unfortunately

desdichado, -a 1 *adj* unfortunate, unlucky, wretched
2 *nm,f* poor devil, wretch; *Fam* **es un d.** he's a poor soul

desdigo *indic pres véase* **desdecir**

desdoblamiento *nm* (**a**) *(enderezamiento)* straightening, unfolding (**b**) *(duplicación)* splitting; **d. de personalidad** split personality

desdoblar *vt* (**a**) *(enderezar)* to straighten (**b**) *(extender)* to unfold (**c**) *(duplicar)* to split; **van a d. esta carretera** they're going to turn this road into a *Br* dual carriageway *o US* divided highway

desdoro *nm* tarnishing; *Fig* blot, stain, dishonour, *US* dishonor

desdramatizar [14] *vt* to play down

deseable *adj* desirable

deseado, -a 1 *pp de* **desear**
2 *adj* desired

desear *vt (con pasión)* to desire; *(querer)* to want; *(anhelar)* to wish (for); **deja mucho que d.** it leaves a lot to be desired; **estoy deseando que vengas** I'm looking forward to your coming; **¿qué desea?** can I help you?; **te deseo lo mejor** I wish you all the very best

desecación *nf (gen)* drying; *Quím* desiccation; **la d. de un pantano** the draining of a marsh

desecar [59] *vt* to desiccate, dry up; **d. una laguna** to drain a lagoon

desechable *adj* disposable, throw-away

desechar *vt* (**a**) *(tirar)* to discard, throw out *o* away; **desechó todas las piezas defectuosas** he threw away all the defective pieces; *Prov* **lo que uno desecha, otro lo ruega** one man's meat is another man's poison (**b**) *(renunciar)* to turn down, refuse; *(idea, proyecto)* to drop, discard; **debería d. esas locas ideas que se le han metido en la cabeza** he should forget all these madcap ideas; **desecha cualquier consejo que pueda darle yo** he brushes aside any advice I give him; **d. esa oferta sería un error** to turn down this offer would be a mistake; **tuvimos que d. el proyecto** we had to drop the plan

desecho *nm* (**a**) *(gen)* reject; **ropa de d.** castoff; *Fig* **es un d. de la sociedad** he is a social outcast (**b**) **desechos** *(basura) Br* rubbish, *US* garbage, trash; *(residuos)* waste

products; **d. radioactivos** radioactive waste (**c**) *CAm Carib (tabaco)* class A tobacco

desembalaje *nm* unpacking

desembalar *vt* to unpack

desembarazado, -a 1 *pp de* **desembarazar**
2 *adj* free and easy, uninhibited, nonchalant

desembarazar [14] **1** *vt (librar)* to free, disencumber; *(vaciar)* to empty
2 desembarazarse *vpr (librarse de)* to get rid (**de** of), rid oneself (**de** of); **intentaré desembarazarme de él lo antes posible** I'll try and get rid of him as soon as possible

desembarazo *nm (desenvoltura)* ease, nonchalance; *(seguridad en sí mismo)* self-assurance, self-confidence

desembarcadero *nm Náut* landing stage, pier, wharf

desembarcar [59] **1** *vt (mercancías)* to unload; *(personas)* to disembark, put ashore
2 *vi* (**a**) *(de barco, avión)* to disembark (**b**) *Am (de autobús, tren)* **d. (de)** to get off
3 desembarcarse *vpr Am* to disembark, land, go ashore

desembarco *nm (mercancías)* landing, unloading; *(personas)* disembarkation

desembargar [38] *vt Jur* to lift *o* raise an embargo

desembargo *nm Jur* lifting *o* raising of an embargo

desembarque *nm véase* **desembarco**

desembarrancar [59] *vt Náut (un barco)* to refloat

desembocadura *nf* (**a**) *(de río)* mouth, outlet (**b**) *(salida)* exit, way out

desembocar [59] *vi (río)* to flow (**en** into); *(calle)* to lead (**en** into), end (**en** at); *Fig* to lead (**en** to), end up (**en** in); **el Ebro desemboca en el Mediterráneo** the river Ebro flows into the Mediterranean; *Fig* **las actuales tensiones internacionales pueden d. en un conflicto armado** current international tension may lead to armed conflict

desembolsar *vt* to pay out

desembolso *nm* expenditure, expense, outgoings *pl*; payment; **d. inicial** down payment

desembozar [14] *vt* to unmask, uncover; *Fig* to uncover, bring out into the open

desembragar [38] *vi Aut* to release *o* disengage the clutch, declutch

desembrague *nm Aut* declutching; *Téc* disengaging

desembrollar *vt Fam* (**a**) *(aclarar)* to clarify, clear up (**b**) *(desenredar)* to disentangle

desembuchar *vt* (**a**) *(aves)* to disgorge (**b**) *Fig (decir)* to blurt out; *Fam Fig* **¡desembucha!** come out with it!

desemejanza *nf* dissimilarity, difference

desempacar [59] *vt* to unpack

desempachar *vt* to relieve from indigestion

desempacho *nm* assurance, self-confidence

desempalmar *vt* to disconnect

desempañar *vt (un cristal)* to wipe the condensation from; *Aut* to demist

desempapelar *vt* (**a**) *(un paquete)* to unwrap (**b**) *(una pared)* to strip

desempaquetar *vt* to unpack, unwrap

desemparejado, -a 1 *pp de* **desemparejar**
2 *adj* without a partner; **un calcetín d.** an odd sock

desemparejar *vt* to unmatch, separate

desempatar *vt Dep* to play a deciding match, play off a tie; *(superar)* to take the lead

desempate *nm Dep* breaking the tie, play-off; **el gol del d.** the deciding goal; **partido de d.** play-off, deciding match

desempedrar [3] *vt* to remove the paving (stones) from, unpave; *Fig* **d. la calle** to roam *o* walk the streets

desempeñar 1 *vt* (**a**) *(recuperar lo empeñado)* to take out of pawn, redeem; **d. a algn** to pay sb's debts (**b**) *(cumplir)* *(obligación)* to discharge, fulfil, *US* fulfill, carry out; *(cargo)* to fill, hold, occupy; **d. un cargo** to hold a post (**c**) *Teat* to play; **desempeña el papel del bufón** he plays the part of the fool

    2 desempeñarse *vpr (cancelar las deudas)* to get out of debt

desempeño *nm* (**a**) *(de lo empeñado)* redeeming; *(deuda)* payment (**b**) *(obligaciones)* carrying out, fulfilment, *US* fulfillment (**c**) *Teat* performance, playing, acting

desempleado, -a 1 *adj* unemployed, out of work
    2 *nm,f* unemployed person; **los desempleados** the unemployed

desempleo *nm* unemployment; **cobrar el d.** to be on the dole

desempolvar *vt* (**a**) *(mueble, jarrón)* to dust (**b**) *(volver a usar)* to unearth, dig up; *Fig* **d. recuerdos** to revive memories

desenamorarse *vpr* to fall out of love (**de** with)

desencadenamiento *nm (de polémica, conflicto)* triggering; **causar el d. de algo** *(accidente, crisis)* to bring sth about; *(conflicto)* to trigger *o* spark off sth

desencadenante 1 *adj* **los factores desencadenantes de …** the factors which brought about …
    2 *nm* **el d. de la tragedia/guerra** what brought about the tragedy/war

desencadenar 1 *vt* (**a**) *(preso, perro)* to unchain (**b**) *(accidente, polémica)* to give rise to; *(pasión, furia)* to unleash; *(conflicto)* to trigger, spark off
    2 desencadenarse *vpr* (**a**) *(preso)* to unchain oneself, get out of one's chains (**b**) *(pasiones)* to erupt; *(polémica, guerra)* to break out (**c**) *(tormenta)* to burst

desencajado, -a 1 *pp de* **desencajar**
    2 *adj (descolocado)* out of place, out of joint; *Fig* **rostro d. por la ira** face distorted by anger

desencajar 1 *vt* to take apart, remove
    2 desencajarse *vpr* (**a**) *(piezas)* to come apart (**b**) *(persona)* to look wild; *(cara)* to become distorted

desencajonar *vt* to take out of a box, unpack

desencallar *vt* to refloat

desencaminar *vt véase* **descaminar**

desencantamiento *nm* disenchantment

desencantar *vt* (**a**) *(desembrujar)* to disenchant (**b**) *(decepcionar)* to disappoint, disillusion

desencanto *nm* disappointment, disillusionment

desencapotarse *vpr (cielo)* to clear

desencarcelar *vt* to release (from prison), free

desenchufar *vt* to unplug, disconnect

desencofrar *vt Constr* to remove the shuttering from

desencolar *vt* to unstick

desenconarse *vpr Fig* to cool off, calm down

desencuadernar 1 *vt* to unbind
    2 desencuadernarse *vpr* to come unbound

desencuentro *nm (en una cita)* failure to meet up; *(desacuerdo)* disagreement

desenfadadamente *adv* casually

desenfadado, -a *adj* carefree, free and easy; **en un tono d.** in a carefree way

desenfado *nm (seguridad en uno mismo)* assurance, self-confidence; *(desenvoltura)* ease, openness

desenfocado, -a 1 *pp de* **desenfocar**
    2 *adj* (**a**) *Fot* out of focus (**b**) *Fig (problema, asunto)* wrongly approached

desenfocar [59] *vt* (**a**) *Fot* to get out of focus (**b**) *Fig* to distort

desenfoque *nm* lack of focus

desenfrenado, -a 1 *pp de* **desenfrenar**
    2 *adj* frantic, uncontrolled; *(vicios, pasiones)* unbridled; **apetito d.** insatiable appetite

desenfrenar 1 *vt Equit* to unbridle
    2 desenfrenarse *vpr (pasiones, vicios)* to let loose, go wild

desenfreno *nm (vicio)* licentiousness, debauchery, unrestraint; *(pasiones)* unleashing

desenfundar *vt* (**a**) *(sacar)* to draw *o* pull out (**b**) *(destapar)* to uncover

desenganchar *vt* (**a**) *(soltar)* to set loose, unhook (**b**) *(desunir)* to uncouple

desengañar 1 *vt* (**a**) **d. a algn** *(de error)* to open sb's eyes, put sb wise (**b**) *(quitar ilusión)* to disillusion
    2 desengañarse *vpr* (**a**) *(dejar de engañarse)* **desengáñate** stop kidding yourself (**b**) *(perder ilusión)* to become disillusioned

desengaño *nm* disappointment; **llevarse** *o* **sufrir un d. con algo** to be disappointed in sth

desengrasar *vt* to degrease, remove the grease from

desenhebrar *vt (una aguja)* to unthread

desenlace *nm* (**a**) *(resultado)* result, outcome; **un feliz d.** a happy end (**b**) *Cin Teat Lit* ending, dénouement

desenlazar [14] *vt* to untie, undo; *Fig* to unravel, solve

desenmarañar *vt (pelo)* to untangle; *(un problema)* to unravel, clear up; *(un asunto)* to sort out

desenmascarar 1 *vt* to unmask
    2 desenmascararse *vpr* (**a**) *(descubrirse)* to take off one's mask (**b**) *Fig (conocerse)* to be revealed, show up

desenredar 1 *vt* to untangle, disentangle
    2 desenredarse *vpr* to get out of, extricate oneself from

desenrollar *vt* to unroll, unwind

desenroscar [59] *vt* to unscrew, uncoil

desensillar *vt (un caballo)* to unsaddle

desentenderse [64] *vpr* (**a**) *(afectar ignorancia)* to ignore (**de** -), pretend not to hear *o* know (**de** about); **se desentiende de nuestros problemas** he ignores our problems (**b**) *(no ocuparse)* to have nothing to do with; **se desentendió del asunto** he wanted nothing to do with the matter

desentendido, -a *nm,f* **hacerse el d.** to pretend one hasn't noticed/heard

desenterrar [3] *vt* (**a**) *(un cadáver)* to exhume, disinter; **d. un tesoro escondido** to dig up a hidden treasure (**b**) *Fig (traer a la memoria)* to revive, recall

desentonar *vi* (**a**) *Mús* to sing out of tune, be out of tune (**b**) *(contrastar)* not to match; **las cortinas desentonan del resto** the curtains don't match the rest (**c**) *(estar fuera de lugar)* to be out of place, seem wrong; **sus modales desentonan en tan selecta compañía** his manners seem out of place in such refined company

desentrañar *vt (destripar)* to disembowel; *Fig (un problema)* to unravel, get to the bottom of, figure out

desentrenado, -a *adj* out of training *o* shape

desentumecer [46] *vt* to put the feeling back into; **d. las piernas** to stretch one's legs

desenvainar *vt (espada)* to draw

desenvoltura *nf* (**a**) *(soltura)* grace, ease (**b**) *(naturalidad)* confidence (**c**) *(desvergüenza)* boldness, insolence

desenvolver [41] *(pp* **desenvuelto**) **1** *vt* to unwrap
    2 desenvolverse *vpr* (**a**) *(manejarse)* to manage, cope;

se **desenvuelve muy bien** he copes very well (**b**) *(desarrollarse)* to go, develop; **la entrevista se desenvolvió con normalidad** the interview went (off) smoothly

desenvuelto, -a 1 *pp de* **desenvolver**
 2 *adj* (**a**) *(comportamiento, movimiento)* natural, easy; *(al hablar)* fluent; **actitud desenvuelta** naturalness (**b**) *(hábil)* resourceful, quick (**c**) *(ágil)* graceful, deft

deseo *nm* desire, wish; **buenos deseos** good intentions; **formular un d.** to make a wish; **se cumplieron sus deseos** his wishes came true

deseoso, -a *adj* eager, desirous, anxious; **estar d. de amistad** to long *o* yearn for friendship; **estar d. de hacer algo** be eager to do sth

desequilibrado, -a 1 *pp de* **desequilibrar**
 2 *adj* unbalanced, off balance
 3 *nm,f* unbalanced person

desequilibrar 1 *vt* to unbalance, throw off balance
 2 desequilibrarse *vpr* to become mentally disturbed

desequilibrio *nm* lack of balance, imbalance; **d. mental** mental disorder

deserción *nf* (**a**) *Mil* desertion (**b**) *(abandono)* abandonment

desertar *vi* (**a**) *Mil* to desert (**b**) *(abandonar) (obligaciones)* to abandon; *(fiesta)* to leave

desértico, -a *adj* desert; **terrenos desérticos** desert lands

desertificación, desertización *nf* desertification

desertizar [14] **1** *vt* to turn into a desert
 2 desertizarse *vpr* to turn into a desert

desertor, -a *nm,f Mil & Fig* deserter

desesperación *nf* despair, desperation; **con total d.** in total despair; **es una d. tener que esperar tanto** it's exasperating *o* unbearable to have to wait so long

desesperado, -a 1 *pp de* **desesperar**
 2 *adj* (**a**) *(sin esperanza)* desperate, hopeless; **en situación desesperada** in a hopeless situation (**b**) *(desazonado)* exasperated, infuriated
 3 *nm,f* desperate person; *Fig* **a la desesperada** as a last hope; *Fig* **como un d.** like a madman; *Fig* **correr como un d.** to run like mad

desesperante *adj* exasperating

desesperanza *nf* despair, hopelessness, desperation

desesperanzar [14] **1** *vt* to make lose hope; **la falta de noticias lo desesperanzó totalmente** the lack of news plunged him into total despair
 2 desesperanzarse *vpr* to despair, lose hope

desesperar 1 *vt* to exasperate
 2 *vi* to have lost (all) hope; **desespero ya de encontrarlo** I've given up all hope of finding it
 3 desesperarse *vpr* (**a**) *(perder la esperanza)* to lose hope, despair (**b**) *(irritarse)* to feel helpless (**c**) *(lamentarse)* to regret

desestabilización *nf* destabilization

desestabilizador, -a *adj* destabilizing

desestabilizar [14] *vt* to destabilize

desestatizar [14] *vt Am* to privatize, sell off

desestimación *nf* refusal, rejection

desestimar *vt (solicitud, recurso)* to refuse, reject

desfachatez *nf* cheek, nerve

desfalcar [59] *vt Fin* to misappropriate, embezzle

desfalco *nm Fin* embezzlement, misappropriation

desfallecer [46] *vi* (**a**) *(desmayarse)* to lose strength, faint; **estoy que desfallezco** I feel faint (**b**) *(desanimarse)* to lose heart

desfallecido, -a 1 *pp de* **desfallecer**
 2 *adj* exhausted, very weak, faint

desfallecimiento *nm* faintness

desfasado, -a 1 *pp de* **desfasar**
 2 *adj* (**a**) *(libro, moda)* outdated; **tu libro está d.** your book is out of date (**b**) *(persona)* old-fashioned, behind the times (**c**) *Téc* out of phase

desfasar 1 *vt Téc* to phase out
 2 desfasarse *vpr* (**a**) *Téc* to change the phase (**b**) *(persona)* to be out of synch; *Argot* to be high

desfase *nm* (**a**) *(diferencia)* gap, imbalance; **d. horario** jet lag; **hay un gran d. entre lo que dice y lo que hace** he says one thing and does something quite different (**b**) *Elec* phase difference

desfavorable *adj* unfavourable, *US* unfavorable

desfavorecer [46] *vt* (**a**) *(perjudicar)* to disadvantage; **la nueva ley de renta desfavorece a los solteros** the new tax law has disadvantages for unmarried people (**b**) *(sentar mal)* not to flatter, not suit; **ese corte de pelo te desfavorece** this haircut doesn't suit you

desfavorecido, -a *adj* (**a**) *(desaventajado)* disadvantaged (**b**) *(feo)* **salí muy d. en la foto** I came out very badly in the photo

desfibrar *vt Téc* to shred

desfiguración *nf* *(de cara)* disfigurement; *(de verdad)* distortion

desfigurado, -a 1 *pp de* **desfigurar**
 2 *adj* *(persona)* disfigured; *(estatua etc)* defaced; *Fig (hecho)* distorted

desfigurar *vt (cara)* to disfigure; *(estatua)* to deface; *Fig (verdad)* to distort; *Fig* **su versión de los hechos defiguraba la realidad** his version of the events did not reflect the truth

desfiladero *nm* defile, narrow pass

desfilar *vi* (**a**) *(gen)* to march in single file, defile (**b**) *Mil* to march, march past, parade (**c**) *(acudir)* to come; **por su casa desfilan todo tipo de personas** all kinds of people are always dropping in at her place (**d**) *(irse)* to leave, file out

desfile *nm* *Mil* parade, march past; **d. de carrozas** procession of floats; *Mil* **d. de la victoria** victory parade; **d. de modas** fashion show

desfloración *nf* deflowering

desflorar *vt* (**a**) *(estropear)* to spoil, ruin (**b**) *(desvirgar)* to deflower (**c**) *(tema)* to touch on, skim over

desfogar [38] **1** *vt* to let out, give vent to; **desfoga sus problemas en el trabajo con sus hijos** he takes his problems at work out on his children
 2 desfogarse *vpr* to let off steam; **se desfoga con la bebida** he drowns his sorrows in drink

desfondar 1 *vt (quitar el fondo)* to knock the bottom out of; *Fig (quitar fuerza)* to whack, tire out
 2 desfondarse *vpr* to collapse; *Fig* to flake out

desfonde *nm* removal *o* knocking out of the bottom; *Fig* exhaustion

desforestación *nf* deforestation

desforestar *vt* to deforest

desgaire *nm* nonchalance, careless; **al d.** nonchalantly, carelessly

desgajar 1 *vt* (**a**) *(una rama)* to tear off; *(una página)* to rip *o* tear out (**b**) *(romper)* to break
 2 desgajarse *vpr* (**a**) *(separarse)* to come off (**b**) *(persona)* to leave, split away (**de** from), break ties (**de** with)

desgalichado, -a *adj Fam* gawky, ungainly

desgana *nf* (**a**) *(inapetencia)* lack of appetite (**b**) *(apatía)* apathy, indifference; **con d.** reluctantly, unwillingly

desganado, -a 1 *pp de* **desganar**
2 *adj* (**a**) *(inapetente)* not hungry; **estar d.** to have no appetite (**b**) *(apático)* apathetic, half-hearted
desganar 1 *vt* to spoil the appetite of
2 desganarse *vpr* (**a**) *(perder el apetito)* to lose one's appetite (**b**) *(desinteresarse)* to lose interest (**de** in), go off (**de** -)
desgañitarse *vpr Fam* to shout oneself hoarse, shout one's head off
desgarbado, -a *adj* ungraceful, ungainly
desgarrador, -a *adj* heart-breaking, heart-rending; *(aterrador)* bloodcurdling
desgarramiento *nm* ripping, tearing
desgarrar *vt* (**a**) *(romper)* to tear, rip (**b**) *Fig (corazón)* to break
desgarriate *nm Méx (desastre)* disaster; *(destrozo)* damage
desgarro *nm* tear, rip
desgarrón *nm* big tear, rip, slash
desgastar 1 *vt (consumir)* to wear out; *Fig* **los diez primeros minutos de la batalla desgastaron nuestras fuerzas** we used up all our strength in the first ten minutes of the battle
2 desgastarse *vpr (consumirse)* to wear out; *Fig (persona)* to wear oneself out
desgaste *nm* wear, wear and tear; *(de metal)* corrosion; *(de cuerdas)* fraying
desglosar *vt (escrito)* to detach; *(gastos)* to break down
desglose *nm* breakdown, separation
desgobernar [3] *vt (país)* to govern badly
desgobierno *nm* misgovernment, mismanagement, mishandling
desgracia *nf* (**a**) *(contrariedad)* misfortune, mishap; **para colmo de desgracias** *o* **para mayor d.** to top it all; **por d.** unfortunately; **¡qué d.!** how awful! (**b**) *(deshonor)* disfavour, *US* disfavor, disgrace; **caer en d.** to lose favour, fall into disgrace
desgraciadamente *adv* unfortunately
desgraciado, -a 1 *pp de* **desgraciar**
2 *adj* unfortunate, unlucky; **una infancia desgraciada** an unhappy childhood
3 *nm,f* unfortunate *o* unlucky person; **ser un pobre d.** to be a poor devil
desgraciar 1 *vt* (**a**) *(echar a perder)* to spoil (**b**) *(herir gravemente)* to injure seriously
2 desgraciarse *vpr* (**a**) *(plan)* to fall through (**b**) *(persona)* to be hurt
desgranar 1 *vt* (**a**) *(guisantes)* to shell; *(trigo)* to thresh; **d. un racimo de uvas** to pick grapes from a bunch (**b**) *Fig (analizar)* to spell out
2 desgranarse *vpr* to come loose
desgravable *adj Fin* tax-deductible
desgravación *nf Fin* deduction; **d. fiscal** tax deduction
desgravar *vt Fin (impuestos)* to deduct
desgreñado, -a 1 *pp de* **desgreñar**
2 *adj* (**a**) *(pelo)* ruffled, tousled, dishevelled, *US* disheveled (**b**) *(persona)* dishevelled, *US* disheveled
desgreñar 1 *vt* to ruffle, dishevel, tousle
2 desgreñarse *vpr* to mess up *o* untidy one's hair
desguace *nm (de barcos)* breaking up; *Aut* scrapping
desguañangar *vt Am Fam* to wreck
desguarnecer [46] *vt* (**a**) *(quitar los adornos de)* to take off, remove, strip off (**b**) *Mil* to leave unprotected, remove the garrison from

desguazar [14]· *vt Náut (un barco)* to break up; *Aut* to scrap
deshabillé *nm* negligée, *US* negligee
deshabitado, -a 1 *pp de* **deshabitar**
2 *adj* uninhabited, unoccupied
deshabitar *vt (lugar, casa)* to leave, abandon, vacate
deshabituar [4] **1** *vt (perder la costumbre de)* to get out of the habit of; *(superar un hábito)* to break the habit of
2 deshabituarse *vpr (perder la costumbre)* to get out of the habit, lose the habit; *(superar un hábito)* to break the habit
deshacer [33] *(pp* **deshecho**) **1** *vt* (**a**) *(un paquete)* to undo; *(una cama)* to unmake; *(una maleta)* to unpack; *(puntadas)* to unpick; *(el camino)* to retrace one's steps; *Fig* **ser el que hace y deshace** to be the boss, rule the roost (**b**) *(destruir)* to destroy, ruin; *Fig* **d. a algn** to be the ruin of sb (**c**) *(acuerdo)* to break off (**d**) *(disolver) (un sólido)* to dissolve; *(helado, chocolate, cera etc)* to melt (**e**) *Inform* to undo
2 deshacerse *vpr* (**a**) *(gen)* to come undone *o* untied (**b**) *(afligirse)* to go to pieces; **se deshizo al morir su madre** he went to pieces when his mother died (**c**) *(disolverse) (un sólido)* to dissolve; *(helado, chocolate, cera etc)* to melt (**d**) *(desvanecerse)* to fade away, disappear (**e**) *(prodigar)* to be full (**en** of); **d. en elogios** to be full of praise; **d. en lágrimas** to cry one's eyes out (**f**) *(esforzarse)* to break one's back, bend over backwards; **d. en atenciones** to be extremely kind; **d. trabajando** to wear oneself out working; **se deshace por complacerme** he would do anything to please me (**g**) *(desembarazarse)* to get rid (**de** of); **deshazte de él** get rid of him (**h**) *(chiflarse)* to be crazy *o* mad (about)
desharrapado, -a 1 *adj* ragged, shabby, tattered
2 *nm,f* shabby person, tramp
deshecho, -a 1 *pp de* **deshacer**
2 *adj* (**a**) *(nudo, paquete)* undone; *(cama)* unmade; *(maleta)* unpacked; *(paquete)* unwrapped (**b**) *(destrozado)* destroyed, disintegrated; **el coche quedó d.** the car was a write-off (**c**) *(roto)* broken, smashed (**d**) *(disuelto)* dissolved; *(derretido)* melted (**e**) *(abatido)* devasted, shattered; **está d. con la enfermedad de su hijo** he's shattered by his son's illness (**f**) *(agotado)* exhausted, tired out, shattered
3 *nm Am (atajo)* short cut
deshelar [3] *vt* to thaw, melt; *(congelador)* to defrost; *(parabrisas)* to de-ice
deshelar [3] *vt* to weed
desheredado, -a 1 *pp de* **desheredar**
2 *adj* disinherited; *Fig* deprived, underprivileged
3 *nm,f* disinherited person; *Fig* deprived *o* under-privileged person; **los desheredados** the deprived
desheredar *vt* to disinherit
deshidratación *nf* dehydration
deshidratado, -a 1 *pp de* **deshidratar**
2 *adj* dehydrated
deshidratar 1 *vt* to dehydrate
2 deshidratarse *vpr* to become dehydrated
deshidrogenar *vt* to dehydrogenate, dehydrogenize
deshielo *nm* (**a**) *(gen)* thaw; *(congelador)* defrosting; *(parabrisas)* de-icing (**b**) *Fig (distensión)* thaw
deshilachado, -a 1 *pp de* **deshilachar**
2 *adj* frayed
deshilachar *vt* to fray
deshilado, -a 1 *pp de* **deshilar**
2 *n* openwork embroidery
deshilar *vt* to unpick
deshilvanado, -a 1 *pp de* **deshilvanar**
2 *adj* (**a**) *Cost* untacked (**b**) *Fig (sin enlace)* disjointed

deshilvanar *vt Cost* to untack

deshinchado, -a 1 *pp de* **deshinchar**
2 *adj* flat, deflated

deshinchar 1 *vt* to deflate, let down
2 deshincharse *vpr* (**a**) *(globo, rueda)* to go down; **ya se me ha deshinchado el brazo** the swelling in my arm has gone down (**b**) *Fig (persona)* to get off one's high horse

deshojar *vt (flor)* to remove o strip the petals of; *(árbol)* to remove o strip the leaves of; *(libro)* to tear the pages out of

deshollinador, -a *nm,f* chimney sweep

deshollinar *vt (chimenea)* to sweep

deshonestidad *nf* (**a**) *(sin honestidad)* dishonesty (**b**) *(impudor)* immodesty, impropriety, indecent

deshonesto, -a *adj* (**a**) *(sin honestidad)* dishonest (**b**) *(inmoral)* immodest, indecent, improper

deshonor *nm,* **deshonra** *nf* dishonour, *US* dishonor, disgrace

deshonrar *vt* (**a**) *(gen)* to dishonour, *US* dishonor (**b**) *(ofender)* to insult (**c**) *(ultrajar)* to slander, defame; *(desprestigiar)* to bring disgrace on

deshonroso, -a *adj* dishonourable, *US* dishonorable, disgraceful, shameful

deshora: a deshora *loc adv* at an unreasonable o inconvenient time; **comer a d.** to eat at odd times

deshuesadora *nf* stoning o boning machine

deshuesar *vt (carne)* to bone; *(fruta)* Br to stone, *US* pit

deshumanización *nf* dehumanization

deshumanizado, -a 1 *pp de* **deshumanizar**
2 *adj* dehumanized

deshumanizar [14] *vt* to dehumanize

desiderata *nf* desiderata

desiderativo, -a *adj* desiderative

desidia *nf* apathy, negligence, slovenliness

desidioso, -a *adj* apathetic, negligent, slovenly

desierto, -a 1 *adj* (**a**) *(deshabitado)* uninhabited (**b**) *(con poca o sin gente)* empty, deserted; **el teatro estaba d.** the theatre was empty (**c**) *(no adjudicado)* void; **el jurado declaró d. el premio** the prize was declared void; **quedar d.** to be declared void
2 *nm* desert; **clamar en el d.** to cry in the desert

designación *nf* (**a**) *(nombre)* name, designation (**b**) *(nombramiento)* appointment, designation

designar *vt* (**a**) *(denominar)* to call, designate (**b**) *(asignar un cargo)* to appoint, assign (**c**) *(fijar)* to assign, fix

designio *nm* intention, plan; **los designios del Señor** God's will

desigual *adj* (**a**) *(gen)* uneven (**b**) *(diferente)* unequal, different (**c**) *(variable)* changeable; **tiempo/carácter d.** changeable weather/temper (**d**) *(no liso)* uneven, rough (**e**) *(irregular)* uneven, irregular, inconsistent

desigualar 1 *vt* to make unequal o uneven
2 desigualarse *vpr* to become unequal o uneven

desigualdad *nf* (**a**) *(gen)* inequality (**b**) *(diferencia)* difference (**c**) *(de carácter)* changeability (**d**) *(en el terreno)* roughness (**e**) *(en la escritura)* unevenness, inconsistency

desilusión *nf* disappointment, disillusionment

desilusionado, -a 1 *pp de* **desilusionar**
2 *adj* disappointed, disillusioned, disheartened

desilusionar 1 *vt* to disappoint, disillusion, dishearten
2 desilusionarse *vpr* to be disappointed, become disillusioned

desimantar *vt* to demagnetize

desincentivar *vt* to discourage

desincrustar *vt (tuberías)* to descale

desinencia *nf Ling* desinence

desinfección *nf* disinfection

desinfectante *adj & nm* disinfectant

desinfectar *vt* to disinfect

desinflado, -a *adj (neumático)* flat

desinflamar *Med* **1** *vt* to reduce the swelling o inflammation in
2 desinflamarse *vpr* to go down, become less swollen o inflamed

desinflar 1 *vt* to deflate; *(una rueda)* to let down
2 desinflarse *vpr* (**a**) *(balón)* to go down; *(una rueda)* to go flat (**b**) *Fam Fig (desanimarse)* to lose interest, cool off

desinformación *nf* misinformation

desinformar *vt* to misinform

desinhibición *nf* lack of inhibition

desinhibido, -a 1 *pp de* **desinhibir**
2 *adj* uninhibited

desinhibir 1 *vt* to free from inhibitions
2 desinhibirse *vpr* to lose one's inhibitions

desinsectación *nf* fumigation

desinsectar *vt (fumigar)* to fumigate

desintegración *nf* disintegration, break up; **d. atómica** atomic disintegration; **d. nuclear** nuclear fission

desintegrar 1 *vt* (**a**) *(objetos, organizaciones)* to disintegrate, break up (**b**) *Fís (un átomo)* to split
2 desintegrarse *vpr* (**a**) *(objetos, organizaciones)* to disintegrate, break up (**b**) *Fís* to split

desinterés *nm* (**a**) *(generosidad)* unselfishness, generosity; **todo lo hace con d.** his motives are completely unselfish (**b**) *(falta de interés)* lack of interest, apathy; **su desinterés por el trabajo es preocupante** his lack of interest in work is worrying

desinteresado, -a 1 *pp de* **desinteresarse**
2 *adj* selfless, unselfish

desinteresarse *vpr* (**a**) *(desentenderse)* to have nothing to do (**de** with) (**b**) *(perder interés)* to lose interest (**de** in), go off (**de** -)

desintoxicación *nf* detoxification; **una cura de d. alcohólica** a drying-out cure

desintoxicar [59] **1** *vt* to detoxify; *(alcohólico)* to dry out
2 desintoxicarse *vpr Med* to detoxify oneself; *(alcohol)* to dry out

desinversión *nf Econ* disinvestment, divestment

desinvertir *vt Econ* to disinvest

desistimiento *nm Jur* abandonment

desistir *vi* to desist, give up; *Jur* to waive

deslavazado, -a *adj* (**a**) *(sin firmeza)* limp (**b**) *(deshilvanado)* disjointed

desleal *adj* disloyal

deslealtad *nf* disloyalty

desleír [56] **1** *vt (sólido)* to dissolve; *(líquido)* to dilute
2 desleírse *vpr* to dissolve

deslenguado, -a *adj (insolente)* insolent, cheeky; *(grosero)* coarse, foul-mouthed

desliar [32] **1** *vt (un paquete)* to unwrap
2 desliarse *vpr* to come unwrapped o undone, open

desligar [38] *vt* (**a**) *(desatar)* to untie, unfasten (**b**) *Fig (independizar)* to separate; **d. a algn de un compromiso** to free o release sb from an obligation; **d. el aspecto político y el económico** to consider the political and economic aspects separately

deslindar *vt* (**a**) *(una propiedad)* to set out the boundaries of (**b**) *Fig (aclarar)* to define, outline

deslinde *nm* setting out of boundaries

deslío *indic pres véanse* **desleír** & **desliar**

desliz *nm* (**a**) *(resbalón)* slip, slide (**b**) *Fig (error)* mistake, error, slip; **cometer** *o* **tener un d.** to slip up, make a slip

deslizamiento *nm* slipping, slip; **un d. de tierra** landslide

deslizante *adj* slippery

deslizar [14] **1** *vt* (**a**) *(pasar)* to slide, slip (**b**) *(decir, hacer)* to slip in; **ella deslizó algunas indirectas sobre su ineficacia** she dropped a few hints about his inefficiency; **le deslizó una nota en el bolso** he slipped a note into her handbag
2 *vi (resbalar)* to slide, slip
3 deslizarse *vpr* (**a**) *(patinar)* to slide; *(sobre agua)* to glide (**b**) *(fluir)* to flow; **las aguas se deslizan plácidamente** the waters flow peacefully by (**c**) *(transcurrir)* to go by, fly; **la mañana se deslizó sin sobresaltos** the morning passed by without incidents (**d**) *(entrar)* to slip into; *(salir)* to slip out of; **se deslizó en los camerinos sin que nadie lo viera** he slipped unseen into the dressing rooms

deslomar 1 *vt* to wear out, exhaust
2 deslomarse *vpr* to wear oneself out, break one's back

deslucido, -a 1 *pp de* **deslucir**
2 *adj* (**a**) *(sin brillo)* faded, dull, lacklustre, *US* lackluster (**b**) *(sin brillantez)* unimpressive, unexciting

deslucir [39] *vt (espectáculo)* to spoil

deslumbrador, -a *adj* (**a**) *(luz)* dazzling (**b**) *(que asombra)* dazzling, impressive

deslumbramiento *nm* dazzle, dazzling

deslumbrante *adj véase* **deslumbrador, -a**

deslumbrar *vt* to dazzle

deslustrar *vt* (**a**) *(quitar brillo)* to take the shine off, dull (**b**) *(desacreditar)* to stain, tarnish

deslúzco *indic pres véase* **deslucir**

desmadejado *adj* tired out, exhausted

desmadejamiento *nm* exhaustion

desmadejar *vt* to tire out, exhaust

desmadrado, -a 1 *pp de* **desmadrarse**
2 *adj Fam* wild, unruly; **los niños están desmadrados hoy** the children are wild today

desmadrarse *vpr Esp Fam* to go wild

desmadre *nm Fam* chaos, havoc, hullabaloo

desmagnetizar [14] *vt* to demagnetize

desmalezar [14] *vt Am* to weed

desmán *nm* outrage, excess

desmanchar *Am* **1** *vt* to clean, remove spots from
2 desmancharse *vpr Andes PRico* (**a**) *(apartarse)* to move away (**b**) *(salir a correr)* to go for a run

desmandado, -a 1 *pp de* **desmandarse**
2 *adj* (**a**) *(persona)* rebellious; **multitud desmandada** unruly crowd (**b**) *(animal)* stray; **un caballo d.** a runaway horse

desmandarse *vpr* to rebel, get out of hand, run wild; *(animal)* to stray from the herd; *(caballo)* to bolt

desmano: a desmano *loc adv* out of the way; **me coge a d.** it is out of my way

desmantelado, -a 1 *pp de* **desmantelar**
2 *adj* (**a**) *(arsenal, instalaciones)* dismantled (**b**) *Náut* dismasted, unrigged

desmantelamiento *nm* (**a**) *(de arsenal, instalaciones)* dismantling (**b**) *Náut* dismasting, unrigging

desmantelar *vt* (**a**) *(arsenal, instalaciones)* to dismantle (**b**) *Náut* to dismast, unrig

desmaquillador, -a 1 *adj* **leche desmaquilladora** cleansing cream *o* milk, make-up remover
2 *nm* make-up remover

desmaquillar(se) *vt & vpr* to remove one's make-up

desmarcarse [59] *vpr* (**a**) *Dep* to lose one's marker (**b**) *(apartarse)* **se desmarcó de la línea oficial del partido** he distanced himself from the official party line

desmarque *nm* (**a**) *Dep* **realizó un buen d.** he lost his marker well (**b**) *(alejamiento)* **su d. de la política del gobierno** his disavowal of government policy

desmayado, -a 1 *pp de* **desmayarse**
2 *adj* unconscious; **caer d.** to faint

desmayarse *vpr* to faint, lose consciousness, swoon

desmayo *nm* faint, fainting fit; **tener un d.** to faint

desmedido, -a *adj* disproportionate, out of all proportion; **ambición desmedida** unbounded ambition

desmedirse [47] *vpr* to go too far, go over the top

desmedrado, -a *adj* tiny, puny, emaciated

desmejorado, -a 1 *pp de* **desmejorar**
2 *adj* poorly, unwell

desmejorar *vi* to deteriorate, go downhill

desmelenado, -a 1 *pp de* **desmelenar**
2 *adj* tousled, ruffled, dishevelled, *US* disheveled

desmelenar 1 *vt (despeinarse)* to dishevel
2 desmelenarse *vpr Fam (desmadrarse)* to let one's hair down

desmembración *nf*, **desmembramiento** *nm* dismemberment; *Fig* separation, division

desmembrar [3] *vt* to dismember; *Fig* to split *o* break up

desmemoriado, -a *adj* forgetful, absent-minded

desmentido *nm* denial

desmentir [62] *vt* (**a**) *(gen)* to deny (**b**) *(contradecir)* to belie, contradict (**c**) *(desmerecer)* not to live up to

desmenuzar [14] *vt* (**a**) *(deshacer)* to break into little pieces, crumble; *(carne)* to chop up (**b**) *Fig (analizar)* to examine in detail; **d. un asunto** to look into a subject carefully

desmerecer [46] *vi* (**a**) *(perder valor)* to lose value (**b**) *(ser inferior)* to compare unfavourably (**de** with), be inferior (**de** to)

desmerecimiento *nm* demerit

desmesura *nf* immoderation, disproportion

desmesuradamente *adv* extremely, disproportionately, excessively

desmesurado, -a *adj* disproportionate, excessive

desmigajar *vt*, **desmigar** [7] *vt (pan)* to crumble

desmilitarización *nf* demilitarization

desmilitarizar [14] *vt* to demilitarize

desmineralización *nf* demineralization

desmineralizar [14] *vt* to demineralize

desmirriado, -a *adj véase* **esmirriado, -a**

desmitificación *nf* **la d. del presidente** the removal of the aura surrounding the president

desmitificador, -a *adj* **revelaciones desmitificadoras de la figura de Gandhi** revelations which shatter the Gandhi myth

desmitificar [59] *vt* **el escándalo desmitificó al presidente** the scandal showed the president had feet of clay

desmontable *adj* that can be taken to pieces; **estantería d.** shelf in kit form

desmontar 1 *vt* (**a**) *(desarmar)* to take to pieces, take down, dismantle (**b**) *(derribar)* to knock down (**c**) *(cortar árboles)* to clear of trees (**d**) *(allanar)* to level (**e**) *(armas)* to uncock
2 *vi (apearse)* to dismount (**de** from), get off (**de** -)

desmoralización *nf* demoralization

desmoralizador, -a *adj* demoralizing

desmoralizar [14] *vt* to demoralize

desmoronamiento *nm* disintegration, decay, crumbling; **el d. de un imperio** the fall of an empire

desmoronar 1 *vt* to disintegrate, destroy; *(una roca)* to erode
2 desmoronarse *vpr* to crumble, fall to pieces; *Fig* **al oír la noticia se desmoronó** he was devastated by the news

desmotivar *vt* to demotivate

desmovilización *nf Mil* demobilization

desmovilizar [14] *vt Mil* to demobilize

desnacionalización *nf Fin* denationalization, privatization

desnacionalizar [14] *vt Fin* to denationalize, privatize

desnatado, -a *adj (leche)* skimmed

desnatar *vt (leche)* to skim

desnaturalización *nf* **(a)** *(de sustancia)* adulteration **(b)** *(destierro)* banishment **(c)** *Quím* denaturation

desnaturalizado, -a 1 *pp de* **desnaturalizar**
2 *adj* **(a)** *(sustancia)* adulterated, distorted **(b)** *Quím* denatured; **alcohol d.** denatured alcohol **(c)** *(descastado)* unnatural, inhuman

desnaturalizar [14] *vt* **(a)** *(alterar)* to adulterate, tamper with **(b)** *Quím* to denature **(c)** *(desterrar)* to banish

desnivel *nm* **(a)** *(cultural, social)* inequality, gap; *Fig* **el d. económico** the economic gap **(b)** *(en el terreno)* drop, difference in height

desnivelación *nf* unevenness, unlevelling

desnivelado, -a 1 *pp de* **desnivelar**
2 *adj* **(a)** *(desigual)* not level, uneven, unequal **(b)** *(desequilibrado)* out of balance

desnivelar *vt* **(a)** *(terreno)* to make uneven **(b)** *(desequilibrar)* to throw out of balance; *(balanza)* to tip

desnucar [59] **1** *vt* to break the neck of
2 desnucarse *vpr* to break one's neck

desnuclearizar [14] *vt* to denuclearize

desnudar 1 *vt* to undress
2 desnudarse *vpr* to get undressed

desnudez *nf* nudity, nakedness

desnudismo *nm* nudism

desnudista *adj & nmf* nudist

desnudo, -a 1 *adj* naked, nude; **con los hombros desnudos** with bare shoulders; **la verdad desnuda** the plain o naked truth
2 *nm Arte* nude

desnutrición *nf* undernourishment, malnutrition

desnutrido, -a 1 *pp de* **desnutrirse**
2 *adj* undernourished

desnutrirse *vpr* to become undernourished

desobedecer [46] *vt* to disobey

desobediencia *nf* disobedience **d. civil** civil disobedience

desobediente 1 *adj* disobedient
2 *nmf* disobedient person

desocupación *nf* **(a)** *(paro)* unemployment **(b)** *(ociosidad)* leisure

desocupado, -a 1 *pp de* **desocupar**
2 *adj* **(a)** *(vacío)* empty, vacant; **¿está d. este asiento?** is this seat free? **(b)** *(ocioso)* free, not busy; **si estás d.** if you're not busy **(c)** *(sin empleo)* unemployed

desocupar 1 *vt* to empty, vacate; *Mil* to evacuate
2 desocuparse *vpr (de un trabajo)* to give up work

desodorante *adj & nm* deodorant

desoír [44] *vt* to ignore, take no notice of, turn a deaf ear to

desojarse *vpr* to strain one's eyes

desolación *nf (aflicción)* desolation; *(pena)* grief

desolado, -a 1 *pp de* **desolar**
2 *adj* **(a)** *(devastado)* devastated, desolated **(b)** *(desconsolado)* inconsolable, disconsolate

desolador, -a *adj* **(a)** *(devastador)* devastating **(b)** *(desconsolador)* desolating

desolar [75] *vt* **(a)** *(devastar)* to devastate **(b)** *(desconsolar)* to desolate, distress

desollar [63] *vt (un animal)* to skin; *Fig* **d. vivo a algn** to tear sb to pieces

desorbitado, -a 1 *pp de* **desorbitar**
2 *adj* **(a)** *(excesivo)* disproportionate; *(exagerado)* exaggerated; **precios desorbitados** exhorbitant prices **(b)** **con los ojos desorbitados** pop-eyed

desorbitar *vt (exagerar)* to get out of proportion, exaggerate; **d. una noticia** to blow a piece of news up out of all proportion

desorden *nm* **(a)** *(desarreglo)* untidiness, disorder, mess; **en d.** in a mess; **¡qué d.!** what a mess! **(b)** *(desarreglo)* irregularity; **evite el d. en las comidas** take meals at regular times ❑ **desórdenes gástricos** stomach disorders **(c)** **desordenes** *(disturbio)* riot *sing*, disorder *sing*; **d. públicos** civil disorder *sing*; **los últimos d. han alterado la vida ciudadana** the recent disturbances have shaken people's lives **(d)** **desordenes** *(excesos)* excesses

desordenado, -a 1 *pp de* **desordenar**
2 *adj* **(a)** *(desarreglado)* messy, untidy; **la casa está toda desordenada** the house is upside down; *Fig* **ideas desordenadas** jumbled (up) o confused ideas **(b)** *Fig (vida)* irregular

desordenar 1 *vt* to make untidy, mess up
2 desordenarse *vpr* to get o become untidy o messed up

desorejado, -a *adj* **(a)** *Andes Pan (que tiene mal oído)* tone-deaf **(b)** *Cuba (derrochador)* wasteful

desorganización *nf* disorganization

desorganizar [14] *vt* to disorganize, disrupt

desorientación *nf* disorientation; *Fig* confusion

desorientado, -a 1 *pp de* **desorientar**
2 *adj* disoriented; *Fig* **tu reacción le dejó d.** your reaction confused him

desorientar 1 *vt* to disorientate; *Fig* to confuse
2 desorientarse *vpr* to lose one's sense of direction, lose one's bearings, be lost o disoriented; *Fig* to get confused

desosar [23] *vt (carne)* to bone; *(fruta) Br* to stone, *US* pit

desovar *vi (insectos)* to lay eggs; *(peces)* to spawn

desove *nm (de insectos)* egg-laying; *(de peces)* spawning

desoxidación *nf* deoxidization

desoxidante 1 *adj* deoxidizing
2 *nm* deoxidizer

desoxidar *vt* to deoxidize

desoxirribonucleico, -a *adj Quím* deoxyribonucleic

despabilado, -a 1 *pp de* **despabilar**
2 *adj* **(a)** *(sin sueño)* wide awake **(b)** *(listo)* quick, smart; **ser muy d.** to be quick on the uptake, have one's wits about one

despabilar 1 *vt* **(a)** *(despertar)* to wake up **(b)** *(avivar el ingenio)* to smarten up, wise up **(c)** *(consumir)* to finish off, eat up
2 *vi (avivar el ingenio)* to get a move on; **como no despabiles te quedas sin el trabajo** get your act together or you'll lose the job

3 despabilarse *vpr* (**a**) *(despertarse)* to wake up (**b**) *(darse prisa)* to hurry up (**c**) *Cuba Fam (marcharse)* to clear off

despachar 1 *vt* (**a**) *(terminar)* to finish; *(resolver)* to get through (**b**) *(enviar)* to send, dispatch (**c**) *(tratar un asunto)* to deal with; **debo d. un negocio con el director** I must settle a matter with the director; **d. la correspondencia** to sort out the mail (**d**) *(en tienda)* to serve; *(entradas)* to issue, sell (**e**) *Fam (comer)* to polish off, get through (**f**) *Fam Fig (despedir)* to send away o packing, sack (**g**) *Fam Fig (matar)* to kill (**h**) *Am (facturar)* to check in
　2 despacharse *vpr (acabar)* to finish off; **d. de algo** to get rid of sth; *Fig* **d. a gusto con algn** to give sb a piece of one's mind

despacho *nm* (**a**) *(acción)* dispatch, handling (**b**) *(comunicación)* dispatch □ **d. diplomático** diplomatic dispatch; **d. telefónico** telephone call; **d. telegráfico** telegram (**c**) *(oficina)* office; **el d. del jefe** the boss's office □ **mesa de d.** desk (**d**) *(en casa)* study (**e**) *(venta)* selling, sale (**f**) *(lugar de venta)* **d. de billetes** ticket office; **d. de localidades** box office; **d. de vino** wine merchant's

despachurrar *Fam* **1** *vt* to squash, crush, flatten
　2 despachurrarse *vpr* to get squashed o crushed

despacio 1 *adv* (**a**) *(lentamente)* slowly; **camina d.** walk slowly (**b**) *esp Am (en voz baja)* quietly
　2 *interj* take it easy!

despacioso, -a *adj* slow, sluggish

despampanante *adj Fam* stunning

despancar [59] *vt SAm (maíz)* to husk

despanzurrar *vt Fam* to squash, crush

desparejado, -a *pp de* **desparejar**
　2 *adj* without a partner; **un calcetín d.** an odd sock

desparejar *vt* to mix up

desparejo, -a *adj* (**a**) *(dispar)* unlike, different (**b**) *Arg Par Urug (desigual)* uneven, uncentred, *US* uncentered, unbalanced

desparpajo *nm* (**a**) *(desenvoltura)* self-assurance, ease; **con d.** in a carefree way, confidently (**b**) *CAm (desorden)* disorder, confusion

desparramar 1 *vt (líquido)* to spill; *(objetos)* to spread, scatter
　2 desparramarse *vpr (líquido)* to spill; *(objetos, personas)* to scatter, spread out

despatarrado, -a 1 *pp de* **despatarrar**
　2 *adj* with legs wide open

despatarrar 1 *vt Fig* to amaze
　2 despatarrarse *vpr (abrir las piernas)* to open one's legs wide, sprawl; *(al caer)* to go sprawling

despavorido, -a *adj* terrified

despechado, -a 1 *pp de* **despecharse**
　2 *adj* bearing a grudge, spiteful

despecharse *vpr* to get angry

despecho *nm* spite; **por d.** out of spite

despechugado, -a *Fam* **1** *pp de* **despechugarse**
　2 *adj* bare chested

despechugarse [38] *vpr Fam* to show o bare one's chest

despectivo, -a *adj* (**a**) *(despreciativo)* derogatory, contemptuous, disparaging; **de forma despectiva** in a derogatory way; **en tono d.** contemptuously (**b**) *Ling* pejorative

despedazar [14] *vt* to cut o tear to pieces

despedida *nf* (**a**) *(adiós)* farewell, goodbye □ **cena de d.** farewell dinner; **d. de soltera** hen party; **d. de soltero** stag party (**b**) *Mús* last verse (of a song)

despedir [47] **1** *vt* (**a**) *(del trabajo)* to sack, fire, dismiss; **¡está Ud. despedido!** you're fired! (**b**) *(decir adiós)* to see

off, say goodbye to; **fue al aeropuerto a despedirlo** he went to see him off at the airport (**c**) *(desprender)* to give off; **esta máquina despide un olor muy desagradable** this machine gives off an awful smell (**d**) *(lanzar)* to shoot; **salir d.** to shoot off (**e**) *(echar)* to chuck o throw out
　2 despedirse *vpr* (**a**) *(decir adiós)* to say goodbye (**de** to); **vino a d.** he came to say goodbye (**b**) *(irse)* to take one's leave, leave; *Fam* **d. a la francesa** to take French leave (**c**) *Fig* to forget, give up; **puedes despedirte de la idea de comprarte el coche** you can forget the idea of buying the car

despegable *adj* detachable

despegado, -a 1 *pp de* **despegar**
　2 *adj* (**a**) *(pieza, etiqueta)* unstuck; **la foto está despegada** the photo has come unstuck (**b**) *Fig* cold, distant, detached

despegar [38] **1** *vt* (**a**) *(pieza, etiqueta)* to unstick (**b**) *CAm Méx (caballos)* to unhitch
　2 *vi Av* to take off
　3 despegarse *vpr* (**a**) *(separarse)* to come unstuck (**b**) *Fig (perder afecto)* to lose affection (**de** for); *(separarse)* to alienate oneself (**de** from), cut oneself off (**de** from)

despego *nm* coldness, detachment; **con d.** with indifference

despegue *nm Av* takeoff □ **pista de d.** runway

despeinado, -a 1 *pp de* **despeinar**
　2 *adj* dishevelled, *US* disheveled, with untidy hair

despeinar 1 *vt* to ruffle; *(peinado)* to mess up
　2 despeinarse *vpr* to ruffle one's hair, make one's hair untidy

despejado, -a 1 *pp de* **despejar**
　2 *adj* (**a**) *(ancho)* wide, spacious; **una frente despejada** a broad forehead (**b**) *(cielo)* clear, cloudless (**c**) *(listo)* clever, bright (**d**) *(despierto)* wide awake

despejar 1 *vt* (**a**) *(desocupar)* to clear (away); **despeja la mesa de papeles** clear those papers off the table; *Ftb* **d. el balón** to clear the ball (**b**) *(aclarar)* to disentangle; **d. la mente** to clear one's head; **d. un enigma** to clear up a mystery (**c**) *(espabilar)* to keep awake; **el paseo te despejará** the walk will wake you up (**d**) *Mat* to find the unknown quantity (**e**) *Inform* to clear
　2 despejarse *vpr* (**a**) *(cielo)* to clear (**b**) *(persona) (despertar)* to wake up; *(espabilarse)* to clear one's head

despeje *nm Dep* clearance

despellejar *vt (a)* *(quitar el pellejo)* to skin (**b**) *Fig (criticar)* to criticize unmercifully, pull to pieces

despelotado, -a *Vulg* **1** *pp de* **despelotarse**
　2 *adj* naked, starkers

despelotarse *vpr Esp Vulg* (**a**) *(desnudarse)* to strip (**b**) *(descojonarse)* to laugh one's head off, die laughing (**c**) *Am (caos)* chaos; **se armó un d.** chaos broke out; **ser un d.** *(proyecto, reunión)* to be chaotic

despelote *nm Vulg* (**a**) *Esp (desnudo)* **hay mucho d. en la playa** there are a lot of people *Br* starkers o *US* buck naked on the beach (**b**) *(descojone)* **tu primo es un d.** your cousin is a good laugh

despenalización *nf* decriminalization

despenalizar [14] *vt* to decriminalize

despensa *nf* (**a**) *(fresquera)* pantry, larder (**b**) *(víveres)* stock of food, provisions *pl*

despeñadero *nm* cliff, precipice

despeñar 1 *vt* to throw over a cliff
　2 despeñarse *vpr* to throw oneself over a cliff

despercudir *vt Am* to liven up, wake up

desperdiciar *vt (gen)* to waste; *(oportunidad)* to throw away

desperdicio nm (**a**) (acto) waste, wasting; Fig **esta película no tiene d.** this film is excellent from start to finish (**b**) **desperdicios** (basura) rubbish sing; (desechos) scraps, leftovers; (residuos) waste sing

desperdigar [38] **1** vt to scatter, disperse
 2 desperdigarse vpr to scatter

desperezarse [14] vpr to stretch (oneself)

desperfecto nm (**a**) (defecto) flaw, imperfection (**b**) (daño) damage; **la lluvia causó algunos desperfectos** the rain caused some damage

despersonalizar [14] vt to depersonalize, make impersonal

despertador nm alarm clock □ **reloj d.** alarm watch

despertar [3] **1** vt to wake (up), awaken; Fig (esperanzas, sentimientos) to raise, arouse
 2 despertarse vpr to wake (up), awaken

despezuñarse vpr Andes Hond PRico (**a**) (caminar de prisa) to walk very quickly, rush (**b**) (esforzarse) to exert oneself, make an effort

despiadado, -a adj merciless, heartless, cruel

despido nm dismissal, sacking □ **d. improcedente** wrongful dismissal

despierto, -a 1 pp de **despertar**
 2 adj (**a**) (desvelado) awake (**b**) (espabilado) quick, sharp, bright

despilfarrador, -a adj & nm,f spendthrift, waster

despilfarrar vt to waste, squander

despilfarro nm wasting, squandering

despintar 1 vt (arrancar la pintura) to take o strip the paint off
 2 despintarse vpr (desteñirse) to fade, lose colour o US color; (por la lluvia) to wash off

despistado, -a 1 pp de **despistar**
 2 adj (**a**) (olvidadizo) absent-minded, scatterbrained (**b**) (confuso) confused; **este asunto me tiene muy d.** this business has got me all muddled up
 3 nm,f absent-minded person, scatterbrain; **hacerse el d.** to pretend not to understand

despistar 1 vt (**a**) (hacer perder la pista) to lose, throw off one's scent (**b**) Fig to mislead, muddle
 2 despistarse vpr (**a**) (perderse) to get lost, lose one's way (**b**) (distraerse) to do absent-mindedly; **me despisté y cogí su bolso en vez del mío** without thinking I took her bag instead of mine (**c**) (olvidarse) to forget about; **no vine porque me despisté** I didn't come because it completely slipped my mind

despiste nm (**a**) (error) mistake, slip; **¡vaya d.!** what a blunder! (**b**) (cualidad) absent-mindedness

desplante nm outspoken o cutting remark

desplazado, -a 1 pp de **desplazar**
 2 adj out of place, misplaced; **sentirse d.** to feel out of place

desplazamiento nm (**a**) (viaje) trip, journey (**b**) Náut displacement (**c**) (traslado) removal, movement

desplazar [14] **1** vt (**a**) (trasladar) to displace, move (**b**) Náut to displace (**c**) Fig (suplantar) to take the place of, supplant
 2 desplazarse vpr (ir) to travel, go

desplegar [43] **1** vt (**a**) (abrir) to unfold, open (out), spread (out) (**b**) Fig (energías etc) to use, deploy
 2 desplegarse vpr (**a**) (abrirse) to unfold, open (out), spread (out) (**b**) Mil to deploy

despliegue nm (**a**) Mil deployment (**b**) Fig (muestra) display, show, manifestation

desplomarse vpr (caer) to collapse; (techo) to fall in

desplome nm collapse

desplumar vt (**a**) (ave) to pluck (**b**) Fam (estafar) to fleece, swindle

despoblación nf depopulation □ **d. forestal** deforestation

despoblado, -a 1 adj unpopulated, deserted
 2 nm deserted spot

despoblar [63] **1** vt to depopulate; **d. de árboles** to deforest
 2 despoblarse vpr to become depopulated

despojar 1 vt (**a**) (quitar) to strip, clear (**de** of) (**b**) Fig to divest, deprive (**de** of) (**c**) Jur to dispossess
 2 despojarse vpr (**a**) (ropa) to take off (**b**) Fig (sentimiento etc) to free oneself (**de** of)

despojo nm (**a**) (acción) deprivation, stripping (**b**) **despojos** (de animal) offal sing; (desperdicios) leftovers, scraps; Constr rubble sing; (cadáver) remains

despolitizar [14] vt to depoliticize

desportillar 1 vt to chip
 2 desportillarse vpr to get chipped

desposado, -a 1 pp de **desposar**
 2 adj Fml newly-wed

desposar Fml **1** vt to marry
 2 desposarse vpr (casarse) to get married (**con** to); (prometerse) to become engaged (**con** to)

desposeer [37] vt to dispossess (**de** of); **d. a algn de su autoridad** to remove sb from authority

desposeído, -a 1 pp de **desposeer**
 2 los desposeídos nmpl the have-nots

desposorios nmpl Fml (boda) marriage sing; (esponsales) engagement sing, betrothal sing

despostar vt Andes RP to cut up

déspota nmf despot

despótico, -a adj despotic

despotismo nm despotism. □ Hist **d. ilustrado** enlightened despotism

despotizar vt Am to tyrannize

despotricar [59] vi to rave (**contra** about), rant (on)

despreciable adj despicable, contemptible; (en cantidad) negligible; (en calidad) worthless

despreciar vt (**a**) (desdeñar) to scorn, despise, look down on (**b**) (rechazar) to reject, spurn (**c**) (menospreciar) to deprecate, belittle

despreciativo, -a adj scornful, contemptuous

desprecio nm (**a**) (desdén) scorn, contempt, disdain (**b**) (desaire) slight, snub

desprender 1 vt (**a**) (separar) to remove, detach (**b**) (soltar) to give off
 2 desprenderse vpr (**a**) (soltarse) to come off o away; Fig **de aquí se desprende que ...** it can be deduced from this that ...; Fig **el enojo se desprende de sus palabras** you can tell she's angry by what she's saying (**b**) (renunciar) to part with, give away; **se desprendió de todos sus bienes** she gave away all her possessions (**c**) Fig (liberarse) to rid oneself (**de** of), free oneself (**de** from); **se desprendió de todas sus dudas** he rid himself of his doubts

desprendido, -a 1 pp de **desprender**
 2 adj Fig generous, unselfish, disinterested

desprendimiento nm (**a**) (acción) loosening, detachment □ Med **d. de retina** detachment of the retina; **d. de tierras** landslide (**b**) Fig (generosidad) generosity, unselfishness

despreocupación nf (**a**) (tranquilidad) unconcern, nonchalance; (indiferencia) indifference (**b**) (descuido) carelessness, negligence

despreocupadamente *adv* in a carefree manner

despreocupado, -a 1 *pp de* **despreocuparse**
  2 *adj* (**a**) *(tranquilo)* unconcerned, unworried; *(indiferente)* indifferent (**b**) *(descuidado)* careless, negligent, sloppy; **tener un estilo d. en el vestir** to dress sloppily o carelessly

despreocuparse *vpr* (**a**) *(tranquilizarse)* to stop worrying (**b**) *(desentenderse)* to be unconcerned, be indifferent (**de** to)

desprestigiar 1 *vt (desacreditar)* to discredit, run down; **su conducta le ha desprestigiado** his behaviour has ruined his reputation
  2 desprestigiarse *vpr* to lose one's prestige, bring discredit on oneself

desprestigio *nm* discredit, loss of reputation; **campaña de d.** smear campaign

despresurización *nf* depressurization; **en caso de d. de la cabina** *(en avión)* if there is a sudden fall in cabin pressure

desprevenido, -a *adj* unprepared, unready; **pillar** o *Esp* **coger a algn d.** to catch sb unawares, take sb by surprise

desproporción *nf* disproportion, lack of proportion

desproporcionado, -a *adj* disproportionate, disproportioned, out of proportion

despropósito *nm* piece of nonsense, silly remark; **decir muchos despropósitos** to talk a lot of nonsense

desproteger [52] *vt Inform (programa)* to hack into

desprotegido, -a *adj* unprotected

desprovisto, -a *adj* lacking (**de** -), without (**de** -), devoid (**de** of); **d. de interés** devoid of interest, uninteresting; **estar d. de** to be lacking in, lack

después *adv* (**a**) *(gen) (tiempo)* afterwards, later; *(entonces)* then; *(luego)* next; **poco d.** soon after; **¿qué pasó d.?** *(entonces)* what happened then?; *(luego)* what happened next?; **vendrá d.** he'll come later (**b**) *(orden)* next, after; **mi calle está d.** my street is next (**c**) **d. de** *(tiempo)* after; *(desde)* since; **d. de la guerra** after the war; **d. de 1975** since 1975 (**d**) **d. de** *(orden)* after; **el 2 está del 1 2** comes after 1; **mi calle está d. de la tuya** my street is the one after yours (**e**) **d. (de) que** after; **d. (de) que amanezca saldremos** we'll go out when the sun is up; **d. (de) que lo hice, me arrepentí** after doing it, I regretted it (**f**) *(al fin y al cabo)* **d. de todo** after all; **d. de todo es un buen chico** when all is said and done, he's a nice guy

despuntado, -a 1 *pp de* **despuntar**
  2 *adj* blunt

despuntar 1 *vt* (**a**) *(embotar)* to blunt, make blunt (**b**) *Náut (cabo, punta)* to round
  2 *vi* (**a**) *(planta)* to sprout; *(flor)* to bud (**b**) *(alba)* to break; **al d. el alba** at daybreak, at dawn (**c**) *Fig (destacar)* to excel, stand out; **despunta por su inteligencia** her intelligence is outstanding

desquiciar 1 *vt* (**a**) *(puerta)* to unhinge, take off its hinges (**b**) *Fig (transtornar)* to upset, unsettle; *(volver loco)* to unhinge
  2 desquiciarse *vpr* (**a**) *(puerta)* to come off its hinges (**b**) *Fig (volverse loco)* to go crazy

desquitarse *vpr* to get even, take revenge; **hoy he perdido pero mañana me desquitaré de esta derrota** I've lost today but I'll make up for my defeat tomorrow·

desquite *nm (satisfacción)* satisfaction; *(venganza)* revenge, retaliation; **tomarse el d.** to have one's revenge, get one's own back

desratización *nf* rodent extermination

desratizar [14] *vt* to clear of rodents

desregulación *nf* deregulation

desregular *vt* to deregulate

desriñonarse *vpr Fam (esforzarse)* to break one's back

destacable *adj* notable, worthy of comment

destacado, -a 1 *pp de* **destacar**
  2 *adj* outstanding, prominent, distinguished

destacamento *nm* (**a**) *Mil* detachment (**b**)· *Am* **d. de policía** *(comisaría)* police station

destacar [59] **1** *vt* (**a**) *Mil* to detach (**b**) *Arte* to make stand out, highlight (**c**) *Fig* to emphasize, point out; **me gustaría d. que ...** I would like to point out that ...
  2 *vi (descollar)* to stand out; **destaca por su bondad** his kindness is exceptional
  3 destacarse *vpr* to stand out

destajo *nm* piecework; **trabajar a d.** to do piecework; *Fig* **hablar a d.** to talk nineteen to the dozen

destapador *nm Am* bottle opener

destapar 1 *vt* (**a**) *(abrir)* to open; *(descubrir)* to uncover; *(botella)* to uncork; *(abrir la tapa)* to take the lid off (**b**) *Fig* to reveal, uncover
  2 *vi Méx (caballo)* to bolt
  3 destaparse *vpr* (**a**) *(desabrigarse)* to get uncovered; **durmiendo me destapé** the sheets slipped off me while I was asleep (**b**) *Fig* to do unexpectedly; **se destapó diciendo que no quería ir** all of a sudden he said he didn't want to go

destape *nm Fam Cin Teat* striptease; **una película de d.** a blue movie

destartalado, -a *adj (desproporcionado)* rambling; *(desvencijado)* tumbledown, ramshackle; *(coche)* rickety

destellar *vi* to flash, sparkle, glitter

destello *nm (resplandor)* flash, sparkle; *(brillo)* gleam, wink; *Fig* glimmer; **a veces tiene destellos de inteligencia** sometimes he shows a glimmer of intelligence

destemplado, -a 1 *pp de* **destemplar**
  2 *adj* (**a**) *Mús* harsh, out of tune, discordant (**b**) *(voz, gesto)* sharp, snappy; **con cajas destempladas** rudely, brusquely (**c**) *(carácter, actitud)* irritable, tetchy (**d**) *Meteor (tiempo)* unpleasant (**e**) *(enfermo)* indisposed, out of sorts

destemplanza *nf* (**a**) *Mús* harshness (**b**) *(irritabilidad)* irritability (**c**) *Meteor* unpleasantness (**d**) *Med (indisposición)* indisposition

destemplar 1 *vt* (**a**) *Mús (desafinar)* to put out of tune (**b**) *Fig (descomponer)* to disturb, upset
  2 destemplarse *vpr* (**a**) *Mús (desafinarse)* to get out of tune (**b**) *Med* to become indisposed o out of sorts (**c**) *Andes Guat Méx (sentir dentera)* to have one's teeth on edge

desteñir [47] **1** *vt* to discolour, *US* discolor
  2 *vi* to lose colour o *US* color, fade; *(color)* to run; **esta tela destiñe** this fabric is not colour fast
  3 desteñirse *vpr* to lose colour o *US* color, fade; **los pantalones se destiñeron** the trousers faded

desternillante *adj* hysterically funny

desternillarse *vi Fam* **d. (de risa)** to split one's sides laughing

desterrado, -a 1 *pp de* **desterrar**
  2 *nm,f* exile

desterrar [3] *vt* to exile, banish; *Fig* **d. la tristeza** to banish sadness

destetar *vt* to wean

destete *nm* weaning

destiempo: a destiempo *loc adv* at the wrong time o moment

destierro *nm* (**a**) *(acción, pena)* exile (**b**) *(lugar)* place of exile

destilación *nf* distillation

destilado, -a 1 *pp de* **destilar**
2 *adj* distilled

destilador, -a 1 *adj* distilling
2 *nm,f* (**a**) *(persona)* distiller (**b**) *(alambique)* still

destilar *vt* (**a**) *(filtrar)* to distil (**b**) *(sangre, pus)* to exude, ooze (**c**) *Fig (revelar)* to exude, reveal; **sus ojos destilaban odio** the look in her eyes was full of hatred

destilería *nf* distillery

destinado, -a 1 *pp de* **destinar**
2 *adj* destined, bound; *Fig* **estar d. al fracaso** to be doomed to failure

destinar *vt* (**a**) *(asignar)* to set aside, assign; **d. una cantidad de dinero para gastos** to allot some money for expenses, put aside some money for expenses (**b**) *(nombrar)* to appoint; **le han destinado a la sucursal de Granada** he has been appointed to the Granada branch (**c**) *Mil (asignar a puesto)* to post

destinatario, -a *nm,f* (**a**) *(de paquete, carta)* addressee (**b**) *(de mercancías)* consignee

destino *nm* (**a**) *(uso)* purpose, use; **una habitación sin d. fijo** an all-purpose room (**b**) *(rumbo)* destination; **el avión con d. a Santiago** the plane to Santiago; **el barco con d. a Dublín** the boat bound for Dublin; **salir con d. a Salamanca** to leave for Salamanca (**c**) *(puesto de trabajo)* position, post; **salió ayer para su d.** he left yesterday to take up his post; **un d. de cartero** a job as a postman (**d**) *(sino)* fate, fortune; **el d. lo quiso así** it was fate, it was fated to be; **la fuerza del d.** the power of destiny

destitución *nf* dismissal from office

destituir [34] *vt* to dismiss o remove from office

destornillador *nm* (**a**) *(herramienta)* screwdriver (**b**) *Fam (combinado)* screwdriver, vodka and orange

destornillar *vt* to unscrew

destrenzar [14] *vt* to unplait

destreza *nf* skill, dexterity; **tener d.** to be skilful

destripar *vt* (**a**) *(animal, persona)* to disembowel; *(pescado)* to gut (**b**) *(despanzurrar)* to cut open; **destripé el cojín** I tore the cushion open

destronamiento *nm* *(de un monarca)* dethronement; *Fig* overthrow

destronar *vt (monarca)* to dethrone; *Fig* to overthrow

destrozado, -a 1 *pp de* **destrozar**
2 *adj* (**a**) *(vestido, zapatos)* ruined; *(jarrón, cámara)* smashed; **estos zapatos están destrozados** these shoes are ruined (**b**) *(moralmente)* shattered, broken (**c**) *(muy cansado)* done in, worn-out, exhausted

destrozar [14] *vt* (**a**) *(romper)* to destroy, ruin, wreck; *(rasgar)* to tear to shreds o pieces; **el huracán destrozó los edificios** the hurricane wrecked the buildings; **el perro me ha destrozado la chaqueta** the dog has torn my jacket to shreds (**b**) *Fig (abatir moralmente)* to crush, shatter (**c**) *Fig (vida, persona)* to ruin; *(corazón)* to break

destrozo *nm* (**a**) *(gen)* destruction (**b**) **destrozos** damage *sing*; **los destrozos ocasionados por la tormenta** the damage caused by the storm

destrucción *nf* destruction

destructivo, -a *adj* destructive

destructor, -a 1 *adj* destructive
2 *nm Náut* destroyer

destruir [34] *vt (gen)* to destroy; *Fig (persona, proyecto)* to ruin

desubicar [59] *vt Andes RP* to confuse

desunión *nf* (**a**) *(división)* separation, division (**b**) *(discordia)* dissension, discord; **la d. entre los trabajadores** the lack of solidarity among the workers

desunir *vt* (**a**) *(dividir)* to separate, pull apart (**b**) *(enemistar)* to set at odds, split; **las diferencias políticas desunen a los países** political differences set countries against each other

desusado, -a *adj* (**a**) *(anticuado)* old-fashioned, outdated (**b**) *(inusitado)* unusual, extraordinary

desuso *nm* disuse; **caer en d.** to fall into disuse; **en d.** obsolete, outdated

desvaído, -a *adj* (**a**) *(color)* faded, pale; *(contorno)* blurred (**b**) *(persona)* drab, dull

desvalido, -a 1 *adj* helpless, destitute
2 *nm,f* destitute person; **los desvalidos** the needy

desvalijamiento *nm* theft, robbery

desvalijar *vt (robar)* to clean out, rob; *(casa, tienda)* to burgle; **me desvalijaron la casa** my house was stripped bare

desvalorización *nf* devaluation, depreciation

desvalorizar [14] *vt* to devalue, depreciate

desván *nm* attic, loft

desvanecer [46] 1 *vt* (**a**) *(disipar)* to cause to vanish, make disappear; *Fig* to dispel; **d. dudas/temores** to dispel doubts/fears (**b**) *(color)* to fade; *(contorno)* to blur
2 **desvanecerse** *vpr* (**a**) *(disiparse)* to vanish, fade away (**b**) *(desmayarse)* to faint

desvanecimiento *nm* (**a**) *(desaparición)* disappearance, dispelling (**b**) *(desmayo)* faint, fainting fit

desvariar [32] *vi* to talk nonsense, rave

desvarío *nm* (**a**) *(delirio)* raving, delirium (**b**) *(disparate)* incoherence, wanderings *pl* of the mind

desvelado, -a 1 *pp de* **desvelar**
2 *adj* awake, wide awake

desvelar 1 *vt (despabilar)* to keep awake, stop from sleeping; **el café me desvela** coffee keeps me awake
2 **desvelarse** *vpr* (**a**) *(desvivirse)* to devote oneself (**por** to); **ella se desvela por el bienestar de todos** she does her utmost to see that everybody is happy (**b**) *(despabilarse)* to stay awake; **si leo novelas me desvelo** if I read novels I can't get to sleep

desvelo *nm* (**a**) *(insomnio)* insomnia, sleeplessness (**b**) **desvelos** *(esfuerzos)* efforts, pains; **su familia es el objeto de todos sus d.** he devotes himself entirely to his family

desvencijado 1 *pp de* **desvencijar**
2 *adj (gen)* broken; *(máquina)* broken-down

desvencijar 1 *vt (romper)* to break; *(máquina)* to break down
2 **desvencijarse** *vpr (romperse)* to fall apart; *(aflojarse)* to become loose

desventaja *nf* disadvantage, drawback; **estar en d.** to be at a disadvantage; **las desventajas de una profesión** the drawbacks of a profession

desventajoso, -a *adj* disadvantageous, unfavourable, *US* unfavorable

desventura *nf* misfortune, bad luck

desventurado, -a 1 *adj* unfortunate, unlucky; **una vida desventurada** an unhappy life
2 *nm,f* unfortunate person, wretch; **los desventurados** the unfortunate; **un pobre d.** a poor wretch

desvergonzado, -a 1 *adj* (**a**) *(sin decoro)* shameless, impudent (**b**) *(descarado)* insolent
2 *nm,f* (**a**) *(sinvergüenza)* shameless person (**b**) *(fresco)* insolent o cheeky person

desvergüenza *nf* (**a**) *(falta de decoro)* impudence, shamelessness (**b**) *(atrevimiento)* cheek, nerve, insolence; **tuvo la d. de negarlo** he had the cheek to deny it (**c**) *(impertinencia)* insolent o rude remark

desvestir [47] **1** vt to undress
2 desvestirse vpr to undress, get undressed
desviación nf deviation; Med **d. de columna** slipped disc; **d. de la norma** deviation from the norm; **d. de una carretera** diversion, detour
desviacionismo nm deviationism
desviacionista adj & nmf deviationist
desviar [32] **1** vt (a) (rio, carretera) to divert; (golpe) to deflect; Fig (tema) to change; Fig (pregunta) to parry, evade; **d. la mirada** to look away (b) (descaminar) to lead away from; **d. del buen camino** to lead astray
2 desviarse vpr (a) (avión, barco) to go off course; (coche) to make a detour (b) (persona, camino) to leave; **nos desviamos de la carretera principal** we left the main road; Fig **d. del objetivo** to lose sight of one's purpose; Fig **d. del tema** to digress
desvinculación nf releasing, freeing
desvincular **1** vt to separate, free
2 desvincularse vpr to separate, cut oneself off; **d. de la familia** to break away from one's family
desvío nm diversion, detour; **d. por obras** diversion due to roadworks; Tel **d. de llamadas** call transfer
desvirgar [38] vt to deflower
desvirtuar [4] vt (a) (debilitar) to impair, spoil (b) (anular) to cancel out, invalidate
desvivirse vpr (a) (gustar mucho) to be mad about; **se desvive por el chocolate** he is mad about chocolate (b) (esforzarse) to do one's utmost; **se desvivieron por ayudarnos** they bent over backwards to help us
detalladamente adv in (great) detail
detallado, -a **1** pp de detallar
2 adj detailed, thorough
detallar vt (a) (narrar con detalle) to relate in detail (b) (precisar) to give the details of; **d. la hora y el día** to give the exact hour and day (c) Com to retail
detalle **1** nm (a) (pormenor, rasgo) detail; **contar con d.** to go into detail; **dar detalles** to give details; **sin entrar en d.** without going into details (b) (delicadeza) nice thought, nicety; **¡qué d.!** how nice!, how sweet!; **tiene muchos detalles** he is very considerate (c) (toque decorativo) touch, ornament
2 al detalle loc adv Com retail; **en este almacén no se vende al d.** we don't sell retail in this warehouse
detallista **1** adj (a) (perfeccionista) perfectionist, discriminating (b) (delicado) thoughtful, considerate
2 nmf Com retailer, retail trader
detección nf detection
detectar vt to detect
detective nmf detective ◻ **d. privado** private detective o eye
detectivesco, -a adj **labor detectivesca** detective work
detector, -a nm,f detector ◻ **d. de incendios** fire detector; **d. de mentiras** lie detector; **d. de un radar** radar scanner
detención nf (a) (paro) stopping, halting, hold-up; **con d.** carefully, thoroughly (b) Jur (arresto) detention, arrest
detener [65] **1** vt (a) (parar) to stop, halt; **d. las negociaciones** to hold up negotiations (b) (retener) to delay; **no quiero detenerle más** I won't keep you any longer (c) Jur (arrestar) to arrest, detain
2 detenerse vpr (a) (pararse) to stop; **se detuvo y la miró** he stopped and looked at her (b) (entretenerse) to hang about, linger
detenidamente adv carefully, thoroughly
detenido, -a **1** pp de detener

2 adj (a) (parado) standing still, stopped (b) (detallado) detailed, thorough; **después de un d. análisis** after a careful analysis
3 nm,f detainee, person under arrest
detenimiento nm **con d.** carefully, thoroughly
detentar vt to hold unlawfully
detergente adj & nm detergent
deteriorado, -a **1** pp de deteriorar
2 adj damaged, worn
deteriorar **1** vt (estropear) to spoil, damage
2 deteriorarse vpr (a) (estropearse) to get damaged, wear out (b) (empeorar) to get worse
deterioro nm (a) (daño) damage; **el d. de la ropa** wear and tear on clothes; **ir en d. de** to harm (b) (empeoramiento) deterioration, worsening; **el d. de las relaciones internacionales** the deterioration of international relations
determinable adj determinable
determinación nf (a) (decisión) decision; **tomar una d.** to make a resolution o a decision (b) (valor) determination, resolution; **con d.** determinedly
determinado, -a **1** pp de determinar
2 adj (a) (preciso) definite, precise; **en el día d.** on the appointed day; **en este caso d.** in this particular case (b) (resuelto) decisive, resolute (c) Ling definite (d) Mat determinate
determinante **1** adj decisive, determinant
2 nm Mat determinant
determinar **1** vt (a) (decidir) to decide on; **han determinado salir el lunes** they have decided to leave on Monday (b) (indicar) to detect, grasp; **podemos d. las razones de su conducta** we can see the reasons for his behaviour (c) (disponer) to stipulate (d) (fijar) to fix, set; **determinaron la fecha de la boda** they fixed the date of the wedding (e) (ocasionar) to bring about; **la nieve determinó el accidente** the accident was caused by the snow; **las grandes manifestaciones determinaron un cambio en la legislación** the massive demonstrations brought about a change in the law
2 determinarse vpr to bring oneself to, make up one's mind to; **no se determinaba a irse** he couldn't make up his mind to go
determinativo, -a adj determinant; Ling determinative
determinismo nm Filos determinism
determinista adj & nmf Filos determinist
detestable adj detestable, respulsive; **un olor d.** an awful smell
detestar vt to detest, hate
detonación nf detonation, explosion
detonador nm detonator
detonante **1** adj detonating, explosive
2 nm detonator; Fig trigger; **el golpe de estado fue el d. de la crisis** the coup d'état triggered off the crisis
detonar vt to detonate, explode
detractor, -a **1** adj slanderous
2 nm,f detractor, slanderer
detrás adv (a) (en el espacio) behind, on o at the back (de of); **el índice está d.** the index is at the back; **ponlo d. de la mesa** put it behind the table; **salió de d.** she came out from behind (b) (después) then, afterwards; **los jugadores salen primero y d. los entrenadores** the players appear first and after them the coaches (c) Fig **d. de** behind; **me pregunto qué hay d. de tanta amabilidad** I wonder what is behind all his kindness (d) Fig **por d.** behind the back; **hablan de él por d.** they are talking about him behind his back

detrimento *nm* detriment, harm; **en d. de** to the detriment of; **sin d. de** without detriment to

detrito *nm,* **detritus** *nm inv Geol* detritus

deuda *nf Fin* debt; **contraer una d.** to get into debt; **estoy en d. contigo** *(monetaria)* I am in debt to you, I owe you money; *(moral)* I am indebted to you; *Fig* **lo prometido es d.** a promise is a promise ❑ **d. del Estado** public debt, government stock; **d. pública** *Br* national debt, *US* public debt

deudo, -a *nm,f* relative

deudor, -a 1 *adj* indebted
2 *nm,f* debtor

devaluación *nf* devaluation

devaluar [4] *vt* to devaluate

devanador *nm Am* winder, reel

devanar 1 *vt (hilo)* to wind; *(alambre)* to coil
2 devanarse *vpr Fam Fig* **d. los sesos** to *Br* rack *o US* cudgel one's brains

devaneo *nm* (a) *(pérdida de tiempo)* waste of time, frivolity (b) *(amorío)* flirting

devastación *nf* devastation

devastador, -a 1 *adj* devastating
2 *nm,f* devastator

devastar *vt* to devastate, ravage

develar *vt Am (revelar)* to reveal, disclose; *(inaugurar)* to unveil

devengado, -a 1 *pp de* **devengar**
2 *adj (sueldo)* due; *(intereses)* accrued

devengar [38] *vt (sueldo)* to earn; *(intereses)* to earn, accrue; **ese dinero no devenga intereses** that money does not earn any interest

devengo 1 *véanse* **devengar** & **devenir²**
2 *nm (cantidad)* amount due

devenir¹ *nm Filos* flow of life

devenir² [69] *vi* to become, turn into

devoción *nf* (a) *Rel* devotion, devoutness; **con d.** devoutly; *Fam* **Mozart no es santo de mi d.** Mozart isn't really my cup of tea (b) *(dedicación, afición)* devotion; **siente una gran d. por su madre** he is devoted to his mother

devocionario *nm* prayer book

devolución *nf* (a) *(restitución)* giving back, return; *Com* refund, repayment; **d. del importe** refund of money; **no se admiten devoluciones** purchases cannot be exchanged (b) *Jur* devolution

devolver [41] *(pp* **devuelto)** **1** *vt* (a) *(restituir)* to give back, return; *Com* to refund, return, repay; **d. la mesa a su lugar** to put the table back in its place; **d. los libros a la biblioteca** to return the books to the library; **d. una visita** to return a visit (b) *(restaurar)* to restore, give back; **d. la paz a un país** to restore peace to a country (c) *(vomitar)* to vomit, throw *o* bring up
2 devolverse *vpr Am salvo RP* to go *o* come back, return

devorador, -a *adj* devouring; **hambre devoradora** ravenous hunger

devorar *vt* (a) *(comer)* to devour (b) *(engullir)* to eat up, gobble up (c) *Fig (consumir)* to devour, consume; **d. un libro** to devour a book; **el fuego devoró la casa** the fire devoured the house; **los celos la devoraban** she was eaten up with jealousy

devoto, -a 1 *adj Rel* pious, devout; **promesa devota** devotional promise; *Fig* **d. de su familia** devoted to his family
2 *nm,f* (a) *Rel* pious person (b) *Fig (seguidor)* devotee

devuelto, -a 1 *pp de* **devolver**

2 *adj* returned, given back; **el dinero d.** the refunded money

dextrina *nf Quím* dextrin, dextrina

deyección *nf* (a) *(de volcán)* ejecta *pl* (b) *Med* dejecta *pl,* faeces *pl*

DF *nm (abrev de* **Distrito Federal**) *(en México)* Mexico City; *(en Venezuela)* Caracas

dg *(abrev de* **decigramo)** dg

DGT *nf (abrev de* **Dirección General de Tráfico**) = Spanish government department responsible for road transport

di (a) *pt indef véase* **dar** (b) *imperat véase* **decir²**

día *nm* (a) *(periodo de tiempo)* day; **al d. siguiente/al otro d.** the following day; **cada d.** each *o* every day; **de un d. para otro** any day now; **del d.** fresh; **d. a d.** day by day; **hoy (en) d.** nowadays; **¿qué d. es hoy?** what's the date today; **todos los días** every day, daily; **un d. sí y otro no** every other day; *Fig* **el d. de mañana** in the future; *Fig* **el d. menos pensado, cualquier d.** when you least expect it, one of these fine days; *Fig* **en su d.** in due course; *Fig* **estar al d.** to be up to date; *Fig* **poner al d.** to bring up to date; *Fig* **un buen d.** one fine day; *Fig* **un d. señalado** a red-letter day; *Fig* **vivir al d.** to live from hand to mouth ❑ **d. de paga** payday; **d. festivo** holiday; **d. laborable** working day; **d. lectivo** teaching day; **d. libre** free day, day off (b) *(luz solar)* daytime; **a la luz del d.** in daylight; **al caer el d.** at dusk; **al despuntar el d.** at dawn, at daybreak; **de d.** by day; **durante el d.** during the daytime; **es de d.** it is daylight (c) *(tiempo atmosférico)* weather, day; **hace buen/mal d.** it's a nice/bad day, the weather is nice/bad today

diabetes *nf Med* diabetes

diabético, -a *adj & nm,f* diabetic

diablesa *nf* she-devil

diablillo *nm Fam* imp

diablo *nm* devil, demon; *Fig* **un pobre d.** a poor devil; *Fam* **¡al d. con los prejuicios!** to hell with prejudice; *Fam* **¿cómo/dónde diablos ...?** how/where on earth ...?; how/where the hell ...?; *Fam* **este niño es un d.** he's a little devil; *Fam* **le mandó al d.** she told him to go to hell; *Fam* **¿qué diablos ...?** what the hell ...?; *Fam* **un jaleo de (todos) los diablos** an almighty racket

diablura *nf* mischief, naughtiness, naughty behaviour

diabólico, -a *adj* (a) *(relativo al diablo)* devilish, diabolic (b) *(muy intrincado)* diabolical

diábolo *nm* diabolo

diácono *nm* deacon; **ordenar de d.** to ordain as a deacon

diacronía *nf* diachrony

diacrónico, -a *adj* diachronic; **lingüística diacrónica** diachronic linguistics

diadema *nf* diadem; *(joya)* tiara

diafanidad *nf* diaphaneity, translucence; *(transparencia)* transparency

diáfano, -a *adj* diaphanous, translucent; *(transparente)* transparent

diafragma *nm (gen)* diaphragm; *Fot* aperture; *Med* cap

diagnosis *nf inv Med* diagnosis

diagnosticar [59] *vt* to diagnose

diagnóstico, -a 1 *adj* diagnostic
2 *nm Med* diagnosis

diagonal *adj & nf* diagonal; **en d.** diagonally

diagrama *nm* diagram ❑ **d. de flujo** flowchart

dial *nm* dial

dialectal *adj* dialectal

dialéctica *nf* dialectic, dialectics *sing*
dialéctico, -a *adj* dialectical; *Filos* **materialismo d.** dialectical materialism
dialecto *nm* dialect
dialectología *nf* dialectology
diálisis *nf inv* dialysis
dialogante *adj* **ser una persona d.** to be open to dialogue
dialogar [38] **1** *vi* to have a conversation, talk
2 *vt* to write in dialogue form
diálogo *nm* dialogue, conversation
diamante *nm* diamond; **d. en bruto** uncut diamond
diamantino, -a *adj* diamond-like, diamantine
diametral *adj* diametrical, diametral
diametralmente *adv* diametrically; **d. opuesto a** diametrically opposed to
diámetro *nm Mat* diameter
diana *nf* (a) *Mil* reveille; **tocar d.** to sound reveille (b) *(blanco)* bull's eye; **hacer d.** to hit the bull's eye
diantre *nm Euf* hell
diapasón *nm Mús* (a) *(instrumento)* tuning fork, diapason (b) *(escala)* diapason, scale, range; **subir/bajar el d.** to raise/lower the tone of one's voice (c) *(de instrumento de cuerda)* fingerboard
diapositiva *nf Fot* slide
diariamente *adv* daily, every day
diario, -a 1 *adj* daily; **a d.** daily, every day; **ropa de d.** everyday clothes
2 *nm* (a) *Prensa* (daily) newspaper; **d. de la mañana/la tarde** morning/evening newspaper (b) *(libro, narración)* diary, journal □ *Náut* **d. de a bordo, d. de navegación** logbook
diarrea *nf Med* diarrhoea, *US* diarrhea; *Fam Fig* **d. verbal** verbal diarrhoea
diáspora *nf* diaspora
diástole *nf Anat* diastole
diatriba *nf* diatribe; **lanzar una d.** to launch an attack
dibujante *nmf* (a) *(artista)* sketcher, drawer; **d. de dibujos animados** cartoonist (b) *Téc* draughtsperson; *(hombre)* draughtsman, *US* draftsman; *(mujer)* draughtswoman, *US* draftswoman
dibujar *vt* (a) *(trazar)* to draw, sketch (b) *Fig (describir)* to describe
2 dibujarse *vpr* to be outlined *o* shown; **en su rostro se dibujó la alegría** her face showed her happiness
dibujo *nm* (a) *(arte)* drawing, sketching □ **d. artístico/técnico** artistic/technical drawing; **d. lineal** draughtsmanship (b) *(figura)* drawing, sketch □ **dibujos animados** cartoons (c) *(muestra)* pattern
dicción *nf* diction
diccionario *nm* dictionary
díceres *nmpl Am (murmuraciones)* gossip *sing*; *(rumores)* rumour *sing*
dicha *nf* (a) *(hecho afortunado, suerte)* good fortune; **nunca es tarde si la d. es buena** better late than never (b) *(alegría)* happiness
dicharachero, -a *adj* talkative and witty *o* funny
dicho, -a 1 *pp de* **decir²**
2 *adj* said; **dicha información** this (piece of) information/ **d. de otro modo** to put it another way; **d. hombre** the said man; **d. sea de paso** let it be said in passing; **d. y hecho** no sooner said than done; **lo d.** what we said; **mejor d.** or rather; **propiamente d.** strictly speaking
3 *nm (refrán)* saying, proverb; *Prov* **del d. al hecho hay**

mucho trecho there's many a slip twixt cup and lip, it is easier said than done
dichoso, -a *adj* (a) *(feliz)* happy, fortunate (b) *Fam (molesto)* damned; **¡este d. trabajo!** this damned job!
diciembre *nm* December; *véase tamb* **noviembre**
dicotomía *nf* dichotomy
dictado 1 *pp de* **dictar**
2 *nm* (a) *(lectura de texto)* dictation; **escribir algo al d.** to take sth down (b) *dictados Fig* dictates; **los dictados de la conciencia** the dictates of conscience
dictador, -a *nm,f* dictator
dictadura *nf* dictatorship
dictáfono® *nm* Dictaphone®
dictamen *nm* (a) *(informe)* report; **la junta directiva emitió su d. final** the board of directors gave their final report (b) *(opinión)* opinion
dictaminar *vi* to pronounce *o* pass judgement, give an opinion (**sobre** on)
dictar *vt* (a) *(texto)* to dictate (b) *(ley)* to enact, decree; *(sentencia)* to pass (c) *(aconsejar)* to suggest, say; **haz lo que el sentido común te dicte** do what common sense tells you (d) *(conferencia, discurso)* to give, deliver
dictatorial *adj* dictatorial
didáctica *nf* didactics *sing*
didáctico, -a *adj* didactic
diecinueve 1 *adj (cardinal)* nineteen; *(ordinal)* nineteenth; **a las d. horas** at nineteen hundred hours
2 *nm inv* (a) *(número)* nineteen (b) *(fecha)* nineteenth; *véase tamb* **ocho**
diecinueveavo, -a 1 *adj* nineteenth
2 *nm,f (de una serie)* nineteenth
3 *nm (parte)* nineteenth; *véase tamb* **octavo, -a**
dieciochesco, -a *adj* eighteenth-century
dieciocho 1 *adj (cardinal)* eighteen; *(ordinal)* eighteenth; **a las d. horas** at eighteen hundred hours
2 *nm* (a) *(número)* eighteen (b) *(fecha)* eighteenth; *véase tamb* **ocho**
dieciséis 1 *adj (cardinal)* sixteen; *(ordinal)* sixteenth; **a las d. horas** at sixteen hundred hours
2 *nm inv* (a) *(número)* sixteen (b) *(fecha)* sixteenth; *véase tamb* **ocho**
dieciseisavo, -a 1 *adj* sixteenth
2 *nm,f (de una serie)* sixteenth
3 *nm (parte)* sixteenth; *véase tamb* **octavo, -a**
diecisiete 1 *adj (cardinal)* seventeen; *(cardinal)* seventeenth; **a las d. horas** at seventeen hundred hours
2 *nm inv* (a) *(número)* seventeen (b) *(fecha)* seventeenth; *véase tamb* **ocho**
diecisieteavo, -a 1 *adj* seventeenth
2 *nm,f (de una serie)* seventeenth
3 *nm (parte)* seventeenth; *véase tamb* **octavo, -a**
diente *nm* tooth; *Arquit* toothing brick; *Téc* cog; **echar los dientes** to teethe; *Fig* **de dientes afuera** without meaning it, hypocritically; *Fig* **hablar entre dientes** to mumble; *Fig* **poner los dientes largos a algn** to make sb green with envy; *Fam* **tener buen d.** to be a good eater □ *Fig* **d. de ajo** clove of garlic; **d. de leche** milk tooth; **d. de león** *(planta)* dandelion; **d. picado** decayed tooth; **dientes postizos** false teeth
diera *subj imperf véase* **dar**
diéresis *nm inv Ling* diaeresis
diesel 1 *adj* diesel
2 *nm* diesel engine
diestra *nf* right hand; **a la d.** on the right
diestramente *adv* skilfully, *US* skillfully

diestro, -a 1 *adj* (**a**) *Literario* on the right-hand side; **estuvo sentado en la parte diestra** he sat on the right-hand side; *Fig Esp* **a d. y siniestro** right, left and centre, wildly (**b**) *(hábil)* skilful, *US* skilful, clever

2 *nm Tau* bullfighter, matador

dieta[1] *nf (régimen)* diet; **estar a d.** to be on a diet

dieta[2] *nf* (**a**) *Pol (asamblea)* diet, assembly (**b**) **dietas** *Com* expenses *o* subsistence allowance

dietética *nf* dietetics *sing*

dietético, -a *adj* dietetic, dietary; **médico d.** dietician

dietista *nmf* dietician

diez 1 *adj (cardinal)* ten; *(ordinal)* tenth; **a las d.** at ten o'clock

2 *nm inv* (**a**) *(número)* ten (**b**) *(fecha)* tenth; *véase tamb* **ocho**

diezmar *vt* to decimate

difamación *nf* defamation, slander; *(escrita)* libel

difamador, -a 1 *adj* defamatory, slanderous; *(escrito)* libellous

2 *nm,f* defamer, slanderer

difamar *vt* to defame, slander; *(por escrito)* to libel

difamatorio, -a *adj* defamatory, slanderous; *(escrito)* libellous

diferencia *nf* difference; **a d. de** unlike; **d. de opinión** disagreement; **hacer d. entre** to make a distinction between

diferenciación *nf* differentiation

diferencial 1 *adj* distinguishing

2 *nm* differential

diferenciar 1 *vt.* (**a**) *(distinguir)* to differentiate, distinguish (**entre** between); **los daltónicos no diferencian entre el verde y el rojo** colour-blind people cannot tell green from red (**b**) *(hacer diferente)* to make different; **¿qué te diferencia de mí?** what makes you different from me?

2 diferenciarse *vpr* (**a**) *(distinguirse)* to differ (**de** from), be different (**de** from) (**b**) *(destacar)* to distinguish oneself, stand out; **se diferencia de las demás por sus rasgos orientales** she stands out from the rest because of her Eastern features

diferendo *nm Andes RP* dispute

diferente 1 *adj* different; **d. de los demás** different from the rest

2 *adv* differently; **pensamos d.** we disagree

diferido, -a 1 *pp de* **diferir**

2 *adj Rad TV,* **retransmisión en d.** recorded transmission

diferir [62] **1** *vt (aplazar)* to postpone, defer, put off; **han diferido la boda** the wedding has been put off

2 *vi (distinguirse)* to be different, differ (**entre, de** from)

difícil *adj* difficult, hard; **d. de complacer** hard to please; **d. de creer/hacer** difficult to believe/do; **es d. que llegue hoy** it is unlikely that she'll arrive today; **tiene un carácter d.** he has a difficult character

dificultad *nf (gen)* difficulty; *(problema)* trouble, problem

dificultar *vt* to make difficult, hinder, restrict, obstruct; **la niebla dificulta la visibilidad** fog reduces visibility

dificultoso, -a *adj* difficult, hard

difteria *nm Med* diphtheria

diftérico, -a *adj Med* diphtheric

difuminar *vt Arte* to blur, soften

difundir 1 *vt (luz, calor)* to diffuse; *Fig (noticia, enfermedad)* to spread

2 difundirse *vpr (luz, calor)* to become diffused; *Fig (noticia, enfermedad)* to spread; **se difundió la noticia de su muerte** the news spread that he had died

difunto, -a 1 *adj* late, deceased; **su difunta madre** her late mother

2 *nm,f* deceased □ **Día de los Difuntos** All Souls' *o* Saints' Day; **misa de difuntos** Requiem Mass

difusión *nf* (**a**) *(de noticia, enfermedad)* spreading; **tener gran d.** to be widely known (**b**) *(calor, luz)* diffusion (**c**) *Rad* broadcast, broadcasting

difuso, -a *adj* (**a**) *(luz)* diffuse (**b**) *Fig (estilo, discurso)* diffuse, wordy

difusor, -a *adj* spreading, propagating; **la agencia difusora de la noticia** the agency which made the news known

digerible *adj* digestible

digerir [62] *vt (comida)* to digest; *(información, hecho)* to assimilate

digestión *nf* digestion □ **corte de d.** sudden indigestion

digestivo, -a 1 *adj* digestive

2 *nm* digestive drink

digitador, -a *nm,f Am* keyboarder

digital *adj* digital; **huellas digitales** fingerprints

digitalización *nf Inform* digitizing

digitalizador *nm Inform* digitizer

digitalizar [14] *vt Inform* to digitize

digitar *vt Am* to key, type

dígito *nm Mat* digit

dignamente *adv* with dignity

dignarse *vpr* to deign (**a** to), condescend (**a** to)

dignatario, -a *nm,f* dignitary

dignidad *nf* (**a**) *(cualidad)* dignity (**b**) *(cargo)* office, post; *(rango)* rank

dignificar [59] *vt* to dignify

digno, -a *adj* (**a**) *(merecedor)* worthy, deserving; **d. de admiración** worthy of admiration; **d. de mención/verse** worth mentioning/seeing (**b**) *(apropiado)* fitting, appropriate (**c**) *(decoroso)* decent, good

digo *indic pres véase* **decir**[2]

digresión *nf* digression

dije[1] *pt indef véase* **decir**[2]

dije[2] *nm* charm, trinket

dilación *nf* delay, hold-up; **sin d.** without delay

dilapidación *nf* wasting, squandering

dilapidar *vt* to waste, squander

dilatación *nf* dilation, expansion

dilatado, -a 1 *pp de* **dilatar**

2 *adj* (**a**) *(agrandado)* dilated; **pupilas dilatadas** dilated pupils (**b**) *(vasto)* vast, extensive; **un hombre de dilatada experiencia** a man of vast experience

dilatar 1 *vt* (**a**) *(agrandar)* to expand; **el calor dilata los cuerpos** heat expands bodies (**b**) *Med* to dilate (**c**) *(prolongar)* to prolong (**d**) *(retrasar)* to delay

2 dilatarse *vpr* (**a**) *(agrandarse)* to expand (**b**) *Med* to dilate

dilatoria *nf* delay, procrastination

dilatorio, -a *adj* delaying

dilema *nm* dilemma

dilentante *nmf* dilettante

diletante *adj & nmf* dilettante

diligencia *nf* (**a**) *(esmero)* diligence, care; **con d.** diligently (**b**) *(gestión)* business (**c**) **diligencias** *Jur* formalities; **hacer unas d.** to go through the formalities; **instruir d.** to start proceedings □ **d. previas** inquiries

diligenciar *vt* to make a formal application (for)

diligente *adj* diligent

dilucidación *nf* elucidation

dilucidar *vt* to elucidate, clarify

diluir [34] **1** *vt* to dilute, dissolve
2 diluirse *vpr* to dilute

diluviar *v impers Meteor* to pour down, pour with rain

diluvio *nm* flood; **el D. (Universal)** the Flood; *Fig* **un d. de consejos** a torrent of advice; *Fig* **un d. de protestas** a storm *o* flood of protests

diluyo *indic pres véase* **diluir**

dimanar *vi* to emanate (**de** from)

dimensión *nf* (**a**) *(tamaño)* dimension, size; **de gran d.** very large (**b**) *Fig (importancia)* importance

dimensional *adj* dimensional

dimes *nmpl Fam* **d. y diretes** *(habladurías)* gossip *sing*; *(discusión)* quibbling *sing*; **andar en d. y diretes** to bicker, quibble

diminutivo, -a *adj & nm* diminutive

diminuto, -a *adj* minute, tiny

dimisión *nm* resignation; **presentar la d.** to hand in one's resignation

dimisionario, -a *adj* outgoing; **el director d.** the outgoing director

dimitir *vi & vt* to resign (**de** from); **d. de un cargo** to give in *o* tender one's resignation

Dinamarca *n* Denmark

dinámica *nf* dynamics *sing*

dinámico, -a *adj* dynamic

dinamismo *nm* dynamism

dinamita *nf* dynamite; **volar con d.** to dynamite

dinamitar *vt* to dynamite, blow up

dinamitero, -a *nm,f* dynamiter

dinamizar [14] *vt* to speed up

dinamo *nf,* **dínamo** *nf Esp Elec* dynamo

dinamómetro *nm* dynamometer

dinar *nm Fin* dinar

dinastía *nf* dynasty

dinástico, -a *adj* dynastic

dineral *nm* fortune; **ella se gastó un d. en la boda** she spent a fortune on the wedding

dinero *nm* money; **andar bien de d.** to have plenty of money; **andar mal** *o* **escaso de d.** to be short of money; **gente de d.** wealthy people ❏ **d. contante (y sonante)** cash; **d. efectivo** *o* **en metálico** cash; **d. falso** counterfeit money; **d. negro** undeclared income/payment; **d. para gastos** pocket money; **d. suelto** loose change

dinosaurio *nm* dinosaur

dintel *nm Arquit* lintel

diñar *vt Fam* to die; **diñarla** to snuff it, kick the bucket

diocesano, -a *adj & nm,f Rel* diocesan

diócesis *nf inv Rel* diocese

diodo *nm Elec* diode

dioptría *nf Med* dioptre, *US* diopter

dios *nm Rel* god, God; **a D. rogando y con el mazo dando** God helps those who help themselves; **a la buena de D.** any old how; **costar algo D. y ayuda** to be very difficult, be a real hassle; **D. los cría y ellos se juntan** birds of a feather flock together; **¡D. mío!** my God!; *Esp* **¡D. nos coja confesados!** God help us!; **hacer algo como D. manda** to do sth properly; **lo hice como D.** I did my very best, I did it as best as I could; **¡por D.!** for goodness sake!; **¡válgame D.!**, **¡vaya por D.!** good heavens!; *Fam* **armar la de D. es Cristo** to raise hell, make an almighty racket; *Fam* **ni D.** nobody; *Fam* **todo D.** everybody

diosa *nf* goddess

dióxido *nm Quím* dioxide; **d. de carbono** carbon dioxide

dioxina *nf Quím* dioxin

diploma *nm* diploma

diplomacia *nf* diplomacy

diplomado, -a 1 *pp de* **diplomarse**
2 *adj* qualified, with a diploma

diplomarse *vpr* to graduate

diplomático, -a 1 *adj* diplomatic; **cuerpo d.** diplomatic corps; **valija diplomática** diplomatic bag
2 *nm,f* diplomat

diplomatura *nf Educ* ≃ diploma, = qualification obtained after three years of university study

díptero, -a 1 *adj* (**a**) *Zool* dipterous (**b**) *Arquit* dipteral
2 *nm,f Zool* dipteran; **los dípteros** Diptera *pl*

díptico *nm* diptych

diptongo *nm Ling* diphthong

diputación *nf* **d. provincial** *Br* ≃ county council, = governing body of each province in Spain

diputado, -a *nm,f Br* ≃ Member of Parliament, M.P., *US* ≃ Representative ❏ **Cámara de Diputados** ≃ *Br* House of Commons, *US* ≃ Congress; **d. provincial** ≃ county councillor, = member of the governing body of a Spanish province

dique *nm Náut* dike ❏ **d. seco** dry dock

dirección *nf* (**a**) *(mando)* direction; **le dieron la d. del proyecto** they put him in charge of the project; **llevar la d. de algo** to run sth (**b**) *Cin Teat* production (**c**) *(dirigentes)* management; **por orden de la d.** by order of the management ❏ **d. comercial** commercial department; **d. general** head office (**d**) *(cargo)* directorship; *(de un partido)* leadership; *(de un colegio)* headship (**e**) *(destino)* destination; **salieron con d. a Soria** they left for Soria (**f**) *(sentido)* way; **calle de d. única** oneway street (**g**) *(señas)* address ❏ **d. electrónica** *(de correo)* e-mail address; *(de página)* web page address (**h**) *Aut Téc* steering ❏ *Esp* **d. asistida** power assisted steering; **'d. prohibida'** 'no entry'

direccional *nm Am Aut* indicator

direccionamiento *nm Inform* addressing

direccionar *vt Inform* to address

directa *nf Aut* top gear

directamente *adv* directly, straight away

directiva *nf* (**a**) *(junta)* board of directors (**b**) *(ley)* directive

directivo, -a 1 *adj* directive; **junta directiva** board of directors
2 *nm,f* director, manager, board member

directo, -a 1 *adj* direct; **emisión en d.** live broadcast
2 *nm Box* straight hit

director, -a *nm,f (gen)* director; *Cin* (film) director; *(de colegio) (hombre)* headmaster; *(mujer)* headmistress; *Univ* principal; *(de editorial)* editor; *(de prisión)* governor ❏ **d. adjunto** associate *o* deputy director; **d. artístico** artistic director; **d. comercial** marketing manager; **d. de cine** movie *o Br* film director; *Teat* **d. de escena** stage manager; **d. ejecutivo** executive director; **d. espiritual** father confessor; **d. general** *Br* managing director, *US* chief executive officer; **d. gerente** managing director; **d. de orquesta** conductor

directorio *nm* (**a**) *(gobierno)* governing body (**b**) *(normas)* instructions *pl* , directive (**c**) *Esp (guía)* directory, guide (**d**) *(junta)* board of directors (**e**) *Inform* directory

directriz 1 *adj* guiding; **líneas directrices** guidelines
2 *nf* (**a**) *(norma)* directive, instruction; **directrices** *(normas)* guidelines (**b**) *Mat* directrix

dirigencia *nf Am* leadership

dirigente 1 *adj* leading; **clase d.** ruling class

2 *nmf* leader; **los dirigentes de la empresa** the company management

dirigible *nm* airship

dirigir [24] **1** *vt* (**a**) *(gen)* to direct (**b**) *(empresa)* to manage; *(negocio, colegio)* to run (**c**) *Cin (película)* to direct; *Teat (obra)* to direct, produce; *Mús (orquesta)* to conduct; **d. un partido** to lead a party; **d. un periódico** to edit a newspaper; **d. una expedición/revuelta** to head an expedition/a revolt (**d**) *(guiar)* to guide; *Aut Náut* to steer (**e**) *(orientar)* to aim; *(acusación)* to level; *(carta, protesta)* to address; **consejos dirigidos a los jóvenes** advice aimed at the young; **d. los ojos hacia abajo** to look down; **estas palabras no van dirigidas a mí** these words are not meant for me (**f**) *(esfuerzos, atención)* to concentrate (**g**) *(apuntar)* to aim, point

2 dirigirse *vpr* (**a**) *(ir)* to go; **¿hacia dónde te diriges?** where are you heading for?; **nos dirigimos hacia el río** we made our way towards the river (**b**) *(escribir)* to write; **diríjase al apartado de correos 42** write to P.O. Box 42 (**c**) *(hablar)* to address, speak; **nunca se dirige a mí** he never speaks to me; **se dirigió a mí al hablar** she looked at me as she spoke

dirigismo *nm Econ* state control

dirimente *adj* (**a**) *(que anula)* nullifying (**b**) *(que zanja)* decisive, final; **un argumento d.** a decisive argument

dirimir *vt* (**a**) *(anular)* to nullify, declare void (**b**) *(zanjar)* to solve, end

discapacidad *nf* disability; **d. física** physical disability

discapacitado, -a 1 *adj* disabled

2 *nm,f* disabled person; **d. físico** physically disabled person

discar [59] *vt Andes RP Tel* to dial

discernimiento *nm* discernment, judgement

discernir [25] *vt* to discern, distinguish, tell; **d. el bien del mal** to tell good from evil

disciplina *nf* (**a**) *(normas, actitud)* discipline (**b**) *(asignatura)* subject

disciplinado, -a *adj* disciplined

disciplinar *vt* to discipline, instruct

disciplinario, -a *adj* disciplinary

discípulo, -a *nm,f* (**a**) *(alumno)* student, pupil (**b**) *(seguidor)* disciple, follower

disc-jockey [dis'jokei] *(pl* **disc-jockeys)** *nmf* disc jockey

disco *nm* (**a**) *Geom* disc, *US* disk (**b**) *Dep* discus (**c**) *Mús* record; **grabar un d.** to make a record ❑ **d. compacto** compact disc (**d**) *Tel* dial (**e**) *(semáforo)* **d. rojo/verde** red/green light (**f**) *Inform* disk ❑ **d. duro/flexible** hard/floppy disk (**g**) *Fam (conversación repetida)* same old story

discóbolo *nm Dep* discus thrower

discografía *nf* records previously released *(by an artist or group)*

discográfico, -a *adj Esp* **casa discográfica** record company; **el mundo d.** the record world

díscolo, -a *adj* rebellious, disobedient

disconforme *adj* in disagreement; **estoy d. con tu opinión** I don't agree with you

disconformidad *nf* disagreement, disconformity

discontinuidad *nf* discontinuity, lack of continuity

discontinuo, -a *adj* discontinuous; *Aut* **línea discontinua** broken line

discordancia *nf* discord

discordante *adj* discordant; **ser la nota d.** to clash

discordar [63] *vi* (**a**) *(desentonar) (colores, opiniones)* to clash; *(instrumentos)* to be out of tune (**b**) *(discrepar)* **d. de algn (en)** to disagree with sb (on *o* about)

discordia *nf* discord; **la manzana de la d.** the bone of contention; **sembrar d.** to sow discord

discoteca *nf* (**a**) *(local)* discotheque, nightclub (**b**) *(colección de discos)* record collection, record library

discotequero, -a *nm,f Fam* nightclubber

discreción *nf* (**a**) *(sensatez)* discretion, tact (**b**) *(a voluntad)* **a d.** freely; **beba agua a d.** drink water at your own discretion

discrecional *adj* not prescribed, optional; **parada d.** request stop; **servicio d. de autobuses** special bus service

discrepancia *nf (desacuerdo)* disagreement; *(diferencia)* discrepancy

discrepante *adj* discrepant, conflicting

discrepar *vi (disentir)* to disagree (**de** with, **en** on); *(diferenciarse)* to be different (**de** from)

discreto, -a 1 *adj* (**a**) *(prudente)* discreet, tactful (**b**) *(moderado)* average, reasonable; **de dimensiones discretas** rather small; **un sueldo d.** a moderate salary (**c**) *(color)* sober (**d**) *(prenda)* modest, sober

2 *nm,f* discreet person

discriminación *nf* discrimination ❑ **d. sexual** sexual discrimination

discriminador, -a 1 *adj (situación, ley)* discriminatory

2 *nm Elec* discriminator

discriminar *vt* (**a**) *(diferenciar)* to discriminate between, distinguish (**b**) *(tratar como inferior)* to discriminate against

discriminatorio, -a *adj* discriminatory

disculpa *nf* excuse; **dar disculpas** to make excuses; **pedir disculpas a algn** to apologize to sb

disculpable *adj* excusable, forgivable

disculpar 1 *vt* to excuse, forgive; **discúlpame ante tus padres** make my apologies to your parents; **disculpe mi inexperiencia** forgive my inexperience

2 disculparse *vpr* to apologize, excuse oneself; **se disculpó por haber llegado tarde** he apologized for arriving late

discurrir 1 *vi* (**a**) *(pensar)* to think, ponder (**b**) *Fig (transcurrir)* to pass, go by; **la conferencia discurrió sin interrupciones** the lecture went off without interruptions (**c**) *Fml (andar)* to walk, wander; **la gente discurría por la plaza** people walked about the square

2 *vt* to think up

discursivo, -a *adj* discursive

discurso *nm* (**a**) *(conferencia)* speech; **dar** *o* **pronunciar un d.** to make a speech (**b**) *(raciocinio)* **d. mental** mental powers (**c**) *(expresión de idea)* discourse; **perder el hilo del d.** to lose the thread of one's argument (**d**) *(transcurso)* course, passing; **el d. del tiempo** the passage of time

discusión *nf* (**a**) *(charla)* discussion (**b**) *(disputa)* argument; **eso no admite d.** that's undeniable

discutible *adj* debatable, questionable

discutir 1 *vt* (**a**) *(hablar)* to discuss, talk about; *(en Parlamento)* **d. un proyecto de ley** to discuss a bill; **un personaje muy discutido** a very controversial character (**b**) *(contradecir)* to question

2 *vi* to argue (about); **están discutiendo de política** they're arguing about politics

disecación *nf (taxidermia)* stuffing

disecar [59] *vt* (**a**) *Med (cortar)* to dissect (**b**) *(taxidermia)* to stuff (**c**) *(planta)* to dry

disección *nf véase* disecación

diseccionar *vt* (**a**) *(cadáver, animal)* to dissect (**b**) *Fig (analizar)* to dissect, analyse in detail

diseminación *nf* dissemination, spreading

diseminar *vt* to disseminate, spread

disensión *nf* dissension, disagreement

disentería *nf Med* dysentery

disentimiento *nm* dissent, disagreement

disentir [62] *vi (discrepar)* to dissent, disagree (**de** with); *(diferir)* to differ, be different; **las dos versiones disienten** the two versions differ

diseñador, -a *nm,f* designer ▫ **d. gráfico** graphic designer; **d. industrial** industrial designer

diseñar *vt* to design

diseño *nm* design ▫ **d. gráfico** graphic design; **d. industrial** industrial design

disertación *nf* dissertation, discourse

disertar *vi* to discourse, lecture (**sobre** on, upon)

disfraz *nm* disguise; *(prenda)* fancy dress; **baile de disfraces** fancy dress ball; *Fig* **bajo el d. de** under the guise of

disfrazar [14] **1** *vt* to disguise; *Fig (ideas, sentimientos)* to disguise, cover up
2 disfrazarse *vpr* to disguise oneself; **d. de pirata** to dress up as a pirate

disfrutar 1 *vi* (**a**) *(gozar)* to enjoy oneself; **disfruta viéndoles felices** she enjoys seeing them happy (**b**) *(poseer)* to enjoy, have (**de** -); **disfruta de una excelente salud** he enjoys excellent health; **¡hay que d. de la vida!** life is for living!
2 *vt* to get, receive; **disfrutan la pensión** they receive a pension

disfrute *nm (goce)* enjoyment; *(aprovechamiento)* benefit

disfunción *nf* dysfunction

disgregación *nf* disintegration, break-up

disgregar [38] *vt* (**a**) *(multitud, manifestación)* to disintegrate, break up (**b**) *(dispersar)* to disperse

disgustado, -a *pp de* disgustar
2 *adj* upset, displeased; **está disgustada con la actitud de su padre** she is upset about her father's reaction; **están muy disgustados con el coche** they are very unhappy with the car

disgustar 1 *vt (molestar)* to upset, make unhappy; **le disgustó mucho que no le saludaras** he was very upset because you didn't say hello to him; **me disgusta que hables así** it upsets me to hear you talk like that
2 disgustarse *vpr* (**a**) *(sentir enfado)* to get upset, be annoyed; **se disgustó porque no se lo dijiste** she was annoyed because you didn't tell her (**b**) *(enemistarse)* to quarrel

disgusto *nm* (**a**) *(enfado)* annoyance, displeasure; **dar un d.** to upset; **llevarse un d.** to get upset; **no sabes qué d. me llevé** you don't know how upset I was (**b**) *(problema, desgracia)* trouble, misfortune; **no gano para disgustos** it's just one thing after another; **¡qué d.!** what a pity!, how sad! (**c**) **a d.** unwillingly; **sentirse** *o* **estar a d.** to feel ill at ease

disidencia *nf* dissidence, disagreement

disidente *adj & nmf* dissident

disidir *vi* to dissent

disimuladamente *adv (con astucia)* craftily; *(escondiéndose)* without being seen, surreptitiously, hiddenly

disimulado, -a 1 *pp de* disimular
2 *adj* (**a**) *(persona)* sly, crafty; **hacerse el d.** to pretend not to see *o* notice (**b**) *(oculto)* hidden, concealed

disimular *vt* to conceal, hide; **con la pintura se**

disimulan las manchas stains don't show under the paint; **ella disimuló su pena** she hid her sorrow

disimulo *nm* pretence, concealment; **tiró el papel al suelo con d.** she surreptitiously dropped the piece of paper on the floor; **la miró con d.** he sneaked a look at her

disipado, -a 1 *pp de* disipar
2 *adj* dissipated, debauched, wasted; **una vida disipada** a life of debauchery

disipar *vt* (**a**) *(humos, niebla)* to drive away; *Fig* to dispel; **d. esperanza** to shatter hopes; **d. temores/dudas** to dispel fears/doubts (**b**) *(derrochar)* to squander

diskette [dis'kete, dis'ket] *nm Inform* diskette, floppy disk

dislate *nm* absurdity, nonsense

dislexia *nf Med* dyslexia

disléxico, -a 1 *adj Med* dyslexic
2 *nm,f Med* dyslexic person

dislocación *nf* dislocation

dislocado, -a 1 *pp de* dislocar
2 *adj (tobillo)* dislocated

dislocar [59] **1** *vt* (**a**) *(hueso)* to dislocate (**b**) *Fig (hechos)* to distort
2 dislocarse *vpr* to dislocate, become dislocated; **d. la muñeca** to dislocate one's wrist

disminución *nf* decrease, drop; **ir en d.** to diminish

disminuido, -a 1 *adj* handicapped
2 *nm,f* handicapped person; **un d. físico/psíquico** a physically/mentally handicapped person

disminuir [34] **1** *vt* to decrease, reduce, diminish; **d. el tamaño/la velocidad** to reduce size/speed
2 *vi* to diminish, drop, fall; **las temperaturas han disminuido** temperatures have dropped

disociable *adj* dissociable

disociación *nf* dissociation

disociar *vt* to dissociate

disolubilidad *nf* solubility

disoluble *adj* soluble, dissoluble

disolución *nf* (**a**) *(desleimiento)* dissolution, dissolving (**b**) *Fig (anulación)* invalidation, cancellation (**c**) *Fig (relajación)* looseness, dissoluteness; **d. de las costumbres** decadence (**d**) *Quím* solution

disoluto, -a 1 *adj* dissolute
2 *nm,f* libertine

disolvente *adj & nm* solvent, dissolvent

disolver [41] *(pp disuelto)* **1** *vt* (**a**) *(en líquido)* to dissolve; **d. un matrimonio/el Parlamento** to dissolve a marriage/Parliament (**b**) *(anular)* to annul
2 disolverse *vpr* to be dissolved; **la manifestación se disolvió pacíficamente** the demonstration broke up peacefully

disonancia *nf Mús* dissonance; *Fig* clash

disonante *adj Mús* dissonant, discordant; *Fig* clashing

dispar *adj* unlike, disparate

disparada *nf* (**a**) *Am (huida)* flight (**b**) *CSur* **a la d.** in a tearing hurry

disparadero *nm* (**a**) *(arma)* trigger (**b**) *Fam* **poner a algn en el d.** to get sb's dander up

disparado, -a *adj* **salir/entrar d.** to shoot out/in

disparador *nm* (**a**) *(de arma)* trigger (**b**) *Fot* shutter release (**c**) *(de reloj)* escapement

disparar 1 *vt (arma de fuego)* to fire; *(bala, flecha)* to shoot; *Ftb* **d. el balón** to shoot the ball; **¡nos disparan!** they are firing at us!
2 *vi (disparatar)* to talk nonsense
3 dispararse *vpr* (**a**) *(arma)* to go off, fire (**b**) *(precios)* to

shoot up (**c**) *(salir corriendo)* to fly o rush off (**d**) *(hablar con volubilidad)* to get carried away

disparatado, -a 1 *pp de* disparatar
  2 *adj* absurd, senseless

disparatar *vi* to talk nonsense

disparate *nm* (**a**) *(desatino)* blunder, nonsense, senseless talk; **no digas disparates** don't talk nonsense (**b**) *(tontería)* foolish act; **ha sido un d. contestar así** you were a fool to answer like that (**c**) *(barbaridad)* enormity; **lo que has hecho es un d.** you've done something terrible; **piden un d.** they are asking an awful lot

disparejo, -a *adj* unequal, uneven

disparidad *nf* disparity, difference

disparo *nm* (**a**) *(de arma)* shot; **se oían disparos** firing o shots o shooting could be heard (**b**) *Dep* shot; **d. a puerta** shot

dispendio *nm* splurge

dispensa *nf* dispensation, exemption

dispensar *vt* (**a**) *(otorgar)* to give, grant; **dispensó una palabra de agradecimiento** he said a few words of thanks (**b**) *(disculpar)* to pardon, forgive; **dispense la molestia** I'm sorry to bother you (**c**) *(eximir)* to exempt, free from an obligation; **me dispensaron (de) la gimnasia** I was exempted from gym class

dispensario *nm Med* dispensary

dispersar 1 *vt* (**a**) *(separar)* to disperse; *(esparcir)* to scatter; **d. la atención/los esfuerzos** to spread one's attention/efforts (**b**) *Mil* to disperse, rout
  2 dispersarse *vpr* to disperse, scatter

dispersión *nf (separación)* dispersion; *(esparcimiento)* scattering

disperso, -a *adj (separado)* dispersed; *(esparcido)* scattered

display [dis'plei] *nm Inform* display

displicencia *nf* indifference, apathy; **con d.** half-heartedly

displicente *adj* indifferent, uninterested; **con un tono d.** showing no emotion, coldly

disponer [50] *(pp* dispuesto) **1** *vt* (**a**) *(arreglar)* to arrange, set out; **dispon las sillas para que todos vean** arrange the chairs so that everyone can see (**b**) *(preparar)* to prepare, get ready (**c**) *(ordenar)* to order; **el alcalde dispuso suspender las fiestas** the Mayor ordered the suspension of the festivities; **la ley dispone que** the law stipulates that
  2 *vi* (**a**) *(tener)* to have at one's disposal; **d. de dinero/tiempo** to have money/time available; **los medios de que dispone** the means available to him (**b**) *(usar)* to make use of, do as one wants with
  3 disponerse *vpr* (**a**) *(prepararse)* to prepare, get ready; **se disponía a marcharse, cuando sonó el teléfono** he was about to leave when the phone rang (**b**) *(mentalmente)* to be prepared, expect; **no me dispongo a perder** I'm not prepared to lose

disponibilidad *nf* availability; *Fin* liquidity; *Com* available stock

disponible *adj* available

disposición *nf* (**a**) *(uso)* disposition, disposal; **a la d. de** at the disposal of; **a su d.** at your disposal o service; **tener la libre d. de algo** to have sth entirely at one's disposal (**b**) *(estado de ánimo)* disposition, frame of mind; *(colocación)* arrangement, layout; **este niño no está en d. de salir** this child isn't up to going out (**c**) *(orden)* order, law; **las disposiciones vigentes** current legislation (**d**) *(aptitud)* talent, gift; **nunca he tenido d. para el dibujo** I have never been any good at drawing

dispositivo *nm* device, gadget □ **d. intrauterino** intrauterine device, IUD

dispuesto, -a 1 *pp de* disponer
  2 *adj* (**a**) *(a punto)* ready; **¿estamos todos dispuestos para salir?** are we all ready to go? (**b**) *(decidido)* determined; **está d. a hablar** he is determined to talk (**c**) *(hábil)* bright, clever, capable (**d**) *(que se presta)* willing, prepared; **está poco d. a ayudar** he is reluctant to help; **estoy d. a lo que sea para conseguirlo** I'll do anything to get it; **la empresa no está dispuesta a ofrecer más dinero** the company is not prepared to offer more money; **siempre está d. a hacer de secretaria** he is always willing to act as secretary (**e**) *(establecido)* established, stipulated; **según lo d. por la ley** in accordance with what the law stipulates

disputa *nf* dispute, argument

disputar 1 *vt* (**a**) *(discutir)* to argue (**b**) *(oponerse a)* to dispute (**c**) *(pretender) (premio)* to contend for (**d**) *Dep (partido)* to play
  2 disputarse *vpr* (**a**) *(pretender)* to contend for; **cinco aspirantes se disputan el puesto** there are five candidates contending for the position (**b**) *Dep* to be played; **el partido se disputa el jueves** the match will be played on Thursday

disquera¹ *nf Am* record company

disquero, -a² *adj Am* record; **la industria disquera** the record o music industry

disquete *nm Inform* diskette, floppy disk

disquetera *nf Inform* disk drive

disquisición *nf* (**a**) *(exposición)* disquisition (**b**) **disquisiciones** digressions; *Fam* **d. filosóficas** rambling *sing*

distancia *nf* (**a**) *(espacio)* distance; **a d.** from a distance; **guardar las distancias** to keep one's distance (**b**) *Fig (diferencia)* difference, gap; **acortar distancias** to bridge the gap; **hay gran d. de una cosa a la otra** the two things are quite different (**c**) *Fot* **d. focal** focal length

distanciamiento *nm* distancing, distance

distanciar 1 *vt* (**a**) *(afectivamente)* to drive apart (**b**) *(en el espacio o tiempo)* to move further apart (**c**) *(rival)* to forge ahead of
  2 distanciarse *vpr* to become separated; *Fig* **d. de los amigos** to distance oneself from one's friends

distante *adj* distant, far-off

distar *vi* (**a**) *(estar a)* to be distant o away; **dista sesenta kilómetros del centro** it's sixty kilometres away from the centre (**b**) *Fig (ser diferente)* to be far from; **dista mucho de ser perfecto** it's far from (being) perfect

distender [64] *vt Fig* to ease, relax; **d. las relaciones internacionales** to ease international relations

distendido, -a 1 *pp de* distender
  2 *adj (informal)* relaxed, informal

distensión *nf* (**a**) *Med (lesión)* strain (**b**) *(calma)* easing, relaxation; *Pol* **d. de las relaciones** détente

distinción *nf* (**a**) *(diferencia)* distinction; **a d. de** unlike; **sin d. de** irrespective of (**b**) *(honor)* distinction; **d. de honor** honour; **de gran d.** highly distinguished (**c**) *(deferencia)* deference, respect; **hacer una d. con algn** to treat sb with special deference (**d**) *(elegancia)* refinement

distinguido, -a 1 *pp de* distinguir
  2 *adj* (**a**) *(ilustre)* distinguished (**b**) *(elegante)* elegant; *(culto)* cultured, of distinction

distinguir [26] **1** *vt* (**a**) *(diferenciar)* to distinguish (**b**) *(ver)* to see, make out; **pude distinguirlo entre la multitud** I saw o distinguished him among the crowd (**c**) *(caracterizar)* to mark, distinguish (**d**) *(mostrar preferencia)* to single out (**e**) *(honrar)* to honour, *US* honor

2 *vi (diferenciar)* to discriminate
3 distinguirse *vpr* (**a**) *(sobresalir)* to distinguish oneself, stand out (**b**) *(verse)* to be visible

distintivo, -a 1 *adj* distinctive, distinguishing; **rasgo d.** characteristic feature
2 *nm* (**a**) *(señal)* distinctive sign *o* mark (**b**) *(característica)* characteristic, emblem; **el d. de una profesión** the emblem *o* symbol of a profession

distinto, -a *adj (diferente)* different; *(varios)* various; **comimos distintos tipos de queso y patés** we ate various sorts of cheese and pâté

distorsión *nf* (**a**) *Med* sprain (**b**) *(de imágenes, sonidos)* distortion; *Fig* **la d. de la verdad** distortion of the truth

distorsionador, -a *adj* (**a**) *(efecto)* distorting (**b**) *(análisis, enfoque)* misleading

distorsionar *vt* to distort

distracción *nf* (**a**) *(pasatiempo)* pastime, hobby; *(recreo)* recreation, entertainment, relaxation; **en Barcelona hay distracciones para todos los gustos** Barcelona offers something for everyone; **mi d. favorita es la música** music is my favourite pastime (**b**) *(error)* slip, oversight; **fue una d. por mi parte** it was an oversight on my part (**c**) *(descuido)* distraction, absent-mindedness; **en un momento de d. cogí tus llaves** in a moment of absent-mindedness I took your keys

distraer [66] **1** *vt* (**a**) *(atención)* to distract; **está prohibido d. al conductor** do not distract the driver; **por lo menos, te distrae de tus preocupaciones** at least it takes your mind off your worries (**b**) *(divertir)* to entertain, amuse (**c**) *Fam Fig (robar)* to embezzle
2 distraerse *vpr* (**a**) *(divertirse)* to amuse oneself (**b**) *(entretenerse)* to relax, pass the time; **necesitas distraerte** you need to relax (**c**) *(abstraerse)* to let one's mind wander; **te distraes mucho** you are so absent-minded

distraído, -a 1 *pp de* distraer
2 *adj* (**a**) *(divertido)* entertaining, fun (**b**) *(inatento)* absent-minded (**c**) *Chile Méx (desaseado)* slovenly, unkempt
3 *nm,f* absent-minded person; **hacerse el d.** to pretend not to notice *o* know

distribución *nf* (**a**) *(reparto, división)* distribution (**b**) *(entrega)* delivery; **la d. del correo** mail delivery (**c**) *(de una casa, un jardín)* layout

distribuidor, -a 1 *adj* distributing, distributive
2 *nm,f (firma)* wholesaler, supplier; **los distribuidores de películas** the film distributors

distribuir [34] *vt* to distribute, deliver; **d. el agua y la electricidad** to supply gas and electricity; **d. el trabajo entre los miembros del equipo** to share the work among everybody in the team

distributivo, -a *adj* distributive

distrito *nm* district □ **d. electoral** ≃ constituency; **d. postal** postal district

disturbar *vt* to disturb

disturbio *nm* riot, disturbance; **disturbios callejeros** riots

disuadir *vt* to dissuade, deter

disuasión *nf* dissuasion, deterrence

disuasivo, -a *adj*, **disuasorio, -a** *adj* dissuasive, deterrent

disuelto, -a *pp de* disolver

disyuntiva *nf* alternative

dita *nf CAm Chile* debt

DIU [diu] *nm Med (abrev de* **dispositivo intrauterino***)* IUD

diuresis *nf Med* diuresis

diurético, -a *adj & nm Med* diuretic

diurno, -a *adj* daytime, daily; *(planta)* diurnal

divagación *nf* digression

divagar [38] *vi* to digress, wander

diván *nm Mueb* divan, couch

díver *adj inv Fam* great fun

divergencia *nf* divergence; **d. de opiniones** diverging opinions

divergente *adj* divergent, diverging

divergir [24] *vi* to diverge

diversidad *nf* diversity, variety

diversificación *nf* diversification

diversificar [59] **1** *vt* to diversify, vary
2 diversificarse *vpr* to be diversified *o* varied

diversión *nf* fun, amusement

diverso, -a *adj (diferente)* different; *(varios)* several, various; **trajo diversos regalos para los niños** he brought various presents for the children

divertido, -a 1 *pp de* divertir
2 *adj* (**a**) *(de risa)* amusing, funny; **una película divertida** a funny film (**b**) *(entretenido)* fun, entertaining; **un tipo muy divertido** a very amusing chap (**c**) *Andes Arg Guat (ebrio)* tipsy

divertimento *nm Mús* divertimento; *(novela, película)* entertainment, divertissement

divertir [62] **1** *vt* to amuse, entertain
2 divertirse *vpr* to enjoy oneself, have a good time; **por divertirme** for fun; **¡que te diviertas!** enjoy yourself!, have fun!

dividendo *nm Mat Com* dividend

dividir 1 *vt* (**a**) *(separar)* to divide, split (**en** into); **la guerra dividió al país** the war divided the country; **los Andes dividen Chile de Argentina** the Andes separate Chile from Argentina (**b**) *Mat* **15 dividido entre 3 son 5** 15 divided by 3 is 5
2 dividirse *vpr* to divide, split up; **el partido se dividió en dos facciones** the party split into two factions

divieso *nm* boil, furuncle

divinidad *nf* (**a**) *Filos* God, divinity (**b**) *(dios pagano)* deity (**c**) *Fam* **¡qué d.!** how gorgeous!

divinización *nf* deification

divinizar [14] *vt* to deify

divino, -a *adj* (**a**) *(de Dios)* divine (**b**) *Fam (bonito)* wonderful, fantastic, gorgeous; **tienen una casa divina** they have a fantastic house

divisa *nf* (**a**) *(emblema)* symbol, emblem (**b**) *Taur* bull owner's emblem (**c**) *(heráldica)* device, motto (**d**) *Com* **divisas** foreign currency *sing*

divisar *vt* to make out, discern

divisibilidad *nf* divisibility

divisible *adj* dividable; *Mat* divisible

división *nf* division; **hay d. de opiniones** opinions are divided; *Ftb* **primera/segunda d.** first/second division □ *Mil* **d. acorazada** *o* **blindada** armoured division

divisor, -a 1 *adj* dividing
2 *nm* divider; *Mat* divisor

divisorio, -a *adj* dividing

divo, -a *nm,f* star; **es una diva (de ópera)** she is a prima donna

divorciado, -a 1 *pp de* divorciar
2 *adj* divorced
3 *nm,f (hombre)* divorcé; *(mujer)* divorcée

divorciar 1 *vt* to divorce
2 divorciarse *vpr* to get divorced; **se divorció de él** she divorced him, she got a divorce from him

divorcio *nm* (**a**) *(separación)* divorce (**b**) *Fig (discrepancia)* discrepancy; **hay un d. entre lo que dice y lo que hace** he says one thing and does another

divulgación *nf* (**a**) *(difusión)* disclosure, spreading; **la d. de una noticia** the publication of a news item (**b**) *(de conocimientos)* popularization

divulgador, -a *adj* (**a**) *(difusor)* broadcasting (**b**) *(propagador)* popularizing

divulgar [38] *vt* (**a**) *(difundir)* to disclose, reveal; *Rad* to broadcast; **las emisoras de radio divulgaron la noticia** the radio stations broadcast the news (**b**) *(propagar)* to popularize

divulgativo, -a *adj* popularizing

dizque *adv Andes Carib Méx Fam* apparently

Djibouti *n* Djibouti, Jibouti

dl *(abrev de* **decilitro***)* dl

dm *(abrev de* **decímetro***)* dm

DNI *nm* *(abrev de* **Documento Nacional de Identidad***)* ID card

Dña. *(abrev de* **doña***)* ≃ Mrs

DO *(abrev de* **Denominación de Origen***)* = certification that a product comes from a particular region and conforms to certain quality standards

do *nm Mús (de solfa)* doh, do; *(de escala diatónica)* C ❑ **do de pecho** high C; *Fam* **dar el do de pecho** to surpass oneself

dóberman *(pl* **dóbermans***) nm Zool* Doberman (pinscher)

dobladillo *nm (de traje, vestido)* hem; *(de pantalón) Br* turn-up, *US* cuff

doblaje *nm Cin* dubbing

doblar 1 *vt* (**a**) *(duplicar)* to double; **me dobla la edad** he is twice as old as I am (**b**) *(plegar)* to fold o turn up (**c**) *(torcer)* to bend (**d**) *Cin Teat (actor, actriz)* to double (**a** for); *(película)* to dub (**e**) *(esquina)* to go round
   2 *vi* (**a**) *(girar)* to turn; **dobla a la derecha/izquierda** turn right/left (**b**) *(campanas)* to toll (**c**) *Cin Teat* to play two roles, double
   3 **doblarse** *vpr* (**a**) *(plegarse)* to fold (**b**) *(torcerse)* to bend (**c**) *(someterse)* to yield, give in

doble 1 *adj* double; **arma de d. filo** double-edged weapon; **una frase de d. sentido** a sentence with a double meaning ❑ **d. moral** double standard; **d. personalidad** split personality; **d. techo** *(de tienda de campaña)* fly sheet; **d. ventana** secondary glazing
   2 *nm* (**a**) *(duplo)* double; **gana el d. que tú** she earns twice as much as you do (**b**) *(toque de campana)* toll (**c**) *Cin* stunt man, double (**d**) *Dep* **dobles** doubles; **d. femeninos/masculinos** ladies'/men's doubles
   3 *nmf Cin (hombre)* stunt man, double; *(mujer)* stunt woman, double
   4 *adv* double; **trabajar d.** to work twice as hard

doblegar [38] 1 *vt* (**a**) *(doblar)* to bend (**b**) *Fig (ceder)* to make give in
   2 **doblegarse** *vpr* to give in

doblemente *adv* (**a**) *(muy)* doubly (**b**) *Fig (con hipocresía)* insincerely, two-facedly

doblete *nm* **hacer d.** to have a second job

doblez 1 *nm (pliegue)* fold
   2 *nm o nf Fig* two-facedness, deceitfulness; **ser una persona sin d.** to be an honest o guileless person

doblón *nm* doubloon

doc *(abrev de* **documento***)* doc

doce 1 *adj (cardinal)* twelve; *(ordinal)* twelfth; **d. casas** twelve houses; **el siglo d./XII** the twelfth/12th century
   2 *nm inv* (**a**) *(número)* twelve (**b**) *(fecha)* twelfth; *véase tamb* **ocho**

doceavo, -a 1 *adj* twelfth
   2 *nm,f (de una serie)* twelfth
   3 *nm (parte)* twelfth; *véase tamb* **octavo, -a**

docena *nf* dozen; **a docenas** by the dozen; *Fig* **d. de fraile** baker's dozen

docencia *nf* teaching; **siempre le ha gustado la d.** he has always liked teaching

docente 1 *adj* teaching; **centros docentes** educational centres; **personal d.** teaching staff
   2 *nmf* teacher

dócil *adj* docile, obedient

docilidad *nf* docility, obedience

doctamente *adv* learnedly

docto, -a 1 *adj* learned
   2 *nm,f* learned person, connoisseur

doctor, -a *nm,f* doctor; **d. en filosofía** doctor in o of philosophy; **la doctora le recetó antibióticos** the doctor prescribed antibiotics for him

doctorado *nm Univ* doctorate, PhD

doctoral *adj* doctoral; **un tono d.** a pedantic way of speaking

doctorarse *vpr Univ* to take o receive one's doctorate

doctrina *nf* doctrine, teachings *pl*

doctrinal *adj* doctrinal

doctrinario, -a *adj & nm,f* doctrinaire

docudrama *nm* docudrama

documentación *nf* documentation; **la d. del coche** the car papers; **la policía le pidió la d.** the police asked to see his papers

documentado, -a 1 *pp de* **documentar**
   2 *adj* (**a**) *(informado)* (informe, estudio) researched; *(persona)* informed (**b**) *(con papeles encima)* having identification; **no pudo entrar porque no iba d.** he couldn't get in because he had no identification with him

documental *adj & nm Cin TV* documentary

documentalista *nmf* archivist

documentar 1 *vt* (**a**) *(libro, informe)* to document (**b**) *(persona)* to give information
   2 **documentarse** *vpr* to research (**sobre** -), get information (**sobre** about o on)

documento *nm también Inform* document ❑ **d. nacional de identidad** identity card

dodecafónico, -a *adj Mús* dodecaphonic

dodotis® *nm inv* disposable *Br* nappy o *US* diaper

dogal *nm* (**a**) *(de caballo)* halter (**b**) *(soga de reo)* hangman's noose

dogma *nm* dogma

dogmático, -a *adj* dogmatic

dogmatismo *nm* dogmatism

dogmatizar [14] *vi* to dogmatize

dogo *nm Zool* bulldog

dólar *nm* dollar

dolencia *nf* ailment; **achaques y dolencias** aches and pains

doler [41] 1 *vi* (**a**) *(físicamente)* to hurt, ache; **me duele la muela/la cabeza** I've got toothache/a headache; **me duelen los ojos** my eyes hurt (**b**) *(sentir pena)* to feel hurt; **estar dolido** to be hurt; **le duele que no le hayas invitado** he is hurt that you didn't invite him (**c**) *(sentir pesar)* to be sorry o sad; **me duele tener que echarte** I'm sorry to have to throw you out
   2 **dolerse** *vpr* (**a**) *(quejarse)* to complain (**de** about) (**b**)

(arrepentirse) to regret (**de** for) (**c**) *(sentir pena)* to suffer (**de** for)

dolido, -a *adj* hurt, upset; **estar/sentirse d.** to be/feel hurt

doliente *adj (enfermo)* ill; *(afligido)* grieving

dolmen *nm* dolmen

dolo *nm Jur* fraud

dolor *nm* (**a**) *Med* pain, ache ❑ **d. de cabeza** headache; **d. de espalda** back pain; **d. de muelas** toothache (**b**) *(padecimiento moral)* grief, sorrow; *(pesar)* regret

dolorido, -a *adj* (**a**) *(dañado)* sore, aching (**b**) *(apenado)* sad, grieved, hurt

dolorosa¹ *nf* (**a**) *Rel* Our Lady of Sorrow (**b**) *Argot (en restaurante)* bill; **tráeme la d.** what's the damage?

doloroso, -a² *adj* painful

doma *nf* taming; *(de caballos)* breaking in

domador, -a *nm,f* tamer ❑ **d. de caballos** horse breaker

domar *vt (animal)* to tame; *(caballo)* to break in; *Fig* to break in

domesticable *adj* trainable

domesticación *nf* domestication, taming

domesticado, -a *adj (animal)* tame

domesticar [59] *vt* to domesticate; *(animal)* to tame; **d. leones para un circo** to train lions for a circus

doméstico, -a 1 *adj* domestic; **animal d.** pet; **servicio d.** domestic help
2 *nm,f* domestic, household servant

domiciliación *Esp nf Fin* payment by standing order

domiciliado, -a 1 *pp de* **domiciliar**
2 *adj* residing, living

domiciliar *vt Esp Fin* to pay by standing order

domiciliario, -a *adj* house; *Jur* **arresto d.** house arrest

domicilio *nm* home, residence; **escriba el nombre y el d.** write your name and address; **servicio a d.** house deliveries; **sin d. fijo** of no fixed abode *o* residence ❑ **d. fijo** permanent address; **d. fiscal** registered office; **d. social** head office

dominación *nf* domination, dominion

dominante *adj* (**a**) *(que domina)* dominant, dominating (**b**) *(déspota)* domineering

dominar 1 *vt* (**a**) *(tener bajo el poder)* to dominate, rule (**b**) *Fig (contener)* to control; **d. el fuego** to contain the fire; **d. la ira/los nervios** to control one's rage/nerves (**c**) *Fig (conocer a fondo)* to master; **d. el francés** to have a good command of French; **d. la fotografía** to be very good at photography; **los estudiantes tienen que d. el verbo 'to be'** students have to master the verb 'to be' (**d**) *(ver)* to see; **desde el balcón se domina la llanura** from the balcony one can see the plain (**e**) *(tener bajo el control)* to overpower, overcome; **le dominó la rabia** he was overcome by rage
2 *vi* (**a**) *(imperar sobre personas o cosas)* to dominate (**b**) *(resaltar)* to stand out (**c**) *Fig (abundar)* to predominate, dominate; **el azul era el color que dominaba** blue was the predominant colour
3 *dominarse* *vpr* to control oneself; **tuve que dominarme para no contestarle mal** I had to restrain myself from answering him angrily

domingas *nfpl Argot* boobs

domingo *nm inv* Sunday; **el traje de los domingos** one's Sunday best ❑ **D. de Resurrección** *o* **Pascua** Easter Sunday; *véase tamb* **viernes**

dominguejo *nm Am* poor devil, wretch

dominguero, -a 1 *adj* Sunday
2 *nm,f Fam* weekend driver

Dominica *n* Dominica

dominical *adj* Sunday; **periódico d.** Sunday newspaper

dominicano, -a *adj & nm,f* Dominican; **República Dominicana** Dominican Republic

dominico, -a *adj Rel* Dominican

dominio *nm* (**a**) *(poder)* control, power; **d. de sí mismo** self-control; **d. de un idioma** command of a language; **d. del mar** command of the sea; **ejercer d.** to exert control; **ser del d. público** to be public knowledge (**b**) *(condominio)* domain (**c**) *(ámbito)* scope, sphere; **el d. de la ciencia** the field *o* sphere of science (**d**) **dominios** dominions; **los d. de la Commonwealth** the dominions of the Commonwealth (**e**) *Inform* domain

dominó *nm (juego)* dominoes *pl*; *(fichas)* set of dominoes

domótica *nf* home automation

don¹ *nm* (**a**) *(regalo)* present, gift (**b**) *(talento)* natural gift, talent; **tiene el d. de sacarme de quicio** he has a knack for getting my goat *nm* ❑ **d. de gentes** gift of the gab

don² *nm (tratamiento)* **Señor D. Jesús Ayerra** Mr Jesús Ayerra; **buenos días D. Jesús** good morning, Mr Ayerra; **D. Fulano de Tal** Mr So-and-So; **d. nadie** a nobody

donación *nf* donation

donador, -a *nm,f* donor

donaire *nm* (**a**) *(garbo)* grace, elegance (**b**) *(ocurrencia graciosa)* wisecrack, witticism

donante *nmf* donor; *Med* **d. de sangre** blood donor

donar *vt Fml* to donate, give; *Med* **d. sangre** to give blood

donativo *nm* donation

doncella *nf* (**a**) *Literario (mujer joven)* maid, maiden (**b**) *(criada)* maid, housemaid

doncellez *nf* maidenhood

donde *adv rel* where, in which; **a** *o* **en d.** where; **de** *o* **desde d.** from where; **d. quieras** wherever you want; **está d. lo dejaste** it is right where you left it; **la casa d. nací** the town where *o* in which I was born; **la fiesta d. nos conocimos** the party where we met; *Fam* **d. las dan las toman** tit for tat; *Fam* **¡vaya por d.!** what do you know?

dónde *adv interr* where; **¿de d. eres?** where are you from?; **no sé d. le vi** I can't remember where I saw him; **¿por d. se va a la playa?** which way is it to the beach?

dondequiera *adv* everywhere; **d. que vaya** wherever I go

dondiego *nm Bot* marvel-of-Peru, four-o'clock ❑ **d. de día** morning glory; **d. de noche** marvel-of-Peru, four-o'clock

donjuán *nm* Don Juan, womanizer; **tiene fama de d.** he has reputation for being a Don Juan *o* a Casanova

donostiarra *Esp* **1** *adj* of *o* from San Sebastián
2 *nmf* person from San Sebastián

dónut® *(pl* **dónuts)** *nm* doughnut

doña *nf (tratamiento)* **Señora D. Mercedes Torres** Mrs Mercedes Torres; **D. Mercedes ha llegado** Mrs Torres has arrived

dopado, -a 1 *pp de* **dopar**
2 *adj (deportista)* = having taken performance-enhancing drugs

dopaje *nm Dep* drug-taking

dopar *vt Dep* to dope, drug

doping ['dopin] *(pl* **dopings)** *nm Dep* doping

doquier *adv,* **doquiera** *adv Literario* **por d. que** everywhere

dorada¹ *nf (pez)* gilthead bream

dorado, -a² **1** *pp de* **dorar**
2 *adj* golden; **con la piel dorada por el sol** suntanned; **los años dorados de la juventud** the golden years of youth

3 *nm* (**a**) *Téc* gilding (**b**) *(pez)* dorado (**c**) **dorados** gilt objects; **crema para limpiar d.** metal polish

dorar *vt* (**a**) *(cubrir con oro)* to gild; *Fig* **d. la píldora** to sugar the pill (**b**) *(tostar)* to brown

dórico, -a 1 *adj* Dorian; *Arquit* **orden d.** Doric order
2 *nm* Doric

dormido, -a 1 *pp de* dormir
2 *adj* asleep; *(soñoliento)* sleepy; **quedarse d.** to fall asleep; **tengo la pierna dormida** my leg has gone numb

dormilón, -ona 1 *adj Fam* sleepyheaded
2 *nm,f* sleepyhead

dormir [27] **1** *vi* to sleep; **¿dormiste bien?** did you sleep well?; **d. con algn** to sleep with sb; **tener ganas de d.** to feel sleepy; *Fam* **d. como un lirón, d. a pierna suelta** to sleep like a log; *Fam Fig* **no te duermas o te quitarán el puesto** don't let the grass grow under your feet
2 *vt* to put to sleep; **d. la siesta** to have an afternoon nap; *Fam* **d. la mona, dormirla** to sleep it off
3 dormirse *vpr* to fall asleep, nod off; **duérmete** go to sleep; **se me ha dormido el brazo** my arm has gone to sleep; *Fig* **d. en los laureles** to rest on one's laurels

dormitar *vi* to doze, snooze

dormitorio *nm* (**a**) *(de una casa)* bedroom (**b**) *(de un colegio, residencia)* dormitory

dorsal 1 *adj* dorsal, spinal, back
2 *nm Dep* number

dorso *nm* back; **instrucciones al d.** instructions over; **ponga la fecha en el d.** write the date on the back; **véase al d.** see overleaf □ **el d. de la mano** the back of the hand

dos 1 *adj (cardinal)* two; **d. amigos** two friends; *(ordinal)* second; **el capítulo d.** the second chapter
2 *nm inv (gen)* two; *(fecha)* second; **de d. en d.** in twos; **el d. de octubre** the second of October; **entre (los) d.** between the two of us/you/them; **los d.** both; **para nosotros/ellos d.** for both of us/them; **¿qué número quieres? — el d.** what number do you want? — number two; *Fam* **cada d. por tres** every other minute; *Fam* **como d. y d. son cuatro** without any doubt; *Fam* **en un d. por tres** in a flash; *véase tamb* **ocho**

doscientos, -as *adj & nm,f (cardinal)* two hundred; *(ordinal)* two hundredth

dosel *nm* canopy

dosificación *nf* dosage

dosificador *nm* dispenser

dosificar [59] *vt* (**a**) *(gen)* to dose (**b**) *(esfuerzos, energías)* to measure

dosis *nf inv* dose; **en pequeñas d.** in small doses

dossier [do'sjer] *(pl* **dossiers** *o* **dossieres)** *nm* dossier

dotación *nf* (**a**) *(acción)* endowment (**b**) *(personal)* personnel, staff; **la d. del barco** the crew of the ship

dotado, -a 1 *pp de* dotar
2 *adj* equipped; **d. de un moderno equipo** provided with modern equipment; *Fam (chico)* **bien d.** good looking; *Vulg (órganos genitales)* well-hung

dotar *vt* (**a**) *(dar dote)* to give a dowry (**b**) *(proveer)* to endow, provide; **d. de** to provide with; **está dotado de un gran oído musical** he's got an excellent ear for music; **d. una oficina** *(de personal)* to staff an office; *(de dinero)* to assign money to an office

dote *nf* (**a**) *(bienes)* dowry (**b**) **dotes** gift *sing*, talent *sing*; **tiene d. para la danza** he is a gifted dancer

doy *indic pres véase* dar

dpt. *(abrev de* **departamento)** Dept

Dr. *(abrev de* **doctor)** Dr

Dra. *(abrev de* **doctora)** Dr

dracma *nf Fin* drachma

draconiano, -a *adj Fig* Draconian, harsh

DRAE ['drae] *nm (abrev de* **Diccionario de la Real Academia Española)** = dictionary of the Spanish Royal Academy

draga *nf* (**a**) *(máquina)* dredge (**b**) *(barco)* dredger

dragado, -a 1 *pp de* dragar
2 *nm* dredging

dragaminas *nm inv* minesweeper

dragar [38] *vt* to dredge

drago *nm Bot* dragon tree

dragón *nm* (**a**) *(fiera)* dragon (**b**) *Hist (soldado)* dragoon

dragonear *Am vi* (**a**) **d. de** *(hacerse pasar por)* to pass oneself off as, pose as (**b**) *(alardear)* to boast

drama *nm* drama

dramático, -a *adj* dramatic; **autor d.** playwright; *Fam* **una situación dramática** a dramatic situation

dramatismo *nm* dramatic nature, drama; **con d.** dramatically

dramatizar [14] *vt Lit Teat* to dramatize

dramaturgia *nf Teat* dramatics *sing*

dramaturgo, -a *nm,f Teat* playwright, dramatist

dramón *nm Fam* melodrama

drástico, -a *adj* drastic

drenaje *nm* drainage; **colector de d.** main drain

drenar *vt* to drain

Dresde *n* Dresden

driblar *vi Dep* to dribble

dribling ['driβlin] *(pl* **driblings)** *nm Dep (habilidad)* dribbling; *(regate)* dribble

dril *nm* (**a**) *(tela)* drill, drilling (**b**) *(mono)* drill

drive [draif] *nm Dep* drive

driver ['draiβer] *(pl* **drivers)** *nm* (**a**) *Inform* driver (**b**) *(en golf)* driver

droga *nf* (**a**) *(limpieza)* household product; *(pintura)* paint (**b**) *(narcótico)* drug □ **d. blanda/dura** soft/hard drug (**c**) *Chile Méx Perú (deuda)* debt; *(trampa)* trap

drogadicción *nf* drug addiction

drogadicto, -a *adj & nm,f* drug addict

drogado, -a 1 *pp de* drogar
2 *adj* drugged (up)
3 *nm,f* drug addict

drogar [38] **1** *vt* to drug
2 drogarse *vpr* to drug oneself, take drugs

drogata *nmf Argot* junkie

drogodependencia *nf* drug dependence, drug addiction

drogodependiente *nmf* drug addict

drogota *nmf Argot véase* **drogata**

droguería *nf* (**a**) *Esp (tienda)* = hardware and household goods shop (**b**) *Col (farmacia)* pharmacy, *Br* chemist's (shop), *US* drugstore (**c**) *Andes CAm RP (distribuidora)* drugs wholesaler

droguero, -a *nm,f* (**a**) *Esp (dependiente)* = shopkeeper in a **droguería** (**b**) *Chile Méx Perú (moroso)* defaulter, bad debtor

dromedario *nm Zool* dromedary

drugstore ['druvstor] *nm* = establishment comprising late-night shop and bar

druida, -esa *nm,f* druid

dto. *(abrev de* **descuento)** discount

dual *adj* dual; *TV* **sistema d.** dual system
dualidad *nf* duality
dualismo *nm* dualism
dualista *adj* dualistic
dubitativo, -a *adj* doubtful
Dublín *n* Dublin
dublinés, -esa 1 *adj* of o from Dublin
2 *nm,f* Dubliner
ducado *nm Hist* (**a**) *(tierras)* dukedom, duchy (**b**) *(moneda)* ducat
ducal *adj* duke's, ducal
ducha *nf* shower; **darse/tomar una d.** to take/have a shower; *Fam Fig* **una d. de agua fría** a hard blow, a kick in the teeth
duchar 1 *vt* to shower, give a shower
2 ducharse *vpr* to shower, have o take a shower
ducho, -a *adj* expert; **estar d. en la materia** to be well versed in the subject
dúctil *adj* ductile
ductilidad *nm* ductility
duda *nf* doubt; **no cabe d., no hay d.** (there is) no doubt; **poner algo en d.** to question sth; **sacar a algn de dudas** to dispel sb's doubts; **salir de dudas** to shed one's doubts; **sin d.** no doubt, without a doubt; **sin la menor d.** without the slightest doubt
dudar 1 *vi* (**a**) *(gen)* to doubt, have doubts (**b**) *(vacilar)* to hesitate; **dudaba entre ir o quedarme** I hesitated whether to go or to stay; **estoy dudando si ir o no** I am not sure whether to go or not (**c**) *(desconfiar)* **d. de algn** to suspect sb; **¿dudas de mi palabra?** don't you trust me?
2 *vt* to doubt; **dudo que llegue a tiempo** I doubt she can come on time; **dudo que sea verdad** I doubt that's true; **lo dudo** I doubt it; **no lo dudé ni un momento** I didn't think twice (about it)
dudoso, -a *adj* (**a**) *(incierto)* uncertain, doubtful (**b**) *(indeciso)* undecided, hesitant; **estoy d.** I'm hesitant (**c**) *(poco honrado)* dubious, suspect (**d**) *(poco seguro)* questionable
duela *nf* stave
duelo[1] *nm (combate)* duel; **batirse en d.** to fight a duel
duelo[2] *nm* (**a**) *(dolor)* grief, affliction (**b**) *(luto)* mourning
duende *nm* (**a**) *(espíritu)* goblin, elf (**b**) *(nomo)* gnome (**c**) *(encanto misterioso)* magic, charm; **Granada es una ciudad con d.** Granada is a magical city; **para cantar flamenco hay que tener d.** a flamenco singer must have a certain magnetism
dueña *nf* owner; *(de casa de huéspedes)* landlady; *Fig* **es muy dueña de hacer de su vida lo que quiera** she can do as she pleases with her life
dueño *nm* owner; *(de casa etc)* landlord; **es el d. y señor** he is lord and master; **¿quién es el d.?** who owns this?; **se ha hecho el d.** he is boss now; *Fig* **hacerse d. de la situación** to get the situation under control; *Fig* **ser d. de sí mismo** to be self-possessed
duermevela *nm* snooze; **en d.** snoozing
Duero *n* **el D.** the Douro
dueto *nm* duet
dulce 1 *adj* (**a**) *(sabor)* sweet (**b**) *(carácter, voz, música)* soft, sweet, gentle (**c**) *(metal)* soft (**d**) *(agua)* fresh; **peces de agua d.** freshwater fish
2 *nm* (**a**) *Culin (pastel)* cake; **fruta en d.** *(escarchada)* glacé fruit; *(confitada)* fruit in heavy syrup; **me encantan los dulces** I have a sweet tooth ◻ **d. de almíbar** preserved fruit; **d. de membrillo** quince jelly (**b**) *(caramelo)* sweet, *US* candy (**c**) *CAm* brown sugar

dulcería *nf* confectionery; *(tienda)* confectioner's
dulcero, -a 1 *adj* sweet-toothed
2 *nm,f* confectioner
dulcificar [59] *vt* (**a**) *(endulzar)* to sweeten (**b**) *Fig* to soften
dulzaina *nf* = type of pipe similar to a clarinet used in folk music
dulzón, -ona *adj* sickly-sweet
dulzor *nm* (**a**) *(de sabor)* sweetness (**b**) *Fig* gentleness, sweetness, softness
dulzura *nf* (**a**) *(de sabor)* sweetness (**b**) *Fig* gentleness, sweetness, softness; **es una d. de niño** he is such a sweet baby/little boy
dumping ['dumpin] *nm Econ* dumping
duna *nf Geog* dune
dúo *nm Mús* duet
duodécimo, -a 1 *adj* twelfth; **duodécima parte** twelfth
2 *nm,f (de una serie)* twelfth
3 *nm (parte)* twelfth; *véase tamb* **octavo, -a**
duodenal *adj Anat Med* duodenal
duodeno *nm Anat* duodenum
dúplex 1 *adj* duplex
2 *nm* (**a**) *Arquit* duplex, duplex apartment (**b**) *Elec* link-up
duplicación *nf* duplication, doubling
duplicado, -a 1 *pp de* **duplicar**
2 *adj* **por d.** in duplicate; **hay que presentar los impresos por d.** all forms must be handed in in duplicate
3 *nm* duplicate, copy
duplicar [59] **1** *vt (gen)* to duplicate; *(cifras)* to double
2 duplicarse *vpr* to double; **el número de parados se ha duplicado** the number of unemployed has doubled
duplicidad *nm* (**a**) *(repetición)* duplication (**b**) *(falsedad)* duplicity
duplo, -a *adj & nm,f* double
duque *nm* duke
duquesa *nf* duchess
durabilidad *nf* durability
durable *adj* durable, lasting
duración *nf* duration, length; **disco de larga d.** long-playing record
duradero, -a *adj* durable, lasting
duralex® *nm* = heat-resistant glass
durante *prep (por)* during, in; *(todo el período)* for; **duerme d. el día** he sleeps during the day; **d. todo el día** all day long; **ha llovido d. la noche** it rained during the night; **la vi tan sólo d. tres o cuatro segundos** I saw her for only three or four seconds; **la vi varias veces d. las vacaciones** I saw her several times during the holidays; **viví en La Coruña d. un año** I lived in La Coruña for a year
durar *vi* (**a**) *(prolongarse)* to last, go on for; *Fig* **Helena no durará ni tres meses en el cargo** Helena won't last more than three months in her job (**b**) *(ropa, calzado)* to wear well, last
durazno *nm Am Bot (fruto)* peach; *(árbol)* peach tree
Durex® *nm Méx Br* Sellotape®, *US* Scotch® tape
dureza *nf* (**a**) *(de objeto, metal, agua)* hardness; *(de carne)* toughness; *(severidad)* harshness, severity; *Fig* **d. de corazón** hardheartedness (**b**) *(callosidad)* corn
durmiente 1 *adj* sleeping; **la bella d.** sleeping beauty
2 *nm Ferroc Br* sleeper, *US* tie

duro, -a 1 *adj* (**a**) *(material, superficie)* hard; *(carne)* tough; *Dep* **juego d.** rough play (**b**) *(penoso)* hard, difficult (**c**) *(áspero)* tough, harsh (**d**) *(resistente)* tough, strong (**e**) *(sin sentimientos)* hardhearted, tough

2 *nm* (**a**) *Esp Antes (moneda)* five peseta coin; *Fam* **¡lo que faltaba para el d.!** just what we o I needed! (**b**) *(persona)* tough guy

3 *adv* hard; **le da d. al trabajo** he works hard; **pégale d.** hit him hard

duty free ['djuti'fri] (*pl* **duty frees**) *nm* duty free shop

dux *nm Hist* doge

d/v *(abrev de* **días vista**) **a diez d/v** due within ten days

DVD (*pl* **DVDs**) *nm* (*abrev de* **Disco Versátil Digital**) DVD

E

E, e [e] *nf (la letra)* E, e

E *(abrev de* **Este)** E

e *conj (delante de palabras que empiecen por* **i** *o* **hi)** *and;* **verano e invierno** summer and winter

ea *interj (para animar)* come on!; *(para indicar resolución)* so there!

EAU *nmpl (abrev de* **Emiratos Árabes Unidos)** UAE

ebanista *nm Carp* cabinet-maker

ebanistería *nf Carp* **(a)** *(arte)* cabinet-making **(b)** *(taller)* cabinet-maker's

ébano *nm* ebony

ebonita *nf* ebonite, vulcanite

ebriedad *nf* inebriation, intoxication, drunkenness

ebrio, -a *adj* inebriated, intoxicated, drunk; *Fig* **e. de ira** furious

Ebro *n* el E. the Ebro

ebullición *nf* boiling; **entrar en e.** to come to the boil; **estar a punto de e.** to be at boiling point; *Fig* **estar en e.** to be boiling over ▫ **punto de e.** boiling point

eccehomo *nm Rel* Ecce Homo; *Fam Fig* **estar hecho un e.** to be a wreck

eccema *nm Med* eczema

ECG *nm (abrev de* **electrocardiograma)** ECG

echado, -a 1 *pp de* **echar**
2 *adj* **(a)** *(tumbado)* **estar e.** to be lying down **(b)** *(arrojado)* thrown; *(descartado)* thrown away; *Fam* **e. pa'lante** go-getting

echador, -a *adj Cuba Méx Ven* bigheaded

echadora *nf* **echadora de cartas** fortune-teller

echar 1 *vt* **(a)** *(lanzar)* to throw; *Fig* **e. algo a suertes** to draw lots for sth; *Fig* **e. maldiciones** to curse; *Fig* **e. pelillos a la mar** to bury the hatchet; *Fig* **e. una mano** to give a hand; *Fig* **e. una mirada/una ojeada** to have a look/a quick look *o* glance **(b)** *(depositar)* to put, drop; **e. dinero en un saco** to put money into a bag **(c)** *(correo) Br* to post, *US* mail **(d)** *(expulsar)* to throw out **(e)** *(despedir)* to sack, dismiss, fire; **le echaron del colegio** he was expelled from school **(f)** **e. por tierra** *o* **abajo** *(derribar) (edificio)* to demolish; *Fig (proyecto)* to ruin **(g)** *(brotar, salir)* to grow; **e. bigotes** to grow a moustache; *Fig* **e. raíces** to put down roots **(h)** *(emanar)* to emit, give out *o* off; **la chimenea echa mucho humo** a lot of smoke is coming out of the chimney **(i)** *(poner) Culin* to put in, add; **e. el cerrojo** to bolt the door; *Aut* **e. el freno** to put the brake on **(j)** *(decir)* **e. la buenaventura** to tell sb's fortune; **e. una regañina** *o* **un sermón a algn** to tell sb off **(k)** *(calcular)* to guess; **e. cuentas** to calculate; **le echó 37 años** he thought she looked 37; *Fam* **échale precio** guess how much I paid **(l)** *(apartar)* to push aside; **echa eso a un lado** push that to one side **(m)** *(servir)* to give, serve up; *(gasolina)* to put in; **me has echado mucho** you've given me a lot **(n)** *Esp Fam (exhibir) Cin TV* to show; **esta noche echan 'Yo, Claudio'** 'I, Claudius' is on tonight **(o)** **e. en cara** *(acusar)* to blame; **no me eches en cara tus errores** don't blame me for your mistakes **(p)** **e. de menos** *o* **en falta** to miss; **echa de menos a su amigo Pepe** he misses his friend Pepe **(q)** *Am (animales)* to urge on
2 *vi* **(a)** **(e. + a +** *infin) (empezar)* to begin to; **echó a correr** he ran off; *(deteriorar)* **e. a perder** to spoil **(b)** *(dar)* **e. de comer** to feed **(c)** *(ir)* **e. por un camino** to follow a path; **e. por la derecha** to go right
3 **echarse** *vpr* **(a)** *(lanzarse)* to throw oneself; *Fig* **la noche se nos echó encima** it was night before we knew it **(b)** *(tumbarse)* to lie down; **e. al suelo** to lie on the floor **(c)** *(apartarse)* **e. a un lado** to move oneself to one side; *Fig* **e. atrás** to have second thoughts, get cold feet **(d)** *Fam* **e. novio/novia** to get a steady boyfriend/girlfriend **(e)** **(e. + a +** *infin) (empezar)* to begin to; **e. a llorar** to burst into tears; **e. a perder** *(comida)* to go bad; *(personas)* to go downhill; **e. a reír** to burst out laughing **(f)** *Fam* **echárselas de** to claim to be; **se las echa de muy listo** he thinks he's very smart

echarpe *nm* shawl, stole

echona *nf Arg Chile Perú* sickle

eclampsia *nf Med* eclampsia

eclecticismo *nm* eclecticism

ecléctico, -a *adj & nm,f* eclectic

eclesial *adj* ecclesiastic, ecclesiastical, church

eclesiástico, -a 1 *adj* ecclesiastic, ecclesiastical, church
2 *nm* clergyman

eclipsar *vt* **(a)** *Astron* to eclipse **(b)** *Fig* to eclipse, outshine
2 eclipsarse *vpr* **(a)** *Astron* to be eclipsed **(b)** *Fig (desaparecer)* to disappear, vanish

eclipse *nm* eclipse

eclíptica *nf* ecliptic

eclosión *nf* **(a)** *Zool* hatching, emergence; *Bot* blossoming **(b)** *Fig* upsurge, flowering, emergence

eclosionar *vi* to break *o* burst out, emerge

eco *nm* **(a)** *Fis* echo **(b)** *Fig* echo, response; **hacer e.** to have an effect, make an impression; **tener e.** to arouse interest ▫ *Prensa* **ecos de sociedad** gossip column *sing*

ecografía *nf Med* scan

ecología *nf* ecology

ecológico, -a *adj* ecological

ecologismo *nm* Green movement

ecologista 1 *adj* ecological; *Pol* **partido e.** ecology party
2 *nmf* ecologist

ecólogo, -a *nm,f* ecologist

economato *nm Com* company store

econometría *nf* econometrics *sing*

economía *nf* (a) *(gen)* economy; **e. doméstica** housekeeping; **la e. británica** the British economy; **e. de mercado** market economy; **e. sumergida** black o hidden economy (b) *(ciencia)* economics (c) *(ahorro)* economy, saving; **hacer economías** to economize (d) *(cualidad)* economy, thrift, thriftiness

económicamente *adv* economically; **viajar e.** to travel cheaply

económico, -a *adj* (a) *(gen)* economic (b) *(barato)* cheap, economical, inexpensive; **resultar e.** to be cheap (c) *(persona)* thrifty, careful with money

› **economista** *nmf* economist

economizar [14] *vt (dinero, tiempo)* to economize, save; *(cosas)* to use sparingly

ecónomo *nm* (a) *Fin* trustee (b) *Rel* acting parish priest

ecosistema *nm* ecosystem

ecotasa *nf* ecotax

ecoturismo *nm* ecotourism

ectoplasma *nm* ectoplasm

ecuación *nf Mat* equation ❑ **e. de segundo grado** quadratic equation; **sistema de ecuaciones** set of equations

Ecuador *n* Ecuador

ecuador *nm* (a) *Geog* equator (b) *Educ Fam* **paso del e. =** trip organised by students celebrating half-way stage in their degree

ecualizador *nm Fis* equalizer

ecuánime *adj* (a) *(temperamento)* equable, even-tempered (b) *(juicio)* impartial, fair

ecuanimidad *nf* (a) *(temperamento)* equanimity (b) *(juicio)* impartiality, fairness

ecuatoguineano, -a 1 *adj* of o from Equatorial Guinea
2 *nm,f* person from Equatorial Guinea

ecuatorial *adj* equatorial

ecuatoriano, -a *adj & nm,f* Ecuadorian, Ecuadoran

ecuestre *adj* equestrian

ecuménico, -a *adj Rel* ecumenic, ecumenical

ecumenismo *nm* ecumenicism, ecumenicalism

eczema *nm Med* eczema

ed. (a) *(abrev de* **edición)** edit. (b) *(abrev de* **editor)** ed.

edad *nf* age; **los menores de e.** minors, children under age; **¿qué e. tienes?** how old are you?; **ya tienes e. para ...** you are old enough to ...; *Euf* **la tercera e.** senior citizens *pl*; *Euf* **una persona de e.** an elderly person ❑ **e. media** Middle Ages *pl*

edecán *nmf Méx (en congreso)* conference usher; *(acompañante)* escort

edema *nm Med* oedema

edén *nm* (a) *Rel* Eden (b) *Fig* paradise, heaven

edénico, -a *adj* idyllic, heavenly

edición *nf* (a) *Impr (publicación)* publication; *(de sellos)* issue; **Ediciones Sánchez** Sanchez Publications (b) *(conjunto de ejemplares)* edition; **agotada la e.** out of stock ❑ **e. anotada** annotated text; **e. pirata** pirate edition

edicto *nm* edict, proclamation

edificable *adj Arquit* **suelo e.** land with planning permission

edificación *nf Arquit* building, construction

edificante *adj* edifying, uplifting

edificar [59] *vt* (a) *(construir)* to build (b) *Fig (enseñar)* to

edify, uplift; **e. con el ejemplo** to teach by example

edificio *nm* building; **E. Cisneros** Cisneros House

edil, -a 1 *nm,f* town councillor
2 *nm Hist* aedile

Edimburgo *n* Edinburgh

Edipo *nm* Oedipus; *Psic* **complejo de E.** Oedipus complex

editar *vt* (a) *(libros, periódicos)* to publish; *(discos)* to release (b) *Inform* to edit

editor, -a 1 *adj* publishing
2 *nm,f* publisher
3 *nm Inform* editor ❑ **e. de textos** text editor

editorial 1 *adj* publishing
2 *nf* publishers, publishing house
3 *nm Prensa* editorial, leader article

editorialista *nmf Prensa* leader writer

edredón *nm* eiderdown, continental quilt, duvet, *US* comforter

educación *nf* (a) *(preparación)* education; **gastos de e.** school o college fees ❑ **e. física** physical education; **e. primaria/secundaria** primary/secondary education **e. sexual** sex education; **e. vial** road safety education (b) *(urbanidad)* upbringing, breeding; **falta de e.** rudeness, discourtesy; **nunca había visto tal falta de e. en la mesa** I'd never seen such bad table manners; **¡qué falta de e.!** how rude!

educado, -a 1 *pp de* **educar**
2 *adj* polite

educador, -a 1 *adj* educating
2 *nm,f* educationalist, teacher

educando, -a *nm,f* pupil, student

educar [59] *vt (enseñar)* to educate, teach; *(entrenar)* to train

educativo, -a *adj* educational; **método e.** teaching method; **sistema e.** education system

edulcorante *nm* sweetener

edulcorar *vt* to add sweeteners to; *Fig* **tener una visión edulcorada de la realidad** to look at the world through rose-tinted glasses

EE.UU. *nmpl (abrev de* **Estados Unidos)** USA

efe *nf* = name of the letter F in Spanish

efebo *nm* Adonis

efectismo *nm* showiness, theatricality

efectista *adj* showy, stagy

efectivamente *adv* quite!, yes indeed!

efectividad *nf* effectiveness; **con e. desde ...** with effect from ..., as from ...

efectivo, -a 1 *adj* (a) *(con resultado)* effective; **medidas efectivas** effective measures; **hacer algo e.** to carry sth out; *Fin* **hacer e. un cheque** to cash a cheque; *Jur* **hacerse e.** to come into effect (b) *(real)* real, actual
2 *nm* (a) *Fin* cash, funds *pl*; **en e.** in cash; **e. en caja** *Br* cash in hand, *US* cash on hand (b) *(plantilla)* personnel (c) *efectivos Mil* forces

efecto *nm* (a) *(resultado)* effect, end result; **surtir e.** to work, do the job, be effective; **tener e.** to take place ❑ **e. dominó** domino effect (b) *(impresión)* impression; **causar o hacer e.** to make an impression; **hace buen e.** it looks good; **no produjo ningún e.** it had no effect (c) *(fin práctico)* aim, object; **a tal e.** to that end; **a efectos de ...** with the object of ... (d) *(efectivamente)* **en e.** quite!, yes indeed! (e) *Dep* spin; *Ftb* **chutar con e.** to bend o swerve the ball; **dar e. a la pelota** to put some spin on the ball (f) *Fin* bill, draft ❑ **e. interbancario** bank draft o bill; **efectos públicos** public bonds (g) *Cin Rad Teat TV* effect; **efectos**

especiales/sonoros special/sound effects (**h**) **efectos** *(artículos)* effects, things ❑ **e. de escritorio** stationery *sing;* **e. personales** personal belongings o effects

efectuar [4] **1** *vt* to carry out, make, do; **e. un pago** to make a payment; *Com* **e. un pedido** to place an order; **e. una suma** to do a sum; **e. un viaje** to make a journey
  2 efectuarse *vpr* to take place

efeméride *nf* (**a**) *(aniversario)* anniversary; *(acontecimiento)* event (**b**) **efemérides** *Prensa* list of the day's anniversaries

efervescencia *nf* (**a**) *(gen)* effervescence; *(de bebida)* fizziness (**b**) *Fig* high spirits *pl*

efervescente *adj* (**a**) *(gen)* effervescent; *(bebidas)* fizzy (**b**) *Fig* vivacious, high-spirited

eficacia *nf (de persona)* efficiency, effectiveness; *(de cosas)* efficacy, effectiveness; *(de rendimiento)* efficiency

eficaz *adj (competente)* efficient; *(cosas)* efficacious, effective; *(rendimiento)* efficient

eficazmente *adv* effectively

eficiencia *nf* efficiency; *Econ* **e. económica** cost-effectiveness

eficiente *adj* efficient

eficientemente *adv* efficiently

efigie *nf* effigy, image

efímero, -a *adj* ephemeral, short-lived, fleeting

efluvio *nm* emanation, flow, effusion; *Fig* **e. de alegría** surge of happiness

efusión *nf* (**a**) *(derramamiento)* effusion, pouring out (**b**) *(manifestación de afecto)* effusiveness

efusivamente *adv* effusively, warmly

efusividad *nf* effusiveness

efusivo, -a *adj* effusive, warm

Egeo *n* **el (Mar) E.** the Aegean Sea

égida *nf* (**a**) *Mit* aegis (**b**) *Fig* protection; **bajo la é. de ...** under the aegis of ...

egipcio, -a *adj & nm,f* Egyptian; **la frontera e.-israelí** the Israeli-Egyptian border

Egipto *n* Egypt

egiptología *nf* Egyptology

egiptólogo, -a *nm,f* Egyptologist

eglefino *nm (pez)* haddock

ego *nm* ego

egocéntrico, -a *adj* egocentric, self-centred, *US* self-centered

egocentrismo *nm* egocentricity

egoísmo *nm* egoism, selfishness

egoísta 1 *adj* egoistic, egoistical, selfish
  2 *nmf* egoist, selfish person

ególatra 1 *adj* egomaniacal
  2 *nmf* egomaniac

egolatría *nf* egomania, self-worship

egotismo *nm* egotism

egotista 1 *adj* egotistic, egoistical
  2 *nmf* egotist

egregio, -a *adj* eminent, illustrious, renowned

egresado, -a *nm,f Am (de escuela)* = student who has completed their studies, *US* graduate (**b**) *(de universidad)* graduate

egresar *vi Am* (**a**) *(de escuela)* to leave school after graduation (**b**) *(de universidad)* to graduate

egreso *nm Am (de universidad)* graduation

eh *interj* (**a**) *(para llamar la atención)* hey (you)! (**b**) *(para preguntar)* ¿eh?, ¿y por qué? really? why's that?; **estaba rico, ¿eh?** it was delicious, wasn't it?

Eire *n* Eire, Republic of Ireland

ej. *(abrev de ejemplo)* e.g.

eje *nm* (**a**) *Téc (de ruedas)* axle; *(de máquinas)* shaft, spindle; *Aut* **e. trasero/delantero** rear/front axle; *Fam Fig* **partir por el e. a algn** to kill sb; **nos han subido el alquiler y nos han partido por el e.** they've put the rent up and it's just about killing us (**b**) *Mat* axis (**c**) *Pol* **E.** Axis (**d**) *Fig* centre, *US* center, core

ejecución *nf* (**a**) *(orden)* carrying out (**b**) *(ajusticiamiento)* execution (**c**) *Mús* performance (**d**) *Jur* seizure

ejecutable *adj* (**a**) *(realizable)* feasible, practicable (**b**) *Inform* executable

ejecutante *nmf Mús* performer

ejecutar *vt* (**a**) *(orden)* to carry out (**b**) *(ajusticiar)* to execute (**c**) *Mús* to perform, play (**d**) *Jur (reclamar)* to seize (**e**) *Inform* to run

ejecutiva *nf (de partido, asociación)* executive

ejecutivo, -a 1 *adj* executive; *Pol* **el poder e.** the executive
  2 *nm,f* executive

ejecutor, -a *nm,f* (**a**) *Jur* executor (**b**) *(verdugo)* executioner

ejecutoria *nf Jur* writ of execution

ejecutorio, -a *adj Jur* executory, enforceable

ejem *interj* ahem, hmm

ejemplar 1 *adj* exemplary, model
  2 *nm* (**a**) *Impr* copy, number, issue; **e. duplicado** duplicate copy (**b**) *(especimen)* specimen ❑ **e. de regalo** *(libro)* complimentary copy

ejemplaridad *nf* exemplariness

ejemplarizar [14] *vt* to set an example to

ejemplificación *nf* illustration, exemplification

ejemplificar [59] *vt* to illustrate, exemplify

ejemplo *nm* example; **dar e.** to set an example; **poner de e.** to give as an example; **por e.** for example; **servir de e.** to serve as an example

ejercer [40] **1** *vt* (**a**) *(practicar)* to practise, *US* practice; **e. una profesión** to follow o practise a profession (**b**) *(usar)* to exercise; *(una influencia)* to exert; **e. el derecho de ...** to exercise one's right to ...
  2 *vi* to work (**de** as)

ejercicio *nm* (**a**) *(gen)* exercise; **e. de una profesión** practice of a profession; **hacer e.** to take o do exercise (**b**) *Educ* exercise; *(en un examen)* question; **cuaderno de ejercicios** exercise book (**c**) *Fin Pol* year; **e. económico** financial o fiscal year

ejercitar 1 *vt (dedicarse)* to practise, *US* practice
  2 ejercitarse *vpr (entrenarse)* to practise, *US* practice; *Mil* to exercise

ejército *nm* army ❑ **E. del Aire** Air Force; **e. profesional** professional army; **E. de Tierra** army *(as opposed to navy and air force)*

ejido *nm* (**a**) *Méx (institución)* = system of cooperative land tenure; *(terreno)* = piece of land farmed by a cooperative; *(sociedad)* = farming cooperative (**b**) *Hist* common land

ejote *nm CAm Méx* green bean

el (*mpl* **los**) *art def* (**a**) *(gen)* the; **el sol, el mar y el cielo** the sun, the sea and the sky (**b**) *(no se traduce)* **el Canadá** Canada; **el Sr. García** Mr. Garcia (**c**) *(el + de)* the one; **el de las once** the eleven o'clock one; **el de Madrid** the one from Madrid (**d**) *(el + de) (no se traduce)* **el de ayer** yesterday's; **el de tu amigo** your friend's (**e**) *(el + que)* the one; **el que quieras** whichever one you want; **el que tienes en la mano** the one you've got in your hand; **el que vino ayer** the one who came yesterday

él *pron pers* (**a**) *(sujeto) (persona)* he; **él me quiere** he loves me (**b**) *(animal, cosa)* it; **él ladró con fuerza** it o he barked loudly (**c**) *(complemento) (persona)* him; **con/sin él** with/without him; **¡es él!** it's him!; **fui a donde él** I went over to him; **hablábamos de él** we were talking about him; **pídeselo a él** ask him for it (**d**) *(animal, cosa)* it; **pon el libro dentro él** put the book in it (**e**) *(posesivo)* **de él** his; **no es mío, es de él** it isn't mine, it's his

elaboración *nf* (**a**) *(de un producto)* manufacture, production; **de e. casera** home-made (**b**) *(de una idea)* working out, development

elaborar *vt* (**a**) *(producto)* to make, manufacture, produce (**b**) *(teoría)* to develop

elasticidad *nf* elasticity, stretch; *Fig* flexibility

elástico, -a 1 *adj* (**a**) *(cuerpo)* elastic; **cama e.** trampoline (**b**) *Fig* flexible; **eso es muy e.** that depends on other factors

  2 *nm* (**a**) *(cinta)* elastic (**b**) **elásticos** braces

ele[1] *interj* eh!

ele[2] *nf* = name of the letter L in Spanish

elección *nf* (**a**) *(opción)* choice; **lo dejo a tu e.** I leave that up to you (**b**) *(de un cargo)* election (**c**) **elecciones** *Pol* elections; **convocar a e.** to call an election; **e. generales** o **legislativas** elections to the national parliament, *Br* ≃ general election, *US* ≃ congressional elections;

eleccionario, -a *adj Am* electoral

electivo, -a *adj* elective; *Pol* **cargo e.** elective office

electo, -a *adj* elect; **el presidente e.** the president elect

elector, -a *nm,f Pol* voter, elector

electorado *nm* electorate, voters *pl*

electoral *adj* *(sistema, distrito, reforma)* electoral; *(campaña, resultado, propaganda)* election

electoralismo *nm Pey* electioneering

electoralista *adj Pey* electioneering

electricidad *nf* electricity ❑ **e. estática** static electricity

electricista *nmf* electrician

eléctrico, -a *adj* electric, electrical

electrificación *nf* electrification

electrificar [59] *vt* to electrify

electrizante *adj Fig* electrifying

electrizar [14] *vt* to electrify; *Fig* **la audiencia quedó electrizada con su actuación** the audience was electrified by his performance

electrocardiograma *nm Med* electrocardiogram

electrochoque *nm Med* electric shock therapy

electrocución *nf* electrocution

electrocutar 1 *vt* to electrocute

  2 electrocutarse *vpr* to be electrocuted

electrodo *nm* electrode

electrodoméstico *nm* (home) electrical appliance

electroencefalograma *nm* electroencephalogram

electrógeno, -a 1 *adj* **grupo e.** generator

  2 *nm* generator

electroimán *nm* electromagnet

electrólisis *nf* electrolysis

electrolito, electrólito *nm* electrolyte

electromagnético, -a *adj* electromagnetic

electromagnetismo *nm* electromagnetism

electromecánica *nf* electromechanics *sing*

electrón *nm* electron

electrónica *nf* electronics *sing*

electrónico, -a *adj* electronic

electroshock [elektro'ʃok] (*pl* **electroshocks**) *nm (terapia)* electric shock therapy

electrostática[1] *nf* electrostatics *sing*

electrostático, -a[2] *adj* electrostatic

elefanta *nf Zool* cow o female elephant

elefante 1 *nm,f* elephant

  2 *nm* **e. marino** elephant seal

elefantiasis *nf Med* elephantiasis

elegancia *nf* elegance, stylishness, smartness

elegante *adj* elegant, stylish, smart

elegantemente *adv* elegantly, stylishly, smartly

elegantoso, -a *adj Am Fam* smart, *Br* posh

elegía *nf* elegy

elegiaco, -a *adj*, **elegíaco, -a** *adj* elegiac

elegibilidad *nf* eligibility

elegible *adj* eligible

elegido, -a 1 *pp de* **elegir**

  2 *adj* (**a**) *(escogido)* chosen (**b**) *Pol* elected

  3 *nm,f* person chosen/elected; **los elegidos** the chosen few

elegir [55] *vt* (**a**) *(optar)* to choose (**b**) *Pol* to elect

elemental *adj* (**a**) *(relativo al elemento)* elemental (**b**) *(básico)* basic, fundamental (**c**) *(muy fácil)* elementary

elemento *nm* (**a**) *(gen)* element (**b**) *(individuo)* type, individual; *Esp Fam* **es un buen e.** he's a good sort (**c**) *(ambiente)* **estar en su e.** to be in one's element (**d**) *(pieza, componente)* component, part (**e**) **elementos** *(fundamentos)* rudiments; **e. de filosofía/geometría** basic principles of philosophy/geometry (**f**) **elementos** *(fuerzas naturales)* elements; **nada puede el hombre contra los e.** man is helpless against the elements

elenco *nm* (**a**) *(catálogo)* index, catalogue (**b**) *Teat* cast (**c**) *(personas)* group of people

elepé *nm Mús* LP (record)

elevación *nf (gen)* elevation, rise; **e. del terreno** rise in the ground, elevation; **la e. del nivel de vida** the rise in the standard of living

elevado, -a 1 *pp de* **elevar**

  2 *adj* (**a**) *(alto)* elevated, raised, high; *(edificio)* tall (**b**) *Fig (pensamiento)* lofty, noble (**c**) *(tono, voz)* angry (**d**) *Mat* **e. al cuadrado** squared; **e. a la cuarta potencia** raised to the power of four

elevador, -a 1 *adj* elevating, hoisting, lifting

  2 *nm Am Br* lift, *US* elevator

elevalunas *nm inv Aut* window mechanism ❑ **e. eléctrico** electric window

elevar 1 *vt* (**a**) *(alzar)* to elevate, raise, lift (**b**) *Mat* to raise; **e. a la cuarta potencia** to raise to the power of four (**c**) *Fig* to exalt

  2 elevarse *vpr* (**a**) *(subir)* to rise; *(llegar a una altura)* to reach; *(erguirse)* to stand (above), tower above (**b**) *(sumar)* to amount o come to; **¿a cuánto se elevan los daños?** how much does the damage amount o come to?

elfo *nm Mit* elf

elidir *Ling* **1** *vt* to elide

  2 elidirse *vpr* to elide, be elided

elijo *indic pres véase* **elegir**

eliminación *nf* elimination

eliminar *vt* (**a**) *(gen)* to eliminate; *(desecho)* to get rid of; *(un factor)* to rule out (**b**) *Fam (matar)* to eliminate, kill

eliminatoria *nf Dep* heat, qualifying round

eliminatorio, -a *adj* qualifying, eliminatory

elipse *nf Mat* ellipse

elipsis *nf inv Ling* ellipsis

elíptico, -a *adj* elliptic, elliptical

elisión *nf Ling* elision

élite *nf,* **elite** *nf* elite, élite

elitismo *nm* elitism

elitista *adj* elitist

elixir *nm* elixir

ella *pron pers f* **(a)** *(sujeto)* she; **e. y yo** she and I **(b)** *(animal, cosa)* it, she; **e. ladró con fuerza** it *o* she barked loudly **(c)** *(complemento)* her; *(animal, cosa)* it, her; **para/con e.** for/ with her; **¡es e.!** it's her!; **pon el libro sobre e.** put the book on it **(d)** *(posesivo)* **de e.** hers; **la casa es de e.** the house is hers; **eso es asunto de e.** that's her affair

ellas *pron pers fpl véase* **ellos**

elle *nf* = name of the digraph Ll in Spanish

ello *pron pers neut* it; **¡a e.!** to work!; **e. es que ...** the fact is that ...; **¡no se hable más de e.!** (and) that's final!

ellos *pron pers mpl* **(a)** *(sujeto)* they **(b)** *(complemento)* them; **con/sin e.** with/without them **(c)** *(posesivo)* **de e.** theirs; **eso es cosa de e.** that's their affair

elocución *nf* elocution

elocuencia *nf* eloquence

elocuente *adj* eloquent

elogiable *adj* praiseworthy

elogiar *vt* to praise, eulogize

elogio *nm* praise, eulogy

elogiosamente *adv* eulogistically, admiringly

elogioso, -a *adj* appreciative, complimentary, eulogistic

elongación *nf* **(a)** *Med* elongation **(b)** *Astron* elongation

elote *nm CAm Méx* corncob, ear of maize *o US* corn

El Salvador *n* El Salvador

elucidación *nf* clarification, elucidation

elucidar *vt* to elucidate, explain

elucubración *nf* **(a)** *(trabajo)* lucubration **(b)** *(divagación)* rambling

elucubrar *vi* **(a)** *(trabajar)* to lucubrate **(b)** *(divagar)* to ramble

eludible *adj* avoidable

eludir *vt* *(responsabilidad, obligación)* to evade; *(la justicia)* to evade; *(perseguidores)* to escape, avoid; **e. una respuesta** to avoid answering

elusivo, -a *adj* evasive

Ema *(abrev de* **Eminecia)** Eminence, Eminency

e-mail ['imeil] *(pl* **e-mails)** *nm Inform* e-mail

emanación *nf* emanation

emanar *vi* **(a)** *(desprenderse)* to emanate **(b)** *(derivar)* to derive *o* come **(de** from)

emancipación *nf* emancipation

emancipado, -a 1 *pp de* **emancipar**
2 *adj* emancipated, free, liberated

emancipador, -a *adj* emancipating, liberating

emancipar 1 *vt* to emancipate, free
2 emanciparse *vpr* to become emancipated *o* liberated *o* free

emasculación *nf* castration, emasculation

embadurnar *vt* to daub, smear **(de** with)

embajada *nf* **(a)** *(oficina, residencia)* embassy **(b)** *(cargo)* ambassadorship, post of ambassador **(c)** *(comunicación)* message **(d)** *Fam* cheeky proposition *o* suggestion

embajador, -a *nm,f* ambassador

embalador, -a *nm,f* packer

embalaje *nm* packing, packaging; **gastos de e.** packing (costs); **papel de e.** wrapping paper

embalar¹ *vt (mercancías)* to pack, wrap

embalar² **1** *vi* to speed up
2 embalarse *vpr* **(a)** *(acelerar)* to speed up **(b)** *Fig (persona)* to get carried away

embaldosado *nm* **(a)** *(trabajo)* tiling **(b)** *(suelo)* tiled floor

embaldosar *vt* to tile

embalsadero *nm* fen, marsh, swamp

embalsamador, -a *nm,f* embalmer

embalsamar *vt* to embalm

embalsar *vt* **(a)** *(llenar de agua)* to dam up **(b)** *Náut (izar a una persona)* to sling *o* lift

embalse *nm* **(a)** *(presa)* dam, reservoir **(b)** *(acción)* damming

embancarse [59] *vt Náut* to run aground

embarazada *nf* pregnant woman, expectant mother

embarazado, -a 1 *pp de* **embarazar**
2 *adj* **(a)** *(preñada)* pregnant **(b)** *(turbado)* embarrassed

embarazar [14] *vt* **(a)** *(dejar preñada)* to make pregnant **(b)** *(dificultar)* to hinder **(c)** *(turbar)* to embarrass

embarazo *nm* **(a)** *(preñez)* pregnancy **(b)** *(obstáculo)* obstacle **(c)** *(turbación)* embarrassment

embarazoso, -a *adj* awkward, troublesome, embarrassing

embarcación *nf* **(a)** *(nave)* boat, craft; **e. de desembarco** landing craft **(b)** *(embarco)* embarkation **(c)** *(viaje)* voyage

embarcadero *nm* pier, quay, jetty

embarcar [59] **1** *vt* **(a)** *(personas)* to embark; *(mercancías)* to ship **(b)** *Fig* involve, implicate; **e. a algn en un asunto** to involve sb in an affair
2 embarcarse *vpr* **(a)** *(barco)* to embark, go on board; *(avión)* to board **(b)** *Fig* to embark

embargar [38] *vt* **(a)** *Jur* to seize, impound **(b)** *Fig* to overwhelm; **le embargaba la emoción** he was overcome by emotion

embargo 1 *nm* **(a)** *Jur* seizure of property **(b)** *Com Náut* embargo
2 sin embargo *loc adv* nevertheless, however, nonetheless

embarque *nm (persona)* boarding; *(mercancías)* loading; **tarjeta de e.** boarding card

embarrado, -a 1 *pp de* **embarrar**
2 *adj* muddy

embarrancar(se) [59] *vi & vpr* **(a)** *Náut* to run aground **(b)** *Fig* to get bogged down

embarrar 1 *vt* **(a)** *(con barro)* to cover with mud **(b)** *Méx (untar)* **e. el pan con mantequilla** to spread butter on the bread **(c)** *Am (calumniar, desacreditar)* to smear **(d)** *CAm Méx RP* **e. a algn en algo** *(en asunto turbio)* to get sb mixed up in sth **(e)** *Carib Chile RP Fam* **embarrarla** *(meter la pata)* to put one's foot in it
2 embarrarse *vpr* to get covered in mud

embarullar *vt* to bungle, mess up

embate *nm* **(a)** *(de las olas)* pounding **(b)** *Fig* outburst

embaucador, -a 1 *adj* deceitful; **palabras embaucadoras** lies
2 *nm,f* deceiver, swindler, cheat

embaucar [59] *vt* to deceive, dupe, swindle, cheat

embeber 1 *vt* **(a)** *(absorber)* to soak up **(b)** *Cost* to take in
2 embeberse *vpr* to become absorbed *o* engrossed **(en** in)

embebido, -a 1 *pp de* **embeber**
2 *adj* engrossed, absorbed

embelecar [59] *vt* to deceive, cheat

embeleco *nm* deception, cheating

embelesado, -a 1 *pp de* **embelesar**
  2 *adj* delighted, fascinated

embelesar *vt* to delight, fascinate

embeleso *nm* **(a)** delight, fascination **(b)** *Cuba (planta)* leadwort

embellecedor, -a 1 *adj* beautifying; **crema e.** beauty cream
  2 *nm Aut* hubcap

embellecer [46] *vt (cosa, sitio)* to embellish, brighten up; *(persona)* to flatter

embellecimiento *nm* embellishment, beautifying

emberrincharse *vpr*, **emberrenchinarse** *vpr Fam* to fly into a tantrum

embestida *nf* **(a)** *(ataque)* onslaught **(b)** *Taur* charge

embestir [47] *vt* **(a)** *Taur* to charge **(b)** *(lanzarse)* to assault; **e. contra** to attack

embijar *vt CAm Méx* to soil, dirty

emblandecer [46] **1** *vt* to soften
  2 emblandecerse *vpr Fig* to relent

emblanquecer [46] *vt* to whiten, bleach

emblema *nm* emblem, badge; *Com* logo

emblemático, -a *adj* emblematic

embobado, -a 1 *pp de* **embobar**
  2 *adj* fascinated

embobamiento *nm* fascination, amazement

embobar 1 *vt* to fascinate, amaze
  2 embobarse *vpr* to be fascinated *o* besotted (**con, de** by)

embocadura *nf* **(a)** *(de un río)* mouth **(b)** *Mús* mouthpiece **(c)** *(bocado)* bit **(d)** *(sabor del vino)* taste, flavour, *US* flavor

embocar [59] *vt* **(a)** *(meter)* to introduce; *(en la boca)* to put into the mouth **(b)** *Golf* to hole

embochinchar *vt Am (alborotar)* to kick up a racket

embolado *nm* **(a)** *Teat* minor role **(b)** *Taur* bull with wooden balls on its horns **(c)** *Esp Fam* fib, lie

embolar¹ *vt Taur* to put wooden balls on the horns of

embolar² *RP Fam* **1** *vt* **(a)** *(aburrir)* to bore **(b)** *(fastidiar)* to annoy
  2 embolarse *vpr (aburrirse)* to get bored

embolia *nf Med* embolism, clot

émbolo *nm Téc* piston

embolsar 1 *vt* **(a)** *(dinero)* to pocket **(b)** *Fig (cobrar)* to collect
  2 embolsarse *vpr* to pocket, earn

embonar *vt Andes Cuba Méx* **(a)** *(ensamblar)* to join **(b)** *(favorecer)* to suit **(c)** *(abonar)* to manure

emboquillado *adj* filter-tipped

emborrachar 1 *vt* to get drunk
  2 emborracharse *vpr* to get drunk

emborrascarse [59] *vpr Meteor* to become stormy *o* overcast

emborronar 1 *vt* **(a)** *(garrapatear)* to blot **(b)** *Fig* to scribble
  2 emborronarse *vpr* to smudge

emboscada *nf* ambush; **tender una e.** to lay an ambush

emboscar [59] *vt* to ambush

embotado, -a 1 *pp de* **embotar**
  2 *adj* dull, blunt, blunted

embotar *vt* to blunt; *Fig (los sentidos)* to dull; *(la mente)* to fuddle

embotellado, -a 1 *pp de* **embotellar**
  2 *adj* bottled
  3 *nm* bottling

embotellador, -a *nm,f (persona)* bottler

embotelladora *nf (máquina)* bottling machine

embotellamiento *nm* **(a)** *(acción)* bottling **(b)** *Aut Fig* traffic jam

embotellar *vt* **(a)** *(meter en botella)* to bottle **(b)** *Aut Fig* to block **(c)** *Fam* to swot up on

embozar [14] **1** *vt* **(a)** *(cubrir el rostro)* to muffle **(b)** *Fig* to play one's cards close to one's chest
  2 embozarse *vpr Fig* to play one's cards close to one's chest

embozo *nm* **(a)** *(prenda)* muffler, mask, covering of the face **(b)** *Fig (recato)* reserve

embragar [38] *vi Aut* to engage the clutch

embrague *nm* clutch

embravecer [46] **1** *vt* to enrage
  2 embravecerse *vpr* **(a)** *(enfadarse)* to become enraged **(b)** *(mar)* to become rough

embravecido, -a *adj* rough

embrear *vt* to tar, pitch

embriagado, -a 1 *pp de* **embriagar**
  2 *adj* intoxicated, drunk, drunken

embriagador, -a *adj* intoxicating

embriagar [38] **1** *vt* to intoxicate, get drunk; *Fig* to transport, enrapture
  2 embriagarse *vpr* to get drunk; *Fig* to be transported *o* enraptured

embriaguez *nf* intoxication, drunkenness; *Fig* intoxication, rapture

embridar *vt (un caballo)* to bridle

embrión *nm* **(a)** *Biol* embryo **(b)** *Fig (de una idea, novela)* beginnings *pl*, embryo; *(de revolución)* seeds *pl*; **en e.** in embryo

embrionario, -a *adj* embryonic, embryonal; **en estado e.** in *o* at the embryonic stage

embrocar [59] *vt Méx* to pull on

embrolladamente *adv* confusedly

embrollado, -a 1 *pp de* **embrollar**
  2 *adj* confused, muddled

embrollar 1 *vt* to confuse, muddle
  2 embrollarse *vpr* to get muddled *o* confused

embrollo *nm* **(a)** *(lío)* muddle, confusion **(b)** *(mentiras)* pack of lies **(c)** *Fig* embarrassing situation

embromar *vt Am (hacer broma)* to tease, play a trick *o* a joke on **(b)** to annoy

embrujado, -a 1 *pp de* **embrujar**
  2 *adj (persona)* bewitched; *(sitio)* haunted

embrujar *vt* **(a)** *(un lugar)* to haunt; *(persona)* to bewitch **(b)** *Fig (fascinar)* to cast a spell on, bewitch

embrujo *nm* spell, charm; *Fig* attraction, fascination

embrutecer [46] **1** *vt* to stultify, make dull
  2 embrutecerse *vpr* to become stultified

embrutecimiento *nm (acción)* stultification

embuchado, -a 1 *pp de* **embuchar**
  2 *adj* **carne e.** processed cold meat *o* meats
  3 *nm* **(a)** *Culin* processed cold meat **(b)** *Fig (asunto engañoso)* cover-up **(c)** *Pol (fraude)* rigging of elections

embuchar 1 *vt* **(a)** *(embutir)* to stuff **(b)** *(aves)* to force-feed **(c)** *(comer)* to stuff oneself with
  2 embucharse *vpr Am* to get angry without reason

embudo *nm* funnel; *Fam* **eso funciona según la ley del e.** there's one law for the rich and another for the poor

embullar *vi Am* to make a din

embuste *nm* lie, trick

embustero, -a 1 *adj* deceitful, lying
2 *nm,f* cheater, liar

embutido *nm* (**a**) *(embuchado)* cold cut, processed cold meat (**b**) *(incrustación)* inlay (**c**) *Am Cost* strip of lace

embutir 1 *vt* (**a**) *(carne)* to stuff (**b**) *(meter)* to stuff *o* cram *o* squeeze (**en** into) (**c**) *(incrustar)* to inlay (**d**) *Fig (resumir)* to condense
2 embutirse *vpr Fam (atiborrarse)* to stuff oneself (**de** with)

eme *nf* (**a**) *(letra)* = name of the letter M in Spanish (**b**) *Fam Euf* sugar; **esto es una e.** this is rubbish; **¡vete a la e.!** eff off!

emergencia *nf* (**a**) *(salida)* emergence (**b**) *(caso imprevisto)* emergency; **en caso de e.** in an emergency

emergente *adj* (**a**) *(saliente)* emergent (**b**) *(resultante)* resulting, consequent

emerger [52] *vi* to emerge

emérito, -a *adj Educ* emeritus

emigración *nf* emigration, migration

emigrado, -a 1 *pp de* **emigrar**
2 *nm,f* emigrant; *Pol* émigré

emigrante *adj & nmf* emigrant

emigrar *vi (gen)* to emigrate; *(aves)* to migrate

emilio *nm Inform Fam* e-mail (message)

eminencia *nf* (**a**) *Geog* height, hill, elevation (**b**) *Fig (mérito)* prominence (**c**) *Fig (persona)* eminence, prominency; **Su E.** His Eminence

eminente *adj* (**a**) *(alto)* high (**b**) *Fig (renombrado)* eminent; **un e. psiquiatra** a top *o* eminent psychiatrist

eminentemente *adv* eminently

emir *nm* emir

emirato *nm* emirate ❑ **Emiratos Arabes Unidos** United Arab Emirates

emisario, -a *nm,f* emissary

emisión *nf* (**a**) *(gen)* emission (**b**) *(de moneda, sello)* issue; **e. de bonos** bond issue; **e. pública** public issue (**c**) *Rad TV (programa)* broadcast; *(transmisión)* broadcasting; **cierre de la e.** close-down; **e. en directo** live transmission

emisor, -a 1 *adj* (**a**) *Rad TV* **centro e.** transmitter, broadcasting station (**b**) *Fin* **banco e.** issuing bank
2 *nm* (**a**) *Rad* radio transmitter (**b**) *Fin* issuer

emisora *nf Rad TV* radio *o* television station

emitir *vt* (**a**) *(gen)* to emit; *(sonidos de los seres vivos)* to utter, emit; *(luz, calor)* to give off (**b**) *(manifestar)* to express; *Jur* **e. el fallo** *o* **la sentencia** to pronounce judgement, pass sentence; **e. un juicio** to express an opinion (**c**) *Rad TV* to transmit (**d**) *(moneda, sello, títulos etc)* to issue

Emmo. *(abrev de* **Eminentísimo)** Most Eminent

emoción *nf* (**a**) *(conmoción, sentimiento)* emotion; **regirse por las emociones** to be ruled by the heart (**b**) *(expectación)* excitement; **la e. del momento** the heat of the moment; **¡qué e.!** how exciting!

emocionado, -a 1 *pp de* **emocionar**
2 *adj* deeply moved *o* touched

emocional *adj* emotional

emocionante *adj* (**a**) *(conmovedor)* moving, touching (**b**) *(agitado)* exciting, thrilling

emocionar 1 *vt* (**a**) *(conmover)* to move, touch; **me emocionó la película** I found the film really moving (**b**) *(excitar)* to thrill; **a los niños les emociona ir en barco** the kids love going out in a boat
2 emocionarse *vpr* (**a**) *(conmoverse)* to be moved to tears (**b**) *(excitarse)* to get excited

emolumento *nm* emolument

emoticón *nm*, **emoticono** *nm Inform* smiley

emotividad *nf* emotiveness

emotivo, -a *adj (palabras)* emotive, stirring, rousing; *(persona)* emotional; *(escena)* moving, touching

empacadora *nf Téc* packing machine

empacar [59] **1** *vt* (**a**) *(mercancias)* to pack (**b**) *Am* to annoy
2 empacarse *vpr* (**a**) *(obstinarse)* to dig one's heels in (**b**) *Fig* to become shy *o* embarrassed (**c**) *Am (animales)* to balk

empachado, -a 1 *pp de* **empachar**
2 *adj* (**a**) *(desmañado)* slow-witted (**b**) *(ahíto)* bloated

empachar 1 *vt* (**a**) *(comer demasiado)* to give indigestion (**b**) *Fig (hartar)* to be fed up; **me empacha tanta televisión** I'm sick of so much television
2 empacharse *vpr* (**a**) *(indigestión)* to stuff oneself (**b**) *(avergonzarse)* to get embarrassed

empacho *nm* (**a**) *(comida)* indigestion, upset stomach (**b**) *Fig* surfeit; **tener un e. de ...** to have had one's fill of ... (**c**) *(vergüenza)* embarrassment; **no tener e. en decir ...** to have no qualms about saying ...; **sin e.** unashamedly

empachoso, -a *adj* (**a**) *(comida)* heavy, indigestible (**b**) *(vergonzoso)* shameful

empadrar *vt Méx (animales)* to mate

empadronamiento *nm* (**a**) *(acción)* census taking (**b**) *(padrón)* census

empadronar 1 *vt* to take a census
2 empadronarse *vpr* to register

empalagar [38] *vi* (**a**) *(dulces)* to pall, cloy (**b**) *Fig (fastidiar)* to bother, pester

empalago *nm* cloying taste

empalagoso, -a *adj* (**a**) *(dulces)* sickly sweet, palling (**b**) *Fig (persona)* smarmy

empalar *vt* to impale

empalizada *nf* fence

empalmar 1 *vt* (**a**) *(unir)* to join; *(cuerdas, cintas)* to splice (**b**) *Fig (planes, ideas)* to combine (**c**) *Ftb* to volley
2 *vi* (**a**) *Ferroc* to connect (**b**) *(suceder a continuación)* to follow on from
3 empalmarse *vpr Esp Vulg* to get a hard-on

empalme *nm* (**a**) *(gen)* connection; *Carp* joint (**b**) *Ferroc* junction; *(en carretera)* intersection, T-junction (**c**) *Cin* splice

empanada *nf Culin* pie; *Fam Fig* **e. mental** muddle

empanadilla *nf Culin* pasty

empanado, -a 1 *pp de* **empanar**
2 *adj Culin* breaded, in breadcrumbs

empanar *vt* (**a**) *Culin (rebozar)* to coat in breadcrumbs (**b**) *(empanada)* to fill

empantanado, -a 1 *pp de* **empantanar**
2 *adj* (**a**) *(inundado)* flooded (**b**) *Fig (atascado)* bogged down

empantanar 1 *vt* (**a**) *(inundar)* to flood (**b**) *Fig (detener)* to bring to a standstill
2 empantanarse *vpr* (**a**) *(inundarse)* to become flooded (**b**) *Fig (trabajo)* to come to a standstill; *(persona)* to be bogged down

empañado, -a 1 *pp de* **empañar**
2 *adj* (**a**) *(cristal)* misty, steamed up (**b**) *(voz)* faint (**c**) *Fig (honor)* tainted, tarnished

empañar 1 *vt* (**a**) *(bebé)* to put a nappy on (**b**) *(cristales)* to steam up (**c**) *Fig (reputación)* to taint, tarnish
2 empañarse *vpr* (**a**) *(cristal)* to steam up (**b**) *Fig (reputación)* to become tainted *o* tarnished

empapado, -a 1 *pp de* **empapar**
2 *adj* soaked, drenched, saturated

empapar 1 *vt* (**a**) *(humedecer)* to soak (**b**) *(absorber)* to soak up

  2 empaparse *vpr* (**a**) *Culin (leche)* to be soaked (**de** in) (**b**) *(persona)* to get soaked (**c**) *Fam Fig* to swot up

empapelado *nm* (**a**) *(papel)* wallpaper (**b**) *(acción)* wallpapering

empapelar *vt* (**a**) *(una pared)* to wallpaper (**b**) *(envolver)* to wrap in paper (**c**) *Fam (acusar) Br* to have up, *US* to bust; **lo empapelaron por estafador** he was had up for fraud

empaque[1] *nm* (**a**) *(acción)* packing (**b**) *(materiales)* packaging

empaque[2] *nm* (**a**) *(aspecto)* bearing, presence (**b**) *Chile Perú PRico (descaro)* cheek, impudence

empaquetador, -a *nm,f* packer

empaquetar *vt* (**a**) *(mercancías)* to pack (**b**) *Fig (personas)* to pack o squeeze in (**c**) *Mil (castigar)* to punish

emparedado, -a 1 *pp de* **emparedar**

  2 *adj* confined, imprisoned

  3 *nm* sandwich

emparedar *vt* to immure

emparejamiento *nm* pairing

emparejar 1 *vt* (**a**) *(juntar) (cosas)* to match; *(personas)* to pair off (**b**) *(nivelar)* to make level

  2 *vi* (**a**) *(ser igual)* to be even (**b**) *(alcanzar)* to catch up

  3 emparejarse *vpr Méx* to manage to get

emparentado, -a 1 *pp de* **emparentar**

  2 *adj* related by marriage (**con** to)

emparentar [3] *vi* to become related by marriage; **e. con una familia** to marry into a family

emparrado *nm Hortic* vine arbour

emparrillar *vt* to grill

empastar *vt (diente)* to fill

empaste *nm (de diente)* filling

empatado, -a *adj* (**a**) *(partido)* drawn; *(equipos)* level; **los dos equipos van empatados en primer lugar** the two are tying for first place (**b**) *(en elecciones, votación)* equally placed, tied

empatar *vt* (**a**) *Dep* to tie, draw; *Ftb* to equalize (**b**) *Am (unir)* to join

empate *nm Dep* draw, tie; *Ftb* **el gol del e.** the equalizer; **e. a tres** three-all draw, *US* tie three to three

empatía *nf* empathy

empavesado *nm* bunting

empavesar *vt* to deck, dress, decorate

empavonarse *vpr CAm* to get dolled up

empecatado, -a *adj* wretched

empecinado, -a 1 *pp de* **empecinarse**

  2 *adj* stubborn

empecinamiento *nm* stubbornness

empecinarse *vpr* to be stubborn, persist

empedarse *vpr Méx RP muy Fam* to get plastered o *Br* pissed

empedernido, -a *adj* confirmed, hardened, inveterate

empedrado, -a 1 *pp de* **empedrar**

  2 *adj (calle)* cobbled

  3 *nm* (**a**) *(adoquines)* cobblestones *pl* (**b**) *(acción)* paving

empedrar [3] *vt* to cobble, pave

empeine *nm* (**a**) *Anat (pubis)* groin; *(del pie)* instep (**b**) *(del zapato)* instep

empeller *vt* to push, jostle, shove

empellón *nm* push, shove; **abrirse paso a empellones** to push one's way through

empelotarse *vpr Andes Cuba Méx* to strip off

empeñar 1 *vt* (**a**) *(cosas)* to pawn, *US* hock; **estar empeñado** to be in debt, *US* be in hock (**b**) *(palabra, honor)* to pledge; **e. su palabra** to pledge o give one's word

  2 empeñarse *vpr* (**a**) *(insistir)* to insist (**en** on), be determined (**en** to) (**b**) *(endeudarse)* to get into debt

empeño *nm* (**a**) *(insistencia)* determination; **poner e. en ello** to put one's mind to it; **¡qué e. tiene!** he's obsessed with it! (**b**) *(deuda)* pledge ❏ **casa de empeños** pawnshop

empeñoso, -a *adj Andes RP* persevering, tenacious

empeoramiento *nm* deterioration, worsening

empeorar 1 *vi* to deteriorate, worsen

  2 *vt* to make worse

  3 empeorarse *vpr* to get worse

empequeñecer [46] *vt (reducir)* to diminish, make smaller; *Fig* to put in the shade, belittle

empequeñecimiento *nm (de tamaño)* diminution, reduction; *Fig* belittling

emperador *nm* (**a**) *(monarca)* emperor (**b**) *(pez espada)* swordfish

emperatriz *nf* empress

emperejilarse *vpr Fam* to get dolled up

emperifollado, -a *adj Fam* dolled up, done up to the nines

emperifollarse *vpr véase* **emperejilarse**

empero *conj Literario* however

emperramiento *nm* stubbornness

emperrarse *vpr* to dig one's heels in, become stubborn

empezar [17] *vt & vi (a hacer algo)* to begin; *(algo)* to start, commence; **empezar a hablar** to begin to speak; **empezaron diciendo que ...** they began by saying that ...

empiece *nm Fam* start, beginning

empinado, -a 1 *pp de* **empinar**

  2 *adj* (**a**) *(alto)* very high (**b**) *Fig (hacia arriba)* steep; *(vertical)* upright (**c**) *Fig (orgulloso)* upright, proud

empinar 1 *vt (cabeza, brazo)* to lift up; *(un vaso)* to raise; *Fam* **e. el codo** to drink (heavily)

  2 empinarse *vpr* (**a**) *(persona)* to stand on tiptoe; *(caballo)* to rear up (**b**) *Fig (árbol, edificio)* to tower

empingorotado, -a *adj* (**a**) *(de clase alta)* upper-class (**b**) *(engreído)* stuck-up, posh

empiparse *vpr Am* to stuff oneself

empíricamente *adv* empirically

empírico, -a *adj* empiric, empirical

empirismo *nm* empiricism

empitonar *vt Taur* to gore

emplastar *vt Med* to apply a poultice to, put a poultice on

emplasto *nm* (**a**) *Med* poultice (**b**) *Fig (componenda)* bad job, botched job; **hacer un e. en algo** to make a poor job of sth, botch sth, make a botch of sth (**c**) *(persona)* sickly person

emplazamiento *nm* (**a**) *(colocación)* site, location (**b**) *Jur* summons *sing*; *Ind* **e. a la huelga** strike call

emplazar[1] [14] *vt Jur* to locate, situate, place

emplazar[2] [14] *vt* (**a**) *Jur* to summons (**b**) *(llamar)* to call together, convene; *Jur* to summons; *Ind* **e. a la huelga** to call out on strike

empleado, -a *nm,f* employee, clerk; **e. de banca** bank clerk ❏ **empleada del hogar** servant, maid

empleador, -a *nm,f* employer

emplear 1 *vt* (**a**) *(dar empleo)* to employ (**b**) *(usar)* to use, employ; *Esp* **lo tiene** o **le está bien empleado** he deserves it, it serves him right (**c**) *(gastar) (dinero)* to spend; *(tiempo)* to invest, spend

  2 emplearse *vpr (palabra)* to be used

empleo nm (a) (oficio) job, occupation; Pol employment; **política de pleno e.** full employment policy; **sin e.** unemployed, out of work, jobless (b) (uso) use; **modo de e.** instructions for use

emplomado nm Constr (ventana) leading; (tejado) lead roof

emplomadura nf RP (empaste) filling

emplomar vt (a) (soldar) to join o seal with lead (b) RP (diente) to fill

emplumar 1 vt (a) (adornar) to put feathers o a feather on (b) (castigar) to tar and feather (c) Fam (castigar) to punish
2 vi (a) (pájaro) to grow feathers (b) Andes PRico to run away, escape

empobrecer [46] **1** vt to impoverish
2 empobrecerse vpr to become impoverished o poor

empobrecimiento nm impoverishment

empollar vt (a) (huevos) to brood, hatch (b) Esp Fam (estudiar) Br to swot up (on), US bone up on

empollón, -ona Esp Fam **1** adj **es muy e.** he's a real Br swot o US grind
2 nm,f Br swot, US grind

empolvado, -a 1 pp de **empolvar**
2 adj dusty

empolvar 1 vt to cover in dust
2 empolvarse vpr to powder; **e. la cara** to powder one's face

emponchado, -a adj Andes Arg (a) (ropa) wearing a poncho (b) (astuto) cunning (c) Fig suspicious

emponzoñar vt to poison

emporcar [67] vt to foul, dirty

emporio nm (a) Com emporium, trading o commercial centre (b) Fig artistic o cultural centre

emporrado, -a Esp **1** pp de **emporrarse**
2 adj Argot (drogado) stoned, high

emporrarse vpr Esp Argot to get high

empotrar vt to fit, build in

emprendedor, -a adj enterprising, resourceful

emprender vt (misión) to tackle; (negocio) to start; (viaje) to set off on; Fam **emprenderla con algn** to pick on sb

empresa nf (a) (acción ardua) enterprise, venture (b) Com Ind firm, business, company, undertaking, enterprise; **la libre e.** free enterprise ❑ **e. conjunta** joint venture; **e. de transportes** haulage firm; **e. matriz** parent company; **e. naviera** shipping company; **e. privada** private company; **la e. privada** the private sector; **e. pública** public sector firm

empresariado nm employers pl

empresarial adj managerial; **ciencias empresariales** business o management studies; **espíritu e.** entrepreneurial spirit

empresario, -a nm,f employer, entrepreneur; (hombre) businessman, manager; (mujer) businesswoman, manager, manageress; **e. de pompas fúnebres** undertaker

empréstito nm Fin debenture loan

empujar vt (a) (puerta) to push (open); (vehículo) to push (b) Fig to force, press; **e. a algn a hacer algo** to push sb into doing sth

empuje nm push, thrust, drive; Fig **necesita un poco de e.** he needs encouragement; Fig **una persona de e.** a person with a lot of go

empujón nm push, shove; **abrirse paso a empujones** to push one's way through; **dar empujones** to push and shove; Fig **a empujones** in fits and starts; **trabajar a empujones** to work in fits and starts; Fig **dar un e. a algo** to give sth a push forward

empuñadura nf (a) (de espada) hilt; **hasta la e.** up to the hilt (b) (de bastón, paraguas) handle, grip

empuñar vt (a) (cuchillo, bastón) to grasp, seize (b) Fig to take up

emú nm Orn emu

emulación nf emulation

emulador, -a adj emulating

emular vt to emulate

émulo, -a nm,f emulator, rival

emulsión nf emulsion

emulsionar vt to emulsify

emulsivo, -a adj emulsifying

en prep (a) (lugar) in, on, at; **en casa** at home; **en el trabajo** at work; **en la mesa** on the table; **en Madrid** in Madrid (b) (tiempo) in, on, at; **cae en martes** it falls on a Tuesday; **en ese momento** at that moment; **en 1940** in 1940; **en verano** in summer (c) (transporte) by, in; **ir en coche/tren** to go by car/train; **ir en avión** to fly; **ir en bici** to cycle (d) (tema, materia) at, in; **bueno en deportes** good at sports; **Doctor en Física** Doctor of Physics; **experto en política** expert in politics (e) **fuiste tonto en creerlo** you were silly to believe it; (con infinitivo) **la conocí en el andar** I recognized her by her walk (f) (modo, manera) **en broma** jokingly; **en camino** on the way; **en francés** in French; **en guerra** at war; **¡en marcha!** let's go!; **en serio** seriously; **en voz baja** softly

enaguas nfpl (prenda) underskirt sing, petticoat sing

enajenación nf distraction, absent-mindedness ❑ **e. mental** mental derangement, insanity

enajenamiento nm véase **enajenación**

enajenar 1 vt (a) Jur (propiedad) to alienate, transfer (b) (turbar) to drive mad
2 enajenarse vpr (a) (de una amistad) to become estranged o alienated (b) (enloquecer) to go mad

enaltecer [46] vt (a) (alabar) to praise, extol (b) (ennoblecer) to do credit to

enamoradizo, -a adj easily infatuated

enamorado, -a 1 adj in love, lovesick
2 nm,f lover, sweetheart; Fig **soy un e. del golf** I love golf, I'm a lover of golf

enamoramiento nm infatuation, falling in love

enamorar 1 vt to win the heart of
2 enamorarse vpr to fall in love (**de** with)

enancar [59] **1** vt (a) Andes Arg Perú (montar) to put on a horse's haunches (b) Arg to follow, be a consequence (**a** of)
2 enancarse vpr (a) Andes Arg Perú (montar) to ride on a horse's haunches (b) Am Fig (entremeterse) to meddle, interfere (c) Méx (encabritarse) to rear up

enanismo nm dwarfism

enano, -a 1 adj dwarf; Bot **frutal e.** dwarf fruit tree
2 nm,f dwarf; Fam **divertirse como un e.** to have a great time

enarbolar 1 vt (a) (izar) to hoist, fly (b) (blandir) (bandera) to wave; (estandarte) to carry; (espada) to brandish
2 enarbolarse vpr (a) (caballo) to rear up (b) Fig (persona) to get angry

enarcar [59] vt (lomo) to arch; (cejas) to raise

enardecedor, -a adj rousing, exciting

enardecer [46] **1** vt (sentimiento) to rouse, stir up; (persona) to fill with enthusiasm
2 enardecerse vpr Fig to become aroused o excited

enardecimiento nm excitement, enthusiasm

enarenar 1 vt to sand
2 enarenarse vpr Náut to run aground

encabestrar *vt (caballo)* to put a halter on

encabezado *nm Chile Méx (en periódico)* headline

encabezamiento *nm (de carta)* heading; *(de periódico)* headline, title; *(preámbulo)* foreword, preamble

encabezar [14] *vt* (**a**) *(carta, lista)* to head; *(periódico)* to title, head, lead (**b**) *(movimiento, rebelión)* to lead; *(carrera)* to lead

encabritarse *vpr* (**a**) *(caballo)* to rear (up); *(barco)* to rise; *(coche, avión)* to stall (**b**) *Fig (enfurecerse)* to get cross

encadenado, -a 1 *pp de* encadenar
  2 *nm* (**a**) *Arquit* buttress (**b**) *Cin* dissolve

encadenamiento *nm* (**a**) *(unión)* connection, linking (**b**) *Lit* concatenation (**c**) *Quím* chaining

encadenar *vt* (**a**) *(poner cadenas en)* to chain, shackle (**b**) *Fig (enlazar)* to link up, connect (**c**) *Fig (atar)* to tie down, chain down; **los niños la encadenan** she's tied to her children

encajar 1 *vt* (**a**) *(ajustar)* to encase, fit in, insert; *Téc* to gear; **e. la puerta** to push the door to (**b**) *Fam (golpe, disparo)* to take, stand; *(acontecimiento, situación)* to drop; *(indirecta, comentario)* to get in; **e. un golpe a algn** to land sb a blow
  2 *vi* (**a**) *(caber)* to fit; **estas piezas no encajan** these pieces don't fit (**b**) *Fig (casar)* to fit (in), correspond, square; **su declaración no encaja con los hechos** his statement doesn't match the facts
  3 encajarse *vpr* (**a**) *(encalarse)* to sink, get stuck (**b**) *(prenda)* to slip on; *(sombrero)* to put on (**c**) *RP (coche)* to get stuck

encaje *nm* (**a**) *(acto)* fit, fitting (**b**) *Téc (hueco)* socket; *(caja)* housing (**c**) *Cost (bordado)* lace

encajonar 1 *vt* (**a**) *(poner en cajas)* to encase, put in a box, pack (**b**) *(meter en un sitio estrecho)* to squeeze in o through (**c**) *Arquit (pared)* to buttress, coffer
  2 encajonarse *vpr* (**a**) *(en sitio estrecho)* to squeeze in o through (**b**) *(río)* to narrow

encalabrinar 1 *vt* (**a**) *(olor, vino)* to go to one's head (**b**) *(irritar)* to irritate, annoy
  2 encalabrinarse *vpr* (**a**) *(irritarse)* to get annoyed (**b**) *(encapricharse)* to become obsessed o infatuated (**c**) *(obstinarse)* to be stubborn

encalado, a 1 *pp de* encalar
  2 *nm* whitewashing

encalambrarse *vpr Am* (**a**) *(aterirse)* to go numb; *(de frío)* to get stiff with cold (**b**) *(tener calambre)* to get cramp

encalar *vt* to whitewash

encalladero *nm Náut* sandbank, reef

encallar *vi* (**a**) *Náut* to run aground (**b**) *Fig* to flounder, fail

encallecer [46] **1** *vi (piel)* to harden, become callous
  2 encallecerse *vpr Fig (persona)* to become hardened o callous

encalmarse *vpr* (**a**) *(viento)* to drop; *(mar)* to become calm (**b**) *(caballo)* to be overheated

encamar *vt (en el suelo)* to stretch out, lie down
  2 encamarse *vpr* (**a**) *(enfermo)* to go to bed (**b**) *Vulg Ofens* **se encama fácilmente** she's an easy lay

encaminar 1 *vt* (**a**) *(guiar)* to direct, guide, set o put on the right road; **estar bien encaminado** to be on the right track (**b**) *(orientar)* to direct, guide
  2 encaminarse *vpr (dirigirse)* to head (**a** for, **hacia** towards)

encamotarse *vpr Andes CAm Fam* to fall in love

encandilado, -a 1 *pp de* encandilar
  2 *adj* (**a**) *(erguido)* erect (**b**) *(deslumbrado)* starry-eyed

encandilar 1 *vt* (**a**) *(deslumbrar)* to dazzle (**b**) *Fig*

(cautivar) to fascinate, daze (**c**) *Fig (deseo, ilusión)* to kindle
  2 encandilarse *vpr (ojos, rostro)* to light up

encanecer [46] *vi* (**a**) *(pelo)* to go grey o US gray (**b**) *(persona)* to grow old

encantado, -a 1 *pp de* encantar
  2 *adj* (**a**) *(contento)* delighted, pleased, charmed; **e. de conocerle** pleased to meet you (**b**) *(distraído)* absent-minded (**c**) *(embrujado)* enchanted, haunted; **casa encantada** haunted house

encantador, -a 1 *adj* charming, delightful
  2 *nm,f* magician, enchanter ❑ **e. de serpientes** snake charmer

encantamiento *nm* spell, charm, enchantment

encantar *vt* (**a**) *(hechizar)* to bewitch, cast a spell on (**b**) *(gustar)* to delight, charm, love; **estoy encantado de haber venido** I'm delighted I came; **me encanta el alpinismo** I love mountaineering

encanto *nm* (**a**) *(hechizo)* spell, charm; *Fig* **como por e.** as if by magic (**b**) *(atractivo)* delight, charm; **esta casa es un e.** this house is lovely; **ser un e.** *(persona)* to be charming (**c**) *(expresión cariñosa)* love, sweetheart; **como tu quieras, e.** whatever you say, darling

encañonar *vt (arma)* to aim o point at; **lo encañonó con un rifle** he pointed a rifle at him

encapotado, -a 1 *pp de* encapotarse
  2 *adj Meteor* overcast, cloudy

encapotarse *vpr Meteor* to become overcast o cloudy

encaprichamiento *nm* infatuation

encapricharse *vpr* to set one's mind (**con** on); *Esp (encariñarse)* to take a fancy (**con** to); *Esp (enamorarse)* to get a crush (**con** on)

encapuchado, -a *adj* hooded

encarado, -a *adj* **bien e.** nice-looking, good-looking; **mal e.** plain

encaramar 1 *vt* (**a**) *(alzar)* to raise, lift up (**b**) *Fig (alabar)* to praise, extol (**c**) *Am (abochornar)* to make blush
  2 encaramarse *vpr* (**a**) *(subirse)* to climb up, get high up (**b**) *Fig (encumbrarse)* to reach a high (social) position (**c**) *Am (abochornarse)* to blush

encarar 1 *vt* (**a**) *(poner de frente)* to bring face to face (**b**) *Fig* to face, confront; **no sabía cómo e. el problema** he didn't know how to deal with the problem (**c**) *(arma)* to point, aim
  2 encararse *vpr* **e. con** o **a** to face up to, bring oneself face to face with

encarcelación *nf* imprisonment, incarceration

encarcelar *vt* to imprison, jail, incarcerate

encarecer [46] **1** *vt* (**a**) *(aumentar precios)* to put up the price of (**b**) *Fig (alabar)* to praise (**c**) *Fig (insistir)* to urge, recommend; **e. a algn que haga algo** to urge sb to do sth
  2 encarecerse *vpr* to go up (in price)

encarecidamente *adv* earnestly, insistently

encarecimiento *nm* (**a**) *(aumento de precios)* increase o rise in price; **el e. de la vida** the rise in the cost of living (**b**) *(insistencia)* insistence; **con e.** earnestly, insistently (**c**) *(alabanza)* extolling, praising

encargado, -a 1 *pp de* encargar
  2 *adj* in charge; **la persona encargada de este asunto** the person in charge of this matter
  3 *nm,f Com (hombre)* manager; *(mujer)* manager, manageress; *(responsable)* person in charge ❑ *Educ* **e. de curso** tutor; *Pol* **e. de negocios** chargé d'affaires

encargar [38] **1** *vt* (**a**) *(encomendar)* to put in charge of, entrust (**b**) *(recomendar)* to advise, recommend (**c**) *Com (pedir)* to order, place an order for; *(libro, cuadro)* to commission; **e. un traje** to have a suit made

2 encargarse *vpr* **e. de** to take charge of, look after, see to, deal with; **yo me encargaré de ella** I'll take care of her

encargo *nm* (**a**) *(recado)* errand; **hacer encargos** to run errands (**b**) *(tarea)* job, assignment (**c**) *(responsabilidad)* responsibility (**d**) *Com* order, commission; *Esp* **hecho de e.** *(a petición)* made to order; *(a la medida)* tailor-made

encariñado, -a 1 *pp de* **encariñarse**
2 *adj* attached (**con** to)

encariñarse *vpr* to become fond (**con** of), get attached (**con** to)

encarnación *nf* incarnation, embodiment; *Fig* **la e. de la bondad** kindness itself o personified

encarnado, -a 1 *pp de* **encarnar**
2 *adj* (**a**) *(hecho carne)* incarnate (**b**) *(rojo)* red; **ponerse e.** to blush, go red

encarnar 1 *vt* (**a**) *(gen)* to personify, embody (**b**) *Teat (personaje, papel)* to play
2 *vi* (**a**) *Rel* to become incarnate (**b**) *Med* to heal
3 encarnarse *vpr Rel* to become incarnate

encarnizadamente *adv* fiercely, cruelly

encarnizado, -a 1 *pp de* **encarnizar**
2 *adj* fierce, bloody

encarnizamiento *nm* fierceness, savagery

encarnizar [14] **1** *vt (enfurecer)* to enrage
2 encarnizarse *vpr* to be brutal o cruel; **e. con algn** to attack sb savagely

encarpetar *vt* to file (away)

encarrilar *vt* (**a**) *(coche, tren)* to put on the road o rails (**b**) *Fig* to direct, guide; **e. bien/mal un asunto** to get off to a good/bad start

encartar 1 *vi Naipes* to lead
2 *vt* (**a**) *Jur (encausar)* to indict (**b**) *(proscribir)* to outlaw, ban, proscribe (**c**) *(implicar)* to implicate; **los encartados en el asunto** those involved in the affair

encarte *nm* (**a**) *Naipes* lead (**b**) *(en una publicación)* free leaflet, booklet

encartuchar *vt Am* to roll up into a cone

encasillado, -a 1 *pp de* **encasillar**
2 *adj (actor, actriz)* typecast
3 *nm (conjunto de casillas)* set of squares o pigeonholes

encasillamiento *nm* pigeonholing

encasillar *vt* (**a**) *(clasificar)* to pigeonhole (**b**) *(actor, actriz)* to typecast

encasquetar 1 *vt (sombrero)* to pull down, put on; *Fig* **e. una idea a algn** to put an idea into sb's head
2 encasquetarse *vpr* (**a**) *(sombrero)* to pull down, put on (**b**) *(empeñarse)* **se le encasquetó en la cabeza la idea de irse de viaje** he got it into his head to go away on a trip

encasquillar 1 *vt Am (caballo)* to shoe
2 encasquillarse *vpr* (**a**) *(arma)* to get jammed (**b**) *Cuba Fam (acobardarse)* to get scared

encausar *vt Jur* to prosecute

encauzamiento *nm* (**a**) *(de agua)* channelling (**b**) *Fig* guidance, orientation

encauzar [14] *vt* (**a**) *(agua)* to channel (**b**) *Fig* to channel, direct, guide

encebollado, -a *adj Culin* with onion; **hígado e.** liver and onions

encefálico, -a *adj Anat* **masa encefálica** brain mass

encefalitis *nf Med* encephalitis

encéfalo *nm Anat* brain

encefalograma *nm Med* encephalogram

encefalopatía *nf Med* **e. espongiforme bovina** bovine spongiform encephalopathy

enceguecer [46] *vt Am* to blind

encelar 1 *vt* to make jealous
2 encelarse *vpr* (**a**) *(sentir celos)* to be jealous (**b**) *Zool (estar en celo)* to be in rut o on heat

encenagado, -a *adj* (**a**) *(lleno de barro)* muddy, covered in mud; **lugar e.** bog (**b**) *Fig (vicioso)* depraved

encendedor *nm (mechero)* lighter

encender [64] **1** *vt* (**a**) *(incendiar)* to light, set fire to, ignite; *(cerilla)* to strike, light; *(vela)* to light; *(luz)* to turn on, switch on, put on; *(gas)* to light, turn on; *(radio)* to switch on, turn on (**b**) *Fig* to inflame, stir up, provoke
2 encenderse *vpr* (**a**) *(incendiarse)* to catch fire, ignite; *(llama)* to flare up; *(luz)* to go o come on (**b**) *Fig* to flare up (**c**) *(cara)* to blush, go red

encendidamente *adv* passionately, ardently

encendido, -a 1 *pp de* **encender**
2 *adj* (**a**) *(ardiendo)* on fire, burning; *(cigarrillo)* lit; *(luz)* on; *(cable)* live (**b**) *(color)* glowing, fiery; *(cara)* red
3 *nm Aut* ignition

encerado, -a 1 *pp de* **encerar**
2 *adj (suelo, mueble)* waxed, polished
3 *nm* (**a**) *(pizarra)* blackboard (**b**) *(barniz de cera)* waxing

encerar *vt* (**a**) *(suelo, mueble)* to wax, polish (**b**) *Méx (iglesia)* to furnish o provide with candles

encerrar [3] **1** *vt* (**a**) *(gen)* to shut in o up; *(con llave)* to lock in o up, put under lock and key; *(vallar)* to enclose; *(confinar)* to confine (**b**) *Fig (contener)* to contain, include; *(implicar)* to involve; **la situación encierra grave peligro** the situation carries a great risk
2 encerrarse *vpr* (**a**) *(gen)* to shut oneself up o in; *(con llave)* to lock oneself in (**b**) *(recluirse)* to go into seclusion o retreat

encerrona *nf* (**a**) *Taur (corrida privada)* private bullfight (**b**) *Fig (trampa)* trap; **preparar** o **tender una e. a algn** to lay a trap for sb

encestar *vi Dep (baloncesto)* to score (a basket)

enceste *nm Dep (baloncesto)* basket

encharcado, -a 1 *pp de* **encharcar**
2 *adj* (**a**) *(terreno)* flooded, swamped (**b**) *(agua)* stagnant

encharcamiento *nm* flooding, swamping

encharcar [59] **1** *vt (terreno)* to flood, swamp
2 encharcarse *vpr* (**a**) *(terreno)* to swamp, get flooded (**b**) *(agua)* *(formar charcos)* to form puddles; *(estancarse)* to become stagnant

enchicharse *vpr Am (emborracharse)* to get drunk (on chicha²)

enchilada *nf Guat Méx Nic Culin* stuffed corn pancake seasoned with chili

enchilar 1 *vt* (**a**) *CAm Méx* to season with chili (**b**) *Méx Fig (molestar)* to annoy
2 *vi CAm, Méx (chile)* to be hot

enchiloso, -a *adj CAm Méx* hot, peppery, spicy

enchironar *vt Esp Argot (encarcelar)* to put away, *Br* bang up

enchisparse *vpr Am* to get drunk

enchivarse *vpr Col Ecuad PRico* to get angry

enchufado, -a 1 *pp de* **enchufar**
2 *adj Fam* **estar e.** to have good connections o contacts, be well in
3 *nm,f Fam (persona)* wirepuller; *(en la escuela)* teacher's pet; **ser un e.** to have good contacts, have friends in the right places

enchufar 1 *vt* (**a**) *Elec* to plug in (**b**) *(unir)* to fit, join, connect (**c**) *Fam* to pull strings for; **ha enchufado a su hermano en la oficina** he got his brother a job in his office
2 enchufarse *vpr Fam* to get in through the back door;

consiguió e. gracias a la influencia de su padre his father's influence got him in

enchufe nm (a) Elec(hembra) socket, point; (macho) plug; **e. bipolar/tripolar** two/three pin plug; **a pilas o e. a la red** battery or mains (**b**) Fam contact; **se lo dieron por e.** he had a friend who put in a good word for him

enchufismo nm Esp Fam string-pulling; **el e. y el amiguismo** the old boy/girl network

encía nf Anat gum

encíclica nf Rel encyclical

enciclopedia nf encyclopaedia, encyclopedia

enciclopédico, -a adj encyclopaedic, encyclopedic

encierro nm (a) Pol (protesta) sit-in (b) Rel (reclusión) retreat (c) (prisión) locking up, confinement (d) Taur bullpen; (recorrido) bull running

encima adv (a) (sobre) on top, above, over; **déjalo e.** put it on top; **llevar algo e.** to have sth on; **¿llevas cambio e.?** do you have any change on you?; Fig **quitarse algo de e.** to get rid of sth (**b**) (además) besides; **se equivocó y e. no quiso reconocerlo** he was wrong and what was more he wouldn't admit it (**c**) **e. de** (sobre) over; Fig (además) besides; **deja la taza e. de la mesa** leave the cup on the table; **e. de que no me pagan me insultan** not only do they not pay, but they insult me as well; Fam **estar algn e. de otro** to be on sb's back (**d**) **por e.** (a más altura) above; (más importante) above; (más allá de) beyond; **aquello estaba por e. de sus posibilidades** it was beyond his capabilities; **él está por e. de mí** he is over me; **leyó el libro muy por e.** he only skipped through the book (**e**) **de e.** top; **el piso de e.** the floor above

encimar vt Chile to add to

encimera nf Esp (de cocina) worktop

encimero, -a adj top; **sábana encimera** top sheet

encina nf Bot holm o evergreen oak, ilex

encinta adj pregnant

encintar vt to adorn with ribbons

encizañar vt & vi to disrupt, cause trouble (among)

enclaustrar 1 vt to cloister, shut up in a convent/monastery; Fig to cloister, shut up
2 enclaustrarse vpr to shut oneself up

enclavar vt (a) (clavar) to nail; (atravesar) to pierce, transfix (b) (ubicar) to locate, place

enclave nm enclave

enclenque 1 adj (débil) weak, puny; (enfermizo) sickly; (delgaducho) skinny
2 nm,f (débil) weak o puny person; (enfermizo) sickly person; (delgaducho) skinny person

enclítico, -a adj Ling enclitic

encocorar 1 vt Fam to annoy, get on the nerves of
2 encocorarse vpr Fam to get annoyed, get one's back up

encoger [52] **1** vi (contraerse) to contract; (prenda) to shrink
2 vt (a) (reducir) to shrink, contract, shorten (b) Fig (amilanar) to intimidate, scare
3 encogerse vpr (a) (contraerse) to contract; (prenda) to shrink; **e. de hombros** to shrug (one's shoulders); Fig **se me encogió el corazón** my heart sank (b) Fig (amilanarse) to cringe; **no se encoge ante nada** she isn't afraid of anything, nothing daunts her

encogido, -a 1 pp de encoger
2 adj (a) (contraído) contracted; (prenda) shrunk, shrunken (b) Fig (tímido) diffident, shy, timid

encogimiento nm (a) (de tela) shrinkage; **e. de hombros** shrug of the shoulders (b) (timidez) diffidence, shyness

encolado, -a 1 pp de encolar
2 nm (a) Arte sizing, pasting; Carp gluing (b) Cin splicing (c) (de vinos) clarification

encolar vt (a) Arte (lienzo, pared) to size, paste; Carp (madera) to glue (b) Cin (película, cinta) to splice (c) (vino) to clarify

encolerizar [14] **1** vt to infuriate, anger, exasperate
2 encolerizarse vpr to lose one's temper, get angry

encomendar [3] **1** vt (encargar) to commend, entrust, put in charge; **le encomendaron una misión** they entrusted him with a mission
2 encomendarse vpr to entrust oneself (a to); **e. a Dios** to put one's trust in God

encomiable adj laudable, praiseworthy

encomiar vt to extol, laud

encomiástico, -a adj eulogistic, laudatory

encomienda nf (a) (encargo) assignment, mission (b) Am (paquete postal) postal parcel

encomio nm praise, tribute, eulogy; **digno de e.** praiseworthy

enconado, -a 1 pp de enconar
2 adj (a) Med inflamed, sore (b) (discusión) bitter, fierce

enconar 1 vt (a) Med (herida) to inflame (b) (exasperar) to anger; **e. el ánimo de algn** to make sb angry
2 enconarse vpr (a) Med (herida) to become inflamed o sore (b) (exasperarse) to get angry o irritated

encono nm spitefulness, ill feeling

encontradizo, -a adj hacerse el e. (con algn) to bump into (sb) accidentally on purpose

encontrado, -a 1 pp de encontrar
2 adj (contrario) conflicting, contrary; **pareceres encontrados** conflicting opinions

encontrar [63] **1** vt (a) (gen) to find; **no lo encuentro** I can't find it (**b**) (persona) to bump into, come across (**c**) (dificultades) to run into, come up against (**d**) (pensar) to find, think; **encuentro que no es justo** I don't think it's fair; (percibir) **te encuentro muy cambiado** you've changed a lot
2 encontrarse vpr (a) (cosas, personas) to meet; **¿dónde nos encontramos?** where shall we meet?; **me encontré con Pilar** I bumped into o met Pilar; **nos encontramos con muchos problemas** we ran into a lot of trouble (**b**) (sentirse) to feel, be; **e. a gusto** to be o feel comfortable; **e. con ganas de o fuerzas para hacer algo** to feel like doing sth (**c**) (estar) to be, find oneself; **me encontraba en París** I was in Paris; Méx **el Sr. López no se encuentra** (no está) Mr Lopez isn't in; **me encuentro en apuros** I am in a bit of trouble

encontronazo nm (a) (choque) collision, crash (b) Fig (de personalidades, ideas) clash

encoñado, -a Esp Vulg **1** pp de encoñarse
2 adj estar e. to be infatuated

encoñarse vpr Esp Vulg to become infatuated (**de** with)

encopetado, -a adj (de alto copete) upper-class, grand; (presumido) haughty, conceited

encorajinarse vpr Fam to get angry, lose one's temper

encorsetar vt (con corsé) to corset; (poner límites) to straitjacket

encorvado, -a 1 pp de encorvar
2 adj (cosa) curved, bent; (persona) bent, stooping

encorvadura nf, **encorvamiento** nm (acción) bending; (de persona) stoop, curvature

encorvar 1 vt to bend
2 encorvarse vpr to stoop o bend (over)

encrespar 1 vt (a) (pelo) to curl, frizz (b) (mar) to make choppy o rough; **el viento encrespó las aguas** the wind whipped up waves on the sea (c) Fig (enfurecer) to infuriate

2 encresparse *vpr* (**a**) *(pelo)* to stand on end (**b**) *(mar)* to get rough (**c**) *Fig (enfurecerse)* to get cross o irritated

encriptación *nf Inform* encryption

encriptar *vt Inform* to encrypt

encrucijada *nf* crossroads *pl*, intersection; *Fig (apuro)* crossroads; **estar en la e.** to be at crisis point, not know which way to turn

encuadernación *nf* (**a**) *(oficio)* bookbinding (**b**) *(cubierta)* binding; **e. en rústica** paperback; **e. en tela** cloth binding ❏ **(taller de) e.** bindery

encuadernador, -a *nm,f* bookbinder

encuadernar *vt* to bind

encuadramiento *nm* framing

encuadrar 1 *vt* (**a**) *(cuadro, imagen)* to frame (**b**) *Fig (encajar)* to fit, insert (**c**) *Fig* to contain, comprise
2 encuadrarse *vpr* (**a**) *Fig (tener como marco)* **la historia se encuadraba en la Inglaterra victoriana** the story was set in Victorian England (**b**) *(incorporarse)* to become part of, join

encuadre *nm Cin TV* framing

encubar *vt (vino)* to vat

encubierta *nf* fraud

encubiertamente *adv (secretamente)* secretly; *(fraudulentamente)* fraudulently

encubierto, -a 1 *pp de* **encubrir**
2 *adj (secreto)* concealed, hidden, secret; *(fraudulento)* fraudulent, underhand

encubridor, -a *nm,f Jur* accessory (after the fact), abettor

encubrimiento *nm* concealment, hiding; *Jur* complicity, abetment

encubrir *(pp* **encubierto)** *vt* (**a**) *(ocultar)* to conceal, hide; *(criminal)* to shelter (**b**) *Jur (ser cómplice en)* to be an accomplice in, abet

encuentro *nm* (**a**) *(acción)* encounter, meeting; **e. casual** o **fortuito** chance meeting; **ir** o **salir al e. de algn** to go out to meet sb (**b**) *(choque)* collision; **e. de opiniones** clash of opinion (**c**) *Dep* meeting, match, clash; **e. amistoso** friendly match (**d**) *Mil* skirmish

encuesta *nf* (**a**) *(sondeo)* (opinion) poll, survey; **hacer una e.** to carry out an opinion poll (**b**) *(investigación)* investigation, inquiry

encuestado, -a *nm,f* person polled

encuestador, -a *nm,f* pollster

encuestar *vt* to poll

encumbrado, -a 1 *pp de* **encumbrar**
2 *adj (eminente)* eminent, distinguished; *(socialmente)* upper-class

encumbramiento *nm* (**a**) *(acción)* rise, raising (**b**) *(posición)* high position, elevated status

encumbrar 1 *vt* to elevate, exalt
2 encumbrarse *vpr* to rise to a high (social) position

encurtidos *nmpl Culin* pickles

encurtir *vt* to pickle

ende: por ende *loc adv* therefore

endeble *adj* weak, puny, feeble

endeblez *nf* weakness, fragility, feebleness

endemia *nf Med* endemic disease

endémico, -a *adj* (**a**) *Med* endemic (**b**) *Fig* chronic

endemoniado, -a *adj* (**a**) *(poseso)* possessed (**b**) *Fig (diabólico; maldito)* wretched

endenantes *adv Am Fam* before

endentar *vt & vi Téc* to enmesh, interlock

enderezamiento *nm (poner derecho)* straightening out o up; *(poner vertical)* setting upright

enderezar [14] **1** *vt* (**a**) *(poner derecho)* to straighten out; *(poner vertical)* to set upright (**b**) *(guiar)* to direct; *Fig* to guide (**c**) *(enmendar)* to put in order, set to rights
2 enderezarse *vpr (ponerse recto)* to straighten up

endeudamiento *nm* borrowing, state of indebtedness ❏ **e. exterior** foreign debt

endeudarse *vpr* to get o fall into debt

endiabladamente *adv* diabolically; *Fig* **e. difícil** extremely difficult

endiablado, -a *adj* (**a**) *(poseso)* possessed (**b**) *(malo)* evil, wicked; *(travieso)* mischievous, devilish (**c**) *(maldito)* wretched, cursed (**d**) *(desenfrenado)* wild

endibia *nf Bot* endive

endilgar [38] *vt Fam* (**a**) *(trabajo)* to palm off onto; **endilgaron el trabajo a Elvira** they lumbered Elvira with the job (**b**) *(golpe)* to land, deal (**c**) *Fig* **nos endilgó un largo discurso** she made us sit through a long speech

endiñar *vt Esp Fam (golpe)* to land; *(tortazo)* to fetch

endiosamiento *nm* conceit, vanity

endiosar 1 *vt* to deify
2 endiosarse *vpr* to become conceited o vain

enditarse *vpr Am* to get into debt

endocrino, -a 1 *adj Biol* endocrine, endocrinal
2 *nm,f Fam* endocrinologist

endocrinología *nf Med* endocrinology

endocrinólogo, -a *nm,f Med* endocrinologist

endogamia *nf* endogamy

endomingarse [38] *vpr Fam* to put on one's Sunday best

endosar *vt* (**a**) *Fin (cheque)* to endorse; **e. una letra de cambio** to endorse a bill of exchange (**b**) *Fam* to lumber; **me han endosado el trabajo más pesado** I've been lumbered with the most boring job

endoscopia *nf Med* endoscopy

endoscopio *nm Med* endoscope

endoso *nm* endorsement; **sin e.** unendorsed

endrina *nf Bot* sloe

endrino, -a 1 *adj (color)* blue-black
2 *nm Bot* sloe, blackthorn

endrogarse [38] *vpr Chile Méx Perú* (**a**) *(endeudarse)* to get into debt (**b**) *(drogarse)* to take drugs, use drugs

endulzar [14] *vt (dulcificar)* to sweeten; *Fig (mitigar)* to alleviate, ease

endurecer [46] **1** *vt* (**a**) *(poner duro)* to harden, make hard (**b**) *Fig (fortalecer)* to harden, toughen; **e. su postura** to take a hard o tough line
2 endurecerse *vpr* (**a**) *(ponerse duro)* to harden, become hard (**b**) *Fig (fortalecerse)* to become hardened o tough

endurecimiento *nm* hardening, toughening

ene *nf* (**a**) *(letra)* = name of the letter N in Spanish (**b**) *(cantidad indeterminada)* x; **un número e. de veces** x number of times

enebro *nm Bot* juniper

eneldo *nm Bot* dill

enema *nm Med* enema

enemigo, -a 1 *adj* enemy, hostile; **barco e.** enemy ship; **soy e. de la bebida** I'm against drink
2 *nm,f* enemy, foe; **somos enemigos declarados** there's no love lost between us

enemistad *nf* hostility, hatred, enmity

enemistar 1 *vt* to set at odds, cause a rift between
2 enemistarse *vpr* to become enemies; **e. con algn** to fall out with sb, become sb's enemy

energético, -a *adj* energy, power

energía *nf* energy ❑ **e. eólica** wind power; **e. hidráulica/ nuclear** water/nuclear power; **e. solar** solar energy *o* power; *Fig* **e. vital** vitality

enérgico, -a *adj* energetic; **decisión enérgica** firm decision; **en tono e.** emphatically

energúmeno, -a *nm,f Fam (hombre)* madman; *(mujer)* madwoman; **ponerse como un e.** to go up the wall

enero *nm* January; **la cuesta de e.** the post-Christmas slump; *véase tamb* **noviembre**

enervante *adj* (a) *Med (debilitante)* enervating (b) *Fam (irritante)* irritating, exasperating, annoying

enervar *vt* (a) *Med (debilitar)* to enervate (b) *Fam (irritar)* to irritate, exasperate, annoy

enésimo, -a *adj* (a) *Mat* nth; **elevado a la enésima potencia** raised to the nth power (b) *Fam* umpteenth; **por enésima vez** for the umpteenth time

enfadadizo, -a *adj* touchy, irritable

enfadado, -a 1 *pp de* **enfadar**
2 *adj esp Esp* angry, cross, annoyed, *US* mad; **estamos enfadados** we're angry with each other; **estoy e. contigo** I'm cross with you; **tener cara de e.** to look angry

enfadar *esp Esp* **1** *vt* to make angry *o* cross *o* annoyed
2 enfadarse *vpr* (a) *(irritarse)* to get angry *o* cross (**con** with); **e. por nada** to make a fuss about nothing (b) *(dos personas)* to fall out

enfado *esp Esp nm* anger, irritation; **fue un e. tonto** she got angry for nothing; **¿se te ha pasado el e.?** have you calmed down?

enfadoso, -a *adj* annoying, irritating

enfangar [38] **1** *vt* to cover with mud
2 enfangarse *vpr* (a) *(hundirse en el fango)* to stick in *o* sink into the mud (b) *(ensuciarse de fango)* to get muddy, get covered in mud (c) *Fig* to get involved in dirty business; **e. en el vicio** to wallow in vice

énfasis *nm inv* (a) *(fuerza)* emphasis, stress; **poner e. en algo** to lay stress on sth (b) *(afectación)* **hablar con e.** to talk in an affected way

enfático, -a *adj* emphatic

enfatizar [14] *vt* to emphasize, stress

enfermar *vi* to become *o* fall ill, be taken ill; **e. de agotamiento** to suffer from exhaustion; **e. del corazón** to have heart trouble

enfermedad *nf* (a) *Med* illness, disease, sickness; **ausentarse por e.** to be away ill *o* sick ❑ **e. contagiosa** contagious disease; **e. laboral** industrial disease; **e. mental** mental illness; **e. profesional** occupational disease; **e. venérea** venereal disease (b) *Fig (mal)* malady, sickness

enfermería *nf* sick bay, infirmary

enfermero, -a *nm,f (mujer)* nurse; *(hombre)* male nurse

enfermizo, -a *adj* unhealthy, sickly; *Fig* **mente enfermiza** morbid mind

enfermo, -a 1 *adj* sick, ill; **caer e.** to be taken ill; *Fam* **esa gente me pone e.** those people make me sick
2 *nm,f* sick person; *(paciente)* patient; **e. grave** seriously ill patient

enfermucho, -a *adj Fam* ailing, sickly; **débil y e.** frail and weak

enfervorizado, -a 1 *pp de* **enfervorizar**
2 *adj* wildly enthusiastic; **la multitud enfervorizada animaba a su equipo** the frenzied crowd cheered on their team

enfervorizar [14] *vt* to arouse passions in, arouse fervour in, enthuse; **sus palabras enfervorizaron a la**

muchedumbre his words aroused the passions of the crowd

enfiestarse *vpr Am* to enjoy oneself

enfilar *vt* (a) *(ir)* to make for; *(calle)* to go along *o* down; *(túnel)* to go through (b) *(dirigir)* to direct

enfisema *nm Med* emphysema

enflaquecer [46] **1** *vt (adelgazar)* to make thin; *(debilitar)* to weaken
2 *vi (adelgazar)* to get thin, lose weight

enflaquecimiento *nm* (a) *(adelgazamiento)* loss of weight (b) *Fig (debilidad)* weakening

enflatarse *vpr* (a) *Am (apenarse)* to sulk (b) *Méx (ponerse de mal humor)* to get into a bad mood

enfocar [59] *vt* (a) *(imagen, objetivo)* to focus; *Fot* **bien/ mal enfocado** in/out of focus (b) *(iluminar)* to shine a light on (c) *Fig* to approach, look at; **e. un tema desde otro punto de vista** to look at a subject from another angle

enfoque *nm* (a) *(acción)* focus, focusing (b) *Fig* approach, angle, point of view

enfrascar [59] **1** *vt* to bottle
2 enfrascarse *vpr (en una actividad)* to become absorbed *o* engrossed (**en** in); *(en la lectura)* to bury oneself (**en** in); **e. en un problema** to get tangled up *o* deeply involved in a problem

enfrentamiento *nm* confrontation

enfrentar 1 *vt* (a) *(encarar)* to bring face to face, confront (b) *(afrontar)* to face, confront
2 enfrentarse *vpr* (a) *(encararse)* to face (**a** -), face up (**a** to), confront (**a** -) (b) *Dep (rival)* to face (**a** -), meet (**a** -); *Box* to take (**a** on) (c) *(pelearse)* to have an argument (**a** with), fall out (**a** with)

enfrente *adv* (a) *(delante)* opposite; **la casa de e.** the house opposite *o* across the road (b) **e. de** opposite (to), facing; **la casa está e. del colegio** the house is opposite the school (c) *Fig* opposed to, against; **estaban uno e. del otro** they were opposed to each other

enfriamiento *nm* (a) *(proceso)* cooling (b) *Med (catarro)* cold, chill; **pillar un e.** to catch a cold *o* chill

enfriar [32] **1** *vt* to cool (down), chill
2 *vi* (a) *Meteor* to get cold *o* colder (b) *Fig* to cool down; **dejar e. algo** to let sth cool down
3 enfriarse *vpr* (a) *(tener frío)* to get *o* go cold; *(resfriarse)* to get *o* catch a cold (b) *(lo que estaba demasiado caliente)* to cool down; *(ponerse demasiado frío)* to go cold; **el agua se ha enfriado un poco, ahora puedes bañar el bebé** the water has cooled down a little, now you can bath the baby; **bebe el café, se está enfriando** drink your coffee, it's getting cold (c) *Fig (pasión, ánimo)* to cool off

enfundar 1 *vt* to put in its case; *(mueble)* to cover; *(espada)* to sheathe
2 enfundarse *vpr (abrigarse)* to wrap oneself up

enfurecer [46] **1** *vt* to enrage, enfuriate
2 enfurecerse *vpr* (a) *(persona)* to get furious (b) *(mar)* to become rough

enfurecido, -a 1 *pp de* **enfurecer**
2 *adj* (a) *(persona)* enraged (b) *(mar)* raging

enfurecimiento *nm* infuriation, temper, rage

enfurruñado, -a *adj* **estar e.** to be sulking

enfurruñamiento *nm Fam* sulking

enfurruñarse *vpr Fam* to sulk

engalanado, -a 1 *pp de* **engalanar**
2 *adj* decked out, festooned

engalanar 1 *vt (calle, balcón)* to deck out, adorn
2 engalanarse *vpr (persona)* to dress up, get dressed up

engallarse *vpr Fig* to be *o* get cocky

enganchado, -a 1 *pp de* **enganchar**
2 *adj Argot (adicto)* hooked; **estar e.** to be hooked (on drugs)
enganchar 1 *vt* **(a)** *(pez)* to hook; *(animales)* to hitch (up), harness; *Ferroc* to couple **(b)** *Fig (pillar)* to hook, rope in
2 engancharse *vpr* **(a)** *(prenderse)* to get caught *o* hooked up; *Argot (hacerse adicto)* to get hooked **(b)** *Mil* to join up
enganche *nm* **(a)** *(gancho)* hook; *(de animales)* hitching, harnessing; *Ferroc* coupling **(b)** *Mil* enlistment, recruitment **(c)** *Méx (depósito)* deposit
enganchón *nm (de ropa, pelo)* snag
engañabobos *nm inv (persona)* con man, confidence trickster; *(trampa)* con trick, trap
engañadizo, -a *adj* gullible
engañar 1 *vt (gen)* to deceive; *(estafar)* to cheat, trick; *(mentir)* to lie, mislead; **las apariencias engañan** appearances can deceive; **me estás engañando** I don't believe you, you're not telling me the truth; *Fig* **e. el hambre** to stave off hunger; *Fam* **engaña a su mujer** he's unfaithful to his wife
2 engañarse *vpr (ilusionarse)* to deceive oneself; *(equivocarse)* to be wrong *o* mistaken; **no nos engañemos** let's not kid ourselves
engañifa *nf Fam* trick; *(estafa)* swindle
engaño *nm* **(a)** *(gen)* deceit; *(estafa)* fraud, trick, swindle; *(mentira)* lie; **aquí no hay e. alguno** it's all above board **(b)** *(error)* mistake, misunderstanding; **estar en un e.** to be mistaken
engañoso, -a *adj (palabras)* deceitful, dishonest; *(apariencias)* deceptive; *(consejo)* misleading
engarce *nm* **(a)** *(de perlas)* threading, stringing **(b)** *(engaste)* setting
engarzar [14] *vt* **(a)** *(collar)* to thread; *(perlas)* to string **(b)** *(engastar)* to mount, set **(c)** *Fig (palabras)* to string together
engastar *vt* to set, mount
engaste *nm* setting, mount
engatusador, -a *Fam* **1** *adj* coaxing, cajoling
2 *nm,f* coaxer
engatusar *vt Fam* to coax, wheedle, get round; **e. a algn para que haga algo** to coax sb into doing sth
engendrar 1 *vt* **(a)** *Biol* to engender, beget **(b)** *Fig* to give rise to, cause; **e. la duda en algn** to plant the seeds of doubt in sb's mind
engendro *nm* **(a)** *Biol (feto)* foetus, *US* fetus **(b)** *(criatura deforme)* malformed child; *Fam (persona fea)* freak **(c)** *Fig Pey* monstrosity; **este cuadro es un e.** this painting is a monstrosity
englobar *vt (incluir)* to include, comprise; *(reunir)* to lump together, put all together
engolado, -a *adj (persona)* arrogant, pompous; *(estilo)* high-flown
engolfarse *vpr Fig* to get absorbed (**en** in)
engolosinar 1 *vt (tentar)* to tempt, entice
2 engolosinarse *vpr* to become fond (**con** of), develop a taste (**con** for)
engomar *vt* to gum, glue, stick
engominar *vt* to put hair cream on
engordar 1 *vt* to fatten (up), make fat
2 *vi* **(a)** *(persona)* to put on weight, get fat; **he engordado tres kilos** I've put on three kilos **(b)** *(comida, bebida)* to be fattening; **el pan engorda** bread is fattening
engorde *nm* fattening (up)
engorro *nm Fam* bother, nuisance
engorroso, -a *adj Fam* awkward, bothersome, tiring; **ser e.** to be a bother *o* a nuisance

engranaje *nm* **(a)** *Téc* gear, gears *pl*, gearing; *(de un reloj)* cogwheel **(b)** *Fig* machinery; **metido en la e. de la política** caught up in the wheels of politics
engranar 1 *vt* **(a)** *Téc* to gear, engage **(b)** *Fig (ideas)* to connect, link
2 *vi (encajar)* to engage, mesh
engrandecer [46] *vt* **(a)** *(aumentar)* to enlarge, magnify **(b)** *Fig (realzar)* to extol, magnify; **viajar engrandece el espíritu** travel broadens the mind **(c)** *Fig (alabar)* to exalt, raise up
engrandecimiento *nm* **(a)** *(aumento)* enlargement, increase **(b)** *Fig (realce)* enhancement **(c)** *Fig (alabanza)* praise
engrapadora *nf Am* stapler
engrapar *vt Am* to staple
engrasar *vt* **(a)** *(lubricar)* to grease, lubricate, oil **(b)** *(manchar)* to make greasy, stain with grease **(c)** *Fam (sobornar)* to bribe
engrase *nm* **(a)** *(acción)* greasing, lubrication, oiling **(b)** *(sustancia)* lubricant
engreído, -a 1 *pp de* **engreír**
2 *adj* vain, conceited, stuck-up
engreimiento *nm* vanity, conceit
engreír [56] **1** *vt Am (mimar)* to spoil, pamper
2 engreírse *vpr* **(a)** *(envanecerse)* to become vain *o* conceited *o* full of oneself **(b)** *Am (encariñarse)* to become fond (**de** of)
engringarse [38] *vpr Am Fam* to adopt American ways
engriparse *vpr CSur* to come down with (the) flu
engrosar [63] **1** *vt (incrementar)* to enlarge; *(cantidad)* to increase, swell
2 *vi (engordar)* to get fat, put on weight
engrudo *nm* paste
enguantado, -a *adj* gloved
enguatar *vt* to pad
engullir *vt* to gobble up, gulp down
enharinar *vt Culin* to (sprinkle with) flour
enhebrar *vt Cost* to thread
enhiesto, -a *adj* upright, erect
enhorabuena *nf* congratulations *pl*; **dar la e. a algn** to congratulate sb; **mi más cordial e.** my warmest congratulations
enhornar *vt Culin* to put into the oven
enigma *nm* enigma, mystery, puzzle
enigmático, -a *adj* enigmatic, mysterious, puzzling
enjabonar *vt* **(a)** *(dar jabón a)* to soap **(b)** *Fig (dar coba a)* to butter up, soft-soap
enjaezar [14] *vt* to harness, saddle up
enjalbegar [38] *vt* to whitewash
enjambre *nm* **(a)** *(de abejas)* swarm **(b)** *Fig* swarm, crowd, throng
enjaretar *vt Fam* to reel off; **le enjaretó un rollo sobre política** he went on and on about politics to him
enjaular *vt* **(a)** *(animal)* to cage **(b)** *Fam* to put inside, put in jail
enjoyar 1 *vt* to adorn with jewels
2 enjoyarse *vpr Fam* to overdo one's jewellery
enjuagar [38] **1** *vt* to rinse
2 enjuagarse *vpr* **e. la boca** to rinse out one's mouth
enjuague *nm* **(a)** *(acción)* rinse; *(líquido)* mouthwash **(b)** *Fig* plot, scheme
enjugar [38] **1** *vt* **(a)** *(secar)* to dry, wipe away; **enjugó sus lágrimas** he dried his tears **(b)** *(pagar) (deuda)* to pay off; *(déficit)* to cancel out

2 enjugarse *vpr (secarse)* to wipe, dry; **se enjugó el sudor de la frente** he wiped o mopped the sweat from his brow

enjuiciamiento *nm* (**a**) *(opinión)* judgement (**b**) *Jur (civil)* lawsuit; *(criminal)* trial, prosecution

enjuiciar *vt* (**a**) *(juzgar)* to judge, examine (**b**) *Jur (juicio civil)* to sue; *(criminal)* to indict, prosecute

enjundia *nf* (**a**) *(grasa)* fat (**b**) *Fig (sustancia)* substance; *(importancia)* importance (**c**) *Fig (vigor)* force, vitality; *(persona)* character

enjundioso, -a *adj* meaty, solid

enjuto, -a *adj* lean, skinny

enlace *nm* (**a**) *(unión)* link, connection; **servir de e., establecer un e.** to link □ **e. químico** chemical bond (**b**) *(casamiento)* marriage (**c**) *Ferroc* connection □ **estación de e.** junction; **vía de e.** crossover (**d**) *(persona)* liaison officer □ *Esp* **e. sindical** shop steward, *US* union delegate (**e**) *Inform* link

enladrillado, -a 1 *pp de* **enladrillar**
2 *adj* brick; **suelo e.** brick floor
3 *nm* brick paving

enladrillar *vt* to pave with bricks

enlatado, -a 1 *pp de* **enlatar**
2 *adj* canned, tinned
3 *nmpl* **enlatados** *Am (comestibles)* groceries

enlatar *vt* (**a**) *(meter en latas)* to can, tin (**b**) *CAm (techo)* to roof with tin

enlazar [14] **1** *vt (unir)* to link, connect, tie (together); **e. una idea con otra** to link one idea with another
2 *vi Ferroc* to connect (**con** with)
3 enlazarse *vpr* (**a**) *(unirse)* to be linked o connected, link (**b**) *(familias)* to become linked by marriage

enlistar *vt Méx* to list

enlodar 1 *vt* (**a**) *(enfangar)* to muddy, cover with mud (**b**) *Fig (reputación)* to stain, besmirch
2 enlodarse *vpr* to get muddy

enloquecedor, -a *adj* maddening

enloquecer [46] **1** *vi (volverse loco)* to go mad
2 *vt* (**a**) *(volver loco)* to drive mad (**b**) *Fam (gustar mucho)* to be mad o wild about; **la enloquece el cine** she's mad on the cinema
3 enloquecerse *vpr (volverse loco)* to go mad, go out of one's mind

enloquecido, -a 1 *pp de* **enloquecer**
2 *adj* mad, crazed

enloquecimiento *nm* madness, insanity

enlosado, -a 1 *pp de* **enlosar**
2 *nm* floor tiling; *(losas)* paving

enlosar *vt* to tile, pave (with tiles)

enlozar [14] *vt Am* to cover o coat with enamel

enlucido, -a 1 *pp de* **enlucir**
2 *nm* plaster

enlucir [39] *vt (pared)* to plaster; *(metal)* to polish

enlutado, -a 1 *pp de* **enlutar**
2 *adj* mourning, in mourning

enlutar 1 *vt* (**a**) *(poner de luto)* to cast o put into mourning (**b**) *Fig (ensombrecer)* to cast a shadow over
2 enlutarse *vpr (estar de luto)* to be in mourning; *(ponerse de luto)* to go into mourning

enmaderar *vt (pared)* to panel; *(suelo)* to lay down floorboards

enmadrado, -a 1 *pp de* **enmadrarse**
2 *adj (niño)* **estar e.** to be tied to one's mother's apron strings

enmadrarse *vpr (niño)* to be tied to one's mother's apron strings

enmarañamiento *nm* (**a**) *(enredo)* entanglement, tangle (**b**) *Fig* confusion, muddle

enmarañar 1 *vt* (**a**) *(pelo)* to tangle (**b**) *Fig (complicar)* to complicate, confuse, muddle up
2 enmarañarse *vpr* (**a**) *(pelo)* to get tangled (**b**) *Fig (complicarse)* to get confused, get into a mess o a muddle

enmarcar [59] *vt (gen)* to frame; *(rodear)* to surround

enmascarado, -a 1 *pp de* **enmascarar**
2 *adj* masked
3 *nm,f* masked person

enmascarar 1 *vt* (**a**) *(poner una máscara)* to mask (**b**) *Fig (ocultar)* to conceal, mask, disguise
2 enmascararse *vpr (ponerse una máscara)* to put on a mask; *(disfrazarse)* to masquerade (**de** as)

enmasillar *vt* to putty

enmendar [3] **1** *vt (corregir)* to correct, put right; *(daño)* to repair, put right; *Jur* to amend
2 enmendarse *vpr (persona)* to reform, mend one's ways

enmendatura *nf* correction

enmienda *nf (corrección)* correction; *(de daño)* repair, indemnity, compensation; *Jur Pol* amendment; **hacer propósito de e.** to turn over a new leaf

enmohecer [46] **1** *vt (metal)* to rust; *Bot* to make mouldy o *US* moldy
2 enmohecerse *vpr (metal)* to rust, get rusty; *Bot* to go mouldy o *US* moldy; *Fig* to go rusty

enmohecido, -a *adj (con moho)* mouldy; *(metal, conocimientos)* rusty

enmontarse *vpr Col Ven (campo)* to turn into a wilderness

enmoquetar *vt Esp RP* to carpet

enmudecer [46] **1** *vi (callar)* to become dumb, lose one's voice
2 enmudecerse *vpr* (**a**) *(estar callado)* to be silent, say nothing (**b**) *(callar)* to become dumb, lose one's voice

enmugrecer [46], *Am* **enmugrar 1** *vt (ensuciar)* to soil, dirty
2 enmugrecerse, *Am* **enmugrarse** *vpr (ensuciarse)* to become soiled o dirty

ennegrecer [46] **1** *vt* to blacken, turn black, darken
2 ennegrecerse *vpr* to turn o go black; *Fig* to get dark, darken

ennoblecer [46] *vt* (**a**) *(hacer noble)* to ennoble (**b**) *Fig (dar esplendor)* to do honour to, be a credit to; **este comportamiento te ennoblece** your behaviour is to your credit

enojadizo, -a *adj esp Am* irritable, touchy, quick-tempered

enojado, -a 1 *pp de* **enojar**
2 *adj esp Am* angry, cross

enojar *esp Am* **1** *vt* to anger, annoy, upset
2 enojarse *vpr* to get angry, lose one's temper, get annoyed o cross

enojo *esp Am nm* anger, annoyance, irritation

enojoso, -a *adj esp Am* annoying, irritating

enología *nf* oenology, study of wine

enólogo, -a *nm,f* oenologist, wine expert

enorgullecer [46] **1** *vt* to fill with pride
2 enorgullecerse *vpr* to be o feel proud; **e. de algo** to pride oneself on sth, be proud of sth

enorgullecimiento *nm* pride

enorme *adj* (**a**) *(grande)* enormous, huge, vast, tremendous (**b**) *Fig (desmedido)* monstrous

enormemente *adv* enormously, greatly, tremendously

enormidad *nf* (**a**) *(grandeza)* enormity, hugeness (**b**) *Fig* *(desmesura)* enormity, monstrousness; *Fam* **nos gustó una e.** we loved it **(c)** *(acto)* wicked o monstrous thing

enquistarse *vpr* **(a)** *Med* to develop into a cyst **(b)** *(odio, costumbre)* to take root, become entrenched; *(proceso)* to become bogged down

enrabiar 1 *vt* to enrage, infuriate
   2 enrabiarse *vpr* to become enraged o infuriated

enraizado, -a *pp de* **enraizar**
   2 *adj* rooted

enraizar [14] **1** *vi Bot (planta)* to take root
   2 enraizarse *vpr (persona)* to put down roots

enramada *nf* **(a)** *(follaje)* foliage, leaves *pl* **(b)** *(cobertizo)* covering of branches

enrarecer [46] **1** *vt (aire)* to rarefy
   2 enrarecerse *vpr* **(a)** *(aire)* to rarefy **(b)** *(escasear)* to become scarce

enrarecido, -a 1 *pp de* **enrarecer**
   2 *adj* rarefied; *Fig* **un ambiente e.** a tense atmosphere

enredadera *nf Bot* climbing plant, creeper

enredador, -a 1 *adj (entrometido)* troublemaking, interfering, meddlesome; *(chismoso)* gossip; **una persona e.** a busybody
   2 *nm,f (entrometido)* troublemaker; *(chismoso)* busybody, gossip

enredar 1 *vt* **(a)** *(animal)* to net, catch in a net **(b)** *(trampa)* to set **(c)** *(enmarañar)* to entangle, tangle up **(d)** *Fig (asunto)* to confuse, complicate; *(trabajo)* to make a mess of **(e)** *Fig (persona)* to involve, implicate **(en** in) **(f)** *Fig (meter cizaña)* **e. a A con B** to set A against B
   2 enredarse *vpr* **(a)** *(enmarañarse)* to get entangled, get tangled (up) o in a tangle **(b)** *Fig (asunto)* to get complicated o confused; *(trabajo)* to get in a mess; **e. en una discusión** to get caught up in an argument **(c)** *Fig (persona)* to get involved **(con** with), have an affair **(con** with)

enredo *nm* **(a)** *(maraña)* tangle **(b)** *Fig (lío)* muddle, mess, mix-up, confusion **(c)** *(amoroso)* love affair **(d)** *Teat* plot **(e)** **enredos** *Fam (trastos)* bits and pieces

enrejado *nm* **(a)** *(reja)* grating, railings *pl*; *(de jaula, celda)* bars *pl*; *(de jardín)* trellis; *(de ventana)* lattice; **e. de alambre** wire netting fence **(b)** *Cost* openwork

enrejar *vt (puerta, ventana)* to put a grating on; *(terreno, área)* to fence, put railings round

enrevesado, -a *adj* complicated, difficult

enriquecedor, -a *adj* enriching

enriquecer [46] **1** *vt* **(a)** *(hacer rico)* to make rich **(b)** *Fig (mejorar)* to enrich
   2 enriquecerse *vpr (hacerse rico)* to get o become rich, prosper

enriquecimiento *nm* enrichment

enristrar *vt (ajos, cebollas)* to string together; *(lanza)* to couch

enrocar [59] *vi Ajedrez* to castle

enrojecer [46] **1** *vt (volver rojo)* to redden, turn red; *(metal)* to make red-hot
   2 *vi (ruborizarse)* to blush
   3 enrojecerse *vpr (ruborizarse)* to blush; *(volverse rojo)* to go red; *(metal)* to get red-hot

enrojecimiento *nm (metal)* reddening, glowing; *(rubor)* blushing

enrolar 1 *vt* to enrol, *US* enroll, sign on, sign up; *Mil* to enlist
   2 enrolarse *vpr* to enrol, *US* enroll, sign on; *Mil* to enlist, join up

enrollable *adj* that rolls up, roll-up; **persiana e.** roller blind

enrollado, -a 1 *pp de* **enrollar**

2 *adj* **(a)** *(en forma de rollo)* rolled up **(b)** *Fam* **estar e. con algn** *(conversando)* to be deep in conversation with sb; *(tener relaciones con)* to go out with sb, see sb **(c)** *Fam* great; **es un tío muy e.** he's a great guy

enrollar 1 *vt (papel)* to roll up; *(hilo)* to wind up; *(cable)* to coil
   2 enrollarse *vpr* **(a)** *Fam (hablar)* to chatter, go on and on; *Esp* **e. como una persiana** to go on and on **(b)** *Esp Fam (tener relaciones)* **e. con algn** *Br* to have it away with sb, *US* get it on with sb **(c)** *Esp Fam* **e. bien** to get on well with people; **e. mal** to be difficult to get on with

enronquecer [46] *vi* to become o go hoarse

enronquecimiento *nm* hoarseness, huskiness

enroque *nm Ajedrez* castling

enroscar [59] **1** *vt* **(a)** *(manguera, cuerda)* to coil up; *(cable)* to twist **(b)** *(tornillo)* to screw in o on
   2 enroscarse *vpr* to coil, wind; *(cable)* to twist, roll up; *(serpiente)* to coil itself

enrostrar *vt Am* to reproach

ensaimada *nf Culin* = kind of spiral pastry from Majorca

ensalada *nf* **(a)** *Culin* salad; **e. de fruta** fruit salad **(b)** *Cuba (refresco)* = mint-flavoured citrus drink

ensaladera *nf* salad bowl

ensaladilla *nf Esp Culin* **e. rusa** Russian salad

ensalmo *nm* spell, incantation, charm; **como por e.** as if by magic

ensalzamiento *nm (enaltecimiento)* exaltation; *(elogio)* praise

ensalzar [14] *vt (enaltecer)* to exalt; *(elogiar)* to praise, extol, *US* extoll

ensamblador *nm* **(a)** *Inform* assembler **(b)** *Carp* joiner

ensambladura *nf Téc* joint

ensamblaje *nm Téc* assembly, joining

ensamblar *vt* to join, assemble

ensanchamiento *nm* widening, broadening

ensanchar 1 *vt (hacer más ancho)* to enlarge, widen, extend, stretch, expand; *Cost (prenda)* to let out
   2 ensancharse *vpr* **(a)** *(hacerse más ancho)* to get wider, spread, stretch, expand **(b)** *Fig (persona)* to get a big head, become conceited

ensanche *nm* enlargement, widening, extension; *(de ciudad)* urban development

ensangrentado, -a 1 *pp de* **ensangrentar**
   2 *adj* bloodstained, bloody

ensangrentar [3] *vt* to stain with blood, cover in blood

ensañamiento *nm* cruelty, brutality

ensañarse *vpr* to be brutal **(con** with), delight in tormenting **(con** -)

ensartar 1 *vt* **(a)** *(perlas)* to string **(b)** *Fig* to reel off, rattle off; **ensartaba una mentira detrás de otra** he reeled off one lie after another **(c)** *Am (engañar)* to rip off
   2 ensartarse *vpr Am (ser engañado)* to be ripped off

ensayar *vt* **(a)** *Teat* to rehearse; *Mús* to practise **(b)** *(experimentar)* to test, try out

ensayismo *nm Filos Lit* essay writing

ensayista *nmf Filos Lit* essayist

ensayo *nm* **(a)** *(prueba)* test, trial, experiment, attempt; **a modo de e.** as an experiment **(b)** *Teat* rehearsal ❑ **e. general** dress rehearsal **(c)** *Filos Lit* essay **(d)** *Rugby* try

enseguida *adv*, **en seguida** *adv (inmediatamente)* at once, straight away; *(poco después)* in a minute, soon; **e. voy** I'll be right there

ensenada *nf* **(a)** *Geog* inlet, cove **(b)** *Arg (corral)* farmyard

enseña *nf* ensign, standard

ensenãdo, -a 1 *pp de* **enseñar**
2 *adj (adiestrado)* trained; *(persona)* educated, instructed
ensenãnte *nmf* teacher
ensenãnza *nf* **(a)** *(educación)* education, teaching, schooling; **dedicarse a la e.** to be a teacher □ **e. laboral** vocational training; **e. primaria/secundaria/superior** primary/secondary/higher education **(b)** *(doctrina)* teaching, doctrine
ensenãr *vt* **(a)** *(instruir)* to teach, instruct, train; *(educar)* to educate; **e. a algn a hacer algo** to teach sb how to do sth **(b)** *(mostrar)* to show; *(señalar)* to point out; **enseña la combinación** her petticoat is showing; **nos enseñó la casa** he showed us over the house; *Fig* **e. los dientes** to bare one's teeth
ensenõrearse *vpr* to take over (**de** -), take possession (**de** of)
enseres *nmpl (bártulos)* belongings, goods; *(material)* equipment *sing*
enseriarse *vpr Carib Perú* to become *o* look serious
ensillar *vt Equit* to saddle (up), put a saddle on
ensimismado, -a 1 *pp de* **ensimismarse**
2 *adj (absorbido)* engrossed; *(abstraído)* lost in thought
ensimismamiento *nm* absorption
ensimismarse *vpr (absorberse)* to become engrossed; *(abstraerse)* to be lost in thought
ensoberbecer [46] **1** *vt* to make arrogant *o* conceited; **el triunfo le ensoberbeció** success went to his head
2 ensoberbecerse *vpr* **(a)** *(causar arrogancia)* to become arrogant *o* conceited **(b)** *Fig (mar)* to get rough
ensombrecer [46] **1** *vt* to cast a shadow over
2 ensombrecerse *vpr* to darken; *Fig* to become gloomy
ensonãción *nf* daydream, pipe dream
ensonãdor, -a 1 *adj* dreamy
2 *nm,f* dreamer
ensonãr *vt* to daydream about
ensopar *vt Am* to soak
ensordecedor, -a *adj* deafening
ensordecer [46] **1** *vt* to deafen
2 *vi* to go deaf
ensordecimiento *nm* deafness
ensortijado, -a 1 *pp de* **ensortijarse**
2 *adj* curly
ensortijarse *vpr* to curl
ensuciar 1 *vt* **(a)** *(manchar)* to (make) dirty **(b)** *Fig (reputación)* to harm, damage
2 ensuciarse *vpr* to get dirty; **e. las manos** to get one's hands dirty
ensueño *nm* dream, fantasy; **unas vacaciones de e.** a dream holiday
entablado 1 *pp de* **entablar**
2 *nm* **(a)** *(entarimado)* planking, planks *pl* **(b)** *(suelo)* wooden floor
entablar 1 *vt* **(a)** *(conversación)* to open, begin; *(amistad)* to strike up; *(negocios)* to start **(b)** *Ajedrez* to set up **(c)** *Jur* **e. acción** *o* **demanda** to take legal action
2 *vi Am (empatar)* to draw
entablillado 1 *pp de* **entablillar**
2 *nm Med* splint
entablillar *vt Med* to splint
entallar *vt Cost* to take in at the waist; **un vestido muy entallado** a close-fitting dress; **una camisa entallada** a fitted shirt
entarimado, -a 1 *pp de* **entarimar**
2 *nm* parquet floor

entarimar *vt* to cover with parquet
ente *nm* **(a)** *(ser)* being **(b)** *(institución)* entity, organization, body **(c)** *Pey* oddball
enteco, -a *adj* puny, weak, frail
entelerido, -a *adj CAm Ven* thin, skinny
entenado, -a *nm,f Méx (hombre)* stepson; *(mujer)* stepdaughter
entendederas *nfpl Fam* brains; **ser duro de e.** to be slow on the uptake; **tener buenas e.** to be quick-witted
entendedor, -a *adj* understanding; *Prov* **a buen e. con pocas palabras bastan** a nod's as good as a wink
entender [64] **1** *vt* **(a)** *(comprender)* to understand; *(darse cuenta)* to realize; **a mi e.** to my way of thinking; **dar a e. que ...** to imply that ...; **hacerse e.** to make oneself understood; **tengo entendido que ...** I understand that ...; *Fam* **no entiendo ni jota** *o RP* **un pito** I don't understand a word **(b)** *(discurrir)* to think, believe **(c)** *(significar)* to mean, intend; **¿qué entiende con eso?** what does he mean by that? **(d)** *(oír)* to hear
2 *vi* **(a)** *(comprender)* to understand **(b)** *(saber)* **e. de** *o* **en** to know about, be an expert in; **entiende de vinos** she knows a lot about wine **(c)** *Jur* to have jurisdiction over
3 entenderse *vpr* **(a)** *(comprenderse)* to be understood, be meant; **¿qué se entiende por esa palabra?** what does that word mean? **(b)** *Fam* to know what one is doing; **yo me entiendo** I have my reasons **(c)** *Fam* to get on (well) (**con** with); **e. con un hombre** to have an affair with a man
entendido, -a 1 *pp de* **entender**
2 *nm,f* expert
entendimiento *nm* **(a)** *(sentido común)* understanding, comprehension, grasp **(b)** *(inteligencia)* mind, intellect, understanding
entenebrecer [46] **1** *vt* to darken, obscure
2 entenebrecerse *vpr* to become *o* get dark
entente *nf* agreement; *Pol* entente (cordiale)
enterado, -a 1 *pp de* **enterar**
2 *adj Esp* knowledgeable, well-informed; **estar e.** to be in the know; **estar e. de ...** to be aware of ...
3 *nm,f Fam* expert; **es un e. de la música** he's a real expert on music
enteramente *adv* entirely, completely
enterar 1 *vt* **(a)** *(informar)* to inform (**de** about, of); *(poner al corriente)* to acquaint (**de** with), tell (**de** about) **(b)** *CAm Col Méx (pagar)* to pay **(c)** *Chile (completar)* to make up
2 enterarse *vpr* to find out; **me he enterado de que ...** I hear that ...; **ni me enteré** I didn't even realize it; **¡toma, para que te enteres!** so now you know!
entereza *nf* **(a)** *(serenidad)* composure, self-possession **(b)** *Fig* integrity, strength of character
enterizo, -a *adj* in one piece, whole
enternecedor, -a *adj* moving, touching
enternecer [46] **1** *vt* to move, touch
2 enternecerse *vpr* to be moved *o* touched
enternecimiento *nm* **(a)** *(cariño)* tenderness **(b)** *(compasión)* pity
entero, -a 1 *adj* **(a)** *(completo)* entire, complete, whole; **por e.** completely **(b)** *Fig (recto, justo)* honest, upright **(c)** *Fig (que tiene entereza)* firm, resolute, unshaken **(d)** *Guat Perú Fam (idéntico)* identical
2 *nm* **(a)** *Mat* whole number **(b)** *Fin* point; **subir/bajar enteros** to go up/down points
enterrador *nm* gravedigger
enterramiento *nm* burial, interment
enterrar [3] **1** *vt* **(a)** *(cadáver)* to bury **(b)** *Fig (olvidar)* to forget about

2 enterrarse *vpr Fig* to bury oneself; **se enterró en vida** he cut himself off from the world

entibiar 1 *vt* **(a)** *(enfriar)* to cool, take the chill off **(b)** *Fig (debilitar)* to cool down

  2 entibiarse *vpr* **(a)** *(enfriarse)* to become lukewarm, cool (down) **(b)** *Fig (debilitarse)* to cool off

entidad *nf* **(a)** *(corporación)* body; *(empresa)* firm, company ❑ **e. bancaria** bank; **e. comercial** company, firm **(b) de e.** of importance, important

entierro *nm* **(a)** *(acción)* burial **(b)** *(ceremonia)* funeral; **asistir a un e.** to go to a funeral; *Argot* **parecer un e. de tercera** to be like a funeral

entintar *vt* **(a)** *Impr* to ink **(b)** *(manchar)* to stain with ink

entlo. *(abrev de* **entresuelo)** first *o US* second floor, mezzanine

entoldado, -a 1 *pp de* **entoldar**
  2 *nm* **(a)** *(toldo)* awning **(b)** *(para fiesta, baile)* marquee

entoldar 1 *vt* **(a)** *(toldo)* to put up **(b)** *(para fiesta, baile)* to put up
  2 entoldarse *vpr Meteor* to become overcast, cloud over

entomología *nf* entomology

entomológico, -a *adj* entomologic, entomological

entomólogo, -a *nm,f* entomologist

entonación *nf* intonation

entonado, -a 1 *pp de* **entonar**
  2 *adj* arrogant

entonar 1 *vt* **(a)** *(nota)* to pitch; *(canción)* to sing; *(voz)* to modulate **(b)** *Med (tonificar)* to tone up
  2 *vi* **(a)** *(cantar)* to sing; *(plegaria)* to sing, sound **(b)** *Fig* to be in harmony, be in tune **(con** with); **no entona** she is out of tune
  3 entonarse *vpr* to give oneself airs

entonces *adv* then; **por aquel e.** at that time; **¿qué hiciste e.?** what did you do then?

entontecer [46] *vt (enloquecer)* to drive mad; *(atontar)* to befuddle

entorchado, -a *nm* braid

entornado, -a 1 *pp de* **entornar**
  2 *adj (ojos etc)* half-closed; *(puerta)* ajar

entornar *vt (ojos etc)* to half-close; *(puerta)* to leave ajar

entorno *nm* environment, surroundings *pl*

entorpecer [46] *vt* **(a)** *(debilitar) (movimientos)* to hinder; *(miembros)* to numb; *(mente)* to cloud **(b)** *Fig (dificultar)* to obstruct, hinder, impede

entorpecimiento *nm* **(a)** *(debilitamiento) (físico)* numbness; *(mental)* haziness **(b)** *Fig (dificultad)* obstruction, stumbling block

entrada *nf* **(a)** *(gen) (entrance, entry; *(puerta)* way in, doorway; **dar e. a** to let *o* allow in ❑ **e. principal** main entrance **(b)** *Teat Cin* admission; *(público)* audience; *(recaudación)* takings *pl* **(c)** *Fig* beginning; *(libro, discurso)* opening; *Fig* **de e.** for a start **(d)** *Culin* entrée **(e)** *Esp Com (en el libro de cuentas)* entry; *(pago inicial)* down payment, deposit; **e. de capital** capital inflow; **derechos de e.** import duty *sing* **(f)** **entradas** *Com (ingresos)* receipts, takings **(g) tener entradas (en la frente)** to have a receding hairline **(h)** *Cuba Méx (paliza)* beating

entrado, -a *adj* **e. el otoño** once we're into autumn; **entrada la noche** once night has set in; **e. en años** elderly; **e. en carnes** portly, rather large

entrador, -a *adj* **(a)** *Méx Perú Ven (animoso)* spirited, energetic **(b)** *CRica RP (agradable)* likeable, charming **(c)** *Chile Perú (entrometido)* meddling, meddlesome

entramado *nm* (wooden) framework

entrambos, -as *adj & pron Fml* both

entrampado, -a *adj Fam (endeudado)* **estar e.** to be up to one's neck in debt

entramparse *vpr* **(a)** *(enredarse)* to get into a mess **(b)** *(endeudarse)* to get into debt

entrante 1 *adj* entering, coming, incoming; **el mes e.** next month
  2 *nm Esp Culin* starter

entrañable *adj* **(a)** *(íntimo)* intimate, close **(b)** *(afectuoso)* affectionate, warm-hearted

entrañablemente *adv* deeply, dearly

entrañar 1 *vt* **(a)** *(ocultar)* to hide **(b)** *(conllevar)* to carry; *(implicar)* to entail
  2 entrañarse *vpr* to get deeply attached **(con** to)

entrañas *nfpl* **(a)** *Anat* entrails, bowels **(b)** *Fig* heart *sing*, core *sing*; **de buenas/malas e.** good-/evil-hearted; **no tener e.** to be heartless; **sacar las e. a algn** to bleed sb dry; **sin e.** heartless; *Fam* **echar las e.** to puke one's guts up

entrar 1 *vi* **(a)** *(introducirse) (viniendo)* to enter, come in; *(yendo)* to enter, go in; **hazle e.** invite him in; *Fig* **entrado en edad** *o* **en años** well on in years; *Fig* **no me entra en la cabeza que ...** I can't believe that ...; *Fam* **esa mujer no me entra** I can't stand that woman; *Fam* **no e. ni salir en algo** to be indifferent to sth; *Fam* **no me entran las matemáticas** I can't get the hang of maths **(b)** *(encajar)* to fit; **no me entra el zapato** that shoe doesn't fit me **(c)** *(periodo, época)* to enter **(d)** *Fig (asociación)* to go into **(e)** *Mús* to come in; **entró el piano** the piano came in **(f)** *Teat* to enter; **entró Macbeth** Macbeth entered **(g)** *(caber)* **en una libra entran tres manzanas** you get three apples to the pound **(h)** *(año etc)* to begin; **el año que entra** next year, the coming year; *Fig* **hasta bien entrada la tarde** well into the evening **(i)** **(e. + a +** *infin)* to begin to do sth; **entra a trabajar en la Embajada** he's starting a new job at the Embassy **(j)** *(venir)* to come over; **me entró dolor de cabeza** I got a headache; **me entraron ganas de reír** I felt like laughing
  2 *vt* to introduce; **e. el coche en el garaje** to put the car into the garage
  3 entrarse *vpr* to get in

entre *prep* **(a)** *(de dos términos)* between; **e. tu y yo** between the two of us; *Fig* **nadar e. dos aguas** to sit on the fence; *Fig* **tener un asunto e. manos** to be tied up with a matter **(b)** *(de más de dos)* among, amongst; **estaba escondido e. los árboles** it was hidden amongst the trees; **estoy e. los aprobados** I've passed **(c)** *(entremedio)* somewhere between; **e. frío y caliente** warmish; **e. gris y azul** greyish-blue **(d)** *(sumando)* counting; **e. el cine y la cena gastamos cinco mil pesos** what with the cinema and dinner we spent five thousand pesos; **e. hombres y mujeres somos veinte** there are twenty of us all together

entreabierto, -a 1 *pp de* **entreabrir**
  2 *adj (ojos etc)* half-open; *(puerta)* ajar

entreabrir *vt (pp* **entreabierto)** *(ojos)* to half open; *(puerta)* to leave ajar

entreacto *nm Teat* interval, intermission

entrecano, -a *adj Br* greying, *US* graying

entrecasa *nf Am* **estar de e.** to be casually dressed; **los guisos de e.** home cooking

entrecejo *nm* space between the eyebrows; *(ceño)* frown; **fruncir el e.** to frown, knit one's brow

entrecerrar [3] *vt* to half-close

entrechocar [59] **1** *vt (espadas)* to clash
  2 *vi (dientes)* to chatter
  3 entrechocarse *vpr* to collide, crash

entrecomillado, -a 1 *pp de* **entrecomillar**
  2 *adj* in quotation marks *o* inverted commas

entrecomillar *vt* to put in quotation marks

entrecortado, -a *adj* (**a**) *(señal, sonido)* intermittent; *(voz)* faltering, hesitant; *(objeto)* partially cut (**b**) *Fig* to cut off, interrupt

entrecot *(pl* entrecots *o* entrecotes*) nm,* **entrecó** *nm Culin* fillet steak

entrecruzarse [14] *vpr* to interweave; **e. los dedos** to clasp one's hands

entrecubiertas *nfpl Náut* between-decks

entredicho *nm* (**a**) *(prohibición)* prohibition, ban; *Jur* injunction (**b**) **estar en e.** to be suspect; **poner algo en e.** to have one's doubts about sth

entredós *nm* (**a**) *Cost* insertion, panel (**b**) *Mueb* cabinet, dresser

entrefino, -a *adj* medium quality

entrega *nf* (**a**) *(gen)* handing over; *(de premios)* presentation; *Com* delivery; **hacer e. de algo** to present *o* deliver *o* hand over sth ❑ **e. contra reembolso** cash on delivery (**b**) *(de posesiones)* surrender; **la e. de armas** the surrender of arms (**c**) *(fascículo)* part, instalment, *US* installment (**d**) *(devoción)* selflessness

entregar [38] **1** *vt* (**a**) *(deberes etc)* to give in, hand in; *(ceder)* to give up; *(dar)* to hand over; *Com* to deliver; **e. algo en mano** to hand sth over (**b**) *Mil (posesiones)* to surrender
2 entregarse *vpr* (**a**) *(dedicarse)* give oneself up; *(rendirse)* to give in, surrender, submit (**b**) **e. a** to devote oneself to; *Pey* to indulge in

entreguerras: de entreguerras *loc adj* periodo/ literatura de e. time/literature between the wars

entrelazar [14] **1** *vt* to entwine, interlace; **e. las manos** to clasp one's hands
2 entrelazarse *vpr* to entwine, interlace

entremedias *adv* in between; *(mientras tanto)* meanwhile, in the meantime; **e. de** between, among

entremés *nm* (**a**) *Teat* interlude, short farce *o* play (**b**) **entremeses** *Culin* hors d'oeuvres

entremeter 1 *vt* to insert, place between
2 entremeterse *véase* entrometerse

entremezclar *vpr* to intermingle, intermix, mix

entrenador, -a *nm,f Dep* trainer, coach

entrenamiento *nm* training

entrenar 1 *vt* to train, coach
2 entrenarse *vpr* (**a**) *Dep* to train (**b**) *Fig* to train, prepare oneself

entrepaño *nm Arquit* alcove, bay; *(de puerta, ventana)* panel; *(de estantería)* shelf

entrepierna *nf* (**a**) *(zona)* crotch, crutch; *Vulg (órganos)* genitals *pl*; *Vulg* **se lo pasó por la e.** he didn't give a shit about it (**b**) *Chile (traje de baño)* bathing *o* swimming trunks

entreplanta *nf* mezzanine

entresacar [59] *vt* to pick out, select; *(pelo, plantas)* to thin out

entresijo *nm* secret, mystery, hidden aspect; **esto tiene muchos entresijos** this is very complicated

entresuelo *nm* mezzanine, first *o US* second floor

entretanto 1 *adv* meanwhile, for the time being
2 *nm* **en el e.** in the meantime

entretecho *nm Chile Col* attic, loft

entretejer *vt* to interweave, intertwine, entwine; **entretejido de seda** interwoven with silk

entretela *nf* (**a**) *Cost* interfacing, interlining (**b**) **entretelas** *Fam* heart *sing*, heartstrings; *(entrañas)* entrails

entretención *nf Am* amusement, entertainment

entretener [65] **1** *vt* (**a**) *(divertir)* to entertain, amuse, distract (**b**) *(retrasar)* to delay; *(detener)* to hold up, detain; **no te entretengo más** I won't keep you any longer (**c**)

(engañar) (hambre) to kill, stave off; *(tiempo)* to while away
2 entretenerse *vpr* (**a**) *(distraerse)* to amuse oneself, while away the time; **me entretengo tocando el piano** I enjoy playing the piano; **sólo para e.** just for fun (**b**) *(retrasarse)* to be delayed, be held up

entretenida *nf* (**a**) *(amante)* mistress, kept woman (**b**) **dar a algn la e.** to try to put sb off

entretenido, -a 1 *pp de* entretener
2 *adj* enjoyable, entertaining

entretenimiento *nm* (**a**) *(distracción)* entertainment, amusement, distraction (**b**) *(mantenimiento)* upkeep, maintenance; **gastos de e.** maintenance costs

entretiempo: de entretiempo *adj* un abrigo de e. lightweight coat

entrever [70] *vt* (**a**) *(vislumbrar)* to glimpse, catch sight of (**b**) *Fig (adivinar)* to guess, suspect; **dejó e. que ...** she hinted that ...

entreverado, -a 1 *pp de* entreverar
2 *adj* mixed, patchy; *Culin* **tocino e.** streaky bacon

entreverar *vt RP* to mix, mix up

entrevés *indic pres véase* entrever

entrevía *nf Ferroc* gauge

entrevista *nf (encuentro)* meeting; *(entrevista)* interview; **hacer una e. a algn** to interview sb ❑ **e. de trabajo** job interview

entrevistado, -a *nm,f* interviewee

entrevistador, -a *nm,f* interviewer

entrevistar 1 *vt* to interview
2 entrevistarse *vpr* **e. con algn** to have an interview *o* a meeting with sb

entristecedor, -a *adj* saddening

entristecer [46] **1** *vt* to sadden, make sad
2 entristecerse *vpr* to be sad (**por** about)

entrometerse *vpr* to meddle, interfere (**en** in), intrude

entrometido, -a 1 *pp de* entrometerse
2 *adj* interfering, nosy
3 *nm,f* meddler, busybody, nosey-parker

entromparse *vpr* (**a**) *Fam* to get sloshed (**b**) *Am* to get cross

entroncamiento *nm* (**a**) *(parentesco)* relationship by marriage (**b**) *Ferroc* junction

entroncar [59] **1** *vt (relacionarse)* to relate, link, connect
2 *vi* to be related to, be connected with; **e. con una familia** to marry into a family

entronización *nf* enthronement

entronizar [14] *vt* (**a**) *(monarca)* to enthrone, put on the throne (**b**) *Fig* to worship, put on a pedestal

entronque *nm véase* entroncamiento

entrucharse *vpr Méx* to meddle, interfere

entuerto *nm* injustice, wrong, injury; **deshacer entuertos** to right wrongs

entumecer [46] **1** *vt* to numb, make numb
2 entumecerse *vpr* to go numb, go dead

entumecido, -a 1 *pp de* entumecer
2 *adj (miembro)* numb, dead

entumecimiento *nm* numbness, deadness

enturbiar 1 *vt* (**a**) *(líquido)* to make cloudy *o* muddy *o* turbid (**b**) *Fig* to cloud, obscure, muddle
2 enturbiarse *vpr* (**a**) *(líquido)* to get muddy, become cloudy (**b**) *Fig* to get confused *o* muddled

entusiasmar 1 *vt* to fill with enthusiasm; *(gustar)* to delight; **me entusiasma Grecia** I love Greece
2 entusiasmarse *vpr* to get excited *o* enthusiastic (**con** about)

entusiasmo *nm* enthusiasm; **con e.** keenly, enthusiastically; **desbordar e.** to be over the moon

entusiasta 1 *adj* enthusiastic, keen (**de** on)
2 *nmf* lover; *Dep* fan, follower, supporter

entusiástico, -a *adj* enthusiastic

enumeración *nf* enumeration, count, reckoning

enumerar *vt* to enumerate, count, reckon

enunciación *nf (teoría)* enunciation; *(palabras)* statement, declaration

enunciado, -a 1 *pp de* **enunciar**
2 *nm (problema)* wording

enunciar *vt (teoría)* to enunciate; *(palabras)* to state, declare

envainar *vt* to sheathe

envalentonamiento *nm* arrogance, boldness

envalentonarse *vpr (ser valiente)* to become bold *o* daring; *(insolentarse)* to become arrogant *o* aggressive

envanecer [46] **1** *vt* to make proud *o* vain
2 envanecerse *vpr* to become conceited *o* proud, give oneself airs

envanecimiento *nm* conceit, vanity

envarado, -a 1 *pp de* **envarar**
2 *adj* numb, stiff

envaramiento *nm* numbness, stiffness

envarar *vt* to stiffen, make stiff

envasado, -a 1 *pp de* **envasar**
2 *adj (en botella)* bottled; *(en paquete)* packed; *(conservas)* canned, tinned; **e. al vacío** vacuum-packed
3 *nm (en botella)* bottling; *(en paquete)* packing; *(de conservas)* canning

envasar *vt (en paquetes)* to pack; *(en botellas)* to bottle; *(enlatar)* to can, tin

envase *nm* (a) *(acto) (gen)* packing; *(en botella)* bottling; *(en lata)* canning (b) *(recipiente)* container; *(botella vacía)* empty; **e. de cartón** carton; **e. plástico** plastic container; **e. sin retorno** nonreturnable container

envejecer [46] **1** *vi* to grow old
2 *vt* to age, make look old

envejecido, -a 1 *pp de* **envejecer**
2 *adj* old, aged, old-looking; **está muy e.** he looks very old

envejecimiento *nm* ageing, growing old

envenenamiento *nm* poisoning; **e. por la comida** food poisoning

envenenar *vt* to poison; *Fig* **la envidia envenenó su mente** envy poisoned his mind

envergadura *nf* (a) *(de pájaro, avión)* span, wingspan; *Náut* breadth (of sail) (b) *Fig* importance, scope; **de gran e.** consequential, far-reaching

envés *nm* (a) *(de tela)* wrong side; *(de página)* back, reverse; *Bot* reverse (b) *(espalda)* back

envestidura *nf* investiture, inauguration

enviado, a 1 *pp de* **enviar**
2 *nm,f* messenger, envoy ❑ *Prensa* **e. especial** special correspondent

enviar [32] *vt* to send; *Com* to remit, dispatch; *(por barco)* to ship; **e. a algn a hacer algo** to send sb to do sth; *Fam* **e. a algn a paseo** to send sb packing

enviciar 1 *vt* to corrupt, spoil
2 *vi Bot* = to produce too many leaves and not enough fruit
3 enviciarse *vpr* to become addicted

envidia *nf* envy; **morirse de e.** to be green with envy; **tener e.** to envy (**de** -)

envidiable *adj* enviable

envidiar *vt* to envy; **no te envidio la suerte** sooner you than me; **no tener nada que e.** to compare favourably (**a** with)

envidioso, -a *adj* envious

envilecer [46] **1** *vt* to degrade, debase
2 *vi* to lose value, be debased

envilecimiento *nm* degradation, debasement

envío *nm* dispatch, shipment; *(remesa)* lot, consignment; *(paquete)* parcel; **gastos de e.** postage and packing; **hacer un e.** to dispatch an order ❑ **e. contra reembolso** cash on delivery

envite *nm* (a) *Naipes* stake, side bet (b) *(ofrecimiento)* offer, bid (c) **al primer e.** right away, straightaway

enviudar *vi (hombre)* to become a widower, lose one's wife; *(mujer)* to become a widow, lose one's husband

envoltorio *nm* (a) *(cosas atadas)* bundle (b) *(cubierta)* wrapper, wrapping; **deshacer el e.** to undo the wrapping; **hacer un e. con algo** to wrap sth up

envoltura *nf* wrapper, wrapping

envolvente *adj* enveloping

envolver [41] *(pp* **envuelto) 1** *vt* (a) *(cubrir) (con papel)* to wrap, wrap up; *(con ropa etc)* to cover, cover up; *Fig* **la niebla envolvía la ciudad** fog enveloped the city (b) *Fig* to imply, involve, mean; *(persona)* to involve, implicate (**en** in); **estaba envuelto en el asesinato** he was involved in the murder
2 envolverse *vpr* (a) *(cubrirse)* to wrap oneself up (**en** in) (b) *Fig* to become involved (**en** in)

enyerbar 1 *vt Col Chile Méx (hechizar)* to cast a spell on
2 enyerbarse *vpr* (a) *Am* to become covered with grass, grass over (b) *Guat Méx (envenenarse)* to poison oneself

enyesado, -a 1 *pp de* **enyesar**
2 *nm* plastering; *Med* plaster cast

enyesar *vt* to plaster; *Med* to put in plaster

enzarzar [14] **1** *vt* (a) *(con zarzas)* to cover with brambles (b) *Fig* to sow discord among, set at odds
2 enzarzarse *vpr* (a) *(con zarzas)* to get entangled in brambles (b) *Fig* to squabble; **e. en una disputa** to get into an argument

enzima *nf Biol* enzyme

eñe *nf* = name of the letter Ñ in Spanish

eoceno, -a *nm Geol* Eocene

eólico, -a *adj* **energía eólica** wind energy

eón *nm* aeon, *US* eon

epatar *vt Argot* to knock dead

E. P. D. *(abrev de* **en paz descanse)** R.I.P.

épica *nf Lit* epic poetry

epicentro *nm* epicentre, *US* epicenter

épico, -a *adj Lit* epic, heroic; **poema é.** epic poem

epicureísmo *nm* Epicureanism

epicúreo, -a *adj* Epicurean

epidemia *nf* epidemic

epidémico, -a *adj* epidemic

epidemiología *nf Med* epidemiology

epidérmico, -a *adj* epidermic; **enfermedad e.** skin disease

epidermis *nf* epidermis, skin

Epifanía *nf Rel* Epiphany, Twelfth Night

epiglotis *nf Anat* epiglottis

epígrafe *nm* (a) *(cita)* epigraph (b) *(título)* heading, title

epigrama *nm Lit* epigram, satirical poem

epilepsia *nf Med* epilepsy

epiléptico, -a *adj & nm,f* epileptic; **ataque e.** epileptic fit

epílogo *nm* (**a**) *(de libro)* epilogue, *US* epilog, final chapter (**b**) *(conclusión)* summary

episcopado *nm Rel* (**a**) *(lugar)* bishopric (**b**) *(época)* episcopate (**c**) *(conjunto de obispos)* episcopacy

episcopal *adj Rel* episcopal

episiotomía *nf Med* episiotomy

episódico, -a *adj* episodic

episodio *nm* (**a**) *Lit* episode (**b**) *(suceso)* event

epistemología *nf* epistemology

epístola *nf Fml* epistle

epistolar *adj Fml* epistolary

epitafio *nm* epitaph

epíteto *nm Lit* epithet; *Fam* **fuertes epitetos** strong words of criticism

epítome *nm* epitome, summary

época *nf* time, age; *Hist* period, epoch; *Agr* season; **hacer é.** to be a landmark; **la é. de las fresas** the strawberry season; **muebles de é.** period furniture; **por aquella é.** about that time

epopeya *nf* (**a**) *Lit* epic poem (**b**) *(hazaña)* heroic action

épsilon (*pl* **épsilons**) *nf* epsilon

equidad *nf* fairness

equidistancia *nf* equidistance

equidistante *adj* equidistant

equidistar *vi* to be equidistant (**de** from)

equilátero, -a *adj Geom* equilateral

equilibrado, -a 1 *pp de* **equilibrar**
2 *adj (dieta)* balanced; *(persona)* sensible

equilibrar 1 *vt* (**a**) *(carga, ruedas, fuerza)* to balance (**b**) *Fig* to balance, adjust
2 equilibrarse *vpr* to balance (**en** on)

equilibrio *nm* (**a**) *(piezas, ruedas, mecanismo)* balance, equilibrium; *(en el circo)* **hacer equilibrios** to do a balancing act; **perder el e.** to lose one's balance (**b**) *Fig (de poder etc)* balance

equilibrismo *nm* balancing act

equilibrista *nmf (en cuerda)* tightrope walker; *(trapecista)*, trapeze artist

equino¹ *nm Zool* sea urchin

equino, -a² *adj* equine, horse

equinoccial *adj* equinoctial

equinoccio *nm* equinox

equipaje *nm* (**a**) *(maletas) Br* luggage, *US* baggage; **hacer el e.** to pack, do the packing □ **e. de mano** hand luggage (**b**) *Náut* crew

equipamiento *nm (acción)* equipping; *(equipo)* equipment

equipar 1 *vt* to equip, furnish; *Náut* to fit out
2 equiparse *vpr* to kit oneself out, equip oneself (**con, de** with)

equiparable *adj* comparable (**a** to, **con** with), applicable (**a, con** to)

equiparación *nf* comparison

equiparar *vt* to compare (**con** with), liken (**con** to)

equipo *nm* (**a**) *Ind* equipment; **gastos de e.** capital expenditure *sing* (**b**) *(ropas, útiles)* outfit, kit □ **e. de alta fidelidad** hi-fi stereo system; **e. de novia** trousseau (**c**) *(personas)* team; *Dep* **e. de fútbol/baloncesto** football/basketball team □ **e. de salvamento** rescue team

equis *nf* (**a**) *(letra)* = name of the letter X in Spanish (**b**) *Mat* a certain amount, x number

equitación *nf* horsemanship, horse *o US* horseback riding

equitador *nm Am* expert in horses, horseman

equitativo, -a *adj* equitable, fair; **trato e.** fair *o* square deal

equivalencia *nf (igual)* equivalence; *(que sustituye)* compensation

equivalente *adj (igual)* equivalent; *(que sustituye)* compensatory

equivaler [68] *vi* (**a**) *(ser igual)* to be equal, be equivalent, amount (**to** a) (**b**) *(significar)* to be tantamount (**a** to); **esta respuesta equivale a una negativa** this answer is tantamount to a refusal

equivocación *nf* error, mistake; **cometiste una e. marchándote** you were wrong to leave

equivocadamente *adv* by mistake

equivocado, -a 1 *pp de* **equivocar**
2 *adj* mistaken, wrong

equívocamente *adv* equivocally

equivocar [59] **1** *vt* to mistake, get wrong, confuse
2 equivocarse *vpr* to be mistaken *o* wrong; *(dirección)* to go wrong, get it wrong; **se equivocó de camino** he went the wrong way; **te has equivocado** you've made a mistake

equívoco, -a 1 *adj* equivocal, misleading, ambiguous
2 *nm* misunderstanding

era¹ *nf* era, age; **e. Cristiana** Christian era

era² *nf* (**a**) *Agr* threshing floor (**b**) *Hortic* bed, plot, patch

era³ *pt indef véase* **ser²**

erario *nm Fin* exchequer, treasury □ **e. público** exchequer

erección *nf* (**a**) *(del pene)* erection (**b**) *(de edificio, monumento)* construction, erection

eréctil *adj* erectile

erecto, -a *adj* upright; *(pene)* erect

eremita *nm* hermit, recluse

eres *indic pres véase* **ser²**

ergonomía *nf* ergonomics *sing*

ergonómico, -a *adj* ergonomic

erguido, -a 1 *pp de* **erguir**
2 *adj* (**a**) *(derecho)* erect, straight, upright (**b**) *Fig (orgulloso)* proud

erguir [28] **1** *vt* to raise up straight, erect, lift up
2 erguirse *vpr* (**a**) *(levantarse)* to straighten up, stand *o* sit up straight (**b**) *Fig (engreírse)* to swell with pride

erial 1 *adj (tierra)* uncultivated, untilled
2 *nm* uncultivated land

erigir [24] **1** *vt* (**a**) *(elevar)* to erect, raise, build (**b**) *Fig (fundar)* to establish, found
2 erigirse *vpr* **e. en algo** to set oneself up in sth

Eritrea *n* Eritrea

erizado, -a 1 *pp de* **erizarse**
2 *adj* bristly, prickly

erizarse [14] *vpr* to bristle, stand on end

erizo *nm* (**a**) *Zool* hedgehog □ **e. de mar** *o* **marino** sea urchin (**b**) *Bot* burr, prickly husk (**c**) *Fam (persona)* surly *o* grumpy person

ermita *nf* hermitage, shrine

ermitaño, -a 1 *nm,f* hermit, recluse
2 *nm Zool* hermit crab

erogación *nf* (**a**) *(distribución)* distribution, division (**b**) *Chile (donativo)* contribution (**c**) *Fin* **erogaciones** expenses, outgoings

erogar [38] *vt* (**a**) *(distribuir)* to distribute, divide, apportion (**b**) *Arg Méx Par (deudas)* to pay

erógeno, -a *adj* erogenous, erogenic

eros *nm inv* eros

erosión *nf* (**a**) *Geol* erosion, wearing away (**b**) *Fig (desgaste)* wear and tear

erosionar *vt Geol* to erode; *(gastar)* to wear away

erótica *nf* **la e. del poder** the thrill of power

erótico, -a *adj* erotic

erotismo *nm* eroticism

erotizar [14] *vt* to eroticize

errabundo, -a *adj* wandering, vagrant

erradamente *adv* mistakenly

erradicación *nf* eradication, extirpation; *(enfermedad)* stamping out

erradicar [59] *vt* to eradicate; *(enfermedad)* to stamp out

errado, -a 1 *pp de* **errar**
2 *adj* mistaken, wrong, erroneous

errante *adj* wandering, vagrant, nomadic

errar [29] **1** *vt* (**a**) *(objetivo)* to miss, get wrong; **e. el camino** to lose one's way (**b**) *Fig (persona)* to fail, fail in one's duties to
2 *vi* (**a**) *(vagar)* to wander, rove, roam (**b**) *(equivocarse)* to err; **e. y porfiar** to persist in error

errata *nf Impr* erratum, misprint; **fe de erratas** errata

errático, -a *adj* erratic, wandering

erre *nf* = name of the letter R in Spanish; **e. que e.** stubbornly, pigheadedly

erróneamente *adv* erroneously, wrongly, falsely

erróneo, -a *adj* erroneous, wrong, false; **juicio e.** faulty judgement

error *nm* error, mistake; **caer en un e.** to make a mistake; **por e.** by mistake, in error □ **e. de cálculo** miscalculation; **e. humano** human error; *Impr* **e. de imprenta** misprint; **e. judicial** miscarriage of justice

eructar *vi* to belch, burp

eructo *nm* belch, burp

erudición *nf* erudition, learning, scholarship

eruditamente *adv* scholarly

erudito, -a 1 *adj* erudite, learned, intellectual
2 *nm,f* scholar, intellectual, expert; **e. a la violeta** pseudo-intellectual

erupción *nf* (**a**) *(de un volcán)* eruption; **entrar en e.** to erupt (**b**) *(en la piel)* rash

es *indic pres véase* **ser²**

esa *adj dem véase* **ese, -a²**

ésa *adj dem véase* **ése, -a**

esbeltez *nf* slimness, slenderness; *(delicadeza)* gracefulness

esbelto, -a *adj* slim, willowy, slender; *(delicado)* graceful

esbirro *nm* (**a**) *(secuaz)* henchman (**b**) *Hist* bailiff

esbozar [14] *vt* to sketch, outline; *Fig* **e. una sonrisa** to force a smile, smile wanly

esbozo *nm* sketch, outline, rough draft

escabechar *vt Culin* to pickle

escabeche *nm Culin* pickle

escabechina *nf* massacre; *Fam Educ* **hacer una e.** to fail everybody

escabel *nm* low stool, footstool

escabrosidad *nf* (**a**) *(aspereza)* unevenness, roughness (**b**) *Fig (dificultad)* toughness, difficulty (**c**) *Fig (indecencia)* coarseness, crudeness

escabroso, -a *adj* (**a**) *(áspero)* uneven, rough (**b**) *Fig (difícil)* tough, difficult (**c**) *Fig (indecente)* coarse, crude

escabullirse *vpr* (**a**) *(entre los dedos)* to slip through (**b**) *(persona)* to slip away, scuttle *o* scurry off

escacharrar *vt Esp Fam* to bust, *Br* knacker

escafandra *nf* diving suit

escafandrista *nmf* diver

escala *nf* (**a**) *(escalera)* ladder, stepladder; **e. de gato** rope ladder (**b**) *(graduación)* scale; *(de colores)* range □ **e. de valores** scale of values; **e. móvil** sliding scale; *Mús* **e. musical** scale; **e. salarial** salary scale (**c**) *(proporción)* scale; **en gran e.** on a large scale (**d**) *Náut* port of call; *Av* stopover; **hacer e. en** to call in at, stop over in □ **e. técnica** refuelling stop

escalada *nf* (**a**) *(de montaña)* climb (**b**) *Fig* escalation, increase; *(de precios)* rise; **la e. del terrorismo** the rise in terrorism

escalador, -a *nm,f* climber, mountaineer

escalafón *nm* *(de personal)* roll, list of officials; *(graduación)* ladder; *(de salarios)* salary *o* wage scale

escalar *vt* (**a**) *(montaña)* to climb, scale (**b**) *Fig (posición social)* to climb (**c**) *(asaltar)* to burgle

escaldado, -a 1 *pp de* **escaldar**
2 *adj* scalded; *Fig* wary, cautious; **salir e.** to get one's fingers burnt; *Prov* **gato e. del agua fría huye** once bitten, twice shy

escaldadura *nf* scald, scalding

escaldar *vt* to scald

escalera *nf* (**a**) *(en edificio)* staircase, stair, stairway □ **e. de caracol** spiral staircase; **e. de incendios** fire escape; **e. mecánica** escalator (**b**) *(escala)* ladder □ **e. doble** *o* **de tijera** stepladder (**c**) *Naipes* run, sequence

escalerilla *nf Náut* gangway; *Av* (boarding) ramp

escalfar *vt Culin* to poach

escalinata *nf Arquit* stoop

escalofriante *adj* hair-raising, bloodcurdling, chilling

escalofrío *nm* shiver, shudder; *(de fiebre)* chill; **me dió un e.** *(de frío)* it made me shiver; *(de miedo, horror)* it gave me the creeps

escalón *nm* (**a**) *(peldaño)* step; *(escala)* rung (**b**) *Fig* degree, level, grade; *Mil* echelon

escalonado, -a 1 *pp de* **escalonar**
2 *adj* at regular intervals, spaced out; *(pelo)* in layers, layered

escalonar *vt* to place at intervals, space out; *Mil* to echelon

escalope *nm Culin* escalope

escalpelo *nm Med* scalpel

escama *nf* (**a**) *Bot Zool* scale; *(de jabón)* flake; **jabón en escamas** soap flakes (**b**) *Fig* resentment, grudge, suspicion

escamado, -a 1 *pp de* **escamar**
2 *adj* (**a**) *(pescado)* scaly (**b**) *Fig* wary, suspicious

escamar 1 *vt* (**a**) *(pescado)* to scale, remove the scales from (**b**) *Fig* to make wary *o* suspicious; **mucho me escama** it smells fishy to me
2 escamarse *vpr* to smell a rat, become suspicious

escamoso, -a *adj* scaly; *(piel)* dry, flaky

escamotear *vt* (**a**) *(truquear)* to whisk away, make vanish (**b**) *Fam Fig (robar)* to lift, pinch; *(engañar)* to diddle out of, do out of (**c**) *(ocultar)* to disregard, avoid

escamoteo *nm* (**a**) *(prestidigitación)* sleight of hand, conjuring (**b**) *(robar)* pilfering; *(mangar)* diddling

escampar 1 *vt* to clear out
2 *vi* to stop raining, clear up

escanciador, -a *nmf* wine waiter

escanciar *vt (vino)* to pour out, serve

escandalera *nf* racket, din, fuss, uproar

escandalizar [14] **1** *vt* to scandalize, shock
2 *vi* to make a racket *o* a din *o* a fuss
3 escandalizarse *vpr* to be shocked (**de** at, by)

escandallar *vt* (**a**) *(fondo del mar)* to sound (**b**) *Com* to fix the price of

escandallo *nm* (**a**) *Náut* sounding lead (**b**) *Com* price fixing, cost accounting

escándalo *nm* (**a**) *(alboroto)* racket, din, fuss, uproar; **armar un e.** to kick up a fuss (**b**) *(asombro)* shock, astonishment (**c**) *(desvergüenza)* scandal, outrage

escandalosamente *adv* scandalously, shockingly, outrageously

escandaloso, -a *adj* (**a**) *(alborotado)* noisy, rowdy (**b**) *(irritante)* scandalous, shocking, outrageous

Escandinavia *n* Scandinavia

escandinavo, -a *adj & nm,f* Scandinavian

escanear *vt Inform Med* to scan

escáner *nm Inform Med (aparato)* scanner; *Med* **hacer un e. a algn** to give sb a scan ❑ **e. (TAC)** CAT scan

escaño *nm* (**a**) *Parl* seat (**b**) *(banco)* bench

escapada *nf* (**a**) *(huida)* escape, flight; *Dep* breakaway; **en una e.** in a jiffy (**b**) *(viaje)* flying visit, quick trip

escapar **1** *vi* to escape, flee, run away; **dejar e. un suspiro** to let out a sigh; **e. a algn** to run away from sb; **escapó de mis manos** it slipped out of my hands
2 escaparse *vpr* (**a**) *(huir)* to escape, run away, get away; **e. con algo** to make off with sth; **e. por un pelo** to have a narrow escape, have a close shave; *Fig* **escapársele a uno algo** to go unnoticed; **este detalle se me había escapado** that detail had escaped my notice (**b**) *(gas etc)* to leak, leak out, escape (**c**) *(autobús, tren)* **se nos escapó el último autobús** we missed the last bus

escaparate *nm* (**a**) *(de tienda)* shop window (**b**) *Col Cuba Ven (armario)* wardrobe

escaparatismo *nm* window dressing

escaparatista *nmf* window dresser

escapatoria *nf* (**a**) *(fuga)* escape, flight; *Fam* **hacer una e.** to get away, skive off (**b**) *(excusa)* way out, loophole

escape *nm* (**a**) *(fuga)* escape, flight, getaway; *Esp* **salir a e.** to rush out (**b**) *(de gas etc)* leak, escape, leakage (**c**) *Téc* exhaust; **tubo de e.** exhaust (pipe)

escaque *nm Ajedrez* square

escaqueado, -a **1** *pp de* **escaquearse**
2 *adj* chequered, *US* checkered

escaquearse *vpr Esp Fam* to shirk, skive off

escarabajo *nm* (**a**) *Zool* beetle, scarab (**b**) *Fam (feo y bajo)* toad (**c**) **escarabajos** scribble *sing*

escaramujo *nm* (**a**) *Bot (rosal silvestre)* wild rose, dog rose; *(fruto)* rosehip (**b**) *Zool* barnacle

escaramuza *nf* (**a**) *Mil* skirmish (**b**) *Fig (riña)* squabble, brush

escarapela *nf* cockade, rosette

escarapelar **1** *vt* (**a**) *Col (manosear)* to rumple (**b**) *Col CRica Ven (descascarar)* to peel; *(desconchar)* to shell
2 *vi Perú (atemorizarse)* to get goose flesh

escarbar *vt* (**a**) *(suelo)* to scratch (**b**) *(dientes)* to pick (**c**) *(fuego)* to poke (**d**) *Fig* to inquire into, investigate

escarceos *nmpl (del caballo)* prancing *sing* ❑ **e. amorosos** romantic adventures, flings

escarcha *nf Meteor* hoarfrost, frost

escarchado, -a **1** *pp de* **escarchar**
2 *adj* (**a**) *Meteor* frosty, frost-covered (**b**) *Culin (fruta)* crystallized, candied

escarchar **1** *vi Meteor* to be frosty *o* freezing
2 *vt* (**a**) *Meteor* to cover in frost (**b**) *Culin (pastel)* to ice; *(fruta)* to crystallize

escarda *nf (azada)* weeding hoe

escardar *vt* to weed

escarlata **1** *adj* scarlet
2 *nf* (**a**) *(color)* scarlet (**b**) *Med* scarlatina, scarlet fever

escarlatina *nf Med* scarlatina, scarlet fever

escarmentar [3] **1** *vt* to punish severely, teach a lesson to
2 *vi* to learn one's lesson; **para que escarmientes** that'll teach you (a lesson)

escarmiento *nm* punishment, lesson; **que esto te sirva de e.** let that be a lesson to you

escarnecer [46] *vt* to scoff at, mock, ridicule

escarnecimiento *nm* mockery, ridicule

escarnio *nm* derision, mockery, ridicule

escarola *nf Bot* curly endive, *US* escarole

escarpa *nf* slope; *Geog Mil* scarp, escarpment

escarpado, -a *adj (inclinado)* steep, sheer; *(abrupto)* craggy

escarpia *nf* spike, hook

escarpín *nm* (**a**) *Am (de bebé)* bootee (**b**) *(de neopreno)* shoe

escasamente *adv* (**a**) *(insuficientemente)* scantly, sparingly, meagerly, *US* meagerly (**b**) *(raramente)* scarcely, hardly, barely

escasear **1** *vt* to be sparing with, skimp on
2 *vi* to be scarce, get scarce; **escasean las provisiones** stores are running low

escasez *nf* (**a**) *(carencia)* scarcity, shortage, lack (**b**) *(mezquindad)* meanness, stinginess

escaso, -a *adj* scarce, scant, limited; *(recursos)* slender; *(dinero)* tight; **andar e. de dinero** to be short of money; **conocimientos escasos** scant knowledge; **e. público** small audience

escatimar *vt (limitar)* to curtail, cut down; *(regatear)* to give sparingly, skimp on; **no escatimó esfuerzo para ...** he spared no efforts to ...

escatología *nf* (**a**) *(sobre excrementos)* scatology (**b**) *Rel* eschatology

escatológico, -a *adj* (**a**) *(de excrementos)* scatological (**b**) *Rel* eschatological

escay *nm* Leatherette

escayola *nf* (**a**) *(estuco)* plaster of Paris, stucco (**b**) *Med* plaster

escayolado, -a **1** *pp de* **escayolar**
2 *adj (brazo, pierna)* in plaster

escayolar *vt Med* to put in plaster, plaster

escena *nf* (**a**) *(acto, fragmento)* scene; **una e. conmovedora** a touching scene; *Fam* **desaparecer de e.** to vanish; *Fam* **hacer** *o* **montar una e.** to make a scene (**b**) *Teat* stage; **entrar en e.** to go on stage; **la segunda e. del primer acto** the second scene of the first act; **poner en e. una obra** to stage a play

escenario *nm* (**a**) *Teat* stage (**b**) *Cin* scenario (**c**) *Fig* scene, setting; **el e. de la tragedia** the scene of the tragedy

escénico, -a *adj* scenic

escenificación *nf (de novela)* dramatization; *(de obra de teatro)* staging

escenificar [59] *vt (novela)* to dramatize; *(obra de teatro)* to stage

escenografía *nf Cin* set design; *Teat* stage design

escenógrafo, -a *nm,f Cin* set designer; *Teat* stage designer

escepticismo *nm* scepticism, *US* skepticism

escéptico, -a *adj & nm,f* sceptic, *US* skeptic

escindible *adj* divisible

escindido, -a 1 *pp de* escindir
2 *adj* un grupo e. a breakaway group

escindir 1 *vt* to split, divide
2 escindirse *vpr* to split (off) (en into)

escisión *nf* (a) *(del átomo)* splitting (b) *(de partido político)* split

esclarecedor, -a *adj* illuminating

esclarecer [46] *vt* (a) *(explicar)* to clear up, shed light on (b) *(entendimiento)* to enlighten

esclarecido, -a 1 *pp de* esclarecer
2 *adj* illustrious, distinguished

esclarecimiento *nm* clearing up, elucidation

esclava *nf* *(brazalete)* bangle

esclavismo *nm* (system of) slavery

esclavista 1 *adj* pro-slavery
2 *nmf* supporter of slavery

esclavitud *nf* slavery, servitude

esclavizar [14] *vt* to enslave

esclavo, -a *adj & nm,f* slave; *Fig* ser e. de algo to be a slave to sth

esclerosis *nf Med*· sclerosis ❑ e. **múltiple** multiple sclerosis

esclusa *nf* lock, sluicegate, floodgate

escoba *nf* brush, broom; **pasar la e.** to sweep up; *Fam* estar como una e. to be as thin as a rake

escobazo *nm* blow with a brush o broom; **echar a algn a escobazos** to boot sb out

escobilla *nf* small brush; *Aut* windscreen wiper blade

escobillar *vt Am* (a) *(cepillar)* to brush (b) *(zapatear)* to tap one's feet quickly on

escobón *nm* large brush o broom

escocedura *nf* (a) *(herida)* sore (b) *(dolor)* soreness, smarting

escocer [15] **1** *vi* to sting, smart; *Fig* to hurt
2 escocerse *vpr* *(piel)* to be sore; *(persona)* to have a rash

escocés, -esa 1 *adj* Scottish, Scots; **falda escocesa** kilt
2 *nm,f* *(hombre)* Scotsman; *(mujer)* Scotswoman

escoch *nm Andes RP véase* **Scotch®**

Escocia *n* Scotland

escoger [52] *vt* to choose, select, pick out; *Pol* to elect; **e. del montón** to choose from the pile; **no hay donde e.** they are all just as bad; **tener donde e.** to have a good choice

escogido, -a 1 *pp de* escoger
2 *adj* chosen, selected; *(en calidad)* choice, select; *Lit* **obras escogidas** selected works

escolanía *nf* (church) choir

escolar 1 *adj* scholastic, school; **curso** o **año e.** school year; **vacaciones escolares** school holidays
2 *nmf* *(niño)* schoolboy; *(niña)* schoolgirl

escolaridad *nf* schooling, education; **libro de e.** school record book

escolarización *nf* schooling

escolarizar [14] *vt* to provide with schools

escolástico, -a *adj* scholastic

escollera *nf* breakwater, jetty

escollo *nm* reef, rock; *Fig* pitfall, snag

escolopendra *nf Zool* centipede

escolta *nf* escort; *Náut* convoy; **dar e.** to escort, accompany ❑ e. **personal** bodyguard

escoltar *vt* to escort, accompany; *Náut* to convoy

escombrera *nf Br* tip, *US* garbage dump

escombros *nmpl* rubble *sing*, debris *sing*

esconder 1 *vt* to hide (de from), conceal (de from)
2 esconderse *vpr* to hide (de from), hide oneself

escondidas: a escondidas *adv* secretly

escondite *nm* (a) *(lugar)* hiding place, hide-out (b) *(juego)* hide-and-seek; **jugar al e.** to play hide-and-seek

escondrijo *nm* hiding place, hide-out

escoñado, -a *adj Vulg* knackered; **esta máquina está escoñada** this machine's had it

escopeta *nf* shotgun; e. **de aire comprimido** air gun; e. **de cañones recortados** sawn-off shotgun

escopetazo *nm* (a) *(tiro)* gunshot (b) *(herida)* gunshot wound (c) *Fig* *(malas noticias)* bombshell

escopeteado, -a *adj Esp Fam* ir o salirse e. to be off like a shot

escoplo *nm* chisel

escora *nf Náut* (a) *(línea de fuerte)* load line (b) *(inclinación)* list

escorar *vi Náut* to list, heel; **el barco va escorado** the boat has a list; e. **a babor** to list to port

escorbuto *nm Med* scurvy

escoria *nf* (a) *(metal)* dross; *(metal, carbón)* slag (b) *Fig* scum, dregs *pl* (c) **escorias** volcanic ash *sing*

escoriación *nf* scraping

escorial *nm* slag heap

escoriar *vt* to scrape

Escorpio *nm Astrol Astron* Scorpio

escorpión *nm Zool* scorpion

escorzar [14] *vt Arte* to foreshorten

escorzo *nm* foreshortening

escota *nf Náut* sheet; **escotas mayores** main sheets

escotado, -a 1 *pp de* escotar[1]
2 *adj Cost* low-cut, low-necked; **ir muy e.** to wear a low-necked dress
3 *nm Cost* low neckline

escotadura *nf Cost* low neckline

escotar[1] *vt* (a) *Cost* to cut a low neckline in, cut out the neck of (b) *(un río)* to draw water from

escotar[2] *vt* to share the cost of; *(pareja)* to go Dutch on

escote[1] *nm Cost* low neckline

escote[2] *nm Esp* pagar a e. to share the cost of; *(pareja)* to go Dutch on

escotilla *nf Náut* hatch, hatchway

escotillón *nm* (a) *Náut* small hatch, scuttle (b) *Teat* trap door

escozor *nm* (a) *(dolor)* stinging, smarting (b) *Fig* *(sentimiento)* pain, grief

escriba *nm* scribe

escribanía *nf* (a) *(escritorio)* writing desk (b) *(material)* writing set (c) *(oficio)* clerkship (d) *(oficina)* clerk's office (e) *Andes CRica RP* *(notaría)* = notary public's position and duties

escribano, -a 1 *nm,f Andes CRica RP* *(notario)* notary (public)
2 *nm Orn* bunting; e. **cerillo** yellowhammer; e. **palustre** reed bunting

escribiente *nmf* clerk

escribir *(pp escrito)* **1** *vt* to write; e. **a mano** to write in longhand; e. **a máquina** to type; **se escribe con g y b** it is spelt with a g and a b
2 escribirse *vpr* to write to each other, correspond

escrito, -a 1 *pp de* **escribir**
2 *adj* written, stated; **declarar por e.** to give a written statement; **e. a mano** handwritten, in longhand; **por e.** in writing, in black and white
3 *nm* **(a)** *(documento)* writing, document, letter, text **(b)** **escritos** *Lit (obras)* writings, works

escritor, -a *nm,f* writer

escritorio *nm* **(a)** *(mueble)* writing desk, bureau **(b)** *esp Am (oficina)* office; **objetos de e.** stationery **(c)** *Inform* desktop

escritura *nf* **(a)** *(de un idioma)* writing, script, alphabet; **e. fonética** phonetic script **(b)** *(de persona)* writing, handwriting; **e. a máquina** typing **(c)** *Jur* deed, document; **e. de propiedad** title deed **(d)** **Sagradas Escrituras** *Rel* Holy Scriptures

escriturar *vt* to formalize legally; *(una propiedad)* to register

escroto *nm Anat* scrotum

escrúpulo *nm* **(a)** *(recelo)* scruple, qualm, doubt; **no tuvo escrúpulos en hacerlo** he had no scruples about doing it; **una persona sin escrúpulos** an unscrupulous person **(b)** *(aprensión)* fussiness; **tener escrúpulos** to be finicky *o* fussy **(c)** *(china)* pebble, stone

escrupulosamente *adv* scrupulously

escrupulosidad *nf* scrupulousness, extreme care

escrupuloso, -a *adj* **(a)** *(minucioso)* scrupulous **(b)** *(quisquilloso)* finicky, fussy

escrutador, -a *adj* scrutinizing, searching, penetrating

escrutar *vt* **(a)** *(examen)* to scrutinize, examine carefully **(b)** *(votos)* to count

escrutinio *nm* **(a)** *(examinar)* examination **(b)** *(votos)* counting of votes

escuadra *nf* **(a)** *(instrumento)* square; **corte a e.** cut at right angles; **e. de dibujo** set square **(b)** *(grupo) Mil* squad; *Mil (de buques)* squadron; *(de coches)* fleet

escuadrar *vt* to square

escuadrilla *nf Mil* squadron

escuadrón *nm Mil Av* squadron

escualidez *nf* **(a)** *(delgadez)* emaciation, extreme thinness **(b)** *(suciedad)* squalor

escuálido, -a *adj* **(a)** *(delgado)* emaciated, extremely thin **(b)** *(sucio)* squalid

escualo *nm (pez)* (spiny) shark

escucha 1 *nf* listening, listening-in; **escuchas telefónicas** phone tapping *sing*; **estar a la e., estar en e.** to be listening out (**de** for)
2 *nm Mil* scout

escuchar 1 *vt* **(a)** *(sonido)* to hear **(b)** *(consejo, aviso)* to listen to, heed, pay attention to
2 escucharse *vpr* to declaim, speak in an affected way

escuchimizado, -a *Esp Fam adj* puny, scrawny

escudar 1 *vt* **(a)** *(amparar con el escudo)* to shield **(b)** *Fig (proteger)* to shield, protect, defend
2 escudarse *vpr* to protect *o* shield oneself; **e. con algo** to hide behind sth, use sth as an excuse; **e. del peligro** to protect oneself from danger

escudería *nf Aut* racing team

escudero *nm Hist* page; *(que llevaba escudo)* squire

escudilla *nf* bowl

escudo *nm* **(a)** *(arma)* shield **(b)** *(blasón)* coat of arms **(c)** *(moneda)* escudo

escudriñar *vt* *(inquirir)* to inquire into, investigate; *(examinar)* to examine, scrutinize

escuela *nf* **(a)** *(establecimiento)* school □ **e. de artes y oficios** Technical College; **e. de Bellas Artes** Art School; **e.**

de conducir driving school; **e. de equitación** riding school; **e. de idiomas** language school; *Am* **e. de manejo** driving school; **e. privada** private school; **e. pública** state school **e. universitaria** = section of a university which awards diplomas in a vocational discipline (e.g. engineering, business) after three years of study **(b)** *(doctrina)* school; **gente de la vieja e.** people of the old school **(c)** *(experiencia)* experience, instruction; **la e. de la vida** the university of life

escuetamente *adv* simply, baldly

escueto, -a *adj* plain, unadorned, bare

escuincle, -a *Méx Fam* **1** *adj* young
2 *nm,f* nipper, kid

escuicar [59] *vt Am (registrar)* to search

esculpir *vt Arte (gen)* to sculpt, sculpture; *(en madera)* to carve; *(en metales)* to engrave

escultismo *nm* scouting

escultor, -a *nm,f (gen) (hombre)* sculptor; *(mujer)* sculptress; *(de madera)* woodcarver; *(de metales)* engraver

escultórico, -a *adj* sculptural

escultura *nf (gen)* sculpture; *(madera)* carving

escultural *adj (en arte)* sculptural; *(persona)* statuesque

escupidera *nf* **(a)** *(recipiente)* spittoon, *US* cuspidor **(b)** *Andes RP (orinal)* chamberpot

escupidor *nm Andes PRico* chamber pot

escupir 1 *vi* **(a)** *(gen)* to spit; **e. a algn** to spit at sb **(b)** *Vulg (confesar)* to come clean, confess
2 *vt* **(a)** *(sujeto: persona, animal)* to spit out **(b)** *Fig (palabras, insultos)* to spit out

escupitajo *nm Vulg* gob, spit, phlegm

escurreplatos *nm inv* dish rack

escurridero *nm* draining board

escurridizo, -a *adj* **(a)** *(resbaladizo)* slippery **(b)** *Fig (elusivo)* elusive, slippery

escurrido, -a 1 *pp de* **escurrir**
2 *adj* **(a)** *(ropa)* tightfitting **(b)** *(mujer)* slim-hipped
3 *nm (de lavadora)* spin-drying programme

escurridor *nm* colander; *(escurreplatos)* dish rack, draining board

escurrir 1 *vt (gen)* to drain; *(ropa)* to wring out; *Culin* to drain
2 *vi (líquido)* to drip, trickle; *(objeto)* to slip, slide; *Fig* **e. el bulto** to dodge the issue
3 escurrirse *vpr* **(a)** *(gen)* to drain **(b)** *(líquido)* to drip, trickle; *(objeto)* to slip, slide **(c)** *(escapar)* to run *o* slip away **(d)** *(decir más de lo debido)* to let sth slip

escúter *nm* (motor) scooter

esdrújula *nf Ling* word stressed on the third-last syllable

esdrújulo, -a *adj Ling* stressed on the third-last syllable

ese¹ *nf* **(a)** *(letra)* = name of the letter S in Spanish **(b)** **eses** zigzags; **hacer e.** to zigzag; *(persona)* to stagger about

ese, -a² *(pl* **esos, -as)** *adj dem* **(a)** *(gen) (singular)* that; **esa casa** that house; *Pey* **el hombre e.** that bloke **(b)** **esos, -as** those; **e. coches** those cars

ése, -a *(pl* **ésos, -as)** *pron dem m,f* **(a)** *(gen) (singular)* that one; *(el anterior)* the former; **coge é. de ahí** take that one there; **entraron Pilar y Elvira, ésa vestida de azul** Pilar and Elvira came in, the former dressed in blue **(b)** **ésos, -as** those (ones); *(los anteriores)* the former (ones); *Fam* **¡ni por ésas!** no way!; *Fam* **¡no me vengas con ésas!** come off it!

esencia *nf* **(a)** *(lo principal, lo básico)* essence; **eso dijo en e.** that's briefly what he said; **quinta e.** quintessence **(b)** *(perfume)* essence, scent

esencial 1 *adj* essential; **lo e.** the main thing
2 *nm* essential

esencialmente *adv* essentially

esfera *nf* (**a**) *(figura)* sphere, globe; **en forma de e.** spherical, globular (**b**) *(del reloj)* face (**c**) *Fig* sphere, plane, field; **eso está fuera de mi e.** that isn't my province

esférico, -a 1 *adj* spherical
2 *nm Ftb* ball

esferoide *nm* spheroid

esfinge *nf* sphinx; *Fig* **parecer una e.** to be inscrutable *o* enigmatic

esfínter *nm Anat* sphincter

esforzado, -a 1 *pp de* **esforzar**
2 *adj (arrojado)* energetic, vigorous; *(valiente)* bold

esforzar [31] **1** *vt (voz, vista)* to strain; **tuve que e. la voz** I had to strain my voice
2 esforzarse *vpr* to exert oneself, make an effort, try hard; **e. por hacer algo** to strive to do sth

esfuerzo *nm* effort, endeavour, *US* endeavor, exertion; *(la imaginación)* stretch; **sin e.** effortlessly

esfumar 1 *vt (contorno)* to soften; *(colores)* to tone down
2 esfumarse *vpr* to fade away, melt away; *(persona)* to disappear, vanish

esgrima *nf Dep* fencing

esgrimidor, -a *nm,f* fencer

esgrimir 1 *vt* (**a**) *(una espada)* to wield, brandish (**b**) *Fig (un argumento)* to put forward
2 *vi* to fence

esguince *nm* (**a**) *Med* sprain; **me hice un e. en el tobillo** I sprained my ankle (**b**) *(ademán)* swerve, dodge; **dar un e.** to swerve, dodge (**c**) *(gesto de disgusto)* frown

eslabón *nm* link; **el e. perdido** the missing link

eslabonamiento *nm* linking

eslabonar *vt* to link together, join; *Fig* to link, connect

eslalon *(pl* **eslalons)** *nm Dep* slalom

eslavo, -a 1 *adj* Slav, Slavonic
2 *nm,f (persona)* Slav
3 *nm (idioma)* Slavonic, Slavic

eslip *(pl* **eslips)** *nm (prenda)* men's briefs *pl,* underpants *pl*

eslogan *nm* slogan; **e. publicitario** catchword

eslora *nf Náut* length; **e. máxima** overall length

eslovaco, -a 1 *adj & nm,f* Slovak, Slovakian
2 *nm (lengua)* Slovak

Eslovaquia *n* Slovakia

Eslovenia *n* Slovenia

esloveno, -a 1 *adj & nm,f* Slovenian
2 *nm (lengua)* Slovenian

esmaltado, -a 1 *pp de* **esmaltar**
2 *adj* enamelled, *US* enameled
3 *nm* enamelling, *US* enameling

esmaltar *vt* (**a**) *(cubrir)* to enamel; *(las uñas)* to varnish (**b**) *Fig (adornar)* to embellish, adorn

esmalte *nm* (**a**) *(barniz)* enamel; *(de uñas)* nail polish *o* varnish (**b**) *Fig (esplendor)* splendour, *US* splendor

esmeradamente *adv* neatly, carefully

esmerado, -a 1 *pp de* **esmerar**
2 *adj (trabajo)* neat, careful; *(persona)* conscientious, painstaking, careful

esmeralda *nf* emerald

esmerar 1 *vt* to polish
2 esmerarse *vpr* to take great pains (over sth), do one's best

esmeril *nm* emery; **papel de e.** emery paper

esmerilado, -a *adj (pulido)* polished with emery; *(translúcido)* frosted

esmerilar *vt (vidrio) (pulir)* to polish with emery; *(deslustrar)* to frost

esmero *nm* painstaking care, neatness

esmirriado, -a *adj Fam* puny, scraggy

esmoquin *nm (prenda) Br* dinner jacket, *US* tuxedo

esnifar *vt Argot (drogas)* to sniff

esnob *(pl* **esnobs) 1** *adj (persona)* snobbish; *(restaurante etc)* posh
2 *nmf* snob

esnobismo *nm* snobbery, snobbishness

ESO ['eso] *nf Esp (abrev de* **Enseñanza Secundaria Obligatoria)** = mainstream secondary education for pupils aged 12-16

eso *pron dem neut* that; **¿cómo es e.?** how come?; **¡e. es!** that's it!; **e. es un rollo** that's a drag; **no es e.** it's not that; **por e.** that's why; **¿y e. qué?** so what?; *Fam* **a e. de las diez** around ten; *Fam* **e. de las Navidades sale muy caro** the whole Christmas deal costs a fortune

esofágico, -a *adj Anat* oesophageal, *US* esophageal

esófago *nm* oesophagus, *US* esophagus, gullet

esos, -as *adj dem pl véase* **ese, -a²**

ésos, -as *pron dem m,fpl véase* **ése, -a**

esotérico, -a *adj* esoteric

esoterismo *nm* esotericism

espabilado, -a 1 *pp de* **espabilar**
2 *adj* (**a**) *(despierto)* wide awake (**b**) *Fig (adulto)* smart, on the ball; *(niño)* bright, sharp, clever; **su hijo es muy e.** her little boy is very bright

espabilar 1 *vt* (**a**) *(una vela)* to snuff out (**b**) *Fig* to wake up, wise up; *(un niño)* to bring forward
2 espabilarse *vpr* to wake up, waken up; *(darse prisa)* to look sharp, hurry up

espachurrar *vt* to squash

espaciado, -a *adj* at regular intervals

espaciador *nm Tip* space-bar

espacial *adj* spatial, spacial

espaciar 1 *vt* to space out
2 espaciarse *vpr* to spread oneself out, stretch out

espacio *nm* (**a**) *(capacidad, extensión)* space; *(de tiempo)* length; **mecanografiado a doble e.** double-spaced ❏ **e. aéreo** air space; **e. verde** green area *(in town or city)*; **e. Web** Web space (**b**) *(hueco libre)* room, space; **nos falta e.** we're short of space; **ocupa mucho e.** it takes up a lot of room (**c**) *Rad TV* programme, *US* program ❏ **e. electoral** party political broadcast; **e. publicitario** advertising slot

espacioso, -a *adj* spacious, roomy; *(movimiento)* slow

espada 1 *nf* (**a**) *(arma)* sword; **desnudar la e.** to draw one's sword; *Fig* **entrar con e. en mano** to come in looking for trouble; *Fig* **e. de dos filos** double-edged sword; **estar entre la e. y la pared** to be between the devil and the deep blue sea ❏ **pez e.** swordfish (**b**) *Naipes* spade; **as de espadas** ace of spades
2 *nm Taur* matador

espadachín *nm* swordsman

espadaña *nf* (**a**) *Arquit* exposed belfry (**b**) *Bot* bulrush

espalda *nf* (**a**) *Anat* back; **espaldas** back *sing;* **a espaldas de algn** behind sb's back; **ancho de espaldas** broad-shouldered; **cargado de espaldas** round-shouldered, stooping; **por la e.** from behind; **volver la e. a** to turn one's back on sb; *Fig* **caerse de espaldas** *(sorprenderse)* to fall flat on one's back; *Fig* **echarse algo a la e.** to take sth on; *Fig* **tener guardadas las espaldas** *(tener protección)* to have good connections; *Fig* **tener las espaldas anchas** to have broad shoulders, be responsible; *Fam* **tira de**

espaldas it knocks you out ▫ *Fam* **e. mojada** *US* wetback (**b**) *Natación* backstroke

espaldar *nm (de silla)* back

espaldarazo *nm* blow to the back; **eso le dio el e. (definitivo)** that finally earned her widespread recognition

espalderas *nfpl* wall bars

espaldilla *nf* (**a**) *Anat* shoulder blade (**b**) *Culin (de ternera etc)* shoulder

espantada *nf (de animales)* stampede; *(de personas)* bolt, stampede; **dar la e.** to stampede, run away

espantadizo, -a *adj* easily frightened

espantajo *nm* (**a**) *(muñeco)* scarecrow (**b**) *Fig (cosa)* sight, fright (**c**) *Fig (persona)* fright, sight; **parecía un auténtico e. tras tres meses en el desierto** he looked a real sight after having spent three months in the desert

espantapájaros *nm inv* scarecrow

espantar 1 *vt* (**a**) *(asustar)* to frighten, scare, scare off (**b**) *(ahuyentar)* to frighten away
2 espantarse *vpr* (**a**) *(asustarse)* to get *o* feel frightened (**de** of), get *o* feel scared (**de** of) (**b**) *(asombrarse)* to be amazed (**de** at) *o* astonished (**de** at)

espanto *nm* (**a**) *(miedo)* fright, terror (**b**) *(asombro)* amazement, astonishment; *Fam* **de e.** dreadful, shocking; *Fam* **hace un frío de e.** it's freezing cold; *Fam* **¡qué e.!** how awful! (**c**) *Am (fantasma)* ghost

espantoso, -a *adj* (**a**) *(horrible)* frightening, dreadful (**b**) *(pasmoso)* amazing, astonishing

España *n* Spain

español, -a 1 *adj* Spanish
2 *nm,f (gen)* Spaniard; *(hombre)* Spanish man; *(mujer)* Spanish woman; **los españoles** the Spanish
3 *nm (idioma)* Spanish

españolada *nf Pey* something pseudo-Spanish

españolismo *nm* (**a**) *(carácter, naturaleza)* Spanishness, Spanish quality (**b**) *(apego, afecto)* love of Spain and Spanish things

españolista 1 *adj* pro-Spanish, Hispanophile
2 *nmf* Hispanophile

españolizar [14] **1** *vt* to make Spanish, hispanicize
2 españolizarse *vpr* to adopt Spanish ways

esparadrapo *nm Br* (sticking) plaster, *US* Band-aid®

esparcido, -a 1 *pp de* **esparcir**
2 *adj* (**a**) *(desparramado)* scattered; *(rumor)* widespread (**b**) *(carácter)* frank, open; *(divertido)* cheerful

esparcimiento *nm* (**a**) *(diseminación)* scattering, spreading (**b**) *Fig* relaxation, amusement, recreation

esparcir [72] **1** *vt (papeles, semillas)* to scatter; *Fig (un rumor)* to spread
2 esparcirse *vpr* (**a**) *(diseminarse)* to spread out, scatter, be scattered (**b**) *(entretenerse)* to relax, amuse oneself

espárrago *nm* (**a**) *Bot* asparagus; **e. triguero** wild asparagus; *Fam* **¡vete a freír espárragos!** get lost! (**b**) *Téc* stud

esparraguera *nf* (**a**) *Bot* asparagus plant (**b**) *Culin* asparagus dish

espartano, -a 1 *adj* Spartan; *Fig* Spartan, austere
2 *nm,f* Spartan

esparto *nm* esparto grass

espasmo *nm* spasm

espasmódico, -a *adj* spasmodic, jerky

espástico, -a *adj Med* spastic

espatarrarse *vpr* to slip and fall with one's legs wide open, sprawl

espátula *nf Culin Med* spatula; *Arte* palette knife; *(de albañil)* bricklayer's trowel; *(de empapelador)* stripping knife

especia *nf* spice

especial *adj* (**a**) *(adecuado)* special; **en e.** especially; **e. para ...** suitable for ...; **sólo en un caso e.** only in special cases; **tiene un sabor e.** it has a distinctive taste (**b**) *(persona)* fussy, finicky (**para** about)

especialidad *nf* speciality, *US* specialty; *Educ US* major, = main subject of degree; **no es de mi e.** it's not in my line

especialista *nmf* (**a**) *(experto)* specialist (**b**) *Cin* stand-in; *(hombre)* stuntman; *(mujer)* stuntwoman

especialización *nf* specialization

especializado, -a 1 *pp de* **especializarse**
2 *adj* specialized; **estar e. en algo** to be a specialist in sth, specialize in sth

especializarse [14] *vpr* to specialize (**en** in)

especialmente *adv (exclusivamente)* specially; *(particularmente)* especially

especie *nf* (**a**) *Biol* species *inv* ▫ **e. protegida** protected species (**b**) *(clase)* kind, sort; **me gusta esa e. de gente** I like that kind of person; **una e. de sopa** a kind of soup (**c**) *(tema, noticia)* matter, idea, notion; **corría entre los refugiados una e. extraña** there was a strange idea going about amongst the refugees (**d**) **en e.** in kind; **pagar en e.** to pay in kind

especiero *nm* spice rack

especificación *nf* specification; **sin e. de hora** without specifying the time

específicamente *adv* specifically

especificar [59] *vt* to specify

especificidad *nf* specificity

específico, -a 1 *adj* specific; **peso e.** specific gravity
2 *nm Med (medicamento)* specific

espécimen *(pl* especímenes*)* *nm* specimen

espectacular *adj* spectacular

espectacularidad *nf* spectacular nature; **su nuevo número de acrobacia es de gran e.** his latest acrobatic feat is really spectacular

espectacularmente *adv* spectacularly

espectáculo *nm* (**a**) *(escena)* spectacle, sight; **dar un e.** to make a scene, make a spectacle of oneself (**b**) *Teat Cin TV* show, performance; **montar un e.** to put on a show

espectador, -a *nm,f Dep* spectator; *(de accidente, espectáculo improvisado)* onlooker; *Teat Cin* member of the audience; **los espectadores** the audience *sing*; *TV* the viewers

espectral *adj* spectral, ghostly

espectro *nm* (**a**) *Fís* spectrum (**b**) *(fantasma)* spectre, *US* specter, ghost, apparition (**c**) *Fig (persona)* ghost; **parece un e.** he looks like a ghost (**d**) *(gama)* range; **un amplio e. de ideologías** a wide range of political opinions

espectrógrafo *nm Fís* spectrograph

espectroscopia *nf Fís* spectroscopy

espectroscopio *nm Fís* spectroscope

especulación *nf* speculation; **e. del suelo** land speculation

especulador, -a *nm,f Fin* speculator

especular 1 *vt (conjeturar)* to speculate about, reflect on
2 *vi* (**a**) *(comerciar)* to speculate (**en** on) (**b**) *(hacer cábalas)* to speculate, guess (**sobre** about)

especulativo, -a *adj* speculative, theoretical

espejear *vi* to shine like a mirror, gleam

espejismo *nm* (**a**) *(imagen)* mirage (**b**) *Fig* mirage, illusion

espejo *nm* (**a**) *(para mirarse)* mirror; *Aut* **e. retrovisor** rear-view mirror (**b**) *Fig* mirror, reflection; **la cara es el e. del alma** one's face is the window of one's soul

espejuelos *nmpl* spectacles

espeleología *nf Dep* potholing, speleology

espeleólogo, -a *nm,f Dep* potholer, speleologist

espeluznante *adj* hair-raising, horrifying

espeluznar *vt* to horrify, terrify

espera *nf* (**a**) *(acción de esperar)* wait, waiting; **en e. de ...** waiting for ...; **estar a la e.** to be waiting o expecting; **sala de e.** waiting room (**b**) *(paciencia)* calm, patience; **tener e.** to have patience

esperanto *nm Ling* Esperanto

esperanza *nf* hope, expectance; **dar esperanzas a algn** to give sb hope; **e. de vida** life expectancy; **estar en estado de buena e.** to be expecting o pregnant; **tener la e. puesta en algo** to have one's hopes pinned on sth

esperanzado, -a *adj* hopeful

esperanzador, -a *adj* encouraging

esperanzar [14] **1** *vt* to give hope to
   2 esperanzarse *vpr* to have hope

esperar 1 *vt* (**a**) *(tener esperanza)* to hope for, expect; **e. la victoria** to hope for victory; **te esperábamos ayer** we were expecting you yesterday (**b**) *(+ que)* to hope (that); **espero que así sea** I hope it's like that; **espero que sí** I hope so; **espero que vengas** I hope you'll come; **no se podía e. menos** it was the least you could hope for (**c**) *(aguardar)* to wait for, await; **espero a mi hermano** I'm waiting for my brother (**d**) *(suponer)* to expect; **espero la visita de un amigo** I'm expecting a friend to call (**e**) *(+ infin)* to hope to; **espero ganar el concurso** I hope to win the competition (**f**) *Fig (bebé)* to expect
   2 *vi* **quien espera desespera** a watched pot never boils; **espera un momento** wait a moment, hold on; **ya puedes e. sentado** you'll be waiting till the cows come home

esperma *nm Biol* sperm ❑ **e. de ballena** spermaceti

espermaticida *adj Med* spermicide

espermatozoide *nm Biol* spermatozoid

espermicida 1 *adj* spermicidal
   2 *nm* spermicide

esperpéntico, -a *adj (grotesco)* grotesque, macabre

esperpento *nm* (**a**) *Lit* = genre created by Don Ramón del Valle-Inclán (1866-1936) (**b**) *(persona)* fright, sight; **va hecho un e.** he looks a real sight (**c**) *(sin sentido)* absurdity, piece of nonsense

espesante *nm* thickener

espesar 1 *vt* to make denser o thicker; *Culin (una salsa)* to thicken
   2 espesarse *vpr* to thicken, get thicker

espeso, -a *adj* (**a**) *(bosque, niebla, muchedumbre)* dense; *(líquido, pared, libro)* thick; *(masa)* stiff (**b**) *Perú Ven Fam (pesado)* **¡no seas e.!** don't be a pain!

espesor *nm* denseness, thickness; **tres metros de e.** three metres thick

espesura *nf* (**a**) *(grosor)* denseness, density (**b**) *(de un bosque)* thicket, overgrown place

espetar *vt* (**a**) *Culin (carne)* to skewer (**b**) *(clavar)* to stab (**c**) *Fig (decir)* to blurt out; **le espetó la sorpresa** he sprang the surprise on him

espía *nmf* spy

espiar [32] *vt* to spy on, watch

espichar *vt Vulg* **espicharla** *(morir)* to kick the bucket

espiche *nm* speech

espiga *nf* (**a**) *(de trigo)* ear (**b**) *Téc* pin; *(de cuchillo)* tang; *(de tornillo)* bolt; *(de clavo)* shank (**c**) *(de campana)* clapper (**d**) *Astron* E. Spica

espigado, -a 1 *pp de* **espigar**
   2 *adj* (**a**) *Bot* ripe (**b**) *(con forma de espiga)* ear-shaped (**c**) *Fig (alto y delgado)* tall, lanky

espigar [38] **1** *vt* to glean; *Fig* **e. datos/noticias** to glean information/news
   2 espigarse *vpr (persona)* to shoot up

espigón *nm* (**a**) *(punta)* sharp point, spike (**b**) *(mazorca)* ear of corn (**c**) *(mar)* breakwater, groyne, spur

espín *nm Fís* spin

espina *nf* (**a**) *Bot* thorn; *Fig* **no hay rosa sin espinas** you've got to take the rough with the smooth (**b**) *(del pez)* bone (**c**) *Anat* **e. dorsal** spinal column, spine, backbone (**d**) *Fig* doubt, worry, suspicion; **ése me da mala e.** I'm suspicious about that one, there's something fishy about that one

espinaca *nf* spinach; *Culin* **espinacas a la crema** creamed spinach

espinal *adj* spinal; **médula e.** spinal marrow

espinazo *nm Anat* spine, backbone; *Fam* **doblar el e.** to bow and scrape

espinilla *nf* (**a**) *Anat* shin (**b**) *(barro)* blackhead

espinillera *nf Dep* shin pad

espino *nm Bot* (**a**) *(planta)* hawthorn; **e. albar** common hawthorn; **e. negro** blackthorn (**b**) *(alambrada)* barbed wire

espinoso, -a *adj también Fig* thorny

espionaje *nm* spying, espionage; **e. industrial** industrial espionage; **novela de e.** spy story

espira *nf* spire

espiración *nf* breathing out, expiration, exhalation

espiral 1 *adj* spiral; **escalera e.** spiral staircase
   2 *nf* spiral; *(de reloj)* hairspring

espirar 1 *vt (respirar)* to breathe out, exhale
   2 *vi* to breathe

espiritismo *nm* spiritualism

espiritista 1 *adj* spiritualistic
   2 *nmf* spiritualist

espíritu *nm* (**a**) *(principio de vida)* spirit; **exhalar el e.** to give up the ghost ❑ **e. de equipo** team spirit (**b**) *(licores)* spirits *pl*; **e. de vino** spirits of wine, alcohol (**c**) *Rel* soul; **el E. Santo** the Holy Ghost; **espíritus malignos** evil spirits (**d**) *(fantasma)* ghost (**e**) *Fig (ánimo)* spirit; **e. de cuerpo** esprit de corps, corporal spirit; **e. combativo** fighting spirit; **e. deportivo** sportsmanship (**f**) *(idea central)* essence, spirit, soul; **el e. de la ley** the spirit of the law

espiritual *adj* spiritual

espiritualidad *nf* spirituality

espiritualismo *nm* spiritualism

espiritualista *adj* spiritualist

espita *nf* spigot, *Br* tap, *US* faucet

espléndidamente *adv* (**a**) *(magníficencia)* splendidly, magnificently, grandly (**b**) *(generosamente)* lavishly, generously

espléndido, -a *adj* (**a**) *(magnífico)* splendid, magnificent, grand (**b**) *(generoso)* lavish, generous

esplendor *nm* (**a**) *(resplandor)* brilliance (**b**) *Fig (lustre)* splendour, *US* splendor, magnificence, grandeur (**c**) *(auge)* glory

esplendoroso, -a *adj* (**a**) *(luz)* brilliant, radiant (**b**) *(grandioso)* magnificent

espliego *nm Bot* lavender

esplín *nm* (*pl* **esplines**) melancholy, depression

espolear *vt* (**a**) *(un caballo)* to spur on (**b**) *Fig (estimular)* to spur on, encourage

espoleta[1] *nf Mil* fuse; **quitar la e. de** to defuse

espoleta[2] *nf Anat (de ave)* wishbone

espolio *nm véase* **expolio**

espolón *nm* (**a**) *(de caballo)* fetlock (**b**) *Geog* spur (**c**) *(malecón)* sea-wall; *Arquit (tajamar)* buttress (**d**) *Náut* ram; **embestir con el e.** to ram

espolvorear *vt* to dust, powder, sprinkle (**de** with)

esponja *nf* sponge; *Fig* **beber como una e., ser una e.** to drink like a fish; *Fam* **pasar la e.** to let it drop, forget about it

esponjar 1 *vt* to fluff up
2 esponjarse *vpr* (**a**) *(tejido)* to go *o* become fluffy (**b**) *(bizcocho)* to rise

esponjosidad *nf (de toalla)* fluffiness; *(de bizcocho)* lightness, fluffiness

esponjoso, -a *adj (tejido)* fluffy; *(bizcocho)* light, fluffy

esponsales *nmpl* betrothal *sing*, engagement *sing*

esponsorizar [14] *vt* to sponsor

espontáneamente *adv* spontaneously

espontaneidad *nf* spontaneity; **obrar/hablar con e.** to act/speak naturally

espontáneo, -a 1 *adj* spontaneous; *(persona)* natural, unaffected; *(discurso)* impromptu, unprepared
2 *nm Taur* = spectator who spontaneously joins in the bullfight

espora *nf Biol* spore

esporádico, -a *adj* sporadic

esposa 1 *nf Am (anillo)* episcopal ring
2 esposas *nfpl (objeto)* handcuffs

esposado, -a 1 *pp de* **esposar**
2 *adj* handcuffed

esposar *vt* to handcuff

esposo, -a *nm,f* spouse; *(hombre)* husband; *(mujer)* wife

espray *(pl* **esprays**) *nm* spray

esprint *(pl* **esprints**) *nm* sprint

esprintar *vi* to sprint

esprínter *(pl* **esprínters**) *nmf* sprinter

espuela *nf* (**a**) *(en el talón)* spur; *Fig (última copa)* one for the road; *Fig* **poner espuelas a algn** to spur sb on (**b**) *Am (de aves)* spur

espuerta *nf* basket; **dinero a espuertas** bags *o* stacks of money

espulgar [38] *vt* (**a**) *(de pulgas, piojos)* to delouse, rid of fleas (**b**) *Fig (examinar)* to scrutinize

espuma *nf* (**a**) *(gen)* foam; *(olas)* surf; *(de cerveza)* froth, head; *(de jabón)* lather; **echarse e.** to foam, froth □ **e. de afeitar** shaving foam (**b**) *(impurezas)* scum

espumadera *nf Culin* spoon for skimming

espumante *nm* foaming agent

espumar 1 *vt* to skim
2 *vi (mar)* to foam; *(jabón)* to lather; *(cerveza)* to froth; *(cava)* to sparkle

espumarajo *nm (de la boca)* foam, froth; **echando espumarajos** foaming at the mouth

espumilla *nf CAm Ecuad* meringue

espumillón *nm* tinsel

espumoso, -a *adj* frothy, foamy, foaming; *(jabón)* lathery; *(vino)* sparkling

espúreo, -a *adj*, **espurio, -a** *adj* (**a**) *(niño)* illegitimate (**b**) *(falso)* spurious, adulterated

esputar *vt* to spit (out)

esputo *nm* sputum, spit

esqueje *nm Bot* cutting

esquela *nf Esp* funeral notice *(in newspaper)*

esquelético, -a *adj* (**a**) *Anat* skeletal; **estructura e.** bone structure (**b**) *(muy flaco)* skinny; **estar e.** to be skin and bones

esqueleto *nm* (**a**) *(de persona)* skeleton; *Fam* **mover el e.** to shake it about (**b**) *Constr* framework (**c**) *CAm Col Méx (formulario)* form

esquema *nm* (**a**) *(resumen)* outline; **seguir un e. fijo** to follow a set pattern (**b**) *(diagrama)* diagram; **dibuja *o* trazar un e.** to draw a diagram

esquemático, -a *adj* schematic, diagrammatic; **corte e.** cross section

esquematizar [14] *vt (un plano)* to sketch; *(unas ideas)* to outline

esquí *(pl* **esquíes** *o* **esquís**) *nm* (**a**) *(objeto)* ski (**b**) *Dep* skiing; **hacer e.** to go skiing □ **e. acuático** water-skiing; **e. de fondo** cross-country skiing; **e. náutico** water-skiing

esquiador, -a *nm,f* skier

esquiar [32] *vi* to ski

esquife *nm Náut* skiff

esquila[1] *nf* small bell, handbell, sheep bell

esquila[2] *nf Agr* sheep shearing

esquilador, -a *nm,f (persona)* sheepshearer

esquiladora *nf (herramienta)* shears *pl*

esquilar *vt (cortar el pelo)* to clip; *(ovejas)* to shear

esquileo *nm* sheepshearing

esquilmar *vt* (**a**) *(cosechar)* to harvest (**b**) *Fig (recursos)* to exhaust

esquimal 1 *adj & nmf* Eskimo
2 *nm (idioma)* Eskimo

esquina *nf* (**a**) *(en calle)* corner; **a la vuelta de la e.** just round the corner; **doblar la e.** to turn the corner; **hacer e. con** to be on the corner of (**b**) *Chile* grocer's, corner shop

esquinado, -a *adj* (**a**) *(con esquinas)* having corners, sharp-cornered (**b**) *Fig (difícil)* touchy, irritable

esquinazo *nm (a) Esp* **dar e. a algn** to give sb the slip (**b**) *Chile (serenata)* serenade

esquinera *nf* cornerpiece, corner cupboard

esquirla *nf* splinter

esquirol *nm Ind* scab, *Br* blackleg

esquite *nm CAm* popcorn

esquivar *vt (a una persona)* to shun, avoid; *(un golpe)* to elude, dodge; **e. hacer algo** to avoid doing sth; **e. un golpe** to dodge a blow

esquivez *nf* coldness, aloofness

esquivo, -a *adj* cold, aloof

esquizofrenia *nf* schizophrenia

esquizofrénico, -a *adj & nm,f* schizophrenic

esquizoide *adj & nmf* schizoid

esta *adj dem véase* **este, -a**[2]

ésta *pron dem f véase* **éste, -a**

estabilidad *nf* stability

estabilización *nf* stabilization

estabilizador, -a 1 *adj* stabilizing; **elemento e.** stabilizing influence *o* factor
2 *nm Av Quím* stabilizer

estabilizante *nm (aditivo)* stabilizer

estabilizar [14] **1** *vt* to stabilize, make stable *o* steady
2 estabilizarse *vpr* to become stable *o* stabilized

estable *adj* stable, steady, balanced

establecer [46] **1** *vt* (**a**) *(gen)* to establish; *(fundar)* to set up, found; *(gente)* to settle; *(récord)* to set (**b**) *(decretar)* to establish, state; **la ley establece que ...** the law states that ...

2 establecerse *vpr (instalarse)* to establish oneself, settle; *Com* to set up in business

establecimiento *nm* (**a**) *(acto)* establishment, setting-up, founding; *(de gente)* settlement (**b**) *(edificio)* establishment; **e. central** head office (**c**) *Jur* statute, ordinance

establo *nm* cow shed, stall, stable

estabulación *nf* rearing of livestock in stables

estabular *vt* to stable

estaca *nf* (**a**) *(madero)* stake, post; *(de tienda de campaña)* peg (**b**) *(garrote)* stick, cudgel

estacada *nf* fence, fencing; *Mil* stockade; *Fig* **dejar a algn en la e.** to leave sb in the lurch; **estar en la e.** to be in a fix

estacar *vt* **1** *Andes CAm Ven (sujetar)* to fasten down with stakes

2 estacarse *vpr CAm Carib Col (clavarse una astilla)* to get a splinter

estacazo *nm* blow with a stick

estación *nf* (**a**) *(del año)* season; **la e. de las lluvias** the rainy season (**b**) *Ferroc Rad* station; **hacer e. en un viaje** to make a stop on a journey ◻ **e. balnearia** spa; **e. de autobuses** bus station; **e. de esquí** ski resort; **e. de metro** *Br* underground station, *US* subway station; **e. de servicio** service station; **e. espacial** space station; **e. metereológica** weather station (**c**) *Rel (de la cruz)* station

estacional *adj* seasonal

estacionamiento *nm* stationing, placing; *Aut (acción)* parking; *(lugar) Br* car park, *US* parking lot; *Fig* **e. del conflicto** stalemate, impasse

estacionar **1** *vt* to station, place; *Aut* to park

2 estacionarse *vpr* (**a**) *Aut* to park (**b**) *(estancarse)* to remain in the same place, be stationary

estacionario, -a *adj* stationary, stable

estadía *nf Am* stay; **planeó una e. de tres días en Lima** he planned a three-day stop in Lima

estadio *nm* (**a**) *Dep* stadium ◻ **e. de fútbol** football stadium *o Br* ground (**b**) *(fase)* stage, phase; **hacer algo por estadios** to do sth in stages

estadista *nmf* (**a**) *Pol (hombre)* statesman; *(mujer)* stateswoman (**b**) *Mat* statistician

estadística *nf (ciencia)* statistics *sing*; **una e.** a figure, a statistic

estadístico, -a 1 *adj* statistical

2 *nm,f* statistician

estado *nm* (**a**) *(situación)* state, condition; **en buen e.** in good condition; **mujer en e.** pregnant woman; *Med* **su e. es grave** his condition is serious ◻ **e. de ánimo** state of mind; **e. de bienestar** welfare state; **e. de excepción** state of emergency; **e. de salud** condition, state of health; **e. de sitio** state of siege; **e. satélite** satellite state; **e. sólido** solid state (**b**) *(relación)* return, summary; **e. de cuentas** statement of accounts (**c**) *(orden social)* status, rank; **e. civil** marital status (**d**) *(clase)* class, estate; **e. noble** noble estate (**e**) *Pol* state ◻ **hombre de e.** statesman; **e. de previsión** welfare state (**f**) *Mil* **E. Mayor general** general staff

Estados Unidos *npl* United States

estadounidense 1 *adj* United States, American; **las universidades estadounidenses** American universities

2 *nmf* United States citizen

estafa *nf* swindle, fraud

estafador, -a *nm,f* racketeer, swindler, trickster

estafar *vt* to swindle, cheat, trick, defraud; *Fam* **te han estafado** you've been done *o* had

estafeta *nf* **e. de Correos** sub post office

estafilococo *nm Biol* staphylococcus

estalactita *nf Geol* stalactite

estalagmita *nf Geol* stalagmite

estalinismo *nm Pol* Stalinism

estalinista *adj & nmf* Stalinist

estallar *vi* (**a**) *(reventar)* to blow up, explode; *(neumático)* to burst; *(bomba)* to explode, go off; *(volcán)* to erupt; *(cristal)* to shatter; **estalló en pedazos** it shattered (**b**) *(rebelión, epidemia)* to break out; **al e. la guerra** when war broke out (**c**) *(restallar)* to crack; **hacer e. el látigo** to crack the whip (**d**) *Fig (sentimientos)* to explode; **e. en sollozos** to burst into tears

estallido *nm* (**a**) *(explosión)* explosion; *(trueno)* crash; *(chasquido)* crack (**b**) *Fig (de una guerra)* outbreak

estambre *nm* (**a**) *Cost* worsted, woollen *o US* woolen yarn (**b**) *Bot* stamen

Estambul *n* Istanbul

estamento *nm (social)* class, stratum

estameña *nf Tex* serge

estampa *nf* (**a**) *(dibujo)* picture (**b**) *Fig (aspecto)* appearance, look, aspect; **ser la viva e. de ...** to be the spitting image of ... (**c**) *(marca)* hallmark (**d**) *Impr* print; *(proceso)* printing; **dar a la e.** to publish

estampación *nf* printing

estampado, -a 1 *pp de* estampar

2 *adj* stamped, printed; *(vestido)* print

3 *nm* (**a**) *(tela)* print (**b**) *(proceso)* printing; *Metal* stamping

estampar *vt* (**a**) *(imprimir, dibujar) (vestidos)* to print; *Metal* to stamp (**b**) *(escribir)* **e. la firma** to sign (**c**) *(dejar impreso)* to engrave, imprint (**d**) *Fam (arrojar)* to hurl (**e**) *Fig (dar)* to plant, place; **le estampó un beso en la frente** she planted a kiss on his forehead

estampida *nf* (**a**) *(estampido)* bang (**b**) *(ganado)* stampede; **de e.** suddenly; **salir de e.** to be *o* go off like a shot

estampido *nm* bang; **dar un e.** to go bang

estampilla *nf* (rubber) stamp; *Am* (postage) stamp

estampillado *nm* rubber stamping

estampillar *vt* to stamp, put a stamp on; *(un documento)* to rubber-stamp

estancado, -a 1 *pp de* estancar

2 *adj* (**a**) *(aguas)* stagnant (**b**) *Fig* static, at a standstill; *(persona)* **quedarse e.** to get stuck *o* bogged down

estancamiento *nm* (**a**) *(de agua)* stagnation (**b**) *Fig* stagnation, standstill

estancar [59] **1** *vt* (**a**) *(aguas)* to hold up, hold back; *(el flujo)* to check (**b**) *Fig (progreso)* to check, block, hold up; *(negociaciones)* to bring to a standstill (**c**) *Com (el mercado)* to corner; *(monopolizar)* to have a state monopoly on

2 estancarse *vpr* (**a**) *(líquido)* to stagnate, become stagnant (**b**) *Fig* to stagnate, get bogged down

estancia¹ *nf* (**a**) *Esp Méx (permanencia)* stay (**b**) *(aposento)* room (**c**) *CSur (hacienda)* ranch, farm

estancia² *nf Lit* stanza

estanciero *nm Andes RP* rancher, farmer

estanco 1 *adj* watertight; **compartimento e.** watertight compartment

2 *nm* (**a**) *Esp (de tabaco)* tobacconist's (**b**) *Andes (de licores) Br* off-licence, *US* liquor store

estándar *(pl estándares)* **1** *adj* standard, standardized; **normas e.** set rules

2 *nm* standard

estandarización *nf* standardization

estandarizar [14] *vt* to standardize

estandarte *nm* standard, banner

estanflación *nf Econ* stagflation

estanque *nm* pool, pond; *Am (depósito)* tank, reservoir; **e. para chapotear** paddling pool

estanquero, -a *nm,f* tobacconist

estante *nm* (**a**) *(tabla)* shelf, rack, stand; **e. para libros** bookcase (**b**) *CAm* post, pillar

estantería *nf* shelves, shelving

estañado, -a 1 *pp de* **estañar**
2 *adj* soldered
3 *nm* tin plating

estañar *vt* (**a**) *(bañar con estaño)* to tin-plate (**b**) *(soldar)* to solder

estaño *nm* tin

estaquilla *nf* (**a**) *(clavo)* tack, spike; *(de tienda de campaña)* tent peg (**b**) *Constr* peg

estar [30] **1** *vi* (**a**) *(existir, hallarse)* to be, be found; *(persona)* to be in; *(en casa)* to be at home; **aquí no está** it is not here; **Dios está en todas partes** God is everywhere; **el mejor vino tinto está en La Rioja** the best red wine is found in La Rioja; **está fuera** she's out; **¿está Jorge?** is Jorge in? (**b**) *(posición)* to be, stand; **estamos en Barcelona** we are in Barcelona; **la casa está en medio de la calle** the house is half-way down the street; *Fig* **los precios están bajos** prices are low (**c**) *(e. + adj) (cualidades transitorias)* to be; **el papel está arrugado** the paper is crumpled; **está enfermo** he's ill; **está vacío** it's empty (**d**) *(e. + ing) (tiempo continuo)* to be; **está escribiendo** she is writing; **estaba comiendo** he was eating (**e**) *(e. + adv)* to be; **en seguida está** it'll be ready in a moment; **está bien** it's all right; **está mal** it's wrong; **ya está** that's done (**f**) *(e. + a) (fecha)* to be; *(precio)* to sell *o* be at; **¿a cuántos estamos?** what's the date?; **estamos a 10 de Enero** it is the 10th of January; **están a 15 pesos la pieza** they're 15 pesos each; **e. al caer** to be just round the corner; **las vacaciones están al caer** the holidays will soon be here; *Fam* **e. a la que salta** to be ready to seize any opportunity; *Fam* **e. a matar** to be at daggers drawn (**g**) *(e. + de) (condiciones transitorias)* **e. de etiqueta** to be in evening dress; *(sobrar)* **e. de más** not to be needed; **e. de paseo** to be out for a walk; **e. de vacaciones** to be (away) on holiday; **e. de viaje** to be (away) on a trip; **estos comentarios están de más** we could do without those comments; **estoy de jefe hoy** I'm the boss today; *Fam* **e. de miedo** to be a real cracker (**h**) *(e. + en) (permanecer)* to be in; *(consistir)* to be; **el problema está en el dinero** the problem is money; **e. en casa** to be in, be at home; *(saber)* **e. en lo cierto** to be right; **e. en todo** not to miss a trick (**i**) *(e. + para)* **e. para algo** to be in the mood for sth; **estará para las seis** it will be finished by six; **hoy no estoy para bromas** I'm in no mood for jokes today (**j**) *(e. + por)* **está por hacer** it is still to be done, it hasn't been done yet; **está por explicar** it remains to be explained; **está por suceder** it is going to happen soon; **e. por algo** to be in favour of it; **estoy por esperar** I'm for waiting (**k**) *(e. + con)* to have; **e. con la gripe** to have the flu, be down with flu; *(de acuerdo)* **estoy con Jaime** I agree with Jaime (**l**) *(e. + que)* **está que se duerme** he is nearly asleep; **estoy que no puedo más** I can't take any more; *Fam* **está que rabia** he's hopping mad; *Fam* **la cosa está que arde** things are really hotting up

2 estarse *vpr* (**a**) *(énfasis)* **se estaba muriendo** he was slowly dying; **¡estáte quieto!** keep still!, stop fidgeting! (**b**) *(permanecer)* to spend, stay; **se estuvo toda la tarde viendo la TV** he spent all afternoon watching TV

estarcido *nm* stencil

estarcir [72] *vt* to stencil

estárter *(pl* **estárters)** *nm Aut* choke

estatal *adj* state; **enseñanza e.** state education; **política e.** government policy

estatalizar [14] *vt* to nationalize

estática *nf* statics *sing*

estático, -a *adj* static

estatismo *nm* (**a**) *Pol* statism, state interventionism (**b**) *(inmovilidad)* stillness

estatizar [14] *vt Am* to nationalize

estatua *nf* statue; **quedarse hecho una e.** to be transfixed

estatuario, -a *adj* statuary; *Fig* statuesque

estatuilla *nf* statuette, figurine

estatuir [34] *vt* to establish, enact, ordain

estatura *nf* stature, height; **¿cuál es su e.?** how tall is she?

estatus *nm inv* status

estatutario *adj* statutory

estatuto *nm Jur* statute; *(de ciudad)* by-law; *Pol* **e. de autonomía** statute of autonomy

este¹ 1 *adj* east, eastern; *(dirección)* easterly; *(viento)* east, easterly
2 *nm* (**a**) *(punto cardinal)* east; **al e. de Bilbao** to the east of Bilbao (**b**) *(viento)* east wind

este, -a² *(pl* **estos, -as)** *adj dem* (**a**) *(gen)* this; **esta casa** this house (**b**) **estos, -as** these; **estas mujeres** these women

éste, -a *(pl* **éstos, -as)** *pron dem m,f* (**a**) *(gen)* this one; *(el anterior)* the former; **coge é.** take this one; **vio a María pero ésta no le dijo nada** he saw María but she didn't say anything to him (**b**) **éstos, -as** these (ones); *(los anteriores)* the former (ones); *Fam* **en éstas** just then; **estábamos viendo la televisión y en éstas sonó el teléfono** we were watching television when suddenly the phone rang

estela¹ *nf* (**a**) *Náut* wake, wash; *Av* vapour *o US* vapor trail; *(de cometa)* tail (**b**) *Fig* trail

estela² *nf* *(lápida)* stele, stela

estelar *adj* (**a**) *Astron* stellar; **poblaciones estelares** star clusters; **luz e.** starlight (**b**) *Cin Teat* star; **la figura e.** the star

estenografía *nf* stenography

estenógrafo, -a *nm,f* stenographer, shorthand writer

estenotipia *nf* (**a**) *(arte)* stenotypy (**b**) *Téc* Stenotype®

estenotipista *nmf* stenotypist

estenotipo *nm* Stenotype®

estentóreo, -a *adj* stentorian, thundering, booming

estepa¹ *nf Geog* steppe

estepa² *nf Bot* rockrose

estepario, -a *adj* pertaining to a steppe

estera *nf* rush mat

esterar *vt* to cover with rush matting

estercolero *nm* dunghill, manure heap; *Fig* pigsty

estéreo *nm,* **estereofonía** *nf* stereo

estereofónico, -a *adj* stereophonic, stereo

estereografía *nf* stereography

estereoscopio *nm* stereoscope

estereotipado, -a 1 *pp de* **estereotipar**
2 *adj Fig* stereotyped, set, standard; **frase estereotipada** hackneyed phrase, cliché

estereotipar *vt* (**a**) *Impr* to stereotype (**b**) *Fig* to stereotype

estereotipo *nm* stereotype

estéril *adj* (**a**) *(persona)* sterile, barren (**b**) *Med* sterile (**c**) *Fig* futile, useless

esterilete *nm Med* coil, IUD

esterilidad *nf* (**a**) *(de persona)* sterility, barrenness (**b**) *Med* sterility (**c**) *Fig* futility, uselessness

esterilización *nf* sterilization

esterilizado, -a 1 *pp de* **esterilizar**
2 *adj* sterilized, sterile

esterilizador, -a 1 *adj* sterilizing
2 *nm,f* sterilizer

esterilizar [14] *vt* to sterilize

esterilla *nf* (**a**) *(tapete)* small mat (**b**) *(tejido)* rush matting, wickerwork; *Am* **silla de e.** wickerwork chair (**c**) *(galón)* gold *o* silver braid

esterlina *adj & nf* sterling; **libra e.** pound (sterling)

esternocleidomastoideo *adj & nm Anat* sternocleidomastoid

esternón *nm Anat* sternum, breastbone

estero *nm* (**a**) *(zona costera)* tideland (**b**) *Am (pantano)* marsh, swamp (**c**) *Ven (charca)* puddle, pool (**d**) *Chile (arroyo)* stream

esteroide *nm* steroid

estertor *nm* death rattle

esteta *nmf* aesthete, *US* esthete

estética *nf* (**a**) *Filos* aesthetics *sing*, *US* esthetics *sing* (**b**) *(belleza)* beauty (**c**) *(estilo)* style; **la e. de los años setenta** the style of the seventies

estetición *(pl* **esteticiéns)** *nmf* beautician

esteticismo *nm* aestheticism, *US* estheticism

esteticista *nmf* beautician

estético, -a *adj* aesthetic, *US* esthetic; *Med* **cirugía estética** plastic surgery

estetoscopio *nm Med* stethoscope

estevado, -a *adj* bow-legged, bandy-legged

esthéticienne [esteti'θjen] *nf* beautician

estiba *nf Náut* stowing, loading

estibador *nm* docker, stevedore

estibar *vt (cargar)* to stow, load

estiércol *nm* manure, dung

estigma *nm* (**a**) *(gen)* stigma; *(marca)* brand, mark; *(de nacimiento)* birthmark (**b**) *Rel* stigmata

estigmatización *nf* (**a**) *(marca)* branding (**b**) *(deshonra)* stigmatization

estigmatizar [14] *vt* (**a**) *(marcar)* to brand, mark (**b**) *(infamar)* to stigmatize

estilar 1 *vt (documento)* to draw up
2 *vi* to be in the habit of; **estila pasearse al anochecer** he usually takes a walk at dusk
3 estilarse *vpr* to be in vogue, be fashionable; **se estilan las camisas huecas** baggy shirts are in

estilete *nm (punzón)* stylus; *(puñal)* stiletto; *Med* probe

estilismo *nm* styling

estilista *nmf* stylist

estilística *nf* stylistics *sing*

estilístico, -a *adj* stylistic

estilización *nf* styling

estilizado, -a *adj (figura, cuerpo)* slim and elegant

estilizar [14] *vt* to stylize

estilo *nm* (**a**) *(gen)* style; *(modo)* manner, fashion; **algo por el e.** something like that; **e. de vida** way of life (**b**) *Ling* speech; **e. directo/indirecto** direct/indirect speech (**c**) *Natación* stroke; **e. braza** breaststroke; **e. mariposa** butterfly stroke; **e. libre** freestyle (**d**) *(punzón)* stylus

estilográfica *nf* fountain pen

estima *nf* (**a**) *(aprecio)* esteem, respect (**b**) *Náut* dead reckoning

estimable *adj* (**a**) *(digno de estimación)* esteemed, reputable, worthy (**b**) *(cantidad)* considerable

estimación *nf* (**a**) *(estima)* esteem, respect; **e. propia** self-esteem (**b**) *(valoración)* estimation, evaluation; *(cálculo)* estimate

estimado, -a 1 *pp de* **estimar**
2 *adj* esteemed, respected; *(en carta)* **E. Señor** Dear Sir; **Estimada Señora** Dear Madam

estimar 1 *vt* (**a**) *(apreciar)* to esteem, respect, admire (**b**) *(valorar)* to estimate; *(un objeto)* to value (**c**) *(juzgar)* to consider, think, reckon; **estimo conveniente dar una explicación** I think an explanation is due
2 estimarse *vpr* to think highly of oneself

estimativo, -a *adj* approximate, estimated

estimulación *nf* stimulation

estimulante 1 *adj* stimulating, encouraging
2 *nm* stimulant

estimular *vt* (**a**) *(excitar)* to stimulate; **e. el apetito** to whet one's appetite (**b**) *(animar)* to encourage

estímulo *nm* (**a**) *Biol Fís* stimulus, stimulation (**b**) *(aliciente)* incentive; *(ánimo)* encouragement

estío *nm* summer

estipendio *nm* stipend, fee, remuneration

estipulación *nf* (**a**) *Jur (cláusula)* stipulation, condition, proviso (**b**) *(acuerdo)* agreement

estipular *vt* (**a**) *(disponer)* to stipulate, establish (**b**) *(acordar)* to agree on

estirado, -a 1 *pp de* **estirar**
2 *adj* (**a**) *(brazos)* stretched out; *(piel)* taut (**b**) *Fig* stiff, excessively formal; *Fam* mean

estiramiento *nm* stretching

estirar 1 *vt* to stretch, draw out, pull out; **e. el cuello** to crane one's neck; **e. las piernas** to stretch one's legs; *Fig* **e. el dinero** to spin one's money out, make one's money go further; *Fam Fig* **e. la pata** to kick the bucket
2 estirarse *vpr (alargarse)* to stretch; *Fig* to shoot up

estirón *nm* pull, jerk, tug; *Fam* **dar** *o* **pegar un e.** to shoot up *o* grow quickly

estirpe *nf* race, stock, pedigree

estival *adj* summer; **época e.** summertime

esto *pron dem neut* this, this thing, this matter; **en e.** just then; **en e. llegó Asunción** at that moment Asunción arrived; **e. es** that is, i.e.; **vendrá tarde, e. es, a las diez** he'll be coming late, I mean, at ten; **e. no lo sabe nadie** nobody knows that; *Fam* **e. de la fiesta** this business about the party

estocada *nf Taur* thrust, stab; *Fig* **la e. final** the coup de grâce

Estocolmo *n* Stockholm

estofa *nf* **de baja e.** *(gente)* low-class; *(cosas)* poor-quality

estofado, -a[1] *Culin* **1** *pp de* **estofar**[1]
2 *adj (carne)* stewed
3 *nm* stew

estofado, -a[2] *Cost* **1** *pp de* **estofar**[2]
2 *adj* quilted
3 *nm* quilting

estofar[1] *vt Culin* to stew

estofar[2] *vt Cost* to quilt

estoicismo *nm* stoicism

estoico, -a 1 *adj* stoic, stoical
2 *nm,f* stoic

estola *nf* stole

estólido, -a *adj* stupid, dense, thick

estomacal 1 *adj* (of the) stomach; **bebida e.** digestive liqueur; **trastorno e.** stomach upset
  2 *nm* digestive liqueur

estómago *nm* stomach; **tener buen e.** to have a strong stomach; *Fig* to be thick-skinned; *Fam* **me revuelve el e.** it turns my stomach □ **dolor de e.** stomach ache

estomatología *nf Med* stomatology

Estonia *n* Estonia

estonio, -a *adj & nm,f* Estonian

estopa *nf (fibra)* tow; *(tela)* burlap □ **e. de acero** steel wool

estoperol *nm Col* tack, stud

estoque *nm Taur* sword

estoquear *vt Taur* to thrust at, stab

estor *nm* (Roman) blind

estorbar 1 *vt* (a) *(dificultar)* to hinder, get in the way; **las obras en la calle estorban la libre circulación de los coches** the road works hold up traffic (b) *(impedir)* to impede, obstruct (c) *(molestar)* to disturb, bother, upset; **la música me estorba cuando quiero estudiar** I can't study when there's music playing
  2 *vi* (a) *(obstaculizar)* to be in the way, block (b) *(persona)* to be a nuisance; **tu hermano no hace más que estorbar** your brother is always getting in the way

estorbo *nm* (a) *(obstáculo)* obstruction, obstacle (b) *(molestia)* hindrance, encumbrance (c) *(persona)* nuisance

estornino *nm Orn* starling

estornudar *vi* to sneeze

estornudo *nm* sneeze

estos, -as *adj dem pl véase* **este, -a²**

éstos, -as *pron dem m,fpl véase* **éste, -a**

estoy *indic pres véase* **estar**

estrábico, -a 1 *adj* squint-eyed
  2 *nm,f* person with a squint

estrabismo *nm Med* strabismus, squint; **tener e.** to have a squint

estrado *nm* stage, platform; *Mús* bandstand; *Jur* **estrados** *(salas)* courtrooms

estrafalario, -a *adj Fam (extraño)* eccentric, weird, outlandish; *(desaliñado)* slovenly

estragar [38] *vt* to ruin, devastate, ravage; *Fig* **e. el paladar** to deaden one's taste buds

estrago *nm* ruin, ravage, waste, havoc; **hacer estragos en** to play havoc with *o* on

estragón *nm Bot Culin* tarragon

estrambótico, -a *adj Fam* outlandish, weird, eccentric, way-out

estrangulación *nf (de persona)* strangling; *Med (de vena, conducto)* strangulation

estrangulador, -a 1 *nm,f (persona)* strangler
  2 *nm Aut* choke

estrangulamiento *nm véase* **estrangulación**

estrangular *vt (ahogar)* to strangle; *Med (vena, conducto)* to strangulate; *Téc (vehículo)* to throttle

estraperlista *nmf* black marketeer

estraperlo *nm* black market; **tabaco de e.** black market cigarettes

Estrasburgo *n* Strasbourg

estratagema *nf Mil* stratagem; *Fam* trick, ruse

estratega *nmf* strategist

estrategia *nf* strategy

estratégico, -a *adj* strategic

estratificación *nf* stratification

estratificar [59] **1** *vt* to stratify
  2 estratificarse *vpr* to be stratified

estrato *nm* (a) *Geol* stratum (b) *Meteor (nube)* stratus (c) *Fig (clase)* stratum, layer, class, level; **estratos sociales** social strata *pl*

estratosfera *nf* stratosphere

estratosférico, -a *adj* (a) *(de la estratosfera)* stratospheric (b) *Fam (precio)* astronomical

estraza *nf* rag, piece of cloth □ **papel de e.** brown paper

estrechamente *adv* (a) *(con estrechez)* narrowly, tightly (b) *Fig (íntimamente)* closely, intimately; **e. unidos** very close; **e. vinculados** closely linked (c) *Fig (con rigidez)* strictly, rigidly

estrechamiento *nm* (a) *(de valle etc)* narrowing; *Cost (de prenda)* taking in; *Aut* **'e. de calzada'** 'road narrows' (b) *(punto estrecho)* narrow point (c) *Fig* tightening; **el estrechamiento de los lazos económicos entre el este y el oeste** the tightening of economic links between east and west

estrechar 1 *vt* (a) *(carretera, valle)* to narrow; *(vestido)* to take in; **e. una falda** to take in a skirt (b) *(abrazar)* to squeeze, hug; *(mano)* to shake; **me estrechó la mano con fuerza** he shook my hand firmly (c) *Fig (obligar)* to compel, constrain (d) *Fig (unir)* to bring closer *o* together; *(lazos)* to tighten; **e. los lazos de amistad** to tighten the bonds of friendship
  2 estrecharse *vpr* (a) *(carretera, valle)* to narrow, become narrower; **el camino se estrecha al llegar al pueblo** as it nears the village the road narrows (b) *(apretarse)* to squeeze together *o* up (c) *Fig* to tighten, get tighter (d) *(dos personas)* to embrace one another, hug; **e. la mano** to shake hands (e) *Fig* to economize, tighten one's belt

estrechez *nf* (a) *(angostura)* narrowness, tightness; *(falta de espacio)* lack of space (b) *Fig (dificultad económica)* want, need; **pasar estrecheces** to be hard up; **vivir en la e.** to live from hand to mouth (c) *Fig (amistad)* closeness, intimacy (d) *Fig (rigidez)* strictness □ **e. de miras** narrow-mindedness (e) *Fig (apuro)* tight spot

estrecho, -a 1 *adj* (a) *(no ancho)* narrow; *(vestido)* tight; *(habitación)* cramped, pokey; *(zapatos)* tight, small (b) *(de dinero)* tight, short (c) *(sin espacio)* packed, jampacked (d) *Fig (relación)* close, intimate; *(lazo)* close (e) *Fig (actitud)* narrow, rigid; *(carácter)* mean; **e. de miras** narrow-minded; *Fam* strait-laced; **¡no te hagas la estrecha!** don't be so coy!
  2 *nm Geog* strait, straits *pl*; **el E. de Gibraltar** the Straits of Gibraltar

estrechura *nf* (a) *(angostura)* narrowness, narrow point (b) *Fig (intimidad)* closeness, intimacy

estregar [43] **1** *vt (con cepillo)* to scrub; *(con trapo etc)* to rub
  2 estregarse *vpr* to rub oneself

estrella *nf (gen)* star; *Fig* **haber nacido con buena e.** to be born under a lucky star; *Fig* **nacer con e.** to be born lucky; *Fig* **tener buena/mala e.** to be lucky/unlucky; *Fig* **ver las estrellas** to see stars □ **e. de cine** movie *o Br* film star; *Zool* **e. de mar** starfish; *Astron* **e. errante, e. fugaz** shooting star

estrellado, -a 1 *pp de* **estrellar**
  2 *adj* (a) *(en forma de estrella)* star-shaped (b) *(cielo)* starry, full of stars, star-spangled (c) *(hecho pedazos)* smashed, shattered

estrellar 1 *vt* (a) *(llenar de estrellas)* to star, cover with stars (b) *Fam (hacer pedazos)* to smash (to pieces), shatter
  2 estrellarse *vpr (hacerse pedazos)* to smash, shatter, crash (**contra** against); *Aut Av (chocar)* to crash (**contra**

into); *Fig* **e. contra un problema** to come up against *o* run into a problem

estrellato *nm* stardom

estrellón *nm Am* crash, collision

estremecedor, -a *adj (que asusta)* startling; *(grito)* bloodcurdling

estremecer [46] **1** *vt (gen)* to shake
2 estremecerse *vpr (temblar)* to shake, tremble, vibrate; *(persona)* to tremble (**ante** at, **de** with); *(de miedo)* to tremble, shudder; *(de frío)* to shiver, tremble

estremecido, -a 1 *pp de* **estremecer**
2 *adj* shaking (**de** with), trembling (**de** with)

estremecimiento *nm (de tierra, edificio)* tremor, vibration; *(de miedo)* trembling, shuddering; *(de frío)* shiver, trembling

estrenar 1 *vt* (**a**) *(gen)* to use for the first time; *(ropa)* to wear for the first time; **e. piso** to move into a new flat (**b**) *Teat (obra)* to perform for the first time, give the first performance of; *Cin (película)* to release, put on release
2 estrenarse *vpr* to start, make one's debut

estreno *nm (de persona)* debut, first appearance; *Teat* first performance; *Cin* premiere, new release; **riguroso e.** world premiere

estreñido, -a *Med* **1** *pp de* **estreñir**
2 *adj* constipated

estreñimiento *nm Med* constipation

estreñir [47] *Med* **1** *vt* to make constipated, constipate
2 estreñirse *vpr* to become constipated

estrépito *nm (estruendo)* din, racket, clatter; *Fig (ostentación)* ostentation, fuss

estrepitosamente *adv* noisily

estrepitoso, -a *adj* noisy, clamorous; *(ruido)* deafening; *Fig (éxito)* resounding; *Fig (fracaso)* spectacular

estreptococo *nm Med* streptococcus

estreptomicina *nf Med* streptomycin

estrés *nm Med* stress

estresado, -a *adj* suffering from stress; **estar e.** to be stressed

estresante *adj* stressful

estresar *vt* to cause stress to; **ese ruido me está estresando** that noise is getting on my nerves

estría *nf* (**a**) *(ranura)* groove; *Arquit* flute, fluting (**b**) *Fam (en la piel)* stretch mark

estriado, -a 1 *pp de* **estriar**
2 *adj* (**a**) *(piel)* stretch-marked (**b**) *(columna)* fluted

estriar [32] **1** *vt* to groove
2 estriarse *vpr (piel)* to become stretch-marked

estribación *nf Geog* spur; **estribaciones** foothills

estribar *vi* (**a**) *(apoyarse)* to rest (**en** on) (**b**) *Fig (basarse)* to lie in, be based on; **su éxito estriba en su capacidad de concentración** her success lies in her powers of concentration

estribillo *nm* (**a**) *(en poesía)* refrain; *(en canción)* chorus (**b**) *(muletilla)* pet phrase *o* saying, catch-phrase

estribo *nm* (**a**) *(de jinete)* stirrup; *Aut* running board, footboard; *(en carruaje)* step; *Fig* **perder los estribos** to lose one's temper, lose one's head (**b**) *Arquit* buttress; *(de puente)* pier, support (**c**) *Geog* spur (**d**) *Anat* stirrup bone

estribor *nm Náut* starboard

estricnina *nf* strychnine

estrictez *nf Am* strictness

estricto, -a *adj* strict, rigorous

estridencia *nf* stridency, shrillness

estridente *adj* strident, shrill

estrofa *nf Lit* stanza, verse, strophe

estrógeno *nm* oestrogen, *US* estrogen

estroncio *nm Quím* strontium

estropajo *nm* scourer; *Fam Fig* **poner a algn como un e.** to pull sb to pieces

estropajoso, -a *adj* (**a**) *(lengua)* furry (**b**) *(habla)* stammering (**c**) *(carne)* gristly, tough (**d**) *(pelo)* strawlike (**e**) *(persona) (andrajoso)* ragged; *(desaliñado)* slovenly

estropear 1 *vt (máquina, cosecha)* to damage; *(fiesta, plan)* to spoil, ruin; *(salud)* to be bad for; *(pelo, manos)* to ruin
2 estropearse *vpr (máquina)* to break down; *(cosecha)* to be *o* get damaged, be spoiled; *(plan, proyecto)* to fail

estropicio *nm Fam* (**a**) *(destrozo)* breakage, smashing, damage; *(ruido)* crash, clatter (**b**) *Fig (desorden)* mess; *(jaleo)* fuss, rumpus; **hacer un e.** to make a right mess of sth

estructura *nf (gen)* structure; *(armazón)* frame, framework

estructuración *nf* structure, organization

estructural *adj* structural

estructurar *vt* to structure, organize

estruendo *nm* (**a**) *(ruido)* din, racket (**b**) *(confusión)* uproar, tumult

estruendoso, -a *adj (ruido)* noisy, deafening; *(aplauso)* thunderous

estrujar 1 *vt* (**a**) *(exprimir)* to squeeze; *(apretar)* to crush; *(ropa)* to wring (**b**) *Fam (explotar)* to drain, bleed dry
2 estrujarse *vpr Fam* **e. los sesos** *o* **el cerebro** to rack one's brains

estrujón *nm* tight squeeze, big hug

estuario *nm Geol* estuary

estucado, -a 1 *pp de* **estucar**
2 *nm* stucco(work)

estucar [59] *vt* to stucco

estuche *nm (caja)* case, box; *(vaina)* sheath □ **e. de aseo** toilet bag

estuco *nm* stucco

estudiado, -a 1 *pp de* **estudiar**
2 *adj (muy pensado) (falso)* affected, studied; *(rebuscado)* elaborate, recherché

estudiantado *nm* students *pl*, student body

estudiante *nmf* student

estudiantil *adj* student, of students

estudiantina *nf* student band

estudiar 1 *vt* (**a**) *(gen)* to study; *(en la universidad)* to read, study; **e. medicina** to study medicine (**b**) *(pensar)* to think about *o* over, ponder; **lo estudiaré** I'll think about it (**c**) *(observar)* to examine, observe; **he estudiado todos sus movimientos** I've observed all his movements
2 *vi* to study; **estudia para médico** he's studying to be a doctor; **este año tiene que e. mucho** he has to work a lot this year

estudio *nm* (**a**) *(gen)* study; *(encuesta)* survey, research; **dedicarse al e. de algo** to study sth; **estar en e.** to be under consideration □ *Com* **e. de mercado** market research; **e. de viabilidad** feasibility study (**b**) *(sala)* studio; *RP (de abogado)* practice □ *Cin* **e. cinematográfico** film studio; *Mús* **e. de grabación** recording studio; *TV* **e. de televisión** television studio (**c**) *(apartamento)* studio *Br* flat *o US* apartment (**d**) **estudios** studies, education *sing*; **dar e. a algn** to pay for sb's education; **hizo sus e. en Europa** she studied in Europe; **tener e.** to be well-educated

estudioso, -a 1 *adj* studious
2 *nm,f* student, scholar

estufa *nf* (**a**) *(calentador)* heater, stove; *(de gas, eléctrica)* fire (**b**) *(invernadero)* hothouse, greenhouse (**c**) *Am (cocina)* stove

estulticia *nf Literario* stupidity, foolishness

estupa *Argot* **1** *nf (grupo)* drug squad
  2 *nmf (persona)* drug squad detective, *US* narc

estupefacción *nf* stupefaction; *(asombro)* astonishment, amazement

estupefaciente *nm* drug, narcotic

estupefacto, -a *adj* astounded, flabbergasted

estupendamente *adv* marvellously, *US* marvelously, wonderfully

estupendo, -a *adj* super, marvellous, *US* marvelous, wonderful; **¡e.!** great!

estupidez *nf* stupidity, stupid thing; **cometer una e.** to do something silly; **¡qué e.!** what a stupid thing to do/say!

estúpido, -a 1 *adj* silly, stupid
  2 *nm,f* berk, idiot

estupor *nm* stupor, amazement, astonishment; **causar e.** to astonish

estupro *nm Jur* rape (of a minor)

esturión *nm (pez)* sturgeon

estuve *pt indef véase* **estar**

esvástica *nf* swastika

ETA *nf (abrev de* **Euskadi Ta Askatasuna**) ETA, terrorist Basque separatist organization

etapa *nf* (**a**) *(fase)* period, stage; **por etapas** in stages; **quemar etapas** to come on in leaps and bounds, progress rapidly (**b**) *Dep* leg, stage

etarra *Pol* **1** *adj* (of) ETA
  2 *nmf* member of ETA

etc. *(abrev de* **etcétera**) etc

etcétera 1 *adv* etcetera, and so on
  2 *nm* list; **y un largo e. de quejas** and a long list of complaints

éter *nm* (**a**) *Quím* ether (**b**) *Literario (espacio celeste)* ether, sky, heavens *pl*

etéreo, -a *adj* ethereal

eternidad *nf* eternity; *Fam* age; **tardaste una e.** you took ages

eternizar [14] **1** *vt* to eternalize, eternize; *Fam* to prolong endlessly, make everlasting
  2 eternizarse *vpr Fam* to be interminable *o* endless; *(persona)* to take ages (**en** over); *(discusión)* to drag on

eterno, -a *adj* eternal, everlasting, endless

Ethernet® [eθer'net] *nf Inform* Ethernet®

ética *nf* ethic, ethics *sing* ❑ **é. profesional** (professional) ethics

ético, -a 1 *adj* ethical
  2 *nm,f* ethicist

etileno *nm* ethylene

etílico, -a *adj* ethylic; **alcohol e.** ethyl alcohol; **en estado e.** intoxicated; **intoxicación etílica** alcohol poisoning

etilo *nm Quím* ethyl

etimología *nf* etymology

etimológico, -a *adj* etymological

etíope *adj & nmf*, **etiope** *adj & nmf* Ethiopian

Etiopía *nf* Ethiopia

etiqueta *nf* (**a**) *(marbete)* label, tag; *Fig* **poner etiquetas a la gente** to label people (**b**) *(ceremonia)* etiquette, formality, ceremony; **de e.** formal; **traje de e.** evening *o* formal dress

etiquetado *nm* labelling

etiquetadora *nf* pricing gun

etiquetar *vt* to label, put a label on

etiquetero, -a *adj* formal, punctilious, ceremonious

etnia *nf* ethnic group; **una persona de e. oriental** a person of Asian extraction

étnico, -a *adj* ethnic

etnocentrismo *nm* ethnocentrism

etnografía *nf* ethnography

etnográfico, -a *adj* ethnographic, ethnographical

etnógrafo, -a *nm,f* ethnographer

etnología *nf* ethnology

etnológico, -a *adj* ethnologic, ethnological

etnólogo, -a *nm,f* ethnologist

etrusco, -a 1 *adj* Etruscan
  2 *nm,f (persona)* Etruscan
  3 *nm (idioma)* Etruscan

ETT (*pl* **ETTs**) *nf (abrev de* **Empresa de Trabajo Temporal**) temping agency

EUA *nmpl (abrev de* **Estados Unidos de América**) USA

eucalipto *nm Bot* eucalyptus

eucaristía *nf Rel* Eucharist

eucarístico, -a *adj* eucharistic, eucharistical

eufemismo *nm* euphemism

eufemístico, -a *adj* euphemistic

eufonía *nf* euphony

eufónico, -a *adj* euphonic, euphonious

euforia *nf* euphoria, elation

eufórico, -a *adj* euphoric, elated

Éufrates *nm* **el É.** the Euphrates

eunuco *nm* eunuch

Eurasia *n* Eurasia

eurasiático, -a *adj* Eurasian

eureka *interj* eureka!

euro *nm (moneda)* euro

euroasiático, -a *adj & nm,f* Eurasian

Eurocámara *nf* European Parliament

eurocomunismo *nm Pol* Eurocommunism

eurocomunista *adj & nmf Pol* Eurocommunist

eurodiputado, -a *nm,f* Euro-MP, MEP

eurodivisa *nf Fin* eurocurrency

Europa *n* Europe ❑ **E. Occidental** Western Europe

europarlamentario, -a *nm,f* Euro-MP, MEP

europeidad *nf* Europeanness

europeísmo *nm* Europeanism

europeísta *adj & nmf* pro-European

europeización *nf* Europeanization

europeizar [14] *vt* to europeanize

europeo, -a *adj & nm,f* European

euscalduna 1 *adj* Basque; *(que habla vasco)* Basque-speaking
  2 *nmf* Basque speaker

Euskadi *n* the Basque Country

euskera *adj & nm*, **eusquera** *adj & nm (idioma)* Basque

eutanasia *nf* euthanasia

evacuación *nf* evacuation

evacuado, -a 1 *pp de* **evacuar**
  2 *adj* evacuated
  3 *nm,f* evacuee

evacuar *vt* (**a**) *(lugar)* to evacuate (**b**) *(llevar a cabo)* to carry out; *Jur* to issue (**c**) *Anat* to empty; **e. el vientre** to have a bowel movement

evadido, -a 1 *pp de* **evadir**
2 *adj* escaped
3 *nm,f* fugitive, escapee
evadir 1 *vt (respuesta, peligro)* to avoid; *(responsabilidad)* to shirk; *(divisas, impuestos)* to evade
2 evadirse *vpr (escaparse)* to escape
evaluable *adj* calculable
evaluación *nf* evaluation □ *Educ* **e. continua** continuous assessment
evaluador, -a *adj* evaluating, evaluative
evaluar [4] *vt* to evaluate, assess
evanescente *adj* evanescent
evangélico, -a *adj Rel* evangelic, evangelical
evangelio *nm* gospel; **el E. según San Juan** the Gospel according to Saint John
evangelismo *nm* evangelism
evangelista *nm* **(a)** *Rel* Evangelist **(b)** *Méx (memorialista)* amanuensis
evangelización *nf* evangelization, evangelizing
evangelizador, -a 1 *adj* evangelizing
2 *nm,f* evangelist
evangelizar [14] *vt* to evangelize, preach the gospel to
evaporable *adj* evaporable
evaporación *nf* evaporation
evaporar 1 *vt* to evaporate
2 evaporarse *vpr* to evaporate; *Fig* to vanish
evasión *nf (fuga)* escape, flight; *Fig* evasion, dodge □ **e. fiscal** *o* **de impuestos** tax evasion; **novela de e.** escapist novel
evasiva *nf* evasive answer; **contestar con evasivas** not to give a straight answer, avoid the issue
evasivo, -a *adj* evasive
evento *nm* eventuality, contingency, unforeseen event; **a todo e.** in any event
eventual 1 *adj* **(a)** *(casual)* chance, possible; *(gastos)* incidental; **circunstancias eventuales** chance circumstances **(b)** *(trabajo, obrero)* casual, temporary, provisional
2 *nm,f (obrero)* temporary worker
eventualidad *nf* eventuality, contingency, chance
eventualmente *adv* by chance
Everest *nm* **el E.** (Mount) Everest
evicción *nf Jur* eviction
evidencia *nf* **(a)** *(claridad)* obviousness, clearness; *(certidumbre)* certainty; **poner algo en e.** to demonstrate sth; **poner a algn en e.** to make a fool of sb, show sb up **(b)** *(prueba)* proof, evidence
evidenciar *vt* to prove, show, demonstrate, make evident *o* obvious
evidente *adj* evident, obvious
evidentemente *adv* evidently, obviously
evitable *adj* avoidable, preventable
evitar 1 *vt (gen)* to avoid; *(prevenir, impedir)* to prevent; *(tentación)* to shun; *(desastre)* to avert; **esto nos evitará muchas molestias** this'll save us a lot of trouble; **quiero e. que sufra** I want to spare him any suffering
2 evitarse *vpr* to avoid one another
evocación *nf* evocation, recollection, recalling
evocador, -a *adj* evocative, evocatory
evocar [59] *vt* **(a)** *(espíritu)* to invoke **(b)** *(recuerdo)* to evoke; *(pasado)* to recall
evolución *nf* **(a)** *(cambio)* evolution; *(desarrollo)* development **(b)** *(vuelta)* turn; *Mil (movimiento)* manoeuvre, *US* maneuver

evolucionar *vi* **(a)** *(cambiar)* to evolve, develop; **e. a pasos agigantados** to take giant strides **(b)** *(dar vueltas)* to turn; *Mil (moverse)* to manoeuvre, *US* maneuver
evolucionismo *nm* evolutionism
evolucionista *adj & nmf* evolutionist
evolutivo, -a *adj* evolutionary, evolving
ex *pref* former, ex-; **ex alumno** former pupil, ex-student; **ex combatiente** ex-serviceman, *US* veteran
exabrupto *nm* sharp comment, sudden outburst; **contestar a algn con un e.** to snap at sb
exacción *nf (de impuestos)* exaction; *(extorsión)* extortion
exacerbación *nf* **(a)** *(agravamiento)* exacerbation, aggravation **(b)** *(irritación)* exasperation
exacerbar *vt* **(a)** *(agravar)* to exacerbate, aggravate **(b)** *(irritar)* to exasperate, irritate
exactamente *adv* exactly, precisely, just so
exactitud *nf (fidelidad)* exactness; *(precisión)* accuracy; **con e.** accurately
exacto, -a *adj (fiel)* exact; *(preciso)* exact, accurate; **¡e.!** precisely!; **para ser e.** to be precise
exageración *nf* exaggeration; **¡qué e.!** come off it!
exageradamente *adv* excessively
exagerado, -a 1 *pp de* **exagerar**
2 *adj* exaggerated; *(historia)* far-fetched; *(castigo)* excessive; **es un tipo e.** he overdoes everything; **precios exagerados** exorbitant prices; **un gesto e.** a flamboyant gesture; **una historia e.** a tall story
exagerar *vt* to exaggerate, *Pey* to overdo, go too far
exaltación *nf* **(a)** *(alabanza)* exaltation, praise **(b)** *(júbilo)* exaltation, elation **(c)** *(enardecimiento)* over-excitement **(d)** *Fam Pol (fanatismo)* fanaticism
exaltado, -a 1 *pp de* **exaltar**
2 *adj (discusión)* impassioned, heated; *(persona)* excitable, hotheaded; **los ánimos estaban exaltados** feelings were running high
3 *nm,f Fam* hothead; *Pol* fanatic, extremist
exaltar 1 *vt* **(a)** *(elevar)* to raise, promote **(b)** *(ensalzar)* to exalt, praise, extol
2 exaltarse *vpr (enardecerse)* to get overexcited, get carried away, get worked up
examen *nm (gen)* examination, exam; *(de problema)* consideration; **aprobar** *o Am* **pasar un e.** to pass an exam; *Esp* **suspender** *o Am* **reprobar un e.** to fail an exam; **hacer un e.** to do an exam; **presentarse a un e.** to take *o* sit an exam □ *Esp* **e. de conducir** driving test; *Educ* **e. de ingreso** entrance examination; *Am* **e. de manejar** driving test; **e. final** final (exam); *Med* **e. médico** checkup **e. oral** oral (exam)
examinador, -a 1 *adj* examining
2 *nm,f* examiner
examinando, -a *nm,f* candidate, examinee
examinar 1 *vt (gen)* to examine; *(inspeccionar)* to go over, inspect, consider
2 examinarse *vpr Esp* to take *o* sit an examination
exangüe *adj* **(a)** *(desangrado)* bloodless **(b)** *Fig (débil)* weak, lifeless
exánime *adj* **(a)** *(muerto)* dead **(b)** *Fig (desmayado)* lifeless; *(muy débil)* worn-out, exhausted
exasperación *nf* exasperation
exasperante *adj* exasperating
exasperar 1 *vt* to exasperate
2 exasperarse *vpr* to become exasperated
Exc. *(abrev de* **Excelencia***)* Excellency
excarcelación *nf* release (from prison)

excarcelar *vt* to release (from prison)

excavación *nf (acción)* excavation, digging; *(lugar)* dig

excavador, -a *nm,f* excavator, digger

excavadora *nf* digger

excavar *vt* to excavate, dig

excedencia *nf Esp (ausencia)* leave (of absence); *(sueldo)* leave pay; *(de profesor)* sabbatical

excedentario, -a *adj* surplus; **la balanza de pagos ha sido excedentaria** the balance of payments has been in surplus

excedente 1 *adj* (**a**) *(excesivo)* excessive; *(que sobra)* excess, surplus (**b**) *(persona)* on leave; *(profesor)* on sabbatical
 2 *nm Com* surplus, excess
 3 *nmf Esp (persona)* person on leave

exceder 1 *vt (superar)* to exceed, surpass; *(sobrepasar)* to excel, outdo; **e. el presupuesto** to overspend; **e. en mucho a ...** to greatly exceed ...
 2 *vi* **e. de** to exceed, surpass
 3 excederse *vpr* to overdo it, go to extremes; **e. a sí mismo** to surpass *o* excel oneself; **e. en sus funciones** to exceed one's duty

excelencia *nf* (**a**) *(cualidad)* excellence; **por e.** par excellence (**b**) *(título)* **Su E.** His/Her Excellency

excelente *adj* excellent, first-rate

excelentísimo, -a *adj (alcalde)* Your Worship; *(embajador)* Your Excellency; *(juez)* Your Honour *o US* Honor

excelso, -a *adj* sublime, lofty

excentricidad *nf* eccentricity

excéntrico, -a *adj* eccentric

excepción *nf* exception; **a** *o* **con e. de** with the exception of, except for; **de e.** exceptional; **la e. confirma la regla** the exception proves the rule; *Pol* **estado de e.** state of emergency

excepcional *adj (extraordinario)* exceptional, outstanding; *(raro)* exceptional, unusual

excepto *adv* except (for), excepting, apart from

exceptuar [4] *vt* to except, exclude, leave out

excesivo, -a *adj* excessive

exceso *nm* (**a**) *(demasía)* excess, surplus; **con e.** too much; **bebe con e.** he drinks too much; **en e.** in excess, excessively □ **e. de equipaje** excess baggage; **e. de velocidad** speeding (**b**) **excesos** excesses; **cometer excesos** to overindulge

excipiente *nm* excipient

excisión *nf Med* excision

excitabilidad *nf* excitability

excitable *adj* excitable, easily worked up

excitación *nf (sentimiento)* excitement; *(acción)* excitation

excitante 1 *adj* exciting; *Med* stimulating
 2 *nm* stimulant

excitar 1 *vt (gen)* to excite; *(emociones)* to arouse, stir up
 2 excitarse *vpr* to get excited, get carried away, get worked up

exclamación *nf* exclamation; *(grito)* cry; **lanzar** *o* **exhalar una e.** to cry out

exclamar *vt & vi* to exclaim, cry out

exclamativo, -a *adj,* **exclamatorio, -a** *adj* exclamatory

exclaustrado, -a 1 *pp de* **exclaustrar**
 2 *nm,f Rel (monje)* secularized monk; *(monja)* secularized nun

exclaustrar *vt Rel* to secularize

excluir [34] *vt* to exclude, shut out; *(rechazar)* to reject

exclusión *nf* exclusion, shutting out; **a e. de** with the exclusion of, excluding, not counting

exclusiva *nf Com* sole right; *Prensa* exclusive

exclusive *adv* exclusively, exclusive; **del ocho de marzo al siete de noviembre e.** from the eighth of March to the seventh of November exclusive

exclusividad *nf* exclusiveness

exclusivismo *nm* exclusionism

exclusivista 1 *adj* exclusive, select
 2 *nm,f* exclusivist

exclusivo, -a *adj* exclusive

excluyente *adj* excluding

Excma. *(abrev de* **Excelentísima***)* Most Excellent

Excmo. *(abrev de* **Excelentísimo***)* Most Excellent

excombatiente *nmf Br (hombre)* ex-serviceman; *(mujer)* ex-servicewoman; *US* war veteran

excomulgar [38] *vt Rel* to excommunicate

excomunión *nf* excommunication

excoriación *nf* excoriation, chafing; *(desolladura)* graze

excoriar 1 *vt* to excoriate, chafe
 2 excoriarse *vpr* to graze oneself

excrecencia *nf* excrescence

excreción *nf* excretion

excremento *nm* excrement

excretar *vi* to excrete

excretor, -a *adj Anat* excretory; **aparato e.** excretory organ

exculpación *nf* exoneration; *Jur* acquittal

exculpar *vt* to exonerate; *Jur* to acquit

exculpatorio, -a *adj* exonerative

excursión *nf* excursion, trip, outing; **hacer una e.** to go on a trip

excursionismo *nm Dep* hiking

excursionista *nmf* tripper; *(a pie)* hiker

excusa *nf (pretexto)* excuse; *(disculpa)* excuse, apology; **presentar** *o* **ofrecer sus excusas** to apologize

excusado, -a 1 *pp de* **excusar**
 2 *adj* (**a**) *(disculpado)* excused, pardoned, forgiven; *(exempt)* extento; **estar e. de** to be exempt from (**b**) *(innecesario)* unnecessary, needless; **e. es decir que ...** needless to say that ...
 3 *nm Euf* **e.** *(retrete)* the bathroom, *Br* the smallest room

excusar 1 *vt* (**a**) *(justificar)* to excuse (**b**) *(disculpar)* to pardon, forgive (**c**) *(eximir)* exempt (**de** from) (**d**) *Esp Fml (evitar)* to avoid, prevent; **así excusamos problemas** this way we avoid problems; **excuso decirte** I don't have to tell you, needless to say
 2 excusarse *vpr (disculparse)* to apologize, excuse oneself

execrable *adj* execrable, abominable

execración *nf* execration

execrar *vt* to execrate, abhor, deplore

exégesis *nf inv* exegesis, explanation

exención *nf* exemption; **e. de impuestos** *o* **fiscal** tax exemption

exento, -a *adj* exempt, free (**de** from); **e. de preocupaciones** carefree; **está e. del servicio militar** he's exempt from military service; **no está e. de peligros** it is not without danger

exequias *nfpl* obsequies, funeral rites

exfoliación *nf* exfoliation

exfoliante 1 *adj* exfoliating
 2 *nm* exfoliating cream/lotion *etc*

exfoliar *vt* to exfoliate

exhalación *nf* (**a**) *(emanación)* exhalation (**b**) *(estrella)* shooting star; *(rayo)* flash of lightning; *Fam Fig* **pasar como una e.** to flash past

exhalar 1 *vt (aire)* to exhale, breathe out; *(gas)* to give off, emit; *(suspiro)* to heave; *(queja)* to utter
  2 exhalarse *vpr (persona)* to rush

exhaustivo, -a *adj* exhaustive, thorough; **de modo e.** thoroughly

exhausto, -a *adj* exhausted

exhibición *nf* éxhibition, show; *Cin* showing ▫ **e. aérea** air show

exhibicionismo *nm* exhibitionism

exhibicionista *nmf* exhibitionist

exhibir 1 *vt* (**a**) *(mostrar)* to exhibit, display, show (**b**) *(ostentar)* to show off (**c**) *Méx (pagar)* to pay
  2 exhibirse *vpr (ostentar)* to show off, make an exhibition of oneself

exhortación *nf* exhortation

exhortar *vt* to exhort

exhumación *nf* exhumation

exhumar *vt* to exhume

exigencia *nf* exigency, demand; *(requisito)* requirement

exigente *adj* demanding, exacting

exigible *adj* payable on demand

exigir [24] *vt (persona)* to demand, insist on; *(situación)* to require, call for; **este problema exige una solución rápida** this problem requires a swift solution; **exige demasiado** he's extremely demanding; **e. buena cualidad en el servicio** to insist upon good service

exigüidad *nf (pequeñez)* smallness; *(escasez)* scantiness, meagreness, scarcity; **e. de recursos** lack of funds

exiguo, -a *adj (pequeño)* small, tiny; *(escaso)* scanty, meagre, *US* meager

exilado, -a *pp & adj & nm,f véase* **exiliado, -a**

exilar *vt véase* **exiliar**

exiliado, -a 1 *pp de* **exiliar**
  2 *adj* exiled, in exile
  3 *nm,f* exile

exiliar 1 *vt* to exile
  2 exilarse *vpr* to go into exile

exilio *nm* (**a**) *(acción)* exile, banishment; **enviar al e.** to send into exile (**b**) *(lugar)* (place of) exile

eximio, -a *adj* distinguished, renowned, eminent

eximir 1 *vt* to exempt, free, excuse (**de** from)
  2 eximirse *vpr* to free oneself (**de** from)

existencia *nf* (**a**) *(vida)* existence, life (**b**) **existencias** *Com* stock *sing*, stocks; **en e.** in stock; **renovar las e.** to restock ▫ **liquidación de e.** clearance sale

existencial *adj Filos* existential

existencialismo *nm Filos* existentialism

existencialista *adj Filos* existentialist

existente *adj* existing, existent; *Com* in stock

existir *vi* to exist, be (in existence); **existen aún muchas dificultades** there are still many difficulties

exitazo *nm Fam* terrific success, smash hit

éxito *nm* success; **con é.** successfully; **no tener é.** to fail, not succeed; **tener é.** to be successful

exitoso, -a *adj* successful

éxodo *nm* exodus

exoneración *nf* exoneration

exonerar *vt* to exonerate

exorbitante *adj* exorbitant, excessive

exorcismo *nm* exorcism

exorcista *nmf* exorcist

exorcizar [14] *vt* to exorcize

exordio *nm* exordium, foreword

exótico, -a *adj* exotic

exotismo *nm* exoticism

expandible *adj Inform* expandible

expandir 1 *vt (dilatar)* to expand; *Fig (divulgar)* to spread
  2 expandirse *vpr (dilatarse)* to expand; *Fig (divulgarse)* to spread

expansión *nf* (**a**) *(de un gas)* expansion; *(crecimiento)* growth (**b**) *Fig (difusión)* spreading (**c**) *Fig (diversión)* relaxation, recreation

expansionarse *vpr* (**a**) *(gas)* to expand (**b**) *Fig (divertirse)* to relax, amuse oneself, let one's hair down

expansionismo *nm* expansionism

expansionista *adj* expansionist

expansivo, -a *adj* (**a**) *(gas)* expansive (**b**) *Fig (persona)* open, frank

expatriación *nf* expatriation

expatriado, -a 1 *pp de* **expatriar**
  2 *adj & nm,f* expatriate

expatriar [32] **1** *vt* to exile, banish
  2 expatriarse *vpr* to leave one's country, emigrate, go into exile

expectación *nf (esperanza)* expectation, expectancy, anticipation; *(emoción)* excitement

expectante *adj* expectant

expectativa *nf* (**a**) *(esperanza)* expectation, expectancy (**b**) *(perspectiva)* prospect; **estar a la e. de** to be on the lookout for, be on the watch for

expectoración *nf* (**a**) *(acción)* expectoration (**b**) *(esputo)* sputum, phlegm

expectorante *nm Farm* expectorant

expectorar *vt & vi* to expectorate

expedición *nf* (**a**) *(gen)* expedition; *(viaje)* expedition; *(personas)* party (**b**) *(envío)* dispatch, shipping; *(conjunto de mercancías)* shipment

expedicionario, -a 1 *adj* expeditionary; *Mil* **cuerpo o grupo e.** expeditionary force
  2 *nm,f* member of an expedition

expedidor, -a *nm,f Com* sender, dispatcher, shipper

expedientar *vt* to make a file on, place under enquiry

expediente *nm* (**a**) *(informe)* dossier, record; *(ficha)* file; *Fam* **cubrir el e.** to keep up appearances ▫ *Educ* **e. académico** student's record (**b**) *Jur* proceedings *pl*, action; **formar e. a** to take proceedings against; **incoar e.** to start proceedings (**c**) *(recurso)* expedient; **recurrir al e. de** to resort to

expedir [47] **1** *vt* (**a**) *(despachar)* *(carta etc)* to send, dispatch; *(mercancías)* to send, dispatch, ship (**b**) *(pasaporte, título)* to issue; *(contrato, documento)* to draw up
  2 expedirse *vpr CSur (manejarse)* to manage

expeditivo, -a *adj* expeditious

expedito, -a *adj (presto)* expeditious, prompt, speedy; *(libre)* free, clear

expeler *vt* to expel, eject, throw out

expendedor, -a 1 *adj* selling, retailing, retail
  2 *nm,f (vendedor)* dealer, seller, retailer; **e. de tabaco** tobacconist
  3 *nm* **e. automático** vending machine

expendeduría *nf Br* tobacconist's, *US* cigar store

expender *vt (al por menor)* to retail, sell; *(gastar)* to spend

expensas *nfpl* **a e. de** at the expense of

experiencia *nf* experience; *(experimento)* experiment; **por e.** from experience ❑ **e. laboral** work experience

experimentación *nf* experimentation, experimenting, testing

experimentado, -a 1 *pp de* **experimentar**
2 *adj (persona)* experienced; *(método)* tested, tried

experimental *adj* experimental

experimentar *vt* **(a)** *(hacer experimentos)* to experiment, test **(b)** *(sentir)* to experience, feel; *(pérdida)* to suffer; *(aumento)* to show; *(cambio)* to undergo; *Med* **e. una mejoría** to improve, make progress **(c)** *(probar)* to test, try out

experimento *nm* experiment, test

experto, -a *adj & nm,f* expert

expiación *nf* expiation, atonement

expiar [32] *vt* to expiate, atone for

expiatorio, -a *adj* expiatory

expiración *nf* expiration, expiry; **fecha de e.** expiry date

expirar *vi* to expire

explanada *nf* esplanade

explanar *vt* **(a)** *(allanar)* to level, grade **(b)** *Fig (explicar)* to explain, elucidate; *(aclarar)* to clear up

explayarse *vpr* **(a)** *(hablar)* to dwell (on), elaborate (on), talk at length (about) **(b)** *(divertirse)* to enjoy oneself **(c)** *(confiarse)* to open one's heart **(con** to)

explicable *adj* explicable, explainable

explicación *nf* explanation; *(motivo)* reason; **sin dar explicaciones** without giving any reason

explicaderas *nfpl Fam* way *sing* of explaining; **tener buenas e.** to be good at explaining things

explicar [59] **1** *vt* to explain, expound
2 explicarse *vpr* **(a)** *(persona)* to explain (oneself); **¿me explico?** do you understand?; **se explica muy bien** he's very articulate **(b)** *(algo)* to understand, make out; **no me lo explico** I can't understand it

explicativo, -a *adj* explanatory

explicitar *vt* to state explicitly

explícito, -a *adj* explicit

exploración *nf* exploration; *Téc* scanning; *Mil* reconnaissance

explorador, -a 1 *adj* exploring, exploratory; *Mil* **avión e.** reconnaissance aircraft
2 *nm,f (persona)* explorer; *(niño)* boy scout; *(niña)* girl guide, *US* girl scout
3 *nm Inform* browser

explorar *vt* to explore; *Med* to probe; *Téc* to scan; *Min* to drill, prospect; *Mil* to reconnoitre; *Fig* **e. el terreno** to see how the land lies; *Inform* to browse

exploratorio, -a *adj* exploratory; *Med* probing

explosión *nf* **(a)** *(estallido)* explosion, blast, blowing up; **hacer e.** to explode; **se oyó una fuerte e.** there was a loud explosion ❑ **e. demográfica** population explosion; **motor de e.** internal combustion engine **(b)** *Fig* outburst

explosionar *vt & vi* to explode, blast, blow up

explosivo, -a 1 *adj* explosive; *Ling* plosive
2 *nm* explosive

explotable *adj (mina)* exploitable, workable; *(terreno)* which can be farmed o cultivated

explotación *nf* **(a)** *(utilización)* exploitation, working; *Agr* cultivation (of land); **e. de recursos** tapping of resources ❑ **e. agrícola** farm; **e. forestal** forestry; **e. minera** mine; **gastos de e.** running costs o expenses **(b)** *Pey (abuso)* exploitation

explotador, -a *nm,f Pey* exploiter

explotar 1 *vt* **(a)** *(gen) (aprovechar)* to exploit; *(mina)* to work; *(recursos)* to tap; *(fábrica)* to operate; *(tierra)* to cultivate **(b)** *Pey (personas, situación)* to exploit
2 *vi (bomba)* to explode, go off

expo *nf (exposición universal)* expo

expoliación *nf* pillaging, plundering

expoliador, -a 1 *adj* pillaging, plundering
2 *nm,f* pillager, plunderer

expoliar *vt* to pillage, plunder

expolio *nm (acción)* pillaging, plundering; *(botín)* plunder, booty

exponencial *adj & nf* exponential

exponente 1 *nmf (persona)* exponent
2 *nm Mat* index, exponent

exponer [50] *(pp* expuesto*)* **1** *vt* **(a)** *(mostrar)* to expose, show, exhibit, display **(b)** *(explicar)* to expound, explain, put forward; *(propuesta)* to set out **(c)** *(arriesgar)* to expose, risk, endanger
2 exponerse *vpr (arriesgarse)* to run the risk **(a** of*)*, expose oneself **(a** to*)*; **no te expongas a tal peligro** don't expose yourself to such a danger; **te expones a perder el trabajo** you run the risk of losing your job

exportable *adj* exportable, for exportation

exportación *nf* exportation, export ❑ **derechos de e.** export duties; **licencia de e.** export licence

exportador, -a 1 *adj* exporting; **países exportadores de petróleo** petroleum exporting countries
2 *nm,f* exporter

exportar *vt también Inform* to export

exposición *nf* **(a)** *Arte* exhibition, show, display ❑ **e. universal** world fair; **sala de exposiciones** gallery **(b)** *(explicación)* account, claim, explanation; *(de hechos, ideas)* exposé **(c)** *Fot* exposure

expositivo, -a *adj* explanatory

expósito, -a *nm,f (niño)* **e.** foundling

expositor, -a *nm,f (de teoría)* exponent; *Arte* exhibitor

exprés *adj* express; **(olla) e.** pressure cooker; **(café) e.** espresso (coffee)

expresado, -a 1 *pp de* expresar
2 *adj* aforesaid, above-mentioned

expresamente *adv (específicamente)* specifically, expressly; *(deliberadamente)* on purpose, deliberately

expresar 1 *vt (gen)* to express; *(manifestar)* to state; *(indicar)* to convey
2 expresarse *vpr* to express oneself

expresión *nf* **(a)** *(gen)* expression; **reducir algo a la mínima e.** to reduce sth to the bare minimum ❑ **e. corporal** free expression **(b)** *(locución)* expression, phrase **(c)** **expresiones** greetings, regards

expresionismo *nm Arte* expressionism

expresionista *adj & nmf Arte* expressionist

expresivamente *adv* affectionately

expresividad *nf* expressiveness

expresivo, -a *adj* **(a)** *(elocuente)* expressive; **mirada expresiva** meaningful glance; **silencio e.** eloquent silence **(b)** *(cariñoso)* warm, affectionate; **es poco e.** he doesn't show his feelings

expreso, -a 1 *adj (especificado)* express; **con el fin e. de** with the express purpose of
2 *nm Ferroc* express (train)
3 *adv* on purpose, deliberately; **lo hizo e. para fastidiar** he did it just to be awkward

exprimidor *nm* squeezer, *US* juicer

exprimir *vt* **(a)** *(limón)* to squeeze; *(zumo)* to squeeze out **(b)** *Fig (persona)* to exploit, bleed dry

expropiación *nf* expropriation ◻ **e. forzosa** expropriation, *Br* compulsory purchase

expropiar *vt* to expropriate

expuesto, -a 1 *pp de* **exponer**
  2 *adj* (**a**) *(sin protección)* exposed (**b**) *(peligroso)* risky, dangerous; **estar e. a** to be exposed to (**c**) *(manifestado)* expressed, stated (**d**) *(exhibido)* on display, exhibited, on show

expulsar *vt* (**a**) *(echar)* to expel, eject, throw out; *Dep (jugador)* to send off; *(de alumno)* to expel; *(de universidad)* to send down, *US* expel (**b**) *(humo etc)* to belch out

expulsión *nf* expulsion, ejection; *Dep* sending off; *(de alumno)* expulsion; *(de universidad)* sending down, *US* expulsion

expulsor, -a 1 *adj* ejecting; **mecanismo e.** ejector mechanism
  2 *nm Téc* ejector

expurgación *nf* expurgation; *Fig* purge, purging

expurgar [38] *vt* to expurgate; *Fig* to purge

exquisitez *nf* exquisiteness; *(manjar)* delicacy, refinement

exquisito, -a *adj (bello)* exquisite; *(delicioso)* delicious; *(gusto)* refined

extasiado, -a 1 *pp de* **extasiarse**
  2 *adj* ecstatic; **quedarse e.** to go into ecstasies *o* raptures

extasiarse [32] *vpr* to go into ecstasies *o* raptures

éxtasis *nm inv* ecstasy, rapture

extemporáneo, -a *adj* (**a**) *(lluvia etc)* unseasonable (**b**) *(inoportuno)* untimely, inappropriate

extender [64] **1** *vt* (**a**) *(gen)* to extend; *(agrandar)* to enlarge (**b**) *(mapa, plano)* to spread (out), open (out); *(mano, brazo)* to stretch (out) (**c**) *(documento)* to draw up; *(cheque)* to make out; *(pasaporte, certificado)* to issue
  2 extenderse *vpr* (**a**) *(en el tiempo)* to extend, last (**b**) *(terreno)* to spread out, stretch; **sus propiedades se extienden hasta el río** his property stretches down to the river (**c**) *(difundirse)* to spread, extend; **el rumor se extendió rápidamente** the rumour spread quickly (**d**) *Fig (hablar demasiado)* to enlarge upon, go on about; **siempre se extiende demasiado en sus clases** she always goes on too much in her classes

extendido, -a 1 *pp de* **extender**
  2 *adj* (**a**) *(gen)* extended; *(mapa, plano)* spread out, open; *(mano, brazo)* outstretched (**b**) *(difundido)* widespread

extensamente *adv* extensively, at length; *(ampliamente)* widely

extensible *adj* extending

extensión *nf (gen)* extension; *(dimensión)* extent, size; *(superficie)* area, expanse; *Mús* range; **de gran e.** very extensive; **en toda la e. de la palabra** in every sense of the word; **por e.** by extension; *Inform Tel* extension

extensivo, -a *adj* extendable, extensive; **hacer extensiva una invitación a algn** to extend an invitation to sb

extenso, -a *adj (amplio)* extensive, long, vast; *(grande)* large; *(largo)* long

extensor, -a 1 *adj* extending; *Anat* **músculo e.** extensor muscle
  2 *nm (aparato)* chest expander

extenuación *nf (agotamiento)* exhaustion; *(debilidad)* weakening; *(enflaquecimiento)* emaciation

extenuado, -a 1 *pp de* **extenuar**
  2 *adj* exhausted, worn-out

extenuante *adj* exhausting

extenuar [4] **1** *vt (agotar)* to exhaust; *(debilitar)* to weaken
  2 extenuarse *vpr* to exhaust oneself

exterior 1 *adj* (**a**) *(de fuera)* outer, exterior, external; *(puerta)* outside; *(pared)* outer; **aspecto e.** outward appearance (**b**) *(política, deuda)* foreign ◻ *Pol* **Ministerio de Asuntos Exteriores** Ministry of Foreign Affairs, *Br* Foreign Office, *US* State Department; **política e.** foreign policy
  2 *nm* (**a**) *(parte de fuera)* exterior, outside (**b**) *(extranjero)* abroad, overseas; **en el e.** abroad, in foreign countries (**c**) *Dep (jugador)* outside (**d**) **exteriores** *Cin* location *sing*

exterioridad *nf* outward *o* external appearance

exteriorización *nf* manifestation, showing, externalization

exteriorizar [14] *vt* to show, reveal, manifest

exteriormente *adv* outwardly

exterminación *nf* extermination, wiping out, destruction

exterminador, -a 1 *adj* exterminating
  2 *nm,f* exterminator

exterminar *vt* to exerminate, wipe out, destroy

exterminio *nm* extermination, wiping out, destruction

externalización *nf Com* outsourcing

externalizar [14] *vt Com* to outsource

externamente *adv* externally, outwardly

externar *vt Méx (emoción, opinión)* to express

externo, -a 1 *adj* external, outward, exterior; **parte externa** outside; *Farm* **de uso e.** for external use only
  2 *nm,f Educ* day pupil

extinción *nf (gen)* extinction; **los bomberos lograron la e. del fuego** the firemen managed to put out the fire

extinguidor *nm Am* fire extinguisher

extinguir [26] **1** *vt (fuego)* to exinguish, put out; *(deuda, raza)* to wipe out
  2 extinguirse *vpr (fuego)* to go out; *(especie)* to become extinct, die out

extinto, -a *adj* extinct

extintor *nm Esp* fire extinguisher

extirpable *adj* (**a**) *Med* removable (**b**) *Fig* eradicable

extirpación *nf* (**a**) *Med* removal, extraction (**b**) *Fig* eradication, stamping out, wiping out

extirpar *vt* (**a**) *Med* to remove, extract (**b**) *Fig* to eradicate, stamp out, wipe out

extorsión *nf* (**a**) *(molestia)* inconvenience, trouble; **si no le causa e.** if it won't put you out (**b**) *(de dinero)* extortion, exaction

extorsionar *vt* (**a**) *(plan)* to mess up (**b**) *(dinero)* to extort, exact

extorsionista *nmf Jur* extortionist

extra¹ 1 *adj* (**a**) *(de más)* extra; **horas e.** overtime; **paga e.** bonus (**b**) *(superior)* **e. especial** top quality
  2 *nm* extra
  3 *nmf Cin Teat* extra
  4 *nf* (**a**) *Fam (paga)* = additional payment of a month's salary or wages in June and December (**b**) *Am (gasolina) Br* 4-star petrol, *US* premium gas

extra² *pref* extra

extracción *nf* (**a**) *(gen)* extraction ◻ **e. social** social extraction (**b**) *(lotería)* draw

extractar *vt* to summarize

extracto *nm* (**a**) *(trozo)* extract, excerpt; *Fin* **e. de cuenta** statement of account (**b**) *(resumen)* summary (**c**) *Quím* extract

extractor *nm* extractor

extracurricular *adj Educ* extracurricular

extradición *nf* extradition; **otorgar la e. de algn** to extadite sb

extraditar *vt* to extradite

extraer [66] *vt* to extract, take out

extraescolar *adj* out of school; **actividad e.** extracurricular activity

extrafino, -a *adj* superfine, best quality; **azúcar e.** castor sugar; **chocolate e.** superfine chocolate

extrajudicial *adj* extrajudicial

extralimitación *nf* abuse

extralimitarse *vpr* to go too far, overstep the mark; **e. en sus funciones** to exceed one's authority

extramatrimonial *adj*, **extramarital** *adj* extramarital

extramuros *adv* outside the city

extranjería *nf* status of foreigners ❑ **ley de e.** law on aliens

extranjerismo *nm* foreign expression

extranjerizar [14] *vt* to introduce foreign customs to

extranjero, -a 1 *adj* foreign, alien
2 *nm,f* foreigner, alien
3 *nm* foreign countries *pl*, abroad; **viajar al e.** to travel *o* go abroad

extranjis: de extranjis *loc adv Esp Fam* secretly, in an underhand way, on the sly

extrañamente *adv* strangely, oddly

extrañamiento *nm* banishment, exile

extrañar 1 *vt* **(a)** *(desterrar)* to banish, exile **(b)** *(sorprender)* to surprise; *(encontrar extraño)* to find strange; **no es de e.** it's hardly surprising, it's no wonder **(c)** *(echar de menos)* to miss; **extraño mi cama** I miss my bed
2 extrañarse *vpr (sorprenderse)* **e. de** to be surprised at, find surprising

extrañeza *nf (sorpresa)* surprise; *(rareza)* strangeness

extraño, -a 1 *adj* strange, odd, queer, peculiar; *Med* **cuerpo e.** foreign body
2 *nm,f* stranger

extraoficial *adj* unofficial, informal; **declaraciones extraoficiales** off-the-record statement

extraordinariamente *adv* extraordinarily, unusually

extraordinario, -a *adj (poco común)* extraordinary, unusual; *(raro)* queer, odd; *(sorprendente)* surprising; *Prensa* **edición extraordinaria** special edition; **hizo un calor e.** it was unusually hot; **no tiene nada de e.** there's nothing special about it

extraplano, -a *adj* super-slim, extra-thin

extrapolación *nf* extrapolation

extrapolar *vt* to extrapolate

extrarradio *nm* outskirts *pl*, suburbs *pl*

extrasensorial *adj* extrasensory

extraterrestre 1 *adj* extraterrestrial
2 *nmf* alien

extraterritorial *adj* extraterritorial

extraterritorialidad *nf* extraterritorial rights

extrauterino, -a *adj Med* extrauterine; **embarazo e.** ectopic pregnancy

extravagancia *nf* extravagance, eccentricity

extravagante *adj* odd, outlandish, strange

extraversión *nf* extroversion

extravertido, -a *adj & nm,f véase* **extrovertido, -a**

extraviado, -a 1 *pp de* **extraviar**
2 *adj (perdido)* lost, missing; **perro e.** stray dog

extraviar [32] **1** *vt* **(a)** *(objeto)* to mislay, lose **(b)** *(persona)* to mislead, lead astray
2 extraviarse *vpr* **(a)** *(objeto)* to be missing, get mislaid **(b)** *(persona)* to get lost, lose one's way

extravío *nm (pérdida)* loss, mislaying; *Fig* deviation, leading astray

extremadamente *adv* extremely

extremado, -a 1 *pp de* **extremar**
2 *adj* extreme

extremar 1 *vt* to carry to extremes *o* to the limit, overdo; **e. la prudencia** to be extremely careful
2 extremarse *vpr* to take great pains, do one's utmost

extremaunción *nf Rel* extreme unction

extremeño, -a 1 *adj* of *o* from Extremadura
2 *nm,f* person from Extremadura

extremidad *nf* **(a)** *(extremo)* end, tip **(b)** *Anat (miembro)* limb, extremity

extremis: in extremis *loc adv* as a last resort

extremismo *nm* extremism

extremista *adj & nmf* extremist

extremo, -a 1 *adj* extreme, utmost
2 *nm (límite)* end, extreme, furthest point; **en e.** very much; **en último e.** as a last resort; **pasar de un e. a otro** to go from one extreme to another
3 *nm,f Dep (jugador)* wing; *Ftb* **e. derecha/izquierda** outside-right/-left

extremoso, -a *adj (persona)* effusive, demonstrative; *(vehemente)* extreme in one's attitudes

extrínseco, -a *adj* extrinsic

extroversión *nf* extroversion

extrovertido, -a *adj & nm,f* extrovert

exuberancia *nf* exuberance

exuberante *adj (gen)* exuberant; *(vegetación)* lush, abundant

exudación *nf* exudation

exudar *vt & vi* to exude, ooze (out)

exultación *nf* exultation

exultante *adj* exultant

exultar *vi* to exult, rejoice; **e. de alegría** to jump for joy

exvoto *nm* votive offering, ex voto

eyaculación *nf* ejaculation; **e. precoz** premature ejaculation

eyacular *vi* to ejaculate

eyección *nf* ejection

eyectable *adj* **asiento e.** ejector seat

eyectar *vt* to eject

eyector *nm* ejector

EZLN *nm Méx (abrev de* **Ejército Zapatista de Liberación Nacional***)* Zapatista Army of National Liberation

F

F, f ['efe] *nf (la letra)* F, f

f. *(abrev de* **folio)** f.

fa *nm Mús* F

fabada *nf Culin* = stew of beans, pork sausage and bacon

fábrica *nf* **(a)** *(industria)* factory, plant ▫ **f. de cerveza** brewery; **f. de conservas** canning plant; **f. de gas** gasworks *sing*; **f. de harina** flour mill; **f. de montaje** assembly plant; **f. de papel** paper mill; **marca de f.** trademark; **precio de f.** factory *o* ex-works price **(b)** *(fabricación)* manufacture **(c)** *Arquit* masonry; **una pared de f.** a stonework wall

fabricación *nf* manufacture, production, making; **de f. casera** home-made; **de f. propia** our own make ▫ **defecto de f.** manufacturing fault; **f. en cadena** mass production; **productos de f. defectuosa** seconds

fabricante *nmf* manufacturer, maker

fabricar [59] *vt* **(a)** *Ind* to manufacture, produce; make; **fabricado en España** made in Spain; **f. algo en serie** to mass-produce sth **(b)** *Fig (inventar)* **f. cuentos/mentiras** to fabricate stories/lies

fabril *adj* manufacturing; **la industria f.** manufacturing industry

fábula *nf* **(a)** *Lit* fable; *Fam* **de f.** smashing, fabulous **(b)** *(mito)* myth, legend **(c)** *Fig (mentira)* invention

fabulación *nf* invention, fantasy

fabular *vi* to make things up

fabulista *nmf Lit* writer of fables

fabuloso, -a *adj* **(a)** *(extraordinario)* fabulous, fantastic **(b)** *Lit* fabulous, mythical

faca *nf* large curved knife

facción *nf* **(a)** *Pol* faction **(b) facciones** *(rasgos)* (facial) features

faccioso, -a 1 *adj* factious, seditious
2 *nm,f* rebel

faceta *nf* facet; *Fig* **este problema presenta muchas facetas** this problem has many sides to it

faceto, -a *adj Méx* finicky, fussy

facha¹ *nf Fam* **(a)** *(aspecto)* appearance, look; **no puedes ir con esa f.** you can't go (looking) like that **(b)** *(mamarracho)* mess, sight; **estar hecho una f.** to look a mess *o* a sight **(c)** *Chile (presunción)* arrogance, presumption

facha² *Esp* **1** *adj Pey* fascist, extreme right-wing
2 *nmf Pey* fascist, extreme right-winger

fachada *nf* **(a)** *Arquit* façade, front; **con f. a** facing, overlooking **(b)** *Fam (apariencia)* outward show, façade, window dressing

fachenda *Fam* **1** *nf (condición)* swankiness, conceit
2 *nmf (persona)* swank, show-off

fachendoso, -a *adj Fam* swanky

fachoso, -a *adj* **(a)** *Fam (desastrado)* scruffy **(b)** *Andes Méx (fanfarrón)* boastful

facial *adj* facial

fácil *adj* **(a)** *(sencillo)* easy; **es muy f. de decir, pero ...** it's easily said, but ...; **f. de comprender/de leer** easy to understand/to read **(b)** *(probable)* likely, probable; **a estas horas no es f. que venga** it's unlikely that he will come at this late hour; **es f. que ...** it's (quite) likely that ... **(c)** *(acomodaticio)* compliant, easygoing **(d)** *Pey (mujer)* easy, loose

facilidad *nf* **(a)** *(simplicidad)* easiness, facility; **ahora tiene mayor f. para viajar** it is easier for him to travel now; **con gran f.** easily; **dar facilidades** to give every facility, make things easy ▫ *Com* **facilidades de pago** easy terms **(b)** *(talento)* talent, gift; **tiene f. para los idiomas** she has a gift for languages

facilitación *nf* **(a)** *(simplificación)* facilitation **(b)** *(abastecimiento)* provision, furnishing

facilitar *vt* **(a)** *(simplificar)* to make easy *o* easier, facilitate **(b)** *(proporcionar)* to provide, supply; **nos facilitarán todo el equipo** they'll provide us with all the equipment **(c)** *(entrevista etc)* to arrange

fácilmente *adv* easily

facilón, -ona *adj Fam* **(a)** *(muy fácil)* dead easy **(b)** *(trivial)* hackneyed, lacking originality; **una canción facilona** a catchy tune

facineroso, -a *nm,f* criminal

facistol 1 *nm (atril)* lectern
2 *adj Carib Méx (petulante)* vain, boastful
3 *nmf Carib Méx (vanidoso)* vain *o* conceited person

facón *nm RP* gaucho knife

facsímil *nm,* **facsímile** *nm* facsimile

factible *adj* feasible, practicable, workable

fáctico, -a *adj* **poderes fácticos** extraparliamentary political powers

factor *nm* **(a)** *(condicionante)* factor **(b)** *Mat* factor **(c)** *Ferroc* luggage clerk

factoría *nf* **(a)** *Com* trading post **(b)** *(fábrica)* factory, mill

factótum *(pl* **factotums)** *nm* **(a)** *(empleado)* factotum **(b)** *(persona entrometida)* busybody

factura *nf* **(a)** *Com* bill, invoice; **pasar** *o* **presentar f. a** to invoice, send a bill to; *Fig* to make (sb) pay; **según f.** as per invoice ▫ **f. pro forma** pro forma invoice **(b)** *Arg Culin* bread and cakes *pl*

facturación *nf* **(a)** *Com* invoicing **(b)** *(de equipajes) (en aeropuerto)* checking-in; *(en estación)* registration

facturar vt (**a**) Com to invoice, charge for (**b**) (equipaje) to register, check in

facultad nf (**a**) (capacidad) faculty, ability □ **facultades mentales** mental powers (**b**) Fml (poder) faculty, power; **tener f. para hacer algo** to be authorized to do sth (**c**) Univ faculty, school; **f. de Derecho** faculty of Law; **f. de Letras** Arts faculty

facultar vt to authorize, empower

facultativo, -a 1 adj (**a**) (no obligatorio) optional (**b**) (profesional) professional; Med medical
  2 nm,f doctor, physician

facundia nf verbosity, wordiness, long-windedness

facundo, -a adj (locuaz) verbose, wordy, long-winded; (parlanchín) talkative

faena nf (**a**) (tarea) task, job; Fam **estar metido en f.** to be hard at work; **faenas de la casa** housework sing, household chores (**b**) Fam (mala pasada) dirty trick (**c**) Taur series of passes (**d**) Cuba Guat Méx (en hacienda) overtime (**e**) Chile (cuadrilla de obreros) group of labourers (**f**) Ecuad (trabajo matinal) morning work (**g**) RP (matanza) slaughtering (of cattle)

faenar vi **1** vi (pescar) to fish
  2 vt RP (ganado) to slaughter

fagocitar vt to engulf, swallow up

fagocito nm Biol phagocyte

fagocitosis nf inv Biol phagocytosis

fagot Mús **1** nm (instrumento) bassoon
  2 nmf (músico) bassoonist

Fahrenheit [faren'xait] adj inv Fahrenheit

faisán nm Orn pheasant

faja nf (**a**) (cinturón) band, belt (**b**) (de mujer) girdle, corset (**c**) (banda) sash (**d**) (correo) **f. (postal)** wrapper (**e**) (franja) strip; **una f. de terreno sin labrar** a strip of unploughed land

fajar 1 vt (**a**) (ceñir) to bind, wrap (**b**) RP Fam (pegar) to thump, beat (**c**) Am (acometer) to attack, assault (**d**) Carib (pedir dinero) to ask for a loan
  2 fajarse vpr Am Fam (pegarse) **se fajaron** they had a scrap

fajín nm Mil sash

fajina nf (**a**) (leña) brushwood, kindling (**b**) Mil mess call

fajo nm (**a**) (de leña, cañas) bundle; **un f. de billetes** a wad of notes (**b**) Am (trago de licor) swig (**c**) Méx (cinturón) belt (**d**) Méx (golpe) blow

falacia nf (**a**) (error) fallacy (**b**) (engaño) deceit, trick (**c**) (hábito de engañar) deceitfulness

falange nf (**a**) Anat phalange, phalanx (**b**) Mil phalanx (**c**) Hist Pol **la F. (Española)** the Falange

falangista adj & nmf Hist Pol Falangist

falaz adj (**a**) (erróneo) fallacious (**b**) (engañoso) deceitful; (falso) false

falca nf (**a**) Méx Ven (canoa) = canoe with a roof (**b**) Col (barcaza) ferryboat (at river crossing)

falda nf (**a**) (prenda) skirt; Fig **está pegado** o **cosido a las faldas de su madre** he is tied to his mother's apron strings; Fam **anda siempre entre faldas** he's always with the girls □ **f. escocesa** kilt; **f. pantalón** culottes pl (**b**) (regazo) lap; **tener un niño en la f.** to have a child on one's lap (**c**) Geog (ladera) slope, hillside (**d**) Culin (corte de carne) brisket (**e**) (de mesa camilla) cover

faldero, -a adj (**a**) (mujeriego) fond of the girls (**b**) (perro) lapdog

faldón nm (**a**) (de ropa) skirt, tail (**b**) Arquit gable

falencia nf Am Com bankruptcy

falibilidad nf fallibility

falible adj fallible

fálico, -a adj phallic

falla[1] nf (defecto) defect, fault

falla[2] nf Geol fault

falla[3] nf Esp (**a**) (figura de cartón) = cardboard figure burnt on Saint Joseph's Day in Valencia (**b**) **las Fallas** = firework celebrations held in Valencia on Saint Joseph's Day

fallar[1] **1** vt (**a**) Jur (sentencia) to pass, pronounce (**b**) (premio) to award
  2 vi (**a**) Jur to pass sentence, pronounce judgement (**b**) (premio) to award a prize

fallar[2] **1** vt Naipes to trump, ruff
  2 vi (**a**) (fracasar) to fail; **he fallado como padre** I have failed as a father; **le falló la puntería** he missed his aim; **me falló el plan** my plan went wrong; **nos falló en el último momento** he let us down at the last minute; **nuestros cálculos fallaron** we were wrong, we miscalculated (**b**) (no funcionar) to fail; **le falló el corazón** he had a heart attack; **le fallaron los frenos** the brakes failed (**c**) (ceder) to give way, collapse

falleba nf latch

fallecer [46] vi Fml to pass away, die

fallecido, -a 1 pp de **fallecer**
  2 adj deceased

fallecimiento nm decease, demise

fallero, -a Esp **1** adj of o relating to **las Fallas**
  2 nm,f (**a**) (constructor) maker of **fallas** (**b**) (organizador) organizer of **las Fallas**

fallido, -a adj unsuccessful, vain; Com **deuda fallida** bad debt

fallo nm (**a**) Esp (error) mistake, blunder; (fracaso) failure (**b**) Esp (defecto) fault, defect (**c**) Jur (sentencia) judgement, sentence (**d**) (de premio) awarding (**e**) Med Téc failure (**f**) Naipes void; **f. en corazones** void in hearts

falo nm phallus

falocracia nf male chauvinism

falócrata nm male chauvinist (pig)

falsario, -a nm,f (**a**) (mentiroso) liar (**b**) (falsificador) forger, counterfeiter

falseamiento nm falsification

falsear 1 vt (**a**) (informe etc) to falsify; (hechos, la verdad) to distort (**b**) (falsificar) to counterfeit, forge (**c**) Constr to bevel
  2 vi (**a**) (flaquear) to give way (**b**) Mús to be out of tune

falsedad nf (**a**) (hipocresía) falseness, hypocrisy; (doblez) duplicity (**b**) (mentira) falsehood, lie

falsete nm Mús falsetto; **voz de f.** falsetto voice

falsía nf (hipocresía) falseness, hypocrisy; (doblez) duplicity

falsificación nf (**a**) (gen) falsification; (de cuadro, firma) forging, forgery; (de moneda) counterfeiting, forgery (**b**) (objeto) forgery

falsificador, -a 1 adj (de cuadro, firma) forging; (de dinero) counterfeiting, forging
  2 nm,f (de cuadro, firma) forger; (de dinero) counterfeiter, forger

falsificar [59] vt (gen) to falsify; (cuadro, firma) to forge; (dinero) to counterfeit, forge

falso, -a adj (**a**) (afirmación, información, rumor) false, untrue; **dar un paso en f.** (tropezar) to trip, stumble; (cometer un error) to make a blunder, make a wrong move; **jurar en f.** to commit perjury □ Ling **f. amigo** false friend; **f. techo** false ceiling (**b**) (persona) insincere, treacherous

falta nf (**a**) (carencia) lack; **por f. de algo** for want o lack of sth; **no hizo por f. de ganas** I didn't go because I didn't feel like it; **sin f.** without fail □ **f. de educación** bad manners; **f.**

de pago nonpayment (**b**) *(escasez)* shortage; **f. de agua** water shortage (**c**) *(ausencia)* absence; **echar algo/a algn en f.** to miss sth/sb; **poner f. a algn** to mark sb absent (**d**) *(error)* mistake; **tu redacción está llena de faltas** you've made a lot of mistakes in your composition ▫ **f. de ortografía** spelling mistake (**e**) *(defecto)* fault, defect; **sacar faltas a algo/a algn** to find fault with sth/sb (**f**) *(mala acción)* misdeed; **coger** o **pillar a algn en f.** to catch sb at fault (**g**) *Med* missed period (**h**) *Jur (infracción)* misdemeanour, *US* misdemeanor ▫ **f. grave/leve** serious/minor offence (**i**) *Dep (en fútbol)* foul; *(en tenis)* fault; **sacar una f.** to take a free kick ▫ **f. personal** personal foul (**j**) **hacer f.** to be necessary; **ahora sólo hace f. que llueva** all we need now is for it to rain; **¡f. hacía!** and about time too!; **hace f. una escalera** we need a ladder; **harán f. dos personas para mover el piano** it'll take two people to move the piano; **me hacen f. más libros** I need more books; **no hace f. que ...** there is no need for ...

faltar *vi* (**a**) *(no estar) (cosa)* to be missing; *(persona)* to be absent; **me falta un bolígrafo** one of my pens is missing; **¿quién falta?** who is missing? (**b**) *(haber poco)* to be lacking o needed, not be enough; **falta (más) agua** we need (more) water, there isn't enough water (**c**) *(no tener)* to lack, not have (enough); **le falta confianza en sí mismo** he lacks confidence in himself; **le falta una mano** he has got only one hand (**d**) *(no acudir)* not to go, miss; **no faltaremos a la fiesta** we won't miss the party; **no faltes** be sure to come (**e**) *(incumplir)* **f. a la verdad** not to tell the truth, lie; **f. a su deber** to fail in one's duty; **f. a su palabra/promesa** to break one's word/promise; **f. en los pagos** not to keep up with one's payments (**f**) *(no respetar)* **faltó a mi dignidad** she slighted me (**g**) *(quedar)* **aún falta mucho por hacer** there is still a lot to be done; **¿cuánto te falta?** how long will you be?, how much more do you have to do?; **¿cuántos kilómetros faltan para Olite?** how many kilometres is it to Olite?, how far is it to Olite?; **falta por ver si lo quiere** whether she wants it or not remains to be seen; **faltó poco para que se liaran a bofetadas** they very nearly came to blows; **ya falta poco para las vacaciones** the holidays will soon be here (**h**) *(locuciones)* **¡lo que me faltaba!** that's all I needed!; **¡no faltaría** o **faltaba más!** *(por supuesto)* (but) of course!; *(por supuesto que no)* think nothing of it!; **¡sólo me faltaba eso!** that's all I needed!, that crowns it all!

falto, -a *adj* lacking, without; **f. de dinero** short of money; **f. de recursos** without resources

faltón, -ona *adj Fam* (**a**) *(informal)* unreliable (**b**) *(grosero)* disrespectful

faltriquera *nf* pouch

falúa *nf Náut* launch

fama *nf* (**a**) *(renombre)* fame, renown; **de f. mundial** world-famous (**b**) *(reputación)* reputation; **tiene buena/ mala f.** it has a good/bad name

famélico, -a *adj* starving, famished

familia *nf* (**a**) *(grupo de personas)* family; **de buena f.** from a good family; **de f. humilde** of humble origin; **viene de f.** it runs in the family; *Fig* **ser como de la f.** to be like one of the family; *Fam* **estar en f.** to be among friends; *Ofens* **acordarse de la f. de algn** to insult sb ▫ **f. de acogida** *(de niño)* foster parents; **f. numerosa** large family; **f. política** in-laws *pl*; *Rel* **la Sagrada F.** the Holy Family (**b**) *(hijos)* children *pl*, offspring *pl*

familiar 1 *adj (de la familia)* family, of the family; **fiesta f.** family party o get-together (**b**) *(conocido)* familiar, well-known; **estos problemas me son familiares** I'm familiar with these problems (**c**) *Ling (informal)* colloquial
2 *nmf* relation, relative

familiaridad *nf* familiarity

familiarizado, -a 1 *pp de* **familiarizar**

2 *adj* familiar, conversant (**con** with); **estar f. con algo** to be familiar o conversant with sth

familiarizar [14] **1** *vt* to familiarize (**con** with)
2 familiarizarse *vpr* to familiarize oneself (**con** with)

famoso, -a 1 *adj* famous, well-known; **sus famosas ocurrencias** her well-known witticisms
2 *nm,f* famous person, celebrity

fan *(pl* **fans)** *nmf* fan, admirer; **soy un f. de las motos** I'm mad on motorbikes

fanal *nm* (**a**) *Náut* beacon (**b**) *(campana)* bell glass

fanático, -a 1 *adj* fanatic, fanatical
2 *nm,f* fanatic

fanatismo *nm* fanaticism

fanatizar [14] *vt* to make a fanatic

fandango *nm* (**a**) *Mús* fandango (**b**) *Fam (jaleo)* row, rumpus

fandanguero, -a *nm,f Fam* reveller, *US* reveler

fanega *nf (medida)* (**a**) *(de capacidad)* = 55.5 litres in Castile, 22.4 litres in Aragon (**b**) *(de superficie)* = 64 square metres in Castile

fanfarria *nf* (**a**) *Mús* fanfare (**b**) *Fam (fanfarronería)* showing off, swanking

fanfarrón, -ona *Fam* **1** *adj* swanky, boastful
2 *nm,f* show-off, swank, braggart

fanfarronada *nf Fam (chulería)* showing off, swanking; *(bravata)* brag, boast

fanfarronear *vi Fam (chulear)* to show off, swank; *(bravear)* to brag, boast

fanfarronería *nf véase* **fanfarronada**

fangal *nm* mire, quagmire, bog

fango *nm* (**a**) *(barro)* mud, mire (**b**) *Fig* degradation

fangoso, -a *adj* muddy, miry

fantasear *vi* to daydream, dream

fantasía *nf (imaginación)* fantasy; *(irrealidad)* fancy; **una joya de f.** a piece of imitation jewellery; *Irón* **tienes mucha f.** tú you're too full of imagination

fantasioso, -a *adj* imaginative

fantasma *nm* (**a**) *(espectro)* ghost, phantom (**b**) *Esp Fam (fanfarrón)* braggart, show-off

fantasmagoría *nf* phantasmagoria

fantasmagórico, -a *adj* phantasmagoric

fantasmal *adj* ghostly

fantástico, -a *adj* fantastic

fantochada *nf Fam* foolish act; *(tontería)* silly thing

fantoche *nm* (**a**) *(títere)* puppet, marionette (**b**) *Pey (fanfarrón)* braggart, show-off (**c**) *Pey (mamarracho)* nincompoop, ninny

faquir *nm* fakir

farallón *nm Geog* crag, rock

faramalla *nf* (**a**) *(charla)* blarney, patter (**b**) *(farfolla)* bauble

farándula *nf* (**a**) *Teat (compañía)* group of strolling players; *(profesión)* acting, the theatre (**b**) *Fam Fig (faramalla)* blarney

farandulero, -a *nm,f* (**a**) *Teat (comediante)* strolling player (**b**) *Fam (trapacero)* bamboozler, trickster

faraón *nm* Pharaoh

faraónico, -a *adj* Pharaonic

FARC [fark] *nfpl abrev de* **Fuerzas Armadas Revolucionarias de Colombia)** Revolutionary Armed Forces of Colombia *(guerrilla group)*

fardar *vi Esp Argot* (**a**) *(presumir)* to show off, swank; **siempre está fardando de novia guapa** he's always boasting about having a beautiful girlfriend (**b**) *(lucir)* to be classy o flash

fardo *nm* bundle, pack

fardón, -ona *adj Esp Argot* classy, flash

farfolla *nf* (**a**) *Bot* husk (**b**) *Fig* worthless thing

farfullar *vt* to gabble, jabber

farfullero, -a *adj* (**a**) *(tartamudo)* gabbling, jabbering (**b**) *(chapucero)* slapdash, shoddy

farináceo, -a *adj* farinaceous

faringe *nf Anat* pharynx

faríngeo, -a *adj* pharyngeal

faringitis *nf Med* pharyngitis

farisaico, -a *adj* (**a**) *Hist* Pharisaic, Pharisaical (**b**) *(falso)* hypocritical

fariseísmo *nm* (**a**) *Hist* Phariseeism (**b**) *(falsedad)* hypocrisy

fariseo, -a *nm,f* (**a**) *Hist* Pharisee (**b**) *(falso)* hypocrite

farmaceuta *nmf Am véase* **farmacéutico, -a**

farmacéutico, -a 1 *adj* pharmaceutical
  2 *nm,f* (**a**) *(licenciado)* pharmacist (**b**) *(en una farmacia)* pharmacist, *Br* chemist, *US* druggist

farmacia *nf* (**a**) *Univ* pharmacology (**b**) *(tienda)* pharmacy, *Br* chemist's (shop), *US* drugstore

fármaco *nm* medicine, medication

farmacología *nf* pharmacology

farmacológico, -a *adj* pharmacological

farmacólogo, -a *nm,f* pharmacologist, pharmacist

faro *nm* (**a**) *(torre)* lighthouse; *(señal)* beacon (**b**) *Aut* headlight, headlamp (**c**) *Fig (guía)* guiding light, guide

farol *nm* (**a**) *(luz)* lantern; *(farola)* streetlight, streetlamp (**b**) *Fam (exageración)* bragging, swank; *(engaño)* bluff; **¡adelante con los faroles!** come on then!, keep it up!; **marcarse** o **tirarse un f.** to brag, boast, swank

farola *nf* streetlight, streetlamp; *(de gas)* gas lamp

farolear *vi Argot (presumir)* to brag, boast, swank

farolero, -a 1 *adj Argot* boastful
  2 *nm,f* show-off

farolillo *nm* (**a**) *(de papel)* Chinese lantern □ *Fig* **el f. rojo** the last to finish (**b**) *Bot* Canterbury bell

farra *nf* (**a**) *Fam (juerga)* binge, spree; **ir de f.** to paint the town red (**b**) *Andes RP* **tomar a algn para la f.** to make fun of sb

fárrago *nm* hotch-potch, jumble

farragoso, -a *adj* confused, rambling

farrear *vi Andes RP* to go out on the town, go on a binge o a spree

farruco, -a *adj Fam* conceited, cocky

farruto, -a *adj Chile* weak, sickly

farsa *nf* (**a**) *Teat* farce (**b**) *Fig* sham, farce; **el referéndum no fue más que una f.** the referendum was nothing but a farce

farsante 1 *adj* lying, deceitful
  2 *nmf* fake, impostor

fas: por fas o por nefas *loc adv* by hook or by crook, by any means

fascículo *nm Impr* fascicle, instalment, *US* installment; **en treinta fascículos semanales** in thirty weekly parts

fascinación *nf* fascination

fascinante *adj*, **fascinador** *adj* fascinating

fascinar *vt* to fascinate, captivate

fascismo *nm Pol* fascism

fascista *adj & nmf Pol* fascist

fase *nf* (**a**) *(etapa)* phase, stage (**b**) *Elec Fís* phase

fastidiado, -a 1 *pp de* **fastidiar**
  2 *adj Esp Fam* (**a**) *(hastiado)* sickened, disgusted (**b**) *(molestado)* annoyed; *(dañado)* damaged, in bad condition; *Fam* **su padre está f.** her father's in a bad way; *Fam* **tiene el estómago f.** he's got a bad stomach

fastidiar 1 *vt* (**a**) *(hastiar)* to sicken, disgust (**b**) *(molestar)* to annoy, bother; *(partes del cuerpo)* to hurt; **me fastidia tener que irme ahora** it's a nuisance to have to leave now; **últimamente me está fastidiando la espalda** my back's been bad lately (**c**) *Esp Fam (estropear)* to damage, ruin; *(planes)* to spoil, upset, mess up
  2 *vi Fam* **¡no fastidies!** you're kidding!
  3 fastidiarse *vpr Esp* (**a**) *(aguantarse)* to put up with it, resign oneself; **¡a f. tocan!** we'll have to grin and bear it!; **y si no te gusta, te fastidias** and if you don't like it you can lump it!; *Fam* **¡que se fastidie!** that's his tough luck! (**b**) *Fam (estropearse)* to get damaged, break down; **se ha fastidiado el tocadiscos** the record player is bust (**c**) *(lastimarse)* to hurt o injure oneself; **me he fastidiado la mano** I've hurt my hand

fastidio *nm* (**a**) *(molestia)* bother, nuisance; **¡qué f.!** what a nuisance! (**b**) *(aburrimiento)* boredom (**c**) *(asco)* repugnance, revulsion

fastidioso, -a *adj* (**a**) *(molesto)* annoying, irksome (**b**) *(aburrido)* boring, tedious

fasto *nm* (**a**) *(lujo)* pomp, display (**b**) **fastos** celebrations

fastuosidad *nf* pomp, lavishness

fastuoso, -a *adj* (**a**) *(cosa)* splendid, lavish (**b**) *(persona)* lavish, ostentatious

fatal 1 *adj* (**a**) *(inexorable)* fateful, inevitable; **ha llegado la hora** o **el momento f.** the time has come (**b**) *(mortal)* deadly, fatal; **dosis f.** lethal dose (**c**) *Esp Fam (muy malo)* awful, horrible, terrible; **tengo una suerte f.** I'm having rotten luck
  2 *adv Esp Fam* very badly, awfully, terribly; **comimos f.** the meal was awful; **lo pasó f.** he had a rotten time; **veo f.** I can't see a thing

fatalidad *nf* (**a**) *(destino)* fate (**b**) *(desgracia)* misfortune

fatalismo *nm* fatalism

fatalista 1 *adj* fatalistic
  2 *nmf* fatalist

fatalmente *adv* (**a**) *(inevitablemente)* inevitably (**b**) *Esp (muy mal)* very badly, awfully, terribly

fatídico, -a *adj* (**a**) *(desastroso)* disastrous, calamitous (**b**) *Fml (profético)* fateful, ominous

fatiga *nf* (**a**) *(cansancio)* fatigue □ **f. crónica** chronic fatigue (**b**) **fatigas** *(esfuerzos)* troubles, difficulties

fatigante *adj* tiring

fatigar [38] **1** *vt* (**a**) *(agotar)* to tire, weary (**b**) *Fig (molestar)* to annoy
  2 fatigarse *vpr* to tire, become tired

fatigosamente *adv* with (great) difficulty, painfully

fatigoso, -a *adj* (**a**) *(que cansa)* tiring, exhausting (**b**) *(en respiración)* laboured, *US* labored

fatuidad *nf* fatuity, fatuousness

fatuo, -a *adj* (**a**) *(necio)* fatuous, foolish (**b**) *(envanecido)* vain, conceited

fauces *nfpl* (**a**) *Anat Zool* fauces, gullet *sing* (**b**) *Fig* jaws

fauna *nf* fauna

fauno *nm Mit* faun

fausto, -a *Fml* **1** *adj Lit* fortunate, auspicious
  2 *nm* pomp, splendour, *US* splendor

fauvismo [fo'βismo] *nm Arte* fauvism

fauvista *nmf Arte* fauvist

favela *nf* shanty

favor *nm* (**a**) *(servicio)* favour, *US* favor, good turn; **a f. de** in favour of; **a mi/su f.** in my/his favour; **estamos seis juegos a uno a f. mío** I'm winning six games to one; **¿puedes hacerme un f.?** can you do me a favour?; **tener algo a su f.** to have sth in one's favour; *Fam* **tiene al presidente a su favor** he has the president on his side (**b**) *por f.* please; **haga el f. de sentarse** please sit down; **¿me da fuego, por f.?** can you give me a light, please?; **¿me harías el f. de correrte un poco?** could you move over a little please?

favorable *adj* favourable, *US* favorable; *(condiciones)* suitable; **se mostró f. al proyecto** he was in favour of the project

favorablemente *adv* **el paciente evoluciona f.** the patient is making good progress

favorecedor, -a *adj* favouring, *US* favoring, favourable, *US* favorable; *(retrato)* flattering; *(vestido)* becoming

favorecer [46] *vt* (**a**) *(beneficiar)* to favour, *US* favor, work in sb's favour *o US* favor; **la oscuridad les favorecía** the darkness was in their favour; **para f. a los más débiles** to help the weakest; **su altura le ha favorecido** being tall has been to her advantage (**b**) *(agraciar)* to flatter, suit; **el bigote le favorece mucho** his moustache really suits him

favorecido, -a 1 *pp de* **favorecer**
  2 *adj* favoured, *US* favored; **está muy f. con ese peinado** that hair style really suits him

favoritismo *nm* favouritism, *US* favoritism

favorito, -a *adj & nm,f* favourite, *US* favorite

fax *(pl* **fax** *o* **faxes)** *nm* (**a**) *(aparato)* fax (machine); **mandar algo por f.** to fax sth (**b**) *(documento)* fax

faxear *vt Fam* to fax

fayuquero, -a *nm,f Méx Fam* dealer in contraband

faz *nf* (**a**) *Literario (cara)* face; **desaparecer de la f. de la tierra** to disappear off the face of the earth (**b**) *(de moneda)* obverse, head (**c**) *Rel* **la Santa** *o* **Sacra F.** the Holy Face

fdo. *(abrev de* **firmado)** signed

fe *nf* (**a**) *(creencia)* faith; **de buena/mala fe** with good/dishonest intentions; **lo hizo de buena fe** he did it in good faith; *Rel* **la fe cristiana** the Christian faith; **tener una fe ciega en algo/algn** to have blind faith in sth/sb (**b**) *Jur (certificado)* certificate ◻ **fe de bautismo/matrimonio** baptism/marriage certificate; **fe de vida** document proving that sb is still alive (**c**) *Impr* **fe de erratas** list of errata

fealdad *nf* ugliness

feamente *adv* in an ugly manner

febrero *nm* February; *véase tamb* **noviembre**

febrífugo, -a *adj & nm Farm* febrifuge

febril *adj* (**a**) *Med* feverish (**b**) *Fig* hectic; **una mente f.** a restless mind

febrilidad *nf* feverishness

fecal *adj Med* faecal

fecha *nf* (**a**) *(día)* date; *Com* **a tres días f.** three days after sight; **con** *o* **de f. 2 de mayo** dated May 2nd; **en f. próxima** at an early date; **fijar la f.** to fix a date; **hasta la f.** so far; **poner la f. a una carta** to date a letter; **sin f.** undated ◻ **f. de nacimiento** date of birth; **f. límite** deadline; **f. tope** deadline (**b**) *(día)* day; **diez fechas después de su publicación** ten days after its publication (**c**) **fechas** *(época)* time *sing*; **en estas f.** in those days; **nos vimos hace un año por estas f.** we met this time last year

fechador *nm* date stamp

fechar *vt* to date, put the date on

fechoría *nf* misdeed, misdemeanour, *US* misdemeanor;

(de niños) mischief; *Fam* **le han hecho una f. en el pelo** they've ruined her hair

fécula *nf* starch

feculento, -a *adj* starchy

fecundable *adj* fertilizable

fecundación *nf* fertilization ◻ **f. in vitro** in vitro fertilization

fecundar *vt* to fertilize, make fertile

fecundidad *nf* (**a**) *(fertilidad)* fertility (**b**) *Fig (productividad)* productivity, fruitfulness

fecundizar [14] *vt* (**a**) *(tierra)* to make fertile (**b**) *Fig* to make fruitful

fecundo, -a *adj* fertile, fecund

federación *nf* federation

federado, -a 1 *pp de* **federar**
  2 *adj* federated

federal *adj & nmf* federal

federalismo *nm* federalism

federalista *adj & nmf* federalist

federar *vt* to federate

federativo, -a *adj* federative

féferes *nmpl Andes Carib Méx* junk *sing*

fehaciente *adj* (**a**) *Fml* authentic, reliable (**b**) *Jur* irrefutable; **documento** *o* **prueba f.** irrefutable proof

felación *nf* fellatio

feldespato *nm Min* feldspar, felspar

felicidad *nf* happiness; **(muchas) felicidades** *(éxitos)* congratulations; *(Navidad)* Merry Christmas; *(cumpleaños)* happy birthday

felicitación *nf* (**a**) *(tarjeta)* greetings card (**b**) **felicitaciones** congratulations

felicitar 1 *vt* to congratulate (**por** on); **f. a algn por su santo** to wish sb a happy Saint's Day; **¡te felicito!** congratulations!
  2 felicitarse *vpr* to congratulate oneself

félido, -a *nm Zool* felid, cat

feligrés, -a *nm,f* parishioner

feligresía *nf* parish, parishioners *pl*

felino, -a *adj & nm Zool* feline

feliz *adj* (**a**) *(contento)* happy; **¡felices Navidades** *o* **Pascuas!** Happy *o* Merry Christmas!; **final f.** happy ending (**b**) *(acertado)* fortunate

felizmente *adv* fortunately, happily; **f. no hubo víctimas** fortunately, there were no casualties

felón, -ona 1 *adj* treacherous, villainous, wicked
  2 *nm,f* traitor, villain

felonía *nf* treachery, villainy

felpa *nf Tex* plush; **oso** *o* **osito de f.** teddy bear

felpudo, -a 1 *adj Tex* plushy, velvety
  2 *nm* mat, doormat

femenino, -a *adj* feminine; **equipo f.** women's team; **sexo f.** female sex

fémina *nf* woman, female

femineidad *nf*, **feminidad** *nf* femininity

feminismo *nm* feminism

feminista *adj & nmf* feminist

feminizar [14] *vt* to make feminine

femoral *adj Anat* femoral

fémur *nm Anat* femur

fenecer [46] *vi Euf (morir)* to pass away, die

fenecimiento *nm Euf (muerte)* decease, death

fenicio, -a *adj & nm,f* Phoenician

fénix *nm inv* (**a**) *Mit* phoenix (**b**) *Fig (genio)* genius, prodigy

fenol *nm Quím* phenol

fenomenal *Fam* **1** *adj* (**a**) *(magnífico)* great, fantastic (**b**) *(enorme)* phenomenal
2 *adv* wonderfully, marvellously; **lo pasamos f.** we had a fantastic time

fenómeno 1 *nm* (**a**) *(suceso)* phenomenon ☐ **fenómenos atmosféricos** atmospheric phenomena (**b**) *(prodigio)* genius (**c**) *(monstruo)* freak
2 *adj Fam* fantastic, terrific, smashing
3 *interj* fantastic!, terrific!

fenomenología *nf* phenomenology

fenotipo *nm* phenotype

feo, -a 1 *adj* (**a**) *(malo)* ugly; **tuvimos un tiempo muy f.** we had horrible weather (**b**) *Fig (alarmante)* nasty; **se está poniendo f.** I don't like the look of this, I don't like the way this is going; **un asunto f.** a nasty affair (**c**) *(indigno)* improper, rude, not nice; **es f. decir palabrotas** it's rude to swear (**d**) *Am (olor, sabor)* unpleasant
2 *nm,f* ugly person
3 *nm Fam* slight, insult; **hacerle un f. a algn** to offend sb

feracidad *nf (tierra)* fertility

feraz *adj* fertile

féretro *nm* coffin

feria *nf* (**a**) *Com* fair ☐ **f. de muestras/del libro** trade/book fair (**b**) *(fiesta)* fair, festival; **la F. de Sevilla** the Seville Festival (**c**) *Méx (monedas)* small change (**d**) *CAm (propina)* tip

feriado, -a *adj* **día f.** holiday

ferial *adj & nm* fair; **recinto f.** fairground

feriante *nmf (vendedor)* stallholder, trader; *(comprador)* fair-goer

feriar *vt Col Guat PRico* to sell off cheap

ferina *adj Med* **tos f.** whooping cough

fermentación *nf* fermentation

fermentar *vi* to ferment

fermento *nm* ferment

ferocidad *nf* ferocity, fierceness

ferodo® *nm* brake lining

Feroe *nfpl* **las (Islas) F.** the Faeroes, the Faeroe Islands

feromona *nf* pheromone

feroz *adj* fierce, ferocious; **el lobo f.** the big bad wolf

ferozmente *adv* fiercely, ferociously

férreo, -a *adj* (**a**) *(de hierro)* ferreous (**b**) *Fig* iron; **voluntad férrea** iron will

ferrería *nf* ironworks *sing*, foundry

ferretería *nf Br* ironmonger's (shop), *US* hardware store

ferretero, -a *nm,f Br* ironmonger, *US* hardware dealer

férrico, -a *adj* ferric

ferrita *nf* ferrite

ferrocarril *nm* railway, *US* railroad

ferroso, -a *adj Quím* ferrous

ferroviario, -a 1 *adj* railway, rail, *US* railroad
2 *nm,f* railway *o US* railroad worker

ferruginoso, -a *adj Min* ferruginous

ferry *(pl* ferries *o* ferrys*)* *nm* ferry

fértil *adj* (**a**) *(mujer, tierra)* fertile (**b**) *Fig* rich, fertile; **imaginación f.** fertile imagination

fertilidad *nf* fertility, fecundity

fertilización *nf* fertilization

fertilizante 1 *adj* fertilizing
2 *nm* fertilizer

fertilizar [14] *vt* to fertilize

férula *nf* ferule, rod; *Fig* **bajo la f. de** under the rule of

ferviente *adj* fervent, passionate

fervor *nm* fervour, *US* fervor

fervoroso, -a *adj* fervent, passionate

festejar *vt* (**a**) *(celebrar)* to celebrate (**b**) *(agasajar)* to wine and dine, entertain (**c**) *(cortejar)* to court, woo (**d**) *Méx Fam (golpear)* to beat, thrash

festejo *nm* (**a**) *(fiesta)* party (**b**) **festejos** festivities

festín *nm* feast, banquet

festinar¹ *vt Am (apresurar)* to speed up

festinar² *vt (agasajar)* to wine and dine, entertain

festival *nm* festival; **f. de cine** film festival

festividad *nf* festivity, celebration

festivo, -a 1 *adj* (**a**) *(alegre)* festive, merry (**b**) *(de fiesta)* **día f.** holiday
2 *nm* holiday

festón *nm Cost* scallop

festonear *vt* to festoon

fetal *adj* foetal, *US* fetal; **posición f.** foetal position

fetén *Esp Fam* **1** *adj* (**a**) *(formidable)* great, *Br* brilliant (**b**) *(auténtico)* hundred per cent, genuine
2 *nf* **la f.** the truth

fetiche *nm* fetish

fetichismo *nm* fetishism

fetichista *adj & nmf* fetishist

fetidez *nf* stink, stench, fetidness

fétido, -a *adj* stinking, fetid

feto *nm* (**a**) *(embrión)* foetus, *US* fetus (**b**) *Fam (persona muy fea)* monster, ugly sod

feúcho, -a *adj Fam* plain, *US* homely

feudal *adj Hist* feudal; **señor f.** feudal lord

feudalismo *nm Hist* feudalism

feudo *nm* fief, feud

FEVE ['feβe] *Esp nf (abrev de* **Ferrocarriles Españoles de Vía Estrecha)** = Spanish narrow-gauge railways

FF.AA. *nfpl (abrev de* **Fuerzas Armadas)** = Spanish armed forces

FF.CC. *(abrev de* **ferrocarriles)** rly

fiabilidad *nf* reliability, trustworthiness

fiable *adj* reliable, trustworthy

fiado, -a 1 *pp de* **fiar**
2 *adj* (**a**) *Com* on credit; **comprar al f.** to buy on credit (**b**) *(confiado)* trusting

fiador, -a 1 *nm,f* guarantor; **salir** *o* **ser f. de algn** *(pagar fianza)* to stand bail for sb; *(avalar)* to vouch for sb
2 *nm* (**a**) *(de escopeta)* safety catch (**b**) *(cerrojo)* bolt

fiambre 1 *adj* (**a**) *Culin (served)* cold (**b**) *Irón* stale, old
2 *nm* (**a**) *Culin Br* cold meat, *US* cold cut; **plato de fiambres** dish of *Br* cold meats *o US* cold cuts (**b**) *Fam (cadáver)* stiff, corpse; **dejar f. a algn** to do sb in

fiambrera *nf* (**a**) *(tartera)* lunch *o* sandwich box (**b**) *RP (fresquera)* meat safe

fianza *nf (depósito)* deposit, security; *Jur* bail; **dejar en libertad bajo f.** to release on bail

fiar [32] **1** *vt* (**a**) *(asegurar)* to guarantee (**b**) *(vender)* to sell on credit (**c**) *(confiar)* to confide, entrust
2 *vi* to trust; **de f.** trustworthy
3 fiarse *vpr* to trust *(de* -); *(en letrero)* **no se fía** no credit given

fiasco *nm* fiasco, failure

fibra *nf* (**a**) *(filamento)* fibre, *US* fiber; *(de madera)* grain ☐ **f. óptica** optic fibre; **f. de vidrio** fibreglass (**b**) *Fig (carácter)* push, go; **es una chica con f.** she's full of go

fibroma *nm Med* fibroma

fibroso, -a *adj* fibrous

ficción *nf* fiction

ficha *nf* **(a)** *(tarjeta)* index card, file card ▫ **f. policial** police record; **f. técnica** specifications *pl*, technical data; *Cin* credits *pl* **(b)** *Tel* token **(c)** *(en juegos)* counter; *Naipes* chip; *Ajedrez* piece, man; *(de dominó)* domino

fichaje *nm Dep* signing (up)

fichar 1 *vt* **(a)** *(archivar)* to put on an index card, to file; **está fichado por la policía** his name is on police files, he has a police record; *Fam* **lo tengo bien fichado** I've got him sized up **(b)** *Dep* to sign up
2 *vi* *(al entrar)* to clock in; *(al salir)* to clock out

fichero *nm* **(a)** *(archivo)* card index **(b)** *Mueb* filing cabinet, file **(c)** *Inform* file

ficticio, -a *adj* fictitious

ficus *nm inv Bot* rubber plant

fidedigno, -a *adj* reliable, trustworthy; **fuentes fidedignas** reliable sources

fideicomisario, -a *nm,f Jur* trustee

fideicomiso *nm Jur* trusteeship; **bajo** *o* **en f.** in trusteeship

fidelidad *nf* **(a)** *(lealtad)* faithfulness, fidelity **(b)** *(exactitud)* accuracy ▫ *Mús* **alta f.** high fidelity, hi-fi

fidelización *nf Com* building of customer loyalty; **programa de f.** loyalty programe

fidelizar [14] *vt Com* **f. a los clientes** to build customer loyalty

fideo *nm Culin* noodle; *Fam Fig* **estar como un f.** to be as thin as a rake

Fidji ['fiji] *n* Fiji

fiduciario, -a *adj & nm,f Jur* fiduciary

fiebre *nf* **(a)** *Med* fever; **tener f.** to have a temperature ▫ **f. amarilla** yellow fever **(b)** *Fig* fever, excitement

fiel 1 *adj* **(a)** *(leal)* faithful, loyal; **es f. a su mujer** he is faithful to his wife **(b)** *(exacto)* accurate, exact; **memoria f.** reliable memory
2 *nm* **(a)** *(de balanza)* needle, pointer **(b)** **los fieles** *Rel* the faithful

fieltro *nm Tex* felt

fiera *nf* **(a)** *(animal)* wild animal *o* beast; **luchó como una f.** she fought like a tiger; *Fam* **estar hecho una f.** to be in a rage ▫ **casa de fieras** menagerie **(b)** *Fig (persona de mal carácter)* beast, brute **(c)** *Fig (genio)* wizard; **es una f. para los idiomas** she's brilliant at languages **(d)** *Taur* bull

fiereza *nf (ferocidad)* ferocity, ferociousness; *(crueldad)* cruelty

fiero, -a *adj (salvaje)* wild; *(feroz)* fierce, ferocious; *Fig (persona)* cruel

fierro *nm Am* iron

fiesta *nf* **(a)** *(vacaciones)* holiday; **ayer fue f.** yesterday was a holiday; **el viernes haré f.** I'll take Friday off; **F. de la Hispanidad** Columbus Day; **F. del Trabajo** Labour *o US* Labor Day **(b)** *Rel* feast ▫ **f. fija/móvil** immovable/ movable feast; **f. de guardar** *o* **precepto** day of obligation **(c)** *(reunión)* party; **estar de f.** to be in a festive mood; **no estar para fiestas** to be in no mood for jokes; **¡tengamos la f. en paz!** cut it out! ▫ **sala de fiestas** dance hall **(d)** *(festividad)* celebration, festivity; **el pueblo está de fiestas** the town is holding its local festivities ▫ *Esp* **f. nacional** bullfighting; **las fiestas de Navidad** Christmas; **las fiestas de San Fermín** the festival of San Fermín

fiestero, -a *nm,f* party animal

FIFA ['fifa] *nf (abrev de* **Federación Internacional de Fútbol Asociación)** FIFA

fifiriche *adj CAm Méx* sickly, weak

figón *nm* cheap restaurant

figura *nf* **(a)** *(de objeto, de persona)* figure; *(forma)* shape; **f. de cerámica** pottery figure; **f. decorativa** figurehead; **tener buena f.** to have a good figure; **una f. de hombre** the shape *o* figure of a man **(b)** *(personaje)* figure; **una f. de las letras** an important literary figure **(c)** *Cin Teat* character **(d)** *Geom* figure, diagram **(e)** *Ling* figure; **f. retórica** figure of speech

figuración *nf* imagination; **son figuraciones tuyas** you're just imagining things

figurado, -a 1 *pp de* **figurar**
2 *adj* figurative; **en sentido f.** figuratively

figurante, -a *nm,f* **(a)** *Teat Cin* extra **(b)** *Fig* figurehead

figurar 1 *vt* **(a)** *(representar)* to represent; **¿qué figuran estas rayas rojas?** what do these red lines represent? **(b)** *(simular)* to simulate, feign, pretend; **figuró estar muerto** he pretended to be dead
2 *vi* **(a)** *(aparecer)* to appear, figure; **su nombre no figura en el listín** her name isn't in the telephone directory **(b)** *(destacar)* to stand out, be important
3 **figurarse** *vpr* **(a)** *(imaginarse)* to imagine, suppose; **nunca me lo hubiera figurado** I would never have suspected it; **ya me lo figuraba** I thought as much **(b)** *interj* **¡figúrate!, ¡figúrese!** just imagine!

figurativo, -a *adj* figurative

figurín *nm* **(a)** *(dibujo)* sketch **(b)** *(revista)* fashion magazine **(c)** *Pey* dandy, fop

figurinista *nmf Teat Cin* costume designer

figurón *nm* **(a)** *Pey* show-off, swank **(b)** *Náut* **f. de proa** figurehead

fija *nf RP Fam* sure thing

fijación *nf* **(a)** *(sujeción)* fixing; *Fot* **baño de f.** fixing bath **(b)** *(amarre)* fastening **(c)** **fijaciones** *(en esquí)* bindings

fijado *nm Fot* fixing

fijador *nm* fixative

fijamente *adv* fixedly; **mirar f.** to stare

fijapelo *nm* hair spray *o* gel

fijar 1 *vt* **(a)** *(sujetar)* to fix, fasten; *(establecer)* to determine; **f. residencia** to take up residence; **f. un sello en** to stick a stamp on; **f. una fecha/un precio** to fix a date/price; *(en letrero)* **prohibido f. carteles** post no bills **(b)** *Carp (puerta)* to hang; *(ventana)* to put in **(c)** *Fot Quím* to fix
2 **fijarse** *vpr* **(a)** *(darse cuenta)* to notice; **se fija en todo** she's very observant; **¿te fijas cómo me contesta?** do you see how he answers me? **(b)** *(poner atención)* to pay attention, watch; **es que no te fijas** you just don't pay attention; **¡fíjate!, ¡fíjese!** (just) fancy that!; **fíjate cómo lo hago yo** watch how I do it; **fíjate en esta foto** look at this photo **(c)** *RP (consultar, mirar)* **f. en un diccionario** to consult a dictionary

fijativo *nm Fot* fixative

fijeza *nf* **(a)** *(insistencia)* insistence, firmness; **mirar algo con f.** to stare at sth **(b)** *(certeza)* certainly; **saber algo con f.** to know sth for certain

Fiji ['fiji] *n* Fiji

fijiano, -a [fi'jiano, -a] *adj & nm,f* Fijian

fijo, -a *adj* **(a)** *(sujeto)* fixed, fastened; **f. a la pared** fixed to the wall **(b)** *(determinado)* **aún no hay fecha fija** the exact date hasn't been fixed yet; **con la mirada fija** staring; **de f.** for certain, for sure **(c)** *(firme)* steady, stable; **asegúrate de que esté bien f.** make sure it is steady **(d)** *(permanente)* permanent; **está f. en Madrid** he's settled in Madrid; **no quiero un empleo f.** I don't want a permanent job; **sin residencia fija** of no fixed abode **(e)** *Fot* fast

fila *nf* (**a**) *(hilera)* line; **en f. de uno, en f. india** in single file; **nos pusieron en f.** we were lined up; **salirse de la f.** to step out of line (**b**) *(de cine, teatro)* row; **en primera f.** in the front row (**c**) **filas** ranks; **cerrar f.** to close ranks; **entrar a engrosar las f. de** to join the ranks of; *Mil* **Juan está en f. ahora** Juan's doing his military service at the moment; **llamar a algn a f.** to call sb up; **romper f.** to break ranks; **¡rompan f.!** fall out!, dismiss!

Filadelfia *n* Philadelphia

filamento *nm* filament

filantropía *nf* philanthropy

filantrópico, -a *adj* philanthropic

filantropismo *nm* philanthropy

filántropo, -a *nm,f* philanthropist

filarmónica *nf* philharmonic (orchestra)

filarmónico, -a *adj* philharmonic

filatelia *nf* philately, stamp collecting

filatélico, -a *adj* philatelic

filatelista *nmf* philatelist, stamp collector

filete *nm* (**a**) *(de carne, pescado)* fillet; *(solomillo)* sirloin (**b**) *Téc (de tornillo)* thread

filfa *nf Fam* hoax

filiación *nf* (**a**) *(datos personales)* particulars *pl* (**b**) *Pol* affiliation

filial 1 *adj* (**a**) *(de hijo)* filial (**b**) *Com* subsidiary; **empresa f.** subsidiary
　2 *nf Com* subsidiary

filibusterismo *nm Fam* filibustering

filibustero, -a *nm,f Fam* filibuster

filiforme *adj* thread-like

filigrana *nf* (**a**) *(en orfebrería)* filigree (**b**) *(en el papel)* watermark (**c**) **filigranas** *Fig* intricacy *sing*, intricate work *sing*

filípica *nf* philippic, tirade

Filipinas *npl* (**las**) **F.** (the) Philippines

filipino, -a *adj & nm,f* Philippine, Filipino

filisteo, -a *adj & nm,f* Philistine

film *(pl* **films**) *nm* movie, *Br* film

filmación *nf* filming, shooting

filmar *vt* to film, shoot

filme *nm* movie, *Br* film

fílmico, -a *adj* movie, *Br* film

filmografía *nf* filmography, films *pl*; **la f. de los años treinta** the films of the thirties

filmoteca *nf (archivo)* film library; *(sala de exhibición)* film institute

filo *nm* (**a**) *(borde)* (cutting) edge; **sacar f. a algo** to sharpen sth; *Fig* **al f. de la medianoche** on the stroke of midnight; *Fig* **arma de doble f.** double-edged argument (**b**) *RP (novio)* boyfriend; *(novia)* girlfriend

filología *nf* philology

filológico, -a *adj* philological

filólogo, -a *nm,f* philologist

filón *nm* (**a**) *Min* seam, vein (**b**) *Fig (buen negocio)* gold mine

filoso, -a *adj* sharp-edged

filosofal *adj* **piedra f.** philosopher's stone

filosofar *vi* to philosophize

filosofía *nf* philosophy; *Fig* **tomar algo con f.** to take sth philosophically

filosófico, -a *adj* philosophical

filósofo, -a *nm,f* philosopher

filoxera *nf* phylloxera

filtración *nf* (**a**) *(de agua)* filtration (**b**) *(de información)* leak

filtrador, -a 1 *adj* filtering
　2 *nm* filter

filtrar 1 *vt* (**a**) *(tamizar)* to filter (**b**) *(información)* to leak
　2 filtrarse *vpr* (**a**) *(penetrar)* to filter, seep (**por** through) (**b**) *(información)* to be leaked

filtro *nm* (**a**) *(de café, cigarrillo, aparato, cámara)* filter □ **cigarrillo con f.** filter *o* filter-tip cigarette; **f. de café** coffee filter (**b**) *Hist (poción)* philtre, love potion

fin *nm* (**a**) *(final)* end; **a fines de mes** at the end of the month; **al f. y al cabo** when all's said and done, in the end; **cuentos sin f.** endless lies; **dar** *o* **poner f. a** to put an end to; **en f.** anyway; **llegar** *o* **tocar a su f.** to come to an end; **no tener f.** to be endless; **noche de F. de Año** New Year's Eve; **¡por** *o* **al f.!** at last! □ **f. de fiesta** grand finale; **f. de semana** weekend (**b**) *(objetivo)* purpose, aim; **a f. de** in order to, so as to; **a f. de que** in order that, so that; **con buen f.** with good intentions; **con el f. de** with the intention of; **con este f.** with this aim; *Prov* **el f. justifica los medios** the end justifies the means

finado, -a 1 *pp de* **finar**
　2 *nm,f* deceased

final 1 *adj* final, last
　2 *nm* (**a**) *(terminación)* end; **al f.** in the end; **al f. del día** at the end of the day; **hasta el f.** until the end □ **f. de línea** terminal; **f. feliz** happy ending (**b**) *Mús* finale
　3 *nf Dep* final □ **cuartos de f.** quarterfinals

finalidad *nf* purpose, aim

finalista 1 *adj* in the final; **equipo f.** team in the final
　2 *nmf* finalist

finalización *nf* *(terminación)* end; *(de contrato)* termination

finalizar [14] *vt & vi* to end, finish

finalmente *adv* finally, eventually

financiación *nf, Am* **financiamiento** *nm* financing

financiar *vt* to finance

financiero, -a 1 *adj* financial
　2 *nm,f* financier

financista *nmf Am* financier

finanzas *nfpl* finances

finar *Fml* **1** *vi* to pass away, die
　2 finarse *vpr* to yearn (**por** for)

finca *nf* (**a**) property, estate □ **f. rústica** country estate; **f. urbana** building (**b**) *(casa de campo)* house in the country (**c**) *Am (plantación)* plantation

finés, -esa *adj & nm,f véase* **finlandés, -esa**

fineza *nf* (**a**) *véase* **finura** (**b**) *(cumplido)* courtesy, compliment

fingido, -a 1 *pp de* **fingir**
　2 *adj* feigned, false; **nombre f.** assumed name

fingimiento *nm* pretence, simulation

fingir [24] **1** *vt* to feign, pretend
　2 fingirse *vpr* to pretend to be

finiquitar *vt Com* (**a**) *(saldar) (cuenta)* to settle; *(deuda)* to discharge (**b**) *(terminar)* to finish, end

finiquito *nm* (**a**) *Com (acción)* settlement (**b**) *(documento)* final discharge

finito, -a *adj* finite

finlandés, -esa 1 *adj* Finnish
　2 *nm,f (persona)* Finn
　3 *nm (idioma)* Finnish

Finlandia *n* Finland

fino, -a 1 *adj* (**a**) *(delicado) (manos)* delicate; *(piel)* smooth; *oro* f. pure gold (**b**) *(alimentos, bebidas)* choice, select (**c**) *(sentidos)* sharp, acute; **olfato f.** keen sense of smell (**d**) *(delgado)* thin (**e**) *(educado)* refined, polite (**f**) *(humor, ironía)* subtle (**g**) *Fam* **estar f.** to be witty o shrewd; **ir f.** to be plastered o stoned
2 *nm (vino)* type of dry sherry

finolis *adj inv Fam* (**a**) *(remilgado)* fussy, finicky (**b**) *(cursi)* affected

finta *nf* feint

fintar *vi* to feint

finura *nf* (**a**) *(calidad)* fineness, excellence (**b**) *(agudeza)* sharpness, acuteness (**c**) *(refinamiento)* refinement, politeness (**d**) *(sutileza)* subtlety

fiordo *nm Geog* fiord, fjord

fique *nm Am Bot* agave fibre

firma *nf* (**a**) *(autógrafo)* signature; **ponga la f. aquí** sign here (**b**) *(empresa)* firm, company

firmamento *nm Astron* firmament

firmante *adj & nmf* signatory; *Fml* **el/la abajo f.** the undersigned

firmar *vt* to sign

firme 1 *adj* (**a**) *(fuerte, sólido)* firm, steady; *Fig* **mantenerse f.** to hold one's ground ❑ **tierra f.** terra firma (**b**) *(color)* fast (**c**) *Jur* **sentencia f.** final judgement (**d**) *Mil* **¡firmes!** attention!
2 *nm Constr* road surface
3 *adv* hard

firmemente *adv* (**a**) *(resistente)* firmly (**b**) *(fuerte)* strongly

firmeza *nf* firmness, steadiness

firulete *nm Andes RP* cheap ornament

fiscal 1 *adj* fiscal, tax
2 *nmf* (**a**) *Jur Br* ≃ public prosecutor, *US* ≃ district attorney (**b**) *Fig* snooper, informer

fiscalía *nf Br* ≃ public prosecutor's office, *US* ≃ district attorney's office

fiscalidad *nf* taxation

fiscalización *nf* supervision, inspection

fiscalizar [14] *vt* to supervise, investigate

fisco *nm* treasury, exchequer

fisgar [38] *vi Fam* to snoop, pry

fisgón, -ona *nm,f (espía)* snooper; *(curioso)* busybody

fisgonear *vi* to snoop, pry

fisgoneo *nm Fam* prying

física *nf* physics *sing*

físicamente *adv* physically

físico, -a 1 *adj* (**a**) *(gen)* physical (**b**) *Cuba Méx Fam (melindroso)* finicky
2 *nm,f (profesión)* physicist
3 *nm (aspecto)* physique

fisiología *nf* physiology

fisiológico, -a *adj* physiological

fisiólogo, -a *nm,f* physiologist

fisión *nf Fis* fission

fisionomía *nf véase* **fisonomía**

fisioterapeuta *nmf Med* physiotherapist

fisioterapia *nf Med* physiotherapy

fisonomía *nf* features *pl*, physiognomy

fisonomista *nmf Fam* **ser buen/mal f.** to be good/no good at remembering faces

fístula *nf Med* fistula

fisura *nf* fissure

fitología *nf* botany

fitoplancton *nm* phytoplankton

fitosanitario, -a *adj* plant health; **control f.** plant health measure

fitoterapia *nf* herbal medicine

FIV *nf Med (abrev de* **fecundación in vitro***)* IVF

Fiyi *n* Fiji

fiyiano, -a *adj & nm,f* Fijian

flaccidez *nf,* **flacidez** *nf* flaccidity, flaccidness, flabbiness

fláccido, -a *adj,* **flácido, -a** *adj* flaccid, flabby

flaco, -a 1 *adj* (**a**) *(delgado)* thin, skinny (**b**) *Fig (débil)* weak; **los números son su punto f.** numbers are his weak point
2 *nm* weak point o spot, weakness

flacucho, -a *adj Pey* skinny

flagelación *nf* flagellation, whipping

flagelar 1 *vt* (**a**) *(azotar)* to flagellate, whip, scourge (**b**) *Fig (criticar)* to flay
2 flagelarse *vpr* to flagellate oneself

flagelo *nm* (**a**) *(látigo)* whip, scourge (**b**) *Fig (calamidad)* scourge, calamity

flagrante *adj* flagrant; **en f. delito** red-handed

flamante *adj* (**a**) *(vistoso)* splendid, brilliant (**b**) *(nuevo)* brand-new

flambear *vt Culin* to flambé

flameado, -a 1 *pp de* **flamear**
2 *adj Culin* flambé

flameante *adj* flamboyant

flamear 1 *vt Culin* to flambé
2 *vi* (**a**) *(llamear)* to flame, blaze (**b**) *(ondear)* to flutter, flap

flamenco, -a 1 *adj* (**a**) *(de Flandes)* Flemish (**b**) *(gitano)* Andalusian gypsy; *Esp Fam* **ponerse f.** to get cocky (**c**) *Mús* flamenco (**d**) *Carib Méx (flaco)* skinny
2 *nm,f (gitano)* Andalusian gypsy
3 *nm* (**a**) *(idioma)* Flemish (**b**) *Mús* flamenco (**c**) *Orn* flamingo

flamencología *nf* study of flamenco

flamencólogo, -a *nm,f* expert in flamenco

flámula *nf* streamer, pennant

flan *nm Culin* caramel custard; **f. de arena** sand pie; *Fig Fam* **estar como un f.** *(físicamente)* to feel tired and washed out; *(anímicamente)* to be easily upset

flanco *nm* flank, side

flanera *nf Culin* custard mould

flanquear *vt* to flank

flaquear *vi* (**a**) *(ceder)* to weaken, give way; **me flaquearon las piernas** my legs gave way (**b**) *(fallar)* to fail; **le flaquea la memoria** his memory is failing (**c**) *(desalentarse)* to lose heart (**d**) *(disminuir)* to decrease, diminish

flaqueza *nf* weakness, frailty

flash [flaʃ] *(pl* **flashes***) nm* (**a**) *Fot* flash, flashlight (**b**) *Fig (noticia)* newsflash

flashback ['flasβak] *(pl* **flashbacks***) nm Cin* flashback

flato *nm* (**a**) *(dolor abdominal)* **tener f.** to have a stitch (**b**) *Am (melancolía)* gloom, melancholy, sadness

flatulencia *nf* flatulence

flatulento, -a *adj* flatulent

flauta *Mús* **1** *nf* flute ❑ **f. de Pan** pipes *pl* of Pan; **f. dulce** recorder; **f. travesera** transverse o cross flute
2 *nmf* flautist, *US* flutist, flute player

flautín *Mús* **1** *nm (instrumento)* piccolo
2 *nmf (músico)* piccolo player

flautista *nmf Mús* flautist, *US* flutist, flute player; **el F. de Hamelín** the Pied Piper (of Hamelin)

flebitis *nf Med* phlebitis

flecha *nf* (**a**) *(arma)* arrow; *(dardo)* dart; *Fig* **salir como una f.** to go off like a shot (**b**) *Aut* arrow; **siga la f.** follow the arrow (**c**) *Arquit* spire, flèche

flechar *vt Fig* to inspire sudden love in

flechazo *nm* (**a**) *Fig (enamoramiento)* love at first sight (**b**) *(disparo)* arrow shot (**c**) *(herida)* arrow wound

fleco *nm* (**a**) *(adorno)* fringe (**b**) *Fig (borde deshilachado)* frayed edge (**c**) *(flequillo)* fringe, *US* bangs *pl*

fleje *nm* (**a**) *Téc* metal strip *o* band (**b**) *(de tonel)* (metal) hoop

flema *nf* phlegm

flemático, -a *adj* phlegmatic

flemón *nm Med* gumboil, abscess

flequillo *nm* fringe, *US* bangs *pl*

fletador, -a *nm,f* charterer, freighter

fletamiento *nm* chartering

fletán *nm* halibut

fletar **1** *vt* (**a**) *(avión, barco)* to charter, freight (**b**) *CSur (mandar)* to send, order to go (**a** to)
2 fletarse *vpr Am Fam (marcharse)* to scram, split

flete *nm* (**a**) *(alquiler)* freightage (**b**) *(carga de un buque)* cargo (**c**) *RP (caballo)* fast horse

fletero, -a *Am* **1** *adj* hire, for hire; **carro f.** hire car
2 *nm (propietario)* owner of vehicles

flexibilidad *nf* flexibility

flexibilización *nf (de normas)* relaxation; *(del mercado de trabajo)* liberalization

flexibilizar [14] *vt (normas)* to make more flexible; *(mercado de trabajo)* to liberalize

flexible *adj* flexible

flexión *nf* (**a**) *(doblegamiento)* flexion (**b**) *Ling* inflection (**c**) *(de brazo)* press-up, *US* push-up

flexionar *vt (músculo)* to flex; *(cuerpo)* to bend

flexo *nm Esp* adjustable table lamp, Anglepoise® lamp

flipado, -a *Esp Argot* **1** *pp de* **flipar**
2 *adj* (**a**) *(asombrado)* flabbergasted, *Br* gobsmacked (**b**) *(drogado)* stoned, high

flipante *adj Esp Argot* great, cool

flipar *Esp Argot* **1** *vi (asombrarse)* to be flabbergasted *o Br* gobsmacked
2 *vt (gustar)* **le flipan las motos** he's crazy about motorbikes
3 fliparse *vpr* to get stoned *o* high

flipe *nm Esp Argot* trip

flirtear *vi* to flirt

flirteo *nm* flirtation, flirting

flojear *vi* (**a**) *(disminuir)* to fall off, go down; **han flojeado las ventas** sales have fallen off (**b**) *(debilitarse)* to weaken, grow weak; **le flojea la memoria** his memory is failing

flojedad *nf* (**a**) *(debilidad)* weakness, slackness (**b**) *(atonía)* flabbiness, limpness

flojera *nf Fam* weakness, faintness

flojo, -a **1** *adj* (**a**) *(suelto)* loose, slack; *Vulg* **me la trae floja** *Br* I couldn't give a toss, *US* I couldn't give a rat's ass (**b**) *(débil)* weak; **está f. en matemáticas** he's weak at mathematics; **un viento muy f.** a light wind (**c**) *Fig (perezoso)* lazy, idle; **una alumna muy floja** a very weak pupil (**d**) *(cobarde)* cowardly
2 *nm,f* lazy person, idler

flor *nf* (**a**) *(en planta)* flower; **en f.** in blossom; *Fig* **en la f. de la vida** in the prime of life; *Fig* **la f. y nata** the cream (of society) ❑ **f. de harina** pure wheat flour; **f. de lis** fleur-de-lis; **f. de Pascua** poinsettia, Christmas flower (**b**) *Fig (piropo)* compliment; **echar flores** to pay compliments (**c**) *(superficie)* **a f. de piel** skin-deep; **a f. de tierra** at ground level

flora *nf* flora ❑ *Med* **f. intestinal** intestinal flora

floración *nf (plantas)* flowering, blooming; *(árboles)* blossoming

floral *adj* floral

floreado, -a **1** *pp de* **florear**
2 *adj* (**a**) *(con flores)* flowered, flowery (**b**) *Lit (estilo)* florid

florear **1** *vt* (**a**) *(adornar)* to adorn with flowers (**b**) *Fam Fig* to pay compliments to
2 *vi* (**a**) *Mús (guitarra)* to play in arpeggio (**b**) *(en esgrima)* to flourish (**c**) *CAm (florecer) (plantas)* to flower, bloom; *(árboles)* to blossom

florecer [46] **1** *vi* (**a**) *Bot (plantas)* to flower, bloom; *(árboles)* to blossom (**b**) *Fig (prosperar)* to flourish, thrive
2 florecerse *vpr* to go mouldy *o US* moldy

floreciente *adj Fig* flourishing, prosperous

florecimiento *nm* (**a**) *Bot (de plantas)* flowering, blooming; *(de árboles)* blossoming (**b**) *Fig (auge)* flourishing, prospering

florero *nm* vase

floresta *nf* wood, thicket

florete *nm* fencing foil

floricultor, -a *nm,f* flower grower

floricultura *nf* flower growing, floriculture

florido, -a *adj* (**a**) *(con flores)* flowery (**b**) *Fig (selecto)* choice, select; **lo más f.** the cream (**c**) *Lit (estilo)* florid

florilegio *nm Lit* anthology

florín *nm (moneda)* florin

floripondio *nm Pey* (**a**) *(flor grande)* large flower, gaudy flower (**b**) *(adorno excesivo)* heavy ornamentation

florista *nmf* florist

floristería *nf* florist's (shop)

floritura *nf* flourish

florón *nm Arquit* rosette, *Espec* fleuron

flota *nf* fleet ❑ **f. pesquera** fishing fleet

flotación *nf* flotation, floating

flotador *nm* (**a**) *(de caña de pescar)* float (**b**) *(de niño)* rubber ring (**c**) *(de cisterna)* ballcock

flotante *adj* floating

flotar *vi* (**a**) *(en líquido)* to float (**b**) *(ondear)* to wave, flutter

flote *nm* **a f.** afloat; **sacar a f. un negocio** to put a business on a sound footing; *Fig* **salir a f.** to get back on one's feet, get out of difficulty

flotilla *nf* flotilla

fluctuación *nf* fluctuation

fluctuante *adj* fluctuating, subject to fluctuation

fluctuar [4] *vi* to fluctuate; *(vacilar)* to hesitate

fluente *adj* flowing, fluid

fluidez *nf* (**a**) *(de sustancia, líquido)* fluidity (**b**) *Fig* fluency

fluido, -a **1** *pp de* **fluir**
2 *adj* (**a**) *(sustancia, líquido)* fluid (**b**) *Fig* fluent
3 *nm* (**a**) *Fís* fluid (**b**) *Elec* current

fluir [34] *vi* to flow

flujo *nm* (**a**) *(movimiento)* flow (**b**) *Mar* rising tide; **f. y reflujo** ebb and flow (**c**) *Fís* flux (**d**) *Med* discharge ❑ *Com* **f. de caja** cash flow; **f. sanguíneo** bloodstream; **f. vaginal** vaginal discharge (**e**) *Inform* stream

fluminense **1** *adj* of *o* from Rio de Janeiro
2 *nmf* person from Rio de Janeiro

flúor *nm* fluorine
fluorescencia *nf* fluorescence
fluorescente *adj* fluorescent
fluorización *nf* fluoridation
fluoruro *nm Quím* fluoride
fluvial *adj* fluvial, river
flux *nm* (a) *Naipes* flush (b) *Carib Col Méx (traje)* suit
FM *nf Rad (abrev de* **Frecuencia Modulada**) FM
FMI *nm Econ (abrev de* **Fondo Monetario Internacional**) IMF
FMLN *nm (abrev de* **Movimiento Farabundo Martí de Liberación Nacional**) FMLN
fobia *nf* phobia
foca *nf* (a) *Zool* seal ❑ **piel de f.** sealskin (b) *Fam (persona)* fat lump
focal *adj* focal; **distancia f.** focal length
focalizar [14] *vt* to focus
focha *nf Orn* coot
foco *nm* (a) *(centro)* centre, *US* center, focal point (b) *Fís Mat* focus (c) *(lámpara)* spotlight, floodlight (d) *Fig* centre (e) *Am* (electric light) bulb (f) *Am (farola)* street light (g) *Am Aut* (car) headlight
fofo, -a *adj (persona)* flabby
fogaje *nm* (a) *Cuba Méx (erupción)* rash (b) *Ecuad (llamarada)* blaze (c) *Carib (sofoco)* stifling heat
fogata *nf* bonfire
fogón *nm* (a) *(cocina)* kitchen range, stove (b) *(de máquina de vapor)* firebox (c) *Chile CRica RP (fogata)* bonfire, camp fire
fogonazo *nm* flash
fogonero *nm* stoker
fogosidad *nf* (a) *(persona)* ardour, *US* ardor, fire (b) *(caballo)* fieriness
fogoso, -a *adj* fiery, spirited
foguear *vt* (a) *(personas, caballos)* to accustom to gunfire (b) *Fig* to harden
fogueo *nm* **cartucho de f.** blank cartridge
foie-gras [fwa'vras] *nm inv* (pâté de) foie-gras
fol. *(abrev de* **folio**) fo., fol.
folclore *nm,* **folclor** *nm* folklore
folclórica *nf Esp* = singer of traditional Spanish songs
folclórico, -a *adj* traditional, popular
fólder *nm Andes CAm Méx (carpeta)* folder
folía *nf* = popular song and dance of the Canary Isles
foliación *nf Bot Impr* foliation
foliar *vt Impr* to foliate, folio, number
folicular *adj* follicular
folículo *nm Bot Anat* follicle
folio *nm (hoja)* folio, leaf; *Impr* **en f.** folio, in folio
folk *nm Mús* folk (music)
folklor *nm* folklore
folklore *nm* folklore
folklórico, -a 1 *adj* (a) *(del folklore)* folkloric, popular, traditional (b) *Fam Pey* quaint
2 *nf (cantante)* flamenco singer
folklorista *nmf* folklorist
folla *nf Esp Vulg* **tener mala f.** *(mala intención)* to be a nasty piece of work
follado, -a 1 *pp de* **follar**
2 *adj Esp muy Fam (con prisa)* **voy f.** I'm rushed of my *Br* bloody *o US* goddamn feet

follaje *nm* (a) *Bot* foliage, leaves (b) *(palabrería)* verbiage, verbosity
follar *Esp Vulg* 1 *vi (copular)* to fuck, screw
2 *vt (suspender)* to fail; **me han follado en mates** I've failed maths
3 **follarse** *vpr* to fuck, screw; **se la folló** he screwed her
folletín *nm* (a) *(relato)* newspaper serial (b) *Fig* melodrama; **¡menudo f.!** what a saga!
folletinesco, -a *adj* melodramatic
folleto *nm (prospecto)* pamphlet, leaflet, brochure; *(explicativo)* instruction leaflet; *(turístico)* brochure
follón *nm Esp Fam* (a) *(alboroto)* rumpus, shindy; **armar (un) f.** to kick up a rumpus (b) *(enredo, confusión)* mess, trouble; **meterse en un f.** to get into a mess; **nos quedó un f. de platos sucios** we were left with a whole load of dirty dishes
follonero, -a *Esp Fam adj & nm,f* **es muy f.** he's a real troublemaker
fomentar *vt* (a) *(favorecer)* to encourage, foster (b) *Carib Méx (organizar)* to open, set up
fomento *nm* (a) *(de cultura, comercio, turismo)* promotion, encouragement, fostering (b) *Med* fomentation
fonación *nf* phonation
fonador, -a *adj* speech; **el aparato f.** the speech apparatus
fonda *nf* (a) *(mesón)* inn (b) *(restaurante)* small restaurant
fondeadero *nm Náut* anchorage
fondeado, -a 1 *pp de* **fondear**
2 *adj* (a) *(barco)* anchored (b) *Am (rico)* well-off, wealthy
fondear 1 *vt* (a) *(sondear)* to sound (b) *(registrar)* to search (c) *Fig (examinar)* to get to the bottom of
2 *vi (barco)* to anchor
3 **fondearse** *vpr Am* to get rich
fondeo *nm* (a) *(sondeo)* sounding (b) *(registro)* search (c) *(anclar)* anchoring
fondillos *nmpl* seat *sing* (of trousers)
fondista *nmf* (a) *(de mesón)* innkeeper (b) *Dep* long-distance runner
fondo *nm* (a) *(parte más baja)* bottom; **a f.** thoroughly; **al f. de la calle** at the bottom of the street; **tocar f.** *Náut* to touch bottom; *Fig* to reach rock bottom; *Fig* **en el f.** deep down, at heart; *Fig* **hay un f. de verdad en sus palabras** there is some truth in what he says ❑ **bajos fondos** dregs of society; **doble f.** false bottom; **f. del mar** seabed; **forma y f.** form and substance; **mar de f.** *Náut* groundswell; *Fig* undercurrent of tension (b) *(parte más lejana)* end, back; **al f. del auditorio** at the back of the auditorium; **al f. del pasillo** at the end of the corridor (c) *(segundo término)* background; **un estampado azul sobre un f. blanco** a blue pattern on a white background ❑ **música de f.** background music (d) *Prensa* **artículo de f.** leading article (e) *Dep* **corredor/carrera de f.** long-distance runner/race; **esquiador/esquí de f.** cross-country skier/skiing (f) *Fin* fund; **cheque sin fondos** bad cheque; **reunir fondos** to raise funds ❑ **f. de comercio** goodwill; **f. común** kitty; **fondos bloqueados** frozen assets; **f. de inversión** investment fund; **f. de inversión mobiliaria** *Br* trust fund, *US* mutual fund; **f. de pensiones** pension fund; **fondos disponibles** available *o* liquid funds; **fondos públicos** public funds
fondón, -ona *adj Fam* big-bottomed, fat
fonema *nm Ling* phoneme
fonendoscopio *nm Med* stethoscope
fonética *nf* phonetics *sing*
fonético, -a *adj* phonetic
fonetista *nmf* phonetician

fónico, -a *adj Ling* phonic

fono *nm Am Fam* phone

fonógrafo *nm* gramophone, *US* phonograph

fonología *nf Ling* phonology

fonológico, -a *adj Ling* phonological

fonoteca *nf* record library

fontana *nf Literario* fountain, spring

fontanería *nf* plumbing

fontanero, -a *nm,f* plumber

footing ['futin] *nm* jogging; **hacer f.** to go jogging

foque *nm Náut* jib

forajido, -a *nm,f* outlaw, desperado

foral *adj* = of *o* relating to the **fueros**

foráneo, -a *adj* alien, foreign

forastero, -a 1 *adj* foreign, alien
  2 *nm,f* outsider, stranger

forcejear *vi* to wrestle, struggle

forcejeo *nm* struggle, struggling

fórceps *nm inv Med* forceps *pl*

forense 1 *adj* forensic, legal
  2 *nmf* **(médico) f.** forensic surgeon

forestal *adj* forest; **repoblación f.** reafforestation

forfait [for'fait, for'fe] *(pl* **forfaits)** *nm* **(a)** *(para esquiar)* ski pass **(b)** *Dep* default **(c)** *(precio invariable)* fixed rate; **a f.** fixed price

forja *nf* **(a)** *(fragua)* forge **(b)** *(forjado)* forging **(c)** *(ferrería)* ironworks *sing,* foundry

forjado, -a 1 *pp de* **forjar**
  2 *adj* wrought
  3 *nm Arquit* forging

forjar 1 *vt* **(a)** *(metales)* to forge **(b)** *Fig* to create, make; **ella sola forjó un imperio** she created an empire single-handed
  2 forjarse *vpr (labrarse)* to forge for oneself; **se ha forjado un buen porvenir** he has forged a fine future for himself; **f. ilusiones** to build up false hopes

forma *nf* **(a)** *(figura)* form, shape; **en f. de L** L-shaped; **¿qué f. tiene?** what shape is it? **(b)** *(manera)* way; **de esta f.** in this way; **de f. que** so that; **de todas formas** anyway, in any case; **no hubo f. de convencerla** there was no way we could convince her □ **f. de pago** method of payment **(c)** *Dep* form; **estar en f.** to be on form; **estar en baja f.** to be off form; **ponerse en f.** to get fit □ **f. física** fitness **(d)** *Rel* **Sagrada F.** Host **(e)** **formas** *(modales)* manners, social conventions; **guardar las f.** to keep up appearances **(f)** **formas** *Fam (de mujer)* curves

formación *nf* **(a)** *(creación)* formation **(b)** *(educación)* upbringing **(c)** *(enseñanza)* education, training □ **f. académica** formal education; **f. musical** musical training; **f. profesional** technical education; **f. universitaria** university education

formal *adj* **(a)** *(serio)* serious, serious-minded; **noviazgo f.** formal engagement **(b)** *(cumplidor)* reliable, dependable **(c)** *(cortés)* polite; **sed formales** behave yourselves

formaldehído *nm Quím* formaldehyde

formalidad *nf* **(a)** *(requisito)* formality **(b)** *(seriedad)* seriousness **(c)** *(fiabilidad)* reliability **(d)** *(trámite)* formality, requisite

formalina *nf Quím* formalin

formalismo *nm* formalism

formalista 1 *adj* formalistic
  2 *nmf* formalist

formalización *nf* formalization

formalizar [14] **1** *vt* **(a)** *(hacer formal)* to formalize **(b)** *Jur (contrato)* to legalize

2 formalizarse *vpr* to become *o* grow serious

formar 1 *vt* **(a)** *(hacer)* to form; **formó un círculo con las sillas** she placed the chairs in a circle **(b)** *(integrar, constituir)* to form, constitute; **f. un comité** to form a commitee; **f. parte de algo** to be a part of sth **(c)** *(educar)* to bring up; *(enseñar)* to educate, train
  2 *vi* to form up; *Mil* **¡a f.!** fall in!
  3 formarse *vpr* **(a)** *(hacerse, crearse)* to be formed, form; **se formó un charco** a puddle formed; **f. una impresión equivocada** to get the wrong impression **(b)** *(educarse)* to be educated *o* trained

formateado, -a *Inform* **1** *pp de* **formatear**
  2 *adj* formatted
  3 *nm (proceso)* formatting

formatear *vt Inform* to format

formateo *nm Inform* formatting

formativo, -a *adj* formative

formato *nm Tip Inform* format; *(del papel)* size

formica® *nf* Formica®

fórmico, -a *adj Quím* formic

formidable *adj* **(a)** *(tremendo)* tremendous, formidable **(b)** *(maravilloso)* wonderful, terrific; **¡f.!** great!

formol *nm Quím* formol

formón *nm Carp* firmer chisel

fórmula *nf* formula; **por pura f.** for form's sake □ **f. de cortesía** polite expression; **f. de tratamiento** form of address; *Aut* **f. uno** formula one

formulación *nf* formulation

formular *vt* **(a)** *(una teoría)* to formulate **(b)** *(quejas, peticiones)* to make; **f. un deseo** to express a desire; **f. una pregunta** to ask a question

formulario, -a 1 *adj* routine; **una visita formularia** a formal visit
  2 *nm* **(a)** *Farm* formulary, collection of formulas **(b)** *(documento)* form; **rellenar un f. de solicitud** to fill in an application (form)

formulismo *nm* formulism

fornicación *nf Fml* fornication

fornicador, -a *Fml* **1** *adj* fornicating
  2 *nm,f* fornicator

fornicar [59] *vi Fml* to fornicate

fornido, -a *adj* strapping, hefty

fornitura *nf* **(a)** *Mil* cartridge belt **(b)** *(accesorios)* accessories *pl* **(c)** *(de un reloj)* spare parts *pl*

foro *nm* **(a)** *Hist* forum **(b)** *Jur (tribunal)* law court, court of justice; *(profesión)* bar, legal profession **(c)** *Teat* back (of the stage) **(d)** *(reunión)* meeting □ *Inform* **f. de discusión** discussion group

forofo, -a *nm,f Fam Esp* fan, supporter

forrado, -a 1 *pp de* **forrar**
  2 *adj* **(a)** *Cost* lined; *(tapizado)* upholstered **(b)** *Fam (rico)* well-heeled, well-off

forraje *nm Agr* fodder, forage

forrajear *vt* to forage for

forrajero, -a *adj Agr* fodder; **plantas forrajeras** fodder crops

forrar 1 *vt* **(a)** *(por dentro)* to line **(b)** *(por fuera)* to cover; *(tapizar)* to upholster
  2 forrarse *vpr* **(a)** *Fam (de dinero)* to make a packet **(b)** *Am Fam (de comida)* to stuff oneself

forro *nm* **(a)** *Cost* lining □ **f. polar** fleece jacket **(b)** *(funda)* cover, case; *(tapizado)* upholstery **(c)** *Fam Fig* **ni por el f.** not in the slightest

fortachón, -ona *adj Fam* strong, strapping

fortalecer [46] **1** *vt* to fortify, strengthen
 2 fortalecerse *vpr* to fortify oneself, become stronger
fortalecimiento *nm* fortification, strengthening
fortaleza *nf* (**a**) *(vigor)* strength, vigour, *US* vigor (**b**) *(de espíritu)* fortitude (**c**) *Mil* fortress, stronghold (**d**) *Chile (hedor)* stench, stink
fortificación *nf* fortification, fortifying
fortificante 1 *adj* fortifying
 2 *nm* fortifier, tonic
fortificar [59] *vt* to fortify, strengthen
fortín *nm* small fort, bunker
fortísimo, -a *adj* (**a**) *(muy fuerte)* very strong (**b**) *Mús* fortissimo
fortuito, -a *adj* fortuitous; **encuentro f.** chance meeting
fortuna *nf* (**a**) *(destino)* fortune, fate ❑ **la rueda de la f.** the wheel of fortune (**b**) *(suerte)* luck; **buena f.** good luck; **mala f.** misfortune; **por f.** fortunately; **probar f.** to try one's luck (**c**) *(capital)* fortune; **heredó una f.** he inherited a fortune
forúnculo *nm Med* boil, furuncle
forzado, -a 1 *pp de* forzar
 2 *adj* (**a**) *(obligado)* forced; **a marchas forzadas** at a brisk pace ❑ **trabajos forzados** hard labour *sing* (**b**) *(rebuscado)* forced, strained; **una risa forzada** a forced laugh
forzar [31] *vt* (**a**) *(obligar, empujar)* to force, compel; **f. a algn a hacer algo** to compel sb to do sth (**b**) *(cerradura, mecanismo)* to force, break open; **forzaron la puerta del coche** they broke the car door open (**c**) *Fml (violar)* to rape
forzoso, -a *adj* (**a**) *(inevitable)* inevitable, unavoidable, inescapable (**b**) *(obligatorio)* obligatory, compulsory; **la asistencia es forzosa** attendance is obligatory; *Av* **aterrizaje f.** forced landing
forzudo, -a *adj* strong brawny
fosa *nf* (**a**) *(sepultura)* grave ❑ **f. común** common grave (**b**) *(hoyo)* pit ❑ **f. marina** oceanic trench; **f. séptica** septic tank (**c**) *Anat* fossa ❑ **fosas nasales** nostrils
fosfatar *vt* *(fertilizar)* to fertilize with phosphates
fosfato *nm* phosphate ❑ **f. de cal** calcium phosphate
fosforecer [46] *vi* to phosphoresce, glow
fosforera *nf* (**a**) *(caja)* matchbox (**b**) *(fábrica)* match factory
fosforero, -a *nm,f* match seller
fosforescencia *nf* phosphorescence
fosforescente *adj* phosphorescent
fosfórico, -a *adj* *Quím* phosphoric
fosforito *adj* *Esp Fam (color, rotulador)* fluorescent
fósforo *nm* (**a**) *Quím* phosphorus (**b**) *(cerilla)* match
fósil *adj & nm* fossil
fosilización *nf* fossilization
fosilizado, -a 1 *pp de* fosilizarse
 2 *adj* fossilized
fosilizarse [14] *vpr* to fossilize, become fossilized
foso *nm* (**a**) *(hoyo)* hole, pit (**b**) *(de fortificación)* moat (**c**) *Teat* pit ❑ **f. de la orquesta** orchestra pit (**d**) *(en garaje)* inspection pit
fotingo *nm Am* battered old car
foto *nf Fam* photo; **sacar fotos** to take photos
fotocélula *nf* photocell, photoelectric cell
fotocomponer [50] *vt Impr* to typeset
fotocomposición *nf Impr* typesetting, *US* photosetting
fotocopia *nf* photocopy, Xerox®; **hacer** *o* **sacar un f. de algo** to photocopy sth

fotocopiadora *nf* photocopier
fotocopiar *vt* to photocopy
fotoeléctrico, -a *adj* photoelectric
fotogenia *nf* photogenic qualities
fotogénico, -a *adj* photogenic
fotograbado *nm* photogravure, photoengraving
fotograbar *vt* to photoengrave
fotografía *nf* (**a**) *(proceso)* photography (**b**) *(retrato)* photograph; **hacer** *o* **sacar fotografías** to take photographs
fotografiar [32] *vt* to photograph, take a photograph of
fotográfico, -a *adj* photographic
fotógrafo, -a *nm,f* photographer; **f. de prensa** press photographer
fotograma *nm* still
fotomatón *nm* automatic coin-operated photo machine
fotometría *nf* photometry
fotómetro *nm* light meter, exposure meter
fotomodelo *nmf* photographic model
fotomontaje *nm Fot* photomontage
fotón *nm Fís* photon
fotonovela *nf* photo story
fotosensible *adj* photosensitive
fotosíntesis *nf* photosynthesis
fototeca *nf Fot* photograph library
foxtrot *(pl* **foxtrots)** *nm Mús* foxtrot
FP *nf Educ (abrev de* **Formación Profesional)** technical education
frac *(pl* **fracs)** *nm (prenda)* dress coat, tails *pl*
fracasado, -a 1 *pp de* fracasar
 2 *adj* unsuccessful
 3 *nm,f (persona)* failure
fracasar *vi* to fail, be unsuccessful
fracaso *nm* failure
fracción *nf* (**a**) *(porción)* fraction, fragment (**b**) *Mat* fraction (**c**) *Pol* faction
fraccionadora *nf Méx (agencia) Br* estate agent's, *US* real estate agent's
fraccionamiento *nm* (**a**) *(división)* division, breaking up (**b**) *Méx (urbanización)* housing estate
fraccionar *vt* to break up, split up, divide into fractions
fraccionario, -a *adj* fractional; **moneda fraccionaria** small change
fractal *nm* fractal
fractura *nf* fracture
fracturar 1 *vt* to fracture
 2 fracturarse *vpr* to fracture; **f. un brazo/una pierna** to fracture one's arm/leg
fragancia *nf* fragrance
fragante *adj* fragrant, scented
fragata *nf Náut* frigate
frágil *adj* (**a**) *(quebradizo)* fragile, breakable (**b**) *(débil)* frail, weak
fragilidad *nf* (**a**) *(de objeto)* fragility (**b**) *(debilidad)* frailty, weakness
fragmentación *nf también Inform* fragmentation
fragmentar 1 *vt (partir)* to fragment; *(dividir)* to divide up; *(disco duro)* to fragment
 2 fragmentarse *vpr* to break up
fragmentario, -a *adj* fragmentary
fragmento *nm* (**a**) *(pedazo)* fragment, piece (**b**) *Lit* passage

fragor *nm* din, roar; *(de trueno)* crash

fragoroso, -a *adj* thunderous, deafening

fragosidad *nf* **(a)** *(terreno)* roughness, unevenness **(b)** *(vegetación)* thickness, denseness

fragoso, -a *adj* thunderous, deafening

fragua *nf* forge

fraguado 1 *pp de* **fraguar**
2 *nm* setting, hardening

fraguar [11] **1** *vt* **(a)** *(metal)* to forge **(b)** *Fig* to think up, fabricate; *(conspiración)* to hatch
2 *vi (endurecerse)* to set, harden

fraile *nm* friar, monk

frailecillo *nm Orn* puffin

frailesco, -a *adj,* **fraileuno, -a** *adj* monkish

frambuesa *nf Bot* raspberry

francachela *nf Fam (comilona)* feast

francamente *adv* frankly

francés, -a 1 *adj* French; **despedirse a la francesa** to take French leave; **tortilla francesa** plain omelette
2 *nm,f (hombre)* Frenchman; *(mujer)* Frenchwoman
3 *nm* **(a)** *(idioma)* French **(b)** *Vulg* blow job

francesilla *nf Bot* buttercup

franchute, -a *nm,f Pey* Frog, Froggy, Frenchy

Francia *n* France

franciscano, -a 1 *adj Rel* Franciscan
2 *nm,f Rel* Franciscan

francmasón, -ona *nm,f* freemason

francmasonería *nf* freemasonry

francmasónico, -a *adj* masonic

franco, -a¹ *adj* **(a)** *(persona)* frank, open **(b)** *(cosa)* clear, obvious **(c)** *Com* free; **f. a bordo** free on board; **f. de aduana** duty-free; **f. de porte y embalaje** post and packaging free; **f. fábrica** ex-works; **puerto f.** free port

franco, -a² *Hist* **1** *adj* Frankish
2 *nm,f (persona)* Frank
3 *nm (idioma)* Frankish

franco³ *nm Fin (moneda)* franc □ **f. suizo** Swiss franc

francófilo, -a *adj & nm,f* francophile

francófono, -a 1 *adj* French-speaking
2 *nm,f* French speaker

francotirador, -a *nm,f Mil* sniper

franela *nf* **(a)** *Tex* flannel **(b)** *Ven (camiseta) Br* vest, *US* undershirt

frangollón, -ona *adj Am (persona)* bungling

franja *nf (banda)* band, strip; *(faja)* fringe; *Cost* fringe, border; *Geog* **la f. de Gaza** the Gaza strip

franqueable *adj* **(a)** *(río, abismo)* crossable, which can be crossed **(b)** *(obstáculo)* surmountable

franquear 1 *vt* **(a)** *(dejar libre)* to free, clear; **f. el paso** to clear the way; **f. la entrada** to allow to enter **(b)** *(atravesar)* to cross; *Fig* **f. una dificultad** to overcome a difficulty **(c)** *(carta)* to frank; **máquina de f.** franking machine; *(en sobre)* **a f. en destino** postage paid
2 franquearse *vpr* **franquearse (con algn)** to open one's heart to sb

franqueo *nm* postage □ **f. pagado** postage paid, postpaid

franqueza *nf* **(a)** *(sinceridad)* frankness, openness **(b)** *(confianza)* familiarity, intimacy

franquicia *nf* exemption; *Com* franchise □ *Com* **f. arancelaria** exemption from customs duty

franquiciado, -a *nm,f Com* franchisee, franchiseholder

franquiciador, -a *nm,f Com* franchiser

franquismo *nm Hist* **el f.** *(régimen)* the Franco regime; *(doctrina)* Franco's doctrine

franquista *Hist* **1** *adj* Francoist, pro-Franco
2 *nmf* Francoist, Franco supporter

frasco *nm* small bottle, flask

frase *nf* **(a)** *Ling (oración)* sentence **(b)** *(expresión)* phrase; **f. hecha** set phrase *o* expression, idiom

fraseología *nf* **(a)** *Ling* phraseology **(b)** *(palabrería)* verbosity

fraternal *adj* brotherly, fraternal

fraternidad *nf* brotherhood, fraternity

fraternizar [14] *vi* to fraternize

fraterno, -a *adj* fraternal, brotherly

fratricida 1 *adj* fratricidal
2 *nmf* fratricide

fratricidio *nm* fratricide

fraude *nm* fraud □ **f. fiscal** tax evasion

fraudulencia *nf* fraudulence

fraudulento, -a *adj* fraudulent

fray *nm Rel* brother; **F. David** Brother David

frazada *nf Am* blanket; **f. eléctrica** electric blanket

frecuencia *nf* **(a)** *(asiduidad)* frequency; **con f.** frequently, often **(b)** *Rad* frequency □ **alta/baja f.** high/low frequency

frecuentación *nf* frequenting

frecuentado, -a 1 *pp de* **frecuentar**
2 *adj* frequented; **un lugar poco f.** a rarely frequented spot

frecuentar *vt* to frequent, visit

frecuente *adj* **(a)** *(repetido)* frequent **(b)** *(usual)* common

frecuentemente *adv* frequently, often

freelance ['frilans] *adj,* **free lance** ['frilans] *adj* freelance

Freetown ['fritaun] *n* Freetown

freeware ['friwer] *nm Inform* freeware

freezer ['friser] *(pl* freezers) *nm Am* freezer

fregadera *nf Am salvo RP Fam* pain, drag

fregadero *nm Esp Méx* (kitchen) sink

fregado, -a¹ 1 *pp de* **fregar**
2 *nm* **(a)** *(lavado)* washing; *(frotar)* scrubbing **(b)** *Fam (riña)* fight, quarrel

fregado, -a² *adj Andes (fastidioso)* tiresome, annoying

fregar [43] *vt* **(a)** *(lavar)* to wash; *(frotar)* to scrub; **f. los platos** to wash up, do the dishes; **f. el suelo** to mop the floor **(b)** *Am Fig* to annoy, irritate

fregón, -ona *adj Am (majadero)* silly, stupid

fregona *nf* **(a)** *Pey (sirvienta)* skivvy **(b)** *Esp (utensilio)* mop

fregotear *vt Fam* to give a quick wipe to

fregoteo *nm Fam* quick wipe

freidora *nf* (deep) fryer

freiduría *nf* fried-fish shop

freír [56] *(pp* frito) **1** *vt* **(a)** *Culin* to fry **(b)** *Fam Fig (exasperar)* to exasperate; **le están friendo a preguntas** they are bombarding him with questions; *Fam Fig* **la mandé a f. espárragos** I told her to go to blazes
2 freírse *vpr* to fry; *Fig* **nos freíamos** it was baking hot

frenada *nf Am* **dar una f.** to brake hard

frenado, -a 1 *pp de* **frenar**
2 *nm* braking

frenar 1 *vt Fig (contener)* to restrain, check
2 *vi (en vehículo)* to brake

frenazo *nm* sudden braking; **dar un f.** to jam on the brakes

frenesí (*pl* **frenesíes**) *nm* frenzy

frenético, -a *adj* (a) *(exaltado)* frenzied, frenetic (b) *(colérico)* wild, mad

frenillo *nm* (a) *Anat* fraenum, *US* frenum (b) *CAm Carib (de cometa)* string *(of kite)*

freno *nm* (a) *Aut* brake; **poner/soltar el f.** to put on/release the brake ❑ **f. de disco** disc brake; **f. de mano** handbrake; **f. de tambor** drum brake; **líquido de frenos** brake fluid (b) *(de caballería)* bit; *Fig* **morder** *o* **tascar el f.** to champ at the bit (c) *Fig* curb, check; **poner f. a algo** to curb sth

frenopatía *nf* psychiatry

frenopático, -a 1 *adj* psychiatric
  2 *nm Fam* loony bin

frente 1 *nm* (a) *(parte delantera)* front; *Arquit* front, façade; **al f. de** at the head of; **chocar de f.** to crash head on; **hacer f. a algo** to face sth, stand up to sth (b) *Mil* front, front line (c) *Meteor* front ❑ **f. frío/cálido** cold/warm front (d) *Pol* front ❑ **f. popular** popular front
  2 *nf Anat* forehead; **arrugar la f.** to frown; **f. a f.** face to face; **no tener dos dedos de f.** to be as thick as two short planks; *Vulg* **adornar la f.** to cuckold, be unfaithful to
  3 *adv* **f. a** in front of, opposite; **viven f. a la estación** they live opposite the station

fresa 1 *adj* (a) red (b) *Méx Fam (esnob)* posh
  2 *nf* (a) *Esp CAm Carib Méx Bot (planta)* strawberry plant; *(fruto)* strawberry (b) *Téc* milling cutter (c) *(de dentista)* drill
  3 *nmf Méx Fam (esnob)* posh person

fresador, -a *nm,f (persona)* milling machine operator

fresadora *nf Téc* milling machine

fresar *vt Téc* to mill

fresca *nf* (a) *(aire fresco)* fresh air, cool air; **tomar la f.** to get some fresh air (b) *Fam (impertinencia)* cheeky remark; **decirle cuatro frescas a algn** to tell sb a few home truths

frescachón, -ona *adj Fam* healthy, robust

frescales *nmf inv Esp Fam* brazen person, cheeky devil

fresco, -a 1 *adj* (a) *(temperatura, aire)* cool, cold; **agua fresca** cold water; **viento f.** cool wind (b) *(tela, vestido)* light, fresh; **esta blusa es muy fresca** this blouse is nice and cool (c) *(aspecto)* healthy, fresh (d) *(comida)* fresh; **fruta fresca** fresh fruit (e) *(reciente)* fresh, new; **las noticias más frescas** the latest news *sing* (f) *Fig (impasible)* cool, calm, unworried; **se quedó tan f.** he didn't bat an eyelid (g) *(desvergonzado)* cheeky, shameless; **la muy fresca se fue sin pagar** she had the nerve to leave without paying; **¡qué f.!** what a nerve!; **¡sí que estamos frescos!** now we're in a fine mess!
  2 *nm* (a) *(frescor)* fresh air, cool air; **al f.** in the cool; **hacer f.** to be chilly; *Fam* **mandar a algn a tomar el f.** to send sb packing (b) *Arte* fresco (c) *Andes CAm Méx (refresco)* soft drink

frescor *nm* coolness, freshness

frescura *nf* (a) *(desvergüenza)* cheek, nerve; **¡qué f.!** what a nerve! (b) *(impertinencia)* impertinence (c) *(calma)* coolness, calmness

fresno *nm Bot* ash tree

fresón *nm Bot (planta)* strawberry plant; *(fruto)* (large) strawberry

fresquera *nf Culin* meat safe

fresquería *nf Am* refreshment stall

freudiano, -a [froi'ðjano] *adj & nm,f Psic* Freudian

frialdad *nf* (a) *(frío)* coldness (b) *Fig* coldness, indifference; **me recibieron con f.** I was given a cool reception

fríamente *adv* coldly, coolly

fricativo, -a *adj Ling* fricative

fricción *nf* (a) *Fís* friction (b) *(friega)* rub, rubbing; *(masaje)* massage (c) *Fig* friction, discord

friccionar *vt* to rub, massage

friega *nf* (a) *(masaje)* rub, rubbing (b) *Am (molestia)* nuisance, annoyance (c) *Am (zurra)* thrashing

friegaplatos *nmf inv (persona)* dishwasher

frigidez *nf* frigidity

frígido, -a *adj* frigid

frigio, -a *adj & nm,f Hist* Phrygian

frigorífico, -a 1 *adj* refrigerating
  2 *nm Esp* (a) *(de uso doméstico)* refrigerator, *Br* fridge, *US* icebox (b) *(cámara)* cold storage room

frijol *nm*, **fríjol** *nm Am* bean

frío, -a 1 *adj* (a) *(a baja temperatura)* cold (b) *Fig* cold, cool, indifferent; **su muerte me dejó f.** *(dejar indiferente)* her death didn't affect me in the least; *(afectar)* I was stunned by her death
  2 *nm* cold; **hace mucho f. hoy** it's very cold today; **pasar f.** to be cold; *Esp* **coger f.** to catch (a) cold; **¡qué f.!** isn't it cold!; *Fam* **hace un f. que pela** it's freezing cold

friolento, -a *adj Am* sensitive to the cold

friolera *nf* (a) *(tontería)* trifle, trinket (b) *Fam (dinero)* **se gastó la f. de dos mil dólares en ello** he spent a mere two thousand dollars on it

friolero, -a *Esp adj* sensitive to the cold; **soy muy f.** I really feel the cold

frisar *vi* **f. con** to approach, border on; **Armando frisa con los cuarenta** Armando is getting on for forty

friso *nm* (a) *Arquit* frieze (b) *(zócalo)* skirting board

frisón, -ona 1 *adj* Friesian
  2 *nm,f (persona)* Friesian
  3 *nm (idioma)* Friesian

fritada *nf* fry, fried dish; *Culin* **f. de pescado** dish of fried fish

fritanga *nf Fam* (a) *Esp* fry-up; **olor a f.** smell of frying (b) *Am Pey (comida grasienta)* greasy food

fritar *vt Am* to fry

frito, -a 1 *pp véase* **freír**
  2 *adj* (a) *Culin* fried ❑ **patatas fritas** chips, *US* French fries (b) *Fam* exasperated, fed up; **me tienes f. con tantas preguntas** I'm sick to death of all your questions (c) *Fam* **quedarse f.** to fall asleep
  3 *nm* fry, piece of fried food; **fritos de calamar** fried squid *sing*

fritura *nf* fry-up, dish of fried food

frivolidad *nf* frivolity

frívolo, -a *adj* frivolous

fronda *nf* (a) *(espesura)* foliage (b) *(de helecho)* frond

frondosidad *nf* foliage, luxuriance

frondoso, -a *adj* leafy, luxuriant

frontal *adj* frontal; *Anat* **hueso f.** frontal bone

frontera *nf* (a) *(división administrativa)* frontier, border (b) *Fig* limit, bounds *pl*

fronterizo, -a *adj* frontier, border; **pueblos fronterizos** border towns

frontero, -a *adj* opposite

frontis *nm*, **frontispicio** *nm* (a) *Arquit (fachada)* façade, front; *(frontón)* pediment (b) *Impr* frontispiece

frontón *nm* (a) *Dep (juego)* pelota (b) *Dep (edificio)* pelota court (c) *Arquit* pediment

frotación *nf*, **frotamiento** *nm* rubbing

frotar 1 *vt* to rub
2 frotarse *vpr* to rub; **f. las manos** to rub one's hands together
frote *nm* rubbing
frotis *nm inv* smear; **f. cervical** cervical smear
fructífero, -a *adj* (a) *Bot* fruit-bearing (b) *Fig* fruitful
fructificar [59] *vi* (a) *Bot* to bear fruit, produce a crop (b) *Fig* to be fruitful
fructosa *nf* fructose
fructuoso, -a *adj* fruitful
frugal *adj* frugal
frugalidad *nf* frugality, frugalness
fruición *nf* pleasure, delight, enjoyment
frunce *nm Cost* gathering; **con frunces** gathered
fruncido, -a 1 *pp de* fruncir
2 *nm* (*en tela*) gathering
fruncir [72] *vt* (a) *Cost* to gather (b) **f. el ceño** to frown, knit one's brow (c) (*labios*) to purse, pucker
fruslería *nf* (a) (*objeto*) trinket (b) *Fam Fig* trifle
frustración *nf* frustration
frustrado, -a 1 *pp de* fustrar
2 *adj* frustrated; **el f. golpe de estado** the attempted coup; **intento f.** unsuccessful attempt
frustrante *adj* frustrating
frustrar 1 *vt* (*intentos, esperanzas*) to frustrate, thwart; (*persona*) to disappoint
2 frustrarse *vpr* (a) (*proyectos, planes*) to fail, go awry (b) (*persona*) to be frustrated o disappointed
frustre *nm Fam* frustration
fruta *nf* (a) (*fruto*) fruit □ **f. del tiempo** fresh fruit; **f. escarchada** candied fruit; **f. de la pasión** passion fruit; **f. prohibida** forbidden fruit; **f. seca** dried fruit (b) *Fig* fruit, product, result
frutal 1 *adj* fruit; **árbol f.** fruit tree
2 *nm* fruit tree
frutería *nf* fruit shop
frutero, -a 1 *adj* fruit; **mercado f.** fruit market
2 *nm,f* fruiterer
3 *nm* fruit dish o bowl
frutícola *adj* **la producción f.** fruit production; **una región f.** a fruit-growing region
frutilla *nf Chile RP Bot* variety of strawberry
fruto *nm* (a) *Bot* fruit; **dar f.** to bear fruit □ **frutos secos** (*nueces, almendras*) nuts; (*pasas, higos pasos*) dried fruit *sing* (b) *Fig* fruit, product, result; **dar f.** to be fruitful; **no dar f.** to be fruitless; **sacar f. de algo** to profit from sth
FSLN *nm* (*abrev de* **Frente Sandinista de Liberación Nacional**) FSLN
FTP *Inform* (*abrev de* **file transfer protocol**) FTP
fu *interj* **ni f. ni fa** so-so, average
fucsia *nf Bot* fuchsia
fuego *nm* (a) (*incandescencia*) fire; **apagar el f.** to put out the fire; **atizar el f.** to poke the fire; **encender un f.** to light a fire; **prender f. a algo** to set fire to sth; *Fig* **jugar con f.** to play with fire; *Fig* **poner las manos en el f. por** to stake one's life on □ **f. de Santelmo** Saint Elmo's fire; **f. fatuo** will-o'-the-wisp, jack-o'-lantern; **fuegos artificiales** fireworks; *Fig* **prueba de f.** trial by fire (b) (*lumbre*) light; **¿me da f., por favor?** have you got a light, please? (c) (*cocina*) burner, ring; **a f. lento** on a low flame; (*al horno*) in a slow oven (d) *Mil* fire; **¡f.!** fire!; **hacer o romper f.** to open fire; *Fig* **estar entre dos fuegos** to be caught between two fires □ **f. cruzado** crossfire; **f. graneado** sustained fire; **f.**

nutrido heavy fire (e) (*ardor*) ardour, *US* ardor, zeal; **atizar el f. de la discordia** to stir up discord
fuel *nm*, **fuel-oil** *nm* fuel oil
fuelle *nm* (a) (*para soplar*) bellows (b) *Mús* (*de gaita*) bag
fuente *nf* (a) (*manantial*) spring (b) (*artificial*) fountain (c) (*recipiente*) dish, serving dish (d) (*origen*) source; **de f. desconocida** from an unknown source; *Elec* **f. de energía** energy source; **fuentes fidedignas** o **bien informadas** reliable sources; **f. de ingresos** source of income; **f. de riqueza** source of wealth (e) *Impr Inform* font
fuer *nm Fml* **a f. de** as a; **a f. de caballero** as a gentleman
fuera¹ *adv* (a) (*en el exterior*) outside, out; **desde f.** from (the) outside; **¡f.!** get out!; *Box* **f. de combate** knocked out; **f. de duda** beyond doubt; **f. de la ley** illegal; **f. de lo normal** extraordinary, very unusual; **f. de lugar** out of place; **f. de peligro** out of danger; **f. de serie** extraordinary; **la puerta de f.** the outer door; **por f.** on the outside; **quédate f.** stay outside; **sal f.** come/go out; *Fig* **estar f. de sí** to be beside oneself (b) (*en otro lugar*) away; **estar f.** to be away; (*en el extranjero*) to be abroad; *Dep* **el equipo de f.** the away team; *Dep* **jugar f.** to play away □ **f. de juego**, *Am* **f. de lugar** offside (c) (*excepto*) except for, apart from; **f. de esto** apart from this
fuera² **1** *subj imperf véase* ir
2 *subj imperf véase* ser²
fueraborda 1 *adj inv* outboard; **motor f.** outboard motor o engine; **lancha f.** outboard, boat with outboard motor
2 *nm inv* (*motor*) outboard motor o engine
3 *nf inv* (*lancha*) outboard, boat with outboard motor
fuero *nm* (a) (*privilegio*) privilege; (*exención*) exemption; **los fueros** = rights and privileges enjoyed by certain Spanish provinces (b) (*jurisdicción*) code of laws (c) *Fig* **en tu f. interno** deep down, in your heart of hearts
fuerte 1 *adj* (a) (*resistente*) (*persona, material*) strong; *Fig* **palabras fuertes** strong words; *Fig* **está muy f. en matemáticas** he's very good at mathematics (b) (*intenso*) severe; **hacía un frío muy f.** it was extremely cold; **padece dolores muy fuertes** he suffers severe pain (c) (*sonido*) loud; **la música está demasiado f.** the music is too loud (d) (*grande*) **el plato f.** the main course; *Fam Fig* the most important event; **una comida f.** a heavy meal; **una f. suma** a large amount of money (e) (*sujeto*) stiff; **este tornillo está muy f.** this screw is stiff
2 *nm* (a) (*fortificación*) fort (b) (*punto fuerte*) forte, strong point; **su f. es la física** she's very good at physics, physics is her strong point
3 *adv* hard; **¡abrázame f.!** hold me tight!; **comer f.** to eat a lot; **¡habla más f.!** speak up!; **¡pégalo f.!** hit it hard!
fuerza *nf* (a) (*fortaleza*) strength, force; **no tengo fuerzas para andar más** I haven't got the energy to walk any further; **sacar fuerzas de flaqueza** to muster up one's courage; *Fig* **a f. de** by dint of, by force of; *Fig* **las fuerzas vivas de la localidad** the local authorities; *Fig* **por la f. de la costumbre** by force of habit □ **f. bruta** brute force; **f. de voluntad** willpower; **f. física** strength; **f. mayor** force majeure (b) *Fis* force □ **f. de gravedad** force of gravity (c) *Mil* force □ **f. aérea** air force; **Fuerzas Armadas** Armed Forces (d) **a la f.** (*obligación*) of necessity; (*violencia*) by force; **por f.** of necessity
fuese 1 *subj imperf véase* ir
2 *subj imperf véase* ser²
fuete *nm Am* whip
fuga *nf* (a) (*escapada*) flight, escape; **darse a la f.** to take flight; **poner en f.** to put to flight □ **f. de cerebros** brain drain; **f. de divisas** flight of capital (b) (*pérdida*) leak (c) *Mús* fugue
fugacidad *nf* fleetingness

fugarse [38] *vpr* to escape, flee; **f. de casa** to run away from home; **se ha fugado con su amante** she has eloped with her lover

fugaz *adj* fleeting, brief

fugitivo, -a 1 *adj* **(a)** *(en fuga)* fleeing **(b)** *Fig (efímero)* ephemeral, fleeting
2 *nm,f* fugitive, runaway

fui 1 *pt indef véase* **ir**
2 *pt indef véase* **ser²**

ful 1 *adj Fam (falso)* bogus, phoney; **policía f.** bogus policeman
2 *nf Argot (mierda)* shit

fulana *nf Pey* whore, tart

fulano, -a 1 *nm,f (hombre)* so-and-so, what's his name; *(mujer)* so-and-so, what's her name; **Doña Fulana de tal** Mrs So-and-so; **f., mengano y zutano** Tom, Dick and Harry
2 *nm Fam* guy, *Br* bloke

fular *nm* foulard, scarf

fulcro *nm Téc* fulcrum

fulero, -a *Fam* **1** *adj* cheating, crooked
2 *nm,f* cheater

fúlgido, -a *adj Literario* shining, glowing, bright

fulgor *nm Literario* **(a)** *(resplandor)* brilliance, glow **(b)** *(esplendor)* splendour, *US* splendor

fulgurante *adj* **(a)** *(que brilla)* brilliant, shining **(b)** *Fig* magnificent, stunning

fulgurar *vi* to shine, glow

full *nm (en póquer)* full house

fullería *nf* cheating; *Naipes* cardsharping; **hacer fullerías** to cheat

fullero, -a 1 *adj* cheating
2 *nm,f Naipes* cheat, cardsharper

fulmar *nm Orn* fulmar

fulminación *nf* fulmination

fulminado, -a 1 *pp de* **fulminar**
2 *adj* struck by lightning

fulminante 1 *adj* **(a)** *(explosivo)* fulminating **(b)** *Fig* staggering; **mirada f.** withering look
2 *nm* fuse, detonator ▫ **cápsula f.** percussion cap

fulminar *vt* **(a)** *(con un rayo)* to strike with lightning **(b)** *Fig* to strike dead; **f. a algn con la mirada** to look daggers at sb

fumador, -a 1 *adj* smoking
2 *nm,f* smoker; **no f.** nonsmoker ▫ **f. pasivo** passive smoker

fumar 1 *vt & vi* to smoke; *(en letrero)* **no fumar** no smoking
2 **fumarse** *vpr* **(a)** *(cigarrillo)* to smoke; **f. un pitillo** to smoke a cigarette **(b)** *Esp Fam* **f. las clases** to play truant o *US* hooky

fumigación *nf* fumigation

fumigador *nm* fumigator

fumigar [38] *vt* to fumigate

funambulista *nmf* tightrope walker

funámbulo, -a *nm,f* tightrope walker

funche *nm Am Culin* maize porridge

función *nf* **(a)** *(actividad, objetivo)* function; **en f. de** according to **(b)** *(cargo)* duties *pl*; **entrar en funciones** to take up one's duties; **estar en funciones** to be in office; **presidente en funciones** acting president **(c)** *Cin Teat* performance; **no hay f.** no performance ▫ **f. benéfica** charity performance; **f. de noche** late performance; **f. de tarde** matinée

funcional *adj* functional

funcionalidad *nf* functional qualities

funcionalismo *nm* functionalism

funcionamiento *nm* functioning, working; **poner algo en f.** to put sth into operation

funcionar *vi* to function, work; **hacer f. una máquina** to operate a machine; **no funciona** *(en letrero)* out of order; *Fam* **así no podemos f.** we can't go on like that

funcionariado *nm (de la Administración central)* civil service; *(profesor, bombero, enfermero)* public sector workers

funcionario, -a *nm,f* **f. (público)** *(de la Administración central)* civil servant; *(profesor, bombero, enfermero)* public sector worker

funda *nf* **(a)** *(flexible)* cover; **f. de almohada** pillow-case **(b)** *(rígida)* case **(c)** *(de arma blanca)* sheath **(d)** *Argot (condón)* French letter

fundación *nf* foundation

fundado, -a 1 *pp de* **fundar**
2 *adj* firm, well-founded, justified; **mal f.** ill-founded

fundador, -a *nm,f* founder

fundamentación *nf* foundation, basis

fundamental *adj* fundamental

fundamentalismo *nm* fundamentalism

fundamentalista *adj & nmf* fundamentalist

fundamentar *vt* **(a)** *Fig* to base **(en** on**) (b)** *Constr* to lay the foundations of

fundamento *nm* **(a)** *(base)* basis, grounds; **sin f.** unfounded **(b)** *(seriedad)* seriousness; *(confianza)* reliability; **una persona de f.** a reliable person **(c)** **fundamentos** *Constr* foundations

fundar 1 *vt* **(a)** *(crear)* to found; *(erigir)* to raise **(b)** *(basar)* to base, found
2 **fundarse** *vpr* **(a)** *(crear, establecer)* to be founded; **la empresa se fundó en 1901** the firm was founded in 1901 **(b)** *(teoría, afirmación)* to be based; *(persona)* to base oneself

fundición *nf* **(a)** *(fusión)* melting **(b)** *(de metales)* smelting, casting ▫ **hierro de f.** cast iron **(c)** *(lugar)* foundry, smelting works *pl* ▫ **f. de acero** steelworks *pl*

fundido *nm Cin TV* fade-in, fade-out

fundidor *nm* caster, smelter

fundir 1 *vt* **(a)** *(un sólido)* to melt **(b)** *Metal* to found, cast; **f. hierro** to smelt iron; **f. una estatua en bronce** to cast a statue in bronze **(c)** *Elec (bombilla)* to blow; *(plomos)* to blow **(d)** *(unir)* to unite, join **(e)** *Am (arruinar)* to ruin
2 **fundirse** *vpr* **(a)** *(derretirse)* to melt **(b)** *Elec* to blow, burn out; **se han fundido los plomos** the fuses have gone **(c)** *(unirse)* to merge **(d)** *Am (arruinarse)* to be ruined

fúnebre *adj* **(a)** *(mortuorio)* funeral **(b)** *(lúgubre)* mournful, lugubrious

funeral 1 *adj* funeral
2 *nm (tamb* **funerales***)* **(a)** *(entierro)* funeral **(b)** *(conmemoración)* memorial service

funerala: a la funerala *loc adv* **(a)** *Fam* **ojo a la f.** black eye **(b)** *Mil* with reversed arms

funeraria *nf* undertaker's, *US* funeral parlor

funerario, -a *adj* funerary, funeral

funesto, -a *adj* ill-fated, fatal; **consecuencias funestas** disastrous consequences

fungible *adj* disposable

fungicida 1 *adj* fungicidal
2 *nm* fungicide

fungir [24] **(a)** *vi Méx* to act **(de** as**) (b)** *CAm Cuba (detentar)* to hold, detain

funicular *nm Ferroc* funicular (railway)

funky ['funki] **1** *adj* **música f.** funk
 2 *nm* funk

fuñir [40] *vt Ven* to mess things up for

furcia *nf Esp Ofens* whore, tart

furgón *nm* **(a)** *Aut* van, wagon, waggon **(b)** *Ferroc* goods wagon *o* waggon, *US* boxcar ❏ **f. de cola** *Br* guard's van, *US* caboose

furgoneta *nf* van

furia *nf* fury, rage; **ponerse hecho una f.** to become furious, fly into a rage

furibundo, -a *adj* furious, enraged

furioso, -a *adj* furious; **ponerse f.** to get angry; **una furiosa tempestad** a raging storm

furor *nm* fury, rage; *Fig* **hacer f.** to be all the rage

furriel *nm Mil* quartermaster

furtivo, -a *adj* furtive, stealthy; **caza furtiva, pesca furtiva** poaching; **cazador/pescador f.** poacher

furúnculo *nm Med* boil

fusa *nf Mús* demisemiquaver, *US* thirty-second note

fuselaje *nm Av* fuselage

fusible 1 *adj* fusible
 2 *nm* fuse

fusil *nm* gun, rifle; **echarse el f. a la cara** to aim one's rifle; **f. ametrallador** automatic rifle

fusilamiento *nm* shooting, execution

fusilar *vt* **(a)** *(ejecutar)* to shoot, execute **(b)** *(plagiar)* to plagiarize

fusilería *nf* **(a)** *(fusiles)* rifles *pl*; **descarga** *o* **fuego de f.** fusillade **(b)** *(fusileros)* fusiliers *pl*

fusilero *nm* fusilier, rifleman

fusión *nf* **(a)** *Fís (metales)* fusion, melting; *(hielo)* thawing, melting ❏ **punto de f.** melting point **(b)** *(de intereses, ideas)* fusion **(c)** *Com* merger, amalgamation

fusionar 1 *vt* to merge
 2 fusionarse *vpr* to merge

fusta *nf* riding whip

fustán *nm Am* (cotton) petticoat *o* underskirt

fuste *nm* **(a)** *Arquit* shaft **(b)** *(importancia)* importance; **un hombre de f.** a man of consequence

fustigar [38] *vt* **(a)** *(caballo)* to whip, lash **(b)** *Fig* to reprimand sharply

fútbol *nm*, *Méx* **futbol** *nm Dep* soccer, *Br* football ❏ **f. americano** American football, *US* football; *Esp* **f. sala** indoor five-a-side

futbolero, -a *nm,f Fam* soccer *o Br* football fan

futbolín *nm Esp Br* table football, *US* foosball

futbolista *nmf Dep* soccer *o Br* football player, *Br* footballer

futbolístico, -a *adj* soccer, *Br* football; **encuentro f.** soccer *o Br* football match

fútil *adj* futile, trivial

futilidad *nf* futility, triviality; **hablar de futilidades** to talk about trivialities

futurismo *nm* futurism

futurista 1 *adj* futuristic
 2 *nmf* futurist

futuro, -a 1 *adj* future
 2 *nm* **(a)** *(tiempo)* future; **en un f. próximo** in the near future **(b)** *Ling* future ❏ **f. perfecto** future perfect

futurología *nf* futurology

futurólogo, -a *nm,f* futurologist

G

G, g [χe] *nf (la letra)* G, g

g *(abrev de* **gramo(s))** g

g/ *Fin (abrev de* **giro)** giro

G8 [χe'otʃo] *(abrev de* **Grupo de los Ocho)** *nm* G8

gabacho, -a *Pey* **1** *adj* **(a)** *Esp (francés)* Froggy **(b)** *Méx (estadounidense)* Yankee, Gringo
2 *nm,f* **(a)** *Esp (francés)* Frog **(b)** *Méx (estadounidense)* Yank, Gringo

gabán *nm* overcoat

gabardina *nf* **(a)** *(prenda)* raincoat **(b)** *Tex* gabardine

gabarra *nf Náut* barge, lighter

gabinete *nm* **(a)** *(despacho)* study; *Fís Quím* laboratory; *Med* **g. de consulta** surgery; **g. de lectura** reading-room **(b)** *(en museo)* section, room; **el g. de monedas** the coin section **(c)** *Pol* cabinet; **g. fantasma** shadow cabinet

gablete *nm Arquit* gable, gable end

Gabón *n* Gabon

gabonés, -esa *adj & nm,f* Gabonese

gacela *nf Zool* gazelle

gaceta *nf* **(a)** *Prensa* gazette; *Fam* **mentir más que la g.** to lie like mad **(b)** *(persona chismosa)* gossip, gossipmonger

gacetilla *nf* **(a)** *Prensa* 'news in brief' **(b)** *(persona chismosa)* gossip, gossipmonger

gacetillero *nm Prensa* **(a)** *(redactor de breves)* editor of 'news in brief' column **(b)** *Fam (periodista)* journalist

gacha *nf* **(a)** *(masa blanda)* paste, mush **(b) gachas** *Culin (papilla)* porridge *sing*, pap *sing*; **g. de avena** oatmeal porridge *sing*; *Fam Fig* **hacerse unas g.** to turn sentimental *o* mushy

gachí *nf Argot (mujer)* bird, chick

gacho, -a *adj* drooping, bent downward; **a gachas** on all fours; **con la cabeza gacha** with one's head bowed; *Fig* **estar con las orejas gachas** to have one's tail between one's legs

gachó *nm Argot* guy, *Br* bloke

gaditano, -a **1** *adj* of *o* from Cadiz
2 *nm,f* person from Cadiz

gaélico, -a **1** *adj* Gaelic
2 *nm (idioma)* Gaelic

gafar *vt Esp Fam* to put a jinx on, bring bad luck to

gafas *nfpl* glasses, spectacles ❑ **g. bifocales** bifocals; **g. graduadas** prescription glasses; **g. de sol** sunglasses

gafe *Esp adj & nmf Fam* **ser g.** to be a jinx

gag *(pl* **gags)** *nm Cin Teat* gag, comic situation

gaguear *vi PRico* to stutter

gaita **1** *nf Mús* bagpipe, bagpipes *pl*; *Fam* **templar gaitas** to smooth things out; *Esp Fam* **¡vaya una g.!** what a drag!

2 *nm,f RP Pey* = sometimes pejorative term used to refer to a Spaniard, especially an immigrant

gaitero, -a **1** *nm,f Mús* piper
2 *adj* **(a)** *(color)* gaudy, flashy **(b)** *(persona)* buffoonish, clownish

gajes *nmpl Fam Irón* **g. del oficio** occupational hazards

gajo *nm* **(a)** *(de uvas)* bunch; *(de frutas)* cluster **(b)** *(de naranja, pomelo etc)* segment **(c)** *(rama desprendida)* torn-off branch **(d)** *Arg Bot (esqueje)* cutting

gala *nf* **(a)** *(vestido)* full dress, best clothes; **de g.** dressed up; *Mil* in full uniform; *(ciudad)* decked out **(b)** *(espectáculo)* gala **(c)** *(lo más selecto)* cream, pride; **hacer g. de** to glory in; **la g. de la sociedad** the cream of society; **la g. del pueblo** the pride of the village; **tener algo a g.** to be proud of sth **(d) galas** finery *sing*; **lucir sus mejores g.** to be dressed in all one's finery

galáctico, -a *adj Astron* galactic

galaico, -a *adj Literario* Galician

galán *nm* **(a)** *(hombre atractivo)* handsome young man; *Hum* ladies' man **(b)** *(pretendiente)* suitor **(c)** *Teat* leading man; **segundo g.** second lead **(d) g. de noche** *Bot* night jasmine **(e) g. de noche** *Mueb* valet

galán, -ana *nf véase* **galano, -a**

galano, -a *adj* smart, elegant

galante *adj* gallant, chivalrous

galanteador, -a *adj* flirtatious, wooing

galantear *vt (mujer)* to court, woo

galantemente *adv* gallantly, politely

galanteo *nm* flirtation, wooing

galantería *nf* **(a)** *(caballerosidad)* gallantry, chivalry **(b)** *(piropo)* compliment

galanura *nf* gracefulness, elegance

galápago *nm* **(a)** *Zool* turtle **(b)** *(lingote)* ingot, pig **(c)** *Hond Perú Ven (silla de montar)* light saddle

Galápagos *npl* **las Islas G.** the Galapagos Islands

galardón *nm* prize

galardonado, -a **1** *pp de* **galardonar**
2 *adj* prizewinning; **el ensayo g.** the (prize)winning essay
3 *nm,f* prizewinner

galardonar *vt* to award a prize to

galaxia *nf Astron* galaxy

galbana *nf Fam* torpor, laziness, apathy; **tener g.** to feel lazy

galena *nf Min* lead sulphide

galeno *nm Fam* doctor

galeón *nm Náut* galleon

galeote *nm* galley slave

galera *nf* (**a**) *Náut* galley; **condenar a galeras** to send to the galleys (**b**) *(carro)* covered wagon (**c**) *Impr* galley proof (**d**) *CAm Méx* hut, shack (**e**) *RP* top hat

galerada *nf* (**a**) *(carro)* wagonload (**b**) *Impr* galley proof

galería *nf* (**a**) *Arquit* covered balcony (**b**) *(local)* **g. de arte** art gallery; **g. comercial** shopping arcade (**c**) *(paso subterráneo)* underground passage, gallery (**d**) *Teat* gallery, gods *pl*; **hablar para la g.** to play to the gallery (**e**) *(para cortinas)* curtain rail

galerista *nmf* gallery owner

galerna *nf*, **galerno** *nm Meteor* = strong north-west wind on northern coast of Spain

galerón *nm Col Ven* = popular song and dance

Gales *n* **el país de G.** Wales

galés, -esa 1 *adj* Welsh
   2 *nm,f (hombre)* Welshman; *(mujer)* Welshwoman; **los galeses** the Welsh
   3 *nm (idioma)* Welsh

galga *nf* boulder, large stone

galgo *nm Zool* greyhound; **¡échale un g.!** you'll be lucky!

galguear *vi RP Fam* to be broke

Galia *n Hist* Gaul

gálibo *nm Téc* gauge

Galicia *n* Galicia

galicismo *nm Ling* gallicism

gálico, -a *adj* Gallic, French

Galilea *n* Galilee

galileo, -a *adj & nm,f* Galilean

galimatías *nm inv Fam* gibberish, rigmarole

gallardear *vi (pavonear)* to strut; *(presumir)* to swagger

gallardete *nm* pennant

gallardía *nf* (**a**) *(gentileza)* gracefulness, poise (**b**) *(arresto)* gallantry, boldness, dash

gallardo, -a *adj* (**a**) *(apuesto)* smart, elegant (**b**) *(valeroso)* gallant, brave

gallear *vi* to swank, show off

gallego, -a 1 *adj* (**a**) *(de Galicia)* Galician (**b**) *Am Pey* Spanish
   2 *nm,f* (**a**) *(de Galicia)* Galician, native of Galicia (**b**) *Am Pey* Spaniard
   3 *nm* (**a**) *(lengua)* Galician (**b**) *Carib (ave)* = gull-like aquatic bird

gallera *nf* coop

galleta *nf* (**a**) *Culin Br* biscuit, *US* cookie (**b**) *Chile (pan)* coarse bread (**c**) *Esp Fam (cachete)* slap, smack (**d**) *Méx Fam (fuerza)* **tiene mucha g.** he's dead strong (**e**) *Ven Fam (desorden)* chaos

gallina 1 *nf Orn* hen, chicken; **acostarse con las gallinas** to go to bed very early; **jugar a la g. ciega** to play blind man's buff; *Fig* **como g. en corral ajeno** like a fish out of water; *Fig* **matar la g. de los huevos de oro** to kill the goose that lays the golden eggs ❏ **g. clueca** broody hen; **g. de agua** coot; **g. de Guinea** guinea fowl; **g. de mar** gurnard
   2 *nmf Fam* coward, chicken

gallinero *nm* (**a**) *(corral)* henhouse, hen run (**b**) *Teat* **el g.** the gods *pl* (**c**) *Fam Fig* bedlam, madhouse

gallineta *nf Am Orn* guinea fowl

gallito *nm Fam Fig (presumido)* cock of the walk; *(peleón)* bully

gallo *nm* (**a**) *Orn* cock, rooster; *Fig* **alzar el g.** to be high and mighty; *Fig* **otro g. me cantara** things would have turned out differently; *Fig* **tener mucho g.** to be very cocky; *Fam Fig* **en menos que un canto de g.** before you could say Jack Robinson ❏ **g. de pelea** fighting cock, gamecock; **g. silvestre** capercaillie, woodgrouse (**b**) *(pez de San Pedro)* John Dory; *(pez plano)* megrim, sail-fluke (**c**) *Fam (persona mandona)* bully (**d**) *Mús* off-key note, squeak (**e**) *Méx* second-hand item (**f**) *Méx* street serenade (**g**) *Chile (de bomberos)* fire engine (**h**) *Box* **peso g.** bantamweight

galo, -a *Hist* **1** *adj* Gallic
   2 *nm,f* Gaul

galocha *nf* = type of clog

galón¹ *nm* (**a**) *(cinta)* braid (**b**) *Mil* stripe, chevron

galón² *nm (medida)* gallon (*Br* 4.55 litres, *US* 3.79 litres)

galopada *nf Equit* gallop

galopante *adj* (**a**) *Equit* galloping (**b**) *Fig (inflación etc)* galloping, escalating; *Med* **tisis g.** galloping consumption

galopar *vi Equit* to gallop

galope *nm Equit* gallop; **a g., de g.** at a gallop; *Fig* very quickly; **llegó a g.** he galloped up; **a g. tendido** at full gallop ❏ **medio g.** canter

galopín *nm* (**a**) *(golfillo)* urchin, ragamuffin (**b**) *(bribón)* rogue

galpón *nm Andes Nic RP* large shack

galvánico, -a *adj Fís* galvanic

galvanismo *nm Fís* galvanism

galvanización *nf* galvanization

galvanizado, -a 1 *pp de* **galvanizar**
   2 *adj* (**a**) *Fís* galvanized, electroplated (**b**) *Fig* galvanized
   3 *nm Fís* electroplating

galvanizar [14] *vt* (**a**) *Fís* to galvanize, electroplate (**b**) *Fig* to galvanize

galvanómetro *nm Fís* galvanometer

gama¹ *nf* (**a**) *Mús (escala)* scale (**b**) *Fig (gradación)* range, gamut, scale; **toda la g. de colores** the whole range of colours

gama² *nf Zool* doe

gamba¹ *nf Zool (grande)* prawn, *US* shrimp; *(pequeño)* shrimp

gamba² *nf Argot (pierna)* leg

gamberrada *nf Esp* act of hooliganism; **hacer una g.** to do some mischief

gamberrismo *nm Esp* hooliganism, vandalism

gamberro, -a *Esp* **1** *adj* loutish, ill-bred
   2 *nm,f* hooligan, lout, *Br* yob

gambeta *nf* (**a**) *(en danza)* cross step (**b**) *Equit* curvet, prance

Gambia *n* (The) Gambia

gambiano, -a *adj & nm,f* Gambian

gambito *nm Ajedrez* gambit

gameto *nm Biol* gamete

gamín, -ina *nm,f Col* street urchin

gamma *nf (letra)* gamma; **rayos g.** gamma rays

gamo *nm Zool* fallow deer

gamonal *nm Andes CAm* village chief

gamonalismo *nm Andes CAm* caciquism

gamuza *nf* (**a**) *Zool* chamois (**b**) *(trapo)* chamois o shammy leather

gana *nf* (**a**) *(deseo)* wish (**de** for); **de buena g.** willingly; **de mala g.** reluctantly, begrudgingly; **lo que te venga en g.** whatever you feel like; **tenerle ganas a algn** to have it in for sb; *Fam* **no me da la real g.** I don't damned well feel like it (**b**) **tener ganas de (hacer) algo** to feel like (doing) sth; **tengo** o **siento ganas de llorar** I feel like crying; *Fam* **tener unas ganas locas de hacer algo** to be longing to do sth (**c**) **entrarle a uno ganas de hacer algo** to feel an urge to do sth; **me entran ganas de pegarle** I really feel like hitting her (**d**) **quedarse con las ganas** not to manage; **se quedó con las ganas de ver el Museo del Prado** he didn't manage to see the Prado Museum (**e**) *(apetito)* appetite; *(hambre)* hunger; **comer con ganas** to eat heartily

ganadería *nf* (**a**) *(crianza de ganado)* stockbreeding (**b**) *(rancho)* stock farm, cattle ranch (**c**) *(conjunto de ganado)* cattle; **la g. extremeña** the livestock of Extremadura (**d**) *(raza)* breed o strain of cattle

ganadero, -a 1 *adj* relating to livestock, cattle; **enfermedad ganadera** cattle disease
   2 *nm,f* stockbreeder, cattle raiser

ganado, -a 1 *pp de* **ganar**
   2 *nm* (**a**) *(animales)* stock, livestock; *(vacas)* cattle; *(ovejas)* flock □ **g. caballar** horses *pl*; **g. de cerda** pigs *pl*; **g. mayor/menor** large/small livestock; **g. vacuno** cattle (**b**) *Fam Fig (gente)* crowd

ganador, -a 1 *adj* winning
   2 *nm,f* winner

ganancia *nf* (**a**) *(rendimiento)* profit, gain; *Com* **g. líquida** net profit; *Com* **margen de g.** profit margin (**b**) *Chile Guat Méx (propina)* tip (**c**) **ganancias** earnings

ganancial *adj Com* relating to profits or earnings; *Jur* **bienes gananciales** joint property

ganancioso, -a *adj* profitable, lucrative; **salir g.** to come out on top

ganapán *nm* (**a**) *(recadero)* messenger; *(factótum)* odd-jobber; *Fam (burro de carga)* dogsbody (**b**) *Fig (hombre tosco)* lout

ganar 1 *vt* (**a**) *(sueldo)* to earn; **gana mil pesos la hora** he earns one thousand pesos an hour; **g. peso** to gain weight (**b**) *(victoria)* to win, **ganamos el concurso/partido** we won the contest/match (**c**) *(conquistar)* to capture; **después de una dura lucha ganaron la ciudad** after a hard battle they captured the city (**d**) *(alcanzar)* to reach; **finalmente ganó la frontera** he finally got to the border (**e**) *(aventajar)* to beat; **le gana en bondad** he's much kinder than her; **le gana en inteligencia** she's much more intelligent than him
   2 *vi* (**a**) *(prosperar)* to thrive, do well; **ganamos con el cambio** we gained with the change; *Fig* **llevar las de g.** to hold the winning cards; *Fig* **no g. para disgustos** to have fate against one (**b**) *(mejorar)* to improve; **gana en destreza cada día** he gets more skilful every day; **has ganado mucho con este corte de pelo** you look much better with this new hairstyle (**c**) **salir ganando (en algo)** to come out on top (in sth)
   3 ganarse *vpr* (**a**) *(conquistar)* to earn; **g. el pan** o **los garbanzos** to earn one's daily bread (**b**) *(merecer)* to deserve; **se lo ha ganado** he deserves it; *Fam Esp* **¡te la vas a ganar!** you're going to get it!

ganchillo *nm* (**a**) *(aguja)* crochet hook (**b**) *(labor)* crochet work; **hacer g.** to crochet

gancho *nm* (**a**) *(gen)* hook; *(para ropa)* peg; **g. de carnicero** butcher's hook; *Fam Fig* **echar el g. a algn** to hook sb (**b**) *(cayado)* shepherd's crook (**c**) *Fam Fig (gracia, atractivo)* attractiveness, charm, sex appeal (**d**) *Fam Fig (cómplice de un timador)* enticer, decoy (**e**) *Andes CAm Méx Ven (percha)* hanger (**f**) *Andes CAm Méx (horquilla)* hairpin (**g**) *Bol Col (imperdible)* safety pin (**h**) *Ecuad (silla)* sidesaddle (**i**) *Méx (labor)* crochet (**j**) *RP Fam (contacto)* **hacerle g. a algn con algn** to fix sb up with sb

ganchudo, -a *adj* hook-shaped

gandalla *nmf Méx Fam* (**a**) *(sinvergüenza)* swine (**b**) *(deshonesto)* crook

gandul, -a 1 *adj* lazy, bone idle
   2 *nm,f* idler, good-for-nothing

gandulear *vi* to idle, slack, loaf around

gandulería *nf* idling, slacking

ganga *nf* bargain, good buy; **precios de g.** bargain prices

ganglio *nm Med* ganglion

gangoso, -a *adj* nasal, twanging

gangrena *nf Med* gangrene

gangrenado, -a 1 *pp de* **gangrenarse**
   2 *adj* gangrenous

gangrenarse *vpr Med* to become gangrenous

gangrenoso, -a *adj Med* gangrenous

gángster ['ganster] *(pl* **gángsters, gángsteres)** *nm* gangster

gangsterismo [ganste'rismo] *nm* gangsterism

ganguear *vi* to speak with a twang

gangueo *nm* nasal accent, twang

gansada *nf Fam* silly thing to say/do; **basta de tus gansadas** enough of your antics/nonsense

gansear *vi* to do/say silly things

ganso, -a 1 *nm,f* (**a**) *Orn* goose; *(macho)* gander; *Mil* **paso de g.** goose-step □ **g. salvaje** wild goose (**b**) *Fam* dolt, idiot; **hacer el g.** to act the goat
   2 *adj* sluggish, lazy, indolent

gánster *(pl* **gánsters** o **gánsteres)** *nm* gangster

gansterismo *nm* gangsterism

ganzúa *nf* (**a**) *(garfio)* picklock (**b**) *(ladrón)* burglar (**c**) *(sonsacador)* prying person, wheedler

gañán *nm* farmhand

gañido, -a 1 *pp de* **gañir**
   2 *nm* yelp

gañir *vi* to yelp

gañote *nm Fam* throat, gullet; **de g.** free

garabatear *vt & vi* to scrawl, scribble

garabato *nm* (**a**) **garabatos** scrawl *sing* (**b**) *(gancho)* hook

garaje *nm* garage

garambaina *nf* (**a**) *(adorno)* cheap finery, frippery (**b**) **garambainas** *Fam* foolery *sing*, nonsense *sing*

garandumba *nf SAm* (**a**) *Náut* large raft (**b**) *(mujer)* large heavy woman

garante *Fin* **1** *adj* acting as guarantor
   2 *nmf* guarantor

garantía *nf* (**a**) *(seguro, promesa)* guarantee, warranty; **bajo g.** under guarantee; **certificado de g.** guarantee (**b**) *Jur (fianza)* bond, security

garantizado, -a 1 *pp de* **garantizar**
   2 *adj* guaranteed, secured

garantizar [14] *vt* (**a**) *(cosa)* to guarantee; *(a persona)* to assure (**b**) *(responder de)* to vouch for

garañón *nm Zool (caballo)* stud horse

garapiña *nf* (**a**) *Culin* sugar coating, icing (**b**) *Am* iced pineapple drink

garapiñar *vt Culin* to coat with sugar; *(fruta)* to candy; **almendra garapiñada** sugared almond

garbanzo *nm Bot* chickpea; *Fam Fig* **en toda tierra de garbanzos** everywhere; *Fam Fig* **ganarse los garbanzos** to earn one's bread and butter; *Fam Fig* **g. negro** black sheep

garbearse *vpr Fam* to take a stroll

garbeo *nm Esp Fam (paseo)* stroll; *(viaje)* trip; **darse un g.** to go for a stroll

garbo *nm* (**a**) *(airosidad al andar)* poise, jauntiness (**b**) *(gracia)* grace, stylishness (**c**) *Fig (generosidad)* generosity, unselfishness

garboso, -a *adj* (**a**) *(gracioso, airoso)* graceful, stylish (**b**) *Fig* generous

garceta *nf Orn* **g. común** little egret

gardenia *nf Bot* gardenia

garduña *nf Zool* marten

garete *nm Náut & Fig* **ir** o **irse al g.** to go adrift

garfio *nm* hook, grapple

gargajear *vi* to clear one's throat noisily, hawk, spit

gargajo *nm* spit, phlegm

garganta *nf* (**a**) *Anat* throat; **dolor de g.** sore throat; *Fam Fig* **le tengo atravesado en la g.** he sticks in my gullet; *Fig* **se me hizo un nudo en la g.** I got a lump in my throat (**b**) *(voz)* voice; **tener buena g:** to have a good singing voice (**c**) *Anat (del pie)* instep (**d**) *(desfiladero)* narrow pass, gorge (**e**) *Arquit (de columna)* neck

gargantilla *nf* short necklace

gárgaras *nfpl* (**a**) *(en la garganta)* gargles, gargling *sing*; **hacer g.** to gargle; *Fam* **mandarle a algn a hacer g.** to tell sb to get lost; *Fam* **¡vete a hacer g.!** get lost! (**b**) *Col Chile Méx (licor)* gargling solution *sing*

gargarismo *nm* (**a**) *(acción)* gargle (**b**) *(líquido)* gargling solution

gargarizar [14] *vi* to gargle

gárgola *nf Arquit* gargoyle

garita *nf* (**a**) *(caseta)* box, cabin, hut; *Mil* **g. de centinela** sentry box (**b**) *(portería)* porter's lodge

garito *nm* gambling den, gaming house

garlar *vi* to chatter, prattle

garlito *nm* (**a**) *(red)* fish trap (**b**) *Fig (celada)* trap; **coger a algn en el g.** to catch sb in the act, catch sb redhanded

garnacha *nf* (**a**) *(uva)* sweet reddish-black grape (**b**) *(vino)* wine made from this grape

garra *nf* (**a**) *Zool* claw; *(de ave)* talon; *Fam Pey (de persona)* hand, paw; *Fig* **caer en las garras de algn** to fall into sb's clutches; *Fig* **echar la g. a algn** to lay (one's) hands on sb (**b**) *Fig (fuerza)* force, power; **tener g.** to be compelling, have character; **una comedia sin g.** a play lacking bite (**c**) *Téc* claw, hook

garrafa *nf* (**a**) *(botella)* carafe (**b**) *RP (de gas)* cylinder

garrafal *adj* monumental, colossal; **un error g.** a terrible blunder; **una mentira g.** a whopping lie

garrafón *nm* demijohn, large carafe

garrapata *nf Ent* tick

garrapatear *vi véase* **garabatear**

garrapato *nm véase* **garabato**

garrapiñar *vt véase* **garapiñar**

garrido, -a *adj* (**a**) *(atractivo)* handsome; **una moza garrida** a pretty young woman (**b**) *(elegante)* smart

garrocha *nf* goad, stick; *Taur* pike, lance

garrotazo *nm* cudgel blow

garrote *nm* (**a**) *(palo grueso)* club, cudgel (**b**) *Jur* garrotte; **dar g. a algn** to garrotte sb (**c**) *Méx (freno)* brake

garrotillo *nm Med* croup

garrulería *nf* garrulity

garrulo, -a *Fam* **1** *adj* coarse, uncouth
2 *nm,f* country bumpkin, yokel, *US* hick

gárrulo, -a *adj* (**a**) *(ave)* twittering (**b**) *Fig (persona)* garrulous

garza *nf Orn* heron ❑ **g. real** grey heron

garzo, -a *adj* blue

gas *nm* (**a**) *(fluido)* gas; **agua con g.** carbonated o fizzy water; *Esp Fam* **a todo g.** flat out ❑ **g. butano** butane gas; *Esp* **g. ciudad** town gas; **g. de escape** exhaust fumes *pl*; **g. hilarante** laughing gas; **g. lacrimógeno** tear gas; **g. mostaza** mustard gas; **g. natural** natural gas; **g. pobre**

producer gas (**b**) **gases** wind, *US* gas; *Med* **tener g. en el estómago** to suffer from flatulence

gasa *nf* (**a**) *Tex* gauze ❑ **g. hidrófila** surgical gauze (**b**) *(pañal)* gauze nappy, *US* gauze diaper

gasear *vt* to gas

gaseoducto *nm* gas pipeline

gaseosa *nf Esp Arg (bebida transparente)* pop, *Br* lemonade; *CAm RP (refresco con gas)* fizzy drink, *US* soda

gaseoso, -a *adj* gaseous, gassy

gásfiter (*pl* **gásfiters** o **gasfiteres**) *nmf Chile Perú* plumber

gasfitería *nf Chile Perú* plumber's (shop)

gasfitero, -a *nm,f Ecuad* plumber

gasificación *nf* gasification

gasificar [59] *vt* to gasify

gasoducto *nm* gas pipeline

gasógeno *nm* gazogene

gasoil *nm*, **gasóleo** *nm* diesel oil

gasolina *nf Aut Br* petrol, *US* gas, *US* gasoline; **poner g.** to fill up (with *Br* petrol o *US* gas)

gasolinera *nf* (**a**) *Aut* petrol o *US* gas station (**b**) *(lancha)* motorboat

gasómetro *nm Téc* gasometer

gastado, -a **1** *pp de* **gastar**
2 *adj* (**a**) *(zapatos etc)* worn-out; *Fig (frase)* meaningless; **ese tema está muy g.** that's a well-worn subject; **este gobierno está ya muy g.** this government is finished (**b**) *(persona)* worn-out, burnt-out

gastador, -a **1** *adj* spendthrift
2 *nm,f* spendthrift, spender
3 *nm Mil* sapper

gastar 1 *vt* (**a**) *(consumir) (dinero, tiempo)* to spend; *(gasolina, electricidad)* to use up, consume; **lo gastó todo en ropa** he spent it all on clothes; **nuestro coche gasta mucha gasolina** our car uses a lot of petrol (**b**) *Fig (malgastar)* to waste; **gasta el tiempo** he wastes his time (**c**) *Esp (usar) (perfume, jabón)* to use; *(ropa)* to wear; **g. unos zapatos** to wear a pair of shoes out; **¿qué número gasta?** what size do you take? (**d**) *(tener)* to have; **g. bigote** to have a moustache; **g. mal genio** to have a bad temper (**e**) *Esp Fig* **una broma a algn** to play a practical joke on sb; **le gastaron una broma pesada** they played a dirty trick on him (**f**) *RP (burlarse de)* to make fun of (**g**) **gastarlas** *Fam* to behave; **ya sé cómo las gastas** I know what you get up to
2 gastarse *vpr* (**a**) *(zapatos etc)* to wear out (**b**) *(gasolina etc)* to run out

gasto *nm* expense; **cubrir gastos** to cover costs; **dinero para gastos** pocket money ❑ **g. público** public expenditure; **gastos diarios** daily expenses; **gastos de mantenimiento** running o maintenance costs; **gastos de representación** entertainment allowance *sing*

gástrico, -a *adj Med* gastric

gastritis *nf Med* gastritis

gastroenteritis *nf Med* gastroenteritis

gastrointestinal *adj Anat* gastrointestinal

gastronomía *nf* gastronomy

gastronómico, -a *adj* gastronomic, gastronomical

gastrónomo, -a *nm,f* gourmet, gastronome

gata *nf Zool* she-cat, cat

gatas: a gatas *loc adv* on all fours; **andar a g.** to crawl

gatear *vi* (**a**) *(andar a gatas)* to crawl (**b**) *(trepar)* to climb (**c**) *Am Fam* to flirt with women

gatera *nf* (**a**) *(puerta)* cat door, cat flap, cat hole (**b**) *Náut* cat hole (**c**) *Andes (persona)* market stallholder

gatillazo *nm Argot Ofens* **pegar g.** to go limp; *(por haber bebido)* to have brewer's droop

gatillo *nm (de armas)* trigger; **apretar el g.** to pull the trigger

gato *nm* (**a**) *Zool* cat, tomcat; *Fam Fig* **aquí hay g. encerrado** there's something fishy going on here; *Fam Fig* **buscarle tres pies al g.** to complicate things unnecessarily; *Fam Fig* **dar g. por liebre** to take sb in, trick sb; *Fam Fig* **ser g. viejo** to be an old hand; *Fam Fig (personas)* **son cuatro gatos** *o RP* **cuatro gatos locos** there are only a few of them; *Prov* **g. escaldado del agua fría huye** once bitten, twice shy ◻ **g. de algalia** civet cat; **g. de Angora** Angora cat; **g. montés** wildcat; **g. siamés** Siamese (cat) (**b**) *Aut Téc* jack (**c**) *Méx Fam Pey (sirviente)* flunkey

GATT [gat] *nm (abrev de* **General Agreement on Tariffs and Trade)** GATT

gatuno, -a *adj* catlike, feline

gauchada *nf Chile RP* (**a**) *(favor)* favour, *US* favor (**b**) *(chiste)* story, joke

gauchear *vi SAm* to live as a gaucho

gaucho, -a 1 *adj* (**a**) *SAm* gaucho; *Fig* coarse, rough (**b**) *RP Fam (simpático)* pleasant, nice
2 *nm,f* (**a**) *SAm* gaucho

gaveta *nf (cajón)* drawer

gavilán *nm Orn* sparrowhawk

gavilla *nf* (**a**) *(de ramillas etc)* sheaf (**b**) *Fig Pey* gang of thugs

gavillero *nm Am* bully, lout

gaviota *nf Orn* seagull, gull ◻ **g. argéntea** herring gull; **g. cana** common gull; **g. enana** little gull; **g. reidora** black-headed gull; **g. tridáctila** kittiwake

gay [gai, gei] *(pl* **gays)** *adj inv & nm* gay, homosexual; **el movimiento g.** the Gay Liberation Movement

gayo, -a *adj Literario* cheerful; **la gaya ciencia** poetry, the art of poetry

gazapo *nm* (**a**) *Zool* young rabbit (**b**) *(error)* error, blunder

gazmoñería *nf* sanctimoniousness

gazmoño, -a *adj* sanctimonious

gaznate *nm* gullet

gazpacho *nm Culin* gazpacho

gazuza *nf Am* hunger; **tener g.** to be starving

GB *(abrev de* **Gran Bretaña)** GB

ge *nf* = name of the letter G in Spanish

géiser *nm* geyser

geisha ['geisa] *nf* geisha

gel *nm* gel ◻ **g. de baño** shower gel, bubble bath; **g. de ducha** shower gel

gelatina *nf (ingrediente)* gelatin, gelatine; *Culin Br* jelly, *US* Jell-O®

gelatinoso, -a *adj* gelatinous, jelly-like

gélido, -a *adj Literario* icy, icy cold

gema *nf* (**a**) *Bot* bud, gemma (**b**) *Min* gem

gemelo, -a 1 *adj & nm,f* twin; **hermanos gemelos** twins; *Fig* **almas gemelas** kindred spirits
2 gemelos *nmpl* (**a**) *(de camisa)* cufflinks (**b**) *(anteojos)* binoculars

gemido, -a 1 *pp de* **gemir**
2 *nm (quejido)* moan, groan; *(gimoteo)* whimper

geminado, -a *adj* geminate

Géminis *nm Astrol Astron* Gemini

gemir [47] *vi* tó moan, groan; *(gimotear)* to whimper

gemología *nf* gemology

gen *nm Biol* gene

genciana *nf Bot* gentian

gendarme *nm* gendarme

gendarmería *nf* gendarmerie

genealogía *nf* genealogy

genealógico, -a *adj* genealogical; **árbol g.** family tree

genealogista *nmf* genealogist

generación *nf* (**a**) *(de personas, tecnología)* generation (**b**) *(creación)* generation

generacional *adj* generation, generational; **la barrera g.** the generation gap

generador, -a 1 *adj* generating
2 *nm Téc* generator

general 1 *adj* general; **en** *o* **por lo g.** in general, generally; **es una costumbre muy g.** it is a very common custom
2 *nm Mil* general

generala *nf Mil* **tocar a g.** to call to arms; **toque a g.** call to arms

generalato *nm Mil* (**a**) *(grado)* generalship (**b**) *(conjunto de generales)* generals *pl*

generalidad *nf* (**a**) *(vaguedad)* generalization; **generalidades** *(principios básicos)* basic principles (**b**) *(mayoría)* majority

generalísimo *nm* generalissimo, supreme commander

generalista *adj (médico)* general

Generalitat [jenerali'tat] *nf Pol* autonomous government *(of the regions of Catalonia, Valencia or the Balearic Islands)*

generalización *nf* (**a**) *(comentario)* generalization (**b**) *(extensión)* spread, spreading

generalizado, -a 1 *pp de* **generalizar**
2 *adj* widespread, common

generalizador, -a *adj* generalizing

generalizar [14] **1** *vt (extender)* to spread
2 generalizarse *vpr* to become widespread *o* common

generalmente *adv* generally

generar *vt* to generate

generativo, -a *adj* generative

generatriz *nf Mat* generatrix

genérico, -a *adj* generic

género *nm* (**a**) *(clase)* kind, sort; **el g. humano** mankind; **ese g. de vida no es para mí** that sort of life is not for me (**b**) *Arte Lit* genre ◻ **g. chico** light opera; **g. dramático** dramatic genre; **g. lírico** opera (**c**) *(mercancía)* article, piece of merchandise; **géneros de punto** knitwear *sing*; **géneros de primera calidad** quality goods (**d**) *Ling* gender (**e**) *Biol* genus

generosidad *nf* generosity, unselfishness

generoso, -a *adj* (**a**) *(dadivoso)* generous (**con, para** to), splendid (**b**) *(vinos)* rich, full-bodied

Génesis *nm Rel* Genesis

génesis *nf inv* genesis

genética *nf* genetics *sing*

genético, -a *adj* genetic

genial *adj* brilliant, inspired, exceptional; *Fam* terrific

genialidad *nf* (**a**) *(idea)* brilliant idea, stroke of genius (**b**) *(acción)* eccentricity (**c**) *(cualidad)* genius

genio *nm* (**a**) *(carácter)* temperament; *(mal carácter)* temper; **es una persona de mucho g.** he has a quick temper; **estar de mal g.** to be in a bad mood; **tener mal g.** to have a bad temper (**b**) *(facultad)* genius; **Mozart fue un g.** Mozart was a genius; *Fam* **eres un g.** you are brilliant (**c**) *(espíritu)* spirit; **el g. español** the Spanish spirit (**d**) *(ser fantástico)* genie

genioso, -a *adj Méx Fam* bad tempered, moody

genital 1 *adj* genital

  2 genitales *nmpl* genitals

genitivo *nm Ling* genitive

Genl. *Mil* (*abrev de* **General**) Gen

genocidio *nm* genocide

genoma *nm* genome

genómico, -a *adj* genomic

genotipo *nm Biol* genotype

Génova *n* Genoa

genovés, -esa *adj & nm,f* Genoese, Genovese

gente *nf* (**a**) (*gen*) people *pl*; **¡cuánta g.!** what a crowd!; **había mucha g.** there were a lot of people; **¡qué g.!** what awful people! ❑ **la g. bien** the well-to-do; **g. de bien** honest people; *Fam Fig* **g. gorda** bigwigs; *Fam* **g. menuda** nippers, kids (**b**) (*familia*) folks, people *pl*; **tengo a mi g. aquí de vacaciones** my folks are here on holiday (**c**) (*personal*) staff (**d**) *Mil* troops

gentil 1 *adj* (**a**) (*pagano*) pagan, heathen; (*no judío*) gentile (**b**) (*apuesto*) charming (**c**) (*amable*) kind

  2 *nmf* Gentile

gentileza *nf* kindness; **esto es una g. de la casa** this is on the house; *Fml* **por g. de** by courtesy of

gentilhombre *nm Hist* gentleman

gentilicio *adj & nm Ling* gentile

gentío *nm* crowd; **¡qué g.!** what a crowd!

gentuza *nf Pey* rabble, riffraff

genuflexión *nf* genuflexion

genuino, -a *adj* (*puro*) genuine; (*verdadero*) authentic

GEO [χeo] *nmpl* (*abrev de* **Grupos Especiales de Operaciones**) = specially trained Spanish police force, *Br* ≃ SAS, *US* ≃ SWAT

geocéntrico, -a *adj* geocentric

geodesia *nf* geodesy

geofísica *nf* (*ciencia*) geophysics *sing*

geofísico, -a 1 *adj* geophysical

  2 *nm,f* geophysicist

geografía *nf* geography ❑ **g. física** physical geography; **g. política** political geography; **g. social** social geography

geográfico, -a *adj* geographic, geographical

geógrafo, -a *nm,f* geographer

geología *nf* geology

geológico, -a *adj* geologic, geological

geólogo, -a *nm,f* geologist

geómetra *nmf* geometer, geometrician

geometría *nf* geometry ❑ **g. del espacio** solid geometry; **g. descriptiva** descriptive geometry

geométrico, -a *adj* geometric, geometrical

geomorfología *nf* geomorphology

geopolítica *nf* geopolitics *sing*

geopolítico, -a *adj* geopolitical

Georgia *n* Georgia

Georgia del Sur *n* South Georgia

georgiano, -a 1 *adj & nm,f* Georgian

  2 *nm* (*lengua*) Georgian

geórgica *nf Lit* georgic

geranio *nm Bot* geranium

gerencia *nf* (**a**) (*actividad, cargo*) management (**b**) (*despacho*) manager's *o* director's office

gerenciar *vt Am* to manage

gerente *nmf* manager, director

geriatra *nmf Med* geriatrician, geriatrist

geriatría *nf Med* geriatrics *sing*

geriátrico, -a 1 *adj* geriatric

  2 *nm* (*hospital*) geriatric hospital; (*residencia*) old folk's home

gerifalte *nm Fam* boss; **vivir como un g.** to live like a king

germanía *nf* thieves' cant

germánico, -a *adj & nm Ling* Germanic

germanismo *nm* Germanism

germanista *nmf* German specialist

germano, -a 1 *adj* German, Germanic

  2 *nm,f* German

germanooccidental *adj & nmf* West German

germanooriental *adj & nmf* East German

germen *nm* (**a**) *Biol* germ ❑ **g. de trigo** wheatgerm (**b**) *Fig* seed, germ, origin

germicida 1 *adj* germicidal

  2 *nm* germicide

germinación *nf* germination

germinal *adj* germinal

germinar *vi* to germinate

gerontología *nf* gerontology

gerontólogo, -a *nm,f* gerontologist

gerundense 1 *adj* of *o* from Gerona

  2 *nmf* person from Gerona

gerundio *nm Ling* gerund

gesta *nf* heroic exploit, gest, geste; *Lit* **cantar de g.** chanson de geste

gestación *nf* (**a**) *Biol* gestation (**b**) *Fig* **en g.** in preparation, in the pipeline

gestar 1 *vt* to gestate

  2 gestarse *vpr Fig* (*proyecto*) to be under way *o* in the pipeline; (*sentimiento*) to grow; (*idea*) to develop

gestatorio, -a *adj* **silla gestatoria** gestatorial chair

gesticulación *nf* gesticulation, gestures *pl*

gesticular *vi* to gesticulate

gestión *nf* (**a**) (*diligencia*) enquiry, search (**b**) (*administración*) administration, management ❑ **g. financiera** financial management (**c**) **gestiones** (*negociaciones*) negotiations; (*medidas*) steps, measures

gestionar *vt* (**a**) *Fin* to take steps to acquire *o* obtain, conduct (**b**) (*negociar*) to negotiate; **están gestionando la entrada del país en la OTAN** they are negotiating the country's entry into NATO

gesto *nm* (**a**) (*mueca*) grimace, face; **hacer gestos** to pull faces; **torcer el g.** to look disappointed; **un g. de tristeza** a sad face (**b**) (*señal*) sign; **hizo un g.** afirmativô con la cabeza he nodded his head in agreement; **tuvo un g. de delicadeza** he made a gesture of kindness

gestor, -a 1 *adj* managing; **actividades gestoras** negotiations

  2 *nm,f* = person who carries out dealings with public bodies on behalf of private customers or companies, combining the roles of solicitor and accountant

gestoría *nf* = office of a **gestor**

gestual *adj* using gestures; **lenguaje g.** sign language

Ghana *n* Ghana

ghanés, -esa *adj & nm,f* Ghanian, Ghanaian

giba *nf* hump, hunch

gibar *vt Esp Fam* to annoy; **lo hace para g.** he does it deliberately

giboso, -a *nm,f* humpback, hunchback

Gibraltar *n* Gibraltar; **el peñón de G.** the Rock of Gibraltar

gibraltareño, -a 1 *adj* of o from Gibraltar
2 *nm,f* Gibraltarian

GIF [gif] *nm Inform (abrev de* **graphics interchange format)** GIF

gigabyte [χiva'βait] *nm Inform* gigabyte

gigante *adj* giant, gigantic

gigante, -a *nm,f (hombre)* giant; *(mujer)* giantess

gigantesco, -a *adj* giant, gigantic, gigantesque

gigantismo *nm Med* gigantism, giantism

gigoló [jiγo'lo] *nm* gigolo

gil, -ila *nm,f CSur Fam* jerk, *Br* twit

gilipollada *nf,* **gilipollez** *nf Esp Ofens* **hacer/decir una g.** to do/say something *Br* bloody o *US* goddamn stupid

gilipollas *nmf inv Esp Ofens Br* prat, *Br* pillock, *US* dork

gimnasia *nf* gymnastics *pl; Fam* **eso sería confundir la g. con la magnesia** it's like chalk and cheese □ **gimnasia rítmica** eurhythmics *sing,* *US* eurythmics *sing*

gimnasio *nm* gymnasium

gimnasta *nmf* gymnast

gimnástico, -a *adj* gymnastic

gimotear *vi* to whine, whimper

gimoteo *nm* whining, whimpering

gincana *nf (carrera de obstáculos)* gymkhana; *(de automóviles)* rally

Ginebra *n* Geneva

ginebra *nf (bebida)* gin

ginebrés, -esa *adj & nm,f,* **ginebrino, -a** *adj & nm,f* Genevan, Genevese

ginecología *nf Med* gynaecology, *US* gynecology

ginecológico, -a *adj Med* gynaecologic, gynaecological, *US* gynecologic, gynecological

ginecólogo, -a *nm,f Med* gynaecologist, *US* gynecologist

gingival *adj* gum; **una afección g.** a gum infection

gingivitis *nf Med* gingivitis

gingko *nm Bot* ginkgo, gingko, maidenhair tree

gin-tonic [jin'tonik] *(pl* **gin-tonics)** *nm,* **gintonic** [jin'tonik] *(pl* **gintonics**) *nm* gin and tonic

gira *nf* excursion, tour; *Teat* tour

girado, -a 1 *pp de* **girar**
2 *nm,f Fin* drawee

girador, -a *nm,f Fin* drawer

giralda *nf* weathercock

girar 1 *vi* **(a)** *(dar vueltas)* to rotate, spin; **el dinero hace g. al mundo** money makes the world go round **(b)** *(torcer)* to turn; **al llegar a la esquina, gira a la derecha** turn right at the corner **(c)** *Fig (versar)* to deal with; **la conversación giraba en torno a ti** the conversation revolved around you **(d)** *Fin (expedir)* to draw
2 *vt* **(a)** *(cambio sentido)* to turn; **g. la cabeza** to turn one's head **(b)** *Fin (giro postal)* to send, remit **(c)** *Fin (cheque)* to draw; **g. contra** to draw on; **g. en descubierto** to overdraw

girasol *nm Bot* sunflower

giratorio, -a *adj* rotating, gyratory; **silla giratoria** swivel chair

giro *nm* **(a)** *(rotación)* rotation; *(vuelta)* turn, turning **(b)** *(cariz)* turn, direction; **dar un nuevo g. a** to put in a new light; **tomar un nuevo g.** to change **(c)** *(frase)* turn of phrase **(d)** *Fin (de letras, órdenes de pago)* draft; *(en efectivo)* money order □ **g. bancario** giro bancario banker's draft; **g. postal** money order; **g. telegráfico** giro, money order **(e)** *Am (ramo)* industry **el g. de la carne** the meat industry

gitanesco, -a *adj* gypsy-like, gipsy-like

gitano, -a 1 *adj* **(a)** *(raza, persona)* gypsy, gipsy **(b)** *Fam (artero)* crafty
2 *nm,f* **(a)** *(persona de raza gitana)* gypsy, gipsy **(b)** *Fig (zalamero)* flatterer **(c)** *Fam (estafador)* fiddler, swindler

glaciación *nf* glaciation

glacial *adj* **(a)** *(época)* glacial **(b)** *Fig* glacial, hostile; **una despedida g.** an icy farewell

glaciar *nm* glacier

gladiador *nm Hist* gladiator

gladiolo *nm,* **gladíolo** *nm Bot* gladiolus

glamour [gla'mur] *nm* glamour

glande *nm Anat* glans penis

glándula *nf Anat* gland

glandular *adj* glandular

glaseado, -a 1 *pp de* **glasear**
2 *nm* glacé

glasear *vt Culin (pastel)* to glaze

glauco, -a *adj Fml* bluish-green, glaucous

glaucoma *nm Med* glaucoma

gleba *nf Hist* land; **siervo de la g.** serf

glicerina *nf Quím* glycerin, glycerine

global *adj* global, comprehensive

globalización *nf* globalization

globalizar [14] *vt* **(a)** *(internacionalizar)* to globalize **(b)** *(generalizar)* to give an overall view of

globalmente *adv* globally, as a whole

globo *nm* **(a)** *(aeróstato, juguete)* balloon □ **g. aerostático** hot air o gas balloon; **g. dirigible** airship **(b)** *(esfera)* globe, sphere □ **g. celeste** globe; **g. terrestre** o **terráqueo** globe **(c)** *Anat* **g. ocular** eyeball **(d)** *(de lámpara)* globe, glass lampshade **(e)** *Argot (condón)* French letter

globular *adj* globular

globulina *nf Biol* globulin

glóbulo *nm* globule □ *Anat* **g. blanco/rojo** white/red corpuscle

gloria *nf* **(a)** *(fama)* honour, *US* honor, glory; **hacer g. de algo** to boast about sth; *Irón* **cubrirse de g.** to make a fool of oneself **(b)** *(persona famosa)* hero **(c)** *Rel (canto)* Gloria; *(cielo)* heaven; *Fam Fig* **estar en la g.** to be in seventh heaven **(d)** *Fam (cosa placentera)* delight; **dar g.** to be a delight; *Fam* **saber/oler a g.** to taste/smell divine

gloriado *nm Am* = punch made from very strong liquor

gloriarse *vpr* **(a)** *(jactarse)* to boast, show off **(b)** *(complacerse)* to take pride **(de** in)

glorieta *nf* **(a)** *(en un jardín)* bower, arbour, *US* arbor **(b)** *(plazoleta)* small square **(c)** *Esp (rotonda)* *Br* roundabout, *US* traffic circle

glorificación *nf* glorification

glorificar [59] **1** *vt* to glorify, exalt
2 glorificarse *vpr véase* **gloriarse**

glorioso, -a *adj* glorious

glosa *nf* marginal note

glosador, -a *nm,f* commentator *(on text)*

glosar *vt* **(a)** *(explicar)* to gloss; *(texto)* to interpret **(b)** *(comentar)* to comment on, speak about

glosario *nm* glossary

glotis *nf Anat* glottis

glotón, -ona 1 *adj* greedy, gluttonous
2 *nm,f* glutton
3 *nm Zool* glutton, wolverine

glotonear *vi* to eat greedily

glotonería *nf* gluttony, greed

glucemia *nf Med* glycemia

glúcido *nm* carbohydrate

glucosa *nf Quím* glucose

gluten *nm* gluten

glúteo, -a 1 *adj Anat* gluteal
  2 *nm* gluteus

gnomo ['nomo] *nm* gnome

gnóstico, -a ['nostiko] *adj & nm,f* gnostic

gobernabilidad *nf* governability

gobernable *adj* governable

gobernación *nf* (a) *(gestión)* governing, government (b) *Méx* G. *(ministerio) Br* ≃ Home Office, *US* ≃ Department of the Interior

gobernador, -a 1 *adj* governing; **la junta gobernadora** the governing board
  2 *nm,f* governor

gobernanta *nf* (a) *(en hotel)* manageress; *Fam* bossy woman (b) *(en casa, institución)* governess

gobernante 1 *adj* ruling; **la clase g.** the ruling class
  2 *nmf* ruler, leader

gobernar [3] **1** *vt* (a) *(gen)* to govern; *(un país)* to govern, rule; *(una familia)* to run; *(un negocio)* to handle, run (b) *(guiar)* to guide; *Náut* to steer (c) *(dominar)* to dominate, boss about (d) *Arg (castigar)* to punish
  2 *vi Náut* to steer
  3 gobernarse *vpr (guiarse)* to manage one's affairs

gobiernista *Andes Méx* **1** *adj* pro-government
  2 *nmf* government supporter

gobierno *nm* (a) *Pol* government; *(edificio)* Government House *o* building ❑ **g. central** central government (b) *(mando)* command, running, handling; **el g. de la casa** the running of the household; **el g. de los asuntos** the handling of affairs (c) *Náut* steering (d) *Náut (timón)* rudder (e) *(locuciones)* **para tu g.** for your own information; **servir de g.** to serve as a guideline

gobio *nm (pez)* gudgeon

goce *nm* pleasure, enjoyment

godo, -a 1 *adj Hist* Gothic
  2 *nm,f Hist* Goth

gofio *nm* (a) *Arg Andes Carib (harina)* roasted *Br* maize *o US* corn meal (b) *CAm Ven (pastel)* = sweet cake made with *Br* maize *o US* corn meal

gogó *nf* go-go dancer

gol *nm Dep* goal; **g. cantado** open goal, sitter; **g. fantasma** controversial goal; **tiro a g.** shot; *Fam Fig* **meter un g. a algn** to pull a fast one on sb

goleada *nf* feast of goals; **ganar por g.** to hammer the opposition

goleador, -a *nm,f* scorer; **el máximo g.** the top scorer

golear *vt Dep* to hammer; **el Torpedo goleó 6-1 al Olympic** Torpedo hammered Olympic 6-1

goleta *nf Náut* schooner

golf *(pl golfs) nm Dep (deporte)* golf; *(terreno)* golf course; **club de g.** golf club; **palo de g.** golf club

golfa *nf Esp Fam Pey* tart, *Br* slag

golfante *adj Fam* rascal

golfear *vi* (a) *(vagabundear)* to loaf around (b) *(hacer gamberradas)* to get up to no good

golfillo, -a *nm,f* street urchin

golfista *nmf* golfer

golfo¹ *nm (gamberro)* lout, *Br* yob; *(pillo)* rogue, wide boy

golfo² *nm Geog* gulf, large bay; **g. de Bengala** Bay of Bengal; **g. de Botnia** Gulf of Bothnia; **g. de Guinea** Gulf of Guinea; **g. de León** Gulf of Lions; **g. de Méjico** Gulf of Mexico; **g. de Vizcaya** Bay of Biscay; **g. Pérsico** Persian Gulf

gollete *nm* (a) *Anat* throat (b) *(de botella)* neck

golondrina *nf* (a) *Orn* swallow (b) *Náut* motorboat (c) *CAm Méx (planta)* spurge (d) *Chile (camioneta)* moving van, *Br* removal van

golondrino *nm* (a) *Orn* young swallow (b) *Fig (vagabundo)* tramp (c) *Med* boil in the armpit (d) *Mil* deserter

golosina *nf* (a) *(caramelo)* sweet, *US* candy (b) *Fig (cosa agradable)* treat

goloso, -a *adj* (a) **ser (un) g.** to have a sweet tooth; *Pey* to be greedy (b) *Fig* mouthwatering, inviting

golpazo *nm* heavy blow

golpe *nm* (a) *(impacto)* blow; **a golpes** by force (b) *Aut* bump, bang, collision (c) *(desgracia)* blow, misfortune; **perder el trabajo fue un duro g.** losing his job was a great blow (d) *(gracia)* witticism, sally; **la película tiene unos golpes muy buenos** the film has some very good bits in it (e) *Fig (sorpresa)* shock (f) *Box* punch; *Box & Fig* **g. bajo** punch below the belt; *Ftb* **g. franco** free kick (g) *(atraco)* raid, job, *US* heist; *Fam* **dar un g.** to do a job (h) *(locuciones)* **de g.**, **de g. y porrazo** all of a sudden; **de un g.** in one go; **errar el g.** to miss; **g. de efecto** coup de théâtre; **g. de estado** coup d'état; **g. de fortuna** stroke of luck; **g. de gracia** coup de grâce; **g. de mano** surprise attack; **g. de suerte** stroke of luck; **g. de vista** quick glance; **no dar ni g.** not to lift a finger; **parar el g.** to soften the blow (i) *Méx (martillo)* sledgehammer (j) *Cuba* **al golpe** *loc adv* instantly

golpear *vt (gen)* to hit; *(cosas)* to knock, beat; *(personas)* to thump, hit, punch; *(una puerta, cabeza)* to bang

golpetear *vt & vi* to bang; **la puerta golpeteaba con el viento** the door was banging in the wind

golpeteo *nm* banging, hammering

golpismo *nm Pol* tendency to coups d'état

golpista 1 *nmf* person involved in a coup d'état
  2 *adj* relating to coups d'état

golpiza *nf Am* thrashing

goma *nf* (a) *(sustancia)* rubber, gum; *(caucho)* rubber; **g. arábiga** gum arabic; **g. de pegar** glue, gum; **suelas de g.** rubber soles (b) *(banda elástica)* rubber band, *Br* elastic band ❑ **g. elástica** elastic (c) **g. de borrar** *Br* rubber, *US* eraser; **g. de mascar** chewing gum (d) *Argot (preservativo)* rubber (e) *Cuba CSur (neumático) Br* tyre, *US* tire

gomaespuma *nf* foam rubber

gomero *nm* (a) *CSur Bot* gum tree (b) *Andes (recolector)* rubber collector

gomina *nf* hair cream

gominola *nf Br* fruit jelly, *US* soft fruit candy

gomoso, -a 1 *adj* sticky
  2 *nm Pey* fop

gónada *nf Anat* gonad

góndola *nf* (a) *(embarcación)* gondola (b) *(carruaje)* carriage

gondolero, -a *nm,f* gondolier

gong *nm*, **gongo** *nm* gong

gongorino, -a *adj Lit* Gongoristic

gongorismo *nm Lit* Gongorism

gonococo *nm Biol* gonococcus

gonorrea *nf Med* gonorrhoea, *US* gonorrhea

gordiano, -a *adj* **nudo g.** Gordian knot

gordinflón, -ona *Fam* **1** *adj* chubby, fat
  2 *nm,f* chubby person, fatty

gordo, -a 1 *adj* (a) *(carnoso)* fat; **ponerse g.** to get fat (b) *(volumen)* thick (c) *(importante)* big; **algo g.** something serious *o* important; **¡qué mentira tan gorda!** what a big liel; *Fig* **el premio g.** the first prize; *Fig* **pez g.** big shot **(d)** *(locuciones)* **estar** *o* **quedarse sin g.** to be broke; **hacer la vista gorda** to turn a blind eye; **me cae g.** I can't stand him; **se armó la gorda** trouble broke out

2 *nm,f* fat person; *Fam* fatty

3 *nm* **(a)** *(tocino)* fat **(b)** *(en lotería)* **el g.** first prize **(c)** *Méx* maize tortilla

gordura *nf* fatness

gorgorito *nm* trill

gorgotear *vi* to gurgle

gorgoteo *nm* gurgle, gurgling

gorguera *nf* ruff; *(de un armadura)* gorget

gorigori *nm Fam* dirge, funeral chant; *Hum* **cantar el g. a algn** to bury sb

gorila *nm* **(a)** *Zool* gorilla **(b)** *Fam Fig (guardaespaldas)* gorilla, henchman, bodyguard

gorjear 1 *vi* to chirp, twitter

2 gorjearse *vpr (bebé)* to crow, gurgle

gorjeo *nm* **(a)** *(de ave)* chirping, twittering **(b)** *(de bebé)* crowing, gurgling

gorra *nf* cap; *(con visera)* peaked cap; *Esp Méx Fam* **de g. free**; *Esp Méx* **comer de g.** to cadge a meal; *Esp Méx* **vivir de g.** to sponge, cadge, be a sponger

gorrear *vi véase* **gorronear**

gorrero, -a *nm,f véase* **gorrón, -ona**

gorrino, -a 1 *adj* dirty, piglike

2 *nm,f* pig

gorrión *nm Orn* sparrow ▫ **g. chillón** rock sparrow; **g. común** house sparrow; **g. moruno** Spanish sparrow

gorro *nm* **(a)** *(para la cabeza)* cap ▫ **g. de baño** *(para piscina)* swimming cap, bathing cap; *(para ducha)* shower cap; **g. de dormir** nightcap; **g. frigio** Phrygian cap **(b)** *Fam* **estar hasta el g.** to have had enough, be up to here **(de** with); **ponerle el g. a algn** *(irritar)* to annoy sb, get on sb's nerves; *(ridiculizar)* to make fun of sb

gorrón, -ona *Esp Méx* **1** *adj* scrounging

2 *nm,f* sponger, scrounger

gorronear *Esp Méx vi* to scrounge, be a parasite

gorronería *nf Esp Fam* sponging, scrounging

góspel *nm Mús* gospel (music)

gota *nf* **(a)** *(gen)* drop; *(de sudor)* bead; **caen cuatro** *o* **unas gotas** it's spitting; **g. a g.** drop by drop; **la g. que colma el vaso** the straw that broke the camel's back; **ni g.** not a bit, nothing at all; **no tengo ni g. de sueño** I am not at all sleepy; **sudar la g. gorda** to sweat blood, work hard; *Med* **(transfusión) g. a g.** drip **(b)** *Med* gout **(c)** *Arquit* gutta

gotear *v impers* to drip; *(lluvia)* to drizzle; **el techo gotea** there's a leak in the ceiling

gotelé *nm* = decorative technique of applying paint to give a roughly textured surface

goteo *nm* dripping

gotera *nf* **(a)** *(agujero)* leak; *(agua)* drip **(b)** *(mancha)* drip mark **(c)** *Andes* **goteras** *(achaques)* aches and pains

gotero *nm* **(a)** *(gota a gota)* (intravenous) drip **(b)** *Am (cuentagotas)* eyedropper

goterón *nm* large drop

gótico, -a 1 *adj Arte Hist* Gothic

2 *nm (estilo)* Gothic

gourmet [gur'met] *(pl* **gourmets**) *nmf* gourmet

goyesco, -a *adj Arte* in the style of Goya

gozada *nf Fam* sheer joy; **¡qué g. de tarde!** what a marvellous evening!

gozar [14] **1** *vt* to enjoy

2 *vi* **(a)** *(divertirse)* to enjoy oneself; **g. con algo** to be

delighted by sth **(b)** *(disfrutar)* to enjoy **(de -)**; **goza de buena salud** he enjoys good health

3 gozarse *vpr* to enjoy; **me gozo con tu presencia** I'm delighted to be with you

gozne *nm* hinge

gozo *nm* **(a)** *(alegría)* joy, pleasure; **dar g.** to be a joy; **no caber en sí de g.** to be beside oneself with joy; **saltar de g.** to jump with joy; *Hum* **todo mi g. en un pozo** that's just my luck **(b) gozos** *Mús Rel* chorus sing in honour of the Virgin

gozoso, -a *adj* **(a)** *(contento)* delighted **(b)** *(que produce alegría)* joyful, happy

g. p., g/p. *(abrev de* **giro postal)** p.o.

grabación *nf* recording

grabado, -a 1 *pp de* **grabar**

2 *nm* **(a)** *(arte)* engraving; **g. al agua fuerte** etching **(b)** *(dibujo)* picture, drawing; **una revista con grabados** an illustrated magazine

grabador, -a 1 *adj* recording

2 *nm,f* engraver

grabadora *nf* tape recorder ▫ **g. de CD** CD writer

grabar *vt* **(a)** *Arte* to engrave **(b)** *(registrar sonidos, imágenes)* to record **(c)** *Fig (fijar en el ánimo)* **g. en la mente** to engrave in one's mind *o* memory; **se me quedó muy grabado** it stuck in my mind **(d)** *Inform* to save

gracejada *nf CAm Méx* dirty trick

gracejo, -a 1 *nm* charm, winsomeness; **con mucho g.** most engagingly

2 *nm,f Méx* clown, joker

gracia *nf* **(a)** *Rel* grace; **estar en g.** to be in a state of grace; . **por la g. de Dios** by the grace of God **(b)** *(favor)* favour, *US* favor, grace; **disfrutaba de la g. del rey** he enjoyed the king's favour **(c)** *(indulto)* pardon; **petición de g.** petition of pardon **(d)** *(buen trato)* graciousness; **caer en g. a algn** to make a good impression on sb **(e)** *Fml (nombre)* **dígame usted su g.** could you give me your name, please? **(f)** *(atractivo)* grace, charm; **la g. de su figura** the charm of her figure **(g)** *(garbo)* grace **(h)** *(chiste)* joke; **a mí no me hace ninguna g.** I don't find it funny at all; **hacer** *o* **tener g.** to be funny; **me hace g.** marvellous, isn't it?; **¡qué g.!** how funny!; **reírle las gracias a algn** to laugh at sb's jokes; **tiene g. que nos encontremos aquí** it's funny that we should meet here; **¡vaya (una) g.!** *(enfado)* oh, no!; **me hace g.** *(desprecio)* it makes me laugh; *Irón* **tú y tus gracias** you and your funny *o* witty remarks **(i)** *Mil & Fig* **tiro de g.** coup de grâce **(j) gracias** *(agradecimiento)* thanks; **g. a** thanks to; *Rel* **acción de g.** thanksgiving; **a Dios g., g. a Dios** thank God, thank goodness; **consiguió el trabajo g. a un amigo** he got the job through a friend; **dar g. a algn** to thank sb; **muchas** *o* **muchísimas g.** thank you very much; *Irón* **y g.** I/ you should be so lucky; **¿en taxi?, en autobús y g.** by taxi? we are lucky we can go by bus! **(k)** *Mit* **lasTres Gracias** theThree Graces

grácil *adj* graceful; *(delicado)* delicate

gracilidad *nf* gracefulness; *(delicadez)* delicateness

gracioso, -a 1 *adj* **(a)** *(divertido)* funny, amusing; **es el chiste más g. que he oído** that's the funniest joke I've ever heard **(b)** *(atractivo)* graceful, charming; **sus graciosos ojos** her charming eyes **(c)** *(monarca británico)* Gracious; **Su Graciosa Majestad** Her Gracious Majesty

2 *nm,f Teat* comic character; *Fam* **no te hagas el g.** I suppose you think you're very funny

grada *nf* **(a)** *(peldaño)* step, stair **(b)** *(asiento colectivo)* tier **(c)** *(tarima)* stand **(d)** *Náut* slipway, building berth **(e)** **gradas** flight *sing* of steps

gradación *nf* **(a)** *Mús* scale **(b)** *(retórica)* climax

gradería *nf. Esp* **graderío** *nm* tiers *pl* of seats, *US* bleachers *pl*

gradiente 1 *nm* gradient, *US* grade
2 *nf Chile Ecuad RP* slope

grado *nm* (**a**) *(gen)* degree; **el g. de humedad/
intensidad** degree of humidity/intensity; **en sumo g.** to
an extreme degree; **en tal g.** so much so □ **g. centígrado**
degree centigrade (**b**) *(fase)* stage (**c**) *Educ (curso)* year, *Br*
form, *US* grade; *(título)* degree (**d**) *Mil* rank (**e**) *(peldaño)*
step (**f**) *Ling* degree (**g**) *(locuciones)* **de buen g.** willingly,
with (a) grace; **de mal g.** unwillingly, with (a) bad grace

graduable *adj* adjustable

graduación *nf* (**a**) *(acción)* grading; *(de la vista)* eye-test;
(de gafas) strength (**b**) *Mil* rank

graduado, -a 1 *pp de* **graduar**
2 *adj* graduated
3 *nm Esp Educ* **g. escolar** *(título)* = basic school-leaving
certificate
4 *nm,f (persona)* graduate

gradual *adj* gradual

graduar [4] **1** *vt* (**a**) *(gen)* to graduate (**b**) *(título,
graduación)* to confer a degree *o* a rank, *US* graduate (**c**)
(medir) to measure; **g. la vista** to test sb's eyes (**d**) *(regular)*
to regulate
2 graduarse *vpr* (**a**) *Educ Mil* to graduate, receive an
academic degree *o* a military rank (**b**) *Esp* **g. la vista** to
have one's eyes tested

graffiti [gra'fiti] *nmpl* graffiti *pl*

grafía *nf* (**a**) *(signo)* graphic symbol; *(escritura)* writing (**b**)
(ortografía) spelling

gráfico, -a 1 *adj* graphic
2 *nm* graph, chart □ **g. de barras** bar chart

grafismo *nm* (**a**) *(diseño gráfico)* graphics *pl* (**b**) *(grafía)*
graphic symbol (**c**) *Fig (fuerza descriptiva)* vividness,
graphicness

grafista *nmf* graphic designer

grafito *nm Min* graphite

grafología *nf* graphology

grafólogo, -a *nm,f* graphologist

gragea *nf Med* pill, tablet

grajilla *nf Orn* jackdaw

grajo, -a 1 *nm,f Orn* rook
2 *nm Andes Carib Fam* body odour

gral. *(abrev de* **General**) gen.

grama *nf Bot* Bermuda grass

gramática *nf* grammar; **g. generativa** transformational
grammar; *Fam Fig* **g. parda** cunning, astuteness

gramatical *adj* grammatical

gramático, -a 1 *adj* grammatical
2 *nm,f* grammarian

gramínea *Bot* **1** *adj* **una planta g.** a grass, *Espec* a
gramineous plant
2 *nf* grass, *Espec* gramineous plant

gramo *nm* gram, gramme

gramófono *nm* gramophone

gramola *nf* gramophone

grampa *nf Am* staple

gran *adj* (**a**) *(superior)* tremendous; **a g. altura** very high;
g. velocidad high speed; **me diste una g. alegría** you've
made me very happy; **un g. susto** a terrible fright (**b**)
(excelente, famoso) great; **una g. persona** a great person; **un
g. libro** a great book; *véase* **grande**

grana¹ *nf (semilla)* seed; *(crecimiento)* seeding

grana² 1 *nf* (**a**) *Ent* cochineal (**b**) *(substancia)* cochineal
2 *adj* scarlet

Granada *n* (**a**) *(ciudad)* Granada (**b**) *(país)* Grenada

granada *nf* (**a**) *Bot* pomegranate (**b**) *Mil* grenade

granadero *nm Mil* grenadier

granadina *nf* (**a**) *Mús* = type of flamenco song from
Granada (**b**) *(bebida)* grenadine

granadino, -a 1 *adj* of *o* from Granada
2 *nm,f* person from Granada

granado, -a 1 *pp de* **granar**
2 *adj* (**a**) *(maduro)* ripened (**b**) *Fig (selecto)* **el** *o* **lo más g.**
the finest (**c**) *Fig (persona)* mature, of a certain age
3 *nm Bot* pomegranate tree

granar *vi Agr* to seed, ripen

granate 1 *adj inv (color)* maroon, dark crimson
2 *nm* (**a**) *Min* garnet (**b**) *(color)* maroon, garnet

granazón *nf* seeding, ripening

Gran Bretaña *n* Great Britain

grande 1 *adj (before singular noun* **gran** *is used)* (**a**)
(tamaño) big, large; **esta chaqueta me está g.** this jacket
is too big for me; *Fig* **¡qué g. eres!** you are really fantastic!
(**b**) *(cantidad)* large; **a lo g.** on a grand scale, in a big way;
Fig **pasarlo en g.** to have a great time; *Fig* **vivir a lo g.** to
live in style (**c**) *RP (fantástico)* great (**d**) *RP (divertido)*
amusing (**e**) *RP (de edad)* old
2 *nmf* (**a**) *(persona)* grown-up, adult (**b**) *(título)* **g. de
España** grandee (**c**) *Pol* **los cuatro grandes** the Big Four
3 *nf RP (en lotería)* first prize

grandeza *nf* (**a**) *(tamaño)* size (**b**) *(importancia)*
greatness; **g. de ánimo** moral courage (**c**) *(generosidad)*
generosity; **g. de alma** magnanimity (**d**) *Esp (dignidad
nobiliaria)* nobility

grandilocuencia *nf* grandiloquence, pomp

grandilocuente *adj* grandiloquent, pompous

grandiosidad *nf* grandeur, splendour, *US* splendor;
gesto de g. grand gesture

grandioso, -a *adj* grandiose, splendid

grandullón, -ona *Fam* **1** *adj* overgrown
2 *nm,f (hombre)* big boy; *(mujer)* big girl

granel: a granel *loc adv* (**a**) *(sin medir exactamente)* loose,
in bulk; **vino a g.** wine in bulk (**b**) *(en abundancia)* tons *o* lots
of; *Fam* **whisky a g.** whisky galore

granero *nm Agr* granary

granítico, -a *adj* granitic, granite

granito *nm* (**a**) *Min* granite (**b**) *(en la piel)* spot, pimple;
aportar su g. de arena to make one's small contribution,
do one's bit

granizada *nf* hailstorm; *Fig* **una g. de insultos** a shower
of insults

granizado *nm* iced drink; **g. de limón** iced lemon
(drink)

granizar [14] *v impers* to hail

granizo *nm* hail, hailstone

granja *nf* farm

granjear 1 *vt* to gain, earn; **su simpatía le granjeó la
amistad de todos** his kindness won him everyone's
affection
2 grangearse *vpr* to gain, earn

granjero, -a *nm,f* farmer

grano *nm* (**a**) *(de cereal, de uva)* grain; **un g. de arena/sal/
trigo** a grain of sand/salt/wheat; **un g. de café** a coffee
bean (**b**) *Med* spot, pimple (**c**) *(locuciones)* **ir al g.** to get to
the point; **ni un g.** not a bit; **no es g. de anís** it's not to be
sniffed at (**d**) **granos** cereals

granuja 1 *nf* grapes *pl*
2 *nmf* (**a**) *(pilluelo)* ragamuffin, urchin (**b**) *(estafador)*
crook, trickster

granujada *nf* foul play, nasty trick

granujería *nf* gang of rogues/urchins

granulación *nf* granulation

granulado, -a 1 *pp de* **granular**
2 *adj* granulated
3 *nm Farm* preparation

granular 1 *adj* granular
2 *vt* to granulate

gránulo *nm* (**a**) *(grano)* granule (**b**) *Farm* small pill

granuloso, -a *adj* (**a**) *(superficie)* granular (**b**) *(piel)* pimply

granzas *nfpl* (**a**) *Agr* chaff *sing* (**b**) *Min* dross *sing*

grao *nm* landing beach, shore

grapa *nf* (**a**) *(para papeles)* staple (**b**) *Constr* cramp (**c**) *(de uvas)* bunch (of grapes) (**d**) *CSur* grappa

grapadora *nf* stapler

grapar *vt* to staple

grasa *nf* grease, fat □ **g. vegetal** vegetable fat

grasiento *adj* greasy, oily

graso, -a *adj* fatty; **alimentos grasos** fatty foods; **pelo g.** greasy hair

grasoso, -a *esp Am adj* greasy, oily

gratén *nm Culin* **al g.** au gratin

gratificación *nf* (**a**) *(satisfacción)* gratification (**b**) *(recompensa)* reward (**c**) *(extra)* bonus

gratificador, -a *adj*, **gratificante** *adj* gratifying, rewarding

gratificar [59] *vt* (**a**) *(satisfacer)* to gratify (**b**) *(recompensar)* to reward

gratinado, -a *adj Culin* au gratin

gratinar *vt Culin* to cook au gratin

gratis *adv* free, for nothing

gratitud *nf* gratitude

grato, -a *adj* (**a**) *(agradable)* pleasant, pleasing; **me es g. anunciarle que ...** I am pleased to inform you that ... (**b**) *Bol Chile (agradecido)* grateful

gratuidad *nf* (**a**) *(ausencia de pago)* **la g. en la enseñanza** free education (**b**) *(arbitrariedad)* gratuitousness

gratuitamente *adv* (**a**) *(de balde)* free, for nothing (**b**) *(sin fundamento)* unfoundedly

gratuito, -a *adj* (**a**) *(de balde)* free (of charge); **entrada gratuita** free entrance (**b**) *(arbitrario)* gratuitous, arbitrary; **afirmación gratuita** unwarranted statement

grava *nf* *(guijas)* gravel; *(piedra)* crushed stone

gravamen *nm Jur* (**a**) *(carga)* burden (**b**) *(impuesto)* tax

gravar *vt Jur* (**a**) *(cargar)* to burden (**b**) *(impuestos)* to tax; **estar gravado** to be mortgaged

grave *adj* (**a**) *(pesado)* heavy (**b**) *(importante)* grave, serious (**c**) *(muy enfermo)* **estar g.** to be seriously ill (**d**) *(de estilo)* solemn (**e**) *(voz, nota)* low (**f**) *Ling* **acento g.** grave accent; **palabra g.** paroxytone

gravedad *nf* (**a**) *(importancia)* graveness, seriousness; **herido de g.** seriously injured (**b**) *Fis* gravity; **centro de g.** centre of gravity; **fuerza de g.** force of gravity

gravidez *nf* pregnancy; **en estado de g.** pregnant

grávido, -a *adj* (**a**) *(lleno)* full (**b**) *(embarazada)* pregnant, gravid

gravilla *nf* fine gravel

gravitación *nf Fis* gravitation

gravitacional *adj Fis* gravitational

gravitar *vi* (**a**) *Fis* to gravitate (**b**) *(apoyarse en)* to rest on; **sobre él gravita el peso de las decisiones** the onus of the decisions rests on him (**c**) *(amenazar)* to loom; **el peligro gravitaba sobre nuestras cabezas** danger loomed over our heads

gravitatorio, -a *adj* gravitational

gravoso, -a *adj* (**a**) *(costoso)* costly, expensive (**b**) *(molesto)* burdensome

graznar *vi* *(gen)* to squawk; *(pato)* to quack; *(cuervo)* to caw

graznido *nm* *(un sonido)* squawk; *(varios)* squawking; *(de pato)* quack; *(de cuervo)* caw

greca *nf Arquit* fret, fretwork

Grecia *n* Greece

grecolatino, -a *adj* Graeco-Latin

grecorromano, -a *adj* Graeco-Roman

greda *nf Min* fuller's earth

gregario, -a *adj* gregarious; **instinto g.** herd instinct

gregoriano, -a *adj* Gregorian; *Mús* **canto g.** Gregorian chant

grelos *nmpl* turnip tops

gremial *adj* union, relating to trade unions; **convenio g.** union agreement

gremialismo *nm* (**a**) *Pey (corporativismo)* = self-interested behaviour, especially of professional groups (**b**) *Am (sindicalismo)* unionism, *Br* trade unionism

gremialista *nmf Am* union member, *Br* trade unionist

gremio *nm* (**a**) *Hist* guild (**b**) *(sindicato)* union (**c**) *(profesión)* profession

greña *nf* lock of entangled hair; *Fam* **andar a la g.** to squabble

greñudo, -a *adj* *(pelo)* tangled; *(persona)* unkempt, dishevelled, *US* disheveled

gres *nm* stoneware; **g. flameado** glazed earthenware

gresca *nf* (**a**) *(bulla)* racket; **armar g.** to kick up a racket (**b**) *(riña)* row

grey *nf* (**a**) *(rebaño)* flock, herd (**b**) *(personas)* group, bunch; *Rel* flock

grial *nm* grail; **el Santo G.** the Holy Grail

griego, -a 1 *adj* Greek
2 *nm,f* Greek
3 *nm* *(idioma)* Greek; *Fam* **hablar en g.** to talk gibberish, *Br* talk double Dutch

grieta *nf* crack; *(en la piel)* chap, crack

grifa *nf* *(droga)* marijuana

grifería *nf* taps *pl*, *US* faucets *pl*, plumbing

grifo, -a¹ 1 *nm* (**a**) *Esp* tap, *US* faucet (**b**) *Perú (gasolinera)* *Br* petrol station, *US* gas station (**c**) *Chile (toma de agua)* (fire) hydrant, *US* fireplug (**d**) *Col Fam (presuntuoso)* **ser g.** to be conceited
2 *adj Méx Fam* **andar g.** *(drogado)* to be stoned o high; *(loco)* to be off one's head

grifo² *nm Mit* griffin, gryphon, griffon

grill [gril] *(pl* **grills)** *nm* grill

grilla *nf* (**a**) *Ent* female cricket (**b**) *Andes (contrariedad)* obstacle (**c**) *Col (riña)* struggle, scuffle

grillado, -a *adj Esp Fam Fig* barmy

grillete *nm* shackle

grillo¹ *nm Ent* cricket

grillo² *nm Bot* sprout

grillo³ *nm* fetters *pl*, shackles *pl*

grima *nf* annoyance, displeasure; **me da g. ...** I can't bear

grímpola *nf* pennant

gringo, -a *Pey* **1** *adj (extranjero)* foreign; *Am* yankee
2 *nm,f* (**a**) *(extranjero)* foreigner; *Am* yankee, gringo (**b**) *Arg (persona)* blond, blonde

gringolandia *nf Am Fam Hum* Yankeeland

gripa *nf Col Méx* flu

gripal *adj Med* related to flu; **una afección g.** flu

griparse *vpr* to seize up

gripe *nf* flu

griposo, -a *adj* **estar g.** to have flu

gris 1 *adj* (**a**) *(color)* grey, *US* gray (**b**) *Fig (mediocre)* mediocre, third-rate (**c**) *Fig (triste)* grey, *US* gray, gloomy
   2 *nm* (**a**) *(color)* grey, *US* gray (**b**) *Esp Argot Antes* cop; **los grises** the fuzz *pl*

grisáceo, -a *adj* greyish

grisalla *nf Méx Arte* chiaroscuro, grisaille

grisma *nf Chile* shred, bit

grisú (*pl* **grisúes**) *nm Min* firedamp

gritar *vt & vi* to shout, yell; **el público gritó al cantante** the singer was booed by the audience; **¡no me grites!** don't shout at me!

griterío *nm* shouting, din

grito *nm* shout, yell; **a voz en g., a g. limpio** *o* **pelado** at the top of one's voice; **dar** *o* **pegar un g.** to shout, scream; **le llamó con un g.** he yelled at him; *Fig* **pedir algo a gritos** to be badly in need of sth; *Fig* **el último g.** the latest craze *o* fashion; *Fig* **poner el g. en el cielo** to raise an outcry, hit the ceiling

gritón, -ona 1 *adj* noisy, loud-mouthed
   2 *nm,f* loudmouth, yeller

groenlandés, -esa 1 *adj* Greenlandic
   2 *nm,f* Greenlander

Groenlandia *n* Greenland

grog (*pl* **grogs**) *nm* grog, punch

grogui *adj* (**a**) *Box* punch-drunk, groggy (**b**) *Fig* groggy, dazed

grosella *nf Bot* redcurrant; **g. negra** blackcurrant; **g. silvestre** gooseberry

grosellero *nm* currant bush; **g. negro** blackcurrant bush

grosería *nf* (**a**) *(ordinariez)* rude word *o* expression; **decir una g.** to say something rude (**b**) *(rusticidad)* rudeness

grosero, -a 1 *adj (tosco)* rough, coarse; *(maleducado)* rude, vulgar
   2 *nm,f* lout, boor

grosor *nm* thickness

grosso modo *adv* roughly, in broad terms

grotesco, -a *adj* grotesque, ludicrous

grúa *nf* (**a**) *Constr* crane, derrick (**b**) *Aut.* breakdown van, *US* tow truck

grueso, -a 1 *adj* thick, heavy; **unas uvas gruesas** some large grapes; **un hombre g.** a fat man; *Mar* **mar gruesa** heavy sea; *Med* **intestino g.** large intestine
   2 *nm* (**a**) *(grosor)* thickness (**b**) *(parte principal)* bulk, main body; **el g. de la población** the bulk of the population

grulla *nf Orn* **g. común** crane

grullo, -a *adj* (**a**) *Guat Méx (gris)* dark grey (**b**) *Méx (gorrón)* spongeing

grumete *nm* cabin boy

grumo *nm* lump; *(leche)* curd

grumoso, -a *adj* lumpy

grunge [grunt∫] *nm Mús* grunge

gruñido *nm* grunt

gruñir *vi* to grunt

gruñón, -ona 1 *adj* grumpy, grumbly, grouchy
   2 *nm,f* grumbler, grouch

grupa *nf* croup, hindquarters *pl*; **montar a la g.** to ride pillion; *Fig* **volver grupas** to go back, retrace one's steps

grupo *nm* (**a**) *(gen)* group; **en g.** together as a group ❑ **g. de discusión** *Inform* discussion group; *(en marketing)* focus group; *Com* **g. de empresas** (corporate) group; *Pol* **g. parlamentario** parliamentary group; *Med* **g. sanguíneo** blood group (**b**) *Téc* unit, set; **g. electrógeno** power plant

grupúsculo *nm* minor group

gruta *nf* grotto, cave

gta. (*abrev de* **glorieta**) *Br* roundabout, *US* traffic circle

gua *interj Am* (**a**) *(temor)* agh! (**b**) *(admiración)* wow!

guaca *nf* (**a**) *Andes CAm (tesoro)* buried treasure (**b**) *Am (hucha)* piggy bank (**c**) *CAm (sepultura)* Indian tomb

guacal *nm* (**a**) *Bot CAm Méx* calabash tree (**b**) *(jaula) Carib Col Méx* calabash basket

guacamayo, -a *nm,f Orn* macaw

guacamole *nm*, *CAm Cuba* **guacamol** *nm Culin* guacamole, avocado sauce

guachafita *nf Col Ven* confusion, uproar

guache *nm* (**a**) *Arte* gouache (**b**) *Col Ven (canalla)* thug (**c**) *Col (maraca)* maraca

guachimán *nm Am* night watchman

guachinango *nm Méx (pez)* red snapper

guacho, -a *adj & nm,f Andes RP* (**a**) orphan (**b**) *(sinvergüenza)* bastard, swine

guaco, -a 1 *adj* (**a**) *Andes (con el labio leporino)* harelipped (**b**) *Méx (mellizo)* twin
   2 *nm* (**a**) *Carib Méx (planta)* guaco (**b**) *Col Ecuad (ave gallinácea)* currasow (**c**) *CAm (ave falcónida)* caracara

guadalajareño, -a 1 *adj* of *o* from Guadalajara
   2 *nm,f* person from Guadalajara

Guadalupe *n* Guadaloupe

guadaña *nf* scythe

guadañar *vt* to mow; *(hierba)* to scythe

guadarnés, -a 1 *nm* tack room
   2 *nm,f (hombre)* stable boy; *(mujer)* stable girl

guagua[1] *nf CAm Carib* bus

guagua[2] *nf Andes* baby, babe

guaina 1 *nmf Am* youngster
   2 *nf Arg* young girl

guaje *nm* (**a**) *(niño)* boy (**b**) *Fam (granuja)* urchin (**c**) *Méx Bot* type of acacia (**d**) *Hond Méx Bot* calabash (**e**) *Hond Méx Fig* idiot (**f**) *CAm Fig (cosa inútil)* trinket; *(persona inútil)* waste of space

guajira *nf* = Cuban popular song about country life

guajiro, -a *nm,f Cuba Fam* peasant

gualdo, -a *adj* yellow; **la bandera roja y gualda** the Spanish flag

gualdrapa *nf* caparison

guanaco, -a *nm,f Am Zool* guanaco

guanajo *nm Carib* turkey

guanche 1 *adj* Guanche
   2 *nmf* Guanche, original inhabitant of the Canary Islands

guando *nm Andes* stretcher

guano *nm* (**a**) *(abono natural)* guano; *(artificial)* manure, fertilizer (**b**) *Cuba (palmera)* palm tree

guantada *nf* slap

guantazo *nm* slap

guante *nm* glove; *Fig* **arrojar el g. a algn** to throw down the gauntlet; *Fig* **más suave que un g.** as meek as a lamb; *Fig* **sentar como un g.** to fit like a glove; *Fam* **echar el g. a algo/algn** to nick sth/catch sb; *Box* **colgar los guantes** to give up boxing

guantear *vt Méx Fam (agarrar)* to collar

guantera *nf Aut* glove compartment

guaperas *inv Esp Fam* **1** *adj* good-looking, *US* cute
 2 *nmf* good-looker

guapetón, -ona *adj Esp Fam* good-looking

guapo, -a **1** *adj* **(a)** *esp Esp (atractivo)* good-looking, *US* cute; *(mujer)* beautiful, pretty; *(hombre)* handsome; **es muy guapa** she's very pretty; **estar g.** to look smart; **¡hola guapa!** hello darling! **(b)** *Esp Fam (muy bueno)* cool, ace
 2 *nm,f* **(a)** good-looking person, good-looker **(b)** *(valiente)* **a ver quién es el g. que ...** let's see who's brave enough to ... **(c)** *Esp Fam (apelativo)* pal, *Br* sunshine; **oye, g., devuélveme mi bolígrafo** listen pal *o Br* sunshine, I want my pen back

guapura *nf* good looks *pl*

guaquear *vt Am* to rob graves

guaraca *nf Andes* sling

guarache *nm Méx* type of sandal

guaragua *nf Andes Mús* swinging

guarango, -a *adj Chile RP* rude, rough, ill-bred

guaraní *(pl* **guaraníes)** **1** *adj* Guarani
 2 *nmf* Guarani
 3 *nm (idioma)* Guarani

guarapo *nm,f Am* **(a)** *(jugo de caña)* juice of sugar cane **(b)** *(licor)* sugar-cane liquor

guarda **1** *nmf* guard, keeper; **Ángel de la G.** Guardian Angel; **g. forestal** forester; **g. jurado** security guard
 2 *nf Impr* endpaper
 3 *nm Arg (cobrador)* tram *o* bus conductor

guardabarrera *nmf Ferroc Br* level crossing keeper, *US* grade crossing keeper

guardabarros *nm inv Esp Bol RP Aut Br* mudguard, *US* fender

guardabosque *nmf* forester

guardacoches *nmf inv* parking attendant

guardacostas *nm inv Naút* coastguard vessel

guardador, -a *adj & nm,f* **ser g.** to like to keep things; **ser g. de la ley** to be law-abiding

guardaespaldas *nmf inv* bodyguard

guardafrenos *nmf inv (hombre)* pointsman, *US* brakeman; *(mujer)* pointswoman, *US* brakewoman

guardagujas *nmf inv Ferroc (hombre)* switchman; *(mujer)* switchwoman

guardameta *nmf Dep* goalkeeper

guardamuebles *nm inv* furniture warehouse

guardapelo *nm* locket

guardapolvo *nm (cubierta)* dust cover; *(mono)* overalls *pl*

guardar **1** *vt* **(a)** *(conservar)* to keep, hold; **g. un buen recuerdo de** to have a pleasant memory of **(b)** *(observar) (la ley)* to observe, abide by; *(un secreto)* to keep; **g. la derecha** to keep to the right; **g. las distancias** to keep one's distance; **g. silencio** to remain silent **(c)** *(poner en un sitio)* to put away; **guárdalo en el cajón** put it in the drawer **(d)** *(reservar)* to save; **guárdame un sitio** keep a seat for me, please; **guárdame un trozo** save a bit for me **(e)** *(proteger)* to protect; **¡Dios guarde a la reina!** God save the Queen! **(f)** *(cuidar)* to look after **(g)** **g. cama** to stay in bed; **g. las formas** to be polite; **g. rencor** to harbour resentment **(h)** *Inform* to save
 2 **guardarse** *vpr* **(a)** *(no dar, retener)* to keep; **me lo guardé en el bolsillo** I put it in my pocket; **puedes guardarte tus consejos** you can keep your advice **(b)** *(abstenerse)* **g. de hacer algo** to avoid doing sth; **g. muy mucho de ...** to take good care not to ...; **me guardé muy bien de hablar** I made sure not to say a word; *Fam* **guardársela a algn** to have it in for sb

guardarropa **1** *nm* **(a)** *(cuarto)* cloakroom **(b)** *(armario)* wardrobe
 2 *nmf* cloakroom attendant

guardarropía *nf Teat* wardrobe for props

guardavallas *nmf inv Am* goalkeeper

guardavía *nmf Ferroc (hombre)* linesman, *US* lineman; *(mujer)* lineswoman, *US* linewoman

guardería *nf* **(a)** **g. infantil** nursery (school) **(b)** *(oficio de guarda)* keeping

guardia **1** *nf* **(a)** *(vigilancia)* watch, lookout, guard; **estar en g.** to be on guard; **mantener la g.** to keep watch; **ponerse en g.** to put oneself on one's guard **(b)** *(tropa)* guard; **g. de asalto** assault guard; **g. municipal** *o* **urbana** traffic police; **la g. civil** the civil guard **(c)** *(turno de servicio)* duty; *Mil* guard duty; **estar de g.** to be on duty; **médico de g.** doctor on duty; **tiene g. de noche** she's on night duty
 2 *nmf (hombre)* policeman; *(mujer)* policewoman; **g. civil** civil guard; **g. de seguridad** security guard; **g. de tráfico** traffic policeman *o* policewoman

guardián, -ana *nm,f* keeper, custodian, watchman

guardilla *nf* attic, garret

guarecer [46] **1** *vt* to shelter, protect
 2 **guarecerse** *vpr* to take shelter *o* refuge **(de** from)

guaricha *nf Am Pey* female, bird

guarida *nf* **(a)** *Zool* haunt, lair **(b)** *(refugio de maleantes)* hide-out

guarismo *nm* digit, number

guarnecer [46] *vt* **(a)** *(poner adornos a)* to decorate, trim; *Culin* to garnish **(b)** *(dotar)* to provide **(con** with) **(c)** *Mil* to garrison **(d)** *Constr* to plaster

guarnecido, -a **1** *pp de* **guarnecer**
 2 *adj* **(a)** *(adornado)* decorated, trimmed; *Culin* garnished **(b)** *(dotado)* equipped **(c)** *Mil* garrisoned
 3 *nm Constr* plaster

guarnición *nf* **(a)** *(adorno)* decoration, trimmings *pl*; *Culin* garnish **(b)** *Mil* garrison **(c)** *(en joyería)* setting **(d)** *(pieza del sable y espada)* guard **(e)** **guarniciones** *Equit* harness *sing*

guarnicionero, -a *nm,f* saddler

guaro *nm CAm* cane liquor

guarrada *nf,* **guarrería** *nf Esp Fam* **(a)** *(suciedad)* filth, muck; **decir guarradas** *o* **guarrerías** to have a foul mouth **(b)** *(acción desaprensiva)* dirty trick

guarro, -a *Esp* **1** *adj* dirty, filthy
 2 *nm,f* pig, dirty pig

guarura *nm Méx Fam* bodyguard

guasa *nf* **(a)** *Fam* mockery; **con g.** jokingly; **estar de g.** to be joking; **le dijo con g. que cantaba muy bien** she told him tongue in cheek that he sang very well **(b)** *Cuba Méx Ven (pez)* jewfish

guasearse *vpr* to tease, make fun **(de** of); **no te guasees de él que es muy tímido** don't take the mickey out of him, he's very shy

guaso, -a *adj* **1** *adj Andes RP* crude, coarse
 2 *nm,f Chile (campesino)* farmer, peasant

guasón, -ona **1** *adj* joking, humorous
 2 *nm,f* joker, humorist

guata *nf Chile* belly, paunch; **echar g.** to get fat

Guatemala *n* Guatemala

guatemalteco, -a *adj & nm,f* Guatemalan

guateque *nm Esp Cuba Méx* party

guay *adj, adv & interj Esp Fam* cool, *US* neat

guayaba *nf* **(a)** *Bot (fruto)* guava **(b)** *Andes CAm Cuba Fig (mentira)* lie

guayabate *nm Méx CAm* guava sweet

guayabear *vi PRico RP* to lie

guayabera *nf Am* = white shirt with pockets, worn outside trousers

guayabero, -a *Am* **1** *adj* lying
  2 *nm,f* liar

guayabo *nm* guava tree

Guayana *n* Guyana

guayanés, -esa *adj & nm,f* Guyanese, Guyanan

gubernamental *adj,* **gubernativo, -a** *adj* government, governmental; **fuerzas gubernamentales** government forces

gubia *nf* gouge

guedeja *nf (cabellera)* mane of hair; *(de león)* mane

guepardo *nm Zool* cheetah

güero, -a *adj Méx* fair-haired

guerra *nf* war, warfare; **en g.** at war; *Fam* **dar g.** to be a real nuisance; *Fam* **tenerle la g. declarada a algn** to be openly against sb □ **g. bacteriológica** germ warfare; **g. civil** civil war; **g. de las galaxias** Star Wars; **g. de guerrillas** guerrilla warfare; **g. fría** cold war; **g. de precios** price war; **g. mundial/nuclear** world/nuclear war; **g. santa** Holy War; **g. sucia** dirty war

guerrear *vi* to war

guerrera *nf* army jacket, trench coat

guerrero, -a **1** *adj* **(a)** *(belicoso)* warlike, warring; **danza guerrera** war dance **(b)** *Fam (niño)* difficult
  2 *nm,f* warrior

guerrilla *nf* **(a)** *(partida armada)* guerrilla force o band **(b)** *(lucha)* guerrilla warfare

guerrillero, -a *nm,f* guerrilla

gueto *nm* ghetto

güevón, -ona *adj & nm,f véase* **huevón, -ona**

güey **1** *nm Méx muy Fam (tonto)* jerk, *Br* plonker
  2 *interj* **¡ay g.!** *(asombro) Br* bloody hell!, *US* goddamn!

guía **1** *nmf (persona)* guide □ **g. turístico** tour guide
  2 *nf* **(a)** *(norma)* guidance, guideline **(b)** *(libro, lista)* directory, guide; *Esp RP* **la g. telefónica** *o* **de teléfonos** the telephone directory **(c)** *Téc* rail, guide **(d)** *(de bicicleta)* handlebar **(e)** *(de bigote)* end, tip **(f)** *(documento)* customs permit **(g)** *Bot* main stem

guiar [32] **1** *vt* **(a)** *(indicar el camino)* to guide, lead **(b)** *(conducir) Aut* to drive; *Náut* to steer; *Av* to pilot; *(caballo, bici)* to ride **(c)** *Agr (plantas)* to train
  2 guiarse *vpr* to be guided, go **(por** by)

guija *nf* **(a)** *(piedra)* pebble **(b)** *Bot* vetch

guijarral *nm* pebbly place

guijarro *nm* pebble, stone

guijo *nm* gravel

guillado, -a **1** *pp de* **guillarse**
  2 *adj Fam* nutty, loony

guillarse *vpr Fam* **(a)** *(chiflarse)* to become a real loony, go bonkers **(b)** *(escabullirse)* to escape; **guillárselas** to clear out

guillotina *nf* guillotine; **ventana de g.** sash window

guillotinar *vt* to guillotine

güinche *nm Am* hoist

guinda *nf Bot* morello (cherry)

guindar *vt* **(a)** *(levantar)* to lift; *Náut* to sway **(b)** *Fam (colgar)* to hang **(c)** *Esp Argot* to nick, lift

guindilla *nf Bot* chilli

guindo *nm Bot* morello (cherry) tree

Guinea *n* Guinea □ **G. Bissau** Guinea-Bissau; **G. Ecuatorial** Equatorial Guinea

guinea *nf* guinea

guineano, -a *adj & nm,f* Guinean

guineo, -a **1** *adj & nm,f* Guinean
  2 *nm* banana

guiñada *nf* **(a)** *(guiño)* wink **(b)** *Náut* yaw, yawing

guiñapo *nm* **(a)** *(andrajo)* tatter, rag **(b)** *Fig (persona)* wreck; **poner a algn como un g.** to pull sb to pieces

guiñar *vt* **(a)** *(el ojo)* to wink; **me guiñó un ojo** he winked at me **(b)** *Náut* to yaw

guiño *nm* wink

guiñol *nm* puppet theatre

guiñolesco, -a *adj* like a puppet show

guión *nm* **(a)** *(esquema)* sketch, outline **(b)** *Cin TV* script □ **g. de cine** film script **(c)** *Ling* hyphen, dash **(d)** *(estandarte)* standard, banner

guionista *nmf Cin TV* scriptwriter

guipar *vt Fam* **(a)** *(ver)* to see **(b)** *(descubrir)* to see through

guipuzcoano, -a **1** *adj* from *o* of Guipúzcoa
  2 *nm,f* person from Guipúzcoa

guiri *nmf Esp Argot* foreigner, tourist

guirigay *(pl* **guirigáis)** *nm Esp Argot* **(a)** *(lenguaje confuso)* gibberish **(b)** *(griterío)* hubbub, commotion

guirlache *nm Culin* almond brittle

guirnalda *nf* garland

guisa *nf* way, manner; **a g. de** as, for; **llevaba una sábana a g. de túnica** she was wearing a sheet as a tunic

guisado *nm Culin* stew

guisante *nm Esp Bot* pea

guisar *esp Esp* *vt* to cook, stew; **tú te lo guisas, tú te lo comes** as you make your bed so must you lie in it

guiso *nm* dish; *(guisado)* stew; **un g. de carne con verduras** a meat and vegetable stew

güisqui *nm* whisky; **g. escocés** Scotch

guita *nf Esp RP Argot* dough, spondulix

guitarra **1** *nf* guitar □ **g. eléctrica** electric guitar
  2 *nmf* guitarist

guitarreo *nm* strumming on the guitar

guitarrero, -a *nm,f (vendedor)* guitar seller; *(fabricante)* guitar maker

guitarrillo *nm* small four-string guitar

guitarrista *nmf* guitarist

guitarro *nm véase* **guitarrillo**

güito *nm* **(a)** *(hueso) Br* stone, *US* pit **(b)** **güitos** = game played with this stone

gula *nf* gluttony

gurí, -isa *nm,f RP* kid, child

guripa *nm Esp Fam* **(a)** *(soldado)* soldier, *Br* squaddie **(b)** *(pillo)* scoundrel **(c)** *(policía)* cop

gurrumino, -a **1** *adj* **(a)** *(enclenque)* sickly, frail **(b)** *Andes (cobarde)* cowardly
  2 *nm,f Méx* kid, youngster

gurú *nm* guru

gusanillo *nm* **(a)** *(gusano)* little worm **(b)** *(locuciones)* **el g. de la conciencia** one's conscience, feelings of guilt; **matar el g.** to drink spirits first thing in the morning

gusano *nm* **(a)** *Zool* worm, earthworm, maggot; *(oruga)* caterpillar; **g. de seda** silkworm **(b)** *Fam (persona despreciable)* worm, despicable person; *(persona insignificante)* poor devil

gusarapo *nm* tiny creature

gustar **1** *vt* **(a)** *(agradar)* to like; **¡así me gusta!** that's what I like!, well done!; **me gusta el champán** I like champagne;

Fig **cuando Ud. guste** as *o* whenever you wish (**b**) *(probar)* to taste, try; **¿Ud. gusta?, ¿gustas?** would you like some?

  2 *vi* **g. de** to enjoy; **gustaba de leer teatro** he enjoyed reading plays

gustativo, -a *adj* gustative; **papilas gustativas** taste buds

gustazo *nm Fam* great pleasure; **darse el g.** to treat oneself; **¡qué g. que mañana sea fiesta!** how wonderful tomorrow is a Bank Holiday!

gustillo *nm (regusto)* aftertaste; **g. ácido** bitter tang; *Fam Fig* **¡qué g. me dio!** how glad I was!; *Fam Fig (satisfacción)* **sentir un g.** to be happy

gusto *nm* (**a**) *(sentido)* taste; **este guiso tiene poco g.** this stew is tasteless (**b**) *(afición, inclinación)* liking, taste; **g. por la música** a taste for music; **gustos sencillos** simple tastes (**c**) *(en fórmulas de cortesía)* pleasure; **con (mucho) g.** with (great) pleasure; **el g. es mío** the pleasure is mine; **tendré**

mucho **g. en acompañarle al aeropuerto** I'd be delighted to take you to the airport; **tengo el g. de comunicarle que ...** it gives me great pleasure to inform you that ... (**d**) *(locuciones)* **tomar** *o Esp* **coger el g. a algo** to take a liking to sth; **dar g. a algn** to please sb; **da g. ver a tanta gente joven** it's a pleasure to see so many young people; **darse el g.** to treat oneself; **eso va a gustos** it's matter of taste; **estar a g.** to feel comfortable *o* at ease; **hacer algo a g.** to enjoy (doing) sth; **hay para todos los gustos** there is sth for everyone; **nunca llueve a g. de todos** you can't please everyone; **por g.** for the sake of it; **¡qué g.!** how lovely!; **ser de buen/mal g.** to be in good/bad taste; **tener buen/mal g.** to have good/bad taste

gustoso, -a *adj* (**a**) *(con placer)* **hacer algo g.** to do sth gladly *o* willingly (**b**) *(sabroso)* tasty

gutural *adj* guttural

Guyana *n* Guyana

guyanés, -esa *adj & nm,f* Guyanese, Guyanan

H, h ['atʃe] *nf (la letra)* H, h; **bomba H** H-bomb, hydrogen bomb

h *(abrev de* **hora(s))** h.

ha¹ *(abrev de* **hectárea(s))** h

ha² *indic pres véase* **haber**

haba *nf* broad bean; *Fig* **en todas partes cuecen habas** it's the same the whole world over; *Fam* **son habas contadas** *(cierto)* it's for sure; *(escaso)* they are few and far between ❑ **h. de las Indias** sweet pea

Habana *n* **La H.** Havana

habanera *nf Mús* = dance and music from Havana

habanero, -a 1 *adj* of o from Havana
2 *nm,f* person from Havana

habano *nm* Havana cigar

hábeas corpus *nm Jur* habeas corpus

haber [1] **1** *v aux* **(a)** *(en tiempos compuestos)* to have; **¡de haberlo sabido!** if only I had known!; **¡haberlo dicho!** why didn't you say so?; **¡he dicho!** and that's that!; **lo había visto** I had seen it; **lo he hecho** I have done it; **me habría gustado** I would have liked it **(b)** *(h. de* + *infin) (obligación)* **has de saber que ...** you should know that ...; **has de ser bueno** you must be good; **¿por qué he de ser yo?** why must it be me?; **¿quién había de ser?** who else could it have been? **(c)** *(h. que* + *infin)* **hay que** one must, you have to; **habrá que ir a verlo** we have to go and see it; **hay que hacer deporte** you've got to do some sport; **hay que hacer las cosas bien** one has to do things well; **hay que trabajar** you've got to work; **no hay que llorar** you mustn't cry; **no hay que tomarlo en serio** you mustn't take it seriously

2 *v impers* **(a)** *(existir, estar)* **hay** there is/are; **hubo** there was/were; **¿cuántos hay?** how many are there?; **habría unas cuarenta personas** there must have been about forty people; **hay un gato en el tejado** there is a cat on the roof; **no hay (nada) como ...** there is nothing like ..., nothing beats ...; **no hay como ser rico** there is nothing like being rich; **no hay nada como tener un buen coche** nothing beats having a good car; **no hay quien lo entienda** it's impossible to understand; **no hay quien te aguante hoy** you're impossible today; **no hay quien trabaje con este ruido** it's impossible for anyone to work with this noise **(b)** *Prensa Rad (tener lugar)* **en el encuentro habido entre ...** in today's game between ...; **habrá una fiesta** there will be a party; **hubo un accidente** there was an accident **(c)** *Literario* **diez años ha** ten years ago **(d)** *(locuciones)* **algo habrá** there must be something in it; **... como hay pocos, donde los haya** few and far between; **había una vez ...** there was once ...; **¡habrase visto** have you ever seen anything like it?, what a cheek!; **¡habráse visto!** well I never!, well really!; **no hay de qué** you're welcome, don't mention

it; **no hay tal** it isn't true; *CAm Col Méx Ven* **¿qué hay?** hello!, hi!, how are things?; *Fam* **eres de lo que no hay** you're impossible; *Fam* **no hay por donde cogerle** he's impossible

3 *vt (tener) Fml* **los hijos habidos en el matrimonio** the children of the marriage; *Fam* **todos los habidos y por h.** every single ...

4 haberse *vpr Fam* **habérselas con algn** to face o confront sb

5 *nm* **(a)** *(gen pl) (bienes)* assets *pl*, property; *(sueldo)* salary, pay, wages *pl* **(b)** *(en balance)* credit; *Fig* **tiene en su h. que ...** it must be said to his credit that ...

habichuela *nf Esp Carib Col* kidney bean

habido, -a *adj* occurred; **los accidentes habidos este verano** the number of accidents this summer

hábil *adj* **(a)** *(diestro)* skilful, *US* skillful; **h. para la costura** good at sewing **(b)** *(astuto)* clever, smart; **maniobra h.** clever move **(c)** *(apto)* usable; **días hábiles** working days; **los muebles dejan poco espacio h.** the furniture leaves little usable space

habilidad *nf* **(a)** *(destreza)* skill; **con gran h.** very skilfully; **tener h. manual** to be good with one's hands; **tener h. para ...** to be good at ... **(b)** *(astucia)* cleverness, smartness **(c) habilidades** *(dotes)* skills

habilidoso, -a *adj* clever, skilful, *US* skillful

habilitación *nf* **(a)** *(de un espacio)* fitting out **(b)** *(capacitación)* entitlement; *(autorización)* authorization **(c)** *(oficina del habilitado)* paymaster's office

habilitado, -a 1 *pp de* **habilitar**
2 *nm,f (hombre)* paymaster; *(mujer)* paymistress

habilitar *vt* **(a)** *(espacio)* to fit out; **h. un garaje para sala de juegos** to fit a garage out as a games room **(b)** *(capacitar)* to entitle, enable; *(autorizar)* to empower, authorize; **h. horas para visitas** to set aside time for visitors **(c)** *Fin (financiar)* to finance

hábilmente *adv* skilfully, *US* skillfully

habitabilidad *nf* habitability; **estar/no estar en condiciones de h.** to be fit/unfit for human habitation

habitable *adj* habitable, inhabitable

habitación *nf* **(a)** *(cuarto)* room; *(dormitorio)* bedroom; **h. individual/doble** single/double room **(b)** *Biol (hábitat)* habitat

habitacional *adj CSur Méx* housing; **un complejo h.** a housing development

habitáculo *nm* **(a)** *(vivienda)* dwelling **(b)** *Biol (hábitat)* habitat

habitante *nmf* inhabitant

habitar 1 *vt (lugar)* to live in, inhabit; **los pueblos primitivos que habitaron la península** the primitive peoples who inhabited the Peninsula; **una casa sin h.** an empty house

2 *vi* to live

hábitat (*pl* **hábitats**) *nm* habitat

hábito *nm* (**a**) *(costumbre)* habit, custom; **adquirir el h. de ...** to get into the habit of ...; **el fumar crea h.** smoking is habit-forming; **la puntualidad es un h. en mí** punctuality is second nature to me; **tener el h. de ...** to be in the habit of ... (**b**) *Rel* habit; **colgar los hábitos** to leave the priesthood; **tomar el h.** *(hombre)* to take holy orders; *(mujer)* to take the veil; **el h. no hace al monje** fine clothes don't make a fair lady, clothes don't make the man

habituación *nf* habituation

habitual *adj* usual, customary, habitual; *(cliente, lector)* regular

habitualmente *adv* *(repetidamente)* usually; *(con regularidad)* regularly

habituar [4] **1** *vt* to accustom (**a** to)

2 habituarse *vpr* to get used (**a** to), become accustomed (**a** to)

habla *nf* (**a**) *(idioma)* language; **h. regional** regional dialect; **países de h. española** Spanish-speaking countries (**b**) *(facultad de hablar)* speech; **perder el h.** to lose one's power of speech; **quedarse sin h.** to be left speechless (**c**) *Tel (comunicación)* **¡al h.!** speaking!; **estar/ponerse al h. con algn** to be/get in touch with sb

habladas *nfpl Am* bragging *sing*, boasting *sing*

hablado, -a 1 *pp de* **hablar**

2 *adj* (**a**) *(dicho)* spoken; **bien h.** well-spoken, nicely spoken; **un chico muy bien h.** a well-spoken young man; **el inglés h.** spoken English; **mal h.** coarse, foul-mouthed; **¡qué mal h. eres!** what a wicked tongue (you've got)! (**b**) *(tratado, discutido)* dealt with; **eso ya está h.** that's been dealt with; **fue un asunto muy h.** it was a widely discussed subject

hablador, -a *adj* (**a**) *(parlanchín)* talkative; *Pey (chismoso)* gossipy, given to gossip (**b**) *Méx R Dom (mentiroso)* lying

habladuría *nf (rumor)* rumour, *US* rumor; *(chisme)* piece of gossip; **son habladurías de la gente** it's just idle gossip

hablante *nmf* speaker; **hay millones de hablantes de español** there are millions of Spanish speakers

hablar 1 *vi* (**a**) *(gen)* to speak, talk; **h. bien/mal de algn** to speak well/badly of sb; **h. claro** to speak plainly; **h. con** *o Am* **a algn** to speak to sb; **h. en nombre de algn** to speak on sb's behalf (**b**) *(mentar, tratar)* to mention; **hablaron de ir a París** they talked of going to Paris; **no se habló de ese tema** that subject wasn't mentioned; **no me hablaste de eso** you never mentioned that (**c**) *(murmurar)* to talk; **a la gente le gusta h.** people will talk; **estás dando que h.** you are making people talk (**d**) *(dar un tratamiento)* to call; **háblame de tú** call me John, Mary *etc* (**e**) *(locuciones)* **h. en broma** to be joking; **h. por h.** to talk for the sake of talking; **eso es h. por h.** take no notice; **¡ni h.!** certainly not!; **de eso ni h.** that's out of the question; **no se hable más de ello** and that's that; *Fig* **es como h. a la pared** I might as well be talking to myself; *Fam* **h. en cristiano** *o* **en plata** to speak plainly; *Fam* **h. por los codos** to be a chatterbox; *Fam* **¡quién fue a h.!** look who's talking!

2 *vt* (**a**) *(tratar un asunto)* to talk over, discuss; **tenemos que hablarlo con el jefe** we'd better talk to the boss (about it) (**b**) *(idioma)* to speak; **habla dos idiomas con soltura** she can speak two languages fluently

3 hablarse *vpr* (**a**) *(comunicarse)* to speak *o* talk to one another; **llevamos meses sin hablarnos** we haven't spoken for months; **no me hablo con el jefe** I don't speak to the boss, I'm not on speaking terms with the boss (**b**) *(correr el rumor)* **se habla de que ...** it's said that ..., there is

talk of ... (**c**) *(en letrero)* **'se habla español'** 'Spanish spoken here'

habón *nm* swelling *o* lump on the skin

hacedero, -a *adj* feasible, practicable, possible

hacedor, -a *nm,f* (**a**) *(creador)* maker; *Rel* **el H.** the Maker (**b**) *Perú (de licor)* = person who makes or sells corn liquor

hacendado, -a 1 *adj* landed

2 *nm,f* (**a**) *(terrateniente)* landowner (**b**) *CSur (ganadero)* rancher

hacendista *nmf* financial expert, tax consultant

hacendoso, -a *adj* house-proud, hardworking

hacer [33] *(pp* **hecho**) **1** *vt* (**a**) *(crear, producir, fabricar)* to make; **h. ruido** to make a noise; **h. sombra** to give shade; **h. un esfuerzo** to make an effort; **h. un poema** to write a poem; **h. una casa** to build a house (**b**) *(arreglar) (uñas)* to do; *(barba)* to trim; *(cama)* to make (**c**) *(obrar, ejecutar)* to do; **eso no se hace** you mustn't do that; **hazme un favor** do me a favour; **¿qué haces?** *(en este momento)* what are you doing?; *(para vivir)* what do you do (for a living)?; **tengo mucho que h.** I have a lot to do (**d**) *(conseguir) (amigos, dinero)* to make (**e**) *(obligar)* to make; **hazle callar/trabajar** make him shut up/work; **no me hagas esperar** don't keep me waiting (**f**) *(creer, suponer)* to think; **le hacía en París** I thought she was in Paris; **te hacía más joven** I thought you were younger (**g**) *(recorrer)* to do; **hice Madrid-París de un tirón** I did Madrid to Paris without stopping; **h. un recorrido de cinco kilómetros** to cover a distance of five kilometres (**h**) *Mat (sumar)* to make; **y con éste hacen cien** and that makes a hundred (**i**) *(ocupar un puesto)* to be; **hago el número seis en la lista** I'm number six on the list (**j**) *(dar aspecto)* to make look; **el negro lo hace más delgado** black makes him look slimmer; **estos pantalones te hacen gorda** these trousers make you look fat (**k**) *(acostumbrar)* to accustom; *Fig* **h. el cuerpo a** to get used to (**l**) *(comportarse como)* to act; **h. el imbécil** to act stupid; *Fam* **h. el indio** to fool around (**m**) *(sustituyendo a otro verbo)* to do; **se negó a ir y yo hice lo mismo** he refused to go and I did the same; **ya no puedo leer como solía hacerlo** I can't read as well as I used to (**n**) *(representar)* to play; **h. el bueno** to play the (part of the) goody (**o**) *(practicar)* to practise; *(pianista)* **h. dedos** to do finger exercises; *(deportista)* **h. piernas** to limber up (**p**) *(locuciones)* **eso está hecho** *(acabado)* that's finished; *(lleva poco tiempo)* that'll only take a minute, that won't take long; **h. burla de** to make fun of; **h. el ridículo** to act the fool; **h. gracia** to amuse; **h. pedazos** to ruin; **h. saber** to make known; **h. tiempo** to kill time; *Fam* **¡buena la has hecho!** you've done it now!; **ha hecho una de las suyas** she's/he's done it again, there she/he goes again

2 *vi* (**a**) *(actuar)* **h. de** to play; **hizo de Desdémona** she played Desdemona; **hizo de padre y madre** he acted as both father and mother (**b**) */h. por* o *para + infin) (procurar)* to try to; **haz por venir** try and come; **h. por h.** to do for the sake of doing (**c**) *(fingirse)* to pretend; **h. como** to act as; **h. algn como que no quiere** to act as though one is not interested; **haz como si no lo supieras** pretend you don't know (**d**) **h. bien/mal** to do the right/wrong thing; **haces mal en no hablar** you're wrong not to talk; **hice bien en ir** I was right to go at; **¡bien hecho!** well done! (**e**) *(servir)* **eso no hace al caso** that has nothing to do with it; **Pepe hace a todo** Pepe can turn his hand to anything (**f**) *(convenir)* to be suitable; **a las ocho si te hace** eight, if that's all right with you; **¿hace?** O.K.? (**g**) *(locuciones)* **a medio h.** half-finished, half-done; **¡así se hace!** that's it!; *Fig* **ser el que hace y deshace** to be the boss

3 *v impers* (**a**) *(clima)* **hace bueno** it's a fine day; **hace calor** it's hot; **no ha hecho verano** we haven't had any summer weather (**b**) *(tiempo transcurrido)* ago; **¿cuánto hace de eso?** how long ago was that?; **hace dos días que no le veo**

I haven't seen him for two days; **hace mucho/poco** a long/ short time ago; **ocurrió hace dos años** it happened two years ago

4 hacerse *vpr* (**a**) *(volverse)* to become; **h. sacerdote** to become a priest; **h. viejo** to grow old; **Paco se ha hecho a sí mismo** Paco's a selfmade man; **poeta no nace, se hace** poets aren't born, they are made (**b**) *(crecer)* to grow; **¡qué grande te has hecho!** haven't you grown! (**c**) *(resultar)* to become, get; **así se hace más fácil** it's easier that way; **la vuelta se me hizo más corta** the return journey felt quicker; **se me hizo imposible ayudarte** I couldn't help you (**d**) *(simular)* to pretend; **se hace el gracioso** he thinks he's funny; *Fig* **h. el sordo** to turn a deaf ear (**e**) *(apropiarse)* **h. con** to get hold of; **me hice con unos patines** I got myself a pair of skates (**f**) *(habituarse)* to get used (**a** to); **enseguida me hago a todo** I soon get used to anything (**g**) *(figurarse)* to imagine; **h. una idea de algo** to imagine sth; **no te hagas ilusiones** don't expect too much; **se me hace que va a llover** I think it's going to rain (**h**) *Náut* **h. a la mar** to put to sea (**i**) *(fabricar)* to make oneself; **me hice un vestido** I made myself a dress (**j**) *(mandar hacer)* to have made *o* built (**k**) *(arreglarse) (uñas)* to have a trim; **h. una permanente** to have a perm (**l**) *Esp muy Fam* **hacérselo con algn** *(tener relaciones sexuales)* to do it with sb, *Br* have it off with sb

hacha *nf* (**a**) *(herramienta)* axe, *US* ax (**b**) *Fam* **ser un h. en algo** to be an ace *o* a wizard at sth

hachazo *nm* blow with an axe, hack; **lo partió de un h.** he chopped it straight down the middle

hache *nf* aitch; *Fam* **¡llámalo h.!** call it what you like, it's all the same; *Fam* **por h. o por be** for one reason or another

hachemita *adj & nmf*, **hachemí** *adj & nmf* Hashemite

hachís [χa'tʃis] *nm* hashish

hacia *prep* (**a**) *(dirección)* towards, to; **h. abajo** down, downwards; **h. acá** this way; **h. adelante** forwards; **h. allá** that way; **h. arriba** up, upwards; **h. atrás** back, backwards; **sentir algo h. algn** to feel sth for *o* towards sb (**b**) *(tiempo)* at about, at around; **h. las tres** at about three o'clock

hacienda *nf* (**a**) *(finca agrícola)* estate, property, *US* ranch (**b**) *(bienes propios)* property, wealth (**c**) *Fin* Treasury; **Delegación de H.** ≃ local Inland Revenue office; **h. pública** public funds *o* finances *pl*; **Ministerio de H.** *Br* ≃ the Treasury, *US* ≃ the Department of the Treasury; **Ministro de H.** ≃ *Br* Chancellor of the Exchequer, *US* ≃ Secretary of the Treasury (**d**) *RP (ganadería)* livestock

hacinamiento *nm (de gente)* overcrowding; *(montón)* piling, heaping

hacinar 1 *vt (amontonar)* to pile up, heap up
  2 hacinarse *vpr (gente)* to be packed (**en** into)

hacker ['χaker] *(pl* **hackers**) *nmf Fam Inform* hacker

hada *nf* fairy ❑ **cuento de hadas** fairy tale; **h. madrina** fairy godmother

hado *nm* destiny, fate

hagiografía *nf* hagiography

hagiógrafo, -a *nm,f* hagiographer, hagiographist

hago *indic pres véase* **hacer**

Haití *n* Haiti

haitiano, -a *adj & nm,f* Haitian, Haytian

hala *interj Esp* (**a**) *(¡ánimo!)* come on! (**b**) *(¡vete!)* clear off!, get out! (**c**) *(¡deprisa!)* go on!, get moving! (**d**) *(¡qué exageración!)* come off it!

halagador, -a *adj* (**a**) *(lisonjero)* flattering (**b**) *(agradable)* gratifying

halagar [38] *vt* (**a**) *(lisonjear)* to flatter; **h. el amor propio** to flatter one's ego (**b**) *(agradar)* to please, gratify; **lo hizo para halagarte** she did it to please you

halago *nm* flattery, compliment

halagüeño, -a *adj* (**a**) *(halagador)* flattering; **en tono h.** flatteringly (**b**) *(prometedor)* promising, encouraging

halar *vt Am salvo RP Náut* to haul, pull

halcón *nm Orn* falcon ❑ **h. peregrino** peregrine (falcon)

halconería *nf* falconry

halconero, -a *nm,f* falconer

hale *interj Esp* get going!, get a move on!

hálito *nm* (**a**) *(aliento)* breath (**b**) *(vapor)* vapour, *US* vapor (**c**) *Literario* gentle breeze

halitosis *nf Med* halitosis

hall [χol] *(pl* **halls**) *nm* (entrance) hall, foyer

hallar 1 *vt (encontrar)* to find; *(averiguar)* to find out; *(descubrir)* to discover
  2 hallarse *vpr (estar)* to be, find oneself; **h. de viaje** to be away (on a trip); **h. presente** to be present

hallazgo *nm* (**a**) *(descubrimiento)* discovery, finding; **'h. de un cadáver'** 'body found'; **sensacional h. de ...** sensational find of ... (**b**) *(cosa encontrada)* find

halo *nm* halo, aura

halógeno, -a *Quím* **1** *adj* halogenous
  2 *nm* halogen

halterofilia *nf Dep* weightlifting

hamaca *nf* (**a**) *(para colgar)* hammock (**b**) *Esp (tumbona) (silla)* deck chair; *(canapé)* sunlounger (**c**) *RP (columpio)* swing (**d**) *RP (mecedora)* rocking chair

hamacar [59] *RP* **1** *vt (en columpio)* to swing, *(en cuna)* to rock
  2 hamacarse *vpr (en columpio)* to swing, *(en cuna)* to rock

hambre *nf* hunger, starvation, famine; **huelga de h.** hunger strike; **morirse de h.** to be starving; **nos están matando de h.** they are starving us to death; **pasar h.** to be hungry, go hungry; **tener h.** to be hungry; **Fig entretener el h.** to stave off hunger; *Fig* **h. y sed de justicia** hunger and thirst for justice; *Fig* **matar el h.** to kill (one's) hunger; *Fig* **sueldos de h.** starvation wages; *Fam* **es más listo que el h.** he's a cunning devil; *Fam Pey* **un muerto de h.** a good-for-nothing

hambriento, -a 1 *adj* (**a**) *(con hambre)* hungry, starving (**b**) *Fig (deseoso)* **h. de** hungry *o* longing for
  2 *nm,f* hungry *o* starving person; **los hambrientos** the hungry

hambruna *nf* famine

hamburguesa *nf* hamburger, burger; **h. de ternera** beefburger

hamburguesería *nf* hamburger joint

hampa *nf* underworld; **el h. barcelonesa** the Barcelona underworld

hampón, -ona 1 *adj* tough, rowdy
  2 *nm,f* tough, thug

hámster ['χamster] *(pl* **hámsters**) *nm Zool* hamster

hándicap ['χandikap] *(pl* **hándicaps**) *nm* handicap

hangar *nm Av* hangar

Hanoi *n* Hanoi

haragán, -ana 1 *adj* lazy, idle
  2 *nm,f* lazybones *inv,* idler

haraganear *vi* to idle, loaf around

harakiri [(χ)ara'kiri] *nm* hara-kiri

harapiento, -a *adj* ragged, in rags

harapo *nm* rag; **hecho un h.** in tatters

haraquiri [χara'kiri] *nm* harakiri

Harare *n* Harare

hardware ['χarwer] *nm Inform* hardware

haré *indic fut véase* **hacer**

harén *nm* harem

harina *nf* flour; *Fam* **eso es h. de otro costal** that's another kettle of fish ❑ **h. de maíz** cornflour, *US* cornstarch; **h. de pescado** fish meal; **h. de trigo** wheat flour; **h. lacteada** malted milk

harinoso, -a *adj* floury

harnero *nm* sieve

hartar 1 *vt* **(a)** *(atiborrar)* to satiate; **el dulce harta enseguida** sweet things soon fill you up **(b)** *(cansar, fastidiar)* to annoy, irritate; **me harta tanto viaje** I'm fed up with all this coming and going; **me hartan los niños** children get on my nerves **(c)** *(llenar)* to overwhelm **(de** with); **le hartaron a golpes** they beat him up; **le hartó a besos** she covered him with kisses

2 hartarse *vpr* **(a)** *(saciar el apetito)* to eat one's fill; **comer hasta h.** to eat oneself sick; **dormir hasta h.** to have one's fill of sleep **(b)** *(cansarse)* to get fed up **(de** with), grow tired **(de** of); **me harto de repetírselo** I'm tired of telling him; **me he hartado de ti** I've had enough of you **(c)** *(de hacer algo)* to do nothing but; **me harté de ver cine** I did nothing but to go the pictures

hartazgo *nm* bellyful; **darse un h. de ...** to stuff oneself with ...

harto, -a 1 *adj* **(a)** *(repleto)* full **(b)** *(cansado)* tired **(de** of), fed up **(de** with); **estoy h. de ser amable con él** I'm tired of being nice to him; **¡me tienes h.!** I'm fed up with you!; **¡ya estoy h.!** I'm fed up!, I'm sick and tired of it!

2 *adv* **(a)** *Esp Fml (muy)* extremely; **es h. frecuente** it's extremely common **(b)** *Am salvo RP (muy)* very, really; *(mucho)* a lot, very much

hartón *nm Esp véase* **hartazgo**

hartura *nf* **(a)** *(hartazgo)* bellyful **(b)** *(abundancia)* plenty, abundance, glut; **tengo tal h. de libros que ...** I've read so many books that ...; **¡qué h.!** what a drag! **(c)** *Fig (de deseo)* fulfilment, *US* fulfillment

hasta 1 *prep* **(a)** *(lugar)* up to, as far as, down to; **¿h. dónde vamos a llegar?** where will it end? **(b)** *(tiempo)* until, till, up to; **h. el domingo** until Sunday; **h. el final** right to the end; **h. junio** until June; **h. la fecha** up to now; **¡h. la vista!** cheerio!, see you!, *US* so long!; **¡h. luego!** see you later!; **no me iré h. no verlo** I won't go until I've seen him **(c)** *(indica cantidad)* up to, as many as; **cabemos h. seis en el ascensor** the lift will take up to six people; **cuenta h. diez** count to ten **(d)** *(incluso)* even; **h. yo lo entiendo** even I can understand it

2 *conj* **h. que** until; **esperaré h. que se vaya** I'll wait until he goes

hastiado, -a 1 *pp de* **hastiar**

2 *adj* disgusted **(de** with), sick **(de** of)

hastial *nm Arquit* gable (end)

hastiar [32] *vt* to weary, sicken

hastío *nm* **(a)** *(repugnancia)* loathing, disgust **(b)** *Fig (tedio)* boredom, weariness

hatajo *nm* **(a)** *(rebaño)* small herd *o* flock **(b)** *Esp Fig Pey* heap, lot, bunch; **un h. de disparates** a load of nonsense; **un h. de ladrones** a gang of thieves; **un h. de mentiras** a pack of lies

hatillo *nm* small bundle

hato *nm* **(a)** *(de ropa, enseres)* bundle; *Fig* **liar el h.** to pack one's bags, get ready to go **(b)** *(rebaño)* herd, flock **(c)** *Carib Col Fam (hacienda)* cattle ranch

Hawai [χa'wai] *n* Hawaii

hawaiano, -a [χawai'ano] *adj & nm,f* Hawaiian

Haya *n* **La H.** The Hague

haya¹ *nf* **(a)** *Bot (árbol)* beech ❑ **h. cobriza** copper beech **(b)** *(madera)* beech (wood)

haya² 1 *subj pres véase* **haber**

2 *imperat véase* **haber**

haz¹ *nm* **(a)** *(de cosas)* bundle; *Agr* sheaf **(b)** *(de luz)* shaft, beam

haz² *nf (cara)* face

haz³ *imperat véase* **hacer**

hazaña *nf* deed, exploit, heroic feat

hazmerreír *nm* laughing stock; **es el h. de la clase** he's the laughing stock of the class

he¹ *adv* **he ahí/aquí ...** there/here you have ...; **he ahí la cuestión** that's the question; **he aquí el problema** this is the problem; **heme/hete aquí** here I am/you are; **heme aquí listo para empezar** here I am ready to start

he² 1 *indic pres véase* **haber**

2 *imperat véase* **haber**

heavy ['χeβi] **1** *adj* **(a)** *Mús* heavy **(b)** *Fam* **¡qué h.!** *(increíble)* (that's) wicked!; *(terrible)* (what a) bummer!

2 *nmf Mús Fam (persona)* heavy metal fan

3 *nm Mús* heavy metal; **h. metal** heavy metal

hebdomadario, -a *adj Prensa* weekly

hebilla *nf* buckle

hebra *nf* *(de hilo)* thread, piece of thread; *Fig* thread; *(de legumbres)* string; *(de carne)* sinew; *(de madera)* grain; *Min (veta)* vein; **pegar la h.** to chat

hebraico, -a *adj* Hebraic, Hebraical, Hebrew

hebraísta *nmf* Hebraist

hebreo, -a 1 *adj* Hebrew

2 *nm,f* Hebrew

3 *nm (idioma)* Hebrew; *Fam* **jurar en h.** to curse and swear

Hébridas *npl* **las (Islas) H.** the Hebrides

hecatombe *nf* **(a)** *Hist* hecatomb **(b)** *(catástrofe)* disaster, catastrophe

hechicería *nf (arte)* witchcraft, sorcery; *(hechizo)* spell, charm

hechicero, -a 1 *adj* bewitching, charming

2 *nm,f (hombre)* wizard, sorcerer; *(mujer)* witch, sorceress

hechizar [14] *vt* **(a)** *(embrujar)* to cast a spell on **(b)** *Fig (fascinar)* to bewitch, charm

hechizo, -a 1 *adj Am (local)* local; *(cosa)* **h. de Méjico** made in Mexico; *(comida)* **producto h.** home-produced

2 *nm* **(a)** *(embrujo)* spell, charm **(b)** *Fig (fascinación)* fascination, charm

hecho, -a 1 *pp de* **hacer**

2 *adj* **(a)** *(llevado a cabo)* made, done; **¡bien h.!** well done!; **eso está h.** that's a sure thing; **está h. un sinvergüenza** he's a cheeky devil; **¡h.!** done!, agreed!; **h. a mano** handmade; **h. a máquina** machine-made; **lo h. h. está** what's done is done; **se puso h. una fiera** he went up the wall, he went mad; *Fam* **a lo h. pecho** as you make your bed, so you must lie on it *o* it's no use crying over spilt milk; *Fam* **dicho y h.** no sooner said than done **(b)** *(carne)* done; **muy h.** *(demasiado)* overdone; *(sin sangre)* well-cooked; **poco h.** *(no suficientemente)* underdone; *(con sangre)* rare **(c)** *(persona)* mature; **un hombre h. y derecho** a real man **(d)** *(frase)* set; *(ropa)* ready-made

3 *nm* **(a)** *(realidad)* fact; **de h.** in fact; **el h. es que ...** the fact is that ... **(b)** *(acto)* act, deed; **h. consumado** fait accompli; *Mil* **h. de armas** feat of arms; *Rel* **Hechos de los Apóstoles** Acts of the Apostles; **hechos son amores** actions speak louder than words **(c)** *(suceso)* event, incident; **el h. tuvo lugar en ...** the incident took place in ...; *Jur* **el lugar de los hechos** the scene of the crime *o* incident; **relato de los hechos acontecidos** account of events

hechura *nf* **(a)** *(forma)* shape; *(corte)* cut **(b)** *(elaboración)* making (**c**) *Fml (obra)* creation, product; **h. de Dios** God's creature

hectárea *nf* hectare

hectolitro *nm* hectolitre, *US* hectoliter

hectómetro *nm* hectometre

heder [64] *vi* (**a**) *(apestar)* to stink, smell foul (**b**) *Fig (fastidiar)* to annoy

hediondez *nf* stink, stench

hediondo, -a *adj* (**a**) *(apestoso)* stinking, foul-smelling, smelly (**b**) *Fig (asqueroso)* repulsive, filthy (**c**) *Fig (molesto)* annoying

hedonismo *nm Filos* hedonism

hedonista *Filos* **1** *adj* hedonistic, hedonic
  2 *nmf* hedonist

hedor *nm* stink, stench

hegeliano, -a [χege'liano] *adj Filos* Hegelian

hegemonía *nf* hegemony

hegemónico, -a *adj (dominante)* dominant; *(clase, partido)* ruling

hégira *nf,* **héjira** *nf* Hegira, Hejira

helada *nf Meteor* frost, freeze; **caer una h.** to freeze ◻ **h. blanca** hoarfrost, white frost

heladera *nf* (**a**) *CSur (nevera)* refrigerator (**b**) *(de helados)* ice-cream machine

heladería *nf* ice-cream parlour

heladero, -a *nm,f* ice-cream seller

helado, -a 1 *pp de* helar
  2 *adj* (**a**) *(muy frío)* frozen, freezing cold; **estoy h. (de frío)** I'm frozen (**b**) *Fig (atónito)* **quedarse h.** to be flabbergasted; **me dejó h.** I couldn't believe it!
  3 *nm* ice cream

helador, -a *adj* icy, freezing; **viento h.** icy wind

helar [3] **1** *vt* (**a**) *(congelar)* to freeze (**b**) *(planta)* to kill by frost
  2 *v impers Meteor* to freeze; **anoche heló** there was a frost last night
  3 helarse *vpr* (**a**) *(congelarse)* to freeze; **se heló el río** the river froze over (**b**) *(planta)* to die from frost (**c**) *(persona)* to freeze to death; **nos vamos a helar** we'll freeze to death; *Fig* **se me heló la sangre** my blood ran cold

helecho *nm Bot* fern, bracken

helénico, -a *adj Hist* Hellenic, Greek

helenismo *nm Hist* Hellenism

helenístico, -a *adj Hist* Hellenistic, Hellenistical

hélice *nf* (**a**) *Av Náut* propeller (**b**) *Anat Arquit Mat* helix

helicoidal *adj* helicoid, spiral

helicóptero *nm Av* helicopter

helio *nm Quím* helium

heliocéntrico, -a *adj Astron* heliocentric

heliotropo *nm Bot* heliotrope

helipuerto *nm Av* heliport

Helsinki *n* Helsinki

Helvecia *n* Helvetia

helvético, -a *adj & nm,f* Helvetian, Swiss

hematíe *nm* red blood corpuscle

hematología *nf Med* haematology, *US* hematology

hematológico, -a *adj* haematological, *US* hematological

hematólogo, -a *nm,f Med* haematologist, *US* hematologist

hematoma *nm Med* haematoma, *US* hematoma, bruise

hembra *nf* (**a**) *Bot Zool* female (**b**) *(mujer)* woman; **una real h.** a fine figure of a woman (**c**) *Téc* female; *(de tornillo)* nut; *(de enchufe)* socket

hembraje *nm Andes RP Agr* female flock o herd

hemeroteca *nf* newspaper library

hemiciclo *nm* (**a**) *(semicírculo)* hemicycle (**b**) *Parl* floor

hemiplejía *nf,* **hemiplejia** *nf* hemiplegia

hemipléjico, -a *adj & nm,f* hemiplegic

hemisférico, -a *adj* hemispheric, hemispherical

hemisferio *nm* hemisphere ◻ **h. norte/sur** northern/ southern hemisphere

hemodiálisis *nf inv* kidney dialysis

hemofilia *nf Med* haemophilia, *US* hemophilia

hemofílico, -a *Med* **1** *adj* haemophilic, *US* hemophilic
  2 *nm,f* haemophiliac, *US* hemophiliac

hemoglobina *nf* haemoglobin, *US* hemoglobin

hemorragia *nf Med* haemorrhage, *US* hemorrhage

hemorrágico, -a *adj* haemorrhagic, *US* hemorrhagic

hemorroides *nfpl Med* haemorrhoids, *US* hemorrhoids

hemos *indic pres véase* haber

henar *nm Agr* loft

henchido, -a *adj* bloated; *Fig* **h. de orgullo** bursting with pride

henchir [47] **1** *vt (llenar)* to stuff, fill, cram; **h. los pulmones de aire fresco** to fill one's lungs with fresh air; *Fig* **henchido de orgullo** swollen with pride
  2 henchirse *vpr (de comida)* to stuff oneself

hender [64] *vt* (**a**) *(resquebrajar)* to crack, cleave, split; *Fig (olas)* to cut (**b**) *Fig (abrirse paso)* to make one's way through

hendido, -a 1 *pp de* hender
  2 *adj* split (open)

hendidura *nf* cleft, crack

hendir [62] *vt véase* hender

heno *nm* hay

hepático, -a *adj* hepatic

hepatitis *nf inv Med* hepatitis

heptagonal *adj* heptagonal

heptágono *nm* heptagon

heráldica *nf* heraldry

heráldico, -a *adj* heraldic

heraldo *nm Hist* herald

herbáceo, -a *adj* herbaceous

herbario 1 *adj* herbal
  2 *nm* (**a**) *(colección)* herbarium (**b**) *(botánico)* herbalist

herbicida *nm* weedkiller, herbicide

herbívoro, -a 1 *adj* herbivorous, grass-eating
  2 *nm,f Zool* herbivore

herbolario, -a 1 *adj Fam Fig* crazy, idiotic
  2 *nm,f (persona)* herbalist
  3 *nm (tienda)* herbalist's (shop)

herboristería *nf* herbalist's (shop)

herboso, -a *adj* grassy

hercio *nm Fís* hertz

hercúleo, -a *adj* Herculean

hércules *nm inv* ox, very strong man

heredad *nf* (**a**) *(finca)* country estate (**b**) *(conjunto de bienes)* private estate

heredado, -a 1 *pp de* heredar
  2 *adj* inherited

heredar *vt* (**a**) *Jur* to inherit; **h. los bienes de algn** to inherit from sb; **esto lo heredé de ...** this came to me from ... (**b**) *Biol (de los padres)* **ha heredado la sonrisa de su madre** she's got her mother's smile

heredero, -a *nm,f (hombre)* heir; *(mujer)* heiress; **h. único** sole heir; **nombrar a algn h.** to make sb one's heir ▫ **príncipe h.** crown prince

hereditario, -a *adj* hereditary

hereje *nmf Rel* heretic

herejía *nf* (**a**) *Rel* heresy (**b**) *Fig (disparate)* ¡**qué h.!** what nonsense!

herencia *nf* (**a**) *Jur* inheritance, legacy (**b**) *Biol* heredity

herético, -a *adj* heretical

herida *nf* (**a**) *(lesión)* wound (**b**) *Fig (pena)* wound, outrage; **lamerse las heridas** to lick one's wounds; **tocar a algn en la h.** to touch sb's sore spot

herido, -a 1 *pp de* **herir**
2 *adj (físicamente)* wounded, injured; *(emocionalmente)* hurt; **caer h.** to be wounded; **h. de gravedad** badly injured; **resultó h. el conductor del camión** the lorry driver was injured; **sentirse h.** to feel hurt
3 *nm,f* wounded o injured person; **no hubo heridos** there were no casualties

herir [62] **1** *vt* (**a**) *(causar heridas a)* to wound, injure, hurt; *Fig* **h. a algn en lo vivo** to cut sb to the quick; *Fig* **h. a algn en su amor propio** to wound sb's pride (**b**) *(golpear)* to beat, hit (**c**) *(vista)* to offend; *(luz)* to dazzle; *(sonido)* to strike
2 herirse *vpr* to injure o hurt oneself; **se ha herido con un cuchillo** he cut himself with a knife

hermafrodita *adj & nmf* hermaphrodite

hermanado, -a 1 *pp de* **hermanar**
2 *adj (semejante)* similar, alike (**b**) *(unido)* joined, united (**c**) *(ciudad)* twin

hermanamiento *nm (unión)* union; *(de ciudades)* twinning

hermanar 1 *vt (unir)* to unite, combine (**b**) *(dos personas)* to unite spiritually (**c**) *(ciudades)* to twin
2 hermanarse *vpr* (**a**) *(combinar)* to combine (**b**) *(dos personas)* to become brothers o sisters in spirit

hermanastro, -a *nm,f (hombre)* stepbrother; *(mujer)* stepsister

hermandad *nf* (**a**) *(grupo)* fraternity, brotherhood, sisterhood; **h. de labradores** farmers' association (**b**) *(relación)* brotherhood; *Fig* close relationship

hermano, -a 1 *adj* (closely) related; **ciudades hermanas** twin towns; **conceptos hermanos** related concepts
2 *nm* (**a**) *(pariente)* brother ▫ **h. gemelo** twin brother; **h. político** brother-in-law; **primo h.** first cousin (**b**) *Rel (fraile)* brother (**c**) **hermanos** brothers and sisters; **eran muchos hermanos** there were a lot of children in the family
3 *nf* (**a**) *(pariente)* sister ▫ **h. gemela** twin sister; **h. política** sister-in-law; **prima h.** first cousin (**b**) *Rel (monja)* sister

hermenéutica *nf* hermeneutics *sing*

hermenéutico, -a *adj* hermeneutic

herméticamente *adv* hermetically; **h. cerrado** hermetically sealed

hermético, -a *adj* (**a**) *(al aire)* hermetic, hermetical, airtight; **cierre h.** hermetic seal, airtight lid (**b**) *Fig* impenetrable, secretive; **persona hermética** secretive person, very reserved person; **un escritor h.** an abstruse writer

hermetismo *nm* hermetism; *Fig* impenetrability, secrecy, secretiveness

hermosear *vt* to beautify, embellish

hermoso, -a *adj* beautiful, lovely

hermosura *nf* beauty; ¡**qué h. de niño!** what a beautiful child!

hernia *nf Med* hernia, rupture

herniado, -a *Med* **1** *pp de* **herniarse**
2 *adj Med* ruptured

herniarse *vpr Med* to rupture oneself

Herodes *nm* Herod; **ir de H. a Pilatos** to go from pillar to post

héroe *nm* hero

heroicidad *nf* (**a**) *(cualidad)* heroism (**b**) *(hecho)* heroic deed

heroico, -a *adj* (**a**) *(del héroe)* heroic; **tiempos heroicos** *(difíciles)* hard times; *(de gestas)* times of heroic deeds (**b**) *Lit* heroic

heroína *nf* (**a**) *(mujer)* heroine (**b**) *(droga)* heroin

heroinomanía *nf* heroin addiction

heroinómano, -a *nm,f* heroin addict

heroísmo *nm* heroism

herpe *nm*, **herpes** *nm Med* herpes *sing*, shingles *sing*

herpético, -a *adj Med* herpetic

herrador *nm* blacksmith

herradura *nf* horseshoe; **en forma de h.** horseshoe-shaped

herraje *nm* iron fittings *pl*, ironwork

herramienta *nf Téc* tool

herrar [3] *vt* (**a**) *(caballo)* to shoe (**b**) *(ganado)* to brand

herrería *nf* forge, smithy, blacksmith's

herrero *nm* (**a**) *(herrador)* blacksmith, smith (**b**) *Am (de caballos)* horseshoer

herrete *nm (metálico)* tag, metal tip

herrumbrarse *vpr* to rust, go rusty

herrumbre *nf* (**a**) *(óxido)* rust (**b**) *(sabor a hierro)* rusty taste

herrumbroso, -a *adj* rusty

hertz [χerts] *(pl* **hertzs**) *nm Fís véase* **hercio**

hertziano, -a *adj Fís* Hertzian; **onda hertziana** Hertzian wave

hervidero *nm* (**a**) *(ebullición)* boiling, bubbling (**b**) *(manantial)* hot spring (**c**) *Fig (lugar)* hotbed; **un h. de intrigas** a nest of intrigue; **un h. de pasiones** a hotbed of passion (**d**) *Fig (muchedumbre)* swarm, throng; **ser un h. de** to be swarming with

hervidor *nm (para agua)* kettle; *(para leche)* milk pan

hervir [62] **1** *vt (hacer bullir)* to boil
2 *vi* (**a**) *(bullir)* to boil; **romper a h.** to come to the boil (**b**) *(mar)* to surge (**c**) *(abundar)* to swarm, seethe (**de** with); **el mercado hervía de gente** the market was teeming with people (**d**) *(ira)* to seethe (**de, en** with); **h. en cólera** to seethe with anger; **h. en deseos de** to be consumed with

hervor *nm* boiling, bubbling; *Culin* **dar un h. a algo** to blanch sth

heteróclito, -a *adj* (**a**) *Ling* heteroclite (**b**) *Fml Fig* heterogeneous, irregular

heterodoxia *nf* heterodoxy

heterodoxo, -a 1 *adj* heterodox, unorthodox
2 *nm,f* heterodox person

heterogeneidad *nf* heterogeneity, heterogeneousness

heterogéneo, -a *adj* heterogeneous

heterosexual *adj & nmf* heterosexual

heterosexualidad *nf* heterosexuality

hexadecimal *adj Inform* hexadecimal

hexaedro *nm* hexahedron, cube

hexagonal *adj* hexagonal

hexágono *nm* hexagon

hexámetro *nm* hexameter

hez *nf* (**a**) *(gen pl) (poso)* sediment, dregs *pl* (**b**) *Fig* scum; *Pey* **la h. de la sociedad** the scum *o* dregs of society (**c**) **heces** *(excrementos)* faeces

hg *(abrev de* **hectogramo***)* hg

hiato *nm Ling* hiatus

hibernación *nf* hibernation

hibernar *vi* to hibernate

hibisco *nm Bot* hibiscus

híbrido, -a *adj & nm,f* hybrid

hice *pt indef véase* **hacer**

hico *nm Carib Col Pan* = cord for suspending a hammock

hidalgo, -a 1 *adj Antes (noble)* noble; *(caballeroso)* gentlemanly
  2 *nm Hist* nobleman, gentleman

hidalguía *nf* nobility; *Fig* chivalry, gentlemanliness

hidra *nf* (**a**) *(culebra acuática)* sea snake (**b**) *(pólipo)* hydra

hidratación *nf* (**a**) *Quím* hydration (**b**) *(de la piel)* moisturizing

hidratado, -a 1 *pp de* **hidratar**
  2 *adj* (**a**) *(piel)* moist (**b**) *Quím* hydrated

hidratante *adj* moisturizing

hidratar *vt* (**a**) *(piel)* to moisturize (**b**) *Quím* to hydrate

hidrato *nm Quím* hydrate □ **h. de carbono** carbohydrate

hidráulica *nf* hydraulics *pl*, fluid mechanics *pl*

hidráulico, -a *adj* hydraulic

hídrico, -a *adj* hydric

hidro- *pref* hydro-

hidroavión *nm* seaplane, *US* hydroplane

hidrocarburo *nm Quím* hydrocarbon

hidrocefalia *nf Med* hydrocephalus, hydrocephaly

hidrodinámica *nf* hydrodynamics *sing*

hidrodinámico, -a *adj* hydrodynamic

hidroeléctrico, -a *adj* hydroelectric

hidrófilo *adj* (**a**) *Bot* hydrophilous (**b**) *(absorbente)* absorbent □ **algodón h.** *Br* cotton wool, *US* cotton

hidrofobia *nf Med* hydrophobia, rabies *sing*

hidrófobo, -a *adj* hydrophobic, rabid

hidrófugo, -a *adj (contra filtraciones)* waterproof; *(contra humedad)* damp-proof

hidrógeno *nm Quím* hydrogen

hidrografía *nf* hydrography

hidrográfico, -a *adj* hydrographic

hidrólisis *nf Quím* hydrolysis

hidrolizado, -a *adj* hydrolyzed

hidrología *nf* hydrology

hidrológico, -a *adj* hydrologic, hydrological; **un plan h.** a plan for managing water resources

hidromasaje *nm* whirlpool bath, Jacuzzi®

hidromecánico, -a *adj* hydrodynamic, water-powered

hidrometría *nf* hydrometry

hidropesía *nf Med* dropsy

hidrópico, -a *Med adj* dropsical, dropsied

hidroplano *nm* (**a**) *(barco)* hydrofoil (**b**) *(avión)* seaplane

hidrosfera *nf* hydrosphere

hidrostática *nf* hydrostatics *sing*

hidrostático, -a *adj* hydrostatic

hidroterapia *nf Med* hydrotherapy

hidrovía *nf Am* waterway

hidróxido *nm* hydroxide

hiedra *nf Bot* ivy

hiel *nf* (**a**) *Anat* bile (**b**) *Fig* bitterness, gall

hielera *nf CSur Méx* cool box, cooler

hielo *nm* ice; *Fig* **romper el h.** to break the ice

hiena *nf Zool* hyaena, hyena

hierático, -a *adj* (**a**) *Hist* hieratic, hieratical (**b**) *(severo, rígido)* rigid

hierba *nf* (**a**) *(planta)* grass; **mala h.** *Bot* weed; *Fig (persona)* bad lot; *Fig* **mala h. nunca muere** ill weeds grow apace; *Fam Hum* **... y otras hierbas** ... among others (**b**) *Culin* herb □ **finas hierbas** mixed herbs; **h. luisa** lemon verbena; **h. mate** maté (**c**) **hierbas** *(veneno)* poison *sing*, potion *sing* (**d**) *Argot (marihuana)* grass

hierbabuena *nf Bot* mint

hierro *nm* (**a**) *(metal)* iron; *Fig* **ser de h.** to be as strong as an ox; *Fig* **voluntad de h.** a will of iron; *Fam Fig* **quitarle h. a un asunto** to play a matter down; *Prov* **quien a h. mata, a h. muere** he who lives by the sword, shall die by the sword □ **h. colado** cast iron; **h. forjado** wrought iron; **h. fundido** wrought iron (**b**) *(punta de arma)* head, point (**c**) *(marca en el ganado)* brand

hi-fi ['ifi] *nf (abrev de* **high fidelity***)* hi-fi

higa *nf* scorn, derision

higadillo *nm (gen pl)* liver; **higadillos de pollo** chicken livers

hígado *nm* (**a**) *Anat* liver; *Fam* **echar los hígados** to go flat out (**b**) *Euf* guts *pl*; **tener hígados** to have guts

higiene *nf* hygiene

higiénico, -a *adj* hygienic □ **papel h.** toilet paper

higienista *nmf* hygienist

higo *nm Bot* fig; *Fig* **de higos a brevas** once in a blue moon; *Fam* **me importa un h.** I couldn't care less; *Fam* **¡y un h.!** not on your life!, nothing doing!; *Fam Fig* **hecho un h.** wizened, crumpled □ **h. chumbo** prickly pear

higuera *nf Bot* fig tree; *Fig* **estar en la h.** to have one's head in the clouds □ **h. chumba** prickly pear

hija *nf* daughter; **h. adoptiva** adopted daughter; **h. mía** darling; **hijas** daughters; **h. única** only daughter; *Pey* **h. de papá** daddy's girl; *Vulg Ofens* **h. de puta** bastard; *véase tamb* **hijo**

hijastro, -a *nm,f (hombre)* stepson; *(mujer)* stepdaughter

hijo *nm* (**a**) *(descendiente)* son, child; **h. adoptivo** adopted child; **h. mío** son, my boy; **h. único** only son; *Fam* **¡h. de mi alma!** my dearest child!; *Fam* **todo h. de vecino** everyone, every mother's son; *Fam Euf* **un h. de tal** a real so-and-so; *Pey* **h. de papá** daddy's boy, rich kid; *Vulg Ofens* **h. de puta** o *Méx* **de la chingada** bastard, son of a bitch (**b**) **hijos** children (**c**) *Fig* brainchild

híjole *interj*, **híjoles** *interj Méx* wow!

hijoputa *nm Vulg Ofens* bastard

hilado, -a 1 *pp de* **hilar**
  2 *adj* spun
  3 *nm* (**a**) *(acción de hilar)* spinning (**b**) *(fibra textil)* spun textile; **fábrica de hilados** spinning mill; **tejidos de h.** spun textiles (**c**) *(hilo)* thread

hilador, -a *nm,f* spinner

hiladora *nf* spinning machine

hilandería *nf* mill; *(de algodón)* cotton mill

hilandero, -a *nm,f* spinner

hilar *vt & vi* (**a**) *(gen)* to spin (**b**) *Fig (idea, plan)* to work out; **h. muy fino** o **delgado** to split hairs

hilarante *adj* hilarious; **gas h.** laughing gas

hilaridad *nf* hilarity, mirth

hilatura *nf* (**a**) *(fábrica)* spinning mill (**b**) *(acción de hilar)* spinning

hilera *nf* line, row; **en h.** in line

hilo *nm* (**a**) thread; *(grueso)* yarn; **cortar al h.** to cut on the grain ❑ **h. dental** dental floss (**b**) *Fig (curso) (historia, discurso)* thread; *(de pensamiento)* train; **coger el h.** to catch *o* get the drift; **estar colgando** *o* **pendiente de un h.** to be hanging by a thread; **perder el h.** to lose the thread; **seguir el h.** to follow the thread (**c**) *Tex* linen; **mantel de h.** linen tablecloth (**d**) *Tel* wire (**e**) *(chorro fino)* trickle, thin stream; *Fig* **un h. de voz** a tiny voice (**f**) *Mús* **h. musical** piped music

hilván *nm Cost* (**a**) *(costura)* Br tacking, *US* basting (**b**) *(hilo)* Br tacking stitch, *US* basting stitch

hilvanar *vt* (**a**) *Cost* Br to tack, *US* baste (**b**) *Fig (bosquejar ideas etc)* to throw together

Himalaya *n* el H. the Himalayas *pl*

himen *nm Anat* hymen

himeneo *nm Lit* (**a**) *(boda)* wedding, marriage (**b**) *(epitamio)* marriage ode

himno *nm* hymn ❑ **h. nacional** national anthem

hincapié *nm* **hacer h. en** *(insistir)* to insist on; *(subrayar)* to emphasize, stress

hincar [59] **1** *vt* (**a**) *(clavar)* to drive (in); **h. el diente a** to sink one's teeth into (**b**) *Argot* **hincarla** to work; **no la hinca en todo el día** he doesn't do a scrap of work all day
2 hincarse *vpr* **h. de rodillas** to kneel (down)

hincha *Fam* **1** *nf (antipatía)* grudge, dislike; **tener h. a algn** to have it in for sb, bear a grudge against sb; **me tiene h.** he's got it in for me
2 *nmf* (**a**) *Ftb* fan, supporter (**b**) *RP Fam (fastidioso, pesado)* pain, bore

hinchable *adj* inflatable

hinchada *nf Ftb Fam* fans *pl*, supporters *pl*

hinchado, -a 1 *pp de* **hinchar**
2 *adj* (**a**) *(gen)* inflated, blown up (**b**) *Med (cara etc)* swollen, puffed up; *(estómago)* bloated; **me siento h.** I feel bloated (**c**) *Fig (persona)* conceited; *(estilo)* bombastic, pompous

hinchar 1 *vt* (**a**) *(inflar)* to inflate, blow up (**b**) *Fig (exagerar)* to inflate, exaggerate
2 hincharse *vpr* (**a**) *Med* to swell (up); **se me hinchan los tobillos** my ankles swell up (**b**) *Fam (hartarse)* to stuff oneself; **me hinché de llorar** I cried for all I was worth (**c**) *(engreírse)* to become conceited *o* bigheaded (**d**) *Fam (enriquecerse)* to make a packet, line one's pockets

hinchazón *nf* (**a**) *Med* swelling (**b**) *Fig (presunción)* vanity, conceit; *(pomposidad)* pomposity, pompousness

hindi *nm* Hindi

hindú (*pl* **hindúes**) *adj & nmf* Hindu

hinduismo *nm* Hinduism

hiniesta *nf Bot* broom

hinojo¹ *nm Bot* fennel

hinojo² *nm Literario* **postrarse de hinojos** to kneel (down)

hip *interj (hipido)* hic!; **¡h.! ¡h.! ¡hurra!** hip, hip, hooray!

hipar *vi* (**a**) *(tener hipo)* to hiccup, hiccough, have the hiccups *o* hiccoughs (**b**) *Fam (desear con ansia)* **h. por algo** to yearn *o* long for sth (**c**) *(lloriquear)* to whine, whimper

híper *nm inv Fam* hypermarket

hiper- *pref Fam (muy)* mega-; **me ha salido hipercaro** it was mega-expensive; **¡es higuapo!** he's a real dish!

hiperactividad *nf* hyperactivity

hiperactivo, -a *adj* hyperactive

hipérbaton (*pl* **hipérbatos** *o* **hiperbatones**) *nm Lit* hyperbaton

hipérbole *nf Lit* hyperbole, exaggeration

hiperbólico, -a *adj Lit* hyperbolic

hipercrítico, -a *adj* hypercritical

hiperenlace *nf Inform* hyperlink

hipermercado *nm* hypermarket

hipermétrope *Med* **1** *adj* long-sighted
2 *nmf* long-sighted person

hipermetropía *nf Med* long-sightedness, *Espec* hypermetropia, *US* hypertropia

hiperrealismo *nm Arte* hyperrealism

hiperrealista *adj & nmf Arte* hyperrealist

hipersensibilidad *nf* hypersensitivity (**a** to)

hipersensible *adj* hypersensitive

hipertensión *nf Med* high blood pressure

hipertenso, -a 1 *adj* with high blood pressure
2 *nm,f* person with high blood pressure

hipertexto *nm Inform* hypertext

hipertextual *adj Inform* **enlace h.** hypertext link

hipertrofia *nf Med* hypertrophy; *Fig (de organización)* overexpansion

hípica *nf (carreras de caballos)* horseracing; *(equitación)* showjumping

hípico, -a *adj* horse, equine; **club h.** riding club; **concurso h.** horse race; **sociedad hípica** racecourse

hipido *nm* hiccup, hiccough

hipismo *nm* horse racing

hipnosis *nf inv* hypnosis

hipnótico, -a *adj* hypnotic

hipnotismo *nm* hypnotism

hipnotizador, -a 1 *adj* hypnotizing
2 *nm,f* hypnotist

hipnotizar [14] *vt* to hypnotize

hipo *nm* (**a**) *(movimiento compulsivo)* hiccup, hiccough; **me ha dado el h.** it's given me hiccups, I've got the hiccups; **quitar el h.** to cure hiccups (**b**) *(deseo)* longing; **tener h. por algo** to be longing for sth

hipoalergénico, -a *adj* hypoallergenic

hipocalórico, -a *adj (alimento, dieta)* low-calorie

hipocampo *nm (pez)* sea horse

hipocondría *nf* hypochondria

hipocondríaco, -a *adj & nm,f,* **hipocondriaco, -a** *adj & nm,f* hypochondriac

hipocrático, -a *adj* **juramento h.** Hippocratic oath

hipocresía *nf* hypocrisy

hipócrita 1 *adj* hypocritical
2 *nmf* hypocrite

hipodérmico, -a *adj* hypodermic

hipódromo *nm* racetrack, racecourse

hipófisis *nf inv* pituitary gland

hipoglucemia *nf* hypoglycaemia, *US* hypoglycemia

hipopótamo *nm Zool* hippopotamus

hipotálamo *nm Anat* hypothalamus

hipoteca *nf* (**a**) *Fin* mortgage (**b**) *Fig (desventaja)* drawback

hipotecable *adj* mortgageable

hipotecar [59] *vt* (**a**) *Fin* to mortgage (**b**) *Fig* to jeopardize

hipotecario, -a *adj Fin* mortgage; **crédito h.** mortgage loan

hipotensión *nf Med* low blood pressure

hipotenso, -a 1 *adj* with low blood pressure
2 *nm,f* person with low blood pressure

hipotensor *nm* hypotensive drug

hipotenusa *nf Geom* hypotenuse

hipótesis *nf inv* hypothesis; **h. de trabajo** work thesis

hipotético, -a *adj* hypothetical, hypothetic

hippy ['χipi] (*pl* **hippies**) *adj & nmf,* **hippie** ['χipi] (*pl* hippies) *adj & nmf* hippy

hiriente *adj* offensive, wounding; *(palabras)* cutting; **en tono h.** offensively

hirsuto, -a *adj* **(a)** *(brazo, pecho)* hirsute, hairy; *(cerdoso)* bristly **(b)** *Fig (hosco)* surly, rough, brusque

hirviente *adj* boiling; *Fig* seething

hisopo *nm* **(a)** *Bot* hyssop **(b)** *Rel* aspergillum, sprinkler **(c)** *Chile (brocha)* brush

hispalense *adj & nmf Fml* of o from Seville

hispánico, -a *adj* Hispanic, Spanish

hispanidad *nf* **(a)** *(carácter hispano)* Spanishness **(b)** *(pueblos de habla española)* Spanish o Hispanic world; **Día de la H.** Columbus Day

hispanismo *nm* **(a)** *(cultural)* Hispanism **(b)** *Ling* Hispanicism

hispanista *nmf* Hispanist

hispanizar [14] *vt* to hispanize, hispanicize

hispano, -a 1 *adj* Spanish, Hispanic, Spanish-American **2** *nm,f* Spaniard, Spanish American, *US* Hispanic

Hispanoamérica *nf* Spanish America, Latin America

hispanoamericano, -a *adj & nm,f* Spanish American, Latin American

hispanoárabe *adj* Hispano-Arabic

hispanófilo, -a *adj & nm,f* Hispanophile

hispanohablante 1 *adj* Spanish-speaking **2** *nmf* Spanish speaker

histamina *nf Biol* histamine

histerectomía *nf* hysterectomy

histeria *nf* hysteria; **un ataque de h.** hysterics *pl; Fam* Fig **h. colectiva** mass hysteria

histérico, -a *adj* hysteric, hysterical; *Fam Fig* **tu lentitud me pone histérica** your slowness drives me mad

histerismo *nm* hysteria; *Fig* hysterics *pl*

histograma *nm* histogram

histología *nf Biol* histology

historia *nf* **(a)** *(estudio del pasado)* history; **esto pasará a la h.** this will go down in history ◻ **h. natural** natural history **(b)** *(narración)* story, tale; *Fam* **¡déjate de historias!** get to the point!; *Fam* **no me vengas con historias** don't come to me with your tales

historiado, -a 1 *pp de* **historiar** **2** *adj Fam (recargado)* over-ornate, florid

historiador, -a *nm,f* historian

historial *nm* **(a)** *Med* medical record, case history **(b)** *(currículum)* curriculum vitae **(c)** *(antecedentes)* background

historiar *vt* **(a)** *Arte* to depict **(b)** *(de viva voz)* to tell the story of; *(acontecimientos)* to recount **(c)** *(escrito)* to write the history of; *(acontecimientos)* to chronicle

historicidad *nf* historicity, historical authenticity

historicismo *nm* historicism

histórico, -a *adj* **(a)** *(de la historia)* historical **(b)** *(auténtico)* factual, true; **una película basada en hechos históricos** a film based on true facts **(c)** *(de gran importancia)* historic, memorable **(d)** *Ling* **presente h.** historical present

historieta *nf* **(a)** *(cuento)* short story, anecdote, tale **(b)** *(tira cómica)* comic strip

historiografía *nf* historiography

historiógrafo, -a *nm,f* historiographer

histrión *nm* **(a)** *Teat* actor **(b)** *Fig (payaso)* clown, buffoon

histriónico, -a *adj* histrionic

histrionismo *nm* histrionics *pl,* theatrical behaviour o *US* behavior

hit [χit] (*pl* hits) *nm* hit

hitita *adj & nmf* Hittite

hitleriano, -a [χitle'rjano] *adj Pol* Hitler, Hitlerite

hitlerismo [χitle'rismo] *nm Pol* Hitlerism

hito *nm* **(a)** *(mojón) (distancias)* milestone; *(límites)* boundary stone **(b)** *(juego)* quoits *pl* **(c)** *(blanco)* bull's-eye; *Fig* target, aim, goal; **dar en el h.** to hit the nail on the head **(d)** *Fig* **mirar de h. en h.** to stare at

hizo *indic indef véase* **hacer**

hl *(abrev de* **hectolitro)** hl

hm *(abrev de* **hectómetro)** hm

Hnos., hnos. *(abrev de* **Hermanos)** Bros.

hobby ['χoβi] (*pl* hobbys) *nm* hobby

hocico *nm* **(a)** *(de animal)* muzzle, snout **(b)** *Pey (de persona)* mug, snout; **caer** o **darse de hocicos** to fall flat on one's face; **poner h.** to grimace; *Fam* **meter los hocicos en algo** to stick o poke one's nose into sth

hockey ['χokei] *nm Dep* hockey ◻ **h. sobre hielo** *Br* ice hockey, *US* hockey; **h. sobre hierba** *Br* hockey, *US* field hockey

hogar *nm* **(a)** *(de la chimenea)* hearth, fireplace **(b)** *Fig (casa)* home; *Fam Fig* **h., dulce h.** home sweet home **(c)** *Fig (familia)* family; **formar** o **crear un h.** to start a family

hogareño, -a *adj (vida)* home, family; *(persona)* home-loving, stay-at-home

hogaza *nf Culin* large loaf (of bread)

hoguera *nf* bonfire; *Euf* **morir en la h.** to be burnt at the stake

hoja *nf* **(a)** *Bot* leaf; *Fig* **h. de parra** cover, alibi **(b)** *(pétalo)* petal **(c)** *(de papel)* sheet, leaf; **una h. en blanco** a blank sheet of paper ◻ **h. informativa** newsletter **(d)** *(de libro)* leaf, page; *Fig* **volver la h.** to change the subject **(e)** *(de metal)* sheet; **batir h.** to beat metal **(f)** *(de cuchillo, espada)* blade ◻ **h. de afeitar** razor blade **(g)** *(impreso)* hand-out, printed sheet; **h. suelta** leaflet **(h)** *(documento)* record ◻ *Com* **h. de ruta** waybill; **h. de servicios** record of service **(i)** *(de puerta o ventana)* leaf; *(de mesa)* leaf, flap; **puerta de dos hojas** double-leaf door **(j)** *Inform* **h. de cálculo** spreadsheet

hojalata *nf* tin, tin plate

hojalatería *nf (taller)* tinsmith's; *(objetos)* tinware; *(oficio)* tinwork

hojalatero *nm* tinsmith

hojaldrado, -a *adj Culin* **pasta hojaldrada** puff pastry

hojaldre *nm Culin* puff pastry

hojarasca *nf* **(a)** *(hojas secas)* fallen o dead leaves *pl* **(b)** *(fronda)* foliage **(c)** *Fig (paja)* rubbish, trash; *(palabras)* verbiage; **tus promesas son h.** your promises are worthless

hojear *vt (libro)* to leaf through, flick through

hojuela *nf* **(a)** *Culin* pancake; *Prov* **miel sobre hojuelas** so much the better **(b)** *(de la aceituna)* pressed olive skins *pl* **(c)** *(hoja de metal)* foil

hola *interj* **(a)** *(saludo)* hello!, hullo!, *US* hi! **(b)** *RP Tel* hello?

holá *interj RP (al teléfono)* hello?

Holanda *n* Holland

holandés, -esa 1 *adj* Dutch **2** *nm,f (hombre)* Dutchman; *(mujer)* Dutchwoman; **los holandeses** the Dutch **3** *nm (idioma)* Dutch

holandesa *nf Impr* = sheet of paper measuring 22 × 28 cm

holding ['χoldin] (*pl* **holdings**) *nm Fin* holding company
holgadamente *adv* (**a**) caber h. to fit (in) easily (**b**) vivir h. to be well-off, be comfortably off
holgado, -a 1 *pp de* **holgar**
2 *adj* (**a**) *(ropa)* loose, baggy (**b**) *(económicamente)* comfortable; **estar en una situación holgada** to be comfortably off, be well off (**c**) *(espacio)* roomy; **ir h.** to have plenty of room; **andar h. de tiempo** to have plenty of spare time
holganza *nf* (**a**) *(ocio)* leisure, idleness (**b**) *(diversión)* pleasure
holgar [16] **1** *vi* (**a**) *(estar ocioso)* to be idle (**b**) *(sobrar)* **huelga decir que ...** it goes without saying that ...; **huelgan las palabras** no comment
2 holgarse *vpr* to be pleased (**con, de** by)
holgazán, -ana 1 *adj* lazy, idle
2 *nm,f* lazybones *inv*, layabout
holgazanear *vi* to laze *o* loaf around
holgazanería *nf* laziness, idleness
holgura *nf* (**a**) *(ropa)* looseness (**b**) *(espacio)* space, roominess; *Téc* play, give; **cabes con h.** there's plenty of room for you (**c**) *(bienestar económico)* affluence, comfort; **vivir con h.** to be comfortably off, be well-off
holístico, -a *adj* holistic
hollar [63] *vt* (**a**) *(pisar)* to tread (on), trample down (**b**) *Fig (humillar)* to humiliate
hollejo *nm Bot* skin, peel
hollín *nm* soot
hollywoodiense [χoliβu'ðjense] *adj* Hollywood; **la vida h.** life in Hollywood, the Hollywood scene
holocausto *nm* holocaust; *Fig* **ofrecer algo en h.** to offer sth as a sacrifice
holografía *nf* holography
holograma *nm* hologram
hombrada *nf* manly action; *Irón* **¡qué h.!** how brave!
hombre 1 *nm* (**a**) *(ser físico)* man; **de h. a h.** man-to-man; **el h. y la mujer** man and woman; **¡h. al agua!** man overboard!; **¡pobre h.!** poor chap!; **ser muy h.** to be every inch a man; **ser otro h.** to be a changed man ❏ **h. anuncio** sandwich man; **h. lobo** werewolf; **h. orquesta** one-man band; **h. rana** frogman; *Fam* **h. del saco** bogeyman (**b**) *(como ser moral)* **h. de bien** good *o* upstanding man; **h. de estado** statesman; **el h. de la calle** the man in the street; **h. de letras** man of letters; **h. de mundo** man of the world; **h. de negocios** businessman; **h. de paja** front man; **h. de palabra** man of his word; **h. de peso** important figure; **h. de pro** *o* **provecho** honest man; **h. masa** the average man (**c**) *(especie)* mankind, man (**d**) *(adulto)* **se está haciendo un h.** he's growing into a man; **te hará un h.** it'll make a man of you (**e**) *Fam (marido)* husband
2 *interj* (**a**) *(saludo)* hey!, hey, there!; *Esp* **¡h., Juan!** hey, Juan!; **¡h., Pepe, tú por aquí!** hello there, Pepe!, fancy seeing you here! (**b**) *(enfático)* **¡sí h.!**, **¡h. claro!** well, of course!, you bet!; **¡h., qué pena!** oh, what a shame! (**c**) *(indica reproche)* **¡anda, h.!** come on!; **¡pero, h.!** but listen! (**d**) *Méx Fam* **n'h.** *(uso enfático)* **¿cómo les fue? — n'h., nos la pasamos súper-bien** how did it go? — man, we had a blast!
hombrear *vi* (**a**) *Méx (dárselas de hombre)* to act the man (**b**) *(empujar)* to push with the shoulders
hombrera *nf* (**a**) *(almohadilla)* shoulder pad (**b**) *(tirante)* shoulder strap (**c**) *Mil* epaulette
hombretón *nm* big *o* well-built fellow
hombría *nf* manliness, virility
hombro *nm* shoulder; **a hombros** on one's shoulders; **arrimar el h.** to lend a hand; **encogerse de hombros** to

shrug one's shoulders; **echarse algo al h.** to shoulder sth; **mirar a algn por encima del h.** to look down one's nose at sb
hombruno, -a *adj (mujer)* mannish, butch
homenaje *nm* homage, tribute; **rendir h. a algn** to pay homage *o* tribute to sb; **una cena de h. al poeta** a dinner in honour of the poet
homenajeado, -a 1 *pp de* **homenajear**
2 *adj* honoured, *US* honored
3 *nm,f* guest of honour *o* *US* honor
homenajear *vt* to pay tribute to, honour
homeópata 1 *adj* homeopathic
2 *nmf* homeopath
homeopatía *nf* homeopathy
homeopático, -a *adj* homeopathic
homérico, -a *adj Lit* Homeric
homicida 1 *nmf (hombre)* murderer; *(mujer)* murderess
2 *adj* homicidal; **el arma h.** the murder weapon
homicidio *nm* homicide; **h. involuntario** manslaughter
homilía *nf Rel* homily, sermon
homínido *nm* hominid
homofobia *nf* homophobia
homofonía *nf Ling* homophony
homófono, -a *adj* homophonous, homophonic
homogeneidad *nf* homogeneity, uniformity
homogeneización *nf* homogenization
homogeneizar [14] *vt* to homogenize, make homogeneous
homogéneo, -a *adj* homogeneous, uniform
homologación *nf* (**a**) *Dep (récord)* ratification (**b**) *(registro)* official approval *o* recognition (**c**) *Jur (muerte etc)* confirmation
homologado, -a 1 *pp de* **homologar**
2 *adj* officially approved *o* recognized; **centro de estudios h.** government recognized school; **productos homologados** authorized products
homologar [38] *vt* (**a**) *Dep (récord)* to ratify (**b**) *(producto)* to give official approval *o* recognition to (**c**) *Jur (confirmar)* to confirm *o* endorse
homólogo, -a 1 *adj Mat Quím* homologous; *(equiparable)* comparable
2 *nm,f (persona con mismas condiciones)* opposite number
homonimia *nf* homonymy
homónimo, -a 1 *adj* homonymous
2 *nm* homonym
homosexual *adj & nmf* homosexual
homosexualidad *nf* homosexuality
honda *nf (arma)* sling
hondo, -a 1 *adj* (**a**) *(profundo)* deep; **plato h.** soup dish (**b**) *Fig (muy íntimo)* profound, deep; *Mús* **cante h.** flamenco song
2 *nm* the depths *pl*, the bottom; **en lo h. del cajón** at the bottom of the drawer
hondonada *nf Geog* hollow, depression
hondura *nf* depth; *Fig* **meterse en honduras** *(profundizar)* to go into too much detail; *(tratar sin conocimiento)* to get out of one's depth, get in over one's head
Honduras *n* Honduras
hondureño, -a *adj & nm,f* Honduran
honestamente *adv* decently, properly
honestidad *nf* (**a**) *(honradez)* honesty, uprightness (**b**) *(pudor)* modesty
honesto, -a *adj* (**a**) *(honrado)* honest, upright; **una**

decisión muy honesta a very sensible decision (**b**) *(recatado)* modest

hongo *nm* (**a**) *Bot* fungus (**b**) *esp Am (comestible)* mushroom; *(no comestible)* toadstool (**c**) **h. nuclear** mushroom cloud (**d**) **(sombrero) h.** *Br* bowler (hat), *US* derby

Honolulú [χonolu'lu] *n* Honolulu

honor *nm* (**a**) *(virtud)* honour, *US* honor; **cuestión de h.** point of honour; **lo juro por mi h.** I swear it upon my honour; **palabra de h.** word of honour (**b**) *(enaltecer)* **en h. a la verdad ...** to be fair ...; **es un h. para mí** it's an honour for me ... (**c**) *(reputación)* **hacer h. a** to live up to; **este vino hace h. a su fama** this wine lives up to its reputation (**d**) **honores** title *sing*, distinction *sing* (**e**) *(fiesta)* **hacer los honores** to do the honours; *Mil* **rendir los honores** with full military honours

honorabilidad *nf* honour, *US* honor

honorable *adj* honourable, *US* honorable

honorar *vt* to honour, *US* honor

honorario, -a 1 *adj* honorary
  2 honorarios *nmpl* fees, fee *sing*, emoluments

honorífico, -a *adj* honorific. **cargo h.** unpaid post

honoris causa *adj* honoris causa

honra *nf* (**a**) *(amor propio)* dignity, self-esteem (**b**) *(fama)* reputation, good name (**c**) *(motivo de orgullo)* honour, *US* honor; **me cabe la h. de ...** I have the honour of ...; **tener a mucha h.** to be very proud of; **¡a mucha h.!** and (I'm) proud of it! (**d**) **honras fúnebres** last honours

honradez *nf* honesty, integrity

honrado, -a 1 *pp de* **honrar**
  2 *adj* (**a**) *(de fiar)* honest (**b**) *(honorable)* honourable, *US* honorable (**c**) *(decente)* upright, respectable

honrar 1 *vt* (**a**) *(respetar)* to honour, *US* honor (**b**) *(enaltecer)* to do credit to; **esas palabras te honran** those words do you credit
  2 honrarse *vpr* to be honoured *o US* honored

honrilla *nf* self-respect, pride; **lo hizo por la negra h.** he did it for the sake of appearances *o* for fear of what people might say

honroso, -a *adj* (**a**) *(respeto)* honourable, *US* honorable (**b**) *(decoroso)* respectable, reputable

hontanar *nm Geol* spring

hora *nf* (**a**) *(del día)* hour; *Fig* time; **¿qué h. es?** what time is it?; **a altas horas de la madrugada** in the small hours; **¡a buenas horas!** and about time too!; **a** *o* **en su h.** at the proper time; **a última h.** at the last moment; **comer entre horas** to eat between meals; **dar la h.** to strike the hour; **h. de acostarse** bedtime; **h. de cenar** dinner time; **h. de comer** lunchtime; *Esp SAm* **la h. de la verdad,** *CAm Méx* **la h. de la h.** the moment of truth; **(trabajo) por horas** (work) paid by the hour; *Fam* **tener horas de vuelo** to be an old hand; *Argot* **ir con la h. pegada al culo** to run around like a blue-arsed fly □ *Esp* **h. punta** *o Am* **pico** rush hour; **horas extras** *o* **extraordinarias** overtime (hours) (**b**) *(cita)* appointment; *(médico etc)* **dar h.** to fix an appointment; **pedir h.** to ask for an appointment (**c**) *Lit* **libro de horas** Book of Hours

horadar *vt (agujerear)* to drill (through), bore (through); *(perforar)* to pierce

horario *nm* (**a**) *(de actividad)* timetable, *US* schedule; **tengo h. de mañanas** I work mornings □ **h. comercial** opening hours; **h. flexible** flexitime; **h. intensivo** = working day without a long break for lunch; **h. laboral** working hours; **h. de trabajo** working hours; **h. de visitas** visiting hours (**b**) *(manecilla de reloj)* hour hand

horca *nf* (**a**) *Agr* pitchfork, hayfork (**b**) *(patíbulo)* gallows *pl*, gibbet (**c**) *(de ajos, cebollas)* string

horcajadas: a horcajadas *loc adv* astride

horchata *nf Culin* = sweet milky drink made from tiger nuts or almonds; *Fig* **tener sangre de h.** to have water in one's veins, be gutless

horchatería *nf* = bar where **horchata** is sold

horcón *nm Am Arquit* support for roof beams

horda *nf* horde, mob; *Fig* gang

horizontal *adj* horizontal

horizontalmente *adv* horizontally

horizonte *nm* horizon; *Fig* **este producto amplia el h. de la informática** this product widens the horizons of computer science

horma *nf* form, mould, *US* mold; *(de zapato)* last; *Fig* **encontrar la h. de su zapato** to meet one's match

hormiga *nf Ent* ant □ **h. blanca** white ant

hormigón *nm Constr* concrete □ **h. armado** reinforced concrete

hormigonera *nf Aut* concrete mixer

hormiguear *vi* (**a**) *(dar sensación de hormigueo)* to itch, tingle; **me hormigueaba la pierna** I had pins and needles in my leg (**b**) *(pulular)* to swarm, teem

hormigueo *nm* pins and needles *pl*, tingling *o* itching sensation; *Fig* anxiety, uneasiness

hormiguero *nm* (**a**) *(de hormigas)* anthill, ants' nest (**b**) *Fig (lugar)* **ser un h.** to be swarming (with people)

hormiguillo *nm* (**a**) *(cosquilleo)* pins and needles *pl*, tingling *o* itching sensation (**b**) *Am Min* amalgamation

hormiguita *nf* small ant; **ser una h.** to be hardworking and thrifty

hormona *nf* hormone

hormonal *adj* hormonal

hornacho *nm Min* excavation

hornacina *nf Arquit* niche

hornada *nf* (**a**) *(pan)* batch (**b**) *Fig* set, batch

hornear *vt* to bake

hornillo *nm* (**a**) *Téc* small furnace (**b**) *(de cocinar)* stove; **h. eléctrico** hotplate (**c**) *Min* blast hole

horno *nm* (*cocina*) oven; *Téc* furnace; *(cerámica, ladrillos)* kiln; **h. de fundición** smelting furnace; *Culin* **pescado al h.** baked fish; *Fam Fig* **esta habitación es un h.** this room is boiling hot; *Fam* **no estar el h. para bollos** not to be the right time □ **alto h.** blast furnace; **h. crematorio** crematorium

horóscopo *nm* horoscope

horqueta *nf Am (en carretera)* fork

horquilla *nf* (**a**) *(para el pelo)* hairpin, *US* bobby pin (**b**) *Agr* pitchfork (**c**) *(de bicicleta)* fork

horrendo, -a *adj* horrifying, horrible

hórreo *nm Agr* granary

horrible *adj* horrible, dreadful, awful

horripilante *adj* hair-raising, scary, creepy

horripilar *vt* to scare stiff, terrify

horro, -a *adj Fml* (**a**) *(carente)* lacking (**b**) *(esclavo)* free

horror *nm* (**a**) *(miedo)* horror, terror; **¡qué h.!** how awful!; *Fam* **tengo h. a las motos** I hate motorbikes (**b**) *Fam Fig (muchísimo)* an awful lot; **cuesta un h.** it costs a bomb; **me gusta horrores** I'm crazy about it; **sufrió horrores** he suffered terribly (**c**) **horrores** *(atrocidades)* atrocities

horrorizar [14] **1** *vt* to horrify, terrify; *Fam* **me horroriza ese traje** I hate that suit
  2 horrorizarse *vpr* to be horrified

horroroso, -a *adj* (**a**) *(que da miedo)* horrifying, terrifying (**b**) *Fam (muy feo)* hideous, ghastly (**c**) *Fam* *(malísimo)* awful, dreadful **(d)** *Fam (muy grande)* **tengo una sed horrorosa** I'm dying of thirst; **me llevé un susto h.** I got an awful fright

hortaliza *nf* vegetable; **hortalizas** vegetables, garden produce *sing*

hortelano, -a 1 *adj* market-gardening, *US* truck-farming
   2 *nm,f* market gardener, *US* truck farmer; *Fig* **ser el perro del h.** to be the dog in the manger

hortensia *nf Bot* hydrangea

hortera *Esp Argot* **1** *adj (decoración, ropa)* tacky, *Br* naff; *(persona)* tasteless
   2 *nmf* person with no taste; **es un h.** he has really tacky *o Br* naff taste

horterada *nf Esp Argot* tacky thing *o* act

hortícola *adj* horticultural

horticultor, -a *nm,f* horticulturist

horticultura *nf* horticulture

hosco, -a *adj* **(a)** *(poco sociable)* surly, sullen **(b)** *(lugar) (tenebroso)* dark, gloomy

hospedaje *nm* **(a)** *(acción de hospedar)* lodging **(b)** *(lugar)* lodgings *pl*, accommodation

hospedar 1 *vt* to put up, lodge
   2 hospedarse *vpr* to stay **(en** at)

hospedería *nf* inn, hostelry

hospiciano, -a *nm,f* orphan, person living in an orphanage

hospicio *nm (para huérfanos)* orphanage; *(para peregrinos)* hospice

hospital *nm* hospital, infirmary □ *Mil* **h. de (primera) sangre** field hospital

hospitalario, -a *adj* **(a)** *(acogedor)* hospitable **(b)** *Med* hospital; **instalaciones hospitalarias** hospital facilities

hospitalidad *nf* hospitality

hospitalización *nf* hospitalization

hospitalizar [14] *vt* to take *o* send into hospital, hospitalize

hosquedad *nf* surliness, sullenness

host [xost] *(pl* hosts) *nm Inform* host

hostal *nm* hostel, cheap hotel

hostelería *nf (negocio)* catering business; *(estudios)* hotel management

hostelero, -a *adj* catering; **sector h.** catering trade

hostería *nf* guesthouse

hostia 1 *nf* **(a)** *Rel* host, Eucharistic wafer **(b)** *Esp Vulg (tortazo)* bash; **darse** *o* **pegarse una h.** to give oneself a real bash, come a cropper; **darle** *o* **pegarle una h. a algn** to belt sb, give sb a belting; **estar de mala h.** to be in a foul mood; **ir a toda h.** *o* **echando hostias** to go flat out; **ser la h.** *(de bueno)* to be *Br* bloody *o US* goddamn amazing; *(de malo)* to be *Br* bloody *o US* goddamn awful
   2 *interj Esp Br* bloody hell!, *US* goddamn it!

hostiar [32] *vt Vulg* to bash, sock

hostigamiento *nm* harassment

hostigar [38] *vt* **(a)** *(caballerías)* to whip **(b)** *Fig (molestar)* to pester **(c)** *(perseguir)* to plague, persecute; *Mil* to harass

hostil *adj* hostile

hostilidad *nf* hostility; *Mil* **romper las hostilidades** to begin hostilities

hostilizar [14] *vt* to harass

hotel *nm* **(a)** *(establecimiento)* hotel **(b)** *(quinta, chalet)* villa, mansion **(c)** *Argot (cárcel)* clink, nick

hotelería *nf Andes RP* hotel and catering industry

hotelero, -a 1 *adj* hotel; **industria hotelera** hotel industry *o* trade
   2 *nm,f* hotel-keeper, hotelier

hoy *adv* **(a)** *(día)* today; **de h. a mañana** very soon; **de h. en adelante** henceforth, from now on; **hasta h.** up till now **(b)** *Fig (presente)* now; **h. (en) día** nowadays; **h. por h.** at the present time; **por h.** for the present

hoya *nf* **(a)** *(hoyo grande)* pit, hole **(b)** *(sepultura)* grave **(c)** *Geog (llano)* dale, valley **(d)** *Am Geog* river basin

hoyo *nm* **(a)** *(agujero)* hole, pit **(b)** *(sepultura)* grave **(c)** *Golf* hole

hoyuelo *nm* dimple

hoz¹ *nf Agr* sickle; *Pol* **la h. y el martillo** the hammer and sickle

hoz² *nf Geog* ravine, gorge

HR *(abrev de* **Hostal Residencia***)* boarding house

HTML *nm Inform (abrev de* **hypertext markup language***)* HTML

HTTP *nm Inform (abrev de* **hypertext transfer protocol***)* HTTP

huacal *nm CAm Col Méx* **(a)** *(jaula)* cage **(b)** *(cajón)* drawer

huaso, -a *nm,f Andes Fam* peasant

hubiera *subj imperf véase* **haber**

hucha *nf Esp* **(a)** *(alcancía)* moneybox, piggy bank **(b)** *Fig (ahorros)* savings *pl*, nest egg

hueco, -a 1 *adj* **(a)** *(vacío)* empty, hollow; **árbol h.** hollow tree; *Fig* **palabras huecas** empty words **(b)** *(sonido)* resonant **(c)** *(esponjoso)* spongy, soft **(d)** *(presumido)* vain, conceited; **ponerse h.** to swell with pride
   2 *nm* **(a)** *(cavidad)* hollow, hole; *Arquit* opening □ **h. del ascensor** lift shaft; **h. de la escalera** stairwell; **h. de la ventana** window recess **(b)** *(sitio no ocupado)* empty space, empty seat; **dejar un h.** to leave a gap; **hacer un h. a algn** to make room for sb; *Fig* **llenar un h.** to fill a gap *o* a need **(c)** *(rato libre)* free time; *(profesor)* free period; **tengo un h. a las cinco, aprovecharé para visitarte** I'm free at five so I'll visit you **(d)** *Fig (vacante)* vacancy

huecograbado *nm Impr* photogravure

huelga *nf Agr* strike; **estar en** *o* **de h.** to be on strike; **hacer** *o* **ir a la h.** to go on strike □ **h. de brazos caídos** go-slow; **h. de celo** work-to-rule; **h. general** general strike; **h. de hambre** hunger strike; **h. salvaje** wildcat strike

huelguista *nmf* striker

huella *nf* **(a)** *(del pie)* footprint; *(de coche)* track; *Fig* **seguir las huellas de algn** to follow in sb's footsteps □ **h. dactilar** fingerprint **h. genética** genetic fingerprint **(b)** *Fig (vestigio)* trace, sign; **dejar h.** to leave one's mark; **huellas de dolor** traces of pain; **no quedó ni h.** there wasn't a trace

huérfano, -a 1 *adj* **(a)** *(persona)* orphan, orphaned; **h. de madre** motherless; **h. de padre** fatherless **(b)** *Fig (carente)* lacking; **h. de cariño** devoid of love
   2 *nm,f* orphan

huero, -a *adj* **(a)** *(huevo)* addled, rotten **(b)** *Fig (hueco)* empty

huerta *nf Agr* **(a)** *(huerto) Br* market garden, *US* truck farm **(b)** *(vega)* = irrigated area used for cultivation

huerto *nm (de verduras)* vegetable garden, kitchen garden; *(de frutales)* orchard; *Fam Fig* **llevarse a algn al h.** *(engañar)* to lead sb up the garden path; *(llevarse a la cama)* to go to bed with sb

huesillo *nm Andes* dried peach

hueso *nm* **(a)** *Anat* bone; **dar con los huesos en tierra** to keel over, collapse; **darle a la sin h.** to talk one's head off; **estar calado** *o* **empapado hasta los huesos** to be soaked (through); **estar en los huesos** to be all skin and bone; **romperle a algn un h.** *o* **los huesos** to give sb a roasting, make mincemeat of sb; **tener los huesos molidos** to be dead beat o exhausted (**b**) *(de fruta) Br* stone, *US* pit (**c**) *Fig (difícil)* hard work; *(profesor)* strict person; **para mí la física es un h.** I find physics a real chore; **un h. duro de roer** a hard nut to crack; **el profesor de música es un h.** the music teacher's a real stickler (**d**) *Fam Fig (de mala calidad)* useless thing (**e**) *Méx Fam (enchufe)* contacts, influence; *(trabajo fácil)* cushy job job

huésped, -a *nm,f* (**a**) *(invitado)* guest; *(en hotel etc)* lodger, boarder ❑ **casa de huéspedes** guesthouse (**b**) *(anfitrión) (hombre)* host; *(mujer)* hostess

hueste *nf* (**a**) *Mil* army, host (**b**) **huestes** *(seguidores)* followers, supporters

huesudo, -a *adj* bony; **rodillas huesudas** knobbly knees

hueva *nf* (**a**) *(de pescado)* roe; **huevas de bacalao** cod roe (**b**) *Méx Fam (aburrimiento)* **¡qué h.!** what a pain o drag!

huevada *nf Andes RP muy Fam* crap

huevazos *nm inv Vulg* wanker

huevear *vi Andes Fam* to muck about

huevera *nf* (**a**) *(copa)* egg cup (**b**) *(caja)* egg box

huevería *nf* egg shop

huevero, -a *nm,f* egg seller

huevo *nm* (**a**) *(de animales)* egg; *Fig* **parecerse como un h. a una castaña** to be as different as chalk and cheese; *Fig* **ser una cosa el h. de Colón** to be easier than it seems ❑ **h. duro** hard-boiled egg; **h. escalfado** poached egg; **h. estrellado** o **frito** fried egg; **h. pasado por agua** soft-boiled egg; **h. de Pascua** Easter egg; *Méx* **h. tibio** soft-boiled egg; **huevos moles** dessert made from egg yolk(s); **huevos revueltos**, *Col* **huevos pericos** scrambled eggs (**b**) *Vulg (gen pl)* balls *pl*; **costar un h.** to cost an arm and a leg; **¡estoy hasta los huevos!** I'm *Br* bloody o *US* goddam sick of it!; **hacer algo por huevos** to do sth even if it kills you; **tener huevos** to have balls; **¡y un h.!** like hell!, *Br* bollocks!, *US* my ass!

huevón, -ona *Vulg* **1** *adj* (**a**) *Cuba Méx (vago)* lazy; **ser muy h.** *Br* to be a lazy sod o git, *US* be goddamn lazy (**b**) *Andes Arg Ven (tonto, torpe)* **ser muy h.** *Br* to be a prat o pillock, *US* be a jerk
2 *nm,f* (**a**) *Cuba Méx (vago)* **ser un h.** *Br* to be a lazy sod o git, *US* be goddamn lazy (**b**) *Andes Arg Ven (tonto, torpe) Br* prat, *US* jerk

hugonote, -a *adj & nm,f Hist* Huguenot

huida *nf* (**a**) *(de persona)* flight, escape (**b**) *(del caballo)* shying, bolting

huidizo, -a *adj (tímido)* shy; *(esquivo)* elusive, fleeting

huipil *nm CAm Méx* embroidered blouse

huir [34] *vi* (**a**) *(escaparse)* to run away (**de** from), flee (**de** -) (**b**) *(evitar)* **h. de** to avoid, keep away from, escape (from); **h. de algn como de la peste** to avoid sb like the plague (**c**) *Lit (tiempo)* to fly

hule *nm (tela impermeable)* oilcloth, oilskin

hulla *nf Min* coal ❑ **h. blanca** water power

hullero, -a *adj Min* coal; **explotación hullera** *(mina)* mine; *(industria)* mining

humanidad *nf* (**a**) *(género humano)* humanity, mankind (**b**) *(cualidad)* humanity, humaneness (**c**) *(bondad)* compassion, kindness (**d**) *(corpulencia)* corpulence (**e**) **humanidades** *Educ* humanities

humanismo *nm* humanism

humanista *nmf* humanist

humanístico, -a *adj* humanistic

humanitario, -a *adj* humanitarian

humanitarismo *nm* humanitarianism

humanización *nf* humanization

humanizar [14] **1** *vt* to humanize
2 humanizarse *vpr* to become more human

humano, -a 1 *adj* (**a**) *(relativo al hombre)* human (**b**) *(compasivo)* humane
2 *nm* human (being)

humarada *nf*, **humareda** *nf* (dense) cloud of smoke

humeante *adj (humo)* smoky, smoking; *(vaho)* steaming

humear 1 *vi* (**a**) *(echar humo)* to smoke; *(arrojar vapor)* to fume, steam, be steaming hot (**b**) *Fig* to smoulder, *US* smolder
2 *vt Am (lugar)* to fumigate

humedad *nf* (**a**) *(de suelo, tierra)* dampness; *(de pared, techo)* damp; **hay mucha h. en la casa** the house is very damp (**b**) *(de labios, ojos)* moistness (**c**) *(de atmósfera)* humidity

humedal *nm* wetland

humedecer [46] **1** *vt* to moisten, dampen
2 humedecerse *vpr* to become damp o moist

humedecimiento *nm* moistening

húmedo, -a *adj* (**a**) *(suelo, tierra, casa)* damp (**b**) *(labios, ojos)* moist (**c**) *(ropa)* damp (**d**) *(clima) (frío)* damp; *(cálido)* humid (**e**) *(aire, atmósfera)* humid

húmero *nm Anat* humerus

humidificador *nm* humidifier

humidificar [59] *vt* to humidify

humildad *nf* humility, humbleness

humilde *adj* humble, modest; **una familia h.** a poor family

humillación *nf* humiliation, humbling

humillante *adj* humiliating, humbling

humillar 1 *vt* to humiliate, humble; **me humilla pedir dinero** I find it humiliating to ask for money
2 humillarse *vpr* **h. ante algn** to humble oneself before sb

humita *nf* (**a**) *Andes Arg Culin* tamale, = paste made of mashed maize and other ingredients, wrapped in maize husks and steamed (**b**) *Chile (pajarita)* bow tie

humo *nm* (**a**) *(producto de combustión)* smoke; *(gas)* fumes *pl*; *(vapor)* vapour, *US* vapor, steam; **echar h.** to smoke; *Fig* **a h. de pajas** thoughtlessly (**b**) **humos** *Fig* conceit *sing*, airs; **bajarle los h. a algn** to put sb in their place, take sb down a peg or two; **¡qué h. tiene!** she gives herself such airs!; **subírsele los h. (a uno)** to become conceited, get on one's high horse

humor *nm* (**a**) *(genio)* mood; *(carácter)* temper; **estar de buen/mal h.** to be in a good/bad mood; **¡qué h. tienes!** what patience you've got!; **tener h. para algo** to feel like (doing) sth, feel in the mood for (doing) sth; **no tengo h. para ir al teatro** I am not in the mood for going to the theatre; **tener un h. de perros** to be in a foul temper (**b**) *(gracia)* humour, *US* humor; **el h. inglés** the English sense of humour; **sentido del h.** sense of humour ❑ **h. negro** black comedy (**c**) *(líquido orgánico)* humour, *US* humor ❑ *Anat* **h. acuoso** aqueous humour

humorada *nf* *(dicho gracioso)* joke, pleasantry; *(extravagancia)* whim, caprice

humorismo *nm* humour, *US* humor

humorista 1 *adj* humorous
2 *nmf* humorist; **h. gráfico** cartoonist

humorístico, -a *adj* humorous, funny

humoso, -a *adj* smoky

humus *nm Agr* humus

hundido, -a 1 *pp de* **hundir**
2 *adj* (**a**) *(embarcación)* sunken; **barco h.** sunken ship;

ojos hundidos deep-set eyes; **mejillas hundidas** hollow cheeks (**b**) *Fig (abatido)* demoralized; **h. en el olvido** long-forgotten; **h. en la miseria** penniless

hundimiento *nm* (**a**) *(de edificio)* collapse (**b**) *(de barco)* sinking (**c**) *(de tierra)* subsidence (**d**) *Fig Fin* crash; slump; *(ruina)* downfall

hundir 1 *vt* (**a**) *(barco)* to sink (**b**) *(hacer caer)* to cause to collapse, ruin; **la nieve hundió el techo** the snow caused the roof to collapse; **vas a h. el suelo** you'll go through the floor (**c**) *(meter)* to submerge; **hundió la cara en la almohada** she buried her face in the pillow (**d**) *Fig (arruinar) (planes etc)* to ruin (**e**) *Fig (abatir)* to demoralize; *(enemigo)* to defeat; **h. a algn en la miseria** to plunge sb into misery

  2 hundirse *vpr* (**a**) *(barco)* to sink (**b**) *(derrumbarse)* to collapse, cave in; **se hundió el imperio** the empire collapsed (**c**) *Fig (arruinarse)* to be ruined (**d**) *(sucumbir)* to be destroyed; **h. en la tristeza** to be consumed by sadness

húngaro, -a 1 *adj* Hungarian
  2 *nm,f (persona)* Hungarian
  3 *nm (idioma)* Hungarian

Hungría *n* Hungary

huno, -a *Hist* **1** *adj* Hunnish
  2 *nm* Hun

huracán *nm* hurricane

huracanado, -a *adj Meteor* hurricane; **vientos huracanados** hurricane winds

huraño, -a *adj Pey* shy, unsociable

hurgar [38] **1** *vt* (**a**) *(remover) (fuego etc)* to poke, rake (**b**) *Fig (fisgar)* to stir up; **h. en** to rummage in (**c**) *Fig (incitar)* to provoke
  2 hurgarse *vpr* **h. las narices** to pick one's nose

hurgón *nm* poker; *(de fuego)* rake

hurgonear *vt* to poke, rake

hurí *(pl* **huríes)** *nf Rel* houri

hurón, -ona 1 *nm Zool* ferret
  2 *nm,f* (**a**) *Fam Fig (fisgón)* busybody, nosey-parker (**b**) *(huraño)* unsociable person

hurra *interj* hurray!, hurrah!

hurtadillas: a hurtadillas *loc adv* stealthily, on the sly

hurtar *vt* (**a**) *(robar)* to steal, pilfer (**b**) *Fig (apartar)* **h. el cuerpo** to dodge (out of the way) (**c**) *(peso)* **h. en el peso de algo** to cheat on the weight of sth

hurto *nm* petty theft, pilfering

húsar *nm Mil* hussar

husillo¹ *nm Téc (tornillo de prensa)* screw

husillo² *nm (conducto de desagüe)* drain

husmeador, -a 1 *adj* (**a**) *(con el olfato)* sniffing (**b**) *Fig (que curiosea)* prying, snooping
  2 *(fisgón)* *nm,f* snooper

husmear 1 *vi* to (begin to) smell high, be smelly
  2 *vt* (**a**) *(rastrear con el olfato)* to sniff out, scent; **h. el peligro** to scent danger (**b**) *Fig (curiosear)* to poke one's nose into, pry into

husmeo *nm* (**a**) *(olfateo)* scenting (**b**) *Fig* prying, snooping

huso *nm* (**a**) *Tex* spindle, bobbin (**b**) *Geog* **h. horario** time zone

huy *interj* (**a**) *(dolor)* ouch!, ow! (**b**) *(asombro)* **¡h., qué feo!** how ugly!; **¡h., qué raro!** that's odd! (**c**) *(reproche)* **¡h., h., h.!** tut, tut, tut!

huyo *indic pres véase* **huir**

huyuyo, -a *adj Am* unsociable, surly

Hz *(abrev de* **hertz)** Hz

I (*pl* **íes**) *nf,* **i** (*pl* **íes**) [i] *nf (la letra)* I, i; **i griega** Y, y

ib. (*abrev de* **ibídem**) ibid., ib.

ibérico, -a *adj* Iberian

ibero, -a, íbero, -a 1 *adj & nm,f* Iberian
  2 *nm (lengua)* Iberian

Iberoamérica *n* Latin America

iberoamericano, -a *adj & nm,f* Latin American

íbice *nm Zool* ibex

ibicenco, -a 1 *adj* of *o* from Ibiza
  2 *nm,f* person from Ibiza

ibíd. (*abrev de* **ibídem**) ibid., ib.

ibis *nf Orn* ibis

iceberg [iθe'βer] (*pl* **icebergs**) *nm* iceberg

ICI ['iθi] *nm* (*abrev de* **Instituto de Cooperación Ibero-americana**) Institute for Latin American co-operation

icono *nm, Am* **ícono** *nm* icon, ikon

iconoclasia *nf* iconoclasm

iconoclasta 1 *adj* iconoclastic
  2 *nmf* iconoclast

iconografía *nf* iconography

iconográfico, -a *adj* iconographical

ictericia *nf Med* jaundice, icterus

ictus *nm inv Med* stroke

I+D ['imas'de] (*abrev de* **investigación y desarrollo**) R&D

íd. (*abrev de* **ídem**) id.

ida *nf* **(a)** *(viaje)* outward journey; **billete de i. y vuelta** *Br* return ticket, *US* round-trip ticket; **idas y venidas** comings and goings; **viaje de i. y vuelta** return journey, *US* round trip **(b)** *(en esgrima)* attack

idea *nf* **(a)** *(gen)* idea; **i. fija** fixed idea; **i. luminosa** *o* **genial** brain wave, *US* brainstorm; **¡qué i.!** what an idea!; *Esp Fam* **tener ideas de bombero** to have madcap ideas **(b)** *(noción)* idea; **hacerse a la i. de** to get used to the idea of; **no tengo la más mínima i.** I haven't the faintest idea; *Fam* **ni i.** no idea, not a clue **(c)** *(opinión)* opinion; **cambiar de i.** to change one's mind; **es de ideas bastante conservadoras** he is quite conservative in his outlook; **¿qué i. tienes de él?** what do you think of him? **(d)** *(intención)* intention; **a mala i.** on purpose; **¿con qué i. lo has hecho?** why did you do it?

ideal 1 *adj* ideal; **la casa i.** the ideal home
  2 *nm* ideal

idealismo *nm* idealism

idealista 1 *adj* idealistic
  2 *nmf* idealist

idealización *nf* idealization

idealizar [14] *vt* to idealize, glorify

idealmente *adv* ideally

idear *vt* **(a)** *(inventar)* to devise, invent **(b)** *(concebir)* to think up, conceive

ideario *nm* ideology, set of ideas

ideático, -a *adj Am (obsesivo)* manic; *(excéntrico)* eccentric

ídem *adv* idem, ditto; *Fam* **i. de í.** exactly the same

idéntico, -a *adj* identical

identidad *nf* **(a)** *(de persona, pueblo)* identity; **carnet de i., documento nacional de i.** identity card **(b)** *(semejanza)* identity, sameness

identificable *adj* identifiable

identificación *nf* identification

identificar [59] **1** *vt* to identify
  2 identificarse *vpr* to identify oneself (**con** with)

ideograma *nm* ideogram, ideograph

ideología *nf* ideology

ideológico, -a *adj* ideologic, ideological

ideólogo, -a *nm,f* ideologist

idílico, -a *adj* idyllic

idilio *nm* **(a)** *Lit* idyll **(b)** *Fig (romance)* romance, love affair

idioma *nm* language; **el i. francés** the French language; *Fig* **hablar el mismo i.** to be on the same wavelength

idiomático, -a *adj* idiomatic; *Ling* **expresión idiomática** idiom

idiosincrasia *nf* idiosyncrasy

idiosincrático, -a *adj* characteristic

idiota 1 *adj* idiotic, stupid
  2 *nmf* idiot, fool; *Fam* **¡i.!** you idiot!

idiotez *nf* **(a)** *(bobería)* idiocy, stupidity **(b)** *Med* imbecility, mental deficiency *o* retardation

idiotizar [14] **1** *vt* to daze
  2 idiotizarse *vpr* to become dazed

ido, -a 1 *pp de* **ir**
  2 *adj* **(a)** *(distraído)* absent-minded; **estar i.** to be miles away **(b)** *Fam (chiflado)* crazy, nuts

idólatra 1 *adj* idolatrous
  2 *nmf (hombre)* idolater; *(mujer)* idolatress

idolatrar *vt* to worship; *Fig* to idolize

idolatría *nf* idolatry

ídolo *nm* idol

idoneidad *nf (adecuación)* suitability; *(aptitud)* aptitude, ability

idóneo, -a *adj* suitable, fit

iglesia *nf* **(a)** *(edificio)* church; **i. parroquial** parish church; *Fam* **llevar a algn a la i.** to lead sb to the altar **(b)**

(institución) the Church; **la i. anglicana** the Anglican Church, the Church of England; **la i. católica** the Catholic Church; **la I. y el Estado** Church and State; *Fam Fig* **¡con la I. hemos topado!** we've really come up against a brick wall now

iglú *(pl* **iglúes)** *nm* igloo

ígneo, -a *adj* igneous

ignición *nf* ignition

ignífugo, -a *adj* fireproof, flameproof

ignominia *nf* ignominy, public shame o disgrace

ignominioso, -a *adj* ignominious, shameful

ignorancia *nf* ignorance

ignorante 1 *adj* **(a)** *(sin instrucción)* ignorant **(b)** *(no informado)* ignorant, unaware **(de** of)
2 *nmf* ignoramus

ignorar *vt* to be ignorant of, not know; **ignoraba que** I had no idea that; **no ignoro que** I am fully aware that

ignoto, -a *adj* unknown, undiscovered

igual 1 *adj* **(a)** *(lo mismo)* the same, alike; **estoy i. de cansado que tú** I'm just as tired as you (are); **los veo todos iguales** they all look the same to me; **es i.** it doesn't matter; *Fam* **nunca he visto cosa i.** I've never seen anything like it **(b)** *(equivalente)* equal; **a partes iguales** into equal parts, fifty-fifty **(c)** *(constante)* even; **la ley es i. para todos** everybody is equal in the eyes of the law **(d)** *Dep (empatados)* even; **ir iguales** to be even o level; **treinta iguales** thirty all **(e)** *Mat* equal; **A es i. a B** A equals B; **tres (multiplicado) por dos i. a seis** three multiplied by o times two makes six **(f)** **al i. que** just like **(g)** **por i.** equally
2 *nmf* equal; **de i. a i.** on an equal footing; **tratar a algn de i. a i.** to treat sb as an equal; **sin i.** unique, unrivalled
3 *nm* **(a)** *Mat* equal o equals sign **(b)** **iguales** *(rango)* equals
4 *adv* probably; **i. se ha quedado dormido** he could easily have overslept

iguala *nf* **(a)** *(contrato)* agreement, contract **(b)** *(cuota)* agreed fee

igualación *nf (de cantidades)* equalization; *(de un terreno)* levelling; *(de madera, metal)* smoothing; *Mat* equating

igualada *nf Dep* draw, tie; **el gol de la igualada** the equalizer

igualado, -a 1 *pp de* **igualar**
2 *adj* equalized; *(terreno)* level; *(material)* smooth; *Dep* even; *(en carreras)* level; **van igualados a dos tantos** the score is now two all

igualar 1 *vt* **(a)** *(gen)* to equalize, make equal **(b)** *(nivelar)* to level; *(pulir)* to smooth **(c)** *Dep* to equalize; **i. el marcador** to equalize **(d)** *Fig (rivalizar con)* to equal; **nadie la iguala en fuerza** his strength cannot be matched o equalled
2 **igualarse** *vpr* **(a)** *(cosas diferentes)* to become equal **(b)** **i. con algn** to place oneself on an equal footing with sb

igualdad *nf (gen)* equality; *(identidad)* sameness; *(terreno)* levelness; *(material)* smoothness; **en i. de condiciones** on equal terms; **i. de salarios/derechos** equal pay/rights

igualitario, -a *adj* egalitarian

igualitarismo *nm* egalitarianism

igualmente *adv* **(a)** equally; *(también)* also, likewise; **son i. de bonitas** they are equally pretty; *Fam* **¡gracias! — ¡i.!** thank you! — the same to you! **(b)** *Esp (posiblemente)* **i. llueve** it could well rain

iguana *nf Zool* iguana

ijada *nf,* **ijar** *nm Anat* flank

ilación *nf* **(a)** *(relación)* inference, connection, relationship **(b)** *(coherencia)* cohesion **(c)** *(de discurso)* thread

ilativo, -a *adj* inferential; *Ling* illative

ilegal *adj* illegal

ilegalidad *nf* illegality

ilegalmente *adv* illegally

ilegibilidad *nf* illegibility, illegibleness

ilegible *adj* illegible, unreadable

ilegítimamente *adv* illegitimately

ilegitimar *vt* to outlaw

ilegitimidad *nf* illegitimacy, illegitimateness

ilegítimo, -a *adj* illegitimate

íleon *nm Anat* ileum

ileso, -a *adj* unhurt, unharmed

iletrado, -a 1 *adj* illiterate, uneducated, uncultured
2 *nm,f* illiterate o uneducated o uncultured person

ilícito, -a *adj* illicit, unlawful

ilimitado, -a *adj* unlimited, limitless, boundless

ilion *nm Anat* ilium

Ilma. *(abrev de* **Ilustrísima)** Your/Her Excellence o Excellency

Ilmo. *(abrev de* **Ilustrísimo)** Your/His Excellence o Excellency

ilocalizable *adj* **se encuentra i.** he cannot be found

ilógico, -a *adj* illogical

Iltre. *(abrev de* **ilustre)** eminent, distinguished

iluminación *nf* **(a)** *(alumbrado)* illumination, lighting; **i. artificial** artificial lighting **(b)** *Fis* illumination **(c)** *(de manuscritos)* illumination

iluminado, -a 1 *pp de* **iluminar**
2 *adj* **(a)** *(con luz)* illuminated, lighted, lit **(b)** *(manuscrito)* illuminated
3 *nm,f (persona)* visionary, illuminate

iluminador, -a 1 *adj* illuminating
2 *nm,f (de manuscritos)* illuminator

iluminar *vt* **(a)** *(con luz)* to illuminate, light (up) **(b)** *(manuscritos)* to illuminate **(c)** *Fig (persona)* to enlighten; *(tema)* to throw light upon

ilusión *nf* **(a)** *(esperanza)* hope; *(esperanza vana)* illusion, illusory hope, delusion; **forjarse** o **hacerse ilusiones** to build up one's hopes; **no te hagas demasiadas ilusiones** you shouldn't bank on it; **no te hagas ilusiones** don't kid yourself, don't raise your hopes **(b)** *(sueño)* dream; **su i. es estar de nuevo en casa** his dream is to be back home **(c)** *esp Esp (emoción)* excitement, thrill; **el viaje me hace mucha i.** I am really looking forward to the trip; **¡qué i.!** how exciting!; **su visita me hizo mucha i.** I was really thrilled by her visit **(d)** **i. óptica** optical illusion

ilusionar 1 *vt* **(a)** *(esperanzar)* to build up hopes **(b)** *(entusiasmar)* to excite, thrill
2 **ilusionarse** *vpr* **(a)** *(esperanzarse)* to build up one's hopes **(b)** *(entusiasmarse)* to be excited o thrilled **(con** about)

ilusionismo *nm* illusionism

ilusionista *nmf* illusionist, conjurer

iluso, -a 1 *adj* easily deceived, gullible
2 *nm,f* dupe

ilusorio, -a *adj* illusory, unreal

ilustración *nf* **(a)** *(grabado)* illustration, picture; *(ejemplo)* illustration **(b)** *(erudición)* learning, erudition; *Hist* **la I.** the Enlightenment

ilustrado, -a 1 *pp de* **ilustrar**
2 *adj* **(a)** *(con dibujos, ejemplos)* illustrated **(b)** *(erudito)* learned, erudite

ilustrador, -a 1 *adj* illustrative
2 *nm,f* illustrator

ilustrar 1 *vt* (**a**) *(gen)* to illustrate (**b**) *(aclarar)* to explain, make clear (**c**) *(instruir)* to enlighten
  2 ilustrarse *vpr* to educate oneself

ilustrativo, -a *adj* illustrative

ilustre *adj* illustrious, distinguished

ilustrísimo, -a *adj* most illustrious; **Vuestra Ilustrísima** Your Grace

imagen *nf* (**a**) *(figura)* image; *Fís* **i. real/virtual** real/virtual image; **ser la viva i. de algn** to be the spitting image of sb (**b**) *Rel* image, statue; *Fam* **quedarse para vestir imágenes** to be left on the shelf (**c**) *TV* picture (**d**) *(apariencia pública)* image; **tener buena/mala i.** to have a good/bad image ❑ **i. corporativa** *o* **de empresa** corporate image; **i. de marca** brand image

imaginable *adj* imaginable, conceivable

imaginación *nf* imagination; **eso son imaginaciones tuyas** you're imagining things; **nunca se me pasó por la i.** it never occurred to me

imaginar 1 *vt* to imagine
  2 imaginarse *vpr* to imagine; **me imagino que sí** I suppose so; *Fam* **¡imagínate!** just imagine!

imaginaria *nf Mil (en dormitorio)* night guard; *(de reserva)* reserve guard

imaginario, -a *adj* imaginary

imaginativo, -a *adj* imaginative

imaginería *nf Rel* religious images *pl*

imaginero *nm* maker of religious images

imán[1] *nm* magnet; *Fam Fig* **tener i.** to have a magnetic personality

imán[2] *nm Rel* imam, imaum

imanación *nf*, **imantación** *nf* magnetization

imanar *vt*, **imantar** *vt* to magnetize

imbatible *adj* unbeatable, invincible

imbatido, -a *adj* unbeaten, undefeated

imbebible *adj* undrinkable

imbécil 1 *adj* stupid, silly
  2 *nmf* idiot, imbecile

imbecilidad *nf* stupidity, imbecility

imberbe *adj* beardless

imborrable *adj* indelible

imbricación *nf* overlap

imbricar [59] *vt* to overlap

imbuir [34] *Fml* **1** *vt* to imbue
  2 imbuirse *vpr* to become imbued (**de** with)

imitable *adj* imitable

imitación *nf* imitation; **a i. de** in imitation of; **joyas de i.** imitation jewellery *sing*

imitador, -a 1 *adj* imitative
  2 *nm,f* imitator

imitamonas *nmf inv Fam* copycat

imitar *vt (gen)* to imitate; *(gestos)* to mimic

impaciencia *nf* impatience

impacientar 1 *vt* to make lose patience, exasperate
  2 impacientarse *vpr* to get *o* grow impatient; **i. por** to grow impatient at

impaciente *adj* impatient; **están impacientes por llegar** they are anxious to arrive; **ponerse i.** to get *o* grow impatient

impacientemente *adv* impatiently

impactante *adj* hard-hitting

impactar 1 *vt (sujeto: noticia)* to have an impact on
  2 *vi (bala)* to hit

impacto *nm* impact; *Mil* hit ❑ **i. ambiental** environmental impact; **i. de bala** bullet hole

impagable *adj* unpayable; *Fig* invaluable

impagado, -a 1 *adj* unpaid
  2 *nm Com Fin* unpaid item, item outstanding

impago, -a 1 *adj* unpaid
  2 *nm* nonpayment

impalpable *adj* impalpable

impar *adj* (**a**) *Mat* odd ❑ **número i.** odd number (**b**) *(sin igual)* unrivalled, *US* unrivaled, unique

imparable *adj Dep* unstoppable

imparcial *adj* impartial, unbiased

imparcialidad *nf* impartiality

imparcialmente *adv* impartially

impartir *vt* to convey, impart; *Rel* **i. su bendición a** to give one's blessing to

impasibilidad *nf* impassiveness

impasible *adj* impassive

impasse [im'pas] *nm* impasse, deadlock

impavidez *nf* (**a**) *(valor)* fearlessness, dauntlessness (**b**) freshness, cheekiness

impávido, -a *adj* (**a**) *(valeroso)* intrepid, fearless, dauntless (**b**) fresh, cheeky

impecable *adj* impeccable

impedido, -a 1 *pp de* **impedir**
  2 *adj* disabled, handicapped, crippled
  3 *nm,f* disabled *o* handicapped person, cripple

impedimenta *nf Mil* impedimenta *pl*

impedimento *nm (gen)* impediment; *(obstáculo)* hindrance, obstacle

impedir [47] *vt (obstaculizar)* to impede, hinder, obstruct; *(imposibilitar)* to prevent, stop, thwart; **i. el paso** to block the way; **una importante reunión me impedirá ir al bautizo** an important meeting will prevent me from going to the christening

impelente *adj Téc* driving, propelling; *Fig (incitante)* inviting, driving, impelling

impeler *vt Téc* to drive, propel; *Fig* to drive, impel, urge

impenetrabilidad *nf* impenetrability

impenetrable *adj* impenetrable; *Fig (secreto, acción)* obscure; *Fig (persona)* reserved, aloof

impenitencia *nf* impenitence

impenitente *adj Rel* impenitent, unrepentant; *Fig Fam (empedernido)* inveterate, confirmed

impensable *adj* unthinkable

impensado, -a *adj* unexpected, unforeseen, out of the blue

impepinable *adj Esp Fam Hum (argumento)* knockdown, unanswerable; **¡eso es i.!** that's for sure!

impepinablemente *adv Fam* as sure as eggs are eggs

imperante *adj* ruling, prevailing

imperar *vi* to rule, prevail

imperativamente *adv* imperatively

imperativo, -a 1 *adj* imperative
  2 *nm Ling* imperative

imperceptible *adj* imperceptible

imperceptiblemente *adv* imperceptibly

imperdible *nm* safety pin

imperdonable *adj* unforgivable, inexcusable

imperecedero, -a *adj* imperishable; *Fig* everlasting, immortal

imperfección *nf* (**a**) *(cualidad)* imperfection (**b**) *(defecto)* defect, fault, flaw, deficiency

imperfecto, -a 1 *adj* (**a**) *(no perfecto)* imperfect, fallible (**b**) *(defectuoso)* defective, faulty, flawed (**c**) *Ling* imperfect; **pretérito i.** (past) imperfect
  2 *nm Ling* imperfect (tense)

imperial *adj* imperial

imperialismo *nm* imperialism

imperialista *adj & nmf* imperialist

impericia *nf (poca habilidad)* lack of skill; *(inexperiencia)* lack of experience, inexperience

imperio *nm* empire; **el i. romano** the Roman Empire; *Fig* haughtiness, arrogance; *Fig* **vale un i.** it's worth a fortune

imperioso, -a *adj* (**a**) *(arrogante)* imperious (**b**) *(indispensable)* urgent, imperative; **una necesidad imperiosa** a pressing need

impermeabilidad *nf* impermeability, imperviousness

impermeabilización *nf* waterproofing

impermeabilizante *adj* waterproofing

impermeabilizar [14] *vt* to waterproof

impermeable 1 *adj (gen)* impermeable, impervious; *(ropa)* waterproof; *Fig* **i. a las críticas** impervious to criticism
  2 *nm* raincoat, *Br* mac

impersonal *adj* impersonal

impersonalidad *nf* impersonality, lacking in character

impertérrito, -a *adj* unmoved, undaunted, fearless

impertinencia *nf (persona)* impertinence; *(palabras)* impertinent remark

impertinente 1 *adj* impertinent, uncalled for, impudent
  2 impertinentes *nmpl* lorgnette *sing*

impertinentemente *adv* impertinently

imperturbable *adj* imperturbable, unruffled

ímpetu *nm* (**a**) *(impulso)* impetus, impulse, momentum (**b**) *(violencia)* violence (**c**) *(fogosidad)* impetuosity, impulsiveness

impetuosidad *nf* (**a**) *(violencia)* violence (**b**) *(fogosidad)* impetuosity, impulsiveness

impetuoso, -a *adj* (**a**) *(violento)* violent; **torrente i.** rushing torrent (**b**) *(fogoso)* impetuous, impulsive

impiedad *nf Rel* impiety; *(falta de compasión)* heartlessness, pitilessness

impío, -a 1 *adj* impious, ungodly, irreligious
  2 *nm,f* infidel

implacable *adj* relentless, implacable, inexorable

implantación *nf* (**a**) *(de costumbres)* implantation; *(de reformas)* introduction (**b**) *Med* implantation

implantar *vt* (**a**) *(costumbres)* to implant, instil, *US* instill; *(reformas)* to introduce; **cuando se implantó la democracia** when democracy was introduced (**b**) *Med* to implant

implante *nm* implant

implementar *vt* to implement

implicación *nf* implication

implicar [59] *vt* (**a**) *(involucrar)* to implicate, involve (**en** in); **la implicó en el asunto** he involved her in the affair (**b**) *(conllevar)* to imply; **eso no implica que no sean buenos amigos** that does not mean that they are not good friends

implícitamente *adv* implicitly

implícito, -a *adj* implicit, implied

implorar *vt* to implore, beseech, beg, entreat

implosión *nf Fís* implosion

impoluto, -a *adj* pure, spotless, immaculate

imponderable *adj & nm* imponderable

imponente *adj* (**a**) *(impresionante)* imposing, impressive (**b**) *Fam (sensacional)* terrific, tremendous, smashing

imponer [50] *(pp* impuesto*)* **1** *vt* (**a**) *(gen)* to impose (**b**) *(exigir)* to demand, exact; *(silencio, obediencia)* to command (**c**) *(dar)* to give; *Mil* to award; **i. un nombre a algn** to give a name to sb (**d**) *(instruir)* to instruct (**en** in); *(informar)* to inform (**de** of) (**e**) *Fin* to deposit (**f**) *Rel* **i. las manos sobre algn** to impose *o* lay hands on sb (**g**) *(un edificio)* to be impressive; *(persona)* to inspire respect
  2 imponerse *vpr* (**a**) *(infundir respeto)* **i. a algn** to command respect from sb, impose one's authority on sb (**b**) *(prevalecer)* to prevail; **se impuso el sentido común** common sense prevailed (**c**) *(ponerse de moda)* to become fashionable; **se ha vuelto a i. la falda corta** short skirts have become fashionable again (**d**) *(asumir)* to assume, take on (**e**) *(ser necesario)* to be necessary (**f**) *(informarse)* **i. de algo** to find out about sth, acquaint oneself with sth

imponible *adj Fin* taxable, subject to taxation; **no i.** tax-free

impopular *adj* unpopular, disliked

impopularidad *nf* unpopularity

importación *nf* (**a**) *(acción)* import, importation; **artículos de i.** imported goods (**b**) **importaciones** imports; **comercio de i.** import trade

importador, -a 1 *adj* importing
  2 *nm,f* importer

importancia *nf* importance, significance; **conceder/dar i. a** to attach/give importance to; **darse i.** to show off; **quitar** *o* **restar i. a algo** to play sth down; **sin i.** unimportant

importante *adj* important, significant; **una suma i.** a considerable sum

importar¹ 1 *vt (valer)* to amount to; **los libros importan dos mil pesos** the books come to two thousand pesos
  2 *vi* (**a**) *(hacer al caso)* to matter; **eso no le importa a usted** that doesn't concern you, that's none of your business; **lo compraré, no importa su precio** I'll buy it whatever the price; **no importa** it doesn't matter; **no me importa decirlo** I don't mind saying it; **¿te importa** *o* **importaría escribirlo?** would you mind writing it down?; *Fam* **me importa un bledo** *o* **un pito** I couldn't care less (**b**) *(implicar)* to involve

importar² *vt* to import

importe *nm Com Fin (valor)* price, cost; *(total)* total, amount

importunar *vt* to bother, pester, importune

importuno, -a *adj* (**a**) *(inoportuno)* inopportune (**b**) *(fastidioso)* bothersome, troublesome, annoying; **temo ser i.** I don't want to be a nuisance

imposibilidad *nf* impossibility

imposibilitado, -a 1 *pp de* imposibilitar
  2 *adj* (**a**) *(inválido)* disabled, crippled (**b**) *(impotente)* helpless, without means; **verse i. para hacer algo** to be unable to do sth, be prevented from doing sth

imposibilitar *vt* (**a**) *(impedir)* to make impossible, prevent (**b**) *(incapacitar)* to disable, cripple

imposible *adj* impossible; **me es i. hacerlo** I can't (possibly) do it; *Fam* **hacer la vida i. a algn** to make life impossible for sb; **hacer lo i.** to do the impossible

imposición *nf* (**a**) *(de disciplina, condiciones, multas)* imposition (**b**) *Fin* deposit; *(impuesto)* tax; **hacer una i.** to deposit money (**c**) **imposiciones** deposits (**d**) *Impr* imposition (**e**) *Rel* **i. de manos** laying on of hands

impositivo, -a *adj* tax, of taxes; **sistema** *o* **método i.** tax system

impositor, -a *nm,f Esp Fin* depositor

impostor, -a *nm,f* (a) *(farsante)* impostor (b) *(calumniador)* slanderer

impostura *nf* (a) *(engaño)* imposture, deception (b) *(calumnia)* slander

impotencia *nf* powerlessness, impotence; *Med* impotence

impotente *adj* powerless, impotent; *Med* impotent; **verse i. para hacer algo** to find oneself powerless to do sth

impracticable *adj* (a) *(inviable)* impracticable, unfeasible, unviable (b) *(camino, carretera)* impassable; *(en letrero)* **carretera i.** road unsuitable for traffic

imprecación *nf* imprecation, curse

imprecar [59] *vt* to imprecate, curse

imprecisión *nf* lack of precision, imprecision, vagueness

impreciso, -a *adj* imprecise, vague

impredecible *adj* unpredictable

impregnación *nf* impregnation

impregnar 1 *vt* to impregnate (**en, de** with)
2 impregnarse *vpr* to become impregnated

impremeditado, -a *adj* unpremeditated

imprenta *nf* (a) *(arte)* printing, art of printing (b) *(taller)* printer's, printing house o works; **tinta de i.** printer's ink (c) *Fig* printed matter; **libertad de i.** freedom of the press

imprescindible *adj* essential, indispensable; **es i. que** it is essential that

impresentable *adj* unpresentable

impresión *nf* (a) *(huella)* impression, imprint; **i. visual** visual impression; **i. dactilar** o **digital** fingerprint (b) *Fig (efecto)* impression; **causar i.** to make an impression (c) *Fig (opinión)* impression; **cambiar impresiones** to exchange impressions (d) *Impr* printing; **una i. de diez mil ejemplares** an edition of ten thousand copies

impresionable *adj* impressionable

impresionante *adj* impressive, striking; *Fam* **un error i.** a terrible mistake

impresionar 1 *vt* (a) *(sorprender)* to impress, make an impression on; *(conmover)* to move, touch; **el accidente la impresionó mucho** she was stunned by the accident; **sus cariñosas palabras me impresionaron** his affectionate words touched me (b) *Fot* to expose; **película sin i.** unexposed film (c) *(grabar discos)* to cut
2 impresionarse *vpr (sorprenderse)* to be impressed; *(conmoverse)* to be moved o touched

impresionismo *nm Arte Lit* impressionism

impresionista *adj & nmf* impressionist

impreso, -a 1 *pp de* **imprimir**
2 *adj* printed; **la letra impresa** the printed word; **lo vi i.** I saw it in print
3 *nm* (a) *(papel, folleto)* printed matter (b) *(formulario)* form; **i. de solicitud** application form (c) **impresos** *(de correos)* printed matter *sing*

impresor, -a *nm,f (persona)* printer

impresora *nf Inform* printer ❑ **i. láser** laser printer

imprevisible *adj* unforeseeable, unpredictable

imprevisión *nf* lack of foresight

imprevisto, -a 1 *adj* unforeseen, unexpected
2 *nm* (a) *(incidente)* unforeseen event; **surgió un i.** something unexpected came up (b) **imprevistos** *(gastos)* incidental expenses

imprimación *nf Arte* (a) *(acción)* priming (b) *(sustancia)* primer, priming material

imprimátur *nm inv Rel* imprimatur

imprimible *adj* printable

imprimir *vt (pp* **impreso)** (a) *Impr Inform* to print (b) *(marcar)* to stamp, imprint, impress (c) *Fig (fijar en el ánimo)* to fix

improbabilidad *nf* improbability, unlikelihood

improbable *adj* improbable, unlikely

ímprobo, -a *adj* (a) *(sin probidad)* dishonest, corrupt (b) *(excesivo)* laborious, very hard; **esfuerzo i.** strenuous effort

improcedencia *nf* (a) *(desacierto)* inappropriateness, unsuitability (b) *Jur* inadmissibility

improcedente *adj* (a) *(inoportuno)* inappropriate, unsuitable (b) *Jur* inadmissible

improductividad *nf* unproductiveness

improductivo, -a *adj* unproductive

impronta *nf* impression; *Fig* mark; **este libro lleva la i. de un gran escritor** this book has the mark of a great writer

impronunciable *adj* unpronounceable

improperio *nm* insult, offensive remark

impropio, -a *adj* (a) *(incorrecto)* improper; **i. de** unbecoming to o for (b) *(inadecuado)* inappropriate, unsuitable

improrrogable *adj* that cannot be prolonged o extended

improvisación *nf* improvisation; *Mús* extemporization

improvisadamente *adv* **se reunieron i.** they had an impromptu meeting

improvisado, -a 1 *pp de* **improvisar**
2 *adj* improvised, impromptu, ad lib; *(reparación, construcción)* makeshift; **discurso i.** impromptu speech

improvisar *vt* to improvise; *Mús* to extemporize

improviso, -a *adj* unforeseen, unexpected; **de i.** unexpectedly, suddenly; *Mús* **tocar de i.** to play impromptu; *Fam* **coger** o **pillar a algn de i.** to catch sb unawares

imprudencia *nf* imprudence, rashness; *(indiscreción)* indiscretion; **i. temeraria** (criminal) negligence

imprudente *adj* imprudent, unwise, rash; *(indiscreto)* indiscreet; **conductor i.** careless driver

impúber 1 *adj* below the age of puberty
2 *nmf* child below the age of puberty

impublicable *adj* unpublishable, unprintable

impudicia *nf*, **impudicicia** *nf (falta de pudor)* immodesty; *(desvergüenza)* shamelessness

impúdico, -a *adj (indecente)* immodest, improper; *(desvergonzado)* shameless

impudor *nm* immodesty; *(desvergüenza)* shamelessness

impuesto, -a 1 *pp de* **imponer**
2 *adj* (a) *(gen)* imposed (b) *(informado)* **estar i. de** o **en** to be informed of, be acquainted with
3 *nm Fin* tax; **libre de impuestos** tax-free; **tienda libre de impuestos** duty-free shop ❑ **i. directo/indirecto** direct/indirect tax; **i. sobre la renta** income tax; **i. sobre el valor** *Am* **agregado** o *Esp* **añadido** value-added tax

impugnable *adj* refutable

impugnación *nf* refutation

impugnar *vt (teoría)* to refute, disprove; *(decisión)* to challenge, contest, oppose

impulsar *vt* to impel, drive forward; *Fig (incitar)* to impel, drive

impulsión *nf* impulsion

impulsividad *nf* impulsiveness

impulsivo, -a *adj* impulsive

impulso *nm* (a) *Fís* impulse, thrust (b) *(velocidad)* momentum; **coger i.** to gather momentum; *Dep* **tomar i.** to take a run up

impulsor, -a 1 *adj* driving; **fuerza impulsora** driving force

2 *nm,f* dynamic force; **él fue el i. del proyecto** he was the driving force behind the project

impune *adj* unpunished

impunemente *adv* with impunity

impunidad *nf* impunity

impureza *nf* impurity

impuro, -a *adj* impure

imputable *adj* attributable

imputación *nf* imputation, charge

imputar *vt* to impute, attribute

inabarcable *adj* too wide *o* large

inabordable *adj* unapproachable, inaccessible

inacabable *adj* interminable, endless

inacabado, -a *adj* unfinished

inaccesible *adj* inaccessible

inacción *nf* inaction, inactivity

inacentuado, -a *adj Ling* unstressed, atonic

inaceptable *adj* unacceptable

inactividad *nf* inactivity; *Fin* lull, stagnation

inactivo, -a *adj* inactive

inadaptable *adj* unadaptable

inadaptación *nf* maladjustment

inadaptado, -a 1 *adj* maladjusted

2 *nm,f* misfit

inadecuación *nf* inadequacy

inadecuado, -a *adj* **(a)** *(insuficiente)* inadequate **(b)** *(inapropiado)* unsuitable, inappropriate

inadmisible *adj* inadmissible

inadvertencia *nf* inadvertence, heedlessness; **por i.** inadvertently, unintentionally

inadvertido, -a *adj* **(a)** *(no visto)* unnoticed, unseen; **pasar i.** to escape notice, pass unnoticed **(b)** *(distraído)* inattentive

inagotable *adj* **(a)** *(recursos etc)* inexhaustible **(b)** *(infatigable)* tireless, indefatigable, unwearying

inaguantable *adj* unbearable, intolerable

inalámbrico, -a *adj* wireless

inalcanzable *adj* unattainable, unachievable

inalienable *adj* inalienable

inalterable *adj* **(a)** *(gen)* unalterable **(b)** *(colour)* fast, permanent **(c)** *(persona) (impasible)* impassive, imperturbable

inalterado, -a *adj* unaltered, unchanged

inamovible *adj* immovable, fixed

inane *adj* inane, empty, pointless

inanición *nf* starvation; *Med* inanition

inanidad *nf* inanity, senselessness

inanimado, -a *adj* inanimate

inapelable *adj* **(a)** *Jur* unappealable, without appeal **(b)** *Fig (irremediable)* inevitable, unavoidable

inapetencia *nf* lack *o* loss of appetite

inapetente *adj* having no appetite

inaplazable *adj* which cannot be postponed; *(urgente)* urgent, pressing

inaplicable *adj* inapplicable

inapreciable *adj* **(a)** *(inestimable)* invaluable, inestimable **(b)** *(insignificante)* insignificant, minimum

inapropiado, -a *adj* inappropriate

inarrugable *adj* crease-resistant

inarticulado, -a *adj* inarticulate

inasequible *adj* **(a)** *(meta)* unattainable, unachievable **(b)** *(persona)* unapproachable, inaccessible **(c)** *(precio)* prohibitive **(d)** *(cuestión, problema)* incomprehensible

inasistencia *nf* absence

inastillable *adj* *(cristal)* shatterproof; *(madera)* splinterproof

inatacable *adj Mil* unassailable; *Fig (argumento, teoría)* irrefutable

inatento, -a *adj* inattentive

inaudible *adj* inaudible

inaudito, -a *adj* **(a)** *(nunca oído)* unheard-of; *(sin precedente)* unprecedented **(b)** *Fig (escandaloso)* outrageous

inauguración *nf* *(gen)* inauguration, opening; *(de una placa, estatua)* unveiling

inaugural *adj* inaugural, opening; **ceremonia i.** inaugural ceremony; *Av* **vuelo i.** maiden flight; *Náut* **viaje i.** maiden voyage

inaugurar *vt* *(gen)* to inaugurate, open; *(placa, estatua)* to unveil; **i. una casa** to have a housewarming party

inca *adj & nmf* Inca

incaico, -a *adj* Inca

incalculable *adj* incalculable, indeterminate

incalificable *adj* indescribable, unspeakable

incandescencia *nf* incandescence

incandescente *adj* incandescent

incansable *adj* tireless, indefatigable, unwearying

incansablemente *adv* tirelessly, indefatigably

incapacidad *nf* **(a)** *(gen)* incapacity, incapability ❑ **i. física** physical disability; **i. laboral** industrial disability *o Br* disablement **(b)** *(incompetencia)* incompetence, inefficiency

incapacitado, -a 1 *pp de* **incapacitar**

2 *adj* **(a)** *(imposibilitado)* incapacitated, disabled **(b)** *(descalificado) (desautorizado)* incapacitated

incapacitar *vt* **(a)** *(sujeto: circunstancias) (para ejercer cargos, votar)* to disqualify **(para** from**)**; *(para trabajar)* to render unfit **(para** for**) (b)** *(sujeto: juez) (para ejercer cargos, votar)* to disqualify, declare disqualified **(para** from**)**; *(para trabajar)* to declare unfit **(para** for *o* to**)**

incapaz *adj* **(a)** *(no capaz)* incapable **(de** of**)**, unfit **(de** for**)**; *Fam* **es i. de matar una mosca** he wouldn't hurt a fly **(b)** *(incompetente)* incompetent, inefficient

incautación *nf Jur* seizure, confiscation

incautamente *adv* incautiously, unwarily

incautarse *vpr Jur* **i. de** to seize, confiscate

incauto, -a 1 *adj* **(a)** *(imprudente)* incautious, unwary **(b)** *(crédulo)* gullible

2 *nm,f* gullible person

incendiado, -a 1 *pp de* **incendiar**

2 *adj* *(que arde)* on fire, burning, in flames; *(destruido)* burnt-out

incendiar 1 *vt* to set on fire, set fire to, set alight, burn down

2 incendiarse *vpr* to catch fire

incendiario, -a 1 *adj* incendiary; *Fig (discurso etc)* inflammatory

2 *nm,f (persona)* arsonist, fireraiser

incendio *nm* fire; **i. forestal** forest fire; **i. intencionado** *o* **provocado** arson

incensario *nm Rel* censer, thurible

incentivar *vt* to give an incentive

incentivo *nm* incentive ❑ **i. fiscal** tax incentive

incertidumbre *nf* uncertainty, doubt

incesante *adj* incessant, never-ending

incesantemente *adv* incessantly

incesto *nm* incest

incestuoso, -a *adj* incestuous

incidencia *nf* (**a**) *(frecuencia, cantidad)* incidence; **hubo una alta i. de muertes en la carretera** there was a high incidence of deaths on the road (**b**) *Fis* incidence (**c**) *(repercusión)* repercussion, consequence, impact, effect; **su discurso tuvo una gran i.** his speech made a great impact (**d**) **por i.** by chance *o* accident

incidental *adj* incidental

incidente *nm* incident; **llegar sin incidentes** to arrive without any problem

incidir *vi* (**a**) *(incurrir)* to fall (**en** into) (**b**) *(afectar)* to affect; *(influir)* to influence (**en** -); **la subida de precios incide más sobre los salarios bajos** the rise in prices has a greater effect on low wages (**c**) *Med* to make an incision

incienso *nm* incense; *Fig (adulación)* flattery

incierto, -a *adj* (**a**) *(dudoso)* uncertain, doubtful (**b**) *(inconstante)* inconstant, unpredictable

incineración *nf (de basuras)* incineration; *(de\cadáveres)* cremation

incinerador *nm* incinerator

incinerar *vt (basura)* to incinerate; *(cadáveres)* to cremate

incipiente *adj* incipient, budding; **el día i.** the dawning day

incisión *nf* incision, cut

incisivo, -a 1 *adj* incisive, sharp, cutting; *Fig* **un comentario i.** a cutting remark
2 *nm Anat* incisor

inciso, -a 1 *adj (estilo)* jerky
2 *nm Ling* interpolated *o* incidental clause; **a modo de i.** in passing, incidentally

incitación *nf* incitement

incitador, -a 1 *adj* inciting
2 *nm,f* inciter

incitante *adj* (**a**) *(instigador)* inciting (**b**) *(provocativo)* provocative

incitar *vt* to incite, urge

incivil *adj* uncivíl, rude

incivilizado, -a *adj* uncivilized

inclasificable *adj* unclassifiable

inclemencia *nf* inclemency, harshness

inclemente *adj* inclement, harsh

inclinación *nf* (**a**) *(desviación)* slope, incline, slant; *(del cuerpo)* stoop (**b**) *(reverencia)* bow; *(señal de asentimiento)* nod (**c**) *Fig (tendencia)* tendency, inclination, propensity, penchant; **tiene i. hacia la música** he has a penchant for music

inclinado, -a 1 *pp de* **inclinar**
2 *adj* inclined, slanting; *Fig* **me siento i. a creerle** I feel inclined to believe him

inclinar 1 *vt* (**a**) *(doblar)* to incline, slant, bend; *(cuerpo)* to bow; *(la cabeza)* to nod (**b**) *Fig (persuadir)* to persuade, incline, induce, dispose
2 inclinarse *vpr* (**a**) *(doblarse)* to lean, slope, incline; **i. hacia adelante** to lean forward (**b**) *(al saludar)* to bow; **i. ante** to bow down to (**c**) *Fig (optar)* **i. a** to be *o* feel inclined to; **me inclino por éste** I'd rather háve this one, I prefer this one

ínclito, -a *adj Lit* distinguished, illustrious

incluido, -a 1 *pp de* **incluir**
2 *adj* (**a**) *(comprendido)* included; **precio todo i.** all-in price; **servicio no i.** service not included (**b**) *(adjunto)* enclosed

incluir [34] *vt* (**a**) *(comprender)* to include; **incluyendo gastos de envío** including postage and packing; **¿me incluiste en la lista?** did you include me in the list? (**b**) *(contener)* to contain, comprise (**c**) *(adjuntar)* to enclose

inclusa *nf* foundling home, orphanage

inclusero, -a *adj & nm,f* foundling, orphan

inclusión *nf* inclusion; **con i. de** including

inclusive *adv* inclusive; **de martes a viernes i.** from Tuesday to Friday inclusive; **hasta la lección ocho i.** up to and including lesson eight

inclusivo, -a *adj* inclusive

incluso 1 *adv* inclusive, inclusively
2 *prep* even

incoar *vt Jur* to initiate

incógnita *nf* (**a**) *Mat* unknown quantity, unknown (**b**) *(misterio)* mystery; **no sé cómo reaccionará, es una i.** I don't know how he will react, he's an unknown quantity

incógnito, -a 1 *adj* incognito, unknown
2 *nm* incognito; **guardar el i.** to remain incognito; **viajar de i.** to travel incognito

incoherencia *nf* incoherence

incoherente *adj* incoherent

incoloro, -a *adj* colourless

incólume *adj Fml* safe, unharmed; **salir i. de un accidente** to escape from an accident without injury

incombustible *adj* incombustible, fireproof

incomestible *adj*, **incomible** *adj* uneatable, inedible

incomodar 1 *vt* (**a**) *(causar molestia)* to inconvenience, put out (**b**) *(fastidiar)* to bother, annoy (**c**) *(enojar, disgustar)* to annoy, anger
2 incomodarse *vpr* (**a**) *(tomarse molestias)* to put oneself out, trouble oneself, go out of one's way; **no te incomodes** don't put yourself out (**b**) *(enojarse, disgustarse)* to get annoyed *o* angry

incomodidad *nf*, **incomodo** *nm* (**a**) *(falta de comodidad)* discomfort (**b**) *(molestia)* inconvenience (**c**) *Euf (malestar)* unrest, uneasiness

incómodo, -a *adj* uncomfortable; **sentirse i.** to feel uncomfortable *o* awkward

incomparable *adj* incomparable

incomparecencia *nf Jur* nonappearance, default

incompatibilidad *nf* incompatibility; *Jur* **i. de caracteres** mutual incompatibility

incompatible *adj* incompatible

incompetencia *nf* incompetence

incompetente *adj & nmf* incompetent

incompleto, -a *adj* incomplete; *(inacabado)* unfinished

incomprendido, -a 1 *adj* misunderstood
2 *nm,f* misunderstood person; **fue siempre un i.** no one ever understood him

incomprensible *adj* incomprehensible

incomprensiblemente *adv* incomprehensibly

incomprensión *nf* lack of understanding, failure to understand; *(poca voluntad)* lack of sympathy

incomprensivo, -a *adj* uncomprehending; *(insolidario)* unsympathetic

incomunicación *nf* (**a**) *(falta de comunicación)* lack of communication (**b**) *Jur* solitary confinement (**c**) *(aislamiento)* isolation

incomunicado, -a 1 *pp de* **incomunicar**
2 *adj* (**a**) *(aislado)* isolated; **el pueblo se quedó i.** the town was cut off (**b**) *(en la cárcel)* in solitary confinement

incomunicar [59] *vt* (**a**) *(aislar) (lugar)* to isolate, cut off;

(habitación) to shut off (**b**) *(recluso)* to place in solitary confinement

inconcebible *adj* inconceivable, unthinkable

inconciliable *adj* irreconcilable

inconcluso, -a *adj* unfinished

incondicional 1 *adj (gen)* unconditional; *(obediencia)* unquestioning, absolute; *(apoyo)* wholehearted; *(amigo)* faithful; *(partidario)* staunch
  2 *nmf (partidario)* staunch supporter; *(amigo)* faithful friend

inconexión *nf (falta de conexión)* disconnection; *(incoherencia)* incoherence

inconexo, -a *adj (sin conexión)* disconnected, unconnected; *(incoherente)* incoherent, confused

inconfesable *adj* shameful, disgraceful, shocking

inconfeso, -a *adj* not pleading guilty, not owning up

inconformismo *nm* nonconformity

inconformista *adj & nmf* nonconformist

inconfundible *adj* unmistakable, obvious

incongruencia *nf* incongruity

incongruente *adj* incongruous

inconmensurable *adj* immeasurable, vast, limitless

inconmovible *adj* firm, unshakable

inconquistable *adj* (**a**) *Mil* inconquerable, invincible (**b**) *Fig (tenaz)* unyielding

inconsciencia *nf Med* unconsciousness; *Fig (desconocimiento)* unawareness; *(irreflexión)* thoughtlessness, irresponsibility

inconsciente 1 *adj (desmayado)* unconscious; *Fig (despreocupado)* unaware (**de** of); *(irreflexivo)* thoughtless, irresponsible
  2 *nmf* unconscious person; *Fig* thoughtless *o* irresponsible person

inconscientemente *adv* unconsciously, unwittingly

inconsecuencia *nf* inconsistency, inconsequence

inconsecuente *adj* inconsistent, inconsequent; **fue i. en sus respuestas** her replies lacked consistency

inconsiderado, -a *adj* inconsiderate, thoughtless

inconsistencia *nf (de líquido)* runniness, wateriness; *(de tela)* flimsiness; *(de argumento)* weakness, insubstantiality

inconsistente *adj (líquido)* runny, watery; *(tela)* flimsy; *(argumento)* weak, insubstantial

inconsolable *nf* inconsolable, disconsolate

inconstancia *nf* inconstancy, fickleness

inconstante *adj* inconstant, fickle; *Meteor* changeable, variable

inconstitucional *adj* unconstitutional

inconstitucionalidad *nf* unconstitutionality

incontable *adj* countless, innumerable, uncountable

incontaminado, -a *adj* unpolluted, uncontaminated

incontenible *adj* uncontrollable, irrepressible; **un ataque de risa i.** a fit of uncontrollable laughter

incontestable *adj* indisputable, unquestionable, undeniable

incontinencia *nf* incontinence

incontinente[1] *adj* (**a**) *(desenfrenado)* lacking in sexual control (**b**) *Med* incontinent

incontinente[2] *adv* at once

incontrolable *adj* uncontrollable

incontrolado, -a *adj* uncontrolled

incontrovertible *adj* incontrovertible, indisputable

inconveniencia *nf* (**a**) *(gen)* inconvenience (**b**)

(impropiedad) unsuitability; *(no aconsejable)* inadvisability (**c**) *(incorrección)* impoliteness; *(dicho grosero)* rude remark; **decir/cometer inconveniencias** to be tactless

inconveniente 1 *adj* (**a**) *(gen)* inconvenient (**b**) *(inapropiado)* unsuitable; *(no aconsejable)* inadvisable (**c**) *(incorrecto)* impolite; *(grosero)* rude, coarse
  2 *nm* (**a**) *(objeción)* objection; **poner inconvenientes a algo** to raise objections to sth (**b**) *(desventaja)* drawback; *(problema)* difficulty; **¿tienes i. en acompañarme?** would you mind coming with me?

incordiar *vt Esp Fam* to bother, pester; **¡no incordies!** don't be such a nuisance!

incordio *nm Esp Fam* nuisance, pain

incorporación *nf* (**a**) *(unir)* incorporation (**b**) *(del cuerpo)* sitting-up

incorporado, -a 1 *pp de* incorporar
  2 *adj* (**a**) *(unido)* incorporated; *Téc* built-in, embodied (**b**) *(en la cama)* sitting up

incorporar 1 *vt* (**a**) *(añadir)* to incorporate (**en** into); *Culin* to mix, blend (**b**) *(levantar)* to help to sit up
  2 incorporarse *vpr* (**a**) *(sociedad)* to join; *(trabajo)* to start; *Mil* **i. a filas** to join up (**b**) *(en la cama)* to sit up

incorpóreo, -a *adj* incorporeal; *(inmaterial)* intangible

incorrección *nf* (**a**) *(falta)* incorrectness, inaccuracy; *(gramatical)* mistake (**b**) *(descortesía)* impoliteness, discourtesy, impropriety; **cometer una i.** to commit a faux pas *o* gaffe

incorrecto, -a *adj* (**a**) *(equivocado)* incorrect, inaccurate (**b**) *(grosero)* impolite, discourteous

incorregible *adj* incorrigible; **has comido demasiado otra vez, eres i.** you've eaten too much again, you'll never change

incorruptible *adj* incorruptible; *Fam* straight

incorrupto, -a *adj* uncorrupted, incorrupt; *(mujer)* chaste

incredulidad *nf* (**a**) *(dificultad en creer)* incredulity, disbelief (**b**) *Rel (falta de fe)* unbelief

incrédulo, -a 1 *adj* (**a**) *(que no cree)* incredulous, disbelieving (**b**) *Rel (sin fe)* unbelieving
  2 *nm,f* (**a**) *(persona que no cree)* disbeliever (**b**) *(persona sin fe)* unbeliever

increíble *adj* incredible, unbelievable

incrementar 1 *vt* to increase
  2 incrementarse *vpr* to increase

incremento *nm (aumento)* increase; *(crecimiento)* growth; **i. de la temperatura** rise in temperature; **i. del coste de vida** rise in the cost of living

increpar *vt Fml* to rebuke, reprimand

incriminación *nf* incrimination

incriminar *vt* to incriminate

incruento, -a *adj* bloodless

incrustación *nf* (**a**) *(en joyería)* inlay; **un marco con incrustaciones de oro** a frame with a gold inlay *o* inlaid with gold (**b**) *(en tuberías, calderas)* scale

incrustar 1 *vt* (**a**) *(introducir, empotrar)* to embed; *Fam Fig* **le dio un golpe que lo incrustó contra la pared** he nearly knocked him through the wall (**b**) *(insertar)* to inlay; **incrustado con** inlaid with
  2 incrustarse *vpr* to become embedded (**en** in); *Fig* **la idea se incrustó en su memoria** the idea engraved itself in his memory

incubación *nf* incubation

incubadora *nf* incubator

incubar *vt* to incubate

incuestionable *adj* unquestionable, indisputable

inculcar [59] *vt (gen)* to inculcate; *(principios, ideas)* to instil (**en** into)

inculpación *nf (gen)* accusation; *Jur* charge

inculpado, -a 1 *pp de* **inculpar**
2 *adj (gen)* accused (**de** of); *Jur* charged (**de** with)
3 *nm,f* **el i., la inculpada** the accused

inculpar *vt (gen)* to accuse (**de** of), blame (**de** for); *Jur* to charge (**de** with)

inculto, -a 1 *adj* (**a**) *(ignorante)* uneducated, uncultured (**b**) *(rudo)* uncouth, uncivilized (**c**) *Agr (terreno)* untilled, uncultivated
2 *nm,f* ignoramus

incultura *nf* (**a**) *(ignorancia)* ignorance, lack of culture (**b**) *(rudeza)* uncouthness

incumbencia *nf* duty, obligation, responsibility, concern; **no es de mi i.** it doesn't come within my province, it isn't my concern

incumbir *vi* to be the duty (**a** of), be incumbent (**a** upon); **esto no te incumbe** this is none of your business; **me incumbe a mí hacerlo** it is my duty to do it, it's my responsibility

incumplido, -a 1 *pp de* **incumplir**
2 *adj* unfulfilled

incumplimiento *nm (de un deber)* non-fulfilment, *US* non-fulfillment; *(de una promesa)* failure to keep; *(de una orden)* failure to execute; **i. de contrato** breach of contract

incumplir *vt* not to fulfil *o US* fulfill; *(deber)* fail to fulfil *o US* fulfill; *(promesa, contrato)* to break; *(orden)* to fail to carry out

incunable *nm Impr* (**a**) *(edición)* incunabulum (**b**) **incunables** incunabula *pl*

incurabilidad *nf* incurability

incurable *adj Med* incurable; *Fig* hopeless, incurable

incurrir *vi* (**a**) *(ganarse)* to incur (**b**) *(cometer)* to commit; **i. en delito** to commit a crime; **i. en (un) error** to fall into error

incursión *nf* raid, incursion

indagación *nf* investigation, inquiry

indagar [38] *vt* to investigate, inquire into

indebidamente *adv* (**a**) *(inapropiadamente)* improperly, unduly (**b**) *(injustamente)* wrongfully, unjustly (**c**) *(ilegalmente)* unlawfully, illegally

indebido, -a *adj* (**a**) *(desconsiderado)* improper, undue (**b**) *(injusto)* wrongful, unjust (**c**) *(ilegal)* unlawful, illegal

indecencia *nf* indecency, obscenity; *Fam Pey* **¡es una i.!** *(indignante)* ¡it's a scandal!

indecente *adj* (**a**) *(obsceno)* indecent; **una persona i.** an obscene person (**b**) *(miserable)* miserable; **una habitación i.** a grotty room (**c**) *(sucio)* filthy; **esta camisa está i.** that shirt is very grubby

indecible *adj* unspeakable; *(inefable)* indescribable; **sufrir lo i.** to suffer terribly

indecisión *nf* indecision, hesitation

indeciso, -a *adj* (**a**) *(por decidir)* undecided (**b**) *(vacilante)* hesitant, irresolute; **es una persona indecisa** he can never make up his mind (**c**) *(resultados etc)* inconclusive

indeclinable *adj* (**a**) *Literario (ineludible)* unavoidable (**b**) *Ling* indeclinable

indecoroso, -a *adj* unseemly

indefectible *adj* unfailing, infallible

indefendible *adj*, **indefensible** *adj* indefensible

indefensión *nf* defencelessness

indefenso, -a *adj* defenceless, helpless

indefinible *adj* indefinable; *(con palabras)* inexpressible

indefinidamente *adv* indefinitely

indefinido, -a *adj* (**a**) *(ilimitado) (tiempo)* indefinite; *(impreciso)* undefined, vague (**b**) *Ling* indefinite

indeformable *adj* which will not lose its shape

indeleble *adj* indelible

indelicadeza *nf* indelicacy, coarseness; *(acto)* tactless act

indemne *adj (persona)* unharmed, unhurt; *(cosa)* undamaged

indemnidad *nf* indemnity

indemnización *nf* (**a**) *(acto)* indemnification (**b**) *Fin (compensación)* indemnity, compensation; **i. por despido** severance pay

indemnizar [14] *vt* to indemnify, compensate (**de, por** for)

indemostrable *adj* indemonstrable

independencia *nf* independence; **con i. de** independently of; **conseguir** *o* **ganar la i.** to gain independence; *Hist* **la guerra de la I.** the War of Independence

independentismo *nm* independence movement

independentista *adj & nmf Pol* independent

independiente *adj (libre)* independent; *(individualista)* self-sufficient; *Pol* **se presenta como candidato i.** he's standing as an independent (candidate)

independientemente *adv* (**a**) *(con independencia)* independently (**de** of) (**b**) *(aparte de)* regardless, irrespective (**de** of)

independizar [14] **1** *vt* to make independent, grant independence to
2 independizarse *vpr* to become independent

indescifrable *adj* indecipherable

indescriptible *adj* indescribable

indeseable *adj & nmf* undesirable

indesmallable *adj (medias)* ladderproof, runproof

indestructible *adj* indestructible

indeterminable *adj* indeterminable

indeterminación *nf* indecision, irresolution

indeterminado, -a *adj* (**a**) *(sin determinar)* indeterminate; *(sin límite)* indefinite; *(impreciso)* vague (**b**) *(persona)* irresolute (**c**) *Ling* indefinite

indexación *nf (gen) & Inform* indexing

indexar *vt (gen) & Inform* to index

India *n* (**la**) **I.** India

indiada *nf Am (indios)* crowd of Indians

indiano, -a 1 *adj Literario* Latin American
2 *nm Hist* = Spanish emigrant who returns to Spain having acquired substantial wealth in Latin America

Indias *npl* (**las**) **I.** the Indies; **las I. Orientales/Occidentales** the East/West Indies

indicación *nf* (**a**) *(señal)* indication, sign (**b**) *(corrección)* hint, suggestion; **hacer algo por i. de algn** to do sth at sb's suggestion (**c**) *(instrucción)* instruction, direction; **indicaciones para el uso** instructions for use (**d**) *(informe)* data, figures *pl*

indicado, -a 1 *pp de* **indicar**
2 *adj* right, suitable, appropriate; **a la hora indicada** at the specified time; **él es el menos i. para llevar la empresa** he's the last person who should run the business; **en el momento menos i.** at the worst possible moment; *Fml* **el cambio de tiempo hace i. el uso de ropas gruesas** owing to the change in weather it's recommended that warm clothes be worn

indicador, -a 1 *adj* indicating; **señales indicadoras de peligro** danger signals
2 *nm* (**a**) *(gen)* indicator ❏ **i. económico** economic indicator (**b**) *Téc* gauge, dial, meter; **i. de presión** pressure gauge; *Aut* **i. del nivel de aceite** (oil) dipstick; *Aut* **i. de velocidad** speedometer

indicar [59] *vt* (**a**) *(señalar)* to indicate, show, point out; **i. algo con el dedo** to point sth out; **¿me podría i. el camino?** could you show me the way? (**b**) *(marcar)* to read (**c**) *(aconsejar)* to show, advise; **indíqueme qué debo hacer** tell me what I should do (**d**) *(esbozar)* to outline

indicativo, -a 1 *adj* (**a**) *(que indica)* indicative (**de** of) (**b**) *Ling* (**modo**) **i.** indicative (mode)
2 *nm* (**a**) *Rad* call sign (**b**) *Ling* indicative

índice *nm* (**a**) *(señal)* indication, sign (**b**) *(en libro)* table of contents; *(de biblioteca)* index, catalogue ❏ **í. alfabético** alphabetical index; **í de materias** table of contents (**c**) *(indica proporción) (evolución)* index; *(razón)* ratio; *(relación, tanto por ciento, en gráfica)* rate ❏ **í. de audiencia** rating; **í. bursátil** stock market index; *Fin* **í. del costo** *o Esp* **coste de la vida** cost of living index; **í. de mortalidad** death rate; **í. de natalidad** birth rate; *Fin* **í. de precios** price index (**d**) *Mat* index (**e**) *Anat* (**dedo**) **í.** index finger, forefinger (**f**) *Rel* **í. expurgatorio** the Index

indicio *nm* (**a**) *(señal)* indication, sign, token (**de** of); **no hay indicios de que vaya a llover** there is no sign that it's going to rain (**b**) *(gen pl) (cantidad pequeña)* trace

índico, -a *adj* Indian; **Océano I.** Indian Ocean

indiferencia *nf* indifference, apathy, disinterest

indiferente *adj* (**a**) *(no importante)* indifferent; **me es i.** it makes no difference to me (**b**) *(actitud) (apatía)* apathetic; *(frialdad)* uninterested; **su esposa le es indiferente** he doesn't care two hoots about his wife

indígena 1 *adj* indigenous, native (**de** to)
2 *nmf* native (**de** of)

indigencia *nf Fml* poverty, indigence

indigenismo *nm* Indianism

indigente *Fml* **1** *adj* needy, poverty-stricken, indigent
2 *nmf* poor person; **los indigentes** the poor, the needy

indigerible *adj Fam (comida)* indigestible, difficult to digest; *Fig (persona, cosa)* hard to stomach

indigestarse *vpr* to cause *o* give indigestion; **se le indigestó la comida** the meal gave her indigestion; *Fam Fig (caer mal)* **ese tipo se me indigesta** I can't stomach that guy

indigestión *nf* indigestion

indigesto, -a *adj* (**a**) *(comida)* indigestible, difficult to digest; **sentirse i.** to be suffering from indigestion (**b**) *Fig (de trato áspero)* surly, brusque

indignación *nf* indignation

indignado, -a 1 *pp de* **indignar**
2 *adj* indignant (**por** at, about)

indignante *adj* outrageous, infuriating

indignar 1 *vt* to infuriate, make angry
2 indignarse *vpr* to be *o* feel indignant (**por** at, about)

indignidad *nf* (**a**) *(cualidad)* unworthiness (**b**) *(acto)* unworthy act

indigno, -a *adj (comportamiento)* unworthy (**de** of); **esta actitud me parece indigna de ti** I didn't expect you to take that attitude; **Raúl es i. de nuestra amistad** Raúl is not worthy of our friendship

índigo *nm* indigo

indio, -a *adj & nm,f* Indian; **en fila india** in single file; **hablar como los indios** to speak (a language) badly; *Fam Esp* **hacer el i.** to act the fool

indirecta *nf Fam (insinuación)* hint, insinuation; **tirar** *o* **lanzar una i.** to drop a hint; **coger la i.** to get the message

indirecto, -a *adj* indirect; *Ling* **estilo i.** indirect *o* reported speech

indisciplina *nf* lack of discipline

indisciplinado, -a 1 *pp de* **indisciplinarse**
2 *adj* undisciplined, unruly

indisciplinarse *vpr* to become undisciplined *o* unruly

indiscreción *nf (gen)* indiscretion; *(comentario)* tactless remark; **si no es i., ¿cómo piensas gastarte el dinero?** I hope you don't mind my asking, but how do you plan to spend the money?

indiscreto, -a 1 *adj* indiscreet, tactless
2 *nm,f* indiscreet person

indiscriminadamente *adv* indiscriminately

indiscriminado, -a *adj* indiscriminate

indiscutible *adj* indisputable, unquestionable

indisociable *adj* inseparable (**de** from)

indisoluble *adj* indissoluble

indispensable *adj* indispensable, essential

indisponer [50] (*pp* **indispuesto**) **1** *vt* (**a**) *(planes)* to upset, spoil; *Med* to upset, make unwell (**b**) *Fig (enemistar)* **i. a una persona contra otra** to set one person against another
2 indisponerse *vpr* (**a**) *Med* to fall ill, become unwell (**b**) *Fig* **i. con algn** to fall out with sb

indisposición *nf* (**a**) *Med* indisposition, illness (**b**) *(reticencia)* unwillingness, disinclination

indispuesto, -a 1 *pp de* **indisponer**
2 *adj* (**a**) *Med* indisposed, unwell (**b**) *Fig (enemistado)* on bad terms (**con** with)

indistintamente *adv* the same; **habla los dos idiomas i.** she speaks both languages equally well

indistinto, -a *adj* (**a**) *(indiferente)* immaterial, inconsequential; **es i. ir en tren o en coche** it makes no difference whether you go by train or car (**b**) *Fin* **cuenta indistinta** joint account (**c**) *(impreciso)* indistinct; *(borroso)* vague

individual 1 *adj* individual; **habitación i.** single room
2 *nm* (**a**) *(mantel)* place mat (**b**) **individuales** *Dep* singles

individualidad *nf* individuality

individualismo *nm* individualism

individualista 1 *adj* individualistic
2 *nmf* individualist

individualización *nf* individualization

individualizar [14] *vt* to individualize

individuo *nm* (**a**) *(persona)* person; *Pey* individual (**b**) *(de especie)* **algunos individuos de la especie** some members of the species; **cada i. ocupa un territorio** each animal occupies its own territory

indivisibilidad *nf* indivisibility

indivisible *adj* indivisible

indiviso, -a *adj* undivided

indización *nf* indexation

indizar [14] *vt* to index

indochino, -a *adj & nm,f* Indo-Chinese

indocumentado, -a 1 *adj* (**a**) without identification papers (**b**) *Esp Fam (ignorante)* ignorant
2 *nm,f Esp Fam (ignorante)* **es un i.** he's a complete ignoramus

indoeuropeo, -a *adj & nm,f* Indo-European

índole *nf* (**a**) *(carácter)* character, nature, disposition (**b**) *(clase, tipo)* kind, sort

indolencia *nf* indolence, laziness

indolente 1 *adj* indolent, lazy
 2 *nmf* idler
indoloro, -a *adj* painless
indomable *adj* **(a)** *(animal)* untameable **(b)** *(pueblo)* ungovernable, unruly; *(niño)* uncontrollable; *(pasión)* indomitable
indómito, -a *adj* **(a)** *(no domado)* untamed; *(indomable)* untamable **(b)** *(pueblo)* unruly; *(persona)* uncontrollable
Indonesia *n* Indonesia
indonesio, -a 1 *adj* Indonesian
 2 *nm,f (persona)* Indonesian
 3 *nm (idioma)* Indonesian
indubitable *adj* indubitable, undoubted, beyond doubt
inducción *nf* induction
inducido, -a 1 *pp de* **inducir**
 2 *adj* induced
 3 *nm Elec* armature
inducir [18] *vt* **(a)** *(incitar, mover)* to lead, induce; **i. en error** to lead into error, mislead **(b)** *(inferir)* to infer, deduce **(c)** *Elec (corriente)* to induce
inductivo, -a *adj* inductive
inductor, -a 1 *adj* **(a)** *(que induce)* inducing **(b)** *Elec* inductive
 2 *nm,f* inducer
 3 *nm Elec* inductor
indudable *adj* indubitable, unquestionable; **es i. que** there is no doubt that
indulgencia *nf* **(a)** *(tolerancia)* indulgence, leniency **(b)** *Rel* indulgence
indulgente *adj* indulgent (**con** towards), lenient (**con** with)
indultar *vt Jur* to pardon; *(eximir)* to exempt
indulto *nm Jur* pardon, amnesty
indumentaria *nf* clothing, clothes *pl*, garments *pl*
industria *nf* industry ◻ **i. alimentaria** food industry; **i. ligera/pesada** light/heavy industry; **i. del ocio** leisure industry
industrial 1 *adj* industrial
 2 *nmf* industrialist, manufacturer
industrialismo *nm* industrialism
industrialización *nf* industrialization
industrializado, -a *adj* industrialized; **países industrializados** industrialized countries
industrializar [14] **1** *vt* to industrialize
 2 industrializarse *vpr* to become industrialized
industrioso, -a *adj* industrious
induzco *indic pres véase* **inducir**
inédito, -a *adj* **(a)** *(libro, texto)* unpublished **(b)** *(nuevo)* completely new; *(desconocido)* unknown
inefable *adj* ineffable, indescribable
ineficacia *nf* *(ineptitud)* inefficiency; *(improducción)* ineffectiveness
ineficaz *adj (inepto)* inefficient; *(improductivo)* ineffective
ineficiencia *nf véase* **ineficacia**
ineficiente *adj véase* **ineficaz**
ineluctable *adj Literario* inevitable, inescapable
ineludible *adj* inescapable, unavoidable
inenarrable *adj* unspeakable, inexpressible
ineptitud *nf* ineptitude, incompetence
inepto, -a 1 *adj* inept, incompetent
 2 *nm,f* incompetent person
inequívoco, -a *adj* unmistakable, unequivocal
inercia *nf* **(a)** *Fís* inertia **(b)** *Fig (pasividad)* inertia,

passivity; *(lentitud)* slowness; **hacer algo por i.** to do sth out of habit
inerme *adj* **(a)** *(desarmado)* unarmed **(b)** *Fig (sin defensas)* defenceless, unprotected **(c)** *Zool* with no prickles/spines/sting
inerte *adj* **(a)** *(gas)* inert **(b)** *Fig (cuerpo)* lifeless
inescrutable *adj Fml* inscrutable; *(impenetrable)* mysterious
inesperadamente *adv (fortuitamente)* unexpectedly; *(imprevistamente)* suddenly
inesperado, -a *adj (fortuito)* unexpected, unforeseen; *(imprevisto)* sudden
inestabilidad *nf* instability, unsteadiness
inestable *adj* unstable, unsteady
inestimable *adj* inestimable, invaluable
inevitable *adj* inevitable, unavoidable
inevitablemente *adv* inevitably, unavoidably
inexactitud *nf* **(a)** *(gen)* incorrectness, inaccuracy **(b)** *(error)* mistake
inexacto, -a *adj* inexact, inaccurate
inexcusable *adj* **(a)** *(imperdonable)* inexcusable, unforgivable **(b)** *(ineludible)* unavoidable, inescapable
inexistencia *nf* non-existence
inexistente *adj* non-existent, inexistent
inexorable *adj* inexorable
inexorablemente *adv* inexorably
inexperiencia *nf* **(a)** *(falta de experiencia)* lack of experience, inexperience **(b)** *(falta de habilidad)* lack of skill
inexperimentado, -a *adj* **(a)** *(persona)* inexperienced **(b)** *(método, invento)* untried
inexperto, -a *adj* **(a)** *(sin experiencia)* inexperienced **(b)** *(inhábil)* inexpert, unskilled
inexplicable *adj* inexplicable
inexplorado, -a *adj* unexplored; *(territorio etc)* uncharted
inexpresable *adj* inexpressible
inexpresivo, -a *adj* inexpressive
inexpugnable *adj* **(a)** *Mil* impregnable **(b)** *Fig* stubborn, hard-headed, unyielding
inextinguible *adj* inextinguishable
inextricable *adj* inextricable
infalibilidad *nf* infallibility
infalible *adj* *(indefectible)* infallible; *(en contenido)* faultless
infamante *adj* shameful
infamar *vt* to defame, slander, discredit
infame *adj* infamous, odious, vile; **tiempo i.** vile weather; **trabajo i.** thankless job
infamia *nf* infamy, disgrace
infancia *nf* childhood, infancy; **ha vuelto a la i.** she is in her second childhood
infanta *nf* infanta, princess
infante *nm* **(a)** *(hijo del rey)* infante, prince **(b)** *Mil* infantryman
infantería *nf Mil* infantry; **la i. de marina** the marines
infanticida 1 *adj* infanticidal
 2 *nmf* infanticide, child-killer
 3 *nm Argot* baby snatcher
infanticidio *nm (acto)* infanticide
infantil *adj* **(a)** *(para niños)* child, children's; **juegos infantiles** children's games; **literatura i.** children's literature; *Med* **parálisis i.** infantile paralysis; **psicología i.**

child psychology (**b**) *(aniñado)* childlike; *Pey* childish, infantile

infantilismo *nm Med* infantilism

infarto *nm* heart attack; *Fam* **me va a dar un i.** it'll be the death of me ❑ **i. cerebral** stroke; **i. de miocardio** heart attack, coronary thrombosis

infatigable *adj* indefatigable, tireless, untiring

infausto, -a *adj Literario* unlucky, ill-fated, ill-starred; **un suceso de infausta memoria** an event which is best left forgotten

infección *nf* infection

infeccioso, -a *adj* infectious

infectar 1 *vt* to infect
  2 infectarse *vpr* to become infected (**de** with)

infecto, -a *adj* (**a**) *(población, zona)* infected (**b**) *(asqueroso)* foul; *(horrendo)* stinking; **olor i.** stench; **tiempo i.** filthy weather

infecundidad *nf* infertility; *(esterilidad)* sterility

infecundo, -a *adj* infertile; *(estéril)* sterile ·

infelicidad *nf* unhappiness; *(infortunio)* misfortune

infeliz 1 *adj* unhappy; *(desdichado)* unfortunate
  2 *nmf Fam* simpleton; **es un pobre i.** he is a poor devil

inferencia *nf* inference

inferior 1 *adj* (**a**) *(más bajo)* lower; **el lado i.** the underside; **labio i.** lower lip (**b**) *(en calidad)* inferior (**a** to); **de calidad i.** of inferior quality (**c**) *(en cantidad)* lower, less; **cualquier número i. a diez** any number less than o under o below ten
  2 *nmf (persona)* subordinate, inferior

inferioridad *nf* inferiority; **estar en i. de condiciones** to be at a disadvantage ❑ **complejo de i.** inferiority complex

inferir [62] *vt Literario* (**a**) *(deducir)* to infer, deduce (**de** from) (**b**) *(causar)* to cause (**c**) *(herida)* to inflict

infernal *adj* infernal, hellish; *Fig* **había un ruido i.** there was a hell of a noise; *Fig* **hace un calor i.** it's as hot as hell

infestar *vt* (**a**) *(animales, plantas)* to infest (**b**) *Fig (llenar)* to overrun, invade; **el lugar estaba infestado de turistas** the place was swarming with tourists (**c**) *(infectar)* to infect

infidelidad *nf* (**a**) *(deslealtad)* infidelity, unfaithfulness (**b**) *(inexactitud)* inaccuracy; **los errores se deben a la i. de la traducción** the mistakes are due to the inaccuracy of the translation

infiel 1 *adj* (**a**) *(desleal)* unfaithful (**b**) *(inexacto)* inaccurate; **si la memoria no me es i.** if my memory doesn't fail me
  2 *nmf Rel* infidel, unbeliever

infielmente *adv* (**a**) *(deslealmente)* unfaithfully (**b**) *(inexactamente)* inaccurately

infiernillo *nm* portable stove; **i. de alcohol** spirit stove

infierno *nm* (**a**) *Rel* hell; **ir al i.** to go to hell (**b**) *(gen pl) Mit* Hades (**c**) *Fig* hell, inferno; **el edificio se convirtió en un i.** the building became an inferno; **en el quinto i.** in the middle of nowhere, at the back of beyond; *Fam* **¡vete al i.!** go to hell!, get lost!

infiltración *nf* infiltration

infiltrado, -a 1 *pp de* **infiltrar**
  2 *nm,f* infiltrator

infiltrar 1 *vt* to infiltrate; *Fig* to drum in, inculcate
  2 infiltrarse *vpr* to infiltrate (**en** into)

ínfimo, -a *adj Fml* (**a**) *(bajo)* lowest; smallest; **a precios ínfimos** at ridiculously low prices (**b**) *(malo)* poorest, worst; **productos de ínfima calidad** goods of the poorest quality

infinidad *nf* (**a**) *(infinito)* infinity; **me pareció esperar una i. (de tiempo)** I seemed to wait for ages (**b**) *(sinfín)*

great number; **en i. de ocasiones** on countless occasions; **tengo una i. de cosas que hacer** I've got a million things to do; **una i. de preguntas** an endless number of questions

infinitamente *adv* infinitely

infinitesimal *adj* infinitesimal

infinitivo, -a *adj & nm Ling* infinitive

infinito, -a 1 *adj* infinite, unlimited, endless
  2 *nm (gen)* infinity
  3 *adv (muchísimo)* infinitely, immensely

inflable *adj* inflatable

inflación *nf Econ* inflation

inflacionario, -a *adj Econ* inflationary

inflacionismo *nm* inflationism

inflacionista *adj véase* **inflacionario, -a**

inflamable *adj* inflammable

inflamación *nf* (**a**) *Med* inflammation (**b**) *(ignición)* ignition, combustion

inflamar 1 *vt* (**a**) *Med* to inflame (**b**) *(encender)* to set on fire, ignite (**c**) *Fig* to excite, arouse; **i. las pasiones** to arouse passions
  2 inflamarse *vpr* (**a**) *Med* to become inflamed (**b**) *(incendiarse)* to catch fire (**c**) *Fig* to become inflamed; **se inflamaron las pasiones** passions became inflamed

inflamatorio, -a *adj* inflammatory

inflar 1 *vt* (**a**) *(hinchar)* to inflate, blow up; *Náut (vela)* to swell (**b**) *Econ* to inflate (**c**) *Fig (exagerar)* to exaggerate (**d**) *(envanecer)* to make conceited
  2 inflarse *vpr* (**a**) *(soplando)* to inflate; *Náut (vela)* to swell (**b**) *(persona)* to get conceited (**con** about); **i. de orgullo** to swell with pride (**c**) *Fam* to eat a lot; **se inflaron de macarrones** they stuffed themselves with macaroni

inflexibilidad *nf* inflexibility

inflexible *adj* inflexible

inflexión *nf* inflection, inflexion

infligir [24] *vt* to inflict

influencia *nf* influence; **ejercer** o **tener i. sobre algn** to have an influence on o upon sb; **tener influencias** to be influential

influenciable *adj* easily influenced

influenciar *vt* to influence

influenza *nf Med* influenza, flu

influir [34] **1** *vt* to influence
  2 *vi* to have influence; **i. en** o **sobre** to influence, have an influence on, affect

influjo *nm* influence

influyente *adj* influential

infografía *nf (en periódico, revista)* graphics

infopista *nf Inform* information highway

información *nf* (**a**) *(conocimiento)* information; **a título de i.** by way of information ❑ **i. privilegiada** privileged information; **oficina de i.** information bureau (**b**) *Prensa (noticia)* **una i.** a piece of news, (some) news *sing*; **i. periodística** newspaper report; *Mil* **servicio de i.** intelligence service (**c**) *Tel Br* directory enquiries *pl, US* information (**d**) *(referencias)* references *pl*

informado, -a 1 *pp de* **informar**
  2 *adj* informed; **bien/mal i.** well-/badly-informed; **de fuentes bien informadas** from reliable sources

informador, -a 1 *adj* informing
  2 *nm,f* informant, informer

informal *adj* (**a**) *(reunión, cena)* informal (**b**) *(comportamiento)* bad, unmannerly, incorrect (**c**) *(persona)* unreliable, untrustworthy

informalidad *nf* (**a**) *(desenfado)* informality (**b**) *(com-*

portamiento) unmannerliness, incorrectness (**c**) *(en persona)* unreliability, untrustworthiness

informalmente *adv* (**a**) *(desenfadado)* informally (**b**) *(de comportamiento)* incorrectly (**c**) *(persona)* unreliably

informante 1 *adj* informing
  2 *nmf* informant

informar 1 *vt (enterar)* to inform (**de** of); *(dar informes)* to report; **el equipo de rescate informó que ...** the rescue party reported that ...
  2 *vi* to report (**de** on); **el científico informó de su descubrimiento** the scientist announced his discovery
  3 informarse *vpr (procurarse noticias)* to find out (**de** about), inform oneself; *(enterarse)* to enquire (**de** about)

informática *nf Inform* computer science, computing; **el mundo de la i.** the computer world

informático, -a *Inform* **1** *adj* computer, computing
  2 *nm,f* (computer) technician

informativo, -a 1 *adj* informative, explanatory
  2 *nm Rad TV* news bulletin

informatizado, -a *adj* computerized

informatizar [14] *vt* to computerize

informe¹ *nm* (**a**) *(documento, estudio)* report; **dar informes sobre** to give information about; **según mis informes** according to my information (**b**) **informes** references; **pedir i. sobre algn** to make enquiries about sb; **'se necesita asistenta con buenos i.'** 'wanted: cleaner with good references'

informe² *adj* shapeless, formless

infortunado, -a *adj* unfortunate, unlucky

infortunio *nm (mala suerte)* misfortune; *(contratiempo)* mishap

infracción *nf (gen)* offence; *(de ley)* infringement, infraction, breach (**de** of)

infractor, -a *nm,f* offender

infraestructura *nf* infrastructure

in fraganti *loc adv* in the act; **coger** *o* **pillar a algn en f.** to catch sb red-handed

infrahumano, -a *adj* subhuman

infranqueable *adj* impassable, insuperable; *Fig* insurmountable

infrarrojo, -a *adj* infrared

infrautilizar [14] *vt* to underuse

infravalorar *vt* to undervalue, underestimate

infrecuente *adj* infrequent; *(extraño)* rare

infringir [24] *vt* to infringe, contravene; **i. una ley** to break a law

infructuosamente *adv* fruitlessly, unsuccessfully

infructuoso, -a *adj* fruitless, unsuccessful

ínfulas *nfpl* conceit *sing*, pretension *sing*; **darse í.** to put on airs

infundado, -a *adj* unfounded, groundless, baseless

infundio *nm* lie, tale, fib; **todo esto son infundios** it's all a pack of lies

infundir *vt (gen)* to infuse; *Fig* to instil, *US* instill; **i. dudas** to give rise to doubt; **i. respeto** to fill with respect

infusión *nf* infusion; **i. de manzanilla** camomile tea

infuso, -a *adj* inspired; *Fam Irón* **tener ciencia infusa** to be a born genius

ingeniar 1 *vt* to invent, devise, think up
  2 ingeniarse *vpr* to manage, find a way; **ingeniárselas para hacer algo** to manage *o* contrive to do sth

ingeniería *nf* engineering □ **i. genética** genetic engineering

ingeniero, -a *nm,f* engineer □ **i. agrónomo** agricultural

engineer; *Esp* **i. de caminos, canales y puertos** civil engineer; **i. de marina** naval architect; **i. de minas/ montes** mining/forestry engineer; **i. de sonido** sound engineer; **i. de telecomunicaciones** electronic engineer; **i. naval** naval architect; **i. químico** chemical engineer; **i. técnico** technician

ingenio *nm* (**a**) *(talento)* talent; *(inventiva)* inventiveness, creativeness; *(chispa)* wit; **aguzar el i.** to sharpen one's wits (**b**) *(persona)* genius (**c**) *(máquina)* machine; *(aparato)* device □ *Ind* **i. de azúcar** sugar mill

ingenioso, -a *adj* ingenious, clever; *(vivaz)* witty; *Fam* **dárselas de i.** to try to be witty

ingente *adj* huge, enormous

ingenuidad *nf* ingenuousness, naïveté

ingenuo, -a 1 *adj* ingenuous, naïve
  2 *nm,f* naïve person

ingerir [62] *vt (comida)* to ingest, consume; *(líquidos, alcohol)* to drink, consume

ingestión *nf* ingestion

Inglaterra *n* England

ingle *nf Anat* groin

inglés, -esa 1 *adj* English
  2 *nm,f (hombre)* Englishman; *(mujer)* Englishwoman; **los ingleses** the English
  3 *nm (idioma)* English

ingobernable *adj Pol* ungovernable; *(incontrolable)* uncontrollable, unmanageable

ingratitud *nf* ingratitude, ungratefulness

ingrato, -a 1 *adj* (**a**) *(persona)* ungrateful (**b**) *(época, noticia)* unpleasant (**c**) *(trabajo)* thankless, unrewarding (**d**) *(tierra)* unproductive
  2 *nm,f* ungrateful person

ingravidez *nf* weightlessness

ingrávido, -a *adj* weightless

ingrediente *nm* ingredient

ingresar 1 *vt* (**a**) *Esp Fin* to deposit, pay in; **i. dinero en una cuenta** to pay money into an account (**b**) *Med* to admit; **i. a algn en el hospital** to admit sb to hospital
  2 *vi* (**a**) **i. en** *(en asociación, ejército)* to join; *(en hospital)* to be admitted to; *(en convento, universidad)* to enter; **i. en un club** to join a club (**b**) *(ser admitido)* to be admitted; *Esp* **ingresó cadáver en el hospital** he was dead on arrival at the hospital

ingreso *nm* (**a**) *Esp Fin* deposit; **hacer un i. en una cuenta** to pay money into an account (**b**) *(entrada)* entry (**en** into); *(admisión)* admission (**en** to); *Med* **su i. en el hospital** his admission to hospital (**c**) **ingresos** *Fin (sueldo, renta)* income *sing*; *(beneficios)* revenue *sing*; **i. anuales** annual income; **i. brutos** gross receipts

inhábil *adj* (**a**) *(torpe)* unskilful, clumsy (**b**) *(incapaz)* unfit; **i. para el trabajo** unfit for work (**c**) *(inadecuado)* unsuitable (**d**) **día i.** non-working day

inhabilidad *nf* (**a**) *(torpeza)* unskilfulness, clumsiness (**b**) *(incapacitación)* unfitness (**para** for) (**c**) *(ineptitud)* ineptitude, incompetence

inhabilitación *nf* (**a**) *Fml (incapacidad)* disablement (**b**) *Jur* disqualification

inhabilitar *vt* (**a**) *Fml (incapacitar)* to disable; **inhabilitado para el trabajo** unfit for work (**b**) *Jur* to disqualify

inhabitable *adj* uninhabitable; *Fam* **vive en una casa i.** she lives in an appalling place

inhabitado, -a *adj* uninhabited

inhalación *nf* inhalation

inhalador *nm Med* inhaler

inhalar *vt* to inhale
inherente *adj* inherent (**a** in)
inhibición *nf* inhibition
inhibir 1 *vt* to inhibit; **sentirse inhibido** to feel inhibited
2 inhibirse *vpr* (**a**) *(cohibirse)* to be *o* feel inhibited (**b**) *(abstenerse)* to keep out (**de** of), keep away (**de** from) (**c**) *Jur (juez)* to stay
inhóspito, -a *adj* inhospitable
inhumación *nf* burial
inhumano, -a *adj* (**a**) *(despiadado)* inhuman; *(desconsiderado)* inhumane (**b**) *Chile (sucio)* filthy
inhumar *vt* to bury
iniciación *nf* (**a**) *(ceremonia)* initiation (**b**) *(introducción)* introduction (**a** to)
iniciado, -a 1 *pp de* **iniciar**
2 *adj* initiated
3 *nm,f* initiate
iniciador, -a 1 *adj* initiatory
2 *nm,f* initiator
inicial *adj & nf* initial; **punto i.** starting point
inicialización *nf Inform* initialization
inicializar [14] *vt Inform* to initialize
iniciar 1 *vt* (**a**) *(introducir)* to initiate; **i. a algn en los misterios** to initiate sb into the mysteries (**b**) *(empezar)* to begin, start; *(discusión)* to initiate; *(una cosa nueva)* to pioneer
2 iniciarse *vpr* (**a**) *(aprender)* **i. en algo** to learn sth (**b**) *(empezar)* to begin, start
iniciático, -a *adj* initiation; **rito i.** initiation rite
iniciativa *nf* initiative; **i. privada** private enterprise; **por i. propia** on one's own initiative
inicio *nm* beginning, start
inicuo, -a *adj* wicked, iniquitous
inigualable *adj* unrivalled
inigualado, -a *adj* unequalled, unparalleled
inimaginable *adj* unimaginable, inconceivable
inimitable *adj* inimitable
ininteligible *adj* unintelligible
ininterrumpidamente *adv* uninterruptedly, continuously
ininterrumpido, -a *adj* uninterrupted, continuous
iniquidad *nf* iniquity
injerencia *nf* interference, meddling (**en** in)
injerir [62] **1** *vt* to insert
2 injerirse *vpr* to interfere, meddle (**en** in)
injertar *vt Agr Med* to graft
injerto *nm* graft; *(acto)* grafting
injuria *nf (insulto)* insult, affront; *(agravio)* offence, *US* offense; *Jur* **delito de injurias** crime of slander
injuriar *vt* (**a**) *(insultar)* to insult; *(ultrajar)* to offend (**b**) *(dañar)* to damage, harm
injurioso, -a *adj (insultante)* insulting; *(ofensivo)* offensive
injustamente *adv* unjustly, unfairly
injusticia *nf* injustice, unfairness
injustificable *adj* unjustifiable
injustificado, -a *adj* unjustified
injusto, -a *adj* unjust, unfair
Inmaculada *nf* **la I.** the Virgin Mary; **la I. Concepción** the Immaculate Conception
inmaculado, -a *adj* immaculate
inmadurez *nf* immaturity

inmaduro, -a *adj* immature
inmarcesible *adj*, **inmarchitable** *adj Fml* unfading, undying
inmaterial *adj* immaterial
inmediaciones *nfpl* neighbourhood *sing*, environs
inmediatamente *adv* immediately, at once
inmediato, -a *adj* (**a**) *(poco después)* immediate, prompt; **de i.** at once (**b**) *(cercano)* close (**a** to), very near (**c**) *(contiguo)* next (**a** to), adjoining; **en la habitación inmediata a la tuya** in the room next to yours
inmejorable *adj* unsurpassable, excellent; **calidad i.** unbeatable quality
inmemorial *adj* immemorial
inmensamente *adv* immensely, vastly
inmensidad *nf* immensity, enormity, vastness; **la i. de los mares** the vastness of the seas
inmenso, -a *adj* immense, vast; **una fortuna inmensa** a huge fortune
inmerecidamente *adv* undeservedly
inmerecido, -a *adj* undeserved, unmerited
inmersión *nf* immersion; *(submarinismo)* dive
inmerso, -a *adj* immersed (**en** in)
inmigración *nf* immigration
inmigrado, -a 1 *pp de* **inmigrar**
2 *adj* immigrant
3 *nm,f* immigrant
inmigrante *adj & nm,f* immigrant
inmigrar *vi* to immigrate
inminencia *nf* imminence
inminente *adj* imminent, impending
inmiscuirse [34] *vpr* to interfere, meddle (**en** in)
inmobiliaria *nf Br* estate agency, *US* real estate agent
inmobiliario, -a *adj* property, *US* real-estate
inmoderadamente *adv* immoderately; *(exageradamente)* excessively
inmoderado, -a *adj* immoderate; *(exagerado)* excessive
inmodestia *nf* immodesty
inmodesto, -a *adj* immodest
inmolación *nf Fml* immolation, sacrifice
inmolar *vt Fml* to immolate, sacrifice
inmoral *adj* immoral
inmoralidad *nf* immorality
inmortal *adj & nm,f* immortal
inmortalidad *nf* immortality
inmortalizar [14] **1** *vt* to immortalize
2 inmortalizarse *vpr* to be immortalized
inmotivado, -a *adj* (**a**) *(sin motivo)* motiveless, unmotivated (**b**) *(sin fundamento)* groundless
inmóvil *adj* (**a**) *(quieto)* motionless, immobile; *(car)* stationary (**b**) *Fig (constante)* determined, steadfast
inmovilidad *nf* immobility
inmovilismo *nm Pol* extreme conservatism
inmovilista *adj & nmf Pol* ultraconservative
inmovilización *nf* (**a**) *(física)* immobilization (**b**) **inmovilizaciones** fixed assets
inmovilizado, -a 1 *pp de* **inmovilizar**
2 *adj* motionless, at a standstill
inmovilizar [14] *vt* (**a**) *(persona, cosa)* to immobilize (**b**) *Fin (capital)* to immobilize, tie up
inmueble 1 *adj* **bienes inmuebles** real estate, landed property
2 *nm* building

inmundicia *nf* (**a**) *(suciedad)* dirt, filth; *Fig* dirtiness (**b**) *(basura) Br* rubbish, *US* garbage

inmundo, -a *adj* dirty, filthy; *Fig* nasty

inmune *adj* immune (**a** to), exempt (**de** from)

inmunidad *nf* immunity (**contra** against) □ **i. diplomática/parlamentaria** diplomatic/parliamentarian immunity

inmunitario, -a *adj Med* immune

inmunización *nf* immunization

inmunizar [14] *vt* to immunize (**contra** against)

inmunodeficiencia *nf Med* immunodeficiency

inmunodeficiente *adj Med* immunodeficient

inmunodepresión *nf Med* immunodepression

inmunodepresor, -a *adj Med* immunosuppressant

inmunología *nf* immunology

inmutabilidad *nf* immutability

inmutable *adj* immutable

inmutarse *vpr* to get upset, be perturbed; **ni se inmutó** he didn't turn a hair

innato, -a *adj* innate, inborn

innecesariamente *adv* unnecessarily

innecesario, -a *adj* unnecessary

innegable *adj* undeniable

innoble *adj* ignoble

innombrable *adj* unmentionable, unspeakable

innominado, -a *adj* nameless

innovación *nf* innovation

innovador, -a 1 *adj* innovatory
  2 *nm,f* innovator

innovar *vt & vi* to innovate

innumerable *adj* innumerable, countless

inobservancia *nf* non-observance (**de** of)

inocencia *nf* (**a**) *(gen)* innocence (**b**) *(ingenuidad)* naïveté

inocentada *nf Fam* practical joke, hoax; **hacer una i. a algn** to play a practical joke on sb

inocente 1 *adj* innocent
  2 *nmf* innocent; *(ingenuo)* naïve; **hacerse el i.** to act innocent □ **día de los Inocentes** Holy Innocents' Day, 28th December, ≃ April Fools' Day

inocentón, -ona 1 *adj* credulous, naïve, gullible
  2 *nm,f (ingenuo)* naïve person; *(tonto)* simpleton

inocuidad *nf* innocuousness, harmlessness

inoculación *nf* inoculation

inocular *vt* to innoculate

inocuo, -a *adj* innocuous, harmless

inodoro, -a 1 *adj* odourless
  2 *nm* toilet, lavatory

inofensivo, -a *adj* inoffensive, harmless

inolvidable *adj* unforgettable

inoperancia *nf* ineffectiveness

inoperante *adj* inoperative, ineffective

inopia *nf Fml* poverty, penury; *Fig* **estar en la i.** to be in the clouds, be miles away

inopinado, -a *adj* unexpected

inoportunamente *adv* inopportunely, inappropriately; *(fuera de tiempo)* at the wrong time

inoportuno, -a *adj* inopportune, inappropriate; *(fuera de tiempo)* untimely; **llegó en un momento muy i.** he turned up at a very awkward moment

inorgánico, -a *adj* inorganic

inoxidable *adj* rustless; **acero i.** stainless steel

inquebrantable *adj Fig (firme)* unshakable; *(infrangible)* unyielding

inquietante *adj* worrying, disturbing

inquietar 1 *vt* to worry, disturb; **me inquieta esta terrible situación económica** I'm deeply concerned about this dire economic situation
  2 inquietarse *vpr* to worry (**por** about)

inquieto, -a *adj* (**a**) *(preocupado)* worried, anxious (**por** about) (**b**) *(agitado)* restless (**c**) *CAm (aficionado)* keen on, fond of

inquietud *nf* (**a**) *(preocupación)* worry, anxiety (**b**) *(agitación)* restlessness

inquilinato *nm* (**a**) *(arriendo)* tenancy; *Jur* lease (**b**) *Col RP* block of flats, tenement

inquilino, -a *nm,f* tenant

inquina *nf Fam (mala voluntad)* ill will, grudge; *(aversión)* dislike; **tener i. a algn** to have a grudge against sb; **tomar i. a algn** to take a dislike to sb

inquirir [5] *vt* to inquire, enquire into, investigate

inquisición *nf* (**a**) *(indagación)* inquiry, investigation (**b**) *Hist* **la I.** the Inquisition

inquisidor, -a 1 *adj* inquiring, inquisitive
  2 *nm,f Hist* inquisitor

inquisitivo, -a *adj* inquisitive

inquisitorial *adj*, **inquisitorio, -a** *adj* inquisitorial

inri *nm Esp Fam* insult; **para más** *o* **mayor i.** to make matters worse, add insult to injury

insaciable *adj* insatiable

insalubre *adj* insalubrious, unhealthy ·

insalubridad *nf* insalubrity, unhealthiness

insalvable *adj (obstáculo)* insuperable, insurmountable

insano, -a *adj* (**a**) *(loco)* insane, mad (**b**) *(insalubre)* unhealthy

insatisfacción *nf* dissatisfaction

insatisfactorio, -a *adj* unsatisfactory, dissatisfactory

insatisfecho, -a *adj* unsatisfied, dissatisfied

inscribir *(pp* **inscrito) 1** *vt* (**a**) *(registrar)* to register, record, enter; **i. a un niño en el registro civil** to register a child's birth (**b**) *(matricular)* to enrol, *US* enroll (**c**) *(grabar)* to inscribe (**d**) *Geom* to inscribe
  2 inscribirse *vpr* (**a**) *(registrarse)* to register; *(hacerse miembro)* to join; **i. en un concurso** to enter for a competition (**b**) *(matricularse)* to enrol, *US* enroll

inscripción *nf* (**a**) *(matriculación)* enrolment, *US* enrollment, registration; *(precio)* registration fee (**b**) *(escrito, dibujo)* inscription

inscrito, -a 1 *pp de* **inscribir**
  2 *adj* (**a**) *(matriculado)* enrolled, registered; **el número de alumnos inscritos ha aumentado** the number of students enrolled has increased (**b**) *(grabado)* inscribed

insecticida 1 *adj* insecticidal, insecticide
  2 *nm* insecticide

insectívoro, -a 1 *adj* insectivorous
  2 *nm* insectivore

insecto *nm* insect

inseguridad *nf* (**a**) *(falta de confianza)* insecurity (**b**) *(duda)* uncertainty (**c**) *(peligro)* lack of safety; **existe una gran i. ciudadana** the city streets are very unsafe

inseguro, -a *adj* (**a**) *(poco confiado)* insecure (**b**) *(dubitativo)* uncertain, doubtful (**c**) *(peligroso)* unsafe; *Fig* **terreno i.** dangerous ground

inseminación *nf* insemination □ **i. artificial** artificial insemination

inseminar *vt* to inseminate

insensatez *nf* foolishness, stupidity; **sólo dice insensateces** he just talks nonsense

insensato, -a 1 *adj* foolish, stupid
2 *nm,f* fool

insensibilidad *nf* (**a**) *(gen)* insensitivity; *(indiferencia)* callousness (**b**) *Med* insensitivity, numbness

insensibilizar [14] **1** *vt* (**a**) *(provocar indiferencia)* to make insensitive (**a** to); **la vida le ha insensibilizado** life has hardened him (**b**) *Med* to desensitize, anaesthetize
2 insensibilizarse *vpr* to become insensitive

insensible *adj* (**a**) *(indiferente)* insensitive (**a** to), unfeeling, callous; **es i. a todo sentimiento humano** she's indifferent to any human feeling (**b**) *Med* insensible, numb (**c**) *(imperceptible)* imperceptible, unnoticeable

inseparable *adj* inseparable; **el trabajo es i. de la fatiga** work and fatigue go together; **son amigos inseparables** they're very close friends

inseparablemente *adv* inseparably

inserción *nf* insertion

insertar *vt también Inform* to insert

inserto, -a *adj* inserted

inservible *adj* useless

insidia *nf* (**a**) *(trampa)* snare, trap (**b**) *(malicia)* maliciousness

insidioso, -a *adj* insidious

insigne *adj* distinguished, famous, illustrious

insignia *nf* (**a**) *(emblema)* badge, decoration (**b**) *(bandera)* flag, banner; *Náut* pennant; **buque i.** flagship

insignificancia *nf* (**a**) *(intrascendencia)* insignificance; **esto demuestra la i. del problema** that shows how silly the problem is (**b**) *(nadería)* trifle

insignificante *adj* insignificant, meaningless

insinuación *nf* insinuation, innuendo, hint; **hacer una i.** to insinuate

insinuante *adj* insinuating; *(atrevido)* suggestive; **una mirada i.** a suggestive glance

insinuar [4] **1** *vt* to insinuate
2 insinuarse *vpr* **i. en** to worm one's way into (**b**) **i. a una mujer** to make advances to a woman

insipidez *nf* insipidness, insipidity; *Fig* dullness, flatness

insípido, -a *adj* insipid; *Fig* dull, flat

insistencia *nf* insistence; *(persistencia)* persistence; **con i.** insistently

insistente *adj (persona)* insistent; *(preguntas)* persistent

insistentemente *adv* insistently

insistir *vi* to insist (**en** on); *(persistir)* to persist (**en** in); **i. en la importancia de** to stress the importance of; **i. en que se haga algo** to insist that sth should be done

in situ *adj & adv* on the spot

insobornable *adj* incorruptible

insociable *adj* unsociable

insolación *nf* (**a**) *Med* sunstroke; **coger una i.** to get sunstroke (**b**) *Meteor* sunlight, sunshine; **horas de i.** hours of sunshine *o* sunlight

insolencia *nf* (**a**) *(descaro)* insolence (**b**) *(inconveniencia)* offence, *US* offense

insolentarse *vpr* to be insolent *o* offensive

insolente 1 *adj* (**a**) *(impertinente)* insolent, offensive (**b**) *(arrogante)* haughty, contemptuous
2 *nmf* (**a**) *(impertinente)* insolent person (**b**) *(arrogante)* haughty *o* contemptuous person

insólito, -a *adj (poco usual)* unusual; *(extraño)* strange, odd

insoluble *adj* insoluble

insolvencia *nf Fin* insolvency

insolvente *adj Fin* insolvent

insomne 1 *adj* sleepless
2 *nmf* insomniac

insomnio *nm* insomnia; **noche de i.** sleepless night

insondable *adj* unfathomable

insonorización *nf* soundproofing

insonorizado, -a 1 *pp de* **insonorizar**
2 *adj* soundproof

insonorizar [14] *vt* to soundproof

insonoro, -a *adj* noiseless

insoportable *adj* unbearable, intolerable

insoslayable *adj* inevitable, unavoidable

insospechado, -a *adj* unsuspected

insostenible *adj* untenable, indefensible

inspección *nf* inspection □ **i. de calidad** quality control inspection

inspeccionar *vt* to inspect

inspector, -a *nm,f* inspector □ **i. de Hacienda** tax inspector; **i. de policía** police inspector

inspiración *nf* (**a**) *(gen)* inspiration (**b**) *(inhalación)* inhalation

inspirado, -a 1 *pp de* **inspirar**
2 *adj* inspired

inspirador, -a *adj* inspiring, inspirational

inspirar 1 *vt* (**a**) *(gen)* to inspire; **i. respeto** to inspire respect (**b**) *(inhalar)* to inhale, breathe in
2 inspirarse *vpr* **i. en** to be inspired by, find inspiration in

instalación *nf* installation □ **i. eléctrica** wiring; **i. sanitaria** plumbing; **instalaciones deportivas** sports facilities

instalador, -a *nm,f* installer, fitter

instalar 1 *vt* (**a**) *(gen) también Inform* to instal, *US* install (**b**) *(equipar)* to fit out, equip (**c**) *(erigir)* to set up
2 instalarse *vpr (persona)* to settle (down), instal *o US* install oneself

instancia *nf* (**a**) *(solicitud)* request, petition; **a instancia(s) de** at the request of (**b**) *(escrito)* application form (**c**) *Jur* **tribunal de primera i.** court of first instance (**d**) **en primera i.** first of all; **en última i.** as a last resort

instantánea *nf Fot* snapshot

instantáneamente *adv* instantaneously, instantly

instantáneo, -a *adj* instantaneous, instant; **café i.** instant coffee

instante *nm* instant, moment; **a cada i.** constantly, all the time; **al i.** immediately, right away; **en este (mismo) i.** right now, at this very moment; **en un i.** in a flash; **por instantes** incessantly, all the time; **¡un i.!** just a moment!

instar *vt* to urge, press

instauración *nf* founding, establishment

instaurador, -a 1 *adj* founding, establishing
2 *nm,f* founder, establisher

instaurar *vt* to found, establish; **i. la monarquía** to establish a *o* the monarchy

instigación *nf* instigation

instigador, -a 1 *adj* instigating
2 *nm,f* instigator

instigar [38] *vt* to instigate; **i. a la rebelión** to incite to rebellion

instintivamente *adv* instinctively

instintivo, -a *adj* instinctive

instinto *nm* instinct; **por i.** instinctively □ **i. de conservación** instinct of self-preservation; **i. maternal** maternal instinct

institución *nf* institution, establishment; *Fig (persona)* **ser una i.** to be an institution □ **i. benéfica** charitable foundation

institucional *adj* institutional

institucionalizado, -a 1 *pp de* **institucionalizar**
2 *adj* institutionalized

institucionalizar [14] *vt* to institutionalize

instituir [34] *vt* to institute; **i. un heredero** to appoint an heir

instituto *nm* **(a)** *(corporación)* institute □ **i. de belleza** beauty salon **(b)** *Esp Educ* high school

institutriz *nf* governess

instrucción *nf* **(a)** *(educación)* education, instruction **(b)** *(gen pl) (indicación)* instruction; **instrucciones para el** *o* **de uso** directions for use; **libro de instrucciones** instruction manual **(c)** *Jur* preliminary investigation; **la i. del sumario** proceedings *pl* □ **juez de i.** examining magistrate **(d)** *Mil* drill, training □ **i. militar** military training

instructivo, -a *adj* instructive

instructor, -a 1 *adj* instructing
2 *nm,f* instructor

instruido, -a 1 *pp de* **instruir**
2 *adj* educated, well-educated

instruir [34] *vt* **(a)** *(gen)* to instruct **(b)** *(enseñar)* to educate, teach **(c)** *Mil* to drill, train **(d)** *(informar)* to inform **(de** of) **(e)** *Jur* to investigate; **i. una causa** to investigate a case

instrumentación *nf* orchestration

instrumental 1 *adj* instrumental
2 *nm* (set of) instruments *pl*, equipment □ **i. médico** surgical instruments

instrumentar *vt Mús* to orchestrate

instrumentista *nmf Mús* **(a)** *(músico)* instrumentalist **(b)** *(fabricante)* instrument maker

instrumento *nm* instrument □ **i. de cuerda/ percusión/viento** stringed/percussion/wind instrument

insubordinación *nf* insubordination

insubordinado, -a 1 *pp de* **insubordinar**
2 *adj* insubordinate
3 *nm,f* insubordinate, rebel

insubordinar 1 *vt (sublevar)* to stir up, incite to rebellion
2 insubordinarse *vpr (sublevarse)* to rebel **(contra** against)

insuficiencia *nf* insufficiency □ *Med* **i. cardiaca/renal** heart/kidney failure

insuficiente 1 *adj* insufficient, inadequate
2 *nm Educ (nota)* fail

insuflar *vt* to insufflate

insufrible *adj* insufferable, unbearable

insular 1 *adj* insular, island; **provincias insulares** island provinces
2 *nmf* islander

insularidad *nf* insularity

insulina *nf Quím* insulin

insulso, -a *adj* insipid, tasteless

insultante *adj* insulting, offensive

insultar *vt* to insult

insulto *nm* insult

insumergible *adj (gen)* unsinkable; *(reloj)* not waterproof

insumisión *nf* **(a)** *Esp Mil* = refusal to do military service or a civilian equivalent **(b)** *(rebeldía)* rebelliousness

insumiso, -a 1 *adj* unsubmissive
2 *nm,f Esp Mil* = person who refuses to do military service or a civilian equivalent

insumos *nmpl Am (bienes)* raw materials; *(suministros)* supplies

insuperable *adj* **(a)** *(en calidad)* unsurpassable **(b)** *(en dificultad)* insurmountable

insurgente *adj & nmf* insurgent

insurrección *nf* insurrection, uprising, revolt

insurrecto, -a *adj & nm,f* insurgent

insustancial *adj* insubstantial

insustituible *adj* irreplaceable

intachable *adj* irreproachable, blameless; **una conducta i.** impeccable behaviour

intacto, -a *adj* intact

intangible *adj* intangible

integración *nf* integration

integral 1 *adj* integral; *Culin* **arroz i.** brown rice; *Mat* **cálculo i.** integral calculus; *Culin* **pan i.** wholemeal bread
2 *nf Mat* integral

íntegramente *adv* wholly, entirely

integrante 1 *adj* integral; **ser parte i. de** to be integral *o* intrinsic to
2 *nmf* member

integrar 1 *vt* **(a)** *(formar)* to compose, make up; **un equipo de fútbol lo integran once jugadores** a football team is made up of eleven players **(b)** *Mat* to integrate
2 integrarse *vpr* to integrate

integridad *nf* integrity

integrismo *nm* reaction □ **i. religioso** religious fundamentalism

integrista *adj & nmf* **(a)** *Pol* reactionary, traditionalist **(b)** *Rel* fundamentalist

íntegro, -a *adj* **(a)** *(entero)* whole, entire; *Cin Lit* **versión íntegra** unabridged version **(b)** *(honrado)* upright, honest

intelecto *nm* intellect

intelectual *adj & nmf* intellectual

intelectualidad *nf* intellectuals *pl*, intelligentsia *pl*

intelectualismo *nm* intellectualism

intelectualizar [14] *vt* to intellectualize

inteligencia *nf* **(a)** *(intelecto)* intelligence □ *Inform* **i. artificial** artificial intelligence; **cociente de i.** intelligence quotient, IQ **(b)** *(comprensión)* understanding; **en la i. de que** on the understanding that

inteligente *adj* intelligent

inteligible *adj* intelligible

intemperie *nf* bad weather; **a la i.** in the open (air), out of doors

intempestivo, -a *adj* untimely, inopportune; **llegaron a una hora intempestiva** they came at a bad time

intención *nf* intention; **buena/mala i.** good/ill will; **con i.** deliberately, on purpose; **con la mejor i.** with the best of intentions; **con segunda/doble i.** with an ulterior motive; **su i. era buena** she had the right idea; **tener la i. de hacer algo** to intend to do sth, have sth in mind

intencionadamente *adv* intentionally, on purpose

intencionado, -a *adj*, **intencional** *adj* intentional, deliberate

intencionalidad *nf* intent

intendencia *nf Mil* ≃ service corps, *US* ≃ quartermaster corps

intendente *nm Mil* quartermaster general

intensidad *nf (gen)* intensity, strength; *(del viento)* force

intensificación *nf* intensification

intensificar [59] **1** *vt* to intensify
2 intensificarse *vpr* to intensify

intensivo, -a *adj* intensive; *Agr* **cultivo i.** intensive farming; *Educ* **curso i.** crash course

intenso, -a *adj* intense; *(luz, corriente)* strong; *(dolor)* acute

intentar *vt* to try, attempt; **¡inténtalo!** try it!, *Fam* give it a go!; **intentó levantarlo solo** he tried to lift it on his own

intento *nm* attempt, try; **al primer i.** at the first attempt; *Pol* **i. de golpe de estado** attempted coup d'état; **i. de suicidio** attempted suicide; **i. fracasado** failed attempt

intentona *nf* (a) *Fam* foolhardy attempt (b) *Pol* putsch

inter- *pref* inter-; **intercontinental** intercontinental

interacción *nf* interaction, interplay

interaccionar *vi* to interact

interactividad *nf* interactivity

interactivo, -a *adj* interactive

interbancario, -a *adj* interbank

intercalación *nf* intercalation, insertion

intercalar *vt* to intercalate, insert

intercambiable *adj* interchangeable

intercambiador *nm* *Esp (de transportes)* transport interchange

intercambiar *vt* to exchange, swap

intercambio *nm* exchange, interchange ❑ **i. comercial/ cultural** commercial/cultural exchange

interceder *vi* to intercede

interceptar *vt* (a) *(atajar)* to intercept (b) *(carretera)* to block; *(tráfico)* to hold up

interceptor *nm* interceptor

intercesión *nf* intercession

intercesor, -a 1 *adj* interceding
  2 *nm,f* intercessor

intercomunicación *nf* intercommunication

intercomunicador *nm* intercom

interconectar *vt* to interconnect

interconexión *nf* interconnection

intercontinental *adj* intercontinental

interdependencia *nf* interdependence

interdicción *nf,* **interdicto** *nm* interdiction, prohibition

interdisciplinar *adj,* **interdisciplinario, -a** *adj* interdisciplinary

interés *nm* (a) *(gen)* interest; **merecer i.** to be interesting; **poner i. en** to take an interest in; **sentir i. por, tener i. en** *o* **por** to be interested in (b) *(provecho personal)* self-interest; **hacer algo (sólo) por i.** to do sth out of self-interest ❑ **i. propio** self-interest; **intereses creados** vested interests (c) *Fin* interest; **con un i. del 11%** at an interest of 11% ❑ **i. bancario** bank interest; **i. compuesto** compound interest; **i. devengado** accrued interest; **i. simple** simple interest

interesado, -a 1 *pp de* interesar
  2 *adj* (a) *(preocupado, curioso)* interested; **las partes interesadas** the interested parties (b) *(egoísta)* selfish, self-interested
  3 *nm,f* interested person; **los interesados** those interested *o* concerned

interesante *adj* interesting; **ser i.** to be interesting; *Fam* **hacerse el i.** to try to attract attention

interesar 1 *vt* (a) *(tener interés)* to interest; **¿te interesa la poesía?** are you interested in poetry? (b) *(conseguir interés)* to interest; **logré interesarle en mi proyecto** I succeeded in interesting him in my project (c) *(afectar)* to concern, involve; **el asunto nos interesa a todos** the matter concerns us all (d) *Med* to affect; **la herida le interesa el hígado** the wound affects her liver
  2 *vi (ser importante)* to be of interest, be important;

interesa *o* **interesaría llegar pronto** it is important to get there early
  3 interesarse *vpr* **i. por** *o* **en** to be interested in; **se interesó por ti** he asked about *o* after you

interestatal *adj* interstate

interfaz *nf Inform* interface

interfecto, -a *nm,f* (a) *Jur* murder victim (b) *Esp Fam Hum* person in question

interferencia *nf (gen)* interference; *Rad TV* jamming

interferir [62] *vt* (a) *(gen)* to interfere with; *(plan)* to upset (b) *Rad TV* to jam

interfono *nm Tel* intercom

intergubernamental *adj* intergovernmental

ínterin 1 *nm* interim; **en el í.** in the meantime
  2 *adv* while

interinamente *adv* temporarily

interinidad *nf* (a) *(temporalidad)* temporariness (b) *(empleo)* temporary employment

interino, -a 1 *adj* (a) *(trabajo, solución)* temporary, provisional, interim (b) *(persona)* acting; **presidente i.** acting president
  2 *nm,f* (a) *(trabajador temporal)* temporary worker (b) *(sustituto)* stand-in

interior 1 *adj* (a) *(gen)* interior, inner, inside; **habitación i.** inner room; **ropa i.** underwear, underclothes (b) *Pol* domestic, internal; **correo i.** inland mail (c) *Geog* inland
  2 *nm* (a) *(gen)* inside, interior, inner part; **pasemos al i.** let's go inside; *Fig* **en su i. no estaba de acuerdo** deep down she disagreed (b) *Geog* interior; *Pol* **Ministerio del I.** *Br* ≃ Home Office, *US* ≃ Department of the Interior; *Pol* **Ministro del I.** *Br* ≃ Home Secretary, *US* ≃ Secretary of the Interior (c) *Ftb (jugador)* inside-forward (d) *Col Ven (calzoncillos) Br* underpants, *US* shorts

interioridad *nf* (a) *(carácter)* inwardness (b) **interioridades** personal affairs, family secrets; *(secretos)* ins and outs; **las i. de la política** the ins and outs of politics; **meterse en i.** to delve

interiorismo *nm* interior design

interiorización *nf (de sentimientos, ideas)* internalization

interiorizar [14] *vt* to internalize

interjección *nf Ling* interjection

interlineado *nm* spacing between the lines

interlocutor, -a *nm,f* speaker, interlocutor; **su i.** the person he was speaking to, the person who spoke to him

interludio *nm* interlude

intermediación *nf* (a) *(en conflicto)* intervention, mediation; **por i. de** through the intervention *o* mediation of (b) *Fin* intermediation

intermediar *vi* to mediate

intermediario, -a 1 *adj* intermediary
  2 *nm,f* intermediary, mediator, go-between; **servir de i.** to act as a mediator
  3 *nm Com* middleman

intermedio, -a 1 *adj* intermediate; **la etapa intermedia** the intervening period, the period in between
  2 *nm* (a) *(intervalo)* interval, intermission (b) *(por medio de)* **por i. de** through, by means of

interminable *adj* interminable, endless

intermitencia *nf* intermittence, intermittency; **con i.** intermittently, on and off

intermitente 1 *adj* intermittent
  2 *nm Esp Col Aut Br* indicator, *US* turn signal

internacional 1 *adj* international, worldwide
  2 *nmf Dep* international
  3 *nf Mús* **la I.** the Internationale

internacionalismo *nm* internationalism

internacionalizar [14] **1** *vt* to internationalize
2 internacionalizarse *vpr* to become internationalized
o international

internacionalmente *adv* internationally

internado, -a 1 *pp de* **internar**
2 *adj* (**a**) *Pol Mil* interned (**b**) *Med* confined
3 *nm* (*colegio*) boarding school

internamiento *nm* (**a**) *Pol* internment (**b**) *Med* confinement

internar 1 *vt* (**a**) *Pol* to intern (**b**) *Med* (*en hospital mental*) to confine
2 internarse *vpr* (**a**) (*penetrar*) to penetrate, advance (**en** into); (**b**) *Dep* to break through

internauta *nmf* Net user

Internet *nf* Internet; **está en I.** it's on the Internet

internista *adj & nmf Med* internist

interno, -a 1 *adj* (**a**) (*de dentro*) internal; *Med* **medicina interna** internal medicine; *Med* **por vía interna** internally (**b**) *Pol* domestic
2 *nm,f* (**a**) (*alumno*) boarder (**b**) *Med* (*enfermo*) intern

interparlamentario, -a *adj Parl* interparliamentary

interpelación *nf Parl* interpellation, appeal

interpelar *vt Parl* to interpellate

interpersonal *adj* interpersonal

interplanetario, -a *adj* interplanetary

Interpol [inter'pol] *nf* (*abrev de* **International Criminal Police Organization**) Interpol

interpolación *nf* interpolation, insertion

interpolar *vt* to interpolate, insert

interponer [50] (*pp* **interpuesto**) **1** *vt* to interpose, insert; *Jur* **i. un recurso** to give notice of appeal
2 interponerse *vpr* to intervene

interposición *nf* interposition, insertion; *Jur* **i. de un recurso** lodging of an appeal

interpretación *nf* (**a**) (*gen*) interpretation; **ha habido una mala i.** there has been a misunderstanding (**b**) *Mús Teat* performance

interpretar *vt* (**a**) (*gen*) to interpret; **i. mal** to misunderstand, misinterpret (**b**) *Teat* (*papel*) to play; (*obra*) to perform; *Mús* (*concierto*) to play, perform; (*canción*) to sing

interpretativo, -a *adj* (**a**) (*de la interpretación artística*) **tiene mucha capacidad interpretativa para los papeles cómicos** he's very good in comic roles; **el pianista tiene un gran estilo i.** he's a very stylish pianist (**b**) (*del significado*) interpretative

intérprete *nmf* (**a**) (*traductor*) interpreter (**b**) *Teat* performer; *Mús* (*cantante*) singer; (*músico*) performer

interpuesto, -a 1 *pp de* **interponer**
2 *adj* interposed

interracial *adj* interracial

interregno *nm* interregnum

interrelación *nf* interrelation

interrelacionar 1 *vt* to interrelate
2 interrelacionarse *vpr* to be interrelated

interrogación *nf* interrogation, questioning

interrogador, -a 1 *adj* (*que interroga*) interrogating, questioning; (*vista*) inquisitive
2 *nmf* (*persona*) interrogator

interrogante 1 *adj* interrogating, questioning
2 *nm* question mark

interrogar [38] *vt* (*gen*) to question; (*testigo etc*) to interrogate

interrogativo, -a *adj & nm* interrogative

interrogatorio *nm* interrogation

interrumpir *vt* (*gen*) to interrupt; (*tráfico*) to block; *Elec* to switch off

interrupción *nf* interruption; **sin i.** uninterruptedly, without a break ▫ **i. del embarazo** termination of pregnancy

interruptor *nm Elec* switch

intersección *nf* intersection

intersticio *nm* (*gen*) interstice, crevice; (*grieta*) crack; (*intervalo*) gap

interurbano, -a *adj* intercity; *Tel* **conferencia interurbana** trunk call, long-distance call

intervalo *nm* (**a**) (*de tiempo*) interval; **a intervalos** at intervals (**b**) (*espacio*) gap

intervención *nf* (**a**) (*participación*) intervention, participation (**en** in), contribution (**en** to); **hacer una i.** to take the floor; *Pol* **política de no i.** non-intervention policy (**b**) *Med* **i. (quirúrgica)** (surgical) operation; **realizar** o **hacer una i. quirúrgica** to perform surgery

intervencionismo *nm* interventionism

intervencionista *adj & nmf* interventionist

intervenir [69] **1** *vi* (*participar*) to intervene (**en** in), take part (**en** in), participate (**en** in), contribute (**en** to); **en esta película intervienen treinta actores** there are thirty actors in this film; **la policía intervino para dispersar la manifestación** the police broke up the demonstration; **no intervino en la discusión** she did not take part in the debate
2 *vt* (**a**) (*confiscar*) to confiscate, seize (**b**) *Tel* (*teléfono*) to tap (**c**) *Med* to operate on

interventor, -a *nm,f* (*financiero*) financial controller; (*de las actas*) scrutineer; (*judicial*) official receiver; (*supervisor*) supervisor, inspector ▫ *Fin* **i. (de cuentas)** auditor

interviú (*pl* **interviús**) *nm* interview

intestinal *adj* intestinal

intestino, -a 1 *adj* (*luchas*) internal, domestic
2 *nm Anat* intestine ▫ **i. delgado/grueso** small/large intestine

intifada *nf* intifada

intimación *nf* announcement, notification

íntimamente *adv* (**a**) (*privadamente*) privately (**b**) (*a fondo*) intimately; **dos fenómenos í. relacionados** two phenomena which are intimately o closely connected (with each other)

intimar 1 *vt* (*notificar*) to notify (**a** to)
2 *vi* (*entablar amistad*) to become close (**con** to)

intimidación *nf* intimidation

intimidad *nf* (*amistad*) intimacy; (*vida privada*) private life; (*privacidad*) privacy; **en la i.** privately, in private

intimidar 1 *vt* to intimidate
2 intimidarse *vpr* to be intimidated, get scared; **no se intimida por nada** she's afraid of nothing

intimidatorio, -a *adj* intimidating, threatening

intimista *adj* **pintor i.** painter of domestic scenes; **novela i.** novel of family life

íntimo, -a 1 *adj* (**a**) (*ambiente, restaurante*) intimate; **higiene íntima** personal hygiene (**b**) (*vida*) private; **una boda íntima** a quiet wedding (**c**) (*amistad*) close
2 *nm,f* close friend, intimate

intitular *vt* to entitle, call

intocable *adj & nmf* untouchable

intolerable *adj* intolerable

intolerancia *nf* intolerance

intolerante 1 *adj* intolerant
  2 *nmf* intolerant person
intoxicación *nf* poisoning; *(por alimentos)* food poisoning
intoxicar [59] *vt* to poison
intra- *pref* intra-; **intrauterino** intrauterine
intraducible *adj* untranslatable
intragable *adj* unpalatable; *Fam* **es una película i.** this film is unbearable
intramuros *adv Literario* within the city (walls)
intramuscular *adj* intramuscular
intranet *nf Inform* intranet
intranquilidad *nf* worry, uneasiness, restlessness
intranquilizador, -a *adj* worrying, upsetting
intranquilizar [14] **1** *vt* to worry, upset, make uneasy
  2 intranquilizarse *vpr* to get worried, be anxious
intranquilo, -a *adj* worried, disquieted, uneasy, restless
intransferible *adj* untransferable, nontransferable
intransigencia *nf* intransigence
intransigente *adj* intransigent
intransitable *adj* impassable
intransitivo, -a *adj Ling* intransitive
intrascendencia *nf* insignificance, unimportance
intrascendente *adj* insignificant, unimportant
intratable *adj* (**a**) *(problema, persona)* intractable, unmanageable (**b**) *(persona)* unsociable, unapproachable
intrauterino, -a *adj* intrauterine
intravenoso, -a *adj Med* intravenous
intrépido, -a *adj* intrepid, bold, daring
intriga *nf* intrigue; *Cin Teat* plot
intrigante 1 *adj* (**a**) *(interesante)* intriguing, interesting (**b**) *Pey (maquinador)* scheming
  2 *nmf (persona)* intriguer
intrigar [38] **1** *vt (interesar)* to intrigue, interest; **esto me tiene muy intrigado** this has got me really intrigued
  2 *vi (maquinar)* to plot, scheme
intrincado, -a *adj* (**a**) *(cuestión, problema)* intricate, complicated (**b**) *(bosque)* dense
intrincar [59] *vt* to complicate, confuse
intríngulis *nm inv Fam* hidden snag, catch; **tiene su i.** there's more to it than meets the eye
intrínseco, -a *adj* intrinsic, inherent
intro *nm Inform* enter (key), return (key)
introducción *nf* introduction
introducir [18] **1** *vt* (**a**) *(gen)* to introduce (**b**) *(poner en uso)* to bring in, introduce (**c**) *(meter)* to insert, put in (**d**) *(problema, discordia)* to cause, create, bring about
  2 introducirse *vpr* (**a**) *(moda, costumbre)* to be introduced (**en** into) (**b**) *(meterse)* to get into, enter; **i. en la alta sociedad** to work one's way into high society
introductor, -a 1 *adj* introductory
  2 *nm,f* introducer
introductorio, -a *adj* introductory
intromisión *nf* meddling, interfering, intrusion
introspección *nf* introspection
introspectivo, -a *adj* introspective
introversión *nf* introversion
introvertido, -a 1 *adj* introverted
  2 *nm,f* introvert
intrusión *nf* intrusion
intrusismo *nm* quackery
intruso, -a 1 *adj* intrusive

  2 *nm,f* (**a**) *(gen)* intruder; *Jur* trespasser (**b**) *(impostor)* quack, impostor
intuición *nf* intuition
intuir [34] *vt* to sense, feel
intuitivamente *adv* intuitively, by intuition
intuitivo, -a *adj* intuitive
inundación *nf* flood, flooding
inundar *vt* to flood, swamp
inusitado, -a *adj* unusual, uncommon
inusual *adj* unusual
inútil 1 *adj* (**a**) *(gen)* useless; *(esfuerzo, intento)* vain, pointless; **es i. que llores** there's no point in crying (**b**) *Mil* unfit (for service)
  2 *nmf Fam* good-for-nothing
inutilidad *nf* uselessness
inutilizado, -a 1 *pp de* inutilizar
  2 *adj* out of action
inutilizar [14] *vt (gen)* to make *o* render useless; *(máquina etc)* to put out of action; **las bombas inutilizaron el alumbrado de la ciudad** the bombing knocked out the lights of the city
invadir *vt* to invade; *Fig* **le invadió la tristeza** she was overcome by sadness; *Fig* **los estudiantes invadieron la calle** students poured out onto the street
invalidación *nf* invalidation
invalidar *vt* to invalidate
invalidez *nf* (**a**) *Jur (nulidad)* invalidity (**b**) *Med (minusvalía)* disablement, disability
inválido, -a 1 *adj* (**a**) *Jur (nulo)* invalid (**b**) *Med (minusválido)* disabled, handicapped
  2 *nm,f Med* disabled *o* handicapped person
invariabilidad *nf* invariability
invariable *adj* invariable, unchanging
invariado, -a *adj* unchanged
invasión *nf* invasion
invasor, -a 1 *adj* invading
  2 *nm,f* invader
invectiva *nf* invective; **una i.** a piece of invective
invencible *adj* (**a**) *Mil* invincible, unbeatable (**b**) *(obstáculo)* insurmountable; *Hist* **la Armada I.** the Spanish Armada
invención *nf* (**invento**) invention; *(hallazgo)* discovery; *(mentira)* fabrication; *Fam* **i. del tebeo** stupid idea
inventar 1 *vt* (**crear**) to invent; *(cuento, historia)* to imagine; *(excusa, mentira)* to make up, concoct, fabricate
  2 inventarse *vpr (excusa, mentira)* to make up, concoct
inventariar [32] *vt* to inventory
inventario *nm* (**a**) *(lista)* inventory (**b**) *(operación)* stocktaking; *Com* **hacer el i.** to do the stocktaking
inventiva *nf* inventiveness; *(imaginación)* imagination
inventivo, -a *adj* inventive, resourceful
invento *nm* invention; *Fam* **¡vaya i.!** what a bright idea!
inventor, -a *nm,f* inventor
invernadero *nm* greenhouse, hothouse, conservatory ❑ **efecto i.** greenhouse effect
invernal *adj* winter, wintry
invernar [3] *vi* (**a**) *(pasar el invierno)* to winter, spend the winter (**en** in) (**b**) *(animales)* to hibernate
inverosímil *adj* unlikely, improbable
inverosimilitud *nf* unlikeliness, improbability
inversión *nf* (**a**) *(gen)* inversion (**b**) *Fin* investment
inversionista *nmf Fin* investor

inverso, -a *adj* inverted, opposite, contrary; **a la inversa** *(al revés)* vice versa, the other way round; *(al contrario)* on the contrary; **en orden i.** in reverse order; **en sentido i.** in the opposite direction; **y a la inversa** and vice versa

inversor, -a *nm,f Fin* investor

invertebrado, -a *adj & nm Zool* invertebrate

invertido, -a 1 *pp de* **invertir**
2 *adj* inverted, reversed
3 *nm,f Pey* queer

invertir [62] **1** *vt* **(a)** *(orden)* to invert, reverse, turn round; *(dirección)* to reverse; **i. los papeles** to exchange roles **(b)** *(tiempo)* to spend **(en** on); *(dinero, esfuerzos)* to invest **(en** in)
2 *vi* **i. en bolsa** to invest in stock

investidura *nf* investiture

investigación *nf* **(a)** *(policíaca etc)* investigation, inquiry **(b)** *(científica)* research

investigador, -a 1 *adj* investigation
2 *nm,f* **(a)** *(detective)* investigator **(b)** *(científico)* researcher, research worker

investigar [38] *vt* **(a)** *(indagar)* to investigate **(b)** *(ciencia)* to do research on

investir [47] *vt* to invest; **i. a algn con** *o* **de algo** to invest sb with sth, confer sth on sb

inveterado, -a *adj* inveterate, deep-rooted

inviable *adj* non-viable, unfeasible

invicto, -a *adj Literario* unconquered, unbeaten

invidencia *nf* blindness

invidente 1 *adj* blind, sightless
2 *nmf* blind person

invierno *nm* winter

inviolabilidad *nf* inviolability

inviolable *adj* inviolable

invisible *adj* invisible

invitación *nf* invitation; *Cin Teat (entrada)* ticket

invitado, -a 1 *pp de* **invitar**
2 *adj* invited; **artista i.** guest artist
3 *nm,f* guest; **tenemos invitados** we have guests

invitar *vt* to invite; **hoy invito yo** the drinks are on me today; **i. a algn a comer** to invite sb to lunch; **me invitó a una copa** he treated me to a drink; *Fig* **esa música invita a bailar** this music makes you want to dance

in vitro *loc adj & adv* in vitro; **fecundación i.** in vitro fertilization

invocación *nf* invocation

invocar [59] *vt* to invoke

involución *nf* **(a)** *Biol* involution **(b)** *Pol* regression, reaction

involucionista *adj & nmf Pol* regressive, reactionary

involucrado, -a 1 *pp de* **involucrar**
2 *adj* involved

involucrar 1 *vt* to involve **(en** in)
2 involucrarse *vpr* to get involved **(en** in)

involuntario, -a *adj* involuntary, unintentional, accidental

involutivo, -a *adj* **(a)** *Biol* involutional **(b)** *Pol* regressive

invulnerabilidad *nf* invulnerability

invulnerable *adj* invulnerable

inyección *nf* injection; **poner una i.** to give an injection ❏ **i. intramuscular/intravenosa** intramuscular/intravenous injection

inyectable 1 *adj* injectable
2 *nm Farm* injection

inyectar *vt* to inject **(en** into); **i. algo a algn** to inject sb with sth

inyector *nm Téc* injector

iodo *nm véase* **yodo**

ión *nm* ion

iónico, -a *adj* ionic

ionización *nf* ionization

ionizador *nm* ionizer

ionizar [14] *vt* to ionize

ionosfera *nf* ionosphere

IPC *nm* (abrev de Esp **Índice de Precios al Consumo** *o Am* **Índice de Precios al Consumidor**) *Br* RPI, *US* CPI

ipso facto *adv* immediately

ir [35] **1** *vi* **(a)** *(gen)* to go; **ir a caballo** to ride; **ir de Bilbao a Madrid** to go from Bilbao to Madrid; **ir de paseo** to go for a walk; **ir de compras/caza** to go shopping/hunting; **ir del brazo/de la mano** to walk arm in arm/hand in hand; **ir despacio** to go slowly; **ir en coche** to go by car, drive; **ir en tren** to go by train; **quiero ir contigo** I want to go with you; **¡vamos!** let's go!; **voy a Lima** I'm going to Lima; **¡ya voy!** (I'm) coming! **(b)** *(río, camino)* to lead; **esta carretera va a la frontera** this road leads to the border **(c)** *(obrar)* **ir con miedo** to be afraid; **ir con prisa** to be in a hurry **(d)** *(funcionar)* to work (properly); **el ascensor no va** the lift is out of order **(e)** *(desenvolverse)* **¿cómo le va el nuevo trabajo?** how is he getting on in his new job?; **¿cómo te va?** how are things?, how are you doing? **(f)** *(sentar bien)* to suit; **el verde te va mucho** green really suits you **(g)** *(combinar)* to match; **el rojo no va muy bien con el verde** red does not go well with green **(h)** *(vestir)* to wear; **ir con falda** to wear a skirt; **ir de blanco/de uniforme** to be dressed in white/in uniform **(i)** *Fam (importar, concernir)* to concern; **en esto te va la reputación** your reputation is at stake here; **eso va por ti también** and the same goes for you; **¿qué te va en ello?** what does it matter to you? **(j)** *Fam (comportarse)* to act; **ir de guapo por la vida** to be a flash Harry **(k)** *(edad)* **ir para los sesenta** to be pushing sixty; **ir por los cincuenta** to be about fifty **(l)** *(carrera, profesión)* **va para abogado** he's studying to be a lawyer **(m)** *Naipes* to go, lead **(n)** *(seguir)* **(ir + por)** **ir por la orilla del río** to follow the riverside; *Esp (ir a buscar)* **ve (a) por agua** go and fetch some water; *(haber llegado)* **voy por la página noventa** I've got as far as page ninety **(o)** *(locuciones)* **a eso iba** I was coming to that; **¡ahí va!** catch!; **dejarse ir** to let oneself go; **en lo que va del** *o Esp* **de mes** so far this month; **ir a parar** to end up; **ir dado** to be in for it; **¡qué va!** of course not!, nothing of the sort!; **¿quién va?** *Mil* who goes there?; *(turno)* whose turn is it?; **va a lo suyo** he looks after his own interests; **¡vamos a ver!** let's see!; **¡vaya!** fancy that; **¡vaya moto!** what a bike!; *Fig* **ir demasiado lejos** to go too far; *Fam* **ir tirando** to get by; **entonces fue y me dijo que no quería hacerlo** then he went and told me that he didn't want to do it; *Fam* **¡vamos anda!** come on!; *Fam* **vas que chutas** you're set; *Vulg* **ir de culo** to be fucked for time **(p)** *Esp Fam (gustar)* **no me va el pop** I'm not a big fan of pop music; **ni me va ni me viene** I don't care one way or the other

2 *v aux* **(a)** *(ir + gerundio)* **ir andando** to go on foot; **ir corriendo** to run; **va mejorando** she's improving **(b)** *(ir + pp)* **ir cansado** to be tired; **ya van rotos tres** three (of them) have already been broken; *Fam Fig* **ir vendido** to be lost **(c)** *(ir + a + inf)* **iba a decir que** I was going to say that; **ir a parar en la cárcel** to end up in jail; **va a llover** it's going to rain; **vas a caerte** you'll fall

3 irse *vpr* **(a)** *(marcharse)* to go away, leave; **me voy** I'm off; **¡vámonos!** let's go!; **¡vete!** go away!; **vete a casa** go home **(b)** *(líquido, gas) (escaparse)* to leak **(c)** *(mano, pie)* to slip; **se le fue el pie** his foot slipped **(d)** *(gastarse)* to go, disappear; **el dinero se va sin que uno se dé cuenta** money just slips away without your noticing it **(e)** *Euf* *(morir)* to pass away, die (**f**) *(locuciones)* **i. a pique** *(barco)* to sink; *Fig* to fall through; **i. abajo** *o* **al traste** to fall through; **i. de la boca** *o* **de la lengua** to tell it all; **i. la mano** to overdo it; *Fam Fig* **i. por las ramas** to get sidetracked

ira *nf* wrath, rage, anger; **descargar la i. en algn** to vent one's wrath on sb

iracundo, -a *adj* (**a**) *(irascible)* irascible (**b**) *(enfadado)* irate, angry

Irak *n véase* **Iraq**

irakí *(pl* **irakíes)** *adj & nmf véase* **iraquí**

Irán *n* Iran

iraní *(pl* **iraníes)** *adj & nmf* Iranian

Iraq *n* Iraq

iraquí *(pl* **iraquíes)** *adj & nmf* Iraqi

irascibilidad *nf* irascibility

irascible *adj* irascible, irritable

iridiscente *adj* iridescent

iris *nm inv Anat* iris ❑ **arco i.** rainbow

irisación *nf (gen pl)* iridiscence

irisado, -a 1 *pp de* **irisar**
2 *adj* iridescent

irisar 1 *vt* to make iridescent
2 *vi* to be iridescent

Irlanda *n* Ireland ❑ **I. del Norte** Northern Ireland

irlandés, -esa 1 *adj* Irish
2 *nm,f (hombre)* Irishman; *(mujer)* Irishwoman; **los irlandeses** the Irish
3 *nm* (**a**) *(idioma)* Irish (**b**) *Fam (café)* Irish coffee

ironía *nf* irony; **con i.** ironically

irónico, -a *adj* ironic

ironizar [14] *vt* to ridicule, be ironical about

IRPF *nm Econ (abrev de* **impuesto sobre la renta de las personas físicas)** income tax

irracional *adj* irrational

irracionalidad *nf* irrationality

irradiación *nf* irradiation

irradiar *vt* (**a**) *(emitir)* to irradiate, radiate (**b**) *Am Fig (expulsar)* to expel

irrazonable *adj* unreasonable

irreal *adj* unreal

irrealidad *nf* unreality

irrealizable *adj* unattainable, unfeasible; *Fig* unreachable

irrebatible *adj* irrefutable

irreconciliable *adj* irreconcilable

irreconocible *adj* unrecognizable

irrecuperable *adj* irretrievable

irrecusable *adj* unimpeachable

irreducible *adj,* **irreductible** *adj* (**a**) *Mat* irreducible (**b**) *(país, pueblo)* unconquerable

irreemplazable *adj* irreplaceable

irreflexión *nf* rashness, impetuosity

irreflexivo, -a *adj (acción)* rash; *(persona)* impetuous

irrefrenable *adj* unrestrained, uncontrollable; **un impulso i.** an irresistible urge

irrefutable *adj* irrefutable

irregular *adj* irregular

irregularidad *nf* irregularity

irrelevancia *nf* unimportance, insignificance

irrelevante *adj* irrelevant

irremediable *adj* irremediable, incurable

irremisible *adj* unpardonable, unforgivable

irremplazable *adj* irreplaceable

irreparable *adj* irreparable

irrepetible *adj* unique, unrepeatable

irreprimible *adj* irrepressible

irreprochable *adj* irreproachable, blameless

irresistible *adj* (**a**) *(impulso, persona)* irresistible (**b**) *(insoportable)* unbearable

irresoluto, -a *adj* irresolute

irrespetuoso, -a *adj* disrespectful

irrespirable *adj* unbreathable

irresponsabilidad *nf* irresponsibility

irresponsable 1 *adj* irresponsible
2 *nmf* irresponsible person

irreverencia *nf* irreverence

irreverente *adj* irreverent

irreversible *adj* irreversible

irrevocable *adj* irrevocable

irrigación *nf* irrigation

irrigar [38] *vt* to irrigate, water

irrisorio, -a *adj* derisory, ridiculous

irritabilidad *nf* irritability

irritable *adj* irritable

irritación *nf* irritation

irritante *adj* irritating

irritar 1 *vt* (**a**) *(enfadar)* to irritate, exasperate (**b**) *Med* to irritate, inflame
2 irritarse *vpr (enfadarse)* to lose one's temper, get angry

irrompible *adj* unbreakable

irrumpir *vi* to burst (**en** into)

irrupción *nf* irruption

isabelino, -a *adj Hist (en España)* Isabelline; *(en Inglaterra)* Elizabethan

ISBN *nm (abrev de* **International Standard Book Number)** ISBN

isla *nf* (**a**) island, isle ❑ **isla desierta** desert island; *Aut* **i. de peatones** traffic island, *US* safety island; **(las) Islas Galápagos** the Galapagos Islands (**b**) *Méx RP (de árboles)* grove (**c**) *Chile (terreno)* flood plain

islam *nm Rel* **el i.** Islam

Islamabad *n* Islamabad

islámico, -a *adj* Islamic

islamismo *nm* Islam

islamizar [14] **1** *vt* to Islamize, convert to Islam
2 islamizarse *vpr* to convert to Islam

islandés, -esa 1 *adj* Icelandic
2 *nm,f (persona)* Icelander
3 *nm (idioma)* Icelandic

Islandia *n* Iceland

isleño, -a 1 *adj* island; **la población isleña** the population of the island
2 *nm,f* islander

isleta *nf* islet

islote *nm* small *o* rocky island

ismo *nm Fam* ism

ISO ['iso] *(abrev de* **International Standards Organization)** ISO

isobara *nf* isobar

isósceles *adj Geom* **triángulo i.** isosceles triangle

isoterma *nf* isotherm

isotérmico, -a *adj,* **isotermo, -a** *adj* **camión i.**

refrigerated *Br* lorry *o US* truck
isotónico, -a *adj* isotonic
isótopo *nm* isotope
Israel *n* Israel
israelí (*pl* israelíes) *adj & nmf* Israeli
israelita *adj & nmf Hist* Israelite
istmo *nm Geog* isthmus ❏ **I. de Panamá** Isthmus of Panama
Italia *n* Italy
italiano, -a 1 *adj* Italian
 2 *nm,f (persona)* Italian
 3 *nm (idioma)* Italian
ítem (*pl* ítems) **1** *nm* item
 2 *adv* item, likewise, also
iteración *nf* iteration

itinerante *adj* itinerant, itinerating
itinerario *nm* itinerary, route
IVA ['iβa] *nm Econ* (*abrev de* **impuesto sobre el valor** *Am* **agregado** *o Esp* **añadido**) *Br* VAT, *US* ≃ sales tax
izar [14] *vt* to hoist, raise
izqda., izqda (*abrev de* **izquierda**) left
izqdo., izqdo (*abrev de* **izquierdo**) left
izquierda *nf* (**a**) *(contrario de derecha)* left; **a la i.** on the left; **girar a la i.** to turn left (**b**) *(mano)* left hand (**c**) *Pol* **la i.** the left; **ser de** *Esp* **izquierdas** *o Am* **i.** to be left-wing
izquierdismo *nm Pol* leftism
izquierdista *Pol* **1** *adj* leftist, left-wing
 2 *nmf* leftist, left-winger
izquierdo, -a *adj* left; **brazo i.** left arm
izquierdoso, -a *adj Fam* leftish

J

J, j [ˈχota] *nf (la letra)* J, j

ja *interj* (**a**) *(al reír)* **¡ja, ja!** ha, ha! (**b**) *(incredulidad)* come on!, come off it!

jabalí *(pl* **jabalíes)** *nm Zool* wild boar

jabalina¹ *nf Zool* female wild boar

jabalina² *nf Dep* javelin

jabato *nm Zool* young wild boar; *Fig* **ser un j.** to be as bold as a lion

jábega *nm Pesca* casting net

jabón *nm* (**a**) soap; *Fam Fig* **dar j. a algn** to soft-soap *o* flatter sb □ **j. de afeitar** shaving soap; **j. de tocador** toilet soap; **j. líquido** liquid soap (**b**) *Méx RP Fam* **dar un j. a algn** *(asustar)* to freak sb

jabonado *nm* (**a**) *(acción)* soaping (**b**) *(ropa)* laundry (**c**) *Fam (reprimenda)* reprimand, ticking off

jabonadura *nf* soaping; **jabonaduras** soapy water *sing,* soapsuds

jabonar *vt véase* **enjabonar**

jaboncillo *nm* (**a**) *(pastilla de jabón)* bar of toilet soap (**b**) *Bot* soapberry

jabonera *nf* soapdish

jabonoso, -a *adj* soapy

jaca *nf Zool* (**a**) *(caballo pequeño)* pony, cob (**b**) *(caballo castrado)* gelding

jacal *nm Méx* hut, shack

jácara *nf* (**a**) *Lit (romance)* picaresque ballad (**b**) *Fam* nuisance, irritation

jacarandá *nm Bot* jacaranda

jacarandoso, -a *adj Fam* cheerful, lively

jacinto *nm* (**a**) *Bot* hyacinth (**b**) *Min* **j. de Ceilán** zircon; **j. occidental** topaz; **j. oriental** ruby

jaco *nm Pey* nag, hack

jacobeo, -a *adj Rel* of Saint James; **peregrinación jacobea** pilgrimage to Santiago de Compostela

jactancia *nf* boastfulness, boasting, bragging

jactancioso, -a 1 *adj* boastful
  2 *nm,f* braggart

jactarse *vpr* to boast, brag (**de** about)

jaculatoria *nf* short prayer

jacuzzi [jaˈkusi] *nm* Jacuzzi®

jade *nm Min* jade

jadeante *adj* panting, breathless

jadear *vi* to pant, gasp

jadeo *nm* panting, gasping

jaez *nm* (**a**) *(del caballo)* harness, trappings *pl* (**b**) *Pey (ralea)* kind, sort; **gente de ese j.** people of that ilk *o* kind

jaguar *nm Zool* jaguar

jai *nf Vulg* woman

jalada *nf* (**a**) *Méx (tirón)* pull; *(suave)* tug; **dar una j. a algo** to pull sth; *(suavemente)* to tug sth (**b**) *Méx Fam (reprimenda)* telling-off; **dar una j. a algn** to tell sb off (**c**) *Perú Fam (aventón) Br* lift, *US* ride; **dar una j. a algn** to give sb a *Br* lift *o US* ride (**d**) *Ven Fam (adulancia)* soft soap; **dar una j. a algn** to soft-soap sb

jalar *Fam* **1** *vt* (**a**) *Am salvo RP (tirar de)* to pull; *(suavemente)* to tug; **lo jaló de la manga** she pulled his sleeve (**b**) *Méx (extender)* to stretch out; **jaló tanto el suéter que lo deformó** she stretched the sweater out of shape (**c**) *Méx Fam (atraer)* **el deporte me jala mucho** I'm crazy about sport *o US* sports, I'm really into sport *o US* sports (**d**) *Méx Fam (convencer)* **lo jalaron para que participara en la campaña** they talked him into joining the campaign (**e**) *Perú Fam (transportar)* to give a *Br* lift *o US* ride; **me jaló hasta la estación** she gave me a *Br* lift *o US* ride to the station (**f**) *Perú Fam (suspender)* to fail, *US* flunk (**g**) *Perú Fam (cobrar)* to sting; **¿cuánto te jalaron por esos zapatos?** how much did they sting you for when you bought those shoes? (**h**) *Ven Fam (succionar)* to suck up (**i**) *Ven Fam (consumir) (energía, combustible)* to guzzle; *(dinero)* to eat up (**j**) *Esp (comer)* to eat, *Br* scoff

  2 *vi* (**a**) *Am salvo RP (tirar)* to pull (**b**) *Am salvo RP (irse)* to go; **jala a la derecha en la tercera calle** take the third street on the right; (**c**) *Méx Fam (trabajar)* to work; **¿en qué jalas?** what are you working on? (**d**) *Méx Fam (robar)* **jalaron con tres computadoras** they made off with *o Br* nicked three computers (**e**) *Méx muy Fam (molestar)* to be a *Br* bloody *o US* goddamn pain (**f**) *Méx Fam (funcionar)* to work (**g**) *Méx Fam (apresurarse)* to get a move on; **dejen de platicar y jálenle, que se hace tarde** stop gabbing and get a move on, it's late (**h**) *Ven Fam (adular)* to crawl

  3 jalarse *vpr* (**a**) *Esp (comerse)* to eat, *Br* scoff (**b**) *Ven (emborracharse)* to get plastered

jalbegar [38] *vt* to whitewash

jale *nm Méx Fam* work

jalea *nf* jelly □ **j. real** royal jelly

jalear *vt* (**a**) *(animar)* to cheer (on), clap and shout (**b**) *Caza* to urge on

jaleo *nm (alboroto)* din, racket; *(escándalo)* fuss, commotion; *(riña)* row; *(confusión)* muddle; **armar j.** to make a racket; **armar un j.** to kick up a fuss; **armarle j. a algn** to start a row with sb

jalón¹ *nm* (**a**) *(estaca)* marker pole; *Fig (hito)* milestone (**b**) *Bol Méx Ven (trecho)* stretch, distance

jalón² *nm* (**a**) *Am salvo RP (tirón)* pull, tug (**b**) *Méx (trago)* shot, tot

jalonar *vt (señalar con estacas)* to stake out; *Fig (marcar)* to mark

Jamaica *n* Jamaica

jamaicano, -a *adj & nm,f, Am* **jamaiquino, -a** *adj & nm,f* Jamaican

jamás *adv* (a) *(f. + indic)* never; **j. he estado allí** I have never been there (b) *(f. + subj)* ever; **el mejor libro que j. se haya escrito** the best book ever written (c) *(locuciones)* **j. de los jamases** never ever, never on your life; **nunca j.** never ever; **por siempre j.** for ever (and ever)

jamba *nf Arquit* jamb

jamelgo *nm Pey* old nag, hack

jamón *nm* ham; **j. de York** *o* **en dulce** boiled ham; **j. serrano** cured ham; *Fam Esp* **¡y un j. (con chorreras)!** nothing doing!, you must be joking!

jamona *Fam* **1** *adj* buxom
2 *nf* buxom woman

Japón *n* **(el) J.** Japan

japonés, -esa **1** *adj* Japanese
2 *nm,f (persona)* Japanese; **los japoneses** the Japanese
3 *nm (idioma)* Japanese

japuta *nf (pez)* Ray's bream

jaque *nm Ajedrez* check; **dar j. a** to check; **dar j. mate a** to checkmate; **estar en j.** to be in check; **j. al rey** check; **j. mate** checkmate; *Fig* **tener** *o* **traer a algn en j.** to intimidate *o* threaten sb

jaquear *vt Ajedrez* to check; *Fig (amenazar)* to harass, threaten

jaqueca *nf* migraine, headache; *Fig* **dar j. a** to bore, be a pain in the neck to

jáquima *nf CAm* drunkenness, drunken bout

jara *nf Bot* rockrose

jarabe *nm* (a) *(bebida)* syrup; **j. para la tos** cough mixture; *Fig Esp* **dar a algn j. de palo** to give sb a hiding; *Fig* **j. de pico** blarney, smooth talk; *Fig* **tener mucho j. de pico** to talk glibly (b) *Mús* Mexican dance

jarana *nf Fam* (a) *(juerga)* wild party, spree; **ir de j.** to go on a spree o a binge (b) *(jaleo)* racket, din; **armar j.** to make a racket (c) *Méx Mús* small guitar (d) *Méx Mús* dance (e) *CAm (deuda)* debt

jaranero, -a **1** *adj* fun-loving, party-loving
2 *nm,f* pleasure seeker, party-lover

jarcia *nf* (a) *Náut* rigging, ropes *pl*; **j. de labor** running rigging; **j. muerta** standing rigging (b) *CAm Cuba Méx (cordel)* rope (c) *Pesca* fishing tackle

jardín *nm Br* garden, *US* yard; **j. botánico** botanical garden; **j. de infancia** nursery school, kindergarten

jardinera *nf* (a) *(mujer)* gardener (b) *(mueble) (para tiestos)* planter, flower stand; *(en una ventana)* window box (c) *(vehículo) (carruaje)* open carriage; *(tranvía)* open tramcar

jardinería *nf* gardening

jardinero *nm* gardener

jareta *nf* (a) *Cost* casing (b) *Náut* cable, rope

jarocho, -a **1** *adj* (a) *(insolente)* rude, uncouth (b) of o from Veracruz
2 *nm,f* person from Veracruz

jarra *nf* pitcher; **j. de leche** milk churn; **j. de cerveza** beer tankard; *Fig* **de** *o* **en jarras** arms akimbo, hands on hips

jarrete *nm (de persona)* back of the knee; *(de animal)* hock

jarretera *nf (liga)* garter; **la Orden de la J.** the Order of the Garter

jarro *nm (recipiente)* jug; *(contenido)* jugful; *Fig* **echar un j. de agua fría a** to pour cold water on

jarrón *nm* vase

Jartum *n* Khartoum

jaspe *nm Min* jasper

jaspeado, -a **1** *pp de* jaspear
2 *adj* mottled, speckled

jaspear *vt* to mottle, speckle

Jauja *nf Fig* promised land; **¡esto es J.!** this is the life! **la tierra de J.** the land of plenty, the land of milk and honey

jaula *nf* (a) *(para animales)* cage; *(embalaje)* crate; *(niños)* playpen; *Min* cage (b) *Carib Col RP Fam (policía)* *Br* Black Maria, *US* paddy wagon

jauría *nf* pack of hounds; *Fig* gang

Java *n* Java

javanés, -a *adj & nm,f* Javanese

jayán, -ana *nm,f (hombre)* big strong man; *(mujer)* big strong woman

jazmín *nm Bot* jasmine

jazz [jas] *nm Mús* jazz

jazzístico, -a [ja'sistiko] *adj Mús* jazz, jazzy

J.C. *(abrev de* Jesucristo*)* J.C.

je *interj* **¡je, je!** ha, ha!

jean [jin] *nm* jeans *pl*

jebe *nm Andes (caucho)* rubber

jeep [jip] *nm Aut* jeep

jefa *nf* female boss, manageress

jefatura *nf* (a) *(cargo, dirección)* leadership; **bajo la j. de** under the leadership of (b) *(sede)* central office; *Mil* headquarters; **j. de policía** police headquarters

jefazo, -a *nm,f Fam* big boss, *esp US* head honcho

jefe *nm* (a) *(persona al mando)* head, chief, boss; *Com* manager; **j. de estación** stationmaster; **j. de redacción** editor-in-chief; **j. de taller** foreman; **j. de ventas** sales manager (b) *Pol* leader; **j. de Estado** Head of State; **j. de gobierno** head of government (c) *Mil* officer in command; **comandante en j.** commander-in-chief; **J. de Estado Mayor** Chief of Staff

Jehová *nm* Jehovah

jején *nm Am* gnat

jengibre *nm Bot* ginger

jenízaro, -a **1** *adj Fig* mixed
2 *nm* janissary

jeque *nm* sheik, sheikh

jerarca *nm* hierarch, chief

jerarquía *nf* (a) *(gen)* hierarchy; **j. social** social hierarchy (b) *(grado)* scale (c) *(categoría)* rank; **de j.** high-ranking

jerárquico, -a *adj* hierarchic, hierarchical

jerarquizar [14] *vt* to structure in a hierarchical manner

jerez *nm* sherry

jerga *nf (técnica)* jargon; *(vulgar)* slang; **la j. legal** legal jargon

jergal *adj (técnico)* of jargon; *(vulgar)* slangy

jergón *nm* straw mattress

jerifalte *nm (persona)* bigwig

jerigonza *nf* (a) *véase* jerga (b) *(extravagancia)* oddness

jeringa *nf Med* syringe; *Aut* **j. de engrase** grease gun

jeringar [38] *vt Fam (molestar)* to pester, annoy

jeringuilla *nf Med* (hypodermic) syringe

jeroglífico, -a **1** *adj* hieroglyphic
2 *nm* hieroglyph, hieroglyphic

jersey *(pl* jerseys *o* jerséis*)* *nm Esp* sweater, *Br* jumper

Jerusalén *n* Jerusalem

Jesucristo *nm* Jesus Christ

jesuita *adj & nmf* Jesuit

jesuítico, -a *adj* Jesuitic; *Fig* cautious, wary

Jesús 1 *nm* Jesus; *Fam* **en un decir J.** in the twinkling of an eye
  2 *interj* (**a**) *(expresa sorpresa)* good heavens! (**b**) *Esp (al estornudar)* bless you!

jet [jet] **1** *nm Av* jet
  2 *nf Esp* **la j.** jet set

jeta *Fam* **1** *nf* (**a**) *(cara)* mug, face; **poner j.** to pull a face (**b**) *(hocico)* snout (**c**) *Esp (descaro)* cheek; **tener j.** to be cheeky, have a nerve; **¡qué j. tienes!** what a cheek you've got!
  2 *nmf Esp* rogue *sing*

jet lag ['jetlag] *nm* jet lag

jet-set ['jetset] *Esp nf. Am nm* jet-set

jíbaro, -a *Am* **1** *adj (indio)* Jivaro; **las tribus jíbaras** the Jivaro tribes
  2 *nm,f* (**a**) *(indio)* Jivaro (**b**) *Ven Fam (traficante)* pusher

jibia *nf (pez)* cuttlefish

jícama *nf Bot* sweet turnip

jícara *nf CAm Méx Ven (bol)* small cup; gourd

jícaro *nm CAm Cuba Bot* calabash tree

jicote *nm CAm Méx Ent* large wasp

jicotera *nf* (**a**) *Am (avispero)* wasps' nest (**b**) *Méx (zumbido)* buzzing of wasps

jiennense 1 *adj* of o from Jaén
  2 *nmf* person from Jaén

jijona *nm Culin* = type of nougat

jilguero, -a *nm,f Orn* goldfinch

jilipollas *nmf inv Fam Ofens véase* **gilipollas**

jineta¹ *nf Zool* genet

jineta² *nf* (**a**) *Equit* **a la j.** with short stirrups (**b**) *Mil (hombrera)* epaulette

jinete *nm* rider, horseman

jinetear *Equit* **1** *vi (montar)* to ride regally
  2 *vt Méx Fam (deuda, pago)* = to delay paying in order to gain interest

jingoísmo *nm* jingoism

jiñar *Esp muy Fam vi Vulg* to shit

jipato, -a *adj Am (persona)* pale

jipi *nm* Panama hat

jira *nf* picnic

jirafa *nf* (**a**) *Zool* giraffe; *Fig* tall person (**b**) *(de micrófono)* boom

jirón *nm* (**a**) *(trozo desgarrado)* shred, strip; *(pedazo suelto)* bit, scrap; **hecho jirones** in shreds o tatters (**b**) *Perú (calle)* street

jitomate *nm Méx* tomato

jiu-jitsu [jiu'jitsu] *nm Dep* jujitsu

JJ OO *nmpl (abrev de* **Juegos Olímpicos)** Olympic Games

jo *interj Esp Fam* bloody hell!

Job [joβ] *nm* Job; **tiene más paciencia que el santo J.** he has the patience of Job

jobar *interj Esp Fam Euf* Jeez!, *Br* flipping heck!

jockey ['jokei] *nm Dep* jockey

jocosidad *nf* humour, *US* humor

jocoso, -a *adj* funny, humorous, comic

jocundo, -a *adj* jovial

joder *Vulg Ofens* **1** *vt* (**a**) *Esp (copular)* to fuck (**b**) *(fastidiar)* to piss off; **jode mucho tener que trabajar en domingo** having to work on Sunday really pisses me off; **¡no me jodas!** come on, don't give me that!; *Esp* **claro que no me importaría ser millonario, ¡no te jode!** o **¡nos ha jodido!** would I like to be a millionaire? no shit! o *Br* too bloody

right I would! (**c**) *(echar a perder)* to fuck up; *Esp* **¡la jodiste!** you screwed it up! (**d**) *(romper)* to screw, *Br* bugger; **ha vuelto a j. el ordenador** he has screwed the computer up again (**e**) *(lastimar)* to screw, *Br* bugger; **tiene el brazo jodido** his arm is screwed o *Br* buggered (**f**) *Esp (quitar, sisar)* **me jodieron seis euros por entrar al museo** it was six fucking euros to get into the museum
  2 joderse *vpr* (**a**) *(fastidiarse)* to put up with it; **¡hay que j.!** you'll just have to grin and bear it!; **¡que se joda!** to hell with him! (**b**) *(echarse a perder)* to fuck up, ruin; **me jodí el domingo por ayudarle a mudarse** I messed up my Sunday by helping her to move house; *Esp* **¡se jodió el invento!** that's the end of that! (**c**) *(lastimarse)* to hurt, fuck up (**d**) *(romperse)* to go bust; **se jodió el día** the weather turned bad
  3 *interj Esp* bloody hell!, fuck!

jodido, -a 1 *pp de* **joder**
  2 *adj Vulg Ofens* (**a**) *(maldito)* fucking (**b**) *(enfermo)* in a bad way; *(cansado)* knackered, exhausted (**c**) *(estropeado, roto)* bust, fucked (**d**) *(difícil)* **es muy j. levantarse a las seis** it's a fucking pain to get up at six

jodienda *nf Esp Vulg Ofens* (**a**) *(coito)* fuck (**b**) *(molestia)* balls-up, mess

jofaina *nf* washbasin

jogging ['joʝin] *nm Dep* jogging; **hacer j.** to jog

Johannesburgo [joχanes'βurɣo] *n* Johannesburg

joker ['joker] *nm Naipes* joker

jolgorio *nm Fam (juerga)* binge; *(algazara)* fun; **ir de j.** to go on a binge; **¡qué j.!** what fun!

jolín *interj,* **jolines** *interj Esp Fam Euf (sorpresa)* gosh!, good grief!; *(enfado)* blast!, damn!

jondo *adj* **cante j.** = traditional flamenco singing

jónico, -a 1 *adj* Ionic, Ionian; *Arquit* Ionic; **el (Mar) J.** the Ionian Sea
  2 *nm,f* Ionian
  3 *nm Ling Lit* Ionic

jope *interj,* **jopé** *interj Esp Fam* Jeez!, *Br* flipping heck!

Jordán *n (río)* Jordan

Jordania *n (país)* Jordan

jordano, -a *adj & nm,f* Jordanian

jornada *nf* (**a**) *(día de trabajo)* working day; **j. de siete horas** seven-hour (working) day; **trabajo de media j /j. completa** part-time/full-time work ❑ **j. electoral** polling day; **j. intensiva** = working day without a lunch break; **j. laboral** working day; **j. partida** working day with a lunch break; (**b**) *(camino recorrido en un día)* day's journey; **de Bilbao a Sevilla hay dos jornadas de camino** it's a two-day journey from Bilbao to Seville (**c**) *Mil* expedition (**d**) *Dep* **los resultados de la j. del sábado** Saturday's results (**e**) *Teat (uso antiguo)* act (**f**) **jornadas** conference *sing*, congress *sing*; **las II J. de Moda Española** the 2nd Conference on Spanish Fashion

jornal *nm (paga)* day's wage; **ganar un buen j.** to earn a good wage; **trabajar a j.** to be paid by the day

jornalero, -a *nm,f* day labourer o *US* laborer

joroba 1 *nf* (**a**) *(deformidad)* curvature, hump (**b**) *Fam (fastidio)* nuisance, drag
  2 *interj* drat!

jorobado, -a 1 *pp de* **jorobar**
  2 *adj* hunchbacked, humpbacked
  3 *nm,f* hunchback, humpback

jorobar *Fam* **1** *vt* (**a**) *(fastidiar)* to annoy, bother; **me joroba** it really gets up my nose (**b**) *(romper)* to smash up, break (**c**) *(estropear) (fiesta, planes)* to mess up; *(máquina, objeto)* to bust, *Br* knacker; **¡no jorobes!** *(fastidio)* stop pestering me!; *(incredulidad)* pull the other one!

2 jorobarse *vpr* (**a**) *(fastidiarse)* to put up with; **¡hay que j.!** that really is the limit! (**b**) *(estropearse)* to break

josefino, -a 1 *adj* of o from San José
2 *nm,f* person from San José

jota[1] *nf* (**a**) *(letra)* name of the letter J in Spanish (**b**) *(cantidad mínima)* jot, scrap; **ni j.** not an iota; **no entiendo ni j.** I don't understand a thing; **no sabe ni j. de latín** he doesn't know the first thing about Latin; **no se ve ni j.** you can't see a thing

jota[2] *nf Mús* Spanish dance and music

joto *nm Méx Fam Pey Br* queer, *US* fag

joule *nm Fís* joule

joven 1 *adj* young; **de aspecto j.** young-looking; **de j.** as a young man o woman
2 *nmf* (*hombre*) youth, young man; *(mujer)* girl, young woman; **los jóvenes** young people, youth

jovencito, -a 1 *adj* very young
2 *nm,f* (*hombre*) boy, youngster; *(mujer)* girl, youngster

jovenzuelo, -a 1 *adj* very young
2 *nm,f* (*hombre*) lad, youngster; *(mujer)* lass, youngster

jovial *adj* jovial, good-humoured, *US* good-humored

jovialidad *nf* joviality, cheerfulness

joya *nf* (**a**) *(pieza de adorno)* jewel, piece of jewellery o *US* jewelry; **joyas de imitación** imitation jewellery *sing* (**b**) *Fig* *(personas)* **ser una j.** to be a real treasure o godsend

joyería *nf* (**a**) *(tienda)* jewellery shop o *US* jewelry store, jeweller's o *US* jeweler's (shop o *US* store) (**b**) *(comercio)* jewellery o *US* jewelry trade

joyero, -a 1 *nm,f* jeweller, *US* jeweler
2 *nm* jewel case o box

Juan *nm* John; **ser un buen J.** to be a simple Simon; **ser un J. Lanas** to be a wimp; *Cuba RP Fam* **J. de los Palotes** anybody (you like), whoever (you like)

juanete *nm* (**a**) *(en el pie)* bunion (**b**) *Náut* topgallant

jubilación *nf* (**a**) *(acción)* retirement; **j. anticipada** early retirement (**b**) *(dinero)* pension

jubilado, -a 1 *pp de* jubilar[2]
2 *adj* retired
3 *nm,f* senior citizen, *Br* pensioner; **los jubilados** retired people

jubilar[1] *adj* **año j.** jubilee

jubilar[2] **1** *vt* (*retirarse*) to retire, pension off; *Fam Fig* to get rid of, ditch
2 *vi Fml* *(alegrarse)* to rejoice
3 jubilarse *vpr* (**a**) *(retirarse)* to retire, go into retirement (**b**) *(alegrarse)* to rejoice (**c**) *Cuba Méx (instruirse)* to learn, become skilled

jubileo *nm* (**a**) *Hist (fiesta)* jubilee (**b**) *Rel (indulgencia)* indulgence; **ganar el j.** to gain an indulgence

júbilo *nm* jubilation, joy

jubiloso, -a *adj* jubilant, joyful

jubón *nm* doublet, jerkin

judaico, -a *adj* Judaic, Jewish

judaísmo *nm* Judaism

judaizar [14] *vi* to Judaize

judas *nm inv* traitor

judeocristiano, -a *adj & nm,f* Judaeo-Christian, *US* Judeo-Christian

judeoespañol, -a *adj & nm,f* Judaeo-Spanish, *US* Judeo-Spanish

judería *nf* (*barrio*) Jewish quarter

judía *nf Bot* bean; **j. blanca/pinta** haricot/kidney bean; *Esp* **j. verde** French bean, green bean

judiada *nf Fam* dirty trick

judicatura *nf* (**a**) *(cuerpo)* judicature (**b**) *(tiempo en el cargo)* judge's term of office

judicial *adj* judicial, juridical

judío, -a 1 *adj* Jewish; *Argot* mean, stingy
2 *nm,f* Jew; **j. converso** converted Jew

judo ['juðo] *nm Dep* judo

judoka [ju'ðoka] *nmf* judoka

juego *nm* (**a**) *(acción de entretenerse o practicar deporte)* play, playing; **a los perros les encanta el j.** dogs love playing; **se vio buen j. en la primera parte** there was some good play in the first half; *Fig* **entrar en j.** (*factor*) to come into play; *Fig* **estar en j.** to be at stake; *Fig* **poner algo en j.** (*arriesgar*) to put sth at stake; *(utilizar)* to bring sth to bear; *Fig* **hacer** o **seguir el j. a algn** to play along with sb; *Fig* **ser un j. de niños** to be child's play □ *Fig* **j. limpio** fair play; *Fig* **j. sucio** foul play (**b**) *(entretenimiento, deporte)* game □ **j. de azar** game of chance; **j. de cartas** card game; *Fig* **j. de manos** sleight of hand; **j. de mesa** board game; *Fig* **j. de palabras** play on words, pun; **j. de rol** fantasy role-playing game; **juegos florales** poetry competition *sing*; **juegos malabares** juggling *sing*; **Juegos Olímpicos** Olympic Games (**c**) *(apuestas)* gambling; **casa de j.** gambling house; **mesa de j.** gambling table, card table; **¡hagan j., señores!** place your bets! (**d**) *Naipes* **tener buen/mal j.** to have a good/bad hand; **descubrir su j.** to show one's hand; *Fig* **descubrirle el j. a algn** to see through sb (**e**) *(conjunto de piezas)* set; *Esp Fig* **a j.** matching; *Fig* **hacer j.** to match □ **j. de café** coffee service; **j. de destornilladores** set of screwdrivers **j. de té** tea service (**f**) *(articulación de piezas)* joint; *(movimiento de las piezas)* movement; *Fig* **este traje me da mucho j.** this dress is very versatile

juerga *nf Fam* partying, *Br* rave-up; **de j.** living it up, having a good time; **ir(se) de j.** to go on a binge; **tener ganas de j.** to feel like living it up, feel like having a good time

juerguista 1 *adv* fun-loving
2 *nmf* fun-loving person, raver

jueves *nm inv* Thursday; **J. Santo** Maundy Thursday; *Fam Fig* **no es nada del otro j.** it's nothing to write home about; *véase tamb* **viernes**

juez *nmf* judge; *Ftb* **j. de banda** linesman; **j. de instrucción** examining magistrate; *Ftb* **j. de línea** linesman; **j. de menores** juvenile court magistrate; *Dep* **j. de meta** finishing line judge; **j. de paz** justice of the peace; **j. de primera instancia** judge of the first instance; *Dep* **j. de salida** starter; *Ten* **j. de silla** umpire

jugada *nf* (**a**) *(gen)* play; *Ajedrez* move; *Bill* shot (**b**) *Fin* **j. de Bolsa** speculation (**c**) *Fam* dirty trick; **hacerle una mala j. a algn** to play a dirty trick on sb

jugador, -a *nm,f* (**a**) *(en deporte)* player; *(apostador)* gambler (**b**) *Fin* **j. de Bolsa** speculator

jugar [36] **1** *vi* (**a**) *(gen)* to play; **j. a(l) fútbol/tenis** to play football/tennis; **¿quién juega?** whose go is it?; *Fig* **j. con dos barajas** to double-deal; *Fig* **j. con fuego** to play with fire; *Fig* **j. sucio** to play dirty (**b**) *(burlarse)* to make fun (**con** of); **j. con los sentimientos de algn** to play with sb's feelings (**c**) *Fin* **j. a la Bolsa** to play the Stock Exchange
2 *vt* (**a**) *(gen)* to play; *Fam Fig* **j. una mala pasada a algn** to play a dirty trick on sb (**b**) *(hacer uso)* (*una pieza*) to move; *(una carta)* to play; **jugó el as** he played the ace (**c**) *(apostar)* to bet, stake
3 jugarse *vpr* (**a**) *(arriesgar)* to risk; *Fam* **j. el pellejo** to risk one's neck (**b**) *(apostar)* to stake, bet; **me juego cien euros** I bet you a hundred euros; *Fig* **j. el todo por el todo** to stake everything one has (**c**) *(engañar)* **jugársela a algn** to pull a fast one on sb, take sb for a ride; **jugársela al marido/a la mujer** to be unfaithful to o two-time one's husband/wife

jugarreta *nf Fam* dirty trick

juglar *nm Hist* minstrel, jester

juglaresco, -a *adj* minstrel

jugo *nm* (**a**) *(líquido)* juice; **jugos gástricos** gastric juices (**b**) *Am (de fruta)* juice (**c**) *Fam (provecho, interés)* meat, substance; **sacar (el) j. a algo/algn** *(aprovechar)* to get the most out of sth/sb

jugosidad *nf* juiciness, succulence

jugoso, -a *adj* (**a**) *(con jugo)* juicy; **un filete j.** a juicy steak (**b**) *Fig (rentable)* profitable; **un negocio j.** a lucrative business (**c**) *Fig (sustancioso)* substantial, meaty

juguete *nm* toy; **pistola de j.** toy gun; *Fig* **ser el j. de algn** to be sb's plaything □ **j. educativo** educational toy

juguetear *vi* to play, frolic

jugueteo *nm* playing, frolicking

juguetería *nf* (**a**) *(tienda)* toyshop (**b**) *(comercio)* toy business

juguetón, -ona *adj* playful, frolicsome

juicio *nm* (**a**) *(facultad mental)* judgement, discernment; *(opinión)* opinion, judgement; **a j. de** in the opinion of; **a mi j.** in my opinion; **dejar algo a j. de algn** to leave sth to sb's discretion; **emitir un j. sobre algo** to express an opinion about sth; **hombre de j.** man of judgement (**b**) *(sensatez)* reason, common sense; **en su sano j.** in one's right mind; **perder el j.** to go mad o insane; **quitar** o **trastornar el j. a algn** to drive sb insane; **tener mucho j.** to be sensible; **tener poco j.** to have little common sense (**c**) *Jur* trial, lawsuit; **j. a puerta abierta** public hearing; **j. contencioso/penal** civil/criminal action; **llevar a algn a j.** to take legal action against sb, sue sb; **suspender un j.** to adjourn a trial (**d**) *Rel* judgement; **J. Final** Last Judgement

juicioso, -a *adj* judicious, sensible, wise

julay *nm Esp Argot* sucker

julepe *nm* (**a**) *Naipes* = kind of card game (**b**) *Fig (castigo)* punishment (**c**) *PRico RP (susto)* fright, scare

julepear *vt* (**a**) *Fam (reñir)* to tell off (**b**) *Fam (cascar)* to give a good beating (**c**) *RP (asustar)* to frighten (**d**) *Méx (fatigar)* to tire, exhaust (**e**) *Col (urgir)* to hurry along

juliana *nf Bot* dameworth

julio¹ *nm* July; *véase tamb* **noviembre**

julio² *nm Fís* joule

juma *nf Fam* binge

jumarse *vpr Fam* to get sloshed o drunk

jumento *nm* ass, donkey

jumera *nf Fam* bender; **agarrar una j.** to go on a bender

juncal 1 *adj* rushlike; *Fig* willowy, graceful
   2 *nm* bed of rushes

juncia *nf Bot* sedge

junco¹ *nm* (**a**) *Bot* rush; **j. de Indias** rattan; **j. oloroso** camel grass (**b**) *(bastón)* walking stick, cane

junco² *nm Náut* junk

jungla *nf* jungle; **j. de asfalto** concrete jungle

junio *nm* June; *véase tamb* **noviembre**

júnior *(pl* **juniors) 1** *adj Dep* júnior
   2 *nm* (**a**) *Rel* junior novice (**b**) *Dep* junior; **campeonato j. de golf** junior golf championship (**c**) *(benjamín)* youngest son

junípero *nm Bot* juniper

junquera *nf* (**a**) *Bot (planta)* rush, bulrush (**b**) *(juncal)* bed of rushes

junquillo *nm* (**a**) *Bot* jonquil (**b**) *Arquit* beading (**c**) *(bastón)* walking stick

junta *nf* (**a**) *(reunión)* meeting, assembly, conference; *(conjunto de personas)* board, council, committee; *(sesión)* session, sitting; **celebrar j.** to hold a meeting; **ser miembro de una j.** to sit on a committee, be on a board □ **j. administrativa** administrative board; **j. de accionistas** shareholders' meeting; **j. de empresa** works council; **j. directiva** board of directors; *Pol* **j. de gobierno** cabinet meeting; **j. general** general meeting (**b**) *Arquit* joint (**c**) *Náut* seam (**d**) *Mil* junta; **j. militar** military junta (**e**) *Téc* joint □ **j. de culata** gasket; **j. de recubrimiento** o **de solapa** lap joint; **j. universal** universal joint

juntamente *adv* (**a**) *(en unión)* jointly, together (**b**) *(al mismo tiempo)* at the same time

juntar 1 *vt* (**a**) *(unir)* to join, put together; *(piezas)* to assemble; **j. dos cosas** to join two things together; **vamos a j. las mesas** let's put the tables together (**b**) *(reunir) (sellos)* to collect; *(dinero)* to raise; *(gente)* to gather (people) together
   2 juntarse *vpr* (**a**) *(unirse a)* to join, get together; *(ríos, caminos)* to meet; **nos juntamos toda la familia** all the family got together; **se juntó al grupo** he joined the group; *Fig* **al final me junté con cinco ofertas de trabajo** eventually I found myself with five job offers (**b**) *(amancebarse)* to live together; **la dejó y se juntó con su amante** he left her and went to live with his mistress

junto, -a 1 *adj* together; **dos camas juntas** two beds placed side by side; **están muy juntos** they are very close together; **todos juntos** all together; **viven juntos** they're living together
   2 *adv* near, close; **demasiado j.** too close together; **llegó j. con su hermana** she came with her sister

juntura *nf* (**a**) *Téc* joint, seam (**b**) *Anat* joint

Júpiter *nm Astron Mit* Jupiter

jura *nf (acción)* oath; *(ceremonia)* swearing in; **j. de bandera** oath of allegiance to the flag

jurado, -a 1 *pp de* **jurar**
   2 *adj* sworn; **declaración jurada** sworn statement; *Fig* **tenérsela jurada a algn** to have it in for sb
   3 *nm* (**a**) *Jur (tribunal)* jury; *(miembro del tribunal)* juror, member of the jury (**b**) *(en un concurso)* panel of judges, jury

juramentado, -a 1 *pp de* **juramentar**
   2 *adj* sworn, sworn-in

juramentar 1 *vt* to swear, swear in
   2 juramentarse *vpr* to take the oath, be sworn in

juramento *nm* (**a**) *Jur* oath; **bajo j.** under oath; **j. de fidelidad** oath of allegiance; **j. falso** perjury; **tomar j. a algn** to swear sb in (**b**) *(blasfemia)* swearword, curse; **soltar juramentos** to curse, blaspheme

jurar 1 *vi* (**a**) *Jur Rel* to swear, take an oath; **j. en falso** to commit perjury; **j. en vano** to take the name of the Lord in vain (**b**) *(blasfemar)* to curse, swear
   2 *vt* to swear; **j. el cargo** to take the oath of office; **j. fidelidad** to pledge allegiance; **j. por Dios** to swear to God
   3 jurarse *vpr* (**a**) *(prometerse)* to swear; **se juraron amor eterno** they swore eternal love to each other (**b**) *Fam* **jurársela(s) a algn** to have it in for sb

jurásico, -a *adj Geol* Jurassic

jurel *nm (pez)* scad, horse mackerel

jurídico, -a *adj* juridical, legal

jurisconsulto *nm* jurist, legal expert

jurisdicción *nf* jurisdiction

jurisdiccional *adj* jurisdictional; **aguas jurisdiccionales** territorial waters

jurisperito *nm* jurist, legal expert

jurisprudencia *nf* jurisprudence

jurista *nmf* jurist, lawyer

justa *nf* (**a**) *Hist* joust, tournament (**b**) *Lit* competition

justamente *adv* (**a**) *(con exactitud)* precisely, exactly; **¡j.!** precisely! (**b**) *(con escasez)* **vive j. con su sueldo** his wage is just enough to live on **(c)** *(con justicia)* fairly, justly

justicia *nf* justice, fairness; **administrar j.** to administer justice; **es de j. que ...** it's only fair o right that ...; **hacer j.** to do justice; **se ha hecho j.** justice has been done; **tomarse la j. por su mano** to take the law into one's own hands

justiciero, -a *adj* severe

justificable *adj* justifiable

justificación *nf* justification

justificado, -a 1 *pp de* **justificar**
2 *adj* justified, well-grounded

justificante *nm* voucher, written proof, document □ **j. médico** doctor's note, sick note

justificar [59] **1** *vt* to justify; **sin nada que lo justifique** without good reason
2 justificarse *vpr* to clear oneself, justify oneself; **j. con algn** to apologize to sb for sth

justificativo, -a *adj* providing evidence, supporting

justillo *nm* jerkin

justiprecio *nm* appraisal, estimate

justo, -a 1 *adj* **(a)** *(gen)* just, fair, right; **un castigo j.** a just punishment; **un trato j.** a fair deal **(b)** *(apretado) (ropa)* tight; **viven muy justos con su sueldo** they just manage to make ends meet on her salary; **estamos justos de tiempo** we're pressed for time **(c)** *(exacto)* right, accurate; **cuatro kilos justos** four kilos exactly; **la palabra justa** the right word; **un cálculo j.** a precise calculation **(d)** *(preciso)*

llegamos en el momento j. en que salían we arrived just as they were leaving **(e) lo j.** just enough o right; **más de lo j.** more than enough
2 *nm,f* just o righteous person; **los justos** the just, the righteous; *Fig* **pagan justos por pecadores** the innocent often have to pay for the sins of the guilty
3 *adv* **(a)** *(exactamente)* exactly, precisely; **es j. lo que mereces** it's just what you deserve; **hice j. lo que me dijiste** I did exactly as you told me **(b)** *(que llega)* just enough; **tengo j. para la entrada** I've got just enough for the ticket; **llegó j.** he just made it

juvenil *adj* youthful, young; *Dep* **el equipo j.** the junior team

juventud *nf* **(a)** *(edad)* youth; **estar en plena j.** to be young **(b)** *(aspecto joven)* youthfulness; **conservar la j.** to keep one's youthful looks **(c)** *(conjunto de jóvenes)* young people; **la j. de hoy** the youth of today

juzgado *nm* court, tribunal; **j. de guardia** court, police court; *Fam Fig* **es de j. de guardia** it's absolutely scandalous!

juzgador, -a 1 *adj* judging
2 *nm,f* judge

juzgar [38] *vt* **(a)** *(gen)* to judge; **a j. por las apariencias** judging by appearances; **j. mal** to misjudge **(b)** *(considerar)* to consider, think; **le juzgo una persona muy inteligente** I consider him to be a very intelligent person

K

K, k [ka] *nf (la letra)* K, k
ka *nf* name of the letter K in Spanish
Kabul *n* Kabul
kafkiano, -a *adj* Kafkaesque
káiser *nm* Kaiser
kaki *adj & nm véase* **caqui**
kamikaze *nm* kamikaze
Kampala *n* Kampala
Kampuchea *n Antes* Kampuchea
kantiano, -a *adj Filos* Kantian
kantismo *nm Filos* Kantianism, Kantism
karaoke *nm* karaoke
kárate *nm Dep* karate
karateka *nmf Dep* person who does karate
kart (*pl* **karts**) *nm* (go-)kart, go-cart
karting *nm* karting, go-cart racing
Katmandú *n* Katmandu, Kathmandu
kayac *nm* kayak, kaiak
Kazajistán *n* Kazak(h)stan
Kenia *n* Kenya
keniano, -a *adj & nm,f,* **keniata** *adj & nmf* Kenyan
kepis *nm inv véase* **quepis**
kermés [ker'mes] (*pl* **kermeses**) *nf,* **kermesse** [ker'mes] (*pl* **kermesses**) *nf* fair, kermesse
keroseno *nm, Am* **kerosén** *nm, Am* **kerosene** *nm véase* **queroseno**
keynesiano, -a *adj Econ* Keynesian
Kg, kg (*abrev de* **kilogramo(s)**) kg
kibbutz [ki'βuts] *nm inv* kibbutz
kif *nm* kif
kikirikí *nm (del gallo)* cock-a-doodle-doo
kilo *nm* (**a**) *(medida)* kilo; *Fam* **pesa un k.** it weighs a ton (**b**) *Esp Antes Fam (millón)* a million pesetas (**c**) *RP Fam (mucho)* **cuesta un k. de plata** it costs loads o a heap of money
kilobyte [kilo'βait] *nm Inform* kilobyte
kilocaloría *nf* kilocalorie
kilociclo *nm* kilocycle
kilogramo *nm* kilogram, kilogramme
kilolitro *nm* kilolitre, *US* kiloliter
kilometraje *nm* ≃ mileage
kilometrar *vt* to measure in kilometres
kilométrico, -a *adj* (**a**) *(distancia)* kilometric, kilo-metrical; **billete k.** multiple-journey ticket (**b**) *Fam (muy largo)* very long; **un sermón k.** a never-ending sermon
kilómetro *nm* kilometre, *US* kilometer
kilovatio *nm* kilowatt ❑ **k. hora** kilowatt-hour
kilovoltio *nm* kilovolt
kilt *nm (prenda)* kilt
kimono *nm véase* **quimono**
kindergarten *nm* nursery, kindergarten
Kingston *n* Kingston
Kinshasa *n* Kinshasa
kiosco *nm véase* **quiosco**
kiosquero, -a *nm,f* = person selling newspapers, drinks etc from a kiosk
Kioto *n* Kyoto
Kirguizistán *n* Kirg(h)izstan
Kiribati *n* Kiribati
kirsch [kirs] *nm* kirsch
kit (*pl* **kits**) *nm (conjunto)* kit, set; *(para montar)* kit
kitsch [kitʃ] *adj inv* kitsch
kiwi *nm* (**a**) *Orn* kiwi (**b**) *Bot (fruto)* kiwi (fruit), Chinese gooseberry
Kleenex® ['klines, 'klineks] *nm* Kleenex®, (paper) tissue
Km, km (*abrev de* **kilómetro(s)**) km, kms
Km/h, km/h (*abrev de* **kilómetros hora**) km/h
knockout [no'kaut] (*pl* **knockouts**) *nm Box* knockout
K.O. ['kao] *nm* (*abrev de* **knockout**) KO; *Fam Fig* **dejar K.O. a algn** to knock sb out
koala *nm Zool* koala (bear)
kopek (*pl* **kopeks**) *nm* kopeck
kosovar 1 *adj* Kosovan
  2 *nmf* Kosovan, Kosovar
Kosovo *n* Kosovo
Kremlin *nm* **el K.** the Kremlin
Krisna *nm Rel* Krishna
Kuala Lumpur *n* Kuala Lumpur
Kurdistán *n* Kurdistan
kurdo, -a 1 *adj* Kurdish
  2 *nm,f (persona)* Kurd
  3 *nm (idioma)* Kurdish
Kuwait [ku'βait] *n* Kuwait
kuwaití [kuβai'ti] *adj & nmf* Kuwaiti
Kw (*abrev de* **kilovatio(s)**) kW, kw
Kw/h (*abrev de* **kilovatios hora**) kWh, kwh, kw-h

L, l ['ele] *nf (la letra)* L, l

l *(abrev de* **litro(s))** l

la¹ 1 *art def f* the; **la mesa** the table

 2 *pron dem f* the one; **la del sombrero rojo** the one in the red hat; *Fam* **a la que puedas vente** come as soon as you can; **la de** the amount of, the number of; **la de gente que había** there were so many people; *véase tamb* **el**

la² *pron pers f* (**a**) *(objeto directo)* her; *(usted)* you; *(cosa)* it; **la invitaré a la fiesta** I'll invite her to the party; **no la dejes abierta** don't leave it open; **ya la avisaremos, señora** we shall notify you, madam; *véase tamb* **le** (**b**) *(objeto indirecto) (a ella) (to)* her; *(a usted) (to)* you; *véase* **laísmo**

la³ *nm Mús* la, lah, A; **concierto en la menor** concerto in A minor

laberíntico, -a *adj* labyrinthine, labyrinthic; *Fig* confusing

laberinto *nm* labyrinth, maze

labia *nf Fam* loquacity; *Pey* glibness; **tener mucha l.** to have the gift of the gab

labiado, -a *adj Bot* labiate

labial *adj & nf Ling* labial

lábil *adj* (**a**) *(inconstante) (volatile); (inestable)* unstable (**b**) *(resbaladizo)* slippery

labilidad *nf* (**a**) *(inestabilidad)* instability (**b**) *(que hace resbalar)* slipperiness (**c**) *(carácter)* fickleness, inconstancy

labio *nm* lip; *Fig* mouth

labiodental *adj & nf Ling* labiodental

labor *nf* (**a**) *(trabajo, tarea)* job, (piece of) work, task; **una l. de equipo** teamwork; **de profesión: sus labores** occupation: housewife (**b**) *Agr* farmwork (**c**) *Cost* needlework, sewing ◻ **labor(es) de punto** knitting *sing* (**d**) *(productos del tabaco)* tobacco goods *pl*

laborable *adj* (**a**) *(no festivo)* **día l.** workday, working day (**b**) *Agr* tillable, arable

laboral *adj* labour, *US* labor; **accidente l.** industrial accident; **jornada l.** working day; *Jur* **juicio l.** industrial relations hearing

laboralista *adj Jur* **abogado l.** industrial relations lawyer

laborar *vi Fml* to work

laboratorio *nm* laboratory

laboriosidad *nf* laboriousness

laborioso, -a *adj* (**a**) *(persona trabajadora)* hardworking, industrious (**b**) *(tarea ardua)* laborious, arduous

laborismo *nm Pol* Labor Movement

laborista *Pol* **1** *adj* Labor; **partido l.** Labor Party
 2 *nmf* Labor (Party) member *o* supporter

labra *nf* carving, cutting

labrado, -a 1 *pp de* **labrar**
 2 *adj* (**a**) *Arte* carved (**b**) *Agr* ploughed, worked (**c**) *Cost* embroidered
 3 *nm* (**a**) *Arte* carving, cutting (**b**) *Cost* embroidery

labrador, -a *nm,f Agr (granjero)* farmer; *(trabajador)* farm worker

labrantío, -a *Agr* **1** *adj* **tierra labrantía** arable land
 2 *nm* arable land

labranza *nf Agr* farming

labrar 1 *vt* (**a**) *(madera)* to carve; *(piedra)* to cut; *(metal)* to work (**b**) *Agr* to till, cultivate; *Fig* **está labrando su triunfo** he is working towards success
 2 labrarse *vpr Fig* to make oneself; **l. un porvenir** to build a future for oneself

labriego, -a *nm,f* farmworker

laburar *vi RP Fam* to work

laburo *nm RP Fam* job

laca *nf* (**a**) *Arte* lacquer (**b**) *(para el pelo)* hair lacquer, hairspray ◻ **l. de uñas** nail polish *o* varnish (**c**) *(resina)* lac; *(manufacturada)* shellac

lacar [59] *vt* to lacquer

lacayo *nm* (**a**) *Hist* lackey, footman (**b**) *Fig* lackey, hanger-on, flunky, flunkey

laceración *nf Fml* laceration

lacerante *adj Fml* sharp; **un grito l.** a heart-rending cry

lacerar¹ *vt Fml* (**a**) *(herir)* to lacerate, tear (**b**) *Fig* to hurt

lacerar² *vi Fml* to suffer

lacero, -a *nm,f* (**a**) *(de reses)* lassoer (**b**) *(de perros sueltos)* dog-catcher (**c**) *(de caza menor)* poacher

lacio, -a *adj* (**a**) *(pelo)* lank, limp (**b**) *(planta)* withered, drooping (**c**) *(sin vigor)* languid, limp

lacón *nm* foreknuckle of pork; *Culin* boiled bacon

lacónico, -a *adj* laconic; *(conciso)* terse

laconismo *nm* terseness

lacra *nf* (**a**) *(señal)* mark, scar (**b**) *Fig* evil, curse; *(tara)* defect; **una l. social** a social scourge, a blot on society (**c**) *Am (costra)* scab

lacrado, -a 1 *pp de* **lacrar¹**
 2 *nm* sealing with wax

lacrar¹ *vt* to seal with sealing wax

lacrar² *vt* to injure the health of; *(contagiar)* to infect; *Fig* to cause harm to

lacre *nm* (**a**) *(para sellar)* sealing wax (**b**) *Cuba (de abeja)* propolis

lacrimal *adj* lachrymal, lacrimal; *Anat* **conductos lacrimales** tear ducts

lacrimógeno, -a *adj* (**a**) gas l. tear gas (**b**) *(lagrimoso) (persona)* tearful; *Fig* una película lacrimógena a tear-jerking film

lacrimoso, -a *adj* tearful

lactancia *nf* lactation; *(amamantamiento)* breast-feeding

lactante 1 *adj* lactational
2 *nmf* unweaned *o* breast-fed baby

lácteo, -a *adj* milk, milky; **productos lácteos** milk *o* dairy products; *Astron* Vía Láctea Milky Way

láctico, -a *adj Quím* lactic

lactosa *nf Quím* lactose, milk sugar

lacustre *adj Fml* lake; **planta l.** lake plant

ladeado, -a *adj (torcido)* tilted, at an angle; **métalo l.** put it in sideways

ladear 1 *vt* (**a**) *(inclinar)* to tilt; *(sesgar)* to slant; *(cabeza)* to lean (**b**) *(desviar)* to divert
2 ladearse *vpr* (**a**) *(inclinarse)* to lean, tilt (**b**) *(apartarse)* to turn away, go off (**c**) *(juntarse)* to join sides (**con** with) (**d**) *Chile Fam (enamorarse)* to fall in love

ladeo *nm* leaning, inclination

ladera *nf Geog* slope, hillside, mountainside

ladilla *nf Ent* crab louse

ladino, -a 1 *adj* (**a**) *(astuto)* cunning, crafty (**b**) *CAm Méx Ven* of mixed race
2 *nm (idioma)* Ladino
3 *nm,f CAm Méx Ven (indio)* Spanish-speaking Indian

lado *nm* (**a**) *(costado, cara, parte lateral)* side; **debe de estar en otro l.** it must be somewhere else (**b**) *(posición)* a un l. aside; al l. close by, nearby; al l. de next to, beside; la casa de al l. the house next door; *Dep* cambiar de l. to change ends; echarse *o* hacerse a un l. to make way; llevar el sombrero de l. to wear one's hat aslant; ponte de l. stand sideways (**c**) *(en direcciones)* direction; ¿por qué l.? which way?; por todos lados on *o* from all sides (**d**) *Fig (locuciones)* dar de l. a algn, *Méx RP* dar a algn por su l. to cold-shoulder sb; dejar algo a un l. *o* de l. to leave *o* set sth aside; l. débil weak point; por un l. ..., por otro l. ... on the one hand ..., on the other hand ...

ladrador, -a *adj* barking

ladrar *vi* to bark, yap; *Fam Fig* ¡para ya de l.! stop growling!, stop yapping at me!

ladrido *nm* bark, yap; *Fam Fig* no me vengas con ladridos don't you growl at me

ladrillo *nm* (**a**) *Constr* brick; fábrica de ladrillos brickworks *pl* □ *Constr* l. visto uncovered brickwork (**b**) *Fam (pesado)* bore, drag

ladrón, -ona 1 *adj* thieving
2 *nm,f* thief, robber; ¡al l.! stop thief!; *Fig* l. de corazones lady-killer
3 *nm* (**a**) *(de canal)* sluicegate (**b**) *Elec* multiple socket

ladronzuelo, -a *nm,f* petty thief

lagar *nm (de vino)* winepress; *(de aceite)* oil press

lagarta *nf* (**a**) *Zool* female lizard (**b**) *Fam Pey (bribona)* minx, sly woman; *(prostituta)* tart, whore

lagartija *nf Zool* small lizard

lagarto *nm* (**a**) *Zool* lizard □ l. de Indias alligator (**b**) *Fam (bribón)* sly *o* crafty fellow

lago *nm* lake

lagópodo *nm Orn* l. escocés red grouse

Lagos *n* Lagos

lágrima *nf* (**a**) *(del ojo)* tear; asomar las lágrimas a los ojos to start crying; derramar lágrimas to shed tears (**b**) *(adorno)* teardrop

lagrimal 1 *adj* lachrymal, lacrimal
2 *nm* corner of the eye

lagrimear *vi* (**a**) *(llorar frecuentemente)* to weep (**b**) *(involuntariamente)* to water

lagrimeo *nm* (**a**) *(frecuente)* weeping, tears *pl* (**b**) *(involuntario)* watering

lagrimoso, -a *adj (persona)* tearful; ojos lagrimosos watery eyes

laguna *nf* (**a**) *Geog* small lake, lagoon (**b**) *Fig (hueco)* gap, hiatus

La Haya *n* The Hague

laicismo *nm* secularism

laico, -a 1 *adj* lay, secular; escuela laica secular school
2 *nm,f* lay person; *(hombre)* layman; *(mujer)* laywoman

laísmo *nm Ling* incorrect use of la, las as indirect objects instead of le, les

laja *nf* (**a**) *Geol* stone slab (**b**) *Hond (arena)* fine sand (**c**) *Ecuad (declive)* bank, slope

lama[1] *nm Rel* lama

lama[2] *nf* (**a**) *(cieno)* mud, slime (**b**) *Am (musgo)* moss

lama[3] *nm Tex* lamé

lambada *nf* lambada

lameculos *nmf inv Ofens* bootlicker, arselicker

lamedura *nf* lick, licking

lamentable *adj* deplorable, regrettable

lamentablemente *adv* regrettably, unfortunately

lamentación *nf* lament, lamentation; Muro de las Lamentaciones Wailing Wall

lamentar 1 *vt* to regret, be sorry about; lamentamos informarle que ... we regret to inform you that *o* of ...
2 lamentarse *vpr* to complain; ¿de qué te lamentas? what are you complaining about?

lamento *nm* moan, wail

lamentoso, -a *adj (quejumbroso)* plaintive, mournful; *(lamentable)* deplorable, regrettable; *(lastimoso)* pitiful

lamer *vt* to lick

lametazo *nm,* **lametón** *nm Fam* lick

lamida *nf* lick

lamido, -a 1 *pp de* lamer
2 *adj Fig* (**a**) *(flaco)* skinny, scrawny (**b**) *(pálido)* pale (**c**) *(afectado)* pretentious, mannered

lámina *nf* (**a**) *(plancha, placa)* sheet, plate; l. de acero steel sheet (**b**) *Impr* plate, illustration (**c**) *Bot* lamina

laminación *nf* (**a**) *(acción)* lamination (**b**) *(de metal)* rolling

laminado, -a 1 *pp de* laminar[1]
2 *adj* (**a**) *(cubierto por láminas)* laminate, laminated (**b**) *(metales)* rolled; acero l. rolled steel, sheet steel
3 *nm* (**a**) *(cubrir con láminas)* lamination (**b**) *(de metales)* rolling □ tren de l. rolling mill

laminadora *nf* rolling mill

laminar[1] *vt* (**a**) *(superficie)* to laminate (**b**) *(metal)* to roll out

laminar[2] *adj* laminar; corriente l. laminar flow

lámpara *nf* (**a**) *(aparato)* lamp, light □ l. de aceite/alcohol oil/spirit lamp; l. de pie standard lamp (**b**) *Elec (bombilla)* bulb (**c**) *Rad* valve (**d**) *Fam (mancha)* oil *o* grease stain

lamparería *nf (fábrica)* lamp factory; *(tienda)* lamp shop

lamparero, -a *nm,f (fabricante)* lamp maker; *(vendedor)* dealer

lamparilla *nf* (**a**) *(lámpara pequeña)* small lamp (**b**) *(en iglesia)* candle

lamparita *nf RP* light bulb

lamparón *nm Fam* oil *o* grease stain

lampazo *nm Bot* burdock

lampiño, -a *adj* hairless

lamprea *nf(pez)* lamprey

lana 1 *nf* wool; *Prov* **ir por l. y volver trasquilado** to be hoist with one's own pertard
2 *nm Andes Méx Fam* dough, cash

lanar *adj* wool, wool-bearing; **ganado l.** sheep

lance *nm* (a) *(lanzar)* throw (b) *(pesca)* catch (c) *Literario (episodio)* episode, event, incident; **l. de fortuna** chance event (d) *(riña)* quarrel, argument ▫ **l. de honor** challenge, duel (e) *Dep* stroke, move (f) **de l.** *(barato)* cheap; *(de segunda mano)* second-hand

lancero *nm* lancer

lanceta *nf* (a) *Med* lancet (b) *Andes Méx* sting

lancha¹ *nf(piedra lisa)* stone slab

lancha² *nf Náut* boat, motorboat, launch ▫ **l. motora** speedboat; **l. neumática** rubber dinghy; **l. patrullera** patrol boat; **l. salvavidas** lifeboat

lanchero *nm* boatman

lanchón *nm Náut* lighter, barge

lancinante *adj* piercing, stabbing

landa *nf* moor, moorland

landó *nm* landau

land rover® [lan'rroβer] *(pl* **land rovers)** *nm* Land Rover®

lanero, -a *adj* wool, woollen, *US* woolen; **la industria lanera** the wool industry

lángaro, -a *adj* (a) *CAm (vagabundo)* vagrant, vagabond (b) *Col Méx (hambriento)* starving

langosta *nf* (a) *Zool* (spiny) lobster (b) *Ent* locust

langostino *nm Zool* prawn

languidecer [46] *vi* to languish

languidez *nf* languor; *(falta de vigor)* listlessness

lánguido, -a *adj* languid; *(sin vigor)* listless, sluggish

lanilla *nf* (a) *(pelusa)* nap (b) *(tela)* flannel

lanolina *nf Farm* lanolin, lanoline

lanoso, -a *adj,* **lanudo, -a** *adj* woolly, fleecy; *(peludo)* furry

lanza *nf* (a) *Mil* spear, lance; *Fig* **estar con la l. en ristre** to be ready for action; *Fig* **romper una l. en favor de algn/de algo** to defend sb/sth (b) *(de carruaje)* shaft

lanzacohetes *nm inv Mil* rocket launcher

lanzada *nf* (a) *(golpe)* lance o spear thrust (b) *(herida)* lance o spear wound

lanzadera *nf* shuttle

lanzado, -a 1 *pp de* **lanzar**
2 *adj Fam* determined, resolute; **ir l.** to speed along, tear along

lanzador, -a 1 *adj* throwing
2 *nm,f* thrower; *(en críquet)* bowler; *(en béisbol)* pitcher

lanzagranadas *nm inv Mil* grenade launcher

lanzallamas *nm inv Mil* flame-thrower

lanzamiento *nm* (a) *(de objeto)* throw, throwing, hurling (b) *Dep (de disco, jabalina)* throw; *(de peso)* put; *(en críquet)* ball, delivery; *(en béisbol)* pitch (c) *Mil (de cohete)* launching; *(de proyectil, torpedo)* firing; *(de bomba)* dropping (d) *Com* launch, launching; **precio de l.** launching price (e) *Náut* launch

lanzamisiles *nm inv* rocket launcher

lanzaplatos *nm inv Dep* (clay pigeon) trap

lanzar [14] **1** *vt* (a) *(arrojar)* to throw, fling, hurl; *(en críquet)* to bowl; *(en béisbol)* to pitch (b) *Fig (grito)* to let out; *(suspiro)* to heave; *(insulto)* to hurl; *(mirada)* to fire (c) *Náut* to launch;

Mil (lanzacohetes, ataque) to launch; *(misil, torpedo)* to fire; *(bomba)* to drop (d) *Com (producto, campaña)* to launch (e) *Inform (programa)* to launch
2 lanzarse *vpr* (a) *(arrojarse)* to fling o hurl oneself; **l. al suelo** to throw oneself to the ground; **l. con paracaídas** to make a parachute jump; **se lanzó al mar** he leapt into the sea (b) *(abalanzarse)* to embark on; **l. a los negocios** to go into business

lanzatorpedos *nm inv Mil* **tubo l.** torpedo tube

Laos *n* Laos

laosiano, -a *adj & nm,f* Laotian

lapa *nf* (a) *Zool* limpet (b) *Pey (persona)* bore; **pegarse como una l.** to cling like a leech

La Paz *n* La Paz

lapicero *nm* (a) *Esp (lápiz)* pencil (b) *Chile (estilográfica)* fountain pen (c) *CAm Perú (bolígrafo)* ballpoint (pen), Biro®

lápida *nf* memorial stone; **l. sepulcral** tombstone

lapidación *nf* stoning, lapidation

lapidar *vt (apedrear)* to throw stones at, lapidate; *(matar)* to stone to death

lapidario, -a *adj & nm,f* lapidary; *Fig* **lenguaje l.** concise language

lapislázuli *nm Min* lapis lazuli

lápiz *nm* pencil ▫ *Arg* **l. de cera** wax crayon; **l. de labios** lipstick; **l. de ojos** eyeliner; *Chile* **l. de pasta** ballpoint pen; *Inform* **l. óptico** light pen; **lápices de colores** coloured pencils, crayons

lapo *nm Esp Argot (gargajo)* spit

lapón, -ona 1 *adj* Lapp
2 *nm,f* Lapp, Laplander
3 *nm (idioma)* Lapp

Laponia *n* Lapland

lapso *nm* (a) *(curso de tiempo)* lapse, space of time (b) *(error)* lapse, slip

lapsus *nm* slip, lapse; **l. de memoria** lapse of memory

laquear *vt* to lacquer

lar *nm* (a) *Mit (gen pl)* lar, household god (b) **lares** *Literario* home *sing*

lardero *adj* **jueves l.** the Thursday before Lent

larga *nf* (a) *Taur* bullfighting pass (b) **dar largas a un asunto** to put a matter off, delay a matter

largamente *adv* (a) *(extensamente)* at length (b) *(generosamente)* generously

largar [38] **1** *vt* (a) *(aflojar)* to let loose; *Náut* **l. amarras** to cast off (b) *Fam (dar)* to give; **le largué una bofetada** I gave him a slap on the face (c) *Fam (soltar, decir)* to come out with; *(grito)* to let out; **¡vaya bronca me ha largado!** he really hauled me over the coals!
2 largarse *vpr* (a) *Fam* to clear off, split; **¡lárgate!** beat it! (b) *CSur (lanzarse a)* to begin (a to)

largo, -a 1 *adj* (a) *(longitud, distancia)* long; *(tiempo)* long, lengthy; **l. tiempo** a long time; **pasamos un mes l. allí** we spent a good month there (b) *(excesivo)* too long; **se hizo l. el día** the day dragged on (c) *(alto)* tall; **cayó cuan l. era** he fell full length (d) *Fam (astuto)* sharp, shrewd (e) *(generoso)* generous, lavish (f) **largos, -as** many; **l. años** many years
2 *nm* (a) *(longitud)* length; **¿cuánto tiene de l.?** how long is it?; **lo até con dos largos de cuerda** I tied it with two lengths of rope (b) *Mús* largo
3 *adv* (a) **l. y tendido** at length (b) **a lo l.** lengthways; **a lo l. de** *(espacio)* along; *(tiempo)* through; **a lo l. y a lo ancho** all over (c) **a la larga** in the long run (d) *Fam* **¡l. (de aquí)!** clear off! (e) **venir de l.** to have a long history (f) *(vestir)* **vestirse de l.** to wear a long dress (g) **ir para l.** to go o walk straight past (h) **tener para l.** to expect a long wait o delay, have a long wait ahead

largometraje *nm Cin* feature film, full-length film

larguero *nm* (**a**) *Arquit* main longitudinal beam (**b**) *(de puerta)* jamb (**c**) *(de cama)* side (**d**) *Ftb* crossbar

largueza *nf* (**a**) *(longitud)* length (**b**) *(liberalidad)* generosity

larguirucho, -a *adj Fam* gangling, lanky, long-legged

largura *nf* length

laringe *nf Anat* larynx

laríngeo, -a *adj* laryngeal

laringitis *nf Med* laryngitis

laringólogo, -a *nm,f Med* laryngologist

larva *nf* larva

larvado, -a *adj Med* masked, larval

las¹ *art def fpl* the; **l. Ramírez** the Ramírez girls *o* sisters; **l. sillas** the chairs; **lávate l. manos** wash your hands; *(no se traduce)* **me gustan l. flores** I like flowers; **l. que** *(personas)* the ones who, those who; *(objetos)* the ones that, those that; **toma l. que quieras** take whichever ones you want; *véase tamb* **la¹** *y* **los¹**

las² *pron pers fpl* (**a**) *(objeto directo) (ellas)* them; *(ustedes)* you; **l. llamaré mañana** I'll call them up tomorrow; **no l. rompas** don't break them; **Pepa es de l. mías** Pepa is on my side; *véase tamb* **los²** (**b**) *(objeto indirecto) (a ellas)* (to) them; *(a ustedes)* (to) you; *véase tamb* **les**

lasaña *nf Culin* lasagna, lasagne

lasca *nf* stone chip

lascivia *nf* lasciviousness, lechery

lascivo, -a *adj* lascivious, lewd, lecherous

láser *nm inv* laser

laserterapia *nf* laser therapy

lasitud *nf* lassitude

laso, -a *adj* (**a**) *(cansado)* tired, weary; *(débil)* languid (**b**) *(pelo, hilo)* straight

lástima *nf* (**a**) *(compasión)* pity; **es una l. que se haya perdido** it's a pity it got lost; **estar hecho una l.** to be a sorry sight; **por l.** out of pity; **¡qué l.!** what a pity!, what a shame!; **tener l. a algn** to feel sorry for sb (**b**) *(quejido)* complaint

lastimado, -a 1 *pp de* **lastimar**
2 *adj* hurt

lastimadura *nf* injury

lastimar 1 *vt* (**a**) *(físicamente)* to hurt, injure (**b**) *(sentimientos)* to hurt
2 lastimarse *vpr* to hurt *o* injure oneself; **se lastimó el tobillo** he hurt his ankle

lastimero, -a *adj* doleful, plaintive

lastimoso, -a *adj* pitiable, pitiful, woeful; **ella ofrecía un aspecto l.** she was a sorry sight

lastrar *vt Náut* to ballast

lastre *nm* (**a**) *Náut* ballast; **largar** *o* **soltar l.** to discharge ballast (**b**) *Fig* dead weight; **el l. de los convencionalismos** the burden of conventionality

lata¹ *nf* (**a**) *(hojalata)* tinplate; **hecho de l.** made of tin (**b**) *(bote de conserva)* tin, *US* can; **espárragos en l.** tinned *o US* canned asparagus

lata² *nf Esp Fam* nuisance, drag; **dar la l.** to be a nuisance *o* a pest; **es una l. tener que ir a la mili** having to do military service is a drag

latear *vt Andes* to pester, be annoying to

latente *adj* latent, dormant

lateral 1 *adj* side, lateral; *Ling* **consonante l.** lateral consonant; **salió por la puerta l.** he went out by the side door
2 *nm* side passage; *Aut* **(carril) l.** side lane

latería *nm Am* tinsmith's (shop)

látex *nm inv Bot* latex

latido *nm (corazón)* beat; *(palpitaciones)* throb, throbbing

latifundio *nm* large landed estate

latifundismo *nm* = distribution and exploitation of land in **latifundios**

latifundista 1 *adj* = of *o* relating to **latifundios**
2 *nmf* = owner of a **latifundio**

latigazo *nm* (**a**) *(golpe)* lash; *(sonido)* crack (**b**) *Esp Argot (trago)* drink, swig (**c**) *Med* whiplash injury

látigo *nm* (**a**) *(fusta)* whip (**b**) *(en parque de atracciones)* **el l.** the whip (**c**) *Ecuad Hond (latigazo)* lash (**d**) *Chile (meta)* finishing post

latigueada *nf Hond (azotaina)* flogging

latiguillo *nm (muletilla)* tag, pet phrase

latín *nm* Latin; **saber mucho l.** to be smart, be nobody's fool, know one's stuff ▫ **l. bajo/vulgar** Low/Vulgar Latin

latinajo *nm Pey (cita)* Latin quotation; *(lengua)* dog Latin

latinidad *nf* (**a**) *(lengua)* Latin (**b**) *(pueblos latinos)* Latin countries *pl*

latinismo *nm* Latinism

latinizar [14] *vt* to Latinize

latino, -a *adj & nm,f* (**a**) *(de país latino)* Latin; **América Latina** Latin America; *Rel* **Iglesia latina** Roman Catholic Church, Latin Church (**b**) *Náut* **vela latina** lateen sail

Latinoamérica *n* Latin America

latinoamericano, -a *adj & nm,f* Latin American

latir *vi* (**a**) *(palpitar)* to beat, throb; *Fig* to be latent (**b**) *Méx Ven (parecer)* **me late que ...** I have a feeling that ...

latitud *nf* (**a**) *Geog* latitude (**b**) **latitudes** region *sing*, area *sing*

lato, -a *adj (extenso)* wide, broad

latón *nm* brass; **un clavo de l.** a brass nail

latoso, -a *Fam* **1** *adj* boring, annoying
2 *nm,f* bore, drag

latrocinio *nm* larceny; **estos precios son un puro l.** those prices are a daylight robbery

laucha *nf* (**a**) *Am* mouse (**b**) *Am Fig* intelligent man (**c**) *Arg Chile (menudo)* shrimp (**d**) *Arg* dirty old man

laúd *nm* (**a**) *Mús* lute (**b**) *Náut* catboat

laudable *adj* laudable, praiseworthy

láudano *nm (droga)* laudanum

laudatorio, -a *adj* laudatory

laudo *nm Jur* finding

laureado, -a 1 *adj* (**a**) *Lit* award-winning; **poeta l.** poet laureate (**b**) *Mil* decorated
2 *nm,f Lit* laureate

laurear *vt* **l. a algn (con)** to honour sb (with)

laurel *nm Bot* laurel, (sweet) bay; *Culin* bay leaf; *Fig* **dormirse en sus laureles** to rest on one's laurels ▫ **l. rosa** oleander

lava *nf Geol* lava

lavable *adj* washable

lavabo *nm* (**a**) *(pila) Br* washbasin, *US* washbowl (**b**) *(cuarto de aseo) Br* lavatory, *US* washroom (**c**) *(retrete)* lavatory, toilet

lavacoches *nmf inv* car washer

lavada *nf* wash, washing

lavadero *nm* (**a**) *(de ropa)* washroom, laundry (**b**) *Min* washery

lavado, -a 1 *pp de* **lavar**
2 *nm* (**a**) *(de manos, ropa)* wash, washing ▫ *Fam Fig* **l. de cerebro** brainwashing; *Med* **l. de estómago** washing out of

the stomach; **l. en seco** dry-cleaning **(b)** *Arte* wash

lavadora *nf* **(a)** *(máquina)* washing machine **(b)** *(persona)* washerwoman

lavafrutas *nm inv* finger bowl

lavamanos *nm inv Br* washbasin, *US* washbowl

lavanda *nf Bot* lavender

lavandera *nf* **(a)** *(mujer)* laundress, washerwoman **(b)** *Orn* **l. blanca** white wagtail; **l. cascadeña** grey wagtail

lavandería *nf* **(a)** *(atendida por personal)* laundry **(b)** *(automática)* launderette, *US* laundromat

lavandero *nm* laundryman, launderer

lavándula *nf Bot* lavender

lavaojos *nm inv* eyebath

lavaplatos *nm inv* **(a)** *(aparato)* dishwasher **(b)** *Chile Col Méx Ven (fregadero)* (kitchen) sink

lavar 1 *vt* to wash; *(cabello)* to shampoo; **l. en seco** to dry-clean

2 lavarse *vpr* to wash oneself; **l. las manos** to wash one's hands; *Fig* **l. las manos de algo** to wash one's hands of sth

lavarropas *nm inv RP* washing machine

lavaseco *nm Andes* dry-cleaner's

lavativa *nf Med* enema

lavatorio *nm* **(a)** *Rel (de la misa)* lavabo **(b)** *(de Semana Santa)* Maundy **(c)** *Andes RP (lavabo) Br* washbasin, *US* washbowl

lavavajillas *nm inv* dishwasher

lavotear *Fam* **1** *vt* to wash hurriedly
2 lavotearse *vpr* to have a quick wash

lavoteo *nm Fam* quick o hurried wash

laxante *adj & nm* laxative

laxar *vt* **(a)** *(ablandar)* to ease, slacken, loosen **(b)** *(vientre)* to loosen

laxativo, -a *adj & nm* laxative

laxitud *nf* laxity, laxness

laxo, -a *adj* lax, loose

laya *nf Fml Pey* kind, ilk; **de toda l.** of all kinds o sorts

lazada *nf* **(a)** *(nudo)* knot **(b)** *(adorno)* bow

lazareto *nm* isolation hospital; *(cuarentena)* quarantine station

lazarillo *nm* blind person's guide; **perro l.** guide dog, *US* seeing eye dog

lazo *nm* **(a)** *(adorno)* bow; **l. de zapato** shoelace **(b)** *(nudo)* knot **l. corredizo** slipknot **(c)** *(para reses)* lasso **(d)** *(trampa)* snare, trap **(e)** *Fig (gen pl) (vínculo)* tie, bond; **lazos de amistad** bonds of friendship; **lazos familiares** o **de sangre** family ties

Lda *(abrev de **licenciada**)* graduate

Ldo *(abrev de **licenciado**)* graduate

le 1 *pron pers mf* **(a)** *(objeto indirecto) (a él)* (to) him; *(a ella)* (to) her; *(a cosa)* (to) it; **lávale la cara** wash his face; **le compraré uno** I'll buy one for her; **no le oigo** I can't hear her; **no quiero verle más** I don't want to see him any more; **¿qué le pasa?** what's the matter with her? **(b)** *(a usted)* you; **no quiero molestarle** I don't wish to disturb you; **ya le llamaré** I'll give you a call
2 *pron pers m Esp (objeto directo) (él)* him; *(usted)* you; *véase tamb* **leísmo**

leal 1 *adj* loyal, faithful
2 *nmf (incondicional)* loyalist

lealtad *nf* loyalty, faithfulness

leasing ['lisin] *(pl **leasings**) nm Fin* leasing

lebrel *nm Zool* greyhound

lección *nf* lesson; *Fig* **dar una l. a algn** to teach sb a

lesson; *Fig* **te servirá de l.** it will be a lesson to you

lechada *nf* whitewash

lechal *adj* sucking; **cordero l.** sucking lamb

lechar *vt Andes (ordeñar)* to milk

leche *nf* **(a)** *(de mujer, hembra)* milk; *Anat* **dientes de l.** milk teeth; *Culin* **l. frita** dessert made of fried milk and flour batter **l. condensada** condensed milk; **l. descremada** o **desnatada** skim o skimmed milk; **l. hidratante** moisturizing lotion **(b)** *Bot* milky sap **(c)** *Fam Fig* **mala l.** bad mood; **tener mala l.** to be spiteful; *Esp* **salió echando leches** he took off like a bat out of hell; **a toda l.** at top speed, flat out **(d)** *Esp Argot (golpe)* knock; **dar** o **pegar una l. a algn** to clobber sb **(e)** *Esp Vulg* semen

lechecillas *nfpl* sweetbreads

lechera *nf* **(a)** *(que vende)* woman who sells milk; *(que ordeña)* milkmaid; **el cuento de la l.** pie in the sky **(b)** *(vasija)* churn **(c)** *RP* milk cow **(d)** *Argot* police car

lechería *nf* dairy, creamery

lechero, -a 1 *adj* **(a)** milk, dairy; **central lechera** dairy co-operative; **vaca lechera** milk cow **(b)** *Bol CAm Méx Perú muy Fam (afortunado) Br* bloody o *US* goddamn lucky
2 *nm* milkman

lecho *nm* bed; **l. del río** river-bed; **l. mortuorio** deathbed; *Fig* **l. de rosas** bed of roses

lechón *nm Zool* **(a)** *(cochinillo)* sucking pig **(b)** *(puerco)* swine, hog

lechona *nf Zool* young sow

lechoso, -a 1 *adj* milky
2 *nm Carib* papaya tree

lechuga *nf* lettuce; *Fam Fig* **(fresco) como una l.** as fresh as a daisy

lechuguino *nm* dandy, fop

lechuza *nf Orn* owl

lecitina *nf* lecithin

lectivo, -a *adj* school; **horas lectivas** teaching hours

lector, -a 1 *nm,f* **(a)** *(de libros)* reader **(b)** *Esp Univ* language assistant
2 *nm Inform (aparato)* **l. de CD-ROM/DVD** CD-ROM/DVD drive; **l. óptico de caracteres** optical character reader

lectorado *nm Esp Univ* = post of language assistant; **hacer un l.** to work as a language assistant

lectura *nf* **(a)** *(de libro, texto)* reading; **dar l. a algo** to read sth; **de mucha l.** well-read; **material de l.** reading matter **(b)** *(interpretación)* interpretation; **hizo una l. marxista de la obra** he gave the work a Marxist interpretation

leer [37] *vt también Inform* to read; **léenos el menú** read out the menu for us; **l. la mano a algn** to read sb's palm; *Fig* **l. entre líneas** to read between the lines

legación *nf* legation

legado, -a 1 *pp de* **legar**
2 *nm* **(a)** *(herencia)* legacy, bequest **(b)** *(representante)* legate; **l. apostólico** papal nuncio

legajo *nm* dossier

legal *adj* **(a)** *Jur* legal, lawful; **requisitos legales** legal formalities **(b)** *Esp Fam (persona)* honest, decent

legalidad *nf* legality, lawfulness; **según la l. (vigente)** according to the law

legalismo *nm* legalism

legalista 1 *adj* legalistic
2 *nmf* legalist

legalización *nf* legalization

legalizar [14] *vt* to legalize; *(documento)* to authenticate

legalmente *adv* legally, lawfully

légamo *nm* slime, ooze

legaña *nf (en ojos)* sleep; *Fig* **quitarse las legañas** to get a move on

legañoso, -a *adj* bleary-eyed

legar [38] *vt* (**a**) *(propiedad etc)* to bequeath; *Fig (tradiciones etc)* to hand down, pass on (**b**) *(enviar como delegado)* to delegate

legatario, -a *nm,f Jur* legatee, heir

legendario, -a *adj* legendary

legible *adj* legible

legión *nf* legion; *Fig* **una l. de admiradores le seguía** a legion of admirers followed her ❑ *Mil* **L. Extranjera** Foreign Legion

legionario, -a 1 *adj* legionary
2 *nm* legionary, legionnaire; *Med* **enfermedad del l.** legionnaire's disease

legionella [leχio'nela] *nf* (**a**) *(enfermedad)* legionnaire's disease (**b**) *(bacteria)* legionella bacterium

legislación *nf* legislation

legislador, -a 1 *adj* legislative
2 *nm,f* legislator

legislar *vi* to legislate, enact

legislativo, -a *adj* legislative

legislatura *nf* (**a**) *(periodo)* legislature (**b**) *Am Pol* legislative body

legitimación *nf Jur* legitimization

legitimar *vt* to legitimize; *(legalizar)* to legalize

legitimidad *nf Jur* legitimacy; *(licitud)* justice

legítimo, -a *adj* (**a**) *Jur* legitimate; **en legítima defensa** in self-defence (**b**) *(auténtico)* authentic, real; **oro l.** pure gold

lego, -a 1 *adj* (**a**) *Rel* lay, secular (**b**) *(ignorante)* ignorant, uninformed; **ser l. en la materia** to know nothing about the subject
2 *nm Rel* lay brother

legua *nf (medida)* league; *Fig* **se nota a la l.** it stands out a mile ❑ **l. marítima** marine league

leguleyo *nm Pey* pettifogger, shyster

legumbre *nf* legume, pod vegetable

leguminosa *nf* pulse, leguminous plant

leguminoso, -a *adj* leguminous

lehendakari [lenda'kari] *nmf* = head of the Basque government

leída *nf* reading

leído, -a 1 *pp de* **leer**
2 *adj* well-read; **ser muy l.** to be very knowledgeable

leísmo *nm Ling* = incorrect use of **le** as a direct object instead of **lo**

leitmotiv [leitmo'tif] *(pl* **leitmotivs)** *nm* leitmotiv, leitmotif

lejanía *nf* distance

lejano, -a *adj* distant, far-off; **parientes lejanos** distant relatives ❑ **el L. Oriente** the Far East

lejía *nf* bleach, lye

lejos 1 *adv* far (away); **a lo l.** in the distance; **de l.** from a distance; **desde l.** from a long way off; **¿está l.?** is it far?; **l. de mí/ti/él ...** far away from me/you/him ...; *Fig* **ir demasiado l.** to go too far; *Fig* **l. de mí hacer tal cosa** how could I do a thing like that?; *Fig* **l. de mejorar, empeora** it gets worse instead of better; *Fig* **llegar l.** to go a long way; *Fig* **más l.** farther o further away; *Fig* **ni de l.** far from it; *Fig* **sin ir más l.** to take an obvious example; *Fam Fig* **l. del mundanal ruido** far from the madding crowd
2 *nm* distant view; *(cuadro)* background

lelo, -a *Fam* **1** *adj* stupid, silly; **quedarse l.** to be stunned o stupefied
2 *nm,f* ninny

lema *nm* (**a**) *(norma)* motto; *(eslogan)* slogan (**b**) *(de diccionario)* headword

lempira *nm* lempira, = standard monetary unit of Honduras

lencería *nf* (**a**) *(ropa interior)* lingerie (**b**) *(ropa blanca)* linen

lendakari *nmf véase* **lehendakari**

lengua *nf* (**a**) *Anat* tongue; **sacar la l. a algn** to stick one's tongue out at sb; *Fig* **andar en lenguas** to be the talk of the town; *Fig* **hacerse lenguas de algo** to praise sth wildly; *Fig* **largo** o **ligero de l.** loose-tongued; *Fig* **l. viperina** o **de víbora** viperous tongue; *Fig* **malas lenguas** gossip *sing*; *Fam Fig* **con la l. fuera** puffing and panting; *Fam Fig* **darle a la l.** to chatter; *Fam Fig* **irse de la l.** to spill the beans; *Fam Fig* **morderse la l.** to hold one's tongue; *Fam Fig* **no tener pelos en la l.** not to mince one's words, be outspoken; *Fam Fig* **tener algo en la punta de la l.** to have sth on the tip of one's tongue; *Fam Fig* **tirarle a algn de la l.** to try to draw sth out of sb; *Fam Fig* **tragarse la l.** to bite one's lip (**b**) *Ling* language, tongue ❑ **l. franca** lingua franca; **l. madre** parent language; **l. materna** native o mother tongue; **l. muerta/viva** dead/living language (**c**) *Geog* neck, spit

lenguado *nm (pez)* sole

lenguaje *nm* (**a**) *(habla)* speech, language; **l. corporal** body language (**b**) *(idioma)* language ❑ **l. literario** literary style; **l. poético** poetic language (**c**) *Inform* language ❑ **l. de alto nivel** high-level language; **l. de programación** program language

lenguaraz *adj (hablador)* talkative, garrulous; *(mal hablado)* foul-mouthed

lengüeta *nf* (**a**) *(de zapato)* tongue, flap (**b**) *Mús* reed (**c**) *RP (charlatán)* chatterbox

lengüetear *vi Carib RP Fam (hablar)* to chatter

Leningrado *n Antes* Leningrad

leninismo *nm Pol* Leninism

leninista *adj & nmf Pol* Leninist

lenitivo, -a 1 *adj* soothing, lenitive
2 *nm* lenitive; *Fig* palliative

lenocinio *nm Fml* procuring, pimping ❑ **casa de l.** brothel

lente *Ópt* **1** *nmf* lens; *Esp* **lentes de contacto** contact lenses
2 *lentes nmpl* glasses, spectacles

lenteja *nf Bot Culin* lentil; *Prov* **venderse por un plato de lentejas** to sell oneself cheap

lentejuela *nf* sequin, spangle

lentilla *nf Esp Ópt* contact lens

lentisco *nm Bot* mastic tree

lentitud *nf* slowness; **con l.** slowly

lento, -a *adj* slow; **fuego l.** low heat; **ser l. de reflejos** to have slow reflexes

leña *nf* (**a**) *(madera)* firewood; **hacer l.** to collect firewood; **l. pequeña** kindling; *Fig* **echar l. al fuego** to add fuel to the fire (**b**) *Fam (golpes)* knocks *pl*; *Dep* rough play; **dar** o **repartir l.** to hit out; *Dep* to play rough

leñador, -a *nm,f* woodcutter, lumberjack

leñazo *nm Argot (golpe)* blow, smash; **se pegaron un l. contra un árbol** they crashed into a tree

leñe *interj Esp Fam* damn it!

leñera *nf* woodshed

leño *nm* (**a**) *(de madera)* log; *Fig* **dormir como un l.** to sleep like a log (**b**) *Fam (persona)* blockhead, half-wit

leñoso, -a *adj* wood-like, ligneous

Leo *nm Astrol Astron* Leo

león (**a**) *nm Zool* lion; *Fig* **se llevó la parte del l.** he got the lion's share; *Prov* **no es tan fiero el l. como lo pintan** he's/she's not as fierce as he's/she's made out to be ❑ *Zool* **l. marino** sea lion (**b**) *Astrol Astron* Leo

leona *nf* (**a**) *Zool* lioness (**b**) *(mujer)* brave woman; *(provocadora)* man-eater

leonado, -a *adj* tawny

leonera *nf* (**a**) *(jaula)* lion's den; *Fig* untidy place *o* room; **¿cómo puedes vivir en esa l.?** how can you live in this mess? (**b**) *Esp Fam (cuarto sucio)* pigsty

leonés, -esa 1 *adj* of *o* from León
2 *nm,f* person from León

leonino, -a *adj* (**a**) *(rostro, aspecto)* leonine, lion-like (**b**) *Jur* **contrato l.** one-sided contract

leontina *nf* watch chain

leopardo *nm Zool* leopard

leotardo *nm* (**a**) *(de gimnasta)* leotard, bodystocking (**b**) *Esp* **leotardos** thick tights

lépero, -a *adj CAm Méx* coarse, vulgar

lepidóptero, -a *Zool* **1** *adj* lepidopterous
2 *nm* lepidopteran

leporino, -a *adj* **labio l.** harelip

lepra *nf Med* leprosy

leprosería *nf* leper colony

leproso, -a 1 *adj* leprous
2 *nm,f* leper

lerdo, -a *adj (torpe)* clumsy; *(poco despierto)* dull, drowsy

leridano, -a 1 *adj* of *o* from Lérida
2 *nm,f* person from Lérida

les 1 *pron pers mfpl* (**a**) *(objeto indirecto) (a ellos)* (to) them; **acéptales el regalo** accept their present; **l. di todo el dinero** I gave them all the money (**b**) *(a ustedes)* (to) you; **l. esperaré** I shall wait for you; **no quiero molestarles** I don't wish to disturb you
2 *pron pers mpl Esp (objeto directo) (ellos)* them; *(ustedes)* you; *véase tamb* **leísmo**

lesbiana *nf* lesbian

lesbianismo *nm* lesbianism

lesión *nf* (**a**) *(daño corporal)* injury, wound (**b**) *(perjuicio)* damage, harm

lesionado, -a 1 *pp de* lesionar
2 *adj* (**a**) *(persona)* injured (**b**) *(algo)* damaged, harmed
3 *nm,f* injured person; **hubo 20 lesionados** there were 20 injured

lesionar 1 *vt* (**a**) *(persona)* to injure; *(algo)* to damage (**b**) *Fig (intereses)* to damage
2 lesionarse *vpr* to get injured

lesivo, -a *adj Fml* harmful, damaging

leso, -a *adj* (**a**) *Jur* **crimen de lesa majestad** lese-majesty, treason; **crimen** *o* **delito de lesa patria** high treason (**b**) *Andes Fam* silly, foolish

Lesoto *n* Lesotho

letal *adj* lethal, deadly

letanía *nf Rel* litany; *Fam Fig* long list

letárgico, -a *adj* lethargic

letargo *nm* lethargy

letón, -ona 1 *adj* Latvian
2 *nm,f* Latvian
3 *nm (idioma)* Latvian, Lettish

Letonia *n* Latvia

letra *nf* (**a**) *Impr Ling* letter; *Fig* **al pie de la l.** to the letter, word for word; *Fig* **mándale cuatro letras** drop her a line;

Prov **la l. con sangre entra** spare the rod and spoil the child ❑ **l. bastardilla** *o* **cursiva** italics *pl*, italic type; **l. de caja alta/baja** capital/small letter; **l. de imprenta** *o* **de molde** print; **l. gótica** Gothic script; **l. itálica** italics *pl*, italic type; **l. mayúscula** *o* **de caja alta** *o* **versal** capital letter; **l. minúscula** small letter; **l. negrilla** semibold type; **l. seminegra** bold type; **l. versal** capital letter; **l. versalita** small capital (**b**) *(modo de escribir)* (hand)writing; **de su puño y l.** in his own hand; **tener buena/mala l.** to have good/bad handwriting (**c**) *Mús (texto)* lyrics *pl*, words *pl* (**d**) *Fin* **l. (de cambio)** bill of exchange, draft; **l. a la vista** sight draft (**e**) **letras** *Univ* arts; **Facultad de L.** Faculty of Arts; **licenciado en L.** arts graduate (**f**) **letras** *(literatura)* letters; **hombre/mujer de l.** man/woman of letters

letrado, -a 1 *adj* learned
2 *nm,f* lawyer

letrero *nm (aviso)* notice, sign; *(cartel)* poster; **l. luminoso** neon sign

letrina *nf* latrine; *Fig* **la playa era una auténtica l.** the beach was like a public toilet

leucemia *nf Med* leukaemia, *US* leukemia

leucémico, -a *Med* **1** *adj* leukaemic, *US* leukemic
2 *nm,f* person suffering from leukaemia *o US* leukemia

leucocito *nm* leucocyte, *US* leukocyte

leva¹ *nf* (**a**) *Mil (reclutamiento)* levy (**b**) *Téc* cam (**c**) *Náut* weighing anchor

leva² *nf* (**a**) *Am (levita)* frock coat (**b**) *CAm Col (engaño)* trick

levadizo, -a *adj* which can be raised, raisable, raiseable; **puente l.** drawbridge

levadura *nf* yeast, leaven ❑ **l. de cerveza** brewer's yeast; *Culin Esp* **l. en polvo** baking powder

levantado, -a 1 *pp de* levantar
2 *adj* up, out of bed

levantador, -a *nm,f* **l. de pesos** *o* **pesas** weightlifter

levantamiento *nm* (**a**) *(suspensión)* raising, lifting; **l. de la veda** opening of the hunting/fishing season (**b**) *Dep* **l. de pesas** weightlifting (**c**) *Mil (insurrección)* uprising, insurrection

levantar 1 *vt* (**a**) *(alzar, elevar)* to raise, lift; *(mano, voz)* to raise; *(ojos)* to look up, raise; *Fig* **l. dudas/temores** to raise doubts/fears; *Fig* **l. un país** to put a country on its feet (**b**) *(obstáculos)* to put up (**c**) *(edificios, monumento)* to erect (**d**) *Pol* to stir up (**e**) *(castigo)* to suspend (**f**) *(recoger)* to clear; **l. la mesa** to clear the table (**g**) *Naipes* **l. las cartas** to cut (the cards) (**h**) *(concluir)* to finish; *(aplazar)* to postpone; **se levanta la sesión** the court will adjourn
2 *vpr* (**a**) *(ponerse de pie)* to stand up, rise (**b**) *(salir de la cama)* to get up, get out of bed; **l. pronto** *o* **temprano** to get up early; *Fig* **l. con el pie izquierdo** to get out of bed on the wrong side (**c**) *(sobresalir)* to stand out, tower (above) (**d**) *Pol* to rise, revolt; **l. en armas** to rise up in arms (**e**) *(viento)* to come up; *(tormenta)* to gather; *Fig* **se levantó una ola de rumores** a flood of rumours arose

levante *nm* (**a**) *Geog (punto cardinal)* east; **(el) L.** (the) Levante, = the regions of Valencia and Murcia (**b**) *(viento)* east wind, Levanter (**c**) *CAm PRico (calumnia)* slander (**d**) *Chile (tasa)* = fee paid by a woodcutter

levantino, -a 1 *adj* of *o* from the **Levante**
2 *nm,f* person from the **Levante**

levantisco, -a *adj* restless, turbulent

levar *vt (ancla)* to weigh; **l. anclas** to set sail

leve *adj (ligero)* light; *Fig (de poca importancia)* slight, unimportant

levedad *nf (ligereza)* lightness; *Fig* slightness; *Fig (de ánimo)* levity

levemente *adv* lightly, slightly

leviatán *nm Rel* leviathan

levita[1] *nm Hist* Levite

levita[2] *nf* frock coat

levitación *nf* levitation

levitar *vi* to levitate

levítico, -a 1 *adj Hist* Levitical; *Fig* clerical
2 *nm Rel* Leviticus

lexema *nm Ling* lexeme

lexicalizar [14] **1** *vt* to lexicalize
2 lexicalizarse *vpr* to become lexicalized

léxico, -a *Ling* **1** *adj* lexical
2 *nm (diccionario)* lexicon; *(vocabulario)* lexicon, vocabulary, word list

lexicografía *nf Ling* lexicography

lexicográfico, -a *adj Ling* lexicographic, lexicographical

lexicógrafo, -a *nm,f Ling* lexicographer

lexicología *nf Ling* lexicology

lexicológico, -a *adj Ling* lexicologic, lexicological

lexicólogo, -a *nm,f Ling* lexicologist

lexicón *nm Ling* lexicon

ley *nf* **(a)** *(gen) & Jur* law; *Parl* bill, act; *Dep* rule, law; **aprobar una l.** to pass a bill; **según/contra la l.** according to/against the law; *Fig* **con todas las de la l.** properly, completely; *Fig* **la l. del más fuerte** the law of the jungle; *Fam* **hecha la l., hecha la trampa** laws are made to be broken; *Fam Fig* **la l. del embudo** one law for oneself and a different one for the others □ **l. constitucional** constitutional law; **la l. de la gravedad** the law of gravity; **l. orgánica** constitutional law; **l. seca** prohibition law, *US* dry law **(b)** *(de un metal)* purity; **oro de l.** pure gold

leyenda *nf* **(a)** *(relato)* legend; **l. negra** black legend **(b)** *(en un mapa)* legend; *(en una moneda)* inscription

liana *nf Bot* liana

liante *nmf Esp Fam (persuasivo)* smooth talker; *(enredador)* stirrer, trouble-maker

liar [32] **1** *vt* **(a)** *(envolver)* to wrap up; *(atar)* to tie up, do up, bind; *(un cigarrillo)* to roll **(b)** *(enredar)* to muddle up; *(confundir)* to confuse **(c)** *(complicar)* to involve, *quise* **liarme en un negocio sucio** he tried to get me mixed up in some shady deal; **l. a bofetadas** to come to blows **(d)** *Esp Fam* **liarla** *(meter la pata)* to mess things up
2 liarse *vpr* **(a)** *(embarullarse)* to get muddled up **(b)** *Esp Fam* to become lovers, have an affair; *(enrollarse)* to get involved with o embroiled in **(c)** *Esp (empezar)* to begin; **l. a hablar** to have a natter **(d)** *Fam (sentimentalmente)* to get involved **(con** with)

libación *nf Lit* libation

libanés, -esa *adj & nm,f* Lebanese

Líbano *n* el L. the Lebanon

libar *vt (néctar)* to suck; *(licor)* to take a sip, swig

libelista *nmf* lampoonist

libelo *nm (escrito difamatorio)* lampoon, satire; *Jur* petition

libélula *nf Ent* dragonfly

liberación *nf* **(a)** *(de país)* liberation; *(de persona)* release, freeing **(b)** *Fin (impuestos)* exemption; *(hipoteca)* redemption

liberado, -a 1 *pp de* **liberar**
2 *adj* liberated, freed; **mujer liberada** liberated woman

liberador, -a 1 *adj* liberating
2 *nm,f* liberator

liberal 1 *adj* **(a)** *(gen)* liberal; *(carácter)* easy-going; *Pol* **Partido L.** Liberal Party; **profesión l.** *(trabajo)* profession **(b)** *(generoso)* generous, liberal
2 *nmf* liberal

liberalidad *nf* generosity, liberality

liberalismo *nm* liberalism

liberalización *nf* liberalization

liberalizar [14] **1** *vt* to liberalize; *Fin* to lift, deregulate
2 liberalizarse *vpr* to become free, become liberal

liberalmente *adv* liberally, freely

liberar 1 *vt (país)* to liberate; *(prisionero)* to free, release
2 liberarse *vpr* to get o become free

liberatorio, -a *adj* liberating, freeing

Liberia *n* Liberia

liberiano, -a *adj & nm,f* Liberian

líbero *nm Ftb* sweeper

libérrimo, -a *adj Lit* entirely o totally free

libertad *nf* **(a)** *(para hacer algo)* freedom, liberty; **en l.** free; *Jur* **(en) l. bajo palabra/fianza** (on) parole/bail; *Jur* **(en) l. condicional** (on) parole; *Jur* **(en) l. provisional** *(bajo fianza)* (on) bail; **(en) l. vigilada** (on) probation; *Fig* **tomarse la l. de decir algo** to take the liberty of saying sth □ **l. de cátedra** academic freedom; **l. de expresión** freedom of speech; **l. de prensa** freedom of the press **(b)** **libertades** liberties; **tomarse (demasiadas) l.** to take liberties

libertador, -a 1 *adj* liberating
2 *nm,f* liberator

libertar *vt (poner en libertad)* to set free, release, liberate, deliver; *(eximir)* to exempt

libertario, -a *adj & nm,f* libertarian

libertinaje *nm* licentiousness

libertino, -a *adj & nm,f* libertine

liberto, -a 1 *adj* emancipated, free
2 *nm,f (hombre)* freedman; *(mujer)* freedwoman

Libia *n* Libya

libidinoso, -a *adj* libidinous, lewd

libido *nf* libido

libio, -a *adj & nm,f* Libyan

libra *nf* **(a)** *Fin* pound; **l. esterlina** pound sterling **(b)** *(medida)* pound **(c)** **L.** *Astrol Astron* Libra

libraco *nm Pey (libro grande)* large, heavy book; *(libro malo)* trashy book

librado, -a 1 *pp de* **librar**
2 *nm,f Fin* drawee

librador, -a *nm,f Fin* drawer

libramiento *nm Fin* order of payment, bill of exchange

librano, -a *Am Astrol* **1** *adj* Libra
2 *nm,f* Libran

libranza *nf véase* **libramiento**

librar 1 *vt* **(a)** *(gen)* to save, free; *Jur* to free, release; *Rel* **¡Dios me o nos libre!** heaven forbid!; **salir bien librado** to get off lightly **(b)** *Com* to draw; **l. una letra** to draw a bill **(c)** *Mil* to fight; **l. batalla** to do o join battle
2 *Esp vi* **(a)** *(no ir a trabajar)* to have off; **libro los martes** I have Tuesdays off **(b)** *(dar a luz)* to give birth
3 librarse *vpr* to escape; **l. de algn** to get rid of sb; **l. de una buena** to have a narrow escape; **l. de una multa** to get out of paying a fine

libre *adj* **(a)** *(no sujeto)* free; *(en servicios)* vacant; **asiento l.** free seat; **entrada l.** admission free, open to the general public; *Natación* **los cien metros libres** the one hundred metres freestyle; **ratos libres** spare time; **traducción l.** free translation; *Econ* **l. cambio** free trade; *Fin* **l. de impuestos** tax-free; *Econ* **l. mercado** free market **l. de preocupa-**

ciones free from worries; (**b**) *Educ* **alumno l.** external student; *Esp* **ir por l.** to do things one's own way

librea *nf* livery, uniform

librecambio *nm*, **librecambismo** *nm Econ* free trade

librecambista *Econ* **1** *adj* free trade
2 *nmf* free-trader

libremente *adv* freely

librepensador, -a 1 *adj* freethinking
2 *nm,f* freethinker

librepensamiento *nm* freethinking, free thought

librería *nf* (**a**) *(tienda)* bookstore, *Br* bookshop (**b**) *Esp Mueb (armario)* bookcase; *(estantería)* bookshelf

librero, -a 1 *nm,f* bookseller
2 *nm Méx CAm Col (estanteria)* bookshelf; *(armario)* bookcase

libresco, -a *adj Pey* bookish

libreta *nf* notebook; **l. (de ahorro)** savings book

libretista *nmf Mús* librettist

libreto *nm* (**a**) *Mús* libretto (**b**) *Am (guión)* script

librillo *nm* small book, booklet; **l. de papel de fumar** packet of cigarette papers

libro *nm* (**a**) *(impreso)* book ❑ *Pol* **l. blanco** White Paper; **l. de bolsillo** paperback; **l. de consulta** reference book; **l. de cuentos** story-book; *Jur* **l. de familia** = book in which births and deaths in the family are registered; **l. de lectura** reader; **l. de reclamaciones** complaints book; **l. de texto** textbook; **l. electrónico** electronic book; *Pol* **l. rojo** White Paper (**b**) *Zool Anat* third stomach (**c**) *Com* **llevar los libros** to keep the books ❑ **l. de caja** cashbook; **l. de contabilidad** accounts book; *Fin* **l. mayor** ledger

Lic. *(abrev de* **licenciado,-a***)* graduate

licantropía *nf Psic* lycanthropy

licántropo *nm Psic* lycanthrope; *(leyenda)* werewolf

licencia *nf* (**a**) *(permiso)* licence, *US* license, permission; *(documento)* permit, licence, *US* license; **dar l. a algn** to grant sb permission; **l. de armas/caza** gun/hunting licence; *Carib Chile Ecuad* **l. de conducir**, *Méx* **l. para conducir** *Br* driving licence, *US* driver's license; *Com* **l. fiscal** business permit; *Com* **l. de importación** import licence; **l. de obras** planning permission; (**b**) *(libertad abusiva)* licence, *US* license, licentiousness ❑ **l. poética** poetic licence (**c**) *Mil* leave; **l. absoluta** discharge (**d**) *Am (en el trabajo)* leave (**e**) *Méx* **con l.** *(con permiso)* if I may, if you'll excuse me; **con l., ¿puedo pasar?** may I come in?

licenciado, -a 1 *pp de* **licenciar**
2 *adj* (**a**) *Univ* graduated (**b**) *Mil* discharged
3 *nm,f Univ* graduate, licentiate, bachelor; *Mil* discharged soldier; **l. en Ciencias** Bachelor of Science; **l. en francés** French graduate

licenciar 1 *vt* (**a**) *(dar permiso a)* to grant a permit o licence o *US* license on; *Mil* to discharge (**b**) *Univ* to confer a degree on
2 licenciarse *vpr Univ* to graduate

licenciatura *nf Univ (título)* (bachelor's) degree; *(ceremonia)* graduation; *(curso)* degree (course)

licencioso, -a *adj* licentious, dissolute

liceo *nm* (**a**) *Hist* Lyceum (**b**) *(sociedad literaria)* literary society (**c**) *(escuela)* secondary school

licitación *nf Com* bid, bidding; *Com* **sacar (algo) a l.** to put (sth) up for auction

licitador *nm Com* bidder

licitar *vt Com (pujar)* to bid for; *(optar)* to tender for

lícito, -a *adj (justo)* just, fair; *(permisible)* allowed; *Jur* lawful, licit

licor *nm* (**a**) *(líquido)* liquid (**b**) *(bebida destilada)* spirits, *US* liquor

licorera *nf* liquor bottle, decanter

licorería *nf Com Br* off-licence, *US* liquor store; *Ind* distillery

licuación *nf* liquefaction

licuado *nm Am (batido)* milk shake

licuadora *nf Esp (para extraer zumo)* juice extractor, juicer; *Am (para batir)* blender, *Br* liquidizer

licuar [4] **1** *vt* to liquefy
2 licuarse *vpr* to liquefy, become liquid

licuefacción *nf* liquefaction

lid *nf (combate)* contest, combat, fight; *Fig* dispute, controversy; *Fig* **experto en esas lides** experienced in these matters

líder *nmf* leader; *Com* **l. del mercado** market leader

liderar *vt* to lead, head

liderato *nm*, **liderazgo** *nm* leadership; *Dep* leader, top o first position

lidia *nf* (**a**) *Taur* bullfight, bullfighting; **toro de l.** fighting bull (**b**) *(lucha)* fight, combat

lidiador *nm Taur* bullfighter

lidiar 1 *vt* (**a**) *Taur* to fight (**b**) *Fig* to deal with
2 *vi* to fight; **l. con** to contend with, fight against

liebre *nf* (**a**) *Zool* hare; *Fig* coward; *Fig* **levantar la l.** to let the cat out of the bag (**b**) *Atlet* pacemaker

Liechtenstein ['liɣenstein] *n* Liechtenstein

liencillo *nm Andes Carib RP Tex* rough cotton cloth

liendre *nf Ent* nit

lienzo *nm* (**a**) *Tex* linen (**b**) *Arte* canvas, painting (**c**) *Arquit (stretch of)* wall

lifting ['liftin] *(pl* **liftings***)* *nm* facelift

liga *nf* (**a**) *Dep Pol* league (**b**) *(para medias) (elástico)* garter; *(colgante) Br* suspender, *US* garter (**c**) *(sustancia pegajosa)* birdlime (**d**) *Bot* mistletoe (**e**) *(mezcla)* mixture (**f**) *(aleación)* alloy

ligado, -a 1 *pp de* **ligar**
2 *adj* connected, linked
3 *nm Impr* ligature; *Mús* slur

ligadura *nf Med Mús* ligature; *Med* **l. de trompas** tubal ligation

ligamento *nm* (**a**) *Anat* ligament (**b**) *Tex* weave

ligar [38] **1** *vt* (**a**) *(unir)* to tie, bind; *Fig* to join; *Fig* **les ligaba la política** they were united by politics (**b**) *(alear)* to alloy (**c**) *Culin* to thicken (**d**) *Med* to bind up (**e**) *Mús* to slur (**f**) *Fam (conquistar)* to pinch (**g**) *Cuba (cosecha)* to contract in advance for
2 *vi* (**a**) *Fam (encontrar pareja)* to score, *Br* pull (**b**) *(concordar)* **l. con** to agree with, be in accordance with (**c**) *Naipes* to combine good cards (**d**) *Carib Guat Perú (deseo)* to have one's desires satisfied (**e**) *RP Ven (en el juego)* to be lucky
3 ligarse *vpr Esp Fam* **ligarse a algn** *Br* to get off with sb, *US* make out with sb

ligazón *nf* (**a**) *(unión)* bond, tie (**b**) *Náut* rib, beam

ligeramente *adv* (**a**) *(levemente)* lightly (**b**) *(un poco)* slightly

ligereza *nf* (**a**) *(livianidad)* lightness, thinness, flimsiness (**b**) *(agilidad)* agility, nimbleness (**c**) *(frivolidad)* rashness, flippancy; *(indiscreción)* indiscretion; **hablar/obrar con l.** to speak/act rashly o without thinking

ligero, -a 1 *adj* (**a**) *(peso)* light, lightweight; **l. como una pluma** as light as a feather; **l. de ropa** lightly clad; *Box* **peso l.** lightweight (**b**) *(ágil)* agile, nimble; *(veloz)* swift, swift; **l. de manos** light-fingered; **paso l.** nimble step, *Mil* quick march (**c**) *(frívolo)* rash, flippant; **de l.** rashly; **tomarse algo a la ligera** to take sth lightly (**d**) *(de poca importancia)* slight
2 *adv (rápido)* fast, swiftly

light [lait] *adj inv (comida)* low-calorie; *(refresco)* diet; *(cigarrillos)* light

lignito *nm Min* lignite

ligón, -ona *Esp Fam* **1** *adj* **es muy l.** he's always getting off with somebody
  2 *nm,f (hombre)* skirt-chaser; *(mujer)* easy pick-up

ligue *nm Esp Fam* pick-up; **ir de l.** to go out to score *o Br* on the pull

liguero, -a 1 *adj Dep* league; **partido l.** league match
  2 *nm Br* suspender belt, *US* garter belt

liguilla *nf Dep* round-robin tournament

lija 1 *nf* **(a)** *(pez)* dogfish **(b)** *Téc* sandpaper
  2 *adj Méx* shrewd, sharp

lijadora *nf Téc* sander, sanding machine

lijar *vt Téc* to sand *o* sandpaper (down)

lila¹ *adj & nm & nf* lilac

lila² *Fam* **1** *adj (tonto)* dumb, stupid
  2 *nmf (tonto)* twit

liliputiense *adj & nmf* Lilliputian

Lima *n* Lima

lima¹ *nf Bot* lime

lima² *nf* **(a)** *(herramienta)* file; *Fig* **come como una l.** he eats like a horse □ **l. de uñas** nailfile **(b)** *Fig* polish, polishing up

limaco *nm Zool* slug

limado *nm (pulimento)* filing

limadura *nf* filing; **limaduras de hierro** iron filings

limar *vt* **(a)** *(desbastar)* to file (down *o* off); *Fig* **l. asperezas** to smooth things over **(b)** *(pulir una obra)* to polish up, put the final touches to

limaza *nf Zool* slug

limbo *nm* **(a)** *Rel* limbo; *Fig* **estar en el l.** to be miles away **(b)** *Mat* limb

limeño, -a 1 *adj* of *o* from Lima
  2 *nm,f* person from Lima

limero *nm Bot* lime (tree)

limitación *nf* limitation, limit

limitado, -a 1 *pp de* **limitar**
  2 *adj* **(a)** *(gen)* limited **(b)** *Euf (poco listo)* dull, dim-witted

limitar 1 *vt* to limit, restrict
  2 *vi* to border; **l. con** to border on
  3 limitarse *vpr* to limit *o* restrict oneself

limitativo, -a *adj* restrictive, limiting

límite 1 *nm* **(a)** *(tope)* limit; **dentro de unos límites** within limits □ **l. de velocidad** speed limit **(b)** *Geog Pol* boundary
  2 *adj inv* **(a)** *(precio, velocidad, edad)* maximum; **fecha l.** deadline **(b)** *(situación)* extreme; *(caso)* borderline

limítrofe *adj* bordering, neighbouring, *US* neighboring

limo *nm* **(a)** *(barro)* mud, slime **(b)** *Andes CAm (árbol)* lime tree

limón *nm Bot* lemon

limonada *nf (sin gas)* lemon squash; *(con gas) Br* lemonade, *US* lemon soda

limonero, -a 1 *adj* lemon; **pera limonera** large variety of pear
  2 *nm* lemon tree

limonita *nf Min* limonite

limosna *nf* alms, charity; **dar (una) l.** to give alms; **pedir l.** to beg

limosnear *vi* to beg

limosnero, -a 1 *adj* charitable
  2 *nm,f Méx* beggar

limoso, -a *adj* slimy, muddy

limpiabarros *nm inv* boot scraper

limpiabotas *nm inv* shoeshine, *Br* bootblack

limpiachimeneas *nm inv* chimney sweep

limpiacristales *nm inv* window cleaner

limpiador, -a 1 *adj* cleaning, cleansing
  2 *nm,f (persona)* cleaner
  3 *nm (producto)* cleaner, cleanser

limpiamente *adv* **(a)** *(con destreza)* cleanly **(b)** *(honradamente)* honestly

limpiametales *nm inv* metal polish

limpiaparabrisas *nm inv Aut Br* windscreen *o US* windshield wiper

limpiar 1 *vt* **(a)** *(gen)* to clean, cleanse; *(con un trapo)* to wipe; *Fig* to cleanse, purify; **l. algo en seco** to dry-clean sth **(b)** *Fam (hurtar)* to pinch, nick; **le limpiaron la cartera** they cleaned out his wallet **(c)** *Méx (castigar)* to beat **(d)** *RP Ven Fam (matar)* to do in, *US* whack
  2 limpiarse *vpr* to clean oneself

limpiavidrios *nm inv Am* window-cleaning fluid

limpidez *nf Lit* limpidity

límpido, -a *adj Lit* limpid

limpieza *nf* **(a)** *(calidad)* cleanness, cleanliness; *Fig (pureza)* purity **(b)** *(acción)* cleaning; **hacer la l.** to do the cleaning □ **l. étnica** ethnic cleansing

limpio, -a 1 *adj* **(a)** *(aseado)* clean, tidy; **l. como una patena** clean as a new pin; **¿tienes las manos limpias?** are your hands clean?; *Fig* **l. de (toda) sospecha** free of suspicion **(b)** *(honrado)* honest, fair; **juego l.** fair play; **un negocio poco l.** a shady business **(c)** *Fin (neto)* net; **l. en l.** net; **gana 1.500 euros limpios** he earns 1,500 euros after tax **(d)** *(claro)* clear; **¿has sacado algo en l. de todo ello?** have you got anything out of all that? **(e)** *Fam (ignorante)* ignorant; **de este tema estoy l.** I don't know a thing about the subject **(f)** *Fam (arruinado)* broke, *Br* skint; **la caída de la bolsa me dejó l.** the stock market crash left me broke
  2 *adv* fairly; **jugar l.** to play fair; **pasar** *Esp* **a** *o Am* **en l., poner en l.** to make a fair copy of, write out neatly

limpión *nm Carib Col* tea towel, tea-cloth, *US* dishtowel

limusina *nf Aut* limousine

linaje *nm* **(a)** *(familia)* lineage **(b)** *(especie)* kind, class

linaza *nf Bot* flaxseed, linseed

lince *nm Zool* lynx; *Fig* **ser un l.** not to miss a thing; *Fig* **tener ojo de l.** to have a sharp eye

linchamiento *nm* lynching

linchar *vt* to lynch

lindamente *adv* neatly, prettily

lindante *adj (limítrofe)* bordering; *Fig (rayano)* bordering on; **una franqueza l. con la grosería** an openness bordering on rudeness

lindar *vi* to adjoin; **l. con** to border on; **Suiza linda con Alemania** Switzerland borders on Germany

linde *nmf* boundary, limit

lindero, -a 1 *adj* bordering, adjoining; **tiene un solar l. con el mío** he has a lot next *o* adjacent to mine
  2 *nm* boundary, limit

lindeza *nf* **(a)** *(belleza)* prettiness **(b)** **lindezas** *Irón (insultos)* insults

lindo, -a 1 *adj esp Am (bonito)* pretty, lovely; **de lo l.** a great deal, in a grand manner
  2 *adv Am* very well, beautifully

línea *nf* **(a)** *(raya, trazo, límite)* line; **en líneas generales** in broad terms; *Fig* **de primera l.** first-rate; *Fig* **leer entre líneas** to read between the lines □ *Aut* **l. continua** solid white line; *Fin* **l. de crédito** credit line, line of credit; **l. de flotación** waterline; **l. de mira** line of fire; **l. de puntos** dotted line; **l. de tiro** line of fire; **l. divisoria** dividing line; **l. recta** straight line; **líneas paralelas** parallel lines (**b**) *Tel* line; **no hay l.** the line's dead (**c**) *Dep* line □ **l. de banda** sideline, touchline; **l. de meta** *(en carrera)* finishing line; *(en fútbol)* goal line; **l. de salida** starting line; **l. de saque** *o* **servicio** base line, service line (**d**) *Com* line □ **l. de productos** line of products (**e**) *(estilo)* style; **de l. clásica** classical; **eso está muy en su l.** that's just his style □ **l. de conducta** course of action (**f**) *(ruta)* **una nueva l. de autobús** a new bus route (**g**) *Av* **l. aérea** airline (**h**) *Inform* **en l.** on-line; **fuera de l.** off-line (**i**) *(silueta)* figure; **guardar la l.** to watch one's weight (**j**) *(familia)* line; **l. directa** unbroken line

lineal *adj* linear; **dibujo l.** line drawing

lineamiento *nm* (**a**) *(contorno)* contour, outline (**b**) *Am (directrices)* outline

linfa *nf* lymph

linfático, -a *adj* lymphatic

lingotazo *nm Esp Fam (de bebida alcohólica)* long swig

lingote *nm* ingot; *(de oro, plata)* bar

lingual *adj & nf* lingual

lingüista *nmf* linguist

lingüística *nf* linguistics *sing*

lingüístico, -a *adj* linguistic

linier *nm Dep* linesman

linimento *nm Farm* liniment

lino *nm* (**a**) *Bot* flax (**b**) *Tex* linen

linóleo *nm* linoleum

linotipia *nf Impr* linotype

linotipista *nmf Impr* linotypist

linotipo *nm Impr* linotype

linterna *nf (de pilas) Br* torch; *US* flashlight; *(farol)* lantern □ **l. mágica** magic lantern

lío *nm* (**a**) *(paquete)* bundle; **un l. de ropa** a bundle of clothes (**b**) *Fam (embrollo)* mess, muddle; *(chisme)* tale; **hacerse un l.** to get mixed up; **meterse en líos** to get into trouble (**c**) *Fam (relación amorosa)* affair

liofilización *nf* freeze-drying

liofilizar [14] *vt* to freeze-dry

lioso, -a *Fam* **1** *adj (persona)* troublemaking; *(asunto)* tangled, confusing
2 *nm,f* troublemaker

lipidia *nf CAm (pobreza)* poverty

lípido *nm Quím* lipid, lipide

liposoluble *adj Quím* fat-soluble

liposucción *nf* liposuction

lipotimia *nf Med* syncope, fainting fit

liquen *nm Bot* lichen

liquidación *nf* (**a**) *(gen)* liquidation (**b**) *Fin* liquidation; *(operación en bolsa)* settlement (**c**) *Com (venta)* clearance sale

liquidado, -a 1 *pp de* **liquidar**
2 *adj* (**a**) *(pagado)* paid, settled (**b**) *(vendido)* sold off *o* up (**c**) *(resuelto)* solved (**d**) *Fam (muerto)* killed

liquidador, -a *nm,f* liquidator

liquidámbar *nm Bot* **l. americano** sweet gum

liquidar *vt* (**a**) *(licuar)* to liquefy (**b**) *Com (deuda)* to liquidate; *(mercancías)* to sell off *o* up; *(cuenta)* to settle (**c**) *Fam (resolver)* to resolve, solve; **hay que l. este problema antes de mañana** we have to solve this problem by tomorrow (**d**) *Fam (eliminar)* to kill, bump off

liquidez *nf Fin* liquidity

líquido, -a 1 *adj* (**a**) *(estado)* liquid (**b**) *Fin* net; **renta líquida** net income (**c**) *Ling* liquid; **consonante líquida** liquid consonant
2 *nm* (**a**) *(fluido)* liquid □ *Med* **l. amniótico** amniotic fluid; **l. de frenos** brake fluid (**b**) *Fin* liquid assets *pl*; **l. imponible** taxable income

lira¹ *nf Mús* lyre

lira² *nf Fin* lira

lírica *nf (género)* lyric poetry

lírico, -a *adj* lyric, lyrical

lirio *nm* iris □ **l. de agua** calla lily; **l. de los valles** lily of the valley

lirismo *nm Lit* lyricism

lirón *nm* dormouse; *Fig* **dormir como un l.** to sleep like a log

lirondo *adj véase* **mondo, -a**

lis *nf* (**a**) *Bot* iris (**b**) *(en heráldica)* fleur-de-lis

Lisboa *n* Lisbon

lisboeta 1 *adj* of *o* from Lisbon
2 *nmf* person from Lisbon

lisiado, -a 1 *pp de* **lisiar**
2 *adj* crippled, disabled
3 *nm,f* cripple, disabled person

lisiar 1 *vt* to maim, cripple
2 lisiarse *vpr* to be maimed

liso, -a *adj* (**a**) *(superficie)* smooth, even; *Esp Dep* **los cien metros lisos** the hundred metres; **lisa y llanamente** purely and simply (**b**) *(pelo)* straight, sleek (**c**) *(colores)* plain (**d**) *Andes CAm Ven (desvergonzado)* cheeky

lisonja *nf (piece of)* flattery

lisonjeador, -a 1 *adj* flattering
2 *nm,f* flatterer

lisonjear *vt* to flatter

lisonjero, -a *adj* (**a**) *(halagador)* flattering (**b**) *(satisfactorio)* gratifying; **no veo el futuro muy l.** the future doesn't look very rosy

lista *nf* (**a**) *(franja)* stripe, band; **a listas** striped (**b**) *(relación)* list, register; **pasar l.** to call the register *o* the roll □ **l. de boda** wedding list; *Inform* **l. de correo** mailing list; **l. de correos** poste restante, *US* general delivery; **l. de espera** waiting list; *Mús* **l. de éxitos** hit parade; **l. de** *Esp* **la compra** *o Am* **las compras** shopping list; **l. de precios** price list; **l. negra** blacklist

listado, -a 1 *pp de* **listar**
2 *adj* striped
3 *nm* enumeration, listing

listar *vt* to list

listillo, -a *nm,f Esp Fam Pey* smart alec(k)

listín *nm Esp Tel* telephone directory

listo, -a *adj* (**a**) *(inteligente)* clever, smart; **dárselas de l.** to think oneself clever; **pasarse de l.** to be too clever by half (**b**) *(diligente)* prompt, quick; *Fam* **¡(pues sí que) estamos listos!** what a fine mess we're in!; *Fam* **¡vas** *o* **estás l.!** you're kidding yourself! (**c**) *(a punto)* ready, prepared; **¿estás l.?** (are you) ready?

listón *nm* (**a**) *Carp* lath (**b**) *Dep (de saltar)* bar; *Fig* **subir el l.** to tighten the conditions, raise the requirements

lisura *nf* (**a**) *(tersura)* smoothness (**b**) *(franqueza)* frankness, straightforwardness

litera *nf (cama)* berth, bunk, couchette (**b**) *(uso antiguo)* litter

literal *adj* literal, exact

literalmente *adv* literally, word for word

literario, -a *adj* literary

literato, -a *nm,f* writer, man/woman of letters

literatura *nf* literature

lítico, -a *adj* lithic

litigación *nf Jur* litigation

litigante *adj & nmf Jur* litigant

litigar [38] **1** *vt Jur* to litigate, go to law
  2 *vi (contender)* to argue, dispute

litigio *nm Jur* litigation, lawsuit; *Fig* dispute; **en l.** in dispute

litigioso, -a *adj Jur* litigious

litio *nm* lithium

litografía *nf* (a) *(técnica)* lithography (b) *(imagen)* lithograph

litografiar [32] *vt* to lithograph

litográfico, -a *adj* lithographic

litógrafo, -a *nm,f* lithographer

litoral 1 *adj* coastal
  2 *nm (costa)* coast, seaboard

litosfera *nf Geol* lithosphere

litro *nm (medida)* litre, *US* liter

Lituania *n* Lithuania

lituano, -a 1 *adj* Lithuanian
  2 *nm,f* Lithuanian
  3 *nm (idioma)* Lithuanian

liturgia *nf* liturgy

litúrgico, -a *adj* liturgical

liviandad *nf* (a) *(ligereza)* lightness (b) *(frivolidad)* unimportance, triviality

liviano, -a *adj* (a) *(de poco peso)* light (b) *(trivial)* trivial, fickle (c) *(lascivo)* lewd

lividecer [46] *vi* to become *o* go livid

lividez *nf* lividness, lividity

lívido, -a *adj* livid

living ['liβin] (*pl* **livings**) *nm* living room

liza *nf* (a) *(lucha)* contest, combat (b) *Hist* lists *pl*

LL, ll ['eʎe, 'eje] *nf (dígrafo)* = formerly fourteenth letter of the Spanish alphabet

llaga *nf Med (úlcera)* sore; *(lesión)* wound; *Fig* **poner el dedo en la l.** to touch a sore spot *o* point

llagar [38] *vt* bring out in sores

llama¹ *nf* (a) *(de fuego, pasión)* flame, blaze; **en llamas** in flames, ablaze (b) *Fig (pasión)* flame, ardour, *US* ardor

llama² *nf Zool* llama

llamada *nf* (a) *(gen)* call; *(telefónica)* (phone) call ❑ **l. de atención** warning; *Tel* **l. interurbana** long-distance call; *Tel* **l. teléfonica** telephone call (b) *Tip (en un escrito)* reference mark

llamado, -a 1 *pp de* **llamar**
  2 *adj* so-called; **el l. Viejo Continente** the so-called Old World
  3 *nm Am* call; *(telefónico)* (phone) call

llamador *nm* (a) *(aldaba)* door knocker (b) *(timbre)* bell

llamamiento *nm* appeal, call

llamar 1 *vt* (a) *(gen)* to call; **l. a algn a voces** to shout to sb; **l. al médico** to call the doctor; **si es niño le llamaremos Juan** if it's a boy we'll call him Juan (b) *(convocar)* to summon, call (c) *(atraer)* to draw, attract; **l. la atención** to attract attention; *Fam* **el dinero llama al dinero** like breeds like
  2 *vi* (a) *Tel (telefonear)* **l. (por teléfono)** to ring up, call; **mañana te llamo** I'll give you a ring tomorrow (b) *(a la puerta)* to knock; **l. a la puerta** to knock at the door; **llaman a la puerta** there's somebody at the door

3 llamarse *vpr* to be called; **¿cómo te llamas?** what's your name?; **me llamo Paco** my name is Paco; **¡eso (sí que) se llama comer!** now that's what I call eating!; *Fig* **l. a engaño** to claim one has been cheated

llamarada *nf* (a) *(llama)* flame, sudden blaze (b) *(del rostro)* sudden flush (c) *Fig (arrebato)* flare-up, outburst

llamativo, -a *adj* (a) *(color, ropa)* loud, gaudy, flashy (b) *(persona)* flashy, showy

llanero, -a *nm,f (hombre)* plainsman; *(mujer)* plains-woman

llaneza *nf (franqueza)* openness, frankness; *(sencillez)* simplicity

llanito, -a *adj & nm,f Esp Fam* Gibraltarian

llano, -a 1 *adj* (a) *(superficie)* flat, level, even (b) *(franco)* open, frank; *(amable)* friendly; *(claro)* clear, easy (c) *(corriente)* simple, common; **el pueblo l.** the common people
  2 *nm (terreno)* plain

llanote, -a *adj Fam* plain-spoken, straightforward

llanta *nf* (a) *Aut (aro metálico)* wheel rim (b) *Am (neumático) Br* tyre, *US* tire; **l. de** *Méx* **refacción** *o Col* **repuesto** spare tyre (c) *Méx Fam (pliegue de grasa)* spare *Br* tyre *o US* tire

llantén *nm Bot* plantain

llantera *nf*, **llantina** *nf Fam* fit of tears, sobbing

llanto *nm* tears *pl*, crying, weeping; **deshacerse en l.** to cry one's heart out

llanura *nf Geog* plain

llave *nf* (a) *(de puerta, cerradura)* key; **cerrar con l.** to lock; **echar la l.** to lock up; **guardar algo bajo l.** to keep sth under lock and key; **llaves en mano** *(piso)* available for immediate occupation ❑ *Aut* **l. de contacto** ignition key; **l. maestra** master key (b) *Téc* spanner, wrench ❑ **l. inglesa** monkey wrench (c) *(de agua, gas) Br* tap, *US* faucet ❑ **l. de paso** stopcock (d) *(de judo, lucha libre)* lock (e) *(de arma)* lock (f) *Tip* curly bracket

llavero *nm* key ring

llavín *nm* small key, latchkey

llegada *nf (gen)* arrival; *Dep* finish

llegar [38] **1** *vi* (a) *(persona, vehículo, medio de transporte)* to arrive, come, reach; **l. a casa** to arrive home; **l. a Madrid** to arrive in Madrid; **estar al l.** to be about to arrive (b) *(alcanzar)* to reach; **¿llegas al techo?** can you reach the ceiling?; **l. a los cincuenta** to reach fifty; **l. a un acuerdo** to reach an agreement; **su estupidez no llega a tanto** he's not that stupid; *Fig* **ella llegó a donde se proponía** she got where she wanted to be (c) *(ser bastante)* to be enough; **la sopa no llega para todos** there isn't enough soup for everyone (d) *(ascender, importar)* to be; **el importe total no llega a 5.000 pesos** the total cost is less than *o* below 5,000 pesos (e) *(locuciones)* **l. a la fama** to become famous; **l. a más** to better oneself; **l. al alma** to affect deeply; **l. al extremo de** to go as far as; **l. a oídos de algn** to hear; *Fig* **l. a las manos** to come to blows; *Fig* **l. lejos** to go far; *Fam* **¡hasta ahí podíamos l.!** that's the limit! (f) *Méx Fam* **voy a llegarle** *(ya me voy)* I'm off home; **¡llégale!** *(no hay problema)* no problem!, don't worry!
  2 *v aux* **l. a** + *infin)* **llegó a decir que ...** he even said that ...; **si llego a saberlo** if only I had known
  3 llegarse *vpr* to stop by, go *o* come round; **llégate al estanco y tráeme tabaco** go to the tobacconist's and get me some cigarettes

llenador, -a *adj CSur (comida)* filling

llenar 1 *vt* (a) *(gen)* to fill; *(formulario)* to fill in; *(superficie)* to cover; *(tiempo)* to fill, occupy; **l. una botella de agua** to fill a bottle with water; **llenaron la pared de cuadros** they covered the wall with pictures (b) *(satisfacer)* to satisfy, meet; **es un trabajo que no llena** it's a job that gives one no sense of fulfilment (**c**) *Fig (de regalos)* to shower (**de** with); *(de insultos)* to heap (**de** on)

2 *vi (comida)* to be filling

3 llenarse *vpr* to fill (up), become full; **las calles se llenan de turistas** the streets are filled with *o* full of tourists

llenito, -a *adj Fam* chubby, tubby

lleno, -a 1 *adj* full (up); **la botella está llena de agua** the bottle is full of water; **l. hasta los bordes** full to the brim; **tengo la agenda llena** I've got a busy day; *Fig* **de l.** entirely, fully; **nos afectó de l.** we were directly affected by it

2 *nm Teat* full house

llevadero, -a *adj* bearable, tolerable

llevar 1 *vt* (**a**) *(transportar)* to carry; **¿llevas dinero encima?** have you got any money on you?; **¿qué llevas en la mano?** what have you got in your hand? (**b**) *(prenda)* to wear; **¿qué llevaba puesto?** what was he wearing? (**c**) *(pelo)* to have; **l. el pelo largo** to have long hair (**d**) *(conducir)* to take, lead; **¿a dónde me llevas?** where are you taking me?; *Fig* **esto me llevó a pensar que ...** this led me to think that ... (**e**) *(soportar)* to bear, put up with; **¿cómo lleva lo de su enfermedad?** how's he bearing up? (**f**) *(pasar tiempo)* **¿cuánto tiempo lleva ahí?** how long has it been there?; **en lo que llevamos de año** so far this year (**g**) *(requerir tiempo)* to take; **me llevó dos horas encontrarte** it took me two hours to find you (**h**) *(encargarse de)* to run; **l. las cuentas** to keep the books; **l. un negocio** to run a business (**i**) *(exceder)* **te llevo tres años** I'm three years older than you; **l. ventaja a algn** to be ahead of sb, have the advantage over sb (**j**) *(tratar)* to treat, handle; **Felipe sabe l. a su tío** Felipe knows how to handle his uncle (**k**) *Mat* to carry over (**l**) *(paso, ritmo)* to keep, mark (**m**) *(locuciones)* **dejarse l. por algo/algn** to be influenced by sth/sb; **l. algo a cabo** *o* **a efecto** to carry sth out; **l. de cabeza** to be tied up with; **l. idea de** to want to; **l. algo a la práctica** to put sth into practice; **l. a (feliz) término** to bring to an (*o* a happy) end

2 *v aux* (**l.** + *participio*) to have + *past participle*; **llevaba escritas seis cartas** I had written six letters; **llevamos andado medio camino** we're half-way there

3 llevarse *vpr* (**a**) *(coger)* to take; *Fam* **l. por delante** to run over (**b**) *(recibir)* to get; **l. un susto** to get a shock; **l. una decepción** to be disappointed; **l. una sorpresa** to be surprised (**c**) *(conseguir)* to win, carry off; **l. la mejor/peor parte** to get the best/worst of it; **l. un premio** to win a prize (**d**) *(arrastrar)* to take away, remove; **la riada se llevó todos los coches** the flood swept away all the cars (**e**) *(estar de moda)* to be fashionable; **se llevan los tonos rojos** red is in fashion (**f**) *(entenderse)* to get on (**con** with); **l. bien con algn** to get on well with sb

llorar 1 *vi* (**a**) *(con lágrimas)* to cry, weep; **ponerse a l.** to start crying; *Fam* **l. a lágrima viva** *o* **a moco tendido** to cry one's heart out; *Prov* **quien bien te quiere te hará l.** you have to be cruel to be kind (**b**) *Fam* to groan, moan; *Vulg* **el que no llora no mama** he who doesn't ask doesn't get

2 *vt* to mourn; **l. la muerte de algn** to mourn sb's death; *Fig* **l. lágrimas de sangre** to regret doing sth

llorera *nf Fam* crying fit

lloriquear *vi* to whimper, snivel

lloriqueo *nm* whimpering, snivelling, *US* sniveling

lloro *nm* tears *pl*, weeping

llorón, -ona 1 *adj* tearful, weeping

2 *nm,f* crybaby

llorona *nf RP* big spur

lloroso, -a *adj* tearful, weeping

llovedera *nf Am* continous rain

llover [41] *v impers* to rain; **¿llueve?** is it raining?; **llueve a cántaros** *o Méx* **duro** it's pouring (down); *Fig* **como llovido**

del cielo out of the blue; **aquel dinero me vino como llovido del cielo** that money was a godsend; *Fig* **ha llovido mucho desde entonces** a lot of water has passed under the bridge since then; *Fam Fig* **llueve sobre mojado** it never rains but it pours

llovizna *nf* drizzle

llovizna *v impers* to drizzle

lloviznoso, -a *adj Am* rainy, wet

lluvia *nf* (**a**) *(precipitación)* rain ❏ **l. ácida** acid rain; **l. de estrellas** shower of shooting stars (**b**) *(de regalos, insultos)* shower; *(de quejas)* string; **recibió una l. de preguntas** he was bombarded with questions (**c**) *CAm CSur (ducha)* shower

lluvioso, -a *adj* rainy; *(clima)* wet

lo[1] *art def neut* the; **lo curioso (del caso) es que ...** the funny thing (about it) is that ...; **lo mejor** the best (part); **lo peor** the worst (part)

lo[2] *pron pers m & neut* (**a**) *(objeto directo)* him; *(usted)* you; *(cosa)* it; **debes hacerlo** you must do it; **lo mataron** they killed him; **¡míralo!** look at it!; **no lo creo** I don't think so; **ya lo sabía** I knew it; *véase tamb* **le** (**b**) **lo que ...** what ...; **lo que pasa** what happens (**c**) **lo cual ...** which ...; **lo cual no se entiende** which doesn't make any sense (**d**) **lo de ...** the affair *o* business of ...; **cuéntame lo del juicio** tell me about the trial (**e**) **lo mío** mine; **lo tuyo** yours; *véase* **loísmo** (**f**) *RP (lugar)* **vamos a lo de Claudio** let's go to Claudio's place

loa *nf* (**a**) *(alabanza)* praise (**b**) *Lit* eulogy

loable *adj* praiseworthy, laudable

loar *vt* to praise

loba *nf Zool* she-wolf; *Fig* whore

lobanillo *nm Med* cyst, wen

lobato *nm Zool* wolf cub

lobbista *nmf RP* lobbyist

lobby ['loβi] (*pl* **lobbies**) *nm* lobby

lobero, -a 1 *adj* wolfish, wolf

2 *nm* wolf hunter

lobezno *nm Zool* wolf cub

lobo *nm Zool* wolf; **como boca de l.** pitch-dark; *Fig* **meterse en la boca del l.** to put one's head in the lion's mouth; *Fam* **el l. feroz** the big bad wolf; *Fam* **¡menos lobos!** that's a tall story! ❏ **l. de mar** *(marinero)* sea dog; *Zool* **l. marino** seal

lóbrego, -a *adj* gloomy, murky

lobreguez *nf* gloom, gloominess, murk

lobular *adj* lobular

lóbulo *nm* lobe

lobuno, -a *adj* wolfish, wolflike, wolf

locación *nf Méx* location

local 1 *adj* local

2 *nm (establecimiento)* premises *pl*, site ❏ **l. comercial** business premises

localidad *nf* (**a**) *(pueblo)* village, town (**b**) *Cin Teat (lugar)* seat; *(billete)* ticket; **reserva de localidades** (advance) booking

localista *adj* regional, local

localización *nf* location, placing, siting

localizador, -a *nm* (**a**) *Inform (de página Web)* URL (**b**) *Méx (buscapersonas)* pager

localizar [14] *vt* (**a**) *(encontrar)* to locate, find, site (**b**) *(fuego, dolor)* to localize

locatario, -a *nm,f* tenant, occupant

locatis *nmf Fam* nutter, crackpot

locativo *nm Ling* locative

loc. cit. (*abrev de* **loco citato**) loc. cit., l.c.

loción *nf* lotion; **l. capilar** hair restorer *o* lotion

loco, -a 1 *adj* mad, crazy; **a lo l.** carelessly, wildly; **l. de amor** madly in love; **l. por los coches** crazy about cars; **volverse l.** to go mad; *Fam* **l. de remate** mad as a hatter; *Fam* **¡ni l.!** I'd sooner die!; *Fam* **traer l. a algn** to drive sb crazy
2 *nm,f (hombre)* madman; *(mujer)* madwoman; **como (un) l.** like crazy; **hacer el l.** to act the fool
3 *nf Argot (afeminado)* queen

locomoción *nf* locomotion

locomotor, -a *adj* locomotive

locomotora *nf* railway engine, locomotive

locomotriz 1 *adj* locomotive
2 *nf* railway engine

locuacidad *nf* loquacity, talkativeness

locuaz *adj* loquacious, talkative

locución *nf* phrase, locution

locuelo, -a *adj Fam* madcap, nutty

locura *nf* **(a)** *(enfermedad)* madness, insanity; **con l.** madly; **¡qué l.!** it's madness! **(b)** *(disparate)* lunacy, act of folly, crazy thing; **cometer** *o* **hacer una l.** to do something foolish

locutor, -a *nm,f Rad* announcer, commentator; *TV* newsreader

locutorio *nm Rel* parlour, *US* parlor; *Rad* studio; *Tel* telephone booth; *(sala de visitas)* visiting room

lodazal *nm* muddy place, mire

lodo *nm* mud; *Fig* **cubrir de l. a algn** to drag sb's name through the mud

lodoso, -a *adj* muddy

logarítmico, -a *adj* logarithmic

logaritmo *nm* logarithm

logia *nf* **(a)** *Arquit* loggia **(b)** *(masónica)* lodge

lógica *nf* logic; **no tiene l.** there's no logic to it

lógicamente *adv* logically

lógico, -a 1 *adj* logical; **era l. que ella se enfadara** it stands to reason that she'd get angry
2 *nm,f* logician

logística *nf* logistics *sing o pl*

logístico, -a *adj* logistic

logopeda *nmf* speech therapist

logopedia *nf* speech therapy, logopaedics *sing*, *US* logopedics *sing*

logotipo *nm* logotype

logrado, -a 1 *pp de* **lograr**
2 *adj* successful

lograr 1 *vt (gen)* to get, obtain; *(premio)* to win; *(ambición)* to achieve; *(deseo)* to fulfil, *US* fulfill; *(hacer algo)* to succeed; **logré que se quedara** I managed to persuade her to stay
2 lograrse *vpr* to succeed, make it, do well

logrero, -a *nm,f* **(a)** *(usurero)* moneylender **(b)** *Am (gorrón)* scrounger

logro *nm* **(a)** *(consecución)* achievement, accomplishment; *(éxito)* success **(b)** *(lucro)* profit **(c)** *(usura)* usury

logroñés, -esa 1 *adj* of o from Logroño
2 *nm,f* person from Logroño

loísmo *nm Ling* = incorrect use of **lo** or **los** as an indirect object instead of **le** or **les**

loma *nf Geog* hill, hillock, rise

lombardo, -a *adj & nm,f* Lombard; **col lombarda** red cabbage

lombriz *nf* worm, earthworm; **l. intestinal** (intestinal) worm

Lomé *n* Lomé

lomo *nm* **(a)** *Anat* back **(b)** *Culin* loin; **a lomo(s)** on the back; **l. (de cerdo)** pork loin; *Fig* **doblar el l.** to toil **(c)** *(de libro)* spine

lona *nf* **(a)** *Tex* canvas **(b)** *Box* canvas

loncha *nf (de queso, jamón)* slice; *(de panceta)* rasher

lonche *nm* **(a)** *Am (comida fría)* (packed) lunch **(b)** *Méx (torta)* filled roll **(c)** *Perú Ven (merienda) (en escuela)* = snack eaten during break-time; *(en casa)* (afternoon) tea

lonchería *nf Am* snack bar

londinense 1 *adj* of o from London
2 *nmf* Londoner

Londres *n* London

longanimidad *nf Fml* forbearance

longaniza *nf Culin* spicy (pork) sausage

longevidad *nf* longevity

longevo, -a *adj* long lived

longitud *nf* **(a)** *(dimensión)* length; **dos metros de l.** two metres long ❑ *Rad* **l. de onda** wavelength **(b)** *Geog* longitude

longitudinal *adj* longitudinal

longitudinalmente *adv* lengthways

longui(s) *nm Esp* **hacerse el l.** to act dumb, keep one's trap shut

lonja¹ *nf (de queso, jamón)* slice; *(de panceta)* rasher

lonja² *nf* **(a)** *(edificio)* exchange; *Esp* **l. de pescado** fish market **(b)** *RP (tira)* thong, strap

lontananza *nf Arte* background; **en l.** in the distance

look [luk] *(pl* **looks***) nm Fam* style

loquera *nf Am Fam* madness

lwᵒquero, -a *nm,f Fam* **los loqueros** the men in white coats.

lord *(pl* **lores***) nm* lord; *Br Parl* **Cámara de los Lores** House of Lords

loro *nm* **(a)** *Orn* parrot; **hablar como un l.** to chatter **(b)** *Fam (charlatán)* chatterbox **(c)** *Esp Fam (aparato de música)* sounds, = radio and/or cassette or CD player **(d)** *Esp Fam* **estar al l.** *(alerta)* to keep one's ears o eyes open; *(enterado)* to be well up (on what's happening); **¡al l.!** get a load of this! **(e)** *Chile Fam (espía)* spy **(f)** *Chile Fam (orinal)* bedpan

los¹ *art def mpl* the; **l. libros** the books; **cierra l. ojos** close your eyes; **esos son l. míos/tuyos** these are mine/yours; **l. García** the Garcías; *véase tamb* **el, las¹** *y* **lo¹**

los² *pron pers mpl* **(a)** *(objeto directo) (ellos)* them; *(ustedes)* you; **¿l. has visto?** have you seen them?; **mañana nos l. comeremos** we will eat them tomorrow; **quiero que l. conozcas** I want you to meet them **(b)** **l.** *(personas)* the ones who, those who; *(objetos)* the ones that, those that; **toma l. que quieras** take whichever ones you want; *véase tamb* **les** *y* **loísmo**

losa *nf* (stone) slab, flag, flagstone; **l. sepulcral** tombstone; *Fam* **estar bajo la l.** to be six feet under

loseta *nf* floor tile, wall tile

lota *nf (pez)* burbot

lote *nm* **(a)** *(porción)* share, portion **(b)** *Com* lot ❑ **l. de Navidad** Christmas box o hamper **(c)** *Inform* batch **(d)** *Esp Fam* **darse** *o* **pegarse el l. (con)** to neck (with), *Br* snog (with)

lotería *nf* lottery; **jugar a la l.** to play the lottery; **tocarle la l. a algn** to win a prize in the lottery; *Fig* **ser una l.** to be a matter of luck, be a complete lottery

lotero, -a *nm,f* lottery-ticket seller

loto *nf Bot* lotus

loza *nf* (**a**) *(cerámica)* pottery (**b**) *(de cocina)* crockery (**c**) *Ven (azulejo)* (glazed) tile

lozanía *nf* (**a**) *(de plantas)* lushness, luxuriance; *(de flores)* freshness (**b**) *(de personas)* vigour, *US* vigor, robustness, liveliness

lozano, -a *adj* (**a**) *(vegetales)* lush, fresh, luxuriant (**b**) *(persona)* robust, lively

LSD *nm* LSD

Luanda *n* Luanda

lubina *nf (pez)* bass

lubricación *nf* lubrication

lubricante 1 *adj* lubricating
  2 *nm* lubricant

lubricar [59] *vt* to lubricate

lubricidad *nf* (**a**) *(deslizamiento)* slipperiness (**b**) *Fig (lujuria)* lewdness

lúbrico, -a *adj* (**a**) *(resbaladizo)* slippery (**b**) *Fig (lujurioso)* lewd

lubrificación *nm* lubrication

lubrificante *adj & nm véase* **lubricante**

lubrificar [59] *vt* to lubricate

lucense 1 *adj* of o from Lugo
  2 *nmf* person from Lugo

lucero *nm* (**a**) *Astron* (bright) star; **l. del alba/de la tarde** morning/evening star (**b**) *(de un animal)* star

lucha *nf* (**a**) *(combate)* fight, struggle ❑ *Pol* **l. de clases** class struggle (**b**) *Dep* wrestling ❑ **l. libre** free-style wrestling

luchador, -a 1 *adj* fighting, battling
  2 *nm,f* (**a**) *(combatiente)* fighter (**b**) *Dep* wrestler

luchar *vi* (**a**) *(combatir)* to fight, struggle; **luchad por la paz** fight for peace (**b**) *Dep* to wrestle

lucidez *nf* lucidity

lucido, -a 1 *pp de* lucir
  2 *adj* brilliant, splendid; *Irón* **estar l.** to be in a fine mess

lúcido, -a *adj* lucid, clear

luciente *adj* shining

luciérnaga *nf Ent* glowworm

Lucifer *nm* Lucifer

lucimiento *nm* brilliance; **con l.** brilliantly

lucio *nm (pez)* pike

lucir [39] **1** *vt* (**a**) *(iluminar)* to illuminate, light up (**b**) *(exhibir)* to show off; *(cualidades, talento)* to display; *(ropas)* to sport; **ella lucía un modelito carísimo** she was wearing a very expensive number
  2 *vi* (**a**) *(brillar)* to shine; *Fig* **así le luce el pelo** it serves him right (**b**) *(aprovechar)* to profit from (**c**) *Am (parecer)* to seem
  3 lucirse *vpr* (**a**) *(hacer buen papel)* to do very well; *Irón (hacer mal papel)* to look a real fool (**b**) *Fam (vestirse bien)* to dress up (**c**) *(presumir)* to show off

lucrar 1 *vt* to gain
  2 lucrarse *vpr* to (make a) profit

lucrativo, -a *adj* lucrative, profitable

lucro *nm* profit, gain; **afán de l.** greed for money

luctuoso, -a *adj* sad, mournful; **un accidente l.** a tragic accident

lucubración *nf* lucubration

lucubrar *vt* to lucubrate

lúcumo *nm Am Bot* canistel

lúdico, -a *adj* **espacios lúdicos** play areas; **actividades lúdicas** leisure activities; **fomentar el espíritu l. en los niños** to encourage children to play

ludópata *nmf* = pathological gambling addict

ludopatía *nf* = pathological addiction to gambling

ludoteca *nf* toy library

luego 1 *adv* (**a**) *(después)* then, next, afterwards; **se quitó el sombrero, l. la chaqueta** he took off his hat and then his jacket (**b**) *(más tarde)* later (on); **déjalo para l.** leave it for later; **¡hasta l.!** so long!; **te veré l.** I'll see you later (**c**) **desde l.** of course (**d**) *Méx (algunas veces)* sometimes (**e**) *Chile Méx Ven (pronto)* soon
  2 *conj* therefore; **pienso, l. existo** I think therefore I am

lueguito *adv Am* immediately, at once

lugar *nm* (**a**) *(sitio)* place, spot; **en l. de** instead of; **en primer l.** in the first place, firstly, first of all; **en tu l.** if I were you; **sin l. a dudas** no room for doubt; **tener l.** to take place; *Fig* **fuera de l.** out of place; *Fig* **l. común** commonplace, platitude (**b**) **dar l. a** to cause, give rise to

lugareño, -a 1 *adj* rural, village
  2 *nm,f* villager; *(hombre)* countryman; *(mujer)* countrywoman

lugarteniente *nmf* lieutenant, deputy

lúgubre *adj* gloomy, dismal, lugubrious

Luisiana *n* Louisiana

lujo *nm* luxury; **impuesto de l.** luxury tax; **no puedo permitirme ese l.** I just can't afford that

lujosamente *adv* luxuriously

lujoso, -a *adj* luxurious

lujuria *nf* (**a**) *(lascivia)* lechery, lust (**b**) *(exceso)* profusion, exuberance

lujurioso, -a 1 *adj* lecherous, lustful
  2 *nm* lecher

lumbago *nm Med* lumbago

lumbar *adj Anat* lumbar

lumbre *nf* (**a**) *(fuego)* fire (**b**) *(resplandor)* brightness, glow (**c**) *Arquit* light, skylight

lumbrera *nf* luminary; *Fig* luminary, eminence

luminaria *nf* light, illumination

luminiscencia *nf* luminiscence

luminiscente *adj* luminiscent

luminosidad *nf* brightness, luminosity

luminoso, -a *adj* luminous; *Fig* bright

lumpen *nm* lumpenproletariat

luna *nf* (**a**) *Astron* moon; *Fig* **estar en la l.** to be woolgathering; *Fig* **quedarse a la l. de Valencia** to be left in the lurch; *Fig* **vivir en la l.** to have one's head in the clouds ❑ **claro de l.** moonlight; **l. creciente** crescent o waxing moon; *Fig* **l. de miel** honeymoon; **l. llena** full moon; **l. menguante** waning moon; **l. nueva** new moon; **media l.** half moon, crescent (**b**) *(vidrio)* window pane; *(espejo)* mirror (**c**) *Fam (talante)* mood; **tener lunas** to be potty

lunación *nf Astron* lunar month

lunar 1 *adj Astron* lunar
  2 *nm* (**a**) *(redondel)* spot; *(en la piel)* mole, beauty spot; **vestido de lunares** spotted dress (**b**) *Fig (defecto)* flaw, blemish

lunático, -a 1 *adj* lunatic
  2 *nm,f* lunatic

lunes *nm inv* Monday; **vendré el l.** I'll come on Monday; *véase tamb* **viernes**

luneta *nf (de vehículo) Br* windscreen, *US* windshield

lunfa *nm*, **lunfardo** *nm Ling* Buenos Aires slang

lupa *nf* magnifying glass

lupanar *nm Fml* brothel
lúpulo *nm Bot* hop, hops *pl*
Lusaka *n* Lusaka
lusitano, -a *adj & nm,f,* **luso, -a** *adj & nm,f* **(a)** *Hist* Lusitanian **(b)** *(portugués)* Portuguese
lustramuebles *nm inv CSur* furniture polish
lustrar *vt* to polish; *(zapatos)* to shine
lustre *nm (brillo)* shine, polish, lustre, *US* luster; *Fig (esplendor)* splendour, *US* splendor, glory; **dar** *o* **sacar l. a algo** to polish sth
lustro *nm* five-year period
lustroso, -a *adj* shiny, glossy
luteranismo *nm Rel* Lutheranism
luterano, -a *adj & nm,f Rel* Lutheran
luto *nm* **(a)** *(vestido)* mourning; **ir de** *o* **llevar l.** to be in mourning **(b)** *Fig* sorrow, grief
luxación *nf Med* dislocation, luxation
Luxemburgo *n* Luxembourg
luxemburgués, -esa 1 *adj* of/from Luxembourg

2 *nm,f* Luxembourger
luz *nf* **(a)** *(gen)* light; **a la l. del día** in broad daylight; **l. del sol/de la luna** sunlight/moonlight; *Fig* **a la l. de** in the light of; *Fig* **a todas luces** obviously; *Fig* **dar a l.** *(parir)* to give birth to; *Fig* **dar l. verde** to give the green light to; *Fig* **sacar a la l.** *(publicar)* to publish; *(revelar)* to bring to light; *Fig* **salir a la l.** *(publicarse)* to come out; *(descubrirse)* to come to light; *Fam Fig* **entre dos luces** tipsy **(b)** *Fam (electricidad)* electricity; **se ha ido la l.** the lights have gone out **(c)** *Arquit (abertura)* opening, window; *(de un puente)* span **(d)** *(lámpara, vela)* light, lamp; *Aut* light ❑ **luces cortas** *o* **de cruce** *Br* dipped headlights, *US* low beams; **luces de posición** sidelights; **luces largas: poner las luces largas** to put one's headlights on *Br* full *o US* high beam **(e)** *Argot* money **(f)** **luces** *(cultura)* culture *sing*; *(inteligencia)* intelligence *sing*; **corto de l.** dim-witted; **el Siglo de las L.** the Age of Enlightenment **(g)** **traje de luces** *Taur* bullfighter's costume
Luzbel *nm* Lucifer, Satan
luzco *indic pres véase* **lucir**
lycra® *nf* Lycra®

M

M, m ['eme] *nf (la letra)* M, m

m (**a**) *(abrev de* **metro(s)**) m (**b**) *(abrev de* **minuto(s)**) min (**c**) *(abrev de* **milla(s)**) mile, miles

m/ *(abrev de* **mi**) my

maca *nf* (**a**) *(defecto)* flaw, blemish (**b**) *(de una fruta)* bruise

macabro, -a *adj* macabre

macaco, -a¹ *adj Chile Cuba Méx Fam* ugly, misshapen

macaco, -a² *nm,f* (**a**) *Zool (mono)* macaque (**b**) *Fam (niño)* kid; *(insulto)* brat

macadam *(pl* **macadams**) *nm,* **macadán** *(pl* **macadanes**) *nm* macadam

macana *nf* (**a**) *Andes Carib Méx (garrote)* wooden *Br* truncheon *o US* billy club (**b**) *Fam CSur Perú Ven (disparate)* stupid thing (**c**) *Fam Andes RP Ven (fastidio)* pain, drag; *(pena)* shame; **¡qué m., acaba de empezar a llover!** what a pain *o* drag, it's just started raining!

macanazo *nm Am* (**a**) *(golpe)* blow (with a club) (**b**) *Fam (disparate)* nonsense, absurdity (**c**) *Fam (fastidio)* nuisance, bore

macanear *Fam* **1** *vt CSur Ven (hacer mal)* to botch, do badly
2 *vi CSur (decir tonterías)* to talk nonsense; *(hacer tonterías)* to be stupid

macanudo, -a *adj* (**a**) *Andes RP (bueno)* great, terrific (**b**) *Andes Ven (grande, fuerte)* **es un tipo m.** he's a great hulk of a man

macaquear **1** *vt CAm (robar)* to steal
2 *vi Arg* to grimace, make faces

macarra *Argot* **1** *adj* loutish, *Br* yobbish
2 *nm* pimp

macarrón *nm* (**a**) *Culin* macaroon (**b**) *Náut* stanchion

macarrones *nmpl Culin* macaroni *sing;* **m. al gratén** macaroni cheese

macarrónico, -a *adj (lenguaje, estilo)* macaronic; **latín m.** pig Latin

macarse [59] *vpr (fruta)* to (start to) go bad

Macedonia *n* Macedonia

macedonia *nf Culin* fruit salad

macedonio, -a *adj & nm,f* Macedonian

maceración *nf* maceration

macerar *vt* to macerate

macero *nm* mace bearer

maceta¹ *nf* (**a**) *(tiesto)* plant pot, flowerpot (**b**) *Méx Fam (cabeza)* head (**c**) *Chile (ramo)* bouquet

maceta² **1** *nf* (**a**) *(martillo)* mallet (**b**) *Chile (ramo)* bouquet
2 *adj Am* (**a**) *(caballo)* useless, slow (**b**) *(persona)* slow-walking

macetero *nm* flowerpot stand *o* holder

machaca *nmf Esp Fam* dogsbody

machacar [59] **1** *vt* (**a**) *(triturar, aplastar)* to crush; *(moler)* to grind, crush (**b**) *Mil (derrotar)* to crush, destroy; *Fig (en una discusión)* to crush, flatten (**c**) *Fam (insistir mucho en)* to harp on about, go on about; **no machaques tanto el asunto** stop going on about it (**d**) *Esp Fam (estudiar con ahinco)* to swot up on, *US* grind away at
2 *vi* (**a**) *Esp Fam (insistir mucho)* to harp on, go on; *Fig* **machacando se aprende el oficio** practice makes perfect; *Fig* **m. en hierro frío** to bang one's head against a brick wall (**b**) *Fam (estudiar con ahinco)* to swot, cram, *US* grind (**c**) *Vulg* **machacársela** *(masturbarse)* to wank, beat one's meat

machacón, -ona *Fam* **1** *adj (repetitivo)* repetitious; *(pesado)* boring, tiresome
2 *nm,f* (**a**) *(pesado)* bore, nuisance (**b**) *(muy estudioso)* swot, *US* grind

machaconería *nf Fam (insistencia)* tiresome insistence

machada *nf Fam* (**a**) *(fanfarronada)* piece of bravado, showing off; **hacer una m.** to show off (**b**) *(necedad)* stupid thing

machamartillo: a machamartillo *loc adv (con firmeza)* firmly; *(con obstinación)* obstinately; **católico a m.** Catholic through and through

machar **1** *vt (machacar)* to grind, crush
2 **macharse** *vpr SAm* to get drunk

machete *nm* machete

machetero, -a *nm,f* (**a**) *(que desbroza)* path clearer (**b**) *Agr* (sugar) cane cutter (**c**) *Méx Anticuado (trabajador)* worker (**d**) *Méx Fam (empollón)* swot

machihembrado *nm Carp (ranura y lengüeta)* tongue and groove *(joint);* *(caja y espiga)* mortise and tenon *(joint)*

machismo *nm* machismo, male chauvinism

machista *adj & nmf* macho, male chauvinist

macho **1** *adj* (**a**) *(animal, planta)* male; **una girafa m.** a male giraffe (**b**) *Téc (pieza)* male (**c**) *(viril)* manly, virile, macho (**d**) *(fuerte)* strong, robust; **vino m.** strong wine
2 *nm* (**a**) *(animal, planta)* male ◻ *Zool* **m. cabrío** he-goat, billy goat (**b**) *Zool (mulo)* he-mule (**c**) *Téc (pieza)* male piece *o* part; *(de enchufe)* plug ◻ **m. de aterrajar** *o* **de roscar** screw tap (**d**) *Cost (de corchete)* hook (**e**) *Fam (hombre viril)* macho, he-man, tough guy; **¿qué te pasa, m.?** what's up with you, man?

machón **1** *nm Arquit* buttress
2 *adj RP (mujer)* mannish

machote¹ *nm CAm Méx (borrador)* rough draft; *(modelo)* example, model

machote² **1** *adj* manly, virile, macho
2 *nm* macho, he-man, tough guy

machucar [59] *vt (aplastar)* to crush

maciega *nf* (**a**) *Am (mala hierba)* weed (**b**) *Arg* grassland, prairie

macilento, -a *adj (flaco)* gaunt, emaciated; *(pálido)* wan, pale; *(triste)* sad

macizo, -a 1 *adj* (**a**) *(sólido)* solid; **de latón m.** of solid brass (**b**) *(persona)* solid, robust; *Fam (atractivo)* smashing

2 *nm* (**a**) *(masa sólida)* mass ❑ *Geog* **m. montañoso** *o* **de montañas** mountain mass, massif (**b**) *(de flores)* bed; *(de árboles)* clump (**c**) *Arquit (de edificios)* group; *(de una pared)* stretch

macramé *nm* macramé

macro *nf Inform* macro

macro- *pref* macro-; **macroeconomía** macroeconomics *sing*

macrobiótica *nf* macrobiotics *sing*

macrobiótico, -a *adj* macrobiotic

macrocosmo *nm* macrocosm

macroeconomía *nf* macroeconomics

macroencuesta *nf* large-scale opinion poll

macrofestival *nm* = large open-air music festival

macroproceso *nm* super-trial *(of important case with many defendants)*

macroscópico, -a *adj* macroscopic

macuco, -a *Chile Fam adj (astuto)* crafty, cunning, sly

mácula *nf* (**a**) *(mancha)* stain, spot (**b**) *(defecto)* flaw, blemish; **sin m.** flawless

macuto *nm* knapsack, haversack

Madagascar *n* Madagascar

madama *nf* (**a**) *Fml* madam (**b**) *SAm Vulg (partera)* midwife

madeira *nm (vino)* Madeira (wine)

madeja *nf (de lana etc)* hank, skein; *Fig* **enredarse la m.** to get complicated

madera *nf* (**a**) *(gen)* wood; *(de construcción)* timber, *US* lumber; **de m.** wood, wooden; *Fam* **¡toca m.!** touch wood!, *US* knock on wood! ❑ **m. contrachapada** plywood; **m. dura** hardwood; **m. fósil** lignite (**b**) *Zool (del casco de las caballerías)* horn, rind (**c**) *Golf* wood (**d**) *Fig (disposición natural)* **tener buena m.** to have what it takes; **tiene m. de músico** he has the makings of a musician (**e**) *Esp muy Fam* **la m.** *(policía)* the pigs

maderable *adj (árbol, bosque)* timber-yielding

maderaje *nm,* **maderamen** *nm* (**a**) *(madera)* timber, wood (**b**) *(conjunto de vigas etc)* timberwork, timbering, woodwork

maderería *nf* timberyard, *US* lumberyard

maderero, -a 1 *adj* timber, *US* lumber; **la industria maderera** the timber industry

2 *nm,f* timber *o US* lumber merchant

madero *nm* (**a**) *(de construcción)* log, piece of timber (**b**) *Esp Argot (policía)* cop; **los maderos** the fuzz *pl*

madona *nf Arte Rel* Madonna

madrás *nm Tex* madras

madrastra *nf* stepmother

madraza *nf* doting mother

madre 1 *nf* (**a**) *(mujer, hembra)* mother; **es m. de tres hijos** she is a mother of three (children); **futura m.** expectant mother, mother-to-be; **va a ser m.** she's going to have a baby; **el día de la M.** Mother's Day; *Fam Fig* **como su m. lo parió** in one's birthday suit, stark naked; *Fam* **éramos ciento y la m.** there were hundreds of us; *Fam* **mentar la m. de algn** to swear at sb; *Vulg Ofens* **la m. que te parió** you bastard!; *Vulg Ofens* **¡tu m.!** up yours! ❑ **m. adoptiva** adoptive mother; **m. biológica** natural mother; **m. de alquiler** surrogate mother; **m. de familia** mother, housewife; **la m. patria** one's motherland; **m. política** mother-in-law; **m. soltera** single mother (**b**) *Rel* mother ❑ **m. superiora** mother superior (**c**) *(de río)* bed; **salirse de m.** *(río)* to burst its banks, overflow; *Fig (persona) (excederse)* to go over the top, go too far; *Fig* **sacar de m. a algn** to make sb lose their patience (**d**) *Fig (origen, raíz)* mother, origin, cradle; *Fig* **ahí está la m. del cordero** *(causa)* there's the real reason; *(dificultad)* there's the rub; *Prov* **el ocio es la m. del vicio** the Devil finds work for idle hands to do (**e**) *(del café)* grounds *pl*, dregs *pl* (**f**) *(acequia)* main channel

2 *interj* **¡m. de Dios!, ¡m. mía!** good heavens!

madrear *vt Méx Fam* (**a**) *(golpear)* **m. a algn** to knock the hell out of sb (**b**) *(estropear)* to bust, jigger

madreperla *nf* (**a**) *(ostra)* pearl oyster (**b**) *(nácar)* mother-of-pearl

madrépora *nf Zool* white coral, madrepore

madreselva *nf Bot* honeysuckle

Madrid *n* Madrid

madrigal *nm Lit Mús* madrigal

madriguera *nf* (**a**) *(de conejo)* burrow, hole; *(de zorro)* den, lair; *(de tejón)* set (**b**) *Fig (de maleantes)* den, hideout

madrileño, -a 1 *adj* of *o* from Madrid, Madrilenian

2 *nm,f* person from Madrid, Madrilenian

madrina *nf* (**a**) *(de bautizo)* godmother (**b**) *(de boda)* ≃ bridesmaid (**c**) *(protectora)* protectress

madroñal *nm* grove of strawberry trees *o* arbutus

madroño *nm Bot* strawberry tree

madrugada *nf* (**a**) *(amanecer)* dawn; **de m.** at daybreak (**b**) *(noche)* early morning; (**a**) **las tres de la m.** (at) three o'clock in the morning

madrugador, -a 1 *adj* early rising

2 *nm,f* early riser

madrugar [38] *vi* (**a**) *(levantarse pronto)* to get up early; *Prov* **no por mucho m. amanece más temprano** time must take its course (**b**) *Fam Fig (adelantarse)* to get there first

madrugón *nm Fam* **darse** *o* **pegarse un m.** to get up unusually early, get up very early

maduración *nf (de fruta, verdura)* ripening; *(de queso, vino)* maturing

madurar 1 *vt* (**a**) *(vino, queso, persona)* to mature; *(fruta)* to ripen (**b**) *Fig (un plan)* to think out

2 *vi* (**a**) *(persona)* to mature (**b**) *(fruta)* to ripen

madurativo, -a *adj* (**a**) *(que hace madurar)* maturing (**b**) *(fruta)* ripening

madurez *nf* (**a**) *(sensatez, juicio)* maturity (**b**) *(de la fruta)* ripeness

maduro, -a *adj* (**a**) *(persona)* mature; **de edad madura** middle-aged (**b**) *(fruta)* ripe

maestranza *nf Mil* (**a**) *(lugar)* arsenal (**b**) *(personal)* staff of an arsenal

maestrazgo *nm Hist* (**a**) *(dignidad)* = office of the grand master of a military order (**b**) *(jurisdicción)* = territory under a grand master's jurisdiction

maestre *nm (de una orden militar)* master

maestría *nf* (**a**) *(habilidad)* mastery, skill (**b**) *Am* master's degree

maestro, -a 1 *adj* (**a**) *(excelente)* excellent; **llave maestra** master key; **obra maestra** masterpiece (**b**) *(principal)* main ❑ **pared maestra** load-bearing wall

2 *nm,f* (**a**) *Educ* teacher ❑ **m. de escuela** schoolteacher (**b**) *(especialista)* master; **es un m. de la escultura** he is a master of sculpture ❏ **m. de ceremonias** master of ceremonies; **m. de obras** foreman (**c**) *Mús* maestro (**d**) *Taur* matador

mafia *nf* mafia

mafioso, -a 1 *adj* of *o* relating to the mafia
  2 *nm,f* member of the mafia, mafioso

maganzón, -ona *Col CRica Fam* **1** *adj (holgazán)* lazy
  2 *nm,f* lazy person

Magdalena *nf* Magdalene; **estar hecho** *o* **llorar como una M.** to cry one's eyes out

magdalena *nf Culin* bun, cake

magenta *adj inv & nm* magenta

magia *nf* magic; **por arte de m.** as if by magic

magiar *adj & nmf* Magyar

mágico, -a *adj* (**a**) *(de la magia)* magic, magical (**b**) *Fig (maravilloso)* wonderful, fascinating

magín *nm Fam* imagination; **ni se me pasó por el m.** it didn't even cross my mind, it never entered my head

magisterio *nm* teaching

magistrado, -a *nm,f* judge

magistral *adj* (**a**) *Educ* of *o* relating to teaching (**b**) *(excelente)* masterly; **un tono m.** a magisterial tone; **una jugada m.** a master stroke

magistratura *nf* magistracy; *Esp* **la M. de Trabajo** ≃ industrial tribunal

magma *nm Geol* magma

magnanimidad *nf* magnanimity

magnánimo, -a *adj* magnanimous

magnate *nm* magnate, tycoon; **un m. de la prensa** a press baron

magnesia *nf* magnesia

magnésico, -a *adj* magnesic

magnesio *nm Quím* magnesium

magnético, -a *adj* magnetic

magnetismo *nm* magnetism

magnetizar [14] *vt* (**a**) *(imantar)* to magnetize (**b**) *(hipnotizar)* to hypnotize

magneto *nm* magneto

magnetofón *nm nm* tape recorder

magnetofónico, -a *adj* magnetic

magnetófono *nm véase* **magnetofón**

magnetoscopio *nm* video recorder

magnicida *nmf* assassin

magnicidio *nm* assassination

magnificar [59] *vt* (**a**) *(ensalzar)* to praise, extol (**b**) *Fig* to magnify

magnificencia *nf* magnificence

magnífico, -a *adj* magnificent, splendid

magnitud *nf* magnitude, dimension; **de primera m.** of the first order

magno, -a *adj Literario* great ❏ **aula magna** main amphitheatre; **Carta Magna** Magna Carta

magnolia *nf Bot* magnolia

mago, -a *nm,f* wizard, magician ❏ **los tres Reyes Magos** the Three Wise Men, the Three Kings

magrear *vt Esp Vulg* to grope

Magreb *nm* **el M.** the Maghreb, = Morocco, Algeria and Tunisia

magrebí *adj & nmf* Maghrebi

magreo *Esp nm Vulg* **se estaban metiendo un buen m.** *Br* they were having a good grope, *US* they were making out in a big way

magro, -a 1 *adj* (**a**) *(sin grasa)* lean (**b**) *(pobre)* meagre, *US* meager
  2 *nm Esp (de cerdo)* lean meat

maguey *nm Bot* maguey

magulladura *nf* bruise, contusion

magullar 1 *vt* to bruise, damage
  2 magullarse *vpr* to get bruised, get damaged

maharajá [maraˈxa] *nm* maharajah

Mahoma *n* Mohammed

mahometano, -a *adj & nm,f Rel* Muslim

mahonesa *nf véase* **mayonesa**

maicena *nf Br* cornflour, *US* cornstarch

mail [ˈmail, ˈmeil] *(pl* **mails**) *nm Inform* e-mail message; **enviar un m. a algn** to e-mail sb

mailing [ˈmeilin] *(pl* **mailings**) *nm Com* mailshot; **hacer un m.** to do a mailshot

maillot [maˈjot] *nm* (**a**) *(bañador)* (lady's) swimming costume (**b**) *Dep* shirt

maitines *nmpl Rel* matins; **tocar a m.** to ring to matins

maître [ˈmetre] *nm Br* head waiter, *US* maître d'

maíz *nm (planta) Br* maize, *US* (Indian) corn; *(utilizado en cocina) Br* sweetcorn, *US* corn ❏ *Col* **m. pira** popcorn; **m. tostado** = toasted, salted maize kernels

maizal *nm Br* maize field, *US* cornfield

majada *nf* (**a**) *(corral)* sheepfold (**b**) *(estiércol)* dung (**c**) *CSur (rebaño)* herd, flock

majaderear *Carib Col* **1** *vt* to pester, bother, annoy
  2 *vi* to be a nuisance *o* pest

majadería *nf* silly thing, absurdity; **decir majaderías** to talk nonsense

majadero, -a 1 *adj* foolish, stupid
  2 *nm,f* fool, idiot

majar *vt* to crush, grind

majara, majareta *Esp Fam* **1** *adj* loony, nutty; **volverse m.** to go crazy
  2 *nmf* loony, nut

majestad *nf* (**a**) *(título)* Majesty; **Su M.** *(usted)* Your Majesty; *(él, ella)* His/Her Majesty (**b**) *(majestuosidad)* grandeur, majesty

majestuosidad *nf* majesty, grandeur, stateliness

majestuoso, -a *adj* majestic, stately

majo, -a *adj (bonito)* pretty, nice; *Esp Fam (simpático)* nice; **tiene un hijo muy m.** she's got a lovely little boy; *Fam* **anda, m., dame un besito** come on, darling, give me a little kiss

majorette [majoˈret] *nf* majorette

majuelo *nm Bot* hawthorn

mal 1 *nm* (**a**) *(maldad)* evil, wrong; **el bien y el m.** good and evil, right and wrong (**b**) *(daño)* harm; **del m. el menos** the lesser of two evils; **el m. está en que ...** the problem is that ...; **m. menor** minor evil; **no le deseo ningún m.** I don't wish him any harm; *Prov* **no hay m. que por bien no venga** every cloud has a silver lining (**c**) *(enfermedad)* illness, disease

  2 *adj* bad; **un m. año** a bad year; *véase tamb* **malo, -a**

  3 *adv* badly, wrong; **caer m.** to create a bad impression; **el actor lo hizo bastante m.** the actor gave a rather poor performance; **encontrarse m.** *(enfermo)* to feel ill; *(desplazado)* to feel uncomfortable; **ir de m. en peor** to go from bad to worse; **m. que bien** one way or another; **menos m. que ...** it's a good job (that) ...; **no está (nada) m.** it is not bad (at all); **no estaría m. un baño en la playa** I fancy a swim in the sea; *(sabor)* **saber m.** to taste bad; *Fig* **me sabe m.** I feel sorry about it; **sentar m.** *(comida)* to disagree with; *Fig (molestar)* to take badly; **su respuesta me sentó muy m.** I didn't like his reply at all; **te oigo/veo**

(muy) m. I can hardly hear/see you; **tomar a m.** *(enfadarse)* to take badly; **no lo tomes a m.** don't get me wrong

malabar *adj* **juegos malabares** juggling *sing*

malabarismo *nm* juggling; **hacer malabarismos** to juggle

malabarista *nmf* **(a)** *(artista)* juggler **(b)** *Chile (ladrón)* clever thief

malacostumbrado, -a 1 *pp de* **malacostumbrar**
2 *adj* spoiled

malacostumbrar *vt* to spoil

málaga *nm (vino)* Malaga wine

malagueña *nf Mús* = Spanish music and dance similar to the **fandango**

malagueño, -a 1 *adj* of o from Malaga
2 *nm,f* person from Malaga

Malaisia *n* Malaysia

malaisio, -a *adj & nm,f* Malaysian

malamente *adv Fam* **(a)** *(mal)* badly **(b)** *(apenas)* hardly

malandanza *nf* misfortune

malandrín, -ina *Hum* **1** *adj* malicious, wicked
2 *nm,f* scoundrel, rogue

malapata *Esp Fam* **1** *nf (mala suerte)* bad luck; *(falta de gracia)* lack of charm
2 *nmf (patoso)* clumsy person; *(gafe)* jinx

malaquita *nf Min* malachite

malaria *nf Med* malaria

Malasia *n* Malaysia

malasio, -a *adj & nm,f* Malaysian

malasombra *nmf Esp (pelma)* pest, nuisance, drag; *(patoso)* clumsy person

malatoba *nm Am Zool* red cockerel o rooster

Malaui *n* Malawi

malaui *adj & nmf* Malawian

malaventura *nf véase* **desventura**

malayo, -a 1 *adj* Malayan, Malay
2 *nm,f (persona)* Malayan, Malay
3 *nm (idioma)* Malay

malbaratar *vt (productos)* to undersell; *(dinero)* to squander

malcarado, -a *adj* grim-faced

malcasado, -a *adj* **(a)** *(infeliz)* unhappily married **(b)** *(infiel)* unfaithful **(c)** *(con persona inferior)* married below one's station

malcomer *vi* to eat badly o poorly

malcriado, -a 1 *adj* ill-mannered, ill-bred, uncivil
2 *nm,f* ill-mannered o uncivil person

malcriar [32] *vt* to spoil

maldad *nf* **(a)** *(gen)* badness, evil **(b)** *(acción perversa)* evil o wicked thing; **cometer maldades** to do evil o wrong **(c)** *Fam (travesura)* mischief; **hacer maldades** to get up to mischief

maldecir [51] **1** *vt* to curse; **maldijo su suerte** she cursed her luck
2 *vi* to curse; **maldice de su familia** he speaks ill of his family

maldiciente 1 *adj* **(a)** *(que se queja)* grumbling, always complaining **(b)** *(malhablado)* foul-mouthed
2 *nmf* grumbler, complainer, moaner

maldición 1 *nf* curse
2 *interj* damnation!

maldito, -a *adj* **(a)** *(embrujado)* damned, cursed; **¡maldita sea!** damn it! **(b)** *Fam (molesto)* damned, bloody; **estos malditos zapatos me están matando** these bloody shoes are killing me

Maldivas *npl* **las M.** the Maldive Islands

maldivo, -a *adj & nm,f* Maldivan

maleabilidad *nf* malleability

maleable *adj* malleable

maleante *adj & nmf* delinquent, criminal

malear 1 *vt Fig* to corrupt, pervert
2 **malearse** *vpr* to go bad; *(pervertirse)* to become corrupted

malecón *nm* **(a)** *(dique)* sea wall **(b)** *(atracadero)* pier, jetty

maledicencia *nf* evil talk

maleducado, -a 1 *adj* bad-mannered
2 *nm,f* bad-mannered person

maleficio *nm (hechizo)* curse, spell

maléfico, -a *adj* evil, harmful

malentendido *nm* misunderstanding

malestar *nm* **(a)** *(molestia)* discomfort; **tengo m. general** I don't feel well **(b)** *Fig (inquietud)* uneasiness; **hay un m. general en el país** there is (a feeling of) unrest throughout the country

maleta 1 *nf (a) (de equipaje)* suitcase, case; **hacer la m.** to pack one's things o case **(b)** *Andes Guat (hatillo)* bundle **(c)** *Chile (alforja)* saddlebag **(d)** *Chile Ven (maletero)* Br boot, US trunk
2 *nm Esp Méx Fam (persona)* bungler

maletero *nm* **(a)** *(mozo)* porter; *(fabricante)* suitcase maker; *(vendedor)* suitcase seller **(b)** *Esp Cuba Aut* boot, US trunk

maletilla *nm Taur* trainee matador

maletín *nm* briefcase

malevolencia *nf* malevolence

malévolo, -a *adj* malevolent

maleza *nf* **(a)** *(arbustos)* thicket, undergrowth **(b)** *(malas hierbas)* weeds *pl*

malformación *nf Med* malformation

malgache *adj & nmf* Madagascan

malgastador, -a 1 *adj* squandering, wasteful
2 *nm,f* spendthrift, squanderer

malgastar *vt* to waste, squander

malgenioso, -a *adj Chile Méx* ill-tempered, irritable

malhablado, -a 1 *adj* foul-mouthed
2 *nm,f* foul-mouthed person

malhadado, -a *adj Literario* ill-fated

malhechor, -a 1 *adj* criminal
2 *nm,f* wrongdoer, criminal

malherir [62] *vt* to wound seriously, injure badly

malhumor *nm* bad temper o mood; **estoy de m.** I am in a bad temper o mood

malhumorado, -a *adj* bad-tempered, cross

Malí *n* Mali

malicia *nf* **(a)** *(mala intención)* malice, maliciousness, spite **(b)** *(astucia)* cunning, craftiness, slyness **(c)** *(maldad)* badness, evil, evilness **(d)** *(sospecha)* suspicion

maliciar *vt,* **maliciarse** *vpr* to feel suspicious about, have one's suspicions about

malicioso, -a 1 *adj* malicious, spiteful
2 *nm,f* malicious o spiteful person

maliense *adj & nmf* Malian

malignidad *nf* malignity

maligno, -a 1 *adj* malignant; **un tumor m.** a malignant tumour
2 *nm* **el m.** *Rel* the devil

malintencionado, -a 1 *adj* ill-intentioned
2 *nm,f* ill-intentioned person

malinterpretar *vt* to misinterpret, misunderstand

malla *nf* (a) *(red)* mesh □ **m. de alambre** wire netting (b) *(prenda)* leotard (c) *Ecuad Perú RP (bañador)* swimsuit, swimming costume (d) *Esp* **mallas** *(de gimnasia)* leotard; *(de ballet)* tights

mallo *nm* (a) *(mazo)* mallet (b) *Dep (juego)* croquet; *(terreno)* croquet lawn

Mallorca *n* Majorca

mallorquín, -ina *adj & nm,f* Majorcan

malmirado, -a *adj* (a) *(desconceptuado)* ill-considered (b) *(desconsiderado)* inconsiderate

malnacido, -a 1 *adj* undesirable, nasty
2 *nm,f* nasty type

malnutrición *nf* malnutrition

malnutrido, -a *adj* undernourished

malo, -a 1 *adj véase tamb* **mal** (a) *(gen)* bad; **estar a malas** to be on bad terms; **hace mucho que no me llama, ¡m.!** he hasn't rung for ages, it's a bad sign; **un año m.** a bad year; **por las malas** by force; *Prov* **más vale m. conocido que bueno por conocer** better the devil you know than the one you don't know (b) *(persona) (malvado)* wicked, bad; *(travieso)* naughty; **ser m.** to be wicked o bad; **no seas m.** don't be naughty (c) *(cosa) (de baja calidad)* bad, poor, cheap; *(falso)* false; **una mala canción/comida** a poor song/meal; **un diamante m.** a false diamond (d) *(perjudicial)* harmful; **el tabaco es m.** tobacco is harmful; **ser m. para ...** not to be any good for ... (e) *(difícil)* difficult, hard; **una montaña mala de escalar** a difficult mountain to climb; **lo m. es que ...** the problem is that ... (f) *(enfermo)* ill, sick; **estar m.** to be sick; *Fam* **ponerse m.** *(enfermar)* to fall ill; *(estropearse)* to go bad; *Euf* **estar mala** to have a period
2 *nm,f Fam* **el m. (de la película)** the baddy o villain

maloca *nf SAm* (a) *(invasión)* = invasion and pillage of Indian territory (b) *(ataque)* Indian raid

malogrado, -a 1 *pp de* **malograr**
2 *adj* (a) *(desaprovechado)* wasted (b) *(difunto)* ill-fated; **el m. James Dean** the ill-fated James Dean

malograr 1 *vt* to waste
2 malograrse *vpr* (a) *(fracasar)* to fail, fall through; **las cosechas se han malogrado** the crops have been ruined (b) *(persona)* to die young

maloliente *adj* foul-smelling, stinking, smelly

malón *nm CSur Hist* Indian raid

malparado, -a *adj* **salir m.** to end up in a sorry state, come off badly

malpensado, -a 1 *adj* nasty-minded
2 *nm,f* nasty-minded person; **ser un m.** to have a twisted mind

malquerencia *nf* (a) *(antipatía)* dislike (b) *(malevolencia)* malevolence

malquistar *vt* **m. a algn contra algn** to set sb against sb

malsano, -a *adj* unhealthy, bad; **una mente malsana** a sick mind

Malta *n* Malta

malta *nf (cebada)* malt

malteado, -a 1 *adj* malted
2 *nm (operación)* malting

maltés, -a *adj & nm,f* Maltese

maltón, -ona *adj Am* big for his/her/its age

maltraer [66] *vi* **llevar** o **traer a algn a m.** to give sb a hard time, ill-treat sb

maltraído, -a 1 *pp de* **maltraer**
2 *adj Andes* shabby, untidy

maltratador, -a *nm, f* abuser, batterer

maltratar *vt* to ill-treat, mistreat

maltrato *nm* ill-treatment, mistreatment □ **m. psicológico** psychological abuse

maltrecho, -a *adj* in a sorry state, wrecked

maltusianismo *nm* Malthusianism

maltusiano, -a *adj & nm,f* Malthusian

malucho, -a *adj Fam* not very well, poorly, off-colour, *US* off-color

malva 1 *adj inv* mauve
2 *nm (color)* mauve
3 *nf Bot* mallow; **como una m.** as quiet as a mouse; *Fam* **criar malvas** to be pushing up the daisies

malvado, -a 1 *adj* evil, wicked
2 *nm,f* villain, evil person

malvasía *nf* (a) *Bot* = variety of sweet grape (b) *(vino)* = dessert wine made with these grapes

malvavisco *nm Bot* marshmallow

malvender *vt* to sell at a loss

malversación *nf* misappropriation, embezzlement

malversador, -a 1 *adj* embezzling
2 *nm,f* embezzler

malversar *vt* to misappropriate, embezzle

Malvinas *npl* **las (Islas M.)** the Falkland Islands

malvivir *vi* to live very badly

mama *nf* (a) *Anat (de mujer)* breast (b) *Zool* udder (c) *Fam (mamá)* mum, mummy

mamá *nf Fam* mum, mummy; *Col Méx* **m. grande** grandma

mamada *nf* (a) *(de bebé)* (breast) feed, (breast) feeding (b) *Vulg (felación)* blow job (c) *Chile Perú (ganga)* bargain

mamadera *nf* (a) *RP (biberón)* (baby's) bottle (b) *Carib (tetina)* rubber nipple

mamado, -a *adj* (a) *Esp RP muy Fam (borracho)* shit-faced, plastered, *Br* pissed (b) *Esp muy Fam (fácil)* **estar m.** to be piss easy (c) *Col Ven Fam (cansado)* beat, *Br* knackered

mamar 1 *vt (leche)* to suck; *Fig* to grow up with
2 *vi* (a) *(bebé)* to suckle; **dar de m.** to breast-feed (b) *Méx Fam* **¡no mames!** *(no fastidies)* come off it!; *(no molestes)* cut it out!
3 mamarse *vpr* (a) *Esp RP muy Fam (emborracharse)* to get plastered (b) *Andes Fam (matar)* **mamarse a algn** to bump sb off, do sb in

mamario, -a *adj* mammary

mamarrachada *nf Fam* (a) *(acción)* ridiculous action, stupid thing to do (b) *(bodrio)* dead loss

mamarracho, -a *nm,f Fam* (a) *(persona)* ridiculous-looking person, mess, sight; **¡vaya m. está hecho!** what a sight he looks! (b) *(obra)* mess, sight

mambo *nm Mús* mambo

mameluco *nm* (a) *Hist* Mameluke (b) *Fig* fool, idiot, dimwit (c) *(ropa) Méx (con mangas) Br* overalls, *US* coveralls; *CSur (de peto) Br* dungarees, *US* overalls; *(para bebé)* rompers

mamífero, -a 1 *adj* mammalian, mammal
2 *nm* mammal

mamografía *nf Med* mammography

mamón, -ona 1 *adj* (a) *(que mama)* unweaned (b) *muy Fam (idiota)* **¡qué m. eres!** you bastard!
2 *nm,f* (a) *(que mama)* unweaned baby (b) *muy Fam (idiota) Br* prat, *US* jerk
3 *nm Bol RP (papaya)* papaya, papaw

mamotreto *nm* (a) *(libro)* great big thick book (b) *(armatoste)* monstrosity

mampara *nf (cancel)* screen

mamporro *nm Fam (bofetada)* punch, clout; *(accidente)* bump

mampostería *nf* masonry, rubblework

mampuesto *nm* (a) *(piedra)* rubble, rough stone (b) *(parapeto)* parapet, ledge (c) *Chile (de arma)* support, rest

mamut *nm Zool* mammoth

maná *nm* (a) *Rel* manna (b) *Bol (dulce) Br* nut sweet, *US* nut candy

manada *nf* (a) *Zool (de vacas, elefantes)* herd; *(de ovejas)* flock; *(de lobos, perros)* pack; *(de leones)* pride (b) *Fam (multitud)* crowd, mob; **en manadas** in crowds

manager ['manajer] *(pl managers) nmf Dep Mús* manager

Managua *n* Managua

managüense 1 *adj* of o from Managua
2 *nmf* person from Managua

manantial *nm* spring, fountain; *Fig (origen)* source, origin, fount; **agua de m.** spring water

manar 1 *vi* (a) *(líquido)* to flow, run (**de** from) (b) *Fig* to abound in
2 *vt* to run with, flow with; **la herida manaba sangre** blood flowed from his wound

manatí *nm Zool* manatee

manazas *nmf inv Fam* clumsy person

mancar [59] **1** *vt* to maim, cripple
2 mancarse *vpr* to become maimed o crippled

mancebo, -a *nm,f (en farmacia)* assistant

mancha *nf* (a) *(de suciedad)* stain, spot; **una m. de tinta/vino** an ink/a wine stain □ **m. solar** sunspot (b) *Fig (defecto)* blemish; **sin m.** unblemished

manchado, -a 1 *pp de* **manchar**
2 *adj* dirty, stained; **un caballo m.** a spotted horse

manchar 1 *vt* to stain, dirty; *Fig* to stain, blemish
2 mancharse *vpr* to get dirty

manchego, -a 1 *adj* of o from La Mancha
2 *nm,f* person from La Mancha
3 *nm* cheese from La Mancha

manchón *nm Fam* large spot o stain

mancilla *nf* stain, blemish

mancillar *vt (honor, fama)* to dishonour, *US* dishonor, stain

manco, -a 1 *adj* (a) *(sin un brazo)* one-armed; *(sin brazos)* armless (b) *(sin una mano)* one-handed; *(sin manos)* handless (c) *Fig (defectuoso)* defective, faulty; *Fam* **no ser m.** *(persona)* to be no fool; *(cosas)* to be no little thing
2 *nm,f* (a) *(sin un brazo)* one-armed/armless person (b) *(sin una mano)* one-handed/handless person

mancomunar 1 *vt (esfuerzos, dinero)* to pool together
2 mancomunarse *vpr* to join together, unite

mancomunidad *nf* community, association

mancornas *nfpl CAm Chile Col Méx Ven* cufflinks

mancuerna *nf* (a) *(pesa)* dumbbell (b) *CAm Chile Col Méx Ven (botón)* cufflink

mandado, -a 1 *pp de* **mandar**
2 *nm (recado)* order, errand; **hacer un m.** to run an errand
3 *nm,f (persona)* person who carries out an order

mandamás *nmf Fam* big boss, *US* head honcho

mandamiento *nm* (a) *(orden)* order, command (b) *Jur* warrant, mandate (c) *Rel* Commandment □ **los Diez Mandamientos** the Ten Commandments

mandangas *nfpl Fam* stories; **no me vengas con m.** who do you think you're trying to kid?

mandar 1 *vt* (a) *(ordenar)* to order; **la ley manda que ...** the law stipulates that ...; **le mandó venir** he ordered him to come; *Esp Méx Fam* **¿mande?** pardon?; *Esp muy Fam* **¡manda huevos!** can you *Br* bloody o *US* goddamn believe it!; *Fam* **me mandó a paseo** she sent me packing, she told me to get lost (b) *(grupo)* to lead, be in charge o command of; *Mil (ejército)* to command; **aquí mando yo** I'm the boss here; **¿quién manda aquí?** who is in charge here? (c) *(enviar)* to send; **lo mandé a comprar caramelos** I sent him to buy some sweets; **m. algo por correo** to post sth, send sth by the post; **m. recuerdos** to send regards
2 mandarse *vpr RP Fam* **m. (a) mudar** to be off, walk out

mandarín *nm Hist* mandarin

mandarina *nf Bot* mandarin (orange), tangerine

mandarinero *nm*, **mandarino** *nm Bot* mandarin orange tree, tangerine tree

mandatario, -a *nm,f* (a) *Jur* mandatory (b) *Pol* president; **el primer m. de la nación** the head of state

mandato *nm* (a) *(orden)* order, command (b) *Jur* writ, warrant □ **m. judicial** warrant (c) *Pol (legislatura)* mandate, term of office

mandíbula *nf* jaw; *Fam* **reír a m. batiente** to laugh one's head off

mandil *nm* (a) *(prenda)* apron (b) *(bayeta)* grooming cloth

mandioca *nf Bot* manioc, tapioca

mando *nm* (a) *(autoridad)* command, control; **ejercer el m., estar al m., tener el m.** to be in charge o control; **entregar el m.** to hand over command; **tomar el m.** to take command (b) *(mandato)* term of office (c) *(gobernante)* authorities *pl*, those in command *pl*; **los mandos del ejército** high-ranking army officers □ **alto m.** high command (d) *Téc (control)* controls *pl* □ **m. a distancia** remote control; **cuadro de mandos** *Av* instrument panel; *Aut* dashboard; **palanca de m.** *Téc* control lever; *(de avión, videojuego)* joystick; **tablero de mandos** *Av* instrument panel; *Aut* dashboard

mandoble *nm* (a) *(golpe)* two-handed blow o sword-stroke (b) *(espada)* large sword (c) *Fam (represión)* telling off

mandolina *nf Mús* mandolin, mandoline

mandón, -ona 1 *adj Fam* bossy, domineering
2 *nm,f Fam* bossy o domineering person
3 *nm Chile (mine)* foreman

mandrágora *nf Bot* mandrake

mandril *nm* (a) *Zool* mandril (b) *Téc* mandrel

manducar [59] *vt & vi Fam* to nosh

maneador *nm Méx RP* leather thong, rein

manecilla *nf (de reloj)* hand

manejabilidad *nf* manageability

manejable *adj (gen)* manageable; *(herramienta)* easy-to-use; *(coche)* manoeuvrable, *US* maneuvrable

manejar 1 *vt* (a) *(manipular)* to handle, operate; *Fig* to handle, deal with; **maneja muy bien las tijeras** she's very handy with a pair of scissors; **manejó la situación muy bien** he dealt with the situation very cleverly (b) *(dirigir)* to run, manage; **ella sola maneja la empresa** she runs the company on her own (c) *Fig (dominar)* to domineer, boss about, push around; **Rosa maneja a su marido** Rosa bosses her husband about (d) *Am Aut (un coche)* to drive
2 manejarse *vpr* to manage; *Fam* **manejárselas** to manage by oneself; **ya te las manejarás** you'll manage somehow

manejo *nm* (a) *(uso)* handling, use; **de fácil m.** easy-to-use (b) *Téc (de una máquina)* running, operation (c) *Fig (de un negocio)* management (d) *Fig* tricks *pl*, trickery (e) *Am Aut (de un coche)* driving

manera *nf* (**a**) *(forma)* way, manner; **a m. de** by way of; **a la m. de** in the manner of; **a mi/tu m.** my/your way, in my/ your own way; **de cualquier m.** *(mal)* carelessly, any old how; *(con facilidad)* easily; *(en cualquier caso)* in any case; **de esta/esa m.** in this/that way; **de la m. que sea** *(pase lo que pase)* whatever happens; *(no importa como)* any way you *etc* like; **de mala m.** *(mal)* badly; *(groseramente)* rudely; **de m. que** so; **te lo advertí, de m. que no te quejes** I warned you, so don't complain now; **de ninguna m.** in no way, certainly not; **de otra m.** *(si no es así)* otherwise; *(de distinto modo)* in a different way; **de tal m. que** in such a way that; **de todas maneras** anyway, at any rate, in any case; **de una m. o de otra** one way or another; **en cierta m.** in a way; **en gran m.** extremely; **sobre m.** very much; **es mi m. de ser** that's the way I am; **no hay m.** it's impossible; **¡qué** *o* **vaya m. de tomarnos el pelo!** that's a fine way to tease us!; **¡y de qué m.!** and how! (**b**) *(clase)* kind, sort (**c**) **maneras** manners; **con buenas m.** politely

manga *nf* (**a**) *(de prenda)* sleeve; **de m. corta/larga** short-/long-sleeved; **en mangas de camisa** in shirt-sleeves; **sin mangas** sleeveless; *Fig* **hacer mangas y capirotes** to act arbitrarily; *Fig* **hacer un corte de mangas a algn** ≃ to give sb *Br* a V-sign *o US* the finger; *Fig* **m. por hombro** messy and untidy; *Fig* **ser de** *o* **tener la m. ancha** *(ser poco estricto)* to be broad-minded; *(ser benevolente)* to be easy-going; *Fig* **sacarse algo de la m.** to pull sth out of one's hat (**b**) *(manguera)* hose, hosepipe ❏ **m. de riego** *(de jardín)* garden *o* watering hose; *(de bombero)* fire hose (**c**) *(red)* casting net ❏ **m. de mariposas** butterfly net (**d**) *Geog* **m. de mar** arm of the sea (**e**) *Náut* breadth (**f**) *(medidor de viento)* windsock, windsleeve (**g**) *Meteor* (*de agua)* waterspout; *(de viento)* whirlwind (**h**) *Dep* leg, round; *Bridge* game; **ir a m.** to go to game (**i**) *Culin* (*filtro)* muslin strainer; *(de pastelero)* icing bag, forcing bag (**j**) *Méx RP* *(turba)* crowd, mob (**k**) *CAm* *(manta)* (sackcloth) blanket (**l**) *Méx (prenda)* oilskin poncho

manganeso *nm Quím* manganese

mangante *Esp Argot* **1** *adj* cadging
  2 *nmf (gorrón)* cadger, scrounger; *(ladrón)* thief

manganzón, -ona *adj Andes CAm Ven Fam* lazy, idle

mangar [38] *vt Esp Argot* to pinch, *Br* nick

manglar *nm* mangrove swamp

mangle *nm* mangrove

mango[1] *nm* (**a**) handle; *(de un hacha)* helve; *(de un látigo)* stock ❏ **m. de la escoba** broomstick (**b**) *RP Fam (dinero)* **no tengo un m.** I haven't got a bean, I'm broke

mango[2] *nm Bot* mango

mangonear *vi* (**a**) *Fam (manipular)* to be bossy, throw one's weight around (**b**) *Fam (entrometerse)* to meddle

mangoneo *nm* (**a**) *Fam* bossing around (**b**) *Fam (entrometimiento)* meddling

mangosta *nf Zool* mongoose

manguear *vt* (**a**) *CSur Méx (ganado)* to drive into a gangway (**b**) *RP Fam (pedir)* to sponge, scrounge; **m. algo a algn** to cadge sth from sb

manguera *nf (de jardín)* garden *o* watering hose, hosepipe; *(de bombero)* fire hose

mangui *Esp Argot* **1** *adj (malo)* bad; *(falso)* false
  2 *nm,f (ladrón)* thief; *(sinvergüenza)* rotter

manguito *nm* (**a**) *(para las manos)* muff; *(para las mangas)* oversleeve (**b**) *Téc* sleeve

maní (*pl* **manises** *o* **maníes**) *nm Andes Carib RP* peanut

manía *nf* (**a**) *Med* mania; *Fam* **sin manías** head-first ❏ **m. depresiva** manic-depressive psychosis; **m. persecutoria** persecution mania *o* complex (**b**) *(costumbre)* habit; **tiene la m. de dejar el coche siempre abierto** he's got this bad habit of leaving the car unlocked (**c**) *(afición exagerada)*

craze; **la m. de las motos** the motorbike craze (**d**) *(ojeriza)* dislike, ill will; **tomarle** *o Esp* **cogerle m. a algn** to take a dislike to sb; **me tiene m.** he has it in for me, he can't stand me

maniaco, -a, maníaco, -a 1 *adj* manic
  2 *nm,f* maniac ❏ **m. depresivo** manic-depressive

maniatar *vt (a una persona)* to tie the hands of

maniático, -a 1 *adj* fussy
  2 *nm,f* fussy person

manicomio *nm Br* mental *o* psychiatric hospital, *US* insane asylum; *Fam* **esta casa es un m.** this place is like a madhouse

manicura *nf* manicure; **hacerse la m.** to have a manicure

manicuro, -a *nm,f* manicurist

manido, -a *adj (asunto)* trite, hackneyed, worn-out

manierismo *nm Arte* mannerism

manierista *Arte* **1** *adj* manneristic
  2 *nmf* mannerist

manifestación *nf* (**a**) *(expresión)* manifestation, expression; **como m. de su amistad** as a sign of his friendship (**b**) *(declaración)* declaration, comment (**c**) *(demostración colectiva)* demonstration

manifestante *nmf* demonstrator

manifestar [3] **1** *vt* (**a**) *(opinión)* to express; **el director manifestó que ...** the director declared that ... (**b**) *(mostrar)* to show, display
  2 manifestarse *vpr* (**a**) *(declararse)* to declare oneself; **se manifestó partidario de la idea** he declared himself in favour of the idea (**b**) *(por la calle)* to demonstrate

manifiesto, -a 1 *adj* evident, clear, obvious, manifest; *(falta)* glaring; **poner de m.** *(revelar)* to reveal, show; *(hacer patente)* to make clear
  2 *nm* manifesto

manigua *nf Carib Col Geog* scrubland

manija *nf* (**a**) *esp Am (manubrio)* handle (**b**) *(maniota)* hobble

Manila *n* Manila

manilargo, -a *adj* (**a**) *(ladrón)* light-fingered (**b**) *(generoso)* generous, open-handed

manileño, -a 1 *adj* of *o* from Manila
  2 *nm,f* person from Manila

manilla *nf* (**a**) *(argolla)* handcuff, manacle (**b**) *(de reloj)* hand

manillar *nm* handlebars *(plural)*

maniobra *nf* (**a**) *Mil* manoeuvre, *US* maneuver; **hacer maniobras** to manoeuvre; **estar de maniobras** to be on manoeuvres (**b**) *Fig (jugada)* move

maniobrabilidad *nf* manoeuvrability, *US* maneuverability

maniobrable *adj* manoeuvrable, *US* maneuverable

maniobrar *vi* to manoeuvre, *US* maneuver

manipulación *nf* manipulation; **m. de mercancías** handling of goods

manipulador, -a 1 *adj* manipulating
  2 *nm,f* manipulator, handler

manipular *vt* (**a**) *(gen)* to manipulate; *(mercancías)* to handle (**b**) *Fig* to interfere with

maniqueísmo *nm* Manicheism

maniqueo, -a *adj & nm,f* Manichean

maniquí 1 *nmf (modelo)* model, mannequin
  2 *nm (muñeco)* dummy; *Fig* puppet

manirroto, -a *adj & nm,f* spendthrift

manitas *nmf inv Esp Fam* (**a**) **m. de plata** clever hands;

ser un m. to be handy, be very good with one's hands (**b**) **hacer m.** to hold hands

manito *nm Méx Fam* pal, *Br* mate, *US* buddy

manivela *nf Téc* crank

manjar *nm* (**a**) dish, food; **un m. exquisito** an exquisite dish; *Fig* **m. de dioses** food fit for the gods (**b**) *Chile (dulce de leche)* = toffee pudding made with caramelized milk

mano¹ *nf* (**a**) *(de persona)* hand; **a m.** *(sin máquina)* by hand; *(asequible)* at hand; **escrito a m.** handwritten; **hecho a m.** handmade; **a m. armada** armed; **a manos de** at the hands of; **a manos llenas** generously; **abrir la m.** *(transigir)* to become more tolerant; *(gastar mucho)* to spend carelessly; **al alcance de la m.** within one's grasp; **alargar la m.** *(para coger algo)* to stretch out one's hand; *(a algn)* to offer one's hand; **alzar la m. contra algn** to *(threaten to)* use violence against sb, raise one's hand to sb; **¡arriba las manos!** hands up!; *Fam* **cargar la m.** to overdo it; *Fam Esp* **coger** *o Am* **agarrar a algn con las manos en la masa** to catch sb red-handed; **cogidos de la m.** holding hands; *Fam* **le das la m. y se toma el codo** give him an inch and he'll take a mile; **dar** *o* **tender la m.** *(para saludar)* to shake hands (**a** with); *(para ayudar)* to offer one's hand (**a** to); *Fam* **echar de algo/algn** to make use of sth/sb; **estrechar la m. a algn** to shake hands with sb; *Fig* **con el corazón en la m.** sincerely; *Fig* **con m. dura** severely, with an iron hand; *Fig* **de mi/tu m.** up to me/you; *Fig* **de la m. de algn** under sb's guidance, under the influence of sb; *Fig* **de primera m.** first-hand; *Fig* **de segunda m.** second-hand; *Fig* **dejar algo en manos de algn** to leave sb in charge of sth; *Fig* **echar una m. a algn** to give sb a hand; *Fig* **en buenas manos** in good hands; *Fig* **hacer lo que está de su m.** to do all in one's power; *Fig* **írsele a algn la m.** to overdo it; *Fig* **írsele a algn algo de las manos** to lose control over sth; *Fam* **¡las manos quietas!** hands off!; *Fig* **m. a m.** *(juntos)* together; *(entrevista)* tête-à-tête; *Fig* **m. sobre m.** idle; *Fig* **¡manos a la obra!** let's get down to work; *Fig* **meter m. a** *(a problema)* to tackle; *Vulg (persona)* to touch up; *Fig* **no estaba en mi m.** **poder ayudarle** I could do nothing to help her; *Fig* **(no) saber lo que se lleva** *o* **trae uno entre manos** (not) to know what's happening o going on; *Fig* **ponerse en manos de algn** to place oneself in sb's hands; *Fig* **ser la m. derecha de algn** to be sb's right hand, be sb's right-hand man; *Fig* **traerse algo entre manos** to be up to sth (**b**) *Zool* forefoot, forepaw ❏ **m. de ave** claw; **m. de cerdo** pig's trotter (**c**) *(de reloj)* hand (**d**) *(lado)* side; **a m. derecha/izquierda** on the right/left(-hand side) (**e**) *(dosis)* dose, series; **m. de jabón** soaping; **m. de pintura** coat of paint (**f**) *(influencia)* influence; **se ve su m. en la decoración** you can see her influence in the decoration (**g**) *(trabajador)* hand, labourer, *US* laborer; **hay que contratar más manos** we have to employ more workers ❏ **m. de obra** labour (force); **m. de obra especializada** skilled labour (**h**) *(habilidad)* skill; **¡qué manos tienes!** you're really clever with your hands!; **tener buena m. para algo** to be good at sth; *Fig* **tener m. izquierda** to be tactful (**i**) *Naipes (grupo de cartas)* hand; *(juego)* game; *(primer jugador)* lead; **echar una m. (de cartas)** to play a game of cards; **yo soy m.** it's my lead (**j**) *(de mortero)* pestle (**k**) *(de papel)* quire (**l**) *Andes CAm Méx (objetos)* = group of four or five objects (**m**) *Am (de plátanos)* bunch (**n**) *CAm Chile Méx (accidente)* mishap, accident

mano² *nmf Am salvo RP Fam Br* mate, *US* buddy

manojo *nm* bunch; **un m. de flores/llaves** a bunch of flowers/keys; *Fam* **ser un m. de nervios** to be a bundle of nerves

manoletina *nf* (**a**) *Taur* = pass with the cape in bullfighting invented by the Spanish bullfighter, Manolete (**b**) *(zapato)* = type of open, low-heeled shoe, often with a bow

manómetro *nm Téc* pressure gauge

manopla *nf* (**a**) *(guante)* mitten (**b**) *Hist* gauntlet

manoseado, -a 1 *pp de* **manosear**
2 *adj* worn(-out); *Fig* hackneyed

manosear *vt (gen)* handle (roughly); *(persona)* to paw

manoseo *nm (gen)* handling, touching; *(de persona)* pawing

manotazo *nm* cuff, slap

manotear 1 *vt* (**a**) to cuff, slap (**b**) *RP (quitar)* to grab
2 *vi* to gesticulate

manoteo *nm* gesticulation

mansalva: a mansalva *loc adv* without risk, safely

mansarda *nf Arquit* attic

mansedumbre *nf* (**a**) *(persona)* meekness, gentleness (**b**) *(animal)* tameness, docility

mansión *nf* mansion; **m. señorial** stately home

manso, -a *adj* (**a**) *(persona)* gentle, meek (**b**) *(animal)* tame, docile (**c**) *Chile Fam (extraordinario)* tremendous

manta 1 *nf* (**a**) *(abrigo)* blanket; **a m.** abundantly; *Fam* lots of; **había gente a m.** there were loads of people; *Fam* **liarse la m. a la cabeza** to take the plunge, go the whole hog; *Fam* **tirar de la m.** to let the cat out of the bag ❏ **m. de viaje** travelling rug; **m. eléctrica** electric blanket (**b**) *(zurra)* beating, hiding (**c**) *(pez)* manta ray, devilfish (**d**) *Méx (algodón)* = coarse cotton cloth
2 *adj Fam* lazy, bone idle
3 *nmf Esp Fam* lazy person, idler

manteado *nm* (**a**) *CAm Méx (tienda)* tent (**b**) *Méx (toldo)* awning

mantear *vt* to toss in a blanket

manteca *nf* (**a**) *Esp (de animal)* fat; *(de la leche)* cream ❏ **m. de cacao/cacahuete** cocoa/peanut butter; **m. de cerdo** lard (**b**) *RP Ven (mantequilla)* butter

mantecado *nm Esp* (**a**) *(pastel)* shortcake (**b**) *(helado)* dairy ice cream

mantecoso, -a *adj (graso)* greasy; *(cremoso)* buttery

mantel *nm* tablecloth

mantelería *nf* table linen

manteleta *nf* shawl

mantenedor, -a *nm,f* president *(of a jury)*

mantener [65] **1** *vt* (**a**) *(conservar)* to keep, keep going; **mantén el fuego encendido** keep the fire burning; **m. la línea** to keep in trim; *(en letrero)* **'mantenga limpia su ciudad'** 'keep your town tidy' (**b**) *(entrevista, reunión)* to have; **m. correspondencia con algn** to correspond with sb; **m. relaciones con algn** *(amorosas)* to be going out with sb; *(amistosas)* to be on friendly terms with sb (**c**) *(ideas, opiniones)* to defend, maintain; **mantuvo su actitud contraria al proyecto** he maintained his opposition to the project (**d**) *(sustentar)* to support, feed; **ella sola mantiene a su familia** she supports the whole family on her own (**e**) *(sostener)* to support, hold up; **esta columna mantiene el techo** this column holds the ceiling up
2 **mantenerse** *vpr* (**a**) *(sostenerse)* to stand; **este edificio se mantiene en pie de milagro** it's a miracle this building is still standing (**b**) *(continuar)* to keep, hold; **m. firme** to hold one's ground; **m. tranquilo/vivo** to keep *o* stay calm/alive; *Fam* **m. en sus trece** to stick to one's guns (**c**) *(sustentarse)* to support oneself

mantenida *nf Pey* kept woman

mantenido, -a 1 *pp de* **mantener**
2 *adj* continuous, constant; **un esfuerzo m.** continuous effort

mantenimiento *nm* (**a**) *Téc* maintenance, upkeep; **servicio de m.** maintenance service (**b**) *(alimento)* sustenance, support

manteo¹ *nm (manteamiento)* tossing in a blanket

manteo² *nm (capa)* mantle

mantequera *nf* butter dish

mantequería *nf* dairy

mantequero, -a *adj* butter; **la industria mantequera** the butter industry

mantequilla *nf* butter ❑ **m. de cacahuete** peanut butter

mantilla *nf* (a) *(de mujer)* mantilla (b) *(de niño)* shawl; *Fig* **estar en mantillas** *(persona)* to be wet behind the ears; *(plan)* to be in its infancy

mantillo *nm* (a) *(humus)* humus (b) *(abono)* leaf mould, *US* leaf mold

manto *nm* (a) *(capa)* cloak, mantle; *Fig* **un m. de silencio** a veil of silence (b) *Min* layer, stratum (c) *Zool* mantle

mantón *nm* shawl ❑ **m. de Manila** embroidered silk shawl

manual 1 *adj* manual; **trabajo m.** manual labour; *Educ* **trabajos manuales** handicrafts
2 *nm (libro)* manual, handbook

manualidades *nfpl (objetos)* craftwork, handicrafts

manubrio *nm* (a) *(manivela)* crank (b) *Am (manillar)* handlebars

manufactura *nf* (a) *(fabricación)* manufacture (b) *(fábrica)* factory

manufacturado, -a 1 *pp de* **manufacturar**
2 *adj* manufactured

manufacturar *vt* to manufacture

manufacturero, -a *adj* manufacturing

manumisión *nf* liberation

manuscrito, -a 1 *adj* handwritten, manuscript
2 *nm* manuscript

manutención *nf* maintenance; **la m. de una familia es cada día más costosa** feeding a family is becoming increasingly expensive

manzana *nf* (a) *Bot* apple ❑ *Fig* **m. de la discordia** bone of contention; **m. podrida** bad apple (b) *Arquit (de casas)* block

manzanal *nm*, **manzanar** *nm* apple orchard

manzanilla *nf* (a) *Bot* camomile (b) *(infusión)* camomile tea (c) *(vino)* manzanilla

manzano *nm Bot* apple tree

maña *nf* (a) *(habilidad)* skill, dexterity; **darse o tener m. para algo** to be good at doing sth; *Prov* **más vale m. que fuerza** brain is better than brawn (b) *(astucia)* trick

mañana 1 *nf* morning; **a las dos de la m.** at two in the morning; **de m.** early in the morning; **por la m.**, *Am* **en la m.** in the morning
2 *nm* tomorrow, the future; **hay que pensar en el m.** one has to think about tomorrow o the future
3 *adv* tomorrow; **¡hasta m.!** see you tomorrow!, till tomorrow!; **m. por la m.** tomorrow morning; **pasado m.** the day after tomorrow

mañanero, -a *adj* (a) *(madrugador)* early rising (b) *(matutino)* morning; **la brisa mañanera** the morning breeze

mañanita 1 *nf* bed jacket
2 **mañanitas** *nfpl Méx* birthday song

maño, -a *adj & nm,f Esp Fam* Aragonese

mañoso, -a *Esp adj* (a) *(hábil)* skilful, *US* skillful, dextrous, deft (b) *(astuto)* crafty, cunning

maoísmo *nm Pol* Maoism

maoísta *adj & nmf Pol* Maoist

maorí *adj & nmf* Maori

mapa *nm* map; **m. mural** wall map; *Fam* **borrar del m.** *(eliminar)* to get rid of; *(matar)* to kill; *Fam* **desaparecer del m.** to vanish (from the face of the earth); *Fam* **como o hecho un m.** badly bruised o cut

mapache *nm Zool* raccoon

mapamundi *nm* (a) *(mapa)* map of the world, world map (b) *(nalgas)* backside, bum, bottom

mapuche 1 *adj* Mapuche
2 *nmf* Mapuche (indian)
3 *nm (lengua)* Mapuche

Maputo *n* Maputo

maqueta *nf* (a) *(miniatura)* scale model, maquette (b) *Impr* dummy (c) *Mús* demo (tape)

maquetación *nf Inform* page layout

maquetador, -a *nm,f Inform* layout editor

maquetar *vt Inform* to do the layout of

maquetista *nmf* maquette maker

maqui *nmf véase* **maquis**

maquiavélico, -a *adj* Machiavellian

maquiavelismo *nm* Machiavellism

maquiladora *nf* = bonded assembly plant set up by a foreign firm near the US border, *US* maquiladora

maquilar *vt CAm Méx (artículos electrónicos)* to assemble; *(ropa)* to make up

maquillador, -a *nm,f* make-up assistant

maquillaje *nm* (a) *(producto)* make-up ❑ **m. de fondo** foundation (b) *(acción)* making-up

maquillar 1 *vt* to make up
2 **maquillarse** *vpr* (a) *(ponerse maquillaje)* to put one's make-up on, make (oneself) up (b) *(llevar maquillaje)* to wear make-up

máquina *nf* (a) *(aparato)* machine; **escrito a m.** typewritten; **hecho a m.** machine-made; *Fam* **a toda m.** at full speed ❑ **m. de afeitar** (electric) razor o shaver; **m. de café** (espresso) coffee machine; **m. de coser** sewing machine; **m. de escribir** typewriter; **m. de fotos** camera; **m. de tren** locomotive; **m. expendedora** vending machine; **m. fotográfica** camera; **m. registradora** cash register; **m.** *Esp* **tragaperras** o *Am* **tragamonedas** slot machine, *Br* fruit machine (b) *Cuba (automóvil)* car

maquinación *nf* machination

maquinador, -a 1 *adj* machinating
2 *nm,f* machinator

maquinal *adj* mechanical

maquinar *vt* to machinate, plot

maquinaria *nf* (a) *(aparatos)* machinery, machines *pl* (b) *(mecanismo) (de reloj, aparato)* mechanism; *(de Estado, partido)* machinery

maquinilla *nf* **m. de afeitar** safety razor; **m. eléctrica** electric razor

maquinismo *nm* mechanization

maquinista *nmf* machinist; *(de tren) Br* engine driver, *US* engineer

maquinizar [14] *vt* to mechanize

maquis *nm inv Mil* guerrilla

mar 1 *nm o f* (a) *(océano, masa de agua)* sea; **en alta m.** on the high seas; **hacerse a la m.** to put (out) to sea, set sail; **m. adentro** out to sea; **por m.** by sea; *Fam* **pelillos a la m.** let bygones be bygones ❑ **m. de fondo** ground swell; *Fig (tensiones)* undercurrent of tension; **m. gruesa** heavy sea; **m. picada** rough sea (b) *Fam (gran cantidad)* **está la m. de guapa** she's looking really beautiful; **la m. de cosas** a lot of things; **me encuentro la m. de bien** I feel great; **llover a mares** to rain cats and dogs; **sudar a mares** to sweat buckets; **sumido en un m. de confusiones** utterly confused; **estar hecho un m. de lágrimas** to cry one's eyes out

2 *nm* **M. de las Antillas** Caribbean Sea; **M. Arábigo** Arabian Sea; **M. de Aral** Aral Sea; **M. de la China Oriental/Meridional** East/South China Sea; **M. del Coral** Coral Sea; **M. de Filipinas** Philippine Sea; **M. de Irlanda** Irish Sea; **M. de Java** Java Sea; **M. del Japón** Japan Sea; **M. Ligur** Ligurian Sea; **M. Muerto** Dead Sea; **M. Negro** Black Sea; **M. de Noruega** Sea of Norway; **M. del Norte** North Sea; **M. Rojo** Red Sea **M. de los Sargazos** Sargasso Sea; **M. de Tasmania** Tasman Sea

marabú *nm Orn* marabou

marabunta *nf* (**a**) *(de hormigas)* plague of ants (**b**) *Fig (multitud)* mob

maraca *nf* (**a**) *Mús* maraca, rattle (**b**) *Chile muy Fam (prostituta)* hooker

maracuyá *nf Bot* passion fruit

marajá *nm* maharajah; **vivir como un m.** to live in the lap of luxury

maraña *nf* (**a**) *(maleza)* thicket (**b**) *Fig (lío)* tangle, mess

marasmo *nm* (**a**) *Med* marasmus (**b**) *Fig (apatía)* apathy; *(estancamiento)* standstill, stagnation

maratón *nm Dep* marathon

maratoniano, -a 1 *adj* marathon
2 *nm,f* marathon runner

maravedí *nm Hist (moneda)* maravedi

maravilla *nf* marvel, wonder; **de m.** wonderfully; **decir maravillas de algo** *o* **algn** to speak enthusiastically about sth *o* sb; **hacer maravillas** to do *o* work wonders; **¡qué m.!** how wonderful!; **¡qué m. de película!** what a wonderful film!; *Fam* **a las mil maravillas** marvellously; *Fam* **venir de maravilla** to be just what one wanted, be a godsend

maravillar 1 *vt* to amaze, astonish; **quedamos maravillados al oírle cantar** we were amazed by his singing, we marvelled at his singing
2 maravillarse *vpr* to marvel (**con** at), wonder (**con** at)

maravilloso, -a *adj* wonderful, marvellous, *US* marvelous

marbete *nm* (**a**) *(etiqueta)* label (**b**) *(perfil)* edge, border

marca *nf* (**a**) *(señal)* mark, sign (**b**) *Com (productos comestibles y del hogar)* brand; *(otros productos)* make; **¿que m. de café/jabón/dentífrico compras?** what brand of coffee/soap/toothpaste do you buy?; **pantalones/zapatos de m.** designer shoes/trousers; *Fam* **de m. mayor** outstanding, enormous ❑ **m. comercial** trademark; **m. de fábrica** trademark; **m. registrada** registered trademark (**c**) *(acción de marcar)* marking; **la m. del ganado** the branding of cattle (**d**) *Dep (récord)* record; **batir la m. mundial** to break the world record

marcación *nf Am* branding iron

marcadamente *adv* markedly; **un espíritu m. liberal** a clearly liberal spirit

marcado, -a 1 *pp de* **marcar**
2 *adj* (**a**) *(pronunciado)* marked (**b**) *(evidente)* distinct, strong; **con marcada diferencia** noticeably different

marcador, -a 1 *adj* marking
2 *nm* (**a**) *(jugador) (defensor)* marker (**b**) *Dep* scoreboard; **inaugurar el m.** to start *o* open the scoring (**c**) *Am (rotulador)* felt-tip pen; *Méx (fluorescente)* highlighter pen

marcaje *nm Dep* marking

marcapasos *nm inv Med* pacemaker

marcar [59] **1** *vt* (**a**) *(poner marca en)* to mark; *(ganado)* to brand; *Com (mercancías)* to put a price on, mark; *Mús* **m. el compás/el paso** to mark rhythm/time; **m. época** to mark an era; **m. un terreno** to mark the land out *o* off; *Fig* **la experiencia lo marcó para siempre** the experience

marked him for life (**b**) *(cabello)* to set (**c**) *(aparato)* to indicate, show; **el contador marca 1.327** the meter reads 1,327; **el reloj marca las tres** the clock says 3 o'clock (**d**) *Dep (gol, puntos)* to score; *(jugador)* to mark; *Fig* **su plan marca un gol para la empresa** her project scores a point for the firm (**e**) *Tel* to dial

2 marcarse *vpr Fam* **m. un farol** to show off, boast; **m. un tanto** to score a triumph

marcha *nf* (**a**) *(partida)* departure; **el día de su m.** the day he went away; **¡en m.!** let's go! (**b**) *(de soldados, manifestantes)* march; **abrir/cerrar la m.** to be first/last in a march *o* procession ❑ **m. antinuclear** antinuclear march; *Dep* **m. atlética** walk, walking race (**c**) *(progreso)* course, progress; **la ecología es una ideología en m.** ecology is on the move; **la m. de los acontecimientos** the course of events; **la m. de las negociaciones/de un negocio** the progress of the negotiations/a business; **hacer algo sobre la m.** to do sth as one goes along (**d**) *(velocidad)* speed; *Esp* **a marchas forzadas** against the clock; **a toda m.** (at) full speed; *Fig* at full blast; **disminuir la m.** to slow down (**e**) *Aut* gear; *Aut* **dar m. atrás** to reverse; *Fig* **han dado m. atrás al proyecto** they have abandoned the project ❑ **m. atrás** reverse (gear); **primera m.** first *o* bottom gear; *Mús* march; **m. fúnebre/militar/nupcial** funeral/military/ wedding march; (**g**) *(funcionamiento)* operation, running; **estar en m.** *(maquinaria)* to be in operation, be on, be working; *(proyecto etc)* to be under way; **poner en m.** *(coche, motor)* to start; *(negocio)* to start up (**h**) *Esp Fam (energía)* go; *(animación)* good humour *o US* humor, good vibrations; **hay mucha m. aquí** it's really lively here; **ir de m.** to go out on the town, have a wild time; **irle la m. a algn** *(ser marchoso)* to be a raver, enjoy living it up; *(ser masoquista)* to be masochist; **¡qué m. llevo hoy!** count me in for anything today!

marchamo *nm* mark, seal

marchante, -a 1 *nm Com* merchant, dealer
2 *nm,f CAm Méx Ven Fam (cliente)* customer, regular client

marchar 1 *vi* (**a**) *(ir)* to go, walk; *Fam* **¡marchando!** on your way!; **¡tres de hamburguesa! — ¡marchando!** three hamburgers! — coming right up! (**b**) *(funcionar)* to work, function; **la radio no marcha** the radio isn't working; *Fig* **el negocio no marcha** the business is doing badly; *Fig* **m. sobre ruedas** to run like clockwork (**c**) *Mil* to march (**d**) *Méx Fam* **¡no marches!** *(no te pases)* cool it!, take it easy!
2 marcharse *vpr (irse)* to leave, depart

marchitamiento *nm* shrivelling, *US* shriveling, withering

marchitar 1 *vt* to shrivel, wither
2 marchitarse *vpr* to shrivel, wither

marchito, -a *adj* shrivelled, *US* shriveled, withered

marchoso, -a *Esp Fam* **1** *adj* fun-loving, wild; **es una gente muy marchosa** they are always living it up; **música marchosa** music with a bit of go
2 *nm,f* raver, fun lover; **es un m.** he's a right raver

marcial *adj* martial; **ley m.** martial law

marcialidad *nf* military manners *o* style

marcianitos *nmpl Fam (juego)* los **m.** space invaders

marciano, -a *adj & nm,f* Martian

marco *nm* (**a**) *(cerco)* frame (**b**) *Fig (fondo)* framework, setting; **en un m. adecuado** in an appropriate setting (**c**) *Fin (moneda)* mark (**d**) *Ftb* goalposts *pl*, goal

marea *nf* (**a**) *Mar* tide; *Fig* **contra viento y m.** come hell or high water ❑ **m. alta/baja** high/low tide ❑ **m. negra** oil slick (**b**) *Fig (multitud)* crowd, mob; **una m. de vendedores** a crowd of salesmen

mareado, -a 1 *pp de* **marear**
2 *adj* (**a**) *(con náuseas)* sick; *(en un avión)* airsick; *(en un*

coche) carsick, travel-sick; **estar m.** to feel sick; *(en el mar)* to feel seasick; *(en un avión)* to feel airsick; *(en un coche)* to feel carsick o travel-sick **(b)** *(aturdido)* dizzy **(c)** *Euf (bebido)* tipsy

mareante *adj* **(a)** *Náut* seafaring **(b)** *(nauseabundo)* sickening, nauseating **(c)** *Fig (pesado)* boring

marear 1 *vt* **(a)** *(provocar náuseas)* to make sick; *(en el mar)* to make seasick; *(en un avión)* to make airsick; *(en un coche)* to make carsick o travel-sick **(b)** *(aturdir)* to make dizzy **(c)** *Fam (cargar)* to annoy, pester

2 marearse *vpr* **(a)** *(tener náuseas)* to get sick; *(en el mar)* to get seasick; *(en un avión)* to get airsick; *(en un coche)* to get carsick o travel-sick **(b)** *(quedar aturdido)* to get dizzy **(c)** *Euf (emborracharse)* to get tipsy

marejada *nf* **(a)** *Mar* swell **(b)** *Fig (descontento)* unrest

marejadilla *nf* slight swell

maremagno *nm*, **maremágnum** *nm* **(a)** *(multitud)* multitude, abundance **(b)** *(confusión)* confusion

maremoto *nm Mar* seaquake

marengo, -a *adj* **gris m.** dark grey

mareo *nm* **(a)** *(náusea)* sickness; *(en el mar)* seasickness; *(en un avión)* airsickness; *(en un coche)* carsickness, travel-sickness **(b)** *(aturdimiento)* dizziness, lightheadedness

marfil *nm* ivory

marfileño, -a 1 *adj* **(a)** *(nacionalidad)* of o from the Ivory Coast **(b)** *(ebúrneo)* ivory-like

2 *nm,f* person from the Ivory Coast

marga *nf Min* marl, loam

margarina *nf Culin* margarine

margarita *nf* **(a)** *Bot* daisy; *Fig* **echar margaritas a los puercos** to cast pearls before swine; *Fig* **deshojar la m.** to play 'he/she loves me, he/she loves me not' **(b)** *Impr* daisy-wheel

margen 1 *nm* **(a)** *(de camino)* side **(b)** *(en papel, página)* margin **(c)** *Com* margin ❑ **m. de beneficio** profit margin **(d)** *(límite)* **dejar algn** o **algo al m.** to leave sb o sth out; **mantenerse al m.** not to get involved ❑ **m. de error** margin of error; **m. de seguridad** degree of certainty **(e)** *(ocasión)* **dar m. a algn para hacer algo** to give sb the occasion to do sth

2 *nf (de río)* bank

marginación *nf* exclusion ❑ **m. social** social exclusion

marginado, -a 1 *pp de* **marginar**

2 *adj* excluded

3 *nm,f* outcast

marginal *adj* **(a)** *(en página)* marginal **(b)** *Pol* fringe; **arte/grupo m.** fringe art/group

marginalidad *nf* **vivir en la m.** to live on the margins of society, be a social outcast

marginalizar [14] *vt* to exclude

marginar *vt* **(a)** *(de un grupo, sociedad)* to leave out, exclude **(b)** *(anotar)* to add marginal notes to **(c)** *(dejar márgenes)* to leave a margin on

maría *nf Argot* **(a)** *Esp Ven (droga)* marijuana, pot **(b)** *Esp Educ Argot (asignatura fácil)* easy subject **(c)** *Fam (ama de casa)* housewife

mariachi *nm Mús* mariachi

mariano, -a *adj* Marian

marica *nm Vulg Ofens Br* poof, *US* fag

Maricastaña *n* **en tiempo de M.** years and years ago, ages ago

maricón *nm Vulg Ofens Br* poof, *US* fag

mariconada *nf Vulg* dirty trick

mariconear *vi Fam* to camp it up

mariconera *nf* (man's) clutch bag

mariconería *nf Vulg* campness; **eso es una m.** that's really *Br* poofy o *US* faggy

maridaje *nm* close association, intimate relationship

maridar 1 *vt Fig (unir)* to marry

2 *vi Literario (casarse)* to marry; *(amancebarse)* to live together, cohabit

marido *nm* husband

marihuana, marijuana *nf* marijuana

marimacho *nm Vulg (mujer)* mannish woman, butch woman; *(niña)* tomboy

marimandón, -ona *nm,f Esp Fam* bossyboots

marimba *nf* **(a)** *(tambor)* type of drum **(b)** *(xilofón)* marimba

marimorena *nf Fam* row, fuss; *Fam* **armar(se) la m.** to kick up a racket

marina *nf* **(a)** *Náut* seamanship **(b)** *Mil* navy ❑ **m. de guerra** navy; **m. mercante** merchant navy **(c)** *Arte (pintura)* seascape **(d)** *Geog (zona costera)* seacoast

marinar *vt* to marinate

marine *nm Mil* marine

marinera *nf Am* marinera, = popular Andean dance

marinería *nf* **(a)** *(profesión)* sailoring **(b)** *(marineros)* seamen *pl*, sailors *pl*

marinero, -a 1 *adj* sea, seafaring; **barco m.** seaworthy ship; **gente marinera** people of the sea; *Culin* **pescado a la marinera** = fish in a tomato and wine sauce with shellfish; **pueblo m.** fishing village o town

2 *nm* sailor, seaman; *Fam* **m. de agua dulce** landlubber

marino, -a 1 *adj* marine; **brisa marina** sea breeze

2 *nm* seaman

marioneta *nf* **(a)** *(muñeco)* marionette, puppet **(b)** **marionetas** puppet show *sing*

mariposa *nf* **(a)** *Ent* butterfly **(b)** *(lamparilla)* oil lamp **(c)** *Natación* butterfly **(d)** *(tuerca)* wing nut **(e)** *Fam (afeminado)* fairy

mariposear *vi* **(a)** *(ser inconstante)* to be fickle **(b)** *(flirtear)* to flirt

mariposón *nm Fam* **(a)** *Ofens (afeminado)* fairy, pansy **(b)** *(galanteador)* flirt

mariquita 1 *nf Ent Br* ladybird, *US* ladybug

2 *nm Fam Ofens (marica)* fairy

marisabidilla *nf Esp Fam* bluestocking, know-all

mariscada *nf* seafood meal

mariscal *nm Mil* marshal; **m. de campo** field marshal

mariscar [59] *vi* to gather shellfish

marisco *nm Culin Zool* shellfish; **'especialidad en pescados y mariscos'** 'seafood a speciality'

marisma *nf Geog* salt-marsh

marismeño, -a *adj* marsh

marisquería *nf* seafood restaurant, shellfish bar

marista *adj & nm Rel* Marist

marital *adj* marital; **vida m.** married life

maritates *nmpl CAm* knick-knacks, trinkets

marítimo, -a *adj* maritime, sea; **ciudad marítima** coastal town; **ruta marítima** sea route; **seguro m.** marine insurance

marjal *nm Geog* marsh, bog

marketing ['marketin] *nm Com* marketing ❑ **m. directo** direct marketing

marlo *nm Am* **(a)** *(espiga de maíz)* cob **(b)** *(tronco de cola)* dock **(c)** *(de planta)* stem

marmita *nf (olla)* cooking pot

marmitón, -ona *nm,f* kitchen helper, scullion

mármol *nm* marble

marmolería *nf* (**a**) *(taller)* marble cutter's workshop (**b**) *(mármoles)* marblework

marmolista *nmf* marble cutter

marmóreo, -a *adj* marmoreal, marble

marmota *nf* (**a**) *Zool* marmot; *Fam* **dormir como una m.** to sleep like a log (**b**) *Fam (dormilón)* sleepyhead (**c**) *Fam (mujer)* charwoman

maroma *nf* (**a**) *(cuerda)* thick rope (**b**) *Náut* cable (**c**) *Andes CAm Carib Méx (volatín)* acrobatic performance

maromear *vi Am salvo RP (hacer volatines)* to do acrobatics on the tightrope

maromo *nm Esp Argot* guy, *Br* bloke

marqués *nm* marquis

marquesa *nf* marchioness

marquesado *nm* marquisate

marquesina *nf Arquit* canopy

marquesote *nm CAm Méx Culin* = type of cake

marquetería *nf* marquetry, inlaid work

marrajo, -a 1 *adj* (**a**) *Taur* vicious, dangerous (**b**) *(astuto)* cunning, sly
2 *nm (pez)* mako shark

marranada *nf,* **marranería** *nf* filthy thing *o* act; **han dejado el piso hecho una m.** they've left the flat like a pigsty; *Fam* **hacer una m. a algn** to play a dirty trick on sb

marrano, -a 1 *adj (sucio)* filthy, dirty
2 *nm,f* (**a**) *Fam (cochino)* dirty pig, slob; *(cabrón)* swine (**b**) *Zool* pig

marrar *vi* to go wrong, fail

marras: de marras *loc adv Fam* **el individuo de m.** the man in question

marrasquino *nm (vino)* maraschino

marrón 1 *adj (color)* brown
2 *nm* (**a**) *(color)* brown (**b**) *Culin* **m. glacé** marron glacé (**c**) *Esp Argot (condena)* sentence; **comerse un m.** to own up; **pillar de m.** to catch red-handed

marroquí *adj & nmf* Moroccan

marroquinería *nf* (**a**) *Ind* leather tanning (**b**) *(artículos de cuero)* leather goods

Marruecos *n* Morocco

marrullería *nf* cajolery, wheedling

marrullero, -a 1 *adj* cajoling, wheedling
2 *nm,f* cajoler, wheedler

Marsella *n* Marseilles

marsopa *nf Zool* porpoise

marsupial *adj & nm Zool* marsupial

marta *nf Zool* (**a**) *(animal)* (pine) marten □ **m. cibellina** sable (**b**) *(piel)* sable

martajar *vt CAm Méx (maíz)* to grind; *Fam* **m. el inglés** to speak broken English

Marte *n Astrol Astron Mit* Mars

martes *nm inv* Tuesday; **M. de Carnaval** Shrove Tuesday, Pancake Tuesday; **m. y trece** ≃ Friday the thirteenth; *Prov* **en m., ni te cases ni te embarques** never take important decisions on a Tuesday; *véase tamb* **viernes**

martillar *vt véase* **martillear**

martillazo *nm* blow with a hammer

martillear *vt* to hammer; *Fig* **m. los oídos** to hammer *o* pound on one's ears

martilleo *nm* hammering

martillo *nm* hammer

martinete[1] *nm Orn* (**a**) *(ave)* night heron (**b**) *(penacho)* plume

martinete[2] *nm* (**a**) *(mazo)* drop hammer (**b**) *(para clavar estacas)* pile-driver (**c**) *Mús (macillo)* hammer

martingala *nf Fam* trick

Martinica *n* Martinique

martín pescador *nm Orn* kingfisher

mártir *nmf* martyr

martirio *nm* (**a**) *Rel* martyrdom (**b**) *Fig (fastidio)* torment

martirizar [14] *vt* (**a**) *(torturar)* to martyr (**b**) *Fig (fastidiar)* to torture, torment

marxismo *nm* Marxism

marxista *adj & nmf* Marxist

marzo *nm* March; *véase tamb* **noviembre**

mas *conj Literario* but

más 1 *adv* (**a**) *(comparativo)* more; **compra otro m.** buy another one; **es m. alta/resuelta que yo** she's taller/more resolute than me; *(mayor)* **hay m. número de niños que de adultos** there are more children than adults; **necesito m. tiempo** I need more time; **no tengo m.** I haven't got any more (**b**) *(con numerales, cantidad)* more than, over; **m. de diez** over ten (**c**) *(superlativo)* most; **es el m. bonito/caro** it's the prettiest/most expensive (**d**) *(en exclamación)* so ..., what a ...; **¡está m. guapa!** she looks so beautiful!; **¡qué casa m. bonita!** what a lovely house! (**e**) *(después de pron interr e indef)* else; **¿algo m.?** anything else?; **no, nada m.** no, nothing else; **¿dónde/qué/quién m.?** where/what/who else?; **nadie/alguien m.** nobody/somebody else (**f**) *(indica suma)* plus; **dos m. dos** two plus *o* and two (**g**) *(locuciones)* **a m. no poder** as much as possible; **a m. tardar** at the latest; **a m. y mejor** a great deal; **cada día** *o* **vez m.** more and more; **cada vez m. caro** more and more expensive, dearer and dearer; **como el que m.** as well as anyone *o* the next man; **cuanto** *o* **mientras m. trabajas, m. ganas** the more you work, the more you earn; **cuanto** *o* **mientras m. lo pienso, menos lo entiendo** the more I think about it, the less I understand it; **cuanto m. mejor** the more the better; **chilló m. que cantó** he screamed rather than sang; **de m.** *(de sobras)* spare, extra; *(que sobra)* too much, too many; **dos de m.** two too many; **estar de m.** to be unnecessary, be surplus to requirements; **traje uno de m.** I brought a spare one; **el que m. y el que menos** everybody; **el m. allá** the beyond; **es m.** what's more, furthermore; **de lo m.** extremely, very, ever so; **es de lo m. guapo** he's ever so handsome; **lo m. posible** as much as possible; **lo m. pronto/tarde** as soon/late as possible; **m. allá** *o* **adelante** further on; **m. allá de** beyond; **m. bien** rather; **m. de la cuenta** too much; **m. de lo normal** more than usual; **(poco) m. o menos** more or less; **m. que** rather than; **m. que nunca** more than ever; **m. aún** even more; **ni m. ni menos** exactly; **no m. de** *o* **que** no more than, only; **por m.** *(con nombre)* however much *o* no matter how much, however many *o* no matter how many; *(con adj, adv, v)* however (much), no matter how (much); **por m. dinero/millones que ahorres no podrás comprarte un castillo** however much money/many millions you save you won't be able to buy a castle; **por m. fuerte que sea** however strong he may be; **por m. que grites no te oirá nadie** no matter how much you shout nobody will hear you; **¿qué m. da?** does it make any difference?, what's the difference?; **quien m., quien menos** everybody; **sin m. ni m.** without reason; **tanto m. cuanto que ...** all the more because ...; **todo lo m.** at the most *o* latest; *Fam* **¡y tú, m.!** same to you!; **los/las m.** the majority, most people; **las m. de las veces** more often than not
2 *nm inv Mat* plus;
3 *adj Fam* **el tuyo es m. vestido que el mío** yours is a better dress than mine

masa *nf* (**a**) *(gen)* mass; **una m. líquida** a liquid mass □ **m. atómica** atomic mass; **m. encefálica** brain (**b**) *(de cosas)* bulk, volume (**c**) *(gente)* mass; **atraer a las masas** to draw the crowds; **en m.** en masse ❑ **medios de comunicación de masas** mass media; **producción en m.** mass production (**d**) *Elec (tierra) Br* earth, *US* ground (**e**) *Constr (mortero)* mortar (**f**) *Culin* dough; *Fig* **con las manos en la m.** red-handed

masacrar *vt* to massacre

masacre *nf* massacre

masaje *nm* massage; **dar masaje(s) (a)** to massage

masajear *vt* to massage, rub

masajista *nmf (hombre)* masseur; *(mujer)* masseuse

mascada *nf* (**a**) *CAm Méx Ven (tabaco)* plug of chewing tobacco (**b**) *CSur (bocado)* mouthful, bite (**c**) *Cuba Méx (pañuelo)* silk handkerchief

mascadura *nf* chewing, mastication

mascar [59] *vt & vi* to chew, masticate

máscara *nf* (**a**) *(para cubrir)* mask; *Fig* **quitar la m. a algn** to unmask sb; *Fig* **quitarse la m.** to reveal oneself ❑ **m. de gas** gas mask; **traje de m.** fancy dress (**b**) **máscaras** masquerade *sing* (**c**) *nmf (persona)* masked person

mascarada *nf* masquerade

mascarilla *nf* (**a**) *(de protección, de oxígeno)* mask ❑ **m. de oxígeno** oxygen mask (**b**) *Med* face mask (**c**) *(cosmética)* face pack

mascarón *nm* (**a**) *(máscara)* large mask (**b**) *Náut* **m. de proa** figurehead

Mascate *n* Muscat

mascota *nf* mascot

masculinidad *nf* masculinity, manliness

masculinizar [14] *vt* to make mannish

masculino, -a 1 *adj* (**a**) *Zool Bot* male; **órganos masculinos** male organs (**b**) *(de hombre)* male, manly; **una voz masculina** a manly voice (**c**) *(para hombre)* men's; **ropa masculina** men's clothes, menswear (**d**) *Ling* masculine
2 *nm Ling* masculine

mascullar *vt* to mumble

masía *nf* traditional Catalan farmhouse

masificación *nf* overcrowding (**de** in)

masificar [59] **1** *vt* to cause overcrowding in
2 masificarse *vpr* to become overcrowded

masilla *nf* putty

masivo, -a *adj* massive

masoca *nm,f Fam* masochist

masón *nm* freemason, mason

masonería *nf* freemasonry, masonry

masónico, -a *adj* masonic

masoquismo *nm* masochism

masoquista 1 *adj* masochistic
2 *nmf* masochist

mastaba *nf Arquit Hist* mastaba

mastectomía *nf Med* mastectomy

máster *(pl* **másters)** *nm* Master's (degree)

masticación *nf* chewing, mastication

masticador, -a *adj* chewing, masticating

masticar [59] *vt* (**a**) *(mascar)* to chew, masticate (**b**) *Fig (ponderar)* to chew o ponder over

mástil *nm* (**a**) *(asta)* mast, pole (**b**) *Náut* mast (**c**) *(de guitarra)* neck

mastín *nm Zool* mastiff

mastitis *nf Med* mastitis

mastodonte *nm* mastodon

mastodóntico, -a *adj* elephantine

mastoides *adj & nf inv Anat* mastoid

mastuerzo 1 *adj (necio)* stupid, foolish, doltish
2 *nm* (**a**) *Bot* cress (**b**) *(necio)* dolt

masturbación *nf* masturbation

masturbar 1 *vt* to masturbate
2 masturbarse *vpr* to masturbate

mata *nf* (**a**) *(matorral)* bush, shrub; **a salto de m.** *(al día)* from one day to the next; *(apresuradamente)* like a shot; *(de cualquier manera)* any old how, haphazardly ❑ **m. de pelo** head of hair (**b**) *(ramita)* sprig; **una m. de tomillo/romero** a sprig of thyme/rosemary

matachín *nm* slaughterer

matadero *nm* slaughterhouse, abattoir; *Fig* **llevar (a algn) al m.** to put sb's life at risk

matador, -a 1 *adj* killing
2 *nm Taur* matador, bullfighter

matadura *nf (harness)* sore

matamoscas *nm inv* (**a**) *(pala)* fly swat (**b**) *(espray)* flyspray

matanza *nf* (**a**) *(masacre)* slaughter. (**b**) *Esp Culin* pork products *pl*

matar 1 *vt* (**a**) *(quitar la vida a)* to kill; *Fig* **m. a algn a disgustos** to drive sb insane; *Fam* **el que la sigue la mata** where there's a will, there's a way; *Fam* **estar a m. con algn** to be at daggers drawn with sb; *Fam* **m. el hambre/el tiempo** to kill hunger/(the) time; *Fam* **matarlas callando** to be a wolf in a sheep's clothing; *Fam* **que me maten si ...** I'll be damned if ... (**b**) *(redondear)* to round, bevel (**c**) *(sello)* to frank (**d**) *(polvo)* to lay (**e**) *(luz, fuego)* to put out (**f**) *(color)* to tone down
2 matarse *vpr* to kill oneself; *Fig* **se mata para sacar a la familia adelante** she kills herself working to support her family

matarife *nm* slaughterer

matarratas *nm inv* (**a**) *(raticida)* rat poison (**b**) *Fam (brebaje)* rotgut

matasanos *nmf inv Fam* quack

matasellar *vt* to cancel, postmark

matasellos *nm inv* (**a**) *(instrumento)* canceller (**b**) *(marca)* postmark

matasiete *nm Fam* bully, braggart

matasuegras *nm inv* paper serpent

matate *nm CAm* string bag

matazón *nf CAm Col Ven (animales)* slaughter, killing; *Fig* toll, carnage

match [matʃ] *nm Dep* match

mate¹ *adj (sin brillo)* matt

mate² *nm Ajedrez* mate ❑ **jaque m.** checkmate

mate³ *nm* (**a**) *Bot* maté; *(bebida)* Paraguayan tea, maté (**b**) *CSur (planta, recipiente)* gourd (**c**) *CSur Fam (cabeza)* nut

matear *vi* to drink maté

matemática *nf,* **matemáticas** *nfpl* mathematics *sing*

matemáticamente *adv* mathematically

matemático, -a 1 *adj* mathematical
2 *nm,f* mathematician

materia *nf* (**a**) *(sustancia)* matter ❑ **m. grasa** fat content; **m. gris** grey matter; **m. orgánica** organic matter **m. prima** raw material (**b**) *(tema)* matter, question; **en m. de** as regards; **entrar en m.** to get to the point (**c**) *Educ (asignatura)* subject

material 1 *adj* material, physical; **daños materiales** damage to property; **el autor m. del hecho** the real instigator of the deed, the person behind the deed; **no tengo tiempo m. para hacerlo** I just haven't got the time to do it

2 *nm* material ❑ **m. escolar/de construcción** teaching/building material *o* materials *pl*; **m. de oficina** office equipment

materialidad *nf* material nature

materialismo *nm* materialism ❑ *Filos* **m. dialéctico** dialectic materialism

materialista *adj & nmf* materialist

materialización *nf* materialization

materializar [14] **1** *vt* (**a**) *(idea, proyecto)* to realize (**b**) *(hacer aparecer)* to produce
2 materializarse *vpr* (**a**) *(idea, proyecto)* to materialize (**b**) *(aparecer)* to appear

materialmente *adv* materially, physically; **es m. imposible** it is quite *o* absolutely impossible

maternal *adj* maternal, motherly

maternidad *nf* maternity, motherhood

materno, -a *adj* maternal; **abuelo m.** maternal grandfather; **lengua materna** native *o* mother tongue

mates *nfpl Fam Br* maths *sing*, *US* math

matinal 1 *adj* morning, matinal
2 *nf* matinée

matinée *nf*, **matiné** *nf* (*por la mañana*) morning showing; *RP* (*por la tarde*) matinée

matiz *nm* (**a**) *(color)* shade, hue, tint; **tres matices de rosa** three shades of pink (**b**) *Fig* shade of meaning, nuance; **un m. irónico** a touch of irony

matización *nf* (**a**) *Arte* blending, harmonization; *(coloreado)* shading, tingeing (**b**) *Fig (de palabras)* nuances *pl*

matizar [14] *vt* (**a**) *Arte (proporcionar)* to blend, harmonize; *(dar color)* to tinge (**b**) *Fig (palabras, discurso)* to tinge; *(voz)* to vary *o* modulate (**c**) *Fig (precisar)* to be more precise *o* explicit about; **convendría m. este tema** we ought to look more closely at this; **esto, hay que matizarlo** it's not as straightforward as that; **¿podría m. sus recientes declaraciones, por favor?** could you clarify your recent statements please?

matojo *nm* shrub, bush; **un m. de hierbas** a tuft of grass

matón, -ona *nm,f Fam* thug, bully

matorral *nm* brushwood, thicket

matraca 1 *nf (ruido)* rattle; *Fam* **dar la m. a algn** *(dar la lata)* to pester *o* bother sb; *(burlarse)* to make fun of sb, laugh at sb
2 *nmf Fam* bore, pest, nuisance

matraquear *vi* (**a**) *(hacer ruido)* to rattle (**b**) *Fam* to pester, be a nuisance

matraqueo *nm* (**a**) *(ruido)* rattling (**b**) *Fam* pestering

matraz *nm Quim* flask

matrero, -a 1 *adj (astuto)* sly, cunning
2 *nm,f* (**a**) *(astuto)* trickster, slyboots (**b**) *Am (bandolero)* bandit, brigand

matriarcado *nm* matriarchy

matriarcal *adj* matriarchal

matricida *nmf (persona)* matricide

matricidio *nm (acto)* matricide

matrícula *nf* (**a**) *(lista)* roll, list (**b**) *(inscripción)* registration ❑ **derechos de m.** registration fee; **m. de honor** top mark; **plazo de m.** registration period (**c**) *Aut (número)* registration number; *(placa) Br* number *o US* license plate (**d**) *Náut* **puerto de m.** port of registry

matriculación *nf* registration

matricular 1 *vt (alumno, vehículo, barco)* to register
2 matricularse *vpr* to register; **me matriculé en (un curso de) inglés** I put my name down for English (classes)

matrimonial *adj* matrimonial; **agencia m.** marriage bureau; **enlace m.** wedding; **vida m.** married life

matrimonio *nm* (**a**) *(institución)* marriage; **contraer m.** to marry ❑ **cama de m.** double bed; **m. civil/religioso** registry office/church wedding (**b**) *(pareja casada)* married couple; **el m. y los niños** the couple and their children; **el m. Romero** Mr and Mrs Romero, the Romeros (**c**) *Andes Carib (boda)* wedding

matriz *nf* (**a**) *Anat* womb, uterus (**b**) *(de talonario)* stub (**c**) *(de documento) (original)* original, master copy (**d**) *Téc* mould, *US* mold (**e**) *Impr Mat* matrix

matrona *nf* (**a**) *(madre respetable)* matron, mature woman (**b**) *Med (comadrona)* midwife (**c**) *(en cárceles, hospitales)* matron (**d**) *(en aduanas)* searcher

matufia *nf RP Fam* trick, fraud

matungo, -a *nm RP Fam* old horse, hack, nag

maturrango, -a *adj* (**a**) *Am (jinete)* poor, incompetent (**b**) *Am Pey* Spanish/European (**c**) *Arg Chile (persona)* clumsy

Matusalén *nm* Methuselah; **más viejo que M.** as old as Methuselah *o* the hills

matute *nm* (**a**) *(contrabando)* smuggling; **de m.** contraband; **hacer m.** to smuggle (**b**) *(género)* contraband, smuggled goods *pl* (**c**) *(casa de juegos)* gambling den

matutino, -a 1 *adj* morning; **estrella matutina** morning star
2 *nm Prensa* morning newspaper

maula 1 *nf* (**a**) *(trasto)* piece of junk; **este coche es una m.** this car is an old crate (**b**) *(retal)* remnant (**c**) *(engaño)* (dirty) trick
2 *nmf Fam* (**a**) *Fig (persona) (moroso)* bad payer; *(tramposo)* slippery *o* tricky customer; *(pesado)* bore (**b**) *(vago)* dead loss, good-for-nothing

maullar [4] *vi* to miaow

maullido *nm* miaowing, miaow

Mauricio *n* Mauritius

Mauritania *n* Mauritania

mauritano, -a *adj & nm,f* Mauritanian

máuser *nf Mil* mauser

mausoleo *nm Arquit* mausoleum

maxilar *Anat* **1** *adj* maxillary
2 *nm* jaw, jawbone

máxima *nf* (**a**) *(sentencia, principio)* maxim (**b**) *Meteor* maximum temperature

maximalismo *nm* maximalism

maximalista *adj & nmf* maximalist

máxime *adv* especially, all the more so

maximizar [14] *vt* to maximize

máximo, -a 1 *adj superl de* **grande** (**a**) *(capacidad, cantidad, temperatura)* maximum; **la máxima puntuación** the highest score (**b**) *Mat* **m. común denominador** highest common factor, *US* highest common denominator
2 *nm* maximum; **al m.** to the utmost; **como m.** *(como mucho)* at the most; *(lo más tarde)* at the latest; **mi paciencia llegó al m.** my patience reached its limit

maya 1 *adj* Mayan
2 *nmf* Maya, Mayan

mayestático, -a *adj* majestic; *Ling* **plural m.** the Royal 'we'

mayo *nm* (**a**) *(mes)* May; *Prov* **hasta el cuarenta de m. no te quites el sayo** ne'er cast a clout till May be out; *véase tamb* **noviembre** (**b**) *(palo)* maypole

mayólica *nf Constr* majolica

mayonesa *nf Culin* mayonnaise

mayor 1 adj (**a**) (comparativo) larger, bigger, greater; (persona) older; (hermanos, hijos) elder; **su casa es m. que la mía** her house is bigger than mine; **Elvira es m. que Pilar** Elvira is older than Pilar; **sus hermanos mayores** her elder brothers (**b**) (superlativo) largest, biggest, greatest; (persona) oldest; (hermanos, hijos) eldest; **el m. enemigo** the greatest enemy; **la m. parte** the majority; **la m. parte de las veces** most times; **el m. de la clase** the oldest in the class; **su hija m.** his eldest daughter (**c**) (adulto) grown-up; **hacerse m.** to grow up; **ser m. de edad** to be of age; Fam **ya eres m.** you're a big boy/girl now (**d**) (maduro) elderly, mature; **un hombre (ya) m.** an elderly man (**e**) (principal) major, main; **calle m.** high o main street; Educ **colegio m.** hall of residence; Com **libro m.** ledger; **plaza m.** main square; **premisa m.** major premise (**f**) Mús major; **do/re/mi m.** C/D/E major (**g**) Com **al por m.** wholesale; Fig (en abundancia) by the score, galore

2 nm (**a**) Mil major (**b**) **mayores** (adultos) grownups, adults; **una película para m.** a film for adults; **respetar a los m.** to show respect for one's elders (**c**) **mayores** (antepasados) ancestors

3 nmf **el/la m.** the oldest; (hermanos, hijos) the eldest

mayoral nm (**a**) (pastor) head shepherd (**b**) Agr (capataz) foreman

mayorazgo nm (**a**) (primogenitura) primogeniture (**b**) (herencia) entailed estate (**c**) (heredero) heir (to an entailed estate) (**d**) Fig (primogénito) first-born, eldest son

mayordomo nm butler

mayoreo nm Am wholesale

mayoría nf majority; **en su m.** in the main; **la gran** o **inmensa m.** the great o vast majority; **la m. de los niños** most children □ **m. absoluta/relativa** absolute/relative majority; **m. de edad** majority

mayorista 1 adj wholesale

2 nmf wholesaler; **precios de m.** wholesale prices

mayoritario, -a adj majority; **un gobierno m.** a majority government

mayúscula nf capital letter

mayúsculo, -a adj (**a**) (enorme) very big, enormous; **un susto m.** a tremendous scare (**b**) Ling (letra) capital

maza nf (**a**) Téc large hammer □ **m. de fraga** drop hammer (**b**) Hist (arma) mace (**c**) (insignia) mace (**d**) Fig bore (**e**) Mús drumstick (**f**) Chile (de rueda) hub

mazacote nm Fam (**b**) (plato) solid mass, stodge (**c**) (objeto, edificio) eyesore, monstrosity

mazamorra nf Perú Culin Br maize porridge, US cornmeal mush

mazapán nm Culin marzipan

mazazo nm blow with a hammer o mace; **caer como un m.** to go down like a ball balloon; **la noticia fue un m.** the news was a heavy blow

mazmorra nf dungeon

mazo nm (**a**) (martillo) mallet (**b**) (manojo) wad, bunch; **un m. de billetes de banco/de papeles** a wad of banknotes/papers (**c**) Fig (pesado) bore, pest

mazorca nf Bot spike; Agr corncob, Br ear of maize

mazurca nf Mús mazurka

m/c, m/cta (abrev de **mi cuenta**) my account

MCCA (abrev de **Mercado Común Centroamericano**) Central American Common Market

me 1 pron pers me; **¿me das un caramelo?** will you give me a sweet?; **no me mires** don't look at me

2 pron reflexivo myself; **me veo en el espejo** I can see myself in the mirror; **me voy/muero** I'm going/dying

meada nf Vulg (**a**) (acción, orina) piss, slash; **echar una m.** to have a piss (**b**) (mancha) urine stain

meadero nm Vulg Br bog, US john

meandro nm meander

meapilas nmf inv Fam Pey holy Joe

mear 1 vi Vulg to (have a) piss

2 mearse vpr to wet oneself; Fig **m. de risa** to piss oneself (laughing)

Meca n (**a**) **la M.** Mecca; Fig **andar de la Ceca a la M.** to go back and forth (**b**) Fig (centro) mecca, centre, US center

mecachis Fam interj Br sugar!, US shoot!

mecánica nf (**a**) (ciencia) mechanics sing □ **m. cuántica** quantum mechanics (**b**) (funcionamiento) mechanics pl

mecanicismo nm mechanism

mecanicista 1 adj mechanistic

2 nmf mechanist

mecánico, -a 1 adj mechanical

2 nm,f mechanic □ **m. dentista** dental technician

mecanismo nm mechanism

mecanización nf mechanization

mecanizar [14] vt to mechanize

mecano® nm Meccano®

mecanografía nf typewriting, typing

mecanografiar [32] vt to type

mecanógrafo, -a nm,f typist

mecatazo nm (**a**) CAm Méx (latigazo) lash, stroke (**b**) CAm Fam (trago) swig

mecate nm (**a**) CAm Méx strip of pita fibre o US fiber; string (**b**) Méx (grosero) coarse o vulgar person

mecedor, -a adj rocking

mecedora nf rocking chair

mecenas nmf inv patron

mecenazgo nm patronage

mecer [40] **1** vt to rock

2 mecerse vpr to swing, rock

mecha nf (**a**) (de vela) wick (**b**) Mil Min fuse; Fam **a toda m.** at full speed; Fam **aguantar m.** to grin and bear it (**c**) Culin lardoon, piece of bacon used to lard meat (**d**) (de pelo) streak; **hacerse mechas** to have one's hair streaked (**e**) Andes Ven (broma) joke

mechar vt (**a**) (carne) to lard (**b**) (pelo) to streak

mechero, -a 1 nm Esp (cigarette) lighter □ **m. de gas** gas lighter

2 nmf Argot shoplifter

mechificar vi Am to mock, scoff

mechón nm (**a**) (de pelo) lock (**b**) (de lana) tuft

meco, -a adj Méx (animal) red o ginger and black

medalla 1 nf medal; Fam **ponerse medallas** to boast

2 nmf Dep (campeón) medallist, US medalist

medallista nmf medallist, US medalist

medallón nm medallion

médano nm (duna) sand dune; (banco) sandbank

media nf (**a**) (prenda) stocking; Am (calcetín) sock; **hacer m.** to knit (**b**) (promedio) average; **una m. de tres litros por día** three litres a day on average (**c**) Mat mean; **m. aritmética/geométrica** arithmetic/geometric mean

mediación nf mediation, intervention; **por m. de un amigo** through a friend

mediado, -a 1 pp de **mediar**

2 adj half-full, half-empty; **está el jarro m.** the jug is half full; **llevo mediada la obra** I'm half-way through the play; **a mediados de mes/semana** about the middle of the month/week

mediador, -a 1 adj mediating

2 nm,f mediator

mediagua *nf Andes CAm (cabaña)* shack, hut

medialuna *nf* **(a)** *(símbolo musulmán)* crescent **(b)** *Culin (pasta)* croissant

mediana *nf Mat* median

medianamente *adv* acceptably, tolerably; **habla francés m. bien** he can get by in French; **sólo entendí m. lo que dijo** I only half understood what he said

medianería *nf* **(a)** *(pared)* party wall **(b)** *Am (aparcería)* partnership

medianero, -a *adj* dividing; *Arquit* **muro m.** dividing fence; *Arquit* **pared medianera** party wall

medianía *nf* **(a)** *(social)* middling position; **vivir en la m.** to have an undistinguished social position **(b)** *Pey (persona)* mediocre person

mediano, -a *adj* **(a)** *(de calidad)* middling, average; **inteligencia mediana** average intelligence **(b)** *(tamaño)* medium-sized; **un coche m.** a medium-sized car **(c)** *Pey (mediocre)* mediocre

medianoche *nf* midnight; **a m.** in the middle of the night

mediante *prep* by means of, with the help of, using; **Dios m.** God willing

mediar *vi* **(a)** *(intervenir)* to mediate, intervene; **m. en favor de** *o* **por algn** to intercede on behalf of sb **(b)** *(tiempo)* to pass; **mediaron tres semanas** three weeks passed; *(distancia)* **median nueve kms entre Tafalla y Olite** it is nine kms from Tafalla to Olite; *Fig* **media un abismo** there is an enormous gap *o* difference **(c)** *(hecho, circunstancia)* to exist; **media el hecho de que es menor de edad** there is the fact that he is a minor **(d)** *(ocurrir)* to intervene, happen, come up; **se iban a casar pero medió el escándalo** they were going to get married, but the scandal intervened **(e)** *(estar en la mitad)* to be in the middle, be half-way through; **mediaba agosto** it was mid-August

mediático,-a *adj* media

mediatización *nf* decisive influence

mediatizar [14] *vt* to exercise *o* have a decisive influence on

medicación *nf* **(a)** *(tratamiento)* medication, medical treatment **(b)** *(medicamentos)* medicines *pl*

medicamento *nm* medicine, medicament

medicamentoso, -a *adj* medicinal

medicar [59] **1** *vt* to administer medicines to, medicate **2 medicarse** *vpr* to take medicines

medicina *nf* medicine; **estudiante de m.** medical student, medic ❑ **m. alternativa** alternative medicine; **m. interna** = branch of medicine which deals with problems of the internal organs, without surgery, *US* internal medicine

medicinal *adj* medicinal

medición *nf* **(a)** *(acción)* measuring **(b)** *(dato)* measurement

médico, -a 1 *adj* medical
2 *nm,f* doctor, physician ❑ **m. de cabecera** family doctor, general practitioner, GP

medida *nf* **(a)** *(cantidad específica)* measure; **a (la) m.** *(ropa)* made-to-measure; *(mueble)* specially made; **pesos y medidas** weights and measures; **tres medidas de arroz** three measures of rice; *Fig* **a la m. de** according to; *Fig* **a m. que** as; **a m. que pasa el tiempo** as time goes by; *Fig* **en gran m.** to a great extent; *Fig* **en la m. en que** in so far as, inasmuch as; *Fig* **en la m. de lo posible** as far as possible; *Fig* **en mayor/menor m.** to a greater/lesser extent; *Fig* **hasta cierta m.** to a certain extent **(b)** *(medición)* measuring, measurement **(c)** *(moderación)* moderation, prudence; **sin m.** immoderately, excessively **(d)** *(disposición)* action, measure; **adoptar** *o* **tomar medidas** to take steps ❑ **m. preventiva** preventive measure; **m. represiva** deterrent **(e)** *Lit* scansion

medidor, -a 1 *adj* measuring
2 *nm Am Téc* meter

medieval *adj* medieval

medievalismo *nm* medievalism

medievalista *nmf* medievalist

medievo *nm* Middle Ages *pl*

medio, -a 1 *adj* **(a)** *(igual a la mitad)* half; **a m. camino** half-way; **clase media** middle class; **dedo m.** middle finger; **m. kilo** half a kilo; **una hora y media** one and a half hours, an hour and a half; *Fig* **media luz** half-light **(b)** *(intermedio)* middle; **a media mañana/tarde** in the middle of the morning/afternoon; **de media edad** middle-aged **(c)** *(promedio)* average; **el hombre m.** the average man; **temperatura media** mean temperature
2 *adv* half; **está m. muerto** he is half dead; **está m. terminado** it's half finished; **a medias** *(incompleto)* unfinished; *(entre dos)* between the two; **lo dejó a medias** he left it half done; **lo pagamos a medias** we went halves on it, we shared the cost; **ir a medias** to go halves
3 *nm* **(a)** *(mitad)* half; **de m. a m.** completely **(b)** *(centro)* middle; **de por m.** in the way; **en m. (de)** *(en el centro)* in the middle (of); *(entre dos)* in between; *(entre varios)* among; **(justo) en m. de la calle** (right) in the middle of the street; **estar/ponerse en m.** to be/put oneself in the way; **la casa del m.** the middle house; **por (el) m.** in *o* down the middle; *Fam* **quitar algo/a algn de en m.** to get sth/sb out of the way **(c)** *(procedimiento)* means, way; **medios de comunicación** (mass) media; **medios de vida** means of support; **no hay m. de ...** there's no way of ...; **por m. de ...** by means of ...; **por sus propios medios** on his own resources; **por todos los medios** by all possible means **(d)** *Biol Fís* medium; **adaptación al m.** adaptation to the environment ❑ **m. ambiente** environment **(e)** *Mat* mean **(f)** *(círculo social)* environment, circle; **en los medios teatrales** in the world of theatre; **encontrarse en su m.** to be in one's element **(g)** *Dep (jugador)* half back **(h)** **medios** *(económicos)* means; **no tener m.** not to have economic resources

medioambiental *adj* environmental

mediocampista *nmf Dep* midfielder

mediocre *adj* mediocre

mediocridad *nf* mediocrity

mediodía *nm* **(a)** *(hora exacta)* midday, noon **(b)** *(período aproximado)* early afternoon, lunchtime; **las tiendas cierran dos o tres horas al m.** shops are closed for two or three hours in the early afternoon *o* at lunchtime **(c)** *(sur)* south

medioevo *nm véase* **medievo**

mediopensionista *nmf* day student

medir [47] **1** *vt* **(a)** *(distancia, superficie, temperatura)* to measure; *Fig* **los boxeadores midieron sus fuerzas** the boxers measured *o* gauged each other's strength **(b)** *(sopesar)* to weigh up; **m. los pros y los contras** to weigh up the pros and cons **(c)** *(moderar)* to weigh; **mide tus palabras** weigh your words **(d)** *Lit (verso)* to scan
2 *vi* to measure, be; **¿cuánto mides?** how tall are you?; **mide 2 metros** he is 2 metres tall; **mide dos metros de alto/ancho/largo** it is two metres high/wide/long
3 medirse *vpr* **m. con algn** to measure oneself against sb

meditabundo, -a *adj* pensive, thoughtful

meditación *nf* meditation

meditar *vt & vi* to meditate, ponder; **m. sobre algo** to ponder over sth

meditativo, -a *adj* meditative

mediterráneo, -a 1 *adj* Mediterranean
  2 *nm* **el M.** the Mediterranean

médium *nmf* medium

medo, -a 1 *adj* Median
  2 *nm,f* Mede

medrar *vi* **(a)** *(plantas, animales)* to thrive, grow **(b)** *Fig* to flourish, do well, prosper

medro *nm* **(a)** *(plantas, animales)* growth **(b)** *Fig* prosperity **(c)** *(mejora)* improvement **(d) medros** progress *sing*, advancement *sing*

medroso, -a 1 *adj* **(a)** *(temeroso)* fearful, faint-hearted **(b)** *(que causa miedo)* frightening
  2 *nm,f* fearful person

médula *nf* **(a)** *Anat* marrow ❏ **m. espinal** spinal cord; **m. ósea** bone marrow **(b)** *Fig (lo más profundo)* marrow, pith; **hasta la m.** to the marrow

medular *adj* of *o* related to the marrow

medusa *nf Zool* jellyfish

mefistofélico, -a *adj* Mephistophelian

mefítico, -a *adj* poisonous, mephitic

mega *nm Fam Inform* megabyte

megabit (*pl* **megabits**) *nm Inform* megabit

megabyte [meɣaˈβait] (*pl* **megabytes**) *nm Inform* megabyte

megaciclo *nm Rad* megacycle

megafonía *nf* **(a)** *(técnica)* sound amplification **(b)** *(equipo)* public-address system, PA system

megáfono *nm* megaphone

megalítico, -a *adj* megalithic

megalito *nm* megalith

megalomanía *nf* megalomania

megalómano, -a *adj* megalomaniac

megatón *nm Fis* megaton

megavatio *nm Fis* megawatt

mejicano, -a *adj & nm,f* Mexican

Méjico *n* Mexico

mejilla *nf* cheek

mejillón *nm Zool* mussel

mejor 1 *adj* **(a)** *(comparativo)* better; **es m. no decírselo** it's better not to tell her; **esta novela es m. que la anterior** this novel is better than his last one; **a falta de algo m.** for want of something better; **pensé que era m. no salir** I thought I'd better stay at home **(b)** *(superlativo)* best; **tu m. amiga** your best friend; **el m. de los dos** the better of the two; **el m. de los tres** the best of the three; **lo m.** the best thing; **lo m. de algo** the best part of sth; **lo m. posible** as well as possible
  2 *adv* **(a)** *(comparativo)* better; **así es m.** that's better; **cada vez m.** better and better; **ella conduce m.** she drives better; **ir a m.** to improve, get better; **m. dicho** or rather; **m. o peor** one way or another; **¡mucho** *o* **tanto m.!** so much the better! **(b)** *(superlativo)* best; **es el que m. canta** he is the one who sings the best; **a lo m.** *(quizás)* perhaps; *(ojalá)* hopefully

mejora *nf* **(a)** *(progreso)* improvement; **m. de sueldo** pay increase, (pay) rise **(b)** *(puja)* higher bid

mejorable *adj* improvable

mejoramiento *nm* improvement

mejorar 1 *vt* to improve, better; **m. la red vial** to improve the road system; **m. una oferta/una puja** to raise an offer/a bid; **m. una marca** *o* **un récord** to break a record
  2 *vi* to improve, get better; **el tiempo ha mejorado** the weather has cleared up; **m. de salud** to improve in health, get better; **m. de situación** to better oneself

3 mejorarse *vpr* to get better; **¡que te mejores!** get well soon!

mejoría *nf* improvement

mejunje *nm* unpleasant mixture *o* brew

melado, -a 1 *adj* honey-coloured, *US* honey-colored
  2 *nm Am* cane syrup

melancolía *nf* melancholy

melancólico, -a 1 *adj* melancholic, melancholy
  2 *nm,f* melancholic person

melanina *nf Biol* melanin

melaza *nf* molasses *pl*

melcocha *nf* honey toffee

melcochudo, -a *adj CAm Cuba* soft, flexible

melé *nf Esp Dep* scrum

melena *nf* **(a)** *(de persona)* (head of) hair ❏ **m. de león** lion's mane **(b) melenas** mop *sing*

melenudo, -a 1 *adj* long-haired
  2 *nm,f* long-haired person

melifluo, -a *adj* mellifluous

melilense 1 *adj* of *o* from Melilla
  2 *nmf* person from Melilla

melindre *nm* **(a)** *Culin (frito)* honey fritter; *(de mazapán)* iced marzipan cake **(b)** *Fig (afectación)* affectation, fussiness; **andarse con melindres** to be finicky *o* fastidious *o* fussy

melindroso, -a 1 *adj* affected, fussy, finicky
  2 *nm,f* affected *o* finicky person

melisa *nf Bot* (lemon) balm

mella *nf* **(a)** *(hendedura)* nick, notch; *(en plato, taza etc)* chip **(b)** *(hueco)* gap, hole; **tantos gastos han hecho m. en mis ahorros** all these expenses have made a hole in my savings **(c)** *Fig* impression; **hacer m.** *(en algn)* to make an impression on; *(en el honor, la reputación etc)* to damage

mellado, -a 1 *pp de* **mellar**
  2 *adj* **(a)** *(hendido)* nicked, notched; *(plato, taza etc)* chipped **(b)** *(sin dientes)* gap-toothed **(c)** *Fig* damaged

mellar *vt* **(a)** *(hacer mellas en)* to nick, notch; *(plato, taza etc)* to chip, take a chip out of **(b)** *Fig (honor)* to cast a slur on; *(orgullo)* to dent

mellizo, -a *adj & nm,f* twin

melocotón *nm esp Esp* peach; *Culin* **melocotones en almíbar** peaches in syrup, tinned peaches

melocotonar *nm esp Esp* peach orchard

melocotonero *nm esp Esp Bot* peach tree

melodía *nf* melody, tune

melódico, -a *adj* melodic

melodioso, -a *adj* melodious, tuneful

melodrama *nm* melodrama

melodramático, -a *adj* melodramatic

melomanía *nf* love of *o* for music

melómano, -a *nm,f* music lover

melón *nm* **(a)** *Bot* melon **(b)** *Hum (cabeza)* nut, bonce **(c)** *Fam (tonto)* ninny **(d)** *Esp muy Fam* **melones** *(pechos)* knockers, *Br* boobs

melonar *nm* melon patch

melopea *nf Esp Fam* **coger** *o* **agarrar/llevar una m.** to get/be drunk *o* pissed

melosidad *nf* sweetness, gentleness

meloso, -a *adj* sweet, honeyed

melva *nf (pez)* frigate mackerel

membrana *nf* membrane

membranoso, -a *adj* membranous

membresía *nf Am* membership

membrete *nm* letterhead

membrillo *nm* (a) *Bot* quince; *(árbol)* quince tree; *(dulce)* quince preserve o jelly (b) *Argot (chivato)* nark

membrudo, -a *adj* brawny, burly

memela *nf Guat Hond Méx* = type of maize tortilla

memez *nf* stupidity; **decir memeces** to talk nonsense

memo, -a *Esp Fam* **1** *adj* silly, stupid
2 *nm,f* nincompoop, ninny

memorable *adj* memorable

memorándum (*pl* **memorándum**) *nm,* **memorando** *nm* notebook

memoria *nf* (a) *(capacidad de recordar)* memory; **aprender/saber algo de m.** to learn/know sth by heart; **borrar de la m.** to banish from memory; **falta de m.** forgetfulness; **hablar de m.** to speak from memory; **hacer m. de algo** to remember o recall sth; **irse de la m.** to slip one's mind; **refrescar la m. a algn** to refresh sb's memory; **traer algo a la m.** to recall sth; **venir a la m.** to come to mind (b) *(recuerdo)* memory, recollection; **de grata/ingrata m.** of happy/unhappy memory (c) *(informe)* report, statement; **m. anual** annual report (d) *(estudio escrito)* essay (e) *(inventario)* inventory, list (f) **memorias** *(biografía)* memoirs (g) *Inform* memory; **m. de acceso aleatorio/de sólo lectura** random access/read-only memory; **m. expandida/extendida/programable** expanded/extended/programmable memory; **m. RAM/ROM** RAM/ROM

memorial *nm* petition, request

memorión, -ona *Fam* **1** *adj* with a very good memory
2 *nm,f* person with a very good memory
3 *nm* very good memory

memorístico, -a *adj* acquired by memory

memorización *nf* memorizing

memorizar [14] *vt* to memorize

mena *nf Min* ore

menaje *nm* furniture and furnishings *pl* ❑ **departamento de m.** hardware and kitchen department; **m. de cocina** kitchen equipment

mención *nf* mention; **digno de m.** worth mentioning; **hacer m. de algo** to mention sth ❑ **m. honorífica** honourable mention

mencionado, -a **1** *pp de* **mencionar**
2 *adj* mentioned; *Fml* **arriba** o **anteriormente m.** aforementioned

mencionar *vt* to mention

menda *pron Esp Fam* yours truly, *Br* muggins; **el** o **mi m. se queda en casa** I'll stay at home; **me lo dijo un m. que pasaba por allí** a bloke who was passing by told me

mendicante *adj & nmf* mendicant

mendicidad *nf* (a) *(acción)* begging (b) *(modo de vida)* beggary

mendigar [38] *vt & vi* to beg

mendigo, -a *nm,f* beggar

mendrugo *nm* (a) *(de pan)* crust (of bread) (b) *Esp Fam (idiota)* fathead, idiot

menear **1** *vt* to shake, move; *(cola)* to wag, waggle; *Fam (caderas, cuerpo)* to wiggle
2 **menearse** *vpr* to move, shake; *Fam* **una tormenta de no te menees** a hell of a storm; *Vulg* **meneársela** to wank

meneo *nm* (a) *(de cola)* wag, waggle; *(de caderas)* wiggle (b) *(paliza)* hiding

menester *nm* (a) *(necesidad)* **haber** o **ser m.** to be necessary; **no es m. que te quedes** there is no need for you to stay; **si hubiera m.** if need be (b) **menesteres** *(asuntos)* business, matters

menesteroso, -a **1** *adj* needy
2 *nm,f* needy person

menestra *nf Culin* vegetable stew

mengano, -a *nm,f Fam* so-and-so, what's-his/her-name; *véase tamb* **fulano, -a**

mengua *nf* (a) *(disminución)* decrease, diminution; **sin m.** without detriment **(de)** to (b) *(falta)* lack, want; **sin m.** complete (c) *(deshonra)* descredit

menguado, -a **1** *pp de* **menguar**
2 *adj* (a) *(reducido)* decreased (b) *(cobarde)* cowardly, spineless; *(miserable)* wretched, miserable
3 *nmf (cobarde)* coward; *(miserable)* wretch
4 *nm Tricot (punto)* decrease

menguante *adj* waning, on the wane ❑ **cuarto m.** last quarter; **luna m.** waning moon

menguar [11] **1** *vt* (a) *(disminuir)* to diminish, reduce (b) *(en calceta)* to decrease
2 *vi* (a) *(disminuir)* to diminish, decrease (b) *(la luna)* to wane

menhir *nm* menhir

meninge *nf Anat* meninx

meningitis *nf Med* meningitis

menisco *nm Anat Fis* meniscus

menopausia *nf Med* menopause

menopáusico, -a *adj* menopausal

menor **1** *adj* (a) *(comparativo)* smaller, lesser; *(persona)* younger; **de m. tamaño** smaller; **mal m.** lesser evil; **ser m. de edad** to be a minor (b) *(superlativo)* smallest, least, slightest; *(persona)* youngest; **sin el m. interés** without the slightest interest; **el m. de los dos** the smaller of the two; **el m. de los tres** the smallest of the three; **es la m.** she's the youngest child (c) *(inferior)* minor; **una obra m.** a minor work (d) *Rel* minor ❑ **órdenes menores** minor orders (e) *Mús* minor; **en la m.** in A minor (f) *Com* **al por m.** retail
2 *nmf* minor; **apto para menores** for all ages

Menorca *n* Minorca

menorquín, -ina *adj & nm,f* Minorcan

menos **1** *adv* (a) *(comparativo)* less, fewer; **m. dinero/leche/tiempo** less money/milk/time; **m. gente/libros/pisos** fewer people/books/flats; **ayer llovió m. que hoy** yesterday it rained less than today; **deberías comer m.** you should eat less; **tiene m. años de lo que parece** he's younger than he looks (b) *(superlativo)* least, fewest; **ayer fue cuando vino m. gente** yesterday was when the fewest people came; **fui el que perdí m. dinero** I lost the least money (c) *(indica resta)* minus; **tres m. uno** three minus one (d) *(locuciones)* **a m. que** unless; **al** o **por lo** o **cuando m.** at least; **cuánto m. lo pienses, mejor** the less you think about it, the better; **cuánto** o **mientras m. comes, más adelgazarás** the less you eat, the more weight you'll lose; **echar a algn de m.** to miss sb; **en m. de ...** in less than ...; **en m. de nada** in no time at all; **eso es lo de m.** that doesn't matter, that's the least of it; **hacer a algn de m.** to disdain o belittle sb; **ir** o **venir a m.** to lose social status; **lo m. que puedes hacer** the least you can do; **los/las m. de** the minority of; **m. de ...** less than ...; **¡m. mal!** thank God!, that's a relief!; **m. aún** even less; **nada m.** no less, no fewer; **nada m. que la mitad de la plantilla perdieron sus puestos de trabajo** no less than half the staff lost their jobs; **¡escribió sesenta cartas, nada m.!** he wrote no fewer than sixty letters!; **ni mucho m.** far from it; **no es para m.** you couldn't expect less; **no puedo por m. de decirle** I can't help telling you; **para no ser m.** not to be left behind; **por m. de nada** for no reason at all; **¿qué m. que decírselo**

personalmente? the least he could have done is to tell her himself; **si al m.** if only; **ya será m.** come off it! **(d)** *Esp RP (con las horas)* to; **son las dos m. diez** it's ten to two; **son m. diez** it's ten to

2 *prep* but, except; **todo m. eso** anything but that

3 *nm Mat* minus

4 *adj Fam* **ésta es m. casa que la tuya** your house is better than this one

menoscabar *vt* **(a)** *(dañar)* to impair, harm, spoil; **tanto trabajo menoscabó su salud** so much work damaged her health **(b)** *(mermar)* to reduce, diminish; **este decreto menoscaba los derechos de los trabajadores** this decree infringes on workers' rights **(c)** *Fig (desacreditar)* to discredit

menoscabo *nm* harm, damage; **ir en m. de algo** to be to the detriment of sth; **sin m.** unimpaired

menospreciable *adj* despicable, contemptible

menospreciar *vt* to show contempt for, scorn, disdain; **m. los consejos de algn** to disregard sb's advice

menosprecio *nm* contempt, scorn, disdain; **con m. de** without regard for

mensaje *nm* message; **el m. de la Corona** the King's/Queen's speech ▫ **m. de texto** text message

mensajería *nf* **(a)** *(de paquetes, cartas)* courier service **(b)** *(por teléfono)* messaging ▫ **m. de imágenes** picture messaging

mensajero, -a *nm,f (portador)* messenger; *(de mensajería)* courier

menstruación *nf* **(a)** *(acción)* menstruation **(b)** *(sangre)* menses *pl*

menstrual *adj* menstrual

menstruar [4] *vi* to menstruate

menstruo *nm* **(a)** *(sangre)* menses *pl* **(b)** *(acción)* menstruation

mensual *adj* monthly; **dos visitas mensuales** two visits a month

mensualidad *nf (pago)* monthly payment; *(sueldo)* monthly salary o wage

mensurable *adj* measurable

menta *nf* **(a)** *Bot* mint ▫ **m. acuática** water mint; **m. de gatos** catmint; **té de m.** mint tea **(b)** *(licor)* crème de menthe

mentado, -a 1 *pp de* **mentar**
2 *adj* **(a)** *(mencionado)* aforementioned **(b)** *Literario (famoso)* famous, well-known

mental *adj* mental; *Fam* **lo suyo es m.** she's not right in her head

mentalidad *nf* mentality; **de m. abierta/cerrada** open-/narrow-minded

mentalizar [14] **1** *vt (concienciar)* to make aware
2 mentalizarse *vpr* **(a)** *(concienciarse)* to become aware **(b)** *(hacerse a la idea)* to come to terms **(a** with); **tienes que mentalizarte** you'll just have to get used to it

mentalmente *adv* mentally

mentar [3] *vt* to mention, name; **ni lo mientes** don't bring the subject up; *Euf* **m. la madre a algn**, *Méx* **m. madres a algn** to insult sb

mente *nf* mind; **no estaba en mi m.** it wasn't my intention (- to); **tenía la m. en blanco** my mind went blank; **traer (algo) a la m.** to bring (sth) to mind; **venir a la m.** to come to mind ▫ **m. abierta/tolerante/cerrada** open/broad/closed mind

mentecato, -a 1 *adj* stupid
2 *nm,f* fool, idiot

mentidero *nm Fam* gossip corner o shop

mentir [62] *vi* to lie, tell lies; **miente más que habla** he lies through his teeth

mentira *nf* lie; **aunque parezca m.** strange as it many seem; **parece m.** it is unbelievable; *Fam Fig* **una m. como una casa** a whopping lie, a whopper ▫ **m. piadosa** white lie

mentirijilla *nf Fam* fib; **de mentirijillas** as a joke, for a laugh, for fun

mentiroso, -a 1 *adj* lying; **un niño m.** a child who tells lies
2 *nm,f* liar

mentís *nm* denial; **dar un m. a (un rumor)** to deny (a rumour)

mentol *nm* menthol

mentolado, -a *adj* mentholated, menthol

mentón *nm Anat* chin

mentor *nm* mentor

menú *(pl* **menús)** *nm* **(a)** *Culin* menu (of the day) ▫ **m. del día** set meal **(b)** *Inform* menu ▫ **m. desplegable** pull-down menu

menudear 1 *vt* to repeat frequently; **menudea sus visitas a esta casa** he visits us quite often
2 *vi* to happen frequently; **los robos menudean en este barrio** burglaries are frequent in this area

menudencia *nf* trifle

menudeo *nm Andes Méx Com* retail

menudillos *nmpl* giblets

menudo, -a 1 *adj* **(a)** *(pequeño)* minute, tiny; **la gente menuda** the little ones *pl*; **lluvia menuda** fine rain **(b)** *(para enfatizar)* what a ...!; **¡m. lío/susto!** what a mess/fright!; **¡m. es el niño!** the little devil!
2 menudos *nmpl (de res)* offal *sing; (de ave)* giblets
3 a menudo *loc adv* often

meñique 1 *adj (muy pequeño)* tiny, very small; **(dedo) m.** little finger
2 *nm (dedo auricular)* little finger

meollo *nm* **(a)** *(miga)* crumb **(b)** *Anat (seso)* brains *pl*; *(médula)* marrow **(c)** *Fig (quid)* essence, pith; **el m. de la cuestión** the heart of the matter **(d)** *Fig (juicio)* intelligence, brains *pl*

meón, -ona *adj* **(a)** *Vulg* who wets himself o herself **(b)** *Fig* baby

mequetrefe *nmf* whippersnapper

mercachifle *nmf* **(a)** *(buhonero)* pedlar **(b)** *Fam Fig (pesetero)* money-grubber

mercadear *vi* to trade

mercader *nmf* merchant

mercadería *nf esp Am* merchandise, goods *pl*

mercadillo *nm* flea market

mercado *nm* market; **acaparar el m.** to corner the market; **abrir m. para un producto** to make a market for a product; **sacar algo al m.** to put sth on the market, market sth ▫ **M. Común** Common Market; *Fin* **m. de capitales** capital market; **m. de divisas** currency market; *Fin* **m. de futuros** futures market; **m. de trabajo** job market; *Fin* **m. de valores** securities market; **m. financiero** financial market; **m. inmobiliario** housing o property market; **m. interbancario** interbank market; **m. laboral** labour market; **m. monetario** money market; **m. negro** black market; **M. Único Europeo** European Single Market

mercadotecnia *nf* marketing

mercancía *nf* merchandise, goods *pl*

mercante *adj* merchant

mercantil *adj* mercantile, commercial; **operaciones mercantiles** commercial transactions

mercantilismo *nm Econ* mercantilism

mercantilista *adj & nmf Econ* mercantilist

mercantilizar [14] *vt* to commercialize

merced *nf Fml* favour, *US* favor, grace; **a m. de** at the mercy of; **m. a** thanks to; *Fml* **nos hizo la m. de ...** he did us the favour of ...

mercenario, -a *adj & nm,f* mercenary

mercería *nf (género) Br* haberdashery, *US* notions *pl*; *(tienda)* haberdasher's (shop), *US* notions store

mercero, -a *nm,f* haberdasher, *US* notions dealer

merchandising [mertʃanˈdaisiŋ] *nm* merchandising

Mercosur *nm (abrev de* **Mercado Común del Sur)** MERCOSUR

mercromina® *nf (para heridas)* mercurochrome®

mercurio *nm* (a) *Quím* mercury, quicksilver (b) *Astrol Astron Mit* Mercury

merecedor, -a *adj* deserving; **ser m. de** to be worthy of, deserve

merecer [46] **1** *vt* to deserve, merit, be worth; **merece la pena visitarlo** it is worth a visit
   2 merecerse *vpr* to deserve

merecido, -a 1 *pp de* **merecer**
   2 *adj* deserved; **ella lo tiene m.** *(recompensa)* she well deserves it; *(castigo)* it serves her right
   3 *nm* deserved punishment, just deserts *pl*

merecimiento *nm* merit, worthiness

merendar [3] **1** *vt* to have as an afternoon snack, have for tea
   2 *vi* to have an afternoon snack, have tea

merendero *nm (establecimiento)* tearoom, snack bar; *(en el campo)* picnic spot

merendola *nf Esp Fam* splendid spread, *Br* slap-up tea

merengue 1 *nm* (a) *Culin (dulce)* meringue (b) *Fam (persona)* weak o lily-livered person (c) *RP (trifulca)* row, fuss
   2 *nmf Esp Fam* = supporter of Real Madrid football club

meretriz *nf Fml* prostitute

merezco *indic pres véase* **merecer**

meridiano, -a 1 *adj* (a) *(del mediodía)* midday, noon (b) *(evidente)* evident, obvious; **de una claridad meridiana** patently clear
   2 *nm* meridian

meridional 1 *adj* southern
   2 *nmf* southerner

merienda *nf* (a) *(comida a media tarde)* afternoon snack, tea; **ir de m.** to go for a picnic □ **m. cena** high tea; *Esp Fam* **m. de negros** bedlam, free-for-all (b) packed lunch

merino, -a 1 *adj Zool* merino
   2 *nm,f Zool* merino (sheep); *(hembra)* merino ewe; *(macho)* merino ram
   3 *nm* (merino) wool

mérito *nm* merit, worth; **atribuirse el m. de algo** to take the credit for sth; **de m.** worthy; **hacer méritos para algo** to strive to deserve sth

meritocracia *nf* meritocracy

meritorio, -a 1 *adj* praiseworthy, meritorious
   2 *nm,f* unpaid trainee

merluza *nf* (a) *(pez)* hake (b) *Esp Fam (borrachera)* **cogerse una m.** to get drunk

merluzo, -a *nm,f Esp Fam* dimwit

merma *nf* decrease, reduction

mermar 1 *vt* to cause to decrease o diminish
   2 *vi* to decrease, diminish
   3 mermarse *vpr* to decrease, diminish

mermelada *nf* jam; **m. de melocotón/fresa** peach/strawberry jam; **m. de naranja/limón** orange/lemon marmalade

mero[1] *nm* (a) *(pez) (del Mediterráneo)* grouper; *(del Atlántico)* halibut (b) *Méx Fam* **el m. m.** the big shot

mero, -a[2] (a) *adj* mere, pure; **por el m. hecho de** through the mere fact of; **una mera coincidencia** a mere coincidence (b) *CAm Méx Fam (propio, mismo)* **¿es usted? — yo m.** is that you? — the very same o it sure is; **viven en el m. centro** they live right in the centre
   2 *adv CAm Méx Fam* (a) *(exactamente)* **aquí m.** right here; **ya m.** right now (b) *(casi)* nearly, almost; **m. me mato** I nearly o almost got killed

merodeador, -a 1 *adj* (a) *Caza Mil* marauding (b) *(paseante)* wandering, prowling
   2 *nm,f* (a) *Caza Mil* marauder (b) *(vagabundo)* prowler

merodear *vi* (a) *Caza Mil* to maraud (b) *(vagar)* to prowl

merodeo *nm* (a) *Caza Mil* marauding (b) *(vagabundeo)* prowling

mes *nm* (a) *(del año)* month; **diez mil pesos al m.** ten thousand pesos a month; **el m. pasado/que viene** last/next month (b) *(mensualidad) (cobro)* monthly salary o wages *pl*; *(pago)* monthly payment; **no ha cobrado el m.** he hasn't been paid for last month (c) *Fam (menstruación)* menstruation; **estar con el m.** to have one's period

mesa *nf* (a) *(mueble)* table; **bendecir la m.** to say grace; **levantarse de la m.** to leave the table; **poner/recoger la m.** to set/clear the table; **sentarse a la m.** to sit down at (the) table; **servir la m.** to wait at table; **ser amante de la buena m.** to be fond of good food; *Fig* **a m. puesta** with free maintenance; *Fig* **a m. y mantel** with free food □ **m. de mezclas** mixing desk; **m. de operaciones** operating table; **m. redonda** *Hist* Round Table; *(reunión)* round table; **m. de trabajo** desk (b) *(junta directiva)* board, executive; **el presidente de la m.** the chairman □ **m. electoral** electoral college

mesada *nf* (a) *Am (pago mensual)* monthly payment, monthly instalment (b) *RP (para adolescentes)* pocket money, *US* allowance (c) *RP (encimera)* worktop

mesana *nf* mizzen

mesar 1 *vt* to tear (at)
   2 mesarse *vpr* to tear (at) one's hair o beard

mescalina *nf* mescalin

mesero, -a *nm,f Col Guat Méx Salv (hombre)* waiter; *(mujer)* waitress

meseta *nf* plateau, tableland, meseta; **la M.** the plateau of Castile

mesiánico, -a *adj* messianic

mesianismo *nm* messianism

mesías *nm inv también Fig* Messiah; **el M.** the Messiah

mesilla *nf* small table □ **m. de noche** bedside table

mesnada *nf* (a) *Hist* armed retinue (b) **mesnadas** followers

mesón *nm* (a) *Hist* inn, tavern (b) *(restaurante)* old-style tavern

mesonero, -a *nm,f Esp* innkeeper

Mesopotamia *n* Mesopotamia

mesopotámico, -a *adj & nm,f* Mesopotamian

mestizaje *nm* crossbreeding

mestizo, -a *adj & nm,f* half-breed, half-caste, mestizo

mesura *nf Fml* moderation, restraint

mesurar 1 *vt* to restrain, temper
   2 mesurarse *vpr* to restrain oneself

meta *nf* (a) *(en carreras) (de caballos)* winning post; *(de coches, bicicletas)* finish, finishing line (b) *Ftb (portería)* goal (c) *Fig (objetivo)* goal, aim, objective

metabólico, -a *adj* metabolic

metabolismo *nm* metabolism

metabolizar [14] *vt* to metabolize

metadona *nf* methadone

metafísica *nf* metaphysics

metafísico, -a *adj* metaphysical

metáfora *nf* metaphor

metafórico, -a *adj* metaphoric, metaphorical

metal *nm* (**a**) *(material)* metal; **metales comunes/ preciosos** base/precious metals; *Fig (dinero)* **el vil m.** filthy lucre (**b**) *(timbre de la voz)* timbre (**c**) *Mús* brass

metálico, -a 1 *adj* metallic

2 *nm* cash; **pagar en m.** to pay (in) cash

metalización *nf* metallization

metalizado, -a 1 *pp de* **metalizar**

2 *adj (pintura)* metallic

metalizar [14] *vt* to metallize

metaloide *nm* metalloid

metalurgia *nf* metallurgy

metalúrgico, -a 1 *adj* metallurgical

2 *nm,f* metallurgist

metamórfico, -a *adj* metamorphic

metamorfismo *nm* metamorphism

metamorfosear *vt* to metamorphose

metamorfosis *nf* metamorphosis

metano *nm* methane

metástasis *nf inv Med* metastasis

metedura *nf Fam* **m. de pata** blunder, *Br* clanger, *US* boner

meteórico, -a *adj* meteoric

meteorito *nm* meteorite

meteoro *nm* meteor

meteorología *nf* meteorology

meteorológico, -a *adj* meteorological

meteorólogo, -a *nm,f* meteorologist; *(hombre)* weatherman

meter 1 *vt* (**a**) *(poner)* to put; **mete los juguetes en la caja** put the toys in the box; **siempre meto mi dinero en el banco** I always put my money in the bank; *Fig* **su familia le metió en la empresa** his family got him a job in the firm; *Fig* **m. la nariz** *o* **las narices en algo** to poke one's nose into sth; *Fam* **a todo m.** *(a toda velocidad)* at full speed; *(intensamente)* intensely; *Fam* **m. mano a algo** to get down to (do) sth; *Fam Fig* **m. la pata** to put one's foot in it, drop a clanger; *Vulg* **m. mano a algn** to grope sb (**b**) *(comprometer)* to involve **(en** in), to get mixed up (**er** in); **a mí no me metas en eso** don't get me mixed up in that; **andar metido en deudas** to be up one's eyes in debt (**c**) *Fam Fig (dar)* to give; **me metieron una multa** I got a ticket; **nos metió el rollo de siempre** he gave us the same old story; **m. miedo a algn** to frighten sb, put the wind up sb; **m. prisa a algn** to hurry sb up (**d**) *(hacer)* to make; **m. ruido** to make a noise (**e**) *Cost (vestido) (de ancho)* to take in; *(de largo)* to take up

2 meterse *vpr* (**a**) *(entrar)* to go *o* come in, get into; **se metió en la casa** he went into the house; **ella se metió en el coche** she got into the car; **métete en la cama** get into bed (**b**) *(introducir)* to put; **métete la camisa (por dentro)** tuck your shirt in; **no te metas los dedos en la nariz** don't pick your nose; *Fig* **métete esto en la cabeza** get this into your head; *Vulg* **que se lo meta donde le quepa** he can shove it up his backside (**c**) *(dedicarse)* to go into; **m. monja** to become a nun; **m. en un conjunto** to join a band; **m. en política** to go into politics (**d**) *(estar, ir a parar)* to be; **¿dónde se ha metido este niño?** where on earth is that child?; **¿dónde te habías metido?** where have you been

(all this time)?; **yo no sabía dónde meterme (de la vergüenza)** (I was so ashamed) I just didn't know where to put myself (**e**) *(entrometerse)* to meddle; **tú no te metas en esto, métete en tus cosas** mind your own business; **m. con algn** *(en broma)* to tease sb; *(en serio)* to lay into sb; **m. donde no llaman** to poke one's nose in; **m. en todo** to poke one's nose into everything; **no m. en nada** *(dejar hacer)* not to interfere; *(no comprometerse)* not to get involved at all, stay out of it

meterete *RP nmf*, **metete** *Andes CAm nmf*, **metiche** *Méx Ven nmf Fam* busybody

meticulosidad *nf* meticulousness

meticuloso, -a *adj* meticulous

metido, -a 1 *pp de* **meter**

2 *adj* (**a**) *Fam* **estar muy m. en algo** to be deeply involved in sth; **m. en años** getting on (in years); **m. en carnes** plump (**b**) *Am (entrometido)* meddlesome

3 *nm Fam* dressing-down; **dar** *o* **pegar un buen m. a un pastel/una paella** to take a good helping of cake/paella

metílico, -a *adj* methylic

metódico, -a *adj* methodical

metodismo *nm Rel* Methodism

metodista *adj & nmf Rel* Methodist

metodizar [14] *vt* to methodize

método *nm* (**a**) *(sistema)* method ❑ **m. anticonceptivo** contraceptive method (**b**) *Educ* course; **m. de música** music course

metodología *nf* methodology

metodológico, -a *adj* methodological

metomentodo *nmf Fam* busybody, *Br* nosey-parker

metonimia *nf Ling* metonymy

metraje *nm Cin (de una película)* length

metralla *nf Mil* shrapnel

metralleta *nf Mil* sub-machine-gun

métrica *nf Lit* metrics *sing*

métrico, -a *adj* (**a**) *(del metro)* metric ❑ **cinta métrica** tape measure; **sistema m.** metric system (**b**) *Lit* metrical

metro *nm* (**a**) *(medida)* metre, *US* meter (**b**) *Fam Br* underground, *US* subway

metrónomo *nm* metronome

metrópoli *nf* metropolis

metropolitano, -a 1 *adj* metropolitan

2 *nm Br* underground, *US* subway

meublé *nm (casa de citas)* brothel; *(apartamento)* flat rented by the hour

mexicanismo [meҳikaˈnismo] *nm* Mexicanism

mexicano, -a [meҳiˈkano] *adj & nm,f* Mexican

México [ˈmeҳiko] *n* Mexico; **ciudad de M.** Mexico City; **Nuevo M.** New Mexico

mezcla *nf* (**a**) *(acción)* mixing, blending (**b**) *(producto)* mixture, blend; **hay tal m. de acentos** there is such a variety of accents ❑ **m. explosiva** *(explosivo)* explosive mixture; *Fig (situación)* explosive situation (**c**) *Rad Cin* mixing; *Aut* mixture

mezclador, -a *nm,f (persona, máquina)* mixer

mezclar 1 *vt* (**a**) *(dos o más cosas)* to mix, blend (**b**) *(desordenar)* to mix up; **mezcló todas las fichas** he mixed up all the index cards; **m. dos temas** to mix two subjects up (**c**) *(involucrar)* to involve, mix up; **mezcló a su hermano en un asunto muy turbio** he got his brother mixed up in some very shady business; **verse mezclado en algo** to find oneself mixed up in sth

2 mezclarse *vpr* (**a**) *(cosas)* to get mixed up; **al caerse, se mezclaron todos los papeles** when they fell, all the papers got mixed up; **aquí se mezcla todo el mundo** *(gente)* all kinds of people mingle here **(b)** *(intervenir)* to get involved; **m. con cierta clase de gente** to mix with a certain kind of people

mezcolanza *nf Fml* strange mixture, hotch-potch; **habla una m. de inglés y español** he speaks a funny mixture of English and Spanish

mezquinar 1 *vt* **(a)** *Am* to be mean o stingy with **(b)** *Arg (esquivar)* to dodge
2 *vi Am* to be mean o stingy

mezquindad *nf* **(a)** *(avaricia)* meanness, stinginess **(b)** *(sordidez)* lowness, baseness **(c)** *(acción)* mean thing, vile deed

mezquino, -a *adj* **(a)** *(avaricioso)* mean, stingy **(b)** *(sórdido)* low, base **(c)** *(escaso)* miserable; **un sueldo m.** a miserable wage

mezquita *nf Rel* mosque

m/f. *(abrev de* **mi favor***)* my favour o *US* favor

m/g *(abrev de* **miligramo***)* mg

MHz *(abrev de* **megahercio***)* MHz

mi¹ *(pl* **mis***) adj* my; **mi casa/trabajo** my house/job; **mis cosas/libros** my things/books

mi² *nm Mús* E; **mi menor** E minor

mí *pron pers* me; **a mí me dio tres** he gave me three; **¡a mí!** help!; **¡(y) a mí qué!** so what!; **compra otro para mí** buy one for me too; **para mí que ...** I think that ...; **por mí ...** *(aprobación)* it's all right with o by me; *(indiferencia)* I don't care; **por mí puede hacer lo que quiera** he can do what he likes for all I care; **por mí mismo** just by myself

mía *adj & pron pos f véase* **mío, -a**

miaja *nf* crumb; *Fig* bit; **no queda ni una m. de comida** there is not a morsel left

miasma *nm* miasma

miau *nm* miaow, mew

mica *nf Min* mica

micción *nf Biol* micturition

Micenas *n* Mycenae

micénico, -a *adj* Mycenaean

michelín *nm Fam* spare tyre o *US* tire

mico, -a 1 *nm* **(a)** *Zool* long-tailed monkey **(b)** *Fig (hombre lujurioso)* randy man, rake **(c)** *Fam Fig (locuciones)* **dar el m.** *(dar un chasco)* to let sb down; *(sorprender)* to come up with sth unexpected; **hecho un m.** ashamed, embarrassed; **ser el último m.** to be of no account; **volverse m. para hacer algo** to (have to) struggle to do sth
2 *nm,f (persona fea)* ape, ugly person

micología *nf Med* mycology

micosis *nf Med* mycosis

micra *nf (medida)* micron

micro 1 *nm Fam (micrófono)* mike
2 *nm* o *nf Arg Bol Chile (autobús)* bus

micro- *pref* micro-; **microcirugía** microsurgery

microbiano, -a *adj* microbic, microbial

microbio *nm* microbe

microbiología *nf* microbiology

microbiológico, -a *adj* microbiological

microbús *nm Aut* minibus

microchip *(pl* **microchips***) nm Inform* microchip

microcircuito *nm* microcircuit

microclima *nm* microclimate

microcomputadora *nf esp Am Inform* microcomputer

microcosmos *nm* microcosmos

microficha *nf* microfiche

microfilm *(pl* **microfilms***) nm* microfilm

micrófono *nm* microphone; **hablar por el m.** to speak over o through the microphone

microlentilla *nf* contact lens

microonda *nf* microwave; **un (horno) microondas** a microwave (oven)

microordenador *nm Esp Inform* microcomputer

microorganismo *nm* microorganism

microprocesador *nm Inform* microprocessor

microscópico, -a *adj* microscopic

microscopio *nm* microscope

microsurco *nm* microgroove

microtecnología *nf* microtechnology

mieditis *nf Fam* jitters *pl*; **tener m.** to have the jitters

miedo *nm* fear; *(recelo)* aprehension; **dar m.** to be scary; **le da m. quedarse sin trabajo** he's worried about losing his job; **me dio m. decírselo** I was afraid to tell her; **me entró muchísimo m.** I felt really frightened; **una película de m.** a horror film; **por m. a** for fear of; **por m. de que te pareciera mal** for fear of upsetting you; **¡qué m.!** how frightening!; **tener m. de algo/algn** to be afraid of sth/sb; *Fig* **morirse de m.** to be scared stiff; *Esp Fam* **de m.** *(fantástico)* great, terrific; *Esp Fam* **lo pasamos de m.** we had a fantastic time □ **m. escénico** stage fright

miedoso, -a 1 *adj* fainthearted, cowardly, timid
2 *nm,f* coward

miel *nf* honey; **dulce como la m.** as sweet as honey; *Fig* **dejar a algn con la m. en los labios** to shatter sb's hopes; *Fig* **m. sobre hojuelas** so much the better □ **luna de m.** honeymoon

mielga *nf* alfalfa

mielina *nf Anat* myelin

miembro *nm* **(a)** *Anat* limb; **m. viril** penis **(b)** *(socio)* member; **estado m.** member state **(c)** *Mat* member **(d)** *Fig (parte)* part, section

mientes *nfpl* **parar m. en** to think of, consider

mientras 1 *adv* **m. (tanto)** meanwhile, in the meantime; **ahora vuelvo, m. (tanto), échale un vistazo a esto** I'll be back in a minute, in the meantime, have a look at this
2 *conj* **(a)** *(al mismo tiempo que)* while, whilst; **Carmen llegó m. comíamos** Carmen arrived while we were eating **(b)** *(durante el tiempo que)* when, while; **m. viví en Berlín** when I lived in Berlin, during the time I lived in Berlin; **m. yo viva no le faltará nada** while I am still alive, she won't go without **(c)** *(por el contrario)* whereas; **él lo admitió, m. que tú lo negaste** he admitted it, whereas you denied it **(d)** *Fam (cuanto más)* **m. más/menos ...** the more/less ...; **m. más se tiene, más se quiere** the more one has, the more one wants

miércoles *nm inv* Wednesday □ **M. de Ceniza** Ash Wednesday; *véase tamb* **viernes**

mierda *nf Vulg* **(a)** *(gen) Fig* shit; **ese libro es una m.** that book is crap; **estar hecho una m.** *(cansado)* to be shagged out; *(abatido)* to be down in the dumps; **irse a la m.** to go to hell; **mandar a la m. a algn** to tell sb to go to hell **(b)** *Fig (porquería)* dirt, filth **(c)** *Esp (borrachera)* **coger** o **pillar una m.** to get drunk

mies *nf* **(a)** *(grano)* corn, grain **(b)** *(cosecha)* harvest time **(c)** **mieses** cornfields

miga *nf* **(a)** *(de pan etc)* crumb; *Fig* **hacer buenas/malas migas con algn** to get on well/badly with sb; *Fig* **hacer migas a algn/algo** to smash sb/sth to bits; *Fam* **hecho migas** *(destrozado físicamente)* smashed to bits; *(destrozado moralmente)* totally destroyed **(b)** *(trocito)* bit **(c)** *Fig (intríngulis)* substance; **la cosa tiene m.** there is more to it than meets the eye **(d)** **migas** breadcrumbs; *Culin* fried breadcrumbs

migaja *nf* (**a**) *(de pan)* crumb (**b**) *Fig* bit, scrap (**c**) **migajas** *(del pan)* crumbs; *Fig* leftovers

migar [38] *vt (desmenuzar)* to crumble; **se miga el pan en la leche** (you) crumble the bread into the milk

migración *nf* migration

migrante *nmf* migrant

migraña *nf Med* migraine

migrar *vi* to migrate

migratorio, -a *adj* migratory

mijo *nm Bot* millet

mil *adj & nm* thousand; **m. pesos** a o one thousand pesos; **m. veces** a thousand times; **que hace m.** the thousandth

milagrería *nf* superstitious belief in miracles

milagrero, -a *adj* (**a**) *(crédulo)* who believes in miracles (**b**) *(milagroso)* miracle-working

milagro *nm* miracle; **de m.** *(en el último momento)* in the nick of time; *(por un pelo)* by the skin of one's teeth; **fue un m. que no se matara** it was a miracle he didn't kill himself; **hacer milagros** to work wonders; *Fam* **ella nos contó su vida y milagros** she told us her life story from beginning to end

milagroso, -a *adj* (**a**) *(de milagro)* miraculous (**b**) *Fig (maravilloso)* wonderful, amazing

milano *nm Orn* kite ▫ **m. real** red kite

milenario, -a 1 *adj* millenarian, millenial **2** *nm* millenium, millenary

milenio *nm* millenium, millenary

milésima *nf* **m. de segundo** millisecond

milésimo, -a *adj & nm,f* thousandth

milhojas *nm inv Culin* millefeuille

mili *nf Esp Antes Fam* military o national service; **hacer la m.** to do one's military service

milibar *nm Fís* millibar

milicia *nf* (**a**) *(grupo armado)* militia (**b**) *(profesión)* military (profession)

miliciano, -a *nm,f (hombre)* militiaman; *(mujer)* woman soldier

miligramo *nm* milligram, milligramme

mililitro *nm* millilitre, *US* milliliter

milimétrico, -a *adj* millimetric

milímetro *nm* millimetre, *US* millimeter

militancia *nf* militancy

militante *adj & nmf* militant

militar 1 *adj* military ▫ **cartilla m.** military record; **tribunal m.** military court **2** *nm* military man, soldier; **los militares** the armed forces **3** *vi* (**a**) *Mil* to serve (**b**) *Pol (de un partido)* to be a militant

militarismo *nm* militarism

militarista 1 *adj* militarist, militaristic **2** *nmf* militarist

militarización *nf* militarization

militarizar [14] *vt* to militarize

milla *nf (medida)* mile

millar *nm* thousand; **millares de personas** thousands of people; *Fig* **a millares** in thousands

millardo *nm* billion, thousand million

millón *nm* million; *(mucho dinero)* **esa casa vale millones** that house is worth a fortune; **tengo millones de cosas que hacer** I've got thousands of things to do; *(mucho)* **un m. de gracias** thanks a million

millonada *nf Fam* fortune, bomb; **me costó una m.** it cost me a bomb

millonario, -a *adj & nm,f* millionaire

millonésimo, -a *adj & nm,f* millionth

milonga *nf Mús* = popular Argentinian song and dance

milpa *nf CAm Méx* field of maize, *US* cornfield

miltomate *nm Bot* (**a**) *Hond Guat Méx* small white tomato (**b**) *Guat Méx* tomato grown in a maize field

mimado, -a 1 *pp de* **mimar** **2** *adj (consentido)* spoiled

mimar *vt (niño, persona)* to spoil, coddle, pamper

mimbre *nm* wicker; **cesta de m.** wicker basket

mimbrera *nf (árbol)* (common) osier

mimético, -a *adj* mimetic

mimetismo *nm* mimicry, mimesis

mimetizar [14] *vt* to copy, imitate

mímica *nf* mimicry

mímico, -a *adj* mimic

mimo *nm* (**a**) *Teat (actor)* mime (**b**) *Fig (zalamería)* coddling, pampering; *Fam* **con gran m.** with love and care

mimosa *nf Bot* mimosa, silver wattle

mimoso, -a *adj* loving, affectionate

mina¹ *nf* (**a**) *Min* mine; **m. de carbón** coal mine ▫ **ingeniero de minas** mining engineer (**b**) *(conducto)* underground passage, tunnel (**c**) *(explosivo)* mine ▫ **campo de minas** minefield (**d**) *(de lápiz)* lead; *(de bolígrafo)* refill (**e**) *Fig (ganga)* gold mine; **este negocio es una m.** this business is a gold mine

mina² *nf RP (mujer)* *Br* bird, *US* chick; *(concubina)* lady friend, lover

minador, -a 1 *adj* mining **2** *nm* (**a**) *(buque)* minelayer (**b**) *(soldado)* sapper

minar *vt* (**a**) *Mil Min* to mine (**b**) *Fig (desgastar)* to undermine

minarete *nm* minaret

mineral *adj & nm* mineral, ore

mineralización *nf* mineralization

mineralizar [14] **1** *vt* to mineralize **2** **mineralizarse** *vpr* to become mineralized

mineralogía *nf* mineralogy

mineralógico, -a *adj* mineralogical

minería *nf* (**a**) *Min* mining (**b**) *Ind* mining industry

minero, -a 1 *adj* mining; **industria/zona minera** mining industry/area **2** *nm,f* miner

mineromedicinal *adj* **aguas mineromedicinales** mineral waters with curative powers

minga *nf Esp Fam* *Br* willy, *US* peter

mingitorio *nm* urinal

miniatura *nf* miniature

miniaturista *nmf* miniaturist

miniaturizar [14] *vt* to miniaturize

MiniDisc® *nm inv* MiniDisc®

minifalda *nf* miniskirt

minifundio *nm* smallholding

minifundista 1 *adj* = of o relating to **minifundios** **2** *nmf* smallholder

minigolf *(pl* **minigolfs)** *nm* (**a**) *(lugar)* crazy golf course (**b**) *(juego)* crazy golf

mínima *nf* minimum temperature

minimalismo *nm Mús* minimalism

minimalista *adj Mús* minimalist

minimizar [14] *vt* to minimize, play down; **el ministro**

minimizó la importancia del incidente the minister played down the incident

mínimo, -a 1 *adj* (**a**) *Mat Téc* minimum, lowest □ **m. común múltiplo** lowest common multiple (**b**) *(muy pequeño)* minute, tiny; **un número m. de personas** a very small number of people
2 *nm* minimum; **al m.** to a minimum; **como m.** at least; **ni lo más m.** not in the least

minino *nm Fam* pussy (cat), kitty

minipímer® (*pl* **minipímers**) *nm o f* liquidizer, blender

ministerial *adj* ministerial

ministerio *nm* (**a**) *Pol Br* ministry, *US* department □ **M. de Asuntos Exteriores** *Br* ≃ Foreign Office, *US* ≃ State Department; **M. de Economía y Hacienda** *Br* ≃ Treasury, *US* ≃ Treasury Department; **M. del Interior** *o* **de la Gobernación** *Br* ≃ Home Office, *US* ≃ Department of the Interior (**b**) *Rel* ministry

ministrable *adj* likely to become a minister

ministro, -a *nm,f* (**a**) *Pol* minister □ **m. de Asuntos Exteriores** *Br* ≃ Foreign Minister, *US* ≃ Secretary of State; **m. de Economía y Hacienda** *Br* ≃ Chancellor of the Exchequer, *US* ≃ Secretary of the Treasury; **m. del Interior** *Br* ≃ Home Secretary, *US* ≃ Secretary of the Interior; **primer m.** Prime Minister (**b**) *Rel* minister

minorar *vt* to reduce, decrease, diminish

minoría *nf* minority □ *Jur* **m. de edad** minority

minorista 1 *adj* retail
2 *nmf* retailer

minoritario, -a *adj* minority; **gobierno m.** minority government

minucia *nf* trifle

minuciosidad *nf* *(meticulosidad)* meticulousness; *(detallismo)* minuteness

minucioso, -a *adj* (**a**) *(persona)* meticulous (**b**) *(informe, trabajo etc)* minute, detailed

minué *nm Mús* minuet

minuendo *nm Mat* minuend

minúscula *nf* small *o* lower-case letter

minúsculo, -a *adj* miniscule, minute; **letra minúscula** lower-case *o* small letter

minusvalía *nf* (**a**) *(física, psíquica)* handicap, disability (**b**) *Econ* depreciation

minusválido, -a 1 *adj* handicapped, disabled
2 *nm,f* handicapped person, disabled person

minusvalorar *vt* to underestimate

minuta *nf* (**a**) *(borrador)* draft (**b**) *(cuenta)* lawyer's bill (**c**) *(menú)* menu

minutero *nm* minute hand

minuto *nm* minute; **al m.** a moment later; **sin perder un m.** without wasting a minute; **vuelvo en un m.** I'll be back in a moment

mío, -a 1 *adj pos* of mine, my; **no es asunto m.** it is none of my business; **un amigo m.** a friend of mine
2 *pron pos* mine; **ese libro es m.** that book is mine; *Fam* **ésta es la mía** this is the chance I've been waiting for; **lo m. son las matemáticas** what I am the best at is mathematics; *Fam* **los míos** my people *o* folks

miocardio *nm Anat* myocardium

miope 1 *adj Ópt* myopic, short-sighted; *Fig* short-sighted; **una política m.** a short-sighted policy
2 *nmf Ópt* myopic *o* short-sighted person; *Fig* short-sighted person

miopía *nf* myopia, short-sightedness

MIR [mir] *nm Esp Med* (*abrev de* **Médico Interno Residente**) *Br* house officer, *US* intern

mira *nf* (**a**) *(en instrumento, arma)* sight □ **m. telescópica** telescopic sight (**b**) *(objetivo)* intention; **con miras a** with a view to; **poner la m. en algo** to aim at; **tener la m. puesta en algo** to have designs on sth; **amplitud de miras** broad-mindedness

mirada *nf* look; **apartar la m.** to look away; **clavar** *o* **fijar la m. en** to fix one's eyes on; **fulminar con la m.** to look daggers at; **lanzar** *o* **echar una m.** to glance at; **levantar la m.** to raise one's eyes; **seguir algo/a algn con la m.** to follow sth/sb with one's eyes; **sostener la m.** to stare at; **volver la m. a** to turn one's eyes towards □ **m. fija** stare; **m. rápida** glance

mirado, -a 1 *pp de* **mirar**
2 *adj* (**a**) *(considerado)* considered; **bien m.** highly regarded *o* respected, well liked; *Fig* all in all; **mal m.** disliked, looked down on (**b**) *(cuidadoso)* careful (**c**) *(cauto)* cautious

mirador *nm* (**a**) *Arquit (balcón)* enclosed balcony (**b**) *(lugar con vista)* viewpoint

miramiento *nm* (**a**) *(cautela)* caution (**b**) *(gen pl)* *(consideración)* consideration, respect; **andarse con miramientos** *(personas)* to treat people with respect; *(cosas)* to handle things carefully; **sin miramientos** without the least consideration

mirar 1 *vt* (**a**) *(dirigir la vista a)* to look at; **le miró a los ojos** he looked him in the eye; **m. a algn de arriba a abajo** to eye sb from head to toe; **m. algo por encima** to glance at sth; **m. una palabra en el diccionario** to look up a word in the dictionary; *Fig* **m. algo** *o* **algn con buenos/malos ojos** to have a good/bad opinion of sth *o* sb; *Fig* **m. a algn por encima del hombro** to look down on sb; *Fam Fig* **de mírame y no me toques** very fragile (**b**) *(vigilar)* to check, watch; **mira bien el cambio antes de irte** check your change before leaving; **¡mira lo que dices/haces!** mind *o* watch what you say/do! (**c**) *(atender)* to look after; **m. por algn** *o* **algo** to look after sb *o* sth; **sólo mira por su interés** he only looks after his own interests (**d**) *(reflexionar)* to think, consider; **gasta el dinero sin m.** he spends money thoughtlessly (**e**) *(tener cuidado)* to be careful; *(procurar)* to see; **mira donde pones los pies** watch where you're putting your feet; **mira que llegue bien/que no le pase nada** see that he arrives all right/that nothing happens to him (**f**) *(comprobar)* to check; **mira si ha llegado tu padre** go and see/ask if your father has arrived; **mira (a ver) si hay carta(s)** go and see/check if there's any mail (**g**) *(dar)* to look, face; **la casa mira al sur** the house faces south; **la cocina mira al jardín** the kitchen looks onto the garden (**h**) *(locuciones)* **mira, haz lo que te parezca** look, do whatever you want; *Esp* **¡mira por dónde!** fancy that!; **mira que si se presenta ahora** just imagine if he turned up now!; **mira que te lo dije** I told you, didn't I?; **¡mira quien habla!** look who's talking!
2 mirarse *vpr* (**a**) *(reflexionar)* to think twice; **ella se lo mirará antes de intentarlo** she'll think twice before trying it (**b**) *(uso reflexivo)* to look at oneself; **m. en el espejo** to look at oneself in the mirror; *Fig* **m. en algn** to think highly of sb (**c**) *(uso recíproco)* to look at each other *o* one another (**d**) *(uso impers)* **si bien se mira** all things considered; **se mire como se mire** whichever way you look at it

miríada *nf* myriad

miriámetro *nm (medida)* myriametre, *US* myriameter

miriápodo *nm* myriapod

mirilla *nf* spyhole, peephole

miriñaque *nm Hist* crinoline

mirlo *nm Orn* **m. (blanco)** blackbird; *Fig* **ser un m. blanco** to be a rare bird

mirón, -ona 1 *adj* (**a**) *(espectador)* onlooking (**b**) *Pey (voyeur)* peeping

2 *nm,f* (**a**) *(espectador)* onlooker (**b**) *Pey* voyeur, peeping Tom

mirra *nf Bot* myrrh

mirto *nm Bot* myrtle

misa *nf* mass; **celebrar** *o* **decir m.** to say mass; **ir a m.** *Rel* to go to mass; *Fam Fig* **lo que yo digo va a m.** what I say goes; *Fam Fig* **no saber de la m. la media** *o* **mitad** to know much less about sth than one thinks □ **m. cantada** sung Mass; **m. de difuntos** Requiem Mass; **m. del gallo** Midnight Mass on Christmas Eve

misal *nm* missal

misantropía *nf* misanthropy

misántropo, -a 1 *adj* misanthropic
2 *nm,f* misanthrope, misanthropist

miscelánea *nf* miscellany

misceláneo, -a *adj* miscellaneous

miserable 1 *adj* (**a**) *(pobre)* miserable, wretched, poor; **una vida m.** a wretched life; **viviendas miserables** very poor dwellings (**b**) *(tacaño)* miserly, mean, stingy (**c**) *(malvado)* wretched, despicable
2 *nmf* (**a**) *(tacaño)* miser (**b**) *(canalla)* wretch, villain

miseria *nf* (**a**) *(pobreza extrema)* extreme poverty (**b**) *(desgracia)* misery, affliction (**c**) *(tacañería)* miserliness, meanness (**d**) *(insignificancia)* pittance; **ganar una m.** to earn next to nothing

misericordia *nf* mercy, compassion

misericordioso, -a *adj* merciful, compassionate

mísero, -a *adj* miserable, wretched; **¡m. de mí!** woe is me!

misil *nm* missile; **m. tierra-aire** surface-to-air missile

misión *nf* (**a**) *(cometido, delegación)* mission □ **m. cumplida** mission accomplished (**b**) *Rel* mission

misionero, -a 1 *adj* mission
2 *nm,f* missionary

misiva *nf Literario* missive

mismamente *adv Fam* just, precisely

mismísimo, -a *adj superl Fam* (**a**) *(preciso)* very; **en el m. centro** right in the centre; **en este m. momento** at this very moment (**b**) *(en persona)* in person; **este niño es el m. demonio** this child is the devil himself; **me lo dijo el m. director** the director himself told me

mismo, -a 1 *adj* (**a**) *(igual, idéntico)* same; **bebemos en el m. vaso** we are sharing the same glass (**b**) *(uso enfático) (propio)* own; **la escuela está en su misma calle** the school is right in the street where he lives; **su misma familia no lo puede entender** even her own family cannot understand it; **yo m.** I myself
2 *pron* same; **éste es el m. que vimos ayer** this is the same one we saw yesterday; **estar en las mismas (de siempre)** to be back to square one; **lo m.** the same (thing); **dar** *o* **ser lo m.** to make no difference; **no es lo m. oir que escuchar** hearing is not the same as listening; **o lo que es lo m.** that is to say; **por eso m.** that is why; **por lo m.** for that reason; **por uno** *o* **sí m.** by oneself; **tres cuartos de lo m.** much of a muchness
3 *adv* (**a**) *(exactamente)* exactly; **ahora m.** right now *o* away; **allí/aquí m.** right there/here; **ayer m.** just *o* only yesterday; **mañana m.** tomorrow! (**b**) *(por ejemplo)* for instance; **aquí m.** here will do; **que venga algn, Juan m.** ask one of them to come, Juan, for instance (**c**) **así m.** likewise

misoginia *nf* misogyny

misógino, -a 1 *adj* misogynous
2 *nm,f* misogynist

miss *nf* Miss; **M. España 1992** Miss Spain 1992

misterio *nm* mystery; **no hay ningún m.** there is no mystery about it; **con m.** mysteriously

misterioso, -a *adj* mysterious

mística *nf* mystical theology

misticismo *nm* mysticism

místico, -a 1 *adj* mystic, mystical
2 *nm,f* mystic

mistificación *nf* trick

mistificar [59] *vt* to trick, cheat

mistral *nm Meteor* mistral

mitad *nf* half, middle; **a/hacia la m. de** in/towards the middle of; **a m. de camino** halfway there; **a m. de precio** half price; **en m. de la reunión** halfway through the meeting; **la m. de un libro/una casa** half a book/a house; **mi otra m.** my better half; **partir algo por la m.** to cut sth in half *o* down the middle; *Fam* **m. y m.** half and half; *Fam* **partir a algn por la m.** to shatter sb's plans *o* expectations

mítico, -a *adj* mythical

mitificar [59] *vt* to mythologize

mitigador, -a 1 *adj* mitigating
2 *nm,f* mitigator

mitigar [38] *vt Fml* to mitigate, palliate, relieve; *(luz)* to reduce

mitin *nm Pol* meeting, rally

mito *nm* myth

mitología *nf* mythology

mitológico, -a *adj* mythological

mitomanía *nf* mythomania

mitómano, -a *adj & nm,f* mythomaniac

mitón *nm* mitt, mitten

mitote *nm Méx* (**a**) *(baile)* Indian dance (**b**) *(fiesta casera)* family party (**c**) *(aspaviento)* fuss

mitra *nf* (**a**) *(tocado)* mitre (**b**) *Fig (rango)* rank of bishop

mitrado 1 *adj* mitred
2 *nm* *(arzobispo)* archbishop; *(obispo)* bishop

mixomatosis *nf Med* myxomatosis

mixteco, -a *adj & nmf* Mixtec

mixtificación *nf véase* **mistificación**

mixtificar [59] *vt véase* **mistificar**

mixto *adj* mixed; *Educ* **colegio m.** coeducational school

mixtura *nf* mixture

mízcalo *nm* milk fungus

m/L. *(abrev de* **mi letra (de crédito))** my credit bill

mnemotecnia *nf* mnemonics *sing*

mnemotécnico, -a *adj* mnemonic

moaré *nm véase* **muaré**

mobiliario *nm* furniture □ **m. urbano** street furniture

moblaje *nm* furniture

moca *nm* mocha, coffee

mocasín *nm* moccasin

mocedad *nf* youth

mocerío *nm* (group of) young people

mocetón, -ona *nm,f (mozo)* strapping lad; *(moza)* strapping lass

mochales *adj inv Esp Fam* crazy, mad

moche *véase* **troche**

mochila *nf* rucksack, backpack

mochilero, -a *nm,f* backpacker

mocho, -a 1 *adj* (**a**) *(extremo, punta)* blunt; *(árbol)* lopped (**b**) *Méx Fam Pey (beato)* holier-than-thou; *(mojigato)* prudish, straitlaced
2 *nm,f Méx Fam Pey (beato)* holy Joe; *(mojigato)* prude
3 *nm (para fregar)* mop

mochuelo *nm* (**a**) *Zool* little owl (**b**) *Fam Fig (fastidio)* bore, boring task; **cargar con el m.** *(con la peor parte)* to get the worst part of a job; *(llevarse las culpas)* to carry the can

moción *nf* motion; **presentar/aprobar una m.** to table/ pass a motion ❏ **m. de censura** motion of censure; **m. de confianza** motion of confidence

mocionar *vt Am* to table a motion

moco *nm* (**a**) *(de la nariz)* mucus, snot; **caérsele a algn los mocos** to have a runny nose; **limpiarse los mocos** to blow one's nose; **llorar a m. tendido** *o* **a m. y baba** to cry one's eyes out (**b**) *(de vela)* drippings (**c**) *(de pavo)* wattle, caruncle; *Fam* **un millón no es m. de pavo** a million is no trifle

mocoso, -a 1 *adj* with a runny nose
  2 *nm,f Fam* brat

moda *nf* (**a**) *(uso, manera)* fashion; **a la m., de m.** in fashion; **la última m.** the latest fashion; **pasado de m.** old-fashioned (**b**) *(furor pasajero)* craze; **la m. de los monopatines** the skateboard craze

modal 1 *adj* modal
  2 modales *nmpl* manners; **¡vaya m.!** what manners!; **buenos/malos m.** good/bad manners

modalidad *nf* form, category ❏ *Dep* **m. deportiva** sport; *Com* **m. de pago** method of payment

modelado *nm* (**a**) *(acción)* modelling, *US* modeling (**b**) *(efecto)* shape

modelador, -a 1 *adj* modelling, *US* modeling
  2 *nm,f* modeller, *US* modeler

modelar 1 *vt* to model, shape
  2 modelarse *vpr* to model oneself (**en** on)

modélico, -a *adj* model, exemplary

modelismo *nm* modelling

modelista *nmf* (**a**) *(operario)* mould *o US* mold maker (**b**) *Cost* pattern maker

modelo 1 *adj* model ❏ **niño m.** model child
  2 *nm* model; **un m. de perfección** a model of perfection; **un nuevo m. de coche** a new model of car
  3 *nmf* (fashion) model ❏ **desfile de modelos** fashion show

módem *(pl* **modems)** *nm Inform* modem

moderación *nf* moderation

moderado, -a 1 *pp de* **moderar**
  2 *adj* moderate; **temperaturas moderadas** mild temperatures
  3 *nm,f Pol* moderate; **los moderados** the moderate wing *sing,* the moderates

moderador, -a 1 *adj* moderating
  2 *nm,f* chairperson; *(hombre)* chairman; *(mujer)* chair-woman

moderar 1 *vt* (**a**) *(gen)* to moderate; *(velocidad)* to reduce; **modera tu lenguaje** moderate your language (**b**) *(debate)* to chair
  2 moderarse *vpr* to control oneself

modernamente *adv* in modern times, these days

modernidad *nf* modernity

modernismo *nm* (**a**) *Lit* modernism (**b**) *Arquit* (Spanish) Art Nouveau

modernista 1 *adj* (**a**) *Lit* modernistic (**b**) *Arquit* (Spanish) Art Nouveau
  2 *nmf* (**a**) *Lit* modernist (**b**) *Arquit* (Spanish) Art Nouveau architect

modernización *nf* modernization

modernizar [14] **1** *vt* to modernize
  2 modernizarse *vpr* to modernize; **este piso necesita**

modernizarse this flat needs modernizing; *Fam* **eres un carca, tienes que modernizarte** you're a square, you have to get up-to-date

moderno, -a *adj* modern

modestia *nf* modesty; **con m.** modestly

modesto, -a 1 *adj* modest
  2 *nm,f* modest person

módico, -a *adj* moderate; **una módica suma** a modest *o* small sum

modificable *adj* modifiable

modificación *nf* modification

modificador, -a *adj* modifying

modificar [59] *vt* to modify

modismo *nm Ling* idiom

modistería *nf Am* boutique

modisto, -a *nm,f* (**a**) *(diseñador)* fashion designer (**b**) *(sastre) (hombre)* tailor; *(mujer)* dressmaker

modo *nm* (**a**) *(manera)* way, manner; **m. de empleo** instructions for use; *Am* **salvo RP** **ni m. pues** there's nothing we can do about it, then; *véase* **manera** (**b**) **modos** manners ❏ **buenos/malos m.** good/bad manners (**c**) *Ling* mood; **m. subjuntivo** subjunctive mood (**d**) *Inform* mode

modorra *nf (somnolencia)* drowsiness

modoso, -a *adj* (**a**) *(recatado)* modest (**b**) *(respetuoso)* well-behaved, well-mannered

modulación *nf* modulation ❏ **m. de frecuencia** frequency modulation

modular[1] *vt* to modulate

modular[2] *adj* modular ❏ **un tresillo m.** a modular suite

módulo *nm* module

modus vivendi *nm inv* way of life

mofa *nf* mockery, ridicule; **en tono de m.** in a gibing tone; **hacer m. de algn/algo** to scoff at sb/sth

mofar *vi,* **mofarse** *vpr* to scoff (**de** at), laugh (**de** at), make fun (**de** of); **no te mofes de ella** don't make fun of her

mofeta *nf* (**a**) *Zool* skunk (**b**) *Min (grisú)* firedamp

moflete *nm* chubby cheek

mofletudo, -a *adj* chubby-cheeked

Mogadiscio *n* Mogadishu

mogol *adj & nmf* Mongol

mogollón *nm Esp Argot* (**a**) *(gran cantidad de)* **m. de** stacks of, piles of; **había un m. de gente** there were thousands of people (**b**) *(confusión)* commotion; *(ruido)* row, din, racket; **con este m. no oigo nada** I can't hear a thing with all this din (**c**) *(acción)* action; **vamos donde está el m.** let's go where the action is, let's go where it's all happening

mohair [mo'er] *nm Tex* mohair

mohín *nm* grimace; **hacer un m.** to make *o* pull a face

mohíno, -a *adj* sulky, upset

moho *nm* (**a**) *(hongo)* mould, *US* mold (**b**) *(de metales)* rust

mohoso, -a *adj* (**a**) *(con hongo)* mouldy, *US* moldy (**b**) *(oxidado)* rusty

moisés *nm* (**a**) *(cuna)* Moses basket, wicker cradle *o* carrycot, *US* bassinet (**b**) **M.** Moses

mojado, -a 1 *pp de* **mojar**
  2 *adj* wet; *(húmedo)* damp

mojama *nf Culin* dried salted tuna

mojar 1 *vt* (**a**) *(con líquido)* to wet; *(humedecer)* to damp; **m. pan en la leche** to dip *o* dunk bread in one's milk (**b**) *Fam (celebrar)* **m. algo** to celebrate sth with a drink

2 mojarse *vpr* (**a**) *(con líquido)* to get wet (**b**) *Fig (comprometerse)* to commit oneself

mojarra *nf* (**a**) *(pez)* two-banded bream (**b**) *Am* short broad-bladed knife

mojicón *nm* (**a**) *(puñetazo en la cara)* punch, slap (**b**) *(bizcocho)* type of sponge cake

mojigatería *nf* sanctimoniousness, affected piety

mojigato, -a 1 *adj* sanctimonious
2 *nm,f* sanctimonious person

mojito *nm* mojito, = cocktail containing rum, sugar, lemon juice and mint

mojón *nm* landmark; **m. kilométrico** ≃ milestone

moka *nm véase* **moca**

mola *nf* (**a**) *Med* mole (**b**) *(pez)* sunfish (**c**) *Col Pan (camisa)* = decorative shirt

molar 1 *adj & nm Anat* molar
2 *vi Esp Argot* (**a**) *(gustar)* **¡cómo me mola esa moto/ese chico!** that motorbike/that guy is really cool!; **me mola esquiar** I'm really into skiing; **hacer surf mola cantidad** surfing is really cool (**b**) *(presumir)* to show off

Moldavia *n* Moldavia

moldavo, -a *adj & nm,f* Moldavian

molde *nm* mould, *US* mold, cast; **letras de m.** printed letters

moldeable *adj* mouldable, *US* moldable

moldeado, -a 1 *pp de* **moldear**
2 *adj* moulded, *US* molded, cast
3 *nm* (**a**) *(de figura, cerámica)* moulding, *US* molding, casting (**b**) *Esp (de pelo)* soft perm

moldeador, -a 1 *adj* moulding, *US* molding, casting
2 *nm Esp (del pelo)* soft perm

moldear *vt* to mould, *US* mold, cast; *(cabello)* to give a soft perm to

moldura *nf* moulding, *US* molding

mole *nf* mass, bulk; *Fam* **este tío es una m.** he's a fat lump

molécula *nf* molecule

molecular *adj* molecular

moler [41] *vt* (**a**) *(triturar)* to grind, mill; **m. la aceituna** to press olives (**b**) *Fam Fig (cansar)* to wear out; **m. a algn a golpes o palos** to beat sb up

molestar 1 *vt* (**a**) *(perturbar)* to disturb, bother, annoy; **los niños le molestan** children get on his nerves; **no quisiera molestarte** I shouldn't like to bother you; **todo le molesta** everything annoys him (**b**) *Fml* to bother; **¿le molestaría esperar fuera?** would you mind waiting outside?; **¿le molestaría llamarme más tarde?** could you possibly phone me later?; **perdone que le moleste ...** I'm sorry to bother you, but ... (**c**) *(causar malestar)* to hurt, trouble; **esta muela me está molestando otra vez** this tooth is troubling me again (**d**) *(ofender levemente)* to offend slightly; **¿te molestó que no viniera a tu fiesta?** are you hurt at my missing your party?

2 molestarse *vpr* (**a**) *(tomarse la molestia)* to bother, take the trouble; **no se moleste, ya lo haré yo** don't bother, I'll do it (**b**) *(ofenderse)* to take offence *o US* offense, get upset; **se molesta por cualquier cosa** he gets annoyed *o* upset over any little thing

molestia *nf* (**a**) *(incomodidad)* bother, nuisance; **no es ninguna m.** it is no trouble at all; **perdone las molestias que le estamos ocasionando** please excuse all the trouble *o* inconvenience we are causing you; **si no (le) es m.** if it is no trouble to you; **tomarse la m. (de hacer algo)** to take the trouble (to do sth) (**b**) *Med (dolor)* trouble, slight pain; **tener molestias de estómago** to have an upset stomach

molesto, -a *adj* annoying, upsetting; **estar m. con algn** to be annoyed *o* upset with sb; **ser m.** to be a nuisance *o* a

bother; **una situación molesta** an embarrassing situation

molestoso, -a *Am salvo RP Fam* **1** *adj* annoying
2 *nm,f* nuisance

molibdeno *nf Quím* molybdenum

molicie *nf* (**a**) *Fig (lujo)* great *o* excessive luxury (**b**) *Literario (blandura)* softness

molido, -a 1 *pp de* **moler**
2 *adj* (**a**) *(pulverizado)* ground, milled (**b**) *Fam (exhausto)* worn-out

molienda *nf* (**a**) *(acción)* grinding, milling; **la m. de la aceituna** the pressing of the olives (**b**) *(temporada)* grinding *o* milling season (**c**) *(cantidad)* quantity being ground *o* milled

molinero, -a 1 *adj* milling
2 *nm,f* miller

molinete *nm* (**a**) *(ventilador)* air extractor, extractor fan (**b**) *(juguete)* toy windmill

molinillo *nm* grinder, mill ❑ **m. de café** coffee grinder

molino *nm* mill ❑ **m. de agua** watermill; **m. de papel** paper mill; **m. de viento** windmill

molla *nf* (**a**) *(parte blanda)* soft fleshy part; *(carne)* lean; *(fruta)* flesh (**b**) *Fig* best part (**c**) *Esp Fam (michelín)* spare tyre, flab

mollar *adj* (**a**) *(tierno)* tender, easy to cut (**b**) *Fig (útil)* very useful (**c**) *(ingenuo)* gullible, credulous, easy to trick (**d**) *Fam (bueno)* good-looking; **es una tía m.** she's a cracker

molledo *nm* (**a**) *Anat* flesh, fleshy part (**b**) *(de pan)* crumb

molleja *nf* (**a**) *(de res)* sweetbread (**b**) *(de ave)* gizzard

mollera *nf Fam* brains *pl*, sense; **duro de m.** *(tonto)* dense, thick; *(testarudo)* pigheaded

molón, -ona *adj Esp Argot (que gusta)* *Br* brilliant, *US* neat; *(elegante)* smart

molturación *nf* grinding, milling

molturar *vt* to grind; *(grano)* to mill

molusco *nm Zool* mollusc, *US* mollusk

momentáneo, -a *adj* momentary

momento *nm* moment; **a cada m.** all the time; **al m.** at once; **de m.** for the time being; **de un m. a otro** any time now; **del m.** current; **dentro de un m.** in a moment; **desde el m. en que** *(tan pronto como)* as soon as; *(puesto que)* since; **desde ese m.** from that time on; **en buen/mal m.** at the right/a bad moment; **en cualquier m.** *(de un momento a otro)* any time now; *(cuando sea)* at any time; **en el m. menos pensado** when least expected; **en este m.** *(ahora mismo)* right now; *(actualmente)* at the moment; **en todo m.** at any moment; **ha llegado el m. de ...** the moment has come to ...; **no es el m. para ...** it's not the right time to ...; **pasar por un buen/mal m.** to go through a good/bad patch; **por el m.** for the moment; **por momentos** by the minute; **sin perder un m.** without delay

momia *nf* mummy

momificación *nf* mummification

momificar [59] **1** *vt* to mummify
2 momificarse *vpr* to become mummified

momio *nm Fam* cushy number

mona *nf* (**a**) *Zool (hembra)* female monkey; *(especie)* Barbary ape; *Prov* **aunque la m. se vista de seda, m. se queda** you can't make a silk purse out of a sow's ear (**b**) *Fam (imitador)* copycat (**c**) *Fam (borrachera)* **coger una m.** to get drunk; **dormir la m.** to sleep it off (**d**) *Naipes* old maid (**e**) *Chile (maniquí)* mannequin

monacal *adj Rel* monastic

monacato *nm Rel* (**a**) *(vida monástica)* monkhood (**b**) *(conjunto de monjes)* monks *pl*

Mónaco *n* Monaco

monada *nf Fam* (**a**) *(zalamería)* caress (**b**) *(gesto afectado)* silly *o* ridiculous way of acting *o* speaking; *(de niño)* sweet little way (**c**) *(preciosidad)* (*niño*) charming little child, poppet; *(chica)* pretty girl; *(cosa)* pretty thing; **su hija es una m.** his daughter is a lovely girl; **¡qué m.!** how cute!; **¡qué m. de chaqueta!** what a beautiful jacket!

monaguillo *nm Rel* altar boy

monarca *nm* monarch

monarquía *nf* monarchy; **m. absoluta/constitucional/parlamentaria** absolute/constitutional/parliamentary monarchy

monárquico, -a 1 *adj* monarchic, monarchical
   2 *nm,f* monarchist

monarquismo *nm* monarchism

monasterio *nm Rel* monastery

monástico, -a *adj Rel* monastic

monda *nf* (**a**) *(acción)* peeling (**b**) *(piel)* peel, skin; **la m. de una naranja** the skin of an orange (**c**) *Esp Fam* **ser la m.** *(extraordinario)* to be amazing; *(divertido)* to be a scream

mondadientes *nm inv* toothpick

mondadura *nf (piel)* peel

mondar 1 *vt* (**a**) *(naranjas, patatas)* to peel; *(frutos secos)* to shell (**b**) *(limpiar)* to clean out, dredge
   2 mondarse *vpr Esp Fam* **m. (de risa)** to laugh one's head off

mondo, -a *adj* bare, plain; *Fam* **con un sueldo m. de veinte mil** with a bare wage of twenty thousand; *Fam* **m. y lirondo** pure and simple

mondongo *nm Am (intestinos)* innards *pl*; *Culin* **hacer el m.** to make sausages

monear *vi Am* to boast, show off

moneda *nf* (**a**) *Fin* currency, money; **acuñar m.** to mint money; *Fig* **ser m. corriente** to be everyday stuff; **la Casa de la M.** ≃ the Royal Mint ❑ **m. de curso legal** legal tender; **m. extranjera** foreign currency; **m. única** single currency (**b**) *(pieza)* coin; *Fig* **pagar a uno con la misma m.** to pay sb back in kind ❑ **m. falsa** counterfeit coin; **m. suelta** small change

monedero *nm* purse ❑ **m. electrónico** electronic purse

monegasco, -a *adj & nm,f* Monegasque

monería *nf véase* **monada**

monetario, -a 1 *adj* monetary
   2 *nm* collection of coins and medals

monetarismo *nm Econ* monetarism

monetarista *adj & nmf Econ* monetarist

mongol 1 *adj* Mongolian
   2 *nmf (persona)* Mongolian
   3 *nm (idioma)* Mongolian

Mongolia *n* Mongolia

mongólico, -a *Med Antes* **1** *adj* mongoloid
   2 *nm,f* mongol

mongolismo *nm Med Antes* mongolism, Down's syndrome

monigote *nm* (**a**) *(figura grotesca)* rag *o* paper doll; **m. de nieve** snowman (**b**) *Pey (persona)* puppet, person with a weak character (**c**) *(dibujo)* rough drawing *o* sketch (of a person)

monitor, -a 1 *nm,f (profesor)* instructor ❑ **m. de esquí** ski instructor
   2 *nm Inform* monitor

monitorear *vt Am* to monitor

monitorizar [14] *vt* to monitor

monja *nf Rel* nun

monje *nm Rel* monk

monjil *adj Pey* nun-like

mono, -a 1 *adj* (**a**) *Fam (bonito)* pretty, lovely, cute, sweet; **¡qué vestido tan m.!** what a lovely dress!; **una niña muy mona** a very pretty little girl (**b**) *Col (rubio)* blonde
   2 *nm* (**a**) *Zool* monkey (**b**) *Pey (persona)* ape, ugly person; *Fam* **m. de imitación** copycat; *Fam* **ser el último m.** to be a nobody (**c**) *(prenda)* *(con mangas)* Br overalls, US coveralls; *(de peto)* Br dungarees, US overalls (**d**) *(dibujo humorístico)* cartoon (**e**) *Esp Argot (droga)* cold turkey, withdrawal symptoms (**f**) *Naipes (comodín)* joker (**g**) *Chile (montón)* pile of produce (**h**) *Col* **meterle a algn los monos** to frighten sb

monocarril *adj & nm* monorail

monocolor *adj* monochrome

monocorde *adj Mús* single-stringed; *Fig* monotonous

monocromático, -a *adj Fís Fot* monochromatic

monocromo, -a *adj & nm* monochrome

monóculo *nm* monocle

monocultivo *nm Agr* monoculture

monoesquí *(pl* **monoesquís** *) nm* monoski

monofásico, -a *adj Elec* single-phase

monogamia *nf* monogamy

monógamo, -a 1 *adj* monogamous
   2 *nm,f* monogamist

monografía *nf* monograph

monográfico, -a *adj* monographic

monograma *nm* monogram

monokini *nm* monokini

monolingüe *adj* monolingual

monolítico, -a *adj* monolithic

monolito *nm* monolith

monologar [38] *vi* to soliloquize

monólogo *nm* monologue

monomando 1 *adj* **grifo m.** mixer tap *(with single control)*
   2 *nm* mixer tap *(with single control)*

monomanía *nf Psic* monomania

monoparental *adj* **familia m.** one-parent *o* single-parent family

monoplano *adj & nm Av* monoplane

monoplaza *adj & nm* single-seater

monopolio *nm* monopoly

monopolización *nf* monopolization

monopolizador, -a 1 *adj* monopolistic
   2 *nm,f* monopolist

monopolizar [14] *vt* to monopolize

monosabio *nm Taur* picador's assistant

monosilábico, -a *adj Ling* monosyllabic

monosílabo, -a *Ling* **1** *adj* monosyllabic
   2 *nm* monosyllable

monoteísmo *nm Filos* monotheism

monoteísta *Filos* **1** *adj* monotheistic
   2 *nmf* monotheist

monotipia *nf Impr* Monotype®

monotonía *nf* monotony

monótono, -a *adj* monotonous

monovolumen *nm Aut* people carrier

monóxido *nm Quím* monoxide ❑ **m. de carbono** carbon monoxide

Monrovia *n* Monrovia

Mons *(abrev de* **Monseñor***)* Mgr, Mgsr

monseñor *nm Rel* monsignor

monserga *nf Esp Fam (aburrido)* boring talk; *(molesto)* annoying talk; **dar la m. a algn** *(aburrir)* to bore sb; *(molestar)* to pester o annoy sb; **déjate de monsergas** don't go on so

monstruo 1 *nm* (a) *(ser fantástico)* monster (b) *(genio)* genius
  2 *adj inv Fam* fantastic; **una fiesta m.** a terrific party

monstruosidad *nf* monstrosity

monstruoso, -a *adj* (a) *(repugnante)* monstrous (b) *(enorme)* massive, huge

monta *nf* (a) *(ir a caballo)* riding; *(subir a caballo)* mounting (b) *Fig (importancia)* value; **de poca m.** of little importance

montacargas *nm inv Br* goods lift, *US* freight elevator

montado, -a 1 *pp de* **montar**
  2 *adj* (a) *Mil* mounted ⛟ **la policía montada** the mounted police (b) *(instalado)* furnished, decorated, fitted out; **una oficina montada con todo lujo** a luxuriously fitted-out office

montador, -a *nm,f* (a) *(operario)* fitter, assembler ⛟ **m. de joyas** setter (b) *Cin TV* film editor (c) *Teat* stager, producer

montaje *nm* (a) *Téc (instalación, ensamblaje)* fitting, assembling ⛟ **cadena de m.** assembly line (b) *Cin* editing and mounting (c) *Teat* staging (d) *Fot* montage (e) *Argot (farsa)* farce, sham; **¡menudo m.!** what a farce!

montante *nm* (a) *Constr Téc* upright (b) *(de puerta)* post (c) *(de ventana)* mullion (d) *Arquit* stanchion (e) *Fin (total)* total amount

montaña *nf* (a) *(elevación)* mountain; **vacaciones en la m.** holidays in the mountains; **hacer una m. (de un grano de arena)** to make a mountain out of a molehill ⛟ **m. rusa** big dipper (b) *Fig (montones)* mountains *pl*, piles *pl*; **una m. de arroz** mountains of rice

montañero, -a *nm,f* mountaineer, climber

montañés, -a 1 *adj* mountain, highland
  2 *nm,f* highlander

montañismo *nm* mountaineering, mountain climbing

montañoso, -a *adj* mountainous

montaplatos *nm inv* service lift, dumb waiter

montar 1 *vi* (a) *(caballo, bicicleta)* to mount, get on; *(avión, autobús, tren)* to get on; *(coche)* to get into (b) *(ir montado)* to ride; **m. a caballo** to ride, go (horse) riding; **m. a pelo** to ride bareback; **m. en avión** to travel by plane; **m. en coche/burro** to ride in a car/on a donkey (c) *Esp (tener importancia)* **tanto monta** it makes no difference, it's all the same
  2 *vt* (a) *(cabalgar)* to ride; **no se atreve a m. ese caballo** he doesn't dare ride that horse (b) *(poner encima)* to put on, mount; **montó al pequeño sobre el burrito** he lifted the little boy onto the donkey (c) *Zool (cubrir)* to mount (d) *(acaballar)* to overlap; **una solapa monta sobre la otra** one lapel overlaps the other (e) *Fin (sumar)* to amount to, come to; **el total monta mil euros** the total amounts to one thousand euros (f) *(máquina etc)* to assemble, put together; *(arma)* to cock; *(joya)* to mount, set; *(tienda)* to put up; *(negocio)* to set up, start; *(casa)* to set up (g) *Esp Culin (claras, nata)* to whip (h) *Cin Fot (película)* to edit, mount; *(fotografía)* to mount (i) *Teat (obra)* to stage, mount; *Esp Fam* **m. un número** o **escándalo** to make a scene
  3 **montarse** *vpr* (a) *(subirse) (avión, autobús, bicicleta)* to get on; *(coche)* to get into (b) *Fam (armarse)* to break out; **menudo jaleo se montó** there was a right to-do (c) *Esp Argot* **montárselo** to have things (nicely) worked out o set up; **qué bien te lo montas** you've got things nicely set up

montaraz *adj* (a) *(montañés)* highland, mountain (b) *(arisco)* harsh, wild

monte *nm* (a) *(montaña)* mountain; *(con nombre propio)* mount; **de m.** wild; **M. Everest** Mount Everest; *Prov* **no todo el m. es orégano** life is not just a bowl of cherries ⛟ *Anat* **m. de Venus** *(de la mano)* mount of Venus; *(del pubis)* mons veneris (b) *(bosque)* woodland ⛟ **m. alto** forest; **m. bajo** scrub, underbrush (c) *Esp Fin* **m. pío** o **de piedad** assistance fund (d) *Méx (pasto)* pasture

montepío *nm Fin* assistance fund

montera *nf Taur* bullfighter's hat; *Prov* **ponerse el mundo por m.** not to give a damn about what people might say

montería *nf* (a) *(caza mayor)* hunting (b) *(arte)* chase, venery

montés, -a *adj (animal)* wild

montevideano, -a *adj & nm,f* Montevidean

Montevideo *n* Montevideo

montículo *nm Geog* hillock

montilla *nm (vino)* montilla, sherry-like wine

monto *nm* total amount, total

montón *nm* (a) *(pila)* heap, pile; **hace un m. de años** many years ago; *Fam* **del m.** run-of-the-mill, nothing special; *Argot* **me gusta un m.** I really love it (b) **montones** stacks, piles, tons; **a m.** lots of; **gana dinero a m.** he earns pots of money

Montreal *n* Montreal

montubio, -a *nm,f Andes* coastal peasant

montuno, -a *adj Carib (rudo)* coarse; *(montaraz)* wild; *(rústico)* rustic

montuoso, -a *adj* mountainous

montura *nf* (a) *(cabalgadura)* mount (b) *(silla de montar)* saddle; **sin m.** bareback (c) *(soporte) (de gafas)* frame; *(de joya)* setting; *(de máquina, telescopio)* mounting, assembly

monumental *adj* monumental

monumento *nm* (a) *Arquit Arte* monument (b) *Fam (hermosura)* babe, *Br* stunner; **es un m.** she is a beauty

monzón *nm Meteor* monsoon

monzónico, -a *adj* monsoon; **lluvias monzónicas** monsoon rains

moña *nf* (a) *Esp Fam (borrachera)* **agarrar una m.** to get smashed (b) *(adorno)* ribbon

moño *nm* (a) *(de pelo)* chignon, bun; *Esp Fam* **estar hasta el m.** to be fed up to the back teeth (b) *(de ave)* crest

moquear *vi* to have a runny nose

moqueo *nm* runny nose

moqueta *nf* (a) *Esp (alfombra)* fitted carpet (b) *Tex* moquette

moquillo *nm* (a) *(de perro)* distemper (b) *(de gallina)* pip

mor: por mor de *loc adv* on account of, for the sake of; **por m. de la verdad, debo decírselo** out of respect for the truth I have to tell him

mora¹ *nf* (a) *(fruto) (de moral)* mulberry; *(de la morera)* white mulberry (b) *(zarzamora)* blackberry (c) *(mujer)* Moorish woman (d) *Bot* mulberry

mora² *nf Jur (retraso)* delay

morada *nf Fml* abode, dwelling; **hacer m.** to stay temporarily

morado, -a 1 *adj* purple; *Esp Fam* **pasarlas moradas** to have a tough time; *Esp* **ponerse m.** to stuff oneself
  2 *nm* purple

morador, -a *nm,f Fml* dweller, inhabitant

moradura *nf véase* **moretón**

moral 1 *adj* moral; **deber m.** moral duty
  2 *nm Bot* mulberry tree

3 *nf* (**a**) *(conjunto de reglas)* morals *pl* (**b**) *(ánimo)* morale, spirits *pl*; **levantar la m. a algn** to cheer sb up, raise sb's spirits; **no tengo m. para verle ahora** I couldn't face seeing him now; *Esp Fam* **tienes más m. que el Alcoyano** what an optimist you are!

moraleja *nf* moral

moralidad *nf* morality

moralismo *nm* moralism

moralista 1 *adj* moralistic
2 *nmf* moralist

moralización *nf* moralization

moralizar [14] *vt & vi* to moralize

morapio *nm Esp Fam (vino)* cheap red wine

morar *vi Fml* to dwell, reside

moratón *nm* bruise

moratoria *nf Jur* moratorium

morbidez *nf* softness, tenderness

mórbido, -a *adj* (**a**) *(suave)* soft, delicate (**b**) *Fml (malsano)* morbid

morbilidad *nf* morbidity, morbidness

morbo *nm Fam* **los cementerios le dan mucho m.** he gets a morbid pleasure out of visiting cemeteries; **esa chica tiene mucho m.** there's something perversely attractive about that girl

morbosidad *nf nm* morbidity

morboso, -a *adj* (**a**) *(enfermo)* sick, ill (**b**) *Fml (malsano)* morbid

morcilla *nf* (**a**) *Culin Br* black pudding, *US* blood sausage; *Esp Fam* **que le den m.** he can drop dead for all I care (**b**) *Teat* improvised part

morcillo *nm* fore knuckle

mordacidad *nf* mordacity

mordaz *adj* mordant

mordaza *nf* gag

mordedor, -a *adj* which bites, vicious

mordedura *nf* bite

morder [41] **1** *vt* (**a**) to bite; **me ha mordido** it has bitten me; *Fig* **m. el anzuelo** to take the bait; *Fam* **el jefe está que muerde** the boss is hopping mad (**b**) *Carib Méx (estafar)* to cheat
2 morderse *vpr* to bite (oneself); **m. las uñas/los labios** to bite one's nails/lips; **m. la lengua** *(sin querer)* to bite one's tongue; *(reprimirse)* to hold one's tongue

mordiente *adj & nm* mordant

mordisco *nm* bite; **dar** *o* **pegar un m.** *(a algo)* to take a bite at *o* out of; *(a algn)* to bite

mordisquear *vt* to nibble (at)

morena *nf (pez)* moray eel

moreno, -a **1** *adj* (**a**) *(pelo)* dark-haired; *(ojos)* dark-eyed; *(piel)* dark-skinned (**b**) *(bronceado)* suntanned, tanned; **ponerse m.** to get a suntan; **en seguida me pongo m.** I go brown very quickly (**c**) *(raza negra)* black; **una cantante morena** a black singer (**d**) *(cosas)* brown; **pan/azúcar m.** brown bread/sugar
2 *nm,f* (**a**) *(persona) (de pelo)* dark-haired person; *(de ojos)* dark-eyed person; *(de piel)* dark-skinned person (**b**) *(de raza negra)* black person (**c**) *(bronceado)* suntan, tan

morera *nf Bot* white mulberry

morería *nf Hist* Moorish quarter; **la m.** the Moors *pl*

moretón *nm Fam* bruise

morfema *nm Ling* morpheme

Morfeo *nm Mit* Morpheus

morfina *nf* morphine

morfinomanía *nf* addiction to morphine

morfinómano, -a **1** *adj* addicted to morphine
2 *nm,f* morphine addict

morfología *nf* morphology

morfológico, -a *adj* morphological

morgue *nf* morgue

moribundo, -a *adj & nm,f* moribund

morigeración *nf* moderation

morigerado, -a **1** *pp de* morigerar
2 *adj* moderate

morigerar *vt* to moderate

morir [27] *(pp* **muerto***)* **1** *vi* (**a**) *(fallecer)* to die; **m. de amor** *o* **pena** to die of a broken heart; **m. de frío** to die of cold; **m. de hambre** to starve to death, die of hunger; **m. de una enfermedad/de cáncer** to die from an illness/from cancer; **¡muera la corrupción!** down with corruption!; **murió en la guerra/de muerte natural** he died in the war/a natural death (**b**) *Fig (terminar)* to end, finish; **los ríos van a m. al mar** rivers end their life in the sea (**c**) *Literario (desaparecer)* to vanish, fade; **las olas morían a sus pies** the waves came in and died by his feet
2 morirse *vpr (fallecer)* to die; **m. de aburrimiento** to be bored to death; **m. de envidia/miedo** to be dying with envy/fear; **m. de frío** to die of cold; *Fig* to freeze to death; **m. de ganas (de hacer algo)** to be dying (to do sth); **m. de hambre** to starve to death; *Fig* to be starving; **m. por algo/algn** to be crazy about sth/sb; **m. de risa** to die laughing; *Fam* **que me muera si …** may I be struck down dead if …

morisco, -a *Hist* **1** *adj* = of *o* relating to Spanish Moors converted to Christianity, Morisco
2 *nm,f* = Spanish Moor converted to Christianity, Morisco

mormón, -ona *adj & nm,f* Mormon

mormonismo *nm* Mormonism

moro, -a **1** *adj* (**a**) *Hist* Moorish (**b**) *Esp Fam Pey (machista)* sexist
2 *nm,f* (**a**) *Hist* Moor; *Fam* **hay moros en la costa** the coast is not clear (**b**) *Esp Fam Pey (árabe)* = term used to refer to Arabs, which is sometimes offensive
3 *nm Esp muy Fam (machista)* sexist pig

morocho, -a **1** *adj* (**a**) *Andes RP (moreno)* dark, swarthy (**b**) *Ven (gemelo)* twin
2 *nm,f* (**a**) *Andes RP (moreno)* dark *o* swarthy person (**b**) *Ven (gemelo)* twin

morosidad *nf* (**a**) *(lentitud)* slowness, sluggishness (**b**) *Com Fin* arrears *pl* (of payment)

moroso, -a *adj* (**a**) *(perezoso)* slow, sluggish, torpid (**b**) *Com Fin* in arrears, slow to pay; **cliente m.** slow *o* bad payer

morral *nm* (**a**) *(para pienso)* nosebag (**b**) *Mil* haversack; *(de cazador)* gamebag

morralla *nf* (**a**) *Pesca* small fish (**b**) *Pey (chusma)* rabble, scum (**c**) *(cosas sin valor)* rubbish, junk (**d**) *Méx (suelto)* loose change

morrear *Esp Fam* **1** *vt* to snog, smooch
2 morrearse *vpr* to snog, smooch

morrena *nf Geol* moraine

morreo *nm Esp Vulg* snog, smooch

morriña *nf Esp* homesickness

morrión *nm Mil* helmet, shako

morro *nm* (**a**) *(hocico)* snout (**b**) *Esp (de avión)* nose; *(de vehículo)* front (**c**) *Esp Fam* **morros** *(labios)* lips; *(boca)* mouth; **estar de morros** to be in a bad mood; **romperle los morros a algn** to smash sb's face in (**d**) *Esp Fam (caradura)* **¡qué m. tiene!, ¡tiene un m. que se lo pisa!** he's got a real nerve!; **por (todo) el m.** *(gratis)* without paying, free; **se presentó allí por (todo) el m.** *(con caradura)* he had the nerve just to walk straight in there

morrocotudo *adj Fam Hum* amazing, terrific; **un lío m.** a tremendous mess

morrón *adj* **pimiento m.** (fleshy) red pepper

morronguear *vi* (**a**) *Am* to suck, sip (**b**) *Arg Chile* to doze, snooze

morroñoso, -a *adj* (**a**) *CAm (áspero)* rough (**b**) *Perú (débil)* weak, sickly

morrudo, -a *adj Fam* thick-lipped

morsa *nf Zool* walrus

morse *nm Téc* morse

mortadela *nf Culin* mortadella

mortaja *nf* (**a**) *(sudario)* shroud (**b**) *Andes Fig (papel de cigarrillo)* cigarette paper

mortal 1 *adj* (**a**) *(no inmortal)* mortal; **los mortales** mortals; **odio/pecado m.** mortal hatred/sin (**b**) *(mortífero)* fatal, lethal, deadly; **un accidente m.** a fatal accident; **veneno m.** lethal *o* deadly poison
 2 *nmf* mortal

mortalidad *nf* mortality; **índice de m.** death rate ❑ **m. infantil** infant mortality

mortandad *nf* mortality, death toll

mortecino, -a *adj* lifeless, colourless, *US* colorless

mortero *nm Culin Mil* mortar

mortífero, -a *adj* deadly, fatal, lethal

mortificación *nf* mortification

mortificar [59] **1** *vt* to mortify
 2 mortificarse *vpr* to mortify oneself

mortuorio, -a *adj* mortuary ❑ **lecho m.** deathbed

moruno, -a *adj* Moorish; *(árabe)* Arab

Mosa *n* Meuse

mosaico, -a 1 *adj Rel* of *o* relating to Moses
 2 *nm* mosaic

mosca *nf* (**a**) *Ent* fly (**b**) *(perilla)* goatee (**c**) *Box* **peso m.** flyweight (**d**) *Argot (dinero)* dough, bread; **aflojar/soltar la m.** to fork out, stump up (**e**) *(locuciones)* **pescar a m.** to fly-fish; *Fam* **con la m. en** *o* **tras la oreja** suspicious; *Esp Fam* **estar m.** *(suspicaz)* to be suspicious; *Esp (enfadado)* to be cross; *Fam* **es incapaz de matar una m.** he's totally harmless, he wouldn't harm a fly; *Fam* **m.** *o* **mosquita muerta** hypocrite; *Fam* **no se oye una m.** you could hear a pin drop; *Fam* **picarle a algn la m.** to start feeling suspicious; *Fam* **por si las moscas** just in case; *Fam* **¿qué m. te ha picado?** what's biting you?

moscada *adj* **nuez m.** nutmeg

moscarda *nf Ent* blowfly, bluebottle

moscardón *nm* (**a**) *Ent* bluebottle, blowfly (**b**) *Fam (pesado)* pest, nuisance

moscatel 1 *adj (vino)* muscat
 2 *nm (vino)* muscatel, muscat

moscón *nm véase* **moscardón**

mosconear *vt* to pester, annoy, bother

moscovita *adj & nmf* Muscovite

Moscú *n* Moscow

mosén *nm Esp Rel* Reverend

mosqueado 1 *pp de* **mosquear**
 2 *adj* (**a**) *(enfadado)* in a huff; **estar m. con algn** to be in a huff with sb (**b**) *(con sospechas)* suspicious

mosquear *Fam* **1** *vt* (**a**) *(enfadar)* **m. a algn** *Br* to get up sb's nose, *US* tick sb off (**b**) *(hacer sospechar)* to make suspicious; **me mosquea que no haya llamado todavía** I'm a bit surprised he hasn't phoned yet
 2 mosquearse *vpr* to get in a huff

mosqueo *nm Fam* (**a**) *(enfado)* annoyance, anger (**b**) *(sospechas)* **tener un m.** to be suspicious

mosquerío *nm*, **mosquero** *nm Am* cloud of flies

mosquete *nm Mil* musket

mosquetero *nm Hist* musketeer

mosquetón *nm* (**a**) *Mil Hist* carbine (**b**) *Téc* snap link *o* hook

mosquitera *nf* mosquito net

mosquitero *nm* (**a**) *(red)* mosquito net (**b**) *Orn* **m. musical** willow warbler; **m. silbador** wood warbler

mosquito *nm Ent* mosquito

mostacho *nm* moustache, *US* mustache

mostajo *nm Bot* common whitebeam

mostaza *nf Bot Culin* mustard

mosto *nm (del vino)* must; *(bebida)* grape juice

mostrador *nm (en tienda)* counter; *(en bar)* bar; *(en aeropuerto)* desk ❑ **m. de facturación** check-in desk; **m. de información** information desk

mostrar [63] **1** *vt* (**a**) *(gen)* to show; **muéstramelo** show it to me (**b**) *(materiales, cualidades)* to display, exhibit (**c**) *(explicar)* to explain, show
 2 mostrarse *vpr* to be, appear, show oneself; **se mostró muy comprensiva** she was very understanding

mostrenco, -a 1 *adj* (**a**) *(sin dueño)* ownerless; **bienes mostrencos** ownerless property (**b**) *Fig (ignorante)* stupid, thick, dense (**c**) *(gordo)* fat
 2 *nm,f* (**a**) *(ignorante)* blockhead, dunce (**b**) *(gordo)* very fat person

mota *nf* (**a**) *(brizna)* mote, speck; **una m. de polvo** a speck of dust (**b**) *(lunar)* dot; **rojo con motas blancas** red with white dots (**c**) *Fig (defecto)* small flaw *o* defect *o* fault (**d**) *CAm Méx Fam (droga)* marijuana

mote[1] *nm (apodo)* nickname; **poner m. a algn** to give sb a nickname; **le pusimos como m. 'el Alto'** we nicknamed him 'Lofty'

mote[2] *nm Andes Culin* stewed *Br* maize *o US* corn

moteado, -a *adj* dotted

motear *vi Perú* to eat 'mote'

motejar *vt* to accuse, brand; **le motejaron de ladrón** they branded him (as) a thief

motel *nm* motel

motero, -a *nm,f Fam* biker

motete *nm* (**a**) *Mús* motet (**b**) *CAm PRico (atado)* bundle

motín *nm (amotinamiento)* mutiny, rising; *(disturbio)* riot, disturbance

motivación *nf* motivation, drive

motivar *vt* (**a**) *(causar)* to cause, give rise to (**b**) *(inducir)* to motivate (**c**) *(razonar)* to explain, justify

motivo *nm* (**a**) *(causa)* motive, cause; *(gen plural)* grounds *pl*; **bajo ningún m.** under no circumstances; **con este** *o* **tal m.** for this reason; **con m. de** on the occasion of; **darle a algn motivos para hacer algo** to give sb reason to do sth; **hay suficientes motivos de divorcio** there are sufficient grounds for divorce; **se ha enfadado con m.** he has every reason to be angry; **sin m.** for no reason at all; *Fml* **Juan Segarra ha sido m. de homenaje** a tribute has been paid to Juan Segarra (**b**) *Arte Mús* motif, leitmotif (**c**) *Chile* **motivos** finickiness

moto *nf Aut* motorbike

motobomba *nf* fire engine

motocarro *nm Aut* three-wheeled delivery van

motocicleta *nf véase* **moto**

motociclismo *nm Aut* motorcycling

motociclista *nmf Aut* motorcyclist

motociclo *nm Aut* motorcycle

motocross [moto'kros] *nm Aut* motocross

motocultivo *nm Agr* mechanized agriculture

motoesquí *(pl* **motoesquís** *o* **motoesquíes)** *nm* snow-bike

motonáutica *nf Náut* motorboating

motonáutico, -a *adj Náut* of *o* relating to motorboating

motonave *nf Náut* motorboat

motonetista *nmf Am* scooter rider

motor, -a 1 *adj* (a) *Téc* motive, motor (b) *Biol* motor
2 *nm* engine, motor ❑ *Inform* **m. de búsqueda** search engine; **m. de explosión** internal combustion engine; **m. de inyección** fuel-injection engine; **m. de reacción** jet engine; **m. diesel** diesel engine; **m. eléctrico** electric motor; **m. fuera borda** *o* **bordo** outboard motor

motora *nf Náut* motorboat

motorismo *nm Aut* motorcycling

motorista *nmf Esp Aut* motorcyclist

motorizado 1 *pp de* **motorizar**
2 *adj* motorized

motorizar [14] **1** *vt* to motorize
2 motorizarse *vpr Fam* to get oneself a car *o* motorbike

motosierra *nf* power saw

motricidad *nf* motivity

motriz *adj f* (a) *Téc* motive ❑ **fuerza m.** motive power (b) *Biol* motor

motu propio *adv*, **motu proprio** *adv* (de) **m.** of one's own accord

mouse [maus] *nm inv Am Inform* mouse

movedizo, -a *adj* (a) *(fácil de mover)* easy to move (b) *(poco firme)* unsteady ❑ **arenas movedizas** quicksand *sing*

mover [41] **1** *vt* (a) *(desplazar, trasladar)* to move; **m. algo de su sitio** to move sth out of its place; **no muevas la cabeza** keep your head still; *Fam* **m. el esqueleto** to dance (b) *(hacer funcionar)* to drive *o* work; **la máquina mueve el tren** the engine pulls the train (c) *(incitar, provocar)* to drive *o* incite; **m. a algn a piedad** to move sb to pity; **movido por la compasión** swayed by compassion; **sólo le mueve su interés por el dinero** it is only money that impels him to do anything
2 moverse *vpr* (a) *(desplazarse, trasladarse)* to move; **no te muevas** don't move (b) *Fam (gestionar)* to take every step, make all possible efforts; **hay que m. para encontrar un trabajo** you have to move heaven and earth to find a job (c) *(darse prisa)* to hurry up; **¡muévete!** get a move on! (d) *Fig (relacionarse)* to move; **ella se mueve entre artistas** she moves in artistic circles

movible *adj* movable

movida *nf Esp RP Argot* (a) *(lío, problema)* problem; **mudarse es una m.** moving house is a real headache; **tener movidas** *o* **una m. con algn** to have a spot of bother with sb (b) *(ambiente, actividad)* scene; **no me va esa m.** it's not my scene

movido, -a 1 *pp de* **mover**
2 *adj* (a) *Fot* blurred (b) *(persona)* active, restless (c) *CAm (enteco)* puny

móvil 1 *adj* movable, mobile; *Tel* mobile
2 *nm* (a) *Tel* mobile (b) *(motivo)* motive, reason; **el m. del crimen** the motive for the murder (c) *Arte* mobile

movilidad *nf* mobility

movilización *nf* mobilization

movilizar [14] *vt (tropas, multitudes, personas)* to mobilize

movimiento *nm* (a) *(desplazamiento)* movement; *Fís Téc* motion; **(poner algo) en m.** (to set sth) in motion; **m. circular/lineal** circular/linear motion ❑ **m. sísmico** earth tremor (b) *(actividad)* movement, activity; **hay mucho m. en el mercado** there is a lot of bustle in the market; **el m.**
de turistas es menor este año the number of tourists has gone down this year (c) *Com Fin (entradas y salidas)* operations *pl* ❑ **m. de caja** turnover, transactions *pl* (d) *(corriente)* movement ❑ **m. literario** literary movement; **m. obrero** working-class movement (e) *Mús (parte de la obra)* movement; *(velocidad del compás)* tempo

moviola *nf Cin TV* editing projector

mozalbete *nm* boy, young lad

Mozambique *n* Mozambique

mozambiqueño, -a *adj & nm,f* Mozambiquean

mozárabe *Hist* **1** *adj* Mozarabic
2 *nmf* Mozarab

mozo, -a 1 *nm,f* (a) *(joven) (hombre)* lad, boy; *(mujer)* lass, young girl; **ser un buen m.** to be a good-looking *o* handsome man
2 *nm* (a) *(de estación)* porter; *(de hotel)* bellboy, *US* bellhop ❑ **m. de comedor** waiter's assistant, *US* busboy; **m. de estación** porter (b) *Esp Mil* conscript

m/p *(abrev de* **mi pagaré)** IOU

MP3 *nm (abrev de* **MPEG-1 Audio Layer-3)** MP3

muaré *nm Tex* moiré

mucamo, -a *nm,f Andes RP* servant

muchacha *nf* (a) *(chica)* (young) girl (b) *Fam (sirvienta)* maid

muchachada *nf* group of children

muchacho *nm* (young) boy, lad; **un gran m.** a good lad

muchedumbre *nf* (a) *(de gente)* crowd (b) *(de cosas)* a great deal of

mucho, -a 1 *adj* (a) *sing (gen en frases afirmativas)* a lot of, lots of; **hace m. calor** it's very hot; **queda m. café** there's a lot of coffee left; **m. tiempo** a long time; **tengo m. sueño/mucha sed** I am very sleepy/thirsty; *(colectivo)* **hay m. tonto suelto** there are lots of idiots around (b) *(gen en frases negativas e interr)* much; **¿bebes m. café?** — **no, no m.** do you drink much coffee? — no, not much (c) *(demasiado)* es **m. coche para mí** this car is far too big *o* expensive for me (d) **muchos, -as** *(gen en frases afirmativas)* a lot of, lots of; **tiene m. años ya** he is very old now; **tienen m. hijos** they have a lot of children (e) *(gen en frases negativas e interr)* **no hizo muchas preguntas** he didn't ask many questions; **¿tienes m. amigos?** have you got many friends?
2 *pron* (a) *(en singular)* a lot; *(en plural)* many, a lot; **¿cuánta leche queda?** — **mucha** how much milk is there left? — a lot (b) **muchos, -as** a lot, many; **¿cuántos libros tienes?** — **m.** how many books have you got? — lots; **m. de los presentes** many of the people here; **m. son los que ...** there are many who ...
3 *adv* (a) *(gran cantidad)* (very) much, a lot; **como m.** at the most; **con m.** by far; **me gusta m.** I like it very much; **m. antes/después** long before/after; **m. mejor/peor** a lot better/worse; **ni con m.** not nearly as; **no es, ni con m., tan bueno como el otro** it is not nearly as good as the other one; **ni m. menos** not in the least; **por m. (que) ...** however much ...; **por m. que te empeñes** however hard you try; **tener a algn en m.** to think a lot of sb; *Fam* **muy m.** very much (b) *(tiempo)* **hace m. que no viene por aquí** he has not been to see us for a long time (c) *(a menudo)* often; **vamos m. al cine** we go to the cinema quite often

mucosa *nf* mucous membrane

mucosidad *nf* mucosity, mucus

mucoso, -a *adj* mucous

múcura *nf Andes Ven* water jar, pitcher

muda *nf* (a) *(de ropa)* change of clothes (b) *Orn Zool (de plumas, pelo)* moult, *US* molt, moulting *o US* molting season; *(serpiente)* slough (c) *(de la voz)* breaking

mudable *adj* (a) *(cambiable)* changeable (b) *(inconstante)* fickle

mudada *nf Andes CAm* (**a**) *(muda)* change of clothes (**b**) *(traslado)* move, removal

mudanza *nf* (**a**) *(cambio)* changing, change (**b**) *(de residencia, piso)* move, removal; **estar de m.** to be moving

mudar 1 *vt* (**a**) *(cambiar)* to change; **le han mudado de oficina** he's been moved to a different office; **m. de opinión** to change one's mind (**b**) *(trasladar)* to change, move; **mudaron su residencia al sur de la ciudad** they went to live in the south of the city (**c**) *(de ropa)* to change (**d**) *(de plumas, pelo)* to moult, *US* molt; *(de piel)* to shed, slough (**e**) *(de voz)* to break

　2 mudarse *vpr* (**a**) *(de lugar)* to change, move; **m. de sitio** to change seats (**b**) *(de ropa)* to change one's clothes (**c**) *(de casa)* to move (house)

mudéjar *adj & nmf Hist* Mudejar

mudez *nf* dumbness

mudo, -a 1 *adj* (**a**) *(que no habla)* dumb; **m. de asombro** dumbfounded; **m. de nacimiento** born dumb (**b**) *Ling* mute (**c**) *Cin* silent ❑ **cine m.** silent films *pl* (**d**) *Fig (callado)* speechless, silent

　2 *nm,f* dumb person

mueble 1 *adj* movable ❑ **bienes muebles** movables

　2 *nm* piece of furniture; **muebles** furniture *sing*; **con/sin muebles** furnished/unfurnished ❑ **m. bar** cocktail cabinet

mueblista *nmf (fabricante)* furniture maker; *(vendedor)* furniture dealer

mueca *nf* (**a**) *(de burla)* mocking face; **hacer muecas** to pull faces (**b**) *(de dolor, asco)* grimace

muela *nf* (**a**) *Anat* molar, tooth; **empastar una m.** to fill a tooth ❑ **dolor de muelas** toothache; **m. del juicio** wisdom tooth ❑ *(de molino)* millstone; *(de afilar)* grindstone

muelle¹ **1** *adj* soft, comfortable

　2 *nm* spring

muelle² *nm* (**a**) *(andén)* loading bay, freight platform (**b**) *Náut* dock

muérdago *nm Bot* mistletoe

muermo *nm Esp Fam (tedio)* **esta fiesta es un m.** this party is a drag; **este tío es un m.** this bloke is a real bore

muerte *nf* (**a**) *(fin de la vida)* death ❑ **m. cerebral** brain death; **m. natural** natural death; **m. súbita** *(en la cuna)* sudden infant death (**b**) *(homicidio)* murder (**c**) *(locuciones)* **a m.** to the death; **a vida o m.** life-and-death; **dar m. a algn** to kill sb; **estar a (las puertas de) la m.** to be dying, be at death's door; **hasta la m.** unto death; **odiar a algn a m.** to loathe sb; *Fam* **de mala m.** lousy, rotten; *Fam* **un susto de m.** the fright of one's life; *Argot* **estar de m.** to be fantastic

muerto, -a 1 *pp de* **morir**

　2 *adj* (**a**) *(sin vida)* dead; **caer m.** to drop dead; **dar a algn por m.** to assume sb to be dead, give sb up for dead; **horas muertas** spare time; **medio m., más m. que vivo** half-dead; **m. de hambre** starving; **m. de frío** frozen to death; **m. de miedo** scared stiff; **m. de pena** broken-hearted; **m. de risa** laughing one's head off; *Am* **estar m. por algn** *(enamorado)* to be head over heels in love with sb; **nacido m.** still-born; **no tener dónde caerse m.** not to have a place to lay one's head ❑ **lengua muerta** dead language; **naturaleza muerta** still life; *Aut* **punto m.** neutral; **en punto m.** out of gear (**b**) *Fam (cansado)* dead tired, dog-tired, exhausted

　3 *nm,f* (**a**) *(difunto)* dead person; *(cadáver)* corpse; **callarse como un m.** not to say a word; **hacer el m.** to float on one's back; **hacerse el m.** to pretend to be dead; **ser un m. de hambre** to be an absolute nobody; *Fam* **cargar con el m.** *(llevar la peor parte)* to be a dogsbody; *(llevarse las culpas)* to carry the can; *Fam* **echarle el m. a algn** to pass the buck to sb; *Ofens* **¡tus muertos!** up yours! (**b**) *(víctima)* fatality,

victim; **hubo dos muertos** there were two fatalities, two (people) died

muesca *nf* (**a**) *Téc (entalladura)* mortise, mortice (**b**) *(incisión)* nick, notch

muestra *nf* (**a**) *(espécimen)* sample, specimen; **botón de m.** sample **m. gratuita** free sample (**b**) *(modelo a copiar)* pattern, model (**c**) *(prueba, señal)* proof, sign; **dar muestras de** to show signs of; **como m. de poder** as a demonstration of power; **m. de cariño/respeto** token of affection/respect; **una m. más de ...** yet another example of ...

muestrario *nm* collection of samples

muestreo *nm* sampling; **m. al azar** random sampling

mugido *nm* (**a**) *(de vaca)* moo; *(de toro)* bellow (**b**) *Lit (estrépito)* howl, roar (**c**) **mugidos** *(de vaca)* mooing *sing*, lowing *sing*; *(de toro)* bellowing *sing*

mugir [24] *vi* (**a**) *(vaca)* to moo, low; *(toro)* to bellow (**b**) *Fig* to bellow (**c**) *Lit* to howl, roar

mugre *nf (suciedad)* filth, grime

mugriento, -a *adj* filthy, grimy

mujer 1 *nf* (**a**) *(hembra adulta)* woman; **dos mujeres** two women ❑ **m. fatal** femme fatale; **m. de la limpieza** cleaning lady; **m. de su casa** housewife; *Euf* **m. de la vida, m. de la vida alegre** prostitute (**b**) *(esposa)* wife; **su futura m.** his bride-to-be; *Fml* **tomar m.** to get married

　2 *interj Esp* **¿te acuerdas de Marisol?, ¡sí, m., nuestra compañera de clase!** do you remember Marisol? you know, she was at school with us!

mujeriego 1 *adj* woman-chasing

　2 *nm* womanizer, woman chaser

mujeril *adj* (**a**) *(femenino)* womanly (**b**) *Pey (cursi)* womanish

mujerío *nm* group of women

mujerona *nf* buxom woman

mujerzuela *nf* prostitute

mújol *nm (pez)* grey mullet

mula *nf* (**a**) she-mule; *Fig* **terco como una m.** as stubborn as a mule (**b**) *Méx (cojín)* shoulder pad (**c**) *Méx (mercancía)* junk, unsaleable goods

muladar *nm* dump, rubbish tip

muladí *Hist* **1** *adj* = of o relating to the Spanish Christians converted to Islam in the Middle Ages

　2 *nmf* = Spanish Christian converted to Islam

mular *adj* mule; **ganado m.** mules *pl*

mulato, -a *adj & nm,f* mulatto

mulero *nm* muleteer

muleta *nf* (**a**) *(prótesis)* crutch (**b**) *Fig (apoyo)* support, prop (**c**) *Taur* muleta

muletilla *nf* (**a**) *Ling (estribillo)* pet word, cliché (**b**) *(bastón)* cross-handled cane

mullido, -a *adj* soft, fluffy

mullir *vt* (**a**) *(lana)* to beat, soften; *(colchón)* to fluff up (**b**) *Agr (tierra)* to break up, hoe

mulo *nm* mule; *Fam* **estar hecho un m.** to be as strong as a horse

multa *nf* fine; *Aut* ticket; **m. de aparcamiento** parking ticket

multar *vt* to fine

multicentro *nm* large shopping mall

multicine *nm* multiplex cinema

multicolor *adj* multicoloured, *US* multicolored

multicopiar *vt* to duplicate

multicopista *nf Esp* duplicator

multicultural *adj* multicultural

multidifusión *nf Inform TV* multicast

multidisciplinario, -a *adj,* **multidisciplinar** *adj* multidisciplinary

multifamiliar *nm Am* block of flats

multiforme *adj* multiform

multigrado *adj* multigrade

multilateral *adj* multilateral

multimedia *adj inv Inform* multimedia

multimillonario, -a *adj & nm,f* multimillionaire

multinacional *adj & nf* multinational

multíparo, -a *adj* multiparous

múltiple *adj* (a) *Mat* multiple (b) **múltiples** *(muchos)* many

multiplicable *adj* multipliable

multiplicación *nf Mat* multiplication

multiplicador, -a 1 *adj* multiplying
2 *nm* (a) *Mat* multiplier (b) *Mil* booster

multiplicando *nm Mat* multiplicand

multiplicar [59] **1** *vt & vi* to multiply (**por** by)
2 multiplicarse *vpr* (a) *(reproducirse, aumentar)* to multiply (b) *Fig (estar en todo)* to be everywhere

multiplicidad *nf* multiplicity

múltiplo, -a *adj & nm* multiple ❑ *Mat* **mínimo común m.** lowest common multiple

multipropiedad *nf* multiple ownership

multipuesto *adj inv Inform* multi-terminal; **red m.** multi-terminal network

multirriesgo *adj inv Seg* **póliza m.** multiple risk policy

multisalas *nm inv (cine)* multiplex cinema

multitarea *adj inv & nf Inform* multitasking

multitud *nf* (a) *(de personas)* crowd (b) *(de cosas)* multitude; **tengo una m. de cosas que hacer** I have thousands of things to do

multitudinario, -a *adj* multitudinous

multiuso *adj inv* multipurpose

multiviaje *adj* **tarjeta m.** season ticket

mundanal *adj,* **mundano, -a** *adj* of this world, mundane; **huir del m. ruido** to get away from it all

mundial 1 *adj* world, worldwide; **campeón m.** world champion; **de fama m.** world-famous
2 *nm* world championship

mundialización *nf* globalization

mundialmente *adv* throughout the world, worldwide

mundillo *nm Fam Irón* circles *pl*, spheres *pl*; **el m. literario** literary circles

mundo *nm* (a) *(la Tierra, el universo, civilización)* world; **el m. de los niños/negocios** the world of children/business; **el fin del m.** the end of the world; **correr** o **ver m.** to see life; **echar** o **traer al m.** to bring into the world; **nada del otro m.** nothing special; **por nada del m.** not for all the tea in China; **se me hundió el m.** my world caved in; **todo el m.** everyone; *Fml* **venir al m.** to come into the world; *Euf* **echarse al m.** to become a prostitute; *Prov* **el m. es un pañuelo** it's a small world ❑ **el otro m.** the hereafter, life after death; **hombre/mujer de m.** man/woman of the world (b) *(baúl)* trunk

mundología *nf* worldliness, experience of the world

mundovisión *nf TV* satellite broadcasting

munición *nf Mil* ammunition ❑ **municiones de boca** provisions; **m. submarina** underwater ordnance

municipal 1 *adj* municipal; **elecciones municipales** local (council) elections
2 *nmf Esp (hombre)* (local) policeman; *(mujer)* (local) policewoman

municipalidad *nf* municipality

municipalizar [14] *vt* to municipalize

municipio *nm* (a) *(circunscripción administrativa)* municipality (b) *(corporación)* local council

munificencia *nf* munificence

muñeca *nf* (a) *Anat* wrist (b) *(juguete, muchacha bonita)* doll (c) *Andes RP Fam* **tener m.** *(enchufe)* to have friends in high places; *(habilidad)* to have the knack

muñeco *nm* (a) *(juguete)* doll ❑ **m. de nieve** snowman; **m. de peluche** cuddly toy; **m. de trapo** rag doll (b) *Fig (marioneta)* puppet

muñequera *nf* wristband

muñequilla *nf Chile* young ear of *Br* maize o *US* corn

muñón *nm Anat* stump

mural *adj & nm* mural

muralla *nf (de una ciudad)* wall

murciano, -a 1 *adj* o from Murcia
2 *nm,f* person from Murcia

murciélago *nm Zool* bat

murga *nf* (a) *Mús* band of street musicians (b) *Esp Fam (tabarra)* bore, pain; **dar la m.** to be a pest o drag

murmullo *nm* murmur, murmuring, whisper, whispering; **el m. de las hojas** the rustling of the leaves

murmuración *nf* gossip, backbiting

murmurador, -a 1 *adj* gossipy
2 *nm,f* gossip

murmurar *vi* (a) *(susurrar)* to whisper; *(refunfuñar)* to mutter, grumble (b) *(criticar)* to gossip, backbite (c) *(producir murmullo)* to murmur

muro *nm* wall ❑ **m. de defensa** dam

murria *nf Fam* sadness, melancholy; **estar con la m.** o **tener m.** to have the blues, be feeling down

murrio, -a *adj Fam* sad, blue

mus *nm Naipes* card game

musa *nf* (a) *Mit* Muse (b) *Lit (inspiración)* muse; **dedicarse a las musas** to write poetry

musaraña *nf Zool* shrew; *Fam* **estar mirando a** o **pensando en las musarañas** to be daydreaming o in the clouds

musculación *nf* body-building

muscular *adj* muscular

musculatura *nf* musculature; **desarrollar la m.** to develop one's muscles

músculo *nm Anat* muscle; **m. estriado/liso** striated/smooth muscle

musculoso, -a *adj* muscular

muselina *nf Tex* muslin; **m. fina** mull

museo *nm* museum; **m. de arte** o **pintura** art gallery

museografía *nf,* **museología** *nf* museology

musgo *nm Bot* moss

musgoso, -a *adj* mossy

música *nf* music; *Fam* **irse con la m. a otra parte** to make oneself scarce; **poner m. a** to set to music ❑ **m. clásica** classical music; **m. étnica** world music; **m. de fondo** background music; *Fig* **m. celestial** high-sounding words, empty promises

musical 1 *adj* musical
2 *nm (comedia)* musical

musicalidad *nf* musicality

músico, -a 1 *adj* musical
2 *nm,f* musician

musicología *nf* musicology

musicólogo, -a *nm,f* musicologist

musitar *vi Literario* to whisper

muslo *nm Anat* thigh

mustang (*pl* **mustangs**) *nm Zool* mustang

mustiarse *vpr* to wilt, wither

mustio, -a *adj* (**a**) *(plantas)* wilted, withered (**b**) *(persona)* sad, gloomy (**c**) *Méx Fam (hipócrita)* two-faced

musulmán, -ana *adj & nm,f* Muslim, Moslem

mutabilidad *nf* mutability

mutable *adj* mutable

mutación *nf (gen)* change; *Biol* mutation

mutante *adj & nmf* mutant

mutar *vt* to mutate

mutilación *nf* mutilation

mutilado, -a 1 *pp de* **mutilar**
  2 *adj* mutilated, crippled, disabled
  3 *nm,f* cripple, disabled person; **m. de guerra** disabled serviceman

mutilar *vt* to mutilate

mutis *nm Teat* exit; **hacer m.** *(callarse)* to shut up; *(irse)* to make oneself scarce; **¡m.!** silence!

mutismo *nm* (**a**) *(silencio)* complete silence (**b**) *Med* mutism

mutua *nf véase* **mutualidad b**

mutualidad *nf* (**a**) *(reciprocidad)* mutuality (**b**) *(asociación) Br* friendly society, *US* mutual benefit society

mutualista 1 *adj* of *o* relating to a *Br* friendly society *o US* mutual benefit society
  2 *nmf* member of a *Br* friendly society *o US* mutual benefit society

mutuo, -a *adj* mutual, reciprocal

muy *adv* very; **m. bueno/malo** very good/bad; **¡m. bien!** very good!; **m. de agradecer** very much to be appreciated; **m. de los catalanes** typically Catalan; **eso es m. de Domingo** that's just like Domingo; *Pey* that's Domingo all over; **m. de mañana/noche** very early/late; **por m. caro/rápido que sea** expensive/fast though it may be; **por m. mal que salgan las cosas** even if the worst comes to the worst; **ser m. hombre/mujer** to be a real man/woman; *Fam* **el m. tonto se lo dijo todo** the silly idiot told her everything; *Fam* **m. mucho** very much

muyahidín *nm inv* mujaheddin

Myanmar *n* Myanmar

N

N, n ['ene] *nf (la letra)* N, n

N (**a**) *(abrev de* **newton**) N (**b**) *(abrev de* **Norte**) N

n. *(abrev de* **nacido, -a**) b.

n/ *(abrev de* **nuestro, -a**) our

nabo *nm* (**a**) *Bot (planta)* turnip (**b**) *Bot .(raíz)* root vegetable (**c**) *Vulg (pene)* tool, *Br* knob

nácar *nm* mother-of-pearl, nacre

nacarado, -a *adj*, **nacarino, -a** *adj* mother-of-pearl, nacreous, pearly

nacatamal *nm CAm* tamale stuffed with pork

nacer [42] *vi* (**a**) *(gen)* to be born; **al n.** at birth; **nació en una familia acomodada** she was born into well-to-do family; **nació para músico** he was born to be a musician; *Fig* **al n. el día** at daybreak *o* dawn; *Fig* **volver a n.** to be born again; *Fam Fig* **n. de pie** to be born under a lucky star; *Fam Fig* **no nací ayer** I wasn't born yesterday (**b**) *(pájaro)* to hatch (out) (**c**) *Bot (brotar)* to sprout, come up (**d**) *(pelo, plumas)* to begin to grow (**e**) *(surgir)* to spring (up) (**f**) *(tener su origen)* to originate, start; **el Ebro nace en Fontibre** the river Ebro rises in Fontibre (**g**) *(derivarse)* to arise; **su actitud nace de su inseguridad** his attitude stems from his lack of confidence

nacido, -a 1 *pp de* **nacer**

2 *adj* born; **n. de padre español** born of a Spanish father; **recién n.** newborn; *Fig* **bien n.** *(de familia ilustre)* of noble birth; *(noble, bondadoso)* of noble mind; *Fig* **mal n.** despicable, mean

3 *nm,f (pl)* **los nacidos en ...** those born in ...

naciente 1 *adj (nuevo)* new, recent; *(creciente)* growing; *(sol)* rising; **su n. amistad** their newly formed friendship

2 *nm (este)* East

nacimiento *nm* (**a**) *(gen)* birth; **de n.** from birth; **sordo de n.** deaf from birth; **de noble n.** of noble birth; *Fam* **ser tonto de n.** to be a complete idiot □ **lugar de n.** birthplace, place of birth (**b**) *Fig (principio)* origin, beginning; *(de río)* source; **el n. de una nueva era** the beginning of a new era (**c**) *(belén)* Nativity scene, crib, crèche

nación *nf* (**a**) *(gen)* nation; **las Naciones Unidas** the United Nations (**b**) *(país, estado)* country, state (**c**) *(pueblo)* people

nacional 1 *adj* (**a**) *(de la nación)* national; **himno n.** national anthem (**b**) *(productos, mercados)* domestic; **vuelos nacionales** domestic flights

2 *nmf* national; *Hist* **los Nacionales** the Francoist forces

nacionalidad *nf* nationality

nacionalismo *nm* nationalism

nacionalista 1 *adj* nationalist, nationalistic

2 *nmf* nationalist

nacionalización *nf* (**a**) *(naturalización)* naturalization (**b**) *(industria)* nationalization

nacionalizar [14] **1** *vt* (**a**) *(naturalizar)* to naturalize (**b**) *Econ (banca, industria)* to nationalize

2 nacionalizarse *vpr* to become naturalized; **n. español** to take up Spanish citizenship

nacionalsocialismo *nm Hist* National Socialism

nacionalsocialista *adj & nf* National Socialist

naco *nm* (**a**) *Méx Fam Pey* **los nacos** *(la gente de pueblo)* the proles, *Br* the plebs (**b**) *Am (de tabaco)* chew, plug

nada 1 *pron* nothing, anything; **antes de n.** first of all; **casi n.** almost nothing; **como si n.** just like that; **de n.** insignificant; **dentro de n.** in a moment; **enfadarse por n.** to get upset for no reason at all; **gracias — de n.** thanks — don't mention it; **n. de eso** nothing of the kind; **¡n. de eso!** not a bit of it!; **n. de excusas** no excuses; **n. de n.** nothing at all; **n. más** only; **n. más verla** as soon as he saw her; **(n. más y) n. menos que** no less than; **nadie sabía n.** nobody knew anything at all; **no es n.** it is nothing; **no hay n. que hacer** nothing can be done; **por n. del mundo** (not) for anything in the world; **¡y n. de ir en moto!** and no riding motorcycles!

2 *adv* not at all; **no me gusta n.** I don't like it at all

3 *nf* nothingness; **salir de la n.** to come out of nowhere

nadador, -a *nm,f* swimmer

nadar *vi* (**a**) *Dep* to swim; *Esp* **n. a braza**, *Am* **n. pecho** to do the breaststroke; *Méx* **n. de dorso**, *Esp* **n. a espalda**, *Andes CAm Carib RP* **n. espalda** to do the backstroke; *Esp* **n. a mariposa**, *Am* **n. mariposa** to do the butterfly; *Fig* **n. en dinero** to be rolling in money; *Fam* **n. y guardar la ropa** to have one's cake and eat it, have the best of both worlds (**b**) *(flotar)* to float

nadería *nf* little something, trifle

nadie 1 *pron* nobody, not ... anybody; **allí no había n.** there was nobody there; **n. de su familia** none of his relatives; **a n. no one came; no se lo digas a n.** don't tell anyone; *Fig* **tú no eres n. para hablarme así** you have no right to talk to me like that

2 *nm* nobody; **ser un (don) n.** to be a nobody

nadir *nm Astron* nadir

nado: a nado *loc adv* swimming; **cruzar** *o* **pasar a n.** to swim across

nafta *nf* (**a**) *Quím* naphtha (**b**) *RP (gasolina) Br* petrol, *US* gasoline

naftalina *nf* naphthalene □ **bola de n.** mothball

naif *(pl* **naïfs**) *adj Arte* naïf

nailon *nm* nylon; **medias de n.** nylons *pl*

naipe *nm* playing card

Nairobi *n* Nairobi

nal. *(abrev de* **nacional**) nat.

nalga *nf Anat* buttock; **nalgas** bottom *sing*, buttocks

Namibia *n* Namibia

nana *nf* (**a**) lullaby; *Fam* **del año de la n.** very old-fashioned; *Fam* **el año de la n.** the year dot (**b**) *Col Méx (niñera)* nanny (**c**) *Col Méx (nodriza)* wet nurse

nanay *interj Fam* no way!

nanosegundo *nm* nanosecond

nanotecnología *nf* nanotechnology

nao *nf Literario* vessel

napa *nf* nappa

napalm *nm Quím* napalm

napia *nf,* **napias** *nfpl Fam Br* conk, *US* schnozzle

napoleónico, -a *adj Hist* Napoleonic

Nápoles *n* Naples

napolitano, -a *adj & nm,f* Neapolitan

naranja 1 *nf Bot* orange; *Fig* **mi media n.** my better half ▫ **n. agria** Seville orange; **n. sanguina** blood orange
2 *adj & nm (color)* orange
3 naranjas *interj Fam* **¡n. (de la China)!** no way!

naranjada *nf* orangeade

naranjal *nm* orange grove

naranjo *nm* orange tree

narcisismo *nm* narcissism, narcism

narcisista 1 *adj* narcissistic
2 *nmf* narcissist

narciso *nm* (**a**) *Bot* narcissus, daffodil (**b**) *Fig (hombre)* narcissist

narco *Fam* **1** *nmf (persona)* drug trafficker
2 *nm (tráfico)* drug trafficking

narcosis *nf Med* narcosis

narcótico, -a 1 *adj* narcotic
2 *nm Med* narcotic; *(droga)* drug

narcotizar [14] *vt Med* to narcotize; *(drogar)* to drug

narcotraficante *nmf* drug trafficker

narcotráfico *nm* drug trafficking

nardo *nm Bot* spikenard, nard

narigón, -ona *nm,f,* **narigudo, -a** *nm,f* person with a big nose

nariz *nf* (**a**) *Anat* nose; *(sentido)* sense of smell; *Fam* **narices** nose *sing* ▫ **n. chata** snub nose; **n. griega** straight nose; **n. respingona** turned-up nose (**b**) *(expresiones) Fig* **darle a algn con la puerta en las narices** to slam a door in sb's face; *Fig* **darse de narices con algn** to bump into sb; *Fig* **darse de narices contra el suelo** to fall flat on one's face; *Fam* **me da en la n. que me quiere engañar** I've got this feeling he wants to cheat me; *Fam* **de narices** *(estupendo)* terrific; *Fam* **en mis (propias) narices** right under my very nose; *Fam* **estar hasta las narices de** to be totally fed up with; *Fam* **hacer lo que le sale a uno de las narices** to do whatever one wants; *Esp Fam* **hinchársele las narices a algn** to get one's back up; *Fam* **meter las narices en algo** to poke one's nose into sth; *Esp Fam* **por narices** because I say so; *Fam* **¿qué narices ...?** what the hell ...?; *Esp Fam* **tener narices** to have a lot of nerve; *Esp Fam* **¡tiene narices la cosa!** this is too much!; *Fam* **tocarle a algn las narices** to get on sb's wick; *Fam* **tocarse las narices** not to do a thing

narizotas *nmf inv Fam* big-nose

narración *nf* narration, narrative, account

narrador, -a *nm,f* narrator

narrar *vt* to narrate, tell

narrativo, -a *adj & nf* narrative

Nª Sªª *(abrev de* **Nuestra Señora**) Our Lady

nasa *nf (pesca)* keepnet

nasal *adj & nf* nasal

nasalización *nf* nasalization

nasalizar [14] *vt* to nasalize

Nassau *n* Nassau

nata *nf* (**a**) *Esp (gen)* cream; **n. batida** whipped cream (**b**) *(de leche hervida)* skin (**c**) *Fig* cream, best

natación *nf Dep* swimming

natal *adj* natal; **mi país n.** my native country; **su pueblo n.** his home town

natalicio, -a 1 *adj* birthday
2 *nm* birthday

natalidad *nf* birth rate

natillas *nfpl Esp Culin* custard *sing*

natividad *nf* Nativity

nativo, -a *adj & nm,f* native

nato, -a *adj* born

natura *nf Literario* nature; **contra n.** against nature

natural 1 *adj* (**a**) *(gen)* natural; *(fruta, flor)* fresh; **de tamaño n.** life-size, life-sized; **en estado n.** in its natural state; **fuerzas naturales** forces of nature; *Jur* **hijo n.** illegitimate child; **luz n.** daylight, sunlight (**b**) *(sin elaboración)* plain; **al n.** *(en la realidad)* in real life; *Culin* in its own juice (**c**) *(espontáneo)* natural, unaffected (**d**) *(comprensible)* natural, usual (**e**) **ser n. de** to come from (**f**) *Mús* natural, *US* cancel
2 *nmf* native, inhabitant; **los naturales de** the natives of, those born in
3 *nm* (**a**) *(temperamento)* nature, disposition; **de n. sencillo** of an unaffected nature (**b**) *Taur* = type of pass with the muleta

naturaleza *nf* (**a**) *(gen)* nature; **dejar obrar a la n.** to let nature take its course; **en plena n.** in the wild, in unspoilt countryside ▫ *Arte* **n. muerta** still life (**b**) *(forma de ser)* nature, character; **es de n. agresiva** he is aggressive by nature; **por n.** by nature (**c**) *(complexión)* physical constitution; **de n. robusta** strongly built

naturalidad *nf* (**a**) *(sencillez)* naturalness; **con la mayor n. del mundo** as if it were the most natural thing in the world; **con n.** naturally, straightforwardly (**b**) *(espontaneidad)* ease, spontaneity

naturalismo *nm* naturalism

naturalista 1 *adj* naturalistic
2 *nmf* naturalist

naturalización *nf* naturalization

naturalizar [14] **1** *vt* to naturalize
2 naturalizarse *vpr* to become naturalized, take up citizenship

naturalmente *adv* naturally; **¡n.!** of course!

naturismo *nm* naturism

naturista 1 *adj* naturistic
2 *nmf* naturist

naufragar [38] *vi* (**a**) *(barco)* to sink, be wrecked; *(persona)* to be shipwrecked (**b**) *Fig (plan)* to fail, fall through; *(persona)* to fail

naufragio *nm* (**a**) *Náut* shipwreck (**b**) *Fig (fracaso)* failure, disaster

náufrago, -a 1 *adj* wrecked, shipwrecked
2 *nm,f* shipwrecked person, castaway

náusea *nf (gen pl)* nausea, sickness; **me da n.** it makes me sick; **sentir náuseas** to feel sick

nauseabundo, -a *adj* nauseating, sickening

náutica *nf* navigation, seamanship

náutico, -a *adj* nautical; **deportes náuticos** water sports

navaja *nf* (**a**) *(cuchillo)* penknife, pocketknife ❑ **n. de afeitar** razor; **n. de monte** hunting knife; **n. de muelle** flick-knife, *US* switchblade (**b**) *Zool (molusco)* razor-shell

navajazo *nm* stab, gash

navajero, -a *nm,f Fam* thug

navajo *adj & nmf (indio)* Navajo

naval *adj* naval

Navarra *n* Navarre

navarro, -a 1 *adj* Navarrese, of *o* from Navarre
2 *nm,f* person from Navarre

nave *nf* (**a**) *Náut* ship, vessel; *Fig* **quemar las naves** to burn one's boats *o* one's bridges (**b**) *Astronáut* **n. espacial** spaceship, spacecraft (**c**) *Arquit (de iglesia)* nave ❑ **n. lateral** aisle (**d**) *Ind* plant, building ❑ **n. industrial** industrial premises *pl*

navegabilidad *nf* (**a**) *(de un río)* navigability (**b**) *(de un barco)* seaworthiness (**c**) *(de un avión)* airworthiness

navegable *adj* navigable

navegación *nf* (**a**) *(arte)* navigation ❑ *Av* **n. aérea** air navigation; **n. fluvial** river navigation (**b**) *(barcos)* shipping

navegador *nm Inform* browser

navegante 1 *adj* sailing; **un pueblo n.** a seafaring people
2 *nmf* navigator

navegar [38] *vi* (**a**) *Náut* to navigate, sail; *Fig* **n. contra corriente** to go against the tide (**b**) *Av* to navigate, fly (**c**) *Inform* **n. por Internet** to surf the Net

Navidad *nf* Christmas; **es N.** it's Christmas (time); **felicitar las Navidades** to wish (sb) happy *o* merry Christmas ❑ **árbol de N.** Christmas tree

navideño, -a *adj* Christmas

naviero, -a 1 *adj* shipping
2 *nm,f (propietario)* shipowner

navío *nm Náut* vessel, ship

nazareno, -a 1 *adj & nm,f* Nazarene
2 *nm Rel* (**a**) **el N.** Jesus of Nazareth (**b**) *(penitente)* = hooded penitent in Holy Week processions

nazco *indic pres véase* nacer

nazi *adj & nmf Pol* Nazi

nazismo *nm Pol* Nazism

NB *(abrev de* **nota bene**) N.B., n.b.

neandertal *nm,* **neanderthal** *nm* neanderthal

neblina *nf Meteor* mist, thin fog

neblinoso, -a *adj Meteor* misty

nebulosa *nf Astron* nebula

nebulosidad *nf Meteor* cloudiness

nebuloso, -a *adj* (**a**) *Meteor* cloudy (**b**) *Fig* nebulous, vague

necedad *nf* (**a**) *(estupidez)* stupidity, foolishness (**b**) *(tontería)* stupid thing to say *o* to do; **son necedades** it's nonsense

necesario, -a *adj* necessary; **es n. hacerlo** it has to be done; **es n. que vayas** you must go; **hacerse n.** *(algo)* to be required; *(persona)* to become vital *o* essential; **no es n. que vayas** there is no need for you to go; **si fuera n.** if need be; **todo lo n.** all that is necessary

neceser *nm (de aseo)* toilet bag *o* case; *(de maquillaje)* make-up bag *o* kit

necesidad *nf* (**a**) *(gen)* necessity, need; **de n.** essential; **artículos de primera n.** essentials; **una herida mortal de n.** a fatal wound; **no hay n. de** there is no need to *o* for; **por n.** of *o* by necessity; **si hubiera n.** if the need arises; **tener n. de** to need (**b**) *(hambre intensa)* starvation, hunger; **morir de n.** to starve to death (**c**) *(pobreza)* poverty, want,

hardship; **quedamos en la mayor n.** we were left in dire need (**d**) *(gen pl) (excrementos)* **hacer sus necesidades** to relieve oneself

necesitado, -a 1 *pp de* necesitar
2 *adj (pobre)* needy, poor; **n. de** in need of
3 *nm,f* needy person; **los necesitados** the needy *pl*

necesitar *vt (gen)* to need; *(en anuncios)* **'se necesita chico'** 'boy wanted'; *Fam* **n. Dios y ayuda** to need all the help one can get; *Fam* **no n. abuela** to blow one's own trumpet

necio, -a 1 *adj* (**a**) *(tonto)* stupid, foolish (**b**) *Méx (susceptible)* touchy
2 *nm,f* fool, idiot

nécora *nf Zool* fiddler crab

necrofilia *nf* necrophilia

necrófilo, -a *adj* necrophiliac

necrología *nf* obituary

necrológico, -a *adj* necrological; **nota necrológica** obituary

necrópolis *nf inv* necropolis

néctar *nm* nectar

nectarina *nf* nectarine

neerlandés, -esa 1 *adj* Dutch, of *o* from the Netherlands
2 *nm,f (persona) (gen)* Netherlander; *(hombre)* Dutchman; *(mujer)* Dutchwoman; **los neerlandeses** the Dutch
3 *nm (idioma)* Dutch

nefando, -a *adj Fml* abominable, odious

nefasto, -a *adj* (**a**) *(que causa desgracia)* unlucky, ill-fated (**b**) *(perjudicial)* harmful, fatal

nefritis *nf inv Med* nephritis

negación *nf* (**a**) *(gen)* negation; **la n. de la realidad** the negation of reality (**b**) *(negativa)* negative, denial, refusal (**c**) *Ling* negative

negado, -a 1 *pp de* negar
2 *adj* dull; **ser n. para algo** to be hopeless *o* useless at sth
3 *nm,f* no-hoper

negar [43] **1** *vt* (**a**) *(gen)* to deny; **n. con la cabeza** to shake one's head; **Engracia niega haberlo robado** Engracia denies having stolen it (**b**) *(no conceder)* to refuse, deny; **le negaron la beca** he didn't get the grant; **nos negaron la entrada** we were turned away
2 **negarse** *vpr* (**a**) *(oponerse)* to refuse (**a** to); **se negó a aceptar la oferta** he turned the offer down; **se niega a entenderlo** he refuses to understand it (**b**) *Culin* to curdle

negativa *nf* negative, denial; **una n. rotunda** a flat refusal

negativo, -a 1 *adj* (**a**) *(respuesta, oración, resultado)* negative (**b**) *Mat* minus
2 *nm Fot* negative

negligé [nevli'je] *nm* negligée

negligencia *nf* negligence, carelessness

negligente 1 *adj* negligent, neglectful, careless
2 *nmf* negligent *o* careless person

negociable *adj* negotiable

negociación *nf* negotiation; **entablar negociaciones con** to open negotiations with ❑ **n. colectiva** collective bargaining

negociado *nm* (**a**) *(sección)* department, section (**b**) *Andes RP (negocio ilícito)* shady deal

negociador, -a 1 *adj* negotiating; **comité n.** negotiating committee
2 *nm,f* negotiator

negociante *nmf* dealer; *(hombre)* businessman; *(mujer)* businesswoman

negociar 1 *vt Fin Pol* to negotiate
  2 *vi (comerciar)* to do business, deal; **negocia en** *o* **con ganado** he trades *o* deals in cattle

negocio *nm* **(a)** *Com Fin (gen)* business; *(transacción)* deal, transaction; *(asunto)* affair; **buen n.** *Com* profitable deal; *Irón* bargain; **el n. del espectáculo** show business; **hablar de negocios** to talk business; **hacer n.** to make a profit; **mal n.** bad deal; *Fig* **n. sucio** shady deal; *Irón* **¡vaya n.!** that was a fine deal! □ **hombre de negocios** businessman; **mujer de negocios** businesswoman **(b)** *RP (tienda)* store

negra *nf* **(a)** *Mús* crotchet, *US* quarter note **(b)** *Fig (mala suerte)* bad luck; **tener la n.** to be very unlucky

negrear *vi* to turn dark *o* black

negrero, -a 1 *adj* of the black slave trade
  2 *nm,f* **(a)** *Hist* slave trader **(b)** *Fig* slave driver

negrita *adj & nf Impr* bold (face)

negro, -a 1 *adj* **(a)** *(gen)* black; **cerveza negra** stout; **n. como la boca del lobo** pitch-black; *Hist* **peste negra** Black Death; *Fig* **lista negra** blacklist **(b)** *(bronceado)* suntanned; **se pone n. enseguida** he tans really quickly **(c)** *Fig (humor)* sad, gloomy; *(suerte)* awful; *(desesperado)* desperate; *(enfadado)* cross; **el lado n. de las cosas** the dark side of things; **estar n. con algo** to be desperate about sth; **la cosa se pone negra** things look bad; **pasarlas negras** to have a rotten time; **poner n. a algn** to drive sb mad; **ponerse n.** to go mad; **verlo todo n.** to be very pessimistic; **vérselas negras para hacer algo** to have a tough time doing sth
  2 *nm,f* **(a)** *(de raza) (hombre)* black man; *(mujer)* black woman; *Fam* **trabajar como un n.** to work like a dog **(b)** *(escritor)* ghostwriter
  3 *nm (color)* black

negroide *adj & nmf* Negroid

negrura *nf* blackness

negruzco, -a *adj* blackish

nemotecnia *nf* mnemonics *sing*

nemotécnico, -a *adj* mnemonic

nene, -a *nm,f* **(a)** *(niño)* baby boy; *(niña)* baby girl **(b)** *(apelativo cariñoso)* darling, baby

nenúfar *nm Bot* water lily

neocelandés, -esa 1 *adj* of *o* from New Zealand
  2 *nm,f* New Zealander

neoclasicismo *nm Arte Lit* neoclassicism

neoclásico, -a *Arte Lit* **1** *adj* neoclassic, neoclassical
  2 *nm,f* neoclassicist

neófito, -a *nm,f* neophyte; *(aprendiz)* beginner

neoliberal *adj & nmf* neoliberal

neoliberalismo *nm* neoliberalism

neolítico, -a *adj & nm* Neolithic

neologismo *nm* neologism

neón *nm* neon

neonazi *adj & nmf* neo-Nazi

neorrealismo *nm Cin* neorealism

neoyorquino, -a 1 *adj* New York, of *o* from New York
  2 *nm,f* New Yorker

neozelandés, -esa *adj & nm,f véase* **neocelandés, -esa**

Nepal *n* Nepal

nepalés, -esa 1 *adj* Nepalese, of *o* from Nepal
  2 *nm,f* Nepalese; **los nepaleses** the Nepalese *pl*

nepotismo *nm* nepotism

Neptuno *n Astron Mit* Neptune

nervio *nm* **(a)** *Anat Bot* nerve; *(de la carne)* tendon, sinew **(b)** *Fig (fuerza, vigor)* nerve, courage; **tener n.** to have character **(c)** *Arquit* rib **(d)** *Impr* band **(e) nervios** nerves; **ataque de n.** a fit of hysterics; **me crispa los n.** it (really)

gets on my nerves; **ponerle a algn los n. de punta** to set sb's nerves on edge; **ser un manojo de n.** to be a bundle of nerves; **tener los n. de acero** to have nerves of steel; **tiene los n. destrozados** he's a nervous wreck

nerviosismo *nm* nervousness, nerves *pl*

nervioso, -a *adj* nervous; **poner n. a algn** to get on sb's nerves; **ponerse n.** to get all excited; **¡qué niño más n.!** what a fidgety child!

nervudo, -a *adj* **(a)** *Anat* sinewy, wiry **(b)** *(fuerte)* strong, vigorous

netiqueta *nf Inform* netiquette

neto, -a *adj* **(a)** *(peso, cantidad)* net **(b)** *(claro)* neat, clear

neumático, -a 1 *nm Br* tyre, *US* tire
  2 *nm* tyre, *US* tire □ **n. de repuesto** *o* **de recambio** spare tyre

neumonía *nf Med* pneumonia

neura *nf Fam* depression; **estar con la n.** to be down in the dumps

neuralgia *nf Med* neuralgia

neurálgico, -a *adj Med* neuralgic

neurastenia *nf Med* neurasthenia

neurasténico, -a *Med* **1** *adj* neurasthenic
  2 *nm,f* neurasthenic person

neurocirugía *nf* neurosurgery

neurocirujano, -a *nm,f* neurosurgeon, brain surgeon

neurología *nf Med* neurology

neurológico, -a *adj* neurological

neurólogo, -a *nm,f Med* neurologist

neurona *nf Anat* neuron

neuronal *adj* neural

neurosis *nf Med* neurosis

neurótico, -a *adj & nm,f Med* neurotic

neurotransmisor *nm* neurotransmitter

neutral *adj* neutral

neutralidad *nf* neutrality

neutralización *nf* neutralization

neutralizar [14] *vt* to neutralize

neutro, -a *adj* **(a)** *Ling* neuter **(b)** *(imparcial)* neutral, impartial **(c)** *(color)* neutral

neutrón *nm Fís* neutron □ **bomba de neutrones** neutron bomb

nevada *nf* snowfall

nevado, -a 1 *pp de* **nevar**
  2 *adj* **(a)** *(gen)* covered with snow; *(montaña)* snow-capped **(b)** *Literario (blanco)* snow-white, snowy

nevar [3] *v impers* to snow

nevera *nf Br* fridge, *US* icebox

nevisca *nf* light snowfall

neviscar [59] *v impers* to snow gently

newton ['njuton] *(pl* **newtons***) nm Fís* newton

nexo *nm* connection, link □ **n. de unión** nexus

ni *conj* **(a)** *(contrastando)* neither, nor; **ni ha venido ni ha llamado** he hasn't come or phoned; **no tengo tiempo ni dinero** I have got neither time nor money; **no vengas ni hoy ni mañana** don't come today or tomorrow **(b)** *(ni siquiera)* not even; **¡ni hablar!** no way!; **ni por dinero** not even for money; **ni se te ocurra** don't even think about it **(c)** *(ni que + subj)* one would think that ...; **¡ni que fuera millonario!** you'd think he was a millionaire!

Niágara *nm* **las cataratas del N.** Niagara Falls

Niamey *n* Niamey

nica *adj CAm Hum* Nicaraguan

Nicaragua *n* Nicaragua

nicaragüense *adj & nmf,* **nicaragüeño, -a** *adj & nm,f* Nicaraguan

nicho *nm* niche

Nicosia *n* Nicosia

nicotina *nf Quím* nicotine

nidada *nf (de huevos)* clutch; *(de crías)* brood

nidal *nm* nest

nidificar [59] *vi* to (build a) nest

nido *nm* (a) *(de animal)* nest; *Fig* **n. de amor** love nest; *Fig* **n. de ladrones** den of thieves □ **cama n.** pull-out bed; **mesa(s) n.** den of tables; *Cost* **n. de abeja** smocking (b) *(escondrijo)* hiding place (c) *(vivero)* hotbed; **un n. de discordia** a hotbed of discord

niebla *nf Meteor* fog; **hay mucha n.** it is very foggy; *Fig* **envuelto en n.** confused, cloudy

nieto, -a *nm,f (niño)* grandson; *(niña)* granddaughter; **mis nietos** my grandchildren

nieve *nf* (a) *Meteor* snow; *Culin* **a punto de n.** (beaten) stiff □ **copo de n.** snowflake (b) *Argot (cocaína)* snow (c) *Carib Méx (helado)* sorbet

NIF [nif] *nm Esp abrev de* **número de identificación fiscal** = identification number for tax purposes

Níger *n* Niger

Nigeria *n* Nigeria

nigeriano, -a *adj & nm,f* Nigerian

nigerino, -a *adj & nm,f* Nigerien

nigromancia *nf* necromancy

nigromante *nmf* necromancer

nihilismo *nm Filos* nihilism

nihilista *Filos* **1** *adj* nihilistic
  2 *nmf* nihilist

Nilo *nm* **el N.** the Nile

nilón *nm Tex* nylon

nimbo *nm* nimbus

nimiedad *nf* (a) *(cualidad)* smallness, triviality (b) *(cosa nimia)* trifle

nimio, -a *adj* (a) *(sin importancia)* insignificant, petty (b) *(minucioso)* overmeticulous, nit-picking

ninfa *nf* (a) *Mit Zool* nymph (b) *Fig (mujer)* nymph, beautiful woman

ninfómana *nf Med* nymphomaniac

ninfomanía *nf Med* nymphomania

ningún *adj (delante de nom sing)* no, not any; **de ningún modo** in no way; *véase tamb* **ninguno, -a**

ninguno, -a **1** *adj* no, not any; **en ninguna parte** nowhere; **ninguna cosa** nothing; **no tiene ninguna gracia** it is not funny at all
  2 *pron* (a) *(persona)* nobody, no one; **n. de ellos** none of them; **n. lo vio** no one saw it (b) *(objeto)* not any, none; **no me gusta** I don't like any of them

niña *nf* (a) *Anat* pupil; *Fig* **es la n. de sus ojos** she's the apple of his eye (b) *véase* **niño, -a**

niñada *nf* (a) *(chiquillada)* childishness, childish behaviour o *US* behavior (b) *(cosa nimia)* trifle

niñato, -a *nm,f Fam Pey* (a) *(inexperto)* amateur, novice (b) *(pijo)* spoiled brat

niñera *nf* nursemaid, nanny

niñería *nf véase* **niñada**

niñez *nf* childhood, infancy

niño, -a *nm,f* (a) *(gen)* child; *(muchacho)* (small) boy; *(muchacha)* (little) girl; **de n.** as a child; **desde n.** from childhood; **es muy niña** she's very young for her age; **n.**

prodigio child prodigy; *Pey* **n. bien** o **de papá** rich boy, rich kid; *Pey* **n. bonito** o **mimado** mummy's o daddy's boy (b) *(bebé)* baby; **esperar un n.** to be expecting a baby (c) *Am salvo RP (tratamiento) (amo)* master; *(ama)* miss (d) **niños** children; *Fig* **juego de n.** child's play

nipón, -ona *adj & nm,f* Japanese; **los nipones** the Japanese

níquel *nm* (a) *Quím* nickel (b) *Carib (moneda)* coin; **níqueles** money

niquelado, -a 1 *pp de* **niquelar**
  2 *adj* nickel-plated
  3 *nm* nickelling, *US* nickeling

niquelar *vt* to nickel

niqui *nm Esp* T-shirt

nirvana *nm Rel* nirvana

níspero *nm Bot (fruto)* medlar; *(árbol)* medlar tree

nitidez *nf* (a) *(trasparencia)* limpidness, transparency (b) *(claridad)* accuracy, precision

nítido, -a *adj* (a) *(transparente)* limpid, transparent (b) *(claridad)* accurate, precise

nitrato *nm Quím* nitrate □ **n. de Chile** Chilean nitrate, Chile saltpetre, nitre

nítrico, -a *adj Quím* nitric

nitrogenado, -a *adj* nitrogenous

nitrógeno *nm* nitrogen

nitroglicerina *nf* nitroglycerine

nivel *nm* (a) *(altura)* level, height; **a n.** levelled; **a n. del mar** at sea level; **al n. de** on a level with (b) *(categoría)* standard, degree; **alto n. de especialización** high degree of specialization; **estar al mismo n. que** to be on a level with □ **n. de vida** standard of living (c) *(instrumento)* level □ **n. de aire** spirit level (d) *Ferroc* **paso a n.** level crossing, *US* grade crossing

nivelación *nf* levelling, *US* leveling

nivelador, -a 1 *adj* levelling, *US* leveling
  2 *nm,f* leveller, *US* leveler

nivelar *vt* to level out o off

níveo, -a *adj Literario* snowy, snow-white

n/L. *(abrev de* **nuestra letra (de crédito))** our L/C

n° *(abrev de* **número)** n

no *(pl* **noes) 1** *adv* (a) *(en frases negativas, respuestas)* no, not; **¡a que no ...!** I bet you don't ...; **aún no** not yet; **¡cómo no!** of course!; **no fumar** no smoking; **no lo hice** I didn't do it; **no sea que** in case; **no sin antes ...** not without first ...; **no sólo ... sino también ...** not only ... but also ...; **te guste o no te guste** whether you like it or not; **¿por qué no?** why not?; **ya no** no longer, not any more (b) *(en frases interrogativas)* **es rubia, ¿no?** she's blonde, isn't she?; **has ido ya, ¿no?** you've been there already, haven't you?; **¿no vienes?** aren't you coming? (c) *(como prefijo negativo)* non-; **la no violencia** nonviolence; **no fumador** nonsmoker; **pacto de no agresión** non-aggression pact (d) *(en frases comparativas)* **es mejor que venga que no que se quede en casa** he'd better off coming along rather than staying at home
  2 *nm* no; **un no rotundo** a definite no

Nobel *nm (premio)* Nobel prize; *(galardonado)* Nobel prize winner

nobiliario, -a *adj* nobiliary, noble

noble 1 *adj* noble; **gas n.** noble gas
  2 *nmf (hombre)* nobleman; *(mujer)* noblewoman; **los nobles** the nobility *sing*

nobleza *nf* (a) *(cualidad)* nobility, honesty, uprightness (b) *(conjunto de nobles)* nobility

noche *nf* night, late evening, night-time; **ayer por la n.**

last night; **buenas noches** *(saludo)* good evening; *(despedida)* good night; **de n.**, *Esp* **por la n.**, *Am* **en la n.** at night; **esta n.** tonight; **hacer n. en** to spend the night at o in; **hacerse de n.** to grow dark; **mañana/el sábado** *Esp* **por la n.** o *Am* **en la n.** tomorrow/Saturday night; **pasar buena/mala n.** to sleep well/badly; *Esp Fam* **pasar una n. toledana** to have a sleepless night, not sleep a wink; **son las nueve de la noche** it's nine p.m.; *Fig* **de la n. a la mañana** overnight ❑ **n. de bodas** wedding night

nochebuena *nf* Christmas Eve

nochecita *nf Am* dusk

nochevieja *nf* New Year's Eve

noción *nf* **(a)** *(gen)* notion, idea **(b)** **nociones** smattering *sing*, basic knowledge *sing*; **n. de español** a smattering of Spanish

nocividad *nf* noxiousness, harmfulness

nocivo, -a *adj* noxious, harmful

noctambulismo *nm* sleepwalking

noctámbulo, -a *nm,f* sleepwalker; *Fam* night-bird

nocturno, -a 1 *adj* **(a)** *(de la noche)* night, evening; **clases nocturnas** evening classes; **vida nocturna** night life; **vuelo n.** night flight **(b)** *Bot Zool* nocturnal
  2 *nm Mús* nocturne

nodriza *nf* **(a)** *(ama)* wet nurse **(b)** *Av Náut* **buque n.** supply ship

nogal *nm Bot* walnut (tree) ❑ **n. negro** black walnut

nogalina *nf* walnut dye

nogueral *nm Bot* walnut grove

nómada 1 *adj* nomadic
  2 *nmf* nomad

nomadismo *nm* nomadism

nomás *adv* **(a)** *Am* just; **así n.** just like that; **hasta allí n.** that far and no further; **¡pase n.!** come right in! **(b)** *Méx* **n. que** as soon as

nombradía *nf* reputation, fame

nombrado, -a 1 *pp de* **nombrar**
  2 *adj* **(a)** *(mencionado)* mentioned; **n. más arriba** aforementioned **(b)** *(designado)* appointed **(c)** *(célebre)* famous, well-known

nombramiento *nm* appointment

nombrar *vt* **(a)** *(mencionar)* to name, mention **(b)** *(designar)* to name, appoint; **n. a algn director** to appoint sb director

nombre *nm* **(a)** *(apelativo)* name; **a n. de** addressed to; **en n. de** on behalf of; **era el presidente sólo de n.** he was the president in name only; **le conozco de n.** I know him by name; **llamar a algn por el n.** to call sb by name; **no tener n.** to be unspeakable; **responder al n. de** to be called; *Fig* **llamar a las cosas por su n.** to call a spade a spade ❑ *Cin Teat* **n. artístico** stage name; *Com* **n. comercial** trade name; **n. de pila** Christian name; *Inform* **n. de usuario** username; **n. y apellidos** full name **(b)** *Ling* noun ❑ **n. común** common noun; **n. propio** proper noun **(c)** *(reputación)* **escritor de n.** famous writer;

nomenclador *nm*, **nomenclátor** *nm*, **nomenclatura** *nf* nomenclature

nomeolvides *nm inv Bot* forget-me-not

nómina *nf* **(a)** *(plantilla)* payroll; **estar en n.** to be on the staff **(b)** *(sueldo)* salary, pay cheque

nominación *nf* nomination

nominal *adj* nominal

nominar *vt* to nominate

nominativo, -a 1 *adj* **(a)** *Com* nominal **(b)** *Ling* nominative
  2 *nm Ling* nominative

non 1 *adj (número)* odd
  2 *nm* **(a)** *Mat* odd number; **pares y nones** odds and evens **(b)** **nones** *Fam (negación)* no; **decir n.** to refuse

nonagenario, -a *adj & nm,f* nonagenarian

nonagésimo, -a 1 *adj* ninetieth; **nonagésima parte** ninetieth; **n. primero** ninety-first; **n. segundo** ninety-second
  2 *nm,f (de una serie)* ninetieth
  3 *nm (parte)* ninetieth; *véase tamb* **octavo, -a**

noneco, -a *adj CAm* thick, dull

nono, -a *adj véase* **noveno, -a**

non plus ultra *nm* **ser el n.** to be the best ever

noquear *vt Box* to knock out

norcoreano, -a *adj & nm,f* North Korean

nordeste *nm véase* **noreste**

nórdico, -a 1 *adj* **(a)** *(del norte)* northern **(b)** *(escandinavo)* Nordic
  2 *nm,f* Nordic person

noreste *nm* **(a)** *Geog* northeast **(b)** *(viento)* north-easterly

noria *nf* **(a)** *(para agua)* water-wheel, noria **(b)** *Esp (de feria)* Br big wheel, US Ferris wheel

norirlandés, -esa 1 *adj* Northern Irish
  2 *nm,f (persona) (hombre)* Northern Irishman; *(mujer)* Northern Irishwoman; **los norirlandeses** the Northern Irish

norma *nf* norm, rule

normal 1 *adj* normal, usual, average; **lo n.** the normal thing, what usually happens
  2 *nf* **(escuela) n.** teacher training college

normalidad *nf* normality; **todo ha vuelto a la n.** everything is back to normal

normalista *nmf Bol Méx* **(a)** *(estudiante)* student teacher **(b)** *(profesor)* teaching graduate

normalización *nf* normalization

normalizar [14] **1** *vt* to normalize, restore to normal
  2 normalizarse *vpr* to return to normal

normando, -a 1 *adj* **(a)** *(de Normandía)* Norman **(b)** *(vikingo)* Norse
  2 *nm,f* **(a)** *(de Normadía)* Norman **(b)** *(vikingo) (hombre)* Norseman; *(mujer)* Norsewoman

normar *vi Am* to set standards o rules

normativa *nf* regulations *pl*

normativo, -a *adj* normative

noroeste *nm* **(a)** *Geog* northwest **(b)** *(viento)* north-westerly

norte *nm* **(a)** *Geog* north; **al n. de** to the north of; **los países del n.** the northern countries **(b)** *Fig* aim, goal; **sin n.** aimless, aimlessly **(c)** *(viento)* northerly wind **(d)** *PRico (llovizna)* drizzle

norteafricano, -a *adj & nm,f* North African

Norteamérica *n* North America

norteamericano, -a *adj & nm,f* (North) American

norteño, -a 1 *adj* northern
  2 *nm,f* Northerner

Noruega *n* Norway

noruego, -a 1 *adj* Norwegian
  2 *nm,f* Norwegian
  3 *nm (idioma)* Norwegian

norvietnamita *adj & nf* North Vietnamese

nos 1 *pron pers (complemento)* us; **n. ha visto** he has seen us; **n. trajo un regalo** he brought us a present
  2 *pron reflexivo* ourselves; **n. queremos mucho** we love each other very much; **n. vamos** we're leaving

nosotros, -as *pron pers pl* **(a)** *(sujeto)* we; **n. lo vimos** we saw it; **somos n.** it is us (**b**) *(complemento)* us; **con n.** with us; **después de n.** after us; **para n.** for us

nostalgia *nf* nostalgia, yearning; *(morriña)* homesickness

nostálgico, -a *adj* nostalgic; *(con morriña)* homesick

nota *nf* (**a**) *(anotación)* note; **tomar n. de algo** *(apuntar)* to note o jot sth down; *Fig (fijarse)* to take note of sth (**b**) *Educ (calificación)* Br mark, US grade; **tener buenas notas** to get good marks (**c**) *(cuenta)* Br bill, US check (**d**) *Fig (detalle)* element, quality; **la n. dominante** the prevailing quality; **la n. elegante** the touch of elegance (**e**) *Mús* note; *Fam* **dar la n.** to make oneself noticed

notabilidad *nf* (**a**) *(cualidad)* notability (**b**) *(persona)* notable

notable 1 *adj (apreciable)* noticeable; *(digno de notar)* oustanding, remarkable
2 *nm* (**a**) *Educ (calificación)* credit (mark) (**b**) **notables** *(personas)* VIPs

notación *nf* notation

notar 1 *vt* (**a**) *(percibir)* to notice, note; **hacer n. algo** to point sth out; **hacerse n.** to draw attention to oneself; **no lo había notado** I hadn't noticed (**b**) *(sentir)* to feel; **noto como que me falta el aire** I feel as if I can't breathe
2 notarse *vpr* (**a**) *(percibirse)* to be noticeable o evident, show; **no se nota** it doesn't show; **se nota que ...** one can see that ... (**b**) *(sentirse)* to feel; **me noto cansado** I feel tired

notaría *nf Esp CAm Carib Méx* (**a**) *(profesión)* = profession of notary (public) (**b**) *(despacho)* notary's office

notariado *nm* (**a**) *(profesión)* = profession of notary (public) (**b**) *(cuerpo de notarios)* notaries *pl*

notarial *adj* notarial

notario, -a *nm,f Esp CAm Carib Méx* notary (public), public solicitor

noticia *nf* news *sing*; **dar la n.** to break the news; **n. bomba** bombshell; **últimas noticias** latest news; **una n.** a piece of news; **una buena n.** good news

noticiario *nm, Am* **noticiero** *nm Rad TV* news bulletin, news *pl*; *Prensa* newspaper

notición *nm Fam* bombshell

notificación *nf* notification; **sin n. previa** without (previous) notice ❑ *Jur* **n. judicial** summons *sing*

notificar [59] *vt* to notify, inform

notoriedad *nf* fame, notoriety, reputation

notorio, -a *adj* (**a**) *(conocido)* noticeable, evident (**b**) *(famoso)* famous, well-known

novatada *nf* (**a**) *(broma)* practical joke *(on newcomer)* (**b**) *(dificultad)* beginner's error; **pagar la n.** to learn the hard way

novato, -a 1 *adj (persona)* inexperienced, green
2 *nm,f* (**a**) *(principiante)* novice, beginner (**b**) *Univ* fresher

novecientos, -as *adj inv* & *nm,f inv (cardinal)* nine hundred; *(ordinal)* nine hundredth

novedad *nf* (**a**) *(cualidad)* newness (**b**) *(cosa nueva)* novelty; **tienda de novedades** fashion shop; **últimas novedades** latest arrivals (**c**) *(cambio)* change, innovation (**d**) *(noticia)* news *pl*; **sin n.** no change, no news; *Mil* nothing to report

novedoso, -a *adj (nuevo)* new, full of novelties

novel 1 *adj* new, inexperienced
2 *nmf* beginner, novice

novela *nf Lit* novel; *(corta)* story ❑ **n. corta** short story; **n. policíaca** detective story

novelar 1 *vt* to novelize, convert into a novel, make a novel out of
2 *vi* to write novels

novelería *nf* gossip

novelero, -a *adj* (**a**) *(aficionado) (a las novedades)* fond of new things; *(a novelas)* fond of novels (**b**) *(fantasioso)* highly imaginative (**c**) *(chismoso)* gossipy

novelesco, -a *adj* (**a**) *(de novela)* novelistic, fictional (**b**) *(extraordinario)* bizarre, fantastic

novelista *nmf* novelist

novelística *nf* novel, fiction

novelístico, -a *adj* novelistic

novelón *nm Fam Pey* = long and badly written novel, pulp novel

novena *nf Rel* novena

noveno, -a 1 *adj* ninth; **novena parte** ninth
2 *nm,f (de una serie)* ninth
3 *nm (parte)* ninth; *véase tamb* **octavo, -a**

noventa *inv* **1** *adj (cardinal)* ninety; *(ordinal)* ninetieth
2 *nm* ninety; *véase tamb* **ochenta** & **ocho**

noventavo, -a *adj* & *nm,f* & *nm véase* **nonagésimo, -a**

novia *nf* (**a**) *(amiga)* girlfriend (**b**) *(prometida)* fiancée (**c**) *(en boda)* bride

noviazgo *nm* engagement; **romper un n.** to break off an engagement

noviciado *nm Rel* noviciate, novitiate

novicio, -a *nm,f Rel* novice

noviembre *nm* November; **a mediados de n.** in the middle of November, in mid-November; **a principios/finales de n.** at the beginning/end of November; **durante el mes de n.** during o in November; **el primero/dieciséis de n.** (on) the first/sixteenth of November; **en n.** in November; **en n. del año pasado/del año que viene** last/next November; **nació el 10 de n. 1955** he was born on 10th November 1955; **todos los años en n.** each o every November

noviero, -a *adj* **desde chiquito fue muy n.** he was never shy of the girls, even as a child

novillada *nf Taur* (**a**) *(corrida)* bullfight with young bulls (**b**) *(conjunto de novillos)* herd of young bulls

novillero, -a *nm,f* (**a**) *Taur* apprentice matador (**b**) *Fam Educ* truant

novillo, -a *nm,f* (**a**) *Zool (toro)* young bull; *(vaca)* young cow (**b**) *Esp Fam Educ* **hacer novillos** to play *Br* truant o *US* hooky

novilunio *nm* new moon

novio *nm* (**a**) *(amigo)* boyfriend (**b**) *(prometido)* fiancé (**c**) *(en boda)* bridegroom; **los novios** the bride and groom

N.S. *(abrev de* **Nuestro Señor**) Our Lord

Ntra Sra *(abrev de* **Nuestra Señora**) Our Lady

ntro. *(abrev de* **nuestro**)

nubarrón *nm Fam* storm cloud

nube *nf* (**a**) *(gen)* cloud; **n. de verano** *Meteor* sudden storm; *Fig (enfado pasajero)* huff; *Fig* **estar** o **vivir en las nubes** to have one's head in the clouds; *Fig* **los precios están por las nubes** prices are sky-high; *Fig* **poner a algn por las nubes** to praise sb to the skies (**b**) *Fig (multitud)* swarm, crowd

nublado, -a 1 *pp de* **nublar**
2 *adj* (**a**) *Meteor* cloudy, overcast (**b**) *Fig* **n. por la pasión** blinded by passion
3 *nm Meteor* thick cloud

nublar 1 *vt Meteor* to cloud
2 nublarse *vpr Meteor* to become cloudy, cloud over; *Fig* **se le nubló la razón** he lost his mind; **se le nubló la vista** his eyes clouded over

nubosidad *nf Meteor* cloudiness

nuboso, -a *adj Meteor* cloudy

nuca *nf Anat* nape, back of the neck

nuclear *adj* nuclear; **central n.** nuclear power station

nuclearizar [14] *vt* **(a)** *Ind* to introduce nuclear power into **(b)** *Mil* to acquire nuclear weapons for

nucleico *adj (ácido)* nucleic

núcleo *nm* **(a)** *Astron Biol Fís Ling* nucleus **(b)** *(parte central)* core ❑ **n. duro** *(de personas)* hard core **(c)** *(lugar)* **un n. de pobreza** an area with an extremely high level of poverty, an area where poverty is concentrated ❑ **n. de población** population centre

nudillo *nm Anat* knuckle

nudismo *nm* nudism

nudista *adj & nmf* nudist

nudo *nm* **(a)** *(lazo)* knot; **hacer un n.** to tie a knot; *Fig* **se me hizo un n. en la garganta** I got a lump in my throat ❑ **n. corredizo** slipknot; **n. gordiano** Gordian knot; **n. marinero** sailor's knot **(b)** *Náut (milla)* knot **(c)** *Bot* knot, node **(d)** *Fig (vínculo)* link, tie **(e)** *(punto principal)* crux, core; **el n. de la cuestión** the heart of the matter **(f)** *(de comunicaciones)* centre, *US* center ❑ *Ferroc* **n. de comunicaciones** junction

nudoso, -a *adj (madera)* knotty, full of knots; *(bastón)* knobbly; **mano nudosa** gnarled hand

nuera *nf* daughter-in-law

nuestro, -a 1 *adj pos* of ours, our; **lo n.** what is ours; **nuestra familia** our family; **un amigo n.** a friend of ours

  2 *pron pos* ours; *Fam* **los nuestros** our side, our people; **es de los nuestros** he is one of us; **este libro es n.** this book is ours

nueva *nf* piece of news; *Fam* **hacerse de nuevas** to pretend not to know, to pretend to be surprised; *Fam* **me cogió de nuevas** it took me by surprise

Nueva Delhi *n* New Delhi

nuevamente *adv* again

Nueva York *n* New York

Nueva Zelanda *n* New Zealand

nueve 1 *adj inv (cardinal)* nine; *(ordinal)* ninth; **a las n.** at nine o'clock

  2 *nm inv* nine; *véase tamb* **ocho**

nuevo, -a 1 *adj (gen)* new; *(adicional)* further; **de n.** again; **es más n. que yo** he hasn't worked here as long as I have; **está (como) n.** it's as good as new; **hay que hacer nuevas indagaciones** we need to carry out further investigation; **n. en el oficio** new to the trade; *Fam* **¿qué hay de n.?** what's new?

  2 *nm,f* newcomer; *(principiante)* beginner; *Univ (novato)* fresher

nuez *nf* **(a)** *Bot* walnut; *Fam* **mucho ruido y pocas nueces** a lot of fuss about nothing ❑ **n. moscada** nutmeg **(b)** *Anat* **n. (de Adán)** Adam's apple

nulidad *nf* **(a)** *(ineptitud)* incompetence; *(persona)* nonentity; **ser una n.** to be hopeless o useless **(b)** *Jur* nullity

nulo, -a *adj* **(a)** *(inepto)* useless, totally incapable; **ser n. para algo** to be hopeless o useless at sth **(b)** *(sin valor)* null and void, invalid; **declarar n.** to nullify; **voto n.** invalid vote

núm. *(abrev de* **número)** n

Numancia *n Hist* Numantia

numantino, -a 1 *adj Hist* Numantian, of Numantia; *Fig (resistencia)* heroic

  2 *nm,f* Numantian

numeración *nf* numeration ❑ **n. arábiga** Arabic numerals *pl*; **n. romana** Roman numerals *pl*

numerador *nm* **(a)** *Mat* numerator **(b)** *(aparato)* numerating machine

numeral *adj & nm* numeral

numerar 1 *vt* to number

  2 numerarse *vpr Mil* to number off

numerario, -a 1 *adj* **profesor n.** teacher on the permanent staff; **profesor no n.** teacher on a temporary contract

  2 *nm* **(a)** *(miembro)* full member **(b)** *(dinero)* cash

numérico, -a *adj* numerical

número *nm* **(a)** *(gen)* number; **en números redondos** in round figures; *Fig* **sin n.** countless ❑ **n. arábigo** Arabic numeral; **n. cardinal** cardinal number; **n. de fax** fax number; *Aut* **n. de matrícula** *Br* registration number, *US* license number; **n. de serie** serial number; **n. de teléfono** (tele)phone number; **n. entero** whole number; **n. impar** odd number; **n. ordinal** ordinal number; **n. par** even number; **n. primo** prime number; **n. quebrado** fraction; **n. romano** Roman numeral **(b)** *Ling* number **(c)** *Prensa* number, issue ❑ **n. atrasado** back number; **n. extraordinario** special edition **(d)** *(de zapatos)* size **(e)** *(en espectáculo)* sketch, act; *Fam* **es todo un n.** he's a real laugh; *Fam Esp* **montar un n.** to make a scene; *Fam* **¡vaya n.!** what a scene!

numeroso, -a *adj* numerous, large

numerus clausus *nm inv Educ* = restriction on number of students in university course

numismática *nf* numismatics *sing*

numismático, -a 1 *adj* numismatic

  2 *nm,f* numismatist

nunca *adv* **(a)** *(en afirmativa)* never; *(en negativa)* ever; **casi n.** hardly ever; **más que n.** more than ever; **n. en la vida** never in my life; **n. jamás** never ever; **n. más** never again; **ser lo n. visto** to be unheard of **(b)** *(en interrogativa)* ever; **¿has visto n. cosa igual?** have you ever seen anything like it?

nunciatura *nf* nunciature

nuncio *nm* nuncio ❑ **n. apostólico** papal nuncio

nupcial *adj* wedding, nuptial; **marcha n.** wedding march

nupcialidad *nf* marriage rate

nupcias *nfpl Fml* wedding *sing*, nuptials; **casarse en segundas n.** to marry again

nurse ['nurse] *nf* nurse, nanny

nutria *nf Zool* otter

nutrición *nf* nutrition

nutricionista *nmf* nutritionist

nutrido, -a 1 *pp de* nutrir

  2 *adj* **(a)** *(alimentado)* nourished; **bien n.** well-nourished; **mal n.** undernourished **(b)** *(numeroso)* large, numerous

nutrir 1 *vt* **(a)** *(alimentar)* to nourish, feed **(b)** *Fig* to encourage, feed **(c)** *(suministrar)* to provide, supply

  2 nutrirse *vpr (alimentarse)* to feed, draw on

nutritivo, -a *adj* nutritious, nourishing; **valor n.** nutritional value

Ñ

Ñ, ñ ['eɲe] *nf (la letra)* fifteenth letter of the Spanish alphabet

ña *nf Am Fam véase* **doña**

ñame *nm CAm Carib Col Bot* yam

ñandú *(pl* **ñandúes)** *nm Orn* rhea

ñandutí *nm Am* nanduti (lace)

ñanga *nf CAm* marsh

ñango, -a *adj* (**a**) *Am (bajo)* short-legged; *(patojo)* lame (**b**) *Méx (flaco)* skinny; *(débil)* weak

ñaño, -a 1 *adj* (**a**) *Col Pan (consentido)* spoiled, pampered (**b**) *Andes (muy amigo)* close, intimate
2 *nm* (**a**) *Chile (hermano)* older brother (**b**) *Perú (niño)* child

ñapa *nf Ven* bonus, little extra

ñatas *nfpl* nose *sing*

ñato, -a *adj Andes RP* snub-nosed

ñeque 1 *adj CAm Andes (vigoroso)* vigorous; *(fuerte)* strong
2 *nm* (**a**) *CAm, Andes (fuerza)* energy (**b**) *CAm Méx (golpe)* blow; *(bofetada)* cuff, punch

ñiquiñaque *nm Fam* (**a**) *(objeto)* junk, rubbish (**b**) *(persona)* good-for-nothing

ñisca *nf* (**a**) *CAm (excremento)* excrement (**b**) *Andes (pizca)* bit, small piece

ño *nm Am Fam véase* **señor, -a**

ñoñería *nf,* **ñoñez** *nf* (**a**) *(sosería)* insipidness, bore (**b**) *(melindrería)* fussiness

ñoño, -a 1 *adj* (**a**) *(soso)* insipid, dull (**b**) *(melindroso)* fussy
2 *nm,f* dull o spineless person

ñoqui *nm* (**a**) *Culin* gnocchi (**b**) *Arg Fam (persona)* = someone who receives a salary but does not turn up for work

ñu *nm Zool* gnu

O

O, o [o] (*pl* **Oes**, **oes**) *nf (la letra)* O, o; *Fig* **no sabe hacer la o con un canuto** he doesn't know a thing, he hasn't got a clue

o *conj* or; **jueves o viernes** Thursday or Friday; **o ... o** either... or; **o sea que** that is, that is to say, so; **o sea que no voy** in other words, I am not coming

O. (*abrev de* **Oeste**) W

oasis *nm inv* oasis

obcecación *nf* blindness; *Fig* obstinacy

obcecado, -a 1 *pp de* **obcecar**
2 *adj* blinded; *Fig* stubborn

obcecar [59] **1** *vt* to make blind; *Fig* **la ira lo obceca** he is blinded by anger
2 obcecarse *vpr* to be blinded; *Fig* to get mixed up

obedecer [46] **1** *vt* (**a**) *(acatar)* to obey; **no obedece a razones** he won't listen to reason; **obedece a tu padre** do as your father says (**b**) *(responder)* to respond to; **el volante no le obedeció** the steering wheel wouldn't turn
2 *vi (provenir)* to be due to; **¿a qué obedece esa actitud?** what's the reason behind this attitude?

obediencia *nf* obedience

obediente *adj* obedient

obelisco *nm* (**a**) *(monumento)* obelisk (**b**) *Tip* obelisk, dagger

obertura *nf Mús* overture

obesidad *nf* obesity

obeso, -a *adj* obese

óbice *nm* obstacle; **eso no es ó. para que yo no ...** that won't prevent me from ...

obispado *nm* (**a**) *(dignidad, diócesis)* bishopric (**b**) *(residencia)* bishop's palace

obispo *nm (prelado)* bishop

óbito *nm Fml* demise, decease

obituario *nm Prensa* obituary

objeción *nf* objection; **o. de conciencia** conscientious objection; **poner una o.** to raise an objection, object

objetar 1 *vt* to argue, object to, point out; **no tengo nada que o.** I have no objections
2 *vi Esp* to register as a conscientious objector

objetivar *vt* to look objectively at, deal with objectively

objetividad *nf* objectivity

objetivo, -a 1 *adj* objective
2 *nm* (**a**) *(fin, meta)* objective, aim, goal (**b**) *Mil* target (**c**) *Cin Fot* lens; **o. zoom** zoom lens

objeto *nm* (**a**) *(gen)* object; **mujer o.** sex object; **objetos perdidos** lost property *sing* (**b**) *(fin)* aim, purpose, object;

con o. de ... in order to ...; **tiene por o. ...** it is designed to ... (**c**) *(tema)* theme, subject, matter (**d**) *Ling* object

objetor, -a 1 *adj* objecting, dissenting
2 *nm,f Mil* objector; **o. de conciencia** conscientious objector

oblea *nf* (**a**) *Rel* wafer (**b**) *Farm* capsule

oblicuo, -a *adj Geom* oblique

obligación *nf* (**a**) *(deber)* obligation; **antes la o. que la devoción** business before pleasure; **cumplir con sus obligaciones** to fulfil one's obligations; **por o.** out of a sense of duty; **tengo o. de ...** I have to ... (**b**) *Fin* bond, debenture □ **obligaciones garantizadas** guaranteed *o* mortgage debentures *o* bonds (**c**) **obligaciones** *(familia)* family *sing*

obligacionista *nmf Fin* bondholder

obligado, -a 1 *pp de* **obligar**
2 *adj* obliged; **verse** *o* **estar o. a** to be obliged to

obligar [38] **1** *vt (forzar)* to compel, force
2 obligarse *vpr* to be under an obligation to, be obliged to

obligatoriedad *nf* obligatory nature

obligatorio, -a *adj* compulsory, obligatory

oblongo, -a *adj* oblong

obnubilado, -a 1 *pp de* **obnubilar**
2 *adj* stunned, dazed

obnubilar *vt* to dazzle

oboe *nm Mús (instrumento)* oboe; *(intérprete)* oboist

oboísta *nmf Mús* oboist

óbolo *nm* (**a**) *Hist* obolus (**b**) *Fig* mite, small contribution

obpo. (*abrev de* **obispo**) bp

obra *nf* (**a**) *(trabajo)* piece of work, work; **por o. (y gracia) de** thanks to; **todo esto es o. suya** this is all his doing (**b**) *Arte* work; *Lit* book; *Mús* work, opus □ **o. de arte** work of art; **o. de teatro** play; **o. maestra** masterpiece; **obras completas** collected *o* complete works (**c**) *(acto)* deed; **obras son amores (y no buenas razones)** actions speak louder than words (**d**) *(institución)* institution, foundation; **o. benéfica** charity (**e**) *Constr* building site (**f**) **obras** *(arreglos)* repairs; **'carretera en o.'** 'roadworks'; **'cerrado por o.'** 'closed for repairs'; **tenemos la casa en o.** we've got the builders in

obrador *nm* workshop

obraje *nm* (**a**) *(manufactura)* manufacture (**b**) *Arg Bol Par* sawmill (**c**) *Méx (carnicería)* butcher's shop

obrar **1** *vi* (**a**) *(proceder)* to act, behave; **o. bien/mal** to do the right/wrong thing; **o. con buena intención** to act in good faith; **o. con ligereza** to act without thinking (**b**) *(estar)* to be; **o. en poder de** to be in the hands of
2 *vt (hacer)* to work

obrerismo *nm* labour *o US* labor movement, labourism, *US* laborism

obrero, -a 1 *adj* working; **clase obrera** working class
2 *nm,f* worker, labourer, *US* laborer ▫ **o.** *Esp* **cualificado** *o Am* **calificado** skilled worker; **o. especializado/no especializado** skilled/unskilled worker; **o. portuario** docker

obscenidad *nf* obscenity

obsceno, -a *adj* obscene

obscurantismo *nm* obscurantism

obscurantista *adj & nmf* obscurantist

obscurecer [46] **1** *vi impers* to get dark
2 *vt* (**a**) *(ensombrecer)* to darken (**b**) *Arte* to shade (**c**) *Fig (ofuscar)* to cloud; *(superar)* to overshadow; **el mal tiempo obscureció la ceremonia** the bad weather put a cloud over the ceremony
3 obscurecerse *vpr (nublarse)* to become cloudy

obscurecimiento *nm* darkening

obscuridad *nf* darkness, gloom; *Fig* obscurity

obscuro, -a *adj* (**a**) *(gen)* dark (**b**) *Fig (origen, idea)* obscure; *(future)* uncertain, gloomy; *(asunto)* shady; *(nublado)* overcast; **sus intenciones son obscuras** his intentions are not clear

obsequiar *vt* to give, offer, present; *Esp* **o. a algn con algo,** *Am* **o. a algn algo** to present sb with sth

obsequio *nm* gift, present

obsequioso, -a *adj* attentive, obliging

observable *adj* observable

observación *nf* (**a**) *(acción de observar)* observation; *Mil* **puesto de o.** observation post (**b**) *(comentario)* observation, remark, comment

observador, -a 1 *adj* observant
2 *nm,f* observer

observancia *nf* observance

observar 1 *vt* (**a**) *(mirar)* to observe, watch (**b**) *(notar)* to notice; **se ha observado un aumento/una mejora de ...** there has been a rise/an improvement in ... (**c**) *(cumplir)* to observe; **hacer o. algo a algn** to point sth out to sb; **o. las buenas costumbres** to be on one's best behaviour

observatorio *nm* observatory ▫ **o. meteorológico** weather station

obsesión *nf* obsession

obsesionar 1 *vt* to obsess; **estoy obsesionado con ello** I can't get it out of my mind
2 obsesionarse *vpr* to get obsessed; **se obsesiona por cualquier tontería** he gets worked up about the slightest thing

obsesivo, -a *adj* obsessive

obseso, -a 1 *adj* obsessed
2 *nm,f* obsessed person; **un o. sexual** a sex maniac

obsoleto, -a *adj* obsolete

obstaculizar [14] *vt* to obstruct, hinder, get in the way of, block

obstáculo *nm* obstacle, hindrance; **poner obstáculos a algo/algn** to hinder sth/sb, put obstacles in the way of sth/sb

obstante: no obstante *loc adv* nevertheless, all the same

obstar *vi* to hinder, prevent; **eso no obsta para que ...** that's no reason not to ..., that doesn't prevent ...

obstetricia *nf Med* obstetrics *sing*

obstinación *nf* obstinacy, stubbornness

obstinado, -a 1 *pp de* **obstinarse**
2 *adj* obstinate, stubborn

obstinarse *vpr* to persist (**en** in)

obstrucción *nf* obstruction; *Med* blockage

obstruccionismo *nm Pol* obstructionism

obstruccionista *nmf Pol* obstructionist

obstruir [34] **1** *vt* (**a**) *(obstaculizar)* to block, obstruct (**b**) *(progreso)* to impede; *(reforma)* to stand in the way of
2 obstruirse *vpr* to get blocked up

obtención *nf* obtaining, securing

obtener [65] **1** *vt* *(alcanzar)* to obtain, get; **o. un crédito** to raise a loan; **o. una victoria** to secure a victory
2 obtenerse *vpr* *(provenir)* to come (**de** from)

obturación *nf* blockage, obstruction

obturador *nm* (**a**) *(gen)* plug, stopper; *Fot* shutter (**b**) *(rueda)* valve

obturar *vt* to block (up), plug (up)

obtuso, -a *adj* obtuse

obús (*pl* **obuses**) *nm* (**a**) *Mil (cañón)* howitzer; *(proyectil)* shell (**b**) *Aut* tyre *o US* tire valve core

obviar 1 *vt* *(evitar)* to obviate, remove; **hay que o. las dificultades** the difficulties have to be overcome
2 *vi* *(oponerse)* to stand in the way (of)

obvio, -a *adj* obvious

oca *nf* (**a**) *Zool* goose (**b**) **la o.** *(juego)* ≃ snakes and ladders *sing*

ocasión *nf* (**a**) *(momento)* occasion; **con o. de ...** on the occasion of ...; **en cierta o.** once; **en contadas ocasiones** on very few occasions (**b**) *(oportunidad)* opportunity, chance; **aprovechar la o.** to make the most of an opportunity; **dar o. a algo** to give rise to sth; **dar o. a algn de ...** to give sb the chance o the opportunity to ...; **si se presenta la o.** if the opportunity arises; **si tienes o.** if you have the chance (**c**) *Com* bargain; **de o.** cheap; **precios de o.** bargain prices

ocasional *adj* (**a**) *(de vez en cuando)* occasional (**b**) *(fortuito)* accidental, chance

ocasionar *vt (causar)* to cause, bring about; *(ser la causa de)* to be the cause of; **o. un revuelo** to cause a stir

ocaso *nm (anochecer)* sunset; *(occidente)* west; *Fig (declive)* fall, decline

occidental 1 *adj* western, occidental
2 *nmf (persona)* westerner, person from the west

occidentalizar [14] *vt* to westernize

occidente *nm* west, Occident; **el O.** the West

occipital *Anat* **1** *adj* occipital
2 *nm* occipital (bone)

occiso, -a *adj Fml* deceased

OCDE *nf (abrev de* **Organización para la Cooperación y el Desarrollo Económico)** OECD

Oceanía *n* Oceania

oceánico, -a *adj* oceanic

océano *nm* ocean

oceanografía *nf* oceanography

oceanográfico, -a *adj* oceanographic

oceanógrafo, -a *nm,f* oceanographer

ocelo *nm Zool* ocellus

ocelote *nm Zool* ocelot

ochava *nf* (**a**) *(octava parte)* eighth (**b**) *(ocho días)* eight days (**c**) *Am (esquina)* corner

ochenta 1 *adj inv (cardinal)* eighty; *(ordinal)* eightieth; **andar por los o.** to be in one's eighties; **durante los años o.** in the eighties; **el o. por ciento del personal** eighty per cent of the staff; **hacía más de o. grados** the temperature was in the eighties; *Aut* **ir a o.** to do *o* be doing eighty (kilometres an hour); **mañana cumplirá o. años** he will be eighty (years old) tomorrow; **unos o. pasajeros/coches** about eighty passengers/cars

2 *nm inv* eighty

ocho 1 *adj inv (cardinal)* eight; *(ordinal)* eighth; **a los o. días** in a week, in a week's time; **cuesta o. dólares** it costs eight dollars; **dieron las o.** the clock struck eight; **el o. de febrero** the eighth of February; **en el siglo o.** in the eighth century; **las o. en punto** eight o'clock precisely o on the dot; **llegará el día o.** he will arrive on the eighth; **o. días** a week; **o. mil** eight thousand; **se marcharon los o.** all eight of them left; **somos o.** there are eight of us; **son las o.** it is eight o'clock; **tiene o. años** he is eight (years old); **un niño de o. años** a boy of eight, an eight-year-old boy; **venga a las o. en punto** come at eight o'clock sharp; **viven en la calle Goya, número o.** they live at number eight Goya Street

2 *nm inv* eight; **el o.** (number) eight; *Naipes* **el o. de corazones** the eight of hearts; **o. más o. son dieciséis** eight and eight are o make sixteen; **o. sobre diez** eight out of ten; *Fig* **ser más chulo que un o.** to be as proud as a peacock

ochocientos, -as 1 *adj inv (cardinal)* eight hundred; *(ordinal)* eight hundredth

2 *nm* eight hundred

ocio *nm* leisure, idleness; **en mis ratos de o.** in my spare o leisure time

ociosidad *nf* idleness

ocioso, -a 1 *adj* **(a)** *(inactivo)* idle; **vida ociosa** life of leisure **(b)** *(inútil)* pointless, useless

2 *nm,f* idler

ocluir [34] **1** *vt* to occlude, obstruct, close (up)

2 ocluirse *vpr* to become obstructed

oclusión *nf* occlusion

oclusivo, -a *adj & nf Ling* occlusive

ocre *nm* ochre, *US* ocher

octaédrico, -a *adj Geom* octahedral

octaedro *nm Geom* octahedron

octagonal *adj Geom* octagonal

octágono *nm Geom* octagon

octanaje *nm* octane number

octano *nm* octane

octava *nf Mús Lit* octave

octavilla *nf* **(a)** *(panfleto)* hand-out, leaflet **(b)** *Lit* octave

octavo, -a 1 *adj* eighth; **quedar en o. lugar** to come eighth; **una octava parte** an eighth; **vivir en el o. piso** to live on the eighth floor

2 *nm,f (de una serie)* eighth; **fue el o. en llegar** he was the eighth to arrive

3 *nm* **(a)** *(parte)* eighth; **tres octavos** three eighths **(b)** *Impr* octavo; **libro en o.** octavo book

octeto *nm Mús* octet, octette

octogenario, -a *adj & nm,f* octogenarian

octogésimo, -a 1 *adj* eightieth; **octogésima parte** eightieth

2 *nm,f (de una serie)* eightieth

3 *nm (parte)* eightieth; *véase tamb* **octavo, -a**

octogonal *adj Geom* octagonal

octógono *nm Geom* octagon

octosílabo, -a 1 *adj* octosyllabic

2 *nm* octosyllable

octubre *nm* October; *véase tamb* **noviembre**

ocular 1 *adj* ocular, eye; **testigo o.** eyewitness

2 *nm Ópt* eyepiece

oculista *nmf Med* ophthalmologist, oculist

ocultación *nf* concealment; *Astron* occultation

ocultar 1 *vt* to conceal, hide; **o. algo a algn** to hide sth from sb

2 ocultarse *vpr* to hide (oneself)

ocultismo *nm* occultism

ocultista *adj & nmf* occultist

oculto, -a *adj* concealed, hidden; **ciencias ocultas** occult sciences; **motivo o.** ulterior motive

ocupa *nmf Fam* squatter

ocupación *nf* **(a)** *(tarea)* occupation, activity **(b)** *Mil* occupation; **o. (ilegal) de viviendas** squatting

ocupacional *adj* occupational

ocupado, -a 1 *pp de* **ocupar**

2 *adj (persona)* busy; *(asiento)* taken; *(aseos)* engaged; *(teléfono)* Br engaged, *US* busy; *(puesto de trabajo)* filled; *Mil* occupied

ocupante *nmf (de una casa)* occupant, occupier; *(ilegal)* squatter; *(de un vehículo)* occupant

ocupar 1 *vt* **(a)** *(apoderarse)* to occupy, take **(b)** *(llenar)* to take up; **ocupa mucho sitio** it takes up a lot of space **(c)** *(estar en)* to be; **María ocupaba el asiento trasero** María was sitting in the back seat **(d)** *(desempeñar)* to hold, fill; **Luis ocupará la presidencia** Luis will be president; **o. un cargo** to hold (an) office o a post **(e)** *(dar que hacer)* to occupy; *(trabajadores)* to employ; **esta empresa ocupa un centenar de obreros** the firm employs a hundred workers; **esto me ocupa totalmente** this takes up all my time **(f)** *(habitar)* to live in, occupy

2 ocuparse *vpr* to occupy; **o. de** o **en** o **con** *(vigilar)* to look after; *(reflexionar)* to look into; **ella se ocupa de la parte técnica** she takes care of the technical side; **o. de un asunto** to deal with a matter; **tú, ocúpate de lo tuyo** you mind your own business

ocurrencia *nf (agudeza)* witty remark, wisecrack; *(idea)* idea; *Irón* bright idea; **¡qué ocurrencias tienes!** what an absurd idea!

ocurrente *adj* bright, witty

ocurrir 1 *vi* to happen, occur; **¿qué ocurre?** what's going on?; **¿qué te ocurre?** what's the matter with you?

2 ocurrirse *vpr* to think; **no se me ocurre nada** I can't think of anything; **¿nunca se te ha ocurrido pensar que ...?** has it never occurred to you that ...?; **que no se le ocurra venir** he'd better stay well away from here; **se me ocurre que ...** it occurs to me that ...; **¡se te ocurre cada cosa!** you do come out with some funny things!

oda *nf Lit* ode

odalisca *nf Hist & Fig* odalisque

odeón *nm Hist* odeum, odeon

odiar *vt* to detest, hate; **odio tener que ...** I hate having to ...

odio *nm* hatred, loathing; **mirada de o.** hateful look; **tener o. a algn** to hate sb

odioso, -a *adj* hateful, detestable

odisea *nf* Odyssey; *Fig* odyssey; *Fam* **fue toda una o.** it was a real hassle; *Fam* **¡menuda o.!** what a saga!

odómetro *nm* odometer

odontología *nf Med* dentistry, odontology

odontológico, -a *adj Med* dental, odontological

odontólogo, -a *nm,f Med* dental surgeon, odontologist

odorífero, -a *adj*, **odorífico, -a** *adj* odoriferous

odre *nm* wineskin

OEA *nf (abrev de* **Organización de Estados Americanos)** OAS

oeste *nm* west; *Náut* westward

ofender 1 *vt* to offend

2 ofenderse *vpr* to get offended **(con, por** by), take offence o *US* offense **(con, por** at)

ofendido, -a 1 *pp de* **ofender**
2 *adj* offended
3 *nm,f* offended party
ofensa *nf* offence, *US* offense
ofensiva *nf Mil* offensive; **tomar la o.** to take the offensive
ofensivo, -a *adj* offensive, rude
ofensor, -a 1 *adj* offending
2 *nm,f Jur* offender
oferta *nf* offer; *Fin Ind (proposición)* bid, tender, proposal; *(suministro)* supply; *Com* **de o.** on (special) offer; **o. pública de adquisición hostil** hostile takeover bid; **o. y demanda** supply and demand
ofertar *vt* **(a)** *(ofrecer)* to offer **(b)** *(vender)* to tender
ofertorio *nm Rel* offertory
off *adj* **(a)** *(desconectado)* off, disconnected **(b)** *(fuera de lugar)* off; *Teat* offstage; **voz en o.** *Teat* voice offstage; *Cin* voice-over **(c)** *Inform* **o. line** off line
office ['ofis] *nm* pantry
offset *(pl* **offsets)** *nm Impr* offset
offside [of'saiδ] *nm Ftb* offside
oficial¹ 1 *adj* official
2 *nmf* **(a)** *Mil Náut* officer **(b)** *(empleado)* clerk
**oficial, -a² ** *nm,f (obrero)* skilled worker
oficialidad *nf* **(a)** *(cualidad)* official character *o* nature **(b)** *Mil* officers *pl*, officialdom
oficialismo *nm Am* **(a)** *(gobernantes)* authorities *pl* **(b)** *(partidarios)* government supporters *pl*
oficialista *Am* **1** *adj* pro-government
2 *nm,f* government supporter
oficializar [14] *vt* to make official
oficiante *nm Rel* officiant
oficiar *vi* **(a)** *Rel* to officiate **(b)** *(hacer de)* to act **(de** as)
oficina *nf* office; **horas de o.** business hours ❑ **o. de correos** post office; **o. de empleo** unemployment office, *Br* Jobcentre, *US* job center; **o. de turismo** tourist office
oficinista *nmf* office worker, clerk
oficio *nm* **(a)** *(ocupación)* job, occupation; *(que requiere especialización)* trade; **aprender un o.** to learn a trade; **ser del o.** to be in the trade; **soy albañil de o.** I'm a bricklayer by trade; *Fam* **gajes del o.** occupational hazards; *Fam* **sin o. ni beneficio** without prospects **(b)** *(comunicación oficial)* official letter *o* note **(c)** *Rel* service; *Hist* **el Santo O.** the Inquisition; **o. de difuntos** office for the dead **(d)** *(función)* role, function **(e)** **oficios** *(acción)* offices
oficioso, -a *adj* **(a)** *(noticia, fuente)* unofficial **(b)** *(persona)* officious
ofidio *nm Zool* snake
ofimática *nf* office automation
ofrecer [46] **1** *vt* **(a)** *(dar) (premio, amistad)* to offer; *(banquete, fiesta)* to hold; *(regalo)* to give **(b)** *(presentar)* to present; **la ciudad ofrecía un aspecto festivo** the town looked in a holiday mood; **la situación ofrece pocas posibilidades** the situation is rather limited; **o. resistencia** to offer resistance
2 ofrecerse *vpr* **(a)** *(prestarse)* to offer, volunteer; **me ofrecí** I volunteered; **me ofrezco para lo que sea** if there's anything I can do **(b)** *(presentarse)* to present itself; **el valle entero se ofrecía ante nuestra vista** the whole valley lay before us **(c)** *(ocurrírsele a uno)* to want; **aquí estoy para lo que se le ofrezca** if there is ever anything you want, don't forget to let me know; **¿qué se le ofrece?** what can I do for you?; **¿se le ofrece algo más?** anything else?, will that be all?
ofrecimiento *nm* offer, offering

ofrenda *nf Rel* offering
ofrendar *vt Rel* to make offerings *o* an offering
ofrezco *indic pres véase* **ofrecer**
oftalmología *nf Med* ophthalmology
oftalmólogo, -a *nm,f Med* ophthalmologist
ofuscación *nf,* **ofuscamiento** *nm* blinding, dazzling
ofuscar [59] *vt* **(a)** *(deslumbrar)* to dazzle **(b)** *Fig (confundir)* to blind
ogro *nm* ogre
oh *interj* oh!
ohm *nm,* **ohmio** *nm Elec* ohm
oídas: de oídas *loc adv* by hearsay; **le conozco de o.** I've heard of him
oído *nm (sentido)* hearing; *Anat (órgano)* ear; **aplicar el o.** to listen carefully; **aprender de o.** to learn by ear; **dar oídos a algo** to listen to sth; **decir algo al o. de algn** to whisper sth in sb's ear; **duro de o.** hard of hearing; **llegar a oídos de algn** to come to sb's attention *o* notice; **ser todo oídos** to be all ears; **taparse los oídos** to close one's ears; **tener buen o.** to have a good ear; *Fig* **hacer oídos sordos** to turn a deaf ear; *Fig* **regalarle el o. a algn** to flatter sb
oír [44] *vt* to hear; **¡oiga Ud.!** now look here!; **¡oye!** hey!; *Tel* **se oye mal** I can't hear you (properly), it's a very bad line; *Fig* **como quien oye llover** it's like water off a duck's back; *Fig* **hacerse o.** to make oneself heard; *Fam* **como lo oyes** believe it or not; *Fam* **o., ver y callar** you haven't seen or heard anything, OK?
OIT *nf (abrev de* **Organización Internacional del Trabajo)** ILO
ojal *nm* buttonhole
ojalá *interj* let's hope so!, I hope so!; **¡o. no lo hubiera visto!** I wish I hadn't seen it; **¡o. sea cierto!** I hope it is true!, if only it were true!
ojeada *nf* glance, quick look; **echar una o.** *(echar una mirada)* to take a quick look **(a** at); *(vigilar)* to keep an eye **(a** on)
ojeador, -a *nm,f Caza* beater
ojear¹ *vt (mirar)* to have a quick look at
ojear² *vt Caza* to beat
ojeo *nm Caza* beating
ojeras *nfpl* rings *o* bags under the eyes
ojeriza *nf* dislike, grudge; **coger o. a algn** to take a dislike to sb
ojeroso, -a *adj* with rings under the eyes, haggard; **triste y o.** sad and weary
ojete *nm* **(a)** *(bordado)* eyelet **(b)** *muy Fam (ano)* arsehole, ring
ojiva *nf* **(a)** *Arquit* ogive **(b)** *Mil* warhead
ojival *adj Arquit* ogival
ojo 1 *nm* **(a)** *Anat* eye; **o. morado** *o Esp* **a la funerala** *o RP* **en compota** black eye; *Esp* **o. de cristal** glass eye; **ojos saltones** bulging eyes; *Fig* **a o. (de buen cubero)** at a rough guess; *Fig* **a ojos vista** clearly, openly; *Fig* **ándate con o.** be careful; *Fig* **calcular** *o* **medir a o.** to guess; *Fig* **en un abrir y cerrar de ojos** in the twinkling of an eye; *Fig* **le bailaban los ojos** his eyes widened with delight; *Fig* **mirar a algn con buenos ojos** to look favourably upon sb; *Fig* **o. por o., diente por diente** an eye for an eye and a tooth for a tooth; *Fig* **ojos que no ven (corazón que no siente)** out of sight, out of mind; *Fig* **pelar los ojos** to keep one's eyes peeled; *Fig* **saltar a los ojos** to be evident; *Fig* **tener buen o.** *o* **o. clínico para algo** to have a good eye for sth; *Fam* **¡dichosos los ojos!** I'm so glad to see you!; *Fam* **no pegué o.** I didn't sleep a wink; *Fam Fig* **costar un o. de la cara** to cost a fortune *o* an arm and a leg; *Fam Fig* **tener**

el **o. echado a algo** to have one's heart set on sth (**b**) *(agujero)* hole; *Cost (de aguja)* eye □ *Náut* **o. de buey** porthole; **o. de la cerradura** keyhole (**c**) *(de un puente)* span **2** *interj* careful!, look out!; **o. con hacer ruido** be careful, not to make a noise

ojota *nf* (**a**) *Andes (sandalia)* sandal (**b**) *RP (chancleta) Br* flip-flop, *US Austral* thong

OK *interj*, **okey** [o'kei] *interj* OK

ola *nf* wave

ole *interj*, **olé** *interj* bravo!

oleada *nf* wave; *Fig* **o. de turistas** influx of tourists

oleaginoso, -a *adj* oleaginous

oleaje *nm* swell

óleo *nm* (**a**) *Arte* oil; **pintura** *o* **cuadro al ó.** oil painting (**b**) *Rel* chrism, oil

oleoducto *nm* pipeline

oleoso, -a *adj* oily

oler [45] **1** *vt* (**a**) *(percibir olor)* to smell (**b**) *Fig (adivinar)* to smell, feel; **huelo algo raro** there is something fishy **2** *vi* (**a**) *(exhalar)* to smell; **huele que apesta** it stinks; **o. a** to smell of; **o. bien/mal** to smell good/bad (**b**) *Fig (parecer)* to smell, smack (**a** of); **huele a mentira** it sounds like a lie; *Fam* **me huele a cuerno quemado** there's something fishy going on here **3 olerse** *vpr Fig* to feel, sense; **me lo olía** I thought as much

olfatear *vt* (**a**) *(oler)* to sniff, smell (**b**) *Fig (indagar)* to nose, pry into; *(sospechar)* to suspect

olfateo *nm* sniffing, smelling; *Fig* snooping

olfativo, -a *adj* olfactory

olfato *nm* sense of smell, olfaction; *Fig* good nose, instinct; *Fig* **tener o. para los negocios** to have a flair for business

oligarca *nmf* oligarch

oligarquía *nf* oligarchy

oligárquico, -a *adj* oligarchic, oligarchical

oligoelemento *nm* trace element

oligofrenia *nf* mental handicap

oligofrénico, -a 1 *adj* mentally retarded **2** *nm,f* mentally retarded person

oligopolio *nm Econ* oligopoly

olimpiada *nf Hist* Olimpiad; *Dep* Olympiad, Olympic Games *pl*; **las olimpiadas** the Olympic Games

olímpico, -a *adj* (**a**) *Dep* Olympic; **Juegos Olímpicos** Olympic Games (**b**) *Fig (altivo)* haughty, lofty; **desprecio o.** utter disdain

olimpismo *nm* Olympic movement

Olimpo *n* el **O.** Mount Olympus

olisquear *vt* to sniff, smell; *Fig* to nose (into), pry into

oliva *nf Bot* olive; **aceite de o.** olive oil

oliváceo, -a *adj* olive-green

olivar *nm Agr* olive grove

olivarero, -a *Agr* **1** *adj* olive; *(del cultivo)* olive-growing **2** *nm,f* olive grower

olivicultura *nf Agr* olive growing

olivo *nm Bot* olive (tree)

olla *nf Culin* saucepan, pot □ **o. exprés** *o* **a presión** pressure cooker

olmeda *nf*, **olmedo** *nm* elm grove

olmo *nm Bot* smooth-leaved elm; *Fig* **pedir peras al o.** to ask the impossible

ológrafo, -a *adj & nm* holograph

olor *nm* smell; **buen/mal o.** nice/nasty smell; **o. corporal**

body odour; *Fig* **o. de santidad** odour of sanctity

oloroso, -a 1 *adj* fragrant, sweet-smelling **2** *nm* full-bodied sherry

OLP *nf (abrev de* **Organización para la Liberación de Palestina**) PLO

olvidadizo, -a *adj* forgetful; **hazte el o.** pretend you've forgotten

olvidado, -a 1 *pp de* olvidar **2** *adj* forgotten; **o. de Dios** godforsaken

olvidar 1 *vt* to forget; **olvidé el paraguas en casa** I've left my umbrella at home; *Fam* **¡olvídame!** leave me alone! **2 olvidarse** *vpr* to forget; **me he olvidado el bolso en tu casa** I've left my handbag at your house; *Fam* **puedes olvidarte de mí** you can leave me out of it; *Fam* **ya puedes olvidarte del coche** you can say goodbye to the car

olvido *nm* (**a**) *(desmemoria)* oblivion; **caer en el o.** to fall into oblivion; **enterrar en el o.** to cast into oblivion (**b**) *(descuido)* forgetfulness, absentmindedness; *(lapsus)* oversight, lapse; **en un momento de o.** in a moment of forgetfulness; **un o. imperdonable** an unforgivable oversight

Omán *n* Oman

ombligo *nm Anat* navel; *Fig* **contemplarse el o.** to contemplate one's navel; *Fam Fig* **encogérsele a uno el o.** to get the wind up

ombudsman *nm* ombudsman

OMC *nf (abrev de* **Organización Mundial del Comercio**) WTO

ominoso, -a *adj* abominable, dreadful

omisión *nf* omission

omiso, -a 1 *pp de* omitir **2** *adj* negligent; **hacer caso o. de** to take no notice of

omitir *vt (pp omiso)* (**a**) *(no decir)* to omit, leave out (**b**) *(dejar de hacer)* to neglect, overlook

ómnibus *nm inv* (**a**) *Esp (tren)* local train (**b**) *Cuba Urug (urbano)* bus; *Andes Cuba Urug (interurbano, internacional) Br* coach, *US* bus

omnímodo, -a *adj* all-embracing, total

omnipotencia *nf* omnipotence

omnipotente *adj* omnipotent, almighty

omnipresencia *nf* omnipresence

omnipresente *adj* omnipresent

omnisciencia *nf* omniscience

omnisciente *adj* omniscient, all-knowing

omnívoro, -a *Zool* **1** *adj* omnivorous **2** *nm,f* omnivore

omóplato *nm*, **omoplato** *nm Anat* shoulder blade

OMS [oms] *nf (abrev de* **Organización Mundial de la Salud**) WHO

onanismo *nm* onanism

ONCE ['onθe] *nf (abrev de* **Organización Nacional de Ciegos Españoles**) = Spanish association for the blind

once 1 *adj inv (cardinal)* eleven; *(ordinal)* eleventh; **a las o.** at eleven o'clock **2** *nm inv* eleven; *Ftb* eleven, team **3 onces** *nfpl Andes (refrigerio)* mid-morning snack, *Br* elevenses; *véase tamb* **ocho**

onceno, -a *adj & nm véase* **undécimo, -a**

oncología *nf Med* oncology

oncológico, -a *adj Med* oncological

oncólogo, -a *nm,f Med* oncologist

onda *nf* (**a**) *(en el agua)* ripple (**b**) *Fís* wave; *Fig* **estar en la misma o. que algn** to be on the same wavelength as sb; *Fam Fig* **estar en la o.** to be with it; *Méx Fam* **¿qué o.?** *(¿qué* *tal?)* how's it going?, how are things? ❑ *Rad* **o. corta** short wave; **o. expansiva** shock wave; **o. hertziana** Hertzian wave; *Rad* **o. larga/media** long/medium wave; **o. sonora** sound wave **(c)** *(en peluquería)* wave **(d)** *Cost* scallop

ondear *vi* **(a)** *(bandera)* to flutter; **o. a media asta** to be flying at half mast **(b)** *(agua)* to ripple

ondina *nf Mit* Nereid

ondulación *nf* undulation, wave; *(agua)* ripple

ondulado, -a 1 *pp de* **ondular**
  2 *adj (pelo)* wavy; *(metal, cartón)* corrugated; *(paisaje)* rolling, undulating

ondulante *adj* undulating

ondular 1 *vt (el pelo)* to wave
  2 *vi (moverse)* to undulate

ondulatorio, -a *adj* wavy; **movimiento o.** wave motion

oneroso, -a *adj* onerous

ONG *nf inv (abrev de* **Organización no Gubernamental)** NGO

ónice *nm Min* onyx

onírico, -a *adj* oneiric, dream, of dreams

ónix *nm Min* onyx

onomástica *nf Esp* saint's day

onomástico, -a *adj* onomastic, name

onomatopeya *nf* onomatopoeia

onomatopéyico, -a *adj* onomatopoeic

ontogénesis *nf,* **ontogenia** *nf Biol* ontogeny, ontogenesis

ontología *nf Filos* ontology

ontológico, -a *adj Filos* ontological

ONU ['onu] *nf (abrev de* **Organización de las Naciones Unidas)** UN(O)

onubense 1 *adj* of o from Huelva
  2 *nmf* person from Huelva

ONUDI [o'nuði] *nf (abrev de* **Organización de las Naciones Unidas para el Desarrollo Industrial)** UNIDO

onza¹ *nf (medida)* ounce

onza² *nm Zool* ounce, snow leopard

onzavo, -a *adj & nm véase* **undécimo, -a**

op. *(abrev de* **opus)** op

OPA ['opa] *nf (abrev de* **oferta pública de adquisición)** takeover bid; **O. hostil** hostile takeover bid

opa *Fam* **1** *adj Andes RP* dumb, *Br* gormless
  2 *interj RP* hello!

opacidad *nf* opaqueness, opacity

opaco, -a *adj* opaque

opalescencia *nf* opalescence

opalescente *adj* opalescent

opalino, -a *adj* opal, opaline, opal-like

ópalo *nm Min* opal

opar *vt (empresa) (intentar adquirir)* to launch a takeover bid for; *(adquirir)* to take over

opción *nf* **(a)** *(elección)* option, choice; *(alternativa)* alternative; **la o. más fácil** the soft option; **no tienes o.** you have no choice **(b)** *(derecho)* right; *(posibilidad)* opportunity, chance

opcional *adj* optional

open *nm Golf* open

OPEP [o'pep] *nf (abrev de* **Organización de los Países Exportadores de Petróleo)** OPEC

ópera *nf Mús* opera ❑ **ó. bufa** comic opera, opera buffa; **ó. prima** *(novela, película)* first work

operable *adj* operable

operación *nf* **(a)** *Med* operation ❑ **o. quirúrgica** surgical operation **(b)** *Fin* transaction, deal; **operaciones bursátiles** stock exchange transactions **(c)** *Mil* manoeuvre, *US* maneuver, operation **(d)** *Mat* operation

operacional *adj* operational

operador, -a 1 *nm Mat* operator; *Inform* operator
  2 *nm,f* **(a)** *(técnico)* operator **(b)** *Med* surgeon **(c)** *Cin (de la cámara) (hombre)* cameraman; *(mujer)* camerawoman; *(del proyector)* projectionist **(d)** *Tel* operator

operante *adj* operative

operar 1 *vt* **(a)** *Med* to operate (a on); **le han operado de las amígdalas** she's had her tonsils out **(b)** *(producir)* to bring about
  2 *vi (hacer efecto)* to operate, work; *Fin* to deal, do business (with); *Mat* **o. con quebrados** to work in fractions
  3 operarse *vpr* **(a)** *Med* to have an operation (**de** for) **(b)** *(producirse)* to occur, come about; **se ha operado una mejoría en el paciente** the patient has shown an improvement

operario, -a *nm,f* operator, worker

operativo, -a *adj* operative

operatorio, -a *adj* operational

opereta *nf Mús* operetta

operístico, -a *adj* operatic

opiáceo, -a *adj* opiate

opinable *adj* debatable, arguable

opinar *vi* to think, give one's opinion, be of the opinion; **tú, ¿qué opinas?** what do you think?; **yo no quiero o.** I'd rather not comment, I'd rather not give an opinion

opinión *nf* **(a)** *(juicio)* opinion, view, point of view; **cambiar de o.** to change one's mind; **soy de la o. de que ...** I'm of the opinion that ... **(b)** *(fama)* reputation

opio *nm (drogas)* opium; **fumadero de o.** opium den

opiómano, -a *nm,f* opium addict

opíparamente *adv* lavishly; **comieron o.** they dined sumptuously

opíparo, -a *adj* lavish

oponente 1 *adj* opposing
  2 *nmf* opponent, opposite number

oponer [50] *(pp* **opuesto) 1** *vt (a un plan, persona)* to oppose; *(resistencia)* to offer; **no tengo nada que o. a tu plan** I've no objections to your plan
  2 oponerse *vpr (estar en contra)* to be opposed, be against; *(ser contrario a)* to be in opposition (**a** to), contradict; **o. a algo** to oppose sth

Oporto *n* Porto

oporto *nm (vino)* port

oportunamente *adv* opportunely

oportunidad *nf* opportunity, chance

oportunismo *nm* opportunism

oportunista *adj & nmf* opportunist

oportuno, -a *adj* **(a)** *(a tiempo)* timely; **¡qué o. fuiste!** that was well-timed! **(b)** *(conveniente)* appropriate; **si te parece o.** if you think it appropriate

oposición *nf* **(a)** *(gen)* opposition **(b)** *(examen)* competitive examination; **está preparando oposiciones para entrar en un banco** he's studying for a bank entrance examination; **ganar** *o* **sacar la o.** to pass a competitive examination

opositar *vi* to sit a competitive examination

opositor, -a *nm,f* **(a)** *(candidato)* candidate for a competitive examination **(b)** *Pol* opponent

opresión *nf* oppression; **o. en el pecho** tightness of the chest

opresivo, -a *adj* oppressive

opresor, -a 1 *adj* oppressive, oppressing
2 *nm,f* oppressor

oprimido, -a 1 *adj* oppressed; *Fig* **con el corazón o.** downhearted
2 *nm,f* **los oprimidos** the oppressed *pl*

oprimir *vt* to squeeze, press; *Fig* to oppress; **oprima el botón** press the button; *Fig* **o. con el poder** to oppress with power

oprobio *nm* ignominy, opprobrium

optar *vi* (a) *(elegir)* to choose (**entre, por** between); **o. entre A y B** to choose between A and B; **o. por** to opt for; **opté por ir yo mismo** I decided to go myself (b) *(aspirar)* to apply (a for); **poder o. a un puesto** to be entitled to apply for a post

optativo, -a *adj* optional; *Ling* optative

óptica *nf* (a) *Fís* optics *sing* (b) *(tienda)* optician's (shop) (c) *(punto de vista)* point of view

óptico, -a 1 *adj* optic, optical; **aparatos ópticos** optical instruments; **nervio ó.** optic nerve
2 *nm,f* optician

optimismo *nm* optimism

optimista 1 *adj* optimistic
2 *nmf* optimist

optimización *nf* optimization

optimizar [14] *vt* to optimize

óptimo, -a *adj* very best, optimum, excellent

opuesto, -a 1 *pp de* **oponer**
2 *adj* (a) *(contrario)* contrary, opposed; **conducta opuesta a las reglas** misconduct; **en direcciones opuestas** in opposite directions; **tenemos gustos opuestos** we have conflicting tastes (b) *(de enfrente)* opposite; **el extremo o.** the other end

opulencia *nf* opulence, luxury; **vivir en la o.** to live a life of luxury

opulento, -a *adj* opulent

opus *nm* Mús opus

opúsculo *nm* booklet; short work

OPV *nf* (abrev de **Oferta Pública de Venta (de acciones)**) offer for sale; *US* public offering

oquedad *nf* hollow, cavity

ora *conj Fml* now; **o. ríe, o. llora** now he laughs, now he cries

oración *nf* (a) *Rel* prayer (b) *Ling* clause, sentence; **partes de la o.** parts of speech ❑ **o. compuesta** complex sentence; **o. principal** main clause; **o. simple** simple sentence; **o. subordinada** subordinate clause (c) *(discurso)* oration, speech

oráculo *nm* oracle

orador, -a *nm,f* speaker, orator; **tiene dotes de o.** he's a gifted speaker

oral *adj* oral; *Med* **por vía o.** to be taken orally

órale *interj Méx Fam* come on!

orangután *nm Zool* orang-outang, orang-utan

orar *vi Rel* to pray

orate *nmf* lunatic; *(hombre)* madman; *(mujer)* madwoman; **casa de orates** lunatic asylum

oratoria *nf* oratory

oratorio¹ *nm* (a) *Mús* oratorio (b) *(capilla)* oratory

oratorio, -a² *adj* oratorical

orbe *nm* (a) *(mundo)* world; **en todo el o.** throughout the world (b) *(bola)* orb

órbita *nf* (a) *Astron Astronáut* orbit; *Fig* orbit; **entrar en ó.** to go into orbit; *Fig* **se sale de la órbita de mis competencias** it lies outside my jurisdiction (b) *Anat* eye socket; **con los ojos fuera de las órbitas** with his eyes popping out of his head

orbital *adj* orbital

orca *nf Zool* orc, killer whale

órdago *nm Fam* **de ó.** fantastic, great; **una riña de ó.** a hell of an argument

orden 1 *nm* (a) *(colocación)* order; **todo en o.** everything in order; **lo encontré todo en o.** everything was in its place (b) *(concierto)* order; **las fuerzas del o.** the forces of law and order; **llamar a algn al o.** to call sb to order; **mantener el o.** to keep order; **sin o. ni concierto** without rhyme or reason ❑ **o. público** law and order (c) *(sucesión)* order; **de primer o.** first-rate; **del o. de ...** in the order of...; **o. del día** agenda, order of the day; **por o. de edad/ estatura** by age/height (d) *Arquit Bot Zool* order; **o. dórico/ jónico** Doric/Ionic order (e) *Mil* drill (f) *Fig (campo)* sphere; **en el o. económico** in the economic sphere
2 *nf* (a) *(mandato)* order; *Mil* **¡a la o.!, ¡a sus órdenes!** sir!; **por o. del señor alcalde** by order of his Lordship the Mayor; *Fig* **está a la o. del día** it's the done thing (b) *Hist Rel* order ❑ **o. militar** military order; **órdenes sagradas** holy orders (c) *Com* order ❑ **o. de compra** purchase order; **o. de pago** money order (d) *Jur* warrant, order ❑ **o. de arresto** *o* **detención** warrant for arrest; **o. de registro** search warrant; **o. judicial** court order

ordenación *nf* (a) *(disposición)* arrangement, organizing (b) *Rel* ordination

ordenada *nf Mat* ordinate

ordenado, -a 1 *pp de* **ordenar**
2 *adj* (a) *(arreglado)* tidy, in order (b) *Rel* ordained

ordenador, -a 1 *adj* ordering
2 *nm Esp Inform* computer ❑ **o. personal** personal computer; **o. portátil** laptop computer

ordenamiento *nm* ordering

ordenanza 1 *nm Mil* orderly; *(en oficina)* messenger
2 **ordenanzas** *nfpl* regulations, code *sing*; **o. municipales** by-laws

ordenar 1 *vt* (a) *(arreglar)* to put in order; *(habitación)* to tidy up; *Fig (encaminar)* to direct; *Fig* **o. las ideas** to collect one's thoughts; *Fig* **o. su vida** to put one's affairs in order (b) *(mandar)* to order to; *Com* **o. un pago** to authorize a payment (c) *Rel* to ordain
2 **ordenarse** *vpr Rel* to be ordained (**de** as), take holy orders

ordeñadora *nf Agr* milking machine

ordeñar *vt Agr* to milk

ordeño *nm Esp Agr* milking

ordinal 1 *adj* ordinal
2 *nm (número)* ordinal

ordinariez *nf (groseria)* vulgarity, coarseness; *(expresión)* rude remark

ordinario, -a *adj* (a) *(corriente)* ordinary, common (b) *(grosero)* vulgar, common

orear 1 *vt (ventilar)* to air
2 **orearse** *vpr (tomar el aire)* to get some fresh air

orégano *nm Bot* oregano, marjoram; *Fig* **no todo el monte es o.** it's not all plain sailing

oreja *nf (gen)* ear; *(de zapato)* flap; *(de sillón)* wing; *Fig* **con las orejas gachas** with one's tail between one's legs; *Fam* **calentarle las orejas a algn** to box sb's ears; *Fam* **con una sonrisa de o. a o.** with a huge grin; *Fam Fig* **verle las orejas al lobo** to have a narrow escape

orejera *nf* (a) *(de gorra)* earflap; *(de sillón)* wing (b) *Am* = earring worn by Indians

orejero, -a *adj* (a) *Am (receloso)* suspicious, distrustful

(b) *Arg (chismoso)* gossiping, scandalmongering

orejón¹ *nm* **(a)** *Culin (dulce)* dried apricot/peach **(b)** *(tirón)* pull on the ear; **darle un o. a algn** to pull sb's ear

orejón, -ona² **1** *adj* **(a)** *(orejudo)* big-eared **(b)** *Col (rudo)* coarse, uncouth
 2 *nm,f (persona)* big-ears

orejudo, -a **1** *adj* big-eared
 2 *nm Zool* long-eared bat

orensano, -a **1** *adj* of o from Orense
 2 *nm,f* person from Orense

orfanato *nm* orphanage

orfandad *nf* orphanhood

orfebre *nm* goldsmith, silversmith

orfebrería *nf* gold o silver work

orfelinato *nm* orphanage

orfeón *nm Mús* choral society

orfeonista *nmf Mús* member of a choral society

organdí (*pl* **organdíes**) *nm Tex* organdie

orgánico, -a *adj* organic

organigrama *nm* organization chart, flow chart, flow diagram; *Inform* flow chart

organillero, -a *nm,f Mús* organ-grinder

organillo *nm Mús* barrel organ, hurdy-gurdy

organismo *nm* **(a)** *(ser viviente)* organism **(b)** *(entidad pública)* organization, body, institution

organista *nmf Mús* organist

organización *nf* organization

organizado, -a **1** *pp de* **organizar**
 2 *adj* organized; **viaje o.** package tour

organizador, -a **1** *adj* organizing
 2 *nm,f* organizer

organizar [14] **1** *vt* **(a)** *(estructurar, ordenar)* to organize **(b)** *Esp (pelea, lío)* to cause
 2 organizarse *vpr* **(a)** *(persona)* to organize oneself **(b)** *Esp (pelea, lío)* to break out, happen suddenly

organizativo, -a *adj* organizing

órgano *nm* **(a)** *Mús* organ **(b)** *Anat* organ

orgasmo *nm* orgasm

orgía *nf* orgy

orgiástico, -a *adj* orgiastic

orgullo *nm* **(a)** *(propia estima)* pride **(b)** *(arrogancia)* arrogance, haughtiness

orgulloso, -a *adj* **(a)** *(satisfecho)* proud **(b)** *(arrogante)* arrogant, haughty

orientación *nf* **(a)** *(dirección)* orientation, direction **(b)** *Arquit (de un edificio)* aspect **(c)** *(enfoque)* approach; **hay que darle una nueva o. al problema** we have to look at the problem in a different way **(d)** *(guía)* guidance; **cursillo de o.** induction course; **estos datos te servirán de o.** this information will give you an idea; **o. profesional** career guidance, vocational guidance

orientador, -a **1** *adj* advising, advisory, guiding
 2 *nm,f* guide, adviser, counsellor

oriental **1** *adj* **(a)** *(del este)* eastern; *(del Lejano Oriente)* oriental **(b)** *Am (uruguayo)* Uruguayan **(c)** *(de Oriente, Venezuela)* of o from Oriente
 2 *nmf* **(a)** *(del Lejano Oriente)* oriental **(b)** *Am (uruguayo)* Uruguayan **(c)** *(persona de Oriente, Venezuela)* person from Oriente

orientar **1** *vt* **(a)** *(dirigir)* to orientate, direct; **charla orientada a los padres** talk aimed at parents; **educación orientada al logro académico** education geared to academic success **(b)** *Arquit (edificios)* to position, place; **una casa orientada al sur** a house facing south **(c)** *(guiar)*

to guide; **el policía les orientó** the policeman gave them directions
 2 orientarse *vpr* **(a)** *(encontrar el camino)* to get one's bearings, find one's way about; *Fig* to get into the swing of things; **los ciegos se orientan por los sonidos** blind people are guided by sounds **(b)** *(dirigirse) (foco)* **o. a** to point towards

orientativo, -a *adj* illustrative, guiding

oriente *nm* **(a)** *(este)* East, Orient; **el Extremo** o **Lejano O.** the Far East; **el O. Medio** the Middle East; **el Próximo O.** the Near East **(b)** *(masonería)* **Gran O.** the Grand Lodge

orificio *nm* hole, opening; *Anat Téc* orifice ❏ **o. de admisión** o **entrada** inlet; **o. de salida** outlet

origen *nm* origin; **dar o. a** to give rise to; **de o. español** of Spanish extraction; **de o. humilde** of humble origins o birth; **en los orígenes de la historia** at the dawn of history; **país de o.** country of origin; **tiene sus orígenes en la Edad Media** it dates back to the Middle Ages

original *adj & nmf* original

originalidad *nf* originality; *Pey* eccentricity

originar **1** *vt* to cause, give rise to
 2 originarse *vpr* to originate, have its origin

originario, -a *adj* *(procedente)* original; *(primigenio)* original; **ser o. de** *(persona)* to come from; *(costumbre)* to originate in

orilla *nf* **(a)** *(borde)* edge; *(del río)* bank; *(del mar)* shore; **a la o. del mar** by the sea, at the seaside **(b)** *Méx RP Ven (arrabales)* outskirts *pl*

orillero, -a *adj Am (persona)* suburban

orillo *nm Tex* selvage, selvedge

orín¹ *nm (herrumbre)* rust

orín² *nm (gen pl)* *(orina)* urine

orina *nf* urine

orinal *nm* chamberpot; *Fam* potty

orinar **1** *vi* to urinate
 2 orinarse *vpr* to wet oneself

Orinoco *nm* **el O.** the Orinoco

oriundo, -a **1** *adj* native of; **ser o. de** to come from, originate from
 2 *nm Ftb* = foreign player of Spanish parentage who plays for a Spanish team

orla *nf* **(a)** *Cost* trimming, edging **(b)** *Esp Univ* graduation photograph

orlar *vt Cost* to put an ornamental edge on

ornamentación *nf* ornamentation, decoration

ornamental *adj* ornamental

ornamentar *vt* to adorn, embellish

ornamento *nm* **(a)** *(adorno)* ornament **(b) ornamentos** *Rel* vestments

ornar *vt Literario* to adorn, embellish

ornato *nm (atavío)* finery; *(adorno)* decoration

ornitología *nf* ornithology

ornitológico, -a *adj* ornithological

ornitólogo, -a *nm,f* ornithologist

ornitorrinco *nm Zool* duck-billed platypus

oro *nm* **(a)** *(metal)* gold; **de o.** gold, golden; *Fig* **libro de o.** visitors' book; *Fig* **tratar algo como o. en** *Esp* **paño** o *Am* **polvo** to handle sth with great care; *Fam Fig* **prometer el o. y el moro** to promise the earth; *Prov* **no es o. todo lo que reluce** all that glitters is not gold ❏ **o. blanco** white gold; **o. de ley** fine gold; **o. negro** oil **(b) oros** *Naipes (baraja española)* ≃ diamonds

orogenia *nf Geol* orogeny, orogenesis

orografía *nf Geog* orography, orology

orográfico, -a *adj Geog* orographic, orological

orondo, -a *adj* **(a)** *(con barriga)* potbellied **(b)** *Fig (ufano)* smug, self-satisfied; **lo dijo y se quedó tan o.** he said it without batting an eyelid

oropel *nm* tinsel

orquesta *nf Mús* orchestra; *(de verbena)* dance band

orquestación *nf Mús* orchestration; *Fig* orchestration, organization

orquestal *adj Mús* orchestral

orquestar *vt Mús* to orchestrate; *Fig* to orchestrate, organize

orquestina *nf Mús* orchestrina

orquídea *nf Bot* orchid

orsay ['orsai] *(pl* **orsays)** *nm Ftb Fam* offside

ortiga *nf Bot* (stinging) nettle

ortigal *nm Bot* nettle field

ortodoncia *nf Med* orthodontics *sing,* orthodontia

ortodoxia *nf* orthodoxy

ortodoxo, -a *adj & nm,f* orthodox

ortografía *nf* orthography, spelling; **faltas de o.** spelling mistakes

ortográfico, -a *adj* orthografic, orthographical; **signos ortográficos** punctuation *sing*

ortopedia *nf* orthopaedics *sing,* US orthopedics *sing*

ortopédico, -a 1 *adj* orthopaedic, US orthopedic; **pierna ortopédica** artificial leg
 2 *nm,f* orthopaedist, US orthopedist

ortopedista *nmf* orthopaedist, US orthopedist

oruga *nf* **(a)** *Zool* caterpillar **(b)** *Bot* rocket **(c)** *Téc* caterpillar

orujo *nm (hollejo)* = grape or olive skins left after pressing; *(bebida)* grape spirit

orza[1] *nf* earthenware jar

orza[2] *nf Náut* luff, luffing

orzar [14] *vi Náut* to luff

orzuelo *nm Med* sty, stye

os *pron pers pl* **(a)** *(complemento directo)* you; **os veo mañana** I'll see you tomorrow **(b)** *(complemento indirecto)* to you; **os escribiré** I'll write to you; **os lo mandaré** I'll send it to you **(c)** *(con verbo reflexivo)* yourselves; **¿no os quejáis?** don't you complain?; **os hacéis daño** you're hurting yourselves; **os organizáis muy bien** you are very well organized; **¡qué pronto os levantáis!** you do get up early! **(d)** *(con verbo recíproco)* each other; **os parecéis** you look alike; **os queréis mucho** you love each other very much

osa *nf* **(a)** *Zool* she-bear **(b)** *Astron* **O. Mayor** Great Bear, US Big Dipper; **O. Menor** Little Bear, US Little Dipper

osadía *nf* **(a)** *(audacia)* daring, boldness, fearlessness **(b)** *(desvergüenza)* impudence

osado, -a *adj* **(a)** *(audaz)* daring, bold, fearless **(b)** *(desvergonzado)* shameless

osamenta *nf* bones *pl,* skeleton

osar *vi* to dare

osario *nm* ossuary

Óscar® *nm Cin* Oscar®

oscense 1 *adj* of o from Huesca
 2 *nmf* person from Huesca

oscilación *nf* **(a)** *Fís* oscillation **(b)** *(de precios)* fluctuation

oscilador *nm Fís* oscillator

oscilante *adj* **(a)** *Fís* oscillating **(b)** *(precios)* fluctuating

oscilar *vi* **(a)** *Fís* to oscillate **(b)** *(variar)* to vary, fluctuate

osciloscopio *nm Fís* oscilloscope

ósculo *nm Literario Hum* kiss

oscurantismo *nm* obscurantism

oscurantista *adj & nmf* obscurantist

oscuras: a oscuras *loc adv* in the dark; **nos quedamos a o.** we were left in darkness

oscurecer [46] *vi impers & vt & vpr véase* **obscurecer**

oscurecimiento *nm véase* **obscurecimiento**

oscuridad *nf véase* **obscuridad**

oscuro, -a *adj véase* **obscuro, -a**

óseo, -a *adj* osseous, bony; **tejido ó.** bone tissue

osera *nf* bear's den

osezno *nm Zool* bear cub

osificación *nf* ossification

osificarse [59] *vpr* to ossify

osito *nm Fam* **o. (de peluche)** teddy bear

Oslo *n* Oslo

osmio *nm Quím* osmium

ósmosis *nf inv,* **osmosis** *nf inv* osmosis

osmótico, -a *adj* osmotic

oso *nm Zool* bear; *Fam Fig* **hacer el o.** to play the fool ❏ **o. blanco** polar bear; **o. hormiguero** anteater; **o. marino** fur seal; **o. panda** panda; **o. polar** polar bear

osobuco *nm Culin* osso bucco

ostensible *adj* ostensible, obvious

ostentación *nf* ostentation; **con o.** ostentatiously; **hacer o. de algo** to show sth off

ostentar *vt* **(a)** *(jactarse)* to show off, flaunt **(b)** *(poseer)* to hold; **ostenta el cargo de** she holds the position of

ostentoso, -a *adj* ostentatious

osteópata *nmf Med* osteopath

osteopatía *nf Med* osteopathy

ostra 1 *nf Zool* oyster; *Fig* **aburrirse como una o.** to be bored stiff
 2 *interj Esp Fam* **¡ostras!** crikey!, US gee!

ostracismo *nm* ostracism

ostrería *nf* oyster restaurant

ostrero, -a 1 *adj* oyster
 2 *nm,f* oyster trader
 3 *nm Orn* oystercatcher

ostrícola *adj* oyster

ostricultura *nf* oyster culture

osuno, -a *adj* bear-like

OTAN ['otan] *nf (abrev de* **Organización del Tratado del Atlántico Norte)** NATO

otario, -a *adj RP* foolish, simple

oteador, -a *nm,f* lookout

otear *vt* to scan, search; **o. el horizonte** to scan the horizon

otero *nm* knoll, hillock

OTI ['oti] *nf (abrev de* **Organización de la Televisión Iberoamericana)**

otitis *nf inv Med* = infection and inflammation of the ear, otitis

otomano, -a *adj & nm,f* Ottoman

otoñal *adj* autumnal, autumn, US fall

otoño *nm* autumn, US fall

otorgamiento *nm (concesión)* granting, authorization; *(de un premio)* award, awarding

otorgar [38] *vt* **(a)** *(conceder)* to grant, give **(a** to); *(premio)* to award **(a** to); **o. un indulto** to grant pardon **(b)** *Jur* to execute, draw up **(c)** *(conferir)* to confer **(a** on)

otorrino, -a *nm,f Fam* ear, nose and throat specialist

otorrinolaringología *nf Med* otolaryngology

otorrinolaringólogo, -a *nm,f* ear, nose and throat specialist, otolaryngologist

otro, -a 1 *adj indef* other, another; **entre otras cosas** amongst other things; **otra cosa** something else; **otra vez** again; **otra vez será** some other time; **o. día** another day **2** *pron indef* other, another; **el o./la otra** the other; **entre otros** among others; **los otros/las otras** the others; **nunca me he visto en otra igual** I just didn't know what to do; **¡otra, otra!** encore!, more!; **o. de mis amigos** another (one) of my friends; **o. tanto** as much; **otros tantos** as many; **que vaya o.** let someone else go; *Fam* **o. que tal** here we go again

otrora *adv Fml* formerly

otrosí *adv Fml* moreover, furthermore

Ottawa [o'tawa] *n* Ottawa

ova *nf Bot* alga

ovación *nf* ovation, cheering, applause

ovacionar *vt* to give an ovation to, applaud

oval *adj,* **ovalado, -a** *adj* oval

óvalo *nm* oval

ovárico, -a *adj Anat* ovarian

ovario *nm Anat* ovary

oveja *nf Zool* sheep, ewe; *Fig* **cada o. con su pareja** every Jack has his Jill; *Fig* **la o. negra (de la familia)** the black sheep (of the family)

ovejuno, -a *adj* sheep

overbooking [oβer'βukin] (*pl* **overbookings**) *nm* overbooking

overol *nm Am (de peto) Br* dungarees, *US* overalls; *(completo)* overalls, *Br* boilersuit; *(para bebé)* rompers

ovetense 1 *adj* of *o* from Oviedo **2** *nmf* person from Oviedo

ovillar *vt (lana)* to wind *o* roll into a ball

ovillo *nm* ball (of wool); *Fig* **hacerse un o.** to curl up into a ball

ovino, -a *adj* ovine; **ganado o.** sheep *pl*

ovíparo, -a *adj Zool* oviparous

ovni *nm* (*abrev de* **objeto volador no identificado**) UFO

ovoide *adj & nm* ovoid

ovulación *nf* ovulation

ovular 1 *adj* ovular **2** *vi* to ovulate

óvulo *nm* ovule

oxálico, -a *adj Quím* oxalic

oxidable *adj Quím* oxidizable

oxidación *nf Quím* oxidation; *(efecto en los metales)* rusting

oxidado, -a 1 *pp de* **oxidar** **2** *adj Quím* oxidized; *(metal)* rusty; *Fig* **su inglés está un poco o.** her English is a bit rusty

oxidante *nm* oxidizer

oxidar 1 *vt Quím* to oxidize; *(efecto en los metales)* to rust **2 oxidarse** *vpr Quím* to oxidize; *(metal)* to rust, go rusty

óxido *nm* (a) *Quím* oxide ❑ **ó. de carbono** carbon monoxide (b) *(orín)* rust

oxigenación *nf Quím* oxygenation

oxigenado, -a *adj* oxygenated

oxigenar 1 *vt* (a) *Quím* to oxygenate (b) *(cabello)* to bleach **2 oxigenarse** *vpr Fig* to get a breath of fresh air

oxígeno *nm* oxygen ❑ **bomba de o.** oxygen cylinder *o* tank

oye *indic pres & imperat véase* **oír**

oyente *nmf* (a) *Rad* listener (b) *Univ* occasional student

ozono *nm Quím* ozone

P

P, p [pe] *nf (la letra)* P, p

p. (*abrev de* **página**) p.

p.a. (**a**) (*abrev de* **por ausencia**) pp (**b**) (*abrev de* **por autorización**) pp

pabellón *nm* (**a**) *Arquit (edificio)* pavilion; *(parte de un edificio)* block, section; *(en hospital)* ward (**b**) *(en parques, jardines)* summerhouse (**c**) *(dosel)* canopy (**d**) *(de la oreja)* **p. auditivo** outer ear (**e**) *(bandera)* flag; **navegaban bajo p. panameño** they sailed under the Panamanian flag (**f**) *(tienda)* bell tent

pábilo *nm,* **pabilo** *nm* wick

pábulo *nm Fml* food, sustenance; *Fig* fuel; **dar p. a** to encourage

paca *nf* bale, pack

pacato, -a *adj* (**a**) *(escrupuloso)* prudish (**b**) *(apaciguado)* moderate, peace-loving

pacense 1 *adj* of o from Badajoz

  2 *nmf* person from Badajoz

paceño, -a 1 *adj* of o from La Paz

  2 *nm,f* person from La Paz

pacer [42] *vt & vi* to graze, pasture

pachá (*pl* **pachás** o **pachaes**) *nm* pasha, pacha; *Fam Fig* **vivir como un p.** to live like a king

pachaco, -a *adj Am (inútil)* useless; *(enclenque)* weak

pachamanca *nf Andes Culin* = meat cooked between hot stones or in a hole in the ground under hot stones

pachanga *nf* celebration, rowdy party

pachanguero, -a *adj Esp Fam (música)* catchy

pacho, -a *adj* (**a**) *CAm Chile Fam (regordete)* chubby (**b**) *CAm (aplanado)* flattened

pachón, -ona 1 *adj Zool* pointer

  2 *nm,f Zool* pointer

  3 *nm Fam* phlegmatic person

pachorra *nf Fam* sluggishness; **tener p.** to be phlegmatic

pachucho, -a *adj Fam* off-colour, *US* off-color

pachulí (*pl* **pachulíes**) *nm Bot* patchouli, pachouli

paciencia *nf* patience; **armarse de p.** to grin and bear it; **perder la p.** to lose (one's) patience; **tener mucha p.** to be very patient; *Prov* **la p. es la madre de la ciencia** if at first you don't succeed, try, try again

paciente *adj & nmf* patient

pacientemente *adv* patiently

pacificación *nf* pacification; *Fig (apaciguamiento)* appeasement

pacificador, -a 1 *adj* pacifying

  2 *nm,f* peacemaker

pacificar [59] **1** *vt* to pacify; *Fig (apaciguar)* to appease, calm

  2 pacificarse *vpr* to calm down

Pacífico *nm* **el (océano) P.** the Pacific (Ocean)

pacífico, -a *adj* peaceful

pacifismo *nm* pacifism

pacifista *adj & nmf* pacifist

paco, -a *nm,f Andes Pan Fam* cop

pacota *nf* (**a**) *Arg (grupo)* gang (**b**) *Méx (objeto)* piece of junk; *(persona)* worthless person

pacotilla *nf Fam* **de p.** shoddy, trashy

pactar *vt* to agree to; **han pactado una tregua** they've agreed to a truce

pacto *nm* agreement, pact; **hacer/romper un p.** to make/break an agreement ❑ **p. electoral** electoral pact; **p. social** social contract

padecer [46] **1** *vt (sufrimiento)* to endure, undergo; *(hambre, injusticia)* to suffer; *(enfermedad)* to suffer from

  2 *vi* to suffer; **p. del corazón/riñón** to suffer from a heart/kidney complaint

padecimiento *nm* suffering

padrastro *nm* (**a**) *(pariente)* stepfather (**b**) *(pellejo)* hangnail

padrazo *nm* easy-going o indulgent father

padre 1 *nm* (**a**) *(gen)* father; **p. de familia** head of family; **p. político** father-in-law; *Fam* **de p. y muy señor mío** tremendous, terrific; *Ofens* **¡tu p.!** up yours! (**b**) *Fig (precursor)* father, creator; *Irón* **¿quién es el p. de la criatura?** who put this together? (**c**) *Rel* father, priest; **el santo p.** the Pope, the Holy Father (**d**) *Rel* God; **P. Eterno** Heavenly Father; *(oración)* **P. Nuestro** Lord's Prayer (**e**) **padres** parents; *(antepasados)* ancestors

  2 *adj Fam* (**a**) *Esp* huge; **llevarse un disgusto p.** to be extremely upset; **pegarse la vida p.** to live like a king (**b**) *Méx (genial)* great, fantastic

padrenuestro *nm Rel* Lord's Prayer

padrillo *nm RP Zool* stallion

padrinazgo *nm* (**a**) *(cargo de padrino)* godfathership (**b**) *Fig (patrocinio)* patronage, sponsorship

padrino *nm* (**a**) *(de bautismo)* godfather; *(de boda)* best man (**b**) *Fig* sponsor, protector (**c**) **padrinos** godparents; *Fig* **hay que tener buenos p.** you have to know the right people

padrísimo, -a *adj Méx Fam* fantastic, great

padrón *nm* (**a**) *(censo)* census (**b**) *CAm Carib Andes Zool* stallion

padrote *nm Méx Fam* pimp

paella *nf Culin* paella, = rice dish made with vegetables, meat and/or seafood

paellera *nf* paella pan

paf *interj* bang!

pág. (*abrev de* **página**) p.

paga *nf* wage; (*niños*) pocket money; *Fig* **esto fue la p. por su comportamiento** she got her just deserts ❑ **p. extra** bonus

pagable *adj* payable

pagadero, -a *adj* payable; *Fin* **cheque p. al portador** cheque payable to bearer

pagado, -a 1 *pp de* **pagar**
2 *adj* (**a**) (*cuenta*) paid (**b**) *Fig* **p. de uno mismo** smug, self-satisfied

pagador, -a 1 *adj* paying
2 *nm,f* payer; (*de banco, institución etc*) cashier

pagaduría *nf* pay office

paganismo *nm* paganism, heathenism

paganizar [14] **1** *vi* to profess paganism
2 *vt* to paganize

pagano, -a *adj & nm,f Rel* pagan, heathen

pagar [38] **1** *vt* to pay; **¿cuánto pagaste por el coche?** how much did you pay for the car?; **p. en metálico** *o* **al contado** to pay cash; *Fig* **¿así pagas lo que ha hecho por ti?** is that how you repay him for what he's done for you?; *Fig* (**ella**) **lo ha pagado caro** she's paid dearly for it; *Fam Fig* **me las pagarás** I'll get you for this, you haven't heard the last of this
2 pagarse *vpr* (**a**) (*uso impers*) to be paid, cost; **¿ a cuánto se pagan las patatas?** how much are (the) potatoes? (**b**) *Fig* (*ufanarse*) to be proud of; **p. de sí mismo** to be full of oneself, to be self-satisfied, to be smug

pagaré *nm Fin* promissory note, IOU; **p. del tesoro** treasury note

página *nf* page; **en la p. 3** on page 3; *Fig* **aquellos hombres escribieron una p. importante de la historia** those men wrote an important chapter in history ❑ *Inform* **p. web** Web page

paginación *nf* pagination

paginar *vt* to paginate, number the pages of

pago¹ *nm* (**a**) *Fin Com* payment; **p. a cuenta** payment on account ❑ **p. adelantado** *o* **anticipado** advance payment; **p. contra entrega** cash on delivery; **p. inicial** down payment (*Fig* return, payment; **en p. por su hospitalidad ...** in return for her hospitality...

pago² *nm* (**a**) (*finca*) estate, property (**b**) (*aldea*) village; **por** *o* **en estos/aquellos pagos** in this/that area

pagoda *nf Arquit* pagoda

paila *nf* (**a**) *Andes CAm Carib* (*sartén*) (frying) pan (**b**) *Chile* (*huevos fritos*) fried eggs

paíño *nm Orn* petrel

paipái *nm* (*pl* **paipáis**), **paipay** *nm* (*pl* **paipay**) *Esp* large palm fan

país *nm* country; **vino del p.** local wine ❑ **p. natal** native country, homeland; **P. Vasco** Basque Country; **los Países Bajos** the Netherlands

paisaje *nm* landscape, scenery

paisajismo *nm* landscape painting

paisajista *nmf Arte* landscape painter

paisajístico, -a *adj* landscape; **belleza paisajística** natural beauty

paisanada *nf Arg* group of peasants

paisanaje *nm* civil population

paisano, -a 1 *adj* of the same country
2 *nm,f* (**a**) (*compatriota*) fellow countryman *o* countrywoman, compatriot (**b**) (*civil*) civilian; **ir de p.** (*policía*) to

be wearing plain clothes; (*militar*) to be wearing civilian clothes; **en traje de p.** (*policía*) in plain clothes; (*militar*) in civilian clothes

Países Bajos *npl* (**los**) P. B. the Netherlands, the Low Countries

paja *nf* (**a**) (*hierba, caña*) straw; **techo de p.** thatched roof; *Fig* **hombre de p.** stooge (**b**) *Fam Fig* (*superfluo*) padding, waffle; *Fig* **meter p.** to waffle; *Fig* **no te enfades por un quítame allá esas pajas** don't make a mountain out of a molehill (**c**) *Vulg* (*masturbación*) *Br* wank, *US* jerkoff; **hacerse una** *o Am* **la p.** to jerk off, *Br* have a wank

pajar *nm* (*almacén*) straw loft; (*en el exterior*) straw rick

pájara *nf* (**a**) (*cometa*) kite (**b**) (*pajarita*) paper bird (**c**) *Fam* (*desfallecimiento*) blackout (**d**) *Fam Pey* (*mujer*) **es una p. de mucho cuidado** she's a crafty old devil

pajarear *vi* (**a**) *Andes Méx* (*caballo*) to shy (**b**) *Chile* (*estar distraído*) to be absent-minded

pajarera *nf* aviary

pajarería *nf* (**a**) (*tienda*) pet shop (**b**) (*pájaros*) flock *o* flight of birds

pajarero, -a 1 *adj Andes Méx* (*caballo*) shy, skittish
2 *nm,f* (*vendedor*) bird dealer

pajarita *nf* (**a**) *Esp* (*prenda*) bow tie (**b**) (*de papel*) paper bird

pájaro *nm* (**a**) *Orn* bird; **a vista de p.** bird's-eye view; *Fig* **matar dos pájaros de un tiro** to kill two birds with one stone; *Fig* **tener la cabeza llena de pájaros** to be scatterbrained; *Prov* **más vale p. en mano que ciento volando** a bird in the hand is worth two in the bush ❑ **p. carpintero** woodpecker; **p. mosca** hummingbird (**b**) *Fam Fig* (*hombre*) chap; (*astuto*) sly person, slyboots *sing*; **p. de cuenta** big shot

pajarraco *nm Pey* (**a**) *Orn* ugly bird (**b**) *Fig* (*astuto*) slyboots *sing*

paje *nm* page

pajita *nf* (drinking) straw

pajizo, -a *adj* (**a**) (*de paja*) (made of) straw (**b**) (*de color de paja*) straw-coloured, *US* straw-colored

pajolero, -a *adj Esp Fam* damn, blessed

pajón, -ona *adj Am* (*hierba*) scrub, coarse grass

pajuerano, -a *nm,f RP Fam Pey* yokel

Pakistán *n* Pakistan

pakistaní *adj & nmf* Pakistani

pala *nf* (**a**) (*herramienta*) (*para recoger*) shovel; (*mecánica*) power shovel; (*de jardinero*) spade; (*recogedor*) dustpan; (*de cocina*) slice; **p. para pescado** fish slice (**b**) *Dep* (*de pingpong, frontón*) bat (**c**) (*de remo, hélice etc*) blade (**d**) (*de zapato*) upper (**e**) *Fam Fig* skill; *Pey* cunning; **tiene buena p.** he is very skilful

palabra *nf* (**a**) (*término, vocablo*) word; **de p.** by word of mouth; **dirigir la p. a algn** to address sb; **juego de palabras** pun; **según las palabras de ...** according to ...; **tener unas palabras con algn** to have a few words with sb; *Fig* **a la primera p.** very soon; *Fig* **comerse las palabras** to swallow one's words; *Fig* **decir la última p.** to have the last word; *Fig* **dejar a algn con la p. en la boca** to cut sb off; *Fig* **ser de pocas palabras** to be a man/woman of few words, not be very talkative; *Fig* **Teresa vio de qué iba el asunto a la primera p.** Teresa knew immediately which way the wind was blowing; *Fam Fig* **ni p. de esto a nadie** don't say a thing to anybody ❑ **p. clave** key word; **palabras mayores** (*insultos*) swearwords; (*de importancia*) big talk *sing* (**b**) (*habla*) speech; **el don de la p.** the faculty of speech (**c**) (*promesa*) word; **cogerle la p. a algn** to take sb at his word; **faltar a la p.** to break one's word; **hombre de p.** man of his word; **p. de honor** word of honour; **tener p.** to keep one's word (**d**) *(lengua)* language; **una mujer de p. clara** a woman who expresses herself clearly (**e**) *(turno para hablar)* right to speak; **dar** *o* **conceder la p. a algn** to give the floor to sb; **tener la p.** to have the floor

palabrear *vt Am Fam* to agree verbally to

palabreja *nf* strange *o* difficult word

palabrería *nf* palaver

palabrota *nf* swearword; **decir palabrotas** to swear

palacete *nm Arquit* small palace, mansion

palaciego, -a *adj* palace, court; **lujo p.** palatial luxury; **intrigas palaciegas** court intrigues

palacio *nm (grande)* palace; *(pequeño)* mansion; *Fig* **las cosas de p. van despacio** it all takes time ❑ **p. de congresos** conference centre; **P. de Justicia** Law Courts *pl*

palada *nf* (**a**) *(paletada)* shovelful (**b**) *(de remo)* stroke

paladar 1 *nm* (**a**) *Anat* palate (**b**) *(sabor)* taste (**c**) *Fig (sensibilidad)* palate
2 *nf o nm Cuba* = small restaurant in a private house

paladear *vt* to savour, *US* savor, relish

paladeo *nm* savouring, *US* savoring, relishing

paladín *nm Literario* champion; *Hist* paladin

paladino, -a *adj* obvious, public

palafito *nm Arquit* lake dwelling

palafrén *nm Literario* palfrey

palafrenero *nm* groom

palanca *nf* (**a**) *Téc* lever; **hacer p.** to (act as a) lever (**b**) *(manecilla)* handle, stick ❑ *Aut* **p. de cambio** gear lever *o* stick, *US* gearshift; **p. de mando** control lever (**c**) *Dep (trampolín)* diving board (**d**) *Am Fam (influencia)* **tener p.** to have friends in high places

palangana 1 *nf* (**a**) *(para lavarse)* washbowl (**b**) *Am (fuente)* serving dish, platter
2 *nm Andes CAm (descarado) Fam* braggart, show-off

palangre *nm Pesca* boulter

palanqueta *nf* crowbar

palatal *adj & nf Anat Ling* palatal

palatino, -a¹ *adj (palatal)* palatal

palatino, -a² *adj (palaciego)* palatine, palace, court

palco *nm Teat* (**a**) *(asiento)* box (**b**) **p. escénico** stage

palenque *nm* (**a**) *(estacada)* fence, palisade (**b**) *(recinto)* arena; **salir al p.** to enter the fray (**c**) *Méx (para peleas de gallos)* cockpit, cockfighting arena (**d**) *Andes RP (para animales)* hitching post

palentino, -a 1 *adj* of *o* from Palencia
2 *nm,f* person from Palencia

paleografía *nf* palaeography, *US* paleography

paleográfico, -a *adj* palaeographic, *US* paleographic

paleógrafo, -a *nm,f* palaeographer, *US* paleographer

paleolítico *adj* palaeolithic, *US* paleolithic

paleontología *nf* palaeontology, *US* paleontology

paleontólogo, -a *nm,f* palaeontologist, *US* paleontologist

Palestina *n* Palestine

palestino, -a *adj & nm,f* Palestinian

palestra *nf* arena; *Fig* **salir** *o* **saltar a la p.** to enter the fray, take the field

paleta *nf* (**a**) *(herramienta) (pala)* small shovel; *(de albañil)* trowel (**b**) *Culin (espátula)* slice (**c**) *Arte (de pintor)* palette (**d**) *Téc (de hélice, ventilador)* blade; *(molino)* wind vane (**e**) *Anat* shoulder blade (**f**) *Dep (de cricket, ping-pong)* bat (**g**) *Inform* ❑ **p. de herramientas** tool box (**h**) *Andes CAm Méx (caramelo)* lollipop; *Bol Col Perú (helado)* Br ice lolly, *US* Popsicle®

paletada *nf (de pala)* shovelful; *(de paleta de albañil)* trowelful

paletilla *nf* (**a**) *Anat* shoulder blade (**b**) *Culin* shoulder; **p. de cordero** shoulder of lamb

paleto, -a *Esp Pey* **1** *adj* coarse, uncouth
2 *nm,f* country bumpkin, yokel, *US* hick

paliacate *nm Méx* big bright scarf

paliar *vt* to alleviate, palliate

paliativo, -a *adj & nm* palliative

palidecer [46] *vi* (**a**) *(persona)* to turn pale (**b**) *Fig (colores)* to fade; *(luz)* to grow dim (**c**) *Fig (disminuir)* to diminish, be on the wane

palidez *nf* paleness, pallor

pálido, -a *adj* pale, pallid; **ponerse** *o* **volverse p.** to turn pale

palillero *nm* toothpick case

palillo *nm* (**a**) *(mondadientes)* toothpick; **palillos chinos** chopsticks; *Fam* **está como un p.** he's as thin as a rake (**b**) *(de hacer punto)* knitting needle (**c**) *Mús* drumstick (**d**) *Taur Fam* banderilla

palio *nm* (**a**) *(dosel)* canopy; *Fig* **recibir a algn bajo p.** to give sb a royal welcome (**b**) *Rel* pallium

palique *nm Esp Fam* chat, small talk; **estar de p.** to have a chat

palisandro *nm Bot* rosewood

paliza *nf* (**a**) *(zurra)* beating; **darle a algn una p.** to beat sb up (**b**) *(derrota)* thrashing; **¡menuda p. os dimos!** we thrashed you! (**c**) *Fam (esfuerzo)* hard grind; **nos dimos una p. tremenda para acabar a tiempo** we slogged our guts out to finish in time (**d**) *Fam (rollo)* drag; **dar la p. (a algn)** to go on and on (to sb)

palma *nf* (**a**) *Anat* palm; *Fig* **conocer algo/a algn como la p. de la mano** to know sth/sb like the back of one's hand (**b**) *Bot* palm tree; *Fig* **llevarse la p.** to win, triumph; *Irón* to take the *Br* biscuit *o US* cake (**c**) **palmas** *(palmadas)* clapping *sing*; *(aplauso)* applause *sing*; **batir palmas** to clap, applaud

palmada *nf* (**a**) *(golpe)* slap; **dar palmadas a algn en la espalda** to give sb a slap on the back (**b**) *(aplauso)* applause, clapping

palmar¹ *nm* palm grove

palmar² *vi Fam* **palmarla** to snuff it, kick it

palmarés *nm* (**a**) *(historial)* service record (**b**) *(vencedores)* list of winners

palmario, -a *adj* obvious, evident

palmatoria *nf* candlestick

palmear 1 *vi* to applaud, clap
2 *vt (espalda etc)* to tap

palmera *nf Bot* palm tree

palmeral *nm Bot* palm grove

palmero, -a 1 *adj* of *o* from La Palma
2 *nm,f* person from La Palma

palmesano, -a 1 *adj* of *o* from Palma de Mallorca
2 *nm,f* person from Palma de Mallorca

palmeta *nf* cane; **el maestro le castigó con la p.** the teacher caned him

palmetazo *nm* caning

palmípedo, -a 1 *nm,f Orn* web-footed bird
2 *adj* web-footed

palmito *nm* (**a**) *Bot* palmetto (**b**) *Culin* palm heart

palmo *nm (medida)* span; **un p. de tierra** a tiny plot of land; *Fig* **p. a p.** inch by inch; *Fam Fig* **con un p. de lengua fuera** out of breath; *Fam Fig* **dejar (a algn) con un p. de narices** to let (sb) down

palmotear *vi* to clap

palmoteo *nm* clapping

palo *nm* (a) *(trozo de madera)* stick; *(vara)* rod; *(pértiga)* pole; *(de escoba)* broomstick; *Fig* **a p. seco** on its own; *Fig* **nos bebimos el vodka a p. seco** we drank the vodka neat; *Prov* **de tal p. tal astilla** like father, like son (**b**) *(golpe)* blow; **dar palos** to hit, strike a blow; *Fig* **dar un p. a algn** to play a dirty trick on sb; *Fig* **la crítica le dio un buen p.** the critics slated him; *Fig* **echar a algn a palos** to throw o kick sb out; *Fig* **p. de ciego** shot in the dark; *Fig* **dar palos de ciego** to grope about in the dark (**c**) *(madera)* wood; **cuchara de p.** wooden spoon (**d**) *Náut (mástil)* mast ❑ **p. de mesana** mizzenmast; **p. mayor** mainmast (**e**) *Golf* club (**f**) *(trazo de letra)* stroke (**g**) *Naipes* suit (**h**) *Dep (de portería)* crossbar, goal post (**i**) *Am (árbol, arbusto)* tree ❑ **p. dulce** liquorice root (**j**) *Carib Fam (trago, copa)* drink

paloma *nf* (a) *Orn* pigeon, dove; **p. de la paz** dove of peace ❑ **p. mensajera** homing o carrier pigeon; **p. torcaz** wood-pigeon; **p. zurita** stock dove (**b**) *Méx (marca)* tick

palomar *nm* pigeon house, dovecote

palometa *nf (pez)* Ray's bream

palomilla *nf* (a) *Ent* grain moth (**b**) *(tuerca)* wing o butterfly nut (**c**) *CAm Chile Méx Fam (chusma)* rabble, riff-raff (**d**) **palomillas** *(olas)* white horses

palomino *nm* (a) *Orn* young pigeon, young dove (**b**) *(mancha)* pigeon droppings *pl*

palomita *nf Fam* **palomitas de maíz** popcorn *sing*

palomo *nm Orn* cock pigeon

palote *nm* (a) *(palo)* stick; *Mús* drumstick (**b**) *(trazo)* = practice stroke used by children learning to write

palpable *adj* palpable, concrete

palpación *nf Med* palpation

palpar *vt* to touch, feel; *Med* to palpate; *Fig* **p. la realidad** to be in touch with reality

palpitación *nf* palpitation, throbbing

palpitante *adj* palpitating, throbbing; *Fig* **una cuestión p.** a life issue

palpitar *vi* to palpitate, throb; *Fig* **en sus palabras palpita el rencor** resentment shows through his words

pálpito *nm esp RP Fam* hunch, feeling

palúdico, -a *Med adj* malarial; **fiebre palúdica** malaria

paludismo *nm Med* malaria

palurdo, -a 1 *adj* uncouth, boorish

  2 *nm,f Pey* country bumpkin, yokel, *US* hick

palustre *adj Geog* marshy, boggy

pambazo *nm Méx Culin* type of bread roll

pamela *nf (prenda)* broad-brimmed hat

pampa *nf* (a) *Geog* pampa, pampas *pl* (**b**) *(negocio)* dishonest

pámpano *nm Bot* vine shoot o tendril

pampeano, -a *adj* of o from the pampa, pampean

pampero, -a 1 *adj* of o from the pampa, pampean

  2 *nm Meteor* = strong wind over the pampas from the Andes

pamplina *nf* (a) *Fam (gen pl) (tontería)* nonsense; **¡déjate de pamplinas!** stop that nonsense! (**b**) *Bot* chickweed

pamplonés, -esa 1 *adj* of o from Pamplona

  2 *nm,f* person from Pamplona

pamplonica *adj* of o from Pamplona

pan *nm* (a) *(alimento)* bread; **barra de p.** French bread; **p. con mantequilla** bread and butter; **p. tierno/duro** fresh/stale bread; *Fig* **llamar al p. p. y al vino vino** to call a spade a spade; *Fam Fig* **con su p. se lo coma** let him stew in his own juice; *Fam Fig* **contigo p. y cebolla** love on a shoestring; *Fam Fig* **es p. comido** it's a piece of cake; *Fam Fig* **ser bueno como un pedazo de p.** o **más bueno que el p.** to be as good as gold, be a treasure ❑ **p. ácimo** unleavened bread; **p. de molde** sliced bread; **p. dulce** *Méx (bollo)* bun; *RP (panetone)* panettone; **p. integral** *Esp* wholemeal o *US* wholewheat bread; *Arg* **p. lactal** sliced bread; **p. rallado** breadcrumbs *pl*; *Col* **p. tajado** sliced bread (**b**) *Fig (alimento)* bread, food; **el p. nuestro de cada día** our daily bread; **ganarse el p.** to make o earn a living (**c**) *(metal)* leaf; **p. de oro** gold leaf

pana *nf Tex* corduroy; **p. lisa** velvet

panacea *nf* panacea

panadería *nf* baker's (shop), bakery

panadero, -a *nm,f* baker

panadizo *nm Med* whitlow

panal *nm* honeycomb

Panamá *n* Panama

panamá *nm (prenda)* Panama hat

panameño, -a *adj & nm,f* Panamanian

panamericanismo *nm* Pan-Americanism

pancarta *nf* placard; *(en la calle)* banner

panceta *nf* bacon

páncreas *nm inv Anat* pancreas

panda[1] *nm Zool* panda

panda[2] *nf Esp (amigos, gente)* crowd, gang; *Pey* gang

pandear 1 *vi* to bend; *(apandar)* to sag

  2 pandearse *vpr* to bend; *(apandarse)* to sag

pandemia *nf Med* pandemic

pandémico *adj Med* pandemic

pandeo *nm* bending; *(apandar)* sagging

pandereta *nf*, **pandero** *nm Mús* tambourine

pandilla *nf Fam véase* **panda**[2]

pando, -a *adj* (a) *(madera)* sagging; *(pared)* not straight; *(viga)* warped (**b**) *Fig (lento)* slow (**c**) *Méx (borracho)* drunk

panecillo *nm Esp* bread roll

panegírico, -a *Literario* **1** *adj* panegyric, panegyrical, eulogistic

  2 *nm* panegyric, eulogy

panel *nm* (a) panel (**b**) *(tablero)* board ❑ **p. do control** control panel

panela *nf* (a) *CAm Col Méx Ven (azúcar)* brown-sugar loaf (**b**) *Méx (queso)* = type of fresh cheese

panera *nf* (a) *(para servir pan)* bread basket (**b**) *(para guardar pan)* Br bread bin, *US* bread box

pánfilo, -a *adj Fam* (a) *(lento)* slow, indolent (**b**) *(bobo)* silly, stupid; *(crédulo)* gullible

panfletario, -a *adj* propagandist

panfletista *nmf* lampoonist, pamphleteer

panfleto *nm* lampoon, political pamphlet

panga *nf Náut (lancha)* launch; *(bote)* barge

pánico *nm* panic; **presa del p.** panic-stricken; **sembrar el p.** to cause panic; *Fam Fig* **de p.** *(estupendo)* great, terrific; *(terrible)* terrible, awful

panificación *nf* bread making

panificadora *nf* (industrial) bakery

panificar [59] *vt* to make bread

panizo *nm Bot* millet; maize

panocha *nf* (a) *Bot* corncob; *(trigo etc)* ear (**b**) *Méx (de melaza)* brown sugar loaf

panoja *nf Bot* corncob; *(trigo etc)* ear

panoli *adj Fam* gullible, idiot

panoplia *nf* (a) *(colección)* panoply (**b**) *(armadura)* suit of armour o *US* armor

panorama *nm* (**a**) *(vista)* panorama, view (**b**) *Fig* panorama; **un negro p.** a gloomy outlook

panorámica *nf Cin TV* panorama

panorámico, -a *adj* panoramic

panqueque *nm Am Culin* pancake

pantagruélico, -a *adj* gargantuan

pantaletas *nfpl CAm Carib Méx* panties, *Br* knickers

pantalla *nf* (**a**) *Cin TV Inform* screen; **la pequeña p.** the small screen; **llevar un libro a la p.** to make a book into a film □ **p. de cristal líquido** liquid crystal display; **p. de radar** radar screen; **p. plana** flat screen (**b**) *(de lámpara)* shade (**c**) *(de chimenea)* fireguard (**d**) *Fig (tapadera)* cover, front; **servir de p.** to act as a decoy (**e**) *Andes RP (abanico)* fan

pantalón *nm,* **pantalones** *nmpl* trousers, *US* pants; *Fam Fig* **bajarse los pantalones** to climb down; *Fam Fig* **llevar los pantalones** to wear the trousers *o US* pants □ **p. bombacho** cossack trousers; **p. corto** *(de niño)* short trousers *o US* pants; *Dep* shorts; **p. vaquero** jeans; *Méx* **pantalones de mezclilla** jeans; *Col, Cuba* **pantalones interiores** panties, *Br* knickers

pantano *nm Geog* (**a**) *(natural)* marsh, bog (**b**) *(artificial)* reservoir

pantanoso, -a *adj* (**a**) *Geog* marshy, boggy (**b**) *Fig (dificultoso)* thorny, difficult

panteísmo *nm Filos* pantheism

panteón *nm* (**a**) *Arquit (tumba)* pantheon, mausoleum □ **p. familiar** family vault (**b**) *(cementerio)* cemetery

pantera *nf Zool* panther

panti *nm Br* tights *pl, US* pantyhose *pl*

pantomima *nf* (**a**) *Teat* pantomime, mime (**b**) *Pey (farsa)* farce

pantorrilla *nf Anat* calf

pants *nmpl Méx (pantalón)* tracksuit bottoms *o US* pants; *(traje)* track *o* jogging suit *sing*

pantufla *nf* slipper

panty *(pl* **pantis)** *nm Br* tights *pl, US* pantyhose *pl*

panza *nf* (**a**) *Fam* belly, paunch (**b**) *(de vasija)* belly (**c**) *Anat Zool* belly

panzada *nf* (**a**) *(en el agua)* belly flop (**b**) *Fam (hartazgo)* bellyful

panzudo, -a *adj* potbellied, paunchy

pañal *nm* (**a**) *(para bebé) Br* nappy, *US* diaper; **un niño de pañales** a baby in nappies; *Fig* **estar en pañales** to be wet behind the ears (**b**) *Fig (origen)* origin, lineage; **ser de humildes pañales** to come from a humble background (**c**) **pañales** *(ropa)* baby clothes

pañería *nf* (**a**) *(tienda) Br* draper's (shop), *US* dry-goods store (**b**) *(persona)* draper

paño *nm* (**a**) *(tela)* cloth, material; *(de lana)* woollen *o US* woolen cloth; *(para polvo)* duster, rag; *(de cocina)* dishcloth; **traje de p.** woollen suit; *Fig* **conocerse el p.** to know one's stuff; *Fig* **paños calientes** half measures; *Fig* **ser el p. de lágrimas de algn** to give sb a shoulder to cry on; *Fam Fig* **ser del mismo p.** to be two of a kind (**b**) **paños** *(ropa)* clothes; **en p. menores** in one's underclothes (**c**) *(de pared)* wall, panel (**d**) *(de un cristal, vidrio)* mist, haze (**e**) *Arte* drapery (**f**) *Teat* **al p.** offstage

pañol *nm Náut* storeroom

pañoleta *nf* (**a**) *(de mujer)* shawl (**b**) *Taur* bullfighter's tie

pañuelo *nm (para la nariz)* handkerchief; *(para los hombros)* shawl; *Fig* **el mundo es un p.** it's a small world

papa¹ *nm* (**a**) *Rel* pope (**b**) *Fam (papá)* dad, daddy

papa² *nf* (**a**) *esp Am* potato □ **p. dulce** sweet potato (**b**) *Fam* **no saber ni p. (de algo)** not to have the faintest idea (about sth)

papá *nm Fam* dad, daddy, *US* pop □ **P. Noel** Santa (Claus), Father Christmas

papachar *vt Méx* to cuddle, pamper

papacho *nm Méx* caress, pat

papada *nf Anat* double chin

papado *nm Rel* papacy

papagayo *nm Orn* parrot

papal *adj Rel* papal

papamoscas *nm inv Orn* flycatcher □ **p. cerrojillo** pied flycatcher; **p. gris** spotted flycatcher

papanatas *nmf inv* sucker, twit

paparrucha *nf Fam* (piece of) nonsense

papaya *nf* papaya *o* papaw fruit

papayo *nm Bot* papaya *o* papaw tree

papear *vi Esp Ven Argot (comer)* to eat, *Br* nosh

papel *nm* (**a**) *(material)* paper; **p. cuadriculado** squared paper; **p. de música** music score (paper); **p. higiénico** toilet paper □ **p. carbón** carbon paper; **p. cebolla** onionskin; **p. de arroz** rice paper; **p. de carta** writing paper, stationery; **p. de China** India paper; **p. de estaño** aluminium *o* tin foil; **p. de estraza** brown paper; **p. de fumar** cigarette paper; **p. de lija** sandpaper; **p. de plata** aluminium *o* tin foil; **p. de seda** silk paper; **p. pintado** wallpaper; **p. secante** blotting paper (**b**) *(hoja)* piece *o* sheet of paper; **hagamos números sobre el p.** let's work it out on paper (**c**) *(carta, credencial)* document (**d**) *Fin* □ **p. moneda** paper money, banknotes *pl*; **p. de pagos** stamped paper; **p. del Estado** government bonds (**e**) *Cin Teat (carácter)* role, part; **esta actriz interpretó el p. de Julieta** this actress played the part of Juliet; *Fig* **el p. de la oposición en la política actual** the role of the opposition in today's politics; *Fig* **María hizo un buen p. en el examen oral** Maria did well in the oral exam (**f**) **papeles** *(documentos, identificación)* documents, identification papers

papela *nf Esp Fam* ID

papeleo *nm Fam* paperwork; **estoy con el p. de la matriculación** I'm going through the registration formalities

papelera *nf* (**a**) *(en despacho)* wastepaper basket *o Br* bin; *(en calle)* litter bin (**b**) *Inform (en Windows)* recycle bin; *(en Macintosh) Br* wastebasket, *US* trash can

papelería *nf* (**a**) *(tienda)* stationer's (**b**) *(material)* stationery (**c**) *(papeles)* sheaf of papers

papelero, -a 1 *adj* paper; **la industria papelera** the paper industry
2 *nm CSur (recipiente)* wastepaper basket *o Br* bin

papeleta *nf* (**a**) *(de rifa, empeño)* ticket; *(de votación)* ballot paper; *(de examen) (tema)* exam paper; *(resultados)* report (**b**) *Fam (dificultad)* tricky problem, difficult job; *(engorro)* drag; **¡menuda p.!** what an awful situation to be in!

papelón *nm* (**a**) *Fam (mal papel)* spectacle; **hacer un p.** to make a fool of oneself, be left looking ridiculous (**b**) *Andes Ven (azúcar)* brown-sugar loaf

papeo *nm Argot* grub

paperas *nfpl Med* mumps

papi *nm Fam* daddy, *US* pop

papila *nf Anat* papilla

papilla *nf* pap, mush; *(de niños)* baby food; *Fam* **echar la primera p.** to be as sick as a dog; *Fam* **estar hecho p.** to be shattered; *Fam* **hacer p. a algn** to make mincemeat of sb

papiro *nm* papyrus

papirotazo *nm* flick

papisa *nf Rel* female pope

papista *nmf* papist; **ser más p. que el papa** to be more Catholic than the Pope

papo *nm* (a) *(papada)* double chin (b) *(bocio)* goitre (c) *Orn (buche)* crop

papú *(pl* **papúes***) adj & nmf* Papuan

Papúa-Nueva Guinea *n* Papua New Guinea

paquebote *nm Náut* packet boat

paquete *nm* (a) *(grande)* package; *(caja)* packet; **un p. de cigarrillos/galletas** a packet of cigarettes/biscuits; *Fam Fig* **meter un p. a algn** to punish sb severely ❏ **p. bomba** parcel bomb; **p. postal** parcel (b) *(conjunto)* package ❏ *Fin* **p. de acciones** share package **p. de medidas** package of measures; **p. turístico** package holiday (c) *Fam (engreimiento)* airs and graces; **ir de p.** to ride pillion (d) *Fam (cosa fastidiosa)* **me ha tocado el p. de hacer ...** I've been lumbered with doing ;.. (e) *Esp Fam (genitales masculinos)* packet, bulge; **marcar p.** to draw attention to one's packet o bulge

paquetería *nf* (a) *(mercancía)* small goods; **empresa de p.** parcel delivery company (b) *RP Fam (elegancia)* smartness, elegance

paquidermo *nm Zool* pachyderm

Paquistán *n* Pakistan

paquistaní *adj & nmf* Pakistani

par 1 *adj* (a) *(igual)* equal (b) *Mat* even
    2 *nm* (a) *(pareja)* pair; *(dos)* couple; *(complementario)* peer; **un p. de terrones** a couple of lumps; **un p. de zapatos/guantes** a pair of shoes/gloves (b) *Mat* even number; **pares y nones** odds and evens (c) *(noble)* peer (d) *(locuciones)* **a la p.** *(juntos)* together; *(al mismo tiempo)* at the same time; *Fin* **a la p. que ...** as well as ...; **de p. en p.** wide open; *Fig* **con el corazón abierto de p. en p.** with open arms; *Fig* **sin p.** matchless

para *prep* (a) *(objeto indirecto)* for, to; **importante p. nosotros** important to us; **p. ti** for you (b) *(dirección)* to, towards; **p. arriba** upwards; **p. delante y p. detrás** backwards and forwards; **salió p. casa** he set off for home (c) *(finalidad)* to, in order to; **bueno p. la salud** good for your health; **p. eso no hace falta que venga** there's no need to come; **¿p. qué?** what for?; **¿p. qué lo quieres?** what do you want it for?; **p. que te compres un regalo** for you to get a present for yourself; **p. terminar antes** as to o in order to finish earlier (d) *(motivo)* **p. que no te enfadaras** so as not to annoy you; **¿p. qué has venido?** why did you come? (e) *(tiempo)* by, for; **hay p. rato** it will be some time before it's over; **¿p. cuánto tienes?** *(tardar)* how long will you be?; *(durar)* how long will it last you?; **p. entonces** by then; **p. la semana próxima** (by) next week; **p. Semana Santa** at Easter (f) *(comparación)* for, considering; **amable p. con todos** kind to everyone; **p. esta época del año** for this time of the year; **p. ser la primera vez** considering it's the first time (g) *(aptitud)* as; **Pedro vale p. arquitecto** Pedro would make a good architect (h) *(locuciones)* **dar p.** to be sufficient; **la comida da p. todos** there is enough food for everybody; **p. sí** to o for oneself; **hacer algo p. sí** to do sth for oneself; **leer un libro p. sí** to read a book to oneself; **ir p. viejo** to be getting old; **no es p. tanto** no need to make such a fuss; **no estoy p. nadie** I don't want to see anybody; **p. eso** for that reason; **p. mí, tenía que haberlo hecho** I think he should have done it

parabién *nm* congratulations *pl*; **dar el p. a algn** to congratulate sb

parábola *nf* (a) *Geom* parabola (b) *Rel* parable

parabólica *nf* satellite dish

parabólico, -a *adj* parabolic

parabrisas *nm inv Aut Br* windscreen, *US* windshield

paraca *nmf Argot* para, parachutist

paracaídas *nm inv* parachute; **lanzar(se)** o **tirar(se) en p.** to parachute

paracaidismo *nm* parachuting

paracaidista *nmf Dep* parachutist; *Mil* paratrooper

parachoques *nm inv* (a) *Aut* bumper, *US* fender (b) *Ferroc* buffer

parada *nf* (a) *(detención)* stop; **hacer p. en ...** to stop at ...; **p. en seco** dead stop ❏ **p. de autobús** bus stop; **p. de taxis** taxi stand o rank; **p. discrecional** request stop (b) *Ftb* save, catch, stop (c) *Andes RP Fam (engreimiento)* airs and graces

paradero *nm* (a) *(lugar)* whereabouts *pl*; **averiguar el p. de algn** to locate sb; **p. desconocido** whereabouts unknown (b) *(desenlace)* end; **tener mal p.** to come to a sticky end (c) *Chile Col Méx Perú (de autobús)* bus stop

paradigma *nm* paradigm

paradigmático, -a *adj* paradigmatic

paradisíaco, -a *adj* heavenly

parado, -a 1 *pp de* parar
    2 *adj* (a) *(inmóvil) (vehículo)* stationary, standing; *(persona)* still, motionless; *(máquina)* at rest; *(fábrica)* at a standstill; **se quedó p.** he remained motionless; *Fig* **salir bien/mal p.** to come off well/badly (b) *Esp (sin trabajo)* unemployed, out of work (c) *Am (de pie)* standing (d) *Chile PRico (orgulloso)* vain, conceited (e) *Esp (pasivo)* lacking in initiative; **ser muy p.** to lack initiative
    3 *nm,f Esp* unemployed person; **los parados** the unemployed *pl*

paradoja *nf* paradox

paradójico, -a *adj* paradoxical

parador *nm* roadside inn; *Esp* **p. nacional** o **de turismo** state-run hotel

paraestatal *adj Pol* semiofficial

parafarmacia *nf* alternative medicines o health remedies

parafernalia *nf* paraphernalia *pl*

parafina *nf Quím* paraffin

parafrasear *vt* to paraphrase

paráfrasis *nf inv* paraphrase

paraguas *nm inv* (a) *(para lluvia)* umbrella (b) *Fam* rubber

Paraguay *n* Paraguay

paraguaya *nf Bot* type of peach

paraguayo, -a *adj & nm,f* Paraguayan

paragüero *nm* umbrella stand

paraíso *nm* (a) *Rel & Fig* paradise ❏ *Fin* **p. fiscal** tax haven; **p. terrenal** heaven on earth (b) *Teat* gods *pl*, gallery

paraje *nm* spot, place

paralela *nf* (a) *Geom* parallel (line) (b) *Dep* **paralelas** parallel bars

paralelamente *adv* parallel; *(comparablemente)* comparably

paralelismo *nm* parallelism; *Fig* similarity

paralelo, -a 1 *adj* parallel; *Fig* **tu situación es paralela a la mía** your position is similar to mine
    2 *nm* parallel; *Elec* **estar en p.** to be in parallel

paralelogramo *nm Geom* parallelogram

parálisis *nm inv Med* paralysis ❏ **p. cerebral** cerebral palsy; **p. infantil** polio

paralítico, -a *adj & nm,f* paralytic

paralización *nf* (a) *Med* paralysis (b) *(detención)* halting, stopping

paralizador, -a *adj*, **paralizante** *adj* paralysing

paralizar [14] **1** *vt* to paralyse; *(circulación)* to stop; **tener una pierna paralizada** to be paralysed in one leg
    2 paralizarse *vpr* (a) *(pararse)* to become paralysed (b) *Fig* to come to a standstill

Paramaribo *n* Paramaribo

paramento *nm* (**a**) *(deoración)* decoration, adornment (**b**) *Arquit* face, facing

parámetro *nm Mat* parameter

paramilitar *adj* paramilitary

páramo *nm* (**a**) *Geog* bleak plain o plateau, moor (**b**) *Col Ecuad Ven (llovizna)* drizzle

parangón *nm Fml* comparison; **sin p.** incomparable

paraninfo *nm Univ* assembly hall, auditorium

paranoia *nf* paranoia

paranoico, -a *adj & nm,f* paranoiac, paranoid

paranormal *adj* paranormal

paraolímpico, -a *adj Dep* **juegos paraolímpicos** Paralympic games, Paralympics

parapente *nm* (**a**) *(deporte) (desde montaña)* paragliding, parapenting; *(a remolque de lancha motora)* parascending (**b**) *(paracaídas)* paraglider

parapetarse *vt* (**a**) *(protegerse)* to take shelter o cover (**b**) *Fig* to take refuge

parapeto *nm* (**a**) *(antepecho)* parapet (**b**) *(de defensa)* barricade

paraplejía *nf Med* paraplegia

parapléjico, -a *adj & nm,f* paraplegic

parar **1** *vt* (**a**) *(detener, interrumpir)* to stop; *Fam* **pararle los pies a algn** to put sb in his/her place (**b**) *Dep* to cut off, intercept; *(tiro)* to save; *(golpe)* to parry (**c**) *Am (levantar)* to raise

2 *vi* (**a**) *(detenerse, interrumpirse)* to stop; **p. de hacer algo** to stop doing sth; **¡para de llorar!** stop crying!; **sin p.** nonstop, without stopping; *Fam* **no p.** to be always on the go; **no paró hasta encontrarme** he didn't give up until he found me (**b**) *(alojarse)* to stay; **nunca he parado en este hotel** I have never stayed at this hotel (**c**) *(llegar)* **¿adónde quieres ir a p.?** what are you getting at?; **¿adónde vamos a ir a p.?** what is the world coming to?; **fue a p. a la basura** it ended up in the dustbin; **todo paró en nada** it all came to nothing (**d**) *Fam (estar)* to be; **nunca paro en casa** I'm never at home

3 **pararse** *vpr* (**a**) *(gen)* to stop; *(coche etc)* to come to a halt; **p. a pensar** to stop to think; **p. en seco** to stop dead, pull up sharply (**b**) *Am (ponerse en pie)* to stand up; *(levantarse de la cama)* to get up

pararrayos *nm inv* lightning conductor, *US* lightning rod

parasicología *nf* parapsychology

parasicológico, -a *adj* parapsychological

parasicólogo, -a *nm,f* parapsychologist

parasitario, -a *adj* parasitic, parasitical

parasitismo *nm* parasitism

parásito, -a **1** *adj* parasitic, parasitical

2 *nm* (**a**) *Biol* parasite; *Fig* **es un p. que vive a costa de sus amigos** he's a parasite who lives off his friends (**b**) **parásitos** *Rad* statics *sing*

parasitología *nf* parasitology

parasol *nm* sunshade, parasol

parcela *nf* (**a**) *(de tierra)* plot (**b**) *Fig (porción)* portion, share; **p. de poder** share of power

parcelación *nf* parcelling out, division into plots

parcelar *vt (tierra)* to parcel out

parche *nm* (**a**) *(de tela, goma)* patch; *(para rueda, vestido)* **poner un p. a** to patch (**b**) *(emplasto)* plaster (**c**) *Pey (chapuza)* botched up o slapdash job; **poner parches** to paper over the cracks (**d**) *Fam* **¡oído al p.!** beware!, look out!

parchís *nm Br* ludo, *US* Parcheesi®

parcial *adj* (**a**) *(no completo)* partial (**b**) *(partidario)* biased

parcialidad *nf* (**a**) *(tendenciosidad)* partiality (**b**) *(prejuicio)* bias, prejudice

parcialmente *adv* partially, partly

parco, -a *adj* (**a**) *(moderado)* sparing, moderate; **p. en palabras** reticent (**b**) *(escaso)* scarce; *(comida)* frugal, scanty

pardela *nf Orn* shearwater

pardiez *interj Anticuado* goodness me!, blimey!

pardillo, -a **1** *adj Esp Fam* (**a**) *(ingenuo)* naive (**b**) *(palurdo)* **ser p.** to be a *Br* bumpkin o *US* hick

2 *nm,f Esp Fam* (**a**) *(ingenuo)* naive person (**b**) *(palurdo) Br* bumpkin, *US* hick

3 *nm Orn* linnet

pardo, -a **1** *adj* greyish-brown, dull brown

2 *nm,f Carib RP (mulato)* mulatto

3 *nm (color)* greyish-brown, dull brown

pardusco, -a *adj* brownish

parecer¹ *nm* (**a**) *(aspecto)* appearance (**b**) *(opinión)* opinion; **cambiar** o **mudar de p.** to change one's mind; **según su p.** according to him

parecer² [46] **1** *vi* (**a**) *(semejar)* to seem, look (like); **a lo que parece** apparently; **así parece** so it seems; **aunque no lo parezca** incredible as it seems; **no parecía que fuera a nevar** it didn't look as if it would snow; **parece difícil** it seems o looks difficult; **parecía (de) cera** it looked like wax; *(uso impers)* **parece que no arranca** it looks as if it won't start; **parece mentira** I can't believe it (**b**) *(estar de acuerdo)* to agree; **como te parezca** whatever you like; **¿te parece?** is that okay with you?, what do you think? (**c**) *(opinar)* to think; **me parece bien/mal** I think it's a good/bad idea; **me parece que sí/no** I think/don't think so; **¿qué te ha parecido?** what did you think of it?

2 **parecerse** *vpr* to be alike, look like; **¿en qué se parecen A y B?** how are A and B alike?; **no se parecen** they're not alike; **se parecen a su madre** they look like their mother

parecido, -a **1** *pp de* parecer²

2 *adj* alike, similar; **ambos son parecidos** they're alike; **éste es muy p. al otro** this looks very much like the other one; **bien p.** good looking

3 *nm* likeness, resemblance; **tener p. con algn** to bear a resemblance to sb

pared *nf* (**a**) *Arquit* wall; *(montaña)* side; **vivir p. por medio** to live next door; *Fig* **entre cuatro paredes** within four walls, confined; *Fig* **las paredes oyen** walls have ears; *Fam Fig* **subirse por las paredes** to be seething (with anger) ❑ **p. maestra** main wall; **p. medianera** party wall (**b**) *Dep* one-two, wall pass

paredón *nm* (**a**) *(muro)* thick wall (**b**) *Fam (de fusilamiento)* execution wall; *Fig* **llevar a algn al p.** to put sb up against the wall

pareja *nf* (**a**) *(par)* pair; **hacer p.** to be two of a kind; **no encuentro la p. de este calcetín** I can't find the other sock; **por parejas** in pairs (**b**) *(de novios)* couple; *(de baile, juegos)* partner; *(hijo e hija)* boy and girl; **hacen buena p.** they make a nice couple, they're well matched ❑ **p. de hecho** unmarried couple (**c**) *(en póker)* pair; **doble p.** two pairs (**d**) *Fig* **correr parejas** o **a las parejas** *(venir juntos)* to come together; *(ser parecidos)* to be on a par

parejero, -a **1** *adj* (**a**) *Am Pey* hanger-on (**b**) *Méx Ven (amigo)* friend

2 *nm CAm Equit* good, fast race-horse

parejo, -a *adj* (**a**) *(parecido)* equal, similar, alike; **por p.** o **un p.** on a par (**b**) *(al mismo nivel)* on the same level, even

parentela *nf Fam* relations *pl*, relatives *pl*

parenteral *adj* **por vía p.** by injection

parentesco *nm* relationship, kinship

paréntesis *nm inv* (**a**) *(signo)* bracket; **abrir/cerrar p.** to open/close brackets; **entre p.** in parentheses *o* brackets (**b**) *Fig* break, interruption; *(digresión)* digression

pareo¹ *nm* wraparound skirt

pareo² *nm (aparejamiento)* pairing, coupling

parezco *indic pres véase* **parecer²**

pargo *nm* porgy

paria *nmf* pariah

parida *nf Esp Fam* **¡menuda p.!** what a lot of nonsense!; **decir paridas** to talk rubbish *o US* garbage

paridad *nf* (**a**) *(equivalencia)* equivalence, parity; *(semejanza)* similarity (**b**) *Fin* parity (of exchange)

parido, -a 1 *pp de* parir
2 *adj Fam* **bien p.** cool

parienta *nf Esp Fam* **la p.** *(cónyuge)* the old lady, *Br* the missus

pariente *nm* relative, relation

parihuela *nf* stretcher

paripé *nm Esp Fam* **hacer el p.** to pretend, put on an act

parir 1 *vi (mujer)* to give birth, have a baby; *(yegua)* to foal; *(vaca)* to calve; *(oveja)* to lamb; *Esp Vulg* **poner algo/a algn a p.** to slag sth/sb off, *US* badmouth sth/sb
2 *vt* to give birth to, bear

París *n* Paris

parisino, -a *adj* Parisian

paritario, -a *adj* joint; **comité p.** joint committee

parka *nf (abrigo)* parka

parking *nm* car park, *US* parking lot

párkinson *nm Med* Parkinson's disease

parlamentar *vi* to negotiate

parlamentario, -a 1 *adj* parliamentary
2 *nm,f* member of parliament, MP, *US* congressman

parlamentarismo *nm* parliamentary system

parlamento *nm* (**a**) *Parl* parliament ❑ **P. Europeo** European Parliament (**b**) *(discurso)* speech

parlanchín, -ina 1 *adj Fam* talkative, chatty
2 *nm,f Fam* chatterbox

parlante 1 *adj* **1** talking; **castellanoparlante** Castilian-speaking
2 *nm Am (altavoz)* speaker

parlar *vi*, **parlotear** *vi* to chat, chatter

parloteo *nm* prattle, chatter

parmesano, -a 1 *adj (queso)* Parmesan
2 *nm Culin* Parmesan cheese

parné *nm Esp Fam* dough, cash

paro *nm* (**a**) *(detención)* stop, stoppage ❑ *Med* **p. cardíaco** cardiac arrest; **p. laboral** industrial action; **p. técnico** *(de máquina)* down time (**b**) *Esp (desempleo)* unemployment; **estar en p.** to be unemployed; **cobrar el p.** to claim *o* receive unemployment benefit (**c**) *esp Am (huelga)* strike; *Am* **hacer p.** to strike

parodia *nf* parody

parodiar *vt* to parody

paroxismo *nm* paroxysm

parpadear *vi (ojos)* to blink, wink; *Fig (luz)* to flicker; *(estrellas)* to twinkle

parpadeo *nm (de ojos)* blinking; *Fig (luz)* flickering; *(estrellas)* twinkling

párpado *nm Anat* eyelid

parque *nm* (**a**) *(terreno)* park ❑ **p. de atracciones** funfair; **p. comercial** *Br* retail park, *US* shopping mall; *Esp* **p. de bomberos** fire station; **p. eólico** wind farm; **p. infantil** playground; **p. nacional** national park; **p. natural** nature reserve; **p. temático** theme park; **p. zoológico** zoological garden, zoo (**b**) *(conjunto de vehículos)* fleet ❑ **p. móvil** fleet (**c**) *Mil* **p. de artillería** artillery depot

parqué *nm Constr* parquet

parqueadero *nm Col Ecuad Pan Ven* car park, *US* parking lot

parquear *Bol Carib Col* **1** *vt* to park
2 parquearse *vpr* to park

parquedad *nf* (**a**) *(moderación)* moderation (**b**) *(escasez)* scantiness

parqueo *nm Bol Col Cuba* parking

parquet *nm véase* **parqué**

parquímetro *nm Aut* parking meter

parra *nf* grapevine; *Fam* **subirse a la p.** to hit the roof

parrafada *nf Fam* (**a**) *(monólogo)* dreary monologue (**b**) *(conversación)* chat; **echar una p.** to have a chinwag

párrafo *nm* paragraph

parral *nm* vine arbour *o US* arbor

parranda *nf Fam* (**a**) *(juerga)* spree; **ir(se) de p.** to go out on the town (**b**) *Mús* = group of singers or musicians

parrandear *vi* to go out on the town

parricida 1 *adj* parricidal
2 *nmf* parricide

parricidio *nm* parricide

parrilla *nf* (**a**) *Culin* grill, gridiron; **carne/pescado a la p.** grilled meat/fish (**b**) *Tec* grate (**c**) *Dep* **p. (de salida)** (starting) grid (**d**) *TV* programme schedule (**e**) *Am (en vehículo)* roof rack

parrillada *nf Culin* mixed grill

párroco 1 *adj* parish
2 *nm* **(cura) p.** parish priest

parroquia *nf* (**a**) *Rel* parish; *(iglesia)* parish church (**b**) *Fam (clientela)* customers *pl*

parroquial *adj* parochial, parish

parroquiano, -a *nm,f* (regular) customer

parsimonia *nf* (**a**) *(calma)* phlegm, calmness (**b**) *(moderación)* carefulness

parsimonioso, -a *adj* (**a**) *(calmado)* unhurried, calm (**b**) *(moderado)* careful, economical, sparing

parte 1 *nf* (**a**) *(pedazo)* part; *Ling* **p. de la oración** part of speech; **primera/última p.** first/last part (**b**) *(en una repartición)* share, portion; **quiero mi p.** I want my share; **yo he hecho mi p.** I've done my bit; *Fig* **la p. del león** the lion's share (**c**) *(lugar)* place, spot; *(zona)* area; *(dirección)* way; **en esta p. del país** in this part of the country; **en** *o* **por todas partes** everywhere; **en otra p.** somewhere else; **en una u otra p.** somewhere *o* other; **se fue por otra p.** he went a different *o* another way; *Fig* **esta discusión no lleva a ninguna p.** arguing like this won't get us anywhere (**d**) *(de un diálogo, lucha, contrato)* party, part; *Jur* party; **ambas partes están de acuerdo** both parties agree; **la parte contraria** opposing party; *Fig* **ser juez y p.** to be one's own judge and jury (**e**) *(bando)* side; **¿de qué p. estás?** which side are you on?; **ponerse de p. de** to side with (**f**) *(parentesco)* side; **por p. de mi madre/padre** on my mother's/father's side (**g**) *Teat (papel)* part, role (**h**) **partes** *Euf (genitales)* private parts (**i**) *(locuciones)* **a una y otra p.** on both sides; **de mi** *o* **por mi p.** as far as I am concerned; **de p. a p.** from one side to the other; **de p. de ...** on behalf of ...; **¿de p. de quién?** your name, please?; *Tel* who's calling?; *Tel* **llamo de p. de tu tío** I'm calling on your uncle's behalf; **en gran p.** to a large extent; **en p.** partly; **por partes** to proceed step by step; **la mayor p.** the majority; **llevar la mejor p.** to have the advantage; **llevar la peor p.** to be at a disadvantage; **llevarse la mejor p.** to come off best; **poner de su p.** to do one's best; **por otra p.**

on the other hand; **tomar p. en** to take part in
  2 *nm (informe)* report; **p. médico** medical bulletin *o* report; **p. metereológico** weather forecast *o* report

partenaire [parte'ner] *nmf (pareja artística)* partner

parterre *nf Esp* flowerbed

partición *nf (reparto)* division, sharing out; *(de herencia)* partition; *(de territorio)* partition; *Inform (de disco duro)* partition

participación *nf* **(a)** *(acto, actividad)* participation; *(pago)* contribution **(b)** *Fin (intereses)* interest, investment; *(acción)* share, *US* stock; **p. en los beneficios** profit-sharing **(c)** *(en lotería)* part of a lottery ticket **(d)** *(notificación)* notice, notification ❑ **p. de boda** wedding invitation

participante 1 *adj* participating
  2 *nmf* participant

participar 1 *vi* **(a)** *(colaborar, intervenir)* to take part, participate **(en** in**)**; **p. en la conversación** to take part in the conversation; **p. en un concurso** to enter a competition **(b)** *Fin* to have a share **(c)** *(compartir)* to share; **no participo de vuestro optimismo/vuestra opinión** I don't share your optimism/view
  2 *vt (notificar)* to notify

participativo, -a *adj* **es muy p. en clase** he participates a lot in class

partícipe 1 *adj* participating
  2 *nmf* participant; **hacer p. de algo** *(notificar)* to inform about sth; *(compartir)* to share sth; *Com Fin* **ser partícipes en un negocio** to be partners in business

participio *nm Ling* participle

partícula *nf* particle

particular 1 *adj* **(a)** *(concreto)* particular; **en este caso p.** in this particular case; **en p.** in particular; **nada de p.** nothing special **(b)** *(no público)* private, personal; **clase/casa p.** private class/home **(c)** *(raro)* peculiar
  2 *nmf (individuo)* private individual
  3 *nm (asunto)* subject, matter; **hablaremos sobre este p. más adelante** we shall deal with this subject in due course

particularidad *nf* **(a)** *(aspecto)* particularity, aspect **(b)** *(peculiaridad)* peculiarity

particularizar [14] **1** *vt* **(a)** *(caracterizar)* to distinguish, characterize **(b)** *(singularizar) (persona)* to single out **(c)** *(detallar)* to give details about
  2 particularizarse *vpr (caracterizarse)* to stand out; *(persona)* to distinguish oneself

particularmente *adv* specially

partida *nf* **(a)** *(salida)* departure **(b)** *(remesa)* batch, consignment; *(pedido)* consignment **(c)** *(juego)* game; **hacer** *o* **echar una p.** to have a game; *Fig* **jugar una mala p. a algn** to play a dirty trick on sb **(d)** *(persona) (banda)* party, gang; **p. de caza** hunting party **(e)** *Fin (entrada)* item; **contabilidad por p. doble** double-entry bookkeeping **(f)** *Jur (certificado)* certificate; **p. de nacimiento** birth certificate

partidario, -a 1 *adj* supporting; **ser/no ser p. de algo** to be for/against sth
  2 *nm,f* supporter, follower; **es p. del aborto** he is in favour of abortion

partidismo *nm* party spirit, bias

partidista *adj* biased, partisan

partido, -a 1 *pp de* **partir**
  2 *adj* split, divided
  3 *nm* **(a)** *Pol* party; **sistema de partidos** party system ❑ **p. político** political party **(b)** *Dep* game, *Br* match ❑ **p. amistoso** friendly game; **p. de vuelta** return match **(c)** *(provecho)* advantage; **sacar p. de** to profit from **(d)** *(resolución)* **tomar p. por** to side with **(e)** *(persona*

casadera) **ser un buen p.** to be a good catch, be eligible **(f)** *Esp* **p. judicial** = area under the jurisdiction of a court of first instance

partir 1 *vt* **(a)** *(dividir)* to split, divide; **pártelo en dos** split it in two **(b)** *(repartir)* to share out; *(distribuir)* distribute **(c)** *(romper, cortar) (frutos secos)* to crack; *(madera)* to cut; *(pan)* to break; *Fig* **me parte el corazón** it breaks my heart; **partirle la cara a algn** to smash sb's face in **(d)** *Fam (desbaratar)* to ruin, spoil; **p. a algn por la mitad** to mess things up for sb
  2 *vi* **(a)** *(marcharse)* to leave, set out *o* off; **p. para** *o* **con rumbo a algún lugar** to set off for somewhere **(b)** *(fecha, antecedente)* **a p. de** starting from; **a p. de ahora** from now on; **a p. de hoy** as of today; **si partimos de la base que** if we assume that
  3 partirse *vpr* to split (up), break (up); *Fam* **p. de risa** to split one's sides laughing

partisano, -a *nm,f Pol Mil* partisan

partitivo, -a *adj & nm Ling* partitive

partitura *nf Mús* score

parto *nm* **(a)** *(alumbramiento)* childbirth, delivery, labour, *US* labor; **estar de p.** to be in labour ❑ **p. natural** natural childbirth; **p. sin dolor** painless childbirth **(b)** *Fig* product, creation; **p. del ingenio** brainchild

parturienta *nf (de parto)* woman in labour *o US* labor; *(que ha parido)* woman who has just given birth

parva *nf Agr* unthreshed grain

parvedad *nf* **(a)** *(pequeñez)* littleness, smallness **(b)** *(escasez)* shortage, sparseness; **p. de medios** limited *o* scant means *pl*

parvo, -a *adj* **(a)** *(pequeño)* little, small **(b)** *(escaso)* sparse

parvulario *nm* nursery school, kindergarten

párvulo, -a *nm,f* infant

pasa *nf Culin* raisin; *Fam Fig* **estar hecho una p.** to be all shrivelled up ❑ **p. de Corinto** currant; *RP* **p. de uva** raisin

pasable *adj* passable, tolerable

pasacalle *nm Mús* lively march

pasada *nf* **(a)** *(paso)* passage, passing; *(con trapo)* rub, clean; **de p.** in passing; **hacer una p./varias pasadas** to pass once/several times; *Fam* **dale otra p.** give it another going *o* run over; *Fam* **deberías dar otra p. con la plancha a estos pantalones** you should give these trousers another run over with the iron **(b)** *Cost* row of stitches **(c)** *(jugarreta)* dirty trick; **hacer una (mala) p. (a algn)** to play a dirty trick (on sb) **(d)** *Esp Fam (exageración)* exaggeration; **eso es una p.** that's a bit much

pasadero, -a 1 *adj (pasable)* passable, tolerable
  2 *nm (piedra)* stepping stone

pasadizo *nm* corridor, passage

pasado, -a 1 *pp de* **pasar**
  2 *adj* **(a)** *(gen)* past; **los pasados días** the past few days; *Fam* **lo p. p. (está)** let bygones be bygones **(b)** *(último)* last; **el año/lunes p.** last year/Monday **(c)** *(anticuado)* dated, old-fashioned; **p. (de moda)** out of date *o* fashion **(d)** *(estropeado) (flor)* faded, withered; *(alimento)* bad; *Fig (noticia)* old hat **(e)** *Culin (cocido)* cooked; **lo quiero muy p.** I want it well done; **p. por agua** *(huevo)* boiled; *Fig (sin sustancia)* insubstantial **(f)** *(después)* after; **pasadas las dos** after two; **p. mañana** the day after tomorrow
  3 *nm* **(a)** *(gen)* past; *Ling* past (tense); **en el p.** in the past; **tu p. no me importa** I don't care about your background **(b)** **pasados** ancestors

pasador *nm* **(a)** *(colador)* colander, strainer **(b)** *(pestillo)* bolt, fastener **(c)** *(prenda)* pin, clasp; *(de corbata)* tiepin; *(para el pelo)* (hair) slide, hairpin; *(para los puños)* cufflink

pasaje *nm* **(a)** *esp Am (para viajar)* ticket **(b)** *(pasajeros)* passengers *pl* (**c**) *Lit Mús (fragmento)* passage (**d**) *(calle)* passage

pasajero, -a 1 *adj* passing, temporary; **aventura pasajera** fling
2 *nm,f* passenger

pasamano *nm*, **pasamanos** *nm inv (barra)* handrail; *(de escalera)* banister, bannister

pasamontañas *nm inv* Balaclava (hood)

pasante *nm (gen)* assistant; *Jur* clerk

pasantía *nf Com* (**a**) *(función)* assistantship (**b**) *(tiempo)* probationary period, apprenticeship

pasaporte *nm* passport; **hacerse** *o* **sacarse el p.** to get one's passport; **renovarse el p.** to renew one's passport; *Esp Fam* **dar (el) p. (a algn)** *(despedir)* to send (sb) packing; *(matar)* to bump (sb) off

pasapurés *nm inv Culin* potato masher

pasar 1 *vt* (**a**) *(gen)* to pass; *(objeto)* to pass on, give, hand over; **pásame la sal** pass (me) the salt (**b**) *(recado, mensaje)* to give; *(página)* to turn (**c**) *(trasladar)* to move; **hemos pasado la televisión al comedor** we have moved the TV set to the dining room; **p. a** *o* **en limpio** to make a clean copy of (**d**) *(introducir)* to insert, put through; *(colar)* to put through; **p. el hilo por el ojo de una aguja** to thread a needle; **p. la sopa por un colador** to strain the soup (**e**) *(cruzar)* to cross; *(barrera)* to pass through *o* over; *(límite)* to go beyond; **es imposible p. la frontera sin pasaporte** one cannot cross the border without a passport (**f**) *(padecer)* to suffer, endure; *(enfermedad)* to get over; **p. frío** to be cold; **p. hambre** to go hungry; *Fam* **pasarlas canutas** *o* **moradas** to go through hell, have a rough time (**g**) *(tiempo)* to spend, pass; **pasamos una semana solos** we spent a week on our own; **p. el rato** to kill time; **pasarlo bien/mal** to have a good/bad time (**h**) *(perdonar)* to forgive, tolerate; *(omitir)* to overlook; **¡esto no hay quien le pase!** nobody could stand for this!; **p. por alto** *o* **por encima** to miss; **pase por esta vez** I'll let you off this time once (**i**) *(sobrepasar)* to go beyond, be over; *(aventajar)* to surpass, beat; **(ella) ha pasado los treinta** she's over thirty; **su hermano ya le pasa 10 cm** his brother is already 10 cm taller than him (**j**) *Aut (adelantar)* to overtake, *US* pass (**k**) *(deslizar)* to run; **le pasó la mano por el pelo** he ran his fingers through his hair; **pásale un trapo** wipe it with a cloth; **p. el cepillo por el pelo** to pass a comb through one's hair (**l**) *Educ (examen)* to pass (**m**) *Cin (película)* to run, show
2 *vi* (**a**) *(ir, moverse)* to pass, go; **déjale p.** let him by; **el tren pasa por Burgos** the train goes via Burgos; **¿ha pasado el autobús?** has the bus gone by?; **ha pasado un hombre** a man has gone past; **pasa por casa mañana** come round to my house tomorrow; **p. de A a B** to go from A to B; **p. de largo** to go by (without stopping); *Fig* **aún podemos p. con menos** we can still manage with less; *Fig* **p. por encima de algn** to walk all over sb; *Fig* **p. por la cabeza** *o* **la imaginación** to cross one's mind; *Fig* **p. sin** to do without; *Fam* **ir pasando** to manage, get by; *Euf* **p. a mejor vida** to pass away (**b**) *(continuar)* **p. a** to go on to; **p. a ser** to become; **pasaron a discutir el siguiente punto** they went on to discuss the next issue (**c**) *(suceder)* to happen; **lo que pasa es que ...** the thing is that ...; **pase lo que pase** whatever happens, come what may; **¿qué le ha pasado?** what has happened to her?; **¿qué pasa aquí?** what's going on here?; **¿qué te pasa?** what's the matter?; **¿qué pasa?** *(¿qué ocurre?)* what's the matter?; *Fam (al saludar a algn)* how's it going?; *Méx Fam* **¿qué pasó?** *(¿qué tal?)* how's it going?; **¿y qué pasa?** so what? (**d**) *(caber)* to go through; **no pasará por la puerta** it won't go through the door *(entrar)* to come *o* go in; **hazle p.** ask him to come in; **pase, por favor** please come in (**f**) *(cesar)* to come to an end; **ya pasó lo peor** the worst is over (**g**) *(ser aceptado)* to pass, be accepted; **puede p.** it's OK, it'll pass (**h**) *Naipes* to pass (**i**)

(persona) **p. por** to be considered; **pasa por sabio** he is considered to be a wise man; **se hace p. por abogado** he passes himself off as a lawyer (**j**) *(exceder)* **p. de** to exceed, go beyond; **pasa de los cincuenta** he's over fifty; **pasan de cien** there are more than a hundred of them; **p. de moda** to go out of fashion; *Fig* **p. de la raya** to go too far; *Fam* **p. de castaño oscuro** to be too much (**k**) *(tiempo)* to pass, go by; **¡cómo pasa el tiempo!** how time passes! (**l**) *Fam (prescindir)* **(ella) pasa de estudiar** she isn't into studying; **pasa de todo** he doesn't give a damn; **yo paso** count me out

3 pasarse *vpr* (**a**) *(al enemigo)* to pass over (**a** to) (**b**) *(acabarse)* **se te ha pasado la hora** your time is over *o* up (**c**) *(dejar escapar)* to miss; **se me pasó la ocasión** I missed my chance *o* opportunity (**d**) *(gastar tiempo)* to spend *o* pass time; **pasárselo bien/mal** to have a good/bad time; **pasárselo en grande** to have a marvellous time; **se pasó la tarde durmiendo** he slept all afternoon (**e**) *(olvidar)* to forget; **se me pasó llamarle** I forgot to call him up (**f**) *(echarse a perder) (flores)* to wither; *(comida)* to go off (**g**) *Fam (excederse)* to go too far; **no te pases** don't overdo it; **no te pases con la sal** don't add too much salt; **p. de (la) raya** *o* **de rosca** to go too far, overstep the mark; **p. de listo** to be too clever by half; **se pasa de generoso** he's too generous (**h**) *(ir)* **p. por** to call in at; **pásate por la oficina en cuanto puedas** call in at the office as soon as you can

pasarela *nf* (**a**) *(puente)* footbridge; *(de barco)* gangway (**b**) *Teat* catwalk

pasatiempo *nm* pastime, amusement, hobby; **mi p. favorito es la lectura** my favourite pastime is reading

pascana *nf Andes (mesón)* inn

pascua *nf* (**a**) *Rel (fiesta cristiana)* Easter; *(fiesta judía)* Passover; **P. de Pentecostés** Whitsun; **P. de Resurrección** *o* **florida** Easter; *Fam* **hacer la p.** to mess things up (**b**) **pascuas** *(Navidad)* Christmas *sing*; **¡felices P.!** Merry Christmas!; *Fam* **de P. a Ramos** once in a blue moon; *Fam* **estar como unas p.** to be (as) happy as Larry, be over the moon; *Fam* **... y santas p.** ... and that's that; **lo hacemos y santas p.** we'll do it and that's that

pascual *adj* Easter; **cordero p.** Paschal lamb

pase *nm* (**a**) *(permiso)* pass, permit (**b**) *Esp (de una película)* showing (**c**) *DepTaur* pass

paseante *nmf* passer-by, stroller

pasear 1 *vt* (**a**) *(persona)* to take for a walk; *(perro)* to walk (**b**) *Fig (exhibir)* to show off (**c**) *CAm (negocio, hacienda)* to ruin
2 *vi* to go for a walk, take a walk
3 pasearse *vpr* to go for a walk

paseíllo *nm Taur* opening parade

paseo *nm* (**a**) *(a pie)* walk; *(en bicicleta, caballo)* ride; *(en coche)* drive; *(en barco)* trip; **dar un p.** to go for a walk *o* a ride; *Fam* **enviar** *o* **mandar (a algn) a p.** to send (sb) packing; *Fam* **¡mándalo todo a p.!** to hell with it all!; *Fam* **¡vete a p.!** get lost! (**b**) *(avenida)* promenade, avenue ❑ **p. marítimo** promenade

pasero *nm Méx* = person who, for a fee, helps people cross the border into the USA illegally

pasillo *nm* (**a**) *(en casa, edificio)* corridor; *(en avión)* aisle ❑ *Av* **p. aéreo** air corridor (**b**) *Col Ecuad Pan (baile, música)* = folk song and dance

pasión *nf* passion; *Rel* **la P.** the Passion; **tener p. por** to have a passion for

pasional *adj* passionate; **crimen p.** crime of passion

pasionaria *nf Bot* passion flower

pasito *adv* gently, softly

pasividad *nf* passivity, passiveness

pasivo, -a 1 *adj* passive; **clases pasivas** pensioners
2 *nm Com* liabilities *pl*

pasma *nf Esp Fam* police; **la p.** the fuzz *pl*

pasmado, -a 1 *pp de* pasmar

  2 *adj (asombrado)* astounded, astonished, amazed; *(atontado)* flabbergasted; **dejar p. a algn** to amaze sb; **quedarse p.** *(asombrado)* to be amazed; *(atontado)* to stand gaping

pasmar 1 *vt* (a) *(asombrar)* to astound, astonish, amaze; *(atontar)* to stun (b) *(enfriar)* to chill

  2 pasmarse *vpr* (a) *(asombrarse)* to be astounded *o* amazed (b) *(estar helado)* to be chilled

pasmarote *nm Fam* twit, dope

pasmo *nm* astonishment, amazement

paso¹ *nm* (a) *(acción)* passage, passing; **a su p. por la ciudad** when he was in town; **de p. tráete un tenedor** bring a fork on your way back; **el p. del tiempo** the passage of time; **estar de p.** to be just passing through; **'prohibido el p.'** 'no entry'; **salir al p. de algn** to go to meet sb; *Fig* **salir al p. de habladurías** to forestall gossip about oneself (b) *(pisada)* step, pace; *(modo de andar)* gait, walk; *(huella)* footprint; *(ruido de andar)* footstep; *(distancia)* pace; **caminar con p. firme** to walk with a firm step; **dar un p. en falso** *(tropezar)* to trip; *Fig* to make a wrong move; *Mil* **llevar el p.** to keep in step; **volver sobre sus pasos** to retrace one's steps; *Fig* **a dos pasos** a short distance away; *Fig* **a p. de tortuga** at a snail's pace; *Fig* **a pasos agigantados** by leaps and bounds; *Fig* **dar el primer p.** to take the first step; *Fig* **seguir los pasos de algn** to follow in sb's steps; *Fig* **seguir los pasos a algn** to keep track of sb (c) *(camino, pasaje)* passage, way; **¡abran p.!** clear the way!; **abrirse p.** to force one's way through; *Aut* **ceda el p.** *Br* give way, *US* yield; **cerrar el p.** to block the way □ *Ferroc* **p. a nivel** *Br* level *o US* grade crossing; **p. de cebra** zebra crossing; **p. elevado** *Br* flyover, *US* overpass; **p. de peatones** pedestrian crossing, *US* crosswalk; **p. subterráneo** *(para peatones) Br* subway, *US* underpass; *(para vehículos)* underpass (d) *Fig (avance)* advance, progress; **un gran p. adelante** an important step forward; **un mal p.** a wrong move (e) *(trámite) (gen pl)* step, move; **dar los pasos necesarios para ...** to take the necessary steps to ... (f) *Geog (de montaña)* mountain pass; *Mar* strait (g) *Rel* Easter procession float

paso, -a² *adj* dried; **ciruela pasa** prune; **uva pasa** raisin

pasodoble *nm Mús* paso doble

pasota *nmf Esp Fam* waster

pasotismo *nm Esp Fam* waster mentality

pasparse *vpr Andes RP (piel)* to get chapped

pasquín *nm Pol* subversive poster

pasta *nf* (a) *(masa)* paste □ **p. de dientes** toothpaste; **p. de madera** wood pulp; **p. dentífrica** toothpaste; **p. de papel** paper pulp (b) *Culin (para pan, pasteles)* dough; *(italiana)* pasta; *Fam* **ser de buena p.** to be good-natured; *Fam* **tener p. de** to have the makings of (c) *(pastelito)* shortcake *Br* biscuit *o US* cookie (d) *Esp Fam (dinero)* dough, bread; **soltar la p.** to cough up the money; **una p.** **(gansa)** a packet, a bomb, a pile

pastaflora *nf Culin* sponge cake

pastaje *nm Col Guat RP* pasture, grass

pastar *vt & vi* to graze, pasture

pastel *nm* (a) *Culin (dulce)* cake; *(de carne, fruta)* pie (b) *Arte* pastel; **dibujo al p.** pastel drawing (c) *Fam Pey (intriga)* shady deal; **descubrir el p.** to spill the beans

pastelería *nf* (a) *(pasteles)* cakes *pl*, pastries *pl*; *(dulces)* confectionery (b) *(tienda)* confectioner's (shop)

pastelero, -a *nm,f* (a) *(cocinero)* pastrycook, confectioner (b) *Pey* crook, shady character

pasteurización *nf*, **pasterización** *nf* pasteurization

pasteurizar [14], *vt*, **pasterizar** [14] *vt* to pasteurize

pastiche *nm* (a) *Arte* pastiche (b) *Fam (chapuza)* botch(-up)

pastilla *nf* (a) *Farm* tablet, pill; *Fam (anticonceptivo)* pill; **pastillas para la tos** cough drops (b) *(de jabón)* bar; *(de chocolate, turrón)* piece (c) *Esp Fam* **a toda p.** at full speed

pastizal *nm* grazing land, pasture

pasto *nm* (a) *(acción)* grazing; *(pastizal)* grazing land, pasture (b) *(sitio)* pasture, *Am (césped)* lawn, grass (c) *Fig (alimento)* food; **es p. de la murmuración** gossip thrives on it; **p. espiritual** spiritual food *o* nourishment; **ser p. de** to be prey to; **ser p. de las llamas** to go up in flames; **su nombre es p. de los periódicos** her name is headline material (d) *Fig* **a todo p.** in great quantities; **había comida a todo p.** there was a pile of food

pastón *nm Esp Fam* **vale un p.** it costs a fortune *o Br* a bomb

pastor, -a 1 *nm,f Agr (hombre)* shepherd; *(mujer)* shepherdess □ **perro p.** sheepdog

  2 *nm Rel (protestante)* pastor, minister

pastoral 1 *adj* pastoral

  2 *nf* (a) *Lit Rel* pastoral (b) *Mús* pastorale

pastorear *vt (pastar)* to graze, pasture

pastoreo *nm* shepherding

pastoril *adj Lit* pastoral

pastoso, -a *adj* (a) *(blando)* pasty; *(arroz)* sticky (b) *(seco)* dry; **tener la boca pastosa** to have a furry tongue (c) *(voz)* mellow

pasudo, -a *Carib Col Méx* **1** *adj (pelo)* curly

  2 *nm,f (persona)* curly-haired person

pata *nf* (a) *Zool (de animal)* leg; *(con garra)* paw; *(pezuña)* hoof (b) *(de mueble)* leg; *Fig* **patas arriba** upside down (c) *Fam (de persona)* leg; **a la p. coja** hopping on one foot; **a p.** on foot; **de cuatro patas** on all fours; *Fig* **estirar la p.** to kick the bucket; *Fig* **mala p.** bad luck; *Fig* **meter la p.** to put one's foot in it; *Fig* **p. de gallo** crow's foot (d) *Fam (despropósito)* silly remark, clanger; *Fam* **a la p. (la) llana** without formalities (e) *Orn (hembra)* duck (f) *Chile Fam* **patas** *(poca vergüenza)* cheek *sing*

patada *nf (puntapié)* kick, stamp; *(paso)* step; **dar patadas en el suelo** to stamp one's feet; **dio una p. al balón** he kicked the ball; *Fig* **en dos patadas** in a jiffy; *Fam* **a patadas** tons of; *Fam* **dar la p. a algn** to give sb the boot; *Fam* **me da cien patadas** I can't stand the sight of ...; *Fam* **sentar como una p. en el estómago** to be like a kick in the teeth; *Fam* **tratar a algn a patadas** to push *o* shove sb around

patagón, -ona *adj & nm,f* Patagonian

Patagonia *n* la P. Patagonia

patalear *vi* (a) *(bebé)* to kick (b) *(de rabia)* to stamp one's feet (with rage) (c) *Fam (protestar)* to kick up a fuss

pataleo *nm* (a) *(de bebé)* kicking (b) *(de rabia)* stamping (c) *Fam (protesta)* angry protest; *Fam* **derecho al p.** right to protest

pataleta *nf Fam* fit, tantrum

patán *nm Pey Br* bumpkin, *US* hick

patasca *nf* (a) *Pan Perú (tumulto)* row, quarrel (b) *Andes Arg Culin* pork and maize *o US* corn stew

patata *nf Esp* potato; *Fam* **ser una p.** to be a duffer □ **patatas fritas** *(de sartén) Br* chips, *US* French fries *o (de bolsa) Br* crisps, *US* (potato) chips; **patatas nuevas** *o* **tempranas** new potatoes

patatal *nm*, **patatar** *nm* potato field

patatero, -a *adj* (a) *(de patatas)* potato (b) *Fam (burdo)* coarse, rough; **un rollo p.** a real bore

patatín: que si patatín que si patatán *loc adv Fam* this, that and the other, and so on and so forth

patatús *nm inv Fam* dizzy spell, queer turn; **me dio un p.** it made my head spin

paté *nm Culin* pâté

patear 1 *vt* (**a**) *(pelota, persona)* to kick; *(pisotear)* to stamp on (**b**) *Fam (tratar mal)* to trample on, treat roughly (**c**) *Teat (abuchear)* to boo, jeer (**d**) *Fam (andar)* to trudge about *o* around

  2 *vi (patalear)* to stamp (one's foot with rage)

  3 patearse *vpr* (**a**) *Fam (andar)* to walk, hoof it (**b**) *(despilfarrar)* to blow; **se pateó la herencia de su tío** he blew all his uncle's fortune

patena *nf* paten; *Esp Fam* **limpio como una p.** as clean as a new pin

patentado, -a *adj* patented

patentar *vt* to patent

patente 1 *adj (evidente)* patent, obvious; **hacer p.** to show clearly

  2 *nf* (**a**) *(autorización)* licence, *US* license, grant, warrant; *(de invención)* patent; *Fig* **p. de corso** total impunity (**b**) *CSur (matrícula) Br* number plate, *US* license plate

pateo *nm* (**a**) *(pataleo)* stamping (**b**) *Teat (abucheo)* boo, booing, jeer, jeering

patera *nf (embarcación)* small boat, dinghy

paternal *adj* paternal, fatherly

paternalismo *nm* paternalism

paternalista *adj* paternalistic

paternidad *nf* paternity, fatherhood

paterno, -a *adj* paternal; **abuelo p.** grandfather on the father's side, paternal grandfather

patético, -a *adj* pathetic, moving

patetismo *nm* pathos *sing*

patibulario, -a *adj* sinister, harrowing

patíbulo *nm* scaffold, gallows *pl*

paticojo, -a *Fam* **1** *adj* lame, gammy-legged

  2 *nm,f* lame person

patidifuso, -a *adj Fam* dumbfounded, flabbergasted; **quedarse p.** to be flabbergasted

patilla *nf* (**a**) *(de gafas)* arm (**b**) **patillas** *(pelo)* sideboards, *US* sideburns

patín *nm* (**a**) *(gen)* skate; *(de ruedas)* roller skate; *(de hielo)* ice skate; *(patinete)* scooter (**b**) *Esp (embarcación)* pedalo

pátina *nf* patina

patinador, -a *nm,f* skater

patinaje *nm Dep* skating ▫ **p. artístico** figure skating; **p. sobre hielo/ruedas** ice-/roller skating

patinar *vi* (**a**) *(con patines)* to skate; *(sobre ruedas)* to roller-skate; *(sobre hielo)* to ice-skate (**b**) *(deslizarse)* to slide; *(resbalar)* to slip; *(vehículo)* to skid (**c**) *Fam (equivocarse)* to put one's foot in it, slip up

patinazo *nm* (**a**) *(resbalón)* skid (**b**) *Fam (equivocación)* blunder, boob; **dar** *o* **pegar un p.** *(patinar)* to skid; *Fam (equivocarse)* to make a boob

patinete *nm* scooter

patio *nm* (**a**) *(de casa)* yard, courtyard, patio; *(de recreo)* playground; *Esp Fam* **¿cómo está el p.?** what's up? (**b**) *Teat* pit ▫ **p. de butacas** stalls *pl*, *US* orchestra

patitieso, -a *adj Fam* (**a**) *(asombrado)* dumbfounded, flabbergasted; **dejar p.** to astound; **quedarse p.** to be flabbergasted *o* dumbfounded (**b**) *(de frío, miedo)* numb, stiff (**c**) *(estirado)* stuck-up, strait-laced

patituerto, -a *adj Fam* bandy-legged

patizambo, -a *adj Fam* knock-kneed

pato *nm Zool* duck; *Fam* **pagar el p.** to carry the can ▫ **p. (macho)** drake; **p. mandarín** mandarin duck; **p. salvaje** *o* **silvestre** wild duck

patochada *nf* blunder, bloomer, boob

patógeno, -a *adj* pathogenic

patojo, -a *nm,f Guat (niño)* kid, youngster

patología *nf* pathology

patológico, -a *adj* pathological

patólogo, -a *nm,f* pathologist

patoso, -a *adj Esp Fam* clumsy, awkward

patota *nf Perú RP Fam* street gang

patraña *nf* lie, fabrication, story

patria *nf* fatherland, native country ▫ **p. adoptiva** country of adoption; **p. celestial** heaven; **p. chica** one's home town *o* region; **madre p.** motherland

patriarca *nm* patriarch

patriarcado *nm* patriarchy

patriarcal *adj* patriarchal

patricio, -a *adj & nm,f* patrician

patrimonial *adj* patrimonial, hereditary

patrimonio *nm* *(bienes)* wealth; *(heredado)* patrimony, inheritance ▫ **p. cultural** cultural heritage; **p. nacional** national wealth

patrio, -a *adj* (**a**) *(nativo)* native; **suelo p.** native soil (**b**) *(paterno)* paternal; *Jur* **patria potestad** paternal authority

patriota *nmf* patriot

patriotería *nf Pey* chauvinism, jingoism

patrioterismo *nm Pey* jingoism, chauvinism

patriotero, -a *Pey* **1** *adj* chauvinistic, jingoistic

  2 *nm,f* chauvinist, jingoist

patriótico, -a *adj* patriotic

patriotismo *nm* patriotism

patrocinador, -a 1 *adj* sponsoring

  2 *nm,f* sponsor

patrocinar *vt* to sponsor, patronize

patrocinio *nm* sponsorship, patronage; **bajo el p. de** sponsored by

patrón, -ona 1 *nm,f* (**a**) *(jefe)* boss; *(amo)* master; *(ama)* owner (**b**) *Esp (de pensión) (hombre)* landlord; *(mujer)* landlady (**c**) *Náut* captain, skipper; *Fig* **donde hay p., no manda marinero** the boss is the boss (**d**) *Rel* patron saint

  2 *nm* (**a**) *Cost Téc* pattern; *Fig* **cortado por el mismo p.** cast in the same mould (**b**) *(medida)* standard; **p. oro** gold standard

patronal 1 *adj* (**a**) *Pol* employers'; **cierre p.** lockout; **clase p.** managerial class (**b**) *Rel* of a patron saint; **fiesta p.** patron saint's day

  2 *nf (asociación)* employers' association; *(dirección)* management

patronato *nm (dirección)* board of trustees; *(con fines benéficos)* trust

patronazgo *nm* patronage

patronear *vt Náut* to skipper

patronímico, -a 1 *adj* patronymic

  2 *nm* patronymic, surname

patrono, -a *nm,f* (**a**) *(jefe)* boss; *(empresario)* owner, employer (**c**) *Rel (santo)* patron saint

patrulla *nf* (**a**) *Mil* patrol; **estar de p.** to be on patrol; **estar de p. en** *o* **por una zona** to patrol an area ▫ **coche p.** patrol car (**b**) *(grupo)* group, band; **p. de rescate** rescue party

patrullar 1 *vt* to patrol

  2 *vi* to be on patrol

patrullero, -a *adj* **1** *patrol, patrolling*
  2 *nm,f Náut* patrol boat; *Av* patrol plane

paulatinamente *adv* gradually, little by little

paulatino, -a *adj* gradual; **de un modo.p.** gradually

pauperización *nf* impoverishment

paupérrimo, -a *adj superl de* **pobre** extremely poor, poverty-stricken

pausa *nf* (**a**) *(descanso)* pause, break; *Mús* rest; **a pausas** at intervals; **sin p.** continuously (**b**) *(calma)* calmness; **con p.** calmly, unhurriedly

pausado, -a *adj* unhurried, calm

pauta *nf* (**a**) *(regla)* ruler; *(para escribir)* writing guide; *(línea)* line, guideline; *Mús* staff (**b**) *Fig (ejemplo)* example, model; **marcar la p.** to set the example o pattern

pautado, -a *adj* ruled, lined; *Mús* **papel p.** ruled paper

pava[1] *nf* (**a**) *Orn* turkey hen; *Fam* **pelar la p.** to court ❏ **p. real** peahen (**b**) *Esp Argot (colilla)* butt (**c**) *Fam (mujer sosa)* bore, dull woman (**d**) *CAm (flequillo) Br* fringe, *US* bangs

pava[2] *nf Arg* kettle

pavada *nf RP Fam (tontería)* stupid thing

pavear *vi* (**a**) *Chile Perú (burlarse)* to (play a) joke (**b**) *RP (pelar la pava)* to court, woo (**c**) *Ecuad Pan (faltar a clase)* to play truant

pavesa *nf* (**a**) *(chispa)* spark (**b**) *(ceniza)* cinder

pavimentación *nf (de calles, carreteras)* paving; *(de una habitación)* flooring

pavimentar *vt (calle, carretera)* to pave; *(habitación)* to floor, lay flooring in

pavimento *nm (de calle, carretera)* paving, pavement; *(de habitación)* flooring

pavo *nm* (**a**) *Orn* turkey; *Fam* **estar en la edad del p.** to be growing up; *Fam* **no ser moco de p.** to be nothing to scoff at; *Fam* **subírsele el p. a algn** to blush ❏ **p. real** peacock (**b**) *Fam (tonto)* twit, ninny

pavón *nm* (**a**) *Orn (pavo real)* peacock (**b**) *Ent* peacock butterfly (**c**) *Metal* bluing

pavonearse *vpr Fam* to show off, strut

pavoneo *nm Fam* showing off, strutting

pavor *nm* terror, dread, panic

pavoroso, -a *adj* terrible, dreadful, frightful

paya *nf Chile* = improvised folk song

payacate *nm Méx Perú* shawl

payador, -a *nm,f CSur* = singer of improvised songs

payar *vi CSur* = to sing improvised songs

payasada *nf* clownish thing to do o say; **hacer payasadas** to act the clown

payasear *vi Am* to act the clown

payaso *nm* clown; **hacer el p.** to act the clown

payés, -esa *nm,f* Catalan o Balearic peasant

payo, -a *adj Esp* non-Gipsy

paz *nf (gen)* peace; *(sosiego)* peacefulness; *(tratado)* peace treaty; **descansar en p.** to rest in peace; **estar en p.** to be at peace; *Fig* to be quits o even; **firmar la p.** to sign a peace treaty; **hacer las paces** to make (it) up; **poner p.** to make peace; **todo lo que quiero es un poco de p.** all I want is some peace and quiet; *Fam* **¡déjame en p.!** leave me alone!

pazguatería *nf* (**a**) *(estupidez)* silliness, stupidity (**b**) *(mojigatería)* prudishness

pazguato, -a **1** *adj* (**a**) *(estúpido)* silly, stupid (**b**) *(mojigato)* prudish
  2 *nm,f* (**a**) *(estúpido)* simpleton, twit (**b**) *(mojigato)* prude

pazo *nm* Galician country house

PBI *nm Perú RP (abrev de* **producto bruto interno***)* GDP

PBN *nm Am (abrev de* **producto bruto nacional***)* GNP

PC *nm (abrev de* **personal computer***)* PC

PCE *nm Pol (abrev de* **Partido Comunista de España***)* Spanish Communist party

PCUS [pe'kus] *nm Pol (abrev de* **Partido Comunista de la Unión Soviética***)* CPSU

PD *(abrev de* **posdata***)* PS

pe *nf* = name of the letter P in Spanish; *Fam* **de pe a pa** from A to Z

peaje *nf Aut* toll

peal *nm Am* lasso

peana *nf* (**a**) *(pedestal)* pedestal, stand (**b**) *Fam (pie)* foot

peatón *nm* pedestrian ❏ **paso de peatones** pedestrian crossing, *US* crosswalk

peatonal *adj* pedestrian; **calle p.** pedestrian street

pebete, -a *nm,f RP* child

peca *nf* freckle

pecado *nm Rel* sin; **hacer** o **cometer un p.** to sin, commit a sin; *Fig* **en el p. lleva la penitencia** every sin carries its own punishment; *Fam* **de mis pecados** of mine; **esta hija de mis pecados** this daughter of mine; *Fam* **sería un p. tirar la comida** it would be a sin to throw the food away ❏ **p. capital** o **mortal** deadly sin; **p. original** original sin

pecador, -a *Rel* **1** *adj* sinful
  2 *nm,f* sinner

pecaminoso, -a *adj Rel* sinful

pecar [59] *vi Rel* to sin; *Fig* **peca de salado** it's a bit too salty; *Fig* **p. por defecto** to fall short of the mark; *Fig* **p. por exceso** to go too far

pecera *nf* fishbowl, fishtank

pechar[1] **1** *vi Fam (apechugar)* **p. con el peor trabajo** to take on the worst job
  2 *vt CSur Fam (dinero)* to scrounge

pechar[2] *vt Andes RP* to shove, push

pechera *nf Cost (de camisa)* (shirt) front; *(de vestido)* front, bosom

pecho *nm* (**a**) *(tórax)* chest; *(de mujer)* breast, bosom, bust; *(de animal)* breast; *Fig (interior)* heart; **dar el p. (a un bebé)** to breast-feed (a baby); **tomar el p.** to be breast-fed; *Fig* **a p. descubierto** defenceless; *Fig* **abrir el p. (a algn)** to open up one's heart (to sb); *Fig* **tomar(se) (algo) a p.** to take (sth) to heart; *Fam* **a lo hecho, p.** it's no use crying over spilt milk; *Fam* **echarse (algo) entre p. y espalda** to tuck (food) away; *Fam* **partirse el p.** *(esforzarse)* to break one's back, slave away; *(reírse)* to split one's sides with laughter (**b**) *Am (en natación)* breaststroke; **nadar p.** to do the breaststroke

pechuga *nf* (**a**) *(de ave)* breast (**b**) *Fam (de mujer)* boob (**c**) *Andes CAm Ven Fam (descaro)* cheek, nerve

pechugón, -ona *adj Fam* big-breasted

pécora *nf Fam* **(mala) p.** *(arpía)* witch, bitch; *(prostituta)* whore, tramp

pecoso, -a *adj* freckled, freckle-faced

pectoral **1** *adj* (**a**) *Anat* pectoral, chest (**b**) *Farm* cough; **jarabe p.** cough syrup
  2 *nm Farm* pectoral, cough medicine

pecuario, -a *adj* livestock; **actividad pecuaria** livestock raising

peculiar *adj* peculiar, characteristic

peculiaridad *nf* peculiarity, characteristic

peculio *nm* one's own money o savings

pecuniario, -a *adj* pecuniary

pedagogía *nf* pedagogy

pedagógico, -a *adj* pedagogic, pedagogical

pedagogo, -a *nm,f* pedagogue, teacher, educator

pedal *nm* (a) *Téc* pedal ❏ *Aut* **p. de embrague** clutch pedal; **p. de freno** footbrake, brake pedal (b) *Esp Fam (borrachera)* bender; **coger un p.** to get sloshed o plastered

pedalear *vi* to pedal

pedaleo *nm* pedalling, *US* pedaling

pedanía *nf* district

pedante 1 *adj* pedantic
  2 *nmf* pedant

pedantería *nf* pedantry

pedazo *nm* piece, bit; **a pedazos** in pieces; **caerse a pedazos** to fall apart o to pieces; **hacer pedazos** to break o tear to pieces, smash (up); *Fig* **hacer pedazos (a algn)** to tear (sb) to pieces; *Fam* **esta chica es un p. de pan** that girl is a pet; *Fam Ofens* **es un p. de animal** o **de alcornoque** he's a blockhead

pederasta *nm* pederast

pederastia *nf* pederasty

pedernal *nm Min* flint; *Fig* **duro como un p.** hard as a rock

pedestal *nm* pedestal; *Fig* **colocar a algn en un p.** to put sb on a pedestal

pedestre *adj* (a) *(a pie)* on foot, walking (b) *Fig (vulgar)* ordinary, pedestrian

pediatra *nmf Med* paediatrician, *US* pediatrician

pediatría *nf Med* paediatrics *sing*, *US* pediatrics *sing*

pediátrico, -a *adj* paediatric, *US* pediatric

pedicuro, -a *nm,f Med Br* chiropodist, *US* podiatrist

pedida *nf Esp* engagement party ❏ **pulsera de p.** engagement bracelet

pedido, -a *pp de* **pedir**
  2 *nm* (a) *Com* order; **hacer un p.** to place an order (b) *Am (petición)* request; **atender un p.** to grant a request

pedigrí *(pl* **pedigríes)** *nm Zool* pedigree

pedigüeño, -a 1 *adj* demanding, insistent
  2 *nm,f* pest, nuisance

pedir [47] *vt* (a) *(gen)* to ask (for); **no se puede p. más** you couldn't ask for more; **p. a una chica en matrimonio** to ask for a girl's hand in marriage; **p. algo a algn** to ask sb for sth; **p. prestado** to borrow; **piden mucho dinero** they're asking (for) a lot of money; **te pido que te quedes** I'm asking you to stay; *Fig* **p. cuentas** to ask for an explanation; *Fam* **p. peras al olmo** to ask for the moon (b) *Com (encargar)* to order; *(en un bar, restaurante)* to order; **no se qué p.** I don't know what to have (c) *Com (precio)* to ask; **¿cuánto piden por esta casa?** how much are they asking for the house? (d) *(mendigar)* to beg; **p. limosna** to beg (e) *Fig (requerir)* to need, require; **esta casa pide a gritos que la restauren** this house is badly in need of repair; **esta enfermedad pide reposo** this illness requires rest

pedo *Fam* **1** *nm* (a) *(ventosidad)* fart, wind; **tirarse un p.** to fart (b) **agarrarse** o *Esp* **cogerse un p.** *(emborracharse)* to get smashed o *Br* pissed (c) *RP* **al p.** *(inútilmente)* for nothing; **de p.** *(de casualidad)* by chance, *Br* by a fluke
  2 *adj inv Esp Méx Fam* **estar p.** to be smashed o *Br* pissed

pedofilia *nf* paedophilia, *US* pedophilia

pedófilo, -a *nm,f* paedophile, *US* pedophile

pedorrera *nf Vulg* string of farts

pedorreta *nf Vulg* raspberry

pedrada *nf* (a) *(lanzamiento)* throw of a stone; *(golpe)* blow from a stone; **a pedradas** (by) throwing stones; **matar a algn a pedradas** to stone sb to death; **pegar una p. a algn** to throw a stone at sb; **rompió la ventana de una p.** he smashed the window with a stone (b) *Fig (expresión mordaz)* wounding remark

pedrea *nf* (a) *(pelea)* stone fight (b) *Esp (en lotería)* small prizes *pl*

pedregal *nm* stony o rocky ground

pedregoso, -a *adj* stony, rocky

pedregullo *nm RP* gravel

pedrera *nf* stone quarry

pedrería *nf* precious stones *pl*, gems *pl*

pedrisco *nm Meteor* hailstorm; *(lluvia de piedras)* shower of stones

pedrusco *nm Fam* rough stone, piece of stone

peeling ['pilin] *(pl* **peelings)** *nm* face mask o pack

pega *nf* (a) *(adhesivo)* glue (b) *Esp Fam (obstáculo)* snag, difficulty; *(objeción)* objection; **a todo le encuentra** o **pone pegas** she finds fault with everything (c) *(falso)* **de p.** fake (d) *Andes Cuba Fam (trabajo)* job

pegada *nf* (a) *Ten* stroke, hit (b) *Box* punch; **tener buena p.** to pack a hard punch

pegadizo, -a *adj* (a) *(pegajoso)* sticky (b) *Mús (canción)* catchy

pegado, -a 1 *pp de* **pegar**
  2 *adj* (a) *(adherido)* stuck (b) *Culin (quemado)* burnt
  3 *nm Med (emplasto)* patch, sticking plaster

pegadura *nf Col Ecuad (burla)* trick

pegajoso, -a *adj* (a) *(pegadizo)* sticky (b) *Fig (persona)* tiresome, hard to get rid of

pegamento *nm* glue

pegapega *nf Col RP* birdlime

pegar¹ [38] **1** *vt* (a) *(adherir)* to stick; *(con pegamento)* to glue; *(póster, cartel)* to put up, fix (up); *Cost (botón)* to sew on; *Fam* **no pegó ojo** he didn't sleep a wink (b) *(arrimar)* to put against, lean against; **pegó la silla a la puerta** he put the chair against the door (c) *Fam Med (contagiar)* to give; *Fig* to give, communicate; **me ha pegado sus manías** I've caught his bad habits (d) *(fuego)* to light (e) *Inform* to paste
  2 *vi* (a) *(adherirse)* to stick (b) *(armonizar)* to match, go; **el azul no pega con el verde, el azul y el verde no pegan** blue and green don't go together; *Fig* **ella no pegaría aquí** she wouldn't fit in here (c) *(estar próximo)* to be next (**a** to) (d) *(sospechar)* *Fam* **me pega que ...** I have a hunch that ...
  3 **pegarse** *vpr* (a) *(adherirse)* to stick; **se ha pegado** it has stuck (b) *Culin (quemarse)* to get burnt (c) *(arrimarse)* to get close; **pégate a mí** stay close to me (d) *Fam Fig* to stick; **p. como una lapa** to stick like a limpet (e) *Med (enfermedad)* to be catching o contagious; *Fig (melodía, acento)* to be catchy; **¿el sarampión se pega?** are measles contagious?

pegar² [38] **1** *vt* (a) *(golpear)* to hit; **p. una bofetada a algn** to slap sb (b) *(dar, realizar)* **p. un grito** to shout; **p. un salto** to jump; **p. un susto a algn** to give sb a fright; **p. un tiro** to shoot (c) *Fam* **dale que te pego** on and on
  2 *vi (golpear)* to hit, beat; **p. duro** to hit hard; **p. en** to strike (against); **p. en el blanco** to hit the target; **pegar en la pared con un palo** to hit the wall with a stick; *Fig* **¡cómo pega el sol!** isn't the sun beating down?; *Fig* **p. fuerte** *Fam (estar de moda)* to be all the rage; *(vino)* to be strong stuff
  3 **pegarse** *vpr* (a) *(pelearse)* to fight (b) *Fam (darse)* to have, get; **p. la buena vida** to live like a king; **p. un hartón de trabajar** to slave o slog away; **p. un tiro** to shoot oneself; **p. una comilona** to have a feast (c) *Esp Fam* **pegársela a algn** to trick o deceive sb; **se la pega a su marido** she's cheating on her husband

pegatina *nf Esp* sticker

pego *nm Esp Fam* **dar el p. a algn** to take sb for a ride, fool sb; **es una baratija pero da el p.** it's a cheap imitation but it looks like the real thing

pegote *nm* (a) *(emplasto)* patch, sticking plaster (b) *Fam (chapuza)* mess, botch-up (c) *Fam (gorrón)* sponger, hanger-on (**d**) *Esp Fam* **tirarse** *o* **marcarse un p.** to tell a tall tale

pegual *nm CSur (cincha)* girth

pehuén *nm Bot* monkey puzzle tree

peinado, -a 1 *pp de* **peinar**
   2 *adj (pelo)* combed; *(relamido)* affected, overdone
   3 *nm* (**a**) *(estilo)* hairdo, hairstyle (**b**) *Tex* combing (**c**) *Argot (policial)* door-to-door search, sweep

peinador, -a 1 *nm,f (persona)* hairdresser
   2 *nm* (**a**) *(bata)* dressing gown, robe (**b**) *Bol Chile Cuba (tocador)* dressing table

peinar 1 *vt* (**a**) *(pelo)* to comb, do; *Fam* **p. canas** to be going grey (**b**) *Argot (policía)* to comb; **la policía peinó el barrio en busca de los atracadores** the cops combed the area for the bank robbers
   2 peinarse *vpr* to comb one's hair

peine *nm* (**a**) *(para pelo)* comb; *Esp Fam Fig* **¡te vas a enterar de lo que vale un p.!** you've got it coming (to you)! (**b**) *Tex* reed

peineta *nf* ornamental comb

peinilla *nf Am* type of cane knife

p.ej. *(abrev de* **por ejemplo)** for example

pejiguera *nf Esp Fam* drag, nuisance

Pekín *n* Peking, Beijing

pela *nf Esp Antes Fam* peseta; **tiene muchas pelas** he has a lot of money, he's loaded

pelada *nf Fam* (**a**) *CSur (calva)* blunder (**b**) *Andes Cuba RP* **la P.** *(muerte)* the Grim Reaper

peladero *nm Andes Ven* barren land, wasteland

peladilla *nf* (**a**) *(dulce)* sugared almond (**b**) *(guijarro)* small pebble

pelado, -a 1 *pp de* **pelar**
   2 *adj* (**a**) *(sin pelo)* hairless; *(calvo)* bald (**b**) *(piel, fruta)* peeled (**c**) *(terreno)* bare (**d**) *(hueso)* clean (**e**) *(cantidad)* bare; *(número)* round (**f**) *Fam (arruinado)* broke, penniless
   3 *nm,f CAm Méx Fam (persona humilde)* common person, *Br* pleb
   4 *nm Esp Fam (corte de pelo)* (short) haircut

peladura *nf* peeling

pelagatos *nmf inv Fam* poor devil, nobody

pelaje *nm* (**a**) *Zool* fur, hair (**b**) *Fam Pey (apariencia)* looks *pl*, appearance (**c**) *Fam (clase)* class, kind, ilk

pelambre *nm* (**a**) *(pelo)* mop (of hair), long *o* thick hair (**b**) *(pelaje)* fur, hair

pelambrera *nf Fam* mop (of hair), long *o* thick hair

pelandusca *nf Fam* whore, tart

pelapatatas *nm inv Esp* potato peeler

pelar 1 *vt* (**a**) *(cortar el pelo)* to cut the hair of; *(fruta)* to peel; *(mariscos)* to shell; *(ave)* to pluck; *Fam* **hace un frío que pela** it's brass monkey weather; *Fam Fig* **ser duro de p.** to be a hard nut (to crack) (**b**) *Fam (robar)* to fleece (**c**) *Méx Fam (hacer caso)* **no me pela** he doesn't pay any attention to me
   2 pelarse *vpr* (**a**) *(cortarse el pelo)* to get one's hair cut (**b**) *(levantarse la piel)* to peel; *Fam* **p. de frío** to freeze (**c**) *Fam* **pelárselas** to do sth fast; **corre que se las pela** he runs like mad (**d**) *Vulg (masturbarse)* **pelársela** to wank, jerk off

peldaño *nm* step; *(de escalera de mano)* rung

pelea *nf (gen)* fight; *(riña)* row, quarrel; **buscar p.** to look for trouble □ **p. de gallos** cockfight

peleado, -a 1 *pp de* **pelear**
   2 *adj* **estar p. (con algn)** not to be on speaking terms (with sb)

pelear 1 *vi (gen)* to fight; *(reñir)* to quarrel; *Fig* to struggle (**por** to)

2 pelearse *vpr* (**a**) *(gen)* to fight; *(reñir)* to quarrel (**b**) *(enemistarse)* to fall out

pelele *nm* (**a**) *(muñeco)* straw puppet; *Fig* puppet; **Juan es solo un p. de Pepe** Juan is just Pepe's yes man (**b**) *Esp (prenda)* rompers *pl*

peleón, -ona *adj* (**a**) *(pendenciero)* quarrelsome, aggressive (**b**) *Fam (vino)* cheap

peletería *nf* (**a**) *Ind* furrier's; *(tienda)* fur shop (**b**) *(pieles)* furs *pl*

peletero, -a 1 *adj* fur; **comercio p.** fur trade
   2 *nm,f* furrier

peliagudo, -a *adj* difficult, tricky, hairy; **pregunta peliaguda** tricky question

pelícano *nm Orn* pelican

pelicorto, -a *adj* short-haired

película *nf* (**a**) *Cin* movie, *Br* film; **echar** *o* **poner una p.** to show a movie; *Fam* **de p.** fabulous □ **p. del Oeste** Western; **p. de miedo** *o* **terror** horror movie *o Br* film; **p. en color/en blanco y negro** colour/black-and-white movie *o Br* film; **p. muda** silent movie *o Br* film; **p. sonora** talkie, talking picture (**b**) *Fot* film (**c**) *(capa)* film (**d**) *Fam (historia increíble)* (tall) story;

peligrar *vi* to be in danger, be threatened; **hacer p.** to endanger, jeopardize

peligro *nm (gen)* danger; *(riesgo)* risk; **con p. de ...** at the risk of ...; **corre (el) p. de ...** to run the risk of ...; **estar en p.** to be in danger; **fuera de p.** out of danger; **poner en p.** to endanger

peligrosidad *nf* danger, dangerousness

peligroso, -a *adj* dangerous, risky

pelillo *nm Esp Fam* **echar pelillos a la mar** to bury the hatchet

pelirrojo, -a 1 *adj* red-haired, ginger-haired
   2 *nm,f* redhead

pelleja *nf* (**a**) *(piel)* skin, hide (**b**) *Fam (persona delgada)* skinny person (**c**) *Fam (prostituta)* whore

pellejerías *nfpl Andes Fam* difficulties

pellejo *nm* (**a**) *(piel)* skin; *Fam* **no quisiera estar en su p.** I wouldn't want to be in his shoes (**b**) *(odre)* wineskin (**c**) *Fam (vida)* life, skin, neck; **arriesgar** *o* **jugarse el p.** to risk one's neck

pelliza *nf* fur jacket

pellizcar [59] *vt* to pinch, nip

pellizco *nm* pinch, nip

pelmazo, -a *Fam* **1** *adj* annoying, tiresome
   2 *nm,f* bore, pain

pelo *nm* (**a**) *(gen)* hair; **a p.** *(en equitación)* bareback; *Fam (desnudo)* stark naked; **cortarse el p.** *(uno mismo)* to cut one's hair; *(en la peluquería)* to have one's hair cut; **llevar el p. largo** to have long hair; *Fig* **no tiene ni un p. de tonto** he's no fool; *Fig* **Sonia no tiene pelos en la lengua** Sonia's very outspoken; *Fig* **soltarse el p.** to let one's hair down; *Fig* **tomar el p. a algn** to pull sb's leg, take the mickey out of sb; *Fig* **traído por los pelos** far-fetched; *Fig* **venir al p.** *(ser oportuno)* to come at right the moment; *(ser útil)* to come in handy; *Fam* **con pelos y señales** in full detail; *Fam* **faltó un p. para que ganase** he very nearly won, he lost by an inch; *Fam* **hasta los pelos** up to here; *Fam* **por los pelos** *o* **un p.** by the skin of one's teeth; *Fam* **se me pusieron los pelos de punta** it gave me the creeps; *Fam* **un hombre de p. en pecho** a tough guy (**b**) *Zool (de animal)* fur, coat, hair (**c**) *Tex (de una tela)* nap, pile (**d**) *(cerda)* bristle

pelón, -ona 1 *adj* (**a**) *(sin pelo)* hairless, bald (**b**) *(arruinado)* broke, skint
   2 *nm RP (fruta)* nectarine

Pelona *nf CAm Col Méx Fam* **la P.** *(la muerte)* the Grim Reaper

pelota 1 nf (**a**) (gen) ball; **jugar a la p.** to play ball; Fam **devolver la p.** to give tit for tat; Esp Fam **hacer la p. a algn** to toady to sb, butter sb up ❑ **p. de fútbol** football; **p. de tenis** tennis ball (**b**) Dep pelota (**c**) Fam (cabeza) nut (**d**) Vulg **pelotas** (testículos) balls; **pillar a algn en p.** to catch sb on the hop; **en p.** Br starkers, US butt-naked; **dejar a algn en p.** to fleece sb; **estoy hasta las p.** I'm pissed off
2 nmf Esp Fam (pelotillero) toady, fawner; **este tío es un p.** he's a real toady

pelotari nm Dep pelota player

pelotazo nm (**a**) (con pelota) kick o throw of a ball (**b**) Esp Fam (copa) swig

pelotear vi Dep to kick a ball around; Ten to knock up

peloteo nm Dep kickabout; Ten knock-up

pelotera nf Fam quarrel, row

pelotilla nf Fam (**a**) Esp **hacer la p. (a algn)** to fawn on (sb) (**b**) (de suciedad) = ball of grime rubbed from skin

pelotillero, -a nm,f Esp Fam toady, fawner

pelotón nm (**a**) Mil squad, party; **p. de ejecución** firing squad (**b**) Fam (grupo) small crowd, bunch (**c**) (amasijo) bundle

pelotudear vi RP Fam to mess about o around

pelotudo, -a adj RP Fam damn stupid

peluca nf wig; **llevar p.** to wear a wig

peluche nf (**a**) (material) plush (**b**) (muñeco) cuddly toy; **osito de p.** teddy bear

peluco nm Argot watch

peludo, -a 1 adj hairy, furry
2 nm RP (**a**) (animal) armadillo

peluquear Am **1** vt to cut the hair of
2 peluquearse vpr to have one's hair cut

peluquería nf (de señoras) hairdresser's (shop); (de caballeros) barber's (shop); **ir a la p.** to go to the hairdresser's/the barber's

peluquero, -a nm,f (de señoras) hairdresser; (de caballeros) barber

peluquín nm toupee; Esp Fam **ni hablar el p.** not on your life

pelusa nf, **pelusilla** nf (**a**) (de tela) fluff; (de planta) down (**b**) Esp Fam (celos) jealousy (among children)

pelvis nf inv Anat pelvis

pena nf (**a**) (castigo) punishment, penalty; **bajo** o **so p. de** under penalty of ❑ **p. de muerte** o **capital** death penalty (**b**) (tristeza) grief, sorrow; **me da p. verte así** it makes me sad to see you like that; **Fig sin p. ni gloria** unmarked (**c**) (lástima) pity; **¡qué p.!** what a pity! (**d**) (dificultad) hardships pl, trouble; **a duras penas** with great difficulty; **merecer** o **valer la p.** to be worth it; **merece la p. intentarlo** it's worth (giving it) a try; **no merece la p.** it's not worth the bother (**e**) CAm Carib Col Méx (vergüenza) embarrassment; **me da p.** I'm embarrassed about it

penacho nm (**a**) (de ave) crest, tuft (**b**) Mil (de plumas) plume

penado, -a 1 pp de **penar**
2 nm,f convict

penal 1 adj penal; Jur **código p.** penal code
2 nm prison, jail, gaol

penalidad nf (gen pl) hardships pl, troubles pl

penalista nmf criminal lawyer

penalización nf sanction, penalization; Dep penalty

penalizar [14] vt to penalize

penalti nm, **penalty** nm Dep penalty; Esp Fam **casarse de p.** to have a shotgun wedding

penar 1 vt to punish

2 vi to be in torment, suffer; **p. por algo/algn** to pine for sth/sb

penca nf Bot fleshy leaf

penco nm (**a**) Fam (jamelgo) nag, jade (**b**) Fam Fig ass, twit

pendejada nf Am muy Fam (acto) Br bloody o US goddamn stupid thing; (dicho) Br bloody o US goddamn stupid remark

pendejear vi Méx Fam to mess about o around

pendejo, -a nm,f (**a**) Méx Fam (cobarde) wet, coward (**b**) Am muy Fam (tonto) jerk, Br tosser (**c**) RP muy Fam Pey (adolescente) spotty teenager
2 nm muy Fam (pelo) pubic hair

pendencia nf quarrel, fight

pendenciero, -a adj quarrelsome, argumentative

pender vi (**a**) (colgar) to hang (**de** from, **sobre** over); Fig **mi vida pende de un hilo** my life is hanging by a thread; Fig **pende sobre nosotros una grave amenaza** a serious threat is hanging over us (**b**) (estar pendiente) to be pending

pendiente 1 adj (**a**) (colgante) hanging (**de** from) (**b**) (por resolver) pending; Educ **asignatura p.** failed subject; Comp **p. de pago** unpaid; **tiene una asignatura p.** he has to resit one exam; **estar p. de** (esperar) to be waiting for; (vigilar) to be on the lookout for
2 nm (joya) earring
3 nf slope; (de un tejado) pitch; **en p.** sloping; **esta p. es muy pronunciada** this slope is very steep; **hacer p.** to slope

pendón nm (**a**) (bandera) banner; Hist pennon (**b**) Esp Fam Pey (mujer) floozy; (hombre) layabout, good-for-nothing

pendonear vi Esp Fam to gad about

pendular adj pendular

péndulo nm pendulum

pene nm Anat penis

penetrabilidad nf penetrability

penetrable adj penetrable

penetración nf (**a**) (gen) penetration (**b**) Fig (perspicacia) insight, perception

penetrante adj (**a**) (gen) penetrating; (frío, voz) piercing; (herida) deep (**b**) Fig (inteligencia) sharp, acute

penetrar 1 vt (gen) to penetrate; (substancia) to permeate; Fig (intención, significado) to grasp, understand; **p. un misterio** to get to the bottom of a mystery
2 vi (gen) to penetrate (**en** in); (entrar) to go o get (**en** in); Fig **frío que penetra en los huesos** cold that gets into one's bones; Fig **un grito penetró en la noche** a scream pierced the night

penicilina nf Med penicillin

península nf Geog peninsula

peninsular 1 adj peninsular
2 nmf person from the (Iberian) Peninsula

penique nm (moneda) penny; **dos peniques** two pence

penitencia nf (**a**) Rel penance; **como** o **en p.** as a penance; **hacer p.** to do penance (**b**) Fam pain, bind; **esto más que un trabajo es una p.** this job is like doing penance

penitenciaría nf prison

penitenciario, -a adj penitentiary, prison

penitente adj & nmf Rel penitent

penoso, -a adj (**a**) (lamentable) sorry, distressing (**b**) (laborioso) laborious, difficult

pensado, -a 1 pp de **pensar**
2 adj thought, thought out; **bien p., creo que me quedaré** on reflection, I think I'll stay; **bien p., no está tan mal** all things considered, it isn't that bad; **en el**

momento menos **p.** when least expected; **este trabajo está poco p.** this paper is badly thought out; **mal p.** evilminded; **tener p.** to have in mind

pensador, -a *nm,f* thinker

pensamiento *nm* (**a**) *(facultad)* thought; **adivinar los pensamientos de algn** to read sb's mind (**b**) *(mente)* mind; **no me pasó por el p.** it didn't cross my mind; *Fig* **como el p.** like a flash; *Fig* **ni por p.** not in the least (**c**) *(máxima)* saying, motto (**d**) *Bot* pansy

pensar [3] *vi* (**gen**) to think (**en** of, about, **sobre** about, over); **¿en qué/quién piensas?** what/who are you thinking about?; **no pensé en ello** I didn't think of it; **p. para sí** *o* **consigo** to think to oneself; *Fig* **sin p.** *(con precipitación)* without thinking; *(involuntariamente)* involuntarily

  2 *vt* (**a**) *(gen)* to think; *(opinar)* to think about; *(considerar)* to think over *o* about; **esto da mucho que pensar** this is food for thought; **(me) lo pensaré** I'll think about it; **pensándolo bien** *o* **mejor** on second thoughts; **p. bien/mal de algn** to think well/badly of sb; **piénsalo bien** think it over; **pienso que ...** I think that ...; **¿qué piensas de esto?** what do you think about this?; **sólo con pensarlo** just the thought of it; *Fam* **¡ni pensarlo!** not on your life! (**b**) *(proponerse)* to intend; **pienso quedarme** I plan to stay (**c**) *(concebir)* to make; **p. un plan** to make a plan; **p. una solución** to find a solution

pensativo, -a *adj* pensive, thoughtful; **estar p.** to be deep in thought

Pensilvania *n* Pennsylvania

pensión *nf* (**a**) *(dinero)* pension, allowance; **cobrar la p.** to draw one's pension ❑ **p. alimenticia** alimony; **p. vitalicia** life annuity (**b**) *(régimen de alojamiento)* board and lodging ❑ **media p.** partial board; **p. completa** full board (**c**) *(residencia)* boarding house (**d**) *(hotel)* guesthouse

pensionado *nm Esp Educ* boarding school

pensionista *nmf* (**a**) *(del estado)* pensioner (**b**) *Esp Educ* boarder

pentaedro *nm* pentahedron

pentagonal *adj* pentagonal

pentágono *nm* pentagon

pentagrama *nm*, **pentágrama** *nm Mús* staff, stave

Pentecostés *nm sing Rel* (**a**) *(cristiano)* Pentecost, Whitsun, Whitsuntide; **domingo de P.** Whit Sunday (**b**) *(judío)* Pentecost

penúltimo, -a *adj & nm,f* next to the last, penultimate

penumbra *nf* penumbra, half-light

penuria *nf* (**a**) *(escasez)* scarcity, shortage (**b**) *(pobreza)* poverty, penury

peña¹ *nf* *(roca)* rock, crag

peña² *nf* (**a**) *Esp Fam (de amigos)* crowd (**b**) *Ftb* pool

peñascal *nm* rocky place

peñasco *nm* rock, crag

peñón *nm* rock ❑ **el P. de Gibraltar** the Rock of Gibraltar

peón *nm* (**a**) *(trabajador)* unskilled labourer *o US* laborer ❑ **p. agrícola** farmhand; **p. de albañil** hod carrier, hodman; **p. caminero** roadman (**b**) *Ajedrez* pawn; *(damas)* man (**c**) *(peonza)* top

peonada *nf* day's work

peonaje *nm* group of labourers *o US* laborers

peonía *nf Bot* peony

peonza *nf* *(spinning)* top

peor 1 *adj* (**a**) *(comparativo)* worse; **A es p. que B** A is worse than B (**b**) *(superlativo)* worst; **el p. de los dos** the worse (of the two); **el p. de los tres** the worst of the three; **en el p. de los casos** if the worst comes to the worst; **éste**

es el **p. de todos** this is the worst of all; **lo p.** the worst (thing)

  2 *adv* (**a**) *(comparativo)* worse; **anda p. que antes** he doesn't walk as well as he used to; **así es p.** that's worse; **cada vez p.** worse and worse; **¡p. para mí o ti!** too bad!; **que p.** worse, still; **¡tanto p.!** so much the worse (**b**) *(superlativo)* worst; **es el que p. canta** he is the one who sings the worst

pepa *nf Am salvo RP (pepita)* pip; *(hueso)* stone, *US* pit

pepenar *vt CAm Méx (recoger)* to collect, gather; *(juntar)* to pick up

pepinazo *nm Fam* (**a**) *(explosión)* blast, explosion (**b**) *Ftb (disparo)* cannonball shot

pepinillo *nm Bot* gherkin

pepino *nm Bot* cucumber; *Fam* **me importa un p.** I don't give a hoot

pepita *nf* (**a**) *(de fruta)* pip, seed (**b**) *(de metal)* nugget

pepito *nm Esp Culin* meat sandwich

pepitoria *nf Culin* fricassee; **pollo en p.** fricassee of chicken

pepona *nf* large paper doll

peque *nm Fam* kid, little 'un

pequeñez *nf* (**a**) *(de tamaño)* smallness, littleness (**b**) *(nimiedad)* trifle; **se preocupa por pequeñeces** he's very nitpicking (**c**) *(mezquindad)* meanness, pettiness; **p. de miras** narrow-mindedness

pequeño, -a 1 *adj* (**a**) *(gen)* small, little (**b**) *(joven)* young (**c**) *(bajo)* short

  2 *nm,f* child; **de p.** as a child; **María es la pequeña** Maria is the youngest; *Fig* **dejar p.** to put in the shade

pequeñoburgués, -esa 1 *adj* petit bourgeois

  2 *nm,f (hombre)* petit bourgeois; *(mujer)* petite bourgeoise

Pequín *n* Peking

pequinés, -esa 1 *adj* Pekinese

  2 *nm,f (persona)* Pekinese

  3 *nm Zool* **(perro) p.** Pekinese

pera 1 *nf* (**a**) *Bot* pear; *Fam* **partir peras con algn** to fall out with sb; *Fam* **poner las peras al cuarto** to give a ticking off; *Esp Fam* **ser la p.** to take the cake ❑ **p. de agua** juicy pear (**b**) *Elec (interruptor)* pearshaped switch (**c**) *(perilla)* goatee (**d**) *(de líquido, aire)* bulb

  2 *adj Esp Fam* posh; **niño p.** spoilt upper-class brat

peral *nm Bot* pear tree

peraltar *vt* (**a**) *Arquit* to stilt (**b**) *(carretera)* to bank

peralte *nm* banking

perca *nf (pez)* perch

percal *nm Tex* percale; *Fig* **conocer el p.** to know one's stuff

percance *nm* mishap, setback; **el viaje discurrió sin p.** the trip went off without a hitch

per cápita *adj & adv* per capita

percatarse *vpr* to notice, realize; **no se percata de nada** he doesn't notice anything

percebe *nm* (**a**) *Zool* (goose) barnacle (**b**) *Fam (persona)* fool, idiot

percepción *nf* perception; **p. extrasensorial** extrasensory perception

perceptible *adj* (**a**) *(sensible)* perceptible (**b**) *Fin* receivable, payable

perceptivo, -a *adj* perceptive

percha *nf (sostén)* perch; *(colgador)* (coat) hanger; *(fijo en la pared)* rack; **cuelga el abrigo en la p.** hang your coat up; *Fam Fig* **tener buena p.** to be well-built

perchero *nm* clothes rack

percherón, -ona *nm,f Zool* shire horse

percibir *vt* (**a**) *(notar)* to perceive, notice; **no se percibía ningún ruido** no noise could be heard (**b**) *(cobrar)* to collect; **percibo un sueldo muy bajo** I'm on a low wage

perclorato *nm Quím* perchlorate

percusión *nf* percussion

percusionista *nmf Mús* percussionist

percusor *nm*, **percutor** *nm (de arma de fuego)* firing pin, hammer

perdedor, -a 1 *adj* losing

  2 *nm,f* loser

perder [64] **1** *vt* (**a**) *(gen)* to lose; **dar algo por perdido** to give sth up as lost; **p. agua** to leak; **p. de vista** to lose sight of; **p. el color** to turn o go pale; **p. el juicio** o **la razón** to go out of one's mind; **p. la esperanza** to lose hope; *Fig* **p. los estribos** to fly off the handle (**b**) *(dejar escapar)* to miss; **ayer volví a p. el tren** yesterday I missed the train again (**c**) *(malgastar)* to waste; **p. tiempo** to waste time (**d**) *(ser la perdición)* to be the ruin o downfall of; **la ambición le perdió** ambition was her downfall

  2 *vi* (**a**) *(gen)* to lose; **echar (algo) a p.** to spoil (sth); **salir perdiendo** to come off worst (**b**) *(desmejorar)* to go off; *(en salud)* to get worse; *(en valor)* to devaluate; **la abuela ha perdido mucho en pocos meses** Grandma has been getting worse over the last few months (**c**) *Tex (desteñirse)* to fade

  3 perderse *vpr* (**a**) *(extraviarse)* to get lost; **me perdí en la oscuridad** I got lost in the darkness (**b**) *(cosas)* to be lost; **nunca se me pierde nada** I never lose anything; **se ha perdido un cuchillo** a knife is missing (**c**) *(no asistir)* to miss; **no te lo pierdas** don't miss it; **te has perdido una buena cena** you missed a good dinner (**d**) *(desaprovecharse)* to go to waste; **con este calor la comida se pierde enseguida** food goes off quickly in this heat (**e**) *Fig (desvanecerse)* to die out; **p. de vista** *(desaparecer)* to fade o disappear into the distance; *(extenderse)* to stretch out as far as the eye can see (**f**) *(entregarse a los vicios)* to be a lost cause; **en cuanto descubrió los placeres de la vida se perdió** as soon as he discovered life's pleasures he was a lost cause; **p. por** to be crazy about

perdición *nf* (**a**) *(ruina moral o material)* undoing, ruin, downfall; **el orgullo será su p.** his pride will be his undoing (**b**) *Rel* damnation, perdition

pérdida *nf* (**a**) *(extravío)* loss; **la p. de algn** the loss of sb; *Esp* **no tiene p.** you can't miss it; **p. del conocimiento** loss of consciousness (**b**) *(de tiempo, esfuerzos)* waste; **intentar convencerlo es una p. absoluta de tiempo** it would be a complete waste of time to try to persuade him (**c**) *(de un fluido)* leak, leakage (**d**) *Fin* loss; **vender con p.** to sell at a loss (**e**) **pérdidas** *Mil* losses (**f**) **pérdidas** *(flujo)* wastage *sing*

perdidamente *adv* madly, desperately

perdido, -a 1 *pp de* **perder**

  2 *adj* (**a**) *(extraviado)* lost; **aquí está el cuchillo p.** here's the lost knife; **lo podemos dar por p.** it is as good as lost; *Fig* **p. en sus pensamientos** lost in thought; *Fig* **un lugar p.** an isolated place (**b**) *(animal, bala)* stray (**c**) *(acabado)* finished; **si me encuentran estoy p.** if they find me I'm done for (**d**) *Esp Fam (sucio)* filthy; **lo dejaron todo p. de barro** the whole place was covered in mud (**e**) *Fam (completo)* absolute; **idiota p.** hopelessly stupid; **loco p.** mad as a hatter (**f**) *(enamorado)* crazy; **estar p. por algn** to be crazy o nuts about sb

  3 *nm,f (depravado)* rake; *(mujer)* whore

perdigón *nm* (**a**) *(proyectil)* pellet; **perdigones** pellets, shot *sing* (**b**) *Orn* young partridge

perdigonada *nf* (**a**) *(disparo)* shot (**b**) *(herida)* shot wound

perdiguero, -a *adj* partidge-hunting; **perro p.** setter

perdiz *nf Orn* partridge; **p. común** red-legged partridge; **p. nival** ptarmigan; **p. pardilla** partridge; *Fig* **fueron felices y comieron perdices** they all lived happily ever after

perdón *nm* pardon, forgiveness; **con p. (sea dicho)** if you will pardon my saying so; **eso no tiene p.** it is unforgivable; **pedir p.** to apologize; **¡p.!** sorry!

perdonable *adj* forgivable, excusable

perdonar *vt* (**a**) *(remitir)* to forgive; **¿me perdonas?** will you forgive me?; **por esta vez te perdono** I'll let you off this time; *Fig* **no perdona (ni) una** he doesn't miss a thing (**b**) *(excusar)* to excuse, pardon; **perdone que le moleste** sorry for bothering you (**c**) *(eximir)* to exempt; **le han perdonado dos años de cárcel** she got two years' remission; **perdonarle la vida a algn** to spare sb's life (**d**) *(aprovechar)* **no p.** to miss; **no perdona oportunidad para** he doesn't miss the chance to

perdonavidas *nm inv Fam* braggart, bully

perdulario, -a 1 *adj* (**a**) *(descuidado)* careless, negligent, sloppy (**b**) *(disoluto)* immoral, dissolute

  2 *nm,f* (**a**) *(descuidado)* careless person (**b**) *(vicioso)* immoral person

perdurable *adj* (**a**) *(eterno)* everlasting (**b**) *(duradero)* durable, long-lasting

perdurar *vi* (**a**) *(durar)* to endure, last (**b**) *(persistir)* to persist, continue to exist

perecedero, -a *adj* perishable; **artículos perecederos** perishables

perecer [46] *vi* to perish, die

peregrinación *nf*, **peregrinaje** *nm* pilgrimage

peregrinamente *adv* peculiarly, strangely

peregrinar *vi* (**a**) *(ir de peregrinaje)* to go on a pilgrimage (**b**) *Fig (errar)* to go to and fro o back and forth

peregrino, -a 1 *adj* (**a**) *(gen)* on a pilgrimage (**b**) *(aves)* migrating (**c**) *Fig (extravagante)* odd, peculiar; **sus ideas son siempre peregrinas** he always has such harebrained ideas

  2 *nm,f* pilgrim

perejil *nm Bot* parsley

perengano *nm Fam* so-and-so, what's his name

perenne *adj* perennial, perpetual, everlasting

perennidad *nf* everlasting quality, perpetuity

perentoriamente *adv* urgently

perentoriedad *nf* peremptoriness, urgency

perentorio, -a *adj* peremptory, urgent, pressing

pereza *nf* laziness, idleness; **me da p. salir** I don't feel like going out; **tener p.** to feel lazy

perezco *indic pres véase* **perecer**

perezosamente *adv* lazily; *(lentamente)* sluggishly

perezoso, -a 1 *adj* (**a**) *(holgazán)* lazy, idle (**b**) *(lento)* sluggish

  2 *nm,f* lazy person, idler

  3 *nm Zool* sloth

perfección *nf* perfection; **hacer algo a la p.** to do sth perfectly o to perfection

perfeccionamiento *nm* (**a**) *(acción)* perfecting (**b**) *(mejora)* improvement

perfeccionar *vt* to perfect; *(mejorar)* improve, make better; **ha ido a Inglaterra a p. su inglés** he's gone to England to improve his English

perfeccionismo *nm* perfectionism

perfeccionista *adj & nmf* perfectionist

perfectamente *adv* (**a**) *(con perfección)* perfectly; **te**

entiendo p. I quite understand (you), I know what you mean (**b**) **¡p.!** *(de acuerdo)* agreed!, all right!

perfectibilidad *nf* perfectibility

perfectible *adj* perfectible

perfectivo, -a *adj* perfective

perfecto, -a *adj* perfect; **nadie es p.** nobody is perfect

perfidia *nf* perfidy, treachery

pérfido, -a 1 *adj* perfidious, treacherous; *Pey* **la pérfida Albión** perfidious Albion
  2 *nm,f* traitor

perfil *nm* (**a**) *(gen)* profile; *(contorno)* outline, contour; **de p.** in profile; **fotografía mi mejor p.** photograph my best side; **vista de p.** side view (**b**) *(trazo)* upstroke (**c**) *Fig (característica)* feature, characteristic (**d**) *Geom* cross section

perfilado, -a 1 *pp de* **perfilar**
  2 *adj* (**a**) *(rostro)* long and thin; *(labios, nariz etc)* well-shaped (**b**) *(dibujado)* outlined (**c**) *Téc* streamlined
  3 *nm* (**a**) *(dibujo)* outline (**b**) *Téc* streamlining

perfilar 1 *vt* (**a**) *(dar forma)* to shape, outline (**b**) *(dibujar)* to draw the outline of (**c**) *(acabar)* to give the finishing touches to (**d**) *Téc* to streamline
  2 perfilarse *vpr* (**a**) *(tomar forma)* to take shape (**b**) *(recortarse)* to stand out

perforación *nf (gen)* perforation; *Min* drilling, boring

perforador, -a *adj (gen)* perforating; *Min* drilling, boring

perforar *vt (gen)* to perforate; *Min* to drill, bore

performance *nf* [per'formans] performance

perfumador *nm* perfume spray

perfumar 1 *vt* to perfume
  2 *vi* to perfume
  3 perfumarse *vpr* to put on perfume; **p. mucho** to use a lot of perfume

perfume *nm* perfume, scent

perfumería *nf* perfumery; *(en grandes almacenes)* perfume counter *o* department

perfumista *nmf* perfume maker *o* seller

perfusión *nf* perfusion

pergamino *nm* (**a**) *(piel)* parchment (**b**) **pergaminos** *(títulos de nobleza)* title deeds

pergeñar *vt (plan)* to sketch, outline; *(texto)* to prepare, draft

pérgola *nf* pergola

pericardio *nm Anat* pericardium

pericarpio *nm Bot* pericarp

pericia *nf* expertise, skill; **la p. del piloto evitó lo peor** the pilot's skill avoided a great disaster

pericial *adj* expert; **informe p.** expert report

periclitar *vi Fml* to decline, wane

perico *nm* (**a**) *Fam Orn* parakeet (**b**) *Esp RP Ven Argot (droga)* snow, cocaine (**c**) *Col (café con leche)* white coffee (**d**) *Carib Guat Méx (charlatán)* big talker

pericote *nm Arg Bol Perú* large rat

periferia *nf (gen)* periphery; *(alrededores de ciudad)* outskirts *pl*

periférico, -a 1 *adj* peripheral
  2 *nm Inform* peripheral device *o* unit

perifollo *nm* (**a**) *Bot* common chervil (**b**) **perifollos** *Pey (adornos)* frills, trimmings

perífrasis *nf inv* periphrasis, long-winded explanation

perifrástico, -a *adj* periphrastic, long-winded, verbose

perilla *nf (barba)* goatee; *Fam* **de perilla(s)** *(oportuno)* at the right moment; *(útil)* very handy; **me viene de perilla(s)** it's just the ticket

perímetro *nm* perimeter

perinatal *adj Med* perinatal

perineo *nm Anat* perineum

periodicidad *nf* periodicity

periódico, -a 1 *adj* (**a**) *(cíclico)* periodic, periodical; *Quím* **tabla periódica** periodic table (**b**) *(publicación)* periodical (**c**) *Med (fiebre)* recurrent
  2 *nm* newspaper

periodismo *nm* journalism

periodista *nmf* journalist, reporter

periodístico, -a *adj* journalistic; **artículo p.** newspaper article

periodo *nm*, **período** *nm* period ❑ **p. de prueba** trial period

peripatético, -a *adj Filos* Peripatetic; *Fig* ridiculous

peripecia *nf* sudden change, vicissitude; **durante la cena nos relató las peripecias de su juventud** over dinner he told us about the ups and downs of his youth

periplo *nm* voyage, tour

peripuesto, -a *adj Fam* dolled-up

periquete *nm Fam* **en un p.** in a jiffy

periquito *nm (salvaje)* parakeet; *(doméstico)* budgerigar

periscópico, -a *adj* periscopic

periscopio *nm* periscope

perisodáctilo, -a *adj & nm Zool* perissodactyl

perista *nm* fence, receiver (of stolen goods)

peristilo *nm Arquit* peristyle

peritaje *nm* (**a**) *(informe)* expert *o* specialist report (**b**) *(estudios)* technical studies *pl*

peritar *vt (vivienda)* to value; *(daños)* to assess the value of

perito, -a 1 *adj* expert
  2 *nm,f* technician, expert; **p. industrial/agrónomo/aeronáutico** ≃ industrial/agricultural/aeronautical expert

peritoneal *adj Anat* peritoneal

peritoneo *nm Anat* peritoneum

peritonitis *nf Med* peritonitis

perjudicado, -a 1 *pp de* **perjudicar**
  2 *adj* harmed, damaged
  3 *nm,f* victim; **el p. siempre soy yo** I am always the loser

perjudicar [59] *vt (dañar)* to harm, injure; *(estropear)* to damage; *(intereses)* to prejudice; *(en paquetes de tabaco)* **'las Autoridades Sanitarias advierten que: el tabaco perjudica seriamente la salud'** 'Government health warning: smoking can seriously damage your health'; **no quiero perjudicarte** I don't want to spoil it for you

perjudicial *adj* prejudicial, detrimental, harmful

perjuicio *nm* prejudice, harm, damage; **en p. de** to the detriment of; **sin p. de** without prejudice to

perjurar *vi* (**a**) *Jur* to commit perjury (**b**) *Fam* to swear a lot; **le juró y perjuró que era verdad** he swore again and again that it was true

perjurio *nm Jur* perjury

perjuro, -a 1 *adj* perjured
  2 *nm,f* perjurer

perla *nf* (**a**) *(joya)* pearl; **p. cultivada** cultured pearl (**b**) *Fig (persona)* gem, jewel (**c**) *Fam* **de perlas** marvellously; **venir de perlas** to be just the thing

perlado, -a *adj (forma)* pearl-shaped; *(color)* pearl-coloured, *US* pearl-colored; *Literario* **p. de sudor** with beads of sweat

permanecer [46] *vi* to remain, stay; **ha permanecido en el puesto durante más de treinta años** he's been in the same job for thirty years

permanencia *nf* (**a**) *(inmutabilidad)* permanency, permanence (**b**) *(estancia)* stay

permanente 1 *adj* permanent; **comisión p.** standing committee; **servicio p.** 24-hour service
2 *nf (en peluquería)* permanent wave, perm; **hacerse la p.** to have one's hair permed

permanentemente *adv* permanently

permanganato *nm Quím* permanganate

permeabilidad *nf* permeability, pervious nature

permeable *adj* permeable, pervious; *Fig (receptivo)* receptive

pérmico, -a *adj & nm Geol* Permian

permisible *adj* permissible

permisión *nf* permission

permisividad *nf* permissiveness

permisivo, -a *adj* permissive

permiso *nm* (**a**) *(autorización)* permission; **con su p.** with your permission, if you don't mind; **pedir p.** to ask permission (**b**) *(documento, licencia)* licence,. *US* license, permit ▫ **p. de conducir** *Br* driving licence, *US* driver's license; **p. de residencia** residence permit; **p. de trabajo** work permit (**c**) *Mil* leave; **estar de p.** to be on leave

permitido, -a 1 *pp de* **permitir**
2 *adj* permitted, allowed

permitir 1 *vt* to permit, allow; **¿me permite?** may I?; **permítame** allow *o* permit me; **si el tiempo lo permite** weather permitting
2 permitirse *vpr* (**a**) *(poder hacer)* to permit *o* allow oneself; **me permito recordarle que** let me remind you that; **no puedo permitirme ese lujo** I can't afford it (**b**) *(uso impers)* to be permitted *o* allowed; *(en letrero)* **'no se permite fumar'** 'no smoking'

permuta *nf* exchange

permutable *adj* permutable

permutación *nf* (**a**) *(cambio)* exchange (**b**) *Mat* permutation

permutar *vt* (**a**) *(cambiar)* to exchange (**b**) *Mat* to permute

pernera *nf* trouser leg, *US* pant leg

pernicioso, -a *adj* pernicious

pernil *nm Culin* ham

pernio *nm* hinge

perno *nm Téc* bolt

pernocta *nf Mil (pase de)* **p.** overnight pass

pernoctar *vi* to stay overnight *o* the night

pero 1 *conj* but; **el dinero hace ricos a los hombres p. no dichosos** money makes men rich but not happy; **p., ¿qué pasa aquí?** now, what's going on here?
2 *nm* fault, objection; **poner** *o* **encontrar peros (a algo/a algn)** to find fault (with sth/with sb)

perogrullada *nf* truism, platitude

perogrullesco *adj* platitudinous

Perogrullo *nm* **una verdad de P.** a truism

perol *nm Culin* large saucepan, pot

peroné *nm Anat* fibula

peronismo *nm Pol* Peronism

peronista *adj & nmf Pol* Peronist

peroración *nf* speech

perorar *vi* to deliver a speech

perorata *nf* boring speech

perpendicular *adj & nf Geom* perpendicular

perpendicularidad *nf Geom* perpendicularity

perpendicularmente *adv* perpendicularly

perpetración *nf* perpetration

perpetrar *vt* to perpetrate, commit

perpetuación *nf* perpetuation

perpetuar [4] **1** *vt* to perpetuate
2 perpetuarse *vpr* to be perpetuated; *(hacer durar)* to go on interminably

perpetuidad *nf* perpetuity; **a p.** in perpetuity

perpetuo, -a *adj* perpetual, everlasting; *Jur* **cadena perpetua** life imprisonment

perplejidad *nf* perplexity, bewilderment

perplejo, -a *adj* perplexed, bewildered; **dejar p.** to perplex, bewilder; **quedar(se) p.** to be perplexed *o* bewildered

perra *nf* (**a**) *Zool* bitch (**b**) *Esp Fam (moneda)* **estar sin una p.** to be broke (**c**) *Esp Fam (idea fija)* obsession; **coger la p. de (hacer algo)** to take it into one's head (to do sth) (**d**) *Esp Fam (rabieta)* tantrum

perrera *nf (para guardar perros)* kennel, kennels *pl*; *Ferroc* dog box

perrería *nf Fam* dirty trick; **hacerle una p. a algn** to play a dirty trick on sb

perrero *nm* dog-catcher

perrito *nm* **p. (caliente)** hot dog

perro, -a 1 *adj Fam* lousy, wretched; **¡perra suerte!** what rotten luck!
2 *nm* (**a**) *Zool* dog; *(en letrero)* **cuidado con el p.** beware of the dog; *Fam Fig* **de perros** lousy; *Fam* **vida de perros** dog's life; *Fig* **¡a otro p. con ese hueso!** *Br* pull the other one!, *US* tell it to the marines!; *Prov* **p. ladrador, poco mordedor** his bark is worse than his bite ▫ **p. callejero** stray dog; **p. faldero** lapdog; **p. guardián** guard dog, watchdog; **p. lobo** alsatian; **p. policía** police dog; *Fig* **p. viejo** old hand (**b**) *Culin* **p. caliente** hot dog (**c**) *Fam (canalla)* rotter, swine (**d**) *Chile (pinza)* *Br* clothes peg, *US* clothes pin

perruno, -a *adj* canine, dog; *(lealtad)* doglike

persa *adj & nmf* Persian

persecución *nf* (**a**) *(seguimiento)* pursuit; **salieron en su p.** they set off in pursuit (of him) (**b**) *Pol (represión)* persecution

per sécula seculorum *adv* for ever and ever

persecutorio, -a *adj* (**a**) *(que sigue)* pursuing (**b**) *(opresor)* persecutory; *Med* **manía persecutoria** persecution mania

perseguidor, -a 1 *adj* (**a**) *(seguidor)* pursuing (**b**) *(represor)* persecuting
2 *nm,f* (**a**) *(el que sigue)* pursuer (**b**) *(opresor)* persecutor

perseguir [61] *vt* (**a**) *(gen)* to pursue, chase; *(seguir)* to run after, follow; *Fig* **me persigue la mala suerte** I'm dogged by bad luck (**b**) *(reprimir)* to persecute (**c**) *Fig (pretender)* to pursue, be after; **¿qué persigues?** what are you aiming at?

perseverancia *nf* perseverance, constancy

perseverante *adj* persevering, constant

perseverar *vi* (**a**) *(persistir)* to persevere, persist; **si perseveras en tu actitud** if you continue to have that attitude (**b**) *(durar)* to last

Persia *n* Persia

persiana *nf* (Persian) blinds *pl*

pérsico, -a 1 *adj* Persian; **golfo P.** Persian Gulf
2 *nm Bot* persicaria, red shank

persignar *Rel* **1** *vt* to cross
2 persignarse *vpr* to cross oneself

persistencia *nf* persistence
persistente *adj* persistent
persistir *vi* to persist
persona *nf* person; **algunas personas** some people; **buena p.** nice person; **en p.** in person; **por p.** per person; *Ling* **la primera p. del plural** the first person plural; *Jur* **p. jurídica** legal entity; *Fam* **p. mayor** grown-up
personaje *nm* (**a**) *(celebridad)* celebrity, personage, important person (**b**) *Cin Lit Teat* character
personal 1 *adj* (**a**) *(particular)* personal, private (**b**) *Ling* personal
 2 *nm* (**a**) *(plantilla)* staff, personnel ❏ **p. docente** teaching staff; **p. sanitario** health workers *pl* (**b**) *Esp Fam (gente)* people
personalidad *nf* personality
personalismo *nm* (**a**) *Filos* personalism (**b**) *Pol (parcialidad)* partiality (**c**) *(egoismo)* egoism
personalista *adj* (**a**) *Filos* personalistic (**b**) *(parcial)* partial (**c**) *(egoísta)* egoistic
personalizar [14] *vt* (**a**) *(aludir)* to personalize (**b**) *(encarnar)* to personify (**c**) *(adaptar)* to become o get personal; *Inform* to customize
personalmente *adv* personally
personarse *vpr* to present oneself, appear in person
personificación *nf* personification
personificar [59] *vt* to personify
perspectiva *nf* (**a**) *(gen)* perspective; **en p.** in perspective; **p. lineal** linear perspective (**b**) *(futuro)* prospect, outlook; **las perspectivas son inmejorables** the perspectives could not be better
perspicacia *nf* keen understanding, insight, perspicacity
perspicaz *adj* sharp, perspicacious
persuadir 1 *vt* to persuade; **estar persuadido de que** to be convinced that
 2 persuadirse *vpr* to become convinced
persuasión *nf* persuasion
persuasiva *nf* persuasiveness
persuasivo, -a *adj* persuasive, convincing
pertenecer [46] *vi* to belong (**a** to)
perteneciente *adj* belonging
pertenencia *nf* (**a**) *(propiedad)* possessions *pl*, property (**b**) *(afiliación)* affiliation, membership (**c**) **pertenencias** personal belongings
pértiga *nf* pole; *Dep* **salto de p.** pole vault
pertinacia *nf* (**a**) *(persistencia)* persistence (**b**) *(obstinación)* obstinacy
pertinaz *adj* (**a**) *(persistente)* persistent (**b**) *(obstinado)* obstinate, stubborn
pertinazmente *adv* (**a**) *(persistentemente)* persistently (**b**) *(obstinadamente)* obstinately
pertinencia *nf* (**a**) *(relación)* pertinence, relevance (**b**) *(adecuado)* appropriateness
pertinente *adj* (**a**) *(relativo)* pertinent, relevant (**b**) *(apropiado)* appropriate; **esta decisión no es p. a mi cargo** it is not up to me to decide
pertrechar 1 *vt* to equip, supply (**de, con** with)
 2 pertrecharse *vpr* to equip oneself
pertrechos *nmpl (equipo)* equipment *sing*; *Mil* ammunition *sing*
perturbación *nf* disturbance; **p. del orden público** breach of the peace; *Med* **p. mental** mental disorder
perturbado, -a 1 *pp de* perturbar
 2 *adj* (**a**) *(confuso)* confused (**b**) *(desequilibrado)* (mentally) deranged o unbalanced

3 *nm,f* mentally deranged o unbalanced person
perturbador, -a 1 *adj* disturbing
 2 *nm,f* troublemaker
perturbar *vt (público)* to disturb; *Med* **p. la mente** to mentally disturb
Perú *n* Peru
peruano, -a *adj & nm,f* Peruvian
perversidad *nf* perversity
perversión *nf* perversion
perverso, -a 1 *adj* perverse, evil
 2 *nm,f* (**a**) *(malvado)* evil o wicked person (**b**) *(depravado)* pervert
pervertido, -a *nm,f* pervert
pervertidor, -a 1 *adj* pervertible
 2 *nm,f* perverter
pervertir [62] **1** *vt* to pervert, corrupt
 2 pervertirse *vpr* to be perverted, become perverted
pervivencia *nf* survival
pervivir *vi* to survive
pesa *nf* weight
pesabebés *nm inv* baby-scales *pl*
pesacartas *nm inv* letter-scales *pl*
pesada *nf* weighing
pesadamente *adv* heavily; *(despacio)* slowly, sluggishly
pesadez *nf* (**a**) *(con peso)* heaviness; *Fig (de estómago)* fullness (**b**) *Fig (lentitud)* slowness, sluggishness (**c**) *Fam (fastidio)* drag, nuisance
pesadilla *nf* nightmare; **de p.** nightmarish
pesado, -a 1 *pp de* pesar
 2 *adj* (**a**) *(gen)* heavy; *(comida)* rich, heavy; *(tiempo)* close, sultry (**b**) *Fig (lento)* slow, sluggish (**c**) *(fatigoso)* hard, tough (**d**) *(aburrido)* tedious, dull; **ponerse p.** to be a pest; **¡qué p. eres!** what a drag you are!
 3 *nm,f* bore, pest
pesadumbre *nf* grief, affliction
pesaje *nm* weighing
pésame *nm* condolence, sympathy; **dar el p.** to offer o express one's condolence o condolences; **mi más sentido p.** my deepest sympathy
pesantez *nf Fís* gravity
pesar 1 *vt* (**a**) *(determinar el peso)* to weigh up (**b**) *(examinar)* to weigh
 2 *vi* (**a**) *(tener gravedad)* to weigh; **¿cuánto pesas?** how much do you weigh?; **pesa cien gramos** it weighs a hundred grams; *Fig* **toda la responsabilidad pesa sobre mí** all the responsibility falls on me (**b**) *(ser pesado)* to be heavy; **A pesa más/menos que B** A is heavier/lighter than B; **pesa demasiado** it's too heavy; **p. poco** to be light (**c**) *Fig (tener importancia)* to play an important part (**d**) *(ser de lamentar)* to be a pity; **mal que te pese** whether you like it or not; **me pesa que no lo aceptes** I'm sorry that you won't accept it; **pese a (que)** in spite of; **pese a quien pese** in spite of everything
 3 pesarse *vpr* to weigh oneself
 4 *nm* (**a**) *(pena)* sorrow, grief (**b**) *(arrepentimiento)* regret; **bien a su p.** much to his regret (**c**) **a p. de** in spite of; **a p. de todo** in spite of everything; **a p. mío/tuyo** against my/your will; **hazlo a p. de lo que digan** do it in spite of what they say
pesaroso, -a *adj* (**a**) *(triste)* sorrowful, sad (**b**) *(arrepentido)* regretful, sorry
pesca *nf* (**a**) *(acción)* fishing; *(con caña)* angling; **ir de p.** to go fishing; **p. de altura** deep-sea fishing; **p. de bajura** coastal fishing; **p. submarina** underwater fishing; *Fam Fig* **andar a la p. de** to fish for; *Fam* **toda la p.** the whole

caboodle (**b**) *(peces)* fish; *(pescado)* catch

pescadería *nf* fish shop, fishmonger's (shop)

pescadero, -a *nm,f* fishmonger

pescadilla *nf (pez)* whiting

pescado *nm* fish; **p. blanco/azul** white/blue fish

pescador, -a 1 *adj* fishing
  2 *nm,f (hombre)* fisherman; *(mujer)* fisherwoman; **p. de caña** angler

pescante *nm* (**a**) *(de carruaje)* coachman's seat (**b**) *Constr* jib, boom (**c**) *Náut* davit

pescar [59] **1** *vt* (**a**) *(peces)* to catch; **ir a p. truchas** to go trout fishing (**b**) *Fam (coger)* to pick up, catch; **le pescó la policía** the police caught him; **no pesca ni un chiste** he doesn't get a single joke; **p. un buen trabajo** to land a good job
  2 *vi* to fish; **ir a p.** to go fishing; **p. con caña** to angle; *Fig* **p. en río revuelto** to fish in troubled waters

pescozada *nf,* **pescozón** *nm* slap on the neck o head

pescuezo *nm Fam* neck; *Hum* **retorcer el p. a algn** to wring sb's neck

pesebre *nm* (**a**) *(cajón)* manger, stall (**b**) *(belén)* Nativity scene

pesero *nm Méx* collective taxi *(with a fixed rate and that travels a fixed route)*

peseta *nf Antes* peseta

pesetero, -a 1 *adj* stingy, money-grubbing, tight
  2 *nm,f* skinflint

pésimamente *adv* awfully, wretchedly, terribly

pesimismo *nm* pessimism

pesimista 1 *adj* pessimistic
  2 *nmf* pessimist

pésimo, -a *adj* very bad, awful, terrible; **de pésima calidad** absolutely useless

peso *nm* (**a**) *(gravedad)* weight; **al p.** by weight; **ganar/perder p.** to put on/lose weight; *Fig* **caer por su propio p.** to be self-evident; *Fig* **de p.** *(persona)* influential; *(razón)* convincing; **me quité un p. de encima** it took a load off my mind ❑ *Fís* **p. atómico** atomic weight; **p. bruto** gross weight; *Fís* **p. específico** specific gravity; **p. muerto** dead weight; **p. neto** net weight (**b**) *Fin (moneda)* peso (**c**) *Dep (de lanzar)* shot; *(de levantar)* weight; **lanzamiento del p.** shot put; **levantamiento de p.** weightlifting ❑ *Box* **p. mosca** flyweight; **p. pesado** heavyweight

pespunte *nm Cost* backstitch

pespuntear *vt Cost* to backstitch

pesquera *nf,* **pesquería** *nf* fishery, fishing ground

pesquero, -a 1 *adj* fishing
  2 *nm* fishing boat

pesquisa *nf* inquiry; **hacer pesquisas** to make inquiries

pestaña *nf* (**a**) *(de párpado)* eyelash, lash (**b**) *(de recortable)* flap (**c**) *Téc* flange

pestañear *vi* to blink; **sin p.** without batting an eyelid

pestañeo *nm* blink, blinking

pestazo *nm Fam* stink, stench

peste *nf* (**a**) *Med* plague; *Hist* **la p. negra** the Black Death; **p. bubónica** bubonic plague; *Fig* **una p. de mosquitos** a plague of mosquitoes (**b**) *(hedor)* stench, stink (**c**) *(cosa mala)* pest, nuisance (**d**) **pestes** *(palabras de enojo)* swearing *sing*, obscenities; **decir o echar pestes** to curse

pesticida *nm* pesticide

pestífero, -a *adj* (**a**) *(dañino)* pestiferous (**b**) *(maloliente)* foul, stinking

pestilencia *nf* (**a**) *(peste)* pestilence (**b**) *(mal olor)* stench, stink

pestilente *adj* (**a**) *(dañino)* pestilent (**b**) *(maloliente)* stinking, foul

pestillo *nm* spring bolt; *(cerrojo)* bolt, latch; *(de la contraventana)* shutter catch

petaca *nf* (**a**) *(para cigarrillos)* cigarette case; *(para picadura)* tobacco pouch; *(para bebidas)* flask (**b**) *Méx (maleta)* suitcase (**c**) *PRico (para lavar)* washing trough (**d**) *(broma)* apple-pie bed (**e**) **petacas** *Méx (nalgas)* buttocks

pétalo *nm Bot* petal

petanca *nf* game of bowls, boules *pl*

petardo *nm* (**a**) *(explosivo)* firecracker, firework; *Mil* petard (**b**) *Fam (persona) (fea)* ugly person, horror; *(inútil)* good-for-nothing, worthless person; *(aburrida)* bore (**c**) *Esp Fam (droga)* joint

petate *nm Mil* luggage; *Fam Esp* **liar el p.** *(marcharse)* to leave, pack up and go; *CAm Méx (morir)* to kick the bucket

petenera *nf Mús* = Andalusian popular song; *Esp Fam* **salir por peteneras** to go off at a tangent

petición *nf* request; *Jur* petition, plea; **a p. de** at the request of; **p. de mano** proposal (of marriage)

peticionante *Am* **1** *adj* petitioning
  2 *nmf* petitioner

peticionar *vt Am* to request

peticionario, -a *nm,f Jur* petitioner

petimetre *nm Pey* dandy

petirrojo *nm Orn* robin (redbreast)

petiso, -a 1 *adj Andes RP Fam* short
  2 *nm RP (caballo)* small horse

peto *nm* (**a**) *(prenda)* bib, bodice (**b**) *Hist (de armadura)* breastplate

pétreo, -a *adj (de piedra)* stone; **una superficie pétrea** a stony surface

petrificación *nf* petrification

petrificar [59] **1** *vt* to petrify
  2 **petrificarse** *vpr* to petrify

petrodólar *nm Fin* petrodollar

petróleo *nm* oil, petroleum; **p. crudo** crude oil; **pozo de p.** oil well

petrolera *nf* oil company

petrolero, -a 1 *adj* oil; **la industria petrolera** the oil industry
  2 *nm Náut* oil tanker

petrolífero, -a *adj* oil; *Geol Min* oil-bearing

petroquímica *nf* petrochemistry

petroquímico, -a *adj* petrochemical

petulancia *nf* arrogance, vanity

petulante *adj* arrogant, vain

petunia *nf Bot* petunia

peúco *nm (de niño)* bootee

peyorativo, -a *adj* pejorative, derogatory

peyote *nm Bot* peyote, mescal

pez[1] *nm Zool* fish; *Fam Fig* **estar como p. en el agua** to be in one's element; *Esp Fam* **estar p. (en algo)** to have no idea (about sth) ❑ **p. cinto** scabbard fish; **p. de San Pedro** John Dory; **p. espada** swordfish; *Fam Fig* **p. gordo** big shot; **p. martillo** hammerhead shark; **p. volador** flying fish

pez[2] *nf* pitch, tar

pezón *nm* (**a**) *Anat* nipple (**b**) *Téc* tip, knob

pezuña *nf Anat Zool* hoof

pH *nm* pH

Phnom Penh [nom'pen] *n* Phnom Penh

piadosamente *adv* (**a**) *(con devoción)* piously (**b**) *(compasivamente)* compassionately

piadoso, -a *adj* (**a**) *(devoto)* pious (**b**) *(compasivo)* compassionate; **mentira piadosa** white lie

pial *nm Am* lasso

pialar *vt Andes RP* to lasso

piamente *adv* (**a**) *(devotamente)* piously (**b**) *(misericordiosamente)* mercifully

pianista *nmf Mús* pianist, piano player

pianístico, -a *adj Mús* pianistic, piano

piano *Mús* **1** *nm* piano ▫ **p. de cola** grand piano; **p. de media cola** baby grand (piano); **p. recto/vertical** upright piano
  2 *adv* (**a**) *Mús* piano (**b**) *Fam (despacio)* slowly, nice and easy

pianoforte *nm Mús* pianoforte, piano

pianola *nf Mús* pianola

piar [32] *vi* to chirp, tweet

piara *nf Zool* herd of pigs

piastra *nf Fin* piastre

PIB *nm Fin (abrev de* **producto** *Esp* **interior** *o Am* **interno bruto)** GDP

pibe, -a *nm,f RP Fam* kid

pica *nf* (**a**) *Hist Mil* pike; *Fig* **poner una p. en Flandes** to bring off sth really difficult (**b**) *Taur* goad (**c**) *Naipes* spade

picacho *nm* mountain peak

picada *nf* (**a**) *RP (tapas)* appetizers, snack (**b**) *RP (carrera)* car race *(in street)* (**c**) *Am (de avión)* nose dive; **hacer un p.** to nose-dive; *Fig* **caer en p.** to plummet

picadero *nm* (**a**) *Equit* riding school (**b**) *Fam (piso)* bachelor pad

picadillo *nm Culin (carne)* minced meat; *(guiso)* type of stew; *Fam* **hacer p. a algn** to make mincemeat of sb

picado, -a 1 *pp de* **picar**
  2 *adj* (**a**) *Culin (pasado)* off, bad; *(vinos)* sour (**b**) *Culin (cortado)* chopped; *(tabaco)* cut; *Esp RP (molido) Br* minced, *US* ground (**c**) *(mordido)* bitten; *(de avispa, abeja)* stung (**d**) *Med (diente)* decayed; **p. de la viruela** pockmarked (**e**) *(mar)* choppy (**f**) *Fam (molesto)* piqued, narked
  3 *nm Esp (de avión)* nose dive; **hacer un p.** to nose-dive; *Fig* **caer en p.** to plummet

picador *nm Taur* mounted bullfighter, picador

picadora *nf Esp RP* mincer

picadura *nf* (**a**) *(de serpiente, insecto)* bite; *(de avispa, abeja)* sting (**b**) *(en una fruta)* spot; *Med (de viruela)* pockmark; *(en un diente)* decay, caries *sing*; *Metal* pitting (**c**) *(tabaco)* cut tobacco

picaflor *nm Am* (**a**) *Orn* hummingbird (**b**) *(persona)* ladykiller

picajoso, -a 1 *adj* touchy
  2 *nm,f* touchy person

picana *nf Am* goad

picanear *vt Am* to goad

picante 1 *adj* (**a**) *Culin* hot, spicy (**b**) *Fig (malicioso)* risqué, spicy
  2 *nm* piquancy, hot spice

picapedrero *nm* stonecutter

picapica *nf* **polvos p.** itching powder *sing*

picapleitos *nmf inv Pey* bad lawyer

picaporte *nm* (**a**) *(aldaba)* door knocker (**b**) *(pomo)* door handle

picar [59] **1** *vt* (**a**) *(punzar) (insectos, serpientes)* to bite; *(avispas, abejas)* to sting; *(espino, barba)* to prickle (**b**) *(espolear)* to spur on; *Taur* to goad, wound (**c**) *(comer) (aves)* to peck (at); *(persona)* to nibble, pick (at) (**d**) *Pesca* to bite (**e**) *(perforar)* to prick, puncture, punch (**f**) *Culin (cortar)* to chop

up; *Esp RP (carne)* to mince (**g**) *Fam (mecanografiar)* to type (up) (**h**) *Fig (incitar)* to incite, goad; **le picaron para que lo dijera** he was forced into saying it; **p. la curiosidad (de algn)** to arouse (sb's) curiosity; **p. el amor propio (de algn)** to wound (sb's) self-esteem (**i**) *Mús* to play staccato
  2 *vi* (**a**) *(escocer)* to itch; *(herida)* to smart; **me pica la nariz** my nose is itching; **me pican los ojos** my eyes are smarting; *Fam* **a quien pique que se rasque** if the cap fits, wear it (**b**) *(calentar el sol)* to burn (**c**) *Culin* to be hot; *(vino)* to be sharp (**d**) *Pesca* to bite (**e**) *Fig (dejarse engañar)* to swallow it
  3 picarse *vpr* (**a**) *(fruta)* to spot, rot; *(vino)* to turn sour; *(ropa)* to become moth-eaten; *(metal)* to pit; *(dientes)* to decay (**b**) *(mar)* to get choppy (**c**) *(sentirse herido)* to take offence *o US* offense; *(enfadarse)* to get cross (**d**) *Fam (drogas)* to shoot up (**e**) *RP* **picárselas** *(largarse)* to scarper

picardía *nf* (**a**) *(bribonería)* naughtiness; *(astucia)* craftiness; **tener mucha p.** to be a crafty old devil (**b**) *(travesura)* dirty trick; *(procacidad)* naughty thing

picaresca *nf* (**a**) *Lit* picaresque literature (**b**) *(falta de honradez)* dishonesty

picaresco, -a *adj* (**a**) *Lit* picaresque (**b**) *(deshonesto)* roguish

pícaro, -a 1 *adj* (**a**) *(travieso)* naughty, mischievous; *(astuto)* sly, crafty (**b**) *(procaz)* risqué
  2 *nm,f* rascal, sly person, rogue

picatoste *nm Culin* crouton

picazón *nf* (**a**) *(que pica)* itch; *(que quema)* smarting, stinging (**b**) *Fig (desazón)* uneasiness, anxiety

picha *nf Esp Vulg* cock, prick

pichana *nf*, **pichanga** *nf Andes* broom

piche 1 *adj CAm* tight-fisted, mean
  2 *nm* (**a**) *Am Fam (miedo)* fear (**b**) *CAm Zool =* kind of armadillo

pichear *vt (en béisbol)* to pitch

pícher *(pl* **píchers)** *nm (en béisbol)* pitcher

pichi *nm Esp (prenda) Br* pinafore (dress), *US* jumper

pichiruche *nm Andes RP Fam* nobody

pichón¹ *nm Orn* young pigeon; **tiro al** *o* **de p.** pigeon shooting

pichón, -ona² *nm,f Fam (persona)* darling, pet

picnic *(pl* **picnics)** *nm* picnic; **ir de p.** to go for a picnic

pico *nm* (**a**) *(de ave)* beak, bill (**b**) *Orn* woodpecker; **p. menor** lesser-spotted woodpecker; **p. picapinos** great spotted woodpecker (**c**) *(punta)* corner (**d**) *(de vasija)* spout; *(de cazuela)* lip (**e**) *(herramienta)* pick, pickaxe, *US* pickax (**f**) *Geog (cima)* peak; *Fig (valor máximo)* peak (**g**) *Fam (boca)* mouth, *esp Br* gob; **abrir el p.** to talk; **cierra el p.** shut your trap; **darse el p.** *(besarse)* to smooch; *(llevarse bien)* to get along well; *Esp* **ir de picos pardos** to paint the town red; **ser** *o* **tener un p. de oro** to have the gift of the gab; **tener mucho p.** to be a great talker (**h**) *(cantidad)* odd amount; **éramos cincuenta y p.** there were fifty odd of us; **llegó a las dos y p.** he arrived just after two; *Fam* **costar un p.** to cost a bomb (**i**) *Fam (drogas)* fix; **meterse un p.** to give oneself a fix (**j**) *Arg Col Fam (beso)* kiss

picoleto *nm Esp Fam* civil guard; **los picoletos** the Civil Guard *sing*

picor *nm (leve)* itch, tingling; *(doloroso)* smarting, stinging

picoso, -a *adj Méx* spicy, hot

picota *nf* pillory; *Fig* **poner a algn en la p.** to pillory sb

picotazo *nm* peck

picotear *vt & vi* (**a**) *(ave)* to peck (**b**) *(comer)* to nibble

picoteo *nm* (**a**) *(de ave)* pecking (**b**) *(de comer)* nibbling

pictografía *nf* pictography

pictográfico, -a *adj* pictographic

pictórico, -a *adj Arte* pictorial

picudo, -a *adj* pointed, beaked

pídola *nf Esp* leapfrog

pie *nm* (**a**) *Anat* foot; **pies** feet; **al p.** close by, at hand; **a los pies de** *o* **al p. de** at the foot of; **a p.** on foot; **a p. firme** steadfastly; **de p.** standing up; **de pies a cabeza** from head to foot; **echar p. a tierra** to get down, dismount; **en p.** standing; **hacer p.** to touch the bottom; **ir a p.** to walk, go on foot; **no se tuvo de p.** he couldn't stand up; **panti sin pies** footless tights; **perder p.** to get out out of one's depth; **poner los pies en** to set foot in; **ponerse de p.** to stand up; **quedar en p.** to remain (standing); **tener los pies planos** to have flat feet; *Fig* **a los pies de algn** at sb's service; *Fig* **a pies juntillas** blindly; *Fig* **al p. de la letra** to the letter, word for word; *Fig* **buscar tres** *o* **cinco pies al gato** to split hairs; *Fig* **con pies de plomo** gingerly, cautiously; *Fig* **dar p. a** to give cause for; *Fig* **el ciudadano de a p.** the man in the street; *Fig (pendiente)* **en p.** pending; *Fig* **en (un) p. de igualdad** on an equal footing; *Fig* **levantarse con el p. izquierdo** to get out of bed on the wrong side; *Fig* **no tener ni pies ni cabeza** to be absurd; *Fig* **pararle los pies a algn** to put sb in his/her place; *Fam Fig* **hacer algo con los pies** to mess o botch sth up; *Fam Fig* **no dar p. con bola** to do everything wrong □ *Med* **p. de atleta** athlete's foot; *Impr* **p. de imprenta** imprint; *Téc* **p. de rey** calliper, *US* caliper (**b**) *(de un instrumento)* stand; *(de una copa)* stem (**c**) *(de un escrito, una página)* foot □ *Inform* **p. de página** footer (**d**) *Impr (de una ilustración)* caption (**e**) *(medida)* foot (**f**) *Teat* cue (**g**) *Lit* foot (**h**) *Chile (anticipo)* down payment

piedad *nf* (**a**) *Rel* devoutness, piety (**b**) *(compasión)* compassion, pity; **por p.** out of pity; **¡por p.!** for pity's sake!; **tenga p. de ellos** have mercy on them (**c**) *Arte* pietà

piedra *nf* (**a**) *(roca)* stone; *(de mechero)* flint; *(de un instrumento)* stand; *(de una copa)* stem (**b**) *(de un escrito, una página)* foot □ *Inform* **p. de página** footer **primera p.** to lay the foundation stone; *Fig* **a tiro de p.** a stone's throw away; *Fam* **menos da una p.** it's better than nothing; *Fam Fig* **me dejó** *o* **me quedé de p.** I was taken aback; *Fam Fig* **no dejar** *o* **quedar p. por mover** to leave no stone unturned; *Hum* **¡que uno no es de p.!** one can only stand so much! □ **p. angular** cornerstone; **p. de afilar** whetstone; **p. de molino** millstone; *Fig* **p. de toque** touchstone; **p. filosofal** philosopher's stone; **p. pómez** pumice (stone); **p. preciosa** precious stone (**b**) *Med* stone, calculus (**c**) *Meteor* hailstone

piel *nf* (**a**) *Anat* skin; *Fig* **dar la p. por algo** to give one's right arm for sth; *Fam* **ser de la p. del diablo** *o* **de Barrabás** to be a little devil (**b**) *(de fruta, de patata)* skin, peel (**c**) *(pelo)* fur; **pieles** fur *sing*; **un abrigo de p.** a fur coat (**d**) *Esp Méx (cuero)* leather; **zapatos/bolso de p.** leather shoes/handbag

     2 *nmf* **p. roja** redskin

piélago *nm Literario* ocean, deep

pienso *nm* fodder, feed; **piensos compuestos** mixed feed *sing*

piercing ['pirsin] *(pl* **piercings)** *nm* body piercing; **hacerse un p. en el ombligo** to have one's navel pierced

pierna *nf Anat* leg; **estirar las piernas** to stretch one's legs; *Culin* **p. de cordero** leg of lamb; *Fig* **estirar la p.** to kick the bucket; *Fam* **dormir a p. suelta** *o* **tendida** to sleep like a log

pieza *nf* (**a**) *(elemento)* piece, part, element; **p. de recambio** spare part, *US* extra; **precio por p.** price per item; *(prenda)* **traje de dos piezas** suit; *Fig* **me dejó** *o* **me quedé de una p.** I was speechless *o* dumbfounded *o* flabbergasted; *Fam* **¡buena p. estás tú hecho!** a fine one you are! (**b**) *(habitación)* room (**c**) *Caza* specimen, piece, head (**d**) *Cost (trozo, remiendo)* patch (**e**) *Tex (de tela)* roll,

piece (**f**) *(juegos)* piece, man (**g**) *Teat* play; **p. corta** sketch (**h**) *Mús* song, piece

piezoelectricidad *nf Fís* piezoelectricity

piezoeléctrico, -a *adj Fís* piezoelectric

pífano *nm Mús* fife

pifia *nf Fam* (**a**) *(error)* blunder, bloomer; **cometer una p.** to put one's foot in it (**b**) *Andes Arg (burla)* joke

pifiar *vi* (**a**) *Fam (equivocarse)* **pifiarla** to put one's foot in it (**b**) *Andes Arg Fam (abuchear)* to boo and hiss

pigmentación *nf* pigmentation

pigmento *nm* pigment

pigmeo, -a *nm,f* Pygmy, Pigmy; *Fig* pygmy, pigmy

pignoración *nf Fin* pledge

pignorar *vt* to pawn

pija *nf esp RP Vulg* cock, prick

pijada *nf Esp Fam* (**a**) *(dicho)* stupid *o* empty remark; **no dice más que pijadas** he talks nothing but rubbish (**b**) *(cosa)* trifle; **se molesta por cualquier p.** he gets annoyed at the slightest thing

pijama *nm (prenda)* pyjamas *pl*

pijo, -a *Esp* **1** *adj Fam Pey* (**a**) *(afectado)* posh; **hablar en plan p.** to talk posh; **un barrio p.** a posh area (**b**) *(tonto)* stupid, foolish

     2 *nm,f Fam Pey (persona)* rich kid

     3 *nm Vulg (pene)* prick, cock

pijotada *nf Esp véase* **pijada**

pijotear *vi Am* to haggle

pijotero, -a *adj Esp Fam* annoying, irritating

pila *nf* (**a**) *Elec* battery □ **p. alcalina** alkaline battery; **p. seca** dry battery (**b**) *(recipiente) (de la cocina)* sink; *(de baño, lavadero)* basin; *(de agua)* small fountain □ *Rel* **p. bautismal** font (**c**) *(montón)* pile, heap; *Fig (muchos)* **piles** *pl*, heaps *pl*, loads *pl*; **una p. de libros** a pile of books; *Fig* **una p. de años** a lot of years

pilar¹ *nm* (**a**) *Arquit* pillar; *Fig (apoyo)* pillar, support (**b**) *(mojón)* milestone; *(poste)* post

pilar² *nm* waterhole

pilastra *nf Arquit* pilaster

pilcha *nf Am* piece of clothing

pilche *nm Andes* wooden bowl

píldora *nf* pill; *Fig* **dorar la p.** to gild the pill; *Fam* **se tragó la p.** he fell for it □ **p. anticonceptiva** contraceptive pill

pileta *nf RP* (**a**) *(piscina)* swimming pool (**b**) *(en baño)* washbasin; *(en cocina)* sink

pilila *nf Fam Br* willy, *US* peter

pillaje *nm* looting, pillage, plunder

pillar **1** *vt* (**a**) *(robar)* to plunder, loot (**b**) *(atrapar)* to catch; *(alcanzar)* to catch up with; **lo pilló un coche** he was run over by a car; **¡te pillé!** caught you!; *Fam* **p. un resfriado** to catch a cold

     2 *vi Esp (lugar)* **me pilla lejos** it's out of the way for me; **me pilla de camino** it's on my way

     3 **pillarse** *vpr* to catch; **p. un dedo/una mano** to catch one's finger/hand; *Fig* **p. los dedos** to come out the loser, lose money

pillastre *nm Fam* rogue, scoundrel, rascal

pillería *nf* (**a**) *(acción)* dirty trick (**b**) *(panda de pillos)* gang of rascals

pillín *nm Fam* little rascal

pillo, -a **1** *adj* (**a**) *(travieso)* naughty (**b**) *(astuto)* sly, cunning

     2 *nm,f* (**a**) *(niño)* naughty child; **¡qué p. eres!** what a naughty boy you are! (**b**) *Pey (adulto)* thug

pilón *nm* (**a**) *(abrevadero)* trough (**b**) *(lavadero)* basin, sink, laundry (**c**) *(pilar)* pillar, column; *(poste)* post

piloncillo *nm Méx* brown sugar *(sold in cone-shaped blocks)*

pilórico, -a *adj Anat* pyloric

píloro *nm Anat* pylorus

piloso, -a *adj* hair

pilotaje *nm* pilotage, piloting

pilotar *vt Av* to pilot, fly; *Aut* to pilot, drive; *Náut* to pilot, steer

pilote *nm Arquit* pile

piloto 1 *nmf Av Náut* pilot; *Aut* driver; **sin p.** pilotless
2 *nm* (**a**) *(luz)* pilot light □ **p. automático** automatic pilot (**b**) *Arg Chile (impermeable)* raincoat
3 *adj* pilot; **casa p.** showhouse; **programa p.** pilot programme

piltra *nf Esp Fam* bed

piltrafa *nf* (**a**) *Fam* weakling; **estar hecho una p.** to be on one's last legs (**b**) **piltrafas** *(residuos)* scraps

pimentero *nm Bot* pepper plant

pimentón *nm* paprika, red pepper

pimienta *nf* pepper; **p. blanca/negra** white/black pepper

pimiento *nm (planta)* pimiento; *(fruto)* pepper; **p. morrón** sweet pepper; *Fam* **me importa un p.** I don't give a damn, I couldn't care less

pimpante *adj Fam* spruce, smart; **más p. que una rosa** as fresh as a daisy

pimpinela *nf Bot* pimpernel

pimplar *vi Esp Fam* to drink, go boozing

pimpollo *nm* (**a**) *Bot* shoot (**b**) *Fam (persona)* dish, smasher

pimpón® *nm Dep* ping-pong, table tennis

PIN *nm (abrev de* **producto interior neto**) NDP

pin *(pl* **pins**) *nm* (**a**) *Fam (insignia)* pin, label badge (**b**) *(de enchufe)* pin

pinacoteca *nf* art gallery

pináculo *nm Arquit* pinnacle

pinar *nm* pine grove, pine wood

pincel *nm* brush, paintbrush; *Fig (estilo)* style

pincelada *nf* brushstroke, stroke of a brush; *Fig* **con cuatro pinceladas ella expresó lo que sentía** in a few words she outlined how she felt

pincha *nmf Esp Fam,* **pinchadiscos** *nmf inv Esp Fam* disc jockey, DJ

pinchar 1 *vt* (**a**) *(punzar)* to prick, prickle; *(desinflar)* to burst; **p. un balón** to burst a ball (**b**) *Fam (incitar)* to prod; *(molestar)* to get at, nag; **deja ya de pincharle** stop getting at him; **hay que pincharla** she needs prodding (**c**) *Med* to inject, give an injection to (**d**) *Fam (teléfono)* to tap (**e**) *Esp Fam* **pinchar discos** to DJ
2 *vi* (**a**) *(rueda)* to get a puncture (**b**) *(barba)* to be prickly (**c**) *Fam (fracasar)* to make a *Br* boob *o US* boo-boo (**d**) *Fam Fig* **ni pincha ni corta** he cuts no ice
3 **pincharse** *vpr* (**a**) *(picarse)* to prick oneself; **me pinché el dedo con un alfiler** I pricked my finger with a pin (**b**) *(rueda)* to get a puncture (**c**) *Fam (inyectarse drogas)* to shoot up

pinchazo *nm* (**a**) *(punzadura)* prick (**b**) *(de dolor)* sudden *o* sharp pain (**c**) *Aut* puncture, blowout

pinche 1 *nmf (ayudante de cocina)* kitchen assistant
2 *adj Méx Fam* damn, *Br* bloody

pinchito *nm Culin* bar snack, aperitif

pincho *nm* (**a**) *(punta)* (sharp) point; *(de planta)* thorn, prickle; *(de animal)* spine; **alambre de pinchos** barbed

wire (**b**) *Culin* bar snack, aperitif; **tomar unos pinchos** to have a snack *o* some starters □ *Esp* **p. moruno** shish kebab

pindonga *nf Esp Fam* gadabout

pindonguear *vi Esp* to gad about

pineda *nf* pine grove, pine wood

pinga *nf Andes Carib Méx muy Fam* prick

pingajo *nm Esp Fam* rag

pingo *nm* (**a**) *Esp Fam (pingajo)* rag; **vas hecho un p.** what a mess you look (**b**) *Fam (persona despreciable)* rotter (**c**) *RP (caballo)* fast horse (**d**) *Chile Perú (caballo malo)* nag

pingonear *vi Fam* to loaf about

ping-pong® [pim'pon] *nm Dep* table tennis, ping-pong

pingüe *adj* abundant, plentiful; **pingües beneficios** fat profits

pingüino *nm Orn* penguin

pinitos *nmpl Fam* first steps; **hacer p.** to take one's first steps

pinnípedo, -a *adj & nm Zool* pinniped, pinnipedian

pino *nm Bot* pine; *Esp* **hacer el p.** to do a handstand; *Esp Fam* **en el quinto p.** in the back of beyond □ **p. albar** Scots pine; **p. insigne** Monterey pine; **p. manso** *o* **piñonero** stone pine

pinol *nm,* **pinole** *nm CAm Méx (harina) Br* maize flour, *US* corn flour

pinrel *nm Esp Fam* foot, hoof; **pinreles** feet *pl,* hooves

pinta[1] *nf* (**a**) *(mota)* dot; *(lunar)* spot (**b**) *Fam (aspecto)* look; **tener buena/mala p.** to look good/bad; **tiene p. de ser interesante** it looks interesting (**c**) *Méx (pintada)* piece of graffiti; **pintas** graffiti *pl* (**d**) *Méx* **irse de p.** *(en la escuela) Br* to play truant, *US* play hooky
2 *nmf Fam* shameless person

pinta[2] *nf (medida)* pint

pintada *nf* (**a**) *(en pared)* piece of graffiti; **pintadas** graffiti *pl* (**b**) *Orn* guinea fowl

pintado, -a 1 *pp de* **pintar**
2 *adj* (**a**) *(coloreado)* painted; *(en letrero)* **recién p.** wet paint; *Fam Fig* **el más p.** the best (person) in town; *Fam Fig* **es su hermana pintada** she's the spitting image of her sister; *Fam Fig* **nos viene que ni p.** it is just the ticket; *Fam Fig* **te está que ni p.** it suits you to a tee (**b**) *(maquillado)* made-up (**c**) *(con manchas)* speckled, mottled

pintamonas *nmf inv Esp Pey* bad painter, dauber

pintar 1 *vt* (**a**) *(dar color)* to paint; **p. con pistola** to spray (**b**) *(dibujar)* to draw, sketch (**c**) *Fig (describir)* to describe, give the full picture of
2 *vi* (**a**) *Naipes* to be trumps (**b**) *Fam (importar)* to count; **yo aquí no pinto nada** *(estoy de más)* I am out of place here; *(no tengo nada que ver)* I have nothing to do with this
3 **pintarse** *vpr* (**a**) *(maquillarse)* to put make-up on (**b**) *Fig (mostrarse)* to show, appear (**c**) **pintárselas** *Fam (arreglarse)* to manage; **se las pinta solo** there is no one like him

pintarraj(e)ar *Fam* **1** *vt* to scribble, daub
2 **pintarraj(e)arse** *vpr* to tart oneself up

pintiparado, -a *adj Fam* just right; **me viene p.** it is just the job, it is just what I need

pinto, -a *adj* spotted, dappled; *Zool* **caballo p.** pinto; *Bot* **judía pinta** pinto bean

pintón, -ona *adj RP (atractivo)* good-looking

pintor, -ona *nm,f* painter; *Fam* **p. de brocha gorda** *(de paredes)* house painter; *Pey* dauber

pintorcito *nm Arg (bata)* apron, pinafore

pintoresco, -a *adj* (**a**) *(lenguaje, estilo)* picturesque (**b**) *(estrafalario)* eccentric, bizarre

pintura *nf* (**a**) *(acción, arte)* painting; **p. a la acuarela** watercolour; **p. al óleo** oil painting; **p. al pastel** pastel drawing; **p. rupestre** cave painting; *Fam Fig* **no la puedo ver ni en p.** I can't stand the sight of her (**b**) *(materia)* paint

pinturero, -a *Fam* **1** *adj* swanky, showy

   2 *nm,f* show-off

pinza *nf* (**a**) *(gen pl)* tweezers *pl; Téc* pincers *pl*, tongs *pl*; **p. de la ropa** clothes peg, *US* clothespin; **p. del pelo** *Br* hairgrip, *US* bobby pin; *Fam* **había que cogerlo con pinzas** he was a wreck; *Fam* **sacarle algo con pinzas a algn** to drag sth out of sb (**b**) *Cost* dart; **un pantalón de pinzas** pleated trousers *o US* pants (**c**) *(de animal)* pincer, nipper

pinzón *nm Orn* chaffinch

piña *nf* (**a**) *Bot (de pino)* pine cone; *(de otros árboles)* cone (**b**) *Bot (ananás)* **p. (americana)** pineapple (**c**) *Fig (grupo)* clan, clique (**d**) *Fam (golpe, puñetazo)* whop, punch

piñata *nf* pot full of sweets

piñón¹ *nm Bot* pine seed *o* nut; *Fam* **estar a partir un p. (con algn)** to be hand in glove (with sb); *Fam* **están a partir un p.** they're thick as thieves

piñón² *nm Téc* pinion; **p. de cambio** bevel pinion

pío¹ *nm (de pájaro, ave)* cheep, chirp; *Fam* **no dijo ni p.** there wasn't a cheep out of him

pío, -a² *adj* pious

piocha *nf Méx (barba)* goatee

piojo *nm* louse; *Fig* **p. resucitado** social climber

piojoso, -a *adj* (**a**) *(con piojos)* lousy; *(sucio)* dirty, filthy (**b**) *Fig (mezquino)* stingy, mean

piolet (*pl* **piolets**) *nm Dep* ice axe *o US* ax

piolín *nm Andes RP* cord

pionero, -a *nm,f* pioneer

piorrea *nf Med* pyorrhoea, *US* pyorrhea

pipa¹ *nf* (**a**) *(de fumar)* pipe; **fumar en p.** to smoke a pipe (**b**) *(tonel)* barrel

pipa² *nf Bot (pepita)* pip; *Fam* **no tener ni para pipas** to be broke; *Fam* **pasárselo p.** to have a great time

pipermín *nm (menta)* peppermint; *(licor)* peppermint liqueur

pipeta *nf Quím* pipette

pipí *nm Fam* pee, *Br* wee-wee; **hacer p.** to pee, *Br* wee-wee

pipián *nm Andes CAm Méx Culin* = type of stew in which the sauce is thickened with ground nuts or seeds

pipiolo, -a *nm,f Fam (niño)* youngster; *(novato)* novice

pipón, -ona *adj RP Fam (lleno)* stuffed

pique *nm* (**a**) *(enfado)* grudge; **tener un p. con algn** to have a grudge against sb (**b**) **a p. de** on the point of (**c**) **irse a p.** *Náut* to sink; *(un plan)* to fall through; *(un negocio)* to go bust

piqué *nm Tex* piqué

piquera *nf* hole

piqueta *nf* (**a**) *(herramienta)* pickaxe, *US* pickax; *(de demolición)* mason's hammer *o* pick (**b**) *(en tienda de campaña)* metal tent-peg (**c**) *Arg Chile (vino)* weak wine

piquete *nm* (**a**) *(estaca)* stake, post (**b**) *(de huelguistas)* picket (**c**) *Mil* **p. de ejecución** firing squad (**d**) *Col (picnic)* picnic

pira *nf* pyre

pirado, -a *Argot* **1** *pp de* **pirarse**

   2 *adj* **estar p. por algo** to be mad about sth

piragua *nf* canoe

piragüismo *nm Dep* canoeing

piragüista *nmf Dep* canoeist

piramidal *adj* pyramidal

pirámide *nf* pyramid; **las pirámides de Egipto** the Egyptian Pyramids

piraña *nf (pez)* piranha

pirarse *vpr Esp RP Argot* to clear off, hop it; **pírate, píratelas** beat it

pirata **1** *adj* (**a**) *(barco, ataque)* pirate (**b**) *(radio, edición, vídeo)* pirate; *(casete, grabación)* bootleg (**c**) *Am (profesional, servicio)* cowboy

   2 *nmf* (**a**) *(del mar)* pirate ▫ **p. del aire** hijacker; **p. informático** cracker, hacker (**b**) *Am (mal profesional)* cowboy

piratear **1** *vi* (**a**) to pirate (**b**) *Inform* to crack

   2 *vt* (**a**) *(avión)* to hijack (**b**) *(plagiar)* to pirate; **p. cintas de vídeo** to pirate videotapes (**c**) *Inform* **p. un programa** *(desproteger)* to crack into a program

pirateo *nm Fam (plagio)* piracy

piratería *nf* piracy ▫ **p. aérea** hijacking; **p. musical** music piracy

pirenaico, -a *adj & nm,f* Pyrenean

pírex *nm* Pyrex®

pirindolo *nm Fam* thingumabob, thingummy, thingamajig

Pirineos *nmpl Geog* Pyrenees

piripi *adj Fam* tipsy, merry; **estar p.** to be drunk

pirita *nf Min* pyrite

piro *nm Esp Argot* **darse el p.** to scarper, *US* split

pirómano, -a *nm,f Med* pyromaniac; *Jur* arsonist

piropear *vt* to shout a compliment at, make a verbal pass at

piropo *nm* compliment, pass; **un desconocido le echó un p. por la calle** a stranger made a pass at her in the street

pirotecnia *nf* pyrotechnics *sing*

pirotécnico, -a **1** *adj* pyrotechnical; **productos pirotécnicos** fireworks

   2 *nm,f* pyrotechnist

pirrar *Fam* **1** *vt* **me pirran las albóndigas** I just adore *o* love meatballs

   2 **pirrarse** *vpr* **p. por algo/algn** to be dead keen on sth/sb

pirueta *nf* pirouette; *Fig* **tuve que hacer piruetas para poder cobrar** I had to go to great lengths to get my money

piruja *nf Col Méx muy Fam (prostituta)* whore, *US* hooker

pirujo, -a *adj CAm* sceptical

pirulí *nm* lollipop

pis *nm Fam Br* pee, wee-wee; **hacer p.** to *Br* pee, wee-wee

pisada *nf* (**a**) *(acción)* step, footstep; **oí pisadas** I heard footsteps; *Fig* **seguir las pisadas de algn** to trail sb (**b**) *(huella)* footprint

pisapapeles *nm inv* paperweight

pisar **1** *vt (gen)* to tread on, step on; *(acelerador)* to press; *Teat* **p. las tablas** *o* **un escenario** to tread the boards; *(en letrero)* **'prohibido p. el césped'** 'keep off the grass'; **¿te pisé?** did I step on your foot?; *Fig* **no p. un lugar** not to set foot in a place; *Fig* **jamás he pisado su casa** I have never set foot in his place; *Fig* **pisarle el terreno a algn** to beat sb to it; *Fig* **pisarle los talones a algn** to tread on sb's heels

   2 *vi* to tread, step; *Fig* **ella no se deja p. por nadie** she can stand up for herself

piscar *vt Méx (maíz)* to harvest, collect

pisciano, -a *adj & nm,f Astrol Am* Pisces

piscícola *adj* piscicultural

piscicultor, -a *nm,f* fish farmer

piscicultura *nf* pisciculture

piscifactoría *nf* fish farm

piscina *nf* swimming pool

Piscis *nm inv Astrol Astron* Pisces

pisco *nm (aguardiente)* Peruvian grape brandy, pisco

piscolabis *nm inv Esp Culin Fam* snack

piso *nm* (**a**) *(suelo)* floor (**b**) *(planta)* floor; **autobús de dos pisos** double-decker bus; **en el tercer p.** on the *Br* third *o US* fourth floor (**c**) *Esp (vivienda)* apartment, flat (**d**) *(de zapato)* sole (**e**) *Chile (taburete)* stool

pisotear *vt (pisar)* to trample on; *(aplastar)* to stamp on; *Fig* **se ha pisoteado el derecho de expresión** freedom of speech has been trampled on

pisotón *nm* stamp (of the foot); **darle un p. a algn** to stamp on sb's toes

pista *nf* (**a**) *(superficie)* track □ **p. de baile** dance floor; *Dep* **p. de carreras** racetrack; **p. de circo** ring; *Dep* **p. de esquí** ski run *o* slope; *Dep* **p. de patinaje** ice rink; *Esp Dep* **p. de tenis** tennis court; *Aut* **p. de tierra** dirt track; **p. forestal** forest track (**b**) *Av* **p. de aterrizaje** landing strip; **p. de despegue** runway (**c**) *Inform Mús* track (**d**) *(rastro)* trail, track; **estar sobre la p.** to be on the right track; **seguir la p. a algn/a algo** to trail sb/sth (**e**) *(indicio)* clue, hint; **dame una p.** give me a clue

pistacho *nm Bot* pistachio nut

pistero, -a *adj CAm* money-grubber

pistilo *nm Bot* pistil

pisto *nm* (**a**) *Culin* ≃ ratatouille (**b**) *Esp Fam* **darse p.** to show off

pistola *nf* (**a**) *(arma)* gun, pistol; **a punta de p.** at gunpoint (**b**) *(para pintar)* spray gun; **pintar a p.** to spray-paint

pistolera *nf* holster

pistolero *nm* gunman, gun, gangster

pistoletazo *nm* gunshot

pistón *nm* (**a**) *Téc (émbolo)* piston (**b**) *(de arma)* cartridge cap (**c**) *Mús* piston

pistonudo, -a *adj Esp Fam* great, fantastic, smashing

pita[1] *nf Bot* agave, pita

pita[2] *nf (gallina)* hen, chicken

pitada *nf* (**a**) *(abucheo)* booing, hissing (**b**) *Am Fam (calada)* drag, puff

pitanza *nf (ración)* ration

pitar 1 *vt* (**a**) *Dep* to referee; **el árbitro pitó (la) falta** the referee called a fault (**b**) *(en señal de desagrado)* to boo, hiss (**c**) *Am Fam (dar una calada a)* to puff (on)
    2 *vi* (**a**) *(tocar el pito)* to blow a whistle; *(del vehículo)* to toot one's horn; *Esp Fam* **irse o salir pitando** to fly off (**b**) *Fam (funcionar)* to work, function; **esto no pita** this doesn't work (**c**) *Chile (burlarse de)* to make fun of

pitido *nm* whistle

pitillera *nf* cigarette case

pitillo *nm* (**a**) *(cigarrillo)* cigarette (**b**) *Col (paja)* drinking straw

pitiminí *(pl* pitiminíes*) nm Bot* fairy rose bush; **rosa de p.** fairy rose

pito *nm* (**a**) *(silbato)* whistle; *Aut* horn; *Fam* **me importa un p.** I don't give a hoot; *Fam* **por pitos o por flautas** for one reason or another; *Fam* **tomar a algn por el p. del sereno** to treat sb as a nobody (**b**) *Orn* **p. real** green woodpecker (**c**) *Fam (cigarrillo)* smoke, *Br* fag (**d**) *(pene) Fam Br* willie, *US* peter; *esp Méx Vulg* cock

pitón *nm* (**a**) *Zool* python (**b**) *(de botijo)* spout (**c**) *(de toro)* horn

pitonisa *nf* fortune-teller

pitorrearse *vpr Esp Fam* **p. de algn** to make fun of sb, *Br* take the mickey out of sb

pitorreo *nm Esp Fam* scoffing, teasing; **¡ya está bien de p.!** give over!

pitorro *nm* spout

pitote *nm Argot* hubbub, din

pitufo, -a *nm,f* Smurf

pituitario, -a *adj Anat* pituitary

pituso, -a 1 *adj* lovely, cute
    2 *nm,f* lovely child

pívot *(pl* pivots*) nmf Dep (en baloncesto)* pivot

pivotar *vi* to pivot

pivote *nm* pivot

píxel *nm Inform* pixel

piyama *nm o nf Am* pyjamas; **un p.** a pair of pyjamas

pizarra *nf* (**a**) *Min Constr* slate (**b**) *Educ (encerado)* blackboard; **salir a la p.** to go up to the blackboard

pizarral *nm* slate quarry

pizarrín *nm* slate pencil

pizarrón *nm Am (en aula) Br* blackboard, *US* chalkboard

pizca *nf* (**a**) *(poco)* little bit, tiny piece; **ni p.** not a bit; **no me hace ni p. de gracia** I don't like it at all; **una p. de sal** a pinch of salt (**b**) *Méx Agr (recolección)* harvest, crop

pizpireta *adj Fam (mujer) (vivaracha)* lively and attractive; *(astuta)* cute, sharp

pizza ['pitsa] *nf Culin* pizza

pizzería [pitse'ria] *nf* pizzeria, pizza parlour *o US* parlor

placa *nf* (**a**) *(lámina)* plate □ **p. de vitrocerámica** *(de cocina)* ceramic hob; *Med* **p. dental** dental plaque; **p. solar** solar panel (**b**) *(conmemorativa)* plaque; *(de policía)* badge (**c**) *Aut* **p. (de matrícula)** *Br* number plate, *US* license plate (**d**) *Geol* plate

placaje *nm Rugby* tackle; **hacer un p. (a un jugador)** to tackle (a player)

placard *(pl* placards*) nm RP* fitted cupboard/wardrobe

placebo *nm Farm* placebo

placenta *nf* placenta

placentario, -a *adj* placental

placentero, -a *adj* pleasant, agreeable

placer[1] *nm Min* placer

placer[2] *nm* pleasure; **ha sido un p. (conocerle)** it's been a pleasure (meeting you); **los placeres de la carne** the pleasures of the flesh; **un viaje de p.** a holiday trip; *Fml* **tengo el p. de** it gives me great pleasure to

placer[3] [48] *vt Fml* to please

placidez *nf* placidity

plácido, -a *adj* placid, easy-going

plaga *nf* (**a**) *(de insectos)* plague; *(calamidad)* calamity (**b**) *Agr* pest, blight; *(de langostas)* plague

plagado, -a 1 *pp de* plagar
    2 *adj* plagued

plagar [38] *vt* to cover, fill; **la cocina estaba plagada de moscas** the kitchen was infested with flies

plagiar *vt* (**a**) *(copiar)* to plagiarize (**b**) *CAm Col Perú Ven (secuestrar)* to kidnap

plagiario, -a *nm,f* (**a**) *(que copia)* plagiarist (**b**) *CAm Col Perú Ven (que secuestra)* kidnapper

plagio *nm* (**a**) *(copia)* plagiarism (**b**) *CAm Col Perú Ven (secuestro)* kidnapping

plaguicida *nm Agr* pesticide

plan *nm* (**a**) *(proyecto)* plan, project; **¿qué planes tienes para mañana?** what are your plans for tomorrow? (**b**) *(programa)* scheme, programme □ *Educ* **p. de estudios** syllabus; *Fin* **p. de inversiones** investment plan; **p. de pensiones** pension plan (**c**) *Med* course of treatment (**d**) *(altitud)* height; *(nivel)* level (**e**) *Fam (actitud)* attitude; *(manera)* way; **en p. de broma** for a laugh; **en p. grande**

on a grand scale; **eso tampoco es p., eso no es p.** that isn't on; **si te pones en ese p.** if you're going to be like that (about it) (**f**) *Fam (ligue, cita)* date

plana *nf* (**a**) *(página)* page; *Fam* **corregirle** *o* **enmendarle la p. a algn** *(criticarle)* to criticize sb's work; *(superarle)* to outdo sb (**b**) *Prensa* page; **a toda p.** full page; **primera p.** front page (**c**) *Mil* **p. mayor** staff

plancha *nf* (**a**) *(de metal)* plate (**b**) *(para planchar)* iron; *(ropa planchada)* ironing (**c**) *Culin* grill; **sardinas a la p.** grilled sardines (**d**) *Impr* plate (**e**) *Fam (equivocación)* blunder, boob; **¡vaya p.!** you've really put your foot in it!

planchado, -a 1 *pp de* **planchar**
    2 *nm* ironing

planchar 1 *vt* to iron
    2 *vi* to do the ironing

planchazo *nm Fam* blunder, boob

plancton *nm Biol* plankton

planeador *nm Av* glider

planeamiento *nm* (**a**) *Av* gliding (**b**) *(proyecto)* planning

planear 1 *vt* to plan
    2 *vi Av* to glide

planeta *nm* planet

planetario, -a 1 *adj* planetary
    2 *nm* planetarium

planicie *nf Geog* plain

planificación *nf* planning ❏ **p. familiar** family planning

planificar [59] *vt* to plan

planilla *nf Am* form

planning ['planin] *(pl* **plannings**) *nm* scheduling

plano, -a 1 *adj* (**a**) *(llano)* flat, even; **de p.** *(llano)* flatly; *(de lleno)* directly (**b**) *Geom Mat* plane
    2 *nm* (**a**) *Geom Mat* plane (**b**) *Arquit* plan, draft; *(mapa)* map; **levantar el p. de la ciudad** to draw a plan of the city (**c**) *Cin* shot; **un primer p.** a close-up; *Fig* **estar en primer p.** to be in the limelight; *Fig* **estar en segundo p.** to be in the background

planta *nf* (**a**) *Bot* plant ❏ **p. de interior** house plant (**b**) *(del pie)* sole (**c**) *(piso)* floor, storey ❏ **p. baja** *Br* ground floor, *US* first floor (**d**) *Arquit (plano)* ground plan (**e**) *(fábrica)* plant ❏ **p. depuradora** purification plant (**f**) *Fam* **de buena p.** good looking

plantación *nf* (**a**) *Agr* plantation (**b**) *(acción)* planting

plantado, -a 1 *pp de* **plantar**
    2 *adj* (**a**) *(planta, árbol)* planted (**b**) *Fam* **bien p.** good looking (**c**) *Fam* **dejar a algn p.** *(no comparecer)* to stand sb up; *(abandonar)* to walk out on sb; **dejarlo todo p.** to give up everything; **no te quedes ahí p.** come on, move

plantar 1 *vt* (**a**) *Agr (árboles, campo)* to plant (**b**) *(poner)* to put, place; **p. la tienda de campaña** to set up tent; **p. un poste** to put in a post; *Fam Fig* **p. a algn de patitas en la calle** to throw sb out; **p. cara a algn** to stand up to sb (**c**) *(pegar)* to plant *o* land (**d**) *Fam (cantar, largar)* to tell off; **le plantó cuatro frescas** he gave him a piece of his mind (**e**) *Fam* **p. a algn** *(no comparecer)* to stand sb up; *(abandonar)* to walk out on sb; **plantó el trabajo** he left his job, just like that
    2 plantarse *vpr* (**a**) *(ponerse, colocarse)* to plant oneself; **se plantó en la puerta** he stood in the doorway (**b**) *(llegar)* to arrive; **en cinco minutos se plantó aquí** he got here in five minutes flat (**c**) *Fig (mantenerse firme)* to stick to stubbornly (**d**) *Naipes* to stick (**e**) *Am (arreglarse)* to get all dressed up

plante *nm Fam* walkout

planteamiento *nm* (**a**) *(exposición)* raising, exposition (**b**) *(enfoque)* approach

plantear 1 *vt* (**a**) *(trazar)* to plan; **debemos p. este**

asunto cuidadosamente we've got to plan this carefully (**b**) *(exponer) (caso)* to state; *(idea, asunto)* to expound; *(problema)* to pose (**c**) *(proponer)* to raise, set up, bring up
    2 plantearse *vpr* (**a**) *(considerar) (problema, situación)* to face; **deberías planteártelo en serio** you ought to think about it seriously (**b**) *(uso impers)* to arise; **se (nos) planteó un problema** we were faced with a problem

plantel *nm Fig* cadre, clique; **cuentan con un buen p. de químicos** they've got a strong chemistry staff

planteo *nm Am (propuesta)* idea

plantificar [59] *vt Fam* to plant; **le plantificó una bofetada** he landed him a punch in the face

plantilla *nf* (**a**) *(patrón)* model, pattern; *(para dibujar)* French curve (**b**) *(personal)* permanent staff, personnel; **estar en p.** to be on the payroll (**c**) *(de zapato)* sole; *(interior)* insole

plantío *nm Agr* field

plantón *nm Fam* long wait; **dar un p. a algn** to stand sb up; **estar de p.** to be kept waiting

plañidera *nf* hired mourner

plañidero, -a *adj* mournful, plaintive

plañido *nm* lamentation; mourning

plañir *vi* to mourn

plaqueta *nf Biol* platelet

plasma *nm Biol* plasma

plasmar *vt* (**a**) *(moldear)* to mould, *US* mold, shape (**b**) *Fig (proyecto, sentimiento)* to capture, grasp

plasta *Fam* **1** *nf* (**a**) *(cosa blanda)* mess; **estos guisantes están hechos una p.** these peas are all mushy (**b**) *(chapuza)* botch-up
    2 *nmf Esp Fam (pesado)* pain, drag **este tío es un p.** this bloke is a drag

plástica *nf* plastic art; **las artes plásticas** the plastic arts

plasticidad *nf* (**a**) *(moldeabilidad)* plasticity (**b**) *(expresividad)* expressiveness

plástico, -a 1 *adj* plastic
    2 *nm* (**a**) *(moldeable)* plastic (**b**) *Argot (disco)* record

plastificado, -a 1 *pp de* **plastificar**
    2 *adj* plastic-coated

plastificar [59] *vt* to coat *o* cover with plastic

plastilina® *nf* Plasticine®

plata *nf* (**a**) *Metal* silver; *(objetos de plata)* silverware; *Fam* **como una p.** as clean as a new pin; *Fam* **hablar en p.** to lay (it) on the line ❏ **p. de ley** sterling silver (**b**) *Am Fam* money

plataforma *nf* (**a**) *(superficie elevada, estrado)* platform; *Ferroc* turntable ❏ *Geog* **p. continental** continental shelf (**b**) *Fig (punto de partida)* stepping stone, springboard (**c**) *Pol* platform (**d**) *Inform* platform

platal *nm Am Fam* **un p.** a fortune, loads of money

platanal *nm*, **platanar** *nm* banana plantation

platanero *nm Bot* banana tree

plátano *nm* (**a**) *(fruta)* banana (**b**) *(árbol)* plane ❏ **p. común** London plane; **p. falso** sycamore; **p. oriental** Oriental plane

platea *nf Teat* (**a**) *(zona)* *Br* stalls, *US* orchestra (**b**) *RP (butaca)* seat in the *Br* stalls *o* *US* orchestra

plateado, -a 1 *pp de* **platear**
    2 *adj* silvered, silver-plated
    3 *nm* silver plating

platear *vt* to silver-plate

platense 1 *adj* *o* from the River Plate
    2 *nmf* person from the River Plate

platería *nf* (**a**) *(oficio)* silversmith's craft (**b**) *(taller)* silversmith's workshop (**c**) *(tienda)* silversmith's (shop)

platero, -a *nm,f* silversmith

plática *nf CAm Méx* chat, talk; **estar de p.** to be chatting

platicador, -a *adj CAm Méx* conversational

platicar [59] *vi CAm Méx* to chat, talk

platicón, -ona *CAm Méx Fam* **1** *adj* talkative **2** *nm,f* chatterbox

platija *nf (pez)* plaice

platillo *nm* (a) *(plato pequeño)* small plate; *(de taza)* saucer (b) *(de balanza)* pan, tray; **pasar el p.** to pass round the hat (c) *Culin* meat and vegetable stew (d) *Mús* cymbal (e) **p. volador** *o Esp* **volante** flying saucer

platina *nf* (a) *(de microscopio)* slide, stage (b) *Téc* worktable (c) *(tocadiscos)* deck; **doble p.** double deck

platino *nm* (a) *Metal* platinum; **rubio p.** platinum blond (b) **platinos** *Aut* contact breaker *sing*, points

plato *nm* (a) *(gen)* plate, dish; **lavar los platos** to do the dishes; *Fam* **pagar los platos rotos** to carry the can; *Fam* **parece que no ha roto un p. en su vida** butter wouldn't melt in his mouth (b) *Culin (parte de una comida)* course; **de primer p.** for starters; **p. fuerte** main course; **una comida de tres platos** a three-course meal ❏ **p. combinado** one-course meal (c) *(guiso)* dish; **un p. español** a Spanish dish; *Fig* **no es p. de mi gusto** it's not my cup of tea (d) *(de balanza)* pan, tray (e) *(de tocadiscos)* turntable (f) *Dep* **tiro al p.** trapshooting

plató *nm* *Cin* (film) set; *TV* floor

platónico, -a *adj* Platonic

platonismo *nm* *Filos* Platonism

platudo, -a *adj Am Fam* loaded, rolling in it

plausibilidad *nf* plausibility

plausible *adj* (a) *(admisible)* plausible, acceptable (b) *(digno de alabanza)* commendable

playa *nf* (a) *(en el mar)* beach; **iremos de vacaciones a la p.** we're spending our holidays at the seaside (b) *Am (en ciudad)* **p. de estacionamiento** *Br* car park, *US* parking lot

play-back ['pleiβak] *(pl play-backs)* *nm* **hacer p.-b.** to mime (the lyrics)

playboy [plei'βoi] *(pl playboys)* *nm* playboy

playera *nf* (a) *(zapatilla) (de deporte)* tennis shoe; *(de lona)* canvas shoe (b) *Méx (camiseta)* T-shirt

playero, -a *adj* beach; **un vestido p.** a beach dress

playo, -a *adj Am (aplanado)* flat

plaza *nf* (a) *(lugar en una población)* square (b) *Com (población)* place, town (c) *(mercado)* market, marketplace (d) *Aut* seat; **un coche de cuatro plazas** a four-seater (car) (e) *(puesto)* post, position; **convocar una p.** to advertise a post; **ocupar una p.** to fill a post *o* vacancy; **p. de garaje** parking space *(in a private garage)*; **p. vacante** vacancy; **plazas limitadas** limited number of (vacant) posts; *Educ* **reservar p.** *(para niño)* to put his/her name down (f) *Taur* **p. de toros** bullring (g) *Mil* **p. fuerte** stronghold

plazo *nm* (a) *(periodo)* time, period; *(término)* time limit; **a corto/largo p.** in the short term/in the long run; **el p. de matrícula acaba mañana** tomorrow is the last day for enrolling; **el p. termina el viernes** Friday is the deadline; **en un p. de quince días** within a fortnight (b) *Fin* instalment, *US* installment; **comprar a plazos** *Br* to buy on hire purchase, *US* buy on an installment plan; **en seis plazos** in six instalments

plazoleta *nf,* **plazuela** *nf* small square

pleamar *nf (mar)* high tide

plebe *nf* masses *pl,* plebs *pl*

plebeyo, -a **1** *adj* plebeian **2** *nm,f* plebeian, pleb

plebiscito *nm* plebiscite

plegable *adj* folding, collapsible; **silla p.** folding chair

plegado, -a **1** *pp de* **plegar** **2** *adj* folded **3** *nm* folding

plegamiento *nm* *Geol* folding

plegar [43] **1** *vt* (a) *(doblar)* to fold (b) *Cost* to pleat **2 plegarse** *vpr* to give way, bow

plegaria *nf Rel* prayer

pleitear *vi Jur* to conduct a lawsuit, plead, sue

pleitesía *nf* tribute, homage

pleito *nm* (a) *(riña)* argument, dispute (b) *Jur* lawsuit, litigation; **poner un p. (a algn)** to sue (sb)

plenario, -a *adj* plenary; **sesión plenaria** plenary session

plenilunio *nm* full moon

plenitud *nf* plenitude, fullness; **en la p. de la vida** in the prime of life

pleno, -a **1** *adj* full; **en plena noche** in the middle of the night; **en plenas facultades** in full possession of one's faculties; **en p. día** in broad daylight; **le dio en plena cara** it hit him right in the face; **la familia en p.** the entire family **2** *nm* plenary meeting

pleonasmo *nm* *Lit* pleonasm

plétora *nf Fig* abundance, plethora

pletórico, -a *adj* abundant, brimming

pleura *nf Anat* pleura

pleuresía *nf,* **pleuritis** *nf inv Med* pleurisy

plexiglás® *nm (plástico)* Perspex®, *US* Plexiglass®

plexo *nm* plexus ❏ **p. solar** solar plexus

plica *nf* sealed envelope

pliego *nm* (a) *(hoja)* sheet *o* piece of paper (b) *(documento)* **p. de cargos** list of charges; **p. de condiciones** bidding specifications (c) *(carta)* sealed letter

pliegue *nm* (a) *(en papel, piel)* fold (b) *Cost* pleat (c) *Geol* fold

plinto *nm* (a) *(de columna)* plinth (b) *Dep* vaulting horse

plisado, -a **1** *pp de* **plisar** **2** *adj* pleated; **falda plisada** pleated skirt

plisar *vt Cost* to pleat

plomada *nf* (a) *(albañil etc)* plumb line (b) *Pesca* weights *pl,* sinkers *pl*

plomazo *nm Fam* bore, drag; **¡qué p.!** what a bore!

plomería *nf Méx RP Ven* plumber's (workshop)

plomero, -a *nm,f Méx RP Ven* plumber

plomífero, -a *adj Fam (aburrido)* boring, tedious

plomizo, -a *adj* lead, leaden; *(color)* lead-colored, *US* lead-colored

plomo *nm* (a) *Metal* lead; **soldadito de p.** tin soldier; *Fam Fig* **andar con pies de p.** to walk with leaden steps (b) *(plomada)* plumb line (c) *Elec (fusible)* fuse; **se han fundido los plomos** the fuses have blown (d) *Fam (pesado)* drag, bore; **este libro es un p.** this book is really boring; **ser un p.** to be a drag *o* a bore (e) **a p.** vertically; **caer a p.** to fall right down; **cayó a p. sobre el suelo** he fell flat on the floor

plóter *(pl ploters),* **plotter** *(pl plotters)* *nm Inform* plotter

pluma *nf* (a) *(de ave)* feather; **ligero como una p.** as light as a feather; **un cojín de plumas** a feather cushion; *Argot* **tener p.** to be camp (b) *(de escribir)* (fountain) pen; *(de ave)* quill (pen); *Carib Méx (bolígrafo)* (ballpoint) pen; *Fig* **dejar correr la p.** to write screeds; *Fig* **ganarse la vida con la p.** to earn one's living as a writer ❏ **p. estilográfica** fountain pen (c) *Dep* **peso p.** featherweight (d) *Carib Col Méx (de agua)* *Br* tap, *US* faucet

plumaje *nm* (**a**) *(de ave)* plumage (**b**) *(de adorno)* plume, crest

plumazo *nm* stroke of the pen; **de un p.** with a stroke of his pen

plúmbeo, -a *adj Pey* boring, tedious

plumero *nm* (**a**) *(para limpiar el polvo)* feather duster (**b**) *(plumier)* pencil case (**c**) *(adorno)* plume; *Fam* **se te ve el p.** I can see through you

plumier *(pl* **plumiers)** *nm* pencil box

plumífero *nm (anorak)* feather-lined anorak

plumilla *nf,* **plumín** *nm* nib

plumón *nm* (**a**) *Orn* down (**b**) *(edredón)* eiderdown; *(anorak)* down-filled anorak; *(saco de dormir)* down-filled sleeping bag (**c**) *Méx (rotulador)* felt-tip pen

plural *adj & nm* plural

pluralidad *nf* plurality

pluralismo *nm* pluralism

pluralizar [14] *vi* (**a**) *(poner plural)* to pluralize (**b**) *(generalizar)* generalize

pluricelular *adj* multicellular

pluriempleado, -a 1 *adj* **estar p.** to have more than one job
  2 *nm,f* = person with more than one job

pluriempleo *nm* moonlighting

plurilingüe *adj* multilingual

pluripartidismo *nm* multiparty system

pluripartidista *adj (democracia, sistema)* multiparty

plurivalente *adj Quím* polyvalent

plus *nm Fin Seg* bonus, bonus payment

pluscuamperfecto *nm Ling* pluperfect

plusmarca *nf* record

plusmarquista *nmf Dep* record breaker

plusvalía *nf Econ* appreciation, capital gain

plutocracia *nf Pol* plutocracy

plutócrata *nmf Pol* plutocrat

Plutón *n* Pluto

plutonio *nm Min* plutonium

pluvial *adj* rain

pluviómetro *nm* rain gauge

pluviosidad *nf* rainfall

PM *nf (abrev de policía militar)* MP

PNB *nm (abrev de producto nacional bruto)* GNP

P.O. *(abrev de por orden)* in order

población *nf* (**a**) *(ciudad)* town; *(pueblo)* village (**b**) *(conjunto de habitantes)* population ◻ **p. flotante** floating population

poblada *nf Andes Ven* (**a**) *(muchedumbre)* crowd (**b**) *(motín)* riot

poblado, -a 1 *pp de* **poblar**
  2 *adj* (**a**) *(habitado)* populated; **un jardín p. de rosas** a garden full of roses; **una zona muy poblada** a densely populated area (**b**) *(peludo)* bushy, thick; **cejas pobladas** bushy eyebrows
  3 *nm (pueblo)* village; *(ciudad)* town

poblador, -a *nm,f* settler

poblano, -a 1 *adj* of o from Puebla
  2 *nm,f* (**a**) *(de Puebla)* person from Puebla (**b**) *Am (lugareño)* villager

poblar [63] **1** *vt* (**a**) *(con gente)* to settle, people; *(con plantas)* to plant (**b**) *(vivir)* to inhabit
  2 poblarse *vpr* (**a**) *(llenarse un lugar)* to become crowded (**b**) *(árboles)* to come into leaf

pobre 1 *adj* poor; **¡p.!** poor thing!; **p. de ti si ...!** you'll be sorry if ...!; **ser p. de espíritu** to be small-minded; **un hombre p.** a poor man; **un p. hombre** a poor devil; **una película p. en primeros planos** a film poor in close-ups
  2 *nmf* poor person, pauper; *(mendigo)* beggar; **¡el p.!** poor thing!; **los pobres** the poor *pl*

pobreza *nf* (**a**) *(indigencia)* poverty (**b**) *(escasez)* scarcity; **p. de recursos naturales** lack of natural resources

pocero *nm* (**a**) *(que hace pozos)* well digger (**b**) *(que limpia pozos)* sewer-man

pochismo *nm Am* = type of Spanish spoken by Mexicans in California

pocho, -a *adj* (**a**) *(fruta)* bad, overripe (**b**) *(persona) (débil)* off-colour, *US* off-color; *(triste)* depressed, down; **ando un poco p.** I'm feeling a bit down (**c**) *Méx Fam* Americanized Mexican, chicano

pochoclo *nm Arg* popcorn

pocholo, -a *adj Esp Fam* lovely, pretty

pocilga *nf* pigsty; *Fam Fig* **su casa parece una p.** his house looks like a pigsty

pocillo *nm* cup

pócima *nf* (**a**) *(medicinal)* potion (**b**) *Pey* concoction, brew

poción *nf* potion

poco, -a 1 *adj* (**a**) *(singular)* little, not much; **hace p. tiempo** a short time ago; **hay p. sitio** there is little space; **p. tiempo** not much time; **¿qué hiciste ayer? — poca cosa** what did you do yesterday? — not much; **tiene p. interés** *(persona)* he's not very interested; *(cosa)* it's not very interesting (**b**) *pocos, -as* few, not many; **pocas cosas** few things; **pocas veces** not very often
  2 *pron* (**a**) *(escasa cantidad)* little, not much; **queda p.** there isn't much left; **ya queda p.** it'll soon be over (**b**) *pocos, -as* few, not many
  3 *adv* not (very) much, little; **ella come p.** she doesn't eat much; **es p. simpático** he's not very nice; **estaré p. aquí** I won't be here long (**c**) *(locuciones)* **a p.** shortly afterwards; **a p. de** shortly after; *Méx* **¿a p. no?** *(¿no es verdad?)* isn't that right?; **dentro de p.** soon; **hace p.** a short while ago; **p. a p.** slowly; **p. antes/después** shortly before/afterwards; **por p.** almost; **por p. se cae** he nearly fell; **por p. que pueda** if I can at all; **y por si fuera p.** and to top it all
  4 *nm* **lo p. que tiene** the little he has; **un p.** a little; **ya sabes lo p. que le gusta** you know how little he likes it

poda *nf* (**a**) *(acción)* pruning (**b**) *(época)* pruning season

podadera *nf* pruning shears *pl,* secateurs *pl*

podar *vt* to prune

podenco *nm Zool* hound

poder¹ *nm* (**a**) *(gen)* power; *Jur* **por poderes** by proxy ◻ *Econ* **p. adquisitivo** purchasing power; **p. legislativo** legislative power (**b**) *Pol* power, authority; **el partido en el p.** the party in power (**c**) *(posesión)* possession; **ayer llegó a mi p.** it reached me yesterday; **estar en p. de algn** to be in the power o the hands of sb (**d**) *(fuerza, vigor)* strength

poder² [49] **1** *vt* (**a**) *(tener la facultad de)* to be able to, can; **no podía valerse** he couldn't manage on his own; **no pudo menos que sonreírse** he couldn't help smiling; **no puedo hablar** I can't speak; **podrías haberme advertido** you could have warned me; *Fig* **no puedo más** I can't take any more; *Fam* **no p. tragar a algn** not to be able to stand o stick sb (**b**) *(tener permiso)* may, might; **¿puedo pasar?** may I come in?; **ya puedes irte** you may go now; *Fam* **¿se puede?** may I (come in)?
  2 *v impers (ser posible)* may, might; **no puede ser** that's impossible; **puede que ellos no lo sepan** they might not know; **puede que tenga razón** maybe he's right
  3 *vi* (**a**) *(aguantar)* to cope (**con** with); **no puede con tanta comida** he can't eat so much food; **no puedo con tanto**

ruido I can't stand so much noise (**b**) *(ser más fuerte que)* to be stronger than; **les puede a todos** he can take on anybody

poderío *nm* (**a**) *(facultad)* authority (**b**) *(poder)* power (**c**) *(bienes)* wealth

poderoso, -a 1 *adj* (**a**) *(con poder)* powerful (**b**) *(eficaz)* effective
  2 *nm,f* (**a**) *(con poder)* powerful person (**b**) *(rico)* rich *o* wealthy person

podiatra *nmf Am* chiropodist, *US* podiatrist

podio *nm,* **pódium** *nm Dep* podium

podología *nf* chiropody, *US* podiatry

podólogo, -a *nm,f* chiropodist, *US* podiatrist

podómetro *nm* pedometer

podré *indic fut véase* **poder²**

podredumbre *nf* (**a**) *(putrefacción)* putrefaction, rottenness (**b**) *Fig (corrupción)* corruption, rottenness

podrido, -a 1 *pp de* **podrir**
  2 *adj* (**a**) *(putrefacto)* rotten, putrid (**b**) *(corrupto)* corrupt; *Fam* **p. de dinero** stinking rich

podrir *vt véase* **pudrir**

poema *nm Lit* poem; **p. en prosa** prose poem; *Fam Fig* **fue todo un p.** *(romántico)* it was like a fairy tale; *(falso)* it was pie in the sky

poesía *nf Lit* (**a**) *(género)* poetry (**b**) *(poema)* poem

poeta *nmf* poet

poético, -a *adj* poetic

poetisa *nf* poetess

póker *nm véase* **póquer**

polaco, -a 1 *adj* Polish
  2 *nm,f* Pole
  3 *nm (idioma)* Polish

polar *adj* polar

polaridad *nf* polarity

polarización *nf* (**a**) *Fís* polarization (**b**) *Fig (concentración)* concentration

polarizar [14] *vt* (**a**) *Fís* to polarize (**b**) *Fig (ánimo, atención)* to concentrate

polca *nf Mús* polka

polea *nf Téc* pulley

polémica *nf* (**a**) *(disputa)* polemic, controversy, dispute (**b**) *(arte)* polemics *sing*

polémico, -a *adj* polemic, controversial

polemista *nmf* polemicist, polemist

polemizar [14] *vi* to argue, debate

polen *nm Bot* pollen

poleo *nm Bot* pennyroyal

polera *nf Arg Chile* polo shirt

poli *Fam* **1** *nmf* cop
  2 *nf* **la p.** the fuzz *pl*

poli- *pref* poly-; **policlínica** polyclinic

polichinela *nm Teat* Punch

policía 1 *nf* police (force); **ha llegado la p.** the police are here ▫ **p. de tráfico** traffic police; **p. militar** military police; **p. secreta** secret police
  2 *nmf (hombre)* policeman; *(mujer)* policewoman

policíaco, -a *adj,* **policiaco, -a** *adj,* **policial** *adj* police; **novela/película policiaca** detective story/film

policromado, -a *adj Arte* polychrome

policromía *nf Arte* polychromy

policromo, -a *adj* polychromatic

policultivo *nm Agr* mixed farming

polideportivo *nm* sports centre *o US* center *o* complex

poliédrico, -a *adj* polyhedral, polyhedric

poliedro *nm* polyhedron

poliéster *nm Quím* polyester

polietileno *nm Br* polythene, *US* polyethylene

polifacético, -a *adj* versatile, many-sided; **es un hombre muy p.** he's a man of many talents

polifonía *nf Mús* polyphony

polifónico, -a *adj Mús* polyphonic

poligamia *nf* polygamy

polígamo, -a 1 *adj* polygamous
  2 *nm,f* polygamist

políglota *adj & nmf* polyglot

poligonal *adj* polygonal

polígono *nm* polygon ▫ **p. industrial** industrial area

polígrafo, -a *nm,f* polygraph

polilla *nf Ent* moth

polimorfismo *nm* polymorphism

polimorfo, -a *adj* polymorphic, polymorphous

Polinesia *n* Polynesia

polinesio, -a *adj & nm,f* Polynesian

polinización *nf Bot* pollination

polinizar [14] *vt Bot* to pollinate

polio *nf,* **poliomielitis** *nf inv Med* polio, poliomyelitis

pólipo *nm* (**a**) *Med* polypus, polyp (**b**) *Zool* polyp

polisílabo *nm Ling* polysyllable

politécnico, -a *adj & nm Educ* polytechnic

politeísta *adj* polytheistic

política *nf* (**a**) *(arte de gobernar)* politics *sing*; **hablar de p.** to talk (about) politics (**b**) *(estrategia)* policy; **la p. de esta empresa** the policy of this firm; **una p. de no agresión** a non-aggression policy; **p. exterior/monetaria** foreign/monetary policy

politicastro *nm Pey* bad politician

político, -a 1 *adj* (**a**) *(de gobierno)* political (**b**) *(pariente)* in-law; **hermano p.** brother-in-law; **su familia política** her in-laws
  2 *nm,f* politician

politiquear *vi* to dabble in politics

politiqueo *nm Pey* petty politics *sing*

politización *nf* politicization

politizar [14] *vt* to politicize

polivalencia *nf* polyvalency

polivalente *adj (vacuna, suero)* polyvalent; *(edificio, sala)* multipurpose

póliza *nf* (**a**) *(sello)* stamp (**b**) *Seg* insurance policy; **suscribir una p.** to take out a policy

polizón *nm Náut* stowaway

polizonte *nm Fam* cop

polla *nf* (**a**) *Orn* young hen ▫ **p. de agua** moorhen (**b**) *Arg (carrera)* horse race (**c**) *Esp Vulg (pene)* prick

pollada *nf (de gallina)* brood

pollear *vi Fam* to become aware of the opposite sex

pollera *nf CSur (prenda)* skirt

pollería *nf* poultry shop

pollero, -a *nm,f* poulterer, poultry farmer

pollino, -a *nm,f* (**a**) *Zool* young ass (**b**) *Fam (persona)* good-for-nothing

pollito *nm* chick

pollo *nm* (**a**) *Orn Culin* chicken; *(pollito)* chick (**b**) *Fam (joven) (chico)* lad; *(chica)* lass

polluelo *nm Orn* chick

polo¹ *nm* (**a**) *(de la Tierra)* pole; *Fig* **ser polos opuestos** to be poles apart; **ser el p. opuesto de algn** to be the complete opposite of sb ❏ **p. magnético** magnetic pole; *Elec* **p. negativo** negative pole; **p. Norte** North Pole; *Elec* **p. positivo** positive pole; **p. Sur** South Pole (**b**) *Fig (centro)* **ser el p. de atención** to be the centre of attraction

polo² *nm* (**a**) *(helado) Br* ice lolly, *US* Popsicle® (**b**) *(prenda)* polo shirt

polo³ *nm Dep* polo ❏ **p. acuático** water polo

Polonia *n* Poland

poltrona *nf* (**a**) *(silla)* easy chair (**b**) **la p. (ministerial)** ministerial office

polución *nf* pollution

polucionar *vt* to pollute

polulo *nm Chile* popcorn

polvareda *nf* (**a**) *(nube)* cloud of dust (**b**) *Fig* uproar, scandal

polvera *nf* powder compact

polvo *nm* (**a**) *(en el aire)* dust; **limpiar** *o* **quitar el p.** to dust; **lleno de p.** covered with dust; *Fin Fig* **limpio de p. y paja** net; *Fam* **estar hecho p.** *(cansado)* to be knackered; *(deprimido)* to be depressed; *Fam* **hacer p. a algn** *(cansar)* to wear sb out; *(frustrar)* to ruin sb's plans (**b**) **en p.** powdered; **leche en p.** powdered milk; **nieve en p.** powdery snow (**c**) *Vulg* screw, *Br* shag; **echar un p.** to have a screw, *Br* have it off (**d**) **polvos** powder *sing*; **p. de talco** talcum powder; *Fam* **p. de la madre Celestina** magic powder

pólvora *nf* *(gen)* gunpowder; *(fuegos artificiales)* fireworks *pl*; *Fig* **gastar p. en salvas** to waste one's efforts; *Fig* **se extendió como un reguero de p.** it spread like wildfire; *Fam* **no haber inventado la p.** to be as thick as two short planks

polvoriento, -a *adj* dusty

polvorín *nm* gunpowder arsenal; **polvorines atómicos** atomic fall-out *sing*

polvorón *nm Culin* = very crumbly shortbread biscuit

polvorosa *nf* **poner pies en p.** to take to one's heels, scarper

pomada *nf Farm* cream, ointment ❏ *RP* **p. para zapatos** shoe polish

pomelo *nm Bot (árbol)* grapefruit tree; *(fruto)* grapefruit

pómez *adj inv Geol* **piedra p.** pumice (stone)

pomo *nm* (**a**) *(de puerta)* knob (**b**) *(de espada)* pommel (**c**) *(frasco)* scent bottle

pompa *nf* (**a**) *(burbuja)* bubble; **p. de jabón** soap bubble (**b**) *(en la ropa)* billow (**c**) *(ostentación)* pomp (**d**) **pompas fúnebres** *(ceremonia)* funeral *sing*; *(servicio público)* undertaker's *sing*

pompis *nm inv Fam* backside, bottom

pomposidad *nf* pomposity

pomposo, -a *adj* pompous

pómulo *nm Anat* (**a**) *(hueso)* cheekbone (**b**) *(mejilla)* cheek

ponchada *nf CSur* **una p. de** loads of; **esa casa le costó una p. (de plata)** that house cost him a packet

ponchar 1 *vt* (**a**) *CAm Carib Méx (rueda)* to puncture (**b**) *Am (en béisbol)* to strike out
2 poncharse *vpr* (**a**) *CAm Carib Méx (rueda)* to get a puncture (**b**) *Am (en béisbol)* to strike out

ponche *nm (bebida)* punch

ponchera *nf* punch bowl

poncho *nm (prenda)* poncho

ponderación *nf* (**a**) *(deliberación)* deliberation; **hablar**
con p. to weigh one's words carefully (**b**) *(equilibrio)* balance; *(moderación)* sense (**c**) *(alabanza)* (high) praise

ponderado, -a 1 *pp de* ponderar
2 *adj* (**a**) *(deliberado)* deliberate (**b**) *(equilibrado)* well-balanced, prudent (**c**) *(alabado)* highly praised

ponderar *vt* (**a**) *(asunto)* to weigh up *o* consider (**b**) *(alabar)* to praise

ponderativo, -a *adj* highly favourable *o US* favorable

pondré *indic fut véase* poner

ponedero *nm* nesting box

ponedor, -a 1 *adj* egg-laying; **gallina ponedora** egg-laying hen
2 *nm (lugar)* nesting box

ponencia *nf* (**a**) *(en conferencia)* paper, communication; *(informe)* report (**b**) *Jur* position of reporter (**c**) *(comisión)* reporting committee

ponente *nmf* *(en conferencia)* speaker; *(informador)* reporter

poner [50] *(pp puesto)* **1** *vt* (**a**) *(gen)* to put; *(colocar)* to place; **pon mucho cuidado** be careful; **p. a un lado** to put aside; **p. al corriente** *(actualizar)* to update; *(informar)* to bring up to date; **p. algo a secar** to put sth to dry; **p. de manifiesto** to show; **p. en duda** to cast doubt on, question; **ponlo aquí** put it here; *Fam* **p. de patitas en la calle** to kick *o* throw out (**b**) *(huevos)* to lay (**c**) *(gesto, mueca)* to make, put on; **p. mala cara** to pull a long face (**d**) *(hacer adquirir condición)* to make; **p. colorado a algn** to make sb blush; **p. triste a algn** to make sb sad; *Ofens* **p. a parir** to get on sb's tits (**e**) *(vestir a algn)* to put; **le pondré el vestido azul** I'll put her blue dress on her; **¿qué llevaba puesto?** what was he wearing? (**f**) *(preparar)* to get ready; **¿has puesto el despertador?** have you set the alarm (clock)?; **p. la mesa** to set the table (**g**) *(suponer)* to suppose; **pongamos que Ana no viene** supposing Ana doesn't turn up; **pongo por caso** for example (**h**) *TV Cin* to be on, show; *Cin* **¿dónde la ponen?** where is it showing?; **¿qué ponen en la tele?** what's on the telly? (**i**) *(conectar)* to turn *o* switch on; **pon la radio** turn the radio on (**j**) *(enviar)* **p. una carta/un telegrama** to send a letter/telegram (**k**) *Esp Tel (con persona)* to put through (**l**) *(escribir)* to write; **pon tu nombre en esta lista** write your name down on this list; **p. por escrito** to write (out); *Esp* **¿qué pone aquí?** what does it say here?; *Esp* **¿qué pone el periódico?** what does the newspaper say? (**m**) *(instalar)* to install, *US* instal; **le han puesto el teléfono** he's had a telephone put in; **p. la luz/el gas** to install electricity/gas (**n**) *(establecer)* to set up; **p. un negocio** to set up a business (**o**) *(dejar)* to leave (sb with); **pongo el dinero en tus manos** I'll leave the money with you (**p**) *(contribuir)* to put in; **cada uno pone 25 pesos** each one pays 25 pesos; **p. de su parte** to do one's bit (**q**) *(alabar)* to praise; *(desacreditar)* to mark; *Fam* **p. a algn por las nubes** to sing sb's praises; *Fam* **p. como un trapo, p. de vuelta y media** to pull to pieces (**r**) *(imponer)* *(multa)* to impose; *(trabajo)* to give, assign (**s**) *(dar nombre a)* to name; **le pusieron como su padre** they named him after his father (**t**) *(dedicar a un trabajo)* to get a job as; **puso a su hijo de mecánico** he got his son a job as a mechanic

2 ponerse *vpr* (**a**) *(colocarse)* to put *o* place oneself; **póngase cómodo** make yourself comfortable; **ponte en contacto con Luis** get in touch with Luis; **ponte más cerca** come closer; **se ha puesto perdido de barro** he's covered in mud (**b**) *(vestirse)* to put on; **ella se puso el jersey** she put her jumper on (**c**) *(volverse)* to become; **se puso muy contento** he was very happy; **p. colorado** to blush (*estados de salud)* to get; **p. bueno** to recover; **p. malo** *o* **enfermo** to become ill (**e**) *(llegar)* to get; **se pusieron allí en nada** they got there in no time (**f**) *Astron* to set; **el sol se pone por el oeste** the sun sets in the west (**g**) *Esp Tel* to answer; **dile que se ponga** ask her to come to the phone, put her on (**h**) **p. a** to start to; **p. a trabajar** to get down to work; **se puso a cantar** he started to sing (**i**) *(exaltarse)* to get upset; **no te pongas así** don't take it like that; **p. a malas con algn** to have a falling out with sb (**j**) **p. de** to get a job as; **p. de taxista** to get a job as a taxi driver (**k**) *Am Fam (parecer)* **se me pone que…** it seems to me that…

poney ['poni] *(pl* **poneis)** *nm Zool* pony

pongo *indic pres véase* **poner**

poni *nm* pony

poniente *nm* (**a**) *(occidente)* West (**b**) *(viento)* westerly (wind)

pontevedrés, -esa 1 *adj* of *o* from Pontevedra
  2 *nm,f* person from Pontevedra

pontificado *nm* pontificate

pontifical *adj* papal

pontificar [59] *vi* to pontificate

pontífice *nm* Pontiff; **el Sumo P.** His Holiness the Pope

pontificio, -a *adj* pontifical

pontón *nm Náut* pontoon

ponzoña *nf* venom, poison

ponzoñoso, -a *adj* venomous, poisonous

pop *adj & nm inv Mús* pop

popa *nf Náut* stern; *Fig* **ir viento en p.** to go smoothly *o* very well

pope *nm Rel* pope

popelín *nm Tex* poplin

popis *nmf inv Méx Fam* posh person

populachero, -a *adj Pey* common, vulgar

populacho *nm Pey* plebs *pl*, masses *pl*

popular *adj* (**a**) *(folklórico)* folk; **arte/música p.** folk art/music (**b**) *(famoso)* popular

popularidad *nf* popularity

popularización *nf* popularization

popularizar [14] *vt* to popularize

popularmente *adv* commonly

populismo *nm* populism

populista *adj & nmf* populist

populoso, -a *adj* densely populated

popurrí *nm Mús* potpourri

popusa *nf Bol Guat Salv (tortilla)* = tortilla filled with cheese or meat

póquer *nm* poker; **p. de ases** *Naipes* four aces *pl*; *(dados)* poker of aces

por *prep* (**a**) *(tiempo)* for; **allá p. mayo** sometime around May; **p. ahora** for the time being; **p. aquel tiempo, p. entonces** at that time; **p. la mañana** in the morning; **p. la noche** at night, during the night; **p. Navidades** for *o* at Christmas; *Am* **fue presidente p. treinta años** he was president for thirty years (**b**) *(lugar)* by; **pasamos p. Soria** we went through Soria; **p. ahí** over there; **p. allí** that way; **p. debajo de** under; **p. dentro** inside; **¿p. dónde vamos?** which way are we taking?; **p. el camino** on *o* along the way; **p. la calle** in the street; **p. la izquierda** on the left (side); **p. mi casa** near my house; **p. todas partes** everywhere, all over (**c**) *(agente, autor)* by; **atropellado p. un coche** run over by a car; **pintado p. Picasso** painted by Picasso (**d**) *(causa)* because of; **es p. eso que …** that's why …, for that reason …; **p. algo será** there must be some reason; **p. otras razones** for other reasons; **p. su culpa** because of him; **p. sus ideas** because of her ideas (**e**) *(medio)* by; **p. avión/correo** by plane/post; **p. escrito** in writing; **p. la fuerza** by force (**f**) *(a cambio de)* for; **cambiar algo p. otra cosa** to exchange sth for sth else; **p. tres mil pesos** for three thousand pesos (**g**) *(distribución)* per; *(uno por uno)* by; **casa**

p. casa from house to house; **clasificado p. autores** classified by author; **p. cabeza** a head, per person; **p. hora/mes** per hour/month; **iba a ochenta p. hora** he was doing eighty an hour (**h**) *Mat* **dos p. tres, seis** two times three is six (**i**) *Mat (porcentaje)* per; **diez p. ciento** ten per cent (**j**) *(finalidad)* for; *(con verbo)* to, in order to; **lo hice p. ti** I did it for you *o* for your sake; **p. lo que** therefore; **p. llegar antes** (in order) to arrive earlier; **p. no molestarle** so as not to bother him (**k**) **p. qué** why (**l**) **estar p.** *(no hecho)* to remain to be; **eso está p. ver** that remains to be seen; **está todo p. hacer** we're right at the beginning (**m**) *(a punto de)* **estar p.** to be about to; **estuve p. llamarte** I almost phoned you (**n**) *(en busca de)* for, to; **baja p. tabaco** go down for some cigarettes; **fue (a) p. el médico** he went to fetch the doctor (**o**) **p. haber** for having; **p. haberse equivocado** for having made a mistake (**p**) *(locuciones)* **p. así decirlo** to say something; **p. cierto** by the way; **¡p. Dios!** for God's sake!; **p. ejemplo** for example *o* instance; **p. favor** please; **p. lo general** in general; **p. lo visto** apparently; **p. más *o* muy … que sea** no matter how … he *o* she is; **p. mí** for my part, as for me; **p. mucho que …** no matter how much …; **p. nada** for nothing; **p. si acaso** just in case; **p. sí mismo** by himself; **p. supuesto** of course; *Fam* **p. las buenas** for the hell of it

porcelana *nf* porcelain, china; **una p.** a piece of china

porcentaje *nm* percentage; *(proporción)* rate

porcentual *adj* percentage

porche *nm* (**a**) *(soportal)* arcade (**b**) *(entrada)* porch

porcino, -a *adj* porcine; pig; **ganado p.** pigs *pl*

porción *nf* portion, part; **una pequeña p.** a small quantity

pordiosear *vi* to beg

pordiosero, -a 1 *adj* begging
  2 *nm,f* beggar

porfía *nf* (**a**) *(lucha)* fight; *(discusión)* argument (**b**) *(obstinación)* obstinacy, pig-headedness, stubbornness; **a p.** in competition

porfiar [32] *vi* (**a**) *(disputar)* to fight (**b**) *(insistir)* to be pigheaded

porfolio *nm Arte* portfolio

pormenor *nm* detail; **venta al p.** retail

pormenorizar [14] *vi* to go into detail

porno *adj inv Fam* pornographic

pornografía *nf* pornography

pornográfico, -a *adj* pornographic; *Cin* X-rated

poro *nm* pore; *Fig* **rezumaba satisfacción por todos los poros** he oozed satisfaction

pororó *nm Am* popcorn

porosidad *nf* porosity, porousness

poroso, -a *adj* porous

poroto *nm Andes RP* kidney bean ❑ *Chile* **p. verde** green bean

porque *conj* (**a**) *(causal)* because; **no estudio p. no me gusta** I don't study because I don't like it (**b**) *(final)* so that, in order that

porqué *nm* reason; **me pregunto el p. de su negativa** I wonder why he refused

porquería *nf* (**a**) *(suciedad)* dirt, filth; **estar hecho una p.** to be really filthy; **la casa está llena de p.** the house is very dirty; **no hagas porquerías** don't be a pig (**b**) *Fam (comida)* rubbish, *US* junk food; **no comas esas porquerías** don't eat that rubbish (**c**) *(cosa de poco valor)* **le compraré cualquier p.** I'll get her any old thing

porqueriza *nf* pigsty

porquerizo *nm* pigman

porra nf (**a**) (de policía) Br truncheon, US nightstick (**b**) Culin = deep-fried pastry sticks (**c**) Esp Fam (apuesta) sweepstake (among friends or work colleagues) (**d**) Méx Dep (hinchada) fans (**e**) Fam (locuciones) **mandar a algn a la p.** to tell sb to go to hell; **¡porras!** damn it!, shit!; **¿qué porras ...?** what on earth ...?; **¡qué vacaciones ni qué porras!** holidays — like hell!; **¡y una p.!** no way!, Br not bloody likely!; **¡vete a la p.!** go to hell!, get lost!

porrada nf Fam (**a**) (golpe) blow o thump (with a truncheon) (**b**) (montón) pile, heap; **una p. de** heaps of, loads of

porrazo nm (golpe) blow, thump; (contra el suelo) bump; **pegarse un p. con algo** to bump into sth; Fig **de golpe y p.** all of a sudden, suddenly

porreta nmf Fam (**a**) (fumador de hachís) dopehead (**b**) (desnudo) **en p.** in the buff, starkers

porrillo: a porrillo loc adv Fam by the score, galore

porrista 1 nmf Méx (hincha) fan, supporter
　2 nf Col Méx (animadora) cheerleader

porro nm Argot joint; **darle al p.** to smoke dope regularly

porrón nm = glass bottle with a spout coming out of its base, used for drinking wine

porta nf Náut port, porthole

portaaviones nm inv Náut aircraft carrier

portabultos nm inv Méx roof rack

portada nf (**a**) (de libro) title page; (de revista) cover; (de periódico) front page; (de disco) sleeve (**b**) Arquit (fachada) front, façade, facade

portadocumentos nm inv Andes RP document wallet

portador, -a 1 adj carrying
　2 nm,f carrier, bearer; Com **páguese al p.** pay the bearer; Med **p. de virus** virus carrier

portaequipajes nm inv Aut Br boot, US trunk

portaestandarte nm Mil standard bearer

portafolios nm inv briefcase

portal nm (**a**) (zaguán) porch, entrance hall (**b**) (puerta de la calle) street door, main door, gateway (**c**) Rel **p. de Belén** Nativity scene (**d**) Inform (página web) portal

portalada nf Arquit large doorway, gateway

portaligas nm inv Am (prenda) Br suspender belt, US garter belt

portamaletas nm inv véase **portaequipajes**

portaminas nm inv propelling pencil

portamonedas nm inv purse

portante nm Fam **tomar** o **coger el p.** to leave, take one's leave

portaobjetos nm inv (de microscopio) slide

portapapeles nm inv Inform clipboard

portar 1 vt to carry
　2 portarse vpr to behave; **portaos bien** be good, behave yourselves; **p. mal** to misbehave; **se portó como un héroe** he acted like a hero

portátil adj portable

portavoz nmf spokesperson; (hombre) spokesman; (mujer) spokeswoman

portazo nm slam of a door; **dar un p.** to slam the door

porte nm (**a**) (aspecto) demeanour, appearance; **un hombre de p. distinguido** a distinguished-looking man (**b**) (transporte) transport, carriage; **portes pagados** carriage paid

porteador, -a nm,f porter

portear vt o carry, transport

portento nm (**a**) (cosa) wonder, marvel (**b**) (persona) genius; **Laura es un p. bailando** Laura is a wonderful dancer

portentoso, -a adj extraordinary, prodigious

porteño, -a 1 adj of o from Buenos Aires
　2 nm,f person from Buenos Aires

portería nf (**a**) (vivienda) porter's house; (garita) porter's lodge (**b**) (empleo) job of porter (**c**) Dep goal

portero, -a nm,f (**a**) (de vivienda) porter, caretaker; (de edificio público) doorman ❑ **p. automático** entryphone (**b**) Dep goalkeeper

pórtico nm (**a**) Arquit (portal) portico, porch (**b**) (con arcadas) arcade

portillo nm (**a**) (abertura) breach, opening, gap; (puerta secundaria) side door o entrance; (postigo) wicket (**b**) Fig (a una solución) opening; **es necesario buscar el p. de este problema** we have to find a solution to this problem

portón nm large door o entrance

portorriqueño, -a adj & nm,f Puerto Rican

portuario, -a adj harbour, US harbor, port; **(trabajador) p.** docker, US longshoreman

Portugal n Portugal

portugués, -esa 1 adj Portuguese
　2 nm,f (persona) Portuguese; **los portugueses** the Portuguese pl
　3 nm (idioma) Portuguese

porvenir nm future; **sin p.** with no prospects; **tener el p. asegurado** to have a secure future

pos: en pos de loc prep (detrás de) behind; (en busca de) after; **va en p. de la fama** he's after fame

pos- pref post-; **posmoderno** post-modern

posada nf (**a**) (fonda) inn; **dar p.** to offer hospitality, take in (**b**) CAm Méx (fiesta) Christmas party

posaderas nfpl Fam buttocks

posadero, -a nm,f innkeeper

posar 1 vi (para fotografía, retrato) to pose, sit
　2 vt to put o lay down; **p. la mirada en algo** to rest one's gaze on sth; **posó su mano sobre la mesa** he laid his hand on the table
　3 posarse vpr (**a**) (aves) to settle, alight; (avión) to land (**b**) (líquido, polvo) to settle

posavasos nm inv coaster

posdata nf postscriptum, postscript

pose nf (**a**) (postura) pose (**b**) (actitud) affected attitude o posturing, posing; **su p. de indiferencia me molesta mucho** I hate her pretending to be indifferent

poseedor, -a 1 adj who possesses
　2 nm,f owner, possessor

poseer [37] vt to possess, own

poseído, -a 1 pp de **poseer**
　2 adj possessed; **poseído de rabia** enraged
　3 nm,f possessed person

posesión nf possession; **estar en p.** to have; **tener en p.** to be in possession of; **tomar p.** (de algo) to take possession (**de** of); (de un cargo) to take up (**de** -)

posesionar 1 vt to give possession of
　2 posesionarse vpr (tomar posesión) to take possession (**de** of); (apropiarse) to seize

posesivo, -a adj & nm possessive

poseso, -a 1 adj possessed
　2 nm,f possessed person; Fig **como un p.** like a madman

posgrado nm véase **postgrado**

posgraduado, -a nm,f véase **postgraduado, -a**

posguerra nf postwar period

posibilidad nf possibility, chance; **no hay ninguna p. de** there is no chance of; **no tienes ninguna p.** you don't stand a chance

posibilitar *vt* to make possible, facilitate

posible 1 *adj* possible; **de ser p.** if possible; **en (la medida de) lo p., dentro de lo p.** as far as possible; **¿es p.?** really?; **es p. que venga** he might come; **hacer lo p.** to do one's best; **lo antes p.** as soon as possible; **¿será p. que no venga?** don't tell me he's not going to come!; **si nos es p.** if we possibly can
2 posibles *nmpl Fam* (economic) means

posiblemente *adv* possibly

posición *nf* position; **p. económica** economic situation; **p. social** social status

posicionamiento *nm* position; **su p. con respecto a algo** his position on sth

posicionarse *vpr* to take a position *o* stance

positivado *nm Fot* developing

positivamente *adv* positively

positivar *vt Fot* (*negativos*) to print

positivismo *nm Filos* positivism

positivista *adj & nmf Filos* positivist

positivo, -a *adj & nm* positive

poso *nm* (**a**) (*sedimento*) dregs *pl*, sediment (**b**) *Fig* (*vestigio*) trace

posponer [50] (*pp* pospuesto) *vt* (**a**) (*relegar*) to put in second place *o* behind, relegate (**b**) (*aplazar*) to postpone, put off

post- *pref* post-; **postnatal** postnatal

posta *nf* (**a**) (*caballos*) relay; (*parada*) staging stop (**b**) **a p.** on purpose; **lo han hecho a p.** they did it on purpose

postal 1 *adj* postal; **paquete p.** parcel (sent by post); **servicio p.** post, mail; **tarjeta p.** postcard
2 *nf* postcard

poste *nm* (*gen*) pole; *Dep* (*larguero*) post; *Fam* **parado como un p.** dead still

póster (*pl* **pósters**) *nm* poster

postergación *nf* (**a**) (*retraso*) delay, delaying; (*aplazamiento*) postponement (**b**) (*relegación*) relegation

postergar [38] *vt* (**a**) (*retrasar*) to delay; (*aplazar*) to postpone (**b**) (*relegar*) to relegate

posteridad *nf* posterity; **pasar a la p.** to go down in history

posterior *adj* (**a**) (*lugar*) posterior, rear; **parte p.** back (**b**) (*tiempo*) later (**a** than), subsequent (**a** to); **el accidente fue p. a la enfermedad** the accident came after the illness

posteriori: a posteriori *loc adv* with hindsight

posterioridad *nf* posteriority; **con p.** later

posteriormente *adv* subsequently, later

postgrado *nm* postgraduate; **estudios de p.** postgraduate studies

postgraduado, -a *nm,f* postgraduate

postigo *nm* (*de puerta*) wicket; (*de ventana*) shutter

postín *nm Fam* boasting, showing-off; **darse p.** to show off, swank; **de p.** posh, swanky

postizo, -a 1 *adj* (**a**) (*artificial*) false, artificial; **dentadura postiza** false teeth *pl*, dentures *pl* (**b**) (*sobrepuesto*) detachable
2 *nm* hairpiece

postoperatorio, -a 1 *adj* postoperative
2 *nm* postoperative period

postor *nm* bidder; **mejor p.** highest bidder

postración *nf* prostration

postrado, -a 1 *pp de* postrar
2 *adj* prostrate; *Fig* **p. por el dolor** prostrate with grief

postrar 1 *vt* to prostrate
2 postrarse *vpr* to prostrate oneself, kneel down

postre *nm Culin* dessert, *Br* pudding; **¿qué hay de p.?** what's for dessert?; *Fig* **a la p.** in the end; *Fig* **para postres** on top of all that

postrero, -a *adj* last

postrimería *nf* (*gen pl*) last part *o* period; **en las postrimerías del siglo pasado** at the end of the last century

postulación *nf* (*de dinero*) collection

postulado, -a 1 *pp de* postular
2 *nm* postulate

postulante *nmf* (**a**) (*de colecta*) collector (**b**) *Rel* postulant

postular *vt* (*dinero*) to collect

póstumo, -a *adj* posthumous

postura *nf* (**a**) (*posición*) position, posture (**b**) *Fig* (*actitud*) attitude; **adoptar una p.** to take *o* adopt an attitude (**c**) (*puja*) bid

postventa *adj*, **posventa** *adj* after-sales; **servicio p.** after-sales service

potable *adj* (**a**) (*agua*) drinkable; **agua no p.** not drinking water; **agua p.** drinking water (**b**) *Fam* (*aceptable*) acceptable

potaje *nm* (**a**) *Culin* hotpot, stew; **p. de legumbres** vegetable stew (**b**) *Fig* (*mezcla*) mixture

potasa *nf* potash

potasio *nm* potassium

pote *nm* pot; (*jarra*) jug; *Fam* **darse p.** to show off

potencia *nf* power; *Mat* **elevar un número a la quinta p.** to raise a number to the power of five; **en p.** potential; **un asesino en p.** he's a potential murderer; *Pol* **las grandes potencias** the superpowers; **un motor de gran p.** a very powerful engine

potenciación *nf* boosting, promotion, strengthening

potencial 1 *adj* potential
2 *nm* (**a**) (*gen*) potential; **p. eléctrico** voltage; **p. humano** manpower (**b**) *Ling* conditional (tense)

potencialidad *nf* potentiality

potencialmente *adv* potentially

potenciar *vt* to boost, promote, strengthen; **p. el comercio** to promote trade

potentado, -a *nm,f* potentate

potente *adj* powerful, strong

potestad *nf* power, authority

potestativo, -a *adj* optional, facultative

potingue *nm Fam Pey* (**a**) (*bebida*) concoction (**b**) (*maquillaje*) make-up, face cream *o* lotion

poto *nm* (**a**) *Perú* (*vasija*) vessel, jug (**b**) *Andes Fam* (*trasero*) bottom, backside

potra¹ *nf Zool* filly

potra² *nf Fam* luck; **tener p.** to be lucky *o Br* jammy

potranco, -a *nm,f* colt

potrero *nm Am* field, pasture

potro *nm* (**a**) *Zool* colt (**b**) (*de herrador*) stanchion (**c**) (*de gimnasia*) horse (**d**) (*de tortura*) rack

poyo *nm* stone bench

poza *nf* puddle

pozal *nm* well bucket

pozo *nm* (**a**) (*gen*) well; **p. de petróleo** oil well; *Fig* **p. de sabiduría** fund of knowledge; *Fig* **p. sin fondo** bottomless pit (**b**) *Min* shaft, pit

pozole *nm CAm Carib Méx* (*guiso*) = stew made with maize kernels, pork or chicken and vegetables

PP *nm Pol* (*abrev de* **Partido Popular**) Spanish conservative party

p.p. (a) (*abrev de* **por poder**) pp **(b)** (*abrev de* **porte pagado**) c/p

práctica *nf* practice; **con la p.** with practice; **en la p.** in practice; **período de prácticas** practical training period; **poner (algo) en p.** to put (sth) into practice; **tener mucha p. en** to have a lot of practice in

practicable *adj* **(a)** *(posible)* feasible **(b)** *(camino, carretera)* passable

prácticamente *adv* practically

practicante 1 *adj Rel* practising, *US* practicing
2 *nmf Med* nurse, medical assistant

practicar [59] **1** *vt (gen)* to practise, *US* practice; *(hacer)* to make; **p. un agujero** to make a hole; **¿practicas algún deporte?** do you go in for any sport?
2 *vi* to do one's practice; **antes de licenciarse practicó durante un mes en una escuela** he taught in a school for a month before graduating

practicidad *nf CSur* **por su p.** because it is very practical

práctico, -a 1 *adj (gen)* practical; *(útil)* handy, useful
2 *nm Náut* coastal pilot

pradera *nf* meadow, prairie

prado *nm* **(a)** *(campo)* meadow, field **(b)** *(paseo)* promenade

Praga *n* Prague

pragmática *nf* pragmatics *sing*

pragmático, -a 1 *adj* pragmatic
2 *nm,f* pragmatist

pragmatismo *nm* pragmatism

pral. (*abrev de* **principal**) first floor, *US* second floor

praliné *nm* praline

praxis *nf inv Fml* praxis

pre- *pref* pre-; **precientífico** prescientific

preacuerdo *nm* draft agreement

preámbulo *nm* **(a)** *(introducción)* preamble **(b)** *(rodeo)* circumlocution; **déjate de preámbulos** stop beating about the bush; **sin (más) p.** getting straight to the point, without further ado

preaviso *nm* previous warning, notice

prebenda *nf* **(a)** *Rel* prebend **(b)** *Fig (chollo)* sinecure, cushy job

preboste *nm* provost

precalentamiento *nm* **(a)** *Téc* preheating **(b)** *Dep* warming up

precalentar [3] *vt* **(a)** *Téc* to preheat **(b)** *Dep* to warm up

precariedad *nf* precariousness

precario, -a *adj* precarious

precaución *nf* caution, precaution; **con p.** cautiously; **por p.** as a precaution; **tomar precauciones** to take precautions

precaver 1 *vt* to guard against
2 precaverse *vpr* to take precautions; **precaverse de** *o* **contra** to guard (oneself) against

precavido, -a 1 *pp de* **precaver**
2 *adj* cautious, prudent; *Prov* **hombre p. vale por dos** forewarned is forearmed

precedencia *nf* precedence, priority

precedente 1 *adj* preceding
2 *nmf* predecessor
3 *nm* precedent; **sentar p.** to establish *o* set up a precedent; **sin p.** unprecedented, unparalleled; **y que no sirva de p.** don't take it as a rule

preceder *vt* to precede, go before

preceptista *nmf* theorist

preceptiva *nf* rules

preceptivo, -a *adj* obligatory, compulsory

precepto *nm* precept, rule; *Rel* **fiestas de p.** days of obligation

preceptor, -a *nm,f Educ* (private) tutor

preces *nfpl Rel* prayers

preciado, -a *adj* valuable, prized

preciarse *vpr* to boast; **me precio de ser su amigo** I'm proud to be his friend

precintado *nm* sealing

precintadora *nf* sealing machine

precintar *vt* to seal

precinto *nm* seal

precio *nm* price; **al p. de** at the cost of; **poner p. (a algo)** to put a price (on sth); **poner p. a la cabeza de algn** to put a price on sb's head; **un p. prohibitivo** a prohibitive price; *Fig* **a cualquier p.** at any price, at all costs; *Fig* **no tener p.** to be priceless ❑ **p. de costo** *o Esp* **coste** cost price; **p. de mercado** market price; **p. fijo** fixed price; **p. simbólico** nominal cost; **p. unitario** unit price

preciosidad *nf* **(a)** *(cualidad)* preciousness **(b)** *(cosa)* lovely thing; **es una p.** it's really lovely **(c)** *(persona)* darling; **¡qué p. de niño!** what a delightful child!

precioso, -a *adj* **(a)** *(valioso)* precious, valuable **(b)** *(hermoso)* lovely, beautiful

preciosura *nf Am* **(a)** *(cosa, persona)* **ser una p.** to be lovely *o* beautiful **(b)** *(como apelativo)* gorgeous

precipicio *nm* precipice, cliff; *Fig (abismo)* abyss

precipitación *nf* **(a)** *(prisa)* haste; *(imprudencia)* rashness; **con p.** *(con prisa)* hastily, hurriedly; *(imprudentemente)* rashly, precipitately **(b)** *Meteor* precipitation, shower

precipitadamente *adv (con prisa)* hastily, hurriedly; *(imprudentemente)* rashly, precipitately

precipitado, -a 1 *pp de* **precipitar**
2 *adj (apresurado)* hasty, hurried; *(imprudente)* rash
3 *nm Quím* precipitate

precipitar 1 *vt* **(a)** *(arrojar)* to throw, hurl down **(b)** *(acelerar)* to hurry, rush; **no precipites los acontecimientos** don't rush things **(c)** *Quím* to precipitate
2 precipitarse *vpr* **(a)** *(arrojarse)* to hurl oneself **(b)** *(actuar precipitadamente)* to hurry, rush; **no nos precipitemos** let's take things easy

precisamente *adv (con precisión)* precisely; *(exactamente)* exactly; **¡p.!** exactly!; **p. por eso** for that very reason

precisar 1 *vt* **(a)** *(determinar)* to determine, give full details of; **no puedo p. cuando** I can't say when exactly **(b)** *(necesitar)* to require, need; **se precisa una gran habilidad** great skill is required
2 *vi (ser necesario)* to be necessary; **p. de algo** to need sth

precisión *nm* **(a)** *(exactitud)* precision, accuracy, exactness; **con p.** precisely, accurately ❑ **instrumento de p.** precision instrument **(b)** *(aclaración)* clarification **(c)** *(necesidad)* need; **tener p. de algo** to need sth

preciso, -a *adj* **(a)** *(necesario)* necessary, essential; **es p. que la llames hoy** you must phone her today **(b)** *(exacto)* accurate, exact; **en este p. momento** at this very moment **(c)** *(claro)* concise, clear; **este informe es muy p.** this report is very clear

precocidad *nf* precocity, precociousness

precocinado, -a *adj* pre-cooked

precolombino, -a *adj* pre-Columbian

preconcebido, -a *adj* preconceived; **ideas preconcebidas** preconceptions

preconcebir [47] *vt* to draw up in advance

preconizar [14] *vt* to recommend, advocate

precoz *adj* **(a)** *(persona)* precocious **(b)** *(fruta)* early

precursor, -a 1 *adj* precursory
   2 *nm,f* precursor
predador, -a 1 *adj* predatory
   2 *nm* predator
predecesor, -a *nm,f* predecessor
predecible *adj* predictable
predecir [51] (*pp* **predicho**) *vt* to foretell, predict
predestinación *nf* predestination
predestinado, -a 1 *pp de* **predestinar**
   2 *adj* predestined
predestinar *vt* to predestine
predeterminación *nf* predetermination
predeterminar *vt* to predetermine
prédica *nf Rel* sermon; *Fam (perorata)* harangue
predicación *nf* preaching
predicado, -a 1 *pp de* **predicar**
   2 *nm Ling* predicate
predicador, -a *nm,f Rel* preacher
predicamento *nm* fame, prestige
predicar [59] *vt* to preach; *Fig* **p. con el ejemplo** to
   practise what one preaches
predicativo, -a *adj* predicative
predicción *nf* prediction, forecast
predice *indic pres véase* **predecir**
predicho, -a *pp de* **predecir**
predigo *indic pres véase* **predecir**
predilección *nf* predilection; **predilecciones y aver-
siones** likes and dislikes; **sentir p. por algo** to prefer sth
predilecto, -a *adj* favourite, *US* favorite, preferred
predio *nm* (**a**) *(finca)* estate, property ▫ **p. rústico**
country estate; **p. urbano** town property (**b**) *Am (edificio)*
building
predisponer [50] (*pp* **predispuesto**) *vt* to predispose
predisposición *nf* predisposition
predispuesto, -a 1 *pp de* **predisponer**
   2 *adj* predisposed
predominancia *nf* predominance
predominante *adj* predominant, predominating; **la
corriente p.** the prevailing current
predominar *vi* to predominate, prevail
predominio *nm* predominance
preeminencia *nf* pre-eminence
preeminente *adj* pre-eminent
preescolar *adj Educ* preschool; **etapa p.** nursery
education
preestablecido, -a *adj* pre-established
preestreno *nm* preview
preexistencia *nf* pre-existence
preexistente *adj* pre-existing
preexistir *vi* to pre-exist
prefabricado, -a 1 *pp de* **prefabricar**
   2 *adj* prefabricated
prefabricar [59] *vt* to prefabricate
prefacio *nm Lit* preface
prefecto *nm* prefect
prefectura *nf* prefecture
preferencia *nf* preference; **con p.** preferably; **de p.**
preferably; *Aut* **p. (de paso)** right of way; **tener p. por
algo** to have a preference for sth
preferente *adj* preferable, preferential
preferentemente *adv* preferably, preferentially

preferible *adj* preferable; **es p. que no vengas** you'd
better not come
preferiblemente *adv* preferably
preferido, -a 1 *pp de* **preferir**
   2 *adj* preferred
   3 *nm,f* favourite, *US* favorite
preferir [62] *vt* to prefer; **prefiere no salir** he'd rather stay
at home; **prefiero el calor al frío** I prefer the heat to the
cold
prefigurar *vt* to prefigure
prefijar *vt* (**a**) *(fijar con antelación)* to fix o arrange in
advance (**b**) *Ling* to prefix
prefijo *nm* (**a**) *Ling* prefix (**b**) *Tel* code, *US* area code
pregón *nm* public announcement
pregonar *vt* (**a**) *(anunciar)* to announce publicly (**b**) *Fig
(divulgar, difundir)* to reveal, disclose
pregonero *nm* town crier
pregunta *nf* question; **contestar a una p.** to answer a
question; **hacer una p.** to ask a question; **p. capciosa** catch
question
preguntar 1 *vt* to ask; **a mí no me lo preguntes** don't
ask me; **p. algo a algn** to ask sb sth; **p. por algn** to ask after
o about sb
   2 preguntarse *vpr* to wonder; **me pregunto si vendrá** I
wonder whether he'll come
preguntón, -ona *Fam* **1** *adj* inquisitive, nosey
   2 *nm,f* busybody, *Br* nosey parker
prehistoria *nf* prehistory
prehistórico, -a *adj* prehistoric
preimpresión *nf Inform* pre-press
prejubilación *nf* = voluntary redundancy before
entitlement to early retirement, with agreed benefits and/
or additional payments, partly funded by the government
prejuiciado, -a *adj Am véase* **prejuicioso**
prejuicio *nm* prejudice; **tener prejuicios** to be
prejudiced, be biased
prejuicioso, -a *adj Am* prejudiced
prejuzgar [38] *vt* to prejudge
prelación *nf* priority, preference
prelado *nm Rel* prelate
preliminar 1 *adj* preliminary
   2 *nm* preliminary; **preliminares** preliminaries
preludiar *vt* (**a**) *Mús* to prelude (**b**) *Fig (anunciar)* to
announce; *(empezar)* to introduce
preludio *nm* (**a**) *Mús* prelude (**b**) *Fig (anuncio)* prelude;
(inicio) introduction
premamá *adj inv (ropa)* maternity
prematrimonial *adj* premarital
prematuro, -a 1 *adj* premature
   2 *nm,f* premature baby
premeditación *nf* premeditation; **con p.** deliberately
premeditadamente *adv* with premeditation
premeditado, -a *adj* premeditated, deliberate
premeditar *vt* to think out in advance
premiación *nf Am (en escuela, club)* prizegiving; *(de cine,
música)* awards ceremony
premiado, -a 1 *pp de* **premiar**
   2 *adj* prize-winning
premiar *vt* (**a**) *(dar un premio)* to award a prize (**a** to) (**b**)
(recompesar) to reward
premier (*pl* **premiers**) *nm Pol* premier
premio *nm* (**a**) *(gen)* prize, award; **dar un p.** to award a
prize ▫ **p. de consolación** consolation prize; **p. en**

metálico prize money; **el P. Nobel** the Nobel Prize winner; *Univ* **p. extraordinario** award with special distinction (**b**) *(recompensa)* reward, recompense (**c**) *(de lotería)* prize; **le tocó un p.** he won a prize ❑ **p. (gordo)** big prize, first prize

premioso, -a *adj* (**a**) *(torpe)* clumsy, awkward (**b**) *(urgente)* urgent

premisa *nf* premise

premolar *adj & nm Anat* premolar

premonición *nf* premonition

premonitorio, -a *adj* premonitory, warning

premunirse *vpr Andes* **p. de** *(armas)* to arm oneself with; *(valor, paciencia)* to summon up

premura *nf* (**a**) *(apremio)* haste; *(urgencia)* urgency; **con p.** urgently (**b**) *(escasez)* shortage, lack; **con p. de tiempo** under time pressure

prenatal *adj* antenatal, prenatal

prenda *nf* (**a**) *(prenda)* garment, article; **prendas interiores** underwear *sing* (**b**) *(garantía)* token, pledge; **dar en p.** to pledge; **en p. de** as a pledge of; *Fam* **no dolerle prendas a uno** to spare no effort *o* expense; *(reconocer un error)* to admit one was wrong; *Fam* **no soltar p.** not to say a word (**c**) *(juego)* **prendas** forfeits (**d**) *(cualidad)* quality, talent (**e**) *Fam (persona)* darling, sweetheart

prendado, -a 1 *pp de* **prendar**
2 *adj* **quedar p. de** to be captivated by

prendar 1 *vt* to captivate, delight; **dejó a todos prendados** everyone was taken by him
2 prendarse *vpr (aficionarse)* to take a fancy (**de** to), be captivated (**de** by); *(enamorarse)* to fall in love (**de** with); **se prendó de ella** he fell for her

prendedor *nm* brooch, pin

prender 1 *vt* (**a**) *(arrestar)* to arrest; *(encarcelar)* to put in prison (**b**) *(sujetar)* to fasten, attach; *(con alfileres)* to pin (**c**) *(fuego)* to set; **p. la lumbre** to start a fire (**d**) *esp Am (luz, interruptor)* to switch on
2 *vi (planta)* to take root; *(fuego)* to catch; **esta leña no prende** this wood won't light; *Fig* **sus ideas prendieron rápidamente en los trabajadores** his ideas quickly caught on with the workers
3 prenderse *vpr* to catch fire

prendido, -a 1 *pp de* **prender**
2 *adj* (**a**) *(sujeto)* fastened, caught (**b**) *Fig (encantado)* enchanted, captivated; **quedar p.** to be captivated

prendimiento *nm* arrest, capture

prenombrado, -a *adj Arg Chile* aforementioned, aforesaid

prensa *nf* (**a**) *Téc (prensadora)* press (**b**) *Impr* printing press; **entrar en p.** to go to press (**c**) *Prensa* press; **la p. diaria** the newspapers *pl*, the dailies *pl*; *Fig* **tener buena/ mala p.** to have a good/a bad press; *Fam* **los chicos de la p.** the gentlemen of the press ❑ **p. del corazón** gossip magazines; **agencia de p.** press agency; **conferencia de p.** press conference

prensado, -a 1 *pp de* **prensar**
2 *adj* pressed, compressed; **madera prensada** chipboard
3 *nm* pressing

prensar *vt* to press

prensil *adj* prehensile

prenupcial *adj* premarital

preñado, -a 1 *adj* (**a**) *(mujer)* pregnant; **preñada de 3 meses** 3 months pregnant (**b**) *Fig (lleno, cargado)* pregnant (**de** with), full (**de** of); **ojos preñados de lágrimas** eyes filled with tears
2 *nm (embarazo)* pregnancy

preñar *vt (mujer)* to make pregnant; *(animal)* to impregnate

preñez *nf* pregnancy

preocupación *nf* (**a**) *(inquietud)* worry, concern (**b**) *(prejuicio)* prejudice

preocupado, -a 1 *pp de* **preocupar**
2 *adj* worried, concerned

preocupante *adj* worrying

preocupar 1 *vt* to worry; **me preocupa que llegue tan tarde** I'm worried about him arriving so late
2 preocuparse *vpr* to worry, get worried (**por** about); **no te preocupes** *(no te inquietes)* don't worry; *(déjalo correr)* never mind

prepa *nf Méx Fam véase* **preparatoria**

prepago *nm* pay-as-you-go; **tarjeta de p.** *(para móvil)* top-up card

preparación *nf (gen)* preparation; *(formación)* training; *(aptitud)* capacity; **p. musical** musical training

preparado, -a 1 *pp de* **preparar**
2 *adj* (**a**) *(dispuesto)* ready, prepared; *Culin* **comidas preparadas** ready-cooked meals; **p. de antemano** prepared (**b**) *(capacitado)* trained, qualified
3 *nm Farm (medicamento)* preparation

preparador, -a *nm,f Dep* coach, trainer

preparar 1 *vt* (**a**) *(gen)* to prepare, get ready; **prepara las maletas** pack your bags; **p. la comida** to get lunch ready; **p. un examen** to prepare for an exam (**b**) *(enseñar)* to train, teach; *Dep (entrenar)* to train, coach
2 prepararse *vpr* (**a**) *(gen)* to prepare oneself, get ready; **me preparaba para salir cuando sonó el teléfono** I was getting ready to leave when the telephone rang; **se prepara una buena tormenta** there's a big storm brewing (**b**) *Dep (entrenarse)* to train; **se está preparando para los Juegos Olímpicos** he's training for the Olympic Games

preparativo *nm* preparation; **hacer los preparativos para** to make preparations for

preparatoria *nf Méx* = three-year course of studies for students aged 14-17, *Br* ≃ Sixth Form studies, *US* ≃ Senior High School studies

preparatorio, -a *adj* preparatory

prepizza *nf RP* pizza base

preponderancia *nf* preponderance, prevalence

preponderante *adj* preponderant

preponderar *vt* to prevail

preposición *nf Ling* preposition

preposicional *adj Ling* prepositional

prepotencia *nf* power, dominance

prepotente *adj* powerful, domineering

prepucio *nm Anat* foreskin

prerrequisito *nm* prerequisite

prerrogativa *nf* prerogative

presa *nf* (**a**) *(captura)* capture, seizure; **hacer p.** to seize; **el fuego hizo p. en su vestido** the fire set light to her dress (**b**) *(cosa)* prey, catch; *Fig* prey; **caer p. de** to fall prey to; **el cazador siempre debe perseguir a su p.** hunters should always stalk their prey; *Fig* **ser p. de** to be a victim of; **p. del pánico** panic-stricken (**c**) *Orn (uña)* claw; *Zool (colmillo)* tusk (**d**) *(embalse)* dam; *(acequia)* channel, ditch

presagiar *vt* to predict, foretell

presagio *nm* (**a**) *(señal)* omen; **buen/mal p.** good/bad omen (**b**) *(premonición)* premonition

presbicia *nf Med Br* long-sightedness, *US* far-sightedness

presbiterianismo *nm Rel* Presbyterianism

presbiteriano, -a *adj & nm,f Rel* Presbyterian

presbiterio *nm* presbytery

presbítero *nm Rel* priest

prescindencia *nf Am* omission; **con p. de** without

prescindir *vi* (**a**) *(pasarse sin)* to do without; **podemos p. del coche** we can do without the car (**b**) *(omitir)* to leave out, omit (**c**) *(desembarazarse)* to get rid of

prescribir *(pp prescrito) vt & vi* to prescribe; **el médico le prescribió unas vacaciones** the doctor advised him to take a holiday

prescripción *nf* prescription; **p. facultativa** medical prescription

prescrito, -a 1 *pp de* **prescribir**
  2 *adj* prescribed

preselección *nf (gen)* short list, short listing; *Dep* seeding

preseleccionar *vt (gen)* to short-list; *Dep* to seed

presencia *nm* (**a**) *(gen)* presence; **en p. de** in the presence of; **hacer acto de p.** to put in an appearance □ **p. de ánimo** presence of mind (**b**) *(aspecto)* presence, look; **de buena p.** distinguished-looking

presencial *adj* **testigo p.** eyewitness

presenciar *vt (estar presente)* to be present at; *(ver)* to witness

presentable *adj* presentable; **no estoy p.** I'm not dressed for it, I'm not dressed for the occasion

presentación *nf (gen)* presentation; *(aspecto)* appearance; *(de personas)* introduction; *(de producto)* launching; **carta de p.** letter of introduction; **hacer las presentaciones** to introduce two or more people; **p. en sociedad** debut, coming out

presentador, -a *nm,f Rad TV* presenter

presentar 1 *vt* (**a**) *(gen)* to present; *(mostrar)* to show, display; *(ofrecer)* to offer; **la habitación presentaba un aspecto desolador** the room looked gloomy; **p. excusas** to excuse oneself; **p. la dimisión** to tender one's resignation; **p. un candidato** to propose sb; **p. un libro/una película** to launch a book/film; **p. una demanda** *o* **una denuncia** to bring an action; *Jur* **p. pruebas** to submit proof; **p. una queja** to lodge a complaint (**b**) *(una persona a otra)* to introduce; **le presento al doctor Ruiz** may I introduce you to Dr Ruiz; **ser presentada en sociedad** to make one's debut, come out
  2 presentarse *vpr* (**a**) *(comparecer)* to present oneself; *(inesperadamente)* to turn *o* come up; **preséntese en mi oficina mañana** report to my office tomorrow; **se presentó sin avisar** he turned up without warning *o* unexpectedly (**b**) *(ocurrir)* to present itself, arise; **si se presenta la ocasión** should the opportunity arise (**c**) *(candidato)* to stand; **p. a unas elecciones** to stand for election, *US* run for office (**d**) *(a examen)* to sit (**a** for) (**e**) *(darse a conocer)* to introduce oneself (**a** to); **p. en sociedad** to make one's debut, come out

presente 1 *adj* present; **estar p. en** to be present at; **hacer p** to declare, state; **hacer p. algo a algn** to remind sb of sth; **la p. (carta)** this letter; **las personas aquí presentes** the people here present; **los presentes** those present; **mejorando lo p.** present company excepted; **¡p.!** here!, present!; **tener p.** *(tener en cuenta)* to bear in mind; *(recordar)* to remember
  2 *nm* (**a**) *(tiempo actual)* present; **al** *o* **de p.** at present; **hasta el p.** up to the present (**b**) *Ling* **(tiempo) p.** present tense; **participio de p.** present participle (**c**) *Fml (regalo)* present, gift

presentimiento *nm* presentiment, premonition; **tengo el p. de que ...** I have the feeling that ...

presentir [62] *vt* to have a presentiment *o* premonition of; **presiento que lloverá** I've got the feeling that it's going to rain

preservación *nf* preservation, protection

preservante *nm Am* preservative

preservar *vt* to preserve, protect (**de** from); (**contra** against)

preservativo, -a 1 *adj* preservative
  2 *nm* sheath, condom

presidencia *nf* (**a**) *Pol* presidency (**b**) *(de una reunión)* *(hombre)* chairmanship; *(mujer)* chairwomanship

presidencial *adj* presidential

presidencialismo *nm Pol* presidential system

presidente, -a *nm,f* (**a**) *Pol (de nación)* president; *(de parlamento)* speaker; **p. del gobierno** Prime Minister, Premier (**b**) *(de reunión)* chairperson, chair; *(hombre)* chairman; *(mujer)* chairwoman

presidiario, -a *nm,f* prisoner, convict

presidio *nm* prison, penitentiary

presidir *vt* (**a**) *Pol (país)* to rule, head; *Fig* **la bondad preside todos sus actos** he is motivated by kindness (**b**) *(reunión)* to chair, preside over

presilla *nf Cost* fastener

presión *nf* pressure; **a** *o* **bajo p.** under pressure; **hacer p.** to press; *Fig (influir)* to pressurize; *Pol* to lobby □ **p. arterial** *o* **sanguínea** blood pressure; **p. atmosférica** atmospheric pressure; *Pol* **grupo de p.** pressure group, lobby

presionar *vt* to press; *Fig* to pressurize, put pressure on

preso, -a 1 *adj* imprisoned
  2 *nm,f* prisoner □ **p. político** political prisoner

prestación *nf* (**a**) *(servicio)* service (**b**) *(ayuda)* help, assistance; *(subsidio)* provision, supply, benefit (**c**) *Téc (gen pl)* performance

prestado, -a 1 *pp de* **prestar**
  2 *adj (a algn)* lent; *(por algn)* borrowed; **dejar p.** to lend; **ese libro está p.** that book is on loan; **pedir p.** to borrow; *Fam* **vivir de p.** to scrounge

prestamiento *nm Méx* loan

prestamista *nmf Fin* moneylender

préstamo *nm* (**a**) *(acción de prestar)* lending; *(acción de pedir prestado)* borrowing (**b**) *(cantidad, cosa)* loan; **pedir un p.** to ask for a loan (**c**) *Ling (palabra)* loanword

prestancia *nf* (**a**) *(excelencia)* excellence, high quality (**b**) *(distinción)* distinction, elegance

prestar 1 *vt* (**a**) *(dejar prestado)* to lend, loan; *(pedir prestado)* to borrow; **¿me prestas diez euros?** could you lend me ten euros?; **¿me prestas tu pluma?** can I borrow your pen? (**b**) *(atención)* to pay; *(ayuda)* to give; *(servicio)* to do, render; *Jur (declaración)* to make; **p. juramento** to make an oath, swear
  2 prestarse *vpr* (**a**) *(ofrecerse)* to offer oneself (**a** to); **se prestó a llevarnos a casa** she (willingly) gave us a lift home (**b**) *(acceder)* to agree; **no te prestes a ese juego** don't get mixed up in that sort of thing (**c**) *(dar motivo)* to cause; **se presta a (crear) malentendidos** it makes for misunderstandings

prestatario, -a *nm,f Fin* borrower

presteza *nf* promptness, diligence; **con p.** promptly

prestidigitación *nf* conjuring, magic

prestidigitador, -a *nm,f* conjuror, magician

prestigiado, -a *adj Chile Méx* prestigious

prestigiar *vt* to give prestige to

prestigio *nm* prestige

prestigioso, -a *adj* prestigious

presto, -a 1 *adj* (**a**) *(dispuesto)* ready, prepared (**b**) *(rápido)* swift, quick, prompt
  2 *adv Mús* presto

presumible *adj* probable, likely

presumido, -a 1 *adj* vain, conceited
2 *nm,f* vain person

presumir 1 *vt (suponer)* to presume, assume, suppose
2 *vi* **(a)** *(vanagloriarse)* to boast, show off; **ella presume de artista** she likes to think she's an artist; **presume de guapo** he fancies himself **(b)** *(ser vanidoso)* to be vain o conceited

presunción *nf* **(a)** *(suposición)* presumption, supposition **(b)** *(vanidad)* vanity, conceit

presuntamente *adv* supposedly

presunto, -a *adj* presumed, supposed; *Jur* **el p. autor del crimen** the alleged criminal

presuntuosidad *nf* vanity, conceit

presuntuoso, -a 1 *adj* **(a)** *(vanidoso)* vain, conceited **(b)** *(pretencioso)* pretentious, showy
2 *nm,f* **(a)** *(vanidoso)* vain o conceited person **(b)** *(pretencioso)* pretentious person, show-off

presuponer [50] *(pp* **presupuesto)** *vt* to presuppose

presuposición *nf* assumption

presupuestar *vt Fin* to budget for; *(importe)* to estimate for

presupuestario, -a *adj* budget, budgetary

presupuesto, -a 1 *pp de* **presuponer**
2 *adj* presupposed
3 *nm* **(a)** *(supuesto)* supposition, assumption **(b)** *Fin* budget; *(cálculo)* estimate; **hacer un p. (de un trabajo)** to give an estimate (for a job)

presurizar [14] *vt* to pressurize

presuroso, -a *adj (rápido)* quick; *(con prisa)* in a hurry

prêt-à-porter [pretapor'te] **1** *adj (ropa, moda)* ready-to-wear, *Br* off-the-peg
2 *nm* ready-to-wear o *Br* off-the-peg clothing

pretencioso, -a 1 *adj* pretentious
2 *nm,f* pretentious person

pretender *vt* **(a)** *(querer)* to want to, mean to; **pretendo acabar pronto** I mean to finish soon **(b)** *(intentar)* to try; **pretende ayudarnos** he's trying to help us; **¿qué pretendes insinuar?** what are you getting at? **(c)** *(afirmar)* to claim; **pretende ser el más rico** he claims to be the richest person around **(d)** *(aspirar a)* to try for; *(cargo)* to apply for **(e)** *(cortejar)* to court, woo

pretendido, -a 1 *pp de* **pretender**
2 *adj* **(a)** *(fingido)* pretended **(b)** *(supuesto)* so-called, would-be

pretendiente, -a 1 *adj* aspiring
2 *nm,f* **(a)** *(de una mujer etc)* suitor **(b)** *Pol (al trono)* pretender **(c)** *(a un cargo)* applicant, candidate

pretensión *nf* **(a)** *(aspiración)* aim, aspiration; **mi única p.** the only thing I want **(b)** *(soberbia)* pretentiousness; **con demasiadas pretensiones** too pretentiously; **tener muchas pretensiones** to be pretentious; **tener pocas pretensiones** to be undemanding; **tenía la p. de que ganaría** he was convinced he was going to win

pretérito, -a 1 *adj* past, former
2 *nm Ling* preterite, simple past tense

pretextar *vt* to plead, allege; **pretextó que tenía dolor de cabeza** he claimed he had a headache

pretexto *nm* pretext, excuse; **con el p. de que …** on the pretext that …

pretil *nm Arquit* parapet

Pretoria *n* Pretoria

preuniversitario, -a *adj* pre-university

prevalecer [46] *vi* **(a)** *(triunfar)* to triumph; *(imponerse)* to prevail; **prevaleció la razón** common sense prevailed **(b)** *Bot (planta)* to take root

prevaleciente *adj* prevailing

prevaler [68] **1** *vi véase* **prevalecer**
2 prevalerse *vpr (valerse, servirse)* to avail oneself **(de** of), take advantage **(de** of); **se prevalió de su autoridad para conseguir lo que quería** he took advantage of his position to achieve his ends

prevaricar [59] *vi Jur* to pervert the course of justice

prevención *nf* **(a)** *(precaución)* prevention; **en p. de** as a precaution against **(b)** *(preparación)* preparation **(c)** *(medida)* precaution; **tomar prevenciones** to take precautions **(d)** *(prejuicio)* prejudice; **tener p. contra algn** to be prejudiced against sb **(e)** *(policial)* police station

prevenido, -a 1 *pp de* **prevenir**
2 *adj* **(a)** *(previsor)* **ser p.** to be cautious **(b)** *(avisado, dispuesto)* **estar p.** to be prepared

prevenir [69] *vt* **(a)** *(preparar)* to prepare, get ready **(b)** *(precaver)* to prevent, forestall; *(evitar)* to avoid; **para p. la gripe** to prevent flu; *Prov* **más vale p. que curar** prevention is better than cure **(c)** *(advertir)* to warn

preventivo, -a *adj* preventive; *(medidas)* precautionary; *Jur* **detención** o **prisión preventiva** remand in custody; *Med* **medicina preventiva** preventive medicine

prever [70] *(pp* **previsto)** *vt* **(a)** *(conjeturar)* to foresee, forecast **(b)** *(planear)* to plan **(c)** *(anticipar)* to make allowances for

previamente *adv* previously

previo, -a *adj* previous, prior; **p. pago de su importe** only on payment; **sin p. aviso** without prior notice

previsible *adj* foreseeable

previsión *nf* **(a)** *(acción de prever)* forecast; *Meteor* **p. del tiempo** weather forecast **(b)** *(precaución)* precaution; **en p. de** as a precaution against

previsional *adj Andes RP* **gastos previsionales** social security spending

previsor, -a *adj* careful, far-sighted

previsto, -a 1 *pp de* **prever**
2 *adj* foreseen, forecast; **todo salió según lo p.** everything turned out as planned o expected

PRI [pri] *nm (abrev de* **Partido Revolucionario Institucional)** = Mexican political party, the governing party from 1929 to 2000

prieto, -a *adj* **(a)** *(apretado)* firm, tight; **de carnes prietas** with a firm body **(b)** *Cuba Méx Fam (moreno)* dark-skinned

priísta *Méx Pol* **1** *adj* relating to the **PRI**
2 *nmf* member/supporter of the **PRI**

prima *nf* **(a)** *(gratificación)* bonus; *(de un seguro)* insurance premium **(b)** *(persona) véase* **primo, -a**

primacía *nf* primacy

primado *nm Rel* primate

primar¹ *vi* to have priority, prevail

primar² *vt* to give a bonus to

primario, -a *adj* primary

primate *nm* **(a)** *Zool* primate **(b)** *(persona)* outstanding person

primavera¹ *nf* **(a)** *(estación)* spring; *Fig* **(ella) tenía quince primaveras** she was fifteen **(b)** *Bot* primrose

primavera² 1 *adj* gullible, naive
2 *nmf* simpleton, sucker, mug

primaveral *adj* spring, spring-like; **hace un tiempo p.** it's like spring

primer *adj (delante de nm) véase* **primero, -a**

primera *nf* **(a)** *(clase)* first class; **viajar en p.** to travel first class **(b)** *Aut (marcha)* first gear **(c) a la p.** at the first attempt; *Fam* **a la p. de cambio** *(así que pueda)* as soon as the opportunity arises; *(inesperadamente)* when least expected; *Fam* **de p.** great, first class; **me viene de p.** it's just the job

primeriza *nf* first-time mother

primerizo, -a 1 *adj* (**a**) *(principiante)* novice (**b**) *(madre)* first-time; *(niño)* first
2 *nm,f* novice

primero, -a 1 *adj* (**a**) *(que precede)* first; *(anterior)* former; **de primera necesidad** basic; **el primer paso es ...** the first thing to do is ...; **es el p. de la clase** he's top of the class; **iré a primera hora de la tarde** I'll go first thing this afternoon; *Prensa* **primera página** front page (**b**) *Fig (fundamental)* first, basic, main; **lo p. es la familia** the family comes first
2 *nm,f* first; **llegar el p.** to arrive first; **no eres el p. en llegar** you're not the first to arrive; **nos vamos a primeros de mes** we shall be leaving at the beginning of the month
3 *adv* (**a**) *(en primer lugar)* first; **cómete eso p.** eat that first (**b**) *(antes, más bien)* rather, sooner; **p. me moriría que pedirle dinero** I'd rather die than ask him for money

primicia *nf* (**a**) *Bot* first fruit (**b**) *Prensa* novelty; **p. informativa** scoop

primigenio, -a *adj* original, primitive

primitivo, -a *adj* (**a**) *(original)* original, first (**b**) *Hist* primitive (**c**) *(tosco)* coarse, rough

primo, -a 1 *adj* (**a**) *(materia)* raw (**b**) *Mat (número)* prime
2 *nm,f* (**a**) *(pariente)* cousin; **p. hermano** first cousin; **p. segundo** second cousin (**b**) *Fam (tonto)* fool, drip, dunce; **hacer el p.** to be taken for a ride

primogénito, -a *adj & nm,f* first-born, eldest

primor *nm* (**a**) *(delicadeza)* delicacy; **con (gran) p.** (very) delicately (**b**) *(belleza)* beauty; **esta niña es un p.** this girl is lovely; *Fam* **dibuja que es un p.** he's a fantastic drawer (**c**) *(habilidad)* care, skill

primordial *adj* essential, basic, fundamental

primoroso, -a *adj* delicate, exquisite

prímula *nf Bot* primula

princesa *nf* princess

principado *nm* principality

principal 1 *adj* main, chief, principal; **lo p. es que ...** the main thing is that ...; *Arquit* **puerta p.** front door
2 *nm* (**a**) *(piso) Br* first floor, *US* second floor (**b**) *(jefe)* chief, boss

príncipe 1 *nm* prince □ **p. azul** Prince Charming; **p. consorte** prince consort; **p. de Gales** Prince of Wales; **p. heredero** crown prince
2 *adj inv* **edición p.** first edition

principesco, -a *adj* princely

principiante 1 *adj* novice
2 *nmf* beginner, learner, novice

principio *nm* (**a**) *(fundamento)* principle; **el p. de Arquímedes** Archimedes' principle; **hombre de principios** man of principles; **no tener principios** to have no principles; **por p.** in principle (**b**) *(comienzo)* beginning, start; **a principio(s) de** at the beginning of; **al p., en un p.** at first, in the beginning; **dar p. a algo** to start sth off; **en p.** in principle (**c**) **principios** *(nociones)* rudiments, basics

pringar [38] **1** *vt* (**a**) *(ensuciar)* to make greasy *o* dirty (**b**) *Fam* **¡ya la has pringado!** now you've done it!
2 *vi Fam* (**a**) *(trabajar)* to work hard (**b**) *(morirse)* to kick the bucket
3 *v impers CAm Méx Ven* to drizzle
4 pringarse *vpr* (**a**) *(ensuciarse)* to get greasy *o* dirty (**b**) *Fam (en asunto sucio)* to get one's hands dirty

pringoso, -a *adj (grasiento)* greasy; *(sucio)* dirty; **manos pringosas** sticky hands

pringue *nm (grasa)* grease; *(suciedad)* dirt, filth

prión *nm* prion

prior, -a *nm,f Rel (hombre)* prior; *(mujer)* prioress

priorato *nm Rel (cargo)* priorate; *(comunidad)* priory

priori: a priori *loc adv* a priori

prioridad *nf* priority; **dar p. a algo** to give priority to sth; **tener p.** to have priority

prioritario, -a *adj* prior, priority; **ser p.** to have priority

priorizar [14] *vt* to give priority to

prisa *nf (prontitud)* hurry, rush; *(velocidad)* speed; **a p.** *véase* **aprisa**; **correr p.** to be urgent; **me corre mucha p.** I need it right away; **date p.** hurry up; **de p.** *véase* **deprisa**; **salió a toda p.** he left in a hurry; **tener p.** to be in a hurry

prisión *nf* prison, jail, gaol; **fue condenado a veinte años de p.** he was given twenty years □ **p. preventiva** remand in custody

prisionero, -a *nm,f* prisoner □ **p. de guerra** prisoner of war

prisma *nm Mat* prism

prismático, -a 1 *adj* prismatic
2 prismáticos *nmpl* binoculars, field glasses

priva *nf Esp Argot* booze

privacidad *nf* privacy

privación *nf* deprivation, privation; **pasar privaciones** to be in great need

privado, -a 1 *pp de* **privar**
2 *adj* private; **vida privada** private life

privar 1 *vt* (**a**) *(despojar)* to deprive (**de** of) (**b**) *(prohibir)* to forbid, ban (**c**) *Fam (gustar)* to like; **no me priva la vida de campo** I don't go for country life
2 *vi* (**a**) *(estar de moda)* to be fashionable *o* popular (**b**) *Esp Fam (beber)* to booze
3 privarse *vpr* (**a**) *(despojarse)* to deprive oneself (**de** of), go without; **no se priva de nada** he really spoils himself (**b**) *Fam (emborracharse)* to get drunk

privativo, -a *adj* exclusive (**de** of)

privatización *nf* privatization

privatizar [14] *vt* to privatize

privilegiado, -a 1 *pp de* **privilegiar**
2 *adj* privileged
3 *nm,f* privileged person

privilegiar *vt (persona)* to favour; *(intereses)* to put first

privilegio *nm* privilege

pro 1 *nm (provecho)* advantage; **en p. de** in favour of; **hombre de p.** man of integrity; **los pros y los contras** the pros and cons
2 *prep (a favor de)* in favour *o US* favor of; **campaña p. desarme** campaign for disarmament, disarmament campaign

pro- *pref* pro-; **prodemocrático** prodemocratic

proa *nf Náut* prow, bows *pl*; **poner la p. a algn** to take a stand against sb; **poner p. a** to set sail for

probabilidad *nf* probability, likelihood; **tiene pocas probabilidades** he stands little chance

probable *adj* probable, likely; **es p. que llueva** it'll probably rain; **es p. que no lo sepa** he's unlikely to know; **lo más p. es que ...** it's very likely that ...

probado, -a 1 *pp de* **probar**
2 *adj* proven; **de probada eficacia** of proven efficiency; **un hecho p.** a proven fact

probador *nm* fitting room

probar [63] **1** *vt* (**a**) *(comprobar)* to test, check; **prueba la puerta a ver si está cerrada con llave** check to see if the door is locked (**b**) *(intentar)* to try; **lo hemos probado todo** we've tried everything (**c**) *(demostrar)* to prove, show; **eso prueba que tenía razón** that shows I was right (**d**) *(comer, beber)* to try; **no había probado este vino** I had never

'tried this wine before; **prueba esta sopa** taste this soup
 2 vi (**a**) (sentar) to suit; **la humedad le prueba mal** dampness is bad for him (**b**) (intentar) to try; **p. a** to attempt o try to; **por p. no se pierde nada** there is no harm in trying; **prueba a levantarlo** try and lift it; **prueba a meterlo de lado** see if it fits sideways
 3 probarse vpr (prenda) to try on

probeta nf Quím test tube ❑ **niño p.** test-tube baby

probidad nf honesty, integrity, decency

problema nm problem, trouble

problemática nf problems pl

problemático, -a adj problematic

probo, -a adj honest, upright, decent

procacidad nf (dicho) rude remark; (hecho) indecent act

procaz adj rude, indecent

procedencia nf (**a**) (origen) origin, source (**b**) (oportunidad, adecuación) adequacy, appropriateness; Jur merits pl

procedente adj (**a**) (originario) coming (**de** from); **el vuelo p. de Sevilla** the flight (coming) from Seville (**b**) (oportuno, adecuado) adequate, appropriate, fitting; Jur proper

proceder 1 vi (**a**) **p. de** (originarse) to come from; **procede del norte** he's from the North (**b**) (actuar) to act, behave; **siempre procede con cautela** he is always careful o cautious (**c**) (ser oportuno) to be advisable o appropriate; **en estas situaciones procede tomar medidas drásticas** under these circumstances it is advisable to take drastic measures (**d**) Jur (ser conforme) to take proceedings (**contra** against); **la protesta no procede** objection overruled (**e**) (ejecutar) (gen uso impers) to proceed; **p. a una votación** to proceed to an election; **se procedió a la elección del presidente** they went on to the election of the chairman
 2 nm (comportamiento) behaviour, US behavior; **de recto p.** upright

procedimiento nm (**a**) (método) procedure, method; **utiliza unos procedimientos poco ortodoxos** he uses unorthodox methods (**b**) Jur (trámites) proceedings pl

proceloso, -a adj Literario tempestuous, stormy

prócer nm great man, notable; **los próceres de la nación** the country's great men

procesado, -a 1 pp de **procesar**
 2 adj (**a**) Jur accused (**b**) Com Tec processed
 3 nm,f Jur accused

procesador nm Inform processor; **p. de datos/textos** data/word processor

procesal adj Jur procedural

procesamiento nm (**a**) Jur prosecution; **auto de p.** indictment (**b**) (elaboración) processing; Inform processing; Inform **p. de datos/textos** data/word processing; Inform **p. por lotes** batch processing

procesar vt (**a**) Jur to prosecute (**b**) (elaborar, transformar) to process; Inform to process

procesión nf procession; Fig **la p. va por dentro** he's putting on a brave face

procesional adj processional

procesionaria adj Ent processionary moth

procesionario nm Rel processional

proceso nm (**a**) (fases sucesivas) process; Inform **p. de datos** data processing; **p. de elaboración del pan** bread-making process; **p. mental** thought process (**b**) (transcurso del tiempo) time; **en el p. de un año** in the course of a year (**c**) Jur trial, suit, hearing

proclama nf proclamation; Rel **p. matrimonial** banns pl

proclamación nf proclamation

proclamar vt to proclaim; **el presidente ha proclamado su inocencia en el escándalo** the president has declared his innocence in the scandal; **no es necesario proclamarlo a los cuatro vientos** you don't need to broadcast it

proclítico, -a adj Ling proclitic

proclive adj prone, apt, inclined; **es muy p. a dejarse llevar por sus sentimientos** he often gets carried away by his emotions

procónsul nm Hist proconsul

procreación nf procreation

procreador, -a 1 adj procreant, procreative
 2 nm,f procreator

procrear vt to procreate

proctología nf Med proctology

proctológico, -a adj Med proctological

proctólogo, -a nm,f Med proctologist

procura nf Am (busca) search, hunt

procuración nf Jur procuration, power of attorney

procurador, -a nm,f Jur procurator

procurar vt (**a**) (intentar) to try, attempt; **hay que p. no molestar a nadie** we have to try not to bother anybody; **procura no hacer ruido** try not to make too much noise; **procura que no te vean** make sure they don't see you (**b**) (proporcionar) (to manage) to get; **ella le procuró un trabajo** she got a job for him

prodigalidad nf (abundancia) lavishness; (profusión) extravagance, prodigality

prodigar [38] **1** vt (despilfarrar) to spend lavishly, lavish
 2 prodigarse vpr (**a**) (ser amable, ayudar) to go out of one's way, be helpful o kind (**b**) (exhibirse) to show off; **cree que para triunfar tiene que p. sus apariciones en público** he thinks he has to be in the public eye more to be successful

prodigio nm (**a**) (suceso sobrenatural) prodigy, miracle; **hacer prodigios** to work wonders (**b**) (niño) child prodigy

prodigiosamente adv prodigiously

prodigioso, -a adj (sobrenatural) prodigious; (maravilloso) wonderful, marvellous, US marvelous, fantastic

pródigo, -a 1 adj (**a**) (derrochador) extravagant, wasteful; Rel **el hijo p.** the prodigal son (**b**) (generoso) generous, lavish; **ella es p. en regalos** she's very generous with presents
 2 nm,f (gastador) spendthrift

producción nf (acción) production, manufacturing; (producto) product; Cin production; **p. en cadena** mass production

producir [18] **1** vt (**a**) (gen) to produce, manufacture, make; (árboles, terrenos) to yield, bear; (rendir) to be profitable; Cin to produce; **el negocio no produce lo que esperábamos** this business is not as profitable as we expected; **el país produce más de lo que puede exportar** the country produces more than it can export (**b**) Fig (originar) to cause, bring about; **los cambios bruscos de tiempo producen enfermedades** sudden changes in the weather cause illnesses
 2 producirse vpr to take place, happen; **las transformaciones políticas se están produciendo a una velocidad inimaginable** the speed with which the political situation is changing is unbelievable

productividad nf productivity

productivo, -a adj productive; (beneficioso) profitable; **las últimas inversiones han resultado muy productivas** the latest investments have been very profitable

producto nm (**a**) (bien, objeto) product; Fig **el éxito es p. del trabajo** success is the product of hard work ❑ **p. alimenticio** foodstuff; **productos agrícolas** farm o agricultural produce; **productos de belleza** cosmetics; **productos de consumo** consumer goods; *Econ* **p.** *Esp* **interior** *o Am* **interno bruto** gross domestic product; **p. químico** chemical **(b)** *Mat* product

productor, -a 1 *adj* productive, producing; **país p. de petróleo** oil-producing country
  2 *nm,f* producer

productora *nf Cin* production company

proemio *nm Lit* proem, introduction, preface

proeza *nf* heroic deed, exploit; **ganar al campeón sería una auténtica p.** to defeat the champion would be a real exploit

prof *(abrev de* **profesor)** *(en colegio, academia)* teacher; *(en universidad) Br* lecturer, *US* professor

prof^a *(abrev de* **profesora)** *(mujer)* teacher

profanación *nf* desecration, profanation

profanador, -a 1 *adj* profanatory, irreverent
  2 *nm,f* profaner

profanamiento *nm* desecration, profanation, irreverence

profanar *vt* to desecrate, profane; **no deberías p. su memoria** you shouldn't desecrate her memory

profano, -a 1 *adj* **(a)** *Rel* profane, secular; *(irreverente)* irreverent **(b)** *(inexperto)* lay, uninitiated
  2 *nm,f (hombre)* layman; *(mujer)* laywoman; **soy p. en la materia** I know nothing about the subject

profe *nmf Fam (de colegio)* teacher; *(de universidad)* lecturer

profecía *nf* **(a)** *(gen)* prophecy **(b) profecías** *Rel* Minor Prophets

proferir [5] *vt* to utter; **p. insultos** to hurl insults

profesar 1 *vt* **(a)** *Rel* to profess; **profesa la religión musulmana** he professes Islam; *Fig* **p. una gran admiración a algn** to have a great admiration for sb **(b)** *(ejercer)* to practise, *US* practice, profess; **profesa como médico** he is a practising doctor
  2 *vi Rel* to profess

profesión *nf* **(a)** *(gen)* profession; **fotógrafo de p.** photographer by profession; **p. liberal** liberal profession; **ser de la p.** to be in the same profession **(b)** *Rel* taking of vows; **p. de fe** profession of faith

profesional *adj & nmf* professional

profesionalidad *nf,* **profesionalismo** *nm* professionalism

profesionalización *nf* professionalization

profesionalizar [14] *vt* to make more professional

profesionalmente *adv* professionally

profeso, -a 1 *Rel adj* professed
  2 *nm,f Rel* professed monk/nun
  3 *adv* **ex p.** intentionally

profesor, -a *nm,f (gen)* teacher; *Univ Br* lecturer, *US* professor ❑ **p. particular** (private) tutor

profesorado *nm* **(a)** *(profesores)* teaching staff, *US* faculty **(b)** *(cargo)* post of teacher

profesoral *adj (gen)* teachers', teaching; *Univ* lecturers'

profeta *nm* prophet

profético, -a *adj* prophetic

profetisa *nf* prophetess

profetizar [14] *vt* to prophesy, foretell

profiláctico, -a *Med* **1** *adj* prophylactic
  2 *nm* condom, *US* prophylactic

profilaxis *nf Med* prophylaxis

prófugo, -a 1 *adj* fugitive, fleeing
  2 *nm,f* fugitive
  3 *nm Mil* deserter

profundamente *adv* deeply

profundidad *nf* **(a)** *(hondura)* depth; **de poca p.** shallow; *Fot* **p. de campo** depth of field; **seis metros de p.** six metres deep *o* in depth **(b)** *Fig (de ideas, pensamientos)* profundity, depth, profoundness; **meterse en profundidades** to get to the bottom

profundizar [14] *vt & vi* **(a)** *(cavar)* to deepen **(b)** *Fig (discurrir)* to study in depth; **p. en un tema** to look deeply into a matter

profundo, -a *adj* **(a)** *(hondo)* deep; **en lo más p.** deep down **(b)** *Fig (intenso)* profound; **un pensamiento p.** a profound thought

profusamente *adv* profusely

profusión *nf* profusion; **con p.** profusely

profuso, -a *adj* profuse

progenie *nf* **(a)** *(casta)* family, lineage **(b)** *(descendientes)* offspring, progeny

progenitor, -a *nm,f (antepasado)* ancestor, progenitor; *(padre)* father; *(madre)* mother; **progenitores** *(padres)* parents

progenitura *nf* offspring, progeny

progesterona *nf Biol* progesterone

programa *nm* programme, *US* program; *Inform* program; **¿cuál es el p. para mañana?** what's the plan for tomorrow? ❑ **p. concurso** quiz (show); **p. electoral** platform; **p. informático** computer program

programable *adj* programable, programmable

programación *nf (gen)* programming, *US* programing; *Rad TV* programme *o US* program planning; *Inform* programming

programador, -a *nm,f Inform* programmer

programar *vt* to programme, *US* program; *Inform* to program; **me gusta p. las vacaciones con antelación** I like to plan my holidays in advance

programático, -a *adj* programmatic

progre *adj & nmf Fam* trendy, lefty

progresar *vi* to progress, make progress

progresía *nf Fam* trendies *pl*

progresión *nf* progression; *Mat* **p. aritmética/geométrica** arithmetic/geometric progression; *Mús* **p. armónica** harmonic progression

progresismo *nm Pol* progressionism

progresista *Pol* **1** *adj* progressive
  2 *nmf* progressist, progressive, member of a progressive party

progresivo, -a *adj* progressive

progreso *nm* progress; **sus progresos son sorprendentes** her progress is surprising

prohibición *nf* prohibition, ban; *Hist* **los años de la p.** the Prohibition years; **p. de fumar** smoking ban

prohibicionista *nmf* prohibitionist; *Hist* Prohibitionist

prohibido, -a 1 *pp de* **prohibir**
  2 *adj* forbidden, prohibited, banned; **está p. fumar aquí** you can't smoke here; **'prohibida la entrada'** 'no admittance'; **p. aparcar/fumar** no parking/smoking

prohibir *vt* to forbid, prohibit, ban; **'se prohíbe pasar'** 'no admittance *o* entry'

prohibitivo, -a *adj* prohibitive, prohibitory

prohijar [32] *vt* to adopt

prohombre *nm* great *o* outstanding man

prójimo, -a 1 *nm,f Fam* person, type; **¡hay cada p. por ahí!** it takes all kinds!; **la prójima** the wife
  2 *nm* one's fellow man, one's neighbour *o US* neighbor; **ama a tu p.** love thy neighbour

pról. *(abrev de* **prólogo)** prologue, *US* prolog

prolapso *nm Med* prolapse, prolapsus

prole *nf* offspring

prolegómeno *nm* introduction, prolegomenon; **dejémonos de prolegómenos y vayamos al grano** let's skip the introduction and get down to business

proletariado *nm* proletariat

proletario, -a *adj & nm,f* proletarian

proliferación *nf* proliferation

proliferar *vi* to proliferate; **tras el cambio político, han proliferado toda clase de partidos** after the political change, all kinds of parties have appeared

prolífico, -a *adj* prolific

prolijidad *nf* verbosity, long-windedness, prolixity

prolijo, -a *adj* **(a)** *(dilatado)* verbose, long-winded, prolix **(b)** *(meticuloso)* excessively meticulous

prologar [38] *vt* to prologue, *US* prolog, introduce

prólogo *nm* prologue, *US* prolog

prolongación *nf* prolonging, extension, prolongation

prolongadamente *adv* at length

prolongado, -a 1 *pp de* **prolongar**
2 *adj* **(a)** *(más largo que ancho)* elongated **(b)** *(largo)* long; **una discusión prolongada** a long discussion

prolongamiento *nm* prolonging, extension, prolongment

prolongar [38] **1** *vt* **(a)** *(alargar)* to prolong, extend **(b)** *(hacer durar)* to prolong; **tuvimos que p. la espera hasta que el avión estuvo preparado** we had to make them wait even longer until the plane was ready
2 prolongarse *vpr* to go on, last longer; **la reunión se prolongó hasta las seis** the meeting went on until six

promediar 1 *vt (repartir)* to average out
2 *vi (interceder)* to mediate

promedio *nm* average; **como p.** on average; **escribe un p. de cinco libros al año** on average, he writes five books a year

promesa *nf* promise; **romper una p.** to break a promise; *Fig* **la joven p. de la música/del baile** the promising young musician/dancer

prometedor, -a *adj* promising

prometer 1 *vt* to promise; **te lo prometo** I promise; *Fig* **p. el oro y el moro** to promise the moon
2 *vi* to be promising; **esto promete** this looks promising
3 prometerse *vpr (pareja)* to get engaged; *Fam* **nos las prometíamos muy felices** we had great expectations

prometido, -a 1 *pp de* **prometer**
2 *adj* promised; **cumplir lo p.** to keep one's word o one's promise; **lo p. es deuda** a promise is a promise
3 *nm,f (hombre)* fiancé; *(mujer)* fiancée

prominencia *nf (protuberancia)* protuberance, bulge; *(elevación)* rise, prominence; *Fig (importancia)* prominence

prominente *adj* **(a)** *(que se eleva)* protruding, projecting; *(elevado, importante)* prominent **(b)** *(ilustre)* illustrious, famous

promiscuidad *nf* promiscuity, promiscuousness

promiscuo, -a *adj* promiscuous

promoción *nf (gen)* promotion; *Com (mejor empleo)* promotion, advancement; *(oferta)* offer; *Educ* **p. universitaria** = class, year or group that graduates at the same time

promocional *adj* promotional

promocionar 1 *vt (cosas)* to promote; *(personas)* to give promotion to; **la publicidad es imprescindible para p. un producto** advertising is essential to promote a product
2 *vi Dep* to promote

3 promocionarse *vpr Fam* to blow one's own trumpet

promontorio *nm Geog* promontory, headland

promotor, -a 1 *adj* promoting
2 *nm,f* promoter ❏ *Com* **p. inmobiliario** *Br* property o *US* real estate developer

promover [41] *vt* **(a)** *(cosas, personas)* to promote; **p. a algn a jefe** to promote sb to manager; *Jur* **p. una querella contra algn** to take legal action against sb **(b)** *(causar)* to cause, give rise to

promulgación *nf Jur* enactment

promulgar [38] *vt Jur* to enact

pronación *nf* pronation

pronombre *nm Ling* pronoun; **p. demostrativo/personal/relativo** demonstrative/personal/relative pronoun

pronominal *adj Ling* pronominal

pronosticador, -a *nm,f* forecaster

pronosticar [59] *vt* to predict, foretell, forecast; *Med* to make a prognosis of

pronóstico *nm* forecast; *Med* prognosis; **de p. grave** seriously ill o injured; **de p. leve** not seriously injured; **de p. reservado** under observation

prontitud *nf* quickness, rapidity, promptness

pronto, -a 1 *adj* quick, fast, prompt; **estar p. para hacer algo** to be ready o willing to do sth
2 *adv* **(a)** *(deprisa)* quickly, rapidly; **al p.** at first; **de p.** suddenly; **por de** o **lo p.** *(para empezar)* to start with; *(de momento)* for the time being **(b)** *(dentro de poco)* soon; **hasta p.** see you soon!; **lo más p. (posible)** as soon as possible; **tan p. como** as soon as **(c)** *Esp (temprano)* early; **salimos p.** we left early
3 *nm (impulso)* sudden impulse; *(de ira)* fit of anger, outburst

prontuario *nm Andes RP Jur* police record

pronunciación *nf* pronunciation

pronunciado, -a 1 *pp de* **pronunciar**
2 *adj* **(a)** *(dicho)* pronounced, uttered **(b)** *Fig (marcado)* pronounced

pronunciamiento *nm* **(a)** *Mil* uprising, insurrection **(b)** *Jur* pronouncement **(c)** *RP (anuncio, declaración)* statement

pronunciar 1 *vt* **(decir)** to pronounce; **pronuncia el inglés como si fuese nativo** he sounds like an English native; **pronunció un discurso histórico** he gave a historic speech
2 pronunciarse *vpr* **(a)** *(definirse)* to state an opinion **(sobre** on); **se pronunció a favor del proyecto** he declared that he was in favour of the project **(b)** *Mil (sublevarse)* to rise up

propagación *nf* propagation, spreading

propagador, -a 1 *adj* propagative
2 *nm,f* propagator

propaganda *nf* **(a)** *Pol* propaganda ❏ **p. electoral** *(folletos)* election literature; *(anuncios, emisiones)* election campaign advertising **(b)** *Com* advertising, publicity

propagandista *nm,f* propagandist

propagandístico, -a *adj* advertising, publicity; **campaña propagandística** advertising campaign; **lo hicieron sólo con fines propagandísticos** it was only a publicity stunt

propagar [38] **1** *vt* to propagate, spread
2 propagarse *vpr* to spread

propalar *vt (secretos)* to spread

propano *nm Quím* propane

proparoxítono, -a *adj Ling* proparoxytone

propasarse *vpr* to go too far; **p. con la bebida** to drink too much

propender *vi* to have a tendency, be inclined

propensión *nf* (**a**) *(inclinación)* tendency, inclination (**b**) *Med* susceptibility

propenso, -a *adj* (**a**) *(inclinado)* prone, inclined (**b**) *Med* susceptible; **soy p. a los catarros** I catch colds very easily

propiamente *adv* really, exactly; **p. dicho** strictly speaking

propiciar *vt* (**a**) *(ganar el favor de)* to win over (**b**) *(causar)* to cause; **su actitud desafiante ha propiciado el enfrentamiento** his defiant manner provoked the confrontation

propiciatorio, -a 1 *adj* propitiatory; **víctima propiciatoria** scapegoat
  2 *nm* (**a**) *(reclinatorio)* prie-dieu (**b**) *Hist* propitiatory, mercy seat

propicio, -a *adj* propitious, apt, suitable; **ser p. a** to be inclined to

propiedad *nf* (**a**) *(posesión)* ownership; *(cosa poseída)* property; **tener (algo) en p.** to own (sth); **una casa p. del estado** a council house ❑ **p. horizontal** joint ownership *(in a block of flats)*; **p. intelectual** copyright; **p. privada** private property (**b**) *(cualidad)* property, quality; **propiedades medicinales** medicinal properties; *Fig* **con p.** properly, appropriately; **emplear una palabra con p.** to use a word properly

propietario, -a 1 *adj* proprietary
  2 *nm,f* owner; **es p. de varias tiendas** he owns several shops

propina *nf* tip; **dar p. (a algn)** to tip (sb); *Fam* **de p.** as a tip

propinar *vt* to give; *Fig* **p. una paliza a algn** to give sb a hiding

propio, -a *adj* (**a**) *(de uno)* own; **en su propia casa** in his own house (**b**) *(indicado)* proper, correct, suitable, appropriate; **es lo p. en estos casos** it is the right thing (to do) in these cases; **juegos propios para su edad** games suitable for their age (**c**) *(particular)* typical, peculiar; **características propias de los ingleses** characteristics peculiar to the English; *Fam* **es muy p. de él** it is very typical of him (**d**) *(mismo) (hombre)* himself; *(mujer)* herself; *(animal, cosa)* itself; **el p. autor** the author himself (**e**) **propios, -as** themselves; **los p. inquilinos** the tenants themselves (**f**) *Ling* proper; **nombre p.** proper noun

proponer [50] *(pp* propuesto) **1** *vt* to propose, put forward, suggest; **me han propuesto para el cargo de presidente** I have been put forward for the post of president; **propongo ir al cine** why don't we go to the cinema?
  2 proponerse *vpr* (**a**) *(intentar)* to intend; **se propone terminar el trabajo mañana** he intends to finish the work tomorrow (**b**) *(decidir)* to decide, be determined; **el nuevo juez se ha propuesto acabar con la delincuencia** the new judge is determined to put a stop to delinquency

proporción *nf* (**a**) *(relación)* proportion; *Mat* proportion; **en p. con** in proportion to (**b**) **proporciones** *(tamaño)* size *sing*; **de grandes p.** huge, massive

proporcionado, -a 1 *pp de* proporcionar
  2 *adj* (**a**) *(que guarda proporción)* proportionate, in proportion (**b**) *(facilitado)* supplied, provided, afforded; **la ayuda humanitaria proporcionada por los países desarrollados** humanitarian help provided by developed countries

proporcional *adj* proportional

proporcionalidad *nf* proportionateness

proporcionalmente *adv* proportionately

proporcionar *vt* (**a**) *(disponer con proporción)* to proportion (**b**) *(dar)* to give; to supply *o* provide with; **le proporcioné un trabajo** I found *o* gave him a job; **le proporcionó una gran alegría** it made her very happy

proposición *nf* (**a**) *(propuesta)* proposition, proposal; **le hizo una p. de matrimonio** he proposed to her (**b**) *Ling (oración)* clause; **p. relativa** relative clause

propósito *nm* (**a**) *(intención)* intention; **ella tenía el p. de cambiar** she was determined to change (**b**) *(objetivo)* purpose, aim; **con el p. de** in order to; **fuera de p.** beside the point (**c**) **a p.** *(por cierto)* by the way; *(adrede)* on purpose, intentionally; **a p. de viajes, ¿has estado en Japón?** speaking of travelling, have you been to Japan?; **hacer algo a p.** to do sth on purpose

propuesta *nf* suggestion, proposal, plan; **a p. de algn** at sb's suggestion

propuesto, -a *pp de* proponer

propugnar *vt* to defend, advocate

propulsar *vt* *(vehículo)* to propel, drive; *Fig (idea)* to promote

propulsión *nf* propulsion; **p. a chorro** jet propulsion; **avión de p. a chorro** jet (plane)

propulsor, -a 1 *adj* propelling
  2 *nm Téc* propellent
  3 *nm,f Fig (persona)* promoter

prorrata *nf* share, pro rata; **a p.** in proportion, pro rata

prorratear *vt* to apportion, *US* prorate

prorrateo *nm* sharing, apportionment, *US* proration

prórroga *nf* (**a**) *(prolongación)* extension; *Dep* extra time, *US* overtime (**b**) *(aplazamiento)* postponement; *Mil* deferment; *Mil* **ha obtenido una p. por estudios** he was allowed to defer because of his studies

prorrogable *adj* that can be extended

prorrogar [38] *vt* (**a**) *(prolongar)* to extend (**b**) *(aplazar)* to postpone; *Mil* to defer

prorrumpir *vi* to burst; **al conocer la noticia prorrumpió en lágrimas** on hearing the news he burst into tears; **p. en gritos** to shout

prosa *nf Lit* prose

prosaico, -a *adj* prosaic

prosaísmo *nm Lit* prosaism, prosaicism

prosapia *nf* lineage, ancestry

proscenio *nm Hist Teat* proscenium

proscribir *(pp* proscrito) *vt (persona)* to exile, banish; *Fig (cosa)* to ban, prohibit

proscrito, -a 1 *pp de* proscribir
  2 *adj (persona)* exiled, banished; *(cosa)* banned
  3 *nm,f* exile, outlaw

prosecución *nf* continuation

proseguir [61] *vt & vi* to carry on, continue; **debemos p. con el trabajo** we must go on with the work

proselitismo *nm* proselytism

proselitista *adj* proselytic

prosélito *nm* proselyte

prosista *nmf Lit* prose writer

prosodia *nf Ling* prosody

prosódico, -a *adj Ling* prosodic

prosopopeya *nf Lit* prosopopoeia, prosopopeia

prospección *nf* (**a**) *Min* prospect; **p. petrolífera** oil prospection (**b**) *Com* survey

prospectar *vt Min* to prospect

prospecto *nm* leaflet, prospectus

prosperar *vi* to prosper, thrive; **nuestro negocio**

prospera we are doing a roaring trade; *Fig* **la idea no prosperó** the idea wasn't accepted

prosperidad *nf* prosperity

próspero, -a *adj* prosperous, thriving; **p. año nuevo** Happy New Year

próstata *nf Anat* prostate (gland)

prosternarse *vpr* to prostrate oneself

prostíbulo *nm* brothel

prostitución *nf* prostitution

prostituir [34] **1** *vt* to prostitute
   2 prostituirse *vpr* to prostitute oneself

prostituta *nf* prostitute

protactinio *nm Quím* protactinium

protagonismo *nm* (a) *Teat Cin* leading role (b) *(importancia)* significance, importance; **acaparar el p.** to steal the limelight, hog the show; *Fig* **(afán de) p.** desire to be in the limelight

protagonista *nmf* (a) *Cin Lit Teat* main character, leading role; **¿quién es el p.?** who plays the lead? (b) *Fig (persona principal)* centre o *US* center of attraction; *(héroe) (hombre)* hero; *(mujer)* heroine

protagonizar [14] *vt Cin Teat* to play the lead in, star in; *Fig* **el niño que protagonizó el suceso** the child involved in the incident

protección *nf* protection □ **p. civil** civil defence

proteccionismo *nm* protectionism

proteccionista *adj & nmf* protectionist

protector, -a 1 *adj* protecting, protective; **sociedad protectora de animales** ≃ Royal Society for the Prevention of Cruelty to Animals
   2 *nm,f (persona)* protector
   3 *nm (objeto) Box* mouthpiece, gumshield □ **p. labial** lip salve; *Inform* **p. de pantalla** screensaver

protectorado *nm Pol* protectorate

proteger [52] *vt* to protect, defend, shield

protegido, -a 1 *pp de* **proteger**
   2 *adj* protected; **p. contra copia/escritura** copy/write protected
   3 *nm,f (hombre)* protégé; *(mujer)* protégée

proteico, -a *adj* proteinous, proteinic

proteína *nf* protein

proteínico, -a *adj* proteinic

prótesis *nf inv* (a) *Med* prosthesis (b) *Ling* prothesis, prosthesis

protesta *nf* protest; *Jur* objection; **presentar una p. formal** to make a formal protest; *Jur* **p. denegada** objection overruled; *Jur* **se admite la p.** objection sustained

protestante *adj & nmf Rel* Protestant

protestantismo *nm Rel* Protestantism

protestar *vi* to protest; *Jur* **¡protesto, su señoría!** objection, Your Honour!; **sin p.** without protest; *Fam* **¡deja ya de p.!** stop moaning, will you!

protesto *nm Com* protest

protestón, -ona 1 *adj Fam* moaning, grumbling
   2 *nm,f* moaner, grumbler

protocolario, -a *adj* formal; **es una invitación protocolaria** the invitation is a pure formality

protocolo *nm* (a) *(reglas)* protocol; *Inform* protocol (b) *Fig (etiqueta)* etiquette, formalities *pl*; **sin protocolos** informally

protohistoria *nf* protohistory

protohistórico, -a *adj* protohistoric

protón *nm Fis* proton

protoplasma *nm Biol* protoplasm

protoplásmico, -a *adj Biol* protoplasmic

prototipo *nm* prototype

protozoo *nm Biol* protozoon, protozoan

protuberancia *nf* protuberance

protuberante *adj* protuberant, bulging

prov. *(abrev de* **provincia)** prov.

provecho *nm* profit, benefit; **¡buen p.!** enjoy your meal!; **de p.** beneficially; **sacar el máximo p. de** to get the most out of; **sacar p. de algo** to benefit from sth; **un hombre de p.** a man with prospects

provechosamente *adv* beneficially

provechoso, -a *adj (beneficioso)* beneficial, useful; *Com (lucrativo)* profitable

provecto, -a *adj Literario* old; **de edad provecta** advanced in years

proveedor, -a *nm,f* supplier, purveyor

proveer [37] *(pp* **provisto)** *vt* (a) *(suministrar)* to supply, provide (b) *(preparar)* to get ready (c) *(dar) (un empleo)* to fill

proveniente *adj (procedente)* coming; *(resultante)* arising, resulting; **el tren p. de Granada** the train from Granada; **su éxito es p. de sus esfuerzos** her success is the result of her efforts

provenir [69] *vi (proceder)* to come; *(originarse)* to arise, result, spring

Provenza *n* Provence

provenzal 1 *adj* Provençal
   2 *nmf (persona)* Provençal
   3 *nm (idioma)* Provençal

proverbial *adj* proverbial

proverbio *nm* (a) *(sentencia)* proverb (b) **proverbios** *(libro de la Biblia)* Proverbs

providencia *nf* (a) *Rel* providence (b) *Jur* ruling, judgement

providencial *adj* providential; **su repentina aparición fue p.** her sudden appearance was a godsend

próvido, -a *adj* provident

provincia *nf* province, ≃ county; **capital de p.** county town; **provincias** the provinces

provincial *adj* provincial; **diputación p.** ≃ county council

provincianismo *nm Pey* provincialism

provinciano, -a *adj Pey* provincial
   2 *nm,f Br* country bumpkin, *US* hick

provisión *nf* (a) *(acción)* provision; *Fin* **p. de fondos** reserve funds (b) **provisiones** *(suministros)* provisions, supplies

provisional *adj* provisional

provisionalmente *adv* provisionally

provisorio, -a *adj Am* provisional

provisto, -a 1 *pp de* **proveer**
   2 *adj (suministrado)* provided; **este automóvil está p. de todos los adelantos técnicos** this car is equipped with the latest in technology

provocación *nf* provocation, instigation, incitement

provocado, -a 1 *pp de* **provocar**
   2 *adj* provoked, caused; *Jur* **incendio p.** arson

provocador, -a 1 *adj* provocative
   2 *nm,f* instigator, agent provocateur

provocante *adj* provoking

provocar [59] **1** *vt* (a) *(incitar)* to provoke (b) *(causar) (accidente, muerte)* to cause, bring about; *(rebelión)* to start; *(sonrisa, burla)* to elicit; **aquello provocó las risas de todos**

that made everyone laugh; **p. un incendio** *(accidentalmente)* to cause o start a fire; *(intencionadamente)* to commit arson (**c**) *(excitar sexualmente)* to lead on

2 *vi Carib Col Méx Fam (apetecer a)* **¿te provoca hacerlo?** would you like to do it?, *Br* do you fancy doing it?

provocativo, -a *adj* provocative; **me miró con actitud provocativa** he looked at me provocatively

proxeneta *nmf* procurer, pimp

proxenetismo *nm* procurement

próximamente *adv (pronto)* soon; *(dentro de poco)* before long; *Cin Teat (en letrero)* 'coming soon'

proximidad *nf* nearness, proximity, closeness; **dada la p. de las elecciones** as elections are coming up; **en las proximidades de** close to, in the vicinity of

próximo, -a *adj* (**a**) *(cerca)* near, close; **las vacaciones están próximas** the holidays will soon start; **p. a la estación** near the station (**b**) *(siguiente)* next; **el p. año/mes** next year/month; **en fecha próxima** shortly; **la próxima parada** the next stop

proyección *nf* (**a**) *(gen)* projection (**b**) *Cin* showing (**c**) *Fig (difusión)* diffusion; *(futuro)* future; **las declaraciones han tenido una gran p. en la prensa** his declarations had wide press coverage; **este joven jugador tiene una gran p.** this young player has a great future

proyectar 1 *vt* (**a**) *(luz)* to project (**b**) *(hacer planes)* to plan; **proyectan mudarse pronto** they are thinking of moving out shortly (**c**) *Cin* to project, show (**d**) *Arquit* to plan; *Téc* to design; *Mat* to project

2 proyectarse *vpr* (**a**) *(sombra, silueta)* to be cast (**b**) *Cin (uso impers)* to show

proyectil *nm* projectile, missile

proyectista *nmf* planner, designer

proyecto *nm (plan)* project, plan; *Téc* plan; *Arquit* design; **p. de acuerdo/de resolución** draft agreement/resolution; *Pol* **p. de ley** bill; **tener algo en p.** to be planning sth; **ella tiene muchos proyectos** she's got a lot of plans

proyector *nm* (**a**) *(de luz)* searchlight; *(foco)* spotlight (**b**) *Cin* projector

prudencia *nf (cuidado)* prudence, discretion; *(moderación)* care; **con p.** *(con cuidado)* with care, cautiously; *(moderadamente)* in moderation, moderately

prudencial *adj (gen)* prudential, discreet; *(moderado)* moderate, careful, cautious; *Fam* **a una distancia p.** at a safe distance

prudenciarse *vpr CAm Col Méx* to be cautious

prudente *adj* prudent, sensible, wise; **a una hora p.** at a reasonable time; **lo más p. sería esperar** the wisest thing (to do) would be to wait

prudentemente *adv* prudently

prueba *nf* (**a**) *(argumento)* proof; *Jur* evidence, proof; **dar pruebas de** to show signs of; **en p. de su amor** as a sign of her love; **la p. de ello es que** the proof of it is that; **tener pruebas de algo** to have proof of sth (**b**) *(examen, ensayo)* test; *Cost* fitting; *Téc* trial; **a p.** on trial; **a p. de agua** waterproof; **a p. de balas** bullet-proof; *Cin* **hacerle una p. a algn** to screen-test sb; **haz la p.** try it ❑ **p. del embarazo** pregnancy test; *Av* **piloto de pruebas** test pilot (**c**) *Fot Impr* proof; **corrección de pruebas** proofreading (**d**) *Dep* event

prurito *nm* (**a**) *Med* itch, pruritus (**b**) *Fig (deseo)* urge

Prusia *n* Prussia

prusiano, -a *adj & nm,f* Prussian

P.S. *(abrev de post scriptum)* PS

psicoanálisis *nm inv Psic* psychoanalysis

psicoanalista *nmf Psic* psychoanalyst

psicoanalítico, -a *adj Psic* psychoanalytic, psychoanalytical

psicoanalizar [14] *vt Psic* to psychoanalyse, *US* psychoanalyze

psicodélico, -a *adj* psychedelic, psychodelic

psicodrama *nm Psic* psychodrama

psicofármaco *nm Farm* psychoactive drug

psicología *nf Psic* psychology

psicológico, -a *adj Psic* psychological

psicólogo, -a *nm,f Psic* psychologist

psiconeurosis *nf inv Psic* psychoneurosis

psicópata *nmf Psic* psychopath, sociopath

psicopatía *nf Psic* psychopathy

psicopático, -a *adj Psic* psychopathic

psicopatología *nf Psic* psychopathology

psicosis *nf inv Psic* psychosis

psicosomático, -a *adj Psic* psychosomatic

psicoterapeuta *nmf Psic* psychotherapist

psicoterapia *nf Psic* psychotherapy

psique *nf* psyche

psiquiatra *nmf Psic* psychiatrist

psiquiatría *nf Psic* psychiatry

psiquiátrico, -a *Psic* **1** *adj* psychiatric; **hospital p.** mental hospital
2 *nm* mental hospital

psíquico, -a *adj* psychic, psychical

psiquis *nf inv* psyche

PSOE [pe'soe, soe] *nm Pol (abrev de* **Partido Socialista Obrero Español)** Spanish political party to the centre-left of the political spectrum

psoriasis *nf inv Med* psoriasis

pta. *Antes (pl* **ptas.)** *(abrev de* **peseta)** peseta

púa *nf* (**a**) *(de plata)* thorn; *(de animal)* quill, spine; *(de tenedor)* prong; *(de alambre)* barb; *(de peine)* tooth; **alambre de púas** barbed wire (**b**) *Mús* plectrum

pub [paβ, paf] *(pl* **pubs)** *nm* pub

púber *adj & nmf,* **púbero, -a** *adj & nm,f* adolescent

pubertad *nf* puberty

púbico, -a *adj* pubic

pubis *nm inv Anat* (**a**) *(vientre)* pubes *pl* (**b**) *(hueso)* pubis

publicación *nf* publication

públicamente *adv* publicly

publicar [59] *vt* (**a**) *Impr (libros)* to publish (**b**) *(difundir)* to publicize; **los periódicos acaban de publicar la noticia** the newspapers have just published the news

publicidad *nf* (**a**) *(hacer público)* publicity; **dar p. a** to publicize (**b**) *Com* advertising; **el mundo de la p.** the world of advertising ❑ **p. directa** direct mailing

publicista *nmf* publicist

publicitario, -a *adj* advertising, publicity; **campaña publicitaria** advertising campaign

público, -a 1 *adj* public; **enemigo p.** public enemy; **en p.** in public; **es del dominio p.** it's common knowledge; **opinión pública** public opinion; **sector p.** public sector, civil service

2 *nm* public, audience; *Dep* spectators *pl*; *TV* viewers *pl*; **abierto al p.** open to the public; **dar o sacar algo al p.** to make sth public; **el p. en general, el gran p.** the general public

publirreportaje *nm (anuncio de televisión)* promotional film; *(en revista)* advertising spread

pucha *interj Andes RP Fam Euf* **¡p.!** *(lamento, enojo) Br* sugar!, *US* shoot!; *(sorpresa)* wow!

pucherazo *nm Fam Pol* electoral fraud; **ha habido p. (en las elecciones)** the elections have been rigged

puchero *nm* (**a**) *(olla)* cooking pot; *(cocido)* stew (**b**) *(llanto)* pout; **hacer pucheros** to pout

pucho *nm* (**a**) *Andes RP (colilla)* cigarette end o butt (**b**) *Chile Ecuad (hijo menor)* youngest child (**c**) **de a puchos** *loc adv Andes RP* bit by bit

pudendo, -a *adj (feo)* ugly; *(asqueroso)* filthy; *Hum* **partes pudendas** private parts

pudibundez *nf* prudishness

pudibundo, -a *adj* prudish

púdico, -a *adj* (**a**) *(casto)* chaste, decent (**b**) *Pey (pudibundo)* prudish

pudiente *adj* rich, wealthy

pudin *nm,* **pudín** *nm* (plum) pudding

pudor *nm* chastity, decency, modesty; *Fig (vergüenza)* shame; *Jur* **actos contra el p.** indecent behaviour

pudoroso, -a *adj* decent, modest; *Fig* shameful

pudridero *nm Br* rubbish dump, *US* garbage dump

pudrir 1 *vt* (**a**) *(descomponer)* to rot, decay (**b**) *Fig (molestar)* to upset, annoy

2 pudrirse *vpr (descomponerse)* to rot, decay; *Fig* to languish; *Fam* **p. de aburrimiento** to be bored to death; *Fam* **¡que se pudra!** let him rot!

pueblada *nf Andes RP (tumulto)* mob; *(motín)* riot

pueblerino, -a 1 *adj* (**a**) *(de pueblo)* village; **la vida pueblerina** village life (**b**) *Pey (tosco)* countrified, provincial

2 *nm,f* (**a**) *(nativo)* villager (**b**) *Pey (paleto)* bumpkin

pueblo *nm* (**a**) *(gente)* people; **el p. español** the Spanish people; **la soberanía del p.** the sovereignty of the people (**b**) *(población) (pequeña)* village; *(grande)* town; *Pey* **ser de p.** to be a *Br* country bumpkin o *US* hick; **un p. de mala muerte** a one-horse town ▫ *Perú* **p. joven,** *Am* **p. nuevo** shanty town

puente *nm* (**a**) *Constr* bridge; **tender un p. sobre un río** to bridge a river; *Fig* **tenderle un p. (de plata) a algn** to give sb an opportunity ▫ *Av* **p. aéreo** *(civil)* air shuttle; *Mil* airlift; **p. basculante** balance o bascule bridge; **p. colgante** suspension bridge; **p. de mando** wheelhouse; **p. de peatones** footbridge; **p. giratorio** swing bridge; **p. levadizo** drawbridge (**b**) *Med (entre dos dientes)* bridge, bridgework (**c**) *(entre dos fiestas)* long weekend; **hacer p. el lunes** to take Monday off (because Tuesday is a bank holiday) (**d**) *(de gafas)* bridge (**e**) *Náut (en barco)* gun deck

puentear *vt Elec* to bridge

puenting *nm* bungee-jumping; **hacer p.** to go bungee-jumping

puercada *nf CAm Méx R Dom* disgusting thing

puerco, -a 1 *adj (sucio)* filthy; *(asqueroso)* disgusting

2 *nm,f* (**a**) *Zool (macho)* pig; *(hembra)* sow (**b**) *Fam (persona)* pig, swine

3 *nm* **p. espín** porcupine

puericultor, -a *nm,f* paediatrician, *US* pediatrician

puericultura *nf* paediatrics *sing,* *US* pediatrics *sing*

pueril *adj* (**a**) *(infantil)* childish, puerile (**b**) *(vano)* useless, vain; **sus esfuerzos fueron pueriles** his efforts were in vain

puerilidad *nf* (**a**) *(propio de niño)* childishness, puerility (**b**) *Fig (insignificancia)* insignificance

puerperal *adj Med* puerperal; **fiebre p.** puerperal fever

puerperio *nm Med* puerperium

puerro *nm Bot* leek

puerta *nf (gen)* door; *(de jardín, de muralla) (verja)* gate; *Aut* **coche de cinco** o **tres puertas** hatchback; *Aut* **coche de cuatro puertas** four-door car, saloon; **de p. en p.** door to door; **las puertas de la ciudad** the gates of the town; **nos encontraremos a la p. del cine** we'll meet outside the cinema; **p. corredera/giratoria** sliding/revolving door; **p. de embarque** *(en aeropuerto)* departure gate; **p. principal/de servicio** main/trademen's entrance; *Fig* **a las puertas, en puertas** imminent; *Fig* **a las puertas de la muerte** at death's door; *Fig* **a p. cerrada** behind closed doors; *Fig* **la p. del éxito** the gateway to success; *Fig* **llamar a la p. de algn** to call on sb for help; *Fig* **por la p. grande** in a grand manner; *Fam* **cogió la p. y se fue** he upped and went; *Fam Fig* **darle a algn con la p. en las narices** o **en la cara** to shut o slam the door in sb's face

puerto *nm* (**a**) *(de mar)* port, harbour, *US* harbor; **tomar p.** to come into port ▫ **p. deportivo** marina; **p. franco** free port; **p. marítimo** seaport (**b**) *(de montaña)* (mountain) pass (**c**) *Inform* port

Puerto España *n* Port of Spain

Puerto Príncipe *n* Port-au-Prince

Puerto Rico *n* Puerto Rico

puertorriqueño, -a *adj & nm,f* Puerto Rican

pues *conj* (**a**) *(puesto que)* as, since; **no pudo contestar, p. ni él mismo lo sabía** he couldn't answer as he didn't even know himself (**b**) *(por lo tanto)* therefore; **la situación requiere, p., una solución inmediata** the situation demands, therefore, a quick solution; **repito, p., que hace lo que debe** therefore, I repeat he is doing what he should (**c**) *(entonces)* so; **no me hiciste caso, p. no te quejes ahora** you didn't listen to me, so don't complain now (**d**) *(para reforzar)* **¡p. claro que no!** of course not!; **¡p. claro que sí!** but of course!; **p. como iba diciendo** well, as I was saying; **¡p. mejor!** so much the better!; **¡p. no!** certainly not!; **¡p. peor!** that's even worse!; **¡p. sí!** of course!; **¿y p.?** so what? (**e**) *(como pregunta)* **¿p.?** why?

puesta *nf* (**a**) *Astron (de un astro)* setting; **p. de sol** sunset (**b**) *Biol (de huevos)* laying; *Fig* **p. a punto** tuning, adjusting; *Fig* **p. al día** updating; *Fig* **p. de largo** coming out, debut; **p. en escena** staging; **p. en marcha** starting-up, start-up; **p. en órbita** putting into orbit; *véase tamb* **puesto, -a**

puestero, -a *nm,f Am* stallholder

puesto, -a 1 *pp de* **poner**

2 *adj (colocado)* set, put; **dejaron la mesa puesta** they didn't clear the table; *Fig* **estar p. en una materia** to be well up in a subject; *Fam Fig* **ir p.** to be high (**b**) *(ropa)* on; **con el abrigo p.** with one's coat on; **¿qué llevaba p.?** what was he wearing?; *Fig* **no tener más que lo p.** to have only what one is standing up in; *Fam* **ir muy p.** to be all dressed up

3 *nm* (**a**) *(lugar)* place; *(asiento)* seat; **devuélvelo a su p.** put it back in its place; **en primer p.** in the first place; **te cambio el p.** shall we change seats?; *Fig (saber)* **estar en su p.** to know one's place (**b**) *(local) (en un mercado)* stall; *(en una exposición)* stand; **p. de flores** flower stall; **p. de periódicos** newspaper stand; **p. de policía** police station; **p. de socorro** first-aid post (**c**) *Mil* post; **p. de vigilancia** sentry post (**d**) *(empleo)* position, post, job; **incorporarse a su p. (de trabajo)** to take up one's duties; **p. de trabajo** job, post; **p. vacante** vacancy (**e**) *RP (de ganado)* cattle station (**f**) *Col Méx (estanco)* tobacconist's

4 puesto que *loc conj* since, as; **tendrás que esperar p. que has llegado tarde** you'll have to wait since you arrived late

puf¹ *(pl* **pufs** *) nm* pouf, pouffe

puf² *interj* ugh!

pufo *nm Fam* trick; **¡menudo p. le metieron!** they pulled a fast one on him!

púgil *nm* boxer, fighter

pugilato *nm* (**a**) *Box* boxing (**b**) *(pugna)* battle, struggle

pugilístico, -a *adj* pugilistic, boxing

pugna *nf* battle, fight; **estar en p. por algo** to be fighting over sth

pugnar *vi* to fight, struggle; **ambos jugadores pugnaban por el balón** both players fought for the ball

puja[1] *nf (pugna)* struggle

puja[2] *nf (acción)* bidding; *(cantidad)* bid

pujante *adj* thriving, prosperous

pujanza *nf* strength, vigour, *US* vigor

pujar[1] *vi* (a) *(hablar mal)* to be inarticulate (b) *(vacilar)* to hesitate (c) *Am (en parto)* to push

pujar[2] *vt* (a) *Naipes* to bid (b) *(en una subasta)* to bid

pujo *nm* (a) *Med* tenesmus (b) *(ansia)* craving, urge; **tener pujos de** to have aspirations to o of

pulcritud *nf* cleanliness, neatness

pulcro, -a *adj* (extremely) clean; (extremely) neat

pulga *nf* flea; *Fam* **buscarle las pulgas a algn** to taunt sb, provoke sb; *Fam* **tener malas pulgas** to be nasty, have a nasty streak

pulgada *nf* inch

pulgar *nm* thumb

Pulgarcito *nm Lit* Tom Thumb

pulgón *nm Ent* plant louse

pulgoso, -a *adj* flea-bitten, flea-ridden

pulido, -a 1 *pp de* pulir

2 *adj* (a) *Téc* polished (b) *Fig (fino)* elegant, refined (c) *(pulcro)* neat, clean

pulimentar *vt* to polish

pulimento *nm (acción)* polishing; *(material, brillo)* polish

pulir 1 *vt* (a) *Téc (metal, madera)* to polish (b) *(perfeccionar, mejorar)* to put the finishing touches to; **necesito p. mi alemán para obtener ese trabajo** I've got to improve my German to get the job (c) *Fam (robar)* to pinch, steal

2 pulirse *vpr Fam (dinero)* to spend, squander; *(acabarse)* to finish; **nos hemos pulido un litro de coñac** we've polished off a litre of brandy

pulla *nf* dig

pullover *nm* pullover, jumper

pulmón *nm Anat* lung; *Med* **p. de acero** iron lung

pulmonar *adj Anat* lung, pulmonary

pulmonía *nf Med* pneumonia

pulóver *nm* pullover

pulpa *nf* pulp

pulpejo *nm* soft o fleshy part

pulpería *nf* (a) *Am (tienda)* grocery store, *Br* grocer's (shop) (b) *(bar)* = Galician snack bar where boiled octopus is served

pulpero *nm* octopus fisherman

púlpito *nm* pulpit

pulpo *nm* octopus

pulposo, -a *adj* pulpy, soft, fleshy

pulque *nm CAm Méx* pulque, = fermented agave cactus juice

pulquería *nf CAm Méx* pulque bar

pulsación *nf (gen)* pulsation; *(latido del corazón)* beat, throb; *(en mecanografía)* stroke, tap; **pulsaciones por minuto** ≃ words per minute

pulsador *nm* push-button

pulsar 1 *vt* (a) *(tocar)* to press; *Fig (tantear)* to sound; **p. las teclas de la máquina de escribir** to tap the typewriter keys; **p. un botón** to press a button; *Fig* **p. la opinión de la gente** to sound out what people think (b) *Mús (tañer)* to play; **p. las cuerdas de la guitarra** to pluck a guitar

2 *vi* to throb, beat, pulse

púlsar *nm Astron* pulsar

pulsera *nf (aro)* bracelet; *(de reloj)* watchstrap; **reloj de p.** wristwatch

pulso *nm* (a) *Anat* pulse; **tomarle el p. a algn** to take sb's pulse; *Fig* **tomar el p. a la opinión** to sound out opinion (b) *(mano firme)* steady hand; **dibujo a p.** freehand drawing; **echarle un p. a algn** to arm-wrestle with sb; **levantar algo a p.** to lift sth with one's bare hands; *Fig* **se lo ha ganado a p.** *(merecido)* he's worked hard for it; *Irón* it serves him right (c) *Fig (tacto)* tact, care, prudence; **tratar algo con mucho p.** to be very tactful when dealing with sth (d) *Col Cuba Méx (pulsera)* bracelet

pulular *vi* to multiply

pulverización *nf (de sólidos)* pulverization; *(de líquidos)* spraying

pulverizador, -a 1 *adj (sólidos)* pulverizing; *(líquidos)* spraying

2 *nm* spray, atomizer; **p. nasal** nasal spray

pulverizar [14] *vt (sólidos)* to pulverize; *(líquidos)* to spray; *Dep (un récord)* to break; *Fig (matar)* to pulverize

pum *interj* bang!

puma *nm Zool* puma

pumba *interj* bang!

puna *nf Andes* (a) *(páramo)* high moor (b) *(mal)* mountain o altitude sickness (c) *(tierra alta)* puna

punción *nf Med* puncture

pundonor *nm* self-respect, self-esteem, dignity

punible *adj* punishable

punición *nf* punishment, punishing

púnico, -a *adj* Punic

punitivo, -a *adj* punitive

punk [paŋk] *(pl* **punks)** *adj nm & nmf* punk

punta 1 *adj* top; **hora p.** rush hour; **velocidad p.** top speed

2 *nf* (a) *(extremo)* tip; *(extremo agudo)* point; **córteme sólo las puntas** I just want the ends trimmed; **de p.** on end; **de p. a cabo, de p. a p.** from one end to the other; **p. del dedo** fingertip; **sacarle p. a un lápiz** to sharpen a pencil; *Fig* **estar de p. con algn** to be at odds with sb; *Fig* **lo tengo en la p. de la lengua** I have it on the tip of my tongue; *Fig* **me pone el pelo de p.** it gives me the creeps; *Fig* **ponerle a algn los nervios de p.** to get on sb's nerves; *Fam* **de p. en blanco** dressed up to the nines; *Fam* **había gente a p. pala** there were thousands of people; *Fam* **siempre le sacas p. a todo lo que digo** you always read too much into what I say (b) *(de cigarrillo) (colilla)* dog-end (c) *(pequeña cantidad)* bit; **una p. de sal** a pinch of salt; *Fig* **tiene una p. de loco** he has a streak of madness (d) *Geog (cabo)* point, foreland, headland (e) *(clavo)* nail (f) *(de grabador)* needle (g) **puntas** *Cost (encaje)* needlework *sing* (h) **de puntas** on tiptoe; **andar de p.** to walk on tiptoe

puntada *nf Cost* stitch; *Fam* **no da p.** *(no hace nada)* he doesn't do a thing; *(no acierta)* he gets nothing right

puntal *nm* (a) *Arquit (madero)* prop; *(en mina)* shore, leg *Fig (soporte)* pillar, support (b) *Andes CAm Méx (aperitivo)* snack

puntapié *nm* kick; **echar a algn a puntapiés** to kick sb out

punteado *nm* (a) *(marcado puntos)* dotting (b) *Mús* plucking

puntear *vt* (a) *(dibujar)* to dot (b) *Mús (guitarra)* to pluck (c) *Col Perú RP (encabezar)* to lead

punteo *nm Mús (de guitarra)* plucking

puntera *nf* (a) *(del zapato)* toe (b) *(remiendo)* steel cap; **zapatos con punteras** steel-capped shoes

puntería *nf* aim; **dirigir la p. (a algo)** to aim (at sth); **rectificar la p.** to change one's aim; **¡qué p.!** that was a good shot!; **tener buena/mala p.** to be a good/bad shot

puntero, -a 1 *adj* outstanding

2 *nm* (**a**) *(para señalar)* pointer (**b**) *Inform* pointer (**c**) *Andes RP Méx (persona)* leader; *(animal)* leading animal

puntiagudo, -a *adj* pointed, sharp

puntilla *nf* (**a**) *Cost (encaje)* lace (**b**) *Taur* dagger; **dar la p.** *Taur* to finish off the bull; *Fig (liquidar)* to give the coup de grâce (**c**) **de puntillas** on tiptoe

puntillismo *nm Arte* pointillism

puntillista *adj Arte* pointillist

puntilloso, -a *adj* punctilious; *Pey* touchy

punto *nm* (**a**) *(gen)* point; **a p.** on the point; **de todo p. imposible** absolutely impossible; *Culin* **en su p.** just right; **estar a p. de hacer algo** to be on the point of doing sth; **estuve a p. de caerme** I almost fell; **has dado en el p.** you've hit the nail on the head; **hasta cierto p.** to a certain *o* some extent; **hasta el p. de** to the point of; **hasta tal p.** to such an extent ❏ **p. cardinal** point of the compass, *Espec* cardinal point; **p. culminante** climax; **p. de apoyo** backup; **p. débil** weak point; **p. de congelación** freezing point; **p. de contacto** point of contact; **p. de ebullición** boiling point; *Geom* **p. de intersección** point of intersection; **p. de partida** starting point; **p. de referencia** point of reference; **p. de vista** viewpoint, opinion; **p. fuerte** strong point; **p. muerto** *Aut* neutral; *Fig (impase)* deadlock; **p. negro** *(grano)* blackhead; *(en carretera)* accident blackspot (**b**) *(marca, señal)* dot; **línea de puntos** dotted line; *Fig* **poner los puntos sobre las íes** to dot one's i's and cross one's t's (**c**) *(apartado, sección)* point; **los puntos del orden del día** the points on the agenda (**d**) *(lugar)* place, spot, point ❏ **p. de encuentro** *o* **de reunión** meeting point; **p. de observación** lookout; *Com* **p. de venta** point of sale; *(tienda)* retail outlet (**e**) *(signo de puntuación)* Br full stop, US period; **dos puntos** colon; *Fig* **con puntos y comas** in great detail ❏ *Bol Perú* **p. acápite** semicolon; **p. final** Br full stop, US period; *Fig* **poner p. final a algo** to put an end to sth; **p. y aparte** Br full stop *o* US period, new paragraph; **p. y coma** semicolon; **p. y seguido** Br full stop *o* US period *(no new paragraph)*; **puntos suspensivos** suspension points (**f**) *(tiempo)* **en p.** sharp, on the dot; **las seis en p.** six o'clock sharp; **llegaron a las tres en p.** they arrived at exactly three o'clock; **ella llegó en p.** she arrived punctually (**g**) *(tanto)* point; **ganar** *o* **marcar diez puntos** to score ten points; *Fig* **ganar/perder (muchos) puntos para algn** to go up/down in sb's estimation (**h**) *Cost Tricot* stitch; **¿cuántos puntos pongo?** how many stitches do I cast on?; **hacer p.** to knit; **un vestido de p.** a knitted dress ❏ **p. de cruz** cross-stitch; **p. del derecho/revés** plain/purl stitch (**i**) *Med* stitch; **le dieron cinco puntos en la cabeza** he had five stitches in his head

puntocom *nf (empresa)* dotcom

puntuable *adj* valid

puntuación *nf* (**a**) *Ling* punctuation; **signos de p.** punctuation marks (**b**) *(en una competición)* scoring; *(número de puntos)* score (**c**) *Educ* Br marking, US grading; *(calificación)* Br mark, US grade; **obtener una buena p.** to get a good mark

puntual 1 *adj* (**a**) *(a la hora)* punctual; **una persona p.** a punctual person (**b**) *(exacto)* exact, accurate, precise (**c**) *(aislado)* specific

2 *adv* punctually; **llegó p.** he arrived punctually *o* on time

puntualidad *nf* punctuality; **la p. es una gran virtud** punctuality is a great virtue

puntualización *nf* clarification

puntualizar [14] *vt* (**a**) *(detallar)* to give full details of,

describe in detail (**b**) *(especificar)* to leave clear; **hay que p. que no estaba solo** it should be pointed out that he wasn't on his own

puntualmente *adv* punctually

puntuar [4] **1** *vt* (**a**) *(al escribir)* to punctuate (**b**) *Educ (calificar)* Br to mark, US grade

2 *vi Dep* to score

punzada *nf* (**a**) *(de dolor)* sudden sharp pain; *Fig (de remordimiento)* pang (**b**) *(pinchazo)* prick

punzante *adj* (**a**) *(que pincha)* sharp, prickly; **objeto p.** sharp object (**b**) *(dolor)* acute, sharp, piercing (**c**) *Fig* biting, cutting, hurtful, spiteful

punzar [14] *vt* to prick; *Fig* to torment

punzón *nm Téc* punch

puñado *nm* handful; **un p. de amigos** a handful of friends; *Fam* **a puñados** by the score, galore

puñal *nm* dagger; *Fig* **ponerle a algn el p. en el pecho** to hold a pistol to sb's head

puñalada *nf* (**a**) *(con puñal)* stab; *Fig* **una p. trapera** a stab in the back (**b**) *Fig (disgusto)* grievous blow

puñeta *nf Fam* annoying thing; **hacerle la p. a algn** to pester sb, annoy sb; **¡puñetas!** damn!; **¡vete a hacer puñetas!** go to hell!

puñetazo *nm* punch; **le tiró al suelo de un sólo p.** he knocked him to the ground with one blow

puñetería *nf Fam* (**a**) *(mala intención)* bloody-mindedness (**b**) *(cosa)* trifle, mere nothing

puñetero, -a *Esp Fam* **1** *adj (cosa)* damn; *(persona)* **no seas p.** don't be awkward *o* bloody-minded

2 *nm,f* pain; **la puñetera de su hermana** his Br bloody *o* US goddamn sister

puño *nm* (**a**) *(mano cerrada)* fist; **apretar los puños** to clench one's fists; **enseñarle a algn el p.** to shake one's fist at sb; *Fig* **comerse los puños** to be starving; *Fig* **de su p. y letra** written in his/her own hand; *Fig* **tener a algn en un p.** to have sb under one's thumb (**b**) *(ropa)* cuff (**c**) *(de espada)* hilt; *(de bastón)* handle

pupa *nf* (**a**) *(en los labios)* cold sore (**b**) *Fam (daño)* pain; **¿te has hecho p.?** have you hurt yourself?

pupila *nf* (**a**) *Anat* pupil (**b**) *(persona)* véase **pupilo, -a**

pupilaje *nm* (**a**) *(de un niño, un huérfano)* tutelage (**b**) *(de alumno)* pupillage (**c**) *Aut* long-term parking; **'se admiten coches a p.'** 'long-term parking available'

pupilente *nm o f Méx* contact lens

pupilo, -a *nm,f* (**a**) *(niño, huérfano)* ward, orphan (**b**) *(alumno)* pupil

pupitre *nm* desk

pupusa *nf CAm Culin* stuffed tortilla

purasangre *adj & nm* thoroughbred

puré *nm Culin* purée; **p. de patata** mashed potatoes; **p. de tomate** tomato purée; **p. de verduras** thick vegetable soup; *Fam* **estoy hecho p.** I'm beat *o* Br knackered

pureza *nf* (**a**) *(calidad de puro)* purity, pureness (**b**) *(castidad)* chastity

purga *nf* (**a**) *Med* purge, purgative (**b**) *Fig (limpieza, depuración)* purge

purgación *nf* (**a**) *Med* purging (**b**) **purgaciones** *Fam* the clap *sing*

purgante *adj & nm* purgative

purgar [38] **1** *vt* (**a**) *Med* to purge (**b**) *(limpiar, depurar)* to purge (**c**) *(expiar)* to purge, expiate; **debe p. sus crímenes** he should pay for his crimes

2 purgarse *vpr* to take a purgative

purgatorio *nm Rel* purgatory

purificación *nf* purification

purificador, -a 1 *adj* purifying
  2 *nm,f Téc* purifier

purificar [59] *vt* to purify

purina *nf Quím* purin, purine

purismo *nm* purism

purista *nmf* purist

puritanismo *nm* puritanism

puritano, -a 1 *adj* puritan, puritanic, puritanical
  2 *nm,f* puritan, Puritan

puro, -a 1 *adj* (**a**) *(sin mezclas)* pure; **aire p.** fresh air; **filosofía pura** pure philosophy (**b**) *(mero)* sheer, mere; **la casa se cayó de p. vieja** the house collapsed out of sheer age; **la pura verdad** the plain truth; **por pura casualidad** by pure chance; **por pura curiosidad** out of sheer curiosity (**c**) *(casto)* chaste, pure
  2 *nm* (**a**) *(cigarro)* cigar ❑ **p. habano** Havana cigar (**b**) *Esp Fam* **meterle un p. a algn** *(regañina)* to give sb a rocket; *(castigo)* to throw the book at sb
  3 *nfpl Andes* **por las puras** just for the sake of it, for no reason

púrpura *adj* purple

purpurado *nm Rel* cardinal

purpúreo, -a *adj* purple

purpurina *nf* purpurin

purulencia *nf* purulence, purulency

purulento, -a *adj* full of pus, purulent

pus *nm* pus

puse *pt indef véase* **poner**

pusilánime *adj* faint-hearted, cowardly

pusilanimidad *nf* faint-heartedness, cowardice

pústula *nf* sore, pimple, spot, pustule

puta *nf Ofens* whore; **de p. madre** great, terrific; **de p. pena** bloody awful; **no tengo ni p. idea** I haven't (got) a bloody clue; **pasarlas putas** to go through hell, have a rotten time

putada *nf Vulg* dirty trick; **¡qué p. que no queden entradas!** what a bummer, the tickets are sold out!; **hacerle una p. a algn** to be a mean bastard to sb;

putativo, -a *adj* putative, supposed

putear *Vulg* **1** *vt* (**a**) *(fastidiar)* **p. a algn** to fuck o piss sb about o around, make sb's life a misery; **¡no me putees!** don't fuck me about! (**b**) *Am (insultar)* **p. a algn** to call sb every name under the sun
  2 *vi* (**a**) *(con prostitutas)* to go whoring (**b**) *Am (hablando)* to eff and blind

puteo *nm Ofens* **es un p.** it's a pain in the *Br* arse o *US* ass

puterío *nm Fam* prostitution

putero, -a *adj Vulg* whoring

puticlub *(pl* **puticlubs** *o* **puticlubes**) *nm Fam* brothel

puto, -a 1 *adj Ofens Br* bloody, *US* goddamn; **de puta m.** *Br* bloody o *US* goddamn brilliant
  2 *nm* rent boy

putrefacción *nf* putrefaction, rotting

putrefacto, -a *adj*, **pútrido, -a** *adj* putrefied, rotten

puya *nf Taur* steel point *(of a lance)*

puyar *vi Chile Col Pan* to work hard

puzzle ['puθle] *nm* puzzle

PVC *nm (abrev de* **cloruro de polivinilo***)* PVC

PVP *nm (abrev de* **precio de venta al público***)* retail price

PYME ['pime] *nf (abrev de* **Pequeña y Mediana Empresa***)* SME

Pza., Plza. *(abrev de* **plaza***)* Sq

Q

Q, q [ku] *nf (la letra)* Q, q

Qatar *n* Qatar

qatarí *(pl* qataríes*) adj & nmf* Qatari

que¹ *pron rel* (**a**) *(sujeto) (persona)* who, that; *(cosa)* that, which; **el chico q. me lo dijo** the boy who told me; **la bomba q. estalló** the bomb that went off; **la moto q. me gusta** the motorbike that I like (**b**) *(sujeto)* **lo q.** what; **eso es lo q. me asusta** that's what frightens me (**c**) *(complemento) (persona)* whom, who; *(cosa)* that, which; **el hombre con el q. hablé** the man who I spoke to; **el libro q. me prestaste** the book (that) you lent me (**d**) *(complemento) (de tiempo, lugar)* when, where; **el jardín en el q. jugábamos** the garden where we used to play; **las ocasiones en q. le visité** the times when I visited him

que² *conj* (**a**) *(con oraciones de sujeto)* that; **dice q. está cansado** he says (that) he's tired; **quiero q. vengas** I want you to come (**b**) *(consecuencia)* that; **habla tan bajo q. no se le oye** he speaks so quietly (that) he can't be heard (**c**) *(causal, consecutiva)* **cuidado q. te vas a caer** careful, you'll fall; **deprisa q. no tenemos mucho tiempo** hurry up, we haven't got much time (**d**) *(énfasis) (no se traduce)* **¡q. no!** no!; **¡q. sí!** yes!; **¡q. te calles!** I said be quiet! (**e**) *(deseo, mandato) (con subj)* **¡q. te diviertas!** enjoy yourself!; **¡q. se atreva!** he wouldn't dare! (**f**) *(copulativa)* and; **corre q. corre** hell for leather (**g**) *(final)* so that; **ven a q. te dé un beso** come and let me give you a kiss (**h**) *(locuciones)* **¿a q. no?** I bet you can't!; **¿a q. no lo adivinas?** I bet you can't guess; **q. yo sepa** as far as I know; **yo q. tú** if I were you; *Fam* **q. si esto o, si lo otro** this, that and the other

qué 1 *pron interr* (**a**) *(interrogativo)* what; **a ver q. dicen** let's see what they say; **no sé q. decir** I don't know what to say; **¿q. hora es?** what time is it?; **¿q. pasa?** what's the matter?; **¿q. quieres?** what do you want?; *Fam* **¿q. tal?, ¿q. hay?** how are things? (**b**) *(cuál)* which; **¿q. libro quieres?** which book do you want? (**c**) *(en exclamativas)* how, so; **¡q. lástima!** what a pity!; *Fam* **¡y q.!** so what? (**d**) *(indica cantidad)* how; **¡q. de coches!** what a lot of cars!

2 *nm* **sin q. ni para** *o* **por** without rhyme or reason

quebrada *nf* (**a**) *Geol (desfiladero)* ravine, gorge (**b**) *Am (arroyo)* stream

quebradero *nm Fig* **q. de cabeza** headache

quebradizo, -a *adj (débil)* fragile; *(rompedero)* brittle

quebrado, -a 1 *pp de* quebrar

2 *adj* (**a**) *(roto)* broken; *(terreno)* uneven, rough; *(voz)* faltering; *Mat* **número q.** fraction; *Culin* **pasta quebrada** puff pastry (**b**) *Fin* bankrupt (**c**) *Méx (pelo)* curly

3 *nm Mat* fraction

quebradura *nf* (**a**) *(grieta)* crack, fissure (**b**) *Med* hernia, rupture

quebrantado, -a *adj* frail

quebrantahuesos *nm inv Orn* lammergeier

quebrantamiento *nm* (**a**) *(gen)* breaking, breaking up; *(de salud)* weakening, deterioration (**b**) *Jur (de una ley)* violation, infringement

quebrantar 1 *vt* (**a**) *(romper)* to break, shatter (**b**) *(violar promesa, ley)* to break (**c**) *Fig (debilitar)* to weaken; *(ánimo)* to break

2 quebrantarse *vpr* (**a**) *(quebrar)* to crack; *(romperse)* to break (**b**) *(salud)* to be shattered

quebranto *nm* (**a**) *(pérdida)* loss; *(daño)* damage (**b**) *(lástima)* pity (**c**) *(aflicción)* grief, affliction (**d**) *Fig (desaliento)* discouragement

quebrar [3] **1** *vt* (**a**) *(romper)* to break (**b**) *(violar promesa, ley)* to break; **q. la ley** to break the law (**c**) *(suavizar)* to soften; *(color)* to make paler (**d**) *(doblar)* to bend

2 *vi* (**a**) *Fin* to go bankrupt; *Fam* to go bust (**b**) *Fig (con amigo)* to fall out, break up

3 quebrarse *vpr* (**a**) *(voz)* to break; *(estar ronco)* to become hoarse (**b**) *Med* to rupture oneself (**c**) *Fig (ánimo)* to break

quechemarín *nm Náut* yawl

quechua 1 *adj* Quechuan

2 *nmf (persona)* Quechua

3 *nm (idioma)* Quechua

queda *nf* **toque de q.** curfew

quedada *nf Argot* trick, joke

quedar 1 *vi* (**a**) *(permanecer)* to remain, stay; **la cama quedó sin hacer** the bed was left unmade; *(en cartas)* **quedamos a la espera de ...** we await ... (**b**) *(resultar en situación o estado)* to remain, be; **¡queda adjudicado!** sold!; **q. a deber algo** to owe sth; **q. en ridículo** to make a fool of oneself; **q. uno bien/mal** to make a good/bad impression; *Fam* **q. como un señor** to create a very good impression (**c**) *(ropa etc) (favorecer)* to look; *(venir a medida)* to fit; **me queda corta** it is too short; **quedaría muy bien allí** it would look very nice there (**d**) *(terminar)* to end; **todo quedó en nada** it all came to nothing; *Fam* **ahí quedó la cosa** that's how it stands (**e**) *(acordar)* to agree (**en** to); **¿en qué quedamos?** so what's it to be? (**f**) *(en un lugar)* to arrange to meet (**g**) *(estar situado)* to be; **¿por dónde queda tu casa?** whereabouts is your house? (**h**) *(faltar)* to be left, remain; **queda poco** there's not much left; *Fig* **no quedó títere con cabeza** nothing was left intact

2 quedarse *vpr* (**a**) *(permanecer)* to be left; **q. sin amigos/trabajo** to lose one's friends/job; **q. sin dinero/pan** to run out of money/bread; *Fam* **q. sin blanca** to be broke; *Fam* **se quedó tan tranquilo** he didn't bat an eyelid (**b**) *(resultar situación o estado)* to be, remain; **q. huérfano** to be left an orphan; *Fig* **me quedé en blanco** my mind went blank (**c**) *(en alojamiento)* to stay; **me quedé en casa todo el día** I stayed at home all day (**d**) *(detenerse)* to stay; *(estarse* *parado)* to stand; **me quedé mirándole** I stood there looking at him; **no te quedes en la puerta** do come in; **q. atrás** to be left behind; *(por propia voluntad)* to stay behind **(e) q. con** *(retener)* to keep; *Fig* to remain; **q. con hambre** to be still hungry; **quédate con la vuelta** keep the change; *Fig* **q. con la boca abierta** to be amazed; *Fig* **q. con las ganas de algo** to go without sth **(f)** *(mar, viento)* to become calm **(g)** *Esp Fam* **q. con algn** to wind sb up

quedo¹ *adv* softly, quietly

quedo, -a² *adj* quiet, still

quehacer *nm* task, chore; **los quehaceres domésticos** housework *sing*, household chores

queja *nf* **(a)** *(disconformidad)* complaint; **no tener q. de algn** to have no complaints about sb; *Jur* **presentar una q.** to lodge a complaint **(b)** *(de dolor)* groan, moan

quejarse *vpr* **(a)** *(expresar dolor)* to suffer, groan **(b)** *(expresar descontento)* to complain **(de** about); **no puedo quejarme** I can't complain; **te quejas de vicio** you're a born complainer

quejica *Fam* **1** *adj* grumpy
2 *nmf* moaner

quejido *nm* groan, cry

quejoso, -a **1** *adj* **estar q. de** *o* **por** to be unhappy *o* dissatisfied with
2 *nm,f* **(a)** *Méx RP Fam Pey (quejica)* whinger **(b)** *Méx Jur (demandante)* plaintiff

quejumbroso, -a *adj* whining; **en tono q.** in an aggrieved tone

quema *nf* burning; *Fig* **huir de la q.** to beat it, flee

quemada *nf Méx véase* **quemadura**

quemadero *nm* **(a)** *Hist* stake **(b)** *(para basura)* incinerator

quemado, -a **1** *pp de* **quemar**
2 *adj* **(a)** *(por fuego)* burnt, burned; **huele a q.** something is burning; **q. por el sol** sunburnt **(b)** *Am (bronceado)* tanned **(c)** *(resentido)* embittered **(d)** *(acabado)* spent, burnt-out; **como actor está q.** as an actor he's a bit of a has-been

quemador *nm (de cocina etc) Br* gas ring, *US* burner

quemadura *nf* **(a)** *(en piel) (por fuego)* burn; *(por agua hirviendo)* scald **(b)** *(en ropa, mueble)* burn mark

quemar **1** *vt* **(a)** *(por sol, fuego, calor)* to burn; *(con líquido hirviendo)* to scald **(b)** *Fam (agotar) (persona)* to burn out **(c)** *Carib Méx (delatar)* to denounce, inform on; *(estafar)* to swindle
2 *vi (estar caliente)* to be burning hot; **este café quema** this coffee's boiling hot
3 quemarse *vpr* **(a)** *(persona)* to burn oneself; *(por el sol)* to get (sun)burnt; *Fig* **q. las pestañas** to burn the midnight oil **(b)** *(objeto)* to be burnt; **se ha quemado el arroz** the rice is burnt **(c)** *Fam (desgastarse)* to burn out **(d)** *Esp Fam (hartarse)* to get fed up **(de** of)

quemarropa: a quemarropa *loc adv* point-blank; **disparar/preguntar a algn a q.** to shoot/ask sb point-blank

quemazón *nf* **(a)** *(calor)* intense heat **(b)** *(comezón)* itch **(c)** *Fig (dicho picante)* cutting word

quepis *nm inv* kepi

quepo *indic pres véase* **caber**

queratina *nf Biol* keratin

querella *nf* **(a)** *(pelea)* dispute **(b)** *(queja)* complaint **(c)** *Jur* charge

querellante *nmf* plaintiff

querellarse *vpr Jur* to bring an action, lodge a complaint

querendón, -ona *adj Am Fam* loving, affectionate

querer¹ *nm* love, affection

querer² [53] **1** *vt* **(a)** *(amar)* to love; **Pepe sabe hacerse q.** Pepe's got winning ways; *Prov* **quien bien te quiere te hará llorar** you've got to be cruel to be kind **(b)** *(desear)* to want; **¿cuánto quieres por la bici?** how much do you want for the bike?; **¡por lo que más quieras!** for Heaven's sake!; **quiere ser médico** he wants to be a doctor **(c)** *(por favor)* would; **¿quieres callarte?** would you be quiet!, please shut up!; **¿quieres ir al cine?** would you like to go to the cinema **(d)** *(significar)* **q. decir** to mean; **¿qué quiere decir?** what does it mean? **(e)** *(ser conveniente)* to need; **estas plantas quieren más agua** these plants need more water
2 *vi* to want; **lo hice sin q.** I didn't mean to do it; **quieras o no** like it or not; **si quieres** if you want (to); **sí, quiero** *(en la boda)* I will; **todo el que quiera** anyone who wants to; *Fig* **el quiero y no puedo** pretentious ideas; *Fig* **q. es poder** where there's a will there's a way; *Fam* **está como quiere** he *o* she is gorgeous
3 quererse *vpr* to love each other

querido, -a **1** *pp de* **querer²**
2 *adj* dear, beloved; *(en carta)* **q. amigo** dear friend
3 *nm,f* **(a)** *(amante) (hombre, mujer)* lover; *(mujer)* mistress **(b)** *(apelativo cariñoso)* darling

queroseno *nm, Am* **querosén** *nm, Am* **querosene** *nm* kerosene, kerosine

querré *indic fut véase* **querer²**

querubín *nm* cherub

quesadilla *nf Culin CAm Méx* = filled fried tortilla

quesera *nf* cheeseboard and cover

quesero, -a **1** *adj* **(a)** *(industria)* cheese **(b)** *(persona)* cheese-loving
2 *nm,f* **(a)** *(que lo hace)* cheese maker **(b)** *(que le gusta)* lover of cheese

queso *nm* **(a)** cheese □ **q. azul** blue cheese; **q. de cabra** goat's cheese; **q. en lonchas** sliced cheese; **q. rallado** grated cheese **(b)** **q. de cerdo** *Br* brawn, *US* headcheese **(c)** *Cost* **medio q.** semicircular ironing board

quetzal [ket'sal] *nm Fin* = standard monetary unit of Guatemala

quevedos *nmpl* pince-nez *pl*

quiché *adj & nmf (de Guatemala)* Quiché

quichua *adj & nm,f véase* **quechua**

quicio *nm* **(a)** *(bisagra)* hinge; *(espacio interior)* jamb; *(de puerta)* doorpost **(b)** *Fig* **estar fuera de q.** to be beside oneself; **sacar a algn de q.** to infuriate sb, make sb's blood boil

quid *(pl* quids) *nm* crux; **ahí está el q. de la cuestión** there's the crux of the matter; **has dado en el q.** you've hit the nail on the head

quiebra *nf* **(a)** *(abertura)* crack, fissure **(b)** *Fin (bancarrota)* bankruptcy, failure; *(crack)* crash **(c)** *Fig (fracaso)* collapse; **la q. de la sociedad** the breakup of society

quiebro *nm* **(a)** *Taur* dodge **(b)** *Ftb* dribbling **(c)** *Mús* trill

quien *pron rel* **(a)** *(sujeto)* who; **fue el jefe q. me lo dijo** it was the boss who told me **(b)** *(complemento)* whom, who; **es a ti a q. quiero** it's you I love; **las personas con quienes trabajo** the people (who) I work with; **su padre, a q. se parece ...** her father, who(m) she resembles ... **(c)** *(indef) (la persona que)* whoever, anyone who; **hay q. dice lo contrario** some people say the opposite; **q. quiera venir que venga** whoever wants to can come; *Fig* **q. más q. menos** everybody

quién *pron interr* **(a)** *(sujeto)* who?; **¿q. sabe?** who knows?; **¿quiénes sois?** who are you? **(b)** *(complemento)* who, whom; **díme con q. has estado** tell me who you've been with; **¿para q. es?** who is it for? (**c**) *(pos)* whose; **¿de q. es esa bici?** whose bike is that?

quienquiera *(pl* **quienesquiera)** *pron indef* whoever; **q. que sea** whoever it may be

quieto, -a *adj* (**a**) *(sin moverse)* still; **estáte q.** keep still! **¡quietos ahí!** don't move!, stay where you are! (**b**) *(sosegado)* calm; **es un chico q.** he's quiet; **mar quieta** calm sea

quietud *nf* (**a**) *(sin movimiento)* stillness (**b**) *(calma)* calm

quihubo *interj CAm Col Méx Ven Fam* how are you doing?

quijada *nf Anat* jawbone; **q. inferior** lower jaw

quijotada *nf* quixotic deed

Quijote *nm* **Don Q.** Don Quixote

quijote *nm* do-gooder

quilate *nm* carat; *Fig* **de muchos quilates** of great value

quilla *nf* (**a**) *Náut* keel (**b**) *Astron (constelación)* Carina

quilo¹ *nm* (**a**) *Biol* chyle (**b**) *Fig* **sudar el q.** to sweat blood

quilo² *nm véase* **kilo**

quilombo *nm RP muy Fam* mess

quimba *nf* (**a**) *Andes (contoneo)* swaying (**b**) *Col Ecuad Ven (calzado)* peasant shoe

quimbar *vi Andes* to sway

quimbombó *nm Cuba* okra, gumbo

quimera *nf* (**a**) *Mit* chimera (**b**) *Fig (ilusión)* fantasy, pipe dream (**c**) *Fig (aprensión)* apprehension (**d**) *(riña)* quarrel

quimérico, -a *adj* unrealistic, fanciful

química *nf* chemistry

químico, -a 1 *adj* chemical
2 *nm,f* chemist

quimioterapia *nf Med* chemotherapy

quimono *nm* kimono

quina *nf Bot* quinine, Peruvian bark; *Fig* **tragar q.** to swallow hard, grin and bear it

quincalla *nf* metal pots and pans *pl*, tinware

quincallería *nf (chatarra)* trinkets *pl*

quincallero, -a *nm,f* (**a**) *(fabricante)* maker of tinware (**b**) *(vendedor)* tinker

quince 1 *adj inv (cardinal)* fifteen; *(ordinal)* fifteenth; **el q. de agosto** the fifteenth of August
2 *nm inv* fifteen; *véase tamb* **ocho**

quinceañero, -a *adj & nm,f* fifteen-year-old

quincena *nf* fortnight, two weeks

quincenal *adj* fortnightly, every two weeks

quincuagenario, -a *adj & nm,f* quinquagenarian

quincuagésimo, -a 1 *adj* fiftieth; **quincuagésima parte** fiftieth
2 *nm,f (de una serie)* fiftieth
3 *nm (parte)* fiftieth; *véase tamb* **octavo, -a**

quinesioterapia *nf* kinesitherapy

quingos *nmpl Col Perú* zigzag *sing*

quiniela *nf Esp* football pools *pl*; **hacer una q.** to do the pools

quinielista *nmf Esp* = person who does the pools

quinientos, -as 1 *adj inv (cardinal)* five hundred; *(ordinal)* five hundredth; **mil q.** one thousand five hundred, fifteen hundred
2 *nm,f* five hundred; *Fam* **a las quinientas** very late

quinina *nf* quinine

quinqué *nm* oil lamp

quinquenal *adj* quinquennial, five-year

quinquenio *nm* quinquennium, five-year period

quinqui *nmf Esp Fam* lout, *Br* yob

quinta *nf* (**a**) *(casa)* country house (**b**) *(reclutar) Mil* conscription, *US* draft; **entrar en quintas** to be called up *o US* drafted (**c**) *Mús* fifth

quintacolumnista *adj & nmf* fifth columnist

quintaesencia *nf* quintessence

quintal *nm (medida)* 46 kg ❑ **q. métrico** ≃ 100 kg

quintar *vt Mil* to conscript, *US* draft

quinteto *nm Mús* quintet

quintillizo, -a *nm,f* quintuplet, quin

Quintín *nm* Quentin; *Fam* **se armó la de San Q.** there was a hell of a row

quinto, -a 1 *adj* fifth; **quinta columna** fifth column
2 *nm,f (de una serie)* fifth
3 *nm* (**a**) *(parte)* fifth; *Esp Fam* **un q. de cerveza** a small beer (**b**) *Mil* conscript, recruit; *véase tamb* **octavo, -a**

quintuplicar [59] **1** *vt* to increase fivefold
2 quintuplicarse *vpr* to increase fivefold

quíntuplo, -a *adj & nm* quintuple

quiosco *nm* (**a**) *(tenderete)* kiosk; **q. de periódicos** newspaper stand (**b**) *RP (de tabaco)* tobacconist's

quiosquero, -a *nm,f* = person selling newspapers, drinks etc from a kiosk

quipe *nm Andes* knapsack

quiquiriquí *(pl* **quiquiriquíes)** *nm* cock-a-doodle-doo

quirófano *nm* operating *Br* theatre *o US* room

quiromancia *nf* palmistry, chiromancy

quiromántico, -a *nm,f* palmist, chiromancer

quiromasaje *nm* (manual) massage

quiromasajista *nmf (hombre)* masseur; *(mujer)* masseuse

quirquincho *nm Andes Arg* armadillo

quirúrgico, -a *adj* surgical

quise *pt indef véase* **querer²**

quisque *pron Fam* **todo** *o* **cada q.** everyone, everybody

quisquilla *nf (marisco)* common prawn

quisquilloso, -a 1 *adj* fussy, finicky, fastidious
2 *nm,f* fusspot

quiste *nm Med* cyst

quita *nf Fin* partial acquittance

quitaesmalte *nm* nail-polish *o* nail-varnish remover

quitamanchas *nm inv* stain remover

quitanieves *adj & nm* **(máquina) q.** snowplough, *US* snowplow

quitar 1 *vt* (**a**) *(gen)* to remove, take out, take off (**b**) *(separar)* to remove, take out; **q. la piel de una manzana** to peel an apple (**c**) *(sacar)* to take off, take out; *(prendas)* to take off; *Med* **q. los puntos** to take out the stitches; **q. tiempo** to take up a lot of time; **quítate el abrigo** take your coat off; **un cuello de quita y pon** a detachable collar; *Fig* **q. importancia a algo** to play sth down; *Fig* **q. las ganas a algn** to put sb off (**d**) *(apartar)* to take away, take off; **quita eso de delante** clear that away; **quítale esa idea de la cabeza** tell him to forget it (**e**) *Esp (la mesa)* to clear (**f**) *(mancha)* to remove (**g**) *(dolor)* to relieve (**h**) *(hipo)* to stop; **le quitó el hipo** it stopped her hiccups; *Fig* it took her breath away (**i**) *(sed)* quench; **te quitará la sed** it will quench your thirst (**j**) *(hambre)* **no lo comas, te quitará el hambre** don't eat it, because it will spoil your appetite (**k**) *(sueño)* **quitarle el sueño a algn** to keep sb awake (**l**) *Mat (descontar)* to take off; *(restar)* to subtract; **de once quita dos** eleven minus two (**m**) *(robar)* to steal, take; **me han quitado el bolso** my handbag's been stolen (**n**) *(coger)* to take; **quítale el sitio a algn** to take sb's place *o* seat (**o**) *(impedir)* to stop, prevent; **eso no le quita valor** that doesn't detract from its value;

eso no quita para que seas educado that's no reason not to be polite (**p**) *(prohibir)* to stop; **me han quitado el fumar** they've stopped me (from) smoking (**q**) *(libertar de cargas)* to relieve, free (**r**) *Fam (radio, agua, electricidad)* to turn off (**s**) *(locuciones)* **no q. ojo a algn** not to take one's eyes off sb; **¡quita!** *(persona)* go away!; *(cosa)* take it away!; **q. la palabra de la boca a algn** to take the words right out of sb's mouth; **yo ni quito ni pongo** it's nothing to do with me; *Fam* **que me quiten lo baila(d)o** they can't take that away from me

2 quitarse *vpr* (**a**) *(apartarse)* to move away; **¡quítate (de ahí)!** come out, get out (of there)! (**b**) *(desaparecer)* to go; *(mancha)* to come out; **la mancha no se quita** the stain won't come out; **se me ha quitado el dolor de cabeza** my headache's gone; **se me han quitado las ganas** I don't feel like it any more (**c**) *(sacarse) (prendas, gafas)* to take off; **q. el bigote** to shave one's moustache off; **q. el sombrero** to tip one's hat; **q. un diente** to have a tooth out; *Fig* **q. años** to lie about one's age (**d**) *(renunciar a) (bebida, fumar etc)* to give up (**e**) *(deshacerse de)* to get rid of; **q. a algn de encima** to get rid of sb

quitasol *nm* parasol, sunshade

quite *nm* (**a**) *(en esgrima)* parry (**b**) *Taur* = distraction of bull by assistants to allow the escape of the bullfighter; *Fig* **estar al q.** to be ready to help

quiteño, -a 1 *adj* of o from Quito
 2 *nm,f* person from Quito

Quito *n* Quito

quiúbole *interj CAm Col Méx Ven Fam* **¿q.?** how's it going?

quizá *adv,* **quizás** *adv* perhaps, maybe; **q. llueva** perhaps it will rain; **q. no** maybe not; **q. sí** maybe

quórum *nm inv* quorum

R

R, r *Esp* ['erre], *Am* ['ere] *nf (la letra)* R, r

rabadilla *nf* (**a**) *Anat* coccyx (**b**) *Culin (de buey)* rump

rabanillo *nm* wild radish

rábano *nm* radish; *Fig* **tomar el r. por las hojas** to get hold of the wrong end of the stick; *Fam* **me importa un r.** I don't give a toss, I couldn't care less; *Fam* **¡un r.!** no way! □ **r. blanco** *o* **picante** horseradish

Rabat *n* Rabat

rabí (*pl* **rabís** *o* **rabíes**) *nm Rel* rabbi

rabia *nf* (**a**) *Med* rabies *sing* (**b**) *Fig (ira)* fury, rage, anger; **me da r.** it makes me mad; **¡qué r.!** how annoying!; **tener r. a algn** not to be able to stand the sight of sb

rabiar *vi* (**a**) *Med* to have rabies (**b**) *Fig (sufrir)* to be in great pain; **r. de dolor** to writhe in pain (**c**) *Fig (enfadarse)* to rage; **estar a r. con algn** to be furious with sb; **está que rabia** he's fuming; **hacer r. a algn** to make sb see red (**d**) *Fig (desear)* **r. por** to long for; **rabiaba por conseguir el cargo** she was dying to get the job (**e**) *Fam* **a r.** a lot, very much; **me gusta a r.** I'm crazy *o Br* mad about it

rabieta *nf Fam* tantrum; **coger una r.** to throw a tantrum

rabillo *nm* (**a**) *(de hoja)* stalk, stem (**b**) *(cizaña)* darnel (**c**) *(del ojo)* corner; **mirar por el r. del ojo** to look out of the corner of one's eye

rabínico, -a *adj* rabbinical

rabino *nm Rel* rabbi

rabiosamente *adv* furiously

rabioso, -a *adj* (**a**) *Med* rabid; **perro r.** rabid dog (**b**) *Fig (enfadado)* furious; **ponerse r.** to fly into a rage (**c**) *(dolor)* terrible, intense (**d**) *(color)* shocking, garish

rabo *nm Anat* tail; *Fig* **aún falta el r. por desollar** the worst is yet to come; *Fam* **irse con el r. entre las piernas** to go away with one's tail between one's legs

rabón, -ona *adj (animal)* bobtailed

rabona *nf RP Fam* **hacerse la r.** *Br* to bunk off, *US* to play hooky

racanear *vi Fam* (**a**) *(holgazanear)* to idle, slack (**b**) *(ser tacaño)* to be stingy

rácano, -a *adj Fam* (**a**) *(holgazán)* idle, lazy (**b**) *(tacaño)* stingy, mean

RACE ['rraθe] *nm Aut (abrev de* **Real Automóvil Club de España**) = Spanish automobile association, *Br* ≃ AA, RAC, *US* ≃ AAA

racha *nf* (**a**) *(de viento)* gust, squall (**b**) *Fam (período)* spell, patch; **a rachas** in fits and starts, on and off; **tener una buena r.** to have a piece of luck; **tener una mala r.** to go through a bad patch (**c**) *Fam (serie)* run, series *sing*; **una r. de accidentes** a string of accidents

racial *adj* racial, race; **disturbios raciales** race riots; **prejuicio r.** racial prejudice

racimo *nm* bunch, cluster; **r. de uvas** bunch of grapes

raciocinio *nm* (**a**) *(razón)* reason (**b**) *(razonamiento)* reasoning

ración *nf* ration, portion, share; *(de comida)* portion, helping; *(en paquete)* **'tres raciones'** 'serves three'; **una r. de patatas fritas, por favor** a portion of French fries *o Br* chips, please

racional *adj* rational

racionalidad *nf* rationality

racionalismo *nm* rationalism

racionalista *adj & nmf* rationalist

racionalización *nf* rationalization

racionalizar [14] *vt* to rationalize

racionalmente *adv* rationally, reasonably

racionamiento *nm* rationing □ **cartilla de r.** ration book, ration card

racionar *vt (limitar)* to ration; *(repartir)* to ration out

racismo *nm* racism, racialism

racista *adj & nmf* racist, racialist

racor *nm Téc* connecter, adapter, adaptor

rada *nf Geog* bay, inlet

radar *nm Téc* radar; **pantalla de r.** radar screen

radiación *nf* radiation □ **r. solar** solar radiation

radiactividad *nf* radioactivity

radiactivo, -a *adj* radioactive

radiado, -a 1 *pp de* **radiar**
2 *adj Bot Zool* radiate

radiador *nm* radiator

radial *adj* (**a**) *(del radio)* radial (**b**) *(en forma de estrella)* radial (**c**) *Am (de la radio)* radio

radiante *adj* radiant (**de** with)

radiar *vt* (**a**) *Fís* to radiate (**b**) *Rad* to broadcast, transmit, radio (**c**) *Med* to X-ray (**d**) *Am (hacer el vacío a)* to cold-shoulder

radicación *nf* (**a**) *(instalación)* taking root, settling down (**b**) *(situación, ubicación)* setting, location

radical 1 *adj* radical
2 *nm Ling Mat* radical, root

radicalismo *nm Pol* radicalism

radicalización *nf* radicalization

radicalizar [14] **1** *vt (conflicto)* to intensify; *(postura)* to harden, make more radical
2 radicalizarse *vpr (conflicto)* to intensify; *(persona, postura)* to become more radical

radicalmente *adv* radically

radicar [59] **1** *vi* (**a**) *(estar, encontrarse)* to be (situated) (**en** in), be rooted (**en** in) (**b**) *Fig* **r. en** to lie in, stem from; **el problema radica en la economía** the problem lies in the economy
2 radicarse *vpr (establecerse)* to settle (down)

radio¹ *nm* (**a**) *Anat Geom* radius; **en un r. de tres kilómetros** within a radius of three kilometres ☐ **r. de acción** field of action, scope, sphere of influence (**b**) *(de rueda)* spoke (**c**) *Am salvo RP (transistor)* radio

radio² *nm Quím* radium

radio³ *nf (medio)* radio; *Esp CSur (aparato)* radio (set); **por r.** by radio; **me enteré por la r.** I heard (about) it on the radio; **poner la r.** to turn on the radio ☐ **r. despertador** clock radio; **r. digital** digital radio; **r. galena** crystal set; *Fam* **r. macuto** bush telegraph, grapevine; **r. pirata** pirate radio station

radioactividad *nf* radioactivity

radioactivo, -a *adj* radioactive

radioaficionado, -a *nm,f* radio ham

radiobaliza *nf* radio beacon

radiocasete *nm* radio cassette

radiocomunicación *nf* radio communication

radiocontrol *nm* remote control

radiodifusión *nf Rad* broadcasting

radioenlace *nm* radio link

radioescucha *nmf Rad* listener

radiofonía *nf* radio *(technology)*

radiofónico, -a *adj* radio; **entrevista radiofónica** radio interview; **espacio** *o* **programa r.** radio programme

radiofrecuencia *nf* radio frequency

radiografía *nf* (**a**) *(técnica)* radiography (**b**) *(imagen)* X-ray, radiograph; **hacerse una r.** to have an X-ray taken

radiografiar [32] *vt* to X-ray

radiología *nf Med* radiology

radiológico, -a *adj* X-ray, radiological; **examen r.** X-ray examination

radiólogo, -a *nm,f Med* radiologist

radiomensaje *nm RP (buscapersonas)* pager

radiómetro *nm* radiometer

radionovela *nf* radio soap opera

radiorreceptor *nm* radio receiver

radioscopia *nf* radioscopy

radioteléfono *nm* radiotelephone

radiotelegrafista *nmf* radio *o* wireless operator

radiotelescopio *nm* radio telescope

radioterapia *nf* radiotherapy, radium therapy

radiotransmisión *nf* radio transmission, broadcasting

radiotransmisor *nm* radio transmitter

radioyente *nmf Rad* listener

RAE ['rrae] *nf (abrev de* **Real Academia Española)**

raer [54] *vt* to scrape (off)

ráfaga *nf* (**a**) *(de viento)* gust, squall (**b**) *(de disparos)* burst (**c**) *(de luz)* flash

rafia *nf Bot* raffia

rafting *nm Dep* rafting

raglán *adj inv Cost* raglan; **mangas r.** raglan sleeves

raid *(pl* **raids)** *nm* raid; *Av* **r. aéreo** *(ataque)* air raid; *(vuelo a gran distancia)* long-distance flight, longhaul flight

raído, -a 1 *pp de* **raer**
2 *adj* worn, threadbare

raigambre *nf* (**a**) *Bot* roots *pl*, root system (**b**) *Fig*

tradition, history; **de honda r.** deep-rooted

raíl *nm,* **rail** *nm Ferroc* rail

raíz *nf* (**a**) *(gen)* root; **arrancar de r.** to pull up by the roots; **echar raíces** *(planta)* to take root; *Fig (establecerse)* to put down roots, settle (down); *Fig* **a r. de** as a result of; *Fig* **cortar algo de r.** to nip sth in the bud (**b**) *Mat* **r. cuadrada/cúbica** square/cube root

raja *nf* (**a**) *(corte)* cut, slit; *(hendidura)* crack, split (**b**) *(tajada) (de melón etc)* slice

rajá *(pl* **rajaes)** *nm* rajah

rajado, -a 1 *pp de* **rajar**
2 *adj* (**a**) *(hendido)* cracked, split (**b**) *Fam (cobarde)* yellow
3 *nm,f Fam (cobarde)* chicken, coward

rajadura *nf* crack, split

rajar 1 *vt* (**a**) *(hender)* to crack, split (**b**) *Esp (melón etc)* to slice (**c**) *Argot (persona)* to cut up; **dame el dinero o te rajo** hand over your money or I'll cut you up (**d**) *Col PRico (aplastar, apabullar)* to crush, defeat (**e**) *Andes RP Fam (echar)* to chuck out
2 *vi Esp Fam (hablar mucho)* to chatter, gabble on; **¡cómo raja el tío!** he doesn't half go on!
3 rajarse *vpr* (**a**) *(partirse)* to crack, split (**b**) *Fam (desistir)* to back out; *(acobardarse)* to chicken out (**c**) *Andes CAm RP (gastar)* to spend lavishly (**d**) *Andes CAm RP (escapar)* to rush *o* run off

rajatabla: a rajatabla *loc adv* to the letter, strictly; **cumplir las normas a r.** to follow the rules to the letter

rajón, -ona *nm,f Fam* (**a**) *CAm Méx (fanfarrón)* braggart (**b**) *CAm Chile Perú (dadivoso)* generous giver (**c**) *Perú (criticón)* gossip

ralea *nf Pey* type, sort, ilk; **son de la misma r.** they are two of a kind, they are birds of a feather

ralentí *nm* (**a**) *Cin* slow motion; **rodar una escena al r.** to film a scene in slow motion (**b**) *Aut* **con el motor al r.** with the engine ticking over

ralentización *nf* slowing down

ralentizar [14] **1** *vt* to slow down
2 ralentizarse *vpr* to slow down

rallado, -a 1 *pp de* **rallar**
2 *adj Culin* grated; **queso r.** grated cheese

rallador *nm* grater

ralladura *nf* grating, gratings *pl*; **ralladuras de limón** grated lemon rind

rallar *vt* to grate

rally ['rrali] *(pl* **rallys)** *nm Aut* rally

ralo, -a *adj* sparse, thin; **dientes ralos** teeth with gaps between them

rama *nf* (**a**) *(de árbol)* branch; **algodón en r.** raw cotton; *Fam* **andarse** *o* **irse por las ramas** to wander off the subject, digress (**b**) *(de ciencia, industria)* branch

Ramadán *nm Rel* Ramadan

ramaje *nm* branches *pl*, foliage

ramal *nm* (**a**) *(de carretera, ferrocarril)* branch (**b**) *(de cuerda)* strand

ramalazo *nm Fam* (passing) fit; **le entró el r. nostálgico** he became all nostalgic; **un r. de locura** a streak of madness

rambla *nf* (**a**) *(cauce)* watercourse, channel (**b**) *(avenida)* boulevard, avenue (**c**) *Urug (muelle)* dock, quayside

ramera *nf* whore, *US* hooker

ramificación *nf* ramification, consequence

ramificarse [59] *vpr* to ramify, branch (out)

ramillete *nm* (**a**) *(de flores)* posy (**b**) *(conjunto)* bunch, group, collection

ramo *nm* (**a**) *(de árbol)* branch; *Rel* **Domingo de Ramos** Palm Sunday (**b**) *(de flores)* bunch, bouquet (**c**) *(de ciencia, industria)* branch; **el r. de la hostelería** the hotel and catering trade

rampa *nf* ramp □ *Astronáut* **r. de lanzamiento** launch pad

rampante *adj (en heráldica)* rampant

ramplón, -ona *adj* coarse, vulgar

ramplonería *nf* coarseness, vulgarity

rana *nf* frog; *Fam* **salir r.** to be a disappointment

ranchera *nf Mús* = popular Mexican song

ranchero, -a *nm,f* rancher, farmer

rancho *nm* (**a**) *Mil (comida)* mess; *Fig* **hacer r. aparte** to go one's own way (**b**) *(granja del Oeste)* ranch (**c**) *Méx (pequeña finca)* = small farmhouse and outbuildings (**d**) *CSur Ven (en la ciudad)* shack, shanty (**e**) *RP (en el campo)* farm labourer's cottage; *(en la playa)* = thatched beachside building

rancio, -a *adj* (**a**) *(comida)* stale; *(mantequilla)* rancid; **saber a r.** to taste rancid; **vino r.** mellow wine (**b**) *(antiguo)* ancient; **de r. abolengo** of ancient lineage

randa 1 *nf (encaje)* lace trimming
    2 *nm Fam (ratero)* pickpocket

rango *nm* (**a**) *(jerarquía)* rank; **de alto r.** high-ranking (**b**) *(jerarquía elevada)* high social standing (**c**) *Andes CAm PRico (esplendidez)* pomp, splendour, *US* splendor

Rangún *n* Rangoon

ranking ['rrankin] *(pl* **rankings)** *nm* ranking, status

ranura *nf* (**a**) *(surco)* groove (**b**) *(de máquina, teléfono)* slot; **introduzca una moneda en la r.** put a coin in the slot

rap *nm Mús* rap

rapacidad *nf* rapacity, rapaciousness

rapado, -a *adj* shaven

rapapolvo *nm Esp Fam* ticking-off, talking-to; **echar un r. a algn** to tick sb off

rapar *vt (afeitar)* to shave; *(pelo)* to crop

rapaz¹ 1 *adj* (**a**) *Zool* predatory; **ave r.** bird of prey (**b**) *Fig (persona)* rapacious, grasping
    2 *nf* bird of prey; **rapaces** *Zool* predators; *Orn* birds of prey

rapaz, -a² *nm,f* youngster; *(muchacho)* lad; *(muchacha)* lass

rape¹ *nm (pez)* angler fish

rape² *nm Fam (pelo)* **cortado al r.** short, close-cropped

rapé *nm* snuff

rapear *vi Mús* to rap

rápel *(pl* **rapels)** *nm Dep* abseiling; **hacer r.** to abseil

rapero, -a *nm,f Mús* rapper

rápidamente *adv* quickly

rapidez *nf* speed, rapidity

rápido, -a 1 *adj* quick, fast, rapid
    2 *adv* quickly; *Fam* **¡y r.!** and hurry up!, and make it snappy!
    3 *nm* (**a**) *Ferroc* fast train, express (**b**) **rápidos** *(de un río)* rapids

rapiña *nf Fam* robbery, theft

raposa *nf* (**a**) *Zool* (female) fox, vixen (**b**) *Fam Fig (persona)* sly old fox

rappel ['rrapel] *(pl* **rappels)** *nm véase* **rápel**

rapsodia *nf Mús* rhapsody

raptar *vt* to kidnap, abduct

rapto *nm* (**a**) *(secuestro)* kidnapping, abduction (**b**) *Fig (arrebato)* outburst, fit; **r. de cólera** fit of anger

raptor, -a *nm,f* kidnapper, abductor

raqueta *nf* (**a**) *(de tenis)* racket; *(de ping-pong)* *Br* bat, *US* paddle (**b**) *(de nieve)* snowshoe (**c**) *(de crupier)* rake

raquítico, -a 1 *adj* (**a**) *Med* rachitic, rickety (**b**) *Fam (escaso)* small, meagre, *US* meager; *(débil)* weak
    2 *nm,f* person with rickets

raquitismo *nm Med* rachitis, rickets *pl*

raramente *adv (rara vez)* rarely, seldom; *(de manera extraña)* oddly, strangely

rareza *nf* (**a**) *(poca frecuencia)* rarity, rareness; *(escasez)* scarcity (**b**) *(peculiaridad)* oddity; *(extravagancia)* eccentricity

rarificar [59] *vt* to rarefy

raro, -a *adj* (**a**) *(poco frecuente)* rare; *(escaso)* scarce; **rara vez** seldom (**b**) *(extraño)* odd, strange, weird; **¡qué r.!** how odd!; *Fam* **es un tío r.** he's a strange guy

ras: a ras de *loc prep* level with; **a r. de tierra** at ground level; **volar a r. de tierra** to fly low

rasante 1 *adj (tiro)* grazing, close; *(vuelo)* low, skimming
    2 *nf (de camino)* slope □ **cambio de r.** brow of a hill

rasar *vt* (**a**) *(rozar)* to graze, skim; *Av* **r. el suelo** to fly low, hedgehop (**b**) *(nivelar)* to level

rasca *nf Esp Fam (frío)* cold

rascacielos *nm inv* skyscraper

rascador *nm* (**a**) *(herramienta)* scraper, rasp (**b**) *(de una caja de cerillas)* striking surface

rascar [59] **1** *vt* (**a**) *(con las uñas)* to scratch (**b**) *(con rascador)* to scrape, rasp (**c**) *Mús (guitarra)* to strum
    2 rascarse *vpr (con las uñas)* to scratch (oneself)

RASD [rrasð] *nf (abrev de* **República Árabe Saharaui Democrática)** Democratic Arab Republic of the Western Sahara

rasera *nf* spatula, fish slice

rasero *nm* leveller; *Fig* **medir con el mismo r.** to treat impartially

rasgado, -a 1 *pp de* **rasgar**
    2 *adj* (**a**) *(desgarrado)* torn (**b**) *(ojos)* slit, almond-shaped; *(boca)* wide

rasgadura *nf* tear, rip

rasgar [38] **1** *vt* to tear, rip
    2 rasgarse *vpr* to tear, rip; *Fig* **r. las vestiduras** to pull one's hair out

rasgo *nm* (**a**) *(trazo)* stroke; *Fig* **explicar a grandes rasgos** to outline, explain briefly (**b**) *(característica)* characteristic, feature, trait; *(de la cara)* feature; **tiene rasgos orientales** he looks Oriental (**c**) *(acto)* act, feat; **en un r. de generosidad** in a moment of generosity

rasgón *nm* tear, rip

rasguear 1 *vt Mús (guitarra)* to strum
    2 *vi (escribir)* to write, scribble

rasgueo *nm* strumming *(of guitar)*

rasguñar 1 *vt* to scratch, scrape
    2 rasguñarse *vpr* to scratch, scrape; **se rasguñó las rodillas al caer** he fell and grazed his knees

rasguño *nm* scratch, scrape

rasilla *nf* (**a**) *Tex (tela)* serge (**b**) *Constr (ladrillo)* tile

raso, -a 1 *adj* (**a**) *(llano)* flat, level; *(liso)* smooth; *(vuelo, lanzamiento)* low; **una cucharada rasa de** a level tablespoonful of (**b**) *Mil* **soldado r.** private (**c**) *(atmósfera)* clear, cloudless; **al r.** in the open (air); **cielo r.** clear sky
    2 *nm Tex* satin

raspa *nf (espina)* bone; *(espina dorsal)* backbone; *Esp Fam* **no dejó ni la r.** he cleaned his plate

raspado *nm* (**a**) *Med* scrape (**b**) *(de pieles)* scraping (**c**) *Méx* *(refresco)* = drink of flavoured crushed ice

raspador *nm (gen)* scraper; *(de caja de cerillas)* striking surface

raspadura *nf* (a) *(ralladura)* scraping, scrapings *pl* (b) *(señal, marca)* scratch, mark

raspar *vt* (a) *(rascar)* to scrape (off) (b) *(borrar)* to scratch out (c) *(al paladar)* to be sharp on; *(la piel)* to be rough on (d) *(hurtar)* to pinch, *Br* nick

rasposo, -a *adj (aspero)* rough, sharp

rasquetear *vt* (a) *Am (caballo)* to brush down, curry (b) *Andes RP (rascar)* to scrape

rasta *adj Fam (rastafari)* Rasta; **pelo** *o* **peinado r.** dreadlocks

rasterizar [14] *vt Inform* to rasterize

rastra *nf* (a) *(huella)* track, trail (b) *Agr (grada)* harrow (c) *(de ajos, cebollas)* string (d) *(para pescar)* trawl net (e) **a rastras** *(arrastrando)* dragging; *Fig (de mal grado)* grudgingly; **lo sacaron del bar a r.** he was dragged out of the bar (f) *RP* = gaucho's leather belt

rastreador *nm* tracker ❏ *Náut* **r. de minas** minesweeper

rastrear 1 *vt* (a) *(seguir el rastro de)* to track, trail (b) *(río)* to drag, dredge (c) *(para pescar)* to trawl (d) *(averiguar)* to find out (e) *Agr* to rake
2 *vi Av (volar bajo)* to fly low, hedgehop

rastreo *nm* (a) *(seguimiento)* tracking, trailing, tracing (b) *(de un río)* dragging, dredging (c) *Pesca* trawling (d) *Agr* raking

rastrero, -a *adj* (a) *(que se arrastra)* creeping, crawling; **pájaro de vuelo r.** low-flying bird (b) *Fig (bajo, despreciable)* vile, base

rastrillada *nf Bol RP* trail, track

rastrillar *vt* (a) *Agr (hojas)* to rake (b) *(cáñamo, lino)* to comb, hackle (c) *Méx (fusil)* to fire

rastrillo *nm* (a) *Agr (herramienta)* rake (b) *(de castillo)* portcullis (c) *(de cáñamo, lino)* comb, hackle (d) *Fam (mercadillo)* flea market; **r. benéfico** *Br* jumble *o US* rummage sale (e) *Méx (cuchilla de afeitar)* razor

rastro *nm* (a) *(huella)* trace, sign; *(en el suelo)* track, trail; **ni r. de** not a trace of; **perder el r. de algn** to lose track of sb; **seguir el r. de algn** to follow sb's trail (b) *(mercado)* **el R.** = the Madrid flea market

rastrojo *nm Agr* (a) *(paja)* stubble (b) *(campo)* stubble field

rasurador *nm*, **rasuradora** *nf Méx* shaver, electric razor

rasurar 1 *vt* to shave
2 rasurarse *vpr* to shave

rata 1 *nf* rat; *Fam* **más pobre que las ratas** as poor as a church mouse
2 *nm Fam* (a) *(ratero)* pickpocket, thief (b) *(tacaño)* mean *o* stingy person

rataplán *nm (del tambor)* drumbeat, rub-a-dub

ratear¹ *vt (repartir)* to share out proportionately, give out pro rata

ratear² *vt Fam (robar)* to swipe, *Br* nick

ratear³ *vi (arrastrarse)* to crawl, creep

ratería *nf* petty theft, pilfering

ratero, -a *nm,f* pickpocket; **r. de hotel** hotel thief

raticida *nm* rat poison

ratificación *nf* ratification

ratificar [59] **1** *vt* to ratify
2 ratificarse *vpr* to be ratified

rato *nm* (a) *(momento, instante)* while, time, moment; **a ratos** at times; **a ratos perdidos** at odd moments; **al poco r.** shortly after; **¿cuánto r. hace que se fue?** how long is it since she left?; **esperar un r.** to wait a while; **hace ya un buen r.** some time ago; **¡hasta otro r.!,** *Méx* **¡nos vemos al r.!** see you (later)!; **hay para r.** it'll take a while; **pasar el r.** to kill time; **pasar un buen/mal r.** to have a good/bad time; **ratos libres** free time *sing* (b) *Esp Fam (mucho)* **un r.** very, a lot; **sabe un r. de música** he knows a lot about music

ratón *nm* (a) *Zool* mouse; *Fam* **r. de biblioteca** bookworm (b) *Esp Inform* mouse

ratonera *nf* (a) *(trampa)* mousetrap; *Fig* **caer en la r.** to fall into the trap (b) *(agujero)* mousehole (c) *Andes RP (casucha)* hovel

ratonero *nm Orn* buzzard

raudal *nm* (a) *(corriente de agua)* torrent, flood (b) *Fig (abundancia)* flood, abundance; **a raudales** in abundance; **la gente entró a raudales** people poured *o* flooded in

raudo, -a *adj Literario* swift, rapid

raya¹ *nf* (a) *(línea)* line; *(de color)* stripe; **camisa a rayas** striped shirt (b) *(guión)* dash (c) *(del pantalón)* crease (d) *Esp Andes RP (del pelo) Br* parting, *US* part; **hacerse la r.** to part one's hair (e) *(límite)* limit; *Fig* **tener a r.** to keep at bay; *Fam* **dar quince** *o* **ciento y r. a algn** to run rings round sb (f) *Argot (de cocaína)* line (g) *Méx (sueldo)* pay, wages (h) *CAm Carib Perú (juego)* hopscotch

raya² *nf (pez)* skate

rayado, -a 1 *pp de* rayar
2 *adj* (a) *(tela)* striped; *(papel)* ruled (b) *(disco, superficie)* scratched (c) *CSur Fam (persona)* **estar r.** to be a headcase *o Br* nutter
3 *nm* stripes *pl*

rayano, -a *adj* bordering; **r. en** bordering on

rayar 1 *vt* (a) *(papel)* to rule, draw lines on (b) *(disco, superficie)* to scratch; **alguien me ha rayado el coche** somebody's scratched my car (c) *Méx RP (detener)* to stop suddenly
2 *vi* (a) *(lindar)* **r. en** to border on; **raya en la locura** it borders on madness; **raya en los cincuenta** he is about *o* around fifty (b) *(alba)* to break; **al r. el alba** at dawn
3 rayarse *vpr* (a) *(disco, superficie)* to get scratched (b) *CSur Fam (volverse loco)* to go crazy *o Br* off one's head

rayo *nm* (a) *(de luz)* ray ❏ **r. láser** laser beam; **un r. de sol** a ray of sunlight; **rayos X** X-rays (b) *(relámpago)* (flash of) lightning; *Fam* **caer como un r.** to drop like a bombshell; *Fam* **echar rayos** to be furious; *Fam* **¡que la parta un r.!, ¡mal r. la parta!** to hell with her!; *Fam* **saber a rayos** to taste awful

rayón *nm Tex* rayon

rayuela *nf* hopscotch

raza *nf* (a) *(humana)* race ❏ **r. blanca** white race; **r. humana** human race; **r. negra** black race (b) *(de animal)* breed; **de r.** *(perro)* pedigree; *(caballo)* thoroughbred (c) *Méx Pey (populacho)* **la r.** the masses *pl*

razón *nf* (a) *(facultad)* reason; **atender a razones, entrar en r.** to listen to reason; **perder la r.** to lose one's reason; **uso de r.** power of reasoning (b) *(motivo)* reason, cause; **con r.** with good reason; **¿cuál es la r.?** what's the reason?; *Pol* **r. de Estado** reasons of state; **r. de más para** all the more reason to; **tener razones para** to have cause to (c) *(mensaje)* message; **mandar r.** to send a message (d) *(justicia)* rightness, justice; **asistirle a algn la r.** to be in the right; **con r. o sin ella** rightly or wrongly; **dar la r. a algn** to admit that sb is right; **no tener r.** to be wrong; **tener r.** to be right (e) *(información)* 'r. aquí' 'enquire within', 'apply within'; 'r. en portería' 'enquiries to caretaker' (f) *Com* **r. social** trade name, firm's name (g) *Mat* ratio, rate; **a r. de** in the ratio of, at the rate of

razonable *adj* reasonable; **dentro de lo r.** within reason

razonablemente *adv* reasonably, rationally

razonado, -a 1 *pp de* **razonar**
  2 *adj* reasoned, well-reasoned

razonamiento *nm* reasoning

razonar 1 *vt (árgumentar)* to reason out
  2 *vi (discurrir)* to reason; *(hablar)* to talk

RDA *nf Antes* (*abrev de* **República Democrática de Alemania**) GDR

RDSI *nf Inform Tel* (*abrev de* **Red Digital de Servicios Integrados**) ISDN

re *nm Mús* re, ray

re- *pref* re-; **reconstruir** to rebuild

reabastecer [46] *vt (de combustible)* to refuel

reabrir (*pp* **reabierto**) *vt* to reopen; *Fig* **r. viejas heridas** to open old wounds

reacción *nf* reaction ❑ **avión de r.** jet (plane); **r. en cadena** chain reaction

reaccionar *vi* to react

reaccionario, -a *adj & nm,f* reactionary

reacio, -a *adj* reluctant, unwilling; **mostrarse r. a hacer algo** to be reluctant to do sth

reactivación *nf* recovery

reactivar *vt* to reactivate

reactivo, -a 1 *adj* reactive
  2 *nm Quím* reagent

reactor *nm* (**a**) *Fís* reactor ❑ **r. nuclear** nuclear reactor (**b**) *Av (avión)* jet (plane)

readaptación *nf (de un enfermo)* rehabilitation; **r. profesional** industrial retraining

readaptarse *vpr* to readapt, readjust

readmisión *nf* readmission

readmitir *vt* to readmit; *(trabajador)* to re-employ

reafirmación *nf* reaffirmation, reassertion

reafirmar *vt* to reaffirm, reassert

reagrupación *nf,* **reagrupamiento** *nm* regrouping

reagrupar 1 *vt* to regroup
  2 reagruparse *vpr* to regroup

reajustar *vt* to readjust

reajuste *nm* readjustment ❑ *Pol* **r. ministerial** cabinet reshuffle

real¹ *adj (efectivo, verdadero)* real; **en la vida r.** in real life; **necesidades reales** real necessities

real² 1 *adj (regio)* royal; *Fig* grand, fine; **la familia r.** the royal family; **palacio r.** royal palace; *Jur* **por r. decreto** by royal decree; *Fam* **porque no me da la r. gana** because I don't feel like it; *Fam* **es una r. moza** she's a good-looking girl
  2 *nm* (**a**) *(moneda)* = old Spanish coin worth one quarter of a peseta; **estar sin un r.** to be penniless; **no vale un r.** it is worthless (**b**) *(feria)* fairground

realce *nm* (**a**) *(relieve)* relief; **bordado de r.** relief embroidery (**b**) *Fig (esplendor)* splendour, *US* splendor, distinction; **dar r. a** to enhance; **poner de r.** to highlight

realengo, -a *adj CAm Carib Méx* ownerless

realeza *nf* royalty

realidad *nf* reality; **en r.** in fact, actually; **la r. es que ...** the fact of the matter is that ... ❑ **r. virtual** virtual reality

realismo *nm* realism ❑ *Lit* **r. mágico** magic(al) realism

realista 1 *adj* realistic
  2 *nmf* realist

realizable *adj (objetivo)* attainable; *(plan, proyecto)* feasible

realización *nf* (**a**) *(de un deseo)* realization, fulfilment, *US* fulfillment (**b**) *(de un proyecto)* execution, carrying out (**c**) *Cin TV* production

realizador, -a *nm,f Cin TV* producer

realizar [14] **1** *vt* (**a**) *(ambición)* to realize, fulfil, *US* fulfill, achieve; *(deseo)* to fulfil, *US* fulfill (**b**) *(plan)* to execute, carry out; **r. un viaje** to make a journey (**c**) *Cin TV* to produce (**d**) *Fin (vender)* to realize
  2 realizarse *vpr* (**a**) *(ambición)* to be realized, be fulfilled, be achieved; *(sueño)* to come true (**b**) *(proyecto)* to be executed, be carried out (**c**) *(persona)* to fulfil *o US* fulfill oneself

realmente *adv (gen)* really; *(en realidad)* actually, in fact; **r. no ha pasado nada** in (actual) fact, nothing has happened; **r. no lo entiendo** I really can't understand it

realojar *vt* to rehouse

realquilado, -a 1 *pp de* **realquilar**
  2 *adj* sublet
  3 *nm,f* = person who sublets from another

realquilar *vt* to sublet

realzar [14] *vt* (**a**) *(pintura)* to highlight (**b**) *Fig (belleza, importancia)* to enhance, heighten; **su modestia realza la nobleza de su gesto** his noble demeanour is heightened by his great modesty

reanimación *nf* (**a**) *(física, moral)* recovery (**b**) *Med* resuscitation

reanimar 1 *vt* (**a**) *(físicamente)* to revive; *(moralmente)* to cheer up (**b**) *Med* to resuscitate
  2 reanimarse *vpr (físicamente)* to revive; *(moralmente)* to cheer up

reanudación *nf* renewal, resumption, re-establishment; **r. de las clases** return to school; **r. de negociaciones** resumption of talks

reanudar 1 *vt* to renew, resume; **r. el paso** *o* **la marcha** to set off again; **r. las clases** to go back to school; **r. negociaciones** to resume negotiations; **r. una amistad** to renew a friendship
  2 reanudarse *vpr* to start again, resume; **se reanudó el trabajo después de la huelga** work was resumed after the strike

reaparecer [46] *vi* to reappear, recur; *(artista)* to make a comeback

reaparición *nf* reappearance, recurrence; *(de artista etc)* comeback

reapertura *nf* reopening

reaprovisionar *vt* to replenish, restock

rearmar Mil 1 *vt* to rearm
  2 rearmarse *vpr* to rearm

rearme *nm* rearmament

reasegurar *vt* to reinsure

reaseguro *nm* reinsurance

reasumir *vt* to reassume, resume

reata *nf* (**a**) *(de caballos, mulas)* single file (**b**) *Méx (para ganado)* lasso

reavivar *vt* to revive

rebaba *nf* rough edge

rebaja *nf* (**a**) *(reducción)* lowering, reduction (**b**) *Com (descuento)* reduction, discount; **nos hicieron una r.** they gave us a discount; **precio de r.** sale price (**c**) *Com* **rebajas** sales; **en r.** in the sales; **'grandes r.'** 'huge reductions'

rebajado, -a 1 *pp de* **rebajar**
  2 *adj* (**a**) *(tierra, techo)* lowered; *(arco)* depressed (**b**) *(precio, mercancía)* reduced (**c**) *(humillado)* humbled
  3 *nm Mil* soldier exempted from duty

rebajar 1 *vt* (**a**) *(tierra)* to lower; *(arco)* to depress (**b**)

tax collection (**b**) *(ingresos)* income, receipts *pl*; *(cantidad recaudada)* takings *pl*, take; *Dep* gate; **hacer una buena r.** to have a good takings (**c**) *(oficina de impuestos)* tax collector's office

recaudador, -a *nm,f* tax collector

recaudar *vt* to collect

recaudería *nf Méx* greengrocer's

recaudo *nm* (**a**) *(recaudación)* collection (**b**) *(precaución)* precaution; **estar a buen r.** to be in safekeeping; **poner algo a buen r.** to put sth in a safe place

recelar *vt* to suspect, distrust

recelo *nm* suspicion, distrust

receloso, -a *adj* suspicious, distrustful

recensión *nf* review

recepción *nf* (**a**) *(de una carta)* receipt (**b**) *(en hotel, oficina)* reception (desk); **pregúntelo en r.** ask at reception (**c**) *(fiesta oficial)* reception (**d**) *Rad* reception

recepcionar *vt Am* to receive

recepcionista *nmf* receptionist

receptáculo *nm* receptacle

receptividad *nf* receptiveness, receptivity

receptivo, -a *adj* receptive

receptor, -a 1 *nm,f (persona)* recipient, receiver
   2 *nm Rad TV* receiver

recesión *nf Econ* recession

recesivo, -a *adj* recessive

receso *nm* recess

receta *nf* (**a**) *Culin* recipe; *Fig* recipe, formula (**b**) *Med* prescription

recetar *vt Med* to prescribe

recetario *nm Med* prescription pad

rechace *nm Dep* point-blank save

rechazar [14] *vt* (**a**) *(gen)* to reject, turn down, resist, refuse; **r. una oferta** to turn down an offer (**b**) *Mil* to repel, repulse, drive back

rechazo *nm* (**a**) *(acción)* rejection, refusal, resistance; *Med* **r. de un órgano** rejection of an organ; *Fig* **de r.** indirectly, as a consequence (**b**) *(negativa)* denial, rejection

rechifla *nf Fam* (**a**) *(silbido)* hissing, booing, catcalls *pl* (**b**) *(mofa)* mockery, jeering

rechiflar *vt* (**a**) *(silbar)* to hiss, boo (**b**) *(mofarse)* to mock, jeer at

rechinar 1 *vi (madera)* to creak; *(metal)* to squeak, screech; *(efecto en el oído)* to grate; *(dientes)* to grind, gnash, grate; **me rechinan los dientes de frío** my teeth are chattering with the cold
   2 rechinarse *vpr CAm Méx (comida)* to burn

rechistar *vi* to clear one's throat; *Fam* **sin r.** that's final

rechoncho, -a *adj Fam* chubby, tubby

rechupete: de rechupete *Fam* **1** *loc adj (comida)* delicious, scrumptious
   2 *loc adv* **pasarlo de r.** to have a brilliant o great time

recibidor *nm* entrance hall

recibimiento *nm* reception, welcome

recibir 1 *vt (gen)* to receive; *(acoger)* to welcome; *(invitados)* to entertain; **fueron a recibirle a la estación** they went to meet him at the station; *(en carta)* **recibe un abrazo de** lots of love from; **r. un premio** to receive an award; **r. una negativa** to be refused, meet with a refusal
   2 *vi (atender visitas)* to receive visitors; **el rey recibe los miércoles** the king receives visitors on Wednesdays
   3 recibirse *vpr Am* to graduate; **r. de abogado** to qualify as a lawyer

recibo *nm* (**a**) *(resguardo)* receipt; *(factura)* invoice, bill (**b**) *(recepción)* reception, receiving; **acusar r. de** to acknowledge receipt of

reciclable *adj* recyclable

reciclado, -a 1 *pp de* **reciclar**
   2 *adj* recycled

reciclaje *nm* (**a**) *(de residuos)* recycling (**b**) *Fam (de profesores)* retraining

reciclar *vt* (**a**) *(residuos)* to recycle (**b**) *Fam (profesores)* to retrain

recién *adv* (**a**) *(con participio)* recently, newly; **café r. hecho** freshly-made coffee; **r. casados** newlyweds; **r. nacido** newborn baby (**b**) *Am (hace poco)* just; **regresó r. ayer** he only o just got back yesterday; **r. me llamaron** they (only) just called me (**c**) *Am (sólo)* only; **r. el martes lo sabremos** we'll only know on Tuesday, we won't know until Tuesday

reciente *adj* recent

recientemente *adv* recently, lately

recinto *nm (cercado)* enclosure; *(zona)* area, grounds *pl*, precinct, precincts *pl*; **r. comercial** shopping precinct; **r. ferial** fairground

recio, -a 1 *adj (robusto)* strong, sturdy; *(grueso)* thick; *(voz)* loud; *(tiempo)* harsh, severe; *Fig* **en lo más r. de la batalla** in the thick of the battle
   2 *adv (con fuerza)* hard, heavily; *Méx* **hablar r.** to talk in a loud voice

recipiente *nm* vessel, receptacle, container

reciprocidad *nf* reciprocity

recíproco, -a *adj* reciprocal

recitación *nf,* **recitado** *nm* recitation

recital *nm Mús* recital; *Lit* reading

recitar *vt* to recite

recitativo *nm* recitative

reclamación *nf* (**a**) *(demanda)* claim, demand (**b**) *(queja)* complaint, protest, objection; **presentar una r.** to lodge a complaint

reclamar 1 *vt* (**a**) *(pedir)* to claim, demand (**b**) *(exigir)* to require, demand
   2 *vi (protestar)* to protest (**contra** against); *(quejarse)* to complain (**contra** about)

reclame *nm Am* advertisement

reclamo *nm* (**a**) *Caza* decoy bird, lure (**b**) *Fig* inducement (**c**) *(anuncio)* advertisement; *(eslogan)* advertising slogan ❏ **r. publicitario** advertising gimmick (**d**) *Am (queja)* complaint; *(reivindicación)* claim

reclinable *adj* reclining

reclinar 1 *vt* to lean (**sobre** on)
   2 reclinarse *vpr* to lean back, recline

reclinatorio *nm* prie-dieu

recluido, -a 1 *pp de* **recluir**
   2 *adj (gen)* shut away, locked away; *(encarcelado)* imprisoned, interned

recluir [34] *vt (gen)* to shut away, lock away; *(encarcelar)* to imprison, intern; *(en institución mental)* to confine

reclusión *nf* (**a**) *(gen)* seclusion; *(encarcelamiento)* imprisonment, internment (**b**) *(lugar)* retreat

recluso, -a 1 *adj* imprisoned; **población reclusa** prison population
   2 *nm,f* prisoner, inmate

recluta *Mil* **1** *nmf (voluntario)* recruit; *(obligatorio)* conscript
   2 *nf (acción)* recruitment, conscription

reclutamiento *nm* (**a**) *(voluntario)* recruitment; *(obligatorio)* conscription (**b**) *(reclutas) (voluntarios)* recruits *pl*; *(voluntarios)* conscripts *pl*

reclutar vt (**a**) (soldado) (voluntariamente) to recruit; (a la fuerza) to conscript (**b**) RP (ganado) to round up

recobrar 1 vt (**a**) (gen) to recover, retrieve; (conocimiento) to regain; **r. el aliento** to get one's breath back (**b**) Mil (plaza) to recapture
. **2 recobrarse** vpr to recover, recuperate

recochinearse vpr Fam to make fun (**de** of), laugh (**de** at)

recochineo nm Fam mockery

recodo nm (de río) twist, turn; (de camino) bend

recogedor nm dustpan

recogepelotas nmf inv Dep (muchacho) ball boy; (muchacha) ball girl

recoger [52] **1** vt (**a**) (coger) to pick up, take back; **recoge el libro del suelo** pick the book up (**b**) (reunir) to gather, collect; **r. datos** to gather information (**c**) (ordenar) to clear up; (limpiar) to clean; **recoge todo esto** clear all of this away; **r. la mesa** to clear the table (**d**) (ir a buscar) to pick up, fetch; **te recogeré a las ocho** I'll pick you up at eight (**e**) Agr to harvest, gather, pick; **r. fruta** to pick fruit (**f**) (albergar) to take in, shelter; **lo recogió un tío** he was taken in by an uncle
2 recogerse vpr (**a**) (irse a casa) to go home; (irse a la cama) to go to bed (**b**) (levantarse) to lift up, pick up; **r. el pelo** to put one's hair up; **se recogió la falda** she gathered up her skirt (**c**) (meditar) to retire, go off alone

recogida nf (gen) collection; Agr (cosecha) harvest, harvesting ❑ **r. de basuras** refuse o Br rubbish o US garbage collection; **r. de equipajes** baggage reclaim

recogido, -a 1 pp de **recoger**
2 adj (**a**) (apartado) secluded, withdrawn; **vida recogida** secluded o quiet life (**b**) (pelo) pinned back, tied back

recogimiento nm withdrawal, recollection; **vivir con r.** to lead a withdrawn o secluded life

recolección nf (**a**) (recogida) collection, gathering (**b**) Agr (cosecha) harvest, harvesting; (temporada) harvest time

recolectar vt (**a**) (reunir) to collect, gather (**b**) Agr to harvest

recolector, -a 1 adj harvesting
2 nm,f (de cosecha) harvester; (de fruta) picker; Am **r. de basura** refuse collector, US garbage collector

recoleto, -a adj (**a**) (lugar) quiet, secluded (**b**) (persona) withdrawn, retiring

recomendable adj recommendable, advisable; **no ser r.** to be unwise

recomendación nf recommendation, reference; **carta de r.** letter of introduction

recomendado, -a 1 pp de **recomendar**
2 adj recommended
3 nm,f (hombre) protégé; (mujer) protégée

recomendar [3] vt to recommend, advise

recomenzar [17] vt to recommence, begin again

recompensa nf reward, recompense; **en r.** as a reward, in return

recompensar vt (**a**) (retribuir) to reward, recompense; **'se recompensará'** 'reward offered' (**b**) (compensar) to compensate

recomponer [50] (pp **recompuesto**) vt to repair, mend, alter

recomposición nf repairing, mending, alteration

recompuesto, -a 1 pp de **recomponer**
2 adj (acicalado) dressed up

reconcentrar 1 vt (**a**) (congregar) to bring together (**b**) (concentrar) to concentrate (**en** on), devote (**en** to); **r. toda la atención en un tema** to give a subject one's full attention

(**c**) Quím to make more concentrated
2 reconcentrarse vpr (ensimismarse) to concentrate, withdraw into oneself

reconciliable adj reconcilable

reconciliación nf reconciliation

reconciliar 1 vt to reconcile
2 reconciliarse vpr to be reconciled

reconcomerse vpr Fam to be consumed (**de** with); **se reconcomía de curiosidad por conocerla** he was itching to meet her

recóndito, -a adj hidden, secret; **en lo más r. del alma** deep down

reconfortante 1 adj comforting
2 nm Med tonic

reconfortar vt (confortar) to comfort; (animar) to cheer up

reconocer [19] **1** vt (**a**) (gen) to recognize; **¿no me reconoces?** don't you recognize me? (**b**) (admitir) to recognize, admit; **hay que reconocerlo** let's face it; **no quiere reconocerlo** he won't admit it (**c**) Med (paciente) to examine (**d**) Mil to reconnoitre
2 reconocerse vpr (**a**) (gen) to recognize each other (**b**) (admitir) to admit; **r. culpable** to admit one's guilt

reconocible adj recognizable

reconocimiento nm (**a**) (gen) también Inform recognition; **en r. de** in recognition o appreciation of (**b**) Med examination, checkup (**c**) Mil reconnaissance

reconquista nf reconquest; Hist **la R.** = the Christian capture of the Iberian Peninsula, freeing it from Moorish rule

reconquistar vt to reconquer, recapture, regain

reconsiderar vt to reconsider

reconstituir [34] vt to reconstitute

reconstituyente nm Med tonic

reconstrucción nf reconstruction

reconstruir [34] vt to reconstruct

reconvención nf reproach, reprimand

reconvenir [69] vt to reproach, reprimand

reconversión nf reconversion; Ind modernization, rationalisation, reorganization

reconvertir [62] vt to reconvert; Ind to modernize

recopilación nf (**a**) (resumen) summary, resumé (**b**) (compendio) compilation, collection

recopilador, -a nm,f compiler

recopilar vt to compile, collect

recopilatorio, -a 1 adj **un disco r.** a compilation (record)
2 nm compilation

recórcholis interj Fam crumbs!

récord (pl **récords**) adj & nm record; **batir un r.** to beat a record; **en un tiempo r.** in record time; **establecer un r.** to set a record; **tener el r.** to hold the record

recordar [63] **1** vt (**a**) (rememorar) to remember; **ahora no lo recuerdo** I can't remember; **si mal no recuerdo, que yo recuerde** as far as I can remember (**b**) (traer a la memoria de otro) to remind; **¿a quién te recuerda?** who does she remind you of?; **r. algo a algn** to remind sb of sth; **recuérdamelo cuando nos veamos** remind me when we next meet
2 vi Méx (despertar) to wake up
3 recordarse vpr Méx (despertarse) to wake up

recordatorio nm (**a**) (aviso) reminder (**b**) Rel (de defunción) notice of death; (de comunión) souvenir of first communion

recordman *nmf Dep* record holder

recorrer *vt* (**a**) *(distancia)* to cover, travel; *(país)* to tour, travel through o round; *(ciudad)* to visit, walk round; **recorrimos media ciudad antes de encontrar un bar abierto** we walked round half the town before we found a bar open (**b**) *(examinar)* to go over, look over; **he recorrido su última novela** I had a look through his latest novel

recorrida *nf Am (ruta, itinerario)* route; *(viaje)* journey

recorrido *nm (distancia)* distance travelled; *(trayecto)* trip, journey; *(itinerario)* itinerary, route; **la maratón tiene un r. accidentado** the marathon course is very hilly; **trenes de largo r.** intercity trains

recortable *adj & nm* cutout; **muñeca r.** cutout doll

recortado, -a 1 *pp de* **recortar**
2 *adj* (**a**) *(cortado)* cut out (**b**) *(borde)* jagged

recortar *vt* (**a**) *(cortar lo sobrante)* to cut out (**b**) *(cortar con arte)* to cut off, trim; *Fig* **el gobierno ha recortado el presupuesto de defensa** the government has cut defence spending

recorte *nm* (**a**) *(acción)* cutting; *(de pelo)* trim, cut; *Fig (disminución)* cut; **r. de las pensiones** cut in pensions; **r. presupuestario/salarial** budget/salary cut (**b**) *(trozo)* cutting, clipping, trimming; **r. de periódico** newspaper cutting, press clipping

recostado, -a 1 *pp de* **recostar**
2 *adj* reclining, leaning, lying

recostar [63] **1** *vt* to lean; **recuéstalo en la puerta** lean it against the door
2 recostarse *vpr (tumbarse)* to lie down; *(sestear)* to take a short rest

recova *nf* (**a**) *Am (mercado)* food market (**b**) *Arg (portal)* doorway, porch

recoveco *nm* (**a**) *(curva)* turn, bend; *Fig* **hablar sin recovecos** to speak plainly (**b**) *(rincón)* nook, corner

recreación *nf* (**a**) *(acción)* recreation (**b**) *(diversión)* recreation, break, amusement

recrear¹ 1 *vt (divertir)* to amuse, entertain
2 recrearse *vpr* to amuse oneself, enjoy oneself; **r. con** to take pleasure o delight in

recrear² *vt (crear de nuevo)* to recreate

recreativo, -a *adj* recreational; **actividades recreativas** recreational activities

recreo *nm* (**a**) *(diversión)* recreation, amusement, entertainment; **viaje de r.** pleasure trip (**b**) *(en el colegio)* break, *Br* playtime, *US* recess

recriminación *nf* recrimination, reproach

recriminar *vt (reprender)* to recriminate; *(reprochar)* to reproach; **le recriminaba su pereza** she reproached him for being lazy

recriminatorio, -a *adj* recriminatory

recrudecerse [46] *vpr* to worsen; **se ha recrudecido el frío** it has grown much colder

recrudecimiento *nm (empeoramiento)* worsening; *(aumento)* heightening, deepening, upsurge; **se teme un r. del temporal para las próximas horas** it's feared that the storm will get worse over the next few hours

recta *nf Geom* straight line; *(de carretera)* straight stretch; *Dep* **la r. final** the home straight

rectal *adj Anat* rectal; **termómetro r.** rectal thermometer

rectamente *adv* honestly

rectangular *adj* rectangular

rectángulo, -a 1 *adj* rectangular; **triángulo r.** right-angled triangle
2 *nm* rectangle

rectificable *adj* rectifiable

rectificación *nf* rectification; *(corrección)* correction, remedy

rectificador, -a 1 *adj* rectifying
2 *nm Elec* rectifier

rectificar [59] *vt* to rectify; *(corregir)* to correct, remedy

rectilíneo, -a *adj* straight; **describir una trayectoria rectilínea** to go in a straight line

rectitud *nf* straightness; *Fig* uprightness, honesty, rectitude

recto, -a 1 *adj* (**a**) *(derecho)* straight; **en línea recta** in a straight line (**b**) *(honesto)* upright, honest (**c**) *Geom* right; **ángulo r.** right angle
2 *nm Anat* rectum
3 *adv* straight (on); **sigue r.** go straight on

rector, -a 1 *adj (principio)* guiding, ruling; *(persona)* leading
2 *nm,f Univ Br* vice-chancellor, *US* president
3 *nm Rel* rector

rectorado *nm Br* vice-chancellorship, *US* presidency

rectoral *adj* rectorial

rectoría *nf* (**a**) *(cargo)* rectorship, rectorate (**b**) *(casa)* rectory

recua *nf (hilera de caballos, mulas)* drove, train; *Fig* string, series

recuadro *nm Impr* box

recubierto, -a *pp de* **recubrir**

recubrimiento *nm* covering

recubrir *(pp* **recubierto**) *vt* to cover

recuento *nm* re-count, count; **hacer r. de votos** to count o re-count the votes

recuerdo *nm* (**a**) *(memoria)* memory, recollection; **tener un buen r. de** to have happy memories of (**b**) *(regalo etc)* souvenir, keepsake; **me trajeron un r. de su viaje** they brought me back a souvenir from their trip (**c**) *recuerdos (saludos)* regards, greetings; **dale r. de mi parte** give him my regards; *(en carta)* **(muchos) r.** best wishes

recular *vi (retrasarse)* to go back, move back; *Fig (ceder)* to back down

recuperable *adj* recoverable, retrievable

recuperación *nf* recovery, retrieval, recuperation; **el enfermo ha experimentado una r. asombrosa** the patient has made an extraordinary recovery

recuperar 1 *vt* (**a**) to recover, retrieve, recoup, regain; **hay que r. las clases perdidas** you must make up the classes you have missed; **r. el afecto de algn** to win back sb's affection; **r. el conocimiento** to regain consciousness; **r. la salud** to recover (one's health) (**b**) *Inform (información)* to recover
2 recuperarse *vpr* to recover, recuperate; **aún no se ha recuperado del susto** he still hasn't got over the shock

recurrencia *nf* recurrence

recurrente 1 *adj* (**a**) *Jur* appealing (**b**) *(repetido)* recurrent
2 *nmf Jur* appealer

recurrir *vi* (**a**) *Jur* to appeal (**b**) **r. a** *(acogerse)* (a algn) to turn to; *(a algo)* to make use of, resort to; **recurrió a mí para que le ayudara** she turned to me for help; **r. a la violencia** to resort to violence

recurso *nm* (**a**) *(medio)* resort; **como último r.** as a last resort (**b**) *Jur* appeal; **r. de apelación** appeal; **r. de casación** high court appeal (**c**) *recursos (medios)* resources, means; **los r. naturales de un país** the natural resources of a country

recusable *adj* objectionable

recusación *nf Jur* challenge, objection

recusar *vt Jur* to challenge, object to

red *nf* (**a**) *(malla)* net, netting; *(para cabello)* hairnet (**b**) *(sistema)* network, system ❑ *Com* **r. comercial** sales network; **r. de espionaje** spy ring; *Com* **r. de supermercados** chain of supermarkets; *Ferroc* **r. ferroviaria** rail o railway network; **r. viaria** road network o system (**c**) *Elec* mains *pl* (**d**) *Inform* network; **la R.** the Net (**e**) *Fig (trampa)* trap; **caer en la r.** to fall into the trap

redacción *nf* (**a**) *(acción de escribir)* writing; *(estilo)* wording (**b**) *Prensa* editing (**c**) *(redactores)* editorial staff; *(oficina)* editorial office (**d**) *(escrito)* composition, essay

redactar *vt* (**a**) *(escribir)* to write; *(carta)* to draft; *(con estilo)* to word (**b**) *Prensa* to edit

redactor, -a *nm,f Prensa* journalist; **r. jefe** editor in chief

redada *nf* (**a**) *(de peces)* catch, haul (**b**) *(policial) (en un solo sitio)* raid; *(en varios lugares a la vez)* round-up

redaño *nm* (**a**) *Anat (mesenterio)* mesentery (**b**) **redaños** *Fam (valor)* guts

redecilla *nf* (**a**) *(de pelo)* hairnet (**b**) *Anat* reticulum

redefinir *vt* to redefine

redención *nf* redemption

redentor, -a 1 *adj* redeeming
2 *nm,f* redeemer; **el R.** the Redeemer

redicho, -a *adj Fam* affected, pretentious

rediez *interj Fam* (**a**) *(enfado)* damn it! (**b**) *(sorpresa)* good heavens!

redil *nm* fold, sheepfold; *Fig* **volver al r.** to return to the fold

redimible *adj* redeemable

redimir 1 *vt* to redeem
2 redimirse *vpr* to redeem oneself

rediós *interj Fam* (**a**) *(asombro)* good heavens! (**b**) *(enfado)* damn!

redistribución *nf* redistribution; **la r. de la riqueza** the redistribution of wealth

redistribuir [34] *vt* to redistribute

rédito *nm Fin* yield, interest

redivivo, -a *adj* resuscitated, revived

redoblar 1 *vt* (**a**) *(intensificar)* to redouble, intensify; **r. los esfuerzos** to redouble one's efforts (**b**) *(torcer)* to bend back, clinch
2 *vi (tambores)* to roll

redoble *nm* roll; **el r. de los tambores** the roll of drums

redoma *nf Quím* flask

redomado, -a *adj* (**a**) *(verdadero)* utter, out-and-out (**b**) *(astuto)* sly

redonda *nf* (**a**) *Mús Br* semibreve, *US* whole note (**b**) *(comarca)* region; **a la r.** around; **no hay ningún hotel en cien millas a la r.** there is not a single hotel within a hundred miles of here

redondeado, -a *adj* rounded

redondear *vt* (**a**) *(poner redondo)* to round, make round (**b**) *(cifra, precio) (al alza)* to round up; *(a la baja)* to round down; **para r. daremos un valor de 10 a la gravedad** in round figures let's give gravity the value of 10

redondel *nm* (**a**) *Fam (círculo)* circle, ring (**b**) *Taur* ring, arena

redondeo *nm (de cifra, precio) (al alza)* rounding up; *(a la baja)* rounding down

redondez *nf* roundness; **en toda la r. de la tierra** in the whole wide world

redondo, -a 1 *adj* (**a**) *(circular)* round; **cara redonda** round face; *Fig* **caer r.** *(caerse)* to collapse; *(morir)* to drop dead; *Fig* **mesa redonda** round table (**b**) *(rotundo)*

categorical; **un no r.** a flat refusal (**c**) *(perfecto)* perfect; **un negocio r.** an excellent business deal (**d**) *(cantidad)* round; **en números redondos** in round figures
2 *nm Culin* topside

reducción *nf (disminución)* reduction

reducido, -a 1 *pp de* **reducir**
2 *adj* (**a**) *(disminuido)* reduced, decreased (**b**) *(limitado)* limited, small

reducir [18] **1** *vt* (**a**) *(disminuir)* to reduce, cut down, break down, decrease, shorten (**b**) *(vencer)* to subdue; **r. al enemigo** to subdue the enemy (**c**) *Med* to set (**d**) *Culin* to boil down (**e**) *Mat* to reduce, convert; **r. las libras a kilogramos** to convert pounds to kilos
2 *vi Aut* to change to a lower gear
3 reducirse *vpr* (**a**) *(disminuirse)* to be reduced, diminish (**b**) *(ahorrar)* to economize

reductible *adj* reducible

reducto *nm Mil* redoubt, stronghold; *Fig* **utilizaremos la fuerza sólo como último r.** we'll use force only as a last resort

reductor, -a *adj* reducing

redundancia *nf* redundancy, superfluousness

redundante *adj* redundant

redundar *vi* (**a**) *(rebosar)* to overflow; *(abundar)* to abound (**b**) **r. en** *(resultar)* to result in, lead to; **redundará en su propio beneficio** it will be to his own advantage

reduplicación *nf* reduplication, redoubling

reduplicar [59] *vt* to reduplicate, redouble

reedición *nf* reprint, reissue

reedificación *nf* rebuilding

reedificar [59] *vt* to rebuild

reeditar *vt* to reprint, reissue

reeducación *nf* re-education

reeducar [59] *vt* to re-educate

reelección *nf Pol* re-election

reelecto, -a *adj Pol* re-elected

reelegir [55] *vt Pol* to re-elect

reembolsable *adj* reimbursable

reembolsar 1 *vt (pagar)* to reimburse; *(deuda)* to repay; *(devolver)* to refund; **la empresa me ha reembolsado los gastos del viaje** the company has reimbursed my travel expenses
2 reembolsarse *vpr (cobrar)* to be paid

reembolso *nm* reimbursement; *(deuda)* repayment; *(devolución)* refund; **contra r.** cash on delivery

reemplazable *adj* replaceable

reemplazar [14] *vt también Inform* to replace (**con** with)

reemplazo *nm* replacement; *Mil* call-up

reemprender *vt* to start again

reencarnación *nf* reincarnation

reencarnarse *vpr* to be reincarnated

reencontrar [63] **1** *vt* to find again
2 reencontrarse *vpr* to meet again

reencuentro *nm* reunion

reengancharse *vpr Mil* to re-enlist

reenganche *nm* re-enlistment

reenviar [32] *vt* (**a**) *(devolver)* to return, send back (**b**) *(reexpedir)* to forward, send on

reenvío *nm* (**a**) *(devolución)* return, sending back (**b**) *(reexpedición)* forwarding

reestreno *nm Teat* revival; *Cin* reshowing, rerun

reestructuración *nf* restructuring, reorganization

reestructurar *vt* to restructure, reorganize

reexpedir [47] *vt* to return

reexportar *vt* to re-export

ref. *(abrev de* **referencia***)* ref

refacción *nf* **(a)** *Andes CAm RP Ven (reforma)* refurbishment; *(reparacion)* restoration **(b)** *Méx (recambio)* spare part

refaccionar *vt Andes CAm Ven (reformar)* to refurbish; *(reparar)* to restore

refajo *nm* petticoat, underskirt

refanfinflar *vt Esp Fam* **me la refanfinfla** I don't care two hoots

refectorio *nm* refectory, dining hall, canteen

referencia *nf* **(a)** *(relación)* reference; **con r. a** with reference to; **hacer r. a** to refer to **(b)** **referencias** *(informes)* references; **en aquella empresa siempre piden r.** that company always asks for references

referendo *(pl* **referendos***) nm,* **referéndum** *(pl* **referéndums***) nm* referendum

referente *adj* **r. a** concerning, regarding

referir [62] **1** *vt* **(a)** *(contar)* to tell, relate; **r. una historia to** tell a story **(b)** *(remitir)* to refer
  2 referirse *vpr (aludir)* to refer **(a** to); **¿a quién te refieres?** who do you mean?; **por lo que se refiere a eso** as for that

refilón: de refilón *loc adv* **(a)** *(oblicuamente)* obliquely; *(de lado)* sideways; **mirar algo de r.** to look at sth out of the corner of one's eye **(b)** *Fig (de pasada)* briefly

refinado, -a 1 *pp de* **refinar**
  2 *adj* refined
  3 *nm* refining; **r. del azúcar** sugar refining

refinamiento *nm* refinement

refinar 1 *vt* **(a)** *(azúcar, alcohol)* to refine **(b)** *Fig (perfeccionar)* to perfect, finish off
  2 refinarse *vpr (perder la vulgaridad)* to polish oneself

refinería *nf* refinery; **r. de petróleo** oil refinery

reflectante *adj Fís* reflective

reflectar *vt Fís* to reflect

reflector, -a 1 *adj* reflecting
  2 *nm* **(a)** *(cuerpo que refleja)* reflector **(b)** *Elec* spotlight, searchlight **(c)** *Astron (telescopio)* reflector, reflecting telescope

reflejar 1 *vt* to reflect
  2 reflejarse *vpr* to be reflected **(en** in); **su imagen se refleja en el espejo** his image is reflected in the mirror

reflejo, -a 1 *adj* **(a)** *(luz, rayo)* reflected **(b)** *(movimiento)* reflex
  2 *nm* **(a)** *(imagen)* reflection **(b)** *(destello)* gleam, glint **(c)** *(de peluquería)* **reflejos** streaks, highlights **(d)** *Anat* reflex; **r. condicionado** conditioned reflex; **tener reflejos** to have good reflexes

réflex 1 *nm inv (sistema)* reflex
  2 *nf inv (cámara)* reflex camera

reflexión *nf* reflection; **con r.** on reflection; **este tipo de decisiones necesitan una profunda r.** this type of decision demands serious consideration

reflexionar *vi* to reflect **(sobre** on), think **(sobre** about)

reflexivo, -a *adj* **(a)** *(persona)* reflective, thoughtful **(b)** *Ling (verbo)* reflexive

reflexología *nf* reflexology

reflotar *vt* to refloat

reflujo *nm* ebb, ebb tide

refocilarse *vpr* **r. haciendo algo** to take delight in doing sth

reforestación *nf* reforestation, *Br* reafforestation

reforestar *vt* to reforest, *Br* reafforest

reforma *nf* **(a)** *(gen)* reform; **r. agraria** agrarian reform; *Pol Fin* **r. fiscal** tax reform **(b)** *Hist* **la R.** the Reformation **(c)** **reformas** *Constr* alterations, repairs, improvements; **'cerrado por r.'** 'closed for alterations' *o* refurbishment'

reformador, -a 1 *adj* reforming
  2 *nm,f* reformer

reformar 1 *vt* to reform; *Constr* to renovate, do up; **r. una casa** to renovate a house
  2 reformarse *vpr (corregirse)* to reform oneself

reformatorio *nm Br* youth custody centre, *US* reformatory

reformismo *nm* reformism

reformista *adj & nmf* reformist

reforzado, -a 1 *pp de* **reforzar**
  2 *adj* reinforced, strengthened

reforzar [31] *vt* to reinforce, strengthen

refracción *nf Fís* refraction; **índice de r.** refractive index; **r. doble** double refraction

refractario, -a *adj* **(a)** *Téc* heat-resistant **(b)** *(persona) (poco dispuesta)* unwilling, reluctant; *(opuesta)* opposed; **r. a cualquier cambio** opposed to all change

refractar *vt Fís* to refract

refrán *nm* proverb, saying; **como dice el r.** as the saying goes

refranero *nm* = collection of proverbs or sayings

refregar [43] *vt* to rub vigorously; *Fig* **r. algo a algn** to rub sth in

refregón *nm* rub, rubbing

refreír [56] *(pp* **refrito***) vt (volver a freír)* to fry again; *(freír demasiado)* to overdo

refrenar 1 *vt* **(a)** *(al caballo)* to rein in **(b)** *(contener)* to restrain, curb, control; **r. las pasiones** to curb one's passions
  2 refrenarse *vpr* to restrain *o* control oneself

refrendar *vt* **(a)** *(firmar)* to endorse, countersign **(b)** *(pasaporte)* to stamp

refrendo *nm* **(a)** *(firma)* endorsement, countersignature **(b)** *(sello)* stamp, visa

refrescante *adj* refreshing

refrescar [59] **1** *vt* **(a)** to refresh, cool; *Fig* **r. el inglés** to brush up one's English; *Fig* **r. la memoria** to refresh one's memory **(b)** *Inform* to refresh
  2 *vi* **(a)** *(del tiempo)* to turn cool **(b)** *(bebida)* to be refreshing
  3 refrescarse *vpr* **(a)** *(tomar el aire)* to take a breath of fresh air **(b)** *(beber)* to have a drink

refresco *nm* **(a)** *(comida)* snack **(b)** *(bebida)* soft drink

refriega *nf (lucha)* scuffle, brawl; *(escaramuza)* skirmish

refrigeración *nf* **(a)** *(enfriamento)* refrigeration, cooling; *(aire acondicionado)* air conditioning **(b)** *(aperitivo)* snack

refrigerado, -a 1 *pp de* **refrigerar**
  2 *adj (enfriado)* refrigerated, cooled; *(con aire acondicionado)* air-conditioned; **local r.** air-conditioned premises

refrigerador *nm* refrigerator, *Br* fridge, *US* icebox

refrigerante 1 *adj* refrigerating, cooling
  2 *nm Quím* refrigerant

refrigerar *vt (enfriar)* to refrigerate; *(con aire acondicionado)* to air-condition

refrigerio *nm* snack, refreshments *pl*

refrito, -a 1 *pp de* **refreír**
  2 *adj* refried
  3 *nm Fam (cosa rehecha)* rehash

refucilo *nm* lightning

refuerzo *nm* **(a)** *(fortalecimiento)* reinforcement, strengthening (**b**) **refuerzos** *Mil* reinforcements

refugiado, -a 1 *pp de* **refugiar**
2 *adj* refugee
3 *nm,f* refugee; **r. político** political refugee

refugiar 1 *vt* to shelter, give refuge to
2 **refugiarse** *vpr* to shelter, take refuge; **r. de la lluvia** to shelter from the rain

refugio *nm* (**a**) *(protección)* refuge, shelter; **r. antiaéreo** air-raid shelter; **r. atómico** (nuclear) fallout shelter; *Fig* **su amistad es un r. para mí** her friendship is a source of comfort to me (**b**) *Aut* (traffic) island

refulgencia *nf* radiance, brilliance

refulgente *adj* radiant, brilliant

refulgir [24] *vi (brillar)* to shine; *(resplandecer)* to glitter, sparkle

refundición *nf* (**a**) *Metal* recasting (**b**) *Lit Teat* adaptation

refundir *vt* (**a**) *Metal* to recast (**b**) *Lit Teat* to adapt

refunfuñar *vi* to grumble, moan, complain

refunfuñón, -ona *Fam* **1** *adj* grumbling, moaning
2 *nm,f* grumbler, moaner

refutable *adj* refutable, disprovable

refutación *nf* refutation, disproof

refutar *vt* to refute, disprove

Reg. *(abrev de* **registro**) reg

regadera *nf* (**a**) *(recipiente)* watering can; *Esp Fam* **estar como una r.** to be as mad as a hatter (**b**) *Col Méx Ven (ducha)* shower

regadío, -a 1 *adj* irrigable
2 *nm* (**a**) *(acción)* irrigation, watering; **cultivo de r.** irrigation farming (**b**) *(tierras)* irrigated land

regalado, -a 1 *pp de* **regalar**
2 *adj* (**a**) *(de regalo)* given as a present; *(gratis)* free (**b**) *(muy barato)* dirt cheap (**c**) *(agradable)* pleasant, comfortable; **lleva una vida regalada** he has *o* leads an easy *o* comfortable life (**d**) *(delicado)* delicate

regalar 1 *vt* (**a**) *(dar)* to give (as a present); **con cada caja te regalan una entrada** there's a free ticket with each packet; **lo regalé** I gave it away; **¿qué quieres que te regale?** what present would you like?; **regálale una corbata** get him a tie (**b**) *(halagar)* to flatter; **r. el oído** to be a pleasure to hear (**c**) *Am salvo RP (prestar)* to lend
2 **regalarse** *vpr* to treat oneself to

regalía *nf* (**a**) *Hist* royal prerogative (**b**) *CAm Carib (regalo)* present

regaliz *nm Bot* liquorice, *US* licorice

regalo *nm* (**a**) *(obsequio)* gift, present; **dar algo de r.** to give sth as a present ❑ **r. de cumpleaños** birthday present (**b**) *(comodidad)* pleasure, comfort; **vivir con gran r.** to live a life of luxury (**c**) *(exquisitez)* delicacy

regañadientes: a regañadientes *loc adv* reluctantly, unwillingly, grudgingly

regañar 1 *vt Fam* to scold, tell off
2 *vi* (**a**) *Esp (reñir)* to argue, quarrel, fall out (**b**) *(refunfuñar)* to grumble, moan, complain

regañina *nf* (**a**) *(represión)* scolding, telling-off (**b**) *(riña)* quarrel, argument

regañón, -ona *Fam* **1** *adj* grumpy, irritable
2 *nm,f* grumbler, moaner

regar [43] *vt* (**a**) *(esparcir agua)* to water (**b**) *(lavar la calle)* to wash down, hose down (**c**) *(esparcir)* to scatter, sprinkle; *(derramar)* to pour (**d**) *(beber)* to wash down (**e**) *Méx Fam* **regarla** *(meter la pata)* to put one's foot in it

regata¹ *nf Agr* irrigation channel

regata² *nf Náut* regatta, boat race

regate *nm* dodge; *Dep* dribble

regateador, -a *nm,f* haggler

regatear¹ 1 *vt* (**a**) *(precio)* to haggle over, barter for (**b**) *(escatimar)* to be sparing with; **no regatearon esfuerzos** they spared no effort
2 *vi* (**a**) *(comerciar)* to haggle, bargain (**b**) *Dep* to dribble

regatear² *vi Náut* to race

regateo *nm* (**a**) *(precios)* haggling, bargaining (**b**) *Dep* dribbling

regato *nm* (**a**) *(charco)* pool (**b**) *(arroyo)* stream

regazo *nm* lap

regencia *nf* regency

regeneración *nf* regeneration

regeneracionismo *nm* = Spanish 19th century political reform movement

regenerador, -a 1 *adj* regenerative
2 *nm,f* regenerator

regenerar *vt* to regenerate

regenerativo, -a *adj* regenerative

regenta *nf Pol* regent

regentar *vt* (**a**) *Pol* to rule, govern (**b**) *(tener un cargo)* to hold (**c**) *(dirigir)* to manage, direct

regente *nmf* (**a**) *Pol (de un país)* regent (**b**) *(administrador) (de tienda)* manager; *(de colegio)* governor (**c**) *Méx (alcalde) (hombre)* mayor; *(mujer)* mayoress

reggae ['rrivi, 'rrevi] *nm Mús* reggae

regicida 1 *adj* regicidal
2 *nmf* regicide

regicidio *nm* regicide

regidor, -a *nm,f* (**a**) *(concejal)* town councillor (**b**) *Teat* stage manager

régimen *(pl* **regímenes**) *nm* (**a**) *Pol* regime, rule, system; **antiguo r.** old regime (**b**) *Med* diet, regime, regimen; **estar a r.** to be on a diet (**c**) *Téc (velocidad)* speed (**d**) *(condiciones)* rules *pl*; **r. tormentoso** stormy weather

regimiento *nm Mil* regiment

regio, -a *adj* (**a**) *(real)* royal, regal (**b**) *Andes RP Fam (genial)* great, fabulous

región *nf* region

regional *adj* regional

regionalismo *nm* regionalism

regionalista *adj & nmf* regionalist

regir [55] **1** *vt* (**a**) *(gobernar)* to govern, rule (**b**) *(dirigir)* to direct, manage
2 *vi (estar vigente)* to be in force, apply, prevail; **el mes que rige** the current month; *Fam* **no r.** to have a screw loose
3 **regirse** *vpr* to be guided, go (**por** by); **siempre me rijo por este diccionario** I always go by what this dictionary says

registrado, -a 1 *pp de* **registrar**
2 *adj* registered, recorded, noted, listed; **marca registrada** registered trademark

registrador, -a 1 *adj* registering, recording
2 *nm,f* registerer, recorder

registrar 1 *vt* (**a**) *(examinar)* to search, inspect, look through; *(cachear)* to frisk; **registraron sus maletas** their suitcases were searched (**b**) *(inscribir)* to register, record, note (**c**) *(grabar)* to record
2 **registrarse** *vpr* (**a**) *(inscribirse)* to register, enrol (**b**) *(detectarse)* to be recorded *o* reported; **se ha registrado un ligero temblor** a slight tremor has been recorded (**c**) *(ocurrir)* to happen

registro *nm* (**a**) *(inspección)* search, inspection, scrutiny (**b**) *(inscripción)* registration, recording (**c**) *(libro)* register; *(oficina)* registry ❑ **r. civil** births, marriages and deaths register; *(oficina)* registry office; **r. de la propiedad** property registry; **r. electoral** electoral roll (**d**) *Mús* register; *(de órgano)* stop; *Fig* **tocar todos los registros** to pull out all the stops (**e**) *Inform (en base de datos)* record

regla *nf* (**a**) *(norma)* rule, regulation, norm, custom; **en r.** in order; **la excepción confirma la r.** the exception confirms the rule; **las reglas del juego** the rules of the game; **por r. general** as a (general) rule; **r. de oro** golden rule; **salir de la r.** to overstep the mark (**b**) *(instrumento)* ruler; **r. de cálculo** slide rule (**c**) *Mat* rule; **r. de tres** rule of three; *Fam* **sabe leer y escribir y las cuatro reglas** he knows the three Rs (**d**) *Med* period; **tener la r.** to have one's period

reglado, -a *adj* ruled, lined

reglaje *nm* adjustment

reglamentación *nf* (**a**) *(acción)* regulation (**b**) *(reglamento)* regulations *pl*, rules *pl*

reglamentar *vt* to regulate

reglamentariamente *adv* in due form, statutorily

reglamentario, -a *adj* statutory, required, prescribed; *Mil* **arma reglamentaria** regulation o standard-issue gun

reglamento *nm* regulations *pl*, rules *pl*

reglar *vt* (**a**) *(regular)* to regulate (**b**) *(ajustar)* to adjust (**c**) *(papel)* to rule, draw lines/a line on

regleta *nf Impr* space

regocijar 1 *vt* to delight, amuse
  2 regocijarse *vpr* to be delighted, rejoice; **r. de** o **con** to delight in, take pleasure in

regocijo *nm* (**a**) *(placer)* delight, joy, happiness (**b**) *(alborozo)* rejoicing, merriment

regodearse *vpr Fam* to delight (**con** in); *(con crueldad)* to take a cruel delight (**con** in)

regodeo *nm Fam* delight; *(cruel)* cruel delight

regodeón, -ona *adj Am* fussy

regordete, -a *adj Fam* plump, tubby, chubby

regrabable *adj Inform* rewritable

regresar 1 *vi (ir)* to go back, return; *(venir)* to come back, return; **¿cuándo regresará?** when will she be back?
  2 *vt Am salvo RP (devolver)* to give back
  3 regresarse *vpr Am salvo RP (ir)* to go back, return; *(venir)* to come back, return

regresión *nf* regression; *(decaimiento)* deterioration, decline; **en vías de r.** on the decline

regresivo, -a *adj* regressive

regreso *nm* return; **a mi r.** on my return; **estar de r.** to be back; **viaje de r.** return journey

regüeldo *nm* burp, belch

reguera *nf (canal)* irrigation channel

reguero *nm* (**a**) *(canal)* irrigation channel (**b**) *(corriente)* trickle of water (**c**) *(señal) (de humo)* trail; *(de sangre)* trickle; **propagarse como un r. de pólvora** to spread like wildfire

regulable *adj* adjustable

regulación *nf* (**a**) *(control)* regulation, control (**b**) *(ajuste)* adjustment

regulador, -a 1 *adj* regulating
  2 *nm* regulator; *Rad TV* **r. de volumen** volume control

regular 1 *vt* (**a**) *(medir)* to regulate, control (**b**) *(ajustar)* to adjust
  2 *adj* (**a**) *(conforme a la regla)* regular; **por lo r.** as a rule; *Ling* **verbo r.** regular verb (**b**) *Fam (mediano)* average, so-so; **¿qué tal la comida? — r.** how was the food? — average

regularidad *nf* regularity; **con r.** regularly

regularización *nf* regularization

regularizar [14] *vt* to regularize

regularmente *adv* (**a**) *(comúnmente)* regularly (**b**) *(medianamente)* so-so

regurgitar *vt* to regurgitate

regusto *nm* aftertaste

rehabilitación *nf* rehabilitation; *(en rango, reputación)* rehabilitation, reinstatement

rehabilitar 1 *vt* to rehabilitate; *(en rango, reputación)* to rehabilitate, reinstate
  2 rehabilitarse *vpr* to rehabilitate oneself

rehacer [33] *(pp* **rehecho)** **1** *vt* (**a**) *(volver a hacer)* to redo, do again (**b**) *(reconstruir)* to remake, rebuild; *Fig* **tendrá que r. su vida** she will have to rebuild her life
  2 rehacerse *vpr* (**a**) *(recuperarse)* to recover, recuperate (**b**) *Fig (dominarse)* to pull oneself together

rehén *(pl* **rehenes)** *nm* hostage

rehilete *nm* (**a**) *(flechilla)* dart (**b**) *(volante)* shuttlecock

rehogar [38] *vt Culin* to brown

rehuir [34] *vt* to shun, avoid; **no rehúyas la pregunta** don't avoid the question

rehusar [4] *vt* to refuse, decline, turn down; **rehusé contestar** I refused to answer

reidor, -a *adj* happy, laughing

Reikiavik *n* Reykjavik

reimplantar *vt* (**a**) *(reintroducir)* to reintroduce (**b**) *Med* to implant again

reimportar *vt* to reimport

reimpresión *nf Impr* (**a**) *(acción)* reprinting (**b**) *(resultado)* reprint

reimprimir *(pp* **reimpreso)** *vt Impr* to reprint

reina *nf* (**a**) *(monarca)* queen; *Zool* **abeja r.** queen bee; **la r. madre** the Queen Mother; *Fig* **r. de belleza** beauty queen (**b**) *Fam (cariño)* love, ducky; **¡gracias, r.!** thanks, love! (**c**) *Ajedrez* queen

reinado *nm* reign

reinante *adj (que reina)* reigning, ruling; *(prevaleciente)* prevailing; **el buen tiempo r.** the current spell of good weather

reinar *vi* to reign; *Fig* **volvió a r. el silencio** silence reigned once more

reincidencia *nf* relapse; *Jur* recidivism

reincidente *adj & nmf* relapsing; *Jur* recidivist

reincidir *vi* to relapse, fall back (**en** into); **r. en el delito** to reoffend

reincorporación *nf* reincorporation; *(a un cargo)* reinstatement, re-employment

reincorporar 1 *vt* to reincorporate; *(a un cargo)* to reinstate, re-employ
  2 reincorporarse *vpr* to rejoin; **se reincorporó al ejército** he rejoined the army

reineta *nf Bot* pippin

reingresar *vi* to return, re-enter, rejoin; **reingresó en el coro** she rejoined the choir

reingreso *nm* return, re-entry

reinicializar [14] *vt*, **reiniciar** *vt Inform (ordenador)* to reboot; *(impresora)* to reset

reino *nm* kingdom; **el r. de los Cielos** the Kingdom of Heaven; **el r. vegetal** the vegetable kingdom

Reino Unido *n* **el R. U.** the United Kingdom

reinserción *nf* adaptation, reintegration; **r. social** social reintegration

reinsertar *vt* to reintegrate

reinstalación *nf* (**a**) *(en lugar)* reinstallation (**b**) *(en puesto)* reinstatement

reinstalar *vt* (**a**) *(en lugar)* to reinstall (**b**) *(en puesto)* to reinstate

reinstaurar *vt* to reestablish

reintegración *nf* (**a**) *(reincorporación)* reinstatement (**b**) *(pago)* refund

reintegrar 1 *vt* (**a**) *(reincorporar)* to reinstate, restore (**b**) *(pagar)* to reimburse, refund
 2 reintegrarse *vpr* to return (**a** to); **se reintegró a su trabajo** she returned to her job

reintegro *nm* (**a**) *(reincorporación)* reinstatement (**b**) *(pago)* reimbursement, refund, repayment (**c**) *(en lotería)* = winning of one's stake

reír [56] **1** *vt* to laugh at; **le ríe todos sus chistes** he laughs at all her jokes
 2 *vi* to laugh; *Irón* **¡no me hagas r.!** don't make me laugh!; *Prov* **quien ríe el último ríe mejor** he who laughs last laughs longest
 3 reírse *vpr* (**a**) *(mostrar alegría)* to laugh; **¡no te rías!** don't laugh!; **r. a carcajadas** to roar with laughter (**b**) *(mofarse)* to laugh (**de** at), make fun (**de** of); **¿de qué te ríes?** what are you laughing at?; **siempre se ríen de mis consejos** they always make fun of my advice

reiteración *nf* reiteration

reiteradamente *adv* repeatedly, reiteratively

reiterar *vt* to reiterate, repeat

reiterativo, -a *adj* repetitive, repetitious, reiterative

reivindicación *nf* claim, demand

reivindicar [59] *vt* to claim, demand; **el atentado fue reivindicado por los terroristas** the terrorists claimed responsibility for the attack

reivindicativo, -a *adj* claiming, demanding

reja¹ *nf Agr* ploughshare, *US* plowshare

reja² *nf (de ventana)* grill, grille, grating, bar; *Fam* **estar entre rejas** to be behind bars

rejego, -a *adj Méx Fam (terco)* pigheaded

rejilla *nf (de ventana)* grill, grille; *(chimeneas)* latticework; *(de horno)* gridiron; *(de ventilador)* grill; *(de silla)* wickerwork; *(para equipaje)* luggage rack; *Aut* **r. del radiador** radiator grille

rejón *nm Taur* lance

rejoneador, -a *nm,f Taur* bullfighter on horseback

rejonear *vt Taur* to fight on horseback

rejoneo *nm Taur* bullfighting on horseback

rejuvenecedor, -a *adj* rejuvenating, rejuvenescent

rejuvenecer [46] **1** *vt* to rejuvenate
 2 rejuvenecerse *vpr* to become rejuvenated

rejuvenecimiento *nm* rejuvenation, rejuvenescence

relación *nf* (**a**) *(correspondencia)* relation, relationship; *(conexión)* connection, link; **con** o **en r.** with regard to; **relaciones diplomáticas** diplomatic relations; **relaciones públicas** public relations; **tener buenas relaciones** to be well connected; **tener relaciones con un chico** to be going out with a boy ◻ **r. calidad-precio** value for money (**b**) *(lista)* list, record; **la r. de los pasajeros** the passenger list (**c**) *(relato)* account, telling (**d**) *Mat* ratio; *Téc* **r. de compresión** compression ratio

relacionado, -a 1 *pp de* **relacionar**
 2 *adj* related, connected, linked; **estar bien r.** to be well connected; **r. con** related to, connected with

relacionar 1 *vt* (**a**) *(poner en relación)* to relate, connect, associate (**con** with) (**b**) *(listar)* to list
 2 relacionarse *vpr* (**a**) *(estar conectado)* to be related, be connected (**b**) *(alternar)* to mix, get acquainted

relajación *nf (gen)* relaxation; *(aflojamiento)* slackening, loosening

relajado, -a 1 *pp de* **relajar**
 2 *adj (gen)* relaxed; *(aflojado)* loose, slack

relajante *adj* relaxing

relajar 1 *vt* (**a**) *(gen)* to relax; *(aflojar)* to loosen, slacken (**b**) *PRico (burlarse de)* to make fun of, mock
 2 relajarse *vpr* (**a**) *(descansar)* to relax; *(viciarse)* to let oneself go (**b**) *(dilatarse)* to slacken, loosen

relajo *nm* (**a**) *Am Fam (alboroto)* **se armó un r.** there was an almighty row; **esta mesa es un r.** this table is a complete mess (**b**) *Méx RP (complicación)* nuisance, hassle; **aquí hacer cualquier trámite es un r.** going through any official procedure here is a hassle (**c**) *CAm Carib Méx (broma)* joke; *Méx* **echar r.** to fool around

relamer 1 *vt* to lick
 2 relamerse *vpr* to lick one's lips

relamido, -a *adj (afectado)* affected; *(pulcro)* prim and proper

relámpago *nm* flash of lightning; *Fig* **guerra r.** blitzkrieg; *Fig* **pasó como un r.** he flashed past; *Fig* **visita r.** lightning visit

relampagueante *adj* flashing

relampaguear *vi impers* to flash

relampagueo *nm* (**a**) *(relámpagos)* lightning (**b**) *(centelleo)* flashing

relanzamiento *nm* relaunch

relanzar [14] *vt* to relaunch

relatar *vt (narrar)* to narrate, relate; *(hacer relación)* to report, tell

relatividad *nf* relativity; *Fís* **teoría de la r.** theory of relativity

relativismo *nm Filos* relativism

relativista *adj & nmf Filos* relativist

relativizar [14] *vt* to play down

relativo, -a 1 *adj* relative; **en lo r. a** with regard to, referring to, concerning; **r. a** relative to
 2 *nm Ling* relative

relato *nm* (**a**) *(cuento)* tale, story (**b**) *(informe)* report, account

relax *nm Fam* (**a**) *(descanso)* relaxation (**b**) *(prostitución)* call-girl service

relé *nm Elec* relay

releer [37] *vt* to reread

relegación *nf* relegation

relegar [38] *vt* to relegate

relente *nm* dew

relevancia *nf* (**a**) *(significancia)* relevance (**b**) *(importancia)* importance

relevante *adj* (**a**) *(significante)* relevant (**b**) *(importante)* important

relevar *vt* (**a**) *(sustituir)* to relieve, take over from; *Mil* to change, relieve (**b**) *(destituir)* to dismiss, remove from office (**c**) *(eximir)* to exempt (**de** from)

relevo *nm* (**a**) *Mil* relief, change *(of the guard)* (**b**) *Dep* relay; **carrera de relevos** relay race

relicario *nm* (**a**) *Rel* reliquary (**b**) *(estuche)* locket; *(caja)* box

relieve *nm Arte* relief; **en r.** in relief; *Fig* **poner de r.** to emphasize

religión *nf* religion; **entrar en r.** to take vows

religiosamente *adv* religiously

religiosidad *nf* religiousness, religiosity

religioso, -a 1 *adj* religious
 2 *nm,f (hombre)* monk; *(mujer)* nun

relinchar *vi* to neigh, whinny

relincho *nm* neigh, whinny

reliquia *nf* relic

rellano *nm* landing

rellenar *vt* (**a**) *(escribir)* to fill in, fill out; **r. un formulario** to fill in a form (**b**) *(llenar del todo)* to cram, pack, stuff (**de** with) (**c**) *Culin (un ave)* to stuff; *(un pastel)* to fill; *Cost (un cojín)* to stuff (**d**) *(volver a llenar)* to refill, fill again

relleno, -a 1 *adj (lleno)* crammed, packed, stuffed (**de** with); *Culin* **pastel r.** cake with a (cream) filling; *Culin* **pavo r.** stuffed turkey

2 *nm Culin (de aves)* stuffing; *(de pasteles)* filling; *Cost* filling, padding

reloj *nm (gen)* clock; *(de pulsera)* watch; **carrera contra r.** race against the clock ◻ **r. de arena** hourglass; **r. de caja** grandfather clock; **r. de pulsera** wristwatch; **r. de sol** sundial; **reloj despertador** alarm clock

relojería *nf* (**a**) *(arte)* watchmaking, clockmaking (**b**) *(tienda, taller)* watchmaker's, clockmaker's ◻ **bomba de r.** time bomb

relojero, -a *nm,f* watchmaker, clockmaker

reluciente *adj* shining, gleaming, glittering

relucir [39] *vi* (**a**) *(brillar)* to shine, gleam, glitter; *Prov* **no es oro todo lo que reluce** all that glitters is not gold (**b**) *(destacarse)* to excel, stand out, shine; **sacar a r. un tema** to bring up a subject

reluctancia *nf Fís* reluctance, reluctancy

relumbrar *vi* to shine, gleam, dazzle

relumbrón *nm* (**a**) *(destello)* flash, glare (**b**) *(ostentación)* flashiness, ostentation; **de r.** flashy

remachar *vt* (**a**) *Téc* to rivet (**b**) *Fig (confirmar)* to stress

remache *nm* rivet

remanente 1 *adj (resto)* residual, remaining; *(extra)* surplus

2 *nm (restos)* remainder, remains; *(extra)* surplus

remangar [38] **1** *vt (mangas, pantalones)* to roll up; *(camisa)* to tuck up

2 remangarse *vpr* **r. la camisa** to tuck up one's shirt; **r. las mangas/los pantalones** to roll up one's sleeves/trousers

remanso *nm* (**a**) *(estanque)* pool; *(agua estancada)* backwater (**b**) *(lugar tranquilo)* quiet place; **r. de paz** oasis of peace

remar *vi Dep* to row

remarcable *adj* remarkable

remarcar [59] *vt* to stress, underline

rematadamente *adv* totally, completely

rematado, -a 1 *pp de* rematar

2 *adj* utter, absolute, out-and-out; **loco r.** as mad as a hatter

rematador, -a *nm,f* (**a**) *Dep* striker (**b**) *Andes RP (en subasta)* auctioneer

rematar 1 *vt* (**a**) *(acabar)* to finish off, round off, complete, put the finishing touches to (**b**) *Com (precios)* to knock down; *(vender más barato)* to sell off cheaply (**c**) *(matar)* to kill, finish off (**d**) *Andes, RP (subastar)* to auction

2 *vi Dep* to take a shot at goal, shoot

remate *nm* (**a**) *(final)* end, finish; **de r.** utter, utterly; **para r.** to crown it all; **por r.** finally, in the end; *Com* **precios de r.** knockdown prices (**b**) *Dep* attempt at goal (**c**) *Andes RP (subasta)* auction

rematista *nmf Perú PRico* auctioneer

rembolsar *vt véase* **reembolsar**

rembolso *nm véase* **reembolso**

remecer [40] *vt Chile Méx* to shake

remedar *vt (imitar)* to imitate, copy; *(con mímica)* to mimic; *(mofarse de)* to mock

remediable *adj* remediable, that can be corrected

remediar *vt* (**a**) *(poner remedio)* to remedy; *(reparar)* to repair, make good (**b**) *(resolver)* to solve; **así no remedias nada** you won't solve anything that way (**c**) *(ayudar)* to help, assist (**d**) *(evitar)* to avoid, prevent; **no pude remediarlo** I couldn't help it

remedio *nm (cura)* remedy, cure; *(solución)* solution; **como último r.** as a last resort; **hay que poner r. a esto** something must be done about this; **no tener más r. que** to have no choice but to; **sin r.** without fail; *Fam* **¡no tienes r.!** you're hopeless! ◻ **r. casero** home remedy

remedo *nm* (**a**) *(imitación)* imitation, copy; *(mímica)* mimicry, mimicking (**b**) *(parodia)* parody; *(burla)* travesty, mockery

remembranza *nf*, **rememoración** *nf* remembrance, recollection

rememorar *vt* to remember, recall

remendar [3] *vt* (**a**) *(corregir)* to mend, repair (**b**) *Cost* to mend; *(ropas)* to patch; *(calcetines)* to darn

remendón, -ona *adj* **zapatero r.** cobbler

remera *nf RP (prenda)* T-shirt

remero, -a *nm,f Dep* rower; *(hombre)* oarsman; *(mujer)* oarswoman

remesa *nf (de mercancías)* consignment, shipment; *(de dinero)* remittance

remezón *nm Andes* earth tremor

remiendo *nm (arreglo)* mend; *(de calcetín)* darn; *(parche)* patch

remilgado, -a *adj (afectado)* affected; *(melindroso)* fussy, finicky; *(mojigato)* prudish

remilgo *nm (amaneramiento)* affectation; *(gazmoñería)* prudishness, primness; **andar con remilgos** to make a fuss, be fussy

reminiscencia *nf* reminiscence

remirado, -a *adj* over-cautious

remirar 1 *vt (volver a mirar)* to have a second look at

2 remirarse *vpr (esmerarse)* to take great care

remise *nm RP* taxi *(in private car without meter)*

remisión *nf* (**a**) *Rel* remission, forgiveness (**b**) *Med* remission (**c**) *(referencia)* reference (**d**) *(envío)* sending

remiso, -a *adj* remiss, negligent

remite *nm (en sobre, paquete)* sender's name and address

remitente *nmf* sender; **'devuélvase al r.'** 'return to sender'

remitir 1 *vt* (**a**) *(enviar)* to send, remit (**b**) *(referir)* to refer; **la nota nos remite a la página tres** the note refers us to page three (**c**) *(perdonar) (pecados)* to forgive (**d**) *(aplazar)* to postpone, adjourn; **tuvimos que r. la reunión hasta el lunes** we had to postpone the meeting until Monday (**e**) *(fiebre, temporal)* to subside

2 remitirse *vpr (atenerse)* to refer (**a** to)

remo *nm* (**a**) *(instrumento)* oar, paddle; **ir a r.** to row (**b**) *(deporte)* rowing; **club de r.** rowing club (**c**) *Anat (brazo)* arm; *(pierna)* leg

remodelación *nf (modificación)* reshaping; *(reorganización)* reorganization; *Pol* **r. ministerial** *o* **del gobierno** cabinet reshuffle

remodelar *vt (modificar)* to reshape; *(reorganizar)* to reorganize

remojar *vt* (**a**) *(empapar)* to soak (**en** in) (**b**) *Fam (celebrar)* to celebrate, drink to

remojo *nm (puesto en agua)* soaking; **dejar** *o* **poner en r.** to soak, leave to soak

remojón nm Fam soaking, drenching

remolacha nf Esp CAm Carib Ecuad RP Br beetroot, US beet; **r. azucarera** (sugar) beet

remolachero, -a adj Esp CAm Carib Ecuad RP Br beetroot, US beet

remolcador nm (a) Náut tug, tugboat (b) Aut breakdown truck, US tow truck

remolcar [59] vt to tow

remolienda nf Chile Perú Fam binge, spree

remolino nm (a) (de agua) whirlpool, eddy; (de aire) whirlwind; (de polvo) whirl, cloud (b) (de pelo) cowlick (c) (de gente) throng

remolón, -ona adj lazy, slack; **hacerse el r.** to shirk, slack

remolonear vi to shirk, slack

remolque nm (a) (acción) towing (b) (vehículo) trailer; **a r.** in tow; Fig **ir a r. de algn** to live in sb's shadow

remontar 1 vt (a) (subir) to go up; **r. el vuelo** to soar; **r. un río** to sail up a river (b) (superar) to overcome
   2 remontarse vpr (a) (pájaro, avión) to soar (b) (datar) to go back, date back (a to); **es una tradición que remonta al siglo XV** it is a tradition which dates back to the 15th century

remoquete nm (a) Fig quip (b) Fam nickname

rémora nf (a) (pez) remora (b) Fig (estorbo) hindrance; (problema) drawback

remorder [41] **1** vt (conciencia) to cause remorse to; (inquietar) to trouble; **me remuerde el haberle mentido** I feel guilty about having lied to her
   2 remorderse vpr (conciencia) to suffer remorse; (inquietarse) to fret

remordimiento nm remorse; **tener remordimientos** to feel remorse

remotamente adv remotely, vaguely; **ni r.** not in the slightest, far from it

remoto, -a adj (a) remote, faraway; Fig **no tengo la más remota idea** I haven't got the faintest idea (b) Inform remote

remover [41] vt (a) (trasladar) to move over (b) (tierra) to turn over (c) (líquido) to shake up (d) (comida etc) to stir; (ensalada) to toss (e) (reavivar) to revive (f) Fig (alterar) to change; **este nuevo problema lo ha removido todo** this new problem has turned everything upside down (g) esp Am (despedir) to dismiss

remozamiento nm (a) (persona) rejuvenation (b) (fachada) modernization; (decoración) redecoration; (limpieza) brightening up

remozar [14] vt (fachada) to modernize; (decorar) to redecorate; (limpiar) to brighten up

remplazable adj véase **reemplazable**

remplazar [14] vt véase **reemplazar**

remplazo nm véase **reemplazo**

remuneración nf remuneration, pay

remunerado, -a 1 pp de **remunerar**
   2 adj paid; **un trabajo bien r.** a well-paid job

remunerar vt to remunerate, pay, reward

renacentista adj Renaissance; **pintura r.** Renaissance painting

renacer [42] vi (a) (flores, hojas) to grow again (b) (sentimiento, interés) to return, revive; **me siento r.** I feel reborn, I feel like I have a new lease of life

renacimiento nm (a) (de flores, hojas) budding (b) (periodo histórico) **el R.** the Renaissance (c) (de sentimiento, interés) revival, return

renacuajo nm (a) Zool tadpole (b) Fam (niño pequeño) shrimp

renal adj renal, kidney; **afección r.** kidney disease

Renania nf Rhineland

renazco indic pres véase **renacer**

rencilla nf quarrel; **rencillas familiares** family quarrels

rencor nm (hostilidad) rancour, US rancor; (resentimiento) resentment; **guardar r. a algn** to bear a grudge against sb, bear sb malice

rencoroso, -a adj (hostil) rancorous; (resentido) resentful; (malicioso) spiteful

rendición nf surrender

rendido, -a 1 pp de **rendir**
   2 adj (a) (sumiso) submissive; (cortés) humble; **admirador r.** devoted admirer (b) (muy cansado) exhausted, worn out

rendidor, -a adj RP (inversión, acciones) profitable; **comprar en grandes cantidades es más r.** buying in bulk is cheaper

rendija nf crack, split

rendimiento nm (a) (producción) yield, output (b) Téc (de máquina, motor) efficiency, performance (c) (sumisión) submissiveness (d) (cansancio) exhaustion, fatigue

rendir [47] **1** vt (a) (vencer) to defeat, conquer (b) (producir) to yield, produce; **por las mañanas rinde más** he's more productive in the morning (c) (cansar) to exhaust, wear out (d) (entregar) to hand over; (restituir) to give back, render; Mil to surrender; **r. las llaves** to hand over the keys; Fig **r. cuentas** to account for one's actions; Fig **r. el alma** to give up the ghost (f) (ofrecer) to offer; **r. culto a** to worship; **r. homenaje a** to pay homage to; **r. honores a la bandera** to salute the flag (g) Mil (bandera) to dip; (armas) to lower
   2 vi (a) (dar beneficios) to pay, be profitable; **este negocio no rinde** this business doesn't pay (b) Am (cundir) to go a long way
   3 rendirse vpr to surrender, give in; **¡me rindo!** I give up!; **r. a la evidencia** to bow to the evidence

renegado, -a 1 pp de **renegar**
   2 adj & nm,f renegade

renegar [43] **1** vt (negar) to deny vigorously
   2 vi (a) (renunciar) to renounce, disown (de -); **r. de su familia** to disown one's family (b) (blasfemar) to swear, curse (c) (quejarse) to grumble, complain

renegrido, -a adj blackened

renglón nm (a) (línea) line; **a r. seguido** immediately afterwards; Fig **leer entre renglones** to read between the lines (b) Com (partida) item (c) **renglones** Fam text sing; **poner cuatro r. a algn** to drop sb a line

rengo, -a adj Andes RP lame

renguear vi Andes RP to limp, hobble

reniego nm (blasfemia) curse, oath

reno nm reindeer

renombrado, -a adj renowned, famous, well-known

renombrar vt Inform to rename

renombre nm renown, fame; **de r.** renowned, famous

renovable adj renewable

renovación nf (a) (de contrato, pasaporte) renewal (b) (de una casa) renovation; (redecoración) redecoration (c) Pol (de un partido) reorganization

renovador, -a 1 adj innovative; Pol reformist
   2 nm,f innovator; Pol reformer

renovar [41] **1** vt (a) (gen) to renew (b) (casa) to renovate; (redecorar) to redecorate (c) Pol (partido) to reorganize
   2 renovarse vpr to be renewed

renquear vi (a) (de la pierna) to limp; (del pie) to hobble (b) Fam to manage, get by; **vamos renqueando** we're just scraping by

renta nf (a) Fin (ingresos) income; **vivir de sus rentas** to live on one's (private) income; **¿ya has presentado la r. este año?** have you filed your tax return this year? □ **impuesto sobre la r.** income tax; **r. fiscal** taxable income; **r. nacional** national income; **r. per cápita** per capita income; **r. pública** government debt; **r. variable** equity securities *pl*; **r. vitalicia** life annuity (**b**) *(beneficio)* interest, return □ **r. fija** fixed interest security (**c**) *(alquiler)* rent

rentabilidad *nf* profitability; *Fin* **tasa de r.** rate of return

rentabilizar [14] *vt* to make profitable

rentable *adj* profitable

rentar *vt* (**a**) *(rendir)* to produce, yield (**b**) *Méx (alquilar)* to rent; **se renta** *(en letrero)* to let

rentero, -a *nm,f* tenant farmer

rentista *nmf* (**a**) *(experto en renta)* financial expert (**b**) *(que vive de rentas)* rentier, person of independent means

renuencia *nf* reluctance, unwillingness

renuevo *nm* (**a**) *Bot* shoot, sprout; **echar renuevos** to sprout (**b**) *(renovación)* renewal

renuncia *nf* (**a**) *(abandono)* giving up (**b**) *(dimisión)* resignation; **presentar la r.** to hand in one's resignation

renunciar *vi* (**a**) *(dejar voluntariamente)* to renounce, give up; *(corona, trono)* to relinquish; **r. a su puesto** to resign (one's post); **r. al alcohol** to give up drinking; **r. a su fe** to renounce one's faith (**b**) *(rechazar)* **r. a hacer algo** to refuse to do sth

reñido, -a *pp de* **reñir**
2 *adj* (**a**) *(enemistado)* on bad terms, at odds; **están reñidos** they are not on speaking terms (**b**) *(encarnizado)* bitter, tough, hard-fought

reñir [47] **1** *vt* (**a**) *(regañar)* to scold, tell off (**b**) *Mil (batalla)* to fight; *(guerra)* to wage
2 *vi* (*discutir*) to quarrel, argue; *(pelear)* to fight; **r. con algn** to fall out with sb; **r. por algo** to fight over sth

reo[1] *nmf* (**a**) *Jur (acusado)* defendant, accused (**b**) *(culpable)* culprit; *(con cargos contra la ley)* offender

reo[2] *nm (pez)* salmon trout

reoca *nf Fam* **ser la r.** *(gracioso)* to be a scream; *(genial)* to be really cool; *(el colmo)* to be the absolute limit

reojo : **de reojo** *loc adv* **mirar algo de r.** to look at sth out of the corner of one's eye

reordenar *vt* to rearrange

reorganización *nf* reorganization; *Pol* **r. ministerial** cabinet reshuffle

reorganizar [14] *vt* to reorganize

reorientar **1** *vt (carrera, empresa, vida)* to give a new direction to; *(energías, interés)* to re-focus (**hacia** on), to redirect (**hacia** towards)
2 **reorientarse** *(carrera, empresa, vida)* to take a new direction; *(energías, interés)* to re-focus (**hacia** on), to be redirected (**hacia** towards)

reostato *nm*, **reóstato** *nm Elec* rheostat

repanchigarse [38] *vpr Fam véase* **repantigarse**

repanocha *nf Fam véase* **reoca**

repantigarse [38] *vpr Fam (acomodarse)* to lounge, loll; *(arrellenarse)* to stretch oneself out

reparable *adj* repairable

reparación *nf* (**a**) *(arreglo)* repair, repairing; **en r.** under repair; **taller de reparaciones** repair shop (**b**) *Fig (desagravio)* reparation, amends *pl*

reparador, -a *adj (descanso, sueño)* refreshing

reparar[1] *vt* (**a**) *(arreglar)* to repair, fix, mend (**b**) *(ofensa, injuria)* to make amends for; *(daño)* to make good (**c**) *(reponer)* to restore, renew (**d**) *(considerar)* to take into account; **repárelo bien** think it over

2 *vi* (**a**) *(darse cuenta)* **r. en** to notice, realize; **reparé en que no llevaba la cartera** I realized I didn't have my wallet on me (**b**) *(hacer caso)* **r. en** to pay attention to; **no r. en gastos** to spare no expense

reparar[2] **1** *vi* (*detenerse*) to stop, stall
2 **repararse** *vpr* (**a**) *(detenerse)* to stop, stall (**b**) *Am (caballo)* to rear (up)

reparo *nm* objection; **no tener reparos en** not to hesitate to; **poner reparos a** to object to, find fault with

repartición *nf* distribution, sharing out

repartidor, -a *nm,f* distributor; **r. de la leche** milkman

repartir **1** *vt* (**a**) *(dividir)* to distribute, divide, share out; **repartámosnos lo que sobra** let's split what's left (**b**) *(entregar)* to give out, hand out; *(correo)* to deliver; **r. premios** to give out prizes; *Fam Fig* **empezó a r. puñetazos a todos los que estaban cerca** he started punching everyone in sight (**c**) *Naipes* to deal
2 **repartirse** *vpr* (**a**) *(dividirse)* to be distributed o divided o shared out (**b**) *(entregarse)* to be given out o handed out; *(correo)* to be delivered

reparto *nm* (**a**) *(división)* distribution, division, sharing out □ *Esp Fin* **r. de beneficios** profit sharing (**b**) *(distribución)* handing out; *(de mercancías)* delivery; **furgoneta de r.** delivery van; **r. de premios** prize-giving (**c**) *Naipes (turno)* deal; *(acción)* dealing (**d**) *Cin Teat* cast

repasar *vt* (**a**) *(volver a pasar por)* to pass by, pass through again (**b**) *(volver a mirar)* to revise, go over (**c**) *Téc (máquina)* to check, overhaul (**d**) *Cost (ropa)* to mend (**e**) *Fam (mirar con descaro)* to look over; **la repasó de arriba a abajo** he looked her up and down

repaso *nm* (**a**) *(revisión)* revision, going over; *(lección)* review; **curso de r.** refresher course (**b**) *Téc (máquina)* checkup, overhaul (**c**) *Cost (ropa)* mending

repatear *vt Fam* to annoy, disgust, turn off; **me repatean los enchufados** I can't stand people who pull strings

repatriación *nf* repatriation

repatriado, -a 1 *pp de* **repatriar**
2 *adj* repatriated
3 *nm,f* repatriate

repatriar [32] *vt* to repatriate

repecho *nm* short steep slope; **a r.** uphill

repelar *Méx* **1** *vt (exasperar)* to exasperate, irritate
2 *vi (rezongar, refunfuñar)* to grumble

repelencia *nf (rechazo)* repulsion

repelente *adj* repulsive, repellent, revolting; *Fam* **niño r.** little know-all

repeler *vt* (**a**) *(rechazar)* to repel, repulse (**b**) *(repugnar)* to disgust; **me repelen los hipócritas** I loathe hypocrites

repeluzno *nm Fam* shiver; **me da r.** it gives me the shivers

repente *nm Fam (movimiento brusco)* sudden movement, start; *(arrebato)* fit, outburst; *(improvisación)* improvisation; **de r.** suddenly, all of a sudden; **un r. de ira** a fit of anger

repentinamente *adv* suddenly

repentino, -a *adj* sudden

repera *nf Fam* **ser la r.** *(gracioso)* to be a scream; *(genial)* to be really cool; *(el colmo)* to be the absolute limit

repercusión *nm* repercussion

repercutir *vi* (**a**) *(resonar)* to resound, echo, reverberate (**b**) *(rebotar)* to rebound (**c**) *Fig* **r. en** to have repercussions on, affect

repertorio *nm* (**a**) *Teat* repertoire, repertory (**b**) *(compilación)* list, index

repesca *nf Fam* second chance; *(examen)* resit; **hacer un examen de r.** to resit an exam

repescar [59] *vt Fam* to give a second chance to; **r. a algn** *(en examen)* to allow sb to resit an exam

repetición *nf* (**a**) *(de acción, dicho)* repetition; *Ftb* **r. de la jugada** action replay (**b**) *(reloj)* repeater (**c**) *Jur* action for recovery (**d**) **arma de r.** repeater, repeating firearm

repetidamente *adv* repeatedly

repetido, -a 1 *pp de* repetir
  2 *adj* repeated; **repetidas veces** repeatedly, countless times

repetidor, -a 1 *adj* repeating; *Educ Fam* **alumno r.** = student who is repeating a year; *Rad TV* **estación repetidora** relay station
  2 *nm Rad TV* relay, booster station; **r. de televisión** television relay
  3 *nm,f Fam Educ* = student who is repeating a year

repetir [47] **1** *vt* to repeat, do again; **no es necesario que me lo repitas** you needn't tell me again
  2 *vi* (**a**) *(volver a servirse)* to have a second helping; **¿quién quiere r. de paella?** who would like some more paella? (**b**) *(venir a la boca)* to repeat; **el pepino repite** cucumber repeats (on you) (**c**) *Educ* to repeat a year
  3 **repetirse** *vpr* (**a**) *(persona)* to repeat oneself (**b**) *(acontecimientos)* to recur; **¡que se repita!** encore!; **¡(y) que no se repita!** (and) don't let it happen again!

repetitivo, -a *adj* repetitive

repicar [59] **1** *vt* (**a**) *(partir a trozos pequeños)* to break up into bits o pieces (**b**) *(las campanas)* to ring
  2 *vi (campanas)* to peal, ring out
  3 **repicarse** *vpr (jactarse)* to boast

repintar 1 *vt (casa, habitación)* to repaint
  2 **repintarse** *vpr (con cosméticos)* to put on layers of make-up

repipi *adj Fam* **niño r.** little know-all

repique *nm (de campanas)* peal, ringing

repiquetear *vt & vi* (**a**) *(repicar)* to peal joyfully; **las campanas repiquetean** the bells are ringing out (**b**) *(tamborilear)* to beat, tap

repiqueteo *nm* (**a**) *(de campanas)* pealing (**b**) *(de tambor)* beating, tapping

repisa *nf* shelf, ledge; **r. de chimenea** mantelpiece

replantar *vt (parque)* to replant; *(planta) (en jardín, huerto)* to transplant; *(en maceta)* to repot

replanteamiento *nm* restatement, reconsideration

replantear 1 *vt (asunto)* to restate, reconsider
  2 **replantearse** *vpr* to reconsider, rethink; **tendrás que replanteártelo todo** you'll have to think it all over again

replegarse [43] *vpr Mil* to fall back, retreat

repleto, -a *adj* full, full up, jam-packed; **r. de** packed with, crammed with; **r. de gente** packed (with people)

réplica *nf* (**a**) *(contestación)* answer, reply; *(objeción)* retort; **el derecho de r.** the right of reply (**b**) *(copia)* replica

replicar [59] **1** *vt (objetar)* to reply, retort
  2 *vi* (**a**) *(poner objeciones)* to argue, answer back; **los niños no replican** little boys don't answer back (**b**) *Jur* to answer

replicón, -ona (**a**) *adj Fam* argumentative, cheeky, bold (**b**) *nm,f* argumentative person

repliegue *nm* (**a**) *(pliegue)* fold, crease; *Fig* recess (**b**) *Mil* withdrawal, retreat

repoblación *nf* repopulation ❑ **r. forestal** reafforestation

repoblar [63] *vt* to repopulate; *(bosque)* to reforest, *Br* reafforest

repollo *nm* cabbage

reponer [50] **1** *vt* (**a**) *(devolver)* to put back, replace, restore (**b**) *Teat (obra)* to put on again; *Cin (película)* to rerun; *TV (programa)* to repeat

  2 **reponerse** *vpr (de susto, enfermedad etc)* to recover, recuperate; **r. de** to recover from, get over

reportaje *nm* (**a**) *Prensa Rad* report; *(noticias)* article, news item; **r. gráfico** illustrated feature (**b**) *Cin TV (documental)* documentary

reportar¹ 1 *vt* (**a**) *(alcanzar)* to bring; **esta relación le reportará muchas ventajas** this relationship will do him a lot of good (**b**) *(refrenar)* to restrain, check
  2 **reportarse** *vpr* to restrain oneself, hold back

reportar² *vt Andes CAm Méx Ven (informar)* to report

reporte *nm Am* report

reportear *Chile Méx* **1** *vt* to report on, cover
  2 *vi* to work as a reporter

reportero, -a *nm,f* reporter ❑ **r. gráfico** press photographer

reposabrazos *nm inv* armrest

reposacabezas *nm inv* headrest

reposado, -a 1 *pp de* reposar
  2 *adj* quiet, peaceful, calm

reposamuñecas *nf* wrist rest

reposapiés *nm inv* footrest

reposar 1 *vt (la cabeza, los pies)* to rest (**en** on)
  2 *vi* (**a**) *(descansar)* to rest, take a rest; *Culin* **deje r. la pasta** leave the dough to stand (**b**) *(enterrar)* to lie, rest, be buried
  3 **reposarse** *vpr (líquido)* to settle

reposición *nf* (**a**) *(restitución)* restoration; *(cambio)* replacement (**b**) *Teat* revival; *Cin* rerun, reshowing; *TV* repeat

repositorio *nm* repository

reposo *nm* rest; **en r.** *(person)* at rest; *Culin* standing

repostar *vt (provisiones)* to stock up on; *Av (combustible)* to refuel; *Aut (gasolina)* to fill up with

repostería *nf* (**a**) *(pastas)* cakes *pl*; *(chocolate, caramelos)* confectionery (**b**) *(tienda) (de pasteles)* cake o pastry shop; *(de chocolate etc)* confectioner's (shop)

repostero, -a 1 *nm,f (de pasteles)* pastrycook; *(de chocolate etc)* confectioner
  2 *nm Andes (armario)* larder, pantry

reprender *vt* to reprimand, scold

reprensión *nf* reprimand, scolding

represa *nf* dam

represalia *nf (gen pl)* reprisals *pl*, retaliation; **tomar represalias** to take reprisals

representación *nf* (**a**) *(símbolo, imagen, ejemplo)* representation; *Com* **tiene una r. de una casa de medias italiana** he represents an Italian hosiery firm (**b**) *Teat* performance

representante 1 *adj* representative
  2 *nmf* (**a**) *(delegado)* representative (**b**) *Teat (hombre)* actor; *(mujer)* actress

representar 1 *vt* (**a**) *(reproducir)* to represent, depict, portray; **el cuadro de la entrada representa el paso por el Mar Rojo** the picture in the hall depicts the crossing of the Red Sea (**b**) *(hacer presente)* to state, express (**c**) *(equivaler)* to represent, stand for; **¿qué representa?** what does it stand for?; **representa muchas horas de trabajo** it has involved many hours of work (**d**) *(importar)* to mean; **representa mucho para mí** it means a lot to me (**e**) *Com (compañía, cliente)* to represent (**f**) *(aparentar)* to appear to be; **una mujer que no representaba más de treinta** a woman who didn't look more than thirty (**g**) *Teat (obra)* to perform; *(actor)* to act
  2 **representarse** *vpr* to imagine, picture

representatividad *nf* representativeness

representativo, -a *adj* representative

represión *nf* repression; **r. sexual** sexual repression

represivo, -a *adj* repressive

represor, -a 1 *adj* repressive
2 *nm,f* oppressor

reprimenda *nf* reprimand

reprimido, -a 1 *pp de* **reprimir**
2 *adj* repressed
3 *nm,f (persona)* repressed person

reprimir *vt* to repress; **r. una pasión** to quench a passion

reprise *nf Aut* acceleration

reprobable *adj* reproachable, reprehensible

reprobación *nf* reprobation, reproof

reprobador, -a *adj* reproachful, reproving

reprobar [63] *vt* **(a)** *(desaprobar) (cosa)* to condemn; *(persona)* to reproach, reprove **(b)** *Am (estudiante, examen)* to fail

réprobo, -a *adj & nm,f* reprobate

reprochable *adj* reproachable

reprochar *vt* to reproach; **r. algo a algn** to reproach sb for sth

reproche *nm* reproach, criticism

reproducción *nf* reproduction; **derechos de r.** copyright; **éste no es el original, es sólo una r.** this isn't the original, it's just a reproduction

reproducir [18] **1** *vt* to reproduce
2 reproducirse *vpr* **(a)** *(repetirse)* to recur, happen again **(b)** *(engendrar)* to reproduce, breed

reproductor, -a 1 *adj (órgano)* reproductive; *(animal)* breeding; **un aparato r. de DVD** a DVD player
2 *nm,f* breeder

reprografía *nf* reprographics *sing*

reptar *vi* to crawl, slither

reptil *nm Zool* reptile

república *nf* republic □ *Fig Pey* **r. bananera** banana republic; **R. Centroafricana** Central African Republic; **R. Checa** Czech Republic

republicanismo *nm* republicanism

republicano, -a *adj & nm,f* republican

repudiar *vt* to repudiate

repudio *nm* repudiation

repuesto, -a 1 *pp de* **reponer**
2 *adj (enfermo)* recovered
3 *nm* **(a)** *(recambio)* spare part, spare; *Aut* **rueda de r.** spare wheel **(b)** *(provisión)* stock

repugnancia *nf* disgust

repugnante *adj* repulsive, disgusting, revolting

repugnar *vi* to disgust, revolt; **me repugna la coliflor** I find cauliflower disgusting

repujado, -a 1 *pp de* **repujar**
2 *adj* embossed, repoussé

repujar *vt* to emboss

repulsa *nf* **(a)** *(rechazo)* rebuff; *Fig* condemnation **(b)** *(reprimenda)* reprimand

repulsión *nf* repulsion, repugnance

repulsivo, -a *adj* repulsive, revolting

repuntar 1 *vi (lluvia, enfermedad)* to (begin to) make itself felt, show the first signs
2 *vt Chile (animales)* to round up

reputación *nf* reputation

reputado, -a 1 *pp de* **reputar**
2 *adj* reputed, reputable

reputar *vt* to consider, deem

requebrar [3] *vt (lisonjear)* to court; *(adular)* to flatter, pay compliments to

requemado, -a 1 *pp de* **requemar**
2 *adj* scorched, burnt

requemar 1 *vt* to scorch, burn; **plantas requemadas por el sol** plants scorched by the sun
2 requemarse *vpr* **(a)** *(quemarse)* to scorch **(b)** *(enfadarse)* to burn with anger

requerimiento *nm* **(a)** *(súplica)* request; **a r. de algn** at sb's request **(b)** *Jur (intimación)* injunction **(c)** *Jur (aviso)* summons *sing*

requerir [62] *vt* **(a)** *(necesitar)* to require; **esto requiere gran destreza** this requires a lot of skill; *Tex* **'no requiere plancha'** 'non-iron' **(b)** *(con autoridad)* to demand, call for; **el ministro requirió su presencia** the minister summoned him **(c)** *(solicitar)* to request **(d)** *Jur (avisar)* to summon **(e)** *(persuadir)* to persuade; *Literario* **r. de amores** to court, woo

requesón *nm* cottage cheese

requete- *pref Fam* really, very, incredibly; **requetebueno** really good, smashing; **requetemoderno** ultra-modern

requeté *nm Hist Mil* Carlist soldier; **los requetés** the Carlist forces

requiebro *nm* flirtatious remark

réquiem *(pl* **réquiems)** *nm Rel Mús* requiem

requintar *vt CAm Col Méx (apretar mucho)* to tighten

requisa *nf* **(a)** *(inspección)* inspection **(b)** *Mil (embargo)* requisition

requisar *vt* **(a)** *Mil* to requisition **(b)** *Fam (apropiarse)* to grab, swipe

requisito *nm* requirement, requisite; **cumplir todos los requisitos** to fulfil all the requirements; **r. previo** prerequisite

requisitoria *nf Jur* requisition, demand

res *nf* beast, animal; *(cabeza de ganado)* head *inv* (of cattle); **r. lanar** sheep *inv*

resabido, -a *adj Pey* pretentious, pedantic

resabio *nm* **(a)** *(mal sabor)* unpleasant *o* bad aftertaste **(b)** *(vicio)* bad habit

resaca *nf* **(a)** *(después de beber)* hangover; **tener r.** to have a hangover **(b)** *Náut* undertow, undercurrent

resalado, -a *adj Fam (vivo)* lively; *(gracioso)* charming, attractive

resaltador *nm Col RP* highlighter

resaltar *vi* **(a)** *(sobresalir)* to project, jut out **(b)** *Fig* to stand out; **hacer r.** to emphasize, stress, underline

resalte *nm,* **resalto** *nm (saliente)* ledge

resarcir [72] *vt* to compensate, indemnify

resbaladizo, -a *adj* **(a)** *(superficie)* slippery **(b)** *Fig* slippery, tricky

resbalar *vi* **(a)** *(deslizarse)* to slide; *(gotas, lágrimas)* to trickle (down); **r. en** *o* **sobre el hielo** to slide *o* slip on the ice **(b)** *(involuntariamente)* to slip; *Aut* to skid **(c)** *Fig (desliz)* to slip up, make a slip

resbalón *nm* slip; **dar un r.** to slip, slide; *Fig* to slip up

resbaloso, -a *adj* slippery

rescatador, -a *nm,f* rescuer

rescatar *vt* **(a)** *(liberar)* to rescue, save **(b)** *Mil (ciudad)* to recapture **(c)** *(recuperar) (objeto)* to recover; *(tiempo)* to make up for

rescate *nm* **(a)** *(salvamento)* rescue; **equipo de r.** rescue team **(b)** *(recuperación)* recovery, recapture **(c)** *(suma)* ransom; **exigir r. por algn** to hold sb to ransom

rescindible *adj (contrato)* cancellable, rescindable

rescindir *vt* to rescind, annul, cancel; **r. el contrato** to cancel the contract

rescisión *nf* rescission, annulment, cancellation

rescoldo *nm* **(a)** *(brasa)* embers *pl* **(b)** *Fig (recelo)* lingering doubt

resecar [59] **1** *vt* **(a)** *(piel)* to dry out **(b)** *(tierra)* to parch
2 resecarse *vpr* **(a)** *(piel)* to dry out **(b)** *(tierra)* to become parched

reseco, -a *adj* **(a)** *(piel, garganta, pan)* very dry **(b)** *(tierra)* parched **(c)** *(flaco)* very thin, skinny

resentido, -a 1 *pp de* **resentirse**
2 *adj (ofendido)* resentful; *(amargado)* bitter; **estar r.** to have a chip on one's shoulder; **estar r. por algo** to be resentful of sth, resent sth
3 *nm,f* resentful person

resentimiento *nm (rencor)* resentment; *(amargura)* bitterness

resentirse [62] *vpr* **(a) r. de** to suffer from, feel the effects of; **aún me resiento de la espalda** I still have trouble with my back **(b)** *(debilitarse)* to be weakened **(c)** *Fig* to become resentful, feel resentment; *(amargarse)* to feel bitter; *(ofenderse)* to feel offended; *(enfadarse)* to get annoyed; **r. por algo** to take offence at sth

reseña *nf* **(a)** *Lit* review; *Prensa* write-up **(b)** *(descripción)* brief description; *(narración breve)* account **(c)** *Mil* review

reseñar *vt* **(a)** *Lit* to review **(b)** *(describir)* to describe; *(acontecimiento)* to give an account of

reserva 1 *nf* **(a)** *(plazas, entradas)* reservation, booking; **'r. de habitaciones'** 'room reservation' **(b)** *(provisión)* reserve; *(existencias)* stock; **reservas de carbón** coal reserves *o* stocks □ *Fin* **r. de divisas** foreign currency reserves *pl* **(c)** *Mil* reserve, reserves *pl* **(d)** *(cautela)* reservation **(e)** *(recato, secreto)* reserve, discretion; **con la mayor r.** in the strictest confidence; **guardar** *o* **tener algo en r.** to keep sth in reserve; **sin reserva(s)** without reservation; **tener reservas sobre algo** to have reservations about sth **(f)** *(vino)* vintage; **un vino de r.** a vintage wine **(g)** *(terreno)* reservation; **r. de indios** Indian reservation **(h)** *(de animales)* reserve □ **r. natural** nature reserve
2 *nmf Dep (sustituto)* reserve, substitute

reservado, -a 1 *pp de* **reservar**
2 *adj* **(a)** *(habitaciones, plazas)* reserved, booked **(b)** *(persona, carácter)* reserved, quiet; *(frío)* distant **(c)** *(asunto)* confidential
3 *nm (de restaurante etc)* private room; *Ferroc* reserved compartment

reservar 1 *vt* **(a)** *(plazas, billetes)* to reserve, book **(b)** *(guardar)* to keep, save **(c)** *(ocultar)* to withhold, keep to oneself
2 reservarse *vpr* **(a)** *(conservarse)* to save oneself **(para** for); **se reserva para la carrera** she's saving herself for the race **(b)** *(guardar para sí)* to withhold; **r. la opinión** to withhold one's opinion, keep one's opinion to oneself

reservista *nmf Mil* reservist

resfriado, -a 1 *pp de* **resfriarse**
2 *adj Med* with a cold; **estar r.** to have a cold; **estoy muy r.** I have a bad *o* heavy cold
3 *nm Med (catarro)* cold; *(de poca importancia)* chill; **coger un r.** to catch (a) cold

resfriarse [32] *vpr Med* to catch (a) cold

resfrío *nm Andes RP Med* cold

resguardar 1 *vt* **(a)** *(proteger)* to protect, shelter **(de** from) **(b)** *(salvaguardar)* to safeguard **(de** against)
2 resguardarse *vpr* **(a)** *(protegerse)* to protect oneself **(b)** *(salvaguardarse)* to safeguard oneself

resguardo *nm* **(a)** *(protección)* protection, shelter **(b)** *(garantía)* safeguard, guarantee **(c)** *(recibo)* receipt, pay-in slip; *(de talonario)* counterfoil, stub; *(vale)* voucher

residencia *nf* **(a)** *(permanencia)* residence; **permiso de r.** residence permit; **tener la r. en** to reside in **(b)** *(lugar)* residence □ **hotel r.** residential hotel; **r. de ancianos** old people's home; *Univ* **r. de estudiantes** *Br* hall of residence, *US* dormitory

residencial *adj* residential

residente 1 *adj* resident; **no r.** non-resident; **médico r.** *Br* house officer, *US* intern
2 *nmf* resident

residir *vi* **(a)** *(vivir)* to reside, live, dwell **(en** in) **(b)** *Fig* to lie **(en** in)

residual *adj* residual; **aguas residuales** sewage *sing*

residuo *nm* **(a)** *Quím* residue **(b)** **residuos** *(material inservible)* waste *sing*, refuse *sing*; **r. radiactivos** radioactive waste *sing*

resignación *nf* resignation, acquiescence

resignadamente *adv* resignedly

resignar 1 *vt* to resign, relinquish
2 resignarse *vpr* to resign oneself **(a** to)

resina *nf* resin

resinoso, -a *adj* resinous

resistencia *nf* **(a)** *(oposición)* resistance; *Pol* **la R.** the Resistance; **oponer r.** to resist; **r. pasiva** passive resistance **(b)** *(aguante, fuerza)* endurance, stamina; *(fortaleza)* strength; **prueba de r.** endurance test **(c)** *Elec* resistance

resistente *adj* **(a)** *(bacteria)* resistant **(a** to); **r. al fuego** fire-resistant **(b)** *(fuerte)* strong, tough, hardy

resistir 1 *vi* **(a)** *(gen)* to resist **(b)** *(soportar)* to hold (out); **¿resistirá este nudo?** will this knot hold? **(c)** *(durar)* to last; **este edificio resiste** this building has stood the test of time
2 *vt* **(a)** *(soportar)* to resist, tolerate; **no lo puedo r. más** I can't stand it any longer; **no puedo r. la tentación** I can't resist temptation **(b)** *(sostener peso etc)* to bear, withstand
3 resistirse *vpr* **(a)** *(forcejear)* to resist; *(oponerse)* to put up resistance **(b)** *(costar esfuerzo)* to struggle; *Fam* **se le resisten las matemáticas** she's having a hard time with maths, maths isn't her strongest subject **(c)** *(negarse)* to refuse; **me resisto a creerlo** I refuse to believe it, I find it hard to believe

resol *nm* glare (of the sun)

resollar [63] *vi* *(respirar)* to breathe heavily; *(con silbido)* to wheeze; *(de cansancio)* to puff and pant; *Fig* **sin r.** without a word

resolución *nf* **(a)** *(de un problema)* solving; *(solución)* solution **(b)** *(decisión)* resolution, decision; **r. fatal** death wish; **r. judicial** court decision; **tomar una r.** to pass a resolution **(c)** *Inform (de imagen)* resolution

resolver [41] *(pp* **resuelto)** **1** *vt* **(a)** *(solucionar)* to solve, resolve; *(asunto)* to settle **(b)** *(decidir)* to resolve, decide; **resolví quedarme** I decided to stay **(c)** *Fís* to dissolve
2 resolverse *vpr* **(a)** *(solucionarse)* to be solved; *(resultar)* to work out **(b)** *(decidirse)* to resolve, decide, make up one's mind **(a** to) **(c)** *(acabar)* to end (up) **(en** in); **todo se resolvió en un altercado** it all ended in a quarrel

resonancia *nf* **(a)** *(repercusión)* resonance; *(eco)* echo □ *Med* **r. magnética** magnetic resonance; **caja de r.** sounding board **(b)** *Fig (notoriedad)* importance; *(consecuencias)* repercussions *pl*; **tener r.** to cause a stir

resonante *adj* resounding; *Fig* important

resonar [63] *vi* *(retumbar)* to resound; *(cristal, metales)* to ring; *(tener eco)* to echo

resoplar *vi* *(respirar)* to breathe heavily; *(de cansancio)* to puff and pant

resoplido *nm* (**a**) *(resollido)* heavy breathing; *(silbido)* wheeze; *(de cansancio)* pant (**b**) *(por enfado)* snort

resorte *nm* (**a**) *(muelle)* spring (**b**) *Fig* means *pl*; **conocer todos los resortes de algo** to know all the ins and outs of sth

respaldar 1 *vt Fig* to support, back (up)
 2 respaldarse *vpr (recostarse)* to lean back (**en** on)

respaldo *nm* (**a**) *(de silla, papel)* back (**b**) *Fig (apoyo)* support, backing

respectar *v* to concern, regard; **por lo que a mí respecta** as far as I'm concerned

respectivamente *adv* respectively

respectivo, -a *adj* respective; **en lo r. a** with regard to, regarding

respecto *nm* proportion, relation; **al r., a este r.** in this respect; **con r. a, a r., al r. de** with regard to; **r. a mí** as for me, as far as I am concerned

respetabilidad *nf* respectability

respetable 1 *adj* (**a**) *(digno)* respectable; **un r. señor de Sanlúcar** a highly respected gentleman from Sanlúcar (**b**) *(considerable)* respectable
 2 *nm Teat Fam* **el r.** the audience

respetar 1 *vt* (**a**) *(venerar, apreciar)* to respect; **hacerse r. de todos** to command everyone's respect (**b**) *Aut* **r. la derecha** to yield to traffic coming from the right
 2 respetarse *vpr* to have self-respect

respeto *nm* (**a**) *(gen)* respect; **falta de r.** lack of respect; **por r. a** out of consideration for (**b**) *(miedo)* fear; **esta oscuridad me inspira r.** this darkness scares me a bit (**c**) **respetos** *Fml* respects; **presentar sus r. a algn** to pay one's respects to sb

respetuoso, -a *adj* respectful

respingar [38] *vi* (**a**) *(caballo)* to shy (**b**) *Fam (falda etc)* to curl up

respingo *nm* (**a**) *(sacudida)* start, jump (**b**) *Fig (enfado)* huff

respingón, -ona *adj (nariz)* snub, upturned

respiración *nf* (**a**) *(acción)* breathing, respiration □ **r. artificial** artificial respiration; **r. boca a boca** mouth-to-mouth resuscitation, the kiss of life (**b**) *(aliento)* breath; **perder la r.** to lose one's breath; **sin r.** breathless; *Fig* **que corta la r.** breathtaking (**c**) *(ventilación)* ventilation

respiradero *nm* (**a**) *Téc* air vent (**b**) *Fig (descanso)* respite

respirador *nm* **r. (artificial)** *(máquina)* respirator, ventilator

respirar 1 *vi* (**a**) *(aire)* to breathe; **r. mal** to breathe with difficulty, gasp; *Fig* **habla sin r.** he talks nonstop (**b**) *Fig* to relieve; **déjame r., ¿vale?** give me a break, will you?; **no poder r. (de trabajo)** to be up to one's eyes in work; **¡por fin respiro!** well, that's a relief!
 2 *vt (absorber)* to breathe (in), inhale; **r. gases tóxicos** to inhale toxic fumes; *Fig* **r. felicidad** to ooze happiness

respiratorio, -a *adj* respiratory; **aparato r.** respiratory system

respiro *nm* (**a**) *(resuello)* breathing (**b**) *(descanso)* breather, break; *(prórroga)* respite; *Fig* **no dar r.** to give no peace o no respite

resplandecer [46] *vi* (*sol*) to shine; *(metal)* to gleam; *(relucir)* to glitter; *(fuego)* to glow; *Fig* **Natalia resplandecía por su belleza** Natalia was radiantly o dazzlingly beautiful

resplandeciente *adj* (**a**) *(brillante)* shining; *(metales)* gleaming; *(reluciente)* glittering; *(fuego)* glowing (**b**) *(esplendoroso)* resplendent, radiant

resplandor *nm* (**a**) *(brillo)* brightness; *(muy intenso)* brilliance; *(de fuego)* glow, blaze (**b**) *(esplendor)* splendour; *US* splendor; *(brillantez)* radiance

responder 1 *vt* to answer; **respondió que sí** she said yes
 2 *vi* (**a**) *(contestar)* **r. a una carta** to reply to a letter; **r. al teléfono** to answer the phone (**b**) *(reaccionar)* to respond; *Med* **r. a un tratamiento** to respond to a course of treatment (**c**) *(corresponder)* to answer; **responde al nombre de Ramón** he goes by the name of Ramón; **r. a una descripción** to fit a description; **r. a una necesidad** to answer o meet a need (**d**) *(rendir)* to produce (**e**) *(avalar)* to guarantee; **r. de algn** to be responsible for sb; **r. por algn** to vouch for sb, act as a guarantor for sb

respondón, -ona *adj Fam* argumentative, cheeky

responsabilidad *nf* responsibility; **cargar con la r. de algo** to take responsibility for sth □ *Jur* **r. civil** civil liability; **r. limitada** limited liability; **r. penal** criminal liability

responsabilizar [14] **1** *vt* to make o hold responsible (**de** for)
 2 responsabilizarse *vpr* to assume o claim responsibility (**de** for)

responsable *adj* responsible; **Andrés es un chico muy r.** Andrés is a very responsible boy; **hacerse r. de algo** to assume responsibility for sth; **la persona r.** *(en trabajo etc)* the person in charge; *(en crimen, robo)* the perpetrator

responso *nm* (**a**) *Rel* prayer for the dead (**b**) *Fam (reprimenda)* ticking-off

responsorio *nm Rel* responsorial psalm

respuesta *nf (gen)* answer, reply; *(reacción)* response; **en r. a** in response to

resquebrajadura *nf* crack

resquebrajarse *vpr* to crack

resquemor *nm (resentimiento)* resentment, ill feeling

resquicio *nm* (**a**) *(abertura)* crack, chink (**b**) *Fig* glimmer; **un r. de esperanza** a glimmer of hope (**c**) *(ocasión)* chance; *(oportunidad)* opportunity; *(posibilidad)* possibility, chance

resta *nf Mat* subtraction

restablecer [46] **1** *vt* to re-establish; **r. el orden** to restore order
 2 restablecerse *vpr* (**a**) *(reinstaurarse)* to be re-established; *(orden etc)* to be restored (**b**) *Med* to recover

restablecimiento *nm* (**a**) *(reinstauración)* re-establishment; *(orden etc)* restoration (**b**) *Med* recovery

restallar *vi* (**a**) *(látigo)* to crack (**b**) *(hacer ruido)* to crack

restallido *nm* crack

restante *adj* remaining; **lo r.** the rest, the remainder, what is left over

restañar *vt (flujo de sangre, herida)* to staunch

restar 1 *vt* (**a**) *Mat* to subtract, take away; **r. seis de diez** to subtract six from ten (**b**) *(quitar)* to reduce, lessen; **r. importancia a algo** to play sth down
 2 *vi (quedar)* to be left, remain; **en todo lo que resta de mes** in what's left of the month

restauración *nf* restoration

restaurador, -a 1 *adj* restoring
 2 *nm,f* restorer

restaurante *nm* restaurant; *Ferroc* **coche r.** restaurant o buffet car

restaurar *vt* (**a**) *(cuadro, edificio)* to restore (**b**) *(en un cargo)* to reinstate

restitución *nf* restitution

restituir [34] *vt (restablecer)* to restore; *(devolver)* to return, give back

resto *nm* (**a**) **el r.** *(lo que queda)* the rest; *Fam* **echar el r.** to give sth all one has got, go all out (**b**) *Mat* remainder (**c**) **restos** remains; *Culin* leftovers □ **r. mortales** mortal remains

restorán *nm RP* restaurant

restregar [43] *vt (frotar)* to rub hard; *(fregar)* to scrub

restricción *nf* restriction

restrictivo, -a *adj* restrictive

restringido, -a *adj* restricted, limited

restringir [24] **1** *vt* to restrict, limit, curb; **r. la libertad de** to restrict the freedom of
 2 restringirse *vpr* to restrict oneself, limit oneself

resucitar *vt* to resuscitate; *Fig (restablecer)* to revive

resuello *nm (acción)* breathing; *(aliento)* breath, gasp

resuelto, -a 1 *pp de* resolver
 2 *adj (decidido)* resolute, determined

resulta *nf* consequence; **de resultas de** as a result of

resultado *nm* result; *(consecuencia)* outcome; **como r.** as a result; **dar buen r.** to work, give results

resultante *adj* resultant, resulting

resultar 1 *vi* **(a)** *(salir)* to (turn out to) be; **toda la confusión resultó ser un malentendido** all the confusion turned out to be because of a misunderstanding; **r. en** *(dar como resultado)* to result in; **resultó ileso** he was uninjured; **intentaré convencerle pero no creo que resulte** I'll try to talk him round, but I don't think it will work **(b)** *(ser)* to be; **resulta sorprendente** it's surprising; **me resultó imposible terminar antes** I was unable to finish earlier; **me resulta muy simpática** I find her very nice; **resulta mejor comprar a granel** it's better to buy in bulk
 2 *v impersonal (suceder)* **al final resultó que tenía razón** in the end it turned out that she was right; **ahora va a r. que la culpa es mía** so now it's suddenly all going to be my fault; **resulta que ha tenido un accidente** it seems he's had an accident

resumen *nm* summary, briefing; **en r.** in short, to sum up

resumir 1 *vt (recapitular)* to summarize; *(concluir)* to sum up
 2 resumirse *vpr* **(a)** *(recapitularse)* to be summed up **(b)** *(venir a ser)* to be reduced to; **el examen se resume en cuatro preguntas tontas** the test boils down to a few silly questions

resurgimiento *nm* resurgence, reappearance

resurgir [24] *vi* **(a)** *(revivir)* to reappear **(b)** *(resucitar)* to resuscitate

resurrección *nf* resurrection; **Domingo de R.** Easter Sunday; *Rel* **la R.** the Resurrection

retablo *nm* altarpiece, reredos *sing*

retacear *vt* **(a)** *(recortar)* to cut out **(b)** *RP (escatimar)* to stint

retaco *nm Fam* short person, shorty, squirt

retador, -a *adj* challenging

retaguardia *nf Mil* rearguard; **ir a la r.** to bring up the rear

retahíla *nf* series *sing*, string; *Irón* **me citó una r. de autores desconocidos** he reeled off the names of a string of little-known authors

retal *nm (desperdicio)* remnant; *(pedazo)* scrap

retama *nf Bot* broom

retamal *nm Bot* broom patch, broom thicket

retar *vt* **(a)** *(desafiar)* to challenge; **r. a duelo** to challenge to a duel **(b)** *RP (reñir)* to tell off **(c)** *Chile (insultar)* to insult, abuse

retardado, -a 1 *pp de* retardar
 2 *adj* delayed, retarded; **dispositivo de efecto r.** delayed-action device

retardar 1 *vt (detener)* to slow down; *(retrasar)* to delay
 2 retardarse *vpr* to be delayed

retardo *nm* delay

retazo *nm* **(a)** *(retal)* remnant; *(pedazo)* scrap **(b)** *(fragmento)* fragment, piece, snippet

retén *nm* **(a)** *(de tropas etc)* reserves *pl*, reinforcements *pl* **(b)** *(previsión)* stock, store

retención *nf (gen)* retention; *Fin* withholding ❑ **r. de haberes** stoppages *pl*; **r. de tráfico** (traffic) hold-up, traffic jam; **r. fiscal** tax

retener [65] **1** *vt* **(a)** *(conservar)* to retain; *(cosa prestada)* to keep back, hold back; **sólo hay que r. las ideas más importantes** one is just meant to take in the main idea **(b)** *Fin (descontar)* to deduct, withhold **(c)** *(detener)* to detain; *(arrestar)* to arrest
 2 retenerse *vpr* to restrain oneself, hold back

retentiva *nf* retentiveness, memory

reticencia *nf* **(a)** *(reserva)* reticence, reserve **(b)** *(retintín)* innuendo, insinuation; **lo dijo con cierta r.** she said it in a rather sarcastic tone

reticente *adj* **(a)** *(reservado)* reticent, reserved **(b)** *(con retintín)* insinuating

retícula *nf*, **retículo** *nm Ópt* reticle

retina *nf Anat* retina

retintín *nm* **(a)** *(tintineo)* ringing; *(ruido)* tinkling **(b)** *(tono sarcástico)* innuendo, sarcastic tone

retinto, -a *adj (color)* dark chestnut

retirada *nf Mil* retreat, withdrawal; **batirse en r.** to beat a retreat

retirado, -a 1 *pp de* retirar
 2 *adj* **(a)** *(alejado)* remote; *(tranquilo)* secluded **(b)** *(jubilado)* retired
 3 *nm,f* retired person, *US* retiree

retirar 1 *vt* **(a)** *(apartar, alejar)* to take away, remove; **le retiraron el carnet de conducir** he had his driving licence taken away; **retira la silla** move your chair back; **r. dinero del banco** to withdraw money from the bank; **r. lo dicho** to take back what one has said **(b)** *(jubilar)* to retire
 2 retirarse *vpr* **(a)** *Mil* to retreat, withdraw **(b)** *(apartarse)* to withdraw, draw back, move back; **no se retire** hold the line, please, don't hang up; **puede r.** you may leave; **r. a su cuarto** to retire to one's bedroom; **retírate de la ventana** come *o* move away from the window **(c)** *(jubilarse)* to retire

retiro *nm* **(a)** *(jubilación)* retirement **(b)** *(pensión)* pension; **cobrar el r.** to receive one's pension **(c)** *(lugar tranquilo)* retreat **(d)** *Rel* **r. (espiritual)** retreat

reto *nm* challenge; **aceptar un r.** to accept a challenge; **lanzar un r. a algn** to challenge sb

retobado, -a *adj* **(a)** *Méx (obstinado)* stubborn, obstinate **(b)** *Méx RP (indómito)* wild, unruly

retobarse *vpr RP* to get angry *o* irritated

retobo *nm* **(a)** *Col Hond (desecho)* refuse **(b)** *Chile Perú (arpillera)* sackcloth

retocado *nm Inform* **r. de imagen** image retouching

retocar [59] *vt* to retouch; *(fotografía etc)* to touch up; *(perfeccionar)* to put the finishing touches to

retomar *vt* to take up again

retoñar *vi* **(a)** *Bot (rebrotar)* to shoot, sprout **(b)** *Fig* to reappear

retoño *nm* **(a)** *Bot (rebrote)* shoot, sprout **(b)** *Fig (niño)* kid

retoque *nm* retouching, touching up; **dar los últimos retoques a** to put the finishing touches to

retorcer [15] **1** *vt* **(a)** *(cuerda, hilo)* to twist; *(ropa)* to wring (out); *Fam* **te voy a r. el pescuezo** I'm going to wring your neck **(b)** *Fig (argumento)* to twist; *(tergiversar)* to distort
 2 retorcerse *vpr* **(a)** *(doblarse)* to twist, become twisted **(b)** *(persona)* **r. de dolor** to writhe in pain; **r. de risa** to

double up with laughter, split one's sides laughing

retorcido, -a 1 *pp de* **retorcer**

2 *adj Fig* twisted; **mente retorcida** warped mind

retorcimiento *nm* (**a**) *(torsión)* twisting (**b**) *Fig* twistedness

retórica *nf Lit* rhetoric

retórico, -a 1 *adj* rhetorical

2 *nm,f* rhetorician

retornable *adj* returnable; **'envase no r.'** 'non-returnable bottle'

retornar 1 *vt (devolver)* to return, give back

2 *vi (volver)* to return, come back, go back

retorno *nm* (**a**) *(trueque)* return (**b**) *(recompensa)* reward

retorta *nf Quím* retort

retortero *nm Fam* **andar al r.** *(estar ocupado)* to be up to one's ears; *(ansioso)* to be climbing the walls; *(enamorado)* to be head over heels; **llevar** *o* **traer a algn al r.** *(tenerlo dominado)* to have sb under one's thumb; *(hacerlo trabajar)* to push sb around

retortijón *nm (dolor)* stomach cramp

retozar [14] *vi* to frolic, romp

retozo *nm* frolic

retozón, -ona *adj* frolicsome, playful

retracción *nf* retraction

retractable *adj* retractable

retractación *nf* retraction, withdrawal; **r. pública** public retraction

retractar 1 *vt* to retract, revoke, withdraw

2 retractarse *vpr* to retract, take back; **me retracto de lo que dije** I take back what I said

retráctil *adj (uña, garra)* retractile; *(tren de aterrizaje)* retractable

retraer [66] **1** *vt* (**a**) *(volver a traer)* to bring back *o* again (**b**) *(disuadir)* to dissuade (**c**) *(echar en cara)* to reproach; **r. algo a algn** to reproach sb for sth

2 retraerse *vpr* (**a**) *(retirarse)* to withdraw; *(por miedo)* to shy away; **r. de la política** to give up politics (**b**) *(refugiarse)* to take refuge

retraído, -a 1 *pp de* **retraer**

2 *adj* (**a**) *(tímido)* shy, reserved (**b**) *(solitario)* solitary; *(recluido)* secluded

retraimiento *nm* (**a**) *(timidez)* shyness, reserve, retiring nature (**b**) *(soledad)* solitude; *(reclusión)* seclusion

retransmisión *nf Rad TV* broadcast, transmission ◻ **r. en diferido** repeat broadcast; **r. en directo** live broadcast

retransmisor *nm Téc* transmitter

retransmitir *vt* (**a**) *(mensaje)* to relay (**b**) *Rad TV* to broadcast; **r. en diferido** to broadcast a recording of; **r. en directo** to broadcast live

retrasado, -a 1 *pp de* **retrasar**

2 *adj* (**a**) *(tren)* late; *(reloj)* slow (**b**) *(persona)* behind; **estar r. en matemáticas** to be behind in maths; **ir r. en los pagos** to be in arrears; **tengo trabajo r.** I'm behind in my work (**c**) *(país)* backward, underdeveloped (**d**) *Med (mental)* retarded, backward

3 *nm,f* **r. (mental)** mentally retarded person

retrasar 1 *vt* (**a**) *(retardar)* to slow down, retard (**b**) *(atrasar)* to delay, put off, postpone (**c**) *(reloj)* to put back

2 *vi* to be late, be behind time; *(reloj)* to be slow

3 retrasarse *vpr* (**a**) *(llegar tarde)* to be late, arrive late, be delayed; *(reloj)* to be slow; **me retrasó el tráfico** the traffic held me up; **¿por qué te has retrasado tanto?** what kept you? (**b**) *(en los estudios)* to fall behind

retraso *nm* (**a**) *(demora)* delay; **el tren llega con r.** the train is late; **llevamos una hora de r.** we are an hour behind schedule; **vamos con r.** we're running late (**b**) *(subdesarrollo)* backwardness, underdevelopment ◻ *Med* **r. mental** mental deficiency, mental retardation

retratar 1 *vt* (**a**) *Arte* to paint a portrait of; *Fot* to photograph, take a photograph of (**b**) *Fig (describir)* to describe, portray, depict

2 retratarse *vpr* (**a**) *Arte* to have one's portrait painted; *Fot* to have one's photograph taken (**b**) *Fam (pagar)* to pay up, cough up

retratista *nmf Arte* portrait painter *o* artist; *Fot* photographer

retrato *nm* (**a**) *Arte* portrait; *Fot* photograph; *Fig* **es el vivo r. de su padre** he is the spitting image of his father ◻ **r. robot** Identikit® picture, *Br* Photofit® picture (**b**) *(descripción)* description, portrayal, depiction

retreparse *vpr (recostarse)* to lean back; *(ponerse cómodo)* to lounge back

retreta *nf Mil* retreat; **tocar r.** to sound the retreat

retrete *nm* lavatory, toilet

retribución *nf (pago)* pay, payment; *(recompensa)* reward, remuneration

retribuir [34] *vt* (**a**) *(pagar)* to pay; *(recompensar)* to reward, remunerate (**b**) *Am (favor)* to return, repay

retributivo, -a *adj* **la política retributiva** pay policy; **un premio r.** a cash prize

retro *adj inv Fam (retrógrado)* reactionary; *(antiguo)* old-fashioned; **la moda r.** the old-fashioned look

retroacción *nf* retroaction

retroactividad *nf (de ley)* retroactivity; *(del pago)* backdating

retroactivo, -a *adj (ley)* retroactive; *(pago)* backdated; **con efecto r.** retroactively

retroalimentación *nf* feedback

retroceder *vi* (**a**) *(recular)* to go back, move back, back away, recede; **hacer r. a algn** to force sb back (**b**) *(echarse atrás)* to back down

retroceso *nm* (**a**) *(movimiento)* backward movement, retirement (**b**) *Med* aggravation, deterioration, worsening (**c**) *Econ* recession (**d**) *(de un arma)* recoil

retrocohete *nm Astronáut* retrorocket

retrógrado, -a 1 *adj* (**a**) *(que retrocede)* retrograde (**b**) *Fig Pol (reaccionario)* reactionary

2 *nm,f (reaccionario)* reactionary

retropropulsión *nf Av* jet propulsion

retroproyector *nm* overhead projector

retrospección *nf* retrospection

retrospectivo, -a *adj & nf* retrospective

retrotraer [66] **1** *vt (relato)* to set in the past; **una historia que nos retrotrae a ...** a story which takes us back to ...

2 retrotraerse *vpr (al pasado)* to cast one's mind back, go back

retrovisor *nm Aut* rear-view mirror

retruécano *nm* pun, play on words

retuerzo *indic pres véase* **retorcer**

retumbante *adj* resounding; *Fig* ostentatious, pretentious

retumbar *vi* (**a**) *(resonar)* to resound, echo (**b**) *(tronar)* to thunder, boom

reuma *nm,* **reúma** *nm Med* rheumatism

reumático, -a *adj & nm,f Med* rheumatic

reumatismo *nm Med* rheumatism

reumatología *nf* rheumatology

reumatólogo, -a *nm,f* rheumatologist

reunificación *nf* reunification

reunificar [59] **1** *vt* to reunify
   2 reunificarse *vpr* to reunify

reunión *nf*(**a**) *(de gente)* meeting, gathering; **asistir a una r.** to attend a meeting; **celebrar una r.** to hold a meeting ❏ *Pol* **r. en la cumbre** summit meeting (**b**) *(de datos, objetos)* collection, gathering

reunir 1 *vt* (**a**) *(congregar)* to assemble, gather together; **r. a toda la familia** to get all the family together (**b**) *(recoger)* to gather (together); *(dinero)* to raise (**c**) *(coleccionar)* to collect (**d**) *(cualidades)* to have, possess; **r. todos los requisitos** to fulfil all the requirements
   2 reunirse *vpr* to meet, gather, get together; **r. con algn** to meet sb

reválida *nf Educ Antes* final examination

revalidación *nf* ratification, confirmation

revalidar *vt* (**a**) *Esp (en deportes)* to successfully defend (**b**) *Am (estudios, diploma)* to validate

revalorización *nf (aumento de valor)* appreciation; *(de moneda)* revaluation

revalorizar [14] **1** *vt (aumentar el valor de)* to increase the value of; *(moneda)* to revalue
   2 revalorizarse *vpr (aumentar de valor)* to appreciate; *(moneda)* to revalue

revancha *nf*(**a**) *(venganza)* revenge; **tomarse la r.** to take revenge (**b**) *Naipes* return game; *Dep* return match

revanchismo *nm* vengefulness, vindictiveness

revanchista 1 *adj* vengeful, vindictive
   2 *nmf* person bent on revenge

revelación *nf* revelation

revelado, -a 1 *pp de* revelar
   2 *nm Fot* developing

revelador, -a 1 *adj* revealing
   2 *nm Fot* developer

revelar *vt* (**a**) *(dar a conocer)* to reveal, disclose; **r. un secreto** to reveal a secret (**b**) *Fot (película)* to develop

revendedor, -a *nm,f* (**a**) *(gen)* seller; *(detallista)* retailer (**b**) *Cin Teat (de entradas)* ticket tout, scalper

revender *vt* (**a**) *(gen)* to resell; *(al por menor)* to retail (**b**) *Cin Teat (entradas)* to tout

revenirse [69] *vpr* (**a**) *(ponerse correoso)* to go soggy (**b**) *(avinagrarse)* to turn sour

reventa *nf*(**a**) *(gen)* resale; *(al por menor)* retail (**b**) *Cin Teat (de entradas)* touting

reventar [3] **1** *vt* (**a**) *(hacer estallar)* to burst, explode; *(neumático)* to puncture, burst (**b**) *(romper)* to break, smash (**c**) *(arruinar)* to ruin, spoil (**d**) *Fig (agotar)* to exhaust, tire out (**e**) *Fam (fastidiar)* to annoy, bother; **le revienta pedir favores** he hates asking for favours (**f**) *Fam (asamblea, celebración)* to disturb, break up
   2 *vi* (**a**) *(estallar)* to burst, explode; **r. de orgullo** to be bursting with pride; **r. de ganas de hacer algo** to be dying to do sth; **reventaba de rabia** he was furious (**b**) *Fam (morir)* to peg out, snuff it
   3 reventarse *vpr* (**a**) *(estallar)* to burst, explode (**b**) *Fam (cansarse)* to tire oneself out

reventón 1 *adj Bot* **clavel r.** large carnation
   2 *nm* (**a**) *(estallido)* burst, explosion (**b**) *(de neumático)* blowout, *Br* puncture, *US* flat (**c**) *Arg Chile Min* outcrop

reverberación *nf* reverberation, reflection

reverberar *vi* to reverberate, reflect

reverbero *nm* (**a**) *(reverberación)* reverberation (**b**) *CAm Cuba Ecuad (cocinilla)* cooking stove

reverdecer [46] *vi* (**a**) *(planta)* to grow green again (**b**) *Fig (revivir)* to revive, come to life again

reverencia *nf* (**a**) *(respeto)* reverence; *Rel* **Su R.** (Your)

Reverence (**b**) *(inclinación)* bow, curtsy; **hacer una r.** to bow, curtsy

reverencial *adj* reverential

reverenciar *vt* to revere, venerate

reverendo, -a *adj & nm,f* reverend

reverente *adj* reverent

reversibilidad *nf* reversibility

reversible *adj* reversible

reversión *nf* (**a**) *(devolución)* reversion (**b**) *(cambio total)* reversal

reverso *nm* reverse, back; *Fig* **el r. de la medalla** the other side of the coin

reverter [64] *vi* to overflow

revertir [62] *vi* (**a**) *(volver)* to revert, return, go back; *Tel* **conferencia a cobro revertido** *Br* reverse-charge call, *US* collect call (**b**) *Jur* to revert (**c**) *(resultar)* to result (**en** in); **r. en beneficio de** to be to the advantage of; **r. en perjuicio de** to be to the detriment of

revés *nm* (**a**) *(reverso)* reverse, back, wrong side, inside; **al o del r.** *(al contrario)* the other way round; *(la parte interior en el exterior)* inside out; *(boca abajo)* upside down; *(la parte de detrás delante)* back to front; **al r. de lo que dicen** contrary to what they say (**b**) *(golpe)* backhander; *(bofetada)* slap; *Ten* backhand (stroke) (**c**) *Fig (contrariedad)* setback, reverse; **los reveses de la vida** life's misfortunes; **reveses de fortuna** setbacks, blows of fate

revestimiento *nm Téc* covering, coating

revestir [47] **1** *vt* (**a**) *(recubrir)* to cover (**de** with), coat (**de** with), line (**de** with) (**b**) *(disfrazar)* to conceal, disguise (**c**) *Fig (tomar)* to take on, acquire; **la herida no reviste importancia** the wound is not serious
   2 revestirse *vpr (virtud, actitud)* to arm oneself (**de** with); **r. de paciencia** to arm oneself with patience, be patient

revisar *vt* (**a**) *(gen)* to revise, check, go through (**b**) *Fin (cuentas)* to check, audit (**c**) *(billetes)* to inspect (**d**) *Aut (coche)* to service, overhaul

revisión *nf* (**a**) *(gen)* revision, checking ❏ *Fin* **r. de cuentas** audit, auditing; *Med* **r. médica** checkup (**b**) *(de billetes)* inspection (**c**) *Aut (de coche)* service, overhaul

revisionismo *nm Pol* revisionism

revisionista *adj & nmf Pol* revisionist

revisor, -a *nm,f* ticket inspector

revista *nf* (**a**) *Prensa (publicación)* magazine, journal, review ❏ **r. del corazón** love story magazine; **r. de modas** fashion magazine; **r. juvenil** teenage magazine; **r. semanal** weekly review (**b**) *(inspección)* inspection; **pasar r. a** to inspect, review (**c**) *Teat* revue; **chica de r.** chorus girl

revistar *vt Mil* to inspect, review

revistero *nm* magazine rack

revitalizar [14] *vt* to revitalize

revival [rri'βaiβal] *nm* revival

revivificar [59] *vt* to revivify, revive

revivir 1 *vi* to revive, come to life again
   2 *vt* to revive, bring back to life

revocable *adj* revocable

revocar [59] *vt* (**a**) *Jur (derogar) (ley)* to revoke, repeal; *(orden)* to cancel, rescind (**b**) *Constr (enlucir)* to plaster, stucco; *(encalar)* to whitewash

revocatoria *nf Am* revocation

revolcar [67] **1** *vt* (**a**) *(derribar)* to knock down, knock over (**b**) *Fam (oponente)* to floor, defeat, crush (**c**) *Fam (examen)* to fail, flunk
   2 revolcarse *vpr* to roll about; **r. en el fango** to wallow in the mud; *Fig* **r. de risa** to split one's sides laughing

revolcón nm (a) Fam (revuelco) fall, tumble (b) Fam (suspenso) failure (c) Vulg (sexual) romp

revolear vi Méx RP to whirl around

revolotear vi to fly about, flutter about, hover

revoloteo nm fluttering, hovering

revoltijo nm, **revoltillo** nm (mezcla) mess, jumble; Fig (confusión) mess; Culin **r. de gambas** scrambled eggs pl with prawns

revoltoso, -a 1 adj (a) (travieso) mischievous, naughty (b) (rebelde) rebellious, unruly
2 nm,f (a) (travieso) mischievous child, handful (b) (rebelde) rebel (c) (alborotador) troublemaker

revolución nf (gen) revolution; Hist **la R. Francesa** the French Revolution; Téc **50 revoluciones por minuto** 50 revolutions per minute

revolucionar vt to revolutionize

revolucionario, -a adj & nm,f revolutionary

revolver [41] (pp **revuelto**) **1** vt (a) (mezclar) to mix; (ensalada) to toss; (líquido) to stir (b) (desordenar) to mess up, disturb; **r. la casa** to turn the house upside down (c) (producir náuseas) to upset; **me revuelve el estómago** it turns my stomach
2 revolverse vpr (a) (agitarse) to roll; (en la cama) to toss and turn (b) (volverse) to turn round; Fig **r. contra algn** to turn against sb (c) (el tiempo) to turn stormy; (el mar) to become rough

revólver nm revolver

revoque nm Constr (a) (enlucido) plastering; (encalado) whitewashing (b) (material) plaster, stucco; (cal) whitewash

revuelco nm fall, tumble, wallow

revuelo nm (a) (revoloteo) fluttering (b) Fig (agitación) stir, commotion, upheaval; **provocar** o **armar un gran r.** to cause a great stir

revuelta nf (a) (insurrección) revolt, riot (b) (curva) bend, turn

revuelto, -a 1 pp de **revolver**
2 adj (a) (desordenado) jumbled, in a mess; (enredado) tangled; Culin **huevos revueltos** scrambled eggs (b) (líquido) cloudy (c) (tiempo) stormy, unsettled; (mar) rough (d) (revoltoso) agitated, annoyed; **la gente está revuelta** people are annoyed (e) (época) turbulent; **están los tiempos muy revueltos** these are turbulent times

revulsión nf Med revulsion

revulsivo, -a adj & nm Med revulsive

rey nm (a) (monarca) king; Fig **a cuerpo de r.** like a king; Fig **vivir a cuerpo de r.** to live like a king; Prov **a r. muerto, r. puesto** off with the old, on with the new Rel **(el día de) Reyes** Epiphany ❑ **el r. de la selva** the king of the jungle; Hist **el R. Sol** the Sun King; CAm Méx **r. de los zopilotes** king vulture; Hist **los Reyes Católicos** the Catholic Monarchs o Kings; **los Reyes de España** the King and Queen of Spain; Rel **los Reyes Magos** the Three Kings, the Three Wise Men (b) Ajedrez Naipes king; **el r. de corazones** the king of hearts

reyerta nf quarrel, brawl, dispute

reyezuelo nm (a) Pey (rey) kinglet (b) Orn ·r. (sencillo) goldcrest

rezagado, -a 1 pp de **rezagar**
2 adj **ir r.** to lag behind; **quedar r.** to be left behind
3 nm,f straggler, latecomer

rezagar [38] **1** vt (dejar atrás) to leave behind; (atrasar) to postpone, delay
2 rezagarse vpr to lag o fall behind

rezar [14] **1** vi (a) (orar) to pray; **r. a Dios** to pray to God (b) (decir) to say, read; **la placa rezaba 'Carbonilla S.A.'** the plate read 'Carbonilla S.A.' (c) (ser aplicable) **r. con** to

concern, apply to; **esto no reza conmigo** that does not concern me
2 vt Rel (oración, misa) to say

rezo nm (a) (acción) praying (b) (oración) prayer

rezongar [38] vi to grumble, moan

rezongón, -ona 1 adj grumbling, griping
2 nm,f grumbler, griper

rezumar 1 vt (líquido) to ooze, exude; Fig **su cara rezumaba alegría** her face exuded happiness
2 vi to ooze out, seep, leak
3 rezumarse vpr to ooze out, seep, leak

RFA nf Antes (abrev de **República Federal de Alemania**) GFR

Rh nf (abrev de **Rhesus**) Rh; **Rh positivo/negativo** rhesus positive/negative

ría nf estuary, river mouth; (en Galicia) ria

riachuelo nm brook, stream

Riad n Riyadh

riada nf flood, flooding

ribazo nm embankment, bank

ribera nf (a) (de río) bank; (del mar) seashore, shore (b) (zona) riverside, waterfront

ribereño, -a 1 adj riverside, waterfront
2 nm,f (persona) riverside o waterfront dweller

ribete nm (a) Cost edging, border (b) **ribetes** (indicios) touch sing, something sing; **tener r. de cómico** to be something of a comic

ribeteado, -a 1 pp de **ribetear**
2 adj Cost edged, bordered

ribetear vt Cost to edge, border

ribonucleico adj Biol **ácido r.** ribonucleic acid

ricacho, -a nm,f, **ricachón, -ona** nm,f Pey filthy o stinking rich person

ricamente adv (lujosamente) richly; Fam **tan r.** very well; **aquí estoy tan r.** I feel great here; **he dormido tan r.** I slept really well

ricino nm Bot castor-oil plant ❑ **aceite de r.** castor oil

rico, -a 1 adj (a) (adinerado) rich, wealthy; **hacerse r.** to get rich (b) (abundante) rich; **r. en proteínas** rich in protein (c) (delicioso) delicious; **esta sopa está muy rica** this soup is very good (d) (bonito) lovely, adorable; **¡qué niño más r.!** what a lovely child! (e) (excelente) rich, magnificent; **una tela muy rica** a sumptuous piece of material (f) (tierra) rich, fertile (g) Fam (tratamiento) pal, Br mate, US buddy; **mira r., haz lo que quieras** look mate, do what you want; **oye r., ¿tú me has tomado por imbécil?** look mush, what do you take me for?
2 nm,f rich person; **los ricos** the rich; **nuevo r.** nouveau riche

rictus nm inv grin; **r. de dolor** wince of pain

ricura nf Fam (a) (de comida) deliciousness (b) (tía buena) smashing girl; **¡qué r.!** what a girl!; **¡qué r. de niño!** what an adorable child! (c) (tratamiento) love; **¡oye, r.!** hey, gorgeous!

ridiculez nf (a) (cualidad) ridiculousness; (objeto) ridiculous thing; **¡qué r.!** how ridiculous! (b) (nimiedad), triviality

ridiculizar [14] vt to ridicule, deride

ridículo, -a 1 adj ridiculous, absurd
2 nm ridicule; **hacer el r., quedar en r.** to make a fool of oneself; **poner en r. a algn** to ridicule sb, make a fool of sb

riego nm Agr watering, irrigation ❑ **boca de r.** hydrant; **r. por aspersión** sprinkling; Anat **r. sanguíneo** blood circulation

riel nm Ferroc rail; **r. de cortina** curtain rail

rielar *vi Literario* to shimmer, gleam; **la luna en el mar riela** the sea shimmers in the moonlight

rienda *nf* rein; *Fig* restraint; *Fig* **aflojar las riendas** to let up, slacken; *Fig* **dar r. suelta a** to give free rein to; *Fig* **empuñar las riendas** to take the reins; *Fig* **llevar las riendas** to hold the reins, be in control

riesgo *nm* risk, danger; **a r. de, con r. de** at the risk of; **correr el r. de** to run the risk of

riesgoso, -a *adj Am* risky

rifa *nf* raffle; **me tocó en una r.** I won it in a raffle

rifar 1 *vt* to raffle (off)
2 rifarse *vpr Fam* **r. algo** to fight over sth

rifle *nm* rifle

Riga *n* Riga

rigidez *nf* (a) *(dureza)* rigidity, stiffness (b) *Fig (severidad)* strictness, inflexibility, firmness

rígido, -a *adj* (a) *(duro)* rigid, stiff (b) *Fig (severo)* strict, inflexible, firm

rigor *nm* (a) *(gen)* rigour, *US* rigor; *(severidad)* severity, strictness; **con r.** rigorously; **de r.** indispensable; **en r.** strictly speaking ❑ **r. mortis** rigor mortis (b) *(aspereza)* rigour, *US* rigor, harshness; **los rigores del invierno** the rigours of winter

rigurosamente *adv* (gen) rigorously; *(meticulosamente)* meticulously; *(severamente)* severely, strictly; **r. cierto** absolutely true

rigurosidad *nf* rigorousness, strictness

riguroso, -a *adj* (gen) rigorous; *(exacto)* exact; *(severo)* severe, strict

rijo *indic pres véase* **regir**

rijoso, -a *adj* (a) *(pendenciero)* quarrelsome (b) *(lujurioso)* lustful

rima *nf Lit* (a) *(gen)* rhyme ❑ **r. imperfecta** half rhyme; **r. perfecta** full rhyme (b) **rimas** *(poema)* poem *sing*

rimar *vt & vi* to rhyme (**con** with)

rimbombante *adj* (gen) ostentatious, showy; *(lenguaje)* pompous, pretentious

rímel *nm* mascara

Rin *n* **el R.** the Rhine

rin *nm Carib Col Méx (llanta)* wheel rim

rincón *nm* corner; *Fam* **vive en un r. de la costa** he lives in a remote spot on the coast

rinconada *nf* corner

rinconera *nf Mueb* corner table

ring [rrin] *(pl* **rings**) *nm Box* ring

ringlera *nf* row, line

ringorrango *nm Fam* (a) *(en la escritura)* rambling (b) *(adorno)* frill, adornment

rinoceronte *nm* rhinoceros

riña *nf* (a) *(pelea)* fight, brawl (b) *(discusión)* row, quarrel, argument

riñón *nm* (a) *Anat* kidney; *Fam Fig* **costar un r.** to cost an arm and a leg; *Fam Fig* **tener el r. bien forrado** *o* **cubierto** to be well off ❑ *Med* **r. artificial** kidney machine (b) *Culin* kidney; **riñones al jerez** kidneys in sherry sauce

riñonada *nf* (a) *(región lumbar)* lower back (b) *Culin (guiso)* kidney stew

riñonera *nf Br* bum bag, *US* fanny pack

río *nm* (a) *(gen)* river; **r. abajo** downstream; **r. arriba** upstream; *Fig* **pescar en r. revuelto** to fish in troubled waters; *Prov* **a r. revuelto, ganancia de pescadores** it's an ill wind that blows nobody any good (b) *Fig* stream; **r. de lágrimas** flood of tears

Río de Janeiro *n* Rio de Janeiro

Río de la Plata *nm* River Plate

rioja *nm* Rioja wine

riojano, -a 1 *adj* of *o* from La Rioja
2 *nm,f* person from La Rioja

rioplatense *adj* of *o* from the River Plate region

R.I.P [rrip] *(abrev de* **requiescat in pace**) RIP

ripiar *vt Carib Cul (destrozar)* to tear to pieces

ripio *nm* (a) *(residuo)* refuse, waste (b) *Constr* rubble, filling (c) *(palabras de relleno)* padding, waffle, verbiage; *Fam* **no perder r.** not to miss a trick (d) *Am (pavimento)* gravel

riqueza *nf* (a) *(cualidad)* richness, wealthiness (b) **riquezas** wealth *sing*, riches

risa *nf* laugh, laughter; **ataque de r.** fit of laughter; **es (cosa) de r.** it's laughable; **me da r.** it makes me laugh; **r. de conejo** forced smile; **tomarse algo a r.** to laugh sth off; *Fig* **morirse** *o* **mondarse** *o* **desternillarse** *o* **troncharse de r.** to die *o* fall about laughing; *Fam* **esta película es una r.** this film is a scream; *Fam* **mi hermano es una r.** my brother is a laugh; *Fam Fig* **tener algo muerto de r.** to have sth sitting; *Fam Fig* **tengo el coche muerto de r.** my car is just sitting there; *Vulg* **mearse de r.** to piss oneself laughing

risco *nm* crag, cliff

risible *adj* laughable

risita *nf* giggle, titter; *(risa falsa)* false laugh

risotada *nf* guffaw

ristra *nf* (a) *(sarta)* string ❑ **r. de ajos** string of garlic; **r. de cebollas** string of onions (b) *Fig* string, series *sing*; **una r. de mentiras** a pack *o* string of lies

ristre *nm* **en r.** at the ready; **máquina en r.** camera at the ready

risueño, -a *adj* (a) *(sonriente)* smiling; **cara risueña** smiling face (b) *(alegre)* cheerful (c) *(prometedor)* bright, promising; **un futuro r.** a bright future

Rita *n Fam* **¡cuéntaselo a R.!** pull the other one!; *Fam* **¡que lo haga R.!** let someone else do it!

rítmico, -a *adj* rhythmic, rhythmical

ritmo *nm* (a) *(gen)* rhythm (b) *(paso)* pace, rate, speed; **llevar un buen r. de trabajo** to work at a good pace

rito *nm* (a) *Rel* rite; **ritos funerarios** funeral rites (b) *(ritual)* ritual (c) *Chile (manta)* heavy poncho

ritual *adj & nm* ritual; **danza r.** ritual dance; *Fig* **ser de r.** to be customary

ritualismo *nm* ritualism

ritualista 1 *adj* ritualistic
2 *nmf* ritualist

rival *adj & nmf* rival

rivalidad *nf* rivalry

rivalizar [14] *vi* to compete

rivera *nf* brook, stream

rizado, -a 1 *pp de* **rizar**
2 *adj* (a) *(pelo)* curly (b) *(mar)* choppy
3 *nm* curling

rizador *nm* curling tongs *pl*, curling iron

rizar [14] **1** *vt* (a) *(pelo)* to curl; *(tela, papel)* to crease; **r. el rizo** *Av* to loop the loop; *Fig* to split hairs (b) *(mar)* to make choppy
2 rizarse *vpr (pelo)* to curl, go curly

rizo *nm* (a) *(de pelo)* curl (b) *(en el agua)* ripple (c) *Tex* terry velvet (d) *Av* loop

rizoma *nm Bot* rhizome

rizoso, -a *adj* naturally curly

RNE *nf (abrev de* **Radio Nacional de España**)

róbalo *nm*, **robalo** *nm (pez)* bass

robar vt (**a**) (objeto) to steal; (banco, persona) to rob; (casa) to break into, burgle; **le robaron la cartera** he had his wallet stolen; **r. un coche** to steal a car; Fig **en aquel supermercado te roban** they really rip you off in that supermarket; Fig **robarle el corazón a algn** to steal sb's heart (**b**) Naipes (carta) to draw

roble nm oak (tree); Fig **fuerte como un r.** as strong as an ox ❑ **r. albar** durmast oak, sessile oak; **r. americano** red oak; **r. cerris** o **turco** Turkey oak

robledal nm, **robledo** nm oak grove o wood

roblón nm rivet

robo nm (gen) robbery, theft; (en casa) burglary; **cometer un r.** to commit a robbery; Fig **estos precios son un r.** these prices are daylight robbery ❑ **r. a mano armada** armed robbery

robot (pl **robots**) nm robot ❑ **r. de cocina** food processor

robótica nf robotics sing

robotización nf automation

robotizar [14] vt to automate

robustecer [46] **1** vt to strengthen
2 robustecerse vpr to gain strength, grow stronger

robustecimiento nm strengthening

robustez nf robustness, strength, sturdiness

robusto, -a adj robust, strong, sturdy

roca nf rock; **cristal de r.** rock crystal; Fig **tener un corazón de r.** to have a heart of stone

rocalla nf pebbles pl, stone chippings pl

Rocallosas nfpl Am **las R.** the Rockies

rocambolesco, -a adj incredible, fantastic, farfetched

roce nm (**a**) (fricción) rubbing; (en la piel) chafing (**b**) (marca) (en la pared) scuff mark; (en la piel) chafe mark, graze (**c**) (contacto ligero) brush, light touch (**d**) Fam (trato entre personas) contact (**e**) Fam (discusión) friction; **ha tenido varios roces con su jefe** she has had a few disagreements with her boss

rochela nf Am din, racket

rociada nf (**a**) (rociadura) spraying, sprinkling (**b**) Fig shower, hail, stream; **una r. de balas** a hail of bullets (**c**) (rocío) dew

rociar [32] **1** vt (**a**) (salpicar) to spray, sprinkle (**b**) (esparcir) to scatter, strew; Fam **r. una comida con vino** to wash down a meal with wine
2 v impers **roció anoche** a dew fell last night

rocín nm (**a**) (caballo) nag, hack (**b**) Fam Fig (zoquete) blockhead, stupid fellow

rocío nm dew

rock nm inv Mús rock; **r. duro** hard rock; **r. and roll** rock and roll

rockero, -a Mús **1** adj rock; **música rockera** rock music
2 nm,f (cantante) rock singer; (músico) rock musician; (fan) rock fan

rococó adj & nm Arte rococo

Rocosas npl **las R.** the Rockies

rocoso, -a adj rocky, stony

roda nf Náut stem

rodada nf tyre o US tire mark

rodado, -a 1 pp de **rodar**
2 adj (**a**) (piedra) smooth, rounded; **canto r.** boulder; Fig **venir r.** to happen at just the right moment (**b**) (vehículo, transporte) on wheels, wheeled; **tráfico r.** road traffic, vehicular traffic (**c**) Fig (persona) experienced
3 nm RP (vehículo) vehicle

rodador nm Am (insecto) gnat

rodaja nf slice; **en rodajas** sliced

rodaje nm (**a**) Cin (filmación) filming, shooting (**b**) Aut running in; **en r.'** 'running in'

rodamiento nm Téc bearing ❑ **r. de bolas** ball bearing

Ródano n **el R.** the Rhone

rodante adj rolling

rodapié nm Br skirting board, US baseboard

rodar [63] **1** vt (**a**) Cin (película, escena) to film, shoot (**b**) Aut (coche) to run in
2 vi (**a**) (gen) to roll, turn; **el camión rodó por la pendiente** the lorry rolled down the hill; **rodó escaleras abajo** he fell down the stairs; Fig **echarlo todo a r.** (estropearlo) to spoil everything; (desistir) to give up (**b**) (rondar) to roam, wander, drift; **no me gusta tener mis papeles rodando por la casa** I don't like having my paperwork all over the house; **r. por el mundo** to roam the world (**c**) Aut to run; **es un coche que rueda bien** it's a car that runs well

Rodas n Rhodes

rodear 1 vt (**a**) (gen) to surround, encircle; **la policía rodeó el edificio** the police surrounded the building; **un bosque rodea la casa** the house is surrounded by a wood (**b**) Am (ganado) to round up
2 rodearse vpr to surround oneself (**de** with); **se rodea de todas las comodidades** he surrounds himself with all kinds of comforts

rodeo nm (**a**) (desvío) detour; **dar un r.** to make a detour (**b**) (al hablar) evasiveness; **andarse con rodeos** to beat about the bush; **no andarse con rodeos** to get straight to the point (**c**) (encierro de ganado) round-up; (espectáculo) rodeo

rodera nf track, tyre o US tire mark

rodete nm (para cargar cosas en la cabeza) (ring-shaped) pad

rodilla nf (**a**) Anat knee; **de rodillas** (arrodillado) kneeling; Fig (humildemente) on bended knees; **doblar** o **hincar la r.** (arrodillarse) to go down on one knee; Fig (humillarse) to humble oneself; **hincarse de rodillas** to kneel down, go down on one's knees (**b**) (trapo) cloth, floorcloth

rodillazo nm blow with the knee; **dar un r. a algn** to knee sb

rodillera nf (**a**) Cost knee patch (**b**) Dep knee pad

rodillo nm roller ❑ **r. de cocina** rolling pin

rododendro nm rhododendron

rodríguez nm inv Fam **estar** o **quedarse de r.** to be left at home while one's family is away on Br holiday o US vacation

roedor, -a adj & nm rodent

roedura nf (**a**) (acción) gnawing (**b**) (marca) gnaw mark

roer [57] vt (**a**) (hueso) to gnaw; (galleta) to nibble at (**b**) Fig to gnaw, nag, torment; **los remordimientos le roen la conciencia** feelings of guilt gnawed at his conscience; Fig **un hueso duro de r.** a hard nut to crack

rogar [16] vt (pedir) to request, ask; (implorar) to beg, implore, plead; **hacerse de r.** to play hard to get; **le rogó que se marchara** he asked her to leave; **'se ruega silencio'** 'silence please'
2 vi (rezar) to pray

rogativas nfpl Rel rogations

roído, -a 1 pp de **roer**
2 adj gnawed, eaten away

roigo indic pres véase **roer**

rojear vi to redden, turn red

rojez nf redness

rojizo, -a adj reddish

(precio) to cut, reduce; *(cantidad)* to make a reduction in; **r. 5.000 pesos** to make a reduction of 5,000 pesos **(c)** *(color)* to tone down, soften; *(intensidad)* to diminish **(d)** *(humillar)* to humiliate **(e)** *(de servicio)* to excuse, exempt **(de** from)
  2 rebajarse *vpr (humillarse)* to humble oneself; **r. a hacer algo** to stoop to doing sth, descend to doing sth; **r. ante algn** to bow before sb

rebaje *nm Mil* exemption

rebanada *nf* slice; **r. de pan** slice of bread

rebanar *vt* **(a)** *(hacer rebanadas)* to slice, cut into slices **(b)** *(cortar)* to cut *o* slice off

rebañar *vt* **(a)** *(comida)* to finish off; **r. el plato (con pan)** to wipe one's plate clean (with bread) **(b)** *Fig (apoderarse de)* to clean out

rebaño *nm* **(a)** *(de ovejas)* flock; *(de otros animales)* herd **(b)** *Rel* flock

rebasar 1 *vt* **(a)** *(exceder)* to exceed, go beyond, surpass; **r. los límites** to overstep the mark **(b)** *(corredor, vehículo)* to pass, overtake
  2 *vi CAm Méx (adelantar)* to overtake

rebatible *adj* refutable

rebatir *vt* to refute

rebato *nm* alarm; **tocar a r.** to sound the alarm

rebeca *nf (prenda)* cardigan

rebeco *nm Zool* chamois

rebelarse *vpr* to rebel, revolt; **r. contra el gobierno** to rebel against the government

rebelde 1 *adj* rebellious; *Fig* **una tos r.** a persistent cough
  2 *nmf* rebel

rebeldía *nf* **(a)** *(insurrección)* rebelliousness **(b)** *Jur* default; **declararse en r.** to default

rebelión *nf* rebellion, revolt

rebenque *nm RP* whip

reblandecer [46] **1** *vt* to soften
  2 reblandecerse *vpr* to soften, become soft

reblandecimiento *nm* softening; **r. cerebral** softening of the brain

rebobinado, -a 1 *pp de* **rebobinar**
  2 *adj* rewound
  3 *nm* rewinding

rebobinar *vt* to rewind

reborde *nm* edge, flange, rim

reborujar *vt Méx* to mix (up)

rebosante *adj* overflowing **(de** with), brimming **(de** with)

rebosar 1 *vi* **(a)** *(recipiente, líquido)* to overflow, brim over **(b)** *Fig* **r. de** to be overflowing *o* brimming with; **rebosaba de salud** she was glowing with health
  2 *vt (estar lleno de)* to be overflowing with; **rebosaba alegría** she was brimming with joy

rebotar 1 *vi* **(a)** *(pelota)* to bounce, rebound **(b)** *(bala)* to ricochet
  2 *vt* **(a)** *(clavo)* to clinch **(b)** *(ataque)* to repel
  3 rebotarse *vpr Fam (persona)* to get *Br* cheesed off *o US* pissed; **se rebota por nada** he gets angry very easily

rebote *nm* **(a)** *(de pelota)* bounce, rebound; **de r.** on the rebound; *Fig* **hacer algo de r.** to do sth on the rebound **(b)** *(de bala)* ricochet

rebozado, -a 1 *pp de* **rebozar**
  2 *adj Culin* coated in breadcrumbs *o* batter

rebozar [14] *vt Culin* to coat in breadcrumbs *o* batter

rebozo *nm* **(a)** *(prenda)* muffler, wrap, shawl **(b)** *Fig (disimulo)* **de r.** secretly, in secret; **sin r.** openly, frankly

rebrotar *vi Bot* to shoot, sprout

rebufo *nm* loud snort

rebullir *vi*, **rebullirse** *vpr* to stir, begin to move

rebuscado, -a 1 *pp de* **rebuscar**
  2 *adj* affected, recherché

rebuscamiento *nm* affectation

rebuscar [59] *vt* to search carefully for

rebuznar *vi* to bray

rebuzno *nm* braying, bray

recabar *vt* **(a)** *(pedir, solicitar)* to ask for, entreat; **r. información** to ask for information **(b)** *(conseguir)* to obtain, manage to get

recadero, -a *nm,f* messenger, errand boy *o* girl

recado *nm* **(a)** *(mandado)* errand; **hacer recados** to run errands **(b)** *(mensaje)* message; **dejar un r.** to leave a message **(c)** *CSur (montura)* saddle and trappings *pl* **(d)** *Nic RDom Culin* mincemeat filling

recaer [13] *vi* **(a)** *Med (enfermo)* to relapse; *Fig (en vicios, equivocaciones)* to backslide, relapse **(b)** *(corresponder)* to fall **(sobre** on); **la responsabilidad recae sobre ella** the responsibility falls on her

recaída *nf Med* relapse; *(en vicios, equivocaciones)* backslide, relapse; **sufrir una r.** to have a relapse

recalar *vi Náut* to sight land

recalcar [59] *vt Fig* to underline, stress, emphasize

recalcitrante *adj* recalcitrant

recalentamiento *nm* overheating

recalentar [3] *vt (comida)* to reheat, warm up; *(calentar demasiado)* to overheat

recamado *nm* embroidery

recamar *vt* to embroider

recámara *nf* **(a)** *(habitación)* dressing room; *CAm Col Méx (dormitorio)* bedroom **(b)** *(de arma)* chamber **(c)** *Fig (cautela)* reserve, caution

recambiar *vt* to change (over)

recambio *nm* **(a)** *(repuesto)* spare (part); **rueda de r.** spare wheel **(b)** *(de tinta)* refill

recapacitar *vi* to think; **recapacita sobre ello antes de decidir** think it over before you decide

recapitalización *nf* recapitalization

recapitulación *nf* recapitulation, summing-up, recap

recapitular *vt* to recapitulate, sum up, recap

recarga *nf* refill

recargable *adj* refillable, rechargeable

recargado, -a 1 *pp de* **recargar**
  2 *adj* **(a)** *(sobrecargado)* overloaded **(b)** *Fig (estilo)* overelaborate, exaggerated, affected

recargar [38] *vt* **(a)** *(volver a cargar)* to reload; *Elec (pila)* to recharge **(b)** *(sobrecargar)* to overload **(c)** *Fin (aumentar)* to increase **(d)** *(adornar con exceso)* to overelaborate, exaggerate

recargo *nm Fin* extra charge, surcharge

recatado, -a 1 *pp de* **recatar**
  2 *adj* **(a)** *(prudente)* prudent, cautious **(b)** *(modesto)* modest, decent

recatar 1 *vt* to hide, cover up
  2 recatarse *vpr* to be cautious, act discreetly; **sin r.** openly

recato *nm* **(a)** *(cautela)* caution, prudence; **sin r.** openly **(b)** *(pudor)* modesty

recauchutado, -a 1 *pp de* **recauchutar**
  2 *nm (de neumático)* retreading

recauchutar *vt (neumático)* to retread

recaudación *nf* **(a)** *(cobro)* collection; **r. de impuestos**

rojo, -a 1 *adj* (**a**) *(encarnado)* red; *Fin* **estar en números rojos** to be in the red; **Mar R.** Red Sea; **ponerse r.** *(gen)* to turn red; *(ruborizarse)* to blush; **r. de ira** red with anger (**b**) *(caliente)* red-hot (**c**) *Pol (comunista)* red, communist; *Hist (en la guerra civil española)* Republican

2 *nm (color)* red; **al r. vivo** *(caliente)* red-hot; *Fig (tenso)* very tense, very heated

3 *nm,f Pol (comunista)* red, communist; *Hist (en la guerra civil española)* Republican

rol *(pl* **roles**) *nm* (**a**) *(lista)* roll, list (**b**) *(papel)* role; **jugar un r.** to play a role

rolar *vi Chile Perú* to mix, socialize

rollizo, -a *adj* chubby, plump

rollo *nm* (**a**) *(cilindro)* roll ❑ **r. de papel higiénico** roll of toilet paper; *Culin* **r. de primavera** spring roll (**b**) *(de grasa)* roll, layer (**c**) *Fam (pesadez)* drag, bore, pain; **es el mismo r. de siempre** it's the same old story; **este libro es un r.** this book is a drag; **este tío es un r.** this guy is a pain in the neck; **un r. de película** a boring movie *o Br* film (**d**) *Esp Fam (asunto, historia)* affair; **no está en el r.** he's not one of us; **tiene un r. con Pedro** she's having a fling with Pedro (**e**) *Ven (rulo)* roller, curler (**f**) *RP Fam (de grasa)* spare *Br* tyre *o US* tire

ROM [rrom] *nf Inform (abrev de* **read-only memory**) ROM

Roma *n* Rome; *Fig* **revolver R. con Santiago** to move heaven and earth; *Prov* **cuando fueres a R. haz lo que vieres** when in Rome do as the Romans do; *Prov* **todos los caminos conducen a R.** all roads lead to Rome

romana *nf (balanza)* steelyard

romance 1 *adj Ling* Romance

2 *nm* (**a**) *(idioma)* Romance; *(español)* Spanish; *Fig* **hablar en r.** to speak plainly (**b**) *Lit* narrative poem, romance, ballad (**c**) *(aventura amorosa)* romance

romancear *vt Chile* to court, woo

romancero *nm Lit* collection of romances

románico, -a *adj & nm* (**a**) *Arte Arquit* Romanesque (**b**) *Ling* Romance

romano, -a *adj & nm,f* Roman

romanticismo *nm* romanticism

romántico, -a *adj & nm,f* romantic

romanza *nf Mús* romance

rombo *nm Geom* rhombus

romboide *nm* rhomboid

romeo *nm* sweetheart

romería *nf Rel* pilgrimage; *(excursión)* trip, excursion

romero, -a¹ *nm,f Rel* pilgrim

romero² *nm Bot* rosemary

romo, -a *adj* (**a**) *(sin punta)* blunt, dull (**b**) *(nariz)* snub

rompecabezas *nm inv* (**a**) *(juego)* (jigsaw) puzzle (**b**) *Fig (problema)* riddle, puzzle; **este caso es un r.** this case is a riddle

rompecorazones *nmf inv Fam* heartbreaker, heart-throb

rompehielos *nm inv Náut* icebreaker

rompehuelgas *nmf inv Am (persona)* scab, *Br* blackleg

rompeolas *nm inv* breakwater, jetty

romper *(pp* **roto**) **1** *vt* (**a**) *(gen)* to break; *(papel, tela)* to tear; *(vajilla, cristal)* to smash, shatter; *(pantalones)* to split; **r. las hojas de un libro** to tear *o* rip out the pages of a book; *Fig* **r. el hielo** to break the ice; *Fam* **r. la cabeza** *o* **crisma** to kill, clobber (**b**) *(relaciones)* to break off; *(contrato)* to break (**c**) *(cerca, límite)* to break through *o* down (**d**) *(gastar)* to wear out (**e**) *Mil* **r. el fuego** to open fire; **r. filas** to break ranks, fall out; **r. las hostilidades** to initiate hostilities (**f**) *(mar, aire)* to cleave

2 *vi* (**a**) *(olas, día)* to break (**b**) *(acabar)* to break (**con** with); **ha roto con su pasado** she broke with her past; **rompió con su novio** she broke it off with her boyfriend (**c**) *(empezar)* **r. a** to burst out; **rompió a llorar** he burst out crying; **r. en** to burst into; **rompió en llanto** she burst into tears

3 romperse *vpr* (**a**) *(gen)* to break; *(papel, tela)* to tear; **se le han roto las gafas** he's broken his glasses; **se me han roto las medias** I've torn my stockings; **se me han roto los vaqueros** my jeans have split; **se rompió por la mitad** it broke *o* split in half; *Fig* **r. la cabeza** to rack one's brains; *Fam (persona)* **de rompe y rasga** determined, resolute (**b**) *(desgastarse)* to wear out

rompible *adj* breakable

rompiente *nm* reef, shoal

rompimiento *nm (rotura)* breaking, breakage; *Fig (de relaciones)* breaking-off

ron *nm* rum

roncar [59] *vi* to snore

roncha *nf* (**a**) *Med (en la piel)* swelling, lump; *Fig* **levantar ronchas** to cause a stir (**b**) *(rodaja)* (round) slice

ronco, -a *adj* hoarse; **quedarse r.** to lose one's voice

ronda *nf* (**a**) *(patrulla)* round, beat, patrol; **hacer la r.** to do one's rounds (**b**) *Mús (conjunto)* group of strolling minstrels; **salir de r.** to go out and sing serenades (**c**) *(carretera) Br* ring road, *US* beltway; *(paseo)* avenue (**d**) *(serie)* round; **pagar una r.** to pay for a round of drinks (**e**) *Naipes* hand, round (**f**) *CSur (corro)* circle, ring

rondador *nm Andes (instrumento)* = type of panpipes

rondalla *nf* (**a**) *Mús* group of strolling minstrels (**b**) *(cuento)* tale, story

rondar 1 *vt* (**a**) *(vigilar)* to patrol, do the rounds of (**b**) *Pey (merodear)* to prowl around, hang about, haunt; **siempre ronda por aquí** he's always prowling around here (**c**) *(cortejar)* to woo, court (**d**) *(estar cerca)* to be about *o* approximately; **debe r. los sesenta** he must be about sixty; **me anda rondando un catarro** I'm getting a cold; **me ronda el sueño** I'm feeling sleepy

2 *vi* (**a**) *(vigilar)* to patrol (**b**) *(merodear)* to prowl around, roam around; **me gusta r. por las tiendas** I like wandering around the shops

rondón: de rondón *loc adv* unexpectedly, unannounced; **colarse de r.** to slip in unnoticed

ronero, -a *adj Cuba* rum; **la producción ronera** rum production

ronquear *vi* to be hoarse

ronquera *nf* hoarseness

ronquido *nm* snore, snoring

ronronear *vi* to purr

ronroneo *nm* purring

ronzal *nm* halter

ronzar [14] *vi* to crunch, munch

roña 1 *nf* (**a**) *(mugre)* filth, dirt (**b**) *(enfermedad de animal)* mange (**c**) *Fam (tacañería)* meanness, stinginess

2 *nmf Fam (tacaño)* scrooge, miser

roñería *nf* meanness, stinginess

roñica *Fam* **1** *adj* mean, stingy

2 *nmf* scrooge, miser

roñoso, -a 1 *adj* (**a**) *(mugriento)* filthy, dirty (**b**) *(animal)* mangy (**c**) *Fam (tacaño)* mean, stingy (**d**) *Carib Méx (ofendido)* resentful

2 *nm,f (tacaño)* scrooge, miser

ropa *nf* (**a**) *(gen)* clothes *pl*, clothing; **quítate la r.** take your clothes off; *Fig* **hay r. tendida** watch what you say; *Fig* **no tocar la r. a algn** not to touch a hair of sb's head; *Prov* **la**

r. sucia se lava en casa one should not wash one's dirty linen in public ❑ **r. blanca** (household) linen; *Cost* **r. hecha** ready-made clothes; **r. interior** underwear; **r. usada** second-hand *o* old clothes (**b**) *Culin* **r. vieja** = meat stew

ropaje *nm* robes *pl*, vestment

ropavejero, -a *nm,f* second-hand clothes dealer

ropero *nm* (**armario**) **r.** wardrobe, *US* (clothes) closet

roque *nm* (**a**) *Ajedrez* rook (**b**) *Fam* **quedarse r.** to fall fast asleep

roquero, -a *adj & nm,f véase* rockero, -a

rorro *nm Fam* baby

rosa 1 *adj inv* (*color*) pink; **clavel r.** pink carnation; **novela r.** romantic novel; *Fig* **verlo todo de color r.** to see everything through rose-tinted spectacles
  2 *nf* (**a**) *Bot* rose; *Fig* **fresco como una r.** as fresh as a daisy; *Fig* **no hay r. sin espinas** there's no rose without a thorn; *Prov* **la vida no es un lecho de rosas** life is not a bed of roses ❑ *Náut* **r. de los vientos** compass (rose); *Bot* **r. silvestre** dog rose (**b**) *Arquit* (*rosetón*) rose window
  3 *nm* (*color*) pink

rosáceo, -a *adj Br* rosy, rose-coloured, *US* rose-colored

rosado, -a 1 *adj* (**a**) (*de color rosa*) pink, rosy (**b**) (*vino*) rosé
  2 *nm* (*vino*) rosé

rosal *nm* rosebush

rosaleda *nf* rose garden

rosario *nm* (**a**) *Rel* rosary, beads *pl*; **rezar el r.** to say the rosary; *Fig* **acabar como el r. de la aurora** to come to an abrupt end, end badly (**b**) (*sarta*) string, series *sing*; **r. de improperios** string of insults

rosbif (*pl* **rosbifs**) *nm* roast beef

rosca *nf* (**a**) (*de tornillo*) thread; **r. de Arquímedes** Archimedes' screw; **tapón de r.** screw-on top; *Fig* **pasarse de r.** to go too far; *Fam* **hacer la r. a algn** to suck up to sb (**b**) (*anillo*) ring; (*espiral*) spiral, coil (**c**) *Culin* (*de pan*) = ring-shaped bread roll; *Méx* (*bizcocho*) sponge cake ❑ *Am* **r. de Reyes** = ring-shaped pastry eaten on 6th January (**d**) *Chile RP Fam* (*discusión*) argument; (*pelea*) fight, clash (**e**) *Chile* (*almohadilla*) pad

rosco *nm* = ring-shaped roll *o* pastry; *Esp Fam* **no comerse un r.** not to get off with anyone

roscón *nm* = ring-shaped bread roll ❑ **r. de Reyes** = ring-shaped pastry eaten on 6th January

rosedal *nm Am* rose garden

roseta *nf* (**a**) (*en las mejillas*) flush (**b**) (*de cintas*) rosette (**c**) (*de regadera*) rose, nozzle (**d**) **rosetas** (*de maíz*) popcorn *sing*

rosetón *nm Arquit* rose window

rosquete *nm Am* large doughnut

rosquilla *nf* = ring-shaped pastry; *Fam Fig* **venderse como rosquillas** to sell like hot cakes

rosticería *nf Méx Nic* grillroom, steak house

rostizar [14] *vt Méx* to spit-roast

rostro *nm* (**a**) (*cara*) face; *Fam* **echarle r.** to be daring *o* cheeky; *Fam* **tener mucho r.** to have a lot of nerve; *Fam* **¡vaya r.!** what a cheek! (**b**) (*pico de ave*) beak

rotación *nf* rotation ❑ *Agr* **r. de cultivos** crop rotation

rotar *vi* (**a**) (*girar*) to rotate, turn (**b**) (*alternar*) to rotate

rotativa *nf* rotary press

rotativo, -a 1 *adj* rotary, revolving
  2 *nm* newspaper

rotatorio, -a *adj* rotary, rotating, revolving

rotisería *nf CSur* delicatessen

roto, -a 1 *pp de* romper
  2 *adj* (**a**) (*gen*) broken; (*papel*) torn; (*gastado*) worn out; (**b**)

(*deshecho*) (*vida*) destroyed; **con el corazón r.** heart-broken (**c**) *Fam* (*exhausto*) shattered (**d**) *Chile Fam Pey* (*ordinario*) common; (*pobre*) penniless
  3 *nm,f Chile Fam* (**a**) (*tipo*) guy; (*mujer*) woman (**b**) *Pey* (*trabajador*) worker; (*persona ordinaria*) common person, *Br* pleb
  4 *nm* (*agujero*) hole, tear

rotonda *nf Arquit* rotunda

rotor *nm* rotor

rótula *nf* (**a**) *Anat* kneecap (**b**) *Téc* ball-and-socket joint

rotulación *nf* lettering

rotulador *nm* felt-tip pen ❑ **r. fluorescente** highlighter (pen)

rotular[1] *vt* to letter, label

rotular[2] *adj Anat* kneecap

rótulo *nm* (**a**) (*letrero*) sign, notice; **r. de neón** neon sign (**b**) (*titular*) title, heading

rotundidad *nf* firmness

rotundo, -a *adj* (**a**) (*terminante*) categorical; **éxito r.** resounding success; **una negativa rotunda** a flat refusal (**b**) (*frase*) well-rounded

rotura *nf* (**a**) (*ruptura*) breaking, breakage, break, crack; *Med* fracture (**b**) (*en un tejido*) tear, rip

roturación *nf Agr* ploughing, *US* plowing

roturadora *nf* plough, *US* plow

roturar *vt* to plough, *US* plow

roulotte [rru'lot] *nf Br* caravan, *US* trailer

royalty [rro'jalti] (*pl* **royalties**) *nm* royalty

rozadura *nf* scratch, chafe mark, abrasion

rozagante *adj Esp* (*satisfecho*) extremely pleased

rozamiento *nm* (*fricción*) rubbing; *Fís* friction

rozar [14] **1** *vt* (**a**) (*frotar*) to rub; (*suavemente*) to brush; **me roza el zapato en la parte de atrás** my shoe is rubbing my heel (**b**) (*pasar cerca de*) to skim, shave; **la bala lo pasó rozando** the bullet missed him by a hair's breadth (**c**) (*estar cerca de*) to border on; **roza los cuarenta** he's almost forty; **su talento roza lo divino** he is touched by genius (**d**) (*desgastar*) to wear out (**e**) *Agr* to clear
  2 *vi* **r. con** (*tocar*) to brush against; (*relacionarse con*) to touch on
  3 rozarse *vpr* (**a**) (*tocarse*) to touch (**b**) (*pasar cerca*) to brush past each other (**c**) (*rasguñarse*) to graze oneself (**con** on); **me rozé la mano con la pared** I grazed my hand on the wall (**d**) (*tener trato*) **rozarse con** to rub shoulders with

r.p.m. (*abrev de* **revoluciones por minuto**) rpm

RR HH (*abrev de* **recursos humanos**) HR

Rte. (*abrev de* **remite, remitente**) sender

RTVE *nf* (*abrev de* **RadioTelevisión Española**)

rúa *nf* street

Ruanda *n* Rwanda

ruandés, -esa *adj & nm,f* Rwandan

rubéola *nf Med* German measles *pl*, rubella

rubí (*pl* **rubíes** *o* **rubís**) *nm Min* ruby

rubia *nf* (*mujer*) blonde ❑ **r. oxigenada** peroxide blonde; **rubia** *Esp* **platino** *o Am* **platinada** platinum blonde

rubiales *nmf inv Esp Fam* (*hombre*) blond; (*mujer*) blonde

rubicundo, -a *adj* rosy, rubicund, reddish

rubio, -a 1 *adj* (*pelo, persona*) fair, blond, blonde; **tabaco r.** Virginia tobacco
  2 *nm* (**a**) (*hombre*) blond (**b**) (*pez*) red gurnard

rublo *nm* (*moneda*) rouble

rubor *nm* blush, flush

ruborizarse [14] *vpr* to blush, go red

ruboroso, -a *adj* blushing, bashful

rúbrica *nf* (**a**) *(trazo)* flourish *(added to a signature)* (**b**) *(título)* title, heading

rubricar [59] *vt* (**a**) *(firmar)* to sign with a flourish; **firmado y rubricado** signed and sealed (**b**) *(respaldar)* to endorse, ratify

rubro *nm Am Fin* item

ruco, -a *adj CAm* worn-out

ruda *nf Bot* rue

rudeza *nf* roughness, coarseness

rudimentario, -a *adj* rudimentary

rudimento *nm* rudiment

rudo, -a *adj* rough, coarse

rueca *nf* distaff

rueda *nf* (**a**) *(gen)* wheel; *Fig* **comulgar con ruedas de molino** to be very gullible; *Fam* **ir sobre ruedas** to go very smoothly ▫ *Andes* **r. de Chicago** *Br* big wheel, *US* Ferris wheel; **r. de la fortuna** *(de hechos)* wheel of fortune; *Méx (noria) Br* big wheel, *US* Ferris wheel; *Aut* **r. delantera** front wheel; *Téc* **r. dentada** cog, cogwheel; *Aut* **r. de recambio** spare wheel; *Chile Urug* **r. gigante** *Br* big wheel, *US* Ferris wheel; *Aut* **r. trasera** rear wheel (**b**) *(corro)* circle, ring ▫ **r. de prensa** press conference (**c**) *(rodaja)* round slice (**d**) *(turno)* round

ruedo *nm* (**a**) *Taur* bullring, arena; **dar la vuelta al r.** to walk round the bullring receiving applause; *Fig* **echarse al r.** to enter the fray (**b**) *(de falda)* hem (**c**) *(estera)* round mat

ruego *nm* request, petition; **'ruegos y preguntas'** 'any other business'

rufián *nm* (**a**) *(granuja)* villain, scoundrel (**b**) *(proxeneta)* pimp

rufianesca *nf* underworld

rufianesco, -a *adj* villainous

rugby *nm Dep* rugby

rugido *nm* (**a**) *(bramido)* roar, bellow; *(viento)* howl (**b**) **rugidos** *(de tripas)* rumbling *sing*

rugir [24] *vi* to roar, bellow; *(viento)* to howl

rugosidad *nf* (**a**) *(cualidad)* roughness (**b**) *(arruga) (de piel)* wrinkle; *(de tejido)* crinkle

rugoso, -a *adj* (**a**) *(áspero)* rough (**b**) *(con arrugas) (piel)* wrinkled; *(tejido)* crinkled

ruibarbo *nm Bot* rhubarb

ruido *nm (gen) & Tel* noise; *(sonido)* sound; *(jaleo)* din, row; *Fig* stir, commotion; **hacer** *o* **meter r.** to make a noise; *Fig* to cause a stir; *Fam Fig* **mucho r. y pocas nueces** much ado about nothing ▫ **r. ambiental** *o* **de fondo** background noise

ruidoso, -a *adj* (**a**) *(que hace ruido)* noisy, loud (**b**) *Fig (sensacional)* sensational

ruin *adj* (**a**) *(vil)* low, contemptible (**b**) *(tacaño)* mean (**c**) *Cuba (en celo) Br* on heat, *US* in heat

ruina *nf* (**a**) *(hundimiento)* ruin, collapse; **amenazar r.** to be about to collapse (**b**) *Fig* downfall, end, fall (**c**) **ruinas** *(de una construcción)* ruins

ruindad *nf* (**a**) *(vileza)* vileness, meanness (**b**) *(acto)* mean act, low trick

ruinoso, -a *adj* (**a**) *Fin* ruinous, disastrous (**b**) *(destartalado)* dilapidated, tumbledown

ruiseñor *nm Orn* nightingale

rular *vi Fam* to go, work; **esta tele no rula** this telly is bust

ruleta *nf* roulette ▫ **r. rusa** Russian roulette

rulo *nm* (**a**) *(rizo)* curl, ringlet (**b**) *(para rizar el pelo)* curler, roller (**c**) *Culin* rolling pin

rulot *(pl* **rulots** *o* **rulotes)** *nf Br* caravan, *US* trailer

ruma *nf Andes Ven* heap, pile

Rumanía *n* Rumania, Roumania

rumano, -a 1 *adj* Rumanian, Roumanian
2 *nm,f (persona)* Rumanian, Roumanian
3 *nm (idioma)* Rumanian, Roumanian

rumba *nf* (**a**) *Mús* rhumba, rumba (**b**) *Carib Perú (juerga)* party

rumbear *vi* (**a**) *(bailar)* to dance the rhumba *o* rumba (**b**) *Am (orientarse)* to get one's bearings (**c**) *Andes RP* **r. para** to be heading for (**d**) *Carib Perú Fam (andar de juerga)* to party

rumbo[1] *nm (dirección)* direction, course; **(con) r. a** bound for, heading for, in the direction of; **marcar el r.** to set course; **perder el r.** *(avión, barco)* to go off course; *Fig (persona)* to lose one's bearings; **poner r. a** to head for

rumbo[2] *nm Fam* (**a**) *(pompa)* pomp, show, lavish display (**b**) *(generosidad)* generosity, lavishness (**c**) *CAm (juerga)* binge

rumboso, -a *adj Fam* sumptuous, lavish

rumia *nf* rumination

rumiante *adj & nm* ruminant

rumiar 1 *vt* (**a**) *(mascar)* to chew (**b**) *Fig (pensar)* to ruminate, reflect on, chew over
2 *vi (mascar)* to ruminate, chew the cud

rumor *nm* (**a**) *(habladuría)* rumour, *US* rumor; **corre el r. de que ...** rumour has it that ... (**b**) *(murmullo)* murmur

rumorearse *v impers* to be rumoured, *US* be rumored; **se rumorea que ...** it is rumoured that ...

rumoroso, -a *adj (arroyo)* murmuring

runfla *nf Méx Fam* gang

runrún *nm* (**a**) *(ruido)* buzz, noise, murmur (**b**) *Fam (rumor)* rumour, *US* rumor

runruneo *nm* buzz, noise, murmur

rupestre *adj* rock; **pintura r.** cave painting

rupia *nf (moneda)* rupee

ruptura *nf (rotura)* breaking, breakage; *Fig (de relaciones)* breaking-off

rural *adj* rural, country; **finca r.** country estate

Rusia *n* Russia

ruso, -a 1 *adj* Russian
2 *nm,f (persona)* Russian
3 *nm (idioma)* Russian

rústica *nf* **en r.** *(encuadernación)* paperback

rústico, -a *adj* rustic, rural

ruta *nf* route, way, road; *Fig* **la r. del éxito** the road to success

rutilante *adj Literario* shining, sparkling, gleaming

rutilar *vi Literario* to shine, sparkle, gleam

rutina *nf* routine; **por r.** as a matter of course

rutinario, -a *adj* (**a**) *(habitual)* routine; **visita rutinaria** routine visit (**b**) *(persona)* unimaginative, pedestrian, dull

Rvda. *(abrev de* **Reverenda**) Rev, Revd

Rvdo. *(abrev de* **Reverendo**) Rev, Revd

S

S, s ['ese] *nf (la letra)* S, s

S *(abrev de* **Sur)** S

S., s. *(abrev de* **San** *o* **Santo)** St

s. **(a)** *(abrev de* **siglo)** c **(b)** *(abrev de* **siguiente)** next, following

s/ (a) *(abrev de* **suyo, -a)**; *véase* **suyo, -a (b)** *(abrev de* **su(s))**; *véase* **su**

S.A. (a) *(abrev de* **Sociedad Anónima)** *Br* ≃ PLC, *US* ≃ Inc **(b)** *(abrev de* **Su Alteza)** H.H.

sábado *nm* Saturday; *véase tamb* **viernes**

sabana *nf* savanna, savannah

sábana *nf* sheet; *Fam* **se me pegaron las sábanas** I overslept ◻ **s. encimera/bajera** top/bottom sheet

sabandija *nf* **(a)** *(animal)* bug, insect, creepy-crawly **(b)** *Fig (persona)* louse

sabañón *nm Med* chilblain

sabático, -a *adj* sabbatical

sabatino, -a *adj* Saturday, = relating to Saturday

sabedor, -a *adj* aware **(de** of), informed **(de** about)

sabelotodo *nmf inv* know-all

saber¹ *nm* knowledge

saber² [58] **1** *vt* **(a)** *(conocer)* to know; **hacer s.** to inform; **para que lo sepas** for your information; **que yo sepa** as far as I know; **¿se puede s. por qué?** may I ask why?; **vete tú a s.** goodness knows; **ya lo sabes todo** now you know all about it; **¡y yo qué sé!** how should I know!; *Fig* **a s.** namely; *Fig* **no sabe por dónde se anda** he hasn't got a clue; *Fig* **no s. dónde meterse** to feel embarrassed; *Fig* **s. más que Lepe** to be nobody's fool; *Fam* **el señor no sé cuántos** Mr so-and-so **(b)** *(tener habilidad)* to be able to, know how to; **¿sabes cocinar?** can you cook?, do you know how to cook?; **¿sabes hablar inglés?** can you speak English? **(c)** *(enterarse)* to learn, find out; **no lo supimos hasta ayer** we only found out yesterday; **¿qué sabes de Marisa?** have you heard from Marisa?

2 *vi* **(a)** *(tener sabor)* to taste **(a** of); **sabe bien** it tastes good; *Fam Fig* **le sabe mal que ...** he is upset *o* annoyed that ... **(b)** *Am (soler)* **s. hacer algo** to be wont to do sth

3 saberse *vpr* to know; **me lo sé todo** I know it all; **ya se sabe** you know how it is

sabido, -a 1 *pp de* **saber²**

2 *adj* known; **como es s.** as everyone knows; **es noticia sabida** it is a well-known fact; **s. es que ...** it is well known that ...

sabiduría *nf* **(a)** *(conocimientos)* knowledge, wisdom **(b)** *(prudencia)* wisdom

sabiendas: a sabiendas *loc adv* knowingly; **a s. de que ...** knowing full well that ...

sabihondo, -a *Fam* **1** *adj* pedantic

2 *nm,f (sabelotodo)* know-all; *(pedante)* pedant

sabio, -a 1 *adj* **(a)** *(con conocimientos)* learned, knowledgeable **(b)** *(prudente)* wise; *(sensato)* sensible

2 *nm,f* **(a)** *(instruido)* learned person, man/woman of learning **(b)** *(poseedor de la sabiduría)* sage, wise person

sabiondo, -a *adj Fam véase* **sabihondo, -a**

sablazo *nm (golpe)* blow with a sabre; *(herida)* sabre wound; *Fam Fig* **dar un s. a algn** to touch sb for money, scrounge some money off *o* from sb

sable *nm* sabre, *US* saber

sableador, -a *nm,f Fam* sponger, scrounger

sablear *vt* to touch for money, scrounge money off

sablista *nmf Fam* sponger, scrounger

sabor *nm* **(a)** *(gusto)* taste, flavour, *US* flavor; **con s. a limón** lemon-flavoured; **sin s.** tasteless **(b)** *Fig (impresión)* feeling; **dejar mal s. (de boca)** to leave a bad taste in one's mouth

saborear *vt* **(a)** *(degustar)* to taste **(b)** *Fig (apreciar)* to savour, *US* savor, relish

saboreo *nm* savouring, *US* savoring

sabotaje *nm* sabotage

saboteador, -a *nm,f* saboteur

sabotear *vt* to sabotage

sabré *indic fut véase* **saber²**

sabroso, -a *adj* **(a)** *(gustoso)* tasty; *(delicioso)* delicious **(b)** *(substancioso)* tidy, considerable **(c)** *(comentario) (gracioso)* juicy, tasty; *(malicioso)* mischievous

sabrosón, -ona *adj Carib Col Méx Fam* **(a)** *(gustoso)* tasty **(b)** *(grato)* pleasant, nice; *(entretenido)* entertaining **(c)** *(contagioso)* contagious **(d)** *(hermoso)* lovely, gorgeous

sabrosura *nf Carib Col Méx Fam* tastiness

sabueso *nm* **(a)** *(perro)* bloodhound **(b)** *Fig (persona)* sleuth

saca *nf* large sack ◻ **s. de correos** *Br* postbag, *US* mailbag

sacacorchos *nm inv* corkscrew

sacacuartos *nm inv Fam* money-waster

sacadineros *Fam* **1** *nm inv* money-waster; *(timo)* racket, swindle

2 *nmf inv (persona)* swindler, fiddler

sacamuelas *nmf inv Fam* dentist; *Fig* **hablar más que un s.** to be a chatterbox

sacapuntas *nm inv* pencil sharpener

sacar [59] **1** *vt* **(a)** *(gen)* to take *o* pull *o* get out; **s. a algn a bailar** to ask sb to dance; **s. brillo a algo** to polish sth, make sth shine; **s. dinero del banco** to withdraw money from the bank; **s. la lengua** to stick one's tongue out; **sacó**

un pañuelo del bolso she took a handkerchief from her bag; *Fig* **s. a algn de sí** to infuriate sb; *Fig* **s. adelante** *(hijos)* to give a good education to; *(negocio)* to help prosper; *Fig* **s. algo a relucir** to bring sth up (in conversation); *Fig* **s. faltas a algo** to find fault with sth; *Fig* **s. fuerzas de flaqueza** to draw strength from nowhere; *Fig* **sacarle los colores a algn** to make sb blush **(b)** *(obtener)* to get; *(premio)* to win; *(dinero)* to get, make; *(conclusiones)* to draw, reach; **¿qué notas has sacado?** what marks did you get?; **s. algo en claro** *o* **en limpio** to make sense of sth **(c)** *(extraer)* to obtain, extract; **s. provecho de algo** to benefit from sth **(d)** *(introducir)* *(nuevo producto)* to bring out; *(nueva moda)* to bring in **(e)** *(publicar)* to publish, bring out **(f)** *(hacer)* *(fotografía)* to take; *(fotocopia)* to make **(g)** *(comprar)* to get, buy; **s. un abono** to buy a season ticket

2 *vi Ten* to serve; *Ftb* to kick off

3 sacarse *vpr* **(a)** *(desvestirse)* to take off **(b)** *(hacerse)* to have taken; **s. una foto** to have a photograph taken

sacarina *nf Quím* saccharin

sacarosa *nf Quím* sucrose

sacerdocio *nm* priesthood

sacerdotal *adj* priestly

sacerdote *nm* priest; **sumo s.** high priest

sacerdotisa *nf* priestess

saciar 1 *vt (satisfacer) (hambre)* to satiate, sate; *(sed)* to quench; *(deseos)* to satisfy; *(ambiciones)* to fulfil, *US* fulfill

2 saciarse *vpr* to satiate oneself, be satiated; **comer/beber hasta s.** to eat/drink one's fill

saciedad *nf* satiation, satiety; **repetir algo hasta la s.** to repeat sth over and over (again)

saco *nm* **(a)** *(bolsa)* sack, bag; *Fig* **no echar algo en s. roto** to take good note of sth ❏ **s. de dormir** sleeping bag; **s. de viaje** overnight bag **(b)** *(contenido)* sackful, bagful **(c)** *Anat* sac **(d)** *Mil* sack; **entrar a s. en una ciudad** to pillage a town **(e)** *Am (abrigo)* coat; *(chaqueta de tela)* jacket; *(chaqueta de punto)* cardigan

sacón, -ona *adj CAm* **(a)** *(acusón)* telltale, sneaking **(b)** *(adulador)* flattering

sacralizar [14] *vt* to consecrate

sacramental *adj Rel* sacramental; *Teat* **auto s.** mystery play

sacramentar *vt Rel* to administer the last rites to

sacramento *nm Rel* sacrament; **el Santísimo S.** the Blessed Sacrament

sacrificar [59] **1** *vt* **(a)** *(ofrecer en sacrificio)* to sacrifice **(b)** *(matar) (reses)* to slaughter

2 sacrificarse *vpr* to make a sacrifice *o* sacrifices; **s. por algo/algn** to sacrifice oneself for sth/sb

sacrificio *nm* sacrifice

sacrilegio *nm* sacrilege

sacrílego, -a *adj* sacrilegious

sacristán, -ana *nm,f Rel* verger, sexton

sacristía *nf Rel* vestry, sacristy

sacro, -a¹ *Anat* **1** *adj* sacrum

2 *nm* **(hueso) s.** sacrum

sacro, -a² *adj (sagrado)* sacred

sacrosanto, -a *adj* sacrosanct

sacudida *nf* **(a)** *(gen)* shake; *(espasmo)* jolt, jerk; **avanzar a sacudidas** to jolt along; **dar una s. a algo** to shake sth **(b)** *(terremoto)* earthquake **(c)** *(conmoción)* shock; **s. eléctrica** electric shock

sacudidor *nm* carpet beater

sacudir 1 *vt* **(a)** *(agitar)* to shake; *(alfombra, sábana)* to shake out **(b)** *(quitar) (arena, polvo)* to shake off **(c)** *(golpear)* to beat **(d)** *(conmover)* to shock, stun

2 sacudirse *vpr (deshacerse de)* to shake off, get rid of; **s. el polvo de la manga** to shake the dust off one's sleeve

S.A. de C.V. *nf Méx (abrev de* **sociedad anónima de capital variable)** variable capital corporation

sádico, -a 1 *adj* sadistic

2 *nm,f* sadist

sadismo *nm* sadism

sadomasoquismo *nm* sadomasochism

sadomasoquista 1 *adj* sadomasochistic

2 *nmf* sadomasochist

saeta *nf* **(a)** *(dardo)* arrow, dart **(b)** *(del reloj etc)* hand, needle **(c)** *Mús Rel* = flamenco song

saetera *nf* loophole

safari *nm* **(a)** *(cacería)* safari **(b)** *(parque)* safari park

saga *nf Lit* saga

sagacidad *nf Fml (listeza)* cleverness, sagacity; *(astucia)* astuteness, shrewdness

sagaz *adj (listo)* clever, sagacious; *(astuto)* astute, shrewd

sagitariano, -a *adj & nm,f Am* Sagittarian

Sagitario *nm Astrol Astron* Sagittarius

sagrado, -a *adj* sacred, holy; **Sagrada Familia** Holy Family; **S. Corazón** Sacred Heart

sagrario *nm Rel* tabernacle

Sáhara ['saɣara], **Sahara** [sa'ara] *nm* **el (desierto del) S.** the Sahara (Desert)

saharaui *adj & nmf* Saharan

sahariana *nf (prenda)* safari shirt *o* jacket

sahariano, -a *adj* Saharan

sahumado, -a *adj Am Fam* tipsy, merry

sahumerio *nm* **(a)** *(substancia)* incense **(b)** *(humo)* aromatic smoke

saín *nm* **(a)** *(grasa)* animal fat; *(de pescado)* fish oil **(b)** *(suciedad)* dirt, grease

sainete *nm* **(a)** *Teat* comic sketch, one-act farce **(b)** *Culin (bocadito)* titbit, *US* tidbit; *(delicia)* delicacy

sajón, -ona *adj & nm,f Hist* Saxon

sal *nf* **(a)** *(cloruro de sodio)* salt ❏ **s. fina** table salt; **s. gema** salt crystals; *Esp* **s. gorda** cooking salt; **s. marina** sea salt **(b)** *Fig (gracia)* wit; *(gentileza)* charm; **la s. de la vida** the spice of life **(c)** *CAm Carib Méx (desgracia)* misfortune, bad luck **(d)** **sales** *(perfumes)* smelling salts ❏ **s. de baño** bath salts

sal *imperat véase* **salir**

sala *nf* **(a)** *(habitación)* room; *(en un hospital)* ward ❏ **s. de espectáculos** *(teatro)* theatre; *(cine)* cinema; **s. de espera** waiting room; **s. de estar** lounge, living room; **s. de exposiciones** exhibition hall; **s. de fiestas** nightclub, discotheque; **s. de lectura** reading room; **s. de operaciones** *Br* operating theatre, *US* operating room; **s. de partos** delivery room **(b)** *Jur* courtroom; *(tribunal)* court

salacot *(pl* **salacots)** *nm* pith helmet, topee

saladero *nm* salting room *o* house

salado, -a 1 *pp de* **salar**

2 *adj* **(a)** *(con sal)* salted; *(con exceso de sal)* salty; **agua salada** salt water **(b)** *Esp (gracioso)* witty, funny; *(encantador)* charming, winsome **(c)** *CAm Carib Méx (desgraciado)* unfortunate **(d)** *CSur Fam (caro)* pricy

saladura *nf* salting

salamanca *nf RP Zool* flat-headed salamander

salamandra *nf Zool* salamander

salamanquesa *nf, Andes* **salamanqueja** *nf Zool* Moorish gecko

salame *nm*, **salami** *nm* (**a**) *CSur (salami)* salami (**b**) *RP Fam (tonto)* idiot

salar *vt* (**a**) *(curar en sal)* to salt (**b**) *(para cocinar)* to salt, add salt to (**c**) *CAm Carib Méx (dar mala suerte)* to bring bad luck to; *(echar a perder)* to ruin, spoil

salarial *adj* salary, wage

salario *nm* salary, wages *pl* ❑ **s. bruto** gross salary; **s. mínimo (interprofesional)** minimum wage **s. neto** net salary

salaz *adj* salacious

salazón *nm* (**a**) *(acción de salar)* salting (**b**) *(carne, pescado)* salted meat *o* fish (**c**) *CAm Cuba Méx Fam (mala suerte)* bad luck

salchicha *nf* sausage

salchichería *nf* pork butcher's (shop)

salchichón *nm* (salami-type) sausage

salchichonería *nf Méx* delicatessen

saldar *vt* (**a**) *Fin (cuenta)* to settle, balance; *(deuda)* to pay off (**b**) *Com (vender barato)* to sell off (**c**) *Fig (diferencias)* to settle, resolve

saldo *nm* (**a**) *Fin* balance, difference ❑ **s. acreedor** credit balance; **s. deudor** debit balance; **s. negativo** negative balance, deficit; **s. positivo** positive balance, surplus (**b**) *(de una deuda)* liquidation, settlement (**c**) *(resto de mercancía)* remnant, remainder, leftover; **a precio de s.** at bargain prices

saldré *indic fut véase* **salir**

saledizo, -a 1 *adj* projecting
   2 *nm* projection, ledge

salero *nm* (**a**) *(recipiente)* saltcellar (**b**) *Fig (gracia)* charm; *(ingenio)* wit; **tener mucho s.** to be very witty

saleroso, -a *adj (agradable)* charming; *(ingenioso)* witty; *(animado)* lively

salesiano, -a *adj & nm,f Rel* Salesian

salgo *indic pres véase* **salir**

sálico, -a *adj* Salic; **ley sálica** Salic Law

salida *nf* (**a**) *(partida)* departure; **el tren tiene su s. a las siete** the train leaves at seven o'clock (**b**) *Dep* start; **línea de s.** starting line; **s. nula** false start (**c**) *(viaje corto)* trip (**d**) *(puerta etc)* exit, way out; **callejón sin s.** dead end; **s. de emergencia/incendios** emergency/fire exit; **tener s. a** to open on to (**e**) *(momento de salir)* coming out; *(de un astro)* rising; **s. del sol** sunrise; **te vi a la s. del cine** I saw you leaving the cinema (**f**) *Com* outlet, market (**g**) *(perspectiva)* opening; **es una carrera sin salidas** it is a career with no openings (**h**) *Fin* outlay, expenditure (**i**) *(recurso)* solution, way out; **no tengo otra s.** I have no other option (**j**) *Fam (ocurrencia)* witty remark, witticism; **s. de tono** improper *o* unfortunate remark (**k**) *Inform* output

salido, -a 1 *pp de* **salir**
   2 *adj* (**a**) *(saliente)* prominent, projecting; **ojos salidos** bulging eyes (**b**) *(animal)* on *o* US in heat; *Vulg (persona)* horny, out for it

saliente 1 *adj* (**a**) *(que sobresale)* projecting, prominent; *Fig* outstanding (**b**) *(cesante)* outgoing
   2 *nm* projection, overhang, ledge

salina *nf* (**a**) *Min* salt mine (**b**) *(instalación)* saltworks *sing*

salinidad *nf* salinity

salino, -a *adj* saline

salir [60] **1** *vi* (**a**) *(de un sitio)* to go out, leave; *(venir de dentro)* to come out; **¿está Marcos? — no, ha salido** is Marcos in? — no, he's gone out; **salió de la habitación** she left the room; **s. disparado** to shoot off; *Fig* **salió en mi defensa** he came to my defence; *Fig* **s. de dudas** to make sure; *Fam* **s. pitando** to rush off (**b**) *(partir)* to leave, depart; **el tren sale a las nueve** the train leaves at nine (**c**) *(novios)* to go out (**con** with) (**d**) *(aparecer)* to appear; **el anuncio que sale en la tele** the advertisement that's on TV; **es una revista que sale los jueves** it's a magazine that comes out on Thursdays; **ha salido una nueva ley** a new law has come in; **la foto salió en todos los periódicos** the photo appeared in all the newspapers (**e**) *(resultar)* to turn out, turn out to be; **¿cómo te salió el examen?** how did your exam go?; **el pequeño les ha salido delincuente** their youngest son turned into a delinquent; **salió presidente** he was elected president; **salió vencedor** he was the winner; **s. ganando** to come out ahead *o* on top; **s. ileso de un accidente** to come out of an accident uninjured (**f**) *(ocurrir)* to happen, occur; **salga lo que salga** whatever happens (**g**) *(ofrecerse)* to come up; **le ha salido un trabajo interesante** an interesting job has come up; **si sale la ocasión** if the opportunity arises (**h**) *(precio)* to cost, come to, work out; **sale a mil pesos** it comes to a thousand pesos; **s. barato/caro** to work out cheap/expensive (**i**) *(proceder)* **s. de** to come from; **el vino sale de la uva** wine comes from grapes (**j**) *(brotar)* to come out; **ha salido una hoja** a leaf has come out; **me salen granos** I'm getting spots (**k**) *(sobresalir)* to project, stick out (**l**) *(parecerse)* **s. a** to take after; **ha salido al abuelo** she takes after her grandfather (**m**) *(solucionar)* to work out; **el crucigrama no me sale** I can't work out the crossword (**n**) *(decir inesperadamente)* **s. con** to come out with; **¡con qué cosas sales!** the things you come out with! (**o**) *(dar)* **s. a** to open onto; **la calle sale a una plaza** the street opens onto a square (**p**) *Inform* to quit, exit
   2 salirse *vpr* (**a**) *(líquido, gas)* to leak (out); *(tornillo etc)* to come off, come out; **se ha salido la leche** the milk has boiled over; *Fig* **s. de lo normal** to be out of the ordinary (**b**) *(salir)* to go out; **s. de la carretera** to go off the road; *Fam* **s. con la suya** to get one's own way

salitre *nm Quim* saltpetre, US saltpeter

saliva *nf* saliva; *Fig* **gastar s.** to waste one's breath; *Fig* **tragar s.** to swallow one's feelings

salivación *nf* salivation

salival *adj* salivary

salivar *vi* to salivate

salivazo *nm* spit

salmantino, -a 1 *adj* of *o* from Salamanca
   2 *nm,f* person from Salamanca

salmo *nm Rel* (**a**) *(alabanza a Dios)* psalm (**b**) **Salmos** *(los de David)* Psalms

salmodia *nf* (**a**) *Rel* psalmody (**b**) *Fam (canturreo)* monotonous singing

salmodiar 1 *vi Rel* to sing psalms
   2 *vt (canturrear)* to sing monotonously

salmón 1 *nm (pescado)* salmon
   2 *adj (color)* salmon pink, salmon

salmonado, -a *adj* (**a**) *(parecido al salmón)* similar to salmon; **trucha salmonada** salmon trout (**b**) *(color)* salmon pink, salmon

salmonella [salmo'nela] *nf Med* salmonella *(bacterium)*

salmonelosis *nf inv Med* salmonellosis, salmonella

salmonete *nm (pescado)* red mullet

salmuera *nf Culin* brine

salobre *adj (agua)* brackish; *(gusto)* salty, briny

salobreño, -a *adj* saline

salobridad *nf* brackishness

Salomón *n* **Islas S.** Solomon Islands

salomónico, -a *adj* Solomonic, Solomonian; *Arquit* **columna salomónica** wreathed column

salón *nm* (**a**) *(en una casa)* lounge, sitting room, drawing room (**b**) *(en edificio público)* hall ❑ **s. de actos** assembly hall; **s. de baile** dance hall (**c**) *(establecimiento)* shop ❑ **s. de belleza** beauty salon; **s. recreativo** amusement arcade; **s. de té** tearoom, teashop (**d**) *(exposición)* show, exhibition ❑ **s. del automóvil** motor show

salpicadera *nf Méx (protección) Dr* mudguard, *US* fender

salpicadero *nm Esp Aut* dashboard

salpicadura *nf* splashing, spattering

salpicar [59] *vt* (**a**) *(rociar)* to splash, spatter; **me salpicó el abrigo de barro** he splashed mud on my coat (**b**) *Fig (esparcir)* to sprinkle; **salpicó su discurso de anécdotas** he sprinkled his speech with anecdotes

salpicón *nm* (**a**) *(acción)* splash, spatter (**b**) *Culin* cocktail ❑ **s. de mariscos** seafood cocktail (**c**) *Col Ecuad (refresco)* fruit juice

salpimentar [3] *vt* (**a**) *Culin* to season (**b**) *Fig (amenizar)* to season, spice

salsa *nf* (**a**) *Culin* sauce; *Fig* **en su (propia) s.** in one's element ❑ **s. bechamel,** *Col CSur* **s. blanca** white sauce; **s. rosa** ≃ Thousand Island dressing; **s. de tomate** ketchup (**b**) *(interés)* spice; **ser la s. de la vida** to make life worth living (**c**) *Mús* salsa

salsera *nf (recipiente)* gravy boat

salsero, -a 1 *adj* salsa
   2 *nm,f* salsa fan

saltador, -a 1 *adj* jumping, leaping
   2 *nm,f Dep* jumper; **s. de altura** high jumper; **s. de pértiga** (pole) vaulter
   3 *nm (cuerda) Br* skipping rope, *US* jump rope

saltamontes *nm inv* grasshopper

saltar 1 *vt* (**a**) *(obstáculo, valla)* to jump (over); **saltó la valla con facilidad** he jumped over the fence easily; *Fig* **estar a la que salta** to be always ready to take a chance (**b**) *(omitir)* to skip, miss out
   2 *vi* (**a**) *(elevarse en el aire)* to jump; **s. a la cuerda** *o Esp* **comba** to skip; **s. de la cama** to jump out of bed; **s. en paracaídas** to parachute; *Fig* **s. a la vista** to be obvious, be as plain as the nose on one's face; *Fig* **s. de alegría** to jump for joy; *Fig* **s. sobre algn** to pounce on sb (**b**) *(romperse)* to break, burst; **el agua caliente hizo s. el cristal** the hot water shattered the glass; **hacer s.** to blow up; **s. en pedazos** to break into little pieces; *Fig* **hacer s. la banca** to break the bank (**c**) *(desprenderse)* to come off; **saltó el corcho** the cork popped out (**d**) *(encolerizarse)* to explode, blow up; **por menos de nada salta** the smallest thing makes him explode
   3 saltarse *vpr* (**a**) *(omitir)* to skip, miss out (**b**) *(no hacer caso)* to ignore; **s. el semáforo** to jump the lights; **s. el turno** *Br* to jump the queue, *US* jump in line; *Fam* **s. algo a la torera** to ignore sth totally (**c**) *(desprenderse)* to come off; **se le saltó un botón** one of his buttons came off; **se me saltaron las lágrimas** tears came to my eyes

saltarín, -a 1 *adj* lively, bouncing
   2 *nm,f* (**a**) *(alegre)* energetic person (**b**) *(persona atolondrada)* madcap

salteado, -a 1 *pp de* **saltear**
   2 *adj* (**a**) *(espaciado)* spaced out (**b**) *(irregular)* irregular (**c**) *Culin* sauté, sautéed

salteador *nm* highwayman

saltear *vt* (**a**) *(asaltar)* to rob; *(a algn)* to hold up (**b**) *(hacer irregularmente)* to do in fits and starts; *(visitas)* to space out; *(partes de un libro)* to skip (**c**) *Culin* to sauté

salterio *nm Rel* Psalter

saltimbanqui *nmf (acróbata)* acrobat, tumbler; *(hombre de circo)* = member of travelling circus

salto *nm* (**a**) *(acción)* jump, leap; *Fig (paso adelante)* leap forward, advance, bound; **dar** *o* **pegar un s.** to jump, leap;

de un s. in a flash; **s. en el vacío** leap in the dark; **subir/bajar de un s.** to jump up/down; *Fig* **a s. de mata** from hand to mouth; *Fig* **a saltos** in leaps and bounds; *Fig* **el corazón me daba saltos** my heart was pounding ❑ **s. de agua** waterfall; **s. de cama** negligée (**b**) *Dep* jump ❑ *Atlet* **s. de altura,** *Am* **s. alto** high jump; *Natación* **s. de la carpa** jack-knife; *Natación* **s. del ángel** swan dive; *Atlet Am* **s. con garrocha** pole vault; *Atlet* **s. de longitud** *Am* **s. largo** long jump; **s. mortal** somersault; *Atlet* **triple s.** hop, step, jump, triple jump (**c**) *Fig (omisión)* gap (**d**) *(despeñadero)* precipice (**e**) *Inform* **s. de página** form feed

saltón, -ona *adj* (**a**) *(ojos)* bulging (**b**) *Chile, Col (comida)* half-cooked

salubre *adj* salubrious, healthy

salubridad *nf* salubrity, salubriousness, healthiness

salud *nf* health; **beber a la s. de algn** to drink to sb's health; *Fig* **creo que aceptan tarjetas pero llevaré algo en efectivo para curarme en s.** I think they accept credit cards, but just to be on the safe side, I'll take some cash; **gozar de buena s.** to be in good health; **rebosar s.** to be glowing with health; *Fam* **¡s.!** cheers!; **tiene una s. de hierro** she has an iron constitution ❑ **s. mental** mental health; **s. pública** public health

saludable *adj* (**a**) *(sano)* healthy, wholesome; **tener un aspecto s.** to look healthy (**b**) *Fig (beneficioso)* good, beneficial

saludar *vt (mostrar respeto)* to greet; *(decir hola a)* to say hello to; *Mil* to salute; **no nos saludamos** we are not on speaking terms; *(en una carta)* **le saluda atentamente** yours faithfully; **saluda de mi parte a** give my regards to

saludes *nfpl CAm Andes Méx* greetings

saludo *nm* greeting; *Mil* salute; **reciba un atento s. de** yours faithfully; **un s. de** best wishes from

salutación *nf* greeting

salva *nf Mil* salvo, volley; *Fig* **s. de aplausos** round of applause

salvable *adj* which can be saved *o* kept *o* preserved

salvación *nf (gen)* salvation; *(rescate)* rescue; *Fig* **no tiene s.** there is no hope for him

salvado *nm Culin* bran

salvador, -a 1 *adj* saving
   2 *nm,f (gen)* saviour; *(rescatador)* rescuer
   3 *nm* (**a**) *Rel* **el S.** the Saviour (**b**) *(país)* **El S.** El Salvador

salvadoreño, -a *adj & nm,f* Salvadoran, Salvadorian

salvaguarda *nf véase* **salvaguardia**

salvaguardar *vt* to safeguard (**de** from), protect (**de** from)

salvaguardia *nf* (**a**) *(documento)* safe-conduct (**b**) *(protección)* safeguard, protection

salvajada *nf* atrocity, savagery, brutal act

salvaje 1 *adj* (**a**) *Bot* wild, uncultivated (**b**) *Zool* wild (**c**) *(pueblo, tribu)* savage, uncivilized (**d**) *Fam (violento)* savage, wild (**e**) *(incontrolado)* wild
   2 *nmf* (**a**) *(habitante primitivo)* savage (**b**) *(bruto)* boor

salvajismo *nm* savagery

salvamanteles *nm inv* table mat

salvamento *nm* rescue

salvapantallas *nm inv Inform* screensaver

salvar 1 *vt* (**a**) *(librar del peligro)* to save, rescue (**de** from); *(barco)* to salvage (**b**) *(superar) (obstáculo)* to clear; *(dificultad)* to get round, overcome (**c**) *(recorrer)* to cover; **salvamos la distancia en menos de dos días** we covered the distance in less than two days (**d**) *(atravesar)* to cross (**e**) *(exceptuar)* to exclude, except; **salvando ciertos errores** except a few mistakes

2 salvarse *vpr* (**a**) *(sobrevivir)* to survive, come out alive; *(escaparse)* to escape (**de** from); **¡sálvese quien pueda!** every man for himself!; *Fam* **s. por los pelos** to have a narrow escape (**b**) *Rel* to be saved, save one's soul.

salvavidas *nm inv* life belt

salve *nf Rel* Hail Mary

salvedad *nf* (**a**) *(excepción)* exception; **con la s. de mis amigos** except for *o* barring my friends (**b**) *(condición)* condition, proviso; **me excusaré con la s. de que él también lo haga** I'll apologize on condition he apologizes too (**c**) *(reserva)* reservation

salvia *nf Bot* sage

salvo, -a 1 *adj* unharmed, safe; **estar a s.** to be safe; **poner algo a s.** to put sth in a safe place; **sano y s.** safe and sound; *Euf* **salva sea la parte** bottom
2 *adv (exceptuando)* except (for); **s. que** unless; **todos s. él** everyone except for him

salvoconducto *nm* safe-conduct

samaritano, -a *adj & nm,f* Samaritan

samba *nf Mús* samba

sambenito *nm* (**a**) *Hist* sanbenito (**b**) *Fig (deshonra)* disgrace; *(descrédito)* stigma; **colgarle un s. a algn** to give sb a bad name

Samoa *n* Samoa

samoano, -a *adj & nm,f* Samoan

samovar *nm* samovar

samurái *nm Hist* samurai

san *adj* saint; **el día de S. Esteban** Boxing Day; **el día de S. José** St Joseph's Day; *véase* **santo, -a**

Sana *n* Sanaa

sanable *adj* curable

sanador, -a 1 *adj* curative
2 *nm,f* curer

sanar 1 *vt (curar)* to cure, heal
2 *vi* (**a**) *(persona)* to recover, get better (**b**) *(herida)* to heal

sanatorio *nm* clinic, nursing home, sanatorium

sanción *nf* (**a**) *(penalización)* sanction (**b**) *(aprobación)* sanction, approval (**c**) *Jur* penalty

sancionable *adj* sanctionable

sancionar *vt* (**a**) *(castigar)* to penalize (**b**) *(aprobar)* to sanction

sanco *nm Am Culin* = type of stew

sancochar *vt Culin* to parboil

sancocho *nm Andes Culin* = stew of beef, chicken or fish, vegetables and green bananas

sanctasanctórum *nm Rel* sancta sanctorum, Holy of holies

sandalia *nf* sandal

sándalo *nm* sandalwood

sandez *nf* piece of nonsense; **decir sandeces** to talk nonsense; **¡qué s.!** what nonsense!

sandía *nf* watermelon

sandinismo *nm* Sandinista movement

sandinista *adj & nmf* Sandinista

sánduche *nm Am* (**a**) *(con pan de molde) (sin tostar)* sandwich; *(tostado)* toasted sandwich (**b**) *(con pan de barra)* sandwich *(made with French bread)*

sandunga *nf* (**a**) *Fam (gracia)* wit (**b**) *Méx (baile)* = regional dance

sandunguero, -a *adj* jolly, fun-loving

sándwich ['sanwitʃ, 'sanwis] *(pl sándwiches) nm* sandwich

sandwichera [sanwi'tʃera] *nf* toasted sandwich maker

saneado, -a 1 *pp de* **sanear**
2 *adj* sound, healthy

saneamiento *nm* (**a**) *(de un terreno)* drainage, draining; *(de un edificio)* cleaning, disinfection (**b**) *Fin* compensation

sanear *vt* (**a**) *(terrenos)* to drain; *(edificios)* to clean, disinfect (**b**) *Fin* to compensate

sanedrín *nm Rel* Sanhedrin

sangrado *nm Impr* indention, indentation, indent

sangrante *adj* (**a**) *(que sangra)* bleeding (**b**) *Fig (flagrante)* flagrant, blatant

sangrar 1 *vt* (**a**) *Med* to bleed (**b**) *(un árbol)* to tap (**c**) *Fam (sacar dinero)* to bleed dry (**d**) *Impr* to indent
2 *vi (emanar sangre)* to bleed

sangre *nf* blood; **de s. caliente** warm-blooded; **de s. fría** cold-blooded; **donar s.** to give blood; *Fig* **a s. fría** in cold blood; *Fig* **a s. y fuego** by fire and sword; *Fig* **no llegó la s. al río** the worst didn't happen; *Fig* **s. fría** sang-froid; *Fig* **subírsele la s. a la cabeza** to see red; *Fig* **tener mala s.** to be evil; *Fam* **lo lleva en la s.** it runs in the family; *Fam Fig* **tener s. de horchata** to have water in one's veins

sangría *nf* (**a**) *Med* bleeding, bloodletting; *Fig* drain (**b**) *(bebida)* sangría (**c**) *Impr* indentation

sangriento, -a *adj* (**a**) *(con sangre)* bloody (**b**) *(cruel)* cruel

sánguche *nm véase* **sánduche**

sanguijuela *nf Zool* leech, bloodsucker

sanguinario, -a *adj* bloodthirsty

sanguíneo, -a *adj* blood

sanguino, -a *adj & nf* blood

sanguinolencia *nf* bloodiness

sanguinolento, -a *adj* bloody, bloodstained; **ojos sanguinolentos** bloodshot eyes

sanidad *nf* (**a**) *(calidad de sano)* health, healthiness (**b**) *(sistema)* public health, sanitation; **Ministerio de S.** Ministry of Health

sanitario, -a 1 *adj* sanitary, health; **centro s.** health centre
2 *nm,f* health officer
3 *nm (instalaciones)* bathroom fitting

San José *n* San José

San Marino *n* San Marino

sano, -a *adj* (**a**) *(bien de salud)* healthy, fit; *(saludable)* healthy, wholesome (**b**) *(libre de error)* good, sound; *(juicio)* right; **filosofía sana** sound philosophy (**c**) *(sincero)* sincere

sansalvadoreño, -a 1 *adj* of *o* from San Salvador
2 *nm,f* person from San Salvador

sánscrito, -a *Ling* **1** *adj* Sanskritic
2 *nm* Sanskrit

sanseacabó *interj Fam* **y s.** and that's that!

sansón *nm Fam* he-man; **estar hecho un s.** to be as strong as an ox

santanderino, -a 1 *adj* of *o* from Santander
2 *nm,f* person from Santander

santería *nf* (**a**) *(beatería)* sanctimoniousness (**b**) *(religión)* santería (**c**) *Am (tienda)* = shop which sells religious objects

santero, -a 1 *adj (beato)* sanctimonious
2 *nm,f* (**a**) *(sacristán)* caretaker, verger (**b**) *(mendigo)* alms collector

Santiago (de Chile) *n* Santiago

Santiago de Compostela *n* Santiago de Compostela

Santiago de Cuba *n* Santiago de Cuba

santiaguero, -a 1 *adj* of *o* from Santiago de Cuba
2 *nm,f* person from Santiago de Cuba

santiagués, -esa 1 *adj* of *o* from Santiago de Compostela

2 *nm,f* person from Santiago de Compostela

santiaguino, -a 1 *adj* of o from Santiago de Chile
  2 *nm,f* person from Santiago de Chile

santiamén *nm Fam* **en un s.** as quick as a flash, in a flash, in no time at all

santidad *nf* saintliness, holiness; **Su S.** His Holiness

santificación *nf* sanctification

santificar [59] *vt Rel* to sanctify, make holy; **s. las fiestas** to keep the Sabbath and holy days

santiguar [11] **1** *vt* to bless, make the sign of the cross over
  2 santiguarse *vpr* to make the sign of the cross, cross oneself

santo, -a 1 *adj* **(a)** *(gen)* holy, sacred **(b)** *(bueno)* saintly; **un s. varón** a saint **(c)** *Fam* blessed; **hace su santa voluntad** he does as he damn well pleases; **todo el s. día** all day long
  2 *nm,f (gen)* saint; *Fig* **desnudar a un s. para vestir a otro** to rob Peter to pay Paul; *Fam* **¡por todos los santos!** for heaven's sake!; *Fam Fig* **Francisco no es s. de mi devoción** I'm not terribly fond of Francisco; *Fam Fig* **quedarse para vestir santos** to be left on the shelf; *Fam Fig* **se me fue el s. al cielo** I clean forgot
  3 *nm* **(a)** *(día onomástico)* saint's day; **hoy es su s.** today is his saint's day; *Fig* **¿a s. de qué?** why on earth? **(b)** *(contraseña)* **s. y seña** password **(c)** *Chile (parche)* patch

Santo Domingo *n* Santo Domingo

santón *nm* **(a)** *Rel* santon **(b)** *(sabio)* sage, wise man

santoral *nm Rel* calendar of saints' feast days

Santo Tomé *n* São Tomé

Santo Tomé y Príncipe *n* Sao Tomé and Príncipe

santuario *nm* **(a)** *(templo)* shrine **(b)** *(lugar venerable)* holy place **(c)** *(de animales)* sanctuary **(d)** *Col (tesoro)* buried treasure

santurrón, -a 1 *adj* sanctimonious
  2 *nm,f* sanctimonious person

santurronería *nf* sanctimoniousness

saña *nf* **(a)** *(crueldad)* cruelty, viciousness; **con s.** viciously **(b)** *(furor)* blind anger, fury; **con s.** furiously

São Paulo *n* São Paulo

sapiencia *nf Fml (sabiduría)* wisdom; *(conocimiento)* knowledge

sapo *nm* **(a)** *Zool* toad; *Fam* **echar sapos y culebras** to rant and rave **(b)** *Chile (suerte)* fluke, stroke of luck **(c)** *Pan, Fam (canalla)* scoundrel, rascal

saponificación *nf Quím* saponification

saponificar [59] *vt Quím* to saponify

saque *nm* **(a)** *Ftb* kick-off ❑ **s. de banda** throw-in; **s. de esquina** corner kick; **s. inicial** kick-off **(b)** *Ten* service **(c)** *Fam* **tener buen s.** to be a big eater

saqueador, -a 1 *adj (en ciudades)* plundering, pillaging; *(en casas)* looting
  2 *nm,f (de ciudades)* plunderer, pillager; *(de casa, tienda)* looter

saquear *vt (ciudad)* to sack, plunder, pillage; *(casas y tiendas)* to loot

saqueo *nm (de ciudades)* sacking, plundering, pillaging; *(de casa, tienda)* looting

S.A.R. *(abrev de* **Su Alteza Real)** H.R.H.

Sarajevo *n* Sarajevo

sarampión *nm Med* measles *pl*

sarao *nm* knees-up; *Fam* **¡vaya s.!** what a mess!

sarape *nm Guat Méx* serape

sarasa *nm Fam Ofens* queer, fairy

sarcasmo *nm* sarcasm

sarcástico, -a *adj* sarcastic

sarcófago *nm* sarcophagus

sarcoma *nm Med* sarcoma

sardana *nf Mús* sardana *(Catalan dance and music)*

sardina *nf (pez)* sardine

sardinero, -a 1 *adj* sardine; **la flota sardinera** the sardine fishing fleet
  2 *nm,f* sardine seller

sardo, -a *adj & nm,f* Sardinian

sardónico, -a *adj* sardonic

sarga *nf Tex* serge, twill

Sargazos *nmpl* **el mar de los S.** the Sargasso Sea

sargento *nmf Mil* sergeant; **s. primero** *Br* staff sergeant, *US* sergeant major; *Fam* **ser un/una s.** to be a tyrant

sari *nm* sari

sarmentoso, -a *adj* bony, scrawny

sarmiento *nm Bot* vine shoot

sarna *nf Med* itch, scabies *sing*; *Zool* mange; *Fam Fig* **s. con gusto no pica** if you want something badly enough you'll put up with anything

sarnoso, -a *adj* itchy, scabby; *Zool* mangy

sarpullido *nm Med* rash

sarraceno, -a *adj & nm,f* Saracen

sarro *nm (sedimento)* deposit; *(en los dientes)* tartar; *(en la lengua, en una pava)* fur

sarta *nf* string; *Fam Fig* **s. de mentiras** string of lies

sartén *nf* frying pan, *US* skillet; *Fig* **tener la s. por el mango** to have the upper hand

sastra *nf* tailoress, female tailor; *Cin Teat* wardrobe mistress

sastre *nm* tailor

sastrería *nf* **(a)** *(tienda)* tailor's (shop) **(b)** *(oficio)* tailoring

Satán *nm,* **Satanás** *nm* Satan

satánico, -a *adj* satanic

satanismo *nm* Satanism

satélite *nm* satellite ❑ **s. artificial** satellite; **s. meteorológico** weather satellite

satén *nm Tex* satin

satinado, -a 1 *pp de* **satinar**
  2 *adj* satiny, glossy, shiny
  3 *nm* gloss, shine

satinar *vt* to gloss, make glossy

sátira *nf Lit & Fig* satire

satírico, -a *adj Lit & Fig* satiric, satirical

satirizar [14] *vt Lit & Fig* to satirize

sátiro *nm Mit & Fig* satyr

satisfacción *nf* satisfaction; **s. de un deseo** fulfilment of a desire

satisfacer [33] *(pp* **satisfecho) 1** *vt* **(a)** *(deseos, necesidades)* to satisfy **(b)** *(cumplir)* to meet, satisfy **(c)** *(deuda)* to pay
  2 satisfacerse *vpr* to be satisfied, satisfy oneself

satisfactorio, -a *adj* satisfactory

satisfecho, -a 1 *pp de* **satisfacer**
  2 *adj* satisfied; **estoy s.** I've had enough to eat; **me doy por s.** that's good enough for me; **s. de sí mismo** self-satisfied, smug

sátrapa *nm Hist* satrap; *Fig* despot, satrap; *Fig* **vivir como un s.** to live like a king

saturación *nf* saturation

saturado, -a 1 *pp de* **saturar**
  2 *adj* saturated

saturar 1 *vt* to saturate
2 saturarse *vpr* to become saturated (**de** with)

saturnismo *nm Med* saturnism, lead poisoning

Saturno *nm Astron Mit* Saturn

sauce *nm Bot* willow ❏ **s. llorón** weeping willow

saúco *nm Bot* elder

saudade *nf* nostalgia, homesickness

saudí *adj & nmf,* **saudita** *adj & nmf* Saudi

sauna *nf* sauna

saurio, -a *adj & nm,f Zool* saurian

savia *nf Bot* sap; *Fig* sap, vitality

saxo *nm Mús Fam* (**a**) *(instrumento)* sax (**b**) *(músico)* saxophonist

saxofón *nm* (**a**) *(instrumento)* saxophone (**b**) *(músico)* saxophonist

saxofonista *nmf* saxophonist

saxófono *nm véase* **saxofón**

saya *nf (falda)* skirt; *(enagua)* petticoat

sayal *nm Tex* sackcloth

sayo *nm* cassock, smock; *Fig* **cortarle un s. a algn** to run sb down; *Fig* **hacer de su capa un s.** to do as one pleases

sazón *nf* (**a**) *(madurez)* ripeness; **en s.** ripe (**b**) *Culin* seasoning; **en s.** in season (**c**) *(época)* **a la s.** at that time

sazonar 1 *vt Culin* to season, flavour, *US* flavor
2 sazonarse *vpr* to ripen

s/c. *(abrev de* **su cuenta***)* your account

scooter [es'kuter] *nm* scooter

Scotch® [es'kotʃ] *nm Andes RP (cinta) Br* Sellotape®, *US* Scotch tape®

scout [es'kaut] *nm (pl* **scouts***)* **1** *adj* **un grupo s.** a Scout troop
2 *nmf (hombre)* (boy) scout; *(mujer)* girl guide

Sdad. *(abrev de* **sociedad***)* Soc

S.E. *(abrev de* **Su Excelencia***)* HE

se¹ *pron* (**a**) *(reflexivo) (a él mismo)* himself; *(a ella misma)* herself; *(a usted mismo)* yourself; *(a ellos mismos)* themselves; *(a ustedes mismos)* yourselves; **todos los días se lava las manos varias veces** she washes her hands several times a day; **María se mira en el espejo** Maria looks at herself in the mirror; **morirse** to die; **no se lo creen** they don't believe it; **ustedes se confunden** you are making a mistake (**b**) *(recíproco)* one another, each other; **se aman** they love one another (**c**) *(voz pasiva)* **el vino se guarda en cubas** wine is kept in casks; **se ha suspendido el partido** the game has been postponed (**d**) *(impersonal)* **nunca se sabe** one never knows; **se dice que** it is said that; **se habla inglés** English spoken

se² *pron pers (dativo) (a él)* him; *(a ella)* her; *(a usted o ustedes)* you; *(a ellos)* them; **se lo diré en cuanto les vea** I'll tell them as soon as I see them; **¿se lo explico?** shall I explain it to you?; **¿se lo has dado ya?** have you given it to him yet?

sé¹ *indic pres véase* **saber²**

sé² *imperat véase* **ser²**

sebáceo, -a *adj* sebaceous; *Anat* **glándulas sebáceas** sebaceous glands

sebo *nm* (**a**) *(para velas)* tallow (**b**) *(grasa)* fat (**c**) *(mugre)* grease, filth (**d**) *Chile (regalo)* = christening present from godparents

seborrea *nf* seborrhoea

seboso, -a *adj* greasy

secadero *nm* drying room

secado *nm* drying

secador *nm* (**a**) *(aparato)* dryer, drier ❏ **s. de pelo** hair-

dryer (**b**) *CAm (trapo) Br* tea towel, *US* dish towel

secadora *nf* clothes dryer, tumble dryer

secamanos *nm inv* hand dryer

secano *nm* dry land; **cultivo de s.** dry farming

secante¹ 1 *adj (que seca)* drying; *(papel)* blotting
2 *nm* (**a**) *(papel)* blotting paper (**b**) *Ftb* spoiler

secante² *adj & nf Geom* secant

secar [59] **1** *vt (gen)* to dry; *(lágrimas, vajilla)* to wipe; *(una hoja)* to blot
2 secarse *vpr* (**a**) *(gen)* to dry; *(persona)* to dry oneself; **déjalo que se seque** leave it to dry; **s. las manos** to dry one's hands (**b**) *(marchitarse)* to dry up, wither

secarropas *nf inv RP* tumble-dryer

sección *nf* (**a**) *(corte)* section, cut; *Geom* section; **s. transversal** cross section (**b**) *(departamento)* section, department (**c**) *Mil* section

seccionar *vt* to section, cut

secesión *nf* secession

secesionismo *nm* secessionism

secesionista *adj & nmf* secessionist

seco, -a *adj* (**a**) *(sin humedad)* dry; **frutos secos** dried fruit; **limpieza en s.** dry-cleaning; *Fig* **a secas** just, only; *Fig* **dejar s.** to kill; *Fig* **Pepe a secas** just plain Pepe (**b**) *(vinos)* dry (**c**) *(personas, carácter)* dry (**d**) *(tono)* curt, sharp (**e**) *(delgado)* skinny; **más s. que un higo** *(delgado)* as thin as a rake; *(viejo)* old and wizened (**f**) *(golpe, ruido)* sharp; *Fig* **a palo s.** simply, on its own; *Fig* **frenar en s.** to pull up sharply; *Fig* **parar en s.** to stop dead

secoya *nf Bot véase* **secuoya**

secreción *nf* secretion

secreta *Fam* **1** *nf* secret police
2 *nmf* secret policeman/policewoman

secretar *vt* to secrete

secretaría *nf* (**a**) *(oficina)* secretary's office; *(organismo)* secretariat; **S. de Estado** = government department under the control of a *Br* junior minister o *US* undersecretary (**b**) *(cargo)* secretaryship, office of secretary

secretariado *nm* (**a**) *(oficina)* secretariat (**b**) *(cargo)* secretaryship (**c**) *Educ* secretarial course

secretario, -a *nm,f* secretary; **s. de Estado** *(en España) Br* junior minister, *US* undersecretary; *(en Estados Unidos)* Secretary of State

secretear *vi* to whisper secrets

secreteo *nm* whispering

secreter *nm Mueb* writing desk, bureau

secreto, -a 1 *adj* secret; **en s.** secretly
2 *nm* (**a**) *(lo oculto)* secret; **guardar un s.** to keep a secret; **s. a voces** open secret ❏ **s. bancario** banking confidentiality; **s. de Estado** state o official secret; **s. profesional** professional secret (**b**) *(sigilo)* secrecy

secta *nf* sect

sectario, -a *adj* sectarian

sectarismo *nm* sectarianism

sector *nm* (**a**) *Geom* sector (**b**) *(parte)* section; **un s. de la opinión pública** a section of public opinion (**c**) *(zona)* area; **un s. de la ciudad** an area of the city (**d**) *Econ* sector; **el s. automovilístico** the motor industry ❏ **s. primario/secundario** primary/secondary sector; **s. servicios** o **terciario** service industries o sector

sectorial *adj* sectoral

secuaz *nmf (seguidor)* supporter, follower; *Pey* underling

secuela *nf* consequence, result

secuencia *nf también Mús Inform* sequence

secuenciador *nm Mús Inform* sequencer

secuencial *adj* sequential

secuenciar *vt* to arrange in sequence

secuestrador, -a *nm,f* (**a**) *(raptor) (de personas)* kidnapper; *(de un avión)* hijacker (**b**) *Jur* sequestrator

secuestrar *vt* (**a**) *(raptar) (personas)* to kidnap; *(aviónes)* to hijack (**b**) *Jur* to sequester, seize, confiscate

secuestro *nm* (**a**) *(rapto) (de personas)* kidnapping; *(de un avión)* highjacking (**b**) *Jur* sequestration, seizure, confiscation

secular 1 *adj* (**a**) *Rel* secular, lay (**b**) *(antiquísimo)* ancient, age-old
 2 *nm* secular

secularización *nf* secularization

secularizar [14] *vt* to secularize

secundar *vt* to support, second

secundario, -a *adj* secondary

secuoya *nf Bot* redwood, sequoia; **s. gigante** giant sequoia

sed *nf* thirst; **dar s.** to make one thirsty; **quitar** *o* **matar la s.** to quench one's thirst; **tener s.** to be thirsty; *Fig* **tener s. de** to thirst for

seda *nf* silk; *Fam Fig* **ir como una s.** to go smoothly ▫ **s. dental** dental floss

sedación *nf Med* sedation

sedal *nm Pesca* fishing line

sedán *nm Aut Br* saloon, *US* sedan

sedante 1 *adj* (**a**) *Farm* sedative (**b**) *(sosegante)* soothing
 2 *nm Farm* sedative

sedar *vt* to sedate

sedativo, -a *adj* sedative

sede *nf* (**a**) *(residencia)* headquarters, central office; *(de gobierno)* seat; **s. social** head office; *Fin* company headquarters (**b**) *Rel* See; **la Santa S.** the Holy See

sedentario, -a *adj* sedentary

sedentarismo *nm* **el s. avanza** people are adopting an increasingly sedentary lifestyle

sedente *adj* seated, sitting

sedería *nf Tex* (**a**) *(comercio)* silk trade (**b**) *(tienda)* silk shop

sedero, -a *adj* silk; **industria sedera** silk industry

sedición *nf* sedition

sedicioso, -a 1 *adj* seditious
 2 *nm,f* rebel

sediento, -a *adj* thirsty; *Fig* **s. de poder** hungry for power

sedimentación *nf* sedimentation

sedimentar 1 *vt* to deposit
 2 sedimentarse *vpr* to settle

sedimentario, -a *adj* sedimentary

sedimento *nm* sediment, deposit

sedoso, -a *adj* silky, silken

seducción *nf* seduction

seducir [18] *vt* *(gen)* to seduce; *(persuadir)* to tempt

seductor, -a 1 *adj* *(gen)* seductive; *(persuasivo)* tempting
 2 *nm,f* seducer

sefardí (*pl* **sefardíes**) **1** *adj* Sephardic
 2 *nmf* Sephardi

sefardita *adj & nmf véase* **sefardí**

segador, -a *nm,f Agr (persona)* reaper, harvester

segadora *nf Agr (máquina)* reaper, harvester ▫ **s. de césped** lawnmower

segar [43] *vt* (**a**) *Agr (maíz etc)* to reap, cut; *(césped)* to mow

(**b**) *Fig (matar)* to mow down (**c**) *Fig (truncar)* to cut off; **s. la juventud de algn** to cut sb down in his prime

seglar 1 *adj* secular, lay
 2 *nmf* lay person; *(hombre)* layman; *(mujer)* laywoman

segmentación *nf* segmentation

segmentar *vt* to segment

segmento *nm* segment

segoviano, -a 1 *adj* of *o* from Segovia
 2 *nm,f* person from Segovia

segregación *nf* (**a**) *(separación)* segregation ▫ **s. racial** racial segregation, apartheid (**b**) *(secreción)* secretion

segregacionismo *nm* racial segregation

segregacionista *adj & nmf* supporter of racial segregation

segregar [38] *vt* (**a**) *(separar)* to segregate (**b**) *(secretar)* to secrete

seguida *nf* rhythm; **en s.** immediately, straight away; **en s. termino** I've nearly finished

seguidamente *adv* next, immediately afterwards

seguidilla *nf Mús* = Spanish type of dance and music

seguido *adv* straight; **todo s.** straight on, straight ahead

seguido, -a 1 *pp de* **seguir**
 2 *adj* (**a**) *(continuo)* continuous; **una línea seguida de casas** a straight line of houses (**b**) *(consecutivo)* consecutive, successive; **tres lunes seguidos** three Mondays in a row; **tres veces seguidas** on three consecutive occasions (**c**) *Am (a menudo)* often

seguidor, -a 1 *adj* following
 2 *nm,f* follower

seguimiento *nm* (**a**) *(persecución)* pursuit; **en s. de** in pursuit of (**b**) *(continuación)* continuation (**c**) *Astronáut* **estación de s. (espacial)** tracking station

seguir [61] **1** *vt* (**a**) *(gen)* to follow (**a** -); **a la tormenta siguió la lluvia** rain followed the storm; **le seguía con la mirada** she follow him with her eyes; **seguí su consejo** I followed her advice; **¡sígame!** follow me!; *Fam* **s. a algn como un perrito** to dog sb *o* sb's footsteps (**b**) *(continuar, proseguir)* to continue; *(un camino)* to continue on; **s. su curso** to take its course; **sigue hablando, te escucho** please carry on, I'm listening (**c**) *(perseguir)* to chase; **nos seguía un policía** a policeman was chasing us (**d**) *Educ (curso)* to do, follow
 2 *vi* (**a**) *(proseguir)* to go on, carry on; **sigue por la avenida hasta llegar a la plaza** go straight along the avenue until you reach the square (**b**) *(continuar)* to continue to be; **sigue con vida** he's still alive
 3 seguirse *vpr* to follow, ensue; **de esto se sigue que ...** it follows that ...

según 1 *prep* (**a**) *(en conformidad con)* according to; **s. la Biblia** according to the Bible; **s. la cara que puso** judging from his reaction; **s. lo que dicen** according to what they say; **s. su opinión** in his opinion (**b**) *(depende)* (**s.** + *que*) depending on; **s. el tiempo que haga** depending on the weather; **s. lo que digan** depending on what they say
 2 *adv* (**a**) *(como)* just as; **estaba s. lo dejé** it was just as I had left it (**b**) *(eventualidad)* depending on; **no sé qué haré, s.** I don't know what I'll do, it depends; **s. estén las cosas** depending on how things stand; **s. y cómo** it all depends (**c**) *(a medida que)* as; **s. iba leyendo me daba cuenta de que ...** as I read on I realized that ...

segundero *nm (de reloj)* second hand

segundo, -a¹ 1 *adj* second; **en s. lugar** in second place; **quedar s.** to come second; *Fig* **decir algo con segundas (intenciones)** to say sth with a double meaning
 2 *nm,f (de una serie)* second (one); *Fam Fig* **el s. de a bordo** the second in command
 3 *nm (parte)* second; *véase tamb* **octavo, -a**

segundo² nm (tiempo) second; **sesenta segundos** sixty seconds

segundón nm second son

segur nm (a) (hacha) axe, US ax (b) (hoz) sickle

seguramente adv (a) (seguro) surely; **sólo hazlo si puedes hacerlo s.** don't do it if you aren't sure about it (b) (probablemente) most probably; **s. no lloverá** it isn't likely to rain

seguridad nf (a) (ausencia de peligro) safety; **de s.** (cinturón, cierre) safety ❑ **s. en el trabajo** safety at work o in the workplace; **s. vial** road safety (b) (protección) security; **cárcel de máxima s.** maximum security prison ❑ **s. ciudadana** public safety; **s. financiera** financial security **S. Social** Social Security (c) (confianza) confidence; **hablar con s.** to speak with confidence; **s. en sí mismo** self-confidence (d) (certeza) certainty; **con toda s.** with absolute certainty; **en la s. de que ...** knowing that ...; **para mayor s.** to be on the safe side; **tener la s. de que ...** to be certain that ...

seguro, -a 1 adj (a) (sin peligro) safe; **método s.** safe method **en sitio s.** in a safe place; **sentirse s.** to feel safe; Fig **ir sobre s.** to play safe (b) (protegido, estable) secure; **un trabajo s.** a secure job (c) (confiado) sure; **estar s. de algo** to be sure about sth **estoy s. de que ...** I am sure that ...; **estar s. de sí mismo** to have self-confidence (d) (cierto) certain; **su nombramiento es s.** he's certain to be given the post; **dar algo por s.** to be sure of sth; **tener por s. que ...** to be sure that ... (e) (firme) steady, firm

2 nm (a) Seg insurance ❑ **s. a todo riesgo** fully comprehensive insurance; **s. contra incendios** fire insurance; **s. contra terceros** third party insurance; **s. de accidentes** accident insurance; **s. de enfermedad** health insurance; **s. médico** medical insurance; **s. de vida** life insurance (b) (dispositivo) safety catch o device; **quitar el s.** to remove the safety catch (c) CAm Méx (alfiler) safety pin

3 adv for sure, definitely **no lo sé s.** I don't know for sure; **s. que vendrá** she's bound o certain o sure to come

seis inv **1** adj (cardinal) six; (ordinal) sixth

2 nm six; **a las s.** at six o'clock; **el s. de mayo** the sixth of May; véase tamb **ocho**

seisavo, -a adj & nm véase **sexto, -a**

seiscientos, -as inv **1** adj (cardinal) six hundred; (ordinal) six hundredth

2 nm (a) (número) six hundred (b) Aut Fam 600 cc SEAT car; véase tamb **ocho**

seísmo nm Geol (terremoto) earthquake; (temblor de tierra) earth tremor

selección nf (a) (gen) selection ❑ Biol **s. natural** natural selection (b) Dep team ❑ **s. nacional** national team

seleccionado nm Dep **el s. cubano** the Cuban (national) team

seleccionador, -a nm,f (a) (gen) selector (b) Dep selector, team manager

seleccionar vt to select

selectividad nf selectivity; Esp Univ **(prueba de) s.** entrance examination

selectivo, -a adj selective

selecto, -a adj select; **ambiente s.** exclusive atmosphere

selector nm selector button; Aut **s. de velocidades** gear lever, US gearshift

selenita nmf moon dweller

self-service [self'serβis] nm self-service cafeteria

sellar vt (a) (documento) to seal; (timbrar) to stamp (b) (pozo, habitación) to close (up); Fig **s. los labios** to seal one's lips (c) Fig to conclude; **sellaron el acto con una comida** they finished off the ceremony with a meal

sello nm (a) (de correos) stamp (b) (para estampar) seal (c) (precinto) seal (d) (carácter distintivo) hallmark, mark; **la calidad es el s. de la casa** quality is the hallmark of our firm (e) (compañía) **s. discográfico** record label; **s. editorial** imprint (f) Andes Ven (de una moneda) reverse

Seltz nm, **seltz** nm **(agua de) S.** Seltzer (water)

selva nf (jungla) jungle; (bosque) forest ❑ **s. tropical** tropical rainforest; **s. virgen** virgin forest

selvático, -a adj woodland

semáforo nm traffic lights pl

semana nf week; **entre s.** during the week; **hoy hace una s.** a week ago (today) ❑ **s. laboral** working week, US work week; **S. Santa** Holy Week, Easter

semanada nf week's work

semanal adj weekly

semanalmente adv every week, once a week; **se publica s.** it's published weekly

semanario 1 adj weekly

2 nm Prensa weekly magazine

semántica nf Ling semantics sing

semántico, -a adj Ling semantic

semblante nm Literario (a) (expresión) countenance; (cara) face; **mudar el s.** to change colour (b) Fig (aspecto) look; **tener buen s.** to look good

semblanza nf Literario portrait

sembrado nm Agr sown field

sembrador, -a nm,f sower

sembradora nf Agr seed drill

sembrar [3] vt (a) Agr (semillas, grano) to sow (b) Fig (esparcir) to scatter, strew; **el camino está sembrado de dificultades** life is fraught with difficulties; **s. el pánico** to spread panic

semejante 1 adj (a) (parecido) similar (b) Pey (comparativo) such; **nunca he visto nada s.** I've never seen anything like it; **s. desvergüenza** such insolence (c) Geom (triángulo) similar

2 nm (prójimo) fellow being; **nuestros semejantes** our fellow beings

semejanza nf similarity, likeness

semejar vt to be like, resemble

semen nm semen

semental nm stud

sementera nf (a) (época) sowing season (b) (tierra sembrada) sown field (c) Fig (origen) breeding ground, source

semestral adj half-yearly; **pagos semestrales** half-yearly payments

semestre nm six-month period, semester

semicircular adj semicircular

semicírculo nm semicircle

semiconductor nm Elec semiconductor

semiconsciente adj semiconscious

semicorchea nf Mús Br semiquaver, US sixteenth note

semidesierto, -a adj half-deserted

semidesnatado, -a adj semi-skimmed

semidesnudo, -a adj half-naked

semidiós, -osa nm,f demigod

semidirecto, -a adj semidirect; Ferroc **un tren s.** an express train

semienterrado, -a adj half-buried

semiesférico, -a adj semispherical

semifinal nf semifinal

semifinalista nmf semifinalist

semifusa *nf Mús Br* hemidemisemiquaver, *US* sixty-fourth note

semilla *nf* seed; *Fig (origen)* **la s. de la discordia** the seeds of discontent

semillero *nm* (**a**) *(para plantar)* seedbed (**b**) *Fig* hotbed, breeding ground

seminal *adj* seminal

seminario *nm* (**a**) *Educ* seminar (**b**) *Rel* seminary

seminarista *nm Rel* seminarist

semioculto, -a *adj* partially hidden

semiología *nf Ling* semiology

semiótica *nf Ling* semiotics *sing*

semiprecioso, -a *adj* semiprecious

semiseco, -a *adj (vino etc)* medium-dry

semita 1 *adj* Semitic
 2 *nmf* Semite

semítico, -a *adj* Semitic

semitismo *nm* Semitism

semitono *nm Mús* semitone

semivocal *Ling* **1** *adj* semivocal
 2 *nf* semivowel

sémola *nf Culin* semolina

sempiterno, -a *adj* everlasting, eternal

Sena *n* **el S.** the Seine

senado *nm* (**a**) *Pol* senate (**b**) *(reunión)* assembly

senador, -a *nm,f* senator

senatorial *adj* senatorial

sencillamente *adv* simply

sencillez *nf* simplicity

sencillo, -a 1 *adj* (**a**) *(sin adornos)* simple, plain (**b**) *(fácil)* simple, easy; **¡es lo más s. del mundo!** it's the easiest thing! (**c**) *(persona) (natural)* natural, unaffected; *(ingenuo)* naïve, gullible; *(incauto)* unwary (**d**) *(no compuesto)* single (**e**) *(billete) Br* single, *US* one-way
 2 *nm* (**a**) *(disco)* single (**b**) *Andes CAm Méx Fam (cambio)* loose change

senda *nf* path

senderismo *nm* hiking, trekking, *Br* hillwalking

sendero *nm* path □ **S. Luminoso** Shining Path

sendos, -as *adj pl* each; **con sendas carteras en la mano** each carrying a briefcase

senectud *nf* old age

Senegal *n* Senegal

senegalés, -esa *adj & nm,f* Senegalese

senil *adj* senile

senilidad *nf* senility

seno *nm* (**a**) *(pecho)* breast, bosom (**b**) *Fig* bosom, heart; **en el s. de la familia** in the bosom of the family (**c**) *(matriz)* womb (**d**) *(cavidad)* cavity, hollow, hole (**e**) *Geog* gulf, bay (**f**) *Mat* sine

sensación *nf* (**a**) *(gen)* sensation, feeling; **s. de calor** feeling of warmth; **tengo la s. de que ...** I have a feeling that ... (**b**) *(impresión)* sensation; **causar s.** to cause a sensation

sensacional *adj* sensational

sensacionalismo *nm* sensationalism

sensacionalista 1 *adj* sensational, sensationalistic; **prensa s.** gutter press
 2 *nmf* sensationalist

sensatez *nf* good sense; **obrar con s.** to act sensibly

sensato, -a *adj* sensible

sensibilidad *nf* (**a**) *(emotividad)* sensibility (**b**) *(percepti-*

vidad, sentido artístico) sensitivity (**c**) *Téc (precisión)* sensitivity

sensibilización *nf* sensitization

sensibilizar [14] *vt* (**a**) *(hacer sensible)* to sensitize (**b**) *Fot (película)* to sensitize (**c**) *Fig (concienciar)* to sensitize, make aware; **s. la opinión pública** to raise public awareness

sensible *adj* (**a**) *(impresionable)* sensitive (**b**) *(delicado)* sensitive; **piel s.** sensitive skin (**c**) *(perceptible)* perceptible (**d**) *(que causa pena, dolor)* heavy, considerable; *Fml* **lamentamos tan s. pérdida** we regret such a sad loss (**e**) *Téc (preciso)* sensitive

sensiblemente *adv* noticeably, considerably

sensiblería *nf* over-sentimentality, mawkishness, gush

sensiblero, -a *adj* over-sentimental, mawkish, gushy

sensitivo, -a *adj* (**a**) *(sensible)* sensitive (**b**) *(de los sentidos)* sense; **órgano s.** sense organ

sensor *nm* sensor

sensorial *adj*, **sensorio, -a** *adj* sensory

sensual *adj (hedónico)* sensuous; *(sexual)* sensual

sensualidad *nf (hedonismo)* sensuousness; *(sexualidad)* sensuality

sentada *nf* (**a**) *(acción)* sitting; **de una s.** in one sitting (**b**) *Fam (protesta)* sit-in (demonstration); **hacer una s.** to hold a sit-in

sentado, -a 1 *pp de* **sentar**
 2 *adj* (**a**) *(en asiento)* seated, sitting (**b**) *(establecido)* established, settled; **dar algo por s.** to take sth for granted; **dejar s. que ...** to make it clear that ... (**c**) *(sensato)* sensible

sentador, -a *adj RP (prenda)* becoming, flattering

sentar [3] **1** *vt* (**a**) *(en silla etc)* to sit, seat (**b**) *(establecer)* to establish; **s. las bases de algo** to lay the foundations of sth
 2 *vi* (**a**) *(color, ropa, peinado)* to suit; **el pelo corto te sienta mal** short hair doesn't suit you (**b**) *(comida)* **s. bien/mal a** to agree/disagree with; **la salsa le sentó mal** the sauce disagreed with him; **la sopa te sentará muy bien** the soup will do you good (**c**) *(agradar)* to please; **le sentó mal la broma** she didn't like the joke; *Fam* **la noticia le sentó como un tiro** the news came as a terrible blow to him
 3 sentarse *vpr* (**a**) *(persona)* to sit, sit down (**b**) *(el tiempo)* to settle (down) (**c**) *(líquidos)* to settle

sentencia *nf* (**a**) *Jur (condena)* sentence; *(decisión)* judgement; **visto para s.** ready for judgement (**b**) *(aforismo)* maxim, saying, motto

sentenciar *vt Jur* to sentence (**a** to)

sentencioso, -a *adj* sententious

sentido, -a 1 *pp de* **sentir**²
 2 *adj* (**a**) *(penoso)* deeply felt; *Fml* **reciba mi más s. pésame** please accept my deepest sympathy (**b**) *(sensible)* sensitive; **es muy s. y se enfada por nada** she's very touchy and loses her temper very easily
 3 *nm* (**a**) *(gen)* sense; **los cinco sentidos** the five senses; *Fig* **hacer algo con los cinco sentidos** to take great pains with sth □ **s. común** common sense; **s. de la orientación** sense of direction; **s. del deber** sense of duty; **s. del humor** sense of humour; **s. del ridículo** sense of the ridiculous; **sexto s.** sixth sense (**b**) *(conciencia)* conscience; **dejar sin s. a algn** to knock sb out; **perder el s.** to faint (**c**) *(significado)* sense, meaning; **doble s.** double meaning; **no lo digo en ese s.** I don't mean it that way; **s. figurado** figurative sense (**d**) *(razón de ser)* meaning, sense; **hablar sin s.** to talk nonsense; **no tiene s.** it doesn't make sense; **¿qué s. tiene ...?** what's the point in ...? (**e**) *(dirección)* direction; **en s. opuesto** in the opposite direction; *Aut* **(de) s. único** one-way

sentimental 1 *adj* sentimental; **vida s.** love life
  2 *nmf* sentimental person

sentimentalismo *nm* sentimentality

sentimentaloide *adj Fam* gooey, over-sentimental, gushy

sentimiento *nm* **(a)** *(gen)* feeling; **buenos sentimientos** sympathy *sing*; **un s. de alegría** a feeling of joy **(b)** *(pesar)* sorrow, grief; *Fml* **le acompaño en el s.** my deepest sympathy

sentir[1] *nm* **(a)** *(sentimiento)* feeling **(b)** *(opinión)* opinion, view

sentir[2] [62] *vt* **(a)** *(gen)* to feel; **no sentí nada** I didn't feel a thing; **s. amor por algn** to feel love for sb; **s. hambre/calor** to feel hungry/hot; *Méx* **s. bonito/feo** to feel well/unwell; *Fig* **dejarse** *o* **hacerse s.** to make itself felt **(b)** *(oír)* to hear **(c)** *(lamentar)* to regret, be sorry about; **lo siento en el alma** I am terribly sorry; **lo siento (mucho)** I'm (very) sorry; **sentí mucho la muerte de tu amigo** I'm very sorry to hear about the death of your friend; **siento molestarle** I'm sorry to bother you **(d)** *(presentir)* to feel, think; **siento que va a ocurrir algo** I think something is going to happen
  2 sentirse *vpr* **(a)** *(encontrarse, considerarse)* to feel; **me siento mal** I feel ill; **¿qué tal te sientes?** how are you feeling?; **s. con ánimos de hacer algo** to feel like doing sth, feel up to sth; **s. ofendido** to feel offended *o* put off **(b)** *Am* *(ofenderse)* to take *Br* offence *o US* offense

seña *nf* **(a)** *(peculiaridad)* mark; **señas personales** *o* **de identidad** description *sing*, (personal) particulars **(b)** *(gesto)* sign; **hablar por señas** to talk in sign language; **hacer señas a algn** to signal to sb **(c)** *(indicio)* sign; **por más señas** specifically **(d)** **señas** *(dirección)* address *sing*

señal *nf* **(a)** *(indicio)* sign, indication; **dar señales de vida** to show signs of life; **en s. de** as a sign of, as a token of; **es buena s.** it's a good sign **(b)** *(gesto etc)* signal, sign; **dar la s.** to give the signal; **hacer señales a algn** to signal to sb; **s. de alarma** alarm signal **(c)** *(placa)* sign ❏ **s. de peligro** danger sign; *Aut* **s. de tráfico** road sign **(d)** *(marca)* mark; *(vestigio)* trace; **deja una s. en la página diez** mark page ten; **dejar s.** to leave a mark; **ni s.** not a trace **(e)** *(cicatriz)* scar, mark **(f)** *Tel* tone; **s. de comunicando** *Br* engaged tone, *US* busy signal; **s. de llamada** ringing tone **(g)** *Com* deposit **(h)** *Rel* **s. de la cruz** sign of the cross; **hacer la s. de la cruz** to make the sign of the cross

señalado, -a 1 *pp de* **señalar**
  2 *adj* **(a)** *(insigne, famoso)* distinguished, famous **(b)** *(fijado)* appointed, fixed; **el día s.** the appointed day; **un día s.** a red-letter day **(c)** *(marcado)* marked, scarred; **tiene la cara señalada** his face is scarred

señalar 1 *vt* **(a)** *(indicar, determinar)* to mark, indicate; *(hacer notar)* to point out; *Fig (apuntar hacia)* to point to; **el aumento del paro señala un decaimiento de la economía** the rise in unemployment is a sure sign of a lull in the economy; **la nieve señala la llegada del invierno** (the) snow marks the beginning of winter; **señálamelo y así lo reconoceré** point it out to me so I'll recognize it; **su derrota señala el fin de una época** his defeat marks the end of an era **(b)** *(marcar)* to mark; **s. algo con una cruz** to mark sth with a cross **(c)** *(con el dedo)* to point at **(d)** *(subrayar)* to stress, underline; **s. la importancia de algo** to stress the importance of sth **(e)** *(fijar) (precio, fecha)* to fix, arrange; **s. la fecha de la boda** to set the date of the wedding **(f)** *(designar)* to appoint; **s. a algn para hacer algo** to appoint sb to do sth **(g)** *(dejar cicatriz)* to mark, scar
  2 señalarse *vpr (sobresalir)* to stand out; *(distinguirse)* to distinguish oneself

señalización *nf* **(a)** *(colocación de señales)* signposting **(b)** *(señales)* road signs *pl*

señalizar [14] *vt (carretera)* to signpost

señero, -a *adj (exclusivo)* unique; *(supremo)* outstanding

señor, -a 1 *adj* **(a)** *(distinguido)* distinguished, grand **(b)** *Fam* fine; **es un s. coche** it's quite a car; **una señora casa** one hell of a house
  2 *nm* **(a)** *(hombre)* man; *(caballero)* gentleman; **el s. de los bigotes** the man with the moustache; **ser todo un s.** to be a real gentleman **(b)** *(amo)* master ❏ **s. de la guerra** warlord; *Hist* **s. feudal** feudal lord **(c)** *Rel* **El S.** the Lord; **ministro del S.** priest; **Nuestro S.** Our Lord **(d)** *(tratamiento de respeto)* sir; **buenos días, s.** good morning, sir; *(en carta)* **muy s. mío** Dear Sir; **¡sí s.!** yes sir! **(e)** *(con apellido)* Mr; **el Sr. Pérez** Mr Pérez **(f)** *(con título) (no se traduce)* **el s. ministro** the Minister

señora *nf* **(a)** *(mujer)* woman; *Fml* lady; **¡señoras y señores!** ladies and gentlemen!; **una s. de unos cincuenta años** a woman in her fifties ❏ **s. de compañía** companion **(b)** *(ama)* mistress; *Hist* lady; **en estos momentos la s. no está en casa** the lady of the house is out at the moment **(c)** *Rel* **Nuestra S.** Our Lady **(d)** *(tratamiento de respeto)* madam; **buenas tardes, s.** good afternoon, madam; *(en carta)* **muy s. mía** Dear Madam **(e)** *(con apellido)* Mrs; **la Sra. González** Mrs González **(f)** *(con título) (no se traduce)* **la s. ministra** the Minister **(g)** *(esposa)* wife; **mi s. no puede venir** my wife cannot come

señorear *vt* **(a)** *(mandar)* to rule, control **(b)** *Fig (dominar)* to tower over

señoría *nf (hombre)* lordship; *(mujer)* ladyship

señorial *adj* stately, majestic; **casa s.** stately home

señorío *nm* **(a)** *(dominio)* dominion, rule **(b)** *(terreno)* estate, domain **(c)** *(majestuosidad)* stateliness **(d)** *(porte distinguido)* distinction; *(elegancia)* elegance

señorita *nf* **(a)** *(joven)* young woman; *Fml* young lady **(b)** *(tratamiento de respeto)* Miss; **¿señora o s.?** Miss or Mrs? **(c)** *(con apellido)* Miss; **S. Muñoz** Miss Muñoz **(d)** *Educ Fam (maestra)* **la s.** the teacher, Miss **(e)** *Fam (puro)* small cigar

señorito *nm* **(a)** *Anticuado (hijo del amo)* master (of the house) **(b)** *Fam Pey (joven rico)* rich kid, daddy's boy

señorón, -ona *adj & nm,f Fam Pey* big shot

señuelo *nm* **(a)** *Caza* decoy **(b)** *Fig (cebo)* bait **(c)** *Arg Bol (novillos)* = group of young lead bulls

sepa *subj pres véase* **saber**[2]

sépalo *nm Bot* sepal

separable *adj* separable, detachable

separación *nf* **(a)** *(de elementos)* separation ❏ *Jur* **s. conyugal** legal separation; *Jur* **s. de bienes** separate estates *(in matrimony)* **(b)** *(espacio)* space, gap

separado, -a 1 *pp de* **separar**
  2 *adj* **(a)** *(apartado)* separate; **por s.** separately, individually; **añadir las claras y las yemas de los huevos por s.** add egg yolks and whites separately **(b)** *(divorciado)* separated

separador, -a *adj* separating

separar 1 *vt* **(a)** *(gen)* to separate; **estaban riñendo y tuvimos que separarlos** they were arguing so we had to separate them; **hemos de s. un caso del otro** we have to consider each case individually; **los separaron de clase** they were put in separate classes **(b)** *(desunir)* to detach, remove; **separa la etiqueta, por favor** take off the label, please **(c)** *(dividir)* to divide, separate; **los separaron en grupos de diez** they were broken up into groups of ten each **(d)** *(guardar)* to set aside; **ha separado un poco de comida para ti** he's put aside some food for you **(e)** *(apartar)* to move away; **separa la silla de la pared** move the chair away from the wall **(f)** *(destituir)* to remove, dismiss
  2 separarse *vpr* **(a)** *(ir por distinto lugar)* to separate, part company; **al llegar a la carretera se separaron** when they

reached the road they went their own ways (**b**) *(matrimonio)* to separate; **sus padres se separaron el año pasado** his parents separated last year (**c**) *(desprenderse)* to separate, come off (**de** from); **se han separado las hojas del libro** the pages have fallen out of the book (**d**) *(apartarse)* to move away; **s. de las viejas amistades** to drift apart from one's old friends (**e**) *(abandonar) (gen negativo)* to part (**de** with); **nunca me separaré de este cuadro** I shall never part with this painting

separata *nf Impr* offprint

separatismo *nm Pol* separatism

separatista *adj & nmf Pol* separatist

sepelio *nm Fml* burial, interment

sepia 1 *nf (pez)* cuttlefish
  2 *adj & nm (color)* sepia

septentrión *nm Fml* north

septentrional *adj* northern

septicemia *nf Med* septicaemia, *US* septicemia

séptico, -a *adj* septic; **fosa séptica** septic tank

septiembre *nm* September; **el 5 de s.** the 5th of September; **en s.** in September; *véase tamb* **noviembre**

séptimo, -a 1 *adj* seventh; **el s. arte** the cinema; **la séptima parte** a seventh; *Fam* **en el s. cielo** in seventh heaven
  2 *nm,f (de una serie)* seventh
  3 *nm (parte)* seventh; *véase tamb* **octavo, -a**

septuagenario, -a *adj & nm,f* septuagenarian

septuagésimo, -a 1 *adj* seventieth; **la septuagésima parte** a seventieth
  2 *nm,f (de una serie)* seventieth; **s. primero** seventy-first; **s. segundo** seventy-second
  3 *nm (parte)* seventieth; *véase tamb* **octavo, -a**

sepulcral *adj* sepulchral; *Fig* **silencio s.** deathly silence

sepulcro *nm* tomb; *Fam* **ser un s.** to keep mum

sepultar *vt* to bury

sepultura *nf* (**a**) *(tumba)* grave (**b**) *(entierro)* burial; **dar s. a algn** to bury sb

sepulturero, -a *nm,f* gravedigger

sequedad *nf* (**a**) *(falta de humedad)* dryness (**b**) *Fig* curtness, abruptness

sequía *nf* (**a**) *(falta de agua)* drought (**b**) *Col (sed)* thirst

séquito *nm* (**a**) *(grupo de acompañantes)* entourage, retinue (**b**) *Pol* group of followers

SER *nf Rad (abrev de* **Sociedad Española de Radiodifusión**)

ser¹ *nm* (**a**) *(ente)* being ❑ **s. humano** human being; **S. Supremo** Supreme Being; **s. vivo** living being (**b**) *(vida)* existence, life; *Fml* **dar el s.** to give life (**c**) *(valor)* core; **esto constituye el s. del espectáculo** this is the heart of the show

ser² [2] *vi* (**a**) *(suceder)* to be; **el estreno será mañana** tomorrow is the opening night (**b**) *(identificar)* to be; **es alto y rubio** he is tall and fair; **Jaime es médico** Jaime is a doctor (**c**) *(clasificar)* to be; **Jaime es el médico** Jaime is the doctor (**d**) *(indica procedencia)* to be, come (**de** from); **¿de dónde eres?** where are you from?; **José María es de San Sebastián** José María is from San Sebastián (**e**) *(indica material)* to be made (**de** of); **la mesa es de madera** the table is made of wood (**f**) *(indica color)* to be; **el edificio es gris** the building is grey (**g**) *(indica posesión)* **s. de** to belong to; **¿de quién es este abrigo?** whose coat is this?; **el perro es de Ricardo** the dog belongs to Ricardo (**h**) **s. para** *(finalidad, adecuación)* to be for; **este jabón es para las manos** this is hand soap; **estos modales no son de caballero** that isn't gentlemanly behaviour (**i**) *(localización tiempo, día, hora)* to be; **es de día** it's daytime; **es invierno** it's winter; **son las dos de la tarde** it's two o'clock *o* p.m (**j**) *(costar)* to be, cost; **¿cuánto es?** how much is it? (**k**) *(causar)* to be, cause; **la bebida fue su perdición** drinking was his downfall (**l**) *(ficción en juegos)* to be; **tú serás la princesa y yo la bruja** you can be the princess and I'll be the witch (**m**) *(consistir en)* to be, lie in, consist of; **el secreto es hacerlo despacio** the secret lies in doing it slowly (**n**) *(devenir)* **s. de** to become of; **¿qué será de mí?** what will become of me? (**o**) *(auxiliar como pasiva)* to be; **el hecho será verificado** the fact is to be verified; **fue asesinado** he was murdered (**p**) *(locuciones)* **a no s. que** unless; **a poder s.** if possible; **como debe s.** as it should be; **¿cómo es eso?, ¿cómo puede s.?** how can that be?; **como sea** anyhow; **de no s. por ...** had it not been for ...; **érase una vez** once upon a time; **es de esperar/desear que ...** it is to be expected/hoped that ...; **es más** furthermore; **es que ...** it's just that ...; **lo que sea** whatever; **no es nada, ha sido una caída tonta** it's all right, it was just a little fall; **no será para tanto** it won't come to that; **o sea** that is (to say); **por si (fuera) poco** to top it all; **no puede s.** it can't be true; **puede s.** it could be, it's possible; **sea como sea** in any case, be that as it may; **siendo así** that being so; **un si es no es** a trifle, a touch; *Fam* **s. de lo que no hay** to be a real winner; *Fam* **muy suyo** to be an eccentric

seráfico, -a *adj* seraphic, angelic

serafín *nm* seraph

serbal *nm Bot* **s. silvestre** rowan, mountain ash

Serbia *n* Serbia

serbio, -a *adj & nm,f* Serbian

serbocroata 1 *adj & nmf* Serbo-Croat
  2 *nm (idioma)* Serbo-Croat

serenar 1 *vt (gen)* to calm, quieten; *(persona)* to calm down
  2 serenarse *vpr* (**a**) *(persona)* to calm down; *(mar)* to grow calm (**b**) *Meteor (tiempo)* to clear up

serenata *nf Mús* serenade

serenidad *nf* serenity, calm; **conservar la s.** to keep calm

sereno¹ *nm* (**a**) *Antes (vigilante)* night watchman (**b**) **dormir al s.** to sleep out in the open

sereno, -a² *adj* (**a**) *(persona)* calm; *(ambiente)* peaceful; *Fam* **estar s.** to be sober (**b**) *Meteor (cielo)* clear; *(tiempo)* fine, good

serial *nm Rad TV* serial

seriamente *adv* seriously

seriar *vt* to serialize

serie *nf* (**a**) *(gen)* series *sing*; **fabricación en s.** mass production; **fabricado en s.** mass-produced; *Fig* **fuera de s.** out of the ordinary, unique (**b**) *(cadena)* series *sing*, succession, string; **una s. de acontecimientos** a string of events (**c**) *Rad TV* serial, series *sing* (**d**) *Dep* series *sing*; **s. mundial** world series

seriedad *nf* (**a**) *(severidad)* seriousness; **con s.** seriously (**b**) *(gravedad)* seriousness, gravity (**c**) *(formalidad)* reliability, dependability; **falta de s.** irresponsibility

serigrafía *nf* serigraphy, silk-screen printing

serio, -a *adj* (**a**) *(severo)* serious; **en s.** seriously; **¿en s.?** are you serious?, do you really mean that?; **hablo en s.** I'm serious; **ponerse s.** to become serious, look serious (**b**) *(grave, importante)* serious, grave; **asunto s.** serious matter (**c**) *(formal)* reliable, dependable, responsible (**d**) *(color)* sober (**e**) *(traje)* formal

sermón *nm* (**a**) *Rel* sermon (**b**) *Fam (represalia)* sermon, lecture, ticking-off

sermonear 1 *vi Rel* to preach
  2 *vt Fam (reprender)* to lecture

seropositivo, -a *Med* **1** *adj* HIV-positive
  2 *nm,f* HIV-positive person

seroso, -a *adj* serous

serpentear *vi (enrollar)* to wind; *(zigzaguear)* to wind one's way, meander

serpenteo *nm (vueltas)* winding; *(zigzag)* meandering

serpentín *nm (tubo)* coil

serpentina *nf* **(a)** *(tira de papel)* streamer **(b)** *Min* serpentine

serpiente *nf* snake □ **s. de cascabel** rattle-snake; **s. pitón** python

serraduras *nfpl* sawdust *sing*

serrallo *nm* harem

serranía *nf* mountainous area *o* country

serranilla *nf Lit* = lyric composition in short verses

serrano, -a 1 *adj* **(a)** *(de la sierra)* mountain, highland **(b)** *Fam (hermoso)* nice; **un cuerpo s.** a shapely figure
  2 *nm,f Am* highlander

serrar [3] *vt* to saw

serrería *nf* sawmill

serrín *nm* sawdust

serrucho *nm* **(a)** *(herramienta)* handsaw **(b)** *Cuba (pez)* sawfish

servicentro *nm CAm CSur* service station

servicial *adj* helpful, obliging, accommodating

servicio *nm* **(a)** *(prestación, asistencia, sistema)* service □ **s. a domicilio** delivery service; **s. de habitaciones** room service; **s. de inteligencia** intelligence service; **s. posventa** after-sales service; **s. secreto** secret service; **servicios sociales** social services **(b)** *(funcionamiento)* service; **entrar en s.** to come into service; **estar fuera de s.** *(máquina)* to be out of order **(c)** *Mil* service; **estar de s.** to be on duty □ **s. militar** military service **(d)** *(favor)* service, favour, *US* favor; **hacer** *o* **prestar s.** to do a favour; *Fam* **hacer un flaco s.** to do more harm than good **(e)** *(empleados domésticos)* servants *pl; (no fijo)* domestic help **(f)** *Dep* service, serve **(g)** *(juego, conjunto)* set □ **s. de té** tea set, tea service **(h)** *Econ* **servicios** *(sector terciario)* services; **una empresa de servicios** a services company **(i)** *Esp* **servicios** *(retrete)* toilet, *US* bathroom

servidor, -a 1 *nm,f* **(a)** *(criado)* servant; *Fml* **s. de usted** at your service; *(en carta)* **su seguro s.** yours faithfully **(b)** *(eufemismo)* myself; **¿quién se ocupa de esto? — s.** who's taking care of it? — I am; **¿Ramón Lopera? — un s.** Ramón Lopera? — yes?
  2 *nm Inform* server

servidumbre *nf* **(a)** *(criados)* servants *pl*, staff *pl* **(b)** *(condición de siervo)* servitude **(c)** *(sujeción a los vicios etc)* compulsion **(d)** *Jur Fin* servitude

servil *adj (humilde)* servile; *(obediente)* subservient

servilismo *nm (humildad)* servility; *(obediencia)* subservience

servilleta *nf* serviette, napkin

servilletero *nm* serviette ring, napkin ring

servir [47] **1** *vt* **(a)** *(gen)* to serve; *Mil* **s. a la patria** to serve one's country **(b)** *(prestar ayuda a)* to help; *(en tienda etc)* **¿en qué puedo servirle?** what can I do for you?, may I help you?; *Fml* **para servirle** at your service **(c)** *(dar comida, bebida a)* to serve, wait on; **¿le sirvo una copa, señor?** would you like a drink, sir?; **s. mesas** to wait at table, *US* wait tables **(d)** *Com (suministrar a)* to supply with; **le serviremos la mercancía lo antes posible** we shall deliver your merchandise as soon as possible
  2 *vi* **(a)** *(gen)* to serve; *Mil* **s. en Ceuta** to serve in Ceuta **(b)** *(camarero etc)* to serve; **s. en la mesa** to wait at table, *US* to wait tables **(c)** *(trabajar de criado)* to be a servant; **ponerse a s.** to go into service; **s. en casa de algn** to be in service at sb's house **(d)** *(valer)* to be useful, be suitable; *(instrumento)*

to be good; **de nada sirve hablar** talking is useless; **mi paraguas no sirve** my umbrella is no good; **no sirve** it's no good; **tu consejo me sirvió de mucho** your advice was very useful to me **(e)** **s. para** to be used for, be for; **¿para qué sirve esto?** what is this (used) for? **(f)** **s. de** to serve as, act as; **s. de aviso** to serve as a warning; **s. de enlace** to act as a go-between **(g)** *Dep* to serve
  3 **servirse** *vpr* **(a)** *(comida etc)* to help oneself; **sírvete tú mismo** help yourself **(b)** **s. de** to use, make use of; *Fig* **se han servido de ti** you've been taken advantage of **(c)** *Fml (carta)* to be kind enough to; **sírvase** *o* **sírvanse comunicarnos su decisión** please inform us of your decision

servodirección *nf* power steering

servofreno *nm Téc* servo brake

servomecanismo *nm* servomechanism

servomotor *nm* servomotor

sésamo *nm* **(a)** *Bot* sesame **(b)** *Lit & Fam* **¡ábrete, s.!** open, sesame!

sesear *vi Ling* to pronounce Spanish **c** (before **e** *o* **i**) and **z** as **s**

sesenta *inv* **1** *adj (cardinal)* sixty; *(ordinal)* sixtieth; **los años s.** the sixties
  2 *nm* sixty; **nací en el s.** I was born in nineteen sixty; *véase tamb* **ocho**

sesentavo, -a 1 *adj* sixtieth
  2 *nm,f (de una serie)* sixtieth
  3 *nm (parte)* sixtieth; *véase tamb* **octavo, -a**

sesentón, -ona *adj & nm,f Fam* sixty-year-old

seseo *nm* pronunciation of Spanish **c** (before **e** *o* **i**) and **z** as **s**

sesera *nf Fam* brains

sesgado, -a *adj* biased, partial; **información sesgada** biased information

sesgar [38] *vt* to cut on the bias

sesgo *nm* **(a)** *Cost* **al s.** on the bias **(b)** *Fig (curso de un asunto)* slant, turn; **tomar un s. favorable/desfavorable** to take a turn for the better/worse

sesión *nf* **(a)** *(reunión)* meeting, session; *Jur* session, sitting; **se abre la s.** the meeting is open; **se cierra la s.** the meeting is adjourned □ **s. plenaria** plenary session **(b)** *Cin* showing □ **s. continua** continuous showing; **s. de noche** late show; **s. de tarde** matinée

seso *nm* **(a)** *Anat* brain **(b)** *Fam Fig* brains *pl*, grey matter; *(juicio)* sense; **beber** *o* **beberse el s.** *o* **los sesos** *(volverse loco)* to lose one's mind; **calentarse** *o* **devanarse los sesos** to rack one's brains; **tener sorbido el s.** *o* **los sesos a algn** *(tener bajo la influencia)* to have sb under one's spell **(c)** **sesos** *Culin* brains

sestear *vi* to have a nap

sesudo, -a *adj* **(a)** *(inteligente)* intelligent, brainy **(b)** *(sensato)* sensible; *(prudente)* wise

set *nm Ten* set

seta *nf Esp (comestible)* mushroom; **s. venenosa** poisonous mushroom

setecientos, -as *inv* **1** *adj (cardinal)* seven hundred; *(ordinal)* seven hundredth
  2 *nm* seven hundred; *véase tamb* **ocho**

setenta *inv* **1** *adj (cardinal)* seventy; *(ordinal)* seventieth; **los años s.** the seventies
  2 *nm* seventy; *véase tamb* **ocho**

setentavo, -a 1 *adj* seventieth
  2 *nm,f (de una serie)* seventieth
  3 *nm (parte)* seventieth; *véase tamb* **octavo, -a**

setentón, -ona *adj & nm,f* seventy-year-old

setiembre *nm véase* **septiembre**

seto *nm* hedge

setter ['seter] (*pl* **setters**) *nm (perro)* setter

seudónimo *nm* pseudonym; *(de escritores)* pen name

Seúl *n* Seoul

s.e.u.o. *(abrev de* **salvo error u omisión)** errors and omissions excepted

severidad *nf* (**a**) *(gravedad)* severity, harshness (**b**) *(rigurosidad)* strictness

severo, -a *adj* (**a**) *(grave)* severe, harsh (**b**) *(riguroso)* strict; **ser s. con algn** to be hard on sb (**c**) *(estilo)* stark, severe

Sevilla *n* Seville

sevillanas *nfpl Mús* = Sevillian folk songs and dance

sevillano, -a 1 *adj* of o from Seville, Sevillian
2 *nm,f* person from Seville, Sevillian

sexagenario, -a *adj & nm,f* sexagenarian

sexagesimal *adj* sexagesimal

sexagésimo, -a 1 *adj* sixtieth; **una sexagésima parte** a sixtieth
2 *nm,f (de una serie)* sixtieth; *véase tamb* **octavo, -a**

sex-appeal [seksa'pil] *nm* sex appeal

sexi *adj véase* **sexy**

sexismo *nm* sexism

sexista *adj* (**a**) *(gen)* sexist (**b**) *(hombre)* male chauvinist

sexo *nm* (**a**) *(género)* sex **el bello s., el s. débil** the weaker sex; **el s. fuerte** the stronger sex (**b**) *(actividad)* sex ❏ **s. oral** oral sex (**c**) *(genitales)* genitals *pl*

sexología *nf* sexology

sexólogo, -a *nm,f* sexologist

sextante *nm Náut* sextant

sexteto *nm Mús* sextet

sexto, -a 1 *adj* sixth
2 *nm,f (de una serie)* sixth
3 *nm (parte)* sixth; *véase tamb* **octavo, -a**

séxtuplo, -a *adj & nm* sextuple

sexuado, -a *adj* sexed

sexual *adj* sexual, sex; **vida s.** sex life

sexualidad *nf* sexuality

sexualmente *adv* sexually

sexy *adj* sexy, with sex appeal

Seychelles [sei'ʃels] *npl* Seychelles

s.f. *(abrev de* **sin fecha)** not dated

s/f. *(abrev de* **su favor)** your favour o *US* favor

sha [sa, ʃa] *nm (título)* shah

shareware ['ʃerwer] *nm Inform* shareware

Shetland *n* **las Islas S.** the Shetland Isles, Shetland *sing*

shock [ʃok] (*pl* **shocks**) *nm Med* shock

short [ʃort] *nm (prenda)* shorts *pl*

show [ʃou, tʃou] (*pl* **shows**) *nm* (**a**) *(espectáculo)* show (**b**) *Fam (exhibición)* show, display; **montar un s.** to put on a show

si¹ *conj* (**a**) *(condicional)* if; **como si** as if; **por si acaso** just in case; **si acaso** if by any chance; **si hubiesen llegado a tiempo** if they had arrived in time; **si llueve, iremos en coche** if it rains, we'll go by car; **si no** if not; **si quieres** if you like, if you wish (**b**) *(disyuntivo)* whether; **dime si te gusta o no** tell me whether you like it or not; **no sé si ir o no** I don't know whether to go or not (**c**) *(protesta, sorpresa)* but; **¡si está llorando!** but she's crying!; **¡si no quiero!** but I don't want to!

si² (*pl* **sis**) *nm Mús* ti, si, B

sí¹ *pron pers* (**a**) *(singular) (él)* himself; *(ella)* herself; *(cosa)* itself; *(plural)* themselves; **de por sí, en sí** in itself; **hablaban entre sí** they were talking among themselves o to each other; **por sí mismo** by himself; **sí mismo** himself (**b**) *(uno mismo)* oneself; **decir para sí** to say to oneself; **estar fuera de sí** to be beside oneself (with anger); **estar sobre sí** to be on one's guard; **volver en sí** to come round, regain consciousness

sí² 1 *adv* (**a**) *(para sustituir a frases afirmativas)* yes; **¡claro que sí!** of course!; **creo que sí** I think so; **dije que sí** I said yes, I accepted, I agreed; **¡eso sí que no!** certainly not!; **porque sí** *(sin razón)* because I o you feel like it; *(por naturaleza)* that's the way it is; **¡que sí!** yes, I tell you!; **un día sí y otro no** every other day (**b**) *(uso enfático) (no se traduce)* **sí que está bien hecho** it certainly is well done; **sí que me gusta** of course I like it
2 *nm* (*pl* **síes**) yes; **dar el sí** to say yes, accept, agree; **síes y noes** yeas and nays

siamés, -esa 1 *adj* Siamese
2 *nm,f (mellizo)* Siamese twin

sibarita 1 *adj* sybarite, sybaritic
2 *nmf* sybarite

sibaritismo *nm* sybaritism

Siberia *n* Siberia

siberiano, -a *adj & nmf* Siberian

sibila *nf Mit* sibyl

sibilante *adj & nf Ling* sibilant

sibilino, -a *adj* (**a**) *Mit* sibylline (**b**) *Fig* cryptic, enigmatic

sicalíptico, -a *adj* suggestive, erotic, pornographic

sicario *nm* hired gunman; *Fam* goon

Sicilia *n* Sicily

siciliano, -a *adj & nm,f* Sicilian

sicoanálisis *nm inv véase* **psicoanálisis**

sicoanalista *nmf véase* **psicoanalista**

sicoanalítico, -a *adj véase* **psicoanalítico, -a**

sicoanalizar [14] *vt véase* **psicoanalizar**

sicodélico, -a *adj véase* **psicodélico, -a**

sicodrama *nm véase* **psicodrama**

sicofanta *nm*, **sicofante** *nm* imposter, fake

sicofármaco *nm véase* **psicofármaco**

sicología *nf véase* **psicología**

sicológico, -a *adj véase* **psicológico, -a**

sicólogo, -a *nm,f véase* **psicólogo, -a**

sicómoro *nm*, **sicomoro** *nm Bot* sycamore

siconeurosis *nf inv véase* **psiconeurosis**

sicópata *nmf véase* **psicópata**

sicopatía *nf véase* **psicopatía**

sicopático, -a *adj véase* **psicopático, -a**

sicopatología *nf véase* **psicopatología**

sicosis *nf inv véase* **psicosis**

sicosomático, -a *adj véase* **psicosomático, -a**

sicote *nm Am* foot odour o *US* odor

sicoterapeuta *nmf véase* **psicoterapeuta**

sicoterapia *nf véase* **psicoterapia**

sida *nm Med (abrev de* **síndrome de inmunodeficiencia adquirida)** AIDS

sidecar [siðe'kar] *nm Aut* sidecar

sideral *adj* sidereal, astral; **espacio s.** outer space

siderurgia *nf Ind* iron and steel industry

siderúrgico, -a *adj Ind* iron and steel; **la industria siderúrgica** the iron and steel industry

sidoso, -a *adj Fam Pey* suffering from AIDS

sidra *nf Br* cider, *US* hard cider

siega *nf Agr* (**a**) *(acción)* reaping, harvesting (**b**) *(temporada)* harvest (time) (**c**) *(mieses)* harvest

siembra *nf Agr* (**a**) *(acción)* sowing (**b**) *(temporada)* sowing time

siempre *adv* (**a**) *(en todo momento, todo el tiempo)* always; **a la hora de s.** at the usual time; **como s.** as usual; **eso es así desde s.** it has always been like that; **para s.** for ever; **para s. jamás** for ever and ever; **s. pasa lo mismo** it's always the same; **s. viene tarde** he is always late; **s. que** *(cada vez que)* whenever; *(a condición de que)* provided, as long as; **s. y cuando** provided, as long as; **son amigos de s.** they are old friends (**b**) *(en cualquier caso, en último extremo)* always; **si no hay autobuses s. podemos ir a pie** if there aren't any buses, we can always walk (**c**) *Am (todavía)* still

siempreviva *nf Bot* everlasting flower, immortelle

sien *nf Anat* temple

siena *adj (color)* sienna, dark yellow

sierpe *nf* (**a**) *Zool Fml* serpent (**b**) *Fig (mal genio)* badtempered person; *(feo)* ugly person

sierra *nf* (**a**) *Téc Carp* saw ❏ **s. circular** circular saw; **s. mecánica** power saw (**b**) *Geog* mountain range, sierra

Sierra Leona *n* Sierra Leone

sierraleonés, -esa *adj & nm,f* Sierra Leonean

siervo, -a *nm,f* (**a**) *(esclavo)* slave; *Rel* **s. de Dios** servant of God (**b**) *Hist* serf

siesta *nf* siesta, nap; **dormir** *o* **echar la s.** to have a siesta *o* an afternoon nap; **no me llames a la hora de la s.** don't call me at siesta time

siete *inv* **1** *adj (cardinal)* seven; *(ordinal)* seventh
2 *nm* (**a**) *(número)* seven; **son las s.** it's seven o'clock; **el s. de abril** the seventh of April, April the seventh; **hablar más que s.** to talk nineteen to the dozen (**b**) *Fam (rasgón)* tear; **me he hecho un s. en los pantalones** I've ripped my trousers *véase tamb* **ocho**

sietemesino, -a **1** *adj* seven-month
2 *nm* (**a**) *(bebé)* seven-month baby, premature baby (**b**) *Fam (enclenque)* weakling (**c**) *Fam (chico presumido)* little squirt

sífilis *nf inv Med* syphilis

sifilítico, -a *adj & nm,f* syphilitic

sifón *nm* (**a**) *(para trasvasar líquidos)* siphon (**b**) *(tubería)* U-bend, trap (**c**) *(botella)* soda siphon (**d**) *(soda)* soda, soda water; **whisky con s.** whisky and soda

sig. *(abrev de* **siguiente)** foll

sigilo *nm* (**a**) *(discreción)* discretion (**b**) *(secreto)* secrecy; **con mucho s.** in great secrecy; *Rel* **s. sacramental** secrecy of the confessional

sigilosamente *adv (mesuradamente)* discreetly; *(secretamente)* secretly; **entró s. en la habitación** she crept *o* slipped into the room

sigiloso, -a *adj* (**a**) *(mesurado)* discreet (**b**) *(asunto)* secret; *(persona)* secretive

sigla *nf* acronym; **EE.UU. son las siglas de Estados Unidos de América** U.S.A. is the abbreviation of United States of America

siglo *nm* century; **por los siglos de los siglos** for ever and ever; *Fam* **hace siglos que no le veo** I haven't seen him for ages ❏ *Hist Lit* **el S. de las luces** the Eighteenth Century; *Hist Lit* **el S. de Oro** the Golden Age

signar **1** *vt* (**a**) *(firmar)* to sign (**b**) *Rel* to make the sign of the cross over
2 signarse *vpr Rel* to make the sign of the cross, cross oneself

signatario, -a *adj & nm,f* signatory; **el s. del documento** the signatory of the document

signatura *nf* (**a**) *Impr* signature (**b**) *(en bibliotecas etc)* catalogue number (**c**) *(firma)* signature

significación *nf* (**a**) *(sentido)* meaning (**b**) *(importancia)* significance

significado, -a **1** *pp de* **significar**
2 *adj (conocido)* well-known; *(importante)* important
3 *nm (sentido)* meaning; **el s. de una palabra** the meaning of a word (**b**) *Ling* signifier

significante *nm Ling* significant, signifier

significar [59] **1** *vt* (**a**) *(querer decir)* to mean; **'persistir' significa insistir en una cosa** 'persistir' means to continue with something (**b**) *(manifestar)* to express, make known
2 significarse *vpr* to stand out

significativamente *adv (con relevancia)* significantly; *(expresivamente, con sentido)* meaningfully

significativo, -a *adj (relevante)* significant; *(expresivo, con sentido)* meaningful; **un gesto s.** a meaningful gesture

signo *nm* (**a**) *(señal)* sign; **cantar es s. de alegría** singing is a (sure) sign of happiness (**b**) *Mat* sign ❏ **s. más** plus sign; **s. menos** minus sign (**c**) *Ling* mark ❏ **s. de admiración, s. de exclamación** *Br* exclamation mark, *US* exclamation point; **s. de interrogación** question mark (**d**) *Astrol (del zodíaco)* (star) sign

sigo *indic pres véase* **seguir**

siguiente *adj* following, next; **¡el s.!** next, please!

sij *adj & nmf Rel* Sikh

sílaba *nf* syllable

silabario *nm* spelling book

silabear *vi* to divide words into syllables

silábico, -a *adj* syllabic

silba *nf* hissing; **el público respondió con una escandalosa s. a ...** the audience hissed and booed at ...

silbar *vi* (**a**) *(producir silbos)* to whistle (**b**) *(abuchear)* to hiss, boo

silbato *nm* whistle

silbido *nm* (**a**) *(acción)* whistle, whistling; *(agudo)* hiss; **el s. del viento** the whistling of the wind ❏ **s. de oídos** ringing in the ears (**b**) *Tel* ring, ringing

silbo *nm (acción)* whistle, whistling; *(voz aguda)* hiss

silenciador *nm* (**a**) *(de arma)* silencer (**b**) *Aut Br* silencer, *US* muffler

silenciar *vt* (**a**) *(acallar) (persona, protestas)* to silence (**b**) *(ocultar, omitir) (hecho, escándalo)* to hush up

silencio *nm* silence; **en s.** in silence; **guardar s.** to keep quiet; **imponer s. a algn** to make sb be quiet; *Fig* **el s. de la prensa es significativo** the silence of the press is meaningful

silencioso, -a *adj (persona)* quiet; *(cosa)* silent; **motor s.** silent motor

sílex *nm inv Min* silex, flint

sílfide *nf Mit* sylph

silicato *nm Quím* silicate

sílice *nf* silica

silicio *nm* silicon

silicona *nf* silicone

silicosis *nf inv Med* silicosis

silla *nf* (**a**) *(asiento)* chair; *Fig* **Don Ramón ocupa una silla en la Academia** Don Ramón holds a seat in the Academy ❏ **s. de ruedas** wheelchair; **s. eléctrica** electric chair; **s. giratoria** swivel chair (**b**) *Equit* **s. (de montar)** saddle

sillar *nm Constr* ashlar

sillería¹ *nf* (**a**) *(sillas)* chairs *pl*, set of chairs (**b**) *(del coro)* choir stalls *pl*

sillería² *nf Constr* ashlar

sillín *nm* saddle

sillón *nm* (**a**) *(butaca)* armchair (**b**) *Equit* side-saddle

silo *nm* silo

silogismo *nm* syllogism

silueta *nf* (**a**) *(contorno)* silhouette, outline (**b**) *(del cuerpo)* figure, shape

silvestre *adj* wild; **plantas silvestres** wild plants

silvicultor, -a *nm,f* forestry expert

silvicultura *nf* forestry

SIM [sim] *nm Tel (abrev de* **subscriber identity module**) SIM; **tarjeta SIM** SIM card

sima *nf Geol* chasm, abyss

simbiosis *nf inv Biol* symbiosis

simbiótico, -a *adj Biol* symbiotic

simbólico, -a *adj* symbolic, symbolical

simbolismo *nm* symbolism

simbolista *adj & nmf* symbolist

simbolizar [14] *vt* to symbolize

símbolo *nm* symbol ❏ **s. sexual** sex symbol

simbología *nf* system of symbols

simetría *nf* symmetry

simétrico, -a *adj* symmetric, symmetrical

simiente *nf Agr* seed

simiesco, -a *adj* simian, apelike

símil *nm* (**a**) *(comparación)* comparison; *(semejanza)* resemblance, similarity (**b**) *Lit* simile

similar *adj* similar

similitud *nf* similarity, resemblance

simio *nm Zool* simian, monkey

simonía *nf* simony

simoníaco, -a 1 *adj* simoniacal
  2 *nm,f* simoniac

simpatía *nf* (**a**) *(agrado)* liking, affection; **cogerle s. a algn** to take a liking to sb; **ganarse la s. de todos** to win everyone's affection; **simpatías y antipatías** likes and dislikes; **le tengo mucha s.** I am very fond of him (**b**) *(solidaridad)* sympathy, solidarity (**c**) *Med* sympathy

simpático, -a *adj* (**a**) *(amable)* nice, likeable; *(agradable)* kind, friendly; *(encantador)* charming; **hacerse el s.** to ingratiate oneself; **me cae s.** I like him (**b**) *Med* sympathetic

simpatizante 1 *adj* sympathetic
  2 *nmf* sympathizer

simpatizar [14] *vi* to get on (**con** with); **simpatizamos al instante** we hit it off from the start

simple 1 *adj* (**a**) *(gen)* simple (**b**) *(fácil)* simple, easy (**c**) *(mero)* mere; **es una s. fórmula** it's a mere formality; **por s. descuido** through sheer carelessness (**d**) *(persona)* simple, simple-minded
  2 *nm* (**a**) *(persona)* simpleton (**b**) *Ten* singles *pl*

simplemente *adv* simply

simpleza *nf* (**a**) *(bobería)* simple-mindedness (**b**) *(tontería)* nonsense

simplicidad *nf* (**a**) *(sencillez)* simplicity (**b**) *(ingenuidad)* naïveté, naïvety

simplificación *nf* simplification

simplificar [59] *vt* to simplify

simplismo *nm* simplism, oversimplification

simplista *adj* simplistic, oversimple

simplón, -ona 1 *adj* simple, naïve
  2 *nm,f* simpleton

simposio *nm* symposium

simulación *nf también Inform* simulation

simulacro *nm* sham, pretence; **un s. de ataque** a mock attack

simulado, -a 1 *pp de* **simular**
  2 *adj* simulated

simulador *nm* simulator ❏ **s. de vuelo** flight simulator

simular *vt* to simulate, pretend, feign; **s. un accidente** to rig an accident

simultáneamente *adv* simultaneously, at the same time

simultanear *vt (hacer al mismo tiempo)* to do simultaneously *o* at the same time; *(combinar)* to combine; **simultanea el trabajo y los estudios** he's working and studying at the same time

simultaneidad *nf* simultaneity

simultáneo, -a *adj* simultaneous

simún *nm Meteor* simoom

sin *prep* without; **está s. lavar** it hasn't been washed; **estamos s. pan** we're out of bread; **iremos sin ti** we'll go without you; **se fue s. pagar** he left without paying; **s. alcohol** alcohol-free; **fuimos, no s. antes preguntar si podíamos** before going, we did ask if we could; **s. más ni más** without further ado; **s. que nadie lo notara** without anyone noticing

sinagoga *nf* synagogue

sinalefa *nf Ling* synaloepha, *US* synalepha

sinapismo *nm* (**a**) *Med* mustard plaster (**b**) *Fam Fig (pesadez)* bore, drag

sinceramente *adv* sincerely

sincerarse *vpr* to open one's heart (**con** to)

sinceridad *nf* sincerity; **con toda s.** in all sincerity

sincero, -a *adj* sincere

síncopa *nf* (**a**) *Ling* syncope (**b**) *Mús* syncopation

sincopado, -a *adj Mús* syncopated

síncope *nm* (**a**) *Med* syncope, fainting, faint (**b**) *Ling* syncope

sincronía *nf* synchrony

sincrónico, -a *adj* synchronic

sincronización *nf* synchronization

sincronizar [14] *vt* to synchronize

síncrono, -a *adj Inform* synchronous

sindicación *nf* (**a**) *(afiliación)* union affiliation (**b**) *(sindicalismo)* unionism, *Br* trade unionism

sindicado, -a *adj* **estar s.** to belong to a (*Br* trade *o US* labor) union, be unionized

sindical *adj* (*Br* trade *o US* labor) union

sindicalismo *nm* unionism, *Br* trade unionism

sindicalista 1 *adj* (*Br* trade *o US* labor) union
  2 *nmf* union member, *Br* trade unionist

sindicar [59] **1** *vt* to unionize
  2 sindicarse *vpr* (**a**) *(afiliarse)* to join a union (**b**) *(formar un sindicato)* to form a union

sindicato *nm Br* trade union, *US* labor union

síndico *nm* (**a**) *Pol* elected representative (**b**) *(depositario)* trustee; *Jur* (official) receiver ❏ **s. de la Bolsa** = Chairman of the Spanish Stock Exchange Commission

síndrome *nm Med* syndrome ❏ **s. de abstinencia** withdrawal symptoms *pl* ; **s. de Down** Down's syndrome; **s. premenstrual** premenstrual syndrome

sinecura *nf* sinecure

sine die 1 *adj* **un aplazamiento s.** an indefinite postponement
  2 *adv* indefinitely

sinergia *nf* synergy

sinestesia *nf* synaesthesia, *US* synesthesia

sinfín *nm* endless number; **un s. de preguntas** an endless number of questions

sinfonía *nf* symphony

sinfónico, -a *adj* symphonic

Singapur *n* Singapore

singladura *nf Náut* day's run

single ['singel] *nm* single

singular 1 *adj* (**a**) *(único, solo)* singular, single (**b**) *(excepcional)* exceptional, unique (**c**) *(raro)* peculiar, odd
2 *nm Ling* singular; **en s.** in the singular; *Fam* **¡habla en s.!** speak for yourself!

singularidad *nf* (**a**) *(unicidad)* singularity (**b**) *(excepcionalidad)* uniqueness (**c**) *(rareza)* peculiarity

singularizar [14] **1** *vt* to single out, distinguish
2 singularizarse *vpr* to stand out, distinguish oneself

sinhueso *nf Fam* tongue; **darle a la s.** to natter

siniestra *nf* left hand

siniestrado, -a *adj* damaged

siniestralidad *nf* accident rate

siniestro, -a 1 *adj* (**a**) *Literario (izquierdo)* left, left-hand (**b**) *(maligno)* sinister, ominous (**c**) *(funesto)* fateful, disastrous
2 *nm (catástrofe)* disaster, catastrophe; *(incendio)* fire

sinnúmero *nm* endless number

sino¹ *nm Fml* fate, destiny

sino² *conj* (**a**) *(para contraponer)* but; **no fui a Madrid, s. a Barcelona** I didn't go to Madrid but to Barcelona; **no sólo ... s. (también)** ... not only... but also ... (**b**) *(solamente)* only; **no quiero s. que me oigan** I only want them to listen (to me) (**c**) *(excepto)* but, except; **no escribo a nadie s. a mi padre** I only write to my father

sínodo *nm Rel* synod

sinonimia *nf* synonymy

sinónimo, -a 1 *adj* synonymous
2 *nm* synonym

sinopsis *nf inv* synopsis

sinóptico, -a *adj* synoptic, synoptical; **cuadro s.** diagram, chart

sinrazón *nf* wrong, injustice

sinsabor *nm (gen pl)* trouble, worry; **mi vida está llena de sinsabores** my life is full of worries

sinsentido *nm* **decir un s.** to say something stupid

sintáctico, -a *adj Ling* syntactic, syntactical

sintagma *nm Ling* **s. nominal/verbal** noun/verb phrase

sintaxis *nf inv Ling* syntax

síntesis *nf inv* synthesis

sintético, -a *adj* synthetic

sintetizador *nm* synthesizer

sintetizar [14] *vt* to synthesize

sintoísmo *nm* Shinto, Shintoism

sintoísta *nmf* Shintoist

síntoma *nm* symptom

sintomático, -a *adj* symptomatic

sintomatología *nf* symptoms *pl*

sintonía *nf* (**a**) *Elec Rad* tuning (**b**) *Mús Rad (de programa)* signature tune (**c**) *Fig* harmony; **estar en s. con algn** to get on well with sb

sintonización *nf* (**a**) *Rad* tuning (**b**) *Fig* harmony

sintonizador *nm Rad* tuner, tuning knob

sintonizar [14] **1** *vt Rad* to tune in; **s. una emisora** to tune in to a radio station

2 *vi Fig (llevarse bien)* to get on well, be on the same wavelength

sinuosidad *nf* (**a**) *(de un camino)* bend, curve (**b**) *(de argumento)* tortuousness (**c**) *(de persona)* deviousness

sinuoso, -a *adj* (**a**) *(camino)* winding (**b**) *(argumento)* tortuous (**c**) *(persona)* devious

sinusitis *nf inv Med* sinusitis

sinvergüenza 1 *adj (desvergonzado)* shameless; *(descarado)* cheeky
2 *nmf (desvergonzado)* scoundrel, rotter; *(caradura)* cheeky devil

sionismo *nm* Zionism

sionista *adj & nmf* Zionist

sioux ['siuks] *o* ['sius] *adj inv & nmf inv* Sioux

sique *nf véase* **psique**

siquiatra *nmf véase* **psiquiatra**

siquiatría *nf véase* **psiquiatría**

siquiátrico, -a *adj véase* **psiquiátrico, -a**

síquico, -a *adj véase* **psíquico, -a**

siquiera 1 *adv (por lo menos)* at least; **dime s. su nombre** at least tell me her name; **ni s.** not even; **ni s. sé su nombre** I don't even know his name
2 *conj (aunque)* although, even though; **ven, s. sea por dos días** do come, even if it's only for two days

sirena *nf* (**a**) *Mit* siren, mermaid (**b**) *(señal acústica)* siren □ **s. de niebla** foghorn

sirga *nf* rope, towrope, towline

sirgar [38] *vt* to tow

Siria *n* Syria

sirimiri *nm Meteor* fine drizzle

sirio, -a *adj & nm,f* Syrian

sirlero, -a *nm,f Argot* mugger

siroco *nm Meteor* sirocco (wind)

sirope *nm* golden syrup; **s. de fresa/chocolate** *(para helado)* strawberry/chocolate sauce

sirviente, -a *nm,f* servant

sisa *nf* (**a**) *(hurto)* petty theft, pilfering, filching (**b**) *Cost* armhole

sisar *vt & vi Esp* to pilfer

sisear *vi* to hiss

siseo *nm* hiss, hissing

sísmico, -a *adj* seismic

sismo *nm* earthquake, tremor

sismógrafo *nm* seismograph

sismología *nf* seismology

sismológico, -a *adj* seismological

sistema *nm* system; **por s.** as a rule □ *Anat* **s. circulatorio** circulatory system; *Mat* **s. de ecuaciones** simultaneous equations *pl*; *Inform* **s. experto** expert system; *Anat* **s. inmunológico** *o* **inmune** immune system; *Mat* **s. métrico decimal** decimal metric system; *Geog* **s. montañoso** mountain chain; *Anat* **s. nervioso** nervous system; *Inform* **s. operativo** operating system; **s. planetario** planetary system; **s. solar** solar system

sistemático, -a *adj* systematic

sistematización *nf* systematization

sistematizar [14] *vt* to systematize

sístole *nf* systole

sitar *nm Mús* sitar

sitiado, -a 1 *pp de* **sitiar**
2 *adj* besieged
3 *nm,f* **los sitiados** those under siege, the besieged

sitiador, -a 1 *adj* besieging
   2 *nm,f* besieger

sitial *nm* seat of honour *o US* honor

sitiar *vt* to besiege, lay siege to

sitio¹ *nm* (**a**) *(lugar)* place; **cambiar de s.** to move; **cambiar de s. con algn** to change places with sb; **ceder el s.** to give up one's place; **en cualquier s.** anywhere; **en todos los sitios** everywhere; *Fig* **quedarse en el s.** to die (**b**) *(espacio)* space, room; **guardar s. a algn** to keep a seat for sb; **hacer s.** to make room; **hay s. para todos** there's room for everyone; **ocupar mucho s.** to take up a lot of space (**c**) *Inform* site ▫ **s. web** web site (**d**) *Méx (granja)* small farm

sitio² *nm Mil* siege; **en estado de s.** in a state of siege; **poner s. a una ciudad** to besiege a town, lay siege to a town

sito, -a *adj Fml* situated, located; **un edificio s. en Sevilla** a building situated in Seville

situación *nf* (**a**) *(circunstancia)* situation; **la s. política** the political situation (**b**) *(posición social etc)* position; **su s. económica es precaria** his financial position is very insecure (**c**) *(emplazamiento)* situation, location

situado, -a 1 *pp de* **situar**
   2 *adj (gen)* situated; *Fig* **estar bien s.** to be comfortably off

situar [4] **1** *vt (en un lugar)* to place, put, situate, locate
   2 situarse *vpr* (**a**) *(en un lugar)* to be placed *o* situated *o* located (**b**) *(abrirse paso)* to get on, do well, be successful

siux *adj & nmf* Sioux

skateboard [es'keidβor] *(pl* **skateboards**) *nm* (**a**) *(tabla)* skateboard (**b**) *(deporte)* skateboarding

skay [es'kai] *nm* Leatherette®

sketch [es'ketʃ] *(pl* **sketches**) *nm Cin Teat* sketch

skin head [es'kinχeð] *(pl* **skin heads**) *nmf* skinhead

S.L. *(abrev de* **Sociedad Limitada**) *Br* ≃ Ltd, *US* ≃ Inc

slalom [es'lalom] *(pl* **slaloms**) *nm Dep véase* **eslalon**

slip [es'lip] *(pl* **slips**) *nm véase* **eslip**

S.M. *(abrev de* **Su Majestad**) Your Majesty

SME *nm Econ (abrev de* **Sistema Monetario Europeo**) EMS

SMI *nm* (**a**) *(abrev de* **sistema monetario internacional**) IMS (**b**) *(abrev de* **salario mínimo interprofesional**) minimum wage

SMS *nm Tel (abrev de* **short message service**) SMS; **un mensaje SMS** an SMS

s/n. *(abrev de* **sin número**)

snob *adj & nmf véase* **esnob**

snobismo *nm véase* **esnobismo**

snowboard [es'nouβor] *(pl* **snowboards**) *nm* (**a**) *(tabla)* snowboard (**b**) *(deporte)* snowboarding

so¹ *prep (bajo)* under; **so pena de** on pain of

so² *nm Fam* **¡so imbécil!** you damned idiot!

so³ *interj (a las caballerías)* whoa!

s/o. *(abrev de* **su orden**) your order

soasar *vt Culin* to roast lightly

soba *nf Fam* (**a**) *(paliza)* hiding, thrashing (**b**) *(manoseo)* fondling, pawing

sobaco *nm* armpit

sobado, -a 1 *pp de* **sobar**
   2 *adj* (**a**) *(desgastado)* worn, shabby; *(libro)* well-thumbed, dog-eared (**b**) *Fig (frase, tema etc)* well-worn

sobajar, *vt,* **sobajear** *vt Andes CAm Méx Ven* to humiliate

sobaquera *nf Cost* dress shield

sobaquina *nf Fam* underarm odour *o US* odor

sobar 1 *vt* (**a**) *(tocar)* to finger, paw; *Fam (persona)* to touch up, fondle (**b**) *Fam (pegar, derrotar)* to give a hiding (**c**) *Méx RP (frotar)* to scrub
   2 *vi Esp Fam Br* to kip, *US* catch some zees

sobe *nm Fam* fondling, touching up

soberanamente *adv* extremely, supremely

soberanía *nf Pol* sovereignty; **bajo la s. de** under the rule of

soberano, -a 1 *adj* (**a**) *Pol (con autoridad)* sovereign; **poder s.** sovereign power (**b**) *Fig (extremo)* extreme, supreme (**c**) *Fam* huge, great
   2 *nm,f (monarca)* sovereign

soberbia *nf* (**a**) *(orgullo)* pride; *(arrogancia)* arrogance, haughtiness (**b**) *(suntuosidad)* sumptuousness, pomp (**c**) *(ira)* anger, rage

soberbiamente *adv* (**a**) *(con arrogancia)* arrogantly (**b**) *(magníficamente)* magnificently, superbly

soberbio, -a *adj* (**a**) *(orgulloso)* proud (**b**) *(arrogante)* arrogant, haughty (**c**) *(suntuoso)* sumptuous, magnificent (**d**) *(magnífico)* splendid, magnificent, superb (**e**) *Fam* huge, great

sobón, -ona *Fam* **1** *adj* given to fondling, randy
   2 *nm,f* randy person; **ser un s.** to be fresh *o* all hands

sobornable *adj* bribable, venal

sobornar *vt* to bribe, suborn

soborno *nm* (**a**) *(acción)* bribery (**b**) *(dinero, regalo)* bribe (**c**) *Bol Chile* **de s.** additional

sobra *nf* (**a**) *(exceso)* excess, surplus; **de s.** *(no necesario)* superfluous; *(excesivo)* more than enough; **estar de s.** to be in the way; **saber algo de s.** to know sth only too well (**b**) **sobras** *(desperdicios)* leftovers

sobradamente *adv* extremely

sobrado, -a 1 *pp de* **sobrar**
   2 *adj (que sobra)* abundant, more than enough; **andar s.** to have a lot to spare; **sobradas veces** repeatedly; **s. de plenty; andar s. de tiempo** to have plenty of time (**c**) *Chile (enorme)* enormous, huge
   3 *adv (demasiado)* too
   4 sobrados *nmpl Andes* leftovers

sobrante 1 *adj* leftover, remaining, spare, surplus
   2 *nm* surplus, excess

sobrar *vi* (**a**) *(haber más de lo necesario)* to be more than enough, be too much; **me sobran ideas** I've got plenty of ideas; **sobran tres sillas** there are three chairs too many (**b**) *(estorbar)* to be in the way; *Fam* **tú sobras aquí** you are not wanted here (**c**) *(quedar)* to be left over; **nos sobró dinero** we had some money left over

sobrasada *nf* = Majorcan spicy pork sausage that can be spread

sobre¹ *nm* (**a**) *(para carta)* envelope (**b**) *(de sopa etc)* packet (**c**) *Fam (cama)* bed; **me voy al s.** I'm off to bed

sobre² *prep* (**a**) *(encima)* on, upon, on top of; **lo dejé s. la silla** I left it on the chair (**b**) *(por encima)* over, above; **volamos s. Francia** we are flying over France (**c**) *(acerca de)* about, on; **un libro s. Cervantes** a book about Cervantes (**d**) *(aproximadamente)* about; **vendré s. las ocho** I'll come at about eight o'clock (**e**) *Fig* upon; **mentira s. mentira** lie upon lie (**f**) **s. todo** especially, above all

sobre- *pref* super-, over-

sobreabundancia *nf* surplus

sobreabundante *adj* excessive

sobreabundar *vi* to abound

sobreactuar [4] *vi* to overact

sobrealimentación *nf* overfeeding

sobrealimentar *vt* to overfeed

sobreañadido *nm* unnecessary addition

sobreañadir *vt* to add on top of

sobrecalentamiento *nm* overheating

sobrecalentar [3] **1** *vt* to overheat
2 sobrecalentarse *vpr* to overheat

sobrecarga *nf* (**a**) *Téc* overload (**b**) *Fig (preocupación)* additional burden, further worry

sobrecargar [38] *vt* (**a**) *Téc* to overload (**b**) *Fig (de preocupaciones, trabajo)* to overburden

sobrecargo *nm Náut* supercargo

sobrecogedor, -a *adj* (**a**) *(que asusta)* frightening (**b**) *(que conmueve)* dramatic, awesome

sobrecoger [52] **1** *vt* (**a**) *(asustar)* to frighten, scare (**b**) *(coger desprevenido)* to startle, take by surprise
2 sobrecogerse *vpr* (**a**) *(asustarse)* to be frightened o scared (**b**) *(sorprenderse)* to be startled (**c**) *(impresionarse)* to be overawed; **s. de** to be seized with, be overcome by

sobrecoste *nm*, **sobrecosto** *nm* extra costs *pl*

sobrecubierta *nf (de libro)* jacket, dust cover

sobredicho, -a *adj Fml* aforementioned, aforesaid, above-mentioned

sobredorar *vt* (**a**) *(metal)* to gild (**b**) *Fig (disimular)* to gloss over

sobredosis *nf inv* overdose

sobreentender [64] **1** *vt (comprender)* to understand; *(deducir)* to deduce
2 sobreentenderse *vpr* to be understood; **se sobre-entiende** that goes without saying

sobreentendido, -a *adj* implied, implicit

sobreesdrújulo, -a *adj véase* **sobresdrújulo, -a**

sobreexceder *vt* to exceed

sobreexcitación *nf* overexcitement

sobreexcitar 1 *vt* to overexcite
2 sobreexcitarse *vpr* to get overexcited

sobreexponer [50] *vt* to overexpose

sobreexposición *nf* overexposure

sobregirar *vt Fin* to overdraw

sobregiro *nm Fin* overdraft

sobrehilado, -a 1 *pp de* **sobrehilar**
2 *nm Cost* whipstitch

sobrehilar *vt* to whipstitch

sobrehumano, -a *adj* superhuman

sobreimpresión *nf Fot Cin* superimposing

sobreimprimir *vt* to superimpose

sobrellevar *vt* to endure, bear

sobremanera *adv* exceedingly

sobremesa *nf* (**a**) *(tertulia)* after-dinner chat; **estar de s.** to have an after-dinner chat (**b**) *Mueb* **lámpara de s.** table lamp

sobrenadar *vi* to float

sobrenatural *adj* supernatural

sobrenombre *nm* nickname

sobrentender [64] *vt véase* **sobreentender**

sobrepaga *nf Fin* bonus

sobreparto *nm* postnatal confinement; **dolores de s.** afterpains

sobrepasar *vt* to exceed, surpass; *(rival)* to beat

sobrepelliz *nf Rel* surplice

sobrepeso *nm (de carga)* overload, excess weight; *(de persona)* excess weight

sobreponer [50] *(pp* **sobrepuesto**) **1** *vt* (**a**) *(poner encima)* to put on top (**b**) *(anteponer)* to put before
2 sobreponerse *vpr* (**a**) *(superar)* to overcome; **s. al dolor** to overcome pain (**b**) *(animarse)* to pull oneself together

sobreprecio *nm Com* surcharge

sobreproducción *nf* excess production, overproduction

sobreproteger [52] *vt* to overprotect

sobrepuesto, -a 1 *pp de* **sobreponer**
2 *adj* superimposed
3 *nm Am (panal)* = honeycomb formed after the hive is full

sobrepujar *vt* to surpass, outdo

sobrero, -a *adj* (**a**) *(sobrante)* surplus, spare (**b**) *Taur (toro)* spare

sobresaliente 1 *adj* (**a**) *(protuberante)* jutting out, sticking out, protruding (**b**) *Fig (que destaca)* outstanding, excellent
2 *nm Educ (en la escuela)* A; *Univ* first
3 *nmf* (**a**) *Taur (torero suplente)* substitute bullfighter (**b**) *Teat (actor suplente)* understudy

sobresalir [60] *vi* (**a**) *(proyectarse)* to jut out, stick out, protrude (**b**) *Fig (destacar)* to stand out, excel

sobresaltar 1 *vt* to startle
2 sobresaltarse *vpr* to be startled, start

sobresalto *nm (movimiento)* start; *(susto)* fright, shock

sobresaturar *vt* to supersaturate

sobrescribir *vt* to overwrite

sobresdrújulo, -a *adj Ling* accented on the syllable preceding the third from the end

sobreseer [37] *vt Jur* to stay; **s. una causa** to stay proceedings

sobreseimiento *nm Jur* stay, dismissal

sobrestante *nm* foreman

sobrestimar *vt* to overestimate

sobresueldo *nm* extra pay, bonus

sobretasa *nf* surcharge

sobretodo *nm* (**a**) *(abrigo)* overcoat (**b**) *(guardapolvo)* overalls *pl*

sobrevalorar *vt* to overestimate

sobrevenir [69] *vi* to happen, occur; **le sobrevino una desgracia** disaster struck (him)

sobreviviente 1 *adj* surviving
2 *nmf* survivor

sobrevivir *vi* to survive; **s. a algn** to outlive sb

sobrevolar [63] *vt Av* to fly over

sobrexceder *vt véase* **sobreexceder**

sobrexcitación *nf véase* **sobreexcitación**

sobrexcitar *vt véase* **sobreexcitar**

sobrexponer *vt véase* **sobreexponer**

sobrexposición *nf véase* **sobreexposición**

sobriedad *nf (moderación)* sobriety, moderation, restraint; *(en la bebida)* soberness

sobrina *nf* niece

sobrino *nm* nephew

sobrio, -a *adj* (**a**) *(estilo, color)* sober, plain (**b**) *(persona)* moderate, restrained; **s. en la bebida** temperate in one's drinking habits (**c**) *(estilo)* concise

socaire *nm Náut* lee; **al s.** to leeward; *Fig* **al s. de** under the protection of

socar [59] *CAm* **1** *vt* (**a**) *(apretar)* to press down, squeeze (**b**) *(molestar)* to annoy, pester
2 socarse *vpr (emborracharse)* to get drunk

socarrar *vt* to scorch, singe

socarrón, -ona 1 *adj* (**a**) *(burlón)* sarcastic, ironical (**b**) *(taimado)* sly, cunning

2 *nm,f* (**a**) *(guasón)* sarcastic *o* ironical person (**b**) *(persona astuta)* sly fox

socarronería *nf* (**a**) *(burlonería)* sarcasm, irony, wry humour *o US* humour (**b**) *(astucia)* slyness

socavar *vt* (**a**) *Min* to dig under (**b**) *Fig* to undermine; **s. la moral de la gente** to weaken people's morale

socavón *nm* (**a**) *Min* gallery, tunnel (**b**) *(bache)* hollow, hole

sociabilidad *nf* sociability, friendliness

sociable *adj* sociable, friendly

social *adj* social; **cambios sociales** social change

socialdemocracia *nf Pol* social democracy

socialdemócrata *Pol* **1** *adj* social democratic
 2 *nmf* social democrat

socialismo *nm Pol* socialism

socialista *adj & nmf* socialist

socialización *nf (gen)* socialization; *(de industria etc)* nationalization

socializar [14] *vt (gen)* to socialize; *(industria etc)* to nationalize

socialmente *adv* socially

sociedad *nf* (**a**) *(de seres vivos)* society; **alta** *o* **buena s.** high society; **presentarse en s.** to make one's debut ❑ **s. de consumo** consumer society (**b**) *Com (empresa)* company ❑ **s. anónima** *Br* public (limited) company, *US* incorporated company; **s. comanditaria** *o* **en comandita** limited partnership; **s. limitada** private limited company; **s. mercantil** (trading) company (**c**) *(asociación)* association, society ❑ *Rel* **S. de Jesús** Society of Jesus; **S. de Naciones** League of Nations; **s. protectora de animales** *Br* ≃ RSPCA, *US* ≃ SPCA

socio, -a *nm,f* (**a**) *(miembro)* member; **hacerse s. de un club** to become a member of a club, join a club (**b**) *Com (asociado)* partner; *(accionista)* shareholder, member ❑ **s. capitalista** *o* **comanditario** *Br* sleeping *o US* silent partner; **s. mayoritario** majority shareholder (**c**) *Fam (amigo)* pal, *Br* mate, *US* buddy

sociocultural *adj* sociocultural

socioeconómico, -a *adj* socioeconomic

sociolingüística *nf* sociolinguistics *sing*

sociolingüístico, -a *adj* sociolinguistic

sociología *nf* sociology

sociológico, -a *adj* sociological

sociólogo, -a *nm,f* sociologist

sociopolítico, -a *adj* sociopolitical

soco, -a *adj Chile PRico (manco)* **es s.** he only has one arm

socollón *nm CAm Cuba* sudden and violent shake

socorrer *vt* to help, assist, come *o* go to the aid of

socorrido, -a **1** *pp de* **socorrer**
 2 *adj* (**a**) *(útil)* handy, useful (**b**) *(abastecido)* well-stocked (**c**) *Fig (frase, argumento)* hackneyed, well-worn

socorrismo *nm* life-saving

socorrista *nmf* life-saver, lifeguard

socorro *nm* (**a**) *(ayuda)* help, aid, assistance; **acudir en s. de algn** to go to sb's aid; **¡s.!** help! ❑ **puesto de s.** first-aid post; **señal de s.** distress signal; **trabajos de s.** rescue work *sing* (**b**) *Mil (provisiones)* supplies *pl*, provisions *pl*

socrático, -a *adj & nm,f Filos* Socratic

soda *nf* (**a**) *Quím* soda (**b**) *(bebida)* soda water

sódico, -a *adj Quím* sodium; **bicarbonato s.** sodium bicarbonate

sodio *nm Quím* sodium

sodomía *nf* sodomy

sodomita *adj & nmf* sodomite

sodomizar [14] *vt* to sodomize

soez *adj* vulgar, crude, rude

sofá *nm* sofa, settee ❑ **s. cama** sofa bed, studio couch

Sofía *n* Sophia

sofisma *nm* sophism

sofista *nmf Filos* sophist

sofisticación *nf* sophistication

sofisticado, -a **1** *pp de* **sofisticar**
 2 *adj* sophisticated

sofisticar [59] *vt* to sophisticate

soflama *nf Pey* harangue

sofocación *nf* (**a**) *(ahogo)* suffocation, stifling sensation (**b**) *(rubor)* blushing (**c**) *(de un incendio)* extinction (**d**) *(de una rebelión)* suppression

sofocado, -a **1** *pp de* **sofocar**
 2 *adj* suffocated

sofocante *adj* suffocating, stifling; **hacía un calor s.** it was unbearably hot

sofocar [59] **1** *vt* (**a**) *(ahogar)* to suffocate, stifle, smother (**b**) *(incendio)* to extinguish, put out (**c**) *(rebelión)* to put down, suppress (**d**) *(avergonzar)* to make blush
 2 sofocarse *vpr* (**a**) *(ahogarse)* to suffocate, stifle (**b**) *(ruborizarse)* to blush (**c**) *(enfadarse)* to get angry *o* upset

sofoco *nm* (**a**) *(ahogo)* suffocation, stifling sensation (**b**) *(vergüenza)* embarrassment; *(disgusto)* shock; **le dio un s.** it gave her quite a turn (**c**) *Med* **sofocos** hot flushes, *US* hot flashes

sofocón *nm Fam* shock; **llevarse un s.** to get into a state

sofreír [56] *vt* to fry lightly, brown

sofrito *nm* = fried tomato and onion sauce

sofrología *nf* relaxation therapy

software ['sofwer] *nm Inform* software

soga *nf* rope, cord; *Fig* **dar s. a algn** *(burlarse)* to make fun of sb; *(seguir la corriente)* to keep sb talking; *Fig* **estar con la s. al cuello** to be in dire straits

soja *nf* soya bean, *US* soybean

sojuzgar [38] *vt* to subjugate

sol[1] *nm* (**a**) *(astro)* sun; *(luz del sol)* sunlight, sunshine; **al ponerse el s.** at sunset; **al salir el s.** at sunrise; **al** *o* **bajo el s.** in the sun; **de s. a s.** from sunrise to sunset; **un día de s.** a sunny day; **hace s.** it's sunny, the sun is shining; **s. y sombra** *Taur* = seats which enjoy some sun and some shade; *(bebida)* = brandy and anisette drink; **tomar el s.** to sunbathe; *Fig* **arrimarse al s. que más calienta** to know which side one's bread is buttered on; *Fig* **no dejar a algn ni a s. ni a sombra** to pester *o* harass sb continually ❑ **s. de medianoche** midnight sun; **s. naciente** rising sun; **s. poniente** setting sun (**b**) *Fam (persona)* darling; **ser un s.** to be a darling (**c**) *Fin* = standard monetary unit of Perú

sol[2] *nm Mús* sol, G

solamente *adv* only; **no s.** not only; **s. con mirarte lo sé** I know just by looking at you; **s. que ...** except that ...

solana *nf (lugar)* sunny spot; *(de una casa)* sun lounge; *(terraza)* veranda, verandah

solano[1] *nm* easterly wind

solano[2] *nm Bot* nightshade

solapa *nf* (**a**) *(de chaqueta)* lapel (**b**) *(de sobre, bolsillo, libro)* flap (**c**) *Fig* pretext

solapadamente *adv* stealthily, in an underhand way

solapado, -a **1** *pp de* **solapar**
 2 *adj (persona)* sly, evasive

solapar **1** *vt Fig (ocultar)* to conceal, cover up
 2 *vi (cubrir en parte)* to overlap

solar¹ *adj* solar; **año s.** solar year; **luz s.** sunlight

solar² *nm* (**a**) *(terreno)* plot; *(en obras)* building site (**b**) *Cuba (casa de vecindad)* tenement

solariego, -a *adj (familia)* ancient and noble; **casa solariega** ancestral home

solario *nm*, **solárium** *nm* solarium

solaz *nm Fml* (**a**) *(descanso)* rest, relaxation; *(esparcimiento)* recreation, entertainment (**b**) *(consuelo)* consolation, solace

solazar [14] **1** *vt* (**a**) *(relajar)* to relax; *(divertir)* to entertain, amuse (**b**) *(consolar)* to console, comfort
  2 solazarse *vpr (relajarse)* to relax; *(divertirse)* to enjoy oneself

soldada *nf* salary, pay

soldadesca *nf* (**a**) *(profesión)* military profession (**b**) *Pey (soldados)* soldiery

soldadesco, -a *adj* soldier-like, soldierly

soldado *nm* soldier ❑ **s. raso** private

soldador, -a 1 *nm,f* welder
  2 *nm* soldering iron

soldadura *nf* (**a**) *(acción)* soldering, welding (**b**) *(trozo, lugar soldado)* soldered joint, weld

soldar [63] **1** *vt (metal)* to solder, weld; **s. por puntos** to spot-weld
  2 soldarse *vpr (huesos)* to knit

soleá *(pl* **soleares)** *nf Mús* = Andalusian song and dance

soleado, -a *adj* sunny

solear *vt* to expose to the sun, put in the sun

solecismo *nm* solecism

soledad *nf* (**a**) *(estado)* solitude; *(sentimiento)* loneliness (**b**) **soledades** *(lugar)* lonely place *sing*

solemne *adj* (**a**) *(majestuoso)* solemn, majestic (**b**) *(serio)* solemn, grave (**c**) *Pey* downright; **es una s. estupidez** it's downright stupid, it's sheer stupidity

solemnidad *nf* (**a**) *(pompa)* solemnity, pomp, formality (**b**) *(ceremonia)* solemn ceremony, ceremonial occasion

solemnizar [14] *vt* to solemnize, celebrate, commemorate

solenoide *nm Elec* solenoid

soler [76] *vi* (**a**) *(en presente)* to be in the habit of, be accustomed to; **solemos ir en coche** we usually go by car; **sueles equivocarte** you are usually wrong (**b**) *(en pasado)* to use to; **solía ser muy criticón** he used to be very critical

solera *nf* (**a**) *(tradición)* tradition; **de s.** old-established; **vino de s.** vintage wine (**b**) *RP (vestido)* sun dress (**c**) *Chile (de acera) Br* kerb, *US* curb

solfa *nf* (**a**) *Mús* solfa, musical notation; *Fam* **poner en s.** to ridicule (**b**) *Fam (paliza)* thrashing, beating

solfear *vt* (**a**) *Mús* to solfa (**b**) *Fam (zurrar)* to thrash, beat (**c**) *Fam (abroncar)* to give a dressing-down to

solfeo *nm Mús* solfa

solicitante 1 *adj* applying
  2 *nmf* applicant

solicitante *nmf* applicant ❑ **s. de asilo** asylum seeker

solicitar *vt* (**a**) *(pedir)* to request, ask for; **s. un trabajo** to apply for a job (**b**) *(persona)* to chase after; **es una persona muy solicitada** he *o* she is much in demand (**c**) *(mujer)* to woo, court

solícito, -a *adj* obliging, attentive

solicitud *nf* (**a**) *(diligencia)* care, attention (**b**) *(petición)* request, petition; *(de trabajo)* application; **a s.** on request

solidaridad *nf* solidarity

solidario, -a *adj* (**a**) *(unido)* united; *(causa)* common (**b**) *Jur* jointly responsible

solidarizar [14] **1** *vt (unir)* to unite

2 solidarizarse *vpr* to show one's solidarity (**con** with); **s. con** *(apoyar)* to support; *(unirse a)* to join

solideo *nm Rel* skullcap

solidez *nf* *(resistencia)* solidity, strength; *(firmeza)* firmness; *Fig (de principio etc)* soundness; *(de color)* fastness

solidificación *nf* solidification

solidificar [59] **1** *vt* to solidify
  2 *vpr* to solidify

sólido, -a 1 *adj (resistente)* solid, strong; *(firme)* firm; *Fig (principio etc)* sound; *(color)* fast
  2 *nm Fís* solid

soliloquio *nm Lit* soliloquy

solio *nm* throne

solista *nmf Mús* soloist

solitaria *nf Med* tapeworm

solitario, -a 1 *adj* (**a**) *(que está solo)* solitary, lone; *(que se siente solo)* lonely; *Av* **vuelo en s.** solo flight (**b**) *(lugar)* deserted, lonely
  2 *nm* (**a**) *(diamante)* solitaire (**b**) *Naipes Br* patience, *US* solitaire

soliviantar *vt* (**a**) *(persona, sentimiento)* to rouse, stir up (**b**) *(irritar)* to irritate

sollozar [14] *vi* to sob

sollozo *nm* sob; **prorrumpir en sollozos** to start sobbing

solo, -a 1 *adj* (**a**) *(sin compañía, sin ayuda)* alone, on one's own, by oneself, by itself; **a solas** alone, by oneself; **café s.** black coffee; **hablar s.** to talk to oneself; **se enciende s.** it switches itself on automatically; **vivir s.** to live alone; **whisky s.** straight whisky (**b**) *(solitario)* lonely; **sentirse s.** to feel lonely (**c**) *(único)* only, sole, single; **ni un s. día** not a single day; **una sola vez** only once, just once; *Fam* **quedarse s.** to have no equal; **se queda s. comiendo** no one can eat like him
  2 *nm* (**a**) *Mús* solo (**b**) *Naipes Br* patience, *US* solitaire (**c**) *Fam (café)* black coffee

sólo *adv*, **solo** *adv* only, just; **con s., s. con** just by; **no s. ... sino (también) ...** not only ... but (also) ...; **no s. dibuja sino que también pinta** she not only draws, but she paints as well; **s. para adultos** for adults only; **s. que** only, but; **tan s. con** just by

solomillo *nm* sirloin

solsticio *nm Astron* solstice

soltar [63] **1** *vt* (**a**) *(desasir)* to release, let go of; **¡suelta!** let go!; **¡suéltame!** let me go!, take your hands off me!; *Fam* **s. la pasta** to cough up (**b**) *(desatar)* to untie, unfasten, loosen; **s. un nudo** to loosen a knot (**c**) *(prisionero)* to release; *(pájaro)* to let out; *(perro)* to unleash (**d**) *(humo, olor)* to give off (**e**) *(dar)* to deal, strike; **le soltó un par de bofetadas** he gave him a few smacks (**f**) *(decir, contar)* to come out with, let slip; **nos soltó un sermón** he started preaching to us; **s. la lengua** to speak freely; **s. un taco** to swear; **s. una carcajada** to burst out laughing
  2 soltarse *vpr (desatarse)* to come untied *o* unfastened *o* loose (**b**) *(perro etc)* to get loose, break loose (**c**) *(desprenderse)* to come off; *(tornillo)* to come loose (**d**) *(adquirir habilidad)* to become proficient, get the knack; **s. en un idioma** to become fluent in a language (**e**) *(desenvolverse)* to lose one's shyness, become self-confident; **le ha costado pero parece que por fin empieza a s.** it's taken him a long time but now it looks as if he's relaxed (**f**) *(relajarse)* to loosen up, let oneself go; **s. a su gusto** to let off steam

soltería *nf* single state; *(de hombre)* bachelorhood; *(de mujer)* spinsterhood

soltero, -a 1 *adj* single, unmarried
  2 *nm,f (hombre)* bachelor, single man; *(mujer)* single

woman; **apellido de soltera** maiden name

solterón, -ona *nm,f Pey (hombre)* old bachelor; *(mujer)* spinster, old maid

soltura *nf (agilidad)* agility; *(seguridad)* confidence, assurance; *(al hablar)* fluency, ease; **hablar un idioma con s.** to speak a language fluently o with ease

solubilidad *nf* solubility

soluble *adj* soluble

solución *nf* (a) *(resolución)* solution; **la s. de un problema** the solution to a problem; **sin s. de continuidad** uninterrupted (b) *Quím* solution ▫ **s. salina** saline solution

solucionar *vt (problema)* to solve; *(asunto, huelga)* to settle

solvencia *nf* (a) *Fin* solvency; *(pago)* settlement (b) *(fiabilidad)* reliability; *(reputación)* good reputation; **fuentes de toda s.** completely reliable sources

solventar *vt (problema)* to solve, resolve; *(deuda, asunto)* to settle

solvente 1 *adj* (a) *Fin* solvent (b) *(fiable)* reliable
 2 *nm Quím* solvent

soma *nm* soma, matter

somalí *adj & nmf* Somali

Somalia *n* Somalia

somanta *nf Fam* beating; **dar una s. a algn** to give sb a thrashing

somático, -a *adj Med* somatic

somatizar [14] *vt Med* to convert into physical symptoms

sombra *nf* (a) *(ausencia de sol)* shade; **a la s.** *(sin sol)* in the shade; *Argot (en la cárcel)* in the nick; **dar s.** to shade, give shade (b) *(silueta proyectada)* shadow; **hacer s.** to cast a shadow; *Fig* **hacer s. a algn** to overshadow sb; *Fig* **no fiarse ni de su s.** to be very distrustful; *Fig* **reírse hasta de la propia s.** to laugh at everything ▫ **s. de ojos** eyeshadow; **sombras chinescas** shadow theatre *sing* (c) *(vestigio)* trace, shadow; **ni por s.** not in the least; **ni s. de** not a trace of; **sin s. de duda** beyond a shadow of doubt (d) *(suerte)* luck; **tener buena s.** *(tener suerte)* to be lucky; *(ser agradable)* to be pleasant; **tener mala s.** *(no tener suerte)* to be unlucky; *(ser desagradable)* to be unpleasant (e) *(espectro)* ghost, shade (f) *Fig (oscuridad)* darkness, obscurity (g) *(mácula)* spot, stain (h) *(clandestinidad)* secrecy; **gobierno en la s.** shadow cabinet; **trabaja en la s.** he works undercover (i) *Chile (sombrilla)* parasol

sombreado *nm* shading

sombrear *vt* to shade, cast a shadow upon

sombrerera *nf* hatbox

sombrerería *nf (para señoras)* milliner's; *(para caballeros)* hatter's

sombrerero, -a *nm,f (para señoras)* milliner; *(para caballeros)* hatter

sombrerete *nm* (a) *(de chimenea)* cowl (b) *Bot (de seta)* cap

sombrero *nm* (a) *(prenda)* hat; **sin s.** hatless, bareheaded; *Fig* **quitarse el s. ante algn** to take one's hat off to sb ▫ **s. canotier** straw hat; **s. cordobés** = wide-brimmed Andalusian hat; **s. de copa** top hat; **s. de jipijapa** Panama hat; **s. de tres picos** three-cornered hat; **s. hongo** *Br* bowler hat, *US* derby (b) *Bot (de seta)* cap

sombrilla *nf* (a) *(quitasol)* parasol, sunshade (b) *Col (paraguas)* umbrella (c) *Méx Fam* **me vale s.** I couldn't care less

sombrío, -a *adj* (a) *(lugar) (oscuro)* dark; *Fig (tenebroso)* sombre, gloomy (b) *Fig (persona)* gloomy, sullen

somero, -a *adj (superficial)* superficial, shallow; *Fig* **hizo una somera exposición del tema** she gave a brief summary of the subject

someter 1 *vt* (a) *(rebeldes)* to subdue, put down; *(rebelión)* to put down, quell; *(pasiones)* to subdue (b) *(exponer, mostrar)* to subject (a lo), expose (a to); **s. a prueba** to put to the test; **s. algo a la autoridad** to refer sth to the authorities; **s. algo a votación** to put sth to the vote (c) *(proposición, idea)* to submit, present
 2 someterse *vpr* (a) *(rendirse)* to surrender, yield; *Fig* **s. a la opinión de algn** to bow to sb's opinion (b) *(recibir)* **s. a** to undergo; **s. a un tratamiento** to undergo treatment

sometimiento *nm* (a) *(dominación)* subjection, subjugation (b) *(presentación)* submission, presentation

somier *nm* spring mattress

somnífero, -a 1 *adj* somniferous, sleep-inducing
 2 *nm* sleeping pill

somnolencia *nf* somnolence, sleepiness, drowsiness

somnoliento, -a *adj* sleepy, drowsy

somormujo *nm Orn* grebe

son *nm* (a) *(sonido)* sound; **al s. del tambor** to the sound of the drum (b) *(rumor)* rumour, *US* rumor (c) *(modo)* manner, way; **a mi s.** my way (d) *(motivo, pretexto)* reason; **¿a s. de qué?** whatever for?; **sin ton ni s.** without rhyme or reason; **venir en s. de paz** to come in peace

sonado, -a 1 *pp de* **sonar**
 2 *adj* (a) *(muy conocido)* famous; *Fam* **hacer una que sea sonada** to cause a great stir (b) *Fam Fig (trastocado)* mad, crazy; **estar s.** *(boxeador)* to be punch-drunk; *(estar loco)* to be off one's rocker

sonaja *nf* (a) *(de pandereta)* small metal disk (b) **sonajas** *(juguete)* rattle *sing*

sonajero *nm* baby's rattle

sonambulismo *nm* somnambulism, sleepwalking

sonámbulo, -a 1 *adj* sleepwalking
 2 *nm,f* somnambulist, sleepwalker

sonante *adj* **dinero contante y s.** hard cash

sonar [63] **1** *vi* (a) *(resonar)* to sound; **s. a** to sound like; **suena bien** it sounds good; *Prov* **cuando el río suena, agua lleva** there's no smoke without fire (b) *(campana, timbre, teléfono)* to ring (c) *(reloj)* to strike; **sonaron las cinco** the clock struck five (d) *(ser conocido, familiar)* **me suena** it sounds familiar, it rings a bell (e) *(pronunciarse)* to be pronounced; **la 'h' no suena** the 'h' is not pronounced; **se escribe como suena** it is written as it's pronounced; **tal y como suena** just as I am telling you
 2 sonarse *vpr (nariz)* to blow one's nose

sónar *nm Náut* sonar

sonata *nf Mús* sonata

sonatina *nf Mús* sonatina

sonda *nf* (a) *Med* sound, probe (b) *Náut* sounding line (c) *Min* drill, bore (d) *Téc* probe; **s. espacial** space probe

sondar *vt* (a) *Med* to sound, probe (b) *Náut* to sound (c) *Min (terreno)* to test, bore; *(roca)* to drill

sondear *vt* (a) *Med* to sound, probe (b) *Náut* to sound (c) *Min (terreno)* to test, bore; *(roca)* to drill (d) *Fig* to test, sound out; **s. la opinión pública** to test public opinion

sondeo *nm* (a) *Med* sounding, probing (b) *Náut* sounding (c) *Min* drilling, boring (d) *(encuesta)* poll; *TV* **s. de audiencia** rating; **s. de la opinión pública** public opinion poll

sonetista *nmf Lit* writer of sonnets

soneto *nm Lit* sonnet

sónico, -a *adj* sonic

sonido *nm* sound; **barrera del s.** sound barrier

soniquete *nm véase* **sonsonete**

sonoridad *nf* sonority

sonorización *nf* (**a**) *Cin (de película)* recording of the soundtrack (**b**) *(amplificación)* amplification (**c**) *Ling (en fonética)* voicing

sonorizar [14] *vt* (**a**) *Cin (película)* to record the soundtrack of (**b**) *(amplificar)* to install amplifying equipment in (**c**) *Ling (en fonética)* to voice

sonoro, -a *adj* (**a**) *Cin* sound; **banda sonora** soundtrack; **efectos sonoros** sound effects; **película sonora** talking picture (**b**) *(resonante)* loud, resounding; **voz sonora** resounding voice (**c**) *Ling* voiced

sonotone® *nm* hearing aid

sonreír [56] **1** *vi* (**a**) *(reír levemente)* to smile; **me sonrió** he smiled at me (**b**) *(ser favorable)* **sonreírle a algn** *(suerte)* to smile on sb
2 sonreírse *vpr* to smile

sonriente *adj* smiling

sonrisa *nf* smile; **dirigir una s. a algn** to smile at sb; **esbozar una s.** to smile

sonrojar 1 *vt* to make blush
2 *vi* **hacer s. a algn** to make sb blush
3 sonrojarse *vpr* to blush

sonrojo *nm* (**a**) *(rubor)* blush, blushing (**b**) *(vergüenza)* shame, embarrassment

sonrosado, -a 1 *pp de* sonrosar
2 *adj* rosy, pink

sonrosar *vt* **el aire fresco le ha sonrosado las mejillas** the fresh air has brought some colour to his cheeks

sonsacar [59] *vt* **s. algo a algn** to extract sth from sb

sonso, -a *adj Am Fam* silly

sonsonete *nm* (**a**) *(voz)* sing-song (voice), monotonous voice (**b**) *(tono)* mocking tone (**c**) *(golpecitos)* rhythmic tapping

soñado, -a 1 *pp de* soñar
2 *adj* of one's dreams, dreamed-of; **que ni s.** marvellous, fantastic

soñador, -a 1 *adj* dreamy, dreaming
2 *nm,f* dreamer

soñar [63] *vt & vi* (**a**) *(dormir)* to dream; **s. con** to dream of o about; *Fig* **¡ni soñarlo!** not on your life!; *Fig* **s. con los angelitos** to have sweet dreams (**b**) *(fantasear)* to daydream, dream; **s. despierto** to daydream

soñarrera *nf Fam*, **soñera** *nf* (**a**) *(sueño profundo)* deep sleep (**b**) *(ganas de dormir)* sleepiness; **cogerse una s.** to feel sleepy

soñoliento, -a *adj* sleepy, drowsy

sopa *nf* soup; *Esp Fig* **comer la s. boba** to be a parasite; *Esp Fig* **dar sopas con honda a algn** to outshine sb; *Fig* **quedar hecho una s.** to get soaked to the skin; *Fam* **estar hasta en la s.** to be everywhere □ *Am* **s. inglesa** trifle; **s. juliana** spring vegetable soup

sopapo *nm* slap; **dar un s. a algn** to slap sb

sopar *vt*, **sopear** *vt Culin* to dunk

sopera *nf* soup tureen

sopero, -a *adj* soup; **cucharada sopera** soup spoon; **plato s.** soup dish

sopesar *vt* to try the weight of; *Fig* to weigh up

sopetón *nm Fam* slap; **de s.** all of a sudden

sopicaldo *nm* thin soup

sopla *interj Fam Br* crikey!, *US* jeez!

soplado, -a 1 *pp de* soplar
2 *adj Fam* (**a**) *(borracho)* drunk, tight, tipsy (**b**) *(engreído)* conceited
3 *nm Téc* glass-blowing

soplador, -a *nm,f* (**a**) **s. (de vidrio)** glass-blower (**b**) *Ecuad Teat* prompter

soplagaitas *nmf inv Fam Pey Br* prat, *US* jerk

soplamocos *nm inv Fam* slap, punch

soplapollas *nmf inv Vulg* berk

soplar 1 *vi* (**a**) *(correr el viento)* to blow (**b**) *Fam (en examen)* **le expulsaron por s.** he was thrown out for whispering the answers
2 *vt* (**a**) *(polvo etc)* to blow away; *(sopa)* to blow on (**b**) *(apagar)* *(vela)* to blow out (**c**) *(llenar de aire)* to blow up (**d**) *Téc (vidrio)* to blow (**e**) *(decir con disimulo)* to whisper o tell the answer to (**f**) *Fam (denunciar)* to split on (**g**) *Esp Fam (robar)* to pinch, *Br* nick
3 soplarse *vpr* (**a**) *(lanzarse aire)* to blow on; **s. los dedos** to blow on one's fingers (**b**) *Esp Fam (beber)* to down; *(comer)* to wolf down

soplete *nm Téc* blowlamp, blowtorch

soplido *nm* blow, puff

soplillo *nm* fan; *Fam* **orejas de s.** sticking out ears, cauliflower ears

soplo *nm* (**a**) *(acción)* blow, puff; *(de viento)* puff, gust; *Fig* **pasar como un s.** to fly past (**b**) *(instante)* moment, minute; **en un s.** in a jiffy (**c**) *Fam (delación)* tip-off; **dar el s.** to squeal, *Br* grass (**d**) *Med* souffle, murmur

soplón, -ona *nm,f Fam (niño) Br* telltale; *US* tattletale; *(delator) Br* grass, *US* rat

soponcio *nm Fam* fainting fit, swoon; **me dio un s.** I passed out, I fainted

sopor *nm* sleepiness, drowsiness

soporífero, -a *adj*, **soporífico, -a** *adj* (**a**) *(que adormece)* soporific, sleep-inducing (**b**) *(aburrido)* boring, dull

soportable *adj* bearable

soportal *nm Arquit* porch; **soportales** arcade *sing*

soportar *vt* (**a**) *(sostener)* to support, bear (**b**) *Fig (tolerar)* to bear, endure; *(aguantar)* to put up with; **no soporto la lluvia** I can't stand rain

soporte *nm* (**a**) *(apoyo)* support (**b**) *(medio) Inform* **s. físico/lógico** hardware/software; **s. publicitario** publicity medium

soprano *nmf Mús* soprano

sor *nf Rel* sister

sorber *vt* (**a**) *(beber)* to sip; *(un huevo)* to suck (**b**) *(absorber)* to soak up, absorb; *Fam* **sorberle el seso a algn** to go to sb's head

sorbete *nm* (**a**) *(postre)* sorbet, sherbet (**b**) *CAm (helado)* ice cream

sorbetería *nf CAm* ice cream parlour o *US* parlor

sorbo *nm* (**a**) *(acción)* sip; **beber a sorbos** to sip (**b**) *(trago)* gulp; **de un s.** in one gulp

sordera *nf* deafness

sordidez *nf* (**a**) *(suciedad)* squalor (**b**) *(mezquindad)* meanness

sórdido, -a *adj* (**a**) *(sucio)* squalid, sordid (**b**) *(mezquino)* mean

sordina *nf* (**a**) *Mús (en trompeta)* mute, sordino; *(en piano)* damper; *Fig* **a la s.** silently, on the quiet (**b**) *(en reloj)* silencer, muffler

sordo, -a 1 *adj* (**a**) *(persona)* deaf; **quedarse s.** to go deaf; **s. como una tapia** stone-deaf; *Fig* **permanecer s. a** to be deaf to (**b**) *(golpe, ruido, dolor)* dull (**c**) *(cólera)* pent-up (**d**) *Ling* voiceless, unvoiced
2 *nm,f* deaf person; **los sordos** the deaf *pl*; *Fam Fig* **hacerse el s.** to turn a deaf ear

sordomudez *nf* deaf-muteness

sordomudo, -a 1 *adj* deaf and dumb, deaf-mute
  2 *nm,f* deaf and dumb person, deaf-mute

sorgo *nm Bot* sorghum

soriano, -a 1 *adj* of o from Soria
  2 *nm,f* person from Soria

soriasis *nf inv Med* psoriasis

sorna *nf (ironía)* sarcasm; *(mofa)* mocking tone

soroche *nm* **(a)** *Andes Arg (mal de altura)* altitude sickness **(b)** *Chile (rubor)* blush, flush

sorprendente *adj* surprising, amazing, astonishing; *(extraordinario)* extraordinary

sorprender 1 *vt* **(a)** *(causar extrañeza)* to surprise, astonish, amaze; **no me sorprendería nada** I wouldn't be at all surprised **(b)** *(coger desprevenido)* to catch unawares, take by surprise; **sorprendieron al ladrón** they caught the burglar in the act **(c)** *(descubrir)* to discover
  2 sorprenderse *vpr* to be surprised; **¿de qué te sorprendes?** why are you so surprised?

sorpresa *nf* surprise; **coger de** o **por s.** to take by surprise; **llevarse una s.** to be surprised

sorpresivo, -a *adj* unexpected, surprising

sortear *vt* **(a)** *(someter a suerte)* to draw o cast lots for; *(rifar)* to raffle (off); *Mil* to draft **(b)** *(evitar)* to avoid, overcome, get round **(c)** *Taur* to dodge

sorteo *nm* draw; *(rifa)* raffle

sortija *nf* **(a)** *(anillo)* ring **(b)** *(rizo)* curl

sortilegio *nm* **(a)** *(hechicería)* sorcery, witchcraft **(b)** *(hechizo)* spell

S.O.S. *nm* SOS; **lanzar un S.O.S.** to send out an SOS

sosa *nf* **(a)** *Bot* saltwort **(b)** *Quím* soda □ **s. cáustica** caustic soda

sosaina *nmf Fam* dull person, bore

sosegado, -a 1 *pp de* **sosegar**
  2 *adj (tranquilo)* calm, quiet; *(pacífico)* peaceful

sosegador, -a *adj* calming

sosegar [43] **1** *vt (aplacar)* to calm, quieten
  2 sosegarse *vpr (tranquilizarse)* to calm down

sosera *nf,* **sosería** *nf* insipidity, dullness

soseras *inv* **1** *adj* dull, boring
  2 *nmf* dull person, bore

sosería *nf* lack of sparkle

sosia *nm* double, lookalike

sosiego *nm (calma)* calmness; *(paz)* peace, tranquility

soslayar *vt* **(a)** *(ladear)* to slant, put on a slant **(b)** *Fig (eludir)* to avoid, dodge

soslayo: de soslayo *loc adv* sideways; **mirar de s.** to look sideways (at)

soso, -a *adj* **(a)** *(comida)* tasteless; **la sopa está sosa** the soup needs more salt **(b)** *Fig (sin gracia)* insipid, dull, flat; **¡qué hombre tan s.!** what a bore (he is)!

sospecha *nf* suspicion; **despertar sospechas** to arouse suspicion; **por encima de toda s.** above suspicion; **s. fundada** well-founded suspicion; **tengo la s. de que ...** I suspect that ...

sospechar 1 *vt (pensar)* to think, suppose, suspect
  2 *vi (desconfiar)* to suspect; **s. de algn** to suspect sb

sospechosamente *adv* suspiciously

sospechoso, -a 1 *adj* suspicious
  2 *nm,f* suspect

sostén *nm* **(a)** *(apoyo)* support **(b)** *(sustento)* sustenance **(c)** *(prenda)* bra, brassière

sostener [65] **1** *vt* **(a)** *(sustentar)* to support, hold up **(b)** *(sujetar)* to hold **(c)** *Fig (aguantar) (dificultades)* to endure, bear, put up with **(d)** *Fig (defender) (teoría, punto de vista)* to

defend, uphold; **s. que ...** to maintain that ... **(e)** *(mantener)* to hold, sustain; **s. la palabra** to keep one's word; **s. una conversación** to have o hold a conversation; **sostenerle la mirada a algn** to stare sb down; *Fig* **s. una familia** to support a family
  2 sostenerse *vpr* **(a)** *(mantenerse)* to support oneself **(b)** *(permanecer)* to stay, remain; **se sostuvo en la presidencia cinco años** he held the presidency for five years

sostenible *adj (objeto, desarrollo)* sustainable; *(idea, argumento)* tenable

sostenido, -a 1 *pp de* **sostener**
  2 *adj* **(a)** *(continuado)* sustained; *(constante)* steady **(b)** *Mús* sharp; **sol s.** G sharp
  3 *nm Mús* sharp

sostenimiento *nm* **(a)** *(apoyo)* support **(b)** *(mantenimiento)* maintenance

sota 1 *nf Naipes* jack, knave
  2 *nm Chile (capataz)* foreman, overseer

sotabanco *nm* attic

sotabarba *nf* **(a)** *(barba)* Newgate frill o fringe **(b)** *(papada)* double chin

sotana *nf Rel* cassock, soutane

sótano *nm* basement, cellar

sotavento *nm Náut* lee, leeward; **Islas de S.** Leeward Islands

soterrado, -a 1 *pp de* **soterrar**
  2 *adj* buried, hidden

soterrar [3] *vt* to bury; *Fig* to hide

soto *nm (arboleda)* grove; *(matorrales)* thicket

sotobosque *nm* undergrowth

soufflé [su'fle] *nm Culin* soufflé

soul *nm Mús* soul (music)

souvenir [suβe'nir] *(pl* **souvenirs)** *nm* souvenir

soviet *nm Pol* soviet

soviético, -a *adj & nm,f* Soviet; **la Unión Soviética** the Soviet Union

soy *indic pres véase* ser[2]

S.P. *(abrev de* **Servicio Público)**

spanglish [es'panglis] *nm* Spanglish

sparring [es'parrin] *(pl* **sparrings)** *nm Box* sparring partner

speaker *nmf Rad TV* presenter, commentator

speed [es'piθ] *nm (droga)* speed

sport [es'por:]: **de sport** *loc adj* casual, sports; **chaqueta de s.** sports jacket; **ropa de s.** casual clothes o wear

spot [es'pot] *(pl* **spots)** *nm TV* commercial, advert, ad

spray [es'prai] *(pl* **sprays)** *nm* spray

sprint [es'prin] *(pl* **sprints)** *nm Dep* sprint

sprintar [esprin'tar] *vi Dep* to sprint

sprinter [es'printer] *(pl* **sprinters)** *nmf Dep* sprinter

squash [es'kwas] *nm inv Dep* squash

Sr. *(abrev de* **Señor)** Mr

Sra. *(abrev de* **Señora)** Mrs

S.R.C., s.r.c. *(abrev de* **se ruega contestación)** R.S.V.P

Sres. *(abrev de* **Señores)** Messrs

Sri Lanka *n* Sri Lanka

Srta. *(abrev de* **Señorita)** Miss

S.S. *Rel (abrev de* **Su Santidad)** H.H.

SS.AA. *(abrev de* **Sus Altezas)** Their Royal Highnesses

SS. MM. *(abrev de* **Sus Majestades)** their Royal Highnesses

s.s.s. *(abrev de* **su seguro servidor)** your humble servant

Sta., sta. (*abrev de* **Santa**) St

stand [es'tan] (*pl* **stands**) *nm Com* stand

standing [es'tandin] *nm* standing; **pisos de alto s.** de luxe *Br* flats *o US* apartments

starter *nm Aut* choke

statu quo [es'tatu'kwo] *nm* status quo

status [es'tatus] *nm inv* status

step [es'tep] (*pl* **steps**) *nm* step (aerobics)

stick [es'tik] (*pl* **sticks**) *nm Dep* stick

Sto., sto. (*abrev de* **Santo**) St

stock [es'tok] (*pl* **stocks**) *nm Com* stock

stop [es'top] (*pl* **stops**) *nm Aut* stop sign

striptease [es'triptis] *nm inv* striptease; **hacer un s.** to strip

su (*pl* **sus**) *adj pos* (*un objeto*) *(de él)* his; *(de ella)* her; *(de usted, ustedes)* your; *(de animales o cosas)* its; *(impersonal)* one's; *(de ellos)* their; **su coche** his/her/your/their car; **su pata** its leg; **sus libros** his/her/your/their books; **sus patas** its legs

suahili [swa'χili] *nm*, **suajili** *nm (lengua)* Swahili

suave *adj* (**a**) *(liso, llano)* smooth (**b**) *(dulce) (luz, voz, música, palabras)* soft (**c**) *Meteor (templado)* mild (**d**) *(tranquilo) (paso)* easy (**e**) *(apacible)* gentle, mild

suavemente *adv* smoothly

suavidad *nf* (**a**) *(lisura)* smoothness (**b**) *(dulzura)* softness (**c**) *Meteor* mildness (**d**) *(tranquilidad)* ease (**e**) *(docilidad)* gentleness

suavizante *nm* (**a**) *(para el pelo)* (hair) conditioner (**b**) *(para la ropa)* fabric softener

suavizar [14] *vt* (**a**) *(alisar)* to smooth (out) (**b**) *(hacer más dulce)* to soften; *Fig* **es necesario s. las tensiones que hay entre ellos** tension between them will have to be eased

Suazilandia *n* Swaziland

suba *nf CSur* price rise

subacuático, -a *adj* underwater

subafluente *nm Geog* tributary

subalimentación *nf* undernourishment

subalimentado, -a 1 *pp de* **subalimentar**
2 *adj* undernourished, underfed

subalimentar *vt* to undernourish

subalquilar *vt* to sublet

subalterno, -a *adj & nm,f* subordinate, subaltern; *Com* clerk

subarrendamiento *nm* sublease

subarrendar [3] *vt* to sublet, sublease

subarrendatario, -a *nm,f* subtenant

subarriendo *nm* sublease

subasta *nf* auction; **sacar a s.** to auction (off)

subastador, -a *nm,f* auctioneer

subastar *vt* to auction (off), sell at auction

subatómico, -a *adj Fís* subatomic

subcampeón *nm* runner-up

subcampeonato *nm* second place, runner-up's position

subcomisión *nf* subcommittee

subconjunto *nm Mat* subset

subconsciencia *nf Psic* subconscious

subconsciente *adj & nm Psic* subconscious

subcontinente *nm* subcontinent

subcontratación *nf* subcontracting

subcontratar *vt* to subcontract

subcontratista *nmf Com Fin* subcontrator

subcontrato *nm Com Fin Jur* subcontract

subcultura *nf* subculture

subcutáneo, -a *adj* subcutaneous

subdelegación *nf* subdelegation

subdelegado, -a *nm,f* subdelegate

subdesarrollado, -a *adj* underdeveloped

subdesarrollo *nm* underdevelopment

subdirección *nf (puesto)* post of assistant manager

subdirector, -a *nm,f* assistant director *o* manager

subdirectorio *nm Inform* subdirectory

súbdito, -a 1 *adj* subject
2 *nm,f* subject, citizen, national; **s. francés** French citizen

subdividir *vt* to subdivide

subdivisión *nf* subdivision

subemplear *vt* to underemploy

subempleo *nm* underemployment

subespecie *nf Biol* subspecies *sing*

subestimar *vt* to underestimate

subfusil *nm Mil* sub-machine-gun

subgénero *nm Biol* subgenus

subgrupo *nm* subgroup

subibaja *nm* seesaw

subida *nf* (**a**) *(ascenso)* ascent, climb; *Dep Aut* hill climb (**b**) *(pendiente)* slope, hill (**c**) *(aumento) (temperatura)* rise; *Com Fin (de precios, salarios)* rise, increase ❑ **s. de precios** price increase (**d**) *Fam (drogas)* high

subido, -a 1 *pp de* **subir**
2 *adj* (**a**) *(alto)* high (**b**) *(intenso)* strong; **de un rojo s.** deep red; **s. de tono** daring, risqué

subidón *nm Fam (de drogas)* high

subíndice *nm Mat* subindex

subinspector, -a *nm,f* deputy inspector

subir 1 *vt* (**a**) *(ascender) (montaña, escaleras)* to climb; *(calle)* to go up (**b**) *(llevar arriba)* to carry up, take up, bring up; **súbame las maletas por favor** carry my suitcases upstairs, please; **súbelo arriba** put it upstairs (**c**) *(levantar)* to lift, raise; **suba la cabeza** raise your head (**d**) *(aumentar)* to raise, put up (**e**) *(dar más volumen a) (radio, televisión)* to turn up; *(voz)* to raise; **si no subes la voz no podré oírte** if you don't raise your voice I won't be able to hear you
2 *vi* (**a**) *(ir arriba)* to go up, come up; **¿subes o bajas?** are you going up *o* coming down?; *Fig* **s. al trono** to ascend the throne (**b**) *(entrar en un vehículo)* **s. a** *(coche)* to get into; *(autobús)* to get on; *(barco, avión, tren)* to board, get on; **s. a bordo** to go aboard (**c**) *(montar)* **s. a** to get on (**d**) *(aumentar)* to rise, go up; *Fam* **s. como la espuma** to rise sky high (**e**) *(totalizar)* **s. a** to amount to, come to; **¿a cuánto sube la cuenta?** what does the bill come to?
3 subirse *vpr* (**a**) *(ir arriba) (árbol)* to climb up; *(piso)* to go up; *Fig* **el champán se le ha subido a la cabeza** the champagne's gone to his head; *Fig* **s. a la parra** to blow one's top; *Fig* **s. por las paredes** to hit the roof, go up the wall; *Fig* **subírsele la sangre a la cabeza** to see red (**b**) *(entrar)* **s.a** *(coche)* to get into; *(autobús, avión, tren)* to get on, board (**c**) *(montar)* to get on (**d**) *(ropa, calcetines)* to pull up; *(cremallera)* to do up; *(mangas)* to roll up

súbitamente *adv* suddenly

súbito, -a *adj* sudden; **de s.** suddenly, all of a sudden

subjefe, -a *nm,f Com* assistant manager

subjetividad *nf* subjectivity, subjectiveness

subjetivismo *nm* subjectivism

subjetivo, -a *adj* subjective

subjuntivo *nm Ling* subjunctive

sublevación *nf*, **sublevamiento** *nm* rising, revolt, rebellion

sublevar 1 *vt* (**a**) *(alzar en sedición)* to stir up, arouse; *(rebelar)* to incite to rebellion (**b**) *Fig (indignar)* to infuriate, enrage
  2 sublevarse *vpr* to rebel, revolt; **los soldados se sublevaron** the soldiers mutinied

sublimación *nf* sublimation

sublimado, -a 1 *pp de* **sublimar**
  2 *adj* sublimated
  3 *nm Quím* sublimate

sublimar *vt* (**a**) *(gen)* to sublimate; *Psic* to sublimate (**b**) *(ensalzar)* to praise, exalt

sublime *adj (excelso)* sublime; *(eminente)* noble, lofty; **lo s.** the sublime

sublimidad *nf* sublimity

subliminal *adj* subliminal

submarinismo *nm* skin-diving

submarinista *nmf* skin-diver

submarino, -a *Náut* **1** *adj* submarine, underwater
  2 *nm (buque)* submarine

submundo *nm* world, scene; **el s. de las drogas** the drugs world *o* scene

subnormal *Med* **1** *adj* subnormal, mentally handicapped
  2 *nmf* mentally handicapped person; *Fam* blockhead, dunderhead

suboficial *nm* (**a**) *Mil* non-commissioned officer (**b**) *Náut* petty officer

suborden *nm Biol* suborder

subordinación *nf* subordination

subordinado, -a 1 *pp de* **subordinar**
  2 *adj* subordinate; *Ling* **oración subordinada** subordinate clause
  3 *nm,f* subordinate

subordinar 1 *vt* to subordinate
  2 subordinarse *vpr* to subordinate oneself

subproducto *nm* by-product

subrayado, -a 1 *adj* underlined
  2 *nm* underlining

subrayar *vt* (**a**) *(hacer una raya)* to underline (**b**) *Fig (recalcar)* to emphasize, stress, underline

subrepticiamente *adv* surreptitiously

subrepticio, -a *adj* surreptitious

subrogar [38] *vt Jur* to subrogate, substitute

subrutina *nf Inform* subroutine

subsahariano, -a *adj* sub-Saharan

subsanable *adj* (**a**) *(remediable)* repairable, that can be mended *o* put right (**b**) *(solucionable)* surmountable

subsanación *nf (de errores)* correction

subsanar *vt* to rectify, put right; **s. un error** to correct a mistake

subscribir *(pp* subscrito*) vt véase* **suscribir**

subscripción *nf véase* **suscripción**

subscriptor, -a *nm,f véase* **suscriptor, -a**

subscrito, -a *pp & adj & nm,f véase* **suscrito, -a**

subsecretaría *nf* (**a**) *(cargo)* undersecretaryship (**b**) *(oficina)* undersecretary's office

subsecretario, -a *nm,f* undersecretary

subsidiar *vt Fml* to subsidize

subsidiariedad *nf* subsidiarity

subsidiario, -a *adj* subsidiary

subsidio *nm* allowance, benefit ❏ **s. de desempleo** *o*

Esp **paro** unemployment *Br* benefit *o US* compensation, dole

subsiguiente *adj* subsequent, succeeding, following

subsistencia *nf* (**a**) *(supervivencia)* subsistence (**b**) **subsistencias** *(provisiones)* food *sing*, provisions, supplies

subsistente *adj* surviving, lasting

subsistir *vi* (**a**) *(conservarse)* to subsist, last, remain (**b**) *(vivir)* to subsist, live on, survive

substancia *nf véase* **sustancia**

substancial *adj véase* **sustancial**

substanciar *vt véase* **sustanciar**

substancioso, -a *adj véase* **sustancioso, -a**

substantivación *nf véase* **sustantivación**

substantivar *vt véase* **sustantivar**

substantivo, -a *adj & nm véase* **sustantivo, -a**

substitución *nf véase* **sustitución**

substituible *adj véase* **sustituible**

substituir *vt véase* **sustituir**

substitutivo *nm véase* **sustitutivo**

substituto, -a *pp & nm,f véase* **sustituto, -a**

substracción *nf véase* **sustracción**

substraendo *nm véase* **sustraendo**

substraer *vt véase* **sustraer**

substrato *nm Geol Filos* substratum

subsuelo *nm* (**a**) *(terreno)* subsoil (**b**) *Andes RP (sótano)* basement

subte *nm RP* metro, *Br* underground, *US* subway

subteniente *nm Mil* second lieutenant

subterfugio *nm (escapatoria)* subterfuge; *(pretexto)* pretext

subterráneo, -a 1 *adj* subterranean, underground
  2 *nm* (**a**) *(túnel)* tunnel, underground passage (**b**) *RP (metro) Br* underground, *US* subway

subtitular *vt* (**a**) *Cin* to subtitle (**b**) *Lit* subhead, subheading

subtítulo *nm Cin* subtitle

subtotal *nm* subtotal

subtropical *adj Geog* subtropical

suburbano, -a 1 *adj* suburban
  2 *nm* suburban train

suburbial *adj* suburban

suburbio *nm (barrio periférico)* suburb; *(barrio pobre)* slums *pl*

subvalorar *vt* to underrate, underestimate, undervalue

subvención *nf* subsidy, grant

subvencionar *vt* to subsidize

subvenir [69] *vt Fin* to meet, defray

subversión *nf* subversion

subversivo, -a *adj* subversive

subvertir [62] *vt* to subvert, upset, overthrow

subyacente *adj* underlying

subyacer [71] *vi* **s. bajo algo** to underlie sth

subyugación *nf* subjugation

subyugador, -a *adj*, **subyugante** *adj* (**a**) *(dominador)* conquering (**b**) *(atrayente)* captivating

subyugar [38] *vt* (**a**) *(dominar)* to subjugate (**b**) *Fig (cautivar)* to captivate

succión *nf* suction

succionar *vt* to suck (in)

sucedáneo, -a 1 *adj* substitute, ersatz
  2 *nm* substitute

suceder 1 *vi* (**a**) *(ocurrir) (uso impers)* to happen, occur; **por lo que pueda s.** just in case; **¿qué sucede?** what's going on?, what's the matter?; **suceda lo que suceda** whatever happens, come what may (**b**) *(seguir)* to follow, succeed; **a la tormenta sucedió la calma** calm followed the storm; **sucedió a su padre como presidente** he succeeded his father as president
2 sucederse *vpr* to follow one another, come after the other

sucedido, -a 1 *pp de* **suceder**
2 *nm Fam* event

sucesión *nf* (**a**) *(serie, conjunto)* series *sing*, succession (**b**) *(al trono)* succession (**c**) *(herencia)* succession, estate, inheritance (**d**) *(descendientes)* issue, heirs *pl; Jur* **derechos de s.** *(al legalizar el testamento)* death duties; *(al heredar)* probate duties

sucesivamente *adv* successively; **y así s.** and so on

sucesivo, -a *adj* (**a**) *(siguiente)* following, successive; **en lo s.** from now on (**b**) *(consecutivo)* consecutive, running

suceso *nm* (**a**) *(acontecimiento)* event, happening, occurrence (**b**) *(hecho delictivo)* crime; *(incidente)* incident; *Prensa* **sección de sucesos** accident and crime reports

sucesor, -a *nm,f* successor

suche 1 *adj Méx, Ven* unripe
2 *nm* (**a**) *Ecuad Perú Bot* white frangipani (**b**) *Chile Nic Fam Pey* menial

suciedad *nf* (**a**) *(porquería)* dirt, filth (**b**) *(calidad de sucio)* dirtiness, filthiness

sucintamente *adv* briefly, concisely

sucinto, -a *adj* brief, concise, succinct

sucio, -a *adj* dirty; *(color)* off, dirty; **un amarillo s.** an off-yellow; *Fig* **en s.** in rough; *Fig* **juego s.** foul play; *Fig* **negocio s.** shady business

sucre *nm Fin* = standard monetary unit of Ecuador

suculento, -a *adj* succulent, juicy

sucumbir *vi* (**a**) *(ceder)* to succumb, yield; **s. a la tentación** to give in to temptation (**b**) *Fml (morir)* to perish

sucursal *nf Com Fin* branch, branch office; *(delegación)* subsidiary

sudaca *nmf Pey* South American

sudadera *nf (prenda)* sweatshirt

Sudáfrica *n* South Africa

sudafricano, -a *adj & nm,f* South African

Sudamérica *n* South America

sudamericano, -a *adj & nm,f* South American

Sudán *n* Sudan

sudanés, -esa *adj & nm,f* Sudanese

sudar *vt* (**a**) *(transpirar)* to sweat, exude; *Fam Fig* **s. la gota gorda** to sweat blood (**b**) *(manchar de sudor)* to stain with sweat (**c**) *(obtener con esfuerzo)* to work hard for
2 *vi* to perspire, sweat; *Fig* **hacer s. a algn** to drive sb hard

sudario *nm* shroud

sudeste 1 *adj (del sudeste)* southeast, southeastern; *(dirección sudeste)* southeasterly
2 *nm* (**a**) *(punto cardinal)* southeast (**b**) *(viento)* southeast wind; *(viento fuerte)* southeasterly

sudista *Hist* **1** *adj* Southern *(in US Civil War)*
2 *nmf* Southerner *(in US Civil War)*

sudoeste 1 *adj (del sudoeste)* southwest, southwestern; *(dirección sudoeste)* southwesterly
2 *nm* (**a**) *(punto cardinal)* southwest (**b**) *(viento)* southwest wind; *(viento fuerte)* southwesterly

sudor *nm* (**a**) *(transpiración)* sweat, perspiration (**b**) *Fig (esfuerzo)* effort, hard work; *Fig* **con el s. de mi frente** by the sweat of my brow; *Fig* **costar muchos sudores** to be a struggle

sudoración *nf* sweating, perspiration

sudorífero, -a *adj* sudoriferous

sudorífico, -a *adj & nm* sudorific

sudoríparo, -a *adj Anat* sudoriferous; **glándulas sudoríparas** sweat glands

sudoroso, -a *adj* sweaty

Suecia *n* Sweden

sueco, -a 1 *adj* Swedish
2 *nm,f (persona)* Swede; *Fam* **hacerse el s.** to pretend not to understand, play dumb
3 *nm (idioma)* Swedish

suegra *nf* mother-in-law

suegro *nm* father-in-law; **mis suegros** my in-laws

suela *nf* (**a**) *(del zapato)* sole; *Fig* **no te llego ni a la s. del zapato** you're one step ahead of me (**b**) *Bill* leather tip

sueldo *nm* salary, wages *pl;* **asesino a s.** hit man; **aumento de s.** pay rise *o US* raise; **estar a s.** to be on a salary □ **s. mínimo** minimum wage

suelo *nm* (**a**) *(superficie)* ground; *(de interior)* floor; **dar consigo en el s.** to fall; **echar al s.** to demolish; **s. de madera** wooden floor; *Fig* **echar por los suelos** to ruin; *Fig* **estar por los suelos** *(precios)* to be rock-bottom; *(ánimos)* to be very low; *Fig* **poner algo por los suelos** to run sth down, tear sth to pieces; *Fam Fig* **besar el s.** to fall flat on one's face (**b**) *(tierra)* soil, earth (**c**) *(territorio)* soil, land; **s. extranjero** foreign soil; **s. patrio** native land (**d**) *(campo, terreno)* land; **s. cultivable** arable land (**e**) *(de carretera)* surface

suelta *nf* freeing, release; **dar rienda s. a** to free, let loose

suelto, -a 1 *adj* (**a**) *(no sujeto)* loose; **esa pieza está suelta** this part has come loose (**b**) *(desatado)* undone, untied; *Fig* **atar cabos sueltos** to tie up loose ends; *Fig* **dinero s.** loose change (**c**) *(en libertad)* free; *(huido)* at large (**d**) *(desaparejado)* odd; **hojas sueltas** loose sheets (of paper); **números sueltos** odd numbers; **se venden sueltos** they are sold singly *o* separately *o* loose (**e**) *(holgado) (prenda)* loose, loose-fitting (**f**) *Lit (estilo)* flowing, easy
2 *nm* (**a**) *(dinero)* (loose) change (**b**) *Prensa* short article, item

sueño *nm* (**a**) *(acto de dormir)* sleep; *(ganas de dormir)* sleepiness; **conciliar el s.** to get to sleep; **entre sueños** while half-asleep; **me caigo de s.** I can't keep my eyes open; **me da s.** it makes me sleepy; **tener el s. ligero** to be a light sleeper; **tener s.** to feel *o* be sleepy; *Fig* **quitar el s.** to keep awake (**b**) *(cosa soñada)* dream; **en sueños** in one's dreams; *Fig* **s. dorado** cherished dream; *Fam* **¡ni en sueños!** I wouldn't dream of it!, not on your life!

suero *nm* (**a**) *Med* serum (**b**) *(de la leche)* whey

suerte *nf* (**a**) *(fortuna)* luck, fortune; *(azar)* chance; **buena/mala s.** good/bad luck; **echar algo** *Esp* **a suertes** *o Am* **a la s.** to draw lots for sth; **estar de s.** to be in luck; **la s. está echada** the die is cast; **por s.** fortunately; **probar s.** to try one's luck; **¡que tengas s.!** good luck!; **trae mala s.** it's unlucky (**b**) *(destino)* fate, destiny (**c**) *(condición)* lot; **mejorar la s. de los pobres** to improve the lot of the poor (**d**) *(género)* kind, sort, type; **toda s. de personas** all kinds of people (**e**) *Taur* stage (of the bullfight) (**f**) *Perú (billete de lotería)* lottery ticket

suertero, -a 1 *adj CSur Fam* lucky
2 *nm,f Perú* lottery ticket seller

suertudo, -a *adj Fam* lucky

suéter *nm* sweater

Suez *n* Suez

sufí (*pl* **sufíes**) **1** *adj* sufic
2 *nmf* sufi

suficiencia *nf* (**a**) *(capacidad)* sufficiency (**b**) *(conveniencia)* suitability, competence (**c**) *(engreimiento)* smugness, complacency

suficiente *adj* (**a**) *(bastante)* sufficient, enough; **hay s. comida para todos** there is enough food for everybody; **tener lo s. para vivir** to have enough to live on (**b**) *(idóneo)* suitable (**c**) *(engreído)* smug, complacent

suficientemente *adv* enough

sufijo, -a *Ling* **1** *adj* suffixal
  2 *nm* suffix

suflé *nm Culin* soufflé

sufragar [38] **1** *vt* (**a**) *(costear) (empresa)* to finance; *(gastos)* to pay, defray (**b**) *(ayudar)* to help, aid
  2 *vi Am* to vote (**por** for)

sufragio *nm* (**a**) *Pol* suffrage □ **s. universal** universal suffrage (**b**) *(ayuda)* help, assistance; *Rel* **misa en s. de ...** mass for the soul of ...

sufragismo *nm Pol* suffragism, suffragist movement

sufragista *Pol* **1** *nmf* suffragist
  2 *nf* suffragette

sufrido, -a 1 *pp de* **sufrir**
  2 *adj* (**a**) *(persona)* patient, long-suffering (**b**) *(tela)* hardwearing (**c**) *(color)* practical, that does not show the dirt

sufridor, -a *adj* easily worried

sufrimiento *nm* suffering

sufrir 1 *vi* *(padecer)* to suffer; **hacer s. a algn** to cause sb pain; **s. del corazón** to have a heart condition
  2 *vt* (**a**) *(tener) (accidente)* to have; *(operación)* to undergo; *(dificultades, cambios)* to experience; **s. dolores de cabeza** to suffer from headaches; **s. hambre** to know hunger; **s. vergüenza** to be ashamed (**b**) *(aguantar)* to bear, put up with (**c**) *(consentir)* to tolerate

sugerencia *nf* suggestion

sugerente *adj* suggestive

sugerir [62] *vt* to suggest

sugestión *nf* suggestion

sugestionable *adj* impressionable, easily influenced

sugestionar *vt* to influence, persuade

sugestivo, -a *adj* (**a**) *(que sugiere)* suggestive (**b**) *(fascinante)* fascinating, alluring

suicida 1 *adj* suicidal; **misión s.** suicide mission
  2 *nmf* *(persona)* suicide

suicidarse *vpr* to commit suicide, kill oneself

suicidio *nm* suicide

sui géneris *adj inv* unusual, individual

suite [suit] *nf* (**a**) *Mús* suite (**b**) *(de hotel)* suite

Suiza *n* Switzerland

suizo, -a 1 *adj* Swiss
  2 *nm,f* *(persona)* Swiss
  3 *nm Esp (bollo)* bun

sujeción *nf* (**a**) *(atadura)* fastening (**b**) *(sometimiento)* subjection

sujetador 1 *adj (que sujeta)* fastening
  2 *nm Esp (prenda)* bra, brassière

sujetalibros *nm inv* bookend

sujetapapeles *nm inv* paper clip

sujetar 1 *vt* (**a**) *(agarrar)* to hold; **¡sujétalo bien!** hold it tightly! (**b**) *(fijar)* to fix, secure, hold down, hold in place; **s. algo con clavos** to nail sth down (**c**) *(someter a disciplina)* to control, restrain (**d**) *(restringir la libertad de)* to tie down
  2 **sujetarse** *vpr* (**a**) *(agarrarse)* to hold on (**b**) *(someterse)* to subject oneself (**a** to)

sujeto, -a 1 *adj* (**a**) *(atado)* fastened, secure; **bien s.** tightly fastened (**b**) *(privado de libertad)* tied down (**c**) *(sometido)* **s. a** subject to, liable to; **s. a cambios** liable to change
  2 *nm* (**a**) *(individuo)* fellow, individual, person (**b**) *Ling* subject (**c**) *(materia)* subject

sulfamida *nf Farm* sulpha drug, sulphonamide

sulfatar *vt Quím* to sulphate

sulfato *nm Quím* sulphate

sulfhídrico, -a *adj Quím* sulphuretted, *US* sulphureted; **ácido s.** hydrogen sulphide

sulfurar 1 *vt* (**a**) *Quím* to sulphurate (**b**) *Fam (exasperar)* to exasperate, burn up, infuriate
  2 **sulfurarse** *vpr Fam* to lose one's temper, blow one's top

sulfúrico, -a *adj Quím* sulphuric

sulfuro *nm Quím* sulphide

sulfuroso, -a *adj Quím* sulphurous

sultán *nm* sultan

sultana *nf* sultana

sultanato *nm* sultanate

suma *nf* (**a**) *(cantidad)* sum, amount (**b**) *Mat* sum, addition; **s. total** sum total (**c**) *(resumen)* summary; **en s.** in short (**d**) *Com* total

sumamente *adv* extremely, highly

sumando *nm Mat* addend

sumar 1 *vt* (**a**) *Mat* to add, add up; **suma y sigue** carried forward; *Fam* and that's not all (**b**) *(valer)* to total, amount to (**c**) *(hacer un resumen de)* to summarize, sum up
  2 **sumarse** *vpr* to join (**a** in); **s. a un partido** to join a party

sumarial *adj Jur* pertaining to an indictment

sumario, -a 1 *adj* summary, brief; *Jur* **juicio s.** summary proceedings *pl*
  2 *nm* (**a**) *Jur* legal proceedings *pl*, indictment (**b**) *(resumen)* summary

sumarísimo, -a *adj Jur* swift, expeditious

sumergible 1 *adj* submergible, submersible
  2 *nm Náut* submarine

sumergir [24] **1** *vt (meter bajo el agua)* to submerge, submerse, immerse; *(hundir)* to sink, plunge
  2 **sumergirse** *vpr* (**a**) *(meterse bajo el agua)* to submerge, go underwater; *(hundirse)* to sink (**b**) *Fig (concentrarse)* to become immersed (**en** in)

sumerio, -a *adj & nm,f Hist* Sumerian

sumidero *nm* drain, sewer

sumiller *(pl* **sumillers)** *nm* sommelier, wine waiter

suministrador, -a *nm,f* supplier

suministrar *vt* to supply, provide; **s. algo a algn** to supply sb with sth

suministro *nm* supply, supplying, provision; **suministros** supplies

sumir 1 *vt (hundir)* to sink, plunge, submerge; *Fig* to plunge; *Fig* **s. a algn en la miseria** to plunge sb into poverty
  2 **sumirse** *vpr Fig* to immerse oneself (**en** in), lose oneself (**en** in)

sumisamente *adv* submissively

sumisión *nf* (**a**) *(acto)* submission (**b**) *(actitud)* submissiveness

sumiso, -a *adj* submissive, obedient

súmmum *nm* summit, acme, peak

sumo, -a *adj* *(supremo)* supreme, highest; *(grande)* greatest; **a lo s.** at (the) most; **con s. cuidado** with extreme care; **en s. grado** to the highest degree; **suma autoridad** supreme authority; **s. sacerdote** high priest

sunita *nm Rel* Sunnite

sunnita 1 *adj* Sunni
2 *nmf* Sunnite, Sunni Moslem

suntuario, -a *adj* sumptuary

suntuosidad *nf* sumptuousness, magnificence

suntuoso, -a *adj* sumptuous, magnificent, splendid

supe *pt indef véase* **saber²**

supeditación *nf* subjection, subordination

supeditar 1 *vt* to subject (**a** to); **estar supeditado a** to be subject to *o* dependent on
2 supeditarse *vpr* to subject oneself (**a** to), bow (**a** to)

súper *Fam* **1** *adj* super, great
2 *nm* (**a**) *(supermercado)* supermarket (**b**) *(gasolina) Br* four-star, *US* regular

superable *adj* superable, surmountable

superabundancia *nf* superabundance

superabundante *adj* superabundant

superabundar *vi* to superabound

superación *nf* (**a**) *(de dificultades, problemas)* overcoming, surpassing (**b**) *(de uno mismo)* self-improvement; **afán de s.** desire to improve *o* better oneself

superado, -a 1 *pp de* **superar**
2 *adj* antiquated, outdated, obsolete; **es una técnica superada** it's an antiquated technique

superar 1 *vt* (**a**) *(ser superior a)* to surpass, exceed, excel (**b**) *(vencer) (obstáculos, dificultades)* to overcome, surmount
2 superarse *vpr* (**a**) *(sobrepasarse)* to excel *o* outdo oneself (**b**) *(mejorarse)* to improve *o* better oneself

superávit *nm Fin* surplus

supercarburante *nm* high octane fuel

superchería *nf* trick, fraud, hoax

superconductividad *nf Fís* superconductivity

superconductor *nm Fís* superconductor

superdotado, -a 1 *adj* exceptionally gifted
2 *nm,f* genius

superestrella *nf* superstar

superestructura *nf* superstructure

superficial *adj* superficial

superficialidad *nf* superficiality, superficialness

superficie *nf* (**a**) *(parte externa)* surface; **la s. de la mesa** the surface of the table; **la s. terrestre** the earth's surface (**b**) *Geom (área)* area; **la s. del triángulo** the area of the triangle

superfino, -a *adj* extra fine

superfluidad *nf* superfluity, superfluousness

superfluo, -a *adj* superfluous

superhéroe *nm* superhero

superhombre *nm* superman

superintendencia *nf* superintendence, superintendency

superintendente *nmf* superintendent

superior 1 *adj* (**a**) *(más alto)* top, upper; **labio s.** upper lip; **parte s.** upper part (**b**) *(mayor)* greater, higher, larger; **una cantidad s. a mil pesos** an amount greater than a thousand pesos (**c**) *(mejor)* superior; **calidad s.** top quality; **ser s. a todos** to surpass everyone; **un vino s.** an excellent wine (**d**) *Educ* higher; **enseñanza s.** higher education
2 *nm* (**a**) *(jefe)* superior; **respetar a los superiores** to respect one's elders (**b**) *Rel* superior

superiora *nf Rel* mother superior

superioridad *nf* (**a**) *(persona con autoridad)* superiority (**b**) *(ventaja)* advantage

superlativo, -a *adj & nm Ling* superlative

supermercado *nm* supermarket

superministro, -a *nm,f* = powerful government minister in charge of more than one department

supernova *nf* supernova

supernumerario, -a *adj & nm,f* supernumerary

superpetrolero *nm Náut* supertanker

superpoblación *nf* overpopulation, overcrowding

superpoblado, -a *adj* overpopulated, overcrowded

superponer [50] *(pp superpuesto)* **1** *vt* to superpose, superimpose; *Fig* to put before
2 superponerse *vpr Fig* to come before

superposición *nf* superposition

superpotencia *nf* superpower

superproducción *nf* (**a**) *Ind* overproduction (**b**) *Cin* mammoth production, blockbuster

supersónico, -a *adj* supersonic

superstición *nf* superstition

supersticioso, -a *adj* superstitious

supervalorar *vt* to overvalue, overrate

superventas *nm inv* best-seller

supervisar *vt* to supervise

supervisión *nf* supervision, control

supervisor, -a *nm,f* supervisor

supervivencia *nf* survival

superviviente 1 *adj* surviving
2 *nmf* survivor

superyó *nm Psic* superego

supino, -a 1 *adj* (**a**) *(boca arriba)* supine, face up (**b**) *Fig (absoluto)* total, absolute; **un s. error** a complete mistake
2 *nm Ling* supine

súpito, -a *adj Am* sudden

suplantación *nf (falsificación)* forgery; **s. de personalidad** impersonation

suplantador, -a *nm,f (falsificador)* forger; *(sustitución de persona)* impersonator

suplantar *vt* to supplant, replace, take the place of

suplementario, -a *adj* supplementary, additional, extra; *Geom* supplementary

suplemento *nm* (**a**) *(añadido)* supplement; *Prensa* **s. dominical** Sunday supplement (**b**) *Com* addition, extra fee; **sin s.** with no extra charge

suplencia *nf* substitution, replacement

suplente *adj & nmf* (**a**) *(sustituto)* substitute, stand-in (**b**) *Teat* understudy (**c**) *Dep* substitute

supletorio, -a 1 *adj* supplementary, additional; **cama supletoria** extra bed; **teléfono s.** extension
2 *nm Tel* extension

súplica *nf* request, entreaty, plea; **a s. de** at the request of

suplicante 1 *adj* beseeching, entreating
2 *nmf* suppliant, supplicant

suplicar [59] *vt & vi* to beseech, implore, beg; **le suplico que se vaya** I beg you to go away *o* leave

suplicatorio *nm Jur (a tribunal superior)* = request by lower court for assistance from a higher court; *(a órgano legislativo)* = request by court for the parliamentary immunity of the accused to be waived

suplicio *nm (tortura)* torture; *(tormento)* torment

suplir *vt* (**a**) *(sustituir)* to replace (**b**) *(compensar)* to make up for

suponer [50] *(pp supuesto)* *vt* (**a**) *(pensar)* to suppose, assume; **supongamos que ...** let's assume that ...; **supongo que sí** I suppose so (**b**) *(significar)* to mean; **el premio supone mucho para mí** the prize means a lot to me (**c**) *(implicar)* to mean, entail, require; **eso va a s. mucho trabajo para su madre** that will mean a lot of work for her mother **(d)** *(adivinar)* to guess; *(imaginar)* to imagine; **me lo suponía** I guessed as much; **¿quién lo iba a s.?** who would have thought it?; **te suponía más viejo** I thought you were older (than that)

suposición *nf* supposition, assumption

supositorio *nm Farm* suppository

supranacional *adj Pol Fin* supranational

suprarrenal *adj* suprarenal

supremacía *nf* supremacy

supremo, -a *adj* supreme; *Literario* **hora suprema** dying moments *pl*, final hour; **jefe s.** commander-in-chief; *Jur* **el Tribunal S.** *Br* ≃ the High Court, *US* ≃ the Supreme Court

supresión *nf* **(a)** *(eliminación) (de una rebelión)* suppression; *(de dificultades)* elimination, removal; *(de una ley, un impuesto)* abolition; *(de restricciones)* lifting; *(de una palabra)* deletion **(b)** *(voluntaria)* omission

suprimir *vt* **(a)** *(eliminar) (una rebelión)* to suppress; *(dificultades)* to eliminate, remove; *(una ley, un impuesto)* to abolish; *(restricciones)* to lift; *(una palabra)* to delete, take *o* leave out **(b)** *(voluntaria)* to omit; **me han suprimido el alcohol** I've been told to cut out alcohol

supuesto, -a 1 *pp de* **suponer**
2 *adj* **(a)** *(asumido)* supposed, assumed; **dar algo por s.** to take sth for granted; **¡por s.!** of course! **(b)** *(pseudo)* so-called, self-styled; **el s. presidente** the self-styled president **(c)** *(falso)* assumed, false; **nombre s.** assumed name
3 *nm (creencia)* supposition, assumption; *(hipótesis)* hypothesis

supuración *nf Med* suppuration

supurar *vi Med* to suppurate, fester

sur *nm* south; **al s. de** (to the) south of; **viento del s.** south wind; *(viento fuerte)* southerly wind

Suramérica *nf véase* **Sudamérica**

suramericano, -a *adj & nm,f véase* **sudamericano, -a**

surcado, -a 1 *pp de* **surcar**
2 *adj* lined, wrinkled; **cara surcada de arrugas** deeply-lined *o* deeply-wrinkled face

surcar [59] *vt* **(a)** *Agr* to plough, *US* plow **(b)** *Fig (viajar)* to cut through; **s. los mares** to ply the seas

surco *nm* **(a)** *Agr* furrow **(b)** *(arruga)* wrinkle **(c)** *(señal) (dejado por una rueda)* rut; *(en un disco)* groove

surcoreano, -a *adj & nm,f* South Korean

sureño, -a 1 *adj* southern
2 *nm,f* southerner

sureste *adj & nm véase* **sudeste**

surf *nm Dep* surfing

surfear *vt & vi Fam Inform* to surf

surfista *Dep* **1** *adj* surf
2 *nmf* surfer

surgir [24] *vi* **(a)** *(aparecer)* to arise, emerge, appear; **continuamente surgen problemas** problems are always cropping up; **surgió de la nada** it came out of nowhere **(b)** *(brotar)* to spring forth, spurt up

Surinam *n* Surinam

surmenaje *nm (mental)* mental fatigue; *(exceso de trabajo)* overwork

suroeste *adj & nm véase* **sudoeste**

surrealismo *nm* surrealism

surrealista 1 *adj* surrealist, surrealistic
2 *nmf* surrealist

surtido, -a 1 *pp de* **surtir**
2 *adj* **(a)** *(variado)* assorted **(b)** *(bien provisto)* well stocked
3 *nm Com* range, selection, assortment

surtidor *nm* **(a)** *(chorro)* jet, spout **(b)** *(fuente)* fountain ❑ **s. de gasolina** *Br* petrol *o US* gas pump

surtir *vt* **(a)** *(proveer)* to supply, provide **(b)** **s. efecto** *(funcionar)* to have the desired effect, work

susceptibilidad *nf (gen)* susceptibility; *(sensibilidad)* sensitivity, touchiness

susceptible *adj (gen)* susceptible; *(sensible)* oversensitive, touchy; **s. de** *(tendente)* liable to; *(capaz)* capable of

suscitar *vt (provocar)* to cause, provoke; *(rebelión)* to stir up, arouse; *(discusión)* to start

suscribir *(pp* **suscrito)** **1** *vt* **(a)** *(adherirse a)* to subscribe to, endorse; **suscribo sus opiniones** I second his opinions **(b)** *Fml (firmar)* to sign; *Fin* to subscribe
2 suscribirse *vpr* to subscribe (**a** to); **acabo de suscribirme al nuevo periódico** I've just taken out a subscription to the new newspaper

suscripción *nf* subscription

suscriptor, -a *nm,f* subscriber

suscrito, -a 1 *pp de* **suscribir**
2 *adj* **(a)** *(abonado)* subscribed; **estar s. a** to subscribe to, have a subscription to **(b)** *(abajo firmado)* undersigned
3 *nm,f* undersigned

susodicho, -a *adj* above-mentioned, aforesaid

suspender 1 *vt* **(a)** *(colgar)* to hang, hang up, suspend **(b)** *(aplazar) (trabajo, acontecimiento)* to delay, postpone, put off; *(reunión)* to adjourn **(c)** *(suprimir) (pagos)* to suspend; *(servicios)* to discontinue **(d)** *Esp Educ* to fail; **me han suspendido** I've failed (the exam) **(e)** *(despedir)* to suspend, remove
2 *vi Esp Educ (alumno)* to fail

suspense *nm Esp* suspense; **mantener a algn en s.** to keep sb guessing *o* in suspense; *Lit* **novela de s.** thriller; *Cin* **película de s.** thriller

suspensión *nf* **(a)** *(levantamiento)* hanging (up), suspension **(b)** *Aut* suspension **(c)** *(aplazamiento)* delay, postponement; *(de una reunión)* adjournment **(d)** *(supresión)* suspension, discontinuation; *Fin Jur* **s. de pagos** suspension of payments

suspensivo, -a *adj* suspensive; *Ling* **puntos suspensivos** row of dots, *US* suspension points

suspenso, -a 1 *adj* **(a)** *(colgado)* hanging, suspended **(b)** *Fig (desconcertado)* baffled, bewildered
2 *nm* **(a)** *Esp Educ* fail **(b)** *Am (suspense)* **mantener a algn en s.** to keep sb guessing *o* in suspense **(c)** **en s.** *(interrumpido)* pending

suspensores *nmpl Andes Br* braces, *US* suspenders

suspensorio *nm Dep* jockstrap

suspicacia *nf* **(a)** *(desconfianza)* mistrust, distrust, wariness **(b)** *(sospecha)* suspicion, suspiciousness

suspicaz *adj* **(a)** *(desconfiado)* untrusting, distrustful **(b)** *(que sospecha)* suspicious

suspirar *vi* to sigh; *Fig* **s. por** to long for

suspiro *nm* sigh; **dar el último s.** to breathe one's last; **deshacerse en suspiros** to heave great sighs

sustancia *nf* **(a)** *(gen)* substance; **sin s.** lacking in substance; *Fam* **persona de poca s.** characterless person **(b)** *(esencia)* essence

sustancial *adj* **(a)** *(gen)* substantial, considerable, important **(b)** *(fundamental)* essential, fundamental

sustanciar *vt* to condense, abridge

sustancioso, -a *adj* **(a)** *(alimentos)* wholesome **(b)** *Fig (libro, discurso)* meaty

sustantivación *nf Ling* nominalization, use as a noun

sustantivar *vt* to use as a noun

sustantivo, -a 1 *adj* substantive
  2 *nm Ling* noun, substantive

sustentación *nf* (**a**) *(soporte)* support (**b**) *(mantenimiento)* sustenance, maintenance

sustentar 1 *vt* (**a**) *(peso)* to support (**b**) *(familia)* to maintain, support (**c**) *(teoría)* to support, defend
  2 sustentarse *vpr* to sustain oneself, live (**de** on)

sustento *nm* (**a**) *(alimento)* sustenance, food; **ganarse el s.** to earn one's living (**b**) *(apoyo)* support

sustitución *nf* substitution, replacement

sustituible *adj* replaceable, expendable

sustituir [34] (*pp* **sustituto**) *vt* (**a**) *(remplazar)* to substitute, replace (**b**) *(hacer las veces de)* to stand in for

sustitutivo *nm* substitute

sustituto, -a *pp de* **sustituir**
  2 *nm,f* substitute, stand-in, replacement

susto *nm* fright, shock, scare; **llevarse** *o* **darse un s.** to get a fright; *Fig* **caerse del s.** to be frightened to death; *Fig* **no pasar del s.** to be just a scare

sustracción *nf* (**a**) *Mat* subtraction (**b**) *(robo)* theft

sustraendo *nm Mat* subtrahend, = amount to be subtracted

sustraer [66] **1** *vt* (**a**) *Mat* to subtract (**b**) *(robar)* to steal, remove
  2 sustraerse *vpr (eludir)* **s. a** *o* **de** *(preguntas)* to evade; *(tentaciones)* to resist

sustrato *nm Geol Filos* substratum

susurrante *adj* whispering

susurrar 1 *vt* to whisper
  2 *vi (persona)* to whisper; *(el agua)* to murmur; *(hojas)* to rustle

susurro *nm (gen)* whisper; *(del agua)* murmur; *(de hojas)* rustle

sutil *adj* (**a**) *(delgado)* thin, fine (**b**) *(delicado) (aroma)* delicate; *(color)* soft; *(brisa)* gentle (**c**) *Fig (diferencia, pregunta)* subtle

sutileza *nf* (**a**) *(finura)* thinness, fineness (**b**) *Fig (dicho)* subtlety

sutilizar [14] **1** *vt* (**a**) *(adelgazar)* to make fine, thin down (**b**) *Fig (pulir)* to polish, refine, perfect
  2 *vi (ser preciso)* to quibble, split hairs

sutilmente *adv Fig* mildly, subtly

sutura *nf Med* suture

suturar *vt Med* to stitch

Suva *n* Suva

suyo, -a *adj & pron pos (de él)* his; *(de ella)* hers; *(de usted, ustedes)* yours; *(de animales o cosas)* its; *(de ellos, ellas)* theirs; **los zapatos que lleva María no son suyos** the shoes Maria is wearing aren't hers; **varios amigos suyos** several friends of his/hers/yours/theirs; *Fam* **es muy s.** he's very aloof; *Fam* **hacer de las suyas** to be up to one's tricks; *Fam* **ir (cada uno) a lo s.** to mind one's own business; *Fam* **salirse con la suya** to get one's own way

svástica [es'βastika] *nf* swastika

Swazilandia *n* Swaziland

swing [swin] *nm Dep Mús* swing

T, t [te] *nf (la letra)* T, t

t *(abrev de* **tonelada(s))** ton, tons

taba *nf* (**a**) *Anat* anklebone (**b**) **jugar a las tabas** to play fivestones

tabacal *nm* tobacco field *o* plantation

tabacalero, -a 1 *adj* tobacco
2 *nm,f (cultivador)* tobacco grower; *(vendedor)* tobacco trader

tabaco *nm* (**a**) *(planta, hoja)* tobacco ❑ **t. picado** shredded tobacco, shag; **t. rubio** Virginia tobacco (**b**) *(cigarrillos)* cigarettes *pl*

tabalear 1 *vi (con los dedos)* to drum
2 *vt (balancear)* to swing, rock

tabanco *nm CAm* attic, loft

tábano *nm Ent* horsefly

tabaquera *nf (caja)* tobacco box; *(para rapé)* snuff box; *(petaca)* tobacco pouch

tabaquería *nf Am Br* tobacconist's (shop), *US* cigar store

tabaquismo *nm Med* nicotinism, nicotine poisoning

tabardillo *nm* (**a**) *Med (insolación)* sunstroke (**b**) *Fam (persona)* nuisance, bore, pain

tabardo *nm Hist* tabard

tabarra *nf Fam* nuisance, bore; **dar la t.** to be a nuisance

tabasco® *nm* Tabasco® (sauce)

taberna *nf* pub, bar; *(antiguamente)* tavern

tabernáculo *nm Rel* tabernacle

tabernario, -a *adj Fam* coarse, rude

tabernero, -a *nm,f* publican; *(hombre)* landlord; *(mujer)* landlady

tabicar [59] *vt* (**a**) *(ventana, puerta)* to wall up (**b**) *(habitación)* to partition off, divide

tabique *nm* (**a**) *(pared)* partition (wall) (**b**) *Anat* **t. nasal** nasal bone

tabla *nf* (**a**) *(gen)* board; *(de madera)* plank, board; *Fig* **a raja t.** strictly, to the letter; *Fig* **hacer t. rasa de algo** to make a clean sweep of sth; *Fig* **t. de salvación** last hope ❑ **t. de lavar** washboard; **t. de planchar** ironing board; *Dep* **t. de surf** surfboard; *Dep* **t. de windsurf** sailboard (**b**) *Arte* panel (**c**) *Cost* pleat; **falda de tablas** pleated skirt (**d**) *(índice)* index; *(lista)* list; *(catálogo)* catalogue ❑ **t. de materias** (table of) contents (**e**) *Mat* table ❑ **t. de multiplicar** multiplication table (**f**) *Agr* plot, bed (**g**) **las tablas** *Teat* the stage *sing*; **pisar las t.** to tread the boards, go on the stage; **tener (muchas) t.** *Teat* to be an experienced actor *o* actress; *Fig* to be an old hand (**h**) **tablas** *Ajedrez* stalemate *sing*, draw *sing*; **quedar en t.** *(juego)* to end in a draw; *Fig (asunto)* to be deadlocked *o* unresolved, reach stalemate (**i**) **tablas** *Taur* fence *sing* (**j**) *Rel* **Tablas de la Ley** Tables of the Law

tablado *nm* (**a**) *(suelo)* wooden floor; *(plataforma)* wooden platform (**b**) *Teat* stage

tablao *nm Fam* = flamenco bar *o* show

tablear *vt* (**a**) *(madera)* to cut into planks (**b**) *(tierra)* to divide into plots (**c**) *Cost* to pleat

tablero *nm* (**a**) *(tablón)* panel, board ❑ *Av* **t. de instrumentos** instrument panel (**b**) *(en juegos)* board ❑ **t. de ajedrez** chessboard (**c**) *(encerado)* blackboard

tableta *nf* (**a**) *(tabla pequeña)* small board (**b**) *(pastilla)* tablet (**c**) *(de chocolate)* bar

tabletear *vi* to rattle

tableteo *nm* rattling, rattle

tablilla *nf (tabla pequeña)* small board

tabloide *nm* tabloid

tablón *nm* (**a**) *(gen)* plank; *(en construcción)* beam ❑ **t. de anuncios** *Br* notice *o US* bulletin board (**b**) *Fam (borrachera)* drunkenness; **agarrar un t.** to get drunk

tabú *(pl* **tabúes** *o* **tabús)** *adj & nm* taboo

tabulación *nf* tabulation

tabulador *nm* tabulator

tabuladora *nf Inform* tabulator

tabular *vt* to tabulate

taburete *nm* stool

TAC [tak] *Med abrev de* **tomografía axial computerizada**
1 *nf (sistema)* CAT
2 *nm (escáner)* CAT scan

tacañería *nf* meanness, stinginess

tacaño, -a 1 *adj* mean, stingy
2 *nm,f* miser

tacatá *nm,* **tacataca** *nm* baby-walker

tacha *nf* (**a**) *(defecto)* flaw, blemish, defect; **sin t.** flawless, without blemish (**b**) *(clavo grande)* large tack; *(decorativo)* large stud

tachadura *nf* crossing out

tachar *vt* (**a**) *(hacer un borrón en)* to cross out (**b**) *Fig* **t. de** to accuse of; **no le puedes t. de ladrón** you can't accuse him of being a thief

tacho *nm* (**a**) *Andes RP (para basura)* *Br* rubbish bin, *US* garbage can; *Fig* **irse al t.** to fail, be unsuccessful (**b**) *RP Fam (taxi)* taxi (**c**) *Am (para dulce)* sugar evaporator (**d**) *Andes RP (metálico, de hojalata)* tin

tachón¹ *nm (borrón)* crossing out

tachón² *nm (tachuela)* large tack; *(decorativo)* large stud

tachonar *vt* to stud, adorn with studs; *Fig* **un cielo tachonado de estrellas** a star-studded sky

tachuela *nf* tack, stud; **clavar algo con tachuelas** to tack sth

tácito, -a *adj* tacit; **regla tácita** unwritten rule

taciturno, -a *adj* **(a)** *(callado)* taciturn, silent **(b)** *(triste)* sullen; *(lunático)* sulky, moody

taco *nm* **(a)** *(tarugo)* plug; *(tapón)* stopper **(b)** *(de bota de fútbol)* stud **(c)** *(bloc de notas)* notepad, writing pad; *(calendario)* tear-off calendar; *(entradas)* book; *(billetes)* wad **(d)** *Esp Culin (de jamón, queso)* cube, piece **(e)** *Bill* cue **(f)** *Culin (tortilla rellena)* taco, = rolled-up tortilla pancake **(g)** *Esp Fam (lío)* mess, muddle; **armarse** *o* **hacerse un t.** to get all mixed up **(h)** *Esp Fam (palabrota)* swearword; **soltar un t., soltar tacos** to swear **(i)** *Esp Fam* **tacos** *(años)* years; **ya he cumplido veinte t.** I've already passed the twenty mark **(j)** *Andes RP (tacón)* heel; **zapatos de t. alto** high heels, high-heeled shoes **(k)** *Chile (atasco)* obstruction, blockage

tacógrafo *nm* tachograph

tacómetro *nm* tachometer

tacón *nm* heel; **zapatos de t.** high-heeled shoes

taconazo *nm* kick with the heel

taconear *vi (pisar)* to tap one's heels; *(golpear)* to stamp one's heels

taconeo *nm (pisada)* heel tapping; *(golpe)* stamping with the heels

táctica *nf* tactic, tactics *pl*, strategy; **su t. consistió en no decir nada hasta el final** her tactic was not to say a word until the end

táctico, -a 1 *adj* tactical
  2 *nm,f* tactician

táctil *adj* tactile

tacto *nm* **(a)** *(sentido)* touch **(b)** *(acción de tocar)* touch, touching; **es agradable al t.** it feels nice **(c)** *Fig (delicadeza)* tact; **¡qué falta de t.!** how tactless!; **tener t.** to be tactful

TAE ['tae] *nf (abrev de* **tasa anual equivalente)** APR

taekwondo [tae'kwondo] *nm Dep* tae kwon do

tafetán *nm, Méx RP* **tafeta** *nm Tex* taffeta

tafilete *nm* morocco leather

tagalo, -a 1 *adj* Tagalog
  2 *nm,f (persona)* Tagalog
  3 *nm (idioma)* Tagalog

tagarote *nm CAm* **(a)** *(potentado)* upright person **(b)** *(mañoso)* cunning *o* sly person

Tahití *n* Tahiti

tahitiano, -a 1 *adj* Tahitian
  2 *nm,f (persona)* Tahitian
  3 *nm (idioma)* Tahitian

tahona *nf* bakery

tahúr *nm* cardsharp, cardsharper

tai-chi *nm* tai chi

taifa *nf Hist* **reinos de taifas** = small Spanish kingdoms after the disintegration of the Caliphate of Cordoba in 1031

taiga *nf* taiga

tailandés, -esa 1 *adj* Thai, Siamese
  2 *nm,f (persona)* Thai, Siamese; **los tailandeses** the Thai *o* Thais
  3 *nm (idioma)* Thai, Siamese

Tailandia *n* Thailand

taimado, -a 1 *adj* **(a)** *(astuto)* sly, crafty **(b)** *Chile (obstinado)* stubborn, obstinate
  2 *nm,f* **(a)** *(astuto)* sly *o* crafty person **(b)** *Chile (obstinado)* stubborn *o* obstinate person

Taipei *n* Taipei

taita *nm Andes Arg Ven Fam* = term of respect for an older male member of the community

Taiwán [tai'wan] *n* Taiwan

taiwanés, -esa [taiwa'nes, -esa] *adj & nm,f* Taiwanese

tajada *nf* **(a)** *(rodaja)* slice; *Fig* **sacar** *o* **llevarse t.** to take one's share **(b)** *(corte)* cut; *(cuchillada)* stab; **dar una t.** to cut **(c)** *Esp Fam (borrachera)* **pillar una t.** to get smashed

tajamar *nm* **(a)** *Andes CAm (dique)* dike, seawall **(b)** *Arg (embalse)* reservoir

tajante *adj* strong, sharp; **orden t.** strict order; **ser de** *o* **tener opiniones tajantes** to be dogmatic

tajar *vt* to cut, chop (off)

Tajo *n* **el T.** the Tagus

tajo *nm* **(a)** *(corte)* cut, slash **(b)** *(para cortar carne)* chopping block *o* board **(c)** *Geog (escarpe)* steep cliff **(d)** *(taburete)* stool **(e)** *Esp Fam (trabajo)* work

tal 1 *adj* **(a)** *(semejante)* such (a), similar; **en tales condiciones** in such conditions; **nunca dije t. cosa** I said no such thing; **de t. manera que** in such a way that **(b)** *(tan grande)* such, so; **es t. su valor que ...** he is so courageous that ...; **lo dijo con t. convecimiento que ...** he said it with such conviction that ... **(c)** *(cosa sin especificar)* such and such; **t. día y a t. hora** such and such a day and at such and such a time **(d)** *(persona)* person called ...; **te llamó un t. García** someone called Garcia phoned you **(e)** *(locuciones)* **como si t. cosa** as if nothing had happened; **t. vez** perhaps, maybe; *Prov* **de t. palo, t. astilla** like father, like son
  2 *pron* *(alguno)* *(cosa)* something; *(persona)* someone, somebody; **t. para cual** two of a kind; **(y) como t.** and therefore *o* as such; **y t. y cual** and so on; *Ofens* **una t.** a prostitute
  3 *adv* **(a)** *(así)* just; **t. cual** just as it is; **lo dejé t. cual** I left it just as I found it; **t. (y) como** just as; **t. (y) como te lo digo** just as I'm telling you; **te lo contamos t. como nos lo contaron a nosotros** we're telling you just like *o* as they told us **(b)** **¿qué t.?** how are things?; **¿qué t. ese vino?** how do you find this wine?
  4 *loc conj* **con t. (de) que** so long as, provided; **con t. de que no hables** so long as you don't talk; **lo que sea con t. de no trabajar** anything to avoid work

tala 1 *nf (acción)* tree felling
  2 *nm Bol RP (árbol)* hackberry tree

taladradora *nf (para pared, madera)* drill; *(para papel)* paper punch

taladrar *vt (gen)* to drill; *(pared)* to bore through; *(billetes)* to punch; *Fig* **t. los oídos** to make an ear-splitting noise

taladro *nm* **(a)** *(herramienta)* drill **(b)** *(agujero)* hole

talaje *nm Chile* pasture

talante *nm* **(a)** *(semblante)* disposition; **tiene un t. pacífico** he's a very calm person **(b)** *(voluntad)* willingness; **de buen t.** willingly; **de mal t.** unwillingly, reluctantly

talar¹ *adj* full-length, long; **vestidura t.** long dress *o* habit

talar² *vt* **(a)** *(árboles)* to fell, cut down **(b)** *(lugar)* to devastate

talasoterapia *nf* thalassotherapy

talco *nm* talc □ **polvos de t.** talcum powder

talega *nf (a) (bolsa)* bag, sack; *(contenido)* bagful, sackful **(b)** *(dinero)* money

talego *nm* **(a)** *(bolsa)* long bag, long sack; *(contenido)* bagful, sackful **(b)** *Esp Argot (cárcel)* slammer, *Br* nick, *US* pen

talento *nm* **(a)** *(inteligencia)* talent, intelligence; **tener t.** to be talented *o* intelligent **(b)** *(aptitud)* gift, talent; **tiene t. para la música** he has a gift for music

talentoso, -a *adj*, **talentudo, -a** *adj* talented, gifted

talero *nm CSur* riding crop

talibán *adj & nm,f* Taliban

talio *nm Quím* thallium

talión *nm* **la ley del t.** an eye for an eye, a tooth for a tooth

talismán *nm* talisman, lucky charm

talla *nf* (**a**) *(escultura)* carving, sculpture (**b**) *(tallado)* cutting, carving; *(metal)* engraving (**c**) *(estatura)* height; *Fig* stature; *Fig* **dar la t.** to be good enough; *Fig* **de (mucha) t.** outstanding (**d**) *(de prenda)* size; **¿qué t. usas?** what size are you?

tallado, -a 1 *pp de* **tallar**
2 *adj (madera)* carved; *(piedra)* cut
3 *nm (de madera)* carving; *(de piedras preciosas)* cutting; *(de metales)* engraving

tallador, -a *nm,f (de madera)* woodcarver; *(de piedras preciosas)* diamond cutter; *(grabador de metales etc)* engraver

tallar *vt* (**a**) *(madera, piedra)* to carve, shape; *(piedras preciosas)* to cut; *(metales)* to engrave (**b**) *(medir)* to measure the height of

tallarines *nmpl* tagliatelle *sing*, noodles *pl*

talle *nm* (**a**) *(cintura)* waist (**b**) *(figura) (de hombre)* build, physique; *(de mujer)* figure, shape (**c**) *Cost* shoulder to waist measurement

taller *nm* (**a**) *(obrador)* workshop, shop □ *Aut* **t. de reparaciones** garage (**b**) *Arte* studio □ **t. de teatro** drama workshop (**c**) *Ind* factory, mill

Tallin *n* Tallin

tallista *nmf (de madera)* wood carver; *(de piedra)* stone cutter

tallo *nm* (**a**) *(de planta, flor)* stem, stalk; *(brote)* sprout, shoot (**b**) *Col (col)* cabbage

talludito, -a *adj* **estar** *o* **ser t.** to be getting on (a bit)

talludo, -a *adj* (**a**) *Bot* leggy, tall (**b**) *(no joven)* middle-aged

talmente *adv Fam* literally, exactly

Talmud *nm* **el T.** the Talmud

talo *nm Bot* thallus

talón *nm* (**a**) *Anat* heel; *(de media, calcetín)* heel; *Fig* **pisarle los talones a algn** to follow close behind sb, be hot on sb's heels □ *Fig* **t. de Aquiles** Achilles' heel (**b**) *Com Fin (cheque)* cheque, *US* check; *(recibo)* receipt; *(matriz)* stub (**c**) *Aut* flange

talonario *nm (de cheques)* cheque *o US* check book; *(de billetes)* book of tickets; *(de recibos)* receipt book

talonear *vi Am Fam* to spur on one's horse

talonera *nf* heelpiece

talud *nm* slope

talvez *adv Am* perhaps, maybe; **¿vienes? — t.** are you coming? — perhaps *o* maybe; **t. vaya** I may go

tamal *nm* (**a**) *Culin* tamale (**b**) *Méx (intriga, embrollo)* intrigue (**c**) *Méx (bulto)* package, bundle

tamango *nm CSur* leather shoe

tamaño, -a 1 *adj* such a big, so big a; **¿cómo puede alguien creer tamaña mentira?** how can anybody believe such a big lie?
2 *nm* size; **de gran t.** large; **del t. de** as large as, as big as

tamarindo *nm Bot* tamarind

tamarisco *nm Bot* tamarisk

tambaleante *adj (persona)* staggering, tottering; *(mueble)* shaky, wobbly

tambalearse *vpr (persona)* to stagger, totter; *(mueble)* to wobble; *Fig* to be shaky; **entró tambaleándose** he staggered in; *Fig* **el gobierno se tambalea** the government is tottering

tambaleo *nm (de persona)* staggering, reeling; *(de mueble)* wobble, wobbling

tambarria *nf Am* binge, spree

tambero, -a *nm,f* (**a**) *RP (granjero)* dairy farmer (**b**) *Andes (dueño) (de una tienda)* storekeeper; *(de un tenderete)* stall holder

también *adv* (**a**) *(igualmente)* too, also, as well; **ellos vienen, y yo t.** they're coming along, and so am I; **¿lo harás?, yo t.** are you going to do it?, so am I; **tú t. puedes venir** you can come too (**b**) *(además)* besides, in addition; **no me apetece y t. es que estoy cansado** I don't like it and besides I'm tired

tambo *nm* (**a**) *RP (granja)* dairy farm (**b**) *Andes (tienda)* shop; *(tenderete)* stall

tambor *nm* (**a**) *Mús (instrumento)* drum; *(persona)* drummer; *Fig* **a t. batiente** triumphantly □ **t. mayor** drum major (**b**) *Téc (de arma)* cylinder, barrel; *(de lavadora)* drum; *(del freno)* drum (**c**) *Cost (para bordar)* tambour, embroidery frame (**d**) *Anat* eardrum (**e**) *(de jabón)* large tub, giant size pack (**f**) *(para enrollar cable)* capstan

tamboril *nm Mús* small drum

tamborilear *vi* (**a**) *Mús* to play the drum (**b**) *(tabalear)* to drum one's fingers

tamborileo *nm* drumming

tamborilero, -a *nm,f* drummer

Támesis *n* **el T.** the Thames

tamil 1 *adj & nmf* Tamil
2 *nm (lengua)* Tamil

tamiz *nm* sieve; **pasar por el t.** to sift, *Fig* to scrutinize

tamizar [14] *vt* (**a**) *(harina, tierra)* to sieve; *(luz)* to filter (**b**) *Fig (seleccionar)* to screen

tampoco *adv (en afirmativas)* nor, neither; *(en negativas)* either, not ... either; **Juan no vendrá y María t.** Juan won't come and neither will María; **la Bolsa no sube, pero t. baja** the stock market isn't going up, but it's not going down either; **¿no fuiste al cine? — yo t.** you didn't go to the cinema? — nor did I; **no lo sé, — yo t.** I don't know, — nor do I

tampón *nm* (**a**) *(de entintar)* inkpad (**b**) *Med* tampon

tam-tam *(pl* **tam-tams***) nm Mús* tom-tom

tan *adv* (**a**) *(tanto)* such, such as; **es t. listo** he's such a clever fellow; **no me gusta t. dulce** I don't like it so sweet; **no sabía que era t. tarde** I didn't know it was so late; **¡qué gente t. agradable!** what nice people!; **¡qué vestido t. bonito!** what a beautiful dress! (**b**) *(comparativo con como)* as ... as; **está t. alto como tú** he's as tall as you (are) (**c**) *(comparativo con que)* so ... (that); **iba t. deprisa que no lo vi** he passed by so fast that I couldn't see him (**d**) **de t.** so; **dejó la nuez sin abrir de t. dura como estaba** the walnut was so hard that he couldn't crack it; **no pudo salir de t. malo como estaba** he couldn't go out because he felt so ill (**e**) **t. siquiera** even, just; **no tienen t. siquiera para comer** they haven't even got enough to eat; **si t. siquiera tuviéramos su teléfono** if only we had her phone number

tana *nf Méx* raffia bag

tanate *nm* (**a**) *CAm Méx (bolso)* leather bag (**b**) *CAm (trasto)* bundle; **cargar con los tanates** to pack one's bags

tanatorio *nm* = building where relatives and friends of a dead person can stand vigil over the deceased in a private room on the night before the burial

tanda *nf* (**a**) *(conjunto)* batch, lot; *(serie)* series *sing*, course; **por tandas** in batches (**b**) *(turno)* shift; **me ha tocado la t. de noche** I've been put on the night shift (**c**) *RP (corte publicitario)* commercial break

tándem *(pl* **tándemes***) nm* (**a**) *(bicicleta)* tandem (**b**) *(dos personas)* team of two

tanga *nm* tanga

tangencial *adj* tangential; **efecto t.** side effect

tangente 1 *nf* tangent; *Fig* **salirse** *o* **escaparse por la t.** to go off at a tangent
  2 *adj Mat* tangent; **líneas tangentes** tangent lines

Tánger *n* Tangier

tangible *adj* tangible

tango *nm Mús* tango

tanguista *nmf Mús* tango singer

tanino *nm* tannin

tanque *nm* (a) *Mil* tank (b) *(depósito)* tank, reservoir (c) *(vehículo cisterna)* tanker

tanqueta *nf Mil* light tank

tanteador *nm* scoreboard

tantear 1 *vt* (a) *(calcular)* to estimate, guess (b) *(probar) (medidas)* to size up; *(pesos)* to feel; **deberías t. los nudos** you should test the knots; **tanteó el cajón para ver si cabía el jarrón** he sized the drawer up to see if the vase would fit in it (c) *Fig (investigar)* to try out, put to the test; **t. a algn** to sound sb out; **t. el terreno** to see how the land lies
  2 *vi Dep* to (keep) score

tanteo *nm* (a) *(cálculo aproximado)* estimate, guess (b) *(prueba)* reckoning, rough estimate; *(de medidas)* sizing up (c) *(sondeo)* trial, test; *(de la actitud de una persona)* sounding (d) *Dep* score; **igualar el t.** to draw

tantito *adv Méx (poquito)* a little bit

tanto, -a 1 *nm* (a) *(punto)* point; **marcar** *o* **apuntarse un t.** to score a point; *Fig* **con aquel hallazgo se apuntó un t. a su favor** that discovery was a feather in his cap (b) *(cantidad imprecisa)* so much, a certain amount; **les pagan (un) t. por cada pieza que venden** they pay them a percentage for each piece they sell; *Com* **t. por ciento** percentage (c) *(poco)* **un t.** a bit; **es un t. ridículo** it's a bit silly; **la casa es un t. pequeña** the house is rather *o* somewhat small
  2 *adj* (a) *(incontables)* so much; *(contables)* so many; **¡ha pasado t. tiempo!** it's been so long!; **no dormí de tanta excitación** I was so excited that I couldn't sleep; **no le des t. dinero** don't give him so much money; **tantas manzanas como puedas** as many apples as you can (b) *(aproximadamente)* odd; **cincuenta y tantas personas** fifty odd people; **en el año sesenta y tantos** in nineteen sixty something
  3 *pron (incontable)* so much; *(contables)* so many; **es una chica de tantas** she's nothing special; **no tengo tantos** I haven't got so many; **otras tantas** as many again; **otro t.** as much again, the same again; **uno de tantos** run-of-the-mill; *Fam* **a las tantas** very late, at an unearthly hour
  4 *adv* (a) *(cantidad)* so much; **estaba rojo de t. llorar** his face was red from crying so much; **no llegará a t.** it won't come to that; **¡te quiero t.!** I love you so much! (b) *(tiempo)* so long; **¿por qué has tardado t.?** what kept you so long? (c) *(frecuencia)* so often; **no vengas t.** don't come so often (d) *(locuciones)* **en** *o* **entre** *o* **mientras t.** meanwhile; **estar al t.** *(informado)* to be informed; *(alerta)* to be on the alert; **no es** *o* **hay para t.** it's not that bad; **no será t.** things can't be as bad as you're making them out to be; **por lo t.** therefore; **t. más/menos** all the more/less; **t. mejor/peor** so much the better/worse; **t. si vienes como si no** whether you come or not; **¡y t.!** oh yes!, and how!; *Fam* **ni t. ni tan poco** *o* **calvo** neither one extreme nor the other

Tanzania *n* Tanzania

tanzano, -a *adj & nm,f* Tanzanian

tañer *vt Mús* to play; **t. campanas** to toll *o* ring bells

tañido *nm (de instrumento)* sound; *(de campanas)* toll, ringing

taoísmo *nm* Taoism

taoísta *adj & nmf* Taoist

tapa *nf* (a) *(cubierta)* lid, top; *Andes RP (de botella)* top; *(de libro)* cover; *(de zapato)* heelplate; *Aut (de cilindro)* head; *Fam Fig* **levantarse** *o* **saltarse la t. de los sesos** to blow one's brains out (b) *Esp Culin (comida)* appetizer, snack

tapabocas *nm inv* scarf, muffler

tapacubos *nm inv Aut* hubcap

tapadera *nf* (a) *(tapa)* cover, lid (b) *Fig (persona)* cover, front

tapadillo *nm* **hacer algo de t.** to do sth secretly

tapado, -a 1 *pp de* **tapar**
  2 *adj* (a) *(cubierto)* covered; *(con tapa)* with the lid on; *(con ropas o mantas)* wrapped (up) (b) *(obstruido)* obstructed, clogged; **tengo la nariz tapada del resfriado** my nose is blocked up with this cold (c) *(oculto)* concealed, hidden (d) *Andes Méx Ven (persona)* stupid, dull
  3 *nm CSur (abrigo)* overcoat

tápalo *nm Méx* shawl

tapaojos *nm inv Andes Méx Ven (anteojeras) Br* blinkers, *US* blinders

tapar 1 *vt* (a) *(gen)* to cover; *(con tapa)* to put the lid *o* top on; *(con ropas o mantas)* to wrap up (b) *(obstruir)* to obstruct; *(tubería)* to block (c) *(ocultar)* to hide; *(vista)* to block; **t. el sol** to block out the sun (d) *(encubrir)* to cover up
  2 taparse *vpr* (a) *(cubrirse)* to cover oneself; *(abrigarse)* to wrap up (b) **t. los oídos** to put one's fingers in one's ears

taparrabos *nm inv* loincloth; *Fam (bañador)* bathing trunks *pl*

tape *nmf RP Pey (indio)* Indian

tapear *vi Esp Fam* to have some tapas

tapeo *nm Esp Fam* **ir de t.** to go out for some tapas; **bar de t.** tapas bar

tapera *nf SAm* ruins *pl*

tapete *nm* (a) *(paño)* runner; *(en mesa de billar, para cartas)* baize; *Fig* **estar sobre el t.** to be under discussion; *Fig* **poner algo sobre el t.** to bring sth up, put sth up for discussion (b) *Am (para el suelo)* carpet

tapia *nf (cerca)* garden wall; *(de adobe)* mud wall, adobe wall; *Fam Fig* **más sordo que una t.** as deaf as a post

tapiar *vt* (a) *(área)* to wall in *o* off (b) *(puerta, ventana etc)* to wall, close up

tapicería *nf* (a) *(arte)* tapestry making; *(tapices)* tapestries (b), *(de mueble, coche)* upholstery (c) *(tienda)* upholsterer's

tapicero, -a *nm,f* (a) *(que hace tapices)* tapestry maker (b) *(de muebles, coches)* upholsterer

tapioca *nf* tapioca

tapir *nm* tapir

tapisca *nf CAm Méx (de maíz) Br* maize harvest, *US* corn harvest

tapiscar [59] *vt CAm Méx* to harvest

tapiz *nm* (a) *(paño)* tapestry (b) *(alfombra)* rug, carpet

tapizado, -a 1 *pp de* **tapizar**
  2 *adj* (a) *(muebles)* upholstered (b) *Fml (cubierto)* covered; **una senda tapizada de hojas** a path carpeted with leaves
  3 *nm* (a) *(de muebles)* upholstering (b) *(colgaduras)* tapestries

tapizar [14] *vt* (a) *(muebles)* to upholster (b) *(cubrir con tapices)* to cover with tapestries

tapón *nm* (a) *(para tapar) (botellas, frascos)* stopper; *(de bañera, lavabo)* plug; *(para el oído)* earplug; *(de botella)* top, cap, cork; **pon el t. al lavabo** put the plug in the basin □ **t. de rosca** screw top, screw-on cap (b) *Fam (persona)* shorty, stubby (c) *(en baloncesto)* block (d) *Aut* traffic jam

taponamiento *nm* blockage, plugging

taponar 1 *vt* (a) *(tubería, hueco)* to plug, stop, obturate; *(el* *paso)* to block; *(poner el tapón en)* to put the plug in **(b)** *Med (herida)* to tampon

2 taponarse *vpr* to get clogged o blocked; **se me han taponado los oídos** my ears are blocked up

taponazo *nm* **(a)** *(ruido)* pop **(b)** *(golpe)* hit, shot; **rompió un cristal de un t.** he broke a window pane with the flying cork

tapujo *nm* deceit, secrecy; **andarse con tapujos** not to come clean (about sth); **sin tapujos** openly

taquear 1 *vi* **(a)** *Am Fam (jugar)* to play o *US* shoot pool **(b)** *Méx (comer)* to eat tacos

2 *vt Am (atiborrar)* to stuff, fill

3 taquearse *vpr Col Ven Fam (de comida)* to stuff oneself

taquería *nf Méx (quiosco)* taco stall; *(restaurante)* taco restaurant

taquicardia *nf Med* tachycardia

taquigrafía *nf* shorthand, stenography

taquigrafiar [32] *vt* to write in shorthand

taquigráfico, -a *adj* written in shorthand; **signos taquigráficos** shorthand symbols

taquígrafo, -a *nm,f* shorthand writer, stenographer

taquilla *nf* **(a)** *(ventanilla)* ticket office, booking office; *Cin Teat* box-office; **un éxito de t.** a box-office hit **(b)** *(recaudación)* takings *pl* **(c)** *(armario)* locker **(d)** *CAm (bar)* bar, tavern **(e)** *Chile (clavo)* small nail, tack

taquillero, -a 1 *adj Fig (film, play)* popular

2 *nm,f* booking o ticket clerk

taquimecanografía *nf* shorthand and typing

taquimecanógrafo, -a *nm,f* shorthand typist

tara *nf* **(a)** *(peso)* tare **(b)** *(defecto)* defect, blemish, fault **(c)** *Col (serpiente)* poisonous snake **(d)** *Ven (langosta)* green grasshopper

tarabilla *nmf Fam (persona)* chatterbox

tarado, -a 1 *pp de* tarar

2 *adj* **(a)** *(defectuoso)* defective, damaged **(b)** *(persona)* handicapped

3 *nm,f Fam* idiot, nitwit

tarambana *adj Fam* madcap

taranta *nf Arg CRica Ecuad* madness

tarantela *nf Mús* tarantella

tarantín *nm CAm Cuba* thingummy, thingumajig

tarántula *nf* tarantula

tarar *vt Com* to tare

tararear *vt* to hum

tarareo *nm* humming

tararira *adj Fam* **estar t.** *(loco)* to be batty o potty; *(borracho)* to be drunk

tarascada *nf Fam* rude retort, snappy answer

tardanza *nf* delay

tardar 1 *vt (emplear tiempo)* to take; **¿cuánto se tarda?** how long does it take?; **tarda una hora en cocerse** it takes an hour to cook; **tardé tres años** it took me three years

2 *vi (demorar)* **a más t.** at the latest; **no tardes** don't be long; **no puede t.** he shouldn't be long, he should be here any moment now; **se tarda más en tren** it takes longer by train; **tarda en llegar** he's late; **tardarás en empezar** it'll be some time before you start

tarde 1 *nf* **(a)** *(hasta las seis)* afternoon; **buenas tardes** good afternoon; **función de t.** matinée; **son las cuatro de la t.** it is four o'clock in the afternoon **(b)** *(después de las seis)* evening; **a las ocho de la t.** at eight o'clock in the evening; **a última hora de la tarde** early this evening; **buenas tardes** good evening

2 *adv* **(a)** *(hora avanzada)* late; **se está haciendo t.** it's getting late; **siento llegar t.** I'm sorry I'm late **(b)**

(demasiado tarde) too late; **es ya t. para ir al cine** it's too late now to go to the cinema **(c)** *(locuciones)* **de t. en t.** very rarely, not very often; **(más) t. o (más) temprano** sooner or later

tardío, -a *adj* late, belated; **fruta tardía** late fruit

tardo, -a (a) *(lento)* slow; **t. en comprender** slow to understand **(b)** *(torpe)* slow

tardón, -ona *nm,f* **(a)** *(impuntual)* = person who is always late **(b)** *(lento)* slowcoach

tarea *nf* job, task; **las tareas de la casa** the chores, the housework *sing*; **tareas escolares** homework *sing*; **una t. poco grata** an unpleasant job (to do)

tareco *nm Am* stuff, things *pl*

tarifa *nf* **(a)** *(precio)* charge; *(de servicio telefónico, postal)* rate; *(en transportes)* fare; *(de médico, abogado)* fee ❏ *Inform* **t. plana** flat rate; **t. reducida** reduced rate, special deal; **t. turística** tourist class rate **(b)** *(lista de precios)* price list **(c)** *Com (arancel)* tariff

tarifar *vt* to put a price on, price

tarima *nf* platform, dais

tarja *nf CAm Méx (tarjeta)* visiting card, *US* calling card

tarjeta *nf* **(a)** *(para presentación, pagos, transporte)* card ❏ **t. de crédito** credit card; **t. de débito** debit card; **t. de embarque** boarding pass; **t. de Navidad** Christmas card; **t. de recarga** top up card; **t. de visita** visiting o *US* calling card; **t. postal** postcard; **t. sanitaria** = card bearing personal indentification number and doctor's address; **t. telefónica** phonecard **(b)** *Dep* **t. amarilla/roja** yellow/red card **(c)** *Inform* **t. de sonido/vídeo** sound/video card

tarjetero *nm* credit-card wallet

tarjetón *nm Col (para votar)* ballot paper

tarot *(pl* **tarots)** *nm* tarot

tarraconense 1 *adj* of o from Tarragona

2 *nmf* person from Tarragona

tarrina *nf (envase)* tub; *Culin* terrine

tarro *nm* **(a)** *(vasija)* jar; **un t. de miel** a jar of honey **(b)** *Esp Fam (cabeza)* nut, *Br* bonce; **comer el t. a algn** to brainwash sb; **está mal del t.** he's off his rocker **(c)** *Chile Fam (sombrero)* top hat **(d)** *Cuba Méx (cuerno)* horn

tarsana *nf Bot CRica Ecuad Perú* soapbark

tarta *nf* cake, tart, pie, flan

tartaja *Fam* **1** *nmf* stammerer, stutterer

2 *adj* **ser t.** to have a stammer o stutter

tartajear *vi* to stammer, stutter

tartajeo *nm (manera de hablar)* stammering, stuttering; *(defecto)* stammer, stutter

tartajoso, -a 1 *adj* stammering, stuttering

2 *nm,f* stammerer, stutterer

tartaleta *nf* tartlet

tartamudear *vi* to stutter, stammer

tartamudeo *nm (manera de hablar)* stuttering, stammering; *(defecto)* stutter, stammer

tartamudez *nf* stutter, stammer

tartamudo, -a 1 *adj* stuttering, stammering

2 *nm,f* stutterer, stammerer

tartana *nf* **(a)** *(carruaje)* trap **(b)** *Fam (coche viejo)* banger, heap

tártaro, -a 1 *adj & nm,f Hist* Tartar

2 *adj Culin* **salsa tártara** tartar sauce

tartera *nf* **(a)** *(fiambrera)* lunch box **(b)** *(cazuela)* baking tin

tartesio, -a *adj & nm,f Hist* Tartessian

tarugada *nf Méx* piece of mischief

tarugo *nm* **(a)** *(de madera)* lump of wood **(b)** *(de pan)* chunk *(of stale bread)* (**c**) *Fam (persona)* blockhead

tarumba *adj Fam* crazy, mad; **estar t.** to be bonkers; **volver t. a algn** to drive sb crazy

tasa *nf* (**a**) *(valoración)* valuation, appraisal (**b**) *(precio)* fee, charge; **tasas académicas** course fees (**c**) *(impuesto)* tax, levy (**d**) *(limite)* limit; *(medida)* measure; **sin t.** without limit (**e**) *(índice)* rate ❑ **t. de cambio** exchange rate; **t. de desempleo** (level of) unemployment; **t. de interés** interest rate; **t. de mortalidad/natalidad** death/birth rate; **t. de paro** (level of) unemployment

tasación *nf* valuation, appraisal

tasador, -a *nm,f* valuer

tasar *vt* (**a**) *(valorar)* to value, appraise; **t. una casa en 100.000 euros** to value a house at 100.000 euros (**b**) *(poner precio a)* to set o fix the price of (**c**) *(articulo)* to tax (**d**) *(regular)* to regulate; *(limitar)* to limit; *(racionar)* to ration

tasca *nf* bar, pub; *Fam* **ir de tascas** to go round a few bars, *Br* go on a pub crawl

Tasmania *n* Tasmania

tasquear *vi* to go round a few bars, *Br* to go on a pub crawl

tata 1 *nf Esp Fam (niñera)* nanny
2 *nm Am Fam (papá)* dad, *US* pop

tatami *nm Dep* tatami, judo/karate mat

tatarabuelo, -a *nm,f (hombre)* great-great-grandfather; *(mujer)* great-great-grandmother; **tatarabuelos** great-great-grandparents

tataranieto, -a *nm,f (hombre)* great-great-grandson; *(mujer)* great-great-granddaughter; **tataranietos** great-great-grandchildren

tate 1 *nm Argot* hashish
2 *interj (cuidado)* look out!, steady!; *(caramba)* good grief!, *Br* crumbs!

tatemar *vt Méx* to roast

tatuador, -a *nm,f* tattooist

tatuaje *nm* (**a**) *(dibujo)* tattoo (**b**) *(procedimiento)* tattooing

tatuar [4] **1** *vt* to tattoo
2 tatuarse *vpr* to have a tattoo o tattoos done; **t. el pecho** to have one's chest tattooed

taúca *nf Bol Ecuad Perú* heap, stack

taumaturgo, -a *nm,f* miracle-worker

taurino, -a *adj* = of o relating to bullfighting; **la fiesta taurina** bullfighting

Tauro *nm Astrol Astron* Taurus

tauromaquia *nf* tauromachy, (art of) bullfighting

tautología *nf* tautology

taxativo, -a *adj* precise, restricted, specific; **de forma taxativa** in a categorical way

taxi *nm* taxi

taxidermia *nf* taxidermy

taxidermista *nmf* taxidermist

taxímetro *nm* taximeter, clock

taxista *nmf* taxi driver

taxonomía *nf* taxonomy

taxonomista *nmf* taxonomist

Tayikistán *n* Tadzhikistan

tayiko, -a 1 *adj & nm,f* Tajik, Tadzhik
2 *nm (lengua)* Tajik, Tadzhik

taza *nf* (**a**) *(para beber)* cup; **una t. de café** *(recipiente)* a coffee cup; *(con café)* a cup of coffee (**b**) *(contenido)* cup, cupful; **tres tazas de azúcar** three cups of sugar (**c**) *(de retrete)* bowl (**d**) *Chile Perú (palangana)* washbasin

tazón *nm* bowl

TC *nm (abrev de* **Tribunal Constitucional***)* constitutional court

te¹ *nf* (**a**) *(letra)* name of the letter T in Spanish (**b**) *Constr* tee

te² *pron pers* (**a**) *(complemento directo)* you; *(complemento indirecto)* (to) you; **no quiero verte** I don't want to see you; **te compraré uno** I'll buy one for you, I'll buy you one; **te lo dije** I told you; **te quiero** I love you (**b**) *(reflexivo)* yourself; *(sin traducción)* **bébetelo todo** drink it up; **lávate** wash yourself; **no te vayas** don't go; **¿te aburres?** are you bored?; **¿te compraste uno?** did you get one for yourself?; **te matarás** you'll kill yourself

té *nm* tea; **t. con limón** lemon tea; **salón de t.** tearoom

tea *nf* torch; *Fam* **cogerse una t.** to get drunk o plastered

teatral *adj* (**a**) *Teat* theatrical, dramatic; **grupo t.** theatre company; **obra t.** play (**b**) *Fig (exagerado)* stagy, *US* stagey, exaggerated; **es muy t.** he's always a bit over the top

teatralidad *nf* showmanship, staginess

teatralizar [14] *vt* to exaggerate

teatrero, -a *adj Fam* **ser t.** to be a drama queen

teatro *nm* (**a**) *(espectáculo)* theatre, *US* theater; **autor de t.** playwright; **obra de t.** play (**b**) *(arte de representar)* theatre, *US* theater, acting; **dejar el t.** to give up the stage; **vive para el t.** she lives for the stage (**c**) *Lit* drama (**d**) *Fig (lugar)* scene, theatre, *US* theater; **el t. de la batalla** the scene of the battle (**e**) *Fig (exageración)* show; **echarle t. a un asunto, hacer t.** to play-act, be melodramatic, put on (such) a show

tebeo *nm Esp* (children's) comic; *Fam* **está más visto que el t.** that's old hat

teca *nf Bot* teak

techado, -a 1 *pp de* **techar**
2 *adj* roofed, covered
3 *nm* roof, covering; **bajo t.** indoors

techar *vt* to roof

techo *nm* (**a**) *Constr* ceiling; *(de coche, tejado)* roof; **viven bajo el mismo t.** they live under the same roof (**b**) *Av (altura máxima)* ceiling (**c**) *Fig* limit, end; **el tema ha tocado t.** the subject has been exhausted, there's nothing more to say about this subject

techumbre *nf* roof, covering, roofing

tecla *nf también Inform* key; *Fig* **dar en la t.** to get it right; *Fig* **tocar teclas** to pull strings; *Fig* **tocas demasiadas teclas** you're trying to do too many things at once

tecladista *nmf Am* keyboard player

teclado *nm* keyboard ❑ *Inform* **t. expandido** expanded keyboard; **t. numérico** (numeric) keypad

teclear *vt & vi (en computadora)* to type; *(en piano)* to play

tecleo *nm (en piano)* playing; *(en máquina de escribir)* clattering

teclista *nmf* keyboard player

técnica *nf* (**a**) *(tecnología)* technics *pl*, technology; **t. mecánica** mechanical engineering (**b**) *(habilidad)* technique, method; **toca bien pero le falta t.** he plays well but he lacks technique

tecnicidad *nf* technicality

tecnicismo *nm Ling* technicality, technical word o expression

técnico, -a 1 *adj* technical; **carrera técnica** technical degree; **vocabulario t.** technical vocabulary
2 *nm,f* technician, technical expert

tecnicolor® *nm* Technicolor®

tecnificación *nf* application of technology

tecnificar [59] *vt* to apply technology to

tecno *nm inv Mús* techno (music)

tecno- *pref* techno-

tecnocracia *nf Pol* technocracy

tecnócrata *nmf* technocrat

tecnocrático, -a *adj* technocratic

tecnología *nf* technology ❏ **t. punta** state-of-the-art technology

tecnológico, -a *adj* technological

tecnólogo, -a *nm,f* technologist

tecomate *nm CAm Méx* = vessel made from a gourd

tectónica *nf* tectonics *sing*

tectónico, -a *adj* tectonic

tedéum *nm inv* Te Deum

tedio *nm* tedium, boredom, monotony

tedioso, -a *adj* tedious, boring, monotonous

teflón® *nm* Teflon®

Tegucigalpa *n* Tegucigalpa

tegucigalpeño, -a 1 *adj* of o from Tegucigalpa
  2 *nm,f* person from Tegucigalpa

tegumento *nm* integument

Teherán *n* Teheran

teína *nf* theine

teísmo *nm* theism

teja *nf Constr* tile

tejadillo *nm* **(a)** *Aut* roof **(b)** *Constr* roof

tejado *nm* roof

tejamanil *nm Carib Col Méx* shingle

tejano, -a 1 *adj* Texan
  2 *nm,f (persona)* Texan
  3 tejanos *nmpl (prenda)* jeans

tejar¹ *nm* tile works *sing*

tejar² *vt* to tile

Tejas *n* Texas

tejedor, -a 1 *adj* **(a)** *(que teje)* weaving **(b)** *Chile Perú Fam (intrigante)* scheming, conniving
  2 *nm,f* **(a)** *(persona que teje)* weaver **(b)** *Chile Perú Fam (persona intrigante)* schemer, conniver

tejemaneje *nm Fam* **(a)** *(mucha actividad)* bustle, fuss; **¿qué es tanto t.?** what's all this fuss about? **(b)** *(maquinación)* intrigue, scheming; **algún t. se deben traer** they must be cooking up something

tejer 1 *vt* **(a)** *(en el telar)* to weave **(b)** *(labor de punto)* to knit **(c)** *(telaraña)* to spin **(d)** *Fig (plan)* to weave, plot, scheme
  2 *vi* **(a)** *(hacer punto)* to knit; *Fig* **t. y destejer** to chop and change **(b)** *(araña)* to spin **(c)** *CSur Perú Fam (conspirar)* to scheme, plot

tejido *nm* **(a)** *(tela)* fabric, textile; **t. de punto** knitted fabric **(b)** *Anat* tissue ❏ **t. muscular** muscle o muscular tissue; **t. nervioso** nervous tissue; **t. óseo** bone tissue **(c)** *Fig* web

tejo¹ *nm* **(a)** *(juego)* hopscotch, = children's game similar to quoits **(b)** *Esp Fam* **tirar los tejos a algn** to make a pass at sb

tejo² *nm Bot* yew (tree)

tejón *nm* badger

tel. *(abrev de* **teléfono)** tel

tela *nf* **(a)** *Tex* material, fabric, cloth; *(de la leche)* skin ❏ **t. de araña** cobweb; **t. metálica** wire netting, mesh gauze **(b)** *Fam (dinero)* dough **(c)** *Arte* painting **(d)** *(locuciones) Fig* **tener t. para rato** to have a lot to do/talk about; *Fig* **poner en t. de juicio** to question; *Fig* **tiene mucha t.** it's not an easy thing

telar *nm* **(a)** *Tex* loom **(b)** *Teat* gridiron

telaraña *nf* cobweb, spider's web

tele *nf Fam* TV, *Br* telly

teleadicto, -a *nm,f* telly addict

teleapuntador *nm Br* Autocue®, *US* Teleprompter®

telearrastre *nm* ski lift

teleaudiencia *nf Am* TV audience, viewers *pl*

telebanca *nf* telephone banking

telebasura *nf Fam* junk TV

telecabina *nf* single cable car

telecomedia *nf* sitcom

telecompra *nf* teleshopping, home shopping

telecomunicación *nf (gen pl)* telecommunication

telecontrol *nm* remote control

telediario *nm Esp* TV television news bulletin

teledifusión *nf* broadcasting

teledirigido, -a 1 *pp de* **teledirigir**
  2 *adj* remote-controlled; **proyectil t.** guided missile

teledirigir [24] *vt* to operate o guide by remote control

telefax *nm* telefax, fax

teleférico *nm* cable car o railway

telefilm *(pl* **telefilms)** *nm*, **telefilme** *nm* TV movie o *Br* film

telefonazo *nm* buzz, *Br* ring; **dar un t. a algn** to give sb a buzz o *Br* ring

telefonear *vt & vi* to telephone, phone; **t. a casa/la oficina** to telephone home/the office

telefonía *nf* telephony

telefónica *nf (empresa)* telecommunications company

telefónicamente *adv* by telephone

telefónico, -a *adj* telephone; **central** o **centralita telefónica** switchboard, telephone exchange

telefonillo *nm* entryphone

telefonista *nmf (telephone)* operator

teléfono *nm* **(a)** *(aparato, sistema)* telephone, phone; **está hablando por t.** she's on the phone; **te llamó por t.** she phoned you ❏ **t. celular** cellular phone, cellphone; **t. fijo** land line (phone); **t. inalámbrico** cordless phone; **t. móvil** mobile phone **(b)** *(número)* telephone number; **t. gratuito** toll-free number, *Br* Freefone® o Freephone® number

telegénico, -a *adj* telegenic

telegrafía *nf* telegraphy

telegrafiar [32] *vt* to telegraph, wire

telegráficamente *adv* by telegraph; *Fam* **hablar/escribir t.** to speak/write telegraphically

telegráfico, -a *adj* telegraphic; **giro t.** giro, money order; **lenguaje t.** telegraphic speech

telegrafista *nmf* telegraphist, telegrapher

telégrafo *nm* **(a)** *(medio, aparato)* telegraph; **poste de t.** telegraph pole **(b)** **telégrafos** post office *sing*

telegrama *nm* telegram, cable

telele *nm Fam* **darle a uno un t.** to have a fit

telemando *nm* remote control (unit)

telemarketing *nm* telesales *pl*, telemarketing

telemática *nf Tec* telematics *sing*

telematizar [14] *vt Inform* to introduce telematics into

telemetría *nf* telemetry

telémetro *nm* telemeter, rangefinder

telenovela *nf* television serial

teleobjetivo *nm Fot* telephoto lens

telepatía *nf* telepathy

telepáticamente *adv* by telepathy

telepático, -a *adj* telepathic

telequinesia *nf* telekinesis

telerruta *nf* = telephone service giving traffic information

telescópico, -a *adj* telescopic

telescopio *nm* telescope

teleserie *nf* TV series

telesilla *nm* chairlift

telespectador, -a *nmf* TV viewer

telesquí *(pl* **telesquís** *o* **telesquíes)** *nm* ski lift

teletexto *nm* teletext

teletienda *nf* home shopping programme

teletipo *nm* Teletype®, teleprinter; **noticia de t.** news from an agency

teletrabajador, -a *nm,f* teleworker

teletrabajo *nm* teleworking

televendedor, -a *nm,f* telesales assistant

televenta *nf* (a) *(por teléfono)* telesales *pl* (b) *(por televisión)* teleshopping, home shopping

televidente *nm,f* TV viewer

televisar *vt* to televise

televisión *nf* (a) *(sistema)* television ❑ **t. digital** digital television; **t. interactiva** interactive television; **t. por cable** cable television; **t. privada/pública** privately owned/public television (b) *(aparato)* television set; **ver la t.** to watch television

televisivo, -a *adj* television; **espacio t.** television programme

televisor *nm* television set

télex *nm inv* telex

telilla *nf* film, skin; **la t. de la leche** the skin of the milk

telón *nm Teat* curtain ❑ *Pol* **t. de acero** Iron Curtain; **t. de fondo** *Teat* backdrop; *Fig* background

telonero, -a *adj* first on stage, support; **grupo t.** support band

telúrico, -a *adj* telluric

tema *nm* (a) *(de libro, de conversación)* topic, subject, theme; *(de examen)* subject; **atenerse al t.** to keep to the point; **le tocó un t. fácil** he was given an easy subject; **por favor no toques este t. otra vez** don't go into that again, please; **salir del t.** to go off at a tangent; **temas de actualidad** current affairs; *Fam* **cada loco con su t.** everyone has his hobbyhorse (b) *Mús* theme (c) *Ling* root, stem, theme; **el t. del verbo decir es dec-** the stem of the verb **decir** is dec-

temario *nm (de examen)* programme; *(de conferencia)* agenda

temática *nf* subject matter

temático, -a *adj* (a) *(de tema)* thematic (b) *Ling (vocal)* thematic

temblar [3] *vi (de frío)* to shiver; *(de miedo)* to tremble (**de** with); *(voz)* to tremble, shake; *(con sacudidas)* to shake; **le tiemblan las manos** he's got shaky hands; **tiemblo ante el futuro** I shudder when I think of the future

tembleque *nm Fam* shaking fit; **sólo de pensarlo me da** *o* **entra (el) t.** I get the shivers just thinking about it

temblequear *vi* (a) *(persona)* to tremble; *(de frío)* to shiver (b) *(suelo, máquina)* to shudder, shake

temblón, -ona 1 *adj Fam* trembling, shaky
2 *nm Bot* álamo t. aspen

temblor *nm* tremor, shudder; **el enfermo tenía temblores** the patient was shaking ❑ **t. de tierra** earth tremor

tembloroso, -a *adj (con sacudidas)* shaking, *(voz)* trembling, quavering, *(de frío)* shivering; *(de miedo)*

trembling; **manos temblorosas** shaky hands

temer 1 *vt* (a) *(tener miedo de)* to fear, be afraid of; **teme al enemigo** he is afraid of the enemy (b) *(sospechar)* to fear, be afraid of; **temo que esté muerto** I fear he's dead; **temo que no podrá recibirte** I'm afraid (that) he won't be able to see you
2 *vi* (a) *(tener miedo)* to be afraid; **era de t.** it had to happen; **no temas** don't be afraid (b) *(preocuparse)* to worry; **no hay nada que t.** there is nothing to worry about
3 temerse *vpr* to fear, be afraid; **¡me lo temía!** I feared this would happen!

temerario, -a *adj* reckless, rash

temeridad *nf* (a) *(actitud)* temerity, rashness (b) *(acto temerario)* reckless act

temeroso, -a *adj* (a) *(receloso)* fearful, timid; **t. de** fearing (that); **t. de Dios** God-fearing (b) *(medroso)* frightful

temible *adj* dreadful, fearful, frightful, frightening; **un ejército t.** a fearsome army

temido, -a 1 *pp de* temer
2 *adj* feared, dreaded; **t. de** *o* **por todos** feared by everybody

temor *nm* (a) *(de Dios)* fear (b) *(recelo)* worry, apprehension; **tener t.** to feel apprehensive; **tus temores son infundados** there's no reason for you to worry

témpano *nm* ice floe; **ser como un t.** to be as cold as ice

témpera *nf Arte* tempera

temperado, -a *adj* temperate

temperamental *adj* temperamental

temperamento *nm* temperament, nature; **tiene buen t.** he is good-natured; **tener t.** to have a strong character

temperancia *nf (calmar)* temperance, moderation, restraint

temperar 1 *vt (calmar)* to temper, mitigate
2 *vi Col Ven (cambiar de aires)* to have a change of air

temperatura *nf* temperature; **¿qué t. hace?** what's the temperature?; *Med* **le ha subido la t.** his temperature has gone up ❑ **t. máxima/mínima** maximum/minimum temperature

tempestad *nf Meteor* storm; *Fig* turmoil, uproar; *Fig* **levantar tempestades** to cause a turmoil; *Fig* **una t. en un vaso de agua** *Br* a storm in a tea cup, *US* a tempest in a teapot ❑ **t. de arena** sandstorm; **t. de nieve** snowstorm, blizzard

tempestuoso, -a *adj* stormy, tempestuous, violent, wild

templado, -a 1 *pp de* templar
2 *adj* (a) *(agua)* lukewarm, warm; *(clima)* mild, temperate; *(temperatura)* mild (b) *(moderado)* moderate; *(sereno)* composed, unruffled; **nervios bien templados** steady nerves (c) *Mús (afinado)* tuned

templanza *nf* (a) *(moderación)* moderation, restraint (b) *(del clima)* mildness

templar 1 *vt* (a) *(algo frío)* to warm up; *(algo caliente)* to cool down (b) *(calmar) (nervios, ánimos)* to calm; *(ira, pasiones)* to restrain; *(voz)* to soften (c) *(tensar)* to tighten up (d) *Mús (instrumento)* to tune (e) *Téc (metal)* to temper (f) *Andes (matar)* to kill
2 templarse *vpr* (a) *(calentarse)* to warm up, get warm (b) *Ecuad Guat Hond (morir)* to die (c) *Chile (enamorarse)* to fall in love

templario *nm Hist* Templar

temple *nm* (a) *(fortaleza)* boldness, courage; *(estado de ánimo)* frame of mind, mood (b) *Téc (de metal)* temper; **dar t. a** to temper (c) *Arte* tempera

templete *nm* (a) *(pabellón)* pavilion, kiosk (b) *(templo pequeño)* small temple

templo *nm* temple; *Fam Fig* **una mentira como un t.** an utter lie; *Fam Fig* **una verdad como un t.** an undeniable fact

temporada *nf* (**a**) *(en artes, deportes, moda)* season; **en plena t.** at the height of the season ❑ **t. alta** high o peak season; **t. baja** low o off season (**b**) *(periodo)* period, time; **por temporadas** on and off

temporal 1 *adj* (**a**) *(transitorio)* temporary, provisional; **bienes temporales** worldly goods (**b**) *Ling* temporal
2 *nm Meteor* storm, tempest; *Fig* **capear el t.** to ride out the storm

temporalidad *nf* temporary nature

temporario, -a *adj Am* temporary

temporero, -a 1 *adj (trabajador)* seasonal, temporary
2 *nm,f* seasonal o temporary worker

temporizador *nm* timer

tempranero, -a *adj* (**a**) *(persona)* early-rising (**b**) *(cosecha)* early

temprano, -a 1 *adj* early
2 *adv* early; **más t.** earlier

tenacidad *nf* (**a**) *(perseverancia)* tenacity, perseverance (**b**) *(resistencia)* toughness

tenacillas *nfpl (para pelo)* curling tongs; *(para vello)* tweezers

tenaz *adj* (**a**) *(perseverante) (persona, actitud)* tenacious (**b**) *(persistente) (mancha, grasa)* stubborn (**c**) *(resistente)* tough (**d**) *Col Fam (terrible)* terrible, awful; **¡uy, t.!** *(¡no me digas!)* you don't say!

tenaza *nf,* **tenazas** *nfpl (herramienta)* pliers, pincers; *(para el fuego)* tongs; *Fam Fig* **esto no se puede coger ni con tenazas** I wouldn't touch it with a barge pole

tenca *nf (pez)* tench

tendal *nm* (**a**) *(cuerda)* clothes line (**b**) *Cuba Ecuad (para café)* drying floor (**c**) *Am Fam (desorden, caos)* **dejaron un t.** they left the place a mess

tendedero *nm* clothes line, drying place

tendencia *nf* tendency, inclination, predisposition, leaning; **tener t. a hacer algo** to tend to do sth, have a tendency to do sth

tendenciosidad *nf* tendentiousness, partiality, bias

tendencioso, -a *adj* tendentious, biased

tendente *adj* directed (**a** at), aimed (**a** at)

tender [64] **1** *vt* (**a**) *(mantel)* to spread; *(red)* to cast; *(puente)* to throw; *(vía, cable)* to lay; *Náut (velas)* to spread (**b**) *(ropa, colada)* to hang out (**c**) *(mano)* to stretch o hold out (**d**) *(emboscada, trampa)* to lay, set (**e**) *(tumbar)* to lay; **estaba tendido en el suelo** he was lying on the floor (**f**) *Constr (pared, techo)* to plaster
2 *vi (tener tendencia)* **t. a** to tend to, have a tendency to
3 tenderse *vpr* (**a**) *(tumbarse)* to lie down, stretch out (**b**) *(caballo)* to run at full gallop

tenderete *nm* (**a**) *(puesto)* market stall (**b**) *(montón)* heap, mess

tendero, -a *nm,f* shopkeeper

tendido, -a 1 *pp de* **tender**
2 *adj* (**a**) *(extendido)* spread o laid out (**b**) *(persona)* lying down; **le dejé t. de un solo puñetazo** I floored him with a single blow (**c**) *(ropa, colada)* hung out; **¿hay ropa tendida?** is there any washing on the line?
3 *nm* (**a**) *(colada)* wash, washing (**b**) *(de vía, cable)* laying; *(de puente)* construction ❑ **t. eléctrico** power lines *pl* (**c**) *Taur (asientos)* front rows *pl*

tendón *nm Anat* tendon, sinew

tenebrismo *nm* tenebrism

tenebrista *adj & nmf Arte* tenebrist

tenebrosidad *nf* darkness, shadiness, obscurity

tenebroso, -a *adj* (**a**) *(sombrío)* dark, gloomy (**b**) *(siniestro)* sinister, shady

tenedor, -a 1 *nm,f Fin* holder ❑ **t. de acciones** shareholder
2 *nm Culin* fork

teneduría *nf* book-keeping

tenencia *nf Jur* tenancy, possession ❑ **t. ilícita de armas** illegal possession of arms

tener [65] **1** *vt* (**a**) *(gen)* to have; **tenemos un examen** we've got an exam; **t. tiempo** to have time, **t. una idea** to have an idea; **tengo algo que deciros** there's something I want to tell you; **tiene los ojos negros** she's got dark eyes; **va a t. un niño** she's going to have a baby, she's expecting; *Fam* **¡ahí (lo) tienes!** so there you are!; *Fam* **¿(con qué) ésas tenemos?** is that so? (**b**) *(poseer)* to have (**c**) *(sostener)* to hold; *(coger)* to take; **lo tienes en la mano** you're holding it; **ten al niño mientras abro** hold the baby while I open the door; **ten, es para ti** take this o here you are, it's for you (**d**) *(sensación, sentimiento)* to be; *(sentir)* to feel; **¿qué tienes?** what's wrong with you?; **t. calor/frío** to be hot/cold; **t. cariño a algn** to be fond of sb; **t. compasión de algn** to take pity on sb; **t. ganas de ...** to feel like ...; **t. ilusión** to be enthusiastic; **t. miedo** to be frightened; *Fam* **no tenerlas todas consigo** *(dudar)* to have one's doubts; *(tener miedo)* to be afraid (**e**) *(mantener)* to keep; **la preocupación me ha tenido despierto toda la noche** I've been up all night with worry; **t. a algn contento** to make sb happy; *Fam* **tenerla tomada con algn** to have it in for sb (**f**) *(medir)* to measure; **la casa tiene cien metros cuadrados** the house is a hundred square metres (**g**) *(contener)* to hold, contain (**h**) *(edad)* to be; **tiene casi treinta (años)** she's almost thirty (years old) (**i**) *(celebrar)* to hold; **t. una reunión** to hold a meeting (**j**) *(considerar)* to consider, think; **me tienen por estúpido** they think I'm a fool; **ten por seguro que lloverá** you can be sure it'll rain
2 *v aux (obligación)* **t. que** to have (got) to; **tengo que irme** I must leave; **tienes/tendrías que verlo** you must/should see it
3 tenerse *vpr* (**a**) *(sostenerse)* to stand up; **no t.** to be tired out; **t. firme** to stand upright (**b**) *(dominarse)* to control oneself (**c**) *(considerarse)* **t. por** to think o consider oneself; **se tiene por muy inteligente** he thinks he's very intelligent

tengo *indic pres véase* **tener**

tenia *nf* tapeworm

teniente *nm* (**a**) *Mil* lieutenant ❑ **t. coronel/general** lieutenant colonel/general (**b**) *(de ayuntamiento)* **t. de alcalde** deputy mayor

tenis *nm* tennis ❑ **t. de mesa** table tennis

tenista *nmf* tennis player

tenístico, -a *adj* tennis; **campeonato t.** tennis championship

Tenochtitlán *n* Tenochtitlan *(Aztec capital)*

tenor¹ *nm Mús* tenor

tenor² *nm* tenor, purport; **a este t.** like this; **a t. de** according to

tenorio *nm* Don Juan, lady-killer, Casanova

tensado, -a 1 *pp de* **tensar**
2 *adj* taut, tautened, tense

tensar *vt (cable, cuerda)* to tauten; *(arco)* to draw

tensión *nf* (**a**) *Téc (de materiales)* stress; *(de gases)* pressure (**b**) *Elec* tension, voltage ❑ **alta/baja t.** high/low voltage (**c**) *Med* **t. arterial** blood pressure; **t. nerviosa** nervous strain (**d**) *(de una situación)* tension, tenseness; *(de una persona)* stress, strain; *(angustia)* anxiety; **en medio de una gran t.** in a very tense situation; **en t.** tense

tenso, -a *adj* (**a**) *(cuerda, cable)* tense, taut (**b**) *(persona)* tense; *(relaciones)* strained

tensor 1 *adj* tensile
   2 *nm* (**a**) *Anat Mat* tensor (**b**) *Téc* turnbuckle

tentación *nf* temptation; **caer en la t.** to succumb o give in to temptation

tentáculo *nm* tentacle

tentador, -a *adj* tempting, enticing

tentar [3] *vt* (**a**) *(palpar)* to feel, touch; **t. el camino** to feel one's way (**b**) *(incitar)* to tempt, entice; *Fam* **¡no me tientes!** don't tempt me!, don't say it twice! (**c**) *(atraer)* to attract, tempt

tentativa *nf* attempt, try ◻ *Jur* **t. de asesinato** attempted murder

tentempié *nm Fam* (**a**) *(comida)* snack, bite (**b**) *(juguete)* tumbler

tentetieso *nm* Weeble®, tumbler (doll)

tenue *adj* (**a**) *(delgado)* thin, light; *(tela)* flimsy, thin; **una t. niebla** a light fog (**b**) *(luz, sonido)* subdued, faint

teñido, -a 1 *pp de* **teñir**
   2 *adj* (**a**) *(gen)* dyed; *(pelo)* tinted, dyed; *Fig* tinged; **una voz teñida de tristeza** a voice tinged with sadness
   3 *nm (acción)* dyeing

teñir [47] **1** *vt* (**a**) *(cambiar el color de)* to dye; *(cambiar el tono de)* to tone down (**b**) *Fig* to tinge (**de** with)
   2 teñirse *vpr (pelo)* to dye one's hair

teocracia *nf* theocracy

teocrático, -a *adj* theocratic

teodolito *nm Téc* theodolite

teologal *adj* theological

teología *nf* theology ◻ **t. de la liberación** liberation theology

teológico, -a *adj* theological

teólogo, -a *nm,f* theologian, theologist

teorema *nm Mat* theorem

teoría *nf* theory; **en t.** theoretically ◻ **t. del caos** chaos theory

teórica *nf* theory, theoretics *sing*

teórico, -a 1 *adj* theoretic, theoretical, hypothetical
   2 *nm,f* theoretician, theorist

teorizador, -a *adj* theorizing

teorizar [14] **1** *vt* to theorize on
   2 *vi* to theorize (**sobre** on)

tepalcate *nm* (**a**) *Guat Méx (vasija)* earthenware jar; *(cacharro)* piece of junk (**b**) *Salv (fragmento)* fragment of pottery

tequiar *vt CAm* to pester

tequila *nm* tequila

terapeuta *nmf* therapist

terapéutica *nf* therapeutics *sing*, therapy

terapéutico, -a *adj* therapeutic

terapia *nf* therapy ◻ **t. de grupo** group therapy; *Méx RP* **t. intensiva** intensive care; **t. ocupacional** occupational therapy

tercer *adj* third; **el t. mundo** the third world; *véase tamb* **tercero, -a**

tercera *nf* (**a**) *(clase)* third class; **viajar en t.** to travel third class (**b**) *Aut (marcha)* third (gear) (**c**) *Mús (intervalo)* third (**d**) *Prov* **a la t. va la vencida** third time lucky

tercerización *nf Am Com* outsourcing

tercerizar [14] *vt Am Com* to outsource

tercermundismo *nm (de países pobres)* underdevelopment; *(de servicios, sistema)* backwardness

tercermundista *adj* third-world

tercero, -a 1 *adj* third
   2 *nm,f (de una serie)* third
   3 *nm* (**a**) *(piso)* **vive en el t.** he lives on the *Br* third o *US* fourth floor (**b**) *(mediador)* mediator; *(persona ajena)* outsider; *Jur* third party; **seguro contra terceros** third party insurance; *véase tamb* **octavo, -a**

terceto *nm* (**a**) *(verso)* tercet (**b**) *Mús* trio

terciado, -a *adj (mediano)* medium-sized

terciar 1 *vt* (**a**) *(dividir)* to divide into three (**b**) *(poner en diagonal)* to place diagonally o crosswise (**c**) *Andes Cuba Méx (aguar)* to water down (**d**) *Col Méx (cargar a la espalda)* to carry on one's back
   2 *vi* (**a**) *(mediar)* to mediate, arbitrate; **t. entre dos enemigos** to mediate between two enemies (**b**) *(participar)* to take part, participate; **t. en el debate** to take part in the debate
   3 terciarse *vpr (ocasión)* to arise; **si se tercia** should the occasion arise

terciario, -a *adj* tertiary

tercio *nm* (**a**) *(parte)* third (**b**) *Mil* division (**c**) *Hist* infantry regiment (**d**) *Taur (suerte)* stage, part *(of a bullfight)* (**e**) *(de cerveza)* medium-size bottle of beer

terciopelo *nm* velvet

terco, -a *adj* stubborn, obstinate

tergal® *nm* = type of polyester fabric

tergiversación *nf* distortion, twisting

tergiversador, -a 1 *adj* distorting
   2 *nm,f* person who distorts the facts

tergiversar *vt (hechos, motivos)* to distort; *(declaraciones, ideas)* to twist

termal *adj* thermal

termas *nfpl (baños)* spa *sing*, hot baths o springs *pl*; *Hist* thermae *pl*

térmico, -a *adj* thermic, thermal

terminación *nf* (**a**) *(acción)* ending, termination (**b**) *(conclusión)* completion (**c**) *(parte final)* end

terminado, -a 1 *pp de* **terminar**
   2 *adj* finished, completed; **dar algo por t.** to consider sth finished

terminal 1 *adj* terminal; **estación t.** terminus
   2 *nf* (**a**) *Elec* terminal; *Inform* terminal (**b**) *(estación)* terminus
   3 *nm Inform* terminal

terminante *adj* (**a**) *(categórico)* categorical, final (**b**) *(dato, resultado)* conclusive, definite, definitive

terminantemente *adv* categorically; **queda** o **está t. prohibido** it is strictly forbidden

terminar 1 *vt (acabar)* to finish, complete
   2 *vi* (**a**) *(acabarse)* to finish, end; **termina en seis/vocal** it ends with a six/vowel; **termina ya** will you finish that (off) now, please; **t. bien** to have a happy ending; **t. de hacer algo** to finish doing sth; **no termina de convencerse** he still isn't quite convinced; **t. mal** *(historia)* to have an unhappy ending; *(relación)* to come to a sticky end; *(personas)* to end up on bad terms (**b**) *(ir a parar)* to end up (**como** as), end (**en** in, with); **terminarás loco** you'll go mad; **terminé rendido** I was exhausted by the end of it; **terminó comprándolo** he ended up buying it; **terminó por caerse** he ended up falling down (**c**) *(eliminar)* **t. con** to put an end to (**d**) *(reñir)* to break up (**con** with)
   3 terminarse *vpr* (**a**) *(acabarse)* to finish, end, be over; **se ha terminado la fiesta** the party is over (**b**) *(agotarse)* to run out

término *nm* (**a**) *(final)* end, finish; **dar t.** to conclude; **llevar algo a buen** o **feliz t.** to carry sth through (successfully); **poner t. a algo** to put an end to sth (**b**)

Ferroc (estación) terminus (**c**) *(límite)* limit, boundary ◻ **t. municipal** district (**d**) *(plazo)* term, time; **en el t. de un día** within the space of a day (**e**) *(palabra)* term, word; *(argumento)* point, term; **en otros términos** in other words; **en términos generales** generally speaking; **invertir los términos** to get *o* put it the wrong way round; *Jur* **los términos de un contrato** the terms of a contract (**f**) *Filos Mat* term; (**por**) **t. medio** on average (**g**) *(lugar, posición)* place; *Arte* **primer t.** foreground; *Fig* **en último t.** as a last resort

terminología *nf* terminology

terminológico, -a *adj* terminological

termita *nf* termite

termo *nm* thermos (flask), flask

termoaislante *adj* heat insulating

termodinámica *nf* thermodynamics *sing*

termodinámico, -a *adj* thermodynamic, thermodynamical

termoeléctrico, -a *adj* thermoelectric

termometría *nf* thermometry

termométrico, -a *adj* thermometric

termómetro *nm* thermometer

termonuclear *adj* thermonuclear

termorregulador *nm* thermostat

termositón *nm* (**a**) *(calentador)* boiler, water heater (**b**) *Téc* thermosiphon

termostato *nm* thermostat

terna *nf Pol* = shortlist of three candidates

ternario, -a *adj* ternary

ternera *nf* (**a**) *Zool* calf (**b**) *Culin* veal

ternero *nm* calf

terneza *nf* tenderness; **ternezas** sweet nothings

ternilla *nf* cartilage

terno *nm* (**a**) *(gen)* set *o* group of three; *(prenda)* three-piece suit (**b**) *Fam (juramento)* swearword

ternura *nf* tenderness, gentleness

terquedad *nf* (**a**) *(obstinación)* stubbornness, obstinacy (**b**) *(dureza)* toughness, hardness

terracota *nf* terracotta

terrado *nm Constr* flat roof, terrace

terral *nm Am* dust cloud

Terranova *n* Newfoundland

terranova *nm Zool* Newfoundland dog

terraplén *nm* embankment

terráqueo, -a *adj* **globo t.** globe

terrario *nm*, **terrarium** *nm* terrarium

terrateniente *nmf Agr* landowner

terraza *nf* (**a**) *(balcón)* balcony (**b**) *(de café)* terrace, patio (**c**) *(azotea)* terrace roof (**d**) *(bancal)* terrace

terrazo *nm* terrazzo

terremoto *nm* earthquake

terrenal *adj* earthly, worldly

terreno, -a 1 *adj* earthly, worldly
2 *nm* (**a**) *(tierra)* (piece of) land, ground; *(solar)* plot, site; *Geol* terrain; *Agr (de cultivo)* soil; *(campo)* field; **ganar/perder t.** to gain/lose ground; **hacer algo sobre el t.** *(en el lugar)* to do sth on the spot; *Fig (improvisar)* to improvise sth; *Fig* **conocer el t.** to be familiar with it; *Fig* **preparar el t.** to pave the way, prepare the ground; *Fig* **saber uno el t. que pisa** to know what one's doing; *Fig* **ser t. abonado (para algo)** to be receptive (to sth) (**b**) *Dep* field, ground ◻ **t. de juego** *Ten* court; *Ftb* field, *Br* pitch (**c**) *Fig* field, sphere; **está en su propio t.** he's on home ground

térreo, -a *adj* earthen

terrestre 1 *adj* (**a**) *(de la tierra)* terrestrial, earthly (**b**) *(por tierra)* by land
2 *nmf (persona)* terrestrial

terrible *adj* terrible, awful

terrícola 1 *adj* land
2 *nmf (persona)* earth dweller; *Lit (en ciencia ficción)* earthling

terrier *(pl* **terriers**) *nm* terrier

territorial *adj* territorial; *Tel* **código t.** area code

territorialidad *nf Jur* territoriality

territorio *nm* territory; **en todo el t. nacional** nationwide, all over the country

terrón *nm* (**a**) *(de tierra)* clod (**b**) *(de azúcar, sal)* lump (**c**) **terrones** *(tierras)* land *sing*

terror *nm (gen)* terror; *Cin* horror; **me da t.** it terrifies me

terrorífico, -a *adj* terrifying, frightening

terrorismo *nm* terrorism

terrorista *adj & nmf* terrorist

terroso, -a *adj* (**a**) *(con tierra)* earthy, containing earth (**b**) *(color)* earth-coloured, *US* earth-colored

terruño *nm* (**a**) *(terreno)* piece of land (**b**) *(patria chica)* homeland, native land

tersar *vt* to make smooth

terso, -a *adj* (**a**) *(liso)* smooth (**b**) *(brillante)* glossy, shining (**c**) *(estilo)* polished, fluent

tersura *nf* (**a**) *(cualidad de liso)* smoothness (**b**) *(brillo)* glossiness, shine (**c**) *(de estilo)* polish, fluency

tertulia *nf* get-together; **estar de t.** to sit around and talk; **hacer t.** to have a get-together ◻ **t. literaria** literary gathering

tertuliano, -a *nm,f Rad* panellist, *US* panelist

tertuliar *vi Am* to hold discussions, debate

tesauro *nm* thesaurus

tesela *nf* tessera

tesina *nf Univ* first degree dissertation

tesis *nf inv* (**a**) *Filos* thesis; *(opinión)* view, theory; **sostener una t.** to hold a view *o* opinion (**b**) *Univ* thesis ◻ **t. doctoral** doctoral thesis

tesitura *nf* (**a**) *Mús* tessitura (**b**) *Fig (estado de ánimo)* mood; *(actitud)* attitude

tesón *nm* tenacity, firmness

tesorería *nf (oficina)* treasurer's office; *(cargo)* treasurer

tesorero, -a *nm,f* treasurer

tesoro *nm* (**a**) *(gen)* treasure (**b**) *(erario)* exchequer ◻ **T. Público** Treasury (**c**) *Fig* treasure; **ese niño es un t.** this child is a gem (**d**) *(diccionario)* thesaurus

test [tes(t)] *(pl* **tests**) *nm Téc* test

testa *nf* head

testado, -a *adj (persona)* testate; *(herencia)* testamentary

testador, -a *nm,f Jur (hombre)* testator; *(mujer)* testatrix

testaferro *nm* front man

testamentaría *nf Jur* testate proceedings *pl*

testamentario, -a 1 *adj* testamentary
2 *nm,f* executor

testamento *nm* (**a**) *Jur* will, testament; **hacer *o* otorgar t.** to make *o* draw up one's will (**b**) *Rel* **Antiguo/Nuevo T.** Old/New Testament

testar *vi* to make *o* draw up one's will

testarazo *nm* butt *o* bump *o* knock on the head

testarudez *nf* stubbornness, obstinacy, pigheadedness

testarudo, -a *adj* stubborn, obstinate, pigheaded

testear *vt CSur* to test

testículo *nm Anat* testicle

testificación *nf* testimony; **es la t. de su talento** it is proof of her talent

testificar [59] *vt & vi* to testify

testigo 1 *nmf (gen)* witness; **poner a algn por t.** to call sb to witness; *Rel* **a Dios pongo por t.** as God is my witness ❏ *Jur* **t. de cargo/descargo** witness for the prosecution/defence; *Jur* **t. ocular, t. presencial** eyewitness; *Rel* **Testigos de Jehová** Jehovah's Witnesses
2 *nm* **(a)** *Fig* evidence, proof **(b)** *Dep (en carreras de relevos)* baton

testimonial *adj* testimonial

testimoniar *vt* **(a)** *Jur (dar testimonio de)* to bear witness to, testify to, attest to **(b)** *Fig (mostrar)* to show, prove, express

testimonio *nm Jur* testimony; *(prueba)* evidence, proof; **dar t.** to give evidence; **levantar falsos testimonios** to commit perjury

testosterona *nf Biol* testosterone

testuz *nm o nf* **(a)** *(frente)* brow **(b)** *(nuca)* nape

teta *nf Fam* **(a)** *(de mujer)* tit, titty, boob; **dar la t.** to breastfeed; **niño de t.** nursing baby; **quitar la t. a** to wean; *Vulg* **es t. de monja** o **novicia** it's delicious; *Vulg* **¡vaya par de tetas!** what a pair of tits! **(b)** *(de vaca)* udder

tetamen *nm Vulg* tits *pl*, boobs *pl*

tétano *nm*, **tetanos** *nm inv Med* tetanus

tetera *nf* teapot

tetero *nm Col Ven* baby's bottle

tetilla *nf* **(a)** *Anat* man's nipple **(b)** *(de biberón)* (rubber) teat **(c) queso de t.** = type of Galician cheese

tetina *nf* (rubber) teat

tetona *Fam* **1** *adj* buxom, busty
2 *nf* busty o buxom woman

tetrabrik® *(pl* **tetrabriks)** *nm* carton

tetralogía *nf* tetralogy

tetraplejía *nf* quadriplegia

tetrapléjico, -a *adj & nm,f* quadriplegic

tétrico, -a *adj* gloomy, dull, dismal

teutón, -ona 1 *adj* **(a)** *(alemán)* German **(b)** *Hist* Teutonic
2 *nm,f* **(a)** *(persona)* German **(b)** *Hist (persona)* Teuton

textil *adj & nm* textile

texto *nm* text ❏ **libro de t.** textbook; *Inform* **t. oculto** hidden text

textual *adj (gen)* textual; *(exacto)* literal; **en palabras textuales** literally

textualmente *adv* literally, word for word

textura *nf* **(a)** *Tex (trama)* texture **(b)** *(en minerales)* structure

tez *nf* complexion

thriller ['θriler] *(pl* **thrillers)** *nm* thriller

ti *pron pers* you; **es para ti** it's for you; **hazlo por ti** do it for your own sake; **lo digo por ti** I am thinking of you; **no sabía nada de ti** I hadn't heard anything from you; **piensas demasiado en ti mismo** you worry too much about yourself, you're always thinking about yourself; **por ti** because of you

tía *nf* **(a)** *(pariente)* aunt; **t. abuela** great-aunt; *Fig* **¡no hay tu t.!** nothing doing! **(b)** *Esp Fam (mujer)* girl, woman; **¡qué t.!** one hell of a woman!; **¡qué t. más imbécil!** what a stupid girl o woman!; **t. buena** gorgeous woman

tianguis *nm inv CAm Méx* open-air market

tiara *nf* tiara

tiarrón, -ona *nm,f Fam* hulk

Tíber *n* el T. the Tiber

Tibet *n* (**el**) **T.** Tibet

tibetano, -a 1 *adj* Tibetan
2 *nm,f (persona)* Tibetan
3 *nm (idioma)* Tibetan

tibia *nf Anat* tibia, shinbone

tibiarse *vpr CAm Ven Fam* to become annoyed o irritated

tibieza *nf (gen)* tepidness, lukewarmness; *Fig* lack of enthusiasm; *Fig* **acogió la victoria con t.** he didn't show any enthusiasm about their victory

tibio, -a *adj* **(a)** *(gen)* tepid, lukewarm; *Fig* **la obra obtuvo una tibia acogida** the play had a lukewarm reception; *Fam* **poner t. a algn** to pull sb to pieces **(b)** *Col Perú Ven (enojado)* annoyed, irritated

tiburón *nm* shark

tic *nm* **(a)** *Med* tic, twitch ❏ **t. nervioso** nervous tic o twitch **(b)** *Fig (mania)* habit

ticholo *nm Arg* small brick

tico, -a *nm,f Am Fam* Costa Rican

tictac *nm* tick-tock, ticking

tiempo *nm* **(a)** *(gen)* time; **a t.** in time; **a su (debido) t.** in due course; **a un t., al mismo t.** at the same time; **al poco t.** soon afterwards; **antes de t.** (too) early o soon; **con el t.** in time, with time; **con t.** in advance; **corre el t.** time flies; **¿cuánto t.?** how long?; **¿cuánto t. hace?** how long ago?; **dar t.** to give time; **¿nos da t. de llegar?** have we got (enough) time to get there?; **de un** o **algún t. a esta parte** for some time now; **demasiado t.** too long; **estar a t. de** to still have time to; **ganar t.** to save time; **hacer t.** to kill time; **perder (el) t.** to waste time; **sin perder t.** at once; **¿qué tal andamos de t.?** how are we doing for time?; **t. atrás** some time ago; **tómate el t. que quieras** take your time; **y si no, al t.** time will tell; *Fig* **dar t. al t.** to let matters take their course; *Fig* **pasar** o **matar (el) t.** to kill time ❏ **t. libre** spare time; *Dep* **t. muerto** time out; *Inform* **t. real** real time **(b)** *(época)* time, period, age; **a través de los tiempos** through the ages; **de t. inmemorial** from time immemorial; **en mis tiempos** in my time; **en otro(s) tiempo(s)** formerly; **eran tiempos difíciles** they were hard times; **¡qué tiempos aquéllos!** those were the days! **(c)** *(temporada)* season; **fuera de t.** *(fuera de temporada)* out of season; *Fig (inoportunamente)* at the wrong moment **(d)** *(meteorológico)* weather; **¿cómo está el t.?** what's the weather like?; **hace buen/mal t.** the weather is good/bad; *Fam Fig* **t. de perros** lousy weather **(e)** *(edad)* age; **¿cuánto** o **qué t. tiene su niño?** how old is your baby o child? **(f)** *Mús* movement, tempo, time **(g)** *Dep (parte, período)* half **(h)** *Ling (del verbo)* tense

tienda *nf* **(a)** *(establecimiento comercial)* shop, *US* store; **ir de tiendas** to go shopping ❏ **t. de alimentación** grocery store, *Br* grocer's (shop); *Méx* **t. de departamentos** department store; **t. virtual** online store o retailer **(b)** *(de campaña)* **t. (de campaña)** tent

tienta *nf* **a tientas** by touch; **andar a tientas** to feel one's way; **buscar (algo) a tientas** to grope (for sth)

tiento *nm* **(a)** *(prudencia)* caution; *(tacto)* tact; **con t.** tactfully **(b)** *(de ciego)* stick **(c)** *(pulso)* steady, hand **(d)** *Fam (trago)* swig; **dar** o **echar un t. a la botella** to take a swig from the bottle

tierno, -a *adj* **(a)** *(blando)* tender, soft **(b)** *(reciente)* fresh; *(persona)* young; **pan t.** fresh bread; **una tierna niña** an innocent young girl **(c)** *(cariñoso)* affectionate, loving; **¡qué niña más tierna!** isn't she a darling! **(d)** *Chile Ecuad (fruto)* unripe

tierra *nf* **(a)** *(superficie sólida)* land; **¡t. a la vista!** land ahoy!; **tocar t.** *Náut* to reach port; *Av* to touch down ❑ **T. del Fuego** Tierra del Fuego; **t. de nadie** noman's-land; **T. Santa** the Holy Land; **t. virgen** virgin land (**b**) *(suelo)* ground; **bajo t.** underground; **dar en t. con algo** to drop *o* throw sth on the ground; *Fig* **echar** *o* **tirar por t. planes** to spoil plans; *Fig* **echar t. encima de un asunto** to hush up an affair; *Fig* **poner t. por medio** to make oneself scarce; *Fig* **t. trágame** I wish the ground would open and swallow me up (**c**) *(materia inorgánica)* earth; *(para nutrir plantas)* soil; **un camino de t.** a dirt track (**d**) *(lugar de origen) (país)* homeland, native land; *(región)* home *o* native region; **vino/ queso de la t.** local wine/cheese ❑ **t. natal** homeland (**e**) *Agr (terreno cultivado)* land; **vivir de la t.** to make a living from the land (**f**) *Elec Br* earth, *US* ground (**g**) *(planeta)* **la T.** the Earth

tierral *nm Am* dust cloud

tieso, -a *adj* (**a**) *(rígido)* stiff, rigid; *(erguido)* upright, erect; **con las orejas tiesas** with its ears pricked up; *Fig* **quedarse t. de frío** to be frozen stiff; *Fam* **dejar t. a algn** *(pasmado)* to leave sb speechless; *(muerto)* to do sb in (**b**) *Fam (engreido)* stiff, starchy, full of oneself (**c**) *Fig (saludable)* in good shape

tiesto *nm* (**a**) *(maceta)* flowerpot (**b**) *Chile (vasija)* pot

tifoideo, -a *adj Med* typhoid

tifón *nm Meteor* (**a**) *(huracán)* typhoon (**b**) *(de agua)* waterspout

tifus *nm inv Med* typhus (fever)

tigre *nm* (**a**) *Zool* tiger (**b**) *Esp Fam (retrete)* *Br* bog, *US* john; *Fam* **oler a t.** to stink

tigresa *nf* (**a**) *Zool* tigress (**b**) *Fig (mujer)* femme fatale

tigrillo *nm Andes CAm Méx Ven (Felis pardalis)* ocelot; *(Felis wiedi)* margay; *(Felis tigrina)* oncilla, tiger cat

TIJ [tiχ] *nm (abrev de* **Tribunal Internacional de Justicia)** ICJ

tijera *nf (gen pl)* (pair of) scissors *pl*; **silla de t.** folding chair

tijereta *nf* (**a**) *Ent* earwig (**b**) *(en fútbol)* (overhead) bicycle kick (**c**) *Andes RP Orn* scissortail

tijeretazo *nm* snip

tila *nf* (**a**) *Bot (flor)* lime *o* linden blossom (**b**) *(infusión)* lime *o* linden blossom tea

tildar *vt* to call, brand; **me tildó de bobo** he called me stupid

tilde *nf* (**a**) *Impr (de la ñ)* tilde; *(acento ortográfico)* written accent (**b**) *Fig (defecto)* fault, flaw

tiliche *nm CAm Méx* trinket

tilico, -a *adj Bol Méx* skinny

tilín *nm (sonido)* ting-a-ling; *Fig* **José le hace t.** she fancies José

tilma *nf Méx* cotton blanket

tilo *nm* lime tree

timador, -a *nm,f* swindler, cheat

timar *vt* to swindle, cheat, trick; **me han timado mil euros** I was cheated out of a thousand euros; **me timó dos euros en el cambio** he shortchanged me by two euros

timba *nf* (**a**) *(garito)* gambling den (**b**) *(partida)* game *o* hand (of cards) (**c**) *CAm Méx Fam (barriga)* belly

timbal *nm* (**a**) *Mús* kettledrum; *(tamboril)* small drum (**b**) *Culin (empanada)* timbale, meat or fish pie

timbalero, -a *nm,f* kettle drummer

timbrado, -a 1 *pp de* **timbrar**
2 *adj* stamped; **papel t.** *(sellado)* stamped paper; *(con membrete)* letterheaded stationery

timbrar *vt (carta)* to stamp, mark; *(documento)* to seal

timbrazo *nm* loud *o* long ring; **dar un t.** to ring the bell

timbre *nm* (**a**) *(de la puerta)* bell; **tocar el t.** to ring the bell (**b**) *(sello) (de documentos)* (official) stamp; *(de impuestos)* seal; *CAm Méx (de correos)* stamp (**c**) *Mús (sonido)* timbre; **t. nasal** twang

timidez *nf* shyness, timidity

tímido, -a *adj* shy, timid; **hizo un t. intento** he made a half-hearted attempt

timo¹ *nm (estafa)* swindle, fiddle, confidence trick; **dar el** *o* **un t.** to cheat, swindle; **¡vaya t.!** what a rip off!; *Fam* **el t. de la estampita** a con trick

timo² *nm Anat* thymus

timón *nm* (**a**) *Náut Av* rudder; *Fig* **empuñar** *o* **llevar el t.** to be at the helm (**b**) *(del arado)* beam (**c**) *Andes Cuba Aut (de vehículo)* steering wheel

timonear *vi* to steer, be at the helm

timonel *nm Náut* steersman, helmsman

timorato, -a *adj* (**a**) *(tímido)* shy, timid (**b**) *(mojigato)* prudish

tímpano *nm* (**a**) *Anat* eardrum (**b**) *Arquit* tympanum (**c**) *Mús (timbal)* kettledrum; *(en orquesta)* timpani *pl*, timps *pl*

tina *nf* (**a**) *(tinaja)* earthenware vat (**b**) *(recipiente)* vat, tub (**c**) *(bañera)* bath, bathtub

tinaco *nm* (**a**) *Méx (tinaja)* (large) pitcher (**b**) *CAm Méx (depósito de agua)* water tank

tinaja *nf* (large) pitcher

tinerfeño, -a 1 *adj* of *o* from Tenerife
2 *nm,f* person from Tenerife

tinglado *nm* (**a**) *(cobertizo)* shed (**b**) *(tablado)* platform, raised floor (**c**) *Fig (embrollo)* mess; **¡menudo t. has armado!** what a terrible mess you've made! (**d**) *Fig (intriga)* intrigue; **¿qué t. se traen?** what's cooking then? (**e**) *Fig (mundillo)* setup, racket; **conocer el t.** to know the setup

tinieblas *nfpl* (**a**) *(oscuridad)* darkness *sing* (**b**) *Fig (ignorancia)* ignorance *sing*, confusion *sing*; **estar en t. (sobre algo)** to be in the dark (about sth)

tino *nm* (**a**) *(prudencia)* (common) sense, good judgement; *(moderación)* moderation; **con t.** wisely; **sacar de t. a algn** to make sb lose their temper, make sb mad; **sin t.** *(imprudentemente)* foolishly; *(sin moderación)* immoderately (**b**) *(puntería)* (good) aim; **tener buen t.** to be a good shot

tinta *nf* (**a**) *(gen)* ink; **escribir con t.** to write in ink; *Fig* **esto ha hecho correr mucha t.** much has been written about this; *Fig* **recargar** *o* **cargar las tintas** to exaggerate; *Fig* **saber algo de buena t.** to have got sth straight from the horse's mouth; *Fig* **sudar t.** to sweat blood ❑ **t. china** Indian ink; **t. simpática** invisible ink (**b**) **tintas** colours, hues; *Fig* **medias t.** ambiguities, half measures

tintar *vt* to dye

tinte *nm* (**a**) *(colorante)* dye; *(proceso)* dyeing (**b**) *(tintorería)* dry-cleaner's; **llevar algo al t.** to have sth dyed (**c**) *Fig (matiz)* shade, colouring, *US* coloring; **una novela con tintes religiosos** a novel with religious overtones (**d**) *Fig (apariencia)* veneer, gloss; **un hombre con un t. de erudición** a man with a touch of learning about him

tintero *nm* inkpot, ink well; *Fig* **se quedó en el t.** it wasn't said

tintinear *vi* (**a**) *(vidrio)* to clink, chink (**b**) *(campanillas)* to jingle, tinkle

tintineo *nm* (**a**) *(de vidrio)* clink, clinking, chink (**b**) *(de campanillas)* jingling, ting-a-ling

tinto 1 *adj* (**a**) *(vino)* red (**b**) *Col Ven (café)* black (**c**) *(teñido)* dyed; *Literario* **t. en sangre** bloodstained
2 *nm (vino)* red wine

tintorera *nf (pez)* blue shark

tintorería *nf* dry-cleaner's

tintorero, -a *nm,f* dry-cleaner

tintorro *nm Fam* cheap red wine, *Br* red plonk

tintura *nf* (a) *(colorante)* dye (b) *(proceso)* dyeing (c) *Farm Quím* tincture ◻ **t. de yodo** iodine

tiña *nf* (a) *Med* tinea, ringworm (b) *Fig (mezquindad)* meanness, stinginess (c) *Fig (pobreza)* misery, poverty

tiñoso, -a *adj* (a) *Med* scabby, mangey, mangy (b) *Fam (mezquino)* mean, stingy

tío *nm* (a) *(pariente)* uncle; **mis tíos** my uncle and aunt; **t. abuelo** great-uncle (b) *Fam* guy, *Br* bloke; **¡eres un t. (grande)!** you're a great guy!; **t. bueno** hunk; **¿vale, t.?** *Br* O.K. mate?, *US* get it man?

tiovivo *nm* merry-go-round, *US* carousel

tiparraco *nm Fam* idiot, twerp

tipazo *nm Fam* good figure

tipear *vt & vi Am* to type

tipejo *nm Fam* idiot, twerp

típico, -a *adj* (a) *(característico)* typical, characteristic; **eso es t. de María** that's just like María; **¡lo t.!** the same old thing! (b) *(de interés turístico)* traditional, picturesque; **un plato t.** a traditional o local dish

tipificación *nf* (a) *(normalización)* standardization (b) *(caracterización)* typification

tipificar [59] *vt* (a) *(normalizar)* to standardize (b) *(caracterizar)* to typify

tipismo *nm* local colour o *US* color, picturesqueness

tiple 1 *nm (voz)* treble, soprano

2 *nmf (persona)* soprano (singer)

tipo¹ *nm* (a) *(clase)* type, kind; **todo t. de** all kind o kinds of; **un nuevo t. de tren** a new type of train (b) *Fin* rate ◻ **t. bancario** o **de descuento** bank rate; **t. de cambio/interés** rate of exchange/interest (c) *Anat (de hombre)* build, physique; *(de mujer)* figure; **tiene buen t.** *(hombre)* he's well-built; *(mujer)* she's got a good figure; *Fig* **aguantar el t.** to keep cool o calm; *Fig* **dar el t.** to fit a description o the bill; *Fig* **jugarse el t.** to risk one's neck (d) *Impr* type

tipo, -a² *nm,f Fam (hombre)* guy, *Br* bloke; *(mujer)* woman; *(mujer joven)* girl; **t. raro** weirdo

tipografía *nf también Inform* typography

tipográfico, -a *adj* typographic, typographical; **error t.** printing error

tipógrafo, -a *nm,f* typographer

tipología *nf* typology

tíquet *(pl* **tíquets)** *nm (billete)* ticket; *(recibo)* receipt

tiquismiquis *Fam* **1** *nmf inv* fusspot; **ser un t.** to be a fusspot

2 *nmpl* (a) *(escrúpulos)* silly scruples; **andarse con t.** to be fussy (b) *(rencillas)* bickering *sing;* **andarse con t.** to be squabbling

tira 1 *nf* (a) *(banda, cinta)* strip; *(tirante)* strap (b) *(de dibujos)* **t. cómica** comic strip (c) *Fam* **la t.** a lot, loads *pl;* **había la t. de gente** there were hundreds of people; **hace la t. que no la veo** I haven't seen her for yonks

2 *nm* **hubo un t. y afloja entre las dos partes** there was a lot of hard bargaining between the two sides

tirabeque *nm Br* mangetout, *US* snow pea

tirabuzón *nm* (a) *(rizo)* ringlet (b) *(sacacorchos)* corkscrew

tirachinas *nm inv Br* catapult, *US* slingshot

tirada *nf* (a) *Impr (impresión)* printing; *(edición)* edition; **t. reducida** limited edition (b) *(distancia)* stretch; **hay una buena t. hasta el pueblo** it's a good few miles to the village (c) *(serie)* (long) series *sing;* **de/en una t.** in one go

tirado, -a 1 *pp de* **tirar**

2 *adj Fam* (a) *(precio)* dirt cheap (b) *(problema, asunto)* dead easy (c) *(abandonado)* **dejar t. a algn** to let sb down

tirador, -a 1 *nm,f (persona)* shooter, marksman; **es un buen t.** he is a good shot

2 *nm* (a) *(de puerta, cajón)* knob, handle; *(cordón)* bell pull (b) *Bol RP* **tiradores** *(para pantalones) Br* braces, *US* suspenders

tiraje *nm Impr* (a) *(impresión)* printing (b) *(distribución)* circulation

tiralíneas *nm inv* tracer, drawing o ruling pen

Tirana *n* Tiranë, Tirana

tiranía *nf* tyranny

tiránico, -a *adj* tyrannic, tyrannical

tiranizar [14] *vt* to tyrannize

tirano, -a *nm,f* tyrant

tirante 1 *adj (tenso)* tight, taut; *Fig* **estar t. con algn** to be at odds with sb; *Fig* **una situación/relación t.** a tense situation/relationship

2 *nm* (a) *Cost (gen pl)* strap (b) *Téc* brace, stay (c) *(de caballería)* trace (d) *Arquit* tie (beam)

tirantez *nf* (a) *(tensión)* tightness, tautness (b) *Fig (de una situación, relación)* tension, strain

tirar 1 *vt* (a) *(echar)* to throw, fling; **¡tírame la pelota!** throw me the ball!; **t. una moneda al aire** to toss a coin (b) *(dejar caer)* to drop; **cuidado, no lo tires** be careful you don't drop it (c) *(desechar)* to throw away; **estos zapatos están para tirarlos** these shoes have had it; *Fig* **t. (el) dinero** to waste o squander money (d) *(derribar)* to knock down; *(líquido)* to spill; *(casa, árbol)* to pull down; **t. la puerta (abajo)** to smash the door in; **t. un vaso/una botella** to knock a glass/bottle over (e) *Impr* to print; **esta revista tira millones de ejemplares** this magazine has a circulation of millions (f) *(hacer) (foto)* to take; *(línea, plano)* to draw (g) *(tiro)* to fire; *(cohete)* to launch; *(bomba)* to drop (h) *(dar) (beso)* to blow; *Ftb (saque)* to take

2 *vi* (a) *(cuerda, puerta)* **t. de** to pull; **t. de una carreta** to draw a cart; *Fig* **tira y afloja** give and take, compromise (b) *(chimenea, estufa)* to draw; **esta estufa no tira** this stove doesn't draw very well (c) *(en juegos)* to have one's move; **tiras tú** it's your move o turn (d) *(funcionar)* to work, run; **¿aún tira tu coche?** does your car still work? (e) *(persona)* to manage, get by o along; **ir tirando** *(espabilarse)* to manage; *(tener buena salud)* to be okay; **yo tiraría con la mitad de lo que tú ganas** I'd make do with half the money you earn (f) *(durar)* to last; **estas cortinas aún tirarán otro año** these curtains will last another year; *Fam* **a todo t.** at the most o latest (g) *(tender)* **t. a** to tend towards; **tira a salado** it's a bit (too) salty (h) *(parecerse)* **t. a** to take after; **tira a su madre** he takes after his mother (i) *(ir)* to go, turn; **tirad a la izquierda y luego todo derecho** turn left and then go straight on; **¡venga, tira ya!** come on, get going!; *Fig* **t. para** to be attracted to; **su hijo también tira para negociante** his son is also attracted to business (j) *(disparar)* to shoot, fire (k) *(sacar, usar)* **t. de** to pull out; **tiró de cartera y nos invitó a todos** he pulled out his wallet and paid for all of us

3 tirarse *vpr* (a) *(lanzarse)* to throw o hurl oneself; **se tiró al agua de cabeza** he dived into the water (b) *(tumbarse)* to lie down (c) *(tiempo)* to spend; **me tiré una hora esperando** I waited (for) a good hour (d) *Vulg (fornicar)* to screw, fuck; **t. a algn** to lay sb

tirita *nf Br* (sticking) plaster, *US* Band-aid®

tiritar *vi* to shiver, shake

tiritona *nf,* **tiritera** *nf* **le dio una t.** he had a fit of shivering

tiro *nm* (a) *(lanzamiento)* throw; **errar el t.** to miss the mark, fail; *Ftb* **t. a gol**, *Am* **t. al arco** shot at goal (**b**) *(disparo, ruido)* shot; **a t.** *(de arma)* within range; *(a mano)* within reach; **dar** o **pegar un t.** to shoot, fire a shot; **pegarse un t.** to shoot oneself; *Fig* **le salió el t. por la culata** it backfired on him; *Fam Fig* **me sentó como un t.** *(hecho)* I felt awful; *(comida)* it made me feel really ill; *Fam Fig* **ni a tiros** not for love or money ❏ **t. al blanco** target shooting; **t. al plato** trapshooting; **t. con arco** archery (**c**) *(galería de tiro)* shooting gallery (**d**) *Cost (de vestido)* shoulder width; *Fig* **de tiros largos** all dressed up (**e**) *(caballerías)* team; **animal de t.** draught animal (**f**) *(de chimenea)* draught, *US* draft; *Min* **t. de mina** mineshaft (**g**) *(de escaleras)* flight

tiroideo, -a *adj* thyroid; **glándula tiroidea** thyroid (gland)

tiroides 1 *adj* thyroid
   2 *nm inv* thyroid (gland)

Tirol *n* (el) **T.** the Tyrol

tirolés, -esa *adj* & *nm,f* Tyrolese, Tyrolean

tirón *nm* pull, tug; **darle un t. de orejas a algn** to tweak sb's ear; *Fam* **de un t.** in one go; *Argot* **dar el t.** to snatch sb's handbag

tironear *vt* to tug (at)

tiroteo *nm* shooting, firing to and fro

Tirreno *n* (Mar) **T.** Tyrrhenian Sea

tirria *nf Fam* dislike; **le tengo t.** I dislike him, I can't stand him

tisana *nf Culin* infusion, tisane

tísico, -a *Med* **1** *adj* tubercular, consumptive
   2 *nm,f* consumptive

tisis *nf inv Med* tuberculosis, consumption

tisú *(pl* tisús) *nm Tex* gold or silver lamé

titán *nm Mit* titan

titánico, -a *adj Mit* titanic

titanio *nm Min* titanium

títere *nm* (**a**) *(marioneta)* puppet, marionette; *Fig* **no dejaron t. con cabeza** no one was spared; *Fig* **no quedó t. con cabeza** everything was upside down (**b**) *Fig (persona)* puppet, dupe

titi *nf Fam Br* bird, *US* broad; **¡hola, t.!** ¡hello gorgeous!

tití *nm (mono)* titi, = small monkey common in Central and South America

titilar *vi* (**a**) *(temblar)* to quiver (**b**) *(luz)* to flicker; *(estrella)* to twinkle

titileo *nm* (**a**) *(temblor)* quivering (**b**) *(de luz)* flickering; *(de estrella)* twinkling

titiritar *vi* to tremble, shiver

titiritero, -a *nm,f* (**a**) *(que maneja títeres)* puppeteer (**b**) *(acróbata ambulante)* travelling o *US* traveling acrobat

titubeante *adj* (**a**) *(indeciso)* hesitant (**b**) *(que se tambalea)* staggering, shaky (**c**) *(al hablar)* stammering

titubear *vi* (**a**) *(dudar)* to hesitate, waver (**b**) *(tambalearse)* to stagger, shake, totter (**c**) *(tartamudear)* to stammer

titubeo *nm* (**a**) *(duda)* hesitation; **sin t.** decisively (**b**) *(temblor)* stagger, staggering, tottering (**c**) *(tartamudeo)* stammering

titulación *nf Educ* qualifications *pl*

titulado, -a 1 *pp de* titular[2]
   2 *adj Educ (licenciado)* graduate; *(diplomado)* qualified

titular[1] 1 *adj* appointed, official; **jugador/juez t.** official player/judge
   2 *nmf (persona)* (office) holder; *Educ* **el t. de cátedra** the professor; *Pol* **el t. de la cartera** the minister
   3 *nm Prensa* headline

titular[2] 1 *vt (poner título)* to call; **¿cómo se titula?** what is it called?

2 titularse *vpr* (**a**) *(tener título)* to be called (**b**) *Educ* to graduate (**en** in)

titularidad *nf* entitlement

título 1 *nm* (**a**) *(de obra)* title ❏ *Cin* **títulos de crédito** credits (**b**) *Educ (licenciatura)* degree; *(diploma)* certificate, diploma, **tener los títulos necesarios** to have the necessary qualifications; (**c**) *(de derecho, obligación) (documento)* deed ❏ **t. de nobleza** title; **t. de propiedad** deeds *pl*; **t. nobiliario** title (**d**) *Fin* security ❏ **t. de deuda pública** government bond, *Br* gilt
   2 a título *loc prep* **a t. individual** on an individual basis; **a t. de amigo** as a friend

tiza *nf* chalk; **una t.** a piece of chalk

tiznado, -a 1 *pp de* tiznar
   2 *adj* sooty, blackened

tiznadura *nf* soot mark, smudge

tiznar 1 *vt* to blacken, soil with soot
   2 tiznarse *vpr* (**a**) *(ponerse negro)* to get blackened (**b**) *Arg (emborracharse)* to get drunk

tizne *nm* soot

tizón *nm* half-burnt stick, brand; *Fig* **negro como un t.** as black as soot o coal

tlapalería *nf Méx* hardware shop

TLC *nm (abrev de* **Tratado de Libre Comercio**) NAFTA

toalla *nf* towel; *Fig* **arrojar** o **tirar la t.** to throw in the towel ❏ *Am* **t. higiénica** *Br* sanitary towel, *US* sanitary napkin

toallero *nm Br* towel rail, *US* towel bar

toallita *nf* (**a**) *(para la cara)* face cloth (**b**) *(refrescante)* towelette (**c**) *(para bebés)* baby o wet wipe

Tobago *n* Tobago

tobera *nf Téc* tuyère, twyer; *Av* nozzle

tobillera *nf* ankle sock o support

tobillo *nm* ankle

tobogán *nm* (**a**) *(para niños, mercancías)* slide, chute (**b**) *(trineo bajo)* toboggan, sledge

toca *nf (sombrero)* headdress; *(de monja)* wimple

tocadiscos *nm inv* record player

tocado[1] *nm* (**a**) *(peinado)* coiffure, hairdo (**b**) *(prenda)* headdress

tocado, -a[2] *adj* (**a**) *(fruta)* bad, rotten (**b**) *Fam (perturbado)* crazy, touched; **t. de la cabeza** touched, not all there (**c**) *Dep* injured

tocador *nm* (**a**) *(mueble)* dressing table; **artículos de t.** toiletries (**b**) *(habitación)* dressing room, boudoir; **t. de señoras** powder room

tocamientos *nmpl* (**a**) *Jur* sexual assault *sing* (**b**) *Euf (masturbación)* touching oneself *sing*

tocante: en lo tocante a *loc adv* regarding

tocar[1] [59] **1** *vt* (**a**) *(gen)* to touch; **por favor no t. la mercancía** please do not handle the goods; **tócalo y verás que suave es** feel it, you'll see how soft it is; *Fig* **me has tocado el corazón** you've touched my heart; *Fig* **no ha tocado ni una coma** he hasn't changed a single comma; *Fam Fig* **toca madera** touch wood (**b**) *(revolver)* to play with, mess about with; **no toques mis cosas** stop fiddling with my things (**c**) *(instrumento, canción)* to play; *(timbre, campanas)* to ring; *(bocina)* to blow, honk; *Mil (diana)* to sound (**d**) *Dep (diana)* to hit; *(en esgrima)* to touch (**e**) *(mencionar)* to touch on; **mejor no t. el tema** let's keep off the subject (**f**) *(afectar)* to concern; **me toca muy de cerca** I'm deeply affected by it; **por lo que a mí me toca** as far as I am concerned

2 *vi* (**a**) *(corresponder)* to be one's turn; **¿a quién le toca jugar/fregar?** whose turn is it to play/do the washing up?

(b) *(caer en suerte)* to win; **¿a cuánto tocamos?** how much did we win?; **le tocó el gordo** *o* **el primer premio** he won the first prize; **le tocó la mili en Málaga** he was posted to Málaga (for his military service) **(c)** *(tener que)* **nos tocó salir a arreglarlo** we had to go out and fix it **(d)** *Av Náut* to call **(en** at), stop over **(en** at) **(e)** *(entrar en contacto)* to touch; **t. con** to be next to; **t. en** to border on; *Fig* **t. a su fin** to be coming to an end **(f)** *(llamar)* **t. a la puerta** to knock at *o* on the door

3 tocarse *vpr* **(a)** *(a uno mismo)* to touch oneself; **t. la nariz** to pick one's nose **(b)** *(una cosa con otra)* to touch each *o* one other; *Fig* **los extremos se tocan** the ends touch one another

tocar² **1** *vt (peinar)* to do the hair of
2 tocarse *vpr (cubrirse)* to cover one's head

tocata **1** *nf Mús* toccata
2 *nm Fam* record player

tocateja: a tocateja *loc adv (pagar)* up front in cash

tocayo, -a *nm,f* namesake

tocho *nm* **(a)** *(hierro)* iron ingot **(b)** *Fam (libro) (grande)* tome; *(aburrido)* boring book

tocinería *nf* pork butcher's

tocino *nm Culin* lard □ **t. ahumado** smoked bacon; **t. de cielo** = sweet made with egg yolk; **t. entreverado** streaky bacon

tocología *nf* obstetrics *sing*

tocólogo, -a *nm Med* tocologist, obstetrician

tocón¹ *nm Bot* stump

tocón, -ona² *nm,f Fam* groper; **ser un t.** to have wandering hands

tocuyo *nm Am Tex* coarse cotton cloth

todavía *adv* **(a)** *(a pesar de ello)* still; **¿y t. te quejas?** and you're still not satisfied? **(b)** *(tiempo)* yet, still; **no mires t.** don't look yet; **t. la quiere** he still loves her; **t. no** not yet **(c)** *(para reforzar)* even, still; **esto t. te gustará más** you'll like *o* enjoy this even more; **t. más/menos** even more/less

todito, -a *adj Fam* all

todo, -a **1** *adj* **(a)** *(sin excluir nada)* all; **t. el mundo** (absolutely) everybody; *Fam* **t. quisqui** *o* **Cristo** *o* **Dios** every Tom, Dick and Harry **(b)** *(entero)* complete, thorough; **es toda una mujer** she is every inch a woman **(c)** *(igual)* (exactly) like; **es t. su padre** he's the image of his father **(d)** *todos (cada)* every; **t. los martes** every Tuesday
2 *nm* **(a)** *(totalidad)* whole
3 *pron* **(a)** *(sin excluir nada)* all, everything; **ante t.** *(sobre todo)* above all; *(en primer lugar)* first of all; **con t.** in spite of everything; **del t.** completely; **después de t.** after all; **eso es t.** that's all, that's it; **estar en t.** to be really with it; **hay de t.** there are all sorts; **lo sé t.** I know all about it; **t. lo contrario** quite the contrary *o* opposite; **t. lo más** at the most; **t. son desgracias para nosotros** we have nothing but misfortune; *Fam* **fue t. uno** it all happened at once; *Fam* **no tenerlas todas consigo** not to be all there; *Fam* **ser t. uno** to be all the same (thing); *Esp* **t. a cien** *(tienda) Br* ≃ pound shop, *US* ≃ nickel-and-dime store **(b)** *(cualquiera)* anybody; **t. aquél** *o* **el que quiera** anybody who wants (to) **(c)** *todos (cada uno)* everybody; **t. salieron perdiendo** they all came off worse
4 *adv* completely, totally; **volvió t. sucio** he was all dirty when he got back

todopoderoso, -a *adj* all-powerful, almighty; **el T.** the Almighty

todoterreno *nm* four-wheel drive, all-terrain vehicle

toga *nf* **(a)** *(de magistrado)* gown, robe **(b)** *Hist* toga

togado, -a **1** *adj* **(a)** *(magistrados)* robed **(b)** *Hist* toga(ed
2 *nm* gentleman of the robe, lawyer

Togo *n* Togo

togolés, -esa *adj & nm,f* Togolese

toilette [twa'let] *(pl* **toilettes) 1** *nm CSur* toilet, lavatory
2 *nf Anticuado* **hacerse la t.** to perform one's toilet(te) *o* ablutions

toisón *nm* fleece; **Orden del T. de Oro** Order of the Golden Fleece

Tokio *n* Tokyo

toldería *nf Am* Indian camp

toldillo *nm Col (para mosquitos)* mosquito *o* fly net

toldo *nm (cubierta)* awning; *(de camión)* tilt, canvas; *(en la playa)* sunshade

toledano, -a 1 *adj* of *o* from Toledo; *Fam* **pasar una noche toledana** to toss and turn all night
2 *nm,f* person from Toledo

tolerable *adj* tolerable

tolerado, -a 1 *pp de* **tolerar**
2 *adj* allowed, tolerated; *Cin Teat* **espectáculo t. para menores** entertainment suitable for children

tolerancia *nf (gen)* tolerance; *(resistencia)* resistance

tolerante *adj* tolerant, lenient

tolerar *vt* to tolerate; *(inconvenientes)* to stand; *(gente)* to put up with; *(comida, bebida)* to take; *(peso)* to bear; **no tolero el desorden** I can't stand untidiness

tolete *nm CAm Carib Col Méx* cudgel, club

tolva *nf* hopper

toma *nf* **(a)** *(acción)* taking □ **t. de agua** outlet, tap; **t. de aire** intake, inlet; *Elec* **t. de corriente** plug, socket; **t. de posesión** takeover; **t. de tierra** *Elec Br* earth, *US* ground; *Av* landing, touchdown **(b)** *Med* dose **(c)** *Mil* capture **(d)** *(grabación)* recording **(e)** *Cin* take, shot **(f)** *Col (cauce)* irrigation ditch **(g)** *Chile (presa)* dam

tomacorriente *nm Am* power point, socket

tomado, -a 1 *pp de* **tomar**
2 *adj* **(a)** *(voz)* hoarse; **tener la voz tomada** to have a hoarse voice **(b)** *Am (borracho)* drunk

tomador, -a *Andes PRico RP* **1** *adj* drinking
2 *nm,f* (heavy) drinker, drunkard

tomadura *nf* taking; *Fam Fig* **t. de pelo** *(engaño)* hoax; *(burla)* tease; *(timo)* rip-off

tomar **1** *vt* **(a)** *(agarrar, recibir)* to take; **me tomó de la cintura** he put his hands round my waist; **toma** here (you are); **toma la primera a la derecha** take the first on the right; **t. decisiones** to make *o* take decisions; **t. a algn de la mano** to take *o* hold sb's hand; **t. el autobús/tren** to catch the bus/train; **t. el sol** *Am* **t. sol** to sunbathe; **t. la palabra** to speak; *Av* **t. tierra** to land; **t. un taxi** to take a taxi; *Fig* **t. las de Villadiego** to beat it; *Fam* **¡toma!** *(sorpresa)* fancy that!; *(enfado)* it serves you right!; *Fam* **¡toma castaña!** take that!; *Fam* **tomarla con algn** to have it in for sb; *Fam Fig* **toma y daca** give and take **(b)** *(ingerir)* *(alimento, medicina, droga)* to take; **¿qué quieres t.?** *(beber)* what would you like (to drink)?; *Esp (comer)* what would you like (to eat)? **(c)** *Mil* to take; **t. una plaza** to capture a position **(d)** *(adquirir)* to acquire; **t. afecto** *o* **cariño a** to become fond of; **t. la costumbre de** to get into the habit of **(e)** *(aceptar)* to accept; **lo toma o lo deja** take it or leave it **(f)** *(entender)* to take; **t. algo a mal** to take sth badly; **t. algo en serio/broma** to take sth seriously/as a joke **(g)** *(considerar)* to take *(por* for); **me tomó por mi hermano** he took me for my brother

2 *vi* **(a)** *(encaminarse)* to go; **t. hacia la derecha** to turn right **(b)** *Am (beber alcohol)* to drink

3 tomarse *vpr* **(a)** *(tiempo, vacaciones, día libre)* to take; **t. la molestia de** to take the trouble to **(b)** *(comer)* to eat; *(beber)* to drink; **¿te has tomado la medicina?** have you taken your medicine? (**c**) *(reaccionar a, interpretar)* to take; **tómatelo con calma** take it easy; **tomarse algo bien/(a) mal** to take sth well/badly; **era una broma, no te lo tomes a mal** it was a joke, don't take it the wrong way; **tomarse algo en serio/a broma** to take sth seriously/as a joke

tomate *nm* (**a**) *Bot* tomato; *(salsa)* tomato sauce; *(de botella)* ketchup, catsup; *Fig* **ponerse como un t.** to go as red as a *Br* beetroot *o US* beet (**b**) *Fam (jaleo)* fuss, commotion; **se armó un buen t.** there was a right to-do (**c**) *Fam (dificultad)* snag, catch; **parece fácil pero tiene t.** it looks easy but there's a catch to it

tomatera *nf* tomato plant

tomavistas *nm inv* cine *o US* movie camera

tómbola *nf* tombola

tomillo *nm* thyme

tomo *nm* volume; *Fam* **de t. y lomo** utter, out-and-out

ton *nm* **sin t. ni son** without rhyme or reason

tonada *nf* (**a**) *Mús* tune, song (**b**) *Am (acento)* accent

tonadilla *nf Mús* ditty, little tune

tonadillero, -a *nm,f* ditty writer *o* singer

tonal *adj* tonal

tonalidad *nf* tonality

tonel *nm* barrel, cask; *Fam Fig* **como un t.** as fat as a pig

tonelada *nf* ton; **t. métrica** tonne, metric ton

tonelaje *nm* tonnage

tonelería *nf* (**a**) *(fabricación)* cooperage, barrel-making (**b**) *(tienda)* barrel shop

tonelero, -a 1 *adj* barrel, cask
2 *nm,f* cooper, barrel-maker

tóner *nm* toner

Tonga *n* Tonga

tongo *nm Box* fix; **hubo t. en el combate** the fight was fixed

tónica *nf* (**a**) *(tendencia)* tendency, trend; **t. general** overall trend (**b**) *(bebida)* tonic (water) (**c**) *Mús* tonic

tónico, -a 1 *adj* (**a**) *Ling* tonic, stressed (**b**) *Mús Med* tonic
2 *nm Med* tonic; *(cosmético)* skin tonic

tonificación *nf* invigoration

tonificante *adj* invigorating

tonificar [59] *vt* to tone up, invigorate

tonillo *nm* (**a**) *(sonsonete)* drone, monotone (**b**) *(deje)* accent, lilt (**c**) *(retintín)* sarcastic tone

tono *nm* tone; **a t. con** in tune *o* harmony with; **bajar de t.** *o* **el t.** to lower one's voice; *Fig (críticas)* to tone down; **dar el t.** to set the tone; **subir de t.** *o* **el t.** to raise one's voice, speak louder; *Mús* **t. mayor/menor** major/minor key; **un t. alto/bajo** a high/low pitch; *Fig* **darse t.** to put on airs; *Fig* **de (buen) t.** *(elegante)* elegant, stylish; *(cortés)* gentlemanly; *Fig* **de mal t.** vulgar; *Fig* **fuera de t.** inappropriate, out of place; *Fig* **sin venir a t.** for no good reason; *Fig* **usa otro t. conmigo** don't use *o* take that tone with me

tontada *nf Fam* (**a**) *(bobada)* silly thing, nonsense (**b**) *(insignificancia)* trifle

tontaina *Fam* **1** *adj* foolish, silly
2 *nmf* fool, nitwit

tontear *vi* (**a**) *(hacer el tonto)* to fool about (**b**) *(galantear)* to flirt

tontería *nf* (**a**) *(calidad de tonto)* stupidity, silliness (**b**) *(dicho, hecho)* silly *o* stupid thing; **decir tonterías** to talk nonsense; **déjate de tonterías** be serious (**c**) *(insignificancia)* trifle; **cómprale una t.** get her a little something

tonto, -a 1 *adj* silly, dumb; **¡qué t. (soy)!** silly me!; *Fam* **ponerse t.** to get stroppy
2 *nm,f* fool, idiot; **hacer el t.** to act the fool; **hacerse el t.** to play dumb; **t. de remate** *o* **de capirote** prize idiot

tontuna *nf Fam* silliness

top *(pl* **tops***) nm (prenda)* top

topacio *nm Min* topaz

topar 1 *vi* (**a**) *(chocar)* to bump; **t. con algo** to come across sth; **t. con algn** to bump into sb; **t. con una dificultad** to come up against a difficulty; **t. con un problema** to run into a problem (**b**) *Andes Méx (en juego)* to wager, bet
2 toparse *vpr* **toparse con** *(persona)* to bump into; *(cosa)* to come across; **se toparon con la policía** they ran into the police

tope 1 *adj* (**a**) *(máximo)* top, maximum; **fecha t.** deadline; **precio t.** top price (**b**) *Esp Fam (fantástico)* fab, *Br* brill; **¡t.! smashing!**
2 *nm* (**a**) *(límite)* limit, end; *Fig* **estar hasta los topes** to be full up; *Fam* **a t.** *(al máximo)* flat out; *(genial)* terrific (**b**) *Téc* stop, check; **t. de puerta** doorstop (**c**) *Ferroc* buffer
3 *adv Esp Fam (muy)* mega, really

topetada *nf*, **topetazo** *nm* butt, bump; **al caernos nos dimos una t.** we fell and bumped into each other

tópico, -a 1 *adj Med Farm* for external use; **uso t.** external use
2 *nm* commonplace, cliché

topless [ˈtoples] *nm inv* topless sunbathing; **en t.** topless; **hacer t.** to go topless

topo *nm* (**a**) *Zool* mole; *Fig* **más ciego que un t.** as blind as a bat (**b**) *(infiltrado)* mole (**c**) *Esp (lunar en tela)* polka dot (**d**) *Col (pendiente)* ear stud

topografía *nf* topography

topográfico, -a *adj* topographic, topographical

topógrafo, -a *nm,f* topographer

topología *nf* topology

toponimia *nf* (**a**) *Ling* toponymy (**b**) *(conjunto de nombres)* place names *pl*

toponímico, -a *adj* toponymic, toponymical

topónimo *nm* place name

toque *nm* (**a**) *(acto)* touch; **dar el último t.** to put the finishing touch; **t. de atención** warning (note); *Ftb* **t. de balón** ball control; *Fam* **dar un t. a algn** *(llamar)* to give sb a shout; *(llamar la atención)* to take sb to task (**b**) *(sonido) (de campanas)* peal, pealing, ringing; *(de trompetas)* blare, sounding; *(de sirena)* hoot; *(de claxon)* honk ▫ **t. de alarma** alarm signal; *Fam* warning; *Mil* **t. de diana** reveille; **t. de difuntos** death knell; **t. de queda** curfew; *Mil* **t. de retreta** tattoo

toquetear *vt* (**a**) *(manosear)* to fiddle with, finger (**b**) *(acariciar)* to fondle

toqueteo *nm* (**a**) *(manoseo)* fiddling, handling (**b**) *(caricias)* fondling, petting

toquilla *nf* (knitted) shawl

torácico, -a *adj Anat* thoracic

tórax *nm Anat* thorax

torbellino *nm* (**a**) *(de viento)* whirlwind (**b**) *Fig (confusión)* whirl, turmoil; **un t. de ideas** a brainstorm (**c**) *(persona)* whirlwind; **eres un t.** you're a real live wire

torcaz *adj Orn* **paloma t.** ringdove, wood pigeon

torcedura *nf* (**a**) *(acción)* twist, twisting (**b**) *Med* sprain

torcer [15] *vt* (**a**) *(gen) (cuerda, hilo)* to twist; *Med* to sprain; *Fig* **no dar su brazo a t.** not to give in; *Fig* **t. el gesto** to look cross (**b**) *(doblar) (metal)* to bend; *(madera)* to warp; *Fig* **t. la esquina** to turn the corner (**c**) *(inclinar) (cuadro)* to slant; **está torcido** it's crooked *o* lopsided (**d**) *(desviar) (el curso)* to change; *(significado)* to distort; *Fig (a algn)* to corrupt, pervert; **t. la vista** to look away

2 *vi* to turn *(left o right)*

3 torcerse *vpr* **(a)** *(doblarse)* to twist, bend **(b)** *Med (tobillo, mano)* to sprain **(c)** *(plan)* to fall through **(d)** *(empeorar)* to take a turn for the worse

torcido, -a 1 *pp de* **torcer**

2 *adj* **(a)** *(que no es recto)* twisted; **lleva la corbata torcida** his tie is crooked **(b)** *(madera)* warped; *(metal)* bent **(c)** *Med* sprained, strained **(d)** *(ladeado)* slanted, crooked, lopsided **(e)** *Guat (desafortunado)* unfortunate

tordo, -a 1 *adj* dapple-grey

2 *nm Orn* thrush; *Arg CAm Chile (estornino)* starling

toreador, -a *nm,f* bullfighter

torear 1 *vt Taur* to fight; *Fam* **t. a algn** to tease o confuse sb; *Fam* **t. un asunto** to tackle a matter skilfully

2 *vi Taur* to fight; **torea bien** he is a good bullfighter

toreo *nm* bullfighting; *Fam* **¡se acabó el t.!** no more fooling around!

torera *nf (chaquetilla)* bolero (jacket); *Fam Fig* **saltarse algo a la t.** to ignore sth completely, pay no heed to sth

torero, -a *Taur* **1** *adj* = of o relating to bullfighting

2 *nm,f* bullfighter, matador

toril *nm* bullpen *(in bullring)*

torito *nm* **(a)** *RP (insecto)* rhinoceros beetle **(b)** *Ecuad (flor)* = variety of orchid **(c)** *Chile (sombrajo)* awning **(d)** *Cuba (pez)* horned boxfish o trunkfish

tormenta *nf Meteor* storm □ **t. de ideas** brainstorming session; **t. de nieve** snowstorm

tormento *nm* **(a)** *(tortura)* torture, torment **(b)** *(padecimiento)* intense suffering, tribulation; *Fam* **ser un t.** to be torture

tormentoso, -a *adj* stormy

tornado *nm Meteor* tornado

tornar *Fml* **1** *vt* **(a)** *(devolver)* to give back, return **(b)** *(convertir)* to transform, turn; **tornó el agua en vino** he turned the water into wine

2 *vi* **(a)** *(regresar)* to return, go back; **t. en sí** to regain consciousness **(b)** *(volver a hacer)* **t. a** to do over, repeat; **t. a leer** to read again

3 tornarse *vpr* to become, turn; **se tornó fiero** it became wild

tornas *nfpl* **volver las t.** to turn the tables

tornasol *nm* **(a)** *Bot* sunflower **(b)** *(colorante)* litmus **(c)** *(irisación)* iridescence

tornasolado, -a *adj* iridescent

torneado, -a 1 *pp de* **tornear**

2 *adj* **(a)** *Téc* lathed, turned on the lathe **(b)** *(cuerpo)* shapely, with soft curves

3 *nm Téc* turning

tornear *vt Téc* to turn

torneo *nm* **(a)** *Hist* tournament **(b)** *Dep* tournament, *US* tourney

tornero, -a *nm,f* turner, lathe operator

tornillo *nm* screw, bolt; *Fam Fig* **apretarle los tornillos a algn** to put the screws on sb; *Fam Fig* **te falta un t.** you've got a screw loose □ **t. de banco** vice, *US* vise, clamp; **t. de orejas** thumbscrew

torniquete *nm* **(a)** *(gen)* turnstile **(b)** *Med* tourniquet

torno *nm* **(a)** *Téc* lathe; **t. de alfarero** potter's wheel **(b)** *(elevador)* winch, windlass **(c)** *(en convento)* revolving window **(d)** **en t. a** *(alrededor de)* around; *(acerca de)* about

toro *nm* **(a)** *Zool* bull; *Taur* **ir a los toros** to go to a bullfight; *Fig* **ver los toros desde la barrera** to watch from the wings; *Fam* **estar hecho un t.** to be a strapping man; *Fam*

fuerte como un t. as strong as an ox □ *Taur* **t. bravo** o **de lidia** fighting bull **(b)** *Cuba (pez)* horned boxfish o trunkfish

toronja *nf* grapefruit

torpe *adj* **(a)** *(sin habilidad)* clumsy **(b)** *(poco inteligente)* dim, thick **(c)** *(movimiento)* slow, awkward

torpedear *vt Mil* to torpedo

torpedero, -a *Mil* **1** *adj* torpedo

2 *nm* torpedo boat

torpedo *nm* **(a)** *Mil* torpedo **(b)** *(pez)* electric ray

torpeza *nf* **(a)** *(física)* clumsiness, ungainliness **(b)** *(mental)* dimness, stupidity **(c)** *(de movimiento)* slowness, heaviness **(d)** *(error)* blunder

torpón, -ona *adj Fam* **(a)** *(falto de habilidad)* clumsy **(b)** *(tonto)* dim, stupid

torrar *vt* to toast

torre *nf* **(a)** *(gen)* tower; *Fig* **t. de marfil** ivory tower **(b)** *Mil Náut* turret □ **t. de vigía** crow's nest **(c)** *Constr* (country) house, villa **(d)** *Ajedrez* rook, castle

torrefacto, -a *adj* dark-roast, high-roast; **café t.** dark-roast o high-roast coffee

torreja *nf* **(a)** *Méx (dulce)* French toast **(b)** *Chile (rodaja)* slice

torrencial *adj* torrential

torrente *nm* **(a)** *(de agua)* mountain stream, torrent; *Anat* **t. sanguíneo** o **circulatorio** bloodstream **(b)** *Fig (abundancia)* flood, stream; **t. en voz** loud strong voice

torreón *nm Mil* fortified tower

torrero *nm* lighthouse keeper

torreta *nf* **(a)** *Arquit* turret, small tower **(b)** *Mil (de tanque)* turret; *Náut (de submarino)* conning tower

torrezno *nm* = rasher of fried bacon

tórrido, -a *adj* torrid

torrija *nf* French toast *(sweetened)*

torsión *nf* **(a)** *(torcedura)* twist, twisting **(b)** *Téc* torsion; **momento de t.** torque

torso *nm* **(a)** *Anat* torso **(b)** *Arte* bust

torta *nf* **(a)** *CSur Ven (dulce)* cake; *Andes CAm Carib RP (salada)* pie; *Esp (de harina)* = flat, round plain cake **(b)** *Méx (sandwich)* filled roll; *(con huevos)* flat omelette, frittata **(c)** *Fam (bofetada)* slap (in the face); *(golpe, accidente)* thump; **pegarse una t.** to get a bump; *Fig* **ni t.** not a thing

tortazo *nm Fam* **(a)** *(bofetada)* slap (in the face) **(b)** *(golpe)* whack, thump; **darse un t.** to crash

tortería *nf Méx* sandwich shop, *US* luncheonette

tortícolis *nf inv* stiff neck, crick in one's neck

tortilla *nf* **(a)** *(de huevo)* omelette, *US* omelet; *Esp* **t. (a la) francesa** (plain) omelette; *Fig* **se volvió la t.** the tables were turned **(b)** *(de maíz)* tortilla

tortillera *nf Vulg* dyke, lesbian

tortillería *nf Am* = shop selling (corn) tortillas

tortita *nf Culin* pancake

tórtola *nf Orn* dove

tortolito, -a *nm,f Fam* lovebird

tortuga *nf (de tierra)* tortoise, *US* turtle; *(de mar)* turtle; *Fig* **a paso de t.** at a snail's pace

tortuosidad *nf* tortuousness

tortuoso, -a *adj* tortuous

tortura *nf* **(a)** *(tormento)* torture **(b)** *(padecimiento)* intense suffering, agony

torturador, -a *nm,f* torturer

torturar 1 *vt* to torture

2 torturarse *vpr* to torture oneself

torvo, -a *adj* grim, fierce

tos *nf* cough, coughing ❑ *Med* **t. ferina** whooping cough

tosco, -a *adj* (**a**) *(basto)* rustic, rough (**b**) *(persona)* uncouth

tosedera *nf SAm* cough

toser *vi* to cough; *Fig* **no hay quien le tosa** he's one step ahead of everyone

tosquedad *nf* roughness, crudeness

tostada *nf* (slice of) toast; *Fam* **olerse la t.** to smell a rat

tostadero *nm* roaster

tostado, -a 1 *pp de* **tostar**
2 *adj* (**a**) *(pan)* toasted; *(café)* roasted (**b**) *(moreno)* tanned, brown (**c**) *(marrón)* brown

tostador, -a *nm,f* *(de pan)* toaster; *(de café)* roaster

tostar [63] **1** *vt (pan)* to toast; *(café)* to roast; *(carne, pescado)* to brown; *Fig (la piel)* to tan
2 tostarse *vpr* to turn *o* get brown

tostón *nm* (**a**) *(pan frito)* crouton (**b**) *Carib (de plátano)* fried plantain chip (**c**) *Fam (tabarra)* bore, drag; **dar el t.** to get on everybody's nerves; **este libro es un t.** this book is a drag

total 1 *adj (completo)* total, overall, complete; *Med* **anestesia t.** general anaesthetic; *Fam* **es un follón t.** it's a complete mess
2 *nm* (**a**) *(todo)* whole; **el t. del ejército** the whole army; **en t.** in all (**b**) *Mat* total, sum
3 *adv* so, in short; **¿t. para qué?** what's the point anyhow?; **t. que ...** so ..., to make a long story short ...; **t., tampoco te hará caso** he won't listen to you, anyway

totalidad *nf* whole, totality; **en su t.** as a whole

totalitario, -a *adj* totalitarian

totalitarismo *nm* totalitarianism, dictatorship

totalitarista *adj* totalitarian

totalizar [14] *(puntos)* *vt* to obtain, to score

tótem *(pl* **tótems** *o* **tótemes)** *nm* totem

totémico, -a *adj* totemic

totopo *nm CAm Méx* tortilla chip

totora *nf Andes RP* totora reed

totuma *nf Am* calabash, gourd

tour [tur] *(pl* **tours)** *nm* tour ❑ **t. operador** tour operator

tournée [tur'ne] *(pl* **tournées)** *nf Teat* tour

toxicidad *nf* toxicity

tóxico, -a 1 *adj* toxic, poisonous
2 *nm* toxicant, poison

toxicología *nf Med* toxicology

toxicológico, -a *adj Med* toxicologic, toxicological

toxicólogo, -a *nm,f Med* toxicologist

toxicomanía *nf Med* drug addiction

toxicómano, -a *Med* **1** *adj* addicted to drugs
2 *nm* drug addict

toxina *nf* toxin

tozudez *nf* obstinacy, stubbornness

tozudo, -a *adj* obstinate, stubborn, headstrong

TPI *nm (abrev de* **Tribunal Penal Internacional)** ICC

traba *nf* (**a**) *(sujeción)* *(de rueda)* chock; *(de caballo)* hobble (**b**) *(enlace)* bond, tie (**c**) *Fig (obstáculo)* hindrance, obstacle, shackle; **poner trabas** to raise objections

trabado, -a 1 *pp de* **trabar**
2 *adj* (**a**) *(sujeto)* fastened (**b**) *(salsa)* smooth (**c**) *(atascado)* jammed (**d**) *(coherente)* coherent

trabajado, -a 1 *pp de* **trabajar**
2 *adj* elaborate, carefully worked

trabajador, -a 1 *adj* (**a**) *(que trabaja)* working (**b**) *(laborioso)* hard-working; **un pueblo t.** an industrious nation

2 *nm,f* worker, labourer, *US* laborer

3 *nm Chile (ave)* heron

trabajar 1 *vt* (**a**) *(dar forma a)* to work (on); **t. el hierro/la madera** to work iron/wood; **t. la tierra** to till the land; *Culin* **t. una pasta** to knead dough (**b**) *(intensificar el trabajo)* to work on; **hay que trabajarlo más** we need to put more work into it; **tienes que t. el francés** you'll have to work harder on your French *o* in French (**c**) *Fam (convencer)* to (try to) persuade; **t. a algn para que haga algo** to talk sb into doing sth
2 *vi* (**a**) *(gen)* to work; **trabaja mucho** he works hard; **t. de camarera** to work as a waitress; **t. en** to work at *o* in; **t. por horas** to be paid by the hour; **trabajo de profesor** I'm a teacher; *Fam* **t. como un condenado** *o* **una bestia** to slave away; *Fam* **t. en balde** to work in vain (**b**) *Cin Teat* to perform, act; **¿quién trabaja en esa película?** who's in that film? (**c**) *Constr (soportar)* to be under stress; **esta viga trabaja mal** this beam is not doing its job properly

trabajo *nm* (**a**) *(ocupación)* work; **ir al t.** to go to work; *Fig Fam* **ser un t. de chinos** to be a finicky job ❑ **t. a destajo** piecework; **t. de campo** field work; **t. de equipo** teamwork; **t. intelectual** mental effort; **t. por turno(s)** shiftwork; **t. social** social work; **t. sucio** dirty work; **trabajos forzados** hard labour *sing*; *Educ* **trabajos manuales** arts and crafts (**b**) *(tarea)* task, job; **ha hecho un buen t.** she's done a good job (**c**) *(empleo)* job; **estoy sin t.** I'm out of work ❑ **t. de media jornada** part-time job; **t. temporal** temporary job (**d**) *Educ (escrito)* essay (**e**) *(esfuerzo)* effort; **con mucho t.** with great effort, **cuesta t. creerlo** it's hard to believe; **puedes ahorrarte el t.** you can save yourself the trouble

trabajoso, -a *adj* (**a**) *(laborioso)* hard, laborious; *(difícil)* difficult (**b**) *Col (exigente)* demanding

trabalenguas *nm inv* tongue twister

trabar 1 *vt* (**a**) *(sujetar)* *(piezas móviles)* to lock, fasten; *(piezas sueltas)* to join, unite; *(mecanismo)* to jam; *(persona)* to shackle; *(las patas de un caballo)* to hobble (**b**) *(impedir)* to hinder; *(un plan)* to obstruct (**c**) *Culin (salsa)* to thicken (**d**) *Fig (iniciar)* to start; **t. amistad/conversación** to strike up a friendship/conversation
2 trabarse *vpr* (**a**) *(cuerdas)* to get tangled up (**b**) *(mecanismo)* to jam, seize up; *Fig* **se le trabó la lengua** he got tongue-tied

trabazón *nf* (**a**) *(ensamblaje)* joining, assembly (**b**) *(enlace)* bond, tie; *Fig (de ideas)* link, coherence

trabilla *nf (de pantalón)* belt loop; *(de chaqueta)* half belt

trabucar [59] **1** *vt* to jumble *o* mix up
2 trabucarse *vpr* to get all mixed up

trabuco *nm (arma)* blunderbuss

traca *nf* string of firecrackers, jumping jack

trácala *nf Méx Ven Fam* trick

tracalero, -a *Méx Ven Fam* **1** *adj* cheating
2 *nm,f* cheat

tracción *nf Téc* traction; *Aut* **t. delantera/trasera** front-/rear-wheel drive; *Aut* **t. en las cuatro ruedas** four-wheel drive

tracto *nm* tract; **t. digestivo** digestive tract

tractor, -a 1 *adj Téc* driving
2 *nm Aut* tractor

tractorista *nmf* tractor driver

tradición *nf* tradition

tradicional *adj* traditional; **es lo t.** it's the traditional thing to do

tradicionalismo *nm* (**a**) *Filos Rel* traditionalism (**b**) *Pol* radical conservatism

tradicionalista *adj & nmf* (**a**) *Filos Rel* traditionalist (**b**) *Pol* radical conservative

traducción *nf* translation ❑ **t. automática** machine translation; **t. directa/inversa** translation from/into a foreign language; **t. simultánea** simultaneous translation

traducir [18] **1** *vt* (**a**) *(gen)* to translate (**a** into) (**b**) *(expresar)* to express, show
2 traducirse *vpr* **t. en** to result in; **la infección se traduce en fiebre** the infection results in a temperature

traductor, -a 1 *adj* translating
2 *nm,f* translator ❑ **t. jurado** sworn translator

traer [66] **1** *vt* (**a**) *(gen)* to bring; **trae** give it to me; **t. (buena) suerte** to bring good luck; *Fig* **t. de cabeza a algn** to drive sb mad (**b**) *(llevar puesto)* to wear; **traía un traje negro** he was wearing a black suit (**c**) *(llevar consigo)* to carry; **¿qué traes en esa bolsa?** what have you got in that bag?; *Fig* **¿qué se traen entre manos?** what are they up to? (**d**) *(causar)* to cause; **traerá como consecuencia ...** it will result in ...; **t. consecuencias** to have serious consequences; **t. consigo** to bring about; **t. problemas** to cause problems (**e**) *(llevar) (noticias)* to feature, carry; **¿qué trae hoy 'El País'?** what's in 'El País' today?
2 traerse *vpr* (**a**) *(llevar consigo)* to bring along; **traéte a tu hermana** bring your sister along (**b**) **traérselas** *(ser de cuidado)* to be really hard o difficult; **el profesor de latín se las trae** the Latin teacher is very hard on us

traficante *nmf* (**a**) *(gen)* dealer, trader; *(productos ilegales)* trafficker ❑ **t. de drogas** drug trafficker o pusher

traficar [59] *vi* (**a**) *(gen)* to deal; *(ilegalmente)* to traffic; **t. con drogas** to traffic in drugs

tráfico *nm* (**a**) *Aut* traffic ❑ **accidente de t.** road o car accident; **t. rodado** road traffic (**b**) *Com* traffic, trade ❑ **t. de armas** arms trafficking; **t. de drogas** drug trafficking

tragacanto *nm Bot* tragacanth

tragaderas *nfpl Fam* throat *sing*; *Fig* **tener buenas t.** *(ser crédulo)* to be gullible; *(tener pocos escrúpulos)* to be too much of a conformist

tragadero *nm* drain

tragaldabas *nmf inv Fam* glutton, pig

tragaleguas *nmf inv Fam* keen walker

tragaluz *nm Arquit* skylight

tragamillas *nmf inv Fam* keen walker

tragamonedas *nf inv Am Fam* slot machine

tragaperras *nf inv* **(máquina) t.** slot machine

tragar [38] **1** *vt* (**a**) *(ingerir)* to swallow; *Fig* **deseaba que lo tragara la tierra** he wished the earth would swallow him up (**b**) *Fam (engullir)* to gobble up, tuck away (**c**) *Fig (absorber)* to swallow up, absorb; *(consumir)* to eat up; **t. millas** to burn up the miles (**d**) *Fig (soportar) (persona)* to stand, stomach; *(suceso)* to stand for, put up with (**e**) *Fig (creer)* to believe, swallow; **t. la píldora** to fall for it, swallow it (**f**) *Fig (disimular)* to hide, keep to oneself; **decidió t. lo que pensaba de él** he decided not to show what he thought about him
2 *vi* (**a**) *(ingerir)* to swallow; **le cuesta t.** he finds it hard to swallow (**b**) *Fam (comer)* **traga que da gusto** he really puts it away
3 tragarse *vpr* (**a**) *(ingerir)* to swallow (**b**) *(absorber)* to swallow up, absorb; *(consumir)* to eat up (**c**) *Fig (creer)* to believe, swallow; **se lo traga todo** she'd fall for anything (**d**) *Fig (disimular)* to hide

tragasables *nmf inv* sword-swallower

tragedia *nf* tragedy; *Irón* **¡qué t.!, se me ha terminado el tabaco** woe is me!, I've run out of cigarettes; **terminar en t.** to end tragically

trágico, -a 1 *adj Teat* tragic; **escritor t.** tragedian; *Fam* **ponerse t.** *(situación)* to become o get tragic; *(persona)* to get all serious
2 *nm,f Teat* tragedian

tragicomedia *nf Cin Teat* tragicomedy

tragicómico, -a *adj* tragicomic

trago *nm* (**a**) *(bebida)* swig, drop; **beberse algo de un t.** to down sth in one go; **echar un t.** *(echar un sorbo)* to take a swig; *(tomar algo)* to have a drink (**b**) *Fam (adversidad)* rough time; **pasar un mal t.** to have a bad time of it; **tener que volver a verle, ¡qué t.!** how awful to have to see him again!

tragón, -ona 1 *adj Fam* greedy, piggy
2 *nm,f* glutton, big eater

traición *nf* treason, betrayal; **a t.** treacherously; **alta t.** high treason

traicionar *vt* (*gen*) to betray; *(delatar)* to give away, betray; *Fig* **le traicionó su acento** his accent gave him away

traicionero, -a *adj* treacherous

traído, -a 1 *pp de* **traer**
2 *adj* (**a**) *(gastado)* threadbare, worn-out (**b**) *(visto)* hackneyed, trite; **t. y llevado** well-worn, hackneyed

traidor, -a 1 *adj* treacherous
2 *nm,f* traitor

traigo *indic pres véase* **traer**

tráiler *(pl* **tráilers)** *nm* (**a**) *Cin* trailer, *US* preview (**b**) *Aut (remolque)* trailer; *(camión) Br* articulated lorry, *US* semitrailer (**c**) *Méx (casa rodante) Br* caravan, *US* trailer

traína *nf Náut* trawl (net)

trainera *nf Náut* trawler

traje¹ *nm* (**a**) *(de hombre)* suit ❑ **t. a medida** tailor-made suit; **t. cruzado** double-breasted suit; **t. de baño** bathing suit o costume, swimsuit; **t. de calle** town clothes *pl*; *Taur* **t. de luces** bullfighter's costume; **t. de paisano** civilian clothes *pl*; **t. espacial** spacesuit (**b**) *(de mujer)* dress ❑ **t. de chaqueta** tailored suit; **t. de gala** dress suit; **t. de novia** wedding dress; **t. largo** o **de noche** evening dress (**c**) *Mil* dress ❑ *Fam* **t. de bonito** formal dress; **t. de campaña** battledress; **t. de ceremonia** full o formal dress; **t. de faena** fatigue dress, undress

traje² *pt indef véase* **traer**

trajeado, -a 1 *pp de* **trajearse**
2 *adj Fam* sharp, dapper

trajearse *vpr* to dress up

trajín *nm Fam* comings and goings *pl*, hustle and bustle

trajinar *vi Fam* to run o bustle about

tralla *nf* (**a**) *(látigo)* whip (**b**) *(cuerda)* rope

trallazo *nm* (**a**) *(golpe)* lash (**b**) *(chasquido)* crack *(of a whip)*

trama *nf* (**a**) *Tex* weft, woof (**b**) *Lit (argumento)* plot

tramado, -a 1 *pp de* **tramar**
2 *adj CAm* (**a**) *(valiente)* brave, valiant (**b**) *(difícil)* intricate

tramar *vt* to plot, cook up; **están tramando algo gordo** something big is on the way; **¿qué tramas?** what are you up to?

tramitación *nf Jur* procedure, steps *pl*; **¿cuánto tarda la t. de pasaporte?** how long does it take to get a passport?

tramitar *vt* (**a**) *(gestionar)* to take the necessary (legal) steps to obtain; **debo t. mi permiso de residencia** I have to obtain my residence permit (**b**) *Fml (despachar)* to convey, transmit (**c**) *Com Jur Fin* to negotiate, carry out, process, transact

trámite *nm* (**a**) *(paso)* step; **¿falta algún t. por cumplir?** are there any more formalities to be gone through?; *Fig* **de puro t.** unimportant, easy (**b**) *Com Jur Fin* procedures *pl*, proceeding

tramo *nm (de carretera, vía)* section, stretch; *(de escalera)* flight

tramontana *nf Meteor* north wind, tramontane

tramoya *nf Teat* **(a)** *(maquinaria)* stage machinery **(b)** *Fig (trama)* plot, scheme

tramoyista *nmf* **(a)** *Teat* stagehand, scene shifter **(b)** *Fig (farsante)* schemer

trampa *nf* **(a)** *(abertura)* trap door, hatch **(b)** *(de caza)* trap, snare; **caer en la t.** to fall into the trap; **tender una t.** to set o lay a trap **(c)** *Mil (emboscada)* ambush **(d)** *(engaño)* fiddle; **hacer trampa(s)** to cheat **(e)** *(truco)* trick; **este juego tiene t.** this game has got a catch; *Fam* **sin t. ni cartón** honest, real

trampear *vi Fam* **(a)** *(engañar)* to fiddle, live by one's wits **(b)** *(ir viviendo)* to get by, manage

trampero, -a *nm,f* trapper

trampilla *nf* trap door, hatch

trampolín *nm* **(a)** *Natación* springboard, diving board **(b)** *Dep* ski jump **(c)** *Fig (medio)* springboard, starting point

tramposo, -a 1 *adj* tricky, deceitful
2 *nm,f* trickster, cheat; *Naipes* cardsharp

tranca *nf* **(a)** *(garrote)* cudgel, club; *Fam* **a trancas y barrancas** with great difficulty **(b)** *(en puerta, ventana)* bar **(c)** *Méx (en verja)* gate

trancar [59] *vt (puerta)* to bar

trancazo *nm* **(a)** *(golpe)* blow *(with a cudgel)*; *Fam* **pegarse un t.** to come a cropper **(b)** *Fam (gripe)* flu; *(resfriado)* cold

trance *nm* **(a)** *(coyuntura)* (critical) moment, juncture; **estar en t. de ...** to be on the point of ...; **pasar por un t.** to hit a bad patch; **en t. mortal** o **de muerte** on the point of death; **sacar a algn de un (mal) t.** to get sb out of a fix; **último t.** final moment; *Fig* **a todo t.** at all costs **(b)** *(éxtasis)* trance

tranco *nm* stride; *Fig* **a trancos** in a hurry

tranquera *nf Am (en alambrado)* gate

tranquilidad *nf* calmness, tranquillity, *US* tranquility; **con t.** calmly; **para mayor t.** to be on the safe side; **para tu t.** for your own peace of mind; **paz y t.** peace and quiet; **perder la t.** to get het up; **pídemelo con toda t.** don't hesitate to ask me; **¡qué t.!** how peaceful!

tranquilizador, -a *adj* calming, reassuring

tranquilizante 1 *adj* calming, reassuring
2 *nm Farm* tranquillizer, *US* tranquilizer

tranquilizar [14] **1** *vt* **(a)** *(calmar)* to tranquillize, *US* tranquilize, calm down **(b)** *(dar confianza a)* to reassure; **me tranquilizó oír tu voz** hearing your voice set my mind at rest
2 tranquilizarse *vpr* **(a)** *(calmarse)* to calm down; **¡tranquilízate!** calm down! **(b)** *(relajarse)* to relax, set one's mind at rest

tranquillo *nm Esp Fam* knack; **coger el t. a algo** to get the knack of sth

tranquilo, -a *adj* **(a)** *(sin inquietud)* calm, tranquil, relaxed; **aguas tranquilas** still waters; **para que estés t.** for your own peace of mind; **tengo la conciencia tranquila** my conscience is clear; *Fam* **déjame t.** leave me alone; *Fam* **quedarse tan t.** not to bat an eyelid; *Fam* **¡t.!** *(no te preocupes)* don't (you) worry!; *(no pierdas la calma)* take it easy! **(b)** *(sin ruidos)* quiet, still, peaceful **(c)** *(persona)* placid, calm, easy-going

transa *nf Méx RP Fam* deal

transacción *nf Fin* transaction, deal

transalpino, -a *adj Geog* transalpine

transandino, -a *adj Geog* transandean

transar *vi Am (transigir)* to compromise, give in; *(negociar)* to come to an arrangement, reach a compromise

transatlántico, -a 1 *adj* transatlantic
2 *nm Náut* (ocean) liner

transbordador *nm Náut* (car) ferry

transbordar 1 *vt* to transfer; *Náut (mercancías)* to transship; *Náut (de orilla a orilla)* to ferry across the river
2 *vi Ferroc* to change trains, *US* transfer

transbordo *nm* **(a)** *Ferroc* change, *US* transfer; **hacer t.** to change o transfer **(b)** *Náut* transshipment

transcendencia *nf véase* **trascendencia**

transcendental *adj véase* **trascendental**

transcendente *adj véase* **trascendente**

transcender *vt & vi véase* **trascender**

transcontinental *adj* transcontinental

transcribir *(pp* **transcrito)** *vt* to transcribe

transcripción *nf* transcription

transcrito *pp de* **transcribir**

transcurrir *vi* **(a)** *(pasar) (el tiempo)* to pass, go by, elapse; **dejé t. cinco minutos antes de volver a llamar** I waited five minutes before phoning again **(b)** *(acontecer)* to take place, go off

transcurso *nm* course, passing; **con el t. de los años** as the years go/went by; **en el t. de ocho días** in the course o space of a week

transeúnte *nmf* **(a)** *(peatón)* pedestrian **(b)** *(residente temporal)* temporary resident

transexual *adj & nmf* transsexual

transexualismo *nm* transsexualism

transferencia *nf (gen)* transference; *Fin* transfer; **t. bancaria** banker's order

transferible *adj* transferable

transferir [62] *vt* **(a)** *(de lugar)* to transfer **(b)** *(aplazar)* to postpone **(c)** *Fin* to transfer, convey **(d)** *Inform* download

transfiguración *nf* transfiguration

transfigurar 1 *vt* to transfigure
2 transfigurarse *vpr* to become transfigured

transformación *nf* transformation

transformador, -a 1 *adj* transforming
2 *nm Elec* transformer

transformar 1 *vt* to transform, change
2 transformarse *vpr* **t. en** to change o turn into; **este sillón se transforma en (una) cama** this armchair converts into a bed

transformista *nmf* quick-change artist

tránsfuga *nmf* **(a)** *Mil* deserter **(b)** *Pol* turncoat

transfusión *nf* transfusion; **t. sanguínea** blood transfusion

transgénico, -a 1 *adj* genetically modified, GM
2 transgénicos *nmpl* GM foods

transgredir *vt* to transgress, break

transgresión *nf* transgression

transgresor, -a *nm,f* transgressor, lawbreaker

transiberiano, -a 1 *adj* Trans-Siberian
2 *nm Ferroc* **el T.** the Trans-Siberian Railway

transición *nf* transition; **período/gobierno de t.** transition period/government; **sin t.** abruptly

transido, -a *adj* deeply affected; **t. de angustia** beset with anxiety; **t. de dolor** racked with pain; **t. de frío** chilled to the bone; **t. de miedo** terrified

transigencia *nf* **(a)** *(concesión)* compromise, yielding **(b)** *(actitud)* lenience, tolerance

transigente *adj* accommodating, lenient, tolerant

transigir [24] *vi* **(a)** *(ceder)* to compromise, yield, give in; **en eso no puedo t.** I cannot possibly agree to that **(b)** *(ser tolerante)* to be tolerant

transistor *nm Elec* transistor

transitable *adj* passable; **la carretera no está t.** *(en malas condiciones)* the road is in bad condition; *(cerrada)* the road is closed to traffic

transitado, -a *pp de* **transitar**
2 *adj* busy; **una carretera muy transitada** a busy o well-travelled road

transitar *vi* to go from place to place, travel (about)

transitivo, -a *adj Ling* transitive

tránsito *nm* (**a**) *(movimiento)* movement, passage; **pasajeros en t.** passengers in transit (**b**) *Aut* traffic; **'cerrado al t.'** 'road closed'; **una calle de (mucho) t.** a busy street (**c**) *Euf (muerte)* death, passing

transitoriedad *nf* transience, transiency

transitorio, -a *adj* transitory, transitional, interim; *Jur* **disposición transitoria** provisional order o ordinance

translación *nf véase* **traslación**

translúcido, -a *adj véase* **traslúcido, -a**

translucir *vt véase* **traslucir**

transmigración *nf* transmigration

transmisión *nf* (**a**) *(paso)* transmission; **t. del pensamiento** thought transmission (**b**) *Jur (de bienes)* transfer(ence) (**c**) *Téc* drive; **t. delantera/trasera** front-/rear-wheel drive (**d**) *Rad TV* transmission, broadcast; *Mil* **(cuerpo de) transmisiones** signal corps *sing*

transmisor, -a *Tel* **1** *adj* transmitting; **estación transmisora** radio station
2 *nm* transmitter

transmitir *vt* (**a**) *(comunicar)* to transmit, pass on; **no me acordé de transmitirle tu recado** I forgot to give him your message (**b**) *Jur* to transfer, hand down (**c**) *Med* to transmit, pass on; **las moscas transmiten microbios** flies carry germs (**d**) *Rad TV* to transmit, broadcast

transmutación *nf* transmutation

transmutar 1 *vt* to transmute
2 transmutarse *vpr* to change (completely), transform

transoceánico, -a *adj* transoceanic

transparencia *nf* (**a**) *(calidad)* transparency (**b**) *Fot* slide

transparentar 1 *vt (emociones etc)* to reveal, betray
2 transparentarse *vpr* (**a**) *(ser transparente)* to be transparent; **esta tela se transparenta** this material is see-through (**b**) *(emociones, intenciones)* to show (through)

transparente 1 *adj* transparent; *Fig* **puedes fiarte de él, es t.** you can trust him, he's straight
2 *nm* (**a**) *(visillo)* net curtain (**b**) *(pantalla)* shade, blind

transpiración *nf* (**a**) *Bot* transpiration (**b**) *(sudoración)* perspiration

transpirar *vi* (**a**) *Bot* to transpire (**b**) *(persona)* to perspire

transpirenaico, -a *adj* trans-Pyrenean, beyond the Pyrenees

transplantar 1 *vt* (**a**) *(gen)* to transplant (**b**) *(trasladar)* to transfer
2 transplantarse *vpr* to uproot oneself, emigrate

transplante *nm* transplant, transplantation; *Med* **t. de corazón/córnea/órganos** heart/eye/organ transplant

transponer [50] *(pp* **transpuesto) 1** *vt* (**a**) *(mudar de sitio)* to transpose, move about (**b**) *(atravesar)* to cross over (**c**) *(trasplantar)* to transplant
2 transponerse *vpr* (**a**) *(esconderse)* to hide; *(el sol)* to set, go down (**b**) *(quedarse dormido)* to doze off

transportador, -a 1 *adj* transporting; **cinta transportadora** conveyor belt
2 *nm* (**a**) *Téc* transporter, conveyor (**b**) *(de dibujo)* protractor

transportar 1 *vt* (**a**) *(gen)* to transport; *(pasajeros)* carry; *(mercancías)* to ship; *Fig* **transportado de felicidad** utterly

happy (**b**) *(ángulo)* to transfer (**c**) *Mús* to transpose
2 transportarse *vpr Fig* to be transported o enraptured

transporte *nm* (**a**) *(medio)* transport ❑ **t. público** public transport (**b**) *(acción)* transport, *US* transportation ❑ **t. aéreo** air freight; **t. de mercancías** freight transport; **t. marítimo** maritime transport

transportista *nmf* carrier

transposición *nf* transposition

transvasar *vt* (**a**) *(líquidos)* to decant (**b**) *(de un río a otro)* to transfer

transvase *nm* (**a**) *(de líquidos)* decanting (**b**) *(de ríos)* transfer

transversal *adj* transverse, cross

transverso, -a *adj* transverse

tranvía *nm* (**a**) *(vehículo)* Br tram, *US* streetcar (**b**) *(sistema de transporte)* tramway

trapacería *nf* trick, fiddle

trapacero, -a 1 *adj* tricky
2 *nm* fiddler, trickster

trapajoso, -a *adj* (**a**) *(ropa)* ragged, tattered (**b**) *(persona)* dowdy, shabby (**c**) *(pronunciación)* badly articulated; **hablar t.** to speak with a thick voice

trapatiesta *nf Fam* racket; **se armó una t.** there was quite an uproar

trapear *vt Andes CAm Méx (suelo)* to mop

trapecio *nm* (**a**) *Geom* trapezium, *US* trapezoid (**b**) *Med (hueso)* trapezium; *(músculo)* trapezius (**c**) *(en gimnasia)* trapeze

trapecista *nmf* trapeze artist

trapense *adj* Trappist

trapería *nf* old-clothes shop

trapero *nm Br* rag-and-bone man, *US* junkman

trapezoide *nm Geom* trapezoid, *US* trapezium

trapichear *vi* to (be on the) fiddle

trapicheo *nm* jiggery-pokery, fiddling; **andar(se) con trapicheos** to be dishonest

trapillo *nm* **de t.** casually dressed

trapisonda *nf Fam* (**a**) *(jaleo)* fuss, to-do, commotion (**b**) *(enredo)* scheme, plot

trapisondear *vi Fam* (**a**) *(reñir)* to kick up a row (**b**) *(liar, enredar)* to scheme

trapitos *nmpl Fam* clothes, rags; **hablar de t.** to talk about clothes

trapo *nm* (**a**) *(viejo, roto)* rag (**b**) *(para limpiar, secar)* cloth, **t. de cocina** *Br* tea towel, *US* dish towel; **t. de polvo** duster; *Fam* **estar hecho un t.** to be worn out; *Fam* **poner a algn como un t. (sucio)** to tear sb apart; *Fam* **lavar los trapos sucios** to wash one's dirty linen (in public); *Fam* **sacar los trapos sucios a relucir** to take the skeletons out of the cupboard (**c**) *Taur* red cape (**d**) *Fam* **trapos** clothes, rags (**e**) *Fam* **a todo t.** flat out

tráquea *nf Anat* trachea, windpipe

traqueotomía *nf Med* tracheotomy

traquetear 1 *vt (agitar)* to shake, bang about
2 *vi (hacer ruido)* to clatter, rattle

traqueteo *nm* (**a**) *(ruido)* rattle, clatter (**b**) *(movimiento)* jolting, bumping

tras *prep* (**a**) *(después de)* after; **t. la muerte de su padre** after his father's death; **uno t. otro** one after the other (**b**) *(detrás)* behind; **sentados uno t. otro** seated one behind the other (**c**) *(en pos de)* after, in pursuit of; **la policía va t. ella** the police are searching for her; **voy t. una vacante de juez** I'm after a vacancy for a judge

trasalpino, -a *adj véase* **transalpino, -a**

trasandino, -a *adj véase* **transandino, -a**

trasatlántico, -a *adj & nm véase* **transatlántico, -a**

trasbordador *nm véase* **transbordador**

trasbordar *vt & vi véase* **transbordar**

trasbordo *nm véase* **transbordo**

trascendencia *nf* **(a)** *(importancia)* importance, significance; **aquel invento tuvo una gran t.** that invention had far-reaching consequences; **sin t.** of little significance **(b)** *Filos* transcendence, transcendency

trascendental *adj,* **trascendente** *adj* **(a)** *(importante)* significant, consequential, far-reaching **(b)** *Filos* transcendent, transcendental

trascender [64] **1** *vt (averiguar)* to discover, bring to light
2 *vi* **(a)** *(darse a conocer)* to become known, leak out; **t. a la opinión pública** to become common knowledge **(b)** *(extenderse)* to spread, have a wide effect; **esperemos que el mal ejemplo no trascienda** let's hope nobody will follow this bad example **(c)** *(exhalar olor)* to smell; **el olor de café trascendía a toda la casa** the smell of coffee wafted all over the house; *Fig* **todo su discurso trasciende a fascismo** his whole speech reeks of fascism **(d)** **t. de** to go beyond, surpass; **esta decisión trasciende de mi competencia** this decision is beyond my powers **(e)** *Filos* to be transcendent o transcendental

trascribir *vt véase* **transcribir**

trascripción *nf véase* **transcripción**

trascrito *pp de* **trascribir**

trascurrir *vi véase* **transcurrir**

trascurso *nm véase* **transcurso**

trasegar [43] *vt* **(a)** *(mudar)* to move about, shuffle **(b)** *(líquidos)* to decant **(c)** *Fam (beber)* to swill

trasero, -a 1 *adj* back, rear; **en la parte trasera** at the back
2 *nm Anat Fam Euf* bottom, *Br* bum, *US* fanny

trasferencia *nf véase* **transferencia**

trasferible *adj véase* **transferible**

trasferir *vt véase* **transferir**

trasfiguración *nf véase* **transfiguración**

trasfigurar *vt véase* **transfigurar**

trasfondo *nm* background; **había un t. de tristeza en sus palabras** there was an undertone of sadness in her words

trasformación *nf véase* **transformación**

trasformador, -a *adj & nm véase* **transformador, -a**

trasformar *vt véase* **transformar**

trasformista *nmf véase* **transformista**

trásfuga *nmf véase* **tránsfuga**

trasfusión *nf véase* **transfusión**

trasgo *nm Mit* goblin, imp

trasgredir *vt véase* **transgredir**

trasgresión *nf véase* **transgresión**

trasgresor, -a *nm,f véase* **transgresor, -a**

trashumancia *nf* transhumance, seasonal migration

trashumante *adj* transhumant

trashumar *vi* to migrate seasonally

trasiego *nm* comings and goings *pl*, hustle and bustle; **t. de personal** reshuffle

traslación *nf* **(a)** *Astron* passage, movement **(b)** *Mat* translation **(c)** *Lit* metaphor

trasladar 1 *vt* **(a)** *(cosa)* to move; *(persona)* to move, transfer; **t. ideas al papel** to put down ideas in writing **(b)** *(acontecimiento)* to postpone, put off; *(reunión, prueba)* to adjourn **(c)** *(traducir)* to translate **(d)** *Fig* to explain
2 trasladarse *vpr (persona, cosa)* to go, move

traslado *nm* **(a)** *(de casa)* move, removal; **¿cuándo haremos el t.?** when are we going to move? **(b)** *(de personal)* transfer **(c)** *(copia)* copy **(d)** *Jur* notification

traslúcido, -a *adj* translucent, semi-transparent

traslucir [39] **1** *vt Fig (sentimientos, intenciones)* to show, reveal; **su tono de voz dejaba t. el miedo** his tone of voice betrayed his fear
2 traslucirse *vpr* **(a)** *(ser traslúcido)* to be translucent **(b)** *(adivinarse)* to show (through); *(revelarse)* to be revealed

trasluz *nm* diffused o reflected light; **mirar algo al t.** to hold sth against the light

trasmano *nm* **a t.** out of reach; **(me) coge a t.** it's out of my way

trasmigración *nf véase* **transmigración**

trasmisión *nf véase* **transmisión**

trasmisor, -a *adj & nm véase* **transmisor, -a**

trasmitir *vt véase* **transmitir**

trasmutación *nf véase* **transmutación**

trasmutar *vt véase* **transmutar**

trasnochado, -a 1 *pp de* **trasnochar**
2 *adj* **(a)** *(desfasado)* old, hackneyed **(b)** *Fig (persona)* bleary-eyed, haggard

trasnochador, -a 1 *adj* given to staying up late
2 *nm,f* night owl

trasnochar *vi* to stay up (very) late

traspapelar 1 *vt (papeles etc)* to mislay, misplace
2 traspapelarse *vpr (documentos etc)* to get mislaid o misplaced

trasparencia *nf véase* **transparencia**

trasparentar *vt véase* **transparentar**

trasparente *adj & nm véase* **transparente**

traspasar *vt* **(a)** *(atravesar)* to go through; *(río)* to cross; *(perforar)* to pierce; **una bala le traspasó el corazón** a bullet went through his heart; *Fig* **estos silbidos te traspasan el oído** that whistling noise is really piercing **(b)** *(comercio, derechos, jugador)* to transfer; **'se traspasa'** 'for sale' **(c)** *Fig (exceder)* to exceed, go beyond; **t. los límites de lo establecido** to go beyond the set limit **(d)** *Fig (afectar)* to transfix

traspaso *nm* **(a)** *(de comercio, derechos)* transfer **(b)** *Com (venta)* sale; **cogió el t. de un comercio** he bought a shop **(c)** *(precio)* takeover fee; **piden 10.000 de t.** they want 10,000 for the takeover

traspatio *nm Am* interior courtyard

traspié *nm* stumble, trip; **dar un t.** to trip; *Fig* to slip up

traspiración *nf véase* **transpiración**

traspirar *vi véase* **transpirar**

traspirenaico, -a *adj véase* **transpirenaico, -a**

trasplantar *vt véase* **trasplantar**

trasplante *nm véase* **trasplante**

trasponer *vt véase* **transponer**

trasportador, -a *adj & nm adj véase* **transportador, -a**

trasportar *vt véase* **transportar**

trasporte *nm véase* **transporte**

trasposición *nf véase* **transposición**

traspuesto, -a 1 *pp de* **trasponer**
2 *adj* **quedarse t.** to nod o doze off

trasquilado, -a 1 *pp de* **trasquilar**
2 *adj* **(a)** *(oveja)* sheared; *Fig* **(ir a por lana y) salir t.** to come out the loser **(b)** *(pelo)* cropped **(c)** *Fam (mermado)* curtailed, cut down

trasquilar *vt* **(a)** *(oveja)* to shear **(b)** *(pelo)* to crop **(c)** *(dinero, recursos)* to cut (back)

trasquilón nm (**a**) Fam (corte de pelo) slash, chop; **con** o **a trasquilones** unevenly cut (**b**) Fam Fig (dinero) loot, catch

trastabillar vi (**a**) (dar traspiés) to stumble, trip (**b**) (tambalearse) to stagger, totter (**c**) (tartamudear) to stutter, stammer

trastabillón nm Am stumble, trip

trastada nf Fam (**a**) (broma pesada) prank (**b**) (mala jugada) dirty trick

trastazo nm Fam whack, wallop, thump; **me di un t. contra un coche** I bumped into a car; **se pegó un t.** he came a cropper

traste[1] nm Mús fret

traste[2] nm (**a**) Andes CAm Carib Méx (de cocina) cooking utensil; **fregar los trastes** to wash the dishes (**b**) CSur Fam (trasero) bottom (**c**) Fig **dar al t. (con un plan)** to ruin (a plan); **irse al t.** to fall through

trastear[1] vt Mús to play

trastear[2] **1** vi (revolver) to rummage about
2 vt (**a**) Taur to tease with the cape (**b**) Fig (manejar) to twist around one's little finger

trastero nm (**cuarto**) **t.** junk room

trastienda nf (**a**) (habitación) back room; Fig **por t.** under the counter (**b**) Fig (astucia) cunning; **tener mucha t.** to be a dark horse

trasto nm (**a**) (que no sirve) piece of junk; (objeto cualquiera) thing; **¿qué hace este t. ahí en medio?** what's this thingamajig o thingummy doing in the way?; **ser un t. viejo** to be useless (**b**) (niño) little devil (**c**) Mueb piece of furniture (**d**) **trastos** tackle sing, gear sing; **los t. de escalar** the climbing gear; **se fue con todos los t. de coser** she went away with the whole sewing kit (**e**) Fam (posesiones) belongings, things; **llévate tus t.** take all your stuff with you; **coger** o **liar los t.** to pack up and leave; **tirarse los t. a la cabeza** to have a blazing o flaming row

trastocar [67] vt véase **trastornar**

trastornado, -a 1 pp de **trastornar**
2 adj mad, unhinged; **esta mujer me tiene t.** this woman has driven me crazy; **mente trastornada** unbalanced mind

trastornar 1 vt (**a**) (revolver) to turn round; Fig to disarrange (**b**) (desordenar) to turn upside down (**c**) (alterar) (planes) to disrupt; (paz, tranquilidad) to disturb; (estómago) to upset; Fig (molestar) to trouble, bother, annoy (**d**) Fig (perturbar) to unhinge; **trastorna a los hombres** she drives men crazy
2 trastornarse vpr to go out of one's mind, go mad

trastorno nm (molestia) trouble, inconvenience; (perturbación) disruption, upset, upheaval; (desorden) confusion ❏ Med **t. estomacal** stomach upset; **t. mental** mental disorder ó disturbance

trastrocamiento nm switch, reversal

trastrocar [67] vt (gen) to switch o change around; (orden) to reverse, invert; (significado, sentido) to change

trasuntar vt Am (**a**) (copiar) to copy, transcribe (**b**) (compendiar) to summarize

trasunto nm Fml copy, replica; **un fiel t. de la realidad** a true representation of reality

trasvasar vt véase **transvasar**

trasvase nm véase **transvase**

trasversal adj véase **transversal**

trasverso, -a adj véase **transverso, -a**

trata nf slave trade o traffic ❏ **t. de blancas** white slave trade

tratable adj easy to get along with, friendly, congenial

tratadista nmf treatise writer, essayist

tratado, -a 1 pp de **tratar**
2 nm (**a**) (estudio) treatise (**b**) (pacto) treaty

tratamiento nm (**a**) (gen) treatment; Med **un t. a base de antibióticos** a course of antibiotics (**b**) Téc processing, treatment (**c**) (título) title; **le debes dar t. de Excelencia** you must address him as Your Excellency (**d**) Inform processing ❏ **t. de datos** data processing; **t. de textos** word processing

tratante nmf dealer

tratar 1 vt (**a**) (asistir, atender) to treat; **nos han tratado muy bien** they were very nice to us; **t. a algn bien/mal** to treat sb well/badly (**b**) Med (enfermedad) to treat (**c**) (asunto) to discuss (**d**) (calificar) to consider, look on; **le trató de loco** he treated him as if he were mad (**e**) (manejar) to handle (**f**) (gestionar) to handle, run (**g**) Inform Téc to process (**h**) Quím to treat
2 vi (**a**) (relacionarse) **he tratado más con la hermana** I'm more acquainted with her sister; **t. con algn** to see o visit sb frequently (**b**) (tener tratos) to deal (**con** with); (negociar) to negotiate (**con** with) (**c**) (intentar) **t. de entenderlo** try to understand (**d**) (llamar) **t. de** to address as; **no es necesario que me trates de usted** you needn't address me as 'usted' (**e**) (versar) **t. de** o **sobre** o **acerca** to be about; **¿de qué trata?** what is it about? (**f**) Com **t. en** to deal in
3 tratarse vpr (**a**) (recíproco) to treat each other (**b**) (llamarse) to address each other; **se tratan de tú** they call each other 'tú' (**c**) (hablarse) to talk to each other, be on speaking terms (**d**) (ser cuestión) **t. de** to be a question of; **se tratará de una media hora** it'll be about half an hour; **sólo se trata de ser más puntual** it's only a matter of being more punctual (**e**) (referirse) **t. de** to be about; **¿de qué se trató durante la cena?** what was the subject during supper?; **se trata de un cuento irlandés** it's an Irish story

tratativas nfpl CSur negotiation sing

trato nm (**a**) (de personas) manner, treatment; (contacto) contact; Pey dealings pl; **no tengo t. con Juan** I have nothing to do with Juan; **tener un t. agradable** to have a pleasant manner; **t. diario** daily contact ❏ **malos tratos** ill-treatment sing; **t. de gentes** a way with people (**b**) (acuerdo) agreement; **hicimos el t. de dejar de fumar** we agreed to stop smoking; **¡t. hecho!** it's a deal! (**c**) Com deal; **cerrar un t.** to close a deal; **estar en tratos con algn** to be negotiating with sb (**d**) (tratamiento) title; **dar a algn el t. de Señoría** to address sb as Your Lordship

trauma nm trauma; Fam **el t. de la mili** the drag of doing military service

traumático, -a adj traumatic

traumatismo nm traumatism

traumatizante adj traumatic

traumatizar [14] vt Med to traumatize; Fam to shock

traumatología nf (hospital) accident ward

traumatólogo, -a nm,f Med traumatologist

travelín nm Cin TV travelling o US traveling shot

través 1 nm (**a**) (de madera) crosspiece, crossbeam (**b**) (inclinación) slant (**c**) Fig (desgracia) misfortune
2 adv (**a**) **a t. de** through; (por dentro) **a t. de ese agujero** through that hole; (por medio de) **lo supe a t. de su mujer** I found out through his wife (**b**) **de t.** (transversalmente) crosswise; **pon los cubiertos de t. en el plato** place the cutlery crosswise on the plate (**c**) (de lado) sideways; **mirar de t.** to look askance at; **ponlo de t. o no pasará** put it sideways or it won't go through
3 prep **al** o **a t.** across, over; **a t. del río** across the river

travesaño nm (**a**) Arquit crosspiece (**b**) Ftb crossbar

travesía nf (**a**) (viaje) voyage; **la t. del Atlántico** the crossing of the Atlantic (**b**) (calle) cross street, passage

travestí (*pl* **travestís** *o* **travestíes**) *nmf*, **travesti** (*pl* **travestis**) *nmf (que se viste de mujer)* transvestite; *(artista)* drag artist

travestirse [47] *vpr* to cross-dress

travestismo *nm* transvestism

travesura *nf* piece of mischief, childish prank; **hacer travesuras** to get into mischief

traviesa *nf Ferroc Br* sleeper, *US* tie

travieso, -a *adj* mischievous, naughty

trayecto *nm* (**a**) *(distancia)* distance, way; **hay un largo t. de aquí a Madrid** it's a long way *o* journey from here to Madrid (**b**) *(recorrido)* route, itinerary; **final de(l) t.** terminus, end of the line

trayectoria *nf* (**a**) *(de proyectil, geométrica)* trajectory (**b**) *Fig (orientación)* line, course; **la impecable t. democrática de nuestro partido** our party's unblemished democratic record

traza *nf* (**a**) *(apariencia)* looks *pl*, appearance; **no llevar** *o* **tener trazas de** not to look as if; **no lleva trazas de curarse** it doesn't look as if he's going to get better (**b**) *Arquit* plan, design (**c**) *(maña)* skill, knack; **este chico no tiene ninguna t. para la pintura** this boy is no good at painting

trazado, -a 1 *pp de* **trazar**
2 *adj* laid out, designed
3 *nm* (**a**) *(plano)* layout, plan (**b**) *(dibujo)* drawing, sketch (**c**) *(de carretera, ferrocarril)* route, course

trazar [14] *vt* (**a**) *(línea, mapa)* to draw; *(parque)* to lay out; *(edificio)* to design; *(esbozo)* to draw (up) (**b**) *(describir)* to sketch; **t. una semblanza (de algn)** to describe *o* depict (sb) (**c**) *Fig (idear)* to draw up the broad lines of

trazo *nm* (**a**) *(línea)* line (**b**) *(de una letra)* stroke (**c**) *(rasgo facial)* feature

trébol *nm* (**a**) *Bot* clover, trefoil (**b**) *Naipes* club (**c**) *(carreteras)* (motorway) interchange

trece *inv* **1** *adj (cardinal)* thirteen; *(ordinal)* thirteenth; **el t. de abril** the thirteenth of April, April the thirteenth; **martes y t.** ≃ Friday 13th
2 *nm* thirteen; *Fig* **estar** *o* **mantenerse** *o* **seguir en sus t.** to stick to one's guns; *véase tamb* **ocho**

treceavo, -a *adj* thirteenth; *véase tamb* **octavo, -a**

trecho *nm* (**a**) *(distancia)* distance, way; **a trechos** in parts *o* places; *Prov* **del dicho al hecho hay un buen t.** there's many a slip 'twixt cup and lip (**b**) *Agr* plot, patch (**c**) *Fam* bit, piece

tregua *nf Mil* truce; *Fig* respite, rest

treinta *inv* **1** *adj (cardinal)* thirty; *(ordinal)* thirtieth; **murió el t. de junio** he died on the thirtieth of June *o* June the thirtieth; **los años t.** the thirties
2 *nm* thirty; *véase tamb* **ochenta** *y* **ocho**

treintañero, -a *adj* & *nm,f Fam* thirtysomething

treintavo, -a 1 *adj* thirtieth
2 *nm (parte)* thirtieth; *véase tamb* **octavo, -a**

treintena *nf* thirty; **una t. de invitados** thirty-odd guests

trekking ['trekin] *nm* hiking

tremebundo, -a *adj* terrible, dreadful

tremendismo *nm Lit* = graphic Spanish post-war realism

tremendista *adj* sensationalist

tremendo, -a *adj* (**a**) *(terrible)* terrible, dreadful, frightful; *Fam* **tomarse algo por la tremenda** to make a great fuss about sth (**b**) *(muy grande)* enormous; *Fig* tremendous

trementina *nf* turpentine □ **esencia de t.** oil *o* spirits of turpentine

tremolina *nf Fam* uproar, shindy

trémolo *nm Mús* tremolo

trémulo, -a *adj Literario (vacilante)* quivering, tremulous; *(luz, llama)* flickering

tren *nm* (**a**) *Ferroc* train; **cambiar de t.** to change (trains), *US* transfer; **coger** *o* **tomar el t.** to catch *o* take the train; **el tren a** *o* **para París** the train to Paris; **iremos en t.** we'll go by train; *Fam Fig* **estar como (para parar) un t.** to be hot stuff *o* very sexy □ **t. correo** mail train; **t. de cercanías** suburban train; **t. de mercancías** *o* **de carga** goods *o* *US* freight train; **t. de pasajeros** passenger train; **t. directo** through train (**b**) *Mil* convoy (**c**) *Téc* set (of gears *o* wheels) □ *Av* **t. de aterrizaje** undercarriage; **t. de lavado** car wash (**d**) *Fig (ritmo)* speed, pace; **vivir a todo t.** to lead a grand life □ **t. de vida** lifestyle

trena *nf Argot* slammer, *Br* nick, *US* pen

trenca *nf (prenda)* duffel *o* duffle coat

trencilla *nf Cost* braided ribbon

trenza *nf* (**a**) *(de pelo) Br* plait, *US* braid; **t. postiza** switch (**b**) *Cost* braid (**c**) *RP (pelea)* quarrel, fight

trenzado, -a 1 *pp de* **trenzar**
2 *adj* (**a**) *(entrelazado)* intertwined (**b**) *Cost* braided (**c**) *(cabello) Br* plaited, *US* braided

trenzar [14] **1** *vt* to intertwine; *(pelo) Br* to plait, *US* braid
2 trenzarse *vpr RP (enredarse, enzarzarse)* to get involved; **trenzarse en una pelea** to get into a fight

trepa *nmf Esp Fam Pey* go-getter, social climber

trepador, -a 1 *adj* **planta trepadora** climber, creeper
2 *nm,f Fam* go-getter, social climber

trepadora *nf Bot* climber, creeper

trepanación *nf Med* trepanation

trepanar *vt Med* to trepan

trépano *nm (en perforaciones)* bit

trepar¹ *vt (persona)* to climb
2 *vi* (**a**) *(persona, planta)* climb (**b**) *Fam Fig (socialmente)* to be a social climber

trepar² *vt* (**a**) *(taladrar)* to drill (**b**) *Cost* to trim

trepidación *nf* vibration, shaking

trepidante *adj* vibrating, shaking; *Fig* **lleva un ritmo de vida t.** he leads a hectic *o* frantic life

trepidar *vi* (**a**) *(vibrar)* to vibrate, shake (**b**) *Chile (vacilar)* to hesitate

tres 1 *adj inv (cardinal)* three; *(ordinal)* third; **el t. de mayo tengo un examen** I've got an examination on May the third; **las t.** three o'clock; *Fam* **como t. y dos son cinco** as sure as eggs are eggs; *Fam* **de t. al cuarto** cheap, of little value; *Fam* **ni a la de t.** there is/was no way
2 *nm* three; **t. en raya** *Br* noughts and crosses, *US* tick-tack-toe; *véase tamb* **ocho**

trescientos, -as 1 *adj inv (cardinal)* three hundred; *(ordinal)* three hundredth; **en (el año) mil t. cuarenta y uno** in (the year) thirteen forty-one
2 *nm* three hundred; *véase tamb* **ochenta** *y* **ocho**

tresillo *nm* (**a**) *Mueb* (three-piece) suite (**b**) *Mús* triplet (**c**) *Naipes* ombre

treta *nf* trick, ruse

tríada *nf* triad

trial *nm Dep* trial; **t. indoor** indoor trial

triangular *adj* triangular

triángulo 1 *adj* triangular
2 *nm* (**a**) *Geom Mús* triangle □ **t. equilátero** equilateral triangle; **t. isósceles** isosceles triangle; **t. rectángulo** right-angled triangle (**b**) *(en relaciones) Fig* **t. amoroso** love triangle

triatlón *nm Dep* triathlon

tribal *adj* tribal, tribe

tribalismo *nm* tribalism

tribu *nf* tribe

tribulación *nf* tribulation

tribuna *nf* (a) *(plataforma)* rostrum, dais; **t. de (la) prensa** press box (b) *Dep* grandstand

tribunal *nm* (a) *Jur* court; **llevar a los tribunales** to take to court ⊐ **T. Constitucional** constitutional court; **t. de apelación** court of appeal; **T. Supremo** *Br* ≃ High Court, *US* ≃ Supreme Court; **t. (tutelar) de menores** juvenile court (b) *(de examen)* board of examiners

tribuno *nm Hist* tribune

tributable *adj* subject *o* liable to tax

tributación *nf* taxation, levy

tributar *vt (impuestos)* to pay; **t. un homenaje** to pay a tribute

tributario, -a 1 *adj* tax; **sistema t.** tax system
  2 *nm,f* taxpayer

tributo *nm* (a) *(impuesto)* tax (b) *Fig Hist* tribute; **t. de amistad** token of friendship

tríceps *nm inv Anat* triceps *sing*

triciclo *nm* tricycle

tricolor *adj* tricolour, *US* tricolor, tricoloured, *US* tricolored

tricornio *nm* (a) *(sombrero)* three-cornered hat, tricorn, tricorne (b) *Argot (guardia civil)* (member of the) civil guard

tricot *nm* knit, tricot

tricotar *vt & vi* to knit; **máquina de t.** knitting machine

tricotosa *nf* knitting machine

tridente *nm* trident

tridimensional *adj* three-dimensional

triedro *nm Geom* trihedron

trienal *adj* triennial

trienio *nm* triennium

trifásico, -a 1 *adj Elec* three-phase
  2 *nm Fam* white coffee with brandy

trifulca *nf Fig* squabble, row, rumpus

trigal *nm* wheat field

trigésimo, -a 1 *adj* thirtieth; **t. primero** thirty-first
  2 *nm,f (de una serie)* thirtieth
  3 *nm (parte)* thirtieth; *véase tamb* **octavo, -a**

trigo *nm* (a) *Bot* wheat; *Fig* **meterse en trigo(s) ajeno(s)** to meddle in sb else's affairs; *Fig* **no ser t. limpio** *(persona)* to be a bad lot; *(asunto)* to be dubious *o* shady (b) *Fam (dinero)* dough

trigonometría *nf* trigonometry

trigonométrico, -a *adj* trigonometric, trigonometrical

trigueño, -a *adj (pelo)* corn-coloured, *US* corn-colored, dark blonde; *(piel)* dark, swarthy; *(persona)* olive-skinned

triguero, -a 1 *adj* wheat; **espárrago t.** wild asparagus
  2 *nm Orn* corn bunting

trilateral *adj* three-sided, trilateral

trilingüe *adj* trilingual

trilita *nf* gelignite

trilla *nf* (a) *Agr* threshing (b) *Andes PRico Fam (paliza)* thrashing, beating

trillado, -a 1 *pp de* **trillar**
  2 *adj Fig (expresión)* overworked, well-worn; **fuera de los caminos trillados** off the beaten track

trillador, -a *nm,f* thresher

trilladora *nf* threshing machine; **t. segadora** combine harvester

trillar *vt Agr* to thresh

trillizo, -a *nm,f* triplet

trillo *nm* (a) *Agr* thresher (b) *CAm Carib (vereda)* path

trillón *nm Br* trillion, *US* quintillion

trilogía *nf* trilogy

trimestral *adj* quarterly, three-monthly, trimestral; **examen t.** end-of-term examination

trimestralmente *adv* quarterly, every three months

trimestre *nm* quarter, trimester; *Educ* term

trimotor *nm Av* three-engined aircraft

trinar *vi* (a) *Orn Mús* to warble (b) *Fam* to rage, fume; **María estaba que trinaba cuando por fin llegué** María was really fuming when I finally arrived

trinca *nf* trio, threesome

trincar [59] **1** *vt Fam (capturar)* to catch
  2 trincarse *vpr* (a) *Ofens* to screw; **t. a una tía** to screw a *Br* bird *o US* chick (b) *Fam* to drink; **se trincó una botella de ron él solito** he put away a bottle of rum all by himself

trinchante *nm* (a) *(cubierto)* carving knife (b) *Mueb* serving *o* side table

trinchar *vt (carne)* to carve, slice (up)

trinche *nm Andes Méx* fork

trinchera *nf Mil* trench

trinchero *nm véase* **trinchante b**

trineo *nm* sled, sledge, sleigh

Trinidad *n* Trinidad

trinidad *nf Rel* trinity; **la Santísima T.** the Blessed *o* Holy Trinity

Trinidad y Tobago *n* Trinidad and Tobago

trinitario, -a *adj & nm,f* Trinitarian

trino *nm* (a) *Orn* warble, trill (b) *Mús* trill

trinomio *nm Mat* trinomial

trinquete¹ *nm Náut* foremast

trinquete² *nm Dep* = pelota played in a closed court

trinquete³ *nm Téc* pawl, ratchet

trío *nm* trio

trip *nm Argot (drogas)* trip

tripa *nf* (a) *(intestino)* gut, intestine; *Fig* **hacer de tripas corazón** to pluck up courage; *Fig* **revolver las tripas** to turn one's stomach (b) *Esp Fam (barriga)* belly, gut; **está echando t.** he's getting a pot belly *o* a bit of a gut (c) *Fam (en lenguaje de niños)* tummy (d) *(de embarazada)* bump, bulge (e) *(de vasija)* belly (f) *Fam* **tripas** *(interior)* insides

tripartito, -a *adj* divided into three, tripartite

tripi *nm Fam (de LSD)* tab

triple *adj & nm* triple; **si aciertas, ganarás el t.** if you win, you'll get back three times your money; **un t. salto mortal** a triple somersault

triplicado, -a 1 *pp de* **triplicar**
  2 *adj* triplicate; **por t.** in triplicate

triplicar [59] *vt* to triple, treble

triplicidad *nf* triplicity

trípode *nm* tripod

Trípoli *n* Tripoli

tripón, -ona *nm,f Fam* potbellied person

tríptico *nm* triptych

triptongo *nm Ling* triphthong

tripudo, -a *adj Fam* paunchy, potbellied

tripulación *nf* crew

tripulante *nmf* crew member

tripular *vt (avión)* to fly; *(barco)* to steer

trique *nm Col Cuba (juego) Br* noughts and crosses, *US* tick-tack-toe

triquinosis *nf inv* trichinosis

triquiñuela *nf Fam* trick, dodge; **andarse con triquiñuelas** to be a trickster, **saberse las triquiñuelas** to know (all) the dodges

triquitraque *nm* clackety-clack, clatter

tris *nm Fig* bit; **en un t.** in a jiffy; **estuve en un t. de llamarte** I nearly called you; **por un t.** by the skin of one's teeth; **no se cayó por un t.** it was pure luck that he didn't fall

trisílabo, -a *Ling* **1** *adj* trisyllabic
  2 *nm* trisyllable

triste *adj* (a) *(infeliz)* sad, unhappy; **es t., pero es verdad** it's sad but true; **poner t. a algn** to make sb sad; **ponerse t.** to become *o* grow sad (b) *(oscuro, sombrío)* dismal, gloomy; **hacer un t. papel** to cut a sorry figure; **t. futuro** bleak future (c) *(único)* single, only; **ni un t. penique** not a single penny (d) *(insignificante)* poor, humble; **su padre era un t. picapedrero** his father was a simple stonecutter

tristeza *nf* sadness; **tristezas** problems, sufferings

tristón, -ona *adj Fam* gloomy, sad

tritón *nm* (a) *Zool* newt (b) *Mit* Triton

trituración *nf* grinding, trituration

triturado, -a *pp de* **triturar**
  2 *adj* ground, crushed; *Fig* **me ha devuelto el libro t.** he's given the book back to me all crumpled up

triturador *nm (de basura)* waste-disposal unit; *(de papeles)* shredder; *(de ajos)* garlic press

trituradora *nf* crushing machine, grinder

triturar *vt* (a) *(machacar)* to grind (up), triturate (b) *Fig (físicamente)* to beat (up); *(moralmente)* to tear apart

triunfador, -a **1** *adj* winning
  2 *nm,f* winner

triunfal *adj* triumphant; **salir t.** to come out the winner *o* on top

triunfalismo *nm* boastfulness; *Pol* jingoism

triunfalista *adj* boastful; *Pol* jingoistic, chauvinist, chauvinistic

triunfar *vi* to triumph, win; **t. en la vida** to succeed in life

triunfo *nm* (a) *(victoria)* triumph, victory; *Dep* win (b) *(éxito)* success (c) *Naipes* trump

triunvirato *nm Hist* triumvirate

trivial *adj* trivial, petty

trivialidad *nf* triviality, pettiness

trivializar [14] *vt* to trivialize, minimize

triza *nf* bit, fragment; **hacer trizas** to tear to shreds; *(gastar)* to wear out; *Fam Fig* **estoy hecho trizas** I feel washed out

trocar [67] **1** *vt* (a) *Com (permutar)* to barter, exchange (b) *(transformar)* to turn (**en** into), convert
  2 trocarse *vpr (mudarse)* to change (**en** into), switch round

trocear *vt* to cut up (into bits *o* pieces)

troche: a troche y moche *loc adv Fam* haphazardly

trofeo *nm* trophy

troglodita *nmf* troglodyte

trola *nf Fam* lie, fib

trole *nm* trolley (pole)

trolebús *nm* trolley bus

trolero, -a *Fam* **1** *adj* lying
  2 *nm* liar, fibber

tromba *nf* waterspout ❑ **t. de agua** violent downpour

trombo *nm Med* thrombus

trombón **1** *nm Mús (instrumento)* trombone ❑ **t. de pistones** *o* **llaves** valve trombone; **t. de varas** slide trombone
  2 *nmf* trombonist

trombosis *nf inv Med* thrombosis

trompa **1** *nf* (a) *Mús* horn (b) *(de elefante)* trunk (c) *(de insecto)* proboscis (d) *Fam Fig* hooter (e) *Anat* tube ❑ **t. de Eustaquio** Eustachian tube, **t. de Faloplo** Fallopian tube (f) *(nube) véase* **tromba** (g) *Fam (borrachera)* **llevar una t., estar t.** to be sloshed *o* plastered
  2 *nmf* horn player

trompada *nf* (a) *(puñetazo)* thump, punch (b) *(choque de personas)* bump, collision (c) *Argot (drogas)* hit

trompazo *nm* bump; **darse** *o* **pegarse un t.** to have a bump, crash

trompeta **1** *nf (instrumento)* trumpet
  2 *nmf* trumpet player

trompetazo *nm* trumpet blast

trompetilla *nf* ear trumpet

trompetista *nmf* trumpet player, trumpeter

trompicar [59] *vi* to trip (up), stumble

trompicón *nm* (a) *(tropezón)* trip, stumble; **a trompicones** in fits and starts; **saqué la carrera a trompicones** I scraped through and got my degree (b) *(golpe)* blow, hit

trompo *nm* spinning top

trompudo, -a *adj Am* (a) *(de labios gruesos)* thick-lipped (b) *(malhumorado)* bad-tempered

tronada *nf* thunder storm

tronado, -a **1** *pp de* **tronar**
  2 *adj* old, broken-down

tronar [63] *vi* to thunder

troncal *adj* **carretera t.** trunk road; **asignatura t.** compulsory *o* core subject

troncha *nf Am* (a) *(tajada)* slice (b) *Fam (suerte)* good luck

tronchante *adj Fam* hilarious, uproarious

tronchar **1** *vt* (a) *(árboles)* to cut down, fell (b) *Fig (esperanzas etc)* to destroy
  2 troncharse *vpr* **t. de risa** to split one's sides laughing

troncho *nm* stem, stalk

tronco *nm* (a) *Anat* trunk, torso (b) *Bot (tallo de árbol)* trunk; *(leño)* log; *Fam Fig* **dormir como un t.** to sleep like a log (c) *Geom* frustum; **t. de cono** truncated cone (d) *(tiro de dos caballos)* team (e) *(linaje)* family stock (f) *Esp Argot (compañero)* pal, *Br* mate, *US* buddy

tronera **1** *nf* (a) *(de fortificación)* loophole; *Náut* porthole (b) *(en billar)* pocket
  2 *nmf Fam (hombre)* rake; *(mujer)* slut, loose woman

trono *nm* throne

tropa *nf* (a) *Mil* soldiers *pl*; **tropas** *(ejército)* troops **tropas de asalto** storm troops (b) *Fam (multitud)* troop, flock (c) *RP (ganado)* herd, drove (d) *RP (caravana de ganado)* convoy

tropecientos, -as *adj inv Fam* hundreds (and hundreds) of, umpteen

tropel *nm* throng, mob; **en t.** in a mad rush

tropelía *nf* (a) *(atropello)* outrage (b) *véase* **tropel** (c) *(delito)* crime

tropero *nm RP* cattle drover

tropezar [17] *vi* (a) *(tropicar)* to trip, stumble (**con** on); **t. con algo** to come across sth; **t. con algn** to run *o* bump into sb; **tropecé con Quique en el concierto** I ran into Quique at the concert (b) *Fig* **t. con** *(dificultades)* to come up against; *(persona)* to disagree with; **el proyecto tropezó con muchos obstáculos** the project ran into many difficulties

tropezón nm (a) (traspié) trip, stumble; **dar un t.** to trip; Fig **a tropezones** in fits and starts (b) Fig (error) slip-up, faux pas (c) Fam (de comida) chunk of meat

tropical adj tropical

trópico nm tropic ❏ **T. de Cáncer** Tropic of Cancer

tropiezo 1 nm (a) (obstáculo) trip (b) Fig (error) blunder, faux pas; (revés) setback, mishap (c) (riña) quarrel
2 indic pres véase **tropezar**

tropilla nf Am drove

troposfera nf Geog troposphere

troquel nm die

troquelar vt to stamp

trotaconventos nf inv Literario procuress, go-between

trotador, -a adj trotting

trotamundos nmf inv globe-trotter

trotar vi (a) (caballo) to trot (b) Fam (andar deprisa) to bustle, run about

trote nm (a) (de caballo) trot; **al t.** at a trot (b) Fam (actividad) chasing about, (hustle and) bustle; **de** o **para todo t.** for everyday use o wear; **ya no está para esos trotes** he can't keep up the pace any more

trotón, -ona adj trotting

troupe [trup] (pl troupes) nf troupe

trova nf Lit medieval poem, lyric

trovador nm troubadour

trovadoresco, -a adj troubadour

Troya n Hist Troy; **caballo de T.** Trojan horse; Fig **aquí** o **allí fue T.** that's where o when the trouble began

troyano, -a adj & nm,f Trojan

trozar vt Am (carne, tronco) to cut up; (res) to butcher

trozo nm piece, chunk; **lo cortó a trozos** he cut it in(to) pieces

trucado, -a adj **una baraja/fotografía trucada** a trick Br pack o US deck/photograph; **dados trucados** (cargados) loaded dice; **el contador del gas estaba t.** the gas meter had been tampered with

trucaje nm Cin trick photography

trucar [59] vt (contador) to tamper with; (motor) to soup up

trucha nf (a) (pez) trout (b) CAm (tenderete) stand, kiosk

trucho, -a adj (a) (falso) bogus (b) (de mala calidad) dodgy, rubbishy

truco nm (a) (ardid) trick; TV Cin gimmick; **este rompecabezas tiene t.** this puzzle has a catch; **t. publicitario** advertising stunt o gimmick (b) (tranquillo) knack; **coger el t. (a algo)** to get the knack o hang (of sth) (c) RP (juego de naipes) = type of card game (d) Chile (golpe) punch, thump

truculencia nf (crueldad) cruelty; (exceso) sensationalism

truculento, -a adj (cruel) cruel; (excesivo) sensationalistic

trueno nm (a) Meteor thunder, thunderclap (b) Fam (joven) madcap

trueque nm Com barter, exchange

trufa nf (a) Bot Culin truffle (b) (bombón) chocolate truffle

trufar vt Culin to stuff with truffles

truhán, -ana nm,f rogue, crook

trullo nm Argot slammer, Br nick, US pen

truncado, -a 1 pp de **truncar**
2 adj truncate, truncated, cut short

truncar [59] **1** vt (a) (cortar) to truncate, Fig cut short; Fig **t. las ilusiones** to shatter hopes (b) Fig (escrito) to leave unfinished, cut off; (sentido) to upset
2 truncarse vpr Fig to cut short

trunco, -a adj Am incomplete

trusa nf (a) Carib (traje de baño) swimsuit (b) Perú (short) briefs pl (c) RP (faja) girdle

trust [trus(t)] (pl **trusts**) nm Fin trust, cartel

tse-tsé adj **mosca t.-t.** tsetse o tzetze fly

tu (pl tus) adj pos your; **tu libro** your book; **tus libros** your books

tú pron you; **de tú a tú** on equal terms; **trátame de tú, por favor** call me 'tú' please

tuareg nmpl Tuareg, Tuaregs

tuba nf Mús tuba

tuberculina nf tuberculin

tubérculo nm (a) Bot tuber (b) Med tubercle

tuberculosis nf inv Med tuberculosis

tuberculoso, -a adj (a) Bot tuberous (b) Med tubercular, tuberculous

tubería nf (a) (de agua) piping, pipes pl, plumbing (b) (de gas, petróleo) pipeline

tubo nm (a) (de análisis etc) tube; Fam Fig **hacer pasar a algn por el t.** to put the screws on sb; Fam Fig **pasar por el t.** to knuckle under; Esp Argot **alucinar por un t.** to flip (out) ❏ **t. de ensayo** test tube (b) (tubería) pipe ❏ Aut **t. de escape** exhaust (pipe) (c) Anat tract ❏ **t. digestivo** digestive tract, alimentary canal (d) Chile (rulo) curl (e) RP Ven (de teléfono) receiver

tubular 1 adj tubular
2 nm bicycle tyre

tucán nm Orn toucan

tuco, -a 1 adj CAm Ecuad PRico one-armed
2 nm Am (trozo) piece
3 nm,f (a) CAm Ecuad PRico (fragmento) piece, fragment (b) Perú (ave) owl

tuerca nf Téc nut

tuerto, -a 1 adj one-eyed, blind in one eye; **quedarse t.** to become o go blind in one eye
2 nm,f one-eyed person
3 nm (agravio) wrong, injustice

tuerzo indic pres véase **torcer**

tueste nm **t. natural** medium roast; **t. torrefacto** high roast

tuétano nm marrow; Fig bones pl, essence; **hasta los tuétanos** through and through; **estaba dolida hasta los tuétanos** she was cut to the bone

tufo nm (a) (mal olor) foul odour o US odor o smell, fug (b) (emanación) fume, vapour, US vapor

tugurio nm (a) (casucha) hovel, shack (b) Fig hole

tul nm Cost tulle

tulipa nf (a) Bot small tulip (b) (lámpara) tulip-shaped lampshade

tulipán nm Bot tulip

tullido, -a 1 pp de **tullir**
2 adj crippled, disabled
3 nm,f cripple

tullir vt (a) (paralizar) to cripple (b) (de cansancio) to wear o tire out

tumba[1] nf grave, tomb; Fig **a t. abierta** (at) full speed; Fam **soy (como) una t.** my lips are sealed

tumba[2] nf Col Cuba (tala) felling

tumbadero nm (a) Cuba Méx PRico (terreno) clearing (b) Ven (corral) branding yard

tumbado, -a 1 pp de **tumbar**
2 adj lying, stretched out; **t. al sol** lying in the sun
3 nm Ecuad ceiling

tumbar 1 vt (a) (derribar) to knock down o over (b) Educ

Fam to fail (**c**) *Col Cuba (talar)* to fell (**d**) *Argot (matar)* to bump off
  2 *vi (caer a tierra)* to fall down
  3 tumbarse *vpr* (**a**) *(acostarse)* to lie down, stretch out (**b**) *(arrellanarse)* to lie back (**c**) *Ofens* to screw, lay
tumbo *nm* jolt, bump; **dar tumbos** to jolt, bump
tumbona *nf* easy chair; *(de lona)* deck chair
tumefacción *nf* swelling
tumefacto, -a *adj* swollen
tumor *nm Med* tumour, *US* tumor ❑ **t. cerebral** brain tumour
túmulo *nm* (**a**) *(en arqueología)* tumulus, barrow (**b**) *Geog* mound (**c**) *(catafalco)* catafalque
tumulto *nm* tumult, commotion
tumultuoso, -a *adj* tumultuous, riotous
tuna *nf* (**a**) *(agrupación musical)* = group of student minstrels (**b**) *Am (higo chumbo)* prickly pear
tunante, -a 1 *adj* **el muy t. se largó sin pagar** the rascal cleared off without paying
  2 *nm,f* rogue, rascal
tunco, -a 1 *adj Méx (manco) (sin una mano)* one-handed; *(sin un brazo)* one-armed
  2 *nm CAm Méx (animal)* pig
tunda *nf Fam* (**a**) *(paliza)* beating, thrashing (**b**) *(trabajo agotador)* exhausting job, drag
tundir *vt* to thrash
tundra *nf Geog* tundra
tunecino, -a *adj & nm,f* Tunisian
túnel *nm* tunnel ❑ *Aut* **t. de lavado** car wash
Túnez *n* (**a**) *(país)* Tunisia (**b**) *(ciudad)* Tunis
túnica *nf (prenda)* tunic
tuno¹ *nm Bot* prickly pear
tuno, -a² 1 *nm,f (bribón)* rogue, rascal
  2 *nm (estudiante)* member of a **tuna**
tuntún: al (buen) tuntún *loc adv* haphazardly, any old how
tupé *nm* (**a**) *(peluca)* toupee (**b**) *Fam (descaro)* nerve, cheek
tupición *nf* (**a**) *Am Fig* confusion (**b**) *Méx (espesura)* dense vegetation
tupido, -a 1 *pp de* **tupir**
  2 *adj* thick, dense
tupir 1 *vt (apretar)* to pack tight, press down
  2 tupirse *vpr* (**a**) *(de comida)* to stuff oneself (**b**) *(confundirse)* to get muddleheaded
turba¹ *nf* (**a**) *(combustible)* peat, turf (**b**) *(abono)* peat (moss)
turba² *nf (muchedumbre)* mob, crowd
turbación *nf* (**a**) *(alteración)* disturbance (**b**) *(preocupación)* anxiety, worry (**c**) *(desconcierto)* confusion, uneasiness
turbado, -a 1 *pp de* **turbar**
  2 *adj* (**a**) *(alterado)* disturbed, unsettled (**b**) *(preocupado)* worried, anxious (**c**) *(desconcertado)* confused, baffled, put off
turbador, -a *adj* (**a**) *(que altera)* disturbing, unsettling (**b**) *(preocupante)* worrying (**c**) *(desconcertante)* confusing, disconcerting, off-putting
turbante *nm (prenda)* turban
turbar 1 *vt* (**a**) *(alterar)* to unsettle; *(paz, tranquilidad)* to disturb; *(agua)* to stir up (**b**) *(preocupar)* to upset, worry (**c**) *(desconcertar)* to baffle, put off
  2 turbarse *vpr* (**a**) *(preocuparse)* to be o become upset (**b**) *(desconcertarse)* to be o become confused, be baffled
turbina *nf Téc* turbine

turbio, -a *adj* (**a**) *(oscurecido)* cloudy, muddy, turbid; *Fig* **lo veo todo t.** I see everything blurry (**b**) *Pey* shady, dubious; **un negocio t.** a shady business (**c**) *Fig (turbulento)* turbulent; **un período t.** an unsettled o turbulent period
turbo *nm* turbocharger
turbodiesel *adj* **motor t.** turbocharged diesel engine
turbonada *nf Meteor* (**a**) *(chubasco)* stormy squall o downpour (**b**) *Arg (viento)* gale
turbopropulsor *nm* turboprop
turborreactor *nm Téc* turbojet (engine)
turbulencia *nf* turbulence
turbulento, -a *adj* turbulent, troubled, unruly
turco, -a 1 *adj* (**a**) *(de Turquía)* Turkish; **cama turca** divan (**b**) *Andes CSur Ven Pey (árabe)* Arab
  2 *nm,f* (**a**) *(de Turquía)* Turk; *Fig* **cabeza de t.** scapegoat (**b**) *Andes CSur Ven Pey (árabe)* Arab
  3 *nm (idioma)* Turkish
turcomano, -a *adj & nm,f* Turkman, Turkoman
turgencia *nf* turgidity, turgidness
turgente *adj*, **túrgido, -a** *adj* turgid
turismo *nm* (**a**) *(actividad)* tourism, touring; **hacer t.** to go touring o sightseeing ❑ **t. de aventura** adventure holidays *pl* ; **t. rural** rural tourism, country holidays *pl*; **casas de t. rural** rural holiday properties (**b**) *(industria)* tourist trade o industry (**c**) *Aut* private car
turista *nmf* tourist; **hacer el t.** to get taken in
turístico, -a *adj* tourist; **lugares de interés t.** tourist sites
Turkmenistán *n* Turkmenistan
turmalina *nf Min* tourmaline
túrmix® *nm* liquidizer, blender
turnar 1 *vt Méx (enviar)* to dispatch
  2 turnarse *vpr* to take turns (**con** with)
turnedó *nm* tournedos
turno *nm* (**a**) *(tanda)* turn, go; **¿a quién le toca el t.?** who's next? (**b**) *(período de trabajo)* shift; **estar de t.** to be on duty; **t. de día/noche** day/night shift
turolense 1 *adj* of o from Teruel
  2 *nmf* person from Teruel
turón *nm* polecat
turquesa *adj & nf* turquoise
Turquestán *n* Turkestan, Turkistan
Turquía *n* Turkey
turro, -a *adj Arg* stupid, idiotic
turrón *nm* = Christmas sweet similar to nougat made with almonds and honey or sugar
turulato, -a *adj Fam* flabbergasted, flummoxed
tururú *adj Fam* touched; **¡t.!** get stuffed!
tusa *nf* (**a**) *CAm Carib Col (mazorca) Br* maize husk, *US* cornhusk (**b**) *Andes Cuba (cigarro)* = cigar rolled in a *Br* maize husk o *US* cornhusk (**c**) *Chile (crines)* mane (**d**) *Col (de viruela)* pockmark (**e**) *CAm (prostituta)* prostitute
tusar *vt Am* to crop
tuso, -a 1 *adj* (**a**) *Col (de viruela)* pockmarked (**b**) *PRico (de rabo corto)* short-tailed; *(sin rabo)* tailless
  2 *interj Am Fam* **¡t.!** *(para llamar al perro)* here, boy!
tute *nm* (**a**) *Naipes* = card game (**b**) *Fam* beating, thrashing; **darse un t.** to wear oneself out
tutear 1 *vt* to address as 'tú'
  2 tutearse *vpr* to address (each other o one another) as **tú**; *Fig* to be on familiar terms
tutela *nf* (**a**) *Jur* guardianship, tutelage; **bajo t.** in ward (**b**)

Fig (protección) protection, guidance; **bajo la t. de** under the protection of

tutelaje *nm Jur* guardianship

tutelar *adj* tutelar, tutelary

tuteo *nm* = use of the 'tú' form of address

tutiplén: a tutiplén *loc adv Fam* in a grand way, **come a t.** he eats like there's no tomorrow

tutor, -a *nm,f* **(a)** *Jur* guardian **(b)** *Educ (en universidad, privado)* tutor; *(en colegio, escuela) Br* form teacher, *US* class teacher

tutoría *nf* **(a)** *Jur* guardianship, tutorship **(b)** *Educ (sesión)* tutorial

tutorial *nm Inform* tutorial

tutú (*pl* **tutús**) *nm* tutu

tutuma *nf Am Fam* calabash, gourd

tuturuto, -a *adj Col Ecuad Ven Fam* stunned, dumbfounded

tuyo, -a 1 *adj pos* yours; **este dinero es t.** this money is yours; **¿es amigo t.?** is he a friend of yours?; **un libro t.** one of your books; **unas amigas tuyas** some friends of yours

2 *pron pos* yours; **éste es el t.** this one is yours; **métete en lo t.** mind your own business; **prométeme que no harás de las tuyas** promise me that you won't get up to your old tricks; *Fam* **los tuyos** *(familiares)* your family; *(amigos)* your friends

TV *(abrev de* **televisión**) TV

TVE *nf (abrev de* **Televisión Española**)

tweed *nm Tex* tweed

twist [twist] *nm Mús* twist

U

U (*pl* **Úes**) *nf*, **u** (*pl* **úes**) [u] *nf (la letra)* U, u

u *conj (delante de palabras que empiecen por* **o** *o* **ho***)* or; **siete u ocho** seven or eight; **ayer u hoy** yesterday or today

UA *nf (abrev de* **Unión Africana***)* AU

Uagadugú *n* Ouagadougou

ubérrimo, -a *adj* very fertile, rich; **vegetación ubérrima** luxuriant vegetation

ubicación *nf* location, position

ubicar [59] **1** *vt* **(a)** *(situar)* to place, position; *(edificio)* to locate **(b)** *Am (encontrar)* to find **(c)** *Chile (candidato)* to nominate
   2 ubicarse *vpr* **(a)** *(edificio)* to be situated, be located **(b)** *(persona)* to get one's bearings; **no me ubico** I haven't got my bearings **(c)** *RP (encontrar empleo)* to find a job, get a position

ubicuidad *nf* ubiquity

ubicuo, -a *adj* ubiquitous, omnipresent

ubre *nf Zool* udder

UCI ['uθi] *nf (abrev de* **unidad de cuidados intensivos***)* ICU

Ucrania *n* Ukraine

ucraniano, -a 1 *adj* Ukrainian
   2 *nm,f (persona)* Ukrainian
   3 *nm (idioma)* Ukrainian

Ud. *(abrev de* **usted***)* you

Uds. *(abrev de* **ustedes***)* you

UE *nf (abrev de* **Unión Europea***)* EU

UEFA ['wefa] *nf (abrev de* **Union of European Football Associations***)* UEFA

UEM [uem] *nf (abrev de* **unión económica y monetaria***)* EMU

UEO *nf (abrev de* **Unión de la Europa Occidental***)* WEU

uf *interj* **(a)** *(alivio)* phew! **(b)** *(repugnancia)* ugh!

ufanarse *vpr* to boast **(de** of)

ufano, -a *adj* **(a)** *(orgulloso)* conceited, arrogant **(b)** *(satisfecho)* satisfied, happy

ufología *nf* ufology

ufólogo, -a *nm,f* ufologist

Uganda *n* Uganda

ugandés, -esa *adj & nm,f* Ugandan

ugetista 1 *adj* (related to the) UGT; **la política u.** UGT policy
   2 *nmf* member of the UGT

UGT *nf (abrev de* **Unión General de Trabajadores***)*

UHT *adj (abrev de* **ultra heat treated***)* UHT

ujier *nm* usher

ukelele *nm Mús* ukelele

Ulan-Bator *n* Ulan-Bator

úlcera *nf Med* ulcer ❑ **u. de estómago** stomach ulcer

ulceración *nf Med* ulceration

ulcerar *Med* **1** *vt* to ulcerate
   2 ulcerarse *vpr Med* to ulcerate

ulceroso, -a *adj Med* ulcerous

ulterior *adj* **(a)** *(más allá)* ulterior, further **(b)** *(siguiente)* subsequent; *(posterior)* later, further

ulteriormente *adv* subsequently, afterwards

ultimación *nf* completion, conclusion

últimamente *adv* lately, recently

ultimar *vt* **(a)** *(terminar)* to conclude, complete; **u. un negocio** to conclude a deal **(b)** *Am Fam (matar)* to kill, finish off

ultimátum *(pl* **ultimátums** *o* **ultimatos***) nm* ultimatum

último, -a *adj* **(a)** *(en el tiempo)* last; *(más reciente)* latest; *(de dos)* latter; **a últimos de mes** towards the end of the month; **la última casa a mano derecha** the last house on the right; **llegar el ú.** to arrive last; **por ú.** finally; *Fig* **estar en las últimas** *(moribundo)* to be at death's door; *(arruinado)* to be down and out; *Fam* **a la última** up to date; **va vestida a la última** she likes to wear the latest fashions; *Fam* **¡es lo ú.!** that really is the limit **(b)** *(en el espacio)* furthest; *(más abajo)* bottom, lowest; *(más arriba)* top, last; *(más atrás)* back, last; **está el ú. de la lista** he's at the bottom of the list; **hasta el ú. pueblo del país** to the last village in the country; **siempre se sienta en la última fila** he always sits in the back row; **vivo en el ú. piso** I live on the top floor **(c)** *(definitivo)* final; **es mi última palabra** that's my final word

ultra *Pol Fam* **1** *adj* extreme right-wing
   2 *nmf* extreme right-winger; **los ultras** the extreme right *sing*

ultra- *pref* ultra-; **ultravirus** ultravirus

ultracongelado, -a *adj* deep-frozen; **ultracongelados** deep-frozen food *sing*

ultraconservador, -a *adj & nm,f* ultraconservative

ultraderecha *nf Pol* extreme right (wing)

ultraderechista *Pol* **1** *adj* extreme right-wing
   2 *nmf* extreme right-winger

ultraísmo *nm* = Spanish and Latin American literary movement of the early 20th century

ultraizquierda *nf Pol* far left

ultraizquierdista *Pol* **1** *adj* far left
   2 *nmf* extreme left-winger

ultrajante *adj* outrageous, insulting, offensive

ultrajar *vt* to outrage, insult, offend

ultraje *nm* outrage, insult, offence, *US* offense

ultraligero *nm* microlight

ultramar *nm* overseas (countries), abroad; **del** *o* **en u.** overseas

ultramarino, -a 1 *adj* overseas
  2 *nm* (**a**) *(tienda)* grocery store, *Br* grocer's (shop) (**b**) **ultramarinos** *(comestibles)* groceries

ultramoderno, -a *adj* ultramodern

ultramontano, -a *adj & nm,f* ultramontane

ultranza: a ultranza 1 *loc adv* (**a**) *(a muerte)* to the death (**b**) *(a todo trance)* at all costs, at any price; **paz a u.** peace at any price
  2 *loc adj (acérrimo)* out-and-out, extreme; **un ecologista a u.** a fanatical ecologist

ultrasecreto, -a *adj* top-secret

ultrasónico, -a *adj* ultrasonic

ultrasonido *nm* ultrasound

ultratumba 1 *adv* beyond the grave
  2 *nf* afterlife

ultravioleta *(pl* **ultravioleta** *o* **ultravioletas)** *adj* ultra-violet

ulular *vi* (**a**) *(viento, animal)* to howl (**b**) *(búho)* to hoot

umbilical *adj* umbilical; **cordón u.** umbilical cord

umbral *nm (de la puerta)* threshold; *Fig* threshold, verge; **en el u. de** on the threshold *o* verge of; **en el u. de la muerte** at death's door

umbrío, -a *adj*, **umbroso, -a** *adj* shady

un, -a *(mpl* **unos**, *fpl* **unas**) **1** *art* (**a**) *(singular)* a, an; **un coche** a car; **un huevo** an egg; **una flor** a flower; **vino un lunes** she came one Monday (**b**) **unos, -as** some; **unas flores** some flowers
  2 *adj (delante de nm sing)* one; **tiene un año** she's one year old; **un chico y dos chicas** one boy and two girls; *véase tamb* **uno, -a**

unánime *adj* unanimous

unanimidad *nf* unanimity; **por u.** unanimously

unción *nf* (**a**) *Rel* unction (**b**) *Fig (devoción)* devotion, fervour, *US* fervor

uncir [72] *vt* to yoke

undécimo, -a 1 *adj* eleventh
  2 *nm,f (de una serie)* eleventh
  3 *nm* (**a**) *(parte)* eleventh; *véase tamb* **octavo, -a**

underground [ander'vraun] *adj inv* underground

UNED [u'neð] *nf (abrev de* **Universidad Nacional de Educación a Distancia)** = distance learning university, *Br* ≃ OU

Unesco [u'nesko] *nf (abrev de* **United Nations Educational, Scientific and Cultural Organization)** UNESCO

ungido, -a 1 *pp de* **ungir**
  2 *adj Rel* anointed

ungir [24] *vt Rel* to anoint

ungüento *nm* ointment

únicamente *adv* only, solely

unicameral *adj Pol* unicameral, single-chamber

Unicef [uni'θef] *nm (abrev de* **United Nations Children's Fund)** UNICEF

unicelular *adj* unicellular, single-cell

unicidad *nf* uniqueness

único, -a *adj* (**a**) *(solo)* only, sole; **es el ú. que tengo** it's the only one I've got; **hijo ú.** only child; **la única vez** the only time; **lo ú. que quiero** the only thing I want (**b**) *(extraordinario)* unique; **un hecho ú. en la historia** an event unique in history

unicornio *nm Mit* unicorn

unidad *nf* (**a**) *(cohesión, acuerdo)* unity; **fracasó por falta de u.** it failed for lack of unity; **necesitamos u. de acción** we need unity of action, we need to act as one (**b**) *(elemento, medida)* unit; **un dólar la u.** one dollar each; **quiero comprar seis unidades** I'd like to buy six ❑ **u. de medida** unit of measurement (**c**) *(sección)* unit ❑ *Inform* **u. central de proceso** central processing unit; *Inform* **u. de CD-ROM** CD-ROM drive; *Mil* **u. de combate** combat unit; **u. de cuidados intensivos** intensive care (unit); *Inform* **u. de disco** disk drive; **u. de vigilancia intensiva** intensive care (unit); *TV Rad* **u. móvil** outside broadcast unit

unidimensional *adj* one-dimensional

unidireccional *adj* unidirectional

unido, -a 1 *pp de* **unir**
  2 *adj* united

unifamiliar *adj* **vivienda u.** detached house

unificación *nf* unification

unificador, -a 1 *adj* unifying
  2 *nm,f* unifier

unificar [59] *vt* to unify

uniformado, -a 1 *pp de* **uniformar**
  2 *adj* in uniform, uniformed

uniformar *vt* (**a**) *(igualar)* to make uniform, standardize (**b**) *(poner un uniforme a)* to put into uniform, give a uniform to

uniforme 1 *adj* (**a**) *(igual)* uniform (**b**) *(superficie)* even
  2 *nm (prenda)* uniform; **usar u.** to wear a uniform ❑ **u. de gala** dress uniform

uniformidad *nf* (**a**) *(igualdad)* uniformity (**b**) *(de superficie)* evenness

uniformización *nf* standardization

uniformizar [14] *vt* to make uniform, standardize

unigénito, -a *Rel* **1** *adj* only-begotten
  2 *nm* **el U.** the Son of God, Jesus Christ

unilateral *adj* unilateral, one-sided; **acuerdo u.** unilateral agreement

unión *nf* (**a**) *(gen)* union; **en u. de** together with; *Prov* **la u. hace la fuerza** united we stand ❑ **U. Africana** African Union; **la U. Europea** the European Union; **u. de hecho** unmarried couple (**b**) *Téc (acoplamiento)* joining, coupling (**c**) *Téc (junta)* joint, coupler

unionismo *nm* unionism

unionista *nmf* unionist

Unión Soviética *n Antes* Soviet Union

unipersonal *adj* single, individual; *Ling* unipersonal

unir 1 *vt (juntar)* to unite, join (together); *(combinar)* to combine (**a** with); **están muy unidos** they are very attached to one another; **la nueva carretera une las dos comarcas** the new road links both districts; **nos une una buena amistad** we are very good friends
  2 unirse *vpr (juntarse)* to unite, join; *(combinarse)* to combine; *Fml* **u. en matrimonio** to be joined in matrimony

unisex *adj inv* unisex

unisexual *adj* unisexual

unísono *nm* harmony, unison; **al u.** in unison

unitario, -a *adj* unitary

Univ. *(abrev de* **Universidad)** university

universal *adj* universal; **acuerdo u.** universal agreement; **historia u.** world history

universalidad *nf* universality

universalismo *nm* universalism

universalización *nf* universalization

universalizar [14] **1** *vt* to universalize

2 universalizarse *vpr* to become universal *o* widespread

universalmente *adv* universally

universidad *nf* university ❑ **u. a distancia** = distance learning university, *Br* ≃ Open University; **u. laboral** technical college

universitario, -a 1 *adj* university; **título u.** university degree

2 *nm,f* university student *o* graduate

universo *nm* universe

unívoco, -a *adj* univocal, unambiguous

uno, -a 1 *adj* (a) *(numeral)* one; **a la una** at one o'clock; **es la una** it is one o'clock; **el número u.** number one; **el tomo u.** volume one; **llegará el día u. de abril** he will arrive on the first of April (b) **unos, -as** some; **habrá unos** *o* **unas veinte** there must be around twenty; **unas cajas** some boxes; **u. libros** some books

2 *pron* (a) *(indefinido, numeral)* one; **de u. en u.** one by one; **se miraron u.** a otro they looked at each other; **una de dos** one of the two; **u. (de ellos), una (de ellas)** one of them; **u. más, u. de tantos** one of many; **u. mismo** oneself; **u. tras otro** one after the other; **u. u otro** one or the other; **u. y otro** both; **unos cuantos** a few; **unos y otros** all (b) *(impersonal)* one, you; **u. tiene que mirar por sus intereses** one has to look after one's own interests (c) *Fam (persona)* someone, somebody; **u. que pasaba por allí** some passer-by; **vive con una** he's living with some woman (d) *Fam (trastada)* dirty trick; **hacerle una a algn** to play a dirty trick on sb (e) *Fam (paliza)* thrashing; **le dieron una buena** he got a really good thrashing

3 *nm inv* one; **el u.** (number) one; **el u. de Mayo** the first of May; **treinta y u.** thirty-one

untadura *nf* (a) *(acción)* smearing (b) *(untura)* grease, ointment

untar 1 *vt* (a) *(piel, cara)* to smear; **u. pan con mantequilla** to spread butter on bread (b) *Fam (sobornar)* to bribe

2 untarse *vpr* (a) *(mancharse)* to get stained *o* smeared (b) *Fam (forrarse)* to line one's pockets, feather one's nest

unto *nm* (a) *(grasa)* grease (b) *Chile (betún)* shoe polish

untuosidad *nf* greasiness, oiliness

untuoso, -a *adj* greasy, oily, slippery

untura *nf* ointment

uña *nf* (a) *Anat* nail; *(del dedo)* fingernail; *(del dedo del pie)* toenail; **hacerse** *o* **arreglarse las uñas** to manicure one's nails; **morderse** *o* **comerse las uñas** to bite one's fingernails; *Fig* **esconder las uñas** to hide one's feelings; *Fig* **estar de uñas** to be at daggers drawn; *Fig* **ser u. y carne** to be inseparable, be hand in glove; *Fam* **tener las uñas largas** to be light-fingered (b) *Zool (garra)* claw; *(pezuña)* hoof; *(del alacrán)* sting

uñero *nm* (a) *Med (inflamación)* whitlow (b) *Med (uña encarnada)* ingrowing toenail

uñeta *nf* *Chile* plectrum

uperisación, uperización *nf* U.H.T. treatment

uperisar, uperizar [14] *vt* to give U.H.T. treatment to

Urales *nmpl* los **U.** the Urals

uralita® *nf* *Constr* = material made of asbestos and cement, usually corrugated and used mainly for roofing

uranio *nm* *Quím* uranium

Urano *nm* *Astron* Uranus

urbanidad *nf* urbanity, politeness

urbanismo *nm* town planning

urbanista *nmf* town planner

urbanístico, -a *adj* town-planning, urban; **conjunto u.** housing development *o* *Br* estate

urbanita *nmf* *Fam* urbanite, townie

urbanización *nf* (a) *(proceso)* urbanization (b) *(conjunto residencial)* housing development *o* *Br* estate

urbanizador, -a 1 *adj* developing

2 *nm,f* developer

urbanizar [14] *vt* to urbanize, develop; **zona sin u.** undeveloped area; **zona urbanizada** built-up area

urbano, -a 1 *adj* urban, city; **guardia u.** (traffic) policeman

2 *nm,f* *Fam (hombre)* (traffic) policeman; *(mujer)* (traffic) policewoman

urbe *nf* large city, metropolis

urdimbre *nf* (a) *Tex* warp (b) *Fig (trama)* intrigue, scheme

urdir *vt* (a) *Tex* to warp (b) *Fig (tramar)* to plot

urea *nf* urea

uremia *nf* *Med* uraemia, uremia

uréter *nm* *Anat* ureter

uretra *nf* *Anat* urethra

urgencia *nf* (a) *(gen)* urgency; *(necesidad)* urgent need; **con u.** urgently (b) *(emergencia)* emergency; **cura de u.** first aid; **en un caso de u.** in an emergency

urgente *adj* urgent; **correo u.** express mail

urgentemente *adv* urgently

urgir [24] *vi* to be urgent *o* pressing; **me urge (tenerlo)** I need it urgently; **urge encontrar una solución** a solution is urgently required

úrico, -a *adj* uric

urinario, -a 1 *adj (de la orina)* urinary

2 *nm (retrete)* urinal, *US* comfort station

URL *nm* *Inform (abrev de* **uniform resource locator***)* URL

urna *nf* (a) *Pol* ballot box; *Fig* **acudir a las urnas** to go to the polls, vote (b) *(vasija)* urn (c) *(caja)* glass case

urogallo *nm* *Orn* capercaillie

urogenital *adj* *Med* urogenital

urología *nf* *Med* urology

urólogo, -a *nm,f* *Med* urologist

urraca *nf* *Orn* magpie

URSS [urs] *nf* *Antes (abrev de* **Unión de Repúblicas Socialistas Soviéticas***)* USSR

ursulina *nf* *Rel* Ursuline nun

urticaria *nf* *Med* hives, urticaria

Uruguay *n* **(el) U.** Uruguay

uruguayo, -a *adj & nm,f* Uruguayan

usado, -a 1 *pp de* usar

2 *adj* (a) *(de segunda mano)* second-hand, used (b) *(gastado)* worn out, old

usanza *nf* *Literario* fashion, custom; **a la antigua u.** in the old style

usar 1 *vt* (a) *(gen)* to use (b) *(prenda)* to wear; **sin u.** new

2 *vi* to make use (de of)

3 usarse *vpr* to be used *o* in fashion; **ya no se usa esta palabra** this word is no longer used

usía *pron pers* *Fml (para hombre)* Your Lordship; *(para mujer)* Your Ladyship

usina *nf* *Andes RP* plant ❑ **u. eléctrica** power station, power plant

USO ['uso] *nf (abrev de* **Unión Sindical Obrera***)*

uso *nm* (a) *(utilización)* use; **en u.** in use; **en u. de** *(utilizando)* using, making use of; *(en virtud de)* by virtue of; **hacer buen u. de** to make good use of; **hacer mal u. de** to misuse; **hacer u. de** to make use of; **hacer u. de la palabra**

to take the floor; **instrucciones de u.** instructions for use; *Farm* **de u. externo** *o* **tópico** for external use only (**b**) *(ejercicio)* exercise; **el u. de un privilegio** the exercise of a privilege (**c**) *(de prenda)* wearing; **es obligatorio el u. de corbata** ties must be worn; **la ropa se gasta con el u.** clothes wear out with use (**d**) *(costumbre)* usage, custom; **al u.** in fashion; **al u. catalán** in the Catalan style *o* manner; **usos y costumbres** habits and customs (**e**) *Ling* usage

usted *pron pers Fml* you; **¡muchas gracias! — ¡a u.!** thank you very much! — you're welcome!; **¿quién es u.?, ¿quiénes son ustedes?** who are you?; **tratar a algn de u.** to use the polite form of address with sb

ustedes *pron pers pl Fml* you; *véase* **usted**

usual *adj* usual, common

usuario, -a *nm,f* user; **los usuarios del teléfono** telephone users

usufructo *nm Jur* usufruct, use

usufructuario, -a *adj & nm,f Jur* usufructuary

usura *nf* usury

usurero, -a *nm,f* usurer

usurpación *nf* usurpation

usurpador, -a 1 *adj* usurping
  2 *nm,f* usurper

usurpar *vt* to usurp

utensilio *nm* (**a**) *(herramienta)* utensil, tool; **utensilios de cocina** kitchen utensils (**b**) *(aparato)* device, implement

uterino, -a *adj Anat* uterine

útero *nm Anat* uterus, womb

UTI ['uti] *nf CSur (abrev de* **Unidad de Tratamiento Intensivo**) ICU

útil 1 *adj (gen)* useful; *(día)* working
  2 *nm (herramienta)* tool, instrument; **útiles de escritorio** writing materials; **útiles de labranza** agricultural implements; *Taur* **útiles de matar** matador's equipment *sing*

utilería *nf Teat* (stage) props

utilidad *nf* (**a**) *(gen)* usefulness, utility (**b**) *(beneficio)* profit (**c**) *Inform* utility (program)

utilitario, -a 1 *adj* utilitarian
  2 *nm Aut (coche)* utility vehicle

utilitarismo *nm Filos* utilitarianism

utilitarista *adj & nm,f Filos* utilitarian

utilizable *adj* usable, fit *o* ready for use

utilización *nf* use, utilization

utilizar [14] *vt* to use, utilize, make use of

utillaje *nm* tools *pl*, equipment

utopía *nf* Utopia

utópico, -a *adj & nm,f* Utopian

uva *nf* grape; *Fam* **estar de mala u.** to be in a bad mood; *Fam* **tener mala u.** *(estar de mal humor)* to be in a bad mood; *(tener mal carácter)* to be a nasty piece of work, be bad-tempered

uve ['uβe] *nf* = name of the letter V in Spanish

UVI ['uβi] *nf* (*abrev de* **unidad de vigilancia intensiva**) ICU

úvula *nf Anat* uvula

Uzbekistán *n* Uzbekistan

uzbeko, -a *adj & nm,f* Uzbek

V

V, v *Esp* ['uβe], *Am* [be'korta] *nf (la letra)* V, v; **v doble** W

V *Elec (abrev de* **voltio(s)**) V

v. (**a**) *(abrev de* **véase**) s.; *(latín)* v (**b**) *(abrev de* **verso**) v

v/ *(abrev de* **visto**) approved

vaca *nf* (**a**) *Zool* cow; *Fig* **las vacas flacas** the lean years; *Fig* **las vacas gordas** the years of plenty; *Fig* **ya vendrán las vacas gordas** the good times will come ❑ **v. lechera** milch cow, dairy cow; **v. marina** sea cow; **v. sagrada** sacred cow; **vacas locas** *(enfermedad)* mad cow disease (**b**) *(carne)* beef (**c**) *Carib Perú RP (fondo común)* kitty

vacacional *adj Br* holiday, *US* vacation; **periodo v.** holiday period

vacaciones *nfpl* holiday *sing, Br* holidays, *US* vacation *sing;* **estar/irse de v.** to be/go on *Br* holiday *o US* vacation; *Fam* **v. a la sombra** time spent in jail ❑ **v. escolares** school holidays; **v. pagadas** paid *Br* holidays *o US* vacation

vacada *nf* herd of cows

vacante 1 *adj* vacant
   2 *nf* vacancy

vacar [59] *vi* to fall *o* become vacant

vaciado 1 *pp de* **vaciar**
   2 *nm* (**a**) *(acción)* emptying, hollowing out (**b**) *Arte* casting, moulding, *US* molding ❑ **v. de yeso** plaster casting; **v. en molde** casting in a mould

vaciar [32] **1** *vt* (**a**) *(recipiente)* to empty; *(contenido)* to pour (away); **la policía mandó v. el local** the police ordered everyone to leave the place (**b**) *(dejar hueco)* to hollow out (**c**) *Arte (moldear)* to cast, mould, *US* mold (**d**) *(afilar)* to sharpen
   2 vaciarse *vpr* (**a**) *(quedar vacío)* to empty (**b**) *Fam (desahogarse)* to let it all out

vacilación *nf* (**a**) *(duda)* hesitation, vacillation (**b**) *(falta de decisión)* irresolution (**c**) *(oscilación)* vacillation, swaying

vacilante *adj* (**a**) *(persona)* hesitant, irresolute (**b**) *(voz)* hesitant, faltering (**c**) *(luz)* flickering (**d**) *(paso, mesa etc)* unsteady, shaky

vacilar 1 *vi* (**a**) *(dudar)* to hesitate; *(al elegir)* to be indecisive; **sin v.** without hesitation (**b**) *(voz, principios, régimen)* to falter (**c**) *(fluctuar) (luz)* to flicker; *(pulso)* to be irregular (**d**) *(oscilar)* to wobble (**e**) *Fam (chulear)* to show off (**f**) *Esp Carib Méx Fam (bromear)* **está vacilando** he's pulling your leg *o* kidding, *Br* he's taking the mickey
   2 *vt Esp Carib Méx Fam* **v. a algn** *(tomar el pelo)* to pull sb's leg, *Br* take the mickey out of sb

vacile *nm Esp Carib Méx Fam (tomadura de pelo)* joke, *Br* wind-up; **estar de v.** *(de broma)* to be kidding *o* joking, *Br* be taking the mickey

vacilón, -a *Fam* **1** *adj* (**a**) *(fanfarrón)* swanky (**b**) *Esp, Carib Méx (bromista)* jokey, teasing (**c**) *CAm Carib Méx (juerguista)* fond of partying; **ser muy v.** to be a party-lover
   2 *nm,f* (**a**) *(fanfarrón)* show-off (**b**) *Esp Carib Méx (bromista)* tease
   3 *nm CAm Carib Méx* (**a**) *(fiesta)* party (**b**) *(tomadura de pelo)* leg-pull

vacío, -a 1 *adj* (**a**) *(gen)* empty; *(hueco)* hollow; *Fig* **palabras vacías** empty words; *Fig* **tener la cabeza vacía** to be empty-headed; *Fig* **volver con las manos vacías** to come back empty-handed (**b**) *(sin ocupar)* vacant, unoccupied
   2 *nm* (**a**) *(abismo, carencia)* void; **se lanzó al v.** he threw himself into the void; **volver de v.** to come back empty-handed; *Fig* **caer en el v.** to fall on deaf ears; *Fig* **hacer el v. a algn** to send sb to Coventry, cold-shoulder sb; *Fig* **sentía un gran v.** he was feeling empty ❑ *Pol* **v. de poder** power vacuum; **v. legal** legal vacuum (**b**) *Fís* vacuum; **en v.** in a vacuum; **envasado al v.** vacuum-packed

vacuidad *nf* vacuity, emptiness

vacuna *nf Med* vaccine

vacunación *nf Med* vaccination

vacunar 1 *vt Med* to vaccinate (**contra** against); *Fig* to inure
   2 vacunarse *vpr* to get oneself vaccinated

vacuno, -a *adj* bovine; **ganado v.** cattle

vacuo, -a *adj* vacuous, empty

vadear *vt (río)* to ford; *Fig (dificultad)* to overcome

vademécum (*pl* **vademécums**) *nm inv* handbook, vademecum

vado *nm* (**a**) *(de un río)* ford (**b**) *Aut* **'v. permanente'** 'keep clear'

Vaduz *n* Vaduz

vagabundear *vi* (**a**) *(vagar)* to wander, roam (**b**) *(holgazanear)* to idle, laze around

vagabundeo *nm* (**a**) *(merodeo)* wandering, roaming (**b**) *(holgazanería)* idling, lazing around

vagabundo, -a 1 *adj (errante)* wandering, roving; *Pey* vagrant; **perro v.** stray dog
   2 *nm,f (trotamundos)* wanderer, rover; *(sin casa)* tramp, *US* hobo; *Pey* vagrant, tramp, *US* bum

vagancia *nf* idleness, laziness, vagrancy

vagar [38] *vi* to wander, roam

vagido *nm* cry *(of a newborn baby)*

vagina *nf Anat* vagina

vaginal *adj Anat* vaginal

vago, -a 1 *adj* (**a**) *(indefinido)* vague (**b**) *(perezoso)* lazy, idle
   2 *nm,f* (**a**) *(holgazán)* idler, slacker, lay-about; **hacer el v.** to laze around (**b**) *Jur* vagrant; *Hist* **ley de vagos y maleantes** vagrancy act

vagón nm Ferroc (**a**) (para pasajeros) carriage, coach, US car (**b**) (para mercancías) truck, wagon, goods van, US freight car, US boxcar ❑ **v. cisterna** tanker

vagoneta nf (**a**) (carro) wagon (**b**) Méx van

vaguada nf Geog valley floor, stream bed

vaguear vi (**a**) (errar) to wander, roam (**b**) (holgazanear) to idle around, laze around

vaguedad nf vagueness; **hablar sin vaguedades** to get straight to the point

vaharada nf puff, breath

vahído nm fainting o dizzy spell

vaho nm (**a**) (aliento) breath (**b**) (vapor) steam, vapour, US vapor (**c**) **vahos** Med inhalation sing

vaina nf (**a**) (de espada) sheath, scabbard (**b**) Bot pod, husk (**c**) Col Perú Ven muy Fam (asunto, tontería) bloody thing; (molestia) pain; **¡qué v.!** what a pisser!

vainica nf Cost hemstitch

vainilla nf vanilla

vaivén nm (**a**) (oscilación) swaying, swinging, to-and-fro movement (**b**) (de la gente) coming and going, bustle (**c**) Fig (cambio) fluctuation, change; **los vaivenes de la vida** life's ups and downs

vajilla nf tableware, crockery, dishes pl; **lavar la v.** to wash the dishes, Br wash up; **una v.** a set of dishes, a dinner service; **v. de porcelana** chinaware

valdré indic fut véase **valer²**

vale nm (**a**) (comprobante) voucher ❑ **v. de comida** luncheon voucher; Fin **v. de compra** credit note; **v. de devolución** credit note; **v. de regalo** gift token (**b**) (pagaré) promissory note, IOU (I owe you)

valedero, -a adj valid

valedor, -a nm,f protector, patron

valencia nf Quím valency

valenciana nf Méx (en pantalón) Br turn-up, US cuff

valenciano, -a 1 adj Valencian
  2 nm,f Valencian
  3 nm Ling Valencian

valentía nf (**a**) (valor) courage, bravery (**b**) (acto valeroso) heroic deed, bold act

valentón, -ona Pey **1** adj bragging, boastful
  2 nm,f braggart

valentonada nf Pey bragging, boasting

valer¹ nm value

valer² [68] **1** vt (**a**) (tener un valor de) to be worth; **no vale nada** it is worthless; **vale una fortuna** it is worth a fortune (**b**) (costar) to cost; **¿cuánto vale?** how much is it?, how much does it cost? (**c**) (ganar) to earn, win, get; **su insolencia le valió una paliza** his insolence earned him a beating (**d**) (proteger) to protect; **¡válgame Dios!** God help me!
  2 vi (**a**) (servir) to be useful, be of use; **no vale para hombre de negocios** he is no use as a businessman; **tienes que hacer v. tus derechos** you must assert your rights (**b**) (ser válido) to be valid, count; **no hay excusa que valga** no excuses; **no vale copiar** copying doesn't count, there's no point in copying (**c**) (ser preferible) **más vale** it is better; **más vale que te vayas ya** you had better leave now; Prov **más vale prevenir que curar** prevention is better than cure; Prov **más vale tarde que nunca** better late than never (**d**) Esp Fam **¿vale?** all right?, O.K.?; **vale** all right, O.K
  3 valerse vpr to use, make use (**de** of); **v. de todos los medios** to try everything; **v. por sí mismo** to be able to manage on one's own

valeriana nf Bot valerian

valeroso, -a adj brave, courageous

valgo indic pres véase **valer²**

valía nf value, worth, merit

validación nf validation

validar vt to validate, make valid

validez nf validity

valido, -a adj & nm favourite, US favorite

válido, -a adj valid

valiente 1 adj (**a**) (valeroso) brave, courageous, bold (**b**) (excelente) fine, excellent, first-class; Irón **¡v. amigo eres tú!** a fine friend you are! (**c**) Pey (bravucón) boasting, bragging
  2 nmf (**a**) (valiente) brave person (**b**) Pey (bravucón) boaster, braggart

valientemente adv bravely, courageously, boldly

valija nf (**a**) (maleta) case, suitcase (**b**) (de correos) mailbag ❑ **v. diplomática** diplomatic bag

valimiento nm Pol favour, US favor, protection

valioso, -a adj valuable, precious

valla nf (**a**) (cerca) fence; (muro) wall; Mil stockade ❑ **v. publicitaria** Br hoarding, US billboard (**b**) Dep hurdle; **los 100 metros vallas** the 100 metres hurdle race (**c**) Col PRico (gallinero) cockpit

valladar nm (**a**) (valla) fence (**b**) Fig (defensa) defence, US defense

vallado nm (valla) fence; Mil stockade

vallar vt to fence (in), build a fence around

valle nm Geog valley; Fig **v. de lágrimas** vale o valley of tears

vallisoletano, -a 1 adj of o from Valladolid
  2 nm,f person from Valladolid

valón, -ona 1 adj Walloon
  2 nm,f (persona) Walloon
  3 nm (idioma) Walloon

valona nf Am (crines) mane

valor nm (**a**) (valía) value, worth; (precio) price; **objetos de v.** valuables; **sin v.** worthless; **una actriz de gran v.** a very talented actress ❑ Fin **v. adquisitivo** purchasing power; **v. alimenticio** food value; Econ **v. añadido**, Am **v. agregado** added value; **v. nominal** face o nominal value (**b**) Mat Mús value (**c**) (importancia) importance; **dar v. a** to attach importance to (**d**) (valentía) courage, valour, US valor; **armarse de v.** to pluck up courage (**e**) (descaro) cheek, nerve; **¡qué v.!** what a nerve! (**f**) Fin **valores** securities ❑ **v. en cartera** investment portfolio sing; **v. inmuebles** real estate sing; **valores del Estado** government securites, Br gilts

valoración nf (**a**) (tasación) valuation, valuing (**b**) (revalorización) appreciation

valorar vt (**a**) (tasar) to value, calculate the value of; Fig **v. a algn en mucho** to hold sb in high esteem (**b**) (aumentar el valor de) to raise the value of

valorización nf (**a**) (tasación) valuation, valuing (**b**) (revalorización) appreciation

valorizar [14] vt (**a**) (tasar) to value (**b**) (revalorizar) to raise the value of

vals nm waltz; **bailar el v.** to waltz

valuar [4] vt to value

valva nf Bot Zool valve

válvula nf valve ❑ **v. de cierre** stopcock; **v. de seguridad** safety valve

vamos 1 indic pres véase **ir**
  2 adv (introduce inciso, matiz o conclusión) **se trata de un amigo, v., de un conocido** he's a friend, well, more of an acquaintance, really; **v., que al final la fiesta fue un desastre** anyway, the party was a disaster in the end

vampiresa *nf* vamp, femme fatale

vampiro *nm* (**a**) *(espectro)* vampire; *Fig* bloodsucker, parasite (**b**) *Zool* vampire bat

vanagloria *nf* vainglory

vanagloriarse *vpr* to boast (**de** of)

vandálico, -a *adj* vandalistic; **un acto v.** an act of vandalism

vandalismo *nm* vandalism

vándalo, -a 1 *adj Hist* Vandal, Vandalic
  2 *nm,f Hist* Vandal; *Fig* vandal

vanguardia *nf* (**a**) *Mil* vanguard, van; *Fig* **ir a la v. de** to be at the forefront of (**b**) *Arte Lit* avant-garde, vanguard

vanguardismo *nm Arte Lit* avant-garde movement

vanguardista *Arte Lit* **1** *adj* avant-garde
  2 *nm,f* avant-gardist

vanidad *nf* vanity, conceit

vanidoso, -a 1 *adj* vain, conceited
  2 *nm,f* vain person

vano, -a 1 *adj* (**a**) *(presuntuoso)* vain, conceited (**b**) *(ilusorio)* vain, futile, useless; **en v.** in vain
  2 *nm,f Arquit* opening, bay

Vanuatú *n* Vanuatu

vapor *nm* (**a**) *(gas)* steam, vapour, *US* vapor; *Culin* **al v.** steamed □ **máquina de v.** steam engine; **v. de agua** water vapour (**b**) *Náut* **(barco de) v.** steamer, steamship; **a todo v.** at full steam, at great speed (**c**) **vapores** *Med* vapours, *US* vapors, hysteria *sing*

vaporización *nf* vaporization

vaporizador *nm* vaporizer, atomizer, spray

vaporizar [14] **1** *vt* to vaporize
  2 vaporizarse *vpr* to vaporize, become vaporized, evaporate

vaporoso, -a *adj* (**a**) *(que despide vapor)* vaporous (**b**) *(tejido)* sheer

vapulear *vt* (**a**) *(zurrar)* to beat, thrash (**b**) *Fig (criticar)* to slate, criticize

vapuleo *nm* (**a**) *(zurra)* beating, thrashing (**b**) *Fig (crítica)* slating, negative criticism

vaquería *nf* (**a**) *(de leche)* dairy (**b**) *Arg (tienda de vaqueros)* jeans shop

vaqueriza *nf* cowshed

vaquerizo, -a 1 *adj* cattle
  2 *nm,f* cowherd

vaquero, -a 1 *adj* cow, cattle; **pantalón v.** jeans *pl*, pair of jeans
  2 *nm* cowherd, *US* cowboy
  3 vaqueros *nmpl (prenda)* jeans, pair *sing* of jeans

vaqueta *nf* cowhide

vaquetón, -ona *adj Méx* barefaced, shameless

vaquilla *nf (vaca)* heifer; *(toro)* young bull

vara *nf* (**a**) *(palo)* pole, rod (**b**) *(bastón de mando)* staff, mace; *Fig* **tener v. alta en** to have a hold on (**c**) *Taur* lance, pike; **poner varas** to thrust at the bull

varadero *nm Náut* shipyard, dry dock

varado, -a 1 *pp de* varar
  2 *adj Náut (encallado)* aground, stranded; *(en el dique seco)* in dry dock; **hay una ballena varada en el puerto** there's a beached whale in the harbour

varapalo *nm* (**a**) *(palo largo)* long pole (**b**) *(golpe)* blow *(with a pole)* (**c**) *Fam (daño)* blow, setback

varar 1 *vt (barco)* to beach, dock
  2 *vi* to run aground
  3 vararse *vpr* (**a**) *(barco, ballena)* to be beached (**b**) *Am (averiarse)* to break down

varazo *nm* blow *(with a stick o pole)*

varear *vt* (**a**) *(fruta)* to knock down *(with a pole)* (**b**) *(golpear)* to beat with a stick

vareo *nm* knocking down *(fruit from trees)*

variabilidad *nf* variability

variable 1 *adj* variable, changeable
  2 *nf Mat* variable

variación *nf* variation □ *Fís* **v. magnética** magnetic declination

variado, -a *pp de* variar
  2 *adj* varied, mixed; **galletas variadas** assorted biscuits

variante 1 *adj* variable
  2 *nf* (**a**) *(versión)* variant (**b**) *(diferencia)* difference

variar [32] **1** *vt (cambiar)* to vary, change
  2 *vi* (**a**) *(cambiar)* to vary, change; *Irón* **para v.** as usual, just for a change (**b**) *(diferir)* to differ, be different

varicela *nf Med* chickenpox, varicella

varicoso, -a *adj* varicose

variedad *nf* (**a**) *(variación)* variety, diversity; *Prov* **en la v. está el gusto** variety is the spice of life (**b**) *Bot Zool* variety (**c**) **variedades** *Teat* variety show *sing* □ **teatro de v.** variety, music hall, *US* vaudeville (theater)

varilla *nf* (**a**) *(vara)* rod, stick (**b**) *(de abanico, paraguas)* rib; *(de corsé)* stay

varillaje *nm (de abanico, paraguas)* ribs *pl*, ribbing

variopinto, -a *adj* diverse, assorted; **un público v.** a mixed audience

varios, -as *adj* several

varita *nf* small stick □ **v. mágica** magic wand

variz *nm Med* varicose vein

varón *nm (hombre)* man; *(chico)* boy; **hijo v.** male child; **sexo v.** male sex; *Fam* **un santo v.** a kind soul

varonil *adj* manly, virile, male

Varsovia *n* Warsaw

vasallaje *nm Hist* vassalage; *Fig* servitude, serfdom, subjection

vasallo, -a *nm,f Hist* vassal; *(súbdito)* subject

vasco, -a 1 *adj* Basque; **el País V.** the Basque Country
  2 *nm,f (persona)* Basque
  3 *nm (idioma)* Basque

vascuence *nm (idioma)* Basque

vascular *adj Anat* vascular

vasectomía *nf Med* vasectomy

vaselina *nf* Vaseline®; *Fam* **dar v. a algn** to soft-soap sb

vasija *nf* vessel, pot, vase, jar

vaso *nm* (**a**) *(para beber)* glass; *Fig* **ahogarse en un v. de agua** to make a mountain out of a molehill (**b**) *(florero)* vase (**c**) *Anat Bot Fís* vessel □ **v. capilar** capillary; **vasos comunicantes** communicating vessels; **vasos sanguíneos** blood vessels

vástago *nm* (**a**) *Bot (brote)* shoot; *Col CRica Ven (de banana)* banana stalk (**b**) *(de una familia)* offspring (**c**) *Téc* rod, stem

vastedad *nf* vastness, immensity

vasto, -a *adj* vast, immense

vate *nm* (**a**) *Lit (poeta)* poet (**b**) *(adivino)* prophet

váter *nm* toilet

Vaticano *n* **(Ciudad del) V.** Vatican (City)

vaticano, -a *adj* Vatican

vaticinador, -a 1 *adj* prophesying, predicting
  2 *nm,f* prophet, seer

vaticinar *vt* to prophesy, predict, foretell

vaticinio *nm* prophesy, prediction

vatio *nm Elec* watt

vaya[1] *interj* well!; **¡v. enredo!** what a mess!; **¡v. por Dios!** goodness me!; **¡v., v.!** well, well!, well I'm blowed!

vaya[2] *subj pres véase* **ir**

VB (*abrev de* **visto bueno**) *(en ejercicios escolares)* = abbreviation equivalent to a tick on a piece of schoolwork

Vd. (*abrev de* **usted**) you

Vda. (*abrev de* **viuda**) widow

Vds. (*abrev de* **ustedes**)

ve 1 *imperat véase* **ir**
   2 *indic pres véase* **ver**[2]

vecinal *adj* local

vecindad *nf* **(a)** *(vecindario)* neighbourhood, *US* neighborhood, vicinity **(b)** *(vecinos)* community, residents *pl*, neighbours *pl*, *US* neighbors *pl* ❏ **casa de v.** block of *Br* flats *o US* apartments **(c)** *Méx (barriada)* = communal dwelling where poor families each live in a single room and share a bathroom and kitchen with others

vecindario *nm* **(a)** *(población)* residents *pl*, inhabitants *pl* **(b)** *(vecindad)* neighbourhood, *US* neighborhood **(c)** *(vecinos)* community, residents, neighbours, *US* neighbors

vecino, -a 1 *adj* neighbouring, *US* neighboring, nearby; **la iglesia está en el pueblo v.** the church is in the next village
   2 *nm,f* **(a)** *(persona)* neighbour, *US* neighbor; **el v. de al lado** the next-door neighbour **(b)** *(residente)* resident; *(habitante)* inhabitant ❏ **asociación de vecinos** residents' association

vector *nm* vector

vectorial *adj* vectorial

veda *nf (prohibición)* prohibition; *(de caza)* close season, *US* closed season; **levantar la v.** to open the season

vedado, -a 1 *pp de* **vedar**
   2 *adj* forbidden, prohibited
   3 *nm* private preserve

vedar *vt* **(a)** *(prohibir)* to forbid, prohibit, ban **(b)** *(impedir)* to prevent

vedette [be'ðet] (*pl* **vedettes**) *nf Cin Teat* star

vega *nf* fertile plain *o* lowland

vegetación *nf* **(a)** *Bot* vegetation **(b)** **vegetaciones** *Med* adenoids

vegetal 1 *adj* vegetable; **el reino v.** the vegetable kingdom ❏ **carbón v.** charcoal
   2 *nm* vegetable, plant

vegetar *vi Bot* to grow; *Fig (persona)* to vegetate

vegetarianismo *nm* vegetarianism

vegetariano, -a *adj & nm,f* vegetarian

vegetativo, -a *adj* vegetative; *Fam* **lleva tres años en estado v.** he has been in a coma for three years

vehemencia *nf* vehemence

vehemente *adj* vehement

vehicular *adj* **lengua v.** teaching language

vehículo *nm* **(a)** *(medio de transporte)* vehicle ❏ **v. pesado** heavy goods vehicle **(b)** *(medio de propagación) (de enfermedad)* carrier; *(de ideas)* vehicle

veinte 1 *adj inv (cardinal)* twenty; *(ordinal)* twentieth; **el v. de junio** (on) the twentieth of June; **los locos años v.** the roaring twenties
   2 *nm inv* twenty; *véase tamb* **ocho**

veinteañero, -a 1 *adj* = in one's (early) twenties
   2 *nm,f* = person in their (early) twenties

veintena *nf (veinte)* twenty; *(unos veinte)* about twenty

veinticinco *nm inv* twenty-five; *véase tamb* **ocho**

veinticuatro *nm inv* twenty-four; *véase tamb* **ocho**

veintidós *nm inv* twenty-two; *véase tamb* **ocho**

veintinueve *nm inv* twenty-nine; *véase tamb* **ocho**

veintiocho *nm inv* twenty-eight; *véase tamb* **ocho**

veintiséis *nm inv* twenty-six; *véase tamb* **ocho**

veintisiete *nm inv* twenty-seven; *véase tamb* **ocho**

veintitantos, -as *nm inv Fam* twenty-odd

veintiuno, -a *nm inv* twenty-one; *véase tamb* **ocho**

vejación *nf,* **vejamen** *nm* **(a)** *(molestia)* vexation **(b)** *(humillación)* humiliation

vejar *vt* **(a)** *(molestar)* to vex, annoy **(b)** *(humillar)* to humiliate

vejatorio, -a *adj* **(a)** *(molesto)* vexatious, annoying **(b)** *(humillante)* humiliating

vejestorio *nm Fam* old codger *o Br* crock

vejete *nm Fam* old guy *o Br* bloke

vejez *nf* old age; *Prov* **a la v., viruelas** there's no fool like an old fool

vejiga *nf Anat* bladder ❏ **v. de la bilis** gall bladder

vela[1] *nf* **(a)** *(candela)* candle; *Fam* **encender una v. a Dios y otra al diablo** to have a foot in both camps; *Fam* **estar a dos velas** to be broke; *Fam* **¿quién te ha dado v. en este entierro?** *Br* who asked you to stick your oar in?, *US* who asked you to butt in? **(b)** *(desvelo)* wakefulness; **pasar la noche en v.** to have a sleepless night **(c)** *(vigilia)* vigil, watch; *(de un muerto)* wake

vela[2] *nf Náut* sail; **a toda v., a velas desplegadas** under full sail, at full speed; **alzar** *o* **largar velas** to set sail; *Fig* **recoger velas** to back down ❏ **v. mayor** mainsail

velada *nf* evening (party)

velado, -a *adj* **(a)** *(oculto)* veiled, hidden **(b)** *Fot* blurred

velador *nm* **(a)** *(mesa)* pedestal table **(b)** *Andes Méx (mesilla de noche)* bedside table **(c)** *Méx RP (lámpara)* bedside lamp

velamen *nm Náut* sails *pl*

velar[1] *adj & nf Ling* velar

velar[2] **1** *vt* **(a)** *(cuidar)* to watch over; **v. a un enfermo** to sit up with a sick person **(b)** *(muerto)* to keep vigil over
   2 *vi* **(a)** *(no dormir)* to stay awake; *(no acostarse)* to stay up **(b)** *(hacer guardia)* to keep watch; *Rel* to keep vigil **(c)** *Fig (cuidar)* **v. por** to look (**por** after), watch (**por** over)

velar[3] **1** *vt* **(a)** *(poner un velo sobre)* to veil; *Fig* to hide, cover **(b)** *Fot* to blur, fog
   2 velarse *vpr Fot* to become blurred *o* fogged

velatorio *nm* vigil, wake

velcro® *nm* Velcro®

veleidad *nf* **(a)** *(inconstancia)* fickleness, inconstancy **(b)** *(capricho)* whim, caprice

veleidoso, -a *adj* fickle, inconstant

velero, -a *Náut* **1** *adj* sailing
   2 *nm* sailing boat *o* ship

veleta 1 *nf* weather vane, weathercock
   2 *nmf Fam* fickle *o* changeable person

vello *nm* hair

vellocino *nm* fleece ❏ *Mit* **V. de Oro** Golden Fleece

vellón *nm* fleece

vellosidad *nf (vello)* down; *(abundancia)* hairiness

velloso, -a *adj,* **velludo, -a** *adj* downy, hairy, fluffy

velo *nm* **(a)** *(prenda)* veil; *Rel* **tomar el v.** to take the veil, become a nun; *Fig* **correr un tupido v. sobre algo** to cover up sth, keep sth quiet **(b)** *Anat* velum ❏ **v. del paladar** soft palate, *Espec* velum

velocidad *nf* **(a)** *(rapidez)* speed, velocity; **a toda v.** at full speed; **le multaron por exceso de v.** he was fined for speeding; *Aut* **v. máxima 60 km** 60 km speed limit ❏ *Av Náut* **v. de crucero** cruising speed; *Inform* **v. de transmisión** bit rate (**b**) *Aut (marcha)* gear; **cambiar la v.** to change gear ❏ **caja de velocidades** gear box

velocímetro *nm* speedometer

velocípedo *nm* velocipede

velocista *nmf* sprinter

velódromo *nm* cycle track, *US* velodrome

velomotor *nm* moped

velón *nm* (**a**) *(lámpara de aceite)* oil lamp (**b**) *Andes RP (vela)* thick candle

velorio *nm* wake

veloz 1 *adj* swift, rapid, quick, fast
  2 *adv* quickly, fast; **el tiempo pasa v.** time flies

vena *nf* (**a**) *Anat* vein (**b**) *Geol Min* vein, seam (**c**) *(de madera)* grain (**d**) *Fig* mood; **le ha dado la v. por irse a la China** he has taken it into his head to go to China; **tener una v. de loco** to have a streak of madness; **tiene v. de músico** he has a gift for music

venablo *nm* javelin, dart; *Fig* **echar venablos** to blow one's top, explode with anger

venado *nm* (**a**) *Zool* deer, stag (**b**) *Culin* venison

venal *adj* (**a**) *(vendible)* venal, which can be bought (**b**) *Pey (sobornable)* venal, corrupt

venalidad *nf* venality

vencedor, -a 1 *adj* (**a**) *Dep* winning (**b**) *Mil* conquering, victorious
  2 *nm,f* (**a**) *Dep* winner, victor (**b**) *Mil* conqueror, victor

vencejo¹ *nm* band, string

vencejo² *nm Orn* swift

vencer [40] **1** *vt* (**a**) *Mil (enemigo)* to conquer, defeat, vanquish; *Dep (rival)* to beat; **v. o morir** do or die (**b**) *(dificultad)* to overcome, surmount; **le venció el sueño** he was overcome by sleep; **no te dejes v.** don't give in
  2 *vi* (**a**) *(pago, deuda)* to fall due, be payable (**b**) *(plazo)* to expire
  3 vencerse *vpr* (**a**) *(controlarse)* to control oneself (**b**) *(doblarse)* to bend, incline

vencido, -a 1 *pp de* **vencer**
  2 *adj* (**a**) *Mil (derrotado)* defeated, vanquished; *Dep* beaten; *Fig* **darse por v.** to give up, admit defeat (**b**) *(pago, deuda)* due, payable; **el alquiler se paga al mes v.** the rent is paid at the end of each month (**c**) *(plazo)* expired; *Fam Fig* **a la tercera va la vencida** third time lucky

vencimiento *nm* (**a**) *(inclinación)* bend, inclination (**b**) *(de un pago, una deuda)* maturity (**c**) *(de un plazo)* expiry, maturity

venda *nf* bandage; *Fig* **tener una v. en los ojos** to be blind, go around with one's eyes closed

vendaje *nm* (**a**) *(vendas)* bandaging (**b**) *Andes Carib (dinero extra)* bonus

vendar *vt* to bandage; *Fig* **v. los ojos a algn** to blindfold sb

vendaval *nm* strong wind, gale

vendedor, -a 1 *adj* selling
  2 *nm,f* (**gen**) seller; *(hombre)* salesman; *(mujer)* saleswoman ❏ **v. ambulante** hawker, street salesman

vender 1 *vt* to sell; **v. a plazos** to sell on credit; **v. al contado** to sell for cash; **v. al por mayor** to (sell) wholesale; **v. al por menor** to (sell) retail
  2 venderse *vpr* (**a**) *(estar en venta)* to be on sale, be sold; **se vende** for sale; **sólo se vende en farmacia** only on sale at chemists; *Fam Fig* **se vende como rosquillas** it's selling like hot cakes (**b**) *(dejarse sobornar)* to sell oneself

vendible *adj* saleable, marketable

vendido, -a 1 *pp de* **vender**
  2 *adj* sold

vendimia *nf* (**a**) *(cosecha)* grape harvest (**b**) *(año de cosecha)* vintage, year

vendimiador, -a *nm,f* grape picker

vendimiar *vt (uvas)* to pick

vendré *indic fut véase* **venir**

Venecia *n* Venice

veneciano, -a *adj & nm,f* Venetian

veneno *nm (químico, vegetal)* poison; *(animal)* venom; *Fig* spite, venom

venenoso, -a *adj* (**a**) *(que envenena)* poisonous (**b**) *Fig* spiteful, venomous

venerable *adj* venerable

veneración *nf* veneration, worship

venerar *vt* to venerate, revere, worship

venéreo, -a *adj Med* venereal

venero *nm* (**a**) *(manantial)* spring (**b**) *Min* seam, vein (**c**) *Fig (fuente)* source, origin; **aquel almanaque es un v. de datos** that almanac is a mine of information

venezolano, -a *adj & nm,f* Venezuelan

Venezuela *n* Venezuela

venga *subj pres véase* **venir**

vengador, -a 1 *adj* avenging
  2 *nm,f* avenger

venganza *nf* vengeance, revenge

vengar [38] **1** *vt* to avenge
  2 vengarse *vpr* to avenge oneself; **v. de algn** to take revenge on sb

vengativo, -a *adj* vengeful, vindictive

vengo *indic pres véase* **venir**

venia *nf* (**a**) *Fml (permiso)* permission; **con la v.** *(al tomar la palabra)* by your leave (**b**) *(perdón)* pardon (**c**) *RP Ven Mil (saludo)* salute

venial *adj* venial

venialidad *nf* veniality

venida *nf* coming, arrival; **idas y venidas** comings and goings

venidero, -a *adj* future, coming; **en lo v.** in the future

venir [69] **1** *vi* (**a**) *(gen)* to come (a to); **el año que viene** next year; **la escena más famosa viene ahora** the most famous scene is next *o* now follows; **la guía viene también en italiano** the guidebook also comes in Italian; **voy y vengo** I'll be right back; *Fig* **eso no viene a cuento** *o* **al caso** that's beside the point; *Fig* **lo veía v.** I could see it coming; *Fig* **me vino la idea de alquilar la casa** I hit on the idea of renting out the house; *Fig* **v. a menos** to come down in the world; *Fig* **v. al mundo** to be born; *Fig* **v. rodado** to come *o* happen at just the right time; *Fam* **a ti no te va ni te viene** it's none of your business; *Fam* **no me vengas con historias** don't come to me with your excuses; *Fam* **¡venga ya!** *(basta)* stop it!, that's quite enough!; *(expresa incredulidad)* come off it! (**b**) *(llegar)* to arrive; **vino a las once** he arrived at eleven (**c**) *(proceder)* **v. de** to come from; **de ahí viene su desgracia** that was his downfall; **la casa le vino de su madre** he inherited the house from his mother (**d**) *(ir bien o mal, ajustarse)* **esos zapatos te vienen grandes** those shoes are too big for you; **v. bien** to be suitable *o* convenient; **el metro me viene muy bien** I find the underground very handy; **v. mal** to be unsuitable *o* inconvenient; **recogerlo hoy me viene mal** it is inconvenient for me to pick it up today; *Fam* **le viene que ni pintado** it suits her down to the ground; *Fam* **me viene de perlas** it's just what I needed, it's just the ticket; *Fam* **no**

les viene en gana trabajar los lunes they don't feel like working on Mondays

2 *v aux* (a) *(v. + a + infin)* **viene a ser lo mismo** it's all the same in the end; **vino a parar en la cárcel** he ended up in jail (b) *(v. + ger)* **venía solicitando este empleo desde hace un año** I've been asking for this job for a year (c) *(v. + pp)* **los cambios de temperatura vienen motivados por los vientos** the changes in temperature are caused by the wind

3 venirse *vpr* (a) *(volver)* to come back, go back (b) **v. abajo** to collapse; *Fig* **el teatro se venía abajo con los aplausos** the applause shook the theatre

venoso, -a *adj* (a) *(sangre)* venous (b) *(manos etc)* veined, veiny (c) *(hoja)* veined, ribbed

venta *nf* (a) *(acción)* sale, selling; **en v.** for sale; **estar a la v.** to be on sale; **poner a la v.** *(casa)* to put up for sale; *(mercancías)* to put on sale ❏ **v. al contado** cash sale; **v. al por mayor** wholesale; **v. al por menor** retail; **v. ambulante** street vending; **v. a plazos** sale by instalments, *Br* hire purchase; **v. por catálogo** mail-order selling (b) *(artículos vendidos)* sales *pl* ❏ **contrato de v.** bill of sale; **departamento de ventas** sales department (c) *(posada)* country inn (d) *Chile (puesto en fiestas)* refreshment stand

ventaja *nf* advantage; **ganó la carrera con tres metros de v.** she won the race by three metres; **llevar v. a** to have the advantage over; **sacar v. a** to be ahead of; **sacar v. de** to profit from, use to one's own advantage, take advantage of; *Ten* **v. para Rodríguez** advantage Rodríguez

ventajista *nmf* opportunist

ventajoso, -a *adj* advantageous

ventana *nf* (a) *Arquit* window; **v. de guillotina** sash window; *Fig* **tirar algo por la v.** to waste sth (b) *Anat (de la nariz)* nostril (c) *Inform* window ❏ **v. de diálogo** dialog *o Br* dialogue box

ventanal *nm* large window

ventanilla *nf* (a) *(de vehículo, de sobre, de banco)* window (b) *Cin Teat* (ticket) window (c) *Anat (de la nariz)* nostril

ventanuco *nm* small window

ventarrón *nm* strong wind, gale

ventear *v impers* to be very windy

ventero, -a *nm,f* innkeeper

ventilación *nf* ventilation; **sin v.** unventilated

ventilador *nm* ventilator, fan

ventilar 1 *vt* (a) *(habitación)* to ventilate, air; *(vestido)* to air (b) *Fig (opinión)* to air; *(cuestión)* to discuss, clear up

2 ventilarse *vpr* (a) *(habitación)* to be ventilated; *(vestido)* to be aired (b) *Fig (opinión)* to be aired; *(cuestión)* to be discussed *o* cleared up (c) *Fam (terminar)* to finish off (d) *(tomar el aire)* to get some fresh air

ventisca *nf* blizzard, snowstorm

ventiscar [59] *v impers,* **ventisquear** *v impers* to blow a blizzard

ventisquero *nm* (a) *(ventisca)* blizzard, snowstorm (b) *(de montaña)* = part of a mountain above the snow line

ventolera *nf (golpe de viento)* gust of wind; *Fam* **darle a uno la v. de hacer algo** to take it into one's head to do sth; *Fam* **darle a uno la v. por algn** to take a fancy to sb

ventosa *nf* (a) *(gen)* suction cup; *Med* cupping glass (b) *Zool* sucker (c) *(abertura)* vent, air hole

ventosear *vi* to break wind

ventosidad *nf* wind, flatulence

ventoso, -a *adj* windy

ventricular *adj* ventricular

ventrículo *nm Anat* ventricle

ventrílocuo, -a 1 *adj* ventriloquistic

2 *nm,f* ventriloquist

ventriloquía *nf* ventriloquism

ventrudo, -a *adj Fam* pot-bellied

ventura *nf* (a) *(felicidad)* happiness; **le deseo toda clase de venturas** I wish you every happiness (b) *(suerte)* luck; *(casualidad)* chance, fortune; **a la buena v.** with no fixed plan; **por v.** *(por casualidad)* by chance; *(por suerte)* fortunately; **echar la buena v. a algn** to tell sb's fortune; **probar v.** to try one's luck

venturoso, -a *adj* lucky, fortunate

Venus 1 *nm Astron Astrol* Venus

2 *nf Mit* Venus ❏ **monte de V.** mount of Venus

veo-veo *nm Fam* **el juego del v.-v.** I-spy

ver¹ *nm* (a) *(vista)* vision, sight (b) *(apariencia)* looks *pl,* appearance; **de buen v.** good-looking

ver² [70] **1** *vt* (a) *(percibir) (imagen)* to see; **déjeme v.** let me see; **lo vi con mis propios ojos** I saw it with my own eyes; **v. la televisión** to watch television; *Fig* **dejarse v.** to appear, become apparent; *Fig* **ni visto ni oído** very quickly; *Fig* **v. venir algo** to see sth coming, expect sth to happen; *Fam* **había un jaleo que no veas** you should have seen the fuss there was; *Fam* **¡habráse visto qué cara más dura!** he's got a nerve!; *Fam* **hasta más** *o* **más v.** see you; *Fam* **¡hay que v.!** it just goes to show!; *Fam* **tengo un hambre que no veo** I'm so starving (b) *Fig (observar, examinar)* to see, have a look at; **a v.** let me see, let's see; **eso está por v.** that remains to be seen; **¿lo ves?** see!; **te veo triste** you look sad; **(ya) veremos** we'll see (c) *Fig (entender)* to understand; **no veo por qué le gusta tanto** I can't see why he likes it so much; **por lo que veo** apparently, it seems; **ya lo veo** I can see that (d) *(visitar)* to see, visit; **ven a verme cuando quieras** come and see me whenever you like (e) *Jur (caso)* to try, hear (f) **tener que v. con** to have something to do with

2 verse *vpr* (a) *(imagen etc)* to be seen; **se ve el mar desde aquí** you can see the sea from here (b) *(encontrarse con algn)* to meet, see each other; *Fig* **vérselas con algn** to deal with sb; *Fam* **Fig no se pueden ni v.** they hate each other (c) *(encontrarse en una situación)* to find oneself; **me veo teniendo que comprarme otro coche** I can see myself having to buy another car (d) **se ve que** apparently

vera *nf* edge, side, border; **a la v. de** beside, next to

veracidad *nf* veracity, truthfulness

veranda *nf* veranda

veraneante *nmf Br* holidaymaker, *US* (summer) vacationer

veranear *vi* to spend one's summer *Br* holidays *o US* vacation

veraneo *nm* summer *Br* holidays *o US* vacation; **su lugar de v. habitual es La Plata** she usually spends the summer in La Plata

veraniego, -a *adj* summer, summery; **temporada veraniega** summer season

veranillo *nm* **v. de San Martín** Indian summer

verano *nm* summer

veras *nfpl* truth *sing;* **de v.** really, seriously; **lo siento de v.** I am truly sorry; **te lo digo de v.** I'm serious, I'm not joking

veraz *adj* truthful

verbal *adj* verbal; **expresión v.** oral expression

verbalizar [14] *vt* to verbalize

verbena *nf* (a) *(fiesta)* street *o* all-night party; **la v. de San Juan** = street party held on the eve of Saint John's Day (b) *Bot* verbena

verbenero, -a *adj* street-party; **ambiente v.** festive atmosphere

verbigracia *adv Fml* for example, for instance

verbo *nm Ling* verb ❏ **v. auxiliar/copulativo/irregular/transitivo** auxiliary/attributive/irregular/transitive verb

verborrea *nf Fam* verbosity, verbal diarrhoea

verbosidad *nf* verbosity, wordiness

verdad *nf* **(a)** *(realidad, afirmación real)* truth; **a decir v.**, **la v. sea dicha** to tell the truth; **de v.** really, truly, seriously; **de v. que no lo sabía** I swear I didn't know; **es v.** it is true; **faltar a la v.** to lie; **¿no es v.?** isn't that so?; **un amigo de v.** a real friend; **una v. a medias** a half truth; *Fam* **decirle a algn las cuatro verdades** to give sb a piece of one's mind; *Fam* **tan de v. como que es de día** it's as true as I'm standing here **(b)** *(confirmación)* isn't it?/aren't you?/don't you? *etc* ...; **debe haber salido, ¿v.?** he must have gone out, mustn't he?; **está muy bien, ¿v.?** it is very good, isn't it?; **hay cuatro, ¿v.?** there are four, aren't there?; **no te gusta, ¿v.?** you don't like it, do you?; **vendrá a la fiesta, ¿v.?** she'll come to the party, won't she?

verdaderamente *adv* truly, really

verdadero, -a *adj* true, real

verde 1 *adj* **(a)** *(colour)* green; **v. botella** bottle green; *Fam Fig* **poner v. a algn** to run sb down, *Br* slag sb off **(b)** *(poco maduro) (fruta)* green, unripe; *(persona)* green, wet behind the ears; *(proyecto, plan)* in its early stages **(c)** *Fam (obsceno)* blue, dirty; **un chiste v.** a dirty joke **(d)** *Pol (ecologista)* green; **el partido v.** the Green Party
2 *nm* **(a)** *(colour)* green **(b)** *(hierba)* grass

verdear *vi (brotar)* to turn green; *(mostrar el color)* to look green

verdecer [46] *vi* to turn *o* go green

verdín *nm* scum

verdor *nm (color)* greenness; *(de plantas)* verdure; *Fig* youthfulness, vigour, *US* vigor

verdoso, -a *adj* greenish

verdugo, -a 1 *nm* **(a)** *(el que ejecuta)* executioner **(b)** *(prenda)* Balaclava (hood)
2 *nmf Fig* tyrant

verduguillo *nm Taur* stiletto

verdulera *nf Pey* coarse *o* foulmouthed woman

verdulería *nf* greengrocer's (shop)

verdulero, -a *nm,f* greengrocer

verdura *nf* **(a)** *(del color)* greenness, greenery **(b)** *(hortaliza)* vegetables *pl*, greens *pl*

verdusco, -a *adj* (dark) greenish

vereda *nf* **(a)** *(camino)* path, lane; *Fig* **meter a algn en v.** to bring sb into line **(b)** *CSur Perú (acera) Br* pavement, *US* sidewalk

veredicto *nm Jur* verdict

verga *nf* **(a)** *Náut* yard **(b)** *Anat Zool* penis **(c)** *(palo)* thin stick

vergel *nm* orchard

vergonzante *adj* shameful, embarrassing

vergonzoso, -a *adj* **(a)** *(penoso)* shameful, disgraceful **(b)** *(tímido)* shy, bashful

vergüenza *nf* **(a)** *(pena)* shame; **es una v.** it's a disgrace; **¿no te da v.?** aren't you ashamed?, have you no shame?; **no tiene v.** he's a shameless person; **¡qué poca v.!** how shameful! **(b)** *(timidez)* shyness, bashfulness; **le da v. cantar en público** she feels shy about singing in public **(c)** *(bochorno)* embarrassment; **se me cayó la cara de v.** I was so embarrassed; *(honor)* **si tuviera v.** if he were a man of honour **(d) vergüenzas** *Fam Euf* private parts

vericueto *nm Geog* rough path

verídico, -a *adj* truthful, true

verificable *adj* verifiable

verificación *nf* verification, checking; *Fin* **v. de cuentas** audit

verificador, -a 1 *adj* verifying, checking
2 *nm,f* tester

verificar [59] **1** *vt* **(a)** *(comprobar)* to verify, check **(b)** *(llevar a cabo)* to perform, carry out
2 verificarse *vpr* **(a)** *(tener lugar)* to take place, occur **(b)** *(resultar verdad)* to come true

verja *nf* **(a)** *(reja)* grating, grille **(b)** *(cerca)* railing, railings *pl* **(c)** *(puerta)* iron gate; **la V. de Gibraltar** the frontier with Gibraltar

vermut *(pl* **vermuts***) nm,* **vermú** *(pl* **vermús***) nm* **(a)** *(bebida)* vermouth **(b)** *(aperitivo)* aperitif **(c)** *esp Andes RP (en cine)* early-evening showing; *(en teatro)* early-evening performance

vernáculo, -a *adj* vernacular; **lengua vernácula** vernacular

verónica *nf* **(a)** *Bot* veronica **(b)** *Taur* = kind of pass with the cape

verosímil *adj (probable)* probable, likely; *(credible)* credible

verosimilitud *nf (probabilidad)* probability, likelihood; *(credibilidad)* credibility, verisimilitude

verraco *nm* male pig, boar

verruga *nf* wart

versado, -a 1 *pp de* **versar**
2 *adj* versed

versal *Impr* **1** *adj* capital
2 *nf* capital (letter)

versalita *Impr* **1** *adj* small capital
2 *nf* small capital (letter)

versallesco, -a *adj Fam Fig (muy galante)* chivalrous; *(afectado)* affected

versar *vi* **(a)** *(tratar)* **v. sobre** to be about, deal with **(b)** *PRico (versificar)* to versify

versátil *adj* **(a)** *(voluble)* changeable, fickle **(b)** *(polifacético)* versatile

versatilidad *nf* **(a)** *(volubilidad)* changeability, fickleness **(b)** *(adaptabilidad)* versatility

versículo *nm Rel* verse, versicle

versificación *nf* versification

versificador, -a *nm,f* versifier

versificar [59] **1** *vt* to versify
2 *vi* to write in verse

versión *nf* **(a)** *(de hecho, obra)* version; *(en música pop)* cover (version) **(b)** *(traducción)* translation, version; **película en v. original** film in the original language; **película inglesa en v. española** English film dubbed in Spanish **(c)** *Cin Teat* adaptation; **la película es una v. de una novela de Torres** the film is based on *o* is an adaptation of a Torres novel

versionar *vt Mús Fam* to cover

verso¹ *nm* **(a)** *(género)* verse; **en v.** in verse ❏ **v. blanco/libre** blank/free verse **(b)** *(unidad rítmica)* line *(of poetry)* **(c)** *Fam (poema)* poem; **hacer versos** to write poems

verso² *nm (de libro)* verso, left-hand page

vértebra *nf Anat* vertebra

vertebrado, -a *adj & nm* vertebrate; *Zool* **los vertebrados** the vertebrates

vertebral *adj* vertebral; *Anat* **columna v.** spinal column, spine

vertebrar *vt* to form the backbone of

vertedero *nm (de basura) Br* rubbish dump *o* tip, *US* garbage dump

verter [64] **1** *vt* (**a**) *(de un recipiente a otro)* to pour (out) (**b**) *(derramar)* to spill (**c**) *(vaciar)* to empty (out) (**d**) *(traducir)* to translate (**e**) *Fig (opiniones etc)* to express, voice
  2 *vi (desembocar)* to flow, run (**a** into)
  3 verterse *vpr* to spill

vertical 1 *adj* vertical; **ponlo v.** put it upright
  2 *nf Geom* vertical (line)
  3 *nm Astron* vertical

verticalidad *nf* verticality, vertical position

vértice *nm Anat Geom* vertex

vertido *nm* (**a**) *(residuo)* waste; **vertidos radiactivos** radioactive waste (**b**) *(acción)* dumping; **v. de residuos** waste dumping

vertiente *nf* (**a**) *(de montaña, tejado)* slope (**b**) *(aspecto)* side, aspect; **desde otra v.** from a different angle (**c**) *CSur (manantial)* spring

vertiginosamente *adv* with dizzying speed

vertiginosidad *nf* dizziness

vertiginoso, -a *adj (mareante)* dizzy; *(rápido)* dizzy, giddy; **venía a una velocidad vertiginosa** he approached at breakneck speed

vértigo *nm* (**a**) *(enfermedad)* vertigo; *(mareo)* dizziness; **la altura me da v.** heights make me feel dizzy; **tener v.** to feel dizzy (**b**) *Fig* frenzy; **de v.** frenzied; **me da v. sólo de pensarlo** I go dizzy just thinking about it

vesícula *nf Bot Med* vesicle; **v. biliar** gall bladder

vesicular *adj* vesicular

vespa® *nf* (motor) scooter

vespertino, -a 1 *adj* evening
  2 *nm Prensa* evening newspaper

vespino® *nm* moped

vestal *nf Mit* vestal (virgin)

vestíbulo *nm* (**a**) *(de casa particular)* hall, entrance; *(de edificio público)* vestibule, entrance hall, foyer, lobby (**b**) *Anat* vestibule

vestido, -a 1 *pp de* vestir
  2 *adj* dressed; **v. de militar** in military uniform; **v. de verano** wearing *o* in summer clothes
  3 *nm (ropa)* clothes *pl*; *(de mujer)* dress; **museo del v.** museum of costume ❑ *Col* **v. de baño** swimsuit; **v. de noche** evening dress; **v. de novia** wedding dress

vestidor *nm* (**a**) *(en casa)* dressing room (**b**) *CAm Méx (en club)* *Br* changing *o US* locker room

vestidura *nf* clothing, clothes *pl*; *Rel* **vestiduras sacerdotales** vestments; *Fam* **rasgarse las vestiduras** to raise an outcry, make a great to-do

vestigio *nm (huella)* vestige, trace, remains *pl*

vestimenta *nf* clothes *pl*, garments *pl*

vestir [47] **1** *vt* (**a**) *(llevar puesto)* to wear; **vestía un traje de pana** he was wearing a corduroy suit (**b**) *(a algn)* to dress; **viste al niño** dress the baby; *Fig Fam* **quedarse para v. santos** to be left on the shelf; *Prov* **vísteme despacio que tengo prisa** more haste less speed (**c**) *(cubrir)* to cover (**de** with)
  2 *vi* (**a**) *(llevar ropa)* to dress; *Fam Hum* **el mismo que viste y calza** the very same, none other (**b**) *Fam* to be classy, look smart; **la seda viste mucho** silk always looks very elegant; **ropa de (mucho) v.** formal dress
  3 vestirse *vpr* (**a**) *(ponerse ropa)* to get dressed, dress; **enseguida me visto** I'll be dressed in a second (**b**) *(comprar prendas)* to buy one's clothes; **se viste en París** he buys his clothes in Paris (**c**) **v. de** to wear, dress in; *(disfrazarse)* to disguise oneself as; **v. de payaso** to dress up as a clown; *Fam* **v. de punta en blanco** to dress up to the nines

vestuario *nm* (**a**) *(conjunto de vestidos)* clothes *pl*, wardrobe; *Teat* wardrobe, costumes *pl*; *Mil* uniform (**b**) *Teat (camerino)* dressing room (**c**) **vestuarios** *Dep* changing room *sing*; *(fábricas etc)* cloakroom *sing*

veta *nf Min* vein, seam; *Fig* streak; *Fig* **tiene una v. de loco** there's a mad streak in him

vetar *vt* to veto, put a veto on

veteado, -a 1 *pp de* vetear
  2 *adj* veined, streaked

vetear *vt (piedras, madera)* to grain, streak

veteranía *nf* seniority, long experience; *(soldado)* long service

veterano, -a 1 *adj* veteran
  2 *nm,f* veteran; *Fam* **es un v. en estas lides** he is an old hand at this

veterinaria *nf* veterinary medicine *o* science

veterinario, -a 1 *adj* veterinary
  2 *nm,f* vet, *Br* veterinary surgeon, *US* veterinarian

veto *nm* veto; **derecho a v.** power *o* right of veto

vetustez *nf Fml (antiguedad)* antiquity; *(vejez)* great age

vetusto, -a *adj Fml (antiguo)* ancient; *(viejo)* very old

vez *nf (gen)* time; *(ocasion, turno)* occasion; **a la vez** at the same time; **a** *o* **algunas veces** sometimes; **alguna que otra v.** on the odd occasion; **Ana habló una v., Paco dos veces y Jorge tres** Ana spoke once, Paco twice and Jorge three times; **cada v.** each *o* every time; **cada v. más** more and more; **cada v. peor** worse and worse; **de una v.** in one go; **de una v. para siempre** once and for all; **de v. en cuando** now and again, every so often, every now and then; **en v. de** instead of; *(en cuentos etc)* **érase** *o* **había una v.** once upon a time; **¿le has visto actuar alguna v.?** have you ever seen him act?; **muchas veces** very often; **otra v.** again; **tal v.** perhaps, maybe

v.g., v.gr. *(abrev de* verbigracia*)* eg

VHF *nf (abrev de* very high frequency*)* VHF

VHS *nm (abrev de* video home system*)* VHS

vía *nf* (**a**) *(camino)* road; *(carril)* lane; *(calle)* street; **v. de circunvalación** bypass, *Br* ring road, *US* beltway; **v. pública** public thoroughfare ❑ *Astron* **V. Láctea** Milky Way (**b**) *Anat* passage, tract, canal; **vías urinarias** urinary tract *sing*; *Farm* **(por) v. oral** to be taken orally (**c**) *Ferroc* track, line; **de v. doble** double-track; **de v. estrecha** narrow-gauge, *Fam Fig* mediocre; **el tren situado en la v. 2** the train standing at platform 2 ❑ **v. férrea** railway track, *US* railroad track; **v. muerta** siding (**d**) *Fig (modo)* way, manner, means; **dar v. libre a** to leave the way open for; **por v. oficial** through official channels; **recurrir a la v. judicial** to go to law; **vías de comunicación** communication channels ❑ *Jur* **v. contenciosa** legal action (**e**) **en vías de** in the process of; **en v. de construcción** under construction; **países en v. de desarrollo** developing countries (**f**) **por v.** *(transportes)* by; *(a través de)* via, through; **Madrid-Londres v. París** Madrid-London via Paris; **por v. aérea/marítima** by air/sea; **por v. terrestre** overland; **transmisión v. satélite** satellite transmission

viabilidad *nf* viability

viabilizar [14] *vt* to make viable

viable *adj* viable

via crucis *nm inv Rel* Way of the Cross, Stations *pl* of the Cross; *Fig* great suffering

viaducto *nm* viaduct

viajante *nmf* commercial traveller *o US* traveler, travelling *o US* traveling salesman *o* saleswoman

viajar *vi* to travel

viaje *nm* (**a**) *(recorrido)* journey, trip; *(largo, en barco)* voyage; **¡buen v.!** bon voyage, have a good trip!; *Irón* too bad!, good riddance!; **estar de v.** to be away (on a trip); **irse** o **marcharse de v.** to go on a journey o trip; *Literario* **el último v.** one's journey's end ❑ **v. de estudios** *(en colegio, universidad)* class trip; **v. de ida** outward journey; **v. de ida y vuelta** *Br* return journey, *US* round trip; **v. de negocios** business trip; **v. de novios** honeymoon; **v. de placer** pleasure trip; **v. en tren** train journey; **v. oficial** official visit **(b)** *(concepto de viajar) (gen pl)* travel; **en sus viajes a la India** on his travels to India ❑ **agencia de viajes** travel agency; **cheque de v.** traveller's cheque; **libro de viajes** travel book **(c)** *(carga)* load; **dos viajes de arena** two loads of sand; *Fam* **de un v.** in one go; *Fam* **¡menudo v. le has pegado a la tarta!** you've had a good go at the cake! **(d)** *Argot (drogas)* trip

viajero, -a 1 *adj* travelling, *US* traveling
  2 *nm,f* **(a)** *(gen)* traveller, *US* traveler **(b)** *(en transporte público)* passenger; **¡viajeros al tren!** all aboard!

vial 1 *adj* road; **seguridad v.** road safety
  2 *nm (frasco)* phial

vianda *nf* **(a)** *Fml (comida)* food **(b)** *Méx RP (tentempié)* packed lunch; *(fiambrera)* lunchbox

viandante *nmf (transeúnte)* pedestrian, passer-by

viaraza *nf Am* **le dio la v. de hacerlo** she took it into her head to do it

viario, -a *adj* road, highway

viático *nm Rel* viaticum

víbora *nf* **(a)** *Zool* viper; *Fig* **lengua de v.** spiteful o venomous tongue **(b)** *(persona mala)* viper

viborear *vi Méx Fam* to bitch, backbite

vibración *nf* vibration; *Ling* rolling, trilling

vibrador *nm* vibrator

vibrante 1 *adj* vibrant, vibrating; *Ling* rolled, trilled
  2 *nf Ling* vibrant

vibrar *vt & vi* to vibrate; *Ling* to roll, trill

vibratorio, -a *adj* vibratory

vicaría *nf* **(a)** *(dignidad)* vicarship, vicariate **(b)** *(residencia, despacho)* vicarage; *Fam* **pasar por la v.** to get married (in church)

vicario, -a 1 *adj* vicarial, substitute
  2 *nm,f* vicar; **el V. de Cristo** the Vicar of Christ

vicealmirante *nm* vice admiral

vicecónsul *nm* vice-consul

vicepresidencia *nf* **(a)** *Pol* vice-presidency **(b)** *(de compañía, comité)* vice-chairmanship

vicepresidente, -a *nm,f* **(a)** *Pol* vice president **(b)** *(de compañía, comité)* vice-chairperson; *(hombre)* vice-chairman; *(mujer)* vice-chairwoman

vicerrector, -a *nm,f* = deputy to the vice-chancellor of a university

vicesecretario, -a *nm,f* assistant secretary

vicetiple *nf* chorus girl

viceversa *adv* vice versa

vichar *vt Am* to spy (on)

viciado, -a 1 *pp de* viciar
  2 *adj* **(a)** *(corrompido)* corrupt **(b)** *(aire) (que huele mal)* foul; *(contaminado)* polluted; *(cargado)* stuffy

viciar 1 *vt* **(a)** *(corromper)* to corrupt; **las malas compañías le viciaron** bad company led him astray **(b)** *(aire)* to pollute, contaminate **(c)** *(anular)* to vitiate, nullify **(d)** *(tergiversar)* to twist, distort
  2 viciarse *vpr* **(a)** *(enviciarse)* to take to vice; *(corromper)* to become corrupted **(b)** *(deformarse)* to go out of shape; **la persiana se ha viciado** the blind is warped

vicio *nm* **(a)** *(corrupción)* vice, corruption **(b)** *(mala costumbre)* bad habit; *(inmoralidad)* vice; **de v.** for no

reason at all, for the sake of it; **quejarse de v.** to complain out of sheer habit **(c)** *(falta física)* defect

vicioso, -a 1 *adj* **(a)** *(persona)* depraved **(b)** *(cosa)* faulty, defective; **círculo v.** vicious circle
  2 *nm,f (persona)* depraved person

vicisitud *nf (gen pl)* vicissitude; **las vicisitudes de la vida** life's ups and downs

víctima *nf* victim; **no hubo víctimas en el accidente** there were no casualties in the accident; **v. propiciatoria** scapegoat

victimar *vt Am* to kill, murder

victimario, -a *nm,f Am* killer, murderer

victoria *nf* victory, triumph; **alzarse con la v.** to come out victorious; **cantar v.** to proclaim a victory

victoriano, -a *adj* Victorian

victoriosamente *adv* triumphantly

victorioso, -a *adj* victorious

victrola *nf Am* gramophone, record player

vicuña *nf Zool* vicuña, vicuna

vid *nf Bot* vine, grapevine

vida *nf* **(a)** *(existencia)* life; **estar con/sin v.** to be alive/dead; **llevar una v. agitada/tranquila** to lead a busy/quiet life; **perder la v.** to die; **quitarle la v. a algn** to take sb's life; **se pasa la v. trabajando** he's always working, he doesn't do anything but work ❑ **v. amorosa** love life; **v. eterna** eternal life; **v. privada** private life **(b)** *(expresiones)* **amargarle la v. a algn** to make sb's life a misery; **cambiar de v.** to change one's lifestyle; **como si le fuera la v. en ello** as if his life depended on it; **costarle algo la v. a algn**, **pagar algn con su v.** to pay for sth with one's life; **dar v. a** to give life to; **daría mi v. por** I would give my right arm for; **de por v.** for life; **una amiga de toda la v.** a lifelong friend; **en la flor de la v.** in the prime of life; **en mi v.** never in my life; **en v. de** during the life of; **entre la v. y la muerte** between life and death; **escapar** o **salir con v.** to come out alive, survive; **ganarse la v.** to earn one's living; **hacerle la v. imposible a algn** to make life impossible for sb; **¡mi v.!**, **¡v. mía!** darling!, my love!; *Euf* **la otra v.** the next life; *Euf* **pasar a mejor v.** to pass away; *Fam* **¡así es la v.!** such is life!, that's life!; *Fam* **contarle a algn su v. y milagros** to tell sb one's life story; *Fam* **darse** o **pegarse la gran v.** to live it up; *Fam* **v. de perros** dog's life; *Fam* **y tu hermana, ¿qué es de su v.?** what about your sister, what's she up to these days?

vidalita *nf Am Mús* = plaintive love song

vidente *nmf* seer, soothsayer

vídeo *nm*, *Am* **video** *nm* video; **grabar en v.** to video-tape, record on video

videoaficionado, -a *nm,f* = person who makes amateur videos

videocámara *nf* camcorder

videocasete *nm* video, videocassette

videocinta *nf* video, videotape

videoclip *(pl* videoclips*)* *nm* (pop) video

videoclub *(pl* videoclubs *o* videoclubes*)* *nm* video club

videoconferencia *nf* videoconference

videoconsola *nf* game console

videojuego *nm* video game

videoportero *nm* video entryphone system

videoteca *nf* video library

videoteléfono *nm* videophone

videoterminal *nm* video terminal

videotexto *nm*, **videotex** *nm inv (por señal de televisión)* teletext; *(por línea telefónica)* videotext, Viewdata®

vidorra *nf Fam* easy life; **pegarse la gran v.** to live like a king

vidorria *nf* (**a**) *Am Pey* dog's life, miserable life (**b**) *Arg Fam* cushy number

vidriado, -a 1 *pp de* **vidriar**
  2 *adj* glazed
  3 *nm* (**a**) *(cerámica)* glazed earthenware (**b**) *(barniz)* glaze (**c**) *(acción)* glazing

vidriar 1 *vt (cerámica)* to glaze
  2 vidriarse *vpr* to become glazed, become glassy; *Fig (asunto)* to become tricky

vidriera *nf* (**a**) *(ventana)* glass window; (**puerta**) v. glass door; *(de galería, balcón)* French window (**b**) *Arquit Arte (ventana de colores)* stained-glass window (**c**) *Am (escaparate)* shop window

vidriería *nf* (**a**) *(fábrica)* glassworks *sing* (**b**) *(tienda)* glass shop

vidriero, -a *nm,f* (**a**) *(fabricante)* glass-maker (**b**) *(que coloca cristales)* glazier

vidrio *nm* (**a**) *(material)* glass ❑ **fibra de v.** fibreglass (**b**) *(de ventana)* window (pane); *Am (de anteojos)* lens; *Am (de automóvil)* window; *Fig Fam* **pagar los vidrios rotos** to carry the can

vidrioso, -a *adj* (**a**) *(quebradizo)* glass-like; *(frágil)* brittle; **ojos vidriosos** glazed eyes (**b**) *(resbaladizo)* slippery (**c**) *Fig* touchy; **asunto v.** delicate matter; **carácter v.** sensitive temperament

vieira *nf (pez)* scallop

vieja *nf Col Méx Ven Fam (mujer, chica)* chick, *Br* bird, *US* broad

viejo, -a 1 *adj* (**a**) *(persona)* old; **es más v. que yo** he's older than me; **estar v.** to look old; **hacerse v.** to grow old; *(en tono afectivo)* **un v. amigo** an old friend; *Fam* **más v. que la nana** *o* **que Matusalén** as old as the hills; *Fam* **ser un gato** *o* **un perro v.** to be a sly old fox (**b**) *(cosa)* old; *(desgastado)* worn out, old; **caerse de v.** to be falling apart (with age) (**c**) *(antiguo)* ancient, old; **viejas costumbres** ancient customs
  2 *nm,f* (**a**) *(anciano) (hombre)* old man; *(mujer)* old woman; **los viejos** elderly people ❑ *Chile* **V. de Pascua** Father Christmas; *Fam* **v. verde** dirty old man (**b**) *Fam (padre, madre)* **mi v.** my *o* the old man; **mi vieja** my *o* the old lady, my old woman; **mis viejos** my folks (**c**) *Am Fam (amigo) (hombre)* pal, *Br* mate, *US* buddy; *(mujer)* girl, *US* girlfriend

Viena *n* Vienna

vienés, -esa *adj & nm,f* Viennese

viento *nm* (**a**) *(aire)* wind; **hace** *o* **sopla mucho v.** it is very windy; **rosa de los vientos** compass rose; *Fig* **beber los vientos por algn** to be crazy about sb; *Fig* **contra v. y marea** come hell or high water; *Fig* **corren malos vientos** it's not the best moment, the time is not right; *Fig* **ir como el v.** to fly like the wind; *Fig* **ir v. en popa** to go splendidly, do very well; *Fam Fig* **mandar a algn a tomar v.** to tell sb where to go; *Prov* **quien siembra vientos recoge tempestades** they that sow the wind shall reap the whirlwind ❑ **vientos alisios** trade winds (**b**) *(rumbo)* direction; *Fig* **gritar algo a los cuatro vientos** to shout sth from the rooftops (**c**) *Caza* scent (**d**) *(cuerda)* rope, guy

vientre *nm* (**a**) *Anat* belly, abdomen; **bajo v.** lower abdomen; **dolor de v** stomach ache; *Fam* belly ache (**b**) *(conjunto de vísceras)* bowels *pl*; **hacer de v.** to have a bowel movement (**c**) *(de mujer embarazada)* womb (**d**) *(de barco, vasija)* belly

viernes *nm inv* Friday; **de v. en ocho días** the Friday after next; **de v. en una semana** a week on Friday, Friday week; **el periódico del v.** Friday's newspaper; **el v.** on Friday; **el v. antepasado** the Friday before last; **el v. pasado** last Friday; **el v. por la mañana/tarde/noche** (on) Friday morning/afternoon/evening *o* night; **el v. próximo** *o* **que viene** next Friday; **el v. siguiente** the following Friday; **este v.** this Friday; **la película del v.** the Friday film; **los v.** on Fridays; **todos los v.** every Friday; **un v. sí y otro no** every other Friday ❑ **V. Santo** Good Friday

Vietnam *n* Vietnam

vietnamita 1 *adj* Vietnamese
  2 *nmf (persona)* Vietnamese
  3 *nm (idioma)* Vietnamese

viga *nf Arquit* (**a**) *(de madera)* beam, rafter; **v. maestra** main beam; **v. transversal** crossbeam (**b**) *(de hierro, acero)* girder

vigencia *nf* validity; **entrar en v.** to come into force *o* effect, become valid; **estar en v.** to be in force, be valid

vigente *adj* in force, valid

vigésimo, -a 1 *adj* twentieth; **vigésima parte** twentieth; **v. primero** twenty-first; **v. segundo** twenty-second
  2 *nm,f (de una serie)* twentieth
  3 *nm (parte)* twentieth; *véase tamb* **octavo, -a**

vigía 1 *nf (atalaya)* watchtower, lookout post
  2 *nmf (gen)* lookout; *(hombre)* watchman; *(mujer)* watch-woman

vigilancia *nf* vigilance, watchfulness; **bajo v.** under surveillance

vigilante 1 *adj (despierto)* vigilant, watchful; *(alerta)* alert
  2 *nm (guarda)* watchman; *(de banco, con armas)* guard; **v. nocturno** night watchman

vigilar 1 *vt (ir con cuidado por)* to watch; *(con armas etc)* to guard; *(supervisar)* to oversee; **vigila al niño** keep an eye on the baby; **vigila que no entren** make sure they don't get in; **vigila que no se salga la leche** take care that the milk doesn't boil over
  2 *vi (gen)* to keep watch; *(observar)* to watch; **v. por** *o* **sobre** to watch over, look after; **v. por el bien público** to guarantee public law and order

vigilia *nf* (**a**) *(no dormir)* vigil, watch; **pasar la noche de v.** to stay awake all night (**b**) *(víspera)* eve; *Rel* vigil (**c**) *Rel (abstinencia)* abstinence; **guardar la v.** to abstain from eating meat (**d**) *(trabajo)* night work *o* study; **este trabajo es fruto de sus vigilias** this work is the product of many sleepless nights

vigor *nm* (**a**) *(fuerza)* vigour, *US* vigor (**b**) *(vigencia)* force, effect; **en v.** in force; **poner en v.** to put into effect

vigorizador, -a *adj (medicamento)* fortifying; *(actividad)* invigorating

vigorizar [14] *vt (medicamento)* to fortify; *(actividad)* to invigorate

vigoroso, -a *adj (robusto)* vigorous; *(colorido)* strong

viguería *nf Arquit* (**a**) *(de madera)* beams *pl* (**b**) *(de metal)* girders *pl*

vigueta *nf Arquit* (**a**) *(de madera)* small beam (**b**) *(de metal)* small girder

VIH *nm (abrev de* **virus de la inmunodeficiencia humana**) HIV

vikingo *nm* Viking

vil *adj Fml (person)* vile, base, despicable; *(act)* vile

vileza *nf* (**a**) *(cualidad)* vileness, baseness (**b**) *(acto)* vile act, despicable deed

vilipendiar *vt Fml* (**a**) *(ofender)* to vilify, revile, insult (**b**) *(despreciar)* to despise; *(rebajar)* to humiliate

vilipendio *nm Fml* (**a**) *(ofensa)* vilification, abuse (**b**) *(desprecio)* scorn, contempt; *(humillación)* humiliation

vilipendioso, -a *adj Fml* (**a**) *(ofensivo)* vilifying (**b**) *(menospreciado)* contemptible; *(humillado)* humiliated

villa nf (**a**) (población) town ◻ Arg Bol **v. miseria** shanty town; **v. olímpica** Olympic village (**b**) (casa) villa, country house

Villadiego nm Fam **tomar las de V.** to clear off, beat it

villancico nm Mús (Christmas) carol

villanía nf Fml (**a**) (cualidad) vileness, baseness (**b**) (acto) vile deed, despicable act, villainy (**c**) (dicho grosero) coarse remark

villano, -a nm,f villain

villorrio nm Pey one-horse town

Vilna n Vilnius

vilo: en vilo loc adv (**a**) (suspendido) in the air, suspended (**b**) (intranquilo) on tenterhooks, in suspense; **tener a algn con el alma en v.** to keep sb on tenterhooks o in suspense

vinagre nm vinegar; Fig bad tempered person

vinagrera nf (**a**) (vasija) vinegar bottle (**b**) **vinagreras** (para aceite y vinagre) cruet set sing (**c**) Andes (ardor de estómago) heartburn

vinagreta nf Culin vinaigrette sauce

vinajera nf Rel cruet (for wine and water)

vinatería nf (**a**) (comercio) wine trade (**b**) (tienda) wine shop

vinatero, -a 1 adj wine
  2 nm,f wine merchant

vinaza nf (vinos) poor quality wine, Br plonk

vincha nf Andes RP hairband

vinculación nf link, connection

vinculante adj Jur binding

vincular 1 vt (**a**) (enlazar) to link; **estar vinculado a** (tener vínculos con) to be linked to, have links with; (depender de) to be linked to (**b**) (obligar) **este tratado vincula a los países firmantes** this treaty is binding for the countries that have signed it
  2 vincularse vpr to link oneself (**a** to)

vínculo nm (**a**) (lazo) (entre hechos, países) link; (personal, familiar) tie, bond; **los unía un v. muy profundo** they shared a very deep bond (**b**) Inform link (**c**) Jur entail

vindicación nf (**a**) (venganza) vengeance, revenge (**b**) (defensa) vindication

vindicar [59] vt (**a**) (vengar) to avenge (**b**) (defensar) to vindicate

vindicativo, -a adj (**a**) (vengativo) vindictive (**b**) (que defiende) vindicatory; (leyes) punitive

vindicatorio, -a adj vindicatory

vinería nf Am wine shop

vinícola adj wine-producing

vinicultor, -a nm,f wine producer

vinicultura nf wine production o growing

vinificación nf wine-making process

vinilo nm vinyl

vino nm wine; **ir de vinos** to go on a drinking spree; Fig **tener mal v.** to become aggressive when drunk; Fam **bautizar el v.** to water down the wine ◻ **v. abocado** fortified wine; **v. añejo** vintage wine; **v. blanco** white wine; **v. clarete** claret; **v. de aguja** slightly sparkling wine; **v. de la casa** house wine; **v. de mesa** table wine; **v. dulce** sweet wine; **v. espumoso** sparkling wine; **v. generoso** o **de postre** full-bodied wine; **v. peleón** cheap wine, Br plonk; **v. rosado** rosé; **v. seco** dry wine; **v. tinto** red wine

vinoso, -a adj wine-like, wine

viña nf vineyard; Prov **de todo hay en la v. del Señor** it takes all sorts (to make a world)

viñador, -a nm,f vine grower

viñedo nm vineyard

viñeta nf (**a**) Impr vignette (**b**) (en tebeo) **historia en viñetas** comic strip, strip cartoon

viola Mús **1** nf viola
  2 nmf viola player

violáceo, -a 1 adj violaceous, violet
  2 violáceas nfpl Bot violaceae pl

violación nf (**a**) (de un derecho, una ley) violation, infringement (**b**) (de una persona) rape

violador, -a n (**a**) (de un derecho, una ley) violator (**b**) (de una persona) rapist (**c**) (de un lugar) violator, trespasser; (de una tumba) desecrator

violar vt (**a**) (un derecho, una ley) to violate, infringe (**b**) (una persona) to rape (**c**) (un lugar) to violate, trespass; (tumba) to desecrate

violencia nf (**a**) (agresividad) violence; **con v.** violently, by force; **la no v.** non-violence ◻ **v. doméstica** domestic violence (**b**) (sentimiento) embarrassment; **si te causa v. ...** if you find it embarrassing ...

violentar 1 vt (**a**) (forzar) to force, break open; (sitio) to break into, enter by force; **v. una cerradura** to force a lock (open); **v. una puerta** to break a door down (**b**) (obligar) to force, use force on (**c**) (enojar) to infuriate (**d**) (texto) to twist, distort
  2 violentarse vpr (**a**) (obligarse) to force oneself; (vencer repugnancia etc) to overcome one's reluctance (**b**) (pasar vergüenza) to be embarrassed; (avergonzarse) to feel ashamed (**c**) (molestarse) to get annoyed

violento, -a adj (**a**) (brutal) violent (**b**) (carácter) violent; **persona de carácter v.** person of a violent nature (**c**) (embarazoso) embarrassing, awkward (**d**) (molesto, incómodo) embarrassed, awkward; **se sentía v. en aquella casa** he felt ill at ease in that house (**e**) (postura) unnatural, forced (**f**) (sentido de un texto) twisted, distorted

violeta 1 adj violet
  2 nm (color) violet
  3 nf Bot violet

violetera nf violet seller

violín Mús **1** nm violin; Méx Fig Fam **pintar a algn un v.** Br to stick two fingers up at sb, US flip sb the bird
  2 nmf violinist; **primer v.** first violin

violinista nmf violinist

violón 1 nm double bass
  2 nmf double bass player

violoncelista nmf, **violonchelista** nmf violoncellist, cellist

violoncelo nm, **violonchelo** nm violoncello, cello

VIP [bip] (pl **VIP** o **VIPs**) nmf (abrev de **very important person**) VIP

viperino, -a adj Zool viperine, viperous; Fig venomous; **lengua viperina** spiteful o venomous tongue

virada nf Náut tack, tacking

viraje nm (**a**) (curva) turn, bend (**b**) (acción de girar) (en coche) turn; Náut tack (**c**) Fig change in direction, volte-face, about-face; Pol change in policy (**d**) Fot toning

viral adj Med viral

virar 1 vi (**a**) Náut to tack, put about; (coche) to turn round (**b**) Fig to change; **v. en redondo** to change completely
  2 vt Fot to tone

virgen 1 adj (**a**) (persona) virgin (**b**) Fig virgin, pure; (en estado natural) unspoiled; (reputación) unsullied; **aceite v.** virgin olive oil; **cinta v.** blank tape; **selva v.** virgin forest; **las Islas Vírgenes** the Virgin Islands
  2 nmf virgin
  3 nf Rel **la (Santísima) V.** the (Blessed) Virgin; Fam **ser un viva la V.** to be a devil-may-care person

virginal 1 *adj* virginal
2 *nm Mús* virginal
virginiano, -a *adj & nm,f Am Astron* Virgo
virginidad *nf* virginity
Virgo *nm Astrol Astron* Virgo
virgo *nm* (a) *(virginidad)* virginity (b) *Anat* hymen
virguería *nf Argot* (a) *(cosa extraordinaria)* gem, marvel; **hacer virguerías** to work wonders, be a dab hand (b) *(adorno exagerado)* frill
virguero, -a *adj Argot* smart, great; **esta camisa es muy virguera** that shirt is the business
vírgula *nf*, **virgulilla** *nf Impr (guión ondulado)* swung dash; *(sobre la ñ)* tilde
vírico, -a *adj* viral
viril *adj* virile, manly; **miembro v.** penis, male member
virilidad *nf* virility
virología *nf Med* virology
virólogo, -a *nm,f Med* virologist
virreina *nf (mujer del virrey)* viceroy's wife; *(la que gobierna)* female viceroy, vicereine
virreinato *nm* viceroyalty
virrey *nm* viceroy
virtual *adj* virtual
virtualidad *nf* potential
virtualmente *adv* virtually
virtud *nf* (a) *(cualidad)* virtue (b) *(propiedad)* property; **hierbas con virtudes curativas** herbs with medicinal properties (c) *(poder, facultad)* power; **tener la v. de** to have the power o ability to; **en v. de** by virtue of
virtuosismo *nm* virtuosity
virtuoso, -a 1 *adj* virtuous
2 *nm,f (genio)* virtuoso
viruela *nf* (a) *Med* smallpox (b) *(cicatrices)* pockmarks *pl*
viruji *nm Fam* fresh air
virulé: a la virulé *Fam* **1** *loc adj* (a) *(torcido)* crooked, twisted (b) **un ojo a la v.** a black eye
2 *loc adv (de cualquier manera)* any old how
virulencia *nf* virulence
virulento, -a *adj* virulent
virus *nm inv también Inform* virus □ **v. del sida** AIDS virus; **v. informático** computer virus
viruta *nf Carp* shaving
vis *nf* **v. cómica** comic sense
visa *nf Am* visa
visado, -a 1 *pp de* visar
2 *adj* endorsed with a visa
3 *nm* visa
visaje *nm* grimace, (wry) face
visar *vt (pasaporte)* to endorse (with a visa); *(documento)* to endorse, approve
víscera *nf Anat* (a) *(órgano)* internal organ (b) **vísceras** *(conjunto de órganos)* viscera, entrails *pl*
visceral *adj* (a) *Anat* visceral (b) *Fig (intenso)* profound, deep-rooted; **reacción v.** gut reaction
viscosidad *nf* viscosity
viscoso, -a *adj* viscous
visera *nf* (a) *(de casco)* visor; **calarse la v.** to pull down one's visor (b) *(de gorra)* peak; **gorra de v.** peaked cap (c) *(pieza suelta de plástico etc)* eye-shade (d) *Cuba (anteojeras)* Br blinkers, US blinders
visibilidad *nf* visibility; **curva con mala v.** blind corner
visible *adj* (a) *(que se puede ver)* visible (b) *(manifiesto)* evident

visiblemente *adv* (a) *(perceptiblemente)* visibly (b) *(claramente)* evidently
visigodo, -a *Hist* **1** *adj* Visigothic
2 *nm,f* Visigoth
visigótico, -a *adj Hist* Visigothic
visillo *nm* small lace o net curtain
visión *nf* (a) *(acción de ver)* vision; *Fig* **v. de conjunto** overall view (b) *(vista)* sight (c) *(aparición)* vision; *Fam* **quedarse como quien ve visiones** to look as if one has seen a ghost (d) *(entendimiento)* vision, view; *(perspicacia)* foresight
visionar *vt Cin* to view *(during production or before release)*
visionario, -a *nm,f (adivino)* visionary; *(iluso)* person who imagines things
visir *nm Hist* vizir, vizier
visita *nf* (a) *(acción)* visit; **estamos de v. en la ciudad** we are visiting the town; **horas de v.** visiting hours; **ir de v. a casa de algn** to pay sb a visit; **tarjeta de v.** visiting card; **v. de cortesía** courtesy visit (b) *(invitado)* visitor, guest; **tenemos v.** we have a visitor (c) *(invitados)* visitors *pl*, guests *pl*; **tenemos v.** we have visitors (d) *Inform (a página Web)* hit
visitación *nf Rel* Visitation
visitador, -a 1 *adj* fond of visiting
2 *nm,f* (a) *(invitado)* person fond of visiting, frequent visitor (b) *Farm (representante)* pharmaceutical salesman o saleswoman
3 *nm (inspector)* inspector
visitante 1 *adj* visiting
2 *nmf* visitor
visitar *vt* (a) *(ir a ver)* to visit; **ven a visitarnos cuando quieras** come and see us whenever you like (b) *(examinar)* *(lugar)* to visit, inspect
vislumbrar *vt* (a) *(ver mal)* to glimpse, catch a glimpse of, see vaguely; **vislumbró dos figuras en la oscuridad** she could make out two shapes in the darkness (b) *Fig (conjeturar)* to begin to see, begin to grasp
vislumbre *nf (gen)* glimpse; *(resplandor tenue)* glimmer; *Fig* glimmer; *Fig* **tener vislumbres de** to have an inkling of
viso *nm* (a) *(reflejo)* sheen (b) *Fig (aspecto)* appearance; **tener visos de** to seem, appear; **una persona de v.** an important person (c) *Cost (forro)* unattached lining
visón *nm Zool* mink
visor *nm* (a) *Fot* viewfinder (b) *(de arma)* sight
víspera *nf* (a) *(día anterior)* day before; *(de festivo)* eve (b) **vísperas** *Rel* vespers
vista *nf* (a) *(gen)* sight, vision, eye, eyes *pl*; **a la v.** visible; **alzar la v.** to look up; *Com Fin* **a tantos días v.** so many days after sight; **apartar la v. de** to look away from; **a primera o simple v.** at first sight, on the face of it; **bajar la v.** to look down; **clavar o fijar la v. en** to stare at; **con vistas a** with a view to; **conocer a algn de v.** to know sb by sight; **corto de v.** short-sighted; **en v. de** in view of, considering; **no le quitó la v. de encima** she didn't take her eyes off him; **perder de v.** to lose sight of; **quítalo de mi v.** take it away; **tener la v. cansada** to be suffering from eyestrain; **tener mala v.** to have poor eyesight; **¡tierra a la v.!** land ahoy!; *Fig* **a la v. de todos** *(abiertamente)* openly; *(públicamente)* in full view of everyone; *Fig* **actuar con mucha v.** to act with great foresight; *Fig* **comer a algn con la v.** to undress sb with one's eyes; *Fig* **es algo que salta a la v.** it sticks out a mile; *Fig* **punto de v.** point of view, viewpoint; *Fig* **tener v. de lince** to have eyes like an eagle; *Fig* **tiene mucha v. para los negocios** she has a good head for business; *Fig* **volver la v. atrás** to look back; *Fam* **¡hasta la v.!** goodbye!, see you!; *Fam Fig* **hacer la v. gorda** to turn a blind eye (b) *(panorama)* view; **París a v. de pájaro** a bird's-eye view o

Paris; **con v. al mar** overlooking the sea (**c**) *(cuadro, dibujo, fotografía)* view; **v. marina** seascape (**d**) *(aspecto)* look, appearance (**e**) *Jur* trial, hearing

vistazo *nm* glance; **dar** *o* **echar un v. a algo** to have a (quick) look at sth; **échale un v. a mi bolso** keep an eye on my handbag

visto, -a 1 *pp de* **ver**[2]
   2 *adj* (**a**) *(dado)* in view of, considering; **está v. que no le interesa** it is obvious that he is not interested; **por lo v.** evidently, apparently; **v. que** in view of the fact that, seeing *o* given that; *Fig* **ni v. ni oído** in a flash (**b**) *(aceptable)* acceptable; **estar bien v.** to be well looked upon, be considered acceptable; **estar mal v.** to be frowned upon (**c**) *(pasado de moda)* old-fashioned; **eso está muy v. ya** there is nothing new about that, that's a very old trick; **este actor está muy v. ya** that actor's becoming a bit passé; **lo nunca v.** something extraordinary, something quite out of the ordinary; *Fam* **esto es lo nunca v.** this really takes the biscuit
   3 *nm* **v. bueno** approval, O.K.; **dar el v. bueno a algo** to approve sth, O.K. sth

vistosidad *nf* brightness, colourfulness, *US* colorfulness

vistoso, -a *adj* (**a**) *(colorido)* bright, colourful, *US* colorful (**b**) *(llamativo)* showy, flashy

visual 1 *adj* visual; **campo v.** field of vision
   2 *nf* (**a**) *Téc* line of sight (**b**) *Argot* sight

visualización *nf* (**a**) *(en general)* visualization (**b**) *Inform* display

visualizador *nm Inform* viewer

visualizar [14] *vt* to visualize

vital *adj* (**a**) *(relativo a la vida)* vital, living; **espacio v.** living space (**b**) *(fundamental)* vital, essential (**c**) *(persona)* lively, vivacious, full of vitality

vitalicio, -a 1 *adj* life, for life; **cargo v.** post held for life; **pensión vitalicia** life annuity *o* pension
   2 *nm (pensión)* life annuity; *(seguro)* life insurance policy

vitalidad *nf* vitality

vitalismo *nm* vitality

vitalista *adj* dynamic

vitalizar [14] *vt* to vitalize

vitamina *nf Biol Quím Med* vitamin

vitaminado, -a *adj Med* vitamin-enriched, with added vitamins

vitamínico, -a *adj Med* vitamin

vitela *nf* vellum

vitelina *nf (proteína)* vitellin

vitelino, -a *adj Biol* vitelline

vitícola *adj* wine-growing, wine-producing, viticultural

viticultor, -a *nm,f* wine grower, viticulturer

viticultura *nf* wine growing, viticulture

vitivinícola *adj (región)* wine-producing; **producción v.** wine production

vito *nm Mús* = Andalusian dance and song

vitola *nf* (**a**) *(medida)* = standard cigar measurement (**b**) *(faja)* cigar band (**c**) *Mil (calibrador)* calibrator

vítor 1 *interj* bravo!, hurrah!
   2 *nm* cheer; **entre vítores de la multitud** amidst the cheers of the crowd

vitorear *vt* (**a**) *(dar vítores a)* to cheer (**b**) *(aplaudir)* to applaud

vitoriano, -a 1 *adj* of *o* from Vitoria
   2 *nm,f* person from Vitoria

vitral *nm* stained-glass window

vítreo, -a *adj* (**a**) *(de vidrio)* vitreous, glass-like, glassy (**b**) *Fís Elec* vitreous

vitrificar [59] *vt* to vitrify

vitrina *nf (armario)* glass *o* display cabinet; *(de exposición)* glass case, showcase; *(escaparate)* shop window

vitriolo *nm* vitriol

vitrocerámica *nf* **cocina (de) v.** ceramic hob

vituallas *nfpl* provisions, food *sing*

vituperable *adj* reprehensible, deserving censure

vituperación *nf* vituperation

vituperar *vt* to vituperate, condemn

vituperio *nm* vituperation, condemnation, censure

viudedad *nf* widower's pension, widow's pension

viudez *nf* widowhood

viudo, -a 1 *adj* widowed; **es v.** he is a widower; **quedó viuda** she was left a widow
   2 *nm,f (hombre)* widower; *(mujer)* widow

viva 1 *interj* hurrah!; **¡v. el novio!** three cheers for the groom!; **¡v. el rey!** long live the king!
   2 *nm* cheer; **dar vivas** to cheer

vivac *nm Mil* bivouac

vivacidad *nf* vivacity, vivaciousness, liveliness

vivalavirgen *nmf inv Fam* devil-may-care person

vivales *nmf inv Fam* crafty devil, smooth operator, clever customer

vivamente *adv* (**a**) *(con viveza)* in a lively fashion (**b**) *(intensamente)* strongly, intensely (**c**) *(profundamente)* deeply, acutely

vivaque *nm Mil* bivouac

vivaquear *vi* to bivouac

vivar *nm* (**a**) *(de conejos)* warren (**b**) *(vivero de peces)* fish farm *o* hatchery

vivaracho, -a *adj Fam* lively, sprightly, vivacious; **ojos vivarachos** sparkling eyes

vivaz *adj* (**a**) *(con vida)* lively, vivacious (**b**) *(perspicaz)* sharp, quick-witted (**c**) *Bot* perennial

vivencia *nf* personal experience

víveres *nmpl* provisions, supplies, food *sing*

vivero *nm* (**a**) *(de plantas)* nursery (**b**) *(de peces, moluscos)* fish farm *o* hatchery (**c**) *Fig (lugar adecuado)* breeding ground, hotbed

viveza *nf* (**a**) *(persona)* liveliness, vivacity; *(color, relato)* vividness; *(ojos)* sparkle (**b**) *(agudeza)* sharpness, quick-wittedness (**c**) *(ardor)* passion, force

vivido, -a 1 *pp de* **vivir**
   2 *adj (real)* real, real-life, true-life; *(experimentado)* based on personal experience

vívido, -a *adj* vivid

vividor, -a *nm,f* (**a**) *(que sabe vivir)* person who makes the most of life (**b**) *Pey* sponger, scrounger

vivienda *nf* (**a**) *(en general)* housing, accommodation; **escasez de v.** housing shortage (**b**) *(morada)* dwelling; *(casa)* house; *(piso)* Br flat, *US* apartment; **un bloque de viviendas** a block of flats; **v. unifamiliar** house *(detached, semi-detached or terraced)*

viviente *adj* living, alive; *Fam* **todo bicho v.** every living creature

vivificador, -a *adj*, **vivificante** *adj* life-giving

vivificar [59] *vt* to give life to, vivify, enliven

vivíparo, -a *adj Biol* viviparous

vivir 1 *nm* life, living; **gente de mal v.** shady characters
   2 *vi* (**a**) *(tener vida)* to be alive, live; **hay que seguir viviendo** life must go on; **no tener con** *o* **de qué v.** to

have nothing to live on; **si pudiera volver a v.** if I could live my life over again; **tú sí que sabes v. bien** you really know how to enjoy life; **vive de milagro** it's a wonder he's still alive; **vive de sus ahorros** she lives off her savings; **viven de la pesca** they make their living by fishing; *Literario* **y vivieron felices y comieron perdices** and they (all) lived happily ever after; *Fig* **no dejar v. a algn** to give sb a hard time; *Fig* **v. a cuerpo de rey** to live like a king; *Fig* **v. al día** to live from day to day; *Fig* **v. del aire** to live on fresh air; *Fam* **vamos viviendo** we are managing, we are getting by; *Fam* **v. a lo grande** to live it up, live in style (**b**) *(habitar)* to live; **vive con sus padres** she lives at home; **vive en Montevideo** he lives in Montevideo; **viven juntos** they live together (**c**) *(durar)* to last

3 *vt (pasar)* to live, live through; **allí viví mi juventud** I spent my youth there; **los que no hemos vivido la guerra** those of us who did not live through the war

vivisección *nf* vivisection

vivito, -a *adj Fam* **v. y coleando** alive and kicking

vivo, -a 1 *adj* (**a**) *(gen)* living, alive, live; **a lo v.** vividly; **de viva voz** verbally, by word of mouth; *TV (programa)* **en v.** live; *Ling* **lengua viva** living language; *Med* **llaga viva** open wound; **materia viva** living matter; *Med* **operar a algn en v.** to operate on sb without an anaesthetic; **su recuerdo sigue v.** the memory of him lives on; **v. o muerto** dead or alive; *Fig* **herir** *o* **tocar a algn en lo más v.** to cut sb to the quick; *Fig Pol* **las fuerzas vivas de un país** the driving forces behind a country; *Fam* **es el v. retrato** *o* **la viva imagen de su madre** she is the spitting image of her mother (**b**) *(fuego, llama)* live, burning; **al rojo v.** red-hot (**c**) *(vivaz)* lively, vivacious (**d**) *(color)* vivid, bright (**e**) *(dolor, deseo etc)* acute, intense, deep (**f**) *(inteligencia)* sharp, quick (**g**) *(descripción, estilo)* lively, graphic (**h**) *(carácter)* quick, irritable; **tiene el genio v.** she's very quick-tempered (**i**) *(listo)* sharp, clever (**j**) *(astuto)* shrewd, sly

2 *nm* (**a**) *(que vive)* living person; **los vivos y los muertos** the living and the dead (**b**) *(persona avispada)* quick-witted person; **un par de vivos** a couple of sharp characters (**c**) *(borde, canto)* border, edge (**d**) *Cost* trimming, border

vizcacha *nf SAm Zool* vizcacha, viscacha

vizcaíno, -a *adj & nm,f* Biscayan

Vizcaya *n* Biscay; **el golfo de V.** the Bay of Biscay

vizcondado *nm (título)* viscounty, viscountcy; *(territorio)* viscounty

vizconde *nm* viscount

vizcondesa *nf* viscountess

V.O. *(abrev de* **versión original***)* original language version; **V.O. subtitulada** subtitled version

vocablo *nm Ling* word, term

vocabulario *nm* vocabulary

vocación *nf* vocation, calling

vocacional *adj* vocational

vocal 1 *adj* vocal

2 *nf Ling* vowel

3 *nmf* member; **v. de una junta** member of a board

vocálico, -a *adj Ling* vocalic

vocalismo *nm Ling* vowel system

vocalista *nmf Mús* vocalist, singer

vocalización *nf* vocalization

vocalizar [14] *vt & vi* to vocalize

vocativo *nm Ling* vocative

voceador, -a 1 *adj* vociferous, loud-mouthed

2 *nm,f* shouter

3 *nm* town crier

vocear 1 *vi (dar voces)* to shout, cry out

2 *vt* (**a**) *(gritar)* to shout, cry out (**b**) *(divulgar)* to publish, proclaim

voceras *nm inv Fam* loudmouth

vocerío *nm* shouting, uproar, hullabaloo

vocero, -a *nm,f* spokesperson, *(hombre)* spokesman; *(mujer)* spokeswoman

vociferador, -a *adj,* **vociferante** *adj* vociferous

vociferante *adj* shouting

vociferar *vt & vi* to vociferate

vocinglero, -a 1 *adj* (**a**) *(que grita mucho)* screaming, shrieking (**b**) *(que dice necedades)* loudmouthed

2 *nm,f* (**a**) *(persona gritona)* screamer, shrieker (**b**) *(persona que dice necedades)* loudmouth

vodevil *nm Teat* vaudeville, music hall

vodevilesco, -a *adj* vaudevillian, music-hall

vodka ['boðka] *nm* vodka

vol. *(abrev de* **volumen***)* vol

volada *nf RP* (**a**) *(ocasión favorable)* event; **aprovechar la v.** to take advantage of the opportunity (**b**) *Fam* **a las voladas** *(rápidamente)* in a flash

voladizo, -a *Arquit* **1** *adj* projecting, jutting out

2 *nm* projection

volado, -a 1 *pp de* volar

2 *adj* (**a**) *Impr* superior (**b**) *Fam* **estar v.** *(intranquilo)* to feel uneasy; *(impaciente)* to be in a hurry

3 *nm RP Ven (de vestido)* ruffle, flounce

volador, -a 1 *adj* flying

2 *nm* (**a**) *(cohete)* rocket (**b**) *(pez)* flying fish (**c**) *(molusco)* = type of squid

voladura *nf Constr* blowing up, demolition; *Min* blasting *(of rocks)*

volandas: en volandas *loc adv (por el aire)* in the air, flying through the air; *Fig (rápidamente)* rapidly, swiftly

volandero, -a *adj* (**a**) *Orn* ready to fly (**b**) *(suspendido)* hanging; *(suelto)* loose (**c**) *(imprevisto)* unexpected, unforeseen (**d**) *(vagabundo)* restless, wandering

volante 1 *adj* (**a**) *(que vuela)* flying (**b**) *(que se desplaza)* flying, mobile; **escuadrón v.** flying squad

2 *nm* (**a**) *Aut* steering wheel; **ir al v.** to be driving; **un as del v.** a motor-racing champion (**b**) *Téc* flywheel; *(de reloj)* balance wheel (**c**) *Cost* flounce; *(adorno)* frill, ruffle (**d**) *Dep* shuttlecock (**e**) *Esp (del médico)* (referral) note

volantín *nm Carib Chile* kite

volapié *nm Taur* = method used in killing the bull

volar [63] **1** *vi* (**a**) *(elevarse)* to fly; **echarse a v.** to fly away, fly off (**b**) *Fig (ir deprisa)* to fly; **cenó volando** he ate his dinner in a rush *o* at top speed; **pasar volando** to fly past; **¡volando!, que no llegamos** jump to it or we'll be late! (**c**) *(noticia)* to spread like wildfire (**d**) *Fam (desaparecer)* to disappear, vanish; **han volado los tres billetes que dejé en el cajón** the three notes I left in the drawer have vanished

2 *vt* (**a**) *(hacer estallar) (edificios)* to blow up, demolish; *(caja fuerte)* to blow open; *Min* to blast (**b**) *Impr* to raise (**c**) *Caza* to flush

3 **volarse** *vpr* (**a**) *(papeles etc)* to blow away (**b**) *(encolerizarse)* to lose one's temper, blow up

volatería *nf* (**a**) *Caza* falconry (**b**) *(conjunto de aves)* fowl *sing,* birds

volátil *adj* volatile

volatilidad *nf* volatility

volatilización *nf* volatilization

volatilizar [14] **1** *vt* to volatilize

2 **volatilizarse** *vpr* to vanish into thin air

volatín *nm* acrobatics *pl*

volatinero, -a *nm,f* acrobat

volcado *nm Inform* **v. de pantalla** screen dump; **v. de pantalla en impresora** hard copy

volcán *nm* volcano

volcánico, -a *adj* volcanic

volcar [67] **1** *vt* (**a**) *(derribar)* to turn over, knock over, upset; *Náut* to capsize (**b**) *(vaciar)* to empty out (**c**) *(turbar la cabeza de)* to make feel dizzy (**d**) *(hacer cambiar de parecer)* to make change one's mind (**e**) *(irritar)* to irritate, annoy
2 *vi* (*coche*) to overturn, turn over; *(barco)* to capsize
3 volcarse *vpr* (**a**) *(vaso, jarra)* to fall over, tip over; *(coche)* to overturn, turn over; *(barco)* to capsize (**b**) *Fig (entregarse a algo)* to do one's utmost; **se volcó para conseguirme una plaza** she really went out of her way to get me a seat

volea *nf* (**a**) *Dep* volley (**b**) *(de carruaje)* whippletree, swingletree

volear *vt Dep* to volley

voleibol *nm Dep* volleyball

voleo *nm* (**a**) *Dep* volley; *Fig* **a(l) v.** at random, haphazardly; *Fig* **de un v.** very quickly, in one go (**b**) *Fam (bofetada)* slap

volframio *nm Quim* wolfram

volitivo, -a *adj* voluntary

volován *nm* vol-au-vent

volquete *nm* dumper truck, *US* dump truck

voltaico, -a *adj* voltaic

voltaje *nm Elec* voltage

volteador, -a *nm,f* acrobat

voltear 1 *vt* (**a**) *(dar la vuelta a)* (heno, crepe, torero) to toss; *(tortilla)* to turn over; *(mesa, silla)* to turn upside-down; *(cabeza, espalda)* to turn (**b**) *Am (derribar)* to knock over
2 voltearse *vpr* (**a**) *Am salvo RP (volverse)* to turn around (**b**) *Méx (volcarse)* to overturn

voltereta *nf* somersault

voltímetro *nm Elec* voltmeter

voltio *nm Elec* volt

volubilidad *nf* (**a**) *(inconstancia)* fickleness, changeableness (**b**) *Bot* volubility

voluble *adj* (**a**) *(inconstante)* fickle, changeable (**b**) *Bot* voluble, twining

volumen *nm* (**a**) *Fís* volume; *(tamaño)* size; *Fig* **de mucho v.** sizeable, important (**b**) *(intensidad)* volume; **baja el v.** turn the volume down (**c**) *(tomo)* volume; **obra en tres volúmenes** three-volume work

voluminoso, -a *adj* voluminous; *(enorme)* massive, bulky

voluntad *nf* (**a**) *(como virtud)* will; **buena v.** good will; **buena v. no le falta** she's very willing; **fuerza de v.** willpower; **hace falta mucha v. para dejar de fumar** it takes a lot of willpower to give up smoking; **tiene mucha v.** he is very strong-willed; **v. férrea** *o* **de hierro** iron will, will of iron (**b**) *(deseo)* wishes *pl*; **a v.** at will; **¿cuánto le doy, entonces? — la v.** how much should I give you, then? — whatever you think right; **ganarse la v. de algn** to win sb over; *Rel* **hágase tu v.** Thy will be done; *Rel* **la v. de Dios** God's will; **lo dejo a tu v.** it is up to you; **no lo dije con v. de** I didn't mean to; **por causas ajenas a nuestra v.** due to reasons beyond our control; **última v.** last wish; *Fam* **siempre hay que hacer su santa v.** everything always has to be done his way

voluntariado *nm (actividad)* voluntary work; *(personas)* volunteers *pl*

voluntariamente *adv* voluntarily

voluntariedad *nf* (**a**) *(intencionalidad)* volition (**b**) *(no aleatoriedad)* voluntary nature

voluntario, -a 1 *adj* voluntary; **ofrecerse v.** to volunteer
2 *nm,f* volunteer

voluntarioso, -a *adj* (**a**) *(de gran voluntad)* willing (**b**) *Pey (testarudo)* wilful, *US* wilfull, headstrong

voluntarismo *nm* will to succeed

voluptuosidad *nf* voluptuousness

voluptuoso, -a *adj* voluptuous

voluta *nf* (**a**) *Arquit* volute, scroll (**b**) *(espiral)* spiral, column; *(de humo, cigarrillo)* (smoke) ring

volver [41] *(pp* **vuelto)** **1** *vt* (**a**) *(dar vuelta a)* to turn (round); *(poner boca abajo)* to turn over *o* upside down; *(lo de fuera dentro)* to turn inside out; *(la parte de atrás delante)* to turn back to front; **v. los ojos hacia** to turn one's eyes towards; **volverle la espalda a algn** to turn one's back on sb; *Fig* **v. la vista atrás** to look back (**b**) *(convertir, hacer)* to turn, change, make; **ha vuelto esta casa en un infierno** it has made this place hell; **la fama le ha vuelto engreído** fame has made him conceited; **me vas a v. loco** you are driving me mad; **vuelve esta frase a pasiva** put this sentence into the passive (**c**) *(torcer)* to turn; **al v. la esquina** on turning the corner (**d**) *Méx* **v. el estómago** to throw up
2 *vi* (**a**) *(regresar)* to return; *(venir)* to come back; *(ir)* to go back; **no quiero v.** I don't want to go back; **v. atrás** to go back; **v. de vacío** to return empty-handed; **v. en sí** to come round, regain consciousness; **v. sobre sus pasos** to retrace one's steps (**b**) **v. a hacer** to do again; **hay que v. a empezar** we've got to start all over again; **vuelve a llover** it's raining again
3 volverse *vpr* (**a**) *(darse la vuelta)* to turn; **la página se volvió** the page turned over; *Fig* **todo se ha vuelto en su contra** everything has gone against him (**b**) *(regresar)* *(venir)* to come back; *(ir)* to go back; *Fig* **v. atrás** to go back on one's word (**c**) *(convertirse)* to become; **se ha vuelto más difícil** she's become more difficult; **se volvió rojo** it turned red; **v. loco** to go mad

vomitar 1 *vi* to vomit, be sick; **tengo ganas de v.** I feel sick, I want to be sick
2 *vt* to vomit, bring up; *Fig* to belch, spew out; **v. sangre** to cough up blood; *Fig* **v. injurias** to hurl insults

vomitivo, -a *adj & nm Med* emetic

vómito *nm (resultado)* vomit; *(acción)* vomiting

vomitona *nf Fam* **echar la v.** to be violently sick

voracidad *nf* voracity, voraciousness

vorágine *nf* vortex, whirlpool

voraz *adj* voracious; *Fig* raging, fierce

vórtice *nm* (**a**) *(torbellino)* vortex, whirlpool (**b**) *(de ciclón)* eye, centre, *US* center

vos *pron pers* (**a**) *Am (tú)* you (**b**) *Hist (usted)* ye, you

V.O.S.E. *nf (abrev de* **versión original subtitulada en español)** = original language version subtitled in Spanish

vosear *vt* to address as 'vos'

voseo *nm* use of 'vos'

Vosgos *n* **los V.** the Vosges

vosotros, -as *pron pers pl Esp* (**a**) *(como sujeto)* you; **v. lo queréis** you want it (**b**) *(con prep)* you; **decididlo entre v.** decide it among yourselves; **no iremos sin vosotras** we won't go without you

votación *nf* (**a**) *(voto)* vote, ballot (**b**) *(acción)* voting; **poner** *o* **someter algo a v.** to put sth to the vote, take a vote on sth; **v. a mano alzada** (voting by a) show of hands

votante 1 *adj* voting
2 *nmf* voter

votar *vi* to vote; **v. a favor/en contra de algo** to vote for/against sth; **v. a** *o* **por algn** to vote (for) sb

voto *nm* (**a**) *(gen)* vote; **diez votos a favor y dos en contra** ten votes for and two against; **por mayoría de votos** by a majority vote; **tener v.** to have the right to vote; *Fam* **tú no tienes ni voz ni v. aquí** you have no say in this matter; **una persona, un v.** one person, one vote ▢ **v. de castigo** vote against one's own party; **v. de censura/confianza** vote of no confidence/confidence; **v. secreto** secret ballot (**b**) *Rel* vow; **hacer v. de castidad/pobreza** to take a vow of chastity/poverty (**c**) *(deseo)* wish; **hago votos por su éxito** I sincerely want him to succeed (**d**) *Chile Cuba Méx RP (papeleta electoral)* ballot paper

vox populi *nf* **ser v. p. que ...** to be common knowledge that ...

voy *indic pres véase* **ir**

voyeur [bwa'jer] (*pl* **voyeurs**) *nmf* voyeur

voyeurismo [bwaje'rismo] *nm* voyeurism

voz *nf* (**a**) *(sonido)* voice; **aclararse la v.** to clear one's throat; **alzar** *o* **levantar la v.** to raise one's voice; **a media voz** in a low voice, softly; **baja la v.** lower your voice; **dar la v. de alarma** to raise the alarm; **de viva v.** verbally; **en v. alta** aloud; **en v. baja** in a low voice; **le está cambiando la v.** his voice is breaking; **v. apagada** weak voice; *Teat* **v. en off** voice offstage; **v. ronca** hoarse voice (**b**) *(grito)* shout; **a v. en cuello** *o* **grito** at the top of one's voice; **a voces** shouting; **dale una v.** give him a shout; **dar voces** to shout; *Fig* **estar pidiendo algo a voces** to be crying out for sth, need sth badly; *Fig* **secreto a voces** open secret (**c**) *(en una reunión)* voice, say; **tener v. y voto** *(opinión)* to have a say; *Pol* to be a voting member (**d**) *(rumor)* rumour, *US* rumor; **corre la v. de que ...** rumour has it that ...; **es v. pública** it's common knowledge (**e**) *Ling (palabra)* word (**f**) *Ling (del verbo)* voice ▢ **v. activa** active voice; **v. pasiva** passive voice (**g**) *Mús* voice; **canción a tres voces** three-part song; **cantar a dos voces** to sing a duet; **llevar la v. cantante** to sing the leading part; *Fig* to rule the roost

vozarrón, -ona *nm,f* powerful *o* big voice

VPO *nf* (*abrev de* **vivienda de protección oficial**) = low-cost home subsidized by the government, *Br* ≃ council house

vudú (*pl* **vudús** *o* **vudúes**) *nm* voodoo

vuelapluma: a vuelapluma *loc adv* **escribir algo a v.** to dash sth off

vuelco *nm* upset, tumble; **dar un v.** *(coche)* to overturn; *Fig (empresa)* to go to ruin; *Fig* **me dio un v. el corazón** my heart missed a beat

vuelo *nm* (**a**) *(acto)* flight; *(acción)* flying; **al v.** in flight; **alzar** *o* **emprender** *o* **levantar el v.** to take flight; **remontar el v.** to soar up; **tomar v.** to grow; *Fig* **cazarlas** *o* **cogerlas al v.** to be quick on the uptake; *Fig* **de alto v.** important, far-reaching; *Fig* **de un v.** in a flash, in no time at all (**b**) *Av* flight; **personal de v.** flight crew; *Fam Fig* **tener muchas horas de v.** to be an old hand at sth ▢ **v. chárter** charter flight; **v. espacial** space flight; **v. libre** hang-gliding; **v. nocturno** night flight; **v. regular** regular flight; **v. sin escala** non-stop flight; **v. sin motor** gliding (**c**) *Orn (plumas)* flight feathers *pl*; *(alas)* wings *pl*; *Fig* **cortarle los vuelos a algn** to clip sb's wings (**d**) *Cost (amplitud)* fullness, flare; **una falda de v.** a full skirt (**e**) *Arquit (voladizo)* projection

vuelta *nf* (**a**) *(giro)* turn, rotation; *(en carreras)* lap, circuit; **dar la v. al mundo** to go round the world; **darle la v. a algo** *(en redondo)* to turn sth round; *(boca abajo)* to turn sth upside down; *(la parte de dentro fuera)* to turn sth inside out; *(la parte posterior delante)* to turn sth back to front; **dio media v. y se fue** she turned round and walked off; *Taur* **v. al ruedo** lap of honour; *Dep* **la v. ciclista a España** the Tour of Spain; **v. de campana** somersault; *Fig* **la cabeza me da vueltas** my head is spinning; *Fig* **no le des más vueltas** stop worrying about it; *Fig* **no tiene v. de hoja** there's no doubt about it; *Fam* **le da cien vueltas a su jefe** her boss couldn't hold a candle to her; *Fam Fig* **buscarle las vueltas a algn** to (try to) find fault with sb; *Fam Fig* **cogerle las vueltas a algn** to have sb figured out; *Fam Fig* **poner a algn de v. y media** to pull sb to pieces (**b**) *(paseo)* walk, stroll; **dar una v. en coche** to go for a drive *o* a spin (in the car); *Fam* **date una v. por casa** drop in and see us (**c**) *(regreso)* return; *(viaje)* return journey, way back; **a la v. de las vacaciones** after the holidays; **a la v.** when he came back; **a v. de correo** by return post; **estar de v.** to be back; *Fam* not to have been born yesterday; **¡hasta la v.!** see you when you/I get back!; **la v. al colegio** back to school; *Dep* **partido de v.** return match; **v. a escena** comeback *(of an artist)* (**d**) *(curva)* bend, turn, curve; **estar a la v. de la esquina** to be just around the corner *o* very close; **una carretera con muchas vueltas** a winding road (**e**) *(parte de atrás)* back, reverse; **ver instrucciones a la v.** for instructions, see back (**f**) *Dep (turno)* round (**g**) *(cambio)* change, alteration; *Fam* **la vida da muchas vueltas** life is full of ups and downs (**h**) *(dinero)* change (**i**) *Tricot* row (**j**) *Cost (forro)* lining

vuelto, -a 1 *pp de* **volver**
2 *adj* **jersey de cuello v.** rollneck sweater
3 *nm* (**a**) *Impr* verso (**b**) *Am (dinero)* change

vuestro, -a *Esp* **1** *adj pos* your; **un amigo v.** a friend of yours; **vuestra majestad** Your Majesty; **v. libro** your book
2 *pron pos* yours; **éstos son los vuestros** these are yours; **lo v.** what is yours, what belongs to you; *Fam* **siempre os salís con la vuestra** you always get your own way

vulcanología *nf Geol* volcanology, vulcanology

vulcanólogo, -a *nm,f Geol* volcanologist, vulcanologist

vulgar *adj* (**a**) *(que carece de delicadeza)* vulgar, coarse, common; **lenguaje v.** coarse language; *(común, general)* common, general; **latín v.** vulgar Latin (**c**) *(ordinario, trivial)* ordinary, banal; **idea v.** commonplace idea (**d**) *(no técnico)* lay; **el término v.** the lay term

vulgaridad *nf* (**a**) *(grosería)* vulgarity, coarseness; **decir vulgaridades** to use bad language (**b**) *(trivialidad)* banality, triviality; **decir vulgaridades** to talk in platitudes

vulgarismo *nm Ling* popular phrase *o* expression, vulgarism

vulgarización *nf* popularization, vulgarization

vulgarizar [14] **1** *vt* (**a**) *(popularizar)* to popularize, spread a knowledge of, vulgarize (**b**) *(hacer vulgar)* to make common
2 vulgarizarse *vpr* to become vulgarized *o* popular *o* common

vulgarmente *adv* (**a**) *(generalmente)* generally (**b**) *(de manera vulgar)* vulgarly

vulgo *nm* **el v.** the common people *pl*; *Pey* the masses

vulnerabilidad *adj* vulnerability

vulnerable *adj* vulnerable

vulneración *nf* (**a**) *(de la reputación)* damaging, harming (**b**) *(de un tratado, un acuerdo)* violation

vulnerar *vt* (**a**) *(deshonrar)* to damage, harm (**b**) *(violar)* *(la ley, un acuerdo)* to violate

vulva *nf Anat* vulva

W

W, w *Esp* [uβe'ðoβle,] *Am* [doβle'βe] *nf (la letra)* W, w
W *(abrev de* **vatio(s))** W
walkie-talkie []*Esp* ['walki'talki,] *Am* ['woki'toki] *(pl* **walkie-talkies)** *nm* walkie-talkie
walkman® ['walman] *(pl* **walkmans)** *nm* Walkman®
WAP [wap] *nm Inform (abrev de* **Wireless Application Protocol)** WAP
Washington ['wasinton] *n* Washington
wáter *Esp* ['bater,] *Am* ['water] *nm Fam* toilet
waterpolista [waterpo'lista] *nmf* water polo player
waterpolo [water'polo] *nm* water polo
watio ['batio] *nm* watt
WC [*Esp* uβe'θe, *Am* doβleβe'se, *Méx* doβleu'se] *nm (abrev de* **water closet)** WC
web [weβ] *(pl* **webs)** *Inform* **1** *nm* o *nf (página Web)* web site

2 *nf (World Wide Web)* **la W.** the Web
Wellington ['welinton] *n* Wellington
western ['wester] *(pl* **westerns)** *nm Cin* western
whiskería [wiske'ria] *nf* = bar where hostesses chat with clients
whisky ['wiski] *(pl* **whiskys)** *nm (escocés)* whisky; *(irlandés, US)* whiskey
windsurf ['winsurf] *nm,* **windsurfing** ['winsurfin] *nm* windsurfing
windsurfista [winsur'fista] *nmf* windsurfer
wireless ['waiales] *adj Inform (tecnología, red)* wireless
wolfram ['bolfram] *nm,* **wolframio** [bol'framjo] *nm Min* wolfram
WWW *(abrev de* **World Wide Web)** WWW

X, x ['ekis] *nf (la letra)* X, x
xenofobia *nf* xenophobia
xenófobo, -a *adj* xenophobic
   2 *nm,f* xenophobe
xerografía *nf* xerography
xerografiar [32] *vt* to photocopy

xilofón *nm* xylophone
xilofonista *nmf* xylophonist
xilófono *nm* xylophone
xilografía *nf (arte)* xylography; *(impresión)* xylograph
xilográfico, -a *adj* xylographic, xylographical

Y

Y, y [i'vrjeva] *nf (la letra)* Y, y

y *conj* (**a**) *(enlace)* and; **Sevilla y Málaga** Seville and Malaga; **son las tres y cuarto** it's a quarter past three; **una chica alta y morena** a tall, dark-haired girl; **y no tardes** and don't be late (**b**) *(diferenciación)* and; **hay políticos y políticos** there are politicians and politicians (**c**) *(repetición)* and; **días y días** (for) days and days (**d**) *(en pregunta)* what about ...?; **¿y López?** what about López?; **¿y los demás?** what about the others?; **y tú, ¿qué opinas?** what do you think? (**e**) **¿y qué?** so what?; **sí, he suspendido, ¿y qué?** yes, I failed the exam, so what? (**f**) **¿y si ...?** what if ...?; **¿y si no llega a tiempo?** what if he doesn't arrive in time?; **¿y si no es verdad?** what if it isn't true? (**g**) **y eso que** although, even though; **sigue engordando y eso que no come nada** she's still putting on weight even though she eats hardly anything (**h**) **¡y tanto!** you bet!, and how!; **¿te hace ilusión? — ¡y tanto!** are you looking forward to it? — you bet I am!; *véase tamb* **e**

ya 1 *adv* (**a**) *(con pasado)* already; **ya lo sabía** I already knew; **ya en la Edad Media** as far back as the Middle Ages (**b**) *(con presente)* now; **es preciso actuar ya** it is vital that we act now; **¿son las nueve ya?** don't tell me it's nine o'clock already!; **ya está aquí** he's already arrived; *(ahora llega)* here he is!; *Fam* **ya caigo** now I get it, now I see (**c**) *(con futuro)* **ya hablaremos luego** we'll talk about it later; **ya nos veremos** see you!; **ya vendrá** she will be here soon; **ya verás** you'll see (**d**) *(ahora mismo)* immediately; **¡hazlo ya!** do it at once!; **¡lo necesito, ya!** I need it this minute!; **pero ya mismo** this very minute! (**e**) **ya no** no longer; **ya no es como antes** it isn't like it used to be; **ya no viene por aquí** he doesn't come round here any more (**f**) *(refuerza el verbo)* **ya entiendo** I see, I understand; **ya era hora** about time too; **ya lo creo** of course, I should think so; **ya lo sé** I know; **ya me dirás** what can you expect?; **ya se acabó** that's the end of it; **ya ves** well, you see; **ya viene** here he comes; **¡ya voy!** coming!; **¡ya está!** there we are!, done!

2 *interj Irón* **te juro que no le he visto — ¡ya, ya!** I swear I haven't seen him — oh yes! *o* yeah, right!

3 *conj* (**a**) *(distributivo)* **ya sea por carta o por fax** (either) by post or by fax (**b**) **ya que** since; **ya que no sabe hablar francés** as he can't speak French; **ya que tengo el coche** since I've got the car

yac *(pl* **yacs)** *nm Zool* yak

yacaré *nm Am Zool* cayman

yacente *adj* lying; **estatua y.** recumbent statue

yacer [71] *vi* to lie, be lying; **aquí yace ...** here lies ...

yacimiento *nm Geol* bed, deposit; **yacimientos petrolíferos** *o* **de petróleo** oilfields

yago *indic pres véase* **yacer**

yagua *nf Andes Carib Méx* (**a**) *(planta)* royal palm (**b**) *(tejido)* = fibrous tissue of the royal palm tree

yagual *nm CAm Méx* = padded ring for carrying loads on the head

yaguar *nm Zool* jaguar

yaguasa *nf CAm* whistling-duck

yaguré *nm Am* skunk

Yakarta *n* Jakarta

yámbico, -a *adj* iambic

yambo *nm* iamb

yanqui *Fam* **1** *adj* American
2 *nmf* Yank

Yanquilandia *n Fam Hum* Gringoland, the States

yantar¹ *nm Anticuado* food, viands *pl*

yantar² *vt Anticuado* to eat

Yaoundé *véase* **Yaundé**

yapa *nf Andes RP Fam (añadidura)* **dar algo de y.** to throw sth in for good measure *o* as an extra

yapar *vt Am* to add for good measure *o* as an extra

yarará *nm* fer-de-lance

yaraví *(pl* **yaravíes** *o* **yaravís)** *nm Am* = type of melancholy Indian song

yarda *nf* yard

Yaundé [jaun'de] *n* Yaoundé

yate *nm Náut* yacht

yaya *nf* (**a**) *Perú (insecto)* mite (**b**) *Cuba PRico (árbol)* lancewood

yayo, -a *nm,f Fam (hombre)* grandad; *(mujer)* grandma

yazgo *indic pres véase* **yacer**

yedra *nf véase* **hiedra**

yegua 1 *nf* (**a**) *(animal)* mare (**b**) *CAm (colilla)* cigar butt
2 *adj CSur Fam* **la muy y.** the old cow

yeguada *nf* (**a**) *(de animales)* herd of horses (**b**) *CAm PRico (disparate)* stupid thing

yeísmo *nm Ling* pronunciation of **ll** as **y**

yeísta *nmf* = person who pronounces Spanish **ll** as **y**

yelmo *nm* helmet

yema *nf* (**a**) *(de huevo)* yolk (**b**) *Bot* bud (**c**) *(del dedo)* fingertip (**d**) *Culin* = sweet made from sugar and egg yolk

Yemen *n* Yemen

yemení *(pl* **yemeníes)** *adj & nmf,* **yemenita** *adj & nmf* Yemeni

yen *nm (moneda)* yen

yerba *nf* (**a**) *véase* **hierba** (**b**) *RP* maté

yerbatero, -a *Andes Carib* **1** *adj* maté; **la industria yerbatera** the maté industry

2 *nm,f* **(a)** *(curandero)* healer **(b)** *(vendedor de hierbas)* herbalist

yerbera *nf RP* = container for maté

Yereván *n* Yerevan

yergo *indic pres véase* **erguir**

yermo, -a 1 *adj* **(a)** *(sin vegetación)* barren, uncultivated **(b)** *(despoblado)* deserted, uninhabited
2 *nm* wasteland

yerno *nm* son-in-law

yerra *nf RP* cattle branding

yerro 1 *nm Literario* mistake, error
2 *indic pres véase* **errar**

yerto, -a *adj* stiff, rigid; **y. de frío** frozen stiff

yesal *nm*, **yesar** *nm* gypsum quarry

yesca *nf* tinder

yesería *nf* **(a)** *Constr* plasterwork, plastering **(b)** *(fábrica)* gypsum kiln

yesero, -a 1 *adj* plaster
2 *nm,f* plasterer

yeso *nm* **(a)** *Geol* gypsum **(b)** *Constr* plaster

yeta *nf RP* bad luck

yeti *nm* yeti, abominable snowman

yeyuno *nm Anat* jejunum

Yibuti *n* Djibouti

yiddish *nm (idioma)* Yiddish

yihad [ji'χaδ] *nf* jihad

yiu-yitsu *nm* jujitsu

yo 1 *pron pers* I; **entre tú y yo** between you and me; **¿quién es? — soy yo** who is it? — it's me; **que yo sepa** as far as I know; **¿quién lo ha cogido? — yo no** who's taken it? — not me; **yo que usted** if I were you; **yo mismo** I myself; **yo soy de los que ...** I'm one of those who ...; **yo soy el culpable** I am to blame; **yo soy quien te lo digo** I'm the one who's telling you
2 *nm Filos Psic* **el yo** the ego, the self

yodado, -a *adj* iodized

yodo *nm* iodine

yoduro *nm* iodide; **y. de plata** silver iodide

yoga *nm* yoga

yogui *nmf*, **yoghi** *nmf* yogi

yogur *(pl* yogures) *nm*, **yogurt** *(pl* yogurts) *nm* yogurt, yoghurt; **y. de piña** pineapple yoghurt; **y. descremado** *o* **desnatado** low-fat yoghurt

yogurtera *nf* yoghurt maker

yola *nf Náut* yawl

yonqui *nmf Argot* junkie, drug addict

yóquey *(pl* yóqueys) *nm Dep* jockey

yoyó *nm* yo-yo

yubarta *nf Zool* finback, rorqual

yuca *nf* **(a)** *Bot* yucca **(b)** *Culin* cassava, manioc

yucal *nm Bot* yucca plantation

Yucatán *n* Yucatan

yucateco, -a 1 *adj* of *o* from Yucatan
2 *nm,f* person from Yucatan

yudo *nm* judo

yudoka *nmf* judoka

yugo *nm Agr* yoke; *Fig* **bajo el y. de la dictadura** under the yoke of the dictatorship; *Fig* **sacudir el y.** to throw off the yoke (of oppression *o* servitude)

Yugoslavia *n* Yugoslavia

yugoslavo, -a *adj & nm,f* Yugoslav, Yugoslavian

yugular *adj Anat* jugular

yunque *nm* anvil; *Fig* rock

yunta *nf* yoke *o* team of oxen

yuntero *nm* ploughman, *US* plowman

yupi *interj Fam* yippee!

yuppie ['jupi] *(pl* yuppies), **yupi** *nmf* yuppie

Yurex® *nm Méx Br* Sellotape®, *US* Scotch® tape

yute *nm Bot Tex* jute

yuxtaponer [50] *(pp* yuxtapuesto) *vt* to juxtapose

yuxtaposición *nf* juxtaposition

yuxtapuesto, -a *pp de* **yuxtaponer**
2 *adj* juxtaposed

yuyero, -a *nm,f Arg* herbalist

yuyo *nm* **(a)** *CSur (mala hierba)* weed; *(medicinal)* medicinal herb **(b)** *Andes (silvestre)* wild herb

Z

Z, z ['θeta] *nf (la letra)* Z, z

zacatal *nm CAm Méx* pasture

zacate *nm CAm Méx* fodder

zacatón *nm CRica Méx Nic* tall pasture grass

zafado, -a 1 *pp de* zafar
2 *adj* (**a**) *Am (loco)* nuts, crazy (**b**) *Andes RP Fam (atrevido)* barefaced, cheeky, *Br* brass-necked

zafar 1 *vi RP Fam (salir bien parado)* to come out on top; **zafamos de milagro** we got away by the skin of our teeth
2 zafarse *vpr* (**a**) *(librarse) (de tarea, obligación)* to get out of it, *(soltarse)* to escape; **z. de** *(persona)* to get rid of; *(obligación)* to get out of (**b**) *RP (articulación)* to become dislocated

zafarrancho *nm* (**a**) *Náut* clearing of the decks ◻ **z. de combate** call to action stations (**b**) *Fam (riña)* row (**c**) *Fam (destrozo)* ravage, destruction

zafio, -a *adj* uncouth, rough, coarse

zafiro *nm Min* sapphire

zafra¹ *nf* (**a**) *(cosecha)* sugar cane harvest *o* crop (**b**) *(fabricación)* sugar making (**c**) *(tiempo)* sugar cane harvest time

zafra² *nf (vasija)* oil can *o* jar

zaga *nf (parte posterior)* rear; **a** *o* **en la z.** behind, at the rear; *Fig* **no irle en z. a algn** to be every bit as good as sb (**b**) *Dep* defence, *US* defense

zagal *nm* (**a**) *(muchacho)* lad (**b**) *(pastor)* shepherd

zagala *nf* (**a**) *(muchacha)* lass (**b**) *(pastora)* shepherdess

zaguán *nm* hall, hallway

zaguero, -a *nm,f Dep* back

zaherir [62] *vt* (**a**) *(sentimientos)* to hurt (**b**) *(reprender)* to reprimand (**c**) *(censurar)* to reproach (**d**) *(burlarse)* to mock

zahones *nmpl* chaps

zahorí *(pl* zahoríes) *nmf* (**a**) *(adivino)* seer, clairvoyant; *(de agua)* water diviner (**b**) *Fig* mind-reader

zahúrda *nf* pigsty, hovel

zaino, -a *adj* (**a**) *(traidor)* treacherous, false (**b**) *(caballo)* chestnut; *(res vacuna)* black

Zaire *n* Zaire

zaireño, -a *adj & nm,f* Zairean

zalamería *nf* flattery, cajolery

zalamero, -a 1 *adj* flattering, fawning
2 *nm,f* flatterer, fawner

zalema *nf* (**a**) *(reverencia)* salaam, bow (**b**) *(zalamería)* flattery, cajolery

zamacuco, -a 1 *nm,f (persona solapada)* crafty person
2 *nm Fam (borrachera)* drunkenness

zamarra *nf (prenda)* sheepskin jacket

zamarro 1 *nm* (**a**) *(zamarra)* sheepskin jacket (**b**) *(piel)* sheepskin (**c**) *Ecuad (pantalón)* jeans *pl*
2 zamarros *nmpl Andes (pantalones)* chaps

zamba *nf Mús* = popular South American dance

zambardo *nm Chile* awkward *o* clumsy person

Zambeze *n* el Z. the Zambezi

Zambia *n* Zambia

zambiano, -a *adj & nm,f* Zambian

zambo, -a 1 *adj (de piernas torcidas)* knock-kneed
2 *nm,f Am* = person who has one Black and one Indian parent

zambomba 1 *nf Mús* = type of rustic percussion instrument
2 *interj Fam* wow!

zambombazo *nm Fam* (**a**) *(explosión)* bang, explosion (**b**) *(golpe)* blow

zambra *nf* (**a**) *Mús* = gypsy dance (**b**) *Fig (algarada)* uproar, racket, din

zambullida *nf* dive, plunge; **darse una z.** to go for a swim, take a dip

zambullir 1 *vt (en el agua) (persona)* to duck; *(cosa)* to dip, plunge
2 zambullirse *vpr* (**a**) *(en el agua)* to dive, plunge (**b**) *Fig (en una actividad)* to lose oneself (**en** in)

Zamora *n* Zamora; *Prov* **no se ganó Z. en una hora** Rome wasn't built in a day

zamorano, -a 1 *adj* of *o* from Zamora
2 *nm,f* person from Zamora

zampabollos *nmf inv Fam* glutton

zampar *Fam* **1** *vt Am (meter)* to shove, stick
2 *vi (comer)* **¡cómo zampa!** look at him stuffing his face!
3 zamparse *vpr Fam (comerse)* to gobble down

zampoña *nf Mús* rustic flute, panpipes *pl*

zanahoria 1 *nf* carrot
2 *nmf Andes RP Ven Fam (ingenuo)* sucker; *(aburrido, sin vicios)* nerd

zanca *nf* leg

zancada *nf* stride; **en dos zancadas** in a flash

zancadilla *nf* (**a**) *(traspiés)* trip; **ponerle** *o* **echarle la z. a algn** to trip sb up (**b**) *Fam (engaño)* ruse, trick

zancadillear *vt* **z. algn** to trip sb up; *Fig* to put a spoke in sb's wheel

zanco *nm* stilt

zancón, -ona *adj Col Méx Ven (traje)* too short

zancuda *nf Orn* wader

zancudo, -a 1 *adj* (**a**) *(persona, animal)* long-legged (**b**) *Orn* wading, **ave zancuda** wading bird, wader
2 *nm Am* mosquito

zanganear *vi* to idle, laze around

zángano, -a 1 *nm,f Fam (persona)* idler, lazybones *inv*
2 *nm Ent* drone

zangolotear *Fam* **1** *vt (sacudir)* to shake, jiggle
2 *vi (moverse)* to fidget, fuss around

zanja *nf* ditch, trench

zanjar *vt* (**a**) *(abrir zanjas)* to dig a ditch o trench in (**b**) *Fig (asunto)* to settle

zapa *nf Mil* sap, trench

zapador *nm Mil* sapper

zapallada *nf Arg* fluke, stroke of luck

zapallo *nm Andes RP (calabaza)* pumpkin; **z. (italiano)** *Br* courgette, *US* zucchini

zapapico *nm* pickaxe, *US* pickax, mattock

zapata *nf* (**a**) *(cuña)* wedge (**b**) *Náut Tec* shoe ❑ *Aut* **z. de freno** brake shoe

zapatazo *nm* blow with a shoe; **dar zapatazos** to stamp one's feet; *Fig* **tratar a algn a zapatazos** to kick sb around

zapateado *nm* = Spanish dance where the dancers stamp their feet rhythmically

zapatear *vi* to tap one's feet

zapateo *nm* foot-tapping, heel-tapping

zapatería *nf* (**a**) *(tienda)* shoe shop (**b**) *(oficio)* shoe-making

zapatero, -a 1 *nm,f* shoemaker, cobbler; *(vendedor)* shoe dealer; **z. remendón** cobbler; *Fam* **¡z., a tus zapatos!** mind your own business!
2 *adj (comida)* hard, undercooked

zapatilla *nf* slipper ❑ **z. de ballet** ballet shoe; **z. de deporte** running o jogging shoe

zapatismo *nm* (**a**) *Pol* Zapatism (**b**) *Hist* = movement led by the Mexican revolutionary Emiliano Zapata

zapatista 1 *adj Pol Hist* Zapatista
2 *nmf Pol* Zapatista, = member of the Zapatista Front, a mainly indigenous insurrectionist group in the Southern Mexican state of Chiapas; *Hist* Zapatista, = follower or supporter of the Mexican revolutionary Emiliano Zapata (1879-1919)

zapato *nm* shoe; **zapatos de tacón** high-heeled shoes; *Fam Fig* **saber dónde le aprieta el z.** to know which side one's bread is buttered on

zape *interj Fam* (**a**) *(al gato)* shoo!, scat! (**b**) *(asombro)* gosh!, crumbs!

zapear *vi Fam* to channel-hop

zapeo *nm Fam* channel-hopping, *US* channel surfing

zapotazo *nm Guat Méx* blow

zapote *nm Bot* sapodilla

zapoteca *adj & nm,f* Zapotec

zapping ['θapin] *nm inv Fam* channel-hopping, *US* channel surfing; **hacer z.** to channel-hop

zar *nm Hist* czar, tsar

zarabanda *nf* (**a**) *Mús* saraband (**b**) *Fam (jaleo)* bustle, confusion, turmoil

zaragata *nf Fam* rumpus, row

zaragate *nm,f* (**a**) *Am (zascandil)* busybody, meddler (**b**) *Méx (truhán)* rascal

Zaragoza *n* Saragossa

zaragozano, -a 1 *adj* o of from Saragossa
2 *nm,f* person from Saragossa

zaramullo, -a 1 *nm,f Am Fam (zascandil)* meddler, busybody
2 *adj CAm Col (remilgado)* fussy, finicky

zaranda *nf* sieve

zarandajas *nfpl Fam* odds and ends, trifles

zarandear 1 *vt* to shake
2 zarandearse *vpr* (**a**) *(bambolearse, agitarse)* to shake; **el vagón se zarandeaba mucho** the carriage was bumping up and down a lot (**b**) *Am (contonearse)* to swing one's hips

zarandeo *nm* (**a**) *(sacudida)* shaking; **le dio un buen z.** she shook him hard (**b**) *Am (contoneo)* swinging of the hips

zarapito *nm Orn* curlew

zarazo, -a *adj Am (fruto)* underripe

zarcillo *nm* (**a**) *Bot (brote)* tendril (**b**) *(pendiente)* earring

zarigüeya *nf Zool* opossum

zarina *nf Hist* czarina, tsarina

zarista *adj & nm,f* czarist, tsarist

zarpa *nf* claw, paw; *Fam* **echar la z.** to grab

zarpar *vi Náut* to weigh anchor, set sail

zarpazo *nm* clawing; **dar** o **pegar un z. a** to claw

zarpear *vt CAm Méx* to splash with mud

zarrapastroso, -a 1 *adj Fam* scruffy
2 *nm,f* scruff

zarza *nf* bramble, blackberry bush

zarzal *nm* bramble patch

zarzamora *nf (zarza)* blackberry bush; *(fruto)* blackberry

zarzaparrilla *nf Bot* sarsaparilla

zarzuela *nf* (**a**) *Mús* = Spanish operetta (**b**) *Culin* = (type of) fish stew

zas *interj* crash!, bang!

zascandil *nm* busybody, meddler

zascandilear *vi* to mess o *Br* faff around

zen *adj inv & nm* Zen

zenit *nm Astron* zenith

zepelín *nm Av* zeppelin

zeta *nf* zed, *US* zee

zigoto *nm* zygote

zigurat *(pl* **zigurats)** *nm* ziggurat

zigzag *(pl* **zigzags** o **zigzagues)** *nm* zigzag

zigzagueante *adj* zigzag

zigzaguear *vi* to zigzag

zigzagueo *nm (de carretera, sendero)* twisting and turning

Zimbabue *n* Zimbabwe

zimbabuo, -a *adj & nm,f* Zimbabwean

zinc *(pl* **zines)** *nm Quím* zinc

zíngaro, -a *adj & nm,f* gypsy

zíper *(pl* **zípers)** *nm CAm Méx Br* zip, *US* zipper

zipizape *nm Fam* row, scuffle

zis, zas *interj* biff!, bash!

zócalo *nm* (**a**) *(de pared)* *Br* skirting board, *US* base (**b**) *(pedestal)* plinth (**c**) *Méx (plaza)* main square (**d**) *Inform* socket

zoco *nm* Moroccan market place, souk

zocotroco *nm Am* (**a**) *(cosa)* hunk, lump (**b**) *(persona)* great fat lump

zodiac® *nf* Zodiac boat, = rubber dinghy with outboard motor

zodiacal *adj Astrol* zodiacal

zodiaco *nm*, **zodíaco** *nm Astrol* zodiac ❑ **signo del z.** sign of the zodiac

zombi *nmf*, **zombie** *nmf* zombie; *Fam* **estar z.** to be crazy

zompopo *nm CAm (hormiga)* = type of large-headed leafcutter ant

zona *nf* zone, area ❏ **z. catastrófica** disaster area; **z. comercial** shopping area; **z. de exclusión** exclusion zone; **z. de guerra** war zone; **z. de libre comercio** free-trade zone; **z. euro** euro zone; *Com* **z. franca** free-trade zone; **z. peatonal** pedestrian precinct; **z. residencial** residential area; **z. verde** park

zonal *adj* **plano z.** map of the area

zoncear *vi Am* to act the fool

zoncería *nf,* **zoncera** *nf Am* silliness, stupidity; **decir/hacer una z.** to say/do something silly

zonda *nm Arg Bol* = hot Andean wind

zonzo, -a *Am Fam* **1** *adj* foolish, silly
  2 *nm,f* fool, idiot

zoo *nm* zoo

zoofilia *nf* bestiality

zoología *nf* zoology

zoológico, -a **1** *adj* zoological; **parque z.** zoo
  2 *nm* zoo

zoólogo, -a *nm,f* zoologist

zoom [θum] (*pl* **zooms**) *nm Cin Fot* zoom

zooplancton *nm* zooplankton

zopenco, -a *Fam* **1** *adj* daft, stupid
  2 *nm,f* dope, half-wit

zopilote *nm CAm Méx* black vulture

zoquete **1** *adj Fam (lerdo)* dull, stupid
  2 *nmf Fam (lerdo)* blockhead
  3 *nm CSur (calcetín)* ankle sock

zorongo *nm* **(a)** *Mús* = Andalusian song and dance **(b)** *(moño)* bun **(c)** *(pañuelo)* kerchief *(worn round the head)*

zorra *nf* **(a)** *Zool* fox, vixen **(b)** *Esp Fam (prostituta)* whore, tart, *US* hooker

. **zorrería** *nf Fam* dirty trick

zorrillo *nm CAm Méx,* **zorrino** *nm Andes RP Zool* skunk

zorro, -a **1** *adj Fam* **(a)** *(astuto)* cunning, sly **(b)** *Esp Fam* bloody; **no tener ni zorra (idea)** not to have the slightest idea
  2 *nm,f Fam (persona)* fox, sly person
  3 *nm* **(a)** *Zool* fox **(b)** *(piel)* fox-fur, fox-skin **(c)** **zorros** *(para el polvo)* duster *sing; Fam* **estar hecho unos z.** to be shattered *o Br* knackered

zorzal *nm* **(a)** *Orn* thrush ❏ **z. alirrojo** redwing **(b)** *Chile (tonto)* simpleton

zote **1** *adj* dim-witted
  2 *nm,f* dimwit

zozobra *nf* **(a)** *Náut (hundimiento)* sinking, capsizing **(b)** *Fig (congoja)* worry, anxiety

zozobrar *vi* **(a)** *Náut (hundirse)* to sink, capsize **(b)** *Fig (persona)* to be anxious, worry **(c)** *Fig (proyecto)* to fail, be ruined

zueco *nm* clog

zulú (*pl* **zulúes**) *adj & nm,f* Zulu

zumba *nf* **(a)** *(burla)* teasing, joking **(b)** *Andes Méx PRico (paliza)* beating, thrashing **(c)** *(cencerro)* bell

zumbado, -a **1** *pp de* **zumbar**
  2 *adj Fam* crazy, mad

zumbador *nm* buzzer

zumbar **1** *vi* to buzz, hum; **me zumban los oídos** my ears are buzzing; *Fam* **salir zumbando** to zoom off
  2 *vt Fam (pegar)* to thrash

zumbido *nm* buzzing, humming

zumbón, -ona **1** *adj* teasing, joking
  2 *nm,f* teaser, joker

zumo *nm Esp* juice; **z. de naranja** orange juice

zunchar *vt* to fasten with a band *o* hoop

zurcido, -a **1** *pp de* **zurcir**
  2 *adj Cost* darned
  3 *nm Cost* darn, mend

zurcir [72] *vt Cost* to darn; *Fam* **¡(anda y) que te zurzan!** go to hell!

zurda *nf (mano)* left hand

zurdazo *nm Dep (disparo)* powerful left-foot shot

zurdo, -a **1** *adj* **(a)** *(persona)* left-handed **(b)** *(mano)* left
  2 *nm,f (persona)* left-handed person

zurra *nf* beating, thrashing

zurrar *vt* **(a)** *(pegar)* to beat, flog; *Fam* **zurrarle la badana a algn** to give sb a good hiding **(b)** *(piel)* to tan

zurriagazo *nm* **(a)** *(latigazo)* lash, stroke **(b)** *Fig (desgracia)* mishap, stroke of bad luck

zurriago *nm* whip

zurrón *nm* shepherd's pouch *o* bag

zutano, -a *nm,f Fam* so-and-so; *(hombre)* what's-his-name; *(mujer)* what's-her-name